County and City Extra
Special Decennial Census Edition

County and City Extra
Special Decennial Census Edition

Editors
Deirdre A. Gaquin
Katherine A. DeBrandt

BERNAN

Lanham, MD

First edition 1992. Special Decennial edition 2002.

ISBN: 0-89059-361-2

ISSN: 1059-9096

Composed and printed by Automated Graphic Systems, Inc., White Plains, MD, on acid-free paper that meets the American National Standards Institute Z39-48 standard.

2003 2002   4 3 2 1

BERNAN
4611-F Assembly Drive
Lanham, MD 20706
800-274-4447
email: info@bernan.com
www.bernan.com

Contents

Page

xi   **Introduction**

xiii   **Column Headings for Tables**

1   **Highlights**

21   **Area Rankings**

83   **Table A. States**

91   **Table B. States and Counties**

443   **Table C. Metropolitan Areas**

487   **Table D. Cities**

629   **Table E. Towns**

687   **Table F. Congressional Districts**

        Appendices
A-1   A. Geographic Concepts and Codes
B-1   B. Metropolitan Statistical Areas and Components
C-1   C. Metropolitan Statistical Areas and Components
               by State
D-1   D. Maps of States and Congressional Districts
E-1   E. Cities by County
F-1   F. Definitions

ABOUT THE EDITORS

Deirdre Gaquin has been a data use consultant to private organizations, government agencies, and universities for 20 years. Prior to that, she was Director of Data Access Services at Data Use & Access Laboratories, a pioneer in private sector distribution of federal statistical data. A former President of the Association of Public Data Users, Ms. Gaquin has served on numerous boards, panels, and task forces concerned with federal statistical data and has worked with four decennial censuses. She holds a Master of Urban Planning (MUP) degree from Hunter College.

Katherine A. DeBrandt is an editor with Bernan Associates. She received her B.A. in political science from Colgate University. She is also an editor of *Education Statistics of the United States*, also published by Bernan.

ACKNOWLEDGMENTS

The editors of *County and City Extra: Special Decennial Census Edition* extend their appreciation to George Hall and Courtenay Slater, the originators of the *County & City Extra*, who initiated the idea for this 2000 Census edition.

We are extremely grateful to Dan Parham, Kara Gottschlich, Jacalyn Houston, and Tamera Wells-Lee who have shepherded this book through the editorial and production processes, with tremendous support from Automated Graphics Systems, Inc. Lorrent Smith prepared the text graphics, and the color county maps were prepared by Bowring Cartographics, Inc.

We are especially grateful to the staff of the Census Bureau who assisted us in obtaining the data, provided excellent resources on their Web site, and patiently answered our questions.

INTRODUCTION

County and City Extra—Special Decennial Census Edition complements Bernan's *County and City Extra*, an annual publication providing the most up-to-date statistical information for every state, county, metropolitan area, and congressional district, and for all cities in the United States with a population of 25,000 or more.

Every 10 years, the United States conducts its Census of Population and Housing, resulting in a wealth of information about every geographic entity in the United States. *County and City Extra—Special Decennial Census Edition* includes information from the 100-percent questionnaire, the information compiled from the questions asked of all people and about every housing unit. Data are included for every state, county, metropolitan area, and congressional district; for every city with a population or 25,000 or more; and for every town with a population of 25,000 or more in the 12 states where towns are important general-purpose governmental entities.

Population items in this volume include sex, age, race, Hispanic or Latino origin, household composition, family relationships, presence of children, and group quarters residency. Housing items include occupancy status, household size, vacancy status, and home ownership. Comparisons with 1990 and 1980 are provided if possible.

Subjects Covered and Volume Organization

Immediately following this introduction is a layout of the column headings to be found in the main data tables, followed by a colored map portfolio, beginning on page xiii. Rankings of states, counties, cities, metropolitan areas, and congressional districts on a number of key demographic and housing characteristics begin on page 21.

The main body of this volume includes six basic tables. Table A, which begins on page 83, contains data for states. Table B, beginning on page 91, contains information for states and counties, while Table C, beginning on page 443, contains similar information for metropolitan areas. Statistics for cities with a 2000 population of 25,000 or more can be found in Table D, beginning on page 487, while Table E, beginning on page 629, includes similar information for towns of 25,000 or

more in Connecticut, Maine, Massachusetts, Michigan, Minnesota, New Hampshire, New Jersey, New York, Pennsylvania, Rhode Island, Vermont, and Wisconsin, states where towns serve as general-purpose local governments. Table F, beginning on page 687, contains data for congressional districts of the 107th Congress. A contents page preceding each of the tables B through F lists the page number where the data for a given geographic area begin. Counties, cities, and towns are listed alphabetically by state. Metropolitan areas are listed alphabetically, except that Primary Metropolitan Statistical Areas (PMSAs) are listed alphabetically within the Consolidated Metropolitan Statistical Area (CMSA) of which they are components. Congressional districts are listed in numeric order within each state.

The Appendices include definitions of geographic concepts (Appendix A); definitions of the data items included in this volume (Appendix F); listing of metropolitan areas with their component counties delineated as of June 30, 1999 listed alphabetically (Appendix B) and within each state (Appendix C); a list of cities by county (Appendix E); and maps showing counties, metropolitan areas, selected places within each state, and congressional districts (Appendix D).

Symbols and Terms

The following symbols are used in this volume:

NA Indicates that data are not available.

X Indicates that data are not applicable or meaningful for this geographic unit.

Figures that are less than half of the unit of measure shown appear in this volume as zero.

Sources

All data in this volume have been compiled from the Census Bureau's compilations of decennial census data. All data are subject to errors arising from factors such as reporting errors, incomplete coverage, nonresponse, imputations, and processing error. Responsibility of the editors and publisher of this volume is limited to reasonable care in the reproduction and presentation of data obtained from sources believed to be reliable.

COLUMN HEADINGS FOR STATES

Table A. States

STATE code	STATE	Population, 2000				Population, 1990			Population and population characteristics, 2000					
									Race (percent)					
									One race					
		Land area, 2000[1] (sq km)	Total persons	Rank	Per square kilometer	Land area, 1990[1] (sq km)	Total persons	Rank	Per square kilometer	White	Black or African American	American Indian or Alaska Native	Asian	Native Hawaiian and other Pacific Islander	Some other race
		1	2	3	4	5	6	7	8	9	10	11	12	13	14

[1] Dry land or land partially or temporarily covered by water.

Table A. States

STATE	Population and population characteristics, 2000 (cont'd)								Population and population characteristics, 1990					
	Race (percent) (cont'd)								Race (percent)					
		Race alone or in combination												
	Two or more races	White	Black	American Indian or Alaska Native	Asian	Native Hawaiian and other Pacific Islander	Some other race	Hispanic[1]	White	Black or African American	American Indian or Alaska Native	Asian and Pacific Islander	Hispanic[1]
	15	16	17	18	19	20	21	22	23	24	25	26	27

[1] Hispanic persons may be of any race.

Table A. States

STATE	Population and population characteristics, 2000											
	Age (percent)											
	Under 5 years	5 to 17 years	18 to 24 years	25 to 34 years	35 to 44 years	45 to 54 years	55 to 64 years	65 to 74 years	75 years and over	Median age (years)	Percent Female
	28	29	30	31	32	33	34	35	36	37	38

Table A. States

STATE	Population and population characteristics, 1990										Population—change, 1980–2000				
	Age (percent)										Total persons			Percent change	
	Under 5 years	5 to 17 years	18 to 24 years	25 to 34 years	35 to 44 years	45 to 54 years	55 to 64 years	65 to 74 years	75 years and over	Percent Female	2000	1990	1980	1990–2000	1980–1990
	39	40	41	42	43	44	45	46	47	48	49	50	51	52	53

[1] Hispanic persons may be of any race.

COLUMN HEADINGS FOR STATES

Table A. States

STATE	Household relationship, 2000																
	In households (percent)										In group quarters (percent)						
					Child		Other relatives		Nonrelatives			Institutionalized population			Noninstitutionalized population		
	Total population	Total in house-holds	House-holder	Spouse	Total	Own child under 18 years	Total	Under 18 years	Total	Unmar-ried partner	Total in group quarters	Correc-tional institu-tions	Nurs-ing homes	Other institu-tions	Col-lege dormi-tories	Mili-tary quar-ters	Other
	54	55	56	57	58	59	60	61	62	63	64	65	66	67	68	69	70

Table A. States

STATE	Households by type, 2000													Households, 1990		
		Family households						Nonfamily households								
			Married couple		Female householder[1]				Householder living alone							
	Total households	Total	With own children under 18 years	Total	With own children under 18 years	Total	With own children under 18 years	Total	Total	65 years and over	Average house-hold size	Average family size	Total house-holds	Female house-holder[1]	House-holder living alone
	71	72	73	74	75	76	77	78	79	80	81	82	83	84	85

[1] No spouse present.

Table A. States

STATE		Housing occupancy, 2000						Housing tenure, 2000				
			Vacant housing units (percent)					Occupied housing units				
	Percent change of households, 1990–2000	Total housing units	Occupied housing units (percent)	Total	For seasonal, recreational, or occasional use	Homeowner vacancy rate (percent)	Rental vacancy rate (percent)	Total	Percent owner-occupied housing units	Percent renter-occupied housing units	Average household size of owner-occupied units	Average household size of renter-occupied units
	86	87	88	89	90	91	92	93	94	95	96	97

COLUMN HEADINGS FOR STATES AND COUNTIES

Table B. States and Counties

STATE/ County code	MSA/ PMSA/ NECMA code[1]	County type[2]	STATE County	Land area, 2000[3] (sq km)	Population, 2000 Total persons	Rank	Per square kilometer	Population, 1990 Land area, 1990[3] (sq km)	Total persons	Rank	Per square kilometer	Population and population characteristics, 2000 — Race (percent) — One race White	Black or African American	American Indian or Alaska Native	Asian	Native Hawaiian and other Pacific Islander	Some other race
				1	2	3	4	5	6	7	8	9	10	11	12	13	14

[1]MSA = Metropolitan Statistical Area. PMSA = Primary MSA. NECMA = New England County Metropolitan Area. See Appendix A for explanation of these concepts. See Appendix B for list of metropolitan areas identified by type, with component counties.
[2]County typology code from the Economic Research Service of USDA. See Appendix A for definition.
[3]Dry land or land partially or temporarily covered by water.

Table B. States and Counties

STATE County	Population and population characteristics, 2000 (cont'd) — Race (percent) (cont'd) — Two or more races	Race alone or in combination White	Black	American Indian or Alaska Native	Asian	Native Hawaiian and other Pacific Islander	Some other race	Hispanic[1]	Population and population characteristics, 1990 — Race (percent) White	Black or African American	American Indian or Alaska Native	Asian and Pacific Islander	Hispanic[1]
	15	16	17	18	19	20	21	22	23	24	25	26	27

[1]Hispanic persons may be of any race.

Table B. States and Counties

STATE County	Population and population characteristics, 2000 — Age (percent) — Under 5 years	5 to 17 years	18 to 24 years	25 to 34 years	35 to 44 years	45 to 54 years	55 to 64 years	65 to 74 years	75 years and over	Median age (years)	Percent Female
	28	29	30	31	32	33	34	35	36	37	38

Table B. States and Counties

STATE County	Population and population characteristics, 1990 — Age (percent) — Under 5 years	5 to 17 years	18 to 24 years	25 to 34 years	35 to 44 years	45 to 54 years	55 to 64 years	65 to 74 years	75 years and over	Percent Female	Population—change, 1980–2000 — Total persons — 2000	1990	1980	Percent change 1990– 2000	1980– 1990
	39	40	41	42	43	44	45	46	47	48	49	50	51	52	53

COLUMN HEADINGS FOR STATES AND COUNTIES

Table B. States and Counties

STATE County	Total population	Household relationship, 2000																
		In households (percent)									In group quarters (percent)						
						Child		Other relatives		Nonrelatives			Institutionalized population			Noninstitutionalized population		
		Total in house-holds	House-holder	Spouse	Total	Own child under 18 years	Total	Under 18 years	Total	Unmar-ried partner	Total in group quarters	Correc-tional institu-tions	Nurs-ing homes	Other institu-tions	Col-lege dormi-tories	Mili-tary quar-ters	Other
	54	55	56	57	58	59	60	61	62	63	64	65	66	67	68	69	70

Table B. States and Counties

STATE County	Households by type, 2000												Households, 1990		
		Family households						Nonfamily households							
				Married couple		Female householder[1]			Householder living alone						
	Total households	Total	With own children under 18 years	Total	With own children under 18 years	Total	With own children under 18 years	Total	Total	65 years and over	Average house-hold size	Average family size	Total house-holds	Female house-holder[1]	House-holder living alone
	71	72	73	74	75	76	77	78	79	80	81	82	83	84	85

[1] No spouse present.

Table B. States and Counties

STATE County	Percent change of households, 1990–2000	Housing occupancy, 2000							Housing tenure, 2000				
					Vacant housing units				Occupied housing units				
		Total housing units	Occupied housing units (percent)	Total	For seasonal, recreational, or occasional use	Homeowner vacancy rate (percent)	Rental vacancy rate (percent)		Total	Percent owner-occupied housing units	Percent renter-occupied housing units	Average household size of owner-occupied units	Average household size of renter-occupied units
	86	87	88	89	90	91	92		93	94	95	96	97

COLUMN HEADINGS FOR METROPOLITAN AREAS

Table C. Metropolitan Areas

CMSA/ MSA/ PMSA/ NECMA code[1]	Area Name	Population, 2000				Population, 1990				Population and population characteristics, 2000					
										Race (percent)					
										One race					
		Land area, 2000[2] (sq km)	Total persons	Rank	Per square kilometer	Land area, 1990[2] (sq km)	Total persons	Rank	Per square kilometer	White	Black or African American	American Indian or Alaska Native	Asian	Native Hawaiian and other Pacific Islander	Some other race
		1	2	3	4	5	6	7	8	9	10	11	12	13	14

[1] MSA = Metropolitan Statistical Area. PMSA = Primary MSA. NECMA = New England County Metropolitan Area. See Appendix A for explanation of these concepts. See Appendix B for list of metropolitan areas identified by type, with component counties.
[2] Dry land or land partially or temporarily covered by water.

Table C. Metropolitan Areas

Area Name	Population and population characteristics, 2000 (cont'd)								Population and population characteristics, 1990				
	Race (percent) (cont'd)								Race (percent)				
	Race alone or in combination												
	Two or more races	White	Black	American Indian or Alaska Native	Asian	Native Hawaiian and other Pacific Islander	Some other race	Hispanic[1]	White	Black or African American	American Indian or Alaska Native	Asian and Pacific Islander	Hispanic[1]
	15	16	17	18	19	20	21	22	23	24	25	26	27

[1] Hispanic persons may be of any race.

Table C. Metropolitan Areas

Area Name	Population and population characteristics, 2000										
	Age (percent)										
	Under 5 years	5 to 17 years	18 to 24 years	25 to 34 years	35 to 44 years	45 to 54 years	55 to 64 years	65 to 74 years	75 years and over	Median age (years)	Percent Female
	28	29	30	31	32	33	34	35	36	37	38

Table C. Metropolitan Areas

Area Name	Population and population characteristics, 1990										Population—change, 1980–2000				
	Age (percent)										Total persons			Percent change	
	Under 5 years	5 to 17 years	18 to 24 years	25 to 34 years	35 to 44 years	45 to 54 years	55 to 64 years	65 to 74 years	75 years and over	Percent Female	2000	1990	1980	1990– 2000	1980– 1990
	39	40	41	42	43	44	45	46	47	48	49	50	51	52	53

COLUMN HEADINGS FOR METROPOLITAN AREAS

Table C. Metropolitan Areas

Area Name	Household relationship, 2000																
	In households (percent)										In group quarters (percent)						
					Child		Other relatives		Nonrelatives			Institutionalized population			Noninstitutionalized population		
	Total population	Total in house-holds	House-holder	Spouse	Total	Own child under 18 years	Total	Under 18 years	Total	Unmar-ried partner	Total in group quarters	Correc-tional institu-tions	Nurs-ing homes	Other institu-tions	Col-lege dormi-tories	Mili-tary quar-ters	Other
	54	55	56	57	58	59	60	61	62	63	64	65	66	67	68	69	70

Table C. Metropolitan Areas

Area Name	Households by type, 2000												Households, 1990		
		Family households						Nonfamily households							
			Married couple		Female householder[1]				Householder living alone						
	Total households	Total	Total	With own children under 18 years	Total	With own children under 18 years	Total	With own children under 18 years	Total	Total	65 years and over	Average house-hold size	Average family size	Total house-holds	Female house-holder[1]	House-holder living alone
	71	72	73	74	75	76	77	78	79	80	81	82	83	84	85

[1]No spouse present.

Table C. Metropolitan Areas

Area Name	Housing occupancy, 2000							Housing tenure, 2000				
				Vacant housing units					Occupied housing units			
	Percent change of households, 1990–2000	Total housing units	Occupied housing units (percent)	Total	For seasonal, recreational, or occasional use	Homeowner vacancy rate (percent)	Rental vacancy rate (percent)	Total	Percent owner-occupied housing units	Percent renter-occupied housing units	Average household size of owner-occupied units	Average household size of renter-occupied units
	86	87	88	89	90	91	92	93	94	95	96	97

COLUMN HEADINGS FOR CITIES

Table D. Cities

STATE Place code	City	Land area, 2000[1] (sq km)	Population, 2000			Population, 1990			Population and population characteristics, 2000					
						Land area, 1990[1] (sq km)			Race (percent)					
									One race					
			Total persons	Rank	Per square kilometer	Land area, 1990[1] (sq km)	Total persons	Rank	Per square kilometer	White	Black or African American	American Indian or Alaska Native	Asian	Native Hawaiian and other Pacific Islander	Some other race
		1	2	3	4	5	6	7	8	9	10	11	12	13	14

[1]Dry land or land partially or temporarily covered by water.

Table D. Cities

City	Population and population characteristics, 2000 (cont'd)								Population and population characteristics, 1990				
	Race (percent) (cont'd)								Race (percent)				
		Race alone or in combination											
	Two or more races	White	Black	American Indian or Alaska Native	Asian	Native Hawaiian and other Pacific Islander	Some other race	Hispanic[1]	White	Black or African American	American Indian or Alaska Native	Asian and Pacific Islander	Hispanic[1]
	15	16	17	18	19	20	21	22	23	24	25	26	27

[1]Hispanic persons may be of any race.

Table D. Cities

City	Population and population characteristics, 2000										
	Age (percent)										
	Under 5 years	5 to 17 years	18 to 24 years	25 to 34 years	35 to 44 years	45 to 54 years	55 to 64 years	65 to 74 years	75 years and over	Median age (years)	Percent Female
	28	29	30	31	32	33	34	35	36	37	38

Table D. Cities

City	Population and population characteristics, 1990										Population—change, 1980–2000				
	Age (percent)										Total persons			Percent change	
	Under 5 years	5 to 17 years	18 to 24 years	25 to 34 years	35 to 44 years	45 to 54 years	55 to 64 years	65 to 74 years	75 years and over	Percent Female	2000	1990	1980	1990–2000	1980–1990
	39	40	41	42	43	44	45	46	47	48	49	50	51	52	53

COLUMN HEADINGS FOR CITIES

Table D. Cities

City	Household relationship, 2000																	
	In households (percent)										In group quarters (percent)							
					Child		Other relatives		Nonrelatives			Institutionalized population				Noninstitutionalized population		
	Total population	Total in house-holds	House-holder	Spouse	Total	Own child under 18 years	Total	Under 18 years	Total	Unmar-ried partner	Total in group quarters	Correc-tional institu-tions	Nurs-ing homes	Other institu-tions	Col-lege dormi-tories	Mili-tary quar-ters	Other
	54	55	56	57	58	59	60	61	62	63	64	65	66	67	00	09	70

Table D. Cities

City	Households by type, 2000												Households, 1990		
		Family households						Nonfamily households							
			Married couple		Female householder[1]				Householder living alone						
	Total households	Total	Total	With own children under 18 years	Total	With own children under 18 years	Total	With own children under 18 years	Total	Total	65 years and over	Average house-hold size	Average family size	Total house-holds	Female house-holder[1]	House-holder living alone
	71	72	73	74	75	76	77	78	79	80	81	82	83	84	85

[1] No spouse present.

Table D. Cities

City	Housing occupancy						Housing tenure					
				Vacant housing units				Occupied housing units				
	Percent change of households, 1990–2000	Total housing units	Occupied housing units (percent)	Total	For seasonal, recreational, or occasional use	Homeowner vacancy rate (percent)	Rental vacancy rate (percent)	Total	Percent owner-occupied housing units	Percent renter-occupied housing units	Average household size of owner-occupied units	Average household size of renter-occupied units
	86	87	88	89	90	91	92	93	94	95	96	97

COLUMN HEADINGS FOR TOWNS

Table E. Towns

STATE MCD code	Town	Population, 2000				Population, 1990				Population and population characteristics, 2000					
										Race (percent)					
										One race					
		Land area, 2000[1] (sq km)	Total persons	Rank within state	Per square kilometer	Land area, 1990[1] (sq km)	Total persons	Rank within state	Per square kilometer	White	Black or African American	American Indian or Alaska Native	Asian	Native Hawaiian and other Pacific Islander	Some other race
		1	2	3	4	5	6	7	8	9	10	11	12	13	14

[1] Dry land or land partially or temporarily covered by water.

Table E. Towns

Town	Population and population characteristics, 2000 (cont'd)								Population and population characteristics, 1990				
	Race (percent) (cont'd)								Race (percent)				
	Two or more races	Race alone or in combination						Hispanic[1]	White	Black or African American	American Indian or Alaska Native	Asian and Pacific Islander	Hispanic[1]
		White	Black	American Indian or Alaska Native	Asian	Native Hawaiian and other Pacific Islander	Some other race						
	15	16	17	18	19	20	21	22	23	24	25	26	27

[1] Hispanic persons may be of any race.

Table E. Towns

Town	Population and population characteristics, 2000										
	Age (percent)										
	Under 5 years	5 to 17 years	18 to 24 years	25 to 34 years	35 to 44 years	45 to 54 years	55 to 64 years	65 to 74 years	75 years and over	Median age (years)	Percent Female
	28	29	30	31	32	33	34	35	36	37	38

Table E. Towns

Town	Population and population characteristics, 1990										Population—change, 1980–2000				
	Age (percent)										Total persons			Percent change	
	Under 5 years	5 to 17 years	18 to 24 years	25 to 34 years	35 to 44 years	45 to 54 years	55 to 64 years	65 to 74 years	75 years and over	Percent Female	2000	1990	1980	1990–2000	1980–1990
	39	40	41	42	43	44	45	46	47	48	49	50	51	52	53

COLUMN HEADINGS FOR TOWNS

Table E. Towns

Town	Household relationship, 2000																
		In households (percent)									In group quarters (percent)						
					Child		Other relatives		Nonrelatives			Institutionalized population			Noninstitutionalized population		
	Total population	Total in house-holds	House-holder	Spouse	Total	Own child under 18 years	Total	Under 18 years	Total	Unmar-ried partner	Total in group quarters	Correc-tional institu-tions	Nurs-ing homes	Other institu-tions	Col-lege dormi-tories	Mili-tary quar-ters	Other
	54	55	56	57	58	59	60	61	62	63	64	65	66	67	68	69	70

Table E. Towns

Town	Households by type, 2000												Households, 1990		
		Family households						Nonfamily households							
				Married couple		Female householder[1]			Householder living alone						
	Total households	Total	With own children under 18 years	Total	With own children under 18 years	Total	With own children under 18 years	Total	Total	65 years and over	Average house-hold size	Average family size	Total house-holds	Female house-holder[1]	House-holder living alone
	71	72	73	74	75	76	77	78	79	80	81	82	83	84	85

[1]No spouse present.

Table E. Towns

Town		Housing occupancy						Housing tenure					
				Vacant housing units					Occupied housing units				
	Percent change of households, 1990–2000	Total housing units	Occupied housing units (percent)	Total	For seasonal, recreational, or occasional use	Homeowner vacancy rate (percent)	Rental vacancy rate (percent)	Total	Percent owner-occupied housing units	Percent renter-occupied housing units	Average household size of owner-occupied units	Average household size of renter-occupied units
	86	87	88	89	90	91	92	93	94	95	96	97

COLUMN HEADINGS FOR CONGRESSIONAL DISTRICTS

Table F. Congressional Districts 107th Congress

STATE District	Population, 2000				Population, 1990				Population and population characteristics, 2000					
									Race (percent)					
											One race			
	Land area, 2000[1] (sq km)	Total persons	Rank	Per square kilometer	Land area, 1990[1] (sq km)	Total persons	Rank	Per square kilometer	White	Black or African American	American Indian or Alaska Native	Asian	Native Hawaiian and other Pacific Islander	Some other race
	1	2	3	4	5	6	7	8	9	10	11	12	13	14

[1] Dry land or land partially or temporarily covered by water.

Table F. Congressional Districts 107th Congress

STATE District	Population and population characteristics, 2000 (cont'd)								Population and population characteristics, 1990				
	Race (percent) (cont'd)								Race (percent)				
		Race alone or in combination											
	Two or more races	White	Black	American Indian or Alaska Native	Asian	Native Hawaiian and other Pacific Islander	Some other race	Hispanic[1]	White	Black or African American	American Indian or Alaska Native	Asian and Pacific Islander	Hispanic[1]
	15	16	17	18	19	20	21	22	23	24	25	26	27

[1] Hispanic persons may be of any race.

Table F. Congressional Districts 107th Congress

STATE District	Population and population characteristics, 2000											
	Age (percent)											
	Under 5 years	5 to 17 years	18 to 24 years	25 to 34 years	35 to 44 years	45 to 54 years	55 to 64 years	65 to 74 years	75 years and over	Median age (years)	Percent Female
	28	29	30	31	32	33	34	35	36	37	38

Table F. Congressional Districts 107th Congress

STATE District	Population and population characteristics, 1990										Population—change, 1980–2000				
	Age (percent)										Total persons			Percent change	
	Under 5 years	5 to 17 years	18 to 24 years	25 to 34 years	35 to 44 years	45 to 54 years	55 to 64 years	65 to 74 years	75 years and over	Percent Female	2000	1990	1980	1990–2000	1980–1990
	39	40	41	42	43	44	45	46	47	48	49	50	51	52	53

COLUMN HEADINGS FOR CONGRESSIONAL DISTRICTS

Table F. Congressional Districts 107th Congress

STATE District	Household relationship, 2000																
	In households (percent)										In group quarters (percent)						
					Child		Other relatives		Nonrelatives			Institutionalized population			Noninstitutionalized population		
	Total population	Total in house-holds	House-holder	Spouse	Total	Own child under 18 years	Total	Under 18 years	Total	Unmar-ried partner	Total in group quarters	Correc-tional institu-tions	Nurs-ing homes	Other institu-tions	Col-lege dormi-tories	Mili-tary quar-ters	Other
	54	55	56	57	58	59	60	61	62	63	64	65	66	67	68	69	70

Table F. Congressional Districts 107th Congress

STATE District	Households by type, 2000													Households, 1990		
		Family households						Nonfamily households								
				Married couple		Female householder[1]			Householder living alone							
	Total households	Total	With own children under 18 years	Total	With own children under 18 years	Total	With own children under 18 years	Total	Total	65 years and over	Average house-hold size	Average family size	Total house-holds	Female house-holder[1]	House-holder living alone
	71	72	73	74	75	76	77	78	79	80	81	82	83	84	85

[1] No spouse present.

Table F. Congressional Districts 107th Congress

STATE District	Housing occupancy							Housing tenure					
				Vacant housing units				Occupied housing units					
	Percent change of households, 1990–2000	Total housing units	Occupied housing units (percent)	Total	For seasonal, recreational, or occasional use	Homeowner vacancy rate (percent)	Rental vacancy rate (percent)	Total	Percent owner-occupied housing units	Percent renter-occupied housing units	Average household size of owner-occupied units	Average household size of renter-occupied units
	86	87	88	89	90	91	92	93	94	95	96	97

Decennial Census Highlights

Page

2   **Highlights of the 2000 Census**

Data Maps by County
9   Population Change, 1990–2000
10   Population Density, 2000
11   Black Population, 2000
12   Hispanic Population, 2000
13   Population Under 18 Years Old, 2000
14   Population 65 Years and Older, 2000
15   Median Age, 2000
16   One-person Households, 2000
17   Families with Children, 2000
18   Owner-occupied Housing, 2000
19   Housing for Seasonal, Recreational, or Occasional
        Use, 2000
20   Persons in Group Quarters, 2000

Highlights

Highlights of the 2000 Census

This book contains data from the 2000 Census for a variety of geographic entities—cities and towns of 25,000 or more population, counties (or their equivalents in states without counties), metropolitan areas (regardless of size), congressional districts, states, and the United States as a whole. Such geographic constructs are often the basic building blocks for several forms of government organization and community services. Often they also serve as the root of many social ties within the United States such as which schools our children attend or the boundaries of what we consider our neighborhood. The discussion that follows has been gleaned from data presented in *County and City Extra—Special Decennial Census Edition.*

A Growing Population

The population of the United States as a whole increased by 13.1 percent between 1990 and 2000, with 19 states exceeding this rate and the remainder growing more slowly. States with the fastest population growth in the 1990's were concentrated in the West, with seven out of the ten fastest growing states located in that region. Heading the list was Nevada, whose population increased by two-thirds during the decade. The big surprise of the 2000 Census was that the United States has about 6 million more people than the estimates had predicted. Every state gained population during the decade, though 1999 estimates had shown declines in three states and the District of Columbia. The census showed gains of less than one percent in West Virginia and North Dakota, but a population loss only in DC—a loss of 5.7 percent compared with a 1999 estimated loss of 14.5 percent.

The constitutional purpose of the census is the reapportionment of the 435 seats in the House of Representatives. Every ten years, these 435 seats are assigned to the states, based on their populations, so that each congressional district includes approximately the same number of people. In this process, numeric gains have more meaning than percentage increases. The map on page 3 shows the shifts that will occur before the next congress is seated in 2003. Arizona, Texas, Georgia, and Florida will each gain two seats, while California, Nevada, Colorado, and North Carolina will each gain a seat. Losing two seats each will be New York and Pennsylvania, and a single seat will be lost by Oklahoma, Mississippi,

Wisconsin, Illinois, Michigan, Indiana, Ohio, and Connecticut. The other 32 states will keep their existing numbers of representatives, but all states will redraw their congressional districts based on the new census.

There is no simple relationship between population size and land area for most of the geographic entities for which data are presented here. At the **state** level, for example, population in 2000 ranged from a high of 33.9 million for California that was almost 69 times the low of 494,000 for Wyoming. (The median population for states—with half having a larger and half a smaller populace—was about four million persons). While California is also one of our largest states in land area (ranking third), Alaska is by far the largest state in area, more than twice the size of Texas, even though its population rank is close to the bottom (48th). Texas is the 2nd largest state in both land area and total population. At the other end of the geographic size spectrum are many of the New England states (with Rhode Island the smallest), as well as Delaware and Hawaii. As a consequence of the differing area size and population rank, New Jersey is the most densely settled state, with about 438 persons per square kilometer of land, while Alaska is the least densely settled, with less than one person (.4) per square kilometer. California, which is the state with the largest population and third largest land area, ranks 13th in terms of population density (with about 84 persons per square kilometer).

Within states, the number and physical size of **counties** varies considerably; Delaware has 3 counties while Texas has over 250 counties. For the approximately 3,140 counties (and county equivalents—see Appendix A) in the United States, population in 2000 ranged from over 9 million in Los Angeles, CA, to 67 in Loving County, TX. Other particularly large counties in terms of population include Cook County, IL (over 5 million population), and Harris county, TX (over 3 million); the former encompassing Chicago and its suburbs, the latter containing Houston. These three counties maintained their top-three rankings from 1990, but the fourth largest county— Maricopa county, AZ (which includes Phoenix)—rose from 7th in population in 1990, while San Diego, CA dropped from 4th to 6th place between 1990 and 2000. There were 34 counties with a population of 1,000,000 or more, which combined contain about one-fourth of the U.S. population. About half of the U.S. population lived in the 150 largest

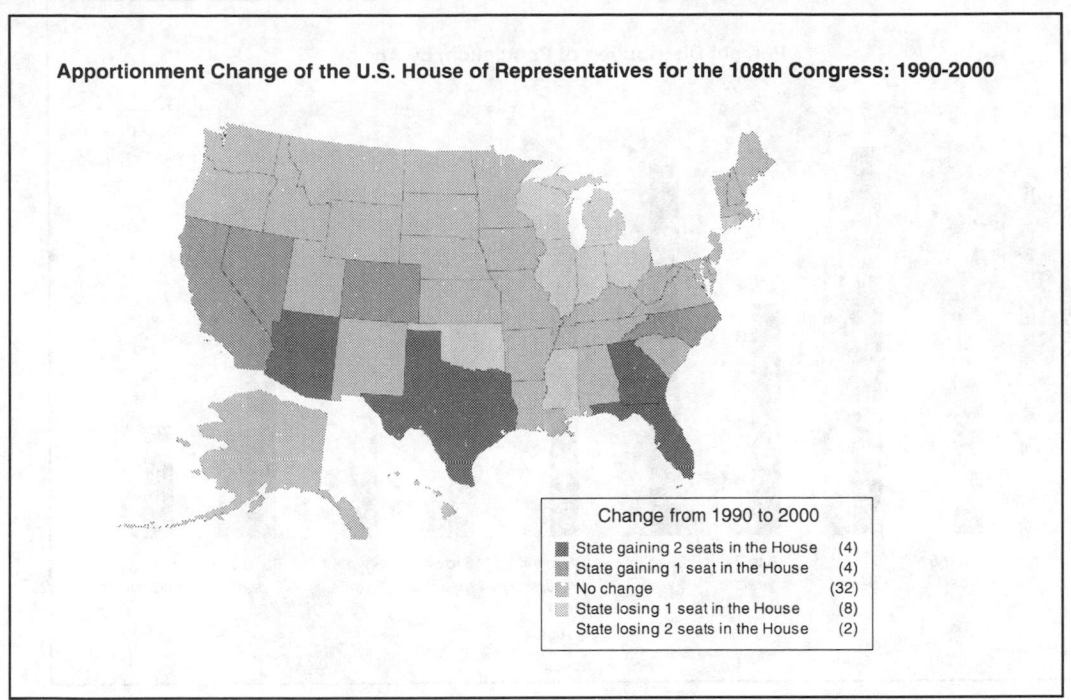

Apportionment Change of the U.S. House of Representatives for the 108th Congress: 1990-2000

Change from 1990 to 2000

- ■ State gaining 2 seats in the House (4)
- State gaining 1 seat in the House (4)
- No change (32)
- State losing 1 seat in the House (8)
- State losing 2 seats in the House (2)

counties, those with a population of about 400,000 or more. At the other extreme, there were 31 counties with fewer than 1,000 people in 2000. The median county population size was just under 25,000.

The nation's fastest growing counties in the 1990's tended to be in or near metropolitan areas in the West or South regions. Douglas County, CO (near Denver), grew by 191 percent, while Forsyth County, GA (near Atlanta), grew by 123 percent. Five counties more than doubled their populations during the decade, all of them near either Denver or Atlanta. The five biggest *numeric* gainers of the decade were Maricopa (AZ), Los Angeles (CA), Clark (NV), Harris (TX), and Orange (CA). Two more California counties (Riverside and San Diego), two Florida counties (Broward and Miami-Dade) and Dallas (TX) complete the top-ten numeric gainers from 1990 to 2000. The largest numeric population loss occurred in Baltimore City (MD), followed closely by two Pennsylvania counties, Philadelphia and Allegheny, which includes Pittsburgh.

In terms of land area, counties range from the nearly 378,000 square kilometers of Yukon-Koyukuk (AK) to New York (NY) with 59 square kilometers, Arlington (VA) with 67 and Bristol (RI) with 64 square kilometers.[1] Counties tend to be larger in the western United States (most of the largest 50 are in that region). The median land area for all U.S. counties was about 1,600 square kilometers in 2000.

While New York county (Manhattan) may have one of the smallest land areas, it had by far the highest population density among U.S. counties in 2000, with over 26,000 persons per square kilometer. No other county approached that density (although three other New York City boroughs were among the top-five counties in population density). San Francisco had the highest density outside of New York City, with Boston (Suffolk, MA), Philadelphia, and Washington, DC among the top ten. The median county only had about 16 persons per square kilometer, with only 105 counties having more than 500 persons per square kilometer. The Nation's largest county in terms of population (Los Angeles) had a population density of 905 persons per square kilometer, ranking only 47th among all U.S. counties.

In 2000, nine **cities** had populations over 1 million persons, topped by New York City with 8 million, Los Angeles with 3.7 million, and Chicago with 2.9 million. California and Texas each have four cities among the nation's 20 largest: Houston, Dallas, San Antonio, and Austin in Texas; and Los Angeles, San Diego, San Jose, and San Francisco in California. No other state has more than one city among the 20 most populous in the country.

---

[1] Several independent cities in Virginia, which are treated as counties for tabulation purposes, were excluded here.

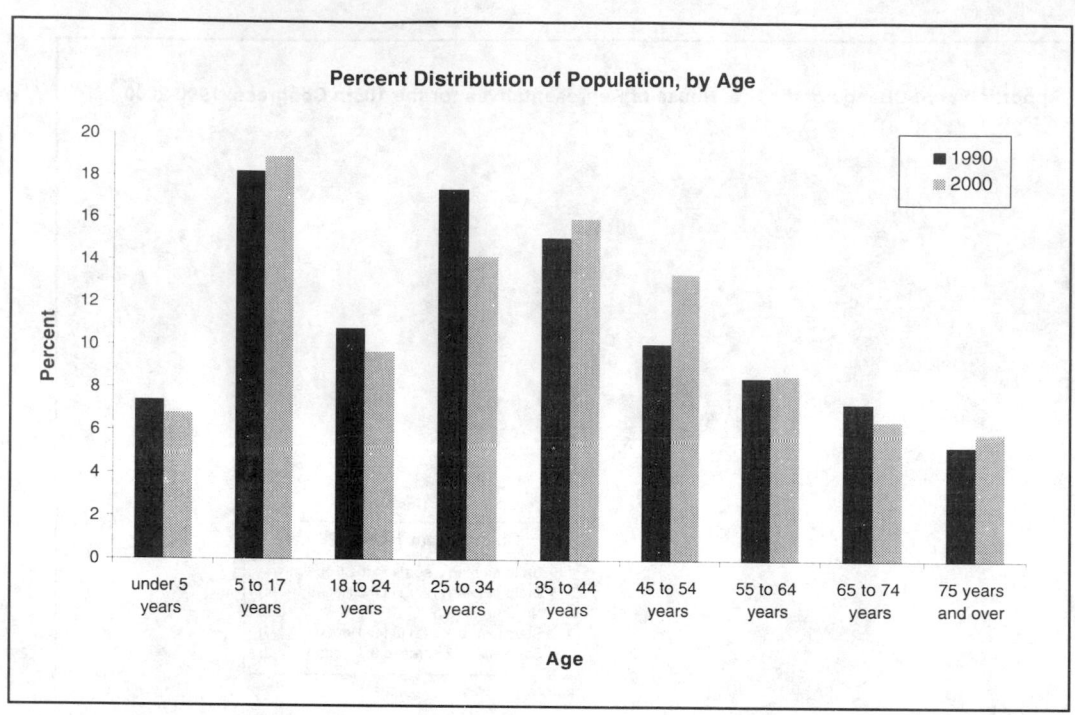

Percent Distribution of Population, by Age

While the majority of these large cities grew in the 1990's, St. Louis lost 12.2 percent of its population, and Baltimore lost 11.5 percent. Also losing more than 10 percent of their populations were Buffalo, NY and Norfolk, VA. Thirteen other large cities lost population in the 1990–2000 period. Large cities are not alone in losing population: about one out of five of the 1,238 U.S. cities with a population of 25,000 or more lost population between 1990 and 2000.

The largest proportionate increase among large cities was in Las Vegas, which grew by more than 85 percent during the decade. This 1990's growth is dwarfed by the percentage increase in many smaller cities, with such places as Gilbert, AZ (near Phoenix, with a 2000 population of 109,697), more than tripling during the 1990–2000 period. Similarly, Henderson, NV, near Las Vegas, nearly doubled in population. Some smaller cities tripled or quadrupled in population. Frisco and Cedar Park, TX, Fishers, IN, and Surprise, AZ had fewer than 10,000 people in 1990, but ten years later had grown to about 30,000.

Juneau, AK, is the nation's largest city in terms of land area, with over 7,000 square kilometers, an area 5.8 times the size of Los Angeles. Twenty cities in the U.S. have land area larger than New York City (which has a land area of about 785 square kilometers). Cities with very large land area tend to be in the West, but some cities with boundaries coextensive with their respective counties (such as the Nashville-Davidson consolidated city in Tennessee

or Indianapolis, IN) also have particularly large land areas. The median land area for all places of 25,000 or more was about 64 square kilometers.

The growth (or declining population) of the largest city in a **metropolitan area** may not correspond to the growth of the metropolitan statistical area (MSA) as a whole. While, for example, Detroit city lost 7.5 percent of its population during the decade, the metropolitan area grew by 4.1 percent between 1990 and 2000. The population of the city of Washington, DC, decreased by more than 5 percent while the metropolitan area as a whole grew by over 16 percent during this same period. It was, however, far from the fastest growing metropolitan area during the 1990's. That distinction went to Las Vegas, Nevada-Arizona MSA, whose population increased by 83 percent between 1990 and 2000. The Atlanta metropolitan area was the fastest growing among the largest 10 metropolitan areas; after dropping 7 percent in the 1980's, the city's population grew by nearly 6 percent in the 1990's, but the MSA as a whole had a population increase of 38.9 percent between 1990 and 2000.

However, 24 MSAs did lose population during the decade, representing about one of every thirteen metropolitan areas in the United States. As a group those experiencing population loss are geographically dispersed, and tend to be relatively small metropolitan areas, although they may have been metropolitan for decades. They include Pine Bluff, AR; Alexandria, LA; Binghamton, NY; and

Muncie, IN, as well as larger metropolitan areas such as Pittsburgh, PA, and Buffalo-Niagara Falls, NY. None of the MSAs that lost population between 1990 and 2000 were in the West region, and about two-thirds of them were in New York, Pennsylvania, and Ohio.

Increasing Diversity

The census measures ethnicity through two separate questions. The first is "Is this person Spanish/Hispanic/Latino?" and the second "What is this person's race?" These are separate questions, and Hispanic persons can be of any race. Other questions concerning ancestry, primary language, and citizenship were asked only on the long form questionnaire, results from which are not yet available and are not included in this volume.

Individuals can identify with more than one race. In the United States as a whole, 77.1 percent of the people were **white**, alone or in combination with other races; 12.9 percent were **black** alone or in combination; 4.2 percent were Asian; 1.5 percent **American Indian or Alaska Native**; .3 percent **Native Hawaiian or other Pacific Islander**; and 6.6 percent checked that they were "**some other race**". This adds to more than 100 percent because of the 2.4 percent of the population who identified with more than one race. The **Hispanic** population is 12.5 percent of the total.

In the 1990 census, each person was asked to select a single racial category. At that time, 80.3 percent considered themselves white, 12.1 percent black, less than 1 percent American Indian or Alaska Native, and 2.9 percent Asian or Pacific Islander. Nine percent were Hispanic. Though all groups increased in population during the 1990's, the white population increased less than the others, resulting in a smaller share of the total.

In fourteen **states**, more than 90 percent of the people were **white**. The highest proportions were the New England states of Vermont, Maine, and New Hampshire. In Hawaii and the District of Columbia, fewer than 40 percent of the people were white. About 300 **counties** are 99 percent white. Located in all regions, these counties tend to have small populations—many with fewer than 1000 people—with only two exceeding 50,000. In about 150 counties, fewer than half the people are white. Many of these are small counties in Alaska, Hawaii, and several states in the South and the Southwest, but they also include many large cities such as Philadelphia, St Louis, and the New York Boroughs of Brooklyn, Queens, and the Bronx.

More than half of the **black** population lived in the southern **states**. In nine states and the District of Columbia, 20 percent or more of the people were black alone or in combination, led by the District of Columbia with over 60 percent. In Jefferson and Claiborne **counties** in Mississippi, and Macon and Greene counties in Alabama, more than 80 percent of the people were black. In about a hundred counties, more than half of the people were black. These were mostly in the South and include large urban counties like the District of Columbia and its suburb Prince George's, MD; Baltimore City, MD; Orleans Parish, LA; (New Orleans); DeKalb, GA (Atlanta); and Shelby, TN (Memphis). More than 2000 counties had black populations of less than 5 percent, including such large counties as Maricopa, AZ (Phoenix); Middlesex, MA (near Boston); Bucks, PA (near Philadelphia); and Santa Clara, CA (San Jose). Among large **cities**, Gary, IN and Detroit, MI were more than 80 percent black, with ten of the 75 largest cities more than half black.

In New Mexico, 42.1 percent of the people were **Hispanic**, making it the **state** with the highest proportion of persons of Hispanic origin, followed by California and Texas, both about 32 percent, and together accounting for fully half of the nation's Hispanic population. Other states with Hispanic populations larger than the national average included the Southwestern states of Arizona, Nevada, and Colorado, as well as Florida, New York, and New Jersey. In about twenty counties, more than 80 percent of the people were Hispanic. Most of these counties were in Texas, and most were near the Mexican border. Starr county tops the list with a 97.5 percent Hispanic population. Several are populous metropolitan counties such as Webb (Laredo), Hidalgo (McAllen), Cameron (Brownsville), and El Paso. Other big cities with large Hispanic populations include Hialeah and Miami in Florida, and several California cities, such as Santa Ana, Anaheim, and Los Angeles. Nearly half (46.5 percent) of the population of Los Angeles is Hispanic. In more than 800 counties, fewer than one percent of the people are Hispanic. These counties are in all regions, but most are in the Midwest, the Northeast and the South.

Under the new option to list more than one race, 2.4 percent of the national population identified with two or more races. However, in Hawaii, 21.4 percent were multiracial, with Alaska a distant second at 5.4 percent. Only 14 states were above the national level of 2.4 percent. Hawaii is the only state with more than 1 percent in the category "Native Hawaiian and Other Pacific Islander" (alone or in combination), 23.3 percent of Hawaii's population.

Another 58 percent in Hawaii were **Asian**, alone or in combination, making Hawaii by far the state with the highest proportion of Asians. Nationally, 4.2 percent marked this category, while California's population was 12.3 percent Asian, and seven more states were above the national average (Washington, New York, New Jersey, Nevada, Alaska, Maryland, and Virginia.) Hawaii's four major counties top the list of counties, with about half or more of their populations checking Asian, alone or in combination. In four large counties in central California—San Francisco, Santa Clara (San Jose), Alameda, and San Mateo—more than one-fifth of the people are Asian, alone or in combination with another race. About 30 counties had populations comprising 10 percent or more Asian people, most of them large urban counties in California, Virginia, and New Jersey.

Nationally, fewer than 1 percent of the population indicated that they were American Indian or Alaska Native. Of the states, Alaska has the largest proportion of native peoples at 15.6 percent. New Mexico, South Dakota, Oklahoma, Montana, Arizona, and North Dakota have between 5 and 10 percent in this group. In 25 counties, at least half of the people are American Indian or Alaska Native, led by Shannon county, SD and Wade Hampton census area in Alaska, both with 95 percent. The group included ten additional counties in the Dakotas and eight in Alaska. Most of these counties had fewer than 10,000 people, but Apache, AZ and McKinley, NM had more than 50,000 people each, with more than three-quarters of their populations American Indian. Among the 75 largest cities, 7.3 percent of the people in Anchorage, AK and 4.8 percent of the people in Tulsa, OK were American Indian or Alaska Native. Flagstaff, AZ-UT is the metropolitan area with the largest American Indian or Alaska Native population, at 27 percent.

An Older Population

In 2000, the median age of the United States population was 35.3, up from 32.9 in 1990. This means that half of the population was older, and half younger. The proportion of people under 18 was about the same in 2000 (25.7 percent) as it was in 1990 (25.6 percent), and the proportion 65 and over was about the same (12.4 in 2000 versus 12.6 in 1990). But large increases in the proportions in the 35- to 54-year-old age groups, coupled with decreases in the proportion aged 18 to 34, increased the median age of the population.

West Virginia had the oldest population, with a median age of 38.9, while Utah had the youngest at 27.1. Utah also had the highest proportion of children under 18 (32.2 percent) with West Virginia having the lowest proportion, except for the District of Columbia, where children under 18 made up only 20 percent of the population, compared with the national level of 25.7. However, the District of Columbia's median age was only 34.6, below the national level of 35.3, because of its high proportion of working age people (46.3 percent)—third after Alaska and Colorado in the percentage aged 25 to 54. Florida had the highest proportion (17.6) of persons aged 65 and over.

Among large counties, five had populations with more than 30 percent under 18: San Bernardino, Fresno, and Riverside, CA; El Paso, TX; and Salt Lake, UT. The metropolitan area with the largest percentage of children under 18 was Laredo, TX with 36.2 percent. San Francisco and New York counties, with very few children, ranked highest in the working age population aged 25 to 54, followed closely by Fairfax county, VA at 50 percent. Fairfax county's proportion of children under 18 (25.4 percent) is only slightly lower than the national average, but its population aged 65 and over was only 7.9 percent, well below the national level of 12.4 percent. Two Florida counties, Palm Beach and Pinellas, had populations with more than 20 percent aged 65 and over. Other large counties that exceeded the national level of the elderly population were located in all regions, but more likely to be in the Northeast, like Allegheny, PA (Pittsburgh), and Erie, NY (Buffalo).

With just over half of its population in the 25-to-54 age group, the San Francisco metropolitan area had the highest proportion in this group. Several other metropolitan areas followed closely: Atlanta, Anchorage, Seattle-Bellevue-Everett, Boulder-Longmont, Denver, San Jose, and Washington, DC. Nine metropolitan areas in Florida, and Barnstable-Yarmouth, MA (Cape Cod) had 20 percent of more of their residents aged 65 and over, with more than a third of the population of Punta Gorda, FL MSA in this older age group.

Our Homes and Families

Most of the people in the United States live in households (97.2 percent). Of the more than 105 million households in the United States, more than two-thirds are family households—people related by birth, marriage, or adoption. The one-third that are nonfamily households are persons living alone or with nonrelatives. The 2.8 percent of people who do not live in households live in group quarters, either institutions or noninstitutional group quarters, such as college dormitories or military barracks.

More than half of all households are family households headed by a married couple, ranging from 63.2 percent of the households in Utah to 22.8 percent of the households in the District of Columbia, where nearly 44 percent of the households consist of a person living alone. Among large counties, the highest proportions of married-couple households are in suburban counties near our largest cities: Nassau (63.1 percent) and Suffolk (62.0) counties (near New York); DuPage, IL (near Chicago, 60.9 percent); Ventura, CA (near Los Angeles, 59.5 percent): and Fairfax, VA (near Washington, DC, 59.4 percent). Low proportions of married-couple family households occur in central city counties such as New York (25.2 percent), Suffolk, MA (Boston, 29.3 percent), and San Francisco (31.6), the three counties that top the list for persons living alone. Fully 48 percent of the households in New York county (Manhattan) are single-person households. Also showing a high proportion of single-person households is Pinellas county, FL, which ranked high on its population aged 65 and over. Female headed family households make up more than 20 percent of households in Bronx and Kings (Brooklyn), NY, Philadelphia, PA, Wayne, MI (Detroit), Essex, NJ, and Shelby, TN (Memphis).

Two-thirds of American households own their own homes, with the highest levels of homeownership in West Virginia, Minnesota, Michigan, and Alabama, and the lowest in the District of Columbia, New York, Hawaii, and California. Among large counties, homeownership is highest in suburban counties of large cities topped by Nassau and Suffolk, NY at about 80 percent, followed closely by Macomb and Oakland, MI, near Detroit, and DuPage, IL, near Chicago. Several of the smaller metropolitan areas in Florida have high homeownership rates, led by Punta Gorda at 83.7 percent. Of the 75 largest cities, only Mesa, AZ has a proportion of homeowners equal to the national level of 66 percent. Of the ten largest cities, only Phoenix, Philadelphia, and San Antonio have homeownership rates of more than half of their households.

Some local areas have very specialized housing patterns. Only 2.8 percent of the population live in group quarters, but there are 30 counties where more than 20 percent of the people live in group quarters. The highest levels (more than 40 percent) are in the Aleutians census areas in Alaska, a sparsely populated area with a large fishing industry. More than 30 percent of people in Williamsburg and Lexington cities (VA) live in college dormitories. In Georgia, almost one-third of the people in Chattahoochee county live in military quarters, and there are 18 counties—half of them in Texas—where more than 20 percent of the people reside in correctional institutions. Among the largest cities, several have multiple colleges and universities, resulting in more than 3 percent of their populations living in dormitories: Raleigh, Pittsburgh, Baton Rouge, Boston, Washington, and Atlanta.

Some housing units are used only occasionally for recreational or seasonal use. In the 3 New England states of Maine, Vermont, and New Hampshire, more than 10 percent of housing units fall into this category. In about 20 counties, more than half of the housing units are for seasonal use, such as the mountain counties of Forest, PA, Hamilton, NY, Daggett, UT, Hinsdale, CO, and Alpine, CA; the island counties of Nantucket and Dukes (Martha's Vineyard), MA; and the lake counties of Lake and Keweenaw, MI and Vilas, WI. Mesa, AZ is the only large city with as many as 10 percent of its housing units held for seasonal use, but the year-round population growth in resort areas has resulted in four small metropolitan areas where more than 20 percent of the housing units are for seasonal use: Barnstable-Yarmouth, MA (Cape Cod) with 32 percent; Atlantic-Cape May, NJ (26.7 percent); Naples, FL (23.8 percent); and Myrtle Beach, SC (20.4 percent).

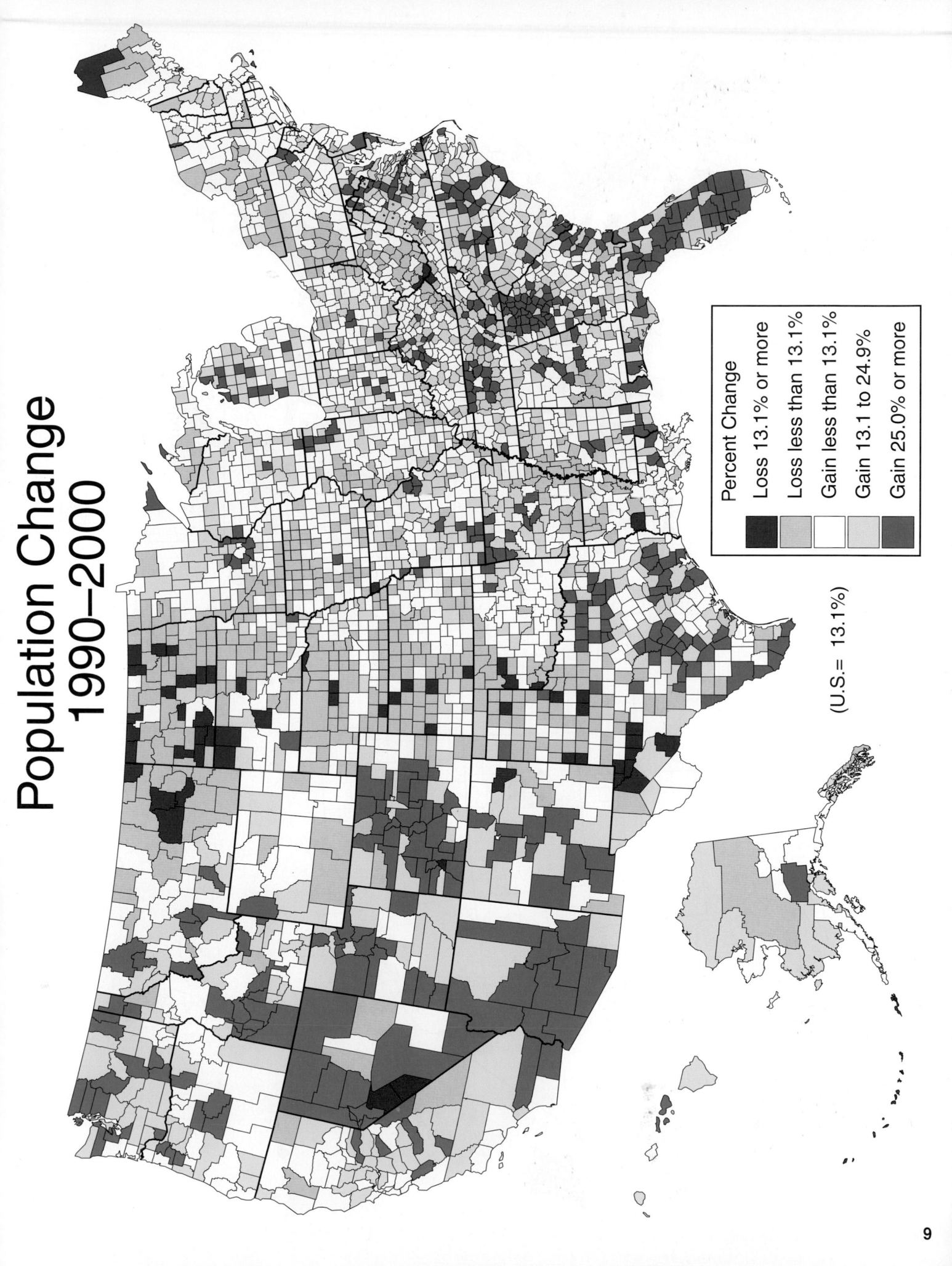

Population Change
1990–2000

Percent Change

Loss 13.1% or more
Loss less than 13.1%
Gain less than 13.1%
Gain 13.1 to 24.9%
Gain 25.0% or more

(U.S.= 13.1%)

9

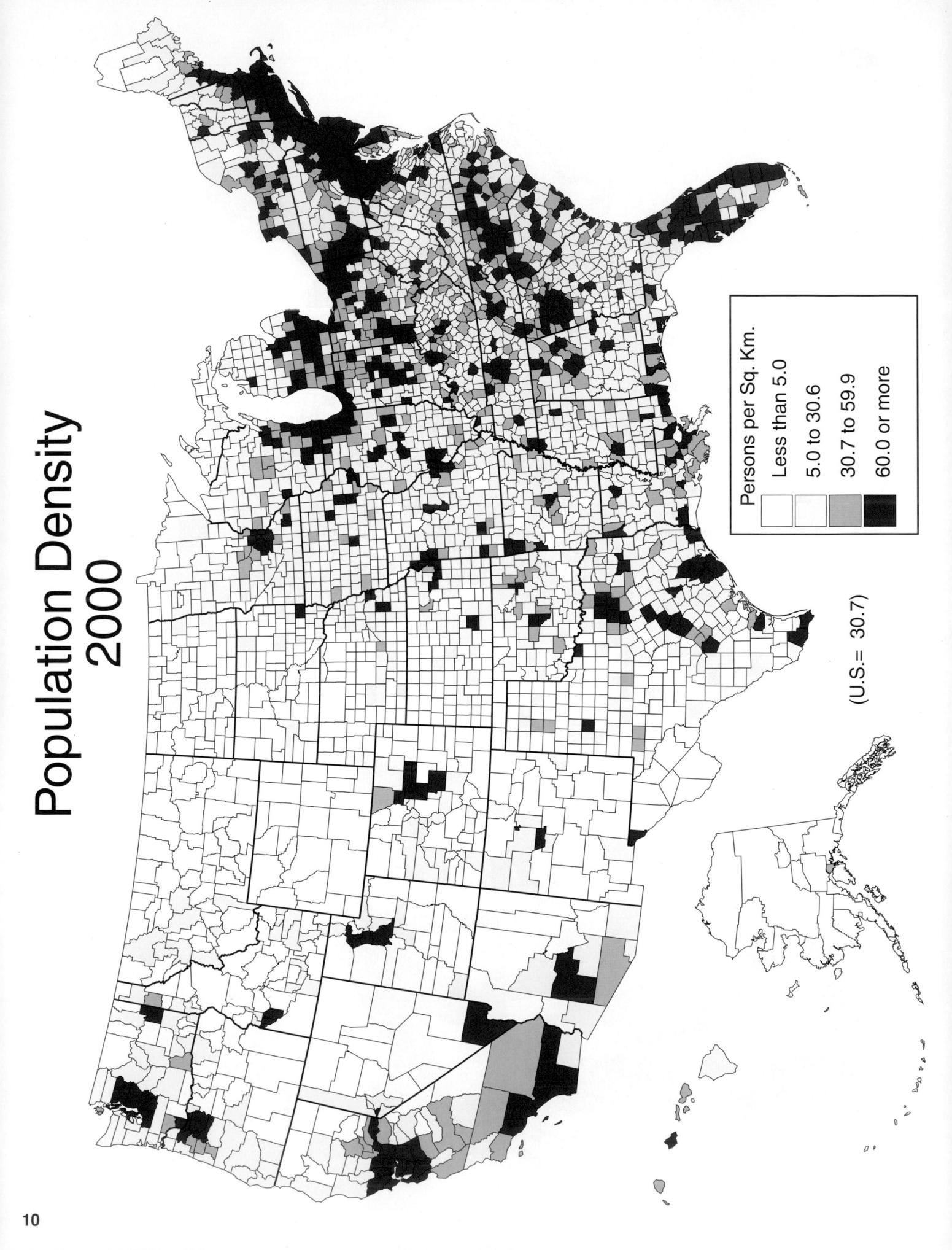

Population Density
2000

Persons per Sq. Km.

Less than 5.0

5.0 to 30.6

30.7 to 59.9

60.0 or more

(U.S. = 30.7)

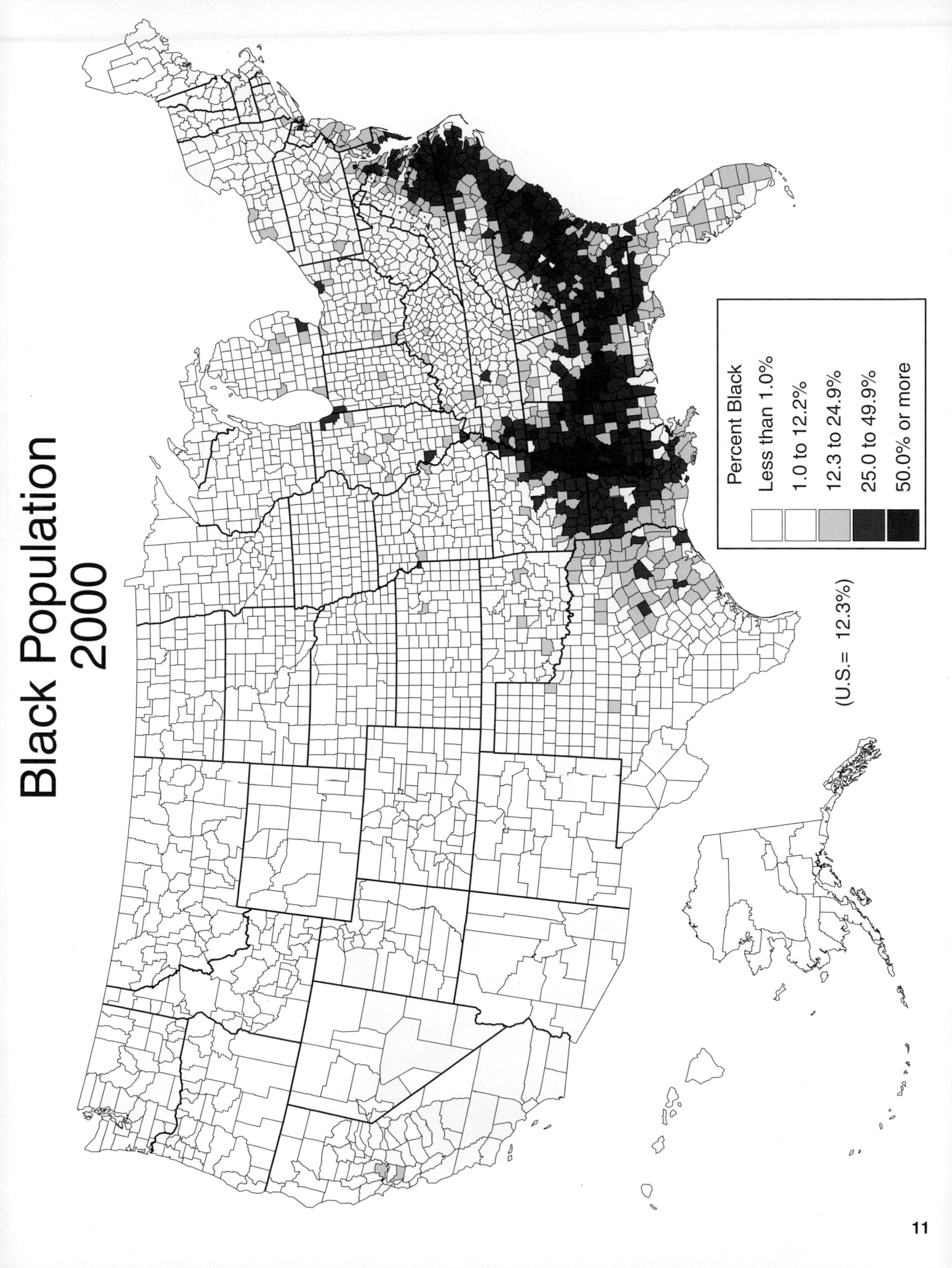

Black Population
2000

Percent Black

Less than 1.0%
1.0 to 12.2%
12.3 to 24.9%
25.0 to 49.9%
50.0% or more

(U.S.= 12.3%)

11

Hispanic Population 2000

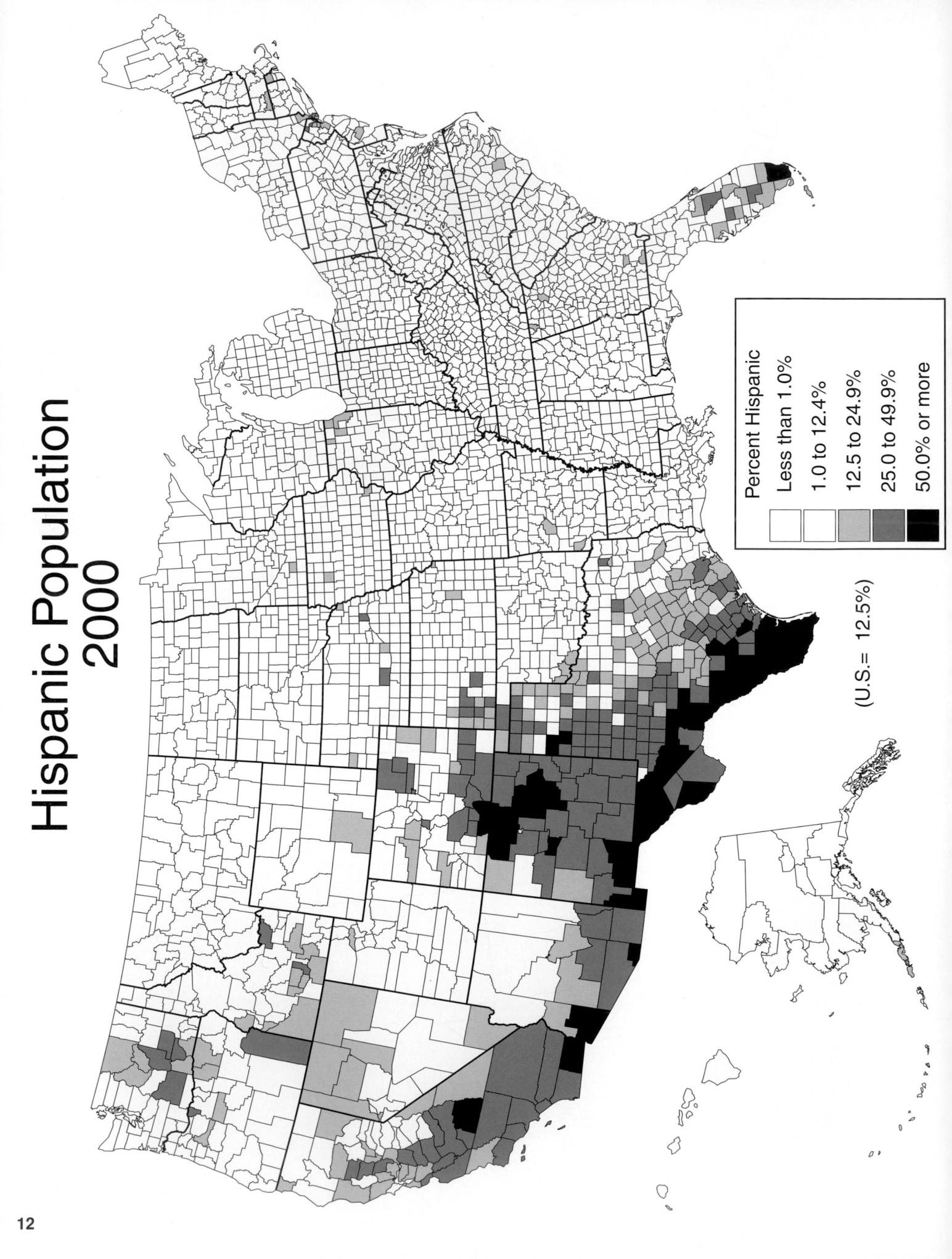

Percent Hispanic

Less than 1.0%
1.0 to 12.4%
12.5 to 24.9%
25.0 to 49.9%
50.0% or more

(U.S.= 12.5%)

Population Under 18 Years Old
2000

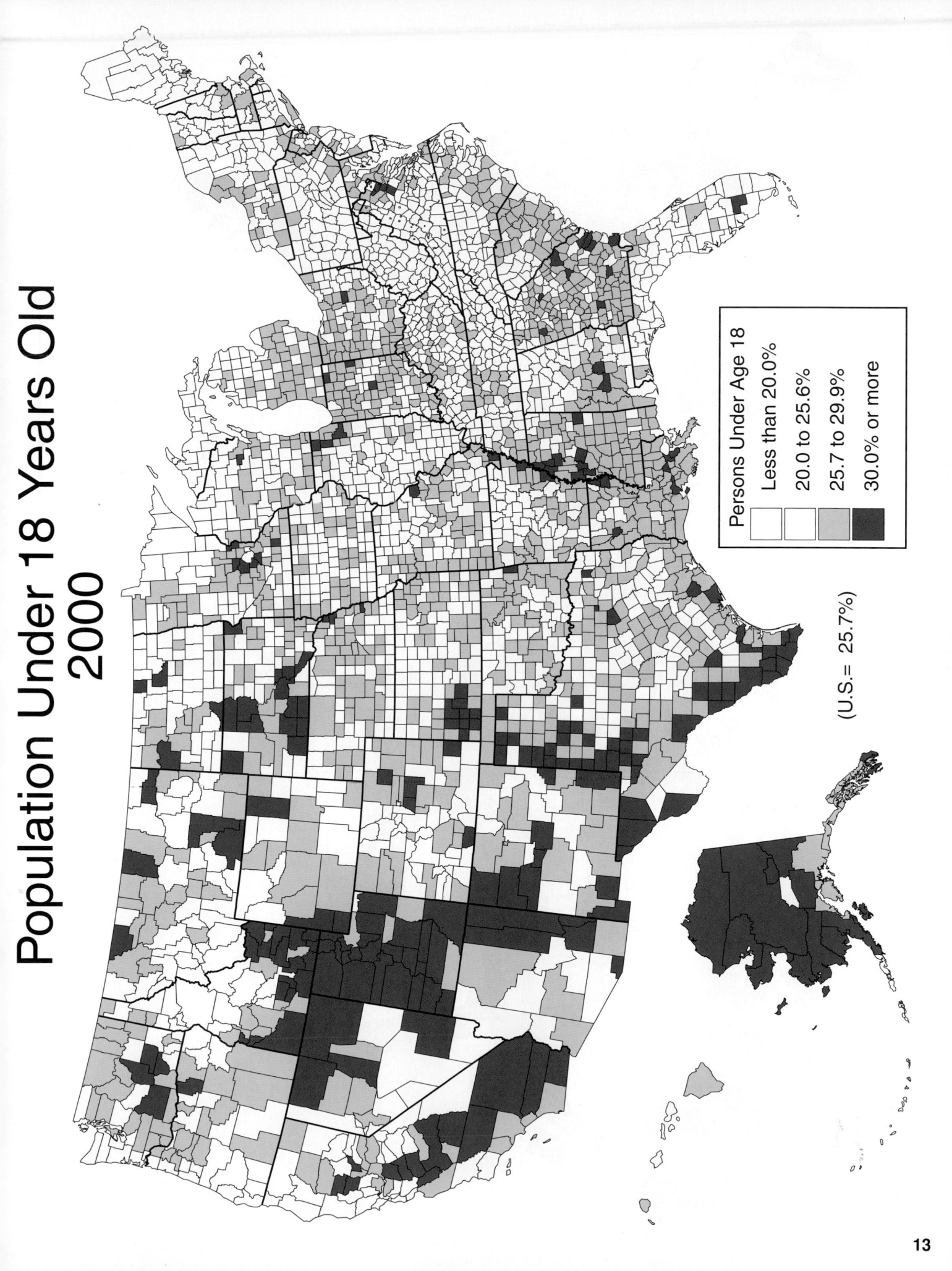

Persons Under Age 18

Less than 20.0%

20.0 to 25.6%

25.7 to 29.9%

30.0% or more

(U.S. = 25.7%)

Population 65 Years and Older
2000

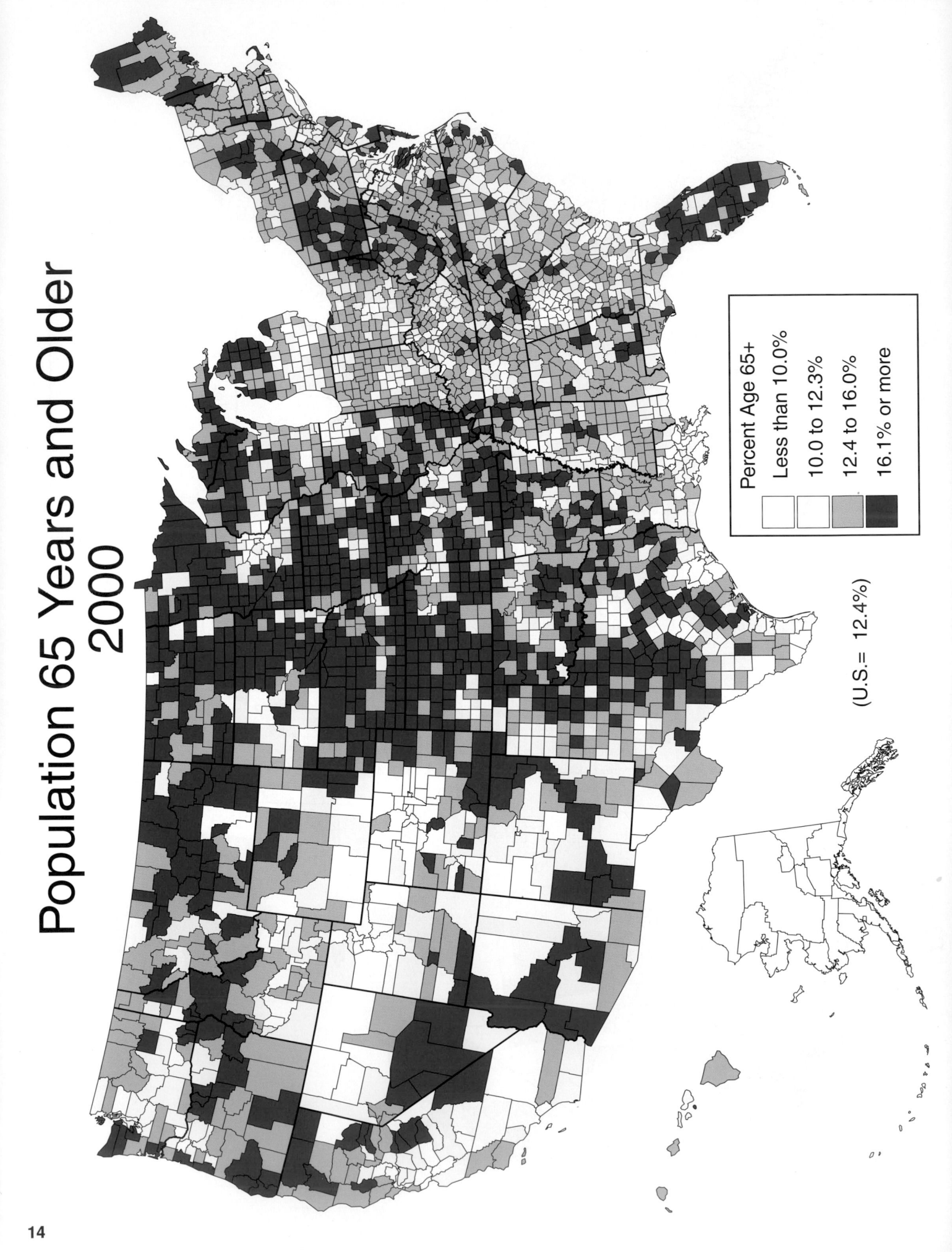

Percent Age 65+

Less than 10.0%
10.0 to 12.3%
12.4 to 16.0%
16.1% or more

(U.S. = 12.4%)

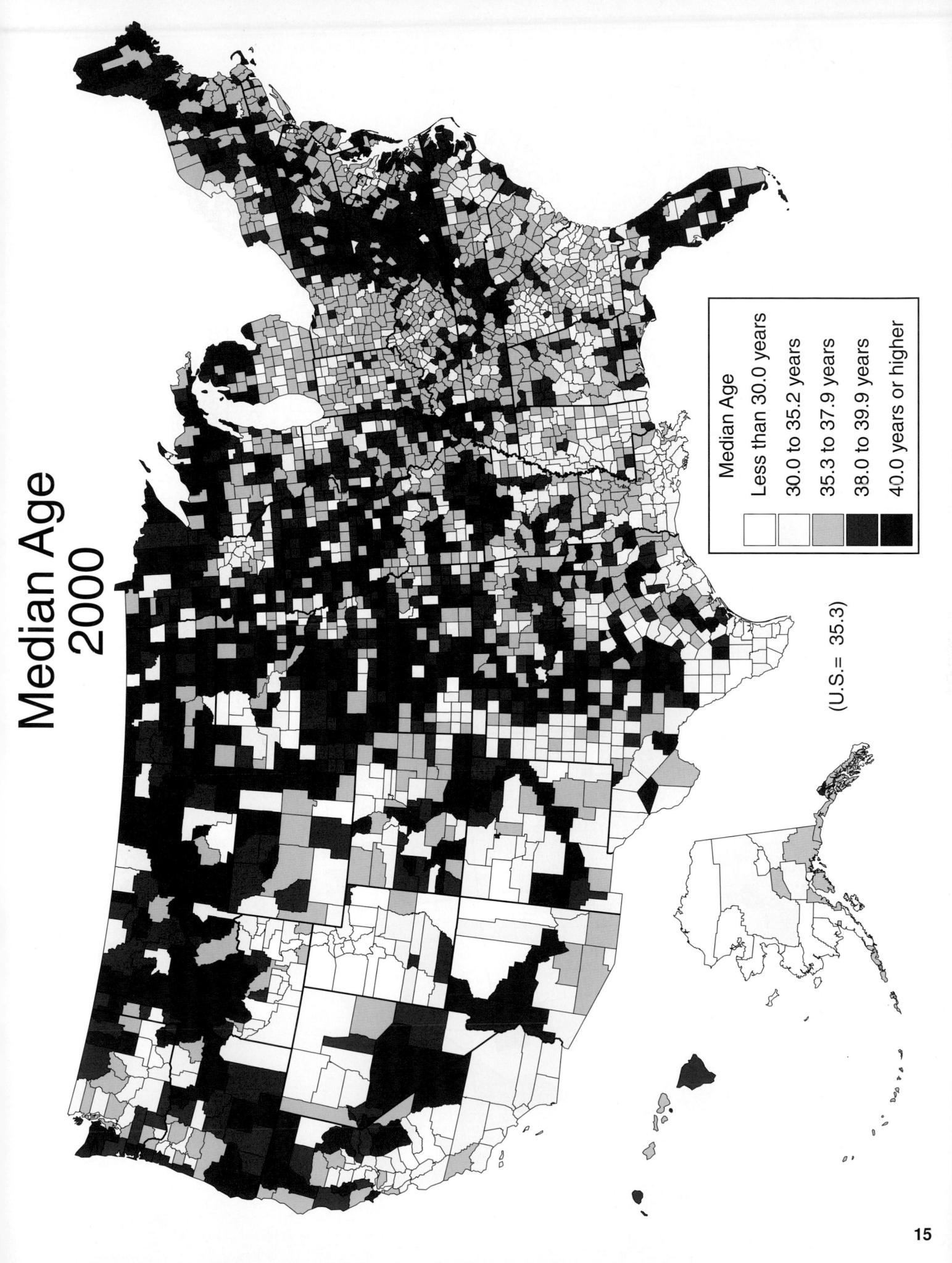

Median Age
2000

Median Age

Less than 30.0 years
30.0 to 35.2 years
35.3 to 37.9 years
38.0 to 39.9 years
40.0 years or higher

(U.S.= 35.3)

15

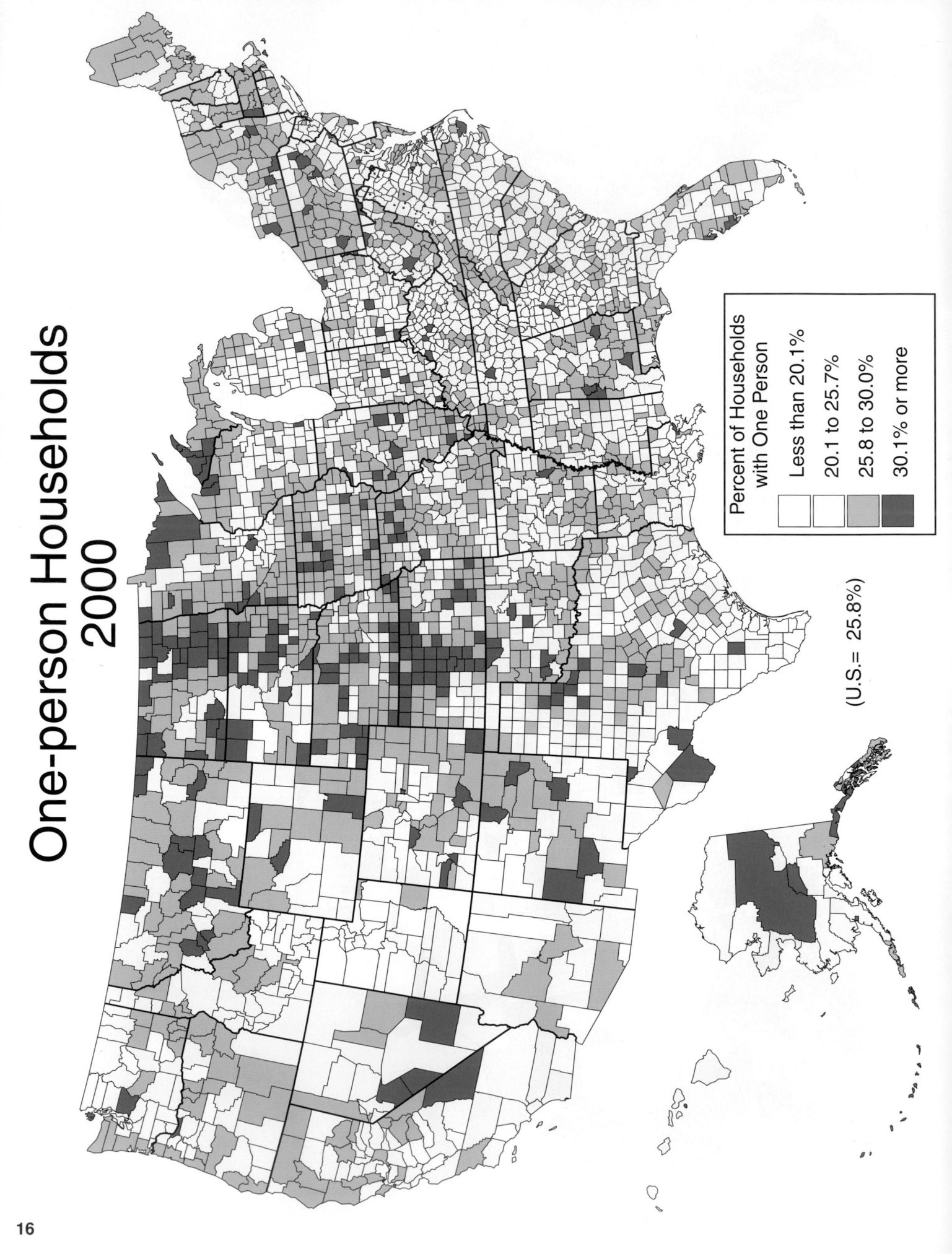

One-person Households
2000

Percent of Households
with One Person

Less than 20.1%

20.1 to 25.7%

25.8 to 30.0%

30.1% or more

(U.S. = 25.8%)

16

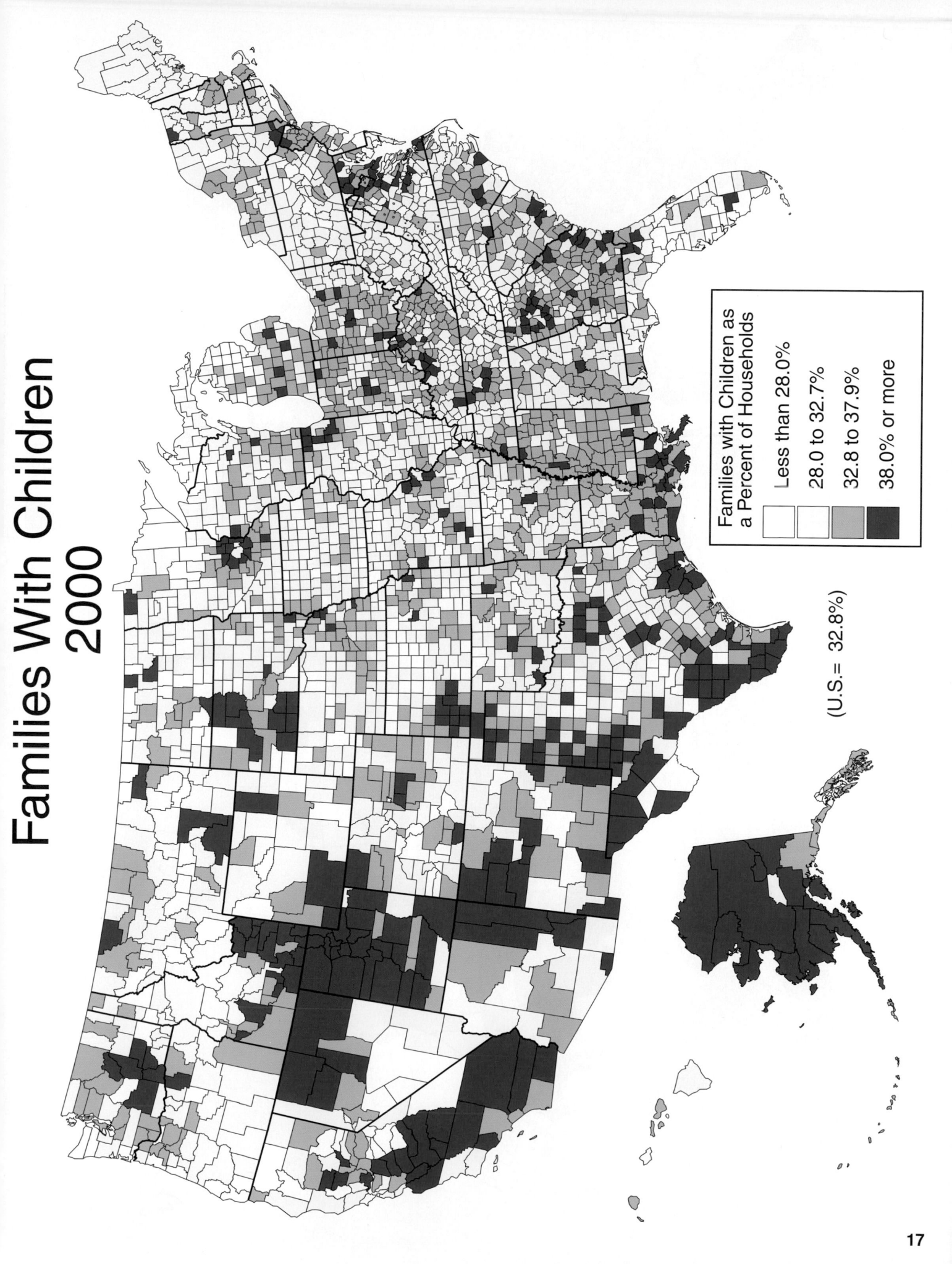

Families With Children
2000

Families with Children as
a Percent of Households

Less than 28.0%

28.0 to 32.7%

32.8 to 37.9%

38.0% or more

(U.S.= 32.8%)

17

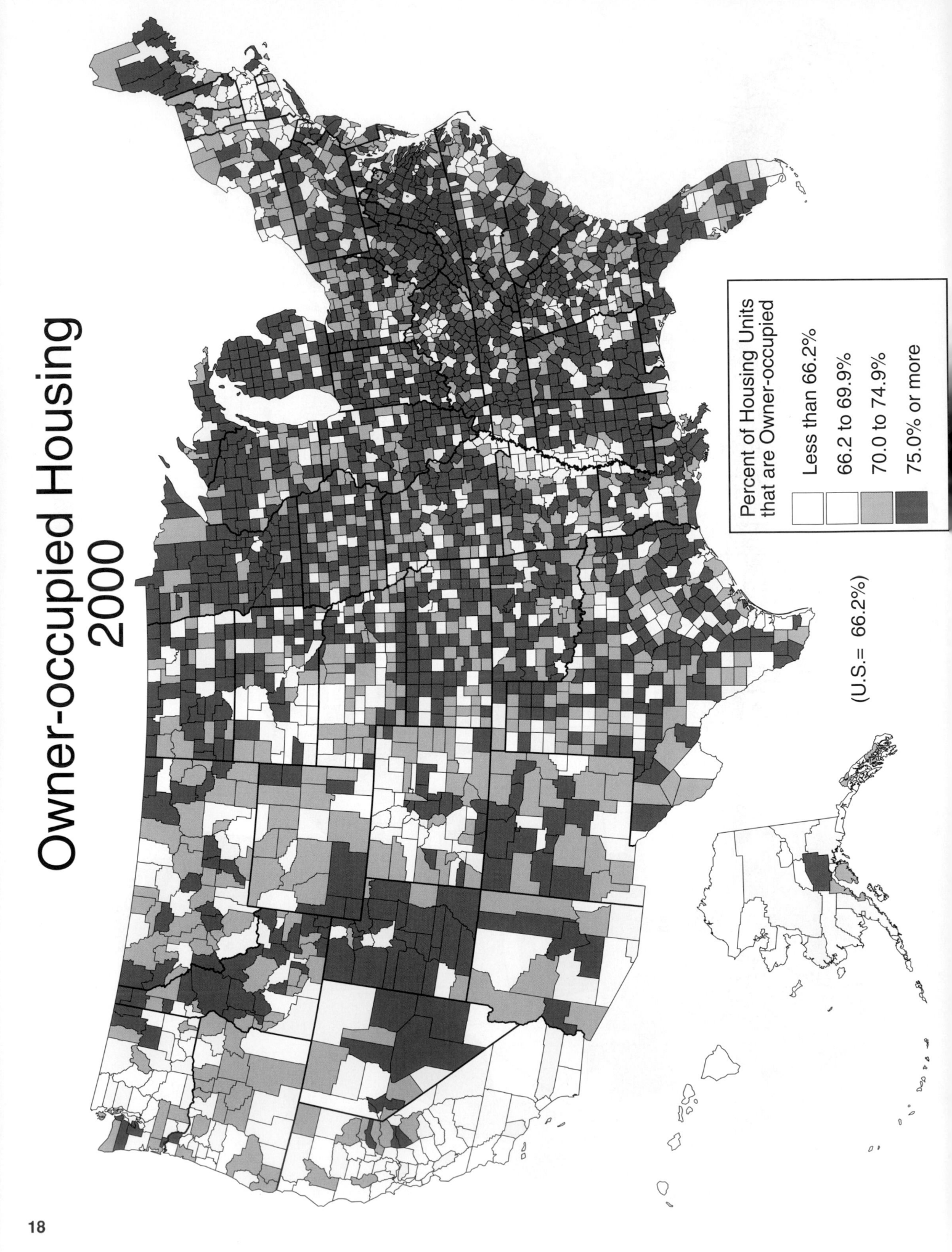

Owner-occupied Housing
2000

Percent of Housing Units
that are Owner-occupied

Less than 66.2%

66.2 to 69.9%

70.0 to 74.9%

75.0% or more

(U.S.= 66.2%)

18

Housing for Seasonal, Recreational, or Occasional Use
2000

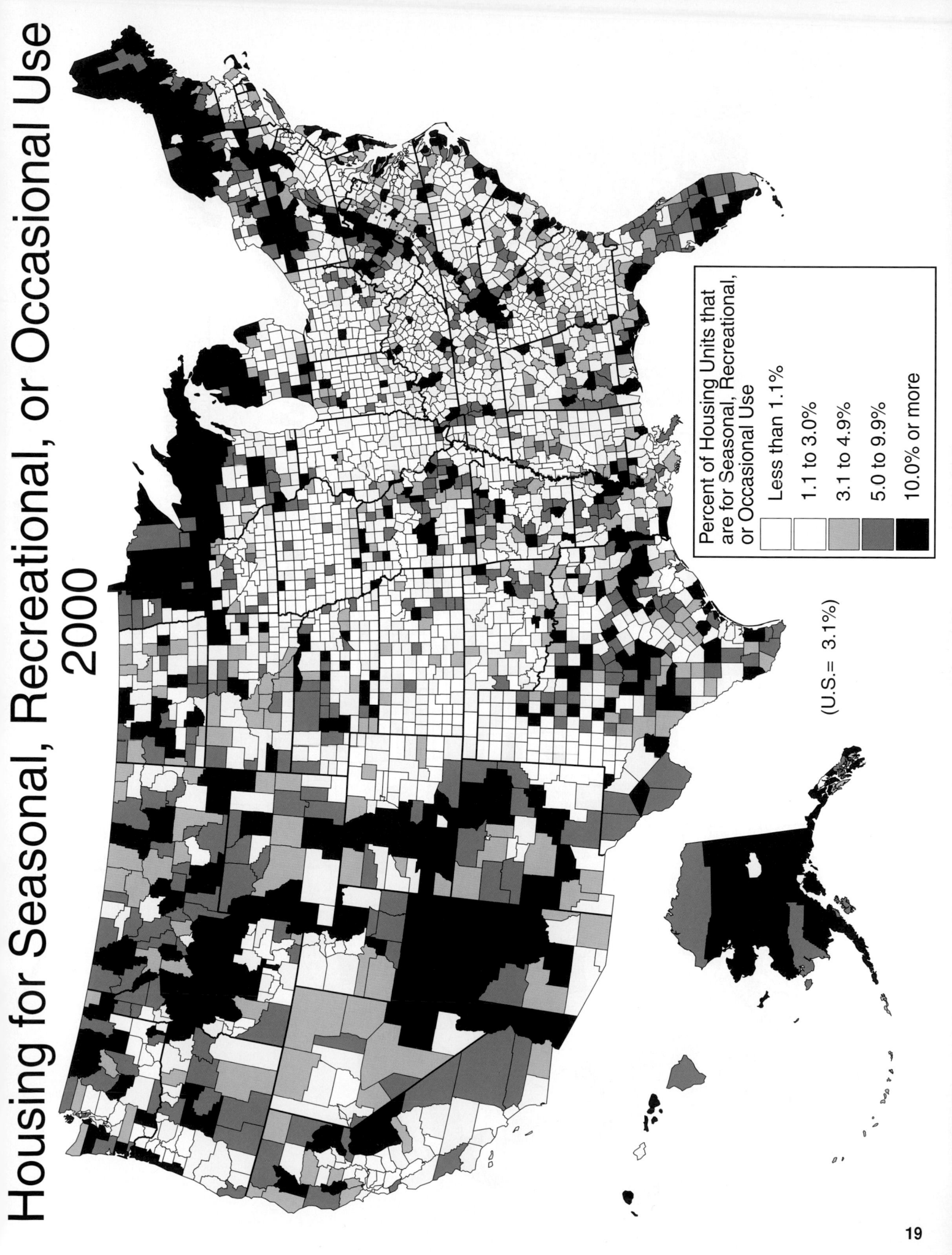

Percent of Housing Units that are for Seasonal, Recreational, or Occasional Use

Less than 1.1%

1.1 to 3.0%

3.1 to 4.9%

5.0 to 9.9%

10.0% or more

(U.S.= 3.1%)

Persons in Group Quarters
2000

Percent of Persons who
Live in Group Quarters

- Less than 1.1%
- 1.1 to 2.7%
- 2.8 to 4.9%
- 5.0% or more

(U.S. = 2.8%)

Area Rankings

Page

Table 1

25   States and the District of Columbia Selected Rankings

25   Population 2,000
25   Total Land Area (Square Kilometers), 2000
25   Population Density (per Square Kilometer), 2000
26   Percent Population Change, 1990-2000
26   Percent White 2000
26   Percent Black 2000
27   Percent American Indian and Alaska Native, 2000
27   Percent Asian, 2000
27   Percent Hispanic, 2000
28   Percent under 18 Years, 2000
28   Percent Age 25 to 54 Years, 2000
28   Percent Age 65 Years and Over, 2000
29   Percent Female-headed Family Households, 2000
29   Percent Living Alone, 2000
29   Percent Married Couple Family Households, 2000
30   Percent of Families with Own Children Under 18 Years, 2000
30   Percent Owner Occupied Housing Units
30   Percent Recreational/Seasonal Housing Units

Table 2

31   75 Largest Counties by 2000 Population Selected Rankings

31   Total Persons, 2000
31   Land Area (Square Kilometers), 2000
31   Population Density (per Square Kilometer), 1999
32   Percent Population Change: 1990-2000
32   Percent White, 2000
32   Percent Black, 2000
33   Percent American Indian and Alaska Native, 2000
33   Percent Asian, 2000
33   Percent Hispanic, 2000
34   Percent Under 18 Years, 2000
34   Percent Age 25 to 54 Years, 2000
34   Percent Age 65 Years and Over, 2000
35   Percent Female-headed Family Households, 2000
35   Percent Living Alone, 2000
35   Percent Married Couple Family Households, 2000
36   Percent of Families with Own Children Under 18 Years, 2000
36   Percent Owner Occupied Housing Units, 2000
36   Percent Recreational/Seasonal Housing Units, 2000

Area Rankings

Page

Table 3

37   All Counties

37   Total Persons, 2000
37   Land Area (Square Kilometers), 2000
37   Population Density (per Square Kilometers), 2000
38   Percent Population Change, 1999-2000
38   Percent White, 2000
38   Percent Black, 2000
39   Percent American Indian and Alaska Native, 2000
39   Percent Asian, 2000
39   Percent Two or More Races, 2000
40   Percent Hispanic, 2000
40   Percent Under 18 Years, 2000
40   Percent Age 25 to 54 Years, 2000
41   Percent Age 65 Years and Over, 2000
41   Percent Female-headed Family Households, 2000
41   Percent Living Alone, 2000
42   Percent Married Couple Family Households, 2000
42   Percent of Families with Own Children Under 18 Years, 2000
42   Percent Change in Households, 1990-2000
43   Percent in Group Quarters, 2000
43   Percent in Dormitories, 2000
43   Percent Owner Occupied Housing Units, 2000
44   Percent Recreational/Seasonal Housing Units, 2000
44   Homeowner Vacancy Rate, 2000
44   Renter Vacancy Rate, 2000

Table 4

45   75 Largest Metropolitan Areas by 2000 Population

45   Total Persons, 2000
45   Land Area (Square Kilometers), 2000
46   Population Density (per Square Kilometer), 2000
46   Percent Population Change, 1990-2000
47   Percent White, 2000
47   Percent Black, 2000
48   Percent American Indian and Alaska Native, 2000
48   Percent Asian, 2000
49   Percent Hispanic, 2000
49   Percent Under 18 Years, 2000
50   Percent Age 25 to 54 Years, 2000
50   Percent Age 65 Years and Over, 2000
51   Percent Female-headed Family Households, 2000
51   Percent Living Alone, 2000
52   Percent Married Couple Family Households, 2000
52   Percent of Families with Own Children Under 18, 2000
53   Percent Owner Occupied Housing Units, 2000

Area Rankings

Page

53   Percent Recreational/Seasonal Housing Units, 2000

Table 5
54   All Metropolitan Areas

54   Total Persons, 2000
54   Land Area (Square Kilometers), 2000
55   Population Density (per Square Kilometer), 2000
55   Percent Population Change, 1990-2000
56   Percent White, 2000
56   Percent Black
57   Percent American Indian and Alaska Native, 2000
57   Percent Asian, 2000
58   Percent Two or More Races, 2000
58   Percent Hispanic, 2000
59   Percent Under 18 Years, 2000
59   Percent Age 25 to 54 Years, 2000
60   Percent Age 65 Years and Over, 2000
60   Percent Female-headed Family Households, 2000
61   Percent Living Alone, 2000
61   Percent Married Couple Family Households, 2000
62   Percent of Families with Own Children Under 18, 2000
62   Percent Change in Households, 1990-2000
63   Percent in Group Quarters, 2000
63   Percent in Dormitories, 2000
64   Percent Owner Occupied Housing Units, 2000
64   Percent Recreational/Seasonal Housing Units, 2000
65   Homeowner Vacancy Rate, 2000
65   Renter Vacancy Rate, 2000

Table 6
66   75 Largest Cities by 2000 Population

66   Total Persons, 2000
66   Land Area (Square Kilometers), 2000
66   Population Density (per Square Kilometer), 2000
67   Percent Population Change, 1990-2000
67   Percent White, 2000
67   Percent Black, 2000
68   Percent American Indian and Alaska Native, 2000
68   Percent Asian, 2000
68   Percent Two or More Races, 2000
69   Percent Hispanic, 2000
69   Percent Under 18 Years, 2000
69   Percent Age 25 to 54 Years, 2000
70   Percent Age 65 Years and Over, 2000
70   Percent Female-headed Family Households, 2000

Area Rankings

Page

70	Percent Living Alone, 2000
71	Percent Married Couple Family Households, 2000
71	Percent of Families with Own Children Under 18 Years, 2000
71	Percent Change in Households, 1990-2000
72	Percent in Group Quarters, 2000
72	Percent in Dormitories, 2000
72	Percent Owner Occupied Housing Units, 2000
73	Percent Recreational/Seasonal Housing Units, 2000
73	Homeowner Vacancy Rate, 2000
73	Renter Vacancy Rate, 2000

Table 7

74	Congressional Districts of the 107th Congress
74	Largest Population, 2000
74	Largest Total Land Area, 2000 (Square Kilometers)
74	Population Density, 2000 (Per Square Kilometer)
75	Percent Population Change, 2000
75	Highest Percent White, 2000
75	Highest Percent Black, 2000
76	Highest Percent American Indian and Alaska Native, 2000
76	Highest Percent Asian Population, 2000
76	Percent Two or More Races, 2000
77	Highest Percent Hispanic, 2000
77	Highest Percent Under 18 Years, 2000
77	Highest Percent Age 25 to 54 Years, 2000
78	Highest Percent Age 65 Years and Over, 2000
78	Highest Percent of Households with Female Householder, 2000
78	Highest Percent Living Alone, 2000
79	Highest Percent Married Couple Family Households, 2000
79	Highest Percent of Families with Own Children Under 18 Years, 2000
79	Highest Percent Change in Households, 1990-2000
80	Highest Percent in Group Quarters, 2000
80	Highest Percent in Dormitories, 2000
80	Highest Percent Owner Occupied Housing Units, 2000
81	Highest Percent Recreational/Seasonal Housing Units, 2000
81	Highest Homeowner Vacancy Rate, 2000
81	Highest Renter Vacancy Rate, 2000

TABLE 1—States and the District of Columbia
Selected Rankings

_	Population, 2000	_	_	_	Total Land Area (Square Kilometers), 2000	_	_	_	Population Density (per Square Kilometer), 2000	_
Popu-lation Rank	State	[col 2] Population	Popu-lation Rank	Land Area Rank	State	[col 1] Land Area	Popu-lation Rank	Density Rank	State	[col 4] Density
X	United States	281 421 906	X	X	United States	9 161 924	X	X	United States	30.7
1	California	33 871 648	48	1	Alaska	1 481 347	50	1	District of Columbia	3 597.9
2	Texas	20 851 820	2	2	Texas	678 051	9	2	New Jersey	438.0
3	New York	18 976 457	1	3	California	403 933	43	3	Rhode Island	387.4
4	Florida	15 982 378	44	4	Montana	376 979	13	4	Massachusetts	312.7
5	Illinois	12 419 293	36	5	New Mexico	314 309	29	5	Connecticut	271.4
6	Pennsylvania	12 281 054	20	6	Arizona	294 312	19	6	Maryland	209.2
7	Ohio	11 353 140	35	7	Nevada	284 448	3	7	New York	155.2
8	Michigan	9 938 444	24	8	Colorado	268 627	45	8	Delaware	154.9
9	New Jersey	8 414 350	51	9	Wyoming	251 489	4	9	Florida	114.4
10	Georgia	8 186 453	28	10	Oregon	248 631	7	10	Ohio	107.0
11	North Carolina	8 049 313	39	11	Idaho	214 314	6	11	Pennsylvania	105.8
12	Virginia	7 078 515	34	12	Utah	212 751	5	12	Illinois	86.3
13	Massachusetts	6 349 097	32	13	Kansas	211 900	1	13	California	83.9
14	Indiana	6 080 485	21	14	Minnesota	206 189	42	14	Hawaii	72.8
15	Washington	5 894 121	38	15	Nebraska	199 099	12	15	Virginia	69.0
16	Tennessee	5 689 283	46	16	South Dakota	196 540	8	16	Michigan	67.6
17	Missouri	5 595 211	47	17	North Dakota	178 647	14	17	Indiana	65.5
18	Wisconsin	5 363 675	17	18	Missouri	178 414	11	18	North Carolina	63.8
19	Maryland	5 296 486	27	19	Oklahoma	177 847	10	19	Georgia	54.6
20	Arizona	5 130 632	15	20	Washington	172 348	16	20	Tennessee	53.3
21	Minnesota	4 919 479	10	21	Georgia	149 976	41	21	New Hampshire	53.2
22	Louisiana	4 468 976	8	22	Michigan	147 121	26	22	South Carolina	51.4
23	Alabama	4 447 100	30	23	Iowa	144 701	22	23	Louisiana	39.6
24	Colorado	4 301 261	5	24	Illinois	143 961	25	24	Kentucky	39.3
25	Kentucky	4 041 769	18	25	Wisconsin	140 663	18	25	Wisconsin	38.1
26	South Carolina	4 012 012	4	26	Florida	139 670	15	26	Washington	34.2
27	Oklahoma	3 450 654	33	27	Arkansas	134 856	23	27	Alabama	33.8
28	Oregon	3 421 399	23	28	Alabama	131 426	17	28	Missouri	31.4
29	Connecticut	3 405 565	11	29	North Carolina	126 161	2	29	Texas	30.8
30	Iowa	2 926 324	3	30	New York	122 283	37	30	West Virginia	29.0
31	Mississippi	2 844 658	31	31	Mississippi	121 488	49	31	Vermont	25.4
32	Kansas	2 688 418	6	32	Pennsylvania	116 074	21	32	Minnesota	23.9
33	Arkansas	2 673 400	22	33	Louisiana	112 825	31	33	Mississippi	23.4
34	Utah	2 233 169	16	34	Tennessee	106 752	30	34	Iowa	20.2
35	Nevada	1 998 257	7	35	Ohio	106 056	33	35	Arkansas	19.8
36	New Mexico	1 819 046	25	36	Kentucky	102 896	27	36	Oklahoma	19.4
37	West Virginia	1 808 344	12	37	Virginia	102 548	20	37	Arizona	17.4
38	Nebraska	1 711 263	14	38	Indiana	92 895	24	38	Colorado	16.0
39	Idaho	1 293 953	40	39	Maine	79 931	40	38	Maine	16.0
40	Maine	1 274 923	26	40	South Carolina	77 983	28	40	Oregon	13.8
41	New Hampshire	1 235 786	37	41	West Virginia	62 361	32	41	Kansas	12.7
42	Hawaii	1 211 537	19	42	Maryland	25 314	34	42	Utah	10.5
43	Rhode Island	1 048 319	49	43	Vermont	23 956	38	43	Nebraska	8.6
44	Montana	902 195	41	44	New Hampshire	23 227	35	44	Nevada	7.0
45	Delaware	783 600	13	45	Massachusetts	20 306	39	45	Idaho	6.0
46	South Dakota	754 844	9	46	New Jersey	19 211	36	46	New Mexico	5.8
47	North Dakota	642 200	42	47	Hawaii	16 635	46	47	South Dakota	3.8
48	Alaska	626 932	29	48	Connecticut	12 548	47	48	North Dakota	3.6
49	Vermont	608 827	45	49	Delaware	5 060	44	49	Montana	2.4
50	District of Columbia	572 059	43	50	Rhode Island	2 706	51	50	Wyoming	2.0
51	Wyoming	493 782	50	51	District of Columbia	159	48	51	Alaska	0.4

Note: Column numbers refer to Table A. States.

TABLE 1—States and the District of Columbia
Selected Rankings

Percent Population Change, 1990-2000				Percent White, 2000				Percent Black, 2000			
Population Rank	Percent Change Rank	State	[col 52] Percent Change	Population Rank	White Rank	State	[col 9] Percent White	Population Rank	Black Rank	State	[col 10] Percent Black
X	X	United States	13.1	X	X	United States	75.1	X	X	United States	12.3
35	1	Nevada	66.3	40	1	Maine	96.9	50	1	District of Columbia	60.0
20	2	Arizona	40.0	49	2	Vermont	96.8	31	2	Mississippi	36.3
24	3	Colorado	30.6	41	3	New Hampshire	96.0	22	3	Louisiana	32.5
34	4	Utah	29.6	37	4	West Virginia	95.0	26	4	South Carolina	29.5
39	5	Idaho	28.5	30	5	Iowa	93.9	10	5	Georgia	28.7
10	6	Georgia	26.4	47	6	North Dakota	92.4	19	6	Maryland	27.9
4	7	Florida	23.5	51	7	Wyoming	92.1	23	7	Alabama	26.0
2	8	Texas	22.8	39	8	Idaho	91.0	11	8	North Carolina	21.6
11	9	North Carolina	21.4	44	9	Montana	90.6	12	9	Virginia	19.6
15	10	Washington	21.1	25	10	Kentucky	90.1	45	10	Delaware	19.2
28	11	Oregon	20.4	38	11	Nebraska	89.6	16	11	Tennessee	16.4
36	12	New Mexico	20.1	21	12	Minnesota	89.4	3	12	New York	15.9
45	13	Delaware	17.6	34	13	Utah	89.2	33	13	Arkansas	15.7
16	14	Tennessee	16.7	18	14	Wisconsin	88.9	5	14	Illinois	15.1
26	15	South Carolina	15.1	46	15	South Dakota	88.7	4	15	Florida	14.6
12	16	Virginia	14.4	14	16	Indiana	87.5	8	16	Michigan	14.2
48	17	Alaska	14.0	28	17	Oregon	86.6	9	17	New Jersey	13.6
33	18	Arkansas	13.7	32	18	Kansas	86.1	7	18	Ohio	11.5
1	19	California	13.6	6	19	Pennsylvania	85.4	2	18	Texas	11.5
44	20	Montana	12.9	7	20	Ohio	85.0	17	20	Missouri	11.2
21	21	Minnesota	12.4	43	20	Rhode Island	85.0	6	21	Pennsylvania	10.0
41	22	New Hampshire	11.4	17	22	Missouri	84.9	29	22	Connecticut	9.1
19	23	Maryland	10.8	13	23	Massachusetts	84.5	14	23	Indiana	8.4
31	24	Mississippi	10.5	24	24	Colorado	82.8	27	24	Oklahoma	7.6
23	25	Alabama	10.1	15	25	Washington	81.8	25	25	Kentucky	7.3
14	26	Indiana	9.7	29	26	Connecticut	81.6	35	26	Nevada	6.8
27	26	Oklahoma	9.7	8	27	Michigan	80.2	1	27	California	6.7
25	28	Kentucky	9.6	16	27	Tennessee	80.2	32	28	Kansas	5.7
18	28	Wisconsin	9.6	33	29	Arkansas	80.0	18	28	Wisconsin	5.7
42	30	Hawaii	9.3	4	30	Florida	78.0	13	30	Massachusetts	5.4
17	30	Missouri	9.3	27	31	Oklahoma	76.2	43	31	Rhode Island	4.5
51	32	Wyoming	8.9	20	32	Arizona	75.5	38	32	Nebraska	4.0
5	33	Illinois	8.6	35	33	Nevada	75.2	24	33	Colorado	3.8
9	33	New Jersey	8.6	45	34	Delaware	74.6	48	34	Alaska	3.5
32	35	Kansas	8.5	5	35	Illinois	73.5	21	34	Minnesota	3.5
46	35	South Dakota	8.5	9	36	New Jersey	72.6	15	36	Washington	3.2
38	37	Nebraska	8.4	12	37	Virginia	72.3	37	36	West Virginia	3.2
49	38	Vermont	8.2	11	38	North Carolina	72.1	20	38	Arizona	3.1
8	39	Michigan	6.9	23	39	Alabama	71.1	30	39	Iowa	2.1
22	40	Louisiana	5.9	2	40	Texas	71.0	36	40	New Mexico	1.9
13	41	Massachusetts	5.5	48	41	Alaska	69.3	42	41	Hawaii	1.8
3	41	New York	5.5	3	42	New York	67.9	28	42	Oregon	1.6
30	43	Iowa	5.4	26	43	South Carolina	67.2	34	43	Utah	0.8
7	44	Ohio	4.7	36	44	New Mexico	66.8	51	43	Wyoming	0.8
43	45	Rhode Island	4.5	10	45	Georgia	65.1	41	45	New Hampshire	0.7
40	46	Maine	3.8	19	46	Maryland	64.0	47	46	North Dakota	0.6
29	47	Connecticut	3.6	22	47	Louisiana	63.9	46	46	South Dakota	0.6
6	48	Pennsylvania	3.4	31	48	Mississippi	61.4	40	48	Maine	0.5
37	49	West Virginia	0.8	1	49	California	59.5	49	48	Vermont	0.5
47	50	North Dakota	0.5	50	50	District of Columbia	30.8	39	50	Idaho	0.4
50	51	District of Columbia	-5.7	42	51	Hawaii	24.3	44	51	Montana	0.3

Note: Column numbers refer to Table A. States.

TABLE 1—States and the District of Columbia
Selected Rankings

Percent American Indian and Alaska Native, 2000

Population Rank	American Indian and Alaska Native Rank	State	[col 11] Percent American Indian and Alaska Native
X	X	United States	0.9
48	1	Alaska	15.6
36	2	New Mexico	9.5
46	3	South Dakota	8.3
27	4	Oklahoma	7.9
44	5	Montana	6.2
20	6	Arizona	5.0
47	7	North Dakota	4.9
51	8	Wyoming	2.3
15	9	Washington	1.6
39	10	Idaho	1.4
35	11	Nevada	1.3
28	11	Oregon	1.3
34	11	Utah	1.3
11	14	North Carolina	1.2
21	15	Minnesota	1.1
1	16	California	1.0
24	16	Colorado	1.0
32	18	Kansas	0.9
38	18	Nebraska	0.9
18	18	Wisconsin	0.9
33	21	Arkansas	0.7
22	22	Louisiana	0.6
40	22	Maine	0.6
8	22	Michigan	0.6
2	22	Texas	0.6
23	26	Alabama	0.5
43	26	Rhode Island	0.5
31	28	Mississippi	0.4
17	28	Missouri	0.4
3	28	New York	0.4
49	28	Vermont	0.4
29	32	Connecticut	0.3
45	32	Delaware	0.3
50	32	District of Columbia	0.3
4	32	Florida	0.3
10	32	Georgia	0.3
42	32	Hawaii	0.3
14	32	Indiana	0.3
30	32	Iowa	0.3
19	32	Maryland	0.3
26	32	South Carolina	0.3
16	32	Tennessee	0.3
12	32	Virginia	0.3
5	44	Illinois	0.2
25	44	Kentucky	0.2
13	44	Massachusetts	0.2
41	44	New Hampshire	0.2
9	44	New Jersey	0.2
7	44	Ohio	0.2
37	44	West Virginia	0.2
6	51	Pennsylvania	0.1

Percent Asian, 2000

Population Rank	Asian Rank	State	[col 12] Percent Asian
X	X	United States	3.6
42	1	Hawaii	41.6
1	2	California	10.9
9	3	New Jersey	5.7
3	4	New York	5.5
15	4	Washington	5.5
35	6	Nevada	4.5
48	7	Alaska	4.0
19	7	Maryland	4.0
13	9	Massachusetts	3.8
12	10	Virginia	3.7
5	11	Illinois	3.4
28	12	Oregon	3.0
21	13	Minnesota	2.9
50	14	District of Columbia	2.7
2	14	Texas	2.7
29	16	Connecticut	2.4
43	17	Rhode Island	2.3
24	18	Colorado	2.2
45	19	Delaware	2.1
10	19	Georgia	2.1
20	21	Arizona	1.8
8	21	Michigan	1.8
6	21	Pennsylvania	1.8
4	24	Florida	1.7
32	24	Kansas	1.7
34	24	Utah	1.7
18	24	Wisconsin	1.7
11	28	North Carolina	1.4
27	28	Oklahoma	1.4
30	30	Iowa	1.3
38	30	Nebraska	1.3
41	30	New Hampshire	1.3
22	33	Louisiana	1.2
7	33	Ohio	1.2
17	35	Missouri	1.1
36	35	New Mexico	1.1
14	37	Indiana	1.0
16	37	Tennessee	1.0
39	39	Idaho	0.9
26	39	South Carolina	0.9
49	39	Vermont	0.9
33	42	Arkansas	0.8
23	43	Alabama	0.7
25	43	Kentucky	0.7
40	43	Maine	0.7
31	43	Mississippi	0.7
47	47	North Dakota	0.6
46	47	South Dakota	0.6
51	47	Wyoming	0.6
44	50	Montana	0.5
37	50	West Virginia	0.5

Percent Hispanic, 2000

Population Rank	Hispanic Rank	State	[col 22] Percent Hispanic
X	X	United States	12.5
36	1	New Mexico	42.1
1	2	California	32.4
2	3	Texas	32.0
20	4	Arizona	25.3
35	5	Nevada	19.7
24	6	Colorado	17.1
4	7	Florida	16.8
3	8	New York	15.1
9	9	New Jersey	13.3
5	10	Illinois	12.3
29	11	Connecticut	9.4
34	12	Utah	9.0
43	13	Rhode Island	8.7
28	14	Oregon	8.0
50	15	District of Columbia	7.9
39	15	Idaho	7.9
15	17	Washington	7.5
42	18	Hawaii	7.2
32	19	Kansas	7.0
13	20	Massachusetts	6.8
51	21	Wyoming	6.4
38	22	Nebraska	5.5
10	23	Georgia	5.3
27	24	Oklahoma	5.2
45	25	Delaware	4.8
11	26	North Carolina	4.7
12	26	Virginia	4.7
19	28	Maryland	4.3
48	29	Alaska	4.1
18	30	Wisconsin	3.6
14	31	Indiana	3.5
8	32	Michigan	3.3
33	33	Arkansas	3.2
6	33	Pennsylvania	3.2
21	35	Minnesota	2.9
30	36	Iowa	2.8
22	37	Louisiana	2.4
26	37	South Carolina	2.4
16	39	Tennessee	2.2
17	40	Missouri	2.1
44	41	Montana	2.0
7	42	Ohio	1.9
23	43	Alabama	1.7
41	43	New Hampshire	1.7
25	45	Kentucky	1.5
31	46	Mississippi	1.4
46	46	South Dakota	1.4
47	48	North Dakota	1.2
49	49	Vermont	0.9
40	50	Maine	0.7
37	50	West Virginia	0.7

Note: Column numbers refer to Table A. States.

TABLE 1—States and the District of Columbia
Selected Rankings

Percent Under 18 Years, 2000				Percent Age 25 to 54 Years, 2000				Percent Age 65 Years and Over, 2000			
Population Rank	Under 18 Years Rank	State	[cols 28 & 29] Percent Under 18 Years	Population Rank	25 to 54 Years Rank	State	[cols 31, 32 & 33] Percent 25 to 54 Years	Population Rank	65 Years and Over Rank	State	[col 35 & 36] Percent 65 Years and Over
X	X	United States	25.7	X	X	United States	43.6	X	X	United States	12.4
34	1	Utah	32.2	48	1	Alaska	47.6	4	1	Florida	17.6
48	2	Alaska	30.4	24	2	Colorado	46.8	6	2	Pennsylvania	15.6
39	3	Idaho	28.5	50	3	District of Columbia	46.3	37	3	West Virginia	15.3
2	4	Texas	28.2	41	4	New Hampshire	45.8	30	4	Iowa	14.9
36	5	New Mexico	28.0	19	5	Maryland	45.7	47	5	North Dakota	14.7
1	6	California	27.3	12	5	Virginia	45.7	43	6	Rhode Island	14.5
22	6	Louisiana	27.3	10	7	Georgia	45.6	40	7	Maine	14.3
31	6	Mississippi	27.3	15	8	Washington	45.2	46	7	South Dakota	14.3
46	9	South Dakota	26.9	13	9	Massachusetts	45.1	33	9	Arkansas	14.0
20	10	Arizona	26.7	9	10	New Jersey	45.0	29	10	Connecticut	13.8
10	11	Georgia	26.5	35	11	Nevada	44.9	38	11	Nebraska	13.6
32	11	Kansas	26.5	11	12	North Carolina	44.6	13	12	Massachusetts	13.5
38	13	Nebraska	26.3	29	13	Connecticut	44.5	17	12	Missouri	13.5
5	14	Illinois	26.2	1	14	California	44.4	44	14	Montana	13.4
8	14	Michigan	26.2	49	15	Vermont	44.3	7	15	Ohio	13.3
21	14	Minnesota	26.2	40	16	Maine	44.2	42	16	Hawaii	13.2
51	17	Wyoming	26.1	3	16	New York	44.2	32	16	Kansas	13.2
14	18	Indiana	25.9	42	18	Hawaii	44.0	9	16	New Jersey	13.2
27	19	Oklahoma	25.8	40	18	Minnesota	44.0	27	16	Oklahoma	13.2
15	20	Washington	25.7	28	18	Oregon	44.0	18	20	Wisconsin	13.1
24	21	Colorado	25.6	16	18	Tennessee	44.0	23	21	Alabama	13.0
19	21	Maryland	25.6	25	22	Kentucky	43.8	20	21	Arizona	13.0
35	21	Nevada	25.6	5	23	Illinois	43.7	45	21	Delaware	13.0
33	24	Arkansas	25.5	8	24	Michigan	43.6	3	24	New York	12.9
17	24	Missouri	25.5	2	24	Texas	43.6	28	25	Oregon	12.8
44	24	Montana	25.5	45	26	Delaware	43.5	49	26	Vermont	12.7
18	24	Wisconsin	25.5	26	27	South Carolina	43.3	25	27	Kentucky	12.5
7	28	Ohio	25.4	18	28	Wisconsin	43.2	14	28	Indiana	12.4
23	29	Alabama	25.3	7	29	Ohio	43.1	8	29	Michigan	12.3
26	30	South Carolina	25.2	43	29	Rhode Island	43.1	16	29	Tennessee	12.3
30	31	Iowa	25.0	51	29	Wyoming	43.1	50	31	District of Columbia	12.2
41	31	New Hampshire	25.0	14	32	Indiana	42.9	5	32	Illinois	12.1
47	31	North Dakota	25.0	37	33	West Virginia	42.8	21	32	Minnesota	12.1
45	34	Delaware	24.9	23	34	Alabama	42.5	26	32	South Carolina	12.1
29	35	Connecticut	24.8	6	34	Pennsylvania	42.5	31	35	Mississippi	12.0
9	35	New Jersey	24.8	17	36	Missouri	42.4	11	35	North Carolina	12.0
3	37	New York	24.7	22	37	Louisiana	42.1	41	37	New Hampshire	11.9
28	37	Oregon	24.7	44	37	Montana	42.1	36	38	New Mexico	11.7
25	39	Kentucky	24.6	36	39	New Mexico	41.9	51	39	Wyoming	11.6
16	39	Tennessee	24.6	32	40	Kansas	41.8	22	40	Louisiana	11.5
42	41	Hawaii	24.5	20	41	Arizona	41.7	39	41	Idaho	11.3
12	41	Virginia	24.5	38	42	Nebraska	41.6	19	41	Maryland	11.3
11	43	North Carolina	24.4	4	43	Florida	41.4	12	43	Virginia	11.2
49	44	Vermont	24.2	27	43	Oklahoma	41.4	15	43	Washington	11.2
6	45	Pennsylvania	23.8	33	45	Arkansas	41.2	35	45	Nevada	11.0
13	46	Massachusetts	23.7	39	45	Idaho	41.2	1	46	California	10.6
40	47	Maine	23.6	31	47	Mississippi	41.1	2	47	Texas	10.0
43	47	Rhode Island	23.6	30	48	Iowa	41.0	24	48	Colorado	9.7
4	49	Florida	22.8	47	49	North Dakota	40.6	10	49	Georgia	9.6
37	50	West Virginia	22.2	46	50	South Dakota	40.3	34	50	Utah	8.5
50	51	District of Columbia	20.1	34	51	Utah	38.6	48	51	Alaska	5.7

Note: Column numbers refer to Table A. States.

TABLE 1—States and the District of Columbia
Selected Rankings

Percent Female-headed Family Households, 2000				Percent Living Alone, 2000				Percent Married Couple Family Households, 2000			
Population Rank	Female Households Rate	State	[col 76] Percent Female Households	Population Rank	Living Alone Rank	State	[col 79] Percent Living Alone	Population Rank	Married Couple Family Households Rank	State	[col 74] Percent Married Couple Family Households
X	X	United States	12.2	X	X	United States	25.8	X	X	United States	51.7
50	1	District of Columbia	18.9	50	1	District of Columbia	43.8	34	1	Utah	63.2
31	2	Mississippi	17.3	47	2	North Dakota	29.3	39	2	Idaho	58.9
22	3	Louisiana	16.6	43	3	Rhode Island	28.6	41	3	New Hampshire	55.3
26	4	South Carolina	14.8	3	4	New York	28.1	30	4	Iowa	55.1
3	5	New York	14.7	13	5	Massachusetts	28.0	51	5	Wyoming	54.8
10	6	Georgia	14.5	6	6	Pennsylvania	27.7	32	6	Kansas	54.7
23	7	Alabama	14.2	38	7	Nebraska	27.6	33	7	Arkansas	54.3
19	8	Maryland	14.1	46	7	South Dakota	27.6	38	8	Nebraska	54.2
36	9	New Mexico	13.2	44	9	Montana	27.4	46	8	South Dakota	54.2
45	10	Delaware	13.1	17	10	Missouri	27.3	2	10	Texas	54.0
43	11	Rhode Island	12.9	7	10	Ohio	27.3	37	10	West Virginia	54.0
16	11	Tennessee	12.9	30	12	Iowa	27.2	25	12	Kentucky	53.9
2	13	Texas	12.7	37	13	West Virginia	27.1	21	13	Minnesota	53.7
1	14	California	12.6	32	14	Kansas	27.0	42	14	Hawaii	53.6
9	14	New Jersey	12.6	40	14	Maine	27.0	14	14	Indiana	53.6
8	16	Michigan	12.5	21	16	Minnesota	26.9	44	14	Montana	53.6
11	16	North Carolina	12.5	5	17	Illinois	26.8	9	17	New Jersey	53.5
42	18	Hawaii	12.4	18	18	Wisconsin	26.8	27	17	Oklahoma	53.5
5	19	Illinois	12.3	27	19	Oklahoma	26.7	47	19	North Dakota	53.4
33	20	Arkansas	12.1	4	20	Florida	26.6	18	20	Wisconsin	53.2
29	20	Connecticut	12.1	29	21	Connecticut	26.4	12	21	Virginia	52.8
7	20	Ohio	12.1	24	22	Colorado	26.3	16	22	Tennessee	52.6
4	23	Florida	12.0	51	22	Wyoming	26.3	48	23	Alaska	52.5
13	24	Massachusetts	11.9	8	24	Michigan	26.2	40	23	Maine	52.5
12	24	Virginia	11.9	49	24	Vermont	26.2	11	23	North Carolina	52.5
25	26	Kentucky	11.8	15	24	Washington	26.2	49	23	Vermont	52.5
17	27	Missouri	11.6	23	27	Alabama	26.1	23	27	Alabama	52.2
6	27	Pennsylvania	11.6	28	27	Oregon	26.1	29	28	Connecticut	52.0
27	29	Oklahoma	11.4	25	29	Kentucky	26.0	17	28	Missouri	52.0
20	30	Arizona	11.1	14	30	Indiana	25.9	15	28	Washington	52.0
14	30	Indiana	11.1	16	31	Tennessee	25.8	20	31	Arizona	51.9
35	30	Nevada	11.1	33	32	Arkansas	25.6	28	31	Oregon	51.9
48	33	Alaska	10.8	36	33	New Mexico	25.4	24	33	Colorado	51.8
37	34	West Virginia	10.7	11	33	North Carolina	25.4	6	34	Pennsylvania	51.7
15	35	Washington	9.9	22	35	Louisiana	25.3	10	35	Georgia	51.5
28	36	Oregon	9.8	12	36	Virginia	25.1	8	36	Michigan	51.4
24	37	Colorado	9.6	45	37	Delaware	25.0	7	36	Ohio	51.4
18	37	Wisconsin	9.6	19	37	Maryland	25.0	45	38	Delaware	51.3
40	39	Maine	9.5	26	37	South Carolina	25.0	5	38	Illinois	51.3
34	40	Utah	9.4	35	40	Nevada	24.9	1	40	California	51.1
32	41	Kansas	9.3	20	41	Arizona	24.8	26	40	South Carolina	51.1
49	41	Vermont	9.3	31	42	Mississippi	24.6	4	42	Florida	50.4
38	43	Nebraska	9.1	9	43	New Jersey	24.5	36	42	New Mexico	50.4
41	43	New Hampshire	9.1	41	44	New Hampshire	24.4	19	44	Maryland	50.2
46	45	South Dakota	9.0	2	45	Texas	23.7	31	45	Mississippi	49.8
21	46	Minnesota	8.9	10	46	Georgia	23.6	35	46	Nevada	49.7
44	46	Montana	8.9	48	47	Alaska	23.5	13	47	Massachusetts	49.0
39	48	Idaho	8.7	1	47	California	23.5	22	48	Louisiana	48.9
51	48	Wyoming	8.7	39	49	Idaho	22.4	43	49	Rhode Island	48.2
30	50	Iowa	8.6	42	50	Hawaii	21.9	3	50	New York	46.6
47	51	North Dakota	7.8	34	51	Utah	17.8	50	51	District of Columbia	22.8

Note: Column numbers refer to Table A. States.

29

TABLE 1—States and the District of Columbia
Selected Rankings

Percent of Families with Own Children Under 18 Years, 2000				Percent Owner Occupied Housing Units				Percent Recreational/Seasonal Housing Units			
Population Rank	Families with Own Children Under 18 Years Rank	State	[col 73] Percent of Families with Own Children Under 18 Years	Population Rank	Owner Occupied Housing Units Rank	State	[col 94] Percent in Owner Occupied Housing Units	Recreational/Seasonal Housing Units Rank	Group Quarters Rank	State	[col 90] Percent Recreational/Seasonal Housing Units
X	X	United States	32.8	X	X	United States	66.2	X	X	United States	3.1
34	1	Utah	42.7	37	1	West Virginia	75.2	40	1	Maine	15.6
48	2	Alaska	39.9	21	2	Minnesota	74.6	49	2	Vermont	14.6
2	3	Texas	36.8	8	3	Michigan	73.8	41	3	New Hampshire	10.3
39	4	Idaho	36.3	23	4	Alabama	72.5	48	4	Alaska	8.2
1	5	California	35.8	39	5	Idaho	72.4	45	5	Delaware	7.6
10	6	Georgia	35.0	45	6	Delaware	72.3	4	6	Florida	6.6
31	7	Mississippi	34.7	30	6	Iowa	72.3	20	7	Arizona	6.5
36	7	New Mexico	34.7	31	6	Mississippi	72.3	18	8	Wisconsin	6.1
22	9	Louisiana	34.5	26	9	South Carolina	72.2	44	9	Montana	5.9
9	10	New Jersey	33.5	40	10	Maine	71.6	42	10	Hawaii	5.6
19	11	Maryland	33.4	34	11	Utah	71.5	8	11	Michigan	5.5
41	11	New Hampshire	33.4	14	12	Indiana	71.4	51	11	Wyoming	5.5
32	13	Kansas	33.2	6	13	Pennsylvania	71.3	39	13	Idaho	5.2
5	14	Illinois	33.0	25	14	Kentucky	70.8	21	14	Minnesota	5.1
21	14	Minnesota	33.0	49	15	Vermont	70.6	36	15	New Mexico	4.1
14	16	Indiana	32.9	17	16	Missouri	70.3	24	16	Colorado	4.0
24	17	Colorado	32.8	4	17	Florida	70.1	26	16	South Carolina	4.0
46	17	South Dakota	32.8	36	18	New Mexico	70.0	34	18	Utah	3.9
8	19	Michigan	32.7	51	18	Wyoming	70.0	37	18	West Virginia	3.9
38	19	Nebraska	32.7	16	20	Tennessee	69.9	11	20	North Carolina	3.8
12	19	Virginia	32.7	41	21	New Hampshire	69.7	13	21	Massachusetts	3.6
15	19	Washington	32.7	33	22	Arkansas	69.4	9	22	New Jersey	3.3
51	19	Wyoming	32.7	11	22	North Carolina	69.4	3	23	New York	3.1
25	24	Kentucky	32.5	32	24	Kansas	69.2	43	24	Rhode Island	3.0
27	25	Oklahoma	32.4	44	25	Montana	69.1	46	24	South Dakota	3.0
23	26	Alabama	32.3	7	25	Ohio	69.1	47	26	North Dakota	2.9
26	26	South Carolina	32.3	27	27	Oklahoma	68.4	6	27	Pennsylvania	2.8
29	28	Connecticut	32.2	18	27	Wisconsin	68.4	17	28	Missouri	2.7
33	29	Arkansas	32.1	46	29	South Dakota	68.2	33	29	Arkansas	2.5
42	29	Hawaii	32.1	12	30	Virginia	68.1	28	29	Oregon	2.5
20	31	Arizona	32.0	20	31	Arizona	68.0	15	29	Washington	2.5
45	32	Delaware	31.9	22	32	Louisiana	67.9	23	32	Alabama	2.4
17	32	Missouri	31.9	19	33	Maryland	67.7	22	33	Louisiana	2.1
18	32	Wisconsin	31.9	10	34	Georgia	67.5	27	33	Oklahoma	2.1
35	35	Nevada	31.8	38	35	Nebraska	67.4	35	33	Texas	2.1
11	35	North Carolina	31.8	24	36	Colorado	67.3	46	36	Nevada	2.0
49	35	Vermont	31.8	5	36	Illinois	67.3	1	37	California	1.9
7	38	Ohio	31.7	29	38	Connecticut	66.8	31	37	Mississippi	1.9
16	38	Tennessee	31.7	47	39	North Dakota	66.6	12	37	Virginia	1.9
3	40	New York	31.6	9	40	New Jersey	65.6	19	40	Maryland	1.8
30	41	Iowa	31.4	15	41	Washington	64.6	29	41	Connecticut	1.7
47	42	North Dakota	31.3	28	42	Oregon	64.3	25	41	Kentucky	1.7
44	43	Montana	31.2	2	43	Texas	63.8	38	43	Nebraska	1.6
28	44	Oregon	30.8	48	44	Alaska	62.5	10	44	Georgia	1.5
13	45	Massachusetts	30.6	13	45	Massachusetts	61.7	16	44	Tennessee	1.5
43	45	Rhode Island	30.6	35	46	Nevada	60.9	14	46	Indiana	1.3
40	47	Maine	30.4	43	47	Rhode Island	60.0	30	46	Iowa	1.3
6	48	Pennsylvania	30.0	1	48	California	56.9	7	48	Ohio	1.0
37	49	West Virginia	28.9	42	49	Hawaii	56.5	32	49	Kansas	0.9
4	50	Florida	28.1	3	50	New York	53.0	50	50	District of Columbia	0.8
50	51	District of Columbia	19.8	50	51	District of Columbia	40.8	5	51	Illinois	0.6

Note: Column numbers refer to Table A. States.

30

TABLE 2—75 Largest Counties by 2000 Population
Selected Rankings

Total Persons, 2000			Land Area (Square Kilometers), 2000				Population Density (per Square Kilometer), 1999			
Population Rank	County	[col 2] Population	Population Rank	Land Area Rank	County	[col 1] Land Area	Population Rank	Density Rank	County	[col 4] Density
1	Los Angeles, CA	9 519 338	13	1	San Bernardino, CA	51 936	17	1	New York, NY	26 054.2
2	Cook, IL	5 376 741	4	2	Maricopa, AZ	23 836	7	2	Kings, NY	13 471.7
3	Harris, TX	3 400 578	53	3	Pima, AZ	23 792	27	3	Bronx, NY	12 226.1
4	Maricopa, AZ	3 072 149	25	4	Clark, NV	20 488	9	4	Queens, NY	7 877.7
5	Orange, CA	2 846 289	16	5	Riverside, CA	18 667	62	5	San Francisco, CA	6 419.3
6	San Diego, CA	2 813 833	58	6	Fresno, CA	15 443	74	6	Suffolk, MA	4 538.2
7	Kings, NY	2 465 326	6	7	San Diego, CA	10 878	18	7	Philadelphia, PA	4 335.9
8	Miami-Dade, FL	2 253 362	1	8	Los Angeles, CA	10 518	59	8	Essex, NJ	2 427.0
9	Queens, NY	2 229 379	12	9	King, WA	5 506	2	9	Cook, IL	2 195.5
10	Dallas, TX	2 218 899	31	10	Palm Beach, FL	5 113	26	10	Nassau, NY	1 796.2
11	Wayne, MI	2 061 162	8	11	Miami-Dade, FL	5 040	39	11	Milwaukee, WI	1 501.9
12	King, WA	1 737 034	64	12	Ventura, CA	4 779	46	12	Bergen, NJ	1 456.5
13	San Bernardino, CA	1 709 434	3	13	Harris, TX	4 478	19	13	Orange, CA	1 391.8
14	Santa Clara, CA	1 682 585	71	14	Pierce, WA	4 348	11	14	Wayne, MI	1 295.5
15	Broward, FL	1 623 018	65	15	Worcester, MA	3 919	41	15	Pinellas, FL	1 271.0
16	Riverside, CA	1 545 387	14	16	Santa Clara, CA	3 343	23	16	Cuyahoga, OH	1 174.4
17	New York, NY	1 537 195	24	17	Bexar, TX	3 229	42	17	Du Page, IL	1 046.5
18	Philadelphia, PA	1 517 550	15	18	Broward, FL	3 122	10	18	Dallas, TX	974.1
19	Middlesex, MA	1 465 396	35	19	Hillsborough, FL	2 722	36	19	Fairfax, VA	947.9
20	Tarrant, TX	1 446 219	37	20	Erie, NY	2 704	66	20	Middlesex, NJ	935.4
21	Alameda, CA	1 443 741	75	21	El Paso, TX	2 624	1	21	Los Angeles, CA	905.1
22	Suffolk, NY	1 419 369	56	22	Travis, TX	2 562	50	22	Marion, IN	838.6
23	Cuyahoga, OH	1 393 978	29	23	Sacramento, CA	2 501	40	23	Westchester, NY	823.8
24	Bexar, TX	1 392 931	2	24	Cook, IL	2 449	52	24	Hamilton, OH	801.2
25	Clark, NV	1 375 765	22	25	Suffolk, NY	2 363	32	25	Hennepin, MN	774.1
26	Nassau, NY	1 334 544	45	26	Orange, FL	2 350	34	26	St. Louis, MO	772.9
27	Bronx, NY	1 332 650	10	27	Dallas, TX	2 278	33	27	Franklin, OH	764.6
28	Allegheny, PA	1 281 666	30	28	Oakland, MI	2 260	3	28	Harris, TX	759.4
29	Sacramento, CA	1 223 499	20	29	Tarrant, TX	2 236	21	29	Alameda, CA	755.9
30	Oakland, MI	1 194 156	19	30	Middlesex, MA	2 133	73	30	Jefferson, KY	695.7
31	Palm Beach, FL	1 131 184	5	31	Orange, CA	2 045	19	31	Middlesex, MA	687.0
32	Hennepin, MN	1 116 200	61	32	Duval, FL	2 004	49	32	Montgomery, MD	680.7
33	Franklin, OH	1 068 978	44	33	Shelby, TN	1 954	28	33	Allegheny, PA	677.8
34	St. Louis, MO	1 016 315	21	34	Alameda, CA	1 910	20	34	Tarrant, TX	646.8
35	Hillsborough, FL	998 948	43	34	Salt Lake, UT	1 910	57	35	Prince George's, MD	637.6
36	Fairfax, VA	969 749	51	36	Hartford, CT	1 905	60	36	Macomb, MI	633.6
37	Erie, NY	950 265	28	37	Allegheny, PA	1 891	70	37	San Mateo, CA	608.0
38	Contra Costa, CA	948 816	38	38	Contra Costa, CA	1 865	22	38	Suffolk, NY	600.7
39	Milwaukee, WI	940 164	68	39	Monroe, NY	1 708	67	39	Montgomery, PA	599.6
40	Westchester, NY	923 459	47	40	Fairfield, CT	1 621	55	40	Fulton, GA	596.1
41	Pinellas, FL	921 482	11	41	Wayne, MI	1 591	48	41	Honolulu, HI	564.2
42	Du Page, IL	904 161	54	42	New Haven, CT	1 569	69	42	Essex, MA	557.8
43	Salt Lake, UT	898 387	48	43	Honolulu, HI	1 553	47	43	Fairfield, CT	544.5
44	Shelby, TN	897 472	63	44	Baltimore, MD	1 550	30	44	Oakland, MI	528.4
45	Orange, FL	896 344	32	45	Hennepin, MN	1 442	54	45	New Haven, CT	525.2
46	Bergen, NJ	884 118	33	46	Franklin, OH	1 398	15	46	Broward, FL	519.9
47	Fairfield, CT	882 567	55	47	Fulton, GA	1 369	72	47	Mecklenburg, NC	510.2
48	Honolulu, HI	876 156	72	48	Mecklenburg, NC	1 363	38	48	Contra Costa, CA	508.7
49	Montgomery, MD	873 341	34	49	St. Louis, MO	1 315	14	49	Santa Clara, CA	503.3
50	Marion, IN	860 454	69	50	Essex, MA	1 297	29	50	Sacramento, CA	489.2
51	Hartford, CT	857 183	49	51	Montgomery, MD	1 283	63	51	Baltimore, MD	486.6
52	Hamilton, OH	845 303	57	52	Prince George's, MD	1 257	43	52	Salt Lake, UT	470.4
53	Pima, AZ	843 746	67	53	Montgomery, PA	1 251	44	53	Shelby, TN	459.3
54	New Haven, CT	824 008	60	54	Macomb, MI	1 244	51	54	Hartford, CT	450.0
55	Fulton, GA	816 006	23	55	Cuyahoga, OH	1 187	8	55	Miami-Dade, FL	447.1
56	Travis, TX	812 280	70	56	San Mateo, CA	1 163	24	56	Bexar, TX	431.4
57	Prince George's, MD	801 515	40	57	Westchester, NY	1 121	68	57	Monroe, NY	430.5
58	Fresno, CA	799 407	52	58	Hamilton, OH	1 055	61	58	Duval, FL	388.7
59	Essex, NJ	793 633	50	59	Marion, IN	1 026	45	59	Orange, FL	381.4
60	Macomb, MI	788 149	36	60	Fairfax, VA	1 023	35	60	Hillsborough, FL	367.0
61	Duval, FL	778 879	73	61	Jefferson, KY	997	37	61	Erie, NY	351.4
62	San Francisco, CA	776 733	42	62	Du Page, IL	864	56	62	Travis, TX	317.0
63	Baltimore, MD	754 292	66	63	Middlesex, NJ	802	12	63	King, WA	315.5
64	Ventura, CA	753 197	26	64	Nassau, NY	743	75	64	El Paso, TX	259.0
65	Worcester, MA	750 963	41	65	Pinellas, FL	725	6	65	San Diego, CA	258.7
66	Middlesex, NJ	750 162	39	66	Milwaukee, WI	626	31	66	Palm Beach, FL	221.2
67	Montgomery, PA	750 097	46	67	Bergen, NJ	607	65	67	Worcester, MA	191.6
68	Monroe, NY	735 343	18	68	Philadelphia, PA	350	71	68	Pierce, WA	161.2
69	Essex, MA	723 419	59	69	Essex, NJ	327	64	69	Ventura, CA	157.6
70	San Mateo, CA	707 161	9	70	Queens, NY	283	4	70	Maricopa, AZ	128.9
71	Pierce, WA	700 820	7	71	Kings, NY	183	16	71	Riverside, CA	82.8
72	Mecklenburg, NC	695 454	74	72	Suffolk, MA	152	25	72	Clark, NV	67.1
73	Jefferson, KY	693 604	62	73	San Francisco, CA	121	58	73	Fresno, CA	51.8
74	Suffolk, MA	689 807	27	74	Bronx, NY	109	53	74	Pima, AZ	35.5
75	El Paso, TX	679 622	17	75	New York, NY	59	13	75	San Bernardino, CA	32.9

Note: Column numbers refer to Table B. States and Counties.

TABLE 2—75 Largest Counties by 2000 Population
Selected Rankings

Percent Population Change: 1990-2000				Percent White, 2000				Percent Black, 2000			
Popu-lation Rank	Percent Change Rank	County	[col 52] Percent Change	Popu-lation Rank	White Rank	County	[col 9] Percent White	Popu-lation Rank	Black Rank	County	[col 10] Percent Black
25	1	Clark, NV	85.6	60	1	Macomb, MI	92.7	57	1	Prince George's, MD	62.7
4	2	Maricopa, AZ	44.8	65	2	Worcester, MA	89.6	44	2	Shelby, TN	48.6
56	3	Travis, TX	40.9	67	3	Montgomery, PA	86.5	55	3	Fulton, GA	44.6
72	4	Mecklenburg, NC	36.0	69	4	Essex, MA	86.4	18	4	Philadelphia, PA	43.2
45	5	Orange, FL	32.3	43	5	Salt Lake, UT	86.3	11	5	Wayne, MI	42.2
16	6	Riverside, CA	32.0	19	6	Middlesex, MA	85.9	59	6	Essex, NJ	41.2
31	7	Palm Beach, FL	31.0	41	6	Pinellas, FL	85.9	7	7	Kings, NY	36.4
15	8	Broward, FL	29.3	22	8	Suffolk, NY	84.6	27	8	Bronx, NY	35.6
53	9	Pima, AZ	26.5	28	9	Allegheny, PA	84.3	72	9	Mecklenburg, NC	27.9
55	10	Fulton, GA	25.8	42	10	Du Page, IL	84.0	61	10	Duval, FL	27.8
43	11	Salt Lake, UT	23.8	30	11	Oakland, MI	82.8	23	11	Cuyahoga, OH	27.4
20	12	Tarrant, TX	23.6	37	12	Erie, NY	82.2	2	12	Cook, IL	26.1
3	13	Harris, TX	20.7	32	13	Hennepin, MN	80.5	39	13	Milwaukee, WI	24.6
13	14	San Bernardino, CA	20.5	54	14	New Haven, CT	79.4	50	14	Marion, IN	24.2
10	15	Dallas, TX	19.8	47	15	Fairfield, CT	79.3	52	15	Hamilton, OH	23.4
58	15	Fresno, CA	19.8	26	15	Nassau, NY	79.3	74	16	Suffolk, MA	22.2
35	15	Hillsborough, FL	19.8	68	18	Monroe, NY	79.1	15	17	Broward, FL	20.5
71	18	Pierce, WA	19.6	31	17	Palm Beach, FL	79.1	10	18	Dallas, TX	20.3
36	19	Fairfax, VA	18.5	46	19	Bergen, NJ	78.4	8	18	Miami-Dade, FL	20.3
38	20	Contra Costa, CA	18.1	71	19	Pierce, WA	78.4	63	20	Baltimore, MD	20.1
5	20	Orange, CA	18.1	73	21	Jefferson, KY	77.4	9	21	Queens, NY	20.0
24	22	Bexar, TX	17.5	4	21	Maricopa, AZ	77.4	34	22	St. Louis, MO	19.0
8	23	Miami-Dade, FL	16.3	51	23	Hartford, CT	76.9	73	23	Jefferson, KY	18.9
42	24	Du Page, IL	15.7	34	24	St. Louis, MO	76.8	3	24	Harris, TX	18.5
61	24	Duval, FL	15.7	12	25	King, WA	75.7	45	25	Orange, FL	18.2
12	26	King, WA	15.2	33	26	Franklin, OH	75.5	33	26	Franklin, OH	17.9
75	27	El Paso, TX	14.9	35	27	Hillsborough, FL	75.2	17	27	New York, NY	17.4
29	28	Sacramento, CA	14.7	53	28	Pima, AZ	75.1	49	28	Montgomery, MD	15.1
49	29	Montgomery, MD	14.5	63	29	Baltimore, MD	74.4	35	29	Hillsborough, FL	15.0
9	30	Queens, NY	14.2	75	30	El Paso, TX	73.9	21	30	Alameda, CA	14.9
6	31	San Diego, CA	12.6	52	31	Hamilton, OH	72.9	40	31	Westchester, NY	14.2
64	31	Ventura, CA	12.6	25	32	Clark, NV	71.6	31	32	Palm Beach, FL	13.8
14	33	Santa Clara, CA	12.4	40	33	Westchester, NY	71.3	68	33	Monroe, NY	13.7
66	34	Middlesex, NJ	11.7	20	34	Tarrant, TX	71.2	37	34	Erie, NY	13.0
33	35	Franklin, OH	11.2	15	35	Broward, FL	70.6	20	35	Tarrant, TX	12.8
57	36	Prince George's, MD	10.9	50	36	Marion, IN	70.5	28	36	Allegheny, PA	12.4
21	37	Alameda, CA	10.7	36	37	Fairfax, VA	69.9	51	37	Hartford, CT	11.7
27	37	Bronx, NY	10.7	64	37	Ventura, CA	69.9	54	38	New Haven, CT	11.3
67	39	Montgomery, PA	10.6	8	39	Miami-Dade, FL	69.7	26	39	Nassau, NY	10.1
30	40	Oakland, MI	10.2	24	40	Bexar, TX	68.9	30	39	Oakland, MI	10.1
60	41	Macomb, MI	9.9	45	41	Orange, FL	68.6	47	41	Fairfield, CT	10.0
63	42	Baltimore, MD	9.0	66	42	Middlesex, NJ	68.4	29	41	Sacramento, CA	10.0
70	43	San Mateo, CA	8.9	56	43	Travis, TX	68.2	1	43	Los Angeles, CA	9.8
44	44	Shelby, TN	8.6	23	44	Cuyahoga, OH	67.4	38	44	Contra Costa, CA	9.4
41	45	Pinellas, FL	8.2	6	45	San Diego, CA	66.5	56	45	Travis, TX	9.3
32	46	Hennepin, MN	8.1	61	46	Duval, FL	65.8	25	46	Clark, NV	9.1
69	47	Essex, MA	8.0	39	47	Milwaukee, WI	65.6	66	46	Middlesex, NJ	9.1
50	48	Marion, IN	7.9	16	47	Riverside, CA	65.6	13	46	San Bernardino, CA	9.1
1	49	Los Angeles, CA	7.4	38	49	Contra Costa, CA	65.5	32	49	Hennepin, MN	9.0
22	49	Suffolk, NY	7.4	49	50	Montgomery, MD	64.8	41	49	Pinellas, FL	9.0
62	51	San Francisco, CA	7.3	5	50	Orange, CA	64.8	36	51	Fairfax, VA	8.6
7	52	Kings, NY	7.2	72	52	Mecklenburg, NC	64.0	62	52	San Francisco, CA	7.8
46	53	Bergen, NJ	7.1	29	52	Sacramento, CA	64.0	67	53	Montgomery, PA	7.5
47	54	Fairfield, CT	6.6	70	54	San Mateo, CA	59.5	24	54	Bexar, TX	7.2
65	55	Worcester, MA	5.8	13	55	San Bernardino, CA	58.9	71	55	Pierce, WA	7.0
40	56	Westchester, NY	5.6	3	56	Harris, TX	58.7	22	56	Suffolk, NY	6.9
2	57	Cook, IL	5.3	10	57	Dallas, TX	58.4	16	57	Riverside, CA	6.2
48	58	Honolulu, HI	4.8	74	58	Suffolk, MA	57.8	6	58	San Diego, CA	5.7
19	58	Middlesex, MA	4.8	2	59	Cook, IL	56.3	12	59	King, WA	5.4
73	60	Jefferson, KY	4.3	17	60	New York, NY	54.4	46	60	Bergen, NJ	5.3
74	61	Suffolk, MA	3.9	58	61	Fresno, CA	54.3	58	60	Fresno, CA	5.3
26	62	Nassau, NY	3.6	14	62	Santa Clara, CA	53.8	4	62	Maricopa, AZ	3.7
17	63	New York, NY	3.3	11	63	Wayne, MI	51.7	70	63	San Mateo, CA	3.5
68	64	Monroe, NY	3.0	62	64	San Francisco, CA	49.7	19	64	Middlesex, MA	3.4
54	65	New Haven, CT	2.5	21	65	Alameda, CA	48.8	42	65	Du Page, IL	3.1
34	66	St. Louis, MO	2.3	1	66	Los Angeles, CA	48.7	75	65	El Paso, TX	3.1
59	67	Essex, NJ	2.0	55	67	Fulton, GA	48.1	53	67	Pima, AZ	3.0
51	68	Hartford, CT	0.6	44	68	Shelby, TN	47.3	14	68	Santa Clara, CA	2.8
23	69	Cuyahoga, OH	-1.3	18	69	Philadelphia, PA	45.0	60	69	Macomb, MI	2.7
37	70	Erie, NY	-1.9	59	70	Essex, NJ	44.5	65	69	Worcester, MA	2.7
39	71	Milwaukee, WI	-2.0	9	71	Queens, NY	44.1	69	71	Essex, MA	2.6
52	72	Hamilton, OH	-2.4	7	72	Kings, NY	41.2	48	72	Honolulu, HI	2.4
11	72	Wayne, MI	-2.4	27	73	Bronx, NY	29.9	64	73	Ventura, CA	1.9
28	74	Allegheny, PA	-4.1	57	74	Prince George's, MD	27.0	5	74	Orange, CA	1.7
18	75	Philadelphia, PA	-4.3	48	75	Honolulu, HI	21.3	43	75	Salt Lake, UT	1.1

Note: Column numbers refer to Table B. States and Counties.

TABLE 2—75 Largest Counties by 2000 Population
Selected Rankings

Percent American Indian and Alaska Native, 2000				Percent Asian, 2000				Percent Hispanic, 2000			
Population Rank	American Indian and Alaska Native Rank	County	[col 11] Percent American Indian and Alaska Native	Population Rank	Asian Rank	County	[col 12] Percent Asian	Population Rank	Hispanic Rank	County	[col 22] Percent Hispanic
53	1	Pima, AZ	3.2	48	1	Honolulu, HI	46.0	75	1	El Paso, TX	78.2
4	2	Maricopa, AZ	1.8	62	2	San Francisco, CA	30.8	8	2	Miami-Dade, FL	57.3
58	3	Fresno, CA	1.6	14	3	Santa Clara, CA	25.6	24	3	Bexar, TX	54.3
71	4	Pierce, WA	1.4	21	4	Alameda, CA	20.4	27	4	Bronx, NY	48.4
16	5	Riverside, CA	1.2	70	5	San Mateo, CA	20.0	1	5	Los Angeles, CA	44.6
13	5	San Bernardino, CA	1.2	9	6	Queens, NY	17.6	58	6	Fresno, CA	44.0
29	7	Sacramento, CA	1.1	66	7	Middlesex, NJ	13.9	13	7	San Bernardino, CA	39.2
32	8	Hennepin, MN	1.0	5	8	Orange, CA	13.6	16	8	Riverside, CA	36.2
27	9	Bronx, NY	0.9	36	9	Fairfax, VA	13.0	64	9	Ventura, CA	33.4
12	9	King, WA	0.9	1	10	Los Angeles, CA	11.9	3	10	Harris, TX	32.9
43	9	Salt Lake, UT	0.9	49	11	Montgomery, MD	11.3	5	11	Orange, CA	30.8
6	9	San Diego, CA	0.9	38	12	Contra Costa, CA	11.0	10	12	Dallas, TX	29.9
64	9	Ventura, CA	0.9	29	12	Sacramento, CA	11.0	53	13	Pima, AZ	29.3
24	14	Bexar, TX	0.8	12	14	King, WA	10.8	56	14	Travis, TX	28.2
25	14	Clark, NV	0.8	46	15	Bergen, NJ	10.7	17	15	New York, NY	27.2
75	14	El Paso, TX	0.8	17	16	New York, NY	9.4	6	16	San Diego, CA	26.7
1	14	Los Angeles, CA	0.8	6	17	San Diego, CA	8.9	9	17	Queens, NY	25.0
39	18	Milwaukee, WI	0.7	58	18	Fresno, CA	8.1	4	18	Maricopa, AZ	24.8
5	18	Orange, CA	0.7	42	19	Du Page, IL	7.9	14	19	Santa Clara, CA	24.0
14	18	Santa Clara, CA	0.7	7	20	Kings, NY	7.5	25	20	Clark, NV	22.0
21	21	Alameda, CA	0.6	74	21	Suffolk, MA	7.0	70	21	San Mateo, CA	21.9
38	21	Contra Costa, CA	0.6	19	22	Middlesex, MA	6.3	2	22	Cook, IL	19.9
10	21	Dallas, TX	0.6	25	23	Clark, NV	5.3	7	23	Kings, NY	19.8
37	21	Erie, NY	0.6	64	23	Ventura, CA	5.3	20	24	Tarrant, TX	19.7
20	21	Tarrant, TX	0.6	3	25	Harris, TX	5.1	21	25	Alameda, CA	19.0
56	21	Travis, TX	0.6	71	26	Pierce, WA	5.1	45	26	Orange, FL	18.8
17	27	New York, NY	0.5	2	27	Cook, IL	4.8	35	27	Hillsborough, FL	18.0
9	27	Queens, NY	0.5	32	27	Hennepin, MN	4.8	38	28	Contra Costa, CA	17.7
3	29	Harris, TX	0.4	26	29	Nassau, NY	4.7	15	29	Broward, FL	16.7
35	29	Hillsborough, FL	0.4	13	29	San Bernardino, CA	4.7	29	30	Sacramento, CA	16.0
7	29	Kings, NY	0.4	18	31	Philadelphia, PA	4.5	40	31	Westchester, NY	15.6
72	29	Mecklenburg, NC	0.4	56	31	Travis, TX	4.5	74	32	Suffolk, MA	15.5
62	29	San Francisco, CA	0.4	40	31	Westchester, NY	4.5	59	33	Essex, NJ	15.4
70	29	San Mateo, CA	0.4	30	34	Oakland, MI	4.1	62	34	San Francisco, CA	14.1
74	29	Suffolk, MA	0.4	10	35	Dallas, TX	4.0	66	35	Middlesex, NJ	13.6
11	29	Wayne, MI	0.4	67	35	Montgomery, PA	4.0	31	36	Palm Beach, FL	12.4
63	37	Baltimore, MD	0.3	57	37	Prince George's, MD	3.9	47	37	Fairfield, CT	11.9
2	37	Cook, IL	0.3	59	38	Essex, NJ	3.7	43	37	Salt Lake, UT	11.9
61	37	Duval, FL	0.3	16	38	Riverside, CA	3.7	51	39	Hartford, CT	11.5
36	37	Fairfax, VA	0.3	20	40	Tarrant, TX	3.6	49	39	Montgomery, MD	11.5
33	37	Franklin, OH	0.3	45	41	Orange, FL	3.4	69	41	Essex, MA	11.0
60	37	Macomb, MI	0.3	47	42	Fairfield, CT	3.3	36	41	Fairfax, VA	11.0
50	37	Marion, IN	0.3	63	43	Baltimore, MD	3.2	22	43	Suffolk, NY	10.5
68	37	Monroe, NY	0.3	33	44	Franklin, OH	3.1	46	44	Bergen, NJ	10.3
49	37	Montgomery, MD	0.3	72	44	Mecklenburg, NC	3.1	54	45	New Haven, CT	10.1
30	37	Oakland, MI	0.3	27	46	Bronx, NY	3.0	26	46	Nassau, NY	10.0
45	37	Orange, FL	0.3	55	46	Fulton, GA	3.0	42	47	Du Page, IL	9.0
18	37	Philadelphia, PA	0.3	61	48	Duval, FL	2.7	39	48	Milwaukee, WI	8.8
41	37	Pinellas, FL	0.3	39	49	Milwaukee, WI	2.6	18	49	Philadelphia, PA	8.5
57	37	Prince George's, MD	0.3	43	49	Salt Lake, UT	2.6	57	50	Prince George's, MD	7.1
22	37	Suffolk, NY	0.3	65	49	Worcester, MA	2.6	65	51	Worcester, MA	6.8
40	37	Westchester, NY	0.3	51	52	Hartford, CT	2.4	48	52	Honolulu, HI	6.7
65	37	Worcester, MA	0.3	68	52	Monroe, NY	2.4	72	53	Mecklenburg, NC	6.5
46	54	Bergen, NJ	0.2	22	52	Suffolk, NY	2.4	55	54	Fulton, GA	5.9
15	54	Broward, FL	0.2	15	55	Broward, FL	2.3	12	55	King, WA	5.5
23	54	Cuyahoga, OH	0.2	69	55	Essex, MA	2.3	71	55	Pierce, WA	5.5
42	54	Du Page, IL	0.2	54	55	New Haven, CT	2.3	68	57	Monroe, NY	5.3
69	54	Essex, MA	0.2	35	58	Hillsborough, FL	2.2	19	58	Middlesex, MA	4.6
59	54	Essex, NJ	0.2	4	58	Maricopa, AZ	2.2	41	58	Pinellas, FL	4.6
47	54	Fairfield, CT	0.2	34	58	St. Louis, MO	2.2	61	60	Duval, FL	4.1
55	54	Fulton, GA	0.2	60	61	Macomb, MI	2.1	32	60	Hennepin, MN	4.1
52	54	Hamilton, OH	0.2	41	61	Pinellas, FL	2.1	50	62	Marion, IN	3.9
51	54	Hartford, CT	0.2	53	63	Pima, AZ	2.0	11	63	Wayne, MI	3.7
48	54	Honolulu, HI	0.2	23	64	Cuyahoga, OH	1.7	23	64	Cuyahoga, OH	3.4
73	54	Jefferson, KY	0.2	28	65	Allegheny, PA	1.7	37	65	Erie, NY	3.3
8	54	Miami-Dade, FL	0.2	11	65	Wayne, MI	1.7	44	66	Shelby, TN	2.6
19	54	Middlesex, MA	0.2	24	67	Bexar, TX	1.6	30	67	Oakland, MI	2.4
66	54	Middlesex, NJ	0.2	52	67	Hamilton, OH	1.6	33	68	Franklin, OH	2.3
26	54	Nassau, NY	0.2	44	67	Shelby, TN	1.6	67	69	Montgomery, PA	2.0
54	54	New Haven, CT	0.2	37	70	Erie, NY	1.5	63	70	Baltimore, MD	1.8
31	54	Palm Beach, FL	0.2	31	70	Palm Beach, FL	1.5	73	70	Jefferson, KY	1.8
44	54	Shelby, TN	0.2	73	72	Jefferson, KY	1.4	60	72	Macomb, MI	1.6
34	54	St. Louis, MO	0.2	50	72	Marion, IN	1.4	34	73	St. Louis, MO	1.4
28	74	Allegheny, PA	0.1	8	72	Miami-Dade, FL	1.4	52	74	Hamilton, OH	1.1
67	74	Montgomery, PA	0.1	75	75	El Paso, TX	1.0	28	75	Allegheny, PA	0.9

Note: Column numbers refer to Table B. States and Counties.

TABLE 2—75 Largest Counties by 2000 Population
Selected Rankings

Percent Under 18 Years, 2000				Percent Age 25 to 54 Years, 2000				Percent Age 65 Years and Over, 2000			
Population Rank	Under 18 Years Rank	County	[cols 28 & 29] Percent Under 18 Years	Population Rank	25 to 54 Years Rank	County	[cols 31, 32, & 33] Percent 25 to 54 Years	Population Rank	65 Years and Over Rank	County	[cols 35 & 36] Percent 65 Years and Over
13	1	San Bernardino, CA	32.3	62	1	San Francisco, CA	54.3	31	1	Palm Beach, FL	23.1
58	2	Fresno, CA	32.1	17	2	New York, NY	51.6	41	2	Pinellas, FL	22.5
75	3	El Paso, TX	32.0	36	3	Fairfax, VA	50.1	28	3	Allegheny, PA	17.8
43	4	Salt Lake, UT	30.5	12	4	King, WA	49.7	15	4	Broward, FL	16.1
16	5	Riverside, CA	30.4	72	5	Mecklenburg, NC	49.4	37	5	Erie, NY	15.9
27	6	Bronx, NY	29.8	55	6	Fulton, GA	48.9	23	6	Cuyahoga, OH	15.6
3	7	Harris, TX	29.0	56	6	Travis, TX	48.9	46	7	Bergen, NJ	15.3
24	8	Bexar, TX	28.5	14	8	Santa Clara, CA	48.4	26	8	Nassau, NY	15.0
64	8	Ventura, CA	28.5	21	9	Alameda, CA	47.8	67	9	Montgomery, PA	14.9
44	10	Shelby, TN	28.2	70	9	San Mateo, CA	47.8	63	10	Baltimore, MD	14.7
20	11	Tarrant, TX	28.1	32	11	Hennepin, MN	47.7	51	11	Hartford, CT	14.6
1	12	Los Angeles, CA	28.0	30	12	Oakland, MI	47.6	54	12	New Haven, CT	14.4
11	12	Wayne, MI	28.0	49	13	Montgomery, MD	47.5	53	13	Pima, AZ	14.2
10	14	Dallas, TX	27.9	19	14	Middlesex, MA	47.2	18	14	Philadelphia, PA	14.1
29	15	Sacramento, CA	27.6	42	15	Du Page, IL	46.9	34	15	St. Louis, MO	14.0
71	16	Pierce, WA	27.2	57	16	Prince George's, MD	46.7	40	16	Westchester, NY	13.9
4	17	Maricopa, AZ	27.0	74	17	Suffolk, MA	46.5	69	17	Essex, MA	13.8
5	17	Orange, CA	27.0	10	18	Dallas, TX	46.4	60	18	Macomb, MI	13.7
7	19	Kings, NY	26.9	20	18	Tarrant, TX	46.4	62	19	San Francisco, CA	13.6
42	20	Du Page, IL	26.8	45	20	Orange, FL	46.3	52	20	Hamilton, OH	13.5
57	21	Prince George's, MD	26.7	3	21	Harris, TX	46.2	73	20	Jefferson, KY	13.5
38	22	Contra Costa, CA	26.6	66	21	Middlesex, NJ	46.2	48	22	Honolulu, HI	13.4
61	23	Duval, FL	26.3	33	23	Franklin, OH	46.1	47	23	Fairfield, CT	13.3
39	23	Milwaukee, WI	26.3	9	24	Queens, NY	46.0	8	23	Miami-Dade, FL	13.3
59	25	Essex, NJ	26.1	5	25	Orange, CA	45.9	65	25	Worcester, MA	13.1
22	25	Suffolk, NY	26.1	61	26	Duval, FL	45.7	39	26	Milwaukee, WI	13.0
2	27	Cook, IL	26.0	50	26	Marion, IN	45.7	68	26	Monroe, NY	13.0
52	28	Hamilton, OH	25.8	38	28	Contra Costa, CA	45.6	19	28	Middlesex, MA	12.7
50	28	Marion, IN	25.8	46	29	Bergen, NJ	45.2	9	28	Queens, NY	12.7
6	28	San Diego, CA	25.8	60	29	Macomb, MI	45.2	16	28	Riverside, CA	12.7
47	31	Fairfield, CT	25.7	25	31	Clark, NV	45.1	70	31	San Mateo, CA	12.4
65	31	Worcester, MA	25.7	22	31	Suffolk, NY	45.1	66	32	Middlesex, NJ	12.3
25	33	Clark, NV	25.6	35	33	Hillsborough, FL	45.0	17	33	New York, NY	12.1
68	33	Monroe, NY	25.6	47	34	Fairfield, CT	44.9	11	33	Wayne, MI	12.1
36	35	Fairfax, VA	25.4	69	35	Essex, MA	44.8	35	35	Hillsborough, FL	12.0
35	35	Hillsborough, FL	25.4	67	35	Montgomery, PA	44.8	59	36	Essex, NJ	11.9
49	35	Montgomery, MD	25.4	71	35	Pierce, WA	44.8	22	37	Suffolk, NY	11.8
18	38	Philadelphia, PA	25.3	65	35	Worcester, MA	44.8	2	38	Cook, IL	11.7
69	39	Essex, MA	25.2	15	39	Broward, FL	44.7	4	39	Maricopa, AZ	11.6
30	39	Oakland, MI	25.2	1	40	Los Angeles, CA	44.6	7	40	Kings, NY	11.5
45	39	Orange, FL	25.2	6	40	San Diego, CA	44.6	38	41	Contra Costa, CA	11.3
34	39	St. Louis, MO	25.2	44	40	Shelby, TN	44.6	30	41	Oakland, MI	11.3
33	43	Franklin, OH	25.1	73	43	Jefferson, KY	44.5	49	43	Montgomery, MD	11.2
72	43	Mecklenburg, NC	25.1	40	43	Westchester, NY	44.5	6	43	San Diego, CA	11.2
40	45	Westchester, NY	25.0	64	45	Ventura, CA	44.3	50	45	Marion, IN	11.1
23	46	Cuyahoga, OH	24.9	63	46	Baltimore, MD	44.2	29	45	Sacramento, CA	11.1
8	47	Miami-Dade, FL	24.8	2	46	Cook, IL	44.2	74	45	Suffolk, MA	11.1
14	47	Santa Clara, CA	24.8	59	48	Essex, NJ	44.1	32	48	Hennepin, MN	11.0
26	49	Nassau, NY	24.7	29	48	Sacramento, CA	44.1	25	49	Clark, NV	10.7
51	50	Hartford, CT	24.6	48	50	Honolulu, HI	44.0	61	50	Duval, FL	10.5
53	50	Pima, AZ	24.6	51	51	Hartford, CT	43.8	24	51	Bexar, TX	10.4
21	52	Alameda, CA	24.5	8	52	Miami-Dade, FL	43.6	12	51	King, WA	10.4
55	52	Fulton, GA	24.5	54	52	New Haven, CT	43.6	21	53	Alameda, CA	10.2
54	54	New Haven, CT	24.4	26	54	Nassau, NY	43.5	71	53	Pierce, WA	10.2
37	55	Erie, NY	24.3	68	55	Monroe, NY	43.4	64	53	Ventura, CA	10.2
73	56	Jefferson, KY	24.2	11	55	Wayne, MI	43.4	27	56	Bronx, NY	10.0
60	57	Macomb, MI	24.1	7	57	Kings, NY	43.3	58	56	Fresno, CA	10.0
67	57	Montgomery, PA	24.1	4	57	Maricopa, AZ	43.3	45	56	Orange, FL	10.0
32	59	Hennepin, MN	24.0	34	57	St. Louis, MO	43.3	44	59	Shelby, TN	9.9
48	60	Honolulu, HI	23.8	24	60	Bexar, TX	43.0	42	60	Du Page, IL	9.8
66	61	Middlesex, NJ	23.7	52	61	Hamilton, OH	42.9	33	60	Franklin, OH	9.8
56	61	Travis, TX	23.7	39	61	Milwaukee, WI	42.9	1	60	Los Angeles, CA	9.8
63	63	Baltimore, MD	23.6	23	63	Cuyahoga, OH	42.6	5	60	Orange, CA	9.8
15	64	Broward, FL	23.5	28	64	Allegheny, PA	42.6	75	64	El Paso, TX	9.7
46	65	Bergen, NJ	23.0	43	65	Salt Lake, UT	42.1	14	65	Santa Clara, CA	9.6
70	66	San Mateo, CA	22.9	37	66	Erie, NY	42.0	72	66	Mecklenburg, NC	8.6
9	67	Queens, NY	22.8	13	66	San Bernardino, CA	42.0	13	66	San Bernardino, CA	8.6
12	68	King, WA	22.5	27	68	Bronx, NY	41.8	55	68	Fulton, GA	8.5
19	68	Middlesex, MA	22.5	53	69	Pima, AZ	41.5	20	69	Tarrant, TX	8.3
28	70	Allegheny, PA	21.9	41	70	Pinellas, FL	41.4	43	70	Salt Lake, UT	8.1
31	71	Palm Beach, FL	21.3	18	71	Philadelphia, PA	41.3	10	71	Dallas, TX	8.0
74	72	Suffolk, MA	20.2	75	72	El Paso, TX	40.6	36	72	Fairfax, VA	7.9
41	73	Pinellas, FL	19.2	16	73	Riverside, CA	40.3	57	73	Prince George's, MD	7.7
17	74	New York, NY	16.7	58	74	Fresno, CA	40.0	3	74	Harris, TX	7.4
62	75	San Francisco, CA	14.6	31	75	Palm Beach, FL	39.5	56	75	Travis, TX	6.8

Note: Column numbers refer to Table B. States and Counties.

TABLE 2—75 Largest Counties by 2000 Population
Selected Rankings

Percent Female-headed Family Households, 2000				Percent Living Alone, 2000				Percent Married Couple Family Households, 2000			
Population Rank	Female Households Rank 1996-98	County	[col 76] Percent Female Households	Population Rank	Living Alone Rate	County	[col 79] Percent Living Alone	Population Rank	Married Couple Family Households Rank	County	[col 74] Percent Married Couple Family Households
27	1	Bronx, NY	30.4	17	1	New York, NY	48.0	26	1	Nassau, NY	63.1
7	2	Kings, NY	22.3	62	2	San Francisco, CA	38.6	22	2	Suffolk, NY	62.0
18	2	Philadelphia, PA	22.3	74	3	Suffolk, MA	36.3	42	3	Du Page, IL	60.9
11	4	Wayne, MI	20.6	41	4	Pinellas, FL	34.1	64	4	Ventura, CA	59.5
59	5	Essex, NJ	20.4	18	5	Philadelphia, PA	33.8	36	5	Fairfax, VA	59.4
44	6	Shelby, TN	20.1	39	6	Milwaukee, WI	33.0	46	6	Bergen, NJ	57.9
57	7	Prince George's, MD	19.6	52	7	Hamilton, OH	32.9	43	7	Salt Lake, UT	57.8
75	8	El Paso, TX	18.0	23	8	Cuyahoga, OH	32.8	67	8	Montgomery, PA	57.2
8	9	Miami-Dade, FL	17.2	28	9	Allegheny, PA	32.7	66	9	Middlesex, NJ	57.0
55	10	Fulton, GA	16.5	55	10	Fulton, GA	32.2	75	10	El Paso, TX	56.7
39	11	Milwaukee, WI	16.3	32	11	Hennepin, MN	31.8	16	11	Riverside, CA	56.5
74	11	Suffolk, MA	16.3	50	11	Marion, IN	31.8	5	12	Orange, CA	55.9
9	13	Queens, NY	16.0	33	13	Franklin, OH	30.9	13	13	San Bernardino, CA	55.8
23	14	Cuyahoga, OH	15.7	37	14	Erie, NY	30.5	47	14	Fairfield, CT	55.5
2	15	Cook, IL	15.6	73	14	Jefferson, KY	30.5	49	15	Montgomery, MD	55.2
61	15	Duval, FL	15.6	12	14	King, WA	30.5	14	16	Santa Clara, CA	54.9
24	17	Bexar, TX	15.5	56	17	Travis, TX	30.1	38	17	Contra Costa, CA	54.5
58	18	Fresno, CA	15.2	15	18	Broward, FL	29.6	48	17	Honolulu, HI	54.5
50	19	Marion, IN	14.9	2	19	Cook, IL	29.4	60	19	Macomb, MI	54.3
13	20	San Bernardino, CA	14.8	31	20	Palm Beach, FL	29.2	30	20	Oakland, MI	54.2
73	21	Jefferson, KY	14.7	68	21	Monroe, NY	28.6	40	21	Westchester, NY	53.9
1	21	Los Angeles, CA	14.7	53	22	Pima, AZ	28.5	70	22	San Mateo, CA	53.0
52	23	Hamilton, OH	14.3	11	23	Wayne, MI	28.3	71	23	Pioroo, WA	52.8
10	24	Dallas, TX	14.1	54	24	New Haven, CT	28.2	20	24	Tarrant, TX	52.6
29	24	Sacramento, CA	14.1	34	25	St. Louis, MO	28.0	58	25	Fresno, CA	52.5
37	26	Erie, NY	13.7	51	26	Hartford, CT	27.9	65	25	Worcester, MA	52.5
3	26	Harris, TX	13.7	7	27	Kings, NY	27.8	4	27	Maricopa, AZ	51.6
45	26	Orange, FL	13.7	72	28	Mecklenburg, NC	27.6	19	28	Middlesex, MA	51.3
54	29	New Haven, CT	13.6	27	29	Bronx, NY	27.4	69	29	Essex, MA	51.1
51	30	Hartford, CT	13.5	63	30	Baltimore, MD	27.3	34	30	St. Louis, MO	51.0
68	31	Monroe, NY	13.4	10	30	Dallas, TX	27.3	31	31	Palm Beach, FL	50.8
35	32	Hillsborough, FL	13.2	30	30	Oakland, MI	27.3	6	32	San Diego, CA	50.7
21	33	Alameda, CA	13.0	69	33	Essex, MA	27.1	3	33	Harris, TX	50.6
33	33	Franklin, OH	13.0	19	33	Middlesex, MA	27.1	24	34	Bexar, TX	50.5
63	35	Baltimore, MD	12.8	44	35	Shelby, TN	27.0	63	35	Baltimore, MD	49.4
34	36	St. Louis, MO	12.7	35	36	Hillsborough, FL	26.9	51	36	Hartford, CT	49.2
17	37	New York, NY	12.6	60	36	Macomb, MI	26.9	25	37	Clark, NV	48.7
15	38	Broward, FL	12.5	59	38	Essex, NJ	26.7	54	38	New Haven, CT	48.6
28	39	Allegheny, PA	12.4	29	38	Sacramento, CA	26.7	35	39	Hillsborough, FL	47.7
69	39	Essex, MA	12.4	61	40	Duval, FL	26.5	72	39	Mecklenburg, NC	47.7
72	39	Mecklenburg, NC	12.4	65	41	Worcester, MA	26.2	8	39	Miami-Dade, FL	47.7
48	42	Honolulu, HI	12.3	21	42	Alameda, CA	26.0	53	39	Pima, AZ	47.7
20	43	Tarrant, TX	12.2	40	43	Westchester, NY	25.7	1	43	Los Angeles, CA	47.6
40	43	Westchester, NY	12.2	67	44	Montgomery, PA	25.6	68	44	Monroe, NY	47.4
16	45	Riverside, CA	12.0	9	44	Queens, NY	25.6	21	45	Alameda, CA	47.0
25	46	Clark, NV	11.8	3	46	Harris, TX	25.1	45	45	Orange, FL	47.0
71	46	Pierce, WA	11.8	20	47	Tarrant, TX	24.9	10	47	Dallas, TX	46.9
53	46	Pima, AZ	11.8	46	48	Bergen, NJ	24.7	9	47	Queens, NY	46.9
6	49	San Diego, CA	11.6	1	49	Los Angeles, CA	24.6	61	49	Duval, FL	46.5
38	50	Contra Costa, CA	11.5	70	49	San Mateo, CA	24.6	37	49	Erie, NY	46.5
47	50	Fairfield, CT	11.5	25	51	Clark, NV	24.5	12	51	King, WA	46.4
65	52	Worcester, MA	11.4	4	51	Maricopa, AZ	24.5	29	51	Sacramento, CA	46.4
26	53	Nassau, NY	10.9	49	53	Montgomery, MD	24.4	28	53	Allegheny, PA	46.1
64	53	Ventura, CA	10.9	71	54	Pierce, WA	24.3	15	53	Broward, FL	46.1
66	55	Middlesex, NJ	10.8	45	55	Orange, FL	24.2	32	55	Hennepin, MN	45.3
22	55	Suffolk, NY	10.8	6	55	San Diego, CA	24.2	73	56	Jefferson, KY	45.2
4	57	Maricopa, AZ	10.7	57	57	Prince George's, MD	24.1	41	57	Pinellas, FL	44.8
5	57	Orange, CA	10.7	24	58	Bexar, TX	24.0	2	58	Cook, IL	44.0
49	59	Montgomery, MD	10.5	47	58	Fairfield, CT	24.0	57	58	Prince George's, MD	44.0
41	59	Pinellas, FL	10.5	8	60	Miami-Dade, FL	23.3	52	60	Hamilton, OH	43.4
43	61	Salt Lake, UT	10.4	38	61	Contra Costa, CA	22.9	33	61	Franklin, OH	43.0
56	61	Travis, TX	10.4	42	61	Du Page, IL	22.9	44	62	Shelby, TN	42.8
60	63	Macomb, MI	10.1	66	63	Middlesex, NJ	22.4	56	63	Travis, TX	42.6
70	63	San Mateo, CA	10.1	48	64	Honolulu, HI	21.6	23	64	Cuyahoga, OH	42.4
14	65	Santa Clara, CA	10.0	36	65	Fairfax, VA	21.4	59	65	Essex, NJ	42.3
32	66	Hennepin, MN	9.9	14	65	Santa Clara, CA	21.4	50	66	Marion, IN	41.2
19	66	Middlesex, MA	9.9	5	67	Orange, CA	21.1	11	67	Wayne, MI	40.7
46	68	Bergen, NJ	9.7	43	68	Salt Lake, UT	20.8	39	68	Milwaukee, WI	39.0
31	68	Palm Beach, FL	9.7	16	69	Riverside, CA	20.7	7	69	Kings, NY	38.6
30	70	Oakland, MI	9.5	58	70	Fresno, CA	20.6	55	70	Fulton, GA	37.3
12	71	King, WA	9.0	64	71	Ventura, CA	18.9	18	71	Philadelphia, PA	32.1
62	72	San Francisco, CA	8.9	26	72	Nassau, NY	18.8	62	72	San Francisco, CA	31.6
67	73	Montgomery, PA	8.8	13	73	San Bernardino, CA	18.4	27	73	Bronx, NY	31.4
36	74	Fairfax, VA	8.6	22	74	Suffolk, NY	18.3	74	74	Suffolk, MA	29.3
42	75	Du Page, IL	7.9	75	75	El Paso, TX	17.8	17	75	New York, NY	25.2

Note: Column numbers refer to Table B. States and Counties.

TABLE 2—75 Largest Counties by 2000 Population
Selected Rankings

Percent of Families with Own Children Under 18 Years, 2000				Percent Owner Occupied Housing Units, 2000				Percent Recreational/Seasonal Housing Units, 2000			
Population Rank	Families with Own Children Under 18 Years Rank	County	[col 73] Percent of Families with Own Children Under 18 Years	Population Rank	Owner Occupied Housing Rank	County	[col 94] Percent in Owner Occupied Housing Units	Recreational/Seasonal Housing Units Rank	Group Quarters Rank	County	[col 90] Percent Recreational/Seasonal Housing Units
75	1	El Paso, TX	44.9	26	1	Nassau, NY	80.3	31	1	Palm Beach, FL	9.5
13	2	San Bernardino, CA	43.7	22	2	Suffolk, NY	79.8	22	2	Suffolk, NY	7.3
58	3	Fresno, CA	41.2	60	3	Macomb, MI	78.9	41	3	Pinellas, FL	7.1
43	4	Salt Lake, UT	40.1	42	4	Du Page, IL	76.4	16	4	Riverside, CA	6.5
64	5	Ventura, CA	39.7	30	5	Oakland, MI	74.7	15	5	Broward, FL	6.3
16	6	Riverside, CA	38.9	31	5	Palm Beach, FL	74.7	13	6	San Bernardino, CA	5.3
27	7	Bronx, NY	38.1	34	7	St. Louis, MO	74.1	4	7	Maricopa, AZ	4.0
3	8	Harris, TX	37.7	67	8	Montgomery, PA	73.5	8	8	Miami-Dade, FL	3.5
42	9	Du Page, IL	37.0	36	9	Fairfax, VA	70.9	53	9	Pima, AZ	2.9
5	9	Orange, CA	37.0	41	10	Pinellas, FL	70.8	17	10	New York, NY	2.4
22	9	Suffolk, NY	37.0	15	11	Broward, FL	69.5	48	11	Honolulu, HI	2.2
1	12	Los Angeles, CA	36.8	38	12	Contra Costa, CA	69.3	25	12	Clark, NV	1.5
20	12	Tarrant, TX	36.8	47	13	Fairfield, CT	69.2	69	12	Essex, MA	1.5
24	14	Bexar, TX	36.6	43	14	Salt Lake, UT	69.0	45	12	Orange, FL	1.5
36	15	Fairfax, VA	36.3	16	15	Riverside, CA	68.9	35	15	Hillsborough, FL	1.4
71	16	Pierce, WA	35.9	49	16	Montgomery, MD	68.7	6	15	San Diego, CA	1.4
38	17	Contra Costa, CA	35.4	63	17	Baltimore, MD	67.6	58	17	Fresno, CA	1.3
26	18	Nassau, NY	35.3	64	17	Ventura, CA	67.6	47	18	Fairfield, CT	1.1
57	18	Prince George's, MD	35.3	4	19	Maricopa, AZ	67.5	62	18	San Francisco, CA	1.1
10	20	Dallas, TX	35.1	46	20	Bergen, NJ	67.2	64	18	Ventura, CA	1.1
49	21	Montgomery, MD	35.0	28	21	Allegheny, PA	67.0	54	21	New Haven, CT	1.0
14	22	Santa Clara, CA	34.9	66	22	Middlesex, NJ	66.7	65	21	Worcester, MA	1.0
47	23	Fairfield, CT	34.2	11	23	Wayne, MI	66.6	5	23	Orange, CA	0.9
66	23	Middlesex, NJ	34.2	32	24	Hennepin, MN	66.2	71	23	Pierce, WA	0.9
44	23	Shelby, TN	34.2	37	25	Erie, NY	65.3	56	23	Travis, TX	0.9
40	26	Westchester, NY	34.0	68	26	Monroe, NY	65.1	30	26	Oakland, MI	0.8
6	27	San Diego, CA	33.9	73	27	Jefferson, KY	64.9	40	26	Westchester, NY	0.8
59	28	Essex, NJ	33.8	13	28	San Bernardino, CA	64.5	12	28	King, WA	0.7
8	28	Miami-Dade, FL	33.8	53	29	Pima, AZ	64.3	26	28	Nassau, NY	0.7
29	30	Sacramento, CA	33.7	51	30	Hartford, CT	64.2	43	28	Salt Lake, UT	0.7
65	31	Worcester, MA	33.6	35	31	Hillsborough, FL	64.1	36	31	Fairfax, VA	0.6
61	32	Duval, FL	33.3	65	31	Worcester, MA	64.1	9	31	Queens, NY	0.6
7	32	Kings, NY	33.3	75	33	El Paso, TX	63.6	70	31	San Mateo, CA	0.6
4	34	Maricopa, AZ	33.0	69	34	Essex, MA	63.5	74	31	Suffolk, MA	0.6
69	35	Essex, MA	32.8	71	34	Pierce, WA	63.5	24	35	Bexar, TX	0.5
11	35	Wayne, MI	32.8	23	36	Cuyahoga, OH	63.2	38	35	Contra Costa, CA	0.5
21	37	Alameda, CA	32.6	61	37	Duval, FL	63.1	37	35	Erie, NY	0.5
30	38	Oakland, MI	32.4	54	37	New Haven, CT	63.1	55	35	Fulton, GA	0.5
45	38	Orange, FL	32.4	44	37	Shelby, TN	63.1	51	35	Hartford, CT	0.5
46	40	Bergen, NJ	32.1	72	40	Mecklenburg, NC	62.3	32	35	Hennepin, MN	0.5
72	40	Mecklenburg, NC	32.1	57	41	Prince George's, MD	61.8	72	35	Mecklenburg, NC	0.5
67	42	Montgomery, PA	32.0	19	42	Middlesex, MA	61.7	19	35	Middlesex, MA	0.5
48	43	Honolulu, HI	31.8	5	43	Orange, CA	61.4	49	35	Montgomery, MD	0.5
68	43	Monroe, NY	31.8	70	43	San Mateo, CA	61.4	28	44	Allegheny, PA	0.4
25	45	Clark, NV	31.7	24	45	Bexar, TX	61.2	63	44	Baltimore, MD	0.4
34	46	St. Louis, MO	31.6	20	46	Tarrant, TX	60.8	46	44	Bergen, NJ	0.4
9	47	Queens, NY	31.5	45	47	Orange, FL	60.7	23	44	Cuyahoga, OH	0.4
35	48	Hillsborough, FL	31.4	40	48	Westchester, NY	60.1	42	44	Du Page, IL	0.4
51	49	Hartford, CT	31.3	52	49	Hamilton, OH	59.9	61	44	Duval, FL	0.4
54	50	New Haven, CT	31.2	12	50	King, WA	59.8	75	44	El Paso, TX	0.4
60	51	Macomb, MI	31.1	14	50	Santa Clara, CA	59.8	33	44	Franklin, OH	0.4
70	51	San Mateo, CA	31.1	50	52	Marion, IN	59.3	3	44	Harris, TX	0.4
2	53	Cook, IL	30.9	18	52	Philadelphia, PA	59.3	73	44	Jefferson, KY	0.4
33	54	Franklin, OH	30.4	25	54	Clark, NV	59.1	1	44	Los Angeles, CA	0.4
63	55	Baltimore, MD	30.2	29	55	Sacramento, CA	58.2	60	44	Macomb, MI	0.4
52	55	Hamilton, OH	30.2	2	56	Cook, IL	57.9	68	44	Monroe, NY	0.4
50	55	Marion, IN	30.2	8	57	Miami-Dade, FL	57.8	14	44	Santa Clara, CA	0.4
19	55	Middlesex, MA	30.2	33	58	Franklin, OH	56.9	34	44	St. Louis, MO	0.4
37	59	Erie, NY	29.6	58	59	Fresno, CA	56.5	21	59	Alameda, CA	0.3
73	59	Jefferson, KY	29.6	6	60	San Diego, CA	55.4	2	59	Cook, IL	0.3
39	61	Milwaukee, WI	29.5	3	61	Harris, TX	55.3	10	59	Dallas, TX	0.3
15	62	Broward, FL	29.3	21	62	Alameda, CA	54.7	52	59	Hamilton, OH	0.3
56	62	Travis, TX	29.3	48	63	Honolulu, HI	54.6	7	59	Kings, NY	0.3
53	64	Pima, AZ	29.2	10	64	Dallas, TX	52.6	50	59	Marion, IN	0.3
32	65	Hennepin, MN	28.8	39	64	Milwaukee, WI	52.6	66	59	Middlesex, NJ	0.3
55	66	Fulton, GA	28.7	55	66	Fulton, GA	52.0	67	59	Montgomery, PA	0.3
23	67	Cuyahoga, OH	28.4	56	67	Travis, TX	51.4	18	59	Philadelphia, PA	0.3
12	68	King, WA	28.4	1	68	Los Angeles, CA	47.9	29	59	Sacramento, CA	0.3
18	69	Philadelphia, PA	27.6	59	69	Essex, NJ	45.6	44	59	Shelby, TN	0.3
28	70	Allegheny, PA	26.4	9	70	Queens, NY	42.8	20	59	Tarrant, TX	0.3
31	71	Palm Beach, FL	24.9	62	71	San Francisco, CA	35.0	11	59	Wayne, MI	0.3
74	72	Suffolk, MA	23.5	74	72	Suffolk, MA	33.9	27	72	Bronx, NY	0.2
41	73	Pinellas, FL	22.1	7	73	Kings, NY	27.1	59	72	Essex, NJ	0.2
17	74	New York, NY	17.1	17	74	New York, NY	20.1	39	72	Milwaukee, WI	0.2
62	75	San Francisco, CA	16.6	27	75	Bronx, NY	19.6	57	72	Prince George's, MD	0.2

Note: Column numbers refer to Table B. States and Counties.

TABLE 3—All Counties
Selected Rankings

Total Persons, 2000			Land Area (Square Kilometers), 2000				Population Density (per Square Kilometer), 2000			
Popu-lation Rank	County	[col 2] Population	Popu-lation Rank	Land Area Rank	County	[col 1] Land Area	Popu-lation Rank	Density Rank	County	[col 4] Density
1	Los Angeles, CA	9 519 338	2734	1	Yukon-Koyukuk, AK	377 878	17	1	New York, NY	26 054.2
2	Cook, IL	5 376 741	2649	2	North Slope, AK	230 035	7	2	Kings, NY	13 471.7
3	Harris, TX	3 400 578	2021	3	Bethel, AK	105 240	27	3	Bronx, NY	12 226.1
4	Maricopa, AZ	3 072 149	2666	4	Northwest Arctic Borough, AK	92 976	9	4	Queens, NY	7 877.7
5	Orange, CA	2 846 289	2429	5	Valdez-Cordova, AK	88 886	62	5	San Francisco, CA	6 419.3
6	San Diego, CA	2 813 833	2765	6	Southeast Fairbanks, AK	64 270	88	6	Hudson, NJ	5 032.9
7	Kings, NY	2 465 326	810	7	Matanuska-Susitna, AK	63 925	74	7	Suffolk, MA	4 538.2
8	Miami-Dade, FL	2 253 362	3078	8	Lake and Peninsula Borough, AK	61 595	18	8	Philadelphia, PA	4 335.9
9	Queens, NY	2 229 379	2514	9	Nome, AK	59 572	94	9	District of Columbia	3 597.9
10	Dallas, TX	2 218 899	13	10	San Bernardino, CA	51 936	421	10	Alexandria City, VA	3 289.3
11	Wayne, MI	2 061 162	2854	11	Dillingham, AK	48 367	82	11	Baltimore city, MD	3 115.6
12	King, WA	1 737 034	463	12	Coconino, AZ	48 219	134	12	Richmond, NY	2 938.6
13	San Bernardino, CA	1 709 434	1333	13	Nye, NV	47 000	291	13	Arlington, VA	2 827.7
14	Santa Clara, CA	1 682 585	2681	14	Wade Hampton, AK	44 531	59	14	Essex, NJ	2 427.0
15	Broward, FL	1 623 018	993	15	Elko, NV	44 493	2	15	Cook, IL	2 195.5
16	Riverside, CA	1 545 387	922	16	Kenai Peninsula, AK	41 474	168	16	St. Louis city, MO	2 176.2
17	New York, NY	1 537 195	344	17	Mohave, AZ	34 477	2406	17	Falls Church City, VA	2 075.4
18	Philadelphia, PA	1 517 550	3074	18	Denali Borough, AK	33 021	106	18	Union, NJ	1 949.8
19	Middlesex, MA	1 465 396	714	19	Apache, AZ	29 021	26	19	Nassau, NY	1 796.2
20	Tarrant, TX	1 446 219	2902	20	Lincoln, NV	27 541	2417	20	Manassas Park City, VA	1 715.0
21	Alameda, CA	1 443 741	1173	21	Sweetwater, WY	27 001	247	21	Norfolk City, VA	1 686.4
22	Suffolk, NY	1 419 369	1902	22	Inyo, CA	26 426	997	22	Charlottesville City, VA	1 668.5
23	Cuyahoga, OH	1 393 978	2636	23	Harney, OR	26 248	39	23	Milwaukee, WI	1 501.9
24	Bexar, TX	1 392 931	532	24	Navajo, AZ	25 779	46	24	Bergen, NJ	1 456.5
25	Clark, NV	1 375 765	1356	25	Malheur, OR	25 607	101	25	Denver, CO	1 397.1
26	Nassau, NY	1 334 544	2015	26	Humboldt, NV	24 988	5	26	Orange, CA	1 391.8
27	Bronx, NY	1 332 650	4	27	Maricopa, AZ	23 836	1244	27	Manassas City, VA	1 351.3
28	Allegheny, PA	1 281 666	53	28	Pima, AZ	23 792	1715	28	Fairfax City, VA	1 343.6
29	Sacramento, CA	1 223 499	1225	29	Fremont, WY	23 782	11	29	Wayne, MI	1 295.5
30	Oakland, MI	1 194 156	2515	30	White Pine, NV	22 989	41	30	Pinellas, FL	1 271.0
31	Palm Beach, FL	1 131 184	2052	31	Idaho, ID	21 976	108	31	Ramsey, MN	1 268.1
32	Hennepin, MN	1 116 200	78	32	Kern, CA	21 085	280	32	Richmond City, VA	1 267.9
33	Franklin, OH	1 068 978	2646	33	Lake, OR	21 072	23	33	Cuyahoga, OH	1 174.4
34	St. Louis, MO	1 016 315	322	34	Yavapai, AZ	21 039	522	34	Portsmouth City, VA	1 169.4
35	Hillsborough, FL	998 948	25	35	Clark, NV	20 488	102	35	Delaware, PA	1 154.9
36	Fairfax, VA	969 749	2961	36	Skagway-Hoonah-Angoon, AK	20 452	2701	36	Lexington City, VA	1 144.5
37	Erie, NY	950 265	2045	37	Carbon, WY	20 451	374	37	Hampton City, VA	1 092.8
38	Contra Costa, CA	948 816	2129	38	San Juan, UT	20 254	42	38	Du Page, IL	1 046.5
39	Milwaukee, WI	940 164	2388	39	Owyhee, ID	19 886	117	39	Orleans, LA	1 035.6
40	Westchester, NY	923 459	3124	40	Yakutat Borough, AK	19 815	115	40	Passaic, NJ	1 018.9
41	Pinellas, FL	921 482	2768	41	Prince of Wales-Outer Ketchikan, AK	19 193	306	41	Newport News City, VA	1 017.8
42	Du Page, IL	904 161	627	42	Fairbanks North Star, AK	19 078	1609	42	Winchester City, VA	982.7
43	Salt Lake, UT	898 387	16	43	Riverside, CA	18 667	10	43	Dallas, TX	974.1
44	Shelby, TN	897 472	3014	44	Aleutians East Borough, AK	18 099	76	44	De Kalb, GA	958.1
45	Orange, FL	896 344	1524	45	Park, WY	17 981	36	45	Fairfax, VA	947.9
46	Bergen, NJ	884 118	1092	46	Tooele, UT	17 950	66	46	Middlesex, NJ	935.4
47	Fairfield, CT	882 567	2951	47	Catron, NM	17 943	1	47	Los Angeles, CA	905.1
48	Honolulu, HI	876 156	676	48	Aroostook, ME	17 279	1104	48	Harrisonburg City, VA	899.3
49	Montgomery, MD	873 341	1895	49	Socorro, NM	17 214	1960	49	Colonial Heights City, VA	889.3
50	Marion, IN	860 454	781	50	Otero, NM	17 163	110	50	Camden, NJ	883.6
51	Hartford, CT	857 183	2271	51	Millard, UT	17 066	542	51	Roanoke City, VA	855.1
52	Hamilton, OH	845 303	2167	52	Kodiak Island, AK	16 990	50	52	Marion, IN	838.6
53	Pima, AZ	843 746	172	53	Washoe, NV	16 426	1676	53	Hopewell City, VA	827.6
54	New Haven, CT	824 008	1010	54	Siskiyou, CA	16 283	40	54	Westchester, NY	823.8
55	Fulton, GA	816 006	275	55	St. Louis, MN	16 123	52	55	Hamilton, OH	801.2
56	Travis, TX	812 280	2536	56	Brewster, TX	16 039	913	56	Bristol, RI	791.4
57	Prince George's, MD	801 515	459	57	Cochise, AZ	15 979	32	57	Hennepin, MN	774.1
58	Fresno, CA	799 407	792	58	Chaves, NM	15 723	34	58	St. Louis, MO	772.9
59	Essex, NJ	793 633	2717	59	Pershing, NV	15 635	33	59	Franklin, OH	764.6
60	Macomb, MI	788 149	58	60	Fresno, CA	15 443	3	60	Harris, TX	759.4
61	Duval, FL	778 879	2767	61	Cherry, NE	15 438	21	61	Alameda, CA	755.9
62	San Francisco, CA	776 733	762	62	Klamath, OR	15 395	1829	62	Fredericksburg City, VA	714.0
63	Baltimore, MD	754 292	1074	63	Rio Arriba, NM	15 171	73	63	Jefferson, KY	695.7
64	Ventura, CA	753 197	2719	64	Wrangell-Petersburg, AK	15 112	89	64	Cobb, GA	689.8
65	Worcester, MA	750 963	1042	65	Box Elder, UT	14 823	19	65	Middlesex, MA	687.0
66	Middlesex, NJ	750 162	2513	66	Beaverhead, MT	14 355	49	66	Montgomery, MD	680.7
67	Montgomery, PA	750 097	473	67	San Juan, NM	14 281	28	67	Allegheny, PA	677.8
68	Monroe, NY	735 343	333	68	Yuma, AZ	14 281	141	68	Virginia Beach City, VA	661.4
69	Essex, MA	723 419	2804	69	Lander, NV	14 228	1566	69	Salem City, VA	651.2
70	San Mateo, CA	707 161	667	70	McKinley, NM	14 112	20	70	Tarrant, TX	646.8
71	Pierce, WA	700 820	307	71	Pinal, AZ	13 907	245	71	Clayton, GA	641.0
72	Mecklenburg, NC	695 454	735	72	Natrona, WY	13 830	57	72	Prince George's, MD	637.6
73	Jefferson, KY	693 604	1125	73	Okanogan, WA	13 644	195	73	Rockland, NY	635.8
74	Suffolk, MA	689 807	2865	74	Garfield, UT	13 401	2028	74	Radford City, VA	634.4
75	El Paso, TX	679 622	2872	75	Phillips, MT	13 311	60	75	Macomb, MI	633.6

Note: Column numbers refer to Table B. States and Counties.

TABLE 3—All Counties
Selected Rankings

Percent Population Change, 1990-2000				Percent White, 2000				Percent Black, 2000			
Population Rank	Percent Change Rank	County	[col 52] Percent Change	Population Rank	White Rank	County	[col 9] Percent White	Population Rank	Black Rank	County	[col 10] Percent Black
311	1	Douglas, CO	191.0	3128	1	Slope, ND	99.7	2467	1	Jefferson, MS	86.5
529	2	Forsyth, GA	123.2	3018	2	Faulk, SD	99.5	1590	2	Macon, AL	84.6
1798	3	Elbert, CO	106.0	2983	2	Hanson, SD	99.5	2302	3	Claiborne, MS	84.1
455	4	Henry, GA	103.2	3010	2	Kidder, ND	99.5	2449	4	Greene, AL	80.3
2121	5	Park, CO	102.4	2815	2	Scott, IL	99.5	1289	5	Petersburg City, VA	79.0
320	6	Loudoun, VA	96.8	3131	2	Thomas, NE	99.5	1713	6	Holmes, MS	78.7
636	7	Paulding, GA	96.3	3112	7	Keya Paha, NE	99.4	2438	7	Hancock, GA	77.8
1406	8	Summit, UT	91.6	2479	7	Tyler, WV	99.4	2195	8	Lowndes, AL	73.4
2720	9	Boise, ID	90.1	3080	9	Campbell, SD	99.3	2103	9	Sumter, AL	73.2
1064	10	Eagle, CO	90.0	1074	0	Dolaware, IA	99.3	2318	10	Bullock, AL	73.1
113	11	Collin, TX	86.2	3009	9	Griggs, ND	99.3	2213	11	Wilcox, AL	71.9
572	12	Washington, UT	86.1	2938	9	Hand, SD	99.3	2356	12	Humphreys, MS	71.5
25	13	Clark, NV	85.6	3023	9	Highland, VA	99.3	2355	13	Allendale, SC	71.0
2456	14	Archuleta, CO	85.2	2202	9	Magoffin, KY	99.3	2510	14	Tunica, MS	70.2
1613	15	Summit, CO	82.8	2259	9	Martin, KY	99.3	1268	15	Sunflower, MS	69.9
1333	16	Nye, NV	82.7	2998	9	McPherson, SD	99.3	2260	16	Noxubee, MS	69.3
2953	17	Custer, CO	81.9	2375	9	Mitchell, IA	99.3	2730	16	Sharkey, MS	69.3
2729	18	San Miguel, CO	80.5	2707	18	Audubon, IA	99.2	1384	18	Coahoma, MS	69.2
232	19	Williamson, TX	79.1	2760	18	Boone, NE	99.2	2436	19	Quitman, MS	68.6
1618	20	Gilmer, GA	75.5	3047	18	Burke, ND	99.2	2301	20	Perry, AL	68.4
2780	21	Teton, ID	74.4	2888	18	Edmunds, SD	99.2	2414	21	Wilkinson, MS	68.2
918	22	Flagler, FL	73.6	1982	18	Fentress, TN	99.2	1167	22	Leflore, MS	67.7
2311	23	Spencer, KY	73.0	2947	18	Franklin, WV	99.2	2494	23	East Carroll, LA	67.3
1264	24	Lyon, NV	72.5	2194	18	Jackson, KY	99.2	117	23	Orleans, LA	67.3
2023	25	Dawson, GA	69.7	2867	18	La Moure, ND	99.2	1185	25	Williamsburg, SC	66.3
3125	26	Hinsdale, CO	69.2	2272	18	Leslie, KY	99.2	1096	26	Bolivar, MS	65.1
876	27	Sumter, FL	68.9	3054	18	Liberty, MT	99.2	771	27	Washington, MS	64.6
1035	28	Rockwall, TX	68.3	3037	18	Logan, ND	99.2	82	28	Baltimore city, MD	64.3
300	29	Hamilton, IN	67.7	2857	18	Owsley, KY	99.2	1787	29	Lee, SC	63.6
1920	30	Bandera, TX	67.1	3136	18	Petroleum, MT	99.2	975	30	Dallas, AL	63.3
92	31	Gwinnett, GA	66.7	2852	18	Pickett, TN	99.2	3043	31	Issaquena, MS	62.8
867	32	Christian, MO	66.3	3084	18	Sheridan, ND	99.2	57	32	Prince George's, MD	62.7
2415	33	Long, GA	66.1	2469	18	Webster, WV	99.2	1979	33	Bamberg, SC	62.5
344	34	Mohave, AZ	65.8	2679	18	Wolfe, KY	99.2	1803	34	Bertie, NC	62.3
580	35	Coweta, GA	65.7	2478	35	Cedar, NE	99.1	2264	35	Sussex, VA	62.1
228	36	Collier, FL	65.3	2475	35	Clinton, KY	99.1	2739	36	Talbot, GA	61.6
976	37	Pike, PA	65.2	2894	35	Emmons, ND	99.1	2835	37	Stewart, GA	61.5
1757	38	Teller, CO	64.9	2070	35	Estill, KY	99.1	229	38	Hinds, MS	61.1
1958	39	Torrance, NM	64.4	3101	35	Garfield, MT	99.1	559	39	Orangeburg, SC	60.9
494	40	Delaware, OH	64.3	3109	35	Golden Valley, MT	99.1	2369	40	Terrell, GA	60.7
1883	41	Teton, WY	63.3	2453	35	Howard, IA	99.1	2755	41	Calhoun, GA	60.6
2937	42	Ouray, CO	63.1	2435	35	Jasper, IL	99.1	2967	42	Clay, GA	60.5
1601	43	Kendall, TX	62.7	2312	35	Lyon, IA	99.1	2179	43	Madison, LA	60.3
1288	44	Iron, UT	62.5	2244	35	Pike, IN	99.1	3061	43	Taliaferro, GA	60.3
1791	45	Fluvanna, VA	61.3	2836	35	Putnam, MO	99.1	539	45	Dougherty, GA	60.1
193	46	Montgomery, TX	61.2	2818	35	Ringgold, IA	99.1	94	46	District of Columbia	60.0
1650	47	Wakulla, FL	61.0	2571	35	Warren, IN	99.1	2328	47	Greensville, VA	59.7
2935	48	Echols, GA	60.8	2843	35	Wells, ND	99.1	1666	48	Hertford, NC	59.6
315	49	Osceola, FL	60.1	3117	35	Wheeler, NE	99.1	2157	49	Macon, GA	59.5
1644	50	Pickens, GA	59.3	3133	50	Blaine, NE	99.0	2627	49	Randolph, GA	59.5
1822	51	Lincoln, NM	58.9	2977	50	Bowman, ND	99.0	2753	49	Warren, GA	59.5
2488	52	Nantucket, MA	58.3	2071	50	Butler, IA	99.0	1689	52	Northampton, NC	59.4
139	53	Denton, TX	58.2	1488	50	Carter, KY	99.0	2098	52	Tallahatchie, MS	59.4
498	54	De Soto, MS	57.9	1998	50	Dickenson, VA	99.0	1619	54	Fairfield, SC	59.1
570	55	Spotsylvania, VA	57.5	3042	50	Divide, ND	99.0	1941	55	Hale, AL	59.0
346	56	Benton, AR	57.3	1246	50	Elk, PA	99.0	1505	55	Phillips, AR	59.0
385	56	Cherokee, GA	57.3	2715	50	Elliott, KY	99.0	2401	57	Kemper, MS	58.1
799	56	Walton, GA	57.3	2933	50	Foster, ND	99.0	849	58	Edgecombe, NC	57.5
166	59	Fort Bend, TX	57.2	1685	50	Franklin, IN	99.0	2163	59	Jefferson Davis, MS	57.4
1589	60	Lincoln, SD	56.4	2275	50	Grundy, IA	99.0	2258	60	Lee, AR	57.2
427	61	Williamson, TN	56.3	1142	50	Holmes, OH	99.0	280	60	Richmond City, VA	57.2
2269	62	Grand, CO	56.2	2620	50	Ida, IA	99.0	996	62	Gadsden, FL	57.1
496	63	Kootenai, ID	55.7	1773	50	Jackson, IA	99.0	1872	63	Brunswick, VA	56.9
322	64	Yavapai, AZ	55.5	985	50	Jefferson, PA	99.0	1694	64	Clay, MS	56.3
980	65	Barrow, GA	55.3	3039	50	Jerauld, SD	99.0	1935	64	Jefferson, GA	56.3
1118	65	Taney, MO	55.3	2342	50	Keokuk, IA	99.0	1235	64	Marion, SC	56.3
2862	67	Gilpin, CO	55.0	2014	50	Lafayette, WI	99.0	2810	67	Emporia City, VA	56.2
577	68	Scott, MN	54.7	1687	50	Lincoln, WV	99.0	1719	68	Hampton, SC	55.7
2717	69	Pershing, NV	54.4	3082	50	Rock, NE	99.0	2725	69	Tensas, LA	55.4
307	69	Pinal, AZ	54.4	2817	50	Van Buren, TN	99.0	2694	70	Charles City County, VA...	54.9
466	71	Deschutes, OR	53.9	3034	50	Worth, MO	99.0	1794	71	Warren, NC	54.5
756	72	Sherburne, MN	53.6	2587	72	Adair, IA	98.9	76	72	De Kalb, GA	54.2
302	73	Rutherford, TN	53.5	2882	72	Adams, IA	98.9	2153	73	Chicot, AR	54.0
1795	74	White, GA	53.3	3027	72	Boyd, NE	98.9	1446	73	Yazoo, MS	54.0
1092	75	Tooele, UT	53.1	2637	72	Calhoun, WV	98.9	2450	75	McCormick, SC	53.9

Note: Column numbers refer to Table B. States and Counties.

TABLE 3—All Counties
Selected Rankings

Percent American Indian and Alaska Native, 2000

Population Rank	American Indian and Alaska Native Rank	County	[col 11] Percent American Indian and Alaska Native
2268	1	Shannon, SD	94.2
2681	2	Wade Hampton, AK	92.5
2874	3	Menominee, WI	87.3
2526	4	Todd, SD	85.6
2918	5	Sioux, ND	84.6
2666	6	Northwest Arctic Borough, AK	82.5
2021	7	Bethel, AK	81.9
3063	8	Buffalo, SD	81.6
714	9	Apache, AZ	76.9
2514	10	Nome, AK	75.2
667	11	McKinley, NM	74.7
2786	12	Dewey, SD	74.2
3078	13	Lake and Peninsula Borough, AK	73.5
2186	14	Rolette, ND	73.0
3025	15	Ziebach, SD	72.3
2734	16	Yukon-Koyukuk, AK	70.9
2854	17	Dillingham, AK	70.1
2649	18	North Slope, AK	68.4
2209	19	Glacier, MT	61.8
2899	20	Corson, SD	60.8
2249	21	Big Horn, MT	59.7
2389	22	Roosevelt, MT	55.8
2129	23	San Juan, UT	55.7
3060	24	Mellette, SD	52.4
2946	25	Bennett, SD	52.1
2670	26	Thurston, NE	52.0
2689	27	Benson, ND	48.0
2997	28	Jackson, SD	47.8
532	29	Navajo, AZ	47.7
2685	30	Blaine, MT	45.4
3102	31	Bristol Bay, AK	43.7
1733	32	Adair, OK	42.5
1532	33	Cibola, NM	40.3
3124	34	Yakutat Borough, AK	39.6
2768	35	Prince of Wales-Outer Ketchikan, AK	38.7
437	36	Robeson, NC	38.0
3014	37	Aleutians East Borough, AK	37.3
473	38	San Juan, NM	36.9
2961	39	Skagway-Hoonah-Angoon, AK	35.0
2923	40	Lyman, SD	33.3
1045	41	Cherokee, OK	32.4
2499	41	Rosebud, MT	32.4
2723	43	Mountrail, ND	30.0
2445	44	Roberts, SD	29.9
2235	45	Swain, NC	29.0
2837	46	Mahnomen, MN	28.6
463	47	Coconino, AZ	28.5
2502	48	Charles Mix, SD	28.3
1391	49	Caddo, OK	24.3
1502	50	Lake, MT	23.8
1187	51	Delaware, OK	22.3
2808	52	McKenzie, ND	21.2
2819	53	Aleutians West Census Area, AK	21.0
1122	54	Beltrami, MN	20.4
1225	55	Fremont, WY	19.7
1139	56	Sequoyah, OK	19.6
2385	57	Latimer, OK	19.4
1155	58	Mayes, OK	19.1
3103	59	Alpine, CA	18.9
2541	60	Sitka, AK	18.6
2659	61	Ferry, WA	18.3
2304	62	Okfuskee, OK	18.2
1561	63	Seminole, OK	17.4
2777	64	Coal, OK	17.3
1977	64	Hill, MT	17.3
2392	66	Nowata, OK	16.6
1309	67	Ottawa, OK	16.5
2095	68	Craig, OK	16.3
575	68	Sandoval, NM	16.3
2150	70	Hughes, OK	16.2
1820	70	McIntosh, OK	16.2
2007	72	Sawyer, WI	16.1
2719	72	Wrangell-Petersburg, AK	16.1
1845	74	Jefferson, OR	15.7
2320	75	Pushmataha, OK	15.6

Percent Asian, 2000

Population Rank	Asian Rank	County	[col 12] Percent Asian
48	1	Honolulu, HI	46.0
818	2	Kauai, HI	36.0
422	3	Maui, HI	31.0
62	4	San Francisco, CA	30.8
363	5	Hawaii, HI	26.7
3014	6	Aleutians East Borough, AK	26.5
14	7	Santa Clara, CA	25.6
2819	8	Aleutians West Census Area, AK	24.6
21	9	Alameda, CA	20.4
70	10	San Mateo, CA	20.0
9	11	Queens, NY	17.6
3140	12	Kalawao, HI	17.0
2167	13	Kodiak Island, AK	16.0
66	14	Middlesex, NJ	13.9
5	15	Orange, CA	13.6
36	16	Fairfax, VA	13.0
150	17	Solano, CA	12.7
1715	18	Fairfax City, VA	12.2
1	19	Los Angeles, CA	11.9
97	20	San Joaquin, CA	11.4
49	21	Montgomery, MD	11.3
649	21	Sutter, CA	11.3
166	23	Fort Bend, TX	11.2
38	24	Contra Costa, CA	11.0
29	24	Sacramento, CA	11.0
12	26	King, WA	10.8
46	27	Bergen, NJ	10.7
321	28	Yolo, CA	9.9
88	29	Hudson, NJ	9.4
17	29	New York, NY	9.4
6	31	San Diego, CA	8.9
108	32	Ramsey, MN	8.8
291	33	Arlington, VA	8.6
190	34	Somerset, NJ	8.4
58	35	Fresno, CA	8.1
42	36	Du Page, IL	7.9
234	37	Howard, MD	7.7
7	38	Kings, NY	7.5
803	38	Yuba, CA	7.5
92	40	Gwinnett, GA	7.2
535	40	Tompkins, NY	7.2
74	42	Suffolk, MA	7.0
113	43	Collin, TX	6.9
264	44	Merced, CA	6.8
133	45	Washington, OR	6.7
308	46	Champaign, IL	6.5
2406	46	Falls Church City, VA	6.5
19	48	Middlesex, MA	6.3
123	48	Morris, NJ	6.3
179	48	Washtenaw, MI	6.3
147	51	Monterey, CA	6.0
2649	52	North Slope, AK	5.9
90	53	Snohomish, WA	5.8
421	54	Alexandria City, VA	5.7
79	54	Multnomah, OR	5.7
134	54	Richmond, NY	5.7
212	57	Anchorage, AK	5.5
83	57	Norfolk, MA	5.5
195	57	Rockland, NY	5.5
1091	57	Whitman, WA	5.5
25	61	Clark, NV	5.3
320	61	Loudoun, VA	5.3
64	61	Ventura, CA	5.3
223	64	Atlantic, NJ	5.1
3	64	Harris, TX	5.1
71	64	Pierce, WA	5.1
642	64	Story, IA	5.1
997	68	Charlottesville City, VA	4.9
167	68	Mercer, NJ	4.9
141	68	Virginia Beach City, VA	4.9
2	71	Cook, IL	4.8
32	71	Hennepin, MN	4.8
1380	73	Juneau, AK	4.7
26	73	Nassau, NY	4.7
13	73	San Bernardino, CA	4.7

Percent Two or More Races, 2000

Population Rank	Two or More Race Rank	County	[col 15] Percent Two or More Races
363	1	Hawaii, HI	28.4
818	2	Kauai, HI	23.8
422	3	Maui, HI	22.2
48	4	Honolulu, HI	19.9
2095	5	Craig, OK	11.4
1139	6	Sequoyah, OK	9.4
2392	7	Nowata, OK	8.2
2837	8	Mahnomen, MN	8.1
3124	9	Yakutat Borough, AK	7.9
2719	10	Wrangell-Petersburg, AK	7.8
1045	11	Cherokee, OK	7.6
1733	12	Adair, OK	7.5
1155	12	Mayes, OK	7.5
2541	12	Sitka, AK	7.5
2768	15	Prince of Wales-Outer Ketchikan, AK	7.1
3078	16	Lake and Peninsula Borough, AK	7.0
1380	17	Juneau, AK	6.9
1009	18	Osage, OK	6.8
1309	18	Ottawa, OK	6.8
2854	20	Dillingham, AK	6.7
1820	21	McIntosh, OK	6.6
2649	21	North Slope, AK	6.6
1187	23	Delaware, OK	6.5
2946	24	Bennett, SD	6.4
712	24	Muskogee, OK	6.4
1119	24	Okmulgee, OK	6.4
703	24	Rogers, OK	6.4
150	24	Solano, CA	6.4
2168	29	Atoka, OK	6.1
2777	29	Coal, OK	6.1
3140	29	Kalawao, HI	6.1
9	29	Queens, NY	6.1
933	29	Washington, OK	6.1
212	34	Anchorage, AK	6.0
97	35	San Joaquin, CA	6.0
2385	36	Latimer, OK	5.9
803	36	Yuba, CA	5.9
27	38	Bronx, NY	5.8
2308	38	Haskell, OK	5.8
29	38	Sacramento, CA	5.8
264	41	Merced, CA	5.7
21	42	Alameda, CA	5.6
88	42	Hudson, NJ	5.6
2429	42	Valdez-Cordova, AK	5.6
627	45	Fairbanks North Star, AK	5.4
1453	45	Geary, KS	5.4
2150	45	Hughes, OK	5.4
2397	45	Johnston, OK	5.4
1243	45	Pontotoc, OK	5.4
132	45	Stanislaus, CA	5.4
830	45	Wagoner, OK	5.4
2158	52	Ketchikan Gateway, AK	5.3
2304	52	Okfuskee, OK	5.3
1561	52	Seminole, OK	5.2
2942	55	Costilla, CO	5.2
727	55	Creek, OK	5.2
3074	55	Denali Borough, AK	5.2
2167	55	Kodiak Island, AK	5.2
440	55	Madera, CA	5.2
1017	55	Pittsburg, OK	5.2
2320	55	Pushmataha, OK	5.2
2961	55	Skagway-Hoonah-Angoon, AK	5.2
321	55	Yolo, CA	5.2
38	64	Contra Costa, CA	5.1
71	64	Pierce, WA	5.1
880	64	San Benito, CA	5.1
3103	67	Alpine, CA	5.0
947	67	Le Flore, OK	5.0
1267	67	McCurtain, OK	5.0
147	67	Monterey, CA	5.0
13	67	San Bernardino, CA	5.0
70	67	San Mateo, CA	5.0
2066	73	Choctaw, OK	4.9
3113	73	Esmeralda, NV	4.9
1	73	Los Angeles, CA	4.9

Note: Column numbers refer to Table B. States and Counties.

TABLE 3—All Counties
Selected Rankings

Percent Hispanic, 2000				Percent Under 18 Years, 2000				Percent Age 25 to 54 Years, 2000			
Population Rank	Hispanic Rank	County	[col 22] Percent Hispanic	Population Rank	Under 18 Years Rank	County	[cols 28 & 29] Percent Under 18 Years	Population Rank	25 to 54 Years Rank	County	[cols 31, 32 & 33] Percent 25 to 54 Years
872	1	Starr, TX	97.5	2681	1	Wade Hampton, AK	46.6	2819	1	Aleutians West Census Area, AK	66.3
961	2	Maverick, TX	95.0	2268	2	Shannon, SD	45.3	3014	2	Aleutians East Borough, AK	62.1
284	3	Webb, TX	94.3	2526	3	Todd, SD	43.9	2729	3	San Miguel, CO	61.2
2608	4	Brooks, TX	91.6	2666	4	Northwest Arctic Borough, AK	41.5	2862	4	Gilpin, CO	58.5
2324	5	Zavala, TX	91.2	3063	5	Buffalo, SD	41.3	2101	5	Pitkin, CO	58.2
2832	6	Jim Hogg, TX	90.0	3025	6	Ziebach, SD	40.7	3074	6	Denali Borough, AK	57.5
96	7	Hidalgo, TX	88.3	2918	7	Sioux, ND	40.3	1613	6	Summit, CO	57.5
2220	8	Duval, TX	88.0	2021	8	Bethel, AK	39.8	421	8	Alexandria City, VA	57.3
1790	9	Willacy, TX	85.7	2129	9	San Juan, UT	39.3	2083	9	West Feliciana, LA	56.4
2422	10	Dimmit, TX	85.0	2786	10	Dewey, SD	38.9	1064	10	Eagle, CO	56.1
2285	11	Zapata, TX	84.8	2874	10	Menominee, WI	38.9	291	11	Arlington, VA	56.0
2656	12	Presidio, TX	84.4	2588	12	Juab, UT	38.6	3134	12	San Juan, CO	55.7
174	13	Cameron, TX	84.3	714	13	Apache, AZ	38.5	1812	13	Routt, CO	55.2
2838	14	Mora, NM	81.6	2854	14	Dillingham, AK	38.2	1883	14	Teton, WY	55.0
2868	15	Guadalupe, NM	81.2	2649	15	North Slope, AK	38.1	2488	15	Nantucket, MA	54.6
1154	16	Santa Cruz, AZ	80.8	667	16	McKinley, NM	37.9	2197	16	Union, FL	54.4
3138	17	Kenedy, TX	79.0	3078	17	Lake and Peninsula Borough, AK	37.8	62	17	San Francisco, CA	54.3
75	18	El Paso, TX	78.2	2348	18	Franklin, ID	37.4	2503	18	Clear Creek, CO	54.2
1392	19	San Miguel, NM	78.0	872	18	Starr, TX	37.4	2328	19	Greensville, VA	53.9
2797	20	La Salle, TX	77.1	2271	20	Millard, UT	37.3	2121	20	Park, CO	53.7
1128	21	Jim Wells, TX	75.7	2514	21	Nome, AK	37.2	2816	21	Crowley, CO	53.5
1002	22	Val Verde, TX	75.5	2899	22	Corson, SD	37.0	311	22	Douglas, CO	52.9
2969	23	Hudspeth, TX	75.0	961	22	Maverick, TX	37.0	3124	23	Yakutat Borough, AK	52.7
2004	24	Frio, TX	73.8	2676	22	Morgan, UT	37.0	2269	24	Grand, CO	52.5
2219	25	Reeves, TX	73.4	2135	25	Duchesne, UT	36.8	2814	25	Hartley, TX	52.2
1074	26	Rio Arriba, NM	72.9	2670	25	Thurston, NE	36.8	320	26	Loudoun, VA	52.0
2993	27	Culberson, TX	72.2	2997	27	Jackson, SD	36.5	3102	27	Bristol Bay, AK	51.9
384	27	Imperial, CA	72.2	2186	28	Rolette, ND	36.4	113	28	Collin, TX	51.6
2942	29	Costilla, CO	67.6	2946	29	Bennett, SD	36.3	17	28	New York, NY	51.6
1520	30	Uvalde, TX	65.9	1839	29	Jefferson, ID	36.3	92	30	Gwinnett, GA	51.3
1360	31	Kleberg, TX	65.4	284	31	Webb, TX	36.2	1286	31	Lassen, CA	51.2
313	32	Dona Ana, NM	63.4	2689	32	Benson, ND	36.1	1380	32	Juneau, AK	50.8
1967	33	Pecos, TX	61.1	1042	32	Box Elder, UT	36.1	1757	32	Teller, CO	50.8
2573	34	Conejos, CO	58.9	2249	34	Big Horn, MT	35.8	1846	34	Blaine, ID	50.7
1147	35	Atascosa, TX	58.6	1142	35	Holmes, OH	35.6	89	34	Cobb, GA	50.7
1397	36	Taos, NM	57.9	532	36	Navajo, AZ	35.5	529	36	Forsyth, GA	50.6
1559	37	Luna, NM	57.7	2376	37	Emery, UT	35.3	856	37	Anderson, TX	50.5
1868	38	Deaf Smith, TX	57.4	96	37	Hidalgo, TX	35.3	1675	37	Powhatan, VA	50.5
8	39	Miami-Dade, FL	57.3	3060	37	Mellette, SD	35.3	2921	39	Concho, TX	50.4
2790	40	Hidalgo, NM	56.0	3110	40	Clark, ID	35.2	1798	39	Elbert, CO	50.4
182	41	Nueces, TX	55.8	241	40	Davis, UT	35.2	2417	41	Manassas Park City, VA	50.3
739	42	Valencia, NM	55.0	2125	42	Gaines, TX	35.1	36	42	Fairfax, VA	50.1
2908	43	Crockett, TX	54.7	1061	43	Bingham, ID	35.0	2406	42	Falls Church City, VA	50.1
24	44	Bexar, TX	54.3	3052	43	Oldham, TX	35.0	385	44	Cherokee, GA	49.9
1338	45	Bee, TX	53.9	1092	43	Tooele, UT	35.0	978	44	Oldham, KY	49.9
2911	46	Sutton, TX	51.7	2734	43	Yukon-Koyukuk, AK	35.0	85	44	Wake, NC	49.9
2582	47	Castro, TX	51.6	2209	47	Glacier, MT	34.9	234	47	Howard, MD	49.8
160	48	Tulare, CA	50.8	1558	48	Uintah, UT	34.7	139	48	Denton, TX	49.7
2965	49	Kinney, TX	50.5	926	49	Franklin, WA	34.6	12	48	King, WA	49.7
333	49	Yuma, AZ	50.5	3067	49	Rich, UT	34.6	2684	48	Liberty, FL	49.7
2970	51	Reagan, TX	49.5	2389	49	Roosevelt, MT	34.6	3125	51	Hinsdale, CO	49.6
732	52	San Patricio, TX	49.4	264	52	Merced, CA	34.5	1406	51	Summit, UT	49.6
2444	53	Parmer, TX	49.2	1850	52	Sevier, UT	34.5	76	53	De Kalb, GA	49.5
417	54	Santa Fe, NM	49.0	1103	54	Finney, KS	34.3	2243	53	Mono, CA	49.5
2678	55	Crosby, TX	48.9	2876	54	Kearny, KS	34.3	644	53	Monroe, FL	49.5
1378	56	Grant, NM	48.8	2970	56	Reagan, TX	34.2	72	56	Mecklenburg, NC	49.4
1895	57	Socorro, NM	48.7	2074	56	Wasatch, UT	34.2	2196	56	New Kent, VA	49.4
3106	58	Terrell, TX	48.6	1995	58	Adams, WA	34.1	636	56	Paulding, GA	49.4
27	59	Bronx, NY	48.4	1717	58	Cassia, ID	34.1	2429	56	Valdez-Cordova, AK	49.4
2092	60	Dawson, TX	48.2	2969	58	Hudspeth, TX	34.1	3141	60	Loving, TX	49.3
1199	61	Hale, TX	47.9	159	58	Utah, UT	34.1	235	60	Marin, CA	49.3
880	61	San Benito, CA	47.9	2324	58	Zavala, TX	34.1	577	60	Scott, MN	49.3
2148	63	Colfax, NM	47.5	2863	63	Martin, TX	33.9	2691	63	Brown, IL	49.2
1786	63	Moore, TX	47.5	174	64	Cameron, TX	33.8	1963	63	Goochland, VA	49.2
2056	65	Karnes, TX	47.4	1252	64	Lagrange, IN	33.8	101	65	Denver, CO	48.9
2728	66	Bailey, TX	47.3	2640	64	Power, ID	33.8	55	65	Fulton, GA	48.9
1995	67	Adams, WA	47.1	3139	67	King, TX	33.7	1244	65	Manassas City, VA	48.9
147	68	Monterey, CA	46.8	1154	67	Santa Cruz, AZ	33.7	200	65	Prince William, VA	48.9
926	69	Franklin, WA	46.7	160	67	Tulare, CA	33.7	56	65	Travis, TX	48.9
1855	70	Colusa, CA	46.5	1786	70	Moore, TX	33.6	212	70	Anchorage, AK	48.8
2628	71	Floyd, TX	45.9	2778	71	Beaver, UT	33.5	300	70	Hamilton, IN	48.8
2653	71	Yoakum, TX	45.9	3097	71	Glasscock, TX	33.5	3031	72	Haines, AK	48.7
1130	73	Medina, TX	45.5	2499	71	Rosebud, MT	33.5	380	72	Shelby, AL	48.7
264	74	Merced, CA	45.3	1807	74	Uinta, WY	33.4	2264	72	Sussex, VA	48.7
2792	74	Saguache, CO	45.3	1868	75	Deaf Smith, TX	33.3	194	75	Boulder, CO	48.6

Note: Column numbers refer to Table B. States and Counties.

TABLE 3—All Counties
Selected Rankings

Percent Age 65 Years and Over, 2000				Percent Female-headed Family Households, 2000				Percent Living Alone, 2000			
Population Rank	65 Years and Over Rank	County	[cols 35 & 36] Percent 65 Years and Over	Population Rank	Female Households Rate	County	[col 76] Percent Female Households	Population Rank	Living Alone Rank	County	[col 79] Percent Living Alone
387	1	Charlotte, FL	34.7	2268	1	Shannon, SD	36.4	3140	1	Kalawao, HI	79.1
2964	2	McIntosh, ND	34.3	2526	2	Todd, SD	31.8	17	2	New York, NY	48.0
600	3	Highlands, FL	33.0	3063	3	Buffalo, SD	31.4	94	3	District of Columbia	43.8
458	4	Citrus, FL	32.2	1713	4	Holmes, MS	31.2	421	4	Alexandria City, VA	43.4
3140	5	Kalawao, HI	32.0	27	5	Bronx, NY	30.4	2701	5	Lexington City, VA	41.0
177	6	Sarasota, FL	31.5	2918	6	Sioux, ND	29.1	291	6	Arlington, VA	40.8
409	7	Hernando, FL	30.8	1384	7	Coahoma, MS	28.7	168	7	St. Louis city, MO	40.3
1950	8	Llano, TX	30.7	2467	8	Jefferson, MS	28.5	101	8	Denver, CO	39.3
3042	9	Divide, ND	29.5	1268	9	Sunflower, MS	28.4	1829	9	Fredericksburg City, VA	39.2
2998	9	McPherson, SD	29.5	2318	10	Bullock, AL	28.2	62	10	San Francisco, CA	38.6
476	11	Indian River, FL	29.2	2438	10	Hancock, GA	28.2	280	11	Richmond City, VA	37.6
918	12	Flagler, FL	28.7	2494	12	East Carroll, LA	27.7	3134	12	San Juan, CO	36.8
2326	13	Lancaster, VA	28.5	2356	12	Humphreys, MS	27.7	2941	13	Nelson, ND	36.3
425	14	Martin, FL	28.3	1167	14	Leflore, MS	27.6	74	13	Suffolk, MA	36.3
3123	15	Harding, NM	28.2	1096	15	Bolivar, MS	27.3	3113	15	Esmeralda, NV	36.0
2875	16	Smith, KS	27.9	2449	16	Greene, AL	27.1	3066	16	Comanche, KS	35.9
2205	17	Sierra, NM	27.7	2302	17	Claiborne, MS	26.9	542	16	Roanoke City, VA	35.9
2941	18	Nelson, ND	27.5	2510	17	Tunica, MS	26.9	2205	16	Sierra, NM	35.9
876	19	Sumter, FL	27.4	2436	19	Quitman, MS	26.8	2294	16	Williamsburg City, VA	35.9
2986	20	Pawnee, NE	27.1	2730	19	Sharkey, MS	26.8	3038	20	Keweenaw, MI	35.8
3037	21	Logan, ND	27.0	2874	21	Menominee, WI	26.6	2101	20	Pitkin, CO	35.8
3126	22	Hooker, NE	26.9	2213	22	Wilcox, AL	26.5	3123	22	Harding, NM	35.3
1153	23	Baxter, AR	26.8	1289	23	Petersburg City, VA	26.1	2885	23	Osborne, KS	35.2
170	23	Pasco, FL	26.8	771	24	Washington, MS	26.0	3074	24	Denali Borough, AK	35.0
2981	25	Cheyenne, KS	26.6	2355	25	Allendale, SC	25.8	82	25	Baltimore city, MD	34.9
1728	25	Curry, OR	26.6	1590	25	Macon, GA	25.8	997	25	Charlottesville City, VA	34.9
3084	25	Sheridan, ND	26.6	2195	27	Lowndes, AL	25.7	806	25	Jackson, Il	34.9
265	28	Lake, FL	26.4	975	28	Dallas, AL	25.4	2922	25	Norton City, VA	34.9
2600	29	Hutchinson, SD	26.3	2301	29	Perry, AL	25.1	1597	29	Staunton City, VA	34.7
2956	30	Decatur, KS	26.2	1505	29	Phillips, AR	25.1	3045	30	Wheatland, MT	34.5
2905	30	Traverse, MN	26.2	82	31	Baltimore city, MD	25.0	2897	31	Clifton Forge City, VA	34.4
2531	32	Hickory, MO	26.1	2260	32	Noxubee, MS	24.7	1609	31	Winchester City, VA	34.4
2281	32	Northumberland, VA	26.1	117	33	Orleans, LA	24.5	1932	33	Bristol City, VA	34.3
2799	32	Republic, KS	26.1	2414	33	Wilkinson, MS	24.5	3008	34	Eddy, ND	34.2
2843	35	Wells, ND	26.0	2157	35	Macon, GA	24.4	2706	34	Galax City, VA	34.2
2928	36	Jewell, KS	25.9	2179	36	Madison, LA	24.2	1931	34	Gogebic, MI	34.2
3066	37	Comanche, KS	25.8	2369	37	Terrell, GA	24.0	2058	34	Martinsville City, VA	34.2
1810	37	La Paz, AZ	25.8	1787	38	Lee, SC	23.8	41	38	Pinellas, FL	34.1
2504	37	Towns, GA	25.8	3025	38	Ziebach, SD	23.8	2756	39	Covington City, VA	34.0
3009	40	Griggs, ND	25.7	1446	40	Yazoo, MS	23.7	942	40	Danville City, VA	33.9
2885	40	Osborne, KS	25.7	1235	41	Marion, SC	23.6	2860	40	Gregory, SD	33.9
3039	42	Jerauld, SD	25.6	2103	42	Sumter, AL	23.5	2406	42	Falls Church City, VA	33.8
2994	42	Rawlins, KS	25.6	2098	42	Tallahatchie, MS	23.5	18	42	Philadelphia, PA	33.8
3072	44	Cottle, TX	25.5	2967	44	Clay, GA	23.4	2218	44	Iron, MI	33.7
2894	44	Emmons, ND	25.5	2755	45	Calhoun, GA	23.2	959	44	Ohio, WV	33.7
1747	44	Gillespie, TX	25.5	539	45	Dougherty, GA	23.2	3064	46	Daniels, MT	33.6
2771	44	Haskell, TX	25.5	1935	47	Jefferson, GA	23.1	3001	46	Towner, ND	33.6
3119	44	Kent, TX	25.5	2258	47	Lee, AR	23.1	2958	48	Ness, KS	33.5
3048	49	De Baca, NM	25.4	2835	47	Stewart, GA	23.1	95	49	Davidson, TN	33.4
136	49	Lee, FL	25.4	1684	50	Burke, GA	22.8	2496	49	Deer Lodge, MT	33.4
2976	51	Elk, KS	25.3	229	51	Hinds, MS	22.7	3042	49	Divide, ND	33.4
2950	51	Rush, KS	25.3	667	51	McKinley, NM	22.7	2774	49	Greer, OK	33.4
3012	53	Hettinger, ND	25.2	2186	51	Rolette, ND	22.7	2522	49	Woods, OK	33.4
2218	53	Iron, MI	25.2	2627	54	Randolph, GA	22.6	2909	54	Baylor, TX	33.3
3047	55	Burke, ND	25.1	996	55	Gadsden, FL	22.5	3061	54	Taliaferro, GA	33.3
2740	55	Washington, KS	25.1	1595	55	Mitchell, GA	22.5	2929	54	Woodson, KS	33.3
3015	57	Potter, SD	25.0	1694	57	Clay, MS	22.4	3105	57	Jones, SD	33.2
2400	57	Sabine, TX	25.0	1185	57	Williamsburg, SC	22.4	117	57	Orleans, LA	33.2
1025	59	Kerr, TX	24.9	2786	59	Dewey, SD	22.3	1951	59	Beadle, SD	33.1
209	59	Manatee, FL	24.9	1379	59	Dillon, SC	22.3	3126	59	Hooker, NE	33.1
3073	61	Garfield, NE	24.8	7	59	Kings, NY	22.3	191	61	Albany, NY	33.0
3002	61	Grant, ND	24.8	18	59	Philadelphia, PA	22.3	2757	61	Bedford City, VA	33.0
2860	61	Gregory, SD	24.8	1426	63	Marlboro, SC	22.2	1590	61	Macon, GA	33.0
2929	61	Woodson, KS	24.8	2753	64	Warren, AL	22.1	39	61	Milwaukee, WI	33.0
3008	65	Eddy, ND	24.7	2153	65	Chicot, AR	22.0	2861	61	Stafford, KS	33.0
2775	66	Thayer, NE	24.6	1941	65	Hale, AL	22.0	2976	66	Elk, KS	32.9
228	67	Collier, FL	24.5	1802	65	Haywood, TN	22.0	52	66	Hamilton, OH	32.9
2747	67	Lincoln, MN	24.5	1308	65	Sumter, GA	22.0	2986	66	Pawnee, NE	32.9
217	67	Marion, FL	24.5	2577	69	Franklin City, VA	21.9	2966	66	Perkins, SD	32.9
2317	70	Alcona, MI	24.4	2324	70	Zavala, TX	21.8	2536	70	Brewster, TX	32.8
3027	71	Boyd, NE	24.3	1693	71	Crisp, GA	21.6	23	70	Cuyahoga, OH	32.8
2891	71	Chautauqua, KS	24.3	2163	71	Jefferson Davis, MS	21.6	2956	70	Decatur, KS	32.8
2965	71	Kinney, TX	24.3	1269	73	Adams, MS	21.5	2617	70	Huerfano, CO	32.8
2958	71	Ness, KS	24.3	849	73	Edgecombe, NC	21.5	2650	70	Russell, KS	32.8
2848	71	Nuckolls, NE	24.3	1726	73	Washington, GA	21.5	1262	70	Silver Bow, MT	32.8

Note: Column numbers refer to Table B. States and Counties.

TABLE 3—All Counties
Selected Rankings

Percent Married Couple Family Households, 2000				Percent of Families with Own Children Under 18 Years, 2000				Percent Change in Households, 1990-2000			
Population Rank	Married Couple Family Households Rank	County	[col 74] Percent in Married Couple Family Households	Population Rank	Families with Own Children Under 18 Years Rank	County	[col 73] Percent of Families with Own Children Under 18 Years	Population Rank	Change in Households Rank	County	[col 86] Percent Change in Households
3139	1	King, TX	79.6	2100	1	Chattahoochee, GA	64.8	311	1	Douglas, CO	192.3
2676	1	Morgan, UT	79.6	2681	2	Wade Hampton, AK	59.7	529	2	Forsyth, GA	116.9
2100	3	Chattahoochee, GA	76.3	2666	3	Northwest Arctic Borough, AK	55.2	2121	3	Park, CO	112.4
1798	4	Elbert, CO	75.1	872	4	Starr, TX	54.7	455	4	Henry, GA	106.7
3067	5	Rich, UT	74.4	284	5	Webb, TX	53.2	2729	5	San Miguel, CO	102.5
311	6	Douglas, CO	73.8	2268	6	Shannon, SD	51.7	1798	6	Elbert, CO	100.5
3135	6	McPherson, NE	73.8	961	7	Maverick, TX	51.6	1333	7	Nye, NV	99.7
2348	8	Franklin, ID	73.6	2021	8	Bethel, AK	51.0	2456	8	Archuleta, CO	98.0
1839	9	Jefferson, ID	72.6	789	9	Liberty, GA	50.5	320	9	Loudoun, VA	96.5
529	10	Forsyth, GA	71.9	166	10	Fort Bend, TX	49.8	572	10	Washington, UT	96.2
564	11	Fayette, GA	71.5	96	11	Hidalgo, TX	49.7	636	11	Paulding, GA	96.1
1142	11	Holmes, OH	71.5	2676	11	Morgan, UT	49.7	1406	12	Summit, UT	96.0
978	11	Oldham, KY	71.5	241	13	Davis, UT	49.5	2720	13	Boise, ID	92.8
1042	14	Box Elder, UT	71.0	2588	14	Juab, UT	49.3	2953	14	Custer, CO	92.2
1035	14	Rockwall, TX	71.0	2918	15	Sioux, ND	48.9	113	15	Collin, TX	89.9
2074	14	Wasatch, UT	71.0	2526	15	Todd, SD	48.9	3140	16	Kalawao, HI	85.5
241	17	Davis, UT	70.8	1565	17	Lee, GA	48.3	2780	17	Teton, ID	85.0
3116	18	Roberts, TX	70.7	159	17	Utah, UT	48.3	1064	18	Eagle, CO	81.3
2271	19	Millard, UT	70.6	2649	19	North Slope, AK	48.1	2023	19	Dawson, GA	80.6
2983	20	Hanson, SD	70.4	2348	20	Franklin, ID	48.0	918	20	Flagler, FL	79.2
3122	21	Banner, NE	70.1	665	21	Coryell, TX	47.7	1618	21	Gilmer, GA	78.8
1850	21	Sevier, UT	70.1	1839	22	Jefferson, ID	47.6	25	22	Clark, NV	78.5
2376	23	Emery, UT	69.8	1092	23	Tooele, UT	47.4	232	23	Williamson, TX	77.8
159	23	Utah, UT	69.8	311	24	Douglas, CO	47.2	2311	24	Spencer, KY	73.4
427	23	Williamson, TN	69.8	3025	24	Ziebach, SD	47.2	1613	25	Summit, CO	72.2
1675	26	Powhatan, VA	69.7	1042	26	Box Elder, UT	47.1	494	26	Delaware, OH	71.6
2895	27	Haskell, KS	69.4	3063	26	Buffalo, SD	47.1	876	27	Sumter, FL	71.5
2327	27	Poquoson City, VA	69.4	2129	28	San Juan, UT	47.0	1822	28	Lincoln, NM	71.3
1357	27	Sioux, IA	69.4	552	29	Stafford, VA	46.9	867	29	Christian, MO	71.1
2655	30	Caribou, ID	69.3	1024	30	Camden, GA	46.8	344	30	Mohave, AZ	70.7
3062	31	Oliver, ND	69.2	2970	30	Reagan, TX	46.8	300	31	Hamilton, IN	69.8
3057	32	Gosper, NE	69.1	384	32	Imperial, CA	46.7	1288	32	Iron, UT	69.5
2588	32	Juab, UT	69.1	414	33	Kings, CA	46.4	1264	33	Lyon, NV	69.4
568	34	Geauga, OH	68.9	2135	34	Duchesne, UT	46.3	1757	34	Teller, CO	69.3
2814	34	Hartley, TX	68.9	880	34	San Benito, CA	46.3	1883	35	Teton, WY	68.3
166	36	Fort Bend, TX	68.8	636	36	Paulding, GA	46.2	3125	36	Hinsdale, CO	67.8
862	36	Kendall, IL	68.8	2074	36	Wasatch, UT	46.2	1920	37	Bandera, TX	67.7
1508	36	Oconee, GA	68.8	2271	38	Millard, UT	46.1	228	38	Collier, FL	66.9
2653	36	Yoakum, TX	68.8	1103	39	Finney, KS	46.0	498	39	De Soto, MS	66.7
339	40	Livingston, MI	68.5	667	39	McKinley, NM	46.0	2937	40	Ouray, CO	66.4
2906	40	Oneida, ID	68.5	2376	41	Emery, UT	45.9	1644	40	Pickens, GA	66.4
636	42	Paulding, GA	68.3	2167	41	Kodiak Island, AK	45.9	580	42	Coweta, GA	66.1
1252	43	Lagrange, IN	68.2	174	43	Cameron, TX	45.8	976	43	Pike, GA	65.5
2970	44	Reagan, TX	68.1	2514	43	Nome, AK	45.8	570	44	Spotsylvania, VA	65.3
2980	45	Sherman, TX	68.0	2415	45	Long, GA	45.6	1035	45	Rockwall, TX	64.4
552	45	Stafford, VA	68.0	1154	45	Santa Cruz, AZ	45.6	1958	46	Torrance, NM	64.1
2135	47	Duchesne, UT	67.9	2417	47	Manassas Park City, VA	45.4	1791	47	Fluvanna, VA	63.5
2303	47	Fremont, ID	67.9	264	47	Merced, CA	45.4	2415	48	Long, GA	62.8
2311	47	Spencer, KY	67.9	577	47	Scott, MN	45.4	193	49	Montgomery, TX	62.5
1385	50	Botetourt, VA	67.8	2854	50	Dillingham, AK	45.3	1650	50	Wakulla, FL	62.2
2920	50	Crane, TX	67.8	2125	50	Gaines, TX	45.3	1601	51	Kendall, TX	61.2
494	52	Delaware, OH	67.7	2969	50	Hudspeth, TX	45.3	1589	52	Lincoln, SD	60.8
2125	52	Gaines, TX	67.7	707	53	Carver, MN	45.2	2269	53	Grand, CO	60.2
2793	52	Gray, KS	67.7	1621	54	Bryan, GA	45.0	427	54	Williamson, TN	60.1
3095	55	Piute, UT	67.6	3110	54	Clark, ID	45.0	1621	55	Bryan, GA	59.5
572	55	Washington, UT	67.6	926	54	Franklin, WA	45.0	92	56	Gwinnett, GA	59.3
579	57	Columbia, GA	67.5	75	57	El Paso, TX	44.9	799	57	Walton, GA	58.6
3097	57	Glasscock, TX	67.5	756	57	Sherburne, MN	44.9	577	58	Scott, MN	58.5
3129	57	Grant, NE	67.5	160	57	Tulare, CA	44.9	1565	59	Lee, GA	58.3
300	57	Hamilton, IN	67.5	1786	60	Moore, TX	44.8	756	60	Sherburne, MN	58.2
851	57	Hancock, IN	67.5	3078	61	Lake and Peninsula Borough, AK	44.7	385	61	Cherokee, GA	58.1
2742	57	Stanton, NE	67.5	1508	61	Oconee, GA	44.7	302	62	Rutherford, TN	57.8
1234	57	Woodford, IL	67.5	1807	61	Uinta, WY	44.7	1795	63	White, GA	57.6
2497	64	Hamilton, NE	67.4	1061	64	Bingham, ID	44.6	166	64	Fort Bend, TX	57.5
840	65	York, VA	67.3	1558	65	Uintah, UT	44.5	2951	65	Catron, NM	56.8
3056	66	Armstrong, TX	67.2	579	66	Columbia, GA	44.4	307	66	Pinal, AZ	56.7
385	66	Cherokee, GA	67.2	1035	66	Rockwall, TX	44.4	322	66	Yavapai, AZ	56.7
1601	66	Kendall, TX	67.2	1142	68	Holmes, OH	44.3	1118	68	Taney, MO	56.6
2778	69	Beaver, UT	67.1	200	69	Prince William, VA	44.2	1810	69	La Paz, AZ	56.4
508	69	Hendricks, IN	67.1	978	70	Oldham, KY	44.1	2862	70	Gilpin, CO	56.2
2440	69	Jefferson, MT	67.1	1995	71	Adams, WA	44.0	466	71	Deschutes, OR	56.1
2312	69	Lyon, IA	67.1	232	72	Williamson, TX	43.9	139	72	Denton, TX	55.8
3107	73	Hayes, NE	67.0	714	73	Apache, AZ	43.8	315	72	Osceola, FL	55.8
2444	73	Parmer, TX	67.0	2186	73	Rolette, ND	43.8	1024	74	Camden, GA	55.5
1659	73	Sanpete, UT	67.0	2324	73	Zavala, TX	43.8	552	74	Stafford, VA	55.5

Note: Column numbers refer to Table B. States and Counties.

TABLE 3—All Counties
Selected Rankings

Percent in Group Quarters, 2000				Percent in Dormitories, 2000				Percent Owner Occupied Housing Units, 2000			
Popu-lation Rank	Group Quarters Rank	County	[col 64] Percent in Group Quarters	Popu-lation Rank	Dormitories Rank	County	[col 68] Percent in Dormitories	Popu-lation Rank	Owner Occupied Housing Units Rank	County	[col 94] Percent in Owner Occupied Housing Units
3014	1	Aleutians East Borough, AK	47.6	2294	1	Williamsburg City, VA	36.3	2317	1	Alcona, MI	89.9
2819	2	Aleutians West Census Area, AK	41.5	2701	2	Lexington City, VA	30.8	1798	2	Elbert, CO	89.6
2294	3	Williamsburg City, VA	37.5	2028	3	Radford City, VA	17.3	3038	3	Keweenaw, MI	88.8
2816	4	Crowley, CO	36.2	1808	4	Prince Edward, VA	15.7	1675	3	Powhatan, VA	88.8
2921	5	Concho, TX	34.5	1104	5	Harrisonburg City, VA	15.2	2196	5	New Kent, VA	88.7
2083	6	West Feliciana, LA	34.1	2192	6	Clay, SD	14.7	2676	6	Morgan, UT	88.3
2701	7	Lexington City, VA	33.0	2302	7	Claiborne, MS	14.5	1893	7	Washington, AL	88.1
2100	8	Chattahoochee, GA	32.8	997	8	Charlottesville City, VA	13.8	529	7	Forsyth, GA	88.0
2197	9	Union, FL	30.9	1322	9	McDonough, IL	13.2	339	8	Livingston, MI	88.0
2610	10	Lake, TN	28.6	1091	10	Whitman, WA	12.5	311	10	Douglas, CO	87.9
2691	11	Brown, IL	28.4	1688	11	Rowan, KY	12.3	1385	11	Botetourt, VA	87.8
786	12	Walker, TX	27.7	782	12	Athens, OH	12.0	1683	12	San Jacinto, TX	87.7
2470	13	Mitchell, TX	27.5	535	13	Tompkins, NY	11.1	2121	13	Park, CO	87.6
2328	14	Greensville, VA	26.6	1044	14	Watauga, NC	11.0	2281	14	Northumberland, VA	87.4
856	15	Anderson, TX	26.5	2461	15	Wayne, NE	10.9	568	15	Geauga, OH	87.2
1286	16	Lassen, CA	26.3	642	16	Story, IA	10.8	1078	16	Chisago, MN	87.1
2814	17	Hartley, TX	25.7	352	17	Hampshire, MA	10.7	2204	16	Greene, MS	87.1
2325	18	De Kalb, MO	23.9	450	17	Monroe, IN	10.7	3095	18	Piute, UT	87.0
1749	18	Jones, TX	23.9	1829	19	Fredericksburg City, VA	10.6	2111	19	Brantley, GA	86.9
1338	20	Bee, TX	23.4	1046	20	Lincoln, LA	10.5	978	19	Oldham, KY	86.9
2056	20	Karnes, TX	23.4	1146	21	Lafayette, MS	10.2	3128	19	Slope, ND	86.9
2630	22	Childress, TX	22.8	1251	22	Latah, ID	10.0	2009	19	Smith, MS	86.9
665	23	Coryell, TX	22.6	621	22	Montgomery, VA	10.0	636	23	Paulding, GA	86.8
2122	23	Lincoln, AR	22.6	1560	24	Adair, MO	9.4	1890	24	Jasper, MS	86.7
2236	25	Madison, TX	22.2	1040	25	Oktibbeha, MS	9.2	801	25	Bedford, VA	86.6
2242	26	Johnson, IL	21.2	1721	26	Winneshiek, IA	9.1	1963	25	Goochland, VA	86.6
2717	27	Pershing, NV	21.1	1696	27	Nodaway, MO	9.0	409	27	Hernando, FL	86.5
1065	28	Union, PA	20.9	362	28	Tippecanoe, IN	8.9	577	27	Scott, MN	86.5
2755	29	Calhoun, GA	20.8	1444	29	Brookings, SD	8.7	876	27	Sumter, FL	86.5
2684	30	Liberty, FL	20.6	397	30	Centre, PA	8.4	2171	30	Dixie, FL	86.4
2264	31	Sussex, VA	20.3	2524	30	Dawes, NE	8.4	564	30	Fayette, GA	86.4
2545	32	Richmond, VA	19.9	806	30	Jackson, IL	8.4	2025	32	Choctaw, AL	86.3
979	33	Fremont, CO	19.8	1326	33	Waller, TX	8.3	2127	33	Gilchrist, FL	86.3
1567	33	Somerset, MD	19.8	774	34	Riley, KS	8.1	1840	34	George, MS	86.2
2668	35	Powell, MT	19.5	1614	35	Clark, AR	8.0	2400	34	Sabine, TX	86.2
2599	36	Lyon, KY	19.1	765	35	Isabella, MI	8.0	2700	36	Bland, VA	86.1
1808	37	Prince Edward, VA	19.0	525	37	Douglas, KS	7.9	2568	36	Franklin, MS	86.1
3007	38	Dickens, TX	18.8	722	38	Payne, OK	7.8	1602	36	Harris, GA	86.1
2203	38	Hamilton, FL	18.8	585	39	De Kalb, IL	7.7	2413	36	Montmorency, MI	86.1
2683	38	Lafayette, FL	18.8	1101	40	Mecosta, MI	7.6	2190	40	Amite, MS	86.0
1104	41	Harrisonburg City, VA	17.8	2439	40	Stevens, MN	7.6	2634	40	Perry, TN	86.0
2028	42	Radford City, VA	17.7	1590	42	Macon, AL	7.5	1477	42	Cass, MN	85.9
1679	42	Tattnall, GA	17.7	917	43	Allegany, NY	7.4	1542	42	Roscommon, MI	85.9
1005	44	Baldwin, GA	17.5	1314	43	Jackson, NC	7.4	834	44	Barry, MI	85.8
2764	44	Wheeler, GA	17.5	836	43	Rice, MN	7.4	1605	44	Jones, GA	85.8
2769	46	Alfalfa, OK	17.4	2552	46	Decatur, IA	7.3	3037	44	Logan, ND	85.8
2772	47	Lincoln, CO	17.3	457	46	Orange, NC	7.3	2495	44	Oscoda, MI	85.8
2550	40	Wilcox, GA	17.2	308	48	Champaign, IL	7.1	2024	48	Benzie, MI	85.7
2204	49	Greene, MS	16.8	350	49	Brazos, TX	7.0	2845	48	Florence, WI	85.7
1544	50	Allen, LA	16.4	1276	49	Calloway, KY	7.0	1516	48	Gladwin, MI	85.7
2192	50	Clay, SD	16.4	747	51	Lynchburg City, VA	6.8	1367	48	Isanti, MN	85.7
2774	52	Greer, OK	16.2	1345	52	Albany, WY	6.7	3062	48	Oliver, ND	85.7
3139	53	King, TX	16.0	881	52	Coles, IL	6.7	272	48	Washington, MN	85.7
1513	54	Bradford, FL	15.9	700	52	Madison, KY	6.7	458	54	Citrus, FL	85.6
1872	55	Brunswick, VA	15.8	2379	52	Rice, KS	6.7	2322	54	Edmonson, KY	85.6
2159	56	Noble, OH	15.7	1357	56	Sioux, IA	6.6	2130	54	Presque Isle, MI	85.6
3045	57	Wheatland, MT	15.6	520	57	Clarke, GA	6.5	1724	54	St. James, LA	85.6
1149	58	Chippewa, MI	15.5	357	57	McLean, IL	6.5	2072	58	Aitkin, MN	85.4
2362	58	Franklin, FL	15.5	1065	59	Union, PA	6.4	1864	59	Adams, WI	85.3
3109	58	Golden Valley, MT	15.5	1115	60	Dunn, WI	6.3	750	59	Clinton, MI	85.3
414	58	Kings, CA	15.5	2164	60	Gunnison, CO	6.3	2877	59	Lake of the Woods, MN	85.3
1268	58	Sunflower, MS	15.5	1217	60	Houghton, MI	6.3	2817	59	Van Buren, TN	85.3
2781	63	Bent, CO	15.4	1405	60	Nicollet, MN	6.3	671	63	Calvert, MD	85.2
997	64	Charlottesville City, VA	15.2	635	64	Grafton, NH	6.2	1791	63	Fluvanna, VA	85.2
2302	64	Claiborne, MS	15.2	2051	65	Chester, TN	6.0	455	63	Henry, GA	85.2
2092	64	Dawson, TX	15.2	1988	65	Seward, NE	6.0	2464	63	Livingston, KY	85.2
2682	67	Luce, MI	15.1	903	67	Clay, MN	5.9	2504	63	Towns, GA	85.2
3124	67	Yakutat Borough, AK	15.1	812	67	Nacogdoches, TX	5.9	2802	68	Big Stone, MN	85.1
1318	69	Prince George, VA	15.0	1567	67	Somerset, MD	5.9	2446	68	Cameron, LA	85.1
774	70	Riley, KS	14.8	1219	70	Addison, VT	5.8	2920	68	Crane, TX	85.1
2438	71	Hancock, GA	14.5	1302	71	Kittitas, WA	5.7	1986	68	Kalkaska, MI	85.1
2450	71	McCormick, SC	14.5	788	71	Otsego, NY	5.7	2094	72	Brown, IN	85.0
1322	71	McDonough, IL	14.5	490	71	Pickens, SC	5.7	2216	72	King William, VA	85.0
1688	74	Rowan, KY	14.3	1852	71	Poweshiek, IA	5.7	2622	72	Ontonagon, MI	85.0
1294	75	Howard, TX	14.2	488	75	Johnson, IA	5.6	1725	72	Wayne, MS	85.0

Note: Column numbers refer to Table B. States and Counties.

TABLE 3—All Counties
Selected Rankings

Percent Recreational/Seasonal Housing Units, 2000				Homeowner Vacancy Rate, 2000				Renter Vacancy Rate, 2000			
Recreational/ Seasonal Housing Units Rank	Group Quarters Rank	County	[col 90] Percent Recreational/ Seasonal Housing Units	Population Rank	Homeowner Vacancy Rank	County	[col 91] Homeowner Vacancy Rate	Population Rank	Renter Vacancy Rank	County	[col 92] Renter Vacancy Rate
2851	1	Forest, PA	75.4	3140	1	Kalawao, HI	100.0	970	1	Worcester, MD	48.8
2822	2	Hamilton, NY	65.4	3139	2	King, TX	40.3	1098	2	Walton, FL	45.5
3114	3	Daggett, UT	63.8	3135	3	McPherson, NE	15.0	2362	3	Franklin, FL	42.3
3125	4	Hinsdale, CO	61.3	3007	4	Dickens, TX	13.4	3067	4	Rich, UT	41.2
3103	5	Alpine, CA	61.1	3088	5	Foard, TX	12.6	3113	5	Esmeralda, NV	40.5
2347	6	Lake, MI	61.0	1471	6	Iosco, MI	11.6	3087	6	Eureka, NV	37.9
3121	7	Mineral, CO	60.1	3137	7	Arthur, NE	11.4	2201	7	Gulf, FL	37.2
3067	8	Rich, UT	59.6	3071	8	Gilliam, OR	10.4	2893	8	Custer, ID	32.5
3078	9	Lake and Peninsula Borough, AK	58.3	3096	8	Motley, TX	10.4	2804	9	Lander, NV	32.4
1734	10	Vilas, WI	56.2	3119	10	Kent, TX	10.3	2269	10	Grand, CO	31.1
2488	11	Nantucket, MA	56.1	3129	11	Grant, NE	9.9	281	11	Horry, SC	30.2
1613	12	Summit, CO	54.7	1613	12	Summit, CO	9.6	2555	12	Mercer, ND	29.8
2091	13	Dukes, MA	53.9	2948	13	Harper, OK	9.5	2655	13	Caribou, ID	28.9
2633	14	Valley, ID	53.7	2898	14	Knox, TX	9.4	846	14	Georgetown, SC	28.6
2733	15	Sullivan, PA	51.8	2982	15	Cimarron, OK	9.2	685	15	Brunswick, NC	28.2
3038	16	Keweenaw, MI	50.5	2965	16	Kinney, TX	9.1	1812	16	Routt, CO	28.1
1398	17	Dare, NC	50.1	2966	17	Perkins, SD	8.8	2847	17	Mineral, NV	27.9
3134	18	San Juan, CO	49.4	3112	18	Keya Paha, NE	8.7	2285	18	Zapata, TX	27.7
2243	19	Mono, CA	49.1	3042	19	Divide, ND	8.5	2520	19	Pocahontas, WV	26.7
2007	20	Sawyer, WI	48.5	3134	19	San Juan, CO	8.5	3065	20	McCone, MT	25.8
2495	21	Oscoda, MI	48.0	3100	21	Harding, SD	8.3	2717	21	Pershing, NV	25.7
1542	21	Roscommon, MI	48.0	3131	22	Thomas, NE	8.1	2822	22	Hamilton, NY	24.8
2317	23	Alcona, MI	47.9	3069	23	Meagher, MT	8.0	3106	23	Terrell, TX	24.4
2839	23	Cook, MN	47.9	3083	23	Wallace, KS	8.0	2653	23	Yoakum, TX	24.4
2413	25	Montmorency, MI	47.5	2769	25	Alfalfa, OK	7.9	1188	25	Camden, MO	24.2
519	26	Cape May, NJ	47.4	3081	25	Irion, TX	7.9	2703	26	Iron, WI	24.1
2072	27	Aitkin, MN	47.1	3114	27	Daggett, UT	7.7	2092	27	Dawson, TX	24.0
2442	28	Forest, WI	46.3	2334	27	Washita, OK	7.7	2515	28	White Pine, NV	23.8
2845	29	Florence, WI	46.2	2841	29	Grant, OK	7.6	1931	29	Gogebic, MI	23.4
1188	30	Camden, MO	46.1	2989	29	Lipscomb, TX	7.6	1294	29	Howard, TX	23.4
2040	31	Burnett, WI	45.0	3136	29	Petroleum, MT	7.6	828	29	Nassau, FL	23.4
1477	31	Cass, MN	45.0	2726	32	Cotton, OK	7.5	3102	32	Bristol Bay, AK	23.2
976	33	Pike, PA	44.3	3028	32	Niobrara, WY	7.5	3116	32	Roberts, TX	23.2
2953	34	Custer, CO	44.0	2912	34	Ellis, OK	7.4	366	34	Bay, FL	22.7
2269	35	Grand, CO	43.9	3067	34	Rich, UT	7.4	519	35	Cape May, NJ	22.5
1023	36	Carroll, NH	42.8	2925	36	Coke, TX	7.3	3003	35	Fallon, MT	22.5
2089	37	Bayfield, WI	42.3	3066	36	Comanche, KS	7.3	390	37	Baldwin, AL	22.3
2784	38	Cameron, PA	42.1	2945	36	Lincoln, KS	7.3	3134	37	San Juan, CO	22.3
2298	39	Mackinac, MI	41.9	3047	39	Burke, ND	7.2	3129	39	Grant, NE	22.2
2143	40	Crawford, MI	40.9	2872	39	Phillips, MT	7.2	2233	40	Andrews, TX	22.0
2121	41	Park, CO	40.5	2961	39	Skagway-Hoonah-Angoon, AK	7.2	3001	41	Towner, ND	21.9
1939	42	Piscataquis, ME	40.0	2779	42	Phillips, KS	7.1	1731	42	Leelanau, MI	21.8
1864	43	Adams, WI	39.9	3122	43	Banner, NE	6.9	2114	42	Lincoln, WY	21.8
1943	43	Avery, NC	39.9	3099	43	Carter, MT	6.9	1525	44	Geneva, AL	21.1
2520	45	Pocahontas, WV	39.5	2950	43	Rush, KS	6.9	3126	44	Hooker, NE	21.1
1822	46	Lincoln, NM	39.4	3084	43	Sheridan, ND	6.9	2243	46	Mono, CA	20.9
1195	47	Oneida, WI	39.2	2880	47	Musselshell, MT	6.8	3042	47	Divide, ND	20.7
3102	48	Bristol Bay, AK	38.9	2878	48	Baca, CO	6.7	1800	48	Beckham, OK	20.4
2741	49	Essex, VT	38.7	3126	48	Hooker, NE	6.7	2802	48	Big Stone, MN	20.4
1894	49	Potter, PA	38.7	3121	48	Mineral, CO	6.7	3074	50	Denali Borough, AK	20.1
1368	51	Clare, MI	38.6	2515	48	White Pine, NV	6.7	3040	50	Dundy, NE	20.1
2703	52	Iron, WI	37.8	3019	52	Renville, ND	6.6	2819	52	Aleutians West Census Area, AK	19.9
1711	52	Ogemaw, MI	37.8	2684	53	Liberty, FL	6.5	3069	53	Meagher, MT	19.8
970	54	Worcester, MD	37.3	2631	53	Valley, MT	6.5	2907	53	Sheridan, MT	19.8
1827	55	Morgan, MO	37.2	2866	55	Hardeman, TX	6.4	2015	55	Humboldt, NV	19.7
2695	56	Grand Isle, VT	37.1	3045	55	Wheatland, MT	6.4	2974	56	Harmon, OK	19.6
3138	57	Kenedy, TX	36.7	3108	55	Wibaux, MT	6.4	465	56	Midland, TX	19.6
1875	58	Hubbard, MN	35.8	2689	58	Benson, ND	6.3	2778	58	Beaver, UT	19.5
3124	59	Yakutat Borough, AK	35.7	2295	58	Blaine, OK	6.3	2790	58	Hidalgo, NM	19.5
1452	60	Door, WI	35.6	3003	58	Fallon, MT	6.3	3047	60	Burke, ND	19.4
956	61	Wayne, PA	35.5	3109	58	Golden Valley, MT	6.3	2423	60	Kiowa, OK	19.4
1986	62	Kalkaska, MI	35.4	2974	58	Harmon, OK	6.3	2374	60	Ward, TX	19.4
2020	63	Washburn, WI	35.3	3054	58	Liberty, MT	6.3	317	63	Okaloosa, FL	19.3
1406	64	Summit, UT	35.0	2931	64	Hall, TX	6.2	2000	63	Scurry, TX	19.3
2865	65	Garfield, UT	34.9	2798	65	Beaver, OK	6.1	1496	63	Wayne, GA	19.3
2877	66	Lake of the Woods, MN	34.7	2981	65	Cheyenne, KS	6.1	449	66	Beaufort, SC	19.2
1810	67	La Paz, AZ	34.6	2994	65	Rawlins, KS	6.1	2437	67	Bacon, GA	19.0
2164	68	Gunnison, CO	34.2	2976	68	Elk, KS	6.0	2292	67	Converse, WY	19.0
1637	69	Antrim, MI	34.1	2557	68	Newton, AR	6.0	1763	67	Crawford, IL	19.0
3090	69	Jackson, CO	34.1	2863	70	Martin, TX	5.9	2470	67	Mitchell, TX	19.0
1415	71	Franklin, ME	33.9	2831	70	Wheeler, TX	5.9	2471	67	Stephens, TX	19.0
2303	71	Fremont, ID	33.9	3021	72	Adams, ND	5.8	2433	72	Quay, NM	18.9
2729	73	San Miguel, CO	33.5	3080	72	Campbell, SD	5.8	2969	73	Hudspeth, TX	18.8
1942	74	Benton, MO	33.4	2509	72	Coleman, TX	5.8	2989	73	Lipscomb, TX	18.8
2776	75	Kane, UT	33.3	2959	72	Edwards, KS	5.8	3108	73	Wibaux, MT	18.8

Note: Column numbers refer to Table B. States and Counties.

TABLE 4—75 Largest Metropolitan Areas by 2000 Population
Selected Rankings

	Total Persons, 2000			Land Area (Square Kilometers), 2000		
Popu-lation Rank	Metropolitan Area	[col 2] Population	Popu-lation Rank	Land Area Rank	Metropolitan Area	[col 1] Land Area
1	Los Angeles-Long Beach, CA	9 519 338	40	1	Las Vegas, NV-AZ	101 964
2	New York, NY	9 314 235	11	2	Riverside-San Bernardino, CA	70 603
3	Chicago, IL	8 272 768	12	3	Phoenix-Mesa, AZ	37 743
4	Boston-Worcester-Lawrence, MA-NH-ME-CT	6 057 826	70	4	Tucson, AZ	23 792
5	Philadelphia, PA-NJ	5 100 931	66	5	Fresno, CA	20 975
6	Washington, DC-MD-VA-WV	4 923 153	6	6	Washington, DC-MD-VA-WV	16 859
7	Detroit, MI	4 441 551	4	7	Boston-Worcester-Lawrence, MA-NH-ME-CT	16 711
8	Houston, TX	4 177 646	17	8	St. Louis, MO-IL	16 555
9	Atlanta, GA	4 112 198	10	9	Dallas, TX	16 021
10	Dallas, TX	3 519 176	9	10	Atlanta, GA	15 861
11	Riverside-San Bernardino, CA	3 254 821	13	11	Minneapolis-St. Paul, MN-WI	15 703
12	Phoenix-Mesa, AZ	3 251 876	75	12	Albuquerque, NM	15 392
13	Minneapolis-St. Paul, MN-WI	2 968 806	8	13	Houston, TX	15 333
14	Orange County, CA	2 846 289	28	14	Kansas City, MO-KS	14 002
15	San Diego, CA	2 813 833	3	15	Chicago, IL	13 111
16	Nassau-Suffolk, NY	2 753 913	27	16	Portland-Vancouver, OR-WA	13 022
17	St. Louis, MO-IL	2 603 607	71	17	Tulsa, OK	12 987
18	Baltimore, MD	2 552 994	22	18	Pittsburgh, PA	11 980
19	Seattle-Bellevue-Everett, WA	2 414 616	19	19	Seattle-Bellevue-Everett, WA	11 457
20	Tampa-St. Petersburg-Clearwater, FL	2 395 997	60	20	Oklahoma City, OK	10 999
21	Oakland, CA	2 392 557	48	21	Austin-San Marcos, TX	10 940
22	Pittsburgh, PA	2 358 695	15	22	San Diego, CA	10 878
23	Miami, FL	2 253 362	35	23	Sacramento, CA	10 569
24	Cleveland-Lorain-Elyria, OH	2 250 871	49	24	Nashville, TN	10 548
25	Denver, CO	2 109 282	1	25	Los Angeles-Long Beach, CA	10 518
26	Newark, NJ	2 032 989	7	26	Detroit, MI	10 093
27	Portland-Vancouver, OR-WA	1 918 009	47	27	Greensboro-Winston-Salem-High Point, NC	10 052
28	Kansas City, MO-KS	1 776 062	5	28	Philadelphia, PA-NJ	9 985
29	San Francisco, CA	1 731 183	25	29	Denver, CO	9 740
30	New Haven-Bridgeport-Stamford-Waterbury-Danbury, CT	1 706 575	37	30	Indianapolis, IN	9 125
31	Fort Worth-Arlington, TX	1 702 625	34	31	Orlando, FL	9 041
32	San Jose, CA	1 682 585	50	32	Raleigh-Durham-Chapel Hill, NC	9 036
33	Cincinnati, OH-KY-IN	1 646 395	58	33	Rochester, NY	8 872
34	Orlando, FL	1 644 561	45	34	New Orleans, LA	8 805
35	Sacramento, CA	1 628 197	43	35	Charlotte-Gastonia-Rock Hill, NC-SC	8 746
36	Fort Lauderdale, FL	1 623 018	33	36	Cincinnati, OH-KY-IN	8 655
37	Indianapolis, IN	1 607 486	38	37	San Antonio, TX	8 615
38	San Antonio, TX	1 592 383	69	38	Albany-Schenectady-Troy, NY	8 345
39	Norfolk-Virginia Beach-Newport News, VA-NC	1 569 541	64	39	Greenville-Spartanburg-Anderson, SC	8 310
40	Las Vegas, NV-AZ	1 563 282	67	40	Birmingham, AL	8 253
41	Columbus, OH	1 540 157	41	41	Columbus, OH	8 136
42	Milwaukee-Waukesha, WI	1 500 741	73	42	Syracuse, NY	7 984
43	Charlotte-Gastonia-Rock Hill, NC-SC	1 499 293	54	43	Memphis, TN-AR-MS	7 787
44	Bergen-Passaic, NJ	1 373 167	62	44	Richmond-Petersburg, VA	7 626
45	New Orleans, LA	1 337 726	31	45	Fort Worth-Arlington, TX	7 557
46	Salt Lake City-Ogden, UT	1 333 914	59	46	Grand Rapids-Muskegon-Holland, MI	7 144
47	Greensboro-Winston-Salem-High Point, NC	1 251 509	24	47	Cleveland-Lorain-Elyria, OH	7 011
48	Austin-San Marcos, TX	1 249 763	57	48	Jacksonville, FL	6 825
49	Nashville, TN	1 231 311	18	49	Baltimore, MD	6 757
50	Raleigh-Durham-Chapel Hill, NC	1 187 941	20	50	Tampa-St. Petersburg-Clearwater, FL	6 615
51	Buffalo-Niagara Falls, NY	1 170 111	74	51	Omaha, NE-IA	6 411
52	Middlesex-Somerset-Hunterdon, NJ	1 169 641	39	52	Norfolk-Virginia Beach-Newport News, VA-NC	6 083
53	Hartford, CT	1 148 618	61	53	Louisville, KY-IN	5 366
54	Memphis, TN-AR-MS	1 135 614	55	54	West Palm Beach-Boca Raton, FL	5 113
55	West Palm Beach-Boca Raton, FL	1 131 184	23	55	Miami, FL	5 040
56	Monmouth-Ocean, NJ	1 126 217	72	56	Ventura, CA	4 779
57	Jacksonville, FL	1 100 491	65	57	Dayton-Springfield, OH	4 360
58	Rochester, NY	1 098 201	46	58	Salt Lake City-Ogden, UT	4 189
59	Grand Rapids-Muskegon-Holland, MI	1 088 514	26	59	Newark, NJ	4 086
60	Oklahoma City, OK	1 083 346	51	60	Buffalo-Niagara Falls, NY	4 059
61	Louisville, KY-IN	1 025 598	53	61	Hartford, CT	3 923
62	Richmond-Petersburg, VA	996 512	42	62	Milwaukee-Waukesha, WI	3 781
63	Providence-Fall River-Warwick, RI-MA	962 886	21	63	Oakland, CA	3 775
64	Greenville-Spartanburg-Anderson, SC	962 441	32	64	San Jose, CA	3 343
65	Dayton-Springfield, OH	950 558	30	65	New Haven-Bridgeport-Stamford-Waterbury-Danbury, CT	3 189
66	Fresno, CA	922 516	36	66	Fort Lauderdale, FL	3 122
67	Birmingham, AL	921 106	16	67	Nassau-Suffolk, NY	3 105
68	Honolulu, HI	876 156	2	68	New York, NY	2 957
69	Albany-Schenectady-Troy, NY	875 583	56	69	Monmouth-Ocean, NJ	2 870
70	Tucson, AZ	843 746	52	70	Middlesex-Somerset-Hunterdon, NJ	2 705
71	Tulsa, OK	803 235	29	71	San Francisco, CA	2 630
72	Ventura, CA	753 197	63	72	Providence-Fall River-Warwick, RI-MA	2 437
73	Syracuse, NY	732 117	14	73	Orange County, CA	2 045
74	Omaha, NE-IA	716 998	68	74	Honolulu, HI	1 553
75	Albuquerque, NM	712 738	44	75	Bergen-Passaic, NJ	1 086

Note: Column numbers refer to Table C. Metropolitan Areas.

TABLE 4—75 Largest Metropolitan Areas by 2000 Population
Selected Rankings

Population Density (per Square Kilometer), 2000				Percent Population Change, 1990-2000			
Population Rank	Density Rank	Metropolitan Area	[col 4] Density	Population Rank	Percent Change Rank	Metropolitan Area	[col 52] Percent Change
2	1	New York, NY	3 150.1	40	1	Las Vegas, NV-AZ	83.3
14	2	Orange County, CA	1 392.1	48	2	Austin-San Marcos, TX	47.7
44	3	Bergen-Passaic, NJ	1 264.0	12	3	Phoenix-Mesa, AZ	45.3
1	4	Los Angeles-Long Beach, CA	905.1	9	4	Atlanta, GA	38.9
16	5	Nassau-Suffolk, NY	886.9	50	5	Raleigh-Durham-Chapel Hill, NC	38.4
29	6	San Francisco, CA	658.2	34	6	Orlando, FL	34.3
21	7	Oakland, CA	633.8	10	7	Dallas, TX	31.5
3	8	Chicago, IL	631.0	55	8	West Palm Beach-Boca Raton, FL	31.0
68	9	Honolulu, HI	564.0	25	9	Denver, CO	30.0
30	10	New Haven-Bridgeport-Stamford-Waterbury-Danbury, CT	535.1	36	10	Fort Lauderdale, FL	29.3
36	11	Fort Lauderdale, FL	519.9	43	11	Charlotte-Gastonia-Rock Hill, NC-SC	29.1
5	12	Philadelphia, PA-NJ	510.9	27	12	Portland-Vancouver, OR-WA	26.6
32	13	San Jose, CA	503.3	70	13	Tucson, AZ	26.5
26	14	Newark, NJ	497.5	8	14	Houston, TX	25.8
23	15	Miami, FL	447.1	11	15	Riverside-San Bernardino, CA	25.7
7	16	Detroit, MI	440.1	31	16	Fort Worth-Arlington, TX	25.1
52	17	Middlesex-Somerset-Hunterdon, NJ	432.4	49	17	Nashville, TN	25.0
42	18	Milwaukee-Waukesha, WI	396.9	46	18	Salt Lake City-Ogden, UT	24.4
63	19	Providence-Fall River-Warwick, RI-MA	395.1	66	19	Fresno, CA	22.1
56	20	Monmouth-Ocean, NJ	392.4	57	20	Jacksonville, FL	21.4
18	21	Baltimore, MD	377.8	75	21	Albuquerque, NM	21.0
4	22	Boston-Worcester-Lawrence, MA-NH-ME-CT	362.5	38	22	San Antonio, TX	20.2
20	23	Tampa-St. Petersburg-Clearwater, FL	362.2	47	23	Greensboro-Winston-Salem-High Point, NC	19.2
24	24	Cleveland-Lorain-Elyria, OH	321.1	35	23	Sacramento, CA	19.2
46	25	Salt Lake City-Ogden, UT	318.4	19	25	Seattle-Bellevue-Everett, WA	18.8
53	26	Hartford, CT	292.8	14	26	Orange County, CA	18.1
6	27	Washington, DC-MD-VA-WV	292.0	13	27	Minneapolis-St. Paul, MN-WI	16.9
51	28	Buffalo-Niagara Falls, NY	288.3	6	28	Washington, DC-MD-VA-WV	16.6
8	29	Houston, TX	272.5	37	29	Indianapolis, IN	16.4
9	30	Atlanta, GA	259.3	23	30	Miami, FL	16.3
15	31	San Diego, CA	258.7	59	31	Grand Rapids-Muskegon-Holland, MI	16.1
39	32	Norfolk-Virginia Beach-Newport News, VA-NC	258.0	64	32	Greenville-Spartanburg-Anderson, SC	15.9
31	33	Fort Worth-Arlington, TX	225.3	20	32	Tampa-St. Petersburg-Clearwater, FL	15.9
55	34	West Palm Beach-Boca Raton, FL	221.2	62	34	Richmond-Petersburg, VA	15.1
10	35	Dallas, TX	219.7	52	35	Middlesex-Somerset-Hunterdon, NJ	14.7
65	36	Dayton-Springfield, OH	218.0	41	36	Columbus, OH	14.5
25	37	Denver, CO	216.6	56	37	Monmouth-Ocean, NJ	14.2
19	38	Seattle-Bellevue-Everett, WA	210.8	21	38	Oakland, CA	13.5
22	39	Pittsburgh, PA	196.9	71	39	Tulsa, OK	13.3
61	40	Louisville, KY-IN	191.1	60	40	Oklahoma City, OK	13.0
33	41	Cincinnati, OH-KY-IN	190.2	54	41	Memphis, TN-AR-MS	12.7
41	42	Columbus, OH	189.3	15	42	San Diego, CA	12.6
13	43	Minneapolis-St. Paul, MN-WI	189.1	72	42	Ventura, CA	12.6
38	44	San Antonio, TX	184.8	32	44	San Jose, CA	12.4
34	45	Orlando, FL	181.9	28	45	Kansas City, MO-KS	12.2
37	46	Indianapolis, IN	176.2	74	46	Omaha, NE-IA	12.1
43	47	Charlotte-Gastonia-Rock Hill, NC-SC	171.4	3	47	Chicago, IL	11.6
57	48	Jacksonville, FL	161.2	67	48	Birmingham, AL	9.7
72	49	Ventura, CA	157.6	2	49	New York, NY	9.0
17	50	St. Louis, MO-IL	157.3	39	50	Norfolk-Virginia Beach-Newport News, VA-NC	8.6
35	51	Sacramento, CA	154.0	61	51	Louisville, KY-IN	8.1
59	52	Grand Rapids-Muskegon-Holland, MI	152.4	29	52	San Francisco, CA	8.0
45	53	New Orleans, LA	151.9	33	53	Cincinnati, OH-KY-IN	7.9
27	54	Portland-Vancouver, OR-WA	147.3	1	54	Los Angeles-Long Beach, CA	7.4
54	55	Memphis, TN-AR-MS	145.8	18	55	Baltimore, MD	7.2
50	56	Raleigh-Durham-Chapel Hill, NC	131.5	4	56	Boston-Worcester-Lawrence, MA-NH-ME-CT	6.5
62	57	Richmond-Petersburg, VA	130.7	26	57	Newark, NJ	6.1
28	58	Kansas City, MO-KS	126.8	44	58	Bergen-Passaic, NJ	5.9
47	59	Greensboro-Winston-Salem-High Point, NC	124.5	16	59	Nassau-Suffolk, NY	5.5
58	60	Rochester, NY	123.8	63	60	Providence-Fall River-Warwick, RI-MA	5.1
49	61	Nashville, TN	116.7	68	61	Honolulu, HI	4.8
64	62	Greenville-Spartanburg-Anderson, SC	115.8	42	61	Milwaukee-Waukesha, WI	4.8
48	63	Austin-San Marcos, TX	114.2	30	63	New Haven-Bridgeport-Stamford-Waterbury-Danbury, CT	4.6
74	64	Omaha, NE-IA	111.8	17	64	St. Louis, MO-IL	4.5
67	65	Birmingham, AL	111.6	7	65	Detroit, MI	4.1
69	66	Albany-Schenectady-Troy, NY	104.9	45	65	New Orleans, LA	4.1
60	67	Oklahoma City, OK	98.5	5	67	Philadelphia, PA-NJ	3.6
73	68	Syracuse, NY	91.7	58	68	Rochester, NY	3.4
12	69	Phoenix-Mesa, AZ	86.2	24	69	Cleveland-Lorain-Elyria, OH	2.2
71	70	Tulsa, OK	61.8	53	69	Hartford, CT	2.2
75	71	Albuquerque, NM	46.3	69	71	Albany-Schenectady-Troy, NY	1.6
11	72	Riverside-San Bernardino, CA	46.1	65	72	Dayton-Springfield, OH	-0.1
66	73	Fresno, CA	44.0	73	73	Syracuse, NY	-1.4
70	74	Tucson, AZ	35.5	22	74	Pittsburgh, PA	-1.5
40	75	Las Vegas, NV-AZ	15.3	51	75	Buffalo-Niagara Falls, NY	-1.6

Note: Column numbers refer to Table C. Metropolitan Areas.

TABLE 4—75 Largest Metropolitan Areas by 2000 Population
Selected Rankings

	Percent White, 2000				Percent Black, 2000		
Population Rank	White Rank	Metropolitan Area	[col 9] Percent White	Population Rank	Black Rank	Metropolitan Area	[col 10] Percent Black
22	1	Pittsburgh, PA	89.5	54	1	Memphis, TN-AR-MS	43.4
69	2	Albany-Schenectady-Troy, NY	89.4	45	2	New Orleans, LA	37.5
73	3	Syracuse, NY	88.9	39	3	Norfolk-Virginia Beach-Newport News, VA-NC	30.9
56	4	Monmouth-Ocean, NJ	88.3	62	4	Richmond-Petersburg, VA	30.2
46	5	Salt Lake City-Ogden, UT	87.6	67	5	Birmingham, AL	30.1
13	6	Minneapolis-St. Paul, MN-WI	86.1	9	6	Atlanta, GA	28.9
59	7	Grand Rapids-Muskegon-Holland, MI	85.7	18	7	Baltimore, MD	27.4
4	8	Boston-Worcester-Lawrence, MA-NH-ME-CT	85.4	6	8	Washington, DC-MD-VA-WV	26.0
74	9	Omaha, NE-IA	85.2	2	9	New York, NY	24.6
27	10	Portland-Vancouver, OR-WA	84.5	7	10	Detroit, MI	22.9
63	11	Providence-Fall River-Warwick, RI-MA	84.4	50	11	Raleigh-Durham-Chapel Hill, NC	22.7
33	12	Cincinnati, OH-KY-IN	84.1	26	12	Newark, NJ	22.3
58	13	Rochester, NY	84.0	57	13	Jacksonville, FL	21.7
51	14	Buffalo-Niagara Falls, NY	83.8	43	14	Charlotte-Gastonia-Rock Hill, NC-SC	20.5
20	15	Tampa-St. Petersburg-Clearwater, FL	82.9	36	14	Fort Lauderdale, FL	20.5
61	16	Louisville, KY-IN	82.8	23	16	Miami, FL	20.3
65	17	Dayton-Springfield, OH	82.3	47	17	Greensboro-Winston-Salem-High Point, NC	20.2
37	18	Indianapolis, IN	82.1	5	18	Philadelphia, PA-NJ	20.1
16	19	Nassau-Suffolk, NY	82.0	3	19	Chicago, IL	18.9
41	20	Columbus, OH	81.3	24	20	Cleveland-Lorain-Elyria, OH	18.5
28	21	Kansas City, MO-KS	80.8	17	21	St. Louis, MO-IL	18.3
53	22	Hartford, CT	80.7	64	22	Greenville-Spartanburg-Anderson, SC	17.5
25	23	Denver, CO	79.4	8	22	Houston, TX	17.5
49	23	Nashville, TN	79.4	42	24	Milwaukee-Waukesha, WI	15.7
30	23	New Haven-Bridgeport-Stamford-Waterbury-Danbury, CT	79.4	49	25	Nashville, TN	15.6
55	26	West Palm Beach-Boca Raton, FL	79.1	10	26	Dallas, TX	15.1
64	27	Greenville-Spartanburg-Anderson, SC	79.0	65	27	Dayton-Springfield, OH	14.2
19	28	Seattle-Bellevue-Everett, WA	78.6	37	28	Indianapolis, IN	13.9
17	29	St. Louis, MO-IL	78.3	61	28	Louisville, KY-IN	13.9
42	30	Milwaukee-Waukesha, WI	77.1	34	28	Orlando, FL	13.9
12	31	Phoenix-Mesa, AZ	77.0	55	31	West Palm Beach-Boca Raton, FL	13.8
24	32	Cleveland-Lorain-Elyria, OH	76.9	41	32	Columbus, OH	13.4
71	33	Tulsa, OK	76.0	33	33	Cincinnati, OH-KY-IN	13.0
60	34	Oklahoma City, OK	75.7	28	34	Kansas City, MO-KS	12.8
70	35	Tucson, AZ	75.1	21	35	Oakland, CA	12.7
34	36	Orlando, FL	75.0	51	36	Buffalo-Niagara Falls, NY	11.7
47	37	Greensboro-Winston-Salem-High Point, NC	74.4	31	37	Fort Worth-Arlington, TX	11.2
31	38	Fort Worth-Arlington, TX	74.3	30	38	New Haven-Bridgeport-Stamford-Waterbury-Danbury, CT	10.6
52	39	Middlesex-Somerset-Hunterdon, NJ	73.9	60	38	Oklahoma City, OK	10.6
40	40	Las Vegas, NV-AZ	73.8	58	40	Rochester, NY	10.3
43	41	Charlotte-Gastonia-Rock Hill, NC-SC	73.6	20	41	Tampa-St. Petersburg-Clearwater, FL	10.2
44	42	Bergen-Passaic, NJ	72.7	1	42	Los Angeles-Long Beach, CA	9.8
57	43	Jacksonville, FL	72.6	53	43	Hartford, CT	9.6
48	44	Austin-San Marcos, TX	72.5	71	44	Tulsa, OK	8.8
5	45	Philadelphia, PA-NJ	72.1	16	45	Nassau-Suffolk, NY	8.5
7	46	Detroit, MI	71.2	74	46	Omaha, NE-IA	8.3
36	47	Fort Lauderdale, FL	70.6	44	47	Bergen-Passaic, NJ	8.1
38	47	San Antonio, TX	70.6	40	47	Las Vegas, NV-AZ	8.1
35	49	Sacramento, CA	70.2	22	47	Pittsburgh, PA	8.1
72	50	Ventura, CA	69.9	48	50	Austin-San Marcos, TX	8.0
23	51	Miami, FL	69.7	52	50	Middlesex-Somerset-Hunterdon, NJ	8.0
75	52	Albuquerque, NM	69.6	11	52	Riverside-San Bernardino, CA	7.7
50	53	Raleigh-Durham-Chapel Hill, NC	69.4	35	52	Sacramento, CA	7.7
18	54	Baltimore, MD	67.3	59	54	Grand Rapids-Muskegon-Holland, MI	7.3
67	54	Birmingham, AL	67.3	38	55	San Antonio, TX	6.6
10	56	Dallas, TX	67.2	73	56	Syracuse, NY	6.5
15	57	San Diego, CA	66.5	69	57	Albany-Schenectady-Troy, NY	6.1
26	58	Newark, NJ	65.9	56	58	Monmouth-Ocean, NJ	5.8
3	59	Chicago, IL	65.8	15	59	San Diego, CA	5.7
62	60	Richmond-Petersburg, VA	64.9	25	60	Denver, CO	5.5
14	61	Orange County, CA	64.8	13	61	Minneapolis-St. Paul, MN-WI	5.3
9	62	Atlanta, GA	63.0	29	61	San Francisco, CA	5.3
39	63	Norfolk-Virginia Beach-Newport News, VA-NC	62.5	66	63	Fresno, CA	5.1
11	64	Riverside-San Bernardino, CA	62.1	4	64	Boston-Worcester-Lawrence, MA-NH-ME-CT	5.0
8	65	Houston, TX	61.1	63	65	Providence-Fall River-Warwick, RI-MA	4.5
6	66	Washington, DC-MD-VA-WV	60.1	19	66	Seattle-Bellevue-Everett, WA	4.4
29	67	San Francisco, CA	58.6	12	67	Phoenix-Mesa, AZ	3.7
45	68	New Orleans, LA	57.3	70	68	Tucson, AZ	3.0
66	69	Fresno, CA	55.4	32	69	San Jose, CA	2.8
21	69	Oakland, CA	55.4	27	70	Portland-Vancouver, OR-WA	2.7
32	71	San Jose, CA	53.8	75	71	Albuquerque, NM	2.5
54	72	Memphis, TN-AR-MS	52.9	68	72	Honolulu, HI	2.4
2	73	New York, NY	48.8	72	73	Ventura, CA	1.9
1	74	Los Angeles-Long Beach, CA	48.7	14	74	Orange County, CA	1.7
68	75	Honolulu, HI	21.3	46	75	Salt Lake City-Ogden, UT	1.1

Note: Column numbers refer to Table C. Metropolitan Areas.

TABLE 4—75 Largest Metropolitan Areas by 2000 Population
Selected Rankings

	Percent American Indian and Alaska Native, 2000				Percent Asian, 2000		
Population Rank	American Indian and Alaska Native Rank	Metropolitan Area	[col 11] Percent American Indian and Alaska Native	Population Rank	Asian Rank	Metropolitan Area	[col 12] Percent Asian
71	1	Tulsa, OK	6.9	68	1	Honolulu, HI	46.0
75	2	Albuquerque, NM	5.6	32	2	San Jose, CA	25.6
60	3	Oklahoma City, OK	4.2	29	3	San Francisco, CA	22.7
70	4	Tucson, AZ	3.2	21	4	Oakland, CA	16.7
12	5	Phoenix-Mesa, AZ	2.2	14	5	Orange County, CA	13.6
66	6	Fresno, CA	1.7	1	6	Los Angeles-Long Beach, CA	11.9
11	7	Riverside-San Bernardino, CA	1.2	52	7	Middlesex-Somerset-Hunterdon, NJ	11.2
35	8	Sacramento, CA	1.1	19	8	Seattle-Bellevue-Everett, WA	9.4
40	9	Las Vegas, NV-AZ	1.0	2	9	New York, NY	9.1
19	9	Seattle-Bellevue-Everett, WA	1.0	35	10	Sacramento, CA	8.9
25	11	Denver, CO	0.9	15	10	San Diego, CA	8.9
27	11	Portland-Vancouver, OR-WA	0.9	44	12	Bergen-Passaic, NJ	8.2
15	11	San Diego, CA	0.9	66	13	Fresno, CA	7.1
72	11	Ventura, CA	0.9	6	14	Washington, DC-MD-VA-WV	6.7
1	15	Los Angeles-Long Beach, CA	0.8	72	15	Ventura, CA	5.3
46	15	Salt Lake City-Ogden, UT	0.8	8	16	Houston, TX	5.2
38	15	San Antonio, TX	0.8	40	17	Las Vegas, NV-AZ	4.7
51	18	Buffalo-Niagara Falls, NY	0.7	3	18	Chicago, IL	4.6
13	18	Minneapolis-St. Paul, MN-WI	0.7	27	18	Portland-Vancouver, OR-WA	4.6
14	18	Orange County, CA	0.7	11	20	Riverside-San Bernardino, CA	4.2
32	18	San Jose, CA	0.7	13	21	Minneapolis-St. Paul, MN-WI	4.1
73	18	Syracuse, NY	0.7	10	22	Dallas, TX	4.0
48	23	Austin-San Marcos, TX	0.6	26	22	Newark, NJ	4.0
10	23	Dallas, TX	0.6	4	24	Boston-Worcester-Lawrence, MA-NH-ME-CT	3.9
31	23	Fort Worth-Arlington, TX	0.6	16	25	Nassau-Suffolk, NY	3.6
21	23	Oakland, CA	0.6	48	26	Austin-San Marcos, TX	3.5
59	27	Grand Rapids-Muskegon-Holland, MI	0.5	5	27	Philadelphia, PA-NJ	3.4
28	27	Kansas City, MO-KS	0.5	9	28	Atlanta, GA	3.3
42	27	Milwaukee-Waukesha, WI	0.5	31	29	Fort Worth-Arlington, TX	3.2
2	27	New York, NY	0.5	25	30	Denver, CO	3.0
74	27	Omaha, NE-IA	0.5	50	31	Raleigh-Durham-Chapel Hill, NC	2.9
63	27	Providence-Fall River-Warwick, RI-MA	0.5	30	32	New Haven-Bridgeport-Stamford-Waterbury-Danbury, CT	2.8
43	33	Charlotte-Gastonia-Rock Hill, NC-SC	0.4	18	33	Baltimore, MD	2.7
47	33	Greensboro-Winston-Salem-High Point, NC	0.4	56	33	Monmouth-Ocean, NJ	2.7
8	33	Houston, TX	0.4	39	33	Norfolk-Virginia Beach-Newport News, VA-NC	2.7
45	33	New Orleans, LA	0.4	34	33	Orlando, FL	2.7
39	33	Norfolk-Virginia Beach-Newport News, VA-NC	0.4	60	37	Oklahoma City, OK	2.5
50	33	Raleigh-Durham-Chapel Hill, NC	0.4	41	38	Columbus, OH	2.4
62	33	Richmond-Petersburg, VA	0.4	7	39	Detroit, MI	2.3
29	33	San Francisco, CA	0.4	36	39	Fort Lauderdale, FL	2.3
9	41	Atlanta, GA	0.3	53	39	Hartford, CT	2.3
18	41	Baltimore, MD	0.3	57	39	Jacksonville, FL	2.3
44	41	Bergen-Passaic, NJ	0.3	63	39	Providence-Fall River-Warwick, RI-MA	2.3
67	41	Birmingham, AL	0.3	46	44	Salt Lake City-Ogden, UT	2.2
3	41	Chicago, IL	0.3	42	45	Milwaukee-Waukesha, WI	2.1
41	41	Columbus, OH	0.3	45	45	New Orleans, LA	2.1
7	41	Detroit, MI	0.3	12	45	Phoenix-Mesa, AZ	2.1
57	41	Jacksonville, FL	0.3	62	45	Richmond-Petersburg, VA	2.1
49	41	Nashville, TN	0.3	70	49	Tucson, AZ	2.0
34	41	Orlando, FL	0.3	43	50	Charlotte-Gastonia-Rock Hill, NC-SC	1.9
58	41	Rochester, NY	0.3	20	50	Tampa-St. Petersburg-Clearwater, FL	1.9
20	41	Tampa-St. Petersburg-Clearwater, FL	0.3	69	52	Albany-Schenectady-Troy, NY	1.8
6	41	Washington, DC-MD-VA-WV	0.3	58	52	Rochester, NY	1.8
4	54	Boston-Worcester-Lawrence, MA-NH-ME-CT	0.2	75	54	Albuquerque, NM	1.7
69	54	Albany-Schenectady-Troy, NY	0.2	59	55	Grand Rapids-Muskegon-Holland, MI	1.6
33	54	Cincinnati, OH-KY-IN	0.2	28	55	Kansas City, MO-KS	1.6
24	54	Cleveland-Lorain-Elyria, OH	0.2	49	55	Nashville, TN	1.6
65	54	Dayton-Springfield, OH	0.2	74	58	Omaha, NE-IA	1.5
36	54	Fort Lauderdale, FL	0.2	38	58	San Antonio, TX	1.5
64	54	Greenville-Spartanburg-Anderson, SC	0.2	73	58	Syracuse, NY	1.5
53	54	Hartford, CT	0.2	55	58	West Palm Beach-Boca Raton, FL	1.5
68	54	Honolulu, HI	0.2	24	62	Cleveland-Lorain-Elyria, OH	1.4
37	54	Indianapolis, IN	0.2	47	62	Greensboro-Winston-Salem-High Point, NC	1.4
61	54	Louisville, KY-IN	0.2	54	62	Memphis, TN-AR-MS	1.4
54	54	Memphis, TN-AR-MS	0.2	23	62	Miami, FL	1.4
23	54	Miami, FL	0.2	17	62	St. Louis, MO-IL	1.4
52	54	Middlesex-Somerset-Hunterdon, NJ	0.2	51	67	Buffalo-Niagara Falls, NY	1.3
16	54	Nassau-Suffolk, NY	0.2	33	68	Cincinnati, OH-KY-IN	1.2
30	54	New Haven-Bridgeport-Stamford-Waterbury-Danbury, CT	0.2	65	68	Dayton-Springfield, OH	1.2
26	54	Newark, NJ	0.2	64	68	Greenville-Spartanburg-Anderson, SC	1.2
5	54	Philadelphia, PA-NJ	0.2	37	68	Indianapolis, IN	1.2
17	54	St. Louis, MO-IL	0.2	71	68	Tulsa, OK	1.2
55	54	West Palm Beach-Boca Raton, FL	0.2	61	73	Louisville, KY-IN	1.1
56	74	Monmouth-Ocean, NJ	0.1	22	73	Pittsburgh, PA	1.1
22	74	Pittsburgh, PA	0.1	67	75	Birmingham, AL	0.8

Note: Column numbers refer to Table C. Metropolitan Areas.

TABLE 4—75 Largest Metropolitan Areas by 2000 Population
Selected Rankings

	Percent Hispanic, 2000				Percent Under 18 Years, 2000		
Population Rank	Hispanic Rank	Metropolitan Area	[col 22] Percent Hispanic	Population Rank	Under 18 Years Rank	Metropolitan Area	[cols 28 & 29] Percent Under 18 Years
23	1	Miami, FL	57.3	66	1	Fresno, CA	31.8
38	2	San Antonio, TX	51.2	46	2	Salt Lake City-Ogden, UT	31.4
1	3	Los Angeles-Long Beach, CA	44.6	11	3	Riverside-San Bernardino, CA	31.3
66	4	Fresno, CA	44.0	8	4	Houston, TX	29.2
75	5	Albuquerque, NM	41.6	72	5	Ventura, CA	28.5
11	6	Riverside-San Bernardino, CA	37.8	38	6	San Antonio, TX	28.4
72	7	Ventura, CA	33.4	59	7	Grand Rapids-Muskegon-Holland, MI	28.3
14	8	Orange County, CA	30.8	54	7	Memphis, TN-AR-MS	28.3
8	9	Houston, TX	29.9	10	9	Dallas, TX	28.0
70	10	Tucson, AZ	29.3	31	9	Fort Worth-Arlington, TX	28.0
15	11	San Diego, CA	26.7	1	9	Los Angeles-Long Beach, CA	28.0
48	12	Austin-San Marcos, TX	26.2	35	12	Sacramento, CA	27.3
2	13	New York, NY	25.1	74	13	Omaha, NE-IA	27.2
12	13	Phoenix-Mesa, AZ	25.1	3	14	Chicago, IL	27.0
32	15	San Jose, CA	24.0	14	14	Orange County, CA	27.0
10	16	Dallas, TX	23.0	13	16	Minneapolis-St. Paul, MN-WI	26.8
40	17	Las Vegas, NV-AZ	20.6	45	16	New Orleans, LA	26.8
25	18	Denver, CO	18.8	12	16	Phoenix-Mesa, AZ	26.8
21	19	Oakland, CA	18.5	71	19	Tulsa, OK	26.7
31	20	Fort Worth-Arlington, TX	18.2	9	20	Atlanta, GA	26.6
44	21	Bergen-Passaic, NJ	17.3	33	20	Cincinnati, OH-KY-IN	26.6
3	22	Chicago, IL	17.1	37	20	Indianapolis, IN	26.6
29	23	San Francisco, CA	16.8	28	20	Kansas City, MO-KS	26.6
36	24	Fort Lauderdale, FL	16.7	7	24	Detroit, MI	26.5
34	25	Orlando, FL	16.5	42	25	Milwaukee-Waukesha, WI	26.4
35	26	Sacramento, CA	14.4	39	25	Norfolk-Virginia Beach-Newport News, VA-NC	26.4
26	27	Newark, NJ	13.3	75	27	Albuquerque, NM	26.3
55	28	West Palm Beach-Boca Raton, FL	12.4	17	27	St. Louis, MO-IL	26.3
52	29	Middlesex-Somerset-Hunterdon, NJ	11.2	57	29	Jacksonville, FL	26.1
30	30	New Haven-Bridgeport-Stamford-Waterbury-Danbury, CT	11.0	25	30	Denver, CO	25.8
46	31	Salt Lake City-Ogden, UT	10.8	15	30	San Diego, CA	25.8
20	32	Tampa-St. Petersburg-Clearwater, FL	10.4	58	32	Rochester, NY	25.7
16	33	Nassau-Suffolk, NY	10.3	73	32	Syracuse, NY	25.7
53	34	Hartford, CT	9.4	26	34	Newark, NJ	25.6
63	35	Providence-Fall River-Warwick, RI-MA	9.2	60	34	Oklahoma City, OK	25.6
6	36	Washington, DC-MD-VA-WV	8.8	41	36	Columbus, OH	25.5
27	37	Portland-Vancouver, OR-WA	7.4	27	36	Portland-Vancouver, OR-WA	25.5
68	38	Honolulu, HI	6.7	43	38	Charlotte-Gastonia-Rock Hill, NC-SC	25.4
60	38	Oklahoma City, OK	6.7	24	38	Cleveland-Lorain-Elyria, OH	25.4
9	40	Atlanta, GA	6.5	16	38	Nassau-Suffolk, NY	25.4
59	41	Grand Rapids-Muskegon-Holland, MI	6.3	21	38	Oakland, CA	25.4
42	41	Milwaukee-Waukesha, WI	6.3	5	38	Philadelphia, PA-NJ	25.4
50	43	Raleigh-Durham-Chapel Hill, NC	6.1	48	43	Austin-San Marcos, TX	25.3
4	44	Boston-Worcester-Lawrence, MA-NH-ME-CT	6.0	18	43	Baltimore, MD	25.3
56	45	Monmouth-Ocean, NJ	5.7	40	43	Las Vegas, NV-AZ	25.3
74	46	Omaha, NE-IA	5.5	6	43	Washington, DC-MD-VA-WV	25.3
28	47	Kansas City, MO-KS	5.2	62	47	Richmond-Petersburg, VA	25.2
19	47	Seattle-Bellevue-Everett, WA	5.2	67	48	Birmingham, AL	25.1
43	49	Charlotte-Gastonia-Rock Hill, NC-SC	5.1	30	48	New Haven-Bridgeport-Stamford-Waterbury-Danbury, CT	25.1
5	49	Philadelphia, PA-NJ	5.1	65	50	Dayton-Springfield, OH	24.8
47	51	Greensboro-Winston-Salem-High Point, NC	5.0	23	50	Miami, FL	24.8
71	52	Tulsa, OK	4.8	56	50	Monmouth-Ocean, NJ	24.8
45	53	New Orleans, LA	4.4	49	50	Nashville, TN	24.8
58	54	Rochester, NY	4.3	34	50	Orlando, FL	24.8
57	55	Jacksonville, FL	3.8	32	50	San Jose, CA	24.8
24	56	Cleveland-Lorain-Elyria, OH	3.3	61	56	Louisville, KY-IN	24.7
13	56	Minneapolis-St. Paul, MN-WI	3.3	70	57	Tucson, AZ	24.6
49	56	Nashville, TN	3.3	51	58	Buffalo-Niagara Falls, NY	24.4
39	59	Norfolk-Virginia Beach-Newport News, VA-NC	3.1	64	58	Greenville-Spartanburg-Anderson, SC	24.4
51	60	Buffalo-Niagara Falls, NY	2.9	52	58	Middlesex-Somerset-Hunterdon, NJ	24.4
7	60	Detroit, MI	2.9	2	58	New York, NY	24.4
69	62	Albany-Schenectady-Troy, NY	2.7	53	62	Hartford, CT	24.2
64	62	Greenville-Spartanburg-Anderson, SC	2.7	50	62	Raleigh-Durham-Chapel Hill, NC	24.2
37	62	Indianapolis, IN	2.7	44	64	Bergen-Passaic, NJ	24.1
54	65	Memphis, TN-AR-MS	2.4	47	65	Greensboro-Winston-Salem-High Point, NC	24.0
62	66	Richmond-Petersburg, VA	2.3	4	66	Boston-Worcester-Lawrence, MA-NH-ME-CT	24.0
73	67	Syracuse, NY	2.1	69	67	Albany-Schenectady-Troy, NY	23.9
18	68	Baltimore, MD	2.0	19	67	Seattle-Bellevue-Everett, WA	23.9
67	69	Birmingham, AL	1.8	68	69	Honolulu, HI	23.8
41	69	Columbus, OH	1.8	63	70	Providence-Fall River-Warwick, RI-MA	23.7
61	71	Louisville, KY-IN	1.6	36	71	Fort Lauderdale, FL	23.5
17	72	St. Louis, MO-IL	1.5	22	72	Pittsburgh, PA	22.3
65	73	Dayton-Springfield, OH	1.2	20	73	Tampa-St. Petersburg-Clearwater, FL	22.0
33	74	Cincinnati, OH-KY-IN	1.1	55	74	West Palm Beach-Boca Raton, FL	21.3
22	75	Pittsburgh, PA	0.7	29	75	San Francisco, CA	18.8

Note: Column numbers refer to Table C. Metropolitan Areas.

TABLE 4—75 Largest Metropolitan Areas by 2000 Population
Selected Rankings

		Percent Age 25 to 54 Years, 2000				Percent Age 65 Years and Over, 2000	
Population Rank	25 to 54 Years Rank	Metropolitan Area	[cols 31, 32 & 33] Percent 25 to 54 Years	Population Rank	65 Years and Over Rank	Metropolitan Area	[cols 35 & 36] Percent 65 Years and Over
29	1	San Francisco, CA	50.9	55	1	West Palm Beach-Boca Raton, FL	23.1
9	2	Atlanta, GA	48.9	20	2	Tampa-St. Petersburg-Clearwater, FL	19.2
19	3	Seattle-Bellevue-Everett, WA	48.7	22	3	Pittsburgh, PA	17.7
25	4	Denver, CO	48.5	56	4	Monmouth-Ocean, NJ	16.9
32	5	San Jose, CA	48.4	36	5	Fort Lauderdale, FL	16.1
6	5	Washington, DC-MD-VA-WV	48.4	51	6	Buffalo-Niagara Falls, NY	15.8
50	7	Raleigh-Durham-Chapel Hill, NC	48.2	24	7	Cleveland-Lorain-Elyria, OH	14.6
48	8	Austin-San Marcos, TX	47.8	63	8	Providence-Fall River-Warwick, RI-MA	14.5
43	9	Charlotte-Gastonia-Rock Hill, NC-SC	47.2	69	9	Albany-Schenectady-Troy, NY	14.3
10	10	Dallas, TX	47.1	70	10	Tucson, AZ	14.2
52	11	Middlesex-Somerset-Hunterdon, NJ	47.0	44	11	Bergen-Passaic, NJ	14.1
13	12	Minneapolis-St. Paul, MN-WI	46.9	53	12	Hartford, CT	14.0
21	12	Oakland, CA	46.9	30	13	New Haven-Bridgeport-Stamford-Waterbury-Danbury, CT	13.9
27	14	Portland-Vancouver, OR-WA	46.8	65	14	Dayton-Springfield, OH	13.5
49	15	Nashville, TN	46.7	5	14	Philadelphia, PA-NJ	13.5
8	16	Houston, TX	46.2	68	16	Honolulu, HI	13.4
62	16	Richmond-Petersburg, VA	46.2	16	16	Nassau-Suffolk, NY	13.4
4	18	Boston-Worcester-Lawrence, MA-NH-ME-CT	45.9	23	18	Miami, FL	13.3
41	18	Columbus, OH	45.9	73	18	Syracuse, NY	13.3
14	18	Orange County, CA	45.9	29	20	San Francisco, CA	13.2
31	21	Fort Worth-Arlington, TX	45.8	58	21	Rochester, NY	12.9
37	22	Indianapolis, IN	45.6	17	22	St. Louis, MO-IL	12.8
18	23	Baltimore, MD	45.3	67	23	Birmingham, AL	12.7
2	23	New York, NY	45.3	4	23	Boston-Worcester-Lawrence, MA-NH-ME-CT	12.7
26	23	Newark, NJ	45.3	61	25	Louisville, KY-IN	12.6
57	26	Jacksonville, FL	45.2	42	25	Milwaukee-Waukesha, WI	12.6
28	26	Kansas City, MO-KS	45.2	47	27	Greensboro-Winston-Salem-High Point, NC	12.5
61	28	Louisville, KY-IN	45.0	34	28	Orlando, FL	12.4
3	29	Chicago, IL	44.9	64	29	Greenville-Spartanburg-Anderson, SC	12.3
7	29	Detroit, MI	44.9	26	30	Newark, NJ	12.2
44	31	Bergen-Passaic, NJ	44.8	18	31	Baltimore, MD	12.1
47	31	Greensboro-Winston-Salem-High Point, NC	44.8	7	31	Detroit, MI	12.1
34	31	Orlando, FL	44.8	12	33	Phoenix-Mesa, AZ	12.0
36	34	Fort Lauderdale, FL	44.7	33	34	Cincinnati, OH-KY-IN	11.9
1	35	Los Angeles-Long Beach, CA	44.6	2	34	New York, NY	11.9
15	35	San Diego, CA	44.6	40	36	Las Vegas, NV-AZ	11.8
54	37	Memphis, TN-AR-MS	44.4	52	36	Middlesex-Somerset-Hunterdon, NJ	11.8
16	37	Nassau-Suffolk, NY	44.4	71	36	Tulsa, OK	11.8
74	37	Omaha, NE-IA	44.4	35	39	Sacramento, CA	11.5
75	40	Albuquerque, NM	44.3	28	40	Kansas City, MO-KS	11.4
67	40	Birmingham, AL	44.3	45	40	New Orleans, LA	11.4
53	40	Hartford, CT	44.3	60	40	Oklahoma City, OK	11.4
30	40	New Haven-Bridgeport-Stamford-Waterbury-Danbury, CT	44.3	75	43	Albuquerque, NM	11.3
39	40	Norfolk-Virginia Beach-Newport News, VA-NC	44.3	62	44	Richmond-Petersburg, VA	11.2
72	40	Ventura, CA	44.3	15	44	San Diego, CA	11.2
33	46	Cincinnati, OH-KY-IN	44.2	57	46	Jacksonville, FL	11.1
40	46	Las Vegas, NV-AZ	44.2	37	47	Indianapolis, IN	10.9
35	46	Sacramento, CA	44.2	59	48	Grand Rapids-Muskegon-Holland, MI	10.8
68	49	Honolulu, HI	44.0	3	49	Chicago, IL	10.7
42	50	Milwaukee-Waukesha, WI	43.8	21	49	Oakland, CA	10.7
64	51	Greenville-Spartanburg-Anderson, SC	43.7	38	49	San Antonio, TX	10.7
45	51	New Orleans, LA	43.7	74	52	Omaha, NE-IA	10.6
23	53	Miami, FL	43.6	11	52	Riverside-San Bernardino, CA	10.6
5	53	Philadelphia, PA-NJ	43.6	27	54	Portland-Vancouver, OR-WA	10.4
69	55	Albany-Schenectady-Troy, NY	43.5	39	55	Norfolk-Virginia Beach-Newport News, VA-NC	10.3
58	56	Rochester, NY	43.4	43	56	Charlotte-Gastonia-Rock Hill, NC-SC	10.2
17	56	St. Louis, MO-IL	43.4	19	56	Seattle-Bellevue-Everett, WA	10.2
71	58	Tulsa, OK	43.3	72	56	Ventura, CA	10.2
60	59	Oklahoma City, OK	43.2	66	59	Fresno, CA	10.1
24	60	Cleveland-Lorain-Elyria, OH	43.1	41	60	Columbus, OH	10.0
59	60	Grand Rapids-Muskegon-Holland, MI	43.1	49	60	Nashville, TN	10.0
12	62	Phoenix-Mesa, AZ	43.0	54	62	Memphis, TN-AR-MS	9.9
63	62	Providence-Fall River-Warwick, RI-MA	43.0	1	63	Los Angeles-Long Beach, CA	9.8
38	64	San Antonio, TX	42.9	14	63	Orange County, CA	9.8
22	65	Pittsburgh, PA	42.5	13	65	Minneapolis-St. Paul, MN-WI	9.6
73	65	Syracuse, NY	42.5	32	65	San Jose, CA	9.6
65	67	Dayton-Springfield, OH	42.4	6	67	Washington, DC-MD-VA-WV	9.1
56	68	Monmouth-Ocean, NJ	42.3	25	68	Denver, CO	9.0
51	69	Buffalo-Niagara Falls, NY	42.1	31	69	Fort Worth-Arlington, TX	8.8
20	70	Tampa-St. Petersburg-Clearwater, FL	41.6	50	70	Raleigh-Durham-Chapel Hill, NC	8.6
70	71	Tucson, AZ	41.5	46	71	Salt Lake City-Ogden, UT	8.3
11	72	Riverside-San Bernardino, CA	41.2	10	72	Dallas, TX	7.7
46	72	Salt Lake City-Ogden, UT	41.2	9	73	Atlanta, GA	7.5
66	74	Fresno, CA	40.2	8	74	Houston, TX	7.4
55	75	West Palm Beach-Boca Raton, FL	39.5	48	75	Austin-San Marcos, TX	7.3

Note: Column numbers refer to Table C. Metropolitan Areas.

TABLE 4—75 Largest Metropolitan Areas by 2000 Population
Selected Rankings

Percent Female-headed Family Households, 2000				Percent Living Alone, 2000			
Population Rank	Female Households Rank	Metropolitan Area	[col 76] Percent Female Households	Population Rank	Living Alone Rank	Metropolitan Area	[col 79] Percent Living Alone
54	1	Memphis, TN-AR-MS	18.9	29	1	San Francisco, CA	32.1
45	2	New Orleans, LA	18.2	2	2	New York, NY	30.8
2	3	New York, NY	18.1	51	3	Buffalo-Niagara Falls, NY	30.2
23	4	Miami, FL	17.2	22	4	Pittsburgh, PA	30.0
18	5	Baltimore, MD	14.9	20	5	Tampa-St. Petersburg-Clearwater, FL	29.7
66	5	Fresno, CA	14.9	36	6	Fort Lauderdale, FL	29.6
39	5	Norfolk-Virginia Beach-Newport News, VA-NC	14.9	69	7	Albany-Schenectady-Troy, NY	29.4
67	8	Birmingham, AL	14.8	24	8	Cleveland-Lorain-Elyria, OH	29.2
38	8	San Antonio, TX	14.8	55	8	West Palm Beach-Boca Raton, FL	29.2
1	10	Los Angeles-Long Beach, CA	14.7	42	10	Milwaukee-Waukesha, WI	28.7
7	11	Detroit, MI	14.6	70	11	Tucson, AZ	28.5
26	12	Newark, NJ	14.4	63	12	Providence-Fall River-Warwick, RI-MA	28.4
62	12	Richmond-Petersburg, VA	14.4	19	12	Seattle-Bellevue-Everett, WA	28.4
5	14	Philadelphia, PA-NJ	14.3	33	14	Cincinnati, OH-KY-IN	28.2
57	15	Jacksonville, FL	14.0	41	15	Columbus, OH	28.1
24	16	Cleveland-Lorain-Elyria, OH	13.8	25	16	Denver, CO	28.0
9	17	Atlanta, GA	13.6	65	17	Dayton-Springfield, OH	27.9
61	17	Louisville, KY-IN	13.6	61	18	Louisville, KY-IN	27.8
51	19	Buffalo-Niagara Falls, NY	13.5	73	18	Syracuse, NY	27.8
17	19	St. Louis, MO-IL	13.5	60	20	Oklahoma City, OK	27.5
11	21	Riverside-San Bernardino, CA	13.4	17	21	St. Louis, MO-IL	27.4
3	22	Chicago, IL	13.3	53	22	Hartford, CT	27.3
8	23	Houston, TX	13.2	4	23	Boston-Worcester-Lawrence, MA-NH-ME-CT	27.2
63	24	Providence-Fall River-Warwick, RI-MA	13.1	7	23	Detroit, MI	27.2
42	25	Milwaukee-Waukesha, WI	12.9	28	25	Kansas City, MO-KS	27.1
75	26	Albuquerque, NM	12.8	45	25	New Orleans, LA	27.1
35	26	Sacramento, CA	12.8	5	25	Philadelphia, PA-NJ	27.1
65	28	Dayton-Springfield, OH	12.7	58	25	Rochester, NY	27.1
64	29	Greenville-Spartanburg-Anderson, SC	12.6	37	29	Indianapolis, IN	27.0
36	30	Fort Lauderdale, FL	12.5	71	29	Tulsa, OK	27.0
30	30	New Haven-Bridgeport-Stamford-Waterbury-Danbury, CT	12.5	74	31	Omaha, NE-IA	26.9
33	32	Cincinnati, OH-KY-IN	12.4	75	32	Albuquerque, NM	26.7
21	32	Oakland, CA	12.4	67	32	Birmingham, AL	26.7
34	32	Orlando, FL	12.4	13	32	Minneapolis-St. Paul, MN-WI	26.7
58	32	Rochester, NY	12.4	48	35	Austin-San Marcos, TX	26.6
6	32	Washington, DC-MD-VA-WV	12.4	18	36	Baltimore, MD	26.4
47	37	Greensboro-Winston-Salem-High Point, NC	12.3	3	36	Chicago, IL	26.4
53	37	Hartford, CT	12.3	47	36	Greensboro-Winston-Salem-High Point, NC	26.4
68	37	Honolulu, HI	12.3	50	36	Raleigh-Durham-Chapel Hill, NC	26.4
49	37	Nashville, TN	12.3	62	36	Richmond-Petersburg, VA	26.4
60	37	Oklahoma City, OK	12.3	6	36	Washington, DC-MD-VA-WV	26.4
43	42	Charlotte-Gastonia-Rock Hill, NC-SC	12.1	49	42	Nashville, TN	26.3
10	42	Dallas, TX	12.1	27	42	Portland-Vancouver, OR-WA	26.3
37	42	Indianapolis, IN	12.1	30	44	New Haven-Bridgeport-Stamford-Waterbury-Danbury, CT	26.1
73	42	Syracuse, NY	12.1	54	45	Memphis, TN-AR-MS	25.5
41	46	Columbus, OH	11.9	64	46	Greenville-Spartanburg-Anderson, SC	25.4
44	47	Bergen-Passaic, NJ	11.8	56	47	Monmouth-Ocean, NJ	25.3
28	47	Kansas City, MO-KS	11.8	35	48	Sacramento, CA	25.2
70	47	Tucson, AZ	11.8	10	49	Dallas, TX	25.1
31	50	Fort Worth-Arlington, TX	11.7	57	50	Jacksonville, FL	24.8
15	51	San Diego, CA	11.6	21	50	Oakland, CA	24.8
71	52	Tulsa, OK	11.5	1	52	Los Angeles-Long Beach, CA	24.6
4	53	Boston-Worcester-Lawrence, MA-NH-ME-CT	11.4	43	53	Charlotte-Gastonia-Rock Hill, NC-SC	24.5
40	53	Las Vegas, NV-AZ	11.4	40	53	Las Vegas, NV-AZ	24.5
74	53	Omaha, NE-IA	11.4	12	55	Phoenix-Mesa, AZ	24.4
22	53	Pittsburgh, PA	11.4	15	56	San Diego, CA	24.2
69	57	Albany-Schenectady-Troy, NY	11.3	31	57	Fort Worth-Arlington, TX	24.0
20	58	Tampa-St. Petersburg-Clearwater, FL	11.2	26	57	Newark, NJ	24.0
50	59	Raleigh-Durham-Chapel Hill, NC	11.0	44	59	Bergen-Passaic, NJ	23.8
59	60	Grand Rapids-Muskegon-Holland, MI	10.9	59	59	Grand Rapids-Muskegon-Holland, MI	23.8
16	60	Nassau-Suffolk, NY	10.9	8	61	Houston, TX	23.6
72	60	Ventura, CA	10.9	34	62	Orlando, FL	23.5
12	63	Phoenix-Mesa, AZ	10.8	39	63	Norfolk-Virginia Beach-Newport News, VA-NC	23.4
14	64	Orange County, CA	10.7	38	63	San Antonio, TX	23.4
48	65	Austin-San Marcos, TX	10.2	9	65	Atlanta, GA	23.3
25	65	Denver, CO	10.2	23	65	Miami, FL	23.3
46	65	Salt Lake City-Ogden, UT	10.2	52	67	Middlesex-Somerset-Hunterdon, NJ	22.3
32	68	San Jose, CA	10.0	68	68	Honolulu, HI	21.6
27	69	Portland-Vancouver, OR-WA	9.9	32	69	San Jose, CA	21.4
52	70	Middlesex-Somerset-Hunterdon, NJ	9.7	14	70	Orange County, CA	21.1
13	70	Minneapolis-St. Paul, MN-WI	9.7	66	71	Fresno, CA	20.1
55	70	West Palm Beach-Boca Raton, FL	9.7	11	72	Riverside-San Bernardino, CA	19.5
56	73	Monmouth-Ocean, NJ	9.6	46	72	Salt Lake City-Ogden, UT	19.5
29	74	San Francisco, CA	9.3	72	74	Ventura, CA	18.9
19	75	Seattle-Bellevue-Everett, WA	9.2	16	75	Nassau-Suffolk, NY	18.6

Note: Column numbers refer to Table C. Metropolitan Areas.

TABLE 4—75 Largest Metropolitan Areas by 2000 Population
Selected Rankings

Percent Married Couple Family Households, 2000				Percent of Families with Own Children Under 18, 2000			
Population Rank	Married Couple Family Households Rank	Metropolitan Area	[col 74] Percent in Married Couple Family Households	Population Rank	Families with Own Children Under 18 Rank	Metropolitan Area	[col 73] Percent of Families with Own Children Under 18
16	1	Nassau-Suffolk, NY	62.5	46	1	Salt Lake City-Ogden, UT	41.6
46	2	Salt Lake City-Ogden, UT	60.3	11	2	Riverside-San Bernardino, CA	41.4
72	3	Ventura, CA	59.5	66	3	Fresno, CA	41.1
52	4	Middlesex-Somerset-Hunterdon, NJ	58.9	72	4	Ventura, CA	39.7
56	5	Monmouth-Ocean, NJ	57.3	8	5	Houston, TX	38.9
11	6	Riverside-San Bernardino, CA	56.1	14	6	Orange County, CA	37.0
14	7	Orange County, CA	55.9	31	7	Fort Worth-Arlington, TX	36.9
44	8	Bergen-Passaic, NJ	55.8	1	8	Los Angeles-Long Beach, CA	36.8
59	9	Grand Rapids-Muskegon-Holland, MI	55.6	38	9	San Antonio, TX	36.6
32	10	San Jose, CA	54.9	10	10	Dallas, TX	36.5
68	11	Honolulu, HI	54.5	59	10	Grand Rapids-Muskegon-Holland, MI	36.5
31	12	Fort Worth-Arlington, TX	54.3	16	12	Nassau-Suffolk, NY	36.2
66	13	Fresno, CA	53.6	9	13	Atlanta, GA	35.8
64	14	Greenville-Spartanburg-Anderson, SC	53.2	39	14	Norfolk-Virginia Beach-Newport News, VA-NC	35.6
8	14	Houston, TX	53.2	54	15	Memphis, TN-AR-MS	35.0
71	16	Tulsa, OK	53.0	52	15	Middlesex-Somerset-Hunterdon, NJ	35.0
43	17	Charlotte-Gastonia-Rock Hill, NC-SC	52.9	32	17	San Jose, CA	34.9
13	18	Minneapolis-St. Paul, MN-WI	52.2	26	18	Newark, NJ	34.7
47	19	Greensboro-Winston-Salem-High Point, NC	52.1	13	19	Minneapolis-St. Paul, MN-WI	34.1
26	19	Newark, NJ	52.1	3	20	Chicago, IL	34.0
38	19	San Antonio, TX	52.1	74	20	Omaha, NE-IA	34.0
10	22	Dallas, TX	52.0	35	20	Sacramento, CA	34.0
30	22	New Haven-Bridgeport-Stamford-Waterbury-Danbury, CT	52.0	15	23	San Diego, CA	33.9
12	24	Phoenix-Mesa, AZ	51.9	23	24	Miami, FL	33.8
74	25	Omaha, NE-IA	51.7	21	25	Oakland, CA	33.7
28	26	Kansas City, MO-KS	51.6	57	26	Jacksonville, FL	33.5
9	27	Atlanta, GA	51.4	37	27	Indianapolis, IN	33.4
34	28	Orlando, FL	51.2	44	28	Bergen-Passaic, NJ	33.3
39	29	Norfolk-Virginia Beach-Newport News, VA-NC	51.1	43	28	Charlotte-Gastonia-Rock Hill, NC-SC	33.3
49	30	Nashville, TN	51.0	33	28	Cincinnati, OH-KY-IN	33.3
27	30	Portland-Vancouver, OR-WA	51.0	71	28	Tulsa, OK	33.3
67	32	Birmingham, AL	50.9	6	28	Washington, DC-MD-VA-WV	33.3
53	32	Hartford, CT	50.9	28	33	Kansas City, MO-KS	33.2
55	34	West Palm Beach-Boca Raton, FL	50.8	75	34	Albuquerque, NM	32.9
37	35	Indianapolis, IN	50.7	45	34	New Orleans, LA	32.9
15	35	San Diego, CA	50.7	62	34	Richmond-Petersburg, VA	32.9
60	37	Oklahoma City, OK	50.6	17	34	St. Louis, MO-IL	32.9
57	38	Jacksonville, FL	50.5	48	38	Austin-San Marcos, TX	32.8
22	38	Pittsburgh, PA	50.5	12	38	Phoenix-Mesa, AZ	32.8
50	38	Raleigh-Durham-Chapel Hill, NC	50.5	30	40	New Haven-Bridgeport-Stamford-Waterbury-Danbury, CT	32.7
33	41	Cincinnati, OH-KY-IN	50.4	7	41	Detroit, MI	32.6
65	42	Dayton-Springfield, OH	50.3	58	41	Rochester, NY	32.6
3	43	Chicago, IL	50.2	73	41	Syracuse, NY	32.6
17	43	St. Louis, MO-IL	50.2	25	44	Denver, CO	32.5
4	45	Boston-Worcester-Lawrence, MA-NH-ME-CT	50.1	49	44	Nashville, TN	32.5
21	46	Oakland, CA	50.0	60	46	Oklahoma City, OK	32.4
58	46	Rochester, NY	50.0	50	46	Raleigh-Durham-Chapel Hill, NC	32.4
35	48	Sacramento, CA	49.7	27	48	Portland-Vancouver, OR-WA	32.3
40	49	Las Vegas, NV-AZ	49.6	67	49	Birmingham, AL	32.2
6	49	Washington, DC-MD-VA-WV	49.6	41	50	Columbus, OH	32.1
25	51	Denver, CO	49.5	18	51	Baltimore, MD	32.0
61	52	Louisville, KY-IN	49.3	56	51	Monmouth-Ocean, NJ	32.0
62	53	Richmond-Petersburg, VA	49.2	64	53	Greenville-Spartanburg-Anderson, SC	31.9
73	53	Syracuse, NY	49.2	34	53	Orlando, FL	31.9
19	55	Seattle-Bellevue-Everett, WA	49.1	5	53	Philadelphia, PA-NJ	31.9
5	56	Philadelphia, PA-NJ	48.8	68	56	Honolulu, HI	31.8
7	57	Detroit, MI	48.6	42	57	Milwaukee-Waukesha, WI	31.7
69	58	Albany-Schenectady-Troy, NY	48.5	4	58	Boston-Worcester-Lawrence, MA-NH-ME-CT	31.5
41	59	Columbus, OH	48.4	53	59	Hartford, CT	31.4
48	60	Austin-San Marcos, TX	48.3	61	59	Louisville, KY-IN	31.4
24	60	Cleveland-Lorain-Elyria, OH	48.3	47	61	Greensboro-Winston-Salem-High Point, NC	31.3
75	62	Albuquerque, NM	48.2	40	62	Las Vegas, NV-AZ	30.9
42	62	Milwaukee-Waukesha, WI	48.2	63	63	Providence-Fall River-Warwick, RI-MA	30.8
20	62	Tampa-St. Petersburg-Clearwater, FL	48.2	65	64	Dayton-Springfield, OH	30.7
18	65	Baltimore, MD	48.0	19	65	Seattle-Bellevue-Everett, WA	30.6
63	65	Providence-Fall River-Warwick, RI-MA	48.0	24	66	Cleveland-Lorain-Elyria, OH	30.4
23	67	Miami, FL	47.7	2	66	New York, NY	30.4
70	67	Tucson, AZ	47.7	69	68	Albany-Schenectady-Troy, NY	30.3
1	69	Los Angeles-Long Beach, CA	47.6	51	69	Buffalo-Niagara Falls, NY	29.9
51	70	Buffalo-Niagara Falls, NY	47.2	36	70	Fort Lauderdale, FL	29.3
36	71	Fort Lauderdale, FL	46.1	70	71	Tucson, AZ	29.2
54	72	Memphis, TN-AR-MS	45.8	22	72	Pittsburgh, PA	27.6
45	73	New Orleans, LA	44.7	20	73	Tampa-St. Petersburg-Clearwater, FL	25.9
29	74	San Francisco, CA	42.0	55	74	West Palm Beach-Boca Raton, FL	24.9
2	75	New York, NY	39.8	29	75	San Francisco, CA	23.6

Note: Column numbers refer to Table C. Metropolitan Areas.

TABLE 4—75 Largest Metropolitan Areas by 2000 Population
Selected Rankings

Percent Owner Occupied Housing Units, 2000				Percent Recreational/Seasonal Housing Units, 2000			
Population Rank	Owner Occupied Housing Units Rank	Metropolitan Area	[col 94] Percent in Owner Occupied Housing Units	Recreational/Seasonal Housing Units Rank	Group Quarters Rank	Metropolitan Area	[col 90] Percent Recreational/Seasonal Housing Units
16	1	Nassau-Suffolk, NY	80.0	55	1	West Palm Beach-Boca Raton, FL	9.5
56	2	Monmouth-Ocean, NJ	78.7	56	2	Monmouth-Ocean, NJ	8.4
59	3	Grand Rapids-Muskegon-Holland, MI	74.9	36	3	Fort Lauderdale, FL	6.3
55	4	West Palm Beach-Boca Raton, FL	74.7	11	4	Riverside-San Bernardino, CA	5.9
7	5	Detroit, MI	72.4	20	5	Tampa-St. Petersburg-Clearwater, FL	5.1
13	5	Minneapolis-St. Paul, MN-WI	72.4	12	6	Phoenix-Mesa, AZ	4.6
64	7	Greenville-Spartanburg-Anderson, SC	71.5	16	7	Nassau-Suffolk, NY	4.2
17	8	St. Louis, MO-IL	71.4	23	8	Miami, FL	3.5
22	9	Pittsburgh, PA	71.3	35	9	Sacramento, CA	3.2
46	9	Salt Lake City-Ogden, UT	71.3	73	10	Syracuse, NY	3.1
52	11	Middlesex-Somerset-Hunterdon, NJ	71.2	40	11	Las Vegas, NV-AZ	2.9
20	12	Tampa-St. Petersburg-Clearwater, FL	70.8	34	11	Orlando, FL	2.9
67	13	Birmingham, AL	70.7	70	11	Tucson, AZ	2.9
5	14	Philadelphia, PA-NJ	69.9	69	14	Albany-Schenectady-Troy, NY	2.7
36	15	Fort Lauderdale, FL	69.5	63	15	Providence-Fall River-Warwick, RI-MA	2.6
47	16	Greensboro-Winston-Salem-High Point, NC	68.7	68	16	Honolulu, HI	2.2
61	17	Louisville, KY-IN	68.6	59	17	Grand Rapids-Muskegon-Holland, MI	2.0
43	18	Charlotte-Gastonia-Rock Hill, NC-SC	68.4	66	18	Fresno, CA	1.7
24	19	Cleveland-Lorain-Elyria, OH	68.3	57	18	Jacksonville, FL	1.7
58	20	Rochester, NY	68.2	58	20	Rochester, NY	1.5
12	21	Phoenix-Mesa, AZ	68.0	39	21	Norfolk-Virginia Beach-Newport News, VA-NC	1.4
28	22	Kansas City, MO-KS	67.9	15	21	San Diego, CA	1.4
37	23	Indianapolis, IN	67.8	4	21	Boston-Worcester-Lawrence, MA-NH-ME-CT	1.4
62	24	Richmond-Petersburg, VA	67.7	53	24	Hartford, CT	1.2
75	25	Albuquerque, NM	67.6	45	24	New Orleans, LA	1.2
73	25	Syracuse, NY	67.6	19	26	Seattle-Bellevue-Everett, WA	1.1
72	25	Ventura, CA	67.6	72	26	Ventura, CA	1.1
57	28	Jacksonville, FL	67.3	48	28	Austin-San Marcos, TX	1.0
65	29	Dayton-Springfield, OH	67.2	67	28	Birmingham, AL	1.0
18	30	Baltimore, MD	66.9	64	28	Greenville-Spartanburg-Anderson, SC	1.0
71	30	Tulsa, OK	66.9	30	28	New Haven-Bridgeport-Stamford-Waterbury-Danbury, CT	1.0
11	32	Riverside-San Bernardino, CA	66.6	29	28	San Francisco, CA	1.0
25	33	Denver, CO	66.5	75	33	Albuquerque, NM	0.9
9	34	Atlanta, GA	66.4	2	33	New York, NY	0.9
53	35	Hartford, CT	66.3	14	33	Orange County, CA	0.9
34	35	Orlando, FL	66.3	38	33	San Antonio, TX	0.9
51	37	Buffalo-Niagara Falls, NY	66.2	13	37	Minneapolis-St. Paul, MN-WI	0.8
33	37	Cincinnati, OH-KY-IN	66.2	26	37	Newark, NJ	0.8
30	37	New Haven-Bridgeport-Stamford-Waterbury-Danbury, CT	66.2	46	37	Salt Lake City-Ogden, UT	0.8
49	40	Nashville, TN	66.0	71	37	Tulsa, OK	0.8
74	40	Omaha, NE-IA	66.0	6	37	Washington, DC-MD-VA-WV	0.8
54	42	Memphis, TN-AR-MS	65.4	10	42	Dallas, TX	0.7
60	43	Oklahoma City, OK	64.7	31	42	Fort Worth-Arlington, TX	0.7
69	44	Albany-Schenectady-Troy, NY	64.6	8	42	Houston, TX	0.7
3	44	Chicago, IL	64.6	17	42	St. Louis, MO-IL	0.7
50	46	Raleigh-Durham-Chapel Hill, NC	64.5	18	46	Baltimore, MD	0.6
70	47	Tucson, AZ	64.3	43	46	Charlotte-Gastonia-Rock Hill, NC-SC	0.6
6	48	Washington, DC-MD-VA-WV	64.0	33	46	Cincinnati, OH-KY-IN	0.6
31	49	Fort Worth-Arlington, TX	63.6	24	46	Cleveland-Lorain-Elyria, OH	0.6
44	50	Bergen-Passaic, NJ	63.4	7	46	Detroit, MI	0.6
38	50	San Antonio, TX	63.4	47	46	Greensboro-Winston-Salem-High Point, NC	0.6
39	52	Norfolk-Virginia Beach-Newport News, VA-NC	63.0	60	46	Oklahoma City, OK	0.6
27	53	Portland-Vancouver, OR-WA	62.9	74	46	Omaha, NE-IA	0.6
41	54	Columbus, OH	62.3	22	46	Pittsburgh, PA	0.6
35	55	Sacramento, CA	62.1	27	46	Portland-Vancouver, OR-WA	0.6
19	56	Seattle-Bellevue-Everett, WA	62.0	50	46	Raleigh-Durham-Chapel Hill, NC	0.6
45	57	New Orleans, LA	61.8	51	57	Buffalo-Niagara Falls, NY	0.5
4	58	Boston-Worcester-Lawrence, MA-NH-ME-CT	61.6	41	57	Columbus, OH	0.5
14	59	Orange County, CA	61.4	25	57	Denver, CO	0.5
40	60	Las Vegas, NV-AZ	61.1	61	57	Louisville, KY-IN	0.5
42	60	Milwaukee-Waukesha, WI	61.1	42	57	Milwaukee-Waukesha, WI	0.5
26	62	Newark, NJ	60.8	9	62	Atlanta, GA	0.4
21	63	Oakland, CA	60.5	44	62	Bergen-Passaic, NJ	0.4
63	64	Providence-Fall River-Warwick, RI-MA	59.9	3	62	Chicago, IL	0.4
32	65	San Jose, CA	59.8	65	62	Dayton-Springfield, OH	0.4
8	66	Houston, TX	59.5	37	62	Indianapolis, IN	0.4
10	67	Dallas, TX	58.9	28	62	Kansas City, MO-KS	0.4
48	68	Austin-San Marcos, TX	58.2	1	62	Los Angeles-Long Beach, CA	0.4
23	69	Miami, FL	57.8	54	62	Memphis, TN-AR-MS	0.4
66	70	Fresno, CA	57.7	52	62	Middlesex-Somerset-Hunterdon, NJ	0.4
15	71	San Diego, CA	55.4	49	62	Nashville, TN	0.4
68	72	Honolulu, HI	54.6	21	62	Oakland, CA	0.4
29	73	San Francisco, CA	49.0	62	62	Richmond-Petersburg, VA	0.4
1	74	Los Angeles-Long Beach, CA	47.9	32	62	San Jose, CA	0.4
2	75	New York, NY	34.7	5	75	Philadelphia, PA-NJ	0.3

Note: Column numbers refer to Table C. Metropolitan Areas.

TABLE 5—All Metropolitan Areas
Selected Rankings

Popu-lation Rank	Metropolitan Area	[col 2] Population	Popu-lation Rank	Land Area Rank	Metropolitan Area	[col 1] Land Area
1	Los Angeles-Long Beach, CA	9 519 338	40	1	Las Vegas, NV-AZ	101 964
2	New York, NY	9 314 235	11	2	Riverside-San Bernardino, CA	70 603
3	Chicago, IL	8 272 768	276	3	Flagstaff, AZ-UT	58 558
4	Boston-Worcester-Lawrence, MA-NH-ME-CT	6 057 826	12	4	Phoenix-Mesa, AZ	37 743
5	Philadelphia, PA-NJ	5 100 931	70	5	Tucson, AZ	23 792
6	Washington, DC-MD-VA-WV	4 923 153	80	6	Bakersfield, CA	21 085
7	Detroit, MI	4 441 551	66	7	Fresno, CA	20 975
8	Houston, TX	4 177 646	179	8	Duluth-Superior, MN-WI	19 514
9	Atlanta, GA	4 112 198	6	9	Washington, DC-MD-VA-WV	16 859
10	Dallas, TX	3 519 176	4	10	Boston-Worcester-Lawrence, MA-NH-ME-CT	16 711
11	Riverside-San Bernardino, CA	3 254 821	17	11	St. Louis, MO-IL	16 555
12	Phoenix-Mesa, AZ	3 251 876	146	12	Reno, NV	16 426
13	Minneapolis-St. Paul, MN-WI	2 968 806	10	13	Dallas, TX	16 021
14	Orange County, CA	2 846 289	9	14	Atlanta, GA	15 861
15	San Diego, CA	2 813 833	13	15	Minneapolis-St. Paul, MN-WI	15 703
16	Nassau-Suffolk, NY	2 753 913	75	16	Albuquerque, NM	15 392
17	St. Louis, MO-IL	2 603 607	8	17	Houston, TX	15 333
18	Baltimore, MD	2 552 994	228	18	Yuma, AZ	14 281
19	Seattle-Bellevue-Everett, WA	2 414 616	28	19	Kansas City, MO-KS	14 002
20	Tampa-St. Petersburg-Clearwater, FL	2 395 997	317	20	Casper, WY	13 830
21	Oakland, CA	2 392 557	3	21	Chicago, IL	13 111
22	Pittsburgh, PA	2 358 695	27	22	Portland-Vancouver, OR-WA	13 022
23	Miami, FL	2 253 362	71	23	Tulsa, OK	12 987
24	Cleveland-Lorain-Elyria, OH	2 250 871	136	24	Visalia-Tulare-Porterville, CA	12 494
25	Denver, CO	2 109 282	22	25	Pittsburgh, PA	11 980
26	Newark, NJ	2 032 989	151	26	Eugene-Springfield, OR	11 795
27	Portland-Vancouver, OR-WA	1 918 009	19	27	Seattle-Bellevue-Everett, WA	11 457
28	Kansas City, MO-KS	1 776 062	189	28	Yakima, WA	11 127
29	San Francisco, CA	1 731 183	60	29	Oklahoma City, OK	10 999
30	New Haven-Bridgeport-Stamford-Waterbury-Danbury, CT	1 706 575	48	30	Austin-San Marcos, TX	10 940
31	Fort Worth-Arlington, TX	1 702 625	15	31	San Diego, CA	10 878
32	San Jose, CA	1 682 585	35	32	Sacramento, CA	10 569
33	Cincinnati, OH-KY-IN	1 646 395	49	33	Nashville, TN	10 548
34	Orlando, FL	1 644 561	1	34	Los Angeles-Long Beach, CA	10 518
35	Sacramento, CA	1 628 197	213	35	Greeley, CO	10 340
36	Fort Lauderdale, FL	1 623 018	7	36	Detroit, MI	10 052
37	Indianapolis, IN	1 607 486	47	37	Greensboro-Winston-Salem-High Point, NC	9 985
38	San Antonio, TX	1 592 383	5	38	Philadelphia, PA-NJ	9 861
39	Norfolk-Virginia Beach-Newport News, VA-NC	1 569 541	217	39	Las Cruces, NM	9 804
40	Las Vegas, NV-AZ	1 563 282	226	40	Redding, CA	9 740
41	Columbus, OH	1 540 157	25	41	Denver, CO	9 219
42	Milwaukee-Waukesha, WI	1 500 741	305	42	Bismarck, ND	9 125
43	Charlotte-Gastonia-Rock Hill, NC-SC	1 499 293	37	43	Indianapolis, IN	9 041
44	Bergen-Passaic, NJ	1 373 167	34	44	Orlando, FL	9 036
45	New Orleans, LA	1 337 726	50	45	Raleigh-Durham-Chapel Hill, NC	8 872
46	Salt Lake City-Ogden, UT	1 333 914	58	46	Rochester, NY	8 827
47	Greensboro-Winston-Salem-High Point, NC	1 251 509	303	47	Grand Forks, ND-MN	8 805
48	Austin-San Marcos, TX	1 249 763	45	48	New Orleans, LA	8 795
49	Nashville, TN	1 231 311	248	49	Bangor, ME	8 746
50	Raleigh-Durham-Chapel Hill, NC	1 187 941	43	50	Charlotte-Gastonia-Rock Hill, NC-SC	8 694
51	Buffalo-Niagara Falls, NY	1 170 111	205	51	Laredo, TX	8 655
52	Middlesex-Somerset-Hunterdon, NJ	1 169 641	282	52	Cincinnati, OH-KY-IN	8 619
53	Hartford, CT	1 148 618	33	53	Grand Junction, CO	8 615
54	Memphis, TN-AR-MS	1 135 614	38	54	San Antonio, TX	8 604
55	West Palm Beach-Boca Raton, FL	1 131 184	125	55	Salinas, CA	8 558
56	Monmouth-Ocean, NJ	1 126 217	178	56	San Luis Obispo-Atascadero-Paso Robles, CA	8 345
57	Jacksonville, FL	1 100 491	69	57	Albany-Schenectady-Troy, NY	8 310
58	Rochester, NY	1 098 201	64	58	Greenville-Spartanburg-Anderson, SC	8 253
59	Grand Rapids-Muskegon-Holland, MI	1 088 514	67	59	Birmingham, AL	8 136
60	Oklahoma City, OK	1 083 346	41	60	Columbus, OH	7 984
61	Louisville, KY-IN	1 025 598	73	61	Syracuse, NY	7 787
62	Richmond-Petersburg, VA	996 512	54	62	Memphis, TN-AR-MS	7 683
63	Providence-Fall River-Warwick, RI-MA	962 886	97	63	Wichita, KS	7 629
64	Greenville-Spartanburg-Anderson, SC	962 441	206	64	Richland-Kennewick-Pasco, WA	7 626
65	Dayton-Springfield, OH	950 558	62	65	Richmond-Petersburg, VA	7 557
66	Fresno, CA	922 516	31	66	Fort Worth-Arlington, TX	7 531
67	Birmingham, AL	921 106	92	67	Little Rock-North Little Rock, AR	7 422
68	Honolulu, HI	876 156	105	68	Johnson City-Kingsport-Bristol, TN-VA	7 328
69	Albany-Schenectady-Troy, NY	875 583	98	69	Mobile, AL	7 279
70	Tucson, AZ	843 746	218	70	Fargo-Moorhead, ND-MN	7 214
71	Tulsa, OK	803 235	212	71	Medford-Ashland, OR	7 190
72	Ventura, CA	753 197	309	72	Rapid City, SD	7 144
73	Syracuse, NY	732 117	59	73	Grand Rapids-Muskegon-Holland, MI	7 089
74	Omaha, NE-IA	716 998	126	74	Santa Barbara-Santa Maria-Lompoc, CA	7 011
75	Albuquerque, NM	712 738	24	75	Cleveland-Lorain-Elyria, OH	7 011

Note: Column numbers refer to Table C. Metropolitan Areas.

TABLE 5—All Metropolitan Areas
Selected Rankings

Population Density (per Square Kilometer), 2000				Percent Population Change, 1990-2000			
Popu-lation Rank	Density Rank	Metropolitan Area	[col 4] Density	Popu-lation Rank	Percent Change Rank	Metropolitan Area	[col 52] Percent Change
86	1	Jersey City, NJ	5 036.2	40	1	Las Vegas, NV-AZ	83.3
2	2	New York, NY	3 150.1	175	2	Naples, FL	65.3
14	3	Orange County, CA	1 392.1	228	3	Yuma, AZ	49.7
44	4	Bergen-Passaic, NJ	1 264.0	94	4	McAllen-Edinburg-Mission, TX	48.5
1	5	Los Angeles-Long Beach, CA	905.1	48	5	Austin-San Marcos, TX	47.7
16	6	Nassau-Suffolk, NY	886.9	156	6	Fayetteville-Springdale-Rogers, AR	47.5
29	7	San Francisco, CA	658.2	119	7	Boise City, ID	46.1
21	8	Oakland, CA	633.8	12	8	Phoenix-Mesa, AZ	45.3
3	9	Chicago, IL	631.0	205	9	Laredo, TX	44.9
141	10	Trenton, NJ	599.4	135	10	Provo-Orem, UT	39.8
68	11	Honolulu, HI	564.0	9	11	Atlanta, GA	38.9
30	12	New Haven-Bridgeport-Stamford-Waterbury-Danbury, CT NECMA...	535.1	50	12	Raleigh-Durham-Chapel Hill, NC	38.4
36	13	Fort Lauderdale, FL	519.9	213	13	Greeley, CO	37.3
5	14	Philadelphia, PA-NJ	510.9	203	14	Myrtle Beach, SC	36.5
32	15	San Jose, CA	503.3	184	15	Wilmington, NC	36.3
26	16	Newark, NJ	497.5	174	16	Fort Collins-Loveland, CO	35.1
23	17	Miami, FL	447.1	34	17	Orlando, FL	34.3
7	18	Detroit, MI	440.1	146	18	Reno, NV	33.3
52	19	Middlesex-Somerset-Hunterdon, NJ	432.4	170	19	Ocala, FL	32.9
42	20	Milwaukee-Waukesha, WI	396.9	283	20	Auburn-Opelika, AL	32.1
63	21	Providence-Fall River-Warwick, RI-MA	395.1	116	21	Fort Myers-Cape Coral, FL	31.6
56	22	Monmouth-Ocean, NJ	392.4	10	22	Dallas, TX	31.5
18	23	Baltimore, MD	377.8	55	23	West Palm Beach-Boca Raton, FL	31.0
4	24	Boston-Worcester-Lawrence, MA-NH-ME-CT	362.5	224	24	Bellingham, WA	30.5
20	25	Tampa-St. Petersburg-Clearwater, FL	362.2	101	25	Colorado Springs, CO	30.2
24	26	Cleveland-Lorain-Elyria, OH	321.1	25	26	Denver, CO	30.0
46	27	Salt Lake City-Ogden, UT	318.4	36	27	Fort Lauderdale, FL	29.3
77	28	Akron, OH	296.5	161	28	Boulder-Longmont, CO	29.3
53	29	Hartford, CT	292.8	43	29	Charlotte-Gastonia-Rock Hill, NC-SC	29.1
91	30	Wilmington-Newark, DE-MD	292.3	217	30	Las Cruces, NM	28.9
6	31	Washington, DC-MD-VA-WV	292.0	147	30	Brownsville-Harlingen-San Benito, TX	28.9
51	32	Buffalo-Niagara Falls, NY	288.3	197	32	Olympia, WA	28.6
149	33	Hamilton-Middletown, OH	275.0	206	33	Richland-Kennewick-Pasco, WA	27.9
8	34	Houston, TX	272.5	251	34	Punta Gorda, FL	27.6
82	35	Gary, IN	266.4	153	35	Fort Pierce-Port St. Lucie, FL	27.2
118	36	Flint, MI	263.3	27	36	Portland-Vancouver, OR-WA	26.6
9	37	Atlanta, GA	259.3	70	37	Tucson, AZ	26.5
79	38	El Paso, TX	259.0	244	38	Santa Fe, NM	26.1
15	39	San Diego, CA	258.7	181	38	Brazoria, TX	26.1
39	40	Norfolk-Virginia Beach-Newport News, VA-NC	258.0	8	40	Houston, TX	25.8
177	41	Galveston-Texas City, TX	242.4	11	41	Riverside-San Bernardino, CA	25.7
186	42	Bremerton, WA	226.2	31	42	Fort Worth-Arlington, TX	25.1
31	43	Fort Worth-Arlington, TX	225.3	235	42	Bryan-College Station, TX	25.1
167	44	South Bend, IN	224.2	49	44	Nashville, TN	25.0
81	45	Allentown-Bethlehem-Easton, PA	223.6	143	45	Salem, OR	24.9
171	46	Santa Cruz-Watsonville, CA	221.7	282	46	Grand Junction, CO	24.8
55	47	West Palm Beach-Boca Raton, FL	221.2	46	47	Salt Lake City-Ogden, UT	24.4
10	48	Dallas, TX	219.7	212	48	Medford-Ashland, OR	23.8
208	49	Racine, WI	218.9	219	48	Sioux Falls, SD	23.8
65	50	Dayton-Springfield, OH	218.0	103	50	Daytona Beach, FL	23.5
190	51	Barnstable-Yarmouth, MA	216.9	260	51	Greenville, NC	23.3
25	52	Denver, CO	216.6	150	52	Springfield, MO	23.2
116	53	Fort Myers-Cape Coral, FL	211.8	155	53	Killeen-Temple, TX	22.6
240	54	Kenosha, WI	211.7	186	54	Bremerton, WA	22.3
19	55	Seattle-Bellevue-Everett, WA	210.8	302	55	Lawrence, KS	22.2
87	56	Springfield, MA	204.7	199	55	Clarksville-Hopkinsville, TN-KY	22.2
22	57	Pittsburgh, PA	196.9	66	57	Fresno, CA	22.1
109	58	Lancaster, PA	191.5	162	58	Tallahassee, FL	21.8
61	59	Louisville, KY-IN	191.1	304	58	Missoula, MT	21.8
33	60	Cincinnati, OH-KY-IN	190.2	233	60	Athens, GA	21.5
41	61	Columbus, OH	189.3	229	60	Charlottesville, VA	21.5
13	62	Minneapolis-St. Paul, MN-WI	189.1	80	62	Bakersfield, CA	21.4
38	63	San Antonio, TX	184.8	57	62	Jacksonville, FL	21.4
128	64	Newburgh, NY-PA	183.4	75	64	Albuquerque, NM	21.0
34	65	Orlando, FL	181.9	115	65	Modesto, CA	20.6
108	66	Melbourne-Titusville-Palm Bay, FL	180.6	258	66	Columbia, MO	20.5
157	67	Fayetteville, NC	179.2	90	66	Sarasota-Bradenton, FL	20.5
37	68	Indianapolis, IN	176.2	276	68	Flagstaff, AZ-UT	20.2
85	69	Toledo, OH	174.9	38	68	San Antonio, TX	20.2
90	70	Sarasota-Bradenton, FL	173.5	191	70	Gainesville, FL	20.0
43	71	Charlotte-Gastonia-Rock Hill, NC-SC	171.4	122	71	Pensacola, FL	19.7
133	72	Reading, PA	168.0	76	72	Tacoma, WA	19.6
140	73	Atlantic-Cape May, NJ	167.9	222	73	Yolo, CA	19.4
187	74	Green Bay, WI	165.6	104	73	Lakeland-Winter Haven, FL	19.4
131	75	York, PA	163.0	108	73	Melbourne-Titusville-Palm Bay, FL	19.4

Note: Column numbers refer to Table C. Metropolitan Areas.

TABLE 5—All Metropolitan Areas
Selected Rankings

	Percent White, 2000				Percent Black, 2000		
Popu-lation Rank	White Rank	Metropolitan Area	[col 9] Percent White	Popu-lation Rank	Black Rank	Metropolitan Area	[col 10] Percent Black
265	1	Altoona, PA	97.6	277	1	Albany, GA	51.0
237	2	Parkersburg-Marietta, WV-OH	97.3	310	2	Pine Bluff, AR	49.6
308	3	Dubuque, IA	97.1	294	3	Sumter, SC	46.7
297	4	Lewiston-Auburn, ME	97.0	117	4	Jackson, MS	45.6
84	5	Scranton-Wilkes-Barre-Hazleton, PA	96.8	54	5	Memphis, TN-AR-MS	43.4
248	6	Bangor, ME	96.6	249	6	Rocky Mount, NC	43.1
185	7	Johnstown, PA	96.3	165	7	Columbus, GA-AL	40.4
273	8	Glens Falls, NY	96.2	272	8	Florence, SC	39.3
154	8	Huntington-Ashland, WV-KY-OH	96.2	148	9	Montgomery, AL	38.9
105	8	Johnson City-Kingsport-Bristol, TN-VA	96.2	152	10	Macon, GA	37.5
242	11	Eau Claire, WI	96.0	45	10	New Orleans, LA	37.5
223	11	St. Cloud, MN	96.0	127	12	Shreveport-Bossier City, LA	37.4
166	13	Portland, ME	95.7	157	13	Fayetteville, NC	34.9
234	14	Wheeling, WV-OH	95.6	160	13	Savannah, GA	34.9
202	15	Burlington, VT	95.4	107	15	Augusta-Aiken, GA-SC	34.4
305	16	Bismarck, ND	95.2	260	16	Greenville, NC	33.6
259	17	Pittsfield, MA	95.0	245	16	Monroe, LA	33.6
179	18	Duluth-Superior, MN-WI	94.9	162	16	Tallahassee, FL	33.6
218	19	Fargo-Moorhead, ND-MN	94.8	286	19	Goldsboro, NC	33.0
267	19	La Crosse, WI-MN	94.8	292	20	Danville, VA	32.6
139	21	Appleton-Oshkosh-Neenah, WI	94.6	99	21	Columbia, SC	32.1
261	22	Steubenville-Weirton, OH-WV	94.5	88	22	Baton Rouge, LA	31.9
150	23	Springfield, MO	94.4	39	23	Norfolk-Virginia Beach-Newport News, VA-NC	30.9
190	24	Barnstable-Yarmouth, MA	94.2	96	24	Charleston-North Charleston, SC	30.8
317	24	Casper, WY	94.2	270	25	Alexandria, LA	30.4
254	26	Jamestown, NY	94.0	62	26	Richmond-Petersburg, VA	30.2
304	26	Missoula, MT	94.0	67	27	Birmingham, AL	30.1
207	28	Cedar Rapids, IA	93.9	225	28	Tuscaloosa, AL	29.3
300	28	Cumberland, MD-WV	93.9	293	29	Jackson, TN	29.2
280	28	Williamsport, PA	93.9	9	30	Atlanta, GA	28.9
271	31	Wausau, WI	93.8	129	31	Lafayette, LA	28.2
306	32	Owensboro, KY	93.7	18	32	Baltimore, MD	27.4
219	32	Sioux Falls, SD	93.7	98	32	Mobile, AL	27.4
299	34	St. Joseph, MO	93.6	289	34	Hattiesburg, MS	26.3
303	35	Grand Forks, ND-MN	93.4	6	35	Washington, DC-MD-VA-WV	26.0
279	36	Sharon, PA	93.1	130	36	Beaumont-Port Arthur, TX	24.8
241	37	Terre Haute, IN	92.9	2	37	New York, NY	24.6
264	38	Billings, MT	92.8	209	38	Lake Charles, LA	24.0
231	38	Joplin, MO	92.8	263	39	Texarkana, TX-Texarkana, AR	23.3
131	38	York, PA	92.8	256	40	Dothan, AL	23.1
287	41	Sheboygan, WI	92.7	7	41	Detroit, MI	22.9
172	42	Binghamton, NY	92.6	283	42	Auburn-Opelika, AL	22.7
251	42	Punta Gorda, FL	92.6	50	42	Raleigh-Durham-Chapel Hill, NC	22.7
135	44	Provo-Orem, UT	92.4	26	44	Newark, NJ	22.3
282	45	Grand Junction, CO	92.3	92	45	Little Rock-North Little Rock, AR	21.9
173	46	Charleston, WV	92.0	57	46	Jacksonville, FL	21.7
159	47	Evansville-Henderson, IN-KY	91.8	144	47	Huntsville, AL	21.0
158	47	Utica-Rome, NY	91.8	199	48	Clarksville-Hopkinsville, TN-KY	20.8
212	49	Medford-Ashland, OR	91.6	155	48	Killeen-Temple, TX	20.8
109	50	Lancaster, PA	91.5	268	50	Dover, DE	20.7
174	51	Fort Collins-Loveland, CO	91.4	233	51	Athens, GA	20.5
121	51	Spokane, WA	91.4	43	51	Charlotte-Gastonia-Rock Hill, NC-SC	20.5
257	51	State College, PA	91.4	36	51	Fort Lauderdale, FL	20.5
78	54	Knoxville, TN	91.3	118	54	Flint, MI	20.4
316	54	Pocatello, ID	91.3	23	55	Miami, FL	20.3
149	56	Hamilton-Middletown, OH	91.2	47	56	Greensboro-Winston-Salem-High Point, NC	20.2
187	57	Green Bay, WI	91.1	246	56	Vineland-Millville-Bridgeton, NJ	20.2
301	57	Kokomo, IN	91.1	5	58	Philadelphia, PA-NJ	20.1
307	59	Elmira, NY	91.0	141	59	Trenton, NJ	19.8
236	59	Janesville-Beloit, WI	91.0	82	60	Gary, IN	19.7
163	61	Erie, PA	90.9	196	61	Longview-Marshall, TX	19.5
278	62	Bloomington, IN	90.8	137	62	Biloxi-Gulfport-Pascagoula, MS	19.3
123	62	Canton-Massillon, OH	90.8	191	62	Gainesville, FL	19.3
215	62	Mansfield, OH	90.8	216	64	Tyler, TX	19.1
314	65	Great Falls, MT	90.7	284	65	Lawton, OK	19.0
281	65	Muncie, IN	90.7	3	66	Chicago, IL	18.9
151	67	Eugene-Springfield, OR	90.6	288	67	Anniston, AL	18.5
274	68	Rochester, MN	90.3	24	67	Cleveland-Lorain-Elyria, OH	18.5
290	69	Iowa City, IA	90.1	239	67	Jacksonville, NC	18.5
176	69	Lincoln, NE	90.1	17	70	St. Louis, MO-IL	18.3
119	71	Boise City, ID	89.9	193	71	Lynchburg, VA	17.9
210	71	Lafayette, IN	89.9	91	72	Wilmington-Newark, DE-MD	17.8
81	73	Allentown-Bethlehem-Easton, PA	89.8	64	73	Greenville-Spartanburg-Anderson, SC	17.5
188	73	Asheville, NC	89.8	8	73	Houston, TX	17.5
112	73	Des Moines, IA	89.8	122	75	Pensacola, FL	16.5

Note: Column numbers refer to Table C. Metropolitan Areas.

TABLE 5—All Metropolitan Areas
Selected Rankings

Percent American Indian and Alaska Native, 2000				Percent Asian, 2000			
Population Rank	American Indian and Alaska Native Rank	Metropolitan Area	[col 11] Percent American Indian and Alaska Native	Population Rank	Asian Rank	Metropolitan Area	[col 12] Percent Asian
276	1	Flagstaff, AZ-UT	27.2	68	1	Honolulu, HI	46.0
309	2	Rapid City, SD	8.1	32	2	San Jose, CA	25.6
168	3	Anchorage, AK	7.3	29	3	San Francisco, CA	22.7
71	4	Tulsa, OK	6.9	21	4	Oakland, CA	16.7
75	5	Albuquerque, NM	5.6	14	5	Orange County, CA	13.6
198	6	Fort Smith, AR-OK	5.1	1	6	Los Angeles-Long Beach, CA	11.9
284	6	Lawton, OK	5.1	95	7	Stockton-Lodi, CA	11.4
189	8	Yakima, WA	4.5	52	8	Middlesex-Somerset-Hunterdon, NJ	11.2
314	9	Great Falls, MT	4.2	100	9	Vallejo-Fairfield-Napa, CA	10.4
60	9	Oklahoma City, OK	4.2	222	10	Yolo, CA	9.9
204	11	Houma, LA	3.9	255	11	Yuba City, CA	9.6
70	12	Tucson, AZ	3.2	86	12	Jersey City, NJ	9.4
264	13	Billings, MT	3.1	19	12	Seattle-Bellevue-Everett, WA	9.4
305	14	Bismarck, ND	3.0	2	14	New York, NY	9.1
316	15	Pocatello, ID	2.9	35	15	Sacramento, CA	8.9
224	16	Bellingham, WA	2.8	15	15	San Diego, CA	8.9
226	16	Redding, CA	2.8	44	17	Bergen-Passaic, NJ	8.2
244	16	Santa Fe, NM	2.8	66	18	Fresno, CA	7.1
302	19	Lawrence, KS	2.6	195	19	Merced, CA	6.8
187	20	Green Bay, WI	2.3	6	20	Washington, DC-MD-VA-WV	6.7
304	20	Missoula, MT	2.3	214	21	Champaign-Urbana, IL	6.5
12	22	Phoenix-Mesa, AZ	2.2	125	22	Salinas, CA	6.0
318	23	Enid, OK	2.1	168	23	Anchorage, AK	5.5
179	24	Duluth-Superior, MN-WI	2.0	72	24	Ventura, CA	5.3
303	24	Grand Forks, ND-MN	2.0	8	25	Houston, TX	5.2
255	24	Yuba City, CA	2.0	76	26	Tacoma, WA	5.1
200	27	Chico-Paradise, CA	1.9	141	27	Trenton, NJ	4.9
247	28	Decatur, AL	1.8	40	28	Las Vegas, NV-AZ	4.7
146	28	Reno, NV	1.8	3	29	Chicago, IL	4.6
66	30	Fresno, CA	1.7	27	29	Portland-Vancouver, OR-WA	4.6
275	30	Sioux City, IA-NE	1.7	315	31	Corvallis, OR	4.5
219	30	Sioux Falls, SD	1.7	271	31	Wausau, WI	4.5
186	33	Bremerton, WA	1.6	186	33	Bremerton, WA	4.4
231	33	Joplin, MO	1.6	197	33	Olympia, WA	4.4
252	33	Pueblo, CO	1.6	146	35	Reno, NV	4.3
136	33	Visalia-Tulare-Porterville, CA	1.6	274	35	Rochester, MN	4.3
228	33	Yuma, AZ	1.6	115	37	Modesto, CA	4.2
80	38	Bakersfield, CA	1.5	11	37	Riverside-San Bernardino, CA	4.2
157	38	Fayetteville, NC	1.5	290	39	Iowa City, IA	4.1
217	38	Las Cruces, NM	1.5	13	39	Minneapolis-St. Paul, MN-WI	4.1
197	38	Olympia, WA	1.5	126	39	Santa Barbara-Santa Maria-Lompoc, CA	4.1
143	38	Salem, OR	1.5	235	42	Bryan-College Station, TX	4.0
156	43	Fayetteville-Springdale-Rogers, AR	1.4	10	42	Dallas, TX	4.0
121	43	Spokane, WA	1.4	26	42	Newark, NJ	4.0
76	43	Tacoma, WA	1.4	257	42	State College, PA	4.0
115	46	Modesto, CA	1.3	4	46	Boston-Worcester-Lawrence, MA-NH-ME-CT	3.9
291	46	Sherman-Denison, TX	1.3	140	47	Atlantic-Cape May, NJ	3.8
218	48	Fargo-Moorhead, ND-MN	1.2	93	48	Ann Arbor, MI	3.7
195	48	Merced, CA	1.2	210	48	Lafayette, IN	3.7
11	48	Riverside-San Bernardino, CA	1.2	16	50	Nassau-Suffolk, NY	3.6
126	48	Santa Barbara-Santa Maria-Lompoc, CA	1.2	48	51	Austin-San Marcos, TX	3.5
111	48	Santa Rosa, CA	1.2	191	51	Gainesville, FL	3.5
221	48	Topeka, KS	1.2	120	51	Madison, WI	3.5
222	48	Yolo, CA	1.2	80	54	Bakersfield, CA	3.4
151	55	Eugene-Springfield, OR	1.1	278	54	Bloomington, IN	3.4
212	55	Medford-Ashland, OR	1.1	5	54	Philadelphia, PA-NJ	3.4
35	55	Sacramento, CA	1.1	171	54	Santa Cruz-Watsonville, CA	3.4
95	55	Stockton-Lodi, CA	1.1	9	58	Atlanta, GA	3.3
97	55	Wichita, KS	1.1	200	58	Chico-Paradise, CA	3.3
248	60	Bangor, ME	1.0	287	58	Sheboygan, WI	3.3
317	60	Casper, WY	1.0	136	58	Visalia-Tulare-Porterville, CA	3.3
40	60	Las Vegas, NV-AZ	1.0	31	62	Fort Worth-Arlington, TX	3.2
169	60	New London-Norwich, CT-RI	1.0	161	63	Boulder-Longmont, CO	3.1
125	60	Salinas, CA	1.0	302	63	Lawrence, KS	3.1
171	60	Santa Cruz-Watsonville, CA	1.0	111	63	Santa Rosa, CA	3.1
19	60	Seattle-Bellevue-Everett, WA	1.0	258	66	Columbia, MO	3.0
246	60	Vineland-Millville-Bridgeton, NJ	1.0	25	66	Denver, CO	3.0
139	68	Appleton-Oshkosh-Neenah, WI	0.9	229	68	Charlottesville, VA	2.9
101	68	Colorado Springs, CO	0.9	176	68	Lincoln, NE	2.9
25	68	Denver, CO	0.9	50	68	Raleigh-Durham-Chapel Hill, NC	2.9
282	68	Grand Junction, CO	0.9	97	68	Wichita, KS	2.9
213	68	Greeley, CO	0.9	224	72	Bellingham, WA	2.8
122	68	Pensacola, FL	0.9	30	72	New Haven-Bridgeport-Stamford-Waterbury-Danbury, CT NECMA	2.8
27	68	Portland-Vancouver, OR-WA	0.9	18	74	Baltimore, MD	2.7
15	68	San Diego, CA	0.9	267	74	La Crosse, WI-MN	2.7

Note: Column numbers refer to Table C. Metropolitan Areas.

TABLE 5—All Metropolitan Areas
Selected Rankings

Percent Two or More Races, 2000				Percent Hispanic, 2000			
Popu-lation Rank	Two or More Races Rank	Metropolitan Area	[col 15] Percent Two or More Races	Popu-lation Rank	Hispanic Rank	Metropolitan Area	[col 22] Percent Hispanic
68	1	Honolulu, HI	19.9	205	1	Laredo, TX	94.3
168	2	Anchorage, AK	6.0	94	2	McAllen-Edinburg-Mission, TX	88.3
95	2	Stockton-Lodi, CA	6.0	147	3	Brownsville-Harlingen-San Benito, TX	84.3
100	4	Vallejo-Fairfield-Napa, CA	5.8	79	4	El Paso, TX	78.2
195	5	Merced, CA	5.7	217	5	Las Cruces, NM	63.4
86	6	Jersey City, NJ	5.6	23	6	Miami, FL	57.3
115	7	Modesto, CA	5.4	132	7	Corpus Christi, TX	54.7
21	7	Oakland, CA	5.4	38	8	San Antonio, TX	51.2
35	9	Sacramento, CA	5.2	136	9	Visalia-Tulare-Porterville, CA	50.8
222	9	Yolo, CA	5.2	228	10	Yuma, AZ	50.5
255	9	Yuba City, CA	5.2	125	11	Salinas, CA	46.8
76	12	Tacoma, WA	5.1	195	12	Merced, CA	45.3
125	13	Salinas, CA	5.0	1	13	Los Angeles-Long Beach, CA	44.6
1	14	Los Angeles-Long Beach, CA	4.9	244	14	Santa Fe, NM	44.4
66	15	Fresno, CA	4.8	66	15	Fresno, CA	44.0
71	15	Tulsa, OK	4.8	75	16	Albuquerque, NM	41.6
284	17	Lawton, OK	4.7	86	17	Jersey City, NJ	39.8
11	17	Riverside-San Bernardino, CA	4.7	311	18	Victoria, TX	39.2
15	17	San Diego, CA	4.7	80	19	Bakersfield, CA	38.4
32	17	San Jose, CA	4.7	252	20	Pueblo, CO	38.0
186	21	Bremerton, WA	4.6	11	21	Riverside-San Bernardino, CA	37.8
2	21	New York, NY	4.6	189	22	Yakima, WA	35.9
136	21	Visalia-Tulare-Porterville, CA	4.6	182	23	Odessa-Midland, TX	35.8
29	24	San Francisco, CA	4.5	126	24	Santa Barbara-Santa Maria-Lompoc, CA	34.2
171	25	Santa Cruz-Watsonville, CA	4.4	72	25	Ventura, CA	33.4
126	26	Santa Barbara-Santa Maria-Lompoc, CA	4.3	115	26	Modesto, CA	31.7
75	27	Albuquerque, NM	4.2	14	27	Orange County, CA	30.8
80	28	Bakersfield, CA	4.1	295	28	San Angelo, TX	30.7
14	28	Orange County, CA	4.1	95	29	Stockton-Lodi, CA	30.5
111	28	Santa Rosa, CA	4.1	8	30	Houston, TX	29.9
40	31	Las Vegas, NV-AZ	4.0	70	31	Tucson, AZ	29.3
200	32	Chico-Paradise, CA	3.9	180	32	Lubbock, TX	27.5
101	32	Colorado Springs, CO	3.9	213	33	Greeley, CO	27.0
60	32	Oklahoma City, OK	3.9	171	34	Santa Cruz-Watsonville, CA	26.8
197	32	Olympia, WA	3.9	15	35	San Diego, CA	26.7
244	32	Santa Fe, NM	3.9	48	36	Austin-San Marcos, TX	26.2
19	32	Seattle-Bellevue-Everett, WA	3.9	222	37	Yolo, CA	25.9
72	32	Ventura, CA	3.9	2	38	New York, NY	25.1
198	39	Fort Smith, AR-OK	3.8	12	38	Phoenix-Mesa, AZ	25.1
155	39	Killeen-Temple, TX	3.8	32	40	San Jose, CA	24.0
23	39	Miami, FL	3.8	10	41	Dallas, TX	23.0
217	42	Las Cruces, NM	3.6	181	42	Brazoria, TX	22.8
226	43	Redding, CA	3.5	206	43	Richland-Kennewick-Pasco, WA	21.3
38	43	San Antonio, TX	3.5	40	44	Las Vegas, NV-AZ	20.6
189	43	Yakima, WA	3.5	255	45	Yuba City, CA	20.1
36	46	Fort Lauderdale, FL	3.4	192	46	Amarillo, TX	19.6
252	46	Pueblo, CO	3.4	175	46	Naples, FL	19.6
178	46	San Luis Obispo-Atascadero-Paso Robles, CA	3.4	100	48	Vallejo-Fairfield-Napa, CA	19.1
151	49	Eugene-Springfield, OR	3.3	246	49	Vineland-Millville-Bridgeton, NJ	19.0
27	49	Portland-Vancouver, OR-WA	3.3	25	50	Denver, CO	18.8
146	49	Reno, NV	3.3	21	51	Oakland, CA	18.5
79	52	El Paso, TX	3.2	31	52	Fort Worth-Arlington, TX	18.2
239	52	Jacksonville, NC	3.2	177	53	Galveston-Texas City, TX	18.0
143	52	Salem, OR	3.2	235	54	Bryan-College Station, TX	17.9
70	52	Tucson, AZ	3.2	194	54	Waco, TX	17.9
228	52	Yuma, AZ	3.2	269	56	Abilene, TX	17.6
132	57	Corpus Christi, TX	3.1	44	57	Bergen-Passaic, NJ	17.3
157	57	Fayetteville, NC	3.1	111	57	Santa Rosa, CA	17.3
206	57	Richland-Kennewick-Pasco, WA	3.1	3	59	Chicago, IL	17.1
25	60	Denver, CO	3.0	29	60	San Francisco, CA	16.8
220	60	Fort Walton Beach, FL	3.0	36	61	Fort Lauderdale, FL	16.7
44	62	Bergen-Passaic, NJ	2.9	146	62	Reno, NV	16.6
212	62	Medford-Ashland, OR	2.9	34	63	Orlando, FL	16.5
34	62	Orlando, FL	2.9	178	64	San Luis Obispo-Atascadero-Paso Robles, CA	16.3
12	62	Phoenix-Mesa, AZ	2.9	155	65	Killeen-Temple, TX	15.7
246	62	Vineland-Millville-Bridgeton, NJ	2.9	143	66	Salem, OR	15.6
6	62	Washington, DC-MD-VA-WV	2.9	35	67	Sacramento, CA	14.4
8	68	Houston, TX	2.8	26	68	Newark, NJ	13.3
63	68	Providence-Fall River-Warwick, RI-MA	2.8	55	69	West Palm Beach-Boca Raton, FL	12.4
121	68	Spokane, WA	2.8	87	70	Springfield, MA	12.2
224	71	Bellingham, WA	2.7	253	71	Wichita Falls, TX	11.8
199	71	Clarksville-Hopkinsville, TN-KY	2.7	101	72	Colorado Springs, CO	11.3
213	71	Greeley, CO	2.7	275	72	Sioux City, IA-NE	11.3
302	71	Lawrence, KS	2.7	52	74	Middlesex-Somerset-Hunterdon, NJ	11.2
169	71	New London-Norwich, CT-RI	2.7	216	74	Tyler, TX	11.2

Note: Column numbers refer to Table C. Metropolitan Areas.

TABLE 5—All Metropolitan Areas
Selected Rankings

Population Rank	Under 18 Years Rank	Metropolitan Area	[cols 28 & 29] Percent Under 18 Years	Population Rank	25 to 54 Years Rank	Metropolitan Area	[cols 31, 32 & 33] Percent 25 to 54 Years
		Percent Under 18 Years, 2000				**Percent Age 25 to 54 Years, 2000**	
205	1	Laredo, TX	36.2	29	1	San Francisco, CA	50.9
94	2	McAllen-Edinburg-Mission, TX	35.3	9	2	Atlanta, GA	48.9
195	3	Merced, CA	34.5	168	3	Anchorage, AK	48.8
135	4	Provo-Orem, UT	34.1	19	4	Seattle-Bellevue-Everett, WA	48.7
147	5	Brownsville-Harlingen-San Benito, TX	33.8	161	5	Boulder-Longmont, CO	48.6
136	6	Visalia-Tulare-Porterville, CA	33.7	25	6	Denver, CO	48.5
79	7	El Paso, TX	32.0	32	7	San Jose, CA	48.4
80	8	Bakersfield, CA	31.9	6	7	Washington, DC-MD-VA-WV	48.4
66	9	Fresno, CA	31.8	50	9	Raleigh-Durham-Chapel Hill, NC	48.2
189	9	Yakima, WA	31.8	48	10	Austin-San Marcos, TX	47.8
46	11	Salt Lake City-Ogden, UT	31.4	86	11	Jersey City, NJ	47.5
11	12	Riverside-San Bernardino, CA	31.3	43	12	Charlotte-Gastonia-Rock Hill, NC-SC	47.2
115	13	Modesto, CA	31.2	10	13	Dallas, TX	47.1
206	14	Richland-Kennewick-Pasco, WA	31.0	52	14	Middlesex-Somerset-Hunterdon, NJ	47.0
95	14	Stockton-Lodi, CA	31.0	13	15	Minneapolis-St. Paul, MN-WI	46.9
182	16	Odessa-Midland, TX	30.3	21	15	Oakland, CA	46.9
255	17	Yuba City, CA	29.9	27	17	Portland-Vancouver, OR-WA	46.8
217	18	Las Cruces, NM	29.7	171	17	Santa Cruz-Watsonville, CA	46.8
168	19	Anchorage, AK	29.2	244	17	Santa Fe, NM	46.8
8	19	Houston, TX	29.2	49	20	Nashville, TN	46.7
311	21	Victoria, TX	29.1	120	21	Madison, WI	46.5
132	22	Corpus Christi, TX	28.9	166	22	Portland, ME	46.3
211	22	Elkhart-Goshen, IN	28.9	8	23	Houston, TX	46.2
228	22	Yuma, AZ	28.9	62	23	Richmond-Petersburg, VA	46.2
128	25	Newburgh, NY-PA	28.8	4	25	Boston-Worcester-Lawrence, MA-NH-ME-CT	46.0
276	26	Flagstaff, AZ-UT	28.7	181	25	Brazoria, TX	46.0
181	27	Brazoria, TX	28.5	202	25	Burlington, VT	46.0
129	27	Lafayette, LA	28.5	101	28	Colorado Springs, CO	45.9
72	27	Ventura, CA	28.5	41	28	Columbus, OH	45.9
119	30	Boise City, ID	28.4	14	28	Orange County, CA	45.9
199	30	Clarksville-Hopkinsville, TN-KY	28.4	31	31	Fort Worth-Arlington, TX	45.8
125	30	Salinas, CA	28.4	93	32	Ann Arbor, MI	45.7
38	30	San Antonio, TX	28.4	146	32	Reno, NV	45.7
277	34	Albany, GA	28.3	37	34	Indianapolis, IN	45.6
59	34	Grand Rapids-Muskegon-Holland, MI	28.3	274	35	Rochester, MN	45.5
204	34	Houma, LA	28.3	99	36	Columbia, SC	45.4
54	34	Memphis, TN-AR-MS	28.3	112	36	Des Moines, IA	45.4
213	38	Greeley, CO	28.2	18	38	Baltimore, MD	45.3
155	38	Killeen-Temple, TX	28.2	187	38	Green Bay, WI	45.3
316	40	Pocatello, ID	28.1	2	38	New York, NY	45.3
294	40	Sumter, SC	28.1	26	38	Newark, NJ	45.3
97	40	Wichita, KS	28.1	111	38	Santa Rosa, CA	45.3
10	43	Dallas, TX	28.0	57	43	Jacksonville, FL	45.2
31	43	Fort Worth-Arlington, TX	28.0	28	43	Kansas City, MO-KS	45.2
1	43	Los Angeles-Long Beach, CA	28.0	106	43	Lexington, KY	45.2
157	46	Fayetteville, NC	27.9	262	46	Hagerstown, MD	45.1
245	46	Monroe, LA	27.9	144	46	Huntsville, AL	45.1
102	48	Fort Wayne, IN	27.8	169	46	New London-Norwich, CT-RI	45.1
275	48	Sioux City, IA-NE	27.8	61	49	Louisville, KY-IN	45.0
284	50	Lawton, OK	27.7	197	49	Olympia, WA	45.0
101	51	Colorado Springs, CO	27.6	186	51	Bremerton, WA	44.9
118	52	Flint, MI	27.5	3	51	Chicago, IL	44.9
117	52	Jackson, MS	27.5	7	51	Detroit, MI	44.9
209	54	Lake Charles, LA	27.4	174	51	Fort Collins-Loveland, CO	44.9
270	55	Alexandria, LA	27.3	219	51	Sioux Falls, SD	44.9
88	55	Baton Rouge, LA	27.3	91	51	Wilmington-Newark, DE-MD	44.9
35	55	Sacramento, CA	27.3	131	51	York, PA	44.9
100	55	Vallejo-Fairfield-Napa, CA	27.3	44	58	Bergen-Passaic, NJ	44.8
268	59	Dover, DE	27.2	47	58	Greensboro-Winston-Salem-High Point, NC	44.8
74	59	Omaha, NE-IA	27.2	34	58	Orlando, FL	44.8
76	59	Tacoma, WA	27.2	76	58	Tacoma, WA	44.8
192	62	Amarillo, TX	27.1	36	62	Fort Lauderdale, FL	44.7
107	62	Augusta-Aiken, GA-SC	27.1	100	62	Vallejo-Fairfield-Napa, CA	44.7
296	62	Kankakee, IL	27.1	313	64	Cheyenne, WY	44.6
152	62	Macon, GA	27.1	177	64	Galveston-Texas City, TX	44.6
3	66	Chicago, IL	27.0	145	64	Hickory-Morganton-Lenoir, NC	44.6
240	66	Kenosha, WI	27.0	230	64	Jackson, MI	44.6
14	66	Orange County, CA	27.0	1	64	Los Angeles-Long Beach, CA	44.6
208	66	Racine, WI	27.0	15	64	San Diego, CA	44.6
274	66	Rochester, MN	27.0	92	70	Little Rock-North Little Rock, AR	44.5
143	66	Salem, OR	27.0	141	70	Trenton, NJ	44.5
134	72	Rockford, IL	26.9	139	72	Appleton-Oshkosh-Neenah, WI	44.4
127	72	Shreveport-Bossier City, LA	26.9	164	72	Dutchess County, NY	44.4
186	74	Bremerton, WA	26.8	54	72	Memphis, TN-AR-MS	44.4
198	74	Fort Smith, AR-OK	26.8	16	72	Nassau-Suffolk, NY	44.4

Note: Column numbers refer to Table C. Metropolitan Areas.

TABLE 5—All Metropolitan Areas
Selected Rankings

Percent Age 65 Years and Over, 2000				Percent Female-headed Family Households, 2000			
Population Rank	65 Years and Over Rank	Metropolitan Area	[cols 35 & 36] Percent 65 Years and Over	Population Rank	Female Households Rank	Metropolitan Area	[col 76] Percent Female Households
251	1	Punta Gorda, FL	34.7	277	1	Albany, GA	21.3
90	2	Sarasota-Bradenton, FL	28.5	54	2	Memphis, TN-AR-MS	18.9
116	3	Fort Myers-Cape Coral, FL	25.4	310	3	Pine Bluff, AR	18.8
153	4	Fort Pierce-Port St. Lucie, FL	24.9	117	4	Jackson, MS	18.7
175	5	Naples, FL	24.5	165	5	Columbus, GA-AL	18.4
170	5	Ocala, FL	24.5	205	6	Laredo, TX	18.3
190	7	Barnstable-Yarmouth, MA	23.1	294	6	Sumter, SC	18.3
55	7	Woct Palm Beach-Boca Raton, FL	23.1	45	8	New Orleans, LA	18.2
103	9	Daytona Beach, FL	22.8	272	9	Florence, SC	18.1
108	10	Melbourne-Titusville-Palm Bay, FL	19.9	2	9	New York, NY	18.1
185	11	Johnstown, PA	19.2	79	11	El Paso, TX	18.0
20	11	Tampa-St. Petersburg-Clearwater, FL	19.2	127	11	Shreveport-Bossier City, LA	18.0
84	13	Scranton-Wilkes-Barre-Hazleton, PA	18.9	245	13	Monroe, LA	17.9
261	14	Steubenville-Weirton, OH-WV	18.5	152	14	Macon, GA	17.7
104	15	Lakeland-Winter Haven, FL	18.3	147	15	Brownsville-Harlingen-San Benito, TX	17.4
279	16	Sharon, PA	18.1	246	16	Vineland-Millville-Bridgeton, NJ	17.3
259	17	Pittsfield, MA	17.9	23	17	Miami, FL	17.2
234	17	Wheeling, WV-OH	17.9	249	18	Rocky Mount, NC	17.1
22	19	Pittsburgh, PA	17.7	270	19	Alexandria, LA	16.8
265	20	Altoona, PA	17.4	148	20	Montgomery, AL	16.7
300	21	Cumberland, MD-WV	17.2	86	21	Jersey City, NJ	16.6
56	22	Monmouth-Ocean, NJ	16.9	107	22	Augusta-Aiken, GA-SC	16.5
292	23	Danville, VA	16.7	118	23	Flint, MI	16.3
228	24	Yuma, AZ	16.6	160	24	Savannah, GA	15.9
158	25	Utica-Rome, NY	16.5	94	25	McAllen-Edinburg-Mission, TX	15.7
89	25	Youngstown-Warren, OH	16.5	98	25	Mobile, AL	15.7
81	27	Allentown-Bethlehem-Easton, PA	16.1	88	27	Baton Rouge, LA	15.6
36	27	Fort Lauderdale, FL	16.1	157	28	Fayetteville, NC	15.5
318	29	Enid, OK	16.0	286	29	Goldsboro, NC	15.4
298	29	Gadsden, AL	16.0	96	30	Charleston-North Charleston, SC	15.3
254	29	Jamestown, NY	16.0	292	30	Danville, VA	15.3
212	29	Medford-Ashland, OR	16.0	289	30	Hattiesburg, MS	15.3
280	29	Williamsport, PA	16.0	293	30	Jackson, TN	15.3
179	34	Duluth-Superior, MN-WI	15.9	129	30	Lafayette, LA	15.3
51	35	Buffalo-Niagara Falls, NY	15.8	263	30	Texarkana, TX-Texarkana, AR	15.3
200	35	Chico-Paradise, CA	15.8	18	36	Baltimore, MD	14.9
183	35	Roanoke, VA	15.8	132	36	Corpus Christi, TX	14.9
172	38	Binghamton, NY	15.7	66	36	Fresno, CA	14.9
307	39	Elmira, NY	15.6	82	36	Gary, IN	14.9
188	40	Asheville, NC	15.5	39	36	Norfolk-Virginia Beach-Newport News, VA-NC	14.9
140	40	Atlantic-Cape May, NJ	15.5	67	41	Birmingham, AL	14.8
173	42	Charleston, WV	15.4	38	41	San Antonio, TX	14.8
105	43	Johnson City-Kingsport-Bristol, TN-VA	15.3	209	43	Lake Charles, LA	14.7
237	43	Parkersburg-Marietta, WV-OH	15.3	217	43	Las Cruces, NM	14.7
285	45	Decatur, IL	15.2	1	43	Los Angeles-Long Beach, CA	14.7
250	45	Florence, AL	15.2	7	46	Detroit, MI	14.6
282	45	Grand Junction, CO	15.2	80	47	Bakersfield, CA	14.5
252	45	Pueblo, CO	15.2	130	47	Beaumont-Port Arthur, TX	14.5
226	45	Redding, CA	15.2	136	47	Visalia-Tulare-Porterville, CA	14.5
291	50	Sherman-Denison, TX	15.1	137	50	Biloxi-Gulfport-Pascagoula, MS	14.4
123	51	Canton-Massillon, OH	15.0	99	50	Columbia, SC	14.4
154	51	Huntington-Ashland, WV-KY-OH	15.0	260	50	Greenville, NC	14.4
203	51	Myrtle Beach, SC	15.0	26	50	Newark, NJ	14.4
133	51	Reading, PA	15.0	62	50	Richmond-Petersburg, VA	14.4
299	55	St. Joseph, MO	14.9	87	50	Springfield, MA	14.4
308	56	Dubuque, IA	14.7	5	56	Philadelphia, PA-NJ	14.3
83	56	Harrisburg-Lebanon-Carlisle, PA	14.7	162	56	Tallahassee, FL	14.3
24	58	Cleveland-Lorain-Elyria, OH	14.6	284	58	Lawton, OK	14.1
273	58	Glens Falls, NY	14.6	195	58	Merced, CA	14.1
193	60	Lynchburg, VA	14.5	57	60	Jacksonville, FL	14.0
142	60	Peoria-Pekin, IL	14.5	95	60	Stockton-Lodi, CA	14.0
63	60	Providence-Fall River-Warwick, RI-MA	14.5	225	60	Tuscaloosa, AL	14.0
241	60	Terre Haute, IN	14.5	256	63	Dothan, AL	13.9
227	64	Benton Harbor, MI	14.4	24	64	Cleveland-Lorain-Elyria, OH	13.8
297	64	Lewiston-Auburn, ME	14.4	268	64	Dover, DE	13.8
215	64	Mansfield, OH	14.4	122	64	Pensacola, FL	13.8
178	64	San Luis Obispo-Atascadero-Paso Robles, CA	14.4	141	64	Trenton, NJ	13.8
69	68	Albany-Schenectady-Troy, NY	14.3	115	68	Modesto, CA	13.7
163	68	Erie, PA	14.3	9	69	Atlanta, GA	13.6
288	70	Anniston, AL	14.2	140	69	Atlantic-Cape May, NJ	13.6
232	70	Lima, OH	14.2	61	69	Louisville, KY-IN	13.6
70	70	Tucson, AZ	14.2	194	69	Waco, TX	13.6
44	73	Bergen-Passaic, NJ	14.1	51	73	Buffalo-Niagara Falls, NY	13.5
262	73	Hagerstown, MD	14.1	17	73	St. Louis, MO-IL	13.5
216	73	Tyler, TX	14.1	288	75	Anniston, AL	13.4

Note: Column numbers refer to Table C. Metropolitan Areas.

TABLE 5—All Metropolitan Areas
Selected Rankings

	Percent Living Alone, 2000				Percent Married Couple Family Households, 2000		
Population Rank	Living Alone Rank	Metropolitan Area	[col 79] Percent Living Alone	Population Rank	Married Couple Family Households Rank	Metropolitan Area	[col 74] % in Married Couple Family Households
278	1	Bloomington, IN	32.4	135	1	Provo-Orem, UT	69.8
29	2	San Francisco, CA	32.1	94	2	McAllen-Edinburg-Mission, TX	65.0
259	3	Pittsfield, MA	31.6	205	3	Laredo, TX	62.6
214	4	Champaign-Urbana, IL	31.4	16	4	Nassau-Suffolk, NY	62.5
179	5	Duluth-Superior, MN-WI	31.0	228	5	Yuma, AZ	62.3
2	6	New York, NY	30.8	181	6	Brazoria, TX	62.2
84	7	Scranton-Wilkes-Barre-Hazleton, PA	30.5	239	7	Jacksonville, NC	61.0
201	7	Springfield, IL	30.5	147	8	Brownsville-Harlingen-San Benito, TX	60.8
51	9	Buffalo-Niagara Falls, NY	30.2	46	9	Salt Lake City-Ogden, UT	60.3
290	9	Iowa City, IA	30.2	109	10	Lancaster, PA	59.9
22	11	Pittsburgh, PA	30.0	271	10	Wausau, WI	59.9
218	12	Fargo-Moorhead, ND-MN	29.9	72	12	Ventura, CA	59.5
221	13	Topeka, KS	29.8	251	13	Punta Gorda, FL	59.2
20	14	Tampa-St. Petersburg-Clearwater, FL	29.7	52	14	Middlesex-Somerset-Hunterdon, NJ	58.9
36	15	Fort Lauderdale, FL	29.6	128	15	Newburgh, NY-PA	58.6
90	15	Sarasota-Bradenton, FL	29.6	206	16	Richland-Kennewick-Pasco, WA	58.3
234	15	Wheeling, WV-OH	29.6	131	16	York, PA	58.3
190	18	Barnstable-Yarmouth, MA	29.5	155	18	Killeen-Temple, TX	58.2
86	18	Jersey City, NJ	29.5	199	19	Clarksville-Hopkinsville, TN-KY	58.1
69	20	Albany-Schenectady-Troy, NY	29.4	247	19	Decatur, AL	58.1
120	20	Madison, WI	29.4	175	19	Naples, FL	58.1
183	20	Roanoke, VA	29.4	136	19	Visalia-Tulare-Porterville, CA	58.1
172	23	Binghamton, NY	29.3	204	23	Houma, LA	58.0
24	24	Cleveland-Lorain-Elyria, OH	29.2	287	23	Sheboygan, WI	58.0
55	24	West Palm Beach-Boca Raton, FL	29.2	195	25	Merced, CA	57.8
191	26	Gainesville, FL	29.1	186	26	Bremerton, WA	57.7
176	26	Lincoln, NE	29.1	156	27	Fayetteville-Springdale-Rogers, AR	57.6
158	26	Utica-Rome, NY	29.1	213	27	Greeley, CO	57.6
173	29	Charleston, WV	28.9	56	29	Monmouth-Ocean, NJ	57.3
285	30	Decatur, IL	28.8	149	30	Hamilton-Middletown, OH	57.0
314	30	Great Falls, MT	28.8	139	31	Appleton-Oshkosh-Neenah, WI	56.9
244	30	Santa Fe, NM	28.8	308	32	Dubuque, IA	56.8
162	30	Tallahassee, FL	28.8	211	32	Elkhart-Goshen, IN	56.8
188	34	Asheville, NC	28.7	119	34	Boise City, ID	56.7
258	34	Columbia, MO	28.7	79	34	El Paso, TX	56.7
300	34	Cumberland, MD-WV	28.7	316	34	Pocatello, ID	56.7
42	34	Milwaukee-Waukesha, WI	28.7	274	34	Rochester, MN	56.7
85	34	Toledo, OH	28.7	311	34	Victoria, TX	56.7
303	39	Grand Forks, ND-MN	28.5	220	39	Fort Walton Beach, FL	56.2
185	39	Johnstown, PA	28.5	145	40	Hickory-Morganton-Lenoir, NC	56.1
302	39	Lawrence, KS	28.5	11	40	Riverside-San Bernardino, CA	56.1
241	39	Terre Haute, IN	28.5	105	42	Johnson City-Kingsport-Bristol, TN-VA	56.0
70	39	Tucson, AZ	28.5	115	42	Modesto, CA	56.0
166	44	Portland, ME	28.4	125	42	Salinas, CA	56.0
63	44	Providence-Fall River-Warwick, RI-MA	28.4	250	45	Florence, AL	55.9
19	44	Seattle-Bellevue-Everett, WA	28.4	198	45	Fort Smith, AR-OK	55.9
87	44	Springfield, MA	28.4	14	45	Orange County, CA	55.9
225	44	Tuscaloosa, AL	28.4	44	48	Bergen-Passaic, NJ	55.8
260	49	Greenville, NC	28.3	232	48	Lima, OH	55.8
297	49	Lewiston-Auburn, ME	28.3	182	48	Odessa-Midland, TX	55.8
33	51	Cincinnati, OH-KY-IN	28.2	237	48	Parkersburg-Marietta, WV-OH	55.8
292	51	Danville, VA	28.2	189	48	Yakima, WA	55.8
281	51	Muncie, IN	28.2	101	53	Colorado Springs, CO	55.6
41	54	Columbus, OH	28.1	59	53	Grand Rapids-Muskegon-Holland, MI	55.6
254	54	Jamestown, NY	28.1	170	53	Ocala, FL	55.6
121	54	Spokane, WA	28.1	164	56	Dutchess County, NY	55.5
140	57	Atlantic-Cape May, NJ	28.0	116	56	Fort Myers-Cape Coral, FL	55.5
138	57	Davenport-Moline-Rock Island, IA-IL	28.0	133	56	Reading, PA	55.5
25	57	Denver, CO	28.0	216	56	Tyler, TX	55.5
304	57	Missoula, MT	28.0	223	60	St. Cloud, MN	55.4
264	61	Billings, MT	27.9	255	60	Yuba City, CA	55.4
65	61	Dayton-Springfield, OH	27.9	282	62	Grand Junction, CO	55.3
307	61	Elmira, NY	27.9	153	63	Fort Pierce-Port St. Lucie, FL	55.2
267	61	La Crosse, WI-MN	27.9	291	63	Sherman-Denison, TX	55.2
167	61	South Bend, IN	27.9	305	65	Bismarck, ND	55.1
299	61	St. Joseph, MO	27.9	231	65	Joplin, MO	55.1
261	61	Steubenville-Weirton, OH-WV	27.9	100	67	Vallejo-Fairfield-Napa, CA	55.0
265	68	Altoona, PA	27.8	32	68	San Jose, CA	54.9
283	68	Auburn-Opelika, AL	27.8	279	69	Sharon, PA	54.8
61	68	Louisville, KY-IN	27.8	123	70	Canton-Massillon, OH	54.7
73	68	Syracuse, NY	27.8	185	70	Johnstown, PA	54.7
318	72	Enid, OK	27.7	134	70	Rockford, IL	54.7
106	72	Lexington, KY	27.7	81	73	Allentown-Bethlehem-Easton, PA	54.6
238	74	Bloomington-Normal, IL	27.6	80	73	Bakersfield, CA	54.6
163	74	Erie, PA	27.6	154	73	Huntington-Ashland, WV-KY-OH	54.6

Note: Column numbers refer to Table C. Metropolitan Areas.

TABLE 5—All Metropolitan Areas
Selected Rankings

Percent of Families with Own Children Under 18, 2000				Percent Change in Households, 1990-2000			
Population Rank	Families with Own Children Under 18 Rank	Metropolitan Area	[col 73] Percent of Families with Own Children Under 18	Population Rank	Change in Households Rank	Metropolitan Area	[col 86] Percent Change in Households
205	1	Laredo, TX	53.2	40	1	Las Vegas, NV-AZ	78.0
94	2	McAllen-Edinburg-Mission, TX	49.7	175	2	Naples, FL	66.9
135	3	Provo-Orem, UT	48.3	94	3	McAllen-Edinburg-Mission, TX	51.6
147	4	Brownsville-Harlingen-San Benito, TX	45.8	228	4	Yuma, AZ	50.5
195	5	Merced, CA	45.4	205	5	Laredo, TX	47.3
79	6	El Paso, TX	44.9	203	6	Myrtle Beach, SC	46.7
136	7	Visalia-Tulare-Porterville, CA	44.9	156	7	Fayetteville-Springdale-Rogers, AR	46.3
239	8	Jacksonville, NC	42.6	119	8	Boise City, ID	45.7
80	9	Bakersfield, CA	42.2	48	9	Austin-San Marcos, TX	44.7
155	10	Killeen-Temple, TX	41.6	184	10	Wilmington, NC	44.6
46	11	Salt Lake City-Ogden, UT	41.6	135	11	Provo-Orem, UT	42.4
11	12	Riverside-San Bernardino, CA	41.4	12	12	Phoenix-Mesa, AZ	41.0
115	13	Modesto, CA	41.2	283	13	Auburn-Opelika, AL	38.1
66	14	Fresno, CA	41.1	174	14	Fort Collins-Loveland, CO	37.9
181	15	Brazoria, TX	40.8	50	15	Raleigh-Durham-Chapel Hill, NC	37.8
199	16	Clarksville-Hopkinsville, TN-KY	40.8	170	16	Ocala, FL	36.6
95	17	Stockton-Lodi, CA	40.5	9	17	Atlanta, GA	36.5
206	18	Richland-Kennewick-Pasco, WA	39.7	276	18	Flagstaff, AZ-UT	34.9
72	19	Ventura, CA	39.7	116	19	Fort Myers-Cape Coral, FL	34.6
189	20	Yakima, WA	39.7	34	20	Orlando, FL	34.4
157	21	Fayetteville, NC	39.4	213	21	Greeley, CO	33.2
125	22	Salinas, CA	39.1	244	22	Santa Fe, NM	33.1
284	23	Lawton, OK	39.0	224	23	Bellingham, WA	32.8
168	24	Anchorage, AK	38.9	147	24	Brownsville-Harlingen-San Benito, TX	32.7
8	25	Houston, TX	38.9	217	25	Las Cruces, NM	32.2
128	26	Newburgh, NY-PA	38.9	251	26	Punta Gorda, FL	31.9
182	27	Odessa-Midland, TX	38.9	197	27	Olympia, WA	31.3
204	28	Houma, LA	38.6	101	28	Colorado Springs, CO	30.9
217	29	Las Cruces, NM	38.4	199	29	Clarksville-Hopkinsville, TN-KY	30.7
255	30	Yuba City, CA	38.0	153	29	Fort Pierce-Port St. Lucie, FL	30.7
100	31	Vallejo-Fairfield-Napa, CA	37.7	43	31	Charlotte-Gastonia-Rock Hill, NC-SC	30.5
119	32	Boise City, ID	37.2	260	32	Greenville, NC	29.8
132	33	Corpus Christi, TX	37.2	161	33	Boulder-Longmont, CO	29.7
213	34	Greeley, CO	37.2	55	33	West Palm Beach-Boca Raton, FL	29.7
311	35	Victoria, TX	37.2	146	35	Reno, NV	29.1
14	36	Orange County, CA	37.0	181	36	Brazoria, TX	28.0
31	37	Fort Worth-Arlington, TX	36.9	10	36	Dallas, TX	28.0
129	38	Lafayette, LA	36.9	302	38	Lawrence, KS	27.7
228	39	Yuma, AZ	36.9	49	39	Nashville, TN	27.6
1	40	Los Angeles-Long Beach, CA	36.8	162	40	Tallahassee, FL	27.4
101	41	Colorado Springs, CO	36.7	25	41	Denver, CO	27.1
38	42	San Antonio, TX	36.6	150	41	Springfield, MO	27.1
10	43	Dallas, TX	36.5	70	43	Tucson, AZ	27.0
59	44	Grand Rapids-Muskegon-Holland, MI	36.5	229	44	Charlottesville, VA	26.6
316	45	Pocatello, ID	36.5	258	44	Columbia, MO	26.6
294	46	Sumter, SC	36.5	282	46	Grand Junction, CO	26.4
211	47	Elkhart-Goshen, IN	36.4	235	47	Bryan-College Station, TX	26.2
16	48	Nassau-Suffolk, NY	36.2	27	48	Portland-Vancouver, OR-WA	25.8
186	49	Bremerton, WA	36.0	155	49	Killeen-Temple, TX	25.7
76	50	Tacoma, WA	35.9	219	49	Sioux Falls, SD	25.7
277	51	Albany, GA	35.8	212	51	Medford-Ashland, OR	25.0
9	52	Atlanta, GA	35.8	304	52	Missoula, MT	24.9
107	53	Augusta-Aiken, GA-SC	35.6	186	53	Bremerton, WA	24.8
209	54	Lake Charles, LA	35.6	99	54	Columbia, SC	24.6
39	55	Norfolk-Virginia Beach-Newport News, VA-NC	35.6	103	54	Daytona Beach, FL	24.6
268	56	Dover, DE	35.5	233	56	Athens, GA	24.4
149	57	Hamilton-Middletown, OH	35.5	206	56	Richland-Kennewick-Pasco, WA	24.4
117	58	Jackson, MS	35.5	220	58	Fort Walton Beach, FL	24.3
88	59	Baton Rouge, LA	35.4	46	58	Salt Lake City-Ogden, UT	24.3
274	60	Rochester, MN	35.2	75	60	Albuquerque, NM	24.1
165	61	Columbus, GA-AL	35.0	106	61	Lexington, KY	24.0
54	62	Memphis, TN-AR-MS	35.0	57	62	Jacksonville, FL	23.9
52	63	Middlesex-Somerset-Hunterdon, NJ	35.0	93	63	Ann Arbor, MI	23.8
223	64	St. Cloud, MN	35.0	36	63	Fort Lauderdale, FL	23.8
32	65	San Jose, CA	34.9	31	65	Fort Worth-Arlington, TX	23.4
275	66	Sioux City, IA-NE	34.9	312	66	Jonesboro, AR	22.9
276	67	Flagstaff, AZ-UT	34.8	191	67	Gainesville, FL	22.8
240	68	Kenosha, WI	34.8	108	67	Melbourne-Titusville-Palm Bay, FL	22.8
269	69	Abilene, TX	34.7	143	69	Salem, OR	22.7
286	70	Goldsboro, NC	34.7	8	70	Houston, TX	22.6
26	71	Newark, NJ	34.7	190	71	Barnstable-Yarmouth, MA	22.2
219	72	Sioux Falls, SD	34.7	290	71	Iowa City, IA	22.2
270	73	Alexandria, LA	34.6	38	73	San Antonio, TX	22.1
102	74	Fort Wayne, IN	34.6	243	74	Panama City, FL	21.8
152	75	Macon, GA	34.6	137	75	Biloxi-Gulfport-Pascagoula, MS	21.7

Note: Column numbers refer to Table C. Metropolitan Areas.

TABLE 5—All Metropolitan Areas
Selected Rankings

	Percent in Group Quarters, 2000				Percent in Dormitories, 2000		
Population Rank	Group Quarters Rank	Metropolitan Area	[col 64] Percent in Group Quarters	Population Rank	Dormitories Rank	Metropolitan Area	[col 68] Percent in Dormitories
239	1	Jacksonville, NC	12.9	278	1	Bloomington, IN	10.7
278	2	Bloomington, IN	11.9	257	2	State College, PA	8.4
257	3	State College, PA	10.9	302	3	Lawrence, KS	7.9
284	4	Lawton, OK	9.0	210	4	Lafayette, IN	7.3
235	5	Bryan-College Station, TX	8.8	214	5	Champaign-Urbana, IL	7.1
210	6	Lafayette, IN	8.7	235	6	Bryan-College Station, TX	7.0
302	6	Lawrence, KS	8.7	238	7	Bloomington-Normal, IL	6.5
246	8	Vineland-Millville-Bridgeton, NJ	8.4	290	8	Iowa City, IA	5.6
214	9	Champaign-Urbana, IL	8.3	258	9	Columbia, MO	5.5
155	9	Killeen-Temple, TX	8.3	315	9	Corvallis, OR	5.5
253	11	Wichita Falls, TX	8.0	233	11	Athens, GA	4.3
238	12	Bloomington-Normal, IL	7.5	281	12	Muncie, IN	4.2
290	13	Iowa City, IA	7.2	229	13	Charlottesville, VA	3.9
262	14	Hagerstown, MD	7.1	191	13	Gainesville, FL	3.9
258	15	Columbia, MO	6.6	303	15	Grand Forks, ND-MN	3.6
300	16	Cumberland, MD-WV	6.5	87	15	Springfield, MA	3.6
164	16	Dutchess County, NY	6.5	225	15	Tuscaloosa, AL	3.6
315	18	Corvallis, OR	6.4	260	18	Greenville, NC	3.5
230	19	Jackson, MI	6.3	141	18	Trenton, NJ	3.5
310	19	Pine Bluff, AR	6.3	218	20	Fargo-Moorhead, ND-MN	3.3
178	19	San Luis Obispo-Atascadero-Paso Robles, CA	6.3	167	20	South Bend, IN	3.3
307	22	Elmira, NY	6.1	114	22	Lansing-East Lansing, MI	3.2
157	22	Fayetteville, NC	6.1	283	23	Auburn-Opelika, AL	3.1
303	22	Grand Forks, ND-MN	6.1	289	23	Hattiesburg, MS	3.1
263	22	Texarkana, TX-Texarkana, AR	6.1	223	23	St. Cloud, MN	3.1
141	26	Trenton, NJ	6.0	162	23	Tallahassee, FL	3.1
229	27	Charlottesville, VA	5.9	266	23	Waterloo-Cedar Falls, IA	3.1
191	27	Gainesville, FL	5.9	202	28	Burlington, VT	2.9
122	27	Pensacola, FL	5.9	106	28	Lexington, KY	2.9
241	27	Terre Haute, IN	5.9	241	28	Terre Haute, IN	2.9
99	31	Columbia, SC	5.8	222	28	Yolo, CA	2.9
281	31	Muncie, IN	5.8	93	32	Ann Arbor, MI	2.8
233	33	Athens, GA	5.6	176	32	Lincoln, NE	2.8
162	33	Tallahassee, FL	5.6	248	34	Bangor, ME	2.6
158	35	Utica-Rome, NY	5.5	267	34	La Crosse, WI-MN	2.6
165	36	Columbus, GA-AL	5.4	293	36	Jackson, TN	2.5
87	36	Springfield, MA	5.4	308	37	Dubuque, IA	2.4
289	38	Hattiesburg, MS	5.3	242	37	Eau Claire, WI	2.4
148	38	Montgomery, AL	5.3	193	37	Lynchburg, VA	2.4
279	38	Sharon, PA	5.3	164	40	Dutchess County, NY	2.3
225	38	Tuscaloosa, AL	5.3	149	40	Hamilton-Middletown, OH	2.3
125	42	Salinas, CA	5.2	269	42	Abilene, TX	2.2
308	43	Dubuque, IA	5.1	50	42	Raleigh-Durham-Chapel Hill, NC	2.2
185	43	Johnstown, PA	5.1	279	42	Sharon, PA	2.2
167	43	South Bend, IN	5.1	161	45	Boulder-Longmont, CO	2.1
266	43	Waterloo-Cedar Falls, IA	5.1	163	45	Erie, PA	2.1
269	47	Abilene, TX	5.0	120	45	Madison, WI	2.1
199	47	Clarksville-Hopkinsville, TN-KY	5.0	304	45	Missoula, MT	2.1
163	47	Erie, PA	5.0	259	45	Pittsfield, MA	2.1
93	50	Ann Arbor, MI	4.9	150	45	Springfield, MO	2.1
176	50	Lincoln, NE	4.9	172	51	Binghamton, NY	2.0
223	52	St. Cloud, MN	4.8	276	51	Flagstaff, AZ-UT	2.0
299	52	St. Joseph, MO	4.8	180	51	Lubbock, TX	2.0
218	54	Fargo-Moorhead, ND-MN	4.7	63	51	Providence-Fall River-Warwick, RI-MA	2.0
260	54	Greenville, NC	4.7	194	51	Waco, TX	2.0
232	54	Lima, OH	4.7	224	56	Bellingham, WA	1.9
193	54	Lynchburg, VA	4.7	73	56	Syracuse, NY	1.9
254	58	Jamestown, NY	4.6	69	58	Albany-Schenectady-Troy, NY	1.8
106	58	Lexington, KY	4.6	174	58	Fort Collins-Loveland, CO	1.8
169	58	New London-Norwich, CT-RI	4.6	312	58	Jonesboro, AR	1.8
280	58	Williamsport, PA	4.6	113	58	Kalamazoo-Battle Creek, MI	1.8
80	62	Bakersfield, CA	4.5	171	58	Santa Cruz-Watsonville, CA	1.8
248	62	Bangor, ME	4.5	300	63	Cumberland, MD-WV	1.7
181	62	Brazoria, TX	4.5	179	63	Duluth-Superior, MN-WI	1.7
267	62	La Crosse, WI-MN	4.5	58	63	Rochester, NY	1.7
259	62	Pittsfield, MA	4.5	126	63	Santa Barbara-Santa Maria-Lompoc, CA	1.7
222	62	Yolo, CA	4.5	99	67	Columbia, SC	1.6
277	68	Albany, GA	4.4	213	67	Greeley, CO	1.6
270	68	Alexandria, LA	4.4	254	67	Jamestown, NY	1.6
234	68	Wheeling, WV-OH	4.4	156	70	Fayetteville-Springdale-Rogers, AR	1.5
130	71	Beaumont-Port Arthur, TX	4.3	64	70	Greenville-Spartanburg-Anderson, SC	1.5
114	71	Lansing-East Lansing, MI	4.3	53	70	Hartford, CT	1.5
194	71	Waco, TX	4.3	297	70	Lewiston-Auburn, ME	1.5
179	74	Duluth-Superior, MN-WI	4.2	316	70	Pocatello, ID	1.5
242	74	Eau Claire, WI	4.2	178	70	San Luis Obispo-Atascadero-Paso Robles, CA	1.5

Note: Column numbers refer to Table C. Metropolitan Areas.

TABLE 5—All Metropolitan Areas
Selected Rankings

Percent Owner Occupied Housing Units, 2000				Percent Recreational/Seasonal Housing Units, 2000			
Population Rank	Owner Occupied Housing Units Rank	Metropolitan Area	[col 94] Percent in Owner Occupied Housing Units	Population Rank	Recreational/Seasonal Housing Units Rank	Metropolitan Area	[col 90] Percent Recreational/Seasonal Housing Units
251	1	Punta Gorda, FL	83.7	190	1	Barnstable-Yarmouth, MA	32.0
16	2	Nassau-Suffolk, NY	80.0	140	2	Atlantic-Cape May, NJ	26.7
170	3	Ocala, FL	79.8	175	3	Naples, FL	23.8
153	4	Fort Pierce-Port St. Lucie, FL	78.8	203	4	Myrtle Beach, SC	20.4
56	5	Monmouth-Ocean, NJ	78.7	276	5	Flagstaff, AZ-UT	18.2
190	6	Barnstable-Yarmouth, MA	77.8	116	6	Fort Myers-Cape Coral, FL	16.1
90	7	Sarasota-Bradenton, FL	76.8	273	7	Glens Falls, NY	15.9
204	8	Houma, LA	76.7	228	8	Yuma, AZ	15.7
110	9	Fort Myers-Cape Coral, FL	76.5	184	9	Wilmington, NC	15.2
230	9	Jackson, MI	76.5	251	10	Punta Gorda, FL	13.2
124	11	Saginaw-Bay City-Midland, MI	76.3	90	11	Sarasota-Bradenton, FL	11.6
279	11	Sharon, PA	76.3	128	12	Newburgh, NY-PA	11.2
103	13	Daytona Beach, FL	76.2	243	12	Panama City, FL	11.2
131	14	York, PA	76.1	153	14	Fort Pierce-Port St. Lucie, FL	10.1
185	15	Johnstown, PA	75.9	147	15	Brownsville-Harlingen-San Benito, TX	9.8
274	15	Rochester, MN	75.9	55	16	West Palm Beach-Boca Raton, FL	9.5
271	17	Wausau, WI	75.7	259	17	Pittsfield, MA	9.4
175	18	Naples, FL	75.6	179	18	Duluth-Superior, MN-WI	9.2
247	19	Decatur, AL	75.5	94	19	McAllen-Edinburg-Mission, TX	9.1
261	19	Steubenville-Weirton, OH-WV	75.5	254	20	Jamestown, NY	9.0
59	21	Grand Rapids-Muskegon-Holland, MI	74.9	166	21	Portland, ME	8.8
55	22	West Palm Beach-Boca Raton, FL	74.7	104	22	Lakeland-Winter Haven, FL	8.4
108	23	Melbourne-Titusville-Palm Bay, FL	74.6	56	22	Monmouth-Ocean, NJ	8.4
237	24	Parkersburg-Marietta, WV-OH	74.5	224	24	Bellingham, WA	8.0
298	25	Gadsden, AL	74.4	248	25	Bangor, ME	7.4
145	26	Hickory-Morganton-Lenoir, NC	74.3	103	25	Daytona Beach, FL	7.4
250	27	Florence, AL	74.2	227	27	Benton Harbor, MI	7.2
105	27	Johnson City-Kingsport-Bristol, TN-VA	74.2	177	28	Galveston-Texas City, TX	6.8
179	29	Duluth-Superior, MN-WI	74.1	36	29	Fort Lauderdale, FL	6.3
181	30	Brazoria, TX	74.0	202	30	Burlington, VT	6.0
133	30	Reading, PA	74.0	178	30	San Luis Obispo-Atascadero-Paso Robles, CA	6.0
102	32	Fort Wayne, IN	73.9	11	32	Riverside-San Bernardino, CA	5.9
193	32	Lynchburg, VA	73.9	98	33	Mobile, AL	5.7
89	32	Youngstown-Warren, OH	73.9	220	34	Fort Walton Beach, FL	5.4
232	35	Lima, OH	73.8	239	35	Jacksonville, NC	5.2
234	36	Wheeling, WV-OH	73.6	171	36	Santa Cruz-Watsonville, CA	5.1
308	37	Dubuque, IA	73.5	20	36	Tampa-St. Petersburg-Clearwater, FL	5.1
104	38	Lakeland-Winter Haven, FL	73.4	158	36	Utica-Rome, NY	5.1
118	39	Flint, MI	73.2	280	39	Williamsport, PA	4.8
94	40	McAllen-Edinburg-Mission, TX	73.1	108	40	Melbourne-Titusville-Palm Bay, FL	4.7
272	41	Florence, SC	73.0	169	40	New London-Norwich, CT-RI	4.7
301	41	Kokomo, IN	73.0	174	42	Fort Collins-Loveland, CO	4.6
203	41	Myrtle Beach, SC	73.0	12	42	Phoenix-Mesa, AZ	4.6
265	44	Altoona, PA	72.9	185	44	Johnstown, PA	4.3
123	44	Canton-Massillon, OH	72.9	170	44	Ocala, FL	4.3
173	44	Charleston, WV	72.9	16	46	Nassau-Suffolk, NY	4.2
154	44	Huntington-Ashland, WV-KY-OH	72.9	244	47	Santa Fe, NM	3.7
207	48	Cedar Rapids, IA	72.7	291	48	Sherman-Denison, TX	3.6
282	48	Grand Junction, CO	72.7	23	49	Miami, FL	3.5
288	50	Anniston, AL	72.5	111	50	Santa Rosa, CA	3.3
7	51	Detroit, MI	72.4	96	51	Charleston-North Charleston, SC	3.2
13	51	Minneapolis-St. Paul, MN-WI	72.4	304	51	Missoula, MT	3.2
223	51	St. Cloud, MN	72.4	35	51	Sacramento, CA	3.2
227	54	Benton Harbor, MI	72.3	137	54	Biloxi-Gulfport-Pascagoula, MS	3.1
300	54	Cumberland, MD-WV	72.3	317	54	Casper, WY	3.1
228	54	Yuma, AZ	72.3	204	54	Houma, LA	3.1
211	57	Elkhart-Goshen, IN	72.2	297	54	Lewiston-Auburn, ME	3.1
142	57	Peoria-Pekin, IL	72.2	73	54	Syracuse, NY	3.1
273	59	Glens Falls, NY	71.9	230	59	Jackson, MI	3.0
215	60	Mansfield, OH	71.8	125	59	Salinas, CA	3.0
98	61	Mobile, AL	71.7	40	61	Las Vegas, NV-AZ	2.9
167	61	South Bend, IN	71.7	34	61	Orlando, FL	2.9
81	63	Allentown-Bethlehem-Easton, PA	71.6	257	61	State College, PA	2.9
285	63	Decatur, IL	71.6	70	61	Tucson, AZ	2.9
149	63	Hamilton-Middletown, OH	71.6	240	65	Kenosha, WI	2.8
209	63	Lake Charles, LA	71.6	69	66	Albany-Schenectady-Troy, NY	2.7
64	67	Greenville-Spartanburg-Anderson, SC	71.5	113	66	Kalamazoo-Battle Creek, MI	2.7
134	67	Rockford, IL	71.5	188	68	Asheville, NC	2.6
119	69	Boise City, ID	71.4	78	68	Knoxville, TN	2.6
287	69	Sheboygan, WI	71.4	63	68	Providence-Fall River-Warwick, RI-MA	2.6
17	69	St. Louis, MO-IL	71.4	309	68	Rapid City, SD	2.6
139	72	Appleton-Oshkosh-Neenah, WI	71.3	80	72	Bakersfield, CA	2.5
138	72	Davenport-Moline-Rock Island, IA-IL	71.3	132	72	Corpus Christi, TX	2.5
22	72	Pittsburgh, PA	71.3	303	72	Grand Forks, ND-MN	2.5
46	72	Salt Lake City-Ogden, UT	71.3	146	72	Reno, NV	2.5

Note: Column numbers refer to Table C. Metropolitan Areas.

TABLE 5—All Metropolitan Areas
Selected Rankings

	Homeowner Vacancy Rate, 2000				Renter Vacancy Rate, 2000		
Popu-lation Rank	Home-owner Vacancy Rate Rank	Metropolitan Area	[col 91] Homeowner Vacancy Rate	Popu-lation Rank	Renter Vacancy Rate Rank	Metropolitan Area	[col 92] Renter Vacancy Rate
284	1	Lawton, OK	4.3	203	1	Myrtle Beach, SC	30.2
184	2	Wilmington, NC	3.4	243	2	Panama City, FL	22.7
203	3	Myrtle Beach, SC	3.2	220	3	Fort Walton Beach, FL	19.3
318	4	Enid, OK	3.1	182	4	Odessa-Midland, TX	18.5
239	5	Jacksonville, NC	2.9	184	5	Wilmington, NC	17.1
231	5	Joplin, MO	2.9	116	6	Fort Myers-Cape Coral, FL	15.2
104	5	Lakeland-Winter Haven, FL	2.9	288	7	Anniston, AL	14.3
243	5	Panama City, FL	2.9	251	8	Punta Gorda, FL	14.2
40	9	Las Vegas, NV-AZ	2.8	147	9	Brownsville-Harlingen-San Benito, TX	14.1
11	9	Riverside-San Bernardino, CA	2.8	209	9	Lake Charles, LA	14.1
288	11	Anniston, AL	2.7	228	9	Yuma, AZ	14.1
300	11	Cumberland, MD-WV	2.7	177	12	Galveston-Texas City, TX	13.3
157	11	Fayetteville, NC	2.7	284	13	Lawton, OK	13.2
116	11	Fort Myers-Cape Coral, FL	2.7	181	14	Brazoria, TX	13.0
170	11	Ocala, FL	2.7	256	15	Dothan, AL	12.9
80	16	Bakersfield, CA	2.6	104	15	Lakeland-Winter Haven, FL	12.9
199	16	Clarksville-Hopkinsville, TN-KY	2.6	98	17	Mobile, AL	12.8
156	16	Fayetteville-Springdale-Rogers, AR	2.6	122	17	Pensacola, FL	12.8
36	16	Fort Lauderdale, FL	2.6	263	19	Texarkana, TX-Texarkana, AR	12.7
175	16	Naples, FL	2.6	152	20	Macon, GA	12.6
277	21	Albany, GA	2.5	90	20	Sarasota-Bradenton, FL	12.6
107	21	Augusta-Aiken, GA-SC	2.5	225	22	Tuscaloosa, AL	12.3
273	21	Glens Falls, NY	2.5	140	23	Atlantic-Cape May, NJ	12.2
303	21	Grand Forks, ND-MN	2.5	144	23	Huntsville, AL	12.2
143	21	Salem, OR	2.5	247	25	Decatur, AL	11.8
276	26	Flagstaff, AZ-UT	2.4	250	26	Florence, AL	11.7
198	26	Fort Smith, AR-OK	2.4	75	27	Albuquerque, NM	11.5
150	26	Springfield, MO	2.4	295	28	San Angelo, TX	11.4
269	29	Abilene, TX	2.3	165	29	Columbus, GA-AL	11.2
140	29	Atlantic-Cape May, NJ	2.3	311	29	Victoria, TX	11.2
283	29	Auburn-Opelika, AL	2.3	97	29	Wichita, KS	11.2
248	29	Bangor, ME	2.3	253	32	Wichita Falls, TX	11.1
278	29	Bloomington, IN	2.3	130	33	Beaumont-Port Arthur, TX	11.0
153	29	Fort Pierce-Port St. Lucie, FL	2.3	285	33	Decatur, IL	11.0
177	29	Galveston-Texas City, TX	2.3	318	33	Enid, OK	11.0
144	29	Huntsville, AL	2.3	78	33	Knoxville, TN	11.0
108	29	Melbourne-Titusville-Palm Bay, FL	2.3	137	37	Biloxi-Gulfport-Pascagoula, MS	10.9
122	29	Pensacola, FL	2.3	153	37	Fort Pierce-Port St. Lucie, FL	10.9
50	29	Raleigh-Durham-Chapel Hill, NC	2.3	158	37	Utica-Rome, NY	10.9
295	29	San Angelo, TX	2.3	107	40	Augusta-Aiken, GA-SC	10.8
241	29	Terre Haute, IN	2.3	292	40	Danville, VA	10.8
253	29	Wichita Falls, TX	2.3	64	40	Greenville-Spartanburg-Anderson, SC	10.8
224	43	Bellingham, WA	2.2	60	40	Oklahoma City, OK	10.8
258	43	Columbia, MO	2.2	127	40	Shreveport-Bossier City, LA	10.8
256	43	Dothan, AL	2.2	241	40	Terre Haute, IN	10.8
220	43	Fort Walton Beach, FL	2.2	277	46	Albany, GA	10.7
64	43	Greenville-Spartanburg-Anderson, SC	2.2	94	46	McAllen-Edinburg-Mission, TX	10.7
312	43	Jonesboro, AR	2.2	148	46	Montgomery, AL	10.7
296	43	Kankakee, IL	2.2	283	49	Auburn-Opelika, AL	10.6
155	43	Killeen-Temple, TX	2.2	118	49	Flint, MI	10.6
78	43	Knoxville, TN	2.2	37	49	Indianapolis, IN	10.6
148	43	Montgomery, AL	2.2	232	49	Lima, OH	10.6
27	43	Portland-Vancouver, OR-WA	2.2	108	49	Melbourne-Titusville-Palm Bay, FL	10.6
251	43	Punta Gorda, FL	2.2	269	54	Abilene, TX	10.5
226	43	Redding, CA	2.2	67	55	Birmingham, AL	10.3
90	43	Sarasota-Bradenton, FL	2.2	239	55	Jacksonville, NC	10.3
20	43	Tampa-St. Petersburg-Clearwater, FL	2.2	217	55	Las Cruces, NM	10.3
158	43	Utica-Rome, NY	2.2	196	55	Longview-Marshall, TX	10.3
172	59	Binghamton, NY	2.1	294	55	Sumter, SC	10.3
43	59	Charlotte-Gastonia-Rock Hill, NC-SC	2.1	102	60	Fort Wayne, IN	10.2
200	59	Chico-Paradise, CA	2.1	201	60	Springfield, IL	10.2
132	59	Corpus Christi, TX	2.1	157	62	Fayetteville, NC	10.1
118	59	Flint, MI	2.1	272	63	Florence, SC	10.0
298	59	Gadsden, AL	2.1	117	63	Jackson, MS	10.0
260	59	Greenville, NC	2.1	105	63	Johnson City-Kingsport-Bristol, TN-VA	10.0
152	59	Macon, GA	2.1	180	63	Lubbock, TX	10.0
23	59	Miami, FL	2.1	234	63	Wheeling, WV-OH	10.0
98	59	Mobile, AL	2.1	88	68	Baton Rouge, LA	9.9
182	59	Odessa-Midland, TX	2.1	172	68	Binghamton, NY	9.9
197	59	Olympia, WA	2.1	96	68	Charleston-North Charleston, SC	9.9
316	59	Pocatello, ID	2.1	312	68	Jonesboro, AR	9.9
263	59	Texarkana, TX-Texarkana, AR	2.1	231	68	Joplin, MO	9.9
119	73	Boise City, ID	2.0	129	68	Lafayette, LA	9.9
186	73	Bremerton, WA	2.0	99	74	Columbia, SC	9.8
292	73	Danville, VA	2.0	132	74	Corpus Christi, TX	9.8

Note: Column numbers refer to Table C. Metropolitan Areas.

TABLE 6—75 Largest Cities by 2000 Population
Selected Rankings

	Total Persons, 2000			Land Area (Square Kilometers), 2000				Population Density (per Square Kilometer), 2000		
Population Rank	City	[col 2] Population	Population Rank	Land Area Rank	City	[col 1] Land Area	Population Rank	Density Rank	City	[col 4] Density
1	New York City, NY	8 008 278	65	1	Anchorage city, AK	4 395.8	1		New York City, NY	10 193.8
2	Los Angeles city, CA	3 694 820	14	2	Jacksonville city, FL	1 962.4	13		San Francisco city, CA	6 424.6
3	Chicago city, IL	2 896 016	29	3	Oklahoma City, OK	1 572.1	72		Jersey City, NJ	6 219.0
4	Houston city, TX	1 953 631	4	4	Houston city, TX	1 500.7	3		Chicago city, IL	4 922.7
5	Philadelphia city, PA	1 517 550	22	5	Nashville-Davidsn consol. city,TN	1 300.9	51		Santa Ana city, CA	4 807.6
6	Phoenix city, AZ	1 321 045	6	6	Phoenix city, AZ	1 229.9	20		Boston city, MA	4 698.1
7	San Diego city, CA	1 223 400	2	7	Los Angeles city, CA	1 214.9	75		Hialeah city, FL	4 546.6
8	Dallas city, TX	1 188 580	9	8	San Antonio city, TX	1 055.6	63		Newark city, NJ	4 440.7
9	San Antonio city, TX	1 144 646	12	9	Indianapolis consolidated city,IN	949.2	5		Philadelphia city, PA	4 337.1
10	Detroit city, MI	951 270	8	10	Dallas city, TX	887.2	47		Miami city, FL	3 922.0
11	San Jose city, CA	894 943	7	11	San Diego city, CA	840.0	21		Washington city, DC	3 597.9
12	Indianapolis consolidated city,IN	791 926	36	12	Kansas City, MO	812.1	34		Long Beach city, CA	3 533.9
13	San Francisco city, CA	776 733	1	13	New York City, NY	785.6	17		Baltimore city, MD	3 111.1
14	Jacksonville city, FL	735 617	27	14	Fort Worth city, TX	757.7	2		Los Angeles city, CA	3 041.3
15	Columbus city, OH	711 470	64	15	Lexington-Fayette, KY	736.9	58		Buffalo city, NY	2 781.8
16	Austin city, TX	656 562	18	16	Memphis city, TN	723.4	41		Oakland city, CA	2 751.3
17	Baltimore city, MD	651 154	16	17	Austin city, TX	651.4	45		Minneapolis city, MN	2 690.7
18	Memphis city, TN	650 100	23	18	El Paso city, TX	645.1	10		Detroit city, MI	2 646.8
19	Milwaukee city, WI	596 974	38	19	Virginia Beach city, VA	643.1	24		Seattle city, WA	2 593.8
20	Boston city, MA	589 141	26	20	Charlotte city, NC	627.5	55		Anaheim city, CA	2 586.9
21	Washington city, DC	572 059	3	21	Chicago city, IL	588.3	19		Milwaukee city, WI	2 399.4
22	Nashville-Davidsn consol. city,TN	569 891	15	22	Columbus city, OH	544.6	33		Cleveland city, OH	2 381.3
23	El Paso city, TX	563 662	30	23	Tucson city, AZ	504.2	52		Pittsburgh city, PA	2 323.4
24	Seattle city, WA	563 374	48	24	Colorado Springs city, CO	481.1	49		St. Louis city, MO	2 170.8
25	Denver city, CO	554 636	43	25	Tulsa city, OK	473.1	59		St. Paul city, MN	2 100.6
26	Charlotte city, NC	540 828	35	26	Albuquerque city, NM	467.9	11		San Jose city, CA	1 976.0
27	Fort Worth city, TX	534 694	31	27	New Orleans city, LA	467.6	70		Stockton city, CA	1 720.3
28	Portland city, OR	529 121	11	28	San Jose city, CA	452.9	73		Norfolk city, VA	1 683.9
29	Oklahoma City, OK	506 132	60	29	Corpus Christi city, TX	400.5	46		Honolulu CDP, HI	1 674.1
30	Tucson city, AZ	486 699	25	30	Denver city, CO	397.2	54		Cincinnati city, OH	1 640.8
31	New Orleans city, LA	484 674	71	31	Birmingham city, AL	388.3	32		Las Vegas city, NV	1 630.1
32	Las Vegas city, NV	478 434	61	32	Aurora city, CO	369.1	40		Sacramento city, CA	1 617.7
33	Cleveland city, OH	478 403	10	33	Detroit city, MI	359.4	68		St. Petersburg city, FL	1 607.7
34	Long Beach city, CA	461 522	50	34	Wichita city, KS	351.6	66		Louisville city, KY	1 592.5
35	Albuquerque city, NM	448 607	5	35	Philadelphia city, PA	349.9	37		Fresno city, CA	1 582.1
36	Kansas City, MO	441 545	28	36	Portland city, OR	347.9	28		Portland city, OR	1 520.9
37	Fresno city, CA	427 652	39	37	Atlanta city, GA	341.2	56		Toledo city, OH	1 502.0
38	Virginia Beach city, VA	425 257	42	38	Mesa city, AZ	323.7	7		San Diego city, CA	1 456.4
39	Atlanta city, GA	416 474	44	39	Omaha city, NE	299.7	25		Denver city, CO	1 396.4
40	Sacramento city, CA	407 018	62	40	Raleigh city, NC	296.8	53		Arlington city, TX	1 341.5
41	Oakland city, CA	399 484	32	41	Las Vegas city, NV	293.5	8		Dallas city, TX	1 339.7
42	Mesa city, AZ	396 375	69	42	Bakersfield city, CA	292.9	15		Columbus city, OH	1 306.4
43	Tulsa city, OK	393 049	57	43	Tampa city, FL	290.2	4		Houston city, TX	1 301.8
44	Omaha city, NE	390 007	37	44	Fresno city, CA	270.3	44		Omaha city, NE	1 301.3
45	Minneapolis city, MN	382 618	40	45	Sacramento city, CA	251.6	67		Riverside city, CA	1 261.3
46	Honolulu CDP, HI	371 657	19	46	Milwaukee city, WI	248.8	42		Mesa city, AZ	1 224.5
47	Miami city, FL	362 470	53	47	Arlington city, TX	248.2	39		Atlanta city, GA	1 220.6
48	Colorado Springs city, CO	360 890	46	48	Honolulu CDP, HI	222.0	74		Baton Rouge city, LA	1 144.8
49	St. Louis city, MO	348 189	24	49	Seattle city, WA	217.2	9		San Antonio city, TX	1 084.4
50	Wichita city, KS	344 284	17	50	Baltimore city, MD	209.3	6		Phoenix city, AZ	1 074.1
51	Santa Ana city, CA	337 977	56	51	Toledo city, OH	208.8	57		Tampa city, FL	1 045.6
52	Pittsburgh city, PA	334 563	67	52	Riverside city, CA	202.3	31		New Orleans city, LA	1 036.5
53	Arlington city, TX	332 969	54	53	Cincinnati city, OH	201.9	16		Austin city, TX	1 007.9
54	Cincinnati city, OH	331 285	33	54	Cleveland city, OH	200.9	50		Wichita city, KS	979.2
55	Anaheim city, CA	328 014	74	55	Baton Rouge city, LA	199.0	30		Tucson city, AZ	965.3
56	Toledo city, OH	313 619	66	56	Louisville city, KY	160.9	35		Albuquerque city, NM	958.8
57	Tampa city, FL	303 447	49	57	St. Louis city, MO	160.4	62		Raleigh city, NC	930.2
58	Buffalo city, NY	292 648	21	58	Washington city, DC	159.0	18		Memphis city, TN	898.7
59	St. Paul city, MN	287 151	68	59	St. Petersburg city, FL	154.4	23		El Paso city, TX	873.8
60	Corpus Christi city, TX	277 454	41	60	Oakland city, CA	145.2	26		Charlotte city, NC	861.9
61	Aurora city, CO	276 393	52	61	Pittsburgh city, PA	144.0	69		Bakersfield city, CA	843.5
62	Raleigh city, NC	276 093	45	62	Minneapolis city, MN	142.2	12		Indianapolis consolidated city,IN	834.3
63	Newark city, NJ	273 546	70	63	Stockton city, CA	141.7	43		Tulsa city, OK	830.8
64	Lexington-Fayette, KY	260 512	73	64	Norfolk city, VA	139.2	48		Colorado Springs city, CO	750.1
65	Anchorage city, AK	260 283	59	65	St. Paul city, MN	136.7	61		Aurora city, CO	748.8
66	Louisville city, KY	256 231	34	66	Long Beach city, CA	130.6	27		Fort Worth city, TX	705.7
67	Riverside city, CA	255 166	55	67	Anaheim city, CA	126.8	60		Corpus Christi city, TX	692.8
68	St. Petersburg city, FL	248 232	20	68	Boston city, MA	125.4	38		Virginia Beach city, VA	661.3
69	Bakersfield city, CA	247 057	13	69	San Francisco city, CA	120.9	71		Birmingham city, AL	625.3
70	Stockton city, CA	243 771	58	70	Buffalo city, NY	105.2	36		Kansas City, MO	543.7
71	Birmingham city, AL	242 820	47	71	Miami city, FL	92.4	22		Nashville-Davidsn consol. city,TN	438.1
72	Jersey City, NJ	240 055	51	72	Santa Ana city, CA	70.3	14		Jacksonville city, FL	374.9
73	Norfolk city, VA	234 403	63	73	Newark city, NJ	61.6	64		Lexington-Fayette, KY	353.5
74	Baton Rouge city, LA	227 818	75	74	Hialeah city, FL	49.8	29		Oklahoma City, OK	321.9
75	Hialeah city, FL	226 419	72	75	Jersey City, NJ	38.6	65		Anchorage city, AK	59.2

Note: Column numbers refer to Table D. Cities.

TABLE 6—75 Largest Cities by 2000 Population
Selected Rankings

Percent Population Change, 1990-2000				Percent White, 2000				Percent Black, 2000			
Population Rank	Percent Change Rank	City	[col 52] Percent Change	Population Rank	White Rank	City	[col 9] Percent White	Population Rank	Black Rank	City	[col 10] Percent Black
32	1	Las Vegas city, NV	85.3	75	1	Hialeah city, FL	88.0	10	1	Detroit city, MI	81.6
69	2	Bakersfield city, CA	40.2	42	2	Mesa city, AZ	81.7	71	2	Birmingham city, AL	73.5
16	3	Austin city, TX	39.1	64	3	Lexington-Fayette, KY	81.0	31	3	New Orleans city, LA	67.3
42	4	Mesa city, AZ	37.1	48	4	Colorado Springs city, CO	80.7	17	4	Baltimore city, MD	64.3
6	5	Phoenix city, AZ	34.2	44	5	Omaha city, NE	78.4	39	5	Atlanta city, GA	61.4
62	6	Raleigh city, NC	30.2	28	6	Portland city, OR	77.9	18	5	Memphis city, TN	61.4
26	7	Charlotte city, NC	28.9	50	7	Wichita city, KS	75.2	21	7	Washington city, DC	60.0
48	8	Colorado Springs city, CO	28.7	23	8	El Paso city, TX	73.3	63	8	Newark city, NJ	53.5
53	9	Arlington city, TX	27.2	65	9	Anchorage city, AK	72.2	49	9	St. Louis city, MO	51.2
61	10	Aurora city, CO	24.4	35	10	Albuquerque city, NM	71.6	33	10	Cleveland city, OH	51.0
55	11	Anaheim city, CA	23.1	60	10	Corpus Christi city, TX	71.6	74	11	Baton Rouge city, LA	50.0
37	12	Fresno city, CA	20.8	68	12	St. Petersburg city, FL	71.4	73	12	Norfolk city, VA	44.1
75	13	Hialeah city, FL	20.4	38	12	Virginia Beach city, VA	71.4	5	13	Philadelphia city, PA	43.2
27	14	Fort Worth city, TX	19.5	6	14	Phoenix city, AZ	71.1	54	14	Cincinnati city, OH	42.9
4	15	Houston city, TX	19.3	56	15	Toledo city, OH	70.2	19	15	Milwaukee city, WI	37.3
9	15	San Antonio city, TX	19.3	30	15	Tucson city, AZ	70.2	58	16	Buffalo city, NY	37.2
25	17	Denver city, CO	18.6	24	17	Seattle city, WA	70.1	3	17	Chicago city, IL	36.8
30	18	Tucson city, AZ	18.3	43	17	Tulsa city, OK	70.1	41	18	Oakland city, CA	35.7
8	19	Dallas city, TX	18.0	32	19	Las Vegas city, NV	69.9	66	19	Louisville city, KY	33.0
35	20	Albuquerque city, NM	16.5	12	20	Indianapolis consolidated city,IN	69.3	26	20	Charlotte city, NC	32.7
64	21	Lexington-Fayette, KY	15.6	61	21	Aurora city, CO	68.9	36	21	Kansas City, MO	31.2
70	21	Stockton city, CA	15.6	29	22	Oklahoma City, OK	68.4	14	22	Jacksonville city, FL	29.0
65	23	Anchorage city, AK	15.0	15	23	Columbus city, OH	67.9	72	23	Jersey City, NJ	28.3
51	23	Santa Ana city, CA	15.0	53	24	Arlington city, TX	67.7	62	24	Raleigh city, NC	27.8
11	25	San Jose city, CA	14.4	9	24	San Antonio city, TX	67.7	52	25	Pittsburgh city, PA	27.1
28	26	Portland city, OR	14.1	52	26	Pittsburgh city, PA	67.0	1	26	New York City, NY	26.6
29	27	Oklahoma City, OK	13.8	22	27	Nashville-Davidsn consol. city,TN	67.0	57	27	Tampa city, FL	26.1
44	27	Omaha city, NE	13.8	59	27	St. Paul city, MN	67.0	8	28	Dallas city, TX	25.9
50	29	Wichita city, KS	13.2	47	29	Miami city, FL	66.6	22	28	Nashville-Davidsn consol. city,TN	25.9
67	30	Riverside city, CA	12.6	16	30	Austin city, TX	65.4	20	30	Boston city, MA	25.3
15	31	Columbus city, OH	12.4	25	31	Denver city, CO	65.3	4	30	Houston city, TX	25.3
22	32	Nashville-Davidsn consol. city,TN	11.6	45	32	Minneapolis city, MN	65.1	12	30	Indianapolis consolidated city,IN	25.3
40	33	Sacramento city, CA	10.2	14	33	Jacksonville city, FL	64.5	15	33	Columbus city, OH	24.5
7	33	San Diego city, CA	10.2	57	34	Tampa city, FL	64.2	56	34	Toledo city, OH	23.5
23	35	El Paso city, TX	9.4	62	35	Raleigh city, NC	63.3	68	35	St. Petersburg city, FL	22.4
1	35	New York City, NY	9.4	66	36	Louisville city, KY	62.9	47	36	Miami city, FL	22.3
14	37	Jacksonville city, FL	9.3	69	37	Bakersfield city, CA	61.9	27	37	Fort Worth city, TX	20.3
24	38	Seattle city, WA	9.1	36	38	Kansas City, MO	60.7	38	38	Virginia Beach city, VA	19.0
57	39	Tampa city, FL	8.4	7	39	San Diego city, CA	60.2	45	39	Minneapolis city, MN	18.0
38	40	Virginia Beach city, VA	8.2	27	40	Fort Worth city, TX	59.7	40	40	Sacramento city, CA	15.5
60	41	Corpus Christi city, TX	7.8	67	41	Riverside city, CA	59.3	43	40	Tulsa city, OK	15.5
34	42	Long Beach city, CA	7.5	26	42	Charlotte city, NC	58.3	29	42	Oklahoma City, OK	15.4
41	43	Oakland city, CA	7.3	55	43	Anaheim city, CA	54.8	34	43	Long Beach city, CA	14.9
13	43	San Francisco city, CA	7.3	20	44	Boston city, MA	54.5	53	44	Arlington city, TX	13.7
43	45	Tulsa city, OK	7.0	58	45	Buffalo city, NY	54.4	64	45	Lexington-Fayette, KY	13.5
12	46	Indianapolis consolidated city,IN	6.7	54	46	Cincinnati city, OH	53.0	61	46	Aurora city, CO	13.4
2	47	Los Angeles city, CA	6.0	8	47	Dallas city, TX	50.8	44	47	Omaha city, NE	13.3
39	48	Atlanta city, GA	5.7	37	48	Fresno city, CA	50.2	59	48	St. Paul city, MN	11.7
59	49	St. Paul city, MN	5.5	19	49	Milwaukee city, WI	50.0	50	49	Wichita city, KS	11.4
18	50	Memphis city, TN	5.1	13	50	San Francisco city, CA	49.7	2	50	Los Angeles city, CA	11.2
72	51	Jersey City, NJ	5.0	4	51	Houston city, TX	49.3	70	50	Stockton city, CA	11.2
3	52	Chicago city, IL	4.0	73	52	Norfolk city, VA	48.4	25	52	Denver city, CO	11.1
45	53	Minneapolis city, MN	3.9	40	53	Sacramento city, CA	48.3	32	53	Las Vegas city, NV	10.4
74	54	Baton Rouge city, LA	3.8	11	54	San Jose city, CA	47.5	16	54	Austin city, TX	10.0
68	55	St. Petersburg city, FL	3.3	2	55	Los Angeles city, CA	46.9	69	55	Bakersfield city, CA	9.2
20	56	Boston city, MA	2.6	74	56	Baton Rouge city, LA	45.7	37	56	Fresno city, CA	8.4
36	57	Kansas City, MO	1.5	34	57	Long Beach city, CA	45.2	24	56	Seattle city, WA	8.4
47	58	Miami city, FL	1.1	5	58	Philadelphia city, PA	45.0	7	58	San Diego city, CA	7.9
63	59	Newark city, NJ	-0.6	1	59	New York City, NY	44.7	13	59	San Francisco city, CA	7.8
46	60	Honolulu CDP, HI	-1.4	49	60	St. Louis city, MO	43.8	67	60	Riverside city, CA	7.4
31	61	New Orleans city, LA	-2.5	70	61	Stockton city, CA	43.3	9	61	San Antonio city, TX	6.8
5	62	Philadelphia city, PA	-4.3	51	62	Santa Ana city, CA	42.7	48	62	Colorado Springs city, CO	6.6
66	63	Louisville city, KY	-4.9	3	63	Chicago city, IL	42.0	28	62	Portland city, OR	6.6
19	64	Milwaukee city, WI	-5.0	33	64	Cleveland city, OH	41.5	65	64	Anchorage city, AK	5.8
33	65	Cleveland city, OH	-5.4	18	65	Memphis city, TN	34.4	6	65	Phoenix city, AZ	5.1
21	66	Washington city, DC	-5.7	72	66	Jersey City, NJ	34.0	60	66	Corpus Christi city, TX	4.7
56	67	Toledo city, OH	-5.8	39	67	Atlanta city, GA	33.2	30	67	Tucson city, AZ	4.3
10	68	Detroit city, MI	-7.5	17	68	Baltimore city, MD	31.6	11	68	San Jose city, CA	3.5
71	69	Birmingham city, AL	-8.5	41	69	Oakland city, CA	31.3	35	69	Albuquerque city, NM	3.1
54	70	Cincinnati city, OH	-9.0	21	70	Washington city, DC	30.8	23	69	El Paso city, TX	3.1
52	71	Pittsburgh city, PA	-9.5	31	71	New Orleans city, LA	28.1	55	71	Anaheim city, CA	2.7
73	72	Norfolk city, VA	-10.3	63	72	Newark city, NJ	26.5	42	72	Mesa city, AZ	2.5
58	73	Buffalo city, NY	-10.8	71	73	Birmingham city, AL	24.1	75	73	Hialeah city, FL	2.4
17	74	Baltimore city, MD	-11.5	46	74	Honolulu CDP, HI	19.7	51	74	Santa Ana city, CA	1.7
49	75	St. Louis city, MO	-12.2	10	75	Detroit city, MI	12.3	46	75	Honolulu CDP, HI	1.6

Note: Column numbers refer to Table D. Cities.

TABLE 6—75 Largest Cities by 2000 Population
Selected Rankings

Percent American Indian and Alaska Native, 2000				Percent Asian, 2000				Percent Two or More Races, 2000			
Population Rank	American Indian and Alaska Native Rank	City	[col 11] Percent American Indian and Alaska Native	Population Rank	Asian Rank	City	[col 12] Percent Asian	Population Rank	Two or More Race Rank	City	[col 15] Percent Two or More Races
65	1	Anchorage city, AK	7.3	46	1	Honolulu CDP, HI	55.9	46	1	Honolulu CDP, HI	14.9
43	2	Tulsa city, OK	4.7	13	2	San Francisco city, CA	30.8	70	2	Stockton city, CA	6.8
35	3	Albuquerque city, NM	3.9	11	3	San Jose city, CA	26.9	40	3	Sacramento city, CA	6.4
29	4	Oklahoma City, OK	3.5	70	4	Stockton city, CA	19.9	65	4	Anchorage city, AK	6.0
30	5	Tucson city, AZ	2.3	40	5	Sacramento city, CA	16.6	72	5	Jersey City, NJ	5.8
45	6	Minneapolis city, MN	2.2	72	6	Jersey City, NJ	16.2	34	6	Long Beach city, CA	5.3
6	7	Phoenix city, AZ	2.0	41	7	Oakland city, CA	15.2	37	7	Fresno city, CA	5.2
42	8	Mesa city, AZ	1.7	7	8	San Diego city, CA	13.6	2	7	Los Angeles city, CA	5.2
37	9	Fresno city, CA	1.6	24	9	Seattle city, WA	13.1	67	9	Riverside city, CA	5.1
69	10	Bakersfield city, CA	1.4	59	10	St. Paul city, MN	12.4	55	10	Anaheim city, CA	5.0
25	11	Denver city, CO	1.3	55	11	Anaheim city, CA	12.0	41	10	Oakland city, CA	5.0
40	11	Sacramento city, CA	1.3	34	11	Long Beach city, CA	12.0	11	10	San Jose city, CA	5.0
51	13	Santa Ana city, CA	1.2	37	13	Fresno city, CA	11.2	1	13	New York City, NY	4.9
50	13	Wichita city, KS	1.2	2	14	Los Angeles city, CA	10.0	7	14	San Diego city, CA	4.8
28	15	Portland city, OR	1.1	1	15	New York City, NY	9.8	47	15	Miami city, FL	4.7
67	15	Riverside city, CA	1.1	51	16	Santa Ana city, CA	8.8	51	16	Santa Ana city, CA	4.6
59	15	St. Paul city, MN	1.1	20	17	Boston city, MA	7.5	24	17	Seattle city, WA	4.5
70	15	Stockton city, CA	1.1	28	18	Portland city, OR	6.3	69	18	Bakersfield city, CA	4.4
24	19	Seattle city, WA	1.0	45	19	Minneapolis city, MN	6.1	20	18	Boston city, MA	4.4
55	20	Anaheim city, CA	0.9	53	20	Arlington city, TX	6.0	45	18	Minneapolis city, MN	4.4
48	20	Colorado Springs city, CO	0.9	67	21	Riverside city, CA	5.7	63	18	Newark city, NJ	4.4
19	20	Milwaukee city, WI	0.9	65	22	Anchorage city, AK	5.5	43	18	Tulsa city, OK	4.4
61	23	Aurora city, CO	0.8	4	23	Houston city, TX	5.3	35	23	Albuquerque city, NM	4.3
58	23	Buffalo city, NY	0.8	38	24	Virginia Beach city, VA	4.9	13	23	San Francisco city, CA	4.3
23	23	El Paso city, TX	0.8	32	25	Las Vegas city, NV	4.8	61	25	Aurora city, CO	4.2
34	23	Long Beach city, CA	0.8	16	26	Austin city, TX	4.7	32	26	Las Vegas city, NV	4.1
2	23	Los Angeles city, CA	0.8	8	27	Philadelphia city, PA	4.5	28	26	Portland city, OR	4.1
9	23	San Antonio city, TX	0.8	61	28	Aurora city, CO	4.4	48	28	Colorado Springs city, CO	3.9
11	23	San Jose city, CA	0.8	69	29	Bakersfield city, CA	4.3	29	28	Oklahoma City, OK	3.9
32	30	Las Vegas city, NV	0.7	3	29	Chicago city, IL	4.3	59	28	St. Paul city, MN	3.9
41	30	Oakland city, CA	0.7	50	31	Wichita city, KS	4.0	30	31	Tucson city, AZ	3.8
44	30	Omaha city, NE	0.7	29	32	Oklahoma City, OK	3.5	25	32	Denver city, CO	3.7
16	33	Austin city, TX	0.6	26	33	Charlotte city, NC	3.4	9	32	San Antonio city, TX	3.7
60	33	Corpus Christi city, TX	0.6	15	34	Columbus city, OH	3.4	75	34	Hialeah city, FL	3.6
27	33	Fort Worth city, TX	0.6	62	35	Raleigh city, NC	3.4	23	35	El Paso city, TX	3.4
7	33	San Diego city, CA	0.6	19	36	Milwaukee city, WI	2.9	6	36	Phoenix city, AZ	3.3
53	37	Arlington city, TX	0.5	48	37	Colorado Springs city, CO	2.8	60	37	Corpus Christi city, TX	3.1
8	37	Dallas city, TX	0.5	25	37	Denver city, CO	2.8	4	37	Houston city, TX	3.1
36	37	Kansas City, MO	0.5	14	37	Jacksonville city, FL	2.8	50	37	Wichita city, KS	3.1
1	37	New York City, NY	0.5	73	37	Norfolk city, VA	2.8	16	40	Austin city, TX	3.0
73	37	Norfolk city, VA	0.5	8	41	Dallas city, TX	2.7	53	41	Arlington city, TX	2.9
20	42	Boston city, MA	0.4	52	41	Pittsburgh city, PA	2.7	3	41	Chicago city, IL	2.9
3	42	Chicago city, IL	0.4	68	41	St. Petersburg city, FL	2.7	57	41	Tampa city, FL	2.9
4	42	Houston city, TX	0.4	21	41	Washington city, DC	2.7	42	44	Mesa city, AZ	2.8
72	42	Jersey City, NJ	0.4	74	45	Baton Rouge city, LA	2.6	8	45	Dallas city, TX	2.7
63	42	Newark city, NJ	0.4	27	45	Fort Worth city, TX	2.6	27	45	Fort Worth city, TX	2.7
62	42	Raleigh city, NC	0.4	64	47	Lexington-Fayette, KY	2.5	19	45	Milwaukee city, WI	2.7
13	42	San Francisco city, CA	0.4	30	47	Tucson city, AZ	2.5	38	45	Virginia Beach city, VA	2.7
57	42	Tampa city, FL	0.4	22	49	Nashville-Davidsn consol. city,TN	2.3	15	49	Columbus city, OH	2.6
38	42	Virginia Beach city, VA	0.4	31	49	New Orleans city, LA	2.3	56	49	Toledo city, OH	2.6
17	51	Baltimore city, MD	0.3	35	51	Albuquerque city, NM	2.2	58	51	Buffalo city, NY	2.5
26	51	Charlotte city, NC	0.3	57	51	Tampa city, FL	2.2	73	51	Norfolk city, VA	2.5
33	51	Cleveland city, OH	0.3	6	53	Phoenix city, AZ	2.0	36	53	Kansas City, MO	2.4
15	51	Columbus city, OH	0.3	49	53	St. Louis city, MO	2.0	21	53	Washington city, DC	2.4
10	51	Detroit city, MI	0.3	39	55	Atlanta city, GA	1.9	10	55	Detroit city, MI	2.3
12	51	Indianapolis consolidated city,IN.	0.3	36	55	Kansas City, MO	1.9	33	56	Cleveland city, OH	2.2
14	51	Jacksonville city, FL	0.3	43	57	Tulsa city, OK	1.8	5	56	Philadelphia city, PA	2.2
22	51	Nashville-Davidsn consol. city,TN	0.3	44	58	Omaha city, NE	1.7	68	56	St. Petersburg city, FL	2.2
5	51	Philadelphia city, PA	0.3	9	59	San Antonio city, TX	1.6	14	59	Jacksonville city, FL	2.0
49	51	St. Louis city, MO	0.3	17	60	Baltimore city, MD	1.5	22	59	Nashville-Davidsn consol. city,TN	2.0
68	51	St. Petersburg city, FL	0.3	54	60	Cincinnati city, OH	1.5	44	61	Omaha city, NE	1.9
56	51	Toledo city, OH	0.3	18	60	Memphis city, TN	1.5	62	61	Raleigh city, NC	1.9
21	51	Washington city, DC	0.3	42	60	Mesa city, AZ	1.5	49	61	St. Louis city, MO	1.9
39	64	Atlanta city, GA	0.2	58	64	Buffalo city, NY	1.4	26	64	Charlotte city, NC	1.7
74	64	Baton Rouge city, LA	0.2	12	64	Indianapolis consolidated city,IN	1.4	54	64	Cincinnati city, OH	1.7
71	64	Birmingham city, AL	0.2	66	64	Louisville city, KY	1.4	66	64	Louisville city, KY	1.7
54	64	Cincinnati city, OH	0.2	33	67	Cleveland city, OH	1.3	12	67	Indianapolis consolidated city,IN	1.6
46	64	Honolulu CDP, HI	0.2	60	67	Corpus Christi city, TX	1.3	64	67	Lexington-Fayette, KY	1.6
64	64	Lexington-Fayette, KY	0.2	63	69	Newark city, NJ	1.2	52	67	Pittsburgh city, PA	1.6
66	64	Louisville city, KY	0.2	23	70	El Paso city, TX	1.1	17	70	Baltimore city, MD	1.5
18	64	Memphis city, TN	0.2	10	71	Detroit city, MI	1.0	31	71	New Orleans city, LA	1.3
47	64	Miami city, FL	0.2	56	71	Toledo city, OH	1.0	39	72	Atlanta city, GA	1.2
31	64	New Orleans city, LA	0.2	71	73	Birmingham city, AL	0.8	74	73	Baton Rouge city, LA	1.0
52	64	Pittsburgh city, PA	0.2	47	74	Miami city, FL	0.7	18	73	Memphis city, TN	1.0
75	75	Hialeah city, FL	0.1	75	75	Hialeah city, FL	0.4	71	75	Birmingham city, AL	0.8

Note: Column numbers refer to Table D. Cities.

TABLE 6—75 Largest Cities by 2000 Population
Selected Rankings

Population Rank	Hispanic Rank	City	[col 22] Percent Hispanic	Population Rank	Under 18 Years Rank	City	[cols 28 & 29] Percent Under 18 Years	Population Rank	25 to 54 Years Rank	City	[cols 31, 32 & 33] Percent 25 to 54 Years
75	1	Hialeah city, FL	90.3	51	1	Santa Ana city, CA	34.2	13	1	San Francisco city, CA	54.3
23	2	El Paso city, TX	76.6	37	2	Fresno city, CA	32.9	24	2	Seattle city, WA	53.1
51	3	Santa Ana city, CA	76.1	69	3	Bakersfield city, CA	32.7	28	3	Portland city, OR	49.5
47	4	Miami city, FL	65.8	70	4	Stockton city, CA	32.4	26	4	Charlotte city, NC	49.1
9	5	San Antonio city, TX	58.7	10	5	Detroit city, MI	31.1	25	5	Denver city, CO	48.9
60	6	Corpus Christi city, TX	54.3	23	5	El Paso city, TX	31.1	65	6	Anchorage city, AK	48.8
55	7	Anaheim city, CA	46.8	55	7	Anaheim city, CA	30.2	16	7	Austin city, TX	48.7
2	8	Los Angeles city, CA	46.5	67	8	Riverside city, CA	30.1	45	8	Minneapolis city, MN	48.5
35	9	Albuquerque city, NM	39.9	65	9	Anchorage city, AK	29.2	62	8	Raleigh city, NC	48.5
37	10	Fresno city, CA	39.9	34	9	Long Beach city, CA	29.2	53	10	Arlington city, TX	48.0
67	11	Riverside city, CA	38.1	6	11	Phoenix city, AZ	29.0	61	10	Aurora city, CO	48.0
4	12	Houston city, TX	37.4	19	12	Milwaukee city, WI	28.7	11	12	San Jose city, CA	47.8
34	13	Long Beach city, CA	35.8	9	13	San Antonio city, TX	28.6	41	13	Oakland city, CA	47.4
30	14	Tucson city, AZ	35.7	33	14	Cleveland city, OH	28.5	39	14	Atlanta city, GA	47.2
8	15	Dallas city, TX	35.6	53	15	Arlington city, TX	28.3	22	14	Nashville-Davidsn consol. city, TN	47.2
6	16	Phoenix city, AZ	34.1	27	15	Fort Worth city, TX	28.3	72	16	Jersey City, NJ	46.9
69	17	Bakersfield city, CA	32.5	60	17	Corpus Christi city, TX	28.2	38	16	Virginia Beach city, VA	46.9
70	17	Stockton city, CA	32.5	63	18	Newark city, NJ	28.0	20	18	Boston city, MA	46.7
25	19	Denver city, CO	31.7	18	19	Memphis city, TN	27.9	15	19	Columbus city, OH	46.5
16	20	Austin city, TX	30.5	61	20	Aurora city, CO	27.6	8	20	Dallas city, TX	46.4
11	21	San Jose city, CA	30.2	38	21	Virginia Beach city, VA	27.5	64	20	Lexington-Fayette, KY	46.4
27	22	Fort Worth city, TX	29.8	4	22	Houston city, TX	27.4	48	22	Colorado Springs city, CO	46.3
63	23	Newark city, NJ	29.5	42	23	Mesa city, AZ	27.3	21	22	Washington city, DC	46.3
72	24	Jersey City, NJ	28.3	40	23	Sacramento city, CA	27.3	7	24	San Diego city, CA	46.0
1	25	New York City, NY	27.0	59	25	St Paul city, MN	27.1	4	25	Houston city, TX	45.7
3	26	Chicago city, IL	26.0	50	25	Wichita city, KS	27.1	2	26	Los Angeles city, CA	45.6
7	27	San Diego city, CA	25.4	14	27	Jacksonville city, FL	26.7	12	27	Indianapolis consolidated city, IN	45.5
32	28	Las Vegas city, NV	23.6	31	27	New Orleans city, LA	26.7	1	27	New York City, NY	45.5
41	29	Oakland city, CA	21.9	48	29	Colorado Springs city, CO	26.5	14	29	Jacksonville city, FL	45.4
40	30	Sacramento city, CA	21.6	8	29	Dallas city, TX	26.5	36	30	Kansas City, MO	45.3
61	31	Aurora city, CO	19.8	2	29	Los Angeles city, CA	26.5	6	31	Phoenix city, AZ	45.1
42	32	Mesa city, AZ	19.7	11	32	San Jose city, CA	26.4	57	32	Tampa city, FL	45.0
57	33	Tampa city, FL	19.3	58	33	Buffalo city, NY	26.3	35	33	Albuquerque city, NM	44.8
53	34	Arlington city, TX	18.3	3	34	Chicago city, IL	26.2	3	33	Chicago city, IL	44.8
20	35	Boston city, MA	14.4	56	34	Toledo city, OH	26.2	55	35	Anaheim city, CA	44.5
13	36	San Francisco city, CA	14.1	32	36	Las Vegas city, NV	25.9	32	35	Las Vegas city, NV	44.5
48	37	Colorado Springs city, CO	12.0	49	37	St. Louis city, MO	25.7	34	35	Long Beach city, CA	44.5
19	37	Milwaukee city, WI	12.0	12	38	Indianapolis consolidated city, IN	25.6	46	38	Honolulu CDP, HI	44.3
29	39	Oklahoma City, OK	10.1	44	38	Omaha city, NE	25.6	27	39	Fort Worth city, TX	44.2
50	40	Wichita city, KS	9.6	29	40	Oklahoma City, OK	25.5	68	39	St. Petersburg city, FL	44.2
5	41	Philadelphia city, PA	8.5	36	41	Kansas City, MO	25.4	29	41	Oklahoma City, OK	44.0
59	42	St. Paul city, MN	7.9	5	42	Philadelphia city, PA	25.3	59	41	St. Paul city, MN	44.0
21	42	Washington city, DC	7.9	71	43	Birmingham city, AL	25.0	44	43	Omaha city, NE	43.8
45	44	Minneapolis city, MN	7.6	41	43	Oakland city, CA	25.0	66	44	Louisville city, KY	43.6
58	45	Buffalo city, NY	7.5	17	45	Baltimore city, MD	24.8	40	45	Sacramento city, CA	43.5
44	45	Omaha city, NE	7.5	43	45	Tulsa city, OK	24.8	50	45	Wichita city, KS	43.5
26	47	Charlotte city, NC	7.4	26	47	Charlotte city, NC	24.7	54	47	Cincinnati city, OH	43.3
33	48	Cleveland city, OH	7.3	72	47	Jersey City, NJ	24.7	43	48	Tulsa city, OK	43.2
43	49	Tulsa city, OK	7.2	57	47	Tampa city, FL	24.7	18	49	Memphis city, TN	43.1
62	50	Raleigh city, NC	7.0	35	50	Albuquerque city, NM	24.6	71	50	Birmingham city, AL	42.9
36	51	Kansas City, MO	6.9	54	51	Cincinnati city, OH	24.5	63	50	Newark city, NJ	42.9
28	52	Portland city, OR	6.8	30	51	Tucson city, AZ	24.5	9	50	San Antonio city, TX	42.9
65	53	Anchorage city, AK	5.7	74	53	Baton Rouge city, LA	24.4	17	53	Baltimore city, MD	42.7
56	54	Toledo city, OH	5.5	1	54	New York City, NY	24.3	51	53	Santa Ana city, CA	42.7
24	55	Seattle city, WA	5.3	15	55	Columbus city, OH	24.2	49	53	St. Louis city, MO	42.7
10	56	Detroit city, MI	5.0	73	56	Norfolk city, VA	24.1	47	56	Miami city, FL	42.6
22	57	Nashville-Davidsn consol. city, TN	4.6	7	57	San Diego city, CA	24.0	60	57	Corpus Christi city, TX	42.4
39	58	Atlanta city, GA	4.5	66	58	Louisville city, KY	23.6	31	57	New Orleans city, LA	42.4
46	59	Honolulu CDP, HI	4.4	75	59	Hialeah city, FL	23.0	30	57	Tucson city, AZ	42.4
14	60	Jacksonville city, FL	4.2	16	60	Austin city, TX	22.5	56	60	Toledo city, OH	42.0
68	60	St. Petersburg city, FL	4.2	39	61	Atlanta city, GA	22.3	69	61	Bakersfield city, CA	41.9
38	60	Virginia Beach city, VA	4.2	22	62	Nashville-Davidsn consol. city, TN	22.2	33	61	Cleveland city, OH	41.9
12	63	Indianapolis consolidated city, IN	3.9	45	63	Minneapolis city, MN	22.0	10	63	Detroit city, MI	41.8
73	64	Norfolk city, VA	3.8	25	64	Denver city, CO	21.9	19	64	Milwaukee city, WI	41.6
64	65	Lexington-Fayette, KY	3.3	47	65	Miami city, FL	21.8	67	65	Riverside city, CA	41.5
31	66	New Orleans city, LA	3.1	68	66	St. Petersburg city, FL	21.5	58	66	Buffalo city, NY	41.3
18	67	Memphis city, TN	3.0	64	67	Lexington-Fayette, KY	21.3	75	66	Hialeah city, FL	41.3
15	68	Columbus city, OH	2.5	28	68	Portland city, OR	21.1	5	66	Philadelphia city, PA	41.3
49	69	St. Louis city, MO	2.0	62	69	Raleigh city, NC	20.8	52	69	Pittsburgh city, PA	40.9
66	70	Louisville city, KY	1.9	21	70	Washington city, DC	20.1	23	70	El Paso city, TX	40.8
17	71	Baltimore city, MD	1.7	52	71	Pittsburgh city, PA	19.9	42	70	Mesa city, AZ	40.8
74	71	Baton Rouge city, LA	1.7	20	72	Boston city, MA	19.7	73	72	Norfolk city, VA	40.6
71	73	Birmingham city, AL	1.6	46	73	Honolulu CDP, HI	19.2	37	73	Fresno city, CA	39.9
54	74	Cincinnati city, OH	1.3	24	74	Seattle city, WA	15.6	70	74	Stockton city, CA	39.2
52	74	Pittsburgh city, PA	1.3	13	75	San Francisco city, CA	14.6	74	75	Baton Rouge city, LA	39.1

Note: Column numbers refer to Table D. Cities.

TABLE 6—75 Largest Cities by 2000 Population
Selected Rankings

Percent Age 65 Years and Over, 2000				Percent Female-headed Family Households, 2000				Percent Living Alone, 2000			
Population Rank	65 Years and Over Rank	City	[cols 35 & 36] Percent 65 Years and Over	Population Rank	Female Households Rate	City	[col 76] Percent Female Households	Population Rank	Living Alone Rank	City	[col 79] Percent Living Alone
46	1	Honolulu CDP, HI	17.8	10	1	Detroit city, MI	31.6	21	1	Washington city, DC	43.8
68	2	St. Petersburg city, FL	17.4	63	2	Newark city, NJ	29.3	54	2	Cincinnati city, OH	42.8
47	3	Miami city, FL	17.0	17	3	Baltimore city, MD	25.0	24	3	Seattle city, WA	40.8
75	4	Hialeah city, FL	16.6	33	4	Cleveland city, OH	24.8	45	4	Minneapolis city, MN	40.3
52	5	Pittsburgh city, PA	16.4	71	5	Birmingham city, AL	24.6	49	4	St. Louis city, MO	40.3
66	6	Louisville city, KY	14.7	31	6	New Orleans city, LA	24.5	52	6	Pittsburgh city, PA	39.4
5	7	Philadelphia city, PA	14.1	18	7	Memphis city, TN	23.8	25	7	Denver city, CO	39.3
49	8	St. Louis city, MO	13.7	58	8	Buffalo city, NY	22.3	13	8	San Francisco city, CA	38.6
13	9	San Francisco city, CA	13.6	5	8	Philadelphia city, PA	22.3	39	9	Atlanta city, GA	38.5
58	10	Buffalo city, NY	13.5	49	10	St. Louis city, MO	21.3	66	10	Louisville city, KY	37.9
71	11	Birmingham city, AL	13.4	19	11	Milwaukee city, WI	21.1	58	11	Buffalo city, NY	37.7
42	12	Mesa city, AZ	13.3	39	12	Atlanta city, GA	20.7	20	12	Boston city, MA	37.1
17	13	Baltimore city, MD	13.2	72	13	Jersey City, NJ	20.2	59	13	St. Paul city, MN	35.9
56	14	Toledo city, OH	13.1	66	14	Louisville city, KY	19.2	68	14	St. Petersburg city, FL	35.6
43	15	Tulsa city, OK	12.8	1	15	New York City, NY	19.1	33	15	Cleveland city, OH	35.2
33	16	Cleveland city, OH	12.5	74	16	Baton Rouge city, LA	19.0	17	16	Baltimore city, MD	34.9
57	16	Tampa city, FL	12.5	3	17	Chicago city, IL	18.9	28	17	Portland city, OR	34.6
54	18	Cincinnati city, OH	12.3	21	17	Washington city, DC	18.9	71	18	Birmingham city, AL	34.4
21	19	Washington city, DC	12.2	73	19	Norfolk city, VA	18.8	15	19	Columbus city, OH	34.1
24	20	Seattle city, WA	12.0	47	20	Miami city, FL	18.7	36	19	Kansas City, MO	34.1
30	21	Tucson city, AZ	11.9	54	21	Cincinnati city, OH	18.6	43	21	Tulsa city, OK	33.9
50	21	Wichita city, KS	11.9	23	22	El Paso city, TX	18.5	5	22	Philadelphia city, PA	33.8
35	21	Albuquerque city, NM	11.9	41	23	Oakland city, CA	17.7	57	23	Tampa city, FL	33.7
36	24	Kansas City, MO	11.8	37	24	Fresno city, CA	17.6	19	24	Milwaukee city, WI	33.5
44	24	Omaha city, NE	11.8	75	25	Hialeah city, FL	17.4	22	25	Nashville-Davidsn consol. city,TN	33.4
31	26	New Orleans city, LA	11.7	70	26	Stockton city, CA	17.3	31	26	New Orleans city, LA	33.2
1	26	New York city, NY	11.7	56	27	Toledo city, OH	17.2	62	27	Raleigh city, NC	33.1
32	28	Las Vegas city, NV	11.6	52	28	Pittsburgh city, PA	16.5	8	28	Dallas city, TX	32.9
29	29	Oklahoma City, OK	11.5	20	29	Boston city, MA	16.4	16	29	Austin city, TX	32.8
28	29	Portland city, OR	11.5	9	30	San Antonio city, TX	16.4	56	29	Toledo city, OH	32.8
40	31	Sacramento city, CA	11.4	34	31	Long Beach city, CA	16.1	3	31	Chicago city, IL	32.6
74	31	Baton Rouge city, LA	11.4	57	31	Tampa city, FL	16.1	41	32	Oakland city, CA	32.5
25	33	Denver city, CO	11.2	14	33	Jacksonville city, FL	16.0	30	33	Tucson city, AZ	32.3
22	33	Nashville-Davidsn consol. city,TN	11.2	36	33	Kansas City, MO	16.0	12	34	Indianapolis consolidated city,IN	32.0
60	35	Corpus Christi city, TX	11.1	69	35	Bakersfield city, CA	15.5	40	34	Sacramento city, CA	32.0
12	36	Indianapolis consolidated city,IN	11.0	60	36	Corpus Christi city, TX	15.4	1	36	New York City, NY	31.9
19	37	Milwaukee city, WI	10.9	40	36	Sacramento city, CA	15.4	44	36	Omaha city, NE	31.9
73	37	Norfolk city, VA	10.9	4	38	Houston city, TX	15.3	74	38	Baton Rouge city, LA	31.7
18	37	Memphis city, TN	10.9	12	39	Indianapolis consolidated city,IN	15.0	64	38	Lexington-Fayette city, KY	31.7
23	40	El Paso city, TX	10.6	8	40	Dallas city, TX	14.9	50	40	Wichita city, KS	31.2
10	41	Detroit city, MI	10.5	67	41	Riverside city, CA	14.8	29	41	Oklahoma City, OK	30.7
41	41	Oakland city, CA	10.5	27	42	Fort Worth city, TX	14.7	35	42	Albuquerque city, NM	30.5
7	41	San Diego city, CA	10.5	15	43	Columbus city, OH	14.5	18	42	Memphis city, TN	30.5
20	44	Boston city, MA	10.4	2	43	Los Angeles city, CA	14.5	47	44	Miami city, FL	30.4
9	44	San Antonio city, TX	10.4	22	45	Nashville-Davidsn consol. city,TN	14.3	73	45	Norfolk city, VA	30.2
3	46	Chicago city, IL	10.3	59	46	St. Paul city, MN	13.9	10	46	Detroit city, MI	29.7
14	46	Jacksonville city, FL	10.3	68	47	St. Petersburg city, FL	13.8	46	46	Honolulu CDP, HI	29.7
59	46	St. Paul city, MN	10.3	30	47	Tucson city, AZ	13.8	4	48	Houston city, TX	29.6
70	49	Stockton city, CA	10.2	26	49	Charlotte city, NC	13.7	34	48	Long Beach city, CA	29.6
64	50	Lexington-Fayette city, KY	10.0	51	50	Santa Ana city, CA	13.5	26	50	Charlotte city, NC	29.5
39	51	Atlanta city, GA	9.7	29	51	Oklahoma City, OK	13.2	72	51	Jersey City, NJ	29.2
72	51	Jersey City, NJ	9.7	55	52	Anaheim city, CA	13.1	27	52	Fort Worth city, TX	28.6
2	51	Los Angeles city, CA	9.7	61	52	Aurora city, CO	13.1	2	53	Los Angeles city, CA	28.5
48	54	Colorado Springs city, CO	9.6	44	54	Omaha city, NE	13.0	7	54	San Diego city, CA	28.0
27	54	Fort Worth city, TX	9.6	35	55	Albuquerque city, NM	12.9	61	55	Aurora city, CO	27.4
37	56	Fresno city, CA	9.3	6	55	Phoenix city, AZ	12.9	48	56	Colorado Springs city, CO	27.0
63	56	Newark city, NJ	9.3	43	55	Tulsa city, OK	12.9	63	57	Newark city, NJ	26.6
34	58	Long Beach city, CA	9.1	38	58	Virginia Beach city, VA	12.4	14	58	Jacksonville city, FL	26.2
45	58	Minneapolis city, MN	9.1	45	59	Minneapolis city, MN	12.3	6	59	Phoenix city, AZ	25.4
67	60	Riverside city, CA	9.0	32	60	Las Vegas city, NV	12.2	9	60	San Antonio city, TX	25.1
26	61	Charlotte city, NC	8.8	46	61	Honolulu CDP, HI	12.1	32	61	Las Vegas city, NV	25.0
15	61	Columbus city, OH	8.8	53	62	Arlington city, TX	11.8	53	62	Arlington city, TX	24.7
69	63	Bakersfield city, CA	8.7	11	63	San Jose city, CA	11.7	42	63	Mesa city, AZ	24.2
8	64	Dallas city, TX	8.6	50	64	Wichita city, KS	11.6	65	64	Anchorage city, AK	23.4
38	65	Virginia Beach city, VA	8.5	65	65	Anchorage city, AK	11.5	37	65	Fresno city, CA	23.3
4	66	Houston city, TX	8.4	64	65	Lexington-Fayette city, KY	11.5	60	66	Corpus Christi city, TX	23.2
62	66	Raleigh city, NC	8.4	62	67	Raleigh city, NC	11.4	70	67	Stockton city, CA	22.9
11	68	San Jose city, CA	8.3	7	67	San Diego city, CA	11.4	69	68	Bakersfield city, CA	21.5
55	69	Anaheim city, CA	8.2	16	69	Austin city, TX	10.8	67	68	Riverside city, CA	21.5
6	70	Phoenix city, AZ	8.1	25	69	Denver city, CO	10.8	38	70	Virginia Beach city, VA	20.4
61	71	Aurora city, CO	7.4	28	69	Portland city, OR	10.8	23	71	El Paso city, TX	19.2
16	72	Austin city, TX	6.7	48	72	Colorado Springs city, CO	10.6	11	72	San Jose city, CA	18.4
53	73	Arlington city, TX	6.1	42	72	Mesa city, AZ	10.6	55	73	Anaheim city, CA	18.1
65	74	Anchorage city, AK	5.5	13	74	San Francisco city, CA	8.9	75	74	Hialeah city, FL	14.7
51	74	Santa Ana city, CA	5.5	24	75	Seattle city, WA	8.1	51	75	Santa Ana city, CA	12.7

Note: Column numbers refer to Table D. Cities.

TABLE 6—75 Largest Cities by 2000 Population
Selected Rankings

Percent Married Couple Family Households, 2000				Percent of Families with Own Children Under 18 Years, 2000				Percent Change in Households, 1990-2000			
Population Rank	Married Couple Family Households Rank	City	[col 74] Percent in Married Couple Family Households	Population Rank	Families with Own Children Under 18 Years Rank	City	[col 73] Percent of Families with Own Children Under 18 Years	Population Rank	Change in Households Rank	City	[col 86] Percent Change in Households
51	1	Santa Ana city, CA	60.6	51	1	Santa Ana city, CA	53.2	32	1	Las Vegas city, NV	77.2
75	2	Hialeah city, FL	57.4	55	2	Anaheim city, CA	43.0	16	2	Austin city, TX	38.3
55	3	Anaheim city, CA	56.3	69	3	Bakersfield city, CA	42.5	42	3	Mesa city, AZ	36.0
11	4	San Jose city, CA	56.0	23	4	El Paso city, TX	42.4	26	4	Charlotte city, NC	35.5
38	5	Virginia Beach city, VA	55.7	70	5	Stockton city, CA	40.8	69	5	Bakersfield city, CA	33.6
23	6	El Paso city, TX	54.6	37	6	Fresno city, CA	40.4	62	6	Raleigh city, NC	31.2
42	7	Mesa city, AZ	52.7	67	7	Riverside city, CA	39.8	48	7	Colorado Springs city, CO	27.7
69	8	Bakersfield city, CA	52.1	65	8	Anchorage city, AK	38.9	6	8	Phoenix city, AZ	25.9
53	9	Arlington city, TX	51.6	38	9	Virginia Beach city, VA	38.8	9	9	San Antonio city, TX	24.1
48	10	Colorado Springs city, CO	51.5	11	10	San Jose city, CA	38.3	53	10	Arlington city, TX	23.9
65	11	Anchorage city, AK	51.1	53	11	Arlington city, TX	38.0	64	11	Lexington-Fayette, KY	21.0
60	12	Corpus Christi city, TX	50.9	75	12	Hialeah city, FL	36.2	28	12	Portland city, OR	19.5
67	13	Riverside city, CA	50.3	60	13	Corpus Christi city, TX	36.1	35	13	Albuquerque city, NM	19.1
32	14	Las Vegas city, NV	48.3	9	14	San Antonio city, TX	35.9	75	13	Hialeah city, FL	19.1
9	15	San Antonio city, TX	48.1	6	15	Phoenix city, AZ	35.7	30	15	Tucson city, AZ	18.6
70	15	Stockton city, CA	48.1	61	16	Aurora city, CO	35.5	61	16	Aurora city, CO	18.5
50	17	Wichita city, KS	47.3	63	17	Newark city, NJ	35.2	15	17	Columbus city, OH	17.3
61	18	Aurora city, CO	46.9	34	18	Long Beach city, CA	35.0	44	18	Omaha city, NE	17.1
6	18	Phoenix city, AZ	46.9	27	19	Fort Worth city, TX	34.7	4	19	Houston city, TX	16.4
14	20	Jacksonville city, FL	46.7	48	20	Colorado Springs city, CO	34.0	27	20	Fort Worth city, TX	15.9
37	21	Fresno city, CA	46.1	10	21	Detroit city, MI	33.9	37	21	Fresno city, CA	15.0
27	22	Fort Worth city, TX	45.8	14	21	Jacksonville city, FL	33.9	65	22	Anchorage city, AK	14.7
29	22	Oklahoma City, OK	45.8	2	23	Los Angeles city, CA	33.5	22	23	Nashville-Davidsn consol. city, TN	14.4
46	24	Honolulu CDP, HI	45.5	42	24	Mesa city, AZ	33.4	29	23	Oklahoma City, OK	14.4
7	25	San Diego city, CA	44.6	4	25	Houston city, TX	33.1	70	25	Stockton city, CA	14.2
44	26	Omaha city, NE	43.8	50	26	Wichita city, KS	32.1	38	26	Virginia Beach city, VA	13.9
35	27	Albuquerque city, NM	43.6	32	27	Las Vegas city, NV	31.9	25	27	Denver city, CO	13.4
26	27	Charlotte city, NC	43.6	18	28	Memphis city, TN	31.3	23	27	El Paso city, TX	13.4
64	29	Lexington-Fayette, KY	43.5	72	29	Jersey City, NJ	31.1	50	29	Wichita city, KS	12.9
4	30	Houston city, TX	43.2	29	30	Oklahoma City, OK	30.8	8	30	Dallas city, TX	12.4
43	31	Tulsa city, OK	43.1	26	31	Charlotte city, NC	30.6	7	31	San Diego city, CA	11.0
2	32	Los Angeles city, CA	41.9	19	32	Milwaukee city, WI	30.5	55	32	Anaheim city, CA	10.7
12	33	Indianapolis consolidated city, IN	40.7	8	33	Dallas city, TX	30.3	14	33	Jacksonville city, FL	10.6
22	34	Nashville-Davidsn consol. city, TN	39.9	73	33	Norfolk city, VA	30.3	11	34	San Jose city, CA	10.5
30	35	Tucson city, AZ	39.7	35	35	Albuquerque city, NM	30.2	60	35	Corpus Christi city, TX	10.4
62	36	Raleigh city, NC	39.5	40	35	Sacramento city, CA	30.2	12	36	Indianapolis consolidated city, IN	9.5
34	37	Long Beach city, CA	39.2	7	35	San Diego city, CA	30.2	24	37	Seattle city, WA	9.2
8	38	Dallas city, TX	38.8	44	38	Omaha city, NE	30.0	18	38	Memphis city, TN	9.1
40	39	Sacramento city, CA	38.4	33	39	Cleveland city, OH	29.9	67	39	Riverside city, CA	8.7
68	40	St. Petersburg city, FL	38.3	12	40	Indianapolis consolidated city, IN	29.8	57	39	Tampa city, FL	8.7
56	41	Toledo city, OH	38.2	56	40	Toledo city, OH	29.8	39	41	Atlanta city, GA	8.0
16	42	Austin city, TX	38.1	1	42	New York City, NY	29.7	13	42	San Francisco city, CA	7.9
28	42	Portland city, OR	38.1	31	43	New Orleans city, LA	29.2	72	43	Jersey City, NJ	7.6
36	44	Kansas City, MO	38.0	59	44	St. Paul city, MN	29.1	1	44	New York City, NY	7.2
1	45	New York City, NY	37.2	30	45	Tucson city, AZ	29.0	40	45	Sacramento city, CA	7.0
73	46	Norfolk city, VA	36.9	3	46	Chicago city, IL	28.9	74	46	Baton Rouge city, LA	6.8
47	47	Miami city, FL	36.6	58	47	Buffalo city, NY	28.6	43	47	Tulsa city, OK	6.6
72	48	Jersey City, NJ	36.4	41	47	Oakland city, CA	28.6	20	48	Boston city, MA	4.8
57	48	Tampa city, FL	36.4	43	49	Tulsa city, OK	28.5	2	48	Los Angeles city, CA	4.8
15	50	Columbus city, OH	36.1	74	50	Baton Rouge city, LA	28.1	46	50	Honolulu CDP, HI	4.3
59	50	St. Paul city, MN	36.1	36	50	Kansas City, MO	28.1	41	50	Oakland city, CA	4.3
74	52	Baton Rouge city, LA	35.8	15	52	Columbus city, OH	28.0	68	52	St. Petersburg city, FL	3.7
3	53	Chicago city, IL	35.1	71	53	Birmingham city, AL	27.7	3	53	Chicago city, IL	3.6
25	54	Denver city, CO	34.7	5	54	Philadelphia city, PA	27.6	36	53	Kansas City, MO	3.6
18	55	Memphis city, TN	34.1	57	54	Tampa city, FL	27.6	47	55	Miami city, FL	3.0
41	56	Oakland city, CA	34.0	64	56	Lexington-Fayette, KY	27.3	34	56	Long Beach city, CA	2.6
24	57	Seattle city, WA	32.7	16	57	Austin city, TX	26.8	51	57	Santa Ana city, CA	1.9
19	58	Milwaukee city, WI	32.2	22	58	Nashville-Davidsn consol. city, TN	26.7	59	58	St. Paul city, MN	1.7
5	59	Philadelphia city, PA	32.1	62	59	Raleigh city, NC	26.5	45	59	Minneapolis city, MN	1.0
66	60	Louisville city, KY	31.6	47	60	Miami city, FL	26.3	31	60	New Orleans city, LA	0.0
13	60	San Francisco city, CA	31.6	66	61	Louisville city, KY	25.7	63	61	Newark city, NJ	-0.2
52	62	Pittsburgh city, PA	31.2	17	62	Baltimore city, MD	25.5	21	62	Washington city, DC	-0.5
71	63	Birmingham city, AL	31.1	49	63	St. Louis city, MO	25.4	66	63	Louisville city, KY	-1.5
63	64	Newark city, NJ	31.0	54	64	Cincinnati city, OH	25.1	56	63	Toledo city, OH	-1.5
31	65	New Orleans city, LA	30.8	28	65	Portland city, OR	24.5	5	65	Philadelphia city, PA	-2.2
45	66	Minneapolis city, MN	29.0	68	66	St. Petersburg city, FL	24.0	19	66	Milwaukee city, WI	-3.5
33	67	Cleveland city, OH	28.5	46	67	Honolulu CDP, HI	23.7	73	67	Norfolk city, VA	-3.7
58	68	Buffalo city, NY	27.6	25	68	Denver city, CO	23.2	54	68	Cincinnati city, OH	-4.0
20	69	Boston city, MA	27.4	20	69	Boston city, MA	22.7	33	69	Cleveland city, OH	-4.6
17	70	Baltimore city, MD	26.7	45	70	Minneapolis city, MN	22.6	71	70	Birmingham city, AL	-6.3
10	70	Detroit city, MI	26.7	39	71	Atlanta city, GA	22.4	52	70	Pittsburgh city, PA	-6.3
54	72	Cincinnati city, OH	26.6	52	72	Pittsburgh city, PA	21.9	17	72	Baltimore city, MD	-6.7
49	73	St. Louis city, MO	26.2	21	73	Washington city, DC	19.8	58	73	Buffalo city, NY	-10.1
39	74	Atlanta city, GA	24.5	24	74	Seattle city, WA	17.9	10	73	Detroit city, MI	-10.1
21	75	Washington city, DC	22.8	13	75	San Francisco city, CA	16.6	49	75	St. Louis city, MO	-10.8

Note: Column numbers refer to Table D. Cities.

71

TABLE 6—75 Largest Cities by 2000 Population
Selected Rankings

Percent in Group Quarters, 2000				Percent in Dormitories, 2000				Percent Owner Occupied Housing Units, 2000			
Population Rank	Group Quarters Rank	City	[col 64] Percent in Group Quarters	Population Rank	Dormitories Rank	City	[col 68] Percent in Dormitories	Population Rank	Owner Occupied Housing Units Rank	City	[col 94] Percent in Owner Occupied Housing Units
73	1	Norfolk city, VA	9.9	62	1	Raleigh city, NC	3.9	42	1	Mesa city, AZ	66.4
39	2	Atlanta city, GA	7.0	52	2	Pittsburgh city, PA	3.7	38	2	Virginia Beach city, VA	65.6
52	3	Pittsburgh city, PA	6.8	74	3	Baton Rouge city, LA	3.4	61	3	Aurora city, CO	63.9
62	4	Raleigh city, NC	6.3	20	3	Boston city, MA	3.4	68	4	St. Petersburg city, FL	63.5
21	5	Washington city, DC	6.2	21	3	Washington city, DC	3.4	14	5	Jacksonville city, FL	63.2
20	6	Boston city, MA	6.0	39	6	Atlanta city, GA	3.2	11	6	San Jose city, CA	61.8
74	7	Baton Rouge city, LA	5.5	64	7	Lexington-Fayette, KY	2.6	50	7	Wichita city, KS	61.6
64	8	Lexington-Fayette, KY	4.9	45	8	Minneapolis city, MN	2.0	23	8	El Paso city, TX	61.4
45	9	Minneapolis city, MN	4.7	22	8	Nashville-Davidsn consol. city,TN	2.0	48	9	Colorado Springs city, CO	60.8
63	9	Newark city, NJ	4.7	24	10	Seattle city, WA	1.9	6	10	Phoenix city, AZ	60.7
24	9	Seattle city, WA	4.7	59	11	St. Paul city, MN	1.8	69	11	Bakersfield city, CA	60.5
22	12	Nashville-Davidsn consol. city,TN	4.2	16	12	Austin city, TX	1.4	35	12	Albuquerque city, NM	60.4
54	13	Cincinnati city, OH	4.1	17	12	Baltimore city, MD	1.4	65	13	Anchorage city, AK	60.1
17	14	Baltimore city, MD	4.0	58	12	Buffalo city, NY	1.4	56	14	Toledo city, OH	59.8
59	15	St. Paul city, MN	3.9	54	12	Cincinnati city, OH	1.4	60	15	Corpus Christi city, TX	59.6
30	15	Tucson city, AZ	3.9	15	12	Columbus city, OH	1.4	44	15	Omaha city, NE	59.6
58	17	Buffalo city, NY	3.8	73	12	Norfolk city, VA	1.4	29	17	Oklahoma City, OK	59.4
7	18	San Diego city, CA	3.7	5	12	Philadelphia city, PA	1.4	5	18	Philadelphia city, PA	59.3
71	19	Birmingham city, AL	3.6	30	12	Tucson city, AZ	1.4	32	19	Las Vegas city, NV	59.1
31	19	New Orleans city, LA	3.6	63	20	Newark city, NJ	1.2	12	20	Indianapolis consolidated city,IN	58.7
5	19	Philadelphia city, PA	3.6	57	20	Tampa city, FL	1.2	9	21	San Antonio city, TX	58.1
66	22	Louisville city, KY	3.3	19	22	Milwaukee city, WI	1.1	36	22	Kansas City, MO	57.7
47	23	Miami city, FL	3.2	67	22	Riverside city, CA	1.1	26	23	Charlotte city, NC	57.5
16	24	Austin city, TX	3.1	7	22	San Diego city, CA	1.1	67	24	Riverside city, CA	56.6
67	24	Riverside city, CA	3.1	66	25	Louisville city, KY	1.0	27	25	Fort Worth city, TX	55.9
49	24	St. Louis city, MO	3.1	31	25	New Orleans city, LA	1.0	18	26	Memphis city, TN	55.8
46	27	Honolulu CDP, HI	3.0	71	27	Birmingham city, AL	0.9	28	26	Portland city, OR	55.8
57	28	Tampa city, FL	2.9	26	27	Charlotte city, NC	0.9	43	28	Tulsa city, OK	55.6
33	29	Cleveland city, OH	2.8	28	27	Portland city, OR	0.9	64	29	Lexington-Fayette, KY	55.3
27	29	Fort Worth city, TX	2.8	43	27	Tulsa city, OK	0.9	22	29	Nashville-Davidsn consol. city,TN	55.3
28	29	Portland city, OR	2.8	46	31	Honolulu CDP, HI	0.8	57	31	Tampa city, FL	55.0
65	32	Anchorage city, AK	2.7	49	31	St. Louis city, MO	0.8	10	32	Detroit city, MI	54.9
19	32	Milwaukee city, WI	2.7	70	31	Stockton city, CA	0.8	59	33	St. Paul city, MN	54.8
44	32	Omaha city, NE	2.7	56	31	Toledo city, OH	0.8	53	34	Arlington city, TX	54.7
43	32	Tulsa city, OK	2.7	44	35	Omaha city, NE	0.7	71	35	Birmingham city, AL	53.7
18	36	Memphis city, TN	2.6	33	36	Cleveland city, OH	0.6	30	36	Tucson city, AZ	53.4
29	36	Oklahoma City, OK	2.6	27	36	Fort Worth city, TX	0.6	25	37	Denver city, CO	52.5
68	36	St. Petersburg city, FL	2.6	2	36	Los Angeles city, CA	0.6	66	37	Louisville city, KY	52.5
15	39	Columbus city, OH	2.5	18	36	Memphis city, TN	0.6	74	39	Baton Rouge city, LA	52.2
13	39	San Francisco city, CA	2.5	35	40	Albuquerque city, NM	0.5	52	40	Pittsburgh city, PA	52.1
26	41	Charlotte city, NC	2.3	3	40	Chicago city, IL	0.5	62	41	Raleigh city, NC	51.6
25	41	Denver city, CO	2.3	48	40	Colorado Springs city, CO	0.5	70	41	Stockton city, CA	51.6
12	41	Indianapolis consolidated city,IN	2.3	12	40	Indianapolis consolidated city,IN	0.5	45	43	Minneapolis city, MN	51.4
1	41	New York City, NY	2.3	34	40	Long Beach city, CA	0.5	75	44	Hialeah city, FL	50.7
34	45	Long Beach city, CA	2.2	1	40	New York City, NY	0.5	37	45	Fresno city, CA	50.6
2	45	Los Angeles city, CA	2.2	13	40	San Francisco city, CA	0.5	17	46	Baltimore city, MD	50.3
40	45	Sacramento city, CA	2.2	25	47	Denver city, CO	0.4	40	47	Sacramento city, CA	50.1
70	45	Stockton city, CA	2.2	72	47	Jersey City, NJ	0.4	55	48	Anaheim city, CA	50.0
56	45	Toledo city, OH	2.2	29	47	Oklahoma City, OK	0.4	7	49	San Diego city, CA	49.5
35	50	Albuquerque city, NM	2.1	9	47	San Antonio city, TX	0.4	51	50	Santa Ana city, CA	49.3
3	50	Chicago city, IL	2.1	68	47	St. Petersburg city, FL	0.4	15	51	Columbus city, OH	49.1
10	50	Detroit city, MI	2.1	53	52	Arlington city, TX	0.3	33	52	Cleveland city, OH	48.5
14	50	Jacksonville city, FL	2.1	60	52	Corpus Christi city, TX	0.3	24	53	Seattle city, WA	48.4
36	50	Kansas City, MO	2.1	37	52	Fresno city, CA	0.3	46	54	Honolulu CDP, HI	46.9
48	55	Colorado Springs city, CO	2.0	14	52	Jacksonville city, FL	0.3	49	54	St. Louis city, MO	46.9
9	55	San Antonio city, TX	2.0	36	52	Kansas City, MO	0.3	31	56	New Orleans city, LA	46.5
60	57	Corpus Christi city, TX	1.9	11	52	San Jose city, CA	0.3	4	57	Houston city, TX	45.8
37	57	Fresno city, CA	1.9	65	58	Anchorage city, AK	0.2	73	58	Norfolk city, VA	45.5
8	59	Dallas city, TX	1.8	4	58	Houston city, TX	0.2	19	59	Milwaukee city, WI	45.3
41	59	Oakland city, CA	1.8	40	58	Sacramento city, CA	0.2	16	60	Austin city, TX	44.8
38	59	Virginia Beach city, VA	1.8	69	61	Bakersfield city, CA	0.1	3	61	Chicago city, IL	43.8
4	62	Houston city, TX	1.7	8	61	Dallas city, TX	0.1	39	62	Atlanta city, GA	43.7
32	62	Las Vegas city, NV	1.7	10	61	Detroit city, MI	0.1	58	63	Buffalo city, NY	43.5
6	62	Phoenix city, AZ	1.7	41	61	Oakland city, CA	0.1	8	64	Dallas city, TX	43.2
51	62	Santa Ana city, CA	1.7	50	61	Wichita city, KS	0.1	41	65	Oakland city, CA	41.4
75	66	Hialeah city, FL	1.6	55	66	Anaheim city, CA	0.0	34	66	Long Beach city, CA	41.0
69	67	Bakersfield city, CA	1.5	61	67	Aurora city, CO	0.0	21	67	Washington city, DC	40.8
72	68	Jersey City, NJ	1.4	23	68	El Paso city, TX	0.0	54	68	Cincinnati city, OH	39.0
50	68	Wichita city, KS	1.4	75	69	Hialeah city, FL	0.0	2	69	Los Angeles city, CA	38.6
55	70	Anaheim city, CA	1.2	32	70	Las Vegas city, NV	0.0	13	70	San Francisco city, CA	35.0
11	70	San Jose city, CA	1.2	42	71	Mesa city, AZ	0.0	47	71	Miami city, FL	34.9
42	72	Mesa city, AZ	1.0	47	72	Miami city, FL	0.0	20	72	Boston city, MA	32.2
23	73	El Paso city, TX	0.9	6	73	Phoenix city, AZ	0.0	1	73	New York City, NY	30.2
61	74	Aurora city, CO	0.8	51	74	Santa Ana city, CA	0.0	72	74	Jersey City, NJ	28.2
53	75	Arlington city, TX	0.7	38	75	Virginia Beach city, VA	0.0	63	75	Newark city, NJ	23.8

Note: Column numbers refer to Table D. Cities.

TABLE 6—75 Largest Cities by 2000 Population
Selected Rankings

Percent Recreational/Seasonal Housing Units, 2000

Recreational/Seasonal Housing Units Rank	Group Quarters Rank	City	[col 90] Percent Recreational/Seasonal Housing Units
42	1	Mesa city, AZ	10.3
68	2	St. Petersburg city, FL	3.9
46	3	Honolulu CDP, HI	3.3
47	4	Miami city, FL	2.0
30	5	Tucson city, AZ	1.7
38	6	Virginia Beach city, VA	1.4
65	7	Anchorage city, AK	1.1
31	7	New Orleans city, LA	1.1
7	7	San Diego city, CA	1.1
13	7	San Francisco city, CA	1.1
60	11	Corpus Christi city, TX	1.0
32	12	Las Vegas city, NV	0.9
1	12	New York City, NY	0.9
6	12	Phoenix city, AZ	0.9
64	15	Lexington-Fayette, KY	0.8
21	15	Washington city, DC	0.8
24	17	Seattle city, WA	0.7
39	18	Atlanta city, GA	0.6
20	18	Boston city, MA	0.6
25	18	Denver city, CO	0.6
57	18	Tampa city, FL	0.6
16	22	Austin city, TX	0.5
17	22	Baltimore city, MD	0.5
48	22	Colorado Springs city, CO	0.5
4	22	Houston city, TX	0.5
45	22	Minneapolis city, MN	0.5
29	22	Oklahoma City, OK	0.5
52	22	Pittsburgh city, PA	0.5
9	22	San Antonio city, TX	0.5
43	22	Tulsa city, OK	0.5
35	31	Albuquerque city, NM	0.4
3	31	Chicago city, IL	0.4
54	31	Cincinnati city, OH	0.4
33	31	Cleveland city, OH	0.4
23	31	El Paso city, TX	0.4
34	31	Long Beach city, CA	0.4
2	31	Los Angeles city, CA	0.4
22	31	Nashville-Davidsn consol. city, TN	0.4
28	31	Portland city, OR	0.4
62	31	Raleigh city, NC	0.4
40	31	Sacramento city, CA	0.4
59	31	St. Paul city, MN	0.4
53	43	Arlington city, TX	0.3
69	43	Bakersfield city, CA	0.3
74	43	Baton Rouge city, LA	0.3
71	43	Birmingham city, AL	0.3
26	43	Charlotte city, NC	0.3
15	43	Columbus city, OH	0.3
8	43	Dallas city, TX	0.3
27	43	Fort Worth city, TX	0.3
12	43	Indianapolis consolidated city, IN	0.3
14	43	Jacksonville city, FL	0.3
72	43	Jersey City, NJ	0.3
36	43	Kansas City, MO	0.3
66	43	Louisville city, KY	0.3
18	43	Memphis city, TN	0.3
73	43	Norfolk city, VA	0.3
41	43	Oakland city, CA	0.3
44	43	Omaha city, NE	0.3
5	43	Philadelphia city, PA	0.3
67	43	Riverside city, CA	0.3
11	43	San Jose city, CA	0.3
49	43	St. Louis city, MO	0.3
56	43	Toledo city, OH	0.3
50	43	Wichita city, KS	0.3
55	66	Anaheim city, CA	0.2
61	66	Aurora city, CO	0.2
58	66	Buffalo city, NY	0.2
10	66	Detroit city, MI	0.2
37	66	Fresno city, CA	0.2
75	66	Hialeah city, FL	0.2
19	66	Milwaukee city, WI	0.2
70	66	Stockton city, CA	0.2
63	74	Newark city, NJ	0.1
51	74	Santa Ana city, CA	0.1

Homeowner Vacancy Rate, 2000

Population Rank	Homeowner Vacancy Rank	City	[col 91] Homeowner Vacancy Rate
58	1	Buffalo city, NY	4.2
39	2	Atlanta city, GA	4.1
17	3	Baltimore city, MD	3.6
49	4	St. Louis city, MO	3.5
73	5	Norfolk city, VA	3.2
47	6	Miami city, FL	2.9
21	6	Washington city, DC	2.9
52	8	Pittsburgh city, PA	2.8
71	9	Birmingham city, AL	2.7
32	10	Las Vegas city, NV	2.5
42	11	Mesa city, AZ	2.4
68	11	St. Petersburg city, FL	2.4
28	13	Portland city, OR	2.3
26	14	Charlotte city, NC	2.2
54	14	Cincinnati city, OH	2.2
34	14	Long Beach city, CA	2.2
31	14	New Orleans city, LA	2.2
29	14	Oklahoma City, OK	2.2
33	19	Cleveland city, OH	2.1
62	19	Raleigh city, NC	2.1
57	19	Tampa city, FL	2.1
69	22	Bakersfield city, CA	2.0
15	22	Columbus city, OH	2.0
60	22	Corpus Christi city, TX	2.0
12	22	Indianapolis consolidated city, IN	2.0
18	22	Memphis city, TN	2.0
22	22	Nashville-Davidsn consol. city, TN	2.0
63	22	Newark city, NJ	2.0
40	22	Sacramento city, CA	2.0
50	22	Wichita city, KS	2.0
35	31	Albuquerque city, NM	1.9
27	31	Fort Worth city, TX	1.9
37	31	Fresno city, CA	1.9
72	31	Jersey City, NJ	1.9
36	31	Kansas City, MO	1.9
5	31	Philadelphia city, PA	1.9
67	31	Riverside city, CA	1.9
14	38	Jacksonville city, FL	1.8
2	38	Los Angeles city, CA	1.8
66	38	Louisville city, KY	1.8
3	41	Chicago city, IL	1.7
25	41	Denver city, CO	1.7
46	41	Honolulu CDP, HI	1.7
1	41	New York City, NY	1.7
74	45	Baton Rouge city, LA	1.6
10	45	Detroit city, MI	1.6
23	45	El Paso city, TX	1.6
4	45	Houston city, TX	1.6
30	45	Tucson city, AZ	1.6
43	45	Tulsa city, OK	1.6
56	51	Toledo city, OH	1.5
38	51	Virginia Beach city, VA	1.5
65	53	Anchorage city, AK	1.4
53	53	Arlington city, TX	1.4
8	53	Dallas city, TX	1.4
6	53	Phoenix city, AZ	1.4
9	53	San Antonio city, TX	1.4
70	53	Stockton city, CA	1.4
19	59	Milwaukee city, WI	1.3
48	60	Colorado Springs city, CO	1.2
24	60	Seattle city, WA	1.2
61	62	Aurora city, CO	1.1
64	62	Lexington-Fayette, KY	1.1
16	64	Austin city, TX	1.0
20	64	Boston city, MA	1.0
75	64	Hialeah city, FL	1.0
41	64	Oakland city, CA	1.0
44	64	Omaha city, NE	1.0
55	69	Anaheim city, CA	0.9
7	70	San Diego city, CA	0.8
13	70	San Francisco city, CA	0.8
51	70	Santa Ana city, CA	0.8
45	73	Minneapolis city, MN	0.7
59	73	St. Paul city, MN	0.7
11	75	San Jose city, CA	0.4

Renter Vacancy Rate, 2000

Population Rank	Renter Vacancy Rank	City	[col 92] Renter Vacancy Rate
29	1	Oklahoma City, OK	12.3
50	2	Wichita city, KS	12.0
35	3	Albuquerque city, NM	11.8
49	3	St. Louis city, MO	11.8
71	5	Birmingham city, AL	11.6
58	6	Buffalo city, NY	11.1
12	7	Indianapolis consolidated city, IN	11.0
33	8	Cleveland city, OH	10.8
42	9	Mesa city, AZ	10.7
46	10	Honolulu CDP, HI	10.2
54	11	Cincinnati city, OH	9.9
36	12	Kansas City, MO	9.6
60	13	Corpus Christi city, TX	9.5
27	14	Fort Worth city, TX	9.1
68	14	St. Petersburg city, FL	9.1
14	16	Jacksonville city, FL	9.0
74	17	Baton Rouge city, LA	8.8
52	17	Pittsburgh city, PA	8.8
56	17	Toledo city, OH	8.8
4	20	Houston city, TX	8.7
43	20	Tulsa city, OK	8.7
26	22	Charlotte city, NC	8.4
32	22	Las Vegas city, NV	8.4
64	22	Lexington-Fayette, KY	8.4
18	22	Memphis city, TN	8.4
15	26	Columbus city, OH	8.3
10	26	Detroit city, MI	8.3
62	26	Raleigh city, NC	8.3
30	29	Tucson city, AZ	8.1
23	30	El Paso city, TX	7.9
31	30	New Orleans city, LA	7.9
6	30	Phoenix city, AZ	7.9
57	33	Tampa city, FL	7.8
17	34	Baltimore city, MD	7.6
66	35	Louisville city, KY	7.5
39	36	Atlanta city, GA	7.2
44	36	Omaha city, NE	7.2
8	38	Dallas city, TX	7.0
5	38	Philadelphia city, PA	7.0
73	40	Norfolk city, VA	6.9
9	40	San Antonio city, TX	6.9
47	42	Miami city, FL	6.6
22	43	Nashville-Davidsn consol. city, TN	6.5
37	44	Fresno city, CA	6.4
69	45	Bakersfield city, CA	6.2
48	45	Colorado Springs city, CO	6.2
28	45	Portland city, OR	6.2
53	48	Arlington city, TX	6.1
19	49	Milwaukee city, WI	6.0
21	50	Washington city, DC	5.9
3	51	Chicago city, IL	5.7
63	52	Newark city, NJ	5.6
40	53	Sacramento city, CA	5.4
65	54	Anchorage city, AK	5.3
67	55	Riverside city, CA	4.8
25	56	Denver city, CO	4.5
70	57	Stockton city, CA	4.3
34	58	Long Beach city, CA	4.2
38	59	Virginia Beach city, VA	4.0
61	60	Aurora city, CO	3.5
16	60	Austin city, TX	3.5
2	60	Los Angeles city, CA	3.5
24	60	Seattle city, WA	3.5
72	64	Jersey City, NJ	3.3
55	65	Anaheim city, CA	3.2
1	65	New York City, NY	3.2
7	65	San Diego city, CA	3.2
20	68	Boston city, MA	3.0
45	69	Minneapolis city, MN	2.8
59	69	St. Paul city, MN	2.8
41	71	Oakland city, CA	2.7
13	72	San Francisco city, CA	2.5
51	73	Santa Ana city, CA	1.9
11	74	San Jose city, CA	1.8
75	75	Hialeah city, FL	1.7

Note: Column numbers refer to Table D. Cities.

TABLE 7—Congressional Districts of the 107th Congress
Selected Rankings

Largest Population, 2000

Population Rank	State/Congressional District	[col 2] Population
1	NV District 2	799 065
2	AZ District 6	696 004
3	AZ District 3	666 168
4	GA District 6	638 800
5	NV District 1	624 837
6	MT At Large	619 439
7	TX District 26	619 391
8	GA District 11	619 374
9	TX District 3	619 370
10	AZ District 1	614 901
11	GA District 9	614 794
12	CO District 5	614 265
13	TX District 21	613 967
14	FL District 19	613 961
15	AZ District 5	613 603
16	VA District 10	610 872
16	TX District 10	610 872
18	FL District 14	610 871
18	FL District 21	610 871
18	TX District 22	610 871
18	DE At Large	610 871
22	FL District 20	606 900
23	FL District 8	602 933
24	GA District 3	602 896
25	TX District 15	602 877
26	TX District 8	602 876
27	AZ District 2	602 842
28	CA District 48	602 839
29	TX District 7	602 832
30	UT District 3	602 774
31	NC District 4	601 643
31	UT District 1	601 643
31	AR District 3	601 643
31	TX District 23	601 643
31	TX District 6	601 643
36	IL District 13	601 642
36	FL District 16	601 642
36	FL District 6	601 642
36	SD At Large	601 642
36	GA District 7	601 642
41	CO District 4	600 957
42	GA District 4	600 876
43	OR District 1	598 056
44	CA District 44	597 921
45	TN District 6	597 690
46	CA District 43	597 688
47	AZ District 4	597 684
48	FL District 4	597 683
49	KS District 3	597 682
50	SC District 2	597 681
51	NC District 2	597 680
51	TN District 7	597 680
53	CA District 4	597 500
53	IN District 6	594 630
53	CO District 3	594 630
53	MD District 6	594 630
53	FL District 7	594 630
53	FL District 9	594 630
53	MN District 6	594 630
53	IL District 14	594 630
53	WA District 2	594 630
53	FL District 15	594 630
53	CA District 47	594 630
53	KY District 6	594 630
65	MD District 5	594 629
65	CA District 51	594 629
67	CA District 10	589 630
68	CA District 20	589 600
69	NJ District 12	589 523
70	CA District 19	589 420
71	VA District 1	589 405
72	TX District 4	589 398
73	KY District 2	589 359
74	ID District 1	589 322
75	CO District 2	588 588

Largest Total Land Area, 2000 (Square Kilometers)

Land Area Rank	State/Congressional District	[col 1] Land Area
1	AK At Large	1 481 346.9
2	MT At Large	376 979.1
3	NV District 2	283 850.8
4	WY At Large	251 488.9
5	SD At Large	196 540.3
6	OR District 2	182 830.5
7	ND At Large	178 646.8
8	NM District 2	174 408.6
9	NE District 3	162 846.9
10	TX District 23	151 274.6
11	CO District 3	147 721.9
12	KS District 1	145 669.0
13	NM District 3	127 698.8
14	UT District 3	123 330.9
15	ID District 2	111 878.2
16	AZ District 3	107 779.2
17	AZ District 6	106 754.6
18	CO District 4	104 330.3
19	ID District 1	102 436.0
20	UT District 1	88 233.2
21	TX District 13	82 231.1
22	CA District 40	77 476.1
23	CA District 2	73 589.3
24	TX District 17	72 843.1
25	ME District 2	70 562.8
26	MN District 7	68 162.6
27	MN District 8	66 868.1
28	OK District 6	66 285.3
29	WA District 4	61 408.0
30	MI District 1	58 958.0
31	TX District 19	52 282.1
32	AR District 4	46 727.2
33	OK District 3	46 520.1
34	IA District 5	46 102.3
35	AZ District 2	45 865.9
36	WA District 5	45 778.2
37	MO District 8	45 243.3
38	TX District 21	44 845.1
39	WI District 7	43 309.9
40	AR District 1	42 986.3
41	MN District 2	42 182.8
42	OR District 4	41 649.3
43	TX District 14	39 824.0
44	TX District 2	36 763.4
45	MO District 4	36 518.7
46	KS District 2	36 185.2
47	IA District 3	35 822.4
48	MO District 6	35 145.8
49	NE District 1	34 701.1
50	LA District 5	33 942.9
51	AZ District 5	32 866.3
52	NY District 24	32 092.7
53	IA District 2	31 753.7
54	MS District 2	31 723.3
55	TX District 28	31 537.2
56	MO District 9	31 455.0
57	FL District 1	30 607.2
58	OK District 2	30 291.4
59	TX District 1	29 949.4
60	AR District 3	29 804.0
61	GA District 8	29 785.3
62	GA District 2	29 678.7
63	TX District 11	29 261.8
64	KY District 1	29 086.5
65	CA District 4	27 988.1
66	CA District 1	27 977.8
67	IL District 19	27 790.5
68	WI District 3	27 552.0
69	PA District 5	27 140.2
70	MS District 1	26 931.2
71	KY District 5	26 744.1
72	LA District 4	26 404.7
73	AL District 2	26 235.3
74	KS District 4	26 028.7
75	MS District 3	25 893.1

Population Density, 2000 (Per Square Kilometer)

Density Rank	State/Congressional District	[col 4] Population Density
1	NY District 15	24 390.5
2	NY District 11	21 108.6
3	NY District 14	18 941.3
4	NY District 8	16 774.7
5	NY District 16	16 185.9
6	NY District 12	14 992.2
7	NY District 10	14 449.0
8	NY District 7	11 864.4
9	NY District 17	11 266.9
10	CA District 8	6 925.9
11	NY District 9	6 881.5
12	NY District 6	6 855.1
13	IL District 4	6 118.7
14	CA District 30	6 038.8
15	MA District 8	5 389.9
16	CA District 35	5 389.6
17	CA District 33	4 852.1
18	CA District 32	4 807.5
19	IL District 5	4 654.6
20	PA District 2	4 527.7
21	NJ District 13	4 435.5
22	IL District 7	4 330.6
23	IL District 9	4 264.6
24	NJ District 10	4 201.0
25	CA District 46	4 078.4
26	NY District 13	3 973.9
27	IL District 1	3 898.7
28	PA District 3	3 897.1
29	PA District 1	3 799.3
30	CA District 26	3 647.6
31	DC Delegate	3 597.9
32	CA District 37	3 294.7
33	CA District 38	3 231.7
34	CA District 9	3 163.6
35	CA District 31	3 069.4
36	NY District 4	2 811.0
37	NJ District 9	2 701.3
38	MI District 14	2 662.5
39	CA District 34	2 637.1
40	CA District 45	2 625.5
41	NY District 18	2 549.2
42	MI District 15	2 429.8
43	NJ District 8	2 365.2
44	CA District 39	2 297.8
45	CA District 12	2 219.1
46	FL District 17	2 123.5
47	MN District 5	2 013.1
48	FL District 18	2 007.2
49	OH District 11	1 970.2
50	WI District 5	1 943.5
51	IL District 3	1 922.4
52	CA District 29	1 915.6
53	CA District 49	1 913.5
54	MD District 7	1 912.9
55	FL District 22	1 906.8
56	CA District 50	1 844.8
57	WA District 7	1 803.9
58	IL District 2	1 726.6
59	CA District 5	1 710.3
60	NV District 1	1 567.5
61	NY District 5	1 565.6
62	AZ District 1	1 520.3
63	VA District 8	1 497.7
64	FL District 10	1 495.0
65	TX District 18	1 492.2
66	MI District 12	1 489.9
67	AZ District 4	1 468.9
68	NY District 3	1 468.2
69	OH District 10	1 423.3
70	MA District 7	1 378.4
71	MO District 1	1 363.0
72	MD District 4	1 298.3
73	IL District 6	1 291.5
74	CA District 42	1 288.9
75	FL District 21	1 283.9

Note: Column numbers refer to Table F. Congressional Districts.

TABLE 7—Congressional Districts of the 107th Congress
Selected Rankings

Percent Population Change, 2000

Percent Change Rank	State/Congressional District	[col 52] Percent Change
1	NV District 2	76.8
2	AZ District 6	63.9
3	AZ District 3	63.3
4	GA District 6	60.0
5	NV District 1	55.8
6	TX District 26	49.7
7	CO District 5	47.6
8	TX District 3	47.1
9	FL District 19	42.4
10	GA District 11	41.9
11	TX District 21	41.5
12	VA District 10	40.9
13	FL District 14	40.6
14	FL District 21	40.4
15	TX District 10	39.7
16	ID District 1	39.6
17	FL District 20	39.3
18	FL District 8	39.1
19	NC District 4	38.6
20	GA District 9	38.2
21	TX District 22	38.1
22	TX District 15	37.8
23	TX District 8	37.4
24	TX District 7	36.7
25	CO District 4	36.3
25	TN District 6	36.3
27	AZ District 1	35.8
28	CA District 48	35.0
29	FL District 16	34.8
30	TX District 23	34.7
31	TN District 7	34.5
32	FL District 6	34.4
33	TX District 6	34.3
34	UT District 3	33.4
35	UT District 1	33.2
36	WA District 2	33.1
37	IL District 13	32.8
38	GA District 3	32.6
39	NC District 2	32.2
40	CO District 3	31.8
40	MN District 6	31.8
42	OR District 1	30.7
43	IN District 6	30.6
44	FL District 4	30.5
45	AZ District 5	29.9
45	CA District 44	29.9
47	AR District 3	29.7
48	WA District 3	29.1
49	CA District 43	29.0
50	WA District 8	28.6
51	FL District 9	28.4
51	FL District 7	28.4
53	CO District 2	27.9
54	FL District 15	27.7
55	GA District 7	27.6
56	CA District 4	27.0
57	AZ District 2	26.7
58	CA District 4	26.4
59	IL District 14	26.1
60	VA District 1	26.0
61	SC District 2	25.8
62	NC District 9	25.5
63	CA District 47	25.2
64	NC District 7	24.9
64	TX District 4	24.9
66	NC District 6	24.8
67	CA District 10	24.7
68	CA District 51	24.6
68	NM District 3	24.6
70	VA District 7	24.3
70	WA District 4	24.3
72	CA District 20	24.1
73	CA District 19	23.8
74	OR District 2	23.5
75	FL District 5	22.6

Highest Percent White, 2000

White Rank	State/Congressional District	[col 9] Percent White
1	KY District 5	97.7
2	PA District 12	97.2
3	ME District 2	97.1
4	PA District 9	97.0
5	ME District 1	96.8
5	VT At Large	96.8
7	WI District 3	96.5
8	WV District 1	96.3
9	PA District 11	96.2
9	TN District 1	96.2
11	IN District 9	96.1
11	NH District 1	96.1
11	WI District 6	96.1
14	PA District 5	96.0
14	WI District 9	96.0
16	NH District 2	95.9
17	OH District 18	95.7
18	MN District 2	95.6
18	OH District 6	95.6
20	IA District 3	95.5
20	IA District 2	95.5
22	KY District 4	95.3
22	MN District 8	95.3
24	IA District 5	95.2
24	WI District 7	95.2
26	VA District 9	95.1
27	PA District 4	95.0
28	MI District 4	94.9
28	PA District 10	94.9
28	PA District 20	94.9
31	MN District 1	94.7
31	NY District 22	94.7
33	WV District 2	94.6
34	OH District 2	94.5
35	IN District 5	94.4
35	MO District 7	94.4
37	NE District 3	94.3
37	OH District 5	94.3
39	IN District 6	94.2
39	MN District 7	94.2
39	WV District 3	94.2
42	IN District 7	94.1
42	NY District 23	94.1
42	TN District 4	94.1
45	MI District 1	94.0
45	NY District 31	94.0
45	OH District 8	94.0
48	MI District 10	93.9
48	MO District 6	93.9
50	OH District 19	93.8
51	IN District 8	93.7
52	IL District 19	93.6
53	PA District 19	93.5
54	MO District 4	93.4
54	NY District 27	93.4
54	PA District 21	93.4
57	IN District 2	93.3
57	NY District 24	93.3
59	MN District 6	93.2
59	MO District 9	93.2
61	MO District 8	93.0
62	OH District 16	92.9
63	WI District 8	92.8
64	OH District 4	92.5
65	IL District 20	92.4
65	ND At Large	92.4
65	PA District 8	92.4
68	IL District 17	92.2
68	MI District 16	92.2
70	NE District 1	92.1
70	WY At Large	92.1
72	IA District 1	92.0
72	KY District 2	92.0
72	OH District 7	92.0
75	OR District 4	91.9

Highest Percent Black, 2000

Black Rank	State/Congressional District	[col 10] Percent Black
1	MI District 14	78.9
2	IL District 2	75.8
3	MD District 7	74.6
4	IL District 1	70.3
5	AL District 7	70.0
6	MI District 15	69.9
7	NY District 11	68.6
8	LA District 2	66.9
9	TN District 9	66.2
10	MS District 2	65.2
11	MD District 4	64.7
12	OH District 11	64.5
13	PA District 2	64.4
14	NY District 10	63.9
15	IL District 7	63.3
16	GA District 5	62.9
17	NJ District 10	60.9
17	SC District 6	60.9
19	FL District 17	60.3
20	DC Delegate	60.0
21	MO District 1	59.9
22	VA District 3	56.6
23	PA District 1	55.4
24	FL District 23	55.3
25	NY District 6	52.5
26	NC District 1	50.5
27	FL District 3	49.7
28	GA District 4	49.5
29	MS District 4	46.9
30	NC District 12	44.6
31	NY District 17	43.6
32	WI District 5	43.3
33	GA District 2	40.5
34	TX District 18	40.4
35	TX District 30	39.3
36	VA District 4	39.1
37	GA District 10	38.5
38	NY District 15	36.7
39	NY District 16	36.0
40	CA District 35	34.6
41	IN District 10	34.3
42	LA District 4	34.0
42	OH District 1	34.0
44	LA District 6	33.6
45	CA District 32	32.9
46	LA District 5	32.6
47	GA District 8	32.3
48	MS District 3	32.1
49	GA District 1	31.1
50	GA District 3	30.6
50	SC District 5	30.6
52	MD District 5	29.1
53	AL District 1	28.6
54	AL District 2	28.0
55	SC District 2	27.7
56	NC District 2	26.9
57	MD District 3	26.8
58	AR District 4	26.6
59	NC District 8	26.4
60	CA District 9	26.2
61	MO District 5	26.1
62	CA District 37	25.9
63	AL District 3	25.3
63	LA District 3	25.3
65	FL District 2	25.2
66	LA District 7	25.0
67	TN District 5	24.9
68	VA District 5	24.0
69	TX District 25	23.8
70	TN District 8	23.5
71	VA District 2	23.1
72	NC District 7	23.0
73	OH District 12	22.8
74	MS District 1	22.4
75	TX District 9	21.7

Note: Column numbers refer to Table F. Congressional Districts.

TABLE 7—Congressional Districts of the 107th Congress
Selected Rankings

Highest Percent American Indian and Alaska Native, 2000

American Indian and Alaska Native Rank	State/Congressional District	[col 11] Percent American Indian and Alaska Native
1	NM District 3	20.3
2	OK District 2	17.0
3	AK At Large	15.6
3	AZ District 6	15.6
5	OK District 3	11.3
6	SD At Large	8.3
7	NC District 7	6.8
8	MT At Large	6.2
9	OK District 1	5.3
10	ND At Large	4.9
11	OK District 6	4.8
12	OK District 4	4.6
13	AZ District 2	4.4
14	NM District 2	4.2
15	OK District 5	4.1
16	NM District 1	3.5
17	WI District 8	2.9
18	CA District 1	2.8
18	WA District 4	2.8
20	MI District 1	2.7
20	MN District 7	2.7
20	NC District 8	2.7
23	AZ District 3	2.6
24	CA District 2	2.4
25	MN District 8	2.3
25	UT District 3	2.3
25	WA District 6	2.3
25	WY At Large	2.3
29	OR District 2	2.1
30	AZ District 1	2.0
31	WA District 2	1.9
32	AZ District 4	1.8
32	CA District 19	1.8
32	NV District 2	1.8
32	WA District 5	1.8
36	CO District 3	1.7
36	MN District 5	1.7
36	WI District 7	1.7
39	CA District 40	1.6
39	CA District 20	1.6
39	CA District 21	1.6
39	LA District 3	1.6
43	NC District 11	1.5
44	ID District 2	1.4
44	OR District 4	1.4
44	WA District 9	1.4
47	AR District 3	1.3
47	CA District 44	1.3
47	CA District 3	1.3
47	CO District 1	1.3
47	ID District 1	1.3
47	KS District 2	1.3
47	OR District 5	1.3
54	AZ District 5	1.2
54	CA District 5	1.2
54	CA District 42	1.2
54	CA District 52	1.2
54	CA District 33	1.2
54	CA District 18	1.2
54	CA District 34	1.2
54	KS District 4	1.2
54	MS District 3	1.2
54	NE District 1	1.2
54	WA District 3	1.2
65	CA District 5	1.1
65	CA District 48	1.1
65	CA District 17	1.1
65	CA District 22	1.1
65	CA District 46	1.1
65	CA District 4	1.1
65	CA District 31	1.1
65	NY District 16	1.1
73	AL District 1	1.0
73	CA District 43	1.0
73	CA District 26	1.0

Highest Percent Asian Population, 2000

Asian Rank	State/Congressional District	[col 12] Percent Asian
1	HI District 1	53.5
2	HI District 2	31.1
3	CA District 12	30.9
4	CA District 13	30.1
5	CA District 8	28.4
6	CA District 31	28.2
7	CA District 16	26.9
8	CA District 30	19.6
9	CA District 28	19.4
10	CA District 14	18.9
11	NY District 5	18.7
12	CA District 39	18.4
13	CA District 15	17.6
14	CA District 9	17.4
15	NY District 7	16.8
16	NY District 12	16.4
17	CA District 5	15.5
18	CA District 45	15.4
19	CA District 36	15.3
20	CA District 46	15.2
21	CA District 7	15.1
22	CA District 41	14.7
23	CA District 50	14.3
24	CA District 47	13.6
25	NY District 9	13.4
26	CA District 27	13.2
26	WA District 7	13.2
28	VA District 11	12.2
29	IL District 9	12.1
30	MD District 8	11.3
30	NJ District 9	11.3
32	CA District 51	11.1
32	NY District 18	11.1
34	NY District 11	11.0
35	NY District 8	10.4
36	TX District 22	10.0
37	NY District 6	9.9
38	CA District 29	9.8
39	NY District 13	9.6
40	NJ District 6	9.4
41	CA District 10	9.3
41	NY District 14	9.3
43	CA District 34	8.9
43	CA District 38	8.9
45	NJ District 7	8.7
45	VA District 8	8.7
47	WA District 1	8.4
48	CA District 37	8.3
49	CA District 49	8.1
50	MN District 4	8.0
50	TX District 3	8.0
52	WA District 9	7.9
53	CA District 32	7.8
53	CA District 24	7.8
53	NJ District 12	7.8
56	IL District 6	7.7
56	WA District 8	7.7
58	CA District 25	7.6
58	MA District 8	7.6
60	IL District 8	7.4
61	CA District 19	7.2
61	TX District 7	7.2
63	CA District 26	6.6
64	CA District 3	6.4
64	NJ District 11	6.4
66	IL District 13	6.2
66	NJ District 5	6.2
68	IL District 5	6.1
69	NJ District 13	6.0
70	IL District 10	5.7
71	OR District 3	5.6
72	MA District 7	5.5
73	MA District 5	5.4
73	TX District 25	5.4
75	CA District 23	5.3

Percent Two or More Races, 2000

Tow or More Races Rank	State/Congressional District	[col 15] Percent Two or More Races
1	HI District 2	25.4
2	HI District 1	16.9
3	NY District 6	8.1
4	CA District 27	6.9
5	OK District 2	6.8
6	NY District 16	6.6
7	CA District 5	6.5
8	CA District 13	6.2
9	CA District 7	6.1
9	NY District 15	6.1
11	CA District 11	6.0
11	NY District 7	6.0
11	NY District 12	6.0
14	NJ District 13	5.8
15	CA District 50	5.7
15	CA District 26	5.7
17	CA District 30	5.5
17	NY District 17	5.5
19	AK At Large	5.4
19	CA District 18	5.4
21	CA District 42	5.3
22	CA District 12	5.2
22	CA District 9	5.2
22	WA District 9	5.2
25	CA District 16	5.1
25	CA District 38	5.1
25	CA District 3	5.1
28	CA District 32	5.0
29	CA District 34	4.9
29	CA District 17	4.9
29	CA District 33	4.9
32	CA District 19	4.8
32	CA District 43	4.8
32	CA District 40	4.8
32	FL District 17	4.8
36	CA District 36	4.7
36	CA District 46	4.7
36	FL District 23	4.7
36	OK District 3	4.7
40	CA District 15	4.6
40	CA District 29	4.6
40	CA District 37	4.6
40	CA District 25	4.6
40	CA District 1	4.6
40	WA District 6	4.6
46	CA District 41	4.5
46	CA District 20	4.5
46	CA District 35	4.5
46	CA District 52	4.5
46	MA District 8	4.5
46	WA District 7	4.5
52	CA District 8	4.4
52	CA District 28	4.4
52	CA District 10	4.4
52	CA District 49	4.4
52	CA District 24	4.4
52	NV District 1	4.4
52	OK District 1	4.4
59	CA District 39	4.3
59	CA District 21	4.3
61	CA District 31	4.2
61	CA District 23	4.2
61	IL District 4	4.2
61	NM District 1	4.2
61	TX District 20	4.2
66	CA District 48	4.1
66	OR District 3	4.1
66	VA District 11	4.1
69	CA District 45	4.0
69	CA District 47	4.0
69	CA District 51	4.0
69	CA District 22	4.0
69	CA District 44	4.0
69	NJ District 10	4.0
69	NY District 10	4.0

Note: Column numbers refer to Table F. Congressional Districts.

TABLE 7—Congressional Districts of the 107th Congress
Selected Rankings

Hispanic Rank	State/Congressional District	[col 22] Percent Hispanic	Under 18 Years Rank	State/Congressional District	[cols 28 & 29] Percent Under 18 Years	25 to 54 Years Rank	State/Congressional District	[cols 31, 32 & 33] Percent 25 to 54 Years
1	CA District 33	86.0	1	CA District 37	36.2	1	CA District 8	55.4
2	TX District 15	78.9	2	CA District 42	35.3	2	NY District 14	54.9
3	TX District 16	78.0	3	CA District 35	34.6	3	CA District 29	53.1
4	FL District 21	77.5	4	CA District 20	34.3	3	VA District 8	53.1
5	CA District 34	72.4	4	NY District 16	34.3	5	WA District 7	52.7
6	FL District 18	70.5	6	UT District 3	33.7	6	GA District 6	52.3
6	TX District 27	70.5	7	TX District 15	33.2	7	NY District 8	50.8
8	IL District 4	70.1	8	TX District 29	33.1	8	TX District 26	50.5
9	TX District 20	67.0	8	UT District 1	33.1	9	TX District 3	50.0
10	TX District 23	66.3	10	CA District 33	33.0	10	TX District 7	49.9
11	CA District 26	65.4	11	CA District 46	32.5	10	GA District 4	49.9
12	TX District 28	65.0	11	TX District 23	32.5	12	IL District 5	49.6
13	CA District 30	64.3	13	AZ District 2	32.2	13	CA District 36	49.5
14	CA District 20	63.7	14	CA District 18	32.1	14	VA District 11	49.4
15	NY District 16	62.9	15	CA District 43	31.7	15	CA District 14	49.2
16	AZ District 2	62.5	16	CA District 26	31.5	16	CA District 15	49.0
17	CA District 46	62.3	17	CA District 50	31.4	16	VA District 10	49.0
18	TX District 29	60.9	17	MI District 14	31.4	18	TX District 10	48.8
19	CA District 31	59.4	17	TX District 16	31.4	18	TX District 6	48.8
20	CA District 37	57.2	20	TX District 28	31.3	20	NC District 4	48.7
21	CA District 35	54.2	21	IL District 4	31.2	21	CO District 6	48.5
22	CA District 50	50.8	22	CA District 21	31.1	22	MN District 6	48.4
22	CA District 42	50.8	22	IL District 2	31.1	22	WA District 1	48.4
24	NY District 15	50.5	22	TX District 27	31.1	24	IL District 8	48.3
25	NY District 12	48.6	25	CA District 34	30.9	24	CA District 12	48.3
26	NM District 2	48.0	25	CA District 41	30.9	26	CA District 49	48.1
27	NJ District 13	47.2	25	TX District 24	30.9	26	NC District 9	48.1
28	NM District 1	42.8	28	FL District 17	30.8	28	CO District 5	48.0
29	CA District 17	42.6	29	CA District 11	30.6	28	CO District 2	48.0
30	CA District 41	40.9	30	AK At Large	30.4	28	CO District 1	48.0
31	CA District 38	40.1	31	WA District 4	30.2	31	WA District 8	47.9
32	CA District 16	39.8	32	CA District 19	30.1	32	MN District 5	47.8
33	NY District 7	39.1	33	CA District 25	30.0	32	MN District 3	47.8
34	CA District 44	38.5	34	MS District 2	29.9	32	TX District 22	47.8
35	CA District 23	37.7	35	MN District 6	29.8	35	AK At Large	47.6
36	CA District 32	37.1	36	MI District 15	29.7	35	CA District 13	47.6
37	CA District 18	36.4	37	CA District 40	29.6	37	CA District 9	47.5
38	NY District 17	35.9	37	UT District 2	29.6	37	MD District 4	47.5
39	NM District 3	35.7	39	NY District 10	29.5	37	OR District 1	47.5
40	CA District 43	35.5	40	CA District 31	29.4	40	GA District 5	47.4
41	TX District 30	34.7	40	ID District 2	29.4	40	OR District 3	47.4
42	TX District 24	34.5	40	TX District 25	29.4	42	MD District 5	47.3
43	CO District 1	33.4	43	TX District 30	29.3	42	IL District 13	47.3
43	TX District 18	33.4	43	TX District 22	29.3	44	NY District 7	47.1
45	CA District 19	32.9	45	IL District 14	29.2	44	IL District 9	47.1
46	CA District 28	31.6	45	NM District 3	29.2	46	MD District 4	47.0
47	CA District 21	31.4	47	FL District 23	29.1	46	NJ District 11	47.0
48	TX District 25	31.1	48	LA District 3	28.9	46	VA District 7	47.0
49	CA District 39	30.4	49	NM District 2	28.8	49	CA District 16	46.9
50	CA District 52	29.7	49	CA District 23	28.8	49	CA District 47	46.9
51	TX District 10	28.8	51	CA District 44	28.7	49	CA District 24	46.9
52	TX District 14	27.9	52	TX District 20	28.6	49	CA District 27	46.9
53	CA District 11	27.8	53	IL District 1	28.5	49	CA District 45	46.9
54	FL District 17	27.4	53	TX District 3	28.5	49	FL District 8	46.9
55	CA District 22	27.0	53	WI District 5	28.5	49	MA District 8	46.9
56	NV District 1	26.6	56	CA District 38	28.4	49	CA District 6	46.9
57	TX District 19	26.1	56	GA District 3	28.4	57	TN District 5	46.8
58	NJ District 8	25.8	58	LA District 2	28.3	57	CA District 10	46.8
59	WA District 4	25.4	58	NY District 11	28.3	57	NJ District 13	46.8
60	CA District 25	25.0	60	CA District 30	28.2	60	NJ District 9	46.7
60	IL District 5	25.0	60	FL District 3	28.2	60	OH District 15	46.7
60	TX District 12	25.0	60	AZ District 6	28.2	62	MA District 7	46.6
63	TX District 13	24.6	63	IL District 13	28.1	63	AZ District 1	46.5
64	IL District 3	24.3	63	IN District 4	28.1	63	IN District 6	46.5
65	CA District 40	23.8	63	LA District 7	28.1	65	MD District 3	46.4
66	TX District 7	23.6	63	MI District 3	28.1	65	CA District 51	46.4
67	CA District 27	23.1	63	CO District 5	28.1	67	DC Delegate	46.3
67	FL District 20	23.1	68	CA District 5	28.0	67	FL District 20	46.3
69	FL District 8	23.0	68	IL District 16	28.0	67	MA District 9	46.3
69	TX District 5	23.0	68	NY District 17	28.0	67	NC District 2	46.3
71	AZ District 1	22.7	68	WA District 8	28.0	67	NJ District 7	46.3
72	CA District 48	22.5	72	CA District 48	27.9	72	MI District 9	46.2
73	TX District 22	22.3	72	VA District 10	27.9	72	MI District 11	46.2
74	CA District 13	22.1	72	CA District 3	27.9	72	NH District 1	46.2
75	CA District 7	21.6	72	TN District 9	27.9	72	MI District 12	46.2

Note: Column numbers refer to Table F. Congressional Districts.

77

TABLE 7—Congressional Districts of the 107th Congress
Selected Rankings

Highest Percent Age 65 Years and Over, 2000			Highest Percent of Households with Female Householder, 2000			Highest Percent Living Alone, 2000		
65 Years and Over Rank	State/Congressional District	[cols 19 & 20] Percent 65 Years and Over	Female Householder Rank	State/Congressional District	[col 76] Percent Female Householder	Living Alone Rank	State/Congressional District	[col 79] Percent Living Alone
1	FL District 13	29.4	1	NY District 16	37.5	1	NY District 14	51.3
2	FL District 14	26.6	2	MI District 14	30.5	2	NY District 8	47.1
3	FL District 19	25.3	3	NY District 10	29.2	3	CA District 29	45.8
4	FL District 22	23.5	4	NY District 11	29.1	4	DC Delegate	43.8
5	FL District 16	23.2	5	IL District 2	29.0	5	CA District 8	41.3
6	FL District 5	22.9	6	MI District 15	28.7	6	FL District 22	40.5
7	FL District 10	22.3	7	NY District 15	27.8	7	WA District 7	39.8
8	FL District 15	20.5	7	PA District 1	27.8	8	IL District 9	39.6
9	FL District 6	20.2	9	FL District 17	27.0	9	PA District 2	38.4
10	PA District 18	19.7	9	IL District 1	27.0	10	MN District 5	38.1
11	FL District 9	19.4	9	NY District 17	27.0	11	CO District 1	37.5
12	PA District 11	18.4	12	MD District 7	26.6	12	CA District 49	36.5
13	AZ District 3	18.2	13	AL District 7	26.1	13	MA District 8	36.4
14	PA District 12	17.9	14	NJ District 10	25.8	14	PA District 14	36.2
15	IA District 5	17.8	15	LA District 2	25.7	15	GA District 5	35.2
16	NC District 11	17.6	16	MS District 2	25.6	16	FL District 10	35.1
16	PA District 20	17.6	17	TN District 9	25.3	17	IL District 7	34.9
18	CA District 44	17.3	18	CA District 35	24.7	18	NY District 15	34.7
18	PA District 4	17.3	19	NY District 6	24.3	18	OH District 11	34.7
20	NE District 3	17.2	20	OH District 11	24.0	18	OH District 1	34.7
21	FL District 18	17.1	21	IL District 7	23.9	21	OH District 5	34.4
22	FL District 12	17.0	22	CA District 37	23.6	22	MO District 1	34.3
23	IL District 19	16.9	23	MO District 1	23.1	23	VA District 8	33.8
24	MA District 10	16.8	24	PA District 2	23.0	24	CA District 9	33.7
24	PA District 14	16.8	25	SC District 6	22.5	24	WI District 5	33.7
26	OH District 19	16.7	26	NY District 12	22.3	26	IN District 10	33.4
26	NJ District 3	16.7	27	FL District 3	22.1	27	MI District 15	33.1
26	OH District 17	16.7	28	FL District 23	22.0	28	MD District 7	32.9
26	PA District 10	16.7	29	VA District 3	21.7	28	OH District 10	32.9
30	IL District 17	16.6	30	MD District 4	21.1	30	MO District 5	32.8
31	PA District 6	16.5	31	GA District 5	20.9	31	TN District 5	32.5
32	KS District 1	16.4	32	TX District 30	20.6	32	PA District 1	32.2
33	IA District 2	16.3	32	WI District 5	20.6	33	NY District 21	32.1
34	NJ District 4	16.2	34	NC District 1	19.3	34	PA District 18	32.0
34	MI District 1	16.2	35	MS District 4	19.1	35	IL District 1	31.8
34	PA District 9	16.2	36	TX District 18	19.0	35	MN District 4	31.8
37	IA District 3	16.0	37	DC Delegate	18.9	37	KY District 3	31.7
37	NY District 5	16.0	38	GA District 2	18.8	38	CA District 32	31.3
39	AZ District 5	15.9	38	NC District 12	18.8	39	TN District 9	30.9
39	NY District 18	15.9	40	CA District 32	18.7	40	FL District 11	30.5
39	NY District 9	15.9	41	CA District 50	18.5	41	OH District 3	30.4
42	NY District 23	15.8	42	TX District 16	18.3	41	OH District 15	30.4
42	WV District 1	15.8	43	IN District 10	18.1	41	TX District 18	30.4
44	WV District 3	15.7	44	CA District 33	17.7	41	TX District 10	30.4
45	PA District 7	15.6	44	GA District 10	17.7	45	CA District 36	30.3
45	PA District 15	15.6	46	NJ District 13	17.6	45	RI District 1	30.3
45	AR District 4	15.6	46	TX District 28	17.6	47	NY District 28	30.2
45	MO District 8	15.6	46	TX District 20	17.6	47	NY District 29	30.2
45	NY District 30	15.6	49	CA District 31	17.4	47	VA District 3	30.2
45	PA District 3	15.6	50	OH District 1	17.3	50	NY District 9	30.1
51	PA District 21	15.5	51	CA District 42	17.2	50	PA District 3	30.1
52	FL District 7	15.4	52	CA District 34	16.9	52	MI District 12	29.8
52	MA District 7	15.4	53	GA District 4	16.8	52	NY District 30	29.8
52	RI District 1	15.4	53	PA District 3	16.8	54	WI District 4	29.7
55	CA District 2	15.3	55	LA District 5	16.7	55	MA District 7	29.6
55	NY District 3	15.3	55	LA District 4	16.7	56	CA District 5	29.5
55	NY District 21	15.3	57	AZ District 2	16.6	56	NY District 17	29.5
58	HI District 1	15.2	57	IL District 4	16.6	58	FL District 13	29.4
58	OR District 4	15.2	59	CA District 30	16.5	58	LA District 2	29.4
58	PA District 13	15.2	59	CA District 20	16.5	58	MA District 9	29.4
58	TX District 1	15.2	59	TX District 29	16.5	58	NY District 26	29.4
58	TX District 17	15.2	62	GA District 8	16.4	62	MO District 3	29.3
62	VA District 5	15.1	62	VA District 4	16.4	62	ND At Large	29.3
62	IL District 20	15.1	64	TX District 27	16.2	64	MD District 3	29.2
62	OH District 18	15.1	65	FL District 21	16.1	65	OK District 1	29.1
62	OR District 2	15.1	65	TX District 24	16.1	66	MI District 13	29.0
67	MN District 7	15.0	67	SC District 5	16.0	66	PA District 11	29.0
67	NY District 31	15.0	68	NY District 7	15.9	68	IL District 15	28.9
67	OK District 3	15.0	68	TX District 25	15.9	68	OH District 9	28.9
67	VA District 6	15.0	70	LA District 6	15.7	70	TX District 5	28.8
67	WI District 7	15.0	70	MS District 3	15.7	71	CA District 27	28.6
72	NJ District 9	14.9	72	AL District 1	15.6	71	NJ District 9	28.6
72	MN District 8	14.9	72	IN District 1	15.6	71	NY District 25	28.6
72	PA District 5	14.9	74	CA District 38	15.5	71	OR District 3	28.6
75	ME District 2	14.8	74	CA District 26	15.5	75	FL District 19	28.5

Note: Column numbers refer to Table F. Congressional Districts.

TABLE 7—Congressional Districts of the 107th Congress
Selected Rankings

Highest Percent Married Couple Family Households, 2000			Highest Percent of Families with Own Children Under 18 Years, 2000			Highest Percent Change in Households, 1990-2000		
Percent Married Couple Family Households Rank	State/Congressional District	[col 74] Percent Married Couple Family Households	Families with Own Children Under 18 Years Rank	State/Congressional District	[col 73] Percent Families with Own Children Under 18 Years	Change in Households Rank	State/Congressional District	[col 86] Percent Change in Households
1	UT District 1	66.3	1	CA District 20	50.3	1	NV District 2	75.9
2	NJ District 5	65.8	2	CA District 37	50.2	2	AZ District 6	71.5
2	UT District 3	65.8	3	CA District 33	49.9	3	AZ District 3	62.8
4	NY District 3	65.5	4	CA District 46	49.1	4	GA District 6	55.6
5	IL District 13	64.4	5	CA District 42	48.9	5	CO District 5	48.0
6	NJ District 12	64.3	6	CA District 41	46.3	6	NC District 7	46.8
7	NJ District 11	63.5	7	TX District 15	46.0	7	NV District 1	46.6
8	WI District 9	62.9	8	UT District 3	45.9	8	TX District 3	46.2
9	MN District 6	62.8	9	CA District 35	45.8	9	VA District 10	44.1
10	TX District 15	62.5	10	TX District 29	45.3	10	FL District 14	43.5
11	VA District 10	62.4	11	CA District 26	44.8	11	GA District 11	43.1
12	IL District 10	62.3	11	TX District 23	44.8	12	TX District 21	40.9
13	CA District 41	62.2	13	CA District 50	44.4	13	NC District 4	40.7
14	TX District 23	62.1	14	CA District 34	44.0	14	TX District 8	40.6
15	GA District 9	62.0	15	NY District 16	43.9	15	TN District 6	40.3
16	TX District 22	61.9	15	UT District 1	43.9	16	TX District 26	40.2
17	IL District 14	61.8	17	CA District 43	43.7	17	ID District 1	39.8
18	NY District 2	61.4	18	TX District 16	43.4	18	FL District 19	39.4
19	PA District 8	61.2	19	CA District 31	43.2	19	MN District 6	38.4
20	OH District 13	61.0	20	TX District 22	42.7	20	FL District 6	37.8
20	WA District 8	61.0	21	CA District 25	42.5	20	TN District 7	37.8
22	IL District 8	60.8	21	CA District 18	42.5	22	GA District 9	37.7
22	MD District 6	60.8	23	IL District 4	42.2	23	FL District 8	37.3
24	MN District 2	60.7	24	MN District 6	41.9	24	TX District 23	37.0
24	NY District 1	60.7	25	IL District 14	40.8	25	TX District 10	36.6
26	CA District 48	60.6	25	TX District 24	40.8	26	TX District 15	36.4
27	NY District 20	60.5	27	CA District 16	40.7	27	UT District 1	36.0
27	TX District 8	60.5	27	TX District 27	40.7	28	IL District 13	35.8
29	NY District 4	60.3	27	TX District 28	40.7	29	TX District 22	35.4
29	PA District 16	60.3	30	FL District 21	40.4	30	FL District 20	34.4
29	TN District 6	60.3	31	AZ District 2	40.2	30	TX District 6	34.4
32	CO District 5	60.2	32	CA District 23	40.0	32	CO District 3	34.2
32	IN District 6	60.2	33	AK At Large	39.9	32	FL District 21	34.2
34	CA District 10	60.1	34	CA District 11	39.8	34	FL District 16	34.1
35	TX District 21	60.0	34	CA District 21	39.8	35	CO District 4	34.0
36	NJ District 7	59.9	36	IL District 13	39.6	35	UT District 3	34.0
37	NY District 5	59.7	36	TX District 3	39.6	35	WA District 2	34.0
38	NY District 19	59.6	38	VA District 10	39.2	38	GA District 3	33.5
39	MI District 2	59.2	39	CA District 48	39.1	39	IN District 6	33.1
39	TX District 4	59.2	40	CO District 5	38.9	40	FL District 4	32.9
41	ID District 1	59.1	40	WA District 8	38.9	41	TX District 7	32.8
41	NJ District 3	59.1	42	LA District 3	38.8	42	NM District 3	32.3
41	OH District 8	59.1	43	GA District 3	38.7	43	AZ District 5	31.9
41	TX District 6	59.1	44	UT District 2	38.6	44	SC District 2	31.6
45	CA District 43	59.0	45	IL District 10	38.4	45	CA District 48	31.5
45	GA District 11	59.0	45	NY District 6	38.4	46	AZ District 1	31.4
47	CA District 39	58.9	47	CA District 19	38.3	47	AR District 3	30.7
47	CA District 46	58.9	47	FL District 17	38.3	48	OR District 1	30.2
47	IL District 16	58.9	49	CA District 30	38.2	48	WA District 8	30.2
47	TN District 7	58.9	49	TX District 8	38.2	50	FL District 15	30.1
51	CA District 23	58.8	51	TX District 25	38.1	51	CA District 4	29.9
52	GA District 6	58.7	52	GA District 13	38.0	52	FL District 9	29.3
53	ID District 2	58.6	52	GA District 6	38.0	53	WA District 3	29.2
53	IN District 5	58.6	52	NY District 2	38.0	54	CO District 2	28.8
55	AL District 4	58.5	55	CA District 28	37.9	55	FL District 7	28.6
55	IN District 9	58.5	56	CA District 39	37.8	56	NC District 2	28.3
57	AZ District 6	58.4	56	WA District 4	37.8	57	NC District 9	28.1
57	CA District 51	58.4	58	GA District 11	37.7	58	VA District 1	27.8
59	FL District 6	58.3	58	TX District 6	37.7	59	SC District 1	27.5
59	KY District 2	58.3	60	CA District 52	37.6	60	NC District 6	26.9
59	MO District 4	58.3	60	IL District 8	37.6	61	GA District 7	26.8
59	OH District 5	58.3	60	MA District 5	37.6	62	IL District 14	25.3
59	TN District 4	58.3	63	NJ District 5	37.6	63	MO District 9	24.3
64	FL District 21	58.2	64	CA District 40	37.5	64	FL District 1	24.1
64	MO District 2	58.2	65	NY District 20	37.4	64	MO District 7	24.1
66	MI District 4	58.1	66	CA District 17	37.2	66	CA District 43	24.0
66	OH District 7	58.1	67	ID District 2	37.1	67	FL District 2	23.9
66	OK District 2	58.1	67	NC District 8	37.1	67	TX District 4	23.9
69	CA District 34	58.0	69	NJ District 12	37.0	69	MD District 5	23.6
69	MD District 8	58.0	70	TN District 7	36.9	69	OR District 2	23.6
69	PA District 9	58.0	71	CA District 10	36.8	71	FL District 5	23.4
72	CA District 20	57.9	71	TX District 7	36.8	71	WI District 9	23.4
72	PA District 19	57.9	73	IL District 16	36.7	73	CA District 44	23.2
72	VA District 7	57.9	73	MD District 6	36.7	73	NC District 11	23.2
72	VA District 1	57.9	73	VA District 11	36.7	73	NM District 2	23.2

Note: Column numbers refer to Table F. Congressional Districts.

TABLE 7—Congressional Districts of the 107th Congress
Selected Rankings

Highest Percent in Group Quarters, 2000			Highest Percent in Dormitories, 2000			Highest Percent Owner Occupied Housing Units, 2000		
Group Quarters Rank	State/Congressional District	[col 64] Percent in Group Quarters	Dormitories Rank	State/Congressional District	[col 68] Percent in Dormitories	Owner Occupied Housing Units Rank	State/Congressional District	[col 94] Percent in Owner Occupied Housing Units
1	CA District 49	7.4	1	MA District 8	5.7	1	MN District 6	84.3
2	CA District 20	7.3	2	IL District 15	3.8	2	NY District 3	83.8
3	MA District 8	7.1	3	DC Delegate	3.4	3	NJ District 3	82.8
4	FL District 2	7.0	3	PA District 5	3.4	4	NJ District 5	81.8
5	NY District 24	6.8	5	IN District 7	3.2	5	IL District 13	81.3
6	NY District 26	6.5	5	NY District 26	3.2	6	MI District 2	80.8
6	PA District 5	6.5	7	IN District 8	3.1	7	NJ District 12	80.7
6	TX District 2	6.5	8	MA District 1	3.0	8	MN District 8	80.5
9	NC District 3	6.4	9	PA District 2	2.8	0	MN District 2	80.1
10	IL District 15	6.3	9	VA District 6	2.8	10	MI District 4	80.0
11	DC Delegate	6.2	11	RI District 1	2.6	11	FL District 6	79.9
11	NY District 15	6.2	12	IA District 3	2.4	12	MI District 5	79.5
11	TX District 13	6.2	12	MI District 13	2.4	13	MI District 10	79.2
14	TX District 11	6.1	12	PA District 14	2.4	13	NY District 1	79.2
15	TX District 17	5.9	15	NY District 21	2.3	15	OH District 13	79.1
16	IN District 7	5.6	16	KY District 6	2.2	16	FL District 16	78.8
16	NY District 23	5.6	16	NY District 23	2.2	16	MI District 1	78.8
18	VA District 6	5.3	16	VA District 9	2.2	18	MI District 11	78.7
19	LA District 5	5.2	16	WI District 3	2.2	19	IL District 8	78.4
20	CA District 22	5.1	20	CT District 2	2.1	20	NY District 2	78.3
20	IN District 8	5.1	20	GA District 5	2.1	21	NJ District 11	78.2
20	PA District 2	5.1	20	MA District 4	2.1	22	PA District 4	78.0
20	PA District 14	5.1	20	MI District 8	2.1	23	AL District 4	77.9
24	IA District 3	5.0	20	NY District 24	2.1	24	FL District 19	77.8
25	FL District 1	4.9	20	PA District 21	2.1	24	NY District 4	77.8
25	NY District 19	4.9	20	VT At Large	2.1	26	FL District 13	77.5
25	NY District 31	4.9	27	NE District 1	2.0	27	MI District 16	77.4
25	PA District 21	4.9	28	CA District 29	1.9	28	FL District 14	77.3
25	VA District 4	4.9	28	CT District 3	1.9	28	LA District 3	77.3
30	CA District 1	4.8	28	NC District 12	1.9	28	MO District 2	77.3
30	CT District 2	4.8	28	NC District 4	1.9	28	PA District 8	77.3
30	GA District 2	4.8	28	NJ District 12	1.9	32	MN District 1	77.2
30	GA District 5	4.8	28	TN District 5	1.9	33	AZ District 3	77.0
30	MA District 1	4.8	34	CA District 49	1.8	33	IL District 10	77.0
30	SC District 2	4.8	34	MN District 7	1.8	35	AZ District 6	76.9
30	VA District 2	4.8	34	NY District 28	1.8	35	GA District 9	76.9
37	CA District 33	4.7	34	WA District 7	1.8	35	OH District 5	76.9
37	KS District 2	4.7	38	IA District 2	1.7	38	FL District 9	76.7
37	NY District 27	4.7	38	MI District 4	1.7	38	TN District 4	76.7
37	SC District 6	4.7	38	MN District 1	1.7	40	IN District 5	76.6
37	TX District 5	4.7	38	MO District 9	1.7	41	FL District 20	76.5
42	MD District 7	4.6	38	NC District 2	1.7	41	IN District 9	76.5
42	NY District 21	4.6	38	NY District 27	1.7	41	KY District 5	76.5
44	GA District 10	4.5	38	NY District 25	1.7	44	IL District 14	76.4
44	WA District 7	4.5	38	NY District 15	1.7	44	MN District 7	76.4
46	MI District 7	4.4	38	NY District 8	1.7	44	MS District 1	76.4
46	NC District 2	4.4	38	SC District 6	1.7	47	MI District 7	76.3
46	OK District 6	4.4	38	VA District 5	1.7	48	IL District 11	76.2
49	CA District 17	4.3	38	WA District 5	1.7	48	OH District 19	76.2
49	NC District 8	4.3	50	CA District 22	1.6	50	NY District 27	76.1
49	OK District 4	4.3	50	IA District 1	1.6	50	PA District 9	76.1
49	OK District 3	4.3	50	MA District 3	1.6	50	TX District 2	76.1
49	RI District 1	4.3	50	MD District 7	1.6	50	VA District 10	76.1
49	VA District 9	4.3	50	ND At Large	1.6	54	FL District 15	76.0
49	WA District 5	4.3	50	NH District 2	1.6	54	IL District 16	76.0
56	GA District 8	4.2	50	NY District 31	1.6	56	IN District 6	75.9
56	IL District 20	4.2	50	OH District 9	1.6	56	OK District 2	75.9
56	IL District 17	4.2	58	AL District 7	1.5	56	PA District 20	75.9
56	MS District 2	4.2	58	IL District 17	1.5	56	WI District 7	75.9
56	WI District 3	4.2	58	IN District 3	1.5	60	WV District 2	75.8
61	GA District 1	4.1	58	MD District 5	1.5	61	MN District 3	75.7
61	MN District 1	4.1	58	MO District 7	1.5	61	PA District 12	75.7
61	MO District 9	4.1	58	NJ District 6	1.5	61	WV District 3	75.7
61	NY District 22	4.1	58	OH District 6	1.5	64	SC District 3	75.6
61	OH District 4	4.1	58	OK District 3	1.5	65	NC District 11	75.5
61	PA District 12	4.1	58	PA District 19	1.5	66	TN District 6	75.4
61	TN District 5	4.1	58	PA District 7	1.5	67	IL District 19	75.3
68	KY District 6	4.0	58	WI District 2	1.5	67	NC District 10	75.3
68	LA District 6	4.0	69	CT District 1	1.4	67	WI District 9	75.3
68	MA District 4	4.0	69	MN District 4	1.4	70	IL District 20	75.2
68	MI District 1	4.0	69	OH District 15	1.4	70	MI District 12	75.2
68	MN District 7	4.0	69	PA District 16	1.4	70	NJ District 4	75.2
68	MN District 5	4.0	69	PA District 15	1.4	73	PA District 19	75.1
68	NC District 12	4.0	69	PA District 1	1.4	74	MD District 6	75.0
68	NE District 1	4.0	69	SC District 3	1.4	74	OH District 18	75.0

Note: Column numbers refer to Table F. Congressional Districts.

TABLE 7—Congressional Districts of the 107th Congress
Selected Rankings

Highest Percent Recreational/Seasonal Housing Units, 2000			Highest Homeowner Vacancy Rate, 2000			Highest Renter Vacancy Rate, 2000		
Recreational/ Seasonal Housing Units Rank	State/Congressional District	[col 90] Percent Recreational/ Seasonal Housing Units	Homeowner Vacancy Rate Rank	State/Congressional District	[col 91] Homeowner Vacancy Rate	Renter Vacancy Rate Rank	State/Congressional District	[col 92] Renter Vacancy Rate
1	MI District 1	23.1	1	NY District 15	5.8	1	FL District 1	19.2
2	MA District 10	19.3	2	CA District 40	3.7	2	SC District 1	17.7
3	FL District 14	18.5	3	OK District 6	3.6	3	NM District 2	14.0
4	MN District 8	18.1	4	GA District 5	3.4	4	FL District 14	13.7
5	ME District 2	17.8	5	CA District 44	3.2	5	NC District 7	13.2
6	NJ District 2	17.7	5	CA District 42	3.2	6	AL District 1	13.1
7	WI District 8	17.4	7	CA District 35	3.1	7	GA District 8	13.0
8	MI District 4	16.7	8	CA District 37	3.0	7	OK District 6	13.0
9	PA District 10	15.8	8	MD District 7	3.0	9	AL District 3	12.7
10	NY District 24	15.7	8	TX District 17	3.0	10	AL District 2	12.4
11	FL District 22	15.5	8	TX District 13	3.0	11	FL District 13	12.3
12	CO District 3	15.2	12	DC Delegate	2.9	12	TX District 17	12.2
13	AZ District 6	14.8	12	MO District 7	2.9	13	AL District 5	12.0
14	PA District 5	14.6	14	AZ District 6	2.8	13	TX District 19	12.0
14	VT At Large	14.6	14	CA District 33	2.8	15	FL District 15	11.9
16	WI District 7	14.0	14	FL District 22	2.8	16	AL District 4	11.8
17	ME District 1	13.4	14	FL District 20	2.8	17	TX District 27	11.8
18	NY District 1	13.2	14	FL District 23	2.8	18	FL District 2	11.6
19	NC District 3	13.0	14	MO District 1	2.8	18	SC District 3	11.6
20	MN District 7	12.5	14	NM District 2	2.8	18	SC District 2	11.6
21	CA District 4	12.1	14	OK District 4	2.8	18	TX District 2	11.6
22	FL District 13	11.3	22	AR District 3	2.7	18	IX District 9	11.6
22	NY District 22	11.3	22	FL District 12	2.7	23	NM District 1	11.5
24	CA District 44	11.2	22	KS District 1	2.7	24	KS District 4	11.4
25	MI District 2	11.1	22	MO District 4	2.7	25	AZ District 6	11.3
26	CA District 40	10.9	22	ND At Large	2.7	25	IN District 10	11.3
26	NH District 1	10.9	22	NE District 3	2.7	25	OK District 4	11.3
28	MO District 4	10.3	22	NV District 2	2.7	28	FL District 9	11.2
28	SC District 1	10.3	22	OK District 3	2.7	28	TX District 15	11.2
30	FL District 16	10.2	30	FL District 14	2.6	30	GA District 1	11.1
31	NJ District 3	9.9	30	MO District 8	2.6	31	AL District 7	10.9
32	NY District 31	9.8	30	NY District 24	2.6	31	GA District 2	10.9
33	NH District 2	9.6	30	NY District 16	2.6	31	LA District 7	10.9
34	NC District 11	9.4	30	OR District 5	2.6	31	TN District 1	10.9
35	MI District 5	8.9	30	VA District 3	2.6	31	TX District 1	10.9
36	HI District 2	8.5	36	AR District 1	2.5	36	AR District 4	10.8
37	AK At Large	8.2	36	AZ District 3	2.5	36	NJ District 3	10.8
38	AZ District 3	7.9	36	CA District 21	2.5	36	OK District 3	10.8
38	MD District 1	7.9	36	FL District 16	2.5	39	FL District 12	10.7
40	FL District 10	7.7	36	FL District 1	2.5	39	MD District 1	10.7
40	NC District 7	7.7	36	FL District 5	2.5	39	MS District 5	10.7
42	DE At Large	7.6	36	FL District 3	2.5	39	OH District 11	10.7
42	TX District 15	7.6	36	FL District 17	2.5	43	AR District 1	10.6
44	FL District 1	7.5	36	NY District 10	2.5	43	FL District 16	10.6
44	WI District 6	7.5	36	UT District 1	2.5	43	TX District 13	10.6
46	FL District 15	7.2	46	AR District 4	2.4	46	FL District 6	10.5
47	FL District 12	7.0	46	CO District 3	2.4	46	LA District 4	10.5
47	TX District 2	7.0	46	FL District 10	2.4	46	MO District 1	10.5
49	NY District 23	6.8	46	IN District 10	2.4	49	FL District 10	10.4
50	FL District 19	6.7	46	MD District 4	2.4	49	MS District 4	10.4
50	UT District 3	6.7	46	MI District 5	2.4	51	GA District 10	10.3
52	NY District 26	6.3	46	NC District 7	2.4	51	NY District 23	10.3
53	CA District 2	6.2	46	NV District 1	2.4	51	OK District 5	10.3
53	TX District 27	6.2	46	NY District 23	2.4	54	AZ District 5	10.2
55	NM District 3	6.1	46	OK District 2	2.4	54	SC District 4	10.2
56	FL District 20	6.0	46	OR District 1	2.4	56	KY District 5	10.1
56	MI District 6	6.0	46	TX District 2	2.4	56	NV District 2	10.1
58	MT At Large	5.9	46	WV District 3	2.4	56	NY District 29	10.1
59	OK District 2	5.8	59	AL District 1	2.3	56	TX District 23	10.1
60	PA District 11	5.7	59	FL District 15	2.3	60	AL District 4	10.0
61	FL District 9	5.6	59	FL District 6	2.3	60	IL District 19	10.0
61	ID District 1	5.6	59	ID District 1	2.3	60	IN District 6	10.0
63	NM District 2	5.5	59	IL District 7	2.3	60	KS District 1	10.0
63	WY At Large	5.5	59	ME District 2	2.3	60	TN District 2	10.0
65	PA District 9	5.4	59	NC District 2	2.3	65	WV District 3	9.9
66	AL District 1	5.3	59	NY District 26	2.3	66	IN District 4	9.8
66	TX District 14	5.3	59	NY District 17	2.3	66	LA District 6	9.8
66	WA District 2	5.3	59	OR District 3	2.3	66	MO District 8	9.8
69	FL District 5	5.2	59	SC District 4	2.3	66	NC District 11	9.8
69	NC District 10	5.2	59	TN District 2	2.3	70	NJ District 1	9.7
69	WV District 2	5.2	59	TX District 11	2.3	70	OH District 3	9.7
72	AZ District 2	5.1	59	WA District 6	2.3	70	WY At Large	9.7
73	GA District 9	5.0	59	WA District 3	2.3	73	FL District 5	9.6
74	ID District 2	4.8	59	WA District 5	2.3	73	FL District 4	9.6
75	OR District 2	4.7	75	CA District 2	2.2	73	OK District 2	9.6

Note: Column numbers refer to Table F. Congressional Districts.

States

(For explanation of symbols, see page xi.)

Table A. States

STATE code	STATE	Land area, 2000[1] (sq km)	Population, 2000 Total persons	Rank	Per square kilometer	Land area, 1990[1] (sq km)	Population, 1990 Total persons	Rank	Per square kilometer	White	Black or African American	American Indian or Alaska Native	Asian	Native Hawaiian and other Pacific Islander	Some other race
		1	2	3	4	5	6	7	8	9	10	11	12	13	14
00	UNITED STATES	9 161 924	281 421 906	X	30.7	9 159 127	248 790 925	X	27.2	75.1	12.3	0.9	3.6	0.1	5.5
01	ALABAMA	131 426	4 447 100	23	33.8	131 443	4 040 389	22	30.7	71.1	26.0	0.5	0.7	0.0	0.7
02	ALASKA	1 481 347	626 932	48	0.4	1 477 268	550 043	50	0.4	69.3	3.5	15.6	4.0	0.5	1.6
04	ARIZONA	294 312	5 130 632	20	17.4	294 333	3 665 339	24	12.5	75.5	3.1	5.0	1.8	0.1	11.6
05	ARKANSAS	134 856	2 673 400	33	19.8	134 875	2 350 624	33	17.4	80.0	15.7	0.7	0.8	0.1	1.5
06	CALIFORNIA	403 933	33 871 648	1	83.9	403 970	29 811 427	1	73.8	59.5	6.7	1.0	10.9	0.3	16.8
08	COLORADO	268 627	4 301 261	24	16.0	268 660	3 294 473	26	12.3	82.8	3.8	1.0	2.2	0.1	7.2
09	CONNECTICUT	12 548	3 405 565	29	271.4	12 550	3 287 116	27	261.9	81.6	9.1	0.3	2.4	0.0	4.3
10	DELAWARE	5 060	783 600	45	154.9	5 062	666 168	46	131.6	74.6	19.2	0.3	2.1	0.0	2.0
11	DISTRICT OF COLUMBIA	159	572 059	50	3 597.9	159	606 900	48	3 817.0	30.8	60.0	0.3	2.7	0.1	3.8
12	FLORIDA	139 670	15 982 378	4	114.4	139 852	12 938 071	4	92.5	78.0	14.6	0.3	1.7	0.1	3.0
13	GEORGIA	149 976	8 186 453	10	54.6	150 010	6 478 149	11	43.2	65.1	28.7	0.3	2.1	0.1	2.4
15	HAWAII	16 635	1 211 537	42	72.8	16 636	1 108 229	41	66.6	24.3	1.8	0.3	41.6	9.4	1.3
16	IDAHO	214 314	1 293 953	39	6.0	214 325	1 006 734	42	4.7	91.0	0.4	1.4	0.9	0.1	4.2
17	ILLINOIS	143 961	12 419 293	5	86.3	143 987	11 430 602	6	79.4	73.5	15.1	0.2	3.4	0.0	5.8
18	INDIANA	92 895	6 080 485	14	65.5	92 904	5 544 156	14	59.7	87.5	8.4	0.3	1.0	0.0	1.6
19	IOWA	144 701	2 926 324	30	20.2	144 716	2 776 831	30	19.2	93.9	2.1	0.3	1.3	0.0	1.3
20	KANSAS	211 900	2 688 418	32	12.7	211 922	2 477 588	32	11.7	86.1	5.7	0.9	1.7	0.0	3.4
21	KENTUCKY	102 896	4 041 769	25	39.3	102 907	3 686 892	23	35.8	90.1	7.3	0.2	0.7	0.0	0.6
22	LOUISIANA	112 825	4 468 976	22	39.6	112 836	4 221 826	21	37.4	63.9	32.5	0.6	1.2	0.0	0.7
23	MAINE	79 931	1 274 923	40	16.0	79 939	1 227 928	38	15.4	96.9	0.5	0.6	0.7	0.0	0.2
24	MARYLAND	25 314	5 296 486	19	209.2	25 316	4 780 753	19	188.8	64.0	27.9	0.3	4.0	0.0	1.8
25	MASSACHUSETTS	20 306	6 349 097	13	312.7	20 300	6 016 425	13	296.4	84.5	5.4	0.2	3.8	0.0	3.7
26	MICHIGAN	147 121	9 938 444	8	67.6	147 136	9 295 287	8	63.2	80.2	14.2	0.6	1.8	0.0	1.3
27	MINNESOTA	206 189	4 919 479	21	23.9	206 207	4 375 665	20	21.2	89.4	3.5	1.1	2.9	0.0	1.3
28	MISSISSIPPI	121 488	2 844 658	31	23.4	121 506	2 575 475	31	21.2	61.4	36.3	0.4	0.7	0.0	0.5
29	MISSOURI	178 414	5 595 211	17	31.4	178 446	5 116 901	15	28.7	84.9	11.2	0.4	1.1	0.1	0.8
30	MONTANA	376 979	902 195	44	2.4	376 991	799 065	44	2.1	90.6	0.3	6.2	0.5	0.1	0.6
31	NEBRASKA	199 099	1 711 263	38	8.6	199 113	1 578 417	36	7.9	89.6	4.0	0.9	1.3	0.0	2.8
32	NEVADA	284 448	1 998 257	35	7.0	284 397	1 201 675	39	4.2	75.2	6.8	1.3	4.5	0.4	8.0
33	NEW HAMPSHIRE	23 227	1 235 786	41	53.2	23 231	1 109 252	40	47.7	96.0	0.7	0.2	1.3	0.0	0.6
34	NEW JERSEY	19 211	8 414 350	9	438.0	19 215	7 747 750	9	403.2	72.6	13.6	0.2	5.7	0.0	5.4
35	NEW MEXICO	314 309	1 819 046	36	5.8	314 334	1 515 069	37	4.8	66.8	1.9	9.5	1.1	0.1	17.0
36	NEW YORK	122 283	18 976 457	3	155.2	122 310	17 990 778	2	147.1	67.9	15.9	0.4	5.5	0.0	7.1
37	NORTH CAROLINA	126 161	8 049 313	11	63.8	126 180	6 632 448	10	52.6	72.1	21.6	1.2	1.4	0.0	2.3
38	NORTH DAKOTA	178 647	642 200	47	3.6	178 695	638 800	47	3.6	92.4	0.6	4.9	0.6	0.0	0.4
39	OHIO	106 056	11 353 140	7	107.0	106 067	10 847 115	7	102.3	85.0	11.5	0.2	1.2	0.0	0.8
40	OKLAHOMA	177 847	3 450 654	27	19.4	177 878	3 145 576	28	17.7	76.2	7.6	7.9	1.4	0.1	2.4
41	OREGON	248 631	3 421 399	28	13.8	248 647	2 842 337	29	11.4	86.6	1.6	1.3	3.0	0.2	4.2
42	PENNSYLVANIA	116 074	12 281 054	6	105.8	116 083	11 882 842	5	102.4	85.4	10.0	0.1	1.8	0.0	1.5
44	RHODE ISLAND	2 706	1 048 319	43	387.4	2 707	1 003 464	43	370.7	85.0	4.5	0.5	2.3	0.1	5.0
45	SOUTH CAROLINA	77 983	4 012 012	26	51.4	77 988	3 486 310	25	44.7	67.2	29.5	0.3	0.9	0.0	1.0
46	SOUTH DAKOTA	196 540	754 844	46	3.8	196 575	696 004	45	3.5	88.7	0.6	8.3	0.6	0.0	0.5
47	TENNESSEE	106 752	5 689 283	16	53.3	106 759	4 877 203	17	45.7	80.2	16.4	0.3	1.0	0.0	1.0
48	TEXAS	678 051	20 851 820	2	30.8	678 358	16 986 335	3	25.0	71.0	11.5	0.6	2.7	0.1	11.7
49	UTAH	212 751	2 233 169	34	10.5	212 816	1 722 850	35	8.1	89.2	0.8	1.3	1.7	0.7	4.2
50	VERMONT	23 956	608 827	49	25.4	23 956	562 758	49	23.5	96.8	0.5	0.4	0.9	0.0	0.2
51	VIRGINIA	102 548	7 078 515	12	69.0	102 558	6 189 197	12	60.3	72.3	19.6	0.3	3.7	0.1	2.0
53	WASHINGTON	172 348	5 894 121	15	34.2	172 447	4 866 669	18	28.2	81.8	3.2	1.6	5.5	0.4	3.9
54	WEST VIRGINIA	62 361	1 808 344	37	29.0	62 384	1 793 477	34	28.7	95.0	3.2	0.2	0.5	0.0	0.2
55	WISCONSIN	140 663	5 363 675	18	38.1	140 672	4 891 954	16	34.8	88.9	5.7	0.9	1.7	0.0	1.6
56	WYOMING	251 489	493 782	51	2.0	251 501	453 589	51	1.8	92.1	0.8	2.3	0.6	0.1	2.5

[1] Dry land or land partially or temporarily covered by water.

STATE	Population and population characteristics, 2000 (cont'd)								Population and population characteristics, 1990				
	Race (percent) (cont'd)								Race (percent)				
	Race alone or in combination												
	Two or more races	White	Black	American Indian or Alaska Native	Asian	Native Hawaiian and other Pacific Islander	Some other race	Hispanic[1]	White	Black or African American	American Indian or Alaska Native	Asian and Pacific Islander	Hispanic[1]
	15	16	17	18	19	20	21	22	23	24	25	26	27
UNITED STATES	2.4	77.1	12.9	1.5	4.2	0.3	6.6	12.5	80.3	12.1	0.8	2.9	9.0
ALABAMA	1.0	72.0	26.3	1.0	0.9	0.1	0.9	1.7	73.6	25.3	0.4	0.5	0.6
ALASKA	5.4	74.0	4.3	19.0	5.2	0.9	2.4	4.1	75.5	4.1	15.6	3.6	3.2
ARIZONA	2.9	77.9	3.6	5.7	2.3	0.3	13.2	25.3	80.8	3.0	5.6	1.5	18.8
ARKANSAS	1.3	81.2	16.0	1.4	1.0	0.1	1.8	3.2	82.7	15.9	0.5	0.5	0.8
CALIFORNIA	4.7	63.4	7.4	1.9	12.3	0.7	19.4	32.4	69.0	7.4	0.8	9.6	25.8
COLORADO	2.8	85.2	4.4	1.9	2.8	0.2	8.5	17.1	88.2	4.0	0.8	1.8	12.9
CONNECTICUT	2.2	83.3	10.0	0.7	2.8	0.1	5.5	9.4	87.0	8.3	0.2	1.5	6.5
DELAWARE	1.7	75.9	20.1	0.8	2.4	0.1	2.6	4.8	80.3	16.9	0.3	1.4	2.4
DISTRICT OF COLUMBIA	2.4	32.2	61.3	0.8	3.1	0.1	5.0	7.9	29.6	65.8	0.2	1.8	5.4
FLORIDA	2.4	79.7	15.5	0.7	2.1	0.2	4.4	16.8	83.1	13.6	0.3	1.2	12.2
GEORGIA	1.4	66.1	29.2	0.6	2.4	0.1	2.9	5.3	71.0	27.0	0.2	1.2	1.7
HAWAII	21.4	39.3	2.8	2.1	58.0	23.3	3.9	7.2	33.4	2.5	0.5	61.8	7.3
IDAHO	2.0	92.8	0.6	2.1	1.3	0.2	5.0	7.9	94.4	0.3	1.4	0.9	5.3
ILLINOIS	1.9	75.1	15.6	0.6	3.8	0.1	6.8	12.3	78.3	14.8	0.2	2.5	7.9
INDIANA	1.2	88.6	8.8	0.6	1.2	0.1	2.0	3.5	90.6	7.8	0.2	0.7	1.8
IOWA	1.1	94.9	2.5	0.6	1.5	0.1	1.6	2.8	96.6	1.7	0.3	0.9	1.2
KANSAS	2.1	87.9	6.3	1.8	2.1	0.1	4.0	7.0	90.1	5.8	0.9	1.3	3.8
KENTUCKY	1.1	91.0	7.7	0.6	0.9	0.1	0.8	1.5	92.0	7.1	0.2	0.5	0.6
LOUISIANA	1.1	64.8	32.9	1.0	1.4	0.1	1.1	2.4	67.3	30.8	0.4	1.0	2.2
MAINE	1.0	97.9	0.7	1.0	0.9	0.1	0.4	0.7	98.4	0.4	0.5	0.5	0.6
MARYLAND	2.0	65.4	28.8	0.7	4.5	0.1	2.5	4.3	71.0	24.9	0.3	2.9	2.6
MASSACHUSETTS	2.3	86.2	6.3	0.6	4.2	0.1	5.1	6.8	89.8	5.0	0.2	2.4	4.8
MICHIGAN	1.9	81.8	14.8	1.3	2.1	0.1	2.0	3.3	83.4	13.9	0.6	1.1	2.2
MINNESOTA	1.7	90.8	4.1	1.6	3.3	0.1	1.8	2.9	94.4	2.2	1.1	1.8	1.2
MISSISSIPPI	0.7	61.9	36.6	0.7	0.8	0.1	0.7	1.4	63.5	35.6	0.3	0.5	0.6
MISSOURI	1.5	86.1	11.7	1.1	1.4	0.1	1.2	2.1	87.7	10.7	0.4	0.8	1.2
MONTANA	1.7	92.2	0.5	7.4	0.8	0.1	0.9	2.0	92.7	0.3	6.0	0.5	1.5
NEBRASKA	1.4	90.8	4.4	1.3	1.6	0.1	3.3	5.5	93.8	3.6	0.8	0.8	2.3
NEVADA	3.8	78.4	7.5	2.1	5.6	0.8	9.7	19.7	84.3	6.6	1.6	3.2	10.4
NEW HAMPSHIRE	1.1	97.0	1.0	0.6	1.6	0.1	0.9	1.7	98.0	0.6	0.2	0.8	1.0
NEW JERSEY	2.5	74.4	14.4	0.6	6.2	0.1	6.9	13.3	79.3	13.4	0.2	3.5	9.6
NEW MEXICO	3.6	69.9	2.3	10.5	1.5	0.2	19.4	42.1	75.6	2.0	8.9	0.9	38.2
NEW YORK	3.1	70.0	17.0	0.9	6.2	0.2	9.1	15.1	74.4	15.9	0.3	3.9	12.3
NORTH CAROLINA	1.3	73.1	22.1	1.6	1.7	0.1	2.8	4.7	75.6	22.0	1.2	0.8	1.2
NORTH DAKOTA	1.2	93.4	0.8	5.5	0.8	0.1	0.6	1.2	94.6	0.6	4.1	0.5	0.7
OHIO	1.4	86.1	12.1	0.7	1.4	0.1	1.1	1.9	87.8	10.6	0.2	0.8	1.3
OKLAHOMA	4.5	80.3	8.3	11.4	1.7	0.1	3.0	5.2	82.1	7.4	8.0	1.1	2.7
OREGON	3.1	89.3	2.1	2.5	3.7	0.5	5.2	8.0	92.8	1.6	1.4	2.4	4.0
PENNSYLVANIA	1.2	86.3	10.5	0.4	2.0	0.1	1.9	3.2	88.5	9.2	0.1	1.2	2.0
RHODE ISLAND	2.7	86.9	5.5	1.0	2.7	0.2	6.6	8.7	91.4	3.9	0.4	1.8	4.6
SOUTH CAROLINA	1.0	68.0	29.9	0.7	1.1	0.1	1.3	2.4	69.0	29.8	0.2	0.6	0.9
SOUTH DAKOTA	1.3	89.9	0.9	9.0	0.8	0.1	0.7	1.4	91.6	0.5	7.3	0.4	0.8
TENNESSEE	1.1	81.2	16.8	0.7	1.2	0.1	1.3	2.2	83.0	16.0	0.2	0.7	0.7
TEXAS	2.5	73.1	12.0	1.0	3.1	0.1	13.3	32.0	75.2	11.9	0.4	1.9	25.5
UTAH	2.1	91.1	1.1	1.8	2.2	1.0	5.1	9.0	93.8	0.7	1.4	1.9	4.9
VERMONT	1.2	97.9	0.7	1.1	1.1	0.1	0.4	0.9	98.6	0.3	0.3	0.6	0.7
VIRGINIA	2.0	73.9	20.4	0.7	4.3	0.1	2.7	4.7	77.4	18.8	0.2	2.6	2.6
WASHINGTON	3.6	84.9	4.0	2.7	6.7	0.7	4.9	7.5	88.5	3.1	1.7	4.3	4.4
WEST VIRGINIA	0.9	95.9	3.5	0.6	0.7	0.0	0.3	0.7	96.2	3.1	0.1	0.4	0.5
WISCONSIN	1.2	90.0	6.1	1.3	1.9	0.1	2.0	3.6	92.2	5.0	0.8	1.1	1.9
WYOMING	1.8	93.7	1.0	3.0	0.8	0.1	3.2	6.4	94.2	0.8	2.1	0.6	5.7

[1] Hispanic persons may be of any race.

Table A. States

STATE	Under 5 years	5 to 17 years	18 to 24 years	25 to 34 years	35 to 44 years	45 to 54 years	55 to 64 years	65 to 74 years	75 years and over	Median age (years)	Percent Female
	Population and population characteristics, 2000										
	Age (percent)										
	28	29	30	31	32	33	34	35	36	37	38
UNITED STATES	6.8	18.9	9.7	14.2	16.0	13.4	8.6	6.5	5.9	35.3	50.9
ALABAMA	6.7	18.6	9.9	13.6	15.4	13.5	9.3	7.1	5.9	35.8	51.7
ALASKA	7.6	22.8	9.1	14.3	18.2	15.1	7.1	3.6	2.1	32.4	48.3
ARIZONA	7.5	19.2	10.0	14.5	15.0	12.2	8.6	7.1	5.9	34.2	50.1
ARKANSAS	6.8	18.7	9.8	13.2	14.9	13.1	9.6	7.4	6.6	36.0	51.2
CALIFORNIA	7.3	20.0	9.9	15.4	16.2	12.8	7.7	5.6	5.0	33.3	50.2
COLORADO	6.9	18.7	10.0	15.4	17.1	14.3	7.9	5.3	4.4	34.3	49.6
CONNECTICUT	6.6	18.2	8.0	13.3	17.1	14.1	9.1	6.8	7.0	37.4	51.6
DELAWARE	6.6	18.3	9.6	13.9	16.3	13.3	9.1	7.2	5.8	36.0	51.4
DISTRICT OF COLUMBIA	5.7	14.4	12.7	17.8	15.3	13.2	8.7	6.3	5.9	34.6	52.9
FLORIDA	5.9	16.9	8.3	13.0	15.5	12.9	9.8	9.1	8.5	38.7	51.2
GEORGIA	7.3	19.2	10.2	15.9	16.5	13.2	8.1	5.3	4.3	33.4	50.8
HAWAII	6.5	18.0	9.5	14.1	15.8	14.1	8.8	7.0	6.2	36.2	49.8
IDAHO	7.5	21.0	10.7	13.1	14.9	13.2	8.3	5.9	5.4	33.2	49.9
ILLINOIS	7.1	19.1	9.8	14.6	16.0	13.1	8.4	6.2	5.9	34.7	51.0
INDIANA	7.0	18.9	10.1	13.7	15.8	13.4	8.7	6.5	5.9	35.2	51.0
IOWA	6.4	18.6	10.2	12.4	15.2	13.4	8.8	7.2	7.7	36.6	50.9
KANSAS	7.0	19.5	10.3	13.0	15.6	13.2	8.2	6.5	6.7	35.2	50.6
KENTUCKY	6.6	18.0	9.9	14.1	15.9	13.8	9.2	6.8	5.7	35.9	51.1
LOUISIANA	7.1	20.2	10.6	13.5	15.5	13.1	8.5	6.3	5.2	34.0	51.6
MAINE	5.5	18.1	8.1	12.4	16.7	15.1	9.7	7.5	6.8	38.6	51.3
MARYLAND	6.7	18.9	8.5	14.1	17.3	14.3	8.9	6.1	5.2	36.0	51.7
MASSACHUSETTS	6.3	17.4	9.1	14.6	16.7	13.8	8.6	6.7	6.8	36.5	51.8
MICHIGAN	6.8	19.4	9.4	13.7	16.1	13.8	8.7	6.5	5.8	35.5	51.0
MINNESOTA	6.7	19.5	9.6	13.7	16.8	13.5	8.2	6.0	6.1	35.4	50.5
MISSISSIPPI	7.2	20.1	10.9	13.4	15.0	12.7	8.6	6.5	5.5	33.8	51.7
MISSOURI	6.6	18.9	9.6	13.2	15.9	13.3	9.1	7.0	6.5	36.1	51.4
MONTANA	6.1	19.4	9.5	11.4	15.7	15.0	9.4	6.9	6.5	37.5	50.2
NEBRASKA	6.8	19.5	10.2	13.0	15.4	13.2	8.3	6.8	6.8	35.3	50.7
NEVADA	7.3	18.3	9.0	15.3	16.1	13.5	9.5	6.6	4.4	35.0	49.1
NEW HAMPSHIRE	6.1	18.9	8.4	13.0	17.9	14.9	8.9	6.3	5.6	37.1	50.8
NEW JERSEY	6.7	18.1	8.0	14.1	17.1	13.8	9.0	6.8	6.4	36.7	51.5
NEW MEXICO	7.2	20.8	9.8	12.9	15.5	13.5	8.7	6.5	5.2	34.6	50.8
NEW YORK	6.5	18.2	9.3	14.5	16.2	13.5	8.9	6.7	6.2	35.9	51.8
NORTH CAROLINA	6.7	17.7	10.0	15.1	16.0	13.5	9.0	6.6	5.4	35.3	51.0
NORTH DAKOTA	6.1	18.9	11.4	12.0	15.3	13.3	8.3	7.1	7.6	36.2	50.1
OHIO	6.6	18.8	9.3	13.4	15.9	13.8	8.9	7.0	6.3	36.2	51.4
OKLAHOMA	6.8	19.0	10.3	13.1	15.2	13.1	9.2	7.0	6.2	35.5	50.9
OREGON	6.5	18.2	9.6	13.8	15.4	14.8	8.9	6.4	6.4	36.3	50.4
PENNSYLVANIA	5.9	17.9	8.9	12.7	15.9	13.9	9.2	7.9	7.7	38.0	51.7
RHODE ISLAND	6.1	17.5	10.2	13.4	16.2	13.5	8.5	7.0	7.5	36.7	52.0
SOUTH CAROLINA	6.6	18.6	10.2	14.0	15.6	13.7	9.3	6.7	5.4	35.4	51.4
SOUTH DAKOTA	6.8	20.1	10.3	12.1	15.3	12.9	8.3	7.0	7.3	35.6	50.4
TENNESSEE	6.6	18.0	9.6	14.3	15.9	13.8	9.4	6.7	5.6	35.9	51.3
TEXAS	7.8	20.4	10.5	15.2	15.9	12.5	7.7	5.5	4.5	32.3	50.4
UTAH	9.4	22.8	14.2	14.6	13.4	10.6	6.4	4.5	4.0	27.1	49.9
VERMONT	5.6	18.6	9.3	12.2	16.7	15.4	9.3	6.7	6.0	37.7	51.0
VIRGINIA	6.5	18.0	9.6	14.6	17.0	14.1	8.9	6.1	5.1	35.7	51.0
WASHINGTON	6.7	19.0	9.5	14.3	16.5	14.4	8.4	5.7	5.5	35.3	50.2
WEST VIRGINIA	5.6	16.6	9.5	12.7	15.1	15.0	10.2	8.2	7.1	38.9	51.4
WISCONSIN	6.4	19.1	9.7	13.2	16.3	13.7	8.5	6.6	6.5	36.0	50.6
WYOMING	6.3	19.8	10.1	12.1	16.0	15.0	9.0	6.3	5.3	36.2	49.7

Table A. States

STATE	Under 5 years	5 to 17 years	18 to 24 years	25 to 34 years	35 to 44 years	45 to 54 years	55 to 64 years	65 to 74 years	75 years and over	Percent Female	2000	1990	1980	1990–2000	1980–1990
					Population and population characteristics, 1990 — Age (percent)						Population—change, 1980–2000 — Total persons			Percent change	
	39	40	41	42	43	44	45	46	47	48	49	50	51	52	53
UNITED STATES	7.4	18.2	10.8	17.4	15.1	10.1	8.5	7.3	5.3	51.3	281 421 906	248 790 925	226 542 204	13.1	9.8
ALABAMA	7.0	19.2	11.0	16.0	14.4	10.4	9.0	7.5	5.5	52.1	4 447 100	4 040 389	3 894 025	10.1	3.8
ALASKA	10.0	21.4	10.2	20.5	18.7	9.8	5.4	2.8	1.2	47.3	626 932	550 043	401 851	14.0	36.9
ARIZONA	8.0	18.8	10.7	17.3	14.4	9.5	8.2	7.9	5.1	50.6	5 130 632	3 665 339	2 716 546	40.0	34.9
ARKANSAS	7.0	19.4	10.1	15.3	13.9	10.4	9.1	8.3	6.6	51.8	2 673 400	2 350 624	2 286 357	13.7	2.8
CALIFORNIA	8.1	18.0	11.5	19.1	15.6	9.8	7.5	6.2	4.3	49.9	33 871 648	29 811 427	23 667 765	13.6	25.7
COLORADO	7.7	18.5	10 2	18.6	17.2	10.2	7.6	5.9	4.1	50.5	4 301 261	3 294 473	2 889 735	30.6	14.0
CONNECTICUT	6.9	15.9	10.5	17.8	15.5	10.8	9.0	7.8	5.8	51.5	3 405 565	3 287 116	3 107 564	3.6	5.8
DELAWARE	7.3	17.2	11.4	17.9	14.8	10.2	9.0	7.4	4.7	51.5	783 600	666 168	594 338	17.6	12.1
DISTRICT OF COLUMBIA	6.2	13.1	13.6	20.0	15.7	10.2	8.4	7.3	5.5	53.4	572 059	606 900	638 432	-5.7	-4.9
FLORIDA	6.6	15.6	9.4	16.4	14.0	10.0	9.8	10.6	7.7	51.6	15 982 378	12 938 071	9 746 961	23.5	32.7
GEORGIA	7.6	19.0	11.4	18.1	15.7	10.3	7.7	6.0	4.1	51.5	8 186 453	6 478 149	5 462 982	26.4	18.6
HAWAII	7.5	17.8	10.9	18.1	16.1	9.8	8.5	7.1	4.2	49.1	1 211 537	1 108 229	964 691	9.3	14.9
IDAHO	8.0	22.7	9.8	15.2	14.8	9.8	7.7	6.9	5.1	50.2	1 293 953	1 006 734	944 127	28.5	6.6
ILLINOIS	7.4	18.4	10.6	17.4	14.9	10.2	8.5	7.3	5.4	51.4	12 419 293	11 430 602	11 427 409	8.6	0.0
INDIANA	7.2	19.1	10.9	16.5	14.8	10.3	8.7	7.3	5.3	51.5	6 080 485	5 544 156	5 490 214	9.7	1.0
IOWA	7.0	18.9	10.2	15.4	14.2	9.9	9.0	8.2	7.2	51.6	2 926 324	2 776 831	2 913 808	5.4	-4.7
KANSAS	7.6	19.1	10.3	16.7	14.6	9.5	8.4	7.5	6.4	51.0	2 688 418	2 477 588	2 364 236	8.5	4.8
KENTUCKY	6.8	19.1	10.9	16.6	14.9	10.4	8.8	7.3	5.4	51.6	4 041 769	3 686 892	3 660 324	9.6	0.7
LOUISIANA	7.9	21.2	11.0	16.7	14.4	9.6	8.1	6.5	4.6	51.9	4 468 976	4 221 826	4 206 116	5.9	0.3
MAINE	7.0	18.2	10.1	16.7	15.7	10.2	8.8	7.5	5.8	51.3	1 274 923	1 227 928	1 125 043	3.8	9.1
MARYLAND	7.5	16.8	10.6	18.8	16.3	10.9	8.3	6.6	4.2	51.5	5 296 486	4 780 753	4 216 933	10.8	13.4
MASSACHUSETTS	6.9	15.6	11.8	18.3	15.3	10.0	8.6	7.6	6.0	52.0	6 349 097	6 016 425	5 737 093	5.5	4.9
MICHIGAN	7.6	18.9	10.8	16.9	15.1	10.2	8.5	7.1	4.9	51.5	9 938 444	9 295 287	9 262 044	6.9	0.4
MINNESOTA	7.7	19.0	10.1	17.8	15.2	9.8	7.9	6.7	5.8	51.0	4 919 479	4 375 665	4 075 970	12.4	7.4
MISSISSIPPI	7.6	21.4	11.4	15.5	13.6	9.6	8.3	7.0	5.5	52.2	2 844 658	2 575 475	2 520 770	10.5	2.2
MISSOURI	7.2	18.5	10.1	16.7	14.4	10.2	8.9	7.7	6.3	51.8	5 595 211	5 116 901	4 916 766	9.3	4.1
MONTANA	7.4	20.4	8.8	15.4	15.9	10.3	8.6	7.6	5.7	50.5	902 195	799 065	786 690	12.9	1.6
NEBRASKA	7.6	19.6	9.9	16.3	14.5	9.5	8.6	7.5	6.7	51.3	1 711 263	1 578 417	1 569 825	8.4	0.5
NEVADA	7.7	17.0	9.9	18.5	16.0	11.3	9.0	7.1	3.5	49.1	1 998 257	1 201 675	800 508	66.3	50.1
NEW HAMPSHIRE	7.6	17.5	10.6	18.5	16.5	10.1	8.0	6.4	4.8	51.0	1 235 786	1 109 252	920 610	11.4	20.5
NEW JERSEY	6.9	16.4	10.1	17.6	15.5	10.9	9.3	7.9	5.5	51.7	8 414 350	7 747 750	7 365 011	8.6	5.0
NEW MEXICO	8.3	21.2	10.0	16.9	15.0	9.7	8.0	6.4	4.3	50.8	1 819 046	1 515 069	1 303 302	20.1	16.2
NEW YORK	7.0	16.7	10.9	17.4	15.1	10.6	9.1	7.5	5.6	52.1	18 976 457	17 990 778	17 558 165	5.5	2.5
NORTH CAROLINA	6.9	17.3	11.8	17.3	15.2	10.5	8.9	7.3	4.8	51.5	8 049 313	6 632 448	5 880 095	21.4	12.8
NORTH DAKOTA	7.5	20.0	10.6	16.3	14.1	8.9	8.4	7.4	6.8	50.2	642 200	638 800	652 717	0.5	-2.1
OHIO	7.2	18.6	10.5	16.5	14.9	10.3	9.0	7.6	5.3	51.8	11 353 140	10 847 115	10 797 603	4.7	0.5
OKLAHOMA	7.2	19.4	10.2	16.2	14.4	10.3	8.9	7.5	6.0	51.3	3 450 654	3 145 576	3 025 487	9.7	4.0
OREGON	7.1	18.4	9.4	15.9	16.7	10.4	8.3	7.9	5.9	50.8	3 421 399	2 842 337	2 633 156	20.4	7.9
PENNSYLVANIA	6.7	16.8	10.3	16.1	14.7	10.2	9.8	9.0	6.4	52.1	12 281 054	11 882 842	11 864 720	3.4	0.2
RHODE ISLAND	6.7	15.8	12.0	17.3	14.7	9.6	8.9	8.5	6.5	52.0	1 048 319	1 003 464	947 154	4.5	5.9
SOUTH CAROLINA	7.4	19.0	11.7	17.0	15.0	10.2	8.4	7.1	4.3	51.6	4 012 012	3 486 310	3 120 729	15.1	11.7
SOUTH DAKOTA	7.8	20.7	9.8	15.7	13.7	9.0	8.6	7.8	6.9	50.8	754 844	696 004	690 768	8.5	0.8
TENNESSEE	6.8	18.1	10.8	16.7	15.2	10.8	8.9	7.3	5.4	51.8	5 689 283	4 877 203	4 591 023	16.7	6.2
TEXAS	8.2	20.3	11.1	18.2	14.9	9.6	7.6	6.0	4.2	50.7	20 851 820	16 986 335	14 225 513	22.8	19.4
UTAH	9.8	26.6	11.0	16.0	13.0	8.0	6.2	5.1	3.6	50.3	2 233 169	1 722 850	1 461 037	29.6	17.9
VERMONT	7.3	18.1	11.2	16.9	16.4	10.2	8.0	6.6	5.2	51.0	608 827	562 758	511 456	8.2	10.0
VIRGINIA	7.2	17.2	11.6	18.4	16.0	10.7	8.1	6.5	4.3	51.0	7 078 515	6 189 197	5 346 797	14.4	15.8
WASHINGTON	7.5	18.4	10.0	17.6	16.5	10.3	7.8	6.9	4.9	50.4	5 894 121	4 866 669	4 132 353	21.1	17.8
WEST VIRGINIA	5.9	18.8	10.0	14.6	15.1	10.7	9.9	8.7	6.3	52.0	1 808 344	1 793 477	1 950 186	0.8	-8.0
WISCONSIN	7.4	19.0	10.5	16.8	14.8	9.8	8.5	7.3	6.0	51.1	5 363 675	4 891 954	4 705 642	9.6	4.0
WYOMING	7.7	22.2	9.1	16.4	16.4	10.0	7.8	6.1	4.3	50.0	493 782	453 589	469 557	8.9	-3.4

[1] Hispanic persons may be of any race.

Table A. States

	Household relationship, 2000																
STATE	In households (percent)										In group quarters (percent)						
					Child		Other relatives		Nonrelatives			Institutionalized population			Noninstitutionalized population		
	Total population	Total in house-holds	House-holder	Spouse	Total	Own child under 18 years	Total	Under 18 years	Total	Unmar-ried partner	Total in group quarters	Correc-tional institu-tions	Nurs-ing homes	Other institu-tions	Col-lege dormi-tories	Mili-tary quar-ters	Other
	54	55	56	57	58	59	60	61	62	63	64	65	66	67	68	69	70
UNITED STATES..............	281 421 906	97.2	37.5	19.4	29.6	22.9	5.6	2.1	5.2	1.9	2.8	0.7	0.6	0.1	0.7	0.1	0.5
ALABAMA......................	4 447 100	97.4	39.1	20.4	29.3	22.3	5.4	2.5	3.3	1.3	2.6	0.8	0.6	0.1	0.7	0.1	0.3
ALASKA.........................	626 932	06.0	35.3	18.6	32.9	27.8	3.9	1.7	6.2	2.6	3.1	0.5	0.1	0.1	0.3	0.6	1.4
ARIZONA.......................	5 130 632	97.9	37.1	19.2	29.2	23.3	6.2	2.6	6.2	2.3	2.1	0.9	0.3	0.1	0.3	0.1	0.5
ARKANSAS....................	2 673 400	97.2	39.0	21.2	28.4	22.5	4.9	2.3	3.7	1.5	2.8	0.8	0.8	0.1	0.7	0.0	0.3
CALIFORNIA...................	33 871 648	97.6	34.0	17.4	31.1	23.7	8.4	2.8	6.8	2.0	2.4	0.7	0.4	0.1	0.4	0.2	0.7
COLORADO....................	4 301 261	97.6	38.6	20.0	28.3	23.4	4.4	1.6	6.4	2.1	2.4	0.7	0.4	0.1	0.5	0.2	0.4
CONNECTICUT..............	3 405 565	96.8	38.2	19.9	29.5	22.7	4.6	1.5	4.7	2.0	3.2	0.6	0.9	0.1	1.1	0.1	0.4
DELAWARE....................	783 600	96.9	38.1	19.5	28.6	22.0	5.1	2.2	5.5	2.3	3.1	0.8	0.6	0.1	1.2	0.0	0.4
DISTRICT OF COLUMBIA....	572 059	93.8	43.4	9.9	22.6	15.5	8.8	3.9	9.1	2.6	6.2	0.5	0.7	0.2	3.4	0.2	1.3
FLORIDA.......................	15 982 378	97.6	39.7	20.0	26.1	20.0	6.0	2.2	5.9	2.3	2.4	0.9	0.6	0.1	0.3	0.1	0.5
GEORGIA......................	8 186 453	97.1	36.7	18.9	29.8	23.2	6.4	2.7	5.3	1.8	2.9	1.0	0.4	0.1	0.6	0.3	0.4
HAWAII.........................	1 211 537	97.0	33.3	17.8	29.0	19.8	10.5	4.0	6.4	1.9	3.0	0.3	0.4	0.4	0.6	0.1	0.4
IDAHO..........................	1 293 953	97.6	36.3	21.4	31.5	26.5	3.4	1.4	5.0	1.7	2.4	0.6	0.4	0.1	0.7	0.1	0.4
ILLINOIS........................	12 419 293	97.4	37.0	19.0	30.7	23.2	6.1	2.3	4.7	1.8	2.6	0.5	0.7	0.1	0.7	0.1	0.4
INDIANA........................	6 080 485	97.1	38.4	20.6	29.6	23.6	3.8	1.6	4.7	2.1	2.9	0.6	0.8	0.1	1.1	0.0	0.3
IOWA...........................	2 926 324	96.4	39.3	21.6	28.4	23.4	2.5	1.0	4.6	1.9	3.6	0.4	1.1	0.2	1.4	0.0	0.4
KANSAS........................	2 688 418	97.0	38.6	21.1	29.5	24.5	3.3	1.4	4.4	1.6	3.0	0.6	0.9	0.1	0.9	0.2	0.3
KENTUCKY....................	4 041 769	97.2	39.4	21.2	28.8	22.3	3.9	1.7	3.9	1.8	2.8	0.7	0.7	0.1	0.6	0.1	0.3
LOUISIANA....................	4 468 976	97.0	37.1	18.1	31.4	23.5	6.3	3.2	4.1	1.9	3.0	1.1	0.7	0.2	1.1	0.1	0.6
MAINE..........................	1 274 923	97.3	40.6	21.3	26.9	21.9	2.6	0.9	5.8	3.0	2.7	0.2	0.7	0.1	1.1	0.1	0.6
MARYLAND....................	5 296 486	97.5	37.4	18.8	29.6	22.6	6.2	2.4	5.5	2.1	2.5	0.7	0.5	0.1	0.7	0.1	0.4
MASSACHUSETTS..............	6 349 097	96.5	38.5	18.9	29.0	21.8	4.5	1.4	5.6	2.1	3.5	0.4	0.9	0.1	1.6	0.0	0.5
MICHIGAN.....................	9 938 444	97.5	38.1	19.6	30.6	23.6	4.4	1.8	4.9	2.0	2.5	0.7	0.5	0.1	0.7	0.0	0.5
MINNESOTA	4 919 479	97.2	38.5	20.7	29.9	24.6	2.8	1.0	5.3	2.0	2.8	0.3	0.8	0.1	0.9	0.0	0.6
MISSISSIPPI	2 844 658	96.6	36.8	18.3	31.1	23.1	6.8	3.6	3.7	1.6	3.4	0.9	0.6	0.2	1.0	0.1	0.3
MISSOURI	5 595 211	97.1	39.2	20.4	29.2	23.1	3.8	1.7	4.5	2.0	2.9	0.6	0.9	0.1	0.8	0.1	0.4
MONTANA	902 195	97.3	39.8	21.3	28.2	23.5	2.9	1.3	5.1	2.0	2.7	0.5	0.7	0.2	0.8	0.0	0.6
NEBRASKA	1 711 263	97.0	38.9	21.1	29.6	24.6	2.8	1.1	4.7	1.7	3.0	0.4	0.9	0.1	1.1	0.0	0.3
NEVADA	1 998 257	98.3	37.6	18.7	28.0	22.6	6.7	2.2	7.4	2.7	1.7	0.8	0.2	0.1	0.1	0.1	0.4
NEW HAMPSHIRE...........	1 235 786	97.1	38.4	21.2	28.8	23.4	3.0	1.0	5.6	2.6	2.9	0.3	0.8	0.1	1.4	0.0	0.3
NEW JERSEY	8 414 350	97.7	36.4	19.5	30.8	22.3	6.5	2.0	4.6	1.8	2.3	0.6	0.6	0.1	0.5	0.0	0.4
NEW MEXICO	1 819 046	98.0	37.3	18.8	31.2	24.5	5.8	2.8	4.9	2.4	2.0	0.6	0.4	0.1	0.4	0.1	0.4
NEW YORK	18 976 457	96.9	37.2	17.3	30.2	21.9	6.7	2.2	5.5	2.0	3.1	0.6	0.7	0.2	0.9	0.0	0.7
NORTH CAROLINA	8 049 313	96.8	38.9	20.4	27.6	21.7	5.1	2.2	4.8	1.8	3.2	0.6	0.6	0.1	0.9	0.5	0.4
NORTH DAKOTA	642 200	96.3	40.0	21.4	28.4	23.8	2.0	0.8	4.5	1.8	3.7	0.2	1.1	0.1	1.6	0.2	0.4
OHIO	11 353 140	97.4	39.2	20.1	29.7	23.2	3.9	1.7	4.4	2.0	2.6	0.6	0.8	0.1	0.8	0.0	0.3
OKLAHOMA	3 450 654	96.7	38.9	20.8	28.7	23.1	4.4	2.1	3.9	1.5	3.3	1.0	0.8	0.1	0.6	0.0	0.3
OREGON	3 421 399	97.7	39.0	20.2	27.4	22.4	4.2	1.5	6.9	2.5	2.3	0.6	0.4	0.1	0.6	0.0	0.6
PENNSYLVANIA	12 281 054	96.5	38.9	20.1	28.9	21.6	4.3	1.6	4.3	1.9	3.5	0.6	0.9	0.2	1.2	0.0	0.6
RHODE ISLAND	1 048 319	96.3	39.0	18.8	29.0	21.8	4.5	1.4	5.1	2.2	3.7	0.3	0.9	0.1	2.0	0.1	0.3
SOUTH CAROLINA............	4 012 012	96.6	38.2	19.5	28.8	21.8	5.9	2.8	4.3	1.8	3.4	0.9	0.5	0.1	1.0	0.4	0.4
SOUTH DAKOTA	754 844	96.2	38.5	20.9	29.5	24.6	3.0	1.4	4.5	1.8	3.8	0.6	1.0	0.3	1.2	0.1	0.6
TENNESSEE	5 689 283	97.4	39.2	20.6	28.3	21.8	5.0	2.2	4.1	1.7	2.6	0.7	0.7	0.1	0.6	0.1	0.3
TEXAS	20 851 820	97.3	35.5	19.1	31.5	24.8	6.8	2.9	4.4	1.6	2.7	1.2	0.5	0.1	0.4	0.2	0.3
UTAH	2 233 169	98.2	31.4	19.8	37.1	29.7	4.7	1.9	5.1	1.1	1.8	0.4	0.3	0.1	0.4	0.1	0.4
VERMONT	608 827	96.6	39.5	20.8	27.5	22.7	2.4	0.8	6.4	3.0	3.4	0.2	0.7	0.1	2.1	0.0	0.4
VIRGINIA.......................	7 078 515	96.7	38.1	20.1	28.1	22.1	5.0	2.0	5.3	1.8	3.3	0.9	0.5	0.1	0.9	0.5	0.3
WASHINGTON	5 894 121	97.7	38.5	20.1	28.7	23.5	4.0	1.5	6.4	2.4	2.3	0.5	0.4	0.1	0.5	0.3	0.6
WEST VIRGINIA	1 808 344	97.6	40.7	22.0	27.2	20.1	3.8	1.6	3.9	1.9	2.4	0.6	0.6	0.1	0.8	0.0	0.3
WISCONSIN	5 363 675	97.1	38.9	20.7	29.4	23.7	3.0	1.1	5.2	2.2	2.9	0.6	0.8	0.1	1.0	0.0	0.5
WYOMING	493 782	97.1	39.2	21.5	28.6	24.0	2.8	1.3	5.0	2.1	2.9	0.8	0.6	0.2	0.8	0.1	0.4

Table A. States

STATE	Households by type, 2000												Households, 1990		
		Family households						Nonfamily households							
				Married couple		Female householder¹			Householder living alone						House-holder
	Total households	Total	With own children under 18 years	Total	With own children under 18 years	Total	With own children under 18 years	Total	Total	65 years and over	Average house-hold size	Average family size	Total house-holds	Female house-holder¹	living alone
	71	72	73	74	75	76	77	78	79	80	81	82	83	84	85
UNITED STATES	105 480 101	68.1	32.8	51.7	23.5	12.2	7.2	31.9	25.8	9.2	2.59	3.14	91 947 410	11.6	24.6
ALABAMA	1 737 080	70.0	32.3	52.2	22.5	14.2	8.1	30.0	26.1	9.8	2.49	3.01	1 506 790	13.4	23.8
ALASKA	221 600	68.7	39.9	52.5	28.5	10.8	7.8	31.3	23.5	4.1	2.74	3.28	188 915	9.6	22.1
ARIZONA	1 901 327	67.7	32.0	51.9	22.6	11.1	6.8	32.3	24.8	8.6	2.64	3.18	1 368 843	10.4	24.7
ARKANSAS	1 042 696	70.2	32.1	54.3	22.7	12.1	7.4	29.8	25.6	10.4	2.49	2.99	891 179	11.1	24.0
CALIFORNIA	11 502 870	68.9	35.8	51.1	26.0	12.6	7.3	31.1	23.5	7.8	2.87	3.43	10 381 206	11.5	23.4
COLORADO	1 658 238	65.4	32.8	51.8	24.4	9.6	6.2	34.6	26.3	7.0	2.53	3.09	1 282 489	9.7	26.6
CONNECTICUT	1 301 670	67.7	32.2	52.0	23.6	12.1	7.0	32.3	26.4	10.1	2.53	3.08	1 230 479	11.4	24.2
DELAWARE	298 736	68.5	31.9	51.3	21.9	13.1	7.7	31.5	25.0	9.1	2.54	3.04	247 497	11.8	23.2
DISTRICT OF COLUMBIA	248 338	46.0	19.8	22.8	8.4	18.9	9.9	54.0	43.8	10.0	2.16	3.07	249 634	19.5	41.5
FLORIDA	6 337 929	66.4	28.1	50.4	19.2	12.0	6.9	33.6	26.6	11.2	2.46	2.98	5 134 869	10.7	25.5
GEORGIA	3 006 369	70.2	35.0	51.5	24.4	14.5	8.6	29.8	23.6	7.0	2.65	3.14	2 366 615	13.9	22.7
HAWAII	403 240	71.2	32.1	53.6	24.0	12.4	5.9	28.8	21.9	7.1	2.92	3.42	356 267	10.5	19.4
IDAHO	469 645	71.5	36.3	58.9	28.1	8.7	5.8	28.5	22.4	8.3	2.69	3.17	360 723	8.0	22.4
ILLINOIS	4 591 779	67.6	33.0	51.3	24.3	12.3	6.9	32.4	26.8	9.6	2.63	3.23	4 202 240	12.0	25.7
INDIANA	2 336 306	68.6	32.9	53.6	23.8	11.1	6.9	31.4	25.9	9.5	2.53	3.05	2 065 355	10.5	24.1
IOWA	1 149 276	67.0	31.4	55.1	23.9	8.6	5.6	33.0	27.2	11.4	2.46	3.00	1 064 325	8.0	25.9
KANSAS	1 037 891	67.6	33.2	54.7	25.1	9.3	6.0	32.4	27.0	10.2	2.51	3.07	944 726	8.6	25.9
KENTUCKY	1 590 647	69.4	32.5	53.9	23.6	11.8	7.0	30.6	26.0	9.8	2.47	2.97	1 379 782	11.6	23.3
LOUISIANA	1 656 053	69.8	34.5	48.9	22.6	16.6	9.8	30.2	25.3	9.0	2.62	3.16	1 499 269	15.6	23.7
MAINE	518 200	65.7	30.4	52.5	21.8	9.5	6.2	34.3	27.0	10.7	2.39	2.90	465 312	9.5	23.3
MARYLAND	1 980 859	68.6	33.4	50.2	23.3	14.1	8.0	31.4	25.0	8.1	2.61	3.13	1 748 991	13.3	22.6
MASSACHUSETTS	2 443 580	64.5	30.6	49.0	22.4	11.9	6.7	35.5	28.0	10.5	2.51	3.11	2 247 110	12.1	25.8
MICHIGAN	3 785 661	68.0	32.7	51.4	23.1	12.5	7.5	32.0	26.2	9.4	2.56	3.10	3 419 331	12.9	23.7
MINNESOTA	1 895 127	66.2	33.0	53.7	25.2	8.9	5.9	33.8	26.9	9.3	2.52	3.09	1 647 853	8.6	25.1
MISSISSIPPI	1 046 434	71.4	34.7	49.8	22.4	17.3	10.1	28.6	24.6	9.6	2.63	3.14	911 374	15.9	23.4
MISSOURI	2 194 594	67.3	31.9	52.0	22.7	11.6	7.1	32.7	27.3	10.3	2.48	3.02	1 961 206	10.6	26.0
MONTANA	358 667	66.2	31.2	53.6	23.0	8.9	5.9	33.8	27.4	10.0	2.45	2.99	306 163	8.6	26.3
NEBRASKA	666 184	66.6	32.7	54.2	24.9	9.1	6.0	33.4	27.6	10.7	2.49	3.06	602 363	8.3	25.7
NEVADA	751 165	66.3	31.8	49.7	22.1	11.1	6.7	33.7	24.9	7.1	2.62	3.14	466 297	10.2	25.7
NEW HAMPSHIRE	474 606	68.2	33.4	55.3	25.4	9.1	5.7	31.8	24.4	8.5	2.53	3.03	411 186	8.5	22.0
NEW JERSEY	3 064 645	70.3	33.5	53.5	25.3	12.6	6.4	29.7	24.5	9.8	2.68	3.21	2 794 711	12.1	23.1
NEW MEXICO	677 971	68.8	34.7	50.4	23.3	13.2	8.3	31.2	25.4	8.2	2.63	3.18	542 709	11.9	23.0
NEW YORK	7 056 860	65.7	31.6	46.6	21.6	14.7	8.1	34.3	28.1	10.1	2.61	3.22	6 639 322	13.8	27.2
NORTH CAROLINA	3 132 013	68.9	31.8	52.5	22.6	12.5	7.3	31.1	25.4	8.6	2.49	2.98	2 517 026	12.3	23.7
NORTH DAKOTA	257 152	64.6	31.3	53.4	24.1	7.8	5.3	35.4	29.3	11.5	2.41	3.00	240 878	7.3	26.5
OHIO	4 445 773	67.3	31.7	51.4	22.4	12.1	7.3	32.7	27.3	10.0	2.49	3.04	4 087 546	11.7	25.0
OKLAHOMA	1 342 293	68.7	32.4	53.5	23.2	11.4	7.0	31.3	26.7	10.1	2.49	3.02	1 206 135	10.4	25.6
OREGON	1 333 723	65.8	30.8	51.9	22.2	9.8	6.2	34.2	26.1	9.1	2.51	3.02	1 103 313	9.2	25.3
PENNSYLVANIA	4 777 003	67.2	30.0	51.7	21.8	11.6	6.2	32.8	27.7	11.6	2.48	3.04	4 495 966	11.3	25.6
RHODE ISLAND	408 424	65.0	30.6	48.2	21.0	12.9	7.8	35.0	28.6	11.4	2.47	3.07	377 977	11.7	26.2
SOUTH CAROLINA	1 533 854	69.9	32.3	51.1	21.8	14.8	8.5	30.1	25.0	8.6	2.53	3.02	1 258 044	14.0	22.4
SOUTH DAKOTA	290 245	67.0	32.8	54.2	24.5	9.0	6.1	33.0	27.6	11.1	2.50	3.07	259 034	8.0	26.4
TENNESSEE	2 232 905	69.3	31.7	52.6	22.4	12.9	7.4	30.7	25.8	9.0	2.48	2.99	1 853 725	12.6	23.9
TEXAS	7 393 354	71.0	36.8	54.0	27.1	12.7	7.6	29.0	23.7	7.3	2.74	3.28	6 070 937	11.6	23.9
UTAH	701 281	76.3	42.7	63.2	35.0	9.4	5.8	23.7	17.8	6.3	3.13	3.57	537 273	9.1	18.9
VERMONT	240 634	65.6	31.8	52.5	23.2	9.3	6.1	34.4	26.2	9.5	2.44	2.96	210 650	9.2	23.4
VIRGINIA	2 699 173	68.5	32.7	52.8	23.9	11.9	6.9	31.5	25.1	8.0	2.54	3.04	2 291 830	11.1	22.9
WASHINGTON	2 271 398	66.0	32.7	52.0	23.8	9.9	6.5	34.0	26.2	8.1	2.53	3.07	1 872 431	9.4	25.4
WEST VIRGINIA	736 481	68.4	28.9	54.0	21.3	10.7	5.7	31.6	27.1	11.9	2.40	2.90	688 557	10.7	24.5
WISCONSIN	2 084 544	66.5	31.9	53.2	23.7	9.6	6.2	33.5	26.8	9.9	2.50	3.05	1 822 118	9.6	24.3
WYOMING	193 608	67.4	32.7	54.8	24.3	8.7	6.0	32.6	26.3	8.8	2.48	3.00	168 839	8.3	24.5

¹No spouse present.

Table A. States

STATE	Percent change of households, 1990–2000	Total housing units	Occupied housing units (percent)	Housing occupancy, 2000 — Vacant housing units (percent) Total	For seasonal, recreational, or occasional use	Homeowner vacancy rate (percent)	Rental vacancy rate (percent)	Housing tenure, 2000 — Occupied housing units Total	Percent owner-occupied housing units	Percent renter-occupied housing units	Average household size of owner-occupied units	Average household size of renter-occupied units
	86	87	88	89	90	91	92	93	94	95	96	97
UNITED STATES.............	14.7	115 904 641	91.0	9.0	3.1	1.7	6.8	105 480 101	66.2	33.8	2.69	2.40
ALABAMA.....................	15.3	1 963 711	88.5	11.5	2.4	2.0	11.8	1 737 080	72.5	27.5	2.57	2.30
ALASKA.......................	17.3	260 978	84.9	15.1	8.2	1.9	7.8	221 600	62.5	37.5	2.89	2.49
ARIZONA......................	38.9	2 189 189	86.9	13.1	6.5	2.1	9.2	1 901 327	68.0	32.0	2.69	2.53
ARKANSAS....................	17.0	1 173 043	88.9	11.1	2.5	2.5	9.6	1 042 696	69.4	30.6	2.54	2.40
CALIFORNIA...................	10.8	12 214 549	94.2	5.8	1.9	1.4	3.7	11 502 870	56.9	43.1	2.93	2.79
COLORADO	29.3	1 808 037	91.7	8.3	4.0	1.4	5.5	1 658 238	67.3	32.7	2.64	2.30
CONNECTICUT................	5.8	1 385 975	93.9	6.1	1.7	1.1	5.6	1 301 670	66.8	33.2	2.67	2.25
DELAWARE....................	20.7	343 072	87.1	12.9	7.6	1.5	8.2	298 736	72.3	27.7	2.61	2.37
DISTRICT OF COLUMBIA....	-0.5	274 845	90.4	9.6	0.8	2.9	5.9	248 338	40.8	59.2	2.31	2.06
FLORIDA.......................	23.4	7 302 947	86.8	13.2	6.6	2.2	9.3	6 337 929	70.1	29.9	2.49	2.39
GEORGIA......................	27.0	3 281 737	91.6	8.4	1.5	1.9	8.2	3 006 369	67.5	32.5	2.71	2.51
HAWAII........................	13.2	460 542	87.6	12.4	5.6	1.6	7.6	403 240	56.5	43.5	3.07	2.71
IDAHO.........................	30.2	527 824	89.0	11.0	5.2	2.2	7.6	469 645	72.4	27.6	2.75	2.52
ILLINOIS......................	9.3	4 885 615	94.0	6.0	0.6	1.5	6.2	4 591 779	67.3	32.7	2.76	2.37
INDIANA......................	13.1	2 532 319	92.3	7.7	1.3	1.8	8.8	2 336 306	71.4	28.6	2.64	2.24
IOWA..........................	8.0	1 232 511	93.2	6.8	1.3	1.7	6.8	1 149 276	72.3	27.7	2.57	2.15
KANSAS......................	9.9	1 131 200	91.8	8.2	0.9	2.0	8.8	1 037 891	69.2	30.8	2.63	2.25
KENTUCKY...................	15.3	1 750 927	90.8	9.2	1.7	1.8	8.7	1 590 647	70.8	29.2	2.55	2.27
LOUISIANA...................	10.5	1 847 181	89.7	10.3	2.1	1.6	9.3	1 656 053	67.9	32.1	2.70	2.44
MAINE.........................	11.4	651 901	79.5	20.5	15.6	1.7	7.0	518 200	71.6	28.4	2.54	2.03
MARYLAND...................	13.3	2 145 283	92.3	7.7	1.8	1.6	6.1	1 980 859	67.7	32.3	2.73	2.35
MASSACHUSETTS............	8.7	2 621 989	93.2	6.8	3.6	0.7	3.5	2 443 580	61.7	38.3	2.72	2.17
MICHIGAN....................	10.7	4 234 279	89.4	10.6	5.5	1.6	6.8	3 785 661	73.8	26.2	2.67	2.24
MINNESOTA	15.0	2 065 946	91.7	8.3	5.1	0.9	4.1	1 895 127	74.6	25.4	2.69	2.03
MISSISSIPPI.................	14.8	1 161 953	90.1	9.9	1.9	1.6	9.2	1 046 434	72.3	27.7	2.59	2.52
MISSOURI....................	11.9	2 442 017	89.9	10.1	2.7	2.1	9.0	2 194 594	70.3	29.7	2.55	2.20
MONTANA....................	17.1	412 633	86.9	13.1	5.9	2.2	7.6	358 667	69.1	30.9	2.63	2.22
NEBRASKA...................	10.6	722 668	92.2	7.8	1.6	1.8	7.6	666 184	67.4	32.6	2.71	2.20
NEVADA......................	61.1	827 457	90.8	9.2	2.0	2.6	9.7	751 165	60.9	39.1	2.70	2.47
NEW HAMPSHIRE...........	15.4	547 024	86.8	13.2	10.3	1.0	3.5	474 606	69.7	30.3	2.81	2.14
NEW JERSEY	9.7	3 310 275	92.6	7.4	3.3	1.2	4.5	3 064 645	65.6	34.4	2.72	2.43
NEW MEXICO	24.9	780 579	86.9	13.1	4.1	2.2	11.6	677 971	70.0	30.0	2.78	2.41
NEW YORK	6.3	7 679 307	91.9	8.1	3.1	1.6	4.6	7 056 860	53.0	47.0	2.54	2.41
NORTH CAROLINA..........	24.4	3 523 944	88.9	11.1	3.8	2.0	8.8	3 132 013	69.4	30.6	2.60	2.37
NORTH DAKOTA.............	6.8	289 677	88.8	11.2	2.9	2.7	8.2	257 152	66.6	33.4	2.62	2.02
OHIO..........................	8.8	4 783 051	92.9	7.1	1.0	1.6	8.3	4 445 773	69.1	30.9	2.55	2.19
OKLAHOMA..................	11.3	1 514 400	88.6	11.4	2.1	2.5	10.6	1 342 293	68.4	31.6	2.59	2.36
OREGON......................	20.9	1 452 709	91.8	8.2	2.5	2.3	7.3	1 333 723	64.3	35.7	2.62	2.36
PENNSYLVANIA..............	6.3	5 249 750	91.0	9.0	2.8	1.6	7.2	4 777 003	71.3	28.7	2.66	2.12
RHODE ISLAND..............	8.1	439 837	92.9	7.1	3.0	1.0	5.0	408 424	60.0	40.0	2.59	2.19
SOUTH CAROLINA...........	21.9	1 753 670	87.5	12.5	4.0	1.9	12.0	1 533 854	72.2	27.8	2.64	2.37
SOUTH DAKOTA.............	12.0	323 208	89.8	10.2	3.0	1.8	8.0	290 245	68.2	31.8	2.57	2.22
TENNESSEE..................	20.5	2 439 443	91.5	8.5	1.5	2.0	8.8	2 232 905	69.9	30.1	2.87	2.29
TEXAS........................	21.8	8 157 575	90.6	9.4	2.1	1.8	8.5	7 393 354	63.8	36.2	3.28	2.53
UTAH.........................	30.5	768 594	91.2	8.8	3.9	2.1	6.5	701 281	71.5	28.5	2.58	2.75
VERMONT....................	14.2	294 382	81.7	18.3	14.6	1.4	4.2	240 634	70.6	29.4		2.11
VIRGINIA.....................	17.8	2 904 192	92.9	7.1	1.9	1.5	5.2	2 699 173	68.1	31.9	2.62	2.36
WASHINGTON................	21.3	2 451 075	92.7	7.3	2.5	1.8	5.9	2 271 398	64.6	35.4	2.65	2.32
WEST VIRGINIA	7.0	844 623	87.2	12.8	3.9	2.2	9.1	736 481	75.2	24.8	2.47	2.17
WISCONSIN..................	14.4	2 321 144	89.8	10.2	6.1	1.2	5.6	2 084 544	68.4	31.6	2.66	2.15
WYOMING....................	14.7	223 854	86.5	13.5	5.5	2.1	9.7	193 608	70.0	30.0	2.58	2.25

States and Counties

(For explanation of symbols, see page xi.)

Page

92	**AL**(Autauga)—**AL**(Walker)
99	**AL**(Washington)—**AR**(Columbia)
106	**AR**(Conway)—**CA**(Amador)
113	**CA**(Butte)—**CO**(Cheyenne)
120	**CO**(Clear Creek)—**CT**(Windham)
128	**DE**(Kent)—**FL**(Santa Rosa)
134	**FL**(Sarasota)—**GA**(Evans)
141	**GA**(Fannin)—**GA**(Randolph)
148	**GA**(Richmond)—**ID**(Clearwater)
155	**ID**(Custer)—**IL**(Iroquois)
162	**IL**(Jackson)—**IL**(Woodford)
169	**IN**(Adams)—**IN**(Pulaski)
176	**IN**(Putnam)—**IA**(Grundy)
183	**IA**(Guthrie)—**KS**(Atchison)
190	**KS**(Barber)—**KS**(Norton)
197	**KS**(Osage)—**KY**(Crittenden)
204	**KY**(Cumberland)—**KY**(Owen)
211	**KY**(Owsley)—**LA**(Plaquemines)
218	**LA**(Pointe Coupee)—**MD**(Talbot)
225	**MD**(Washington)—**MI**(Lapeer)
232	**MI**(Leelanau)—**MN**(Goodhue)
239	**MN**(Grant)—**MN**(Yellow Medicine)
246	**MS**(Adams)—**MS**(Stone)
253	**MS**(Sunflower)—**MO**(Jackson)
260	**MO**(Jasper)—**MO**(Wright)
267	**MO**(St. Louis City)—**NE**(Banner)
274	**NE**(Blaine)—**NE**(Pierce)
281	**NE**(Platte)—**NJ**(Hunterdon)
288	**NJ**(Mercer)—**NY**(Fulton)
295	**NY**(Genesee)—**NC**(Cherokee)
302	**NC**(Chowan)—**NC**(Surry)
309	**NC**(Swain)—**ND**(Walsh)
316	**ND**(Ward)—**OH**(Noble)
323	**OH**(Ottawa)—**OK**(Kingfisher)
330	**OK**(Kiowa)—**OR**(Marion)
337	**OR**(Morrow)—**PA**(Pike)
344	**PA**(Potter)—**SC**(Spartanburg)
351	**SC**(Sumter)—**SD**(Todd)
358	**SD**(Tripp)—**TN**(Marion)
365	**TN**(Marshall)—**TX**(Burnet)
372	**TX**(Caldwell)—**TX**(Grimes)
379	**TX**(Guadalupe)—**TX**(Martin)
386	**TX**(Mason)—**TX**(Titus)
393	**TX**(Tom Green)—**VT**(Caledonia)
400	**VT**(Chittenden)—**VA**(Loudoun)
407	**VA**(Louisa)—**VA**(Lynchburg City)
414	**VA**(Manassas City)—**WV**(Boone)
421	**WV**(Braxton)—**WI**(Crawford)
428	**WI**(Dane)—**WY**(Carbon)
435	**WY**(Converse)—**WY**(Weston)

Table B—States and Counties

Table B. States and Counties

STATE/ County code	MSA/ PMSA/ NECMA code[1]	County type[2]	STATE County	Population, 2000				Population, 1990				Population and population characteristics, 2000					
												Race (percent)					
												One race					
				Land area, 2000[3] (sq km)	Total persons	Rank	Per square kilometer	Land area, 1990[3] (sq km)	Total persons	Rank	Per square kilometer	White	Black or African American	American Indian or Alaska Native	Asian	Native Hawaiian and other Pacific Islander	Some other race
				1	2	3	4	5	6	7	8	9	10	11	12	13	14
00 000	...		UNITED STATES.........	9 161 924	281 421 906	X	30.7	9 159 127	248 790 925	X	27.2	75.1	12.3	0.9	3.6	0.1	5.5
01 000	...		ALABAMA	131 426	4 447 100	X	33.8	131 443	4 040 389	X	30.7	71.1	26.0	0.5	0.7	0.0	0.7
01 001	5240	2	Autauga...............	1 544	43 671	1 022	28.3	1 544	34 222	1 160	22.2	80.7	17.1	0.4	0.5	0.0	0.4
01 003	5160	2	Baldwin...............	4 135	140 415	390	34.0	4 135	98 280	467	23.8	87.1	10.3	0.6	0.4	0.0	0.5
01 005	...	6	Barbour...............	2 292	29 038	1 424	12.7	2 292	25 417	1 450	11.1	51.3	46.3	0.5	0.3	0.0	0.9
01 007	...	6	Bibb...................	1 614	20 826	1 743	12.9	1 612	16 598	1 878	10.3	76.7	22.2	0.2	0.1	0.0	0.3
01 009	1000	2	Blount................	1 672	51 024	909	30.5	1 672	39 248	1 019	23.5	95.1	1.2	0.5	0.1	0.0	2.1
01 011	...	6	Bullock...............	1 619	11 714	2 318	7.2	1 619	11 042	2 289	6.8	25.3	73.1	0.4	0.2	0.0	0.4
01 013	...	7	Butler................	2 012	21 399	1 718	10.6	2 012	21 892	1 584	10.9	58.4	40.8	0.2	0.2	0.0	0.1
01 015	0450	3	Calhoun...............	1 576	112 249	478	71.2	1 576	116 032	396	73.6	78.9	18.5	0.4	0.6	0.1	0.6
01 017	...	5	Chambers..............	1 547	36 583	1 200	23.6	1 547	36 876	1 079	23.8	60.9	38.1	0.1	0.2	0.0	0.1
01 019	...	6	Cherokee..............	1 433	23 988	1 593	16.7	1 433	19 543	1 696	13.6	92.8	5.5	0.3	0.1	0.0	0.3
01 021	...	6	Chilton...............	1 797	39 593	1 124	22.0	1 798	32 458	1 202	18.1	86.7	10.6	0.3	0.2	0.0	1.5
01 023	...	9	Choctaw...............	2 366	15 922	2 025	6.7	2 366	16 018	1 922	6.8	55.1	44.1	0.2	0.0	0.0	0.1
01 025	...	7	Clarke................	3 207	27 867	1 454	8.7	3 208	27 240	1 382	8.5	55.9	43.0	0.2	0.2	0.0	0.2
01 027	...	9	Clay..................	1 567	14 254	2 145	9.1	1 567	13 252	2 116	8.5	82.6	15.7	0.3	0.1	0.0	0.5
01 029	...	6	Cleburne..............	1 451	14 123	2 151	9.7	1 451	12 730	2 164	8.8	94.7	3.7	0.3	0.1	0.0	0.3
01 031	...	4	Coffee................	1 759	43 615	1 026	24.8	1 759	40 240	994	22.9	77.1	18.4	0.9	0.9	0.1	0.9
01 033	2650	3	Colbert...............	1 540	54 984	859	35.7	1 540	51 666	818	33.5	81.5	16.6	0.4	0.2	0.0	0.3
01 035	...	7	Conecuh...............	2 204	14 089	2 155	6.4	2 204	14 054	2 052	6.4	55.4	43.6	0.2	0.1	0.0	0.1
01 037	...	8	Coosa.................	1 690	12 202	2 282	7.2	1 690	11 063	2 287	6.5	63.9	34.2	0.3	0.0	0.0	0.6
01 039	...	7	Covington.............	2 678	37 631	1 171	14.1	2 680	36 478	1 091	13.6	86.2	12.4	0.5	0.2	0.0	0.2
01 041	...	6	Crenshaw..............	1 579	13 665	2 187	8.7	1 579	13 635	2 089	8.6	73.8	24.8	0.4	0.1	0.0	0.2
01 043	...	6	Cullman...............	1 913	77 483	654	40.5	1 913	67 613	657	35.3	96.8	1.0	0.4	0.2	0.0	0.6
01 045	2180	3	Dale..................	1 453	49 129	928	33.8	1 453	49 633	845	34.2	74.4	20.4	0.6	1.1	0.1	1.3
01 047	...	4	Dallas................	2 540	46 365	975	18.3	2 540	48 130	867	18.9	35.6	63.3	0.1	0.3	0.0	0.1
01 049	...	6	De Kalb...............	2 015	64 452	754	32.0	2 015	54 651	788	27.1	92.6	1.7	0.8	0.2	0.1	3.1
01 051	5240	2	Elmore................	1 609	65 874	741	40.9	1 610	49 210	854	30.6	77.0	20.6	0.4	0.4	0.0	0.5
01 053	...	6	Escambia..............	2 454	38 440	1 151	15.7	2 454	35 518	1 111	14.5	64.4	30.8	3.0	0.2	0.0	0.4
01 055	2880	3	Etowah................	1 385	103 459	514	74.7	1 385	99 840	460	72.1	82.9	14.7	0.3	0.4	0.0	0.7
01 057	...	6	Fayette...............	1 626	18 495	1 869	11.4	1 626	17 962	1 790	11.0	86.9	11.9	0.2	0.2	0.0	0.3
01 059	...	6	Franklin..............	1 646	31 223	1 370	19.0	1 646	27 814	1 357	16.9	89.7	4.2	0.3	0.1	0.1	4.6
01 061	...	6	Geneva................	1 493	25 764	1 525	17.3	1 493	23 647	1 507	15.8	87.1	10.6	0.8	0.1	0.0	0.6
01 063	...	8	Greene................	1 673	9 974	2 449	6.0	1 673	10 153	2 373	6.1	19.1	80.3	0.1	0.1	0.0	0.1
01 065	...	6	Hale..................	1 667	17 185	1 941	10.3	1 667	15 498	1 953	9.3	39.8	59.0	0.2	0.2	0.0	0.3
01 067	...	6	Henry.................	1 455	16 310	2 003	11.2	1 455	15 374	1 966	10.6	65.7	32.3	0.2	0.1	0.0	1.0
01 069	2180	3	Houston...............	1 503	88 787	587	59.1	1 503	81 331	559	54.1	73.1	24.6	0.4	0.6	0.0	0.4
01 071	...	6	Jackson...............	2 794	53 926	869	19.3	2 794	47 796	879	17.1	91.9	3.7	1.8	0.2	0.0	0.4
01 073	1000	2	Jefferson.............	2 882	662 047	77	229.7	2 882	651 520	71	226.1	58.1	39.4	0.2	0.9	0.0	0.6
01 075	...	9	Lamar.................	1 567	15 904	2 027	10.1	1 567	15 715	1 941	10.0	86.9	12.0	0.1	0.1	0.0	0.4
01 077	2650	3	Lauderdale............	1 734	87 966	593	50.7	1 734	79 661	572	45.9	88.4	9.8	0.3	0.4	0.0	0.4
01 079	2030	3	Lawrence..............	1 796	34 803	1 258	19.4	1 796	31 513	1 230	17.5	77.8	13.4	5.4	0.1	0.0	0.3
01 081	0580	4	Lee...................	1 577	115 092	469	73.0	1 577	87 146	524	55.3	74.1	22.7	0.2	1.6	0.0	0.5
01 083	3440	2	Limestone.............	1 471	65 676	742	44.6	1 471	54 135	794	36.8	83.8	13.3	0.5	0.4	0.0	1.1
01 085	...	8	Lowndes...............	1 859	13 473	2 195	7.2	1 860	12 658	2 171	6.8	25.9	73.4	0.1	0.1	0.0	0.1
01 087	...	6	Macon	1 581	24 105	1 590	15.2	1 581	24 928	1 465	15.8	14.0	84.6	0.2	0.4	0.0	0.1
01 089	3440	2	Madison...............	2 085	276 700	205	132.7	2 085	238 912	209	114.6	72.1	22.8	0.8	1.9	0.1	0.6
01 091	...	7	Marengo...............	2 531	22 539	1 668	8.9	2 531	23 084	1 534	9.1	47.3	51.7	0.1	0.2	0.0	0.4
01 093	...	7	Marion	1 920	31 214	1 371	16.3	1 920	29 830	1 302	15.5	94.8	3.6	0.3	0.2	0.0	0.4
01 095	...	4	Marshall..............	1 469	82 231	630	56.0	1 469	70 832	625	48.2	93.4	1.5	0.5	0.2	0.0	3.2
01 097	5160	2	Mobile................	3 194	399 843	148	125.2	3 194	378 643	134	118.5	63.1	33.4	0.7	1.4	0.0	0.4
01 099	...	7	Monroe................	2 657	24 324	1 582	9.2	2 657	23 968	1 493	9.0	57.7	40.1	1.0	0.3	0.0	0.1
01 101	5240	2	Montgomery............	2 045	223 510	253	109.3	2 046	209 085	239	102.2	48.8	48.6	0.3	1.0	0.0	0.4
01 103	2030	3	Morgan................	1 508	111 064	487	73.6	1 508	100 043	458	66.3	85.1	11.2	0.7	0.4	0.1	1.3
01 105	...	7	Perry.................	1 863	11 861	2 301	6.4	1 864	12 759	2 161	6.8	30.9	68.4	0.1	0.0	0.0	0.1
01 107	...	6	Pickens...............	2 283	20 949	1 739	9.2	2 283	20 699	1 645	9.1	55.9	43.0	0.1	0.1	0.0	0.2
01 109	...	6	Pike..................	1 738	29 605	1 412	17.0	1 738	27 595	1 369	15.9	60.8	36.6	0.7	0.4	0.0	0.3
01 111	...	7	Randolph..............	1 505	22 380	1 674	14.9	1 505	19 881	1 684	13.2	76.4	22.2	0.2	0.2	0.0	0.3
01 113	1800	2	Russell...............	1 661	49 756	919	30.0	1 661	46 860	893	28.2	56.7	40.8	0.4	0.4	0.1	0.6
01 115	1000	2	St. Clair.............	1 641	64 742	751	39.5	1 642	49 811	843	30.3	90.0	8.1	0.4	0.2	0.0	0.4
01 117	1000	2	Shelby................	2 058	143 293	380	69.6	2 059	99 363	462	48.3	89.8	7.4	0.3	1.0	0.0	0.8
01 119	...	7	Sumter................	2 344	14 798	2 103	6.3	2 344	16 174	1 913	6.9	25.9	73.2	0.1	0.1	0.0	0.2
01 121	...	4	Talladega.............	1 915	80 321	639	41.9	1 916	74 109	608	38.7	67.0	31.5	0.2	0.2	0.0	0.2
01 123	...	6	Tallapoosa............	1 859	41 475	1 068	22.3	1 860	38 826	1 028	20.9	73.5	25.4	0.3	0.2	0.0	0.2
01 125	8600	3	Tuscaloosa............	3 430	164 875	326	48.1	3 432	150 500	310	43.9	68.1	29.3	0.2	0.9	0.0	0.6
01 127	...	6	Walker................	2 057	70 713	702	34.4	2 058	67 670	656	32.9	92.2	6.2	0.3	0.2	0.0	0.3

[1]MSA = Metropolitan Statistical Area. PMSA = Primary MSA. NECMA = New England County Metropolitan Area. See Appendix A for explanation of these concepts. See Appendix B for list of metropolitan areas identified by type, with component counties.
[2]County typology code from the Economic Research Service of USDA. See Appendix A for definition.
[3]Dry land or land partially or temporarily covered by water.

Table B. States and Counties

STATE County	Two or more races	White	Black	American Indian or Alaska Native	Asian	Native Hawaiian and other Pacific Islander	Some other race	Hispanic[1]	White	Black or African American	American Indian or Alaska Native	Asian and Pacific Islander	Hispanic[1]
	Population and population characteristics, 2000 (cont'd)								**Population and population characteristics, 1990**				
	Race (percent) (cont'd)								**Race (percent)**				
		Race alone or in combination											
	15	16	17	18	19	20	21	22	23	24	25	26	27
UNITED STATES	2.4	77.1	12.9	1.5	4.2	0.3	6.6	12.5	80.3	12.1	0.8	2.9	9.0
ALABAMA......................	1.0	72.0	26.3	1.0	0.9	0.1	0.9	1.7	73.6	25.3	0.4	0.5	0.6
Autauga	0.9	81.5	17.3	0.9	0.7	0.1	0.5	1.4	79.3	20.0	0.2	0.4	0.7
Baldwin	1.0	88.1	10.5	1.1	0.5	0.0	0.8	1.8	86.0	12.9	0.6	0.2	1.0
Barbour	0.7	51.7	46.7	0.8	0.5	0.1	1.1	1.6	55.5	44.0	0.2	0.2	0.5
Bibb...............................	0.5	77.1	22.3	0.6	0.1	0.0	0.4	1.0	78.7	21.0	0.2	0.1	0.2
Blount............................	1.0	96.0	1.3	1.1	0.3	0.0	2.3	5.3	97.8	1.3	0.3	0.1	0.7
Bullock	0.7	25.7	73.5	0.7	0.3	0.0	0.5	2.7	27.5	72.3	0.1	0.1	0.6
Butler	0.4	58.7	41.0	0.4	0.2	0.0	0.1	0.7	59.6	40.2	0.1	0.1	0.3
Calhoun	1.0	79.7	18.8	0.8	0.8	0.1	0.8	1.6	80.0	18.6	0.3	0.7	1.1
Chambers	0.6	61.3	38.4	0.4	0.3	0.0	0.2	0.8	63.9	35.9	0.1	0.0	0.3
Cherokee	0.8	93.6	5.8	0.7	0.3	0.1	0.5	0.9	92.9	6.6	0.3	0.1	0.3
Chilton	0.7	87.3	10.8	0.7	0.3	0.0	1.7	2.9	88.3	11.3	0.2	0.1	0.4
Choctaw	0.4	55.5	44.4	0.3	0.1	0.0	0.2	0.7	55.6	44.2	0.1	0.1	0.3
Clarke	0.5	56.3	43.3	0.5	0.2	0.0	0.2	0.6	57.0	42.7	0.2	0.1	0.4
Clay	0.8	83.4	15.8	0.9	0.2	0.0	0.6	1.8	83.3	16.3	0.2	0.1	0.2
Cleburne	0.8	95.5	3.8	0.8	0.2	0.0	0.5	1.4	94.9	4.6	0.2	0.1	0.3
Coffee	1.7	78.5	18.9	1.7	1.3	0.2	1.2	2.7	81.3	17.2	0.4	0.8	1.2
Colbert	0.9	82.3	16.9	0.9	0.3	0.1	0.5	1.1	82.9	16.6	0.3	0.2	0.4
Conecuh	0.6	56.0	43.7	0.6	0.2	0.1	0.1	0.7	57.4	42.2	0.3	0.1	0.6
Coosa	0.9	64.7	34.4	0.8	0.1	0.0	0.9	1.3	65.5	34.2	0.3	0.0	0.2
Covington	0.6	86.8	12.5	0.9	0.3	0.0	0.3	0.8	86.5	13.1	0.2	0.1	0.4
Crenshaw	0.7	74.4	25.1	0.8	0.2	0.0	0.3	0.6	73.7	26.0	0.2	0.1	0.2
Cullman	1.0	97.8	1.1	1.0	0.3	0.1	0.9	2.2	98.7	0.8	0.2	0.2	0.4
Dale	2.1	76.1	21.0	1.5	1.6	0.3	1.8	3.3	79.3	17.8	0.5	1.5	2.4
Dallas.............................	0.5	35.9	63.6	0.3	0.4	0.1	0.3	0.6	41.8	57.8	0.1	0.3	0.3
De Kalb	1.6	94.1	1.8	1.9	0.3	0.1	3.5	5.6	96.9	1.9	0.9	0.1	0.4
Elmore	1.0	77.9	21.0	1.0	0.5	0.1	0.6	1.2	76.9	22.4	0.3	0.3	0.5
Escambia	1.1	65.4	31.0	3.7	0.4	0.0	0.6	1.0	68.5	28.3	2.9	0.2	0.5
Etowah...........................	0.9	83.7	14.9	0.8	0.5	0.1	0.9	1.7	85.4	13.8	0.3	0.4	0.3
Fayette	0.5	87.4	12.1	0.4	0.2	0.0	0.4	0.8	87.5	12.2	0.1	0.1	0.4
Franklin	1.0	90.5	4.4	0.7	0.2	0.1	5.0	7.4	95.1	4.5	0.2	0.1	0.4
Geneva	0.7	87.8	10.8	1.2	0.2	0.1	0.7	1.8	87.5	11.9	0.4	0.1	0.5
Greene	0.3	19.2	80.5	0.2	0.2	0.0	0.2	0.6	19.4	80.6	0.0	0.0	0.2
Hale	0.6	40.2	59.3	0.4	0.3	0.1	0.4	0.9	40.4	59.5	0.1	0.1	0.4
Henry	0.7	66.3	32.5	0.6	0.2	0.0	1.1	1.5	64.5	35.1	0.2	0.0	0.6
Houston	0.9	73.8	24.9	0.8	0.8	0.1	0.6	1.3	75.6	23.3	0.4	0.6	0.6
Jackson..........................	2.0	93.8	3.9	3.4	0.3	0.1	0.5	1.1	93.5	4.1	2.1	0.2	0.4
Jefferson........................	0.8	58.7	39.7	0.5	1.1	0.1	0.8	1.6	64.2	35.1	0.1	0.5	0.4
Lamar.............................	0.5	87.3	12.2	0.4	0.1	0.0	0.5	1.3	87.8	11.8	0.2	0.1	0.5
Lauderdale......................	0.8	89.1	10.1	0.7	0.4	0.0	0.5	1.0	89.8	9.7	0.2	0.2	0.4
Lawrence........................	3.1	80.7	13.6	8.2	0.2	0.0	0.4	1.1	77.9	15.2	6.7	0.1	0.3
Lee	0.9	74.9	22.9	0.6	1.9	0.1	0.7	1.4	74.5	23.4	0.2	1.8	0.6
Limestone	0.9	84.6	13.6	0.9	0.5	0.1	1.3	2.6	86.2	13.2	0.3	0.3	0.5
Lowndes.........................	0.4	26.1	73.7	0.3	0.2	0.0	0.1	0.6	25.2	74.7	0.1	0.0	0.5
Macon	0.7	14.3	85.3	0.5	0.5	0.0	0.2	0.7	13.8	85.6	0.1	0.4	0.4
Madison	1.9	73.6	23.4	1.7	2.3	0.1	0.9	1.9	77.1	20.1	0.7	1.8	1.2
Marengo	0.5	47.6	52.0	0.4	0.2	0.0	0.3	1.0	49.0	50.9	0.0	0.0	0.3
Marion............................	0.7	95.4	3.8	0.7	0.3	0.1	0.5	1.2	96.4	3.2	0.2	0.1	0.2
Marshall	1.1	94.4	1.7	1.1	0.4	0.1	3.6	5.7	97.9	1.5	0.3	0.2	0.4
Mobile............................	1.0	63.9	33.7	1.1	1.6	0.1	0.7	1.2	67.3	31.1	0.5	0.9	0.8
Monroe...........................	0.8	58.4	40.4	1.4	0.3	0.0	0.3	0.8	59.7	39.1	0.9	0.2	0.4
Montgomery....................	0.9	49.5	49.0	0.5	1.3	0.1	0.6	1.2	57.1	41.8	0.2	0.7	0.8
Morgan...........................	1.2	86.2	11.5	1.4	0.6	0.1	1.5	3.3	89.1	10.1	0.3	0.4	0.6
Perry	0.5	31.1	68.8	0.2	0.3	0.1	0.2	0.9	35.3	64.4	0.1	0.1	0.3
Pickens	0.6	56.4	43.3	0.4	0.3	0.1	0.3	0.7	58.0	41.8	0.1	0.1	0.2
Pike	1.4	61.8	37.1	1.5	0.5	0.1	0.5	1.2	64.6	34.6	0.5	0.2	0.4
Randolph	0.6	77.0	22.4	0.5	0.3	0.0	0.4	1.2	76.1	23.6	0.1	0.1	0.3
Russell	1.1	57.5	41.3	0.8	0.6	0.2	0.9	1.5	60.8	38.6	0.2	0.2	0.6
St. Clair..........................	0.9	90.8	8.3	0.9	0.3	0.0	0.5	1.1	90.3	9.1	0.3	0.2	0.4
Shelby............................	0.7	90.5	7.5	0.6	1.2	0.0	0.9	2.0	91.3	7.8	0.3	0.6	0.5
Sumter	0.5	26.2	73.6	0.3	0.2	0.0	0.3	1.1	29.4	70.3	0.0	0.2	0.5
Talladega	0.7	67.6	31.8	0.5	0.3	0.1	0.4	1.0	68.8	30.7	0.2	0.2	0.7
Tallapoosa	0.5	73.9	25.6	0.5	0.2	0.1	0.3	0.6	73.4	26.3	0.2	0.1	0.2
Tuscaloosa	0.8	68.8	29.6	0.6	1.1	0.1	0.8	1.3	72.7	26.2	0.2	0.8	0.6
Walker............................	0.9	93.0	6.3	0.7	0.3	0.0	0.6	0.9	93.2	6.5	0.1	0.2	0.3

[1] Hispanic persons may be of any race.

Table B. States and Counties

STATE County	Population and population characteristics, 2000										
	Age (percent)										
	Under 5 years	5 to 17 years	18 to 24 years	25 to 34 years	35 to 44 years	45 to 54 years	55 to 64 years	65 to 74 years	75 years and over	Median age (years)	Percent Female
	28	29	30	31	32	33	34	35	36	37	38
UNITED STATES	6.8	18.9	9.7	14.2	16.0	13.4	8.6	6.5	5.9	35.3	50.9
ALABAMA	6.7	18.6	9.9	13.6	15.4	13.5	9.3	7.1	5.9	35.8	51.7
Autauga	6.9	21.7	8.0	13.1	17.6	12.9	9.6	6.1	4.1	35.1	51.4
Baldwin	6.1	18.3	7.5	12.1	15.6	14.0	10.9	8.8	6.7	39.0	51.0
Barbour	6.2	19.3	9.3	14.0	15.6	13.5	8.8	7.0	6.3	35.8	48.4
Bibb	7.0	18.4	9.5	15.6	15.3	13.1	9.6	6.4	5.2	34.7	48.4
Blount	6.9	18.5	8.4	14.0	15.2	13.5	10.6	7.4	5.5	36.4	50.1
Bullock	6.3	19.8	10.3	13.7	15.6	12.8	8.3	5.9	7.3	35.0	47.6
Butler	6.3	20.5	8.6	10.9	14.2	13.5	9.6	8.2	8.2	37.7	53.2
Calhoun	6.2	17.4	10.4	12.9	15.0	14.2	9.8	8.0	6.2	37.2	52.2
Chambers	6.6	18.0	8.6	13.0	14.0	13.6	9.9	8.2	8.0	37.7	52.8
Cherokee	6.0	16.2	7.6	13.1	14.5	14.3	12.4	9.4	6.5	40.0	50.8
Chilton	6.9	18.8	9.1	13.8	15.2	13.3	10.1	7.2	5.6	35.9	50.5
Choctaw	6.9	19.1	7.9	12.0	14.2	13.9	11.3	7.9	6.7	37.9	53.0
Clarke	7.5	20.6	8.5	12.7	14.9	12.5	10.0	7.3	6.2	35.5	52.7
Clay	6.2	17.7	8.0	12.7	14.7	13.2	11.0	8.6	8.0	38.7	51.2
Cleburne	6.1	18.2	8.2	13.6	14.9	14.2	11.1	7.8	5.9	37.5	50.2
Coffee	6.2	18.5	8.9	13.0	15.1	14.0	10.2	7.7	6.4	37.2	51.2
Colbert	6.1	17.7	8.1	12.7	15.1	13.9	11.0	8.3	7.1	38.7	52.1
Conecuh	6.2	19.7	8.3	11.7	14.1	14.0	10.3	8.5	7.2	38.0	52.7
Coosa	6.2	17.5	8.6	13.5	15.5	13.8	10.4	8.3	6.2	37.7	48.9
Covington	5.9	17.6	8.1	11.6	14.5	13.4	10.9	9.2	8.7	39.8	52.2
Crenshaw	5.9	18.8	7.9	11.9	14.5	13.8	10.1	8.5	8.6	38.8	52.7
Cullman	6.4	17.9	8.8	13.3	15.1	13.5	10.4	8.0	6.6	37.5	50.7
Dale	7.5	19.1	9.6	15.0	15.3	12.6	9.2	6.8	5.1	34.3	50.4
Dallas	7.4	21.2	9.4	11.6	14.6	12.8	9.1	7.4	6.5	35.3	54.5
De Kalb	6.8	17.9	9.2	14.1	15.0	13.4	9.9	7.5	6.3	36.3	51.1
Elmore	6.6	19.1	8.8	15.1	17.0	13.9	8.8	5.9	4.8	35.3	49.4
Escambia	6.2	17.9	9.7	13.5	15.4	13.5	10.2	7.3	6.4	36.9	49.3
Etowah	6.4	17.4	8.7	13.0	14.3	14.1	10.0	8.5	7.5	38.3	52.1
Fayette	6.0	17.9	8.2	12.3	14.2	14.0	11.2	8.3	7.8	39.0	51.7
Franklin	6.4	18.1	9.2	13.7	14.3	13.0	10.4	8.2	6.6	36.7	50.9
Geneva	5.6	18.4	7.5	12.3	14.5	13.8	11.5	8.7	7.6	39.3	51.4
Greene	7.7	21.5	8.9	10.7	14.3	13.3	8.9	7.8	6.9	35.9	53.1
Hale	8.2	21.4	9.1	12.0	14.7	12.6	8.5	6.9	6.6	34.4	52.8
Henry	6.2	17.8	8.4	12.2	13.5	14.8	10.6	8.5	7.8	39.3	52.5
Houston	6.8	19.1	8.2	13.2	15.6	13.8	9.6	7.4	6.3	36.7	52.5
Jackson	6.3	17.9	8.3	13.7	15.0	14.2	11.2	7.8	5.6	37.6	51.3
Jefferson	6.5	18.3	9.6	14.0	15.7	13.8	8.5	7.1	6.6	36.0	52.9
Lamar	5.8	17.8	8.7	12.9	14.8	13.3	10.8	8.6	7.3	38.2	51.7
Lauderdale	5.9	17.1	10.1	13.0	14.9	13.7	10.2	8.1	6.9	37.6	52.2
Lawrence	6.3	19.4	8.4	14.3	15.9	13.5	10.2	6.9	5.2	35.9	51.0
Lee	6.3	17.0	22.7	14.5	13.6	11.0	6.8	4.6	3.5	27.5	50.8
Limestone	6.6	18.3	8.8	14.9	17.2	13.8	9.4	6.4	4.7	35.8	49.2
Lowndes	7.5	22.7	9.1	12.0	15.1	12.3	9.1	6.8	5.4	33.9	53.2
Macon	6.5	18.7	16.9	11.0	12.0	12.4	8.6	6.8	7.2	32.0	54.1
Madison	6.8	18.8	9.4	13.8	17.7	13.4	9.2	6.4	4.4	35.7	51.2
Marengo	6.8	21.7	8.0	11.6	14.4	13.1	9.8	7.8	6.7	36.4	53.1
Marion	6.0	16.5	8.2	13.3	14.9	13.6	11.6	8.4	7.4	38.9	50.5
Marshall	6.7	18.2	8.5	13.7	15.3	13.0	10.4	8.0	6.2	36.9	51.3
Mobile	7.3	20.1	10.0	13.3	15.3	13.1	8.7	6.5	5.5	34.4	52.2
Monroe	7.5	20.8	8.6	12.5	14.3	13.1	9.4	7.2	6.6	35.4	52.4
Montgomery	6.9	18.9	11.7	14.5	15.3	12.9	8.0	6.2	5.6	33.5	52.4
Morgan	6.6	18.8	8.4	13.6	16.4	14.1	9.7	7.0	5.4	36.6	51.0
Perry	7.6	22.2	11.1	10.8	12.7	11.1	9.5	7.8	7.1	33.3	54.4
Pickens	6.8	20.5	8.5	11.6	14.1	12.8	9.9	8.6	7.1	36.9	53.2
Pike	6.5	17.9	15.8	12.7	13.3	12.0	9.2	6.4	6.2	32.5	52.8
Randolph	6.6	18.5	8.7	12.4	14.3	13.2	10.3	8.5	7.4	37.7	51.7
Russell	7.1	19.5	9.1	13.7	15.1	12.9	9.5	7.5	5.6	35.4	52.4
St. Clair	6.6	18.8	7.9	14.3	16.4	14.1	10.2	7.0	4.7	36.4	49.6
Shelby	7.5	18.8	8.2	15.8	17.9	15.0	8.4	5.1	3.4	34.9	51.0
Sumter	7.2	21.9	12.2	11.9	13.5	11.6	7.9	6.7	7.2	32.1	54.1
Talladega	6.3	18.6	9.0	13.6	15.3	14.0	9.8	7.4	5.9	36.6	51.1
Tallapoosa	6.2	18.0	7.6	12.3	14.5	14.1	10.9	8.7	7.9	39.3	52.5
Tuscaloosa	6.4	17.0	16.5	13.9	14.1	13.0	7.8	6.3	5.0	31.9	51.9
Walker	6.4	17.1	8.6	13.1	14.9	14.2	10.9	8.2	6.6	38.3	51.8

Table B. States and Counties

STATE County	Population and population characteristics, 1990										Population—change, 1980-2000				
	Age (percent)										Total persons			Percent change	
	Under 5 years	5 to 17 years	18 to 24 years	25 to 34 years	35 to 44 years	45 to 54 years	55 to 64 years	65 to 74 years	75 years and over	Percent Female	2000	1990	1980	1990–2000	1980–1990
	39	40	41	42	43	44	45	46	47	48	49	50	51	52	53
UNITED STATES	7.4	18.2	10.8	17.4	15.1	10.1	8.5	7.3	5.3	51.3	281 421 906	248 790 925	226 542 204	13.1	9.8
ALABAMA	7.0	19.2	11.0	16.0	14.4	10.4	9.0	7.5	5.5	52.1	4 447 100	4 040 389	3 894 025	10.1	3.8
Autauga	7.8	21.7	9.7	16.2	14.8	11.4	8.5	5.7	4.1	51.3	43 671	34 222	32 259	27.6	6.1
Baldwin	6.9	19.1	8.5	14.7	14.4	11.0	10.3	9.2	6.0	51.4	140 415	98 280	78 556	42.9	25.1
Barbour	7.4	21.9	9.3	14.4	14.2	9.2	8.8	8.2	6.4	52.5	29 038	25 417	24 756	14.2	2.7
Bibb	7.1	21.9	10.8	14.9	13.7	10.7	8.5	6.7	6.0	51.1	20 826	16 598	15 723	25.5	5.4
Blount	6.7	18.8	10.0	15.1	14.7	12.0	9.5	7.4	5.6	51.2	51 024	39 248	36 459	30.0	7.6
Bullock	8.6	22.0	9.2	15.3	12.9	8.6	7.3	8.5	7.6	51.7	11 714	11 042	10 596	6.1	4.2
Butler	7.5	22.6	8.6	13.5	12.9	9.2	8.9	8.8	8.0	53.2	21 399	21 892	21 680	-2.3	1.0
Calhoun	6.4	18.6	12.9	15.9	14.5	10.2	9.1	7.4	5.0	51.7	112 249	116 032	119 761	-3.3	-3.1
Chambers	6.6	19.6	10.0	14.1	13.4	10.0	9.6	9.2	7.7	52.9	36 583	36 876	39 191	-0.8	-5.9
Cherokee	5.8	18.2	9.8	14.4	14.3	11.9	10.8	8.9	5.8	50.8	23 988	19 543	18 760	22.7	4.2
Chilton	6.8	20.0	9.6	15.2	14.0	11.1	9.6	7.8	6.1	51.4	39 593	32 458	30 612	22.0	6.0
Choctaw	7.1	22.3	9.5	14.1	13.2	11.0	8.9	7.5	6.4	52.6	15 922	16 018	16 839	-0.6	-4.9
Clarke	7.2	22.8	10.4	14.6	12.9	10.5	8.5	7.1	6.0	52.2	27 867	27 240	27 702	2.3	-1.7
Clay	5.9	19.1	9.4	14.2	12.9	11.2	10.0	8.6	8.3	52.0	14 254	13 252	13 703	7.6	-3.3
Cleburne	6.7	19.3	10.2	15.1	13.9	11.8	9.6	7.7	5.7	50.9	14 123	12 730	12 595	10.9	1.1
Coffee	6.7	19.0	10.0	15.9	14.8	11.2	9.4	7.6	5.6	51.1	43 615	40 240	38 533	8.4	4.4
Colbert	6.6	17.7	9.6	15.1	14.2	11.8	10.4	9.0	5.7	52.0	54 984	51 666	54 519	6.4	-5.2
Conecuh	6.7	21.2	8.8	14.0	12.7	9.5	9.7	9.3	8.0	52.8	14 089	14 054	15 884	0.2	-11.5
Coosa	7.1	18.9	10.3	15.2	12.9	10.5	10.6	8.3	6.2	50.9	12 202	11 063	11 377	10.3	-2.8
Covington	6.4	19.0	9.0	14.1	13.2	10.7	10.4	9.5	7.7	52.7	37 631	36 478	36 850	3.2	-1.0
Crenshaw	6.6	20.2	8.8	13.3	13.1	10.0	9.7	10.0	8.3	52.6	13 665	13 635	14 110	0.2	-3.4
Cullman	6.6	18.6	9.9	15.2	14.1	11.2	10.0	8.2	6.2	51.4	77 483	67 613	61 642	14.6	9.7
Dale	8.6	19.3	13.1	19.7	13.3	9.2	7.4	5.5	3.9	49.5	49 129	49 633	47 821	-1.0	3.8
Dallas	8.0	23.3	10.0	14.3	12.8	9.3	8.5	7.5	6.2	54.4	46 365	48 130	53 981	-3.7	-10.8
De Kalb	6.2	19.3	9.7	15.0	14.3	11.1	9.9	8.2	6.4	51.7	64 452	54 651	53 658	17.9	1.9
Elmore	6.8	19.2	10.5	17.1	15.3	10.8	8.6	6.7	5.0	49.4	65 874	49 210	43 390	33.9	13.4
Escambia	6.5	20.2	9.9	15.3	14.0	10.9	9.4	7.6	6.3	50.8	38 440	35 518	38 440	8.2	-7.6
Etowah	6.0	18.6	9.7	14.2	14.6	10.8	10.3	9.4	6.5	52.7	103 459	99 840	103 057	3.6	-3.1
Fayette	6.1	19.5	9.6	13.9	14.0	11.1	9.5	8.6	7.7	52.3	18 495	17 962	18 809	3.0	-4.5
Franklin	6.5	18.4	9.6	14.5	13.7	11.6	10.4	8.6	6.8	52.2	31 223	27 814	28 350	12.3	-1.9
Geneva	6.4	18.5	9.5	13.7	13.4	11.4	10.4	9.2	7.6	51.8	25 764	23 647	24 253	9.0	-2.5
Greene	7.8	25.2	8.8	13.6	11.9	8.4	8.8	7.4	8.2	54.1	9 974	10 153	11 021	-1.8	-7.9
Hale	8.0	23.5	8.9	14.3	12.2	8.9	8.2	8.3	7.7	53.3	17 185	15 498	15 604	10.9	-0.7
Henry	6.6	20.1	9.4	13.3	14.1	10.4	9.8	9.0	7.3	52.7	16 310	15 374	15 302	6.1	0.5
Houston	7.4	20.3	9.5	16.0	15.0	10.6	8.9	7.3	5.1	52.5	88 787	81 331	74 632	9.2	9.0
Jackson	6.2	19.5	9.7	15.1	15.0	12.2	9.8	7.5	5.1	51.7	53 926	47 796	51 407	12.8	-7.0
Jefferson	6.9	18.1	9.9	16.8	15.3	9.9	9.2	8.0	6.0	53.3	662 047	651 520	671 371	1.6	-3.0
Lamar	6.4	19.0	9.7	14.4	13.6	11.1	10.1	8.2	7.5	52.2	15 904	15 715	16 453	1.2	-4.5
Lauderdale	6.4	17.6	11.4	15.2	14.2	11.1	9.9	8.4	5.9	52.3	87 966	79 661	80 546	10.4	-1.1
Lawrence	7.3	20.1	11.0	16.1	13.7	11.1	8.8	7.0	4.9	50.8	34 803	31 513	30 170	10.4	4.5
Lee	6.2	15.7	26.0	15.6	12.5	8.6	6.7	5.0	3.6	50.4	115 092	87 146	76 283	32.1	14.2
Limestone	6.8	18.3	10.7	18.2	14.8	11.1	8.8	6.5	4.8	50.0	65 676	54 135	46 005	21.3	17.7
Lowndes	9.0	25.7	10.5	14.4	11.6	8.5	7.6	6.7	6.0	53.7	13 473	12 658	13 253	6.4	-4.5
Macon	7.2	19.4	18.4	12.6	11.7	7.9	7.4	8.4	6.9	53.7	24 105	24 928	26 829	-3.3	-7.1
Madison	7.3	17.3	11.6	19.9	14.8	11.3	8.8	5.6	3.3	50.7	276 700	238 912	196 966	15.8	21.3
Marengo	7.8	22.5	9.5	13.8	13.0	9.7	9.2	7.7	6.9	52.8	22 539	23 084	25 047	-2.4	-7.8
Marion	6.3	18.2	10.2	14.3	13.9	11.8	9.9	8.2	7.0	51.1	31 214	29 830	30 041	4.6	-0.7
Marshall	6.5	18.2	9.5	15.4	14.4	11.6	10.4	8.1	5.9	52.1	82 231	70 832	65 622	16.1	7.9
Mobile	7.8	20.7	10.4	16.3	14.6	10.0	8.3	7.0	4.8	52.6	399 843	378 643	364 980	5.6	3.7
Monroe	7.8	23.0	10.0	14.6	13.2	9.8	8.5	7.1	6.1	51.7	24 324	23 968	22 651	1.5	5.8
Montgomery	7.7	19.7	11.3	17.0	15.0	9.6	8.0	6.7	4.9	52.9	223 510	209 085	197 038	6.9	6.1
Morgan	6.9	19.1	9.4	16.9	15.4	11.4	9.1	6.9	4.8	51.3	111 064	100 043	90 231	11.0	10.9
Perry	7.6	23.7	12.6	12.0	10.7	9.1	8.4	7.7	8.1	53.4	11 861	12 759	15 012	-7.0	-15.0
Pickens	7.1	21.4	9.0	13.6	12.1	10.2	10.3	8.7	7.7	53.3	20 949	20 699	21 481	1.2	-3.6
Pike	6.7	18.2	18.4	13.4	11.7	9.2	7.8	7.7	6.9	53.1	29 605	27 595	28 050	7.3	-1.6
Randolph	6.4	19.7	9.7	14.4	13.0	10.0	10.2	9.2	7.4	51.6	22 380	19 881	20 075	12.6	-1.0
Russell	7.5	19.1	10.6	15.9	13.8	10.8	9.6	7.6	5.1	52.2	49 756	46 860	47 356	6.2	-1.0
St. Clair	7.2	19.4	9.7	16.3	15.2	11.3	9.3	7.1	4.5	49.8	64 742	49 811	41 205	30.0	20.9
Shelby	8.0	19.3	10.3	19.4	17.9	10.5	6.9	4.6	3.0	51.1	143 293	99 363	66 298	44.2	49.9
Sumter	7.6	23.1	14.0	14.1	11.1	7.8	7.7	7.4	7.2	53.8	14 798	16 174	16 908	-8.5	-4.3
Talladega	6.9	20.8	10.6	14.8	14.5	10.2	9.3	7.6	5.3	51.7	80 321	74 109	73 826	8.4	0.4
Tallapoosa	6.4	19.1	9.7	14.0	13.9	10.5	10.2	9.1	7.0	53.0	41 475	38 826	38 766	6.8	0.2
Tuscaloosa	6.4	17.3	17.5	15.7	14.2	9.2	8.3	6.6	4.8	51.7	164 875	150 500	137 541	9.6	9.4
Walker	6.2	19.0	9.8	14.9	14.5	11.4	9.7	8.2	6.2	52.0	70 713	67 670	68 660	4.5	-1.4

Table B. States and Counties

STATE County		Household relationship, 2000															
		In households (percent)										In group quarters (percent)					
					Child		Other relatives		Nonrelatives				Institutionalized population			Noninstitutionalized population	
	Total population	Total in house-holds	House-holder	Spouse	Total	Own child under 18 years	Total	Under 18 years	Total	Unmar-ried partner	Total in group quarters	Correc-tional institu-tions	Nurs-ing homes	Other institu-tions	Col-lege dormi-tories	Mili-tary quar-ters	Other
	54	55	56	57	58	59	60	61	62	63	64	65	66	67	68	69	70
UNITED STATES	281 421 906	97.2	37.5	19.4	29.6	22.9	5.6	2.1	5.2	1.9	2.8	0.7	0.6	0.1	0.7	0.1	0.5
ALABAMA	4 447 100	97.4	39.1	20.4	29.3	22.3	5.4	2.5	3.3	1.3	2.6	0.8	0.6	0.1	0.7	0.1	0.3
Autauga	43 671	99.4	36.6	22.1	32.6	25.6	5.2	2.5	2.9	1.3	0.6	0.2	0.2	0.0	0.0	0.0	0.2
Baldwin	140 415	98.4	39.4	23.4	28.2	22.2	4.2	1.9	3.2	1.4	1.6	0.6	0.4	0.1	0.2	0.0	0.3
Barbour	29 038	90.6	35.8	17.2	28.4	21.5	6.5	3.4	2.7	1.2	9.4	8.5	0.6	0.2	0.0	0.0	0.0
Bibb................................	20 826	94.1	35.6	20.8	29.4	22.1	5.6	2.8	2.6	1.3	5.9	4.3	0.5	0.1	0.0	0.0	1.0
Blount.............................	51 024	98.8	37.8	24.7	29.3	22.8	4.7	2.0	2.4	1.0	1.2	0.2	0.6	0.0	0.0	0.0	0.3
Bullock	11 714	87.1	34.0	12.1	29.6	21.7	8.0	4.0	3.3	1.3	12.9	11.9	1.0	0.0	0.0	0.0	0.0
Butler	21 399	98.8	39.2	18.7	31.2	23.0	6.7	3.5	2.9	1.5	1.2	0.1	1.0	0.0	0.0	0.0	0.1
Calhoun	112 249	97.8	40.4	21.1	27.5	20.4	5.4	2.6	3.5	1.4	2.2	0.3	0.4	0.1	1.0	0.0	0.4
Chambers	36 583	98.6	39.7	19.3	29.0	20.4	7.8	3.8	2.8	1.5	1.4	0.5	0.9	0.0	0.0	0.0	0.1
Cherokee	23 988	98.5	40.5	24.9	26.4	19.7	4.6	2.1	2.1	1.1	1.5	0.3	1.1	0.0	0.0	0.0	0.1
Chilton	39 593	99.1	38.6	23.2	29.3	22.9	4.8	2.2	3.2	1.2	0.9	0.4	0.3	0.0	0.0	0.0	0.1
Choctaw..........................	15 922	99.2	40.0	20.8	29.9	22.3	6.4	3.4	2.1	1.1	0.8	0.2	0.6	0.0	0.0	0.0	0.1
Clarke.............................	27 867	98.6	38.0	20.4	32.1	24.2	6.3	3.6	1.8	1.1	1.4	0.2	0.6	0.4	0.0	0.0	0.1
Clay................................	14 254	98.1	40.4	22.9	27.7	21.4	4.8	2.1	2.3	1.2	1.9	0.3	1.4	0.0	0.0	0.0	0.1
Cleburne	14 123	99.2	39.6	24.3	28.4	22.0	4.4	1.9	2.6	1.4	0.8	0.2	0.5	0.0	0.0	0.0	0.1
Coffee	43 615	98.2	39.9	22.5	28.5	22.2	4.3	2.0	3.0	1.2	1.8	0.8	0.8	0.1	0.0	0.0	0.1
Colbert............................	54 984	98.9	40.9	22.9	28.3	21.1	4.7	2.2	2.2	1.1	1.1	0.1	0.6	0.1	0.1	0.0	0.1
Conecuh..........................	14 089	99.4	41.1	19.6	30.9	22.4	5.6	3.0	2.2	1.2	0.6	0.0	0.4	0.1	0.0	0.0	0.0
Coosa	12 202	96.8	38.4	21.0	27.7	20.0	6.6	3.3	3.0	1.4	3.2	2.8	0.3	0.1	0.0	0.0	0.0
Covington........................	37 631	98.6	41.6	22.5	27.6	21.1	4.5	2.2	2.4	1.3	1.4	0.3	0.9	0.0	0.0	0.0	0.2
Crenshaw........................	13 665	98.8	40.8	20.7	29.6	21.7	5.5	2.5	2.3	1.1	1.2	0.1	1.1	0.0	0.0	0.0	0.0
Cullman...........................	77 483	98.7	39.6	24.1	28.3	22.1	4.0	1.6	2.7	1.1	1.3	0.1	0.7	0.1	0.1	0.0	0.2
Dale................................	49 129	96.6	38.4	21.1	30.1	24.3	3.9	1.9	3.0	1.3	3.4	0.1	0.8	0.0	0.0	2.4	0.1
Dallas	46 365	98.8	38.5	15.6	33.1	23.3	9.2	4.8	2.5	1.4	1.2	0.0	0.3	0.1	0.4	0.0	0.3
De Kalb	64 452	98.7	39.0	23.2	28.7	22.3	4.7	1.9	3.1	1.3	1.3	0.1	0.8	0.0	0.0	0.0	0.4
Elmore	65 874	91.9	34.5	21.2	29.1	23.0	4.8	2.3	2.4	1.1	8.1	7.1	0.9	0.1	0.0	0.0	0.0
Escambia........................	38 440	92.2	37.2	19.2	27.6	20.8	5.4	2.9	2.8	1.4	7.8	4.0	0.6	0.1	0.2	0.0	2.9
Etowah............................	103 459	98.0	40.2	21.8	28.0	20.7	5.2	2.4	2.8	1.2	2.0	0.4	0.8	0.2	0.1	0.0	0.5
Fayette............................	18 495	98.2	40.5	23.2	28.0	21.4	4.3	2.0	2.2	1.0	1.8	0.3	0.9	0.0	0.4	0.0	0.3
Franklin	31 223	98.7	39.3	23.2	28.7	22.1	4.6	1.9	2.9	1.0	1.3	0.2	0.9	0.0	0.0	0.0	0.2
Geneva	25 764	98.9	40.7	22.9	28.0	21.4	4.7	2.2	2.7	1.5	1.1	0.2	0.7	0.0	0.0	0.0	0.2
Greene............................	9 974	99.2	39.4	14.3	33.5	23.5	9.5	5.4	2.5	1.3	0.8	0.2	0.6	0.0	0.0	0.0	0.0
Hale................................	17 185	98.3	37.3	17.0	34.2	25.3	7.5	3.9	2.3	1.4	1.7	0.6	0.9	0.1	0.0	0.0	0.0
Henry	16 310	98.9	40.0	21.6	28.7	20.8	6.2	2.9	2.5	1.3	1.1	0.1	0.9	0.0	0.0	0.0	0.1
Houston	88 787	98.7	40.4	21.2	29.5	23.3	4.6	2.1	3.1	1.5	1.3	0.4	0.6	0.1	0.0	0.0	0.1
Jackson	53 926	98.9	40.1	23.6	28.4	21.5	4.3	2.0	2.5	1.3	1.1	0.2	0.4	0.3	0.0	0.0	0.1
Jefferson.........................	662 047	97.6	39.8	18.3	29.5	21.5	6.4	2.9	3.6	1.3	2.4	0.5	0.6	0.1	0.7	0.0	0.5
Lamar..............................	15 904	98.7	40.7	23.8	28.6	21.6	3.7	1.6	2.0	0.9	1.3	0.3	0.9	0.0	0.0	0.0	0.0
Lauderdale	87 966	98.1	41.0	22.9	27.8	21.2	3.4	1.4	2.9	1.1	1.9	0.2	0.7	0.1	0.7	0.0	0.2
Lawrence.........................	34 803	99.3	38.9	23.5	30.4	23.1	4.4	2.3	2.0	1.1	0.7	0.2	0.4	0.0	0.0	0.0	0.0
Lee	115 092	96.1	39.7	17.5	25.9	20.9	4.6	2.0	8.4	1.5	3.9	0.2	0.3	0.2	3.1	0.0	0.2
Limestone	65 676	96.0	37.6	22.6	29.3	22.8	4.1	1.7	2.4	1.2	4.0	3.3	0.5	0.0	0.1	0.0	0.0
Lowndes..........................	13 473	99.7	36.4	15.6	35.0	24.0	10.0	6.0	2.6	1.6	0.3	0.2	0.0	0.0	0.0	0.0	0.1
Macon	24 105	90.5	37.1	11.8	28.6	20.0	8.6	4.7	4.4	1.5	9.5	0.2	1.6	0.2	7.5	0.0	0.1
Madison	276 700	97.4	39.7	21.2	29.1	23.3	4.1	1.8	3.2	1.3	2.6	0.3	0.3	0.1	1.4	0.2	0.3
Marengo..........................	22 539	99.1	38.9	18.8	32.4	24.6	6.7	3.6	2.3	1.2	0.9	0.1	0.7	0.0	0.0	0.0	0.1
Marion.............................	31 214	97.1	40.7	23.8	26.6	20.5	3.9	1.7	2.2	1.1	2.9	1.9	0.9	0.0	0.1	0.0	0.1
Marshall	82 231	98.8	39.6	22.9	28.0	22.2	5.0	2.1	3.3	1.3	1.2	0.3	0.7	0.0	0.0	0.0	0.2
Mobile	399 843	98.0	37.6	18.6	31.7	23.7	6.6	3.2	3.5	1.5	2.0	0.3	0.5	0.2	0.7	0.0	0.3
Monroe............................	24 324	99.0	38.6	20.2	32.1	24.7	6.0	3.3	2.1	1.2	1.0	0.2	0.8	0.0	0.0	0.0	0.0
Montgomery.....................	223 510	94.6	38.5	16.9	29.4	22.2	6.2	3.0	3.7	1.5	5.4	1.2	0.5	0.2	1.3	1.6	0.6
Morgan............................	111 064	98.5	39.3	22.5	29.5	23.1	4.3	1.8	2.8	1.2	1.5	0.6	0.6	0.0	0.0	0.0	0.3
Perry...............................	11 861	96.0	36.5	14.8	33.6	24.1	8.8	4.9	2.3	1.4	4.0	0.1	1.2	0.0	2.7	0.0	0.0
Pickens	20 949	99.0	38.6	19.2	31.7	22.8	7.3	4.1	2.2	1.0	1.0	0.0	0.9	0.0	0.0	0.0	0.0
Pike	29 605	96.0	40.3	17.6	27.6	21.0	6.0	3.0	4.5	1.4	4.0	0.3	0.0	0.0	3.6	0.0	0.2
Randolph	22 380	97.4	38.6	21.7	28.8	21.8	5.8	2.9	2.6	1.3	2.6	0.3	1.7	0.0	0.5	0.0	0.0
Russell............................	49 756	98.6	39.7	17.6	30.7	22.6	6.9	3.4	3.7	1.9	1.4	0.6	0.6	0.0	0.0	0.0	0.2
St. Clair...........................	64 742	97.1	37.3	23.4	29.0	22.8	4.7	2.1	2.6	1.3	2.9	2.2	0.6	0.0	0.0	0.0	0.1
Shelby.............................	143 293	98.8	38.1	24.3	30.2	24.6	3.4	1.3	2.8	1.0	1.2	0.1	0.2	0.1	0.6	0.0	0.1
Sumter............................	14 798	98.3	38.6	14.1	30.4	23.5	9.2	5.2	3.7	1.7	1.7	0.2	0.8	0.0	0.7	0.0	0.0
Talladega	80 321	95.4	38.2	20.0	28.5	21.1	5.9	3.1	2.8	1.3	4.6	2.9	0.5	0.5	0.4	0.0	0.3
Tallapoosa	41 475	97.9	40.2	21.3	27.9	20.9	5.9	2.8	2.7	1.4	2.1	0.3	1.6	0.1	0.0	0.0	0.1
Tuscaloosa	164 875	94.7	39.1	18.5	27.1	20.7	5.0	2.3	5.0	1.4	5.3	0.3	0.7	0.5	3.6	0.0	0.2
Walker.............................	70 713	98.6	40.1	22.6	28.0	20.6	5.3	2.5	2.6	1.2	1.4	0.4	0.8	0.0	0.1	0.0	0.1

STATE County	Households by type, 2000												Households, 1990		
		Family households						Nonfamily households							House-holder living alone
				Married couple		Female householder¹			Householder living alone					Female house-holder¹	
	Total households	Total	With own children under 18 years	Total	With own children under 18 years	Total	With own children under 18 years	Total	Total	65 years and over	Average house-hold size	Average family size	Total house-holds		
	71	72	73	74	75	76	77	78	79	80	81	82	83	84	85
UNITED STATES	105 480 101	68.1	32.8	51.7	23.5	12.2	7.2	31.9	25.8	9.2	2.59	3.14	91 947 410	11.6	24.6
ALABAMA	1 737 080	70.0	32.3	52.2	22.5	14.2	8.1	30.0	26.1	9.8	2.49	3.01	1 506 790	13.4	23.8
Autauga	16 003	77.2	39.1	60.3	29.5	13.1	7.5	22.8	19.9	7.6	2.71	3.12	11 826	12.2	17.7
Baldwin	55 336	72.8	31.5	59.3	24.0	10.2	5.9	27.2	23.3	9.5	2.50	2.94	37 044	10.0	21.4
Barbour	10 409	71.0	33.3	47.9	20.1	19.1	11.2	29.0	26.5	12.1	2.53	3.04	9 218	16.5	25.4
Bibb	7 421	75.2	34.4	58.4	25.8	12.7	6.8	24.8	22.1	9.4	2.64	3.08	5 745	11.3	20.3
Blount	19 265	76.9	34.3	65.5	28.3	7.9	4.2	23.1	20.8	9.5	2.62	3.02	14 644	7.9	19.0
Bullock	3 986	68.5	33.5	35.5	14.0	28.2	17.3	31.5	28.9	12.3	2.56	3.13	3 787	25.9	27.0
Butler	8 398	69.9	32.5	47.7	20.0	18.2	10.7	30.1	27.5	13.5	2.52	3.06	7 935	16.2	25.0
Calhoun	45 307	69.1	29.5	52.2	20.7	13.4	7.1	30.9	26.9	10.7	2.42	2.94	42 983	12.4	23.2
Chambers	14 522	70.2	29.3	48.5	18.6	17.4	9.1	29.8	27.0	12.4	2.48	3.01	13 786	15.7	23.9
Cherokee	9 719	74.1	28.9	61.4	22.7	9.2	4.3	25.9	23.9	10.4	2.43	2.86	7 466	8.9	20.4
Chilton	15 287	74.2	34.4	60.1	26.7	10.5	5.9	25.8	22.9	10.2	2.57	3.00	12 114	10.1	21.1
Choctaw	6 363	71.9	32.5	52.0	21.4	16.0	9.2	28.1	26.5	11.6	2.48	2.99	5 747	14.5	23.8
Clarke	10 578	72.8	35.4	53.9	24.4	15.7	9.3	27.2	25.5	11.9	2.60	3.13	9 506	14.8	23.0
Clay	5 765	71.1	30.8	56.7	22.9	10.5	5.9	28.9	26.7	13.1	2.43	2.93	5 003	9.9	23.0
Cleburne	5 590	73.8	32.8	61.4	26.2	8.7	4.5	26.2	23.0	10.3	2.51	2.95	4 776	8.1	20.0
Coffee	17 421	71.7	32.1	56.4	23.2	12.1	7.3	28.3	24.9	10.2	2.46	2.93	15 260	10.7	21.7
Colbert	22 461	71.4	30.5	56.0	22.4	12.1	6.5	28.6	26.1	11.5	2.42	2.92	20 096	11.3	22.9
Conecuh	5 792	68.0	30.9	47.7	19.2	16.2	9.9	32.0	30.1	13.5	2.42	3.01	5 259	15.4	24.8
Coosa	4 682	72.8	30.0	54.8	21.2	13.5	6.9	27.2	24.3	9.8	2.52	2.98	4 017	11.8	21.3
Covington	15 640	69.0	29.5	54.1	21.5	11.3	6.3	31.0	28.6	14.1	2.37	2.90	14 444	11.3	25.7
Crenshaw	5 577	69.8	31.0	50.7	20.9	15.4	8.2	30.2	28.2	14.7	2.42	2.96	5 262	14.2	26.7
Cullman	30 706	73.2	32.1	60.8	25.5	8.7	4.7	26.8	24.0	10.4	2.49	2.94	25 605	8.2	20.6
Dale	18 878	72.2	36.0	55.0	24.9	13.6	9.0	27.8	24.3	8.8	2.51	2.99	17 574	11.7	21.1
Dallas	17 841	70.0	33.5	40.4	16.9	25.4	14.8	30.0	27.8	11.6	2.57	3.15	17 033	23.7	25.4
De Kalb	25 113	73.4	33.2	59.5	25.7	9.9	5.5	26.6	23.8	10.8	2.53	2.98	20 968	9.2	21.8
Elmore	22 737	77.2	37.4	61.4	28.3	12.0	7.1	22.8	20.0	7.7	2.66	3.07	16 532	11.2	19.4
Escambia	14 297	70.6	32.0	51.7	21.7	15.1	8.5	29.4	26.4	11.4	2.48	2.99	12 899	14.3	24.2
Etowah	41 615	70.8	29.9	54.2	21.3	13.1	7.1	29.2	26.3	12.4	2.44	2.93	38 675	11.8	24.3
Fayette	7 493	71.3	30.8	57.3	23.2	10.6	5.7	28.7	26.6	13.5	2.42	2.92	6 859	9.7	23.1
Franklin	12 259	73.0	32.5	59.2	24.9	10.4	5.9	27.0	24.5	12.1	2.51	2.97	10 850	9.0	23.3
Geneva	10 477	71.2	30.6	56.4	22.5	11.0	6.1	28.8	26.3	12.3	2.43	2.92	9 231	9.9	24.2
Greene	3 931	67.4	32.7	36.4	14.8	27.1	16.6	32.6	30.8	12.3	2.52	3.16	3 512	25.5	26.1
Hale	6 415	71.8	36.5	45.6	21.0	22.0	13.7	28.2	26.4	10.9	2.63	3.19	5 397	20.3	24.4
Henry	6 525	72.5	30.5	53.9	21.1	14.7	7.7	27.5	25.3	12.3	2.47	2.95	5 769	13.5	23.3
Houston	35 834	70.1	33.0	52.5	22.4	14.1	8.8	29.9	26.4	10.1	2.45	2.95	30 844	13.3	24.1
Jackson	21 615	73.2	31.5	59.0	23.9	10.5	5.7	26.8	24.3	10.5	2.47	2.92	18 020	9.3	20.7
Jefferson	263 265	66.8	30.8	46.1	20.1	17.2	9.3	33.2	28.7	9.9	2.45	3.04	251 479	15.7	26.5
Lamar	6 468	72.9	31.4	58.6	23.4	10.9	6.3	27.1	25.4	12.1	2.43	2.89	6 005	9.5	23.6
Lauderdale	36 088	69.7	30.4	55.8	22.7	10.8	6.3	30.3	26.4	11.0	2.39	2.89	30 905	10.1	23.4
Lawrence	13 538	75.3	34.7	60.5	26.8	11.2	6.1	24.7	22.6	9.5	2.55	2.99	11 410	10.4	19.5
Lee	45 702	59.7	29.7	44.1	20.9	11.8	7.1	40.3	27.8	5.7	2.42	3.03	33 097	11.1	26.1
Limestone	24 688	73.8	34.8	60.0	27.1	10.4	5.9	26.2	23.4	8.9	2.55	3.02	19 685	9.8	20.7
Lowndes	4 909	73.1	35.4	42.9	18.6	25.7	14.8	26.9	24.6	9.4	2.73	3.28	4 056	26.3	21.0
Macon	8 950	61.9	28.4	31.7	12.2	25.8	14.4	38.1	33.0	11.9	2.44	3.13	8 483	24.2	29.3
Madison	109 955	68.5	33.0	53.4	24.1	11.8	7.2	31.5	27.2	7.4	2.45	3.00	91 208	10.5	24.0
Marengo	8 767	71.6	34.7	48.4	21.4	19.4	11.6	28.4	26.5	12.1	2.55	3.08	8 156	17.8	24.2
Marion	12 697	71.2	30.4	58.4	23.3	9.5	5.3	28.8	26.5	12.7	2.39	2.87	11 521	8.8	23.0
Marshall	32 547	72.3	32.4	57.8	24.2	10.7	6.3	27.7	24.6	10.9	2.50	2.96	27 761	10.1	22.8
Mobile	150 179	71.1	34.4	49.5	22.3	17.7	10.4	28.9	24.8	8.8	2.61	3.13	136 899	16.7	23.3
Monroe	9 383	72.4	35.6	52.3	24.2	16.1	9.5	27.8	25.7	11.1	2.57	3.09	8 412	15.0	22.8
Montgomery	86 068	66.0	32.2	43.8	19.3	18.6	11.2	34.0	29.5	9.4	2.46	3.06	77 173	17.2	26.7
Morgan	43 602	72.1	33.5	57.4	25.0	11.2	6.6	27.9	24.8	9.4	2.51	2.99	37 799	10.3	22.1
Perry	4 333	70.3	33.8	40.4	16.5	25.1	15.0	29.7	27.9	12.0	2.63	3.23	4 201	22.5	25.0
Pickens	8 086	71.6	32.6	49.8	20.5	18.2	10.5	28.4	26.4	12.5	2.56	3.11	7 568	16.3	24.1
Pike	11 933	64.1	29.7	43.6	18.2	16.8	10.0	35.9	29.8	11.0	2.38	2.98	10 314	15.6	28.0
Randolph	8 642	72.0	31.1	56.2	22.7	12.2	6.6	28.0	25.6	11.5	2.52	3.02	7 553	11.6	24.0
Russell	19 741	68.0	32.0	44.4	18.7	18.9	10.9	32.0	28.0	10.6	2.49	3.05	17 499	17.4	24.5
St. Clair	24 143	76.4	35.1	62.8	27.6	10.0	5.6	23.6	20.8	8.2	2.60	3.01	17 666	9.0	18.5
Shelby	54 631	74.3	36.7	63.6	31.0	8.1	4.5	25.7	21.7	5.2	2.59	3.04	35 985	8.0	19.5
Sumter	5 708	64.2	31.9	36.7	16.5	23.5	13.7	35.8	31.2	12.3	2.55	3.26	5 545	23.2	26.6
Talladega	30 674	71.4	32.1	52.4	21.6	15.2	8.6	28.6	25.9	10.6	2.50	3.00	26 448	14.2	21.9
Tallapoosa	16 656	70.9	29.9	53.0	20.3	14.3	8.0	29.1	26.5	11.6	2.44	2.94	14 700	13.9	23.4
Tuscaloosa	64 517	64.6	30.3	47.2	20.6	14.0	8.3	35.4	28.4	8.3	2.42	3.00	55 354	13.0	25.8
Walker	28 364	72.2	30.7	56.3	22.9	11.9	5.8	27.8	25.3	11.2	2.46	2.93	25 554	10.7	21.9

¹No spouse present.

Table B. States and Counties

STATE County	Percent change of households, 1990–2000	Total housing units	Occupied housing units (percent)	Vacant housing units — Total	For seasonal, recreational, or occasional use	Homeowner vacancy rate (percent)	Rental vacancy rate (percent)	Occupied housing units — Total	Percent owner-occupied housing units	Percent renter-occupied housing units	Average household size of owner-occupied units	Average household size of renter-occupied units
	86	87	88	89	90	91	92	93	94	95	96	97
UNITED STATES	14.7	115 904 641	91.0	9.0	3.1	1.7	6.8	105 480 101	66.2	33.8	2.69	2.40
ALABAMA	15.3	1 963 711	88.5	11.5	2.4	2.0	11.8	1 737 080	72.5	27.5	2.57	2.30
Autauga	35.3	17 662	90.6	9.4	0.9	1.8	14.6	16 003	80.8	19.2	2.71	2.71
Baldwin	49.4	74 285	74.5	25.5	16.0	3.3	22.3	55 336	79.5	20.5	2.55	2.29
Barbour	12.9	12 461	83.5	16.5	3.2	2.2	12.0	10 409	73.1	26.9	2.59	2.37
Bibb	29.2	8 345	88.9	11.1	1.5	1.4	9.3	7 421	80.2	19.8	2.70	2.39
Blount	31.6	21 158	91.1	8.9	1.2	1.2	11.4	19 265	83.4	16.6	2.65	2.47
Bullock	5.3	4 727	84.3	15.7	4.7	1.2	7.5	3 986	74.5	25.5	2.55	2.58
Butler	5.8	9 957	84.3	15.7	2.7	2.2	11.9	8 398	76.2	23.8	2.57	2.35
Calhoun	5.4	51 322	88.3	11.7	0.5	2.7	14.3	45 307	72.5	27.5	2.48	2.28
Chambers	5.3	16 256	89.3	10.7	1.1	1.3	12.3	14 522	75.7	24.3	2.51	2.39
Cherokee	30.2	14 025	69.3	30.7	22.7	1.8	11.4	9 719	81.7	18.3	2.44	2.41
Chilton	26.2	17 651	86.6	13.4	4.8	1.8	9.9	15 287	82.3	17.7	2.58	2.51
Choctaw	10.7	7 839	81.2	18.8	6.7	1.2	9.8	6 363	86.3	13.7	2.52	2.24
Clarke	11.3	12 631	83.7	16.3	4.1	1.0	12.7	10 578	81.2	18.8	2.64	2.41
Clay	15.2	6 612	87.2	12.8	2.4	1.4	9.4	5 765	77.2	22.8	2.51	2.16
Cleburne	17.0	6 189	90.3	9.7	1.2	1.4	10.8	5 590	80.4	19.6	2.54	2.36
Coffee	14.2	19 837	87.8	12.2	1.0	2.6	14.3	17 421	71.4	28.6	2.49	2.38
Colbert	11.8	24 980	89.9	10.1	1.8	2.0	11.0	22 461	75.7	24.3	2.49	2.21
Conecuh	10.1	7 265	79.7	20.3	5.7	1.8	18.6	5 792	81.0	19.0	2.45	2.29
Coosa	16.6	6 142	76.2	23.8	12.9	2.0	11.1	4 682	84.8	15.2	2.55	2.39
Covington	8.3	18 578	84.2	15.8	2.9	3.3	16.7	15 640	77.7	22.3	2.39	2.32
Crenshaw	6.0	6 644	83.9	16.1	3.1	1.7	12.3	5 577	76.7	23.3	2.47	2.25
Cullman	19.9	35 233	87.2	12.8	3.1	2.3	13.3	30 706	78.0	22.0	2.55	2.29
Dale	7.4	21 779	86.7	13.3	0.8	2.5	15.1	18 878	64.3	35.7	2.48	2.57
Dallas	4.7	20 450	87.2	12.8	1.2	2.1	8.6	17 841	65.7	34.3	2.59	2.52
De Kalb	19.8	28 051	89.5	10.5	1.9	1.6	9.7	25 113	78.7	21.3	2.55	2.46
Elmore	37.5	25 733	88.4	11.6	3.7	2.2	12.2	22 737	81.3	18.7	2.70	2.51
Escambia	10.8	16 544	86.4	13.6	1.2	1.6	17.3	14 297	77.1	22.9	2.51	2.38
Etowah	7.6	45 959	90.5	9.5	0.5	2.1	9.8	41 615	74.4	25.6	2.48	2.31
Fayette	9.2	8 472	88.4	11.6	1.2	1.7	11.1	7 493	77.3	22.7	2.50	2.15
Franklin	13.0	13 749	89.2	10.8	1.7	1.9	13.4	12 259	74.3	25.7	2.52	2.50
Geneva	13.5	12 115	86.5	13.5	1.3	2.1	21.1	10 477	80.6	19.4	2.44	2.41
Greene	11.9	5 117	76.8	23.2	11.1	2.4	4.4	3 931	75.6	24.4	2.53	2.49
Hale	18.9	7 756	82.7	17.3	7.8	1.2	5.1	6 415	80.2	19.8	2.68	2.46
Henry	13.1	8 037	81.2	18.8	9.1	2.7	10.0	6 525	80.9	19.1	2.49	2.38
Houston	16.2	39 571	90.6	9.4	0.7	2.1	11.6	35 834	69.5	30.5	2.51	2.30
Jackson	20.0	24 168	89.4	10.6	2.3	1.6	11.5	21 615	77.9	22.1	2.52	2.27
Jefferson	4.7	288 162	91.4	8.6	0.5	1.9	10.2	263 265	66.5	33.5	2.57	2.23
Lamar	7.7	7 517	86.0	14.0	2.1	1.4	11.0	6 468	76.8	23.2	2.48	2.25
Lauderdale	16.8	40 424	89.3	10.7	2.1	2.1	12.1	36 088	73.2	26.8	2.49	2.13
Lawrence	18.7	15 009	90.2	9.8	1.4	1.5	11.4	13 538	83.0	17.0	2.59	2.36
Lee	38.1	50 329	90.8	9.2	1.2	2.3	10.6	45 702	62.1	37.9	2.62	2.09
Limestone	25.4	26 897	91.8	8.2	0.9	1.6	10.0	24 688	77.3	22.7	2.60	2.38
Lowndes	21.0	5 801	84.6	15.4	3.1	0.8	6.5	4 909	83.3	16.7	2.76	2.61
Macon	5.5	10 627	84.2	15.8	1.3	1.7	16.0	8 950	67.3	32.7	2.50	2.32
Madison	20.6	120 288	91.4	8.6	0.6	2.5	12.6	109 955	69.9	30.1	2.58	2.16
Marengo	7.5	10 127	86.6	13.4	3.1	1.1	8.8	8 767	79.2	20.8	2.59	2.41
Marion	10.2	14 416	88.1	11.9	0.7	2.5	16.7	12 697	77.8	22.2	2.46	2.14
Marshall	17.2	36 331	89.6	10.4	1.9	2.2	11.6	32 547	74.7	25.3	2.51	2.46
Mobile	9.7	165 101	91.0	9.0	1.1	1.6	10.2	150 179	68.8	31.2	2.68	2.44
Monroe	11.5	11 343	82.7	17.3	6.0	2.1	13.1	9 383	80.4	19.6	2.61	2.41
Montgomery	11.5	95 437	90.2	9.8	0.3	2.4	10.1	86 068	64.1	35.9	2.52	2.34
Morgan	15.4	47 388	92.0	8.0	0.4	1.8	11.9	43 602	73.1	26.9	2.58	2.31
Perry	3.1	5 406	80.2	19.8	6.3	0.8	8.4	4 333	74.0	26.0	2.64	2.61
Pickens	6.8	9 520	84.9	15.1	4.7	1.0	5.7	8 086	79.3	20.7	2.61	2.38
Pike	15.7	13 981	85.4	14.6	1.2	2.1	15.4	11 933	67.2	32.8	2.46	2.21
Randolph	14.4	10 285	84.0	16.0	5.5	1.9	11.0	8 642	79.2	20.8	2.54	2.46
Russell	12.8	22 831	86.5	13.5	1.0	2.3	16.6	19 741	62.5	37.5	2.54	2.39
St. Clair	36.7	27 303	88.4	11.6	4.2	1.3	12.0	24 143	83.7	16.3	2.63	2.45
Shelby	51.8	59 302	92.1	7.9	1.8	2.3	10.1	54 631	81.0	19.0	2.71	2.09
Sumter	2.9	6 953	82.1	17.9	5.2	1.7	8.7	5 708	72.3	27.7	2.65	2.29
Talladega	16.0	34 469	89.0	11.0	3.0	1.6	10.7	30 674	76.3	23.7	2.55	2.34
Tallapoosa	13.3	20 510	81.2	18.8	8.1	2.4	16.3	16 656	76.3	23.7	2.49	2.29
Tuscaloosa	16.6	71 429	90.3	9.7	0.7	1.7	12.3	64 517	63.5	36.5	2.58	2.14
Walker	11.0	32 417	87.5	12.5	1.9	1.8	14.1	28 364	80.0	20.0	2.50	2.30

STATE/ County code	MSA/ PMSA/ NECMA code[1]	County type[2]	STATE County	Population, 2000				Population, 1990				Population and population characteristics, 2000					
												Race (percent)					
												One race					
				Land area, 2000[3] (sq km)	Total persons	Rank	Per square kilometer	Land area, 1990[3] (sq km)	Total persons	Rank	Per square kilometer	White	Black or African American	American Indian or Alaska Native	Asian	Native Hawaiian and other Pacific Islander	Some other race
				1	2	3	4	5	6	7	8	9	10	11	12	13	14
			ALABAMA—Cont'd														
01 129	...	8	Washington	2 799	18 097	1 893	6.5	2 799	16 694	1 869	6.0	65.0	26.9	7.1	0.1	0.0	0.0
01 131	...	9	Wilcox	2 302	13 183	2 213	5.7	2 302	13 568	2 096	5.9	27.5	71.9	0.1	0.1	0.0	0.1
01 133	...	6	Winston	1 591	24 843	1 563	15.6	1 592	22 053	1 573	13.9	97.3	0.4	0.5	0.1	0.0	0.9
02 000	...		ALASKA	1 481 347	626 932	X	0.4	1 477 268	550 043	X	0.4	69.3	3.5	15.6	4.0	0.5	1.6
02 013	...	NA	Aleutians East Borough	18 099	2 697	3 014	0.1	18 091	2 464	3 023	0.1	24.0	1.7	37.3	26.5	0.3	7.4
02 016		NA	Aleutians West Census Area	11 388	5 465	2 819	0.5	11 401	9 478	2 436	0.8	40.0	3.0	21.0	24.6	0.6	7.3
02 020	0380	3	Anchorage	4 396	260 283	212	59.2	4 397	226 338	218	51.5	72.2	5.8	7.3	5.5	0.9	2.2
02 050	...	7	Bethel	105 240	16 006	2 021	0.2	106 416	13 660	2 085	0.1	12.5	0.4	81.9	1.0	0.1	0.2
02 060	...	NA	Bristol Bay	1 308	1 258	3 102	1.0	1 345	1 410	3 100	1.0	52.5	0.6	43.7	0.2	0.5	0.1
02 068	...	NA	Denali Borough	33 021	1 893	3 074	0.1	33 414	1 682	3 086	0.1	85.7	1.4	4.8	1.5	0.4	1.0
02 070	...	NA	Dillingham	48 367	4 922	2 854	0.1	47 829	4 010	2 917	0.1	21.6	0.4	70.1	0.6	0.0	0.5
02 090	...	5	Fairbanks North Star	19 078	82 840	627	4.3	19 069	77 720	583	4.1	77.8	5.8	6.9	2.1	0.3	1.7
02 100	...	9	Haines	6 070	2 392	3 031	0.4	6 105	2 117	3 061	0.3	82.5	0.1	11.5	0.7	0.1	0.4
02 110	...	5	Juneau	7 036	30 711	1 380	4.4	6 717	26 752	1 399	4.0	74.8	0.8	11.4	4.7	0.4	1.1
02 122	...	5	Kenai Peninsula	41 474	49 691	922	1.2	41 644	40 802	982	1.0	86.2	0.5	7.5	1.0	0.2	0.8
02 130	...	7	Ketchikan Gateway	3 194	14 070	2 158	4.4	3 159	13 828	2 072	4.4	74.3	0.5	15.0	4.3	0.2	0.4
02 150	...	7	Kodiak Island	16 990	13 913	2 167	0.8	16 738	13 309	2 113	0.8	59.7	1.0	14.6	16.0	0.8	2.8
02 164	...	NA	Lake and Peninsula Borough	61 595	1 823	3 078	0.0	61 208	1 666	3 088	0.0	18.8	0.1	73.5	0.2	0.2	0.3
02 170	...	6	Matanuska-Susitna	63 925	59 322	810	0.9	63 957	39 683	1 008	0.6	87.6	0.7	5.5	0.7	0.1	0.9
02 180	...	7	Nome	59 572	9 196	2 514	0.2	59 603	8 288	2 538	0.1	19.3	0.4	75.2	0.7	0.0	0.2
02 185	...	NA	North Slope	230 035	7 385	2 649	0.0	227 559	5 986	2 760	0.0	17.1	0.7	68.4	5.9	0.8	0.5
02 188	...	NA	Northwest Arctic Borough	92 976	7 208	2 666	0.1	92 884	6 106	2 743	0.1	12.3	0.2	82.5	0.9	0.1	0.4
02 201	...	NA	Prince of Wales-Outer Ketchikan	19 193	6 146	2 768	0.3	18 970	6 278	2 726	0.3	53.1	0.1	38.7	0.4	0.0	0.5
02 220	...	NA	Sitka	7 444	8 835	2 541	1.2	7 463	8 588	2 504	1.2	68.5	0.3	18.6	3.8	0.4	0.9
02 232	...	NA	Skagway-Hoonah-Angoon	20 452	3 436	2 960	0.2	20 660	3 679	2 941	0.2	58.1	0.1	35.0	0.4	0.1	1.0
02 240	...	NA	Southeast Fairbanks	64 270	6 174	2 765	0.1	67 325	5 925	2 766	0.1	79.0	2.0	12.7	0.7	0.1	0.7
02 261	...	7	Valdez-Cordova	88 886	10 195	2 429	0.1	95 688	9 920	2 392	0.1	75.9	0.3	13.3	3.6	0.3	1.1
02 270	...	9	Wade Hampton	44 531	7 028	2 681	0.2	44 351	5 789	2 779	0.1	4.7	0.1	92.5	0.1	0.0	0.0
02 280	...	7	Wrangell-Petersburg	15 112	6 684	2 719	0.4	15 044	7 042	2 654	0.5	73.0	0.2	16.1	1.6	0.1	1.1
02 282	...	NA	Yakutat Borough	19 815	808	3 124	0.0	17 586	725	3 129	0.0	50.4	0.1	39.6	1.2	0.7	0.0
02 290	...	NA	Yukon-Koyukuk	377 878	6 551	2 734	0.0	406 944	6 798	2 676	0.0	24.3	0.1	70.9	0.4	0.0	0.4
04 000	...		ARIZONA	294 312	5 130 632	X	17.4	294 333	3 665 339	X	12.5	75.5	3.1	5.0	1.8	0.1	11.6
04 001	...	5	Apache	29 021	69 423	714	2.4	29 023	61 591	709	2.1	19.5	0.2	76.9	0.1	0.1	1.8
04 003	...	4	Cochise	15 979	117 755	459	7.4	15 980	97 624	471	6.1	76.7	4.5	1.1	1.6	0.3	12.1
04 005	2620	5	Coconino	48 219	116 320	463	2.4	48 224	96 591	477	2.0	63.1	1.0	28.5	0.8	0.1	4.1
04 007	...	4	Gila	12 348	51 335	901	4.2	12 349	40 216	995	3.3	77.8	0.4	12.9	0.4	0.1	6.6
04 009	...	7	Graham	11 990	33 489	1 300	2.8	11 991	26 554	1 405	2.2	67.1	1.9	14.9	0.6	0.0	13.3
04 011	...	7	Greenlee	4 784	8 547	2 564	1.8	4 784	8 008	2 565	1.7	74.2	0.5	1.7	0.2	0.0	20.0
04 012	...	7	La Paz	11 655	19 715	1 810	1.7	11 654	13 844	2 068	1.2	74.2	0.8	12.5	0.4	0.1	9.4
04 013	6200	0	Maricopa	23 836	3 072 149	4	128.9	23 838	2 122 101	7	89.0	77.4	3.7	1.8	2.2	0.1	11.9
04 015	4120	2	Mohave	34 477	155 032	344	4.5	34 479	93 497	495	2.7	90.1	0.5	2.4	0.8	0.1	4.0
04 017	...	5	Navajo	25 779	97 470	532	3.8	25 780	77 674	586	3.0	45.9	0.9	47.7	0.3	0.0	3.1
04 019	8520	2	Pima	23 792	843 746	53	35.5	23 794	666 957	68	28.0	75.1	3.0	3.2	2.0	0.1	13.3
04 021	6200	1	Pinal	13 907	179 727	391	12.9	13 908	116 397	395	8.4	70.4	2.8	7.8	0.6	0.1	15.7
04 023	...	6	Santa Cruz	3 205	38 381	1 154	12.0	3 206	29 676	1 309	9.3	76.0	0.4	0.7	0.5	0.1	19.7
04 025	...	4	Yavapai	21 039	167 517	322	8.0	21 040	107 714	429	5.1	91.9	0.4	1.6	0.5	0.1	3.6
04 027	9360	3	Yuma	14 281	160 026	333	11.2	14 282	106 895	432	7.5	68.3	2.2	1.6	0.9	0.1	23.6
05 000	...		ARKANSAS	134 856	2 673 400	X	19.8	134 875	2 350 624	X	17.4	80.0	15.7	0.7	0.8	0.1	1.5
05 001	...	7	Arkansas	2 560	20 749	1 750	8.1	2 560	21 653	1 595	8.5	75.2	23.4	0.2	0.4	0.0	0.2
05 003	...	7	Ashley	2 386	24 209	1 588	10.1	2 386	24 319	1 485	10.2	69.8	27.1	0.2	0.2	0.0	1.7
05 005	...	7	Baxter	1 436	38 386	1 153	26.7	1 436	31 186	1 239	21.7	97.8	0.1	0.5	0.3	0.0	0.2
05 007	2580	3	Benton	2 191	153 406	346	70.0	2 184	97 530	472	44.7	90.9	0.4	1.6	1.1	0.1	4.1
05 009	...	7	Boone	1 531	33 948	1 281	22.2	1 531	28 297	1 345	18.5	97.6	0.1	0.7	0.3	0.0	0.3
05 011	...	7	Bradley	1 685	12 600	2 255	7.5	1 685	11 793	2 229	7.0	63.4	28.6	0.2	0.1	0.0	7.0
05 013	...	9	Calhoun	1 627	5 744	2 806	3.5	1 627	5 826	2 777	3.6	74.5	23.4	0.2	0.0	0.0	0.9
05 015	...	7	Carroll	1 632	25 357	1 550	15.5	1 642	18 623	1 758	11.3	93.6	0.1	0.9	0.4	0.1	3.3
05 017	...	7	Chicot	1 668	14 117	2 153	8.5	1 668	15 713	1 942	9.4	43.2	54.0	0.1	0.4	0.0	1.4
05 019	...	7	Clark	2 241	23 546	1 614	10.5	2 242	21 437	1 606	9.6	74.3	22.0	0.5	0.6	0.0	1.4
05 021	...	7	Clay	1 656	17 609	1 922	10.6	1 656	18 107	1 785	10.9	98.1	0.2	0.7	0.1	0.0	0.2
05 023	...	6	Cleburne	1 432	24 046	1 592	16.8	1 433	19 411	1 710	13.5	98.2	0.1	0.5	0.1	0.0	0.1
05 025	...	8	Cleveland	1 548	8 571	2 561	5.5	1 548	7 781	2 597	5.0	84.8	13.2	0.3	0.1	0.0	0.7
05 027	...	7	Columbia	1 984	25 603	1 531	12.9	1 984	25 691	1 432	12.9	62.1	36.1	0.3	0.3	0.0	0.5

[1] MSA = Metropolitan Statistical Area. PMSA = Primary MSA. NECMA = New England County Metropolitan Area. See Appendix A for explanation of these concepts. See Appendix B for list of metropolitan areas identified by type, with component counties.
[2] County typology code from the Economic Research Service of USDA. See Appendix A for definition.
[3] Dry land or land partially or temporarily covered by water.

Table B. States and Counties

	Population and population characteristics, 2000 (cont'd)								Population and population characteristics, 1990				
	Race (percent) (cont'd)								Race (percent)				
	Race alone or in combination												
STATE County	Two or more races	White	Black	American Indian or Alaska Native	Asian	Native Hawaiian and other Pacific Islander	Some other race	Hispanic¹	White	Black or African American	American Indian or Alaska Native	Asian and Pacific Islander	Hispanic¹
	15	16	17	18	19	20	21	22	23	24	25	26	27
ALABAMA—Cont'd													
Washington	0.9	65.7	27.1	7.7	0.2	0.0	0.1	0.9	65.8	27.7	6.4	0.1	0.3
Wilcox	0.2	27.6	72.0	0.3	0.2	0.0	0.1	0.7	31.0	68.9	0.0	0.0	0.3
Winston	0.8	98.1	0.4	1.0	0.2	0.1	1.1	1.5	99.4	0.3	0.2	0.1	0.3
ALASKA	5.4	74.0	4.3	19.0	5.2	0.9	2.4	4.1	75.5	4.1	15.6	3.6	3.2
Aleutians East Borough	2.9	26.4	1.7	38.6	27.7	0.5	8.0	12.6	33.6	0.6	42.3	18.8	7.3
Aleutians West Census Area	3.5	42.8	3.3	22.5	26.1	1.0	8.2	10.5	67.1	7.0	11.4	10.3	7.8
Anchorage	6.0	77.2	7.2	10.4	7.1	1.4	3.3	5.7	80.7	6.4	6.4	4.8	4.1
Bethel	3.9	15.8	0.7	85.5	1.4	0.1	0.5	0.9	15.4	0.5	83.3	0.7	0.6
Bristol Bay	2.4	54.3	0.6	45.1	1.0	1.0	0.5	0.6	63.4	2.7	32.3	0.9	2.3
Denali Borough	5.2	90.9	1.5	8.6	2.1	0.5	1.7	2.5	NA	NA	NA	NA	NA
Dillingham	6.7	27.2	0.5	76.2	1.3	0.2	1.4	2.3	25.4	0.2	72.9	0.7	1.2
Fairbanks North Star	5.4	82.6	7.0	9.9	3.2	0.6	2.6	4.2	82.0	7.1	6.9	2.6	3.7
Haines	4.6	86.9	0.3	15.6	1.1	0.2	0.7	1.4	85.1	0.0	13.2	0.8	1.3
Juneau	6.9	80.5	1.4	16.6	6.7	0.7	1.8	3.4	80.6	1.1	12.9	4.3	2.8
Kenai Peninsula	3.9	89.8	0.8	10.2	1.6	0.4	1.4	2.2	90.9	0.5	7.2	1.0	1.8
Ketchikan Gateway	5.3	79.2	0.8	19.1	5.3	0.4	0.9	2.6	81.8	0.4	13.7	3.6	2.1
Kodiak Island	5.2	64.0	1.1	17.6	17.5	1.5	3.7	6.1	69.8	1.0	16.0	11.2	5.0
Lake and Peninsula Borough	7.0	25.3	0.2	79.7	0.4	0.4	1.0	1.2	23.3	0.0	75.6	0.7	1.9
Matanuska-Susitna	4.6	91.9	1.1	8.6	1.4	0.4	1.5	2.5	93.1	0.8	4.9	0.7	1.9
Nome	4.2	23.2	0.6	79.1	1.0	0.1	0.5	1.0	24.4	0.1	74.2	0.7	1.3
North Slope	6.6	22.4	1.2	73.8	7.2	1.3	1.0	2.4	21.3	0.7	72.5	4.8	2.1
Northwest Arctic Borough	3.7	15.6	0.5	85.8	1.2	0.2	0.6	0.8	13.8	0.2	85.2	0.8	0.6
Prince of Wales-Outer Ketchikan	7.1	59.6	0.4	45.3	1.2	0.3	0.8	1.7	61.5	0.1	37.6	0.4	1.9
Sitka	7.5	75.0	0.8	24.7	5.2	0.7	1.7	3.3	74.0	0.5	20.9	3.9	2.4
Skagway-Hoonah-Angoon	5.2	62.7	0.4	39.5	1.2	0.3	1.4	2.8	NA	NA	NA	NA	NA
Southeast Fairbanks	4.8	83.7	2.3	15.9	1.1	0.4	1.5	2.7	79.0	4.9	13.0	1.4	3.0
Valdez-Cordova	5.6	81.1	0.5	17.3	4.6	0.6	1.7	2.8	82.9	0.6	12.5	3.3	2.7
Wade Hampton	2.5	7.0	0.2	94.9	0.2	0.1	0.1	0.3	6.0	0.2	93.3	0.4	0.3
Wrangell-Petersburg	7.8	80.0	0.6	22.6	3.3	0.4	1.7	2.0	78.7	0.2	19.4	1.3	1.7
Yakutat Borough	7.9	56.7	0.2	46.8	4.0	1.9	0.4	0.7	NA	NA	NA	NA	NA
Yukon-Koyukuk	3.9	27.9	0.3	74.4	0.7	0.1	0.6	1.2	42.3	1.0	55.7	0.6	1.0
ARIZONA	2.9	77.9	3.6	5.7	2.3	0.3	13.2	25.3	80.8	3.0	5.6	1.5	18.8
Apache	1.4	20.6	0.4	77.8	0.2	0.1	2.4	4.5	20.2	0.2	77.6	0.2	4.2
Cochise	3.7	79.8	5.3	2.1	2.5	0.5	13.8	30.7	81.7	5.2	0.8	2.3	29.1
Coconino	2.4	65.1	1.4	29.7	1.1	0.2	5.0	10.9	64.0	1.5	29.2	0.9	10.0
Gila	1.8	79.4	0.5	13.8	0.6	0.1	7.5	16.6	76.5	0.2	13.0	0.3	18.6
Graham	2.1	68.9	2.1	15.6	0.8	0.1	14.8	27.0	77.6	1.9	14.9	0.4	25.2
Greenlee	3.5	77.4	0.6	2.7	0.3	0.1	22.4	43.1	85.4	0.3	2.3	0.2	43.2
La Paz	2.7	76.2	1.1	14.2	0.5	0.2	10.6	22.4	74.7	0.9	17.4	0.7	22.7
Maricopa	2.9	79.8	4.3	2.5	2.7	0.3	13.5	24.8	84.8	3.5	1.8	1.7	16.3
Mohave	2.1	92.0	0.7	3.3	1.1	0.2	4.9	11.1	95.0	0.3	2.3	0.6	5.3
Navajo	1.9	47.6	1.1	48.8	0.5	0.1	3.9	8.2	44.0	0.9	52.0	0.3	7.3
Pima	3.2	77.8	3.7	4.0	2.7	0.2	15.1	29.3	78.7	3.1	3.0	1.8	24.5
Pinal	2.7	72.6	3.1	8.7	0.9	0.2	17.3	29.9	74.9	3.1	9.3	0.4	29.3
Santa Cruz	2.6	78.4	0.5	1.0	0.7	0.1	22.0	80.8	74.7	0.3	0.2	0.6	78.2
Yavapai	1.9	93.7	0.6	2.5	0.8	0.2	4.3	9.8	95.7	0.3	1.6	0.5	6.4
Yuma	3.2	71.1	2.6	2.2	1.4	0.3	25.8	50.5	75.5	2.9	1.3	1.3	40.6
ARKANSAS	1.3	81.2	16.0	1.4	1.0	0.1	1.8	3.2	82.7	15.9	0.5	0.5	0.8
Arkansas	0.7	75.7	23.6	0.6	0.5	0.1	0.3	0.8	77.7	21.9	0.2	0.2	0.3
Ashley	1.0	70.6	27.3	0.6	0.3	0.1	2.1	3.2	72.0	27.2	0.2	0.2	0.9
Baxter	1.0	98.8	0.2	1.2	0.5	0.1	0.3	1.0	99.3	0.0	0.4	0.2	0.5
Benton	1.8	92.6	0.5	2.7	1.3	0.1	4.6	8.8	97.4	0.1	1.5	0.5	1.4
Boone	0.9	98.5	0.2	1.3	0.4	0.1	0.5	1.1	99.1	0.0	0.6	0.2	0.6
Bradley	0.8	64.0	28.9	0.5	0.2	0.0	7.2	8.3	67.9	30.9	0.1	0.0	1.6
Calhoun	0.9	75.2	23.8	0.8	0.2	0.1	1.1	1.5	74.8	24.8	0.1	0.1	0.5
Carroll	1.6	95.2	0.2	1.9	0.5	0.1	3.8	9.7	98.7	0.0	0.8	0.3	1.0
Chicot	0.9	43.8	54.3	0.5	0.7	0.1	1.6	2.9	42.6	56.4	0.1	0.4	1.0
Clark	1.2	75.3	22.6	1.0	0.8	0.1	1.6	2.4	76.2	22.9	0.3	0.4	0.6
Clay	0.8	98.9	0.2	1.3	0.2	0.0	0.3	0.8	99.6	0.0	0.2	0.1	0.4
Cleburne	0.9	99.1	0.2	1.1	0.2	0.1	0.3	1.2	99.4	0.0	0.4	0.1	0.5
Cleveland	0.8	85.6	13.4	0.7	0.4	0.1	0.7	1.6	85.9	13.6	0.2	0.2	0.6
Columbia	0.8	62.6	36.4	0.7	0.5	0.1	0.6	1.1	64.5	35.0	0.2	0.2	0.3

¹Hispanic persons may be of any race.

STATE County	Under 5 years	5 to 17 years	18 to 24 years	25 to 34 years	35 to 44 years	45 to 54 years	55 to 64 years	65 to 74 years	75 years and over	Median age (years)	Percent Female
	28	29	30	31	32	33	34	35	36	37	38
ALABAMA—Cont'd											
Washington	7.2	21.4	8.6	12.8	14.6	13.3	9.6	7.0	5.4	34.9	51.0
Wilcox	8.1	22.6	9.1	11.9	13.6	12.2	8.8	7.1	6.6	33.8	53.4
Winston	6.2	17.5	7.9	13.6	15.1	14.0	11.5	8.0	6.2	38.0	51.0
ALASKA	7.6	22.8	9.1	14.3	18.2	15.1	7.1	3.6	2.1	32.4	48.3
Aleutians East Borough	4.3	12.5	10.2	17.4	24.8	19.9	8.2	1.9	0.7	37.0	35.1
Aleutians West Census Area	4.7	12.5	7.8	22.0	25.6	18.7	6.4	1.7	0.5	36.1	35.7
Anchorage	7.7	21.5	9.6	15.4	18.5	14.9	7.0	3.4	2.1	32.4	49.4
Bethel	10.0	29.8	9.7	13.5	15.4	10.6	5.8	3.2	2.0	25.3	46.9
Bristol Bay	7.1	24.2	5.9	11.4	23.4	17.1	7.1	2.8	1.0	36.0	45.5
Denali Borough	5.2	18.6	6.7	14.3	22.5	20.7	9.0	2.2	0.9	37.6	41.8
Dillingham	9.7	28.5	7.7	12.1	16.8	12.7	6.8	3.7	2.0	28.9	47.8
Fairbanks North Star	8.1	22.0	12.2	16.3	17.0	13.8	6.0	2.9	1.7	29.5	47.8
Haines	5.4	20.3	5.3	10.1	18.1	20.5	9.9	6.2	4.3	40.7	49.4
Juneau	6.5	20.9	8.1	14.0	18.8	18.0	7.7	3.5	2.6	35.3	49.6
Kenai Peninsula	6.6	23.3	6.9	11.4	18.3	17.6	8.7	4.8	2.6	36.3	48.0
Ketchikan Gateway	6.9	21.3	7.5	12.7	18.7	16.3	8.7	4.5	3.3	36.0	48.9
Kodiak Island	8.9	23.5	8.3	14.8	19.1	14.3	6.2	3.2	1.6	31.6	47.1
Lake and Peninsula Borough	8.0	29.8	8.5	9.6	18.4	12.5	7.7	3.6	1.9	29.2	46.8
Matanuska-Susitna	7.0	25.2	7.4	11.7	19.4	16.0	7.4	4.0	1.9	34.1	48.0
Nome	8.6	28.6	9.3	13.3	15.7	12.3	6.3	3.5	2.4	27.6	46.0
North Slope	9.5	28.6	9.5	13.4	16.7	12.1	5.9	2.7	1.4	27.0	47.1
Northwest Arctic Borough	10.7	30.8	10.0	14.0	14.1	10.5	5.0	3.4	1.6	23.9	46.6
Prince of Wales- Outer Ketchikan	7.4	23.6	7.5	11.9	18.1	16.6	9.2	4.0	1.7	34.7	45.5
Sitka	6.4	20.8	9.4	13.1	17.8	15.5	8.7	5.1	3.3	35.2	49.0
Skagway-Hoonah-Angoon	5.2	21.6	7.1	11.6	17.9	18.9	10.4	4.5	2.8	37.8	46.2
Southeast Fairbanks	7.1	25.7	7.6	11.1	16.7	16.0	9.8	4.3	1.7	33.7	48.3
Valdez-Cordova	6.7	23.0	7.0	11.5	19.4	18.5	8.0	3.9	2.2	36.1	46.8
Wade Hampton	10.6	36.0	9.7	13.3	12.4	8.2	4.9	3.2	1.8	20.0	47.8
Wrangell-Petersburg	6.7	23.0	5.7	11.5	17.5	17.0	9.1	5.0	4.5	37.2	48.0
Yakutat Borough	4.8	23.3	5.3	11.6	20.9	20.2	8.5	4.0	1.4	37.2	40.7
Yukon-Koyukuk	7.1	27.9	8.7	10.7	16.2	14.5	7.6	4.8	2.5	31.1	45.7
ARIZONA	7.5	19.2	10.0	14.5	15.0	12.2	8.6	7.1	5.9	34.2	50.1
Apache	9.1	29.4	9.4	11.5	13.6	11.0	7.7	5.0	3.3	27.0	50.4
Cochise	6.8	19.6	9.3	11.9	14.1	13.1	10.6	8.7	6.1	36.9	49.6
Coconino	7.3	21.5	14.4	14.0	15.2	13.4	7.3	4.3	2.7	29.6	50.1
Gila	6.1	19.0	6.4	9.2	13.1	13.7	12.7	11.2	8.6	42.3	50.8
Graham	7.8	22.3	12.0	13.5	13.8	10.9	7.9	6.5	5.4	30.9	47.1
Greenlee	8.3	23.4	7.5	12.5	15.7	14.1	8.5	5.9	4.0	33.6	47.8
La Paz	4.9	16.2	6.1	8.6	11.8	12.2	14.4	16.6	9.2	46.8	48.7
Maricopa	7.9	19.1	10.2	15.9	15.5	11.9	7.8	6.1	5.5	33.0	50.0
Mohave	6.0	17.1	6.5	10.0	13.3	13.1	13.6	12.3	8.2	42.9	50.3
Navajo	8.6	26.9	8.8	11.4	13.9	11.7	8.7	6.2	3.8	30.2	50.3
Pima	6.6	18.0	10.9	13.5	14.9	13.1	8.8	7.5	6.7	35.7	51.1
Pinal	6.7	18.4	8.7	13.1	14.1	11.9	10.8	10.0	6.2	37.1	46.7
Santa Cruz	8.7	25.0	8.2	12.3	14.4	12.3	8.5	6.3	4.5	31.8	52.2
Yavapai	5.2	16.0	7.1	9.2	13.2	14.5	12.9	12.1	9.9	44.5	51.0
Yuma	7.9	21.0	10.0	12.5	13.1	9.9	9.0	10.0	6.6	33.9	49.5
ARKANSAS	6.8	18.7	9.8	13.2	14.9	13.1	9.6	7.4	6.6	36.0	51.2
Arkansas	6.6	18.3	8.3	11.8	14.5	14.3	10.1	8.2	8.0	38.7	52.4
Ashley	6.7	20.1	8.3	13.1	14.1	13.5	10.4	7.3	6.5	36.2	51.7
Baxter	4.5	14.5	5.8	8.8	12.2	13.2	14.2	14.2	12.6	48.1	52.0
Benton	7.6	19.0	8.6	14.3	15.1	11.9	9.2	8.0	6.4	35.3	50.7
Boone	6.3	17.7	8.2	12.3	14.2	13.5	11.2	8.8	7.8	38.9	51.8
Bradley	5.9	17.6	9.7	12.4	14.0	12.5	10.4	8.8	8.7	38.0	50.6
Calhoun	5.3	19.3	7.0	11.7	16.5	13.1	11.2	8.1	7.8	39.2	51.9
Carroll	6.4	17.5	8.1	11.5	14.6	14.5	11.5	8.8	7.0	39.4	50.7
Chicot	6.9	20.5	8.6	12.5	13.8	12.4	9.8	8.4	7.0	36.2	51.5
Clark	6.0	15.7	20.0	11.6	12.2	11.3	8.6	7.4	7.2	31.8	51.9
Clay	6.0	17.1	7.7	11.7	13.6	12.8	11.8	10.0	9.4	40.5	51.7
Cleburne	5.1	16.2	6.6	10.1	14.0	13.0	13.9	12.1	9.0	43.7	51.6
Cleveland	6.5	19.6	7.9	12.9	14.8	13.4	11.3	7.5	6.1	36.9	51.2
Columbia	6.1	19.0	12.3	11.7	13.6	11.9	9.5	8.0	7.9	35.7	52.4

Table B. States and Counties

STATE County	Under 5 years	5 to 17 years	18 to 24 years	25 to 34 years	35 to 44 years	45 to 54 years	55 to 64 years	65 to 74 years	75 years and over	Percent Female	2000	1990	1980	1990–2000	1980–1990
	39	40	41	42	43	44	45	46	47	48	49	50	51	52	53
ALABAMA—Cont'd															
Washington	7.4	23.1	9.9	15.1	13.5	10.5	8.5	6.7	5.3	51.2	18 097	16 694	16 821	8.4	-0.8
Wilcox	7.9	20.1	0.2	12.8	11.4	8.5	8.3	8.3	7.5	53.5	13 183	13 568	14 755	-2.8	-8.0
Winston	6.4	18.2	9.9	14.9	14.3	12.1	10.1	8.2	5.0	51.2	24 843	22 053	21 953	12.7	0.5
ALASKA	10.0	21.4	10.2	20.5	18.7	9.8	5.4	2.8	1.2	47.3	626 932	550 043	401 851	14.0	36.9
Aleutians East Borough	7.3	14.9	16.2	26.6	17.4	9.6	5.7	2.1	0.3	35.8	2 697	2 464	1 643	9.5	50.0
Aleutians West Census Area	8.2	11.6	23.2	30.9	16.8	5.9	2.5	0.6	0.3	34.2	5 465	9 478	6 125	-42.3	54.7
Anchorage	9.5	20.0	10.6	21.5	19.2	10.3	5.3	2.7	1.0	48.6	260 283	226 338	174 431	15.0	29.8
Bethel	13.7	25.4	10.8	18.7	13.5	8.1	5.0	3.0	1.8	47.6	16 006	13 660	10 999	17.2	24.2
Bristol Bay	8.7	18.4	10.5	27.9	18.0	9.0	4.5	2.2	0.8	40.1	1 258	1 410	1 094	-10.8	28.9
Denali Borough	NA	NA	NA	NA	NA	NA	NA	NA	NA	NA	1 893	1 682	0	12.5	NA
Dillingham	14.0	23.5	8.6	19.1	15.5	8.4	5.7	3.2	1.9	48.3	4 922	4 010	3 232	22.7	24.1
Fairbanks North Star	10.4	20.9	13.0	21.8	17.9	8.3	4.4	2.3	1.0	46.6	82 840	77 720	53 983	6.6	44.0
Haines	7.3	20.6	6.3	16.8	20.6	12.2	7.6	6.1	2.5	46.6	2 392	2 117	1 680	13.0	26.0
Juneau	9.0	20.3	8.0	19.3	21.5	11.2	5.5	3.3	1.8	49.3	30 711	26 752	19 528	14.8	37.0
Kenai Peninsula	9.3	23.5	7.4	17.8	20.2	10.5	6.3	3.7	1.3	47.0	49 691	40 802	25 282	21.8	61.4
Ketchikan Gateway	8.8	21.1	8.7	18.2	18.7	11.5	6.5	4.2	2.4	47.8	14 070	13 828	11 316	1.8	22.2
Kodiak Island	10.5	20.5	10.8	22.7	19.3	8.5	4.5	2.2	1.0	44.4	13 913	13 309	9 939	4.5	33.9
Lake and Peninsula Borough	12.8	25.2	8.1	20.8	13.4	8.2	6.5	3.5	1.6	45.4	1 823	1 666	1 384	9.4	20.5
Matanuska-Susitna	9.8	25.6	6.1	17.8	20.4	9.9	5.8	3.3	1.4	48.1	59 322	39 683	17 816	49.5	122.7
Nome	12.9	25.4	9.2	18.5	15.0	8.5	5.5	3.0	2.1	45.9	9 196	8 288	6 537	11.0	26.8
North Slope	13.9	23.5	9.4	19.6	15.2	9.6	5.5	2.1	1.2	45.5	7 385	5 986	4 199	23.4	42.4
Northwest Arctic Borough	15.7	27.4	10.5	17.7	12.2	6.7	5.2	2.5	2.1	47.3	7 208	6 106	4 831	18.0	26.5
Prince of Wales-Outer Ketchikan	9.3	23.0	8.4	19.2	19.1	11.7	5.8	2.4	1.1	43.5	6 146	6 278	3 822	-2.1	64.3
Sitka	8.9	21.8	9.2	19.6	17.5	11.2	6.1	3.4	2.3	47.6	8 835	8 588	7 803	2.9	10.1
Skagway-Hoonah-Angoon	NA	NA	NA	NA	NA	NA	NA	NA	NA	NA	3 436	3 679	NA	-6.6	NA
Southeast Fairbanks	10.2	25.5	8.4	18.5	18.3	10.2	5.2	2.6	1.2	46.1	6 174	5 925	5 676	4.2	4.2
Valdez-Cordova	8.9	20.3	8.1	19.6	21.1	11.1	6.4	3.2	1.4	45.0	10 195	9 920	8 348	2.8	19.2
Wade Hampton	18.0	27.9	11.1	16.3	10.7	6.4	5.2	3.1	1.4	48.1	7 028	5 789	4 665	21.4	24.1
Wrangell-Petersburg	9.8	21.1	7.6	18.5	18.6	10.6	6.7	4.5	2.7	46.4	6 684	7 042	6 167	-5.1	14.2
Yakutat Borough	NA	NA	NA	NA	NA	NA	NA	NA	NA	NA	808	725	NA	11.4	NA
Yukon-Koyukuk	11.0	23.9	7.3	18.8	18.1	10.2	6.0	2.8	1.9	43.5	6 551	6 798	7 873	-3.6	-14.7
ARIZONA	8.0	18.8	10.7	17.3	14.4	9.5	8.2	7.9	5.1	50.6	5 130 632	3 665 339	2 716 546	40.0	34.9
Apache	12.2	29.5	10.5	15.0	11.7	8.3	6.1	4.0	2.7	50.9	69 423	61 591	52 108	12.7	18.2
Cochise	7.7	20.5	10.0	15.5	14.0	10.2	9.3	8.1	4.7	49.1	117 755	97 624	85 686	20.6	13.9
Coconino	8.9	22.0	17.0	17.1	14.9	8.4	5.8	3.7	2.0	50.2	116 320	96 591	75 008	20.4	28.8
Gila	7.1	19.6	6.7	11.6	12.9	10.8	11.9	12.2	7.2	51.1	51 335	40 216	37 080	27.6	8.5
Graham	8.8	24.4	10.7	14.1	12.6	8.6	8.1	7.3	5.3	48.7	33 489	26 554	22 862	26.1	16.1
Greenlee	7.5	26.7	6.2	13.9	14.5	10.5	9.4	7.2	4.0	49.4	8 547	8 008	11 406	6.7	-29.8
La Paz	7.8	18.8	7.6	13.0	12.3	10.2	11.3	12.2	6.9	48.7	19 715	13 844	12 557	42.4	10.2
Maricopa	8.0	18.2	10.7	18.5	14.8	9.6	7.7	7.4	5.1	50.7	3 072 149	2 122 101	1 509 175	44.8	40.6
Mohave	6.5	16.1	6.8	13.2	12.8	11.1	13.1	14.2	6.5	50.2	155 032	93 497	55 865	65.8	67.4
Navajo	11.1	27.3	9.4	15.0	12.6	9.0	7.3	5.3	2.9	50.2	97 470	77 674	67 629	25.5	14.9
Pima	7.5	17.4	11.8	17.1	14.7	9.3	8.4	8.2	5.5	51.1	843 746	666 957	531 443	26.5	25.5
Pinal	8.3	21.0	9.2	15.2	13.5	9.6	9.4	8.8	4.9	48.7	179 727	116 397	90 918	54.4	28.0
Santa Cruz	9.3	25.1	9.5	14.6	13.5	9.2	8.2	6.7	3.9	52.4	38 381	29 676	20 459	29.3	45.1
Yavapai	5.6	16.0	7.0	11.3	13.5	10.4	12.5	15.2	8.6	51.1	167 517	107 714	68 145	55.5	58.1
Yuma	8.5	21.1	11.4	16.0	12.4	8.3	8.4	8.9	4.9	49.1	160 026	106 895	76 205	49.7	40.3
ARKANSAS	7.0	19.4	10.1	15.3	13.9	10.4	9.1	8.3	6.6	51.8	2 673 400	2 350 624	2 286 357	13.7	2.8
Arkansas	6.8	20.6	7.8	14.0	14.3	10.1	9.5	9.0	7.8	52.8	20 749	21 653	24 175	-4.2	-10.4
Ashley	7.1	21.0	9.4	14.1	13.7	11.0	9.1	8.0	6.6	52.0	24 209	24 319	26 538	-0.5	-8.4
Baxter	4.7	14.8	6.0	10.6	11.7	10.1	13.0	16.5	12.7	52.4	38 386	31 186	27 409	23.1	13.8
Benton	6.8	18.0	8.9	15.0	13.4	9.9	10.1	10.9	7.0	51.2	153 406	97 530	78 115	57.3	24.8
Boone	6.4	18.4	8.9	14.3	13.5	10.9	10.4	9.2	8.0	52.2	33 948	28 297	26 067	20.0	8.6
Bradley	6.6	19.2	8.9	13.1	12.5	10.5	10.2	9.9	8.9	52.5	12 600	11 793	13 803	6.8	-14.6
Calhoun	7.1	19.8	8.8	15.3	13.0	10.3	9.1	8.9	7.6	51.7	5 744	5 826	6 079	-1.4	-4.2
Carroll	6.1	18.2	7.8	13.5	14.4	11.2	10.7	10.2	7.9	51.7	25 357	18 623	16 203	36.2	15.1
Chicot	7.9	24.4	9.3	12.4	11.3	9.4	9.1	8.1	8.1	54.0	14 117	15 713	17 793	-10.2	-11.7
Clark	5.9	16.5	18.3	12.9	11.8	9.3	8.7	8.7	8.0	52.6	23 546	21 437	23 326	9.8	-8.1
Clay	5.7	17.3	8.3	13.1	12.2	11.3	11.4	10.9	9.8	52.2	17 609	18 107	20 616	-2.8	-12.2
Cleburne	5.2	16.5	6.9	13.0	12.2	11.9	13.3	12.4	8.5	51.5	24 046	19 411	16 909	23.9	14.8
Cleveland	6.5	19.8	9.4	13.5	14.3	11.9	9.7	7.9	7.0	51.4	8 571	7 781	7 868	10.2	-1.1
Columbia	7.0	19.2	11.5	14.4	12.1	9.7	9.3	8.5	8.3	53.1	25 603	25 691	26 644	-0.3	-3.6

Table B. States and Counties

STATE County	Total population	Total in house-holds	House-holder	Spouse	Child Total	Child Own child under 18 years	Other relatives Total	Other relatives Under 18 years	Nonrelatives Total	Nonrelatives Unmar-ried partner	Total in group quarters	Correc-tional institu-tions	Nurs-ing homes	Other institu-tions	Col-lege dormi-tories	Mili-tary quar-ters	Other
	54	55	56	57	58	59	60	61	62	63	64	65	66	67	68	69	70
ALABAMA—Cont'd																	
Washington	18 097	99.5	37.1	21.9	33.0	25.3	5.6	3.1	2.0	1.0	0.5	0.0	0.4	0.0	0.0	0.0	0.1
Wilcox	13 183	97.7	36.2	14.4	35.3	24.9	9.6	5.3	2.2	1.1	2.3	1.2	0.7	0.0	0.3	0.0	0.0
Winston	24 843	98.8	40.7	24.3	27.6	21.8	3.7	1.5	2.5	1.2	1.2	0.3	0.8	0.0	0.0	0.0	0.1
ALASKA	626 932	96.9	35.3	18.6	32.9	27.8	3.9	1.7	6.2	2.6	3.1	0.5	0.1	0.1	0.3	0.6	1.4
Aleutians East Borough	2 697	52.4	19.5	8.6	18.5	15.2	2.3	1.3	3.6	2.2	47.6	0.0	0.0	0.0	0.0	0.0	47.6
Aleutians West Census Area	5 465	58.5	23.2	10.2	18.4	16.0	1.9	0.6	4.8	1.8	41.5	0.0	0.0	0.0	0.0	1.2	40.3
Anchorage	260 283	97.3	36.4	18.6	31.5	26.7	3.8	1.5	6.9	2.7	2.7	0.4	0.1	0.2	0.2	0.8	1.0
Bethel	16 006	98.5	26.4	13.3	45.6	34.2	8.8	4.7	4.4	2.3	1.5	1.1	0.0	0.2	0.1	0.0	0.2
Bristol Bay	1 258	100.0	39.0	19.2	35.0	30.2	1.7	0.9	5.2	3.9	0.0	0.0	0.0	0.0	0.0	0.0	0.0
Denali Borough	1 893	94.5	41.5	20.1	26.4	23.0	2.0	0.5	4.5	2.9	5.5	0.0	0.0	0.0	0.0	5.5	0.0
Dillingham	4 922	99.3	31.1	15.9	40.9	33.3	7.1	3.9	4.5	2.2	0.7	0.0	0.0	0.0	0.0	0.0	0.5
Fairbanks North Star	82 840	96.3	35.9	19.6	32.2	28.1	2.5	1.2	5.9	2.4	3.7	0.3	0.1	0.0	0.9	1.9	0.5
Haines	2 392	99.8	41.4	22.4	28.6	24.2	2.1	1.1	5.3	2.6	0.2	0.0	0.0	0.0	0.0	0.0	0.2
Juneau	30 711	97.8	37.6	19.2	29.5	24.9	3.5	1.3	8.0	3.0	2.2	0.5	0.1	0.1	0.4	0.0	1.0
Kenai Peninsula	49 691	97.3	37.1	20.6	32.2	28.0	2.4	1.1	5.1	2.5	2.7	1.7	0.2	0.0	0.2	0.1	0.6
Ketchikan Gateway	14 070	98.4	38.4	19.7	30.9	26.0	3.7	1.5	5.7	2.6	1.6	0.4	0.5	0.0	0.0	0.3	0.5
Kodiak Island	13 913	97.6	31.8	19.0	34.6	29.5	5.4	2.0	6.8	2.1	2.4	0.0	0.1	0.0	0.0	0.6	1.6
Lake and Peninsula Borough	1 823	100.0	32.3	15.6	39.8	33.0	7.4	3.8	4.9	2.4	0.0	0.0	0.0	0.0	0.0	0.0	0.0
Matanuska-Susitna	59 322	98.3	34.7	20.4	34.5	29.8	3.1	1.3	5.7	2.6	1.7	1.0	0.1	0.1	0.0	0.0	0.5
Nome	9 196	97.6	29.3	12.4	40.6	31.4	9.2	4.9	6.1	3.3	2.4	1.0	0.0	0.3	0.0	0.2	0.9
North Slope	7 385	98.6	28.6	12.4	41.2	32.2	9.5	4.8	7.0	3.4	1.4	0.0	0.0	0.0	0.2	0.0	1.2
Northwest Arctic Borough	7 208	95.6	24.7	11.8	44.4	35.0	9.3	5.6	5.4	3.1	4.4	0.0	0.0	0.2	0.0	0.0	4.2
Prince of Wales-Outer Ketchikan	6 146	98.8	36.8	18.7	33.5	27.7	4.0	2.3	5.7	3.7	1.2	0.0	0.0	0.0	0.0	0.0	1.2
Sitka	8 835	96.9	37.1	19.6	30.0	24.4	4.3	2.0	5.9	2.8	3.1	0.0	1.1	0.3	0.9	0.2	0.5
Skagway-Hoonah-Angoon	3 436	99.4	39.8	19.6	30.0	23.6	4.3	2.5	5.6	3.1	0.6	0.0	0.0	0.0	0.0	0.0	0.6
Southeast Fairbanks	6 174	95.2	34.0	19.8	34.3	29.6	3.0	1.5	4.1	2.3	4.8	0.0	0.0	0.0	0.0	0.8	4.0
Valdez-Cordova	10 195	98.2	38.1	19.8	31.4	27.6	3.5	1.5	5.4	2.6	1.8	0.0	0.1	0.0	0.5	0.2	0.9
Wade Hampton	7 028	99.9	22.8	10.8	52.3	39.9	9.8	6.2	4.2	2.2	0.1	0.0	0.0	0.0	0.0	0.0	0.1
Wrangell-Petersburg	6 684	99.0	38.7	21.0	31.7	27.7	3.1	1.4	4.4	2.5	1.0	0.1	0.3	0.0	0.0	0.1	0.6
Yakutat Borough	808	84.9	32.8	12.6	27.8	23.3	4.8	2.1	6.8	3.7	15.1	0.0	0.0	0.0	0.0	0.0	15.1
Yukon-Koyukuk	6 551	99.0	35.2	13.0	37.1	30.1	7.1	3.6	6.6	4.2	1.0	0.0	0.0	0.0	0.0	0.0	1.0
ARIZONA	5 130 632	97.9	37.1	19.2	29.2	23.3	6.2	2.6	6.2	2.3	2.1	0.9	0.3	0.1	0.3	0.1	0.5
Apache	69 423	98.2	28.8	14.2	41.7	31.2	11.0	6.8	2.5	1.6	1.8	0.8	0.2	0.3	0.3	0.0	0.3
Cochise	117 755	95.2	37.3	20.5	28.6	23.1	4.9	2.4	3.8	1.8	4.8	2.0	0.4	0.0	0.1	1.9	0.3
Coconino	116 320	97.3	34.8	17.3	31.0	24.8	6.5	3.4	7.8	2.6	2.7	0.1	0.1	0.1	2.1	0.0	0.3
Gila	51 335	98.2	39.2	21.6	26.7	21.0	6.3	3.4	4.4	1.9	1.8	0.8	0.8	0.0	0.0	0.0	0.2
Graham	33 489	90.3	30.2	17.3	32.7	25.7	6.2	3.7	4.0	1.5	9.7	8.4	0.4	0.0	0.8	0.0	0.1
Greenlee	8 547	99.7	36.5	21.3	34.0	28.3	4.7	2.7	3.2	1.6	0.3	0.3	0.0	0.1	0.0	0.0	0.0
La Paz	19 715	98.6	42.4	23.0	22.9	18.2	5.0	2.4	5.2	2.6	1.4	1.3	0.0	0.0	0.0	0.0	0.1
Maricopa	3 072 149	98.5	36.9	19.0	29.5	23.8	6.4	2.4	6.0	2.3	1.5	0.5	0.3	0.1	0.2	0.0	0.5
Mohave	155 032	99.2	40.5	22.3	24.9	20.2	5.2	2.1	6.3	2.8	0.8	0.2	0.3	0.1	0.0	0.0	0.1
Navajo	97 470	97.7	30.8	17.1	37.3	28.9	9.2	5.7	3.4	1.8	2.3	1.5	0.2	0.3	0.1	0.0	0.2
Pima	843 746	97.4	39.4	18.8	27.6	21.6	5.5	2.3	6.1	2.5	2.6	0.8	0.2	0.1	0.8	0.1	0.6
Pinal	179 727	91.5	34.1	19.4	26.6	21.0	6.5	3.3	4.9	2.3	8.5	7.5	0.1	0.1	0.2	0.0	0.6
Santa Cruz	38 381	99.5	30.8	18.9	37.6	28.6	9.6	4.6	2.7	1.2	0.5	0.1	0.0	0.1	0.0	0.0	0.3
Yavapai	167 517	97.8	41.9	23.0	23.0	18.7	4.0	1.6	5.9	2.3	2.2	0.1	0.8	0.3	0.6	0.0	0.4
Yuma	160 026	96.3	33.6	21.0	31.9	25.5	6.2	3.0	3.6	1.7	3.7	1.7	0.4	0.0	0.1	1.0	0.3
ARKANSAS	2 673 400	97.2	39.0	21.2	28.4	22.5	4.9	2.3	3.7	1.5	2.8	0.8	0.8	0.1	0.7	0.0	0.3
Arkansas	20 749	98.3	40.8	21.6	27.6	21.6	5.2	2.7	3.1	1.6	1.7	0.3	1.2	0.0	0.0	0.0	0.2
Ashley	24 209	99.0	38.8	22.0	29.7	23.1	5.8	3.2	2.7	1.3	1.0	0.2	0.8	0.0	0.0	0.0	0.0
Baxter	38 386	98.2	44.4	26.2	21.6	17.3	2.9	1.1	3.0	1.5	1.8	0.1	1.2	0.3	0.0	0.0	0.3
Benton	153 406	98.6	37.9	23.9	29.0	24.5	4.0	1.6	3.7	1.5	1.4	0.2	0.5	0.1	0.6	0.0	0.1
Boone	33 948	98.2	40.8	24.3	26.8	21.9	3.4	1.5	3.0	1.3	1.8	0.1	0.9	0.3	0.0	0.0	0.5
Bradley	12 600	94.0	38.4	20.0	27.1	19.9	5.7	2.9	2.8	1.0	6.0	0.1	2.0	0.6	0.0	0.0	3.2
Calhoun	5 744	98.0	40.3	22.4	28.0	21.8	4.6	2.4	2.5	1.3	2.0	0.4	1.6	0.0	0.0	0.0	0.0
Carroll	25 357	99.1	40.2	23.0	26.4	21.4	4.6	1.9	4.9	1.9	0.9	0.1	0.6	0.0	0.0	0.0	0.1
Chicot	14 117	94.9	36.9	16.1	29.3	21.7	9.2	5.1	3.4	1.8	5.1	3.8	0.9	0.2	0.0	0.0	0.2
Clark	23 546	90.1	37.8	18.8	24.3	19.4	4.1	1.8	5.0	1.2	9.9	0.2	1.0	0.0	8.0	0.0	0.7
Clay	17 609	99.0	42.1	23.8	26.4	20.8	3.6	1.8	3.1	1.6	1.0	0.2	0.8	0.0	0.0	0.0	0.0
Cleburne	24 046	98.9	42.4	26.2	24.1	19.3	3.3	1.5	2.9	1.4	1.1	0.1	0.8	0.0	0.0	0.0	0.3
Cleveland	8 571	99.2	38.2	24.0	29.4	22.9	5.3	2.8	2.3	1.0	0.8	0.0	0.0	0.0	0.0	0.0	0.8
Columbia	25 603	95.6	39.0	19.1	28.4	21.1	6.1	3.2	3.2	1.1	4.4	0.1	0.9	0.1	2.9	0.0	0.3

Table B. States and Counties

STATE County	Households by type, 2000												Households, 1990		
	Family households						Nonfamily households								
		Married couple			Female householder[1]			Householder living alone							
	Total households	Total	With own children under 18 years	Total	With own children under 18 years	Total	With own children under 18 years	Total	Total	65 years and over	Average household size	Average family size	Total households	Female householder[1]	Householder living alone
	71	72	73	74	75	76	77	78	79	80	81	82	83	84	85
ALABAMA—Cont'd															
Washington	6 705	75.2	37.9	59.1	29.1	12.5	7.1	24.8	22.8	10.1	2.69	3.17	5 709	12.7	19.2
Wilcox	4 776	70.7	36.0	39.8	18.0	26.5	15.8	29.3	27.5	11.9	2.70	3.31	4 415	23.4	23.9
Winston	10 107	72.1	31.8	59.6	24.6	9.1	5.3	27.9	25.6	11.4	2.43	2.89	8 544	8.3	21.5
ALASKA	221 600	68.7	39.9	52.5	28.5	10.8	7.8	31.3	23.5	4.1	2.74	3.28	188 915	9.6	22.1
Aleutians East Borough	526	65.4	39.2	44.1	23.6	14.4	11.0	34.6	27.4	3.4	2.69	3.30	533	9.6	22.5
Aleutians West Census Area	1 270	58.0	35.4	44.0	26.5	7.6	4.7	42.0	32.0	2.1	2.52	3.26	1 845	5.1	14.3
Anchorage	94 822	67.6	38.9	51.1	27.3	11.5	8.3	32.4	23.4	3.8	2.67	3.19	82 702	10.1	22.9
Bethel	4 226	75.1	51.0	50.2	36.2	15.2	9.1	24.9	19.9	2.8	3.73	4.41	3 605	14.7	18.2
Bristol Bay	490	61.4	38.2	49.2	29.0	6.1	4.3	38.6	31.2	2.9	2.57	3.33	407	6.1	27.0
Denali Borough	785	57.7	31.0	48.4	24.5	4.5	3.7	42.3	35.0	1.4	2.28	3.03	NA	NA	NA
Dillingham	1 529	72.3	45.3	51.1	31.5	15.0	9.7	27.7	23.3	3.6	3.20	3.84	1 215	13.3	18.6
Fairbanks North Star	29 777	68.9	41.3	54.7	30.8	9.3	7.1	31.1	23.6	3.6	2.68	3.20	26 693	8.1	22.4
Haines	991	66.0	31.6	54.0	23.1	7.3	5.4	34.0	27.1	7.2	2.41	2.94	791	5.1	24.4
Juneau	11 543	66.2	36.7	51.2	26.3	10.5	7.3	33.8	24.4	4.3	2.60	3.10	9 902	10.2	23.6
Kenai Peninsula	18 438	69.0	38.0	55.4	27.8	9.0	6.9	31.0	24.7	5.1	2.62	3.15	14 250	8.4	21.8
Ketchikan Gateway	5 399	67.3	36.8	51.5	25.7	11.3	8.1	32.7	26.1	6.2	2.56	3.10	5 030	9.2	24.0
Kodiak Island	4 424	73.6	45.9	59.7	36.1	8.8	6.3	26.4	19.9	3.7	3.07	3.52	4 083	8.1	18.4
Lake and Peninsula Borough	588	71.1	44.7	48.5	29.9	9.7	6.1	28.9	24.7	3.9	3.10	3.74	509	11.0	21.6
Matanuska-Susitna	20 556	73.2	42.3	58.9	31.7	9.1	6.9	26.8	20.3	4.1	2.84	3.29	13 394	8.7	19.0
Nome	2 693	70.5	45.8	42.4	28.2	15.3	9.6	29.5	23.2	3.3	3.33	4.01	2 371	14.6	21.7
North Slope	2 109	72.3	48.1	43.3	29.5	18.3	11.9	27.7	21.4	1.9	3.45	4.05	1 673	14.8	20.8
Northwest Arctic Borough	1 780	78.9	55.2	47.9	33.8	19.7	13.9	21.1	16.6	2.1	3.87	4.36	1 526	17.8	17.6
Prince of Wales- Outer Ketchikan	2 262	67.9	37.6	50.8	25.7	10.0	7.1	32.1	26.0	5.0	2.68	3.25	2 061	9.1	21.4
Sitka	3 278	67.7	36.2	53.0	26.4	10.3	6.8	32.3	24.5	5.4	2.61	3.15	2 939	9.1	20.9
Skagway-Hoonah-Angoon	1 369	63.3	30.8	49.3	22.4	8.4	4.9	36.7	30.1	5.6	2.50	3.14	NA	NA	NA
Southeast Fairbanks	2 098	71.8	39.4	58.2	30.4	8.6	5.8	28.2	23.5	5.5	2.80	3.34	1 909	7.0	19.7
Valdez-Cordova	3 884	65.9	37.3	52.1	27.4	8.5	6.2	34.1	27.0	4.9	2.58	3.18	3 425	7.5	24.2
Wade Hampton	1 602	80.9	59.7	47.4	37.1	20.3	13.9	19.1	16.0	1.8	4.38	4.95	1 368	15.8	16.9
Wrangell-Petersburg	2 587	68.2	36.7	54.3	26.7	9.2	6.8	31.8	26.3	7.5	2.56	3.11	2 514	7.6	22.9
Yakutat Borough	265	60.0	32.8	38.5	18.5	12.1	8.7	40.0	32.1	4.9	2.59	3.30	NA	NA	NA
Yukon-Koyukuk	2 309	64.1	38.9	36.9	21.7	16.9	11.4	35.9	30.5	6.2	2.81	3.53	2 748	12.6	27.7
ARIZONA	1 901 327	67.7	32.0	51.9	22.6	11.1	6.8	32.3	24.8	8.6	2.64	3.18	1 368 843	10.4	24.7
Apache	19 971	76.4	43.8	49.3	28.5	21.4	12.2	23.6	21.2	6.9	3.41	4.04	15 981	20.4	16.8
Cochise	43 893	70.1	32.0	55.1	22.5	11.1	7.1	29.9	25.3	10.1	2.55	3.07	34 546	10.2	23.3
Coconino	40 448	66.6	34.9	49.7	24.2	12.2	7.8	33.4	22.1	4.5	2.80	3.36	29 918	11.5	19.9
Gila	20 140	70.0	26.3	55.1	17.8	10.8	6.3	30.0	25.8	12.3	2.50	2.99	15 438	8.8	24.3
Graham	10 116	75.3	39.0	57.2	27.9	13.4	8.4	24.7	20.9	9.9	2.99	3.47	7 930	12.2	19.9
Greenlee	3 117	72.7	39.2	58.3	29.8	9.0	5.8	27.3	24.5	7.3	2.73	3.26	2 809	8.0	22.7
La Paz	8 362	67.2	21.2	54.2	13.6	8.2	5.1	32.8	26.6	12.9	2.32	2.79	5 348	9.5	24.6
Maricopa	1 132 886	67.4	33.0	51.6	23.7	10.7	6.6	32.6	24.5	7.9	2.67	3.21	807 560	10.2	25.0
Mohave	62 809	69.1	25.1	55.1	16.8	9.3	5.6	30.9	24.1	11.3	2.45	2.87	36 801	7.5	21.8
Navajo	30 043	76.8	40.5	55.5	27.7	16.3	9.8	23.2	19.9	7.2	3.17	3.68	22 189	15.3	16.8
Pima	332 350	63.8	29.2	47.7	19.7	11.8	7.1	36.2	28.5	9.4	2.47	3.06	261 792	10.9	27.8
Pinal	61 364	73.7	29.8	56.9	19.5	11.5	7.1	26.3	21.1	9.2	2.68	3.09	39 154	11.4	19.9
Santa Cruz	11 809	80.5	45.6	61.3	34.6	15.4	9.0	19.5	16.5	7.1	3.23	3.66	8 808	14.9	16.6
Yavapai	70 171	66.6	23.8	55.0	16.9	8.1	4.8	33.4	26.7	12.4	2.33	2.79	44 778	7.0	24.9
Yuma	53 848	77.4	36.9	62.3	27.0	11.2	7.6	22.6	18.5	8.9	2.86	3.27	35 791	9.4	19.0
ARKANSAS	1 042 696	70.2	32.1	54.3	22.7	12.1	7.4	29.8	25.6	10.4	2.49	2.99	891 179	11.1	24.0
Arkansas	8 457	70.6	31.4	53.0	21.0	13.9	8.6	29.4	26.1	12.4	2.41	2.89	8 389	12.1	25.8
Ashley	9 384	73.6	33.6	56.8	24.0	13.0	7.7	26.4	23.9	11.2	2.55	3.02	8 890	11.9	21.9
Baxter	17 052	69.2	22.0	59.0	16.2	7.7	4.6	30.8	27.5	15.1	2.21	2.65	13 486	6.1	24.5
Benton	58 212	74.7	34.4	63.0	27.1	8.2	5.3	25.3	21.1	8.5	2.60	3.01	37 555	6.9	20.0
Boone	13 851	71.2	30.7	59.5	23.4	8.8	5.6	28.8	25.6	11.2	2.41	2.88	11 131	7.9	23.2
Bradley	4 834	70.1	29.5	52.2	20.0	14.5	8.0	29.9	27.6	13.9	2.45	2.96	4 545	10.5	25.2
Calhoun	2 317	70.3	31.2	55.6	23.2	11.3	6.2	29.7	27.3	12.6	2.43	2.94	2 185	10.5	24.0
Carroll	10 189	69.8	29.2	57.1	21.5	8.6	5.5	30.2	25.2	10.3	2.47	2.93	7 550	8.4	24.4
Chicot	5 205	70.0	31.7	43.7	17.3	22.0	12.6	30.0	26.9	13.0	2.58	3.12	5 557	21.7	26.8
Clark	8 912	65.3	29.8	49.8	20.6	12.2	7.6	34.7	27.6	12.4	2.38	2.91	7 907	11.2	27.4
Clay	7 417	68.4	28.3	56.6	21.9	8.6	4.7	31.6	28.4	16.7	2.35	2.87	7 504	7.7	26.5
Cleburne	10 190	72.7	26.3	61.7	20.1	7.9	4.7	27.3	24.4	12.3	2.33	2.74	7 926	6.7	22.0
Cleveland	3 273	76.8	34.9	62.7	26.9	9.9	5.9	23.2	21.4	10.0	2.60	3.00	2 868	9.5	19.5
Columbia	9 981	67.6	30.1	48.9	20.1	15.1	8.4	32.4	29.2	13.8	2.45	3.03	9 638	13.8	26.8

[1] No spouse present.

104 AL(Washington)—AR(Columbia)

Table B. States and Counties

STATE County	Housing occupancy, 2000							Housing tenure, 2000				
	Percent change of households, 1990–2000	Total housing units	Occupied housing units (percent)	Vacant housing units		Homeowner vacancy rate (percent)	Rental vacancy rate (percent)	Occupied housing units			Average household size of owner-occupied units	Average household size of renter-occupied units
				Total	For seasonal, recreational, or occasional use			Total	Percent owner-occupied housing units	Percent renter-occupied housing units		
	86	87	88	89	90	91	92	93	94	95	96	97
ALABAMA—Cont'd												
Washington	17.4	8 123	82.5	17.5	5.3	1.8	10.8	6 705	88.1	11.9	2.72	2.45
Wilcox	8.2	6 183	77.2	22.8	10.9	0.8	4.4	4 776	83.3	16.7	2.72	2.60
Winston	18.3	12 502	80.8	19.2	9.5	2.0	14.4	10 107	80.1	19.9	2.48	2.20
ALASKA	17.3	260 978	84.9	15.1	8.2	1.9	7.8	221 600	62.5	37.5	2.89	2.49
Aleutians East Borough	-1.3	724	72.7	27.3	11.0	0.3	8.7	526	58.2	41.8	2.93	2.35
Aleutians West Census Area	-31.2	2 234	56.8	43.2	3.7	3.3	19.9	1 270	27.8	72.2	2.91	2.37
Anchorage	14.7	100 368	94.5	5.5	1.1	1.4	5.3	94 822	60.1	39.9	2.81	2.46
Bethel	17.2	5 188	81.5	18.5	9.8	2.0	6.2	4 226	61.1	38.9	4.16	3.06
Bristol Bay	20.4	979	50.1	49.9	38.9	3.9	23.2	490	50.0	50.0	2.94	2.19
Denali Borough	NA	1 351	58.1	41.9	30.5	3.2	20.1	785	65.1	34.9	2.53	1.80
Dillingham	25.8	2 332	65.6	34.4	27.1	1.7	7.2	1 529	60.4	39.6	3.56	2.65
Fairbanks North Star	11.6	33 291	89.4	10.6	3.0	1.6	9.3	29 777	54.0	46.0	2.81	2.52
Haines	25.3	1 419	69.8	30.2	21.2	3.7	17.0	991	70.0	30.0	2.47	2.26
Juneau	16.6	12 282	94.0	6.0	1.5	0.9	5.7	11 543	63.7	36.3	2.78	2.29
Kenai Peninsula	29.4	24 871	74.1	25.9	18.3	2.9	14.4	18 438	73.7	26.3	2.74	2.30
Ketchikan Gateway	7.3	6 218	86.8	13.2	3.9	2.2	11 7	5 399	60.7	39.3	2.76	2.26
Kodiak Island	8.4	6 150	85.8	14.2	6.0	2.6	7.2	4 424	54.8	45.2	3.23	2.88
Lake and Peninsula Borough	15.5	1 557	37.8	62.2	58.3	1.2	10.5	588	68.2	31.8	3.25	2.79
Matanuska-Susitna	53.5	27 329	75.2	24.8	19.2	1.9	7.0	20 556	78.9	21.1	2.91	2.56
Nome	13.6	3 649	73.8	26.2	19.2	1.6	10.3	2 693	58.1	41.9	3.71	2.80
North Slope	26.1	2 538	83.1	16.9	5.8	3.5	10.1	2 109	48.9	51.1	4.03	2.90
Northwest Arctic Borough	16.6	2 540	70.1	29.9	22.2	1.6	5.0	1 780	56.0	44.0	4.39	3.21
Prince of Wales-Outer Ketchikan	9.8	3 055	74.0	26.0	10.5	3.7	11.3	2 262	69.8	30.2	2.78	2.45
Sitka	11.5	3 650	89.8	10.2	4.6	1.5	5.2	3 278	58.1	41.9	2.78	2.39
Skagway-Hoonah-Angoon	NA	2 108	64.9	35.1	22.3	7.2	14.8	1 369	62.9	37.1	2.63	2.27
Southeast Fairbanks	9.9	3 225	65.1	34.9	16.4	4.1	12.2	2 098	68.5	31.5	2.82	2.76
Valdez-Cordova	13.4	5 148	75.4	24.6	13.9	2.5	11.6	3 884	67.9	32.1	2.70	2.32
Wade Hampton	17.1	2 063	77.7	22.3	13.4	1.9	4.5	1 602	66.7	33.3	4.71	3.72
Wrangell-Petersburg	2.9	3 284	78.8	21.2	9.9	1.7	13.1	2 587	70.4	29.6	2.65	2.34
Yakutat Borough	NA	499	53.1	46.9	35.7	1.3	5.3	265	59.6	40.4	2.98	2.01
Yukon-Koyukuk	-16.0	3 917	58.9	41.1	28.9	3.2	13.5	2 309	67.3	32.7	2.96	2.50
ARIZONA	38.9	2 189 189	86.9	13.1	6.5	2.1	9.2	1 901 327	68.0	32.0	2.69	2.53
Apache	25.0	31 621	63.2	36.8	20.7	2.0	13.5	19 971	74.3	25.7	3.42	3.40
Cochise	27.1	51 126	85.9	14.1	3.8	2.9	12.0	43 893	67.3	32.7	2.55	2.56
Coconino	35.2	53 443	75.7	24.3	17.1	2.2	6.5	40 448	61.4	38.6	2.93	2.60
Gila	30.5	28 189	71.4	28.6	20.3	3.2	11.3	20 140	78.7	21.3	2.47	2.61
Graham	27.6	11 430	88.5	11.5	2.5	2.7	10.6	10 116	73.2	26.8	2.98	3.03
Greenlee	11.0	3 744	83.3	16.7	3.3	3.4	11.2	3 117	50.6	49.4	2.65	2.82
La Paz	56.4	15 133	55.3	44.7	34.6	3.7	14.8	8 362	78.0	22.0	2.22	2.69
Maricopa	40.3	1 250 231	90.6	9.4	4.0	1.8	8.7	1 132 886	67.5	32.5	2.74	2.54
Mohave	70.7	80 062	78.5	21.5	12.4	3.7	9.2	62 809	73.6	26.4	2.38	2.64
Navajo	35.4	47 413	63.4	36.6	27.4	2.8	9.6	30 043	75.4	24.6	3.17	3.18
Pima	27.0	366 737	90.6	9.4	2.9	1.8	9.2	332 350	64.3	35.7	2.59	2.26
Pinal	56.7	81 154	75.6	24.4	14.5	4.0	16.8	61 364	77.4	22.6	2.61	2.93
Santa Cruz	34.1	13 036	90.6	9.4	2.5	2.1	8.2	11 809	68.0	32.0	3.30	3.10
Yavapai	56.7	81 730	85.9	14.1	7.4	2.7	7.6	70 171	73.4	26.6	2.32	2.36
Yuma	50.5	74 140	72.6	27.4	15.7	1.8	14.1	53 848	72.3	27.7	2.83	2.96
ARKANSAS	17.0	1 173 043	88.9	11.1	2.5	2.5	9.6	1 042 696	69.4	30.6	2.54	2.40
Arkansas	0.8	9 672	87.4	12.6	3.2	1.7	8.6	8 457	67.9	32.1	2.42	2.40
Ashley	5.6	10 615	88.4	11.6	2.9	2.5	11.9	9 384	76.0	24.0	2.56	2.53
Baxter	26.4	19 891	85.7	14.3	6.9	3.2	8.8	17 052	79.7	20.3	2.21	2.20
Benton	55.0	64 281	90.6	9.4	2.7	2.6	8.0	58 212	72.2	27.8	2.61	2.57
Boone	24.4	15 426	89.8	10.2	1.7	3.2	9.0	13 851	73.3	26.7	2.46	2.26
Bradley	6.4	5 930	81.5	18.5	7.4	1.7	10.6	4 834	72.7	27.3	2.48	2.36
Calhoun	6.0	3 012	76.9	23.1	13.3	1.4	13.9	2 317	82.3	17.7	2.44	2.38
Carroll	35.0	11 828	86.1	13.9	4.4	3.7	11.7	10 189	73.0	27.0	2.45	2.51
Chicot	-6.3	5 974	87.1	12.9	2.5	1.8	9.0	5 205	69.8	30.2	2.56	2.60
Clark	12.7	10 166	87.7	12.3	2.1	2.2	8.7	8 912	65.7	34.3	2.45	2.25
Clay	-1.2	8 498	87.3	12.7	2.5	3.6	10.7	7 417	74.9	25.1	2.36	2.32
Cleburne	28.6	13 732	74.2	25.8	17.9	3.1	10.4	10 190	80.4	19.6	2.34	2.30
Cleveland	14.1	3 834	85.4	14.6	5.4	1.1	7.2	3 273	82.2	17.8	2.63	2.46
Columbia	3.6	11 566	86.3	13.7	1.3	3.6	12.0	9 981	71.4	28.6	2.50	2.33

Table B. States and Counties

STATE/ County code	MSA/ PMSA/ NECMA code[1]	County type[2]	STATE County	Population, 2000				Population, 1990				Population and population characteristics, 2000 — Race (percent) — One race					
				Land area, 2000[3] (sq km)	Total persons	Rank	Per square kilometer	Land area, 1990[3] (sq km)	Total persons	Rank	Per square kilometer	White	Black or African American	American Indian or Alaska Native	Asian	Native Hawaiian and other Pacific Islander	Some other race
				1	2	3	4	5	6	7	8	9	10	11	12	13	14
			ARKANSAS—Cont'd														
05 029	...	6	Conway	1 440	20 336	1 770	14.1	1 441	19 151	1 724	13.3	84.3	13.1	0.5	0.2	0.0	0.7
05 031	3700	5	Craighead	1 841	82 148	631	44.6	1 841	68 956	642	37.5	89.3	7.0	0.3	0.6	0.0	0.9
05 033	2720	3	Crawford	1 542	53 247	879	34.5	1 542	42 493	946	27.6	92.2	0.9	2.0	1.2	0.0	1.5
05 035	4920	1	Crittenden	1 580	50 866	912	32.2	1 581	49 939	842	31.6	50.9	47.1	0.2	0.5	0.0	0.7
05 037	...	6	Cross	1 595	19 526	1 816	12.2	1 595	19 225	1 718	12.1	74.8	23.7	0.2	0.3	0.0	0.2
05 039	...	7	Dallas	1 729	9 210	2 511	5.3	1 729	9 614	2 423	5.6	57.0	41.0	0.2	0.2	0.0	1.0
05 041	...	7	Desha	1 981	15 341	2 068	7.7	1 981	16 798	1 860	8.5	50.5	46.3	0.4	0.3	0.0	1.7
05 043	...	7	Drew	2 145	18 723	1 860	8.7	2 145	17 369	1 829	8.1	70.3	27.2	0.3	0.4	0.0	1.0
05 045	4400	2	Faulkner	1 677	86 014	605	51.3	1 677	60 006	724	35.8	88.3	8.5	0.5	0.7	0.0	0.7
05 047	...	6	Franklin	1 579	17 771	1 913	11.3	1 579	14 897	1 995	9.4	96.2	0.6	0.8	0.3	0.1	0.7
05 049	...	9	Fulton	1 601	11 642	2 323	7.3	1 601	10 037	2 381	6.3	97.7	0.2	0.7	0.2	0.0	0.1
05 051	...	4	Garland	1 754	88 068	591	50.2	1 756	73 397	613	41.8	88.9	7.8	0.6	0.5	0.0	0.7
05 053	...	6	Grant	1 636	16 464	1 992	10.1	1 636	13 948	2 061	8.5	95.5	2.5	0.4	0.1	0.0	0.6
05 055	...	7	Greene	1 496	37 331	1 182	25.0	1 496	31 804	1 218	21.3	97.4	0.1	0.4	0.2	0.0	0.5
05 057	...	6	Hempstead	1 888	23 587	1 608	12.5	1 888	21 621	1 597	11.5	63.3	30.4	0.4	0.2	0.0	4.2
05 059	...	6	Hot Spring	1 593	30 353	1 389	19.1	1 593	26 115	1 418	16.4	87.3	10.3	0.4	0.2	0.0	0.4
05 061	...	7	Howard	1 521	14 300	2 140	9.4	1 522	13 569	2 094	8.9	73.6	21.9	0.4	0.5	0.0	2.8
05 063	...	7	Independence	1 978	34 233	1 274	17.3	1 978	31 192	1 238	15.8	94.9	2.0	0.5	0.6	0.0	0.6
05 065	...	9	Izard	1 504	13 249	2 208	8.8	1 504	11 364	2 264	7.6	96.4	1.4	0.6	0.1	0.0	0.3
05 067	...	7	Jackson	1 641	18 418	1 873	11.2	1 641	18 944	1 739	11.5	80.6	17.6	0.3	0.2	0.0	0.4
05 069	6240	3	Jefferson	2 292	84 278	617	36.8	2 292	85 487	537	37.3	48.5	49.6	0.2	0.7	0.0	0.3
05 071	...	7	Johnson	1 715	22 781	1 655	13.3	1 715	18 221	1 777	10.6	93.7	1.4	0.6	0.3	0.0	2.6
05 073	...	8	Lafayette	1 364	8 559	2 563	6.3	1 364	9 643	2 420	7.1	62.1	36.5	0.4	0.2	0.0	0.2
05 075	...	7	Lawrence	1 519	17 774	1 911	11.7	1 519	17 455	1 824	11.5	97.8	0.4	0.6	0.1	0.0	0.1
05 077	...	6	Lee	1 558	12 580	2 258	8.1	1 558	13 053	2 136	8.4	41.4	57.2	0.2	0.3	0.0	0.5
05 079	...	8	Lincoln	1 454	14 492	2 122	10.0	1 454	13 690	2 082	9.4	64.9	32.9	0.4	0.1	0.0	1.0
05 081	...	6	Little River	1 377	13 628	2 188	9.9	1 377	13 966	2 059	10.1	74.5	21.3	1.5	0.2	0.0	0.9
05 083	...	6	Logan	1 839	22 486	1 672	12.2	1 839	20 557	1 651	11.2	96.5	1.0	0.7	0.1	0.0	0.4
05 085	4400	2	Lonoke	1 984	52 828	882	26.6	1 983	39 268	1 018	19.8	91.0	6.4	0.5	0.4	0.0	0.5
05 087	...	8	Madison	2 167	14 243	2 146	6.6	2 168	11 618	2 247	5.4	95.9	0.1	1.2	0.1	0.1	1.5
05 089	...	9	Marion	1 548	16 140	2 013	10.4	1 548	12 001	2 219	7.8	97.5	0.1	0.8	0.2	0.0	0.1
05 091	8360	3	Miller	1 616	40 443	1 106	25.0	1 616	38 467	1 041	23.8	74.0	23.0	0.6	0.4	0.0	0.5
05 093	...	4	Mississippi	2 326	51 979	893	22.3	2 327	57 525	756	24.7	64.4	32.7	0.3	0.4	0.0	1.1
05 095	...	7	Monroe	1 571	10 254	2 421	6.5	1 571	11 333	2 272	7.2	59.4	38.8	0.3	0.1	0.0	0.3
05 097	...	9	Montgomery	2 023	9 245	2 508	4.6	2 023	7 841	2 589	3.9	95.4	0.3	1.1	0.4	0.0	1.6
05 099	...	7	Nevada	1 606	9 955	2 451	6.2	1 606	10 101	2 377	6.3	66.9	31.2	0.4	0.1	0.0	0.9
05 101	...	9	Newton	2 131	8 608	2 557	4.0	2 132	7 666	2 605	3.6	97.4	0.1	0.6	0.2	0.0	0.4
05 103	...	7	Ouachita	1 897	28 790	1 428	15.2	1 897	30 574	1 262	16.1	59.7	38.6	0.3	0.2	0.0	0.3
05 105	...	8	Perry	1 427	10 209	2 427	7.2	1 427	7 969	2 574	5.6	95.6	1.7	1.0	0.1	0.0	0.4
05 107	...	7	Phillips	1 794	26 445	1 505	14.7	1 794	28 830	1 336	16.1	39.2	59.0	0.2	0.3	0.0	0.4
05 109	...	9	Pike	1 562	11 303	2 349	7.2	1 562	10 086	2 379	6.5	92.0	3.5	0.6	0.2	0.0	2.6
05 111	...	6	Poinsett	1 963	25 614	1 530	13.0	1 963	24 664	1 475	12.6	91.0	7.1	0.2	0.2	0.0	0.7
05 113	...	7	Polk	2 226	20 229	1 778	9.1	2 226	17 347	1 830	7.8	94.7	0.2	1.5	0.2	0.1	1.7
05 115	...	5	Pope	2 103	54 469	865	25.9	2 103	45 883	906	21.8	93.7	2.6	0.7	0.6	0.0	0.9
05 117	...	8	Prairie	1 673	9 539	2 486	5.7	1 673	9 518	2 432	5.7	84.8	13.7	0.4	0.2	0.0	0.3
05 119	4400	2	Pulaski	1 996	361 474	163	181.1	1 997	349 569	147	175.0	64.0	31.9	0.4	1.2	0.0	1.1
05 121	...	7	Randolph	1 688	18 195	1 887	10.8	1 688	16 558	1 883	9.8	97.0	1.0	0.5	0.1	0.0	0.3
05 123	...	6	St. Francis	1 642	29 329	1 420	17.9	1 642	28 497	1 343	17.4	48.4	49.0	0.2	0.6	0.0	0.4
05 125	4400	2	Saline	1 874	83 529	622	44.6	1 877	64 183	684	34.2	95.3	2.2	0.5	0.6	0.0	0.4
05 127	...	6	Scott	2 315	10 996	2 366	4.7	2 315	10 205	2 371	4.4	93.5	0.2	1.4	1.0	0.0	2.6
05 129	...	9	Searcy	1 728	8 261	2 585	4.8	1 728	7 841	2 589	4.5	97.3	0.0	0.8	0.1	0.0	0.4
05 131	2720	3	Sebastian	1 389	115 071	470	82.8	1 389	99 590	461	71.7	82.3	6.2	1.6	3.5	0.0	3.7
05 133	...	6	Sevier	1 461	15 757	2 035	10.8	1 461	13 637	2 088	9.3	79.6	4.9	1.8	0.1	0.1	11.8
05 135	...	7	Sharp	1 565	17 119	1 948	10.9	1 565	14 109	2 046	9.0	97.1	0.5	0.7	0.1	0.0	0.2
05 137	...	9	Stone	1 571	11 499	2 335	7.3	1 571	9 775	2 407	6.2	97.3	0.1	0.8	0.1	0.0	0.1
05 139	...	5	Union	2 691	45 629	988	17.0	2 691	46 719	895	17.4	66.1	32.0	0.2	0.4	0.0	0.5
05 141	...	8	Van Buren	1 843	16 192	2 008	8.8	1 843	14 008	2 054	7.6	96.8	0.3	0.8	0.2	0.0	0.4
05 143	2580	3	Washington	2 460	157 715	338	64.1	2 461	113 409	405	46.1	88.0	2.2	1.3	1.5	0.5	4.3
05 145	...	4	White	2 678	67 165	731	25.1	2 678	54 676	787	20.4	93.5	3.6	0.4	0.3	0.0	0.8
05 147	...	7	Woodruff	1 519	8 741	2 551	5.8	1 519	9 520	2 431	6.3	67.9	30.8	0.2	0.1	0.1	0.2
05 149	...	7	Yell	2 403	21 139	1 727	8.8	2 403	17 759	1 800	7.4	86.6	1.5	0.6	0.7	0.0	9.0
06 000	...		CALIFORNIA	403 933	33 871 648	X	83.9	403 970	29 811 427	X	73.8	59.5	6.7	1.0	10.9	0.3	16.8
06 001	5775	0	Alameda	1 910	1 443 741	21	755.9	1 910	1 304 347	21	682.9	48.8	14.9	0.6	20.4	0.6	8.9
06 003	...	9	Alpine	1 913	1 208	3 103	0.6	1 913	1 113	3 109	0.6	73.7	0.6	18.9	0.3	0.1	1.4
06 005	...	6	Amador	1 536	35 100	1 247	22.9	1 535	30 039	1 294	19.6	85.8	3.9	1.8	1.0	0.1	5.0

[1] MSA = Metropolitan Statistical Area. PMSA = Primary MSA. NECMA = New England County Metropolitan Area. See Appendix A for explanation of these concepts. See Appendix B for list of metropolitan areas identified by type, with component counties.
[2] County typology code from the Economic Research Service of USDA. See Appendix A for definition.
[3] Dry land or land partially or temporarily covered by water.

Table B. States and Counties

STATE County	Population and population characteristics, 2000 (cont'd) Race (percent) (cont'd) Race alone or in combination Two or more races	White	Black	American Indian or Alaska Native	Asian	Native Hawaiian and other Pacific Islander	Some other race	Hispanic[1]	Population and population characteristics, 1990 Race (percent) White	Black or African American	American Indian or Alaska Native	Asian and Pacific Islander	Hispanic[1]
	15	16	17	18	19	20	21	22	23	24	25	26	27
ARKANSAS—Cont'd													
Conway	1.2	85.4	13.5	1.1	0.4	0.1	1.0	1.8	84.3	15.0	0.4	0.2	0.6
Craighead	1.1	90.2	8.0	0.8	0.8	0.1	1.2	2.1	93.5	5.5	0.3	0.6	0.6
Crawford	2.2	94.3	1.1	3.5	1.5	0.1	1.9	3.3	96.4	0.9	1.5	0.9	1.1
Crittenden	0.6	51.4	47.3	0.5	0.6	0.1	0.8	1.4	56.4	42.9	0.2	0.4	0.7
Cross	0.7	75.4	23.9	0.6	0.5	0.0	0.4	0.9	74.6	24.9	0.2	0.2	0.6
Dallas	0.6	57.4	41.3	0.4	0.3	0.1	1.1	1.9	61.1	38.5	0.2	0.1	0.3
Desha	0.8	51.1	46.6	0.7	0.5	0.1	1.9	3.2	56.6	42.5	0.3	0.2	0.9
Drew	0.9	71.0	27.5	0.7	0.5	0.1	1.2	1.8	72.1	27.4	0.2	0.1	0.5
Faulkner	1.2	89.5	8.8	1.1	0.9	0.1	0.9	1.8	91.1	8.0	0.4	0.4	0.6
Franklin	1.4	97.5	0.7	1.7	0.4	0.1	1.1	1.7	98.3	0.7	0.7	0.2	1.2
Fulton	1.2	98.8	0.3	1.6	0.3	0.0	0.2	0.5	99.3	0.1	0.5	0.1	0.3
Garland	1.5	90.2	8.2	1.4	0.7	0.1	1.0	2.6	91.0	7.6	0.7	0.3	1.1
Grant	0.7	96.2	2.6	0.9	0.2	0.1	0.7	1.1	96.7	2.7	0.3	0.2	0.6
Greene	1.3	98.7	0.2	1.5	0.3	0.1	0.6	1.2	99.4	0.1	0.2	0.1	0.5
Hempstead	1.6	64.6	31.0	1.2	0.3	0.1	4.6	8.3	68.9	29.9	0.3	0.2	1.3
Hot Spring	1.3	88.5	10.6	1.3	0.3	0.1	0.6	1.3	88.3	11.0	0.5	0.1	0.4
Howard	0.9	74.3	22.1	0.9	0.6	0.0	3.0	5.1	77.4	21.5	0.4	0.4	0.7
Independence	1.3	96.1	2.3	1.3	0.8	0.1	0.8	1.5	97.3	1.9	0.3	0.4	0.6
Izard	1.1	97.5	1.5	1.5	0.2	0.1	0.4	1.0	99.1	0.1	0.6	0.2	0.6
Jackson	1.0	81.5	17.7	0.8	0.3	0.0	0.7	1.3	84.9	14.6	0.3	0.1	0.3
Jefferson	0.8	49.0	49.9	0.5	0.8	0.1	0.4	1.0	56.0	43.1	0.3	0.4	0.5
Johnson	1.4	95.0	1.5	1.4	0.5	0.1	3.0	6.7	96.8	1.7	0.6	0.4	1.2
Lafayette	0.6	62.6	36.7	0.6	0.3	0.1	0.3	1.0	61.0	38.5	0.2	0.2	0.4
Lawrence	1.0	98.8	0.5	1.3	0.2	0.1	0.3	0.7	98.7	0.5	0.7	0.1	0.3
Lee	0.4	41.7	57.4	0.3	0.4	0.1	0.6	2.2	41.7	57.4	0.1	0.4	1.3
Lincoln	0.7	65.6	33.2	0.8	0.2	0.0	1.1	1.8	62.9	36.0	0.5	0.1	1.1
Little River	1.7	76.1	21.6	2.5	0.3	0.0	1.2	1.7	77.5	21.0	0.8	0.1	1.1
Logan	1.3	97.7	1.2	1.6	0.3	0.0	0.5	1.2	97.7	1.3	0.6	0.1	0.7
Lonoke	1.1	92.0	6.7	1.0	0.7	0.1	0.7	1.7	90.1	9.0	0.4	0.3	0.6
Madison	1.1	97.0	0.2	2.1	0.1	0.1	1.6	3.1	98.4	0.0	1.2	0.1	1.0
Marion	1.2	98.7	0.2	1.8	0.3	0.1	0.2	0.8	99.2	0.0	0.4	0.2	0.4
Miller	1.4	75.3	23.4	1.3	0.5	0.0	1.0	1.6	76.6	22.4	0.4	0.4	0.8
Mississippi	1.1	65.3	33.2	0.7	0.6	0.1	1.3	2.2	70.7	27.8	0.3	0.6	1.3
Monroe	1.1	60.3	39.4	0.7	0.3	0.1	0.4	1.3	60.5	39.0	0.2	0.2	0.3
Montgomery	1.2	96.6	0.4	2.2	0.5	0.0	1.6	2.5	98.4	0.1	1.2	0.1	0.7
Nevada	0.6	67.4	31.5	0.7	0.2	0.0	0.9	1.5	67.9	31.6	0.3	0.0	0.6
Newton	1.3	98.7	0.2	1.5	0.3	0.0	0.6	1.1	98.9	0.0	0.7	0.2	0.6
Ouachita	0.8	60.4	39.0	0.7	0.4	0.0	0.4	0.7	64.4	35.1	0.1	0.2	0.4
Perry	1.1	96.7	1.9	1.7	0.2	0.0	0.6	1.2	97.6	1.5	0.5	0.2	0.6
Phillips	0.8	39.7	59.4	0.6	0.4	0.1	0.6	1.4	44.8	54.6	0.1	0.2	0.8
Pike	1.1	93.1	3.7	1.3	0.2	0.0	2.8	3.6	95.4	3.7	0.6	0.1	0.6
Poinsett	0.7	91.7	7.3	0.6	0.2	0.0	0.9	1.4	92.4	7.2	0.2	0.1	0.5
Polk	1.7	96.3	0.2	2.9	0.3	0.1	2.0	3.5	98.2	0.0	1.1	0.2	1.7
Pope	1.4	95.0	2.8	1.5	0.8	0.1	1.2	2.1	96.2	2.5	0.7	0.4	0.9
Prairie	0.6	85.4	14.0	0.8	0.2	0.0	0.4	0.8	85.8	13.6	0.4	0.0	0.4
Pulaski	1.4	65.1	32.5	0.9	1.6	0.1	1.4	2.4	72.2	26.4	0.3	0.8	0.9
Randolph	1.1	98.1	1.1	1.3	0.2	0.1	0.5	0.8	98.6	0.9	0.3	0.1	0.5
St. Francis	1.4	49.6	49.4	0.5	0.7	0.1	1.3	4.9	51.7	47.4	0.2	0.4	0.7
Saline	1.0	96.2	2.3	1.1	0.8	0.1	0.6	1.3	96.9	2.1	0.4	0.4	0.6
Scott	1.3	94.8	0.3	2.3	1.1	0.0	2.8	5.7	98.3	0.0	1.0	0.5	0.4
Searcy	1.3	98.6	0.1	1.8	0.3	0.0	0.6	1.0	98.8	0.0	0.8	0.2	0.4
Sebastian	2.7	84.7	6.7	3.1	3.9	0.1	4.3	6.7	89.1	5.7	1.4	3.3	1.4
Sevier	1.6	81.1	5.2	2.8	0.2	0.1	12.3	19.7	88.6	5.8	1.6	0.1	4.6
Sharp	1.4	98.5	0.6	1.8	0.2	0.0	0.4	1.0	98.6	0.5	0.7	0.1	0.4
Stone	1.6	98.9	0.2	2.1	0.2	0.1	0.2	1.1	99.1	0.1	0.6	0.2	0.4
Union	0.8	66.7	32.3	0.6	0.6	0.1	0.6	1.1	69.4	30.1	0.2	0.2	0.5
Van Buren	1.5	98.2	0.4	1.8	0.4	0.1	0.7	1.3	98.8	0.3	0.5	0.2	0.7
Washington	2.2	89.9	2.6	2.3	1.9	0.7	4.9	8.2	95.9	1.5	1.3	0.9	1.3
White	1.3	94.8	3.9	1.2	0.4	0.1	1.1	1.9	96.0	3.1	0.4	0.2	0.7
Woodruff	0.8	68.5	31.2	0.7	0.1	0.1	0.2	0.8	68.3	31.4	0.2	0.1	0.2
Yell	1.6	88.1	1.6	1.4	0.9	0.1	9.6	12.7	96.7	2.1	0.4	0.6	1.0
CALIFORNIA	4.7	63.4	7.4	1.9	12.3	0.7	19.4	32.4	69.0	7.4	0.8	9.6	25.8
Alameda	5.6	53.1	16.2	1.6	22.6	1.2	11.4	19.0	59.6	17.9	0.7	15.1	14.2
Alpine	5.0	77.1	1.2	22.9	1.5	0.6	2.1	7.8	72.4	0.5	25.2	0.4	6.6
Amador	2.4	88.0	4.1	3.0	1.5	0.2	5.8	8.9	89.5	5.6	1.6	0.7	8.4

[1] Hispanic persons may be of any race.

STATE County	Under 5 years	5 to 17 years	18 to 24 years	25 to 34 years	35 to 44 years	45 to 54 years	55 to 64 years	65 to 74 years	75 years and over	Median age (years)	Percent Female
	28	29	30	31	32	33	34	35	36	37	38
ARKANSAS—Cont'd											
Conway	6.5	19.0	0.3	11.7	15.0	13.0	10.5	8.5	7.6	37.9	51.5
Craighead	6.9	17.2	14.0	14.4	14.3	12.8	8.8	6.2	5.5	33.0	51.6
Crawford	7.4	20.8	8.4	13.2	16.1	13.3	9.5	6.5	4.8	35.1	50.6
Crittenden	8.4	22.7	9.4	13.8	15.3	12.3	8.2	5.3	4.6	32.0	52.4
Cross	6.7	21.1	8.5	12.3	15.1	13.0	9.6	7.2	6.5	35.9	51.5
Dallas	6.1	20.0	8.3	10.9	13.6	14.4	9.7	8.4	8.6	38.4	51.5
Desha	7.5	21.4	9.0	11.3	13.9	13.1	9.6	7.2	7.0	35.5	53.3
Drew	6.7	19.1	12.6	12.8	14.4	12.4	9.1	6.9	5.9	34.0	51.5
Faulkner	6.9	18.7	15.3	14.6	15.5	12.0	7.5	5.2	4.3	31.0	51.2
Franklin	6.5	19.4	8.5	12.2	14.6	12.8	10.4	8.0	7.8	37.6	50.5
Fulton	5.5	17.3	6.4	10.2	13.4	13.8	13.2	11.4	8.8	43.0	51.0
Garland	5.5	15.8	7.3	11.1	14.1	13.5	11.6	11.4	9.8	42.5	51.4
Grant	6.4	19.5	8.0	13.3	16.3	14.0	10.3	6.7	5.4	36.6	50.4
Greene	6.7	18.5	9.1	13.8	14.9	13.0	10.0	7.6	6.3	36.2	51.2
Hempstead	7.5	19.8	9.6	12.8	14.5	12.4	9.3	7.3	7.0	35.2	51.6
Hot Spring	6.3	18.8	8.2	11.8	14.6	14.0	10.6	8.6	7.2	38.4	51.2
Howard	6.7	20.1	8.6	12.8	15.1	12.2	9.5	7.3	7.8	36.1	51.2
Independence	6.4	18.1	9.2	12.2	15.4	13.8	10.3	7.7	6.8	37.7	50.9
Izard	5.1	15.8	7.1	11.0	14.0	12.7	13.1	11.0	10.2	42.6	49.3
Jackson	5.7	16.4	11.5	11.5	14.6	13.4	10.4	8.6	7.9	38.2	52.3
Jefferson	6.9	19.4	10.8	12.8	15.1	13.4	8.7	6.6	6.3	35.1	51.1
Johnson	6.7	18.5	9.7	13.0	14.6	12.6	10.2	7.8	7.0	36.4	50.3
Lafayette	6.0	19.4	8.1	10.6	13.8	13.2	11.2	8.8	9.0	39.3	51.6
Lawrence	6.3	17.6	9.6	12.1	13.8	12.5	10.7	8.8	8.6	38.2	51.6
Lee	6.4	19.6	10.2	14.4	14.3	12.4	8.7	7.1	6.9	34.6	47.3
Lincoln	5.7	16.5	12.4	15.9	17.3	12.5	7.9	5.9	5.9	34.7	41.3
Little River	6.9	18.3	8.4	12.1	13.7	14.2	11.4	7.9	7.1	38.2	51.4
Logan	6.5	19.4	7.5	12.0	14.7	13.2	10.7	8.2	7.8	38.0	50.4
Lonoke	7.1	21.6	8.0	13.7	17.2	12.9	9.0	5.6	4.8	34.7	50.8
Madison	6.4	20.4	7.5	11.6	15.4	14.0	10.3	7.6	6.8	37.7	50.1
Marion	5.0	17.1	6.0	9.2	14.2	14.5	14.1	11.2	8.8	44.1	50.5
Miller	7.4	19.1	9.7	13.9	14.6	12.9	9.2	6.9	6.3	34.9	51.3
Mississippi	8.1	21.5	9.9	13.0	14.5	12.3	8.5	6.6	5.7	33.1	52.1
Monroe	6.9	21.0	7.6	10.2	13.6	13.0	10.4	8.7	8.6	38.3	53.1
Montgomery	6.1	17.4	6.2	10.8	14.1	13.3	13.0	10.5	8.4	41.5	51.0
Nevada	6.4	18.8	8.7	12.1	14.0	13.7	10.1	7.9	8.2	37.7	51.5
Newton	5.8	19.1	7.6	10.5	14.5	14.9	12.8	7.8	7.0	40.1	49.4
Ouachita	6.1	19.7	8.0	11.0	14.6	13.9	9.7	8.7	8.2	38.7	52.7
Perry	6.3	19.0	7.4	12.8	15.2	13.5	11.0	8.2	6.5	38.0	50.4
Phillips	8.5	23.7	9.4	10.5	12.8	11.8	9.4	7.6	6.4	33.0	54.1
Pike	6.4	18.6	7.3	12.1	14.3	12.8	11.7	8.1	8.9	38.9	50.7
Poinsett	6.8	19.3	8.9	12.7	14.4	13.1	10.6	7.7	6.6	36.6	51.4
Polk	6.7	18.9	7.9	11.7	13.3	13.0	11.5	9.0	8.0	38.6	50.8
Pope	6.5	19.0	11.6	13.1	15.1	12.9	9.0	6.8	6.0	34.8	50.9
Prairie	6.0	18.0	7.5	11.4	14.7	13.8	11.4	8.7	8.6	40.1	50.8
Pulaski	7.2	18.1	9.6	15.2	15.9	14.2	8.5	6.0	5.5	35.0	52.1
Randolph	6.0	18.6	8.3	11.5	14.2	13.4	10.9	9.2	7.8	38.8	51.0
St. Francis	7.7	20.3	9.9	13.7	15.4	12.8	8.5	6.4	5.5	33.8	48.6
Saline	6.4	19.0	7.7	13.7	16.4	13.8	10.4	7.3	5.1	36.8	50.5
Scott	7.3	19.2	8.1	12.1	14.4	12.5	11.8	8.1	6.6	37.3	49.5
Searcy	5.5	17.1	6.9	10.4	14.0	14.5	12.2	10.3	9.0	42.3	50.5
Sebastian	7.4	18.7	9.2	14.0	15.5	13.2	9.1	6.6	6.4	35.5	51.2
Sevier	7.8	20.4	9.5	14.2	13.5	12.1	9.3	6.9	6.3	33.6	50.2
Sharp	5.5	16.4	6.3	10.1	12.6	12.8	12.7	13.1	10.5	44.3	52.0
Stone	5.5	16.8	7.1	9.4	14.2	14.4	14.1	10.9	7.7	43.1	50.8
Union	6.4	19.5	8.3	11.8	15.1	13.4	9.4	7.8	8.3	37.7	52.2
Van Buren	5.1	16.4	6.6	9.8	13.2	12.8	12.7	12.5	10.8	44.2	50.8
Washington	7.4	17.7	15.3	15.6	14.6	12.0	7.5	5.2	4.7	30.8	49.9
White	6.3	18.1	12.8	12.7	14.5	12.6	9.3	7.2	6.6	35.1	51.2
Woodruff	7.0	19.0	8.4	10.8	13.7	14.3	10.1	8.1	8.6	38.4	52.8
Yell	6.5	19.3	8.9	13.6	14.7	12.2	9.8	7.7	7.4	36.1	50.1
CALIFORNIA	7.3	20.0	9.9	15.4	16.2	12.8	7.7	5.6	5.0	33.3	50.2
Alameda	6.8	17.7	9.6	16.7	17.2	13.9	7.8	5.2	5.0	34.5	50.9
Alpine	5.0	17.8	10.4	10.2	17.3	19.0	10.3	6.2	3.7	39.3	47.4
Amador	4.2	16.4	6.9	9.9	16.3	16.2	12.1	9.8	8.2	42.7	44.9

Population and population characteristics, 2000

Age (percent)

Table B. States and Counties

	Population and population characteristics, 1990										Population—change, 1980–2000				
	Age (percent)										Total persons			Percent change	
STATE County	Under 5 years	5 to 17 years	18 to 24 years	25 to 34 years	35 to 44 years	45 to 54 years	55 to 64 years	65 to 74 years	75 years and over	Percent Female	2000	1990	1980	1990–2000	1980–1990
	39	40	41	42	43	44	45	46	47	48	49	50	51	52	53
ARKANSAS—Cont'd															
Conway	7.0	20.2	8.7	14.6	12.7	10.5	9.9	9.2	7.2	52.1	20 336	19 151	19 505	6.2	-1.8
Craighead	7.0	17.7	14.4	16.2	13.9	10.3	8.4	6.8	5.4	51.9	82 148	68 956	63 239	19.1	9.0
Crawford	7.5	21.5	8.9	16.1	14.5	11.1	8.4	6.8	5.1	51.1	53 247	42 493	36 892	25.3	15.2
Crittenden	8.8	23.1	10.2	16.2	13.6	9.9	7.6	6.1	4.5	52.8	50 866	49 939	49 499	1.9	0.9
Cross	7.5	22.7	9.4	14.3	13.4	10.5	8.3	7.6	6.3	52.0	19 526	19 225	20 434	1.6	-5.9
Dallas	6.6	19.9	8.2	13.2	13.6	10.3	9.8	9.5	8.8	52.1	9 210	9 614	10 515	-4.2	-8.6
Desha	8.0	23.7	9.2	14.1	13.0	9.4	7.8	7.6	7.2	53.3	15 341	16 798	19 760	-8.7	-15.0
Drew	7.0	20.8	12.5	14.5	13.5	10.0	8.3	7.1	6.4	51.9	18 723	17 369	17 910	7.8	-3.0
Faulkner	7.0	18.6	16.4	16.5	14.0	9.5	7.3	6.1	4.6	51.6	86 014	60 006	46 192	43.3	29.9
Franklin	6.4	19.8	9.0	14.1	13.5	10.7	9.5	9.1	7.7	50.4	17 771	14 897	14 705	19.3	1.3
Fulton	5.8	17.8	7.3	11.9	13.0	11.1	12.0	12.2	9.0	52.2	11 642	10 037	9 975	16.0	0.6
Garland	5.8	15.8	7.8	13.0	13.1	10.5	11.9	12.9	9.2	52.4	88 068	73 397	70 531	20.0	4.1
Grant	6.8	20.0	9.0	15.1	15.0	12.4	8.8	7.1	5.7	50.8	16 464	13 948	13 008	18.0	7.2
Greene	6.7	18.5	9.6	14.5	13.9	11.5	9.9	8.6	6.9	51.6	37 331	31 804	30 744	17.4	3.4
Hempstead	7.0	20.6	8.3	15.0	13.0	10.1	9.3	8.4	8.2	52.5	23 587	21 621	23 635	9.1	-8.5
Hot Spring	6.5	19.4	8.4	13.8	14.2	10.9	10.3	9.6	7.1	51.7	30 353	26 115	26 819	16.2	-2.6
Howard	6.9	20.8	8.9	14.2	12.8	10.5	8.7	8.6	8.6	52.0	14 300	13 569	13 459	5.4	0.8
Independence	6.5	19.7	9.2	14.9	14.5	10.9	9.5	8.1	6.6	51.4	34 233	31 192	30 147	9.7	3.5
Izard	5.6	16.0	6.7	11.5	11.7	11.0	11.8	14.3	11.6	52.0	13 249	11 364	10 768	16.6	5.5
Jackson	6.3	19.4	7.9	14.1	13.6	11.0	10.1	9.5	8.2	52.3	18 418	18 944	21 646	-2.8	-12.5
Jefferson	7.3	21.0	11.5	15.0	13.7	9.8	8.3	7.5	6.0	51.9	84 278	85 487	90 718	-1.4	-5.8
Johnson	6.3	18.5	10.6	14.3	12.5	10.4	10.0	9.2	8.1	51.3	22 781	18 221	17 423	25.0	4.6
Lafayette	6.4	21.3	9.1	13.1	12.5	10.8	9.1	9.2	8.5	52.3	8 559	9 643	10 213	-11.2	-5.6
Lawrence	6.3	18.4	9.7	13.6	12.8	10.8	9.9	9.8	8.9	52.0	17 774	17 455	18 447	1.8	-5.4
Lee	8.2	25.5	8.7	11.4	11.9	9.4	9.3	8.3	7.4	52.8	12 580	13 053	15 539	-3.6	-16.0
Lincoln	6.0	17.3	10.8	21.6	15.1	9.6	7.6	6.1	5.9	41.2	14 492	13 690	13 369	5.9	2.4
Little River	6.8	21.3	9.5	14.1	13.9	11.3	9.0	7.7	6.4	51.5	13 628	13 966	13 952	-2.4	0.1
Logan	6.8	20.2	8.6	14.0	13.2	10.9	9.3	9.0	8.0	50.7	22 486	20 557	20 144	9.4	2.1
Lonoke	7.0	22.4	8.6	16.1	14.9	11.4	7.9	6.5	5.1	50.9	52 828	39 268	34 518	34.5	13.8
Madison	7.1	19.8	8.2	13.6	14.0	11.1	9.9	9.2	7.2	50.9	14 243	11 618	11 373	22.6	2.2
Marion	5.2	16.8	6.5	11.7	12.8	11.4	12.8	13.5	9.3	51.3	16 140	12 001	11 334	34.5	5.9
Miller	7.5	20.9	9.9	15.2	13.7	10.1	8.8	7.8	6.2	52.2	40 443	38 467	37 766	5.1	1.9
Mississippi	8.9	22.4	11.0	16.4	13.1	8.8	7.6	6.5	5.2	51.7	51 979	57 525	59 517	-9.6	-3.3
Monroe	7.6	21.9	8.0	13.1	11.6	10.0	9.8	9.6	8.4	53.1	10 254	11 333	14 052	-9.5	-19.3
Montgomery	5.7	17.4	7.8	12.6	12.5	12.0	12.1	11.4	8.5	50.7	9 245	7 841	7 771	17.9	0.9
Nevada	6.4	20.7	8.8	13.3	13.5	10.0	8.9	9.6	8.7	52.2	9 955	10 101	11 097	-1.4	-9.0
Newton	6.4	21.5	7.7	13.2	14.3	12.1	9.7	8.9	6.1	49.9	8 608	7 666	7 756	12.3	-1.2
Ouachita	7.0	20.0	8.1	14.6	14.0	9.9	10.0	8.9	7.6	52.8	28 790	30 574	30 541	-5.8	0.1
Perry	6.2	19.1	9.1	13.6	13.6	11.3	10.8	9.9	6.3	50.8	10 209	7 969	7 266	28.1	9.7
Phillips	9.0	25.2	8.6	12.6	11.5	9.4	8.6	8.1	7.0	54.3	26 445	28 830	34 772	-8.3	-17.1
Pike	6.7	19.5	8.3	13.8	12.9	11.1	9.5	10.1	8.2	51.3	11 303	10 086	10 373	12.1	-2.8
Poinsett	7.2	19.5	9.3	14.6	13.3	11.4	9.5	8.7	6.6	51.9	25 614	24 664	27 032	3.9	-8.8
Polk	6.5	19.2	7.9	12.4	12.8	11.1	10.7	10.3	9.0	51.3	20 229	17 347	17 007	16.6	2.0
Pope	7.3	19.0	12.8	15.7	14.4	10.0	8.3	6.9	5.5	50.6	54 469	45 003	38 964	18.7	17.8
Prairie	6.7	19.2	8.5	14.3	13.3	11.3	10.2	9.4	7.2	50.9	9 539	9 518	10 140	0.2	-6.1
Pulaski	7.5	18.7	10.1	18.4	15.7	10.1	7.9	6.6	4.9	52.4	361 474	349 569	340 597	3.4	2.6
Randolph	6.5	19.1	8.6	13.5	12.8	11.2	11.0	9.5	7.7	51.7	18 195	16 558	16 834	9.9	-1.6
St. Francis	8.4	24.5	8.8	13.9	13.2	9.5	8.3	7.4	6.0	53.6	29 329	28 497	30 858	2.9	-7.7
Saline	6.7	20.6	8.9	16.5	15.7	11.6	8.9	6.7	4.4	50.6	83 529	64 183	53 156	30.1	20.7
Scott	7.2	18.3	9.1	14.0	12.0	12.1	10.5	8.8	8.0	50.9	10 996	10 205	9 685	7.8	5.4
Searcy	5.9	18.5	7.4	11.8	13.9	11.2	11.6	10.9	8.9	51.2	8 261	7 841	8 847	5.4	-11.4
Sebastian	7.3	18.8	9.6	16.4	14.7	10.7	8.5	7.8	6.2	51.7	115 071	99 590	95 172	15.5	4.6
Sevier	6.4	19.7	9.1	14.9	13.6	10.6	9.2	8.8	7.6	50.6	15 757	13 637	14 060	15.5	-3.0
Sharp	4.9	16.7	6.6	10.7	11.3	10.0	12.6	15.5	11.6	52.5	17 119	14 109	14 607	21.3	-3.4
Stone	5.7	18.6	6.6	13.1	13.9	12.4	12.3	10.1	7.3	51.1	11 499	9 775	9 022	17.6	8.3
Union	7.2	20.3	8.4	15.0	14.0	9.7	8.9	9.0	7.6	52.7	45 629	46 719	48 573	-2.3	-3.8
Van Buren	5.1	17.2	6.8	11.0	11.9	10.4	13.7	15.1	8.7	50.7	16 192	14 008	13 357	15.6	4.9
Washington	6.9	17.8	15.2	16.8	14.4	9.8	7.7	6.3	4.9	50.6	157 715	113 409	100 494	39.1	12.9
White	6.5	18.6	13.4	14.2	13.1	10.6	9.0	8.1	6.6	51.5	67 165	54 676	50 835	22.8	7.6
Woodruff	7.3	21.5	8.6	13.6	13.3	9.5	8.6	9.3	8.3	53.0	8 741	9 520	11 222	-8.2	-15.2
Yell	6.9	18.8	9.1	14.5	12.9	11.3	10.1	9.3	7.2	51.3	21 139	17 759	17 026	19.0	4.3
CALIFORNIA	8.1	18.0	11.5	19.1	15.6	9.8	7.5	6.2	4.3	49.9	33 871 648	29 811 427	23 667 765	13.6	25.7
Alameda	7.5	16.2	11.2	19.6	17.2	10.3	7.4	6.2	4.4	50.7	1 443 741	1 304 347	1 105 379	10.7	15.5
Alpine	7.1	18.2	9.1	19.0	18.2	11.5	9.3	4.3	3.2	47.0	1 208	1 113	1 097	8.5	1.5
Amador	4.9	13.9	10.3	16.0	15.9	10.6	10.8	10.9	6.7	43.7	35 100	30 039	19 314	16.8	55.5

Table B. States and Counties

STATE County	Total population	Total in house-holds	House-holder	Spouse	Child Total	Child Own child under 18 years	Other relatives Total	Other relatives Under 18 years	Nonrelatives Total	Nonrelatives Unmarried partner	Total in group quarters	Correctional institutions	Nursing homes	Other institutions	College dormitories	Military quarters	Other
	54	55	56	57	58	59	60	61	62	63	64	65	66	67	68	69	70
ARKANSAS—Cont'd																	
Conway	20 336	98.3	39.2	22.2	28.9	22.2	5.1	2.4	2.9	1.4	1.7	0.3	0.8	0.0	0.0	0.0	0.7
Craighead	82 148	96.6	39.3	21.0	27.5	21.9	4.1	1.7	4.6	1.5	3.4	0.3	0.8	0.0	1.8	0.0	0.5
Crawford	53 247	99.1	37.0	23.0	31.7	25.5	4.3	2.1	3.1	1.4	0.9	0.1	0.5	0.0	0.0	0.0	0.2
Crittenden	50 866	98.8	36.3	16.6	33.3	25.7	8.7	4.9	3.8	2.0	1.2	0.5	0.6	0.0	0.0	0.0	0.2
Cross	19 526	98.5	37.9	20.9	30.8	23.9	6.0	3.3	2.9	1.4	1.5	0.3	0.9	0.0	0.0	0.0	0.3
Dallas	9 210	94.7	38.2	19.5	26.8	19.6	7.2	4.3	2.9	1.5	5.3	1.5	2.1	0.0	0.0	0.0	1.7
Desha	15 341	99.1	38.6	17.9	32.1	24.5	7.3	3.9	3.1	1.6	0.9	0.0	0.8	0.0	0.0	0.0	0.0
Drew	18 723	96.5	39.2	20.1	28.8	22.6	4.6	2.3	3.8	1.6	3.5	0.4	0.3	0.0	1.9	0.0	1.0
Faulkner	86 014	95.3	37.1	21.0	28.8	23.6	3.4	1.4	4.9	1.4	4.7	0.2	0.5	0.0	3.2	0.0	0.9
Franklin	17 771	97.3	38.7	22.9	28.8	22.9	3.9	1.9	2.9	1.5	2.7	0.0	1.2	0.0	0.0	0.0	1.5
Fulton	11 642	98.9	41.3	25.8	25.8	20.6	3.6	1.7	2.4	1.0	1.1	0.1	0.9	0.0	0.0	0.0	0.1
Garland	88 068	97.9	42.9	22.8	23.9	18.8	4.3	1.9	3.9	1.7	2.1	0.4	0.8	0.3	0.3	0.0	0.3
Grant	16 464	98.9	37.9	24.5	29.5	23.4	4.2	2.0	2.8	1.4	1.1	0.4	0.6	0.0	0.0	0.0	0.1
Greene	37 331	98.4	39.5	23.4	28.7	22.8	3.8	1.8	3.1	1.5	1.6	0.2	0.9	0.0	0.1	0.0	0.3
Hempstead	23 587	98.9	38.0	19.5	30.2	23.2	6.9	3.3	4.2	1.7	1.1	0.2	0.8	0.0	0.0	0.0	0.1
Hot Spring	30 353	98.8	39.5	23.4	28.4	22.3	4.6	2.2	2.9	1.3	1.2	0.0	0.8	0.1	0.0	0.0	0.3
Howard	14 300	97.4	38.3	21.1	29.9	23.9	4.9	2.4	3.2	1.4	2.6	0.3	1.9	0.0	0.0	0.0	0.4
Independence	34 233	97.3	39.3	23.2	28.0	22.0	4.0	1.9	2.7	1.3	2.7	0.3	0.9	0.1	1.1	0.0	0.3
Izard	13 249	94.3	41.1	24.1	23.3	18.9	3.3	1.5	2.5	1.2	5.7	4.2	1.4	0.1	0.0	0.0	0.0
Jackson	18 418	91.0	37.8	19.8	25.2	19.0	5.2	2.5	2.9	1.3	9.0	7.4	1.4	0.0	0.0	0.0	0.2
Jefferson	84 278	93.7	36.3	17.2	29.7	21.8	7.5	3.9	3.1	1.4	6.3	3.9	0.9	0.1	1.2	0.0	0.2
Johnson	22 781	97.4	38.4	22.3	28.2	22.7	4.5	1.8	4.1	1.6	2.6	0.2	0.6	0.0	1.5	0.0	0.3
Lafayette	8 559	98.6	40.1	20.3	27.9	20.6	7.4	4.0	2.9	1.5	1.4	0.4	1.0	0.0	0.0	0.0	0.0
Lawrence	17 774	96.9	40.0	23.1	27.7	21.8	3.5	1.7	2.7	1.5	3.1	0.2	1.4	0.0	1.3	0.0	0.2
Lee	12 580	86.1	33.2	14.3	27.3	20.2	8.8	5.2	2.4	1.3	13.9	13.1	0.6	0.0	0.0	0.0	0.2
Lincoln	14 492	77.4	29.4	16.0	24.5	18.8	5.0	2.9	2.5	1.3	22.6	20.8	1.7	0.0	0.0	0.0	0.0
Little River	13 628	98.7	40.1	22.3	28.3	21.8	5.3	2.9	2.7	1.4	1.3	0.1	0.9	0.0	0.0	0.0	0.3
Logan	22 486	97.9	38.7	22.7	28.9	22.9	4.4	2.2	3.2	1.4	2.1	0.1	0.8	0.7	0.0	0.0	0.5
Lonoke	52 828	98.8	36.5	23.1	32.1	26.1	4.3	2.2	2.9	1.3	1.2	0.1	1.0	0.0	0.0	0.0	0.1
Madison	14 243	99.4	38.4	24.2	30.0	24.4	4.0	1.8	2.9	1.2	0.6	0.0	0.6	0.0	0.0	0.0	0.0
Marion	16 140	99.1	42.0	25.7	24.8	19.9	3.5	1.5	3.1	1.4	0.9	0.0	0.8	0.0	0.0	0.0	0.1
Miller	40 443	97.3	38.7	19.7	30.2	23.2	5.4	2.7	3.4	1.5	2.7	1.5	0.7	0.1	0.0	0.0	0.4
Mississippi	51 979	98.4	37.2	18.6	32.2	25.1	6.9	3.9	3.5	1.8	1.6	0.8	0.6	0.0	0.0	0.0	0.2
Monroe	10 254	98.7	40.0	18.5	30.2	23.5	6.6	3.9	3.4	1.6	1.3	0.3	1.1	0.0	0.0	0.0	0.0
Montgomery	9 245	98.8	40.9	25.6	25.7	21.0	3.8	1.8	2.8	1.2	1.2	0.0	1.0	0.0	0.0	0.0	0.1
Nevada	9 955	97.0	39.1	20.3	29.3	22.0	5.6	2.7	2.7	1.2	3.0	0.2	1.6	0.0	0.0	0.0	1.1
Newton	8 608	99.2	40.7	24.4	28.7	23.0	3.2	1.5	2.2	1.0	0.8	0.0	0.6	0.0	0.0	0.0	0.2
Ouachita	28 790	98.6	40.3	20.2	29.1	22.2	6.4	3.3	2.6	1.3	1.4	0.1	0.7	0.0	0.0	0.0	0.6
Perry	10 209	98.5	39.1	23.9	28.5	22.7	4.1	1.9	2.9	1.4	1.5	0.2	0.8	0.2	0.0	0.0	0.3
Phillips	26 445	98.8	36.7	14.8	34.2	25.7	9.7	5.9	3.4	1.7	1.2	0.3	0.6	0.0	0.0	0.0	0.0
Pike	11 303	98.4	39.8	24.3	27.8	22.7	4.0	1.8	2.4	1.2	1.6	0.1	1.4	0.1	0.0	0.0	0.0
Poinsett	25 614	98.5	39.1	21.4	29.3	22.4	5.5	3.0	3.2	1.7	1.5	0.6	1.0	0.0	0.0	0.0	0.0
Polk	20 229	99.0	39.8	24.0	28.2	23.3	4.0	1.7	3.0	1.1	1.0	0.1	0.8	0.0	0.0	0.0	0.0
Pope	54 469	96.8	38.0	22.3	28.8	23.3	3.9	1.7	3.8	1.4	3.2	0.1	0.7	0.2	1.7	0.0	0.5
Prairie	9 539	98.5	40.8	23.1	27.2	20.9	4.9	2.7	2.5	1.2	1.5	0.2	1.3	0.0	0.0	0.0	0.0
Pulaski	361 474	97.7	40.9	18.8	28.4	22.2	5.3	2.4	4.3	1.7	2.3	0.6	0.5	0.2	0.2	0.3	0.5
Randolph	18 195	98.3	39.9	23.3	28.1	22.1	4.2	1.9	2.8	1.5	1.7	0.1	1.3	0.3	0.0	0.0	0.1
St. Francis	29 329	90.8	34.2	16.1	30.4	23.3	7.1	4.0	3.0	1.6	9.2	8.3	0.6	0.0	0.0	0.0	0.3
Saline	83 529	97.9	38.0	24.3	28.9	23.2	3.7	1.6	2.9	1.3	2.1	0.3	1.0	0.3	0.0	0.0	0.6
Scott	10 996	99.1	39.3	23.4	28.5	23.5	4.3	2.1	3.5	1.4	0.9	0.0	0.9	0.0	0.0	0.0	0.0
Searcy	8 261	99.4	42.6	25.0	26.3	21.0	3.4	1.4	2.0	1.1	0.6	0.1	0.6	0.0	0.0	0.0	0.0
Sebastian	115 071	98.0	39.4	20.6	29.1	23.4	4.7	1.9	4.2	1.8	2.0	0.5	0.6	0.4	0.0	0.0	0.5
Sevier	15 757	98.9	36.2	21.5	30.6	24.8	6.5	2.7	4.1	1.4	1.1	0.0	0.8	0.0	0.0	0.0	0.2
Sharp	17 119	98.7	42.1	25.2	25.0	19.8	3.6	1.6	2.7	1.3	1.3	0.0	1.1	0.0	0.0	0.0	0.2
Stone	11 499	98.8	41.5	25.8	25.2	20.1	3.7	1.7	2.5	1.2	1.2	0.3	0.9	0.0	0.0	0.0	0.1
Union	45 629	97.8	39.4	20.2	29.2	22.4	6.0	3.1	3.0	1.4	2.2	0.3	1.6	0.0	0.0	0.0	0.2
Van Buren	16 192	98.3	42.2	24.9	24.3	19.0	4.0	1.9	3.0	1.6	1.7	0.2	1.4	0.0	0.0	0.0	0.1
Washington	157 715	96.2	38.1	20.0	27.4	22.7	4.4	1.6	6.3	1.9	3.8	0.2	0.8	0.3	2.4	0.0	0.2
White	67 165	94.7	37.4	22.4	27.7	22.1	4.0	1.8	3.1	1.3	5.3	0.2	0.9	0.1	3.7	0.0	0.3
Woodruff	8 741	98.4	40.4	19.6	29.1	22.0	6.3	3.4	3.0	1.5	1.6	0.1	1.3	0.0	0.0	0.0	0.2
Yell	21 139	98.0	37.5	21.9	28.2	22.5	6.1	2.5	4.3	1.5	2.0	0.2	1.3	0.0	0.0	0.0	0.6
CALIFORNIA	33 871 648	97.6	34.0	17.4	31.1	23.7	8.4	2.8	6.8	2.0	2.4	0.7	0.4	0.1	0.4	0.2	0.7
Alameda	1 443 741	98.1	36.3	17.0	28.7	21.4	8.5	2.6	7.6	2.3	1.9	0.4	0.4	0.1	0.4	0.0	0.6
Alpine	1 208	99.9	40.0	17.5	24.5	18.1	5.8	3.5	12.1	3.0	0.1	0.0	0.0	0.0	0.0	0.0	0.0
Amador	35 100	86.9	36.4	21.4	21.8	17.5	3.5	1.5	3.9	1.8	13.1	10.1	0.4	2.2	0.0	0.0	0.3

Table B. States and Counties

STATE County	Total households	Family households Total	With own children under 18 years	Married couple Total	With own children under 18 years	Female householder¹ Total	With own children under 18 years	Nonfamily households Total	Householder living alone Total	65 years and over	Average household size	Average family size	1990 Total households	Female householder¹	Householder living alone
	71	72	73	74	75	76	77	78	79	80	81	82	83	84	85
ARKANSAS—Cont'd															
Conway	7 967	72.0	31.4	56.7	23.2	11.5	6.2	28.0	25.4	12.1	2.51	2.99	7 179	10.9	23.5
Craighead	32 301	68.4	32.3	53.3	23.7	11.4	6.9	31.6	25.2	9.1	2.46	2.96	26 285	10.5	23.5
Crawford	19 702	76.9	37.5	62.2	28.3	10.9	6.9	23.1	20.0	8.2	2.68	3.07	15 251	9.9	17.9
Crittenden	18 471	72.4	37.4	45.8	21.4	21.3	13.3	27.6	23.7	8.0	2.72	3.23	17 120	18.7	21.3
Cross	7 391	73.7	34.7	55.2	24.2	14.1	8.4	26.3	23.5	11.1	2.60	3.07	6 754	12.8	20.8
Dallas	3 519	69.1	29.6	51.0	20.3	13.8	7.8	30.9	28.3	13.9	2.48	3.03	3 600	11.6	25.3
Desha	5 922	70.8	34.6	46.5	19.5	19.9	13.0	29.2	26.9	12.7	2.57	3.10	5 957	17.5	24.3
Drew	7 337	69.4	33.5	51.3	22.8	14.2	8.7	30.6	26.0	10.5	2.46	2.97	6 342	13.6	23.7
Faulkner	31 882	70.4	35.7	56.7	27.2	10.2	6.5	29.6	22.5	6.9	2.57	3.04	21 325	9.3	20.5
Franklin	6 882	72.1	32.4	59.2	25.1	8.8	5.0	27.9	24.6	12.4	2.51	2.99	5 578	8.0	22.2
Fulton	4 810	73.0	27.4	62.4	21.4	7.8	4.5	27.0	24.4	12.8	2.39	2.83	4 010	7.0	23.3
Garland	37 813	66.8	25.1	53.2	17.4	10.1	6.0	33.2	28.8	13.5	2.28	2.78	30 836	9.5	27.6
Grant	6 241	76.6	35.6	64.7	29.0	8.5	4.9	23.4	20.4	9.0	2.61	3.00	5 118	7.2	19.1
Greene	14 750	72.6	33.1	59.2	25.3	9.7	5.6	27.4	24.0	11.0	2.49	2.95	12 325	8.5	22.0
Hempstead	8 959	71.2	33.4	51.4	22.2	15.3	9.1	28.8	25.5	11.7	2.60	3.09	8 212	13.4	25.0
Hot Spring	12 004	73.6	31.8	59.2	23.5	10.6	6.2	26.4	23.5	11.1	2.50	2.94	10 115	10.0	23.2
Howard	5 471	71.7	34.1	55.2	24.7	12.7	7.5	28.3	25.7	12.6	2.55	3.04	4 975	11.5	23.4
Independence	13 467	71.8	32.1	59.0	25.0	9.2	5.1	28.2	25.5	11.7	2.47	2.95	11 840	8.2	22.8
Izard	5 440	69.3	25.5	50.7	19.5	7.5	4.3	30.7	27.8	15.1	2.30	2.78	4 684	6.9	24.2
Jackson	6 971	69.3	27.7	52.2	18.9	13.1	7.1	30.7	27.9	14.4	2.40	2.92	7 361	12.2	25.0
Jefferson	30 555	70.4	33.1	47.4	19.9	18.8	11.2	29.6	26.2	10.6	2.59	3.13	30 001	16.0	24.2
Johnson	8 738	71.4	32.4	58.1	24.7	9.5	5.6	28.6	24.6	11.6	2.54	3.01	7 059	8.6	24.4
Lafayette	3 434	69.2	27.9	50.6	18.7	14.4	7.3	30.8	28.4	14.6	2.46	3.00	3 584	13.9	26.6
Lawrence	7 108	70.5	30.8	57.7	23.4	9.6	5.6	29.5	26.7	14.2	2.42	2.92	6 857	9.3	24.9
Lee	4 182	70.8	31.2	43.2	15.6	23.1	13.5	29.2	27.2	13.8	2.59	3.14	4 578	20.1	25.6
Lincoln	4 265	73.4	34.8	54.3	23.7	14.8	8.6	26.6	23.5	10.6	2.63	3.11	3 796	14.0	23.4
Little River	5 465	71.6	31.4	55.6	22.1	12.3	7.0	28.4	26.3	12.0	2.46	2.95	5 150	11.5	22.1
Logan	8 693	72.5	32.9	58.7	24.8	10.1	5.9	27.5	24.4	12.5	2.53	3.00	7 628	8.6	23.6
Lonoke	19 262	78.0	40.3	63.3	31.4	10.6	6.7	22.0	19.0	7.6	2.71	3.09	13 866	9.4	18.5
Madison	5 463	74.7	33.9	63.0	27.1	7.9	4.8	25.3	22.4	10.4	2.59	3.03	4 970	6.2	20.7
Marion	6 776	71.9	26.0	61.3	19.6	7.4	4.8	28.1	24.9	12.4	2.36	2.79	4 970	6.8	23.3
Miller	15 637	70.9	34.0	50.9	22.0	16.0	9.9	29.1	25.6	10.7	2.52	3.02	14 273	14.9	23.7
Mississippi	19 349	71.9	36.0	50.0	22.6	17.4	11.0	28.1	24.7	10.7	2.64	3.15	20 420	15.3	22.4
Monroe	4 105	66.6	29.3	46.1	17.6	16.7	9.7	33.4	30.1	15.1	2.47	3.07	4 361	15.8	28.7
Montgomery	3 785	72.6	28.0	62.6	23.0	7.0	3.5	27.4	24.5	12.2	2.41	2.85	3 062	6.9	23.2
Nevada	3 893	69.9	31.4	51.9	21.7	14.0	7.8	30.1	27.8	13.7	2.48	3.02	3 798	12.3	26.0
Newton	3 500	71.3	32.2	60.0	25.4	7.7	4.7	28.7	26.0	10.9	2.44	2.94	2 818	6.1	20.5
Ouachita	11 613	69.5	30.8	50.0	20.1	15.6	8.8	30.5	28.0	13.5	2.45	2.99	11 712	13.0	25.8
Perry	3 989	73.7	32.6	61.1	25.5	8.7	5.1	26.3	23.2	10.4	2.52	2.96	3 055	6.9	22.8
Phillips	9 711	69.7	34.2	40.3	16.4	25.1	15.7	30.3	27.6	13.0	2.69	3.29	10 183	22.1	26.8
Pike	4 504	72.5	32.1	60.9	25.4	8.3	4.8	27.5	25.2	13.4	2.47	2.94	3 855	6.8	22.5
Poinsett	10 026	72.1	32.6	54.6	22.8	13.2	7.5	27.9	24.8	11.7	2.52	2.99	9 368	11.4	23.1
Polk	8 047	72.0	31.9	60.4	25.1	8.4	5.0	28.0	25.0	12.3	2.49	2.97	6 827	7.5	24.0
Pope	20 701	72.5	34.3	58.6	26.1	10.2	6.2	27.5	23.0	9.1	2.55	3.00	16 828	8.7	21.8
Prairie	3 894	71.8	30.6	56.6	22.3	11.1	6.2	28.2	25.6	13.2	2.41	2.88	3 661	8.9	24.1
Pulaski	147 942	64.7	30.5	45.9	19.3	15.1	9.3	35.3	30.0	8.8	2.39	2.98	137 209	13.5	27.5
Randolph	7 265	72.2	30.7	58.4	23.1	9.9	5.6	27.8	24.7	12.1	2.46	2.93	6 445	8.5	23.1
St. Francis	10 043	72.0	35.3	46.9	20.0	20.8	13.2	28.0	25.1	10.8	2.65	3.17	9 958	19.2	23.8
Saline	31 778	77.1	35.4	63.8	27.3	9.7	5.9	22.9	19.6	7.5	2.57	2.94	23 037	8.1	17.6
Scott	4 323	72.2	32.6	59.5	25.1	8.5	5.2	27.8	24.8	11.4	2.52	2.98	3 957	8.1	22.0
Searcy	3 523	70.0	27.9	58.5	21.5	7.7	4.5	30.0	28.0	14.3	2.33	2.83	3 117	5.5	23.6
Sebastian	45 300	67.8	32.8	52.4	23.4	11.3	7.1	32.2	27.5	10.0	2.49	3.04	39 298	9.8	26.7
Sevier	5 708	74.0	36.4	59.3	27.7	10.0	6.1	26.0	22.8	11.0	2.73	3.19	5 118	8.8	23.2
Sharp	7 211	71.3	25.8	59.9	19.5	8.1	4.5	28.7	25.6	14.4	2.34	2.79	5 819	6.5	24.0
Stone	4 768	72.6	26.9	62.3	21.4	7.1	3.8	27.4	24.8	11.2	2.38	2.82	3 866	7.0	22.0
Union	17 989	70.3	32.2	51.3	21.5	15.2	8.7	29.7	26.9	12.1	2.48	3.00	17 819	13.0	25.8
Van Buren	6 825	70.4	25.2	59.1	19.1	7.7	4.1	29.6	26.4	14.4	2.33	2.79	5 698	6.5	22.8
Washington	60 151	65.6	32.5	52.3	24.5	9.4	5.9	34.4	25.8	7.1	2.52	3.07	43 372	8.1	24.4
White	25 148	73.2	33.0	59.9	25.3	9.5	5.6	26.8	23.4	10.5	2.53	2.98	19 823	8.5	21.4
Woodruff	3 531	69.1	30.9	48.6	19.8	16.7	9.2	30.9	28.2	14.2	2.44	2.97	3 630	16.3	26.8
Yell	7 922	73.4	33.6	58.5	25.1	10.1	6.1	26.6	23.2	11.8	2.61	3.04	6 907	8.4	22.8
CALIFORNIA	11 502 870	68.9	35.8	51.1	26.0	12.6	7.3	31.1	23.5	7.8	2.87	3.43	10 381 206	11.5	23.4
Alameda	523 366	64.8	32.6	47.0	23.5	13.0	7.0	35.2	26.0	7.3	2.71	3.31	479 518	12.9	26.8
Alpine	483	61.1	25.5	43.9	16.6	11.0	5.2	38.9	27.7	5.4	2.50	2.96	450	10.2	29.8
Amador	12 759	71.1	26.2	58.9	18.7	8.7	5.4	28.9	23.9	11.3	2.39	2.81	10 518	6.0	22.3

¹No spouse present.

Table B. States and Counties

STATE County	Percent change of households, 1990-2000	Total housing units	Occupied housing units (percent)	Vacant housing units Total	For seasonal, recreational, or occasional use	Homeowner vacancy rate (percent)	Rental vacancy rate (percent)	Occupied housing units Total	Percent owner-occupied housing units	Percent renter-occupied housing units	Average household size of owner-occupied units	Average household size of renter-occupied units
	86	87	88	89	90	91	92	93	94	95	96	97
ARKANSAS—Cont'd												
Conway	11.0	9 028	88.2	11.8	2.5	1.9	10.0	7 967	78.1	21.9	2.55	2.38
Craighead	22.9	35 133	91.9	8.1	0.4	2.2	9.9	32 301	63.9	36.1	2.54	2.31
Crawford	29.2	21 315	92.4	7.6	0.9	2.2	7.3	19 702	75.9	24.1	2.70	2.61
Crittenden	7.9	20 507	90.1	9.9	1.7	1.8	9.0	18 471	60.3	39.7	2.77	2.64
Cross	9.4	8 030	92.0	8.0	0.6	2.1	6.5	7 391	70.8	29.2	2.62	2.55
Dallas	-2.3	4 401	80.0	20.0	7.2	3.5	11.0	3 519	73.8	26.2	2.51	2.40
Desha	-0.6	6 663	88.9	11.1	2.0	2.1	6.8	5 922	63.5	36.5	2.55	2.59
Drew	15.7	8 287	88.5	11.5	1.9	2.0	10.3	7 337	69.0	31.0	2.52	2.33
Faulkner	49.5	34 546	92.3	7.7	0.9	2.6	8.7	31 882	68.6	31.4	2.70	2.28
Franklin	23.4	7 673	89.7	10.3	1.7	2.2	9.0	6 882	78.1	21.9	2.53	2.43
Fulton	20.0	5 973	80.5	19.5	9.3	3.9	9.8	4 810	81.1	18.9	2.40	2.37
Garland	22.6	44 953	84.1	15.9	6.1	2.8	14.5	37 813	71.1	28.9	2.31	2.20
Grant	21.9	6 960	89.7	10.3	2.1	1.9	11.0	6 241	80.4	19.6	2.63	2.51
Greene	19.7	16 161	91.3	8.7	0.3	2.2	11.4	14 750	71.3	28.7	2.54	2.36
Hempstead	9.1	10 166	88.1	11.9	2.7	2.0	5.9	8 959	69.3	30.7	2.57	2.67
Hot Spring	18.7	13 384	89.7	10.3	2.0	2.1	8.6	12 004	77.9	22.1	2.50	2.49
Howard	10.0	6 297	86.9	13.1	2.0	2.1	10.3	5 471	72.2	27.8	2.57	2.47
Independence	13.7	14 841	90.7	9.3	0.9	1.9	8.5	13 467	74.4	25.6	2.52	2.34
Izard	16.1	6 591	82.5	17.5	5.3	4.8	11.1	5 440	80.2	19.8	2.32	2.19
Jackson	-5.3	7 956	87.6	12.4	0.4	3.2	15.1	6 971	69.6	30.4	2.39	2.43
Jefferson	1.8	34 350	89.0	11.0	1.1	1.6	8.5	30 555	66.2	33.8	2.59	2.57
Johnson	23.8	9 926	88.0	12.0	2.9	2.8	8.7	8 738	73.1	26.9	2.55	2.52
Lafayette	-4.2	4 560	75.3	24.7	12.6	2.8	8.1	3 434	78.6	21.4	2.45	2.49
Lawrence	3.7	8 085	87.9	12.1	3.0	2.8	7.9	7 108	71.1	28.9	2.43	2.41
Lee	-8.7	4 768	87.7	12.3	1.9	2.4	11.1	4 182	63.7	36.3	2.55	2.67
Lincoln	12.4	4 955	86.1	13.9	2.6	2.3	7.9	4 265	76.1	23.9	2.64	2.61
Little River	6.1	6 435	84.9	15.1	3.8	3.0	10.0	5 465	76.5	23.5	2.50	2.35
Logan	14.0	9 942	87.4	12.6	2.7	3.1	9.4	8 693	77.1	22.9	2.56	2.45
Lonoke	38.9	20 749	92.8	7.2	0.7	1.8	6.9	19 262	75.9	24.1	2.74	2.61
Madison	24.4	6 537	83.6	16.4	3.3	3.4	7.2	5 463	79.1	20.9	2.59	2.60
Marion	36.3	8 235	82.3	17.7	7.6	3.6	11.0	6 776	80.1	19.9	2.36	2.34
Miller	9.6	17 727	88.2	11.8	1.1	2.7	14.3	15 637	68.0	32.0	2.54	2.46
Mississippi	-5.2	22 310	86.7	13.3	0.3	2.4	18.1	19 349	58.9	41.1	2.65	2.64
Monroe	-5.9	5 067	81.0	19.0	9.0	2.9	6.6	4 105	65.0	35.0	2.47	2.45
Montgomery	23.6	5 048	75.0	25.0	11.5	3.7	7.8	3 785	82.9	17.1	2.42	2.40
Nevada	2.5	4 751	81.9	18.1	4.2	2.0	4.9	3 893	74.8	25.2	2.50	2.42
Newton	24.2	4 316	81.1	18.9	5.5	6.0	8.6	3 500	81.5	18.5	2.48	2.26
Ouachita	-0.8	13 450	86.3	13.7	1.9	2.6	11.4	11 613	71.4	28.6	2.46	2.41
Perry	30.6	4 702	84.8	15.2	5.5	2.6	10.1	3 989	82.2	17.8	2.54	2.44
Phillips	-4.6	10 859	89.4	10.6	1.1	2.9	10.5	9 711	56.2	43.8	2.58	2.83
Pike	16.8	5 536	81.4	18.6	7.3	4.5	10.0	4 504	78.9	21.1	2.46	2.50
Poinsett	7.0	11 051	90.7	9.3	1.7	1.9	8.5	10 026	66.8	33.2	2.53	2.49
Polk	17.9	9 236	87.1	12.9	3.0	3.7	13.3	8 047	78.4	21.6	2.50	2.46
Pope	23.0	22 851	90.6	9.4	1.2	2.4	10.2	20 701	71.2	28.8	2.62	2.37
Prairie	6.4	4 790	81.3	18.7	9.9	1.8	11.2	3 894	73.1	26.9	2.45	2.32
Pulaski	7.8	161 135	91.8	8.2	0.5	1.8	9.5	147 942	60.9	39.1	2.49	2.23
Randolph	12.7	8 268	87.9	12.1	3.7	2.4	9.0	7 265	74.4	25.6	2.51	2.31
St. Francis	0.9	11 242	89.3	10.7	0.7	2.1	11.2	10 043	63.2	36.8	2.65	2.67
Saline	37.9	33 825	93.9	6.1	0.8	1.4	8.4	31 778	80.7	19.3	2.60	2.47
Scott	9.2	4 924	87.8	12.2	2.4	2.2	6.9	4 323	74.3	25.7	2.52	2.51
Searcy	13.0	4 292	82.1	17.9	3.3	2.2	10.1	3 523	77.7	22.3	2.37	2.20
Sebastian	15.3	49 311	91.9	8.1	0.6	2.4	8.2	45 300	63.5	36.5	2.58	2.34
Sevier	11.5	6 434	88.7	11.3	1.6	2.8	10.3	5 708	74.1	25.9	2.70	2.83
Sharp	23.9	9 342	77.2	22.8	12.5	5.8	11.2	7 211	80.3	19.7	2.33	2.38
Stone	23.3	5 715	83.4	16.6	6.9	2.7	8.2	4 768	78.1	21.9	2.42	2.25
Union	1.0	20 676	87.0	13.0	2.0	2.3	11.8	17 989	72.9	27.1	2.51	2.39
Van Buren	19.8	9 164	74.5	25.5	13.7	3.7	10.5	6 825	81.1	18.9	2.36	2.23
Washington	38.7	64 330	93.5	6.5	0.6	2.5	5.9	60 151	59.5	40.5	2.64	2.35
White	26.9	27 613	91.1	8.9	0.8	2.8	9.7	25 148	72.9	27.1	2.59	2.36
Woodruff	-2.7	4 089	86.4	13.6	4.2	2.1	7.4	3 531	65.4	34.6	2.44	2.43
Yell	14.7	9 157	86.5	13.5	3.6	2.8	8.2	7 922	72.9	27.1	2.57	2.74
CALIFORNIA	10.8	12 214 549	94.2	5.8	1.9	1.4	3.7	11 502 870	56.9	43.1	2.93	2.79
Alameda	9.1	540 183	96.9	3.1	0.3	0.7	2.5	523 366	54.7	45.3	2.86	2.52
Alpine	7.3	1 514	31.9	68.1	61.1	0.9	8.4	483	68.3	31.7	2.49	2.51
Amador	21.3	15 035	84.9	15.1	10.8	1.9	4.4	12 759	75.5	24.5	2.38	2.44

Table B. States and Counties

STATE/County code	MSA/PMSA/NECMA code[1]	County type[2]	STATE County	Land area, 2000[3] (sq km)	Total persons	Rank	Per square kilometer	Land area, 1990[3] (sq km)	Total persons	Rank	Per square kilometer	White	Black or African American	American Indian or Alaska Native	Asian	Native Hawaiian and other Pacific Islander	Some other race
					Population, 2000				Population, 1990			Population and population characteristics, 2000 — Race (percent) — One race					
				1	2	3	4	5	6	7	8	9	10	11	12	13	14
			CALIFORNIA—Cont'd														
06 007	1620	3	Butte	4 246	203 171	270	47.8	4 247	182 120	266	42.9	84.5	1.4	1.9	3.3	0.1	4.8
06 009	...	6	Calaveras	2 642	40 554	1 100	15.3	2 642	31 998	1 211	12.1	91.2	0.7	1.7	0.9	0.1	2.1
06 011	...	6	Colusa	2 980	18 804	1 855	6.3	2 981	16 275	1 906	5.5	64.3	0.5	2.3	1.2	0.4	26.7
06 013	5775	0	Contra Costa	1 865	948 816	38	508.7	1 866	803 731	47	430.7	65.5	9.4	0.6	11.0	0.4	8.1
06 015	...	7	Del Norte	2 610	27 507	1 466	10.5	2 610	23 460	1 517	9.0	78.9	4.3	6.4	2.3	0.1	3.9
06 017	6920	1	El Dorado	4 431	156 299	342	35.3	4 433	125 995	368	28.4	89.7	0.5	1.0	2.1	0.1	3.5
06 019	2840	2	Fresno	15 443	799 407	58	51.8	15 445	667 479	67	43.2	54.3	5.3	1.6	8.1	0.1	25.9
06 021	...	6	Glenn	3 405	26 453	1 503	7.8	3 406	24 798	1 471	7.3	71.8	0.6	2.1	3.4	0.1	18.2
06 023	...	5	Humboldt	9 253	126 518	429	13.7	9 254	119 118	389	12.9	84.7	0.9	5.7	1.7	0.2	2.4
06 025	...	4	Imperial	10 813	142 361	384	13.2	10 813	109 303	421	10.1	49.4	4.0	1.9	2.0	0.1	39.1
06 027	...	7	Inyo	26 426	17 945	1 902	0.7	26 397	18 281	1 775	0.7	80.1	0.2	10.0	0.9	0.1	4.6
06 029	0680	2	Kern	21 085	661 645	78	31.4	21 087	544 981	88	25.8	61.6	6.0	1.5	3.4	0.1	23.2
06 031	...	4	Kings	3 603	129 461	414	35.9	3 599	101 469	450	28.2	53.7	8.3	1.7	3.1	0.2	28.3
06 033	...	6	Lake	3 258	58 309	820	17.9	3 259	50 631	832	15.5	86.2	2.1	3.0	0.8	0.2	4.1
06 035	...	6	Lassen	11 803	33 828	1 286	2.9	11 804	27 598	1 368	2.3	80.8	8.8	3.3	0.7	0.4	3.2
06 037	4480	0	Los Angeles	10 518	9 519 338	1	905.1	10 515	8 863 052	1	842.9	48.7	9.8	0.8	11.9	0.3	23.5
06 039	2840	2	Madera	5 532	123 109	440	22.3	5 539	88 090	518	15.9	62.2	4.1	2.6	1.3	0.2	24.4
06 041	7360	0	Marin	1 346	247 289	235	183.7	1 346	230 096	212	170.9	84.0	2.9	0.4	4.5	0.2	4.5
06 043	...	8	Mariposa	3 758	17 130	1 947	4.6	3 759	14 302	2 031	3.8	88.9	0.7	3.5	0.7	0.1	2.7
06 045	...	4	Mendocino	9 088	86 265	603	9.5	9 089	80 345	568	8.8	80.8	0.6	4.8	1.2	0.1	8.6
06 047	4940	3	Merced	4 995	210 554	264	42.2	4 996	178 403	272	35.7	56.2	3.8	1.2	6.8	0.2	26.1
06 049	...	7	Modoc	10 215	9 449	2 491	0.9	10 216	9 678	2 414	0.9	85.9	0.7	4.2	0.6	0.1	5.7
06 051	...	7	Mono	7 885	12 853	2 243	1.6	7 885	9 956	2 390	1.3	84.2	0.5	2.4	1.1	0.1	9.5
06 053	7120	2	Monterey	8 604	401 762	140	46.7	8 604	355 660	144	41.3	55.9	3.7	1.0	6.0	0.4	27.8
06 055	8720	0	Napa	1 952	124 279	433	63.7	1 953	110 765	417	56.7	80.0	1.3	0.8	3.0	0.2	10.9
06 057	...	4	Nevada	2 480	92 033	555	37.1	2 480	78 510	576	31.7	93.4	0.3	0.9	0.8	0.1	1.9
06 059	5945	0	Orange	2 045	2 846 289	5	1 391.8	2 045	2 410 668	5	1 178.8	64.8	1.7	0.7	13.6	0.3	14.8
06 061	6920	1	Placer	3 637	248 399	233	68.3	3 637	172 796	280	47.5	88.6	0.8	0.9	2.9	0.2	3.4
06 063	...	6	Plumas	6 614	20 824	1 745	3.1	6 615	19 739	1 689	3.0	91.8	0.6	2.5	0.5	0.1	1.8
06 065	6780	0	Riverside	18 667	1 545 387	16	82.8	18 669	1 170 413	26	62.7	65.6	6.2	1.2	3.7	0.3	18.7
06 067	6920	0	Sacramento	2 501	1 223 499	29	489.2	2 501	1 066 789	29	426.5	64.0	10.0	1.1	11.0	0.6	7.5
06 069	...	6	San Benito	3 598	53 234	880	14.8	3 598	36 697	1 082	10.2	65.2	1.1	1.2	2.4	0.2	24.9
06 071	6780	0	San Bernardino	51 936	1 709 434	13	32.9	51 960	1 418 380	16	27.3	58.9	9.1	1.2	4.7	0.3	20.8
06 073	7320	0	San Diego	10 878	2 813 833	6	258.7	10 890	2 498 016	4	229.4	66.5	5.7	0.9	8.9	0.5	12.8
06 075	7360	0	San Francisco	121	776 733	62	6 419.3	121	723 959	55	5 983.1	49.7	7.8	0.4	30.8	0.5	6.5
06 077	8120	2	San Joaquin	3 624	563 598	97	155.5	3 625	480 628	101	132.6	58.1	6.7	1.1	11.4	0.3	16.3
06 079	7460	3	San Luis Obispo	8 558	246 681	236	28.8	8 559	217 162	229	25.4	84.6	2.0	0.9	2.7	0.1	6.2
06 081	7360	0	San Mateo	1 163	707 161	70	608.0	1 163	649 623	72	558.6	59.5	3.5	0.4	20.0	1.3	10.2
06 083	7480	2	Santa Barbara	7 089	399 347	149	56.3	7 093	369 608	139	52.1	72.7	2.3	1.2	4.1	0.2	15.2
06 085	7400	0	Santa Clara	3 343	1 682 585	14	503.3	3 344	1 497 577	14	447.8	53.8	2.8	0.7	25.6	0.3	12.1
06 087	7485	0	Santa Cruz	1 153	255 602	220	221.7	1 155	229 734	214	198.9	75.1	1.0	1.0	3.4	0.1	15.0
06 089	6690	3	Shasta	9 804	163 256	329	16.7	9 805	147 036	320	15.0	89.3	0.8	2.8	1.9	0.1	1.7
06 091	...	8	Sierra	2 469	3 555	2 949	1.4	2 469	3 318	2 970	1.3	94.2	0.2	1.9	0.2	0.1	1.0
06 093	...	7	Siskiyou	16 283	44 301	1 010	2.7	16 284	43 531	931	2.7	87.1	1.3	3.9	1.2	0.1	2.8
06 095	8720	0	Solano	2 148	394 542	150	183.7	2 145	339 469	150	158.3	56.4	14.9	0.8	12.7	0.8	8.0
06 097	7500	0	Sonoma	4 082	458 614	125	112.4	4 082	388 222	130	95.1	81.6	1.4	1.2	3.1	0.2	8.4
06 099	5170	2	Stanislaus	3 869	446 997	132	115.5	3 871	370 522	137	95.7	69.3	2.6	1.3	4.2	0.3	16.8
06 101	9340	3	Sutter	1 561	78 930	649	50.6	1 561	64 409	677	41.3	67.5	1.9	1.6	11.3	0.2	13.0
06 103	...	6	Tehama	7 643	56 039	842	7.3	7 643	49 625	846	6.5	84.8	0.6	2.1	0.8	0.1	8.3
06 105	...	6	Trinity	8 233	13 022	2 230	1.6	8 233	13 063	2 134	1.6	88.9	0.4	4.8	0.5	0.1	2.0
06 107	8780	2	Tulare	12 494	368 021	160	29.5	12 495	311 932	160	25.0	58.1	1.6	1.6	3.3	0.1	30.8
06 109	...	6	Tuolumne	5 790	54 501	863	9.4	5 790	48 456	863	8.4	89.4	2.1	1.8	0.7	0.2	2.9
06 111	8735	0	Ventura	4 779	753 197	64	157.6	4 781	669 016	66	139.9	69.9	1.9	0.9	5.3	0.2	17.7
06 113	9270	0	Yolo	2 624	168 660	321	64.3	2 622	141 212	337	53.9	67.7	2.0	1.2	9.9	0.3	13.8
06 115	9340	3	Yuba	1 633	60 219	803	36.9	1 633	58 234	744	35.7	70.6	3.2	2.6	7.5	0.2	9.9
08 000	...		COLORADO	268 627	4 301 261	X	16.0	268 660	3 294 473	X	12.3	82.8	3.8	1.0	2.2	0.1	7.2
08 001	2080	0	Adams	3 087	363 857	162	117.9	3 087	265 038	186	85.9	77.3	3.0	1.2	3.2	0.1	11.7
08 003	...	7	Alamosa	1 872	14 966	2 093	8.0	1 872	13 617	2 091	7.3	71.2	1.0	2.3	0.8	0.2	20.3
08 005	2080	0	Arapahoe	2 080	487 967	116	234.6	2 080	391 572	129	188.3	79.9	7.7	0.7	3.9	0.1	4.5
08 007	...	9	Archuleta	3 497	9 898	2 456	2.8	3 495	5 345	2 815	1.5	88.3	0.4	1.4	0.3	0.0	7.0
08 009	...	9	Baca	6 619	4 517	2 878	0.7	6 620	4 556	2 867	0.7	93.7	0.0	1.2	0.2	0.1	3.0
08 011	...	9	Bent	3 921	5 998	2 781	1.5	3 921	5 048	2 836	1.3	79.5	3.7	2.2	0.6	0.0	10.3
08 013	1125	0	Boulder	1 923	291 288	194	151.5	1 923	225 339	221	117.2	88.5	0.9	0.6	3.1	0.1	4.7
08 015	...	7	Chaffee	2 625	16 242	2 005	6.2	2 625	12 684	2 167	4.8	90.9	1.6	1.1	0.4	0.0	4.2
08 017	...	9	Cheyenne	4 614	2 231	3 049	0.5	4 614	2 397	3 031	0.5	92.9	0.5	0.8	0.1	0.0	5.1

[1] MSA = Metropolitan Statistical Area. PMSA = Primary MSA. NECMA = New England County Metropolitan Area. See Appendix A for explanation of these concepts. See Appendix B for list of metropolitan areas identified by type, with component counties.
[2] County typology code from the Economic Research Service of USDA. See Appendix A for definition.
[3] Dry land or land partially or temporarily covered by water.

STATE County	Population and population characteristics, 2000 (cont'd) Race (percent) (cont'd) Race alone or in combination								Population and population characteristics, 1990 Race (percent)				
	Two or more races	White	Black	American Indian or Alaska Native	Asian	Native Hawaiian and other Pacific Islander	Some other race	Hispanic[1]	White	Black or African American	American Indian or Alaska Native	Asian and Pacific Islander	Hispanic[1]
	15	16	17	18	19	20	21	22	23	24	25	26	27
CALIFORNIA—Cont'd													
Butte	3.9	88.0	1.9	3.6	4.1	0.3	6.3	10.5	90.7	1.3	1.8	2.8	7.5
Calaveras	3.3	94.3	1.0	3.5	1.4	0.3	3.0	6.8	95.7	0.6	2.1	0.6	5.4
Colusa	4.5	68.1	0.7	3.3	1.9	0.7	30.0	46.5	76.4	0.6	2.1	2.2	33.3
Contra Costa	5.1	69.7	10.3	1.6	12.9	0.8	10.4	17.7	76.0	9.3	0.7	9.0	11.4
Del Norte	4.1	82.6	4.6	9.1	3.0	0.3	4.8	13.9	86.1	3.7	6.4	1.9	10.3
El Dorado	3.0	92.4	0.8	2.2	2.9	0.3	4.5	9.3	94.5	0.5	1.1	1.9	7.0
Fresno	4.7	58.0	5.9	2.6	9.2	0.3	29.0	44.0	63.3	5.0	1.1	8.6	35.5
Glenn	3.9	75.3	0.8	3.3	3.9	0.3	20.5	29.6	85.4	0.6	2.1	3.3	20.0
Humboldt	4.4	88.8	1.4	8.3	2.3	0.4	3.5	6.5	90.6	0.8	5.5	1.9	4.2
Imperial	3.6	52.4	4.3	2.4	2.6	0.2	41.9	72.2	67.3	2.4	1.7	2.0	65.8
Inyo	4.1	83.8	0.4	12.0	1.3	0.2	6.6	12.6	86.3	0.4	10.0	1.0	8.4
Kern	4.1	65.1	6.6	2.6	4.2	0.3	25.6	38.4	69.6	5.5	1.3	3.0	28.0
Kings	4.8	57.8	8.9	2.5	4.0	0.4	31.4	43.6	64.2	8.1	1.1	3.5	34.1
Lake	3.5	89.4	2.6	4.8	1.3	0.4	5.2	11.4	91.8	1.8	2.3	0.9	7.2
Lassen	2.7	83.3	9.1	4.6	1.1	0.6	4.1	13.8	87.7	6.2	3.1	1.1	10.4
Los Angeles	4.9	52.8	10.5	1.5	13.1	0.5	26.9	44.6	56.8	11.2	0.5	10.8	37.8
Madera	5.2	66.7	4.7	4.0	1.9	0.4	27.8	44.3	71.9	2.8	1.6	1.4	34.5
Marin	3.5	87.1	3.5	1.1	5.8	0.4	5.9	11.1	88.7	3.6	0.3	4.1	7.8
Mariposa	3.4	92.1	0.8	5.6	1.2	0.3	3.5	7.8	92.4	0.9	4.5	0.9	4.9
Mendocino	3.9	84.3	1.0	6.6	1.8	0.3	10.1	16.5	89.6	0.6	4.1	1.2	10.3
Merced	5.7	60.9	4.5	2.3	8.0	0.5	29.8	45.3	67.4	4.8	0.8	8.5	32.6
Modoc	2.8	88.6	1.0	5.8	1.0	0.2	6.4	11.5	91.0	0.8	4.2	0.4	7.2
Mono	2.2	86.2	0.7	3.2	1.7	0.3	10.3	17.7	92.7	0.4	3.7	1.3	11.3
Monterey	5.0	60.0	4.5	1.9	7.7	0.8	30.4	46.8	63.8	6.4	0.8	7.8	33.6
Napa	3.7	83.3	1.6	1.8	3.9	0.5	12.8	23.7	88.9	1.1	0.7	3.3	14.4
Nevada	2.6	95.9	0.5	2.2	1.3	0.3	2.7	5.7	97.3	0.2	1.1	0.8	4.2
Orange	4.1	68.3	2.1	1.3	14.9	0.6	17.1	30.8	78.6	1.8	0.5	10.3	23.4
Placer	3.2	91.5	1.1	1.9	3.9	0.4	4.5	9.7	93.7	0.6	1.1	2.2	8.0
Plumas	2.6	94.3	0.8	4.2	0.9	0.2	2.4	5.7	94.2	0.8	3.1	0.6	4.6
Riverside	4.4	69.3	7.0	2.1	4.6	0.5	21.2	36.2	76.4	5.4	1.0	3.6	26.3
Sacramento	5.8	68.5	11.4	2.5	13.0	1.1	9.8	16.0	75.1	9.3	1.2	9.3	11.7
San Benito	5.1	69.6	1.5	2.2	3.7	0.5	28.0	47.9	69.8	0.6	1.0	2.2	45.8
San Bernardino	5.0	63.1	10.0	2.2	5.7	0.5	23.8	39.2	73.0	8.1	0.9	4.2	26.7
San Diego	4.7	70.3	6.6	1.6	10.5	0.9	15.1	26.7	74.9	6.4	0.8	7.9	20.4
San Francisco	4.3	53.0	8.6	1.2	32.6	0.8	8.5	14.1	53.6	10.9	0.5	29.1	13.9
San Joaquin	6.0	62.7	7.5	2.3	13.6	0.8	19.5	30.5	73.5	5.6	1.1	12.4	23.4
San Luis Obispo	3.4	87.7	2.4	2.1	3.6	0.3	7.6	16.3	89.2	2.6	1.0	2.9	13.3
San Mateo	5.0	63.5	4.1	1.1	22.1	2.0	12.6	21.9	71.9	5.4	0.5	16.8	17.6
Santa Barbara	4.3	76.4	2.8	2.2	5.2	0.4	17.5	34.2	77.2	2.8	0.9	4.4	26.6
Santa Clara	4.7	57.6	3.4	1.3	27.5	0.7	14.5	24.0	68.9	3.8	0.6	17.5	21.0
Santa Cruz	4.4	78.9	1.5	2.1	4.7	0.4	17.2	26.8	83.9	1.1	0.8	3.7	20.4
Shasta	3.5	92.5	1.1	4.8	2.4	0.3	2.5	5.5	93.8	0.7	2.7	1.8	3.8
Sierra	2.4	96.6	0.3	3.1	0.6	0.3	1.7	6.0	95.7	0.2	2.2	0.4	5.5
Siskiyou	3.6	90.5	1.6	6.2	1.6	0.3	3.7	7.6	92.1	1.6	4.1	0.9	5.9
Solano	6.4	61.3	16.6	2.0	15.4	1.5	10.3	17.6	66.8	13.5	0.9	12.8	13.4
Sonoma	4.1	85.2	2.0	2.4	4.1	0.5	10.2	17.3	90.6	1.4	1.1	2.8	10.6
Stanislaus	5.4	73.9	3.2	2.5	5.5	0.8	19.9	31.7	80.2	1.7	1.1	5.2	21.8
Sutter	4.6	71.0	2.4	3.0	13.0	0.4	15.2	22.2	76.9	1.6	1.5	9.4	16.4
Tehama	3.4	88.0	0.9	3.8	1.2	0.2	9.5	15.8	91.9	0.5	1.9	0.7	10.3
Trinity	4.4	93.1	0.5	8.1	0.9	0.4	1.6	4.0	92.9	0.4	4.8	0.8	3.3
Tulare	4.6	62.0	2.0	2.5	4.0	0.3	34.0	50.8	65.7	1.5	1.3	4.3	38.8
Tuolumne	2.8	92.2	2.3	3.4	1.2	0.4	3.6	8.2	90.4	3.2	2.0	0.8	7.7
Ventura	3.9	73.3	2.4	1.8	6.5	0.5	19.7	33.4	79.1	2.3	0.7	5.2	26.4
Yolo	5.2	72.0	2.6	2.2	11.7	0.6	16.4	25.9	75.9	2.2	1.2	8.4	20.0
Yuba	5.9	75.7	4.0	5.2	8.9	0.5	12.0	17.4	78.2	4.2	2.9	8.4	11.6
COLORADO	2.8	85.2	4.4	1.9	2.8	0.2	8.5	17.1	88.2	4.0	0.8	1.8	12.9
Adams	3.5	80.3	3.5	2.1	3.8	0.3	13.6	28.2	86.7	3.3	0.9	2.6	18.6
Alamosa	4.2	74.6	1.3	3.8	1.3	0.3	22.9	41.4	82.4	0.5	0.9	0.9	38.6
Arapahoe	3.2	82.6	8.7	1.4	4.8	0.3	5.7	11.8	89.2	5.9	0.5	2.8	5.6
Archuleta	2.6	90.9	0.6	2.4	0.4	0.1	8.4	16.8	87.3	0.1	2.0	0.5	23.3
Baca	1.8	95.5	0.1	2.6	0.2	0.1	3.3	7.0	94.8	0.0	1.4	0.2	5.6
Bent	3.8	83.0	3.9	3.5	0.9	0.0	12.7	30.2	90.9	0.7	0.7	0.6	27.2
Boulder	2.2	90.5	1.2	1.2	3.7	0.2	5.5	10.5	93.3	0.9	0.6	2.4	6.7
Chaffee	1.7	92.5	1.7	1.9	0.6	0.1	4.9	8.6	95.4	1.6	0.9	0.3	9.5
Cheyenne	0.6	93.5	0.5	1.1	0.1	0.0	5.4	8.1	98.4	0.0	0.2	0.1	3.5

[1]Hispanic persons may be of any race.

STATE County	Under 5 years	5 to 17 years	18 to 24 years	25 to 34 years	35 to 44 years	45 to 54 years	55 to 64 years	65 to 74 years	75 years and over	Median age (years)	Percent Female
	28	29	30	31	32	33	34	35	36	37	38
CALIFORNIA—Cont'd											
Butte	5.7	18.3	13.6	11.4	13.4	13.2	8.6	7.5	8.3	35.8	51.0
Calaveras	4.4	18.4	5.5	7.7	14.7	16.9	14.2	10.7	7.5	44.6	50.4
Colusa	8.1	23.5	10.3	12.6	14.4	12.0	7.8	5.9	5.4	31.5	49.2
Contra Costa	7.0	19.6	7.7	13.3	17.3	15.0	8.9	5.8	5.5	36.4	51.2
Del Norte	5.5	19.5	8.0	14.4	17.7	13.7	8.5	6.7	5.8	36.4	44.8
El Dorado	5.7	20.4	6.8	10.0	17.8	17.1	9.8	7.0	5.4	39.4	50.1
Fresno	8.5	23.6	11.1	14.0	14.5	11.5	6.9	5.2	4.8	29.9	49.9
Glenn	7.5	23.2	8.7	12.1	14.7	12.1	8.6	6.8	6.2	33.7	49.4
Humboldt	5.6	17.6	12.4	12.7	14.8	15.7	8.8	6.3	6.1	36.3	50.6
Imperial	7.7	23.8	9.9	14.7	15.7	11.3	6.8	5.9	4.1	31.0	47.8
Inyo	5.4	19.0	5.8	8.3	15.1	16.2	11.1	10.0	9.1	42.8	51.2
Kern	8.4	23.5	10.2	14.1	15.7	11.6	7.1	5.2	4.2	30.6	48.7
Kings	8.1	20.9	11.8	17.9	17.1	10.8	6.1	4.1	3.3	30.2	42.6
Lake	5.3	18.8	6.0	9.2	14.4	15.3	11.5	10.5	9.0	42.7	50.6
Lassen	5.0	16.9	10.8	18.1	18.8	14.3	7.1	5.0	4.0	34.6	37.2
Los Angeles	7.7	20.3	10.3	16.6	15.9	12.1	7.3	5.2	4.6	32.0	50.6
Madera	7.7	22.0	9.9	13.7	15.4	12.5	7.9	6.2	4.8	32.7	52.1
Marin	5.4	14.9	5.5	12.9	18.0	18.4	11.3	6.8	6.7	41.3	50.4
Mariposa	4.4	17.2	6.9	9.4	15.6	16.1	13.1	9.8	7.4	42.9	48.8
Mendocino	6.0	19.6	8.1	11.2	14.4	16.9	10.2	6.9	6.6	38.9	50.3
Merced	8.9	25.6	10.3	13.4	14.4	10.9	7.0	5.3	4.2	29.0	50.2
Modoc	5.6	20.1	5.7	9.3	14.0	16.0	11.7	9.6	8.0	41.8	49.4
Mono	5.7	17.3	10.3	15.0	18.4	16.1	9.6	5.2	2.4	36.0	45.1
Monterey	7.8	20.6	10.9	15.9	15.4	12.3	7.1	5.3	4.7	31.7	48.2
Napa	6.1	18.1	8.5	12.5	15.2	14.8	9.5	7.0	8.4	38.3	50.1
Nevada	4.7	18.4	6.1	8.7	15.3	17.9	11.4	9.1	8.4	43.1	50.4
Orange	7.6	19.4	9.4	16.4	16.8	12.7	7.9	5.2	4.6	33.3	50.2
Placer	6.4	20.1	6.9	11.8	17.3	15.2	9.3	7.0	6.1	38.0	50.9
Plumas	4.5	18.2	6.0	8.0	14.6	17.3	13.5	10.2	7.6	44.2	50.0
Riverside	7.9	22.5	9.2	13.2	15.7	11.4	7.5	6.7	6.0	33.1	50.2
Sacramento	7.3	20.3	9.5	14.7	16.3	13.1	7.7	5.8	5.3	33.8	51.1
San Benito	8.8	23.4	8.8	14.6	16.9	12.4	6.9	4.5	3.6	31.4	49.4
San Bernardino	8.4	23.9	10.3	14.2	15.9	11.9	6.8	4.8	3.8	30.3	50.1
San Diego	7.1	18.7	11.3	15.8	16.3	12.5	7.3	5.7	5.5	33.2	49.7
San Francisco	4.1	10.5	9.1	23.2	17.2	13.9	8.4	6.9	6.7	36.5	49.2
San Joaquin	8.0	23.0	10.0	13.4	15.4	12.2	7.4	5.4	5.2	31.9	50.0
San Luis Obispo	5.0	16.6	13.6	11.4	15.6	14.7	8.6	7.3	7.1	37.3	48.6
San Mateo	6.4	16.5	7.9	15.9	17.4	14.5	9.0	6.3	6.1	36.8	50.6
Santa Barbara	6.5	18.4	13.3	13.9	15.1	12.3	7.8	6.3	6.4	33.4	50.0
Santa Clara	7.1	17.7	9.3	17.8	17.6	13.0	8.0	5.2	4.4	34.0	49.3
Santa Cruz	6.1	17.7	11.9	14.4	16.5	15.9	7.6	4.8	5.1	35.0	50.1
Shasta	5.9	20.2	8.2	10.3	15.0	14.7	10.5	7.9	7.3	38.9	51.3
Sierra	4.1	19.2	4.8	8.8	15.2	17.2	13.0	9.5	8.2	43.7	49.5
Siskiyou	5.1	18.9	6.7	8.3	14.4	16.8	11.6	9.5	8.6	43.0	50.9
Solano	7.3	21.1	9.2	14.2	17.1	14.0	7.6	5.1	4.4	33.9	49.6
Sonoma	6.0	18.4	8.8	12.7	16.5	16.1	8.8	6.0	6.7	37.5	50.8
Stanislaus	8.0	23.2	9.8	13.6	15.4	12.1	7.4	5.5	5.0	31.7	50.8
Sutter	7.3	21.7	9.2	13.2	15.0	12.5	8.8	6.8	5.6	34.1	50.5
Tehama	6.3	21.1	7.8	10.8	14.8	13.0	10.2	8.4	7.5	37.8	50.6
Trinity	4.2	18.6	5.1	7.9	14.9	18.4	13.7	10.3	6.9	44.6	49.0
Tulare	8.9	24.8	10.6	13.6	14.0	11.2	7.0	5.2	4.6	29.2	50.0
Tuolumne	4.5	16.2	7.6	10.4	15.0	16.3	11.5	10.2	8.3	42.9	47.3
Ventura	7.5	21.0	9.0	13.8	16.9	13.6	8.1	5.3	4.9	34.2	50.1
Yolo	6.5	18.7	18.3	14.0	14.2	12.0	6.9	4.8	4.6	29.5	51.1
Yuba	8.2	22.8	10.7	13.1	14.9	11.7	7.9	6.0	4.7	31.4	49.6
COLORADO	6.9	18.7	10.0	15.4	17.1	14.3	7.9	5.3	4.4	34.3	49.6
Adams	8.4	20.1	10.3	17.1	16.9	12.3	7.1	4.7	3.1	31.4	49.3
Alamosa	6.9	20.3	15.9	12.2	14.5	13.1	7.5	5.1	4.5	30.6	50.2
Arapahoe	6.9	19.8	8.6	15.5	17.6	15.2	7.8	4.6	3.9	34.5	50.7
Archuleta	5.4	20.0	6.3	9.5	16.6	18.2	12.2	8.1	3.8	40.8	49.3
Baca	5.9	18.6	5.9	9.0	13.7	13.6	10.9	10.6	11.8	42.9	50.3
Bent	5.9	17.8	9.3	13.4	15.8	13.3	8.5	8.2	7.7	37.3	43.7
Boulder	6.0	16.9	13.4	16.0	17.6	15.0	7.2	4.2	3.6	33.4	49.4
Chaffee	4.4	15.3	7.7	12.1	15.9	16.0	11.5	9.9	7.1	41.8	46.8
Cheyenne	6.4	22.4	7.1	9.2	17.0	13.8	7.5	7.4	9.2	37.9	49.8

STATE County	Under 5 years	5 to 17 years	18 to 24 years	25 to 34 years	35 to 44 years	45 to 54 years	55 to 64 years	65 to 74 years	75 years and over	Percent Female	2000	1990	1980	1990–2000	1980–1990
	Population and population characteristics, 1990										**Population—change, 1980–2000**				
	Age (percent)										**Total persons**			**Percent change**	
	39	40	41	42	43	44	45	46	47	48	49	50	51	52	53
CALIFORNIA—Cont'd															
Butte	6.8	16.8	13.8	14.5	13.9	8.7	8.4	10.1	7.2	51.0	203 171	182 120	143 851	11.6	26.6
Calaveras	6.5	18.3	5.1	12.6	16.1	11.8	11.9	11.6	6.1	50.4	40 554	31 998	20 710	26.7	54.5
Colusa	8.2	22.6	8.8	15.1	14.4	9.4	8.7	7.8	5.1	48.9	18 804	16 275	12 791	15.5	27.2
Contra Costa	7.6	17.6	9.0	17.5	17.6	11.8	8.1	6.6	4.3	51.0	948 816	803 731	656 331	18.1	22.5
Del Norte	7.4	19.6	9.2	18.9	14.3	9.5	8.2	8.0	4.9	45.7	27 507	23 460	18 217	17.3	28.8
El Dorado	7.4	19.0	6.8	16.2	19.0	10.8	8.9	7.7	4.1	50.0	156 299	125 995	85 812	24.1	46.8
Fresno	9.4	22.0	11.3	17.1	14.1	8.8	7.1	6.1	4.3	50.4	799 407	667 479	514 621	19.8	29.7
Glenn	8.4	22.1	8.5	14.9	14.2	9.5	8.4	8.0	6.0	50.1	26 453	24 798	21 350	6.7	16.1
Humboldt	7.2	18.5	11.1	16.4	17.0	9.6	7.9	7.2	5.1	50.3	126 518	119 118	108 525	6.2	9.8
Imperial	9.1	25.1	10.2	15.4	13.3	8.6	8.1	6.5	3.7	50.8	142 361	109 303	92 110	30.2	18.7
Inyo	6.5	17.7	5.7	13.3	15.9	11.3	11.0	10.7	7.8	51.0	17 945	18 281	17 895	-1.8	2.2
Kern	9.6	21.8	10.0	18.2	14.3	9.0	7.2	5.9	3.8	49.6	661 645	544 981	403 089	21.4	35.2
Kings	9.3	21.1	12.7	21.1	14.1	8.1	6.0	4.6	3.1	46.0	129 461	101 469	73 738	27.6	37.6
Lake	6.7	17.2	5.7	12.3	14.4	9.8	11.1	13.9	8.7	51.1	58 309	50 631	36 366	15.2	39.2
Lassen	6.6	18.1	11.5	19.8	16.6	9.2	7.8	6.5	3.8	41.6	33 828	27 598	21 661	22.6	27.4
Los Angeles	8.3	17.9	12.3	19.8	15.1	9.5	7.3	5.7	4.0	50.1	9 519 338	8 863 052	7 477 239	7.4	18.5
Madera	8.3	22.8	9.1	14.7	14.8	9.6	8.5	7.5	4.8	49.8	123 109	88 090	63 116	39.8	39.6
Marin	5.9	13.2	7.6	17.1	20.7	14.1	9.2	7.3	5.0	50.5	247 289	230 096	222 592	7.5	3.4
Mariposa	6.2	16.6	6.5	14.2	15.3	11.8	11.7	11.2	6.3	49.5	17 130	14 302	11 108	19.8	28.8
Mendocino	7.3	20.0	7.6	14.1	17.9	11.0	8.5	8.0	5.5	50.2	86 265	80 345	66 738	7.4	20.4
Merced	10.2	23.8	10.8	17.4	13.2	8.3	7.0	5.7	3.5	49.5	210 554	178 403	134 558	18.0	32.6
Modoc	6.5	20.6	6.3	13.1	15.3	10.9	10.4	10.3	6.6	49.0	9 449	9 678	8 610	-2.4	12.4
Mono	8.2	16.3	9.5	22.4	19.7	10.4	7.3	4.1	2.1	45.6	12 853	9 956	8 577	29.1	16.1
Monterey	8.8	18.7	13.1	19.5	14.7	8.4	7.0	5.8	4.0	48.1	401 762	355 660	290 444	13.0	22.5
Napa	6.7	16.5	9.2	15.2	16.0	11.0	8.8	9.0	7.5	50.4	124 279	110 765	99 199	12.2	11.7
Nevada	6.2	18.0	5.6	12.3	18.5	10.9	10.4	11.5	6.6	50.8	92 033	78 510	51 645	17.2	52.0
Orange	7.7	16.8	12.5	20.1	15.6	10.6	7.5	5.4	3.8	49.6	2 846 289	2 410 668	1 932 921	18.1	24.7
Placer	7.3	18.9	7.7	15.8	18.2	11.7	8.4	7.2	4.8	50.5	248 399	172 796	117 247	43.8	47.4
Plumas	6.4	19.1	5.0	12.5	16.7	11.4	11.9	11.0	5.9	50.3	20 824	19 739	17 340	5.5	13.8
Riverside	9.0	19.5	9.8	18.1	14.1	8.6	7.6	7.9	5.3	50.0	1 545 387	1 170 413	663 199	32.0	76.5
Sacramento	8.1	18.3	10.3	19.4	15.9	9.7	7.8	6.5	4.1	51.1	1 223 499	1 066 789	783 381	14.7	32.9
San Benito	8.7	22.3	10.0	17.1	15.3	9.3	7.4	6.0	3.9	49.5	53 234	36 697	25 005	45.1	46.8
San Bernardino	9.8	21.2	10.9	19.2	15.0	8.6	6.5	5.3	3.5	49.9	1 709 434	1 418 380	895 016	20.5	58.5
San Diego	7.8	16.6	13.5	20.0	15.2	8.8	7.1	6.5	4.4	49.0	2 813 833	2 498 016	1 861 846	12.6	34.2
San Francisco	4.9	11.2	10.3	21.9	17.9	10.3	8.8	7.9	6.6	49.9	776 733	723 959	678 974	7.3	6.6
San Joaquin	8.8	20.8	10.4	17.3	14.9	9.3	7.4	6.5	4.6	49.4	563 598	480 628	347 342	17.3	38.4
San Luis Obispo	6.4	15.5	14.5	16.9	15.8	8.8	7.9	8.4	5.7	48.4	246 681	217 162	155 435	13.6	39.7
San Mateo	6.9	15.0	9.5	18.9	17.0	11.5	8.9	7.3	5.0	50.7	707 161	649 623	587 329	8.9	10.6
Santa Barbara	7.3	15.9	14.6	18.2	14.5	9.3	7.8	6.9	5.4	49.8	399 347	369 608	298 694	8.0	23.7
Santa Clara	7.5	16.5	11.4	21.2	16.3	10.9	7.5	5.3	3.4	49.3	1 682 585	1 497 577	1 295 071	12.4	15.6
Santa Cruz	7.2	16.6	12.2	17.7	18.8	9.7	6.6	6.1	5.2	50.3	255 602	229 734	188 141	11.3	22.1
Shasta	7.7	19.8	8.1	14.7	15.6	11.0	9.1	8.6	5.5	51.0	163 256	147 036	115 613	11.0	27.2
Sierra	6.9	19.3	4.5	12.8	17.1	12.2	9.7	10.2	7.2	49.8	3 555	3 318	3 073	7.1	8.0
Siskiyou	6.7	20.0	6.7	12.7	16.4	10.7	10.3	9.9	6.6	50.8	44 301	43 531	39 732	1.8	9.6
Solano	8.7	20.0	10.3	19.4	17.2	9.5	6.6	5.2	3.0	48.8	394 542	339 469	235 203	16.2	44.3
Sonoma	7.3	17.4	8.9	16.8	18.4	10.4	7.4	7.5	5.9	51.0	458 614	388 222	299 681	18.1	29.5
Stanislaus	9.1	21.5	9.8	17.6	14.7	9.3	7.2	6.3	4.5	50.8	446 997	370 522	265 900	20.6	39.3
Sutter	8.4	20.1	9.4	16.2	14.2	10.7	9.0	7.0	4.8	50.5	78 930	64 409	52 246	22.5	23.3
Tehama	7.3	19.9	7.4	14.0	13.7	10.7	10.2	10.0	6.8	50.0	56 039	49 625	38 888	12.9	27.6
Trinity	6.8	19.6	5.8	12.7	17.9	11.0	11.2	9.8	5.2	49.0	13 022	13 063	11 858	-0.3	10.2
Tulare	9.3	23.7	10.2	16.1	13.6	9.0	7.2	6.2	4.6	50.1	368 021	311 932	245 738	18.0	26.9
Tuolumne	5.7	16.7	7.8	16.0	16.5	10.2	10.6	10.6	5.9	47.0	54 501	48 456	33 928	12.5	42.8
Ventura	8.0	19.3	10.7	18.1	16.4	10.7	7.4	5.5	3.9	49.6	753 197	669 016	529 174	12.6	26.4
Yolo	7.3	16.8	18.8	17.7	14.3	8.9	6.8	5.6	4.0	50.4	168 660	141 212	113 374	19.4	24.6
Yuba	10.4	21.3	10.7	17.3	13.0	8.8	7.9	6.5	4.0	50.0	60 219	58 234	49 733	3.4	17.1
COLORADO	7.7	18.5	10.2	18.6	17.2	10.2	7.6	5.9	4.1	50.5	4 301 261	3 294 473	2 889 735	30.6	14.0
Adams	8.7	20.4	9.9	19.7	16.0	9.9	7.8	4.9	2.7	50.4	363 857	265 038	245 944	37.3	7.8
Alamosa	8.6	20.6	16.0	15.8	14.3	8.9	6.6	4.9	4.4	50.4	14 966	13 617	11 799	9.9	15.4
Arapahoe	7.9	19.3	8.8	19.4	19.1	11.1	6.9	4.8	2.6	51.2	487 967	391 572	293 300	24.6	33.5
Archuleta	8.3	21.3	5.5	14.2	17.1	10.6	11.4	8.2	3.4	49.0	9 898	5 345	3 664	85.2	45.9
Baca	6.6	18.7	5.7	12.7	14.3	10.4	11.0	11.6	9.0	50.5	4 517	4 556	5 419	-0.9	-15.9
Bent	6.7	19.6	5.9	11.8	14.8	10.5	11.8	10.8	8.0	48.0	5 998	5 048	5 945	18.8	-15.1
Boulder	7.0	16.0	14.5	19.6	18.7	10.2	6.2	4.3	3.3	49.9	291 288	225 339	189 625	29.3	18.8
Chaffee	5.5	17.3	8.4	15.3	15.7	10.6	10.7	9.7	6.8	46.4	16 242	12 684	13 227	28.1	-4.1
Cheyenne	9.0	22.5	5.8	17.2	13.7	8.1	7.9	7.8	7.9	49.1	2 231	2 397	2 153	-6.9	11.3

Table B. States and Counties

STATE County	Total population	Total in house-holds	House-holder	Spouse	Child Total	Child Own child under 18 years	Other relatives Total	Other relatives Under 18 years	Nonrelatives Total	Nonrelatives Unmarried partner	Total in group quarters	Institutionalized Correctional institutions	Institutionalized Nursing homes	Institutionalized Other institutions	Noninstitutionalized College dormitories	Noninstitutionalized Military quarters	Noninstitutionalized Other
	54	55	56	57	58	59	60	61	62	63	64	65	66	67	68	69	70
CALIFORNIA—Cont'd																	
Butte	203 171	97.1	39.2	18.3	26.5	21.4	4.3	1.8	8.9	2.5	2.9	0.3	0.5	0.0	1.3	0.0	0.8
Calaveras	40 554	99.0	40.6	23.9	25.3	20.0	4.3	1.9	4.8	2.2	1.0	0.5	0.2	0.1	0.0	0.0	0.2
Colusa	18 804	97.6	32.4	19.3	35.0	27.8	6.8	2.4	4.0	1.6	2.4	0.4	0.5	0.6	0.0	0.0	0.9
Contra Costa	948 816	98.8	36.3	19.8	30.7	23.8	6.4	2.2	5.7	2.0	1.2	0.2	0.3	0.1	0.2	0.0	0.5
Del Norte	27 507	86.1	33.3	16.7	26.4	21.9	4.5	1.9	5.2	2.3	13.9	12.9	0.3	0.2	0.0	0.0	0.5
El Dorado	156 299	99.3	37.7	22.7	29.4	23.9	4.0	1.5	5.6	2.2	0.7	0.2	0.2	0.0	0.0	0.0	0.3
Fresno	799 407	97.8	31.6	16.6	35.6	27.9	8.2	3.3	5.8	2.0	2.2	0.9	0.4	0.1	0.2	0.0	0.6
Glenn	26 453	98.5	34.7	19.6	34.1	27.7	5.6	2.2	4.6	2.2	1.5	0.8	0.3	0.1	0.0	0.0	0.3
Humboldt	126 518	96.8	40.5	17.4	25.8	20.6	4.0	1.7	9.1	3.5	3.2	0.4	0.4	0.0	1.2	0.0	1.1
Imperial	142 361	92.2	27.7	16.0	35.5	26.3	9.7	4.5	3.4	1.4	7.8	6.9	0.2	0.2	0.0	0.0	0.4
Inyo	17 945	99.1	42.9	21.4	26.6	22.4	3.9	1.6	4.3	2.2	0.9	0.0	0.8	0.0	0.0	0.0	0.1
Kern	661 645	95.5	31.5	17.2	34.6	28.0	7.2	3.1	4.9	2.0	4.5	3.6	0.3	0.1	0.0	0.1	0.4
Kings	129 461	84.5	26.6	15.4	31.7	25.7	6.2	2.6	4.5	1.7	15.5	14.1	0.3	0.0	0.0	0.8	0.4
Lake	58 309	98.1	41.1	19.6	25.8	20.8	5.1	2.4	6.5	2.9	1.9	0.5	0.4	0.1	0.0	0.0	0.9
Lassen	33 828	73.7	28.5	15.9	23.2	19.8	2.6	1.3	3.6	1.7	26.3	25.5	0.3	0.0	0.1	0.0	0.4
Los Angeles	9 519 338	98.2	32.9	15.7	32.3	23.9	10.6	3.4	6.7	2.0	1.8	0.3	0.4	0.1	0.4	0.0	0.6
Madera	123 109	93.4	29.4	17.9	32.3	25.4	8.3	3.2	5.6	1.8	6.6	5.8	0.3	0.1	0.0	0.0	0.4
Marin	247 289	95.4	40.7	19.7	23.5	18.9	3.4	0.8	8.0	2.5	4.6	2.6	0.7	0.1	0.2	0.0	1.0
Mariposa	17 130	91.7	38.6	21.5	23.5	19.3	3.8	1.6	4.2	2.1	8.3	0.8	0.2	0.2	0.0	0.0	7.2
Mendocino	86 265	97.5	38.6	18.8	27.6	22.2	5.4	2.2	7.2	3.0	2.5	0.5	0.4	0.1	0.0	0.0	1.6
Merced	210 554	98.6	30.3	17.5	38.0	30.3	8.0	3.2	4.8	2.0	1.4	0.3	0.2	0.0	0.0	0.0	0.8
Modoc	9 449	95.6	40.0	21.9	26.1	22.4	3.5	1.7	4.1	1.9	4.4	1.7	0.8	0.1	0.0	0.0	1.8
Mono	12 853	97.2	40.0	20.2	24.2	21.1	4.0	1.4	8.8	2.8	2.8	0.3	0.0	0.0	0.0	0.8	1.7
Monterey	401 762	94.8	30.2	16.9	31.1	24.0	10.0	3.5	6.6	1.7	5.2	3.0	0.2	0.1	0.4	0.6	0.9
Napa	124 279	95.8	36.5	19.4	27.5	21.4	6.3	1.9	6.0	2.0	4.2	0.2	0.5	1.8	0.7	0.0	1.0
Nevada	92 033	99.1	40.1	23.1	26.2	21.0	3.5	1.4	6.1	2.2	0.9	0.2	0.4	0.2	0.0	0.0	0.2
Orange	2 846 289	98.5	32.9	18.4	31.1	23.6	8.9	2.6	7.3	1.6	1.5	0.2	0.3	0.1	0.3	0.0	0.6
Placer	248 399	98.8	37.6	22.3	30.1	24.6	3.7	1.3	5.1	2.0	1.2	0.1	0.5	0.1	0.1	0.0	0.4
Plumas	20 824	99.1	43.2	24.0	24.7	20.8	2.7	1.3	4.5	2.1	0.9	0.2	0.6	0.0	0.0	0.0	0.1
Riverside	1 545 387	97.8	32.8	18.5	33.2	26.4	7.8	3.1	5.5	2.0	2.2	1.1	0.3	0.1	0.2	0.0	0.6
Sacramento	1 223 499	97.9	37.1	17.2	30.8	24.3	6.4	2.4	6.4	2.5	2.1	0.5	0.4	0.1	0.1	0.0	0.9
San Benito	53 234	99.0	29.8	19.6	36.0	28.1	8.2	3.2	5.3	1.7	1.0	0.2	0.2	0.0	0.0	0.0	0.5
San Bernardino	1 709 434	97.4	30.9	17.2	35.4	27.9	8.5	3.5	5.3	1.9	2.6	1.0	0.3	0.3	0.1	0.4	0.6
San Diego	2 813 833	96.6	35.3	17.9	29.3	22.7	6.8	2.3	7.2	2.1	3.4	0.4	0.3	0.1	0.5	1.5	0.7
San Francisco	776 733	97.5	42.4	13.4	19.0	12.0	9.0	2.0	13.6	3.2	2.5	0.2	0.2	0.1	0.5	0.0	1.5
San Joaquin	563 598	96.7	32.2	17.5	34.1	26.8	7.6	3.1	5.2	2.0	3.3	1.3	0.5	0.2	0.3	0.0	1.0
San Luis Obispo	246 681	93.7	37.6	19.0	24.6	19.5	4.1	1.4	8.4	2.0	6.3	3.0	0.4	0.8	1.5	0.0	0.6
San Mateo	707 161	98.5	35.9	19.1	27.7	20.1	8.6	2.3	7.2	1.9	1.5	0.3	0.5	0.1	0.1	0.0	0.5
Santa Barbara	399 347	95.8	34.2	17.6	27.7	21.8	6.9	2.4	9.4	1.8	4.2	1.0	0.4	0.1	1.7	0.1	0.8
Santa Clara	1 682 585	98.2	33.6	18.5	28.9	21.5	9.4	2.6	7.9	1.8	1.8	0.3	0.3	0.1	0.6	0.0	0.5
Santa Cruz	255 602	96.5	35.7	17.1	27.0	21.0	6.2	2.0	10.6	2.8	3.5	0.3	0.5	0.1	1.8	0.0	0.9
Shasta	163 256	97.9	38.9	20.6	28.5	23.1	4.4	1.9	5.6	2.3	2.1	0.4	0.4	0.2	0.4	0.0	0.7
Sierra	3 555	99.0	42.8	22.7	25.9	21.5	2.3	1.0	5.3	2.6	1.0	0.1	0.8	0.0	0.0	0.0	0.1
Siskiyou	44 301	98.4	41.9	21.7	26.4	21.0	3.6	1.6	4.9	2.2	1.6	0.4	0.3	0.1	0.2	0.0	0.5
Solano	394 542	96.0	33.1	18.4	32.1	24.7	7.1	2.8	5.3	2.0	4.0	2.5	0.5	0.1	0.0	0.5	0.5
Sonoma	458 614	97.6	37.6	18.9	27.7	21.8	5.4	1.7	7.9	2.7	2.4	0.3	0.4	0.1	0.3	0.1	1.3
Stanislaus	446 997	98.3	32.5	18.2	34.9	27.2	7.6	3.0	5.2	2.0	1.7	0.2	0.5	0.1	0.1	0.0	0.8
Sutter	78 930	98.2	34.2	19.5	32.8	25.7	6.9	2.6	4.7	1.8	1.8	0.6	0.7	0.1	0.0	0.0	0.4
Tehama	56 039	98.2	37.5	20.5	29.7	24.1	5.2	2.3	5.3	2.3	1.8	0.5	0.5	0.1	0.0	0.0	0.7
Trinity	13 022	98.1	42.9	21.6	25.0	20.6	3.4	1.5	5.2	2.8	1.9	1.3	0.0	0.2	0.0	0.0	0.4
Tulare	368 021	98.4	30.0	17.4	37.1	29.2	8.7	3.6	5.2	1.9	1.6	0.3	0.4	0.3	0.0	0.0	0.6
Tuolumne	54 501	91.1	38.5	21.0	23.3	18.5	3.4	1.5	4.9	2.3	8.9	7.8	0.3	0.1	0.2	0.0	0.5
Ventura	753 197	98.2	32.3	19.2	32.7	24.9	7.8	2.7	6.2	1.6	1.8	0.3	0.3	0.0	0.2	0.2	0.8
Yolo	168 660	95.5	35.2	16.8	28.0	22.6	5.3	1.9	10.3	2.0	4.5	0.2	0.5	0.1	2.9	0.0	0.8
Yuba	60 219	97.8	34.1	18.1	33.3	27.1	6.2	2.8	6.1	2.2	2.2	0.6	0.1	0.1	0.0	0.9	0.5
COLORADO	4 301 261	97.6	38.6	20.0	28.3	23.4	4.4	1.6	6.4	2.1	2.4	0.7	0.4	0.1	0.5	0.2	0.4
Adams	363 857	99.1	35.2	19.0	31.5	25.1	7.1	2.7	6.4	2.3	0.9	0.4	0.4	0.0	0.0	0.0	0.2
Alamosa	14 966	93.4	36.5	18.5	30.3	25.2	3.4	1.5	4.7	1.8	6.6	0.5	0.8	0.0	4.8	0.0	0.6
Arapahoe	487 967	99.0	39.1	20.0	29.9	24.7	4.4	1.4	5.5	2.1	1.0	0.3	0.4	0.1	0.0	0.0	0.2
Archuleta	9 898	99.2	40.2	24.1	27.4	23.5	3.3	1.5	4.2	2.0	0.8	0.2	0.4	0.0	0.0	0.0	0.2
Baca	4 517	98.1	42.2	24.0	27.3	23.1	2.1	0.9	2.5	1.2	1.9	0.0	1.7	0.0	0.0	0.0	0.0
Bent	5 998	84.6	33.4	17.9	26.2	21.3	3.9	2.0	3.2	1.4	15.4	11.6	3.6	0.0	0.0	0.0	0.3
Boulder	291 288	97.1	39.4	19.3	25.5	21.6	3.2	1.0	9.8	2.4	2.9	0.2	0.4	0.0	2.1	0.0	0.2
Chaffee	16 242	91.6	40.5	23.0	22.2	18.4	2.4	1.0	3.6	1.7	8.4	7.8	0.5	0.0	0.0	0.0	0.1
Cheyenne	2 231	98.7	39.4	23.4	32.3	27.8	1.7	0.6	1.9	0.8	1.3	0.0	1.3	0.0	0.0	0.0	0.0

Table B. States and Counties

STATE County	Households by type, 2000												Households, 1990		
	Total households	Family households		Married couple		Female householder[1]		Nonfamily households	Householder living alone		Average household size	Average family size	Total households	Female householder[1]	Householder living alone
		Total	With own children under 18 years	Total	With own children under 18 years	Total	With own children under 18 years	Total	Total	65 years and over					
	71	72	73	74	75	76	77	78	79	80	81	82	83	84	85
CALIFORNIA—Cont'd															
Butte	79 566	62.1	28.4	46.7	10.8	11.2	7.1	37.9	27.2	11.1	2.48	3.02	71 665	9.7	25.4
Calaveras	16 469	71.3	26.7	58.9	19.3	8.6	5.2	28.7	23.3	10.1	2.44	2.85	12 649	7.1	21.2
Colusa	6 097	75.1	41.4	59.6	32.3	9.6	6.0	24.9	21.5	10.1	3.01	3.51	5 612	9.3	22.5
Contra Costa	344 129	70.4	35.4	54.5	26.7	11.5	6.5	29.6	22.9	8.0	2.72	3.23	300 288	10.8	22.3
Del Norte	9 170	68.6	33.5	50.0	20.8	13.6	9.4	31.4	25.3	10.1	2.58	3.08	7 987	10.8	23.0
El Dorado	58 939	73.0	34.2	60.1	26.0	8.9	5.7	27.0	20.1	7.3	2.63	3.04	46 845	7.8	18.3
Fresno	252 940	73.8	41.2	52.5	28.2	15.2	9.6	26.2	20.6	7.8	3.09	3.59	220 933	13.9	21.0
Glenn	9 172	73.4	38.1	56.7	27.5	10.9	7.2	26.6	22.0	10.7	2.84	3.33	8 821	10.0	23.2
Humboldt	51 238	59.8	28.5	43.1	17.6	11.8	7.7	40.2	28.9	9.2	2.39	2.95	46 420	10.6	26.2
Imperial	39 384	79.9	46.7	57.7	33.4	17.1	10.6	20.1	17.1	8.1	3.33	3.77	32 842	15.0	18.0
Inyo	7 703	64.1	27.9	49.8	18.4	9.9	6.7	35.9	31.4	13.6	2.31	2.88	7 565	8.7	29.0
Kern	208 652	75.0	42.2	54.6	29.1	14.5	9.7	25.0	20.3	7.8	3.03	3.50	181 480	12.3	20.3
Kings	34 418	78.4	46.4	58.0	32.9	14.3	9.8	21.6	17.0	6.8	3.18	3.56	29 082	12.9	17.4
Lake	23 974	64.1	26.6	47.7	16.2	11.3	7.3	35.9	29.0	13.4	2.39	2.92	20 805	9.5	26.3
Lassen	9 625	70.4	35.9	55.8	25.5	10.3	7.3	29.6	24.5	9.2	2.59	3.08	8 543	9.5	21.3
Los Angeles	3 133 774	68.2	36.8	47.6	25.9	14.7	8.2	31.8	24.6	7.1	2.98	3.61	2 989 552	13.1	25.0
Madera	36 155	79.1	40.2	60.9	29.4	12.2	7.5	20.9	16.5	7.7	3.18	3.52	28 370	10.9	17.0
Marin	100 650	60.3	27.5	48.4	20.9	8.5	4.9	39.7	29.8	9.6	2.34	2.90	95 006	8.5	28.4
Mariposa	6 613	67.9	25.6	55.8	18.6	8.0	4.6	32.1	26.5	11.2	2.37	2.86	5 604	7.1	23.9
Mendocino	33 266	65.7	31.4	48.9	20.6	11.7	7.7	34.3	27.0	10.4	2.53	3.04	30 419	10.7	24.6
Merced	63 815	78.0	45.4	57.8	32.5	14.1	9.2	22.0	17.7	7.4	3.25	3.69	55 331	12.5	17.7
Modoc	3 784	67.4	29.1	54.6	20.5	8.8	6.3	32.6	28.1	12.7	2.39	2.91	3 711	8.0	25.1
Mono	5 137	61.2	28.7	50.6	21.8	6.5	4.4	38.8	26.6	4.3	2.43	2.98	3 961	6.1	25.0
Monterey	121 236	72.5	39.1	56.0	29.6	11.6	6.9	27.5	21.2	8.2	3.14	3.65	112 965	10.4	20.4
Napa	45 402	67.6	31.4	53.2	23.3	9.9	5.7	32.4	25.8	11.6	2.62	3.16	41 312	9.2	24.7
Nevada	36 894	70.3	28.7	57.6	20.9	8.8	5.4	29.7	22.8	9.8	2.47	2.88	30 758	7.6	20.8
Orange	935 287	71.4	37.0	55.9	29.1	10.7	5.7	28.6	21.1	7.2	3.00	3.48	827 066	9.7	20.7
Placer	93 382	72.5	35.0	59.4	27.2	9.2	5.7	27.5	21.3	8.1	2.63	3.06	64 101	8.7	19.5
Plumas	9 000	67.2	26.4	55.4	18.2	8.0	5.8	32.8	27.5	10.1	2.29	2.77	8 125	8.1	24.1
Riverside	506 218	73.6	38.9	56.5	28.6	12.0	7.4	26.4	20.7	9.3	2.98	3.47	402 067	9.6	20.6
Sacramento	453 602	65.6	33.7	46.4	22.2	14.1	8.7	34.4	26.7	8.0	2.64	3.24	394 530	13.0	25.3
San Benito	15 885	81.2	46.3	65.7	37.3	10.5	6.2	18.8	14.1	5.4	3.32	3.64	11 422	9.8	16.0
San Bernardino	528 594	76.5	43.7	55.8	31.0	14.8	9.3	23.5	18.4	6.6	3.15	3.58	464 737	12.1	19.0
San Diego	994 677	66.7	33.9	50.7	24.8	11.6	6.8	33.3	24.2	7.9	2.73	3.29	887 403	10.8	22.9
San Francisco	329 700	44.0	16.6	31.6	12.2	8.9	3.4	56.0	38.6	9.8	2.30	3.22	305 584	9.9	39.3
San Joaquin	181 629	74.2	40.5	54.3	28.5	14.0	8.8	25.8	20.7	8.4	3.00	3.48	158 156	12.7	20.9
San Luis Obispo	92 739	63.2	28.2	50.4	20.7	9.1	5.5	36.8	26.0	10.3	2.49	3.01	80 281	8.5	23.8
San Mateo	254 103	67.4	31.1	53.0	24.6	10.1	4.7	32.6	24.6	8.4	2.74	3.29	241 914	9.8	25.1
Santa Barbara	136 622	65.5	32.4	51.4	24.5	10.0	5.7	34.5	24.3	9.4	2.80	3.33	129 802	9.3	23.0
Santa Clara	565 863	69.9	34.9	54.9	27.8	10.0	5.1	30.1	21.4	5.9	2.92	3.41	520 180	10.3	21.7
Santa Cruz	91 139	62.7	31.9	48.0	23.2	10.2	6.1	37.3	25.1	8.2	2.71	3.25	83 566	9.6	24.1
Shasta	63 426	69.4	31.7	53.0	21.1	11.9	7.7	30.6	24.7	10.2	2.52	2.98	55 966	11.0	22.3
Sierra	1 520	64.9	27.6	53.1	19.5	7.9	5.6	35.1	29.0	11.5	2.32	2.83	1 336	5.7	26.3
Siskiyou	18 556	65.9	27.6	51.7	18.3	10.1	6.8	34.1	28.6	12.8	2.35	2.87	17 306	9.6	25.7
Solano	130 403	74.7	39.9	55.7	28.5	13.8	8.5	25.3	19.6	6.5	2.90	3.33	113 429	11.5	18.5
Sonoma	172 403	65.2	31.9	50.3	23.3	10.4	6.1	34.8	25.7	10.0	2.60	3.12	149 011	9.8	24.6
Stanislaus	145 146	75.5	41.2	56.0	29.6	13.7	8.4	24.5	19.4	7.9	3.03	3.47	125 375	11.5	19.9
Sutter	27 033	73.8	37.9	57.0	27.6	11.7	7.4	26.2	21.2	8.6	2.87	3.35	23 111	10.9	21.6
Tehama	21 013	70.9	32.9	54.6	22.5	11.6	7.3	29.1	24.0	11.5	2.62	3.08	18 704	9.9	22.3
Trinity	5 587	64.9	25.4	50.5	15.9	10.1	6.9	35.1	29.5	11.1	2.29	2.80	5 156	8.4	24.6
Tulare	110 385	78.9	44.9	58.1	31.8	14.5	9.4	21.1	17.1	7.7	3.28	3.67	97 861	12.8	18.1
Tuolumne	21 004	67.8	26.1	54.4	17.7	9.6	6.0	32.2	26.0	11.7	2.36	2.82	17 959	8.5	22.5
Ventura	243 234	75.2	39.7	59.5	31.0	10.9	6.2	24.8	18.9	7.4	3.04	3.46	217 298	9.8	17.5
Yolo	59 375	63.1	33.6	47.6	24.4	11.1	6.9	36.9	23.3	7.3	2.71	3.25	50 972	10.2	23.1
Yuba	20 535	72.1	38.1	53.2	26.1	13.3	8.6	27.9	21.7	8.2	2.87	3.34	19 776	12.8	20.6
COLORADO	1 658 238	65.4	32.8	51.8	24.4	9.6	6.2	34.6	26.3	7.0	2.53	3.09	1 282 489	9.7	26.6
Adams	128 156	71.9	37.8	53.8	27.1	12.1	7.5	28.1	21.2	5.5	2.81	3.27	96 353	12.2	21.7
Alamosa	5 467	66.8	35.3	50.5	24.5	11.7	7.9	33.2	27.3	8.7	2.56	3.14	4 721	12.3	24.7
Arapahoe	190 909	65.9	34.9	51.2	25.8	10.6	7.0	34.1	27.0	5.9	2.53	3.11	154 710	10.1	26.3
Archuleta	3 980	72.2	31.6	59.8	23.1	8.2	5.9	27.8	22.1	6.0	2.47	2.89	2 010	8.0	19.8
Baca	1 905	66.6	28.4	56.8	22.8	7.5	4.2	33.4	30.4	15.7	2.33	2.90	1 872	5.0	28.4
Bent	2 003	69.3	32.5	53.5	22.2	11.4	7.8	30.7	27.2	12.2	2.53	3.07	1 865	8.7	28.6
Boulder	114 680	60.0	30.7	48.9	23.7	7.7	5.1	40.0	26.3	5.5	2.47	3.03	88 402	7.9	26.3
Chaffee	6 584	66.3	25.2	56.7	19.1	6.8	4.4	33.7	28.4	11.2	2.26	2.77	4 848	7.2	27.5
Cheyenne	880	68.5	34.1	59.3	28.9	5.7	3.0	31.5	29.0	12.4	2.50	3.12	904	5.1	29.0

[1] No spouse present.

Table B. States and Counties

STATE County	Percent change of households, 1990–2000	Total housing units	Occupied housing units (percent)	Total	For seasonal, recreational, or occasional use	Homeowner vacancy rate (percent)	Rental vacancy rate (percent)	Total	Percent owner-occupied housing units	Percent renter-occupied housing units	Average household size of owner-occupied units	Average household size of renter-occupied units
	86	87	88	89	90	91	92	93	94	95	96	97
CALIFORNIA—Cont'd												
Butte	11.0	85 523	93.0	7.0	1.6	2.1	5.2	79 566	60.7	39.3	2.48	2.48
Calaveras	30.2	22 946	71.8	28.2	23.7	2.1	6.2	16 469	78.7	21.3	2.42	2.51
Colusa	8.6	6 774	90.0	10.0	4.6	2.3	3.0	6 097	63.2	36.8	2.94	3.13
Contra Costa	14.6	354 577	97.1	2.9	0.5	0.8	2.7	344 129	69.3	30.7	2.78	2.59
Del Norte	14.8	10 434	87.9	12.1	3.2	3.0	10.6	9 170	63.8	36.2	2.53	2.52
El Dorado	25.8	71 278	82.7	17.3	13.5	1.2	5.8	58 939	74.7	25.3	2.67	2.52
Fresno	14.5	270 767	93.4	6.6	1.3	1.6	5.5	252 940	56.5	43.5	3.02	3.18
Glenn	4.0	9 982	91.9	8.1	1.4	1.5	8.2	9 172	63.8	36.2	2.76	2.99
Humboldt	10.4	55 912	91.6	8.4	3.1	1.7	4.7	51 238	57.6	42.4	2.45	2.30
Imperial	19.9	43 891	89.7	10.3	4.7	1.4	4.9	39 384	58.3	41.7	3.36	3.30
Inyo	1.8	9 042	85.2	14.8	6.1	1.8	6.9	7 703	65.9	34.1	2.31	2.31
Kern	15.0	231 564	90.1	9.9	2.5	2.6	8.2	208 652	62.1	37.9	3.02	3.04
Kings	18.3	36 563	94.1	5.9	0.3	1.8	5.6	34 418	55.9	44.1	3.14	3.22
Lake	15.2	32 528	73.7	26.3	16.8	4.1	10.3	23 974	70.6	29.4	2.30	2.60
Lassen	12.7	12 000	80.2	19.8	8.5	4.1	13.4	9 625	68.3	31.7	2.60	2.56
Los Angeles	4.8	3 270 909	95.8	4.2	0.4	1.6	3.3	3 133 774	47.9	52.1	3.13	2.85
Madera	27.4	40 387	89.5	10.5	4.3	1.7	4.5	36 155	66.2	33.8	3.01	3.52
Marin	5.9	104 990	95.9	4.1	1.8	0.7	2.2	100 650	63.6	36.4	2.42	2.21
Mariposa	18.0	8 826	74.9	25.1	16.4	2.4	7.7	6 613	69.8	30.2	2.36	2.40
Mendocino	9.4	36 937	90.1	9.9	5.4	1.4	3.3	33 266	61.3	38.7	2.49	2.60
Merced	15.3	68 373	93.3	6.7	1.2	1.4	4.2	63 815	58.7	41.3	3.14	3.42
Modoc	2.0	4 807	78.7	21.3	4.8	5.1	9.3	3 784	70.7	29.3	2.33	2.54
Mono	29.7	11 757	43.7	56.3	49.1	2.1	20.9	5 137	60.0	40.0	2.39	2.50
Monterey	7.3	131 708	92.0	8.0	3.0	1.4	2.9	121 236	54.6	45.4	3.10	3.18
Napa	9.9	48 554	93.5	6.5	3.2	1.3	2.8	45 402	65.1	34.9	2.58	2.71
Nevada	19.9	44 282	83.3	16.7	13.4	1.3	3.1	36 894	75.8	24.2	2.49	2.41
Orange	13.1	969 484	96.5	3.5	0.9	0.9	3.0	935 287	61.4	38.6	2.96	3.05
Placer	45.7	107 302	87.0	13.0	9.2	1.2	6.4	93 382	73.2	26.8	2.71	2.42
Plumas	10.8	13 386	67.2	32.8	25.0	2.9	9.9	9 000	70.0	30.0	2.30	2.27
Riverside	25.9	584 674	86.6	13.4	6.5	2.5	7.2	506 218	68.9	31.1	3.00	2.96
Sacramento	15.0	474 814	95.5	4.5	0.3	1.4	4.8	453 602	58.2	41.8	2.71	2.54
San Benito	39.1	16 499	96.3	3.7	0.8	1.0	2.7	15 885	68.2	31.8	3.26	3.44
San Bernardino	13.7	601 369	87.9	12.1	5.3	3.1	7.3	528 594	64.5	35.5	3.18	3.08
San Diego	12.1	1 040 149	95.6	4.4	1.4	1.0	3.1	994 677	55.4	44.6	2.78	2.68
San Francisco	7.9	346 527	95.1	4.9	1.1	0.8	2.5	329 700	35.0	65.0	2.73	2.06
San Joaquin	14.8	189 160	96.0	4.0	0.3	1.2	3.8	181 629	60.4	39.6	2.96	3.06
San Luis Obispo	15.5	102 275	90.7	9.3	6.0	1.1	3.2	92 739	61.5	38.5	2.53	2.44
San Mateo	5.0	260 576	97.5	2.5	0.6	0.5	1.8	254 103	61.4	38.6	2.83	2.59
Santa Barbara	5.3	142 901	95.6	4.4	1.4	0.8	2.8	136 622	56.1	43.9	2.76	2.85
Santa Clara	8.8	579 329	97.7	2.3	0.4	0.5	1.8	565 863	59.8	40.2	3.00	2.80
Santa Cruz	9.1	98 873	92.2	7.8	5.1	0.8	2.5	91 139	60.0	40.0	2.71	2.70
Shasta	13.3	68 810	92.2	7.8	2.3	2.2	5.9	63 426	66.1	33.9	2.53	2.51
Sierra	13.8	2 202	69.0	31.0	22.1	0.7	11.3	1 520	70.7	29.3	2.38	2.17
Siskiyou	7.2	21 947	84.5	15.5	6.7	3.0	9.2	18 556	67.2	32.8	2.32	2.41
Solano	15.0	134 513	96.9	3.1	0.3	0.9	3.7	130 403	65.2	34.8	2.96	2.80
Sonoma	15.7	183 153	94.1	5.9	3.3	0.8	2.4	172 403	64.1	35.9	2.61	2.57
Stanislaus	15.8	150 807	96.2	3.8	0.3	1.3	3.2	145 146	61.9	38.1	3.03	3.03
Sutter	17.0	28 319	95.5	4.5	0.4	1.5	4.8	27 033	61.5	38.5	2.90	2.82
Tehama	12.3	23 547	89.2	10.8	3.7	2.3	8.6	21 013	67.6	32.4	2.58	2.71
Trinity	8.4	7 980	70.0	30.0	20.6	3.8	8.5	5 587	71.3	28.7	2.25	2.37
Tulare	12.8	119 639	92.3	7.7	2.3	1.8	5.8	110 385	61.5	38.5	3.18	3.43
Tuolumne	17.0	28 336	74.1	25.9	20.7	2.2	6.9	21 004	71.3	28.7	2.36	2.38
Ventura	11.9	251 712	96.6	3.4	1.1	0.9	2.6	243 234	67.6	32.4	3.03	3.08
Yolo	16.5	61 587	96.4	3.6	0.4	0.9	3.4	59 375	53.1	46.9	2.76	2.67
Yuba	3.8	22 636	90.7	9.3	1.8	1.8	6.7	20 535	54.1	45.9	2.73	3.03
COLORADO	29.3	1 808 037	91.7	8.3	4.0	1.4	5.5	1 658 238	67.3	32.7	2.64	2.30
Adams	33.0	132 594	96.7	3.3	0.2	1.0	4.4	128 156	70.6	29.4	2.86	2.69
Alamosa	15.8	6 088	89.8	10.2	1.2	1.8	10.9	5 467	64.0	36.0	2.73	2.25
Arapahoe	23.4	196 835	97.0	3.0	0.3	0.9	4.3	190 909	68.0	32.0	2.67	2.23
Archuleta	98.0	6 212	64.1	35.9	23.4	4.0	11.0	3 980	76.8	23.2	2.48	2.41
Baca	1.8	2 364	80.6	19.4	1.9	6.7	15.2	1 905	76.1	23.9	2.32	2.36
Bent	7.4	2 366	84.7	15.3	1.0	3.6	15.0	2 003	68.0	32.0	2.53	2.53
Boulder	29.7	119 900	95.6	4.4	1.7	0.8	3.4	114 680	64.7	35.3	2.59	2.23
Chaffee	35.8	8 392	78.5	21.5	15.9	2.6	8.1	6 584	73.4	26.6	2.32	2.10
Cheyenne	-2.7	1 105	79.6	20.4	2.2	5.2	17.2	880	74.3	25.7	2.57	2.31

Table B. States and Counties

STATE/ County code	MSA/ PMSA/ NECMA code[1]	County type[2]	STATE County	Population, 2000				Population, 1990				Population and population characteristics, 2000					
												Race (percent)					
												One race					
				Land area, 2000[3] (sq km)	Total persons	Rank	Per square kilometer	Land area, 1990[3] (sq km)	Total persons	Rank	Per square kilometer	White	Black or African American	American Indian or Alaska Native	Asian	Native Hawaiian and other Pacific Islander	Some other race
				1	2	3	4	5	6	7	8	9	10	11	12	13	14
			COLORADO—Cont'd														
08 019	...	8	Clear Creek	1 024	0 322	2 503	9.1	1 024	7 619	2 608	7.4	96.4	0.3	0.7	0.4	0.0	1.0
08 021	...	9	Conejos	3 334	8 400	2 573	2.5	3 334	7 453	2 618	2.2	72.8	0.2	1.7	0.2	0.1	21.5
08 023	...	9	Costilla	3 178	3 663	2 942	1.2	3 178	3 190	2 984	1.0	60.9	0.8	2.5	1.0	0.1	29.5
08 025	...	8	Crowley	2 043	5 518	2 816	2.7	2 044	3 946	2 921	1.9	82.9	7.0	2.6	0.8	0.0	4.8
08 027	...	8	Custer	1 914	3 503	2 953	1.8	1 914	1 926	3 071	1.0	95.9	0.4	1.1	0.3	0.0	0.7
08 029	...	7	Delta	2 958	27 834	1 455	9.4	2 958	20 980	1 631	7.1	92.3	0.5	0.8	0.3	0.0	4.3
08 031	2080	0	Denver	397	554 636	101	1 397.1	397	467 549	106	1 177.7	65.3	11.1	1.3	2.8	0.1	15.6
08 033	...	9	Dolores	2 763	1 844	3 077	0.7	2 764	1 504	3 096	0.5	95.3	0.1	2.0	0.4	0.1	0.6
08 035	2080	1	Douglas	2 176	175 766	311	80.8	2 176	60 391	717	27.8	92.8	1.0	0.4	2.5	0.1	1.4
08 037	...	7	Eagle	4 372	41 659	1 064	9.5	4 372	21 928	1 581	5.0	85.4	0.3	0.7	0.8	0.1	10.8
08 039	...	8	Elbert	4 794	19 872	1 798	4.1	4 794	9 646	2 419	2.0	95.2	0.6	0.6	0.4	0.1	1.3
08 041	1720	2	El Paso	5 507	516 929	107	93.9	5 508	397 014	125	72.1	81.2	6.5	0.9	2.5	0.2	4.7
08 043	...	6	Fremont	3 970	46 145	979	11.6	3 971	32 273	1 207	8.1	89.5	5.3	1.5	0.5	0.1	1.2
08 045	...	7	Garfield	7 633	43 791	1 021	5.7	7 634	29 974	1 299	3.9	90.0	0.4	0.7	0.4	0.1	6.5
08 047	...	8	Gilpin	388	4 757	2 862	12.3	388	3 070	2 995	7.9	94.4	0.5	0.8	0.7	0.2	1.5
08 049	...	9	Grand	4 783	12 442	2 269	2.6	4 791	7 966	2 575	1.7	95.2	0.5	0.4	0.7	0.1	2.0
08 051	...	7	Gunnison	8 388	13 956	2 164	1.7	8 389	10 273	2 362	1.2	95.1	0.5	0.7	0.5	0.0	1.4
08 053	...	9	Hinsdale	2 895	790	3 125	0.3	2 895	467	3 136	0.2	97.3	0.0	1.5	0.3	0.0	0.4
08 055	...	6	Huerfano	4 120	7 862	2 617	1.9	4 121	6 009	2 756	1.5	81.0	2.7	2.7	0.4	0.1	9.4
08 057	...	9	Jackson	4 178	1 577	3 090	0.4	4 178	1 605	3 090	0.4	96.2	0.3	0.8	0.1	0.0	1.5
08 059	2080	0	Jefferson	2 000	527 056	105	263.5	2 000	438 430	113	219.2	90.6	0.9	0.8	2.3	0.1	3.2
08 061	...	9	Kiowa	4 587	1 622	3 088	0.4	4 587	1 688	3 085	0.4	96.1	0.5	1.1	0.0	0.1	1.4
08 063	...	7	Kit Carson	5 597	8 011	2 605	1.4	5 597	7 140	2 639	1.3	87.3	1.7	0.5	0.3	0.0	9.2
08 065	...	7	Lake	976	7 812	2 623	8.0	976	6 007	2 757	6.2	77.6	0.2	1.3	0.3	0.1	18.0
08 067	...	7	La Plata	4 383	43 941	1 018	10.0	4 383	32 284	1 206	7.4	87.3	0.3	5.8	0.4	0.1	3.9
08 069	2670	3	Larimer	6 737	251 494	227	37.3	6 738	186 136	260	27.6	91.4	0.7	0.7	1.6	0.1	3.4
08 071	...	7	Las Animas	12 361	15 207	2 075	1.2	12 362	13 765	2 076	1.1	82.6	0.4	2.5	0.4	0.2	10.0
08 073	...	8	Lincoln	6 698	6 087	2 772	0.9	6 698	4 529	2 871	0.7	86.3	5.0	0.9	0.6	0.0	5.7
08 075	...	7	Logan	4 762	20 504	1 761	4.3	4 762	17 567	1 817	3.7	91.7	2.0	0.6	0.4	0.1	3.8
08 077	2995	5	Mesa	8 619	116 255	464	13.5	8 619	93 145	498	10.8	92.3	0.5	0.9	0.5	0.1	3.7
08 079	...	9	Mineral	2 268	831	3 121	0.4	2 268	558	3 133	0.2	93.6	0.2	0.9	0.3	0.0	0.1
08 081	...	7	Moffat	12 282	13 184	2 211	1.1	12 283	11 357	2 266	0.9	90.0	0.3	0.9	0.3	0.0	3.2
08 083	...	7	Montezuma	5 275	23 830	1 598	4.5	5 276	18 672	1 752	3.5	81.7	0.1	11.2	0.2	0.1	4.3
08 085	...	7	Montrose	5 803	33 432	1 301	5.8	5 804	24 423	1 480	4.2	90.0	0.3	1.0	0.4	0.1	5.7
08 087	...	6	Morgan	3 329	27 171	1 476	8.2	3 329	21 939	1 580	6.6	79.7	0.3	0.8	0.2	0.2	16.4
08 089	...	6	Otero	3 271	20 311	1 772	6.2	3 271	20 185	1 665	6.2	79.0	0.8	1.4	0.7	0.1	15.1
08 091	...	9	Ouray	1 400	3 742	2 937	2.7	1 404	2 295	3 039	1.6	95.1	0.1	0.9	0.3	0.1	0.5
08 093	...	8	Park	5 700	14 523	2 121	2.5	5 700	7 174	2 636	1.3	95.1	0.5	0.9	0.4	0.0	4.7
08 095	...	9	Phillips	1 781	4 480	2 883	2.5	1 781	4 189	2 898	2.4	93.0	0.2	0.3	0.4	0.0	2.4
08 097	...	7	Pitkin	2 513	14 872	2 101	5.9	2 514	12 661	2 170	5.0	94.3	0.5	0.3	1.1	0.0	3.5
08 099	...	7	Prowers	4 249	14 483	2 123	3.4	4 249	13 347	2 110	3.1	78.6	0.3	1.2	0.4	0.0	17.2
08 101	6560	3	Pueblo	6 187	141 472	388	22.9	6 187	123 051	374	19.9	79.5	1.9	1.6	0.7	0.1	12.9
08 103	...	9	Rio Blanco	8 342	5 986	2 783	0.7	8 343	6 051	2 751	0.7	95.0	0.1	0.8	0.3	0.0	2.0
08 105	...	7	Rio Grande	2 361	12 413	2 270	5.3	2 364	10 770	2 310	4.6	73.9	0.3	1.3	0.2	0.0	21.4
08 107	...	7	Routt	6 116	19 690	1 812	3.2	6 117	14 088	2 049	2.3	96.9	0.1	0.5	0.4	0.1	0.7
08 109	...	9	Saguache	8 206	5 917	2 792	0.7	8 207	4 619	2 865	0.6	71.3	0.1	2.1	0.5	0.4	23.0
08 111	...	9	San Juan	1 003	558	3 134	0.6	1 003	745	3 127	0.7	97.1	0.0	0.7	0.2	0.0	0.7
08 113	...	9	San Miguel	3 332	6 594	2 728	2.0	3 332	3 653	2 944	1.1	93.6	0.3	0.8	0.7	0.1	3.4
08 115	...	9	Sedgwick	1 420	2 747	3 011	1.9	1 420	2 690	3 014	1.9	90.5	0.5	0.1	0.8	0.1	6.0
08 117	...	9	Summit	1 575	23 548	1 613	15.0	1 575	12 881	2 148	8.2	91.8	0.7	0.5	0.9	0.1	4.0
08 119	...	6	Teller	1 443	20 555	1 757	14.2	1 443	12 468	2 183	8.6	94.9	0.5	1.0	0.6	0.1	1.0
08 121	...	9	Washington	6 529	4 926	2 853	0.8	6 530	4 812	2 855	0.7	96.4	0.0	0.6	0.1	0.0	2.0
08 123	3060	3	Weld	10 340	180 936	305	17.5	10 341	131 821	350	12.7	81.7	0.6	0.9	0.8	0.1	13.3
08 125	...	7	Yuma	6 127	9 841	2 462	1.6	6 128	8 954	2 475	1.5	94.2	0.1	0.3	0.1	0.0	4.1
09 000	...		CONNECTICUT	12 548	3 405 565	X	271.4	12 550	3 287 116	X	261.9	81.6	9.1	0.3	2.4	0.0	4.3
09 001	5483	2	Fairfield	1 621	882 567	47	544.5	1 621	827 645	42	510.6	79.3	10.0	0.2	3.3	0.0	4.7
09 003	3283	0	Hartford	1 905	857 183	51	450.0	1 905	851 783	38	447.1	76.9	11.7	0.2	2.4	0.0	6.4
09 005	...	4	Litchfield	2 383	182 193	301	76.5	2 383	174 092	278	73.1	95.8	1.1	0.2	1.2	0.0	0.7
09 007	3283	1	Middlesex	956	155 071	343	162.2	956	143 196	332	149.8	91.3	4.4	0.2	1.6	0.0	1.0
09 009	5483	2	New Haven	1 569	824 008	54	525.2	1 569	804 219	46	512.6	79.4	11.3	0.2	2.3	0.0	4.5
09 011	5523	2	New London	1 725	259 088	215	150.2	1 725	254 957	195	147.8	87.0	5.3	1.0	2.0	0.1	2.1
09 013	3283	1	Tolland	1 062	136 364	395	128.4	1 062	128 699	360	121.2	92.3	2.7	0.2	2.3	0.0	1.1
09 015	...	4	Windham	1 328	109 091	495	82.1	1 328	102 525	449	77.2	91.3	1.9	0.5	0.8	0.0	3.6

[1]MSA = Metropolitan Statistical Area. PMSA = Primary MSA. NECMA = New England County Metropolitan Area. See Appendix A for explanation of these concepts. See Appendix B for list of metropolitan areas identified by type, with component counties.
[2]County typology code from the Economic Research Service of USDA. See Appendix A for definition.
[3]Dry land or land partially or temporarily covered by water.

Table B. States and Counties

	Population and population characteristics, 2000 (cont'd)								Population and population characteristics, 1990				
STATE County	Race (percent) (cont'd)								Race (percent)				
		Race alone or in combination											
	Two or more races	White	Black	American Indian or Alaska Native	Asian	Native Hawaiian and other Pacific Islander	Some other race	Hispanic[1]	White	Black or African American	American Indian or Alaska Native	Asian and Pacific Islander	Hispanic[1]
	15	16	17	18	19	20	21	22	23	24	25	26	27
COLORADO—Cont'd													
Clear Creek	1.2	97.5	0.4	1.3	0.6	0.1	1.3	3.9	97.7	0.3	0.4	0.5	3.3
Conejos	3.6	76.1	0.3	2.6	0.3	0.1	24.3	58.9	85.7	0.2	0.4	0.3	59.9
Costilla	5.2	65.5	1.2	4.1	1.4	0.4	32.8	67.6	83.5	0.3	0.6	1.3	76.9
Crowley	1.8	84.7	7.1	3.6	1.0	0.0	5.4	22.5	87.7	6.6	1.8	0.8	23.1
Custer	1.6	97.4	0.6	2.1	0.6	0.0	1.1	2.5	97.9	0.0	1.4	0.2	2.9
Delta	1.8	94.0	0.6	1.7	0.5	0.0	5.0	11.4	96.0	0.3	0.6	0.3	9.1
Denver	3.7	68.3	12.1	2.2	3.4	0.2	17.7	31.7	72.1	12.8	1.2	2.4	23.0
Dolores	1.7	96.8	0.3	2.6	0.5	0.2	1.3	3.9	96.1	0.0	2.7	0.1	3.2
Douglas	1.9	94.5	1.3	0.8	3.2	0.2	2.0	5.1	97.2	0.7	0.4	0.8	3.2
Eagle	1.9	87.2	0.5	1.0	1.1	0.1	12.1	23.2	91.6	0.2	0.5	0.5	13.3
Elbert	1.8	96.9	0.9	1.4	0.7	0.2	1.8	3.9	97.6	0.5	0.7	0.4	2.2
El Paso	3.9	84.5	7.7	2.0	3.6	0.5	6.0	11.3	86.0	7.2	0.8	2.5	8.7
Fremont	1.8	91.2	5.5	2.6	0.7	0.1	1.7	10.3	94.7	2.6	1.0	0.3	8.5
Garfield	1.8	91.7	0.7	1.3	0.7	0.2	7.4	16.7	97.2	0.3	0.7	0.4	5.6
Gilpin	1.9	96.1	0.7	2.0	0.9	0.2	2.0	4.2	97.5	0.5	1.2	0.4	3.6
Grand	1.1	96.3	0.6	0.8	0.9	0.1	2.4	4.4	97.4	0.2	0.4	0.5	3.1
Gunnison	1.7	96.7	0.7	1.4	0.8	0.1	2.1	5.0	97.4	0.6	0.7	0.5	3.6
Hinsdale	0.5	97.8	0.1	1.8	0.3	0.0	0.5	1.5	99.1	0.2	0.6	0.0	0.9
Huerfano	3.7	84.4	3.0	4.6	0.5	0.1	11.2	35.1	92.7	0.4	1.3	0.2	40.4
Jackson	1.3	97.5	0.3	1.4	0.3	0.0	2.0	6.5	92.2	0.0	1.6	0.1	7.4
Jefferson	2.2	92.6	1.2	1.5	2.8	0.2	4.1	10.0	94.6	0.7	0.6	1.7	7.0
Kiowa	0.8	96.7	0.5	1.7	0.1	0.1	1.8	3.1	97.6	0.0	0.7	0.0	3.3
Kit Carson	0.9	88.1	1.8	0.9	0.4	0.0	9.6	13.7	95.2	0.1	0.3	0.2	6.6
Lake	2.6	80.0	0.3	2.2	0.6	0.1	19.5	36.1	91.3	0.2	0.8	0.3	23.9
La Plata	2.3	89.3	0.6	6.9	0.7	0.1	4.7	10.4	89.9	0.2	5.0	0.6	11.1
Larimer	2.2	93.5	1.0	1.4	2.1	0.2	4.2	8.3	94.5	0.6	0.6	1.5	6.6
Las Animas	3.8	86.2	0.6	3.7	0.7	0.3	12.6	41.5	86.6	0.2	0.9	0.5	44.2
Lincoln	1.6	87.8	5.2	1.7	0.6	0.1	6.3	8.5	98.1	0.1	0.6	0.3	1.7
Logan	1.4	93.0	2.3	1.1	0.5	0.2	4.4	11.9	95.9	0.1	0.3	0.2	7.9
Mesa	2.0	94.2	0.7	1.8	0.8	0.1	4.4	10.0	94.7	0.4	0.7	0.7	8.1
Mineral	2.2	99.0	0.4	2.4	0.0	0.4	0.2	2.0	98.0	0.0	0.9	0.0	4.8
Moffat	1.8	95.3	0.4	1.8	0.5	0.0	3.8	9.5	96.2	0.1	0.8	0.4	6.1
Montezuma	2.4	84.0	0.3	12.6	0.3	0.1	5.1	9.5	85.4	0.1	11.5	0.2	8.6
Montrose	2.5	92.1	0.5	2.1	0.6	0.1	7.1	14.9	95.8	0.3	0.6	0.3	11.2
Morgan	2.5	81.8	0.5	1.4	0.4	0.3	18.1	31.2	88.1	0.3	0.6	0.4	18.4
Otero	3.0	81.7	1.0	2.5	1.0	0.2	16.8	37.6	82.9	0.6	1.0	0.6	35.2
Ouray	1.7	98.0	0.2	2.1	0.7	0.1	0.9	4.1	98.0	0.0	0.4	0.1	4.5
Park	1.8	96.8	0.8	1.9	0.7	0.1	1.7	4.3	98.0	0.6	0.7	0.2	2.9
Phillips	1.3	94.3	0.4	0.9	0.6	0.1	5.2	11.8	99.6	0.0	0.0	0.2	4.1
Pitkin	1.3	95.6	0.6	0.7	1.5	0.1	2.9	6.5	97.4	0.3	0.4	1.1	3.8
Prowers	2.3	80.7	0.4	2.0	0.5	0.0	18.8	32.9	85.4	0.3	0.7	0.3	23.2
Pueblo	3.4	82.4	2.3	2.6	1.0	0.2	15.1	38.0	84.8	1.8	0.8	0.6	35.8
Rio Blanco	1.7	96.7	0.4	1.6	0.4	0.1	2.6	4.9	97.2	0.2	0.7	0.4	4.0
Rio Grande	2.8	76.5	0.4	2.1	0.4	0.1	23.5	41.7	89.8	0.1	0.8	0.1	40.3
Routt	1.3	98.1	0.3	1.1	0.7	0.2	1.1	3.2	98.8	0.1	0.5	0.3	2.5
Saguache	3.1	74.1	0.3	3.3	0.6	0.1	24.7	45.3	80.1	0.2	3.0	0.2	45.6
San Juan	0.9	97.7	0.0	1.3	0.2	0.4	1.4	7.3	95.4	0.1	0.5	0.3	15.8
San Miguel	1.1	94.6	0.4	1.2	1.0	0.1	3.7	6.7	98.8	0.1	0.4	0.3	2.8
Sedgwick	2.0	92.4	0.7	0.7	0.9	0.1	7.2	11.4	97.2	0.4	0.6	1.2	8.6
Summit	2.1	93.8	0.8	0.9	1.2	0.1	5.4	9.8	97.6	0.2	0.6	0.7	2.5
Teller	2.0	96.8	0.8	2.0	1.0	0.1	1.4	3.5	97.8	0.2	0.9	0.4	2.6
Washington	0.9	97.0	0.1	1.0	0.3	0.1	2.3	6.3	98.1	0.0	0.3	0.2	2.9
Weld	2.7	84.1	0.8	1.6	1.2	0.2	14.8	27.0	88.9	0.4	0.6	0.9	20.9
Yuma	1.2	95.3	0.2	0.8	0.1	0.1	4.6	12.9	97.9	0.0	0.4	0.1	3.2
CONNECTICUT	2.2	83.3	10.0	0.7	2.8	0.1	5.5	9.4	87.0	8.3	0.2	1.5	6.5
Fairfield	2.5	81.1	10.9	0.5	3.7	0.1	6.3	11.9	84.6	9.8	0.1	2.1	8.6
Hartford	2.3	78.5	12.6	0.6	2.8	0.1	7.7	11.5	83.5	10.2	0.2	1.6	8.4
Litchfield	1.1	96.8	1.4	0.5	1.4	0.1	1.0	2.1	97.9	0.9	0.2	0.8	1.1
Middlesex	1.6	92.6	5.1	0.6	1.9	0.1	1.5	3.0	93.9	4.2	0.2	1.1	2.0
New Haven	2.2	81.0	12.2	0.7	2.7	0.1	5.6	10.1	85.5	10.2	0.2	1.3	6.3
New London	2.7	89.1	6.5	1.9	2.5	0.2	2.8	5.1	91.9	4.8	0.5	1.3	3.3
Tolland	1.4	93.5	3.2	0.6	2.6	0.1	1.5	2.8	95.4	2.0	0.2	1.9	1.7
Windham	1.9	93.0	2.4	1.2	1.1	0.1	4.3	7.1	95.9	1.1	0.3	0.7	4.2

[1] Hispanic persons may be of any race.

Table B. States and Counties

STATE County	Population and population characteristics, 2000 Age (percent)									Median age (years)	Percent Female
	Under 5 years	5 to 17 years	18 to 24 years	25 to 34 years	35 to 44 years	45 to 54 years	55 to 64 years	65 to 74 years	75 years and over		
	28	29	30	31	32	33	34	35	36	37	38
COLORADO—Cont'd											
Clear Creek	5.7	16.8	5.6	12.0	20.6	21.6	10.6	4.4	2.6	40.2	47.9
Conejos	7.9	24.3	8.5	10.3	13.3	12.4	8.5	8.3	6.6	34.2	50.4
Costilla	5.7	19.4	6.6	9.1	14.2	15.4	12.9	9.8	7.0	42.1	50.0
Crowley	4.4	14.4	9.9	17.9	21.7	13.9	6.9	5.7	5.1	36.6	32.7
Custer	5.5	17.0	4.5	7.1	16.2	19.8	15.1	10.1	4.7	44.9	49.0
Delta	5.8	18.3	6.3	9.6	14.0	14.9	11.6	10.2	9.5	42.3	49.8
Denver	6.8	15.1	10.7	20.5	15.6	12.8	7.2	5.5	5.7	33.1	49.5
Dolores	5.0	16.9	6.8	10.8	15.5	15.9	11.9	9.4	7.7	42.4	48.3
Douglas	9.6	21.9	4.8	16.3	21.7	14.9	6.6	2.7	1.4	33.7	50.1
Eagle	7.1	16.4	11.4	23.1	19.0	14.0	6.0	2.1	0.9	31.2	45.2
Elbert	6.6	23.6	5.5	10.2	22.6	17.6	7.9	3.7	2.2	37.2	49.8
El Paso	7.6	20.0	10.5	14.9	17.6	13.4	7.3	4.9	3.8	33.0	49.8
Fremont	4.8	15.8	7.5	15.1	18.3	14.5	9.5	7.7	6.8	38.8	42.8
Garfield	7.5	19.7	9.0	15.2	17.8	14.8	7.3	4.9	3.9	34.2	48.6
Gilpin	5.7	15.5	5.8	16.4	21.0	21.1	9.0	3.9	1.8	38.3	47.0
Grand	5.8	16.0	9.0	16.0	18.7	17.8	9.0	5.4	2.3	36.9	47.0
Gunnison	4.6	13.3	21.1	18.3	14.6	14.1	7.0	4.2	2.7	30.4	45.8
Hinsdale	6.1	13.4	4.7	10.9	18.6	20.1	14.6	8.1	3.5	43.9	48.6
Huerfano	4.4	16.6	7.3	11.3	16.0	15.3	12.1	8.3	8.7	41.7	45.7
Jackson	5.6	19.9	5.4	10.1	16.8	16.4	12.7	8.1	5.0	40.5	49.7
Jefferson	6.3	19.0	8.1	13.6	18.5	16.1	8.8	5.4	4.3	36.8	50.2
Kiowa	6.0	19.9	7.3	9.4	15.3	14.2	10.4	7.5	10.1	39.7	50.0
Kit Carson	6.1	20.6	7.5	11.9	17.1	12.3	9.9	7.1	7.5	37.4	47.1
Lake	7.8	19.0	12.8	17.7	15.5	13.3	7.4	4.1	2.5	30.5	46.3
La Plata	5.1	17.6	13.9	12.7	16.3	16.4	8.7	5.3	4.1	35.6	49.1
Larimer	6.1	17.7	14.2	14.4	16.3	14.2	7.6	5.1	4.5	33.2	50.0
Las Animas	5.6	18.7	7.9	10.1	14.0	15.2	10.7	8.9	9.1	40.9	51.1
Lincoln	5.0	18.9	7.1	14.2	18.8	12.5	9.2	6.9	7.3	37.8	43.3
Logan	6.3	18.4	10.8	12.3	16.0	13.0	8.7	7.3	7.2	36.5	47.2
Mesa	6.3	18.8	9.4	11.4	15.4	14.4	9.3	7.9	7.3	38.1	51.0
Mineral	4.5	16.0	4.7	8.1	16.7	17.1	15.6	10.5	6.9	45.0	49.0
Moffat	6.8	21.7	8.6	12.4	17.5	15.2	8.5	5.2	4.1	35.4	48.1
Montezuma	6.9	20.6	7.1	11.2	15.1	15.0	10.3	7.7	6.2	38.0	50.8
Montrose	6.8	20.0	7.2	10.9	14.9	14.3	10.7	7.8	7.4	38.8	50.8
Morgan	8.5	21.9	8.5	13.1	15.1	11.9	8.0	6.5	6.6	33.5	49.9
Otero	6.5	20.4	8.9	10.6	13.8	13.5	9.9	8.6	7.8	37.7	51.1
Ouray	4.8	17.7	4.1	9.9	17.3	19.7	14.4	8.0	4.2	43.4	49.5
Park	5.7	17.8	5.1	11.2	22.2	20.3	10.3	5.2	2.1	40.0	48.3
Phillips	6.9	20.0	6.3	10.3	15.0	12.7	9.4	9.1	10.3	39.8	51.7
Pitkin	4.1	12.5	7.7	19.5	18.9	19.8	10.7	4.7	2.1	38.4	46.5
Prowers	7.9	22.2	10.7	12.5	14.0	12.4	7.8	6.4	6.3	32.4	49.7
Pueblo	6.7	19.1	9.4	12.4	14.8	13.5	8.9	8.0	7.2	36.7	51.1
Rio Blanco	5.7	20.8	9.2	11.2	16.3	15.7	9.9	6.3	4.9	37.5	49.5
Rio Grande	7.0	21.2	8.0	10.7	14.6	14.0	9.8	7.6	7.1	37.3	50.7
Routt	5.5	17.1	10.1	17.3	19.2	18.7	7.1	3.0	2.1	35.0	46.2
Saguache	6.8	21.6	7.9	10.5	15.5	16.6	10.3	6.1	4.7	36.9	49.6
San Juan	4.7	15.4	4.3	11.8	16.3	27.6	12.9	4.3	2.7	43.7	47.5
San Miguel	4.5	13.1	9.9	23.6	19.7	17.9	7.9	2.3	1.0	34.2	45.3
Sedgwick	5.6	17.1	6.6	10.3	13.2	13.7	11.3	11.0	11.1	43.2	50.0
Summit	5.3	12.0	15.7	25.7	18.5	13.3	6.1	2.6	0.7	30.8	41.8
Teller	5.7	20.2	5.6	9.9	21.3	19.6	10.1	5.3	2.2	39.4	49.3
Washington	6.2	20.3	6.3	10.0	14.8	13.6	10.6	9.7	8.5	40.2	49.2
Weld	7.8	20.4	13.2	14.3	15.4	12.6	7.4	4.8	4.1	30.9	49.9
Yuma	6.6	21.7	7.1	11.5	14.5	12.9	9.3	8.2	8.1	37.3	50.8
CONNECTICUT	6.6	18.2	8.0	13.3	17.1	14.1	9.1	6.8	7.0	37.4	51.6
Fairfield	7.3	18.4	7.0	13.4	17.5	14.0	9.2	6.8	6.5	37.3	51.7
Hartford	6.4	18.2	7.8	13.1	16.6	14.1	9.1	7.1	7.5	37.7	51.9
Litchfield	5.9	18.8	5.7	11.6	18.1	15.8	9.9	7.0	7.3	39.6	51.1
Middlesex	6.2	17.0	7.3	13.2	17.9	15.3	9.5	6.7	6.9	38.6	51.3
New Haven	6.4	18.0	8.7	13.6	16.3	13.7	8.7	6.8	7.6	37.0	52.0
New London	6.3	18.1	8.6	13.6	17.6	13.9	8.9	6.7	6.3	37.0	50.5
Tolland	5.9	17.2	12.9	12.9	17.8	14.5	8.7	5.4	4.7	35.7	49.9
Windham	6.1	19.0	9.6	13.1	17.2	14.1	8.6	6.1	6.2	36.3	50.7

Table B. States and Counties

STATE County	Under 5 years	5 to 17 years	18 to 24 years	25 to 34 years	35 to 44 years	45 to 54 years	55 to 64 years	65 to 74 years	75 years and over	Percent Female	2000	1990	1980	1990–2000	1980–1990
	39	40	41	42	43	44	45	46	47	48	49	50	51	52	53
COLORADO—Cont'd															
Clear Creek	7.0	19.0	5.5	16.1	24.8	12.9	7.5	4.6	2.6	48.1	9 322	7 619	7 308	22.4	4.3
Conejos	8.5	26.2	7.3	12.9	12.8	8.9	9.4	8.0	6.0	50.3	8 400	7 453	7 794	12.7	-4.4
Costilla	7.2	21.3	7.7	13.1	12.8	10.5	11.0	9.6	6.7	50.0	3 663	3 190	3 071	14.8	3.9
Crowley	5.6	15.4	9.0	21.8	16.1	9.1	8.4	7.6	7.0	37.6	5 518	3 946	2 988	39.8	32.1
Custer	5.9	20.6	4.0	12.4	15.7	13.8	12.9	9.2	5.6	49.9	3 503	1 926	1 528	81.9	26.0
Delta	5.9	18.6	5.9	11.5	13.8	10.8	11.1	12.3	10.1	50.7	27 834	20 980	21 225	32.7	-1.2
Denver	7.4	14.6	9.8	20.5	16.5	9.1	8.2	7.6	6.2	51.3	554 636	467 549	492 686	18.6	-5.1
Dolores	6.4	21.1	6.3	14.1	14.0	12.2	11.2	8.5	6.1	49.2	1 844	1 504	1 658	22.6	-9.3
Douglas	9.5	21.5	5.6	20.0	22.0	11.7	5.5	2.8	1.3	49.8	175 766	60 391	25 153	191.0	140.1
Eagle	8.9	16.7	10.0	27.2	21.9	8.3	3.8	2.2	1.0	47.3	41 659	21 928	13 320	90.0	64.6
Elbert	7.3	23.4	5.3	16.4	21.2	11.7	6.9	4.4	3.3	49.9	19 872	9 646	6 850	106.0	40.8
El Paso	8.5	19.1	12.2	19.6	16.1	9.6	7.0	5.0	3.0	49.8	516 929	397 014	309 424	30.2	28.3
Fremont	5.5	17.1	7.5	15.5	15.3	10.2	10.0	10.1	8.7	48.1	46 145	32 273	28 676	43.0	12.5
Garfield	8.1	19.5	8.5	18.4	18.7	9.6	7.2	5.8	4.2	49.1	43 791	29 974	22 514	46.1	33.1
Gilpin	6.2	17.7	4.7	18.1	26.3	12.6	7.2	4.6	2.6	47.1	4 757	3 070	2 441	55.0	25.8
Grand	6.6	18.7	8.4	20.9	19.7	9.1	8.9	5.1	2.5	46.9	12 442	7 966	7 475	56.2	6.6
Gunnison	6.5	14.3	23.5	17.9	16.9	8.6	6.0	3.8	2.6	47.0	13 956	10 273	10 689	35.9	-3.0
Hinsdale	3.9	14.6	4.7	17.3	20.3	12.4	14.1	9.0	3.6	47.3	790	467	408	69.2	14.5
Huerfano	6.0	19.8	6.0	11.5	13.6	10.9	11.2	11.2	9.8	51.3	7 862	6 009	6 440	30.8	-6.7
Jackson	7.4	18.2	7.9	15.7	16.6	12.8	10.7	5.7	5.0	46.7	1 577	1 605	1 863	-1.7	-13.8
Jefferson	7.6	18.9	8.4	18.5	18.9	11.8	7.7	5.0	3.0	50.7	527 056	438 430	371 753	20.2	17.9
Kiowa	6.0	22.7	4.6	13.3	14.8	10.2	8.8	11.1	8.5	51.2	1 622	1 688	1 936	-3.9	-12.8
Kit Carson	7.7	21.5	6.0	15.0	13.6	10.4	9.7	8.8	7.4	50.5	8 011	7 140	7 599	12.2	-6.0
Lake	8.2	19.6	10.2	19.1	17.3	9.9	7.6	4.9	3.3	48.4	7 812	6 007	8 830	30.0	-32.0
La Plata	6.9	18.7	14.4	15.3	17.7	9.6	7.4	6.0	4.0	49.6	43 941	32 284	27 195	36.1	18.7
Larimer	7.3	18.0	14.3	17.9	16.9	9.4	6.5	5.5	4.1	50.5	251 494	186 136	149 184	35.1	24.8
Las Animas	6.4	19.0	8.7	12.0	13.7	10.0	10.3	10.1	9.7	51.3	15 207	13 765	14 897	10.5	-7.6
Lincoln	7.6	18.7	5.8	15.4	12.1	10.6	10.3	10.4	9.1	51.0	6 087	4 529	4 663	34.4	-2.9
Logan	7.0	19.7	8.8	15.1	13.8	10.1	9.9	8.5	7.1	51.2	20 504	17 567	19 800	16.7	-11.3
Mesa	7.1	19.8	8.8	14.9	15.7	10.2	9.1	8.6	5.9	51.5	116 255	93 145	81 530	24.8	14.2
Mineral	8.8	13.6	3.6	19.4	14.9	12.9	11.8	9.7	5.4	48.6	831	558	804	48.9	-30.6
Moffat	8.6	23.8	6.9	17.3	17.5	10.5	7.4	4.6	3.4	49.4	13 184	11 357	13 133	16.1	-13.5
Montezuma	8.3	22.9	7.2	14.4	15.2	10.2	9.4	7.6	4.8	51.3	23 830	18 672	16 510	27.6	13.1
Montrose	6.4	21.0	6.2	13.1	15.2	11.6	10.0	9.5	6.9	51.2	33 432	24 423	24 352	36.9	0.3
Morgan	8.3	21.4	7.8	15.7	13.5	9.3	8.9	7.8	7.3	51.0	27 171	21 939	22 513	23.8	-2.5
Otero	7.3	21.6	7.8	13.4	13.3	10.0	9.5	9.0	8.1	51.8	20 311	20 185	22 567	0.6	-10.6
Ouray	5.5	19.3	4.3	12.5	19.0	15.5	10.0	8.5	4.6	49.5	3 742	2 295	1 925	63.1	19.2
Park	6.6	20.6	4.2	17.3	22.6	13.1	8.2	5.4	2.0	48.8	14 523	7 174	5 333	102.4	34.5
Phillips	6.7	19.6	5.4	13.4	12.8	10.1	10.9	10.0	11.0	52.8	4 480	4 189	4 542	6.9	-7.8
Pitkin	5.6	11.2	8.9	24.7	26.1	13.0	6.0	3.1	1.3	47.5	14 872	12 661	10 338	17.5	22.5
Prowers	8.2	23.0	8.5	15.0	14.3	9.7	8.5	7.1	5.6	51.2	14 483	13 347	13 070	8.5	2.1
Pueblo	6.9	19.5	9.2	14.9	14.6	9.8	10.0	8.8	6.4	51.6	141 472	123 051	125 972	15.0	-2.3
Rio Blanco	7.5	22.6	9.1	15.6	16.5	11.2	7.9	5.5	4.1	49.2	5 986	6 051	6 255	-1.1	-3.3
Rio Grande	7.8	22.4	7.6	14.2	14.1	10.1	9.3	8.0	6.6	50.6	12 413	10 770	10 511	15.3	2.5
Routt	7.1	18.1	10.1	20.9	23.6	9.4	5.1	3.6	2.1	46.5	19 690	14 088	13 404	39.8	5.1
Saguache	8.2	23.5	7.9	15.5	15.1	9.8	7.5	7.5	4.9	48.7	5 917	4 619	3 935	28.1	17.4
San Juan	6.3	23.5	7.0	16.1	23.2	10.6	6.8	5.5	0.9	44.3	558	745	833	-25.1	-10.6
San Miguel	7.0	15.6	8.6	23.2	25.8	10.4	5.0	2.3	2.0	47.0	6 594	3 653	3 192	80.5	14.4
Sedgwick	5.3	19.0	5.0	12.4	13.6	10.1	11.6	11.9	11.2	51.3	2 747	2 690	3 266	2.1	-17.6
Summit	7.3	13.2	12.6	30.6	21.3	7.9	4.8	1.8	0.5	45.6	23 548	12 881	8 848	82.8	45.6
Teller	7.6	21.3	5.1	16.8	22.4	11.6	8.0	5.0	2.2	49.2	20 555	12 468	8 034	64.9	55.2
Washington	6.5	20.6	5.8	13.8	13.7	10.5	11.5	10.0	7.6	50.0	4 926	4 812	5 304	2.4	-9.3
Weld	7.9	20.2	13.2	16.4	15.3	9.6	7.2	5.7	4.5	50.6	180 936	131 821	123 438	37.3	6.8
Yuma	6.6	22.3	6.0	13.8	14.2	10.6	9.6	8.8	8.0	51.1	9 841	8 954	9 682	9.9	-7.5
CONNECTICUT	6.9	15.9	10.5	17.8	15.5	10.8	9.0	7.8	5.8	51.5	3 405 565	3 287 116	3 107 564	3.6	5.8
Fairfield	6.9	15.7	9.5	17.1	15.7	12.0	9.8	7.7	5.6	51.8	882 567	827 645	807 143	6.6	2.5
Hartford	6.8	15.8	10.4	17.9	15.3	10.6	9.2	8.1	6.0	51.9	857 183	851 783	807 766	0.6	5.4
Litchfield	6.9	16.5	8.6	16.8	17.1	11.4	8.7	7.9	6.2	51.0	182 193	174 092	156 769	4.7	11.1
Middlesex	6.7	15.3	10.2	18.3	16.9	11.1	8.5	7.3	5.8	51.2	155 071	143 196	129 017	8.3	11.0
New Haven	7.0	15.7	10.7	18.0	15.1	10.1	8.7	8.4	6.3	52.0	824 008	804 219	761 325	2.5	5.6
New London	7.4	16.1	12.0	19.3	14.9	9.9	8.4	7.0	4.9	49.4	259 088	254 957	238 409	1.6	6.9
Tolland	6.8	15.7	16.2	17.7	16.6	10.7	7.3	5.4	3.6	50.0	136 364	128 699	114 823	6.0	12.1
Windham	7.4	18.3	11.0	17.6	15.2	10.2	7.8	7.0	5.5	51.3	109 091	102 525	92 312	6.4	11.1

Table B. States and Counties

STATE County	Total population	In households (percent) Total in households	Householder	Spouse	Child Total	Child Own child under 18 years	Other relatives Total	Other relatives Under 18 years	Nonrelatives Total	Nonrelatives Unmarried partner	In group quarters (percent) Total in group quarters	Institutionalized population Correctional institutions	Nursing homes	Other institutions	Noninstitutionalized population College dormitories	Military quarters	Other
	54	55	56	57	58	59	60	61	62	63	64	65	66	67	68	69	70
COLORADO—Cont'd																	
Clear Creek	9 322	99.5	43.1	23.6	25.1	21.3	2.2	0.8	5.7	2.4	0.5	0.5	0.0	0.0	0.0	0.0	0.0
Conejos	8 400	99.4	35.5	20.0	36.7	28.9	4.8	2.8	2.5	1.4	0.6	0.1	0.4	0.1	0.0	0.0	0.1
Costilla	3 663	100.0	41.0	21.6	28.9	21.6	5.2	2.9	3.3	1.8	0.0	0.0	0.0	0.0	0.0	0.0	0.0
Crowley	5 518	63.8	24.6	13.6	20.2	16.9	3.1	1.5	2.4	1.2	36.2	35.4	0.7	0.0	0.0	0.0	0.0
Custer	3 503	99.5	42.2	27.3	24.1	20.4	3.1	1.5	2.8	1.3	0.5	0.2	0.0	0.0	0.0	0.0	0.3
Delta	27 834	96.7	39.7	24.0	26.5	22.1	3.4	1.3	3.1	1.4	3.3	1.8	0.4	0.1	0.0	0.0	1.0
Denver	554 636	97.7	43.1	15.0	23.8	18.6	7.3	2.7	8.6	2.8	2.3	0.5	0.5	0.1	0.4	0.0	0.8
Dolores	1 844	100.0	42.6	24.6	26.1	20.1	2.8	1.5	4.0	1.7	0.0	0.0	0.0	0.0	0.0	0.0	0.0
Douglas	175 766	99.7	34.7	25.6	34.4	30.7	2.1	0.6	3.0	1.3	0.3	0.1	0.1	0.0	0.0	0.0	0.1
Eagle	41 659	99.2	36.4	18.2	24.2	21.3	4.7	1.2	15.7	2.5	0.8	0.1	0.0	0.0	0.0	0.0	0.7
Elbert	19 872	99.8	34.1	25.6	33.5	28.5	3.3	1.2	3.4	1.4	0.2	0.0	0.1	0.0	0.0	0.0	0.0
El Paso	516 929	97.0	37.2	20.7	30.3	25.4	3.6	1.5	5.2	1.8	3.0	0.3	0.4	0.1	0.3	1.6	0.3
Fremont	46 145	80.2	33.0	18.6	22.7	18.8	2.7	1.2	3.2	1.4	19.8	18.4	1.1	0.0	0.0	0.0	0.3
Garfield	43 791	98.1	37.1	21.3	28.7	25.0	4.3	1.4	6.6	2.1	1.9	0.5	0.8	0.0	0.4	0.0	0.2
Gilpin	4 757	99.5	42.9	22.7	22.8	19.7	2.7	1.0	8.3	3.5	0.5	0.5	0.0	0.0	0.0	0.0	0.0
Grand	12 442	96.8	40.8	22.3	23.4	20.4	2.0	0.6	8.3	2.5	3.2	0.2	0.1	0.2	0.0	0.0	2.7
Gunnison	13 956	93.0	40.5	17.9	19.6	17.1	1.6	0.4	13.5	3.2	7.0	0.2	0.0	0.1	6.3	0.0	0.4
Hinsdale	790	100.0	45.4	27.7	20.8	18.5	1.4	0.5	4.7	2.0	0.0	0.0	0.0	0.0	0.0	0.0	0.0
Huerfano	7 862	88.3	39.2	19.0	23.1	18.4	3.2	1.6	3.8	1.9	11.7	9.6	1.7	0.4	0.0	0.0	0.1
Jackson	1 577	99.4	41.9	23.0	27.8	24.0	2.8	0.8	3.8	2.0	0.6	0.3	0.0	0.0	0.0	0.0	0.4
Jefferson	527 056	98.5	39.1	21.6	29.1	23.6	3.4	1.2	5.4	2.0	1.5	0.3	0.4	0.1	0.2	0.0	0.4
Kiowa	1 622	98.5	41.0	23.6	27.8	23.4	3.5	2.0	2.6	1.4	1.5	0.0	1.2	0.0	0.0	0.0	0.3
Kit Carson	8 011	93.4	37.3	22.2	29.3	25.5	2.2	0.9	2.3	1.2	6.6	5.8	0.5	0.0	0.0	0.0	0.3
Lake	7 812	98.7	38.1	19.3	28.6	24.4	4.8	1.9	7.9	2.3	1.3	0.1	0.2	0.1	0.9	0.0	0.1
La Plata	43 941	95.8	39.5	19.7	25.0	21.0	3.0	1.0	8.7	2.7	4.2	0.5	0.3	0.1	2.9	0.0	0.4
Larimer	251 494	97.2	38.6	20.7	26.6	22.4	2.8	0.9	8.4	2.2	2.8	0.1	0.4	0.0	1.8	0.0	0.4
Las Animas	15 207	97.4	40.6	20.3	28.0	21.6	4.8	2.2	3.8	2.0	2.6	0.3	1.0	0.0	0.7	0.0	0.5
Lincoln	6 087	82.7	33.8	18.7	25.7	22.6	2.2	1.0	2.2	1.1	17.3	15.9	1.5	0.0	0.0	0.0	0.0
Logan	20 504	90.3	36.8	20.2	26.9	22.5	2.9	1.4	3.5	1.4	9.7	6.8	0.9	0.2	1.6	0.0	0.2
Mesa	116 255	97.2	39.4	21.8	27.5	22.8	3.5	1.4	5.0	1.9	2.8	0.4	0.3	0.2	0.6	0.0	1.3
Mineral	831	99.9	45.4	25.9	22.0	18.5	3.5	1.8	3.1	1.6	0.1	0.0	0.0	0.0	0.0	0.0	0.0
Moffat	13 184	97.6	37.8	22.2	30.7	26.7	2.6	1.0	4.4	1.9	2.4	0.3	0.0	0.0	0.0	0.0	2.0
Montezuma	23 830	98.2	38.6	21.8	29.8	24.9	4.1	2.0	3.8	1.8	1.8	0.4	0.8	0.0	0.0	0.0	0.6
Montrose	33 432	98.4	39.0	23.0	29.0	24.4	3.5	1.5	3.7	1.6	1.6	0.3	0.2	0.1	0.0	0.0	1.0
Morgan	27 171	98.2	35.1	21.0	32.1	27.1	5.8	2.5	4.3	1.6	1.8	0.4	1.3	0.0	0.0	0.0	0.1
Otero	20 311	97.2	39.0	20.5	30.1	23.9	4.4	2.2	3.2	1.7	2.8	0.1	1.3	0.3	0.8	0.0	0.3
Ouray	3 742	99.5	42.1	25.8	25.0	21.3	2.2	0.9	4.3	1.8	0.5	0.0	0.0	0.0	0.0	0.0	0.3
Park	14 523	99.5	40.6	26.0	25.9	22.2	2.1	0.8	4.9	2.5	0.5	0.5	0.0	0.0	0.0	0.0	0.1
Phillips	4 480	98.0	39.8	24.3	28.6	25.2	2.6	1.0	2.8	1.2	2.0	0.0	1.7	0.2	0.0	0.0	0.1
Pitkin	14 872	97.8	45.8	17.7	18.3	15.9	1.9	0.5	14.1	3.0	2.2	0.1	0.0	0.0	0.0	0.0	2.1
Prowers	14 483	97.9	36.6	20.0	32.1	27.2	4.8	2.2	4.3	1.7	2.1	0.4	0.7	0.0	0.7	0.0	0.2
Pueblo	141 472	97.1	38.6	19.3	29.5	22.6	5.1	2.4	4.6	2.0	2.9	0.7	0.6	0.6	0.3	0.0	0.5
Rio Blanco	5 986	96.1	38.5	23.1	29.2	25.1	2.2	0.9	3.1	1.3	3.9	0.3	0.0	0.2	2.4	0.0	1.0
Rio Grande	12 413	98.0	37.9	21.9	31.1	25.4	4.1	2.4	3.0	1.8	2.0	0.1	1.2	0.1	0.0	0.0	0.6
Routt	19 690	98.7	40.4	20.4	24.6	21.7	1.5	0.5	11.7	2.8	1.3	0.2	0.2	0.0	0.7	0.0	0.1
Saguache	5 917	99.4	38.9	20.5	31.5	25.9	4.5	1.8	4.1	2.0	0.6	0.3	0.0	0.0	0.0	0.0	0.9
San Juan	558	99.1	48.2	21.1	21.9	17.9	3.0	1.3	4.8	1.8	0.9	0.0	0.0	0.0	0.0	0.0	0.9
San Miguel	6 594	99.7	45.7	17.5	18.9	16.7	1.8	0.5	15.8	4.1	0.3	0.3	0.0	0.0	0.0	0.0	0.3
Sedgwick	2 747	97.9	42.4	25.1	25.9	21.4	2.4	1.2	2.1	1.0	2.1	0.0	1.8	0.0	0.0	0.0	0.3
Summit	23 548	96.1	38.7	17.0	17.8	15.6	2.8	0.6	19.7	2.9	3.9	0.2	0.0	0.0	0.0	0.0	3.7
Teller	20 555	99.4	38.9	25.0	28.4	24.1	2.7	1.2	4.5	2.0	0.6	0.3	0.2	0.0	0.0	0.0	0.1
Washington	4 926	99.2	40.4	24.5	29.4	25.0	2.3	0.9	2.6	0.9	0.8	0.2	0.5	0.0	0.0	0.0	0.0
Weld	180 936	97.2	35.0	20.1	30.7	25.3	5.4	2.2	6.1	1.8	2.8	0.4	0.4	0.1	1.6	0.0	0.3
Yuma	9 841	98.6	38.6	23.0	30.5	26.4	3.8	1.6	2.7	1.3	1.4	0.1	1.1	0.0	0.0	0.0	0.2
CONNECTICUT	3 405 565	96.8	38.2	19.9	29.5	22.7	4.6	1.5	4.7	2.0	3.2	0.6	0.9	0.1	1.1	0.1	0.4
Fairfield	882 567	98.0	36.7	20.4	30.6	23.6	5.4	1.7	4.8	1.6	2.0	0.3	0.7	0.1	0.6	0.0	0.3
Hartford	857 183	96.9	39.1	19.2	29.4	22.5	4.7	1.6	4.5	2.1	3.1	0.7	1.2	0.0	0.8	0.0	0.4
Litchfield	182 193	98.6	39.3	22.5	29.4	23.0	3.3	1.0	4.2	2.1	1.4	0.0	0.9	0.1	0.0	0.0	0.3
Middlesex	155 071	96.0	39.6	21.5	27.0	21.4	3.2	1.1	4.7	2.1	4.0	0.0	1.0	0.8	1.6	0.0	0.6
New Haven	824 008	96.6	38.7	18.8	29.5	22.2	5.0	1.7	4.6	2.1	3.4	0.5	1.0	0.1	1.3	0.0	0.4
New London	259 088	95.4	38.5	20.2	28.2	22.5	3.4	1.2	5.1	2.4	4.6	1.4	0.8	0.1	1.1	0.8	0.4
Tolland	136 364	91.9	36.2	21.0	27.2	22.0	2.4	0.8	4.9	2.1	8.1	2.0	0.3	0.1	5.5	0.0	0.1
Windham	109 091	96.5	37.7	19.7	29.3	23.0	3.7	1.4	6.0	3.0	3.5	0.5	1.0	0.0	1.6	0.0	0.4

Table B. States and Counties

STATE County	Households by type, 2000												Households, 1990		
		Family households						Nonfamily households							
				Married couple		Female householder[1]			Householder living alone						
	Total households	Total	With own children under 18 years	Total	With own children under 18 years	Total	With own children under 18 years	Total	Total	65 years and over	Average household size	Average family size	Total households	Female householder[1]	Householder living alone
	71	72	73	74	75	76	77	78	79	80	81	82	83	84	85
COLORADO—Cont'd															
Clear Creek	4 019	64.9	28.2	54.6	21.3	6.9	4.5	35.1	27.2	4.3	2.31	2.81	3 153	6.2	27.5
Conejos	2 980	74.2	38.5	56.3	27.8	12.7	7.8	25.8	23.7	11.5	2.80	3.33	2 492	10.6	21.6
Costilla	1 503	68.5	28.5	52.6	20.0	11.3	5.8	31.5	28.1	11.6	2.44	2.98	1 192	11.9	23.9
Crowley	1 358	70.5	34.5	55.1	24.4	11.0	7.6	29.5	25.7	13.0	2.59	3.12	1 165	9.0	27.0
Custer	1 480	72.8	25.5	64.6	20.1	5.4	3.7	27.2	23.8	7.9	2.36	2.77	770	5.5	23.4
Delta	11 058	71.8	29.0	60.3	22.0	7.9	4.9	28.2	24.8	12.4	2.43	2.89	8 372	6.7	24.5
Denver	239 235	49.9	23.2	34.7	15.0	10.8	6.4	50.1	39.3	9.4	2.27	3.14	210 952	11.5	40.4
Dolores	785	69.0	24.5	57.7	18.0	8.5	4.7	31.0	26.2	10.4	2.35	2.82	581	3.1	24.3
Douglas	60 924	81.8	47.2	73.8	41.6	5.7	4.1	18.2	13.3	1.9	2.88	3.19	20 844	5.5	12.4
Eagle	15 148	59.5	32.7	50.0	26.6	5.6	4.0	40.5	20.9	1.9	2.73	3.17	8 354	7.0	22.0
Elbert	6 770	83.5	42.8	75.1	37.4	5.7	3.8	16.5	12.2	3.1	2.93	3.19	3 377	4.9	14.7
El Paso	192 409	69.6	36.7	55.6	27.5	10.2	6.9	30.4	23.9	6.1	2.61	3.11	146 965	9.8	23.7
Fremont	15 232	68.9	30.0	56.3	21.8	9.2	5.9	31.1	26.9	12.5	2.43	2.93	11 713	9.5	26.4
Garfield	16 229	69.5	37.2	57.6	29.0	7.8	5.6	30.5	22.8	6.3	2.65	3.11	11 266	7.6	22.3
Gilpin	2 043	61.9	26.9	53.0	20.5	5.7	4.5	38.1	26.8	3.7	2.32	2.81	1 308	5.4	27.2
Grand	5 075	63.4	28.1	54.7	22.1	5.2	3.9	36.6	24.8	4.8	2.37	2.85	3 168	5.1	23.9
Gunnison	5 649	52.5	24.1	44.2	18.5	5.4	4.0	47.5	27.2	4.6	2.30	2.84	3 855	5.7	26.8
Hinsdale	359	68.8	23.4	61.0	17.6	4.7	3.6	31.2	24.8	3.1	2.20	2.60	214	2.8	28.5
Huerfano	3 082	62.3	25.0	48.4	16.7	10.4	6.2	37.7	32.8	14.1	2.25	2.85	2 446	11.2	30.2
Jackson	661	67.0	29.2	54.9	21.5	7.9	5.7	33.0	28.4	10.1	2.37	2.91	632	4.6	25.0
Jefferson	206 067	68.2	33.4	55.1	25.4	9.1	5.7	31.8	24.5	6.3	2.52	3.03	166 545	9.2	22.1
Kiowa	665	68.0	28.9	57.6	22.4	6.6	4.5	32.0	29.8	15.2	2.40	2.97	657	5.5	26.9
Kit Carson	2 990	69.6	33.6	59.4	27.5	6.3	4.2	30.4	27.2	12.5	2.50	3.07	2 785	6.2	25.7
Lake	2 977	64.3	33.9	50.7	25.5	8.4	5.6	35.7	26.3	5.6	2.59	3.15	2 382	8.4	27.5
La Plata	17 342	62.8	29.6	49.9	21.4	8.7	5.7	37.2	24.8	6.1	2.43	2.92	11 976	8.8	23.6
Larimer	97 164	65.0	31.7	53.6	24.5	7.9	5.3	35.0	23.4	6.3	2.52	2.99	70 472	7.6	23.0
Las Animas	6 173	66.3	28.8	49.9	19.5	11.6	6.8	33.7	29.7	14.3	2.40	2.97	5 421	12.2	29.3
Lincoln	2 058	67.5	33.7	55.3	25.4	8.4	5.9	32.5	29.0	13.0	2.44	3.04	1 817	6.4	28.5
Logan	7 551	67.1	31.9	54.8	24.2	8.6	5.6	32.9	28.5	12.4	2.45	3.02	6 978	7.4	27.5
Mesa	45 823	68.9	31.4	55.3	22.7	9.8	6.3	31.1	25.1	10.3	2.47	2.94	36 250	9.8	24.8
Mineral	377	66.6	22.3	57.0	18.0	5.8	2.4	33.4	28.1	9.8	2.20	2.70	247	5.7	30.4
Moffat	4 983	71.8	38.2	58.7	28.4	8.2	6.5	28.2	23.6	8.1	2.58	3.05	4 178	7.4	23.5
Montezuma	9 201	70.8	33.3	56.4	24.2	10.6	6.9	29.2	24.6	9.3	2.54	3.04	6 762	10.4	21.5
Montrose	13 043	71.4	32.5	59.0	24.5	8.7	5.6	28.6	24.3	11.3	2.52	3.00	9 405	8.1	22.5
Morgan	9 539	73.1	37.9	59.7	29.6	9.0	5.8	26.9	23.0	10.9	2.80	3.29	8 139	7.9	24.6
Otero	7 920	69.1	32.2	52.7	21.9	12.0	7.7	30.9	27.8	12.9	2.49	3.04	7 593	11.7	25.7
Ouray	1 576	71.3	28.6	61.4	22.1	6.5	4.4	28.7	23.5	5.5	2.36	2.77	947	5.2	24.3
Park	5 894	71.6	30.2	64.1	25.1	4.4	3.1	28.4	21.1	3.2	2.45	2.86	2 775	4.0	19.9
Phillips	1 781	69.6	32.9	61.2	27.4	5.6	3.4	30.4	27.5	14.3	2.47	3.01	1 712	6.5	28.9
Pitkin	6 807	46.8	21.1	38.7	15.7	5.3	3.7	53.2	35.8	3.5	2.14	2.77	5 877	5.4	35.4
Prowers	5 307	70.2	37.4	54.6	27.3	10.9	7.2	29.8	25.4	11.5	2.67	3.21	4 984	10.6	25.7
Pueblo	54 579	68.4	31.5	50.1	20.7	13.3	8.1	31.6	26.6	11.1	2.52	3.04	47 057	13.7	25.8
Rio Blanco	2 306	71.4	35.6	60.1	27.5	7.8	5.8	28.6	24.8	8.7	2.60	2.98	2 181	5.9	22.1
Rio Grande	4 701	72.7	35.1	57.8	25.3	11.2	7.3	27.3	24.1	10.3	2.59	3.08	3 930	10.8	21.8
Routt	7 953	60.1	31.1	50.6	24.2	5.8	4.4	39.9	24.4	3.7	2.44	2.92	5 483	6.5	23.3
Saguache	2 300	67.7	33.4	52.7	24.1	11.0	7.4	32.3	26.9	7.7	2.56	3.15	1 643	11.0	23.4
San Juan	269	58.7	23.8	43.9	13.0	8.9	7.8	41.3	36.8	4.8	2.06	2.63	287	7.7	26.1
San Miguel	3 015	47.2	22.8	38.3	16.5	5.4	4.3	52.8	32.7	2.5	2.18	2.77	1 489	6.4	26.5
Sedgwick	1 165	68.9	26.4	59.1	20.7	6.6	4.2	31.1	29.4	13.6	2.31	2.83	1 141	5.2	28.7
Summit	9 120	52.3	24.0	44.0	19.1	4.4	3.1	47.7	21.6	1.6	2.48	2.86	5 295	4.6	23.7
Teller	7 993	74.1	33.6	64.2	27.2	6.6	4.3	25.9	19.6	4.0	2.56	2.94	4 720	6.6	19.3
Washington	1 989	70.8	31.3	60.7	25.2	6.4	3.8	29.2	26.2	11.6	2.46	2.97	1 915	4.8	26.1
Weld	63 247	71.5	37.2	57.6	28.6	9.4	6.1	28.5	21.0	6.9	2.78	3.25	47 470	9.1	22.3
Yuma	3 800	69.6	33.3	59.6	27.3	6.8	4.4	30.4	27.4	13.3	2.55	3.13	3 472	5.6	26.9
CONNECTICUT	1 301 670	67.7	32.2	52.0	23.6	12.1	7.0	32.3	26.4	10.1	2.53	3.08	1 230 479	11.4	24.2
Fairfield	324 232	70.4	34.2	55.5	26.8	11.5	6.1	29.6	24.0	9.4	2.67	3.18	305 011	11.3	22.9
Hartford	335 098	66.4	31.3	49.2	21.5	13.5	8.1	33.6	27.9	10.7	2.48	3.05	324 691	12.7	25.0
Litchfield	71 551	69.3	32.1	57.2	25.5	8.6	4.8	30.7	25.3	10.2	2.51	3.03	66 371	8.4	23.1
Middlesex	61 341	66.2	30.3	54.4	24.0	8.8	4.9	33.8	27.2	10.0	2.43	2.98	54 651	9.0	24.4
New Haven	319 040	66.0	31.2	48.6	21.6	13.6	7.9	34.0	28.2	11.0	2.50	3.08	304 730	12.5	25.9
New London	99 835	67.3	32.4	52.5	23.4	11.0	6.9	32.7	26.4	9.5	2.48	3.00	93 245	9.6	23.1
Tolland	49 431	69.1	33.3	58.0	26.6	8.0	4.9	30.9	23.5	7.7	2.54	3.03	44 309	7.6	20.1
Windham	41 142	68.6	33.5	52.3	23.4	11.9	7.6	31.4	24.3	9.6	2.56	3.04	37 471	10.8	22.2

[1] No spouse present.

Table B. States and Counties

STATE County	Percent change of households, 1990–2000	Total housing units	Occupied housing units (percent)	Vacant housing units Total	For seasonal, recreational, or occasional use	Homeowner vacancy rate (percent)	Rental vacancy rate (percent)	Occupied housing units Total	Percent owner-occupied housing units	Percent renter-occupied housing units	Average household size of owner-occupied units	Average household size of renter-occupied units
	86	87	88	89	90	91	92	93	94	95	96	97
COLORADO—Cont'd												
Clear Creek	27.5	5 128	78.4	21.6	17.9	1.2	5.4	4 019	76.1	23.9	2.38	2.10
Conejos	19.6	3 886	76.7	23.3	14.0	2.0	5.8	2 980	78.8	21.2	2.85	2.63
Costilla	26.1	2 202	68.3	31.7	20.3	1.5	4.1	1 503	78.2	21.8	2.43	2.46
Crowley	16.6	1 542	88.1	11.9	1.2	2.8	13.1	1 358	72.5	27.5	2.61	2.55
Custer	92.2	2 989	49.5	50.5	44.0	4.9	6.4	1 480	79.2	20.8	2.36	2.36
Delta	32.1	12 374	89.4	10.6	3.7	2.3	7.8	11 058	77.5	22.5	2.44	2.42
Denver	13.4	251 435	95.1	4.9	0.6	1.7	4.5	239 235	52.5	47.5	2.41	2.10
Dolores	35.1	1 193	65.8	34.2	24.1	5.2	11.7	785	76.8	23.2	2.34	2.39
Douglas	192.3	63 333	96.2	3.8	0.7	1.2	9.3	60 924	87.9	12.1	2.95	2.33
Eagle	81.3	22 111	68.5	31.5	26.8	2.4	7.7	15 148	63.7	36.3	2.76	2.67
Elbert	100.5	7 113	95.2	4.8	0.5	1.5	4.5	6 770	89.6	10.4	2.96	2.64
El Paso	30.9	202 428	95.1	4.9	0.7	1.3	6.0	192 409	64.7	35.3	2.72	2.40
Fremont	30.0	17 145	88.8	11.2	5.0	2.3	8.2	15 232	75.9	24.1	2.46	2.34
Garfield	44.1	17 336	93.6	6.4	2.8	1.6	3.7	16 229	65.2	34.8	2.70	2.54
Gilpin	56.2	2 929	69.8	30.2	21.8	2.1	13.4	2 043	78.4	21.6	2.37	2.12
Grand	60.2	10 894	46.6	53.4	43.9	3.9	31.1	5 075	68.2	31.8	2.43	2.25
Gunnison	46.5	9 135	61.8	38.2	34.2	2.4	5.5	5 649	58.3	41.7	2.41	2.15
Hinsdale	67.8	1 304	27.5	72.5	61.3	4.9	13.1	359	64.9	35.1	2.21	2.18
Huerfano	26.0	4 599	67.0	33.0	21.1	4.2	12.6	3 082	70.7	29.3	2.27	2.22
Jackson	4.6	1 145	57.7	42.3	34.1	4.3	7.4	661	67.6	32.4	2.28	2.56
Jefferson	23.7	212 488	97.0	3.0	0.7	0.6	3.6	206 067	72.5	27.5	2.63	2.22
Kiowa	1.2	817	81.4	18.6	3.9	5.8	9.9	665	71.3	28.7	2.43	2.34
Kit Carson	7.4	3 430	87.2	12.8	0.8	2.8	14.6	2 990	71.9	28.1	2.51	2.48
Lake	25.0	3 913	76.1	23.9	15.0	3.9	8.8	2 977	68.2	31.8	2.65	2.45
La Plata	44.8	20 765	83.5	16.5	11.8	1.6	5.5	17 342	68.4	31.6	2.54	2.19
Larimer	37.9	105 392	92.2	7.8	4.6	1.2	4.1	97 164	67.7	32.3	2.62	2.29
Las Animas	13.9	7 629	80.9	19.1	8.2	3.3	8.8	6 173	70.6	29.4	2.43	2.34
Lincoln	13.3	2 406	85.5	14.5	1.6	3.3	9.5	2 058	69.0	31.0	2.50	2.32
Logan	8.2	8 424	89.6	10.4	0.9	2.4	12.0	7 551	69.9	30.1	2.53	2.28
Mesa	26.4	48 427	94.6	5.4	1.0	1.7	5.8	45 823	72.7	27.3	2.52	2.32
Mineral	52.6	1 119	33.7	66.3	60.1	6.7	3.9	377	74.0	26.0	2.22	2.14
Moffat	19.3	5 635	88.4	11.6	4.0	1.5	12.0	4 983	72.1	27.9	2.68	2.34
Montezuma	36.1	10 497	87.7	12.3	4.6	2.0	9.9	9 201	74.8	25.2	2.56	2.49
Montrose	38.7	14 202	91.8	8.2	1.4	2.1	7.7	13 043	74.9	25.1	2.55	2.45
Morgan	17.2	10 410	91.6	8.4	3.2	1.6	5.5	9 539	68.4	31.6	2.84	2.71
Otero	4.3	8 813	89.9	10.1	0.3	3.1	8.9	7 920	69.1	30.9	2.55	2.37
Ouray	66.4	2 146	73.4	26.6	12.7	4.6	8.3	1 576	73.4	26.6	2.38	2.31
Park	112.4	10 697	55.1	44.9	40.5	3.3	8.5	5 894	87.6	12.4	2.47	2.33
Phillips	4.0	2 014	88.4	11.6	1.1	4.3	10.7	1 781	75.6	24.4	2.51	2.31
Pitkin	15.8	10 096	67.4	32.6	27.0	2.4	7.7	6 807	59.2	40.8	2.29	1.92
Prowers	6.5	5 977	88.8	11.2	1.0	2.4	12.0	5 307	66.2	33.8	2.70	2.61
Pueblo	16.0	58 926	92.6	7.4	1.0	1.8	8.5	54 579	70.4	29.6	2.57	2.38
Rio Blanco	5.7	2 855	80.8	19.2	8.0	3.1	15.8	2 306	70.6	29.4	2.55	2.35
Rio Grande	19.6	6 003	78.3	21.7	12.7	2.3	8.8	4 701	70.7	29.3	2.60	2.56
Routt	45.0	11 217	70.9	29.1	17.6	1.7	28.1	7 953	69.2	30.8	2.52	2.28
Saguache	40.0	3 087	74.5	25.5	11.7	3.2	6.9	2 300	69.3	30.7	2.56	2.54
San Juan	-6.3	632	42.6	57.4	49.4	8.5	22.3	269	67.7	32.3	2.06	2.05
San Miguel	102.5	5 197	58.0	42.0	33.5	2.6	14.4	3 015	51.6	48.4	2.27	2.09
Sedgwick	2.1	1 387	84.0	16.0	1.4	4.4	13.3	1 165	73.0	27.0	2.36	2.17
Summit	72.2	24 201	37.7	62.3	54.7	9.6	18.0	9 120	58.9	41.1	2.49	2.46
Teller	69.3	10 362	77.1	22.9	15.1	3.0	10.6	7 993	80.9	19.1	2.59	2.41
Washington	3.9	2 307	86.2	13.8	2.1	3.8	9.8	1 989	73.6	26.4	2.46	2.46
Weld	33.2	66 194	95.5	4.5	0.3	1.7	4.0	63 247	68.6	31.4	2.85	2.63
Yuma	9.4	4 295	88.5	11.5	1.4	2.7	7.4	3 800	70.8	29.2	2.53	2.60
CONNECTICUT	5.8	1 385 975	93.9	6.1	1.7	1.1	5.6	1 301 670	66.8	33.2	2.67	2.25
Fairfield	6.3	339 466	95.5	4.5	1.1	0.9	4.0	324 232	69.2	30.8	2.77	2.44
Hartford	3.2	353 022	94.9	5.1	0.5	0.9	6.3	335 098	64.2	35.8	2.62	2.22
Litchfield	7.8	79 267	90.3	9.7	5.8	1.3	5.1	71 551	75.2	24.8	2.66	2.06
Middlesex	12.2	67 285	91.2	8.8	5.2	1.0	4.7	61 341	72.1	27.9	2.59	1.99
New Haven	4.7	340 732	93.6	6.4	1.0	1.3	6.4	319 040	63.1	36.9	2.66	2.22
New London	7.1	110 674	90.2	9.8	4.7	1.3	6.4	99 835	66.7	33.3	2.60	2.23
Tolland	11.6	51 570	95.9	4.1	1.2	0.7	4.0	49 431	73.5	26.5	2.72	2.03
Windham	9.8	43 959	93.6	6.4	1.7	1.3	5.4	41 142	67.4	32.6	2.70	2.27

Table B. States and Counties

STATE/ County code	MSA/ PMSA/ NECMA code[1]	County type[2]	STATE County	Population, 2000				Population, 1990				Population and population characteristics, 2000 Race (percent) One race					
				Land area, 2000[3] (sq km)	Total persons	Rank	Per square kilometer	Land area, 1990[3] (sq km)	Total persons	Rank	Per square kilometer	White	Black or African American	American Indian or Alaska Native	Asian	Native Hawaiian and other Pacific Islander	Some other race
				1	2	3	4	5	6	7	8	9	10	11	12	13	14
10 000	...		DELAWARE	5 060	783 600	X	154.9	5 062	666 168	X	131.6	74.6	19.2	0.3	2.1	0.0	2.0
10 001	2190	3	Kent	1 527	126 697	426	83.0	1 530	110 993	414	72.5	73.5	20.7	0.6	1.7	0.0	1.3
10 003	9160	2	New Castle	1 104	500 265	112	453.1	1 104	441 946	112	400.3	73.1	20.2	0.2	2.6	0.0	2.2
10 005	...	6	Sussex	2 428	156 638	341	64.5	2 429	113 229	407	46.6	80.3	14.9	0.6	0.7	0.0	2.0
11 000	...		DISTRICT OF COLUMBIA	159	572 059	X	3 597.9	159	606 900	X	3 817.0	30.8	60.0	0.3	2.7	0.1	3.8
11 001	8840	0	District of Columbia	159	572 059	94	3 597.9	159	606 900	76	3 817.0	30.8	60.0	0.3	2.7	0.1	3.8
12 000	...		FLORIDA	139 670	15 982 378	X	114.4	139 852	12 938 071	X	92.5	78.0	14.6	0.3	1.7	0.1	3.0
12 001	2900	3	Alachua	2 264	217 955	259	96.3	2 264	181 596	268	80.2	73.5	19.3	0.2	3.5	0.0	1.4
12 003	...	6	Baker	1 516	22 259	1 682	14.7	1 516	18 486	1 763	12.2	84.0	13.9	0.4	0.4	0.0	0.2
12 005	6015	3	Bay	1 978	148 217	366	74.9	1 978	126 994	365	64.2	84.2	10.6	0.8	1.7	0.1	0.7
12 007	...	6	Bradford	759	26 088	1 513	34.4	759	22 515	1 554	29.7	76.3	20.8	0.3	0.6	0.1	0.7
12 009	4900	2	Brevard	2 637	476 230	120	180.6	2 638	398 978	124	151.2	86.8	8.4	0.4	1.5	0.1	1.1
12 011	2680	0	Broward	3 122	1 623 018	15	519.9	3 131	1 255 531	23	401.0	70.6	20.5	0.2	2.3	0.1	3.0
12 013	...	8	Calhoun	1 469	13 017	2 231	8.9	1 470	11 011	2 291	7.5	79.9	15.8	1.3	0.5	0.1	1.0
12 015	6580	3	Charlotte	1 796	141 627	387	78.9	1 797	110 975	415	61.8	92.6	4.4	0.2	0.9	0.0	0.8
12 017	...	4	Citrus	1 512	118 085	458	78.1	1 512	93 513	494	61.8	95.0	2.4	0.4	0.8	0.0	0.4
12 019	3600	2	Clay	1 557	140 814	389	90.4	1 557	105 986	437	68.1	87.4	6.7	0.5	2.0	0.1	1.3
12 021	5345	3	Collier	5 246	251 377	228	47.9	5 246	152 099	305	29.0	86.1	4.5	0.3	0.6	0.1	6.2
12 023	...	6	Columbia	2 064	56 513	838	27.4	2 065	42 613	943	20.6	79.7	17.0	0.5	0.7	0.0	1.0
12 027	...	6	De Soto	1 651	32 209	1 341	19.5	1 651	23 865	1 497	14.5	73.3	12.7	1.6	0.4	0.0	10.5
12 029	...	9	Dixie	1 823	13 827	2 171	7.6	1 824	10 585	2 329	5.8	88.8	9.0	0.5	0.2	0.0	0.4
12 031	3600	2	Duval	2 004	778 879	61	388.7	2 004	672 971	63	335.8	65.8	27.8	0.3	2.7	0.1	1.3
12 033	6080	2	Escambia	1 715	294 410	192	171.7	1 719	262 445	191	152.7	72.4	21.4	0.9	2.2	0.1	0.9
12 035	2020	2	Flagler	1 256	49 832	918	39.7	1 256	28 701	1 338	22.9	87.3	8.8	0.3	1.2	0.0	1.0
12 037	...	7	Franklin	1 410	11 057	2 362	7.8	1 383	8 967	2 473	6.5	81.2	16.3	0.5	0.2	0.0	0.4
12 039	8240	3	Gadsden	1 337	45 087	996	33.7	1 337	41 116	978	30.8	38.7	57.1	0.2	0.3	0.0	2.8
12 041	...	8	Gilchrist	904	14 437	2 127	16.0	904	9 667	2 417	10.7	90.5	7.0	0.4	0.2	0.0	0.7
12 043	...	8	Glades	2 004	10 576	2 391	5.3	2 003	7 591	2 610	3.8	77.0	10.5	4.9	0.3	0.0	5.6
12 045	...	6	Gulf	1 436	13 332	2 201	9.3	1 463	11 504	2 256	7.9	79.9	16.9	0.6	0.4	0.0	0.5
12 047	...	9	Hamilton	1 333	13 327	2 203	10.0	1 334	10 930	2 303	8.2	58.8	37.7	0.4	0.2	0.0	1.7
12 049	...	6	Hardee	1 651	26 938	1 486	16.3	1 651	19 499	1 702	11.8	70.7	8.3	0.7	0.3	0.1	18.0
12 051	...	6	Hendry	2 985	36 210	1 208	12.1	2 985	25 773	1 429	8.6	66.1	14.7	0.8	0.4	0.0	14.7
12 053	8280	0	Hernando	1 239	130 802	409	105.6	1 239	101 115	454	81.6	92.9	4.1	0.3	0.6	0.0	1.0
12 055	...	6	Highlands	2 663	87 366	600	32.8	2 664	68 432	645	25.7	83.5	9.3	0.4	1.0	0.0	4.1
12 057	8280	0	Hillsborough	2 722	998 948	35	367.0	2 722	834 054	41	306.4	75.2	15.0	0.4	2.2	0.1	4.7
12 059	...	7	Holmes	1 250	18 564	1 867	14.9	1 250	15 778	1 936	12.6	89.8	6.5	1.0	0.4	0.0	0.8
12 061	...	4	Indian River	1 303	112 947	476	86.7	1 303	90 208	507	69.2	87.4	8.2	0.2	0.7	0.0	2.1
12 063	...	6	Jackson	2 372	46 755	966	19.7	2 372	41 375	972	17.4	70.2	26.6	0.7	0.4	0.0	0.8
12 065	...	6	Jefferson	1 548	12 902	2 241	8.3	1 548	11 296	2 275	7.3	59.3	38.3	0.4	0.3	0.0	0.6
12 067	...	9	Lafayette	1 406	7 022	2 683	5.0	1 406	5 578	2 792	4.0	79.3	14.4	0.7	0.1	0.0	4.3
12 069	5960	1	Lake	2 469	210 528	265	85.3	2 469	152 104	304	61.6	87.5	8.3	0.3	0.8	0.0	1.9
12 071	2700	2	Lee	2 081	440 888	136	211.9	2 081	335 113	154	161.0	87.7	6.6	0.3	0.8	0.0	3.1
12 073	8240	3	Leon	1 727	239 452	240	138.7	1 727	192 493	249	111.5	66.4	29.1	0.3	1.9	0.0	0.8
12 075	...	8	Levy	2 897	34 450	1 266	11.9	2 897	25 912	1 426	8.9	85.9	11.0	0.5	0.4	0.0	1.0
12 077	...	8	Liberty	2 165	7 021	2 684	3.2	2 165	5 569	2 793	2.6	76.4	18.4	1.8	0.1	0.0	2.1
12 079	...	7	Madison	1 792	18 733	1 859	10.5	1 792	16 569	1 882	9.2	57.5	40.3	0.3	0.3	0.0	0.5
12 081	7510	2	Manatee	1 919	264 002	209	137.6	1 920	211 707	237	110.3	86.4	8.2	0.3	0.9	0.1	2.8
12 083	5790	3	Marion	4 089	258 916	217	63.3	4 090	194 835	247	47.6	84.2	11.5	0.4	0.7	0.0	1.7
12 085	2710	2	Martin	1 439	126 731	425	88.1	1 439	100 900	455	70.1	89.9	5.3	0.3	0.6	0.1	2.7
12 086	5000	0	Miami-Dade	5 040	2 253 362	8	447.1	5 036	1 937 194	10	384.7	69.7	20.3	0.2	1.4	0.0	4.6
12 087	...	4	Monroe	2 582	79 589	644	30.8	2 583	78 024	580	30.2	90.7	4.8	0.4	0.8	0.0	1.5
12 089	3600	2	Nassau	1 688	57 663	828	34.2	1 688	43 941	927	26.0	90.0	7.7	0.4	0.5	0.0	0.3
12 091	2750	3	Okaloosa	2 423	170 498	317	70.4	2 424	143 777	330	59.3	83.4	9.1	0.6	2.5	0.1	1.3
12 093	...	6	Okeechobee	2 005	35 910	1 222	17.9	2 006	29 627	1 311	14.8	79.3	7.9	0.5	0.7	0.0	9.6
12 095	5960	0	Orange	2 350	896 344	45	381.4	2 351	677 491	62	288.2	68.6	18.2	0.3	3.4	0.1	6.0
12 097	5960	1	Osceola	3 424	172 493	315	50.4	3 424	107 728	428	31.5	77.2	7.4	0.5	2.2	0.1	9.1
12 099	8960	2	Palm Beach	5 113	1 131 184	31	221.2	5 269	863 503	37	163.9	79.1	13.8	0.2	1.5	0.1	3.0
12 101	8280	0	Pasco	1 929	344 765	170	178.7	1 930	281 131	176	145.7	93.7	2.1	0.4	0.9	0.0	1.5
12 103	8280	0	Pinellas	725	921 482	41	1 271.0	726	851 659	39	1 173.1	85.9	9.0	0.3	2.1	0.1	1.1
12 105	3980	2	Polk	4 855	483 924	119	99.7	4 856	405 382	122	83.5	79.6	13.5	0.4	0.9	0.0	3.8
12 107	...	6	Putnam	1 870	70 423	705	37.7	1 870	65 070	673	34.8	77.9	17.0	0.4	0.4	0.0	2.9
12 109	3600	2	St. Johns	1 577	123 135	439	78.1	1 577	83 829	547	53.2	90.9	6.3	0.3	1.0	0.1	0.5
12 111	2710	2	St. Lucie	1 483	192 695	285	129.9	1 483	150 171	312	101.3	79.1	15.4	0.2	0.9	0.1	2.4
12 113	6080	2	Santa Rosa	2 634	117 743	460	44.7	2 631	81 961	554	31.2	90.7	4.2	1.0	1.3	0.1	0.7

[1] MSA = Metropolitan Statistical Area. PMSA = Primary MSA. NECMA = New England County Metropolitan Area. See Appendix A for explanation of these concepts. See Appendix B for list of metropolitan areas identified by type, with component counties.
[2] County typology code from the Economic Research Service of USDA. See Appendix A for definition.
[3] Dry land or land partially or temporarily covered by water.

Table B. States and Counties

STATE County	Population and population characteristics, 2000 (cont'd) Race (percent) (cont'd) Race alone or in combination								Population and population characteristics, 1990 Race (percent)				
	Two or more races	White	Black	American Indian or Alaska Native	Asian	Native Hawaiian and other Pacific Islander	Some other race	Hispanic[1]	White	Black or African American	American Indian or Alaska Native	Asian and Pacific Islander	Hispanic[1]
	15	16	17	18	19	20	21	22	23	24	25	26	27
DELAWARE	1.7	75.9	20.1	0.8	2.4	0.1	2.6	4.8	80.3	16.9	0.3	1.4	2.4
Kent	2.2	75.1	21.8	1.3	2.2	0.1	1.9	3.2	78.7	18.6	0.6	1.3	2.3
New Castle	1.6	74.3	21.0	0.6	2.9	0.1	2.8	5.3	80.4	16.5	0.2	1.6	2.7
Sussex	1.4	81.3	15.6	1.0	0.9	0.1	2.5	4.4	81.0	16.8	0.6	0.5	1.3
DISTRICT OF COLUMBIA	2.4	32.2	61.3	0.8	3.1	0.1	5.0	7.9	29.6	65.8	0.2	1.8	5.4
District of Columbia	2.4	32.2	61.3	0.8	3.1	0.1	5.0	7.9	29.6	65.8	0.2	1.8	5.4
FLORIDA	2.4	79.7	15.5	0.7	2.1	0.2	4.4	16.8	83.1	13.6	0.3	1.2	12.2
Alachua	2.0	75.1	20.0	0.8	4.1	0.1	2.1	5.7	77.5	19.0	0.2	2.5	3.7
Baker	1.0	84.9	14.2	0.9	0.6	0.1	0.4	1.9	84.3	15.0	0.3	0.3	1.1
Bay	1.9	85.8	11.2	1.5	2.3	0.2	1.0	2.4	86.3	10.8	0.7	1.8	1.8
Bradford	1.2	77.3	21.2	0.8	0.8	0.2	1.0	2.4	78.6	20.2	0.4	0.4	1.9
Brevard	1.8	88.3	9.0	0.9	2.0	0.2	1.7	4.6	89.8	7.9	0.3	1.3	3.1
Broward	3.4	72.4	22.2	0.5	2.8	0.2	5.4	16.7	81.7	15.4	0.2	1.4	8.6
Calhoun	1.5	81.2	16.1	2.0	0.8	0.1	1.3	3.8	83.2	15.1	1.2	0.1	1.1
Charlotte	1.1	93.5	4.8	0.5	1.1	0.1	1.2	3.3	95.0	3.8	0.2	0.7	2.5
Citrus	1.1	96.0	2.6	0.9	0.9	0.1	0.6	2.7	96.7	2.4	0.3	0.4	1.8
Clay	2.0	89.1	7.3	1.1	2.6	0.2	1.9	4.3	92.2	5.2	0.3	1.7	2.6
Collier	2.2	87.4	5.5	0.5	0.8	0.1	7.9	19.6	91.4	4.6	0.3	0.4	13.6
Columbia	1.4	80.9	17.5	1.2	0.9	0.1	1.0	2.7	80.8	18.0	0.2	0.6	1.5
De Soto	1.4	74.5	13.1	2.0	0.5	0.1	11.3	24.9	80.2	15.6	0.4	0.4	9.6
Dixie	1.0	89.7	9.2	1.0	0.3	0.1	0.7	1.8	90.6	8.7	0.3	0.2	0.9
Duval	2.0	67.3	28.5	0.8	3.3	0.2	2.0	4.1	72.8	24.4	0.3	1.9	2.6
Escambia	2.2	74.1	22.0	1.8	2.9	0.2	1.2	2.7	76.6	20.0	1.0	1.9	1.9
Flagler	1.5	88.5	9.4	0.7	1.5	0.1	1.5	5.1	90.0	8.2	0.2	1.0	4.4
Franklin	1.3	82.4	16.6	1.2	0.3	0.1	0.7	2.4	86.7	12.4	0.5	0.2	0.7
Gadsden	0.9	39.3	57.5	0.5	0.4	0.1	3.2	6.2	40.6	57.7	0.2	0.2	2.3
Gilchrist	1.3	91.6	7.3	1.1	0.3	0.0	1.0	2.8	90.6	8.5	0.3	0.2	1.6
Glades	1.6	78.3	10.8	5.6	0.5	0.1	6.3	15.1	78.9	12.1	5.7	0.2	8.0
Gulf	1.6	81.1	17.4	1.5	0.6	0.2	0.8	2.0	80.4	18.8	0.5	0.2	0.7
Hamilton	1.2	59.5	38.2	0.9	0.4	0.1	2.1	6.4	59.0	38.9	0.4	0.2	2.7
Hardee	2.0	72.1	8.9	1.1	0.4	0.1	19.5	35.7	84.0	5.3	0.4	0.2	23.4
Hendry	3.2	68.8	15.2	1.2	0.6	0.1	17.4	39.6	72.1	16.7	2.1	0.4	22.3
Hernando	1.1	93.8	4.4	0.7	0.9	0.1	1.4	5.0	95.0	3.9	0.2	0.4	2.9
Highlands	1.5	84.7	9.8	0.8	1.2	0.1	5.0	12.1	87.3	10.0	0.3	0.6	5.1
Hillsborough	2.6	77.1	15.8	0.9	2.7	0.2	6.1	18.0	82.8	13.2	0.3	1.4	12.8
Holmes	1.5	91.2	6.7	2.0	0.5	0.1	1.1	1.9	93.4	5.0	1.1	0.3	1.1
Indian River	1.2	88.4	8.6	0.5	1.0	0.1	2.7	6.5	90.3	8.5	0.2	0.5	3.0
Jackson	1.4	71.3	27.1	1.4	0.5	0.1	1.1	2.9	72.7	26.2	0.6	0.2	2.4
Jefferson	1.1	60.2	38.6	0.9	0.5	0.1	0.9	2.2	56.1	43.4	0.2	0.2	1.2
Lafayette	1.2	80.1	14.7	1.3	0.3	0.1	4.7	9.1	83.0	14.1	0.3	0.2	4.1
Lake	1.2	88.4	8.6	0.7	1.0	0.1	2.4	5.6	89.2	9.3	0.3	0.4	2.8
Lee	1.6	88.9	7.1	0.6	1.0	0.1	3.9	9.5	91.4	6.6	0.2	0.6	4.5
Leon	1.5	67.5	29.7	0.7	2.3	0.1	1.2	3.5	73.6	24.2	0.3	1.4	2.4
Levy	1.3	87.1	11.2	1.2	0.6	0.1	1.3	3.9	86.2	12.4	0.4	0.5	1.9
Liberty	1.1	77.4	18.7	2.4	0.3	0.1	2.4	4.5	80.9	17.6	0.5	0.2	1.9
Madison	1.0	58.3	40.7	0.8	0.4	0.1	0.8	3.2	57.6	41.7	0.3	0.1	1.4
Manatee	1.4	87.5	8.6	0.6	1.1	0.1	3.5	9.3	89.9	7.7	0.2	0.6	4.5
Marion	1.4	85.3	12.0	1.0	0.9	0.1	2.3	6.0	85.8	12.8	0.3	0.5	3.0
Martin	1.1	90.7	5.6	0.6	0.8	0.2	3.3	7.5	91.3	6.0	0.2	0.5	4.7
Miami-Dade	3.8	72.3	21.6	0.4	1.8	0.2	7.6	57.3	72.9	20.5	0.2	1.4	49.2
Monroe	1.8	92.1	5.2	0.9	1.1	0.1	2.5	15.8	92.1	5.4	0.3	0.8	12.3
Nassau	1.0	91.0	7.9	0.9	0.7	0.1	0.6	1.5	88.9	10.3	0.3	0.3	1.1
Okaloosa	3.0	85.9	9.9	1.4	3.7	0.3	2.0	4.3	87.1	9.0	0.5	2.5	3.1
Okeechobee	2.0	81.0	8.3	1.0	0.9	0.1	10.8	18.6	84.3	6.4	0.5	0.5	11.8
Orange	3.4	70.9	19.5	0.8	4.0	0.3	8.1	18.8	79.6	15.2	0.3	2.1	9.6
Osceola	3.6	80.0	8.4	0.9	2.8	0.2	11.4	29.4	89.3	5.5	0.3	1.5	11.9
Palm Beach	2.4	80.4	14.9	0.5	1.9	0.2	4.6	12.4	84.8	12.5	0.1	1.0	7.7
Pasco	1.4	94.9	2.3	0.9	1.2	0.1	2.0	5.7	96.3	1.9	0.3	0.5	3.3
Pinellas	1.6	87.2	9.4	0.7	2.4	0.1	1.8	4.6	90.5	7.7	0.2	1.1	2.4
Polk	1.7	80.9	14.1	0.8	1.2	0.1	4.7	9.5	84.4	13.4	0.3	0.6	4.1
Putnam	1.2	78.9	17.3	0.9	0.6	0.1	3.4	5.9	79.9	18.3	0.2	0.4	2.6
St. Johns	1.0	91.8	6.5	0.6	1.2	0.1	0.8	2.6	90.1	8.7	0.2	0.6	2.3
St. Lucie	1.8	80.3	16.2	0.6	1.2	0.1	3.4	8.2	81.3	16.4	0.2	0.7	4.0
Santa Rosa	2.0	92.5	4.6	1.9	1.9	0.2	1.0	2.5	93.6	4.0	0.9	1.2	1.5

[1] Hispanic persons may be of any race.

Table B. States and Counties

STATE County	Population and population characteristics, 2000										
	Age (percent)									Median age (years)	Percent Female
	Under 5 years	5 to 17 years	18 to 24 years	25 to 34 years	35 to 44 years	45 to 54 years	55 to 64 years	65 to 74 years	75 years and over		
	28	29	30	31	32	33	34	35	36	37	38
DELAWARE	6.6	18.3	9.6	13.9	16.3	13.3	9.1	7.2	5.8	36.0	51.4
Kent	7.2	20.0	10.1	13.5	16.2	12.5	8.7	6.6	5.0	34.4	51.8
New Castle	6.7	18.3	10.3	14.8	16.7	13.4	8.3	6.2	5.4	35.0	51.4
Sussex	5.8	16.8	7.0	11.4	15.0	13.6	12.0	10.9	7.6	41.1	51.1
DISTRICT OF COLUMBIA	5.7	14.4	12.7	17.8	15.3	13.2	8.7	6.3	5.9	34.6	52.9
District of Columbia	5.7	14.4	12.7	17.8	15.3	13.2	8.7	6.3	5.9	34.6	52.9
FLORIDA	5.9	16.9	8.3	13.0	15.5	12.9	9.8	9.1	8.5	38.7	51.2
Alachua	5.1	15.0	23.2	14.4	13.3	12.2	7.1	5.0	4.6	29.0	51.2
Baker	7.0	20.5	9.9	14.1	16.6	13.8	8.9	5.8	3.4	34.0	47.5
Bay	6.1	18.0	8.7	13.3	16.9	13.7	10.0	7.9	5.4	37.4	50.5
Bradford	5.5	16.4	9.5	14.8	17.3	13.8	9.7	7.0	5.9	37.2	44.1
Brevard	5.2	16.8	6.8	10.6	16.5	13.3	11.0	10.9	9.0	41.4	51.0
Broward	6.3	17.2	7.2	14.2	17.2	13.3	8.4	7.2	8.9	37.8	51.7
Calhoun	5.9	17.3	9.0	16.0	15.4	12.5	9.8	7.3	6.6	36.2	46.0
Charlotte	3.7	12.0	4.5	7.6	11.2	11.8	14.5	18.4	16.3	54.3	52.2
Citrus	3.8	13.4	4.6	7.7	11.4	12.1	14.8	17.4	14.8	52.6	52.0
Clay	6.6	21.4	7.9	12.7	17.6	14.7	9.3	5.6	4.2	35.9	50.8
Collier	5.3	14.5	6.6	11.2	13.3	11.7	12.7	14.0	10.5	44.1	49.9
Columbia	6.4	18.9	9.0	12.3	15.4	13.7	10.3	8.0	5.9	37.3	49.3
De Soto	5.8	16.9	11.2	14.1	12.6	10.4	10.1	10.6	8.4	36.5	43.8
Dixie	5.6	16.5	7.9	11.8	14.8	13.5	12.7	10.7	6.5	40.7	46.7
Duval	7.2	19.1	9.6	15.5	16.9	13.3	7.9	5.6	4.9	34.1	51.5
Escambia	6.1	17.4	12.2	13.7	15.3	12.9	9.2	7.3	6.1	35.4	50.3
Flagler	4.1	13.8	4.8	8.1	12.3	13.2	15.1	17.1	11.6	50.4	52.1
Franklin	4.6	13.4	7.6	14.0	16.8	14.5	13.3	8.9	6.8	40.8	43.5
Gadsden	6.7	19.7	9.5	13.3	15.6	13.8	9.2	6.8	5.4	35.5	52.4
Gilchrist	5.7	18.7	14.2	10.8	14.0	12.5	10.3	7.9	5.7	35.4	47.1
Glades	5.8	16.3	7.6	13.3	13.7	11.5	13.0	11.9	6.9	40.2	45.1
Gulf	5.1	16.7	6.8	12.7	16.7	14.2	11.8	9.6	6.6	40.3	46.6
Hamilton	6.3	17.2	10.8	15.6	16.2	13.8	8.9	6.4	4.8	35.1	42.5
Hardee	7.7	19.9	11.0	14.5	13.7	10.7	8.4	7.9	6.0	32.7	45.6
Hendry	7.8	22.2	13.3	14.8	13.5	10.4	7.8	5.9	4.2	29.5	44.4
Hernando	4.5	14.4	5.4	8.4	12.0	11.8	12.6	16.3	14.5	49.5	52.5
Highlands	4.8	14.3	6.3	8.6	10.8	10.2	12.0	17.1	15.9	50.0	51.2
Hillsborough	6.9	18.5	9.3	15.1	16.6	13.3	8.4	6.4	5.6	35.1	51.1
Holmes	5.5	17.5	8.8	14.4	14.9	13.1	10.9	7.9	6.9	37.5	47.0
Indian River	4.7	14.6	6.0	9.2	13.0	12.2	11.2	14.6	14.6	47.0	51.6
Jackson	5.5	16.9	9.7	13.9	15.7	13.8	10.0	7.7	6.8	37.6	47.5
Jefferson	5.3	17.4	8.2	12.4	16.5	15.6	10.1	7.7	6.7	39.4	49.0
Lafayette	5.5	16.1	10.7	17.9	16.1	11.9	9.4	7.1	5.3	34.8	40.2
Lake	5.2	15.1	5.8	10.2	13.5	11.6	12.2	14.4	12.0	45.1	51.6
Lee	5.2	14.4	6.2	10.5	13.4	12.4	12.4	13.7	11.7	45.2	51.1
Leon	5.7	15.6	21.4	14.7	14.2	13.1	7.0	4.4	3.9	29.5	52.3
Levy	5.7	17.9	6.9	10.9	14.2	13.7	12.8	10.3	7.6	41.1	51.6
Liberty	5.5	16.3	9.4	18.7	18.9	12.1	8.9	6.2	4.0	35.0	40.8
Madison	5.7	19.5	9.2	13.6	14.7	12.9	9.8	7.5	7.0	36.3	48.2
Manatee	5.6	15.1	6.5	11.0	13.7	12.3	10.9	12.5	12.4	43.6	51.7
Marion	5.2	16.2	6.4	10.2	13.6	12.1	11.8	13.6	10.9	43.8	51.7
Martin	4.4	14.2	5.3	8.9	14.0	13.0	11.9	14.2	14.1	47.3	50.9
Miami-Dade	6.5	18.3	9.1	15.0	16.1	12.5	9.2	7.2	6.1	35.6	51.7
Monroe	4.3	12.7	6.3	12.9	18.2	18.4	12.5	8.5	6.1	42.6	46.8
Nassau	6.2	18.9	7.2	12.3	16.5	15.0	11.3	7.9	4.7	38.3	50.7
Okaloosa	6.4	18.4	9.6	13.9	17.2	13.1	9.3	7.4	4.7	36.1	49.5
Okeechobee	6.3	18.9	9.5	12.8	14.2	11.5	10.4	9.5	6.8	36.7	46.4
Orange	6.8	18.4	10.9	16.6	17.1	12.6	7.5	5.5	4.5	33.3	50.5
Osceola	6.8	20.0	9.3	14.6	16.3	12.9	8.7	6.4	5.0	34.6	50.7
Palm Beach	5.6	15.7	6.6	11.8	15.2	12.5	9.6	10.8	12.3	41.8	51.7
Pasco	5.3	14.9	5.8	10.4	13.7	12.1	11.0	12.9	13.9	44.9	52.0
Pinellas	4.9	14.3	6.4	11.8	15.6	14.0	10.4	10.5	12.0	43.0	52.4
Polk	6.4	18.0	8.3	12.3	14.2	12.3	10.3	9.9	8.4	38.6	50.9
Putnam	6.1	18.4	7.7	10.4	13.8	13.4	11.6	10.8	7.6	40.5	50.6
St. Johns	5.4	17.7	7.0	10.8	16.8	15.8	10.7	8.8	7.1	40.6	51.4
St. Lucie	5.6	17.0	6.6	10.6	14.5	12.3	10.7	12.3	10.4	42.0	51.2
Santa Rosa	6.5	20.0	7.2	13.0	18.2	14.1	9.9	6.9	4.1	36.8	49.8

Table B. States and Counties

STATE County	Under 5 years	5 to 17 years	18 to 24 years	25 to 34 years	35 to 44 years	45 to 54 years	55 to 64 years	65 to 74 years	75 years and over	Percent Female	2000	1990	1980	1990–2000	1980–1990
	39	40	41	42	43	44	45	46	47	48	49	50	51	52	53
DELAWARE	7.3	17.2	11.4	17.9	14.8	10.2	9.0	7.4	4.7	51.5	783 600	666 168	594 338	17.6	12.1
Kent	8.4	18.8	11.9	17.8	14.2	10.1	8.4	6.1	4.2	51.1	126 697	110 993	98 219	14.1	13.0
New Castle	7.2	16.8	12.1	18.5	15.2	10.3	8.6	7.0	4.4	51.6	500 265	441 946	398 115	13.2	11.0
Sussex	6.8	17.1	8.5	15.5	14.1	10.2	11.1	10.6	6.2	51.0	156 638	113 229	98 004	38.3	15.5
DISTRICT OF COLUMBIA	6.2	13.1	13.6	20.0	15.7	10.2	8.4	7.3	5.5	53.4	572 059	606 900	638 432	-5.7	-4.9
District of Columbia	6.2	13.1	13.6	20.0	15.7	10.2	8.4	7.3	5.5	53.4	572 059	606 900	638 432	-5.7	-4.9
FLORIDA	6.6	15.6	9.4	16.4	14.0	10.0	9.8	10.6	7.7	51.6	15 982 378	12 938 071	9 746 961	23.5	32.7
Alachua	6.5	15.3	22.0	18.1	14.4	8.2	6.3	5.5	3.8	50.9	217 955	181 596	151 369	20.0	20.0
Baker	7.8	22.7	10.3	18.3	15.4	10.2	7.4	4.8	3.2	47.8	22 259	18 486	15 289	20.4	20.9
Bay	7.3	18.1	9.9	17.8	14.5	10.8	9.6	7.7	4.3	50.7	148 217	126 994	97 740	16.7	29.9
Bradford	6.3	17.7	9.4	19.4	15.3	10.9	8.8	7.3	4.8	44.8	26 088	22 515	20 023	15.9	12.4
Brevard	6.6	15.3	8.8	17.5	13.6	10.5	11.0	10.8	5.8	50.6	476 230	398 978	272 959	19.4	46.2
Broward	6.3	14.1	8.2	17.1	14.8	9.9	8.8	10.6	10.1	52.1	1 623 018	1 255 531	1 018 257	29.3	23.3
Calhoun	7.1	19.0	10.5	15.9	13.5	10.8	8.7	7.8	6.7	48.2	13 017	11 011	9 294	18.2	18.5
Charlotte	4.4	11.2	5.8	10.8	10.3	8.7	15.0	20.9	12.9	51.8	141 627	110 975	58 460	27.6	89.8
Citrus	4.7	12.9	5.5	10.5	10.7	9.7	14.6	19.8	11.5	52.2	118 085	93 513	54 703	26.3	70.9
Clay	7.6	21.2	9.6	16.8	17.3	11.7	7.4	5.2	3.3	50.7	140 814	105 986	67 052	32.9	58.1
Collier	6.0	13.9	7.8	14.6	12.8	10.0	12.1	14.4	8.4	50.4	251 377	152 099	85 971	65.3	76.9
Columbia	7.3	20.6	9.2	15.1	14.2	10.6	9.6	8.5	4.8	50.9	56 513	42 613	35 399	32.6	20.4
De Soto	6.9	16.9	9.3	14.9	12.8	9.9	10.1	11.8	7.6	48.4	32 209	23 865	19 039	35.0	25.3
Dixie	6.7	17.8	8.6	14.4	13.7	11.8	12.3	9.9	4.9	48.2	13 827	10 585	7 751	30.6	36.6
Duval	8.1	17.8	11.3	19.4	15.2	9.5	7.9	6.5	4.2	51.2	778 879	672 971	571 003	15.7	17.9
Escambia	7.4	17.9	12.1	17.1	14.1	10.5	9.1	7.4	4.5	51.4	294 410	262 445	233 794	12.2	12.4
Flagler	5.1	13.9	6.2	11.4	12.0	9.7	16.0	19.1	6.4	52.1	49 832	28 701	10 913	73.6	163.0
Franklin	6.3	17.7	7.7	13.3	12.7	12.4	11.8	10.7	7.3	51.2	11 057	8 967	7 661	23.3	17.0
Gadsden	7.7	21.9	10.0	15.6	14.1	9.8	8.4	7.2	5.4	52.5	45 087	41 116	41 674	9.7	-1.3
Gilchrist	6.7	18.3	13.6	13.6	13.3	10.4	10.4	9.0	4.8	47.2	14 437	9 667	5 767	49.3	67.6
Glades	6.4	18.0	7.0	12.2	11.8	11.8	13.1	13.0	6.7	49.3	10 576	7 591	5 992	39.3	26.7
Gulf	6.1	18.4	9.1	15.4	12.6	11.3	11.8	9.2	6.1	49.8	13 332	11 504	10 658	15.9	7.9
Hamilton	7.4	21.5	11.3	16.9	14.1	9.6	7.9	6.5	4.9	47.6	13 327	10 930	8 761	21.9	24.8
Hardee	7.8	21.4	10.0	13.8	12.7	9.8	9.4	9.4	5.8	49.3	26 938	19 499	20 357	38.2	-4.2
Hendry	9.0	22.4	10.4	15.7	13.0	10.2	8.4	6.8	4.2	49.3	36 210	25 773	18 599	40.5	38.6
Hernando	5.0	13.5	5.9	10.5	10.8	9.1	14.5	21.1	9.6	52.1	130 802	101 115	44 469	29.4	127.4
Highlands	5.1	13.6	5.7	10.6	9.7	8.2	13.6	20.6	12.9	52.6	87 366	68 432	47 526	27.7	44.0
Hillsborough	7.3	17.0	10.7	18.7	15.4	10.3	8.4	7.4	4.8	51.3	998 948	834 054	646 939	19.8	28.9
Holmes	6.2	18.7	9.5	14.9	13.7	11.6	9.7	9.1	6.6	49.2	18 564	15 778	14 723	17.7	7.2
Indian River	5.5	13.9	6.9	12.9	12.0	9.1	12.5	17.1	10.1	51.7	112 947	90 208	59 896	25.2	50.6
Jackson	5.9	19.0	11.1	15.3	14.1	10.5	9.3	8.2	6.7	49.3	46 755	41 375	39 154	13.0	5.7
Jefferson	7.4	21.6	9.0	13.8	14.5	9.9	9.1	8.2	6.6	52.2	12 902	11 296	10 703	14.2	5.5
Lafayette	5.8	18.9	11.1	19.7	14.4	10.3	8.9	6.9	4.0	42.4	7 022	5 578	4 035	25.9	38.2
Lake	5.6	14.3	6.8	12.2	11.4	9.6	12.6	16.2	11.3	52.1	210 528	152 104	104 870	38.4	45.0
Lee	5.9	13.6	7.3	14.1	12.5	9.5	12.1	15.3	9.4	51.7	440 888	335 113	205 266	31.6	63.3
Leon	6.4	16.0	20.5	18.0	15.7	8.9	6.2	5.0	3.2	51.9	239 452	192 493	148 655	24.4	29.5
Levy	6.4	17.8	7.9	13.2	13.1	10.9	11.7	12.3	6.6	52.2	34 450	25 912	19 870	32.9	30.4
Liberty	6.0	18.2	11.1	19.7	14.7	9.7	9.3	6.8	4.5	43.0	7 021	5 569	4 260	26.1	30.7
Madison	7.8	19.7	10.7	16.1	13.0	10.0	8.5	7.7	6.4	48.8	18 733	16 569	14 894	13.1	11.2
Manatee	5.8	13.4	7.3	13.7	12.0	8.8	11.0	15.6	12.5	52.7	264 002	211 707	148 445	24.7	42.6
Marion	6.3	15.8	7.7	13.8	12.5	9.8	11.9	14.4	7.7	51.8	258 916	194 835	122 488	32.9	59.1
Martin	5.1	12.5	6.7	13.6	12.7	9.7	12.2	16.7	10.8	50.9	126 731	100 900	64 014	25.6	57.6
Miami-Dade	7.2	16.9	10.0	17.1	14.4	10.9	9.4	7.5	6.4	52.1	2 253 362	1 937 194	1 625 509	16.3	19.2
Monroe	5.7	11.6	7.8	17.8	17.3	12.1	11.8	10.5	5.4	47.5	79 589	78 024	63 188	2.0	23.5
Nassau	7.4	19.7	9.2	16.6	15.7	12.0	9.3	6.4	3.7	50.5	57 663	43 941	32 894	31.2	33.6
Okaloosa	7.8	18.1	11.0	19.8	14.6	10.4	9.1	6.3	3.0	49.4	170 498	143 777	109 920	18.6	30.8
Okeechobee	7.7	19.5	9.1	14.8	12.4	9.7	10.7	10.7	5.5	48.9	35 910	29 627	20 264	21.2	46.2
Orange	7.4	16.5	12.7	20.5	14.9	9.4	8.0	6.5	4.1	50.4	896 344	677 491	470 865	32.3	43.9
Osceola	7.3	17.9	10.0	17.0	14.7	10.3	8.9	8.3	5.6	50.1	172 493	107 728	49 287	60.1	118.6
Palm Beach	6.2	13.5	7.5	15.8	13.6	9.3	9.8	13.5	10.9	52.0	1 131 184	863 503	576 758	31.0	49.7
Pasco	5.2	12.7	6.7	11.8	10.9	8.6	11.9	18.9	13.4	52.6	344 765	281 131	193 661	22.6	45.2
Pinellas	5.2	12.5	7.5	14.9	13.6	9.7	10.5	13.5	12.5	53.3	921 482	851 659	728 531	8.2	16.9
Polk	7.0	17.1	9.2	14.7	13.1	10.0	10.3	11.3	7.3	51.5	483 924	405 382	321 652	19.4	26.0
Putnam	6.8	18.6	8.0	13.6	12.9	10.2	11.8	11.7	6.4	51.2	70 423	65 070	50 549	8.2	28.7
St. Johns	6.4	15.9	9.0	15.5	15.5	10.8	10.4	10.4	6.1	51.5	123 135	83 829	51 303	46.9	63.4
St. Lucie	7.0	16.1	7.6	15.3	12.8	9.1	11.1	13.7	7.3	51.1	192 695	150 171	87 182	28.3	72.3
Santa Rosa	7.8	19.4	9.2	18.2	15.3	11.6	9.0	6.1	3.4	50.2	117 743	81 961	55 988	43.7	45.8

Table B. States and Counties

STATE County	Total population	Total in households	House-holder	Spouse	Child Total	Child Own child under 18 years	Other relatives Total	Other relatives Under 18 years	Nonrelatives Total	Nonrelatives Unmarried partner	Total in group quarters	Correctional institutions	Nursing homes	Other institutions	College dormitories	Military quarters	Other
	54	55	56	57	58	59	60	61	62	63	64	65	66	67	68	69	70
DELAWARE	783 600	96.9	38.1	19.5	28.6	22.0	5.1	2.2	5.5	2.3	3.1	0.8	0.6	0.1	1.2	0.0	0.4
Kent	126 697	97.1	37.3	19.7	30.4	24.3	4.7	2.2	5.1	2.5	2.9	0.1	0.9	0.1	1.4	0.3	0.2
New Castle	500 265	96.5	37.8	18.7	29.1	22.1	5.2	2.2	5.7	2.3	3.5	0.9	0.5	0.1	1.5	0.0	0.5
Sussex	156 638	97.8	40.0	21.9	25.5	19.6	5.1	2.3	5.3	2.4	2.2	1.0	0.7	0.2	0.0	0.0	0.4
DISTRICT OF COLUMBIA	572 059	93.8	43.4	9.9	22.6	15.5	8.8	3.9	9.1	2.6	6.2	0.5	0.7	0.2	3.4	0.2	1.3
District of Columbia	572 059	93.8	43.4	9.9	22.6	15.5	8.8	3.9	9.1	2.6	6.2	0.5	0.7	0.2	3.4	0.2	1.3
FLORIDA	15 982 378	97.6	39.7	20.0	26.1	20.0	6.0	2.2	5.9	2.3	2.4	0.9	0.6	0.1	0.3	0.1	0.5
Alachua	217 955	94.1	40.2	15.6	22.6	18.0	4.3	1.6	11.5	2.4	5.9	0.7	0.2	0.2	3.9	0.0	0.9
Baker	22 259	90.5	31.6	19.5	30.6	24.0	5.2	2.6	3.5	1.6	9.5	6.1	0.7	2.3	0.0	0.0	0.3
Bay	148 217	97.7	40.2	20.9	27.3	21.5	4.3	1.9	5.1	2.3	2.3	1.1	0.5	0.1	0.0	0.4	0.3
Bradford	26 088	84.1	32.6	18.0	24.8	18.9	4.9	2.3	3.8	1.8	15.9	14.6	1.0	0.0	0.0	0.0	0.4
Brevard	476 230	98.0	41.6	22.0	25.1	19.7	4.1	1.6	5.1	2.3	2.0	0.5	0.5	0.3	0.2	0.0	0.4
Broward	1 623 018	98.8	40.3	18.6	27.4	21.0	6.4	2.1	6.0	2.6	1.2	0.4	0.3	0.1	0.0	0.0	0.4
Calhoun	13 017	86.8	34.3	17.9	25.8	20.1	4.9	2.5	3.8	1.7	13.2	11.2	1.7	0.0	0.0	0.0	0.3
Charlotte	141 627	98.2	45.1	26.7	18.4	13.9	3.7	1.3	4.3	2.1	1.8	0.8	0.9	0.0	0.0	0.0	0.1
Citrus	118 085	98.2	44.6	26.0	19.6	15.2	3.7	1.4	4.3	2.2	1.8	0.2	1.0	0.1	0.0	0.0	0.4
Clay	140 814	98.9	35.7	22.7	31.8	25.5	4.4	1.9	4.2	1.8	1.1	0.2	0.5	0.0	0.0	0.0	0.4
Collier	251 377	98.1	41.0	23.8	21.7	17.4	5.4	1.7	6.3	2.1	1.9	0.3	0.6	0.1	0.0	0.0	1.0
Columbia	56 513	94.8	37.0	19.9	27.7	21.7	5.8	2.9	4.4	2.1	5.2	3.7	0.7	0.3	0.1	0.0	0.4
De Soto	32 209	90.0	33.4	18.5	22.5	18.0	6.6	2.5	9.1	1.9	10.0	5.0	0.2	1.6	0.0	0.0	3.2
Dixie	13 827	92.0	37.6	20.7	23.7	18.8	5.1	2.5	4.8	2.5	8.0	7.4	0.4	0.0	0.0	0.0	0.2
Duval	778 879	98.0	39.0	18.1	29.5	23.2	5.6	2.5	5.7	2.4	2.0	0.4	0.5	0.0	0.3	0.5	0.3
Escambia	294 410	92.5	37.7	18.0	26.8	20.5	5.0	2.4	4.9	1.9	7.5	2.6	0.8	0.3	1.5	2.1	0.2
Flagler	49 832	99.1	42.7	26.8	21.2	15.9	4.5	1.6	3.9	1.9	0.9	0.1	0.7	0.1	0.0	0.0	0.1
Franklin	11 057	84.5	37.0	19.4	20.1	15.7	4.0	1.9	3.8	2.1	15.5	14.2	1.2	0.0	0.0	0.0	0.1
Gadsden	45 087	94.6	35.2	15.6	30.3	21.0	9.3	4.9	4.1	2.0	5.4	2.7	0.6	1.5	0.0	0.0	0.5
Gilchrist	14 437	90.8	34.8	20.5	26.7	21.5	4.5	2.1	4.3	2.0	9.2	7.9	1.2	0.0	0.0	0.0	0.1
Glades	10 576	91.4	36.4	21.2	22.9	18.5	5.8	2.8	5.0	2.3	8.6	6.8	0.0	0.0	0.0	0.0	1.8
Gulf	13 332	89.5	37.0	20.5	24.1	18.3	4.9	2.6	2.9	1.4	10.5	9.2	0.8	0.1	0.0	0.0	0.3
Hamilton	13 327	81.2	31.2	15.7	24.4	18.8	6.5	3.6	3.5	1.6	18.8	17.7	0.5	0.4	0.0	0.0	0.3
Hardee	26 938	92.9	30.3	18.2	28.8	22.1	8.8	4.2	6.8	1.5	7.1	4.7	0.3	0.5	0.0	0.0	1.7
Hendry	36 210	92.5	30.0	16.7	30.4	24.8	7.8	3.5	7.6	2.0	7.5	3.5	0.6	0.3	0.0	0.0	3.2
Hernando	130 802	98.4	42.4	25.6	21.9	16.6	4.4	1.6	4.1	2.1	1.6	0.6	0.6	0.1	0.0	0.0	0.4
Highlands	87 366	98.5	42.9	24.5	20.9	16.4	4.7	2.0	5.5	1.9	1.5	0.3	0.9	0.0	0.1	0.0	0.2
Hillsborough	998 948	98.3	39.2	18.7	28.3	22.3	5.9	2.3	6.3	2.6	1.7	0.3	0.3	0.1	0.4	0.0	0.5
Holmes	18 564	90.7	37.3	20.7	25.9	20.5	3.8	1.7	3.0	1.5	9.3	7.7	1.0	0.3	0.0	0.0	0.2
Indian River	112 947	98.0	43.5	23.7	21.6	16.8	4.4	1.7	4.7	2.0	2.0	0.6	0.5	0.0	0.1	0.0	0.7
Jackson	46 755	86.8	35.5	18.3	25.6	19.2	4.6	2.2	2.8	1.4	13.2	10.4	0.5	1.3	0.4	0.0	0.7
Jefferson	12 902	92.0	36.4	18.6	26.3	18.7	7.0	3.3	3.7	1.8	8.0	6.1	1.1	0.2	0.0	0.0	0.6
Lafayette	7 022	81.2	30.5	18.1	24.0	18.7	4.6	2.1	4.0	1.5	18.8	17.5	0.8	0.0	0.0	0.0	0.5
Lake	210 528	98.2	42.0	24.7	22.5	17.8	4.5	1.8	4.4	2.0	1.8	0.7	0.7	0.1	0.0	0.0	0.3
Lee	440 888	98.7	42.8	23.7	21.9	17.4	4.5	1.6	5.8	2.5	1.3	0.3	0.6	0.1	0.1	0.0	0.3
Leon	239 452	94.3	40.3	16.0	24.0	19.2	4.2	1.6	9.7	2.2	5.7	1.1	0.5	0.1	3.6	0.0	0.4
Levy	34 450	98.2	40.3	21.5	25.7	20.0	5.6	2.8	5.2	2.5	1.8	1.1	0.4	0.1	0.0	0.0	0.2
Liberty	7 021	79.4	31.6	16.4	24.0	19.1	3.7	1.9	3.6	1.9	20.6	19.0	0.0	0.5	0.0	0.0	1.0
Madison	18 733	90.9	35.4	17.3	27.4	20.4	6.9	3.5	3.9	1.7	9.1	7.5	1.1	0.4	0.0	0.0	0.0
Manatee	264 002	97.7	42.6	22.5	22.6	17.9	4.7	1.8	5.3	2.4	2.3	0.5	0.8	0.1	0.0	0.0	0.9
Marion	258 916	97.3	41.2	22.9	23.8	18.6	4.8	2.0	4.6	2.2	2.7	1.5	0.6	0.1	0.1	0.0	0.4
Martin	126 731	97.4	43.6	24.0	21.2	16.9	3.6	1.2	5.0	2.1	2.6	1.3	0.7	0.1	0.1	0.0	0.5
Miami-Dade	2 253 362	98.0	34.5	16.5	30.0	21.0	10.8	3.3	6.2	2.0	2.0	0.7	0.4	0.2	0.3	0.0	0.4
Monroe	79 589	98.3	44.1	20.6	19.3	15.4	4.4	1.2	9.9	3.8	1.7	0.7	0.3	0.0	0.0	0.1	0.5
Nassau	57 663	98.8	38.1	23.3	28.2	22.1	4.9	2.2	4.2	1.9	1.2	0.3	0.5	0.1	0.0	0.0	0.3
Okaloosa	170 498	96.8	38.9	21.8	27.7	22.6	3.4	1.5	4.9	1.8	3.2	1.4	0.5	0.2	0.0	0.9	0.2
Okeechobee	35 910	94.2	35.1	19.5	26.0	20.6	6.6	2.9	7.0	2.3	5.8	4.1	0.5	1.1	0.0	0.0	0.1
Orange	896 344	97.9	37.5	17.6	28.4	22.1	6.5	2.5	7.8	2.7	2.1	0.7	0.4	0.2	0.4	0.0	0.4
Osceola	172 493	98.6	35.4	19.8	30.3	23.5	6.9	2.6	6.2	2.4	1.4	0.5	0.5	0.1	0.1	0.0	0.2
Palm Beach	1 131 184	98.3	41.9	21.3	24.3	19.0	5.2	1.7	5.7	2.3	1.7	0.4	0.6	0.1	0.3	0.0	0.4
Pasco	344 765	98.4	42.8	23.4	23.2	18.1	4.2	1.5	4.9	2.5	1.6	0.2	0.8	0.0	0.1	0.0	0.4
Pinellas	921 482	97.5	45.0	20.2	22.3	17.2	4.2	1.5	5.8	2.7	2.5	0.4	1.0	0.1	0.2	0.0	0.8
Polk	483 924	97.4	38.7	21.0	26.7	20.8	6.0	2.7	5.0	2.2	2.6	1.0	0.6	0.2	0.4	0.0	0.5
Putnam	70 423	98.0	39.5	20.9	27.1	21.0	6.0	2.9	4.6	2.2	2.0	0.9	0.5	0.0	0.0	0.0	0.6
St. Johns	123 135	98.2	40.3	22.9	26.1	21.1	3.7	1.5	5.2	2.2	1.8	0.3	0.6	0.1	0.6	0.0	0.3
St. Lucie	192 695	98.6	39.9	22.1	25.3	19.7	5.7	2.3	5.6	2.4	1.4	0.4	0.4	0.0	0.1	0.0	0.5
Santa Rosa	117 743	97.8	37.2	23.1	29.8	24.2	3.8	1.6	3.9	1.7	2.2	1.4	0.3	0.1	0.0	0.1	0.2

Table B. States and Counties

	Households by type, 2000												Households, 1990		
	Family households						Nonfamily households								
			Married couple		Female householder[1]			Householder living alone							
STATE County	Total households	Total	With own children under 18 years	Total	With own children under 18 years	Total	With own children under 18 years	Total	Total	65 years and over	Average household size	Average family size	Total households	Female householder[1]	Householder living alone
	71	72	73	74	75	76	77	78	79	80	81	82	83	84	85
DELAWARE	298 736	68.5	31.9	51.3	21.9	13.1	7.7	31.5	25.0	9.1	2.54	3.04	247 497	11.8	23.2
Kent	47 224	71.2	35.5	52.9	23.9	13.8	8.9	28.8	23.0	8.4	2.61	3.06	39 655	11.9	21.2
New Castle	188 935	67.3	32.5	49.6	22.6	13.4	7.7	32.7	25.7	8.5	2.56	3.09	164 161	12.1	24.0
Sussex	62 577	70.1	27.1	54.9	18.4	11.3	6.7	29.9	24.3	11.1	2.45	2.88	43 681	10.9	22.3
DISTRICT OF COLUMBIA	248 338	46.0	19.8	22.8	8.4	18.9	9.9	54.0	43.8	10.0	2.16	3.07	249 634	19.5	41.5
District of Columbia	248 338	46.0	19.8	22.8	8.4	18.9	9.9	54.0	43.8	10.0	2.16	3.07	249 634	19.5	41.5
FLORIDA	6 337 929	66.4	28.1	50.4	19.2	12.0	6.9	33.6	26.6	11.2	2.46	2.98	5 134 869	10.7	25.5
Alachua	87 509	54.6	25.2	38.8	16.3	12.3	7.4	45.4	29.1	6.4	2.34	2.94	71 258	12.0	28.1
Baker	7 043	79.5	41.2	61.7	30.3	13.1	8.0	20.5	17.1	6.9	2.86	3.20	5 554	12.4	15.8
Bay	59 597	67.9	30.6	52.0	20.8	12.0	7.5	32.1	26.0	8.8	2.43	2.92	48 938	11.1	23.0
Bradford	8 497	72.9	31.9	55.4	22.0	13.3	7.7	27.1	22.9	9.7	2.58	3.01	7 193	12.3	20.4
Brevard	198 195	66.8	26.5	53.0	18.5	10.2	6.0	33.2	26.9	11.6	2.35	2.84	161 365	9.1	23.7
Broward	654 445	62.9	29.3	46.1	20.1	12.5	7.2	37.1	29.6	12.4	2.45	3.07	528 442	10.0	29.5
Calhoun	4 468	70.1	32.5	52.3	22.7	13.5	7.3	29.9	26.5	12.4	2.53	3.02	3 793	13.3	24.3
Charlotte	63 864	69.1	17.4	59.2	12.2	7.2	3.8	30.9	26.0	16.7	2.18	2.56	48 933	6.0	23.0
Citrus	52 634	69.0	19.0	58.3	13.1	7.6	4.3	31.0	26.1	15.6	2.20	2.60	40 573	6.8	23.1
Clay	50 243	78.4	39.6	63.8	30.3	10.7	6.9	21.6	16.9	5.5	2.77	3.11	36 663	9.1	15.2
Collier	102 973	69.2	22.7	58.1	16.5	7.2	4.0	30.8	24.5	11.9	2.39	2.79	61 703	7.1	22.6
Columbia	20 925	71.3	32.1	53.7	21.9	12.9	7.6	28.7	23.8	9.8	2.56	3.02	15 611	13.0	22.7
De Soto	10 746	71.4	26.5	55.5	18.0	10.3	6.1	28.6	21.0	11.4	2.70	3.00	8 222	10.9	22.1
Dixie	5 205	70.3	27.4	54.9	18.8	10.6	5.9	29.7	23.9	11.6	2.44	2.87	3 916	10.0	22.4
Duval	303 747	66.4	33.3	46.5	21.4	15.6	9.7	33.6	26.5	7.8	2.51	3.06	257 245	13.7	26.0
Escambia	111 049	66.8	29.9	47.8	18.9	15.1	9.0	33.2	26.9	9.7	2.45	2.98	98 608	14.2	23.6
Flagler	21 294	73.6	21.1	62.8	15.4	8.1	4.4	26.4	21.6	12.0	2.32	2.67	11 880	7.1	18.9
Franklin	4 096	66.6	24.8	52.5	16.7	9.8	5.7	33.4	28.7	11.8	2.28	2.77	3 628	9.6	25.4
Gadsden	15 867	72.0	32.6	44.5	18.1	22.5	12.2	28.0	23.9	9.5	2.69	3.18	13 405	22.5	21.5
Gilchrist	5 021	74.0	32.9	59.0	24.0	11.2	7.1	26.0	21.1	8.7	2.61	3.01	3 284	9.4	19.0
Glades	3 852	71.8	25.8	58.3	17.9	8.6	5.1	28.2	22.7	11.4	2.51	2.91	2 885	7.0	22.1
Gulf	4 931	71.7	28.4	55.5	20.0	11.9	6.1	28.3	25.5	11.4	2.42	2.87	4 324	11.1	22.6
Hamilton	4 161	72.0	32.9	50.3	21.0	16.8	9.3	28.0	24.1	9.1	2.60	3.07	3 488	18.4	22.2
Hardee	8 166	76.6	34.9	60.0	25.9	11.1	6.1	23.4	18.0	9.4	3.06	3.40	6 391	10.4	17.6
Hendry	10 850	75.0	40.2	55.7	28.4	12.5	8.3	25.0	18.6	7.3	3.09	3.44	8 402	12.1	17.6
Hernando	55 425	72.2	21.8	60.4	15.4	8.7	4.8	27.8	23.3	14.7	2.32	2.70	42 300	6.9	19.7
Highlands	37 471	68.8	20.0	57.2	13.5	8.5	4.9	31.2	26.3	16.7	2.30	2.70	29 544	7.0	24.2
Hillsborough	391 357	65.2	31.4	47.7	21.1	13.2	8.0	34.8	26.9	8.1	2.51	3.07	324 872	11.9	25.3
Holmes	6 921	70.7	30.9	55.6	22.3	10.8	6.2	29.3	26.1	12.4	2.43	2.92	5 800	11.2	23.6
Indian River	49 137	66.6	21.7	54.5	15.0	8.9	5.1	33.4	28.2	16.1	2.25	2.72	38 057	7.8	23.9
Jackson	16 620	69.8	30.9	51.5	20.4	14.4	8.4	30.2	27.0	12.8	2.44	2.95	14 465	12.9	25.3
Jefferson	4 695	70.4	29.2	51.0	19.9	15.1	7.4	29.6	25.2	10.2	2.53	3.03	3 982	16.7	22.1
Lafayette	2 142	74.3	34.0	59.2	25.4	9.2	5.5	25.7	22.0	10.1	2.66	3.06	1 721	10.7	19.6
Lake	88 413	70.7	23.4	58.9	16.7	8.5	4.9	29.3	24.6	13.7	2.34	2.75	63 616	8.0	23.8
Lee	188 599	67.7	22.4	55.5	15.4	8.7	5.1	32.3	25.8	13.1	2.31	2.73	140 124	8.2	23.0
Leon	96 521	56.3	27.7	39.8	18.0	13.0	8.0	43.7	29.7	5.8	2.34	2.95	74 828	12.3	27.0
Levy	13 867	69.8	27.4	53.4	17.9	11.8	7.0	30.2	24.9	11.6	2.44	2.88	10 079	11.1	22.4
Liberty	2 222	69.9	34.2	51.8	22.7	13.2	8.9	30.1	25.9	10.6	2.51	3.00	1 706	11.3	21.9
Madison	6 629	70.6	31.9	48.9	19.7	17.5	10.0	29.4	25.4	11.6	2.57	3.06	5 522	17.1	22.9
Manatee	112 460	65.6	23.0	52.7	15.7	9.4	5.5	34.4	28.4	15.0	2.29	2.78	91 060	8.4	27.0
Marion	106 755	69.9	24.7	55.6	16.5	10.7	6.3	30.1	25.0	13.0	2.36	2.79	78 177	10.3	22.9
Martin	55 288	65.5	21.5	55.0	15.7	7.4	4.2	34.5	29.0	16.0	2.23	2.71	43 022	6.5	25.0
Miami-Dade	776 774	70.6	33.8	47.7	22.6	17.2	9.1	29.4	23.3	8.6	2.84	3.35	692 355	14.9	24.9
Monroe	35 086	58.1	20.8	46.8	14.7	7.3	4.3	41.9	28.8	8.2	2.23	2.73	33 583	6.4	27.8
Nassau	21 980	75.2	32.8	61.2	25.0	9.9	5.7	24.8	20.1	7.7	2.59	2.97	16 192	9.5	21.2
Okaloosa	66 269	70.2	33.1	56.2	24.3	10.2	6.6	29.8	23.5	7.5	2.49	2.94	53 313	9.5	20.9
Okeechobee	12 593	71.6	30.4	55.5	20.9	10.7	6.5	28.4	21.5	10.1	2.69	3.07	10 214	9.3	19.1
Orange	336 286	65.5	32.4	47.0	21.8	13.7	8.2	34.5	24.2	6.5	2.61	3.14	254 852	11.6	23.7
Osceola	60 977	73.9	36.4	56.1	25.8	12.8	7.9	26.1	19.1	7.0	2.79	3.18	39 150	9.5	19.2
Palm Beach	474 175	64.1	24.9	50.8	17.5	9.7	5.7	35.9	29.2	14.6	2.34	2.89	365 558	8.6	27.5
Pasco	147 566	67.1	23.5	54.6	16.7	8.9	4.9	32.9	27.3	15.9	2.30	2.77	121 674	7.3	25.7
Pinellas	414 968	58.6	22.1	44.8	14.5	10.5	5.9	41.4	34.1	15.5	2.17	2.77	380 508	9.4	31.9
Polk	187 233	70.7	29.0	54.4	19.6	12.0	7.1	29.3	24.1	11.1	2.52	2.96	155 969	10.8	22.4
Putnam	27 839	69.9	28.1	52.8	18.3	12.9	7.5	30.1	25.1	11.9	2.48	2.95	25 070	11.8	23.1
St. Johns	49 614	68.7	29.2	56.8	22.3	8.9	5.2	31.3	24.3	9.4	2.44	2.90	33 426	9.3	24.1
St. Lucie	76 933	70.5	26.3	55.3	17.6	11.1	6.5	29.5	23.5	12.4	2.47	2.89	58 174	9.9	20.3
Santa Rosa	43 793	76.1	36.5	62.2	27.8	10.2	6.5	23.9	19.3	6.6	2.63	3.00	29 900	9.8	18.3

[1] No spouse present.

Table B. States and Counties

| STATE County | Percent change of households, 1990-2000 | Total housing units | Occupied housing units (percent) | Vacant housing units | | Homeowner vacancy rate (percent) | Rental vacancy rate (percent) | Occupied housing units | Percent owner-occupied housing units | Percent renter-occupied housing units | Average household size of owner-occupied units | Average household size of renter-occupied units |
				Total	For seasonal, recreational, or occasional use			Total				
	86	87	88	89	90	91	92	93	94	95	96	97
DELAWARE	20.7	343 072	87.1	12.9	7.6	1.5	8.2	298 736	72.3	27.7	2.61	2.37
Kent	19.1	50 481	93.5	6.5	0.7	1.6	6.7	47 224	70.0	30.0	2.66	2.49
New Castle	15.1	199 521	94.7	5.3	0.4	1.2	7.4	188 935	70.1	29.9	2.67	2.29
Sussex	43.3	93 070	67.2	32.8	26.8	2.1	13.4	62 577	80.7	19.3	2.41	2.60
DISTRICT OF COLUMBIA	-0.5	274 845	90.4	9.6	0.8	2.9	5.9	248 338	40.8	59.2	2.31	2.06
District of Columbia	-0.5	274 845	90.4	9.6	0.8	2.9	5.9	248 338	40.8	59.2	2.31	2.06
FLORIDA	23.4	7 302 947	86.8	13.2	6.6	2.2	9.3	6 337 929	70.1	29.9	2.49	2.39
Alachua	22.8	95 113	92.0	8.0	0.7	2.0	7.9	87 509	54.9	45.1	2.51	2.14
Baker	26.8	7 592	92.8	7.2	1.3	0.8	7.7	7 043	81.2	18.8	2.90	2.69
Bay	21.8	78 435	76.0	24.0	11.2	2.9	22.7	59 597	68.6	31.4	2.48	2.33
Bradford	18.1	9 605	88.5	11.5	2.3	1.9	12.6	8 497	79.0	21.0	2.61	2.48
Brevard	22.8	222 072	89.2	10.8	4.7	2.3	10.6	198 195	74.6	25.4	2.40	2.23
Broward	23.8	741 043	88.3	11.7	6.3	2.6	6.5	654 445	69.5	30.5	2.49	2.35
Calhoun	17.8	5 250	85.1	14.9	4.1	2.7	14.3	4 468	80.2	19.8	2.50	2.63
Charlotte	31.9	79 758	80.1	19.9	13.2	2.2	14.2	63 864	83.7	16.3	2.16	2.28
Citrus	29.7	62 204	84.6	15.4	8.3	2.6	13.4	52 634	85.6	14.4	2.19	2.27
Clay	37.0	53 748	93.5	6.5	1.5	1.4	8.2	50 243	77.9	22.1	2.82	2.59
Collier	66.9	144 536	71.2	28.8	23.8	2.6	9.8	102 973	75.6	24.4	2.31	2.65
Columbia	34.0	23 579	88.7	11.3	1.8	1.9	13.2	20 925	77.2	22.8	2.60	2.44
De Soto	30.7	13 608	79.0	21.0	13.3	2.7	8.5	10 746	74.7	25.3	2.48	3.35
Dixie	32.9	7 362	70.7	29.3	18.7	3.4	16.6	5 205	86.4	13.6	2.42	2.60
Duval	18.1	329 778	92.1	7.9	0.4	1.8	9.0	303 747	63.1	36.9	2.62	2.32
Escambia	12.6	124 647	89.1	10.9	2.5	2.2	11.8	111 049	67.3	32.7	2.48	2.40
Flagler	79.2	24 452	87.1	12.9	7.9	2.0	9.5	21 294	84.0	16.0	2.30	2.43
Franklin	12.9	7 180	57.0	43.0	19.0	4.2	42.3	4 096	79.2	20.8	2.31	2.18
Gadsden	18.4	17 703	89.6	10.4	1.3	1.8	9.7	15 867	78.0	22.0	2.66	2.79
Gilchrist	52.9	5 906	85.0	15.0	6.5	2.5	7.3	5 021	86.3	13.7	2.61	2.64
Glades	33.5	5 790	66.5	33.5	24.2	3.8	17.4	3 852	81.7	18.3	2.43	2.85
Gulf	14.0	7 587	65.0	35.0	16.8	3.5	37.2	4 931	81.0	19.0	2.43	2.40
Hamilton	19.3	4 966	83.8	16.2	3.9	1.3	14.5	4 161	77.4	22.6	2.59	2.64
Hardee	27.8	9 820	83.2	16.8	9.5	1.5	9.2	8 166	73.4	26.6	2.92	3.45
Hendry	29.1	12 294	88.3	11.7	4.3	2.4	7.5	10 850	72.4	27.6	3.00	3.31
Hernando	31.0	62 727	88.4	11.6	5.7	2.4	8.7	55 425	86.5	13.5	2.30	2.47
Highlands	26.8	48 846	76.7	23.3	12.6	3.9	14.6	37 471	79.7	20.3	2.22	2.60
Hillsborough	20.5	425 962	91.9	8.1	1.4	1.9	8.9	391 357	64.1	35.9	2.63	2.29
Holmes	19.3	7 998	86.5	13.5	1.9	2.2	9.5	6 921	81.5	18.5	2.42	2.50
Indian River	29.1	57 902	84.9	15.1	9.1	2.2	8.9	49 137	77.6	22.4	2.25	2.27
Jackson	14.9	19 490	85.3	14.7	3.4	2.0	15.8	16 620	77.9	22.1	2.45	2.41
Jefferson	17.9	5 251	89.4	10.6	1.7	1.8	15.7	4 695	80.9	19.1	2.55	2.45
Lafayette	24.5	2 660	80.5	19.5	10.0	1.4	9.6	2 142	80.6	19.4	2.54	3.18
Lake	39.0	102 830	86.0	14.0	6.5	2.6	11.6	88 413	81.5	18.5	2.33	2.40
Lee	34.6	245 405	76.9	23.1	16.1	2.7	15.2	188 599	76.5	23.5	2.29	2.38
Leon	29.0	103 974	92.8	7.2	0.7	1.8	8.1	96 521	57.0	43.0	2.53	2.09
Levy	37.6	16 570	83.7	16.3	6.5	2.9	15.4	13 867	83.6	16.4	2.42	2.52
Liberty	30.2	3 156	70.4	29.6	3.8	6.5	17.9	2 222	81.8	18.2	2.52	2.47
Madison	20.0	7 836	84.6	15.4	3.6	1.8	13.1	6 629	78.4	21.6	2.57	2.57
Manatee	23.5	138 128	81.4	18.6	12.2	2.5	10.1	112 460	73.8	26.2	2.26	2.39
Marion	36.6	122 663	87.0	13.0	4.3	2.7	9.8	106 755	79.8	20.2	2.35	2.42
Martin	28.5	65 471	84.4	15.6	10.3	2.3	9.5	55 288	79.8	20.2	2.20	2.34
Miami-Dade	12.2	852 278	91.1	8.9	3.5	2.1	5.7	776 774	57.8	42.2	3.00	2.63
Monroe	4.5	51 617	68.0	32.0	23.9	3.0	11.5	35 086	62.4	37.6	2.23	2.23
Nassau	35.7	25 917	84.8	15.2	5.4	1.5	23.4	21 980	80.6	19.4	2.64	2.39
Okaloosa	24.3	78 593	84.3	15.7	5.4	2.2	19.3	66 269	66.4	33.6	2.51	2.45
Okeechobee	23.3	15 504	81.2	18.8	7.5	2.6	10.4	12 593	74.8	25.2	2.57	3.02
Orange	32.0	361 349	93.1	6.9	1.5	1.7	7.1	336 286	60.7	39.3	2.74	2.41
Osceola	55.8	72 293	84.3	15.7	9.1	2.3	11.0	60 977	67.7	32.3	2.81	2.74
Palm Beach	29.7	556 428	85.2	14.8	9.5	2.0	8.7	474 175	74.7	25.3	2.34	2.37
Pasco	21.3	173 717	84.9	15.1	8.6	2.3	11.4	147 566	82.4	17.6	2.30	2.31
Pinellas	9.0	481 573	86.2	13.8	7.1	2.3	10.2	414 968	70.8	29.2	2.22	2.03
Polk	20.0	226 376	82.7	17.3	8.4	2.9	12.9	187 233	73.4	26.6	2.51	2.53
Putnam	11.0	33 870	82.2	17.8	8.7	3.0	10.0	27 839	80.0	20.0	2.46	2.54
St. Johns	48.4	58 008	85.5	14.5	7.4	2.3	12.8	49 614	76.4	23.6	2.52	2.18
St. Lucie	32.2	91 262	84.3	15.7	9.9	2.3	11.8	76 933	78.0	22.0	2.39	2.74
Santa Rosa	46.5	49 119	89.2	10.8	2.0	2.6	16.8	43 793	80.4	19.6	2.65	2.56

Table B. States and Counties

STATE/ County code	MSA/ PMSA/ NECMA code[1]	County type[2]	STATE County	Land area, 2000[3] (sq km)	Total persons	Rank	Per square kilometer	Land area, 1990[3] (sq km)	Total persons	Rank	Per square kilometer	White	Black or African American	American Indian or Alaska Native	Asian	Native Hawaiian and other Pacific Islander	Some other race
				1	2	3	4	5	6	7	8	9	10	11	12	13	14
			FLORIDA—Cont'd														
12 115	7510	2	Sarasota	1 480	325 957	177	220.2	1 481	277 776	178	187.6	92.6	4.2	0.2	0.8	0.0	1.1
12 117	5960	0	Seminole	798	365 196	161	457.0	708	287 521	170	360.3	82.4	9.5	0.3	2.5	0.0	3.1
12 119	...	6	Sumter	1 413	53 345	876	37.8	1 413	31 577	1 228	22.3	82.6	13.8	0.5	0.4	0.1	1.2
12 121	...	7	Suwannee	1 781	34 844	1 256	19.6	1 781	26 780	1 397	15.0	84.5	12.1	0.4	0.5	0.0	1.1
12 123	...	7	Taylor	2 699	19 256	1 830	7.1	2 699	17 111	1 845	6.3	77.8	19.0	1.0	0.4	0.0	0.3
12 125	...	8	Union	622	13 442	2 197	21.6	622	10 252	2 363	16.5	73.6	22.8	0.7	0.3	0.0	1.0
12 127	2020	2	Volusia	2 857	443 343	135	155.2	2 864	370 737	136	129.4	86.1	9.3	0.3	1.0	0.0	1.8
12 129	...	8	Wakulla	1 571	22 863	1 650	14.6	1 571	14 202	2 037	9.0	86.1	11.5	0.6	0.2	0.0	0.3
12 131	...	6	Walton	2 739	40 601	1 098	14.8	2 739	27 759	1 360	10.1	88.4	7.0	1.3	0.5	0.0	0.8
12 133	...	6	Washington	1 502	20 973	1 738	14.0	1 502	16 919	1 855	11.3	81.7	13.7	1.5	0.4	0.1	0.6
13 000	...		GEORGIA	149 976	8 186 453	X	54.6	150 010	6 478 149	X	43.2	65.1	28.7	0.3	2.1	0.1	2.4
13 001	...	7	Appling	1 317	17 419	1 928	13.2	1 318	15 744	1 937	11.9	76.8	19.6	0.2	0.3	0.0	2.5
13 003	...	9	Atkinson	876	7 609	2 635	8.7	876	6 213	2 731	7.1	66.8	19.6	0.4	0.1	0.0	12.0
13 005	...	7	Bacon	738	10 103	2 437	13.7	738	9 566	2 426	13.0	81.5	15.7	0.1	0.3	0.0	1.5
13 007	...	8	Baker	889	4 074	2 913	4.6	889	3 615	2 949	4.1	47.4	50.4	0.2	0.0	0.0	1.3
13 009	...	4	Baldwin	669	44 700	1 005	66.8	669	39 530	1 012	59.1	54.2	43.4	0.2	1.0	0.0	0.5
13 011	...	8	Banks	605	14 422	2 128	23.8	605	10 308	2 358	17.0	93.2	3.2	0.3	0.6	0.1	2.0
13 013	0520	1	Barrow	420	46 144	980	109.9	420	29 721	1 306	70.8	84.8	9.7	0.3	2.2	0.0	1.5
13 015	0520	1	Bartow	1 190	76 019	659	63.9	1 191	55 915	774	46.9	87.8	8.7	0.3	0.5	0.0	1.6
13 017	...	7	Ben Hill	652	17 484	1 924	26.8	652	16 245	1 911	24.9	63.3	32.6	0.2	0.3	0.0	2.9
13 019	...	7	Berrien	1 172	16 235	2 006	13.9	1 172	14 153	2 041	12.1	85.5	11.4	0.3	0.3	0.1	1.5
13 021	4680	2	Bibb	647	153 887	345	237.8	648	150 137	313	231.7	50.1	47.3	0.2	1.1	0.0	0.5
13 023	...	6	Bleckley	563	11 666	2 321	20.7	563	10 430	2 346	18.5	73.2	24.6	0.1	0.9	0.0	0.5
13 025	...	9	Brantley	1 151	14 629	2 111	12.7	1 151	11 077	2 285	9.6	94.4	4.0	0.1	0.1	0.0	0.3
13 027	...	7	Brooks	1 278	16 450	1 993	12.9	1 279	15 398	1 964	12.0	57.4	39.3	0.3	0.3	0.0	1.8
13 029	7520	2	Bryan	1 144	23 417	1 621	20.5	1 144	15 438	1 959	13.5	82.8	14.1	0.3	0.8	0.1	0.6
13 031	...	6	Bulloch	1 767	55 983	843	31.7	1 768	43 125	936	24.4	68.7	28.8	0.1	0.8	0.0	0.8
13 033	...	6	Burke	2 151	22 243	1 684	10.3	2 151	20 579	1 660	9.6	46.9	51.0	0.2	0.3	0.0	0.6
13 035	...	6	Butts	483	19 522	1 818	40.4	483	15 326	1 970	31.7	69.2	28.8	0.4	0.3	0.0	0.3
13 037	...	8	Calhoun	726	6 320	2 755	8.7	726	5 013	2 841	6.9	38.3	60.6	0.1	0.1	0.0	0.4
13 039	...	6	Camden	1 631	43 664	1 024	26.8	1 632	30 167	1 291	18.5	75.0	20.1	0.5	1.0	0.1	1.4
13 043	...	7	Candler	639	9 577	2 482	15.0	640	7 744	2 599	12.1	65.4	27.1	0.2	0.3	0.0	6.2
13 045	0520	1	Carroll	1 292	87 268	601	67.5	1 293	71 422	620	55.2	80.5	16.3	0.3	0.6	0.0	1.1
13 047	1560	2	Catoosa	420	53 282	878	126.9	420	42 464	947	101.1	96.4	1.3	0.3	0.7	0.0	0.4
13 049	...	8	Charlton	2 022	10 282	2 419	5.1	2 022	8 496	2 513	4.2	68.6	29.3	0.4	0.3	0.1	0.1
13 051	7520	2	Chatham	1 135	232 048	248	204.4	1 141	216 774	230	190.0	55.3	40.5	0.2	1.7	0.1	0.9
13 053	1800	2	Chattahoochee	644	14 882	2 100	23.1	644	16 934	1 853	26.3	58.1	29.9	0.8	1.8	0.5	5.2
13 055	...	7	Chattooga	812	25 470	1 541	31.4	813	22 236	1 569	27.4	86.7	11.2	0.1	0.1	0.0	0.8
13 057	0520	1	Cherokee	1 097	141 903	385	129.4	1 098	90 204	508	82.2	92.4	2.5	0.4	0.8	0.0	2.6
13 059	0500	3	Clarke	313	101 489	520	324.2	313	87 594	520	279.9	64.9	27.3	0.2	3.1	0.0	3.1
13 061	...	9	Clay	506	3 357	2 967	6.6	506	3 364	2 966	6.6	38.4	60.5	0.1	0.3	0.1	0.0
13 063	0520	0	Clayton	369	236 517	245	641.0	369	181 436	269	491.7	37.9	51.6	0.3	4.5	0.1	3.5
13 065	...	7	Clinch	2 096	6 878	2 699	3.3	2 096	6 160	2 736	2.9	68.9	29.5	0.5	0.1	0.0	0.1
13 067	0520	0	Cobb	881	607 751	89	689.8	881	447 745	111	508.2	72.4	18.8	0.3	3.1	0.0	3.6
13 069	...	7	Coffee	1 551	37 413	1 179	24.1	1 552	29 592	1 314	19.1	68.2	25.9	0.3	0.6	0.0	4.0
13 071	...	7	Colquitt	1 430	42 053	1 057	29.4	1 430	36 645	1 084	25.6	67.8	23.5	0.3	0.2	0.0	7.1
13 073	0600	2	Columbia	751	89 288	579	118.9	751	66 031	664	87.9	82.7	11.2	0.3	3.4	0.1	0.8
13 075	...	7	Cook	593	15 771	2 033	26.6	593	13 456	2 104	22.7	67.9	29.1	0.2	0.4	0.0	1.5
13 077	0520	1	Coweta	1 146	89 215	580	77.8	1 148	53 853	798	46.9	78.9	18.0	0.2	0.7	0.0	1.2
13 079	...	8	Crawford	842	12 495	2 265	14.8	842	8 991	2 471	10.7	72.9	23.8	0.4	0.2	0.0	1.8
13 081	...	6	Crisp	709	21 996	1 693	31.0	709	20 011	1 677	28.2	54.1	43.4	0.2	0.7	0.0	1.0
13 083	1560	2	Dade	451	15 154	2 081	33.6	450	13 183	2 125	29.3	97.5	0.6	0.5	0.4	0.0	0.2
13 085	...	8	Dawson	547	15 999	2 023	29.2	547	9 429	2 440	17.2	97.2	0.4	0.4	0.4	0.0	0.7
13 087	...	6	Decatur	1 546	28 240	1 442	18.3	1 546	25 517	1 447	16.5	57.1	39.9	0.2	0.3	0.0	1.6
13 089	0520	0	De Kalb	695	665 865	76	958.1	695	546 174	87	785.9	35.8	54.2	0.2	4.0	0.0	3.5
13 091	...	7	Dodge	1 296	19 171	1 836	14.8	1 297	17 607	1 813	13.6	69.0	29.4	0.2	0.2	0.0	0.8
13 093	...	6	Dooly	1 018	11 525	2 332	11.3	1 018	9 901	2 398	9.7	46.0	49.5	0.2	0.4	0.1	2.9
13 095	0120	3	Dougherty	854	96 065	539	112.5	854	96 321	479	112.8	37.8	60.1	0.2	0.6	0.0	0.5
13 097	0520	0	Douglas	516	92 174	553	178.6	516	71 120	622	137.8	77.3	18.5	0.4	1.2	0.0	1.2
13 099	...	6	Early	1 324	12 354	2 277	9.3	1 324	11 854	2 227	9.0	50.3	48.1	0.2	0.2	0.1	0.4
13 101	...	9	Echols	1 047	3 754	2 935	3.6	1 047	2 334	3 036	2.2	77.1	6.9	1.1	0.1	0.0	13.7
13 103	7520	2	Effingham	1 242	37 535	1 176	30.2	1 242	25 687	1 435	20.7	84.7	13.0	0.3	0.5	0.0	0.5
13 105	...	6	Elbert	955	20 511	1 759	21.5	955	18 949	1 738	19.8	66.9	30.9	0.2	0.2	0.0	1.1
13 107	...	7	Emanuel	1 776	21 837	1 699	12.3	1 777	20 546	1 652	11.6	63.7	33.3	0.1	0.2	0.0	2.1
13 109	...	8	Evans	479	10 495	2 398	21.9	479	8 724	2 491	18.2	61.7	33.0	0.2	0.3	0.0	4.2

[1] MSA = Metropolitan Statistical Area. PMSA = Primary MSA. NECMA = New England County Metropolitan Area. See Appendix A for explanation of these concepts. See Appendix B for list of metropolitan areas identified by type, with component counties.
[2] County typology code from the Economic Research Service of USDA. See Appendix A for definition.
[3] Dry land or land partially or temporarily covered by water.

Table B. States and Counties

STATE County	Population and population characteristics, 2000 (cont'd)								Population and population characteristics, 1990				
	Race (percent) (cont'd)								Race (percent)				
	Race alone or in combination												
	Two or more races	White	Black	American Indian or Alaska Native	Asian	Native Hawaiian and other Pacific Islander	Some other race	Hispanic[1]	White	Black or African American	American Indian or Alaska Native	Asian and Pacific Islander	Hispanic[1]
	15	16	17	18	19	20	21	22	23	24	25	26	27
FLORIDA—Cont'd													
Sarasota	1.0	93.5	4.5	0.5	1.0	0.1	1.5	4.3	94.6	4.3	0.2	0.5	2.1
Seminole	2.2	84.2	10.2	0.8	3.0	0.1	4.1	11.2	88.2	8.5	0.3	1.7	6.5
Sumter	1.5	83.8	14.1	1.1	0.6	0.1	1.8	6.3	82.6	16.2	0.5	0.2	2.4
Suwannee	1.3	85.7	12.4	1.1	0.7	0.1	1.4	4.9	84.1	14.7	0.4	0.2	1.6
Taylor	1.4	79.0	19.3	1.8	0.6	0.1	0.6	1.5	80.6	18.0	0.9	0.2	1.0
Union	1.5	74.8	23.3	1.4	0.5	0.2	1.5	3.5	75.1	23.2	0.6	0.4	3.3
Volusia	1.4	87.3	9.7	0.8	1.3	0.1	2.4	6.6	88.6	9.0	0.2	0.7	4.0
Wakulla	1.2	87.2	11.8	1.2	0.4	0.1	0.6	1.9	86.1	12.9	0.7	0.2	0.6
Walton	2.1	90.3	7.3	2.6	0.7	0.1	1.1	2.2	91.1	6.8	1.5	0.5	0.9
Washington	2.0	83.5	14.1	2.8	0.6	0.2	0.9	2.3	82.9	14.5	1.6	0.5	1.1
GEORGIA	1.4	66.1	29.2	0.6	2.4	0.1	2.9	5.3	71.0	27.0	0.2	1.2	1.7
Appling	0.6	77.3	19.8	0.5	0.4	0.0	2.6	4.5	78.5	20.8	0.1	0.3	0.9
Atkinson	1.1	67.5	19.8	0.9	0.3	0.0	12.5	17.0	71.3	26.7	0.0	0.0	2.5
Bacon	0.9	82.3	16.1	0.5	0.4	0.0	1.6	3.4	83.9	15.5	0.1	0.2	0.9
Baker	0.6	47.9	50.6	0.4	0.0	0.1	1.6	2.7	48.3	51.5	0.0	0.1	0.6
Baldwin	0.7	54.6	43.8	0.5	1.2	0.1	0.7	1.4	56.8	42.3	0.1	0.7	0.9
Banks	0.7	93.8	3.3	0.7	0.7	0.1	2.2	3.4	95.8	3.5	0.2	0.3	0.5
Barrow	1.4	85.9	10.1	0.8	2.5	0.1	2.0	3.2	87.4	11.3	0.2	0.8	0.9
Bartow	1.1	88.8	9.0	0.7	0.7	0.1	1.9	3.3	90.2	9.0	0.2	0.3	0.9
Ben Hill	0.8	63.9	32.9	0.5	0.4	0.0	3.1	4.6	68.3	31.3	0.1	0.2	0.5
Berrien	0.9	86.3	11.6	0.8	0.4	0.1	1.7	2.4	87.7	11.6	0.2	0.2	2.0
Bibb	0.8	50.7	47.7	0.4	1.3	0.1	0.7	1.3	57.5	41.7	0.1	0.5	0.6
Bleckley	0.6	73.8	24.8	0.4	1.0	0.1	0.6	0.9	76.7	22.4	0.1	0.8	0.4
Brantley	1.1	95.4	4.2	1.0	0.2	0.1	0.5	1.0	94.2	5.4	0.3	0.0	0.3
Brooks	0.9	58.1	39.7	0.9	0.5	0.2	1.9	3.1	57.8	41.5	0.2	0.2	1.6
Bryan	1.3	83.8	14.7	0.9	1.2	0.3	0.8	2.0	84.3	14.9	0.2	0.5	0.9
Bulloch	0.8	69.3	29.1	0.3	1.0	0.1	1.0	1.9	73.0	26.0	0.1	0.5	0.8
Burke	1.0	47.7	51.3	0.6	0.5	0.1	0.9	1.4	47.4	52.3	0.1	0.1	0.3
Butts	0.9	70.0	29.2	0.8	0.4	0.1	0.6	1.4	63.7	35.5	0.2	0.3	0.7
Calhoun	0.5	38.6	60.8	0.3	0.2	0.0	0.6	3.0	40.8	58.9	0.2	0.0	0.2
Camden	1.9	76.6	20.8	1.0	1.6	0.2	1.9	3.6	77.2	20.2	0.5	1.3	2.1
Candler	0.8	66.0	27.4	0.4	0.4	0.0	6.5	9.2	67.6	31.1	0.1	0.1	1.8
Carroll	1.1	81.5	16.8	0.6	0.8	0.1	1.5	2.6	83.5	15.7	0.2	0.3	0.8
Catoosa	0.9	97.3	1.4	0.8	0.9	0.1	0.6	1.2	98.5	0.8	0.2	0.4	0.5
Charlton	1.2	69.6	29.7	1.0	0.5	0.1	0.3	0.8	71.7	27.7	0.4	0.1	0.4
Chatham	1.3	56.2	41.0	0.6	2.1	0.2	1.3	2.3	60.2	38.1	0.2	1.1	1.3
Chattahoochee	3.8	60.7	31.6	1.5	2.7	0.9	6.8	10.4	59.6	30.9	0.6	2.8	10.6
Chattooga	1.0	87.6	11.6	0.5	0.2	0.1	1.1	2.1	90.9	8.7	0.2	0.1	0.3
Cherokee	1.3	93.6	2.7	0.9	1.1	0.1	3.1	5.4	97.2	1.9	0.3	0.3	1.2
Clarke	1.4	66.1	27.8	0.5	3.6	0.1	3.5	6.3	70.7	26.2	0.2	2.5	1.7
Clay	0.7	38.7	60.9	0.7	0.3	0.1	0.0	1.0	38.9	60.8	0.1	0.1	0.6
Clayton	2.1	39.2	52.7	0.8	5.0	0.2	4.4	7.5	72.4	23.8	0.3	2.8	2.1
Clinch	0.8	69.7	29.9	1.0	0.1	0.0	0.1	0.8	72.3	27.3	0.1	0.1	1.0
Cobb	1.9	73.8	19.5	0.7	3.5	0.1	4.4	7.7	87.5	9.9	0.2	1.8	2.1
Coffee	0.9	69.0	26.2	0.5	0.7	0.1	4.5	6.8	72.9	25.4	0.1	0.4	1.9
Colquitt	1.1	68.6	23.8	0.6	0.6	0.1	7.6	10.8	73.8	24.2	0.2	0.1	4.3
Columbia	1.6	84.0	11.6	0.7	4.0	0.2	1.1	2.6	86.0	11.0	0.2	2.3	1.5
Cook	0.8	68.5	29.5	0.5	0.6	0.1	1.7	3.1	69.2	30.0	0.3	0.2	1.6
Coweta	1.0	79.8	18.3	0.6	0.9	0.0	1.5	3.1	76.7	22.6	0.2	0.3	0.7
Crawford	1.0	73.7	24.2	0.9	0.3	0.1	2.0	2.4	67.7	30.7	0.4	0.2	1.7
Crisp	0.7	54.6	43.8	0.3	0.9	0.1	1.2	1.7	58.9	40.7	0.2	0.1	0.3
Dade	0.8	98.3	0.7	1.1	0.5	0.0	0.3	0.9	98.7	0.8	0.3	0.2	0.5
Dawson	1.0	98.1	0.5	1.1	0.4	0.1	0.9	1.6	98.9	0.0	0.9	0.1	0.4
Decatur	0.7	57.7	40.2	0.5	0.4	0.1	1.9	3.2	59.7	39.5	0.3	0.2	1.9
De Kalb	2.1	37.0	55.3	0.7	4.5	0.1	4.7	7.9	53.6	42.2	0.2	3.0	2.9
Dodge	0.5	69.3	29.6	0.4	0.3	0.0	0.9	1.3	71.7	27.6	0.1	0.2	0.8
Dooly	0.9	46.6	49.8	0.5	0.7	0.2	3.2	4.7	50.4	49.0	0.0	0.4	0.8
Dougherty	0.7	38.3	60.5	0.5	0.7	0.1	0.7	1.3	48.8	50.2	0.3	0.5	0.8
Douglas	1.4	78.5	19.2	0.8	1.5	0.1	1.6	2.9	91.0	7.9	0.2	0.5	1.1
Early	0.8	50.7	48.5	0.6	0.4	0.2	0.6	1.2	55.5	44.1	0.3	0.1	0.4
Echols	1.0	78.1	7.0	1.7	0.1	0.0	14.1	19.7	86.0	11.3	1.7	0.1	1.9
Effingham	1.0	85.6	13.3	0.8	0.7	0.1	0.8	1.4	85.3	14.1	0.2	0.2	0.7
Elbert	0.7	67.6	31.0	0.4	0.3	0.1	1.3	2.4	69.4	30.2	0.0	0.3	0.7
Emanuel	0.5	64.1	33.5	0.3	0.4	0.0	2.3	3.4	67.0	32.5	0.1	0.2	0.4
Evans	0.6	62.2	33.1	0.4	0.4	0.1	4.5	6.0	64.8	34.0	0.0	0.2	1.2

[1] Hispanic persons may be of any race.

STATE County	Under 5 years	5 to 17 years	18 to 24 years	25 to 34 years	35 to 44 years	45 to 54 years	55 to 64 years	65 to 74 years	75 years and over	Median age (years)	Percent Female
	Population and population characteristics, 2000										
	Age (percent)										
	28	29	30	31	32	33	34	35	36	37	38
FLORIDA—Cont'd											
Sarasota	3.9	12.3	5.0	8.9	12.7	12.8	12.8	15.2	16.3	50.5	52.6
Seminole	6.3	19.0	8.4	14.2	17.8	15.0	8.7	5.9	4.8	36.2	51.0
Sumter	4.0	12.1	5.9	10.7	12.5	11.3	16.1	17.8	9.6	49.2	46.9
Suwannee	6.0	18.0	8.5	11.1	14.0	13.6	11.8	9.4	7.6	39.7	51.2
Taylor	5.9	18.7	8.2	13.0	15.4	14.3	10.5	8.3	5.8	37.8	48.9
Union	5.5	16.4	8.7	17.8	21.9	14.7	7.5	4.7	2.7	35.7	35.3
Volusia	4.9	15.4	8.2	10.9	14.4	13.3	10.9	11.3	10.8	42.4	51.4
Wakulla	5.9	19.7	7.6	13.4	18.3	14.9	9.8	6.4	3.9	36.8	48.2
Walton	5.3	16.3	7.1	12.2	16.2	14.6	12.3	9.6	6.3	40.5	48.7
Washington	6.0	17.3	7.7	13.1	15.4	13.4	11.2	8.4	7.3	38.8	48.6
GEORGIA	7.3	19.2	10.2	15.9	16.5	13.2	8.1	5.3	4.3	33.4	50.8
Appling	7.3	19.8	9.0	13.3	15.3	13.7	9.8	6.6	5.2	35.4	50.7
Atkinson	9.5	20.9	10.9	15.2	14.4	11.2	8.6	5.1	4.1	30.7	50.5
Bacon	7.5	18.7	9.9	14.2	13.9	13.7	9.4	7.5	5.3	34.8	51.0
Baker	7.2	20.1	10.0	12.7	14.2	13.0	9.0	7.6	6.1	35.0	53.7
Baldwin	5.1	16.6	14.5	14.9	16.3	13.2	8.7	6.0	4.6	34.2	46.0
Banks	7.5	18.6	8.9	14.5	16.1	13.8	9.9	6.2	4.3	35.2	49.5
Barrow	8.3	20.2	8.5	17.7	16.8	11.9	7.5	4.9	4.1	32.5	50.3
Bartow	7.8	20.1	8.3	16.2	16.9	13.1	8.3	5.5	3.9	33.7	50.6
Ben Hill	7.3	20.2	9.7	13.1	13.9	13.2	9.3	6.7	6.6	34.8	52.1
Berrien	7.1	20.2	8.6	13.9	14.8	12.8	10.1	6.9	5.5	35.2	50.9
Bibb	7.4	19.1	10.1	13.8	15.1	13.3	8.4	6.6	6.1	34.7	54.0
Bleckley	6.4	20.2	11.3	12.0	14.5	12.4	9.7	7.4	6.1	35.1	51.8
Brantley	7.4	21.0	8.5	13.9	16.0	13.7	9.5	6.4	3.7	34.6	49.8
Brooks	6.5	20.4	8.9	12.6	14.3	12.7	9.6	7.4	7.6	36.3	52.0
Bryan	7.7	23.4	8.0	13.4	18.6	14.2	7.5	4.3	3.0	33.3	50.5
Bulloch	5.8	16.5	26.2	12.1	12.7	10.5	7.0	5.0	4.3	26.1	51.3
Burke	8.0	23.3	9.1	12.2	15.1	13.1	8.4	5.8	5.1	33.0	52.5
Butts	6.3	17.8	9.2	15.1	17.9	14.0	9.5	5.9	4.3	35.9	46.7
Calhoun	6.0	16.0	11.3	15.6	17.7	13.3	7.5	6.2	6.3	35.6	43.5
Camden	8.7	23.0	12.9	17.2	16.7	10.5	5.8	3.2	2.0	28.2	48.3
Candler	7.2	19.7	9.4	12.8	13.2	13.0	9.5	7.2	8.0	35.6	49.8
Carroll	7.1	18.9	12.9	14.8	15.1	12.5	8.8	5.5	4.5	32.5	51.3
Catoosa	6.8	19.0	8.1	14.7	16.1	13.7	9.7	7.1	4.8	35.8	51.6
Charlton	6.5	20.9	10.6	14.3	17.4	11.5	9.1	5.6	4.1	33.4	47.1
Chatham	6.7	18.3	11.2	14.6	15.0	12.8	8.6	6.8	6.1	34.4	51.8
Chattahoochee	8.4	20.0	27.9	23.7	12.7	3.5	1.9	1.2	0.6	23.2	36.8
Chattooga	6.5	16.4	10.0	14.8	15.2	13.0	9.9	7.8	6.5	36.5	48.4
Cherokee	8.2	20.0	7.7	15.9	19.8	14.2	7.5	3.9	2.7	34.0	49.8
Clarke	5.2	12.6	31.3	16.4	11.0	9.5	5.9	4.1	3.9	25.4	51.2
Clay	6.6	19.2	8.0	9.1	11.9	14.9	10.8	10.1	9.4	41.9	54.5
Clayton	8.3	21.6	10.4	18.4	16.9	12.0	6.4	3.6	2.3	30.2	51.4
Clinch	7.3	20.5	8.6	13.7	15.3	13.6	9.1	6.8	5.0	34.9	50.3
Cobb	7.2	18.8	9.0	18.1	18.4	14.2	7.3	4.0	3.0	33.2	50.4
Coffee	7.8	20.4	11.0	15.1	15.3	12.3	8.2	5.5	4.4	32.1	50.4
Colquitt	7.6	19.9	10.3	14.2	13.8	12.3	9.0	6.7	6.2	33.7	50.5
Columbia	6.9	22.7	7.3	12.4	18.6	15.8	8.3	4.7	3.3	35.4	51.1
Cook	7.7	20.5	9.1	13.6	14.3	12.1	9.7	7.1	5.9	34.3	52.0
Coweta	8.2	20.6	7.6	16.2	17.2	13.4	8.4	4.9	3.6	33.6	50.5
Crawford	6.7	20.9	7.9	14.1	17.5	14.0	9.7	5.4	3.8	35.2	49.9
Crisp	7.8	21.2	9.2	12.7	14.3	13.1	8.7	6.9	6.1	34.4	53.0
Dade	5.9	18.0	11.8	12.9	15.0	14.3	10.2	7.2	4.8	36.1	51.0
Dawson	7.0	18.0	7.6	14.7	17.7	14.6	11.0	6.3	3.0	36.2	49.8
Decatur	7.7	20.9	9.1	13.2	14.8	12.6	8.6	7.2	6.1	34.4	52.4
De Kalb	7.1	17.5	10.9	19.5	17.2	12.8	6.9	4.3	3.7	32.3	51.5
Dodge	6.2	19.7	8.7	14.1	15.4	13.1	9.6	7.1	6.2	35.8	48.8
Dooly	6.8	18.8	10.3	13.9	15.9	13.6	8.9	6.1	5.7	35.1	47.7
Dougherty	7.6	20.0	12.2	13.8	13.8	12.7	8.2	6.4	5.2	32.2	53.4
Douglas	7.3	20.3	8.9	15.6	17.9	14.2	8.2	4.5	3.1	33.8	50.9
Early	7.1	21.6	7.8	11.6	14.3	12.2	9.7	7.8	8.0	36.4	53.4
Echols	8.0	21.3	12.5	16.4	14.3	11.1	7.2	5.7	3.4	29.7	46.3
Effingham	7.6	22.3	8.2	14.0	18.1	13.5	8.2	4.7	3.3	33.6	50.3
Elbert	6.4	19.5	8.4	12.8	14.4	13.6	10.0	8.0	6.9	37.2	52.0
Emanuel	6.8	21.1	10.4	11.9	14.1	13.1	9.4	6.8	6.5	34.9	51.9
Evans	6.9	20.6	10.2	13.8	15.2	12.2	8.5	6.6	6.0	34.0	51.4

Table B. States and Counties

STATE County	Under 5 years	5 to 17 years	18 to 24 years	25 to 34 years	35 to 44 years	45 to 54 years	55 to 64 years	65 to 74 years	75 years and over	Percent Female	Total persons 2000	1990	1980	Percent change 1990–2000	1980–1990
	39	40	41	42	43	44	45	46	47	48	49	50	51	52	53
FLORIDA—Cont'd															
Sarasota	4.6	11.2	6.2	12.0	12.0	9.5	12.4	17.9	14.2	53.2	325 957	277 776	202 251	17.3	37.3
Seminole	7.0	18.4	9.6	18.3	17.4	11.1	8.0	6.3	4.0	51.1	365 196	287 521	179 752	27.0	60.0
Sumter	6.0	16.2	8.7	13.1	11.5	10.0	12.3	14.6	7.7	49.8	53 345	31 577	24 272	68.9	30.1
Suwannee	6.2	20.3	8.4	13.1	13.3	11.1	10.7	9.3	7.6	51.7	34 844	26 780	22 287	30.1	20.2
Taylor	7.8	20.4	8.8	15.4	13.4	10.6	10.3	8.0	5.2	51.5	19 256	17 111	16 532	12.5	3.5
Union	6.6	19.1	9.0	23.9	17.4	9.6	7.0	4.8	2.7	38.2	13 442	10 252	10 166	31.1	0.8
Volusia	5.7	14.0	9.5	14.8	13.0	9.4	10.9	13.3	9.5	51.6	443 343	370 737	258 762	19.6	43.3
Wakulla	7.0	21.3	8.1	14.9	16.5	11.4	9.1	6.8	4.8	51.1	22 863	14 202	10 887	61.0	30.4
Walton	6.3	17.5	7.7	14.5	13.4	11.5	12.6	10.4	6.1	50.9	40 601	27 759	21 300	46.3	30.3
Washington	6.4	18.8	8.7	13.1	13.2	11.3	10.9	10.1	7.5	51.6	20 973	16 919	14 509	24.0	16.6
GEORGIA	7.6	19.0	11.4	18.1	15.7	10.3	7.7	6.0	4.1	51.5	8 186 453	6 478 149	5 462 982	26.4	18.6
Appling	6.9	22.2	10.0	15.3	14.6	10.4	8.4	7.1	5.1	51.8	17 419	15 744	15 565	10.6	1.2
Atkinson	8.0	22.0	10.9	15.1	13.3	11.0	7.9	7.1	4.7	51.4	7 609	6 213	6 141	22.5	1.2
Bacon	7.5	22.3	10.4	14.7	14.2	10.1	8.5	7.4	4.8	52.5	10 103	9 566	9 379	5.6	2.0
Baker	7.4	22.4	10.2	14.7	13.4	9.6	9.0	7.5	5.7	54.0	4 074	3 615	3 808	12.7	-5.1
Baldwin	6.0	17.1	13.3	19.4	15.1	10.2	8.0	6.3	4.4	48.3	44 700	39 530	34 000	13.1	14.0
Banks	6.6	19.0	10.5	10.1	15.8	11.3	8.2	6.9	4.5	49.5	14 422	10 308	8 702	39.9	18.5
Barrow	8.5	19.5	10.5	18.8	14.1	10.0	7.7	6.2	4.8	51.1	46 144	29 721	21 354	55.3	39.2
Bartow	8.2	19.3	10.9	17.8	15.1	10.7	8.0	6.1	4.0	50.7	76 019	55 915	40 760	36.0	37.2
Ben Hill	8.0	22.7	8.8	14.5	14.1	9.6	8.2	7.8	6.2	54.0	17 484	16 245	16 000	7.6	1.5
Berrien	7.6	20.0	10.4	15.1	13.9	10.9	9.3	7.4	5.3	51.3	16 235	14 153	13 525	14.7	4.6
Bibb	7.6	19.0	10.8	16.7	14.6	9.7	8.7	7.6	5.3	53.4	153 887	150 137	150 256	2.5	0.0
Bleckley	6.8	19.6	12.6	14.5	13.2	10.9	9.1	7.9	5.5	51.9	11 666	10 430	10 767	11.9	-3.1
Brantley	7.6	22.8	10.3	15.6	15.4	10.8	8.5	5.5	3.5	50.3	14 629	11 077	8 701	32.1	27.3
Brooks	8.4	21.5	10.0	14.4	12.6	9.3	8.8	8.1	7.1	52.8	16 450	15 398	15 255	6.8	0.9
Bryan	8.5	24.0	9.6	17.0	17.4	9.7	6.7	4.7	2.5	50.7	23 417	15 438	10 175	51.7	51.7
Bulloch	6.4	16.4	25.7	13.9	12.0	8.4	7.0	5.9	4.3	51.4	55 983	43 125	35 785	29.8	20.5
Burke	9.1	24.1	9.7	15.7	13.4	9.0	7.6	6.6	4.9	52.8	22 243	20 579	19 349	8.1	6.4
Butts	7.0	18.8	11.0	17.9	15.3	10.3	8.2	6.6	5.0	47.1	19 522	15 326	13 665	27.4	12.2
Calhoun	7.2	21.9	9.1	14.2	12.9	8.8	9.0	8.6	8.4	54.8	6 320	5 013	5 717	26.1	-12.3
Camden	10.4	20.0	14.1	23.8	14.5	7.4	4.8	3.2	1.9	46.7	43 664	30 167	13 371	44.7	125.6
Candler	7.4	19.8	10.0	13.4	13.7	10.5	8.9	9.1	7.3	52.5	9 577	7 744	7 518	23.7	3.0
Carroll	7.3	19.5	14.2	16.5	14.4	10.4	7.4	5.8	4.4	51.6	87 268	71 422	56 346	22.2	26.8
Catoosa	6.7	19.3	9.8	16.0	15.8	12.1	9.6	6.7	4.2	51.7	53 282	42 464	36 991	25.5	14.8
Charlton	9.1	21.9	10.0	16.8	12.5	10.6	8.5	5.9	4.5	51.4	10 282	8 496	7 343	21.0	15.7
Chatham	7.9	18.5	11.1	17.4	14.3	9.6	8.5	7.8	5.0	52.1	232 048	216 774	202 226	7.0	7.2
Chattahoochee	8.0	19.9	31.8	23.5	11.6	2.6	1.3	0.9	0.5	34.1	14 882	16 934	21 732	-12.1	-22.1
Chattooga	6.8	18.8	10.1	14.5	13.7	10.9	10.3	8.9	5.9	52.0	25 470	22 236	21 856	14.5	1.8
Cherokee	9.1	19.0	9.3	21.6	17.8	10.2	6.0	4.2	2.8	49.7	141 903	90 204	51 699	57.3	74.5
Clarke	6.0	14.0	28.9	17.0	12.3	7.4	5.7	4.9	3.7	52.3	101 489	87 594	74 498	15.9	17.6
Clay	7.3	21.9	9.0	13.0	12.9	8.3	9.5	10.0	8.2	55.2	3 357	3 364	3 553	-0.2	-5.3
Clayton	8.3	19.6	11.7	20.7	16.6	10.6	6.6	3.8	2.0	51.3	236 517	181 436	150 357	30.4	20.7
Clinch	7.9	22.1	10.3	14.9	14.3	10.2	8.8	6.9	4.7	51.7	6 878	6 160	6 660	11.7	-7.5
Cobb	7.6	17.7	10.4	21.3	19.0	11.2	6.5	4.1	2.2	50.8	607 751	447 745	297 718	35.7	50.4
Coffee	8.1	21.9	11.2	16.3	14.0	10.1	7.5	6.5	4.5	51.9	37 413	29 592	26 894	26.4	10.0
Colquitt	7.3	21.0	10.6	14.5	13.6	10.4	8.5	8.1	6.0	51.5	42 053	36 645	35 376	14.8	3.6
Columbia	8.2	22.3	8.9	18.0	19.3	11.0	6.4	3.9	2.0	50.1	89 288	66 031	40 118	35.2	64.6
Cook	7.9	20.8	10.6	14.3	12.9	10.8	8.9	7.9	5.9	51.9	15 771	13 456	13 490	17.2	-0.3
Coweta	8.4	20.1	9.7	16.9	15.5	11.1	8.0	5.9	4.2	51.7	89 215	53 853	39 268	65.7	37.1
Crawford	7.9	20.4	10.1	17.6	14.6	11.6	7.7	5.8	4.3	50.6	12 495	8 991	7 684	39.0	17.0
Crisp	7.7	22.3	9.0	14.3	14.1	9.7	9.0	7.8	6.2	54.2	21 996	20 011	19 489	9.9	2.7
Dade	6.7	19.3	12.1	15.8	14.8	11.8	8.6	6.7	4.2	51.2	15 154	13 183	12 318	15.0	6.7
Dawson	7.7	20.0	9.3	18.8	15.4	11.3	8.6	6.1	2.8	49.5	15 999	9 429	4 774	69.7	97.5
Decatur	7.5	22.2	10.1	15.4	13.8	9.3	8.6	7.6	5.4	52.3	28 240	25 517	25 495	10.7	0.0
De Kalb	7.1	16.7	11.7	20.9	17.2	10.5	7.5	5.2	3.3	52.1	665 865	546 174	483 024	21.9	13.1
Dodge	7.0	18.9	10.6	15.3	14.1	10.9	9.1	8.1	6.1	50.9	19 171	17 607	16 955	8.9	3.8
Dooly	7.8	22.4	8.9	13.9	13.1	10.2	8.7	8.3	6.7	54.5	11 525	9 901	10 826	16.4	-8.5
Dougherty	8.4	22.0	11.9	15.5	14.4	9.5	8.1	6.2	4.0	53.1	96 065	96 321	100 710	-0.3	-4.4
Douglas	7.9	20.5	10.6	18.5	17.5	11.2	6.8	4.3	2.8	50.4	92 174	71 120	54 573	29.6	30.3
Early	7.7	22.4	9.2	12.9	13.2	9.6	9.1	8.3	7.6	53.9	12 354	11 854	13 158	4.2	-9.9
Echols	7.5	22.4	10.4	16.7	13.6	10.4	9.2	6.1	3.9	48.9	3 754	2 334	2 297	60.8	1.6
Effingham	8.0	23.0	10.0	17.8	15.5	10.7	7.1	5.0	2.9	49.9	37 535	25 687	18 327	46.1	40.2
Elbert	7.2	19.6	9.4	14.7	13.8	10.9	9.3	8.3	6.8	52.3	20 511	18 949	18 758	8.2	1.0
Emanuel	7.8	22.6	9.2	14.3	13.6	9.8	8.3	8.4	6.0	52.4	21 837	20 546	20 795	6.3	-1.2
Evans	8.0	21.3	9.6	15.5	13.1	9.5	8.6	7.9	6.4	51.4	10 495	8 724	8 428	20.3	3.5

Table B. States and Counties

	Household relationship, 2000																
	In households (percent)										In group quarters (percent)						
					Child		Other relatives		Nonrelatives			Institutionalized population			Noninstitutionalized population		
STATE County	Total population	Total in house-holds	House-holder	Spouse	Total	Own child under 18 years	Total	Under 18 years	Total	Unmar-ried partner	Total in group quarters	Correc-tional institu-tions	Nurs-ing homes	Other institu-tions	Col-lege dormi-tories	Mili-tary quar-ters	Other
	54	55	56	57	58	59	60	61	62	63	64	65	66	67	68	69	70
FLORIDA—Cont'd																	
Sarasota	325 957	90.0	46.0	24.2	19.0	14.7	3.6	1.1	5.2	2.3	2.0	0.2	1.2	0.0	0.2	0.0	0.3
Seminole	365 196	99.0	38.2	20.7	29.5	23.1	4.9	1.8	5.6	2.3	1.0	0.3	0.3	0.0	0.0	0.0	0.4
Sumter	53 345	88.3	39.0	23.7	17.9	13.7	4.1	1.9	3.6	1.7	11.7	11.2	0.5	0.0	0.0	0.0	0.0
Suwannee	34 844	98.1	38.6	21.8	26.7	20.4	6.1	2.8	4.9	1.8	1.9	0.4	1.1	0.0	0.0	0.0	0.4
Taylor	19 256	93.7	37.3	19.6	27.1	20.8	5.3	2.9	4.5	2.2	6.3	5.7	0.5	0.0	0.0	0.0	0.0
Union	13 442	69.1	25.0	14.5	23.7	19.1	3.2	1.8	2.7	1.3	30.9	30.2	0.0	0.2	0.0	0.0	0.5
Volusia	443 343	96.7	41.7	21.0	23.4	17.7	4.8	1.8	5.8	2.5	3.3	0.6	0.9	0.2	1.0	0.0	0.6
Wakulla	22 863	95.0	37.0	21.1	28.8	23.2	4.3	1.9	3.8	2.1	5.0	4.5	0.4	0.0	0.0	0.0	0.1
Walton	40 601	95.6	40.8	21.6	24.2	19.1	4.2	1.9	4.8	2.3	4.4	3.5	0.8	0.0	0.0	0.0	0.1
Washington	20 973	93.1	37.8	21.2	26.3	20.6	4.4	2.1	3.4	1.7	6.9	5.3	0.9	0.2	0.0	0.0	0.5
GEORGIA	8 186 453	97.1	36.7	18.9	29.8	23.2	6.4	2.7	5.3	1.8	2.9	1.0	0.4	0.1	0.6	0.3	0.4
Appling	17 419	98.6	37.9	21.5	29.5	23.0	5.9	2.9	3.8	1.6	1.4	0.1	0.7	0.5	0.0	0.0	0.0
Atkinson	7 609	99.4	35.7	19.7	32.6	26.1	6.8	3.3	4.6	2.0	0.6	0.1	0.1	0.0	0.0	0.0	0.4
Bacon	10 103	98.5	37.9	20.9	29.2	22.0	6.4	3.3	4.0	1.7	1.5	0.4	1.0	0.0	0.0	0.0	0.1
Baker	4 074	99.7	37.2	17.7	32.5	22.2	8.7	4.5	3.6	1.8	0.3	0.1	0.0	0.0	0.0	0.0	0.2
Baldwin	44 700	82.5	33.0	14.5	24.9	18.0	5.1	2.5	5.0	1.9	17.5	11.1	1.4	2.5	2.2	0.0	0.3
Banks	14 422	100.0	37.2	24.3	29.8	23.3	5.4	2.4	3.3	1.6	0.0	0.0	0.0	0.0	0.0	0.0	0.0
Barrow	46 144	99.0	35.4	21.4	31.7	25.5	6.0	2.4	4.5	2.0	1.0	0.2	0.4	0.0	0.0	0.0	0.4
Bartow	76 019	98.8	35.7	22.1	31.1	24.7	5.9	2.7	3.9	1.8	1.2	0.6	0.4	0.0	0.0	0.0	0.1
Ben Hill	17 484	97.9	38.2	18.0	30.4	23.4	6.9	3.3	4.5	1.8	2.1	0.6	1.1	0.3	0.0	0.0	0.2
Berrien	16 235	99.1	38.6	21.7	30.2	24.2	4.8	2.2	3.7	1.9	0.9	0.2	0.8	0.0	0.0	0.0	0.0
Bibb	153 887	96.5	38.8	16.4	30.2	22.6	6.8	3.3	4.4	1.9	3.5	1.1	0.8	0.3	1.1	0.0	0.2
Bleckley	11 666	94.5	37.5	19.4	29.4	22.4	5.4	2.7	2.9	1.4	5.5	0.2	0.9	0.9	3.3	0.0	0.1
Brantley	14 629	99.4	37.2	22.6	31.3	25.1	4.7	2.3	3.7	1.8	0.6	0.1	0.5	0.0	0.0	0.0	0.0
Brooks	16 450	97.6	37.4	18.1	30.3	22.4	7.6	3.8	4.2	1.7	2.4	0.2	1.6	0.0	0.0	0.0	0.7
Bryan	23 417	99.4	34.5	22.2	34.8	28.3	4.7	2.3	3.2	1.6	0.6	0.3	0.3	0.0	0.0	0.0	0.0
Bulloch	55 983	93.6	37.1	16.3	24.8	19.7	4.7	2.1	10.7	1.7	6.4	0.4	0.0	0.0	5.0	0.0	1.0
Burke	22 243	98.7	35.7	16.2	34.8	26.1	8.2	4.6	3.9	2.0	1.3	0.3	0.0	0.0	0.0	0.0	1.0
Butts	19 522	90.2	33.1	18.8	28.1	20.3	6.7	3.3	3.5	1.8	9.8	9.2	0.5	0.0	0.0	0.0	0.1
Calhoun	6 320	79.2	31.0	12.9	26.0	17.9	6.9	3.9	2.3	1.3	20.8	19.6	1.0	0.0	0.0	0.0	0.2
Camden	43 664	95.8	33.7	20.9	33.7	29.4	3.3	1.6	4.2	1.6	4.2	0.2	0.2	0.0	0.0	3.8	0.0
Candler	9 577	95.7	35.2	18.6	29.3	22.2	7.2	4.0	5.4	1.4	4.3	0.4	3.8	0.0	0.0	0.0	0.1
Carroll	87 268	96.3	36.2	20.4	29.3	22.9	5.5	2.4	5.0	1.8	3.7	0.6	0.5	0.0	2.4	0.0	0.2
Catoosa	53 282	99.2	38.3	23.2	30.0	23.4	4.5	2.0	3.1	1.5	0.8	0.2	0.4	0.0	0.0	0.0	0.1
Charlton	10 282	89.0	32.5	18.0	29.4	23.0	6.0	3.4	3.2	1.4	11.0	10.2	0.7	0.0	0.0	0.0	0.0
Chatham	232 048	96.5	38.7	17.5	28.3	21.3	6.7	3.2	5.3	1.9	3.5	1.0	0.5	0.1	0.7	0.7	0.5
Chattahoochee	14 882	67.2	19.7	15.0	29.4	27.3	2.1	0.9	1.1	0.5	32.8	0.0	0.0	0.0	0.0	32.8	0.0
Chattooga	25 470	93.4	37.6	20.2	26.6	19.9	5.4	2.4	3.7	1.8	6.6	5.9	0.6	0.0	0.0	0.0	0.1
Cherokee	141 903	99.3	34.9	23.4	32.0	26.2	4.7	1.6	4.3	1.5	0.7	0.1	0.3	0.0	0.3	0.0	0.1
Clarke	101 489	91.9	39.1	12.8	19.9	15.4	5.2	1.9	15.0	2.1	8.1	0.6	0.6	0.0	6.5	0.2	0.2
Clay	3 357	98.3	40.1	16.3	28.5	19.9	10.1	5.3	3.2	1.8	1.7	0.0	1.7	0.0	0.0	0.0	0.0
Clayton	236 517	98.6	34.8	15.9	33.2	25.9	8.5	3.4	6.3	2.2	1.4	0.6	0.2	0.0	0.0	0.3	0.2
Clinch	6 878	94.8	36.5	18.9	29.8	23.4	6.6	3.9	3.0	1.6	5.2	3.0	1.3	0.0	0.0	0.0	0.9
Cobb	607 751	98.8	37.4	20.3	29.6	23.9	5.2	1.6	6.2	1.7	1.2	0.4	0.3	0.0	0.1	0.0	0.4
Coffee	37 413	96.1	35.7	19.1	30.5	24.2	6.5	3.3	4.3	1.9	3.9	2.7	0.6	0.0	0.4	0.0	0.2
Colquitt	42 053	97.0	36.8	18.8	30.1	23.6	6.8	3.0	4.4	1.8	3.0	0.8	0.6	0.1	0.0	0.0	1.5
Columbia	89 288	99.2	34.9	23.5	34.3	27.7	3.9	1.6	2.6	1.2	0.8	0.1	0.2	0.0	0.0	0.0	0.5
Cook	15 771	98.5	37.3	19.9	31.0	24.1	6.6	3.4	3.7	1.7	1.5	0.2	0.6	0.0	0.0	0.0	0.7
Coweta	89 215	99.1	35.2	22.0	32.2	25.6	5.9	2.6	3.8	1.4	0.9	0.5	0.3	0.0	0.0	0.0	0.0
Crawford	12 495	99.1	35.7	21.6	31.5	24.1	6.2	3.0	4.1	1.7	0.9	0.2	0.7	0.0	0.0	0.0	0.0
Crisp	21 996	97.9	37.9	17.0	32.0	24.7	7.0	3.6	4.0	2.1	2.1	0.8	1.0	0.0	0.0	0.0	0.3
Dade	15 154	94.9	37.2	23.3	28.2	21.8	4.1	1.7	2.2	1.1	5.1	0.2	0.5	0.0	4.1	0.0	0.3
Dawson	15 999	99.4	37.9	24.9	28.1	22.5	4.9	2.1	3.6	1.6	0.6	0.5	0.0	0.0	0.0	0.0	0.1
Decatur	28 240	97.5	36.8	18.0	31.9	24.3	7.2	3.8	3.5	1.8	2.5	0.9	0.7	0.5	0.0	0.0	0.3
De Kalb	665 865	97.9	37.4	15.0	27.6	20.5	9.1	3.4	8.8	2.3	2.1	0.5	0.3	0.2	0.6	0.0	0.5
Dodge	19 171	91.2	36.8	18.4	28.1	21.3	4.9	2.4	2.9	1.5	8.8	5.5	1.0	1.8	0.0	0.0	0.6
Dooly	11 525	89.0	33.9	15.3	29.0	21.6	7.1	3.5	3.6	1.8	11.0	10.1	0.8	0.0	0.0	0.0	0.2
Dougherty	96 065	95.3	37.0	15.1	30.9	22.6	7.8	4.1	4.5	2.0	4.7	1.1	0.5	0.0	1.2	0.2	1.6
Douglas	92 174	99.1	35.6	21.0	31.6	24.5	6.0	2.4	4.9	1.8	0.9	0.6	0.3	0.0	0.0	0.0	0.0
Early	12 354	97.9	38.0	17.1	31.4	23.2	8.3	4.5	3.1	1.8	2.1	0.4	1.1	0.4	0.0	0.0	0.1
Echols	3 754	100.0	33.7	19.7	31.2	25.3	5.4	2.2	10.0	1.6	0.0	0.0	0.0	0.0	0.0	0.0	0.0
Effingham	37 535	99.3	35.0	22.5	33.7	27.2	4.8	2.2	3.3	1.6	0.7	0.4	0.3	0.0	0.0	0.0	0.1
Elbert	20 511	98.7	39.0	20.3	30.1	22.2	6.1	3.2	3.2	1.5	1.3	0.3	0.9	0.0	0.0	0.0	0.1
Emanuel	21 837	96.3	36.8	18.5	30.6	23.2	6.2	3.1	4.2	1.6	3.7	1.1	0.7	0.9	0.0	0.0	1.0
Evans	10 495	94.4	36.0	17.6	29.3	22.8	6.7	3.5	4.8	2.1	5.6	3.9	0.8	0.5	0.0	0.0	0.4

Table B. States and Counties

STATE County	Households by type, 2000												Households, 1990		
	Family households						Nonfamily households								
				Married couple		Female householder[1]			Householder living alone							House-holder living alone
	Total households	Total	With own children under 18 years	Total	With own children under 18 years	Total	With own children under 18 years	Total	Total	65 years and over	Average house-hold size	Average family size	Total house-holds	Female house-holder[1]	
	71	72	73	74	75	76	77	78	79	80	81	82	83	84	85
FLORIDA—Cont'd															
Sarasota	149 937	63.0	18.3	52.7	12.9	7.7	4.1	37.0	30.4	16.9	2.13	2.61	125 493	7.3	27.7
Seminole	139 572	69.7	33.9	54.3	25.2	11.5	6.7	30.3	22.9	6.6	2.59	3.07	107 657	10.1	21.2
Sumter	20 779	72.4	18.8	60.9	12.5	8.4	4.6	27.6	23.5	13.8	2.27	2.62	12 119	10.9	23.4
Suwannee	13 460	72.0	29.5	56.5	21.1	11.2	6.2	28.0	23.3	11.0	2.54	2.96	10 034	11.3	23.2
Taylor	7 176	71.5	31.6	52.5	20.2	14.4	8.8	28.5	24.2	10.6	2.51	2.95	6 401	12.2	21.4
Union	3 367	77.4	41.8	57.7	28.7	15.0	10.1	22.6	19.5	7.1	2.76	3.13	2 658	12.4	18.7
Volusia	184 723	65.0	24.1	50.4	16.2	10.9	6.0	35.0	27.9	13.6	2.32	2.82	153 416	9.5	26.4
Wakulla	8 450	73.8	35.6	57.1	25.0	12.4	7.9	26.2	22.0	7.0	2.57	2.99	5 210	12.5	19.0
Walton	16 548	67.2	26.4	53.0	18.2	10.1	5.8	32.8	27.1	10.1	2.35	2.83	11 294	10.1	24.5
Washington	7 931	71.2	30.3	56.2	21.7	11.4	6.6	28.8	25.1	12.0	2.46	2.93	6 443	11.1	23.2
GEORGIA	3 006 369	70.2	35.0	51.5	24.4	14.5	8.6	29.8	23.6	7.0	2.65	3.14	2 366 615	13.9	22.7
Appling	6 606	73.5	34.5	56.6	25.1	12.5	7.2	26.5	23.2	9.8	2.60	3.04	5 834	11.8	24.6
Atkinson	2 717	72.9	38.8	55.1	28.0	12.8	7.8	27.1	23.3	9.1	2.78	3.27	2 210	12.1	23.4
Bacon	3 833	73.4	33.0	55.2	23.1	14.1	7.7	26.6	23.6	9.5	2.60	3.03	3 442	15.7	21.6
Baker	1 514	72.3	33.1	47.7	20.7	19.5	10.2	27.7	25.1	10.8	2.68	3.20	1 300	16.9	25.1
Baldwin	14 758	66.7	31.0	43.9	18.1	18.2	10.7	33.3	25.6	7.8	2.50	3.02	12 165	17.9	22.8
Banks	5 364	77.6	35.6	65.4	29.4	7.9	4.0	22.4	19.2	7.7	2.69	3.06	3 775	7.5	19.2
Barrow	16 354	76.7	39.9	60.3	30.7	11.6	6.8	23.3	18.6	6.7	2.79	3.17	10 676	10.8	18.9
Bartow	27 176	77.4	38.2	61.9	29.7	11.1	6.2	22.6	18.7	6.7	2.76	3.14	20 091	10.7	19.2
Ben Hill	6 673	69.4	33.2	47.2	20.3	17.4	10.5	30.6	26.7	11.9	2.57	3.09	5 972	16.9	25.2
Berrien	6 261	72.5	34.9	56.2	25.3	11.7	7.1	27.5	23.6	10.0	2.57	3.03	5 149	11.1	21.5
Bibb	59 667	66.7	31.9	42.3	17.6	20.6	12.4	33.3	28.2	9.8	2.49	3.06	56 307	19.1	26.4
Bleckley	4 372	71.4	32.9	51.8	21.5	15.5	9.3	28.6	25.5	11.0	2.52	3.02	3 816	14.0	23.2
Brantley	5 436	76.4	38.2	60.9	28.8	10.6	6.3	23.6	20.4	7.7	2.68	3.06	3 811	10.1	16.5
Brooks	6 155	71.0	31.6	48.3	19.8	18.1	9.7	29.0	25.2	11.0	2.61	3.11	5 392	18.1	22.7
Bryan	8 089	80.5	45.0	64.4	34.4	11.9	8.1	19.5	16.4	5.8	2.88	3.22	5 070	10.9	14.5
Bulloch	20 743	59.5	29.7	44.1	20.8	11.8	7.2	40.5	24.6	6.8	2.53	3.08	14 984	11.9	23.3
Burke	7 934	73.1	38.4	45.4	21.5	22.8	14.4	26.9	23.6	9.5	2.77	3.27	7 037	21.9	22.4
Butts	6 455	75.4	34.5	57.0	24.6	13.9	7.5	24.6	20.9	8.0	2.73	3.15	4 696	14.6	18.6
Calhoun	1 962	68.7	31.2	41.7	17.1	23.2	12.7	31.3	28.7	12.7	2.55	3.15	1 794	20.4	27.4
Camden	14 705	77.4	46.8	62.2	35.7	11.7	8.7	22.6	17.7	4.0	2.84	3.22	9 459	10.6	17.0
Candler	3 375	71.9	33.7	52.8	23.3	14.3	8.0	28.1	23.9	11.4	2.72	3.17	2 828	14.7	25.4
Carroll	31 568	72.9	35.2	56.3	25.9	12.3	7.2	27.1	21.2	7.6	2.66	3.09	25 370	11.7	21.1
Catoosa	20 425	75.4	35.4	60.6	26.9	11.0	6.4	24.6	21.3	8.5	2.59	3.00	15 745	10.3	19.3
Charlton	3 342	74.8	37.6	55.4	26.1	15.0	9.0	25.2	21.8	8.5	2.74	3.20	2 911	14.0	19.7
Chatham	89 865	66.1	30.4	45.2	18.7	17.0	9.9	33.9	27.1	9.4	2.49	3.05	81 111	16.0	25.9
Chattahoochee	2 932	89.5	64.8	76.3	54.9	10.1	7.7	10.5	8.9	2.3	3.41	3.64	2 884	7.4	7.5
Chattooga	9 577	71.4	30.8	53.7	21.6	12.6	6.5	28.6	25.2	12.4	2.49	2.94	8 467	12.6	22.6
Cherokee	49 495	79.2	41.4	67.2	34.7	8.3	5.0	20.8	16.0	4.1	2.85	3.18	31 309	7.4	14.1
Clarke	39 706	49.6	22.5	32.6	13.4	13.3	7.9	50.4	29.7	5.8	2.35	2.95	33 170	13.3	28.8
Clay	1 347	68.9	25.7	40.7	11.6	23.4	12.6	31.1	27.8	13.2	2.45	2.99	1 210	21.3	26.3
Clayton	82 841	72.0	40.7	45.7	24.1	20.3	13.6	28.0	21.8	3.6	2.84	3.30	65 523	14.1	19.9
Clinch	2 512	72.6	36.5	51.7	23.8	16.9	10.6	27.4	24.6	9.2	2.60	3.09	2 173	14.4	21.9
Cobb	227 487	68.8	35.8	54.3	27.6	10.7	6.5	31.2	23.2	4.1	2.64	3.14	171 288	9.1	22.5
Coffee	13 354	73.3	37.3	53.5	25.9	15.2	9.0	26.7	22.6	8.9	2.69	3.14	10 541	15.3	22.0
Colquitt	15 495	71.4	34.6	51.0	22.6	15.5	9.6	28.6	24.9	11.2	2.63	3.12	12 980	16.0	22.8
Columbia	31 120	81.5	44.4	67.5	35.8	10.6	6.8	18.5	15.4	5.1	2.85	3.18	21 841	9.4	13.5
Cook	5 882	72.8	34.8	53.3	23.8	15.3	8.9	27.2	24.0	10.5	2.64	3.12	4 825	13.5	23.1
Coweta	31 442	78.6	39.9	62.5	30.9	12.2	7.2	21.4	17.6	5.7	2.81	3.17	18 930	13.1	17.9
Crawford	4 461	77.5	37.5	60.5	28.2	12.6	6.9	22.5	18.8	6.3	2.78	3.14	3 069	12.9	18.8
Crisp	8 337	70.4	34.8	44.8	18.5	21.6	14.2	29.6	26.1	11.1	2.58	3.10	7 287	20.5	24.8
Dade	5 633	75.7	33.3	62.7	27.1	9.5	4.6	24.3	21.7	8.2	2.55	2.97	4 661	9.2	18.4
Dawson	6 069	77.2	33.7	65.7	27.4	8.2	4.4	22.8	18.6	5.0	2.62	2.98	3 360	8.0	16.0
Decatur	10 380	72.7	35.4	49.0	22.0	19.5	11.1	27.3	24.3	10.4	2.65	3.14	8 962	18.2	23.2
De Kalb	249 339	62.8	31.0	40.1	18.7	17.6	10.2	37.2	26.9	5.2	2.62	3.20	208 690	15.0	25.2
Dodge	7 062	69.2	32.2	50.0	21.6	15.2	8.5	30.8	27.8	11.6	2.48	3.02	6 387	14.9	25.2
Dooly	3 909	70.8	33.6	45.1	18.8	20.5	12.4	29.2	25.9	11.4	2.62	3.14	3 557	19.5	25.7
Dougherty	35 552	68.3	32.9	40.9	16.8	23.2	14.1	31.7	26.8	8.9	2.58	3.13	34 163	22.0	23.3
Douglas	32 822	75.9	38.6	58.9	28.6	12.7	7.6	24.1	18.4	4.4	2.78	3.17	24 277	9.9	15.0
Early	4 695	70.2	32.0	45.0	17.7	20.8	12.1	29.8	26.9	12.7	2.58	3.13	4 263	17.4	25.0
Echols	1 264	74.1	38.1	58.6	28.8	10.8	6.7	25.9	18.7	9.1	2.97	3.26	816	9.6	18.8
Effingham	13 151	79.8	43.0	64.3	33.7	11.1	6.8	20.2	16.9	6.0	2.84	3.18	8 759	10.6	16.2
Elbert	8 004	72.1	32.0	51.9	21.0	15.7	8.7	27.9	25.0	11.6	2.53	3.01	7 115	14.2	23.6
Emanuel	8 045	71.5	34.3	50.1	21.7	17.1	10.6	28.5	25.0	11.1	2.61	3.10	7 420	16.2	24.2
Evans	3 778	70.9	34.9	49.0	22.3	16.4	9.7	29.1	25.0	9.9	2.62	3.10	3 144	16.3	24.8

[1] No spouse present.

STATE County	Percent change of households, 1990–2000	Total housing units	Occupied housing units (percent)	Vacant housing units — Total	For seasonal, recreational, or occasional use	Homeowner vacancy rate (percent)	Rental vacancy rate (percent)	Occupied housing units — Total	Percent owner-occupied housing units	Percent renter-occupied housing units	Average household size of owner-occupied units	Average household size of renter-occupied units
	86	87	88	89	90	91	92	93	94	95	96	97
FLORIDA—Cont'd												
Sarasota	19.5	182 467	82.2	17.0	11.2	1.9	14.8	149 937	79.1	20.9	2.14	2.11
Seminole	29.6	147 079	94.9	5.1	0.8	1.3	6.2	139 572	69.5	30.5	2.71	2.31
Sumter	71.5	25 195	82.5	17.5	9.1	2.2	15.7	20 779	86.5	13.5	2.22	2.55
Suwannee	34.1	15 679	85.8	14.2	3.8	2.3	12.1	13 460	80.9	19.1	2.52	2.61
Taylor	12.1	9 646	74.4	25.6	13.7	3.3	15.3	7 176	79.8	20.2	2.52	2.47
Union	26.7	3 736	90.1	9.9	1.3	1.8	14.8	3 367	74.6	25.4	2.76	2.75
Volusia	20.4	211 938	87.2	12.8	7.4	2.0	8.1	184 723	75.3	24.7	2.35	2.22
Wakulla	62.2	9 820	86.0	14.0	5.2	1.8	13.9	8 450	84.2	15.8	2.59	2.49
Walton	46.5	29 083	56.9	43.1	26.4	4.1	45.5	16 548	79.0	21.0	2.34	2.37
Washington	23.1	9 503	83.5	16.5	6.6	1.8	15.2	7 931	81.9	18.1	2.45	2.50
GEORGIA	27.0	3 281 737	91.6	8.4	1.5	1.9	8.2	3 006 369	67.5	32.5	2.71	2.51
Appling	13.2	7 854	84.1	15.9	2.9	1.7	15.6	6 606	79.1	20.9	2.58	2.67
Atkinson	22.9	3 171	85.7	14.3	1.0	2.7	15.8	2 717	74.4	25.6	2.76	2.85
Bacon	11.4	4 464	85.9	14.1	1.0	1.6	19.0	3 833	74.9	25.1	2.57	2.66
Baker	16.5	1 740	87.0	13.0	1.8	1.3	11.5	1 514	77.7	22.3	2.67	2.72
Baldwin	21.3	17 173	85.9	14.1	4.4	1.8	12.2	14 758	66.5	33.5	2.59	2.32
Banks	42.1	5 808	92.4	7.6	1.1	1.4	7.8	5 364	80.9	19.1	2.70	2.62
Barrow	53.2	17 304	94.5	5.5	0.2	2.5	4.7	16 354	75.5	24.5	2.82	2.71
Bartow	35.3	28 751	94.5	5.5	0.4	1.9	6.0	27 176	75.3	24.7	2.79	2.69
Ben Hill	11.7	7 623	87.5	12.5	1.0	3.0	15.0	6 673	66.7	33.3	2.59	2.51
Berrien	21.6	7 100	88.2	11.8	1.1	1.9	11.9	6 261	75.4	24.6	2.58	2.54
Bibb	6.0	67 194	88.8	11.2	0.3	2.5	13.9	59 667	58.8	41.2	2.57	2.38
Bleckley	14.6	4 866	89.8	10.2	1.2	1.6	13.3	4 372	76.1	23.9	2.55	2.44
Brantley	42.6	6 490	83.8	16.2	6.0	1.3	14.4	5 436	86.9	13.1	2.71	2.46
Brooks	14.2	7 118	86.5	13.5	2.3	1.8	11.8	6 155	76.9	23.1	2.61	2.59
Bryan	59.5	8 675	93.2	6.8	1.0	1.7	8.3	8 089	77.9	22.1	2.95	2.64
Bulloch	38.4	22 742	91.2	8.8	1.3	1.7	8.4	20 743	58.1	41.9	2.67	2.33
Burke	12.7	8 842	89.7	10.3	1.2	1.3	8.1	7 934	76.0	24.0	2.81	2.64
Butts	37.5	7 380	87.5	12.5	5.6	2.5	7.9	6 455	76.6	23.4	2.77	2.58
Calhoun	9.4	2 305	85.1	14.9	1.6	2.2	8.6	1 962	71.8	28.2	2.57	2.50
Camden	55.5	16 958	86.7	13.3	3.0	2.5	12.5	14 705	63.3	36.7	2.88	2.78
Candler	19.3	3 893	86.7	13.3	4.4	1.0	11.0	3 375	73.1	26.9	2.68	2.81
Carroll	24.4	34 067	92.7	7.3	0.8	1.8	7.7	31 568	70.5	29.5	2.72	2.52
Catoosa	29.7	21 794	93.7	6.3	0.5	1.6	9.5	20 425	77.1	22.9	2.64	2.41
Charlton	14.8	3 859	86.6	13.4	2.6	2.2	14.9	3 342	80.8	19.2	2.79	2.51
Chatham	10.8	99 683	90.2	9.8	1.1	1.7	9.7	89 865	60.4	39.6	2.57	2.37
Chattahoochee	1.7	3 316	88.4	11.6	0.3	1.9	3.9	2 932	27.0	73.0	2.73	3.66
Chattooga	13.1	10 677	89.7	10.3	1.6	2.0	12.1	9 577	75.3	24.7	2.50	2.43
Cherokee	58.1	51 937	95.3	4.7	0.5	1.9	7.3	49 495	83.9	16.1	2.87	2.75
Clarke	19.7	42 126	94.3	5.7	0.4	1.6	4.9	39 706	42.0	58.0	2.45	2.27
Clay	11.3	1 925	70.0	30.0	19.1	2.5	6.0	1 347	74.5	25.5	2.42	2.53
Clayton	25.5	86 461	95.1	4.9	0.2	1.6	6.1	82 243	60.6	39.4	2.93	2.69
Clinch	15.6	2 837	88.5	11.5	1.2	1.6	13.6	2 512	72.6	27.4	2.66	2.41
Cobb	32.8	237 522	95.8	4.2	0.2	1.4	5.8	227 487	68.2	31.8	2.76	2.39
Coffee	26.7	15 610	85.5	14.5	1.1	2.6	18.2	13 354	74.4	25.6	2.74	2.57
Colquitt	19.4	17 554	88.3	11.7	0.7	1.9	13.5	15 495	66.7	33.3	2.62	2.65
Columbia	42.5	33 321	93.4	6.6	1.0	2.9	9.1	31 120	82.1	17.9	2.88	2.69
Cook	21.9	6 558	89.7	10.3	0.8	3.3	9.9	5 882	74.9	25.1	2.64	2.64
Coweta	66.1	33 182	94.8	5.2	0.5	1.9	6.0	31 442	78.0	22.0	2.84	2.70
Crawford	45.4	4 872	91.6	8.4	0.9	2.1	6.3	4 461	84.6	15.4	2.78	2.75
Crisp	14.4	9 559	87.2	12.8	2.9	1.8	10.3	8 337	60.5	39.5	2.53	2.66
Dade	20.9	6 224	90.5	9.5	1.7	0.9	9.2	5 633	80.3	19.7	2.61	2.33
Dawson	80.6	7 163	84.7	15.3	11.0	2.1	5.1	6 069	81.4	18.6	2.64	2.54
Decatur	15.8	11 968	86.7	13.3	1.6	2.1	13.6	10 380	72.5	27.5	2.66	2.64
De Kalb	19.5	261 231	95.4	4.6	0.3	1.6	4.7	249 339	58.5	41.5	2.66	2.55
Dodge	10.6	8 186	86.3	13.7	1.6	2.3	11.4	7 062	73.7	26.3	2.52	2.34
Dooly	9.9	4 499	86.9	13.1	2.5	1.8	10.6	3 909	71.3	28.7	2.60	2.68
Dougherty	4.1	39 656	89.7	10.3	0.4	2.6	11.0	35 552	53.5	46.5	2.57	2.58
Douglas	35.2	34 825	94.2	5.8	0.2	1.9	7.5	32 822	74.8	25.2	2.87	2.52
Early	10.1	5 338	88.0	12.0	1.9	1.0	6.9	4 695	72.4	27.6	2.57	2.60
Echols	54.9	1 482	85.3	14.7	2.6	1.0	16.6	1 264	75.7	24.3	2.83	3.40
Effingham	50.1	14 169	92.8	7.2	0.6	2.1	9.2	13 151	82.6	17.4	2.85	2.76
Elbert	12.5	9 136	87.6	12.4	3.1	1.7	8.0	8 004	75.9	24.1	2.56	2.43
Emanuel	8.4	9 419	85.4	14.6	2.2	1.9	9.6	8 045	71.1	28.9	2.61	2.62
Evans	20.2	4 381	86.2	13.8	2.8	3.2	13.4	3 778	71.5	28.5	2.61	2.66

Table B. States and Counties

STATE/County code	MSA/PMSA/NECMA code[1]	County type[2]	STATE County	Land area, 2000[3] (sq km)	Total persons	Rank	Per square kilometer	Land area, 1990[3] (sq km)	Total persons	Rank	Per square kilometer	White	Black or African American	American Indian or Alaska Native	Asian	Native Hawaiian and other Pacific Islander	Some other race
					Population, 2000				Population, 1990			Population and population characteristics, 2000 — Race (percent) — One race					
				1	2	3	4	5	6	7	8	9	10	11	12	13	14
			GEORGIA—Cont'd														
13 111	...	9	Fannin	999	19 798	1 801	19.8	999	15 992	1 923	16.0	98.0	0.1	0.5	0.2	0.0	0.2
13 113	0520	1	Fayette	510	91 263	564	178.9	511	62 415	696	122.1	83.9	11.5	0.2	2.4	0.0	0.8
13 115	...	4	Floyd	1 329	90 565	569	68.1	1 329	81 251	561	61.1	81.3	13.3	0.3	0.9	0.1	2.9
13 117	0520	1	Forsyth	585	98 407	529	168.2	585	44 083	925	75.4	95.0	0.7	0.3	0.8	0.0	2.3
13 119	...	8	Franklin	682	20 285	1 775	29.7	682	16 650	1 873	24.4	89.5	8.8	0.2	0.3	0.0	0.4
13 121	0520	0	Fulton	1 369	816 006	55	596.1	1 369	648 776	73	473.9	48.1	44.6	0.2	3.0	0.0	2.6
13 123	...	8	Gilmer	1 105	23 456	1 618	21.2	1 105	13 368	2 108	12.1	93.6	0.3	0.5	0.2	0.3	3.8
13 125	...	9	Glascock	373	2 556	3 022	6.9	373	2 357	3 035	6.3	90.6	8.3	0.0	0.0	0.0	0.1
13 127	...	5	Glynn	1 094	67 568	725	61.8	1 094	62 496	695	57.1	70.7	26.5	0.3	0.6	0.1	0.9
13 129	...	6	Gordon	921	44 104	1 015	47.9	920	35 067	1 130	38.1	89.7	3.5	0.3	0.5	0.1	5.0
13 131	...	6	Grady	1 187	23 659	1 604	19.9	1 187	20 279	1 662	17.1	64.6	30.1	0.9	0.3	0.0	3.2
13 133	...	6	Greene	1 006	14 406	2 131	14.3	1 006	11 793	2 229	11.7	53.0	44.4	0.2	0.2	0.1	1.5
13 135	0520	0	Gwinnett	1 121	588 448	92	524.9	1 121	352 910	146	314.8	72.7	13.3	0.3	7.2	0.0	4.3
13 137	...	7	Habersham	720	35 902	1 223	49.9	721	27 622	1 367	38.3	88.9	4.5	0.3	1.9	0.1	3.0
13 139	...	6	Hall	1 020	139 277	392	136.5	1 020	95 434	484	93.6	80.8	7.3	0.3	1.3	0.2	8.8
13 141	...	9	Hancock	1 226	10 076	2 438	8.2	1 226	8 908	2 479	7.3	21.5	77.8	0.2	0.1	0.0	0.1
13 143	...	6	Haralson	731	25 690	1 528	35.1	731	21 966	1 578	30.0	93.0	5.4	0.3	0.3	0.0	0.2
13 145	1800	2	Harris	1 201	23 695	1 602	19.7	1 201	17 788	1 798	14.8	78.4	19.5	0.4	0.5	0.0	0.3
13 147	...	6	Hart	601	22 997	1 642	38.3	601	19 712	1 691	32.8	79.1	19.4	0.2	0.5	0.0	0.2
13 149	...	8	Heard	767	11 012	2 364	14.4	767	8 628	2 500	11.2	87.5	10.8	0.3	0.1	0.1	0.5
13 151	0520	1	Henry	836	119 341	455	142.8	836	58 741	741	70.3	81.4	14.7	0.2	1.8	0.0	0.8
13 153	4680	2	Houston	976	110 765	489	113.5	976	89 208	514	91.4	70.6	24.8	0.3	1.6	0.1	1.0
13 155	...	7	Irwin	924	9 931	2 455	10.7	924	8 649	2 498	9.4	72.0	25.9	0.1	0.3	0.0	1.2
13 157	...	6	Jackson	887	41 589	1 066	46.9	887	30 005	1 295	33.8	89.0	7.8	0.2	1.0	0.0	1.1
13 159	...	8	Jasper	959	11 426	2 339	11.9	960	8 453	2 517	8.8	71.0	27.3	0.2	0.2	0.0	0.6
13 161	...	7	Jeff Davis	863	12 684	2 248	14.7	864	12 032	2 216	13.9	81.2	15.1	0.2	0.4	0.0	2.4
13 163	...	8	Jefferson	1 367	17 266	1 935	12.6	1 367	17 408	1 827	12.7	42.1	56.3	0.1	0.2	0.0	0.8
13 165	...	7	Jenkins	906	8 575	2 560	9.5	906	8 247	2 544	9.1	56.3	40.5	0.2	0.2	0.1	2.1
13 167	...	9	Johnson	788	8 560	2 562	10.9	788	8 329	2 532	10.6	62.4	37.0	0.1	0.1	0.0	0.2
13 169	4680	2	Jones	1 020	23 639	1 605	23.2	1 020	20 739	1 643	20.3	75.0	23.3	0.2	0.5	0.0	0.2
13 171	...	6	Lamar	479	15 912	2 026	33.2	479	13 038	2 138	27.2	67.8	30.4	0.3	0.4	0.0	0.3
13 173	...	9	Lanier	484	7 241	2 661	15.0	484	5 531	2 798	11.4	71.6	25.6	0.6	0.4	0.0	0.6
13 175	...	6	Laurens	2 104	44 874	1 001	21.3	2 105	39 988	1 000	19.0	63.4	34.5	0.2	0.8	0.0	0.4
13 177	0120	3	Lee	921	24 757	1 565	26.9	922	16 250	1 909	17.6	82.2	15.5	0.2	0.8	0.0	0.5
13 179	...	4	Liberty	1 344	61 610	789	45.8	1 345	52 745	804	39.2	46.6	42.8	0.5	1.8	0.4	4.4
13 181	...	8	Lincoln	547	8 348	2 576	15.3	547	7 442	2 620	13.6	64.3	34.4	0.4	0.2	0.0	0.2
13 183	...	9	Long	1 038	10 304	2 415	9.9	1 039	6 202	2 732	6.0	68.4	24.3	0.4	1.2	0.0	3.9
13 185	...	5	Lowndes	1 306	92 115	554	70.5	1 306	75 981	591	58.2	62.0	34.0	0.4	1.2	0.0	1.1
13 187	...	7	Lumpkin	737	21 016	1 735	28.5	737	14 573	2 015	19.8	94.0	1.5	1.0	0.4	0.1	1.6
13 189	0600	2	McDuffie	673	21 231	1 723	31.5	673	20 119	1 669	29.9	60.8	37.5	0.2	0.3	0.0	0.3
13 191	...	9	McIntosh	1 123	10 847	2 377	9.7	1 123	8 634	2 499	7.7	61.3	36.8	0.4	0.3	0.0	0.3
13 193	...	6	Macon	1 045	14 074	2 157	13.5	1 045	13 114	2 130	12.5	37.4	59.5	0.2	0.6	0.0	1.5
13 195	0500	3	Madison	735	25 730	1 526	35.0	737	21 050	1 626	28.6	89.0	8.5	0.2	0.3	0.0	1.0
13 197	...	8	Marion	951	7 144	2 674	7.5	951	5 590	2 701	5.9	60.8	34.1	0.4	0.2	0.2	3.0
13 199	...	6	Meriwether	1 303	22 534	1 669	17.3	1 304	22 411	1 559	17.2	56.1	42.2	0.3	0.2	0.1	0.3
13 201	...	9	Miller	733	6 383	2 750	8.7	733	6 280	2 725	8.6	70.3	28.9	0.2	0.0	0.1	0.2
13 205	...	6	Mitchell	1 326	23 932	1 595	18.0	1 326	20 275	1 663	15.3	49.6	47.9	0.2	0.3	0.1	1.3
13 207	...	6	Monroe	1 025	21 757	1 706	21.2	1 025	17 113	1 844	16.7	70.4	27.9	0.3	0.3	0.0	0.2
13 209	...	9	Montgomery	635	8 270	2 584	13.0	635	7 379	2 623	11.6	69.7	27.2	0.1	0.2	0.0	2.1
13 211	...	6	Morgan	906	15 457	2 053	17.1	906	12 883	2 147	14.2	69.7	28.5	0.1	0.3	0.0	0.4
13 213	...	7	Murray	892	36 506	1 202	40.9	892	26 147	1 415	29.3	95.3	0.6	0.3	0.3	0.0	2.6
13 215	1800	2	Muscogee	560	186 291	295	332.7	560	179 280	271	320.1	50.4	43.7	0.4	1.5	0.0	1.9
13 217	0520	1	Newton	716	62 001	784	86.6	716	41 808	960	58.4	75.3	22.2	0.2	0.7	0.0	0.6
13 219	0500	3	Oconee	481	26 225	1 508	54.5	481	17 618	1 812	36.6	89.6	6.4	0.2	1.4	0.0	1.5
13 221	...	8	Oglethorpe	1 142	12 635	2 253	11.1	1 143	9 763	2 408	8.5	78.3	19.8	0.2	0.2	0.0	0.6
13 223	0520	1	Paulding	812	81 678	636	100.6	812	41 611	967	51.2	90.6	7.0	0.3	0.4	0.0	0.6
13 225	4680	2	Peach	391	23 668	1 603	60.5	391	21 189	1 621	54.2	51.3	45.4	0.3	0.3	0.0	1.8
13 227	0520	1	Pickens	601	22 983	1 644	38.2	601	14 432	2 023	24.0	96.2	1.3	0.4	0.2	0.0	1.0
13 229	...	7	Pierce	889	15 636	2 047	17.6	888	13 328	2 111	15.0	86.9	10.9	0.3	0.2	0.1	1.0
13 231	...	8	Pike	566	13 688	2 185	24.2	566	10 224	2 368	18.1	83.6	14.8	0.2	0.4	0.0	0.4
13 233	...	6	Polk	806	38 127	1 161	47.3	806	33 815	1 170	42.0	80.5	13.3	0.2	0.3	0.0	4.6
13 235	...	6	Pulaski	641	9 588	2 481	15.0	641	8 108	2 554	12.6	63.0	34.3	0.3	0.3	0.1	1.2
13 237	...	6	Putnam	892	18 812	1 853	21.1	892	14 137	2 043	15.8	67.5	29.9	0.2	0.7	0.0	0.8
13 239	...	9	Quitman	392	2 598	3 020	6.6	393	2 210	3 054	5.6	52.1	46.9	0.2	0.0	0.0	2.6
13 241	...	9	Rabun	961	15 050	2 088	15.7	961	11 648	2 241	12.1	94.9	0.8	0.4	0.4	0.0	2.6
13 243	...	7	Randolph	1 112	7 791	2 626	7.0	1 112	8 023	2 562	7.2	38.9	59.5	0.3	0.2	0.1	0.5

[1] MSA = Metropolitan Statistical Area. PMSA = Primary MSA. NECMA = New England County Metropolitan Area. See Appendix A for explanation of these concepts. See Appendix B for list of metropolitan areas identified by type, with component counties.
[2] County typology code from the Economic Research Service of USDA. See Appendix A for definition.
[3] Dry land or land partially or temporarily covered by water.

STATE County	Population and population characteristics, 2000 (cont'd)								Population and population characteristics, 1990				
	Race (percent) (cont'd)								Race (percent)				
	Race alone or in combination												
	Two or more races	White	Black	American Indian or Alaska Native	Asian	Native Hawaiian and other Pacific Islander	Some other race	Hispanic[1]	White	Black or African American	American Indian or Alaska Native	Asian and Pacific Islander	Hispanic[1]
	15	16	17	18	19	20	21	22	23	24	25	26	27
GEORGIA—Cont'd													
Fannin	1.0	99.0	0.2	1.3	0.3	0.0	0.3	0.7	99.6	0.0	0.2	0.1	0.4
Fayette	1.2	84.9	11.9	0.6	2.8	0.1	1.1	2.8	92.5	5.4	0.1	1.7	1.6
Floyd	1.1	82.3	13.6	0.7	1.1	0.0	3.3	5.5	85.3	13.7	0.2	0.5	1.0
Forsyth	0.9	95.9	0.8	0.6	1.0	0.0	2.7	5.6	98.8	0.0	0.2	0.2	1.4
Franklin	0.8	90.2	9.1	0.6	0.4	0.0	0.6	0.9	89.5	10.1	0.2	0.2	0.5
Fulton	1.5	49.1	45.2	0.5	3.4	0.1	3.2	5.9	47.8	49.9	0.2	1.3	2.1
Gilmer	1.4	94.7	0.3	1.3	0.3	0.3	4.5	7.7	99.2	0.3	0.1	0.1	0.8
Glascock	0.7	90.8	8.5	0.7	0.5	0.0	0.2	0.5	87.2	12.6	0.1	0.0	0.3
Glynn	1.1	71.5	26.9	0.6	0.9	0.1	1.2	3.0	73.6	25.5	0.2	0.5	0.9
Gordon	1.0	90.6	3.7	0.7	0.7	0.1	5.3	7.4	95.5	3.8	0.2	0.4	0.6
Grady	0.8	65.3	30.5	1.3	0.4	0.0	3.4	5.2	67.4	31.5	0.4	0.1	1.4
Greene	0.6	53.4	44.7	0.5	0.3	0.1	1.6	2.9	49.7	49.9	0.1	0.0	0.8
Gwinnett	2.2	74.3	13.9	0.7	7.8	0.1	5.4	10.9	90.9	5.2	0.2	2.9	2.4
Habersham	1.4	89.8	4.8	0.9	2.2	0.2	3.6	7.7	91.7	5.6	0.3	1.9	1.2
Hall	1.4	82.0	7.5	0.7	1.5	0.2	9.5	19.6	87.1	8.6	0.2	0.7	4.8
Hancock	0.4	21.7	78.0	0.3	0.1	0.0	0.3	0.5	20.2	79.4	0.1	0.0	0.7
Haralson	0.8	93.8	5.6	0.7	0.4	0.0	0.3	0.6	93.0	6.5	0.1	0.2	0.4
Harris	0.9	79.2	19.7	0.8	0.7	0.1	0.5	1.1	73.7	25.7	0.3	0.2	0.5
Hart	0.6	79.6	19.6	0.4	0.6	0.0	0.4	0.9	79.4	20.3	0.1	0.2	0.4
Heard	0.7	88.1	11.1	0.6	0.2	0.1	0.7	1.1	86.0	13.5	0.1	0.3	0.8
Henry	1.1	82.3	15.1	0.6	2.1	0.1	1.1	2.3	88.7	10.3	0.2	0.6	0.8
Houston	1.7	71.9	25.3	0.8	2.2	0.1	1.4	3.0	76.3	21.7	0.3	1.2	1.6
Irwin	0.5	72.3	26.0	0.3	0.4	0.0	1.4	2.0	69.3	30.4	0.1	0.2	0.6
Jackson	1.0	89.9	8.1	0.6	1.2	0.0	1.3	3.0	89.8	9.7	0.2	0.2	0.5
Jasper	0.8	71.7	27.5	0.5	0.2	0.0	0.8	2.1	64.8	34.8	0.2	0.1	0.7
Jeff Davis	0.6	81.7	15.2	0.5	0.5	0.1	2.6	5.1	83.8	15.2	0.1	0.2	1.2
Jefferson	0.5	42.4	56.5	0.3	0.2	0.0	1.0	1.5	44.0	55.7	0.1	0.1	0.2
Jenkins	0.7	56.9	40.8	0.4	0.3	0.1	2.2	3.3	58.3	41.4	0.1	0.2	0.2
Johnson	0.3	62.7	37.0	0.3	0.2	0.0	0.1	0.9	65.7	34.1	0.0	0.1	0.4
Jones	0.7	75.6	23.6	0.5	0.7	0.1	0.4	0.7	73.9	25.6	0.2	0.2	0.4
Lamar	0.9	68.5	30.8	0.7	0.4	0.0	0.5	1.1	65.6	34.1	0.1	0.1	0.4
Lanier	1.2	72.7	25.9	1.1	0.7	0.1	0.8	1.7	71.9	26.6	0.7	0.4	1.2
Laurens	0.6	63.9	34.8	0.4	0.9	0.1	0.5	1.2	66.2	33.3	0.1	0.3	0.5
Lee	0.7	82.8	15.7	0.5	1.0	0.1	0.7	1.2	80.0	19.3	0.2	0.3	0.7
Liberty	3.4	48.9	44.6	1.1	2.6	0.7	5.8	8.2	54.9	39.2	0.5	2.3	6.1
Lincoln	0.6	64.7	34.5	0.7	0.3	0.0	0.3	1.0	61.8	38.0	0.0	0.1	0.8
Long	1.9	69.9	25.0	1.1	1.0	0.4	4.6	8.4	75.5	21.6	0.4	0.7	3.0
Lowndes	1.3	63.0	34.5	0.8	1.6	0.1	1.4	2.7	66.6	31.9	0.3	0.9	1.3
Lumpkin	1.5	95.5	1.6	2.0	0.5	0.1	1.8	3.5	96.1	1.6	1.6	0.3	1.5
McDuffie	0.8	61.3	37.9	0.5	0.6	0.1	0.5	1.3	63.2	36.4	0.2	0.1	0.4
McIntosh	0.9	62.0	37.3	0.8	0.3	0.0	0.4	0.9	56.5	43.1	0.2	0.1	0.7
Macon	0.8	37.9	59.8	0.6	0.7	0.1	1.7	2.6	40.9	58.7	0.1	0.2	0.4
Madison	1.0	89.9	8.6	0.7	0.5	0.1	1.3	2.0	90.5	8.8	0.1	0.3	0.9
Marion	1.4	62.0	34.5	1.2	0.4	0.3	3.1	5.8	58.1	41.3	0.3	0.2	0.4
Meriwether	0.7	56.7	42.4	0.6	0.3	0.1	0.6	0.8	55.1	44.6	0.1	0.1	0.5
Miller	0.3	70.6	29.0	0.4	0.1	0.1	0.3	0.7	72.3	27.5	0.1	0.1	0.3
Mitchell	0.7	50.1	48.2	0.5	0.4	0.1	1.5	2.1	51.4	47.6	0.3	0.1	1.3
Monroe	0.7	70.9	28.2	0.7	0.6	0.0	0.3	1.3	67.8	31.6	0.2	0.2	0.6
Montgomery	0.6	70.3	27.4	0.3	0.4	0.1	2.3	3.3	69.8	28.3	0.1	0.2	2.0
Morgan	0.9	70.3	29.0	0.5	0.5	0.1	0.8	1.6	64.9	34.6	0.1	0.2	0.9
Murray	0.9	96.1	0.8	0.7	0.4	0.0	2.9	5.5	99.3	0.2	0.2	0.2	0.5
Muscogee	1.9	51.8	44.6	0.8	2.0	0.3	2.5	4.5	59.0	38.0	0.3	1.4	3.0
Newton	1.0	76.1	22.6	0.5	0.9	0.1	0.9	1.9	76.9	22.4	0.2	0.3	0.9
Oconee	0.9	90.3	6.6	0.5	1.7	0.1	1.8	3.2	91.7	7.5	0.2	0.5	1.0
Oglethorpe	0.8	79.0	20.2	0.6	0.4	0.1	0.6	1.4	74.7	24.8	0.2	0.1	0.7
Paulding	1.2	91.6	7.3	0.8	0.6	0.1	0.8	1.7	95.4	4.0	0.3	0.2	0.6
Peach	0.8	51.9	45.7	0.6	0.5	0.1	2.1	4.2	50.6	47.5	0.3	0.3	1.8
Pickens	0.8	97.0	1.3	0.9	0.3	0.0	1.2	2.0	97.8	1.7	0.2	0.1	0.3
Pierce	0.7	87.5	11.2	0.5	0.3	0.1	1.1	2.3	87.7	11.8	0.2	0.1	0.8
Pike	0.6	84.1	15.0	0.5	0.5	0.0	0.5	1.2	79.4	20.1	0.1	0.2	0.5
Polk	0.9	81.3	13.7	0.5	0.4	0.1	5.0	7.7	84.5	14.2	0.2	0.3	1.4
Pulaski	0.8	63.7	34.6	0.7	0.5	0.2	1.3	2.8	66.6	32.5	0.1	0.2	1.0
Putnam	0.9	68.0	30.3	0.6	0.8	0.1	1.2	2.2	65.8	33.6	0.1	0.3	0.7
Quitman	0.5	52.5	47.2	0.6	0.0	0.0	0.2	0.5	49.5	50.1	0.3	0.1	0.0
Rabun	0.9	95.7	1.0	1.0	0.5	0.1	2.7	4.5	98.9	0.4	0.3	0.1	0.6
Randolph	0.4	39.3	59.7	0.5	0.3	0.2	0.6	1.2	41.3	57.9	0.0	0.6	0.5

[1] Hispanic persons may be of any race.

STATE County	Population and population characteristics, 2000										
	Age (percent)									Median age (years)	Percent Female
	Under 5 years	5 to 17 years	18 to 24 years	25 to 34 years	35 to 44 years	45 to 54 years	55 to 64 years	65 to 74 years	75 years and over		
	28	29	30	31	32	33	34	35	36	37	38
GEORGIA—Cont'd											
Fannin	5.4	15.6	7.0	11.2	13.7	15.2	13.0	11.1	7.9	43.1	51.7
Fayette	5.8	23.3	6.5	9.3	18.4	18.2	9.6	4.9	4.0	38.2	51.1
Floyd	6.6	18.0	10.8	13.6	14.9	12.8	9.3	7.4	6.5	35.7	51.6
Forsyth	9.5	18.4	6.1	16.8	20.3	13.5	8.3	4.3	2.8	34.6	49.3
Franklin	6.3	17.6	9.6	12.7	14.6	13.0	10.8	8.4	6.9	37.6	51.5
Fulton	7.0	17.5	11.0	18.6	16.9	13.4	7.3	4.4	4.1	32.7	50.8
Gilmer	7.2	17.2	8.5	13.6	14.9	13.8	11.8	8.3	4.9	37.3	49.3
Glascock	6.8	17.1	7.7	12.1	14.7	12.9	10.5	8.5	9.7	39.6	52.0
Glynn	6.5	18.8	8.2	12.3	15.3	14.4	10.1	7.8	6.7	37.9	52.2
Gordon	7.2	18.9	9.5	15.8	15.6	13.1	9.3	6.1	4.5	34.1	50.2
Grady	7.0	20.2	9.0	13.0	14.9	13.1	9.5	7.0	6.2	35.5	52.5
Greene	6.7	18.4	8.7	11.0	13.2	14.1	13.4	8.4	6.0	39.1	52.1
Gwinnett	8.0	20.2	8.7	17.8	19.7	13.8	6.5	3.2	2.2	32.5	49.6
Habersham	6.3	17.2	11.1	13.3	15.1	13.1	10.0	7.8	6.0	36.4	48.7
Hall	8.2	18.7	10.8	16.7	15.5	12.4	8.1	5.4	4.0	32.2	49.1
Hancock	5.8	18.3	9.9	14.7	16.3	13.8	9.3	7.0	5.0	35.8	46.6
Haralson	6.8	19.2	8.1	14.1	15.1	13.3	10.3	7.2	5.8	36.1	51.2
Harris	5.9	19.7	6.3	12.0	17.3	16.4	10.5	6.9	5.0	38.5	50.6
Hart	6.3	17.2	7.7	12.5	14.8	13.8	11.2	9.3	7.2	39.2	50.8
Heard	7.9	20.8	7.6	15.0	15.6	12.8	9.1	6.2	4.8	34.1	50.9
Henry	8.1	21.1	7.4	16.3	18.6	13.2	7.8	4.5	2.9	33.4	50.7
Houston	7.0	21.2	9.5	14.0	17.8	13.1	8.2	5.7	3.6	34.0	50.8
Irwin	6.8	22.0	9.2	12.5	13.6	12.2	9.7	7.4	6.6	34.6	50.9
Jackson	7.3	19.4	8.7	15.3	16.5	13.0	9.5	5.6	4.8	34.6	49.9
Jasper	7.0	20.3	7.9	13.0	15.6	14.6	9.8	6.8	5.0	36.3	51.0
Jeff Davis	7.7	19.5	9.3	13.5	14.8	13.8	9.6	6.9	5.0	35.0	50.9
Jefferson	7.2	21.2	9.0	12.7	14.4	12.9	8.9	6.8	6.9	34.9	52.9
Jenkins	7.1	21.4	9.2	11.8	14.7	13.4	8.9	7.3	6.2	35.4	52.1
Johnson	6.8	23.3	8.9	11.1	13.2	11.5	9.5	8.0	7.6	34.9	50.7
Jones	6.5	20.6	7.9	13.2	17.4	14.4	9.6	6.0	4.3	36.1	51.2
Lamar	6.1	18.4	11.4	13.2	14.7	14.0	9.6	7.0	5.6	35.7	52.1
Lanier	7.2	20.2	11.0	14.2	16.3	11.8	8.7	6.2	4.5	33.3	49.3
Laurens	6.9	19.9	9.1	12.9	15.0	13.5	9.3	6.9	6.4	35.8	51.9
Lee	7.3	23.4	8.5	14.7	18.5	14.7	6.7	3.8	2.5	32.6	49.5
Liberty	10.4	21.6	17.9	19.1	14.8	8.0	4.3	2.4	1.5	25.0	47.3
Lincoln	5.4	19.0	7.2	11.9	15.6	14.7	11.6	9.1	5.5	39.3	51.3
Long	11.0	22.1	14.2	16.6	14.4	10.1	5.8	3.5	2.3	26.5	49.5
Lowndes	7.2	19.0	15.1	15.9	15.4	11.4	7.1	5.0	4.0	30.2	50.3
Lumpkin	6.4	17.9	15.4	13.6	15.4	12.5	9.1	5.6	4.1	32.5	50.9
McDuffie	7.1	20.7	8.6	13.2	15.3	13.9	9.3	6.4	5.5	35.2	52.8
McIntosh	6.6	21.5	7.2	12.3	14.6	14.7	11.4	7.1	4.7	37.0	50.5
Macon	7.1	20.5	9.7	12.4	15.2	13.5	8.7	6.7	6.0	35.1	50.4
Madison	6.9	19.4	8.2	14.1	16.5	14.0	9.9	6.3	4.7	35.8	50.9
Marion	6.5	21.9	8.6	12.7	16.0	14.5	9.2	5.7	4.8	35.2	50.8
Meriwether	6.7	19.9	9.0	12.3	14.8	13.5	10.1	7.0	6.6	36.4	52.2
Miller	6.0	20.3	7.0	12.0	14.2	12.8	10.7	8.2	8.9	38.2	52.9
Mitchell	7.2	20.1	9.9	14.1	15.3	12.7	8.9	6.3	5.5	34.0	49.1
Monroe	6.3	19.9	8.3	13.1	17.2	15.0	9.8	6.0	4.4	36.4	50.2
Montgomery	6.8	18.2	12.8	14.5	15.7	12.3	9.1	6.1	4.5	33.6	48.8
Morgan	6.6	19.9	7.8	12.9	15.8	14.2	10.2	6.8	5.7	36.8	51.6
Murray	8.1	19.9	9.5	16.4	16.7	12.9	8.6	5.1	2.9	32.6	50.0
Muscogee	7.3	19.5	11.9	14.6	15.2	12.2	7.5	6.5	5.2	32.6	51.4
Newton	7.9	19.7	8.9	16.3	15.8	12.7	8.8	5.7	4.2	33.3	51.4
Oconee	6.9	23.3	7.0	12.4	17.8	15.7	8.3	4.6	3.9	35.2	50.7
Oglethorpe	6.9	18.9	7.8	13.3	16.7	13.5	10.5	7.0	5.4	36.8	51.4
Paulding	9.4	21.3	7.6	19.8	18.6	11.0	6.4	3.6	2.3	31.2	50.0
Peach	6.5	19.6	14.9	13.2	14.3	12.7	9.0	5.8	4.0	31.8	51.6
Pickens	6.3	17.2	7.7	14.0	15.8	13.9	11.9	8.2	5.0	37.9	51.1
Pierce	6.7	20.0	8.5	13.1	15.0	14.2	10.4	6.8	5.3	36.2	50.8
Pike	7.0	20.6	8.0	13.2	17.0	13.5	9.8	6.2	4.7	35.7	50.0
Polk	7.2	18.9	9.7	14.1	14.7	12.6	9.6	7.2	6.0	35.1	50.2
Pulaski	6.4	16.7	9.3	14.9	16.2	13.4	9.9	7.0	6.2	36.7	57.4
Putnam	6.1	17.1	7.7	12.5	14.5	14.8	13.1	9.0	5.1	39.6	50.8
Quitman	6.1	17.9	7.2	9.8	13.8	13.9	11.5	11.7	8.2	42.0	52.9
Rabun	5.7	16.1	7.0	11.7	13.6	14.6	13.1	10.7	7.5	42.0	50.7
Randolph	7.1	20.2	11.0	10.4	13.8	12.8	9.1	7.5	8.0	36.1	53.8

Table B. States and Counties

	Population and population characteristics, 1990										Population—change, 1980–2000				
	Age (percent)										Total persons			Percent change	
STATE County	Under 5 years	5 to 17 years	18 to 24 years	25 to 34 years	35 to 44 years	45 to 54 years	55 to 64 years	65 to 74 years	75 years and over	Percent Female	2000	1990	1980	1990–2000	1980–1990
	39	40	41	42	43	44	45	46	47	48	49	50	51	52	53
GEORGIA—Cont'd															
Fannin	5.8	17.4	7.9	13.2	14.2	11.0	12.6	11.1	6.8	51.8	19 798	15 992	14 748	23.8	8.4
Fayette	7.0	22.2	0.1	14.2	20.0	13.7	6.7	4.6	2 5	50.6	91 263	62 415	29 043	46.2	114.9
Floyd	6.7	17.3	11.4	15.4	14.1	10.7	9.8	8.4	6.2	52.4	90 565	81 251	79 800	11.5	1.8
Forsyth	7.7	18.1	9.8	18.5	17.0	11.9	8.0	5.5	3.4	49.9	98 407	44 083	27 958	123.2	57.7
Franklin	6.5	17.3	10.8	14.2	13.5	11.6	10.6	9.2	6.4	52.2	20 285	16 650	15 185	21.8	9.6
Fulton	7.4	16.8	12.0	19.6	16.8	10.3	7.0	5.6	4.4	52.3	816 006	648 776	589 904	25.8	10.0
Gilmer	6.5	18.7	9.6	14.7	14.4	11.8	10.9	8.0	5.6	50.8	23 456	13 368	11 110	75.5	20.3
Glascock	5.5	18.0	8.8	14.7	13.4	11.5	10.4	9.0	8.8	53.3	2 556	2 357	2 382	8.4	-1.0
Glynn	7.3	18.7	9.5	15.9	14.5	10.9	9.2	8.4	5.5	52.5	67 568	62 496	54 981	8.1	13.7
Gordon	7.1	19.9	10.5	16.7	14.9	11.7	8.5	6.3	4.4	50.8	44 104	35 067	30 070	25.8	16.6
Grady	7.3	21.0	9.8	15.1	13.5	10.2	8.7	7.9	6.6	52.5	23 659	20 279	19 845	16.7	2.2
Greene	7.6	23.1	9.2	13.7	13.4	10.1	8.7	8.1	6.1	53.4	14 406	11 793	11 391	22.2	3.5
Gwinnett	8.6	19.3	9.6	22.9	19.4	10.2	5.2	3.0	1.7	50.3	588 448	352 910	166 808	66.7	111.6
Habersham	6.3	17.3	13.8	15.1	13.8	10.7	9.8	7.8	5.4	48.9	35 902	27 622	25 020	30.0	10.4
Hall	7.5	18.1	11.2	17.9	15.1	11.0	8.3	6.5	4.3	50.7	139 277	95 434	75 649	45.9	26.2
Hancock	7.8	23.5	9.8	14.5	13.1	9.0	8.5	7.7	6.0	54.6	10 076	8 908	9 466	13.1	-5.9
Haralson	7.5	19.0	10.3	15.5	14.0	11.2	9.3	7.6	5.8	52.0	25 690	21 966	18 422	17.0	19.2
Harris	6.4	18.9	8.7	15.1	16.2	11.5	9.9	8.4	4.9	50.7	23 695	17 788	15 464	33.2	15.0
Hart	6.8	18.0	9.7	14.6	13.6	10.8	10.5	9.3	6.6	51.8	22 997	19 712	18 585	16.7	6.1
Heard	7.2	21.2	10.3	15.8	14.2	11.2	8.1	7.0	5.0	51.2	11 012	8 628	6 520	27.6	32.3
Henry	8.1	19.6	9.6	18.8	16.3	11.4	8.0	5.1	3.3	50.6	119 341	58 741	36 309	103.2	61.8
Houston	8.2	20.0	10.1	19.1	15.3	11.1	8.3	5.3	2.5	50.9	110 765	89 208	77 605	24.2	15.0
Irwin	7.9	20.8	9.7	14.0	12.4	10.6	9.1	8.4	7.2	53.0	9 931	8 649	8 988	14.8	-3.8
Jackson	7.2	19.3	10.2	16.7	14.7	11.4	8.4	7.0	5.0	50.4	41 589	30 005	25 343	38.6	18.4
Jasper	7.4	20.8	8.8	14.8	15.4	10.0	9.3	7.8	5.9	51.8	11 426	8 453	7 553	35.2	11.9
Jeff Davis	7.4	20.7	11.2	15.5	14.6	10.7	8.9	6.7	4.4	50.7	12 684	12 032	11 473	5.4	4.9
Jefferson	8.1	22.1	10.8	14.1	13.3	9.0	8.0	8.0	6.6	53.8	17 266	17 408	18 403	-0.8	-5.4
Jenkins	8.1	21.4	9.3	14.5	13.3	9.9	9.3	8.6	5.6	53.0	8 575	8 247	8 841	4.0	-6.7
Johnson	7.7	21.6	9.4	14.8	12.0	9.8	9.3	8.6	6.7	53.5	8 560	8 329	8 660	2.8	-3.8
Jones	7.6	20.3	9.7	17.3	16.3	11.7	7.7	5.9	3.4	51.4	23 639	20 739	16 579	14.0	25.1
Lamar	6.9	19.5	11.0	15.0	14.3	10.8	9.2	7.8	5.6	52.7	15 912	13 038	12 215	22.0	6.7
Lanier	8.0	21.2	10.6	15.8	13.6	10.5	8.5	6.4	5.4	51.4	7 241	5 531	5 654	30.9	-2.2
Laurens	7.4	20.7	9.7	15.3	14.1	10.0	8.9	8.3	5.6	52.1	44 874	39 988	36 990	12.2	8.1
Lee	7.5	24.6	9.6	18.7	18.1	9.1	5.9	4.2	2.3	49.2	24 757	16 250	11 684	52.4	39.1
Liberty	11.4	19.0	23.0	23.4	11.2	5.2	3.2	2.3	1.4	44.6	61 610	52 745	37 583	16.8	40.3
Lincoln	6.7	20.0	9.7	14.4	13.9	10.8	10.3	8.9	5.3	51.7	8 348	7 442	6 716	12.2	10.8
Long	10.3	20.0	15.8	16.7	13.1	8.9	6.7	5.5	3.0	49.7	10 304	6 202	4 524	66.1	37.1
Lowndes	8.2	19.8	14.8	17.7	14.0	9.0	6.9	5.6	3.9	51.0	92 115	75 981	67 972	21.2	11.8
Lumpkin	6.8	17.5	16.4	17.1	13.6	10.2	8.2	5.9	4.3	50.4	21 016	14 573	10 762	44.2	35.4
McDuffie	8.0	21.4	9.7	15.5	15.0	10.1	8.5	7.2	4.7	52.8	21 231	20 119	18 546	5.5	8.5
McIntosh	7.5	20.5	9.6	15.6	13.8	10.6	9.6	7.6	5.2	51.6	10 847	8 634	8 046	25.6	7.3
Macon	7.9	23.7	9.7	14.5	13.7	9.3	7.5	7.4	6.4	53.5	14 074	13 114	14 003	7.3	-6.3
Madison	7.2	19.4	10.1	17.0	15.5	11.4	8.3	6.3	4.7	51.1	25 730	21 050	17 747	22.2	18.6
Marion	7.7	20.9	9.8	16.3	14.2	10.7	7.5	7.6	5.3	52.0	7 144	5 590	5 297	27.8	5.5
Meriwether	7.8	21.3	10.5	14.9	13.3	10.1	8.5	7.8	5.7	52.2	22 534	22 411	21 229	0.5	5.6
Miller	6.8	20.7	9.3	13.4	12.2	11.6	9.3	8.9	7.8	52.6	6 383	6 280	7 038	1.6	-10.8
Mitchell	7.8	23.9	10.1	14.3	12.8	9.9	8.1	7.3	5.8	53.1	23 932	20 275	21 114	18.0	-4.0
Monroe	7.0	20.0	10.2	16.1	15.9	11.0	8.5	6.4	4.9	51.0	21 757	17 113	14 610	27.1	17.1
Montgomery	6.6	19.4	13.9	16.5	13.7	9.6	8.1	6.8	5.5	50.7	8 270	7 379	7 011	12.1	5.2
Morgan	7.4	20.2	9.6	16.2	14.3	10.7	8.3	7.4	5.8	51.8	15 457	12 883	11 572	20.0	11.3
Murray	7.6	20.7	11.3	18.6	14.9	11.1	7.6	4.9	3.3	50.5	36 506	26 147	19 685	39.6	32.8
Muscogee	8.2	18.8	12.5	18.1	13.9	9.1	8.6	6.5	4.3	51.4	186 291	179 280	170 108	3.9	5.4
Newton	8.1	19.8	11.8	16.5	14.3	10.8	8.1	6.1	4.5	52.1	62 001	41 808	34 666	48.3	20.6
Oconee	7.9	20.8	9.0	16.9	18.1	11.2	6.9	5.1	4.1	51.3	26 225	17 618	12 427	48.9	41.8
Oglethorpe	7.3	18.8	9.9	16.5	15.0	11.4	9.0	6.8	5.3	51.8	12 635	9 763	8 929	29.4	9.3
Paulding	9.3	19.8	10.7	21.1	15.4	9.7	6.7	4.4	2.9	50.1	81 678	41 611	26 110	96.3	59.4
Peach	7.1	20.1	15.1	15.4	13.6	10.3	8.3	6.0	4.0	52.4	23 668	21 189	19 151	11.7	10.6
Pickens	7.2	17.9	10.1	15.8	14.4	11.5	9.8	8.1	5.4	51.1	22 983	14 432	11 652	59.3	23.9
Pierce	6.7	21.5	9.7	14.7	15.2	11.4	9.1	7.0	4.7	51.5	15 636	13 328	11 897	17.3	12.0
Pike	7.3	20.0	9.3	15.7	14.4	11.8	9.0	7.1	5.3	50.6	13 688	10 224	8 937	33.9	14.4
Polk	7.1	19.3	10.2	15.2	13.6	11.0	9.4	8.0	6.1	52.0	38 127	33 815	32 382	12.8	4.4
Pulaski	6.7	20.3	8.8	13.9	13.5	11.3	10.0	8.7	6.9	53.2	9 588	8 108	8 950	18.3	-9.4
Putnam	6.8	19.0	9.8	15.8	13.9	11.6	10.8	7.8	4.5	51.0	18 812	14 137	10 295	33.1	37.3
Quitman	7.3	18.5	10.1	13.0	12.0	10.4	11.2	11.2	6.3	53.6	2 598	2 210	2 357	17.6	-6.2
Rabun	5.8	16.2	8.6	13.1	14.5	11.9	11.8	10.6	7.6	51.7	15 050	11 648	10 466	29.2	11.3
Randolph	7.1	22.2	11.5	12.9	12.2	8.3	8.6	9.5	7.8	54.5	7 791	8 023	9 599	-2.9	-16.4

Table B. States and Counties

STATE County	Total population	In households (percent) Total in house-holds	House-holder	Spouse	Child Total	Child Own child under 18 years	Other relatives Total	Other relatives Under 18 years	Nonrelatives Total	Nonrelatives Unmarried partner	In group quarters (percent) Total in group quarters	Institutionalized population Correctional institutions	Institutionalized population Nursing homes	Institutionalized population Other institutions	Noninstitutionalized population College dormitories	Noninstitutionalized population Military quarters	Other
	54	55	56	57	58	59	60	61	62	63	64	65	66	67	68	69	70
GEORGIA—Cont'd																	
Fannin	19 798	99.3	42.3	25.3	24.9	18.6	4.3	1.9	2.5	1.3	0.7	0.1	0.6	0.0	0.0	0.0	0.0
Fayette	91 263	99.4	34.5	24.7	34.2	27.4	3.8	1.4	2.1	0.8	0.6	0.2	0.4	0.0	0.0	0.0	0.0
Floyd	90 565	95.9	37.6	20.2	27.9	21.4	5.9	2.5	4.4	1.6	4.1	1.0	0.8	0.3	1.8	0.0	0.2
Forsyth	98 407	99.3	35.1	25.2	31.2	26.3	4.0	1.2	3.7	1.1	0.7	0.1	0.3	0.0	0.0	0.0	0.3
Franklin	20 285	97.1	38.9	22.2	27.6	21.2	5.1	2.1	3.3	1.5	2.9	0.3	0.7	0.2	1.7	0.0	0.0
Fulton	816 006	96.2	39.4	14.7	27.0	20.9	7.2	2.9	7.9	2.2	3.8	0.9	0.2	0.0	1.7	0.0	1.0
Gilmer	23 456	99.3	38.7	23.6	27.1	21.4	5.2	2.1	4.6	1.6	0.7	0.3	0.4	0.0	0.0	0.0	0.0
Glascock	2 556	95.9	39.3	23.0	26.8	21.0	4.4	2.4	2.4	1.2	4.1	0.0	0.0	0.0	0.0	0.0	4.1
Glynn	67 568	98.1	40.3	19.9	27.6	21.6	5.7	2.8	4.7	1.9	1.9	0.4	0.3	0.0	0.0	0.0	1.2
Gordon	44 104	99.0	36.7	22.1	29.5	22.9	6.2	2.5	4.6	1.6	1.0	0.3	0.5	0.0	0.0	0.0	0.1
Grady	23 659	98.8	37.2	19.8	30.2	23.0	7.4	3.5	4.3	1.9	1.2	0.3	0.6	0.0	0.0	0.0	0.3
Greene	14 406	98.6	38.0	19.4	29.1	20.3	8.1	4.1	4.0	1.7	1.4	0.3	0.9	0.0	0.0	0.0	0.2
Gwinnett	588 448	98.9	34.4	21.0	31.9	26.1	6.1	1.6	5.5	1.5	1.1	0.5	0.2	0.0	0.0	0.0	0.4
Habersham	35 902	94.8	36.9	22.5	26.7	20.6	5.2	2.1	3.5	1.3	5.2	3.5	0.3	0.0	1.0	0.0	0.4
Hall	139 277	98.4	34.0	20.5	29.8	23.3	8.2	2.8	5.9	1.5	1.6	0.6	0.2	0.3	0.2	0.0	0.3
Hancock	10 076	85.5	32.1	12.2	28.9	18.7	9.8	5.0	2.4	1.4	14.5	13.6	0.8	0.0	0.0	0.0	0.1
Haralson	25 690	98.7	38.2	22.1	29.6	22.8	5.1	2.5	3.7	1.8	1.3	0.2	0.8	0.0	0.0	0.0	0.2
Harris	23 695	99.1	37.2	24.1	30.0	22.0	5.3	2.4	2.5	1.1	0.9	0.4	0.4	0.0	0.0	0.0	0.1
Hart	22 997	97.7	39.6	22.5	27.6	20.5	5.1	2.5	2.9	1.5	2.3	1.2	0.4	0.0	0.0	0.0	0.7
Heard	11 012	99.0	36.7	21.3	31.3	25.0	6.0	3.1	3.7	2.1	1.0	0.2	0.7	0.0	0.0	0.0	0.1
Henry	119 341	99.4	34.7	23.0	32.9	26.5	5.2	2.2	3.6	1.4	0.6	0.2	0.2	0.0	0.0	0.0	0.2
Houston	110 765	97.8	36.9	20.7	32.1	25.6	4.4	2.1	3.7	1.6	2.2	0.2	0.5	0.0	0.0	1.3	0.2
Irwin	9 931	96.3	36.7	20.4	30.5	23.2	5.5	2.8	3.3	1.5	3.7	0.2	1.2	2.2	0.0	0.0	0.1
Jackson	41 589	98.1	36.2	21.9	30.3	23.7	5.8	2.4	3.9	1.9	1.9	1.0	0.2	0.4	0.0	0.0	0.3
Jasper	11 426	99.3	36.5	20.8	30.4	22.8	7.4	3.7	4.2	2.0	0.7	0.2	0.6	0.0	0.0	0.0	0.0
Jeff Davis	12 684	99.2	38.1	21.5	30.4	24.1	5.3	2.6	4.0	1.9	0.8	0.1	0.6	0.0	0.0	0.0	0.0
Jefferson	17 266	97.3	36.7	16.2	32.4	23.4	8.6	4.5	3.4	1.8	2.7	1.1	0.5	0.0	0.0	0.0	1.1
Jenkins	8 575	98.5	37.5	17.2	31.1	23.3	8.8	4.6	4.0	2.1	1.5	0.2	0.0	0.0	0.0	0.0	1.3
Johnson	8 560	92.7	36.6	18.2	29.9	22.0	5.9	3.1	2.1	1.2	7.3	0.1	1.8	5.3	0.0	0.0	0.1
Jones	23 639	98.5	36.6	21.5	32.3	24.3	5.1	2.4	2.9	1.5	1.5	0.3	1.1	0.0	0.0	0.0	0.1
Lamar	15 912	94.8	35.9	19.4	29.1	20.5	6.9	3.5	3.6	1.7	5.2	1.0	0.7	0.1	3.4	0.0	0.0
Lanier	7 241	96.2	35.8	19.7	31.3	23.9	5.5	2.9	3.8	1.8	3.8	2.8	1.0	0.0	0.0	0.0	0.0
Laurens	44 874	97.2	38.1	19.1	31.1	23.5	5.7	2.8	3.3	1.7	2.8	1.0	0.8	0.7	0.0	0.0	0.3
Lee	24 757	96.8	33.2	21.9	34.8	28.2	4.2	2.1	2.7	1.3	3.2	2.9	0.2	0.0	0.0	0.0	0.1
Liberty	61 610	92.2	31.5	18.8	33.5	29.3	4.0	2.1	4.6	1.4	7.8	0.0	0.3	0.0	0.0	7.5	0.0
Lincoln	8 348	99.1	38.9	20.7	29.4	20.6	7.2	3.5	2.8	1.6	0.9	0.9	0.0	0.0	0.0	0.0	0.0
Long	10 304	100.0	34.7	19.1	34.5	29.2	5.8	2.8	6.0	2.1	0.0	0.0	0.0	0.0	0.0	0.0	0.0
Lowndes	92 115	92.6	35.4	17.2	29.2	23.1	5.2	2.5	5.5	1.7	7.4	4.5	0.4	0.2	1.5	0.6	0.1
Lumpkin	21 016	93.6	35.9	20.6	26.9	21.4	4.6	1.7	5.6	1.8	6.4	0.3	0.5	0.6	4.9	0.0	0.2
McDuffie	21 231	98.4	37.5	18.7	31.8	24.2	6.8	3.3	3.6	2.0	1.6	0.6	0.0	1.4	0.0	0.0	1.0
McIntosh	10 847	98.5	38.7	20.2	28.7	22.0	6.7	3.9	4.1	2.2	1.5	0.1	0.0	1.4	0.0	0.0	0.0
Macon	14 074	93.0	34.3	14.7	32.1	22.7	9.0	4.5	2.9	1.5	7.0	5.2	1.8	0.0	0.0	0.0	0.0
Madison	25 730	99.4	38.1	23.1	30.1	23.4	4.8	2.4	3.3	1.7	0.6	0.1	0.5	0.0	0.0	0.0	0.0
Marion	7 144	98.8	37.3	19.3	31.1	24.7	6.3	3.1	4.7	1.7	1.2	0.3	0.9	0.0	0.0	0.0	0.0
Meriwether	22 534	98.1	36.6	17.9	30.3	20.9	9.8	5.1	3.4	1.8	1.9	0.2	0.9	0.7	0.0	0.0	0.1
Miller	6 383	97.9	39.0	19.8	29.7	22.7	6.7	3.3	2.8	1.6	2.1	0.2	1.7	0.0	0.0	0.0	0.2
Mitchell	23 932	91.8	33.7	15.7	30.1	21.7	8.5	4.4	3.8	1.9	8.2	6.7	0.7	0.6	0.0	0.0	0.2
Monroe	21 757	97.1	35.5	21.2	31.0	22.8	6.4	3.1	3.1	1.7	2.9	2.2	0.7	0.0	0.0	0.0	0.0
Montgomery	8 270	90.9	35.3	18.8	28.2	22.1	5.0	2.3	3.6	1.7	9.1	5.7	0.0	0.0	3.3	0.0	0.1
Morgan	15 457	98.9	36.0	21.2	31.0	22.4	7.6	3.8	3.2	1.6	1.1	0.2	0.3	0.0	0.0	0.0	0.0
Murray	36 506	99.4	36.4	22.1	31.0	24.7	5.8	2.6	4.1	2.0	0.6	0.2	0.3	0.0	0.0	0.0	0.0
Muscogee	186 291	95.1	37.5	16.7	30.2	23.1	6.2	3.1	4.4	1.8	4.9	1.0	0.6	0.1	0.2	2.6	0.4
Newton	62 001	98.3	35.5	21.0	31.2	24.1	6.8	3.1	3.8	1.7	1.7	0.2	0.5	0.0	0.9	0.0	0.1
Oconee	26 225	99.1	34.5	23.7	34.5	28.6	3.5	1.3	2.9	1.2	0.9	0.1	0.3	0.0	0.0	0.0	0.6
Oglethorpe	12 635	99.1	38.4	22.0	29.4	22.5	5.9	2.8	3.4	1.7	0.9	0.1	0.3	0.0	0.0	0.0	0.6
Paulding	81 678	99.4	34.4	23.5	33.6	28.2	4.5	1.9	3.4	1.5	0.6	0.3	0.0	0.3	0.0	0.0	0.0
Peach	23 668	95.5	35.6	16.7	30.2	21.9	7.4	3.6	5.5	1.6	4.5	0.4	0.0	0.0	3.7	0.0	0.5
Pickens	22 983	99.1	39.0	24.7	27.0	21.0	4.6	1.8	3.7	1.6	0.9	0.2	0.7	0.0	0.0	0.0	0.0
Pierce	15 636	99.3	38.1	22.5	30.9	24.0	5.0	2.2	2.8	1.4	0.7	0.1	0.6	0.0	0.0	0.0	0.1
Pike	13 688	97.7	34.7	22.7	31.3	23.6	6.2	3.1	2.7	1.2	2.3	1.4	0.5	0.4	0.0	0.0	0.1
Polk	38 127	97.8	36.8	20.6	28.7	21.7	7.3	3.3	4.5	1.6	2.2	1.0	0.8	0.3	0.0	0.0	0.1
Pulaski	9 588	88.5	35.5	17.4	26.7	19.7	5.8	3.0	3.1	1.7	11.5	10.5	1.1	0.0	0.0	0.0	0.0
Putnam	18 812	98.6	39.3	22.3	26.9	20.0	6.1	2.8	3.9	2.0	1.4	1.0	0.4	0.0	0.0	0.0	0.0
Quitman	2 598	100.0	40.3	20.2	28.1	19.5	8.4	4.3	3.0	1.3	0.0	0.0	0.0	0.0	0.0	0.0	0.0
Rabun	15 050	98.1	41.7	24.0	24.6	19.1	3.9	1.4	3.9	1.5	1.9	0.2	0.8	0.0	0.0	0.0	0.9
Randolph	7 791	96.1	37.3	15.3	30.8	21.3	9.6	5.4	3.1	1.5	3.9	0.3	1.0	0.0	2.5	0.0	0.0

Table B. States and Counties

STATE County	Households by type, 2000 — Total households	Family households: Total	Family households: With own children under 18 years	Married couple: Total	Married couple: With own children under 18 years	Female householder[1]: Total	Female householder[1]: With own children under 18 years	Nonfamily households: Total	Householder living alone: Total	Householder living alone: 65 years and over	Average household size	Average family size	Households, 1990: Total households	Households, 1990: Female householder[1]	Households, 1990: Householder living alone
	71	72	73	74	75	76	77	78	79	80	81	82	83	84	85
GEORGIA—Cont'd															
Fannin	8 369	71.8	25.9	59.8	20.1	8.9	4.3	28.2	25.6	12.8	2.35	2.80	6 334	8.3	22.1
Fayette	31 524	82.4	43.1	71.5	36.6	8.3	5.0	17.6	15.0	6.5	2.88	3.20	21 054	6.8	12.5
Floyd	34 028	71.2	32.1	53.6	23.0	13.0	7.0	28.8	24.5	10.8	2.55	3.02	30 518	12.6	23.6
Forsyth	34 565	81.3	41.7	71.9	36.6	6.6	3.7	18.7	14.8	4.0	2.83	3.12	15 938	7.0	16.3
Franklin	7 888	72.2	31.1	57.2	23.3	10.5	5.6	27.8	24.6	11.6	2.50	2.96	6 365	9.9	23.3
Fulton	321 242	57.8	28.7	37.3	17.5	16.5	9.7	42.2	32.2	6.7	2.44	3.15	257 140	18.5	31.0
Gilmer	9 071	73.8	30.9	61.1	24.2	8.4	4.6	26.2	22.2	8.6	2.57	2.96	5 072	9.0	20.4
Glascock	1 004	71.3	32.8	58.7	25.8	9.6	5.1	28.7	26.3	11.9	2.44	2.94	867	9.7	22.6
Glynn	27 208	67.6	30.2	49.5	19.5	14.6	8.9	32.4	27.2	10.1	2.44	2.95	23 947	14.0	23.6
Gordon	16 173	75.8	35.8	60.4	27.4	11.1	6.2	24.2	20.3	8.1	2.70	3.08	12 778	10.3	19.8
Grady	8 797	74.0	34.1	53.1	22.7	16.2	9.2	26.0	22.4	10.7	2.66	3.08	7 354	15.2	22.3
Greene	5 477	73.8	29.2	51.0	16.6	18.3	10.7	26.2	23.0	10.1	2.59	3.02	4 083	19.4	23.9
Gwinnett	202 317	75.3	42.3	61.2	34.1	10.0	6.3	24.7	18.4	3.1	2.88	3.28	126 971	8.3	17.7
Habersham	13 259	74.3	32.0	60.9	24.9	9.3	5.2	25.7	22.4	9.6	2.57	2.98	9 966	8.5	21.2
Hall	47 381	76.0	37.1	60.2	28.8	10.8	6.0	24.0	19.2	6.7	2.89	3.26	34 721	11.1	20.0
Hancock	3 237	71.4	31.3	38.0	14.1	28.2	15.3	28.6	26.1	10.8	2.66	3.22	2 969	26.5	24.4
Haralson	9 826	73.2	33.5	57.7	24.9	11.3	6.2	26.8	23.0	10.2	2.58	3.03	8 248	10.9	22.2
Harris	8 822	79.2	34.8	64.8	27.3	10.7	5.6	20.8	17.9	7.7	2.66	3.02	6 454	11.1	19.1
Hart	9 106	72.6	29.0	56.8	20.9	12.0	6.1	27.4	24.4	10.6	2.47	2.92	7 459	12.1	22.0
Heard	4 043	75.2	37.7	57.9	27.6	12.1	6.9	24.8	21.3	8.7	2.70	3.12	3 093	11.8	19.8
Henry	41 373	80.5	42.9	66.4	34.7	10.3	6.2	19.5	15.4	4.0	2.87	3.19	20 012	8.9	13.2
Houston	40 911	73.9	38.4	56.0	27.1	14.0	9.1	26.1	22.1	6.2	2.65	3.10	32 433	12.3	20.6
Irwin	3 644	74.0	35.2	55.5	24.6	14.4	8.2	26.0	23.1	11.3	2.62	3.07	3 142	15.6	23.9
Jackson	15 057	76.3	36.3	60.5	27.8	10.8	5.9	23.7	19.7	7.3	2.71	3.10	10 721	10.2	19.5
Jasper	4 175	74.8	34.6	56.8	24.9	13.3	7.2	25.2	21.4	7.7	2.72	3.14	3 036	14.1	21.2
Jeff Davis	4 828	74.4	35.7	56.5	25.7	13.6	7.5	25.6	22.3	9.1	2.61	3.02	4 357	13.6	20.0
Jefferson	6 339	71.7	34.3	44.2	19.4	23.1	12.9	28.3	25.7	11.2	2.65	3.17	6 093	22.2	24.6
Jenkins	3 214	70.6	33.7	45.9	20.7	19.7	10.8	29.4	25.6	11.3	2.63	3.16	2 951	17.8	23.4
Johnson	3 130	71.6	32.3	49.7	19.8	18.2	10.7	28.4	26.6	12.7	2.53	3.06	3 010	17.1	24.8
Jones	8 659	77.0	37.5	58.7	27.6	13.3	7.3	23.0	20.2	7.1	2.69	3.09	7 300	12.8	18.4
Lamar	5 712	75.0	32.2	54.0	21.3	16.3	8.9	25.0	21.6	8.9	2.64	3.05	4 669	15.1	21.4
Lanier	2 593	74.5	37.6	55.0	26.5	13.7	8.2	25.5	21.8	9.4	2.69	3.12	1 965	15.1	21.3
Laurens	17 083	71.3	33.8	50.3	21.5	17.1	10.3	28.7	25.7	10.3	2.55	3.06	14 514	15.8	23.2
Lee	8 229	82.6	48.3	65.8	37.0	13.0	9.0	17.4	14.3	4.3	2.91	3.21	5 199	13.2	15.0
Liberty	19 383	78.1	50.5	59.6	36.9	14.8	11.1	21.9	16.6	3.2	2.93	3.29	15 136	12.1	14.8
Lincoln	3 251	73.2	30.6	53.2	21.5	15.5	7.3	26.8	23.7	10.4	2.55	3.01	2 702	14.1	21.9
Long	3 574	74.9	45.6	55.0	31.9	14.5	10.2	25.1	19.6	5.2	2.88	3.28	2 196	9.9	20.4
Lowndes	32 654	68.1	35.3	48.5	23.4	15.9	9.9	31.9	24.2	7.6	2.61	3.14	26 311	15.2	21.8
Lumpkin	7 537	71.2	32.9	57.5	25.5	9.4	5.1	28.8	22.0	6.5	2.61	3.04	4 976	8.8	19.3
McDuffie	7 970	73.5	36.3	49.7	22.1	19.2	11.8	26.5	23.2	9.4	2.62	3.08	7 270	17.7	21.4
McIntosh	4 202	71.7	31.0	52.2	20.6	14.7	7.8	28.3	24.2	8.8	2.54	3.00	3 186	16.9	22.9
Macon	4 834	72.1	34.5	42.7	18.9	24.4	13.5	27.9	25.2	10.4	2.71	3.25	4 388	23.8	22.6
Madison	9 800	74.8	34.6	60.6	26.6	10.6	5.9	25.2	21.5	8.0	2.61	3.04	7 740	9.7	18.9
Marion	2 668	71.7	35.3	51.6	23.1	15.1	9.7	28.3	24.3	10.5	2.65	3.12	1 962	16.2	20.0
Meriwether	8 248	72.9	31.5	49.0	19.9	18.4	9.0	27.1	23.8	10.6	2.68	3.18	7 637	17.8	22.1
Miller	2 487	71.0	31.5	50.7	20.7	15.5	8.5	29.0	26.7	13.6	2.51	3.03	2 336	13.7	23.7
Mitchell	8 063	73.6	34.4	46.6	19.1	22.5	13.1	26.4	23.3	9.5	2.72	3.19	6 798	21.4	20.8
Monroe	7 719	77.8	35.8	59.6	26.5	13.8	7.1	22.2	18.9	7.4	2.74	3.12	5 838	13.7	19.4
Montgomery	2 919	70.7	34.0	53.1	24.1	13.5	7.7	29.3	25.6	10.2	2.57	3.08	2 493	13.0	24.0
Morgan	5 558	77.4	34.8	58.9	25.4	14.6	7.4	22.6	19.4	7.8	2.75	3.15	4 399	15.5	19.4
Murray	13 286	77.2	39.0	60.8	29.2	11.1	6.7	22.8	18.8	6.0	2.73	3.10	9 363	9.5	17.4
Muscogee	69 819	68.3	34.6	44.7	20.7	19.6	11.8	31.7	26.7	9.4	2.54	3.08	65 858	17.9	24.5
Newton	21 997	77.8	37.7	59.2	27.4	14.1	8.1	22.2	18.3	6.6	2.77	3.14	14 401	13.3	18.3
Oconee	9 051	80.9	44.7	68.8	37.0	9.4	6.1	19.1	15.5	5.3	2.87	3.21	6 156	9.0	16.0
Oglethorpe	4 849	73.0	33.6	57.3	25.0	11.5	6.3	27.0	23.0	9.0	2.58	3.05	3 581	12.5	20.6
Paulding	28 089	81.5	46.2	68.3	38.1	9.0	5.6	18.5	14.6	3.8	2.89	3.20	14 326	8.5	13.7
Peach	8 436	71.1	33.6	47.0	20.1	19.6	11.6	28.9	22.6	7.8	2.68	3.14	7 142	19.4	20.0
Pickens	8 960	75.8	31.1	63.5	24.3	8.8	4.8	24.2	20.5	7.7	2.54	2.91	5 386	8.4	19.5
Pierce	5 958	74.5	34.7	59.0	26.3	11.6	6.6	25.5	23.1	9.8	2.61	3.06	4 807	10.5	20.4
Pike	4 755	79.6	37.0	65.4	30.2	10.5	4.9	20.4	17.5	7.5	2.81	3.18	3 526	9.0	18.3
Polk	14 012	73.8	32.9	55.9	23.9	13.1	6.9	26.2	22.7	10.5	2.66	3.09	12 519	13.0	22.6
Pulaski	3 407	68.7	30.4	48.9	19.4	15.7	9.1	31.3	27.9	13.5	2.49	3.04	3 098	16.3	27.2
Putnam	7 402	74.0	28.5	56.8	19.0	12.8	7.2	26.0	22.0	7.8	2.50	2.90	5 229	13.4	21.4
Quitman	1 047	72.2	26.0	50.2	15.2	18.7	9.4	27.8	24.9	12.3	2.48	2.95	857	19.5	25.0
Rabun	6 279	69.3	26.5	57.4	20.3	8.1	4.1	30.7	26.8	11.7	2.35	2.82	4 630	8.9	22.4
Randolph	2 909	67.8	30.3	40.9	16.3	22.6	12.3	32.2	30.0	14.8	2.57	3.20	2 815	21.1	27.5

[1] No spouse present.

Table B. States and Counties

STATE County	Percent change of households, 1990–2000	Total housing units	Occupied housing units (percent)	Housing occupancy, 2000 — Vacant housing units — Total	For seasonal, recreational, or occasional use	Homeowner vacancy rate (percent)	Rental vacancy rate (percent)	Housing tenure, 2000 — Occupied housing units — Total	Percent owner-occupied housing units	Percent renter-occupied housing units	Average household size of owner-occupied units	Average household size of renter-occupied units
	86	87	88	89	90	91	92	93	94	95	96	97
GEORGIA—Cont'd												
Fannin	32.1	11 134	75.2	24.8	17.4	2.5	10.8	8 369	82.6	17.4	2.37	2.25
Fayette	49.7	32 726	96.3	3.7	0.4	1.3	7.6	31 524	86.4	13.6	2.92	2.57
Floyd	11.5	36 615	92.9	7.1	0.4	1.6	8.4	34 028	66.8	33.2	2.58	2.49
Forsyth	116.9	36 505	94.7	5.3	2.0	1.6	4.1	34 565	88.0	12.0	2.82	2.88
Franklin	23.9	9 303	84.8	15.2	6.3	2.0	6.8	7 888	79.3	20.7	2.53	2.37
Fulton	24.9	348 632	92.1	7.9	0.5	2.7	7.1	321 242	52.0	48.0	2.60	2.28
Gilmer	78.8	11 924	76.1	23.9	15.5	2.9	9.6	9 071	78.1	21.9	2.50	2.80
Glascock	15.8	1 192	84.2	15.8	4.9	1.0	13.4	1 004	80.0	20.0	2.50	2.20
Glynn	13.6	32 636	83.4	16.6	6.9	2.2	15.1	27 208	65.5	34.5	2.47	2.37
Gordon	26.6	17 145	94.3	5.7	0.5	1.3	5.8	16 173	71.8	28.2	2.67	2.77
Grady	19.6	9 991	88.0	12.0	1.3	2.2	10.8	8 797	73.4	26.6	2.64	2.71
Greene	34.1	6 653	82.3	17.7	10.7	1.6	4.6	5 477	76.4	23.6	2.58	2.65
Gwinnett	59.3	209 682	96.5	3.5	0.2	1.2	5.7	202 317	72.4	27.6	2.98	2.60
Habersham	33.0	14 634	90.6	9.4	0.8	2.2	8.9	13 259	76.2	23.8	2.57	2.55
Hall	36.5	51 046	92.8	7.2	1.6	2.5	5.6	47 381	71.1	28.9	2.81	3.09
Hancock	9.0	4 287	75.5	24.5	12.4	1.3	9.6	3 237	76.4	23.6	2.68	2.60
Haralson	19.1	10 719	91.7	8.3	0.6	1.9	9.9	9 826	75.1	24.9	2.61	2.48
Harris	36.7	10 288	85.8	14.2	8.4	1.7	7.5	8 822	86.1	13.9	2.67	2.60
Hart	22.1	11 111	82.0	18.0	10.3	1.9	7.0	9 106	80.8	19.2	2.49	2.37
Heard	30.7	4 512	89.6	10.4	2.4	1.3	10.2	4 043	77.4	22.6	2.70	2.67
Henry	106.7	43 166	95.8	4.2	0.3	1.9	6.1	41 373	85.2	14.8	2.91	2.62
Houston	26.1	44 509	91.9	8.1	0.6	2.1	11.2	40 911	68.5	31.5	2.69	2.55
Irwin	16.0	4 149	87.8	12.2	1.0	1.7	14.2	3 644	76.8	23.2	2.63	2.61
Jackson	40.4	16 226	92.8	7.2	0.4	2.2	8.9	15 057	74.9	25.1	2.73	2.64
Jasper	37.5	4 806	86.9	13.1	6.9	1.4	4.1	4 175	79.0	21.0	2.72	2.71
Jeff Davis	10.8	5 581	86.5	13.5	0.9	2.3	17.2	4 828	77.4	22.6	2.62	2.57
Jefferson	4.0	7 221	87.8	12.2	1.1	1.4	11.0	6 339	72.2	27.8	2.68	2.57
Jenkins	8.9	3 907	82.3	17.7	4.8	1.5	11.3	3 214	73.3	26.7	2.64	2.59
Johnson	4.0	3 634	86.1	13.9	1.0	1.4	10.0	3 130	79.8	20.2	2.54	2.50
Jones	18.6	9 272	93.4	6.6	0.5	1.5	12.2	8 659	85.8	14.2	2.71	2.59
Lamar	22.3	6 145	93.0	7.0	0.9	1.3	7.2	5 712	72.4	27.6	2.68	2.55
Lanier	32.0	3 011	86.1	13.9	1.5	1.5	15.3	2 593	76.2	23.8	2.73	2.53
Laurens	17.7	19 687	86.8	13.2	1.2	1.8	15.4	17 083	71.3	28.7	2.58	2.50
Lee	58.3	8 813	93.4	6.6	0.3	2.2	8.0	8 229	78.3	21.7	2.93	2.85
Liberty	28.1	21 977	88.2	11.8	1.6	3.8	9.1	19 383	50.7	49.3	2.91	2.95
Lincoln	20.3	4 514	72.0	28.0	21.0	1.8	6.4	3 251	81.7	18.3	2.57	2.42
Long	62.8	4 232	84.5	15.5	1.3	2.7	17.4	3 574	66.2	33.8	2.93	2.79
Lowndes	24.1	36 551	89.3	10.7	0.7	2.2	13.0	32 654	60.8	39.2	2.69	2.49
Lumpkin	51.5	8 263	91.2	8.8	2.3	1.1	8.3	7 537	72.3	27.7	2.68	2.42
McDuffie	9.6	8 916	89.4	10.6	1.4	1.4	8.0	7 970	71.3	28.7	2.65	2.55
McIntosh	31.9	5 735	73.3	26.7	17.9	2.2	11.0	4 202	83.6	16.4	2.57	2.38
Macon	10.2	5 495	88.0	12.0	1.7	1.8	10.5	4 834	73.0	27.0	2.75	2.61
Madison	26.6	10 520	93.2	6.8	0.9	1.3	8.5	9 800	80.2	19.8	2.64	2.50
Marion	36.0	3 130	85.2	14.8	2.7	2.5	5.5	2 668	78.1	21.9	2.65	2.61
Meriwether	8.0	9 211	89.5	10.5	1.2	1.5	6.9	8 248	74.2	25.8	2.69	2.65
Miller	6.5	2 770	89.8	10.2	1.8	1.3	9.4	2 487	77.0	23.0	2.51	2.52
Mitchell	18.6	8 880	90.8	9.2	0.8	1.7	5.1	8 063	72.0	28.0	2.74	2.67
Monroe	32.2	8 425	91.6	8.4	1.6	1.0	9.0	7 719	79.5	20.5	2.77	2.59
Montgomery	17.1	3 492	83.6	16.4	3.7	2.5	16.5	2 919	77.9	22.1	2.60	2.48
Morgan	26.3	6 128	90.7	9.3	3.5	1.7	4.9	5 558	77.5	22.5	2.76	2.71
Murray	41.9	14 320	92.8	7.2	0.5	1.0	10.0	13 286	73.7	26.3	2.75	2.68
Muscogee	6.0	76 182	91.6	8.4	0.3	1.7	10.5	69 819	56.4	43.6	2.57	2.49
Newton	52.7	23 033	95.5	4.5	0.6	1.6	5.1	21 997	77.7	22.3	2.76	2.79
Oconee	47.0	9 528	95.0	5.0	0.3	1.9	5.3	9 051	80.2	19.8	2.92	2.66
Oglethorpe	35.4	5 368	90.3	9.7	1.4	1.1	11.3	4 849	82.6	17.4	2.63	2.33
Paulding	96.1	29 274	96.0	4.0	0.3	1.2	6.6	28 089	86.8	13.2	2.92	2.69
Peach	18.1	9 093	92.8	7.2	0.6	1.3	7.3	8 436	68.4	31.6	2.69	2.65
Pickens	66.4	10 687	83.8	16.2	9.2	2.1	7.4	8 960	82.1	17.9	2.56	2.46
Pierce	23.9	6 719	88.7	11.3	1.7	1.6	12.5	5 958	80.6	19.4	2.64	2.46
Pike	34.9	5 068	93.8	6.2	1.1	1.4	5.2	4 755	81.6	18.4	2.86	2.62
Polk	11.9	15 059	93.0	7.0	0.4	1.2	6.3	14 012	71.3	28.7	2.61	2.78
Pulaski	10.0	3 944	86.4	13.6	1.1	2.0	9.4	3 407	73.6	26.4	2.48	2.53
Putnam	41.6	10 319	71.7	28.3	22.0	1.6	7.2	7 402	79.3	20.7	2.49	2.58
Quitman	22.2	1 773	59.1	40.9	29.3	4.5	10.4	1 047	81.1	18.9	2.48	2.47
Rabun	35.6	10 210	61.5	38.5	30.1	2.7	11.7	6 279	79.5	20.5	2.34	2.39
Randolph	3.3	3 402	85.5	14.5	2.9	1.7	7.9	2 909	68.9	31.1	2.62	2.47

STATE/ County code	MSA/ PMSA/ NECMA code[1]	County type[2]	STATE County	Population, 2000				Population, 1990				Population and population characteristics, 2000					
												Race (percent)					
												One race					
				Land area, 2000[3] (sq km)	Total persons	Rank	Per square kilometer	Land area, 1990[3] (sq km)	Total persons	Rank	Per square kilometer	White	Black or African American	American Indian or Alaska Native	Asian	Native Hawaiian and other Pacific Islander	Some other race
				1	2	3	4	5	6	7	8	9	10	11	12	13	14
			GEORGIA—Cont'd														
13 245	0600	2	Richmond	839	199 775	277	238.1	839	189 719	253	226.1	45.6	49.8	0.3	1.5	0.1	1.0
13 247	0520	1	Rockdale	338	70 111	709	207.4	339	54 091	795	159.6	75.7	18.2	0.3	1.9	0.1	2.5
13 249	...	9	Schley	434	3 766	2 932	8.7	434	3 590	2 951	8.3	65.8	31.3	0.2	0.1	0.2	1.4
13 251	...	6	Screven	1 679	15 374	2 062	9.2	1 680	13 842	2 069	8.2	53.6	45.3	0.1	0.3	0.1	0.2
13 253	...	6	Seminole	617	9 369	2 501	15.2	617	9 010	2 468	14.6	61.7	34.7	0.2	0.2	0.0	2.8
13 255	0520	1	Spalding	513	58 417	819	113.9	513	54 457	792	106.2	66.5	31.1	0.2	0.7	0.0	0.7
13 257	...	7	Stephens	464	25 435	1 545	54.8	464	23 436	1 519	50.5	85.7	12.0	0.3	0.6	0.1	0.4
13 259	...	8	Stewart	1 188	5 252	2 835	4.4	1 188	5 654	2 788	4.8	37.1	61.5	0.2	0.2	0.0	0.1
13 261	...	6	Sumter	1 257	33 200	1 308	26.4	1 257	30 232	1 285	24.1	48.2	49.0	0.3	0.6	0.0	1.3
13 263	...	8	Talbot	1 018	6 498	2 739	6.4	1 019	6 524	2 706	6.4	36.8	61.6	0.2	0.3	0.0	0.3
13 265	...	9	Taliaferro	506	2 077	3 061	4.1	506	1 915	3 073	3.8	38.2	60.3	0.0	0.0	0.0	0.7
13 267	...	7	Tattnall	1 253	22 305	1 679	17.8	1 253	17 722	1 802	14.1	60.5	31.4	0.1	0.3	0.1	6.6
13 269	...	8	Taylor	978	8 815	2 544	9.0	978	7 642	2 606	7.8	55.4	42.6	0.1	0.2	0.0	0.9
13 271	...	7	Telfair	1 142	11 794	2 306	10.3	1 143	11 000	2 293	9.6	59.7	38.4	0.0	0.2	0.0	1.2
13 273	...	6	Terrell	869	10 970	2 369	12.6	869	10 653	2 322	12.3	37.9	60.7	0.2	0.3	0.0	0.1
13 275	...	6	Thomas	1 420	42 737	1 043	30.1	1 420	38 943	1 024	27.4	59.0	38.9	0.3	0.4	0.1	0.5
13 277	...	7	Tift	686	38 407	1 152	56.0	687	34 998	1 133	50.9	65.3	28.0	0.2	1.0	0.0	4.6
13 279	...	7	Toombs	950	26 067	1 514	27.4	950	24 072	1 490	25.3	69.2	24.2	0.2	0.5	0.0	5.3
13 281	...	9	Towns	432	9 319	2 504	21.6	431	6 754	2 680	15.7	98.8	0.1	0.2	0.3	0.0	0.2
13 283	...	7	Treutlen	520	6 854	2 704	13.2	520	5 994	2 758	11.5	65.7	33.1	0.1	0.3	0.0	0.3
13 285	...	4	Troup	1 072	58 779	816	54.8	1 072	55 532	779	51.8	65.8	31.9	0.2	0.6	0.1	0.7
13 287	...	7	Turner	741	9 504	2 489	12.8	741	8 703	2 492	11.7	56.4	41.0	0.1	0.3	0.0	1.8
13 289	4680	2	Twiggs	933	10 590	2 390	11.4	933	9 806	2 403	10.5	54.9	43.7	0.2	0.1	0.0	0.2
13 291	...	9	Union	835	17 289	1 933	20.7	836	11 993	2 220	14.3	97.9	0.6	0.3	0.2	0.0	0.2
13 293	...	7	Upson	843	27 597	1 464	32.7	843	26 300	1 411	31.2	70.6	27.9	0.3	0.4	0.0	0.3
13 295	1560	2	Walker	1 157	61 053	797	52.8	1 156	58 310	743	50.4	94.4	3.8	0.3	0.3	0.0	0.4
13 297	0520	1	Walton	853	60 687	799	71.1	853	38 586	1 038	45.2	83.0	14.4	0.3	0.7	0.0	0.6
13 299	...	7	Ware	2 337	35 483	1 233	15.2	2 338	35 471	1 112	15.2	69.7	28.0	0.2	0.5	0.0	1.0
13 301	...	8	Warren	739	6 336	2 753	8.6	740	6 078	2 748	8.2	39.5	59.5	0.2	0.1	0.0	0.3
13 303	...	7	Washington	1 762	21 176	1 726	12.0	1 762	19 112	1 726	10.8	45.7	53.2	0.2	0.3	0.0	0.2
13 305	...	7	Wayne	1 670	26 565	1 496	15.9	1 670	22 356	1 561	13.4	76.7	20.3	0.2	0.4	0.0	1.3
13 307	...	8	Webster	543	2 390	3 032	4.4	543	2 263	3 046	4.2	50.5	47.0	0.1	0.0	0.0	1.6
13 309	...	9	Wheeler	771	6 179	2 764	8.0	771	4 903	2 844	6.4	64.6	33.2	0.1	0.1	0.0	1.2
13 311	...	9	White	626	19 944	1 795	31.9	626	13 006	2 141	20.8	95.2	2.2	0.4	0.5	0.2	0.5
13 313	...	4	Whitfield	751	83 525	623	111.2	751	72 462	617	96.5	80.9	3.8	0.4	0.9	0.0	12.0
13 315	...	9	Wilcox	985	8 577	2 559	8.7	985	7 008	2 658	7.1	62.6	36.2	0.1	0.2	0.0	0.5
13 317	...	6	Wilkes	1 221	10 687	2 386	8.8	1 221	10 597	2 328	8.7	55.1	43.1	0.2	0.2	0.0	0.5
13 319	...	8	Wilkinson	1 157	10 220	2 425	8.8	1 157	10 228	2 367	8.8	58.0	40.7	0.2	0.1	0.0	0.4
13 321	...	6	Worth	1 476	21 967	1 695	14.9	1 476	19 744	1 687	13.4	68.7	29.6	0.4	0.2	0.0	0.6
15 000	...		HAWAII	16 635	1 211 537	X	72.8	16 636	1 108 229	X	66.6	24.3	1.8	0.3	41.6	9.4	1.3
15 001	...	5	Hawaii	10 433	148 677	363	14.3	10 433	120 317	383	11.5	31.5	0.5	0.4	26.7	11.2	1.1
15 003	3320	2	Honolulu	1 553	876 156	48	564.2	1 554	836 231	40	538.1	21.3	2.4	0.2	46.0	8.9	1.3
15 005	...	NA	Kalawao	34	147	3 140	4.3	34	130	3 140	3.8	25.9	0.0	0.0	17.0	48.3	2.7
15 007	...	5	Kauai	1 612	58 463	818	36.3	1 612	51 177	823	31.7	29.5	0.3	0.4	36.0	9.1	0.9
15 009	...	5	Maui	3 002	128 094	422	42.7	3 002	100 374	457	33.4	33.9	0.4	0.4	31.0	10.7	1.4
16 000	...		IDAHO	214 314	1 293 953	X	6.0	214 325	1 006 734	X	4.7	91.0	0.4	1.4	0.9	0.1	4.2
16 001	1080	2	Ada	2 732	300 904	188	110.1	2 733	205 775	242	75.3	92.9	0.6	0.7	1.7	0.1	1.7
16 003	...	9	Adams	3 534	3 476	2 955	1.0	3 535	3 254	2 979	0.9	96.3	0.1	1.4	0.1	0.0	0.9
16 005	6340	5	Bannock	2 883	75 565	663	26.2	2 883	66 026	665	22.9	91.3	0.6	2.9	1.0	0.2	2.1
16 007	...	7	Bear Lake	2 516	6 411	2 749	2.5	2 516	6 084	2 747	2.4	97.7	0.1	0.5	0.1	0.0	1.1
16 009	...	8	Benewah	2 010	9 171	2 501	4.6	2 010	7 937	2 579	3.9	88.7	0.1	8.9	0.2	0.1	0.3
16 011	...	7	Bingham	5 425	41 735	1 061	7.7	5 426	37 583	1 056	6.9	82.4	0.2	6.7	0.4	0.0	8.0
16 013	...	7	Blaine	6 850	18 991	1 846	2.8	6 850	13 552	2 097	2.0	90.7	0.1	0.3	0.7	0.1	6.4
16 015	...	8	Boise	4 927	6 670	2 720	1.4	4 927	3 509	2 956	0.7	95.2	0.1	0.9	0.3	0.1	1.3
16 017	...	6	Bonner	4 501	36 835	1 193	8.2	4 500	26 622	1 402	5.9	96.6	0.1	0.9	0.3	0.0	0.4
16 019	...	5	Bonneville	4 839	82 522	628	17.1	4 840	72 207	618	14.9	92.8	0.5	0.6	0.8	0.1	3.7
16 021	...	9	Boundary	3 286	9 871	2 459	3.0	3 286	8 332	2 531	2.5	95.2	0.2	2.0	0.6	0.1	0.9
16 023	...	9	Butte	5 783	2 899	2 999	0.5	5 783	2 918	3 004	0.5	94.7	0.3	0.7	0.2	0.0	2.4
16 025	...	9	Camas	2 784	991	3 111	0.4	2 784	727	3 128	0.3	95.2	1.2	0.3	0.2	0.0	0.9
16 027	1080	2	Canyon	1 527	131 441	406	86.1	1 527	90 076	510	59.0	83.1	0.3	0.9	0.8	0.1	12.2
16 029	...	7	Caribou	4 574	7 304	2 655	1.6	4 574	6 963	2 663	1.5	96.1	0.1	0.2	0.1	0.1	2.2
16 031	...	7	Cassia	6 647	21 416	1 717	3.2	6 647	19 532	1 698	2.9	84.7	0.2	0.8	0.4	0.1	12.1
16 033	...	9	Clark	4 570	1 022	3 110	0.2	4 571	762	3 126	0.2	74.2	0.1	1.0	0.2	0.0	23.5
16 035	...	7	Clearwater	6 375	8 930	2 532	1.4	6 375	8 505	2 510	1.3	94.8	0.1	2.0	0.4	0.1	0.6

[1] MSA = Metropolitan Statistical Area. PMSA = Primary MSA. NECMA = New England County Metropolitan Area. See Appendix A for explanation of these concepts. See Appendix B for list of metropolitan areas identified by type, with component counties.
[2] County typology code from the Economic Research Service of USDA. See Appendix A for definition.
[3] Dry land or land partially or temporarily covered by water.

Table B. States and Counties

STATE County	Population and population characteristics, 2000 (cont'd)								Population and population characteristics, 1990				
	Race (percent) (cont'd)								Race (percent)				
	Race alone or in combination												
	Two or more races	White	Black	American Indian or Alaska Native	Asian	Native Hawaiian and other Pacific Islander	Some other race	Hispanic[1]	White	Black or African American	American Indian or Alaska Native	Asian and Pacific Islander	Hispanic[1]
	15	16	17	18	19	20	21	22	23	24	25	26	27
GEORGIA—Cont'd													
Richmond	1.8	46.8	50.7	0.7	2.0	0.2	1.5	2.8	55.1	42.0	0.3	1.7	2.0
Rockdale	1.3	76.8	18.7	0.6	2.1	0.1	3.0	6.0	90.4	8.1	0.2	1.0	1.1
Schley	1.1	66.6	31.7	0.8	0.3	0.3	1.8	2.4	64.6	34.1	0.1	0.0	1.5
Screven	0.5	53.9	45.5	0.3	0.4	0.1	0.4	1.0	54.9	44.9	0.1	0.1	0.4
Seminole	0.4	62.1	34.8	0.4	0.2	0.0	3.0	3.7	66.9	32.7	0.2	0.1	0.6
Spalding	0.9	67.2	31.4	0.5	0.9	0.1	0.9	1.6	70.3	29.0	0.2	0.4	0.6
Stephens	0.9	86.6	12.4	0.6	0.8	0.1	0.6	1.0	87.3	12.0	0.1	0.4	0.6
Stewart	0.8	37.7	62.1	0.6	0.4	0.1	0.3	1.5	36.1	63.3	0.3	0.3	0.5
Sumter	0.6	48.7	49.3	0.5	0.7	0.1	1.4	2.7	52.6	46.5	0.3	0.4	0.6
Talbot	0.8	37.3	62.1	0.7	0.3	0.1	0.4	1.3	37.3	62.3	0.2	0.0	0.8
Taliaferro	0.7	38.7	60.7	0.1	0.2	0.1	0.9	0.9	38.4	60.9	0.1	0.2	1.1
Tattnall	0.9	61.3	31.8	0.4	0.4	0.1	7.0	8.4	68.2	29.2	0.1	0.3	3.1
Taylor	0.8	56.1	42.9	0.3	0.3	0.0	1.2	1.8	56.2	43.2	0.0	0.1	0.8
Telfair	0.5	60.0	38.7	0.1	0.3	0.1	1.3	1.8	65.5	34.3	0.1	0.1	0.4
Terrell	0.7	38.4	61.0	0.5	0.6	0.1	0.3	1.2	39.9	59.9	0.1	0.1	0.4
Thomas	0.9	59.6	39.2	0.7	0.6	0.1	0.7	1.7	61.5	37.9	0.3	0.2	0.7
Tift	0.9	66.0	28.3	0.5	1.1	0.0	5.0	7.7	71.3	26.8	0.1	0.5	3.5
Toombs	0.7	69.7	24.4	0.4	0.6	0.0	5.6	8.9	73.1	23.4	0.2	0.6	3.4
Towns	0.4	99.2	0.2	0.4	0.4	0.0	0.3	0.7	99.7	0.0	0.2	0.1	0.3
Treutlen	0.6	66.2	33.3	0.2	0.4	0.0	0.5	1.2	66.8	33.1	0.0	0.0	0.3
Troup	0.8	66.5	32.2	0.5	0.7	0.1	0.9	1.7	69.2	30.1	0.1	0.5	0.5
Turner	0.4	56.6	41.1	0.3	0.4	0.0	1.9	2.6	58.9	40.6	0.1	0.2	0.4
Twiggs	0.9	55.6	43.9	0.6	0.3	0.0	0.5	1.1	53.9	45.9	0.1	0.1	0.5
Union	0.7	98.6	0.6	0.7	0.4	0.0	0.4	0.9	99.4	0.2	0.2	0.2	0.4
Upson	0.5	71.0	28.1	0.5	0.5	0.1	0.4	1.2	71.9	27.7	0.1	0.3	0.4
Walker	0.8	95.2	4.0	0.7	0.4	0.1	0.5	0.9	95.6	3.8	0.2	0.2	0.4
Walton	0.9	83.9	14.7	0.7	0.9	0.0	0.9	1.9	80.8	18.4	0.2	0.4	0.9
Ware	0.7	70.2	28.3	0.4	0.6	0.1	1.1	1.9	73.3	26.0	0.2	0.3	0.5
Warren	0.5	39.9	59.7	0.3	0.2	0.0	0.4	0.8	39.7	60.2	0.0	0.1	0.0
Washington	0.4	46.0	53.5	0.3	0.4	0.1	0.3	0.6	48.1	51.7	0.1	0.1	0.3
Wayne	1.0	77.5	20.6	0.6	0.6	0.0	1.6	3.8	80.0	19.5	0.2	0.2	0.8
Webster	0.8	51.3	47.1	0.6	0.0	0.0	1.8	2.8	49.8	50.0	0.2	0.0	0.0
Wheeler	0.8	64.9	33.5	0.5	0.3	0.0	1.5	3.5	68.4	30.1	0.1	0.1	2.1
White	1.1	96.2	2.3	1.1	0.6	0.2	0.6	1.6	96.3	2.8	0.3	0.5	0.8
Whitfield	1.9	82.7	4.2	0.7	1.1	0.1	13.2	22.1	93.2	4.0	0.2	0.4	3.2
Wilcox	0.4	62.9	36.4	0.2	0.2	0.0	0.6	1.6	67.9	31.7	0.1	0.0	0.4
Wilkes	0.9	55.9	43.4	0.5	0.3	0.1	0.7	2.0	53.3	46.3	0.2	0.1	0.4
Wilkinson	0.7	58.4	41.1	0.4	0.2	0.0	0.7	1.0	57.8	42.1	0.0	0.1	0.3
Worth	0.6	69.2	29.7	0.6	0.3	0.0	0.7	1.1	68.6	30.6	0.3	0.2	1.1
HAWAII	21.4	39.3	2.8	2.1	58.0	23.3	3.9	7.2	33.4	2.5	0.5	61.8	7.3
Hawaii	28.4	52.1	1.2	3.3	47.7	31.0	4.9	9.5	39.7	0.5	0.7	57.1	9.3
Honolulu	19.9	35.2	3.4	1.8	61.6	21.6	3.7	6.7	31.6	3.1	0.4	63.0	6.8
Kalawao	6.1	31.3	0.0	0.0	18.4	50.3	6.8	4.1	23.1	0.0	0.0	76.9	8.5
Kauai	23.8	46.4	0.9	2.4	54.3	24.2	4.2	8.2	34.6	0.4	0.3	62.7	10.9
Maui	22.2	48.9	1.0	2.1	47.7	25.8	4.6	7.8	39.6	0.5	0.5	57.7	7.8
IDAHO	2.0	92.8	0.6	2.1	1.3	0.2	5.0	7.9	94.4	0.3	1.4	0.9	5.3
Ada	2.2	94.9	1.0	1.4	2.4	0.3	2.4	4.5	96.7	0.5	0.7	1.4	2.7
Adams	1.2	97.3	0.1	2.2	0.2	0.1	1.3	1.6	98.4	0.1	1.3	0.0	1.2
Bannock	2.0	93.1	0.9	3.6	1.5	0.3	2.7	4.7	93.5	0.7	2.5	1.1	4.1
Bear Lake	0.5	98.1	0.2	0.8	0.1	0.1	1.2	2.4	98.6	0.0	0.4	0.1	2.2
Benewah	1.8	90.4	0.3	10.3	0.3	0.1	0.5	1.5	91.7	0.1	7.6	0.4	1.6
Bingham	2.1	84.4	0.4	7.3	0.9	0.1	9.1	13.3	86.3	0.1	7.0	0.7	9.6
Blaine	1.6	92.1	0.3	0.8	1.2	0.1	7.2	10.7	97.7	0.1	0.4	0.8	2.9
Boise	2.0	97.2	0.2	2.1	0.7	0.2	1.7	3.4	97.8	0.1	1.0	0.4	2.4
Bonner	1.7	98.2	0.2	2.0	0.6	0.1	0.7	1.6	98.5	0.1	0.8	0.3	1.3
Bonneville	1.5	94.2	0.7	1.2	1.1	0.1	4.2	6.9	95.9	0.4	0.5	1.0	4.2
Boundary	1.1	96.1	0.2	2.8	0.8	0.1	1.1	3.4	95.4	0.0	1.8	0.3	3.7
Butte	1.8	96.0	0.8	2.0	0.5	0.2	2.5	4.1	96.9	0.0	0.8	0.2	3.5
Camas	2.2	97.3	1.5	1.8	0.8	0.1	1.0	5.5	97.9	0.3	1.1	0.4	0.6
Canyon	2.6	85.5	0.5	1.7	1.3	0.3	13.5	18.6	89.3	0.2	0.8	1.1	13.1
Caribou	1.2	97.2	0.2	0.5	0.4	0.4	2.7	4.0	98.0	0.1	0.3	0.2	2.8
Cassia	1.9	86.4	0.2	1.4	0.8	0.1	13.2	18.7	90.0	0.0	0.9	0.5	13.4
Clark	1.0	75.1	0.5	1.1	0.2	0.1	24.0	34.2	90.3	0.0	0.7	0.0	10.4
Clearwater	2.0	96.7	0.2	3.3	0.6	0.2	1.0	1.8	97.1	0.1	2.1	0.2	1.3

[1] Hispanic persons may be of any race.

Table B. States and Counties

STATE County	Under 5 years	5 to 17 years	18 to 24 years	25 to 34 years	35 to 44 years	45 to 54 years	55 to 64 years	65 to 74 years	75 years and over	Median age (years)	Percent Female
	28	29	30	31	32	33	34	35	36	37	38
GEORGIA—Cont'd											
Richmond	7.1	19.7	12.0	14.8	15.0	12.6	7.9	6.0	4.8	32.3	51.8
Rockdale	6.4	21.1	8.8	13.0	17.5	15.2	8.8	5.3	3.9	35.4	50.3
Schley	8.5	20.8	8.2	13.5	14.0	13.0	11.0	6.3	4.8	34.5	52.1
Screven	6.6	21.3	8.9	11.5	15.0	13.6	9.1	7.4	6.6	36.2	52.2
Seminole	7.2	18.9	8.6	11.9	14.5	12.2	10.8	8.8	6.9	37.5	52.4
Spalding	7.5	19.8	9.2	14.1	15.3	13.3	9.2	6.3	5.4	34.6	51.8
Stephens	6.1	17.3	10.5	12.7	13.9	13.6	10.2	8.0	7.6	37.5	52.0
Stewart	6.4	18.5	8.0	11.7	13.5	13.7	9.6	8.6	9.9	38.8	52.2
Sumter	7.9	19.9	11.9	13.9	13.5	12.5	8.1	6.0	6.4	32.6	53.1
Talbot	5.9	18.2	7.7	11.6	15.3	16.0	10.8	8.7	5.7	39.5	53.3
Taliaferro	6.3	17.8	7.6	10.9	13.7	12.9	11.9	9.5	9.4	40.2	51.8
Tattnall	6.1	16.8	11.2	17.7	16.9	11.8	8.2	6.0	5.2	33.9	42.4
Taylor	7.1	19.8	9.0	13.1	15.0	12.6	10.2	6.6	6.7	35.7	51.2
Telfair	6.0	16.5	10.3	14.4	15.6	13.8	8.5	7.4	7.5	36.8	47.4
Terrell	7.7	20.6	9.5	11.5	14.5	13.0	10.2	6.6	6.4	35.4	53.1
Thomas	6.7	20.4	8.1	12.7	15.5	13.5	9.4	7.1	6.6	36.3	52.9
Tift	7.7	19.5	11.6	13.9	14.4	12.6	8.5	6.3	5.4	33.0	51.4
Toombs	7.7	20.8	9.2	13.2	14.6	12.7	9.5	6.5	5.7	34.2	52.3
Towns	4.4	11.9	9.1	9.6	10.9	13.0	15.3	14.9	10.9	48.6	52.7
Treutlen	7.4	18.6	11.9	13.6	13.6	12.6	9.1	6.8	6.4	33.9	50.3
Troup	7.2	20.6	9.2	13.6	14.8	13.6	8.3	6.5	6.1	34.6	52.3
Turner	7.7	21.7	10.2	12.8	13.5	12.6	8.5	6.8	6.2	33.3	51.9
Twiggs	6.7	20.3	9.4	13.1	16.0	13.4	9.9	6.6	4.7	35.4	52.1
Union	4.8	15.2	6.6	10.3	13.3	13.8	14.4	12.7	8.9	44.8	50.9
Upson	6.5	19.0	8.3	12.6	15.2	13.4	10.1	7.7	7.2	37.4	52.5
Walker	6.6	18.2	8.7	13.2	15.6	13.8	10.2	7.7	6.2	37.1	51.5
Walton	8.1	20.3	8.1	15.4	16.8	13.1	8.6	5.4	4.3	33.9	51.3
Ware	6.4	18.4	9.1	13.6	14.6	13.5	9.1	7.9	7.5	36.8	50.6
Warren	6.8	19.5	8.7	11.1	14.4	13.7	9.7	8.1	8.0	37.8	53.6
Washington	6.3	20.6	8.8	13.2	17.1	12.7	8.6	6.4	6.2	35.6	55.1
Wayne	6.6	19.3	8.6	14.6	16.1	14.2	9.2	6.8	4.5	35.5	48.0
Webster	7.1	18.2	8.2	13.0	14.7	14.2	9.9	7.9	6.9	37.5	49.7
Wheeler	5.9	16.4	10.2	15.4	16.2	14.6	8.5	5.9	6.7	36.1	43.8
White	6.2	16.9	9.2	12.6	15.2	13.8	11.5	8.5	6.1	38.3	50.5
Whitfield	8.2	19.2	10.0	15.7	15.1	12.7	8.9	5.9	4.4	33.0	49.7
Wilcox	6.2	16.5	9.6	14.6	16.6	14.0	8.8	6.9	6.6	36.7	44.7
Wilkes	5.8	18.1	8.0	11.9	14.8	13.1	11.1	8.6	8.5	39.0	52.2
Wilkinson	7.3	20.0	9.0	12.6	15.5	12.8	9.8	7.5	5.5	35.8	52.5
Worth	7.0	21.6	8.1	12.2	15.2	14.0	9.9	6.6	5.3	35.7	52.1
HAWAII	6.5	18.0	9.5	14.1	15.8	14.1	8.8	7.0	6.2	36.2	49.8
Hawaii	6.1	20.0	8.2	10.8	15.4	16.4	9.5	7.3	6.2	38.6	49.9
Honolulu	6.5	17.3	10.1	14.9	15.7	13.4	8.7	7.1	6.3	35.7	49.7
Kalawao	0.0	2.0	1.4	6.1	12.2	21.1	25.2	23.8	8.2	58.6	50.3
Kauai	6.2	20.2	7.1	11.6	15.7	16.1	9.4	7.0	6.8	38.4	50.0
Maui	6.7	18.8	7.7	13.8	17.1	15.5	8.9	6.0	5.4	36.8	49.8
IDAHO	7.5	21.0	10.7	13.1	14.9	13.2	8.3	5.9	5.4	33.2	49.9
Ada	7.7	19.6	10.3	15.9	16.7	13.6	7.2	4.6	4.5	32.8	49.9
Adams	4.0	19.9	4.6	7.1	15.5	17.5	15.2	9.9	6.2	44.4	48.7
Bannock	8.1	20.0	14.6	13.7	13.5	12.7	7.4	5.2	4.9	29.8	50.6
Bear Lake	6.9	26.0	7.4	8.9	13.6	12.5	9.2	8.1	7.5	35.8	50.4
Benewah	6.5	20.4	6.8	10.7	14.8	15.0	11.6	8.2	6.0	39.2	49.0
Bingham	8.8	26.2	9.7	11.4	13.9	11.8	7.8	5.7	4.6	29.7	50.0
Blaine	5.9	18.2	7.7	14.5	18.1	18.1	9.8	5.0	2.8	37.4	48.1
Boise	6.6	20.3	4.7	9.5	17.6	18.5	11.8	7.0	4.0	40.4	48.7
Bonner	5.7	19.8	6.7	9.6	15.8	17.9	11.4	7.6	5.5	40.8	49.9
Bonneville	8.2	23.9	9.5	12.2	14.9	13.0	7.9	5.4	4.7	31.8	50.1
Boundary	7.0	22.2	6.9	10.1	14.3	16.5	9.7	8.0	5.4	38.3	49.6
Butte	6.6	22.5	6.3	9.8	14.1	14.1	11.6	9.0	6.0	38.8	49.7
Camas	4.3	20.4	6.6	10.0	18.2	13.7	13.8	7.2	5.9	39.7	48.8
Canyon	9.1	21.8	10.7	14.5	13.8	11.5	7.5	5.5	5.5	30.5	50.3
Caribou	7.5	24.2	8.2	10.1	14.4	13.0	9.0	7.2	6.4	35.0	50.2
Cassia	8.7	25.4	9.0	11.1	13.4	11.5	8.1	6.3	6.4	31.1	49.7
Clark	8.9	26.3	8.0	12.4	15.1	10.2	9.9	5.4	3.8	30.7	47.5
Clearwater	4.8	18.2	5.9	10.4	15.9	16.0	13.1	8.9	6.7	41.7	46.9

Table B. States and Counties

STATE County	Under 5 years (39)	5 to 17 years (40)	18 to 24 years (41)	25 to 34 years (42)	35 to 44 years (43)	45 to 54 years (44)	55 to 64 years (45)	65 to 74 years (46)	75 years and over (47)	Percent Female (48)	2000 (49)	1990 (50)	1980 (51)	1990–2000 (52)	1980–1990 (53)
GEORGIA—Cont'd															
Richmond	8.0	19.1	12.8	18.4	14.4	9.3	8.0	6.1	3.9	51.5	199 775	189 719	181 629	5.3	4.5
Rockdale	7.6	20.8	9.7	17.2	17.1	12.0	7.6	5.0	3.0	50.7	70 111	54 091	36 570	29.6	47.9
Schley	7.4	20.9	11.6	13.9	13.4	12.0	7.6	7.9	5.5	51.8	3 766	3 590	3 433	4.9	4.6
Screven	7.9	21.3	8.9	14.9	14.1	9.3	8.6	8.5	6.4	52.6	15 374	13 842	14 043	11.1	-1.4
Seminole	6.8	19.5	11.0	14.8	12.8	9.9	10.4	9.0	5.8	50.6	9 369	9 010	9 057	4.0	-0.5
Spalding	7.9	20.2	10.3	16.4	14.6	10.5	8.3	6.9	4.9	52.1	58 417	54 457	47 899	7.3	13.7
Stephens	6.7	17.5	11.7	14.5	14.3	11.1	9.2	9.2	5.8	51.7	25 435	23 436	21 761	8.5	7.7
Stewart	6.7	20.7	10.2	13.9	12.7	9.5	9.1	9.8	7.4	51.9	5 252	5 654	5 896	-7.1	-4.1
Sumter	8.0	21.2	12.5	15.1	13.2	9.2	7.4	7.0	6.3	53.9	33 200	30 232	29 360	9.8	3.0
Talbot	6.9	20.1	9.4	15.8	14.7	10.1	9.5	7.1	6.4	52.6	6 498	6 524	6 536	-0.4	-0.2
Taliaferro	6.9	20.8	8.5	13.4	11.5	10.7	9.0	10.3	8.9	52.8	2 077	1 915	2 032	8.5	-5.8
Tattnall	6.6	17.6	10.3	19.1	14.2	10.4	8.4	7.8	5.6	46.3	22 305	17 722	18 134	25.9	-2.3
Taylor	7.2	20.8	10.4	15.0	12.4	11.1	8.6	8.6	5.8	53.2	8 815	7 642	7 902	15.3	-3.3
Telfair	6.9	20.8	9.4	14.4	13.1	8.9	9.1	9.5	8.0	54.2	11 794	11 000	11 445	7.2	-3.9
Terrell	7.9	21.8	8.9	14.1	12.7	10.4	9.2	8.3	6.7	54.1	10 970	10 653	12 017	3.0	-11.4
Thomas	7.6	21.0	9.1	15.2	13.9	10.4	8.9	8.0	5.9	53.5	42 737	38 943	38 098	9.7	2.2
Tift	7.9	20.8	12.3	15.9	14.2	9.7	7.8	6.5	4.8	51.3	38 407	34 998	32 862	9.7	6.5
Toombs	7.9	21.5	9.4	15.8	14.3	10.5	8.0	7.2	5.3	52.5	26 067	24 072	22 592	8.3	6.6
Towns	4.6	12.8	11.3	11.7	11.9	9.9	13.9	13.8	10.1	51.5	9 319	6 754	5 638	38.0	19.8
Treutlen	7.1	21.3	10.2	14.1	12.9	10.1	8.9	8.3	7.0	53.9	6 854	5 994	6 087	14.3	-1.5
Troup	7.8	20.1	10.4	15.7	14.4	9.3	8.6	7.7	6.0	52.9	58 779	55 532	50 003	5.8	11.1
Turner	8.2	23.1	10.4	13.1	12.7	10.0	8.6	7.9	6.2	52.7	9 504	8 703	9 510	9.2	-8.5
Twiggs	7.9	22.6	9.9	16.6	13.3	10.2	8.3	6.6	4.5	52.0	10 590	9 806	9 354	8.0	4.8
Union	5.6	16.6	8.7	12.9	13.6	11.2	12.9	10.8	7.6	50.3	17 289	11 993	9 390	44.2	27.7
Upson	6.8	18.6	9.7	15.2	13.4	10.8	9.5	9.0	7.0	52.7	27 597	26 300	25 998	4.9	1.2
Walker	6.5	19.2	9.4	15.6	14.7	11.5	9.7	8.0	5.3	51.5	61 053	58 310	56 470	4.7	3.3
Walton	7.8	20.0	10.6	17.0	14.6	11.0	7.9	6.5	4.7	51.6	60 687	38 586	31 211	57.3	23.6
Ware	6.9	19.9	9.4	14.7	14.4	9.9	9.7	8.7	6.4	51.7	35 483	35 471	37 180	0.0	-4.6
Warren	8.2	20.0	9.3	14.7	13.0	9.3	9.0	8.4	8.1	54.6	6 336	6 078	6 583	4.2	-7.7
Washington	8.0	21.4	9.3	16.1	13.8	9.5	8.1	7.4	6.3	53.0	21 176	19 112	18 842	10.8	1.4
Wayne	7.7	21.3	9.3	15.3	15.1	10.4	9.1	6.8	4.9	51.4	26 565	22 356	20 750	18.8	7.7
Webster	6.8	20.8	9.8	15.1	13.5	9.8	9.7	8.7	5.8	53.3	2 390	2 263	2 341	5.6	-3.3
Wheeler	7.5	21.3	9.7	12.5	14.0	10.5	8.4	9.3	6.9	51.5	6 179	4 903	5 155	26.0	-4.9
White	6.0	17.0	10.1	14.2	14.5	12.3	10.9	8.9	6.0	51.3	19 944	13 006	10 120	53.3	28.5
Whitfield	7.1	19.0	11.4	17.2	15.4	11.5	8.5	6.0	3.9	50.8	83 525	72 462	65 775	15.3	10.2
Wilcox	7.3	21.1	9.1	12.9	13.5	9.8	9.0	9.9	7.4	52.9	8 577	7 008	7 682	22.4	-8.8
Wilkes	6.5	20.0	8.4	14.6	13.4	10.5	9.5	9.7	7.3	52.3	10 687	10 597	10 951	0.8	-3.2
Wilkinson	7.7	21.7	10.6	16.4	13.1	10.3	8.7	6.7	4.8	52.4	10 220	10 228	10 368	-0.1	-1.4
Worth	8.2	22.1	10.0	15.3	14.2	10.6	7.9	7.0	4.6	51.8	21 967	19 744	18 064	11.3	9.3
HAWAII	7.5	17.8	10.9	18.1	16.1	9.8	8.5	7.1	4.2	49.1	1 211 537	1 108 229	964 691	9.3	14.9
Hawaii	7.9	20.8	7.5	15.0	17.6	9.9	8.9	7.8	4.8	49.6	148 677	120 317	92 053	23.6	30.7
Honolulu	7.4	17.1	11.9	18.7	15.6	9.8	8.5	7.0	4.0	49.1	876 156	836 231	762 565	4.8	9.7
Kalawao	0.0	0.0	0.8	6.9	11.5	18.5	28.5	20.0	13.8	38.5	147	130	144	13.1	-9.7
Kauai	7.8	19.8	8.3	16.0	17.0	9.8	8.3	7.7	5.4	49.3	58 463	51 177	39 082	14.2	30.9
Maui	7.8	19.0	8.5	17.7	17.8	9.9	7.9	7.0	4.3	49.0	128 094	100 374	70 847	27.6	41.7
IDAHO	8.0	22.7	9.8	15.2	14.8	9.8	7.7	6.9	5.1	50.2	1 293 953	1 006 734	944 127	28.5	6.6
Ada	7.7	20.6	9.8	17.7	16.9	10.0	6.8	6.0	4.4	50.8	300 904	205 775	173 125	46.2	18.9
Adams	7.4	21.1	5.9	13.7	15.1	12.0	10.3	8.6	6.0	48.5	3 476	3 254	3 347	6.8	-2.8
Bannock	8.4	24.1	10.9	15.8	14.8	9.0	6.9	5.9	4.3	50.4	75 565	66 026	65 421	14.4	0.9
Bear Lake	8.9	28.5	5.9	12.8	11.3	9.1	8.5	8.6	6.4	50.6	6 411	6 084	6 931	5.4	-12.2
Benewah	7.5	22.1	7.6	13.4	15.8	11.4	9.1	7.2	5.9	49.3	9 171	7 937	8 292	15.5	-4.3
Bingham	9.4	29.2	7.9	14.1	13.0	9.0	7.4	5.9	4.2	49.8	41 735	37 583	36 489	11.0	3.0
Blaine	7.5	19.1	7.3	20.0	22.1	11.1	6.3	4.2	2.5	48.1	18 991	13 552	9 841	40.1	37.7
Boise	7.0	21.3	6.3	14.3	17.8	12.0	10.4	7.5	3.5	47.3	6 670	3 509	2 999	90.1	17.0
Bonner	7.0	21.5	5.8	13.2	17.7	10.9	9.6	8.7	5.6	50.3	36 835	26 622	24 163	38.4	10.2
Bonneville	9.5	25.7	9.0	16.1	14.1	9.5	7.2	5.4	3.6	49.7	82 522	72 207	65 980	14.3	9.4
Boundary	7.6	24.8	7.6	13.1	16.2	9.3	9.2	6.7	5.6	49.0	9 871	8 332	7 289	18.5	14.3
Butte	7.4	27.7	4.9	12.5	14.3	10.6	9.7	7.4	5.4	49.6	2 899	2 918	3 342	-0.7	-12.7
Camas	7.8	21.9	4.8	13.1	15.4	13.5	9.9	7.6	6.1	46.6	991	727	818	36.3	-11.1
Canyon	8.2	22.5	9.9	14.4	13.9	9.7	7.7	7.6	6.1	50.7	131 441	90 076	83 756	45.9	7.5
Caribou	8.1	29.9	6.2	13.3	13.1	9.7	8.1	6.5	5.2	49.8	7 304	6 963	8 695	4.9	-19.9
Cassia	9.2	27.4	8.2	13.4	12.7	8.7	8.0	7.2	5.2	49.7	21 416	19 532	19 427	9.6	0.5
Clark	7.0	23.5	7.6	15.4	12.7	13.0	8.7	8.0	4.2	45.1	1 022	762	798	34.1	-4.5
Clearwater	5.3	20.0	6.0	14.6	15.4	12.9	10.8	9.0	6.0	47.8	8 930	8 505	10 390	5.0	-18.1

Table B. States and Counties

STATE County		Household relationship, 2000															
		In households (percent)										In group quarters (percent)					
						Child		Other relatives		Nonrelatives			Institutionalized population			Noninstitutionalized population		
	Total population	Total in house-holds	House-holder	Spouse	Total	Own child under 18 years	Total	Under 18 years	Total	Unmar-ried partner	Total in group quarters	Correc-tional institu-tions	Nurs-ing homes	Other institu-tions	Col-lege dormi-tories	Mili-tary quar-ters	Other
	54	55	56	57	58	59	60	61	62	63	64	65	66	67	68	69	70
GEORGIA—Cont'd																	
Richmond	199 775	94.5	37.0	15.5	30.3	22.7	6.9	3.5	4.8	2.0	5.5	1.2	0.2	0.1	0.4	2.2	1.3
Rockdale	70 111	98.4	34.3	21.1	31.9	24.4	6.3	2.4	4.8	1.5	1.6	0.6	0.4	0.0	0.0	0.0	0.6
Schley	3 766	99.7	38.1	19.8	32.0	25.8	6.5	3.2	3.3	1.7	0.3	0.2	0.0	0.0	0.0	0.0	0.1
Screven	15 374	98.0	37.7	18.1	31.6	23.6	7.4	3.8	3.3	1.9	2.0	1.0	0.0	0.0	0.0	0.0	1.0
Seminole	9 369	96.8	38.1	19.5	28.4	21.0	7.8	4.2	2.9	1.6	3.2	0.2	0.7	0.0	0.0	0.0	2.3
Spalding	58 417	98.5	36.8	18.5	30.7	22.8	7.9	3.8	4.5	2.1	1.5	0.6	0.6	0.1	0.0	0.0	0.1
Stephens	25 435	96.3	39.1	22.1	27.3	21.2	4.5	1.8	3.3	1.4	3.7	0.3	0.7	0.3	2.2	0.0	0.2
Stewart	5 252	94.9	38.2	15.1	28.0	18.5	10.0	5.4	3.6	1.9	5.1	0.8	1.6	2.7	0.0	0.0	0.0
Sumter	33 200	95.4	36.2	16.1	31.4	23.4	7.6	4.0	4.1	1.7	4.6	1.0	1.8	0.0	1.6	0.0	0.1
Talbot	6 498	99.7	39.1	18.3	30.6	19.3	8.9	4.4	2.9	1.6	0.3	0.3	0.0	0.0	0.0	0.0	0.0
Taliaferro	2 077	98.9	41.9	16.5	28.7	19.7	8.7	4.0	3.2	1.9	1.1	0.0	1.1	0.0	0.0	0.0	0.0
Tattnall	22 305	82.3	31.6	16.2	24.9	19.6	5.2	2.6	4.5	1.5	17.7	16.5	1.0	0.0	0.0	0.0	0.1
Taylor	8 815	95.3	37.2	16.9	30.6	21.7	7.4	3.9	3.1	1.7	4.7	2.4	0.8	0.0	0.0	0.0	1.6
Telfair	11 794	86.9	35.1	17.0	25.8	18.7	6.2	3.3	2.9	1.5	13.1	11.3	1.9	0.0	0.0	0.0	0.0
Terrell	10 970	98.1	36.5	16.1	32.4	22.8	9.4	5.1	3.7	2.3	1.9	1.0	0.7	0.0	0.0	0.0	0.2
Thomas	42 737	97.3	38.2	18.3	30.2	23.0	6.7	3.4	4.0	1.8	2.7	0.8	0.8	0.5	0.0	0.0	0.6
Tift	38 407	96.1	36.2	18.6	30.0	23.4	6.7	3.1	4.5	1.8	3.9	0.5	0.8	0.4	1.6	0.0	0.7
Toombs	26 067	98.2	37.9	18.5	30.7	24.4	6.5	3.4	4.6	1.7	1.8	0.3	1.3	0.1	0.0	0.0	0.1
Towns	9 319	94.6	42.9	26.6	19.4	15.2	2.7	0.8	2.9	1.4	5.4	0.0	1.2	0.0	3.9	0.0	0.4
Treutlen	6 854	94.3	36.9	18.5	29.9	22.1	6.2	3.2	2.8	1.4	5.7	4.5	1.0	0.0	0.0	0.0	0.2
Troup	58 779	97.4	37.3	18.3	30.9	23.6	7.0	3.5	3.9	1.7	2.6	0.8	0.2	0.5	0.6	0.0	0.4
Turner	9 504	98.3	36.1	18.1	32.2	24.4	8.3	4.4	3.6	1.7	1.7	0.8	0.7	0.0	0.0	0.0	0.3
Twiggs	10 590	98.7	36.2	18.8	32.0	21.7	8.6	4.8	3.1	1.6	1.3	0.4	0.9	0.0	0.0	0.0	0.0
Union	17 289	97.4	41.4	26.0	24.0	18.3	3.5	1.3	2.6	1.1	2.6	1.4	0.9	0.0	0.0	0.0	0.3
Upson	27 597	98.4	38.9	19.7	29.5	21.7	6.8	3.2	3.5	1.7	1.6	0.4	1.0	0.0	0.0	0.0	0.1
Walker	61 053	98.4	38.7	22.3	29.0	21.9	5.3	2.4	3.0	1.5	1.6	0.9	0.7	0.0	0.0	0.0	0.0
Walton	60 687	99.1	35.1	22.0	32.2	25.1	6.1	2.7	3.6	1.7	0.9	0.3	0.6	0.0	0.0	0.0	0.0
Ware	35 483	93.7	38.0	19.1	27.6	21.1	6.0	3.1	3.0	1.5	6.3	4.2	1.5	0.2	0.0	0.0	0.4
Warren	6 336	98.2	38.4	16.2	30.9	21.1	8.8	4.5	3.9	2.3	1.8	0.0	1.7	0.0	0.0	0.0	0.2
Washington	21 176	93.1	35.1	16.4	30.9	22.3	7.9	4.0	2.8	1.5	6.9	5.1	0.5	0.2	0.0	0.0	1.1
Wayne	26 565	91.9	35.1	19.8	29.2	23.1	4.7	2.3	3.0	1.5	8.1	7.4	0.5	0.0	0.0	0.0	0.2
Webster	2 390	99.9	38.1	19.4	29.7	20.7	9.4	4.4	3.2	1.8	0.1	0.1	0.0	0.0	0.0	0.0	0.0
Wheeler	6 179	82.5	32.5	16.9	24.7	19.1	5.3	2.8	3.0	1.4	17.5	16.3	1.0	0.1	0.0	0.0	0.1
White	19 944	97.4	38.8	24.3	27.0	21.2	4.1	1.6	3.2	1.6	2.6	0.3	0.7	0.0	1.5	0.0	0.1
Whitfield	83 525	99.1	35.2	20.9	30.3	23.7	8.1	2.9	4.6	1.5	0.9	0.1	0.4	0.1	0.0	0.0	0.3
Wilcox	8 577	82.8	32.5	16.9	26.1	19.4	5.0	3.0	2.2	1.3	17.2	14.7	2.0	0.0	0.0	0.0	0.5
Wilkes	10 687	98.7	40.4	19.0	28.6	20.2	7.3	3.4	3.4	1.7	1.3	0.4	0.7	0.0	0.0	0.0	0.2
Wilkinson	10 220	99.2	37.4	18.9	31.6	22.4	8.1	4.4	3.2	1.6	0.8	0.2	0.6	0.0	0.0	0.0	0.1
Worth	21 967	99.1	36.9	20.5	31.9	24.4	6.7	3.6	3.0	1.6	0.9	0.1	0.0	0.0	0.0	0.0	0.8
HAWAII	1 211 537	97.0	33.3	17.8	29.0	19.8	10.5	4.0	6.4	1.9	3.0	0.3	0.2	0.1	0.4	1.2	0.8
Hawaii	148 677	98.1	35.6	18.0	29.3	21.7	8.2	3.5	7.0	2.8	1.9	0.1	0.4	0.1	0.6	0.0	0.6
Honolulu	876 156	96.5	32.7	17.8	29.0	19.1	11.0	4.0	6.0	1.6	3.5	0.3	0.2	0.1	0.4	1.6	0.9
Kalawao	147	100.0	78.2	12.9	4.1	2.0	2.0	0.0	2.7	0.0	0.0	0.0	0.0	0.0	0.0	0.0	0.0
Kauai	58 463	98.9	34.5	18.6	30.6	22.1	9.0	3.7	6.1	2.4	1.1	0.2	0.2	0.2	0.0	0.0	0.5
Maui	128 094	98.9	34.0	17.3	28.5	20.7	10.5	4.1	8.7	2.8	1.1	0.3	0.0	0.0	0.1	0.0	0.5
IDAHO	1 293 953	97.6	36.3	21.4	31.5	26.5	3.4	1.4	5.0	1.7	2.4	0.6	0.4	0.4	0.6	0.1	0.4
Ada	300 904	97.6	37.7	20.8	30.2	25.7	3.1	1.0	5.8	2.1	2.4	1.3	0.4	0.1	0.3	0.0	0.3
Adams	3 476	98.9	40.9	25.9	26.1	22.2	2.2	0.9	3.8	2.0	1.1	0.5	0.4	0.0	0.0	0.0	0.2
Bannock	75 565	97.0	36.0	20.4	32.2	26.2	3.3	1.4	5.1	1.7	3.0	0.7	0.4	0.0	1.5	0.0	0.4
Bear Lake	6 411	99.1	35.2	23.6	37.1	32.0	1.4	0.6	1.8	0.8	0.9	0.0	0.5	0.0	0.0	0.0	0.3
Benewah	9 171	98.5	39.0	22.8	29.0	24.3	3.4	1.9	4.3	2.6	1.5	0.3	1.0	0.1	0.0	0.0	0.1
Bingham	41 735	99.0	31.9	21.3	39.0	32.2	4.4	2.2	2.5	1.1	1.0	0.3	0.1	0.3	0.0	0.0	0.3
Blaine	18 991	98.1	41.0	21.0	26.2	22.9	2.7	0.7	7.3	2.8	1.9	0.1	0.4	0.0	0.0	0.0	1.3
Boise	6 670	98.9	39.2	24.5	27.4	24.1	3.1	1.5	4.6	2.3	1.1	0.1	0.0	0.4	0.0	0.0	0.6
Bonner	36 835	99.2	39.9	23.4	27.8	23.4	3.0	1.3	5.1	2.4	0.8	0.2	0.3	0.0	0.0	0.0	0.3
Bonneville	82 522	98.6	34.8	21.6	35.9	30.2	3.1	1.3	3.2	1.3	1.4	0.4	0.2	0.3	0.0	0.0	0.4
Boundary	9 871	97.9	37.6	23.0	31.0	26.8	2.7	1.2	3.6	1.6	2.1	0.2	0.5	0.0	0.0	0.0	1.5
Butte	2 899	99.3	37.6	23.7	32.4	27.0	3.2	1.5	2.4	1.4	0.7	0.2	0.6	0.0	0.0	0.0	0.0
Camas	991	99.7	40.0	26.0	26.9	22.9	2.7	1.0	4.0	1.7	0.3	0.0	0.0	0.3	0.0	0.0	0.0
Canyon	131 441	97.8	34.2	20.8	33.4	28.2	4.8	2.0	4.5	1.7	2.2	0.3	0.5	0.2	0.8	0.0	0.4
Caribou	7 304	99.1	35.0	24.3	35.1	29.9	2.7	1.2	2.0	0.9	0.9	0.1	0.4	0.0	0.0	0.0	0.4
Cassia	21 416	98.5	33.0	21.5	38.0	32.2	3.5	1.6	2.5	1.2	1.5	0.6	0.5	0.0	0.0	0.0	0.4
Clark	1 022	100.0	33.3	20.5	38.8	33.4	4.0	1.2	3.3	1.7	0.0	0.0	0.0	0.0	0.0	0.0	0.0
Clearwater	8 930	93.3	38.7	23.4	24.8	21.3	2.9	1.2	3.5	1.9	6.7	5.7	0.5	0.1	0.0	0.0	0.4

Table B. States and Counties

STATE County	Total households	Family households Total	With own children under 18 years	Married couple Total	With own children under 18 years	Female householder[1] Total	With own children under 18 years	Nonfamily households Total	Householder living alone Total	65 years and over	Average household size	Average family size	Total households	Female householder[1]	Householder living alone
	71	72	73	74	75	76	77	78	79	80	81	82	83	84	85
GEORGIA—Cont'd															
Richmond	73 920	67.0	33.6	41.8	18.7	20.8	12.7	33.0	27.7	8.5	2.55	3.13	68 675	18.0	26.1
Rockdale	24 052	78.5	39.1	61.6	29.5	12.4	7.5	21.5	16.9	5.3	2.87	3.20	18 337	9.9	14.4
Schley	1 435	72.6	36.3	52.1	24.7	15.7	9.1	27.4	24.8	11.3	2.62	3.11	1 315	13.5	24.6
Screven	5 797	70.8	33.7	48.0	21.0	18.3	10.5	29.2	26.5	11.4	2.60	3.14	5 048	17.1	24.5
Seminole	3 573	72.7	29.9	51.1	18.5	17.9	9.5	27.3	24.3	11.5	2.54	3.01	3 137	16.5	23.8
Spalding	21 519	73.3	34.0	50.3	21.2	18.2	10.4	26.7	22.3	8.5	2.67	3.12	19 426	16.6	19.9
Stephens	9 951	71.0	30.5	56.6	22.6	11.1	6.2	29.0	25.5	11.3	2.46	2.94	8 949	10.7	23.8
Stewart	2 007	67.2	27.7	39.5	14.0	23.1	12.0	32.8	29.5	14.5	2.48	3.07	1 982	21.4	25.5
Sumter	12 025	70.7	34.5	44.5	19.3	22.0	13.3	29.3	25.0	8.9	2.64	3.15	10 484	21.7	24.3
Talbot	2 538	71.9	28.2	46.8	16.0	20.2	10.2	28.1	25.4	10.3	2.55	3.06	2 345	20.2	23.2
Taliaferro	870	64.3	26.8	39.3	13.4	20.0	11.0	35.7	33.3	16.8	2.36	3.00	727	16.4	31.6
Tattnall	7 057	69.1	33.0	51.1	22.7	13.4	8.0	30.9	26.7	11.9	2.60	3.12	5 845	14.1	24.6
Taylor	3 281	69.6	30.8	45.5	18.7	20.1	10.7	30.4	27.6	11.1	2.56	3.12	2 804	18.9	24.1
Telfair	4 140	69.4	31.1	48.4	20.2	16.7	8.6	30.6	28.4	13.6	2.48	3.01	4 017	17.1	26.0
Terrell	4 002	72.8	33.3	44.1	17.1	24.0	14.0	27.2	24.3	10.2	2.69	3.18	3 738	21.5	23.7
Thomas	16 309	70.3	32.7	47.9	20.2	18.4	10.7	29.7	25.8	10.6	2.55	3.06	14 323	17.9	23.3
Tift	13 919	72.6	35.4	51.4	22.8	16.9	10.3	27.4	23.3	9.0	2.65	3.10	12 184	15.7	22.4
Toombs	9 877	69.1	34.7	48.7	22.6	15.6	9.7	30.9	27.0	10.6	2.59	3.13	8 804	15.4	24.8
Towns	3 998	70.7	20.8	61.9	16.2	6.3	3.0	29.3	26.0	13.1	2.20	2.61	2 812	6.5	25.3
Treutlen	2 531	72.1	33.2	50.2	21.3	17.3	9.8	27.9	25.3	12.0	2.55	3.05	2 158	17.0	23.8
Troup	21 920	71.2	34.6	49.1	22.3	17.9	10.4	28.8	24.9	10.2	2.61	3.12	20 371	16.2	23.4
Turner	3 435	73.9	35.7	50.0	21.8	18.6	11.3	26.1	23.2	10.4	2.72	3.19	3 043	18.9	22.1
Twiggs	3 832	74.7	33.4	52.0	22.2	17.5	8.8	25.3	22.3	8.7	2.73	3.20	3 296	16.8	20.2
Union	7 159	72.8	24.8	62.9	19.6	7.1	3.8	27.2	24.2	12.0	2.35	2.77	4 709	7.5	20.8
Upson	10 722	71.7	31.7	50.7	20.6	16.9	9.0	28.3	25.2	11.6	2.53	3.01	9 911	15.5	24.0
Walker	23 605	74.0	32.6	57.8	24.2	12.0	6.2	26.0	22.9	10.4	2.54	2.98	21 697	10.8	20.1
Walton	21 307	79.8	39.2	62.7	29.5	12.8	7.5	20.2	16.6	6.2	2.82	3.16	13 433	12.0	17.4
Ware	13 475	69.0	30.7	50.3	20.5	14.8	8.3	31.0	27.9	12.3	2.47	3.01	13 046	16.1	25.4
Warren	2 435	69.5	30.6	42.1	15.5	22.1	12.7	30.5	27.4	12.6	2.55	3.09	2 130	21.9	22.9
Washington	7 435	72.4	34.6	46.7	20.8	21.5	11.8	27.6	24.8	10.6	2.65	3.17	6 739	19.7	23.8
Wayne	9 324	74.4	35.9	56.5	25.3	14.0	8.5	25.6	22.6	9.4	2.62	3.06	7 922	13.3	21.1
Webster	911	74.1	31.9	50.9	21.8	16.8	7.4	25.9	23.5	12.1	2.62	3.07	798	16.4	21.6
Wheeler	2 011	69.4	32.6	52.1	22.8	13.0	7.8	30.6	27.8	14.8	2.54	3.08	1 786	13.2	24.7
White	7 731	74.8	31.2	62.7	24.5	8.7	4.7	25.2	21.7	8.6	2.51	2.91	4 907	7.8	20.8
Whitfield	29 385	75.4	36.8	59.5	28.7	10.8	5.6	24.6	20.6	8.2	2.82	3.24	26 859	10.9	20.3
Wilcox	2 785	71.0	32.5	52.1	22.3	15.0	8.4	29.0	26.7	13.3	2.55	3.09	2 511	14.3	25.5
Wilkes	4 314	68.8	29.1	47.1	18.5	17.3	8.9	31.2	28.1	13.8	2.45	2.98	4 022	16.1	25.1
Wilkinson	3 827	73.3	33.7	50.6	21.3	18.4	10.2	26.7	24.1	10.4	2.65	3.13	3 619	17.0	21.8
Worth	8 106	75.5	36.3	55.7	24.5	15.7	9.7	24.5	21.5	9.0	2.68	3.12	6 895	15.3	19.5
HAWAII	403 240	71.2	32.1	53.6	24.0	12.4	5.9	28.8	21.9	7.1	2.92	3.42	356 267	10.5	19.4
Hawaii	52 985	69.6	32.2	50.6	21.3	13.2	7.7	30.4	23.1	8.0	2.75	3.24	41 461	11.5	20.6
Honolulu	286 450	71.8	31.8	54.5	24.6	12.3	5.3	28.2	21.6	7.0	2.95	3.46	265 304	10.5	19.2
Kalawao	115	19.1	1.7	16.5	0.9	2.6	0.9	80.9	79.1	31.3	1.28	2.27	62	0.0	62.9
Kauai	20 183	72.2	34.0	53.9	24.0	12.8	7.1	27.8	21.4	7.7	2.87	3.34	16 295	9.8	17.4
Maui	43 507	68.7	33.0	50.9	23.4	12.0	6.6	31.3	21.9	6.3	2.91	3.41	33 145	9.9	19.8
IDAHO	469 645	71.5	36.3	58.9	28.1	8.7	5.8	28.5	22.4	8.3	2.69	3.17	360 723	8.0	22.4
Ada	113 408	68.2	36.2	55.1	27.7	9.4	6.2	31.8	23.8	6.7	2.59	3.11	77 471	9.2	23.6
Adams	1 421	72.6	28.0	63.3	21.3	5.7	4.2	27.4	23.2	9.9	2.42	2.83	1 251	4.9	20.5
Bannock	27 192	70.7	36.5	56.7	27.8	10.0	6.5	29.3	22.8	7.6	2.69	3.20	23 412	8.8	23.9
Bear Lake	2 259	75.7	38.8	66.9	33.1	6.4	4.4	24.3	22.2	12.1	2.81	3.33	2 005	4.4	22.1
Benewah	3 580	70.9	31.3	58.4	23.2	7.7	4.8	29.1	24.0	10.4	2.52	2.99	2 991	7.8	21.8
Bingham	13 317	80.4	44.6	66.7	35.8	9.8	6.2	19.6	17.1	7.7	3.10	3.52	11 513	9.2	16.5
Blaine	7 780	62.2	31.9	51.2	24.2	7.2	5.3	37.8	27.3	5.5	2.40	2.96	5 506	7.2	28.0
Boise	2 616	72.6	30.7	62.5	23.7	5.8	3.9	27.4	21.8	6.1	2.52	2.93	1 357	5.2	22.5
Bonner	14 693	69.9	30.6	58.6	22.8	7.5	5.1	30.1	24.0	8.2	2.49	2.94	10 269	7.2	23.2
Bonneville	28 753	74.6	40.6	62.0	32.1	9.3	6.3	25.4	21.4	7.8	2.83	3.33	24 289	7.8	20.3
Boundary	3 707	72.8	34.1	61.4	26.2	7.5	5.3	27.2	23.1	8.5	2.61	3.07	2 857	7.4	21.0
Butte	1 089	73.7	32.8	63.2	26.8	7.4	5.0	26.3	23.6	10.9	2.64	3.14	997	6.5	22.6
Camas	396	72.5	30.8	65.2	26.0	4.5	3.3	27.5	22.2	8.3	2.49	2.92	275	4.0	20.7
Canyon	45 018	75.4	39.8	60.7	30.4	10.1	6.6	24.6	19.8	8.4	2.85	3.28	31 288	9.3	21.2
Caribou	2 560	77.3	39.6	69.3	34.2	5.2	3.8	22.7	20.4	10.3	2.83	3.29	2 262	3.7	19.7
Cassia	7 060	77.7	42.4	65.2	34.1	8.8	5.9	22.3	19.5	9.5	2.99	3.46	6 373	7.2	20.4
Clark	340	75.6	45.0	61.8	35.0	7.1	5.3	24.4	20.0	8.5	3.01	3.52	277	4.7	26.0
Clearwater	3 456	71.8	28.9	60.5	21.2	6.9	4.7	28.2	24.0	10.0	2.41	2.84	3 213	6.6	21.6

[1] No spouse present.

Table B. States and Counties

STATE County	Percent change of households, 1990–2000	Housing occupancy, 2000						Housing tenure, 2000			Average household size of owner-occupied units	Average household size of renter-occupied units
		Total housing units	Occupied housing units (percent)	Vacant housing units				Occupied housing units				
				Total	For seasonal, recreational, or occasional use	Homeowner vacancy rate (percent)	Rental vacancy rate (percent)	Total	Percent owner-occupied housing units	Percent renter-occupied housing units		
	86	87	88	89	90	91	92	93	94	95	96	97
GEORGIA—Cont'd												
Richmond	7.6	82 312	89.8	10.2	0.3	2.6	10.7	73 920	58.0	42.0	2.62	2.46
Rockdale	31.2	25 082	95.9	4.1	0.3	1.2	5.4	24 052	74.5	25.5	2.88	2.83
Schley	9.1	1 612	89.0	11.0	2.1	0.9	6.4	1 435	70.4	23.6	2.58	2.73
Screven	14.8	6 853	84.6	15.4	2.4	1.7	7.2	5 797	77.9	22.1	2.64	2.44
Seminole	13.9	4 742	75.3	24.7	16.4	2.0	10.2	3 573	80.5	19.5	2.48	2.77
Spalding	10.8	23 001	93.6	6.4	0.2	1.3	7.5	21 519	62.8	37.2	2.66	2.70
Stephens	11.2	11 652	85.4	14.6	4.9	1.9	10.4	9 951	72.7	27.3	2.51	2.33
Stewart	1.3	2 354	85.3	14.7	5.3	2.4	8.4	2 007	72.9	27.1	2.49	2.46
Sumter	14.7	13 700	87.8	12.2	2.6	2.0	8.3	12 025	64.0	36.0	2.72	2.49
Talbot	8.2	2 871	88.4	11.6	3.4	1.6	10.7	2 538	82.6	17.4	2.55	2.55
Taliaferro	19.7	1 085	80.2	19.8	3.4	2.0	5.6	870	76.9	23.1	2.34	2.42
Tattnall	20.7	8 578	82.3	17.7	2.7	2.7	17.6	7 057	70.6	29.4	2.57	2.69
Taylor	17.0	3 978	82.5	17.5	4.6	1.2	17.4	3 281	76.9	23.1	2.60	2.43
Telfair	3.1	5 083	81.4	18.6	3.0	3.0	13.1	4 140	78.4	21.6	2.49	2.43
Terrell	7.1	4 460	89.7	10.3	1.5	1.9	8.5	4 002	66.3	33.7	2.68	2.70
Thomas	13.9	18 285	89.2	10.8	0.7	2.7	12.7	16 309	70.0	30.0	2.57	2.51
Tift	14.2	15 411	90.3	9.7	0.7	2.6	12.2	13 919	67.3	32.7	2.69	2.57
Toombs	12.2	11 371	86.9	13.1	1.7	2.1	13.6	9 877	65.5	34.5	2.60	2.57
Towns	42.2	6 282	63.6	36.4	27.3	3.4	14.1	3 998	85.2	14.8	2.20	2.20
Treutlen	17.3	2 865	88.3	11.7	1.6	0.9	4.1	2 531	74.8	25.2	2.62	2.35
Troup	7.6	23 824	92.0	8.0	0.7	1.7	7.7	21 920	64.5	35.5	2.64	2.56
Turner	12.9	3 916	87.7	12.3	2.2	1.9	14.2	3 435	71.6	28.4	2.76	2.62
Twiggs	16.3	4 291	89.3	10.7	1.1	1.7	11.4	3 832	82.6	17.4	2.73	2.72
Union	52.0	10 001	71.6	28.4	20.4	2.5	12.0	7 159	82.3	17.7	2.37	2.30
Upson	8.2	11 616	92.3	7.7	0.7	1.4	6.8	10 722	69.8	30.2	2.56	2.47
Walker	8.8	25 577	92.3	7.7	0.5	1.3	10.9	23 605	76.9	23.1	2.57	2.47
Walton	58.6	22 500	94.7	5.3	0.3	2.0	6.2	21 307	76.5	23.5	2.85	2.75
Ware	3.3	15 831	85.1	14.9	0.9	2.3	18.7	13 475	70.3	29.7	2.49	2.42
Warren	14.3	2 767	88.0	12.0	2.4	1.1	5.9	2 435	77.0	23.0	2.61	2.37
Washington	10.3	8 327	89.3	10.7	1.9	1.5	10.0	7 435	74.0	26.0	2.62	2.51
Wayne	17.7	10 827	86.1	13.9	2.0	2.6	19.3	9 324	76.5	23.5	2.62	2.62
Webster	14.2	1 115	81.7	18.3	7.4	1.5	4.0	911	81.7	18.3	2.62	2.62
Wheeler	12.6	2 447	82.2	17.8	6.0	1.4	8.5	2 011	77.5	22.5	2.56	2.44
White	57.6	9 454	81.8	18.2	10.6	2.2	15.1	7 731	79.2	20.8	2.52	2.47
Whitfield	9.4	30 722	95.6	4.4	0.2	0.9	5.6	29 385	67.6	32.4	2.76	2.94
Wilcox	10.9	3 320	83.9	16.1	4.1	1.9	12.6	2 785	79.9	20.1	2.57	2.48
Wilkes	7.3	5 022	85.9	14.1	3.8	2.1	5.2	4 314	75.5	24.5	2.49	2.32
Wilkinson	5.7	4 449	86.0	14.0	1.1	2.6	9.4	3 827	82.5	17.5	2.67	2.55
Worth	17.6	9 086	89.2	10.8	2.3	1.0	8.6	8 106	76.2	23.8	2.69	2.66
HAWAII	13.2	460 542	87.6	12.4	5.6	1.6	8.2	403 240	56.5	43.5	3.07	2.71
Hawaii	27.8	62 674	84.5	15.5	8.1	1.9	7.6	52 985	64.5	35.5	2.79	2.69
Honolulu	8.0	315 988	90.7	9.3	2.2	1.6	8.6	286 450	54.6	45.4	3.13	2.74
Kalawao	85.5	172	66.9	33.1	18.0	100.0	0.0	115	0.0	100.0	0.00	1.28
Kauai	23.9	25 331	79.7	20.3	15.2	1.2	6.1	20 183	61.4	38.6	3.01	2.63
Maui	31.3	56 377	77.2	22.8	17.3	1.2	7.2	43 507	57.6	42.4	3.13	2.62
IDAHO	30.2	527 824	89.0	11.0	5.2	2.2	7.6	469 645	72.4	27.6	2.75	2.52
Ada	46.4	118 516	95.7	4.3	0.4	1.8	5.1	113 408	70.7	29.3	2.71	2.30
Adams	13.6	1 982	71.7	28.3	16.8	3.5	17.7	1 421	79.1	20.9	2.41	2.46
Bannock	16.1	29 102	93.4	6.6	0.9	2.1	8.4	27 192	70.7	29.3	2.83	2.36
Bear Lake	12.7	3 268	69.1	30.9	22.3	2.8	12.8	2 259	83.1	16.9	2.86	2.57
Benewah	19.7	4 238	84.5	15.5	8.2	1.8	8.2	3 580	78.5	21.5	2.55	2.40
Bingham	15.7	14 303	93.1	6.9	0.7	1.7	9.4	13 317	79.3	20.7	3.17	2.85
Blaine	41.3	12 186	63.8	36.2	30.6	2.0	13.6	7 780	68.9	31.1	2.42	2.35
Boise	92.8	4 349	60.2	39.8	33.2	4.5	12.1	2 616	83.4	16.6	2.51	2.57
Bonner	43.1	19 646	74.8	25.2	19.2	2.4	7.7	14 693	77.9	22.1	2.53	2.34
Bonneville	18.4	30 484	94.3	5.7	1.2	1.6	5.9	28 753	74.7	25.3	2.96	2.44
Boundary	29.8	4 095	90.5	9.5	3.1	1.8	9.1	3 707	78.3	21.7	2.66	2.41
Butte	9.2	1 290	84.4	15.6	2.9	4.4	14.7	1 089	77.0	23.0	2.76	2.26
Camas	44.0	601	65.9	34.1	22.8	4.7	16.0	396	77.5	22.5	2.47	2.58
Canyon	43.9	47 965	93.9	6.1	0.5	2.5	6.9	45 018	73.3	26.7	2.87	2.82
Caribou	13.2	3 188	80.3	19.7	8.1	2.2	28.9	2 560	79.5	20.5	2.88	2.62
Cassia	10.8	7 862	89.8	10.2	1.3	2.7	11.3	7 060	72.6	27.4	2.99	2.99
Clark	22.7	521	65.3	34.7	24.0	3.3	14.2	340	67.9	32.1	2.98	3.06
Clearwater	7.6	4 144	83.4	16.6	7.1	2.9	13.3	3 456	78.0	22.0	2.43	2.34

Table B. States and Counties

STATE/ County code	MSA/ PMSA/ NECMA code[1]	County type[2]	STATE County	Population, 2000				Population, 1990				Population and population characteristics, 2000					
												Race (percent)					
												One race					
				Land area, 2000[3] (sq km)	Total persons	Rank	Per square kilometer	Land area, 1990[3] (sq km)	Total persons	Rank	Per square kilometer	White	Black or African American	American Indian or Alaska Native	Asian	Native Hawaiian and other Pacific Islander	Some other race
				1	2	3	4	5	6	7	8	9	10	11	12	13	14
			IDAHO—Cont'd														
16 037	...	9	Custer	12 757	4 342	2 893	0.3	12 757	4 133	2 902	0.3	97.3	0.0	0.6	0.0	0.0	1.2
16 039	...	6	Elmore	7 971	29 130	1 423	3.7	7 971	21 205	1 620	2.7	85.4	3.2	0.9	1.7	0.2	5.4
16 041	...	7	Franklin	1 723	11 329	2 348	6.6	1 724	9 232	2 452	5.4	95.1	0.1	0.3	0.1	0.0	3.4
16 043	...	7	Fremont	4 835	11 819	2 303	2.4	4 835	10 937	2 300	2.3	91.4	0.2	0.5	0.4	0.1	5.9
16 045	...	6	Gem	1 457	15 181	2 077	10.4	1 457	11 844	2 228	8.1	93.8	0.1	0.7	0.4	0.1	3.2
16 047	...	7	Gooding	1 893	14 155	2 149	7.5	1 893	11 633	2 244	6.1	87.6	0.2	0.8	0.2	0.1	8.2
16 049	...	7	Idaho	21 976	15 511	2 052	0.7	21 977	13 768	2 074	0.6	94.1	0.1	2.9	0.3	0.0	0.9
16 051	...	7	Jefferson	2 836	19 155	1 839	6.8	2 836	16 543	1 887	5.8	90.9	0.3	0.5	0.2	0.1	6.8
16 053	...	7	Jerome	1 554	18 342	1 878	11.8	1 554	15 138	1 978	9.7	87.0	0.2	0.7	0.3	0.0	9.8
16 055	...	4	Kootenai	3 225	108 685	496	33.7	3 225	69 795	635	21.6	95.8	0.2	1.2	0.5	0.1	0.6
16 057	...	7	Latah	2 789	34 935	1 251	12.5	2 789	30 617	1 260	11.0	93.9	0.6	0.7	2.1	0.1	0.8
16 059	...	7	Lemhi	11 821	7 806	2 625	0.7	11 822	6 899	2 671	0.6	96.6	0.1	0.6	0.2	0.0	0.8
16 061	...	9	Lewis	1 241	3 747	2 936	3.0	1 241	3 516	2 955	2.8	92.2	0.3	3.8	0.4	0.1	0.9
16 063	...	9	Lincoln	3 122	4 044	2 917	1.3	3 122	3 308	2 975	1.1	86.5	0.5	1.2	0.4	0.0	9.4
16 065	...	7	Madison	1 221	27 467	1 469	22.5	1 221	23 674	1 505	19.4	95.5	0.2	0.3	0.6	0.2	2.2
16 067	...	7	Minidoka	1 967	20 174	1 782	10.3	1 968	19 361	1 712	9.8	78.1	0.3	0.9	0.4	0.0	17.8
16 069	...	5	Nez Perce	2 199	37 410	1 180	17.0	2 199	33 754	1 172	15.3	91.6	0.3	5.3	0.7	0.1	0.5
16 071	...	9	Oneida	3 109	4 125	2 906	1.3	3 109	3 492	2 957	1.1	97.5	0.1	0.3	0.1	0.1	1.4
16 073	...	8	Owyhee	19 886	10 644	2 388	0.5	19 887	8 392	2 521	0.4	76.9	0.2	3.2	0.5	0.1	16.5
16 075	...	7	Payette	1 055	20 578	1 756	19.5	1 055	16 434	1 897	15.6	90.3	0.1	0.9	0.9	0.0	5.6
16 077	...	7	Power	3 640	7 538	2 640	2.1	3 641	7 086	2 648	1.9	83.8	0.1	3.3	0.3	0.0	11.1
16 079	...	7	Shoshone	6 822	13 771	2 175	2.0	6 822	13 931	2 063	2.0	95.8	0.1	1.5	0.2	0.1	0.5
16 081	...	9	Teton	1 166	5 999	2 780	5.1	1 167	3 439	2 960	2.9	91.3	0.2	0.6	0.2	0.2	6.7
16 083	...	5	Twin Falls	4 986	64 284	759	12.9	4 986	53 580	801	10.7	92.5	0.2	0.7	0.8	0.1	3.8
16 085	...	9	Valley	9 526	7 651	2 633	0.8	9 527	6 109	2 741	0.6	96.4	0.0	0.7	0.3	0.0	1.1
16 087	...	7	Washington	3 772	9 977	2 448	2.6	3 772	8 550	2 509	2.3	87.6	0.1	0.7	1.0	0.1	8.2
17 000	...		ILLINOIS	143 961	12 419 293	X	86.3	143 987	11 430 602	X	79.4	73.5	15.1	0.2	3.4	0.0	5.8
17 001	...	5	Adams	2 219	68 277	721	30.8	2 219	66 090	662	29.8	95.1	3.1	0.2	0.4	0.0	0.3
17 003	...	7	Alexander	612	9 590	2 480	15.7	612	10 626	2 324	17.4	63.0	34.9	0.3	0.4	0.0	0.5
17 005	...	6	Bond	985	17 633	1 921	17.9	985	14 991	1 988	15.2	90.7	7.4	0.5	0.3	0.0	0.4
17 007	6880	2	Boone	728	41 786	1 059	57.4	729	30 806	1 249	42.3	90.1	0.9	0.3	0.5	0.0	6.7
17 009	...	9	Brown	792	6 950	2 691	8.8	792	5 836	2 776	7.4	80.3	18.2	0.1	0.1	0.1	0.7
17 011	...	7	Bureau	2 250	35 503	1 232	15.8	2 250	35 688	1 107	15.9	96.8	0.3	0.2	0.5	0.0	1.3
17 013	...	8	Calhoun	657	5 084	2 846	7.7	657	5 322	2 816	8.1	98.8	0.0	0.3	0.2	0.0	0.2
17 015	...	7	Carroll	1 151	16 674	1 976	14.5	1 151	16 805	1 859	14.6	96.9	0.5	0.2	0.4	0.0	0.8
17 017	...	6	Cass	974	13 695	2 184	14.1	974	13 437	2 105	13.8	94.9	0.4	0.2	0.3	0.0	3.3
17 019	1400	3	Champaign	2 582	179 669	308	69.6	2 583	173 025	279	67.0	78.8	11.2	0.2	6.5	0.0	1.3
17 021	...	6	Christian	1 836	35 372	1 238	19.3	1 836	34 418	1 153	18.7	96.3	2.1	0.2	0.4	0.0	0.5
17 023	...	6	Clark	1 299	17 008	1 952	13.1	1 299	15 921	1 929	12.3	98.8	0.2	0.2	0.1	0.0	0.1
17 025	...	7	Clay	1 215	14 560	2 116	12.0	1 215	14 460	2 019	11.9	98.5	0.1	0.2	0.5	0.0	0.2
17 027	7040	1	Clinton	1 228	35 535	1 230	28.9	1 228	33 944	1 165	27.6	94.2	3.9	0.2	0.3	0.0	0.8
17 029	...	5	Coles	1 316	53 196	881	40.4	1 317	51 644	819	39.2	95.4	2.3	0.2	0.8	0.0	0.4
17 031	1600	0	Cook	2 449	5 376 741	2	2 195.5	2 449	5 105 044	2	2 084.5	56.3	26.1	0.3	4.8	0.0	9.9
17 033	...	7	Crawford	1 149	20 452	1 763	17.8	1 149	19 464	1 704	16.9	93.6	4.5	0.3	0.3	0.0	0.5
17 035	...	9	Cumberland	896	11 253	2 353	12.6	896	10 670	2 320	11.9	98.8	0.1	0.2	0.2	0.0	0.2
17 037	1600	1	De Kalb	1 642	88 969	585	54.2	1 643	77 932	582	47.4	88.5	4.6	0.2	2.3	0.1	2.7
17 039	...	6	De Witt	1 030	16 798	1 970	16.3	1 030	16 516	1 891	16.0	97.8	0.5	0.2	0.3	0.0	0.5
17 041	...	6	Douglas	1 080	19 922	1 797	18.4	1 080	19 464	1 704	18.0	97.3	0.3	0.2	0.3	0.0	1.3
17 043	1600	0	Du Page	864	904 161	42	1 046.5	866	781 689	49	902.6	84.0	3.1	0.2	7.9	0.0	3.1
17 045	...	6	Edgar	1 615	19 704	1 811	12.2	1 615	19 595	1 693	12.1	97.1	1.8	0.2	0.2	0.0	0.3
17 047	...	9	Edwards	576	6 971	2 688	12.1	576	7 440	2 621	12.9	98.9	0.1	0.1	0.4	0.0	0.1
17 049	...	7	Effingham	1 240	34 264	1 272	27.6	1 240	31 704	1 222	25.6	98.7	0.2	0.2	0.3	0.0	0.2
17 051	...	6	Fayette	1 856	21 802	1 702	11.7	1 856	20 893	1 634	11.3	94.0	4.9	0.1	0.2	0.0	0.3
17 053	...	6	Ford	1 258	14 241	2 147	11.3	1 259	14 275	2 032	11.3	98.2	0.2	0.1	0.3	0.0	0.4
17 055	...	7	Franklin	1 067	39 018	1 138	36.6	1 067	40 319	992	37.8	98.6	0.2	0.2	0.2	0.0	0.1
17 057	...	6	Fulton	2 242	38 250	1 159	17.1	2 242	38 080	1 050	17.0	95.1	3.6	0.2	0.2	0.0	0.3
17 059	...	8	Gallatin	838	6 445	2 743	7.7	838	6 909	2 670	8.2	98.4	0.3	0.7	0.1	0.0	0.1
17 061	...	6	Greene	1 407	14 761	2 105	10.5	1 407	15 317	1 971	10.9	98.1	0.7	0.2	0.1	0.0	0.2
17 063	1600	1	Grundy	1 088	37 535	1 176	34.5	1 088	32 337	1 205	29.7	97.1	0.2	0.2	0.3	0.0	1.3
17 065	...	7	Hamilton	1 127	8 621	2 556	7.6	1 127	8 499	2 511	7.5	98.2	0.7	0.3	0.1	0.0	0.1
17 067	...	7	Hancock	2 058	20 121	1 785	9.8	2 058	21 373	1 615	10.4	98.7	0.2	0.2	0.2	0.0	0.1
17 069	...	9	Hardin	462	4 800	2 859	10.4	462	5 189	2 826	11.2	95.4	2.8	0.0	0.5	0.1	0.5
17 071	...	9	Henderson	981	8 213	2 590	8.4	981	8 096	2 555	8.3	98.5	0.3	0.1	0.1	0.0	0.2
17 073	1960	2	Henry	2 132	51 020	910	23.9	2 132	51 159	824	24.0	96.2	1.1	0.1	0.2	0.0	1.3
17 075	...	6	Iroquois	2 892	31 334	1 365	10.8	2 892	30 787	1 252	10.6	95.9	0.7	0.2	0.3	0.0	2.1

[1]MSA = Metropolitan Statistical Area. PMSA = Primary MSA. NECMA = New England County Metropolitan Area. See Appendix A for explanation of these concepts. See Appendix B for list of metropolitan areas identified by type, with component counties.
[2]County typology code from the Economic Research Service of USDA. See Appendix A for definition.
[3]Dry land or land partially or temporarily covered by water.

Table B. States and Counties

STATE County	\(2000\) Two or more races (15)	White (16)	Black (17)	American Indian or Alaska Native (18)	Asian (19)	Native Hawaiian and other Pacific Islander (20)	Some other race (21)	Hispanic[1] (22)	\(1990\) White (23)	Black or African American (24)	American Indian or Alaska Native (25)	Asian and Pacific Islander (26)	Hispanic[1] (27)
IDAHO—Cont'd													
Custer	0.9	98.2	0.0	1.4	0.1	0.0	1.2	4.2	97.8	0.0	0.8	0.5	2.2
Elmore	3.3	88.3	3.8	1.8	2.6	0.5	6.6	12.0	80.1	3.7	0.8	2.1	7.5
Franklin	0.9	95.9	0.1	0.6	0.2	0.1	4.0	5.2	98.1	0.1	0.4	0.1	2.6
Fremont	1.6	92.9	0.4	1.1	0.5	0.2	6.6	10.6	93.9	0.1	0.6	0.3	7.0
Gem	1.8	95.4	0.2	1.6	0.7	0.2	3.8	6.9	95.6	0.1	1.2	0.4	5.2
Gooding	2.8	90.3	0.5	1.3	0.5	0.1	10.1	17.1	93.6	0.1	0.4	0.3	8.8
Idaho	1.7	95.7	0.1	4.0	0.5	0.1	1.4	1.6	97.1	0.0	2.5	0.2	0.9
Jefferson	1.3	92.1	0.3	0.9	0.5	0.2	7.4	10.0	94.5	0.0	0.7	0.2	7.0
Jerome	1.9	88.8	0.3	1.4	0.4	0.1	11.0	17.2	94.5	0.1	0.8	0.4	6.7
Kootenai	1.6	97.4	0.3	2.1	0.8	0.2	0.9	2.3	98.1	0.1	1.0	0.5	1.5
Latah	1.8	95.6	0.8	1.4	2.6	0.2	1.1	2.1	96.0	0.6	0.7	2.3	1.5
Lemhi	1.7	98.2	0.2	1.5	0.5	0.1	1.2	2.2	98.2	0.0	0.7	0.3	2.0
Lewis	2.2	94.2	0.4	5.0	0.5	0.1	1.9	1.9	94.5	0.1	4.8	0.5	1.2
Lincoln	1.9	88.4	0.7	2.3	0.6	0.0	10.1	13.4	97.7	0.1	0.7	0.4	5.9
Madison	1.0	96.4	0.3	0.6	0.9	0.3	2.5	3.9	96.1	0.2	0.5	1.3	3.2
Minidoka	2.5	80.4	0.4	1.6	0.7	0.1	19.6	25.5	85.4	0.2	1.0	0.5	19.3
Nez Perce	1.6	93.1	0.4	6.3	0.9	0.2	0.7	1.9	93.9	0.1	5.0	0.6	1.2
Oneida	0.5	98.0	0.1	0.4	0.4	0.2	1.4	2.3	98.3	0.1	0.5	0.2	1.6
Owyhee	2.7	79.4	0.3	4.5	0.6	0.2	17.8	23.1	82.6	0.3	3.3	0.9	16.8
Payette	2.3	92.5	0.3	1.8	1.4	0.1	6.5	11.9	92.6	0.1	1.2	1.0	7.3
Power	1.4	84.9	0.2	3.7	0.5	0.1	12.0	21.7	86.9	0.1	2.9	0.6	13.2
Shoshone	1.7	97.5	0.2	2.7	0.5	0.2	0.8	1.9	97.8	0.1	1.3	0.3	1.8
Teton	0.8	92.1	0.2	0.9	0.3	0.2	7.1	11.8	97.7	0.1	0.4	0.0	6.9
Twin Falls	2.0	94.4	0.3	1.4	1.0	0.2	4.8	9.4	95.6	0.1	0.6	1.0	5.8
Valley	1.4	97.8	0.1	1.3	0.6	0.1	1.6	2.0	98.0	0.1	1.0	0.4	1.8
Washington	2.4	89.8	0.2	1.5	1.4	0.2	9.4	13.8	89.6	0.1	0.5	1.5	10.7
ILLINOIS	1.9	75.1	15.6	0.6	3.8	0.1	6.8	12.3	78.3	14.8	0.2	2.5	7.9
Adams	1.0	96.0	3.5	0.4	0.5	0.0	0.5	0.8	96.7	2.6	0.1	0.4	0.4
Alexander	0.9	63.7	35.4	0.7	0.5	0.0	0.7	1.4	66.4	32.9	0.2	0.5	0.5
Bond	0.7	91.4	7.6	0.8	0.4	0.1	0.5	1.4	96.6	2.9	0.2	0.1	0.5
Boone	1.5	91.5	1.2	0.7	0.8	0.0	7.4	12.5	95.3	0.4	0.1	0.5	6.7
Brown	0.5	80.8	18.3	0.3	0.3	0.1	0.8	3.9	90.2	9.4	0.2	0.1	1.8
Bureau	0.9	97.6	0.5	0.5	0.6	0.1	1.6	4.9	98.5	0.1	0.2	0.5	2.8
Calhoun	0.5	99.3	0.1	0.8	0.2	0.0	0.2	0.6	99.5	0.0	0.2	0.3	0.2
Carroll	1.0	97.9	0.7	0.7	0.6	0.2	1.0	2.0	98.3	0.7	0.2	0.4	1.8
Cass	0.8	95.7	0.5	0.5	0.4	0.0	3.7	8.5	99.6	0.1	0.1	0.2	0.4
Champaign	2.0	80.4	12.0	0.7	7.1	0.1	1.8	2.9	84.7	9.6	0.2	4.6	2.0
Christian	0.5	96.8	2.3	0.4	0.4	0.1	0.5	1.0	99.3	0.2	0.1	0.3	0.3
Clark	0.6	99.4	0.4	0.4	0.2	0.1	0.2	0.3	99.5	0.1	0.2	0.2	0.3
Clay	0.4	98.9	0.2	0.5	0.5	0.0	0.3	0.6	99.6	0.0	0.1	0.2	0.4
Clinton	0.5	94.7	4.0	0.4	0.5	0.1	0.9	1.6	96.3	3.0	0.1	0.3	1.0
Coles	0.9	96.2	2.6	0.5	1.0	0.1	0.7	1.4	97.2	1.8	0.2	0.7	0.8
Cook	2.5	58.3	26.7	0.6	5.3	0.1	11.5	19.9	62.8	25.8	0.2	3.7	13.6
Crawford	0.7	94.3	4.8	0.5	0.5	0.0	0.7	1.7	99.2	0.3	0.2	0.2	0.4
Cumberland	0.5	99.3	0.2	0.5	0.3	0.0	0.3	0.6	99.6	0.0	0.1	0.2	0.4
De Kalb	1.6	89.8	5.0	0.6	2.7	0.1	3.4	6.6	93.6	2.7	0.2	2.2	3.0
De Witt	0.7	98.5	0.7	0.5	0.4	0.0	0.6	1.3	99.2	0.2	0.2	0.3	0.5
Douglas	0.7	97.9	0.4	0.4	0.4	0.0	1.6	3.5	99.1	0.1	0.1	0.2	1.5
Du Page	1.7	85.5	3.4	0.4	8.5	0.1	3.9	9.0	91.5	2.0	0.1	5.1	4.4
Edgar	0.4	97.5	1.9	0.4	0.2	0.0	0.3	0.8	99.4	0.3	0.1	0.1	0.3
Edwards	0.4	99.2	0.2	0.3	0.5	0.1	0.1	0.5	99.5	0.1	0.1	0.3	0.4
Effingham	0.5	99.1	0.2	0.4	0.4	0.0	0.4	0.7	99.4	0.0	0.1	0.3	0.4
Fayette	0.5	94.6	5.0	0.4	0.3	0.0	0.3	0.8	96.4	2.9	0.2	0.2	0.7
Ford	0.8	98.9	0.4	0.4	0.4	0.0	0.6	1.2	99.2	0.3	0.1	0.3	0.6
Franklin	0.7	99.3	0.2	0.6	0.3	0.0	0.2	0.6	99.4	0.1	0.3	0.2	0.3
Fulton	0.5	95.7	3.7	0.4	0.3	0.0	0.4	1.2	97.5	1.8	0.2	0.3	0.6
Gallatin	0.5	98.8	0.4	0.9	0.2	0.0	0.1	0.9	99.0	0.6	0.1	0.2	0.2
Greene	0.6	98.6	0.9	0.6	0.2	0.1	0.3	0.5	99.4	0.1	0.3	0.1	0.3
Grundy	0.9	97.9	0.3	0.5	0.5	0.0	1.6	4.1	98.5	0.1	0.1	0.3	2.3
Hamilton	0.5	98.8	0.8	0.5	0.4	0.0	0.2	0.6	99.6	0.0	0.1	0.2	0.3
Hancock	0.6	99.2	0.3	0.5	0.3	0.1	0.2	0.5	99.5	0.1	0.1	0.2	0.3
Hardin	0.7	96.0	2.9	0.5	0.6	0.1	0.5	1.1	97.6	1.6	0.3	0.3	0.6
Henderson	0.8	99.3	0.4	0.4	0.1	0.2	0.3	0.9	99.3	0.1	0.4	0.1	0.7
Henry	1.0	97.1	1.5	0.4	0.4	0.0	1.6	2.9	97.7	1.3	0.1	0.3	1.6
Iroquois	0.8	96.7	0.8	0.5	0.4	0.1	2.4	3.9	97.9	0.5	0.1	0.2	2.1

[1] Hispanic persons may be of any race.

Table B. States and Counties

STATE County	Population and population characteristics, 2000 — Age (percent)										
	Under 5 years	5 to 17 years	18 to 24 years	25 to 34 years	35 to 44 years	45 to 54 years	55 to 64 years	65 to 74 years	75 years and over	Median age (years)	Percent Female
	28	29	30	31	32	33	34	35	36	37	38
IDAHO—Cont'd											
Custer	5.4	20.2	4.8	9.7	16.2	16.9	12.4	8.3	6.2	41.2	48.9
Elmore	8.4	19.6	13.9	18.7	17.3	9.1	5.9	4.1	3.0	29.1	44.8
Franklin	10.0	27.4	9.3	11.7	12.5	10.1	7.4	5.5	6.2	27.7	50.2
Fremont	8.5	24.7	9.3	11.0	13.7	11.5	9.0	7.1	5.3	31.9	48.6
Gem	7.0	20.9	7.6	11.0	14.3	13.3	10.2	7.7	7.9	37.5	50.3
Gooding	7.8	21.9	8.7	11.5	13.6	11.8	9.4	7.8	7.6	35.1	49.0
Idaho	5.3	19.7	6.3	8.3	15.0	16.0	12.3	9.4	7.6	42.3	49.1
Jefferson	8.9	27.4	9.6	11.0	14.5	11.8	7.5	5.1	4.2	28.8	49.4
Jerome	8.2	23.3	8.9	12.2	14.8	12.3	7.9	6.5	5.8	32.9	48.9
Kootenai	6.9	20.3	8.7	12.6	15.5	14.5	9.4	6.6	5.7	36.1	50.5
Latah	5.4	14.9	24.5	14.6	12.4	11.9	7.0	4.5	5.0	27.9	48.2
Lemhi	5.1	20.4	5.5	8.0	14.7	16.7	12.8	8.7	8.1	42.7	50.2
Lewis	4.8	20.6	5.3	8.8	15.0	14.0	13.1	9.6	8.9	42.5	49.5
Lincoln	7.5	22.8	9.0	11.6	13.9	13.3	8.8	7.1	5.9	34.3	48.4
Madison	7.1	19.0	39.9	7.6	8.3	7.1	4.8	3.1	3.0	20.7	52.4
Minidoka	8.0	23.6	9.1	11.0	14.1	12.0	8.9	6.8	6.4	33.5	50.0
Nez Perce	6.0	17.7	10.0	12.0	14.7	13.7	9.3	8.0	8.5	38.1	50.8
Oneida	7.4	24.6	7.7	9.2	13.9	12.6	8.7	7.3	8.6	36.0	49.2
Owyhee	7.8	24.1	8.5	12.1	14.4	12.0	8.9	6.6	5.5	32.9	47.8
Payette	7.6	23.1	7.9	12.3	14.3	12.1	9.5	6.7	6.5	34.4	50.4
Power	8.4	25.4	8.4	11.8	13.6	13.6	8.4	5.6	4.7	31.6	49.8
Shoshone	5.6	17.3	6.7	10.3	15.2	15.4	12.0	9.1	8.3	41.8	50.1
Teton	8.5	23.3	8.1	16.2	17.6	13.3	5.6	4.2	3.3	31.3	47.0
Twin Falls	7.3	20.6	10.4	11.8	14.2	12.8	8.6	6.9	7.4	34.9	50.9
Valley	4.3	19.3	4.4	8.4	16.5	18.6	13.6	9.1	5.8	43.5	48.6
Washington	6.7	20.7	7.2	9.7	13.6	13.5	10.8	9.0	8.7	39.2	51.1
ILLINOIS	7.1	19.1	9.8	14.6	16.0	13.1	8.4	6.2	5.9	34.7	51.0
Adams	6.2	18.7	8.8	11.7	14.7	13.0	9.3	8.2	9.4	38.3	51.9
Alexander	6.3	19.6	7.7	12.3	14.3	13.1	9.8	8.6	8.3	38.0	50.4
Bond	5.6	16.3	11.6	13.8	15.6	13.5	8.8	7.5	7.3	36.8	46.2
Boone	7.6	22.2	7.7	13.3	16.6	13.0	9.0	5.8	4.9	34.5	50.0
Brown	4.0	13.7	12.6	19.2	18.3	11.7	7.8	6.0	6.7	35.2	36.4
Bureau	5.9	18.8	7.4	11.3	14.9	13.9	10.0	8.2	9.5	39.6	51.4
Calhoun	5.3	17.6	7.6	11.0	14.9	12.8	11.6	10.0	9.2	40.5	49.8
Carroll	5.5	18.7	6.6	10.5	14.9	13.7	10.7	10.0	9.3	40.8	50.6
Cass	6.8	18.5	8.4	12.9	14.9	13.0	9.7	7.7	8.0	37.2	50.3
Champaign	5.8	15.3	23.1	14.7	13.5	11.4	6.6	5.1	4.7	28.6	49.7
Christian	6.1	18.0	7.6	12.2	15.9	13.1	9.8	8.3	8.9	38.9	50.1
Clark	6.0	18.9	7.4	11.4	15.2	12.9	10.2	8.6	9.4	39.2	51.4
Clay	5.9	18.0	8.0	11.6	14.3	13.0	10.0	8.7	10.4	39.7	52.0
Clinton	6.1	18.8	9.3	13.1	17.0	12.6	8.7	7.7	6.8	36.6	48.4
Coles	5.3	14.4	23.5	11.1	12.7	11.8	7.9	6.6	6.7	30.8	52.3
Cook	7.2	18.8	9.9	16.2	15.5	12.5	8.2	6.1	5.6	33.6	51.6
Crawford	5.5	17.3	8.6	13.0	15.9	13.3	9.8	8.5	8.1	38.6	48.2
Cumberland	6.3	20.1	8.0	12.5	15.0	12.9	9.3	7.7	8.2	37.2	51.1
De Kalb	6.2	16.9	22.0	13.5	14.1	10.8	6.6	4.8	5.0	28.4	50.4
De Witt	6.2	18.4	7.8	12.3	16.0	13.2	10.3	7.7	8.2	38.5	51.1
Douglas	6.9	20.1	8.0	11.4	15.4	12.7	9.4	8.1	7.8	37.4	51.4
Du Page	7.3	19.5	8.2	14.6	17.8	14.5	8.2	5.0	4.8	35.2	50.7
Edgar	5.7	18.1	8.3	11.6	15.4	13.4	9.8	8.3	9.4	39.3	51.3
Edwards	5.7	17.4	8.0	11.5	14.6	13.9	10.4	9.0	9.5	40.5	51.6
Effingham	7.2	21.4	8.2	12.1	16.1	12.6	8.5	6.9	7.0	35.7	50.5
Fayette	6.1	17.7	9.0	13.3	16.1	12.5	9.4	8.0	7.9	37.5	47.9
Ford	6.4	19.4	6.9	10.7	15.6	12.4	9.1	8.9	10.5	39.4	52.1
Franklin	5.6	17.3	7.9	11.8	14.3	13.4	10.9	8.9	9.8	40.3	52.1
Fulton	5.6	16.4	8.7	13.0	15.0	13.2	9.8	8.7	9.6	39.2	48.7
Gallatin	5.2	17.0	8.2	11.5	13.9	13.3	12.7	8.9	9.3	40.7	51.5
Greene	6.2	19.2	8.8	11.5	14.9	12.2	9.6	8.6	8.9	37.9	50.9
Grundy	6.6	20.0	8.3	13.1	17.1	13.8	8.7	6.1	6.2	36.3	50.3
Hamilton	5.9	18.0	7.9	10.5	14.2	13.5	10.8	9.3	9.9	40.6	51.7
Hancock	5.6	19.0	7.1	10.8	14.7	14.3	10.2	8.9	9.4	40.3	51.5
Hardin	5.5	15.0	7.8	11.3	15.0	15.1	11.8	9.9	8.7	42.1	49.9
Henderson	5.7	17.4	7.5	10.4	15.8	14.1	12.4	9.2	7.5	41.0	50.6
Henry	6.0	19.3	7.7	11.0	15.4	14.3	10.0	8.0	8.3	39.1	51.0
Iroquois	6.1	19.3	7.1	10.7	15.0	13.3	10.3	8.7	9.4	39.6	51.0

Table B. States and Counties

STATE County	Under 5 years	5 to 17 years	18 to 24 years	25 to 34 years	35 to 44 years	45 to 54 years	55 to 64 years	65 to 74 years	75 years and over	Percent Female	2000	1990	1980	1990–2000	1980–1990
	39	40	41	42	43	44	45	46	47	48	49	50	51	52	53
IDAHO—Cont'd															
Custer	8.0	22.6	5.3	14.7	17.0	11.7	8.7	7.3	4.7	48.4	4 342	4 133	3 385	5.1	22.1
Elmore	10.5	21.0	12.3	21.0	13.6	8.1	8.0	4.6	2.9	47.8	29 130	21 205	21 565	37.4	-1.7
Franklin	9.3	30.4	7.5	12.2	11.3	8.3	7.1	7.2	6.7	49.7	11 329	9 232	8 895	22.7	3.8
Fremont	8.7	29.2	8.3	13.0	12.2	9.1	8.1	6.6	4.7	49.1	11 819	10 937	10 813	8.1	1.1
Gem	7.1	21.1	7.3	13.1	13.1	11.0	9.4	10.4	7.5	50.1	15 181	11 844	11 972	28.2	-1.1
Gooding	7.3	22.9	6.7	13.4	12.6	10.2	9.5	9.3	8.0	50.1	14 155	11 633	11 874	21.7	-2.0
Idaho	6.6	21.3	6.0	13.6	15.0	11.3	10.5	8.7	6.9	49.2	15 511	13 768	14 769	12.7	-6.8
Jefferson	10.0	30.4	7.8	13.4	12.8	9.0	6.8	5.7	4.1	49.2	19 155	16 543	15 304	15.8	8.1
Jerome	8.2	23.9	7.1	14.7	13.8	9.6	8.6	8.4	5.7	50.0	18 342	15 138	14 840	21.2	2.0
Kootenai	7.1	20.0	8.4	14.6	16.4	11.2	8.9	8.0	5.4	50.9	108 685	69 795	59 770	55.7	16.8
Latah	6.5	16.4	22.9	16.8	13.6	8.3	5.9	4.9	4.7	49.0	34 935	30 617	28 749	14.1	6.5
Lemhi	6.9	20.6	5.8	11.9	15.2	11.9	10.2	10.9	6.6	50.4	7 806	6 899	7 460	13.1	-7.5
Lewis	7.4	20.8	6.0	13.7	13.2	11.3	10.2	10.2	7.3	49.2	3 747	3 516	4 118	6.6	-14.6
Lincoln	7.1	24.3	7.8	12.4	14.7	9.7	9.6	8.1	6.3	49.1	4 044	3 308	3 436	22.2	-3.7
Madison	8.1	24.1	34.0	10.0	8.3	5.8	3.9	3.2	2.6	52.6	27 467	23 674	19 480	16.0	21.5
Minidoka	8.4	26.7	7.6	14.4	12.9	9.6	7.9	8.0	4.5	49.8	20 174	19 361	19 718	4.2	-1.8
Nez Perce	6.5	18.4	9.2	15.0	14.7	10.7	9.4	9.0	7.1	50.9	37 410	33 754	33 220	10.8	1.6
Oneida	9.5	27.7	5.3	13.0	11.3	8.2	7.3	9.5	8.2	50.3	4 125	3 492	3 258	18.1	7.2
Owyhee	8.4	24.7	9.9	13.4	12.5	9.7	8.6	7.1	5.7	47.8	10 644	8 392	8 272	26.8	1.5
Payette	7.9	22.5	7.8	13.0	13.4	10.8	8.6	8.8	7.3	50.8	20 578	16 434	15 825	25.2	3.8
Power	8.5	26.5	7.9	14.1	15.2	9.5	8.0	5.8	4.4	50.3	7 538	7 086	6 844	6.4	3.5
Shoshone	5.7	20.1	7.4	13.3	15.1	11.5	10.2	9.5	7.3	50.2	13 771	13 931	19 226	-1.1	-27.5
Teton	9.7	23.9	8.8	15.4	15.1	8.9	7.2	6.9	4.2	47.3	5 999	3 439	2 897	74.4	18.7
Twin Falls	7.7	22.2	8.4	14.2	14.1	9.8	8.3	8.4	6.9	51.0	64 284	53 580	52 927	20.0	1.2
Valley	6.9	21.0	4.8	12.9	19.7	11.9	10.0	8.8	4.0	49.0	7 651	6 109	5 604	25.2	9.0
Washington	6.9	22.1	6.2	11.6	12.9	10.1	10.3	10.6	9.3	51.7	9 977	8 550	8 803	16.7	-2.9
ILLINOIS	7.4	18.4	10.6	17.4	14.9	10.2	8.5	7.2	5.4	51.4	12 419 293	11 430 602	11 427 409	8.6	0.0
Adams	7.0	18.8	9.1	14.5	13.5	10.0	9.5	9.3	8.3	52.5	68 277	66 090	71 622	3.3	-7.7
Alexander	8.4	20.4	7.9	13.5	12.0	9.8	9.8	9.6	8.5	53.0	9 590	10 626	12 264	-9.7	-13.4
Bond	6.3	18.2	11.2	14.2	13.5	9.3	9.7	9.1	8.3	51.7	17 633	14 991	16 224	17.6	-7.6
Boone	7.6	20.3	9.5	15.7	15.5	11.6	8.2	6.6	5.1	50.6	41 786	30 806	28 630	35.6	7.6
Brown	5.6	16.4	10.8	19.3	14.1	9.1	7.9	8.3	8.5	43.7	6 950	5 836	5 411	19.1	7.9
Bureau	6.5	19.9	7.9	13.8	13.9	10.4	9.4	9.7	8.5	52.2	35 503	35 688	39 114	-0.5	-8.8
Calhoun	6.2	18.1	8.4	13.2	12.3	10.9	11.1	10.2	9.7	50.0	5 084	5 322	5 867	-4.5	-9.3
Carroll	6.4	18.7	7.5	13.7	13.6	10.7	10.7	10.2	8.4	51.6	16 674	16 805	18 779	-0.8	-10.5
Cass	6.6	19.4	8.4	14.5	13.8	10.5	9.7	9.2	8.0	51.4	13 695	13 437	15 084	1.9	-10.9
Champaign	6.8	15.0	22.7	18.9	13.6	7.9	6.4	5.0	3.8	49.4	179 669	173 025	168 392	3.8	2.8
Christian	6.9	18.4	8.3	14.5	13.6	10.5	9.9	9.4	8.5	52.8	35 372	34 418	36 446	2.8	-5.6
Clark	6.5	18.1	8.0	14.7	13.0	10.4	10.0	10.3	9.1	52.0	17 008	15 921	16 913	6.8	-5.9
Clay	6.3	19.2	7.8	14.3	13.3	10.2	9.6	10.0	9.4	52.7	14 560	14 460	15 283	0.7	-5.4
Clinton	6.9	20.1	9.7	17.1	13.9	9.6	9.0	7.5	6.2	49.1	35 535	33 944	32 617	4.7	4.1
Coles	5.5	15.2	23.0	13.7	12.3	8.7	7.9	7.4	6.4	52.9	53 196	51 644	52 260	3.0	-1.2
Cook	7.5	17.6	10.7	18.5	14.6	10.1	8.7	7.3	5.1	51.9	5 376 741	5 105 044	5 253 628	5.3	-2.8
Crawford	6.4	18.4	7.6	14.6	13.7	10.5	10.5	9.7	8.6	51.7	20 452	19 464	20 818	5.1	-6.5
Cumberland	7.5	20.5	8.9	14.8	13.1	10.0	9.4	8.8	6.8	50.7	11 253	10 670	11 062	5.5	-3.5
De Kalb	6.3	15.1	25.2	15.6	12.5	8.4	6.6	5.6	4.6	50.8	88 969	77 932	74 628	14.2	4.4
De Witt	6.8	18.9	8.1	15.6	13.5	11.1	9.4	9.2	7.5	51.0	16 798	16 516	18 108	1.7	-8.8
Douglas	7.3	20.9	7.6	15.1	13.5	10.1	10.2	8.6	6.6	51.6	19 922	19 464	19 774	2.4	-1.6
Du Page	8.2	18.2	9.5	19.5	17.3	11.1	7.5	5.2	3.5	50.7	904 161	781 689	658 858	15.7	18.6
Edgar	6.4	19.2	7.7	13.5	13.7	10.7	10.0	10.2	8.8	52.6	19 704	19 595	21 725	0.6	-9.8
Edwards	6.3	18.3	7.9	14.0	14.1	10.2	9.3	10.6	9.3	52.1	6 971	7 440	7 961	-6.3	-6.5
Effingham	8.7	21.4	8.4	16.4	13.6	9.4	8.1	7.5	6.4	51.3	34 264	31 704	30 944	8.1	2.5
Fayette	6.4	18.5	8.7	15.9	13.2	9.9	9.4	9.4	8.5	49.2	21 802	20 893	22 167	4.4	-5.7
Ford	6.6	19.3	7.1	14.4	13.2	10.0	10.4	9.8	9.3	52.2	14 241	14 275	15 265	-0.2	-6.5
Franklin	6.1	17.9	8.6	13.5	13.6	10.7	9.4	11.1	9.1	52.6	39 018	40 319	43 201	-3.2	-6.7
Fulton	5.8	18.6	8.4	14.4	14.0	9.9	9.9	10.0	8.9	50.9	38 250	38 080	43 687	0.4	-12.8
Gallatin	5.9	17.8	8.6	12.5	13.3	12.2	10.1	10.2	9.4	52.2	6 445	6 909	7 590	-6.7	-9.0
Greene	6.9	19.6	8.2	14.0	12.5	9.9	10.0	10.0	8.9	51.4	14 761	15 317	16 661	-3.6	-8.1
Grundy	7.3	20.4	8.8	16.4	15.4	10.6	8.2	7.2	5.7	50.4	37 535	32 337	30 582	16.1	5.7
Hamilton	5.9	18.1	7.0	13.4	12.8	10.6	10.4	11.5	10.2	52.6	8 621	8 499	9 172	1.4	-7.3
Hancock	6.3	19.4	7.3	13.8	13.8	10.2	10.5	10.0	8.7	52.5	20 121	21 373	23 877	-5.9	-10.5
Hardin	5.4	18.4	9.0	13.8	14.2	10.7	11.0	10.2	7.4	49.8	4 800	5 189	5 383	-7.5	-3.6
Henderson	6.3	19.2	6.9	14.1	14.0	10.4	10.7	9.6	6.7	51.1	8 213	8 096	9 114	1.4	-11.2
Henry	6.7	20.2	7.9	13.8	14.6	11.0	9.5	8.8	7.6	51.2	51 020	51 159	57 968	-0.3	-11.7
Iroquois	6.5	19.4	7.3	14.0	13.5	10.7	10.3	10.0	8.3	51.6	31 334	30 787	32 976	1.8	-6.6

Table D. States and Counties

STATE County	Total population	Total in house-holds	House-holder	Spouse	Child Total	Child Own child under 18 years	Other relatives Total	Other relatives Under 18 years	Nonrelatives Total	Nonrelatives Unmarried partner	Total in group quarters	Correctional institutions	Nursing homes	Other institutions	College dormitories	Military quarters	Other
	54	55	56	57	58	59	60	61	62	63	64	65	66	67	68	69	70
IDAHO—Cont'd																	
Custer	4 342	98.4	40.8	24.5	27.6	24.4	1.8	0.8	3.7	1.8	1.6	0.1	0.0	0.0	0.0	0.0	1.5
Elmore	29 130	86.1	31.2	20.0	29.4	26.3	2.6	1.3	2.8	1.1	13.9	0.1	0.1	11.0	0.0	2.3	0.4
Franklin	11 329	99.3	30.7	22.6	41.6	35.6	2.8	1.5	1.6	0.6	0.7	0.1	0.0	0.3	0.0	0.0	0.2
Fremont	11 819	97.3	32.9	22.3	36.5	30.3	3.5	1.5	2.1	0.9	2.7	1.0	0.2	1.2	0.0	0.0	0.2
Gem	15 181	98.7	36.5	23.1	30.9	25.3	4.2	1.8	3.9	1.5	1.3	0.2	0.7	0.1	0.0	0.0	0.4
Gooding	14 155	98.6	35.6	22.1	31.9	26.9	4.4	1.7	4.6	1.5	1.4	0.1	0.7	0.4	0.0	0.0	0.2
Idaho	15 511	96.5	39.2	23.8	27.3	23.1	2.9	1.3	3.3	1.8	3.5	1.9	0.6	0.0	0.0	0.0	0.9
Jefferson	19 155	99.6	30.8	22.4	41.2	34.5	3.3	1.5	1.9	0.8	0.4	0.1	0.0	0.0	0.0	0.0	0.3
Jerome	18 342	99.4	34.3	21.9	34.2	28.8	4.9	2.0	4.1	1.5	0.6	0.1	0.1	0.0	0.0	0.0	0.4
Kootenai	108 685	98.7	38.0	22.3	29.9	25.0	3.2	1.3	5.4	2.0	1.3	0.2	0.5	0.2	0.0	0.0	0.4
Latah	34 935	88.8	37.4	18.9	22.3	19.3	1.7	0.6	8.6	1.8	11.2	0.1	0.9	0.0	10.0	0.0	0.2
Lemhi	7 806	99.7	42.0	24.2	27.8	23.9	2.3	1.1	3.3	1.7	0.3	0.2	0.0	0.0	0.0	0.0	0.2
Lewis	3 747	99.1	41.5	24.0	27.0	23.3	2.9	1.5	3.7	1.9	0.9	0.2	0.0	0.0	0.0	0.0	0.7
Lincoln	4 044	99.1	35.8	22.0	32.9	28.1	4.1	1.6	4.3	1.5	0.9	0.0	0.8	0.0	0.0	0.0	0.1
Madison	27 467	94.9	26.0	15.6	30.2	25.1	1.9	0.6	21.3	0.3	5.1	0.2	0.3	0.1	4.4	0.0	0.0
Minidoka	20 174	99.3	34.6	22.3	35.0	28.7	4.3	2.2	3.2	1.2	0.7	0.0	0.4	0.2	0.0	0.0	0.1
Nez Perce	37 410	98.2	40.9	21.6	26.6	21.6	3.5	1.5	5.7	2.5	1.8	0.1	1.0	0.0	0.4	0.0	0.3
Oneida	4 125	98.9	34.7	23.8	35.9	30.5	2.6	1.1	1.9	0.6	1.1	0.0	0.6	0.0	0.0	0.0	0.4
Owyhee	10 644	99.3	34.9	21.3	34.5	29.4	5.0	2.1	3.6	1.4	0.7	0.2	0.4	0.0	0.0	0.0	0.1
Payette	20 578	99.4	35.8	22.2	33.5	28.1	4.3	1.9	3.7	1.7	0.6	0.1	0.2	0.0	0.0	0.0	0.2
Power	7 538	99.3	34.0	21.5	36.0	30.7	4.6	2.4	3.2	1.4	0.7	0.3	0.4	0.0	0.0	0.0	0.0
Shoshone	13 771	98.6	42.9	22.6	25.8	21.1	2.7	1.3	4.6	2.6	1.4	0.3	1.0	0.1	0.0	0.0	0.1
Teton	5 999	99.5	34.6	20.9	34.6	30.1	3.8	1.1	5.6	2.2	0.5	0.1	0.0	0.0	0.0	0.0	0.4
Twin Falls	64 284	97.8	37.1	21.5	31.0	25.7	3.7	1.5	4.5	1.8	2.2	0.4	0.7	0.0	0.3	0.0	0.8
Valley	7 651	99.1	41.9	25.6	25.5	22.1	2.2	1.1	3.9	2.0	0.9	0.2	0.6	0.0	0.0	0.0	0.1
Washington	9 977	98.5	37.7	22.9	30.8	25.2	3.8	1.7	3.3	1.4	1.5	0.3	0.9	0.0	0.0	0.0	0.3
ILLINOIS	12 419 293	97.4	37.0	19.0	30.7	23.2	6.1	2.3	4.7	1.8	2.6	0.5	0.7	0.1	0.7	0.1	0.4
Adams	68 277	96.0	39.3	21.3	28.9	23.0	2.6	1.2	3.8	1.9	4.0	0.4	2.4	0.1	0.8	0.0	0.3
Alexander	9 590	93.8	39.7	17.5	29.0	22.7	4.9	2.7	2.6	1.4	6.2	4.9	0.8	0.0	0.0	0.0	0.5
Bond	17 633	86.3	34.9	20.6	25.4	20.3	2.5	1.1	2.9	1.4	13.7	9.2	0.9	0.0	3.5	0.0	0.1
Boone	41 786	99.2	34.9	22.4	33.8	27.6	4.2	1.5	3.8	1.7	0.8	0.1	0.6	0.0	0.0	0.0	0.0
Brown	6 950	71.6	30.3	16.8	20.7	16.6	1.6	0.7	2.3	1.3	28.4	27.5	0.9	0.0	0.0	0.0	0.0
Bureau	35 503	98.6	39.9	23.2	29.5	23.1	2.6	1.1	3.3	1.8	1.4	0.0	1.0	0.0	0.0	0.0	0.4
Calhoun	5 084	98.9	40.2	24.5	29.2	21.7	2.3	0.8	2.6	1.6	1.1	0.0	1.1	0.0	0.0	0.0	0.0
Carroll	16 674	98.5	40.7	23.8	27.6	22.2	2.8	1.3	3.6	1.9	1.5	0.1	1.2	0.0	0.0	0.0	0.2
Cass	13 695	98.5	39.0	21.8	28.8	22.8	3.7	1.6	5.2	2.2	1.5	0.0	1.3	0.0	0.0	0.0	0.3
Champaign	179 669	91.7	39.3	17.1	23.2	19.4	2.7	1.1	9.5	2.0	8.3	0.2	0.6	0.0	7.1	0.0	0.3
Christian	35 372	94.9	39.4	21.8	27.5	21.9	2.8	1.3	3.4	1.7	5.1	3.4	1.2	0.3	0.0	0.0	0.3
Clark	17 008	98.5	41.0	23.3	29.1	23.3	2.4	1.1	2.8	1.7	1.5	0.1	1.3	0.0	0.0	0.0	0.0
Clay	14 560	96.7	40.1	22.6	28.2	22.1	2.5	1.1	3.3	1.8	3.3	0.0	2.1	0.4	0.0	0.0	0.8
Clinton	35 535	93.3	35.9	21.6	30.8	23.5	2.2	0.9	2.8	1.5	6.7	4.4	1.1	0.9	0.0	0.0	0.2
Coles	53 196	91.4	39.6	18.3	22.7	18.2	2.2	0.9	8.6	1.8	8.6	0.2	1.2	0.2	6.7	0.0	0.3
Cook	5 376 741	98.3	36.7	16.1	31.0	22.0	9.1	3.4	5.3	1.8	1.7	0.2	0.6	0.1	0.4	0.0	0.4
Crawford	20 452	92.3	38.3	22.2	26.4	21.0	2.4	1.1	3.0	1.6	7.7	6.1	0.9	0.1	0.0	0.0	0.6
Cumberland	11 253	98.8	38.8	23.1	31.2	24.5	2.2	1.1	3.5	1.8	1.2	0.1	1.1	0.0	0.0	0.0	0.0
De Kalb	88 969	91.2	35.6	18.1	26.4	21.6	2.9	1.0	8.2	1.9	8.8	0.1	0.7	0.0	7.7	0.0	0.2
De Witt	16 798	98.4	40.3	22.9	28.5	22.5	3.0	1.4	3.8	2.1	1.6	0.3	1.1	0.0	0.0	0.0	0.2
Douglas	19 922	98.5	38.0	23.2	31.7	25.4	2.9	1.2	2.6	1.3	1.5	0.1	1.2	0.0	0.0	0.0	0.2
Du Page	904 161	98.3	36.0	21.9	32.4	25.3	4.4	1.1	3.6	1.3	1.7	0.1	0.8	0.0	0.5	0.0	0.2
Edgar	19 704	96.0	40.0	21.6	27.6	21.7	3.1	1.5	3.8	2.2	4.0	2.0	1.7	0.0	0.0	0.0	0.2
Edwards	6 971	99.0	41.7	24.6	27.9	21.7	2.2	0.9	2.7	1.6	1.0	0.0	0.6	0.0	0.0	0.0	0.4
Effingham	34 264	98.6	37.9	21.9	33.8	27.3	2.1	0.9	2.9	1.6	1.4	0.1	1.0	0.0	0.0	0.0	0.3
Fayette	21 802	91.9	37.4	21.2	27.5	21.9	2.6	1.4	3.2	1.9	8.1	6.7	0.7	0.4	0.0	0.0	0.3
Ford	14 241	97.2	39.6	22.9	29.2	24.0	2.5	1.1	2.9	1.6	2.8	0.2	2.6	0.0	0.0	0.0	0.0
Franklin	39 018	98.6	42.1	22.3	27.5	20.9	3.4	1.4	3.4	1.7	1.4	0.1	1.1	0.0	0.0	0.0	0.2
Fulton	38 250	93.3	38.9	22.0	26.1	20.0	2.7	1.4	3.6	1.8	6.7	5.2	1.4	0.1	0.0	0.0	0.1
Gallatin	6 445	98.9	42.3	23.2	27.2	20.5	3.7	1.6	2.5	1.6	1.1	0.0	0.8	0.0	0.0	0.0	0.3
Greene	14 761	97.8	39.0	22.2	29.6	23.1	3.5	1.8	3.4	1.9	2.2	1.1	1.1	0.0	0.0	0.0	0.0
Grundy	37 535	99.1	38.1	22.7	31.7	24.9	2.9	1.2	3.8	2.0	0.9	0.1	0.8	0.0	0.0	0.0	0.0
Hamilton	8 621	97.6	40.2	23.7	28.6	22.0	2.9	1.5	2.3	1.3	2.4	0.0	1.9	0.0	0.0	0.0	0.5
Hancock	20 121	98.2	40.1	23.6	28.7	22.9	2.1	1.0	3.6	1.8	1.8	0.1	1.2	0.0	0.0	0.0	0.5
Hardin	4 800	95.1	41.4	23.7	25.0	18.7	2.9	1.3	2.2	1.2	4.9	3.2	1.2	0.3	0.0	0.0	0.3
Henderson	8 213	99.1	41.0	24.4	27.4	21.2	2.7	1.3	3.6	2.1	0.9	0.1	0.7	0.0	0.0	0.0	0.2
Henry	51 020	98.8	39.3	23.6	29.9	23.6	2.6	1.2	3.4	1.8	1.2	0.2	0.8	0.1	0.0	0.0	0.1
Iroquois	31 334	97.8	39.0	23.1	29.1	23.2	3.2	1.5	3.4	1.8	2.2	0.0	1.5	0.5	0.0	0.0	0.1

Table B. States and Counties

	Households by type, 2000												Households, 1990		
	Family households						Nonfamily households								
				Married couple		Female householder[1]			Householder living alone						
STATE County	Total households	Total	With own children under 18 years	Total	With own children under 18 years	Total	With own children under 18 years	Total	Total	65 years and over	Average household size	Average family size	Total households	Female householder[1]	Householder living alone
	71	72	73	74	75	76	77	78	79	80	81	82	83	84	85
IDAHO—Cont'd															
Custer	1 770	67.6	29.9	60.1	24.5	4.4	3.1	32.4	27.7	11.3	2.41	2.96	1 561	4.9	24.1
Elmore	9 092	75.3	43.0	64.1	34.9	7.5	5.7	24.7	20.7	6.4	2.76	3.21	7 136	6.3	18.6
Franklin	3 476	82.7	48.0	73.6	42.5	5.8	3.4	17.3	10.0	8.9	3.24	3.64	2 824	4.9	18.5
Fremont	3 885	78.0	39.5	67.9	33.5	6.9	4.1	22.0	19.5	8.5	2.96	3.40	3 453	6.5	19.5
Gem	5 539	75.4	34.0	63.4	27.1	8.4	4.7	24.6	20.8	9.9	2.70	3.12	4 424	7.8	22.0
Gooding	5 046	73.7	36.1	61.9	29.2	7.6	4.7	26.3	22.0	11.5	2.76	3.22	4 320	6.6	24.7
Idaho	6 084	70.6	29.2	60.8	23.0	6.3	4.0	29.4	25.3	11.7	2.46	2.95	5 187	5.4	24.0
Jefferson	5 901	82.7	47.6	72.6	41.2	6.8	4.5	17.3	15.2	7.4	3.23	3.62	4 871	6.6	15.4
Jerome	6 298	76.3	39.1	63.8	31.3	7.6	5.2	23.7	19.5	8.7	2.89	3.33	5 325	7.2	21.0
Kootenai	41 308	71.8	34.9	58.6	26.0	9.2	6.2	28.2	21.9	8.3	2.60	3.03	26 942	8.5	23.0
Latah	13 059	59.5	27.9	50.5	22.2	6.1	4.0	40.5	26.3	6.3	2.38	2.93	11 229	6.1	25.6
Lemhi	3 275	67.7	28.6	57.8	22.4	6.9	4.6	32.3	27.7	12.4	2.38	2.91	2 769	6.9	26.4
Lewis	1 554	67.6	27.5	57.8	21.1	6.4	4.6	32.4	28.1	14.5	2.39	2.92	1 393	6.2	25.8
Lincoln	1 447	72.6	37.7	61.5	31.0	5.5	3.4	27.4	22.9	10.2	2.77	3.27	1 191	4.3	24.5
Madison	7 129	68.1	39.0	60.1	34.1	5.7	3.7	31.9	12.7	5.6	3.66	3.70	5 801	5.5	11.5
Minidoka	6 973	76.9	38.9	64.4	31.4	8.2	5.0	23.1	20.0	9.6	2.87	3.32	6 472	7.7	19.0
Nez Perce	15 286	66.4	29.0	52.8	20.6	9.3	5.9	33.6	26.7	11.3	2.40	2.90	13 618	8.3	26.7
Oneida	1 430	76.4	38.4	68.5	33.1	4.5	3.0	23.6	22.5	11.9	2.85	3.35	1 159	4.2	23.0
Owyhee	3 710	74.3	37.8	61.2	29.5	8.7	6.0	25.7	21.8	9.5	2.85	3.35	2 820	7.7	23.5
Payette	7 371	75.6	37.7	62.0	28.8	9.3	6.1	24.4	20.6	9.5	2.78	3.21	6 040	9.0	21.9
Power	2 560	76.9	40.9	63.4	31.6	8.8	6.4	23.1	20.3	8.8	2.92	3.38	2 370	7.4	19.2
Shoshone	5 906	65.3	26.7	52.7	18.2	8.1	5.3	34.7	29.4	13.6	2.30	2.82	5 691	8.9	27.4
Teton	2 078	70.5	39.7	60.3	34.0	5.8	3.5	29.5	21.3	5.3	2.87	3.43	1 123	3.7	20.4
Twin Falls	23 853	71.1	34.7	58.0	26.3	9.2	5.9	28.9	23.6	10.4	2.64	3.13	19 737	8.0	23.4
Valley	3 208	70.2	28.1	60.9	21.4	5.4	3.9	29.8	24.8	7.9	2.36	2.81	2 404	6.1	22.5
Washington	3 762	72.8	32.7	60.7	26.0	8.2	4.9	27.2	23.5	13.3	2.61	3.10	3 257	7.0	24.6
ILLINOIS	4 591 779	67.6	33.0	51.3	24.3	12.3	6.9	32.4	26.8	9.6	2.63	3.23	4 202 240	12.0	25.7
Adams	26 860	67.0	31.1	54.2	23.1	9.8	6.3	33.0	28.5	13.2	2.44	3.00	25 515	9.3	27.7
Alexander	3 808	65.0	30.0	44.1	17.1	17.5	11.2	35.0	32.3	15.3	2.36	2.99	4 234	18.0	29.9
Bond	6 155	70.6	32.1	59.1	25.0	8.1	5.0	29.4	25.6	12.8	2.47	2.97	5 652	7.7	25.1
Boone	14 597	77.1	40.1	64.2	32.2	8.7	5.7	22.9	19.0	8.0	2.84	3.24	10 950	8.3	18.7
Brown	2 108	65.5	29.1	55.3	22.4	6.8	4.4	34.5	30.8	13.9	2.36	2.96	1 991	6.1	29.2
Bureau	14 182	69.7	30.7	58.1	23.8	8.0	4.8	30.3	27.0	14.0	2.47	2.99	13 790	7.6	25.8
Calhoun	2 046	70.3	29.0	60.8	24.5	5.7	2.6	29.7	26.5	14.4	2.46	2.98	2 048	5.2	24.5
Carroll	6 794	68.9	28.9	58.4	22.4	7.4	4.7	31.1	27.3	13.9	2.42	2.93	6 638	7.2	25.4
Cass	5 347	69.0	32.0	55.8	24.1	9.2	5.7	31.0	26.1	13.0	2.52	3.01	5 195	8.3	25.6
Champaign	70 597	55.7	27.2	43.6	19.5	9.2	6.1	44.3	31.4	7.8	2.33	2.96	63 900	8.4	28.7
Christian	13 921	68.1	30.4	55.3	22.6	9.1	5.6	31.9	28.4	14.7	2.41	2.94	13 591	8.4	27.0
Clark	6 971	69.0	31.2	56.9	23.6	8.7	5.4	31.0	28.1	14.0	2.40	2.94	6 394	7.6	26.3
Clay	5 839	68.6	30.6	56.4	23.1	8.6	5.2	31.4	27.9	14.8	2.41	2.94	5 708	7.9	26.1
Clinton	12 754	72.3	35.1	60.1	28.2	8.4	4.9	27.7	24.2	11.9	2.60	3.10	11 583	8.0	22.2
Coles	21 043	57.4	26.1	46.2	19.2	8.3	5.2	42.6	31.2	11.2	2.31	2.91	18 957	8.1	28.2
Cook	1 974 181	64.3	30.9	44.0	21.1	15.6	8.0	35.7	29.4	9.3	2.68	3.38	1 879 488	15.4	28.2
Crawford	7 842	69.5	30.6	57.8	23.6	8.6	5.3	30.5	26.8	14.0	2.41	2.91	7 792	7.4	26.3
Cumberland	4 368	70.6	33.2	57.5	26.2	7.6	4.7	29.4	25.5	14.0	2.55	3.06	4 029	7.4	24.1
De Kalb	31 674	63.0	32.5	50.9	25.0	8.5	5.6	37.0	25.5	7.9	2.56	3.11	26 413	7.3	25.2
De Witt	6 770	69.2	30.9	56.8	23.2	8.5	5.3	30.8	26.8	12.6	2.44	2.95	6 488	8.0	25.6
Douglas	7 574	72.3	33.5	61.1	26.8	7.9	4.7	27.7	24.7	12.3	2.59	3.10	7 206	7.0	23.0
Du Page	325 601	72.0	37.0	60.9	31.5	7.9	4.2	28.0	22.9	6.8	2.73	3.27	279 344	7.3	20.4
Edgar	7 874	67.6	29.9	54.0	21.3	9.6	6.0	32.4	28.5	14.7	2.40	2.93	7 859	8.9	27.8
Edwards	2 905	69.8	29.8	59.0	23.4	8.2	4.8	30.2	27.5	14.6	2.37	2.88	3 016	6.4	26.7
Effingham	13 001	70.6	36.3	57.8	28.1	9.1	6.0	29.4	26.1	11.6	2.60	3.16	11 465	8.4	23.8
Fayette	8 146	69.4	31.9	56.6	24.2	8.5	5.1	30.6	27.2	13.6	2.46	2.98	7 719	7.7	26.1
Ford	5 639	69.2	31.7	57.8	24.5	8.0	5.1	30.8	28.0	15.3	2.45	2.99	5 602	7.1	26.7
Franklin	16 408	66.9	28.2	53.0	20.3	10.1	5.8	33.1	29.8	15.8	2.34	2.89	16 564	9.2	28.9
Fulton	14 877	68.9	28.6	56.5	21.2	8.8	5.2	31.1	28.3	14.5	2.40	2.90	14 893	8.9	26.8
Gallatin	2 726	67.4	28.3	54.8	21.0	9.8	5.8	32.6	29.4	16.1	2.34	2.90	2 784	8.9	26.8
Greene	5 757	70.8	32.5	57.0	24.7	9.2	5.1	29.2	25.7	14.1	2.51	3.00	5 910	8.2	25.8
Grundy	14 293	71.9	35.3	59.6	27.6	8.6	5.4	28.1	23.5	9.4	2.60	3.09	11 979	6.8	22.8
Hamilton	3 462	70.4	30.0	59.0	23.5	7.9	4.5	29.6	27.3	15.8	2.43	2.95	3 476	7.2	27.8
Hancock	8 069	69.5	30.5	58.9	24.3	7.6	4.4	30.5	26.9	13.8	2.45	2.96	8 409	7.2	25.7
Hardin	1 987	68.8	28.4	57.2	22.2	8.8	4.7	31.2	28.6	15.9	2.30	2.81	2 049	10.2	27.7
Henderson	3 365	70.6	28.6	59.6	22.1	7.1	4.1	29.4	25.3	12.4	2.42	2.88	3 237	6.3	26.1
Henry	20 056	71.3	31.8	60.0	24.9	8.0	5.0	28.7	25.1	13.2	2.51	3.00	19 514	7.9	24.0
Iroquois	12 220	71.3	31.3	59.2	24.2	8.5	5.0	28.7	25.2	13.4	2.51	2.99	11 788	7.2	24.1

[1] No spouse present.

Table B. States and Counties

STATE County	Percent change of households, 1990–2000	Total housing units	Occupied housing units (percent)	Vacant housing units Total	For seasonal, recreational, or occasional use	Homeowner vacancy rate (percent)	Rental vacancy rate (percent)	Total	Percent owner-occupied housing units	Percent renter-occupied housing units	Average household size of owner-occupied units	Average household size of renter-occupied units
	86	87	88	89	90	91	92	93	94	95	96	97
IDAHO—Cont'd												
Custer	13.4	2 983	59.3	40.7	25.0	5.1	32.5	1 770	74.9	25.1	2.35	2.60
Elmore	27.4	10 527	86.4	13.6	4.7	3.0	9.3	9 092	57.4	42.6	2.72	2.81
Franklin	23.1	3 872	89.8	10.2	4.3	2.3	4.6	3 476	80.8	19.2	3.28	3.06
Fremont	12.5	6 890	56.4	43.6	33.9	3.5	15.2	3 885	84.4	15.6	2.99	2.78
Gem	25.2	5 888	94.1	5.9	0.6	2.3	7.1	5 539	79.8	20.2	2.68	2.79
Gooding	16.8	5 505	91.7	8.3	1.6	2.0	5.3	5 046	72.3	27.7	2.67	3.00
Idaho	17.3	7 537	80.7	19.3	10.5	3.0	12.7	6 084	77.2	22.8	2.48	2.38
Jefferson	21.1	6 287	93.9	6.1	0.8	1.9	7.0	5 901	84.9	15.1	3.28	2.97
Jerome	18.3	6 713	93.8	6.2	0.7	1.9	5.4	6 298	70.0	30.0	2.80	3.10
Kootenai	53.3	46 607	88.6	11.4	6.4	2.2	7.8	41 308	74.5	25.5	2.66	2.40
Latah	16.3	13 838	94.4	5.6	0.7	1.9	4.5	13 059	58.7	41.3	2.56	2.12
Lemhi	18.3	4 154	78.8	21.2	11.0	3.4	11.7	3 275	76.2	23.8	2.38	2.34
Lewis	11.6	1 795	86.6	13.4	3.0	2.8	10.6	1 554	74.6	25.4	2.42	2.29
Lincoln	21.5	1 651	87.6	12.4	2.2	3.2	9.2	1 447	74.8	25.2	2.76	2.81
Madison	22.9	7 630	93.4	6.6	0.9	1.6	7.0	7 129	59.1	40.9	3.57	3.78
Minidoka	7.7	7 498	93.0	7.0	0.4	1.7	11.0	6 973	76.9	23.1	2.83	3.00
Nez Perce	12.2	16 203	94.3	5.7	1.4	1.3	5.4	15 286	68.8	31.2	2.49	2.20
Oneida	23.4	1 755	81.5	18.5	6.5	3.0	5.6	1 430	82.4	17.6	2.87	2.78
Owyhee	31.6	4 452	83.3	16.7	6.8	3.3	10.0	3 710	69.6	30.4	2.81	2.94
Payette	22.0	7 949	92.7	7.3	0.7	2.3	9.3	7 371	74.1	25.9	2.79	2.73
Power	8.0	2 844	90.0	10.0	1.0	3.4	6.1	2 560	74.6	25.4	2.91	2.97
Shoshone	3.8	7 057	83.7	16.3	5.4	4.2	15.4	5 906	72.6	27.4	2.31	2.27
Teton	85.0	2 632	79.0	21.0	13.5	2.4	9.7	2 078	73.5	26.5	2.89	2.83
Twin Falls	20.9	25 595	93.2	6.8	0.8	2.3	7.5	23 853	68.3	31.7	2.66	2.59
Valley	33.4	8 084	39.7	60.3	53.7	4.8	17.5	3 208	78.9	21.1	2.38	2.30
Washington	15.5	4 138	90.9	9.1	1.5	2.9	7.4	3 762	73.7	26.3	2.61	2.62
ILLINOIS	9.3	4 885 615	94.0	6.0	0.6	1.5	6.2	4 591 779	67.3	32.7	2.76	2.37
Adams	5.3	29 386	91.4	8.6	1.2	1.9	9.5	26 860	73.7	26.3	2.56	2.11
Alexander	-10.1	4 591	82.9	17.1	2.3	4.1	13.8	3 808	71.8	28.2	2.37	2.34
Bond	8.9	6 690	92.0	8.0	0.6	2.6	7.1	6 155	79.7	20.3	2.53	2.25
Boone	33.3	15 414	94.7	5.3	0.6	2.5	5.8	14 597	78.6	21.4	2.91	2.59
Brown	5.9	2 456	85.8	14.2	5.0	3.0	8.2	2 108	74.1	25.9	2.47	2.05
Bureau	2.8	15 331	92.5	7.5	0.5	2.2	8.2	14 182	76.0	24.0	2.51	2.32
Calhoun	-0.1	2 681	76.3	23.7	13.4	2.7	9.2	2 046	80.7	19.3	2.51	2.26
Carroll	2.4	7 945	85.5	14.5	7.3	3.0	11.4	6 794	76.7	23.3	2.46	2.27
Cass	2.9	5 784	92.4	7.6	1.0	1.5	8.4	5 347	74.9	25.1	2.50	2.60
Champaign	10.5	75 280	93.8	6.2	0.3	1.6	6.9	70 597	55.7	44.3	2.53	2.09
Christian	2.4	14 992	92.9	7.1	0.4	1.9	9.3	13 921	76.2	23.8	2.47	2.22
Clark	9.0	7 816	89.2	10.8	1.4	2.1	14.0	6 971	77.5	22.5	2.45	2.24
Clay	2.3	6 394	91.3	8.7	0.6	2.9	9.2	5 839	79.9	20.1	2.48	2.14
Clinton	10.1	13 805	92.4	7.6	1.3	1.0	4.3	12 754	80.2	19.8	2.69	2.24
Coles	11.0	22 768	92.4	7.6	0.9	1.9	8.2	21 043	61.9	38.1	2.45	2.08
Cook	5.0	2 096 121	94.2	5.8	0.3	1.4	5.3	1 974 181	57.9	42.1	2.84	2.45
Crawford	0.6	8 785	89.3	10.7	0.6	3.3	19.0	7 842	80.3	19.7	2.45	2.25
Cumberland	8.4	4 876	89.6	10.4	2.7	2.5	9.2	4 368	82.1	17.9	2.58	2.37
De Kalb	19.9	32 988	96.0	4.0	0.3	1.7	3.8	31 674	59.5	40.5	2.76	2.28
De Witt	4.3	7 282	93.0	7.0	0.7	1.9	9.8	6 770	75.0	25.0	2.54	2.16
Douglas	5.1	8 005	94.6	5.4	0.4	1.5	6.2	7 574	76.9	23.1	2.65	2.39
Du Page	16.6	335 621	97.0	3.0	0.4	0.8	4.8	325 601	76.4	23.6	2.88	2.23
Edgar	0.2	8 611	91.4	8.6	0.7	2.3	8.0	7 874	74.6	25.4	2.44	2.30
Edwards	-3.7	3 199	90.8	9.2	0.8	2.1	9.8	2 905	81.2	18.8	2.42	2.18
Effingham	13.4	13 959	93.1	6.9	1.4	1.6	8.3	13 001	76.0	24.0	2.74	2.16
Fayette	5.5	9 053	90.0	10.0	2.3	1.9	8.7	8 146	79.8	20.2	2.50	2.31
Ford	0.7	6 060	93.1	6.9	0.4	2.4	5.7	5 639	76.2	23.8	2.50	2.31
Franklin	-0.9	18 105	90.6	9.4	1.0	2.3	8.8	16 408	77.7	22.3	2.38	2.22
Fulton	-0.1	16 240	91.6	8.4	1.7	1.5	4.7	14 877	76.4	23.6	2.45	2.23
Gallatin	-2.1	3 071	88.8	11.2	1.7	4.8	7.4	2 726	81.1	18.9	2.35	2.28
Greene	-2.6	6 332	90.9	9.1	0.9	2.4	5.2	5 757	76.2	23.8	2.54	2.41
Grundy	19.3	15 040	95.0	5.0	0.9	1.5	5.7	14 293	72.4	27.6	2.73	2.27
Hamilton	-0.4	3 983	86.9	13.1	1.0	1.8	6.0	3 462	81.4	18.6	2.46	2.32
Hancock	-4.0	8 909	90.6	9.4	1.3	2.8	10.4	8 069	80.4	19.6	2.50	2.26
Hardin	-3.0	2 494	79.7	20.3	9.1	3.9	11.2	1 987	80.4	19.6	2.33	2.17
Henderson	4.0	4 126	81.6	18.4	11.5	2.5	7.3	3 365	78.8	21.2	2.43	2.37
Henry	2.8	21 270	94.3	5.7	0.4	1.6	6.1	20 056	78.7	21.3	2.58	2.27
Iroquois	3.7	13 362	91.5	8.5	2.2	3.0	5.6	12 220	76.4	23.6	2.55	2.39

Table B. States and Counties

STATE/ County code	MSA/ PMSA/ NECMA code[1]	County type[2]	STATE County	Population, 2000				Population, 1990				Population and population characteristics, 2000					
												Race (percent)					
												One race					
				Land area, 2000[3] (sq km)	Total persons	Rank	Per square kilometer	Land area, 1990[3] (sq km)	Total persons	Rank	Per square kilometer	White	Black or African American	American Indian or Alaska Native	Asian	Native Hawaiian and other Pacific Islander	Some other race
				1	2	3	4	5	6	7	8	9	10	11	12	13	14
			ILLINOIS—Cont'd														
17 077	...	5	Jackson	1 523	59 612	806	39.1	1 523	61 067	713	40.1	80.8	13.0	0.3	3.0	0.1	1.0
17 079	...	7	Jasper	1 280	10 117	2 435	7.9	1 281	10 609	2 327	8.3	99.1	0.1	0.1	0.2	0.0	0.2
17 081	...	7	Jefferson	1 479	40 045	1 113	27.1	1 479	37 020	1 072	25.0	89.9	7.8	0.2	0.5	0.0	0.4
17 083	7040	1	Jersey	956	21 668	1 709	22.7	956	20 539	1 653	21.5	98.1	0.5	0.2	0.3	0.0	0.2
17 085	...	6	Jo Daviess	1 557	22 289	1 681	14.3	1 557	21 821	1 589	14.0	98.7	0.2	0.1	0.2	0.0	0.3
17 087	...	9	Johnson	893	12 878	2 242	14.4	896	11 347	2 268	12.7	83.5	14.2	0.3	0.1	0.0	1.1
17 089	1600	0	Kane	1 348	404 119	146	299.8	1 349	317 471	159	235.3	79.3	5.8	0.3	1.8	0.0	10.6
17 091	3740	3	Kankakee	1 753	103 833	511	59.2	1 755	96 255	480	54.8	79.9	15.5	0.2	0.7	0.0	2.4
17 093	1600	1	Kendall	830	54 544	862	65.7	830	39 413	1 014	47.5	92.9	1.3	0.2	0.9	0.0	3.4
17 095	...	4	Knox	1 855	55 836	845	30.1	1 855	56 393	770	30.4	89.9	6.3	0.2	0.7	0.0	1.6
17 097	1600	0	Lake	1 159	644 356	84	556.0	1 160	516 418	90	445.2	80.1	6.9	0.3	3.9	0.0	6.7
17 099	...	4	La Salle	2 939	111 509	484	37.9	2 940	106 913	431	36.4	95.0	1.5	0.2	0.5	0.0	1.7
17 101	...	7	Lawrence	963	15 452	2 054	16.0	963	15 972	1 925	16.6	98.0	0.8	0.1	0.1	0.0	0.3
17 103	...	7	Lee	1 879	36 062	1 214	19.2	1 879	34 392	1 154	18.3	92.7	4.9	0.1	0.6	0.0	0.8
17 105	...	6	Livingston	2 703	39 678	1 120	14.7	2 703	39 301	1 017	14.5	92.3	5.2	0.2	0.3	0.0	1.2
17 107	...	6	Logan	1 601	31 183	1 372	19.5	1 601	30 798	1 250	19.2	91.7	6.6	0.2	0.5	0.0	0.4
17 109	...	5	McDonough	1 526	32 913	1 322	21.6	1 526	35 244	1 124	23.1	92.9	3.5	0.1	2.0	0.0	0.5
17 111	1600	0	McHenry	1 563	260 077	213	166.4	1 565	183 241	262	117.1	93.9	0.6	0.2	1.5	0.0	2.8
17 113	1040	3	McLean	3 065	150 433	357	49.1	3 066	129 180	358	42.1	89.2	6.2	0.2	2.1	0.0	1.0
17 115	2040	3	Macon	1 504	114 706	472	76.3	1 504	117 206	394	77.9	83.5	14.1	0.2	0.6	0.0	0.3
17 117	...	6	Macoupin	2 237	49 019	931	21.9	2 237	47 679	880	21.3	98.0	0.8	0.2	0.2	0.0	0.1
17 119	7040	0	Madison	1 878	258 941	216	137.9	1 878	249 238	200	132.7	90.2	7.3	0.3	0.6	0.0	0.5
17 121	...	7	Marion	1 482	41 691	1 063	28.1	1 482	41 561	969	28.0	94.0	3.8	0.2	0.6	0.0	0.2
17 123	...	6	Marshall	1 000	13 180	2 214	13.2	1 000	12 846	2 151	12.8	98.2	0.3	0.2	0.3	0.0	0.3
17 125	...	6	Mason	1 396	16 038	2 019	11.5	1 396	16 269	1 907	11.7	98.8	0.1	0.3	0.2	0.0	0.1
17 127	...	7	Massac	619	15 161	2 079	24.5	619	14 752	2 003	23.8	92.6	5.5	0.2	0.3	0.0	0.3
17 129	7880	3	Menard	814	12 486	2 266	15.3	814	11 164	2 280	13.7	98.8	0.4	0.2	0.2	0.0	0.2
17 131	...	6	Mercer	1 453	16 957	1 955	11.7	1 453	17 290	1 834	11.9	98.4	0.3	0.1	0.2	0.0	0.4
17 133	7040	1	Monroe	1 006	27 619	1 461	27.5	1 006	22 422	1 557	22.3	98.8	0.1	0.2	0.3	0.0	0.3
17 135	...	6	Montgomery	1 823	30 652	1 383	16.8	1 823	30 728	1 256	16.9	94.9	3.7	0.2	0.2	0.0	0.5
17 137	...	4	Morgan	1 473	36 616	1 198	24.9	1 473	36 397	1 093	24.7	92.3	5.4	0.2	0.5	0.0	0.7
17 139	...	6	Moultrie	869	14 287	2 141	16.4	869	13 930	2 064	16.0	98.9	0.2	0.2	0.1	0.0	0.1
17 141	6880	2	Ogle	1 965	51 032	908	26.0	1 966	45 957	904	23.4	95.3	0.4	0.2	0.4	0.0	2.5
17 143	6120	2	Peoria	1 605	183 433	298	114.3	1 605	182 827	263	113.9	79.4	16.1	0.2	1.7	0.0	0.9
17 145	...	7	Perry	1 142	23 094	1 639	20.2	1 142	21 412	1 610	18.7	89.6	8.0	0.2	0.3	0.0	1.1
17 147	...	6	Piatt	1 140	16 365	1 999	14.4	1 140	15 548	1 950	13.6	98.8	0.2	0.1	0.1	0.0	0.1
17 149	...	7	Pike	2 150	17 384	1 929	8.1	2 151	17 577	1 816	8.2	97.4	1.5	0.2	0.2	0.0	0.1
17 151	...	9	Pope	961	4 413	2 886	4.6	961	4 373	2 885	4.6	93.3	3.8	0.8	0.3	0.0	0.5
17 153	...	9	Pulaski	520	7 348	2 652	14.1	520	7 523	2 614	14.5	66.5	31.0	0.1	0.9	0.0	0.3
17 155	...	9	Putnam	414	6 086	2 773	14.7	414	5 730	2 784	13.8	97.6	0.6	0.3	0.3	0.0	0.6
17 157	...	6	Randolph	1 498	33 893	1 284	22.6	1 498	34 583	1 149	23.1	88.7	9.3	0.2	0.2	0.0	0.8
17 159	...	7	Richland	933	16 149	2 012	17.3	933	16 545	1 886	17.7	98.2	0.3	0.1	0.6	0.0	0.2
17 161	1960	2	Rock Island	1 105	149 374	361	135.2	1 105	148 723	318	134.6	85.5	7.5	0.3	1.0	0.0	3.8
17 163	7040	0	St. Clair	1 719	256 082	219	149.0	1 719	262 852	190	152.9	67.9	28.8	0.3	0.9	0.0	0.8
17 165	...	7	Saline	993	26 733	1 493	26.9	993	26 551	1 406	26.7	94.1	4.1	0.3	0.2	0.0	0.3
17 167	7880	3	Sangamon	2 249	188 951	292	84.0	2 249	178 386	273	79.3	87.4	9.7	0.2	1.1	0.0	0.4
17 169	...	7	Schuyler	1 133	7 189	2 667	6.3	1 133	7 498	2 616	6.6	98.8	0.2	0.1	0.1	0.0	0.2
17 171	...	9	Scott	650	5 537	2 814	8.5	650	5 644	2 789	8.7	99.5	0.0	0.1	0.1	0.0	0.0
17 173	...	6	Shelby	1 965	22 893	1 649	11.7	1 965	22 261	1 565	11.3	98.9	0.2	0.1	0.2	0.0	0.1
17 175	...	8	Stark	746	6 332	2 754	8.5	746	6 534	2 704	8.8	98.6	0.1	0.2	0.2	0.0	0.1
17 177	...	4	Stephenson	1 461	48 979	934	33.5	1 461	48 052	870	32.9	89.3	7.7	0.2	0.7	0.0	0.6
17 179	6120	2	Tazewell	1 681	128 485	420	76.4	1 681	123 692	372	73.6	97.4	0.9	0.3	0.5	0.0	0.3
17 181	...	7	Union	1 078	18 293	1 881	17.0	1 078	17 619	1 811	16.3	96.3	0.8	0.4	0.3	0.0	1.2
17 183	...	4	Vermilion	2 329	83 919	620	36.0	2 329	88 257	516	37.9	85.8	10.6	0.2	0.6	0.0	1.4
17 185	...	7	Wabash	579	12 937	2 237	22.3	579	13 111	2 131	22.6	97.9	0.4	0.2	0.4	0.0	0.3
17 187	...	7	Warren	1 405	18 735	1 858	13.3	1 405	19 181	1 721	13.7	95.6	1.6	0.2	0.3	0.1	1.1
17 189	...	6	Washington	1 457	15 148	2 082	10.4	1 457	14 965	1 990	10.3	98.6	0.3	0.2	0.2	0.0	0.1
17 191	...	7	Wayne	1 849	17 151	1 946	9.3	1 849	17 241	1 839	9.3	98.7	0.2	0.1	0.3	0.0	0.1
17 193	...	6	White	1 282	15 371	2 063	12.0	1 282	16 522	1 890	12.9	98.2	0.3	0.3	0.2	0.0	0.2
17 195	...	4	Whiteside	1 774	60 653	800	34.2	1 774	60 186	721	33.9	92.8	1.0	0.3	0.4	0.0	4.1
17 197	1600	0	Will	2 168	502 266	111	231.7	2 169	357 313	143	164.7	81.8	10.5	0.2	2.2	0.0	3.6
17 199	...	5	Williamson	1 097	61 296	794	55.9	1 099	57 733	753	52.5	95.3	2.5	0.3	0.5	0.0	0.4
17 201	6880	2	Winnebago	1 331	278 418	203	209.2	1 331	252 913	198	190.0	82.5	10.5	0.3	1.7	0.0	3.1
17 203	6120	2	Woodford	1 367	35 469	1 234	25.9	1 368	32 653	1 198	23.9	98.5	0.3	0.2	0.3	0.0	0.1

[1]MSA = Metropolitan Statistical Area. PMSA = Primary MSA. NECMA = New England County Metropolitan Area. See Appendix A for explanation of these concepts. See Appendix B for list of metropolitan areas identified by type, with component counties.
[2]County typology code from the Economic Research Service of USDA. See Appendix A for definition.
[3]Dry land or land partially or temporarily covered by water.

STATE County	Population and population characteristics, 2000 (cont'd)								Population and population characteristics, 1990				
	Race (percent) (cont'd)								Race (percent)				
	Race alone or in combination												
	Two or more races	White	Black	American Indian or Alaska Native	Asian	Native Hawaiian and other Pacific Islander	Some other race	Hispanic[1]	White	Black or African American	American Indian or Alaska Native	Asian and Pacific Islander	Hispanic[1]
	15	16	17	18	19	20	21	22	23	24	25	26	27
ILLINOIS—Cont'd													
Jackson	1.8	82.3	13.7	0.9	3.4	0.1	1.4	2.4	85.1	10.4	0.2	3.6	1.8
Jasper	0.3	99.4	0.1	0.2	0.3	0.0	0.2	0.5	99.7	0.0	0.1	0.2	0.3
Jefferson	1.2	90.9	8.2	0.7	0.7	0.0	0.6	1.3	94.2	5.2	0.2	0.3	0.4
Jersey	0.7	98.8	0.7	0.6	0.4	0.0	0.3	0.7	99.1	0.5	0.2	0.2	0.5
Jo Daviess	0.5	99.2	0.3	0.4	0.3	0.0	0.4	1.5	99.6	0.1	0.1	0.1	0.4
Johnson	0.8	84.3	14.3	0.7	0.3	0.1	1.3	2.9	90.2	9.2	0.2	0.1	1.7
Kane	2.2	81.2	6.3	0.6	2.2	0.1	11.9	23.7	84.9	6.0	0.2	1.4	13.7
Kankakee	1.4	81.1	16.0	0.6	0.9	0.1	2.9	4.8	83.3	15.0	0.2	0.7	2.0
Kendall	1.3	94.1	1.6	0.5	1.1	0.1	4.0	7.5	96.5	0.5	0.2	0.6	4.6
Knox	1.4	91.1	7.0	0.6	0.8	0.0	1.9	3.4	92.9	5.1	0.2	0.6	2.5
Lake	2.0	81.8	7.5	0.6	4.4	0.1	7.6	14.4	87.3	6.7	0.2	2.4	7.5
La Salle	1.0	96.0	1.8	0.5	0.7	0.0	2.1	5.2	97.1	1.1	0.2	0.5	3.0
Lawrence	0.7	98.7	1.0	0.5	0.2	0.0	0.4	0.9	98.7	0.9	0.2	0.1	0.4
Lee	0.9	93.6	5.2	0.5	0.8	0.0	1.0	3.2	94.6	3.6	0.2	0.5	2.1
Livingston	0.8	93.1	5.3	0.4	0.5	0.0	1.5	2.7	93.0	5.4	0.2	0.3	2.1
Logan	0.6	92.2	6.8	0.4	0.7	0.1	0.5	1.6	94.9	4.2	0.1	0.5	1.1
McDonough	1.0	93.8	3.8	0.5	2.3	0.1	0.6	1.5	93.6	3.6	0.2	2.3	1.0
McHenry	1.1	94.9	0.8	0.4	1.7	0.1	3.2	7.5	97.6	0.2	0.2	0.7	3.3
McLean	1.4	90.4	6.8	0.5	2.3	0.1	1.3	2.5	93.7	4.3	0.2	1.3	1.3
Macon	1.4	84.7	14.9	0.5	0.7	0.1	0.5	1.0	87.2	12.1	0.1	0.4	0.5
Macoupin	0.6	98.6	0.9	0.5	0.3	0.1	0.3	0.6	98.7	0.8	0.2	0.2	0.4
Madison	1.1	91.2	7.7	0.7	0.8	0.1	0.7	1.5	92.4	6.5	0.3	0.6	1.1
Marion	1.1	95.0	4.3	0.7	0.7	0.1	0.4	0.9	95.4	3.7	0.3	0.6	0.6
Marshall	0.7	98.9	0.5	0.5	0.4	0.0	0.4	1.0	99.3	0.1	0.2	0.2	0.6
Mason	0.5	99.3	0.2	0.6	0.3	0.0	0.2	0.5	99.5	0.0	0.2	0.2	0.4
Massac	1.2	93.6	6.0	0.7	0.4	0.0	0.4	0.8	93.6	5.9	0.3	0.2	0.3
Menard	0.4	99.0	0.5	0.4	0.3	0.0	0.3	0.8	99.4	0.1	0.3	0.1	0.3
Mercer	0.7	99.0	0.4	0.4	0.3	0.0	0.5	1.3	99.2	0.2	0.2	0.2	0.6
Monroe	0.5	99.2	0.1	0.4	0.4	0.0	0.3	0.7	99.3	0.1	0.2	0.3	0.7
Montgomery	0.5	95.3	3.8	0.4	0.3	0.1	0.6	1.1	97.5	1.8	0.2	0.2	0.8
Morgan	1.0	93.2	5.8	0.5	0.6	0.0	0.8	1.4	95.0	4.1	0.1	0.4	0.8
Moultrie	0.5	99.4	0.3	0.4	0.2	0.1	0.2	0.5	99.7	0.1	0.2	0.1	0.3
Ogle	1.1	96.3	0.7	0.5	0.6	0.1	2.9	6.0	97.7	0.1	0.2	0.3	3.0
Peoria	1.7	80.8	17.1	0.6	1.9	0.1	1.3	2.1	84.4	13.6	0.2	1.2	1.4
Perry	0.8	90.3	8.3	0.6	0.4	0.1	1.2	1.8	97.6	1.9	0.1	0.3	0.6
Piatt	0.6	99.4	0.3	0.4	0.2	0.0	0.2	0.6	99.7	0.1	0.1	0.1	0.2
Pike	0.6	97.9	1.6	0.5	0.4	0.0	0.2	0.5	99.6	0.0	0.1	0.2	0.4
Pope	1.4	94.6	4.1	1.8	0.4	0.0	0.6	0.9	93.1	6.1	0.3	0.1	1.3
Pulaski	1.1	67.4	31.7	0.6	1.0	0.0	0.6	1.5	66.9	32.8	0.1	0.1	0.4
Putnam	0.5	98.1	0.9	0.5	0.3	0.1	0.8	2.8	98.0	0.2	0.1	0.1	2.4
Randolph	0.8	89.4	9.6	0.5	0.4	0.1	0.9	1.5	91.2	8.2	0.2	0.2	1.0
Richland	0.6	98.7	0.4	0.3	0.8	0.1	0.3	0.8	99.4	0.1	0.1	0.3	0.4
Rock Island	1.9	87.2	8.3	0.7	1.3	0.1	4.5	8.6	89.7	7.1	0.2	0.7	5.4
St. Clair	1.3	69.0	29.3	0.6	1.3	0.1	1.1	2.2	71.5	27.1	0.2	0.8	1.5
Saline	1.0	95.0	4.5	0.7	0.3	0.0	0.5	1.0	95.9	3.5	0.2	0.2	0.5
Sangamon	1.2	88.5	10.3	0.6	1.3	0.1	0.6	1.1	90.8	8.1	0.2	0.8	0.7
Schuyler	0.5	99.3	0.2	0.5	0.2	0.0	0.3	0.5	99.7	0.0	0.1	0.1	0.1
Scott	0.2	99.7	0.1	0.3	0.1	0.0	0.1	0.2	99.8	0.0	0.1	0.1	0.3
Shelby	0.4	99.3	0.2	0.4	0.3	0.0	0.2	0.5	99.7	0.1	0.1	0.1	0.2
Stark	0.8	99.4	0.1	0.7	0.3	0.0	0.3	0.9	99.4	0.1	0.1	0.3	0.5
Stephenson	1.5	90.7	8.5	0.4	0.9	0.1	1.0	1.5	92.7	6.4	0.1	0.6	0.6
Tazewell	0.7	98.1	1.0	0.6	0.6	0.0	0.4	1.0	99.1	0.2	0.2	0.3	0.7
Union	1.0	97.3	1.0	0.9	0.4	0.1	1.5	2.6	98.3	0.7	0.2	0.3	1.0
Vermilion	1.3	87.0	11.2	0.6	0.7	0.0	1.9	3.0	89.5	8.9	0.2	0.6	1.6
Wabash	0.8	98.7	0.6	0.5	0.6	0.1	0.3	0.7	98.8	0.3	0.1	0.6	0.6
Warren	1.1	96.6	2.1	0.4	0.5	0.1	1.5	2.7	97.1	1.9	0.1	0.4	1.1
Washington	0.5	99.1	0.4	0.5	0.3	0.0	0.2	0.7	99.3	0.3	0.2	0.2	0.3
Wayne	0.5	99.2	0.3	0.5	0.4	0.0	0.1	0.6	99.4	0.1	0.2	0.3	0.4
White	0.9	99.1	0.4	0.9	0.3	0.0	0.2	0.7	99.2	0.2	0.2	0.2	0.4
Whiteside	1.4	94.1	1.4	0.6	0.6	0.0	4.8	8.8	94.9	0.7	0.1	0.3	7.4
Will	1.6	83.2	11.0	0.6	2.6	0.1	4.3	8.7	84.9	10.7	0.2	1.3	5.6
Williamson	1.0	96.3	2.8	0.7	0.7	0.1	0.5	1.2	97.2	2.0	0.2	0.4	0.8
Winnebago	1.9	84.1	11.2	0.7	2.0	0.1	3.8	6.9	88.0	9.2	0.3	1.2	3.1
Woodford	0.6	99.1	0.4	0.5	0.4	0.1	0.3	0.7	99.2	0.2	0.2	0.3	0.7

[1] Hispanic persons may be of any race.

Table B. States and Counties

STATE County	Population and population characteristics, 2000										
	Age (percent)										
	Under 5 years	5 to 17 years	18 to 24 years	25 to 34 years	35 to 44 years	45 to 54 years	55 to 64 years	65 to 74 years	75 years and over	Median age (years)	Percent Female
	28	29	30	31	32	33	34	35	36	37	38
ILLINOIS—Cont'd											
Jackson	5.0	14.2	26.0	14.2	11.7	10.9	6.9	5.5	5.5	27.5	49.0
Jasper	5.7	20.2	8.6	10.8	15.7	13.3	9.3	7.0	8.6	38.1	50.6
Jefferson	5.9	18.4	8.8	13.1	15.3	13.8	9.5	7.4	7.9	37.6	49.0
Jersey	5.9	19.5	9.9	11.3	16.3	13.1	9.7	7.5	6.9	37.3	51.1
Jo Daviess	5.6	17.6	6.7	10.6	14.7	14.7	12.1	9.6	8.3	41.6	49.9
Johnson	4.7	13.7	11.4	17.4	16.7	12.4	10.3	7.6	6.0	36.7	40.2
Kane	8.7	21.5	9.1	15.0	16.8	13.2	7.2	4.4	4.0	32.2	49.7
Kankakee	7.0	20.1	9.7	12.9	15.3	13.2	8.8	6.7	6.3	35.2	51.1
Kendall	8.0	21.5	7.5	14.6	17.8	13.8	8.3	4.5	4.0	34.1	50.3
Knox	5.8	16.3	9.8	12.0	14.4	14.1	10.0	8.5	9.1	39.4	50.2
Lake	8.2	21.2	8.9	13.7	17.9	13.9	7.7	4.8	3.8	33.8	49.7
La Salle	6.3	18.8	8.1	11.9	16.1	13.1	9.2	7.9	8.5	38.1	50.5
Lawrence	5.5	17.2	7.6	11.3	14.8	13.4	10.0	9.3	10.8	40.8	52.4
Lee	5.5	18.7	7.8	12.9	17.4	14.0	9.0	7.5	7.2	37.9	48.7
Livingston	6.0	19.0	8.2	13.1	16.4	13.2	8.7	7.4	7.9	37.3	50.6
Logan	5.4	16.5	11.6	13.5	16.1	12.9	8.9	7.1	7.9	37.0	50.0
McDonough	4.4	13.3	27.6	10.3	11.2	11.2	7.9	6.7	7.5	29.0	51.2
McHenry	8.1	22.1	7.1	14.1	19.3	13.8	7.5	4.4	3.7	34.2	49.8
McLean	6.5	17.0	18.6	14.2	15.0	12.2	6.9	5.0	4.7	30.5	51.7
Macon	6.4	18.2	9.8	11.6	14.8	14.4	9.6	7.9	7.3	38.0	52.3
Macoupin	5.7	18.9	8.3	11.3	15.3	13.5	9.4	8.4	9.1	38.9	51.3
Madison	6.3	18.6	9.4	12.9	16.0	13.4	9.1	7.4	6.8	36.9	51.8
Marion	6.4	19.1	8.1	11.5	15.0	13.3	10.0	7.8	8.8	38.4	51.8
Marshall	5.5	18.0	7.2	11.1	14.5	14.4	10.5	9.0	9.8	40.9	51.0
Mason	5.7	18.7	7.7	11.3	15.0	13.7	10.5	8.4	8.9	39.5	51.0
Massac	6.2	16.8	7.9	12.2	15.3	13.0	10.8	8.6	9.2	39.6	52.2
Menard	5.8	20.8	6.8	11.2	17.7	14.6	10.0	6.6	6.6	38.0	51.0
Mercer	5.7	19.1	7.3	11.0	15.6	14.5	10.9	7.9	8.1	39.5	50.8
Monroe	6.5	19.9	7.4	12.0	18.6	13.5	8.7	7.2	6.2	37.5	50.8
Montgomery	5.8	18.0	8.3	13.4	16.0	12.8	8.9	8.0	9.0	38.1	48.4
Morgan	5.4	17.3	11.1	11.8	15.3	13.6	9.7	7.6	8.0	37.8	50.3
Moultrie	6.5	19.2	7.9	11.0	14.9	13.3	9.5	8.2	9.5	38.7	51.8
Ogle	6.3	21.1	7.2	12.0	16.8	13.6	9.5	6.9	6.5	37.2	50.4
Peoria	6.9	18.3	10.4	13.2	14.4	13.8	8.9	7.0	7.1	36.0	51.9
Perry	5.3	16.7	10.3	13.5	15.6	13.2	9.3	7.8	8.2	37.6	46.9
Piatt	6.2	19.0	6.8	10.7	16.9	14.5	10.4	7.9	7.6	39.6	51.2
Pike	5.8	18.3	7.8	11.6	14.1	13.4	9.8	8.6	10.6	39.8	50.5
Pope	4.8	16.7	10.2	9.7	14.1	14.0	12.7	9.4	8.3	41.1	49.4
Pulaski	6.1	21.0	8.3	10.6	14.7	12.6	9.1	8.6	8.8	37.7	52.2
Putnam	5.9	19.2	7.0	10.7	16.0	14.1	11.2	8.2	7.6	39.6	50.6
Randolph	5.4	16.7	9.6	14.2	16.2	13.4	8.9	7.4	8.2	37.6	46.2
Richland	6.1	18.4	8.3	11.4	15.2	12.5	10.4	8.8	8.8	39.1	51.7
Rock Island	6.4	17.4	10.0	12.3	15.0	14.1	9.7	7.6	7.5	37.8	51.4
St. Clair	6.9	20.8	8.9	12.9	16.3	13.1	8.0	7.0	6.2	35.3	52.2
Saline	5.8	18.2	8.2	10.9	14.2	13.1	10.5	9.1	9.9	39.9	51.9
Sangamon	6.4	18.5	8.1	13.3	16.5	14.8	8.9	6.8	6.7	37.3	52.3
Schuyler	5.8	17.3	7.1	11.4	14.9	13.9	10.3	9.5	9.9	40.9	50.4
Scott	6.3	18.8	7.8	11.3	16.0	13.0	10.2	8.2	8.3	38.8	51.7
Shelby	5.8	19.2	7.6	11.0	15.2	13.1	10.3	8.9	8.9	39.3	50.6
Stark	6.3	18.8	6.8	11.2	14.0	13.6	10.2	8.7	10.4	39.9	51.8
Stephenson	6.1	19.1	7.6	11.9	15.7	13.4	9.9	8.0	8.4	38.5	51.8
Tazewell	6.2	18.2	8.1	12.8	15.8	14.4	9.6	8.0	6.9	38.1	50.8
Union	5.2	17.9	7.5	11.4	15.3	13.8	11.4	8.2	9.3	40.3	51.4
Vermilion	6.6	18.3	8.4	12.4	14.8	13.5	9.9	8.2	7.8	38.0	50.8
Wabash	5.7	18.5	9.1	10.8	15.5	14.1	9.2	8.4	8.6	39.0	51.2
Warren	5.6	17.5	12.4	10.7	13.9	13.8	9.8	8.0	8.3	37.8	51.6
Washington	5.7	19.7	7.6	11.2	16.1	13.4	9.6	7.9	8.9	38.8	50.6
Wayne	6.0	17.7	7.9	11.4	14.4	13.0	10.8	9.2	9.6	39.9	51.3
White	5.1	16.4	7.7	10.2	15.0	13.6	11.0	9.7	11.2	42.0	52.3
Whiteside	6.4	18.6	8.2	11.8	15.2	14.0	9.8	8.1	8.0	38.5	51.0
Will	8.4	21.6	8.1	14.8	18.1	13.2	7.4	4.5	3.8	33.3	50.1
Williamson	6.0	17.0	8.6	12.9	15.0	13.6	10.5	8.1	8.4	38.8	51.6
Winnebago	7.1	19.3	8.4	13.8	16.0	13.8	8.9	6.6	6.1	35.9	51.1
Woodford	6.6	20.1	8.7	10.6	15.6	14.6	9.1	6.8	8.0	37.8	51.2

Table B. States and Counties

STATE County	Under 5 years	5 to 17 years	18 to 24 years	25 to 34 years	35 to 44 years	45 to 54 years	55 to 64 years	65 to 74 years	75 years and over	Percent Female	2000	1990	1980	1990–2000	1980–1990
	39	40	41	42	43	44	45	46	47	48	49	50	51	52	53
ILLINOIS—Cont'd															
Jackson	5.5	13.5	28.3	16.1	11.9	7.5	6.4	5.8	5.0	48.6	59 612	61 067	61 649	-2.4	-0.9
Jasper	7.3	21.0	7.5	15.1	12.9	9.6	9.0	9.3	8.3	51.1	10 117	10 609	11 318	-4.6	-6.3
Jefferson	7.4	19.5	8.4	15.0	14.4	10.0	9.0	9.1	7.4	52.0	40 045	37 020	36 558	8.2	1.3
Jersey	6.9	19.9	10.7	15.3	13.7	10.4	9.2	7.8	6.0	51.1	21 668	20 539	20 538	5.5	0.0
Jo Daviess	6.4	19.8	7.8	14.2	13.9	10.9	10.3	9.7	7.0	50.7	22 289	21 821	23 520	2.1	-7.2
Johnson	4.8	15.0	10.1	18.6	15.5	11.2	9.3	8.7	6.8	42.2	12 878	11 347	9 624	13.5	17.9
Kane	8.8	21.0	9.9	17.9	16.1	10.0	7.0	5.3	4.0	50.4	404 119	317 471	278 405	27.3	14.0
Kankakee	7.6	20.6	9.9	15.3	14.3	10.1	8.6	7.9	5.8	51.6	103 833	96 255	102 926	7.9	-6.5
Kendall	7.7	22.3	9.1	16.1	16.9	12.1	7.2	5.3	3.4	50.0	54 544	39 413	37 202	38.4	5.9
Knox	6.0	17.9	9.4	14.4	14.7	10.5	10.0	9.2	7.9	51.0	55 836	56 393	61 607	-1.0	-8.5
Lake	8.5	19.1	10.9	18.0	16.9	10.8	7.5	5.1	3.3	49.4	644 356	516 418	440 388	24.8	17.3
La Salle	6.8	18.7	8.8	15.1	13.5	10.2	9.7	9.4	7.8	51.1	111 509	106 913	112 033	4.3	-4.6
Lawrence	6.0	17.7	7.7	14.2	13.2	9.8	10.3	10.1	10.8	53.2	15 452	15 972	17 807	-3.3	-10.3
Lee	6.9	19.0	8.6	16.9	14.8	10.1	9.1	8.0	6.7	49.6	36 062	34 392	36 328	4.9	-5.3
Livingston	6.6	18.3	8.7	17.5	14.3	9.8	8.9	8.1	7.7	49.8	39 678	39 301	41 381	1.0	-5.0
Logan	6.4	17.4	10.2	16.7	14.2	10.3	8.8	8.3	7.7	49.9	31 183	30 798	31 802	1.3	-3.2
McDonough	5.0	13.4	28.5	12.9	11.0	8.1	7.4	7.1	6.6	50.3	32 913	35 244	37 467	-6.6	-5.9
McHenry	8.6	20.5	8.4	18.0	17.3	10.9	6.9	5.4	4.0	50.0	260 077	183 241	147 897	41.9	23.9
McLean	6.6	16.5	20.7	16.3	14.0	8.6	6.9	5.7	4.8	52.3	150 433	129 180	119 149	16.5	8.4
Macon	6.8	19.1	9.3	14.8	14.9	10.8	9.6	8.2	6.3	52.3	114 706	117 206	131 375	-2.1	-10.8
Macoupin	6.4	19.4	8.7	14.0	13.6	9.8	10.0	9.5	8.5	52.1	49 019	47 679	49 384	2.8	-3.5
Madison	7.2	18.4	9.7	16.5	14.5	10.4	9.5	7.9	6.0	52.0	258 941	249 238	247 661	3.9	0.6
Marion	7.0	19.6	8.3	14.9	13.6	10.3	9.2	9.0	8.0	52.4	41 691	41 561	43 523	0.3	-4.5
Marshall	5.9	19.3	7.9	13.0	14.0	10.7	9.7	10.5	9.0	51.8	13 180	12 846	14 479	2.6	-11.3
Mason	6.6	19.4	8.0	13.9	13.9	11.0	9.7	9.6	7.9	51.3	16 038	16 269	19 492	-1.4	-16.5
Massac	5.8	18.0	8.0	14.6	12.8	10.9	10.6	10.3	9.0	53.0	15 161	14 752	14 990	2.8	-1.6
Menard	6.9	20.6	7.0	14.9	15.6	11.1	8.9	7.7	7.4	51.9	12 486	11 164	11 700	11.8	-4.6
Mercer	6.6	20.0	7.8	14.1	14.5	11.6	9.3	8.8	7.4	51.5	16 957	17 290	19 286	-1.9	-10.3
Monroe	7.3	19.4	8.4	16.8	14.4	10.7	9.5	7.2	6.2	50.8	27 619	22 422	20 117	23.2	11.5
Montgomery	6.6	18.8	8.3	15.8	13.6	9.4	9.2	9.6	8.7	50.2	30 652	30 728	31 686	-0.2	-3.0
Morgan	6.3	18.1	11.0	15.6	13.8	10.2	9.2	8.3	7.5	51.4	36 616	36 397	37 502	0.6	-2.9
Moultrie	6.9	19.4	7.2	14.0	13.7	10.3	9.3	9.1	10.1	52.4	14 287	13 930	14 546	2.6	-4.2
Ogle	7.3	20.1	8.3	16.0	14.5	10.9	8.9	7.7	6.4	51.0	51 032	45 957	46 338	11.0	-0.8
Peoria	7.0	19.0	10.8	15.2	14.7	10.2	8.9	7.9	6.3	52.1	183 433	182 827	200 466	0.3	-8.8
Perry	6.8	19.6	8.6	14.4	14.2	10.0	9.4	9.1	7.9	51.9	23 094	21 412	21 714	7.9	-1.4
Piatt	6.2	19.5	7.3	15.2	15.0	11.7	9.7	8.6	6.8	51.3	16 365	15 548	16 581	5.3	-6.2
Pike	6.4	18.4	7.9	13.2	13.3	9.9	10.2	10.6	10.0	51.9	17 384	17 577	18 896	-1.1	-7.0
Pope	5.1	18.0	12.3	13.6	12.6	10.7	9.4	10.1	8.3	46.5	4 413	4 373	4 404	0.9	-0.7
Pulaski	7.2	21.6	7.8	13.7	11.5	9.7	9.7	9.9	8.9	53.4	7 348	7 523	8 840	-2.3	-14.9
Putnam	6.9	19.3	7.8	14.7	14.1	12.2	9.5	9.0	6.4	49.8	6 086	5 730	6 085	6.2	-5.8
Randolph	6.1	18.2	9.8	17.7	14.6	9.8	8.5	7.9	7.4	46.7	33 893	34 583	35 652	-2.0	-3.0
Richland	6.8	19.2	8.0	15.2	12.7	10.8	9.9	8.9	8.6	52.3	16 149	16 545	17 587	-2.4	-5.9
Rock Island	6.9	18.6	9.6	15.2	14.6	10.6	9.6	8.5	6.5	51.9	149 374	148 723	166 759	0.4	-10.8
St. Clair	8.0	20.5	9.9	16.8	14.2	9.2	8.8	7.2	5.5	52.2	256 082	262 852	267 531	-2.6	-1.7
Saline	6.1	18.1	8.1	13.5	13.0	10.7	10.1	10.5	9.9	52.8	26 733	26 551	28 448	0.7	-6.7
Sangamon	7.2	18.3	8.7	17.1	16.0	10.3	8.7	7.5	6.3	52.9	188 951	178 386	176 070	5.9	1.3
Schuyler	6.0	18.8	7.7	14.1	13.5	10.3	10.3	10.1	9.2	51.3	7 189	7 498	8 365	-4.1	-10.4
Scott	6.5	19.7	7.7	14.9	13.1	10.5	9.7	8.9	8.9	52.2	5 537	5 644	6 142	-1.9	-8.1
Shelby	6.8	19.0	8.0	14.4	13.2	10.5	10.2	9.8	8.1	50.8	22 893	22 261	23 923	2.8	-6.9
Stark	6.2	19.5	7.1	13.6	13.5	10.7	10.1	10.2	9.2	52.0	6 332	6 534	7 389	-3.1	-11.6
Stephenson	7.1	18.7	8.7	15.5	14.1	10.7	9.2	8.8	7.1	51.7	48 979	48 052	49 536	1.9	-3.0
Tazewell	6.8	19.6	8.7	15.2	15.3	11.1	10.0	7.4	5.8	51.5	128 485	123 692	132 078	3.9	-6.3
Union	6.1	17.1	8.2	14.1	14.2	11.5	9.8	9.9	9.0	51.3	18 293	17 619	17 765	3.8	-0.8
Vermilion	6.7	19.2	8.4	15.0	14.4	10.6	9.8	9.1	6.8	51.3	83 919	88 257	95 222	-4.9	-7.3
Wabash	6.5	19.5	9.1	15.0	14.2	9.9	9.7	8.9	7.3	52.0	12 937	13 111	13 713	-1.3	-4.4
Warren	6.4	19.5	10.4	13.5	13.5	10.2	9.3	9.1	8.2	51.8	18 735	19 181	21 943	-2.3	-12.6
Washington	6.7	19.6	7.5	14.9	13.4	10.0	9.3	9.8	8.8	51.3	15 148	14 965	15 472	1.2	-3.3
Wayne	6.3	18.2	8.4	14.0	12.6	10.9	10.2	10.2	9.3	51.9	17 151	17 241	18 059	-0.5	-4.5
White	6.1	17.6	7.0	14.4	13.2	10.4	10.5	10.7	9.9	52.9	15 371	16 522	17 864	-7.0	-7.5
Whiteside	7.0	19.9	8.7	15.0	14.4	10.6	9.7	8.4	6.5	51.3	60 653	60 186	65 970	0.8	-8.8
Will	8.2	21.6	10.0	17.4	16.8	10.5	6.8	5.1	3.5	50.1	502 266	357 313	324 460	40.6	10.1
Williamson	6.4	17.6	9.0	15.3	14.5	11.1	9.2	9.4	7.5	51.9	61 296	57 733	56 538	6.2	2.1
Winnebago	7.6	18.6	9.5	17.0	15.3	10.6	8.8	7.4	5.3	51.5	278 418	252 913	250 884	10.1	0.8
Woodford	7.2	21.7	8.4	14.1	15.6	10.4	8.6	7.4	6.7	51.1	35 469	32 653	33 320	8.6	-2.0

Table B. States and Counties

STATE County	Total population	In households (percent) Total in households	Householder	Spouse	Child Total	Child Own child under 18 years	Other relatives Total	Other relatives Under 18 years	Nonrelatives Total	Nonrelatives Unmarried partner	In group quarters (percent) Total in group quarters	Institutionalized population Correctional institutions	Institutionalized population Nursing homes	Institutionalized population Other institutions	Noninstitutionalized population College dormitories	Noninstitutionalized population Military quarters	Other
	54	55	56	57	58	59	60	61	62	63	64	65	66	67	68	69	70
ILLINOIS—Cont'd																	
Jackson	59 612	89.6	40.6	16.0	21.5	17.3	2.7	1.0	8.8	2.1	10.4	0.5	0.6	0.5	8.4	0.0	0.4
Jasper	10 117	99.2	38.8	24.2	31.7	24.7	2.0	0.9	2.5	1.6	0.8	0.1	0.7	0.0	0.0	0.0	0.0
Jefferson	40 045	93.6	38.4	21.2	27.6	22.0	2.9	1.4	3.5	1.8	6.4	5.0	0.8	0.3	0.0	0.0	0.3
Jersey	21 668	95.9	37.4	22.5	30.4	23.5	2.7	1.1	3.0	1.7	4.1	0.0	1.4	0.3	2.3	0.0	0.1
Jo Daviess	22 289	99.1	41.4	24.1	27.7	21.9	2.3	0.8	3.6	1.8	0.9	0.1	0.7	0.0	0.0	0.0	0.2
Johnson	12 878	78.8	32.5	20.2	21.2	16.7	2.7	1.2	2.1	1.2	21.2	20.5	0.4	0.0	0.0	0.0	0.3
Kane	404 119	98.4	33.1	20.3	34.1	27.3	6.5	2.2	4.3	1.6	1.6	0.2	0.6	0.4	0.2	0.0	0.3
Kankakee	103 833	96.1	36.8	19.4	30.8	24.2	4.5	2.1	4.5	2.1	3.9	0.2	1.2	0.9	1.0	0.0	0.6
Kendall	54 544	99.6	34.5	23.7	34.9	27.7	3.6	1.4	3.0	1.4	0.4	0.1	0.3	0.0	0.0	0.0	0.0
Knox	55 836	92.2	39.5	20.3	25.1	19.8	3.0	1.4	4.3	2.2	7.8	3.3	1.6	0.1	1.9	0.0	0.9
Lake	644 356	96.7	33.6	21.2	33.2	27.4	4.9	1.5	3.8	1.4	3.3	0.1	0.5	0.3	0.3	1.6	0.4
La Salle	111 509	97.1	38.9	21.7	30.0	23.3	3.0	1.3	3.5	1.8	2.9	1.5	1.1	0.0	0.0	0.0	0.3
Lawrence	15 452	96.2	40.8	22.4	26.7	20.8	2.9	1.4	3.4	1.9	3.8	0.1	3.1	0.0	0.0	0.0	0.7
Lee	36 062	91.7	36.8	20.5	28.1	22.4	2.3	1.1	4.0	2.1	8.3	6.3	1.3	0.0	0.0	0.0	0.7
Livingston	39 678	90.9	36.2	20.6	28.2	23.2	2.4	1.1	3.5	1.7	9.1	6.7	1.3	0.1	0.0	0.0	1.0
Logan	31 183	86.3	35.6	19.7	25.3	20.2	2.3	1.1	3.4	1.6	13.7	7.7	1.4	1.3	3.0	0.0	0.3
McDonough	32 913	85.5	37.6	17.7	20.7	16.5	1.8	0.7	7.7	1.7	14.5	0.1	1.1	0.0	13.2	0.0	0.1
McHenry	260 077	99.4	34.4	22.9	34.9	28.7	3.7	1.1	3.6	1.5	0.6	0.1	0.3	0.0	0.0	0.0	0.2
McLean	150 433	92.5	37.7	19.2	26.3	22.1	2.3	0.9	6.9	1.8	7.5	0.1	0.6	0.1	6.5	0.0	0.2
Macon	114 706	96.9	40.6	20.6	28.2	22.1	3.6	1.8	4.3	1.9	3.1	0.5	0.9	0.1	1.4	0.0	0.3
Macoupin	49 019	97.6	39.3	22.8	29.1	22.7	2.9	1.4	3.4	1.9	2.4	0.1	1.6	0.0	0.7	0.0	0.1
Madison	258 941	97.8	39.4	20.9	29.7	22.7	3.6	1.6	4.2	2.1	2.2	0.1	0.9	0.1	0.8	0.0	0.3
Marion	41 691	97.7	39.9	21.2	29.2	22.9	3.7	1.8	3.7	1.9	2.3	0.1	1.5	0.6	0.0	0.0	0.2
Marshall	13 180	97.9	39.6	24.1	28.7	22.1	2.2	0.8	3.3	1.6	2.1	0.0	1.9	0.0	0.0	0.0	0.1
Mason	16 038	98.6	39.8	23.2	28.6	22.2	2.9	1.4	4.0	1.9	1.4	0.1	1.0	0.0	0.0	0.0	0.2
Massac	15 161	97.8	41.3	22.9	27.2	21.0	3.6	1.5	2.8	1.6	2.2	0.2	1.8	0.1	0.0	0.0	0.2
Menard	12 486	98.5	39.0	23.7	31.2	25.4	1.7	0.7	2.9	1.6	1.5	0.2	1.2	0.0	0.0	0.0	0.0
Mercer	16 957	98.7	39.1	24.8	29.2	22.8	2.7	1.4	2.9	1.6	1.3	0.2	1.0	0.1	0.0	0.0	0.1
Monroe	27 619	98.6	37.2	24.3	32.2	25.2	2.3	0.9	2.5	1.4	1.4	0.0	1.3	0.0	0.0	0.0	0.1
Montgomery	30 652	91.7	37.5	21.1	27.2	21.9	2.6	1.2	3.2	1.8	8.3	6.6	1.6	0.0	0.0	0.0	0.1
Morgan	36 616	90.8	38.3	20.2	25.8	20.6	2.5	1.1	4.0	1.9	9.2	2.9	1.5	1.4	2.8	0.0	0.6
Moultrie	14 287	96.7	37.8	24.0	30.1	24.1	2.4	1.1	2.5	1.4	3.3	0.1	2.7	0.0	0.0	0.0	0.6
Ogle	51 032	98.8	37.8	23.1	31.4	25.6	3.0	1.2	3.5	1.9	1.2	0.2	0.9	0.1	0.0	0.0	0.1
Peoria	183 433	96.2	39.7	19.3	28.6	22.4	3.8	1.9	4.9	2.0	3.8	0.4	1.0	0.2	1.4	0.0	0.7
Perry	23 094	89.4	36.8	20.4	26.3	20.1	2.8	1.3	3.1	1.7	10.6	9.5	0.8	0.1	0.0	0.0	0.2
Piatt	16 365	98.8	39.6	25.0	29.3	23.7	2.2	1.1	2.7	1.5	1.2	0.1	1.0	0.0	0.0	0.0	0.1
Pike	17 384	95.8	39.6	23.1	27.9	22.4	2.3	1.1	2.9	1.6	4.2	2.4	1.5	0.0	0.0	0.0	0.2
Pope	4 413	93.5	40.1	23.2	25.3	18.8	2.3	1.0	2.6	1.3	6.5	0.0	1.2	0.0	0.0	0.0	5.3
Pulaski	7 348	96.0	39.4	18.7	29.9	23.1	5.1	2.7	3.0	1.3	4.0	2.5	0.7	0.0	0.0	0.0	0.8
Putnam	6 086	99.8	39.7	24.6	29.9	23.1	2.5	1.1	3.0	1.5	0.2	0.0	0.1	0.0	0.0	0.0	0.0
Randolph	33 893	87.9	35.7	20.0	26.4	20.4	2.7	1.2	3.2	1.6	12.1	9.4	1.5	0.9	0.0	0.0	0.4
Richland	16 149	99.1	41.2	23.0	28.7	23.1	2.3	0.9	3.9	1.9	0.9	0.1	0.6	0.1	0.0	0.0	0.1
Rock Island	149 374	96.9	40.6	20.0	27.8	21.4	3.7	1.7	4.7	2.2	3.1	0.8	0.8	0.1	1.0	0.0	0.3
St. Clair	256 082	98.1	37.8	18.2	32.5	24.5	5.4	2.6	4.2	2.0	1.9	0.4	1.0	0.0	0.1	0.2	0.3
Saline	26 733	95.6	41.1	21.4	26.5	20.5	3.5	1.5	3.0	1.5	4.4	0.3	2.1	2.1	0.0	0.0	0.0
Sangamon	188 951	98.2	41.7	20.1	28.7	22.9	3.2	1.4	4.6	2.3	1.8	0.2	0.6	0.1	0.2	0.0	0.6
Schuyler	7 189	98.5	41.4	24.7	26.6	21.3	2.6	1.1	3.4	1.8	1.5	0.1	1.1	0.0	0.0	0.0	0.3
Scott	5 537	99.0	40.1	23.4	29.8	23.7	2.6	1.2	3.1	2.0	1.0	0.0	1.0	0.0	0.0	0.0	0.0
Shelby	22 893	98.7	39.6	24.2	29.7	23.2	2.6	1.3	2.7	1.4	1.3	0.0	1.1	0.0	0.0	0.0	0.2
Stark	6 332	98.2	39.9	23.9	29.4	23.7	2.3	1.0	2.6	1.5	1.8	0.0	1.8	0.0	0.0	0.0	0.0
Stephenson	48 979	98.3	40.4	22.4	29.1	23.4	2.6	1.2	3.8	2.0	1.7	0.2	1.1	0.0	0.0	0.0	0.4
Tazewell	128 485	97.4	39.2	23.2	28.9	22.6	2.6	1.2	3.5	1.8	2.6	1.3	0.8	0.1	0.0	0.0	0.3
Union	18 293	95.0	39.9	22.2	27.2	21.4	3.0	1.2	2.8	1.4	5.0	0.0	1.6	0.1	0.0	0.0	3.3
Vermilion	83 919	96.3	39.8	20.2	28.2	22.4	3.8	1.9	4.3	2.2	3.7	2.4	1.0	0.1	0.0	0.0	0.2
Wabash	12 937	98.6	40.1	23.0	29.2	22.4	2.8	1.4	3.5	1.8	1.4	0.0	1.2	0.0	0.0	0.0	0.1
Warren	18 735	93.5	38.2	21.6	27.1	21.2	2.7	1.2	3.8	2.0	6.5	0.0	1.3	0.1	4.7	0.0	0.3
Washington	15 148	98.3	38.6	23.8	30.6	23.7	2.3	0.9	3.0	1.6	1.7	0.0	1.2	0.2	0.0	0.0	0.3
Wayne	17 151	98.8	41.6	24.3	27.7	22.0	2.4	1.2	2.7	1.5	1.2	0.2	0.8	0.0	0.0	0.0	0.2
White	15 371	97.2	42.5	24.1	25.1	19.5	2.7	1.4	2.8	1.6	2.8	0.4	1.6	0.6	0.0	0.0	0.2
Whiteside	60 653	97.9	39.0	22.5	29.0	22.7	3.4	1.7	4.0	2.1	2.1	0.2	1.1	0.1	0.2	0.0	0.5
Will	502 266	98.1	33.4	21.6	35.2	27.7	4.6	1.8	3.3	1.5	1.9	0.9	0.5	0.1	0.2	0.0	0.2
Williamson	61 296	97.3	41.4	22.1	27.3	21.2	3.1	1.3	3.5	1.7	2.7	1.2	1.2	0.2	0.0	0.0	0.2
Winnebago	278 418	98.2	38.8	20.3	30.0	23.7	4.3	1.9	4.8	2.3	1.8	0.3	0.8	0.2	0.1	0.0	0.4
Woodford	35 469	96.9	36.1	24.3	32.2	25.4	2.0	0.9	2.3	1.1	3.1	0.0	1.8	0.0	1.1	0.0	0.1

Table B. States and Counties

STATE County	Total households	Family households Total	With own children under 18 years	Married couple Total	With own children under 18 years	Female householder[1] Total	With own children under 18 years	Nonfamily households Total	Householder living alone Total	65 years and over	Average household size	Average family size	1990 Total households	Female householder[1]	Householder living alone
	71	72	73	74	75	76	77	78	79	80	81	82	83	84	85
ILLINOIS—Cont'd															
Jackson	24 215	52.3	24.4	39.3	16.2	9.7	6.5	47.7	34.9	9.3	2.21	2.89	23 466	8.9	32.1
Jasper	3 930	72.5	32.9	62.3	27.0	7.0	4.1	27.5	24.7	13.2	2.55	3.06	3 962	6.2	22.8
Jefferson	15 374	68.7	31.1	55.3	22.7	9.9	6.2	31.3	27.6	13.0	2.44	2.96	14 606	10.1	26.3
Jersey	8 096	72.4	34.6	60.1	27.1	9.1	5.6	27.6	23.9	11.8	2.57	3.05	7 344	8.1	22.0
Jo Daviess	9 218	68.2	27.3	58.2	21.8	6.5	3.8	31.8	27.5	12.7	2.40	2.92	8 371	7.0	23.9
Johnson	4 183	73.0	30.6	62.3	24.6	7.1	4.2	27.0	24.2	12.1	2.43	2.87	3 725	6.7	24.1
Kane	133 901	75.8	41.6	61.2	33.3	10.0	6.1	24.2	19.6	6.7	2.97	3.43	107 176	9.9	19.9
Kankakee	38 182	70.1	34.4	52.8	23.8	13.1	8.2	29.9	24.9	10.4	2.61	3.12	34 623	12.5	24.3
Kendall	18 798	79.6	41.7	68.8	35.5	7.5	4.4	20.4	16.4	6.1	2.89	3.27	13 301	7.0	16.1
Knox	22 056	65.4	27.7	51.4	18.8	10.6	6.9	34.6	29.6	14.1	2.33	2.87	21 909	9.6	28.3
Lake	216 297	75.8	42.1	63.2	34.7	9.2	5.7	24.2	19.7	6.2	2.88	3.33	173 966	8.7	18.5
La Salle	43 417	68.7	31.7	55.7	24.0	9.2	5.5	31.3	27.4	13.3	2.49	3.04	41 284	8.7	26.4
Lawrence	6 309	67.4	28.7	54.9	21.3	9.0	5.2	32.6	29.2	15.0	2.36	2.89	6 320	9.0	27.4
Lee	13 253	69.0	32.2	55.9	23.8	9.3	6.0	31.0	26.5	12.1	2.49	3.01	12 475	8.0	25.1
Livingston	14 374	69.2	32.9	56.8	24.8	8.8	5.8	30.8	26.8	12.5	2.51	3.04	13 737	7.8	24.7
Logan	11 113	68.2	31.2	55.3	23.0	9.3	5.9	31.8	27.8	13.9	2.42	2.94	11 033	8.6	26.9
McDonough	12 360	57.4	24.3	47.1	18.1	7.5	4.6	42.6	31.8	12.1	2.28	2.87	12 255	7.5	29.6
McHenry	89 403	77.5	42.9	66.5	36.6	7.6	4.5	22.5	18.0	6.1	2.89	3.31	62 940	7.1	16.9
McLean	56 746	62.5	31.5	50.9	24.0	8.8	5.9	37.5	27.6	8.1	2.45	3.03	46 796	8.3	26.1
Macon	46 561	66.5	29.6	50.7	19.7	12.2	7.9	33.5	28.8	11.6	2.39	2.93	45 996	11.4	26.4
Macoupin	19 253	70.8	31.4	58.1	23.6	8.9	5.5	29.2	25.6	13.7	2.48	2.97	18 176	8.9	24.3
Madison	101 953	68.7	32.2	53.0	22.9	11.8	7.1	31.3	26.3	11.2	2.48	3.00	94 857	11.2	23.9
Marion	16 619	69.1	31.4	53.3	21.5	11.6	7.2	30.9	27.2	13.5	2.45	2.97	16 272	10.7	26.7
Marshall	5 225	71.2	29.6	60.8	23.6	6.7	4.0	28.8	25.0	12.6	2.47	2.95	4 900	6.0	23.6
Mason	6 389	71.4	30.5	58.4	22.7	9.0	5.3	28.6	24.9	13.0	2.48	2.93	6 342	7.9	24.2
Massac	6 261	69.0	29.9	55.5	22.2	10.0	5.9	31.0	28.0	14.1	2.37	2.88	5 908	10.2	26.7
Menard	4 873	72.9	36.1	60.7	27.7	9.1	6.3	27.1	23.8	10.3	2.52	2.99	4 199	8.0	22.0
Mercer	6 624	74.2	32.1	63.5	25.6	7.2	4.4	25.8	22.8	11.6	2.53	2.96	6 572	6.8	22.8
Monroe	10 275	75.7	37.7	65.3	31.7	7.3	4.1	24.3	21.3	9.6	2.65	3.09	8 189	6.4	21.0
Montgomery	11 507	68.9	31.9	56.1	23.7	8.9	5.7	31.1	27.8	14.7	2.44	2.97	11 480	8.0	25.8
Morgan	14 039	65.9	30.0	52.7	21.7	10.0	6.4	34.1	29.3	13.1	2.37	2.92	13 678	8.8	28.6
Moultrie	5 405	73.6	33.0	63.3	26.9	7.1	4.3	26.4	23.6	12.0	2.56	3.03	5 122	7.0	23.0
Ogle	19 278	73.5	35.5	61.3	27.7	8.3	5.4	26.5	22.5	9.8	2.62	3.07	17 132	7.1	22.2
Peoria	72 733	64.8	29.9	48.6	19.7	12.9	8.4	35.2	29.7	11.0	2.43	3.01	70 797	12.3	28.1
Perry	8 504	68.7	30.1	55.3	22.2	9.7	5.7	31.3	27.9	14.6	2.43	2.96	8 306	9.1	25.5
Piatt	6 475	73.0	32.6	63.3	26.8	6.8	4.4	27.0	23.7	11.8	2.50	2.96	5 934	6.5	21.7
Pike	6 876	69.5	30.5	58.5	24.1	7.8	4.5	30.5	27.8	16.1	2.42	2.94	7 016	6.9	26.5
Pope	1 769	69.0	27.5	57.8	21.0	7.6	4.9	31.0	27.9	13.3	2.33	2.84	1 611	7.3	26.3
Pulaski	2 893	67.1	31.2	47.4	19.7	15.8	9.5	32.9	30.0	15.5	2.44	3.03	2 957	14.1	29.4
Putnam	2 415	72.4	30.5	62.1	24.8	7.0	4.1	27.6	24.6	12.3	2.52	2.99	2 204	6.8	22.9
Randolph	12 084	69.2	31.3	56.0	23.4	9.2	5.6	30.8	26.9	13.8	2.46	2.99	11 949	8.3	25.3
Richland	6 660	68.1	30.5	55.8	24.2	8.8	5.9	31.9	27.7	13.9	2.40	2.92	6 503	8.1	26.0
Rock Island	60 712	64.5	28.9	49.1	19.4	11.6	7.5	35.5	30.2	12.5	2.38	2.97	59 317	11.5	28.6
St. Clair	96 810	69.5	34.5	48.1	21.9	17.1	10.3	30.5	25.9	10.3	2.59	3.13	95 333	16.4	24.4
Saline	10 992	65.8	28.9	51.9	21.1	10.2	5.9	34.2	31.3	16.0	2.32	2.90	10 839	10.0	30.1
Sangamon	78 722	63.4	30.5	48.2	21.0	11.7	7.5	36.6	31.0	10.6	2.36	2.97	72 146	11.3	29.4
Schuyler	2 975	69.6	28.7	59.7	23.1	7.1	3.9	30.4	27.3	13.7	2.38	2.87	3 002	7.0	25.1
Scott	2 222	70.3	33.8	58.3	26.5	8.3	5.1	29.7	26.1	13.8	2.47	2.98	2 190	8.4	24.3
Shelby	9 056	71.8	31.0	61.2	24.6	7.1	4.4	28.2	25.4	13.3	2.50	2.99	8 563	6.1	22.7
Stark	2 525	69.9	30.3	60.0	25.1	7.0	3.7	30.1	27.1	15.0	2.46	3.00	2 512	6.2	25.3
Stephenson	19 785	68.1	30.7	55.4	22.4	9.5	6.4	31.9	27.6	12.6	2.43	2.97	18 920	8.3	26.0
Tazewell	50 327	71.3	31.8	59.2	24.4	8.7	5.5	28.7	24.8	10.7	2.49	2.96	47 171	8.3	22.8
Union	7 290	68.2	30.3	55.6	22.8	9.5	5.8	31.8	28.4	14.9	2.38	2.93	6 838	8.0	27.0
Vermilion	33 406	66.8	30.1	50.6	19.9	12.2	7.8	33.2	28.9	13.5	2.42	2.96	34 072	11.2	27.0
Wabash	5 192	69.1	30.9	57.2	24.0	8.7	5.0	30.9	27.0	13.6	2.46	2.98	5 032	7.9	25.3
Warren	7 166	69.3	29.8	56.5	21.9	8.8	5.5	30.7	26.7	12.7	2.44	2.94	7 393	8.4	27.5
Washington	5 848	72.5	33.5	61.7	27.4	7.1	4.2	27.5	24.3	13.3	2.55	3.02	5 658	5.8	25.3
Wayne	7 143	69.6	29.8	58.3	23.0	8.3	5.1	30.4	27.6	14.8	2.37	2.88	6 935	7.1	25.4
White	6 534	67.0	26.8	56.6	20.7	7.6	4.5	33.0	29.8	16.6	2.29	2.82	6 845	7.3	28.0
Whiteside	23 684	70.8	31.5	57.5	23.2	9.5	6.1	29.2	25.1	11.8	2.51	2.99	22 740	8.3	23.6
Will	167 542	78.2	42.7	64.8	35.3	9.6	5.5	21.8	17.8	6.0	2.94	3.36	116 933	9.9	17.7
Williamson	25 358	66.9	29.5	53.4	21.5	10.2	6.2	33.1	28.9	13.3	2.35	2.89	23 120	9.4	27.5
Winnebago	107 980	68.2	32.9	52.3	23.0	11.8	7.6	31.8	26.3	9.6	2.53	3.06	96 727	10.9	24.5
Woodford	12 797	76.6	35.4	67.5	30.0	6.6	4.1	23.4	20.5	10.4	2.69	3.12	11 395	6.0	19.5

[1] No spouse present.

Table B. States and Counties

| STATE County | Percent change of households, 1990–2000 | Total housing units | Occupied housing units (percent) | Vacant housing units | | Homeowner vacancy rate (percent) | Rental vacancy rate (percent) | Occupied housing units | | | Average household size of owner-occupied units | Average household size of renter-occupied units |
| | | | | Total | For seasonal, recreational, or occasional use | | | Total | Percent owner-occupied housing units | Percent renter-occupied housing units | | |
	86	87	88	89	90	91	92	93	94	95	96	97
ILLINOIS—Cont'd												
Jackson	3.2	26 844	90.2	9.8	0.5	1.8	11.2	24 215	53.3	46.7	2.42	1.96
Jasper	-0.8	4 294	91.5	8.5	0.7	1.6	11.7	3 930	83.2	16.8	2.62	2.24
Jefferson	5.3	16 990	90.5	9.5	1.0	2.2	7.6	15 374	74.6	25.4	2.54	2.14
Jersey	10.2	8 918	90.8	9.2	4.2	1.5	5.9	8 096	77.7	22.3	2.65	2.29
Jo Daviess	10.1	12 003	76.8	23.2	16.4	2.1	12.8	9 218	77.3	22.7	2.46	2.18
Johnson	12.3	5 046	82.9	17.1	9.2	2.0	4.8	4 183	84.7	15.3	2.47	2.18
Kane	24.9	138 998	96.3	3.7	0.3	1.2	5.2	133 901	76.0	24.0	3.08	2.63
Kankakee	10.3	40 610	94.0	6.0	0.9	2.2	6.0	38 182	69.4	30.6	2.69	2.43
Kendall	41.3	19 519	96.3	3.7	0.4	1.5	6.0	18 798	84.1	15.9	2.97	2.47
Knox	0.7	23 717	93.0	7.0	1.2	1.6	7.7	22 056	71.6	28.4	2.42	2.12
Lake	24.3	225 919	95.7	4.3	1.1	1.1	5.0	216 297	77.8	22.2	2.97	2.56
La Salle	5.2	46 438	93.5	6.5	0.8	1.7	7.7	43 417	75.0	25.0	2.58	2.24
Lawrence	-0.2	7 014	89.9	10.1	1.2	2.5	13.2	6 309	77.0	23.0	2.39	2.26
Lee	6.2	14 310	92.6	7.4	1.0	2.1	9.3	13 253	73.9	26.1	2.58	2.24
Livingston	4.6	15 297	94.0	6.0	0.6	1.9	7.2	14 374	74.1	25.9	2.59	2.27
Logan	0.7	11 872	93.6	6.4	0.2	1.9	6.0	11 113	71.3	28.7	2.48	2.26
McDonough	0.9	13 289	93.0	7.0	0.4	2.3	6.9	12 360	63.1	36.9	2.40	2.06
McHenry	42.0	92 908	96.2	3.8	1.0	1.2	4.0	89 403	83.2	16.8	2.98	2.48
McLean	21.3	59 972	94.6	5.4	0.4	1.8	6.6	56 746	66.5	33.5	2.63	2.11
Macon	1.2	50 241	92.7	7.3	0.3	1.6	11.0	46 561	71.6	28.4	2.46	2.21
Macoupin	5.9	21 097	91.3	8.7	2.2	1.8	7.7	19 253	79.0	21.0	2.52	2.34
Madison	7.5	108 942	93.6	6.4	0.2	1.6	8.6	101 953	73.8	26.2	2.59	2.18
Marion	2.1	18 022	92.2	7.8	0.6	1.6	7.4	16 619	76.6	23.4	2.51	2.27
Marshall	6.6	5 914	88.3	11.7	4.1	2.3	8.0	5 225	80.1	19.9	2.52	2.27
Mason	0.7	7 033	90.8	9.2	2.5	1.8	7.7	6 389	76.8	23.2	2.48	2.45
Massac	6.0	6 951	90.1	9.9	0.7	2.6	10.8	6 261	78.6	21.4	2.41	2.22
Menard	16.1	5 285	92.2	7.8	1.5	2.4	7.6	4 873	78.9	21.1	2.60	2.26
Mercer	0.8	7 109	93.2	6.8	1.5	1.4	4.8	6 624	79.7	20.3	2.56	2.38
Monroe	25.5	10 749	95.6	4.4	1.1	0.7	3.2	10 275	80.2	19.8	2.78	2.12
Montgomery	0.2	12 525	91.9	8.1	0.7	2.3	7.6	11 507	78.4	21.6	2.49	2.28
Morgan	2.6	15 291	91.8	8.2	0.5	1.6	11.5	14 039	70.4	29.6	2.48	2.09
Moultrie	5.5	5 743	94.1	5.9	0.5	1.9	4.6	5 405	78.5	21.5	2.62	2.34
Ogle	12.5	20 420	94.4	5.6	1.0	1.4	6.3	19 278	74.5	25.5	2.72	2.32
Peoria	2.7	78 204	93.0	7.0	0.2	1.6	9.7	72 733	67.7	32.3	2.54	2.19
Perry	2.4	9 457	89.9	10.1	2.2	1.9	8.0	8 504	78.6	21.4	2.50	2.15
Piatt	9.1	6 798	95.2	4.8	0.4	1.2	4.3	6 475	80.2	19.8	2.57	2.22
Pike	-2.0	8 011	85.8	14.2	4.3	2.1	7.3	6 876	77.1	22.9	2.46	2.29
Pope	9.8	2 351	75.2	24.8	14.2	2.5	17.6	1 769	82.2	17.8	2.39	2.09
Pulaski	-2.2	3 353	86.3	13.7	2.1	4.0	8.1	2 893	75.6	24.4	2.46	2.39
Putnam	9.6	2 888	83.6	16.4	11.6	2.1	5.4	2 415	82.6	17.4	2.58	2.21
Randolph	1.1	13 328	90.7	9.3	1.9	1.5	11.4	12 084	79.4	20.6	2.52	2.23
Richland	2.4	7 468	89.2	10.8	1.1	2.9	14.8	6 660	76.5	23.5	2.46	2.22
Rock Island	2.4	64 489	94.1	5.9	0.4	1.3	7.4	60 712	69.7	30.3	2.49	2.13
St. Clair	1.5	104 446	92.7	7.3	0.2	1.6	7.1	96 810	67.0	33.0	2.66	2.47
Saline	1.4	12 360	88.9	11.1	1.2	2.2	8.1	10 992	76.5	23.5	2.37	2.17
Sangamon	9.1	85 459	92.1	7.9	0.3	2.0	10.3	78 722	70.0	30.0	2.48	2.08
Schuyler	-0.9	3 304	90.0	10.0	2.8	1.4	6.5	2 975	78.8	21.2	2.42	2.24
Scott	1.5	2 464	90.2	9.8	2.3	1.7	6.9	2 222	77.6	22.4	2.48	2.41
Shelby	5.8	10 060	90.0	10.0	1.7	2.3	7.1	9 056	81.0	19.0	2.53	2.34
Stark	0.5	2 725	92.7	7.3	0.8	2.6	6.5	2 525	77.2	22.8	2.50	2.32
Stephenson	4.6	21 713	91.1	8.9	0.9	1.8	12.4	19 785	74.8	25.2	2.52	2.17
Tazewell	6.7	52 973	95.0	5.0	0.4	1.4	7.4	50 327	76.1	23.9	2.61	2.11
Union	6.6	7 894	92.3	7.7	0.8	1.7	5.6	7 290	75.4	24.6	2.48	2.08
Vermilion	-2.0	36 349	91.9	8.1	0.4	2.2	10.2	33 406	71.7	28.3	2.47	2.28
Wabash	3.2	5 758	90.2	9.8	1.6	2.7	9.7	5 192	75.3	24.7	2.54	2.20
Warren	-3.1	7 787	92.0	8.0	1.7	2.2	7.7	7 166	74.6	25.4	2.49	2.31
Washington	3.4	6 385	91.6	8.4	1.5	2.3	7.0	5 848	81.1	18.9	2.59	2.37
Wayne	3.0	7 950	89.8	10.2	1.6	3.2	10.0	7 143	79.4	20.6	2.42	2.20
White	-4.5	7 393	88.4	11.6	2.2	2.8	10.5	6 534	78.0	22.0	2.33	2.14
Whiteside	4.2	25 025	94.6	5.4	0.6	1.5	6.3	23 684	74.5	25.5	2.58	2.29
Will	43.3	175 524	95.5	4.5	0.2	1.7	7.0	167 542	83.1	16.9	3.04	2.46
Williamson	9.7	27 703	91.5	8.5	1.0	1.8	9.3	25 358	73.6	26.4	2.45	2.09
Winnebago	11.6	114 404	94.4	5.6	0.3	1.4	7.6	107 980	70.0	30.0	2.65	2.24
Woodford	12.3	13 487	94.9	5.1	0.7	1.3	4.7	12 797	82.8	17.2	2.77	2.29

Table B. States and Counties

STATE/ County code	MSA/ PMSA/ NECMA code[1]	County type[2]	STATE County	Population, 2000				Population, 1990				Population and population characteristics, 2000					
												Race (percent)					
												One race					
				Land area, 2000[3] (sq km)	Total persons	Rank	Per square kilometer	Land area, 1990[3] (sq km)	Total persons	Rank	Per square kilometer	White	Black or African American	American Indian or Alaska Native	Asian	Native Hawaiian and other Pacific Islander	Some other race
				1	2	3	4	5	6	7	8	9	10	11	12	13	14
18 000	...		INDIANA	92 895	6 080 485	X	65.5	92 904	5 544 156	X	59.7	87.5	8.4	0.3	1.0	0.0	1.6
18 001	2760	2	Adams	879	33 625	1 295	38.3	879	31 095	1 243	35.4	97.3	0.1	0.2	0.2	0.0	1.5
18 003	2760	2	Allen	1 702	331 849	176	195.0	1 702	300 836	164	176.8	83.1	11.3	0.4	1.4	0.0	2.0
18 005	...	4	Bartholomew	1 054	71 435	692	67.8	1 054	63 657	687	60.4	94.2	1.8	0.1	1.9	0.0	1.0
18 007	...	8	Benton	1 052	9 421	2 493	9.0	1 052	9 441	2 439	9.0	96.9	0.2	0.1	0.1	0.0	1.3
18 009	...	6	Blackford	428	14 048	2 160	32.8	428	14 067	2 051	32.9	98.4	0.1	0.3	0.2	0.0	0.2
18 011	3480	1	Boone	1 095	46 107	982	42.1	1 095	38 147	1 049	34.8	97.9	0.4	0.3	0.5	0.0	0.4
18 013	...	8	Brown	809	14 957	2 094	18.5	809	14 080	2 050	17.4	98.2	0.2	0.2	0.2	0.0	0.4
18 015	...	6	Carroll	964	20 165	1 783	20.9	964	18 809	1 747	19.5	97.6	0.2	0.2	0.1	0.0	1.4
18 017	...	6	Cass	1 069	40 930	1 082	38.3	1 069	38 413	1 042	35.9	93.7	1.3	0.3	0.5	0.0	3.2
18 019	4520	2	Clark	971	96 472	536	99.4	972	87 774	519	90.3	90.3	6.6	0.3	0.6	0.0	0.8
18 021	8320	3	Clay	926	26 556	1 499	28.7	926	24 705	1 473	26.7	98.4	0.3	0.2	0.1	0.0	0.2
18 023	3920	3	Clinton	1 049	33 866	1 285	32.3	1 049	30 974	1 246	29.5	94.4	0.3	0.1	0.2	0.0	4.2
18 025	...	8	Crawford	792	10 743	2 380	13.6	792	9 914	2 393	12.5	98.3	0.2	0.4	0.1	0.1	0.3
18 027	...	7	Daviess	1 115	29 820	1 402	26.7	1 116	27 533	1 373	24.7	97.5	0.4	0.2	0.2	0.0	1.0
18 029	1640	1	Dearborn	790	46 109	981	58.4	791	38 835	1 027	49.1	98.7	0.6	0.2	0.3	0.0	0.2
18 031	...	6	Decatur	965	24 555	1 573	25.4	965	23 645	1 508	24.5	98.5	0.0	0.1	0.7	0.0	0.4
18 033	2760	2	De Kalb	940	40 285	1 108	42.9	940	35 324	1 120	37.6	97.8	0.3	0.2	0.3	0.0	0.7
18 035	5280	3	Delaware	1 019	118 769	456	116.6	1 019	119 659	386	117.4	90.7	6.7	0.2	0.7	0.1	0.5
18 037	...	7	Dubois	1 114	39 674	1 121	35.6	1 114	36 616	1 086	32.9	97.5	0.1	0.1	0.2	0.0	1.5
18 039	2330	3	Elkhart	1 201	182 791	299	152.2	1 201	156 198	300	130.1	86.4	5.2	0.3	0.9	0.0	5.4
18 041	...	7	Fayette	557	25 588	1 535	45.9	557	26 015	1 420	46.7	97.2	1.7	0.1	0.3	0.0	0.1
18 043	4520	2	Floyd	383	70 823	701	184.9	383	64 404	678	168.2	93.2	4.4	0.2	0.5	0.0	0.5
18 045	...	6	Fountain	1 025	17 954	1 901	17.5	1 025	17 808	1 797	17.4	98.7	0.1	0.2	0.2	0.0	0.3
18 047	...	6	Franklin	1 000	22 151	1 685	22.2	1 000	19 580	1 694	19.6	99.0	0.0	0.2	0.2	0.0	0.1
18 049	...	7	Fulton	954	20 511	1 759	21.5	954	18 840	1 744	19.7	96.2	0.8	0.4	0.4	0.0	1.1
18 051	...	6	Gibson	1 266	32 500	1 332	25.7	1 266	31 913	1 215	25.2	96.5	1.9	0.2	0.5	0.0	0.2
18 053	...	4	Grant	1 072	73 403	681	68.5	1 072	74 169	607	69.2	89.2	7.2	0.4	0.6	0.0	1.0
18 055	...	6	Greene	1 403	33 157	1 311	23.6	1 404	30 410	1 274	21.7	98.6	0.1	0.3	0.2	0.0	0.2
18 057	3480	0	Hamilton	1 031	182 740	300	177.2	1 031	108 936	423	105.7	94.4	1.5	0.2	2.4	0.0	0.5
18 059	3480	1	Hancock	793	55 391	851	69.8	793	45 527	909	57.4	98.4	0.1	0.2	0.4	0.0	0.2
18 061	4520	2	Harrison	1 257	34 325	1 270	27.3	1 257	29 890	1 301	23.8	98.4	0.4	0.3	0.2	0.0	0.2
18 063	3480	1	Hendricks	1 058	104 093	508	98.4	1 058	75 717	594	71.6	96.7	1.1	0.3	0.7	0.0	0.4
18 065	...	6	Henry	1 018	48 508	939	47.7	1 018	48 139	866	47.3	98.0	0.9	0.2	0.2	0.0	0.3
18 067	3850	3	Howard	759	84 964	614	111.9	759	80 827	564	106.5	89.7	6.5	0.4	1.0	0.0	0.8
18 069	2760	2	Huntington	991	38 075	1 162	38.4	991	35 427	1 116	35.7	98.2	0.2	0.4	0.3	0.0	0.3
18 071	...	7	Jackson	1 319	41 335	1 070	31.3	1 319	37 730	1 054	28.6	96.1	0.5	0.2	0.8	0.1	1.5
18 073	...	6	Jasper	1 450	30 043	1 395	20.7	1 450	24 823	1 468	17.1	98.0	0.3	0.2	0.2	0.0	0.6
18 075	...	6	Jay	994	21 806	1 700	21.9	994	21 512	1 603	21.6	97.6	0.3	0.2	0.3	0.0	0.8
18 077	...	6	Jefferson	936	31 705	1 352	33.9	936	29 797	1 304	31.8	96.2	1.5	0.2	0.6	0.0	0.4
18 079	...	7	Jennings	977	27 554	1 465	28.2	977	23 661	1 506	24.2	97.5	0.7	0.2	0.3	0.0	0.2
18 081	3480	0	Johnson	829	115 209	468	139.0	829	88 109	517	106.3	97.0	0.8	0.2	0.8	0.0	0.5
18 083	...	5	Knox	1 336	39 256	1 132	29.4	1 336	39 884	1 007	29.9	96.4	1.9	0.2	0.5	0.0	0.3
18 085	...	6	Kosciusko	1 392	74 057	673	53.2	1 392	65 294	671	46.9	94.6	0.6	0.3	0.6	0.0	2.9
18 087	...	8	Lagrange	983	34 909	1 252	35.5	983	29 477	1 317	30.0	96.7	0.2	0.1	0.3	0.0	1.9
18 089	2960	0	Lake	1 287	484 564	118	376.5	1 287	475 594	103	369.5	66.7	25.3	0.3	0.8	0.0	5.0
18 091	...	4	La Porte	1 549	110 106	493	71.1	1 550	107 066	430	69.1	86.3	10.1	0.3	0.5	0.0	1.3
18 093	...	6	Lawrence	1 162	45 922	986	39.5	1 163	42 836	940	36.8	97.9	0.4	0.3	0.3	0.0	0.3
18 095	3480	3	Madison	1 171	133 358	402	113.9	1 171	130 669	355	111.6	89.9	7.9	0.2	0.4	0.0	0.6
18 097	3480	0	Marion	1 026	860 454	50	838.6	1 027	797 159	48	776.2	70.5	24.2	0.3	1.4	0.0	2.0
18 099	...	6	Marshall	1 151	45 128	994	39.2	1 151	42 182	955	36.6	95.5	0.3	0.3	0.3	0.0	2.5
18 101	...	7	Martin	871	10 369	2 407	11.9	871	10 369	2 351	11.9	98.9	0.2	0.1	0.1	0.0	0.1
18 103	...	6	Miami	973	36 082	1 211	37.1	973	36 897	1 077	37.9	93.7	3.0	1.1	0.3	0.0	0.5
18 105	1020	3	Monroe	1 021	120 563	450	118.1	1 021	108 978	422	106.7	90.8	3.0	0.3	3.4	0.0	0.9
18 107	...	6	Montgomery	1 307	37 629	1 172	28.8	1 307	34 436	1 152	26.3	96.8	0.8	0.2	0.4	0.0	1.1
18 109	3480	1	Morgan	1 053	66 689	733	63.3	1 053	55 920	773	53.1	98.6	0.1	0.2	0.2	0.0	0.4
18 111	...	8	Newton	1 041	14 566	2 115	14.0	1 041	13 551	2 098	13.0	97.3	0.2	0.3	0.2	0.1	1.1
18 113	...	6	Noble	1 065	46 275	977	43.5	1 065	37 877	1 052	35.6	94.0	0.4	0.2	0.4	0.0	4.0
18 115	1640	1	Ohio	225	5 623	2 812	25.0	225	5 315	2 818	23.6	98.7	0.5	0.1	0.1	0.0	0.1
18 117	...	7	Orange	1 035	19 306	1 828	18.7	1 035	18 409	1 769	17.8	97.9	0.6	0.3	0.2	0.0	0.2
18 119	...	6	Owen	998	21 786	1 705	21.8	998	17 281	1 835	17.3	98.2	0.3	0.4	0.2	0.0	0.2
18 121	...	6	Parke	1 152	17 241	1 938	15.0	1 152	15 410	1 963	13.4	96.4	2.1	0.2	0.2	0.0	0.2
18 123	...	7	Perry	988	18 899	1 849	19.1	988	19 107	1 727	19.3	97.6	1.4	0.2	0.1	0.0	0.1
18 125	...	8	Pike	871	12 837	2 244	14.7	871	12 509	2 181	14.4	99.1	0.1	0.1	0.1	0.0	0.1
18 127	2960	1	Porter	1 083	146 798	370	135.5	1 083	128 932	359	119.1	95.3	0.9	0.2	0.9	0.0	1.3
18 129	2440	2	Posey	1 058	27 061	1 480	25.6	1 058	25 968	1 422	24.5	98.0	0.9	0.3	0.2	0.0	0.2
18 131	...	9	Pulaski	1 123	13 755	2 176	12.2	1 123	12 780	2 157	11.4	97.5	0.9	0.2	0.2	0.0	0.3

[1] MSA = Metropolitan Statistical Area. PMSA = Primary MSA. NECMA = New England County Metropolitan Area. See Appendix A for explanation of these concepts. See Appendix B for list of metropolitan areas identified by type, with component counties.
[2] County typology code from the Economic Research Service of USDA. See Appendix A for definition.
[3] Dry land or land partially or temporarily covered by water.

Table B. States and Counties

STATE County	Population and population characteristics, 2000 (cont'd)								Population and population characteristics, 1990				
	Race (percent) (cont'd)								Race (percent)				
	Race alone or in combination												
	Two or more races	White	Black	American Indian or Alaska Native	Asian	Native Hawaiian and other Pacific Islander	Some other race	Hispanic¹	White	Black or African American	American Indian or Alaska Native	Asian and Pacific Islander	Hispanic¹
	15	16	17	18	19	20	21	22	23	24	25	26	27
INDIANA	1.2	88.6	8.8	0.6	1.2	0.1	2.0	3.5	90.6	7.8	0.2	0.7	1.8
Adams	0.7	98.0	0.2	0.4	0.3	0.1	1.7	3.3	98.2	0.1	0.1	0.2	2.6
Allen	1.8	84.7	12.1	0.8	1.7	0.1	2.6	4.2	87.8	10.1	0.3	0.9	1.9
Bartholomew	1.0	95.0	2.2	0.4	2.1	0.1	1.2	2.2	97.0	1.6	0.2	1.0	0.7
Benton	1.4	98.2	0.4	1.0	0.2	0.1	1.5	2.6	99.4	0.1	0.2	0.0	1.1
Blackford	0.8	99.2	0.3	0.9	0.2	0.0	0.3	0.6	99.4	0.0	0.3	0.1	0.6
Boone	0.6	98.5	0.5	0.5	0.6	0.0	0.5	1.2	99.1	0.2	0.2	0.2	0.7
Brown	0.8	98.9	0.4	0.7	0.4	0.0	0.5	0.9	99.2	0.1	0.3	0.1	0.7
Carroll	0.5	98.2	0.3	0.4	0.1	0.0	1.6	2.9	99.5	0.1	0.1	0.0	0.6
Cass	0.9	94.5	1.5	0.6	0.7	0.1	3.5	7.1	98.3	0.9	0.4	0.3	0.6
Clark	1.4	91.6	7.3	0.7	0.8	0.1	1.0	1.9	93.7	5.4	0.2	0.4	0.6
Clay	0.7	99.0	0.5	0.6	0.2	0.1	0.3	0.6	99.3	0.5	0.2	0.1	0.3
Clinton	0.8	95.1	0.4	0.4	0.3	0.1	4.6	7.3	99.0	0.1	0.2	0.2	1.5
Crawford	0.6	98.8	0.2	0.6	0.2	0.0	0.5	0.9	99.5	0.1	0.3	0.1	0.2
Daviess	0.5	98.0	0.6	0.5	0.3	0.1	1.1	2.1	99.4	0.4	0.1	0.1	0.3
Dearborn	0.7	98.7	0.8	0.5	0.4	0.0	0.3	0.6	99.0	0.6	0.1	0.2	0.3
Decatur	0.5	99.0	0.1	0.4	0.8	0.0	0.2	0.5	99.1	0.2	0.1	0.5	0.4
De Kalb	0.7	98.5	0.4	0.5	0.4	0.1	0.8	1.7	99.1	0.1	0.3	0.2	0.9
Delaware	1.1	91.8	7.2	0.6	0.9	0.1	0.6	1.1	93.0	6.0	0.2	0.5	0.7
Dubois	0.5	98.0	0.2	0.3	0.3	0.0	1.7	2.8	99.6	0.1	0.1	0.2	0.7
Elkhart	1.8	88.0	5.8	0.7	1.2	0.1	6.1	8.9	93.8	4.5	0.3	0.6	1.9
Fayette	0.7	97.8	1.9	0.4	0.4	0.0	0.2	0.5	97.9	1.7	0.1	0.3	0.3
Floyd	1.1	94.3	5.0	0.6	0.7	0.1	0.7	1.1	95.4	4.1	0.1	0.3	0.4
Fountain	0.5	99.2	0.2	0.5	0.3	0.0	0.4	1.1	99.5	0.0	0.1	0.2	0.5
Franklin	0.5	99.5	0.1	0.4	0.3	0.0	0.1	0.5	99.6	0.1	0.2	0.1	0.3
Fulton	1.2	97.4	1.0	0.8	0.5	0.1	1.5	2.3	98.5	0.8	0.2	0.2	0.7
Gibson	0.7	97.1	2.3	0.4	0.6	0.0	0.3	0.7	97.6	1.9	0.1	0.3	0.4
Grant	1.5	90.6	7.9	0.9	0.7	0.1	1.4	2.4	91.4	6.8	0.4	0.5	2.0
Greene	0.6	99.2	0.2	0.7	0.3	0.0	0.3	0.8	99.5	0.0	0.2	0.2	0.5
Hamilton	0.9	95.2	1.8	0.4	2.8	0.1	0.7	1.6	98.0	0.6	0.1	1.1	0.7
Hancock	0.6	99.0	0.2	0.5	0.5	0.0	0.3	0.9	99.2	0.1	0.1	0.4	0.7
Harrison	0.6	98.9	0.5	0.6	0.3	0.0	0.2	1.0	99.2	0.4	0.2	0.1	0.4
Hendricks	0.9	97.5	1.3	0.6	0.9	0.1	0.5	1.1	98.4	0.9	0.2	0.4	0.5
Henry	0.5	98.5	1.0	0.4	0.3	0.0	0.4	0.8	98.6	1.0	0.2	0.2	0.4
Howard	1.5	91.1	7.2	0.8	1.2	0.1	1.1	2.0	93.3	5.4	0.3	0.6	1.3
Huntington	0.7	98.8	0.3	0.7	0.4	0.0	0.4	1.0	98.8	0.1	0.4	0.4	0.8
Jackson	0.7	96.8	0.7	0.5	0.9	0.1	1.8	2.7	98.8	0.4	0.2	0.5	0.3
Jasper	0.7	98.6	0.4	0.5	0.3	0.0	0.8	2.4	98.8	0.4	0.2	0.2	1.3
Jay	0.7	98.3	0.3	0.5	0.5	0.1	1.1	1.8	99.1	0.1	0.1	0.3	0.7
Jefferson	1.1	97.3	1.8	0.7	0.8	0.1	0.6	1.0	97.9	1.2	0.2	0.4	0.4
Jennings	1.1	98.5	1.0	0.6	0.4	0.0	0.7	0.7	98.7	0.9	0.1	0.2	0.4
Johnson	0.7	97.6	1.0	0.4	1.0	0.1	0.6	1.4	98.1	1.0	0.2	0.6	0.7
Knox	0.7	97.0	2.1	0.5	0.6	0.1	0.4	0.8	98.1	1.2	0.2	0.4	0.5
Kosciusko	1.1	95.6	0.8	0.6	0.7	0.0	3.4	5.0	98.1	0.5	0.2	0.5	1.9
Lagrange	0.7	97.5	0.3	0.5	0.4	0.0	2.1	3.1	98.9	0.1	0.2	0.3	1.2
Lake	1.9	68.3	25.9	0.7	1.1	0.1	6.0	12.2	70.3	24.5	0.2	0.6	9.4
La Porte	1.5	87.6	10.8	0.8	0.6	0.1	1.7	3.1	89.9	8.9	0.2	0.4	1.5
Lawrence	0.8	98.7	0.5	0.7	0.4	0.0	0.5	0.9	99.3	0.3	0.2	0.2	0.3
Madison	1.0	90.8	8.3	0.7	0.5	0.0	0.8	1.5	91.6	7.6	0.2	0.3	0.7
Marion	1.6	71.8	25.0	0.7	1.8	0.1	2.4	3.9	77.2	21.3	0.2	1.0	1.1
Marshall	1.0	96.5	0.5	0.6	0.5	0.0	2.9	5.9	98.4	0.2	0.2	0.4	2.0
Martin	0.5	99.5	0.3	0.4	0.3	0.0	0.1	0.4	99.5	0.1	0.1	0.1	0.1
Miami	1.4	95.0	3.4	1.9	0.6	0.1	0.7	1.3	94.3	3.0	1.5	0.6	1.5
Monroe	1.6	92.3	3.5	0.7	3.9	0.1	1.2	1.9	94.3	2.6	0.2	2.5	1.3
Montgomery	0.7	97.4	0.9	0.5	0.6	0.1	1.2	1.6	98.6	0.6	0.2	0.4	0.5
Morgan	0.7	99.3	0.2	0.7	0.4	0.0	0.3	0.7	99.5	0.0	0.2	0.2	0.4
Newton	0.8	98.1	0.2	0.7	0.3	0.1	1.3	2.9	99.2	0.1	0.3	0.2	1.3
Noble	0.9	94.9	0.5	0.6	0.5	0.1	4.4	7.1	98.9	0.2	0.2	0.3	1.7
Ohio	0.5	99.1	0.6	0.4	0.3	0.0	0.1	0.4	98.9	0.8	0.2	0.2	0.1
Orange	0.7	98.6	0.8	0.7	0.2	0.0	0.4	0.6	98.9	0.7	0.2	0.1	0.3
Owen	0.8	99.0	0.4	0.8	0.3	0.0	0.3	0.8	99.3	0.3	0.3	0.1	0.3
Parke	0.7	97.1	2.2	0.7	0.3	0.0	0.3	0.6	98.8	0.8	0.3	0.1	0.6
Perry	0.5	98.0	1.6	0.4	0.2	0.1	0.2	0.7	98.5	1.1	0.2	0.2	0.3
Pike	0.4	99.5	0.2	0.3	0.2	0.0	0.1	0.6	99.7	0.0	0.1	0.2	0.3
Porter	1.3	96.6	1.1	0.7	1.2	0.1	1.8	4.8	98.0	0.4	0.2	0.7	3.0
Posey	0.6	98.5	1.1	0.5	0.3	0.0	0.2	0.4	98.5	1.1	0.1	0.1	0.4
Pulaski	0.8	98.2	1.0	0.6	0.3	0.1	0.5	1.4	98.9	0.5	0.2	0.2	0.8

¹Hispanic persons may be of any race.

Table B. States and Counties

STATE County	Population and population characteristics, 2000										
	Age (percent)									Median age (years)	Percent Female
	Under 5 years	5 to 17 years	18 to 24 years	25 to 34 years	35 to 44 years	45 to 54 years	55 to 64 years	65 to 74 years	75 years and over		
	28	29	30	31	32	33	34	35	36	37	38
INDIANA	7.0	18.9	10.1	13.7	15.8	13.4	8.7	6.5	5.9	35.2	51.0
Adams	8.0	23.1	9.1	12.3	14.0	12.0	8.1	6.0	7.4	32.9	50.6
Allen	7.7	20.0	9.4	14.2	15.8	13.6	7.9	5.9	5.5	34.1	51.1
Bartholomew	7.4	19.2	7.7	13.9	15.8	14.2	9.8	6.6	5.5	36.2	50.9
Benton	6.6	21.2	7.1	12.5	15.4	12.1	9.4	7.3	8.3	36.7	50.4
Blackford	6.5	18.2	7.5	12.7	14.8	14.2	10.7	8.3	7.1	38.5	50.8
Boone	7.3	21.0	6.3	12.1	18.0	14.5	8.9	5.8	6.0	36.9	51.2
Brown	5.3	18.0	6.3	11.1	16.8	17.1	12.5	7.6	5.2	40.8	49.8
Carroll	6.8	19.5	7.4	12.8	15.9	13.8	9.9	7.2	6.7	37.2	50.1
Cass	7.0	18.9	8.7	12.9	15.5	13.2	9.4	7.3	7.2	36.7	49.7
Clark	6.7	17.5	9.0	14.4	16.3	14.5	9.4	6.8	5.6	36.5	51.4
Clay	6.6	19.5	8.6	12.3	15.5	13.2	9.3	7.6	7.5	37.1	51.5
Clinton	7.1	20.2	8.8	13.0	15.4	12.7	8.4	6.9	7.5	35.6	50.7
Crawford	6.3	19.2	8.4	12.4	16.0	14.6	10.4	7.2	5.4	37.3	49.7
Daviess	7.6	21.3	8.6	11.8	14.4	12.7	9.0	7.2	7.5	35.5	50.7
Dearborn	6.8	20.8	7.7	12.6	17.5	14.3	9.0	6.3	4.9	36.2	50.5
Decatur	7.5	18.8	8.9	13.7	15.6	13.0	9.3	7.0	6.3	35.8	50.6
De Kalb	7.6	20.4	8.6	13.7	16.6	13.3	8.3	5.9	5.5	34.7	50.2
Delaware	5.9	16.2	16.9	12.4	13.2	12.5	9.4	7.1	6.4	33.8	52.0
Dubois	7.2	20.2	7.9	12.9	16.9	13.4	8.7	6.7	6.2	36.1	50.5
Elkhart	8.1	20.8	9.5	14.5	15.3	12.8	8.1	5.6	5.2	33.0	50.3
Fayette	6.4	17.9	8.6	12.8	14.3	14.7	9.9	8.1	7.3	38.0	51.5
Floyd	6.5	19.3	8.4	12.8	17.1	14.6	8.9	6.5	5.8	36.8	51.8
Fountain	6.6	19.6	7.2	12.5	15.4	12.6	10.5	8.2	7.4	37.7	50.4
Franklin	7.0	21.2	7.6	12.8	16.4	13.6	9.0	6.8	5.7	35.9	50.1
Fulton	6.6	19.4	7.7	12.0	15.6	13.1	10.2	8.0	7.3	37.9	50.6
Gibson	6.4	18.4	8.4	12.3	15.9	13.6	9.5	8.0	7.5	38.0	51.1
Grant	5.9	17.7	11.8	11.5	14.3	13.6	10.3	8.0	6.9	37.4	52.0
Greene	6.2	18.5	7.7	12.6	15.6	13.9	10.1	7.8	7.4	38.1	50.8
Hamilton	9.1	21.7	5.6	15.2	19.7	13.9	7.3	4.2	3.2	34.1	50.8
Hancock	6.8	19.8	6.8	12.5	17.5	15.3	10.2	6.4	4.9	37.4	50.6
Harrison	6.5	19.5	8.7	12.5	17.7	14.5	9.2	6.5	5.0	36.6	50.2
Hendricks	7.3	20.7	7.0	13.8	18.5	14.2	8.7	5.4	4.4	35.6	49.9
Henry	6.2	17.9	7.5	12.6	15.2	14.3	10.5	8.3	7.4	38.7	51.8
Howard	7.0	18.6	8.3	13.1	15.1	14.3	10.3	7.3	6.0	37.1	51.6
Huntington	6.7	19.5	9.9	12.3	15.8	13.1	8.7	6.6	7.5	36.2	51.3
Jackson	7.0	18.5	8.8	14.5	15.8	12.9	9.2	7.0	6.3	35.8	50.7
Jasper	6.9	20.5	10.1	12.5	15.3	13.2	9.1	6.8	5.7	35.0	50.4
Jay	7.3	19.7	7.7	12.9	14.4	13.1	10.2	7.5	7.2	36.7	51.0
Jefferson	6.2	18.2	10.6	12.5	16.0	13.6	9.8	7.1	6.0	36.6	50.5
Jennings	7.5	20.2	8.2	14.7	15.7	13.5	9.5	6.1	4.6	34.6	50.3
Johnson	7.5	19.7	8.7	14.2	16.6	13.7	8.6	5.7	5.3	34.9	51.0
Knox	5.9	17.1	13.6	11.0	14.4	13.2	9.5	7.6	7.7	36.7	50.4
Kosciusko	7.5	20.3	8.7	13.4	15.6	13.4	9.2	6.2	5.7	35.1	50.1
Lagrange	9.8	24.0	10.3	12.9	13.3	11.5	8.3	5.7	4.4	29.5	49.4
Lake	7.1	19.6	9.3	12.7	15.6	13.7	8.9	7.0	6.0	35.9	51.8
La Porte	6.5	18.1	8.6	13.6	16.1	14.5	9.2	7.1	6.4	37.1	48.7
Lawrence	6.5	18.1	7.7	12.9	15.2	14.5	10.4	8.1	6.7	38.2	51.3
Madison	6.4	17.4	9.1	13.3	15.0	13.9	10.0	7.8	7.1	37.4	50.7
Marion	7.4	18.4	10.0	16.5	16.5	12.7	7.6	5.8	5.3	33.6	51.7
Marshall	7.3	20.8	8.7	12.5	15.5	13.3	8.7	6.9	6.4	35.5	50.3
Martin	6.3	18.9	7.4	12.3	15.2	15.1	10.5	7.8	6.4	38.5	49.4
Miami	6.4	19.5	8.1	13.5	16.4	14.1	9.2	7.0	5.9	36.6	49.2
Monroe	5.1	12.9	27.7	14.7	12.6	11.1	6.7	4.9	4.3	27.6	50.9
Montgomery	6.7	19.3	9.0	12.5	16.0	12.8	9.8	7.2	6.7	36.6	50.1
Morgan	7.2	20.0	7.7	13.5	17.1	14.3	9.5	6.2	4.5	36.0	50.3
Newton	6.2	20.2	7.9	12.2	16.2	14.2	10.2	6.8	6.0	37.3	50.3
Noble	8.0	21.0	9.2	14.3	15.7	12.9	7.9	5.8	5.2	33.3	49.6
Ohio	5.9	19.0	7.8	11.8	16.8	14.2	10.8	7.6	6.1	38.4	50.8
Orange	6.7	19.0	8.0	12.4	15.6	13.4	10.1	7.9	6.9	37.5	50.8
Owen	6.3	20.3	7.2	11.9	16.9	14.3	10.3	7.6	5.3	37.6	50.3
Parke	5.5	18.4	7.3	12.2	16.5	14.3	11.2	8.1	6.6	38.9	52.3
Perry	5.4	17.5	9.8	12.5	16.6	14.2	9.1	7.7	7.2	38.0	48.3
Pike	6.1	17.8	7.7	12.2	16.0	13.8	11.0	8.1	7.2	38.8	50.0
Porter	6.5	19.3	9.8	12.5	16.4	15.5	9.2	5.9	5.0	36.3	50.9
Posey	6.3	21.0	7.4	11.4	17.6	14.5	9.4	6.8	5.6	37.4	50.2
Pulaski	6.1	20.8	7.4	11.6	15.7	13.3	9.7	7.8	7.5	37.8	49.6

Table B. States and Counties

STATE County	Population and population characteristics, 1990 Age (percent) Under 5 years	5 to 17 years	18 to 24 years	25 to 34 years	35 to 44 years	45 to 54 years	55 to 64 years	65 to 74 years	75 years and over	Percent Female	Population—change, 1980–2000 Total persons 2000	1990	1980	Percent change 1990–2000	1980–1990
	39	40	41	42	43	44	45	46	47	48	49	50	51	52	53
INDIANA	7.2	19.1	10.9	16.5	14.8	10.3	8.7	7.3	5.3	51.5	6 080 485	5 544 156	5 490 214	9.7	1.0
Adams	8.7	23.0	9.9	15.0	13.3	9.2	7.4	7.3	6.2	51.0	33 625	31 095	29 619	8.1	5.0
Allen	7.9	19.8	10.0	17.5	15.6	9.8	8.1	6.6	4.8	51.5	331 849	300 836	294 335	10.3	2.2
Bartholomew	7.2	18.7	9.5	16.0	15.8	12.2	9.0	6.7	4.8	51.4	71 435	63 657	65 088	12.2	-2.2
Benton	7.4	20.8	7.7	14.6	13.1	10.2	9.5	9.4	7.2	51.1	9 421	9 441	10 218	-0.2	-7.6
Blackford	6.9	18.5	8.8	14.8	14.1	11.5	10.1	8.7	6.5	51.5	14 048	14 067	15 570	-0.1	-9.7
Boone	7.5	19.9	7.5	16.1	16.3	11.5	8.3	6.8	6.0	51.8	46 107	38 147	36 446	20.9	4.7
Brown	6.2	18.5	7.8	15.0	16.6	12.8	10.4	7.9	4.8	50.0	14 957	14 080	12 377	6.2	13.8
Carroll	7.0	19.5	8.5	15.0	14.5	11.2	9.6	8.8	6.0	51.0	20 165	18 809	19 722	7.2	-4.6
Cass	6.7	19.7	8.2	15.3	14.5	10.8	9.5	8.9	6.3	52.0	40 930	38 413	40 936	6.6	-6.2
Clark	6.6	19.1	9.6	16.9	15.8	10.9	9.1	7.1	5.0	52.3	96 472	87 774	88 838	9.9	-1.2
Clay	6.8	19.3	8.6	15.0	13.5	10.2	9.6	9.2	7.7	52.0	26 556	24 705	24 862	7.5	-0.6
Clinton	7.4	20.2	8.4	15.4	14.1	10.0	8.9	8.4	7.1	51.7	33 866	30 974	31 545	9.3	-1.8
Crawford	6.9	20.6	9.1	14.9	14.4	10.6	9.2	7.6	6.6	50.4	10 743	9 914	9 820	8.4	1.0
Daviess	7.9	21.0	8.5	14.6	13.5	9.5	8.9	8.9	7.1	51.6	29 820	27 533	27 836	8.3	-1.1
Dearborn	7.4	21.2	8.9	15.6	15.6	10.8	8.6	7.0	4.9	51.0	46 109	38 835	34 291	18.7	13.3
Decatur	7.3	21.6	9.3	15.8	13.9	10.2	8.5	7.4	6.0	50.7	24 555	23 645	23 841	3.8	-0.8
De Kalb	7.7	21.2	9.3	17.1	14.7	9.8	8.1	6.6	5.3	51.0	40 285	35 324	33 606	14.0	5.1
Delaware	6.1	16.0	19.0	13.9	13.0	10.6	8.8	7.3	5.4	52.5	118 769	119 659	128 587	-0.7	-6.9
Dubois	8.1	20.1	9.3	17.8	14.4	9.8	8.3	6.6	5.7	50.9	39 674	36 616	34 238	8.4	6.9
Elkhart	8.5	20.0	10.2	16.6	15.2	10.3	8.0	6.4	4.8	51.1	182 791	156 198	137 330	17.0	13.7
Fayette	6.2	20.3	9.3	13.9	15.1	10.9	9.6	8.4	6.1	51.6	25 588	26 015	28 272	-1.6	-8.0
Floyd	6.9	19.5	9.1	16.1	16.1	10.7	8.8	7.4	5.4	52.3	70 823	64 404	61 205	10.0	5.2
Fountain	6.7	19.2	8.6	14.3	13.2	11.6	9.8	9.5	7.2	51.7	17 954	17 808	19 033	0.8	-6.4
Franklin	7.4	22.1	9.0	15.3	14.5	10.3	8.9	6.9	5.5	50.5	22 151	19 580	19 612	13.1	-0.2
Fulton	6.8	19.8	7.6	15.3	13.5	10.8	10.1	9.1	6.9	51.4	20 511	18 840	19 335	8.9	-2.6
Gibson	6.6	19.1	8.7	15.4	14.1	10.5	9.8	8.5	7.2	52.0	32 500	31 913	33 156	1.8	-3.7
Grant	6.5	18.3	11.3	14.2	14.2	11.6	10.2	8.1	5.7	51.9	73 403	74 169	80 934	-1.0	-8.4
Greene	6.4	19.0	8.5	14.7	14.2	11.0	9.7	9.1	7.3	51.5	33 157	30 410	30 416	9.0	0.0
Hamilton	8.2	20.9	7.6	17.5	18.5	11.7	7.5	5.0	3.2	51.1	182 740	108 936	82 027	67.7	32.8
Hancock	6.6	21.0	8.7	15.0	17.1	12.6	8.6	6.1	4.3	50.8	55 391	45 527	43 939	21.7	3.6
Harrison	6.8	21.4	8.7	16.0	16.1	10.8	8.7	6.5	4.9	50.4	34 325	29 890	27 276	14.8	9.6
Hendricks	7.0	20.9	8.7	16.6	16.9	12.0	8.2	6.0	3.7	49.6	104 093	75 717	69 804	37.5	8.5
Henry	6.1	18.5	9.0	14.9	14.9	11.8	10.1	8.5	6.2	52.0	48 508	48 139	53 336	0.8	-9.7
Howard	7.1	19.5	9.1	15.6	15.2	12.2	9.6	7.0	4.8	52.2	84 964	80 827	86 896	5.1	-7.0
Huntington	7.5	20.2	9.7	16.3	14.0	9.9	8.3	7.7	6.5	51.5	38 075	35 427	35 596	7.5	-0.5
Jackson	6.9	20.1	9.3	16.1	14.3	10.7	9.0	7.4	6.2	51.5	41 335	37 730	36 523	9.6	3.3
Jasper	7.1	21.6	11.2	14.7	14.2	10.7	8.1	7.2	5.1	50.5	30 043	24 823	26 138	21.0	-4.5
Jay	7.0	19.5	9.2	14.4	13.8	11.3	9.6	8.7	6.6	51.4	21 806	21 512	23 239	1.4	-7.4
Jefferson	6.4	18.6	11.6	15.4	14.5	11.0	9.0	7.8	5.7	51.3	31 705	29 797	30 419	6.4	-2.0
Jennings	7.0	20.0	9.9	16.2	15.0	11.6	8.8	6.8	4.7	50.5	27 554	23 661	22 854	16.5	3.5
Johnson	7.1	20.0	10.4	16.6	16.4	11.2	7.8	5.8	4.8	51.5	115 209	88 109	77 240	30.8	14.1
Knox	6.1	17.0	14.9	14.0	12.9	9.7	9.3	8.4	7.5	51.4	39 256	39 884	41 838	-1.6	-4.7
Kosciusko	8.2	20.6	9.6	16.3	14.7	10.3	8.4	7.0	4.9	51.0	74 057	65 294	59 555	13.4	9.6
Lagrange	10.0	25.1	10.3	14.7	13.1	9.2	7.5	6.0	4.2	50.1	34 909	29 477	25 550	18.4	15.4
Lake	7.2	20.8	9.5	16.0	14.5	10.4	9.3	7.7	4.6	52.0	484 564	475 594	522 917	1.9	-9.0
La Porte	6.7	18.7	9.5	16.6	15.7	10.6	9.2	7.9	5.2	49.1	110 106	107 066	108 632	2.8	-1.4
Lawrence	6.5	19.0	9.2	14.9	14.8	11.5	9.7	8.1	6.4	51.6	45 922	42 836	42 472	7.2	0.9
Madison	6.4	18.3	10.4	14.8	14.2	11.2	9.5	8.2	5.8	51.1	133 358	130 669	139 336	2.1	-6.2
Marion	7.9	17.6	10.5	20.1	14.6	9.3	8.3	6.8	4.9	52.5	860 454	797 159	765 233	7.9	4.2
Marshall	7.7	20.8	8.6	15.7	14.6	10.2	9.0	7.4	5.9	50.9	45 128	42 182	39 155	7.0	7.7
Martin	7.0	20.1	9.1	15.2	14.4	10.9	9.5	8.6	5.3	50.7	10 369	10 369	11 001	0.0	-5.7
Miami	7.9	20.5	10.5	16.8	14.5	9.8	8.4	6.8	4.8	50.7	36 082	36 897	39 820	-2.2	-7.3
Monroe	5.5	12.9	29.0	16.8	12.8	8.0	6.5	4.9	3.7	51.7	120 563	108 978	98 787	10.6	10.3
Montgomery	7.0	18.2	10.4	16.0	13.8	11.0	9.3	7.9	6.4	50.4	37 629	34 436	35 501	9.3	-3.0
Morgan	7.1	20.8	9.6	16.1	15.6	11.9	8.6	6.1	4.2	50.9	66 689	55 920	51 999	19.3	7.5
Newton	7.0	21.9	8.1	15.1	14.5	11.2	8.8	7.3	6.0	50.8	14 566	13 551	14 844	7.5	-8.7
Noble	8.1	21.2	9.6	16.1	14.7	9.9	8.2	6.9	5.2	50.7	46 275	37 877	35 443	22.2	6.9
Ohio	6.9	19.3	8.8	16.6	13.9	11.1	9.5	7.6	6.4	51.4	5 623	5 315	5 114	5.8	3.9
Orange	7.0	19.7	8.6	15.2	14.3	10.4	9.5	8.8	6.4	51.3	19 306	18 409	18 677	4.9	-1.4
Owen	7.0	19.8	8.7	15.0	14.8	11.3	10.2	7.7	5.7	50.7	21 786	17 281	15 841	26.1	9.1
Parke	6.5	18.6	8.6	14.4	14.4	11.4	10.7	8.8	7.1	51.5	17 241	15 410	16 372	11.9	-5.9
Perry	6.3	19.6	9.9	16.8	14.0	9.7	9.1	8.4	6.2	49.5	18 899	19 107	19 346	-1.1	-1.2
Pike	6.3	18.2	8.5	15.2	14.3	11.6	10.2	8.6	7.1	50.8	12 837	12 509	13 465	2.6	-7.1
Porter	6.8	20.8	10.8	15.6	16.9	11.2	8.0	6.0	3.8	51.1	146 798	128 932	119 816	13.9	7.6
Posey	7.6	20.4	8.4	16.6	15.8	10.6	8.6	6.8	5.2	50.6	27 061	25 968	26 414	4.2	-1.7
Pulaski	7.6	21.1	8.4	14.9	13.3	9.7	9.5	8.9	6.7	50.7	13 755	12 780	13 258	7.6	-4.6

STATE County	Total population	Total in house-holds	House-holder	Spouse	Child Total	Child Own child under 18 years	Other relatives Total	Other relatives Under 18 years	Nonrelatives Total	Nonrelatives Unmarried partner	Total in group quarters	Correctional institutions	Nursing homes	Other institutions	College dormitories	Military quarters	Other
	54	55	56	57	58	59	60	61	62	63	64	65	66	67	68	69	70
INDIANA	6 080 485	97.1	38.4	20.6	29.6	23.6	3.8	1.6	4.7	2.1	2.9	0.6	0.8	0.1	1.1	0.0	0.3
Adams	33 625	98.7	35.1	21.7	37.0	29.6	2.4	1.0	2.6	1.2	1.3	0.1	1.0	0.0	0.0	0.0	0.2
Allen	331 849	98.3	38.8	20.0	31.4	25.5	3.5	1.5	4.6	2.1	1.7	0.2	0.7	0.1	0.2	0.0	0.4
Bartholomew	71 435	98.7	39.1	22.9	29.8	24.5	3.0	1.4	3.9	1.8	1.3	0.2	0.9	0.1	0.0	0.0	0.1
Benton	9 421	97.8	37.8	22.5	31.5	26.0	2.5	1.3	3.6	1.7	2.2	0.5	1.7	0.0	0.0	0.0	0.0
Blackford	14 048	98.7	40.5	23.0	28.6	22.6	3.0	1.5	3.5	2.0	1.3	0.5	0.8	0.0	0.0	0.0	0.0
Boone	46 107	98.2	37.0	23.9	31.7	26.7	2.5	1.0	3.0	1.6	1.8	0.1	1.4	0.0	0.0	0.0	0.2
Brown	14 957	99.1	39.4	25.5	27.3	21.6	3.3	1.3	3.5	1.8	0.9	0.2	0.6	0.0	0.0	0.0	0.1
Carroll	20 165	98.9	38.3	24.3	30.1	24.5	3.0	1.2	3.3	1.6	1.1	0.1	0.9	0.0	0.0	0.0	0.0
Cass	40 930	97.2	38.4	21.5	28.6	22.9	3.6	1.4	5.1	1.9	2.8	0.2	0.7	1.5	0.0	0.0	0.4
Clark	96 472	98.4	40.2	20.9	28.5	21.7	4.2	1.8	4.5	2.2	1.6	0.3	1.0	0.0	0.0	0.0	0.3
Clay	26 556	98.8	38.5	23.0	30.3	23.8	3.5	1.5	3.5	1.7	1.2	0.1	0.9	0.0	0.0	0.0	0.1
Clinton	33 866	97.5	37.0	21.8	30.5	25.0	3.9	1.6	4.2	1.9	2.5	0.4	2.0	0.0	0.0	0.0	0.1
Crawford	10 743	99.1	38.9	23.0	29.3	23.0	3.6	1.8	4.2	2.4	0.9	0.1	0.7	0.0	0.0	0.0	0.1
Daviess	29 820	98.2	36.5	21.8	33.8	27.1	3.0	1.3	3.0	1.5	1.8	0.1	1.5	0.0	0.0	0.0	0.2
Dearborn	46 109	98.9	36.5	22.8	32.6	25.6	3.4	1.5	3.5	1.8	1.1	0.3	0.5	0.1	0.0	0.0	0.2
Decatur	24 555	98.8	38.2	23.0	30.6	24.3	3.3	1.4	3.7	2.1	1.2	0.2	0.9	0.0	0.0	0.0	0.1
De Kalb	40 285	98.9	37.6	22.3	31.8	25.9	3.1	1.4	4.2	2.1	1.1	0.2	0.7	0.2	0.0	0.0	0.1
Delaware	118 769	94.2	39.7	19.3	25.0	19.9	3.1	1.4	7.1	2.1	5.8	0.1	1.0	0.2	4.2	0.0	0.2
Dubois	39 674	98.0	37.3	23.1	32.4	26.2	2.1	0.7	3.1	1.5	2.0	0.2	1.2	0.0	0.0	0.0	0.6
Elkhart	182 791	98.5	36.2	20.6	31.7	26.1	4.7	1.9	5.4	2.2	1.5	0.3	0.6	0.0	0.4	0.0	0.2
Fayette	25 588	98.0	39.9	22.2	27.9	21.6	4.0	1.9	4.1	2.2	2.0	0.4	1.2	0.1	0.0	0.0	0.3
Floyd	70 823	98.5	38.8	21.5	30.6	23.8	3.5	1.4	4.1	2.0	1.5	0.1	1.1	0.1	0.0	0.0	0.1
Fountain	17 954	99.0	39.2	23.2	29.8	24.1	3.2	1.4	3.6	1.8	1.0	0.2	0.8	0.0	0.0	0.0	0.0
Franklin	22 151	98.4	35.5	23.4	33.4	26.3	3.1	1.4	2.9	1.5	1.6	0.3	0.6	0.0	0.0	0.0	0.7
Fulton	20 511	99.3	39.4	23.4	29.2	23.8	3.1	1.4	4.1	2.0	0.7	0.1	0.6	0.0	0.0	0.0	0.1
Gibson	32 500	97.9	39.5	23.0	29.6	23.1	2.8	1.3	3.1	1.7	2.1	0.3	0.9	0.1	0.6	0.0	0.1
Grant	73 403	93.8	38.6	20.7	26.7	21.1	3.7	1.9	4.1	1.9	6.2	0.3	1.0	0.4	4.1	0.0	0.3
Greene	33 157	98.4	40.3	23.4	28.4	22.7	2.6	1.1	3.7	1.9	1.6	0.2	1.2	0.0	0.0	0.0	0.2
Hamilton	182 740	99.1	36.1	24.4	34.0	29.8	1.9	0.6	2.8	1.4	0.9	0.2	0.4	0.1	0.0	0.0	0.2
Hancock	55 391	99.2	37.4	25.3	31.0	24.9	2.8	1.2	2.7	1.4	0.8	0.2	0.6	0.0	0.0	0.0	0.1
Harrison	34 325	99.0	37.6	23.5	30.6	23.9	3.5	1.5	3.7	1.9	1.0	0.3	0.6	0.1	0.0	0.0	0.2
Hendricks	104 093	96.9	35.8	24.0	31.7	26.3	2.5	1.0	2.9	1.5	3.1	2.3	0.6	0.0	0.0	0.0	0.2
Henry	48 508	98.6	40.2	23.5	28.3	22.0	3.3	1.5	3.4	1.8	1.4	0.3	0.8	0.1	0.0	0.0	0.2
Howard	84 964	98.6	41.0	21.6	29.2	23.4	3.2	1.5	3.6	1.8	1.4	0.2	0.8	0.2	0.0	0.0	0.2
Huntington	38 075	96.2	37.4	22.2	30.3	24.2	2.7	1.3	3.6	1.7	3.8	0.2	1.7	0.1	1.4	0.0	0.4
Jackson	41 335	98.7	38.8	22.6	29.3	23.3	3.6	1.5	4.3	2.0	1.3	0.1	1.1	0.0	0.0	0.0	0.1
Jasper	30 043	96.7	35.6	23.3	31.6	25.1	3.3	1.6	3.0	1.6	3.3	0.2	0.7	0.2	2.2	0.0	0.0
Jay	21 806	99.0	38.5	22.7	31.1	24.8	3.1	1.3	3.6	2.0	1.0	0.2	0.6	0.0	0.0	0.0	0.3
Jefferson	31 705	94.2	38.3	21.1	27.5	22.1	3.1	1.4	4.1	2.2	5.8	0.7	1.0	0.9	3.1	0.0	0.1
Jennings	27 554	98.1	36.8	22.3	30.6	24.8	4.1	2.0	4.2	2.2	1.9	0.2	0.5	0.0	0.0	0.0	1.3
Johnson	115 209	96.9	36.8	22.8	30.8	25.4	2.9	1.2	3.5	1.7	3.1	0.3	0.8	0.1	0.6	0.0	1.3
Knox	39 256	93.6	39.6	20.4	26.8	21.1	2.6	1.0	4.2	1.9	6.4	0.1	1.3	0.3	4.1	0.0	0.6
Kosciusko	74 057	98.1	36.8	22.4	31.3	25.6	3.3	1.4	4.3	2.0	1.9	0.3	1.2	0.1	0.0	0.0	0.3
Lagrange	34 909	99.4	32.2	21.9	39.6	32.2	2.9	1.4	2.8	1.3	0.6	0.0	0.4	0.0	0.0	0.0	0.1
Lake	484 564	98.8	37.5	18.3	32.8	23.3	6.3	2.8	4.1	1.9	1.2	0.2	0.6	0.0	0.2	0.0	0.2
La Porte	110 106	94.1	37.3	20.1	28.4	22.0	4.1	1.8	4.3	2.2	5.9	5.0	0.6	0.1	0.0	0.0	0.2
Lawrence	45 922	98.4	40.4	23.6	28.0	22.5	3.1	1.6	3.3	1.8	1.6	0.3	1.1	0.0	0.0	0.0	0.1
Madison	133 358	96.0	39.8	20.9	27.3	21.4	3.7	1.8	4.3	2.2	4.0	2.1	0.8	0.1	0.8	0.0	0.2
Marion	860 454	97.8	40.9	16.9	28.4	22.7	5.2	2.3	6.4	2.8	2.2	0.5	0.7	0.2	0.4	0.0	0.4
Marshall	45 128	98.5	36.6	22.4	32.0	25.9	3.7	1.4	3.8	1.7	1.5	0.1	0.8	0.0	0.0	0.0	0.6
Martin	10 369	99.0	40.3	22.8	30.1	23.5	2.6	1.2	3.2	1.7	1.0	0.5	0.5	0.0	0.0	0.0	0.0
Miami	36 082	95.9	38.0	22.0	29.4	23.8	2.9	1.4	3.6	1.9	4.1	3.4	0.4	0.0	0.0	0.0	0.1
Monroe	120 563	88.1	38.9	16.2	20.0	16.6	2.2	0.8	10.7	2.3	11.9	0.2	0.4	0.3	10.7	0.0	0.3
Montgomery	37 629	96.8	38.8	22.4	28.6	24.1	2.8	1.2	4.3	2.1	3.2	0.2	1.1	0.0	1.8	0.0	0.1
Morgan	66 689	99.0	36.6	23.9	31.2	24.9	3.7	1.7	3.5	1.8	1.0	0.3	0.6	0.1	0.0	0.0	0.1
Newton	14 566	98.7	36.7	23.1	31.0	24.2	4.1	1.6	3.8	1.9	1.3	0.3	1.0	0.0	0.0	0.0	0.0
Noble	46 275	98.6	36.1	21.7	32.4	26.5	4.0	1.7	4.4	2.0	1.4	0.6	0.8	0.0	0.0	0.0	0.1
Ohio	5 623	99.2	39.1	23.4	29.6	23.0	3.3	1.4	3.7	1.9	0.8	0.0	0.8	0.0	0.0	0.0	0.0
Orange	19 306	98.4	39.5	22.7	29.3	23.8	3.3	1.5	3.5	2.2	1.6	0.4	0.9	0.0	0.0	0.0	0.2
Owen	21 786	98.7	38.0	23.7	29.4	24.1	3.6	1.8	4.0	2.0	1.3	0.2	0.9	0.0	0.0	0.0	0.2
Parke	17 241	93.2	37.2	22.3	27.6	22.1	2.8	1.2	3.2	1.6	6.8	4.6	1.9	0.0	0.0	0.0	0.3
Perry	18 899	94.1	38.5	21.8	27.9	21.2	2.8	1.2	3.1	1.9	5.9	4.9	0.8	0.0	0.0	0.0	0.2
Pike	12 837	98.7	39.9	23.8	28.6	21.9	3.1	1.4	3.3	1.7	1.3	0.3	0.9	0.0	0.0	0.0	0.1
Porter	146 798	97.6	37.2	22.3	31.0	23.9	3.1	1.3	4.0	1.9	2.4	0.1	0.6	0.1	1.3	0.0	0.3
Posey	27 061	99.0	37.7	24.0	32.0	25.6	2.5	1.2	2.9	1.6	1.0	0.2	0.8	0.0	0.0	0.0	0.0
Pulaski	13 755	97.3	37.6	23.1	30.7	24.8	2.8	1.5	3.1	1.7	2.7	1.4	1.1	0.0	0.0	0.0	0.2

Table B. States and Counties

STATE County	Households by type, 2000												Households, 1990		
	Family households						Nonfamily households								
				Married couple		Female householder[1]			Householder living alone						
	Total households	Total	With own children under 18 years	Total	With own children under 18 years	Total	With own children under 18 years	Total	Total	65 years and over	Average household size	Average family size	Total households	Female householder[1]	Householder living alone
	71	72	73	74	75	76	77	78	79	80	81	82	83	84	85
INDIANA	2 336 306	68.6	32.9	53.6	23.8	11.1	6.9	31.4	25.9	9.5	2.53	3.05	2 065 355	10.5	24.1
Adams	11 818	73.3	37.5	61.7	30.1	8.3	5.4	26.7	24.0	11.6	2.81	3.37	10 470	7.6	20.9
Allen	128 745	67.0	34.1	51.5	24.1	11.7	7.8	33.0	27.4	8.8	2.53	3.11	113 333	10.9	24.9
Bartholomew	27 936	71.8	33.9	58.6	25.8	9.7	6.1	28.2	24.0	8.8	2.52	2.98	24 192	9.2	21.7
Benton	3 558	71.6	35.2	59.5	27.1	8.5	5.6	28.4	24.5	12.8	2.50	3.09	3 524	7.3	23.9
Blackford	5 690	70.8	30.8	56.8	22.2	10.0	6.2	29.2	25.9	12.0	2.44	2.91	5 436	8.6	23.2
Boone	17 081	75.0	38.0	64.4	31.4	7.8	4.8	25.0	21.1	8.6	2.65	3.09	13 922	6.9	19.7
Brown	5 897	75.2	29.9	64.8	24.1	6.5	3.5	24.8	20.6	7.3	2.51	2.89	5 370	5.7	20.4
Carroll	7 718	73.7	33.2	63.5	27.0	6.5	3.8	26.3	22.8	10.5	2.59	3.04	7 067	6.1	21.4
Cass	15 715	69.5	31.7	55.9	23.7	9.4	5.7	30.5	25.9	11.8	2.53	3.01	14 659	9.7	24.5
Clark	38 751	68.5	31.4	52.1	21.9	12.5	7.4	31.5	26.3	9.3	2.45	2.95	33 292	12.2	23.3
Clay	10 216	72.8	33.6	59.7	25.8	9.4	5.6	27.2	23.8	12.3	2.57	3.03	9 382	8.6	24.0
Clinton	12 545	72.2	35.2	58.9	26.9	9.0	5.7	27.8	23.6	11.1	2.63	3.10	11 450	8.4	22.1
Crawford	4 181	73.1	32.5	59.1	24.0	9.5	5.8	26.9	22.5	9.4	2.55	2.96	3 660	8.1	22.4
Daviess	10 894	71.8	35.5	59.8	28.1	8.7	5.3	28.2	25.0	12.3	2.69	3.24	10 012	8.3	24.2
Dearborn	16 832	75.9	37.4	62.5	29.2	9.6	6.0	24.1	20.1	8.1	2.71	3.13	13 642	9.1	19.2
Decatur	9 389	73.3	34.1	60.1	26.2	9.2	5.4	26.7	22.8	9.6	2.58	3.03	8 427	8.6	20.9
De Kalb	15 134	72.1	36.3	59.3	28.0	8.8	5.7	27.9	23.4	9.3	2.63	3.11	12 725	8.3	21.3
Delaware	47 131	63.0	27.8	48.5	19.0	10.9	6.9	37.0	28.2	10.4	2.37	2.90	45 177	10.6	25.9
Dubois	14 813	72.5	37.1	61.8	30.6	7.4	4.6	27.5	23.5	9.9	2.63	3.13	13 023	6.7	21.9
Elkhart	66 154	72.0	36.4	56.8	26.6	10.5	7.0	28.0	22.6	8.4	2.72	3.18	56 713	9.1	21.6
Fayette	10 199	70.1	30.8	55.6	22.0	10.2	6.2	29.9	25.8	12.3	2.46	2.94	9 945	11.0	24.1
Floyd	27 511	71.6	34.7	55.4	24.9	12.4	7.7	28.4	23.5	8.7	2.54	3.00	24 085	12.6	21.9
Fountain	7 041	71.6	32.6	59.1	25.3	8.0	4.7	28.4	24.8	12.6	2.52	3.00	6 858	7.3	23.8
Franklin	7 868	77.9	37.6	66.0	31.0	8.0	4.5	22.1	19.0	8.8	2.77	3.17	6 636	6.8	18.2
Fulton	8 082	71.0	31.8	59.5	24.5	7.5	4.6	29.0	24.9	12.0	2.52	2.99	7 345	7.6	24.2
Gibson	12 847	70.8	32.1	58.1	24.3	9.2	5.7	29.2	25.7	12.1	2.48	2.98	12 299	7.9	24.5
Grant	28 319	69.1	29.5	53.7	19.9	11.5	7.2	30.9	26.7	11.5	2.43	2.92	27 701	11.4	23.7
Greene	13 372	70.0	31.7	58.0	24.3	8.4	5.3	30.0	26.5	12.4	2.44	2.92	11 910	8.2	24.8
Hamilton	65 933	77.1	43.7	67.5	37.3	7.0	4.7	22.9	18.6	5.0	2.75	3.16	38 834	6.9	17.0
Hancock	20 718	78.0	36.7	67.5	30.4	7.4	4.5	22.0	18.8	7.6	2.65	3.02	15 959	6.8	17.0
Harrison	12 917	75.2	36.0	62.4	28.2	8.8	5.4	24.8	20.7	8.4	2.63	3.04	10 618	8.3	18.2
Hendricks	37 275	78.0	39.6	67.1	32.6	7.7	4.9	22.0	18.3	6.6	2.71	3.08	26 109	7.1	16.4
Henry	19 486	71.7	30.7	58.4	23.0	9.9	5.7	28.3	24.8	11.9	2.45	2.91	18 642	9.3	22.8
Howard	34 800	67.7	31.3	52.7	21.7	11.5	7.5	32.3	28.2	10.3	2.41	2.95	31 523	11.3	25.0
Huntington	14 242	72.2	34.4	59.4	26.4	9.1	5.7	27.8	23.6	9.7	2.57	3.04	12 830	8.1	21.9
Jackson	16 052	72.1	33.7	58.1	25.7	9.9	5.7	27.9	23.5	10.1	2.54	2.98	14 032	9.1	21.2
Jasper	10 686	76.9	36.4	65.4	29.8	7.7	4.4	23.1	19.9	9.3	2.72	3.13	8 527	7.5	19.1
Jay	8 405	71.6	32.3	58.8	24.9	9.1	5.3	28.4	24.8	12.2	2.57	3.06	8 161	8.4	23.7
Jefferson	12 148	69.4	32.0	55.0	23.1	10.6	6.7	30.6	25.7	10.1	2.46	2.94	10 897	10.5	23.4
Jennings	10 134	75.0	36.4	60.7	27.6	9.5	5.8	25.0	20.6	8.2	2.67	3.07	8 351	8.7	20.0
Johnson	42 434	74.5	37.4	62.0	29.5	9.0	5.8	25.5	21.2	7.3	2.63	3.06	31 354	8.6	19.3
Knox	15 552	65.2	30.0	51.6	21.6	10.2	6.4	34.8	29.7	13.3	2.36	2.93	15 145	9.5	27.9
Kosciusko	27 283	73.3	35.6	60.9	27.8	8.3	5.3	26.7	21.9	8.0	2.66	3.11	23 449	7.2	20.1
Lagrange	11 225	78.9	40.6	64.2	34.5	6.9	3.9	21.1	18.0	7.5	3.09	3.54	9 209	5.7	16.6
Lake	181 633	69.9	32.8	48.7	21.5	16.6	9.3	30.1	25.8	9.6	2.64	3.19	170 748	15.9	23.2
La Porte	41 050	69.7	31.8	53.8	22.6	11.7	7.1	30.3	25.2	10.5	2.52	3.02	38 488	10.9	23.6
Lawrence	18 535	70.9	31.4	58.5	24.0	9.0	5.4	29.1	25.5	11.5	2.44	2.91	16 235	8.3	22.5
Madison	53 052	68.3	29.9	52.5	20.3	11.8	7.3	31.7	27.2	11.7	2.41	2.91	49 804	11.4	24.9
Marion	352 164	60.6	30.2	41.2	18.4	14.9	9.3	39.4	31.8	8.7	2.39	3.03	319 471	13.8	29.3
Marshall	16 519	73.8	35.8	61.3	28.3	8.3	5.2	26.2	22.3	10.0	2.69	3.15	15 146	7.5	21.0
Martin	4 183	68.8	31.6	56.5	24.5	8.2	4.9	31.2	27.6	12.3	2.45	3.00	3 836	7.9	23.9
Miami	13 716	71.5	33.7	57.2	24.9	9.8	6.4	28.5	24.6	10.1	2.52	3.00	13 484	8.6	21.2
Monroe	46 898	52.7	24.3	41.8	17.5	8.1	5.1	47.3	32.4	7.2	2.27	2.87	39 351	8.3	28.5
Montgomery	14 595	70.2	33.4	57.6	25.0	8.6	5.9	29.8	25.3	11.0	2.50	2.97	13 235	7.8	24.4
Morgan	24 437	77.9	36.9	65.2	29.4	8.6	5.0	22.1	18.4	7.3	2.70	3.06	19 600	8.4	16.2
Newton	5 340	74.9	34.2	63.1	27.4	7.8	4.3	25.1	20.9	9.4	2.69	3.12	4 839	7.5	20.4
Noble	16 696	73.6	37.4	60.2	29.0	9.0	5.9	26.4	21.9	8.6	2.73	3.19	13 418	8.1	19.8
Ohio	2 201	72.1	31.9	59.9	24.4	8.5	5.2	27.9	23.2	10.2	2.53	3.00	1 980	7.6	21.6
Orange	7 621	70.1	32.4	57.6	24.9	8.6	5.2	29.9	26.2	12.0	2.49	3.00	6 950	8.8	22.8
Owen	8 282	74.8	33.6	62.3	25.9	8.5	5.2	25.2	21.3	8.9	2.60	3.00	6 394	7.5	19.6
Parke	6 415	72.1	30.5	59.9	23.1	8.3	5.1	27.9	24.1	11.6	2.51	2.97	5 845	8.3	23.6
Perry	7 270	69.8	30.6	56.7	23.2	9.0	5.0	30.2	26.7	12.7	2.45	2.96	6 845	9.1	23.0
Pike	5 119	71.9	30.6	59.8	23.6	8.4	4.8	28.1	24.9	11.8	2.47	2.94	4 925	7.5	23.5
Porter	54 649	72.7	35.0	59.8	27.6	9.2	5.4	27.3	22.2	8.0	2.62	3.08	45 159	8.4	19.6
Posey	10 205	74.6	36.4	63.5	29.5	7.8	4.9	25.4	22.1	10.0	2.63	3.08	9 508	7.2	20.4
Pulaski	5 170	73.1	33.9	61.4	26.8	7.3	4.6	26.9	23.5	11.4	2.59	3.06	4 722	6.4	23.8

[1]No spouse present.

Table B. States and Counties

STATE County	Percent change of households, 1990–2000	Total housing units	Occupied housing units (percent)	Housing occupancy, 2000 — Vacant housing units — Total	For seasonal, recreational, or occasional use	Homeowner vacancy rate (percent)	Rental vacancy rate (percent)	Housing tenure, 2000 — Occupied housing units — Total	Percent owner-occupied housing units	Percent renter-occupied housing units	Average household size of owner-occupied units	Average household size of renter-occupied units
	86	87	88	89	90	91	92	93	94	95	96	97
INDIANA	13.1	2 532 319	92.3	7.7	1.3	1.8	8.8	2 336 306	71.4	28.6	2.64	2.24
Adams	12.9	12 404	95.3	4.7	0.4	1.0	6.9	11 818	77.0	23.0	3.02	2.10
Allen	13.6	138 905	92.7	7.3	0.3	1.8	10.8	128 745	71.0	29.0	2.69	2.15
Bartholomew	15.5	29 853	93.6	6.4	0.8	1.9	8.5	27 936	74.3	25.7	2.60	2.32
Benton	1.0	3 818	93.2	6.8	0.3	2.5	6.3	3 558	75.8	24.2	2.62	2.51
Blackford	4.7	6 155	92.4	7.6	0.8	1.9	8.4	5 690	78.7	21.3	2.49	2.23
Boone	22.7	17 929	95.3	4.7	0.4	1.2	7.2	17 081	78.7	21.3	2.77	2.22
Brown	9.8	7 163	82.3	17.7	13.1	1.7	5.7	5 897	85.0	15.0	2.54	2.35
Carroll	9.2	8 675	89.0	11.0	6.0	1.1	4.8	7 718	79.7	20.3	2.60	2.53
Cass	7.2	16 620	94.6	5.4	0.6	1.0	4.5	15 715	73.7	26.3	2.54	2.51
Clark	16.4	41 176	94.1	5.9	0.6	1.6	8.0	38 751	70.0	30.0	2.55	2.22
Clay	8.9	11 097	92.1	7.9	1.0	1.8	7.9	10 216	79.1	20.9	2.64	2.28
Clinton	9.6	13 267	94.6	5.4	0.3	1.5	5.8	12 545	72.9	27.1	2.65	2.59
Crawford	14.2	5 138	81.4	18.6	10.6	2.0	7.8	4 181	82.9	17.1	2.58	2.39
Daviess	8.8	11 898	91.6	8.4	1.9	1.9	9.0	10 894	78.6	21.4	2.80	2.29
Dearborn	23.4	17 791	94.6	5.4	0.9	1.0	7.9	16 832	78.6	21.4	2.82	2.31
Decatur	11.4	9 992	94.0	6.0	1.1	1.4	6.3	9 389	73.2	26.8	2.65	2.41
De Kalb	18.9	16 144	93.7	6.3	0.8	1.9	9.1	15 134	81.5	18.5	2.72	2.26
Delaware	4.3	51 032	92.4	7.6	0.4	1.7	9.0	47 131	67.2	32.8	2.44	2.23
Dubois	13.7	15 511	95.5	4.5	0.8	1.0	5.4	14 813	78.0	22.0	2.78	2.07
Elkhart	16.6	69 791	94.8	5.2	0.5	1.7	6.7	66 154	72.2	27.8	2.81	2.49
Fayette	2.6	10 981	92.9	7.1	0.6	1.8	9.0	10 199	71.5	28.5	2.52	2.30
Floyd	14.2	29 087	94.6	5.4	0.3	1.6	7.1	27 511	72.5	27.5	2.66	2.22
Fountain	2.7	7 692	91.5	8.5	1.7	2.1	7.9	7 041	77.9	22.1	2.58	2.33
Franklin	18.6	8 596	91.5	8.5	3.6	1.1	6.1	7 868	81.4	18.6	2.85	2.42
Fulton	10.0	9 123	88.6	11.4	4.8	1.9	11.2	8 082	78.4	21.6	2.57	2.35
Gibson	4.5	14 125	91.0	9.0	1.8	1.7	10.8	12 847	77.9	22.1	2.57	2.16
Grant	2.2	30 560	92.7	7.3	0.3	1.6	10.0	28 319	73.2	26.8	2.52	2.19
Greene	12.3	15 053	88.8	11.2	2.4	2.5	9.0	13 372	80.0	20.0	2.50	2.20
Hamilton	69.8	69 478	94.9	5.1	0.4	1.5	11.7	65 933	80.9	19.1	2.88	2.17
Hancock	29.8	21 750	95.3	4.7	0.3	1.4	10.5	20 718	81.4	18.6	2.74	2.28
Harrison	21.7	13 699	94.3	5.7	0.6	1.2	7.1	12 917	84.1	15.9	2.68	2.35
Hendricks	42.8	39 229	95.0	5.0	0.4	1.4	10.1	37 275	83.0	17.0	2.79	2.31
Henry	4.5	20 592	94.6	5.4	0.5	1.8	6.1	19 486	77.0	23.0	2.52	2.23
Howard	10.4	37 604	92.5	7.5	0.7	1.8	10.2	34 800	71.7	28.3	2.49	2.19
Huntington	11.0	15 269	93.3	6.7	0.4	1.6	9.5	14 242	77.1	22.9	2.65	2.32
Jackson	14.4	17 137	93.7	6.3	0.5	2.0	6.1	16 052	74.3	25.7	2.58	2.44
Jasper	25.3	11 236	95.1	4.9	0.5	1.5	4.4	10 686	77.5	22.5	2.79	2.47
Jay	3.0	9 074	92.6	7.4	0.3	2.0	9.3	8 405	77.7	22.3	2.63	2.35
Jefferson	11.5	13 386	90.8	9.2	2.4	1.9	8.8	12 148	74.6	25.4	2.55	2.19
Jennings	21.4	11 469	88.4	11.6	4.0	2.1	8.4	10 134	79.1	20.9	2.71	2.51
Johnson	35.3	45 095	94.1	5.9	0.6	2.0	10.1	42 434	76.5	23.5	2.77	2.18
Knox	2.7	17 305	89.9	10.1	0.8	2.6	12.5	15 552	69.0	31.0	2.46	2.14
Kosciusko	16.4	32 188	84.8	15.2	10.5	1.9	6.4	27 283	79.0	21.0	2.73	2.43
Lagrange	21.9	12 938	86.8	13.2	9.0	1.3	6.3	11 225	81.5	18.5	3.21	2.56
Lake	6.4	194 992	93.1	6.9	0.3	1.6	7.0	181 633	69.0	31.0	2.74	2.41
La Porte	6.7	45 621	90.0	10.0	4.0	1.8	8.3	41 050	75.2	24.8	2.60	2.29
Lawrence	14.2	20 560	90.2	9.8	1.9	2.1	9.3	18 535	78.9	21.1	2.51	2.16
Madison	6.5	56 939	93.2	6.8	0.4	1.7	8.6	53 052	74.2	25.8	2.47	2.25
Marion	10.2	387 183	91.0	9.0	0.3	2.0	11.0	352 164	59.3	40.7	2.54	2.18
Marshall	9.1	18 099	91.3	8.7	3.8	1.3	6.3	16 519	76.8	23.2	2.75	2.49
Martin	9.0	4 729	88.5	11.5	3.8	1.6	8.5	4 183	81.2	18.8	2.53	2.11
Miami	1.7	15 299	89.7	10.3	0.6	1.7	10.6	13 716	76.0	24.0	2.56	2.39
Monroe	19.2	50 846	92.2	7.8	1.9	2.3	6.8	46 898	54.0	46.0	2.48	2.02
Montgomery	10.3	15 678	93.1	6.9	0.6	1.7	8.5	14 595	73.4	26.6	2.57	2.30
Morgan	24.7	25 908	94.3	5.7	0.6	1.5	7.5	24 437	79.7	20.3	2.77	2.43
Newton	10.4	5 726	93.3	6.7	0.9	2.4	6.1	5 340	79.9	20.1	2.73	2.54
Noble	24.4	18 233	91.6	8.4	2.8	2.3	6.9	16 696	78.0	22.0	2.82	2.42
Ohio	11.2	2 424	90.8	9.2	3.6	1.2	11.5	2 201	77.6	22.4	2.62	2.24
Orange	9.7	8 348	91.3	8.7	1.7	2.0	9.9	7 621	79.1	20.9	2.58	2.14
Owen	29.5	9 853	84.1	15.9	7.0	2.4	7.1	8 282	81.6	18.4	2.63	2.44
Parke	9.8	7 539	85.1	14.9	7.9	2.1	6.7	6 415	80.2	19.8	2.54	2.35
Perry	6.2	8 223	88.4	11.6	3.7	1.7	9.5	7 270	79.3	20.7	2.56	2.03
Pike	3.9	5 611	91.2	8.8	1.3	1.4	10.6	5 119	82.5	17.5	2.53	2.21
Porter	21.0	57 616	94.9	5.1	1.1	1.4	6.9	54 649	76.7	23.3	2.75	2.21
Posey	7.3	11 076	92.1	7.9	1.7	1.6	12.4	10 205	81.8	18.2	2.69	2.31
Pulaski	9.5	5 918	87.4	12.6	6.1	2.3	8.6	5 170	80.6	19.4	2.61	2.48

Table B. States and Counties

STATE/County code	MSA/PMSA/NECMA code[1]	County type[2]	STATE County	Population, 2000				Population, 1990				Population and population characteristics, 2000					
												Race (percent) One race					
				Land area, 2000[3] (sq km)	Total persons	Rank	Per square kilometer	Land area, 1990[3] (sq km)	Total persons	Rank	Per square kilometer	White	Black or African American	American Indian or Alaska Native	Asian	Native Hawaiian and other Pacific Islander	Some other race
				1	2	3	4	5	6	7	8	9	10	11	12	13	14
			INDIANA—Cont'd														
18 133	...	6	Putnam	1 244	36 019	1 216	29.0	1 244	30 315	1 279	24.4	94.9	2.9	0.3	0.5	0.0	0.4
18 135	...	6	Randolph	1 173	27 401	1 470	23.4	1 173	27 148	1 385	23.1	98.1	0.3	0.2	0.2	0.0	0.6
18 137	...	6	Ripley	1 156	26 523	1 501	22.9	1 156	24 616	1 476	21.3	98.3	0.0	0.3	0.4	0.0	0.5
18 139	...	6	Rush	1 057	18 261	1 882	17.3	1 058	18 129	1 781	17.1	97.7	0.6	0.2	0.5	0.0	0.2
18 141	7800	3	St. Joseph	1 185	265 559	208	224.1	1 185	247 052	203	208.5	82.4	11.5	0.4	1.3	0.1	2.5
18 143	4520	2	Scott	493	22 960	1 645	46.6	493	20 991	1 630	42.6	98.6	0.0	0.2	0.2	0.0	0.4
18 145	3480	1	Shelby	1 069	43 445	1 029	40.6	1 069	40 307	993	37.7	97.3	0.8	0.2	0.6	0.0	0.5
18 147	...	8	Spencer	1 033	20 391	1 767	19.7	1 033	19 490	1 703	18.9	97.7	0.6	0.2	0.2	0.0	0.7
18 149	...	6	Starke	801	23 556	1 611	29.4	801	22 747	1 546	28.4	97.5	0.2	0.2	0.2	0.0	0.7
18 151	...	6	Steuben	800	33 214	1 306	41.5	800	27 446	1 378	34.3	97.2	0.4	0.3	0.4	0.0	0.9
18 153	...	6	Sullivan	1 158	21 751	1 707	18.8	1 158	18 993	1 735	16.4	94.1	4.3	0.3	0.1	0.0	0.3
18 155	...	8	Switzerland	573	9 065	2 523	15.8	573	7 738	2 600	13.5	98.8	0.2	0.2	0.1	0.0	0.3
18 157	3920	3	Tippecanoe	1 294	148 955	362	115.1	1 295	130 598	356	100.8	88.9	2.5	0.3	4.5	0.0	2.5
18 159	3850	3	Tipton	674	16 577	1 985	24.6	674	16 119	1 916	23.9	98.3	0.1	0.2	0.3	0.0	0.3
18 161	...	8	Union	418	7 349	2 651	17.6	418	6 976	2 662	16.7	98.7	0.2	0.3	0.2	0.0	0.2
18 163	2440	2	Vanderburgh	608	171 922	316	282.8	608	165 058	289	271.5	89.3	8.2	0.2	0.8	0.0	0.4
18 165	8320	3	Vermillion	665	16 788	1 971	25.2	665	16 773	1 863	25.2	98.4	0.3	0.2	0.1	0.0	0.2
18 167	8320	3	Vigo	1 045	105 848	501	101.3	1 045	106 107	436	101.5	90.7	6.0	0.3	1.2	0.0	0.4
18 169	...	7	Wabash	1 070	34 960	1 250	32.7	1 070	35 069	1 129	32.8	97.4	0.4	0.7	0.4	0.0	0.4
18 171	...	8	Warren	945	8 419	2 571	8.9	945	8 176	2 548	8.7	99.1	0.1	0.1	0.2	0.0	0.4
18 173	2440	2	Warrick	995	52 383	892	52.6	995	44 920	913	45.1	97.5	1.0	0.1	0.6	0.0	0.2
18 175	...	6	Washington	1 332	27 223	1 474	20.4	1 332	23 717	1 502	17.8	98.8	0.1	0.1	0.2	0.0	0.2
18 177	...	5	Wayne	1 045	71 097	699	68.0	1 045	71 951	619	68.9	92.0	5.1	0.1	0.5	0.0	0.7
18 179	2760	2	Wells	958	27 600	1 462	28.8	958	25 948	1 423	27.1	98.3	0.2	0.2	0.2	0.0	0.4
18 181	...	6	White	1 309	25 267	1 556	19.3	1 309	23 265	1 527	17.8	95.2	0.2	0.3	0.2	0.0	3.2
18 183	2760	2	Whitley	869	30 707	1 381	35.3	869	27 651	1 365	31.8	98.4	0.2	0.4	0.2	0.0	0.3
19 000	...		IOWA	144 701	2 926 324	X	20.2	144 716	2 776 831	X	19.2	93.9	2.1	0.3	1.3	0.0	1.3
19 001	...	8	Adair	1 474	8 243	2 587	5.6	1 475	8 409	2 519	5.7	98.9	0.1	0.1	0.2	0.0	0.2
19 003	...	9	Adams	1 097	4 482	2 882	4.1	1 097	4 866	2 846	4.4	98.9	0.1	0.4	0.2	0.0	0.0
19 005	...	7	Allamakee	1 656	14 675	2 110	8.9	1 657	13 855	2 067	8.4	95.9	0.1	0.2	0.3	0.0	2.8
19 007	...	7	Appanoose	1 285	13 721	2 181	10.7	1 285	13 743	2 077	10.7	98.2	0.4	0.2	0.3	0.0	0.3
19 009	...	7	Audubon	1 148	6 830	2 707	5.9	1 148	7 334	2 627	6.4	99.2	0.1	0.1	0.2	0.0	0.0
19 011	...	6	Benton	1 855	25 308	1 552	13.6	1 856	22 429	1 556	12.1	98.8	0.2	0.1	0.2	0.0	0.1
19 013	8920	3	Black Hawk	1 469	128 012	423	87.1	1 469	123 798	371	84.3	88.4	8.0	0.2	1.0	0.0	0.9
19 015	...	6	Boone	1 480	26 224	1 509	17.7	1 480	25 186	1 455	17.0	98.5	0.4	0.2	0.2	0.0	0.3
19 017	...	6	Bremer	1 134	23 325	1 628	20.6	1 134	22 813	1 541	20.1	98.2	0.5	0.1	0.5	0.0	0.1
19 019	...	6	Buchanan	1 480	21 093	1 732	14.3	1 480	20 844	1 638	14.1	98.4	0.3	0.2	0.4	0.0	0.2
19 021	...	7	Buena Vista	1 489	20 411	1 765	13.7	1 489	19 965	1 679	13.4	88.0	0.4	0.1	4.3	0.0	5.8
19 023	...	8	Butler	1 503	15 305	2 071	10.2	1 503	15 731	1 939	10.5	99.0	0.1	0.1	0.2	0.0	0.2
19 025	...	9	Calhoun	1 477	11 115	2 357	7.5	1 477	11 508	2 255	7.8	98.1	0.7	0.2	0.2	0.0	0.3
19 027	...	6	Carroll	1 475	21 421	1 716	14.5	1 475	21 423	1 608	14.5	98.9	0.2	0.2	0.2	0.0	0.3
19 029	...	6	Cass	1 462	14 684	2 108	10.0	1 462	15 128	1 979	10.3	98.8	0.2	0.1	0.1	0.0	0.2
19 031	...	6	Cedar	1 501	18 187	1 889	12.1	1 501	17 444	1 825	11.6	98.5	0.2	0.2	0.3	0.0	0.3
19 033	...	5	Cerro Gordo	1 472	46 447	974	31.6	1 472	46 733	894	31.7	96.3	0.8	0.2	0.7	0.0	0.9
19 035	...	7	Cherokee	1 495	13 035	2 229	8.7	1 495	14 098	2 048	9.4	98.3	0.3	0.2	0.4	0.0	0.4
19 037	...	7	Chickasaw	1 307	13 095	2 221	10.0	1 307	13 295	2 115	10.2	98.7	0.1	0.0	0.3	0.0	0.3
19 039	...	6	Clarke	1 117	9 133	2 519	8.2	1 117	8 287	2 539	7.4	96.6	0.1	0.3	0.4	0.0	2.0
19 041	...	7	Clay	1 473	17 372	1 930	11.8	1 474	17 585	1 815	11.9	98.1	0.2	0.1	0.8	0.0	0.3
19 043	...	9	Clayton	2 017	18 678	1 862	9.3	2 017	19 054	1 730	9.4	98.9	0.1	0.2	0.1	0.0	0.2
19 045	...	4	Clinton	1 800	50 149	914	27.9	1 800	51 040	827	28.4	95.9	1.9	0.2	0.6	0.0	0.3
19 047	...	7	Crawford	1 850	16 942	1 956	9.2	1 850	16 775	1 862	9.1	93.1	0.8	0.3	0.5	0.0	4.6
19 049	2120	2	Dallas	1 519	40 750	1 090	26.8	1 519	29 755	1 305	19.6	94.7	0.7	0.2	0.7	0.0	2.8
19 051	...	7	Davis	1 303	8 541	2 565	6.6	1 304	8 312	2 533	6.4	98.3	0.2	0.2	0.2	0.0	0.2
19 053	...	9	Decatur	1 377	8 689	2 552	6.3	1 379	8 338	2 530	6.0	96.5	1.0	0.2	0.6	0.1	0.5
19 055	...	6	Delaware	1 497	18 404	1 874	12.3	1 497	18 035	1 789	12.0	99.3	0.1	0.1	0.1	0.0	0.1
19 057	...	5	Des Moines	1 078	42 351	1 048	39.3	1 078	42 614	942	39.5	93.7	3.6	0.2	0.6	0.0	0.7
19 059	...	7	Dickinson	987	16 424	1 996	16.6	987	14 909	1 992	15.1	98.9	0.2	0.2	0.2	0.0	0.1
19 061	2200	3	Dubuque	1 575	89 143	583	56.6	1 575	86 403	528	54.9	97.1	0.9	0.1	0.6	0.1	0.5
19 063	...	7	Emmet	1 025	11 027	2 363	10.8	1 025	11 569	2 251	11.3	97.4	0.2	0.3	0.3	0.0	1.3
19 065	...	6	Fayette	1 893	22 008	1 691	11.6	1 893	21 843	1 587	11.5	97.7	0.5	0.1	0.4	0.0	0.4
19 067	...	7	Floyd	1 296	16 900	1 959	13.0	1 297	17 058	1 847	13.2	98.1	0.2	0.1	0.4	0.1	0.4
19 069	...	7	Franklin	1 508	10 704	2 383	7.1	1 509	11 364	2 264	7.5	94.9	0.1	0.2	0.2	0.0	4.1
19 071	...	9	Fremont	1 324	8 010	2 606	6.0	1 324	8 226	2 546	6.2	98.0	0.0	0.2	0.2	0.0	1.0
19 073	...	7	Greene	1 472	10 366	2 408	7.0	1 472	10 045	2 380	6.8	98.2	0.1	0.2	0.2	0.0	0.7
19 075	...	8	Grundy	1 302	12 369	2 275	9.5	1 302	12 029	2 217	9.2	99.0	0.1	0.0	0.3	0.0	0.2

[1]MSA = Metropolitan Statistical Area. PMSA = Primary MSA. NECMA = New England County Metropolitan Area. See Appendix A for explanation of these concepts. See Appendix B for list of metropolitan areas identified by type, with component counties.
[2]County typology code from the Economic Research Service of USDA. See Appendix A for definition.
[3]Dry land or land partially or temporarily covered by water.

Table B. States and Counties

STATE County	Population and population characteristics, 2000 (cont'd)								Population and population characteristics, 1990				
	Race (percent) (cont'd)								Race (percent)				
	Race alone or in combination												
	Two or more races	White	Black	American Indian or Alaska Native	Asian	Native Hawaiian and other Pacific Islander	Some other race	Hispanic[1]	White	Black or African American	American Indian or Alaska Native	Asian and Pacific Islander	Hispanic[1]
	15	16	17	18	19	20	21	22	23	24	25	26	27
INDIANA—Cont'd													
Putnam	0.9	95.7	3.2	0.7	0.7	0.1	0.6	1.1	96.3	2.7	0.3	0.5	0.6
Randolph	0.7	98.8	0.4	0.5	0.3	0.0	0.7	1.2	99.3	0.2	0.2	0.1	0.7
Ripley	0.4	98.7	0.1	0.6	0.5	0.0	0.6	0.9	99.5	0.1	0.2	0.2	0.3
Rush	0.8	98.5	0.8	0.6	0.6	0.0	0.4	0.5	98.7	0.8	0.1	0.3	0.3
St. Joseph	2.0	84.1	12.3	0.9	1.7	0.1	3.1	4.7	87.8	9.8	0.3	1.0	2.1
Scott	0.5	99.1	0.1	0.4	0.3	0.0	0.5	1.0	99.3	0.1	0.1	0.2	0.7
Shelby	0.7	97.9	0.9	0.5	0.7	0.1	0.6	1.1	98.6	0.8	0.2	0.4	0.3
Spencer	0.5	98.2	0.7	0.5	0.3	0.0	0.8	1.5	99.0	0.6	0.2	0.2	0.5
Starke	1.0	98.5	0.3	0.7	0.4	0.0	1.1	2.2	98.7	0.3	0.4	0.2	1.6
Steuben	0.8	98.0	0.5	0.7	0.5	0.0	1.1	2.1	98.9	0.2	0.2	0.5	0.7
Sullivan	0.8	94.9	4.5	0.8	0.2	0.1	0.5	0.8	99.5	0.1	0.2	0.1	0.3
Switzerland	0.4	99.2	0.3	0.5	0.1	0.0	0.4	0.9	99.4	0.2	0.2	0.1	0.3
Tippecanoe	1.4	90.1	2.8	0.7	4.8	0.1	2.9	5.3	93.4	2.0	0.2	3.7	1.6
Tipton	0.7	99.0	0.2	0.4	0.4	0.1	0.5	1.2	99.2	0.1	0.1	0.3	0.8
Union	0.4	99.1	0.3	0.5	0.3	0.1	0.2	0.3	99.1	0.3	0.2	0.3	0.4
Vanderburgh	1.1	90.3	8.8	0.5	1.0	0.1	0.6	1.0	91.6	7.5	0.2	0.6	0.5
Vermillion	0.8	99.2	0.4	0.7	0.3	0.1	0.3	0.6	99.5	0.1	0.2	0.2	0.4
Vigo	1.4	91.9	6.7	0.7	1.5	0.1	0.6	1.2	92.7	5.6	0.3	1.1	0.9
Wabash	0.7	98.1	0.5	1.0	0.5	0.1	0.5	1.2	98.3	0.4	0.7	0.4	0.9
Warren	0.4	99.5	0.1	0.4	0.2	0.0	0.2	0.4	99.6	0.0	0.2	0.2	0.3
Warrick	0.5	98.0	1.2	0.3	0.8	0.1	0.2	0.6	98.6	0.8	0.2	0.3	0.4
Washington	0.6	99.3	0.2	0.5	0.2	0.0	0.3	0.7	99.6	0.1	0.1	0.1	0.5
Wayne	1.4	93.4	5.9	0.6	0.7	0.1	0.9	1.4	93.9	5.3	0.2	0.4	0.5
Wells	0.6	99.0	0.3	0.5	0.3	0.0	0.5	1.4	99.3	0.0	0.2	0.2	1.0
White	0.9	96.1	0.2	0.6	0.3	0.1	3.6	5.3	99.4	0.0	0.2	0.2	0.8
Whitley	0.6	98.9	0.3	0.7	0.3	0.1	0.4	0.9	99.4	0.1	0.3	0.1	0.5
IOWA	1.1	94.9	2.5	0.6	1.5	0.1	1.6	2.8	96.6	1.7	0.3	0.9	1.2
Adair	0.5	99.4	0.1	0.3	0.3	0.0	0.4	0.7	99.6	0.0	0.1	0.2	0.4
Adams	0.4	99.3	0.1	0.5	0.2	0.0	0.2	0.6	99.6	0.1	0.1	0.1	0.4
Allamakee	0.7	96.5	0.2	0.4	0.5	0.1	3.0	3.5	99.5	0.0	0.2	0.2	0.3
Appanoose	0.7	98.8	0.5	0.6	0.3	0.0	0.3	1.0	98.8	0.6	0.2	0.3	0.5
Audubon	0.4	99.5	0.3	0.3	0.2	0.0	0.0	0.5	99.9	0.0	0.0	0.1	0.3
Benton	0.5	99.3	0.4	0.4	0.2	0.0	0.2	0.6	99.5	0.1	0.1	0.2	0.4
Black Hawk	1.5	89.8	8.6	0.5	1.2	0.1	1.5	1.8	91.8	6.9	0.2	0.8	0.7
Boone	0.4	98.9	0.5	0.4	0.3	0.0	0.3	0.8	99.3	0.2	0.1	0.3	0.4
Bremer	0.6	98.8	0.7	0.2	0.7	0.0	0.3	0.6	99.0	0.3	0.0	0.6	0.3
Buchanan	0.5	98.9	0.4	0.5	0.5	0.0	0.3	0.6	99.3	0.2	0.1	0.2	0.5
Buena Vista	1.4	89.1	0.6	0.3	4.7	0.1	6.6	12.5	97.5	0.3	0.1	2.0	0.8
Butler	0.5	99.5	0.2	0.3	0.3	0.1	0.2	0.6	99.7	0.0	0.1	0.2	0.2
Calhoun	0.5	98.5	0.9	0.4	0.3	0.0	0.5	0.9	99.3	0.3	0.1	0.2	0.3
Carroll	0.3	99.2	0.3	0.2	0.4	0.0	0.3	0.5	99.5	0.0	0.1	0.3	0.3
Cass	0.3	99.2	0.4	0.3	0.1	0.0	0.3	0.7	99.6	0.1	0.1	0.1	0.3
Cedar	0.6	99.0	0.3	0.4	0.4	0.1	0.4	0.9	99.4	0.1	0.1	0.3	0.6
Cerro Gordo	1.2	97.4	1.2	0.4	0.9	0.1	1.3	2.8	97.9	0.6	0.1	0.6	2.1
Cherokee	0.4	98.7	0.4	0.3	0.5	0.1	0.4	1.0	99.3	0.1	0.3	0.2	0.4
Chickasaw	0.6	99.3	0.1	0.3	0.3	0.1	0.5	0.6	99.8	0.0	0.0	0.1	0.3
Clarke	0.6	97.2	0.2	0.6	0.4	0.1	2.1	4.0	99.6	0.0	0.1	0.3	0.2
Clay	0.5	98.6	0.3	0.3	1.0	0.1	0.4	1.1	99.2	0.0	0.2	0.5	0.3
Clayton	0.4	99.3	0.2	0.4	0.2	0.0	0.3	0.8	99.7	0.0	0.1	0.1	0.3
Clinton	1.1	96.9	2.3	0.6	0.7	0.0	0.5	1.3	97.7	1.4	0.2	0.4	0.6
Crawford	0.8	93.8	0.9	0.6	0.6	0.0	4.9	8.7	98.8	0.4	0.2	0.5	0.6
Dallas	0.8	95.5	1.0	0.4	0.9	0.1	3.1	5.4	99.3	0.2	0.1	0.2	0.6
Davis	0.8	99.1	0.3	0.7	0.3	0.1	0.3	0.7	99.2	0.0	0.3	0.3	0.5
Decatur	1.1	97.5	1.2	0.7	1.0	0.4	0.7	1.7	98.3	0.4	0.2	0.9	0.5
Delaware	0.3	99.6	0.1	0.2	0.2	0.0	0.2	0.7	99.6	0.1	0.1	0.2	0.4
Des Moines	1.2	94.8	4.2	0.6	0.8	0.1	0.9	1.7	95.8	3.1	0.2	0.5	1.2
Dickinson	0.4	99.3	0.3	0.4	0.2	0.0	0.2	0.7	99.5	0.1	0.1	0.2	0.3
Dubuque	0.8	97.8	1.1	0.4	0.7	0.1	0.7	1.2	98.8	0.4	0.1	0.5	0.5
Emmet	0.5	97.9	0.4	0.5	0.4	0.0	1.4	4.3	99.3	0.2	0.1	0.3	0.5
Fayette	0.8	98.4	0.7	0.4	0.5	0.1	0.7	1.5	99.2	0.2	0.1	0.2	0.9
Floyd	0.6	98.6	0.4	0.3	0.6	0.2	0.5	1.3	99.4	0.0	0.1	0.3	0.5
Franklin	0.5	95.4	0.2	0.4	0.2	0.0	4.3	6.0	99.0	0.1	0.1	0.1	1.3
Fremont	0.5	98.5	0.1	0.5	0.3	0.0	1.0	2.2	99.4	0.0	0.1	0.2	0.6
Greene	0.6	98.8	0.3	0.4	0.3	0.0	0.9	1.7	99.5	0.0	0.1	0.3	0.3
Grundy	0.5	99.5	0.1	0.2	0.4	0.0	0.3	0.6	99.6	0.1	0.1	0.2	0.3

[1] Hispanic persons may be of any race.

Table B. States and Counties

STATE County	Under 5 years	5 to 17 years	18 to 24 years	25 to 34 years	35 to 44 years	45 to 54 years	55 to 64 years	65 to 74 years	75 years and over	Median age (years)	Percent Female
	28	29	30	31	32	33	34	35	36	37	38
INDIANA—Cont'd											
Putnam	6.1	17.4	13.2	13.0	16.3	12.3	9.3	7.0	5.3	35.1	48.0
Randolph	6.7	18.5	7.9	12.3	15.0	13.6	10.2	8.3	7.5	38.2	51.0
Ripley	7.4	20.7	7.7	13.2	15.7	12.8	9.2	6.9	6.5	35.7	50.9
Rush	6.8	19.9	7.5	12.9	16.0	13.1	9.1	7.7	7.1	36.9	50.9
St. Joseph	7.0	18.7	11.8	13.2	14.8	13.1	7.8	6.7	6.9	34.4	51.7
Scott	7.4	18.9	9.2	14.5	15.8	13.5	9.7	6.3	4.7	35.1	50.4
Shelby	6.8	19.9	8.0	13.2	17.4	13.6	9.0	6.5	5.7	36.2	50.5
Spencer	6.3	20.2	7.3	12.4	16.7	14.3	9.9	7.2	5.7	37.3	49.9
Starke	6.5	20.3	8.0	12.3	15.5	13.2	10.3	7.8	6.1	37.0	50.5
Steuben	6.6	19.0	10.4	13.1	15.4	13.9	9.7	6.6	5.3	35.5	49.5
Sullivan	5.6	17.0	9.4	14.3	16.2	14.1	9.4	7.2	6.9	37.3	46.5
Switzerland	6.3	20.0	8.5	12.2	15.8	13.8	10.8	7.2	5.4	36.8	49.6
Tippecanoe	5.9	15.1	25.4	14.6	12.5	10.9	6.5	4.6	4.5	27.2	48.7
Tipton	6.1	18.9	7.2	12.7	15.4	14.8	10.4	7.1	7.4	38.4	51.1
Union	7.0	20.3	7.7	12.9	15.6	13.3	10.3	6.9	6.0	36.5	50.4
Vanderburgh	6.2	16.9	11.5	12.7	15.4	13.3	8.7	7.6	7.7	36.9	52.6
Vermillion	6.3	17.5	8.1	12.6	14.9	14.7	10.2	7.7	8.1	38.9	51.3
Vigo	6.1	16.8	14.3	12.9	14.3	12.9	8.4	6.9	7.3	34.9	50.9
Wabash	5.9	18.6	10.3	11.7	14.5	13.6	9.7	7.6	8.1	37.5	51.5
Warren	6.0	20.0	6.6	12.4	15.5	14.3	11.2	7.5	6.4	38.2	49.3
Warrick	6.6	20.3	7.2	12.2	17.5	15.7	9.7	5.8	5.0	37.3	50.9
Washington	6.7	19.8	8.7	13.5	16.2	13.7	9.3	6.4	5.6	35.8	50.0
Wayne	6.2	18.0	9.2	12.7	14.8	13.5	9.9	8.2	7.5	37.7	52.0
Wells	6.6	20.7	8.3	11.5	16.6	13.3	8.9	7.0	7.1	36.8	50.7
White	6.4	19.4	7.8	12.4	15.3	13.8	10.0	7.9	6.9	37.6	50.8
Whitley	6.8	19.9	8.1	12.4	16.4	14.5	8.8	6.7	6.3	36.9	50.4
IOWA	6.4	18.6	10.2	12.4	15.2	13.4	8.8	7.2	7.7	36.6	50.9
Adair	5.4	18.5	6.9	9.3	15.1	12.9	9.8	9.4	12.7	41.8	51.0
Adams	5.5	18.4	6.3	9.5	14.6	13.2	11.0	10.0	11.4	41.9	50.8
Allamakee	5.9	19.6	7.0	10.6	15.0	13.1	10.5	8.9	9.5	39.7	49.9
Appanoose	5.6	18.2	7.8	10.7	14.4	13.0	10.5	9.3	10.7	40.6	52.2
Audubon	5.8	20.1	5.0	9.2	13.5	12.3	10.6	10.6	12.9	42.4	52.1
Benton	6.5	20.9	6.8	12.0	17.3	12.4	8.7	7.5	8.0	37.2	50.0
Black Hawk	6.1	17.0	15.7	11.9	13.3	13.6	8.4	6.8	7.2	34.4	52.0
Boone	6.0	18.8	8.4	11.5	15.6	14.2	9.1	7.8	8.6	38.6	51.0
Bremer	5.5	18.6	12.0	9.9	14.0	13.6	10.3	7.3	8.7	38.1	51.7
Buchanan	6.9	21.7	8.1	11.2	15.1	13.4	9.1	7.0	7.5	36.4	50.3
Buena Vista	5.9	19.5	12.2	10.7	14.7	12.7	7.5	7.9	9.0	36.4	49.9
Butler	5.5	18.9	6.4	10.5	14.4	14.4	9.8	9.1	11.0	41.3	51.0
Calhoun	5.1	17.9	6.4	9.9	14.9	13.5	10.1	9.8	12.3	42.4	50.5
Carroll	6.0	20.9	7.4	10.3	15.6	12.4	8.6	8.7	9.9	38.7	51.3
Cass	5.4	18.3	6.8	9.7	15.1	13.4	10.5	9.6	11.2	41.6	51.5
Cedar	6.1	19.3	6.9	11.3	16.4	14.3	9.5	7.6	8.7	39.2	50.6
Cerro Gordo	5.9	17.8	9.0	11.0	15.4	14.0	9.2	8.7	9.0	39.3	51.9
Cherokee	5.5	19.1	6.8	8.9	15.1	14.3	10.0	10.0	10.3	41.7	50.7
Chickasaw	5.7	20.4	6.9	10.0	15.7	13.0	10.4	8.6	9.3	39.7	50.0
Clarke	6.4	19.9	7.6	11.0	15.5	13.4	9.1	8.2	8.8	38.6	50.8
Clay	6.1	18.6	8.0	11.1	15.8	13.8	8.7	8.5	9.5	39.4	51.7
Clayton	5.8	19.6	6.5	10.6	15.5	13.7	9.9	9.2	9.4	40.2	50.6
Clinton	6.4	19.2	8.2	11.4	15.7	13.5	9.8	7.7	8.1	38.2	51.5
Crawford	6.4	20.2	8.1	10.9	14.9	12.9	9.6	8.2	9.0	38.2	49.8
Dallas	8.3	19.9	6.9	14.7	17.5	13.6	8.0	5.5	5.6	35.1	50.6
Davis	7.1	20.1	7.4	10.7	14.5	12.9	10.0	8.4	9.0	38.5	50.5
Decatur	5.5	17.5	16.3	9.2	12.4	12.0	9.5	8.6	9.0	36.4	51.1
Delaware	6.4	22.6	7.0	10.9	16.7	12.3	9.2	7.5	7.5	37.1	50.4
Des Moines	6.3	18.1	8.5	11.6	14.6	14.6	9.7	7.9	8.8	38.9	51.7
Dickinson	5.3	16.6	6.6	9.9	14.0	15.6	11.2	10.7	9.9	43.3	51.3
Dubuque	6.6	18.9	10.2	12.0	15.3	13.4	8.9	7.3	7.4	36.5	51.4
Emmet	5.5	18.8	10.1	9.9	13.9	13.3	9.3	8.6	10.8	39.6	51.4
Fayette	6.0	19.0	8.6	10.3	14.7	12.6	9.8	9.0	10.0	39.4	50.6
Floyd	6.2	18.9	7.0	10.8	13.7	13.7	10.5	8.6	10.6	40.3	51.7
Franklin	5.6	18.6	7.3	10.0	14.1	13.9	10.0	9.8	10.7	41.3	50.9
Fremont	5.6	19.5	6.0	10.0	14.3	14.6	10.2	9.3	10.6	41.2	51.2
Greene	5.8	19.8	6.1	9.5	14.8	13.1	9.3	9.6	12.0	41.0	51.2
Grundy	5.4	19.8	6.3	9.8	15.3	13.7	10.4	8.8	10.4	40.8	51.1

Table B. States and Counties

	Population and population characteristics, 1990										Population—change, 1980–2000				
	Age (percent)										Total persons			Percent change	
STATE County	Under 5 years	5 to 17 years	18 to 24 years	25 to 34 years	35 to 44 years	45 to 54 years	55 to 64 years	65 to 74 years	75 years and over	Percent Female	2000	1990	1980	1990–2000	1980–1990
	39	40	41	42	43	44	45	46	47	48	49	50	51	52	53
INDIANA—Cont'd															
Putnam	6.0	17.1	16.2	15.3	13.4	10.2	9.2	7.0	5.7	48.7	36 019	30 315	29 163	18.8	4.0
Randolph	6.5	19.3	8.9	14.4	14.2	11.0	10.3	8.6	6.7	51.6	27 401	27 148	29 997	0.9	-9.5
Ripley	7.4	21.2	9.2	15.3	14.0	10.2	8.6	7.6	6.6	51.0	26 523	24 616	24 398	7.7	0.9
Rush	6.9	21.0	9.2	15.0	13.8	10.1	9.3	8.2	6.5	51.6	18 261	18 129	19 604	0.7	-7.5
St. Joseph	7.3	18.0	12.4	15.9	14.5	9.1	8.8	8.0	6.1	51.8	265 559	247 052	241 617	7.5	2.2
Scott	7.2	20.6	10.0	15.9	14.4	11.5	8.5	6.5	5.3	51.5	22 960	20 991	20 422	9.4	2.8
Shelby	7.3	20.0	9.2	16.7	15.0	10.7	8.9	6.9	5.3	51.4	43 445	40 307	39 887	7.8	1.1
Spencer	6.9	20.4	8.6	16.3	14.8	10.8	9.1	7.2	5.8	50.0	20 391	19 490	19 361	4.6	0.7
Starke	7.3	20.7	9.3	15.4	13.1	10.2	9.6	8.2	6.2	50.8	23 556	22 747	21 997	3.6	3.4
Steuben	7.2	18.9	11.0	15.5	14.5	10.7	9.2	7.8	5.3	50.1	33 214	27 446	24 694	21.0	11.1
Sullivan	6.1	19.4	8.2	13.6	14.7	10.5	9.7	9.8	8.0	52.1	21 751	18 993	21 107	14.5	-10.0
Switzerland	6.6	20.4	8.2	14.5	13.8	11.7	9.8	8.2	6.9	50.9	9 065	7 738	7 153	17.1	8.2
Tippecanoe	6.3	14.7	26.0	16.3	12.7	8.1	6.4	5.4	4.1	49.3	148 955	130 598	121 702	14.1	7.3
Tipton	6.3	19.8	8.6	14.8	15.0	11.7	8.9	8.0	6.8	51.4	16 577	16 119	16 819	2.8	-4.2
Union	6.7	21.3	9.0	15.0	14.7	11.1	8.4	7.5	6.4	51.5	7 349	6 976	6 860	5.3	1.7
Vanderburgh	6.9	16.9	10.1	16.9	14.2	9.8	9.4	8.8	6.9	52.9	171 922	165 058	167 515	4.2	-1.5
Vermillion	6.0	18.9	8.6	14.3	14.5	11.3	9.2	9.4	7.9	52.6	16 788	16 773	18 229	0.1	-8.0
Vigo	6.2	16.7	14.7	15.4	13.9	9.3	8.5	8.5	6.6	51.0	105 848	106 107	112 385	-0.2	-5.6
Wabash	6.7	19.5	11.0	14.7	13.8	10.4	9.1	7.9	6.9	51.6	34 960	35 069	36 640	-0.3	-4.3
Warren	7.0	19.2	8.3	13.9	14.7	12.1	9.9	8.8	6.1	50.7	8 419	8 176	8 976	3.0	-8.9
Warrick	7.0	21.3	8.6	16.0	17.4	11.7	7.7	6.0	4.3	50.8	52 383	44 920	41 474	16.6	8.3
Washington	6.8	20.6	9.4	16.0	14.3	10.7	8.7	7.7	5.8	50.3	27 223	23 717	21 932	14.8	8.1
Wayne	6.6	18.6	10.2	14.7	13.9	10.9	9.9	8.5	6.6	52.3	71 097	71 951	76 058	-1.2	-5.4
Wells	7.7	20.7	8.5	16.4	14.4	10.2	8.5	7.5	6.0	51.5	27 600	25 948	25 401	6.4	2.2
White	6.8	20.2	7.8	15.0	14.6	9.9	9.9	9.3	6.5	51.7	25 267	23 265	23 867	8.6	-2.5
Whitley	7.5	20.9	8.8	15.8	15.5	9.7	8.9	7.1	5.8	50.9	30 707	27 651	26 215	11.1	5.5
IOWA	7.0	18.9	10.2	15.4	14.2	9.9	9.0	8.2	7.2	51.6	2 926 324	2 776 831	2 913 808	5.4	-4.7
Adair	6.6	18.5	6.3	13.3	11.7	10.0	10.1	11.2	12.4	51.9	8 243	8 409	9 509	-2.0	-11.6
Adams	7.0	17.4	5.8	13.5	12.4	10.9	11.3	11.2	10.5	50.9	4 482	4 866	5 731	-7.9	-15.1
Allamakee	7.2	20.1	6.7	13.8	12.9	9.9	10.0	10.1	9.4	51.1	14 675	13 855	15 108	5.9	-8.3
Appanoose	6.3	18.8	7.6	13.5	12.6	9.9	9.8	10.9	10.5	52.4	13 721	13 743	15 511	-0.2	-11.4
Audubon	6.9	18.6	5.6	12.0	12.1	10.5	11.2	11.7	11.4	52.0	6 830	7 334	8 559	-6.9	-14.3
Benton	7.4	20.4	7.4	15.4	13.6	10.0	9.3	8.8	7.8	51.0	25 308	22 429	23 649	12.8	-5.2
Black Hawk	6.7	18.7	13.9	14.1	14.6	9.8	8.6	7.7	5.9	52.4	128 012	123 798	137 961	3.4	-10.3
Boone	6.6	17.9	7.7	15.1	15.0	10.1	9.6	8.9	9.1	52.3	26 224	25 186	26 184	4.1	-3.8
Bremer	6.0	19.2	11.7	12.7	13.8	11.2	8.6	8.6	8.1	51.4	23 325	22 813	24 820	2.2	-8.1
Buchanan	7.8	23.0	7.3	14.3	13.7	9.9	8.5	8.7	6.9	51.0	21 093	20 844	22 900	1.2	-9.0
Buena Vista	7.1	18.8	11.4	14.4	12.8	8.0	9.5	9.3	8.6	51.5	20 411	19 965	20 774	2.2	-3.9
Butler	6.2	20.1	6.5	12.9	13.7	9.9	10.1	10.6	9.9	51.3	15 305	15 731	17 668	-2.7	-11.0
Calhoun	6.0	19.1	5.2	12.6	13.1	9.9	10.4	12.2	11.6	52.4	11 115	11 508	13 542	-3.4	-15.0
Carroll	7.9	21.8	7.2	14.5	12.5	9.0	9.4	9.3	8.4	51.7	21 421	21 423	22 951	0.0	-6.7
Cass	6.4	19.3	6.0	13.7	13.2	10.3	10.2	10.3	10.7	52.4	14 684	15 128	16 932	-2.9	-10.7
Cedar	6.3	20.3	6.9	14.8	14.9	10.5	9.5	9.0	7.8	51.2	18 187	17 444	18 635	4.3	-6.4
Cerro Gordo	6.8	18.0	8.9	15.8	14.2	9.7	9.8	9.1	7.8	52.7	46 447	46 733	48 458	-0.6	-3.6
Cherokee	6.6	20.5	6.0	13.5	13.8	9.9	11.1	9.6	8.9	51.7	13 035	14 098	16 238	-7.5	-13.2
Chickasaw	6.7	21.4	6.5	14.4	13.1	10.7	9.3	9.3	8.6	50.4	13 095	13 295	15 437	-1.5	-13.9
Clarke	6.8	19.4	6.9	14.3	14.0	10.1	10.0	8.7	9.9	52.2	9 133	8 287	8 612	10.2	-3.8
Clay	7.1	20.2	7.4	15.0	14.5	9.5	9.7	9.0	7.5	52.4	17 372	17 585	19 576	-1.2	-10.2
Clayton	7.0	20.9	6.7	14.2	13.0	10.0	10.2	9.4	8.7	50.8	18 678	19 054	21 098	-2.0	-9.7
Clinton	7.0	19.7	8.1	15.1	14.2	10.6	9.4	8.9	7.1	52.0	50 149	51 040	57 122	-1.7	-10.6
Crawford	7.0	20.5	7.8	14.2	13.1	10.4	9.7	9.3	8.1	51.1	16 942	16 775	18 935	1.0	-11.4
Dallas	7.1	20.8	7.1	15.8	15.8	10.5	8.3	7.7	6.9	51.2	40 750	29 755	29 513	37.0	0.8
Davis	7.3	19.9	7.5	13.7	12.9	10.4	9.6	8.9	9.9	51.1	8 541	8 312	9 104	2.8	-8.7
Decatur	6.1	17.2	14.0	12.1	11.3	9.1	9.6	10.1	10.4	51.7	8 689	8 338	9 794	4.2	-14.9
Delaware	7.8	22.9	7.4	15.7	12.7	9.7	9.1	8.2	6.5	50.9	18 404	18 035	18 933	2.0	-4.7
Des Moines	6.6	19.1	8.4	14.5	15.0	10.7	9.5	8.7	7.5	52.2	42 351	42 614	46 203	-0.6	-7.8
Dickinson	5.5	18.0	6.0	12.8	14.9	10.4	11.6	11.7	9.1	52.1	16 424	14 909	15 629	10.2	-4.6
Dubuque	7.0	20.1	10.8	15.2	14.1	10.0	8.7	7.6	6.5	51.7	89 143	86 403	93 745	3.2	-7.8
Emmet	6.1	20.4	9.3	12.5	13.3	9.3	10.2	9.7	9.1	51.6	11 027	11 569	13 336	-4.7	-13.2
Fayette	6.8	19.6	7.9	13.6	13.0	9.9	9.9	10.0	9.2	51.4	22 008	21 843	25 488	0.8	-14.3
Floyd	6.6	19.4	7.4	12.5	13.3	11.2	10.1	10.4	9.3	52.4	16 900	17 058	19 597	-0.9	-13.0
Franklin	6.4	19.3	6.2	13.4	13.8	10.1	10.6	10.1	9.9	51.6	10 704	11 364	13 036	-5.8	-12.8
Fremont	6.3	19.8	6.3	12.2	13.7	9.7	10.5	11.2	10.4	52.7	8 010	8 226	9 401	-2.6	-12.5
Greene	6.3	18.4	6.1	12.8	13.1	9.8	10.9	10.9	11.6	52.5	10 366	10 045	12 119	3.2	-17.1
Grundy	6.4	19.1	5.8	13.1	14.0	11.3	10.2	10.6	9.4	52.0	12 369	12 029	14 366	2.8	-16.3

Table B. States and Counties

STATE County	Total population	Total in house-holds	House-holder	Spouse	Child Total	Child Own child under 18 years	Other relatives Total	Other relatives Under 18 years	Nonrelatives Total	Nonrelatives Unmarried partner	Total in group quarters	Correctional institutions	Nursing homes	Other institutions	College dormitories	Military quarters	Other
	54	55	56	57	58	59	60	61	62	63	64	65	66	67	68	69	70
INDIANA—Cont'd																	
Putnam	36 019	87.9	34.4	21.5	26.4	21.8	2.6	1.2	3.0	1.5	12.1	5.8	0.9	0.1	5.3	0.0	0.1
Randolph	27 401	98.9	39.9	23.5	29.1	23.3	2.8	1.3	3.5	2.0	1.1	0.3	0.7	0.0	0.0	0.0	0.1
Ripley	26 523	98.7	37.1	22.7	32.5	26.2	3.1	1.4	3.2	1.7	1.3	0.1	0.9	0.0	0.0	0.0	0.3
Rush	18 261	98.5	37.9	23.1	31.0	24.8	3.0	1.3	3.5	1.9	1.5	0.2	1.1	0.1	0.0	0.0	0.1
St. Joseph	265 559	94.9	37.9	19.0	29.2	23.2	4.0	1.8	4.8	2.1	5.1	0.2	0.8	0.1	3.3	0.0	0.6
Scott	22 960	99.1	38.5	22.2	30.1	23.6	4.1	2.0	4.2	2.3	0.9	0.3	0.5	0.0	0.0	0.0	0.2
Shelby	43 445	98.5	38.1	22.6	30.3	24.4	3.3	1.5	4.3	2.3	1.5	0.3	0.7	0.0	0.0	0.0	0.5
Spencer	20 391	98.2	37.1	24.1	31.6	24.9	2.7	1.2	2.7	1.5	1.8	0.3	0.7	0.0	0.0	0.0	0.8
Starke	23 556	98.7	37.1	22.0	31.4	24.2	4.2	1.9	4.0	2.1	1.3	0.2	1.1	0.0	0.0	0.0	0.0
Steuben	33 214	97.2	38.4	21.9	28.6	23.5	3.2	1.3	5.2	2.6	2.8	0.3	0.4	0.0	1.9	0.0	0.1
Sullivan	21 751	89.5	35.9	20.9	26.5	20.5	2.9	1.3	3.2	1.5	10.5	9.5	0.8	0.0	0.0	0.0	0.2
Switzerland	9 065	99.0	37.9	22.3	30.5	23.8	4.0	1.9	4.3	2.5	1.0	0.0	0.9	0.0	0.0	0.0	0.1
Tippecanoe	148 955	89.8	37.1	17.4	23.5	19.6	2.8	0.9	9.2	2.0	10.2	0.2	0.8	0.1	8.9	0.0	0.1
Tipton	16 577	98.8	39.0	24.3	29.5	23.2	2.6	1.2	3.3	1.7	1.2	0.2	0.9	0.0	0.0	0.0	0.2
Union	7 349	98.9	38.0	23.8	30.7	25.1	3.3	1.6	3.1	1.7	1.1	0.2	0.7	0.0	0.0	0.0	0.2
Vanderburgh	171 922	95.9	41.1	19.5	26.1	21.0	3.5	1.6	4.9	2.1	4.1	0.3	1.1	0.3	2.0	0.0	0.5
Vermillion	16 788	98.2	40.3	23.1	28.6	22.1	2.9	1.2	3.3	1.9	1.8	0.2	1.4	0.2	0.0	0.0	0.1
Vigo	105 848	92.3	38.7	18.6	26.2	20.6	3.4	1.5	5.3	2.3	7.7	1.8	1.0	0.4	4.1	0.0	0.4
Wabash	34 960	94.4	37.8	22.3	27.9	22.1	2.8	1.3	3.6	1.7	5.6	0.2	2.2	0.5	2.2	0.0	0.4
Warren	8 419	98.7	38.2	24.8	29.3	24.0	2.9	1.4	3.4	2.0	1.3	0.3	1.1	0.0	0.0	0.0	0.0
Warrick	52 383	98.7	37.1	24.8	31.5	25.3	2.6	1.1	2.7	1.4	1.3	0.2	1.0	0.0	0.0	0.0	0.1
Washington	27 223	98.8	37.7	22.7	30.8	24.4	3.5	1.5	4.0	2.0	1.2	0.2	0.9	0.0	0.0	0.0	0.1
Wayne	71 097	96.8	40.0	21.2	27.5	21.7	3.6	1.7	4.6	2.3	3.2	0.2	1.1	0.4	1.2	0.0	0.2
Wells	27 600	98.3	37.7	23.3	32.1	25.7	2.3	1.0	2.9	1.6	1.7	0.3	1.3	0.0	0.0	0.0	0.1
White	25 267	98.8	38.5	23.2	28.8	23.5	3.6	1.5	4.6	2.1	1.2	0.3	0.8	0.0	0.0	0.0	0.1
Whitley	30 707	98.5	38.1	23.4	30.9	24.9	2.6	1.2	3.5	1.8	1.5	0.4	0.5	0.3	0.0	0.0	0.2
IOWA	2 926 324	96.4	39.3	21.6	28.4	23.4	2.5	1.0	4.6	1.9	3.6	0.4	1.1	0.2	1.4	0.0	0.4
Adair	8 243	97.6	41.2	24.5	27.2	22.8	1.7	0.7	3.0	1.8	2.4	0.0	2.1	0.0	0.0	0.0	0.2
Adams	4 482	97.3	41.7	24.2	26.6	22.6	1.9	0.8	3.0	1.8	2.7	0.4	1.0	0.0	0.0	0.0	1.2
Allamakee	14 675	97.2	39.0	22.8	28.8	24.0	2.6	0.7	4.1	1.7	2.8	0.5	1.8	0.1	0.0	0.0	0.4
Appanoose	13 721	98.4	42.1	22.4	27.3	22.1	2.6	1.1	4.0	2.2	1.6	0.1	1.2	0.1	0.0	0.0	0.4
Audubon	6 830	97.4	40.6	24.9	28.3	24.9	1.4	0.6	2.1	1.3	2.6	0.1	2.5	0.0	0.0	0.0	0.0
Benton	25 308	98.8	38.5	24.1	31.0	25.9	1.6	0.8	3.5	1.8	1.2	0.1	1.0	0.0	0.0	0.0	0.1
Black Hawk	128 012	94.9	38.8	19.5	26.7	21.2	2.9	1.3	7.0	2.1	5.1	0.2	0.9	0.1	3.1	0.0	0.7
Boone	26 224	96.3	39.6	23.0	28.2	23.1	2.0	0.8	3.7	1.8	3.7	0.0	2.0	0.4	0.0	0.0	1.2
Bremer	23 325	93.7	38.0	23.8	27.8	23.0	1.2	0.5	3.0	1.3	6.3	0.0	1.2	0.3	4.6	0.0	0.1
Buchanan	21 093	98.1	37.6	22.8	32.6	26.9	1.8	0.8	3.2	1.8	1.9	0.1	0.9	0.7	0.0	0.0	0.3
Buena Vista	20 411	93.2	36.7	21.1	28.0	23.5	3.1	1.1	4.3	1.5	6.8	0.1	1.5	0.3	4.6	0.0	0.3
Butler	15 305	98.1	40.3	25.4	28.6	23.4	1.5	0.6	2.3	1.4	1.9	0.1	1.8	0.0	0.0	0.0	0.0
Calhoun	11 115	93.9	40.6	23.5	25.9	21.9	1.5	0.7	2.4	1.3	6.1	3.7	1.9	0.0	0.0	0.0	0.5
Carroll	21 421	97.5	39.6	22.6	31.0	26.1	1.3	0.5	3.0	1.3	2.5	0.1	1.5	0.8	0.0	0.0	0.1
Cass	14 684	96.8	41.7	23.6	26.8	22.6	1.7	0.6	3.1	1.8	3.2	0.1	1.5	0.0	0.0	0.0	1.5
Cedar	18 187	98.4	39.3	24.2	29.4	24.1	1.9	0.8	3.7	2.0	1.6	0.0	1.2	0.1	0.0	0.0	0.2
Cerro Gordo	46 447	96.9	41.7	21.6	27.5	22.4	1.9	0.8	4.2	2.1	3.1	0.2	1.3	0.1	0.8	0.0	0.8
Cherokee	13 035	97.1	41.3	23.6	27.7	23.0	1.4	0.7	3.1	1.7	2.9	0.1	1.9	0.9	0.0	0.0	0.0
Chickasaw	13 095	98.3	39.6	24.1	30.2	25.2	1.4	0.5	3.0	1.8	1.7	0.0	1.3	0.0	0.0	0.0	0.4
Clarke	9 133	98.3	39.2	22.7	29.5	24.4	2.9	1.2	4.0	2.2	1.7	0.1	0.9	0.3	0.0	0.0	0.4
Clay	17 372	98.3	41.8	23.3	27.8	23.6	1.6	0.6	3.9	2.1	1.7	0.1	1.4	0.2	0.0	0.0	0.1
Clayton	18 678	97.4	39.5	23.6	29.1	24.2	1.8	0.5	3.5	1.9	2.6	0.0	1.7	0.0	0.0	0.0	0.8
Clinton	50 149	98.0	40.1	21.9	29.4	23.9	2.6	1.2	4.0	2.2	2.0	0.1	0.5	0.3	0.4	0.0	0.8
Crawford	16 942	96.2	38.0	22.2	28.5	24.0	3.0	1.1	4.5	2.0	3.8	0.1	1.5	0.3	0.0	0.0	1.8
Dallas	40 750	98.9	38.2	23.2	31.4	26.9	2.3	0.9	3.7	1.9	1.1	0.1	1.1	0.0	0.0	0.0	0.0
Davis	8 541	97.8	37.5	23.6	31.4	25.7	2.1	0.8	3.3	1.5	2.2	0.1	1.9	0.0	0.0	0.0	0.1
Decatur	8 689	91.1	38.4	20.9	25.1	21.3	2.6	1.0	4.2	1.5	8.9	0.0	1.2	0.0	7.3	0.0	0.4
Delaware	18 404	98.6	37.1	23.8	33.5	28.0	1.5	0.5	2.7	1.5	1.4	0.0	1.3	0.0	0.0	0.0	0.1
Des Moines	42 351	97.8	40.8	21.5	28.5	22.5	2.7	1.2	4.3	2.2	2.2	0.3	1.2	0.2	0.1	0.0	0.5
Dickinson	16 424	98.3	43.2	25.0	25.1	20.9	1.6	0.6	3.4	1.9	1.7	0.0	1.6	0.0	0.0	0.0	0.1
Dubuque	89 143	94.9	37.8	21.5	30.2	24.4	1.9	0.7	3.5	1.6	5.1	0.1	1.2	0.1	2.4	0.0	1.3
Emmet	11 027	95.1	40.4	22.2	26.8	21.8	1.9	0.7	3.9	1.7	4.9	0.2	1.9	1.1	1.4	0.0	0.3
Fayette	22 008	96.2	39.9	22.7	28.4	23.8	1.8	0.7	3.5	1.8	3.8	0.3	1.2	0.2	1.6	0.0	0.4
Floyd	16 900	97.1	40.4	23.3	28.5	23.9	1.7	0.7	3.1	1.8	2.9	0.0	1.9	0.3	0.0	0.0	0.7
Franklin	10 704	98.0	40.7	24.0	27.7	23.0	2.1	0.8	3.6	1.7	2.0	0.0	1.9	0.0	0.0	0.0	0.1
Fremont	8 010	97.8	39.9	23.5	28.3	23.5	2.3	0.9	3.8	1.9	2.2	0.2	1.8	0.0	0.0	0.0	0.2
Greene	10 366	97.6	40.6	23.3	29.2	24.6	1.9	0.7	2.8	1.5	2.4	0.1	2.2	0.0	0.0	0.0	0.1
Grundy	12 369	98.6	40.3	25.7	28.8	24.2	1.5	0.7	2.2	1.1	1.4	0.0	1.3	0.0	0.0	0.0	0.1

Table B. States and Counties

STATE County	Households by type, 2000												Households, 1990		
		Family households						Nonfamily households							
				Married couple		Female householder[1]			Householder living alone						
	Total households	Total	With own children under 18 years	Total	With own children under 18 years	Total	With own children under 18 years	Total	Total	65 years and over	Average household size	Average family size	Total households	Female householder[1]	Householder living alone
	71	72	73	74	75	76	77	78	79	80	81	82	83	84	85
INDIANA—Cont'd															
Putnam	12 374	73.7	34.0	62.4	26.8	7.7	5.0	26.3	22.4	9.4	2.56	2.99	9 996	6.9	21.7
Randolph	10 937	71.3	31.5	58.9	24.0	8.7	5.2	28.7	25.0	11.9	2.48	2.95	10 451	8.4	22.9
Ripley	9 842	73.9	36.7	61.3	29.2	8.7	5.2	26.1	22.7	10.7	2.66	3.13	8 778	7.6	22.2
Rush	6 923	72.9	34.3	60.8	27.1	8.4	5.0	27.1	23.3	11.3	2.60	3.06	6 504	8.2	21.1
St. Joseph	100 743	66.3	32.0	50.0	22.1	12.4	7.8	33.7	27.9	10.7	2.50	3.07	92 365	11.4	26.4
Scott	8 832	73.5	35.0	57.6	25.5	11.3	6.7	26.5	22.5	8.9	2.58	2.99	7 593	11.2	20.1
Shelby	16 561	72.8	34.7	59.2	26.1	9.3	5.9	27.2	22.7	9.5	2.58	3.02	14 761	8.2	21.0
Spencer	7 569	76.0	35.4	65.0	29.3	7.2	3.9	24.0	20.8	10.0	2.65	3.07	6 962	6.7	20.8
Starke	8 740	73.8	33.7	59.4	25.3	9.9	5.9	26.2	22.4	10.2	2.66	3.10	8 141	9.2	21.1
Steuben	12 738	70.0	32.6	57.0	24.0	8.5	5.6	30.0	24.3	9.1	2.53	3.00	10 194	6.9	22.8
Sullivan	7 819	71.3	31.9	58.1	24.5	9.3	5.4	28.7	25.3	13.1	2.49	2.96	7 364	7.5	25.6
Switzerland	3 435	73.9	33.0	58.7	23.8	10.2	6.1	26.1	21.7	9.2	2.61	3.03	2 839	7.0	23.0
Tippecanoe	55 226	58.7	28.5	46.9	21.3	8.3	5.5	41.3	28.0	7.4	2.42	3.01	45 618	7.9	25.4
Tipton	6 469	73.4	32.5	62.3	26.2	7.7	4.3	26.6	23.1	11.2	2.53	2.97	6 026	7.7	21.8
Union	2 793	74.2	35.3	62.6	28.3	8.2	5.0	25.8	22.4	10.3	2.60	3.05	2 576	8.7	21.2
Vanderburgh	70 623	62.9	28.7	47.5	19.5	11.9	7.3	37.1	31.0	12.1	2.33	2.93	66 780	11.4	29.2
Vermillion	6 762	69.7	30.8	57.3	23.6	9.0	5.4	30.3	26.6	12.9	2.44	2.94	6 638	8.8	27.2
Vigo	40 998	63.6	29.6	48.0	20.0	11.7	7.3	36.4	30.0	11.9	2.38	2.96	39 804	10.7	28.3
Wabash	13 215	71.1	31.4	59.0	24.1	8.5	5.1	28.9	24.9	10.8	2.50	2.97	12 630	7.6	22.4
Warren	3 219	75.3	33.3	64.9	26.9	6.8	4.0	24.7	21.2	10.5	2.58	2.98	3 015	6.0	19.1
Warrick	19 438	78.1	37.7	66.9	30.9	8.2	5.0	21.9	18.6	7.5	2.66	3.03	15 817	7.7	16.8
Washington	10 264	73.9	35.0	60.2	26.9	9.2	5.4	26.1	22.2	9.0	2.62	3.05	8 664	9.0	21.2
Wayne	28 469	67.8	30.1	52.8	20.8	11.4	7.1	32.2	27.4	11.8	2.42	2.92	27 587	11.3	24.9
Wells	10 402	73.3	35.1	61.9	28.0	8.3	5.2	26.7	23.3	10.2	2.61	3.09	9 438	7.5	20.9
White	9 727	72.9	32.4	60.4	24.8	8.4	5.1	27.1	22.6	11.2	2.57	2.99	8 926	7.1	23.5
Whitley	11 711	73.5	34.5	61.3	26.9	8.3	5.2	26.5	22.4	9.5	2.58	3.03	10 010	6.8	20.3
IOWA	1 149 276	67.0	31.4	55.1	23.9	8.6	5.6	33.0	27.2	11.4	2.46	3.00	1 064 325	8.0	25.9
Adair	3 398	68.4	29.2	59.5	23.1	5.7	4.1	31.6	28.1	15.9	2.37	2.89	3 419	4.8	27.6
Adams	1 867	66.2	28.0	58.0	22.8	5.5	3.5	33.8	30.0	17.6	2.34	2.91	2 005	4.5	28.5
Allamakee	5 722	68.7	30.6	58.4	24.6	6.6	3.9	31.3	27.5	14.3	2.49	3.02	5 268	5.7	27.1
Appanoose	5 779	65.8	28.4	53.1	20.5	8.8	5.5	34.2	29.9	15.4	2.34	2.89	5 609	8.5	28.8
Audubon	2 773	69.5	30.1	61.4	24.7	5.6	3.9	30.5	28.2	16.7	2.40	2.94	2 936	4.5	26.8
Benton	9 746	72.4	34.9	62.7	28.4	6.5	4.4	27.6	23.4	11.7	2.56	3.04	8 518	6.8	23.5
Black Hawk	49 683	64.3	29.5	50.2	20.6	10.8	7.2	35.7	27.1	10.9	2.45	2.97	46 932	10.4	25.6
Boone	10 374	68.8	31.2	58.0	24.5	7.8	5.1	31.2	26.7	11.8	2.44	2.95	9 827	7.2	25.8
Bremer	8 860	71.4	32.0	62.5	26.0	6.2	4.4	28.6	24.7	12.7	2.47	2.95	8 394	5.0	24.0
Buchanan	7 933	71.5	34.5	60.7	27.5	7.4	4.9	28.5	24.7	12.5	2.61	3.13	7 506	7.4	23.6
Buena Vista	7 499	68.3	31.9	57.5	24.9	7.2	5.0	31.7	27.0	13.2	2.54	3.08	7 515	5.4	27.5
Butler	6 175	72.4	30.9	62.8	25.0	6.3	4.0	27.6	25.0	14.5	2.43	2.90	6 036	5.4	23.8
Calhoun	4 513	66.8	27.8	57.9	22.1	6.6	4.3	33.2	30.5	17.8	2.31	2.87	4 684	5.1	30.8
Carroll	8 486	66.8	32.9	57.0	26.5	6.8	4.7	33.2	29.6	15.5	2.46	3.07	7 964	6.3	27.0
Cass	6 120	66.9	29.3	56.6	22.1	7.2	5.1	33.1	29.8	15.9	2.32	2.87	6 177	5.5	29.6
Cedar	7 147	71.9	33.3	61.6	26.6	6.7	4.3	28.1	23.7	11.9	2.51	2.96	6 684	6.1	23.2
Cerro Gordo	19 374	64.0	29.1	51.9	21.2	9.1	6.0	36.0	30.9	13.5	2.32	2.91	19 061	8.5	29.3
Cherokee	5 378	66.9	29.1	57.3	22.7	6.5	4.4	33.1	29.5	15.3	2.35	2.91	5 514	6.0	27.8
Chickasaw	5 192	70.2	31.9	60.7	25.4	6.3	4.4	29.8	26.1	13.7	2.48	3.00	5 040	5.8	24.9
Clarke	3 584	69.7	32.1	57.8	24.4	8.3	5.7	30.3	25.9	13.3	2.50	3.01	3 343	6.8	26.8
Clay	7 259	65.8	30.7	55.6	23.7	6.8	4.9	34.2	29.8	13.7	2.35	2.92	7 074	6.7	27.9
Clayton	7 375	69.6	30.9	59.7	24.6	6.1	4.0	30.4	26.3	13.3	2.47	2.98	7 218	5.2	25.2
Clinton	20 105	68.0	31.8	54.6	23.3	9.8	6.4	32.0	27.4	12.2	2.44	2.98	19 757	9.2	25.6
Crawford	6 441	69.7	31.6	58.5	24.6	7.0	4.8	30.3	26.2	13.1	2.53	3.03	6 397	6.2	27.2
Dallas	15 584	71.7	37.2	60.6	29.7	8.0	5.5	28.3	23.6	8.2	2.59	3.08	11 204	7.7	22.1
Davis	3 207	71.3	32.0	62.7	26.6	5.2	3.1	28.7	25.0	13.8	2.61	3.13	3 093	5.6	23.3
Decatur	3 337	64.4	28.0	54.3	21.2	7.2	5.2	35.6	30.3	15.5	2.37	2.96	3 207	5.6	29.8
Delaware	6 834	73.6	36.7	64.1	30.7	6.2	4.1	26.4	23.0	11.2	2.66	3.15	6 389	6.3	21.8
Des Moines	17 270	66.8	29.6	52.7	20.6	10.5	6.9	33.2	28.6	12.6	2.40	2.94	16 874	9.9	27.0
Dickinson	7 103	67.0	26.1	57.8	20.3	6.7	4.4	33.0	28.6	13.7	2.27	2.78	6 160	6.1	27.7
Dubuque	33 690	68.6	33.1	56.8	25.9	8.7	5.5	31.4	26.7	10.8	2.51	3.07	30 799	8.5	24.4
Emmet	4 450	65.4	27.9	55.0	21.6	7.8	4.8	34.6	30.3	15.3	2.36	2.93	4 461	6.9	26.7
Fayette	8 778	67.8	30.4	56.8	23.4	7.4	4.9	32.2	28.2	15.0	2.41	2.96	8 490	5.9	27.4
Floyd	6 828	69.0	30.5	57.7	22.9	7.7	5.6	31.0	28.0	14.6	2.40	2.92	6 721	6.7	26.6
Franklin	4 356	68.5	29.3	58.9	23.2	6.4	4.2	31.5	27.6	15.4	2.41	2.93	4 579	5.7	27.7
Fremont	3 199	70.1	30.2	58.9	23.1	8.2	5.2	29.9	26.3	14.9	2.45	2.93	3 217	6.5	26.1
Greene	4 205	68.0	30.7	57.3	23.4	7.2	4.9	32.0	29.1	16.6	2.41	2.97	4 195	6.0	29.4
Grundy	4 984	71.9	30.7	63.8	25.6	5.5	3.4	28.1	25.5	14.2	2.45	2.94	4 776	4.7	24.8

[1] No spouse present.

Table B. States and Counties

STATE County	Percent change of households, 1990–2000	Total housing units	Occupied housing units (percent)	Vacant housing units — Total	For seasonal, recreational, or occasional use	Homeowner vacancy rate (percent)	Rental vacancy rate (percent)	Occupied housing units — Total	Percent owner-occupied housing units	Percent renter-occupied housing units	Average household size of owner-occupied units	Average household size of renter-occupied units
	86	87	88	89	90	91	92	93	94	95	96	97
INDIANA—Cont'd												
Putnam	23.8	13 505	91.6	8.4	3.0	2.0	5.2	12 374	78.6	21.4	2.63	2.28
Randolph	4.7	11 775	92.9	7.1	0.7	1.8	7.5	10 937	75.9	24.1	2.51	2.30
Ripley	12.1	10 482	93.9	6.1	1.2	1.5	6.1	9 842	76.8	23.2	2.76	2.33
Rush	6.4	7 337	94.4	5.6	0.5	1.6	3.7	6 923	74.1	25.9	2.65	2.46
St. Joseph	9.1	107 013	94.1	5.9	0.4	1.5	7.3	100 743	71.7	28.3	2.62	2.21
Scott	16.3	9 737	90.7	9.3	0.5	1.9	10.3	8 832	75.9	24.1	2.62	2.45
Shelby	12.2	17 633	93.9	6.1	0.5	1.8	7.5	16 561	73.4	26.6	2.65	2.39
Spencer	8.7	8 333	90.8	9.2	1.4	1.7	12.4	7 569	83.2	16.8	2.72	2.29
Starke	7.4	10 201	85.7	14.3	9.2	1.7	5.6	8 740	80.9	19.1	2.69	2.55
Steuben	25.0	17 337	73.5	26.5	21.0	2.3	8.7	12 738	78.1	21.9	2.60	2.29
Sullivan	6.2	8 804	88.8	11.2	1.0	3.0	12.2	7 819	79.8	20.2	2.55	2.25
Switzerland	21.0	4 226	81.3	18.7	10.8	2.4	4.9	3 435	77.9	22.1	2.67	2.41
Tippecanoe	21.1	58 343	94.7	5.3	0.3	1.6	5.6	55 226	55.9	44.1	2.62	2.18
Tipton	7.4	6 848	94.5	5.5	0.6	0.8	6.2	6 469	79.9	20.1	2.60	2.24
Union	8.4	3 077	90.8	9.2	1.7	1.4	8.0	2 793	75.3	24.7	2.66	2.43
Vanderburgh	5.8	76 300	92.6	7.4	0.4	2.1	8.0	70 623	66.8	33.2	2.49	2.03
Vermillion	1.9	7 405	91.3	8.7	1.1	2.1	8.3	6 762	79.5	20.5	2.49	2.22
Vigo	3.0	45 203	90.7	9.3	0.5	2.5	11.5	40 998	67.5	32.5	2.50	2.13
Wabash	4.6	14 034	94.2	5.8	0.6	1.2	6.2	13 215	75.9	24.1	2.57	2.28
Warren	6.8	3 477	92.6	7.4	2.0	1.9	5.4	3 219	81.1	18.9	2.61	2.46
Warrick	22.9	20 546	94.6	5.4	0.5	1.3	8.7	19 438	83.3	16.7	2.74	2.27
Washington	18.5	11 191	91.7	8.3	2.2	1.1	7.0	10 264	81.1	18.9	2.68	2.36
Wayne	3.2	30 468	93.4	6.6	0.4	1.7	8.6	28 469	68.7	31.3	2.48	2.29
Wells	10.2	10 970	94.8	5.2	0.4	1.2	5.7	10 402	80.9	19.1	2.71	2.18
White	9.0	12 083	80.5	19.5	14.6	2.0	6.4	9 727	76.6	23.4	2.56	2.59
Whitley	17.0	12 545	93.4	6.6	2.4	1.6	8.3	11 711	83.3	16.7	2.67	2.17
IOWA	8.0	1 232 511	93.2	6.8	1.3	1.7	6.8	1 149 276	72.3	27.7	2.57	2.15
Adair	-0.6	3 690	92.1	7.9	0.6	2.3	7.4	3 398	75.0	25.0	2.39	2.29
Adams	-6.9	2 109	88.5	11.5	1.0	1.8	6.9	1 867	74.7	25.3	2.39	2.19
Allamakee	8.6	7 142	80.1	19.9	15.1	1.9	6.7	5 722	76.4	23.6	2.54	2.33
Appanoose	3.0	6 697	86.3	13.7	3.3	3.3	9.4	5 779	74.0	26.0	2.42	2.11
Audubon	-5.6	2 995	92.6	7.4	1.1	1.6	7.4	2 773	79.2	20.8	2.37	2.51
Benton	14.4	10 377	93.9	6.1	1.2	1.5	6.6	9 746	79.4	20.6	2.64	2.27
Black Hawk	5.9	51 759	96.0	4.0	0.2	0.8	5.0	49 683	68.9	31.1	2.54	2.25
Boone	5.6	10 968	94.6	5.4	0.3	1.6	6.1	10 374	75.8	24.2	2.56	2.03
Bremer	5.6	9 337	94.9	5.1	0.9	1.5	5.4	8 860	78.2	21.8	2.56	2.12
Buchanan	5.7	8 697	91.2	8.8	0.5	1.3	6.8	7 933	78.2	21.8	2.66	2.42
Buena Vista	-0.2	8 145	92.1	7.9	0.6	2.1	7.5	7 499	70.4	29.6	2.60	2.39
Butler	2.3	6 578	93.9	6.1	0.9	1.5	5.2	6 175	80.4	19.6	2.47	2.28
Calhoun	-3.7	5 219	86.5	13.5	3.7	3.7	11.5	4 513	77.4	22.6	2.39	2.05
Carroll	6.6	9 019	94.1	5.9	0.2	1.8	7.7	8 486	74.4	25.6	2.60	2.05
Cass	-0.9	6 590	92.9	7.1	0.7	2.7	8.0	6 120	74.6	25.4	2.41	2.06
Cedar	6.9	7 570	94.4	5.6	0.8	1.5	5.5	7 147	76.8	23.2	2.57	2.29
Cerro Gordo	1.6	21 488	90.2	9.8	5.0	1.5	6.2	19 374	71.5	28.5	2.46	1.97
Cherokee	-2.5	5 850	91.9	8.1	0.5	1.9	9.5	5 378	73.7	26.3	2.42	2.18
Chickasaw	3.0	5 593	92.8	7.2	0.9	1.5	8.0	5 192	80.2	19.8	2.55	2.18
Clarke	7.2	3 934	91.1	8.9	0.9	1.9	7.8	3 584	72.4	27.6	2.57	2.33
Clay	2.6	7 828	92.7	7.3	0.9	1.6	6.2	7 259	69.1	30.9	2.49	2.04
Clayton	2.2	8 619	85.6	14.4	8.3	2.0	9.7	7 375	76.5	23.5	2.54	2.23
Clinton	1.8	21 585	93.1	6.9	0.8	1.4	9.6	20 105	72.9	27.1	2.55	2.14
Crawford	0.7	6 958	92.6	7.4	0.2	2.3	7.6	6 441	73.0	27.0	2.58	2.38
Dallas	39.1	16 529	94.3	5.7	0.4	2.6	6.2	15 584	76.3	23.7	2.71	2.19
Davis	3.7	3 530	90.8	9.2	1.8	1.9	7.7	3 207	79.7	20.3	2.70	2.22
Decatur	4.1	3 833	87.1	12.9	3.0	2.1	10.6	3 337	71.1	28.9	2.48	2.10
Delaware	7.0	7 682	89.0	11.0	6.1	1.4	9.3	6 834	77.8	22.2	2.74	2.37
Des Moines	2.3	18 643	92.6	7.4	0.9	1.9	8.9	17 270	74.2	25.8	2.51	2.09
Dickinson	15.3	11 375	62.4	37.6	32.3	2.8	10.9	7 103	78.0	22.0	2.33	2.06
Dubuque	9.4	35 505	94.9	5.1	0.5	1.0	8.4	33 690	73.5	26.5	2.68	2.03
Emmet	-0.2	4 889	91.0	9.0	1.2	2.4	8.8	4 450	75.1	24.9	2.42	2.17
Fayette	3.4	9 505	92.4	7.6	0.8	1.7	8.2	8 778	75.7	24.3	2.46	2.26
Floyd	1.6	7 317	93.3	6.7	0.7	2.0	7.7	6 828	74.1	25.9	2.47	2.20
Franklin	-4.9	4 763	91.5	8.5	0.5	2.9	8.9	4 356	75.0	25.0	2.45	2.30
Fremont	-0.6	3 514	91.0	9.0	1.6	3.2	7.1	3 199	74.5	25.5	2.49	2.33
Greene	0.2	4 623	91.0	9.0	0.7	2.6	5.4	4 205	75.6	24.4	2.45	2.27
Grundy	4.4	5 304	94.0	6.0	0.7	1.8	5.0	4 984	79.9	20.1	2.51	2.21

Table B. States and Counties

STATE/ County code	MSA/ PMSA/ NECMA code[1]	County type[2]	STATE County	Land area, 2000[3] (sq km)	Total persons	Rank	Per square kilometer	Land area, 1990[3] (sq km)	Total persons	Rank	Per square kilometer	White	Black or African American	American Indian or Alaska Native	Asian	Native Hawaiian and other Pacific Islander	Some other race
					Population, 2000				Population, 1990			Population and population characteristics, 2000 — Race (percent) — One race					
				1	2	3	4	5	6	7	8	9	10	11	12	13	14
			IOWA—Cont'd														
19 077	...	8	Guthrie	1 530	11 353	2 346	7.4	1 530	10 935	2 301	7.1	98.6	0.1	0.1	0.1	0.0	0.4
19 079	...	7	Hamilton	1 494	16 438	1 994	11.0	1 494	16 071	1 919	10.8	96.7	0.2	0.2	1.5	0.0	0.6
19 081	...	7	Hancock	1 479	12 100	2 290	8.2	1 479	12 638	2 174	8.5	97.7	0.1	0.1	0.3	0.0	1.4
19 083	...	7	Hardin	1 474	18 812	1 853	12.8	1 475	19 094	1 728	12.9	97.1	0.6	0.1	0.3	0.0	1.2
19 085	...	6	Harrison	1 805	15 666	2 042	8.7	1 805	14 730	2 004	8.2	98.7	0.1	0.2	0.2	0.0	0.2
19 087	...	7	Henry	1 125	20 336	1 770	18.1	1 125	19 226	1 717	17.1	94.8	1.5	0.2	1.9	0.0	0.5
19 089	...	7	Howard	1 226	9 932	2 453	8.1	1 226	9 809	2 401	8.0	99.1	0.1	0.2	0.2	0.0	0.1
19 091	...	7	Humboldt	1 125	10 381	2 404	9.2	1 125	10 756	2 311	9.6	98.6	0.1	0.1	0.2	0.1	0.4
19 093	...	8	Ida	1 118	7 837	2 620	7.0	1 118	8 365	2 527	7.5	99.0	0.1	0.1	0.2	0.0	0.2
19 095	...	8	Iowa	1 519	15 671	2 041	10.3	1 519	14 630	2 010	9.6	98.7	0.2	0.1	0.3	0.0	0.4
19 097	...	6	Jackson	1 647	20 296	1 773	12.3	1 648	19 950	1 681	12.1	99.0	0.1	0.1	0.1	0.1	0.1
19 099	...	6	Jasper	1 891	37 213	1 186	19.7	1 891	34 795	1 140	18.4	97.6	0.8	0.2	0.4	0.1	0.3
19 101	...	7	Jefferson	1 128	16 181	2 010	14.3	1 128	16 310	1 902	14.5	96.0	0.6	0.2	1.7	0.0	0.5
19 103	3500	3	Johnson	1 591	111 006	488	69.8	1 592	96 119	482	60.4	90.1	2.9	0.3	4.1	0.0	1.0
19 105	...	6	Jones	1 490	20 221	1 779	13.6	1 490	19 444	1 706	13.0	96.7	1.8	0.3	0.2	0.0	0.2
19 107	...	9	Keokuk	1 500	11 400	2 341	7.6	1 500	11 624	2 246	7.7	99.0	0.1	0.1	0.2	0.0	0.2
19 109	...	7	Kossuth	2 520	17 163	1 944	6.8	2 520	18 591	1 759	7.4	98.8	0.1	0.1	0.3	0.0	0.3
19 111	...	5	Lee	1 340	38 052	1 163	28.4	1 340	38 687	1 036	28.9	94.2	2.8	0.3	0.4	0.1	1.0
19 113	1360	3	Linn	1 858	191 701	286	103.2	1 858	168 767	284	90.8	93.9	2.6	0.2	1.4	0.0	0.5
19 115	...	8	Louisa	1 041	12 183	2 284	11.7	1 041	11 592	2 249	11.1	93.9	0.3	0.2	0.2	0.0	4.6
19 117	...	6	Lucas	1 115	9 422	2 492	8.5	1 115	9 070	2 463	8.1	98.4	0.1	0.1	0.3	0.0	0.4
19 119	...	6	Lyon	1 522	11 763	2 312	7.7	1 522	11 952	2 223	7.9	99.1	0.1	0.1	0.2	0.0	0.1
19 121	...	6	Madison	1 453	14 019	2 162	9.6	1 453	12 483	2 182	8.6	98.6	0.1	0.3	0.2	0.0	0.3
19 123	...	7	Mahaska	1 479	22 335	1 677	15.1	1 479	21 532	1 602	14.6	97.2	0.6	0.2	0.9	0.0	0.3
19 125	...	6	Marion	1 435	32 052	1 344	22.3	1 436	30 001	1 296	20.9	97.5	0.4	0.2	1.0	0.0	0.2
19 127	...	5	Marshall	1 482	39 311	1 129	26.5	1 482	38 276	1 046	25.8	90.4	0.9	0.3	0.8	0.1	6.0
19 129	...	6	Mills	1 131	14 547	2 118	12.9	1 131	13 202	2 122	11.7	98.0	0.3	0.3	0.3	0.0	0.4
19 131	...	7	Mitchell	1 215	10 874	2 375	8.9	1 215	10 928	2 304	9.0	99.3	0.2	0.1	0.2	0.0	0.1
19 133	...	6	Monona	1 795	10 020	2 443	5.6	1 795	10 034	2 383	5.6	98.3	0.1	0.8	0.1	0.0	0.1
19 135	...	7	Monroe	1 123	8 016	2 603	7.1	1 123	8 114	2 553	7.2	98.4	0.2	0.4	0.4	0.0	0.1
19 137	...	6	Montgomery	1 098	11 771	2 310	10.7	1 098	12 076	2 212	11.0	98.2	0.1	0.3	0.2	0.0	0.7
19 139	...	4	Muscatine	1 136	41 722	1 062	36.7	1 136	39 907	1 006	35.1	90.7	0.7	0.3	0.8	0.0	6.1
19 141	...	7	O'Brien	1 484	15 102	2 084	10.2	1 484	15 444	1 958	10.4	98.0	0.3	0.2	0.5	0.0	0.5
19 143	...	7	Osceola	1 033	7 003	2 686	6.8	1 033	7 267	2 630	7.0	98.0	0.1	0.3	0.2	0.0	0.8
19 145	...	7	Page	1 385	16 976	1 954	12.3	1 385	16 870	1 858	12.2	96.1	1.7	0.5	0.5	0.0	0.5
19 147	...	7	Palo Alto	1 460	10 147	2 434	7.0	1 460	10 669	2 321	7.3	98.6	0.1	0.2	0.3	0.0	0.2
19 149	...	6	Plymouth	2 237	24 849	1 562	11.1	2 237	23 388	1 520	10.5	98.2	0.3	0.1	0.3	0.1	0.5
19 151	...	9	Pocahontas	1 496	8 662	2 554	5.8	1 496	9 525	2 430	6.4	98.5	0.2	0.2	0.2	0.0	0.3
19 153	2120	2	Polk	1 475	374 601	156	254.0	1 475	327 140	156	221.8	88.3	4.8	0.3	2.6	0.1	2.2
19 155	5920	2	Pottawattamie	2 472	87 704	596	35.5	2 472	82 628	550	33.4	96.0	0.8	0.4	0.5	0.0	1.3
19 157	...	7	Poweshiek	1 515	18 815	1 852	12.4	1 515	19 033	1 733	12.6	96.7	0.5	0.2	1.1	0.0	0.5
19 159	...	9	Ringgold	1 393	5 469	2 818	3.9	1 393	5 420	2 806	3.9	99.1	0.1	0.2	0.2	0.0	0.4
19 161	...	9	Sac	1 491	11 529	2 331	7.7	1 491	12 324	2 192	8.3	98.5	0.3	0.1	0.1	0.0	0.5
19 163	1960	2	Scott	1 186	158 668	334	133.8	1 186	150 973	309	127.3	88.5	6.1	0.3	1.6	0.0	1.6
19 165	...	6	Shelby	1 530	13 173	2 215	8.6	1 530	13 230	2 118	8.6	98.7	0.1	0.1	0.3	0.0	0.2
19 167	...	7	Sioux	1 989	31 589	1 357	15.9	1 989	29 903	1 300	15.0	97.3	0.2	0.1	0.6	0.0	1.2
19 169	...	4	Story	1 484	79 981	642	53.9	1 484	74 252	606	50.0	91.1	1.8	0.2	5.1	0.0	0.6
19 171	...	6	Tama	1 868	18 103	1 892	9.7	1 868	17 419	1 826	9.3	90.4	0.3	6.1	0.2	0.0	1.9
19 173	...	9	Taylor	1 383	6 958	2 690	5.0	1 383	7 114	2 643	5.1	97.7	0.0	0.1	0.3	0.1	1.1
19 175	...	7	Union	1 099	12 309	2 279	11.2	1 099	12 750	2 163	11.6	98.4	0.2	0.2	0.3	0.0	0.3
19 177	...	9	Van Buren	1 256	7 809	2 624	6.2	1 257	7 676	2 603	6.1	98.6	0.1	0.3	0.3	0.1	0.2
19 179	...	5	Wapello	1 118	36 051	1 215	32.2	1 118	35 696	1 106	31.9	96.3	0.9	0.3	0.6	0.0	1.1
19 181	2120	2	Warren	1 481	40 671	1 094	27.5	1 481	36 033	1 098	24.3	98.1	0.3	0.2	0.4	0.0	0.3
19 183	...	6	Washington	1 473	20 670	1 753	14.0	1 473	19 612	1 692	13.3	97.0	0.3	0.2	0.2	0.0	1.5
19 185	...	9	Wayne	1 361	6 730	2 716	4.9	1 361	7 067	2 650	5.2	98.8	0.1	0.1	0.1	0.1	0.2
19 187	...	5	Webster	1 852	40 235	1 109	21.7	1 853	40 342	991	21.8	93.4	3.4	0.3	0.7	0.0	1.1
19 189	...	7	Winnebago	1 037	11 723	2 316	11.3	1 037	12 122	2 206	11.7	97.4	0.2	0.2	0.7	0.0	1.0
19 191	...	7	Winneshiek	1 786	21 310	1 721	11.9	1 786	20 847	1 636	11.7	97.9	0.5	0.1	0.8	0.0	0.2
19 193	7720	3	Woodbury	2 260	103 877	510	46.0	2 260	98 276	468	43.5	87.5	2.0	1.7	2.4	0.0	4.4
19 195	...	9	Worth	1 036	7 909	2 614	7.6	1 036	7 991	2 567	7.7	98.4	0.3	0.1	0.1	0.0	0.4
19 197	...	7	Wright	1 504	14 334	2 137	9.5	1 504	14 269	2 033	9.5	95.9	0.2	0.2	0.2	0.0	2.9
20 000	...		KANSAS	211 900	2 688 418	X	12.7	211 922	2 477 588	X	11.7	86.1	5.7	0.9	1.7	0.0	3.4
20 001	...	7	Allen	1 303	14 385	2 134	11.0	1 303	14 638	2 008	11.2	94.8	1.6	0.8	0.3	0.0	0.9
20 003	...	6	Anderson	1 510	8 110	2 597	5.4	1 510	7 803	2 594	5.2	97.4	0.3	0.7	0.2	0.0	0.3
20 005	...	6	Atchison	1 120	16 774	1 972	15.0	1 120	16 932	1 854	15.1	91.6	5.3	0.6	0.3	0.1	0.5

[1] MSA = Metropolitan Statistical Area. PMSA = Primary MSA. NECMA = New England County Metropolitan Area. See Appendix A for explanation of these concepts. See Appendix B for list of metropolitan areas identified by type, with component counties.
[2] County typology code from the Economic Research Service of USDA. See Appendix A for definition.
[3] Dry land or land partially or temporarily covered by water.

Table B. States and Counties

STATE County	Population and population characteristics, 2000 (cont'd) Race (percent) (cont'd)								Population and population characteristics, 1990 Race (percent)				
	Race alone or in combination												
	Two or more races	White	Black	American Indian or Alaska Native	Asian	Native Hawaiian and other Pacific Islander	Some other race	Hispanic[1]	White	Black or African American	American Indian or Alaska Native	Asian and Pacific Islander	Hispanic[1]
	15	16	17	18	19	20	21	22	23	24	25	26	27
IOWA—Cont'd													
Guthrie	0.6	99.2	0.2	0.4	0.3	0.1	0.5	1.1	99.5	0.1	0.2	0.1	0.3
Hamilton	0.8	97.4	0.4	0.4	1.7	0.0	0.9	1.4	08.9	0.1	0.1	0.6	0.7
Hancock	0.4	98.1	0.1	0.2	0.5	0.0	1.5	2.5	99.1	0.0	0.0	0.2	1.0
Hardin	0.5	97.6	0.7	0.3	0.4	0.1	1.4	2.4	98.7	0.6	0.1	0.3	0.6
Harrison	0.6	99.3	0.3	0.6	0.3	0.0	0.3	0.7	99.5	0.1	0.1	0.3	0.3
Henry	1.1	95.7	1.8	0.6	2.2	0.1	0.7	1.3	97.3	1.1	0.2	1.1	0.7
Howard	0.4	99.5	0.2	0.3	0.3	0.0	0.2	0.6	99.6	0.1	0.1	0.2	0.2
Humboldt	0.5	99.0	0.2	0.2	0.4	0.1	0.6	1.0	99.5	0.1	0.1	0.3	0.3
Ida	0.4	99.4	0.2	0.2	0.4	0.0	0.2	0.5	99.6	0.0	0.1	0.2	0.3
Iowa	0.4	99.0	0.2	0.2	0.4	0.0	0.5	1.0	99.6	0.0	0.1	0.2	0.3
Jackson	0.5	99.4	0.2	0.3	0.2	0.1	0.2	0.6	99.6	0.1	0.1	0.1	0.5
Jasper	0.6	98.1	1.0	0.5	0.6	0.1	0.4	1.0	99.0	0.2	0.2	0.5	0.6
Jefferson	0.9	96.8	0.8	0.4	2.0	0.0	0.8	1.8	98.3	0.6	0.1	0.9	0.9
Johnson	1.5	91.5	3.4	0.6	4.6	0.1	1.4	2.5	93.3	2.1	0.2	4.0	1.5
Jones	0.8	97.4	2.1	0.6	0.3	0.0	0.5	1.1	98.0	1.5	0.2	0.1	0.5
Keokuk	0.4	99.3	0.1	0.3	0.3	0.1	0.3	0.5	99.5	0.1	0.2	0.2	0.2
Kossuth	0.3	99.1	0.2	0.3	0.4	0.0	0.3	0.8	99.3	0.0	0.0	0.3	0.5
Lee	1.2	95.4	3.4	0.7	0.5	0.1	1.3	2.4	95.6	2.9	0.2	0.3	1.9
Linn	1.4	95.2	3.3	0.6	1.7	0.1	0.7	1.4	96.7	2.0	0.2	0.8	0.9
Louisa	0.9	94.8	0.4	0.4	0.3	0.0	5.1	12.6	96.7	0.7	0.3	0.2	3.7
Lucas	0.6	99.1	0.1	0.3	0.3	0.0	0.8	0.9	99.3	0.0	0.2	0.2	0.6
Lyon	0.4	99.5	0.2	0.4	0.2	0.1	0.1	0.4	99.5	0.0	0.1	0.1	0.1
Madison	0.7	99.2	0.2	0.7	0.3	0.1	0.3	0.7	99.4	0.0	0.3	0.1	0.5
Mahaska	0.8	97.9	0.8	0.5	1.1	0.0	0.4	0.9	98.8	0.2	0.1	0.8	0.4
Marion	0.6	98.1	0.6	0.5	1.2	0.1	0.4	0.8	98.5	0.3	0.1	0.9	0.5
Marshall	1.4	91.7	1.3	0.6	1.0	0.1	6.7	9.0	97.9	0.7	0.3	0.8	0.8
Mills	0.8	98.8	0.4	0.8	0.4	0.0	0.5	1.2	99.3	0.2	0.2	0.1	0.5
Mitchell	0.2	99.5	0.2	0.1	0.2	0.0	0.2	0.6	99.7	0.0	0.0	0.2	0.4
Monona	0.6	98.9	0.2	1.0	0.2	0.0	0.7	0.7	99.5	0.0	0.3	0.1	0.3
Monroe	0.5	98.9	0.4	0.6	0.5	0.0	0.1	0.5	99.1	0.2	0.2	0.4	0.2
Montgomery	0.4	98.6	0.1	0.6	0.3	0.0	0.7	1.3	99.7	0.0	0.1	0.1	0.4
Muscatine	1.4	92.0	0.9	0.7	1.0	0.1	6.8	11.9	94.6	0.5	0.2	0.8	7.3
O'Brien	0.5	98.4	0.4	0.3	0.6	0.1	0.6	1.8	99.3	0.1	0.2	0.3	0.3
Osceola	0.5	98.6	0.2	0.4	0.3	0.0	1.1	1.8	99.5	0.0	0.1	0.2	0.2
Page	0.8	96.8	1.8	0.8	0.6	0.1	0.7	1.6	98.3	0.5	0.3	0.5	1.2
Palo Alto	0.6	99.2	0.2	0.5	0.4	0.0	0.3	0.8	99.5	0.1	0.2	0.2	0.2
Plymouth	0.6	98.7	0.5	0.3	0.4	0.1	0.6	1.3	99.5	0.0	0.1	0.2	0.2
Pocahontas	0.6	99.0	0.4	0.4	0.3	0.1	0.5	0.9	99.6	0.0	0.1	0.2	0.3
Polk	1.7	89.8	5.4	0.6	3.0	0.1	2.8	4.4	92.7	4.5	0.3	1.8	1.9
Pottawattamie	1.1	97.0	1.1	0.8	0.7	0.1	1.6	3.3	98.3	0.6	0.3	0.3	1.8
Poweshiek	0.9	97.6	0.8	0.5	1.4	0.1	0.6	1.2	98.3	0.5	0.1	0.3	0.4
Ringgold	0.4	99.5	0.2	0.4	0.2	0.0	0.2	0.2	99.4	0.0	0.2	0.3	0.3
Sac	0.6	99.1	0.4	0.2	0.3	0.1	0.5	1.0	99.6	0.0	0.1	0.2	0.4
Scott	1.8	90.2	6.9	0.8	1.9	0.1	2.1	4.1	92.3	5.3	0.3	0.9	2.8
Shelby	0.5	99.1	0.2	0.5	0.4	0.0	0.3	0.7	99.6	0.0	0.2	0.2	0.3
Sioux	0.5	97.8	0.3	0.3	0.7	0.0	1.4	2.6	99.0	0.1	0.1	0.7	0.2
Story	1.1	92.1	2.1	0.4	5.6	0.1	0.9	1.5	93.1	1.6	0.1	4.7	1.1
Tama	1.2	91.5	0.4	6.8	0.2	0.1	2.3	3.8	94.5	0.2	4.7	0.4	0.7
Taylor	0.7	98.4	0.0	0.3	0.4	0.1	1.5	3.8	99.4	0.0	0.1	0.3	0.6
Union	0.6	99.0	0.3	0.4	0.3	0.0	0.5	1.0	99.2	0.1	0.2	0.4	0.3
Van Buren	0.6	99.2	0.2	0.6	0.3	0.1	0.3	0.8	99.5	0.1	0.1	0.2	0.4
Wapello	0.8	97.0	1.1	0.6	0.8	0.0	1.2	2.2	98.3	0.8	0.3	0.5	0.6
Warren	0.8	98.8	0.4	0.5	0.5	0.1	0.5	1.1	99.0	0.2	0.1	0.4	0.8
Washington	0.7	97.7	0.5	0.4	0.3	0.1	1.7	2.7	98.9	0.5	0.1	0.3	1.0
Wayne	0.6	99.4	0.2	0.4	0.3	0.1	0.3	0.7	99.6	0.0	0.1	0.2	0.4
Webster	1.1	94.5	3.9	0.7	0.8	0.0	1.4	2.3	96.7	2.2	0.3	0.4	1.2
Winnebago	0.5	97.8	0.3	0.3	1.0	0.0	1.1	2.0	98.7	0.3	0.1	0.6	0.8
Winneshiek	0.5	98.3	0.6	0.3	0.9	0.0	0.4	0.8	98.7	0.2	0.0	0.9	0.3
Woodbury	2.0	89.2	2.7	2.4	2.8	0.1	5.0	9.1	93.7	1.9	1.7	1.3	2.8
Worth	0.7	99.1	0.4	0.5	0.2	0.0	0.5	1.6	99.1	0.2	0.0	0.2	1.1
Wright	0.6	96.5	0.3	0.4	0.3	0.0	3.1	4.9	99.3	0.1	0.1	0.3	0.6
KANSAS	2.1	87.9	6.3	1.8	2.1	0.1	4.0	7.0	90.1	5.8	0.9	1.3	3.8
Allen	1.7	96.3	2.1	1.8	0.5	0.0	1.1	1.9	96.5	1.8	0.7	0.3	1.8
Anderson	0.9	98.3	0.6	1.3	0.4	0.0	0.4	1.1	98.3	0.5	0.9	0.1	0.7
Atchison	1.6	93.1	6.1	1.3	0.5	0.2	0.7	1.9	92.1	5.7	0.5	0.8	2.2

[1]Hispanic persons may be of any race.

Table B. States and Counties

STATE County	Population and population characteristics, 2000										
	Age (percent)										
	Under 5 years	5 to 17 years	18 to 24 years	25 to 34 years	35 to 44 years	45 to 54 years	55 to 64 years	65 to 74 years	75 years and over	Median age (years)	Percent Female
	28	29	30	31	32	33	34	35	36	37	38
IOWA—Cont'd											
Guthrie	5.5	18.0	6.3	9.6	15.2	14.0	10.9	10.2	10.3	41.9	50.6
Hamilton	6.4	19.0	7.1	11.3	15.8	13.1	9.3	8.7	9.3	39.1	50.5
Hancock	6.1	20.4	6.6	9.9	15.6	13.9	9.5	8.1	9.8	39.7	50.8
Hardin	5.7	19.0	8.4	9.4	14.4	12.9	9.5	9.0	11.6	40.6	51.1
Harrison	6.0	20.2	6.8	10.9	16.1	12.8	9.6	8.5	9.2	38.9	50.9
Henry	6.0	18.7	9.0	13.0	16.2	13.7	8.8	6.7	8.0	37.1	49.4
Howard	6.0	20.3	6.8	10.5	14.9	12.0	9.3	9.2	11.0	39.5	50.8
Humboldt	5.4	19.4	7.0	9.0	15.6	12.8	9.7	9.7	11.3	41.3	51.1
Ida	5.5	20.0	6.1	9.4	14.6	13.5	9.2	10.2	11.6	41.5	51.6
Iowa	6.2	20.2	6.3	11.1	16.8	13.1	9.3	7.9	9.2	38.8	51.3
Jackson	5.9	20.1	7.0	10.7	15.9	13.2	10.0	8.7	8.6	39.1	50.7
Jasper	6.2	18.4	7.4	12.5	16.1	13.8	9.6	8.2	7.8	38.5	49.6
Jefferson	5.4	19.0	7.6	10.2	14.2	21.1	8.7	6.3	7.5	41.1	51.1
Johnson	5.8	14.3	23.4	16.6	14.1	12.2	6.1	3.9	3.5	28.4	50.2
Jones	5.6	18.5	7.9	12.4	16.5	13.7	9.5	8.0	7.8	38.5	47.8
Keokuk	5.9	19.8	7.0	10.3	15.2	12.4	9.1	9.1	11.0	40.0	51.5
Kossuth	5.4	20.4	6.1	9.0	15.3	13.4	10.2	9.6	10.5	41.3	51.2
Lee	6.0	18.4	7.8	11.0	15.7	14.8	9.9	8.0	8.6	39.5	50.5
Linn	7.0	18.3	10.1	14.3	15.9	13.6	8.5	6.2	6.1	35.2	51.0
Louisa	7.2	20.5	7.9	12.9	15.7	12.5	9.2	7.2	6.8	35.9	50.3
Lucas	6.0	19.3	7.3	10.4	14.2	12.6	10.8	9.1	10.2	39.9	51.4
Lyon	6.7	21.3	7.6	10.6	14.1	12.7	8.2	9.1	9.7	38.1	50.4
Madison	7.0	20.1	6.9	11.9	15.5	14.2	9.3	6.7	8.4	37.9	50.7
Mahaska	6.6	19.1	9.4	11.9	14.9	13.1	8.6	7.6	8.8	37.2	50.2
Marion	6.3	19.1	10.2	11.4	15.1	13.0	9.1	7.3	8.6	37.2	50.4
Marshall	6.5	18.8	8.1	11.9	14.4	14.3	9.6	8.0	8.4	38.6	50.2
Mills	6.3	20.4	7.0	11.5	16.7	15.8	9.7	6.5	6.1	38.1	49.8
Mitchell	6.1	20.4	6.1	9.4	14.8	11.9	9.7	9.8	11.8	40.6	51.1
Monona	5.3	17.9	6.2	9.1	14.2	12.7	10.6	10.7	13.2	43.0	51.5
Monroe	6.4	19.0	7.2	11.1	13.9	13.0	10.0	9.1	10.5	39.7	51.3
Montgomery	6.1	18.9	6.5	11.0	14.5	13.8	8.9	9.4	10.9	40.4	52.6
Muscatine	6.9	20.0	8.6	12.9	15.9	13.9	8.9	6.5	6.5	36.1	50.5
O'Brien	5.9	18.9	7.8	9.6	14.5	12.9	9.2	9.7	11.4	40.7	51.1
Osceola	5.9	20.2	7.2	9.8	16.4	12.1	9.5	9.0	9.9	39.7	51.3
Page	5.6	17.7	7.9	11.4	14.9	13.5	9.3	9.2	10.6	40.2	49.3
Palo Alto	5.4	18.6	9.5	9.1	14.1	12.3	9.6	10.3	11.0	40.7	51.4
Plymouth	6.6	21.7	7.2	10.8	15.7	13.6	8.5	7.9	8.0	37.8	50.3
Pocahontas	4.9	20.5	5.3	7.9	15.6	13.6	10.5	9.7	12.0	42.5	50.9
Polk	7.5	18.2	9.4	15.8	16.4	13.5	8.0	5.7	5.4	34.4	51.5
Pottawattamie	6.6	19.4	9.1	12.7	15.9	13.7	9.0	7.4	6.3	36.5	51.1
Poweshiek	5.5	17.1	12.8	10.0	14.4	13.0	9.5	8.1	9.6	38.4	52.0
Ringgold	5.9	18.2	6.9	8.2	13.2	12.6	11.1	11.3	12.7	43.2	51.5
Sac	5.6	18.5	6.6	9.3	14.3	13.2	9.6	10.2	12.5	42.1	51.1
Scott	6.9	19.6	9.3	13.7	15.7	14.3	8.7	6.1	5.7	35.4	51.1
Shelby	5.9	20.5	5.7	9.4	15.8	13.0	9.3	9.5	10.9	40.5	51.1
Sioux	6.6	20.5	15.2	9.9	13.6	11.4	7.7	7.1	7.9	32.8	51.0
Story	5.2	13.9	28.3	13.4	12.0	10.9	6.4	4.7	5.1	26.5	48.9
Tama	6.9	19.6	7.0	11.0	14.2	12.6	9.9	8.8	9.9	39.1	50.9
Taylor	5.5	18.4	7.5	9.7	13.7	12.7	10.1	9.7	12.7	41.6	51.5
Union	5.9	17.4	8.7	10.6	14.7	14.1	9.8	8.5	10.1	40.1	52.1
Van Buren	5.6	19.2	7.0	10.3	14.1	13.8	11.0	8.8	10.3	40.8	50.1
Wapello	5.9	17.3	9.7	11.4	14.6	13.7	9.5	8.7	9.0	39.2	51.3
Warren	6.8	20.2	9.7	11.7	16.5	14.2	9.0	6.0	5.9	36.0	51.4
Washington	6.7	19.4	7.0	11.2	15.6	13.4	8.9	7.8	10.1	38.8	51.8
Wayne	5.0	18.8	5.9	8.9	14.5	12.1	10.9	10.6	13.2	43.0	52.2
Webster	6.3	18.2	11.1	11.0	14.5	13.0	8.6	8.3	9.1	37.7	49.9
Winnebago	5.6	18.5	9.8	9.7	14.5	14.3	8.8	8.5	10.5	39.8	51.1
Winneshiek	5.1	17.9	16.7	9.4	14.8	11.9	8.5	7.4	8.3	35.7	50.8
Woodbury	7.6	19.7	10.2	13.6	14.7	13.0	7.8	6.7	6.7	34.2	51.0
Worth	5.7	18.6	6.5	10.5	15.8	13.8	9.7	8.8	10.6	40.7	50.4
Wright	5.7	18.8	6.5	10.0	14.6	13.7	9.6	9.2	12.0	41.4	51.0
KANSAS	7.0	19.5	10.3	13.0	15.6	13.2	8.2	6.5	6.7	35.2	50.6
Allen	5.9	19.3	9.8	9.9	14.2	13.3	9.6	8.4	9.6	38.8	51.1
Anderson	6.2	20.0	7.0	10.0	14.6	11.7	10.4	9.1	11.0	39.6	50.8
Atchison	6.4	20.3	11.3	10.6	13.8	12.1	9.3	7.9	8.4	36.2	51.7

Table B. States and Counties

| | Population and population characteristics, 1990 | | | | | | | | | | Population—change, 1980–2000 | | | | |
| | Age (percent) | | | | | | | | | | Total persons | | | Percent change | |
STATE County	Under 5 years	5 to 17 years	18 to 24 years	25 to 34 years	35 to 44 years	45 to 54 years	55 to 64 years	65 to 74 years	75 years and over	Percent Female	2000	1990	1980	1990–2000	1980–1990
	39	40	41	42	43	44	45	46	47	48	49	50	51	52	53
IOWA—Cont'd															
Guthrie	5.8	19.1	6.0	12.3	13.3	10.7	11.7	11.1	9.9	52.0	11 353	10 935	11 983	3.8	-8.7
Hamilton	6.6	18.8	6.9	14.6	13.8	10.3	10.5	10.0	8.4	51.5	16 438	16 071	17 862	2.3	-10.0
Hancock	7.2	21.0	6.5	14.6	13.7	9.5	9.4	9.3	8.8	51.4	12 100	12 638	13 833	-4.3	8.6
Hardin	5.9	19.1	7.9	13.0	12.9	9.7	10.2	10.6	10.6	51.6	18 812	19 094	21 776	-1.5	-12.3
Harrison	7.0	19.9	7.0	14.1	12.6	10.1	9.9	9.8	9.7	51.8	15 666	14 730	16 348	6.4	-9.9
Henry	6.6	18.6	9.9	15.5	14.8	9.9	8.2	8.4	8.2	50.1	20 336	19 226	18 890	5.8	1.8
Howard	6.9	19.9	6.0	13.7	11.7	9.7	10.4	10.4	11.3	51.4	9 932	9 809	11 114	1.3	-11.7
Humboldt	6.6	18.9	6.0	13.4	12.8	10.0	11.2	11.4	9.6	51.6	10 381	10 756	12 246	-3.5	-12.2
Ida	7.5	20.4	5.8	13.7	12.9	9.0	10.6	10.3	10.0	51.6	7 837	8 365	8 908	-6.3	-6.1
Iowa	7.2	18.4	6.7	15.4	13.5	9.9	10.0	9.8	9.1	51.7	15 671	14 630	15 429	7.1	-5.2
Jackson	7.1	20.8	7.7	14.3	13.0	10.4	10.1	8.8	7.8	51.0	20 296	19 950	22 503	1.7	-11.3
Jasper	6.4	19.2	7.6	15.1	14.6	10.7	10.4	8.7	7.3	51.2	37 213	34 795	36 425	6.9	-4.5
Jefferson	6.5	17.9	7.2	14.3	21.2	10.1	8.0	7.4	7.3	51.2	16 181	16 310	16 316	-0.8	0.0
Johnson	6.4	13.7	24.8	20.3	14.5	7.5	5.4	4.1	3.4	50.5	111 006	96 119	81 717	15.5	17.6
Jones	6.5	19.2	9.0	15.9	14.3	10.0	9.1	8.4	7.6	48.3	20 221	19 444	20 401	4.0	-4.7
Keokuk	6.5	19.5	6.6	14.2	12.4	9.7	10.4	10.2	10.6	51.5	11 400	11 624	12 921	-1.9	-10.0
Kossuth	7.0	21.1	5.7	13.9	12.8	10.1	10.4	9.8	9.2	51.4	17 163	18 591	21 891	-7.7	-15.1
Lee	6.6	19.2	7.9	15.0	14.6	10.4	9.5	9.2	7.6	51.1	38 052	38 687	43 106	-1.6	-10.3
Linn	7.1	18.1	11.0	17.2	15.5	10.6	8.4	6.8	5.4	51.4	191 701	168 767	169 775	13.6	-0.6
Louisa	6.9	20.4	8.6	15.3	14.4	10.3	9.1	7.7	7.3	49.7	12 183	11 592	12 055	5.1	-3.8
Lucas	6.3	18.3	7.1	12.9	12.9	10.9	10.9	10.4	10.3	52.3	9 422	9 070	10 313	3.9	-12.1
Lyon	7.9	22.3	7.0	13.1	12.8	8.7	10.3	9.3	8.7	51.1	11 763	11 952	12 896	-1.6	-7.3
Madison	6.7	20.9	7.1	13.4	14.6	10.4	8.9	8.9	9.1	51.3	14 019	12 483	12 597	12.3	-0.9
Mahaska	7.1	19.0	9.5	14.7	13.6	9.3	9.1	9.6	8.1	51.3	22 335	21 532	22 867	3.7	-5.8
Marion	6.6	19.0	11.5	14.1	13.8	9.9	9.0	8.5	7.7	50.3	32 052	30 001	29 669	6.8	1.1
Marshall	6.5	18.5	8.1	14.2	14.9	10.8	10.5	9.5	9.4	51.1	39 311	38 276	41 652	2.7	-8.1
Mills	6.3	21.1	7.4	15.1	16.8	10.7	8.9	7.3	6.4	50.4	14 547	13 202	13 406	10.2	-1.5
Mitchell	6.5	19.5	6.6	13.0	12.0	9.9	10.5	10.7	11.2	51.4	10 874	10 928	12 329	-0.5	-11.4
Monona	6.0	18.5	5.6	12.3	12.3	10.4	11.1	11.5	12.3	52.4	10 020	10 034	11 692	-0.1	-14.2
Monroe	6.3	19.0	7.2	13.6	13.1	9.7	10.4	10.8	9.8	51.9	8 016	8 114	9 209	-1.2	-11.9
Montgomery	6.0	18.6	6.8	13.5	13.7	9.3	10.3	10.2	11.6	52.9	11 771	12 076	13 413	-2.5	-10.0
Muscatine	7.4	20.5	9.0	16.3	14.9	10.3	8.3	7.2	6.2	51.1	41 722	39 907	40 436	4.5	-1.3
O'Brien	6.6	20.1	6.8	13.7	12.6	9.1	10.5	10.3	10.4	51.9	15 102	15 444	16 972	-2.2	-9.0
Osceola	7.4	19.9	7.0	14.2	12.2	9.3	10.6	9.5	9.8	51.5	7 003	7 267	8 371	-3.6	-13.2
Page	5.9	19.1	7.1	13.2	13.7	9.9	10.2	10.5	10.5	51.6	16 976	16 870	19 063	0.6	-11.5
Palo Alto	6.4	20.3	7.4	12.7	11.7	9.4	11.5	9.9	10.6	51.7	10 147	10 669	12 721	-4.9	-16.1
Plymouth	7.3	21.7	8.6	13.8	13.3	9.4	9.7	8.3	8.0	50.9	24 849	23 388	24 743	6.2	-5.5
Pocahontas	6.8	19.2	5.0	13.3	12.4	10.6	10.8	11.3	10.5	51.6	8 662	9 525	11 369	-9.1	-16.2
Polk	7.6	17.5	11.0	18.7	15.6	10.0	8.1	6.5	5.1	52.3	374 601	327 140	303 170	14.5	7.9
Pottawattamie	7.5	19.8	8.9	16.3	14.1	10.3	9.7	7.7	5.7	51.9	87 704	82 628	86 561	6.1	-4.5
Poweshiek	6.1	18.4	12.5	13.7	13.3	10.0	9.1	8.7	8.0	51.9	18 815	19 033	19 306	-1.1	-1.4
Ringgold	5.4	18.6	5.5	11.7	12.4	10.1	12.2	12.1	12.1	52.4	5 469	5 420	6 112	0.9	-11.3
Sac	6.8	19.8	5.8	13.2	12.6	9.1	10.8	11.0	11.0	51.2	11 529	12 324	14 118	-6.5	-12.7
Scott	7.8	20.2	9.8	16.7	15.7	10.3	8.1	6.6	4.8	51.6	158 668	150 973	160 022	5.1	-5.7
Shelby	6.7	20.4	6.3	13.4	12.8	9.7	10.4	10.4	9.9	51.2	13 173	13 230	15 043	-0.4	-12.1
Sioux	7.7	22.2	12.7	13.2	12.3	8.7	8.3	7.9	6.8	51.5	31 589	29 903	30 813	5.6	-3.0
Story	5.9	13.9	28.7	16.1	12.2	7.6	6.0	5.0	4.6	48.3	79 981	74 252	72 326	7.7	2.7
Tama	6.5	19.6	7.3	13.4	12.8	10.7	10.3	9.8	9.7	51.6	18 103	17 419	19 533	3.9	-10.8
Taylor	6.1	19.5	6.0	11.6	12.7	9.3	10.6	11.8	12.4	52.7	6 958	7 114	8 353	-2.2	-14.8
Union	6.3	19.6	8.5	13.6	13.9	9.8	9.2	9.6	9.7	53.0	12 309	12 750	13 858	-3.5	-8.0
Van Buren	7.1	19.1	6.8	13.1	12.8	10.5	10.1	10.5	9.9	50.7	7 809	7 676	8 626	1.7	-11.0
Wapello	6.5	17.5	8.9	14.0	14.1	9.9	10.5	9.8	8.9	52.3	36 051	35 696	40 241	1.0	-11.3
Warren	7.2	21.1	10.2	15.1	16.1	11.4	8.0	5.9	5.0	51.3	40 671	36 033	34 878	12.9	3.3
Washington	7.4	19.4	7.2	15.0	13.7	9.6	9.1	9.2	9.4	51.9	20 670	19 612	20 141	5.4	-2.6
Wayne	6.3	17.1	5.7	12.2	11.6	9.5	11.3	13.1	13.1	52.8	6 730	7 067	8 199	-4.8	-13.8
Webster	7.3	18.7	8.7	14.6	13.5	9.6	10.1	9.3	8.4	52.3	40 235	40 342	45 953	-0.3	-12.2
Winnebago	6.5	18.9	9.4	13.7	13.8	9.2	9.2	9.0	10.1	51.6	11 723	12 122	13 010	-3.3	-6.8
Winneshiek	6.8	17.8	16.3	14.1	12.0	8.9	8.7	8.2	7.3	51.1	21 310	20 847	21 876	2.2	-4.7
Woodbury	7.6	20.5	9.7	15.6	14.2	8.9	8.8	8.1	6.6	51.9	103 877	98 276	100 884	5.7	-2.6
Worth	6.3	18.5	6.7	13.5	13.3	10.5	10.4	9.9	10.9	51.4	7 909	7 991	9 075	-1.0	-11.9
Wright	6.7	17.7	6.4	13.4	13.2	9.8	10.6	11.4	10.7	52.4	14 334	14 269	16 319	0.5	-12.6
KANSAS	7.6	19.1	10.3	16.7	14.6	9.5	8.4	7.5	6.4	51.0	2 688 418	2 477 588	2 364 236	8.5	4.8
Allen	6.9	20.3	8.3	13.8	12.9	9.4	9.4	9.6	9.4	51.9	14 385	14 638	15 654	-1.7	-6.5
Anderson	6.6	19.8	7.0	12.8	11.9	10.1	9.8	10.9	11.1	51.8	8 110	7 803	8 749	3.9	-10.8
Atchison	7.0	20.6	10.7	14.0	12.1	9.6	9.2	8.5	8.4	51.2	16 774	16 932	18 397	-0.9	-8.0

Table B. States and Counties

STATE County	Total population	Total in house-holds	House-holder	Spouse	Child Total	Own child under 18 years	Other relatives Total	Under 18 years	Nonrelatives Total	Unmar-ried partner	Total in group quarters	Correc-tional institu-tions	Nurs-ing homes	Other institu-tions	Col-lege dormi-tories	Mili-tary quar-ters	Other
	54	55	56	57	58	59	60	61	62	63	64	65	66	67	68	69	70
IOWA—Cont'd																	
Guthrie	11 353	97.7	40.9	24.5	26.5	21.9	2.4	1.0	3.4	1.8	2.3	0.1	2.3	0.0	0.0	0.0	0.0
Hamilton	16 438	98.7	40.7	23.6	29.3	24.2	1.8	0.7	3.4	1.9	1.3	0.0	1.2	0.0	0.0	0.0	0.1
Hancock	12 100	98.3	39.6	24.1	30.1	25.5	1.7	0.7	2.8	1.7	1.7	0.0	1.6	0.0	0.0	0.0	0.1
Hardin	18 812	95.4	40.5	23.2	26.6	22.3	1.9	0.8	3.2	1.7	4.6	0.1	1.8	1.1	1.0	0.0	0.7
Harrison	15 666	98.0	39.0	23.2	30.1	24.6	2.4	1.1	3.3	1.7	2.0	0.0	2.0	0.0	0.0	0.0	0.1
Henry	20 336	92.2	37.5	21.6	27.8	23.2	1.9	0.8	3.4	1.8	7.8	5.0	0.9	0.6	1.2	0.0	0.1
Howard	9 932	97.3	40.0	22.7	30.1	25.5	1.4	0.4	3.1	1.7	2.7	0.0	1.6	0.0	0.0	0.0	1.1
Humboldt	10 381	98.5	41.4	23.7	28.6	23.7	1.6	0.6	3.1	1.5	1.5	0.1	1.2	0.3	0.0	0.0	0.0
Ida	7 837	98.0	41.0	24.4	28.6	24.3	1.4	0.6	2.6	1.4	2.0	0.1	1.2	0.0	0.0	0.0	0.7
Iowa	15 671	98.2	39.3	23.6	30.4	25.4	1.7	0.6	3.2	1.8	1.8	0.1	1.6	0.0	0.0	0.0	0.2
Jackson	20 296	98.5	39.8	23.2	30.4	24.7	1.9	0.7	3.3	1.9	1.5	0.0	1.2	0.0	0.0	0.0	0.3
Jasper	37 213	95.5	39.5	23.4	27.7	23.2	1.8	0.9	3.1	1.8	4.5	2.7	1.2	0.0	0.0	0.0	0.5
Jefferson	16 181	96.1	41.1	21.8	27.2	23.0	1.8	0.7	4.1	2.0	3.9	0.1	1.4	0.0	1.7	0.0	0.7
Johnson	111 006	92.8	39.7	17.4	22.6	19.2	1.9	0.5	11.2	2.4	7.2	0.8	0.4	0.2	5.6	0.0	0.2
Jones	20 221	92.3	37.4	22.1	27.3	22.6	1.8	0.7	3.7	1.9	7.7	6.5	0.9	0.1	0.0	0.0	0.2
Keokuk	11 400	98.4	40.2	23.7	29.4	24.4	1.8	0.8	3.2	1.8	1.6	0.1	1.4	0.1	0.0	0.0	0.0
Kossuth	17 163	98.2	40.6	24.6	29.6	25.1	1.1	0.4	2.3	1.2	1.8	0.0	1.5	0.0	0.0	0.0	0.3
Lee	38 052	95.8	39.8	21.4	28.0	22.4	2.6	1.2	3.9	2.1	4.2	2.5	1.1	0.3	0.0	0.0	0.3
Linn	191 701	97.4	40.0	21.3	28.5	23.6	2.4	0.9	5.2	2.2	2.6	0.2	0.7	0.0	1.1	0.0	0.6
Louisa	12 183	98.6	37.1	22.7	30.7	25.1	4.0	1.8	4.2	2.0	1.4	0.1	1.1	0.0	0.0	0.0	0.2
Lucas	9 422	97.8	40.4	22.9	28.5	23.5	2.3	1.0	3.6	1.9	2.2	0.1	1.5	0.2	0.0	0.0	0.4
Lyon	11 763	98.3	37.6	25.2	32.6	27.2	1.2	0.5	1.6	0.9	1.7	0.0	1.7	0.0	0.0	0.0	0.0
Madison	14 019	97.9	38.0	24.3	30.8	25.9	2.0	0.8	2.9	1.7	2.1	0.1	2.0	0.0	0.0	0.0	0.1
Mahaska	22 335	97.4	39.8	23.3	28.7	24.3	1.9	0.8	3.7	1.8	2.6	0.2	1.0	0.0	1.3	0.0	0.1
Marion	32 052	93.9	37.5	22.9	28.9	24.2	1.8	0.8	2.8	1.4	6.1	0.0	1.0	0.8	3.3	0.0	1.0
Marshall	39 311	96.8	39.0	21.6	28.1	23.1	3.5	1.4	4.6	2.0	3.2	0.2	2.7	0.1	0.1	0.0	0.1
Mills	14 547	95.2	36.6	22.6	30.2	24.6	2.5	1.3	3.3	1.7	4.8	0.1	0.8	2.7	0.0	0.0	1.2
Mitchell	10 874	97.4	39.5	24.0	30.3	25.6	1.2	0.6	2.4	1.3	2.6	0.0	2.3	0.0	0.0	0.0	0.2
Monona	10 020	97.3	42.0	22.9	26.0	21.3	2.6	1.1	3.8	2.1	2.7	0.1	2.6	0.0	0.0	0.0	0.0
Monroe	8 016	97.8	40.3	22.6	29.2	23.7	2.4	1.1	3.2	1.6	2.2	0.1	1.8	0.2	0.0	0.0	0.1
Montgomery	11 771	97.9	41.5	22.6	27.9	23.4	2.3	1.0	3.6	2.0	2.1	0.1	2.0	0.0	0.0	0.0	0.1
Muscatine	41 722	98.3	38.0	22.0	30.3	24.6	3.8	1.6	4.2	2.2	1.7	0.2	1.0	0.0	0.0	0.0	0.5
O'Brien	15 102	96.1	39.7	24.2	28.2	24.0	1.3	0.5	2.6	1.1	3.9	0.1	2.8	0.7	0.2	0.0	0.1
Osceola	7 003	98.3	39.7	24.6	30.2	25.2	1.6	0.5	2.2	1.2	1.7	0.1	1.5	0.0	0.0	0.0	0.1
Page	16 976	91.8	39.5	21.9	25.4	20.9	1.9	0.8	3.1	1.7	8.2	4.7	1.6	0.4	0.0	0.0	1.4
Palo Alto	10 147	96.0	40.6	22.8	27.6	23.1	1.3	0.4	3.7	1.7	4.0	0.1	2.1	0.5	0.9	0.0	0.4
Plymouth	24 849	98.5	37.7	23.9	32.7	27.2	1.5	0.7	2.6	1.3	1.5	0.1	1.1	0.2	0.0	0.0	0.1
Pocahontas	8 662	98.1	41.8	24.3	28.1	24.4	1.3	0.5	2.7	1.5	1.9	0.1	1.7	0.0	0.0	0.0	0.0
Polk	374 601	97.6	39.8	20.3	28.7	23.7	3.5	1.4	5.3	2.3	2.4	0.3	0.7	0.2	0.7	0.0	0.5
Pottawattamie	87 704	98.1	38.6	20.7	29.7	23.3	4.1	1.8	5.0	2.3	1.9	0.3	0.8	0.2	0.4	0.0	0.2
Poweshiek	18 815	92.3	39.3	21.9	25.4	21.5	1.5	0.6	4.1	1.7	7.7	0.0	1.7	0.0	5.7	0.0	0.2
Ringgold	5 469	97.2	41.0	24.5	27.0	22.7	1.9	0.8	2.8	1.4	2.8	0.0	2.6	0.0	0.0	0.0	0.1
Sac	11 529	97.5	41.2	24.0	28.0	23.2	1.3	0.4	3.1	1.5	2.5	0.1	2.2	0.1	0.0	0.0	0.1
Scott	158 668	97.9	39.3	20.5	30.0	24.3	3.2	1.5	4.9	2.3	2.1	0.2	0.7	0.2	0.6	0.0	0.4
Shelby	13 173	97.7	39.3	24.5	30.1	25.5	1.3	0.5	2.6	1.5	2.3	0.1	1.8	0.3	0.0	0.0	0.1
Sioux	31 589	91.6	33.9	23.5	31.5	26.4	1.0	0.3	1.8	0.5	8.4	0.1	1.4	0.0	6.6	0.0	0.3
Story	79 981	88.0	36.7	18.2	21.4	18.3	1.6	0.4	9.9	1.7	12.0	0.1	0.7	0.0	10.8	0.0	0.5
Tama	18 103	97.3	38.8	22.9	29.0	23.9	3.2	1.5	3.4	1.9	2.7	0.2	1.8	0.6	0.0	0.0	0.2
Taylor	6 958	97.4	40.6	24.0	26.9	22.3	2.4	1.1	3.5	1.8	2.6	0.1	1.8	0.0	0.0	0.0	0.8
Union	12 309	97.6	42.6	22.6	26.2	22.0	2.1	0.8	4.2	2.1	2.4	0.1	1.3	0.0	0.5	0.0	0.5
Van Buren	7 809	98.4	40.7	23.7	28.6	23.2	1.9	0.8	3.4	1.9	1.6	0.0	1.1	0.0	0.0	0.0	0.5
Wapello	36 051	97.1	41.0	21.6	26.7	21.2	3.0	1.3	4.8	2.4	2.9	0.2	1.0	0.1	1.0	0.0	0.4
Warren	40 671	95.8	36.2	23.3	31.0	25.6	2.2	1.0	3.1	1.6	4.2	0.1	1.5	0.0	2.5	0.0	0.2
Washington	20 670	97.6	39.0	23.5	29.9	24.8	2.1	0.8	3.2	1.6	2.4	0.1	1.9	0.2	0.0	0.0	0.3
Wayne	6 730	98.0	41.9	24.4	27.3	22.5	2.3	1.0	2.2	1.1	2.0	0.1	1.8	0.0	0.0	0.0	0.1
Webster	40 235	93.9	39.5	20.4	27.6	22.7	2.4	1.1	4.0	1.9	6.1	3.1	1.7	0.4	0.7	0.0	0.1
Winnebago	11 723	95.5	40.5	23.0	27.5	23.2	1.3	0.4	3.1	1.5	4.5	0.0	1.7	0.0	2.4	0.0	0.4
Winneshiek	21 310	89.2	36.3	21.4	26.7	22.3	1.2	0.4	3.6	1.4	10.8	0.0	1.4	0.2	9.1	0.0	0.1
Woodbury	103 877	97.3	37.7	19.6	30.6	24.9	4.1	1.6	5.4	2.2	2.7	0.2	0.8	0.2	0.9	0.0	0.5
Worth	7 909	98.5	41.4	24.1	28.1	23.2	1.7	0.6	3.2	1.8	1.5	0.1	1.4	0.0	0.0	0.0	0.0
Wright	14 334	97.8	41.4	23.8	27.2	23.2	1.8	0.6	3.6	1.6	2.2	0.0	2.0	0.0	0.0	0.0	0.2
KANSAS	2 688 418	97.0	38.6	21.1	29.5	24.5	3.3	1.4	4.4	1.6	3.0	0.6	0.9	0.1	0.9	0.2	0.3
Allen	14 385	97.5	40.1	21.9	28.7	22.9	2.9	1.5	3.9	1.7	2.5	0.1	1.2	0.0	0.3	0.0	0.9
Anderson	8 110	98.4	39.7	23.8	29.3	24.5	2.8	1.3	2.8	1.3	1.6	0.2	0.9	0.4	0.0	0.0	0.1
Atchison	16 774	93.7	37.4	20.3	29.0	23.6	3.1	1.5	4.0	1.7	6.3	0.1	0.9	0.8	3.1	0.0	1.3

Table B. States and Counties

STATE County	Households by type, 2000												Households, 1990		
	Family households						Nonfamily households								
				Married couple		Female householder[1]			Householder living alone						Household-holder living alone
	Total households	Total	With own children under 18 years	Total	With own children under 18 years	Total	With own children under 18 years	Total	Total	65 years and over	Average household size	Average family size	Total households	Female householder[1]	Householder living alone
	71	72	73	74	75	76	77	78	79	80	81	82	83	84	85
IOWA—Cont'd															
Guthrie	4 641	70.0	27.9	60.0	21.7	6.6	3.9	30.0	26.1	14.1	2.39	2.86	4 407	6.0	26.1
Hamilton	6 692	68.7	30.6	57.9	24.0	7.6	4.7	31.3	27.5	13.6	2.43	2.95	6 358	6.8	25.0
Hancock	4 795	70.4	32.6	60.9	26.5	6.0	4.2	29.6	26.5	13.7	2.48	3.01	4 867	5.6	24.9
Hardin	7 628	66.7	29.5	57.1	23.0	6.5	4.5	33.3	29.4	15.7	2.35	2.91	7 611	5.5	28.0
Harrison	6 115	70.4	32.3	59.3	25.4	7.6	5.0	29.6	26.1	13.7	2.51	3.02	5 656	6.8	25.7
Henry	7 626	69.1	32.8	57.7	25.0	8.2	5.6	30.9	26.8	12.2	2.46	2.98	7 089	7.0	25.8
Howard	3 974	66.7	31.1	56.8	25.0	6.6	4.4	33.3	29.5	15.6	2.43	3.03	3 856	5.1	28.5
Humboldt	4 295	67.1	29.7	57.4	23.4	6.4	4.1	32.9	29.8	16.3	2.38	2.94	4 339	5.4	26.6
Ida	3 213	68.0	29.4	59.5	24.3	5.9	3.6	32.0	29.3	15.9	2.39	2.95	3 222	4.3	26.4
Iowa	6 163	69.8	32.8	60.1	26.8	6.6	4.3	30.2	25.9	12.5	2.50	3.03	5 713	6.0	24.9
Jackson	8 078	69.2	32.0	58.2	25.1	7.7	4.9	30.8	27.0	13.8	2.47	3.01	7 527	7.5	24.8
Jasper	14 689	69.9	31.7	59.3	24.7	7.4	4.9	30.1	26.1	11.8	2.42	2.92	13 632	6.6	23.7
Jefferson	6 649	64.4	31.1	53.1	23.0	8.0	6.0	35.6	30.4	10.7	2.34	2.93	6 309	7.4	28.2
Johnson	44 080	53.5	26.5	43.9	20.7	6.8	4.4	46.5	30.2	5.6	2.34	2.97	36 067	6.7	27.8
Jones	7 560	70.1	31.0	59.0	24.0	7.9	5.2	29.9	25.3	12.5	2.47	2.95	6 917	7.1	23.6
Keokuk	4 586	68.8	30.5	59.0	24.4	6.5	4.0	31.2	27.8	15.8	2.45	2.99	4 573	6.3	25.9
Kossuth	6 974	68.7	30.9	60.4	25.8	5.8	3.8	31.3	28.7	15.5	2.42	2.98	7 194	5.1	27.3
Lee	15 161	67.6	30.4	53.7	21.5	10.3	6.7	32.4	28.3	13.5	2.41	2.93	14 936	9.7	26.8
Linn	76 753	65.6	31.8	53.2	23.8	9.0	6.0	34.4	27.5	8.9	2.43	2.99	65 501	8.5	25.0
Louisa	4 519	73.4	35.0	61.3	27.2	8.2	5.2	26.6	22.5	10.4	2.66	3.11	4 296	7.3	22.0
Lucas	3 811	67.2	28.3	56.7	21.9	7.0	4.3	32.8	28.7	14.6	2.42	2.98	3 766	6.6	29.9
Lyon	4 428	73.7	34.8	67.1	30.8	4.4	2.7	26.3	24.3	13.7	2.61	3.13	4 289	4.0	22.4
Madison	5 326	73.7	34.8	63.9	28.5	7.0	4.7	26.3	22.7	11.7	2.58	3.04	4 715	6.4	23.6
Mahaska	8 880	69.2	32.4	58.6	25.1	7.5	5.1	30.8	26.6	12.4	2.45	2.96	8 306	6.9	25.0
Marion	12 017	71.0	33.0	61.2	26.6	6.9	4.5	29.0	25.6	11.9	2.50	3.02	10 815	6.5	24.7
Marshall	15 338	68.2	31.1	55.4	22.6	9.3	6.3	31.8	26.9	12.2	2.48	3.00	14 890	8.3	26.0
Mills	5 324	74.0	34.8	61.7	26.7	8.9	6.1	26.0	22.3	10.1	2.60	3.04	4 665	8.9	22.7
Mitchell	4 294	69.5	30.1	60.8	24.6	5.7	3.7	30.5	27.6	15.4	2.47	3.02	4 253	4.7	26.7
Monona	4 211	65.0	26.7	54.5	20.7	7.1	3.8	35.0	31.0	17.5	2.31	2.88	4 098	6.6	28.7
Monroe	3 228	68.5	30.5	56.2	23.0	8.6	5.5	31.5	28.0	15.3	2.43	2.97	3 196	7.6	27.9
Montgomery	4 886	66.7	29.7	54.4	21.7	8.7	5.8	33.3	29.5	14.7	2.36	2.91	4 955	7.4	29.0
Muscatine	15 847	71.2	34.8	57.9	26.1	9.3	6.1	28.8	24.1	9.9	2.59	3.07	14 806	9.2	23.0
O'Brien	6 001	68.7	30.4	61.0	25.5	4.9	3.1	31.3	28.0	14.7	2.42	2.97	5 980	4.6	27.1
Osceola	2 778	69.9	31.7	62.0	26.9	5.1	3.3	30.1	27.6	15.1	2.48	3.03	2 817	4.5	26.6
Page	6 708	66.5	28.2	55.5	21.3	8.1	5.3	33.5	29.9	15.4	2.32	2.87	6 687	7.3	28.7
Palo Alto	4 119	64.9	28.5	56.3	23.4	5.9	3.4	35.1	30.4	16.1	2.37	2.96	4 183	5.1	29.5
Plymouth	9 372	72.6	35.7	63.3	29.5	6.2	4.1	27.4	24.0	12.0	2.61	3.12	8 417	5.6	23.6
Pocahontas	3 617	67.2	29.5	58.3	23.6	5.9	4.1	32.8	30.2	17.8	2.35	2.91	3 820	4.4	27.9
Polk	149 112	64.8	32.2	51.0	23.8	10.3	6.5	35.2	28.1	8.6	2.45	3.04	129 237	10.2	27.0
Pottawattamie	33 844	69.8	32.3	53.6	22.6	11.8	7.3	30.2	24.9	10.0	2.54	3.03	31 262	11.2	23.3
Poweshiek	7 398	66.0	29.0	55.8	22.1	7.4	5.2	34.0	29.2	13.9	2.35	2.88	7 158	6.4	25.9
Ringgold	2 245	68.5	27.7	59.7	22.0	5.5	3.8	31.5	28.6	17.8	2.37	2.90	2 218	5.0	27.6
Sac	4 746	67.4	28.6	58.3	22.8	6.2	4.0	32.6	29.4	16.4	2.37	2.92	4 914	5.4	28.1
Scott	62 334	67.2	33.2	52.3	23.4	11.4	7.7	32.8	26.9	9.0	2.49	3.04	57 438	11.1	24.9
Shelby	5 173	71.6	32.6	62.3	26.6	6.8	4.7	28.4	25.2	13.6	2.49	2.99	5 024	5.4	24.7
Sioux	10 693	75.4	36.8	69.4	33.1	4.2	2.7	24.6	22.2	11.4	2.71	3.19	9 925	3.7	22.0
Story	29 383	58.0	27.3	49.6	22.3	5.9	3.7	42.0	26.7	7.6	2.39	2.94	25 941	5.8	25.4
Tama	7 018	70.8	31.6	59.2	24.4	8.0	5.1	29.2	25.3	13.7	2.51	3.01	6 768	6.6	24.8
Taylor	2 824	67.7	28.0	59.0	22.6	5.9	3.6	32.3	27.8	16.1	2.40	2.94	2 859	5.6	27.7
Union	5 242	64.0	27.5	53.1	20.0	8.0	5.6	36.0	31.3	14.4	2.29	2.87	5 173	8.5	28.9
Van Buren	3 181	68.0	28.7	58.3	22.4	6.0	3.9	32.0	28.0	15.7	2.41	2.96	3 056	5.7	27.0
Wapello	14 784	66.3	28.8	52.7	20.4	9.9	6.4	33.7	28.2	13.4	2.37	2.89	14 555	9.4	27.1
Warren	14 708	76.2	37.8	64.5	30.0	8.8	5.9	23.8	19.9	8.7	2.65	3.05	12 659	8.0	18.3
Washington	8 056	69.9	31.4	60.3	25.8	6.7	3.9	30.1	26.4	12.5	2.50	3.04	7 454	6.4	25.9
Wayne	2 821	68.0	27.3	58.2	20.9	6.4	4.4	32.0	29.8	17.9	2.34	2.89	2 953	4.7	28.5
Webster	15 878	64.9	30.2	51.8	21.7	9.5	6.4	35.1	30.3	13.1	2.38	2.97	15 963	9.1	27.9
Winnebago	4 749	67.0	30.6	56.9	23.8	7.2	5.1	33.0	29.4	14.7	2.36	2.91	4 704	6.0	28.2
Winneshiek	7 734	67.1	30.9	58.9	26.1	5.5	3.5	32.9	27.6	12.3	2.46	3.03	7 256	5.1	25.6
Woodbury	39 151	67.5	34.0	51.9	24.0	11.3	7.5	32.5	26.6	11.2	2.58	3.13	36 899	10.5	25.9
Worth	3 278	69.1	30.4	58.1	23.8	7.3	4.5	30.9	27.6	14.3	2.38	2.88	3 239	5.8	27.2
Wright	5 940	66.3	28.4	57.3	22.5	6.2	4.2	33.7	30.2	16.3	2.36	2.92	5 899	5.6	28.3
KANSAS	1 037 891	67.6	33.2	54.7	25.1	9.3	6.0	32.4	27.0	10.2	2.51	3.07	944 726	8.6	25.9
Allen	5 775	67.4	29.8	54.6	21.5	8.9	5.7	32.6	28.5	14.4	2.43	2.98	5 705	7.7	27.3
Anderson	3 221	70.3	31.0	59.9	25.0	6.9	4.0	29.7	26.8	15.6	2.48	3.00	3 067	6.6	26.3
Atchison	6 275	68.2	32.4	54.3	23.7	10.0	6.6	31.8	27.6	12.8	2.51	3.05	6 129	9.4	26.3

[1] No spouse present.

Items 71—85

Table B. States and Counties

STATE County	Percent change of households, 1990–2000	Total housing units	Occupied housing units (percent)	Vacant housing units Total	For seasonal, recreational, or occasional use	Homeowner vacancy rate (percent)	Rental vacancy rate (percent)	Total	Percent owner-occupied housing units	Percent renter-occupied housing units	Average household size of owner-occupied units	Average household size of renter-occupied units
	86	87	88	89	90	91	92	93	94	95	96	97
IOWA—Cont'd												
Guthrie	5.3	5 467	84.9	15.1	5.2	2.4	8.2	4 641	79.6	20.4	2.43	2.22
Hamilton	5.3	7 082	94.5	5.5	0.3	1.8	5.0	6 692	72.8	27.2	2.53	2.15
Hancock	-1.5	5 164	92.9	7.1	1.1	1.8	6.3	4 795	78.2	21.8	2.53	2.32
Hardin	0.2	8 318	91.7	8.3	1.0	2.2	9.5	7 628	74.6	25.4	2.41	2.19
Harrison	8.1	6 602	92.6	7.4	0.6	2.5	7.4	6 115	76.6	23.4	2.58	2.28
Henry	7.6	8 246	92.5	7.5	0.9	1.7	9.5	7 626	73.0	27.0	2.58	2.12
Howard	3.1	4 327	91.8	8.2	0.8	1.1	9.3	3 974	79.2	20.8	2.52	2.11
Humboldt	-1.0	4 645	92.5	7.5	0.3	2.2	8.2	4 295	76.0	24.0	2.46	2.13
Ida	-0.3	3 506	91.6	8.4	0.4	1.4	8.1	3 213	73.2	26.8	2.46	2.20
Iowa	7.9	6 545	94.2	5.8	0.4	1.3	7.0	6 163	77.9	22.1	2.62	2.06
Jackson	7.3	8 949	90.3	9.7	4.6	1.4	5.3	8 078	76.0	24.0	2.56	2.21
Jasper	7.8	15 659	93.8	6.2	0.6	1.7	8.9	14 689	75.7	24.3	2.53	2.09
Jefferson	5.4	7 241	91.8	8.2	0.8	1.8	9.2	6 649	67.2	32.8	2.49	2.03
Johnson	22.2	45 831	96.2	3.8	0.4	1.9	2.9	44 080	56.6	43.4	2.58	2.02
Jones	9.3	8 126	93.0	7.0	0.8	1.9	7.4	7 560	75.9	24.1	2.53	2.26
Keokuk	0.3	5 013	91.5	8.5	0.5	3.0	7.5	4 586	78.7	21.3	2.49	2.28
Kossuth	-3.1	7 605	91.7	8.3	0.7	2.3	12.6	6 974	77.8	22.2	2.49	2.15
Lee	1.5	16 612	91.3	8.7	0.7	1.6	9.8	15 161	75.5	24.5	2.50	2.11
Linn	17.2	80 551	95.3	4.7	0.6	1.6	5.6	76 753	72.7	27.3	2.58	2.03
Louisa	5.2	5 133	88.0	12.0	5.5	1.2	7.9	4 519	77.3	22.7	2.66	2.64
Lucas	1.2	4 239	89.9	10.1	1.2	2.4	8.1	3 811	78.3	21.7	2.50	2.11
Lyon	3.2	4 758	93.1	6.9	0.4	2.6	9.4	4 428	81.8	18.2	2.65	2.42
Madison	13.0	5 661	94.1	5.9	0.7	1.3	7.8	5 326	78.0	22.0	2.67	2.24
Mahaska	6.9	9 551	93.0	7.0	1.2	1.4	8.5	8 880	71.1	28.9	2.53	2.24
Marion	11.1	12 755	94.2	5.8	0.8	1.3	7.5	12 017	75.6	24.4	2.65	2.05
Marshall	3.0	16 324	94.0	6.0	0.5	1.7	7.5	15 338	73.7	26.3	2.56	2.26
Mills	14.1	5 671	93.9	6.1	1.1	2.3	5.1	5 324	79.5	20.5	2.67	2.32
Mitchell	1.0	4 594	93.5	6.5	1.3	1.5	5.8	4 294	81.6	18.4	2.53	2.17
Monona	2.8	4 660	90.4	9.6	1.4	2.7	8.4	4 211	76.0	24.0	2.35	2.20
Monroe	1.0	3 588	90.0	10.0	1.0	1.5	9.9	3 228	78.4	21.6	2.49	2.21
Montgomery	-1.4	5 399	90.5	9.5	0.7	2.1	8.7	4 886	73.1	26.9	2.41	2.21
Muscatine	7.0	16 786	94.4	5.6	1.4	1.1	5.6	15 847	75.4	24.6	2.65	2.38
O'Brien	0.4	6 509	92.2	7.8	0.3	2.2	8.5	6 001	76.9	23.1	2.47	2.23
Osceola	-1.4	3 012	92.2	7.8	0.4	2.3	7.1	2 778	77.5	22.5	2.51	2.38
Page	0.3	7 302	91.9	8.1	0.6	2.3	8.5	6 708	71.6	28.4	2.43	2.05
Palo Alto	-1.5	4 631	88.9	11.1	2.1	2.1	12.5	4 119	74.1	25.9	2.42	2.20
Plymouth	11.3	9 880	94.9	5.1	0.3	1.6	7.4	9 372	77.5	22.5	2.73	2.21
Pocahontas	-5.3	3 988	90.7	9.3	0.7	1.8	8.0	3 617	79.3	20.7	2.39	2.21
Polk	15.4	156 447	95.3	4.7	0.3	1.5	6.1	149 112	68.8	31.2	2.62	2.07
Pottawattamie	8.3	35 761	94.6	5.4	0.3	1.4	8.4	33 844	71.1	28.9	2.64	2.31
Poweshiek	3.4	8 556	86.5	13.5	7.4	1.8	7.1	7 398	71.9	28.1	2.45	2.08
Ringgold	1.2	2 789	80.5	19.5	11.5	2.5	5.9	2 245	75.7	24.3	2.41	2.25
Sac	-3.4	5 460	86.9	13.1	5.5	2.8	10.9	4 746	76.8	23.2	2.41	2.23
Scott	8.5	65 649	95.0	5.0	0.4	1.5	7.3	62 334	70.6	29.4	2.63	2.17
Shelby	3.0	5 459	94.8	5.2	0.4	1.7	5.3	5 173	77.0	23.0	2.55	2.28
Sioux	7.7	11 260	95.0	5.0	0.3	1.4	6.4	10 693	80.5	19.5	2.81	2.28
Story	13.3	30 630	95.9	4.1	0.3	1.5	4.1	29 383	58.3	41.7	2.60	2.11
Tama	3.7	7 583	92.5	7.5	0.9	2.2	8.8	7 018	77.5	22.5	2.55	2.35
Taylor	-1.2	3 199	88.3	11.7	0.6	2.8	9.7	2 824	76.4	23.6	2.39	2.43
Union	1.3	5 657	92.7	7.3	0.7	1.1	7.6	5 242	72.1	27.9	2.39	2.05
Van Buren	4.1	3 581	88.8	11.2	4.2	1.7	6.1	3 181	79.7	20.3	2.46	2.25
Wapello	1.6	15 873	93.1	6.9	1.3	1.7	6.6	14 784	75.6	24.4	2.43	2.17
Warren	16.2	15 289	96.2	3.8	0.4	1.0	6.3	14 708	79.9	20.1	2.79	2.10
Washington	8.1	8 543	94.3	5.7	0.6	1.4	6.9	8 056	75.3	24.7	2.62	2.15
Wayne	-4.5	3 357	84.0	16.0	3.5	3.0	8.6	2 821	79.3	20.7	2.40	2.11
Webster	-0.5	16 969	93.6	6.4	0.4	1.6	7.4	15 878	71.3	28.7	2.51	2.05
Winnebago	1.0	5 065	93.8	6.2	0.8	1.6	6.9	4 749	76.1	23.9	2.43	2.12
Winneshiek	6.6	8 208	94.2	5.8	1.1	0.8	5.5	7 734	73.5	26.5	2.59	2.09
Woodbury	6.1	41 394	94.6	5.4	0.3	1.5	7.7	39 151	68.6	31.4	2.70	2.32
Worth	1.2	3 534	92.8	7.2	0.8	2.1	8.9	3 278	79.0	21.0	2.44	2.13
Wright	0.7	6 559	90.6	9.4	2.5	2.3	6.7	5 940	74.2	25.8	2.42	2.20
KANSAS	9.9	1 131 200	91.8	8.2	0.9	2.0	8.8	1 037 891	69.2	30.8	2.63	2.25
Allen	1.2	6 449	89.5	10.5	1.2	2.3	8.8	5 775	75.0	25.0	2.49	2.25
Anderson	5.0	3 596	89.6	10.4	2.0	2.6	11.4	3 221	80.0	20.0	2.51	2.37
Atchison	2.4	6 818	92.0	8.0	0.7	1.4	9.9	6 275	73.3	26.7	2.59	2.28

Table B. States and Counties

STATE/ County code	MSA/ PMSA/ NECMA code[1]	County type[2]	STATE County	Land area, 2000[3] (sq km)	Population, 2000 Total persons	Rank	Per square kilometer	Land area, 1990[3] (sq km)	Population, 1990 Total persons	Rank	Per square kilometer	Population and population characteristics, 2000 Race (percent) One race White	Black or African American	American Indian or Alaska Native	Asian	Native Hawaiian and other Pacific Islander	Some other race
				1	2	3	4	5	6	7	8	9	10	11	12	13	14
			KANSAS—Cont'd														
20 007	...	9	Barbor	2 937	5 307	2 829	1.8	2 938	5 874	2 773	2.0	97.1	0.4	0.6	0.1	0.0	0.9
20 009	...	7	Barton	2 315	28 205	1 445	12.2	2 316	29 382	1 318	12.7	93.0	1.1	0.5	0.2	0.0	3.5
20 011	...	7	Bourbon	1 650	15 379	2 061	9.3	1 650	14 966	1 989	9.1	94.1	3.1	0.8	0.4	0.0	0.3
20 013	...	7	Brown	1 478	10 724	2 381	7.3	1 478	11 128	2 281	7.5	86.9	1.6	8.8	0.2	0.0	0.7
20 015	9040	2	Butler	3 698	59 482	808	16.1	3 699	50 580	833	13.7	94.9	1.4	0.9	0.4	0.0	0.7
20 017	...	9	Chase	2 010	3 030	2 992	1.5	2 010	3 021	2 998	1.5	96.9	1.0	0.6	0.1	0.0	0.6
20 019	...	9	Chautauqua	1 662	4 359	2 891	2.6	1 662	4 407	2 880	2.7	93.8	0.3	3.6	0.1	0.0	0.3
20 021	...	6	Cherokee	1 521	22 605	1 665	14.9	1 521	21 374	1 614	14.1	92.3	0.6	3.5	0.2	0.0	0.5
20 023	...	9	Cheyenne	2 641	3 165	2 981	1.2	2 642	3 243	2 980	1.2	97.9	0.1	0.1	0.3	0.0	1.0
20 025	...	9	Clark	2 524	2 390	3 032	0.9	2 525	2 418	3 029	1.0	95.8	0.3	1.1	0.1	0.0	1.9
20 027	...	7	Clay	1 668	8 822	2 543	5.3	1 668	9 158	2 455	5.5	97.7	0.6	0.4	0.1	0.0	0.3
20 029	...	7	Cloud	1 853	10 268	2 420	5.5	1 854	11 023	2 290	5.9	98.3	0.3	0.3	0.3	0.0	0.1
20 031	...	7	Coffey	1 631	8 865	2 537	5.4	1 632	8 404	2 520	5.1	97.0	0.2	0.5	0.3	0.0	0.5
20 033	...	9	Comanche	2 042	1 967	3 066	1.0	2 042	2 313	3 038	1.1	98.0	0.1	0.3	0.1	0.2	0.6
20 035	...	4	Cowley	2 917	36 291	1 205	12.4	2 917	36 915	1 076	12.7	90.1	2.7	2.0	1.5	0.0	1.4
20 037	...	4	Crawford	1 536	38 242	1 160	24.9	1 536	35 582	1 109	23.2	93.3	1.8	0.9	1.1	0.1	1.1
20 039	...	9	Decatur	2 314	3 472	2 956	1.5	2 314	4 021	2 915	1.7	97.9	0.5	0.1	0.1	0.1	0.4
20 041	...	7	Dickinson	2 196	19 344	1 826	8.8	2 197	18 958	1 737	8.6	96.4	0.6	0.5	0.3	0.0	0.4
20 043	...	8	Doniphan	1 016	8 249	2 586	8.1	1 016	8 134	2 551	8.0	94.8	2.0	1.2	0.3	0.0	0.4
20 045	4150	3	Douglas	1 183	99 962	525	84.5	1 184	81 798	556	69.1	86.1	4.2	2.6	3.1	0.1	1.2
20 047	...	9	Edwards	1 611	3 449	2 959	2.1	1 611	3 787	2 931	2.4	92.5	0.3	0.5	0.3	0.0	5.6
20 049	...	8	Elk	1 676	3 261	2 976	1.9	1 678	3 327	2 968	2.0	95.1	0.2	1.0	0.2	0.1	1.2
20 051	...	7	Ellis	2 331	27 507	1 466	11.8	2 331	26 004	1 421	11.2	96.1	0.7	0.2	0.8	0.0	1.3
20 053	...	9	Ellsworth	1 854	6 525	2 737	3.5	1 854	6 586	2 700	3.6	93.7	3.6	0.5	0.2	0.0	1.1
20 055	...	5	Finney	3 372	40 523	1 103	12.0	3 367	33 070	1 188	9.8	69.1	1.3	1.0	2.9	0.1	23.0
20 057	...	5	Ford	2 845	32 458	1 334	11.4	2 845	27 463	1 377	9.7	74.9	1.6	0.6	2.1	0.1	18.2
20 059	...	6	Franklin	1 486	24 784	1 564	16.7	1 486	21 994	1 576	14.8	95.0	1.2	0.9	0.3	0.0	0.8
20 061	...	5	Geary	996	27 947	1 453	28.1	995	30 453	1 271	30.6	64.1	22.0	0.8	3.2	0.4	4.1
20 063	...	9	Gove	2 775	3 068	2 987	1.1	2 775	3 231	2 981	1.2	97.9	0.1	0.2	0.1	0.0	0.7
20 065	...	9	Graham	2 327	2 946	2 995	1.3	2 327	3 543	2 954	1.5	94.9	3.2	0.3	0.3	0.0	0.4
20 067	...	7	Grant	1 489	7 909	2 614	5.3	1 489	7 159	2 637	4.8	77.0	0.2	0.9	0.4	0.0	19.5
20 069	...	9	Gray	2 250	5 904	2 793	2.6	2 251	5 396	2 809	2.4	92.3	0.2	0.5	0.1	0.1	5.4
20 071	...	9	Greeley	2 015	1 534	3 093	0.8	2 015	1 774	3 079	0.9	93.1	0.2	0.3	0.1	0.1	5.2
20 073	...	6	Greenwood	2 952	7 673	2 632	2.6	2 952	7 847	2 587	2.7	96.5	0.1	0.8	0.1	0.0	0.8
20 075	...	9	Hamilton	2 581	2 670	3 017	1.0	2 581	2 388	3 032	0.9	81.6	0.5	0.5	0.6	0.0	15.1
20 077	...	7	Harper	2 076	6 536	2 736	3.1	2 076	7 124	2 641	3.4	97.2	0.2	0.8	0.1	0.0	0.4
20 079	9040	2	Harvey	1 397	32 869	1 323	23.5	1 397	31 028	1 245	22.2	91.0	1.6	0.5	0.5	0.0	4.2
20 081	...	9	Haskell	1 495	4 307	2 895	2.9	1 495	3 886	2 925	2.6	85.1	0.2	0.6	0.6	0.0	11.4
20 083	...	9	Hodgeman	2 227	2 085	3 059	0.9	2 227	2 177	3 055	1.0	97.3	0.9	0.2	0.0	0.0	0.5
20 085	...	6	Jackson	1 698	12 657	2 251	7.5	1 701	11 525	2 254	6.8	90.2	0.5	6.8	0.2	0.0	0.5
20 087	...	8	Jefferson	1 389	18 426	1 871	13.3	1 389	15 905	1 931	11.5	96.7	0.4	0.9	0.2	0.0	0.4
20 089	...	9	Jewell	2 355	3 791	2 928	1.6	2 355	4 251	2 893	1.8	98.8	0.0	0.3	0.1	0.0	0.1
20 091	3760	0	Johnson	1 235	451 086	131	365.3	1 235	355 021	145	287.5	91.1	2.6	0.3	2.8	0.0	1.5
20 093	...	9	Kearny	2 256	4 531	2 876	2.0	2 253	4 027	2 913	1.8	80.3	0.6	0.9	0.3	0.1	15.7
20 095	...	6	Kingman	2 236	8 673	2 553	3.9	2 237	8 292	2 536	3.7	97.5	0.2	0.6	0.2	0.0	0.3
20 097	...	9	Kiowa	1 871	3 278	2 975	1.8	1 871	3 660	2 942	2.0	97.2	0.2	0.6	0.3	0.0	1.0
20 099	...	7	Labette	1 680	22 835	1 651	13.6	1 681	23 693	1 504	14.1	89.3	4.7	1.9	0.3	0.0	1.2
20 101	...	9	Lane	1 858	2 155	3 055	1.2	1 858	2 375	3 034	1.3	97.7	0.0	0.0	0.1	0.0	0.5
20 103	3760	1	Leavenworth	1 200	68 691	718	57.2	1 200	64 371	679	53.6	84.2	10.4	0.7	1.1	0.1	1.2
20 105	...	9	Lincoln	1 862	3 578	2 945	1.9	1 862	3 653	2 944	2.0	98.3	0.1	0.5	0.1	0.0	0.3
20 107	...	8	Linn	1 551	9 570	2 483	6.2	1 551	8 254	2 543	5.3	97.5	0.6	0.5	0.1	0.0	0.4
20 109	...	9	Logan	2 779	3 046	2 991	1.1	2 779	3 081	2 994	1.1	96.7	0.6	0.2	0.2	0.0	0.7
20 111	...	5	Lyon	2 204	35 935	1 220	16.3	2 204	34 732	1 144	15.8	83.3	2.3	0.5	2.0	0.0	9.8
20 113	...	7	McPherson	2 330	29 554	1 413	12.7	2 331	27 268	1 381	11.7	96.5	0.8	0.3	0.3	0.1	0.8
20 115	...	6	Marion	2 443	13 361	2 200	5.5	2 443	12 888	2 146	5.3	97.1	0.5	0.6	0.2	0.0	0.5
20 117	...	7	Marshall	2 338	10 965	2 370	4.7	2 338	11 705	2 232	5.0	98.1	0.2	0.4	0.2	0.0	0.3
20 119	...	9	Meade	2 534	4 631	2 871	1.8	2 534	4 247	2 894	1.7	91.1	0.4	0.5	0.2	0.0	6.2
20 121	3760	1	Miami	1 494	28 351	1 436	19.0	1 494	23 466	1 516	15.7	96.0	1.5	0.5	0.2	0.0	0.4
20 123	...	7	Mitchell	1 813	6 932	2 692	3.8	1 813	7 203	2 632	4.0	97.6	0.5	0.4	0.3	0.0	0.2
20 125	...	5	Montgomery	1 671	36 252	1 207	21.7	1 671	38 816	1 030	23.2	85.8	6.1	3.2	0.5	0.0	1.1
20 127	...	9	Morris	1 806	6 104	2 770	3.4	1 806	6 198	2 733	3.4	97.5	0.3	0.3	0.2	0.0	0.7
20 129	...	9	Morton	1 890	3 496	2 954	1.8	1 891	3 480	2 958	1.8	88.4	0.2	1.1	1.1	0.0	7.5
20 131	...	9	Nemaha	1 860	10 717	2 382	5.8	1 862	10 446	2 343	5.6	98.3	0.5	0.2	0.1	0.1	0.2
20 133	...	7	Neosho	1 481	16 997	1 953	11.5	1 481	17 035	1 848	11.5	94.9	0.9	1.0	0.3	0.0	1.1
20 135	...	9	Ness	2 784	3 454	2 958	1.2	2 784	4 033	2 912	1.4	98.2	0.1	0.2	0.1	0.0	0.3
20 137	...	7	Norton	2 274	5 953	2 788	2.6	2 274	5 947	2 765	2.6	93.3	4.0	0.4	0.4	0.0	1.0

[1] MSA = Metropolitan Statistical Area. PMSA = Primary MSA. NECMA = New England County Metropolitan Area. See Appendix A for explanation of these concepts. See Appendix B for list of metropolitan areas identified by type, with component counties.
[2] County typology code from the Economic Research Service of USDA. See Appendix A for definition.
[3] Dry land or land partially or temporarily covered by water.

Table B. States and Counties

STATE County	Population and population characteristics, 2000 (cont'd)								Population and population characteristics, 1990				
	Race (percent) (cont'd)								Race (percent)				
	Race alone or in combination												
	Two or more races	White	Black	American Indian or Alaska Native	Asian	Native Hawaiian and other Pacific Islander	Some other race	Hispanic[1]	White	Black or African American	American Indian or Alaska Native	Asian and Pacific Islander	Hispanic[1]
	15	16	17	18	19	20	21	22	23	24	25	26	27
KANSAS—Cont'd													
Barber	1.0	98.1	0.6	1.1	0.2	0.0	1.1	2.0	98.6	0.2	0.5	0.1	1.2
Barton	1.6	94.5	1.5	1.0	0.3	0.0	4.2	8.3	96.6	1.2	0.5	0.4	2.8
Bourbon	1.3	95.3	3.4	1.6	0.5	0.1	0.5	1.3	96.5	2.8	0.4	0.1	0.5
Brown	1.8	88.7	2.0	9.9	0.3	0.0	1.0	2.3	91.6	1.2	6.5	0.1	1.7
Butler	1.7	96.6	1.7	1.9	0.6	0.1	0.9	2.2	97.5	0.7	0.9	0.3	1.5
Chase	0.8	97.7	1.2	1.1	0.2	0.0	0.7	1.7	99.1	0.2	0.4	0.0	1.3
Chautauqua	1.8	95.7	0.5	5.0	0.3	0.0	0.5	1.4	95.3	0.5	3.4	0.3	1.0
Cherokee	2.9	95.1	0.9	6.0	0.3	0.1	0.6	1.3	95.6	0.5	3.6	0.1	0.8
Cheyenne	0.5	98.3	0.1	0.3	0.6	0.2	1.1	2.6	99.4	0.2	0.0	0.3	0.6
Clark	0.9	96.7	0.4	1.6	0.1	0.0	2.1	4.0	97.4	0.0	1.1	0.3	1.7
Clay	0.9	98.6	0.7	0.9	0.3	0.1	0.4	0.8	99.1	0.2	0.2	0.3	0.4
Cloud	0.7	99.0	0.4	0.7	0.3	0.0	0.3	0.6	99.0	0.3	0.2	0.0	0.7
Coffey	1.4	98.4	0.4	1.5	0.5	0.0	0.8	1.5	98.9	0.1	0.6	0.2	0.7
Comanche	0.9	98.6	0.2	0.7	0.4	0.2	0.9	1.8	99.0	0.3	0.5	0.0	0.6
Cowley	2.3	92.2	3.2	3.3	1.8	0.1	1.8	3.6	92.9	2.9	1.9	0.9	3.0
Crawford	1.6	94.8	2.2	1.8	1.3	0.1	1.4	2.4	96.3	1.3	0.9	1.2	0.9
Decatur	0.9	98.7	0.5	0.6	0.3	0.1	0.7	1.0	99.5	0.0	0.2	0.0	0.3
Dickinson	1.4	97.7	0.8	1.1	0.6	0.0	1.1	2.3	98.1	0.6	0.3	0.3	1.8
Doniphan	1.3	96.0	2.4	1.9	0.4	0.0	0.6	1.2	96.4	1.9	1.2	0.2	0.6
Douglas	2.7	88.5	5.2	3.6	3.7	0.2	1.8	3.3	89.1	4.1	2.6	3.2	2.6
Edwards	0.8	93.3	0.4	0.7	0.3	0.0	6.1	9.7	96.3	0.1	0.3	0.2	5.2
Elk	2.3	97.3	0.3	2.9	0.3	0.2	1.4	2.2	97.3	0.2	1.7	0.1	1.8
Ellis	0.9	96.9	1.0	0.6	0.9	0.0	1.4	2.4	98.6	0.4	0.2	0.6	0.8
Ellsworth	1.2	94.7	3.9	1.2	0.4	0.0	1.1	3.6	96.4	2.0	0.4	0.2	2.8
Finney	2.8	71.5	1.6	1.5	3.2	0.2	24.9	43.3	80.0	1.3	0.8	3.6	25.3
Ford	2.6	77.1	2.0	1.2	2.2	0.2	19.9	37.7	83.3	1.7	0.6	2.4	14.9
Franklin	1.7	96.7	1.6	2.1	0.4	0.0	1.1	2.6	96.4	1.3	0.9	0.5	2.1
Geary	5.4	68.2	24.6	1.8	4.9	0.7	5.7	8.5	68.8	23.6	0.7	4.0	6.1
Gove	1.0	98.9	0.3	0.7	0.2	0.0	0.8	1.2	99.6	0.1	0.2	0.1	0.3
Graham	0.8	95.6	3.5	1.0	0.4	0.0	0.5	0.8	96.2	2.9	0.4	0.3	0.6
Grant	2.1	78.9	0.3	1.5	0.5	0.0	20.9	34.7	84.6	0.0	1.1	0.6	21.6
Gray	1.5	93.7	0.3	1.0	0.2	0.2	6.1	9.8	95.8	0.1	0.4	0.0	4.2
Greeley	1.0	94.1	0.4	0.6	0.1	0.1	5.7	11.5	95.1	0.6	0.1	0.1	6.0
Greenwood	1.6	98.1	0.3	1.9	0.2	0.0	1.1	1.7	98.4	0.1	1.0	0.0	1.2
Hamilton	1.7	83.2	0.6	0.9	0.7	0.1	16.1	20.6	94.0	0.2	0.3	1.2	5.8
Harper	1.2	98.3	0.4	1.5	0.2	0.1	0.6	1.1	98.8	0.2	0.6	0.1	1.5
Harvey	2.1	93.0	2.2	1.2	0.7	0.1	5.0	8.0	94.4	1.8	0.5	0.7	5.2
Haskell	2.1	87.2	0.2	1.3	0.8	0.1	12.6	23.6	87.8	0.1	0.6	0.1	14.3
Hodgeman	1.1	98.4	1.2	0.7	0.0	0.0	0.8	2.7	98.2	1.0	0.1	0.0	1.5
Jackson	1.8	92.0	0.7	8.3	0.3	0.0	0.5	1.5	92.9	0.4	6.3	0.1	1.1
Jefferson	1.4	98.1	0.5	1.8	0.3	0.1	0.6	1.3	98.1	0.5	0.8	0.4	0.8
Jewell	0.7	99.4	0.1	0.9	0.1	0.1	0.2	0.7	99.6	0.0	0.3	0.1	0.2
Johnson	1.5	92.5	3.0	0.8	3.2	0.1	2.0	4.0	95.4	1.9	0.4	1.6	2.0
Kearny	2.1	82.4	0.9	1.3	0.4	0.1	17.2	26.6	89.4	0.1	0.6	0.1	16.7
Kingman	1.2	98.5	0.2	1.5	0.4	0.0	0.4	1.4	99.0	0.1	0.3	0.1	0.9
Kiowa	0.7	97.9	0.4	1.1	0.4	0.1	1.3	2.0	98.4	0.2	0.5	0.3	1.1
Labette	2.6	91.7	5.4	3.4	0.5	0.0	1.6	3.1	92.7	4.3	1.7	0.4	2.2
Lane	1.6	99.1	0.2	1.1	0.3	0.1	0.9	1.4	99.1	0.0	0.2	0.0	1.9
Leavenworth	2.2	86.0	11.2	1.6	1.5	0.3	1.7	3.8	85.5	11.1	0.6	1.5	3.4
Lincoln	0.8	99.0	0.2	1.1	0.2	0.1	0.3	1.0	99.5	0.0	0.3	0.0	0.4
Linn	1.1	98.5	0.9	1.1	0.2	0.1	0.3	0.9	98.8	0.4	0.5	0.1	0.4
Logan	1.6	98.3	0.9	0.8	0.5	0.0	1.1	1.6	98.9	0.4	0.3	0.0	0.8
Lyon	2.2	85.2	2.7	1.1	2.3	0.1	10.8	16.7	91.6	2.1	0.6	2.0	6.1
McPherson	1.2	97.6	1.1	0.9	0.5	0.2	1.0	1.9	97.8	0.8	0.4	0.5	1.2
Marion	1.1	98.1	0.7	1.1	0.3	0.2	0.8	1.9	98.4	0.6	0.3	0.2	0.9
Marshall	0.8	98.9	0.3	0.8	0.4	0.1	0.3	0.8	99.4	0.1	0.3	0.1	0.4
Meade	1.5	92.6	0.6	1.3	0.2	0.0	6.9	10.9	96.4	0.0	0.3	0.3	4.7
Miami	1.4	97.2	1.9	1.3	0.3	0.0	0.6	1.6	96.5	2.4	0.6	0.2	1.2
Mitchell	0.9	98.4	0.7	1.0	0.4	0.0	0.4	0.9	98.9	0.6	0.2	0.1	0.4
Montgomery	3.3	88.8	6.8	5.6	0.6	0.1	1.6	3.1	90.2	6.3	2.3	0.4	1.9
Morris	0.9	98.3	0.4	0.9	0.4	0.0	0.9	2.2	98.4	0.3	0.5	0.2	1.5
Morton	1.7	90.0	0.4	1.5	1.3	0.0	8.4	14.1	94.7	0.1	0.9	1.1	10.1
Nemaha	0.6	98.9	0.7	0.5	0.1	0.1	0.3	0.7	99.3	0.4	0.1	0.2	0.1
Neosho	1.9	96.7	1.2	2.1	0.5	0.1	1.4	2.9	97.1	1.1	0.8	0.2	2.1
Ness	0.9	99.1	0.1	0.9	0.2	0.0	0.6	1.5	99.6	0.0	0.1	0.1	0.6
Norton	0.7	94.0	4.1	0.8	0.6	0.1	1.1	2.4	96.3	2.3	0.3	0.3	1.4

[1] Hispanic persons may be of any race.

Table B. States and Counties

STATE County	Population and population characteristics, 2000										
	Age (percent)										
	Under 5 years	5 to 17 years	18 to 24 years	25 to 34 years	35 to 44 years	45 to 54 years	55 to 64 years	65 to 74 years	75 years and over	Median age (years)	Percent Female
	28	29	30	31	32	33	34	35	36	37	38
KANSAS—Cont'd											
Barber	5.0	19.9	5.8	8.3	14.9	14.1	10.5	10.4	11.1	42.6	52.0
Barton	6.4	19.6	9.0	9.9	15.3	12.9	9.1	8.8	9.1	38.6	51.6
Bourbon	6.1	19.6	9.5	10.6	13.5	12.9	9.4	8.5	9.7	38.0	51.8
Brown	6.4	20.0	7.4	10.0	14.1	13.3	9.4	8.4	11.0	39.8	51.7
Butler	6.9	21.7	8.3	11.6	17.2	13.9	7.8	6.3	6.3	35.9	49.8
Chase	6.0	18.1	6.5	10.7	15.8	13.9	10.2	8.8	9.9	40.3	49.0
Chautauqua	4.5	18.9	6.1	7.9	13.0	12.3	13.0	10.4	13.9	44.7	51.7
Cherokee	6.9	19.6	8.4	12.1	14.8	12.8	10.2	7.3	7.8	37.0	51.5
Cheyenne	4.7	19.1	5.1	9.0	13.8	13.2	8.6	12.7	13.9	44.2	50.7
Clark	6.1	20.5	4.9	9.3	13.8	13.4	10.2	9.6	12.2	42.1	51.1
Clay	5.4	19.6	6.7	10.0	13.9	14.3	9.4	9.3	11.5	41.3	50.2
Cloud	4.9	17.4	10.4	9.1	12.7	12.4	9.8	9.3	14.0	41.4	52.5
Coffey	5.9	20.9	6.5	10.4	16.0	14.4	9.6	7.1	9.1	39.2	51.0
Comanche	5.6	16.5	4.5	8.3	12.8	13.8	12.7	10.9	14.9	46.9	51.7
Cowley	6.4	19.7	9.9	11.3	14.7	12.9	9.3	7.7	8.2	37.0	51.1
Crawford	6.4	16.5	16.4	12.2	12.9	11.9	8.3	6.5	8.9	33.8	51.3
Decatur	4.5	19.1	4.7	8.3	14.6	12.9	9.6	12.6	13.6	44.3	50.6
Dickinson	5.7	20.0	6.3	10.2	16.1	13.2	9.9	9.1	9.5	40.0	51.3
Doniphan	6.4	18.9	11.8	10.7	14.0	13.6	8.4	7.7	8.5	36.8	50.3
Douglas	5.6	14.8	26.4	15.2	13.1	11.2	5.8	4.1	3.9	26.6	50.3
Edwards	5.9	18.8	6.7	10.4	14.7	12.4	10.4	9.8	11.0	41.0	50.6
Elk	4.2	18.2	5.8	7.9	12.1	13.8	12.6	11.7	13.6	46.0	52.2
Ellis	5.8	16.7	18.4	11.6	13.6	12.3	7.3	7.1	7.2	32.7	51.1
Ellsworth	4.2	17.2	7.3	10.6	16.5	14.0	9.8	8.9	11.5	41.8	47.2
Finney	10.5	23.8	11.0	15.9	15.2	10.7	6.0	3.7	3.3	28.1	49.0
Ford	9.4	21.7	11.2	15.4	14.0	10.7	6.6	5.2	5.8	29.9	48.3
Franklin	6.8	20.7	8.9	12.0	16.2	12.4	8.9	6.9	7.1	36.0	50.4
Geary	9.4	20.2	13.6	15.2	14.8	10.6	6.8	5.1	4.3	29.1	50.7
Gove	5.9	20.2	5.4	7.7	14.3	13.7	10.0	11.1	11.5	42.6	51.2
Graham	4.5	18.0	5.3	7.3	15.8	12.9	12.5	12.2	11.5	44.4	51.3
Grant	8.7	24.1	8.7	13.2	15.5	13.0	7.2	5.5	4.1	31.4	49.8
Gray	7.8	23.8	8.3	12.7	14.5	12.5	7.7	5.7	7.0	33.0	50.0
Greeley	6.7	21.5	6.8	8.5	18.8	12.1	7.9	9.3	8.4	38.6	50.4
Greenwood	5.5	18.2	6.5	9.1	14.1	13.3	10.4	11.0	11.8	42.6	51.2
Hamilton	6.9	21.5	7.2	11.0	14.3	12.1	8.7	9.0	9.4	37.6	50.6
Harper	5.6	19.0	6.6	8.6	13.4	13.1	10.4	9.9	13.3	42.9	51.6
Harvey	6.6	19.4	9.1	11.3	15.2	13.1	8.5	7.8	9.0	37.6	51.4
Haskell	9.1	23.8	9.1	12.7	15.2	12.3	7.3	5.9	4.7	30.8	49.2
Hodgeman	4.8	24.1	4.7	8.5	16.7	12.9	9.2	9.3	9.7	39.8	50.7
Jackson	6.9	21.3	6.8	11.3	15.4	13.8	9.6	7.4	7.5	37.4	50.8
Jefferson	6.4	21.0	7.0	10.8	17.1	14.7	10.2	6.6	6.2	38.0	49.3
Jewell	4.6	17.4	4.4	7.5	13.9	15.3	10.9	12.9	13.0	46.2	50.5
Johnson	7.5	19.6	7.6	15.0	17.8	14.8	7.7	5.1	4.9	35.2	51.2
Kearny	8.8	25.5	8.3	11.7	15.3	11.9	7.3	5.9	5.2	31.6	48.9
Kingman	6.1	21.3	5.8	9.3	15.5	12.5	10.0	8.8	10.8	40.2	51.0
Kiowa	5.5	18.5	8.2	8.8	13.0	15.1	9.5	10.6	10.7	42.1	50.9
Labette	6.2	19.5	8.7	11.2	14.6	13.1	9.4	7.9	9.5	37.9	51.1
Lane	5.3	20.1	5.4	9.7	14.9	13.7	10.4	9.3	11.2	41.6	49.9
Leavenworth	7.0	19.7	8.2	13.8	19.3	14.1	8.1	5.3	4.5	35.6	46.8
Lincoln	5.2	18.3	5.5	8.5	14.4	14.6	9.9	10.9	12.6	43.7	51.0
Linn	6.3	18.7	6.7	9.7	14.5	14.4	11.3	9.6	8.7	40.8	50.0
Logan	6.4	19.0	7.2	9.4	15.0	13.1	9.2	9.8	10.9	40.7	51.6
Lyon	6.9	18.9	16.2	12.8	14.4	11.8	7.3	5.4	6.3	30.9	50.7
McPherson	5.9	19.5	10.3	10.1	15.1	13.2	8.5	7.6	9.7	38.1	51.0
Marion	5.5	19.3	7.9	9.0	14.5	12.5	10.2	9.3	11.8	41.0	51.3
Marshall	5.0	20.0	6.6	8.3	15.3	13.2	9.6	10.0	12.0	41.7	50.8
Meade	7.9	21.6	6.9	12.4	14.2	11.1	8.1	8.9	9.0	36.1	50.5
Miami	6.9	21.1	7.3	12.0	17.8	13.9	9.2	6.3	5.6	36.7	50.5
Mitchell	5.1	19.4	8.5	8.6	14.0	13.7	9.3	9.8	11.6	41.1	50.7
Montgomery	6.0	19.0	8.6	10.8	13.9	13.3	10.0	8.4	9.9	39.2	51.8
Morris	5.7	19.6	5.6	9.2	14.7	14.2	10.1	10.1	11.0	42.0	50.8
Morton	8.1	21.3	8.0	11.4	15.9	12.0	9.4	7.5	6.4	36.2	51.4
Nemaha	7.1	21.4	6.0	9.5	14.6	11.2	8.2	9.2	12.8	39.1	50.8
Neosho	6.0	19.7	8.9	10.7	14.7	12.9	9.6	8.5	9.1	38.4	51.7
Ness	5.1	17.8	4.6	8.0	16.0	13.7	10.5	10.8	13.5	43.9	50.4
Norton	4.8	17.3	7.7	11.9	16.4	12.9	9.4	8.6	11.0	40.1	45.0

Table B. States and Counties

STATE County	Population and population characteristics, 1990										Population—change, 1980–2000				
	Age (percent)										Total persons			Percent change	
	Under 5 years	5 to 17 years	18 to 24 years	25 to 34 years	35 to 44 years	45 to 54 years	55 to 64 years	65 to 74 years	75 years and over	Percent Female	2000	1990	1980	1990–2000	1980–1990
	39	40	41	42	43	44	45	46	47	48	49	50	51	52	53
KANSAS—Cont'd															
Barber	6.7	20.0	5.4	14.4	12.6	9.0	10.5	11.4	10.0	52.0	5 307	5 874	6 548	-9.7	-10.3
Barton	7.6	19.4	8.0	15.4	13.4	9.5	10.0	9.1	7.6	51.8	28 205	29 382	31 343	-4.0	-6.3
Bourbon	7.2	18.7	8.4	13.3	13.0	9.3	9.6	9.9	10.5	53.0	15 379	14 966	15 969	2.8	-6.3
Brown	7.3	20.1	6.7	13.6	12.2	8.9	9.3	10.3	11.4	52.1	10 724	11 128	11 955	-3.6	-6.9
Butler	7.6	21.3	7.9	15.4	15.6	9.9	9.1	7.3	6.1	50.9	59 482	50 580	44 782	17.6	12.9
Chase	6.5	18.4	5.8	13.2	12.6	10.1	10.1	11.6	11.6	50.4	3 030	3 021	3 309	0.3	-8.7
Chautauqua	6.1	17.4	5.5	12.0	10.9	11.4	10.3	13.8	12.7	51.4	4 359	4 407	5 016	-1.1	-12.1
Cherokee	6.7	19.7	8.9	13.6	13.4	10.8	9.3	9.4	8.3	52.3	22 605	21 374	22 304	5.8	-4.2
Cheyenne	6.2	17.9	4.7	11.3	13.8	8.5	13.4	12.8	11.3	52.1	3 165	3 243	3 678	-2.4	-11.8
Clark	5.5	19.6	4.9	12.2	13.3	9.9	10.6	11.3	12.8	51.5	2 390	2 418	2 599	-1.2	-7.0
Clay	6.5	19.1	6.3	12.2	13.7	9.2	10.2	11.0	12.0	51.6	8 822	9 158	9 802	-3.7	-6.6
Cloud	6.0	16.9	9.4	12.0	11.7	9.6	9.6	11.1	13.6	53.0	10 268	11 023	12 494	-6.8	-11.8
Coffey	6.7	20.5	6.5	14.5	14.2	9.7	8.3	9.3	10.4	50.5	8 865	8 404	9 370	5.5	-10.3
Comanche	6.6	17.8	5.6	12.0	11.8	10.3	9.8	11.6	14.5	52.1	1 967	2 313	2 554	-15.0	-9.4
Cowley	7.0	19.5	9.2	14.7	13.8	10.1	9.4	8.2	8.1	51.5	36 291	36 915	36 824	-1.7	0.2
Crawford	6.1	17.2	13.2	14.3	12.4	8.9	8.2	9.6	10.0	52.0	38 242	35 582	37 916	7.5	-6.2
Decatur	7.0	18.9	4.0	13.7	11.7	9.0	11.4	11.4	13.1	51.4	3 472	4 021	4 509	-13.7	-10.8
Dickinson	6.8	19.3	6.7	14.0	13.0	10.1	10.2	9.6	10.3	51.9	19 344	18 958	20 175	2.0	-6.0
Doniphan	6.6	19.5	10.4	13.3	13.5	9.5	9.1	9.4	8.7	50.9	8 249	8 134	9 268	1.4	-12.2
Douglas	6.3	14.2	28.0	17.6	13.1	7.3	5.5	4.4	3.7	50.2	99 962	81 798	67 640	22.2	20.9
Edwards	5.9	19.1	5.3	14.1	11.7	10.2	10.3	11.9	11.5	51.7	3 449	3 787	4 271	-8.9	-11.3
Elk	5.9	15.6	5.7	10.0	10.7	10.9	11.6	13.8	15.9	52.2	3 261	3 327	3 918	-2.0	-15.1
Ellis	6.8	19.1	14.9	15.4	14.1	8.3	8.0	7.3	6.0	51.0	27 507	26 004	26 098	5.8	-0.4
Ellsworth	5.6	18.0	7.3	14.8	13.2	9.0	9.7	10.2	12.0	48.2	6 525	6 586	6 640	-0.9	-0.8
Finney	10.6	23.6	11.5	19.2	14.0	7.7	5.8	4.4	3.3	49.2	40 523	33 070	23 825	22.5	38.8
Ford	9.0	20.0	12.2	16.8	13.1	8.8	7.6	7.0	5.6	49.5	32 458	27 463	24 315	18.2	12.9
Franklin	8.0	20.0	9.0	15.6	13.1	9.8	8.8	7.7	7.9	51.6	24 784	21 994	22 062	12.7	-0.3
Geary	11.1	18.4	17.2	19.8	12.2	7.3	6.2	4.6	3.0	48.7	27 947	30 453	29 852	-8.2	2.0
Gove	6.8	20.1	5.5	13.2	13.2	9.3	11.8	10.0	10.1	50.4	3 068	3 231	3 726	-5.0	-13.3
Graham	6.0	20.2	4.5	13.6	12.1	11.0	12.2	9.5	10.9	50.9	2 946	3 543	3 995	-16.9	-11.3
Grant	9.0	25.5	8.5	16.5	14.7	9.4	7.7	5.0	3.7	50.0	7 909	7 159	6 977	10.5	2.6
Gray	8.6	23.4	7.4	15.1	14.9	9.5	7.7	6.8	6.5	50.9	5 904	5 396	5 138	9.4	5.0
Greeley	8.6	22.2	5.6	17.2	12.5	8.1	10.1	9.0	6.7	50.3	1 534	1 774	1 845	-13.5	-3.8
Greenwood	6.0	17.8	6.4	12.1	12.3	9.1	11.0	12.6	12.7	51.5	7 673	7 847	8 764	-2.2	-10.5
Hamilton	6.8	19.0	5.6	14.2	13.2	10.3	11.1	9.2	10.6	52.5	2 670	2 388	2 514	11.8	-5.0
Harper	6.6	18.7	5.7	12.9	12.6	9.6	10.7	11.0	12.2	51.8	6 536	7 124	7 778	-8.3	-8.4
Harvey	6.9	19.5	9.6	14.5	14.4	9.8	9.0	8.0	8.4	51.5	32 869	31 028	30 531	5.9	1.6
Haskell	9.0	23.6	7.9	17.6	14.1	9.9	7.7	6.0	4.3	49.5	4 307	3 886	3 814	10.8	1.9
Hodgeman	8.1	20.0	4.3	14.8	12.2	10.0	11.5	9.0	10.0	50.4	2 085	2 177	2 269	-4.2	-4.1
Jackson	7.3	21.3	7.6	13.9	13.9	10.9	8.8	8.1	8.1	50.9	12 657	11 525	11 644	9.8	-1.0
Jefferson	6.8	20.6	7.1	15.1	14.9	11.7	8.9	7.9	6.8	49.7	18 426	15 905	15 207	15.9	4.6
Jewell	6.5	17.4	4.5	11.9	12.5	9.4	13.1	11.8	13.0	50.5	3 791	4 251	5 241	-10.8	-18.9
Johnson	7.9	18.9	8.4	19.1	18.1	10.7	7.5	5.8	3.6	51.7	451 086	355 021	270 269	27.1	31.4
Kearny	9.3	24.1	7.7	16.2	14.5	8.7	8.2	6.3	5.1	49.2	4 531	4 027	3 435	12.5	17.2
Kingman	7.1	20.6	5.8	13.7	12.9	9.9	10.2	10.4	9.5	51.4	8 673	8 292	8 960	4.6	-7.5
Kiowa	6.5	19.4	6.5	12.3	13.5	9.3	11.4	10.7	10.4	52.1	3 278	3 660	4 046	-10.4	-9.5
Labette	7.2	19.4	8.9	14.5	13.2	9.5	8.9	9.4	9.1	52.0	22 835	23 693	25 682	-3.6	-7.7
Lane	6.7	20.8	5.0	13.3	13.0	10.3	10.1	10.7	10.0	49.5	2 155	2 375	2 472	-9.3	-3.9
Leavenworth	7.0	19.7	8.2	19.1	19.8	9.7	7.0	5.5	4.1	44.9	68 691	64 371	54 809	6.7	17.4
Lincoln	5.6	18.3	4.4	11.6	13.3	9.2	11.7	11.7	14.3	52.3	3 578	3 653	4 145	-2.1	-11.9
Linn	6.3	19.2	6.7	12.2	12.3	10.2	11.1	11.7	10.2	50.9	9 570	8 254	8 234	15.9	0.2
Logan	6.8	19.7	5.7	13.4	13.0	9.5	11.7	10.6	9.5	50.7	3 046	3 081	3 478	-1.1	-11.4
Lyon	7.7	19.1	16.3	16.6	13.4	8.0	6.7	6.0	6.2	51.2	35 935	34 732	35 108	3.5	-1.1
McPherson	7.0	19.1	10.1	14.3	13.9	9.4	8.9	8.5	8.9	51.4	29 554	27 268	26 855	8.4	1.5
Marion	5.8	17.6	8.4	12.2	12.3	9.7	10.5	11.2	12.2	52.1	13 361	12 888	13 522	3.7	-4.7
Marshall	7.1	19.4	5.4	13.6	11.9	9.4	10.3	10.8	12.2	51.1	10 965	11 705	12 787	-6.3	-8.5
Meade	6.9	20.3	6.2	13.8	13.5	9.6	10.7	9.3	9.8	50.9	4 631	4 247	4 788	9.0	-11.3
Miami	7.2	20.6	7.7	15.7	14.8	11.1	9.1	7.0	6.8	50.8	28 351	23 466	21 618	20.8	8.5
Mitchell	6.3	20.4	6.9	12.5	13.7	8.7	9.5	9.3	12.6	51.7	6 932	7 203	8 117	-3.8	-11.3
Montgomery	7.2	18.7	8.5	13.7	12.9	10.3	9.5	10.0	9.4	52.8	36 252	38 816	42 281	-6.6	-8.2
Morris	6.5	18.6	6.1	13.0	12.9	9.6	11.1	11.1	11.0	51.2	6 104	6 198	6 419	-1.5	-3.4
Morton	7.8	22.6	7.1	15.5	13.5	10.0	9.9	7.5	6.1	50.8	3 496	3 480	3 454	0.5	0.8
Nemaha	7.9	20.8	6.5	14.0	11.7	8.4	10.1	9.9	10.7	50.6	10 717	10 446	11 211	2.6	-6.8
Neosho	7.0	18.8	8.2	14.2	13.0	9.9	9.9	9.7	9.3	52.0	16 997	17 035	18 967	-0.2	-10.2
Ness	5.9	20.4	4.5	14.4	12.6	9.1	10.8	10.6	11.7	50.8	3 454	4 033	4 498	-14.4	-10.3
Norton	5.7	16.5	7.8	14.3	12.8	10.1	10.4	10.3	12.1	48.0	5 953	5 947	6 689	0.1	-11.1

Table B. States and Counties

		In households (percent)										In group quarters (percent)						
					Child		Other relatives		Nonrelatives			Institutionalized population				Noninstitutionalized population		
STATE County	Total population	Total in house-holds	House-holder	Spouse	Total	Own child under 18 years	Total	Under 18 years	Total	Unmar-ried partner	Total in group quarters	Correc-tional institu-tions	Nurs-ing homes	Other institu-tions	Col-lege dormi-tories	Mili-tary quar-ters	Other
	54	55	56	57	58	59	60	61	62	63	64	65	66	67	68	69	70
KANSAS—Cont'd																	
Barber	5 307	98.8	42.1	24.7	28.0	23.7	1.6	0.8	2.4	0.9	1.2	0.0	1.2	0.0	0.0	0.0	0.0
Barton	28 205	97.3	40.4	22.3	29.0	24.5	2.3	0.9	3.3	1.5	2.7	0.2	1.2	0.2	0.9	0.0	0.3
Bourbon	15 379	97.9	40.1	21.8	28.7	23.5	3.3	1.6	3.9	1.5	2.1	0.1	1.0	0.2	0.6	0.0	0.2
Brown	10 724	98.1	40.3	22.5	29.8	24.6	2.5	1.1	3.2	1.7	1.9	0.1	1.7	0.1	0.0	0.0	0.0
Butler	59 482	96.6	36.2	22.6	32.1	26.8	2.7	1.2	3.0	1.2	3.4	1.8	1.2	0.0	0.3	0.0	0.1
Chase	3 030	96.3	41.1	22.4	27.1	22.1	2.2	1.2	3.3	1.5	3.7	2.3	1.4	0.0	0.0	0.0	0.0
Chautauqua	4 359	96.5	41.2	23.6	26.7	21.7	2.7	1.4	2.2	1.1	3.5	0.1	3.4	0.0	0.0	0.0	0.0
Cherokee	22 605	98.5	39.3	22.2	29.7	23.5	3.7	1.9	3.6	1.6	1.5	0.1	1.1	0.0	0.1	0.0	0.2
Cheyenne	3 165	98.3	43.0	25.8	26.1	22.8	1.8	0.6	1.6	0.7	1.7	0.0	1.7	0.0	0.0	0.0	0.0
Clark	2 390	98.1	41.0	24.7	28.4	24.9	2.2	1.1	1.9	0.8	1.9	0.0	1.9	0.0	0.0	0.0	0.0
Clay	8 822	98.1	41.0	24.6	28.0	23.5	1.8	0.8	2.7	1.3	1.9	0.3	1.6	0.0	0.0	0.0	0.0
Cloud	10 268	93.6	40.5	22.3	25.2	21.1	2.2	0.8	3.4	1.2	6.4	0.1	3.3	0.0	2.1	0.0	1.0
Coffey	8 865	98.1	39.4	23.9	29.3	25.2	2.3	1.1	3.2	1.4	1.9	0.1	1.3	0.0	0.0	0.0	0.5
Comanche	1 967	96.4	44.3	24.1	24.0	20.5	1.7	0.9	2.3	0.8	3.6	0.0	3.6	0.0	0.0	0.0	0.0
Cowley	36 291	95.0	38.7	21.3	28.5	23.7	3.1	1.5	3.4	1.5	5.0	1.6	0.9	0.0	1.6	0.0	0.7
Crawford	38 242	95.3	40.5	19.4	26.0	21.1	2.9	1.1	6.4	2.0	4.7	0.2	1.5	0.1	2.5	0.0	0.4
Decatur	3 472	96.5	43.0	24.5	26.1	22.4	1.2	0.4	1.7	0.9	3.5	0.1	2.8	0.5	0.0	0.0	0.0
Dickinson	19 344	98.3	40.9	23.6	28.6	24.1	2.1	1.0	3.1	1.6	1.7	0.1	1.6	0.0	0.0	0.0	0.0
Doniphan	8 249	95.3	38.5	21.7	29.7	23.7	2.4	1.2	3.0	1.5	4.7	0.1	1.1	0.0	3.6	0.0	0.0
Douglas	99 962	91.3	38.5	16.6	22.6	19.2	2.4	0.8	11.1	2.1	8.7	0.1	0.5	0.0	7.9	0.0	0.3
Edwards	3 449	98.2	42.2	23.7	27.7	23.3	2.4	0.9	2.2	1.2	1.8	0.1	1.4	0.2	0.0	0.0	0.1
Elk	3 261	97.4	43.3	24.3	24.7	20.4	3.2	1.8	1.8	0.8	2.6	0.2	2.4	0.0	0.0	0.0	0.0
Ellis	27 507	95.4	40.7	20.3	26.0	21.3	2.0	0.6	6.4	1.5	4.6	0.1	1.0	0.0	3.0	0.0	0.4
Ellsworth	6 525	87.3	38.0	21.8	23.6	19.7	1.8	0.8	2.2	1.1	12.7	9.6	2.3	0.5	0.0	0.0	0.3
Finney	40 523	98.6	32.0	19.1	36.2	31.0	6.1	2.3	5.2	1.7	1.4	0.2	0.4	0.1	0.5	0.0	0.3
Ford	32 458	97.6	33.4	19.4	32.4	27.6	6.8	2.3	5.7	1.6	2.4	0.2	1.3	0.0	0.3	0.0	0.5
Franklin	24 784	97.6	38.1	22.2	30.2	25.4	2.9	1.5	4.2	1.9	2.4	0.2	1.1	0.0	0.9	0.0	0.2
Geary	27 947	97.8	37.4	21.3	31.5	27.1	3.3	1.7	4.3	1.7	2.2	0.1	0.6	0.1	0.0	1.3	0.1
Gove	3 068	98.3	40.6	25.7	29.4	25.3	1.2	0.6	1.3	0.7	1.7	0.0	1.6	0.2	0.0	0.0	0.0
Graham	2 946	97.7	42.9	25.5	25.9	22.0	1.6	0.4	1.9	1.1	2.3	0.0	1.5	0.0	0.0	0.0	0.8
Grant	7 909	99.1	34.7	23.0	35.7	30.9	3.4	1.5	2.2	1.0	0.9	0.1	0.8	0.0	0.0	0.0	0.0
Gray	5 904	97.6	34.6	23.4	35.0	30.4	2.3	0.8	2.2	0.8	2.4	0.0	2.3	0.0	0.0	0.0	0.0
Greeley	1 534	98.2	39.2	24.0	30.7	27.1	2.0	0.7	2.3	1.4	1.8	0.0	1.8	0.0	0.0	0.0	0.0
Greenwood	7 673	97.5	42.1	23.8	25.5	21.4	2.7	1.3	3.3	1.7	2.5	0.2	1.6	0.3	0.0	0.0	0.4
Hamilton	2 670	98.4	39.5	22.5	30.6	26.5	3.1	1.3	2.8	1.5	1.6	0.1	1.5	0.0	0.0	0.0	0.0
Harper	6 536	97.4	42.4	23.5	26.5	22.8	2.5	1.2	2.6	1.1	2.6	0.2	2.1	0.3	0.0	0.0	0.0
Harvey	32 869	95.6	38.3	23.1	28.6	24.0	2.8	1.2	2.9	1.2	4.4	0.2	1.8	0.4	1.8	0.0	0.2
Haskell	4 307	99.2	34.4	23.9	35.8	31.1	3.3	1.3	1.8	0.8	0.8	0.1	0.7	0.0	0.0	0.0	0.0
Hodgeman	2 085	98.3	38.2	24.8	31.7	27.8	1.8	1.1	1.8	1.0	1.7	0.0	1.6	0.0	0.0	0.0	0.0
Jackson	12 657	98.2	37.3	23.3	31.5	26.2	3.0	1.5	3.0	1.5	1.8	0.6	1.1	0.0	0.0	0.0	0.1
Jefferson	18 426	98.6	37.1	24.2	31.2	25.5	3.0	1.5	3.1	1.6	1.4	0.3	1.1	0.0	0.0	0.0	0.1
Jewell	3 791	98.8	44.7	26.0	24.6	20.7	1.5	0.8	2.0	1.0	1.2	0.1	1.0	0.0	0.0	0.0	0.1
Johnson	451 086	98.9	38.7	22.9	30.8	26.0	2.6	0.8	4.0	1.4	1.1	0.0	0.7	0.1	0.1	0.0	0.1
Kearny	4 531	99.0	34.0	22.2	36.4	31.6	3.7	2.1	2.7	1.1	1.0	0.2	0.8	0.0	0.0	0.0	0.0
Kingman	8 673	97.7	38.9	24.1	30.2	25.6	2.3	1.1	2.3	1.0	2.3	0.1	2.1	0.1	0.0	0.0	0.0
Kiowa	3 278	96.7	41.6	24.8	26.8	23.0	1.7	0.6	1.7	0.6	3.3	0.1	1.7	0.0	1.5	0.0	0.0
Labette	22 835	96.2	40.3	21.0	28.5	23.6	2.8	1.3	3.6	1.7	3.8	1.1	1.5	0.0	0.1	0.0	1.1
Lane	2 155	98.9	42.2	25.0	27.4	23.7	2.1	1.0	2.3	1.1	1.1	0.2	0.9	0.0	0.0	0.0	0.0
Leavenworth	68 691	90.3	33.6	20.6	30.0	24.8	3.2	1.5	3.0	1.4	9.7	8.0	0.5	0.2	0.3	0.3	0.3
Lincoln	3 578	97.9	42.7	24.8	26.0	22.2	1.7	0.7	2.6	1.3	2.1	0.0	2.1	0.0	0.0	0.0	0.0
Linn	9 570	98.6	39.8	24.9	27.6	22.7	3.3	1.8	3.0	1.6	1.4	0.1	1.0	0.0	0.0	0.0	0.3
Logan	3 046	98.1	40.8	24.2	29.2	24.6	2.3	0.7	1.7	1.0	1.9	0.0	1.9	0.0	0.0	0.0	0.0
Lyon	35 935	95.5	38.1	19.3	28.1	23.7	3.5	1.3	6.5	2.1	4.5	0.3	0.8	0.0	3.0	0.0	0.3
McPherson	29 554	94.5	37.9	23.7	28.4	24.2	1.7	0.7	2.8	1.1	5.5	0.0	2.2	0.0	3.1	0.0	0.2
Marion	13 361	94.3	38.3	24.4	27.4	23.3	1.7	0.8	2.5	1.0	5.7	0.0	2.4	0.0	2.3	0.0	0.9
Marshall	10 965	97.8	40.7	24.3	28.6	24.0	1.7	0.6	2.5	1.2	2.2	0.1	1.6	0.4	0.0	0.0	0.1
Meade	4 631	97.5	37.3	24.1	31.7	28.1	2.4	1.0	1.9	0.7	2.5	0.7	1.7	0.1	0.0	0.0	0.0
Miami	28 351	97.4	36.6	23.2	31.4	26.0	2.9	1.3	3.3	1.6	2.6	0.4	0.9	0.8	0.0	0.0	0.5
Mitchell	6 932	95.0	41.1	23.5	26.5	22.9	1.3	0.4	2.6	1.2	5.0	0.1	2.2	1.1	1.4	0.0	0.1
Montgomery	36 252	97.5	41.1	21.8	27.6	22.6	3.5	1.7	3.5	1.6	2.5	0.2	1.3	0.0	0.8	0.0	0.3
Morris	6 104	98.8	41.6	25.3	28.1	24.0	2.0	0.9	1.8	1.0	1.2	0.1	1.2	0.0	0.0	0.0	0.0
Morton	3 496	98.4	37.4	24.0	32.0	27.9	3.1	1.3	1.9	0.9	1.6	0.1	1.5	0.0	0.0	0.0	0.0
Nemaha	10 717	95.4	36.9	22.9	32.1	27.6	1.7	0.6	1.7	0.8	4.6	0.1	4.2	0.0	0.0	0.0	0.4
Neosho	16 997	97.2	39.6	22.8	29.0	24.0	2.2	1.1	3.6	1.7	2.8	0.2	1.5	0.0	0.9	0.0	0.2
Ness	3 454	97.7	43.9	25.0	25.6	21.9	1.1	0.5	2.0	1.1	2.3	0.0	2.2	0.0	0.0	0.0	0.1
Norton	5 953	86.7	38.1	21.1	24.0	21.0	1.6	0.6	2.0	1.0	13.3	11.7	1.3	0.1	0.0	0.0	0.3

STATE County	Households by type, 2000												Households, 1990		
		Family households						Nonfamily households							
				Married couple		Female householder[1]			Householder living alone						
	Total households	Total	With own children under 18 years	Total	With own children under 18 years	Total	With own children under 18 years	Total	Total	65 years and over	Average household size	Average family size	Total households	Female householder[1]	Householder living alone
	71	72	73	74	75	76	77	78	79	80	81	82	83	84	85
KANSAS—Cont'd															
Barber	2 235	67.6	28.7	58.7	23.2	6.5	4.1	32.4	29.9	17.0	2.35	2.91	2 358	4.9	27.9
Barton	11 393	66.1	31.3	55.1	23.9	7.8	5.3	33.9	30.2	14.3	2.41	3.01	11 561	7.7	27.3
Bourbon	6 161	67.0	30.5	54.5	22.5	9.2	5.9	33.0	29.0	14.9	2.44	3.01	5 897	8.4	28.3
Brown	4 318	68.3	31.4	55.8	22.7	9.2	6.4	31.7	28.8	15.7	2.44	2.99	4 347	6.1	29.1
Butler	21 527	74.6	37.9	62.6	30.0	8.3	5.6	25.4	21.9	9.4	2.67	3.13	18 488	7.5	20.5
Chase	1 246	65.6	28.3	54.6	22.2	7.6	3.8	34.4	31.1	14.9	2.34	2.92	1 214	5.4	26.9
Chautauqua	1 796	68.8	26.2	57.3	19.6	7.9	4.6	31.2	29.4	16.4	2.34	2.87	1 835	6.7	30.9
Cherokee	8 875	70.3	32.4	56.6	24.1	9.7	5.8	29.7	26.3	13.0	2.51	3.02	8 396	9.6	26.3
Cheyenne	1 360	67.6	27.6	60.1	22.4	5.1	3.5	32.4	30.8	17.3	2.29	2.85	1 389	4.8	30.5
Clark	979	69.1	30.2	60.3	24.6	6.2	3.9	30.9	29.6	17.0	2.39	2.95	1 006	3.7	31.4
Clay	3 617	69.6	30.5	59.9	24.0	6.1	4.3	30.4	27.7	15.4	2.39	2.91	3 641	4.8	27.0
Cloud	4 163	64.8	27.1	55.1	21.0	6.6	4.3	35.2	30.8	15.9	2.31	2.89	4 483	5.5	29.9
Coffey	3 489	71.0	33.2	60.7	26.2	6.9	4.7	29.0	26.0	12.6	2.49	2.99	3 311	5.6	26.0
Comanche	872	62.0	24.4	54.4	19.8	6.2	3.7	38.0	35.9	21.2	2.18	2.81	950	5.4	30.5
Cowley	14 039	68.5	32.2	55.2	23.4	9.6	6.4	31.5	27.9	13.2	2.46	3.00	14 047	8.8	26.2
Crawford	15 504	60.9	28.5	47.9	20.4	9.3	5.8	39.1	30.6	13.4	2.35	2.96	14 606	8.4	31.7
Decatur	1 494	65.7	25.8	57.0	20.8	5.6	3.3	34.3	32.8	17.5	2.24	2.83	1 651	5.2	30.5
Dickinson	7 903	68.6	31.1	57.9	23.6	7.7	5.5	31.4	28.1	14.1	2.40	2.94	7 542	6.5	27.0
Doniphan	3 173	68.8	32.6	56.4	25.0	8.7	5.6	31.2	27.6	14.2	2.48	3.03	3 074	7.7	25.5
Douglas	38 486	55.0	27.4	43.1	19.9	8.5	5.6	45.0	28.5	5.8	2.37	2.97	30 138	7.6	27.0
Edwards	1 455	65.7	28.7	56.3	22.5	6.0	4.0	34.3	32.0	17.3	2.33	2.94	1 585	4.9	30.9
Elk	1 412	65.4	24.4	56.0	19.0	6.1	3.3	34.6	32.9	18.6	2.25	2.84	1 436	5.2	31.5
Ellis	11 193	60.5	28.8	50.0	22.5	7.8	4.8	39.5	30.1	10.8	2.35	2.96	10 096	7.7	29.0
Ellsworth	2 481	66.1	27.9	57.2	22.0	6.2	4.3	33.9	31.4	17.3	2.30	2.88	2 522	5.5	31.7
Finney	12 948	75.3	46.0	59.8	35.2	10.5	7.8	24.7	19.6	6.3	3.09	3.55	10 836	9.3	19.4
Ford	10 852	72.4	40.9	57.9	31.7	9.2	6.5	27.6	22.7	9.5	2.92	3.42	9 872	8.2	24.4
Franklin	9 452	71.1	34.7	58.1	26.0	8.9	6.1	28.9	24.8	11.3	2.56	3.04	8 308	7.6	24.2
Geary	10 458	72.5	39.6	56.9	28.5	12.3	9.0	27.5	22.5	7.8	2.61	3.07	10 676	10.2	19.6
Gove	1 245	69.2	28.4	63.5	25.0	3.5	2.0	30.8	29.7	17.5	2.42	3.01	1 284	3.7	27.3
Graham	1 263	67.1	27.4	59.5	22.9	5.9	3.9	32.9	30.1	16.7	2.28	2.84	1 435	5.1	28.2
Grant	2 742	76.5	43.6	66.4	36.6	7.1	5.1	23.5	21.0	8.2	2.86	3.34	2 393	6.9	17.8
Gray	2 045	76.1	42.0	67.7	36.3	5.6	3.8	23.9	21.2	9.4	2.82	3.31	1 913	5.2	22.5
Greeley	602	68.8	34.2	61.1	30.2	4.5	2.7	31.2	28.6	12.8	2.50	3.10	656	4.6	24.2
Greenwood	3 234	66.6	27.1	56.5	20.7	6.6	4.2	33.4	30.3	16.8	2.31	2.86	3 285	6.1	31.1
Hamilton	1 054	67.9	33.9	56.9	26.6	7.6	5.1	32.1	29.4	15.8	2.49	3.09	986	7.3	32.4
Harper	2 773	65.2	27.7	55.3	21.7	6.9	4.3	34.8	32.1	17.9	2.30	2.90	3 007	6.1	31.3
Harvey	12 581	71.0	32.8	60.2	26.0	7.7	5.1	29.0	25.8	11.6	2.50	3.00	11 581	7.0	25.2
Haskell	1 481	77.9	43.6	69.4	38.2	5.9	3.8	22.1	20.1	9.2	2.88	3.35	1 372	4.3	21.1
Hodgeman	796	73.0	34.7	65.1	29.4	4.4	2.8	27.0	24.7	14.2	2.58	3.09	826	3.4	23.8
Jackson	4 727	74.2	35.2	62.3	27.8	8.2	5.1	25.8	22.7	11.5	2.63	3.09	4 277	6.3	23.2
Jefferson	6 830	76.0	35.7	65.2	28.9	7.0	4.4	24.0	20.1	9.3	2.66	3.07	5 778	5.2	20.1
Jewell	1 695	64.8	23.7	58.1	20.1	4.8	2.8	35.2	32.4	18.1	2.21	2.80	1 806	4.5	28.5
Johnson	174 570	69.7	36.0	59.2	29.7	7.8	4.9	30.3	24.5	6.7	2.56	3.09	136 433	7.8	23.0
Kearny	1 542	77.8	43.5	65.1	34.7	8.3	6.0	22.2	20.2	8.5	2.91	3.35	1 379	7.5	20.2
Kingman	3 371	71.8	32.4	61.9	26.3	7.1	4.4	28.2	26.0	13.8	2.51	3.03	3 175	6.0	25.1
Kiowa	1 365	67.7	27.7	59.6	22.6	5.3	3.4	32.3	30.5	15.5	2.32	2.89	1 466	5.1	29.4
Labette	9 194	66.5	31.2	52.1	21.8	10.2	6.8	33.5	29.8	14.3	2.39	2.95	9 377	9.3	29.0
Lane	910	67.4	29.5	59.1	23.7	5.1	3.4	32.6	30.3	16.5	2.34	2.91	966	5.1	29.6
Leavenworth	23 071	74.6	38.9	61.4	30.3	9.5	6.4	25.4	21.7	8.1	2.69	3.15	19 715	9.0	20.2
Lincoln	1 529	68.0	27.1	58.1	21.0	6.4	4.0	32.0	29.6	16.4	2.29	2.81	1 531	4.2	29.7
Linn	3 807	72.2	28.9	62.7	23.5	6.2	3.7	27.8	24.0	13.0	2.48	2.94	3 215	5.6	24.1
Logan	1 243	68.9	29.5	59.3	24.7	6.3	3.1	31.1	28.6	14.8	2.40	2.98	1 221	5.2	28.3
Lyon	13 691	63.1	32.6	50.8	24.2	8.4	5.9	36.9	28.5	9.8	2.51	3.12	13 059	7.7	28.3
McPherson	11 205	71.1	33.0	62.5	27.3	6.0	4.0	28.9	25.5	11.8	2.49	2.99	10 230	5.3	25.5
Marion	5 114	72.1	30.5	63.8	25.5	5.5	3.4	27.9	25.2	14.2	2.46	2.94	4 975	4.9	26.6
Marshall	4 458	67.9	30.2	59.7	25.3	5.4	3.4	32.1	29.5	17.0	2.40	2.98	4 689	4.9	29.8
Meade	1 728	72.5	36.4	64.7	31.5	4.9	3.0	27.5	25.6	13.6	2.61	3.16	1 667	3.8	27.6
Miami	10 365	75.2	37.0	63.5	29.2	8.0	5.4	24.8	21.0	8.8	2.66	3.09	8 402	7.3	21.8
Mitchell	2 850	65.4	27.8	57.3	22.8	5.3	3.4	34.6	31.2	16.2	2.31	2.91	2 846	4.5	30.5
Montgomery	14 903	66.8	29.8	53.0	21.0	10.1	6.6	33.2	29.7	14.7	2.37	2.93	15 670	9.2	28.9
Morris	2 539	70.0	30.2	60.7	24.4	6.6	4.3	30.0	28.0	14.9	2.37	2.90	2 528	5.6	26.4
Morton	1 306	73.6	36.6	64.2	30.9	6.8	4.6	26.4	24.3	9.2	2.63	3.15	1 290	5.3	23.8
Nemaha	3 959	69.8	34.0	61.9	29.9	5.1	3.1	30.2	28.0	16.0	2.58	3.20	3 996	4.3	28.1
Neosho	6 739	69.5	31.5	57.4	23.7	8.5	5.4	30.5	27.1	13.8	2.45	2.96	6 748	7.2	27.3
Ness	1 516	64.5	26.1	57.1	21.4	4.7	2.7	35.5	33.5	18.3	2.23	2.83	1 670	4.7	30.3
Norton	2 266	64.9	28.2	55.5	21.8	7.0	4.8	35.1	32.3	17.9	2.28	2.89	2 330	5.0	31.3

[1]No spouse present.

Table B. States and Counties

STATE County	Percent change of households, 1990–2000	Total housing units	Occupied housing units (percent)	Vacant housing units Total	For seasonal, recreational, or occasional use	Homeowner vacancy rate (percent)	Rental vacancy rate (percent)	Occupied housing units Total	Percent owner-occupied housing units	Percent renter-occupied housing units	Average household size of owner-occupied units	Average household size of renter-occupied units
	86	87	88	89	90	91	92	93	94	95	96	97
KANSAS—Cont'd												
Barber	-5.2	2 740	81.6	18.4	3.8	4.6	14.6	2 235	75.3	24.7	2.36	2.30
Barton	-1.5	12 888	88.4	11.6	0.5	3.1	12.5	11 393	72.1	27.9	2.46	2.27
Bourbon	4.5	7 135	86.3	13.7	4.1	2.1	9.2	6 161	74.0	26.0	2.52	2.22
Brown	-0.7	4 815	89.7	10.3	0.7	3.2	8.0	4 318	71.4	28.6	2.51	2.26
Butler	16.4	23 176	92.9	7.1	0.7	2.3	9.8	21 527	77.7	22.3	2.77	2.32
Chase	2.6	1 529	81.5	18.5	8.5	3.6	5.1	1 246	73.3	26.7	2.37	2.25
Chautauqua	-2.1	2 169	82.8	17.2	5.1	3.0	10.3	1 796	82.1	17.9	2.36	2.27
Cherokee	5.7	10 031	88.5	11.5	1.2	2.8	13.1	8 875	76.1	23.9	2.54	2.41
Cheyenne	-2.1	1 636	83.1	16.9	0.9	6.1	7.5	1 360	77.2	22.8	2.27	2.35
Clark	-2.7	1 111	88.1	11.9	0.9	4.0	9.8	979	76.4	23.6	2.37	2.48
Clay	-0.7	4 084	88.6	11.4	1.1	2.1	13.6	3 617	76.7	23.3	2.44	2.22
Cloud	-7.1	4 838	86.0	14.0	1.2	4.4	15.5	4 163	74.3	25.7	2.39	2.07
Coffey	5.4	3 876	90.0	10.0	1.9	2.4	10.3	3 489	78.3	21.7	2.57	2.23
Comanche	-8.2	1 088	80.1	19.9	2.4	7.3	7.3	872	73.9	26.1	2.22	2.05
Cowley	-0.1	15 673	89.6	10.4	0.6	2.2	12.6	14 039	70.8	29.2	2.52	2.30
Crawford	6.1	17 221	90.0	10.0	0.7	2.4	9.2	15 504	64.4	35.6	2.44	2.18
Decatur	-9.5	1 821	82.0	18.0	3.2	4.2	17.7	1 494	76.0	24.0	2.30	2.05
Dickinson	4.8	8 686	91.0	9.0	0.5	3.1	9.9	7 903	74.8	25.2	2.49	2.16
Doniphan	3.2	3 489	90.9	9.1	0.8	1.5	8.8	3 173	74.5	25.5	2.54	2.29
Douglas	27.7	40 250	95.6	4.4	0.4	1.7	3.8	38 486	51.9	48.1	2.63	2.10
Edwards	-8.2	1 754	83.0	17.0	1.6	5.8	12.4	1 455	77.7	22.3	2.31	2.38
Elk	-1.7	1 860	75.9	24.1	7.8	6.0	12.4	1 412	81.1	18.9	2.28	2.12
Ellis	10.9	12 078	92.7	7.3	0.4	1.6	6.9	11 193	63.3	36.7	2.56	1.98
Ellsworth	-1.6	3 228	76.9	23.1	9.4	3.2	13.8	2 481	79.6	20.4	2.35	2.08
Finney	19.5	13 763	94.1	5.9	0.3	1.4	7.8	12 948	64.8	35.2	3.24	2.79
Ford	9.9	11 650	93.2	6.8	0.3	1.7	8.5	10 852	64.8	35.2	2.97	2.83
Franklin	13.8	10 229	92.4	7.6	1.2	2.1	6.7	9 452	73.5	26.5	2.63	2.37
Geary	-2.0	11 959	87.4	12.6	0.5	2.9	12.8	10 458	50.5	49.5	2.54	2.69
Gove	-3.0	1 423	87.5	12.5	1.5	3.7	10.7	1 245	79.8	20.2	2.44	2.33
Graham	-12.0	1 553	81.3	18.7	3.2	5.5	16.7	1 263	79.5	20.5	2.36	1.97
Grant	14.6	3 027	90.6	9.4	0.4	2.2	16.5	2 742	74.6	25.4	2.94	2.63
Gray	6.9	2 181	93.8	6.2	0.3	1.5	4.6	2 045	72.7	27.3	2.82	2.80
Greeley	-8.2	712	84.6	15.4	1.4	3.2	8.3	602	74.4	25.6	2.38	2.85
Greenwood	-1.6	4 273	75.7	24.3	7.9	4.0	7.7	3 234	75.2	24.8	2.32	2.28
Hamilton	6.9	1 211	87.0	13.0	0.7	3.7	14.1	1 054	69.4	30.6	2.44	2.60
Harper	-7.8	3 270	84.8	15.2	1.9	4.6	9.4	2 773	74.3	25.7	2.37	2.10
Harvey	8.6	13 378	94.0	6.0	0.4	1.7	7.3	12 581	71.9	28.1	2.62	2.20
Haskell	7.9	1 639	90.4	9.6	0.7	3.5	9.8	1 481	72.2	27.8	2.81	3.07
Hodgeman	-3.6	945	84.2	15.8	2.0	3.4	12.3	796	78.5	21.5	2.63	2.39
Jackson	10.5	5 094	92.8	7.2	0.8	1.9	8.3	4 727	80.6	19.4	2.68	2.42
Jefferson	18.2	7 491	91.2	8.8	3.3	2.1	7.0	6 830	84.8	15.2	2.69	2.50
Jewell	-6.1	2 103	80.6	19.4	4.1	2.0	9.6	1 695	79.4	20.6	2.24	2.09
Johnson	28.0	181 612	96.1	3.9	0.4	1.1	6.5	174 570	72.3	27.7	2.75	2.04
Kearny	11.8	1 657	93.1	6.9	0.4	1.6	7.6	1 542	73.3	26.7	2.98	2.73
Kingman	6.2	3 852	87.5	12.5	2.1	1.6	8.2	3 371	77.8	22.2	2.55	2.40
Kiowa	-6.9	1 643	83.1	16.9	2.1	4.2	12.9	1 365	71.8	28.2	2.35	2.25
Labette	-2.0	10 306	89.2	10.8	0.8	2.7	9.7	9 194	73.2	26.8	2.44	2.25
Lane	-5.8	1 065	85.4	14.6	1.4	4.9	10.4	910	77.3	22.7	2.34	2.35
Leavenworth	17.0	24 401	94.5	5.5	0.3	1.5	5.9	23 071	67.0	33.0	2.69	2.69
Lincoln	-0.1	1 853	82.5	17.5	2.5	7.3	6.7	1 529	78.3	21.7	2.33	2.14
Linn	18.4	4 720	80.7	19.3	11.5	1.8	7.4	3 807	82.6	17.4	2.48	2.47
Logan	1.8	1 423	87.4	12.6	1.8	3.1	13.2	1 243	76.3	23.7	2.46	2.23
Lyon	4.8	14 757	92.8	7.2	0.5	1.6	8.2	13 691	61.0	39.0	2.70	2.21
McPherson	9.5	11 830	94.7	5.3	0.3	1.5	6.6	11 205	74.0	26.0	2.61	2.15
Marion	2.8	5 882	86.9	13.1	3.7	3.4	10.9	5 114	79.9	20.1	2.54	2.15
Marshall	-4.9	4 999	89.2	10.8	0.9	2.2	12.7	4 458	79.5	20.5	2.48	2.10
Meade	3.7	1 968	87.8	12.2	1.6	4.3	10.7	1 728	74.4	25.6	2.60	2.66
Miami	23.4	10 984	94.4	5.6	0.6	1.7	6.0	10 365	78.6	21.4	2.76	2.33
Mitchell	0.1	3 340	85.3	14.7	2.8	2.6	10.9	2 850	74.6	25.4	2.43	1.97
Montgomery	-4.9	17 207	86.6	13.4	1.0	3.4	16.1	14 903	71.6	28.4	2.42	2.24
Morris	0.4	3 160	80.3	19.7	11.1	1.8	7.6	2 539	78.0	22.0	2.43	2.17
Morton	1.2	1 519	86.0	14.0	1.3	3.7	13.0	1 306	71.3	28.7	2.66	2.58
Nemaha	-0.9	4 340	91.2	8.8	0.8	3.2	7.6	3 959	80.8	19.2	2.70	2.07
Neosho	-0.1	7 461	90.3	9.7	1.4	2.5	8.4	6 739	74.6	25.4	2.50	2.30
Ness	-9.2	1 835	82.6	17.4	1.4	5.3	12.3	1 516	76.0	24.0	2.28	2.07
Norton	-2.7	2 673	84.8	15.2	1.8	4.7	7.5	2 266	77.8	22.2	2.33	2.10

STATE/ County code	MSA/ PMSA/ NECMA code[1]	County type[2]	STATE County	Population, 2000				Population, 1990				Population and population characteristics, 2000					
												Race (percent)					
												One race					
				Land area, 2000[3] (sq km)	Total persons	Rank	Per square kilometer	Land area, 1990[3] (sq km)	Total persons	Rank	Per square kilometer	White	Black or African American	American Indian or Alaska Native	Asian	Native Hawaiian and other Pacific Islander	Some other race
				1	2	3	4	5	6	7	8	9	10	11	12	13	14
			KANSAS—Cont'd														
20 139	...	6	Osage	1 822	16 712	1 975	9.2	1 822	15 248	1 974	8.4	97.3	0.2	0.7	0.2	0.1	0.4
20 141	...	9	Osborne	2 311	4 452	2 885	1.9	2 312	4 867	2 845	2.1	98.6	0.1	0.2	0.2	0.0	0.1
20 143	...	9	Ottawa	1 868	6 163	2 766	3.3	1 868	5 634	2 790	3.0	97.5	0.5	0.4	0.1	0.0	0.3
20 145	...	7	Pawnee	1 953	7 233	2 662	3.7	1 953	7 555	2 611	3.9	91.0	5.0	1.0	0.6	0.0	1.2
20 147	...	7	Phillips	2 295	6 001	2 779	2.6	2 295	6 590	2 699	2.9	98.3	0.2	0.3	0.4	0.0	0.0
20 149	...	6	Pottawatomie	2 187	18 209	1 886	8.3	2 187	16 128	1 915	7.4	96.3	0.7	0.6	0.3	0.0	0.6
20 151	...	7	Pratt	1 904	9 647	2 474	5.1	1 904	9 702	2 412	5.1	95.3	1.0	0.4	0.5	0.0	1.7
20 153	...	9	Rawlins	2 770	2 966	2 994	1.1	2 770	3 404	2 964	1.2	98.5	0.3	0.3	0.1	0.0	0.1
20 155	...	4	Reno	3 249	64 790	749	19.9	3 249	62 389	697	19.2	91.6	2.9	0.6	0.4	0.0	2.7
20 157	...	7	Republic	1 855	5 835	2 799	3.1	1 856	6 482	2 711	3.5	98.6	0.3	0.2	0.2	0.0	0.3
20 159	...	7	Rice	1 882	10 761	2 379	5.7	1 882	10 610	2 326	5.6	94.7	1.2	0.6	0.3	0.0	1.8
20 161	...	5	Riley	1 579	62 843	774	39.8	1 579	67 139	658	42.5	84.8	6.9	0.6	3.2	0.2	1.9
20 163	...	9	Rooks	2 301	5 685	2 809	2.5	2 301	6 039	2 752	2.6	97.1	1.1	0.4	0.2	0.0	0.4
20 165	...	9	Rush	1 860	3 551	2 950	1.9	1 860	3 842	2 928	2.1	98.5	0.3	0.4	0.1	0.0	0.3
20 167	...	7	Russell	2 291	7 370	2 650	3.2	2 291	7 835	2 591	3.4	97.6	0.5	0.6	0.3	0.0	0.3
20 169	...	5	Saline	1 864	53 597	871	28.8	1 864	49 301	851	26.4	89.2	3.1	0.5	1.7	0.0	3.3
20 171	...	7	Scott	1 858	5 120	2 842	2.8	1 859	5 289	2 820	2.8	95.5	0.1	0.5	0.1	0.0	2.8
20 173	9040	2	Sedgwick	2 588	452 869	130	175.0	2 591	403 662	123	155.8	79.4	9.1	1.1	3.3	0.1	4.2
20 175	...	7	Seward	1 656	22 510	1 670	13.6	1 656	18 743	1 748	11.3	65.4	3.8	0.8	2.9	0.1	23.8
20 177	8440	3	Shawnee	1 424	169 871	319	119.3	1 424	160 976	297	113.0	82.9	9.0	1.2	1.0	0.0	3.2
20 179	...	9	Sheridan	2 322	2 813	3 005	1.2	2 322	3 043	2 997	1.3	98.6	0.1	0.1	0.1	0.1	0.4
20 181	...	7	Sherman	2 735	6 760	2 714	2.5	2 735	6 926	2 667	2.5	93.8	0.4	0.3	0.2	0.2	4.1
20 183	...	9	Smith	2 319	4 536	2 875	2.0	2 319	5 078	2 834	2.2	98.8	0.1	0.2	0.0	0.1	0.2
20 185	...	9	Stafford	2 051	4 789	2 861	2.3	2 052	5 365	2 812	2.6	95.0	0.1	0.4	0.1	0.0	3.0
20 187	...	9	Stanton	1 761	2 406	3 029	1.4	1 761	2 333	3 037	1.3	84.4	0.6	1.2	0.2	0.0	12.5
20 189	...	7	Stevens	1 884	5 463	2 820	2.9	1 884	5 048	2 836	2.7	83.0	0.9	0.9	0.2	0.0	13.3
20 191	...	6	Sumner	3 061	25 946	1 519	8.5	3 061	25 841	1 428	8.4	94.6	0.7	1.1	0.2	0.1	1.3
20 193	...	7	Thomas	2 784	8 180	2 595	2.9	2 784	8 258	2 542	3.0	97.1	0.4	0.3	0.3	0.0	1.0
20 195	...	9	Trego	2 301	3 319	2 971	1.4	2 301	3 694	2 940	1.6	97.8	0.2	0.4	0.5	0.1	0.2
20 197	...	8	Wabaunsee	2 065	6 885	2 696	3.3	2 065	6 603	2 698	3.2	97.2	0.5	0.5	0.1	0.1	0.6
20 199	...	9	Wallace	2 367	1 749	3 083	0.7	2 367	1 821	3 076	0.8	94.6	0.6	0.8	0.2	0.0	2.5
20 201	...	9	Washington	2 327	6 483	2 740	2.8	2 327	7 073	2 649	3.0	98.9	0.1	0.3	0.0	0.0	0.1
20 203	...	9	Wichita	1 861	2 531	3 024	1.4	1 861	2 758	3 012	1.5	86.3	0.1	0.7	0.1	0.0	10.5
20 205	...	7	Wilson	1 486	10 332	2 411	7.0	1 486	10 289	2 360	6.9	96.8	0.4	0.9	0.3	0.0	0.5
20 207	...	9	Woodson	1 297	3 788	2 929	2.9	1 297	4 116	2 905	3.2	97.0	0.8	0.9	0.1	0.0	0.2
20 209	3760	0	Wyandotte	392	157 882	337	402.8	392	162 026	293	413.3	58.2	28.3	0.7	1.6	0.0	8.2
21 000	...		KENTUCKY	102 896	4 041 769	X	39.3	102 907	3 686 892	X	35.8	90.1	7.3	0.2	0.7	0.0	0.6
21 001	...	7	Adair	1 054	17 244	1 936	16.4	1 054	15 360	1 967	14.6	96.0	2.6	0.2	0.3	0.0	0.2
21 003	...	7	Allen	896	17 800	1 910	19.9	897	14 628	2 011	16.3	97.6	1.1	0.2	0.1	0.0	0.4
21 005	...	6	Anderson	525	19 111	1 842	36.4	525	14 571	2 016	27.8	96.5	2.3	0.1	0.1	0.0	0.2
21 007	...	9	Ballard	651	8 286	2 581	12.7	651	7 902	2 581	12.1	95.3	2.9	0.1	0.2	0.0	0.1
21 009	...	7	Barren	1 272	38 033	1 164	29.9	1 272	34 001	1 163	26.7	94.3	4.1	0.1	0.4	0.0	0.4
21 011	...	8	Bath	724	11 085	2 359	15.3	724	9 692	2 413	13.4	96.9	1.8	0.2	0.0	0.0	0.4
21 013	...	7	Bell	934	30 060	1 394	32.2	934	31 506	1 231	33.7	96.0	2.4	0.2	0.3	0.0	0.1
21 015	1640	0	Boone	638	85 991	607	134.8	638	57 589	755	90.3	95.2	1.5	0.2	1.3	0.0	0.7
21 017	4280	2	Bourbon	755	19 360	1 825	25.6	755	19 236	1 716	25.5	90.4	6.9	0.1	0.1	0.0	1.4
21 019	3400	2	Boyd	415	49 752	920	119.9	415	51 096	825	123.1	96.0	2.5	0.2	0.3	0.0	0.1
21 021	...	7	Boyle	471	27 697	1 458	58.8	470	25 590	1 439	54.4	87.8	9.7	0.2	0.6	0.0	0.2
21 023	...	8	Bracken	526	8 279	2 583	15.7	526	7 766	2 598	14.8	98.5	0.6	0.3	0.1	0.0	0.2
21 025	...	9	Breathitt	1 283	16 100	2 016	12.5	1 283	15 703	1 943	12.2	98.7	0.4	0.1	0.3	0.0	0.1
21 027	...	9	Breckinridge	1 483	18 648	1 863	12.6	1 483	16 312	1 901	11.0	95.8	2.9	0.2	0.1	0.0	0.2
21 029	4520	2	Bullitt	775	61 236	796	79.0	775	47 567	881	61.4	98.1	0.4	0.3	0.3	0.0	0.2
21 031	...	9	Butler	1 109	13 010	2 232	11.7	1 109	11 245	2 278	10.1	97.9	0.5	0.2	0.2	0.0	0.6
21 033	...	6	Caldwell	899	13 060	2 226	14.5	899	13 232	2 117	14.7	93.9	4.8	0.1	0.2	0.0	0.4
21 035	...	7	Calloway	1 000	34 177	1 276	34.2	1 000	30 735	1 254	30.7	93.5	3.6	0.2	1.3	0.0	0.5
21 037	1640	0	Campbell	393	88 616	588	225.5	393	83 866	546	213.4	96.6	1.6	0.2	0.5	0.0	0.3
21 039	...	9	Carlisle	499	5 351	2 825	10.7	499	5 238	2 824	10.5	97.8	1.0	0.4	0.1	0.0	0.1
21 041	...	6	Carroll	337	10 155	2 431	30.1	337	9 292	2 445	27.6	95.2	1.9	0.2	0.2	0.0	1.4
21 043	3400	2	Carter	1 063	26 889	1 488	25.3	1 064	24 340	1 484	22.9	99.0	0.1	0.2	0.1	0.0	0.1
21 045	...	9	Casey	1 154	15 447	2 055	13.4	1 154	14 211	2 035	12.3	98.3	0.3	0.3	0.1	0.1	0.3
21 047	1660	3	Christian	1 868	72 265	688	38.7	1 868	68 941	643	36.9	69.9	23.7	0.5	0.9	0.3	2.2
21 049	4280	2	Clark	659	33 144	1 313	50.3	659	29 496	1 316	44.8	93.6	4.8	0.2	0.2	0.0	0.5
21 051	...	9	Clay	1 220	24 556	1 572	20.1	1 220	21 746	1 591	17.8	93.9	4.8	0.2	0.1	0.0	0.2
21 053	...	9	Clinton	511	9 634	2 475	18.9	511	9 135	2 457	17.9	99.1	0.1	0.2	0.0	0.1	0.1
21 055	...	7	Crittenden	938	9 384	2 498	10.0	938	9 196	2 454	9.8	98.2	0.7	0.1	0.1	0.0	0.1

[1]MSA = Metropolitan Statistical Area. PMSA = Primary MSA. NECMA = New England County Metropolitan Area. See Appendix A for explanation of these concepts. See Appendix B for list of metropolitan areas identified by type, with component counties.
[2]County typology code from the Economic Research Service of USDA. See Appendix A for definition.
[3]Dry land or land partially or temporarily covered by water.

STATE County	Population and population characteristics, 2000 (cont'd)								Population and population characteristics, 1990				
	Race (percent) (cont'd)								Race (percent)				
		Race alone or in combination											
	Two or more races	White	Black	American Indian or Alaska Native	Asian	Native Hawaiian and other Pacific Islander	Some other race	Hispanic[1]	White	Black or African American	American Indian or Alaska Native	Asian and Pacific Islander	Hispanic[1]
	15	16	17	18	19	20	21	22	23	24	25	26	27
KANSAS—Cont'd													
Osage	1.2	98.4	0.4	1.4	0.3	0.2	0.6	1.5	98.6	0.2	0.7	0.1	1.2
Osborne	0.8	99.4	0.2	0.5	0.3	0.0	0.4	0.4	99.3	0.1	0.4	0.1	0.3
Ottawa	1.1	98.6	0.8	0.8	0.3	0.0	0.6	1.3	99.4	0.1	0.3	0.1	0.6
Pawnee	1.3	92.2	5.5	1.3	0.7	0.0	1.6	4.2	93.7	3.2	0.4	0.8	3.4
Phillips	0.7	98.9	0.3	0.8	0.5	0.0	0.2	0.7	99.0	0.2	0.2	0.4	0.5
Pottawatomie	1.5	97.7	1.0	1.4	0.5	0.1	0.9	2.3	98.0	0.6	0.7	0.4	1.5
Pratt	1.1	96.3	1.2	0.9	0.6	0.1	2.0	3.1	96.5	1.2	0.7	0.3	1.9
Rawlins	0.7	99.2	0.5	0.7	0.2	0.0	0.1	0.8	99.4	0.1	0.2	0.2	0.8
Reno	1.8	93.2	3.4	1.3	0.6	0.1	3.3	5.7	93.9	2.7	0.6	0.3	4.0
Republic	0.5	99.0	0.4	0.5	0.2	0.0	0.4	0.9	99.5	0.0	0.2	0.2	0.2
Rice	1.4	96.0	1.4	1.2	0.4	0.0	2.3	5.6	96.3	1.1	0.5	0.2	2.6
Riley	2.4	86.8	7.7	1.3	4.0	0.4	2.5	4.6	83.2	10.1	0.7	3.6	4.2
Rooks	0.7	97.8	1.3	0.8	0.3	0.1	0.5	1.1	98.9	0.6	0.2	0.1	0.4
Rush	0.5	99.0	0.4	0.8	0.2	0.0	0.2	1.0	99.3	0.0	0.1	0.1	0.9
Russell	0.7	98.3	0.7	1.1	0.4	0.0	0.3	0.9	98.7	0.5	0.4	0.1	0.6
Saline	2.1	91.1	3.9	1.3	2.0	0.1	3.9	6.0	93.9	3.1	0.5	1.1	2.5
Scott	1.0	96.4	0.3	0.7	0.2	0.0	3.3	6.3	97.3	0.1	0.2	0.4	2.6
Sedgwick	2.8	81.8	10.0	2.2	3.9	0.2	5.0	8.0	85.5	8.9	1.1	2.2	4.3
Seward	3.3	68.1	4.3	1.5	3.3	0.2	26.0	42.1	77.3	5.9	0.8	2.4	19.5
Shawnee	2.7	85.2	10.2	2.2	1.3	0.1	4.0	7.3	87.7	8.3	1.1	0.7	4.8
Sheridan	0.6	99.2	0.2	0.2	0.1	0.1	0.7	1.5	99.2	0.0	0.3	0.2	0.9
Sherman	1.0	94.8	0.5	0.8	0.4	0.2	4.5	8.4	94.8	0.2	0.1	0.2	6.8
Smith	0.5	99.2	0.2	0.6	0.0	0.1	0.3	0.7	99.7	0.1	0.1	0.1	0.1
Stafford	1.4	96.4	0.4	1.0	0.4	0.0	3.3	5.4	98.2	0.2	0.5	0.2	2.1
Stanton	1.1	85.3	0.6	1.5	0.5	0.0	13.1	23.7	86.4	0.1	0.7	0.3	16.8
Stevens	1.6	84.5	1.2	1.5	0.2	0.1	14.2	21.7	90.2	0.5	0.8	0.3	10.9
Sumner	2.1	96.6	0.9	2.3	0.3	0.1	1.8	3.6	96.2	0.5	1.1	0.3	3.4
Thomas	0.9	98.0	0.6	0.8	0.4	0.0	1.1	1.8	98.2	0.4	0.2	0.4	1.2
Trego	1.0	98.7	0.2	1.3	0.5	0.1	0.2	0.8	99.3	0.1	0.2	0.5	0.2
Wabaunsee	1.0	98.2	0.7	1.0	0.2	0.1	0.8	1.9	98.3	0.6	0.4	0.1	1.8
Wallace	1.3	95.7	1.0	1.4	0.3	0.1	3.0	4.8	98.0	0.3	0.3	0.2	4.3
Washington	0.5	99.4	0.3	0.5	0.2	0.0	0.1	0.6	99.7	0.1	0.1	0.0	0.3
Wichita	2.4	88.5	0.2	1.3	0.4	0.0	12.1	18.4	89.0	0.0	0.3	0.3	11.8
Wilson	1.2	97.9	0.5	1.7	0.4	0.1	0.7	1.7	98.6	0.2	0.7	0.2	0.7
Woodson	1.1	98.0	1.0	1.6	0.1	0.0	0.5	1.4	98.6	0.4	0.7	0.1	0.6
Wyandotte	2.9	60.5	29.4	1.7	2.0	0.1	9.5	16.0	67.1	27.5	0.7	1.2	6.8
KENTUCKY	1.1	91.0	7.7	0.6	0.9	0.1	0.8	1.5	92.0	7.1	0.2	0.5	0.6
Adair	0.8	96.7	2.8	0.6	0.3	0.0	0.3	0.8	96.7	3.0	0.1	0.2	0.6
Allen	0.7	98.2	1.3	0.5	0.2	0.0	0.5	0.8	98.7	1.1	0.1	0.0	0.2
Anderson	0.7	97.2	2.6	0.5	0.2	0.0	0.2	0.8	96.7	3.0	0.0	0.1	0.5
Ballard	1.4	96.7	3.1	1.1	0.3	0.0	0.2	0.6	96.7	3.0	0.2	0.1	0.5
Barren	0.6	94.9	4.4	0.4	0.5	0.0	0.4	0.9	94.7	4.9	0.1	0.2	0.3
Bath	0.7	97.5	2.1	0.6	0.1	0.0	0.4	0.8	96.9	2.9	0.1	0.1	0.3
Bell	0.8	96.8	2.6	0.7	0.5	0.1	0.3	0.6	97.0	2.6	0.1	0.3	0.2
Boone	1.0	96.1	1.8	0.6	1.5	0.1	1.0	2.0	98.5	0.6	0.2	0.6	0.6
Bourbon	1.0	91.4	7.4	0.5	0.3	0.0	1.6	2.6	91.0	8.6	0.1	0.1	0.4
Boyd	0.9	96.8	2.9	0.6	0.4	0.0	0.3	1.1	97.5	2.0	0.1	0.3	0.9
Boyle	1.1	88.8	10.2	0.6	0.7	0.0	0.8	1.4	90.0	9.5	0.1	0.3	0.4
Bracken	0.4	98.8	0.7	0.4	0.1	0.0	0.3	0.5	99.3	0.6	0.1	0.0	0.2
Breathitt	0.4	99.1	0.4	0.4	0.3	0.1	0.1	0.7	99.6	0.2	0.1	0.1	0.2
Breckinridge	0.9	96.7	3.2	0.7	0.1	0.0	0.2	0.7	96.1	3.6	0.2	0.1	0.3
Bullitt	0.8	98.8	0.5	0.8	0.4	0.0	0.3	0.6	99.1	0.4	0.2	0.2	0.3
Butler	0.6	98.5	0.6	0.6	0.3	0.0	0.6	1.0	99.2	0.5	0.2	0.1	0.3
Caldwell	0.6	94.4	5.0	0.4	0.3	0.1	0.5	0.6	93.8	5.8	0.3	0.1	0.2
Calloway	0.9	94.3	3.8	0.5	1.6	0.1	0.7	1.4	96.2	3.1	0.1	0.4	0.5
Campbell	0.8	97.3	1.8	0.5	0.7	0.0	0.4	0.9	98.5	1.0	0.1	0.3	0.4
Carlisle	0.6	98.3	1.1	0.8	0.1	0.0	0.3	0.8	98.6	1.1	0.2	0.1	0.4
Carroll	1.0	96.1	2.3	0.6	0.3	0.1	1.6	3.2	97.5	2.1	0.2	0.2	0.2
Carter	0.4	99.4	0.2	0.5	0.2	0.0	0.1	0.6	99.7	0.1	0.1	0.1	0.2
Casey	0.7	99.0	0.4	0.6	0.2	0.1	0.5	1.3	99.3	0.3	0.2	0.1	0.3
Christian	2.4	71.8	24.8	1.1	1.4	0.5	3.0	4.8	71.7	24.6	0.4	1.3	3.4
Clark	0.7	94.3	5.0	0.5	0.3	0.0	0.7	1.2	94.0	5.5	0.3	0.1	0.3
Clay	0.7	94.6	5.0	0.6	0.2	0.0	0.3	1.4	98.1	1.5	0.2	0.1	0.2
Clinton	0.3	99.4	0.1	0.5	0.1	0.1	0.1	1.2	99.8	0.1	0.0	0.1	0.4
Crittenden	0.7	99.0	0.8	0.6	0.2	0.0	0.2	0.5	98.9	0.8	0.1	0.1	0.3

[1] Hispanic persons may be of any race.

Table B. States and Counties

STATE County	Population and population characteristics, 2000										
	Age (percent)										
	Under 5 years	5 to 17 years	18 to 24 years	25 to 34 years	35 to 44 years	45 to 54 years	55 to 64 years	65 to 74 years	75 years and over	Median age (years)	Percent Female
	28	29	30	31	32	33	34	35	36	37	38
KANSAS—Cont'd											
Osage	6.5	20.6	6.4	10.3	16.7	13.5	10.2	7.8	8.0	38.9	51.0
Osborne	4.6	19.2	5.5	7.6	14.7	12.7	10.0	10.6	15.1	44.0	50.8
Ottawa	5.7	20.0	5.8	10.2	16.5	13.8	10.4	8.5	9.1	40.1	50.0
Pawnee	5.6	18.5	7.3	10.4	15.0	14.4	10.2	8.4	10.1	40.5	47.2
Phillips	5.5	19.0	5.7	9.5	13.6	14.4	10.4	9.6	12.2	42.5	51.3
Pottawatomie	7.4	22.0	7.7	11.7	16.1	13.3	8.3	6.7	6.8	35.9	50.5
Pratt	5.9	18.6	9.4	9.2	14.8	13.6	9.2	8.9	10.3	40.2	51.5
Rawlins	4.5	19.5	3.8	7.1	14.4	14.1	11.0	12.1	13.5	45.4	50.0
Reno	6.4	18.1	9.3	11.6	15.3	13.7	9.2	7.9	8.4	38.2	49.8
Republic	4.5	17.8	4.5	7.8	14.3	14.1	10.9	11.4	14.7	45.7	51.8
Rice	5.8	18.8	13.3	9.1	13.7	11.9	9.4	8.8	9.2	37.6	52.0
Riley	5.7	13.1	34.5	15.1	10.7	8.5	4.8	3.6	3.9	23.9	46.7
Rooks	5.6	19.6	6.4	10.3	15.3	11.9	9.6	9.9	11.5	40.5	50.5
Rush	4.8	17.3	5.5	8.9	14.1	13.9	10.3	11.9	13.4	44.6	51.5
Russell	5.0	17.4	5.8	8.8	14.5	13.4	10.9	11.1	13.0	44.1	51.9
Saline	6.9	19.3	9.4	12.9	15.6	13.4	8.6	7.1	6.8	36.1	50.7
Scott	6.1	21.1	6.6	10.1	15.2	14.6	9.8	7.6	8.9	39.2	50.7
Sedgwick	7.9	20.3	9.5	14.2	16.1	13.1	7.5	5.9	5.4	33.6	50.6
Seward	9.6	22.4	11.7	15.7	14.7	10.6	6.3	4.6	4.3	29.0	48.7
Shawnee	6.8	18.5	8.8	12.8	15.6	14.6	9.1	7.1	6.6	37.1	51.6
Sheridan	5.0	21.4	5.8	8.0	15.7	13.8	10.1	10.6	9.6	41.5	50.0
Sherman	6.1	18.5	11.8	10.4	13.5	12.8	10.0	8.7	8.3	37.8	48.9
Smith	4.3	17.4	4.7	7.7	14.4	13.1	10.5	12.2	15.7	46.0	51.9
Stafford	5.7	20.6	5.4	8.9	15.6	12.8	9.7	10.0	11.2	41.0	51.2
Stanton	7.9	23.0	8.4	12.6	15.8	11.3	8.1	7.6	5.3	33.8	49.0
Stevens	8.2	23.0	8.3	12.0	15.8	11.1	8.3	6.4	7.0	33.6	51.2
Sumner	6.6	21.9	7.5	10.3	15.9	13.7	8.7	7.5	8.0	37.6	50.8
Thomas	6.7	19.6	13.5	9.9	14.5	12.9	8.2	7.1	7.6	35.3	51.4
Trego	5.1	18.8	5.5	7.9	15.6	13.2	10.1	11.0	13.0	43.5	52.3
Wabaunsee	6.2	20.5	6.2	10.1	16.6	14.5	10.3	8.4	7.2	39.5	49.4
Wallace	5.6	23.5	6.5	8.3	15.2	13.7	9.0	9.0	9.0	39.5	50.3
Washington	5.7	18.0	5.4	8.9	14.0	12.4	10.6	10.8	14.3	43.6	49.8
Wichita	8.3	20.4	7.3	11.7	13.9	13.0	9.3	8.0	8.0	36.7	48.9
Wilson	5.8	19.6	7.4	9.6	14.2	13.2	10.3	9.4	10.6	40.6	51.5
Woodson	5.0	16.7	7.4	8.5	13.6	13.9	10.0	11.5	13.3	44.1	50.8
Wyandotte	8.1	20.4	10.4	14.5	15.0	12.1	7.7	6.2	5.6	32.5	51.2
KENTUCKY	6.6	18.0	9.9	14.1	15.9	13.8	9.2	6.8	5.7	35.9	51.1
Adair	6.1	17.4	10.7	13.0	14.8	13.1	10.3	7.9	6.7	36.9	51.5
Allen	6.6	19.3	8.9	13.4	15.0	13.1	10.0	7.6	6.1	36.2	51.0
Anderson	7.5	19.1	7.4	15.0	17.4	13.8	8.9	5.8	5.0	35.5	51.1
Ballard	6.0	17.0	7.6	12.6	15.1	14.2	11.2	8.4	7.8	39.6	50.6
Barren	6.4	17.8	8.2	13.1	15.7	13.6	10.2	7.9	7.1	38.0	51.9
Bath	6.6	17.5	8.6	13.4	15.4	14.0	9.8	7.8	6.9	37.4	50.6
Bell	6.1	18.3	9.0	13.5	15.2	13.9	10.3	7.4	6.4	37.0	52.2
Boone	8.0	20.7	8.5	15.5	18.0	13.6	7.7	4.9	3.2	33.4	50.6
Bourbon	6.5	18.6	8.1	12.7	15.9	14.7	10.1	7.2	6.4	37.6	51.4
Boyd	5.5	16.3	8.3	13.0	15.7	14.8	10.8	8.7	6.9	39.7	51.0
Boyle	5.6	17.1	11.0	13.3	15.3	14.2	9.5	7.4	6.7	36.9	50.4
Bracken	6.6	18.9	8.4	13.4	16.1	13.2	9.8	7.5	6.0	36.8	50.5
Breathitt	5.8	19.7	10.0	13.1	15.9	14.3	9.7	6.7	4.9	35.9	50.7
Breckinridge	6.3	18.6	8.2	11.7	15.0	15.0	11.0	8.2	6.0	38.5	50.4
Bullitt	7.2	19.9	8.6	15.1	17.6	14.4	9.3	5.1	2.8	34.5	50.3
Butler	6.3	19.0	9.5	13.3	15.9	13.1	10.2	6.9	6.0	36.3	50.3
Caldwell	5.5	16.9	7.0	12.1	14.2	14.8	11.5	9.3	8.7	41.2	51.9
Calloway	4.9	13.8	19.8	12.1	12.6	12.0	9.8	7.3	7.7	34.5	51.8
Campbell	6.9	18.7	9.8	14.2	16.4	13.0	8.4	6.7	5.9	35.2	51.8
Carlisle	5.9	17.4	7.8	12.6	13.8	14.0	10.1	9.6	8.7	39.5	51.2
Carroll	6.7	18.7	9.1	14.0	15.9	13.8	9.4	7.0	5.4	35.9	49.7
Carter	6.4	18.1	10.8	13.5	14.9	13.5	10.3	7.1	5.4	35.8	51.0
Casey	6.3	18.2	8.2	13.0	14.5	13.9	10.8	8.3	6.8	37.8	51.1
Christian	9.9	18.4	15.8	17.6	12.5	9.3	6.7	5.2	4.5	27.9	48.4
Clark	6.5	18.3	8.1	14.1	16.2	14.7	9.7	6.9	5.6	36.8	51.7
Clay	5.7	19.7	9.2	16.0	16.5	13.4	9.1	5.9	4.4	34.6	47.2
Clinton	6.3	16.4	8.6	12.7	15.0	13.8	12.2	8.2	6.8	39.0	51.8
Crittenden	5.4	17.8	8.0	11.4	14.7	13.9	12.5	8.3	8.0	40.1	51.6

Table B. States and Counties

STATE County	Under 5 years (39)	5 to 17 years (40)	18 to 24 years (41)	25 to 34 years (42)	35 to 44 years (43)	45 to 54 years (44)	55 to 64 years (45)	65 to 74 years (46)	75 years and over (47)	Percent Female (48)	2000 (49)	1990 (50)	1980 (51)	1990–2000 (52)	1980–1990 (53)
KANSAS—Cont'd															
Osage	6.8	20.2	6.6	14.9	13.9	10.1	9.9	8.8	8.8	51.3	16 712	15 248	15 319	9.6	-0.5
Osborne	6.8	17.4	4.7	11.7	11.6	9.3	11.4	12.6	14.4	52.1	4 452	4 867	5 959	-8.5	-18.3
Ottawa	6.5	19.0	5.5	13.8	13.4	10.2	11.0	9.6	11.1	51.6	6 163	5 634	5 971	9.4	-5.6
Pawnee	6.0	19.9	6.4	13.8	14.6	10.5	9.6	10.4	8.8	49.5	7 233	7 555	8 065	-4.3	-6.3
Phillips	6.5	18.6	5.1	12.4	13.5	10.3	10.4	11.4	11.7	51.4	6 001	6 590	7 406	-8.9	-11.0
Pottawatomie	8.2	21.3	8.2	16.1	14.5	9.2	8.0	7.3	7.3	50.2	18 209	16 128	14 782	12.9	9.1
Pratt	6.4	19.4	7.6	13.8	13.8	9.8	10.2	9.7	9.5	51.6	9 647	9 702	10 275	-0.6	-5.6
Rawlins	6.1	20.3	5.0	12.8	13.1	10.0	11.3	10.7	10.6	50.6	2 966	3 404	4 105	-12.9	-17.1
Reno	6.9	18.6	8.8	15.6	14.4	10.1	9.3	8.6	7.7	50.9	64 790	62 389	64 983	3.8	-4.0
Republic	6.1	16.7	4.2	11.9	11.6	10.0	11.8	13.1	14.7	52.2	5 835	6 482	7 569	-10.0	-14.4
Rice	7.2	19.1	8.0	13.1	12.1	10.0	10.4	9.7	10.4	52.2	10 761	10 610	11 900	1.4	-10.8
Riley	7.5	14.1	33.2	19.1	10.8	5.1	4.0	3.5	2.8	45.0	62 843	67 139	63 505	-6.4	5.7
Rooks	7.3	19.4	5.7	14.0	12.3	9.3	10.4	10.7	11.0	51.7	5 685	6 039	7 006	-5.9	-13.8
Rush	5.8	17.0	4.5	12.6	12.3	9.6	13.1	12.9	12.3	51.7	3 551	3 842	4 516	-7.6	-14.9
Russell	5.5	17.6	5.4	13.3	12.9	9.8	11.8	12.1	11.6	51.8	7 370	7 835	8 868	-5.9	-11.6
Saline	7.4	18.9	9.4	16.9	14.6	10.0	8.7	7.8	6.3	51.7	53 597	49 301	48 905	8.7	0.8
Scott	7.7	21.3	6.7	14.4	14.6	10.2	9.0	8.4	7.8	50.4	5 120	5 289	5 782	-3.2	-8.5
Sedgwick	8.5	19.2	9.8	18.7	15.0	9.2	8.2	6.8	4.6	51.0	452 869	403 662	367 088	12.2	10.0
Seward	9.2	22.1	11.3	18.5	13.4	8.5	7.6	5.4	4.0	49.5	22 510	18 743	17 071	20.1	9.8
Shawnee	7.2	18.7	9.2	17.0	15.5	10.2	9.1	7.2	5.9	51.8	169 871	160 976	154 916	5.5	3.9
Sheridan	7.3	21.4	4.6	13.7	13.3	9.6	12.3	9.2	8.7	49.1	2 813	3 043	3 544	-7.6	-14.1
Sherman	7.8	18.7	9.2	13.5	13.0	10.8	10.3	9.2	7.5	51.1	6 760	6 926	7 759	-2.4	-10.7
Smith	5.3	17.1	4.1	11.7	11.8	9.7	12.4	12.7	15.2	52.0	4 536	5 078	5 947	-10.7	-14.6
Stafford	7.0	18.7	5.5	12.9	12.9	9.7	10.1	11.5	11.7	51.9	4 789	5 365	5 694	-10.7	-5.8
Stanton	9.2	23.0	7.5	16.8	12.2	10.8	9.7	5.8	5.1	50.3	2 406	2 333	2 339	3.1	-0.3
Stevens	8.6	22.0	7.4	15.9	13.3	10.3	8.3	8.1	6.2	51.0	5 463	5 048	4 736	8.2	6.6
Sumner	7.6	21.4	6.7	14.4	14.1	9.8	9.3	8.7	8.0	51.3	25 946	25 841	24 928	0.4	3.7
Thomas	7.5	20.8	11.3	14.6	13.7	9.0	8.4	8.0	6.6	51.3	8 180	8 258	8 451	-0.9	-2.3
Trego	5.7	20.4	4.4	13.2	12.7	9.4	10.4	11.5	12.2	50.7	3 319	3 694	4 165	-10.2	-11.3
Wabaunsee	6.8	20.2	6.9	14.1	13.6	10.4	10.3	9.4	8.2	50.6	6 885	6 603	6 867	4.3	-3.8
Wallace	8.0	21.1	8.0	13.6	13.1	9.3	10.5	8.6	7.8	49.1	1 749	1 821	2 045	-4.0	-11.0
Washington	5.9	18.6	5.6	11.7	11.2	9.2	11.4	12.0	14.3	51.0	6 483	7 073	8 543	-8.3	-17.2
Wichita	8.6	23.1	6.1	14.4	14.2	9.4	9.2	7.4	7.7	50.3	2 531	2 758	3 041	-8.2	-9.3
Wilson	6.6	19.0	6.3	12.3	13.1	10.2	10.5	11.2	10.8	52.1	10 332	10 289	12 128	0.4	-15.2
Woodson	6.0	18.0	5.2	12.0	12.9	8.3	11.2	13.3	13.1	51.5	3 788	4 116	4 600	-8.0	-10.5
Wyandotte	8.3	20.1	9.8	17.5	13.5	9.1	8.6	7.4	5.6	52.3	157 882	162 026	172 335	-2.6	-6.0
KENTUCKY	6.8	19.1	10.9	16.6	14.9	10.4	8.8	7.3	5.4	51.6	4 041 769	3 686 892	3 660 324	9.6	0.7
Adair	5.8	18.8	11.2	14.4	13.5	11.1	9.6	8.9	6.8	51.1	17 244	15 360	15 233	12.3	0.8
Allen	7.0	19.4	8.9	14.2	13.3	11.1	9.9	9.2	6.9	51.5	17 800	14 628	14 128	21.7	3.5
Anderson	7.1	19.4	9.2	16.8	16.0	10.9	8.2	6.8	5.6	51.2	19 111	14 571	12 567	31.2	15.9
Ballard	5.6	17.8	8.6	13.9	14.4	11.8	9.8	9.5	8.6	51.2	8 286	7 902	8 798	4.9	-10.2
Barren	6.4	18.5	8.7	15.6	14.0	11.0	10.0	8.7	7.3	52.6	38 033	34 001	34 009	11.9	0.0
Bath	6.5	18.6	9.4	15.5	14.5	10.5	9.7	8.0	7.2	51.3	11 085	9 692	10 025	14.4	-3.3
Bell	6.6	20.5	10.5	15.6	14.4	10.4	8.7	7.7	5.5	51.8	30 060	31 506	34 330	-4.6	-8.2
Boone	8.1	21.3	9.4	18.3	16.7	10.4	7.5	5.0	3.3	51.2	85 991	57 589	45 842	49.3	25.6
Bourbon	6.9	19.3	9.5	15.6	15.2	11.0	8.9	7.8	5.9	51.5	19 360	19 236	19 405	0.6	-0.9
Boyd	5.8	17.6	8.5	15.6	15.3	11.7	10.7	8.7	6.1	51.5	49 752	51 096	55 513	-2.6	-7.9
Boyle	5.9	18.2	11.2	14.8	15.1	10.7	9.6	8.2	6.3	50.9	27 697	25 590	25 066	8.2	2.3
Bracken	6.6	19.4	9.5	14.9	13.4	10.7	10.1	8.4	7.0	51.6	8 279	7 766	7 738	6.6	0.4
Breathitt	6.7	22.0	11.1	15.5	15.2	10.1	8.4	6.0	4.9	50.5	16 100	15 703	17 004	2.5	-7.7
Breckinridge	6.4	20.2	8.4	14.3	14.5	11.2	9.8	8.9	6.2	50.4	18 648	16 312	16 861	14.3	-3.3
Bullitt	7.2	22.1	10.7	17.4	16.7	11.9	7.2	4.4	2.5	50.2	61 236	47 567	43 346	28.7	9.7
Butler	6.5	20.1	9.2	15.1	14.1	11.4	8.7	8.2	6.6	50.5	13 010	11 245	11 064	15.7	1.6
Caldwell	6.1	17.7	8.6	13.3	14.0	10.9	10.6	10.1	8.8	52.8	13 060	13 232	13 473	-1.3	-1.8
Calloway	5.3	14.2	20.3	13.2	12.5	9.9	8.5	8.9	7.2	51.9	34 177	30 735	30 031	11.2	2.3
Campbell	7.7	19.1	10.3	17.3	14.2	9.6	8.9	7.6	5.3	52.2	88 616	83 866	83 317	5.7	0.7
Carlisle	5.8	18.3	8.9	13.0	13.4	10.9	11.0	9.9	8.8	51.9	5 351	5 238	5 487	2.2	-4.5
Carroll	6.8	20.4	9.0	15.7	14.0	10.9	9.4	8.2	5.7	51.5	10 155	9 292	9 270	9.3	0.2
Carter	6.2	20.5	11.5	14.8	14.2	11.3	8.8	7.2	5.5	51.0	26 889	24 340	25 060	10.5	-2.9
Casey	6.5	20.1	9.0	14.2	14.2	10.9	10.0	8.4	6.7	51.2	15 447	14 211	14 818	8.7	-4.1
Christian	8.6	17.4	17.9	19.7	12.0	7.8	6.7	5.4	4.5	46.1	72 265	68 941	66 878	4.8	3.1
Clark	6.7	19.1	9.3	16.1	16.0	11.2	9.0	7.2	5.3	51.9	33 144	29 496	28 322	12.4	4.1
Clay	7.5	22.8	10.8	16.5	14.2	9.8	7.7	6.0	4.6	50.7	24 556	21 746	22 752	12.9	-4.4
Clinton	6.0	18.8	9.2	15.2	13.9	11.7	9.8	8.6	6.7	52.3	9 634	9 135	9 321	5.5	-2.0
Crittenden	6.2	18.7	8.7	14.1	13.5	11.6	9.5	9.4	8.2	51.7	9 384	9 196	9 207	2.0	-0.1

Table B. States and Counties

STATE County	Total population	Total in house-holds	House-holder	Spouse	Child Total	Own child under 18 years	Other relatives Total	Under 18 years	Nonrelatives Total	Unmarried partner	Total in group quarters	Correctional institutions	Nursing homes	Other institutions	College dormitories	Military quarters	Other
	54	55	56	57	58	59	60	61	62	63	64	65	66	67	68	69	70
KANSAS—Cont'd																	
Osage	16 712	98.6	38.8	23.7	29.8	25.0	2.9	1.4	3.4	1.6	1.4	0.0	1.3	0.0	0.0	0.0	0.1
Osborne	4 452	97.3	43.6	23.7	26.6	23.0	1.3	0.5	2.1	1.2	2.7	0.1	2.5	0.0	0.0	0.0	0.1
Ottawa	6 163	96.9	39.4	24.2	28.2	24.3	2.0	1.0	3.0	1.7	3.1	0.9	1.1	0.7	0.0	0.0	0.3
Pawnee	7 233	87.5	37.9	20.8	24.5	21.1	1.9	1.0	2.4	1.4	12.5	4.8	0.8	3.3	0.0	0.0	3.5
Phillips	6 001	97.6	41.6	25.6	27.0	23.4	1.7	0.8	1.7	1.0	2.4	0.1	1.8	0.5	0.0	0.0	0.0
Pottawatomie	18 209	98.5	37.2	23.2	32.9	27.9	2.2	1.0	2.9	1.4	1.5	0.0	0.6	0.1	0.4	0.0	0.3
Pratt	9 647	96.6	41.1	23.3	27.8	23.2	1.7	0.7	2.7	1.0	3.4	0.4	0.6	0.5	1.9	0.0	0.0
Rawlins	2 966	98.1	42.8	25.5	26.9	23.2	1.3	0.6	1.7	0.6	1.9	0.0	1.7	0.0	0.0	0.0	0.2
Reno	64 790	95.0	39.4	22.0	27.3	22.6	2.7	1.2	3.7	1.6	5.0	3.2	1.3	0.1	0.4	0.0	0.1
Republic	5 835	97.6	43.8	25.8	25.0	21.6	1.2	0.4	1.8	1.0	2.4	0.1	2.3	0.0	0.0	0.0	0.0
Rice	10 761	91.8	37.6	22.3	27.2	23.0	2.2	1.1	2.5	1.3	8.2	0.2	1.0	0.1	6.7	0.0	0.0
Riley	62 843	85.2	35.2	16.3	20.6	17.9	1.9	0.6	11.2	1.3	14.8	0.0	0.6	0.1	8.1	5.6	0.5
Rooks	5 685	96.5	41.5	23.0	28.0	24.3	1.8	0.7	2.2	1.3	3.5	1.9	1.5	0.0	0.0	0.0	0.0
Rush	3 551	97.5	43.6	24.4	24.9	21.2	2.0	0.8	2.6	1.5	2.5	0.0	2.5	0.0	0.0	0.0	0.0
Russell	7 370	97.2	43.5	23.2	25.0	21.0	1.9	0.8	3.5	1.9	2.8	0.3	1.8	0.3	0.0	0.0	0.5
Saline	53 597	97.3	40.0	21.2	28.5	24.0	2.9	1.2	4.8	2.1	2.7	0.4	0.8	0.2	0.8	0.0	0.6
Scott	5 120	98.3	39.9	24.4	30.1	25.9	2.0	0.9	2.0	1.2	1.7	0.1	1.5	0.0	0.0	0.0	0.0
Sedgwick	452 869	98.6	39.0	20.2	31.3	25.8	4.1	1.8	4.1	1.6	1.4	0.4	0.5	0.0	0.1	0.1	0.3
Seward	22 510	98.2	33.0	19.6	33.8	28.8	6.7	2.5	5.1	1.5	1.8	0.3	0.7	0.0	0.6	0.0	0.2
Shawnee	169 871	97.1	40.6	20.1	28.2	22.9	3.6	1.7	4.6	2.0	2.9	0.8	1.1	0.6	0.2	0.0	0.3
Sheridan	2 813	98.4	40.0	25.5	30.2	25.4	1.2	0.5	1.6	0.6	1.6	0.0	1.6	0.0	0.0	0.0	0.0
Sherman	6 760	98.0	40.8	22.8	27.6	23.5	2.2	0.8	4.6	1.3	2.0	0.2	0.9	0.0	0.0	0.0	0.9
Smith	4 536	97.6	43.1	26.1	24.4	20.5	1.5	0.5	2.5	1.1	2.4	0.0	2.1	0.2	0.0	0.0	0.1
Stafford	4 789	98.4	42.0	23.5	28.9	25.0	1.4	0.7	2.6	0.9	1.6	0.0	1.4	0.1	0.0	0.0	0.2
Stanton	2 406	97.7	35.7	22.7	32.4	28.7	3.7	1.3	3.3	1.4	2.3	1.4	0.9	0.0	0.0	0.0	0.0
Stevens	5 463	98.9	36.4	23.0	34.0	29.2	3.5	1.6	2.0	0.8	1.1	0.1	1.0	0.0	0.0	0.0	0.0
Sumner	25 946	98.4	38.1	22.8	31.6	26.2	3.0	1.6	2.9	1.2	1.6	0.1	1.2	0.2	0.0	0.0	0.1
Thomas	8 180	96.6	39.4	22.1	29.5	25.3	1.4	0.5	4.0	1.3	3.4	0.1	1.3	0.0	2.0	0.0	0.0
Trego	3 319	96.7	42.5	24.7	26.2	21.8	1.4	0.7	1.8	1.1	3.3	0.0	2.3	1.0	0.0	0.0	0.0
Wabaunsee	6 885	98.4	38.2	24.6	30.1	24.9	2.6	1.1	2.8	1.4	1.6	0.0	1.6	0.0	0.0	0.0	0.0
Wallace	1 749	98.6	38.5	24.5	31.5	27.6	1.8	0.7	2.2	0.7	1.4	0.0	1.4	0.0	0.0	0.0	0.0
Washington	6 483	96.9	41.2	24.5	27.5	22.8	1.9	0.6	1.7	0.7	3.1	0.0	2.3	0.4	0.0	0.0	0.4
Wichita	2 531	99.0	38.2	24.9	31.2	27.0	3.0	1.3	1.7	0.7	1.0	0.0	1.0	0.0	0.0	0.0	0.0
Wilson	10 332	97.7	40.7	23.2	28.0	23.5	2.7	1.2	3.0	1.4	2.3	0.3	1.3	0.0	0.0	0.0	0.7
Woodson	3 788	97.0	43.3	23.3	25.5	20.0	2.1	1.1	2.7	1.1	3.0	1.8	1.2	0.0	0.0	0.0	0.0
Wyandotte	157 882	99.0	37.8	15.9	31.7	24.1	7.8	3.5	5.7	2.1	1.0	0.2	0.5	0.0	0.0	0.0	0.3
KENTUCKY	4 041 769	97.2	39.4	21.2	28.8	22.3	3.9	1.7	3.9	1.8	2.8	0.7	0.7	0.1	0.8	0.2	0.3
Adair	17 244	95.6	39.1	22.5	28.0	21.6	3.2	1.3	2.8	1.2	4.4	0.3	0.6	0.2	3.1	0.0	0.2
Allen	17 800	98.8	38.8	23.5	29.7	23.7	3.8	1.6	3.0	1.5	1.2	0.2	0.9	0.1	0.0	0.0	0.0
Anderson	19 111	99.3	38.3	24.0	30.2	24.6	3.3	1.5	3.4	1.8	0.7	0.0	0.6	0.0	0.0	0.0	0.2
Ballard	8 286	98.1	41.0	24.4	26.7	21.0	2.9	1.5	3.1	1.7	1.9	0.7	1.1	0.0	0.0	0.0	0.2
Barren	38 033	98.3	40.3	23.5	28.1	22.3	3.4	1.4	2.9	1.5	1.7	0.3	1.3	0.0	0.0	0.0	0.0
Bath	11 085	99.0	40.1	23.1	28.4	21.8	4.0	1.7	3.3	1.7	1.0	0.0	1.0	0.0	0.0	0.0	0.0
Bell	30 060	97.4	39.9	20.4	29.6	21.7	5.4	2.3	2.1	1.2	2.6	1.1	1.0	0.1	0.2	0.0	0.3
Boone	85 991	99.3	36.4	22.4	33.4	26.8	3.4	1.3	3.8	1.7	0.7	0.3	0.3	0.0	0.0	0.0	0.0
Bourbon	19 360	99.0	39.7	21.7	29.3	22.8	4.0	1.6	4.3	1.9	1.0	0.4	0.6	0.0	0.0	0.0	0.1
Boyd	49 752	95.8	40.2	22.4	26.4	19.4	3.9	1.6	2.9	1.4	4.2	3.0	0.4	0.1	0.0	0.0	0.6
Boyle	27 697	90.9	38.2	20.5	25.4	20.2	3.6	1.6	3.1	1.6	9.1	4.6	0.7	0.4	3.2	0.0	0.1
Bracken	8 279	99.3	39.0	22.3	30.1	22.9	4.3	2.0	3.6	1.8	0.7	0.0	0.7	0.0	0.0	0.0	0.0
Breathitt	16 100	97.5	38.3	21.1	30.7	22.2	4.7	2.2	2.8	1.5	2.5	0.1	0.8	0.6	1.0	0.0	0.1
Breckinridge	18 648	98.5	39.3	23.4	28.0	22.5	3.9	1.8	3.1	1.6	1.5	0.8	0.2	0.1	0.0	0.0	0.4
Bullitt	61 236	99.6	36.2	23.7	31.9	24.6	4.3	2.0	3.5	1.9	0.4	0.1	0.2	0.0	0.0	0.0	0.1
Butler	13 010	98.2	38.9	23.4	29.1	22.8	3.8	1.6	3.0	1.6	1.8	0.3	1.2	0.3	0.0	0.0	0.0
Caldwell	13 060	98.2	41.6	23.7	26.5	20.2	3.7	1.8	2.7	1.4	1.8	0.2	1.5	0.1	0.0	0.0	0.0
Calloway	34 177	91.2	40.6	20.7	21.7	17.3	2.5	0.9	5.8	1.5	8.8	0.4	1.2	0.0	7.0	0.0	0.1
Campbell	88 616	97.7	39.2	19.7	30.8	23.5	4.0	1.7	4.0	1.9	2.3	0.2	0.9	0.0	0.9	0.0	0.3
Carlisle	5 351	98.9	41.3	24.1	28.1	21.8	3.1	1.3	2.2	1.3	1.1	0.0	1.1	0.0	0.0	0.0	0.0
Carroll	10 155	97.5	38.8	20.3	28.4	22.5	4.4	2.0	5.6	2.7	2.5	1.1	0.7	0.0	0.0	0.0	0.7
Carter	26 889	97.7	38.5	23.3	29.5	22.3	3.5	1.5	2.9	1.6	2.3	0.1	0.4	0.0	1.5	0.0	0.2
Casey	15 447	98.7	40.5	22.7	28.8	22.0	4.0	1.7	2.7	1.4	1.3	0.0	0.8	0.4	0.0	0.0	0.1
Christian	72 265	91.6	34.4	19.6	30.8	26.1	3.5	1.7	3.3	1.3	8.4	0.5	0.9	0.3	0.0	6.4	0.3
Clark	33 144	98.7	39.3	22.7	29.0	22.3	4.5	2.0	3.3	1.7	1.3	0.5	0.6	0.0	0.0	0.0	0.2
Clay	24 556	91.1	34.8	20.4	29.1	21.9	4.5	2.1	2.3	1.3	8.9	7.1	0.5	1.1	0.0	0.0	0.1
Clinton	9 634	99.3	42.4	23.5	27.4	21.1	3.1	1.0	2.8	1.5	0.7	0.1	0.5	0.0	0.0	0.0	0.0
Crittenden	9 384	98.6	40.8	24.0	28.4	21.4	3.3	1.5	2.1	1.2	1.4	0.2	1.2	0.0	0.0	0.0	0.0

Table B. States and Counties

STATE County	Households by type, 2000												Households, 1990		
		Family households						Nonfamily households							
				Married couple		Female householder[1]			Householder living alone						Householder living alone
	Total households	Total	With own children under 18 years	Total	With own children under 18 years	Total	With own children under 18 years	Total	Total	65 years and over	Average household size	Average family size	Total households	Female householder[1]	
	71	72	73	74	75	76	77	78	79	80	81	82	83	84	85
KANSAS—Cont'd															
Osage	6 490	73.0	33.8	61.0	25.7	8.1	5.3	27.0	23.5	11.5	2.54	2.99	5 806	6.6	23.1
Osborne	1 940	62.3	25.9	54.5	21.1	5.2	3.4	37.7	35.2	18.3	2.23	2.90	2 057	5.4	31.4
Ottawa	2 430	70.7	31.6	61.4	24.7	6.3	4.9	29.3	25.7	13.4	2.46	2.96	2 266	5.7	26.6
Pawnee	2 739	65.2	29.2	54.8	22.4	7.3	4.7	34.8	32.2	15.6	2.31	2.91	2 923	7.2	31.6
Phillips	2 496	69.0	28.3	61.5	24.0	5.5	3.2	31.0	28.6	15.8	2.35	2.89	2 695	4.9	28.9
Pottawatomie	6 771	72.8	36.4	62.4	29.7	7.2	4.8	27.2	23.2	9.7	2.65	3.15	5 938	6.0	22.6
Pratt	3 963	66.6	30.0	56.7	22.8	7.5	5.5	33.4	30.4	14.6	2.35	2.93	3 937	5.9	29.1
Rawlins	1 269	66.7	27.5	59.5	23.3	4.9	2.5	33.3	31.4	17.6	2.29	2.88	1 361	4.6	29.0
Reno	25 498	67.9	30.3	55.9	22.4	8.7	5.7	32.1	27.9	12.1	2.41	2.94	24 239	8.4	26.7
Republic	2 557	65.9	25.6	58.8	20.8	4.8	3.2	34.1	31.8	18.0	2.23	2.80	2 769	3.6	31.4
Rice	4 050	69.9	31.2	59.1	24.2	7.2	4.9	30.1	27.8	15.3	2.44	2.97	4 165	6.5	27.9
Riley	22 137	55.4	27.8	46.2	22.4	6.8	4.4	44.6	27.5	6.1	2.42	2.99	21 280	6.4	23.6
Rooks	2 362	65.9	29.1	55.4	22.4	7.2	4.8	34.1	31.8	18.5	2.32	2.93	2 444	5.5	29.9
Rush	1 548	65.5	26.6	56.1	20.5	5.8	3.9	34.5	31.7	18.0	2.24	2.80	1 642	4.4	30.4
Russell	3 207	63.0	25.4	53.4	18.7	7.1	5.0	37.0	32.8	16.8	2.23	2.83	3 371	6.1	32.1
Saline	21 436	66.3	32.1	52.9	23.2	9.7	6.5	33.7	28.3	10.7	2.43	2.98	19 826	9.3	27.3
Scott	2 045	70.2	33.3	61.0	26.6	6.7	4.9	29.8	27.3	13.6	2.46	3.01	2 022	4.9	24.5
Sedgwick	176 444	66.7	34.4	51.7	24.9	10.9	7.1	33.3	28.2	8.7	2.53	3.14	156 571	10.2	26.7
Seward	7 419	74.2	43.5	59.6	33.9	10.0	7.1	25.8	20.6	7.8	2.98	3.46	6 614	10.3	21.1
Shawnee	68 920	64.8	30.7	49.6	21.0	11.6	7.6	35.2	29.8	10.0	2.39	2.98	63 768	10.5	27.6
Sheridan	1 124	70.8	30.4	63.8	26.1	4.5	2.9	29.2	27.6	14.8	2.46	3.01	1 171	3.1	25.2
Sherman	2 758	64.6	29.2	55.8	23.4	6.0	4.1	35.4	29.2	14.4	2.40	3.00	2 733	7.5	27.1
Smith	1 953	67.7	25.6	60.6	20.9	4.7	3.0	32.3	30.2	18.6	2.27	2.78	2 165	4.5	30.0
Stafford	2 010	64.4	29.9	55.9	24.0	5.9	4.2	35.6	33.0	17.2	2.34	2.99	2 203	5.4	29.9
Stanton	858	74.4	40.2	63.5	33.4	6.8	4.4	25.6	22.6	9.0	2.74	3.21	831	5.9	21.9
Stevens	1 988	73.3	38.8	63.1	32.2	7.1	4.6	26.7	24.3	12.1	2.72	3.27	1 885	5.4	24.6
Sumner	9 888	71.7	34.5	59.9	26.9	8.0	5.2	28.3	25.6	12.4	2.58	3.10	9 689	6.7	24.5
Thomas	3 226	65.9	32.9	56.1	26.4	6.9	4.8	34.1	28.4	11.7	2.45	3.04	3 124	6.5	25.9
Trego	1 412	66.3	27.3	58.1	22.5	6.3	3.5	33.7	31.4	17.7	2.27	2.86	1 464	4.6	27.0
Wabaunsee	2 633	74.4	33.5	64.3	27.2	6.3	4.3	25.6	23.0	10.8	2.57	3.01	2 482	5.0	23.0
Wallace	674	70.8	33.8	63.6	28.8	4.0	3.1	29.2	27.6	13.6	2.56	3.12	677	3.7	26.3
Washington	2 673	66.6	26.6	59.4	23.3	4.2	2.3	33.4	31.2	17.8	2.35	2.96	2 862	3.9	29.9
Wichita	967	74.8	35.1	65.3	28.6	5.8	4.4	25.2	23.7	10.0	2.59	3.07	996	5.4	22.5
Wilson	4 203	67.8	29.6	57.1	22.7	7.8	5.2	32.2	29.1	15.8	2.40	2.96	4 194	6.2	28.7
Woodson	1 642	64.1	25.8	53.8	18.9	7.4	4.9	35.9	33.3	19.4	2.24	2.83	1 699	5.7	30.8
Wyandotte	59 700	65.6	32.6	42.1	18.9	17.8	10.9	34.4	28.9	10.0	2.62	3.24	61 514	16.4	27.5
KENTUCKY	1 590 647	69.4	32.5	53.9	23.6	11.8	7.0	30.6	26.0	9.8	2.47	2.97	1 379 782	11.6	23.3
Adair	6 747	71.2	31.5	57.6	24.0	10.2	5.6	28.8	26.2	13.0	2.44	2.93	5 800	9.5	22.4
Allen	6 910	74.0	34.1	60.6	26.5	9.8	5.7	26.0	23.1	10.4	2.55	2.99	5 595	8.6	22.1
Anderson	7 320	75.5	37.0	62.8	29.2	9.2	5.7	24.5	20.5	8.4	2.59	2.99	5 438	9.0	20.0
Ballard	3 395	71.1	30.7	59.6	24.2	8.0	4.5	28.9	25.8	12.7	2.39	2.85	3 191	7.6	25.2
Barren	15 346	71.3	31.7	58.3	24.3	9.8	5.8	28.7	25.6	11.6	2.44	2.91	13 136	9.5	23.0
Bath	4 445	71.9	32.3	57.7	24.1	10.3	6.3	28.1	25.3	12.0	2.47	2.93	3 659	10.1	22.1
Bell	12 004	71.0	31.9	51.0	22.1	15.7	8.1	29.0	26.8	11.4	2.44	2.95	11 512	15.6	22.0
Boone	31 258	75.0	39.8	61.6	31.7	9.8	6.0	25.0	20.2	6.2	2.73	3.17	20 127	9.5	18.4
Bourbon	7 681	70.9	32.8	54.7	22.9	12.3	7.6	29.1	24.8	11.1	2.49	2.95	7 250	12.2	21.2
Boyd	20 010	70.5	28.9	55.7	20.8	11.6	6.5	29.5	26.5	12.2	2.38	2.86	19 876	10.9	24.0
Boyle	10 574	69.5	31.0	53.7	21.7	12.5	7.6	30.5	27.1	12.1	2.38	2.87	9 483	11.3	24.4
Bracken	3 228	72.7	33.5	57.3	25.0	10.7	6.3	27.3	23.9	11.3	2.55	3.00	2 872	9.7	21.9
Breathitt	6 170	73.6	34.1	55.0	24.5	14.2	7.6	26.4	23.8	9.0	2.54	3.00	5 555	13.3	19.6
Breckinridge	7 324	72.5	31.0	59.6	23.9	8.9	5.1	27.5	24.6	11.6	2.51	2.97	6 159	8.8	22.8
Bullitt	22 171	80.0	39.0	65.4	30.1	10.4	6.5	20.0	16.4	5.4	2.75	3.07	15 965	9.2	13.5
Butler	5 059	73.3	34.4	60.3	27.1	9.3	5.5	26.7	23.7	10.3	2.52	2.98	4 180	8.6	21.4
Caldwell	5 431	70.0	28.5	57.1	21.6	9.8	5.3	30.0	27.5	14.0	2.36	2.85	5 274	10.2	25.6
Calloway	13 862	62.0	25.8	51.0	19.2	8.1	5.0	38.0	29.7	11.4	2.25	2.79	11 607	7.8	27.1
Campbell	34 742	66.5	32.5	50.3	23.2	12.3	7.3	33.5	28.6	9.9	2.49	3.09	31 169	11.7	25.3
Carlisle	2 208	71.3	30.6	58.5	22.9	9.3	5.6	28.7	26.3	13.1	2.40	2.88	2 106	8.4	25.1
Carroll	3 940	69.1	33.1	52.4	22.7	11.7	7.5	30.9	25.3	10.1	2.51	2.98	3 505	12.0	24.4
Carter	10 342	74.9	33.5	60.5	25.8	10.7	5.8	25.1	22.3	9.8	2.54	2.95	8 679	10.6	19.2
Casey	6 260	70.6	31.0	56.1	23.6	10.8	5.4	29.4	26.8	12.6	2.44	2.94	5 436	9.7	22.1
Christian	24 857	73.8	41.1	57.0	30.0	13.6	9.1	26.2	22.5	8.5	2.66	3.12	21 636	12.9	20.6
Clark	13 015	73.4	33.4	57.9	24.6	12.1	7.0	26.6	22.8	9.4	2.51	2.95	10 973	11.0	20.1
Clay	8 556	75.3	36.9	58.6	28.0	12.4	6.8	24.7	22.5	9.0	2.62	3.06	7 367	12.5	16.2
Clinton	4 086	68.8	29.8	55.5	22.6	9.7	5.3	31.2	28.4	12.8	2.34	2.85	3 591	10.7	24.1
Crittenden	3 829	70.7	29.6	58.8	23.1	8.9	5.2	29.3	27.0	13.8	2.42	2.93	3 646	8.2	25.6

[1]No spouse present.

Table B. States and Counties

STATE County	Percent change of households, 1990–2000	Total housing units	Occupied housing units (percent)	Housing occupancy, 2000 — Vacant housing units — Total	For seasonal, recreational, or occasional use	Homeowner vacancy rate (percent)	Rental vacancy rate (percent)	Housing tenure, 2000 — Occupied housing units — Total	Percent owner-occupied housing units	Percent renter-occupied housing units	Average household size of owner-occupied units	Average household size of renter-occupied units
	86	87	88	89	90	91	92	93	94	95	96	97
KANSAS—Cont'd												
Osage	11.8	7 018	92.5	7.5	1.6	2.0	8.1	6 490	79.8	20.2	2.60	2.31
Osborne	-5.7	2 419	80.2	19.8	0.7	4.0	14.9	1 940	78.8	21.2	2.27	2.10
Ottawa	7.2	2 755	88.2	11.8	1.1	2.8	11.9	2 430	82.1	17.9	2.54	2.10
Pawnee	-6.3	3 114	88.0	12.0	0.9	2.8	12.8	2 739	74.2	25.8	2.36	2.17
Phillips	-7.4	3 088	80.8	19.2	1.8	7.1	18.1	2 496	77.9	22.1	2.40	2.14
Pottawatomie	14.0	7 311	92.6	7.4	0.9	1.4	8.3	6 771	78.4	21.6	2.73	2.36
Pratt	0.7	4 633	85.5	14.5	0.8	2.6	11.8	3 963	73.4	26.6	2.43	2.13
Rawlins	-6.8	1 565	81.1	18.9	2.4	6.1	12.5	1 269	76.8	23.2	2.30	2.27
Reno	5.2	27 625	92.3	7.7	0.5	1.9	10.1	25 498	70.7	29.3	2.51	2.18
Republic	-7.7	3 113	82.1	17.9	1.2	4.6	11.8	2 557	79.0	21.0	2.29	2.00
Rice	-2.8	4 609	87.9	12.1	1.8	2.5	9.4	4 050	76.6	23.4	2.48	2.32
Riley	4.0	23 397	94.6	5.4	0.5	2.0	4.1	22 137	47.2	52.8	2.56	2.30
Rooks	-3.4	2 758	85.6	14.4	2.4	5.2	10.7	2 362	77.1	22.9	2.36	2.19
Rush	-5.7	1 928	80.3	19.7	2.9	6.9	17.8	1 548	82.0	18.0	2.26	2.12
Russell	-4.9	3 871	82.8	17.2	1.5	4.0	15.9	3 207	75.2	24.8	2.27	2.11
Saline	8.1	22 695	94.5	5.5	0.3	1.6	7.4	21 436	69.0	31.0	2.54	2.18
Scott	1.1	2 291	89.3	10.7	1.3	2.4	10.1	2 045	74.4	25.6	2.50	2.35
Sedgwick	12.7	191 133	92.3	7.7	0.3	1.8	11.5	176 444	66.2	33.8	2.68	2.23
Seward	12.2	8 027	92.4	7.6	0.4	1.9	9.6	7 419	64.1	35.9	3.04	2.87
Shawnee	8.1	73 768	93.4	6.6	0.2	1.3	7.3	68 920	67.4	32.6	2.53	2.12
Sheridan	-4.0	1 263	89.0	11.0	2.0	2.9	10.0	1 124	82.3	17.7	2.48	2.39
Sherman	0.9	3 184	86.6	13.4	1.1	2.5	17.1	2 758	68.9	31.1	2.47	2.25
Smith	-9.8	2 326	84.0	16.0	0.6	4.5	8.7	1 953	79.6	20.4	2.31	2.09
Stafford	-8.8	2 458	81.8	18.2	4.0	4.9	12.9	2 010	77.8	22.2	2.34	2.34
Stanton	3.2	1 007	85.2	14.8	0.3	4.7	14.0	858	67.8	32.2	2.72	2.78
Stevens	5.5	2 265	87.8	12.2	0.4	2.0	11.6	1 988	75.6	24.4	2.74	2.66
Sumner	2.1	10 877	90.9	9.1	1.2	2.7	10.2	9 888	76.6	23.4	2.66	2.34
Thomas	3.3	3 562	90.6	9.4	0.5	2.3	7.7	3 226	69.0	31.0	2.60	2.12
Trego	-3.6	1 723	82.0	18.0	6.2	2.7	13.3	1 412	81.1	18.9	2.30	2.15
Wabaunsee	6.1	3 033	86.8	13.2	5.5	2.8	7.9	2 633	83.1	16.9	2.61	2.40
Wallace	-0.4	791	85.2	14.8	0.6	8.0	6.1	674	77.3	22.7	2.55	2.57
Washington	-6.6	3 142	85.1	14.9	1.4	2.3	13.0	2 673	79.5	20.5	2.39	2.20
Wichita	-2.9	1 119	86.4	13.6	2.1	1.9	14.9	967	74.0	26.0	2.62	2.50
Wilson	0.2	4 937	85.1	14.9	2.9	3.2	8.1	4 203	78.1	21.9	2.44	2.28
Woodson	-3.4	2 076	79.1	20.9	8.3	3.6	11.8	1 642	81.4	18.6	2.28	2.06
Wyandotte	-2.9	65 892	90.6	9.4	0.3	1.8	8.3	59 700	62.9	37.1	2.69	2.50
KENTUCKY	15.3	1 750 927	90.8	9.2	1.7	1.8	8.7	1 590 647	70.8	29.2	2.55	2.27
Adair	16.3	7 792	86.6	13.4	2.8	1.8	10.4	6 747	80.2	19.8	2.48	2.32
Allen	23.5	8 057	85.8	14.2	3.7	2.4	8.5	6 910	79.0	21.0	2.56	2.49
Anderson	34.6	7 752	94.4	5.6	1.0	1.1	8.6	7 320	79.7	20.3	2.61	2.51
Ballard	6.4	3 837	88.5	11.5	1.6	3.7	8.5	3 395	81.9	18.1	2.44	2.17
Barren	16.8	17 095	89.8	10.2	1.9	2.2	10.2	15 346	72.3	27.7	2.49	2.30
Bath	21.5	4 994	89.0	11.0	2.7	2.2	6.4	4 445	79.8	20.2	2.48	2.42
Bell	4.3	13 341	90.0	10.0	0.7	1.7	9.5	12 004	67.6	32.4	2.49	2.33
Boone	55.3	33 351	93.7	6.3	0.9	2.3	7.9	31 258	74.3	25.7	2.89	2.28
Bourbon	5.9	8 349	92.0	8.0	0.6	2.1	7.4	7 681	65.5	34.5	2.53	2.42
Boyd	0.7	21 976	91.1	8.9	0.5	2.0	12.5	20 010	72.9	27.1	2.45	2.20
Boyle	11.5	11 418	92.6	7.4	0.7	1.5	8.9	10 574	69.3	30.7	2.44	2.24
Bracken	12.4	3 715	86.9	13.1	2.0	3.0	4.1	3 228	76.9	23.1	2.57	2.46
Breathitt	11.1	6 812	90.6	9.4	1.4	1.0	7.5	6 170	76.5	23.5	2.58	2.43
Breckinridge	18.9	9 890	74.1	25.9	16.7	2.6	10.7	7 324	81.7	18.3	2.54	2.37
Bullitt	38.9	23 160	95.7	4.3	0.3	1.2	6.3	22 171	83.9	16.1	2.78	2.59
Butler	21.0	5 815	87.0	13.0	3.1	1.5	8.3	5 059	79.6	20.4	2.57	2.33
Caldwell	3.0	6 126	88.7	11.3	1.4	2.9	9.2	5 431	77.4	22.6	2.38	2.31
Calloway	19.4	16 069	86.3	13.7	5.8	2.5	9.6	13 862	68.4	31.6	2.36	2.02
Campbell	11.5	36 898	94.2	5.8	0.5	1.7	6.9	34 742	69.0	31.0	2.65	2.14
Carlisle	4.8	2 490	88.7	11.3	1.4	3.3	10.8	2 208	83.8	16.2	2.42	2.28
Carroll	12.4	4 439	88.8	11.2	2.4	3.4	8.6	3 940	66.7	33.3	2.56	2.41
Carter	19.2	11 534	89.7	10.3	1.4	1.4	8.6	10 342	81.0	19.0	2.58	2.38
Casey	15.2	7 242	86.4	13.6	2.3	1.4	7.4	6 260	80.9	19.1	2.45	2.36
Christian	14.9	27 182	91.4	8.6	0.4	2.5	7.1	24 857	55.3	44.7	2.56	2.79
Clark	18.6	13 749	94.7	5.3	0.3	1.4	5.7	13 015	68.7	31.3	2.56	2.41
Clay	16.1	9 439	90.6	9.4	1.0	1.1	7.8	8 556	74.7	25.3	2.66	2.49
Clinton	13.8	4 888	83.6	16.4	4.2	1.9	11.9	4 086	77.1	22.9	2.39	2.17
Crittenden	5.0	4 410	86.8	13.2	2.8	2.7	10.6	3 829	80.5	19.5	2.44	2.33

Table B. States and Counties

STATE/ County code	MSA/ PMSA/ NECMA code[1]	County type[2]	STATE County	Land area, 2000[3] (sq km)	Total persons	Rank	Per square kilometer	Land area, 1990[3] (sq km)	Total persons	Rank	Per square kilometer	White	Black or African American	American Indian or Alaska Native	Asian	Native Hawaiian and other Pacific Islander	Some other race
				1	2	3	4	5	6	7	8	9	10	11	12	13	14
			KENTUCKY—Cont'd														
21 057	...	9	Cumberland	792	7 147	2 673	9.0	792	6 784	2 678	8.6	95.3	3.4	0.1	0.0	0.1	0.2
21 059	5990	3	Daviess	1 198	91 545	560	76.4	1 198	87 189	522	72.8	93.7	4.3	0.1	0.4	0.0	0.4
21 061	...	9	Edmonson	784	11 644	2 322	14.9	784	10 357	2 353	13.2	98.4	0.6	0.4	0.1	0.0	0.1
21 063	...	8	Elliott	606	6 748	2 715	11.1	606	6 455	2 713	10.7	99.0	0.0	0.1	0.0	0.0	0.0
21 065	...	6	Estill	658	15 307	2 070	23.3	658	14 614	2 012	22.2	99.1	0.1	0.2	0.0	0.0	0.1
21 067	4280	2	Fayette	737	260 512	211	353.5	737	225 366	220	305.8	81.0	13.5	0.2	2.5	0.0	1.2
21 069	...	7	Fleming	909	13 792	2 173	15.2	909	12 292	2 197	13.5	97.3	1.4	0.1	0.2	0.0	0.3
21 071	...	7	Floyd	1 021	42 441	1 047	41.6	1 021	43 586	930	42.7	97.7	1.3	0.1	0.2	0.1	0.1
21 073	...	4	Franklin	545	47 687	957	87.5	545	44 143	923	81.0	88.0	9.4	0.1	0.7	0.0	0.6
21 075	...	7	Fulton	541	7 752	2 629	14.3	541	8 271	2 540	15.3	75.1	23.2	0.1	0.3	0.0	0.3
21 077	1640	1	Gallatin	256	7 870	2 616	30.7	256	5 393	2 810	21.1	96.7	1.6	0.2	0.2	0.0	0.3
21 079	...	6	Garrard	599	14 792	2 104	24.7	599	11 579	2 250	19.3	95.7	3.1	0.1	0.0	0.0	0.4
21 081	1640	1	Grant	673	22 384	1 673	33.3	673	15 737	1 938	23.4	98.3	0.3	0.2	0.3	0.1	0.3
21 083	...	7	Graves	1 439	37 028	1 189	25.7	1 439	33 550	1 176	23.3	92.7	4.4	0.2	0.2	0.0	1.3
21 085	...	7	Grayson	1 305	24 053	1 591	18.4	1 305	21 050	1 626	16.1	98.3	0.5	0.2	0.1	0.0	0.2
21 087	...	9	Green	748	11 518	2 333	15.4	748	10 371	2 350	13.9	96.2	2.6	0.1	0.1	0.0	0.3
21 089	3400	2	Greenup	896	36 891	1 192	41.2	897	36 766	1 081	41.0	98.1	0.6	0.2	0.4	0.0	0.1
21 091	...	8	Hancock	489	8 392	2 574	17.2	489	7 864	2 585	16.1	98.0	0.8	0.3	0.2	0.0	0.2
21 093	...	4	Hardin	1 626	94 174	545	57.9	1 627	89 240	513	54.8	82.0	11.9	0.4	1.8	0.2	1.3
21 095	...	7	Harlan	1 210	33 202	1 307	27.4	1 210	36 574	1 088	30.2	95.6	2.6	0.5	0.3	0.0	0.1
21 097	...	6	Harrison	802	17 983	1 898	22.4	802	16 248	1 910	20.3	95.6	2.5	0.3	0.1	0.0	0.6
21 099	...	9	Hart	1 077	17 445	1 926	16.2	1 077	14 890	1 996	13.8	92.6	6.2	0.2	0.1	0.0	0.2
21 101	2440	2	Henderson	1 140	44 829	1 003	39.3	1 140	43 044	937	37.8	91.2	7.1	0.2	0.3	0.0	0.4
21 103	...	8	Henry	749	15 060	2 087	20.1	749	12 823	2 153	17.1	94.0	3.3	0.2	0.3	0.0	1.3
21 105	...	9	Hickman	633	5 262	2 834	8.3	633	5 566	2 794	8.8	88.4	9.9	0.3	0.1	0.0	0.2
21 107	...	7	Hopkins	1 426	46 519	972	32.6	1 426	46 126	900	32.3	92.0	6.2	0.2	0.3	0.0	0.1
21 109	...	8	Jackson	897	13 495	2 194	15.0	897	11 955	2 222	13.3	99.2	0.1	0.2	0.0	0.0	0.0
21 111	4520	2	Jefferson	997	693 604	73	695.7	997	665 123	69	667.1	77.4	18.9	0.2	1.4	0.0	0.7
21 113	4280	2	Jessamine	448	39 041	1 137	87.1	448	30 508	1 268	68.1	94.4	3.1	0.2	0.6	0.0	0.5
21 115	...	7	Johnson	677	23 445	1 620	34.6	677	23 248	1 528	34.3	98.6	0.3	0.1	0.3	0.0	0.1
21 117	1640	0	Kenton	419	151 464	354	361.5	421	142 005	335	337.3	94.0	3.8	0.1	0.6	0.0	0.4
21 119	...	9	Knott	912	17 649	1 919	19.4	912	17 906	1 793	19.6	98.3	0.7	0.1	0.2	0.0	0.1
21 121	...	7	Knox	1 004	31 795	1 350	31.7	1 004	29 676	1 309	29.6	97.8	0.8	0.3	0.2	0.0	0.1
21 123	...	7	Larue	682	13 373	2 199	19.6	682	11 679	2 239	17.1	94.6	3.5	0.2	0.2	0.0	0.3
21 125	...	7	Laurel	1 128	52 715	884	46.7	1 128	43 438	932	38.5	97.7	0.6	0.4	0.3	0.0	0.1
21 127	...	8	Lawrence	1 085	15 569	2 049	14.3	1 085	13 998	2 057	12.9	98.9	0.1	0.3	0.1	0.0	0.1
21 129	...	9	Lee	544	7 916	2 613	14.6	544	7 422	2 622	13.6	94.4	3.8	0.3	0.1	0.0	0.1
21 131	...	9	Leslie	1 046	12 401	2 272	11.9	1 046	13 642	2 087	13.0	99.2	0.1	0.1	0.1	0.0	0.0
21 133	...	7	Letcher	878	25 277	1 554	28.8	878	27 000	1 389	30.8	98.7	0.5	0.1	0.3	0.0	0.0
21 135	...	8	Lewis	1 255	14 092	2 154	11.2	1 255	13 029	2 139	10.4	98.9	0.2	0.2	0.0	0.0	0.1
21 137	...	7	Lincoln	871	23 361	1 625	26.8	872	20 096	1 671	23.0	96.1	2.5	0.1	0.1	0.0	0.4
21 139	...	9	Livingston	819	9 804	2 464	12.0	819	9 062	2 465	11.1	98.5	0.1	0.4	0.0	0.0	0.3
21 141	...	7	Logan	1 439	26 573	1 495	18.5	1 439	24 416	1 481	17.0	90.7	7.6	0.2	0.2	0.0	0.3
21 143	...	9	Lyon	559	8 080	2 599	14.5	559	6 624	2 693	11.8	91.9	6.7	0.3	0.2	0.0	0.4
21 145	...	5	McCracken	650	65 514	746	100.8	650	62 879	693	96.7	86.8	10.9	0.2	0.5	0.1	0.4
21 147	...	9	McCreary	1 108	17 080	1 949	15.4	1 108	15 603	1 946	14.1	98.0	0.6	0.4	0.0	0.0	0.2
21 149	...	8	McLean	659	9 938	2 452	15.1	659	9 628	2 422	14.6	98.6	0.4	0.2	0.0	0.0	0.3
21 151	4280	2	Madison	1 141	70 872	700	62.1	1 141	57 508	757	50.4	93.0	4.4	0.3	0.7	0.0	0.3
21 153	...	9	Magoffin	801	13 332	2 201	16.6	801	13 077	2 133	16.3	99.3	0.2	0.2	0.1	0.0	0.0
21 155	...	7	Marion	897	18 212	1 885	20.3	898	16 499	1 892	18.4	89.2	9.1	0.1	0.4	0.0	0.4
21 157	...	7	Marshall	790	30 125	1 393	38.1	790	27 205	1 383	34.4	98.6	0.1	0.2	0.1	0.0	0.2
21 159	...	9	Martin	598	12 578	2 259	21.0	598	12 526	2 180	20.9	99.3	0.0	0.1	0.1	0.1	0.0
21 161	...	6	Mason	624	16 800	1 969	26.9	625	16 666	1 871	26.7	90.9	7.2	0.1	0.4	0.0	0.6
21 163	...	6	Meade	799	26 349	1 506	33.0	799	24 170	1 488	30.3	92.4	4.1	0.6	0.5	0.1	0.8
21 165	...	9	Menifee	528	6 556	2 732	12.4	528	5 092	2 832	9.6	97.6	1.4	0.1	0.0	0.0	0.1
21 167	...	6	Mercer	650	20 817	1 746	32.0	650	19 148	1 725	29.5	94.3	3.7	0.2	0.5	0.0	0.6
21 169	...	9	Metcalfe	753	10 037	2 441	13.3	753	8 963	2 474	11.9	97.3	1.6	0.2	0.1	0.0	0.1
21 171	...	7	Monroe	857	11 756	2 313	13.7	857	11 401	2 261	13.3	95.6	2.8	0.1	0.0	0.0	0.9
21 173	...	6	Montgomery	514	22 554	1 667	43.9	514	19 561	1 695	38.1	95.1	3.5	0.2	0.1	0.0	0.3
21 175	...	9	Morgan	987	13 948	2 165	14.1	988	11 648	2 241	11.8	94.6	4.4	0.2	0.2	0.0	0.1
21 177	...	7	Muhlenberg	1 230	31 839	1 349	25.9	1 230	31 318	1 235	25.5	94.2	4.6	0.1	0.1	0.0	0.2
21 179	...	6	Nelson	1 095	37 477	1 178	34.2	1 095	29 710	1 308	27.1	92.8	5.5	0.1	0.5	0.0	0.4
21 181	...	8	Nicholas	509	6 813	2 710	13.4	509	6 725	2 685	13.2	98.3	0.8	0.2	0.1	0.0	0.2
21 183	...	6	Ohio	1 538	22 916	1 647	14.9	1 538	21 105	1 625	13.7	97.7	0.7	0.2	0.2	0.0	0.4
21 185	4520	2	Oldham	490	46 178	978	94.2	490	33 263	1 185	67.9	93.6	4.2	0.0	0.4	0.0	0.4
21 187	...	8	Owen	912	10 547	2 394	11.6	912	9 035	2 466	9.9	97.0	1.1	0.3	0.2	0.0	0.5

[1]MSA = Metropolitan Statistical Area. PMSA = Primary MSA. NECMA = New England County Metropolitan Area. See Appendix A for explanation of these concepts. See Appendix B for list of metropolitan areas identified by type, with component counties.
[2]County typology code from the Economic Research Service of USDA. See Appendix A for definition.
[3]Dry land or land partially or temporarily covered by water.

Table B. States and Counties

STATE County	Two or more races	White	Black	American Indian or Alaska Native	Asian	Native Hawaiian and other Pacific Islander	Some other race	Hispanic[1]	White	Black or African American	American Indian or Alaska Native	Asian and Pacific Islander	Hispanic[1]
	15	16	17	18	19	20	21	22	23	24	25	26	27
KENTUCKY—Cont'd													
Cumberland	0.9	96.1	3.9	0.5	0.2	0.2	0.3	0.6	95.2	4.5	0.2	0.1	0.3
Daviess	0.9	94.6	4.8	0.4	0.6	0.0	0.6	0.9	95.4	4.2	0.1	0.3	0.4
Edmonson	0.5	98.8	0.7	0.7	0.1	0.0	0.1	0.6	98.1	1.6	0.1	0.1	0.2
Elliott	0.8	99.9	0.1	0.6	0.2	0.0	0.1	0.6	99.9	0.0	0.0	0.0	0.2
Estill	0.5	99.6	0.2	0.5	0.1	0.0	0.2	0.5	99.9	0.1	0.0	0.0	0.3
Fayette	1.6	82.4	14.1	0.6	2.8	0.1	1.7	3.3	84.5	13.4	0.2	1.6	1.1
Fleming	0.7	98.0	1.7	0.5	0.2	0.0	0.3	0.7	98.1	1.8	0.0	0.1	0.5
Floyd	0.4	98.1	1.4	0.4	0.3	0.1	0.2	0.6	99.0	0.7	0.1	0.2	0.3
Franklin	1.2	89.0	10.0	0.6	0.9	0.1	0.7	1.1	91.7	7.5	0.2	0.5	0.4
Fulton	0.9	76.0	23.6	0.4	0.4	0.0	0.6	0.7	81.0	18.6	0.1	0.2	0.3
Gallatin	1.0	97.7	1.9	0.6	0.5	0.1	0.6	1.0	95.9	1.7	0.1	0.1	0.1
Garrard	0.6	96.3	3.4	0.3	0.1	0.0	0.5	1.3	95.9	3.9	0.1	0.1	0.3
Grant	0.5	98.8	0.3	0.5	0.4	0.1	0.4	1.0	99.6	0.2	0.1	0.1	0.2
Graves	1.1	93.8	4.8	0.7	0.3	0.0	1.6	2.4	95.2	4.5	0.1	0.1	0.3
Grayson	0.7	98.9	0.7	0.6	0.2	0.0	0.3	0.8	99.3	0.3	0.2	0.2	0.4
Green	0.7	96.8	2.8	0.5	0.2	0.0	0.4	0.9	96.3	3.4	0.1	0.1	0.6
Greenup	0.6	98.7	0.7	0.6	0.5	0.0	0.2	0.6	99.1	0.4	0.1	0.3	0.2
Hancock	0.6	98.5	1.0	0.5	0.3	0.0	0.2	0.8	98.3	1.2	0.2	0.2	0.4
Hardin	2.4	84.0	12.8	1.0	2.5	0.4	1.9	3.4	85.1	11.1	0.4	2.1	2.8
Harlan	1.0	96.5	2.9	1.0	0.4	0.0	0.3	0.7	96.4	3.3	0.1	0.1	0.3
Harrison	0.8	96.4	2.8	0.6	0.2	0.0	0.8	1.2	96.7	2.9	0.1	0.1	0.3
Hart	0.7	93.3	6.4	0.6	0.2	0.1	0.2	0.9	92.6	7.2	0.1	0.1	0.4
Henderson	0.9	92.0	7.5	0.4	0.5	0.0	0.6	1.0	92.4	7.1	0.2	0.3	0.4
Henry	0.9	94.8	3.7	0.5	0.5	0.0	1.5	2.3	95.6	4.2	0.1	0.1	0.2
Hickman	1.2	89.6	10.4	0.9	0.1	0.0	0.3	1.0	90.7	9.0	0.1	0.0	0.3
Hopkins	0.9	92.8	6.6	0.5	0.4	0.0	0.5	0.9	92.9	6.6	0.1	0.3	0.4
Jackson	0.5	99.7	0.1	0.6	0.1	0.0	0.1	0.5	99.8	0.0	0.1	0.0	0.3
Jefferson	1.4	78.6	19.5	0.6	1.7	0.1	1.1	1.8	81.9	17.1	0.2	0.7	0.7
Jessamine	1.1	95.5	3.5	0.6	0.8	0.1	0.8	1.3	96.0	3.2	0.2	0.4	0.6
Johnson	0.6	99.2	0.3	0.5	0.4	0.0	0.1	0.6	99.4	0.1	0.1	0.3	0.2
Kenton	1.0	94.9	4.3	0.5	0.8	0.1	0.6	1.1	96.4	2.9	0.1	0.4	0.5
Knott	0.6	98.8	0.9	0.5	0.2	0.0	0.2	0.6	99.2	0.6	0.1	0.1	0.2
Knox	0.8	98.6	0.9	0.8	0.3	0.1	0.2	0.6	98.6	1.0	0.2	0.1	0.3
Larue	1.1	95.7	4.0	0.8	0.2	0.0	0.5	1.0	95.5	4.2	0.2	0.1	0.5
Laurel	0.9	98.5	0.8	1.0	0.5	0.0	0.2	0.6	98.9	0.6	0.3	0.2	0.4
Lawrence	0.6	99.5	0.2	0.6	0.1	0.0	0.2	0.4	99.5	0.2	0.2	0.2	0.2
Lee	0.7	95.7	3.8	0.9	0.1	0.0	0.1	0.4	99.6	0.4	0.1	0.0	0.1
Leslie	0.5	99.6	0.2	0.4	0.2	0.0	0.1	0.6	99.8	0.1	0.1	0.1	0.3
Letcher	0.4	99.1	0.5	0.3	0.3	0.0	0.1	0.4	99.0	0.7	0.1	0.1	0.2
Lewis	0.5	99.5	0.3	0.5	0.1	0.0	0.1	0.4	99.6	0.2	0.2	0.0	0.2
Lincoln	0.7	96.8	2.7	0.5	0.2	0.0	0.5	0.9	96.5	3.1	0.2	0.1	0.2
Livingston	0.6	99.1	0.2	0.9	0.1	0.0	0.4	0.8	99.6	0.2	0.2	0.1	0.3
Logan	1.0	91.6	8.0	0.6	0.3	0.0	0.4	1.1	91.1	8.5	0.2	0.1	0.3
Lyon	0.5	92.4	6.8	0.6	0.3	0.0	0.5	0.7	92.9	6.5	0.3	0.2	0.4
McCracken	1.2	87.9	11.4	0.7	0.7	0.1	0.5	1.1	89.4	10.1	0.2	0.3	0.5
McCreary	0.7	98.7	0.7	1.0	0.1	0.0	0.3	0.6	98.8	0.8	0.4	0.0	0.2
McLean	0.5	99.1	0.4	0.6	0.1	0.0	0.4	0.8	99.4	0.5	0.1	0.0	0.2
Madison	1.2	94.1	5.0	0.7	0.9	0.0	0.5	1.0	94.1	5.1	0.1	0.6	0.3
Magoffin	0.3	99.6	0.2	0.4	0.1	0.0	0.1	0.4	99.8	0.0	0.1	0.0	0.1
Marion	0.8	89.9	9.5	0.4	0.5	0.1	0.5	0.8	90.8	8.9	0.1	0.1	0.3
Marshall	0.8	99.3	0.2	0.8	0.2	0.0	0.3	0.8	99.6	0.0	0.2	0.1	0.4
Martin	0.5	99.8	0.1	0.5	0.1	0.1	0.0	0.6	99.8	0.1	0.1	0.1	0.2
Mason	0.9	91.7	7.6	0.4	0.4	0.0	0.7	1.0	92.1	7.6	0.1	0.1	0.5
Meade	1.4	93.6	4.5	1.1	0.9	0.3	1.1	2.2	87.5	9.9	0.4	1.1	2.4
Menifee	0.7	98.3	1.4	0.7	0.1	0.1	0.2	1.1	97.9	1.7	0.1	0.1	0.5
Mercer	1.0	94.9	4.2	0.5	0.6	0.1	0.8	1.3	95.1	4.3	0.1	0.4	0.5
Metcalfe	0.6	97.9	1.8	0.6	0.1	0.0	0.2	0.5	97.2	2.5	0.2	0.1	0.3
Monroe	0.6	96.1	3.0	0.4	0.0	0.0	1.0	1.4	96.7	3.1	0.1	0.1	0.6
Montgomery	0.8	95.8	3.7	0.5	0.3	0.1	0.5	1.1	95.5	4.2	0.1	0.1	0.3
Morgan	0.6	95.2	4.5	0.6	0.2	0.1	0.2	0.6	99.0	0.9	0.1	0.1	0.4
Muhlenberg	0.7	94.9	4.9	0.5	0.2	0.0	0.3	0.7	95.6	4.1	0.1	0.1	0.3
Nelson	0.6	93.4	5.8	0.4	0.6	0.0	0.5	1.1	93.5	6.1	0.1	0.2	0.4
Nicholas	0.2	98.5	0.9	0.4	0.2	0.1	0.2	0.5	98.3	1.3	0.1	0.3	0.2
Ohio	0.7	98.4	0.9	0.6	0.3	0.0	0.6	1.0	98.8	0.8	0.2	0.1	0.4
Oldham	1.0	94.5	4.5	0.6	0.6	0.0	0.7	1.3	95.7	3.6	0.2	0.4	0.6
Owen	0.9	97.9	1.3	0.7	0.4	0.0	0.7	1.0	98.0	1.7	0.2	0.1	0.2

[1] Hispanic persons may be of any race.

Table B. States and Counties

STATE County	Under 5 years	5 to 17 years	18 to 24 years	25 to 34 years	35 to 44 years	45 to 54 years	55 to 64 years	65 to 74 years	75 years and over	Median age (years)	Percent Female
	28	29	30	31	32	33	34	35	36	37	38
KENTUCKY—Cont'd											
Cumberland	5.6	18.0	6.9	11.8	15.1	13.1	11.7	9.7	8.2	40.1	51.9
Daviess	6.7	19.1	9.0	12.6	15.8	13.7	9.2	7.3	6.5	36.8	51.9
Edmonson	6.0	17.6	9.0	12.8	14.9	13.8	11.5	8.3	6.1	38.0	50.6
Elliott	6.5	18.9	9.1	12.7	14.8	14.3	10.5	7.1	6.2	37.0	51.2
Estill	6.0	18.1	9.1	14.1	15.1	13.6	10.6	7.4	6.1	36.7	51.6
Fayette	6.2	15.1	14.6	17.1	16.1	13.2	7.6	5.3	4.7	33.0	50.9
Fleming	6.7	18.7	8.4	14.1	14.9	14.0	9.9	7.3	6.0	36.3	51.0
Floyd	5.9	17.7	9.4	14.3	16.0	14.9	9.6	6.8	5.4	36.7	50.8
Franklin	6.1	16.5	9.7	14.4	16.1	15.4	9.6	6.7	5.7	37.0	51.6
Fulton	6.5	18.4	8.9	11.5	14.0	13.3	10.0	8.5	9.1	38.5	53.3
Gallatin	7.5	21.0	7.7	14.4	16.6	13.3	9.1	5.4	4.9	34.6	50.3
Garrard	6.1	18.2	8.1	13.9	17.0	13.6	10.0	7.4	5.7	37.1	50.8
Grant	8.0	20.7	9.4	15.5	16.0	12.2	8.7	5.2	4.4	32.7	50.7
Graves	6.6	17.9	8.3	12.6	14.8	13.5	10.3	7.7	8.3	38.1	51.3
Grayson	6.3	18.2	9.0	13.0	15.0	13.8	10.7	8.0	6.0	37.5	50.5
Green	5.4	17.3	8.1	11.6	15.2	14.1	11.3	8.7	8.2	40.0	50.8
Greenup	5.8	17.8	7.9	12.4	15.5	14.7	11.3	8.5	6.1	39.2	51.9
Hancock	7.1	19.6	8.5	13.5	15.5	14.6	10.2	6.1	4.9	35.9	50.6
Hardin	7.2	20.4	10.6	14.2	17.3	12.7	7.9	5.6	4.0	33.5	49.5
Harlan	6.1	18.9	8.5	12.5	15.0	15.3	9.8	7.4	6.6	37.8	52.1
Harrison	6.3	18.7	8.2	13.7	16.1	13.9	9.7	7.0	6.4	37.1	51.3
Hart	6.6	19.2	8.6	12.6	15.6	13.2	10.3	7.7	6.2	36.9	50.8
Henderson	6.4	18.2	8.4	13.4	16.6	14.5	9.4	7.3	5.9	37.2	51.7
Henry	6.8	18.6	7.9	13.2	16.6	14.5	10.2	6.6	5.7	37.3	50.2
Hickman	5.4	16.7	6.9	11.9	14.7	13.8	12.1	8.7	9.7	40.9	52.3
Hopkins	6.1	18.0	8.3	12.8	15.4	14.4	10.2	7.5	7.2	38.3	52.4
Jackson	6.6	19.4	9.8	14.2	15.1	13.4	9.5	6.5	5.4	34.9	50.7
Jefferson	6.7	17.5	8.9	14.1	16.3	14.1	8.7	7.2	6.3	36.7	52.2
Jessamine	7.4	19.0	11.6	15.0	16.1	13.5	7.8	5.2	4.3	32.9	50.9
Johnson	6.1	17.9	8.8	13.4	15.4	15.4	10.3	7.1	5.5	37.4	51.8
Kenton	7.3	19.0	9.2	15.3	16.7	13.5	7.9	5.9	5.1	34.5	51.0
Knott	6.0	18.5	10.8	13.1	16.0	14.8	9.5	6.2	5.2	35.9	50.7
Knox	7.1	19.1	9.7	13.7	14.4	13.3	9.9	6.5	6.2	35.3	51.8
Larue	6.3	18.7	7.7	12.2	16.1	13.6	10.4	7.9	7.1	38.2	51.2
Laurel	7.1	18.3	9.2	14.5	16.0	13.9	9.6	6.7	4.8	35.5	51.1
Lawrence	5.9	19.4	8.8	13.8	14.9	14.4	10.4	7.0	5.5	36.5	50.7
Lee	5.2	17.5	9.0	14.7	15.7	13.8	9.9	7.9	6.4	37.4	47.8
Leslie	6.1	18.5	9.2	13.9	17.0	14.5	9.4	6.6	4.8	36.4	51.3
Letcher	5.7	18.0	9.2	12.6	16.1	15.4	10.4	7.1	5.5	37.9	51.1
Lewis	6.4	19.0	9.1	14.0	15.4	13.7	9.9	6.8	5.6	35.9	50.3
Lincoln	6.8	18.9	8.4	14.2	15.6	12.9	10.2	7.2	5.8	36.0	50.9
Livingston	5.3	17.1	7.5	12.5	15.7	14.9	12.1	8.2	6.7	39.8	50.6
Logan	6.8	18.8	8.4	12.9	15.6	13.4	10.2	7.2	6.6	37.0	51.8
Lyon	3.8	12.0	7.5	14.8	18.1	14.4	12.5	9.4	7.4	41.5	42.8
McCracken	6.1	17.3	7.9	12.4	15.7	14.8	9.9	8.1	7.9	39.2	52.5
McCreary	6.7	20.9	9.8	13.9	14.4	13.7	10.0	6.1	4.5	34.2	50.8
McLean	6.6	17.6	8.3	13.0	14.6	14.1	11.2	7.5	7.0	38.1	50.9
Madison	6.4	15.5	18.8	15.3	14.2	12.1	8.0	5.4	4.3	30.7	51.7
Magoffin	7.0	19.7	10.1	14.2	16.0	13.5	8.9	5.9	4.7	34.3	50.7
Marion	6.7	18.6	9.9	14.1	16.2	13.4	8.3	6.8	6.0	35.4	49.4
Marshall	5.1	16.7	7.5	11.7	15.3	14.2	12.1	9.4	8.1	40.9	51.0
Martin	7.0	21.1	9.5	13.5	15.8	14.8	8.5	5.8	3.9	34.1	50.5
Mason	6.3	17.8	8.0	13.0	15.4	14.6	9.3	8.1	7.4	38.1	51.6
Meade	8.7	21.0	9.1	15.4	17.3	12.3	8.0	5.1	3.0	32.2	49.9
Menifee	5.8	19.1	10.1	12.9	15.2	13.9	11.2	7.1	4.7	36.3	49.6
Mercer	6.4	18.0	7.4	13.2	15.9	14.1	10.4	7.7	6.9	38.2	51.5
Metcalfe	6.4	18.3	8.2	13.1	15.5	12.8	10.7	8.5	6.5	37.7	51.2
Monroe	6.3	17.6	8.9	12.5	15.2	13.2	11.1	8.3	7.0	38.2	51.5
Montgomery	7.0	17.9	8.7	14.7	15.4	14.2	9.2	6.9	6.0	36.0	51.4
Morgan	5.4	17.0	10.6	15.6	17.3	13.5	8.8	6.6	5.2	35.8	44.8
Muhlenberg	6.0	16.7	9.2	12.7	15.2	14.1	10.7	8.1	7.4	38.7	50.5
Nelson	7.4	20.3	8.7	13.8	17.0	13.8	8.5	5.9	4.7	34.9	50.8
Nicholas	6.2	17.4	8.3	13.2	15.1	14.0	10.5	7.7	7.6	38.4	51.6
Ohio	6.3	18.6	8.6	12.9	14.6	13.8	10.8	7.4	7.0	37.5	50.9
Oldham	6.6	20.8	6.9	12.5	20.6	16.8	8.7	4.2	2.9	36.7	46.7
Owen	6.1	19.5	8.4	12.2	15.7	14.0	10.1	7.5	6.5	37.5	49.9

Table B. States and Counties

	Population and population characteristics, 1990										Population—change, 1980-2000				
	Age (percent)										Total persons			Percent change	
STATE County	Under 5 years	5 to 17 years	18 to 24 years	25 to 34 years	35 to 44 years	45 to 54 years	55 to 64 years	65 to 74 years	75 years and over	Percent Female	2000	1990	1980	1990–2000	1980–1990
	39	40	41	42	43	44	45	46	47	48	49	50	51	52	53
KENTUCKY—Cont'd															
Cumberland	6.1	17.7	8.6	14.7	12.9	10.6	11.4	9.7	8.4	52.8	7 147	6 784	7 289	5.4	-6.9
Daviess	7.3	19.9	9.7	16.1	14.5	10.4	9.3	7.5	5.4	52.2	91 545	87 189	85 949	5.0	1.4
Edmonson	6.1	20.2	10.3	13.7	13.7	12.0	10.4	8.2	5.5	50.7	11 644	10 357	9 962	12.4	4.0
Elliott	7.0	22.1	10.3	15.2	14.1	10.4	8.4	6.8	5.7	50.4	6 748	6 455	6 908	4.5	-6.6
Estill	6.1	20.5	10.6	15.1	14.0	10.9	9.0	7.4	6.4	52.0	15 307	14 614	14 495	4.7	0.8
Fayotto	6.8	15.6	14.6	20.3	15.9	9.5	7.4	5.8	4.1	52.2	260 512	225 366	204 165	15.6	10.4
Fleming	6.3	19.0	10.0	15.0	13.9	10.6	9.6	8.5	7.0	51.0	13 792	12 292	12 323	12.2	-0.3
Floyd	7.1	21.7	10.2	15.8	15.3	10.0	8.3	6.8	4.7	51.2	42 441	43 586	48 764	-2.6	-10.6
Franklin	6.4	17.8	10.1	16.6	16.7	11.3	9.1	7.2	5.0	52.0	47 687	44 143	41 830	8.0	5.5
Fulton	6.2	18.8	8.9	13.5	12.6	9.7	9.9	10.6	9.8	54.2	7 752	8 271	8 971	-6.3	-7.8
Gallatin	7.6	20.8	9.4	15.3	14.9	11.1	8.3	7.0	5.5	50.4	7 870	5 393	4 842	45.9	11.4
Garrard	6.0	18.1	8.9	15.8	14.1	11.3	10.3	8.4	7.1	51.7	14 792	11 579	10 853	27.7	6.7
Grant	7.3	21.5	9.9	15.9	14.2	11.5	8.1	6.8	4.8	50.8	22 384	15 737	13 308	42.2	18.3
Graves	6.2	18.1	8.4	14.5	14.1	11.1	9.4	9.9	8.4	52.2	37 028	33 550	34 049	10.4	-1.5
Grayson	6.3	19.8	9.2	15.0	14.1	11.1	10.0	8.5	6.0	51.2	24 053	21 050	20 854	14.3	0.9
Green	5.6	17.6	8.4	14.9	13.7	11.3	10.6	9.9	8.0	51.4	11 518	10 371	11 043	11.1	-6.1
Greenup	5.7	19.9	9.0	14.5	15.9	12.5	10.3	7.6	4.6	51.7	36 891	36 796	39 132	0.3	-6.1
Hancock	7.2	22.0	9.2	15.5	16.2	11.3	8.2	6.2	4.2	49.9	8 392	7 864	7 742	6.7	1.6
Hardin	8.2	20.1	16.2	18.5	13.8	8.8	6.7	4.6	3.1	47.4	94 174	89 240	88 911	5.5	0.4
Harlan	7.0	21.8	9.9	15.2	15.1	9.8	8.4	7.6	5.3	51.8	33 202	36 574	41 889	-9.2	-12.7
Harrison	6.5	20.2	8.8	15.0	14.2	10.6	9.2	8.2	7.4	51.6	17 983	16 248	15 166	10.7	7.1
Hart	6.5	19.5	9.0	15.1	13.8	11.1	9.7	9.2	6.1	51.8	17 445	14 890	15 402	17.2	-3.3
Henderson	6.9	19.7	9.2	16.8	15.2	10.7	8.8	7.3	5.5	52.1	44 829	43 044	40 849	4.1	5.4
Henry	6.8	18.5	9.2	15.6	14.5	11.8	9.3	8.2	6.0	50.9	15 060	12 823	12 740	17.4	0.7
Hickman	6.2	16.9	7.7	14.3	13.1	11.0	9.9	10.4	10.5	52.8	5 262	5 566	6 065	-5.5	-8.2
Hopkins	6.7	19.4	8.9	15.5	15.2	10.7	8.9	8.1	6.6	52.0	46 519	46 126	46 174	0.9	-0.1
Jackson	7.0	21.6	10.1	15.3	14.3	10.0	8.4	7.5	5.7	50.6	13 495	11 955	11 996	12.9	-0.3
Jefferson	6.8	17.6	9.7	17.4	15.4	10.2	9.4	7.8	5.6	52.8	693 604	665 123	684 638	4.3	-2.9
Jessamine	7.4	20.0	12.2	18.2	16.1	10.2	7.2	5.2	3.5	51.0	39 041	30 508	26 065	28.0	17.0
Johnson	6.1	21.1	10.1	15.7	15.8	10.9	8.5	6.9	4.9	51.1	23 445	23 248	24 432	0.8	-4.8
Kenton	8.1	19.5	10.1	18.2	15.1	9.5	8.0	6.7	4.8	51.9	151 464	142 005	137 058	6.7	3.6
Knott	6.6	22.7	11.5	16.5	15.1	9.8	7.4	6.1	4.4	50.8	17 649	17 906	17 940	-1.4	-0.2
Knox	7.1	21.3	11.3	14.9	14.1	10.5	7.8	7.3	5.7	52.0	31 795	29 676	30 239	7.1	-1.9
Larue	6.1	18.9	8.1	15.2	14.1	11.7	9.9	9.0	7.1	51.2	13 373	11 679	11 922	14.5	-2.0
Laurel	6.7	20.9	10.2	16.5	15.2	10.5	8.6	6.6	4.8	51.0	52 715	43 438	38 982	21.4	11.4
Lawrence	6.5	21.8	9.7	15.0	14.5	10.6	8.9	7.4	5.6	50.7	15 569	13 998	14 121	11.2	-0.9
Lee	6.9	20.9	9.6	14.8	14.0	10.0	9.6	7.7	6.7	51.7	7 916	7 422	7 754	6.7	-4.3
Leslie	7.6	22.7	10.7	17.2	14.8	9.7	7.9	5.2	4.1	50.5	12 401	13 642	14 882	-9.1	-8.3
Letcher	6.2	22.5	9.6	16.0	15.3	10.3	8.4	6.9	4.8	51.5	25 277	27 000	30 687	-6.4	-12.0
Lewis	6.2	21.5	9.9	15.3	14.1	10.7	8.7	7.8	5.7	50.2	14 092	13 029	14 545	8.2	-10.4
Lincoln	6.8	19.8	9.8	15.5	13.8	10.7	9.3	8.3	5.9	50.7	23 361	20 096	19 053	16.2	5.2
Livingston	5.7	17.1	9.0	15.4	15.2	11.9	10.2	8.9	6.6	51.0	9 804	9 062	9 219	8.2	-1.7
Logan	6.5	19.8	8.7	15.3	13.8	11.4	9.5	8.4	6.7	51.9	26 573	24 416	24 138	8.8	1.2
Lyon	3.9	12.5	8.8	19.2	15.3	11.8	10.8	9.8	7.9	43.8	8 080	6 624	6 490	22.0	2.1
McCracken	6.2	18.1	8.2	15.6	15.1	10.7	9.8	9.0	7.2	53.0	65 514	62 879	61 310	4.2	2.6
McCreary	7.5	22.9	11.1	14.6	14.4	10.2	8.1	6.7	4.5	50.9	17 080	15 603	15 634	9.5	-0.2
McLean	6.1	18.9	9.4	14.0	14.9	11.8	9.2	8.7	7.0	50.8	9 938	9 628	10 090	3.2	-4.6
Madison	5.9	16.5	21.5	15.5	13.5	9.5	7.3	5.9	4.4	52.4	70 872	57 508	53 352	23.2	7.8
Magoffin	7.2	23.8	11.1	16.7	14.2	9.7	7.1	6.0	4.2	50.6	13 332	13 077	13 515	1.9	-3.2
Marion	6.5	20.9	10.3	16.7	14.4	9.6	8.6	7.0	6.0	50.1	18 212	16 499	17 910	10.4	-7.9
Marshall	5.9	17.3	7.7	14.4	14.2	12.0	11.2	9.9	7.4	51.2	30 125	27 205	25 637	10.7	6.1
Martin	7.6	24.2	10.7	16.8	15.5	9.3	7.3	5.3	3.4	51.0	12 578	12 526	13 925	0.4	-10.0
Mason	6.7	18.9	9.2	15.2	14.0	10.0	10.0	9.2	6.7	52.0	16 800	16 666	17 760	0.8	-6.2
Meade	10.1	23.0	9.8	22.5	13.3	8.3	6.2	4.2	2.7	50.3	26 349	24 170	22 854	9.0	5.8
Menifee	6.6	20.9	11.2	15.4	14.2	10.8	8.8	7.6	4.6	49.9	6 556	5 117	5 092	28.8	-0.5
Mercer	6.1	18.4	9.1	15.0	14.8	11.6	10.0	8.5	6.5	52.2	20 817	19 148	19 011	8.7	0.7
Metcalfe	6.2	18.5	9.6	15.0	13.4	11.2	10.4	8.8	6.9	52.1	10 037	8 963	9 484	12.0	-5.5
Monroe	6.1	18.7	8.9	15.1	13.6	11.6	9.9	8.5	7.6	52.2	11 756	11 401	12 353	3.1	-7.7
Montgomery	6.3	20.0	9.9	15.1	15.8	10.7	9.2	7.4	5.6	51.8	22 554	19 561	20 046	15.3	-2.4
Morgan	6.5	21.0	9.5	16.6	14.7	10.1	9.1	6.7	5.7	48.8	13 948	11 648	12 103	19.7	-3.8
Muhlenberg	6.1	19.6	9.9	14.6	14.4	10.9	9.3	8.5	6.7	51.8	31 839	31 318	32 238	1.7	-2.9
Nelson	7.4	21.7	9.7	17.1	15.0	9.9	7.9	6.4	4.8	51.4	37 477	29 710	27 584	26.1	7.7
Nicholas	5.8	19.7	8.8	14.4	14.3	11.2	9.9	9.0	7.0	51.6	6 813	6 725	7 157	1.3	-6.0
Ohio	6.7	20.4	8.6	14.3	14.1	11.2	9.2	8.4	7.0	51.9	22 916	21 105	21 765	8.6	-3.0
Oldham	6.5	22.1	8.2	17.0	20.5	12.4	6.5	4.1	2.6	47.9	46 178	33 263	27 795	38.8	19.7
Owen	6.2	20.5	8.2	15.1	14.1	10.6	9.9	8.5	6.9	50.3	10 547	9 035	8 924	16.7	1.2

Table B. States and Counties

STATE County		Household relationship, 2000														
		In households (percent)									In group quarters (percent)					
					Child		Other relatives		Nonrelatives			Institutionalized population			Noninstitutionalized population		
	Total population	Total in house-holds	House-holder	Spouse	Total	Own child under 18 years	Total	Under 18 years	Total	Unmar-ried partner	Total in group quarters	Correc-tional institu-tions	Nurs-ing homes	Other institu-tions	Col-lege dormi-tories	Mili-tary quar-ters	Other
	54	55	56	57	58	59	60	61	62	63	64	65	66	67	68	69	70
KENTUCKY—Cont'd																	
Cumberland	7 147	98.5	41.6	22.1	27.4	21.0	4.4	2.1	3.0	1.6	1.5	0.0	1.4	0.0	0.0	0.0	0.1
Daviess	91 545	97.2	39.4	21.1	29.9	23.4	3.3	1.6	3.5	1.7	2.8	0.2	1.0	0.3	0.5	0.0	0.9
Edmonson	11 644	98.6	39.9	24.8	27.6	21.3	3.6	1.5	2.7	1.4	1.4	0.0	0.8	0.0	0.0	0.0	0.6
Elliott	6 748	99.2	39.1	23.5	30.2	23.2	3.9	1.6	2.5	1.4	0.8	0.0	0.8	0.0	0.0	0.0	0.0
Estill	15 307	99.1	39.9	22.1	29.7	21.8	4.4	1.9	3.0	1.8	0.9	0.2	0.6	0.0	0.0	0.0	0.1
Fayette	260 512	95.1	41.6	18.1	24.2	19.4	3.8	1.4	7.5	2.2	4.9	1.1	0.5	0.1	2.6	0.0	0.5
Fleming	13 792	99.1	38.9	23.4	30.3	23.4	3.4	1.5	3.0	1.7	0.9	0.0	0.7	0.0	0.0	0.0	0.1
Floyd	42 441	97.5	39.8	22.5	29.2	21.7	4.1	1.6	2.0	1.2	2.5	1.6	0.4	0.1	0.0	0.0	0.4
Franklin	47 687	96.2	41.7	20.3	26.1	20.4	3.8	1.6	4.2	2.1	3.8	1.1	0.2	0.0	1.4	0.0	1.2
Fulton	7 752	96.7	41.8	18.5	28.0	21.5	5.8	3.2	2.6	1.6	3.3	2.4	0.8	0.0	0.0	0.0	0.1
Gallatin	7 870	98.7	36.9	21.4	31.6	25.8	4.4	2.0	4.4	2.7	1.3	0.0	1.3	0.0	0.0	0.0	0.0
Garrard	14 792	99.3	38.8	24.3	28.7	22.2	4.1	1.7	3.4	1.5	0.7	0.0	0.6	0.0	0.0	0.0	0.0
Grant	22 384	99.2	36.5	22.0	32.3	26.1	4.0	1.9	4.4	2.3	0.8	0.0	0.8	0.0	0.0	0.0	0.0
Graves	37 028	97.9	40.1	23.2	28.1	22.2	3.5	1.5	3.0	1.3	2.1	0.4	1.1	0.1	0.1	0.0	0.3
Grayson	24 053	98.7	39.9	23.5	28.6	22.3	3.3	1.5	3.3	1.8	1.3	0.6	0.7	0.0	0.0	0.0	0.0
Green	11 518	98.6	40.9	24.4	27.2	20.6	3.3	1.4	2.9	1.4	1.4	0.0	1.1	0.1	0.0	0.0	0.2
Greenup	36 891	98.8	39.4	24.6	28.8	21.6	3.7	1.5	2.3	1.2	1.2	0.3	0.9	0.0	0.0	0.0	0.0
Hancock	8 392	99.1	38.3	24.7	31.0	25.1	2.7	1.2	2.5	1.4	0.9	0.1	0.5	0.0	0.0	0.0	0.2
Hardin	94 174	95.8	36.6	21.2	31.2	25.3	3.4	1.5	3.4	1.7	4.2	0.6	0.5	0.2	0.0	2.8	0.1
Harlan	33 202	98.9	40.0	21.7	30.2	22.4	4.9	2.2	2.0	1.0	1.1	0.2	0.8	0.1	0.0	0.0	0.0
Harrison	17 983	98.7	39.0	22.6	29.3	22.6	4.1	1.9	3.7	2.0	1.3	0.0	1.3	0.0	0.0	0.0	0.0
Hart	17 445	98.6	38.8	22.0	30.1	23.1	4.3	2.1	3.3	1.8	1.4	0.6	0.8	0.0	0.0	0.0	0.0
Henderson	44 829	98.2	40.4	22.0	28.7	22.3	3.5	1.7	3.6	2.0	1.8	0.7	0.8	0.0	0.0	0.0	0.3
Henry	15 060	99.6	38.8	22.8	29.2	22.8	4.7	2.0	4.1	2.1	0.4	0.0	0.4	0.0	0.0	0.0	0.0
Hickman	5 262	97.1	41.6	23.5	26.4	20.2	3.6	1.6	2.1	1.1	2.9	0.6	2.3	0.0	0.0	0.0	0.0
Hopkins	46 519	98.3	40.5	22.8	28.3	21.9	3.9	1.7	2.9	1.5	1.7	0.3	1.2	0.0	0.0	0.0	0.2
Jackson	13 495	99.2	39.3	23.7	30.0	23.6	3.7	1.7	2.5	1.5	0.8	0.2	0.4	0.0	0.0	0.0	0.2
Jefferson	693 604	98.2	41.4	18.7	28.5	21.6	4.7	2.1	4.8	2.2	1.8	0.4	0.7	0.1	0.4	0.0	0.4
Jessamine	39 041	95.4	35.5	22.0	30.2	24.3	3.7	1.6	4.0	1.7	4.6	0.3	0.8	0.0	3.0	0.0	0.4
Johnson	23 445	97.8	38.8	23.5	28.9	21.7	4.2	1.8	2.4	1.3	2.2	0.5	0.5	0.0	0.0	0.0	1.2
Kenton	151 464	98.8	39.2	19.7	31.3	24.1	4.0	1.7	4.6	2.2	1.2	0.2	0.5	0.1	0.1	0.0	0.4
Knott	17 649	96.8	38.1	21.9	30.2	21.9	4.4	2.1	2.2	1.1	3.2	0.0	0.5	0.0	1.9	0.0	0.9
Knox	31 795	98.0	39.1	21.2	30.3	23.3	5.0	2.3	2.5	1.3	2.0	0.2	1.0	0.1	0.7	0.0	0.1
Larue	13 373	98.4	39.4	23.4	29.0	22.7	3.7	1.7	2.9	1.6	1.6	0.5	0.9	0.0	0.0	0.0	0.1
Laurel	52 715	98.7	38.6	23.4	29.8	23.3	4.1	1.9	2.8	1.5	1.3	0.6	0.6	0.0	0.0	0.0	0.0
Lawrence	15 569	99.1	38.2	23.4	30.6	22.9	4.2	1.8	2.7	1.2	0.9	0.0	0.9	0.0	0.0	0.0	0.9
Lee	7 916	91.0	37.7	20.7	27.3	20.7	3.3	1.6	2.0	1.2	9.0	7.5	1.5	0.0	0.0	0.0	0.0
Leslie	12 401	99.1	39.4	23.0	29.8	22.3	4.5	1.9	2.4	1.4	0.9	0.1	0.8	0.0	0.0	0.0	0.0
Letcher	25 277	99.1	39.9	23.3	29.8	21.5	4.1	1.8	2.1	1.1	0.9	0.1	0.7	0.0	0.0	0.0	0.0
Lewis	14 092	98.5	38.5	23.2	29.9	23.1	3.7	1.6	3.2	1.9	1.5	0.4	0.8	0.0	0.0	0.0	0.3
Lincoln	23 361	99.0	39.4	23.1	29.6	23.5	3.6	1.5	3.3	1.8	1.0	0.4	0.5	0.0	0.0	0.0	0.1
Livingston	9 804	98.6	40.8	24.6	26.7	20.2	3.6	1.7	2.9	1.6	1.4	0.2	1.1	0.0	0.0	0.0	0.1
Logan	26 573	98.8	39.5	22.6	29.3	23.0	4.1	2.0	3.3	1.5	1.2	0.4	0.6	0.0	0.0	0.0	0.2
Lyon	8 080	80.9	35.9	21.5	19.3	14.7	2.4	1.0	2.0	1.2	19.1	17.0	2.1	0.0	0.0	0.0	0.0
McCracken	65 514	98.0	42.3	21.6	27.2	21.3	3.4	1.5	3.3	1.6	2.0	0.7	1.1	0.1	0.0	0.0	0.2
McCreary	17 080	97.5	38.2	20.8	31.2	24.1	4.5	2.1	2.9	1.5	2.5	0.3	0.4	0.2	0.0	0.0	1.7
McLean	9 938	98.8	40.1	24.1	28.3	21.9	3.5	1.8	2.9	1.5	1.2	0.0	1.2	0.0	0.0	0.0	0.0
Madison	70 872	92.5	38.3	20.3	25.2	20.1	3.3	1.2	5.3	1.9	7.5	0.3	0.5	0.0	6.7	0.0	0.0
Magoffin	13 332	98.7	37.7	23.3	31.9	24.5	3.9	1.8	1.9	1.1	1.3	0.0	1.3	0.0	0.0	0.0	0.0
Marion	18 212	93.7	36.3	19.5	30.8	23.2	3.5	1.7	3.5	2.1	6.3	4.8	1.2	0.0	0.0	0.0	0.3
Marshall	30 125	98.1	41.2	25.3	26.4	20.2	2.9	1.1	2.3	1.2	1.9	0.6	1.2	0.0	0.0	0.0	0.1
Martin	12 578	99.3	38.0	22.6	32.5	25.6	3.8	1.9	2.4	1.4	0.7	0.0	0.0	0.0	0.0	0.0	0.7
Mason	16 800	98.0	40.8	22.1	27.9	22.0	3.6	1.5	3.6	2.0	2.0	0.7	1.1	0.0	0.0	0.0	0.2
Meade	26 349	99.6	35.9	23.0	33.4	27.3	3.9	1.9	3.3	1.8	0.4	0.1	0.2	0.0	0.0	0.0	0.1
Menifee	6 556	96.3	38.7	24.2	26.9	21.2	3.4	1.5	3.1	1.8	3.7	0.0	1.0	0.2	0.0	0.0	2.6
Mercer	20 817	99.3	40.5	23.4	28.5	22.2	4.0	1.6	3.0	1.5	0.7	0.0	0.5	0.0	0.0	0.0	0.2
Metcalfe	10 037	98.7	40.0	23.2	28.3	22.0	3.8	1.8	3.3	1.7	1.3	0.0	1.0	0.0	0.0	0.0	0.3
Monroe	11 756	98.9	40.3	23.2	28.2	21.4	4.3	1.9	2.9	1.3	1.1	0.1	1.0	0.0	0.0	0.0	0.0
Montgomery	22 554	98.2	39.5	22.8	28.5	22.5	3.9	1.7	3.6	2.0	1.8	0.6	0.8	0.0	0.0	0.0	0.3
Morgan	13 948	86.8	34.1	21.3	26.4	20.3	2.9	1.2	2.2	1.0	13.2	11.9	0.6	0.5	0.0	0.0	0.2
Muhlenberg	31 839	95.2	38.8	23.2	26.8	20.0	4.0	1.9	2.4	1.3	4.8	2.9	1.1	0.0	0.0	0.0	0.8
Nelson	37 477	98.1	37.2	21.2	32.9	25.6	3.0	1.4	3.8	2.2	1.9	0.3	0.9	0.0	0.0	0.0	0.7
Nicholas	6 813	98.5	39.8	22.9	27.5	20.9	4.5	2.0	3.8	1.8	1.5	0.0	1.5	0.0	0.0	0.0	0.0
Ohio	22 916	98.5	38.8	23.8	29.5	22.8	3.8	1.7	2.7	1.4	1.5	0.2	1.2	0.0	0.0	0.0	0.1
Oldham	46 178	91.6	32.2	23.0	31.7	26.0	2.7	1.1	2.0	1.1	8.4	7.6	0.5	0.2	0.0	0.0	0.2
Owen	10 547	99.0	38.7	23.5	29.8	23.4	3.5	1.6	3.4	2.0	1.0	0.0	1.0	0.1	0.0	0.0	0.0

Table B. States and Counties

STATE County	Households by type, 2000												Households, 1990		
	Family households						Nonfamily households								
			Married couple		Female householder¹			Householder living alone							
	Total households	Total	With own children under 18 years	Total	With own children under 18 years	Total	With own children under 18 years	Total	Total	65 years and over	Average household size	Average family size	Total households	Female householder¹	Householder living alone
	71	72	73	74	75	76	77	78	79	80	81	82	83	84	85
KENTUCKY—Cont'd															
Cumberland	2 976	68.5	29.4	53.0	21.4	11.2	5.8	31.5	28.9	14.5	2.37	2.89	2 714	12.7	24.0
Daviess	36 033	68.9	32.9	53.6	23.8	11.8	7.2	31.1	27.1	11.1	2.47	3.00	33 036	11.5	24.8
Edmonson	4 648	74.5	31.8	62.2	25.4	8.9	4.9	25.5	22.4	9.6	2.47	2.88	3 843	9.3	18.6
Elliott	2 638	73.0	33.4	60.0	26.6	9.7	5.3	27.0	24.7	11.0	2.54	3.02	2 324	12.0	19.3
Estill	6 108	72.6	32.3	55.4	23.0	12.9	7.2	27.4	24.6	10.7	2.48	2.94	5 357	12.9	20.5
Fayette	108 288	58.1	27.3	43.5	18.9	11.5	6.9	41.9	31.7	7.5	2.29	2.90	89 529	12.2	29.1
Fleming	5 367	73.9	34.8	60.3	27.2	9.6	5.4	26.1	23.3	11.0	2.55	2.99	4 626	9.0	22.6
Floyd	16 881	72.7	33.0	56.5	24.5	12.3	6.8	27.3	25.2	10.2	2.45	2.93	15 664	12.1	19.5
Franklin	19 907	64.5	29.5	48.7	20.3	12.2	7.3	35.5	30.4	10.6	2.30	2.86	17 385	12.0	27.0
Fulton	3 237	65.3	29.3	44.4	16.4	18.0	11.4	34.7	32.3	16.2	2.32	2.92	3 378	14.5	29.4
Gallatin	2 902	73.6	37.0	58.0	27.9	10.7	6.1	26.4	22.0	8.2	2.68	3.11	1 941	9.6	20.7
Garrard	5 741	75.5	33.4	62.6	26.3	9.4	5.4	24.5	21.1	9.5	2.56	2.95	4 435	9.8	20.0
Grant	8 175	76.1	39.6	60.1	29.5	11.1	7.2	23.9	19.8	8.2	2.72	3.10	5 585	9.5	19.5
Graves	14 841	71.2	31.5	58.9	23.6	10.0	6.2	28.8	26.2	12.7	2.44	2.92	13 377	8.8	24.8
Grayson	9 596	72.6	32.1	58.9	24.0	10.0	6.2	27.4	24.1	10.7	2.47	2.91	7 991	8.9	21.5
Green	4 706	71.8	29.9	59.7	23.0	8.5	4.9	28.2	25.4	13.2	2.41	2.87	4 089	8.0	22.4
Greenup	14 536	75.9	32.0	62.3	24.7	10.4	5.7	24.1	21.7	10.0	2.51	2.91	13 414	9.1	18.1
Hancock	3 215	75.8	36.4	64.4	29.2	8.3	5.3	24.2	21.2	8.9	2.59	3.01	2 795	7.9	17.6
Hardin	34 497	73.5	38.4	57.8	28.1	11.9	8.0	26.5	22.8	7.5	2.62	3.07	29 358	10.2	18.6
Harlan	13 291	71.1	32.2	54.3	24.0	13.2	6.7	28.9	27.0	12.6	2.47	3.00	13 269	13.3	21.9
Harrison	7 012	72.2	33.5	58.0	25.2	10.3	6.1	27.8	24.0	11.2	2.53	2.99	6 086	10.4	22.5
Hart	6 769	71.1	32.6	56.8	24.7	10.4	5.8	28.9	25.3	12.0	2.54	3.05	5 740	9.9	22.8
Henderson	18 095	69.5	32.4	54.4	23.3	11.6	7.1	30.5	26.4	10.6	2.43	2.93	16 558	11.4	23.5
Henry	5 844	74.1	33.8	58.7	24.7	10.4	6.2	25.9	22.0	9.9	2.57	2.97	4 896	9.8	21.8
Hickman	2 188	70.5	28.2	56.5	20.4	10.8	6.4	29.5	27.6	13.0	2.34	2.82	2 188	9.7	23.8
Hopkins	18 820	71.2	31.6	56.3	23.0	11.9	7.0	28.8	25.8	11.5	2.43	2.91	17 760	11.1	23.0
Jackson	5 307	74.5	35.5	60.2	27.7	10.3	5.7	25.5	23.0	9.3	2.52	2.96	4 381	10.6	20.2
Jefferson	287 012	63.8	29.6	45.2	19.0	14.7	8.7	36.2	30.5	10.3	2.37	2.97	264 138	14.5	27.5
Jessamine	13 867	76.9	38.8	61.9	29.6	11.1	7.0	23.1	18.5	6.5	2.69	3.05	10 601	10.1	16.6
Johnson	9 103	75.4	34.1	60.5	26.1	11.3	6.3	24.6	22.3	9.0	2.52	2.93	8 469	10.9	20.5
Kenton	59 444	66.4	33.4	50.1	24.2	12.1	7.1	33.6	27.8	9.0	2.52	3.11	52 690	12.2	25.2
Knott	6 717	74.3	34.4	57.6	25.8	12.6	6.6	25.7	23.6	9.3	2.54	3.00	6 086	12.6	18.2
Knox	12 416	72.0	34.4	54.3	24.8	13.6	7.4	28.0	25.7	10.6	2.51	3.01	10 718	14.8	20.9
Larue	5 275	73.3	32.5	59.2	24.4	10.5	6.2	26.7	23.7	11.2	2.49	2.94	4 503	9.0	22.4
Laurel	20 353	75.5	35.2	60.6	26.8	11.4	6.6	24.5	21.7	8.2	2.56	2.97	15 585	11.2	17.7
Lawrence	5 954	75.2	35.0	61.3	27.6	10.5	5.8	24.8	22.4	10.0	2.59	3.02	5 007	10.4	20.2
Lee	2 985	71.1	32.6	54.8	23.6	12.8	7.0	28.9	26.6	11.8	2.41	2.91	2 760	12.1	21.7
Leslie	4 885	75.1	35.5	58.3	26.7	12.9	6.6	24.9	22.4	8.7	2.52	2.94	4 711	12.7	16.0
Letcher	10 085	74.0	32.3	58.4	24.9	11.5	5.5	26.0	24.1	10.1	2.48	2.94	9 731	11.8	19.7
Lewis	5 422	74.7	35.1	60.4	27.0	9.7	5.4	25.3	22.5	10.0	2.56	2.98	4 713	9.7	19.7
Lincoln	9 206	73.1	33.7	58.6	25.3	10.3	5.9	26.9	23.6	10.5	2.51	2.95	7 431	9.7	20.2
Livingston	3 996	72.4	29.5	60.4	23.6	7.9	4.0	27.6	24.4	11.0	2.42	2.86	3 593	7.5	22.7
Logan	10 506	72.1	33.3	57.2	24.7	11.2	6.4	27.9	25.0	11.4	2.50	2.96	9 302	9.9	23.0
Lyon	2 898	70.5	25.1	59.2	18.9	8.1	4.8	29.5	26.8	12.2	2.26	2.70	2 355	7.3	27.2
McCracken	27 736	66.5	29.6	51.1	20.3	12.2	7.5	33.5	29.7	12.3	2.31	2.86	25 625	11.7	27.0
McCreary	6 520	72.9	35.7	54.5	25.0	13.8	8.0	27.1	24.7	8.4	2.55	3.03	5 479	14.4	20.1
McLean	3 984	72.3	32.3	60.0	25.0	8.7	5.2	27.7	24.7	11.4	2.47	2.93	3 672	8.2	21.6
Madison	27 152	67.1	31.5	53.1	23.1	10.7	6.7	32.9	25.2	7.6	2.42	2.90	20 012	10.6	21.8
Magoffin	5 024	76.8	37.5	61.9	29.7	11.2	5.9	23.2	21.4	8.2	2.62	3.04	4 440	10.5	16.8
Marion	6 613	71.9	35.6	53.8	25.0	13.7	8.2	28.1	24.4	10.1	2.58	3.06	5 688	12.7	21.3
Marshall	12 412	72.5	29.2	61.4	22.8	7.9	4.7	27.5	25.0	11.9	2.38	2.83	10 789	6.9	21.5
Martin	4 776	75.8	39.2	59.5	29.4	12.5	7.5	24.2	21.8	8.3	2.62	3.05	4 300	12.2	16.6
Mason	6 847	68.6	31.3	54.2	23.3	11.1	6.3	31.4	27.6	12.8	2.41	2.92	6 537	11.5	25.3
Meade	9 470	78.1	42.2	64.1	33.2	9.7	6.3	21.9	18.4	6.5	2.77	3.15	8 080	7.9	14.4
Menifee	2 537	74.9	32.0	62.4	24.8	8.8	5.2	25.1	22.1	9.1	2.49	2.88	1 842	9.6	19.8
Mercer	8 423	71.7	31.8	58.0	24.1	10.4	5.9	28.3	25.1	11.6	2.45	2.93	7 413	9.9	22.1
Metcalfe	4 016	71.8	32.3	58.1	24.6	10.0	5.4	28.2	25.2	12.3	2.47	2.93	3 433	8.9	22.0
Monroe	4 741	71.3	31.1	57.4	24.1	10.4	5.3	28.7	26.3	12.6	2.45	2.94	4 505	10.1	23.9
Montgomery	8 902	72.3	33.6	57.7	24.9	11.2	6.8	27.7	23.9	10.5	2.49	2.93	7 312	10.8	20.9
Morgan	4 752	75.1	34.8	62.4	27.8	9.2	5.0	24.9	22.6	10.3	2.55	2.97	4 089	9.4	19.6
Muhlenberg	12 357	73.3	30.7	59.7	23.9	10.4	5.3	26.7	24.3	12.6	2.45	2.90	11 683	9.9	21.5
Nelson	13 953	73.6	38.0	56.9	27.5	12.1	7.7	26.4	22.3	7.5	2.64	3.08	10 417	11.8	19.7
Nicholas	2 710	72.0	31.5	57.5	23.6	10.0	5.2	28.0	24.6	12.0	2.48	2.92	2 621	9.4	23.9
Ohio	8 899	74.0	33.0	61.2	26.1	9.2	5.0	26.0	23.2	11.1	2.54	2.98	7 816	8.3	20.8
Oldham	14 856	82.1	44.1	71.5	37.6	7.8	4.8	17.9	14.9	4.8	2.85	3.17	10 673	8.5	13.8
Owen	4 086	73.3	33.4	60.7	25.9	8.0	4.6	26.7	23.1	10.7	2.55	3.00	3 412	8.2	22.8

¹No spouse present.

Table B. States and Counties

STATE County	Percent change of households, 1990–2000	Total housing units	Occupied housing units (percent)	Vacant housing units — Total	For seasonal, recreational, or occasional use	Homeowner vacancy rate (percent)	Rental vacancy rate (percent)	Occupied housing units — Total	Percent owner-occupied housing units	Percent renter-occupied housing units	Average household size of owner-occupied units	Average household size of renter-occupied units
	86	87	88	89	90	91	92	93	94	95	96	97
KENTUCKY—Cont'd												
Cumberland	9.7	3 567	83.4	16.6	5.5	2.2	9.0	2 976	77.6	22.4	2.38	2.30
Daviess	9.1	38 432	93.8	6.2	0.4	1.7	7.0	36 033	70.3	29.7	2.57	2.22
Edmonson	20.9	6 104	76.1	23.9	17.8	1.6	8.3	4 648	85.6	14.4	2.50	2.30
Elliott	13.5	3 107	84.9	15.1	2.0	2.0	7.0	2 638	82.3	17.7	2.56	2.40
Estill	14.0	6 824	89.5	10.5	1.5	1.7	10.4	6 108	74.0	26.0	2.53	2.34
Fayette	21.0	116 167	93.2	6.8	0.8	1.1	8.4	108 288	55.3	44.7	2.47	2.07
Fleming	16.0	6 120	87.7	12.3	2.7	1.9	7.1	5 367	78.9	21.1	2.57	2.47
Floyd	7.8	18 551	91.0	9.0	0.8	1.4	9.1	16 881	76.3	23.7	2.48	2.36
Franklin	14.5	21 409	93.0	7.0	0.6	1.4	9.5	19 907	64.8	35.2	2.42	2.09
Fulton	-4.2	3 697	87.6	12.4	0.3	3.0	17.4	3 237	64.3	35.7	2.38	2.21
Gallatin	49.5	3 362	86.3	13.7	5.1	3.6	8.8	2 902	76.8	23.2	2.78	2.32
Garrard	29.4	6 414	89.5	10.5	1.8	2.4	10.5	5 741	76.4	23.6	2.58	2.49
Grant	46.4	9 306	87.8	12.2	4.8	2.3	7.5	8 175	74.2	25.8	2.77	2.55
Graves	10.9	16 340	90.8	9.2	0.6	2.1	11.4	14 841	77.9	22.1	2.48	2.31
Grayson	20.1	12 802	75.0	25.0	17.0	1.9	10.4	9 596	77.3	22.7	2.51	2.34
Green	15.1	5 420	86.8	13.2	0.8	1.9	12.1	4 706	78.2	21.8	2.47	2.22
Greenup	8.4	15 977	91.0	9.0	1.3	2.0	9.0	14 536	81.6	18.4	2.54	2.36
Hancock	15.0	3 600	89.3	10.7	1.5	1.6	18.2	3 215	82.4	17.6	2.64	2.35
Hardin	17.5	37 673	91.6	8.4	0.5	2.4	9.4	34 497	66.9	33.1	2.66	2.52
Harlan	0.2	15 017	88.5	11.5	0.8	2.0	11.7	13 291	73.5	26.5	2.52	2.33
Harrison	15.2	7 660	91.5	8.5	1.2	1.9	6.8	7 012	70.5	29.5	2.61	2.35
Hart	17.9	8 045	84.1	15.9	4.5	2.2	12.3	6 769	77.3	22.7	2.59	2.38
Henderson	9.3	19 466	93.0	7.0	0.5	1.4	7.0	18 095	67.3	32.7	2.55	2.19
Henry	19.4	6 381	91.6	8.4	1.8	1.9	5.6	5 844	77.6	22.4	2.56	2.58
Hickman	0.0	2 436	89.8	10.2	1.0	1.8	6.7	2 188	81.4	18.6	2.36	2.25
Hopkins	6.0	20 668	91.1	8.9	0.6	2.2	10.1	18 820	74.7	25.3	2.48	2.29
Jackson	21.1	6 065	87.5	12.5	2.0	1.6	7.9	5 307	80.1	19.9	2.55	2.40
Jefferson	8.7	305 835	93.8	6.2	0.4	1.5	7.6	287 012	64.9	35.1	2.50	2.14
Jessamine	30.8	14 646	94.7	5.3	0.4	1.8	5.2	13 867	67.1	32.9	2.71	2.63
Johnson	7.5	10 236	88.9	11.1	1.0	1.6	10.5	9 103	76.5	23.5	2.56	2.37
Kenton	12.8	63 571	93.5	6.5	0.4	1.7	8.3	59 444	66.4	33.6	2.72	2.11
Knott	10.4	7 579	88.6	11.4	1.3	1.6	10.3	6 717	79.6	20.4	2.56	2.48
Knox	15.8	13 999	88.7	11.3	0.6	1.7	12.5	12 416	71.4	28.6	2.57	2.36
Larue	17.1	5 860	90.0	10.0	0.9	1.7	6.2	5 275	80.2	19.8	2.54	2.33
Laurel	30.6	22 317	91.2	8.8	0.9	1.9	9.1	20 353	77.0	23.0	2.61	2.39
Lawrence	18.9	7 040	84.6	15.4	4.5	1.9	11.1	5 954	78.1	21.9	2.62	2.48
Lee	8.2	3 321	89.9	10.1	1.8	0.7	6.3	2 985	76.6	23.4	2.46	2.27
Leslie	3.7	5 502	88.8	11.2	1.4	1.3	13.3	4 885	82.3	17.7	2.55	2.36
Letcher	3.6	11 405	88.4	11.6	0.9	2.4	9.0	10 085	80.9	19.1	2.50	2.40
Lewis	15.0	6 173	87.8	12.2	4.2	2.1	5.2	5 422	81.2	18.8	2.57	2.51
Lincoln	23.9	10 127	90.9	9.1	0.8	2.1	8.2	9 206	78.9	21.1	2.54	2.41
Livingston	11.2	4 772	83.7	16.3	5.1	1.8	9.2	3 996	85.2	14.8	2.44	2.28
Logan	12.9	11 875	88.5	11.5	2.3	2.2	12.1	10 506	75.2	24.8	2.54	2.39
Lyon	23.1	4 189	69.2	30.8	22.8	3.8	12.7	2 898	81.8	18.2	2.29	2.11
McCracken	8.2	30 361	91.4	8.6	0.4	2.3	10.7	27 736	68.7	31.3	2.41	2.10
McCreary	19.0	7 405	88.0	12.0	2.2	1.8	10.7	6 520	75.7	24.3	2.59	2.44
McLean	8.5	4 392	90.7	9.3	1.8	1.7	6.4	3 984	80.3	19.7	2.49	2.37
Madison	35.7	29 595	91.7	8.3	0.4	2.4	9.4	27 152	59.7	40.3	2.56	2.20
Magoffin	13.2	5 447	92.2	7.8	1.0	0.7	5.1	5 024	82.0	18.0	2.66	2.45
Marion	16.3	7 277	90.9	9.1	1.0	1.9	10.3	6 613	78.1	21.9	2.64	2.38
Marshall	15.0	14 730	84.3	15.7	8.7	1.9	12.0	12 412	82.6	17.4	2.42	2.19
Martin	11.1	5 551	86.0	14.0	1.2	2.8	12.1	4 776	79.4	20.6	2.66	2.45
Mason	4.7	7 754	88.3	11.7	0.9	2.8	12.4	6 847	67.4	32.6	2.45	2.32
Meade	17.2	10 293	92.0	8.0	1.1	2.0	6.6	9 470	73.8	26.2	2.77	2.77
Menifee	37.7	3 710	68.4	31.6	24.0	2.3	6.0	2 537	81.4	18.6	2.51	2.40
Mercer	13.6	9 289	90.7	9.3	3.4	1.6	7.9	8 423	74.6	25.4	2.47	2.41
Metcalfe	17.0	4 592	87.5	12.5	1.4	2.9	7.0	4 016	79.3	20.7	2.49	2.40
Monroe	5.2	5 288	89.7	10.3	1.3	1.4	9.3	4 741	75.2	24.8	2.48	2.36
Montgomery	21.7	9 682	91.9	8.1	0.3	1.9	8.6	8 902	71.4	28.6	2.53	2.38
Morgan	16.2	5 487	86.6	13.4	2.8	1.7	8.0	4 752	79.8	20.2	2.60	2.34
Muhlenberg	5.8	13 675	90.4	9.6	0.8	1.9	10.4	12 357	82.8	17.2	2.48	2.30
Nelson	33.9	14 934	93.4	6.6	0.9	1.5	8.2	13 953	78.0	22.0	2.69	2.43
Nicholas	3.4	3 051	88.8	11.2	1.6	1.3	11.4	2 710	74.7	25.3	2.51	2.37
Ohio	13.9	9 909	89.8	10.2	1.8	1.5	8.7	8 899	80.3	19.7	2.57	2.39
Oldham	39.2	15 541	95.6	4.4	1.1	1.7	4.4	14 856	86.9	13.1	2.92	2.39
Owen	19.8	5 345	76.4	23.6	13.2	3.7	8.9	4 086	78.3	21.7	2.58	2.47

Table B. States and Counties

STATE/ County code	MSA/ PMSA/ NECMA code[1]	County type[2]	STATE County	Land area, 2000[3] (sq km)	Total persons	Rank	Per square kilometer	Land area, 1990[3] (sq km)	Total persons	Rank	Per square kilometer	White	Black or African American	American Indian or Alaska Native	Asian	Native Hawaiian and other Pacific Islander	Some other race
				Population, 2000				Population, 1990				Population and population characteristics, 2000 — Race (percent) — One race					
				1	2	3	4	5	6	7	8	9	10	11	12	13	14
			KENTUCKY—Cont'd														
21 189	...	9	Owsley	513	4 858	2 857	9.5	513	5 036	2 840	9.8	99.2	0.1	0.1	0.0	0.0	0.0
21 191	1640	1	Pendleton	727	14 390	2 133	19.8	725	12 062	2 213	16.6	98.4	0.5	0.2	0.1	0.0	0.4
21 193	...	7	Perry	886	29 390	1 417	33.2	886	30 283	1 280	34.2	97.3	1.6	0.1	0.5	0.0	0.0
21 195	...	7	Pike	2 040	68 736	716	33.7	2 040	72 584	616	35.6	98.3	0.5	0.1	0.4	0.0	0.1
21 197	...	6	Powell	467	13 237	2 210	28.3	467	11 686	2 236	25.0	98.6	0.6	0.1	0.1	0.0	0.1
21 199	...	7	Pulaski	1 714	56 217	841	32.8	1 714	49 489	849	28.9	97.5	1.1	0.2	0.4	0.0	0.2
21 201	...	9	Robertson	259	2 266	3 044	8.7	259	2 124	3 060	8.2	98.6	0.0	0.0	0.0	0.0	0.2
21 203	...	6	Rockcastle	822	16 582	1 984	20.2	822	14 803	2 000	18.0	98.8	0.1	0.2	0.1	0.0	0.0
21 205	...	7	Rowan	727	22 094	1 688	30.4	727	20 353	1 658	28.0	96.0	1.6	0.2	0.9	0.0	0.4
21 207	...	9	Russell	657	16 315	2 002	24.8	657	14 716	2 005	22.4	98.3	0.6	0.1	0.1	0.0	0.2
21 209	4280	2	Scott	737	33 061	1 317	44.9	739	23 867	1 496	32.3	91.9	5.4	0.3	0.5	0.0	0.8
21 211	...	6	Shelby	995	33 337	1 304	33.5	995	24 824	1 467	24.9	86.6	8.8	0.3	0.4	0.1	2.4
21 213	...	6	Simpson	612	16 405	1 997	26.8	612	15 145	1 976	24.7	87.8	10.2	0.2	0.5	0.1	0.3
21 215	...	7	Spencer	481	11 766	2 311	24.5	482	6 801	2 675	14.1	97.5	1.1	0.2	0.1	0.0	0.3
21 217	...	7	Taylor	699	22 927	1 646	32.8	699	21 146	1 622	30.3	93.6	5.1	0.1	0.2	0.0	0.3
21 219	...	8	Todd	975	11 971	2 296	12.3	975	10 940	2 298	11.2	89.3	8.8	0.2	0.2	0.0	0.9
21 221	...	8	Trigg	1 148	12 597	2 256	11.0	1 148	10 361	2 352	9.0	88.3	9.8	0.2	0.3	0.0	0.2
21 223	...	8	Trimble	386	8 125	2 596	21.0	386	6 090	2 745	15.8	97.9	0.3	0.4	0.1	0.0	0.7
21 225	...	6	Union	894	15 637	2 046	17.5	894	16 557	1 884	18.5	85.0	12.9	0.2	0.1	0.0	0.4
21 227	...	5	Warren	1 412	92 522	551	65.5	1 412	77 720	583	55.0	87.0	8.6	0.2	1.4	0.1	1.3
21 229	...	7	Washington	779	10 916	2 373	14.0	779	10 441	2 344	13.4	90.6	7.5	0.2	0.3	0.0	0.6
21 231	...	7	Wayne	1 190	19 923	1 796	16.7	1 190	17 468	1 823	14.7	97.0	1.5	0.2	0.1	0.0	0.5
21 233	...	6	Webster	867	14 120	2 152	16.3	867	13 955	2 060	16.1	93.6	4.7	0.1	0.1	0.1	0.8
21 235	...	7	Whitley	1 140	35 865	1 224	31.5	1 140	33 326	1 182	29.2	98.4	0.3	0.1	0.2	0.0	0.1
21 237	...	9	Wolfe	577	7 065	2 679	12.2	577	6 503	2 710	11.3	99.2	0.2	0.1	0.0	0.0	0.1
21 239	4280	2	Woodford	494	23 208	1 632	47.0	494	19 955	1 680	40.4	92.1	5.4	0.1	0.3	0.0	1.1
22 000	...		LOUISIANA	112 825	4 468 976	X	39.6	112 836	4 221 826	X	37.4	63.9	32.5	0.6	1.2	0.0	0.7
22 001	3880	2	Acadia	1 697	58 861	813	34.7	1 697	55 882	775	32.9	80.7	18.2	0.2	0.2	0.0	0.2
22 003	...	6	Allen	1 980	25 440	1 544	12.8	1 980	21 226	1 619	10.7	71.9	24.6	1.7	0.6	0.0	0.2
22 005	0760	2	Ascension	755	76 627	656	101.5	755	58 214	745	77.1	77.4	20.3	0.3	0.3	0.0	1.0
22 007	...	6	Assumption	877	23 388	1 624	26.7	877	22 753	1 545	25.9	67.2	31.5	0.3	0.2	0.0	0.2
22 009	...	6	Avoyelles	2 156	41 481	1 067	19.2	2 156	39 159	1 020	18.2	68.5	29.5	1.0	0.2	0.0	0.3
22 011	...	6	Beauregard	3 005	32 986	1 320	11.0	3 005	30 083	1 293	10.0	84.2	12.9	0.7	0.6	0.0	0.3
22 013	...	6	Bienville	2 100	15 752	2 036	7.5	2 100	16 232	1 912	7.7	54.9	43.8	0.3	0.2	0.0	0.3
22 015	7680	2	Bossier	2 174	98 310	530	45.2	2 172	86 088	531	39.6	74.7	20.8	0.5	1.3	0.1	1.0
22 017	7680	2	Caddo	2 284	252 161	224	110.4	2 285	248 253	201	108.6	52.9	44.6	0.4	0.7	0.0	0.4
22 019	3960	3	Calcasieu	2 774	183 577	297	66.2	2 774	168 134	285	60.6	73.6	24.0	0.3	0.6	0.0	0.4
22 021	...	8	Caldwell	1 371	10 560	2 393	7.7	1 371	9 806	2 403	7.2	80.4	17.9	0.5	0.1	0.0	0.5
22 023	...	8	Cameron	3 401	9 991	2 446	2.9	3 401	9 260	2 448	2.7	93.7	3.9	0.4	0.4	0.0	0.9
22 025	...	7	Catahoula	1 822	10 920	2 372	6.0	1 823	11 065	2 286	6.1	71.8	27.1	0.2	0.1	0.0	0.2
22 027	...	6	Claiborne	1 955	16 851	1 964	8.6	1 954	17 405	1 828	8.9	51.7	47.4	0.1	0.1	0.0	0.1
22 029	...	7	Concordia	1 802	20 247	1 777	11.2	1 804	20 828	1 639	11.5	60.7	37.7	0.2	0.2	0.0	0.5
22 031	...	6	De Soto	2 272	25 494	1 540	11.2	2 272	25 668	1 436	11.3	56.0	42.2	0.5	0.1	0.1	0.5
22 033	0760	2	East Baton Rouge	1 180	412 852	145	349.9	1 180	380 105	132	322.1	56.2	40.1	0.2	2.1	0.0	0.5
22 035	...	7	East Carroll	1 092	9 421	2 493	8.6	1 092	9 709	2 411	8.9	31.6	67.3	0.2	0.3	0.0	0.3
22 037	...	6	East Feliciana	1 174	21 360	1 720	18.2	1 174	19 211	1 720	16.4	51.8	47.1	0.2	0.2	0.0	0.2
22 039	...	7	Evangeline	1 720	35 434	1 237	20.6	1 721	33 274	1 184	19.3	70.4	28.6	0.2	0.1	0.0	0.2
22 041	...	7	Franklin	1 615	21 263	1 722	13.2	1 615	22 387	1 560	13.9	67.2	31.6	0.3	0.2	0.0	0.1
22 043	...	8	Grant	1 671	18 698	1 861	11.2	1 671	17 526	1 818	10.5	85.4	11.9	0.9	0.1	0.0	0.4
22 045	...	4	Iberia	1 490	73 266	684	49.2	1 490	68 297	647	45.8	65.1	30.8	0.3	1.9	0.0	0.6
22 047	...	6	Iberville	1 602	33 320	1 305	20.8	1 602	31 049	1 244	19.4	49.3	49.7	0.2	0.3	0.0	0.1
22 049	...	6	Jackson	1 476	15 397	2 059	10.4	1 476	15 859	1 932	10.7	71.0	27.9	0.3	0.2	0.0	0.2
22 051	5560	0	Jefferson	794	455 466	128	573.6	792	448 306	110	566.0	69.8	22.9	0.4	3.1	0.0	2.0
22 053	...	6	Jefferson Davis	1 689	31 435	1 362	18.6	1 690	30 722	1 257	18.2	80.6	17.8	0.4	0.2	0.0	0.2
22 055	3880	2	Lafayette	699	190 503	288	272.5	699	164 762	290	235.7	73.4	23.8	0.3	1.1	0.0	0.5
22 057	3350	3	Lafourche	2 809	89 974	574	32.0	2 810	85 860	535	30.6	82.9	12.6	2.3	0.7	0.0	0.6
22 059	...	7	La Salle	1 616	14 282	2 142	8.8	1 616	13 662	2 084	8.5	86.1	12.2	0.6	0.2	0.0	0.2
22 061	...	4	Lincoln	1 221	42 509	1 046	34.8	1 221	41 745	963	34.2	57.4	39.8	0.2	1.3	0.0	0.5
22 063	0760	2	Livingston	1 678	91 814	558	54.7	1 678	70 523	629	42.0	94.3	4.2	0.4	0.2	0.0	0.2
22 065	...	7	Madison	1 616	13 728	2 179	8.5	1 617	12 463	2 184	7.7	37.9	60.3	0.2	0.2	0.0	0.3
22 067	...	6	Morehouse	2 057	31 021	1 377	15.1	2 057	31 938	1 214	15.5	55.8	43.4	0.1	0.2	0.0	0.1
22 069	...	6	Natchitoches	3 252	39 080	1 135	12.0	3 254	37 254	1 065	11.4	57.9	38.4	1.1	0.4	0.0	0.9
22 071	5560	0	Orleans	468	484 674	117	1 035.6	468	496 938	98	1 061.8	28.1	67.3	0.2	2.3	0.0	0.9
22 073	5200	3	Ouachita	1 581	147 250	368	93.1	1 582	142 191	334	89.9	64.5	33.6	0.2	0.6	0.0	0.3
22 075	5560	1	Plaquemines	2 187	26 757	1 492	12.2	2 188	25 575	1 440	11.7	69.8	23.4	2.1	2.6	0.0	0.7

[1]MSA = Metropolitan Statistical Area. PMSA = Primary MSA. NECMA = New England County Metropolitan Area. See Appendix A for explanation of these concepts. See Appendix B for list of metropolitan areas identified by type, with component counties.
[2]County typology code from the Economic Research Service of USDA. See Appendix A for definition.
[3]Dry land or land partially or temporarily covered by water.

Table B. States and Counties

	Population and population characteristics, 2000 (cont'd)								Population and population characteristics, 1990				
	Race (percent) (cont'd)								Race (percent)				
	Race alone or in combination												
STATE County	Two or more races	White	Black	American Indian or Alaska Native	Asian	Native Hawaiian and other Pacific Islander	Some other race	Hispanic¹	White	Black or African American	American Indian or Alaska Native	Asian and Pacific Islander	Hispanic¹
	15	16	17	18	19	20	21	22	23	24	25	26	27
KENTUCKY—Cont'd													
Owsley	0.5	99.0	0.2	0.3	0.1	0.0	0.2	0.7	99.6	0.3	0.1	0.0	0.3
Pendleton	0.4	98.8	0.5	0.4	0.2	0.0	0.4	0.7	99.3	0.4	0.2	0.1	0.2
Perry	0.4	97.7	1.8	0.3	0.5	0.0	0.1	0.5	97.9	1.7	0.1	0.2	0.2
Pike	0.6	98.9	0.5	0.4	0.5	0.1	0.2	0.7	99.3	0.4	0.1	0.2	0.3
Powell	0.6	99.1	0.7	0.5	0.2	0.0	0.1	0.7	99.0	0.7	0.1	0.1	0.4
Pulaski	0.7	98.1	1.2	0.6	0.4	0.0	0.3	0.8	98.3	1.2	0.2	0.2	0.4
Robertson	1.1	99.2	0.1	0.4	0.0	0.5	0.8	0.9	99.8	0.2	0.0	0.0	0.2
Rockcastle	0.6	99.4	0.2	0.8	0.2	0.0	0.1	0.6	99.7	0.0	0.1	0.1	0.4
Rowan	1.0	96.9	1.8	0.7	1.1	0.1	0.5	1.1	97.7	1.5	0.2	0.5	0.4
Russell	0.6	98.9	0.7	0.5	0.2	0.0	0.3	0.9	99.2	0.6	0.1	0.0	0.3
Scott	1.1	93.0	5.7	0.6	0.7	0.0	1.1	1.6	93.0	6.3	0.1	0.4	0.4
Shelby	1.3	87.8	9.4	0.7	0.5	0.2	2.8	4.5	89.5	9.9	0.1	0.4	0.4
Simpson	0.9	88.7	10.7	0.4	0.6	0.1	0.4	0.9	88.6	11.0	0.2	0.2	0.3
Spencer	0.8	98.3	1.4	0.7	0.1	0.1	0.3	1.1	98.1	1.7	0.0	0.2	0.1
Taylor	0.7	94.2	5.4	0.4	0.2	0.0	0.5	0.8	94.7	5.1	0.1	0.1	0.2
Todd	0.7	89.9	9.0	0.4	0.4	0.1	1.1	1.7	88.6	11.0	0.2	0.1	0.5
Trigg	1.2	89.4	10.2	0.8	0.3	0.0	0.5	0.9	87.8	11.8	0.1	0.1	0.3
Trimble	0.7	98.5	0.4	0.8	0.2	0.0	0.8	1.4	99.6	0.0	0.3	0.0	0.5
Union	1.4	85.9	13.6	0.7	0.3	0.1	0.8	1.6	84.0	15.4	0.2	0.3	0.7
Warren	1.4	88.3	9.0	0.6	1.6	0.2	1.8	2.7	90.7	8.2	0.1	0.8	0.6
Washington	0.8	91.4	7.9	0.5	0.5	0.0	0.7	1.6	90.8	8.7	0.1	0.2	0.5
Wayne	0.8	97.7	1.7	0.7	0.1	0.0	0.6	1.5	97.9	1.8	0.2	0.0	0.3
Webster	0.7	94.2	4.9	0.4	0.1	0.1	0.9	1.9	93.9	5.6	0.2	0.2	0.2
Whitley	0.8	99.1	0.5	0.7	0.3	0.1	0.2	0.7	99.0	0.6	0.2	0.2	0.3
Wolfe	0.3	99.6	0.3	0.3	0.0	0.0	0.1	0.5	99.7	0.1	0.1	0.0	0.1
Woodford	0.9	92.9	5.8	0.5	0.4	0.0	1.2	3.0	93.0	6.5	0.1	0.1	0.5
LOUISIANA	1.1	64.8	32.9	1.0	1.4	0.1	1.1	2.4	67.3	30.8	0.4	1.0	2.2
Acadia	0.5	81.2	18.4	0.4	0.2	0.0	0.3	0.9	81.5	18.2	0.1	0.1	0.7
Allen	1.0	72.7	24.9	2.3	0.7	0.1	0.5	4.5	76.8	21.2	1.4	0.2	3.2
Ascension	0.7	78.0	20.5	0.5	0.4	0.0	1.3	2.5	76.4	22.8	0.2	0.3	1.6
Assumption	0.6	67.7	31.7	0.5	0.3	0.0	0.4	1.2	67.1	32.3	0.2	0.3	1.3
Avoyelles	0.7	69.0	29.8	1.4	0.2	0.0	0.4	1.0	72.3	27.0	0.3	0.1	1.6
Beauregard	1.2	85.3	13.3	1.3	0.8	0.1	0.6	1.4	83.9	14.9	0.4	0.5	1.4
Bienville	0.6	55.3	44.0	0.5	0.3	0.0	0.4	0.9	56.2	43.5	0.1	0.1	0.5
Bossier	1.7	76.1	21.3	1.1	1.7	0.1	1.4	3.1	77.9	20.2	0.4	1.1	2.1
Caddo	1.0	53.6	45.0	0.8	0.9	0.1	0.7	1.5	59.0	40.1	0.2	0.4	1.0
Calcasieu	1.0	74.5	24.4	0.7	0.8	0.1	0.7	1.3	76.2	22.9	0.2	0.4	1.1
Caldwell	0.6	81.0	18.0	0.8	0.2	0.0	0.6	1.5	81.2	17.9	0.1	0.1	1.6
Cameron	0.7	94.3	4.1	0.6	0.5	0.0	1.2	2.2	93.8	5.4	0.2	0.3	1.5
Catahoula	0.6	72.3	27.3	0.6	0.2	0.1	0.2	0.9	73.5	26.0	0.1	0.0	0.6
Claiborne	0.5	52.1	47.6	0.4	0.2	0.1	0.1	0.8	53.5	46.2	0.2	0.1	0.2
Concordia	0.6	61.2	38.0	0.4	0.4	0.1	0.6	1.5	63.2	36.5	0.1	0.1	0.6
De Soto	0.7	56.5	42.4	0.9	0.2	0.1	0.6	1.6	55.2	44.0	0.2	0.0	1.5
East Baton Rouge	0.9	56.9	40.5	0.5	2.3	0.1	0.8	1.8	63.3	34.8	0.2	1.4	1.5
East Carroll	0.4	31.9	67.4	0.3	0.4	0.0	0.3	1.2	34.6	64.8	0.0	0.2	1.2
East Feliciana	0.5	52.2	47.3	0.4	0.4	0.0	0.3	0.7	52.2	47.3	0.1	0.1	1.0
Evangeline	0.5	70.8	28.8	0.4	0.2	0.0	0.3	1.0	73.3	26.1	0.1	0.1	0.8
Franklin	0.6	67.6	31.8	0.6	0.3	0.1	0.3	0.8	68.2	31.4	0.1	0.1	0.5
Grant	1.3	86.6	12.1	1.7	0.3	0.1	0.5	1.1	84.8	14.5	0.5	0.2	0.9
Iberia	1.2	66.0	31.3	0.7	2.2	0.1	1.1	1.5	68.7	29.5	0.2	1.2	1.9
Iberville	0.5	49.6	49.9	0.4	0.3	0.0	0.3	1.0	53.2	46.3	0.2	0.2	1.9
Jackson	0.4	71.4	28.0	0.4	0.3	0.0	0.3	0.6	70.5	29.2	0.2	0.1	0.3
Jefferson	1.7	71.2	23.2	0.8	3.5	0.1	2.9	7.1	78.3	17.6	0.4	2.2	5.9
Jefferson Davis	0.8	81.3	18.2	0.6	0.3	0.0	0.4	1.0	80.5	19.0	0.2	0.1	0.7
Lafayette	0.9	74.1	24.2	0.6	1.3	0.1	0.8	1.7	76.1	22.4	0.2	1.0	1.6
Lafourche	1.0	83.7	12.8	2.9	0.8	0.1	0.8	1.4	84.3	12.5	2.2	0.8	1.5
La Salle	0.6	86.8	12.3	1.1	0.3	0.0	0.3	0.8	89.8	9.2	0.6	0.3	0.3
Lincoln	0.8	58.0	40.2	0.4	1.4	0.0	0.8	1.2	59.0	39.7	0.1	0.8	0.9
Livingston	0.7	95.0	4.3	0.8	0.3	0.0	0.3	1.1	94.0	5.6	0.2	0.2	0.9
Madison	1.1	38.3	60.6	0.4	0.2	0.6	1.1	2.1	39.8	59.5	0.1	0.1	1.0
Morehouse	0.4	56.1	43.6	0.3	0.3	0.0	0.2	0.7	58.2	41.5	0.1	0.1	0.4
Natchitoches	1.3	58.8	38.9	1.6	0.6	0.0	1.5	1.4	60.9	37.6	0.5	0.4	1.3
Orleans	1.3	28.9	67.9	0.5	2.5	0.1	1.5	3.1	34.9	61.9	0.2	1.9	3.5
Ouachita	0.7	65.0	33.8	0.5	0.8	0.1	0.5	1.2	68.1	31.0	0.2	0.5	0.8
Plaquemines	1.4	70.9	23.6	2.8	3.0	0.1	1.2	1.6	72.4	23.2	1.9	2.0	2.3

¹Hispanic persons may be of any race.

Table B. States and Counties

STATE County	Population and population characteristics, 2000										
	Age (percent)										
	Under 5 years	5 to 17 years	18 to 24 years	25 to 34 years	35 to 44 years	45 to 54 years	55 to 64 years	65 to 74 years	75 years and over	Median age (years)	Percent Female
	28	29	30	31	32	33	34	35	36	37	38
KENTUCKY—Cont'd											
Owsley	5.5	19.1	8.9	12.3	14.7	13.8	10.7	8.1	6.9	38.2	49.5
Pendleton	6.7	21.6	8.5	13.9	17.3	12.6	8.8	6.0	4.5	34.5	49.9
Perry	5.8	18.5	9.1	14.4	16.3	15.0	9.7	6.4	4.8	36.3	51.4
Pike	6.1	17.6	9.2	14.0	16.0	15.1	9.8	7.1	5.2	37.1	51.2
Powell	6.8	19.8	9.5	14.2	15.9	13.7	9.6	6.3	4.3	34.8	50.2
Pulaski	5.9	17.5	8.0	13.2	15.4	14.1	10.8	8.5	6.6	38.5	51.1
Robertson	5.5	18.3	6.7	12.2	15.0	13.6	11.9	8.5	8.4	39.5	51.3
Rockcastle	6.0	18.5	8.8	14.7	15.3	13.4	10.2	7.5	5.8	36.3	50.5
Rowan	5.4	14.8	23.5	12.9	13.0	11.4	8.6	5.9	4.5	29.8	51.4
Russell	5.5	17.0	7.5	12.7	14.8	14.1	11.8	9.1	7.3	39.9	51.6
Scott	7.6	18.7	11.8	16.0	16.6	12.9	7.5	4.8	4.0	32.4	51.1
Shelby	6.9	18.3	8.7	14.4	17.0	14.5	9.4	5.9	4.9	35.9	51.3
Simpson	7.5	18.8	8.5	13.7	15.4	13.4	9.5	6.6	6.6	35.9	51.2
Spencer	7.3	19.7	7.7	15.2	18.3	14.0	8.7	5.2	3.9	35.1	49.5
Taylor	6.0	17.4	10.4	11.5	15.4	13.6	10.5	8.6	6.6	38.1	51.9
Todd	7.5	19.1	8.7	13.3	15.1	12.6	9.8	7.4	6.5	35.9	51.3
Trigg	5.9	17.1	6.8	12.1	14.6	14.2	12.8	9.7	6.9	40.5	50.8
Trimble	6.7	19.7	7.7	14.8	16.1	14.4	9.2	6.0	5.4	35.7	50.8
Union	6.2	19.1	13.8	11.5	14.0	13.8	8.7	6.8	6.0	34.5	49.6
Warren	6.4	16.7	16.2	14.2	15.0	12.9	8.2	5.6	4.8	32.3	51.0
Washington	5.8	19.4	8.8	12.3	15.6	13.3	9.8	7.6	7.4	37.1	50.9
Wayne	6.7	18.6	8.9	13.5	14.6	13.5	10.5	7.8	5.9	36.6	50.6
Webster	6.0	18.1	8.9	12.9	15.0	14.0	10.1	7.9	7.1	37.8	51.1
Whitley	6.3	19.4	10.8	12.9	14.4	13.2	10.0	7.0	6.0	35.4	51.7
Wolfe	6.7	19.3	9.4	12.4	16.1	13.6	9.9	6.8	5.9	36.4	50.4
Woodford	6.2	19.1	7.9	13.0	18.1	15.6	9.5	5.8	4.6	37.1	51.8
LOUISIANA	7.1	20.2	10.6	13.5	15.5	13.1	8.5	6.3	5.2	34.0	51.6
Acadia	7.8	22.0	9.6	12.3	15.1	12.2	8.7	6.7	5.5	33.7	51.7
Allen	6.4	18.2	9.3	16.4	17.0	12.0	8.8	6.8	5.0	34.8	44.2
Ascension	8.2	21.9	9.5	15.3	17.3	12.8	7.4	4.4	3.3	32.0	50.8
Assumption	7.0	21.5	9.8	13.0	15.7	13.2	9.0	6.0	4.9	34.2	51.6
Avoyelles	6.8	20.0	9.2	13.7	15.3	12.4	9.0	7.1	6.6	35.2	50.9
Beauregard	7.0	20.5	8.6	13.2	15.5	13.5	9.8	6.9	5.0	35.5	49.8
Bienville	6.5	20.8	8.0	10.8	13.9	12.4	10.1	8.7	8.9	38.0	52.3
Bossier	7.6	20.4	9.7	14.0	16.6	12.7	8.6	6.1	4.3	33.8	51.0
Caddo	6.9	19.9	10.2	12.9	14.5	13.3	8.7	7.0	6.6	35.1	52.7
Calcasieu	7.2	20.2	10.3	13.0	15.7	13.2	8.6	6.8	5.1	34.5	51.3
Caldwell	6.1	18.6	9.6	13.3	15.2	13.3	10.0	7.5	6.4	36.7	49.3
Cameron	6.7	21.7	9.4	12.2	17.5	12.6	9.4	6.6	4.0	35.0	49.8
Catahoula	6.5	19.3	10.0	11.7	15.1	13.5	9.5	7.9	6.5	36.7	49.8
Claiborne	6.0	19.6	8.0	12.4	14.5	12.6	9.7	8.7	8.6	37.7	50.1
Concordia	7.3	20.5	8.9	10.7	15.0	13.3	9.7	8.3	6.3	36.9	51.2
De Soto	7.0	21.4	8.3	11.5	14.8	13.5	9.5	7.5	6.6	36.3	52.4
East Baton Rouge	7.0	19.1	14.4	14.0	14.7	13.1	7.7	5.3	4.6	31.5	52.1
East Carroll	7.6	22.7	11.5	13.2	14.0	10.8	7.7	6.8	5.7	30.9	48.9
East Feliciana	6.5	19.2	13.8	13.8	16.9	14.4	9.3	5.9	4.7	35.8	46.2
Evangeline	7.9	21.6	9.6	12.6	15.0	11.8	8.6	7.0	5.8	33.7	50.1
Franklin	7.2	20.7	9.1	11.8	14.0	12.1	9.8	7.9	7.4	35.9	52.3
Grant	7.4	20.8	7.9	13.0	15.2	13.0	10.0	7.0	5.7	35.5	51.0
Iberia	8.0	22.0	9.6	12.8	15.6	12.3	8.2	6.1	5.3	33.3	51.9
Iberville	6.5	19.7	10.5	14.3	16.7	13.2	8.3	6.0	4.8	34.4	50.1
Jackson	6.5	18.8	9.3	11.7	13.9	13.0	10.6	8.1	8.0	37.6	52.3
Jefferson	6.6	18.7	9.1	14.2	16.1	14.2	9.1	6.6	5.3	35.9	52.0
Jefferson Davis	7.6	21.7	9.1	12.2	15.0	11.9	9.1	7.3	6.0	34.5	51.9
Lafayette	7.3	20.1	11.7	14.6	16.6	12.9	7.3	5.5	4.0	32.4	51.5
Lafourche	6.9	20.4	10.5	13.7	16.0	12.7	8.6	6.4	4.8	34.1	51.2
La Salle	6.1	20.0	9.4	12.4	14.7	13.0	9.6	8.0	6.8	36.4	49.9
Lincoln	6.0	16.1	25.7	11.5	11.7	10.5	7.1	5.6	5.7	26.5	51.5
Livingston	7.5	22.0	9.1	14.8	16.7	13.1	8.3	5.1	3.4	32.8	50.4
Madison	8.2	24.4	11.2	12.6	12.9	11.7	7.4	6.2	5.4	29.8	49.2
Morehouse	7.0	20.5	9.5	12.2	14.3	12.8	8.6	8.1	7.0	35.6	52.3
Natchitoches	7.1	18.9	17.9	11.6	12.7	11.7	8.1	6.4	5.7	30.2	52.5
Orleans	6.9	19.8	11.4	14.5	14.8	13.1	7.8	6.0	5.7	33.1	53.1
Ouachita	7.2	20.7	12.0	13.5	14.4	12.2	8.1	6.5	5.4	32.3	52.8
Plaquemines	7.4	21.8	9.2	13.6	16.9	12.7	8.6	6.1	3.7	33.7	50.2

STATE County	Under 5 years	5 to 17 years	18 to 24 years	25 to 34 years	35 to 44 years	45 to 54 years	55 to 64 years	65 to 74 years	75 years and over	Percent Female	2000	1990	1980	1990–2000	1980–1990
	39	40	41	42	43	44	45	46	47	48	49	50	51	52	53
KENTUCKY—Cont'd															
Owsley	6.3	20.2	10.2	14.2	13.9	10.7	9.0	8.3	7.1	49.4	4 858	5 036	5 709	-3.5	-11.8
Pendleton	8.0	21.0	10.0	16.6	13.6	9.8	8.0	6.9	5.2	51.1	14 390	12 062	10 989	19.3	9.5
Perry	6.4	22.0	10.9	16.2	15.6	10.2	8.1	6.1	4.4	51.2	29 390	30 283	33 763	-2.9	-10.3
Pike	6.3	21.5	10.3	16.4	15.7	10.4	8.7	6.5	4.1	51.1	68 736	72 584	81 123	-5.3	-10.5
Powell	7.3	22.4	10.3	15.9	14.8	10.9	7.9	6.0	4.5	50.9	13 237	11 686	11 101	13.3	5.3
Pulaski	6.2	18.4	9.6	15.5	14.5	11.3	10.2	8.3	5.9	51.4	56 217	49 489	45 803	13.6	8.0
Robertson	6.0	18.0	9.7	14.2	13.4	11.3	9.8	10.0	7.5	51.1	2 266	2 124	2 270	6.7	-6.4
Rockcastle	6.7	20.0	10.8	15.5	13.8	10.8	9.1	7.3	6.0	50.7	16 582	14 803	13 973	12.0	5.9
Rowan	5.7	14.9	27.9	13.6	11.8	8.9	7.2	5.6	4.4	52.0	22 094	20 353	19 049	8.6	6.8
Russell	5.9	17.7	9.5	15.2	13.8	11.2	10.6	9.4	6.7	51.9	16 315	14 716	13 708	10.9	7.4
Scott	6.8	20.0	12.3	16.3	15.5	10.4	7.9	6.1	4.8	51.6	33 061	23 867	21 813	38.5	9.4
Shelby	6.4	18.8	9.3	15.6	16.0	11.7	9.0	7.2	5.9	52.2	33 337	24 824	23 328	34.3	6.4
Simpson	7.2	19.4	9.5	15.7	14.7	10.6	8.5	8.0	6.4	51.7	16 405	15 145	14 673	8.3	3.2
Spencer	6.6	20.3	9.2	16.8	14.7	10.9	9.3	7.0	5.1	50.0	11 766	6 801	5 929	73.0	14.7
Taylor	6.4	18.5	9.9	16.0	14.2	11.1	9.9	8.0	6.1	51.7	22 927	21 146	21 178	8.4	-0.2
Todd	6.9	19.4	9.5	15.6	12.9	10.2	9.5	9.0	7.0	51.7	11 971	10 940	11 874	9.4	-7.9
Trigg	5.8	17.0	8.0	12.9	13.3	11.9	11.8	11.8	7.6	51.3	12 597	10 361	9 384	21.6	10.4
Trimble	7.1	19.3	9.0	15.2	15.2	11.5	8.8	7.8	6.1	51.0	8 125	6 090	6 253	33.4	-2.6
Union	6.0	22.5	15.1	13.6	13.7	8.9	7.9	7.0	5.3	48.7	15 637	16 557	17 821	-5.6	-7.1
Warren	6.4	17.9	15.6	16.1	14.7	10.4	7.8	6.3	4.8	52.1	92 522	77 720	71 828	19.0	8.2
Washington	6.9	20.1	9.5	15.7	13.3	10.2	8.8	8.7	6.8	52.1	10 916	10 441	10 764	4.5	-3.0
Wayne	6.5	20.5	9.8	14.7	14.2	10.5	9.7	8.2	5.8	50.8	19 923	17 468	17 022	14.1	2.6
Webster	6.2	20.1	8.7	14.5	13.9	10.3	9.7	8.6	8.0	51.9	14 120	13 955	14 832	1.2	-5.9
Whitley	6.8	20.3	12.3	14.5	13.9	10.9	8.4	7.3	5.6	52.2	35 865	33 326	33 396	7.6	-0.2
Wolfe	6.3	22.5	8.8	16.4	14.6	10.6	8.9	6.9	4.9	50.3	7 065	6 503	6 698	8.6	-2.9
Woodford	7.2	19.2	9.4	16.6	17.3	11.9	7.8	6.1	4.5	52.2	23 208	19 955	17 778	16.3	12.2
LOUISIANA	7.9	21.2	11.0	16.7	14.4	9.6	8.1	6.5	4.6	51.9	4 468 976	4 221 826	4 206 116	5.9	0.3
Acadia	8.5	23.5	9.5	15.7	12.9	9.7	8.3	6.8	5.1	52.4	58 861	55 882	56 427	5.3	-1.0
Allen	7.5	21.2	9.1	16.1	14.0	10.0	9.1	7.2	5.7	49.4	25 440	21 226	21 408	19.9	-0.9
Ascension	8.5	23.5	10.6	17.8	15.2	9.8	6.7	4.8	3.2	51.0	76 627	58 214	50 068	31.6	16.3
Assumption	8.2	23.5	10.7	16.2	13.4	9.6	7.6	6.3	4.5	51.5	23 388	22 753	22 084	2.8	3.0
Avoyelles	7.7	21.7	9.4	14.7	13.0	9.6	9.0	8.3	6.7	51.8	41 481	39 159	41 393	5.9	-5.4
Beauregard	7.8	21.4	10.2	16.2	14.6	10.2	8.6	6.3	4.6	49.6	32 986	30 083	29 692	9.6	1.3
Bienville	7.4	20.8	8.8	13.5	11.9	9.6	9.7	8.9	9.4	52.3	15 752	16 232	16 387	-3.0	-2.5
Bossier	8.4	20.8	10.5	18.1	14.6	10.4	8.2	5.6	3.5	51.4	98 310	86 088	80 721	14.2	6.6
Caddo	7.9	20.7	9.6	15.7	14.3	9.8	8.8	7.5	5.8	53.3	252 161	248 253	252 437	1.6	-1.7
Calcasieu	7.8	21.4	10.2	16.5	14.5	10.0	8.9	6.6	4.3	51.4	183 577	168 134	167 223	9.2	0.5
Caldwell	7.2	21.7	9.0	14.3	13.1	10.5	9.1	8.0	7.1	51.2	10 560	9 806	10 761	7.7	-8.9
Cameron	8.5	22.1	9.4	17.8	13.1	9.8	9.4	6.0	4.0	50.2	9 991	9 260	9 336	7.9	-0.8
Catahoula	7.9	22.7	8.7	14.9	13.1	9.8	9.5	7.4	6.0	51.6	10 920	11 065	12 287	-1.3	-9.9
Claiborne	6.8	18.7	9.8	15.1	13.0	9.3	9.5	8.9	8.7	49.3	16 851	17 405	17 095	-3.2	1.8
Concordia	7.5	23.1	9.1	14.4	13.2	10.1	10.1	7.5	5.0	52.6	20 247	20 828	22 981	-2.8	-9.4
De Soto	8.0	21.8	9.3	14.8	13.2	9.6	8.8	7.8	6.7	52.6	25 494	25 668	25 727	-0.7	-1.5
East Baton Rouge	7.7	19.8	13.9	17.5	15.3	9.4	7.2	5.7	3.5	52.0	412 852	380 105	366 191	8.6	3.8
East Carroll	9.6	26.5	9.7	13.3	10.6	8.1	8.6	7.3	6.4	53.0	9 421	9 709	11 772	-3.0	-17.5
East Feliciana	7.9	21.9	9.9	17.4	14.8	9.7	7.6	6.1	4.7	47.9	21 360	19 211	19 015	11.2	1.0
Evangeline	8.6	22.9	9.5	14.7	12.3	9.6	9.1	7.6	5.8	52.1	35 434	33 274	33 343	6.5	-0.2
Franklin	7.7	23.1	9.5	13.5	12.4	9.6	9.1	8.1	7.2	52.7	21 263	22 387	24 141	-5.0	-7.3
Grant	7.9	21.9	9.4	15.5	12.9	10.2	8.6	7.6	6.1	51.8	18 698	17 526	16 703	6.7	4.9
Iberia	8.8	23.3	10.3	16.6	13.3	9.2	7.8	6.2	4.4	51.8	73 266	68 297	63 752	7.3	7.1
Iberville	8.2	21.6	10.7	17.4	14.2	9.3	7.7	6.4	4.5	51.6	33 320	31 049	32 159	7.3	-3.5
Jackson	6.8	21.7	9.0	13.2	12.9	10.4	9.3	8.9	8.0	52.3	15 397	15 859	17 321	-2.9	-9.3
Jefferson	7.3	19.6	10.2	17.9	15.8	10.6	8.4	6.4	3.8	51.9	455 466	448 306	454 592	1.6	-1.4
Jefferson Davis	8.1	23.0	9.0	15.4	12.8	9.7	9.2	7.4	5.4	51.8	31 435	30 722	32 168	2.3	-4.5
Lafayette	8.5	20.6	12.1	19.0	15.1	8.9	7.5	4.9	3.4	51.5	190 503	164 762	150 017	15.6	9.8
Lafourche	8.3	21.8	12.1	17.3	13.7	9.6	7.8	5.8	3.6	51.1	89 974	85 860	82 483	4.8	4.1
La Salle	6.6	20.8	8.7	14.2	14.0	10.3	9.8	8.6	7.0	52.6	14 282	13 662	17 004	4.5	-19.7
Lincoln	6.2	16.7	27.8	13.4	10.8	7.7	6.6	5.9	4.9	51.5	42 509	41 745	39 763	1.8	5.0
Livingston	8.0	23.4	10.0	17.2	15.7	10.2	7.3	5.2	3.0	50.5	91 814	70 523	58 806	30.2	19.9
Madison	8.7	26.0	9.1	13.0	12.2	8.8	8.2	7.4	6.5	53.8	13 728	12 463	15 682	10.2	-20.5
Morehouse	7.7	23.0	9.6	14.1	12.7	8.8	9.5	8.2	6.4	53.0	31 021	31 938	34 803	-2.9	-8.2
Natchitoches	7.6	22.3	14.7	13.4	12.2	8.8	8.0	7.2	5.9	52.7	39 080	37 254	39 863	4.9	-8.0
Orleans	7.8	19.7	11.4	16.9	14.3	8.9	8.0	7.4	5.6	53.5	484 674	496 938	557 927	-2.5	-10.9
Ouachita	8.0	21.3	12.6	15.7	13.6	9.4	8.1	6.4	4.8	52.8	147 250	142 191	139 241	3.6	2.1
Plaquemines	8.4	22.9	10.7	18.2	13.8	9.7	8.3	5.1	2.8	49.4	26 757	25 575	26 049	4.6	-1.8

Table B. States and Counties

STATE County	Total population	Total in households	Householder	Spouse	Child Total	Own child under 18 years	Other relatives Total	Under 18 years	Nonrelatives Total	Unmarried partner	Total in group quarters	Correctional institutions	Nursing homes	Other institutions	College dormitories	Military quarters	Other
	54	55	56	57	58	59	60	61	62	63	64	65	66	67	68	69	70
KENTUCKY—Cont'd																	
Owsley	4 858	98.0	39.0	21.3	29.9	21.7	5.5	2.7	2.3	1.7	2.0	0.0	1.9	0.0	0.0	0.0	0.0
Pendleton	14 390	98.8	35.9	22.6	32.3	25.7	4.3	2.0	3.7	2.0	1.2	0.1	0.4	0.0	0.0	0.0	0.7
Perry	29 390	98.7	39.0	22.1	30.4	21.7	4.7	2.1	2.5	1.4	1.3	0.2	0.7	0.3	0.0	0.0	0.2
Pike	68 736	98.6	40.2	23.6	29.0	21.6	3.8	1.6	2.0	1.1	1.4	0.2	0.6	0.1	0.4	0.0	0.2
Powell	13 237	99.1	38.1	22.2	30.7	23.5	4.7	2.3	3.4	1.9	0.9	0.2	0.5	0.0	0.0	0.0	0.1
Pulaski	56 217	97.8	40.4	23.7	27.2	21.2	3.5	1.4	3.0	1.5	2.2	0.3	0.8	0.8	0.0	0.0	0.3
Robertson	2 266	96.9	38.2	22.0	28.5	21.3	4.4	2.0	3.8	1.7	3.1	0.0	2.7	0.0	0.0	0.0	0.4
Rockcastle	16 582	98.1	39.5	22.8	29.2	22.2	3.9	1.8	2.7	1.6	1.9	0.5	1.1	0.0	0.0	0.0	0.2
Rowan	22 094	85.7	35.9	18.8	23.4	18.5	2.8	1.0	4.8	1.6	14.3	0.5	0.5	0.4	12.3	0.0	0.6
Russell	16 315	99.0	42.5	23.5	26.6	20.3	3.4	1.5	2.9	1.6	1.0	0.1	0.7	0.1	0.0	0.0	0.2
Scott	33 061	95.6	36.6	21.6	29.9	24.4	3.3	1.3	4.2	1.9	4.4	0.4	0.6	0.0	3.4	0.0	0.1
Shelby	33 337	95.5	36.3	22.1	28.5	22.6	4.2	1.8	4.4	1.8	4.5	2.3	1.0	0.0	0.0	0.0	1.2
Simpson	16 405	98.6	39.1	22.2	29.5	23.6	4.0	1.9	3.7	1.8	1.4	0.6	0.7	0.0	0.0	0.0	0.1
Spencer	11 766	99.0	36.1	24.5	31.1	24.7	3.6	1.8	3.6	2.0	1.0	0.0	0.9	0.0	0.0	0.0	0.1
Taylor	22 927	97.1	40.3	22.7	27.9	21.5	3.4	1.5	2.8	1.3	2.9	0.0	0.6	0.0	2.3	0.0	0.1
Todd	11 971	98.9	38.2	22.4	30.7	24.1	4.5	2.0	3.1	1.6	1.1	0.3	0.8	0.0	0.0	0.0	0.0
Trigg	12 597	99.1	41.4	24.9	27.0	21.2	3.2	1.4	2.6	1.5	0.9	0.1	0.8	0.0	0.0	0.0	0.0
Trimble	8 125	99.3	38.6	23.4	29.8	24.0	3.3	1.7	4.1	2.2	0.7	0.0	0.7	0.0	0.0	0.0	0.0
Union	15 637	91.1	36.5	20.6	27.3	20.6	4.0	2.1	2.6	1.4	8.9	0.2	0.6	0.5	0.0	0.0	7.6
Warren	92 522	94.0	38.2	19.6	26.3	20.8	3.9	1.6	6.0	1.9	6.0	0.4	0.7	0.1	4.4	0.0	0.4
Washington	10 916	96.9	37.8	22.5	30.2	22.8	3.6	1.4	2.9	1.4	3.1	0.0	1.1	0.6	0.9	0.0	0.5
Wayne	19 923	99.1	39.7	23.4	29.8	23.2	3.4	1.5	2.8	1.5	0.9	0.1	0.5	0.2	0.0	0.0	0.0
Webster	14 120	98.2	39.4	23.2	28.7	21.7	3.8	1.8	3.1	1.4	1.8	0.5	1.2	0.1	0.0	0.0	0.0
Whitley	35 865	96.6	38.4	21.1	29.8	23.2	4.5	2.1	2.8	1.3	3.4	0.1	0.9	0.2	1.9	0.0	0.2
Wolfe	7 065	97.8	39.9	20.8	29.8	22.9	4.2	1.8	3.1	1.8	2.2	0.0	1.4	0.0	0.0	0.0	0.7
Woodford	23 208	98.4	38.3	23.7	29.5	23.6	3.6	1.3	3.3	1.5	1.6	0.4	0.3	0.2	0.6	0.0	0.1
LOUISIANA	4 468 976	97.0	37.1	18.1	31.4	23.5	6.3	3.2	4.1	1.9	3.0	1.1	0.7	0.2	0.6	0.1	0.3
Acadia	58 861	98.3	35.9	19.6	34.6	26.7	4.9	2.6	3.3	1.9	1.7	0.4	1.1	0.1	0.0	0.0	0.1
Allen	25 440	83.6	31.8	17.2	27.9	21.8	4.2	2.2	2.4	1.3	16.4	15.3	1.0	0.0	0.0	0.0	0.1
Ascension	76 627	99.2	34.8	20.9	34.9	27.0	5.2	2.6	3.3	1.8	0.8	0.3	0.4	0.1	0.0	0.0	0.1
Assumption	23 388	99.1	35.2	20.0	33.8	23.9	7.1	4.1	3.0	1.9	0.9	0.2	0.5	0.0	0.0	0.0	0.2
Avoyelles	41 481	92.5	35.5	18.4	30.6	23.6	5.0	2.7	3.0	1.9	7.5	5.6	1.8	0.1	0.0	0.0	0.1
Beauregard	32 986	96.4	36.7	22.2	30.4	24.6	4.3	2.3	2.8	1.4	3.6	2.7	0.7	0.1	0.0	0.0	0.1
Bienville	15 752	97.6	38.8	18.1	30.7	22.7	7.2	4.0	2.9	1.4	2.4	0.3	2.0	0.0	0.0	0.0	0.0
Bossier	98 310	97.9	37.3	20.3	31.4	24.9	4.9	2.6	4.0	1.7	2.1	0.3	0.6	0.3	0.0	0.8	0.1
Caddo	252 161	97.5	38.9	16.4	30.4	22.2	7.5	3.9	4.3	1.9	2.5	0.7	0.9	0.2	0.3	0.0	0.5
Calcasieu	183 577	97.5	37.4	19.7	31.6	24.2	5.0	2.5	3.9	1.8	2.5	0.7	0.7	0.3	0.6	0.0	0.3
Caldwell	10 560	93.3	37.3	20.7	27.8	21.3	4.7	2.7	2.8	1.6	6.7	5.0	1.0	0.2	0.0	0.0	0.5
Cameron	9 991	99.3	36.0	22.4	32.4	25.4	4.9	2.4	3.7	1.8	0.7	0.2	0.1	0.0	0.0	0.0	0.3
Catahoula	10 920	95.3	37.4	20.4	28.9	21.9	6.0	3.3	2.6	1.6	4.7	3.6	1.1	0.0	0.0	0.0	0.0
Claiborne	16 851	93.1	37.2	17.5	29.1	21.4	6.5	3.7	2.7	1.5	6.9	5.5	1.3	0.0	0.0	0.0	0.1
Concordia	20 247	96.6	37.1	18.2	30.8	22.8	7.7	4.5	2.7	1.4	3.4	2.3	0.8	0.4	0.0	0.0	0.0
De Soto	25 494	98.7	38.0	18.5	31.9	23.7	7.4	4.1	2.9	1.5	1.3	0.4	0.7	0.1	0.0	0.0	0.1
East Baton Rouge	412 852	96.5	37.9	16.9	30.2	22.6	6.1	3.0	5.4	1.8	3.5	0.4	0.6	0.3	1.9	0.0	0.4
East Carroll	9 421	88.8	31.5	12.6	32.6	23.9	9.2	6.1	2.8	1.8	11.2	9.6	1.6	0.0	0.0	0.0	0.1
East Feliciana	21 360	86.6	31.4	16.4	28.7	20.5	8.0	4.6	2.2	1.2	13.4	7.9	2.5	0.0	0.0	0.0	3.0
Evangeline	35 434	95.0	35.9	18.8	33.4	26.6	4.5	2.5	2.4	1.6	5.0	3.4	0.9	0.4	0.0	0.0	0.2
Franklin	21 263	96.3	36.5	19.5	31.0	23.4	6.7	4.0	2.7	1.5	3.7	1.4	2.1	0.0	0.0	0.0	0.1
Grant	18 698	98.8	37.8	21.6	31.3	25.0	5.2	2.8	2.9	1.6	1.2	0.1	0.9	0.0	0.0	0.0	0.1
Iberia	73 266	97.8	34.6	18.4	34.3	25.7	6.8	3.7	3.6	2.0	2.2	0.5	0.8	0.1	0.0	0.0	0.8
Iberville	33 320	89.9	32.0	15.9	31.1	21.4	8.1	4.4	2.8	1.6	10.1	9.3	0.7	0.0	0.0	0.0	0.1
Jackson	15 397	98.2	39.5	20.9	29.9	22.0	5.4	2.8	2.5	1.2	1.8	0.1	1.5	0.1	0.0	0.0	0.0
Jefferson	455 466	99.0	38.7	18.7	30.7	21.8	6.8	3.0	4.3	2.1	1.0	0.2	0.4	0.1	0.0	0.0	0.3
Jefferson Davis	31 435	98.7	36.5	20.7	33.3	25.9	5.0	2.9	3.1	1.6	1.3	0.2	0.9	0.0	0.0	0.0	0.1
Lafayette	190 503	97.5	38.0	18.7	31.6	24.9	4.1	1.9	5.1	2.3	2.5	0.5	0.6	0.1	0.9	0.0	0.4
Lafourche	89 974	98.1	35.6	21.1	32.2	24.2	5.3	2.6	3.9	2.1	1.9	0.2	0.5	0.1	0.8	0.0	0.2
La Salle	14 282	93.5	37.0	21.8	27.6	21.5	4.7	2.4	2.4	1.1	6.5	3.3	1.4	1.7	0.0	0.0	0.0
Lincoln	42 509	87.5	35.8	15.9	25.1	19.2	4.8	2.3	5.8	1.3	12.5	0.2	0.8	0.8	10.5	0.0	0.2
Livingston	91 814	99.4	35.5	22.4	33.6	26.7	4.4	2.1	3.5	1.7	0.6	0.2	0.3	0.1	0.0	0.0	0.1
Madison	13 728	89.3	32.6	13.4	31.6	23.7	8.7	5.4	3.0	1.8	10.7	4.4	1.2	3.5	0.0	0.0	1.7
Morehouse	31 021	96.9	36.7	18.0	31.0	22.2	8.4	4.9	2.8	1.5	3.1	1.4	1.6	0.0	0.0	0.0	0.1
Natchitoches	39 080	93.3	36.5	16.5	29.5	22.3	5.9	3.2	4.9	1.4	6.7	0.8	0.5	0.3	5.0	0.0	0.1
Orleans	484 674	96.4	38.8	12.0	30.7	21.2	9.4	4.9	5.5	2.3	3.6	1.3	0.6	0.1	1.0	0.1	0.6
Ouachita	147 250	96.6	37.5	17.9	31.4	24.0	6.0	3.2	3.9	1.8	3.4	0.5	0.8	0.4	1.3	0.0	0.4
Plaquemines	26 757	97.3	33.7	19.4	33.4	24.6	7.3	4.0	3.5	1.9	2.7	1.2	0.3	1.0	0.0	0.1	0.2

Table B. States and Counties

STATE County	Total households	Family households Total	With own children under 18 years	Married couple Total	With own children under 18 years	Female householder[1] Total	With own children under 18 years	Nonfamily households Total	Householder living alone Total	65 years and over	Average household size	Average family size	Households, 1990 Total households	Female householder[1]	Householder living alone
	71	72	73	74	75	76	77	78	79	80	81	82	83	84	85
KENTUCKY—Cont'd															
Owsley	1 894	73.3	32.6	54.8	23.2	12.7	7.1	26.7	24.5	10.7	2.51	2.98	1 848	11.0	19.6
Pendleton	5 170	76.8	39.0	62.8	30.5	9.6	5.6	23.2	20.1	8.3	2.75	3.14	4 332	8.7	20.7
Perry	11 460	74.1	34.2	56.7	25.4	13.2	6.8	25.9	23.3	9.3	2.53	2.98	10 598	12.4	19.0
Pike	27 612	73.8	33.7	58.8	25.9	11.4	6.1	26.2	24.1	9.8	2.46	2.90	26 148	11.0	18.6
Powell	5 044	75.0	36.1	58.2	26.5	12.4	7.0	25.0	21.8	8.3	2.60	3.02	4 057	12.1	17.8
Pulaski	22 719	71.9	31.2	58.5	23.4	10.1	6.0	28.1	24.9	10.8	2.42	2.87	18 866	9.8	21.7
Robertson	866	71.8	31.1	57.6	23.8	9.1	4.4	28.2	24.7	11.1	2.54	3.00	820	6.3	27.7
Rockcastle	6 544	72.8	33.6	57.9	25.2	11.4	6.5	27.2	24.4	10.7	2.49	2.95	5 464	10.7	20.7
Rowan	7 927	65.8	30.5	52.4	22.8	10.2	5.9	34.2	27.0	9.2	2.39	2.91	6 755	10.9	24.2
Russell	6 941	69.1	29.0	55.3	21.4	10.2	5.5	30.9	28.0	12.9	2.33	2.82	5 896	10.1	23.8
Scott	12 110	74.2	38.5	58.8	28.6	11.5	7.6	25.8	21.0	7.0	2.61	3.01	8 501	10.9	19.9
Shelby	12 104	75.4	34.7	61.0	26.5	10.6	6.2	24.6	20.2	8.0	2.63	3.00	9 048	10.7	20.1
Simpson	6 415	72.3	33.8	56.8	24.6	11.5	7.0	27.7	24.2	10.4	2.52	2.97	5 767	11.9	22.7
Spencer	4 251	79.0	38.4	67.9	31.9	7.6	4.5	21.0	17.1	6.0	2.74	3.08	2 451	7.5	18.5
Taylor	9 233	71.0	30.9	56.4	22.3	11.5	6.9	29.0	26.0	12.2	2.41	2.89	8 216	9.6	22.4
Todd	4 569	73.7	33.5	58.7	25.4	11.6	6.3	26.3	23.0	11.1	2.59	3.05	4 104	10.5	22.3
Trigg	5 215	72.2	29.1	60.2	22.1	8.4	5.1	27.8	25.0	11.6	2.39	2.84	4 104	8.5	22.8
Trimble	3 137	73.2	35.4	60.6	27.7	8.5	5.3	26.8	22.0	9.1	2.57	3.00	2 246	6.9	18.3
Union	5 710	71.5	32.1	56.5	23.7	11.4	6.6	28.5	26.1	12.4	2.50	2.99	5 580	11.2	23.1
Warren	35 365	66.2	31.4	51.4	22.6	11.2	6.9	33.8	26.1	8.3	2.46	2.97	28 819	10.8	24.6
Washington	4 121	73.3	33.1	59.5	25.4	10.0	5.6	26.7	24.0	11.4	2.57	3.03	3 709	10.2	19.9
Wayne	7 913	73.4	33.4	58.9	25.4	10.6	5.9	26.6	23.9	10.4	2.49	2.94	6 517	10.3	19.8
Webster	5 560	72.9	31.9	58.9	24.2	10.3	5.8	27.1	24.3	11.9	2.49	2.94	5 372	10.1	23.5
Whitley	13 780	71.8	33.7	54.9	24.4	13.0	7.3	28.2	25.2	10.2	2.52	3.01	12 153	13.8	21.8
Wolfe	2 816	70.2	33.6	52.3	23.4	12.5	7.0	29.8	27.0	9.7	2.45	2.96	2 451	12.4	22.9
Woodford	8 893	74.7	35.0	61.9	27.8	9.7	5.7	25.3	21.0	7.5	2.57	2.99	7 223	9.2	18.1
LOUISIANA	1 656 053	69.8	34.5	48.9	22.6	16.6	9.8	30.2	25.3	9.0	2.62	3.16	1 499 269	15.6	23.7
Acadia	21 142	74.1	38.5	54.5	26.8	14.9	9.0	25.9	22.6	10.3	2.74	3.22	19 285	14.5	20.9
Allen	8 102	73.2	36.9	54.0	25.7	15.2	9.0	26.8	24.3	11.1	2.62	3.12	7 080	13.5	21.3
Ascension	26 691	77.9	42.5	60.1	31.6	13.3	8.3	22.1	18.3	5.9	2.85	3.25	19 337	13.1	16.8
Assumption	8 239	76.6	37.9	56.8	27.0	14.9	8.4	23.4	20.3	9.2	2.81	3.26	7 397	13.2	18.3
Avoyelles	14 736	71.8	36.3	51.7	24.0	15.7	9.8	28.2	25.0	11.9	2.60	3.11	13 480	14.4	22.5
Beauregard	12 104	75.0	36.2	60.6	27.7	10.9	6.5	25.0	22.2	9.1	2.63	3.07	10 362	9.9	20.5
Bienville	6 108	69.0	31.0	46.7	18.9	17.7	9.8	31.0	28.8	14.1	2.52	3.09	5 852	15.5	26.2
Bossier	36 628	72.7	36.9	54.6	25.7	14.1	8.9	27.3	22.9	7.8	2.63	3.09	30 718	12.8	21.2
Caddo	97 974	66.3	30.9	42.2	17.3	19.8	11.5	33.7	28.9	10.5	2.51	3.11	93 248	18.3	27.1
Calcasieu	68 613	71.5	35.6	52.6	24.4	14.7	9.0	28.5	24.0	8.9	2.61	3.11	60 328	13.2	22.2
Caldwell	3 941	71.5	32.1	55.4	23.4	12.6	7.2	28.5	25.4	11.7	2.50	2.99	3 575	13.2	22.6
Cameron	3 592	75.3	39.0	62.2	31.5	9.0	5.3	24.7	20.9	8.6	2.76	3.21	3 153	7.9	17.0
Catahoula	4 082	73.3	32.7	54.7	22.1	14.5	8.3	26.7	24.3	11.3	2.55	3.02	3 927	12.8	22.8
Claiborne	6 270	69.2	29.7	47.1	17.7	17.6	9.8	30.8	28.5	14.8	2.50	3.07	6 065	15.0	27.2
Concordia	7 521	72.2	33.0	49.0	20.3	19.0	10.5	27.8	25.3	11.5	2.60	3.12	7 341	18.5	21.8
De Soto	9 691	71.9	33.5	48.7	20.7	18.6	10.6	28.1	25.4	11.6	2.60	3.11	9 129	18.0	23.7
East Baton Rouge	156 365	65.6	32.8	44.7	20.8	16.8	10.0	34.4	26.9	7.2	2.55	3.14	138 620	15.3	24.9
East Carroll	2 969	72.1	36.5	40.0	16.8	27.7	17.7	27.9	25.6	11.3	2.82	3.40	3 129	27.5	24.3
East Feliciana	6 699	75.1	35.6	52.4	23.6	18.0	9.9	24.9	22.5	8.5	2.76	3.26	5 589	18.8	19.6
Evangeline	12 736	71.9	38.0	52.3	25.6	15.5	10.2	28.1	25.8	11.9	2.64	3.19	11 795	13.4	23.3
Franklin	7 754	73.6	33.9	53.3	22.8	16.5	9.1	26.4	23.9	12.2	2.64	3.13	7 776	15.8	22.6
Grant	7 073	74.6	36.5	57.2	25.8	12.9	8.2	25.4	22.6	10.1	2.61	3.06	6 261	12.2	21.2
Iberia	25 381	75.5	39.5	53.2	26.1	17.2	10.6	24.5	21.1	8.7	2.82	3.28	22 847	15.5	19.3
Iberville	10 674	75.1	36.2	49.6	23.2	20.4	10.9	24.9	21.9	8.5	2.81	3.29	9 875	19.4	20.7
Jackson	6 086	70.7	31.7	52.8	22.2	14.4	7.9	29.3	27.0	13.5	2.48	3.01	5 817	13.1	25.2
Jefferson	176 234	68.2	31.9	48.2	21.3	15.4	8.5	31.8	26.7	8.4	2.56	3.13	166 398	13.5	24.9
Jefferson Davis	11 480	74.3	37.2	56.8	26.6	13.7	8.4	25.7	22.6	10.7	2.70	3.18	10 669	12.3	20.9
Lafayette	72 372	67.5	36.2	49.2	24.6	14.0	9.2	32.5	25.4	6.9	2.57	3.12	60 411	12.7	24.6
Lafourche	32 057	75.8	37.8	59.1	28.2	12.4	7.2	24.2	19.6	7.8	2.75	3.17	28 835	11.8	17.3
La Salle	5 291	71.8	33.6	59.0	27.3	9.8	5.0	28.2	25.7	13.0	2.52	3.03	5 086	9.7	23.6
Lincoln	15 235	63.6	30.0	44.5	19.1	15.3	9.3	36.4	27.0	9.4	2.44	3.01	13 669	13.7	26.1
Livingston	32 630	78.3	41.6	63.1	32.1	10.7	6.6	21.7	18.2	6.5	2.80	3.17	23 814	9.7	16.5
Madison	4 469	70.3	35.4	41.2	18.1	24.2	14.9	29.7	26.6	11.0	2.74	3.35	4 252	24.1	25.4
Morehouse	11 382	73.1	33.3	49.1	20.1	19.8	11.2	26.9	24.4	11.6	2.64	3.14	10 961	18.1	22.3
Natchitoches	14 263	66.6	33.0	45.3	20.8	17.7	10.7	33.4	27.1	10.9	2.56	3.14	12 644	18.1	25.3
Orleans	188 251	60.0	29.2	30.8	13.3	24.5	14.0	40.0	33.2	9.7	2.48	3.23	188 235	24.1	32.2
Ouachita	55 216	69.4	34.2	47.7	21.2	17.9	11.0	30.6	25.8	9.3	2.58	3.12	50 518	17.0	24.1
Plaquemines	9 021	77.6	39.5	57.5	28.7	14.6	7.9	22.4	18.6	7.1	2.89	3.30	8 213	12.4	17.1

[1]No spouse present.

Table B. States and Counties

STATE County	Percent change of households, 1990–2000	Total housing units	Occupied housing units (percent)	Vacant housing units		Homeowner vacancy rate (percent)	Rental vacancy rate (percent)	Occupied housing units			Average household size of owner-occupied units	Average household size of renter-occupied units
				Total	For seasonal, recreational, or occasional use			Total	Percent owner-occupied housing units	Percent renter-occupied housing units		
	86	87	88	89	90	91	92	93	94	95	96	97
KENTUCKY—Cont'd												
Owsley	2.5	2 247	84.3	15.7	1.9	0.8	7.3	1 894	78.5	21.5	2.57	2.31
Pendleton	19.3	5 756	89.8	10.2	2.5	1.7	9.0	5 170	77.9	22.1	2.79	2.61
Perry	8.1	12 741	89.9	10.1	1.3	1.7	13.1	11 460	77.4	22.6	2.57	2.39
Pike	5.6	30 923	89.3	10.7	0.5	2.1	9.7	27 612	78.7	21.3	2.51	2.26
Powell	24.3	5 526	91.3	8.7	1.0	1.0	8.2	5 044	74.0	26.0	2.64	2.49
Pulaski	20.4	27 181	83.6	16.4	7.7	2.4	12.0	22 719	76.0	24.0	2.46	2.28
Robertson	5.6	1 034	83.8	16.2	3.4	1.9	6.9	866	78.1	21.9	2.51	2.63
Rockcastle	19.8	7 353	89.0	11.0	1.0	2.2	7.3	6 544	79.5	20.5	2.53	2.31
Rowan	17.4	8 985	88.2	11.8	1.9	2.3	13.5	7 927	69.8	30.2	2.48	2.18
Russell	17.7	9 064	76.6	23.4	14.7	2.4	10.8	6 941	79.5	20.5	2.35	2.25
Scott	42.5	12 977	93.3	6.7	0.5	2.2	8.2	12 110	69.8	30.2	2.69	2.41
Shelby	33.8	12 857	94.1	5.9	0.6	1.7	5.8	12 104	72.8	27.2	2.63	2.64
Simpson	11.2	7 016	91.4	8.6	0.3	2.5	10.7	6 415	71.8	28.2	2.56	2.43
Spencer	73.4	4 555	93.3	6.7	0.7	1.8	7.5	4 251	82.6	17.4	2.77	2.58
Taylor	12.4	10 180	90.7	9.3	1.0	1.5	10.9	9 233	72.3	27.7	2.45	2.29
Todd	11.3	5 121	89.2	10.8	1.7	1.7	10.8	4 569	76.6	23.4	2.58	2.62
Trigg	27.1	6 698	77.9	22.1	15.0	3.1	7.0	5 215	81.5	18.5	2.39	2.40
Trimble	39.7	3 437	91.3	8.7	1.6	2.2	8.2	3 137	80.7	19.3	2.58	2.54
Union	2.3	6 234	91.6	8.4	0.5	1.1	8.7	5 710	77.9	22.1	2.57	2.25
Warren	22.7	38 350	92.2	7.8	0.4	1.9	10.4	35 365	64.0	36.0	2.56	2.29
Washington	11.1	4 542	90.7	9.3	2.8	1.7	4.0	4 121	80.0	20.0	2.60	2.44
Wayne	21.4	9 789	80.8	19.2	10.4	2.0	8.2	7 913	76.5	23.5	2.51	2.44
Webster	3.5	6 250	89.0	11.0	0.7	1.3	7.8	5 560	78.1	21.9	2.52	2.41
Whitley	13.4	15 288	90.1	9.9	0.7	1.7	11.4	13 780	72.6	27.4	2.57	2.38
Wolfe	14.9	3 264	86.3	13.7	2.5	1.1	5.3	2 816	73.9	26.1	2.49	2.35
Woodford	23.1	9 374	94.9	5.1	0.4	1.2	5.8	8 893	72.4	27.6	2.62	2.42
LOUISIANA	10.5	1 847 181	89.7	10.3	2.1	1.6	9.3	1 656 053	67.9	32.1	2.70	2.44
Acadia	9.6	23 209	91.1	8.9	1.0	1.1	9.9	21 142	72.2	27.8	2.77	2.66
Allen	14.4	9 157	88.5	11.5	2.7	1.6	12.0	8 102	76.1	23.9	2.65	2.53
Ascension	38.0	29 172	91.5	8.5	0.7	2.1	13.9	26 691	82.3	17.7	2.89	2.66
Assumption	11.4	9 635	85.5	14.5	7.5	0.9	5.9	8 239	84.0	16.0	2.84	2.67
Avoyelles	9.3	16 576	88.9	11.1	3.6	1.3	6.4	14 736	74.4	25.6	2.63	2.54
Beauregard	16.8	14 501	83.5	16.5	5.5	2.5	14.0	12 104	79.8	20.2	2.66	2.50
Bienville	4.4	7 830	78.0	22.0	8.9	2.8	8.7	6 108	77.9	22.1	2.51	2.53
Bossier	19.2	40 286	90.9	9.1	1.1	1.9	10.9	36 628	69.5	30.5	2.66	2.55
Caddo	5.1	108 296	90.5	9.5	0.7	1.7	10.9	97 974	63.8	36.2	2.55	2.43
Calcasieu	13.7	75 995	90.3	9.7	0.9	1.7	14.1	68 613	71.6	28.4	2.68	2.44
Caldwell	10.2	5 035	78.3	21.7	10.2	2.7	11.5	3 941	79.2	20.8	2.51	2.46
Cameron	13.9	5 336	67.3	32.7	24.9	1.7	18.4	3 592	85.1	14.9	2.78	2.65
Catahoula	3.9	5 351	76.3	23.7	15.4	1.7	5.5	4 082	83.1	16.9	2.55	2.53
Claiborne	3.4	7 815	80.2	19.8	7.6	2.3	10.1	6 270	75.8	24.2	2.45	2.66
Concordia	2.5	9 148	82.2	17.8	10.5	1.7	6.5	7 521	76.1	23.9	2.57	2.69
De Soto	6.2	11 204	86.5	13.5	2.9	2.3	9.3	9 691	76.7	23.3	2.60	2.59
East Baton Rouge	12.8	169 073	92.5	7.5	0.3	1.5	9.4	156 365	61.6	38.4	2.69	2.32
East Carroll	-5.1	3 303	89.9	10.1	1.7	1.3	8.4	2 969	62.1	37.9	2.71	2.99
East Feliciana	19.9	7 915	84.6	15.4	4.8	1.5	8.8	6 699	82.4	17.6	2.79	2.64
Evangeline	8.0	14 258	89.3	10.7	3.3	1.7	6.4	12 736	69.4	30.6	2.68	2.57
Franklin	-0.3	8 623	89.9	10.1	2.6	1.6	6.0	7 754	76.3	23.7	2.60	2.77
Grant	13.0	8 531	82.9	17.1	5.8	1.5	12.9	7 073	81.7	18.3	2.61	2.63
Iberia	11.1	27 844	91.2	8.8	1.1	1.1	7.9	25 381	73.4	26.6	2.86	2.72
Iberville	8.1	11 953	89.3	10.7	3.5	2.0	9.3	10 674	77.4	22.6	2.86	2.64
Jackson	4.6	7 338	82.9	17.1	6.7	2.1	12.3	6 086	77.2	22.8	2.47	2.52
Jefferson	5.9	187 907	93.8	6.2	1.0	1.2	7.2	176 234	63.9	36.1	2.71	2.30
Jefferson Davis	7.6	12 824	89.5	10.5	1.7	2.4	9.9	11 480	74.9	25.1	2.72	2.64
Lafayette	19.8	78 122	92.6	7.4	0.5	1.3	10.4	72 372	66.0	34.0	2.73	2.24
Lafourche	11.2	35 045	91.5	8.5	2.6	0.9	8.0	32 057	78.0	22.0	2.82	2.52
La Salle	4.0	6 273	84.3	15.7	5.3	1.8	10.3	5 291	83.3	16.7	2.53	2.52
Lincoln	11.5	17 000	89.6	10.4	0.9	1.5	12.7	15 235	60.0	40.0	2.56	2.26
Livingston	37.0	36 212	90.1	9.9	2.3	1.4	11.5	32 630	83.7	16.3	2.83	2.60
Madison	5.1	4 979	89.8	10.2	3.4	1.7	5.8	4 469	61.9	38.1	2.62	2.94
Morehouse	3.8	12 711	89.5	10.5	2.0	1.5	8.3	11 382	71.5	28.5	2.61	2.71
Natchitoches	12.8	16 890	84.4	15.6	4.8	1.8	9.4	14 263	64.5	35.5	2.59	2.49
Orleans	0.0	215 091	87.5	12.5	1.1	2.2	7.9	188 251	46.5	53.5	2.60	2.37
Ouachita	9.3	60 154	91.8	8.2	0.7	1.4	9.0	55 216	64.1	35.9	2.62	2.50
Plaquemines	9.8	10 481	86.1	13.9	5.2	1.3	8.9	9 021	78.9	21.1	2.93	2.74

Table B. States and Counties

STATE/ County code	MSA/ PMSA/ NECMA code[1]	County type[2]	STATE County	Population, 2000				Population, 1990				Population and population characteristics, 2000 — Race (percent) — One race					
				Land area, 2000[3] (sq km)	Total persons	Rank	Per square kilometer	Land area, 1990[3] (sq km)	Total persons	Rank	Per square kilometer	White	Black or African American	American Indian or Alaska Native	Asian	Native Hawaiian and other Pacific Islander	Some other race
				1	2	3	4	5	6	7	8	9	10	11	12	13	14
			LOUISIANA—Cont'd														
22 077	...	6	Pointe Coupee	1 444	22 763	1 658	15.8	1 444	22 540	1 553	15.6	60.9	37.8	0.2	0.3	0.0	0.3
22 079	0220	3	Rapides	3 425	126 337	430	36.9	3 426	131 556	352	38.4	66.5	30.4	0.7	0.9	0.0	0.4
22 081	...	8	Red River	1 008	9 622	2 477	9.5	1 006	9 526	2 429	9.5	57.9	40.9	0.3	0.1	0.0	0.2
22 083	...	6	Richland	1 446	20 981	1 737	14.5	1 447	20 629	1 648	14.3	61.0	38.0	0.1	0.2	0.0	0.2
22 085	...	7	Sabine	2 241	23 459	1 617	10.5	2 241	22 646	1 551	10.1	72.7	16.9	7.8	0.1	0.0	0.3
22 087	5560	0	St. Bernard	1 204	67 229	728	55.8	1 205	66 631	660	55.3	88.3	7.6	0.5	1.3	0.0	0.7
22 089	5560	0	St. Charles	735	48 072	951	65.4	735	42 437	948	57.7	72.4	25.2	0.3	0.6	0.0	0.6
22 091	...	8	St. Helena	1 058	10 525	2 395	9.9	1 058	9 874	2 399	9.3	46.5	52.4	0.1	0.1	0.0	0.1
22 093	5560	1	St. James	637	21 216	1 724	33.3	638	20 879	1 635	32.7	50.0	49.4	0.1	0.0	0.0	0.1
22 095	5560	1	St. John the Baptist	567	43 044	1 036	75.9	567	39 996	998	70.5	52.6	44.8	0.3	0.5	0.0	0.9
22 097	3880	2	St. Landry	2 405	87 700	597	36.5	2 405	80 312	570	33.4	56.5	42.1	0.1	0.2	0.0	0.3
22 099	3880	2	St. Martin	1 916	48 583	938	25.4	1 916	44 097	924	23.0	65.9	32.0	0.3	0.9	0.0	0.9
22 101	...	7	St. Mary	1 587	53 500	875	33.7	1 588	58 086	747	36.6	62.8	31.8	1.4	1.6	0.0	0.9
22 103	5560	0	St. Tammany	2 212	191 268	287	86.5	2 213	144 500	328	65.3	87.0	9.9	0.4	0.7	0.0	0.6
22 105	...	4	Tangipahoa	2 047	100 588	521	49.1	2 047	85 709	536	41.9	69.8	28.4	0.2	0.4	0.0	0.5
22 107	...	9	Tensas	1 560	6 618	2 725	4.2	1 561	7 103	2 645	4.6	43.4	55.4	0.0	0.1	0.0	0.3
22 109	3350	3	Terrebonne	3 250	104 503	506	32.2	3 251	96 982	474	29.8	74.1	17.8	5.3	0.8	0.0	0.5
22 111	...	6	Union	2 273	22 803	1 654	10.0	2 273	20 796	1 640	9.1	69.8	27.9	0.2	0.3	0.0	1.3
22 113	...	6	Vermilion	3 040	53 807	870	17.7	3 040	50 055	841	16.5	82.7	14.2	0.3	1.8	0.0	0.3
22 115	...	5	Vernon	3 441	52 531	888	15.3	3 441	61 961	704	18.0	73.7	17.1	1.5	1.6	0.3	2.5
22 117	...	6	Washington	1 734	43 926	1 019	25.3	1 734	43 185	935	24.9	67.4	31.5	0.2	0.2	0.0	0.1
22 119	7680	2	Webster	1 542	41 831	1 058	27.1	1 543	41 989	956	27.2	65.5	32.8	0.3	0.2	0.0	0.2
22 121	0760	2	West Baton Rouge	495	21 601	1 714	43.6	495	19 419	1 709	39.2	62.8	35.5	0.2	0.2	0.0	0.5
22 123	...	9	West Carroll	931	12 314	2 278	13.2	931	12 093	2 209	13.0	79.9	18.9	0.3	0.1	0.0	0.3
22 125	...	8	West Feliciana	1 052	15 111	2 083	14.4	1 052	12 915	2 145	12.3	48.6	50.5	0.2	0.2	0.0	0.0
22 127	...	7	Winn	2 462	16 894	1 961	6.9	2 462	16 498	1 893	6.7	66.3	32.0	0.5	0.2	0.1	0.3
23 000	...		MAINE	79 931	1 274 923	X	16.0	79 939	1 227 928	X	15.4	96.9	0.5	0.6	0.7	0.0	0.2
23 001	4243	3	Androscoggin	1 218	103 793	512	85.2	1 218	105 259	438	86.4	97.0	0.7	0.3	0.6	0.0	0.3
23 003	...	5	Aroostook	17 279	73 938	676	4.3	17 280	86 936	525	5.0	96.8	0.4	1.4	0.5	0.0	0.2
23 005	6403	3	Cumberland	2 164	265 612	207	122.7	2 164	243 135	206	112.4	95.7	1.1	0.3	1.4	0.0	0.3
23 007	...	6	Franklin	4 397	29 467	1 415	6.7	4 398	29 008	1 329	6.6	98.0	0.2	0.4	0.4	0.0	0.2
23 009	...	6	Hancock	4 112	51 791	895	12.6	4 116	46 948	891	11.4	97.6	0.3	0.4	0.4	0.0	0.2
23 011	...	4	Kennebec	2 247	117 114	462	52.1	2 247	115 904	397	51.6	97.3	0.3	0.4	0.6	0.0	0.2
23 013	...	7	Knox	947	39 618	1 123	41.8	947	36 310	1 095	38.3	98.3	0.2	0.2	0.4	0.0	0.1
23 015	...	9	Lincoln	1 181	33 616	1 296	28.5	1 180	30 357	1 276	25.7	98.5	0.2	0.3	0.4	0.0	0.1
23 017	...	6	Oxford	5 382	54 755	860	10.2	5 383	52 602	806	9.8	98.3	0.2	0.3	0.4	0.0	0.1
23 019	0733	3	Penobscot	8 795	144 919	377	16.5	8 796	146 601	321	16.7	96.6	0.5	1.0	0.7	0.0	0.1
23 021	...	6	Piscataquis	10 272	17 235	1 939	1.7	10 273	18 653	1 755	1.8	97.8	0.2	0.5	0.3	0.0	0.1
23 023	...	6	Sagadahoc	658	35 214	1 241	53.5	658	33 535	1 177	51.0	96.5	0.9	0.3	0.6	0.1	0.4
23 025	...	7	Somerset	10 170	50 888	911	5.0	10 171	49 767	844	4.9	98.0	0.2	0.4	0.3	0.0	0.1
23 027	...	6	Waldo	1 890	36 280	1 206	19.2	1 890	33 018	1 190	17.5	97.3	0.2	0.4	0.2	0.0	0.2
23 029	...	7	Washington	6 652	33 941	1 282	5.1	6 653	35 308	1 121	5.3	93.5	0.3	4.4	0.3	0.0	0.4
23 031	...	4	York	2 566	186 742	294	72.8	2 567	164 587	291	64.1	97.6	0.4	0.2	0.7	0.0	0.2
24 000	...		MARYLAND	25 314	5 296 486	X	209.2	25 316	4 780 753	X	188.8	64.0	27.9	0.3	4.0	0.0	1.8
24 001	1900	3	Allegany	1 102	74 930	666	68.0	1 102	74 946	600	68.0	93.0	5.3	0.2	0.5	0.0	0.2
24 003	0720	0	Anne Arundel	1 077	489 656	114	454.6	1 077	427 239	117	396.7	81.2	13.6	0.3	2.3	0.1	0.9
24 005	0720	0	Baltimore	1 550	754 292	63	486.6	1 550	692 134	60	446.5	74.4	20.1	0.3	3.2	0.0	0.5
24 009	8840	1	Calvert	557	74 563	671	133.9	557	51 372	822	92.2	83.9	13.1	0.3	0.9	0.0	0.5
24 011	...	6	Caroline	829	29 772	1 404	35.9	829	27 035	1 388	32.6	81.7	14.8	0.4	0.5	0.0	1.3
24 013	0720	1	Carroll	1 163	150 897	356	129.7	1 163	123 372	373	106.1	95.7	2.3	0.2	0.8	0.0	0.3
24 015	9160	2	Cecil	902	85 951	608	95.3	902	71 347	621	79.1	89.3	3.9	0.3	0.7	0.0	0.5
24 017	8840	1	Charles	1 194	120 546	451	101.0	1 194	101 154	453	84.7	68.5	26.1	0.8	1.8	0.1	0.7
24 019	...	7	Dorchester	1 444	30 674	1 382	21.2	1 444	30 236	1 283	20.9	69.4	28.4	0.2	0.7	0.0	0.4
24 021	8840	1	Frederick	1 717	195 277	283	113.7	1 717	150 208	311	87.5	89.3	6.4	0.2	1.7	0.0	0.9
24 023	...	8	Garrett	1 678	29 846	1 401	17.8	1 679	28 138	1 347	16.8	98.8	0.4	0.1	0.2	0.0	0.1
24 025	0720	0	Harford	1 140	218 590	258	191.7	1 141	182 132	265	159.6	86.8	9.3	0.2	1.5	0.1	0.7
24 027	0720	0	Howard	653	247 842	234	379.5	653	187 328	258	286.9	74.3	14.4	0.2	7.7	0.0	1.1
24 029	...	6	Kent	724	19 197	1 833	26.5	724	17 842	1 796	24.6	79.6	17.4	0.1	0.5	0.0	1.0
24 031	8840	0	Montgomery	1 283	873 341	49	680.7	1 281	762 875	51	595.5	64.8	15.1	0.3	11.3	0.0	5.0
24 033	8840	0	Prince George's	1 257	801 515	57	637.6	1 260	722 705	56	573.6	27.0	62.7	0.3	3.9	0.1	3.4
24 035	0720	1	Queen Anne's	964	40 563	1 099	42.1	964	33 953	1 164	35.2	89.0	8.8	0.2	0.6	0.0	0.4
24 037	...	4	St. Mary's	936	86 211	604	92.1	936	75 974	592	81.2	81.6	13.9	0.3	1.8	0.1	0.6
24 039	...	7	Somerset	847	24 747	1 566	29.2	848	23 440	1 518	27.6	56.4	41.1	0.4	0.5	0.0	0.5
24 041	...	6	Talbot	697	33 812	1 287	48.5	697	30 549	1 264	43.8	82.0	15.4	0.2	0.8	0.1	0.8

[1] MSA = Metropolitan Statistical Area. PMSA = Primary MSA. NECMA = New England County Metropolitan Area. See Appendix A for explanation of these concepts. See Appendix B for list of metropolitan areas identified by type, with component counties.
[2] County typology code from the Economic Research Service of USDA. See Appendix A for definition.
[3] Dry land or land partially or temporarily covered by water.

Table B. States and Counties

STATE County	Population and population characteristics, 2000 (cont'd)							Population and population characteristics, 1990				
	Race (percent) (cont'd)							Race (percent)				
	Race alone or in combination											
	Two or more races	White	Black	American Indian or Alaska Native	Asian	Native Hawaiian and other Pacific Islander	Some other race	Hispanic[1]	White	Black or African American	American Indian or Alaska Native	Asian and Pacific Islander	Hispanic[1]
	15	16	17	18	19	20	21	22	23	24	25	26	27

STATE County	15	16	17	18	19	20	21	22	23	24	25	26	27
LOUISIANA—Cont'd												
Pointe Coupee	0.6	61.3	38.1	0.4	0.3	0.0	0.5	1.1	58.5	41.1	0.1	0.1	0.7
Rapides	1.0	67.3	30.8	1.2	1.0	0.1	0.7	1.4	70.7	28.0	0.4	0.7	1.2
Red River	0.6	58.3	41.2	0.5	0.3	0.1	0.3	1.0	61.3	38.2	0.2	0.1	0.6
Richland	0.5	61.3	38.2	0.4	0.3	0.0	0.3	1.1	63.1	36.5	0.1	0.1	1.0
Sabine	2.2	74.7	17.1	9.5	0.3	0.0	0.5	2.7	79.2	17.6	2.8	0.1	4.6
St. Bernard	1.5	89.7	7.9	1.0	1.8	0.1	1.2	5.1	93.3	4.7	0.5	0.9	6.3
St. Charles	0.9	73.2	25.5	0.6	0.7	0.0	0.9	2.8	74.6	24.2	0.3	0.4	2.5
St. Helena	0.7	47.0	52.7	0.4	0.3	0.1	0.4	1.0	47.9	51.9	0.1	0.0	0.5
St. James	0.4	50.3	49.5	0.3	0.1	0.0	0.2	0.6	50.2	49.6	0.0	0.1	0.5
St. John the Baptist	1.0	53.3	45.1	0.5	0.7	0.1	1.3	2.9	62.6	36.1	0.3	0.4	2.4
St. Landry	0.7	57.0	42.5	0.4	0.3	0.0	0.5	0.9	59.2	40.3	0.1	0.2	0.8
St. Martin	0.7	66.4	32.3	0.5	1.0	0.0	0.4	0.8	65.5	33.0	0.2	0.7	1.1
St. Mary	1.5	64.1	32.1	2.0	1.8	0.0	1.6	2.2	64.9	31.6	1.4	1.7	1.9
St. Tammany	1.3	88.2	10.3	0.9	1.0	0.1	1.0	2.5	87.8	11.0	0.4	0.5	2.2
Tangipahoa	0.8	70.4	28.6	0.6	0.5	0.1	0.7	1.5	70.7	28.6	0.2	0.3	1.1
Tensas	0.7	43.7	55.9	0.4	0.3	0.0	0.5	1.3	46.3	53.3	0.2	0.1	0.6
Terrebonne	1.5	75.3	18.1	6.2	1.0	0.1	0.9	1.6	77.4	16.5	5.1	0.7	1.4
Union	0.5	70.2	28.1	0.4	0.3	0.1	1.4	2.0	71.8	27.9	0.1	0.1	0.6
Vermilion	0.8	83.3	14.5	0.5	2.0	0.1	0.4	1.4	84.4	13.9	0.2	1.4	1.2
Vernon	3.4	76.5	18.1	2.8	2.4	0.6	3.4	5.9	74.0	20.8	0.7	2.4	5.5
Washington	0.5	67.8	31.7	0.5	0.3	0.0	0.2	0.8	68.7	31.0	0.1	0.1	0.6
Webster	0.9	66.2	33.1	0.8	0.3	0.1	0.4	0.9	68.0	31.6	0.2	0.1	0.5
West Baton Rouge	0.8	63.4	35.8	0.6	0.3	0.1	0.8	1.4	63.5	36.0	0.2	0.1	1.1
West Carroll	0.4	80.3	18.9	0.5	0.2	0.0	0.6	1.3	82.7	16.7	0.3	0.0	1.0
West Feliciana	0.4	49.0	50.6	0.4	0.3	0.0	0.1	1.0	43.9	55.4	0.4	0.1	1.6
Winn	0.9	67.0	32.4	0.9	0.3	0.1	0.2	0.9	69.7	29.5	0.4	0.1	0.9
MAINE	1.0	97.9	0.7	1.0	0.9	0.1	0.4	0.7	98.4	0.4	0.5	0.5	0.6
Androscoggin	1.2	98.1	1.0	0.8	0.8	0.1	0.5	1.0	98.5	0.5	0.2	0.5	0.7
Aroostook	0.8	97.5	0.5	1.8	0.6	0.1	0.3	0.6	97.3	1.1	0.9	0.5	0.6
Cumberland	1.1	96.7	1.4	0.7	1.7	0.1	0.6	1.0	98.1	0.6	0.3	0.9	0.6
Franklin	0.8	98.7	0.3	0.9	0.6	0.1	0.3	0.5	99.2	0.1	0.3	0.3	0.4
Hancock	1.1	98.7	0.4	1.0	0.6	0.1	0.4	0.6	99.0	0.2	0.4	0.3	0.6
Kennebec	1.0	98.4	0.5	0.9	0.8	0.0	0.3	0.7	98.9	0.2	0.3	0.4	0.4
Knox	0.8	99.0	0.4	0.7	0.5	0.0	0.2	0.6	99.3	0.2	0.3	0.2	0.4
Lincoln	0.6	99.1	0.3	0.7	0.5	0.0	0.2	0.5	99.4	0.1	0.3	0.1	0.4
Oxford	0.8	99.0	0.3	0.7	0.5	0.0	0.2	0.5	99.4	0.1	0.2	0.3	0.4
Penobscot	1.0	97.5	0.7	1.4	0.9	0.1	0.4	0.6	98.0	0.4	0.9	0.6	0.5
Piscataquis	1.0	98.8	0.3	1.0	0.4	0.1	0.5	0.5	99.1	0.1	0.4	0.3	0.4
Sagadahoc	1.2	97.6	1.3	0.8	0.9	0.1	0.6	1.1	97.8	1.0	0.2	0.7	1.0
Somerset	0.9	98.8	0.4	0.9	0.5	0.0	0.3	0.5	99.2	0.1	0.3	0.2	0.3
Waldo	1.1	99.0	0.4	1.2	0.4	0.1	0.3	0.6	99.3	0.1	0.2	0.2	0.5
Washington	1.1	94.5	0.4	5.1	0.5	0.0	0.7	0.8	95.5	0.2	4.0	0.2	0.4
York	0.8	98.3	0.6	0.6	0.9	0.1	0.3	0.7	98.7	0.3	0.2	0.7	0.6
MARYLAND	2.0	65.4	28.8	0.7	4.5	0.1	2.5	4.3	71.0	24.9	0.3	2.9	2.6
Allegany	0.7	93.7	5.7	0.4	0.7	0.1	0.3	0.8	97.3	2.0	0.1	0.4	0.4
Anne Arundel	1.7	82.6	14.2	0.8	2.8	0.1	1.3	2.6	85.7	11.8	0.3	1.8	1.6
Baltimore	1.4	75.4	20.8	0.6	3.6	0.1	1.1	1.8	84.9	12.3	0.2	2.2	1.2
Calvert	1.3	85.1	13.6	0.8	1.2	0.1	0.6	1.5	83.4	15.7	0.2	0.6	1.0
Caroline	1.3	82.7	15.4	0.9	0.7	0.1	1.7	2.7	82.7	16.5	0.2	0.3	0.9
Carroll	0.7	96.4	2.5	0.5	1.0	0.0	0.5	1.0	96.7	2.4	0.2	0.6	0.7
Cecil	1.2	94.5	4.3	0.8	0.9	0.1	0.8	1.5	94.5	4.5	0.2	0.4	0.9
Charles	2.1	70.2	27.1	1.4	2.4	0.1	1.1	2.3	79.3	18.2	0.8	1.3	1.7
Dorchester	0.9	70.0	28.9	0.5	0.8	0.0	0.7	1.3	71.3	27.9	0.2	0.5	0.6
Frederick	1.5	90.6	7.0	0.6	2.1	0.1	1.2	2.4	93.1	5.3	0.2	1.0	1.1
Garrett	0.4	99.2	0.5	0.3	0.2	0.0	0.1	0.4	99.4	0.4	0.1	0.1	0.4
Harford	1.5	88.0	9.9	0.6	1.9	0.1	1.0	1.9	89.3	8.5	0.3	1.4	1.5
Howard	2.2	76.0	15.5	0.7	8.4	0.1	1.7	3.0	83.2	11.8	0.2	4.3	2.0
Kent	1.2	80.6	17.8	0.5	0.7	0.1	1.6	2.8	78.9	19.8	0.2	0.4	2.6
Montgomery	3.4	67.3	16.3	0.8	12.3	0.2	6.8	11.5	76.7	12.2	0.2	8.2	7.4
Prince George's	2.6	28.5	64.3	1.0	4.4	0.1	4.5	7.1	43.1	50.7	0.3	3.9	4.1
Queen Anne's	0.9	89.8	9.1	0.5	0.9	0.0	0.6	1.1	88.1	11.3	0.1	0.4	0.6
St. Mary's	1.7	83.0	14.5	0.9	2.4	0.1	0.9	2.0	84.4	13.5	0.4	1.2	1.6
Somerset	1.2	57.2	41.7	0.9	0.7	0.0	0.7	1.3	60.9	38.2	0.2	0.4	1.0
Talbot	0.8	82.6	15.7	0.4	1.0	0.2	0.9	1.8	81.3	18.0	0.1	0.3	0.5

[1] Hispanic persons may be of any race.

Table B. States and Counties

STATE County	Population and population characteristics, 2000										
	Age (percent)										
	Under 5 years	5 to 17 years	18 to 24 years	25 to 34 years	35 to 44 years	45 to 54 years	55 to 64 years	65 to 74 years	75 years and over	Median age (years)	Percent Female
	28	29	30	31	32	33	34	35	36	37	38
LOUISIANA—Cont'd											
Pointe Coupee	6.9	20.4	8.8	11.5	15.5	13.8	9.3	7.7	6.2	36.7	51.4
Rapides	7.1	20.2	9.5	12.6	15.3	13.2	9.2	7.1	6.0	35.5	52.2
Red River	7.5	22.6	9.3	11.1	13.7	12.3	9.2	7.3	7.1	34.6	52.4
Richland	7.4	19.9	9.9	11.8	14.9	12.1	8.9	7.6	7.4	35.8	53.0
Sabine	6.5	19.7	8.3	11.0	13.5	12.8	11.6	9.2	7.3	38.2	51.1
St. Bernard	6.3	18.9	9.2	13.1	16.1	13.9	8.7	7.9	5.9	36.6	51.7
St. Charles	7.3	23.0	8.3	12.7	18.7	13.7	7.3	5.4	3.6	34.2	51.2
St. Helena	7.5	21.5	9.1	11.9	14.3	13.9	9.4	7.0	5.5	35.0	52.0
St. James	7.0	22.5	9.8	12.2	16.0	12.8	8.6	6.4	4.8	34.0	51.8
St. John the Baptist	8.0	23.1	9.7	13.5	16.7	13.3	7.8	4.5	3.3	32.0	51.5
St. Landry	7.8	21.7	9.2	11.8	14.6	12.3	9.1	7.4	6.0	34.6	52.2
St. Martin	7.7	21.8	9.6	13.4	16.2	12.6	8.6	5.7	4.5	33.4	50.9
St. Mary	7.4	22.3	8.7	12.6	16.1	12.8	9.1	6.4	4.6	34.3	51.3
St. Tammany	7.1	21.4	7.3	12.0	17.8	15.5	8.8	5.7	4.3	36.3	51.0
Tangipahoa	7.2	20.5	12.7	13.1	14.6	13.0	8.2	6.0	4.6	32.3	51.8
Tensas	6.6	19.9	10.0	10.2	14.8	14.2	8.8	7.8	7.8	37.3	50.5
Terrebonne	7.4	21.8	10.1	13.7	16.2	12.7	8.4	5.7	4.1	33.0	50.9
Union	7.0	18.7	9.1	12.3	14.2	13.2	10.6	8.1	6.8	37.3	51.4
Vermilion	7.1	20.9	9.4	12.4	15.8	12.2	8.6	7.1	6.4	35.1	51.6
Vernon	9.5	19.7	14.7	17.9	13.6	9.8	7.0	4.8	3.2	28.3	47.8
Washington	7.2	19.6	9.5	12.2	14.5	13.0	9.6	7.6	6.7	36.1	51.2
Webster	6.5	19.1	8.6	11.5	14.5	13.0	10.6	8.6	7.7	38.1	52.1
West Baton Rouge	7.0	21.0	9.9	13.6	17.0	13.2	8.5	5.7	4.1	34.0	50.9
West Carroll	6.0	19.6	9.7	11.6	14.9	12.4	10.2	7.9	7.6	37.2	49.5
West Feliciana	4.6	15.7	8.7	17.6	22.4	16.4	7.4	4.3	2.9	36.6	34.4
Winn	6.3	18.5	9.6	13.6	15.3	13.3	9.4	7.1	6.9	36.2	47.4
MAINE	5.5	18.1	8.1	12.4	16.7	15.1	9.7	7.5	6.8	38.6	51.3
Androscoggin	5.9	18.0	9.1	13.2	16.5	13.9	9.0	7.1	7.3	37.2	51.5
Aroostook	5.0	17.6	7.9	10.9	15.4	15.3	10.9	9.2	7.8	40.7	51.2
Cumberland	5.8	17.5	8.4	13.9	17.5	14.9	8.7	6.6	6.7	37.6	51.6
Franklin	5.1	18.4	11.1	10.7	15.7	14.6	10.2	7.8	6.4	38.2	51.7
Hancock	4.9	17.4	7.4	11.3	16.2	16.3	10.5	8.6	7.4	40.7	51.1
Kennebec	5.5	18.4	8.5	11.9	16.7	15.2	9.7	7.4	6.8	38.7	51.5
Knox	5.3	17.1	6.3	11.7	15.7	16.2	10.5	8.5	8.7	41.4	51.2
Lincoln	4.8	17.9	5.5	10.1	15.5	16.1	12.0	9.6	8.6	42.6	51.2
Oxford	5.3	18.9	6.5	10.8	17.0	15.2	10.3	8.6	7.5	40.2	51.2
Penobscot	5.4	17.5	11.3	12.5	16.5	14.6	9.2	7.2	5.8	37.2	51.2
Piscataquis	4.8	18.6	5.7	10.2	15.8	16.2	11.3	9.0	8.4	42.1	50.9
Sagadahoc	6.1	19.7	6.6	12.7	17.8	15.3	9.6	6.4	5.9	38.0	50.9
Somerset	5.7	19.0	7.0	12.3	16.4	15.0	10.3	7.8	6.5	38.9	51.0
Waldo	5.6	18.6	7.5	11.9	15.9	16.6	10.2	7.6	6.0	39.3	50.9
Washington	5.1	17.8	8.0	11.2	15.1	14.9	10.7	9.1	8.2	40.5	51.2
York	5.9	18.9	6.9	12.4	17.6	15.2	9.5	7.3	6.3	38.5	51.4
MARYLAND	6.7	18.9	8.5	14.1	17.3	14.3	8.9	6.1	5.2	36.0	51.7
Allegany	5.0	15.5	11.2	12.4	14.4	13.2	10.3	9.0	8.9	39.1	50.2
Anne Arundel	6.8	18.5	8.1	14.8	18.0	14.6	9.3	5.7	4.3	36.0	50.2
Baltimore	6.0	17.6	8.5	13.4	16.4	14.4	9.0	7.4	7.3	37.7	52.6
Calvert	6.8	22.8	6.4	12.2	19.5	14.9	8.5	4.9	4.0	35.9	50.7
Caroline	6.2	20.6	7.7	12.4	16.5	13.6	9.5	7.1	6.4	37.0	51.1
Carroll	6.7	21.0	7.0	11.9	18.7	15.0	8.9	5.7	5.1	36.9	50.6
Cecil	6.9	20.7	7.5	13.9	17.2	14.3	9.0	6.0	4.5	35.5	50.4
Charles	7.1	21.6	7.6	14.4	18.8	14.0	8.7	4.5	3.3	34.6	51.2
Dorchester	5.4	17.9	6.7	11.3	15.5	14.2	11.3	9.4	8.3	40.7	52.7
Frederick	7.2	20.4	7.4	13.8	18.9	14.6	8.1	5.2	4.5	35.6	50.8
Garrett	6.1	19.0	7.8	12.1	15.5	13.6	10.9	8.0	6.9	38.3	50.7
Harford	7.2	20.7	6.8	13.1	18.4	14.6	9.0	5.9	4.2	36.2	51.0
Howard	7.4	20.7	6.3	14.7	19.6	15.5	8.4	4.2	3.3	35.5	50.9
Kent	4.6	16.1	10.9	9.5	14.2	13.6	11.7	9.9	9.4	41.3	52.1
Montgomery	6.9	18.5	6.9	14.5	17.8	15.2	8.9	5.7	5.5	36.8	52.1
Prince George's	7.2	19.5	10.4	15.7	17.3	13.7	8.4	4.6	3.1	33.3	52.2
Queen Anne's	6.4	19.0	5.8	11.6	18.4	14.9	10.9	7.4	5.5	38.8	50.2
St. Mary's	7.2	20.7	8.9	14.4	18.1	13.2	8.3	5.0	4.0	34.2	49.5
Somerset	4.8	13.7	15.7	13.4	16.1	12.9	9.3	7.8	6.3	36.5	46.6
Talbot	5.2	16.5	5.6	10.3	14.9	14.8	12.3	10.5	9.9	43.3	52.3

Table B. States and Counties

STATE County	Population and population characteristics, 1990										Population—change, 1980–2000				
	Age (percent)									Percent Female	Total persons			Percent change	
	Under 5 years	5 to 17 years	18 to 24 years	25 to 34 years	35 to 44 years	45 to 54 years	55 to 64 years	65 to 74 years	75 years and over		2000	1990	1980	1990–2000	1980–1990
	39	40	41	42	43	44	45	46	47	48	49	50	51	52	53
LOUISIANA—Cont'd															
Pointe Coupee	7.8	22.5	9.3	15.7	13.6	9.6	8.7	7.2	5.6	51.9	22 763	22 540	24 045	1.0	-6.3
Rapides	7.7	21.4	10.3	16.5	13.8	9.9	8.4	7.0	5.0	52.1	126 337	131 556	135 282	-4.0	-2.8
Red River	8.4	22.7	9.2	14.3	11.8	9.3	8.7	8.7	6.8	52.7	9 622	9 526	10 433	1.0	-10.0
Richland	7.7	23.0	9.1	14.5	12.1	9.1	8.9	8.3	7.3	53.1	20 981	20 629	22 187	1.7	-7.0
Sabine	7.7	20.8	8.6	13.5	12.1	10.3	10.4	9.7	6.8	51.4	23 459	22 646	25 280	3.6	-10.4
St. Bernard	7.4	19.8	10.1	16.8	14.9	9.9	9.7	7.5	3.8	52.0	67 229	66 631	64 097	0.9	4.0
St. Charles	9.2	22.3	8.9	19.3	15.6	9.5	7.7	4.6	2.8	51.1	48 072	42 437	37 259	13.3	13.9
St. Helena	8.8	22.7	10.2	14.8	13.2	9.5	8.5	6.5	5.7	52.1	10 525	9 874	9 827	6.6	0.5
St. James	8.7	23.1	10.8	16.8	13.6	9.4	7.8	5.6	4.2	52.1	21 216	20 879	21 495	1.6	-2.9
St. John the Baptist	9.6	24.5	9.2	19.2	15.4	9.0	6.0	4.2	2.9	51.1	43 044	39 996	31 924	7.6	25.3
St. Landry	8.4	23.4	9.6	14.9	12.7	9.7	9.0	7.0	5.3	52.4	87 700	80 312	84 128	9.2	-4.5
St. Martin	8.9	23.4	10.7	17.0	13.7	9.6	7.3	5.7	3.6	51.4	48 583	44 097	40 214	10.2	9.7
St. Mary	8.8	23.3	10.1	17.1	13.4	9.9	7.7	5.6	3.9	51.2	53 500	58 086	64 253	-7.9	-9.6
St. Tammany	8.0	22.4	7.9	16.3	17.7	11.0	7.8	5.7	3.2	50.7	191 268	144 500	110 869	32.4	30.3
Tangipahoa	7.8	22.5	12.2	15.3	14.0	9.3	7.9	6.3	4.8	52.2	100 588	85 709	80 698	17.4	6.2
Tensas	8.0	24.4	7.8	13.3	12.8	8.2	8.7	9.3	7.6	54.4	6 618	7 103	8 525	-6.8	-16.7
Terrebonne	8.7	23.7	10.4	17.4	14.2	9.9	7.5	5.2	3.2	51.0	104 503	96 982	94 393	7.8	2.7
Union	7.2	20.8	9.0	13.8	13.4	10.5	9.7	8.8	6.7	52.0	22 803	20 796	21 167	9.7	-1.8
Vermilion	8.0	22.7	9.1	16.0	13.0	9.4	8.6	7.3	5.8	51.5	53 807	50 055	48 458	7.5	3.3
Vernon	10.6	18.7	21.6	20.3	11.4	6.5	5.1	3.5	2.4	45.0	52 531	61 961	53 475	-15.2	15.9
Washington	7.0	21.8	9.0	14.9	13.7	10.0	9.3	8.5	5.9	51.7	43 926	43 185	44 207	1.7	-2.3
Webster	7.1	20.2	8.7	14.4	13.0	10.4	10.0	9.1	7.1	52.7	41 831	41 989	43 631	-0.4	-3.8
West Baton Rouge	8.1	21.7	10.8	17.8	14.4	10.3	7.8	5.7	3.5	51.5	21 601	19 419	19 086	11.2	1.7
West Carroll	7.2	21.9	8.5	13.6	12.8	10.7	9.4	8.8	7.1	52.2	12 314	12 093	12 922	1.8	-6.4
West Feliciana	5.2	14.6	9.0	26.9	22.1	9.3	6.2	4.0	2.9	32.1	15 111	12 915	12 186	17.0	6.0
Winn	7.3	20.6	9.9	14.6	13.3	10.1	9.1	8.7	6.5	50.5	16 894	16 498	17 253	2.4	-5.7
MAINE	7.0	18.2	10.1	16.7	15.7	10.2	8.8	7.5	5.8	51.3	1 274 923	1 227 928	1 125 043	3.8	9.1
Androscoggin	7.4	18.4	10.9	17.0	14.5	9.8	8.6	7.4	6.0	51.6	103 793	105 259	99 509	-1.4	5.8
Aroostook	7.0	18.7	10.2	17.0	15.2	9.9	9.2	7.3	5.5	49.5	73 938	86 936	91 344	-15.0	-4.8
Cumberland	7.0	16.5	10.8	18.2	16.3	9.9	8.3	7.2	5.8	51.9	265 612	243 135	215 789	9.2	12.7
Franklin	6.9	19.3	12.0	15.2	14.9	10.6	8.8	6.8	5.5	51.8	29 467	29 008	27 447	1.6	5.7
Hancock	6.8	17.3	8.8	15.7	16.0	10.4	9.6	8.2	7.1	51.0	51 791	46 948	41 781	10.3	12.4
Kennebec	6.7	18.5	10.2	15.9	16.0	10.4	8.9	7.5	5.9	51.8	117 114	115 904	109 889	1.0	5.5
Knox	6.7	17.7	7.5	14.6	16.6	10.3	9.6	9.4	7.6	51.5	39 618	36 310	32 941	9.1	10.2
Lincoln	6.6	18.5	6.9	14.1	16.3	10.9	10.2	9.2	7.3	51.3	33 616	30 357	25 691	10.7	18.2
Oxford	7.2	19.2	7.6	15.9	15.0	10.4	9.6	8.5	6.5	51.3	54 755	52 602	49 043	4.1	7.3
Penobscot	6.5	17.7	13.4	16.6	15.2	10.1	8.8	6.5	5.0	51.1	144 919	146 601	137 015	-1.1	7.0
Piscataquis	6.1	20.0	7.5	14.0	15.4	10.9	10.0	9.0	7.1	51.2	17 235	18 653	17 634	-7.6	5.8
Sagadahoc	8.1	18.5	9.1	18.8	16.6	10.5	7.3	6.2	4.9	50.6	35 214	33 535	28 795	5.0	16.5
Somerset	7.0	20.4	8.8	15.7	15.3	10.6	9.1	7.3	5.7	51.1	50 888	49 767	45 049	2.3	10.5
Waldo	7.1	19.9	8.5	15.0	16.8	10.4	9.3	7.5	5.6	50.9	36 280	33 018	28 414	9.9	16.2
Washington	6.4	19.2	9.0	14.4	14.3	10.4	10.1	9.0	7.2	51.0	33 941	35 308	34 963	-3.9	1.0
York	7.4	18.7	8.7	17.6	16.4	10.0	8.5	7.2	5.4	51.3	186 742	164 587	139 739	13.5	17.8
MARYLAND	7.5	16.8	10.6	18.8	16.3	10.9	8.3	6.6	4.2	51.5	5 296 486	4 780 753	4 216 933	10.8	13.4
Allegany	5.8	16.0	11.9	13.0	13.1	10.7	11.0	10.6	8.0	52.9	74 930	74 946	80 548	0.0	-7.0
Anne Arundel	7.4	17.2	10.9	18.7	16.8	11.9	8.2	5.7	3.1	49.7	489 656	427 239	370 775	14.6	15.2
Baltimore	6.8	15.0	9.9	18.0	15.8	10.7	9.8	8.6	5.4	52.3	754 292	692 134	655 615	9.0	5.6
Calvert	7.9	20.5	8.6	17.4	18.0	11.4	7.2	5.6	3.3	50.4	74 563	51 372	34 638	45.1	48.3
Caroline	7.6	18.7	8.8	16.1	14.6	10.5	9.2	8.3	6.1	51.5	29 772	27 035	23 143	10.1	16.8
Carroll	7.8	18.8	9.3	17.2	17.4	11.7	7.6	5.8	4.4	50.8	150 897	123 372	96 356	22.3	28.0
Cecil	7.9	19.5	10.1	16.7	16.2	10.9	8.5	6.5	3.8	50.1	85 951	71 347	60 430	20.5	18.1
Charles	8.5	20.9	10.7	19.2	16.7	11.3	6.3	4.1	2.4	50.3	120 546	101 154	72 751	19.2	39.0
Dorchester	6.7	16.2	8.6	15.6	14.1	10.8	10.8	10.1	7.2	52.6	30 674	30 236	30 623	1.4	-1.3
Frederick	7.9	18.5	10.4	18.3	17.4	10.7	7.3	5.6	3.8	50.8	195 277	150 208	114 792	30.0	30.9
Garrett	6.9	20.1	9.3	15.7	14.1	10.8	9.2	8.0	5.8	51.2	29 846	28 138	26 490	6.1	6.2
Harford	8.1	18.7	10.1	18.7	16.9	11.5	7.8	5.4	2.9	50.1	218 590	182 132	145 930	20.0	24.8
Howard	8.1	17.8	8.9	20.9	19.3	12.3	6.5	3.8	2.3	50.2	247 842	187 328	118 572	32.3	58.0
Kent	6.2	15.1	12.1	14.5	13.2	11.1	10.9	10.2	6.7	51.6	19 197	17 842	16 695	7.6	6.9
Montgomery	7.5	16.0	8.9	19.7	17.7	11.7	8.2	6.1	4.1	51.8	873 341	762 875	579 053	14.5	30.7
Prince George's	7.6	16.8	13.0	20.7	16.6	11.1	7.2	4.5	2.4	51.5	801 515	722 705	665 071	10.9	9.5
Queen Anne's	7.3	17.3	7.9	16.8	16.1	11.7	10.1	8.1	4.7	50.6	40 563	33 953	25 508	19.5	33.1
St. Mary's	8.9	19.4	11.9	20.3	14.9	9.7	6.5	5.1	3.2	49.1	86 211	75 974	59 895	13.5	26.8
Somerset	5.3	14.9	13.7	18.3	13.6	9.4	9.9	8.6	6.3	47.0	24 747	23 440	19 188	5.6	22.2
Talbot	6.3	14.7	7.5	14.8	14.2	11.1	11.3	11.7	8.4	52.6	33 812	30 549	25 604	10.7	19.3

Table B. States and Counties

STATE County	Total population	In households (percent) Total in house-holds	House-holder	Spouse	Child Total	Child Own child under 18 years	Other relatives Total	Other relatives Under 18 years	Nonrelatives Total	Nonrelatives Unmar-ried partner	In group quarters (percent) Total in group quarters	Institutionalized population Correc-tional institu-tions	Institutionalized population Nurs-ing homes	Institutionalized population Other institu-tions	Noninstitutionalized population Col-lege dormi-tories	Noninstitutionalized population Mili-tary quar-ters	Other
	54	55	56	57	58	59	60	61	62	63	64	65	66	67	68	69	70
LOUISIANA—Cont'd																	
Pointe Coupee	22 763	98.5	36.9	19.8	32.1	23.2	6.9	3.7	2.9	1.8	1.5	0.5	1.0	0.0	0.0	0.0	0.0
Rapides	126 337	95.6	37.3	18.5	30.6	23.4	5.8	3.0	3.4	1.7	4.4	1.1	1.1	0.5	0.4	0.0	1.3
Red River	9 622	97.1	35.5	18.3	32.7	24.4	7.6	4.4	3.0	1.5	2.9	0.6	1.6	0.7	0.0	0.0	0.0
Richland	20 981	94.4	35.7	17.9	31.0	22.9	6.9	3.9	2.9	1.6	5.6	3.2	1.7	0.0	0.0	0.0	0.7
Sabine	23 459	98.2	39.3	21.9	29.6	23.0	4.8	2.7	2.6	1.4	1.8	0.5	1.1	0.0	0.0	0.0	0.1
St. Bernard	67 229	98.8	37.4	19.9	31.6	22.1	6.1	2.7	3.9	2.1	1.2	0.4	0.6	0.0	0.0	0.0	0.1
St. Charles	48 072	99.1	34.2	20.6	35.5	27.0	5.6	2.9	3.2	1.8	0.9	0.2	0.5	0.1	0.0	0.0	0.1
St. Helena	10 525	99.3	36.8	18.0	32.9	23.2	9.1	5.3	2.6	1.4	0.7	0.0	0.6	0.0	0.0	0.0	0.1
St. James	21 216	98.8	33.0	18.2	36.4	23.9	8.9	5.0	2.3	1.4	1.2	0.4	0.5	0.3	0.0	0.0	0.0
St. John the Baptist	43 044	99.0	33.2	18.6	36.7	26.7	7.4	4.0	3.2	1.8	1.0	0.7	0.3	0.0	0.0	0.0	0.0
St. Landry	87 700	98.3	36.9	18.2	34.3	25.7	6.0	3.3	3.0	1.8	1.7	0.3	0.9	0.3	0.0	0.0	0.2
St. Martin	48 583	98.4	35.3	19.3	34.5	25.9	5.7	3.0	3.6	2.2	1.6	0.9	0.6	0.1	0.0	0.0	0.1
St. Mary	53 500	98.8	36.1	18.4	33.2	25.0	7.2	4.1	3.9	2.2	1.2	0.5	0.3	0.1	0.0	0.0	0.2
St. Tammany	191 268	98.8	36.2	22.2	32.6	25.9	4.4	2.0	3.4	1.7	1.2	0.3	0.5	0.3	0.0	0.0	0.2
Tangipahoa	100 588	96.7	36.3	18.2	31.5	23.8	6.4	3.3	4.3	1.8	3.3	0.5	0.6	0.2	1.3	0.0	0.6
Tensas	6 618	92.6	36.5	15.7	28.7	20.7	8.4	5.2	3.3	1.7	7.4	6.4	1.1	0.0	0.0	0.0	0.0
Terrebonne	104 503	98.6	34.4	19.6	33.9	25.0	6.5	3.5	4.2	2.2	1.4	0.5	0.5	0.2	0.0	0.0	0.2
Union	22 803	98.0	38.8	21.5	29.4	22.1	5.7	3.2	2.6	1.4	2.0	0.6	1.3	0.1	0.0	0.0	0.0
Vermilion	53 807	98.6	36.9	20.5	32.7	25.2	4.8	2.4	3.7	2.1	1.4	0.3	1.0	0.1	0.0	0.0	0.1
Vernon	52 531	93.6	34.8	21.3	31.3	26.7	3.5	1.9	2.7	1.1	6.4	0.5	0.4	0.1	0.0	5.3	0.1
Washington	43 926	95.9	37.5	18.5	30.2	22.3	6.8	3.9	3.0	1.5	4.1	3.0	0.8	0.2	0.0	0.0	0.5
Webster	41 831	97.8	39.4	19.6	29.1	21.5	6.4	3.4	3.2	1.6	2.2	0.7	1.1	0.0	0.0	0.0	0.5
West Baton Rouge	21 601	97.4	35.5	18.3	33.3	23.7	6.9	3.8	3.4	1.8	2.6	2.0	0.5	0.0	0.0	0.0	0.1
West Carroll	12 314	93.6	36.2	20.9	28.4	22.0	5.8	3.1	2.2	1.1	6.4	4.7	1.6	0.0	0.0	0.0	0.1
West Feliciana	15 111	65.9	24.1	13.0	22.9	17.7	4.1	2.2	1.8	0.9	34.1	33.2	0.8	0.0	0.0	0.0	0.0
Winn	16 894	89.5	35.1	18.2	27.5	20.7	6.2	3.6	2.5	1.4	10.5	9.1	1.1	0.0	0.0	0.0	0.3
MAINE	1 274 923	97.3	40.6	21.3	26.9	21.9	2.6	0.9	5.8	3.0	2.7	0.2	0.7	0.1	1.1	0.1	0.6
Androscoggin	103 793	96.5	40.5	20.1	27.2	22.2	2.9	0.9	5.9	3.2	3.5	0.1	1.3	0.1	1.5	0.0	0.5
Aroostook	73 938	96.9	41.1	22.8	26.3	20.9	2.4	0.8	4.3	2.5	3.1	0.1	1.1	0.1	0.9	0.0	0.9
Cumberland	265 612	96.8	40.7	20.4	26.7	21.9	2.7	0.8	6.4	2.8	3.2	0.3	0.6	0.1	1.3	0.1	0.7
Franklin	29 467	96.2	40.1	21.0	26.1	21.9	2.4	0.8	6.6	3.2	3.8	0.1	0.8	0.0	2.8	0.0	0.2
Hancock	51 791	97.5	42.2	22.6	24.9	20.7	2.1	0.7	5.6	3.1	2.5	0.0	0.7	0.1	1.2	0.2	0.3
Kennebec	117 114	96.9	40.7	21.0	27.2	22.3	2.4	0.9	5.6	3.2	3.1	0.2	0.9	0.1	1.5	0.0	0.5
Knox	39 618	96.8	41.9	21.9	25.3	20.9	2.2	0.8	5.5	3.1	3.2	1.9	0.9	0.0	0.0	0.1	0.3
Lincoln	33 616	98.8	42.1	23.6	25.7	21.1	2.3	0.8	5.0	2.8	1.2	0.0	0.4	0.0	0.0	0.0	0.7
Oxford	54 755	98.5	40.8	22.0	27.3	22.3	2.7	1.0	5.8	3.3	1.5	0.1	1.1	0.0	0.0	0.0	0.8
Penobscot	144 919	95.5	40.1	20.6	25.8	21.0	2.5	0.8	6.5	3.0	4.5	0.2	0.6	0.1	2.6	0.0	0.8
Piscataquis	17 235	98.9	42.2	22.8	26.2	21.7	2.6	0.8	5.1	2.7	1.1	0.1	0.7	0.0	0.0	0.0	0.3
Sagadahoc	35 214	99.2	40.1	21.9	29.1	24.2	2.7	1.0	5.4	2.8	0.8	0.0	0.4	0.0	0.0	0.0	0.4
Somerset	50 888	98.2	40.3	21.8	27.5	22.4	2.6	1.0	6.0	3.5	1.8	0.1	0.7	0.0	0.2	0.0	0.7
Waldo	36 280	98.6	40.6	22.4	27.1	22.4	2.8	1.1	5.7	3.4	1.4	0.1	0.4	0.0	0.7	0.0	0.2
Washington	33 941	97.3	41.6	21.7	25.9	20.9	2.9	1.2	5.2	2.8	2.7	0.5	0.9	0.0	0.8	0.1	0.4
York	186 742	98.7	39.9	22.0	28.5	23.1	2.9	1.0	5.4	2.8	1.3	0.0	0.5	0.1	0.2	0.1	0.4
MARYLAND	5 296 486	97.5	37.4	18.8	29.6	22.6	6.2	2.4	5.5	2.1	2.5	0.7	0.5	0.1	0.7	0.1	0.4
Allegany	74 930	91.8	39.1	19.8	24.8	18.5	3.4	1.3	4.7	1.9	8.2	4.3	1.2	0.4	2.0	0.0	0.3
Anne Arundel	489 656	96.7	36.5	20.9	29.5	22.8	4.8	1.9	5.1	2.1	3.3	1.4	0.4	0.1	0.1	1.0	0.4
Baltimore	754 292	97.7	39.8	19.6	28.0	21.1	5.1	1.9	5.2	2.2	2.3	0.2	0.5	0.2	0.9	0.0	0.5
Calvert	74 563	99.2	34.1	22.1	33.8	26.8	5.1	2.2	4.1	1.8	0.8	0.2	0.4	0.0	0.0	0.0	0.2
Caroline	29 772	98.5	37.3	20.3	29.8	23.5	5.6	2.5	5.5	2.6	1.5	0.2	0.9	0.0	0.0	0.0	0.3
Carroll	150 897	97.6	34.8	23.2	32.4	25.9	3.8	1.3	3.4	1.6	2.4	0.5	0.6	0.3	0.7	0.0	0.3
Cecil	85 951	98.6	36.3	21.3	31.4	24.9	4.7	2.1	4.9	2.5	1.4	0.2	0.5	0.2	0.0	0.0	0.5
Charles	120 546	98.9	34.6	20.1	33.4	25.7	5.7	2.5	5.2	2.2	1.1	0.5	0.3	0.0	0.0	0.0	0.3
Dorchester	30 674	97.8	41.4	19.7	26.3	19.9	5.7	2.7	4.7	2.7	2.2	0.5	0.9	0.2	0.0	0.0	0.6
Frederick	195 277	97.6	35.9	21.9	31.6	25.6	3.8	1.4	4.4	2.0	2.4	0.2	0.7	0.1	0.9	0.1	0.4
Garrett	29 846	97.9	38.5	23.4	29.4	23.0	3.1	1.2	3.6	1.9	2.1	0.2	1.1	0.4	0.1	0.0	0.3
Harford	218 590	99.3	36.4	22.5	32.6	25.9	4.0	1.5	3.7	1.8	0.7	0.2	0.3	0.0	0.0	0.1	0.1
Howard	247 842	98.5	36.3	22.0	32.2	26.6	3.8	1.1	4.2	1.7	1.5	0.4	0.2	0.1	0.0	0.0	0.7
Kent	19 197	93.0	39.9	20.6	23.7	18.4	4.1	1.8	4.7	2.3	7.0	0.3	1.1	0.4	3.9	0.0	1.4
Montgomery	873 341	98.9	37.2	20.5	29.9	23.6	5.7	1.4	5.6	1.5	1.1	0.1	0.5	0.0	0.0	0.0	0.4
Prince George's	801 515	97.8	35.8	15.7	30.9	22.4	8.9	3.6	6.5	2.1	2.2	0.2	0.3	0.1	1.2	0.1	0.3
Queen Anne's	40 563	98.7	37.8	23.5	29.0	23.1	4.2	1.8	4.2	2.2	1.3	0.7	0.4	0.0	0.0	0.0	0.2
St. Mary's	86 211	96.8	35.5	20.5	31.5	25.5	4.2	1.9	5.0	2.2	3.2	0.2	0.7	0.0	1.1	0.7	0.5
Somerset	24 747	80.2	33.8	15.6	21.5	15.4	5.2	2.5	4.1	1.8	19.8	12.9	0.8	0.0	5.9	0.0	0.2
Talbot	33 812	98.2	42.3	23.0	24.7	19.6	4.1	1.6	4.1	2.1	1.8	0.3	1.0	0.0	0.1	0.0	0.4

Column header spanning: **Household relationship, 2000** — *In households (percent)* (columns 55–63), *In group quarters (percent)* (columns 64–70).

Table B. States and Counties

STATE County	Households by type, 2000												Households, 1990		
		Family households						Nonfamily households							
				Married couple		Female householder[1]			Householder living alone						House-holder living alone
	Total households	Total	With own children under 18 years	Total	With own children under 18 years	Total	With own children under 18 years	Total	Total	65 years and over	Average house-hold size	Average family size	Total house-holds	Female house-holder[1]	
	71	72	73	74	75	76	77	78	79	80	81	82	83	84	85
LOUISIANA—Cont'd															
Pointe Coupee	8 397	73.5	35.2	53.7	24.7	15.3	8.4	26.5	23.4	11.1	2.67	3.17	7 736	15.2	21.5
Rapides	47 120	70.3	34.6	49.7	22.4	16.8	10.1	29.7	26.0	10.3	2.56	3.09	45 941	15.3	23.0
Red River	3 414	74.0	35.7	51.5	23.1	18.6	11.0	26.0	23.1	11.5	2.74	3.23	3 321	16.6	23.6
Richland	7 490	73.2	34.3	50.2	21.4	18.8	10.6	26.8	24.0	12.4	2.65	3.14	7 079	16.8	22.2
Sabine	9 221	71.5	31.4	55.7	22.2	12.0	7.2	28.5	26.0	12.8	2.50	3.00	8 361	12.0	24.1
St. Bernard	25 123	72.8	33.7	53.4	24.1	14.6	7.3	27.2	22.9	10.1	2.64	3.12	23 156	13.1	18.3
St. Charles	16 422	79.7	43.4	60.4	31.9	14.7	8.8	20.3	16.7	5.4	2.90	3.27	14 333	12.6	17.6
St. Helena	3 873	71.9	34.0	48.9	22.2	18.4	9.4	28.1	25.4	10.4	2.70	3.27	3 328	16.1	22.9
St. James	6 992	79.4	38.9	55.3	26.7	19.3	10.2	20.6	18.4	7.7	3.00	3.43	6 432	18.2	15.6
St. John the Baptist	14 283	79.2	43.0	56.1	29.3	18.1	10.9	20.8	17.5	6.0	2.98	3.38	12 710	15.1	16.2
St. Landry	32 328	71.8	36.1	49.3	23.0	17.9	10.7	28.2	25.4	11.4	2.67	3.21	27 477	16.5	21.8
St. Martin	17 164	75.6	39.7	54.6	26.8	15.9	10.0	24.4	20.7	7.9	2.78	3.22	14 634	14.7	18.4
St. Mary	19 317	72.9	36.7	51.0	24.1	16.5	9.7	27.1	23.2	8.7	2.74	3.23	19 456	15.4	20.5
St. Tammany	69 253	76.1	39.3	61.4	30.6	11.0	6.5	23.9	19.7	6.7	2.73	3.15	50 346	10.4	18.5
Tangipahoa	36 558	70.5	35.3	49.9	23.6	16.2	9.6	29.5	24.0	8.4	2.66	3.19	29 663	16.4	23.1
Tensas	2 416	67.7	30.0	43.1	17.0	20.2	10.6	32.3	29.3	14.9	2.54	3.14	2 515	20.6	25.2
Terrebonne	35 997	76.1	39.2	57.0	28.1	14.1	8.2	23.9	19.3	7.3	2.86	3.29	31 837	12.8	17.4
Union	8 857	72.4	31.3	55.3	22.2	13.7	7.6	27.6	24.9	11.0	2.52	3.01	7 528	12.9	21.4
Vermilion	19 832	72.9	37.1	55.5	26.6	13.0	8.0	27.1	23.1	10.9	2.67	3.16	17 762	12.4	21.8
Vernon	18 260	75.1	42.3	61.2	33.1	10.7	7.2	24.9	22.0	7.3	2.69	3.15	19 111	8.1	17.4
Washington	16 467	70.7	32.7	49.3	21.2	17.1	9.4	29.3	26.6	12.5	2.56	3.09	15 475	16.5	23.9
Webster	16 501	70.1	30.4	49.7	19.4	16.3	9.0	29.9	27.0	12.9	2.48	2.99	15 849	15.0	25.2
West Baton Rouge	7 663	74.9	37.6	51.5	25.0	18.2	9.8	25.1	21.5	7.1	2.74	3.20	6 606	17.3	19.1
West Carroll	4 458	72.9	33.3	57.8	25.2	12.3	6.5	27.1	24.8	13.8	2.59	3.09	4 394	10.2	23.8
West Feliciana	3 645	74.2	38.9	54.1	26.8	15.6	9.6	25.8	23.1	8.2	2.73	3.24	2 741	17.9	22.4
Winn	5 930	71.4	32.6	51.8	22.1	15.3	8.3	28.6	26.2	12.9	2.55	3.07	5 787	13.8	24.6
MAINE	518 200	65.7	30.4	52.5	21.8	9.5	6.2	34.3	27.0	10.7	2.39	2.90	465 312	9.5	23.3
Androscoggin	42 028	64.7	30.9	49.6	20.6	10.8	7.5	35.3	28.3	11.0	2.38	2.91	40 017	10.9	24.4
Aroostook	30 356	67.3	28.4	55.6	21.3	8.1	5.0	32.7	27.6	13.1	2.36	2.86	31 366	8.6	21.7
Cumberland	107 989	62.7	30.1	50.1	22.3	9.5	6.0	37.3	28.4	10.2	2.38	2.95	94 512	9.8	25.2
Franklin	11 806	65.6	29.5	52.4	20.5	9.2	6.3	34.4	25.8	10.5	2.40	2.88	10 778	9.0	22.3
Hancock	21 864	65.1	28.2	53.5	20.5	8.1	5.4	34.9	27.9	11.6	2.31	2.81	18 342	8.2	24.0
Kennebec	47 683	65.7	31.2	51.6	21.6	10.0	6.9	34.3	27.6	10.6	2.38	2.89	43 889	9.9	24.2
Knox	16 608	64.6	28.3	52.2	20.2	9.0	5.9	35.4	29.0	12.7	2.31	2.83	14 344	9.2	26.0
Lincoln	14 158	67.4	28.2	56.1	20.9	7.7	5.1	32.6	26.7	12.1	2.35	2.82	11 968	7.5	23.6
Oxford	22 314	68.0	30.4	54.1	21.3	9.5	6.3	32.0	25.6	11.0	2.42	2.87	20 064	9.8	22.4
Penobscot	58 096	65.1	30.1	51.5	21.3	9.9	6.5	34.9	26.7	10.0	2.38	2.88	54 063	9.9	22.6
Piscataquis	7 278	66.7	28.6	54.1	20.1	8.4	5.6	33.3	27.8	14.0	2.34	2.83	7 194	8.3	23.3
Sagadahoc	14 117	68.3	33.2	54.6	24.0	9.6	6.6	31.7	25.2	9.3	2.47	2.96	12 581	9.3	21.6
Somerset	20 496	68.9	31.6	54.2	21.6	10.1	6.8	31.1	24.6	10.2	2.44	2.87	18 513	10.0	21.2
Waldo	14 726	68.3	30.7	55.2	21.7	9.0	6.2	31.7	24.9	9.6	2.43	2.88	12 415	9.3	21.7
Washington	14 118	65.9	28.0	52.1	19.3	9.5	5.9	34.1	28.3	13.1	2.34	2.84	13 418	10.0	23.6
York	74 563	68.2	32.2	55.0	23.8	9.5	6.2	31.8	24.9	9.7	2.47	2.96	61 848	8.9	21.4
MARYLAND	1 980 859	68.6	33.4	50.2	23.3	14.1	8.0	31.4	25.0	8.1	2.61	3.13	1 748 991	13.3	22.6
Allegany	29 322	64.4	26.5	50.6	18.9	10.3	5.8	35.6	30.1	15.2	2.35	2.90	29 634	11.0	27.7
Anne Arundel	178 670	72.3	34.9	57.2	26.4	11.1	6.3	27.7	21.3	6.4	2.65	3.09	149 114	10.0	18.2
Baltimore	299 877	66.2	30.2	49.4	21.0	12.8	7.2	33.8	27.3	10.1	2.46	3.00	268 280	11.1	23.4
Calvert	25 447	79.2	41.7	64.8	33.4	9.9	5.8	20.8	16.3	5.7	2.91	3.26	16 986	9.4	14.2
Caroline	11 097	73.5	34.8	54.3	23.4	13.6	8.1	26.5	21.5	9.4	2.64	3.03	9 983	11.6	21.7
Carroll	52 503	78.3	39.7	66.5	33.0	8.3	4.8	21.7	17.5	7.4	2.81	3.18	42 248	7.7	16.0
Cecil	31 223	74.6	37.0	58.0	27.2	11.1	6.9	25.4	19.9	7.1	2.71	3.12	24 725	10.2	17.9
Charles	41 668	77.5	41.1	58.0	29.2	14.5	9.1	22.5	17.2	5.2	2.86	3.21	32 950	11.9	14.2
Dorchester	12 706	66.9	27.3	47.5	16.5	15.5	8.9	33.1	28.2	13.5	2.36	2.86	12 117	14.7	25.8
Frederick	70 060	74.1	38.6	61.1	30.8	9.4	5.7	25.9	20.1	6.7	2.72	3.16	52 570	8.7	18.0
Garrett	11 476	72.8	32.6	60.7	25.7	8.4	4.8	27.2	23.5	10.6	2.55	3.00	10 110	8.8	20.4
Harford	79 667	75.8	38.7	61.9	30.4	10.2	6.1	24.2	19.7	6.8	2.72	3.14	63 193	9.2	16.9
Howard	90 043	73.1	40.0	60.5	32.5	9.5	5.9	26.9	20.8	4.6	2.71	3.18	68 337	8.4	19.2
Kent	7 666	67.0	26.3	51.7	17.3	11.1	6.3	33.0	27.8	13.7	2.33	2.81	6 702	10.7	24.8
Montgomery	324 565	69.1	35.0	55.2	27.7	10.5	5.9	30.9	24.4	7.7	2.66	3.19	282 228	9.4	22.3
Prince George's	286 610	69.1	35.3	44.0	21.4	19.6	11.3	30.9	24.1	4.9	2.74	3.25	258 011	16.3	21.6
Queen Anne's	15 315	75.4	33.3	62.2	25.8	9.5	5.4	24.6	19.6	7.9	2.62	2.99	12 489	8.5	17.8
St. Mary's	30 642	72.8	38.3	57.8	29.0	10.6	6.6	27.2	21.3	5.7	2.72	3.17	25 500	9.1	18.1
Somerset	8 361	65.1	25.9	46.1	16.3	15.1	7.8	34.9	29.4	12.9	2.37	2.92	7 977	14.8	25.7
Talbot	14 307	67.3	26.4	54.4	19.1	9.8	5.5	32.7	27.8	13.0	2.32	2.82	12 677	9.9	25.3

[1] No spouse present.

Table B. States and Counties

STATE County	Percent change of households, 1990–2000	Total housing units	Occupied housing units (percent)	Vacant housing units		Homeowner vacancy rate (percent)	Rental vacancy rate (percent)	Occupied housing units			Average household size of owner-occupied units	Average household size of renter-occupied units
				Total	For seasonal, recreational, or occasional use			Total	Percent owner-occupied housing units	Percent renter-occupied housing units		
	86	87	88	89	90	91	92	93	94	95	96	97
LOUISIANA—Cont'd												
Pointe Coupee	8.5	10 297	81.5	18.5	10.2	1.6	9.0	8 397	77.7	22.3	2.69	2.59
Rapides	2.6	52 038	90.5	9.5	0.8	1.6	9.7	47 120	68.0	32.0	2.60	2.48
Red River	2.8	3 988	85.6	14.4	1.5	2.3	7.6	3 414	76.3	23.7	2.70	2.84
Richland	5.8	8 335	89.9	10.1	3.0	1.8	7.1	7 490	72.2	27.8	2.61	2.73
Sabine	10.3	13 671	67.4	32.6	22.7	2.9	10.8	9 221	81.0	19.0	2.51	2.46
St. Bernard	8.5	26 790	93.8	6.2	1.4	1.1	5.7	25 123	74.6	25.4	2.71	2.46
St. Charles	14.6	17 430	94.2	5.8	0.7	1.1	7.6	16 422	81.4	18.6	2.95	2.70
St. Helena	16.4	5 034	76.9	23.1	10.4	1.5	8.3	3 873	84.9	15.1	2.72	2.56
St. James	8.7	7 605	91.9	8.1	0.4	1.1	8.2	6 992	85.6	14.4	3.03	2.83
St. John the Baptist	12.4	15 532	92.0	8.0	0.8	1.4	11.2	14 283	81.0	19.0	3.03	2.79
St. Landry	17.7	36 216	89.3	10.7	2.4	1.4	8.4	32 328	70.7	29.3	2.69	2.60
St. Martin	17.3	20 245	84.8	15.2	7.9	1.1	10.4	17 164	81.7	18.3	2.82	2.64
St. Mary	-0.7	21 650	89.2	10.8	1.9	1.1	11.8	19 317	73.9	26.1	2.79	2.58
St. Tammany	37.6	75 398	91.8	8.2	1.6	1.8	10.8	69 253	80.5	19.5	2.81	2.40
Tangipahoa	23.2	40 794	89.6	10.4	1.5	1.7	9.6	36 558	73.3	26.7	2.74	2.44
Tensas	-3.9	3 359	71.9	28.1	14.9	2.9	9.2	2 416	69.1	30.9	2.47	2.68
Terrebonne	13.1	39 928	90.2	9.8	3.6	1.0	8.5	35 997	75.6	24.4	2.95	2.59
Union	17.7	10 873	81.5	18.5	8.1	1.5	7.7	8 857	81.2	18.8	2.53	2.50
Vermilion	11.7	22 461	88.3	11.7	4.2	1.3	8.6	19 832	77.1	22.9	2.70	2.60
Vernon	-4.5	21 030	86.8	13.2	1.8	3.1	8.6	18 260	56.7	43.3	2.58	2.84
Washington	6.4	19 106	86.2	13.8	1.8	1.6	10.4	16 467	76.4	23.6	2.58	2.50
Webster	4.1	18 991	86.9	13.1	2.4	2.0	9.3	16 501	74.5	25.5	2.48	2.49
West Baton Rouge	16.0	8 370	91.6	8.4	1.1	0.8	11.8	7 663	78.8	21.2	2.78	2.62
West Carroll	1.5	4 980	89.5	10.5	1.1	2.3	9.5	4 458	78.9	21.1	2.58	2.59
West Feliciana	33.0	4 485	81.3	18.7	9.3	1.7	11.2	3 645	74.5	25.5	2.78	2.61
Winn	2.5	7 502	79.0	21.0	9.2	1.6	16.2	5 930	74.8	25.2	2.53	2.62
MAINE	11.4	651 901	79.5	20.5	15.6	1.7	7.0	518 200	71.6	28.4	2.54	2.03
Androscoggin	5.0	45 960	91.4	8.6	3.1	1.4	8.2	42 028	63.4	36.6	2.59	2.02
Aroostook	-3.2	38 719	78.4	21.6	13.1	2.9	12.5	30 356	73.0	27.0	2.52	1.93
Cumberland	14.3	122 600	88.1	11.9	8.8	0.7	3.7	107 989	66.8	33.2	2.58	1.97
Franklin	9.5	19 159	61.6	38.4	33.9	1.7	8.9	11 806	76.1	23.9	2.50	2.07
Hancock	19.2	33 945	64.4	35.6	31.4	1.9	5.9	21 864	75.7	24.3	2.40	2.03
Kennebec	8.6	56 364	84.6	15.4	10.2	1.6	8.9	47 683	71.2	28.8	2.53	2.01
Knox	15.8	21 612	76.8	23.2	18.8	1.3	5.9	16 608	74.0	26.0	2.43	1.98
Lincoln	18.3	20 849	67.9	32.1	28.1	1.9	9.3	14 158	83.0	17.0	2.39	2.11
Oxford	11.2	32 295	69.1	30.9	25.3	1.8	10.7	22 314	77.0	23.0	2.51	2.11
Penobscot	7.5	66 847	86.9	13.1	7.4	2.3	6.2	58 096	69.8	30.2	2.56	1.98
Piscataquis	1.2	13 783	52.8	47.2	40.0	4.0	13.6	7 278	79.5	20.5	2.44	1.99
Sagadahoc	12.2	16 489	85.6	14.4	10.2	1.0	6.0	14 117	72.1	27.9	2.57	2.23
Somerset	10.7	28 222	72.6	27.4	20.9	2.9	11.4	20 496	77.8	22.2	2.52	2.15
Waldo	18.6	18 904	77.9	22.1	16.2	1.8	7.7	14 726	79.8	20.2	2.50	2.14
Washington	5.2	21 919	64.4	35.6	24.5	4.3	13.3	14 118	77.7	22.3	2.42	2.04
York	20.6	94 234	79.1	20.9	17.6	0.9	5.4	74 563	72.6	27.4	2.60	2.14
MARYLAND	13.3	2 145 283	92.3	7.7	1.8	1.6	6.1	1 980 859	67.7	32.3	2.73	2.35
Allegany	-1.1	32 984	88.9	11.1	1.7	2.9	10.4	29 322	70.2	29.8	2.43	2.14
Anne Arundel	19.8	186 937	95.6	4.4	1.0	1.0	4.2	178 670	75.5	24.5	2.72	2.43
Baltimore	11.8	313 734	95.6	4.4	0.4	1.3	5.7	299 877	67.6	32.4	2.61	2.13
Calvert	49.8	27 576	92.3	7.7	3.6	1.6	6.4	25 447	85.2	14.8	2.97	2.55
Caroline	11.2	12 028	92.3	7.7	0.8	2.0	5.7	11 097	74.1	25.9	2.67	2.55
Carroll	24.3	54 260	96.8	3.2	0.2	1.2	4.3	52 503	82.0	18.0	2.92	2.30
Cecil	26.3	34 461	90.6	9.4	4.1	1.5	6.8	31 223	75.0	25.0	2.78	2.52
Charles	26.5	43 903	94.9	5.1	1.0	1.6	5.0	41 668	78.2	21.8	2.91	2.67
Dorchester	4.9	14 681	86.5	13.5	4.2	2.2	6.8	12 706	70.1	29.9	2.39	2.31
Frederick	33.3	73 017	96.0	4.0	0.4	1.5	5.2	70 060	75.9	24.1	2.84	2.35
Garrett	13.5	16 761	68.5	31.5	23.8	2.7	14.3	11 476	77.9	22.1	2.60	2.35
Harford	26.1	83 146	95.8	4.2	0.4	1.1	5.5	79 667	78.0	22.0	2.82	2.38
Howard	31.8	92 818	97.0	3.0	0.4	0.9	4.2	90 043	73.8	26.2	2.89	2.22
Kent	14.4	9 410	81.5	18.5	10.2	2.4	8.6	7 666	70.4	29.6	2.39	2.19
Montgomery	15.0	334 632	97.0	3.0	0.5	0.9	3.3	324 565	68.7	31.3	2.79	2.39
Prince George's	11.1	302 378	94.8	5.2	0.2	2.3	4.8	286 610	61.8	38.2	2.84	2.56
Queen Anne's	22.6	16 674	91.8	8.2	3.9	1.4	4.8	15 315	83.4	16.6	2.66	2.41
St. Mary's	20.2	34 081	89.9	10.1	3.6	1.9	8.1	30 642	71.8	28.2	2.80	2.52
Somerset	4.8	10 092	82.8	17.2	5.8	2.8	8.3	8 361	69.6	30.4	2.40	2.31
Talbot	12.9	16 500	86.7	13.3	6.7	1.8	6.5	14 307	71.6	28.4	2.39	2.14

Table B. States and Counties

STATE/ County code	MSA/ PMSA/ NECMA code[1]	County type[2]	STATE County	Population, 2000				Population, 1990				Population and population characteristics, 2000 Race (percent) One race					
				Land area, 2000[3] (sq km)	Total persons	Rank	Per square kilometer	Land area, 1990[3] (sq km)	Total persons	Rank	Per square kilometer	White	Black or African American	American Indian or Alaska Native	Asian	Native Hawaiian and other Pacific Islander	Some other race
				1	2	3	4	5	6	7	8	9	10	11	12	13	14
			MARYLAND—Cont'd														
24 043	3180	3	Washington	1 187	131 923	404	111.1	1 187	121 393	379	102.3	89.7	7.8	0.2	0.8	0.0	0.5
24 045	...	5	Wicomico	977	84 644	615	86.6	977	74 339	605	76.1	72.6	23.3	0.2	1.7	0.0	0.8
24 047	...	7	Worcester	1 226	46 543	970	38.0	1 226	35 028	1 132	28.6	81.2	16.7	0.2	0.6	0.0	0.4
24 510	0720	0	Baltimore city	209	651 154	82	3 115.6	209	736 014	53	3 521.6	31.6	64.3	0.3	1.5	0.0	0.7
25 000	...		MASSACHUSETTS	20 306	6 349 097	X	312.7	20 300	6 016 425	X	296.4	84.5	5.4	0.2	3.8	0.0	3.7
25 001	0743	3	Barnstable	1 024	222 230	256	217.0	1 025	186 605	259	182.1	94.2	1.8	0.6	0.6	0.0	1.1
25 003	6323	3	Berkshire	2 412	134 953	399	56.0	2 412	139 352	342	57.8	95.0	2.0	0.1	1.0	0.0	0.6
25 005	1123	2	Bristol	1 440	534 678	104	371.3	1 440	506 325	94	351.6	91.0	2.0	0.2	1.3	0.0	3.1
25 007	...	9	Dukes	269	14 987	2 091	55.7	269	11 639	2 243	43.3	90.7	2.4	1.7	0.5	0.1	1.5
25 009	1123	0	Essex	1 297	723 419	69	557.8	1 290	670 080	65	519.4	86.4	2.6	0.2	2.3	0.0	6.2
25 011	...	4	Franklin	1 818	71 535	691	39.3	1 819	70 086	632	38.5	95.4	0.9	0.3	1.0	0.0	0.7
25 013	8003	2	Hampden	1 602	456 228	127	284.8	1 602	456 310	109	284.8	79.1	8.1	0.3	1.3	0.1	8.8
25 015	8003	2	Hampshire	1 370	152 251	352	111.1	1 370	146 568	322	107.0	91.1	2.0	0.2	3.4	0.1	1.5
25 017	1123	0	Middlesex	2 133	1 465 396	19	687.0	2 133	1 398 468	18	655.6	85.9	3.4	0.2	6.3	0.0	2.1
25 019	...	7	Nantucket	124	9 520	2 488	76.8	124	6 012	2 755	48.5	87.8	8.3	0.0	0.6	0.0	1.6
25 021	1123	0	Norfolk	1 035	650 308	83	628.3	1 035	616 087	75	595.3	89.0	3.2	0.1	5.5	0.0	0.8
25 023	1123	1	Plymouth	1 712	472 822	121	276.2	1 711	435 276	114	254.4	88.7	4.6	0.2	0.9	0.0	3.1
25 025	1123	0	Suffolk	152	689 807	74	4 538.2	152	663 906	70	4 367.8	57.8	22.2	0.4	7.0	0.1	8.2
25 027	1123	2	Worcester	3 919	750 963	65	191.6	3 919	709 711	59	181.1	89.6	2.7	0.3	2.6	0.0	2.9
26 000	...		MICHIGAN	147 121	9 938 444	X	67.6	147 136	9 295 287	X	63.2	80.2	14.2	0.6	1.8	0.0	1.3
26 001	...	9	Alcona	1 747	11 719	2 317	6.7	1 747	10 145	2 374	5.8	98.0	0.2	0.6	0.2	0.0	0.1
26 003	...	7	Alger	2 377	9 862	2 460	4.1	2 377	8 972	2 472	3.8	87.8	6.1	3.3	0.3	0.0	0.4
26 005	3000	2	Allegan	2 143	105 665	503	49.3	2 143	90 509	505	42.2	93.5	1.3	0.5	0.6	0.0	2.8
26 007	...	7	Alpena	1 487	31 314	1 366	21.1	1 487	30 605	1 261	20.6	98.2	0.2	0.4	0.3	0.0	0.1
26 009	...	9	Antrim	1 235	23 110	1 637	18.7	1 235	18 185	1 779	14.7	97.0	0.2	1.1	0.2	0.1	0.3
26 011	...	8	Arenac	950	17 269	1 934	18.2	950	14 906	1 994	15.7	95.4	1.8	0.9	0.3	0.0	0.2
26 013	...	9	Baraga	2 341	8 746	2 550	3.7	2 342	7 954	2 577	3.4	78.6	5.0	12.0	0.3	0.0	0.4
26 015	...	6	Barry	1 440	56 755	834	39.4	1 440	50 057	840	34.8	97.4	0.2	0.5	0.3	0.0	0.5
26 017	6960	2	Bay	1 151	110 157	492	95.7	1 151	111 723	411	97.1	94.9	1.3	0.5	0.5	0.0	1.2
26 019	...	9	Benzie	832	15 998	2 024	19.2	832	12 200	2 201	14.7	96.4	0.3	1.6	0.2	0.0	0.4
26 021	0870	3	Berrien	1 479	162 453	330	109.8	1 479	161 378	294	109.1	79.7	15.9	0.4	1.1	0.0	1.1
26 023	...	6	Branch	1 314	45 787	987	34.8	1 314	41 502	970	31.6	93.4	2.6	0.5	0.4	0.0	1.4
26 025	3720	2	Calhoun	1 836	137 985	394	75.2	1 836	135 982	345	74.1	83.9	10.9	0.6	1.1	0.0	1.3
26 027	...	6	Cass	1 275	51 104	905	40.1	1 275	49 477	850	38.8	89.2	6.1	0.8	0.5	0.0	1.2
26 029	...	7	Charlevoix	1 080	26 090	1 512	24.2	1 080	21 468	1 605	19.9	96.3	0.2	1.5	0.2	0.1	0.4
26 031	...	7	Cheboygan	1 853	26 448	1 504	14.3	1 853	21 398	1 611	11.5	94.8	0.2	2.5	0.2	0.0	0.1
26 033	...	7	Chippewa	4 043	38 543	1 149	9.5	4 043	34 604	1 148	8.6	75.9	5.5	13.3	0.5	0.0	0.4
26 035	...	7	Clare	1 468	31 252	1 368	21.3	1 468	24 952	1 464	17.0	97.4	0.3	0.7	0.3	0.0	0.3
26 037	4040	2	Clinton	1 480	64 753	750	43.8	1 480	57 893	749	39.1	96.4	0.6	0.4	0.5	0.0	0.8
26 039	...	9	Crawford	1 446	14 273	2 143	9.9	1 446	12 260	2 199	8.5	96.4	1.5	0.6	0.3	0.0	0.2
26 041	...	7	Delta	3 030	38 520	1 150	12.7	3 031	37 780	1 053	12.5	95.8	0.1	2.2	0.3	0.0	0.1
26 043	...	7	Dickinson	1 985	27 472	1 468	13.8	1 985	26 831	1 395	13.5	98.0	0.1	0.5	0.4	0.0	0.1
26 045	4040	2	Eaton	1 493	103 655	513	69.4	1 493	92 879	499	62.2	90.3	5.3	0.4	1.1	0.0	1.2
26 047	...	7	Emmet	1 212	31 437	1 361	25.9	1 212	25 040	1 461	20.7	94.3	0.5	3.1	0.4	0.0	0.2
26 049	2640	2	Genesee	1 657	436 141	137	263.2	1 657	430 459	116	259.8	75.3	20.4	0.6	0.8	0.0	0.8
26 051	...	6	Gladwin	1 313	26 023	1 516	19.8	1 313	21 896	1 583	16.7	97.6	0.1	0.6	0.3	0.0	0.3
26 053	...	7	Gogebic	2 854	17 370	1 931	6.1	2 854	18 052	1 788	6.3	94.2	1.8	2.2	0.2	0.0	0.3
26 055	...	7	Grand Traverse	1 205	77 654	653	64.4	1 205	64 273	682	53.3	96.5	0.4	0.9	0.5	0.0	0.5
26 057	...	6	Gratiot	1 477	42 285	1 050	28.6	1 477	38 982	1 022	26.4	92.0	3.7	0.5	0.3	0.0	1.8
26 059	...	6	Hillsdale	1 551	46 527	971	30.0	1 551	43 431	933	28.0	97.6	0.4	0.4	0.3	0.0	0.3
26 061	...	7	Houghton	2 620	36 016	1 217	13.7	2 620	35 446	1 113	13.5	95.5	0.9	0.5	1.8	0.0	0.2
26 063	...	7	Huron	2 167	36 079	1 212	16.6	2 167	34 951	1 135	16.1	98.0	0.2	0.3	0.4	0.0	0.3
26 065	4040	2	Ingham	1 448	279 320	202	192.9	1 448	281 912	151	194.7	79.5	10.9	0.5	3.7	0.1	2.4
26 067	...	6	Ionia	1 485	61 518	791	41.4	1 485	57 024	764	38.4	92.0	4.6	0.6	0.3	0.0	1.0
26 069	...	7	Iosco	1 422	27 339	1 471	19.2	1 422	30 209	1 288	21.2	96.9	0.4	0.7	0.5	0.1	0.2
26 071	...	9	Iron	3 021	13 138	2 218	4.3	3 021	13 175	2 126	4.4	96.3	1.1	1.0	0.2	0.0	0.2
26 073	...	4	Isabella	1 487	63 351	765	42.6	1 487	54 624	789	36.7	91.5	1.9	2.8	1.4	0.0	0.7
26 075	3520	3	Jackson	1 830	158 422	335	86.6	1 830	149 756	316	81.8	88.5	7.9	0.4	0.5	0.0	0.8
26 077	3720	2	Kalamazoo	1 455	238 603	242	164.0	1 455	223 411	223	153.5	84.6	9.7	0.4	1.8	0.0	1.3
26 079	...	9	Kalkaska	1 453	16 571	1 986	11.4	1 453	13 497	2 102	9.3	97.5	0.2	0.8	0.2	0.0	0.1
26 081	3000	2	Kent	2 217	574 335	93	259.1	2 218	500 631	97	225.7	83.1	8.9	0.5	1.9	0.1	3.3
26 083	...	9	Keweenaw	1 401	2 301	3 038	1.6	1 402	1 701	3 083	1.2	95.0	3.5	0.1	0.1	0.0	0.2
26 085	...	9	Lake	1 470	11 333	2 347	7.7	1 470	8 583	2 506	5.8	84.7	11.2	1.0	0.2	0.0	0.6
26 087	2160	1	Lapeer	1 694	87 904	595	51.9	1 695	74 768	602	44.1	96.2	0.8	0.4	0.4	0.0	1.1

[1] MSA = Metropolitan Statistical Area. PMSA = Primary MSA. NECMA = New England County Metropolitan Area. See Appendix A for explanation of these concepts. See Appendix B for list of metropolitan areas identified by type, with component counties.
[2] County typology code from the Economic Research Service of USDA. See Appendix A for definition.
[3] Dry land or land partially or temporarily covered by water.

Table B. States and Counties

STATE County	Population and population characteristics, 2000 (cont'd)								Population and population characteristics, 1990				
	Race (percent) (cont'd)								Race (percent)				
	Two or more races	Race alone or in combination						Hispanic¹	White	Black or African American	American Indian or Alaska Native	Asian and Pacific Islander	Hispanic¹
		White	Black	American Indian or Alaska Native	Asian	Native Hawaiian and other Pacific Islander	Some other race						
	15	16	17	18	19	20	21	22	23	24	25	26	27
MARYLAND—Cont'd													
Washington	1.0	90.7	8.2	0.5	1.0	0.1	0.6	1.2	92.9	6.0	0.2	0.7	0.7
Wicomico	1.3	73.6	24.0	0.5	2.0	0.1	1.2	2.2	76.3	22.3	0.2	0.9	0.8
Worcester	1.0	82.0	17.1	0.5	0.8	0.1	0.6	1.3	77.8	21.3	0.2	0.5	0.8
Baltimore city	1.5	32.6	65.2	0.8	1.8	0.1	1.2	1.7	39.1	59.2	0.3	1.1	1.0
MASSACHUSETTS	2.3	86.2	6.3	0.6	4.2	0.1	5.1	6.8	89.8	5.0	0.2	2.4	4.8
Barnstable	1.7	95.6	2.4	1.0	0.8	0.1	1.9	1.3	96.2	1.5	0.6	0.5	1.2
Berkshire	1.2	96.1	2.5	0.5	1.3	0.1	0.8	1.7	97.0	1.8	0.2	0.7	1.0
Bristol	2.3	92.8	2.8	0.6	1.5	0.2	4.5	3.6	95.3	1.6	0.2	0.9	2.7
Dukes	3.2	93.5	3.3	2.7	0.7	0.2	3.1	1.0	94.3	2.9	2.2	0.4	1.0
Essex	2.1	88.1	3.4	0.5	2.7	0.1	7.4	11.0	92.0	2.4	0.2	1.5	7.2
Franklin	1.6	96.8	1.4	1.0	1.4	0.1	1.1	2.0	97.9	0.7	0.3	0.7	1.2
Hampden	2.3	80.8	9.0	0.7	1.6	0.2	10.2	15.2	85.0	7.5	0.2	0.9	10.0
Hampshire	1.8	92.6	2.6	0.7	3.9	0.1	2.0	3.4	93.8	1.7	0.2	3.1	2.7
Middlesex	2.2	87.6	4.0	0.4	6.9	0.1	3.3	4.6	92.1	2.9	0.1	3.7	3.4
Nantucket	1.6	88.9	9.0	0.3	0.9	0.1	2.5	2.2	96.3	2.5	0.1	0.3	0.8
Norfolk	1.4	90.1	3.6	0.4	5.9	0.1	1.4	1.8	94.6	2.0	0.1	2.9	1.4
Plymouth	2.5	90.1	6.0	0.6	1.2	0.1	4.7	2.4	93.4	3.8	0.2	0.8	2.2
Suffolk	4.4	60.2	24.4	0.9	7.6	0.3	11.3	15.5	66.1	22.5	0.3	5.0	11.0
Worcester	1.8	91.1	3.2	0.6	3.0	0.1	3.9	6.8	93.8	2.1	0.2	1.6	4.6
MICHIGAN	1.9	81.8	14.8	1.3	2.1	0.1	2.0	3.3	83.4	13.9	0.6	1.1	2.2
Alcona	0.9	98.9	0.2	1.3	0.3	0.0	0.1	0.7	98.8	0.3	0.6	0.3	0.5
Alger	2.0	89.8	6.2	5.1	0.4	0.0	0.6	1.0	93.9	2.4	3.4	0.3	0.5
Allegan	1.3	94.7	1.6	1.1	0.7	0.1	3.2	5.7	95.9	1.6	0.6	0.5	3.2
Alpena	0.7	98.9	0.4	0.8	0.4	0.1	0.2	0.6	99.2	0.1	0.3	0.3	0.5
Antrim	1.2	98.2	0.4	1.7	0.3	0.1	0.5	1.2	98.4	0.1	1.2	0.1	0.5
Arenac	1.3	96.6	2.0	1.8	0.4	0.1	0.4	1.4	98.4	0.1	0.9	0.3	1.1
Baraga	3.8	82.1	5.4	15.1	0.5	0.0	0.8	0.9	87.6	0.6	11.5	0.1	0.4
Barry	1.1	98.5	0.4	1.1	0.4	0.0	0.7	1.5	98.7	0.2	0.4	0.3	1.0
Bay	1.5	96.4	1.7	1.2	0.6	0.0	1.6	3.9	96.4	1.1	0.6	0.4	3.1
Benzie	1.2	97.6	0.4	2.4	0.2	0.0	0.6	1.5	97.2	0.2	1.9	0.3	1.1
Berrien	1.6	81.0	16.7	1.0	1.4	0.1	1.6	3.0	82.6	15.4	0.4	0.9	1.7
Branch	1.7	94.9	2.9	1.2	0.6	0.0	2.1	3.0	97.1	1.7	0.5	0.4	1.1
Calhoun	2.1	85.8	11.9	1.5	1.3	0.1	1.7	3.2	87.3	10.6	0.5	0.8	1.9
Cass	2.1	91.1	7.0	1.9	0.7	0.0	1.6	2.4	90.6	7.5	0.9	0.4	1.3
Charlevoix	1.2	97.5	0.4	2.4	0.3	0.1	0.5	1.0	97.8	0.1	1.8	0.2	0.5
Cheboygan	2.0	96.7	0.4	4.2	0.4	0.1	0.3	0.8	97.4	0.1	2.2	0.3	0.4
Chippewa	4.4	79.8	6.2	16.9	0.8	0.1	0.8	1.6	81.9	6.3	11.0	0.4	0.8
Clare	1.0	98.4	0.4	1.4	0.3	0.0	0.4	1.1	98.8	0.2	0.6	0.2	0.5
Clinton	1.2	97.5	0.9	1.0	0.7	0.1	1.1	2.6	97.9	0.4	0.5	0.3	2.2
Crawford	1.1	97.4	1.7	1.3	0.4	0.0	0.4	1.0	96.3	2.2	1.2	0.3	0.6
Delta	1.4	97.2	0.2	3.4	0.4	0.0	0.2	0.5	97.5	0.0	2.1	0.3	0.4
Dickinson	0.8	98.8	0.2	0.9	0.6	0.1	0.3	0.7	98.9	0.1	0.5	0.4	0.4
Eaton	1.7	91.8	5.8	1.1	1.3	0.1	1.7	3.2	94.3	3.6	0.5	0.6	2.4
Emmet	1.5	95.7	0.6	4.1	0.6	0.1	0.4	0.9	96.3	0.5	2.7	0.3	0.5
Genesee	2.2	77.1	21.3	1.6	1.1	0.1	1.2	2.3	78.2	19.6	0.7	0.7	2.1
Gladwin	1.1	98.7	0.3	1.2	0.3	0.0	0.5	1.0	99.1	0.1	0.5	0.2	0.6
Gogebic	1.2	95.4	1.9	3.0	0.4	0.0	0.5	0.9	96.9	1.3	1.6	0.1	0.4
Grand Traverse	1.1	97.5	0.6	1.5	0.7	0.0	0.7	1.5	98.0	0.4	0.9	0.5	0.8
Gratiot	1.6	93.4	4.1	1.2	0.5	0.0	2.4	4.4	97.0	0.8	0.4	0.3	3.8
Hillsdale	1.0	98.5	0.5	0.9	0.5	0.0	0.6	1.2	98.8	0.3	0.3	0.3	0.9
Houghton	1.0	96.4	1.1	1.1	2.0	0.1	0.4	0.7	97.2	0.4	0.4	1.7	0.5
Huron	0.8	98.8	0.4	0.7	0.5	0.0	0.5	1.6	99.1	0.1	0.3	0.2	1.1
Ingham	3.0	82.0	12.2	1.4	4.2	0.1	3.4	5.8	84.1	9.9	0.7	2.7	4.8
Ionia	1.5	93.2	5.0	1.4	0.6	0.1	1.4	2.8	93.2	5.3	0.4	0.2	2.1
Iosco	1.3	98.1	0.6	1.4	0.7	0.1	0.4	1.0	95.9	2.1	0.8	0.9	1.2
Iron	1.2	97.4	1.2	1.9	0.3	0.0	0.4	0.6	98.9	0.0	0.8	0.2	0.5
Isabella	1.7	93.0	2.4	3.6	1.6	0.1	1.1	2.2	95.6	1.2	1.9	0.8	1.3
Jackson	1.7	90.1	8.7	1.1	0.7	0.1	1.2	2.2	90.5	8.0	0.4	0.4	1.5
Kalamazoo	2.2	86.5	10.8	1.2	2.2	0.1	1.8	2.6	88.4	8.9	0.5	1.4	1.8
Kalkaska	1.1	98.6	0.4	1.5	0.4	0.1	0.3	0.9	98.7	0.1	0.8	0.2	0.6
Kent	2.2	85.0	9.8	1.1	2.2	0.1	4.1	7.0	88.7	8.1	0.6	1.1	2.9
Keweenaw	1.1	95.9	3.7	0.8	0.3	0.0	0.3	0.8	99.2	0.1	0.2	0.4	0.4
Lake	2.4	86.8	12.3	2.3	0.3	0.1	0.9	1.7	85.5	13.4	0.9	0.1	0.7
Lapeer	1.2	97.3	1.0	1.0	0.6	0.0	1.4	3.1	97.7	0.6	0.4	0.4	2.0

¹Hispanic persons may be of any race.

Table B. States and Counties

STATE County	Population and population characteristics, 2000										
	Age (percent)										
	Under 5 years	5 to 17 years	18 to 24 years	25 to 34 years	35 to 44 years	45 to 54 years	55 to 64 years	65 to 74 years	75 years and over	Median age (years)	Percent Female
	28	29	30	31	32	33	34	35	36	37	38
MARYLAND—Cont'd											
Washington	6.1	17.3	8.1	14.4	16.9	13.8	9.2	7.4	6.7	37.4	48.9
Wicomico	6.3	18.5	11.8	12.2	15.8	13.7	8.9	7.0	5.8	35.8	52.3
Worcester	4.9	15.7	6.2	11.1	15.3	13.9	12.9	11.9	8.2	43.0	51.2
Baltimore city	6.4	18.4	10.9	14.3	15.6	12.8	8.4	6.9	6.3	35.0	53.4
MASSACHUSETTS	6.3	17.4	9.1	14.6	16.7	13.8	8.6	6.7	6.8	36.5	51.8
Barnstable	4.8	15.7	5.2	9.7	15.3	14.8	11.5	11.9	11.2	44.6	52.7
Berkshire	5.2	17.2	8.4	10.9	15.4	14.9	10.0	8.6	9.4	40.5	52.2
Bristol	6.4	18.2	8.5	14.0	16.5	13.5	8.7	6.9	7.3	36.7	52.0
Dukes	5.5	17.2	5.5	11.6	18.0	18.6	9.2	7.6	6.8	40.7	51.1
Essex	6.7	18.5	7.5	13.1	17.3	14.4	8.7	6.8	7.0	37.5	52.1
Franklin	5.2	18.3	7.8	11.8	16.7	16.9	9.0	6.7	7.5	39.5	51.6
Hampden	6.5	19.5	9.2	12.6	15.7	13.4	8.5	7.0	7.5	36.4	52.1
Hampshire	4.6	15.0	19.3	11.8	15.0	14.6	7.6	5.7	6.3	34.4	53.4
Middlesex	6.3	16.2	9.0	16.1	17.3	13.8	8.6	6.5	6.2	36.4	51.6
Nantucket	5.5	13.7	7.4	19.6	20.9	14.1	8.3	5.7	4.8	36.7	48.7
Norfolk	6.4	17.0	7.0	14.1	17.5	14.5	9.1	7.2	7.2	38.1	52.2
Plymouth	7.0	19.8	7.2	12.9	17.5	14.7	9.2	6.0	5.8	36.8	51.3
Suffolk	5.6	14.6	15.1	20.6	14.9	11.0	7.2	5.6	5.5	31.7	51.8
Worcester	6.7	19.0	8.4	13.7	17.4	13.7	8.1	6.3	6.8	36.3	51.1
MICHIGAN	6.8	19.4	9.4	13.7	16.1	13.8	8.7	6.5	5.8	35.5	51.0
Alcona	4.3	14.7	4.6	7.9	13.0	14.1	16.9	14.0	10.4	49.0	49.4
Alger	4.6	16.0	7.3	12.4	16.3	15.3	11.0	8.9	8.2	41.2	46.2
Allegan	7.2	21.6	8.0	12.9	17.2	13.6	8.4	5.8	5.3	35.2	50.1
Alpena	5.5	18.2	7.8	10.2	16.3	14.0	10.9	9.0	8.1	40.4	51.4
Antrim	5.7	18.6	6.3	10.3	15.0	13.7	12.8	10.2	7.3	41.1	50.0
Arenac	5.3	18.0	7.8	10.9	15.9	13.6	12.0	9.6	7.0	40.1	48.7
Baraga	5.6	17.4	7.3	13.7	14.7	14.5	10.7	7.1	9.2	39.0	47.4
Barry	6.6	20.5	7.5	12.2	16.8	14.6	9.9	6.7	5.1	36.9	50.1
Bay	6.1	18.4	8.3	12.3	15.9	14.6	9.8	7.3	7.4	38.4	51.4
Benzie	5.9	17.5	6.2	11.3	15.7	14.2	11.6	9.9	7.6	40.8	50.5
Berrien	6.5	19.5	8.3	12.1	15.4	14.1	9.6	7.5	6.9	37.4	51.5
Branch	6.3	19.2	8.4	13.3	16.5	13.6	9.5	7.0	6.1	36.7	49.4
Calhoun	6.5	19.5	8.9	13.0	15.3	14.0	9.2	7.2	6.5	36.4	51.4
Cass	6.1	19.5	7.4	11.6	16.0	15.2	10.7	7.7	5.9	38.5	50.0
Charlevoix	6.5	19.4	6.5	11.5	16.0	14.2	11.1	8.2	6.8	39.1	50.5
Cheboygan	5.9	17.8	6.2	11.2	14.6	13.8	12.5	10.0	8.0	41.3	50.4
Chippewa	5.4	15.9	11.9	14.6	17.1	13.4	8.9	7.0	5.7	36.2	44.3
Clare	5.8	18.6	7.1	10.9	14.0	13.4	12.9	10.2	7.0	40.5	50.7
Clinton	6.9	21.2	7.3	11.9	17.3	15.1	9.5	6.0	4.9	36.7	50.3
Crawford	5.4	19.1	6.3	10.8	15.9	13.9	12.0	9.9	6.7	40.6	49.0
Delta	5.5	18.4	7.9	10.4	15.6	15.1	10.3	8.8	8.2	40.4	50.9
Dickinson	5.5	19.6	6.3	10.8	16.4	14.3	9.0	8.5	9.6	40.0	50.8
Eaton	6.4	19.8	9.1	12.6	16.2	15.4	9.2	6.0	5.3	36.4	51.4
Emmet	6.2	19.2	7.1	11.9	16.2	15.7	9.5	7.5	6.8	38.9	50.8
Genesee	7.3	20.2	8.9	13.6	16.0	13.7	8.7	6.6	5.0	35.0	51.9
Gladwin	5.5	17.7	6.5	10.4	13.7	13.6	14.2	11.1	7.2	42.3	50.4
Gogebic	4.6	15.9	8.3	10.5	14.0	13.4	10.8	10.1	12.5	42.9	49.7
Grand Traverse	6.1	19.3	7.9	12.5	17.2	15.1	8.8	6.6	6.4	37.7	51.2
Gratiot	5.9	17.9	11.6	13.7	15.7	12.8	8.8	6.5	7.1	35.6	48.0
Hillsdale	6.5	19.9	10.0	11.5	15.3	13.6	9.9	7.3	6.0	36.5	50.2
Houghton	5.4	16.4	19.1	10.1	12.5	12.0	8.9	7.0	8.5	34.0	46.8
Huron	5.5	18.7	6.5	10.4	14.7	13.8	11.0	9.9	9.6	41.2	50.5
Ingham	6.3	17.1	18.5	14.4	14.2	12.9	7.1	4.9	4.5	30.4	51.7
Ionia	6.9	20.0	11.5	14.7	16.3	12.8	7.7	5.4	4.7	32.9	46.5
Iosco	4.7	17.7	5.4	9.0	14.4	13.5	13.8	12.4	9.1	44.2	51.0
Iron	4.3	16.3	6.0	8.6	14.3	14.2	11.2	11.5	13.7	45.4	50.6
Isabella	5.2	15.1	29.4	11.5	12.2	10.7	6.7	4.9	4.2	25.1	52.2
Jackson	6.6	19.1	8.1	13.6	16.8	14.2	8.8	6.6	6.2	36.6	49.0
Kalamazoo	6.5	17.6	15.2	13.5	14.7	13.2	7.9	5.8	5.5	32.7	51.6
Kalkaska	6.4	19.1	7.6	12.1	16.5	13.6	10.9	8.1	5.6	38.0	49.7
Kent	7.8	20.5	10.5	14.9	16.2	12.7	7.1	5.3	5.1	32.5	50.8
Keweenaw	4.5	18.0	6.4	8.1	13.3	16.1	13.3	11.6	8.7	44.9	46.2
Lake	5.2	16.7	8.0	9.2	13.5	13.5	14.1	12.0	7.7	43.1	47.8
Lapeer	6.7	21.3	7.7	12.8	18.2	14.7	9.2	5.5	4.1	35.9	49.4

Table B. States and Counties

STATE County	Under 5 years (39)	5 to 17 years (40)	18 to 24 years (41)	25 to 34 years (42)	35 to 44 years (43)	45 to 54 years (44)	55 to 64 years (45)	65 to 74 years (46)	75 years and over (47)	Percent Female (48)	2000 (49)	1990 (50)	1980 (51)	1990–2000 (52)	1980–1990 (53)
MARYLAND—Cont'd															
Washington	6.7	16.0	10.6	17.8	15.0	10.6	9.5	8.1	5.7	49.5	131 923	121 393	113 086	8.7	7.3
Wicomico	7.0	17.3	12.2	16.5	15.1	10.2	8.8	7.6	5.3	52.1	84 644	74 339	64 540	13.9	15.2
Worcester	6.5	15.4	8.1	16.1	14.4	10.5	11.7	10.8	6.5	51.9	46 543	35 028	30 809	32.0	13.4
Baltimore city	7.7	16.7	11.2	18.7	14.3	9.1	8.5	7.9	5.8	53.3	651 154	736 014	786 741	-11.5	-6.4
MASSACHUSETTS	6.9	15.6	11.8	18.3	15.3	10.0	8.6	7.6	6.0	52.0	6 349 097	6 016 425	5 737 093	5.5	4.9
Barnstable	6.4	14.6	7.5	14.6	14.9	9.4	10.6	12.5	9.5	52.8	222 230	186 605	147 925	19.1	26.1
Berkshire	6.3	16.5	10.9	15.1	14.7	10.1	9.6	9.3	7.6	52.1	134 953	139 352	145 110	-3.2	-4.0
Bristol	7.1	17.4	10.8	16.8	14.8	10.0	8.7	8.3	6.1	52.2	534 678	506 325	474 641	5.6	6.7
Dukes	7.1	16.1	5.9	16.4	20.1	9.5	9.0	9.1	6.6	51.5	14 987	11 639	8 942	28.8	30.2
Essex	7.3	16.4	9.9	17.4	15.7	10.3	8.8	7.9	6.2	52.3	723 419	670 080	633 688	8.0	5.7
Franklin	7.2	17.5	9.0	16.5	17.8	9.7	7.9	8.2	6.4	51.6	71 535	70 086	64 317	2.1	9.0
Hampden	7.4	17.6	11.0	16.7	14.2	9.5	8.8	8.5	6.3	52.5	456 228	456 310	443 018	0.0	3.0
Hampshire	5.4	13.8	22.4	15.7	15.4	8.6	7.0	6.8	4.8	52.8	152 251	146 568	138 813	3.9	5.6
Middlesex	6.5	14.3	12.0	19.7	15.7	10.4	8.8	7.0	5.5	51.9	1 465 396	1 398 468	1 367 034	4.8	2.3
Nantucket	7.0	13.9	7.8	20.4	18.6	9.7	9.1	7.1	6.6	50.0	9 520	6 012	5 087	58.3	18.2
Norfolk	6.5	14.6	10.6	18.1	15.8	10.9	9.5	7.8	6.3	52.5	650 308	616 087	606 587	5.6	1.6
Plymouth	7.6	18.7	10.3	16.8	16.5	10.9	7.8	6.6	5.0	51.2	472 822	435 276	405 437	8.6	7.4
Suffolk	6.4	12.9	16.6	22.6	13.6	8.4	7.4	6.6	5.5	51.9	689 807	663 906	650 142	3.9	2.1
Worcester	7.5	16.9	11.2	17.9	15.1	9.5	8.1	7.7	6.0	51.3	750 963	709 711	646 352	5.8	9.8
MICHIGAN	7.6	18.9	10.8	16.9	15.1	10.2	8.5	7.1	4.9	51.5	9 938 444	9 295 287	9 262 044	6.9	0.4
Alcona	5.1	16.0	6.2	11.4	11.4	11.3	14.5	14.4	9.7	50.2	11 719	10 145	9 740	15.5	4.2
Alger	6.1	18.8	8.1	13.9	15.1	10.6	10.0	10.1	7.1	48.6	9 862	8 972	9 225	9.9	-2.7
Allegan	8.3	21.4	8.9	17.1	15.2	9.9	7.8	6.6	4.9	50.5	105 665	90 509	81 555	16.7	11.0
Alpena	6.6	19.8	8.0	15.1	13.9	11.2	10.4	8.6	6.4	51.5	31 314	30 605	32 315	2.3	-5.3
Antrim	6.9	18.8	7.3	14.3	13.6	10.4	11.2	10.4	7.0	51.1	23 110	18 185	16 194	27.1	12.3
Arenac	6.7	20.0	7.8	14.5	13.2	10.4	11.2	9.7	6.5	51.1	17 269	14 906	14 706	15.9	1.4
Baraga	6.7	19.8	8.5	12.3	14.6	10.5	8.1	10.8	8.8	49.7	8 746	7 954	8 484	10.0	-6.2
Barry	7.4	20.6	8.4	15.7	15.8	11.5	9.0	6.8	4.8	50.0	56 755	50 057	45 781	13.4	9.3
Bay	7.1	19.2	9.6	15.9	15.1	10.9	8.9	7.9	5.5	51.6	110 157	111 723	119 881	-1.4	-6.8
Benzie	7.0	17.3	7.5	14.5	14.2	11.2	11.2	10.3	6.9	50.7	15 998	12 200	11 205	31.1	8.9
Berrien	7.4	19.6	9.7	15.5	14.4	10.4	9.3	8.0	5.7	52.1	162 453	161 378	171 276	0.7	-5.8
Branch	7.7	20.2	8.6	16.1	14.5	10.6	9.1	7.7	5.6	51.1	45 787	41 502	40 188	10.3	3.3
Calhoun	7.4	19.3	9.8	15.3	15.0	10.4	9.4	7.7	5.6	51.6	137 985	135 982	141 579	1.5	-4.0
Cass	7.1	19.9	8.9	15.1	15.1	11.1	9.7	7.9	5.2	50.9	51 104	49 477	49 499	3.3	0.0
Charlevoix	7.6	19.4	7.9	15.7	15.1	10.4	9.6	8.4	6.0	51.0	26 090	21 468	19 907	21.5	7.8
Cheboygan	6.7	19.4	7.5	13.3	13.9	10.7	11.1	10.3	7.1	51.7	26 448	21 398	20 649	23.6	3.6
Chippewa	6.1	17.3	13.6	18.3	14.8	8.9	8.6	7.2	5.4	44.5	38 543	34 604	29 029	11.4	19.2
Clare	7.3	18.9	8.2	14.0	12.3	10.1	11.6	10.9	6.8	51.6	31 252	24 952	23 822	25.2	4.7
Clinton	7.5	21.3	9.5	16.4	16.2	11.9	8.0	5.4	3.9	50.2	64 753	57 893	55 893	11.8	3.6
Crawford	7.3	18.8	8.2	16.1	13.5	10.3	10.8	8.9	6.0	48.8	14 273	12 260	9 465	16.4	29.5
Delta	6.7	20.3	8.3	14.5	14.8	10.4	9.7	8.7	6.6	51.3	38 520	37 780	38 947	2.0	-3.0
Dickinson	6.8	19.2	7.1	14.9	14.7	9.6	9.5	9.9	8.4	50.9	27 472	26 831	25 341	2.4	5.9
Eaton	7.1	20.5	9.9	16.1	17.0	11.5	7.9	5.7	4.2	51.4	103 655	92 879	88 337	11.6	5.1
Emmet	7.5	19.2	8.0	16.2	16.3	10.0	8.7	7.8	6.3	51.5	31 437	25 040	22 992	25.5	8.9
Genesee	7.8	20.3	10.3	16.9	15.0	10.8	8.7	6.1	4.1	52.1	436 141	430 459	450 449	1.3	-4.4
Gladwin	7.2	19.2	8.0	13.3	12.3	10.4	12.3	10.9	6.5	50.8	26 023	21 896	19 957	18.8	9.7
Gogebic	5.7	16.6	8.5	12.2	12.6	9.7	10.7	12.7	11.2	50.9	17 370	18 052	19 686	-3.8	-8.3
Grand Traverse	7.6	19.5	9.1	17.1	17.1	9.6	7.8	6.8	5.4	51.3	77 654	64 273	54 899	20.8	17.1
Gratiot	6.9	20.2	11.3	15.0	14.1	10.2	8.4	7.3	6.4	51.4	42 285	38 982	40 448	8.5	-3.6
Hillsdale	7.7	20.5	10.5	15.1	13.8	10.3	8.9	7.4	5.8	50.9	46 527	43 431	42 071	7.1	3.2
Houghton	6.0	16.4	19.5	12.2	11.7	8.7	7.7	9.1	8.8	47.3	36 016	35 446	37 872	1.6	-6.4
Huron	7.0	19.9	8.0	14.1	13.3	9.4	10.1	10.5	7.8	51.0	36 079	34 951	36 459	3.2	-4.1
Ingham	7.4	16.9	19.6	17.9	14.8	8.6	6.3	5.0	3.7	52.0	279 320	281 912	275 520	-0.9	2.3
Ionia	7.7	20.5	13.1	17.6	14.5	9.3	7.2	5.7	4.4	46.7	61 518	57 024	51 815	7.9	10.1
Iosco	8.3	18.0	10.4	17.0	12.2	8.5	10.5	8.9	6.2	50.0	27 339	30 209	28 349	-9.5	6.6
Iron	5.4	16.9	5.1	11.5	12.7	9.4	12.0	14.9	12.1	52.1	13 138	13 175	13 635	-0.3	-3.4
Isabella	6.5	16.4	28.6	14.3	12.0	7.5	6.3	5.0	3.4	52.2	63 351	54 624	54 110	16.0	0.9
Jackson	7.3	18.5	9.5	17.6	15.7	10.3	8.8	7.2	5.1	49.2	158 422	149 756	151 495	5.8	-1.1
Kalamazoo	7.3	17.1	15.5	16.9	15.1	9.8	7.6	6.0	4.6	51.9	238 603	223 411	212 378	6.8	5.2
Kalkaska	7.7	21.6	7.9	16.0	13.9	10.0	9.5	8.2	5.1	49.9	16 571	13 497	10 952	22.8	23.2
Kent	8.7	19.5	10.9	18.8	14.9	9.0	7.4	6.1	4.7	51.6	574 335	500 631	444 506	14.7	12.6
Keweenaw	4.9	15.0	4.7	10.5	13.6	10.2	11.7	14.9	14.5	51.1	2 301	1 701	1 963	35.3	-13.3
Lake	6.7	18.4	6.3	11.7	11.4	10.4	13.7	12.9	8.4	51.0	11 333	8 583	7 711	32.0	11.3
Lapeer	7.3	22.3	9.7	16.3	16.6	11.6	7.6	5.2	3.5	49.9	87 904	74 768	70 038	17.6	6.8

Table B. States and Counties

STATE County	Total population	In households (percent)			Child		Other relatives		Nonrelatives		In group quarters (percent)	Institutionalized population			Noninstitutionalized population		
		Total in house-holds	House-holder	Spouse	Total	Own child under 18 years	Total	Under 18 years	Total	Unmar-ried partner	Total in group quarters	Correc-tional institu-tions	Nurs-ing homes	Other institu-tions	Col-lege dormi-tories	Mili-tary quar-ters	Other
	54	55	56	57	58	59	60	61	62	63	64	65	66	67	68	69	70
MARYLAND—Cont'd																	
Washington	131 923	92.9	37.7	20.3	27.0	21.3	3.4	1.4	4.4	2.4	7.1	5.5	0.9	0.2	0.0	0.0	0.6
Wicomico	84 644	96.3	38.1	18.7	27.9	21.9	4.9	2.3	6.7	2.5	3.7	0.0	0.7	0.5	2.0	0.0	0.5
Worcester	46 543	98.5	42.3	22.5	23.7	18.0	4.8	2.1	5.3	2.4	1.5	0.5	0.8	0.0	0.0	0.0	0.1
Baltimore city	651 154	96.0	39.6	10.6	27.3	18.4	11.0	5.5	7.6	2.8	4.0	1.2	0.6	0.1	1.4	0.0	0.6
MASSACHUSETTS	6 349 097	96.5	38.5	18.9	29.0	21.8	4.5	1.4	5.6	2.1	3.5	0.4	0.9	0.1	1.6	0.0	0.5
Barnstable	222 230	97.4	42.7	22.3	24.6	18.9	3.1	1.0	4.8	2.1	2.6	0.1	1.0	0.1	0.3	0.0	1.0
Berkshire	134 953	95.5	41.5	19.9	26.4	20.5	2.8	0.9	4.8	2.4	4.5	0.2	1.3	0.2	2.1	0.0	0.7
Bristol	534 678	97.4	38.4	19.8	30.8	22.7	4.2	1.4	4.2	2.2	2.6	0.2	0.9	0.1	1.0	0.0	0.3
Dukes	14 987	98.7	42.8	19.5	26.0	21.3	2.9	0.9	7.5	2.7	1.3	0.2	0.7	0.0	0.0	0.0	0.4
Essex	723 419	97.7	38.1	19.4	30.8	23.2	4.7	1.5	4.6	2.0	2.3	0.2	1.0	0.1	0.8	0.0	0.3
Franklin	71 535	98.0	41.2	19.7	27.5	21.7	2.8	1.0	6.7	3.2	2.0	0.3	0.9	0.1	1.2	0.0	0.6
Hampden	456 228	96.8	38.4	17.6	31.0	23.5	4.7	1.8	5.0	2.4	3.2	0.4	1.0	0.2	1.2	0.0	0.3
Hampshire	152 251	88.0	36.8	17.4	23.7	18.3	2.5	0.8	7.6	2.6	12.0	0.2	0.7	0.2	10.7	0.0	0.2
Middlesex	1 465 396	96.4	38.3	19.6	28.2	21.0	4.3	1.1	6.0	1.8	3.6	0.3	0.8	0.1	2.1	0.0	0.4
Nantucket	9 520	92.0	38.9	17.8	22.0	18.2	2.3	0.5	11.1	2.8	8.0	0.0	0.5	0.0	0.9	0.0	7.5
Norfolk	650 308	97.3	38.3	20.8	29.9	22.2	3.9	1.0	4.4	1.5	2.7	0.5	0.9	0.1	0.4	0.0	0.3
Plymouth	472 822	97.5	35.6	20.3	33.0	24.6	4.6	1.6	4.0	1.9	2.5	0.8	0.8	0.3	2.9	0.0	0.9
Suffolk	689 807	94.7	40.4	11.8	24.9	17.5	7.1	2.2	10.5	2.5	5.3	0.4	0.8	0.3	2.9	0.0	0.9
Worcester	750 963	96.6	37.8	19.9	30.3	23.8	3.8	1.2	4.8	2.2	3.4	0.5	1.0	0.2	1.2	0.0	0.4
MICHIGAN	9 938 444	97.5	38.1	19.6	30.6	23.6	4.4	1.8	4.9	2.0	2.5	0.7	0.5	0.1	0.7	0.0	0.5
Alcona	11 719	98.3	43.8	26.3	21.7	17.1	2.9	1.4	3.6	1.9	1.7	0.3	0.8	0.0	0.0	0.0	0.6
Alger	9 862	90.0	38.4	21.9	24.0	19.1	2.2	0.9	3.6	2.0	10.0	8.6	0.7	0.0	0.0	0.0	0.8
Allegan	105 665	98.2	36.1	22.2	32.6	26.6	3.1	1.4	4.2	2.1	1.8	0.2	0.6	0.0	0.0	0.0	1.1
Alpena	31 314	98.2	40.9	22.7	28.5	22.2	2.3	0.9	3.8	2.1	1.8	0.2	0.4	0.0	0.1	0.0	1.0
Antrim	23 110	98.8	39.9	24.3	27.3	22.3	3.2	1.3	4.0	2.0	1.2	0.2	0.5	0.1	0.0	0.0	0.5
Arenac	17 269	95.3	38.9	22.1	27.5	21.4	2.7	1.1	4.2	2.3	4.7	3.3	0.7	0.0	0.0	0.0	0.7
Baraga	8 746	91.0	38.3	19.7	26.6	21.1	2.7	1.2	3.7	2.3	9.0	7.0	0.9	0.0	0.0	0.0	1.1
Barry	56 755	99.2	37.1	23.8	31.2	25.1	3.1	1.3	4.1	2.1	0.8	0.1	0.4	0.0	0.0	0.0	0.3
Bay	110 157	98.4	39.9	21.4	30.2	22.5	2.9	1.3	4.0	2.1	1.6	0.2	0.5	0.0	0.0	0.0	0.9
Benzie	15 998	98.3	40.6	24.0	26.5	21.5	2.8	1.2	4.3	2.3	1.7	0.2	0.6	0.2	0.0	0.0	0.6
Berrien	162 453	97.3	39.1	20.0	29.3	23.0	4.3	2.1	4.5	2.1	2.7	0.3	0.4	0.2	0.5	0.0	1.2
Branch	45 787	93.2	35.7	20.0	29.0	23.2	3.6	1.5	4.9	2.3	6.8	5.2	0.7	0.1	0.0	0.0	0.9
Calhoun	137 985	97.0	39.2	19.5	29.1	23.1	4.1	2.0	5.1	2.4	3.0	0.5	0.6	0.3	0.8	0.0	0.8
Cass	51 104	98.5	38.5	22.4	29.0	22.5	4.2	2.0	4.5	2.3	1.5	0.3	0.4	0.0	0.0	0.1	0.4
Charlevoix	26 090	98.9	39.9	23.3	29.1	24.2	2.5	1.1	4.1	2.0	1.1	0.1	0.5	0.0	0.1	0.1	0.3
Cheboygan	26 448	98.6	41.0	23.8	27.0	21.9	2.8	1.2	4.1	2.2	1.4	0.3	0.6	0.0	0.1	0.0	0.3
Chippewa	38 543	84.5	35.0	18.0	24.7	20.0	2.2	0.8	4.7	2.1	15.5	12.5	0.3	0.2	2.1	0.0	0.5
Clare	31 252	98.4	40.6	22.4	27.1	21.9	3.3	1.5	5.0	2.7	1.6	0.6	0.6	0.0	0.0	0.0	0.5
Clinton	64 753	98.8	36.5	23.5	33.1	26.6	2.3	0.9	3.3	1.6	1.2	0.2	0.6	0.1	0.0	0.0	0.3
Crawford	14 273	96.7	39.4	22.7	27.4	22.2	2.9	1.3	4.4	2.3	3.3	2.1	0.6	0.1	0.0	0.0	0.3
Delta	38 520	98.5	41.1	22.9	28.6	22.4	2.1	0.9	3.9	2.1	1.5	0.2	0.9	0.0	0.0	0.0	0.6
Dickinson	27 472	98.3	41.4	22.7	28.8	23.8	1.8	0.7	3.6	2.0	1.7	0.2	0.9	0.0	0.0	0.0	0.6
Eaton	103 655	98.3	38.8	21.8	30.4	24.2	3.0	1.3	4.3	2.1	1.7	0.2	0.4	0.0	0.6	0.0	0.4
Emmet	31 437	97.7	40.0	22.4	28.6	23.7	2.4	1.0	4.4	2.1	2.3	0.6	0.7	0.0	0.2	0.0	0.7
Genesee	436 141	98.8	38.9	18.5	31.9	24.4	4.6	2.3	4.9	2.4	1.2	0.2	0.4	0.0	0.1	0.0	0.5
Gladwin	26 023	98.7	40.6	24.5	26.9	21.5	2.7	1.2	3.9	2.0	1.3	0.2	0.6	0.0	0.0	0.0	0.4
Gogebic	17 370	94.1	42.7	21.0	24.5	18.9	2.2	0.7	3.7	1.9	5.9	2.6	1.5	0.1	0.0	0.0	1.7
Grand Traverse	77 654	97.7	39.1	21.8	29.1	24.0	2.4	0.8	5.3	2.1	2.3	0.3	0.7	0.0	0.3	0.0	1.0
Gratiot	42 285	88.0	34.3	19.8	27.6	22.1	2.3	1.0	4.0	1.9	12.0	7.3	1.6	0.0	2.4	0.0	0.7
Hillsdale	46 527	96.8	37.3	22.3	29.8	24.0	3.1	1.3	4.4	2.0	3.2	0.1	0.5	0.0	1.8	0.0	0.7
Houghton	36 016	91.4	38.3	18.2	26.2	21.0	1.8	0.6	6.9	1.7	8.6	0.8	1.0	0.0	6.3	0.0	0.5
Huron	36 079	98.1	40.5	23.7	28.7	22.8	2.4	0.9	2.9	1.6	1.9	0.2	0.7	0.1	0.0	0.0	1.0
Ingham	279 320	94.0	38.9	16.7	26.5	21.4	3.4	1.4	8.5	2.4	6.0	0.2	0.4	0.1	5.0	0.0	0.4
Ionia	61 518	90.6	33.5	19.7	30.7	24.9	2.5	1.1	4.3	2.2	9.4	8.5	0.5	0.0	0.0	0.0	0.4
Iosco	27 339	98.6	42.9	23.7	25.0	20.4	2.6	1.2	4.3	2.3	1.4	0.2	1.0	0.0	0.0	0.0	0.3
Iron	13 138	95.6	43.8	22.1	24.2	19.3	2.2	0.7	3.4	2.0	4.4	2.0	1.8	0.0	0.2	0.0	0.3
Isabella	63 351	90.4	35.4	16.1	23.3	18.9	2.3	0.9	13.3	2.2	9.6	0.3	0.4	0.3	8.0	0.0	0.7
Jackson	158 422	93.7	36.7	19.8	29.0	23.1	3.5	1.7	4.7	2.3	6.3	4.6	0.7	0.0	0.5	0.0	0.5
Kalamazoo	238 603	95.3	39.2	18.7	27.0	22.2	2.9	1.2	7.6	2.3	4.7	0.2	0.6	0.1	3.0	0.0	0.8
Kalkaska	16 571	98.8	38.8	22.8	28.7	23.2	3.0	1.4	5.5	2.6	1.2	0.3	0.5	0.0	0.0	0.0	0.4
Kent	574 335	97.8	37.1	19.4	32.0	26.1	3.8	1.4	5.5	2.0	2.2	0.2	0.7	0.1	0.7	0.0	0.5
Keweenaw	2 301	92.3	43.4	22.4	22.5	17.6	1.4	0.4	2.6	1.8	7.7	0.2	0.0	5.6	0.0	0.0	2.0
Lake	11 333	94.7	41.5	21.8	23.0	18.4	3.5	1.7	5.0	2.6	5.3	1.6	0.7	2.9	0.0	0.0	0.2
Lapeer	87 904	97.9	35.0	23.0	33.0	26.0	3.4	1.4	3.5	1.7	2.1	1.2	0.3	0.0	0.0	0.0	0.6

Table B. States and Counties

STATE County	Households by type, 2000												Households, 1990		
		Family households						Nonfamily households							
				Married couple		Female householder[1]			Householder living alone						
	Total households	Total	With own children under 18 years	Total	With own children under 18 years	Total	With own children under 18 years	Total	Total	65 years and over	Average house-hold size	Average family size	Total house-holds	Female house-holder[1]	House-holder living alone
	71	72	73	74	75	76	77	78	79	80	81	82	83	84	85
MARYLAND—Cont'd															
Washington	49 726	68.6	31.3	54.0	22.2	10.7	6.7	31.4	26.0	11.1	2.46	2.96	44 762	9.7	23.6
Wicomico	32 218	67.6	32.3	49.2	21.1	14.1	8.8	32.4	24.8	9.8	2.53	3.00	27 772	13.2	23.5
Worcester	19 694	67.4	24.5	53.2	16.6	10.8	6.1	32.6	26.3	11.6	2.33	2.79	14 142	11.5	24.7
Baltimore city	257 996	57.0	25.5	26.7	10.0	25.0	13.3	43.0	34.9	11.3	2.42	3.16	276 484	24.6	30.5
MASSACHUSETTS	2 443 580	64.5	30.6	49.0	22.4	11.9	6.7	35.5	28.0	10.5	2.51	3.11	2 247 110	12.1	25.8
Barnstable	94 822	64.4	24.3	52.2	17.8	9.4	5.7	35.6	29.5	14.4	2.28	2.82	77 586	9.8	27.2
Berkshire	56 006	62.7	27.5	48.0	18.8	11.0	6.7	37.3	31.6	13.9	2.30	2.89	54 315	10.8	27.5
Bristol	205 411	68.5	33.0	51.6	23.2	13.0	7.8	31.5	26.5	11.0	2.54	3.08	187 668	12.5	23.8
Dukes	6 421	59.0	28.4	45.4	20.2	9.8	6.0	41.0	32.0	11.1	2.30	2.91	5 003	8.7	31.5
Essex	275 419	67.2	32.8	51.1	23.9	12.4	7.2	32.8	27.1	10.9	2.57	3.15	251 285	12.4	25.2
Franklin	29 466	62.5	29.5	47.9	20.4	10.6	6.9	37.5	29.0	10.9	2.38	2.95	27 640	10.5	26.1
Hampden	175 288	66.0	31.9	45.8	19.8	15.9	10.1	34.0	28.4	11.9	2.52	3.10	169 906	15.4	25.6
Hampshire	55 991	60.4	28.2	47.4	20.7	9.8	6.0	39.6	28.6	10.2	2.39	2.96	50 052	9.9	24.8
Middlesex	561 220	64.3	30.2	51.3	24.2	9.9	4.9	35.7	27.1	9.5	2.52	3.11	519 527	10.5	25.2
Nantucket	3 699	56.9	26.9	47.4	20.6	8.0	4.8	43.1	29.8	8.0	2.37	2.90	2 597	7.4	31.4
Norfolk	248 827	66.7	31.2	54.2	26.0	9.5	4.3	33.3	26.8	10.8	2.54	3.14	227 798	10.0	24.5
Plymouth	168 361	72.7	36.3	57.0	27.9	11.9	6.6	27.3	22.2	9.0	2.74	3.23	149 519	11.9	20.1
Suffolk	278 722	49.9	23.5	29.3	12.6	16.3	9.4	50.1	36.3	9.5	2.34	3.17	264 061	16.6	34.8
Worcester	283 927	67.8	33.6	52.5	24.8	11.4	6.9	32.2	26.2	10.4	2.56	3.11	260 153	11.2	23.9
MICHIGAN	3 785 661	68.0	32.7	51.4	23.1	12.5	7.5	32.0	26.2	9.4	2.56	3.10	3 419 331	12.9	23.7
Alcona	5 132	69.5	20.4	60.1	15.2	5.8	3.0	30.5	26.6	14.2	2.24	2.67	4 261	7.5	24.6
Alger	3 785	68.3	27.0	57.0	20.1	7.6	4.5	31.7	26.8	12.6	2.35	2.83	3 337	8.5	24.3
Allegan	38 165	74.4	37.4	61.4	29.0	9.1	5.9	25.6	20.7	7.8	2.72	3.15	31 709	8.6	19.3
Alpena	12 818	67.8	29.4	55.3	21.8	9.0	5.4	32.2	27.8	13.3	2.40	2.93	11 838	9.1	24.6
Antrim	9 222	72.8	29.7	61.0	22.4	7.9	4.9	27.2	23.4	10.5	2.47	2.89	6 980	8.5	21.5
Arenac	6 710	70.3	29.0	57.0	20.4	9.0	5.8	29.7	25.5	12.3	2.45	2.92	5 642	9.4	22.7
Baraga	3 353	66.3	29.1	51.5	20.0	10.1	6.3	33.7	29.5	13.6	2.37	2.93	3 065	10.2	28.0
Barry	21 035	76.0	35.2	64.1	27.5	7.7	4.9	24.0	19.5	7.7	2.68	3.06	17 763	7.7	17.7
Bay	43 930	68.4	30.7	53.7	22.0	10.9	6.6	31.6	27.2	11.3	2.47	3.00	42 188	11.0	24.1
Benzie	6 500	70.7	28.8	59.2	21.8	7.7	4.9	29.3	24.1	10.8	2.42	2.86	4 772	7.3	22.6
Berrien	63 569	68.2	31.2	51.2	20.9	13.2	8.3	31.8	27.1	10.8	2.49	3.01	61 025	13.3	24.4
Branch	16 349	70.8	33.2	56.0	23.9	9.9	6.2	29.2	24.2	10.4	2.61	3.08	14 921	9.9	22.3
Calhoun	54 100	67.0	31.7	49.6	20.8	13.0	8.3	33.0	27.8	10.5	2.47	3.01	51 812	13.1	25.3
Cass	19 676	72.7	31.0	58.2	22.5	9.9	5.8	27.3	22.6	9.4	2.56	2.98	18 239	10.4	20.3
Charlevoix	10 400	70.3	31.8	58.4	23.9	8.1	5.3	29.8	25.2	10.5	2.48	2.96	8 243	8.7	23.0
Cheboygan	10 835	69.9	28.6	58.0	21.0	8.6	5.6	30.1	25.8	11.8	2.41	2.87	8 201	9.6	22.1
Chippewa	13 474	66.5	30.4	51.5	20.4	10.7	7.4	33.5	27.5	10.7	2.42	2.93	11 541	10.0	25.4
Clare	12 686	69.0	27.9	55.3	18.8	9.4	6.1	31.0	26.2	11.7	2.42	2.89	9 698	10.5	22.5
Clinton	23 653	76.0	37.4	64.3	30.0	8.4	5.5	24.0	19.8	7.1	2.70	3.12	20 212	7.8	17.2
Crawford	5 625	71.8	30.0	57.6	20.7	9.7	6.4	28.2	24.0	10.5	2.45	2.87	4 441	9.6	21.0
Delta	15 836	67.5	29.7	55.8	22.4	8.3	5.4	32.5	28.0	13.0	2.40	2.93	14 531	8.9	25.7
Dickinson	11 386	66.6	31.0	54.9	23.3	8.4	5.6	33.4	29.4	14.9	2.37	2.93	10 633	8.3	26.2
Eaton	40 167	70.3	33.8	56.3	24.8	10.3	6.7	29.7	24.5	8.4	2.54	3.03	34 027	9.4	21.2
Emmet	12 577	67.8	31.7	55.0	24.0	8.5	5.6	32.2	26.9	10.0	2.44	2.97	9 516	9.0	24.2
Genesee	169 825	68.3	33.7	47.4	20.7	16.3	10.5	31.7	26.6	9.0	2.54	3.07	161 296	16.7	23.9
Gladwin	10 561	72.1	27.1	60.5	19.8	8.0	5.0	27.9	24.0	11.2	2.43	2.85	8 357	8.6	21.7
Gogebic	7 425	61.7	24.4	49.1	17.2	9.3	5.4	38.3	34.2	18.5	2.20	2.81	7 449	9.2	31.8
Grand Traverse	30 396	68.2	32.8	55.7	24.8	9.2	5.9	31.8	25.0	9.0	2.49	2.99	23 965	9.2	22.5
Gratiot	14 501	71.7	34.0	57.6	24.7	10.2	6.7	28.3	23.7	10.7	2.57	3.02	13 659	9.5	21.5
Hillsdale	17 335	72.4	32.9	59.9	25.0	8.4	5.4	27.6	22.9	9.3	2.60	3.05	15 637	8.7	21.1
Houghton	13 793	59.0	26.1	47.5	19.4	8.0	4.8	41.0	32.6	13.8	2.39	3.04	13 172	8.4	31.5
Huron	14 597	69.5	29.0	58.6	22.8	7.4	4.2	30.5	27.3	14.1	2.42	2.95	13 268	8.1	24.2
Ingham	108 593	58.7	29.8	43.0	19.8	12.1	7.9	41.3	30.2	7.7	2.42	3.04	102 648	12.3	26.3
Ionia	20 606	73.5	38.1	58.7	28.1	10.1	6.9	26.5	21.9	8.9	2.70	3.15	18 447	9.7	20.6
Iosco	11 727	67.0	24.9	55.2	17.4	8.4	5.3	33.0	28.6	14.0	2.30	2.79	11 588	7.7	23.7
Iron	5 748	62.9	23.7	50.4	16.3	8.4	5.2	37.1	33.7	19.4	2.19	2.76	5 655	7.5	31.0
Isabella	22 425	58.0	28.4	45.4	20.3	8.9	5.9	42.0	23.8	7.3	2.55	3.03	17 591	9.4	20.6
Jackson	58 168	70.2	33.5	53.8	22.9	12.0	7.8	29.8	24.6	9.6	2.55	3.03	53 660	11.5	23.2
Kalamazoo	93 479	62.0	30.4	47.7	21.1	11.0	7.4	38.0	28.0	8.5	2.43	3.00	83 702	10.9	24.7
Kalkaska	6 428	72.1	31.7	58.6	22.9	9.0	6.0	27.9	22.3	8.2	2.55	2.95	4 934	8.8	20.3
Kent	212 890	67.7	35.8	52.3	26.1	11.6	7.6	32.3	25.6	8.0	2.64	3.20	181 740	11.5	23.0
Keweenaw	998	60.6	20.9	51.6	15.7	5.7	3.8	39.4	35.8	17.4	2.13	2.76	777	6.3	34.5
Lake	4 704	64.9	23.0	52.4	15.4	8.7	5.4	35.1	29.6	13.8	2.28	2.79	3 536	9.8	27.9
Lapeer	30 729	77.7	38.3	65.7	31.2	8.1	4.8	22.3	18.5	6.9	2.80	3.19	24 659	8.9	15.7

[1] No spouse present.

Table B. States and Counties

STATE County	Percent change of households, 1990–2000	Total housing units	Occupied housing units (percent)	Vacant housing units		Homeowner vacancy rate (percent)	Rental vacancy rate (percent)	Occupied housing units			Average household size of owner-occupied units	Average household size of renter-occupied units
				Total	For seasonal, recreational, or occasional use			Total	Percent owner-occupied housing units	Percent renter-occupied housing units		
	86	87	88	89	90	91	92	93	94	95	96	97
MARYLAND—Cont'd												
Washington	11.1	52 972	93.9	6.1	0.9	1.6	5.1	49 726	65.6	34.4	2.57	2.27
Wicomico	16.0	34 401	93.7	6.3	0.8	1.5	4.6	32 218	66.5	33.5	2.55	2.49
Worcester	39.3	47 360	41.6	58.4	37.3	1.9	48.8	19 694	75.0	25.0	2.33	2.32
Baltimore city	-6.7	300 477	85.9	14.1	0.5	3.6	7.6	257 996	50.3	49.7	2.57	2.27
MASSACHUSETTS	8.7	2 621 989	93.2	6.8	3.6	0.7	3.5	2 443 580	61.7	38.3	2.72	2.17
Barnstable	22.2	147 083	64.5	35.5	32.0	1.4	7.4	94 822	77.8	22.2	2.34	2.09
Berkshire	3.1	66 301	84.5	15.5	9.4	1.7	8.2	56 006	66.9	33.1	2.47	1.95
Bristol	9.5	216 918	94.7	5.3	0.9	0.8	5.5	205 411	61.6	38.4	2.78	2.15
Dukes	28.3	14 836	43.3	56.7	53.9	1.3	3.6	6 421	71.3	28.7	2.39	2.09
Essex	9.6	287 144	95.9	4.1	1.5	0.5	3.0	275 419	63.5	36.5	2.75	2.24
Franklin	6.6	31 939	92.3	7.7	3.0	1.4	3.6	29 466	66.9	33.1	2.56	2.02
Hampden	3.2	185 876	94.3	5.7	0.9	1.0	5.3	175 288	61.9	38.1	2.64	2.32
Hampshire	11.9	58 644	95.5	4.5	1.7	0.7	2.9	55 991	65.0	35.0	2.59	2.03
Middlesex	8.0	576 681	97.3	2.7	0.5	0.5	2.3	561 220	61.7	38.3	2.76	2.12
Nantucket	42.4	9 210	40.2	59.8	56.1	2.4	3.9	3 699	63.1	36.9	2.51	2.13
Norfolk	9.2	255 154	97.5	2.5	0.5	0.4	2.5	248 827	69.7	30.3	2.80	1.96
Plymouth	12.6	181 524	92.7	7.3	4.7	0.6	3.2	168 361	75.6	24.4	2.89	2.26
Suffolk	5.6	292 520	95.3	4.7	0.6	0.9	2.9	278 722	33.9	66.1	2.54	2.24
Worcester	9.1	298 159	95.2	4.8	1.0	0.8	4.3	283 927	64.1	35.9	2.76	2.19
MICHIGAN	10.7	4 234 279	89.4	10.6	5.5	1.6	6.8	3 785 661	73.8	26.2	2.67	2.24
Alcona	20.4	10 584	48.5	51.5	47.9	2.6	11.0	5 132	89.9	10.1	2.24	2.27
Alger	13.4	5 964	63.5	36.5	30.9	3.2	12.5	3 785	82.5	17.5	2.41	2.05
Allegan	20.4	43 292	88.2	11.8	7.3	1.6	7.7	38 165	82.9	17.1	2.78	2.40
Alpena	8.3	15 289	83.8	16.2	10.8	1.6	6.5	12 818	79.1	20.9	2.49	2.05
Antrim	32.1	15 090	61.1	38.9	34.1	1.7	10.0	9 222	84.9	15.1	2.49	2.37
Arenac	18.9	9 563	70.2	29.8	23.8	2.6	13.3	6 710	84.6	15.4	2.48	2.31
Baraga	9.4	4 631	72.4	27.6	21.9	2.1	6.0	3 353	77.7	22.3	2.45	2.10
Barry	18.4	23 876	88.1	11.9	7.9	1.3	5.8	21 035	85.8	14.2	2.73	2.36
Bay	4.1	46 423	94.6	5.4	0.8	1.1	7.9	43 930	79.3	20.7	2.58	2.04
Benzie	36.2	10 312	63.0	37.0	30.8	2.3	15.4	6 500	85.7	14.3	2.45	2.26
Berrien	4.2	73 445	86.6	13.4	7.2	1.9	8.1	63 569	72.3	27.7	2.54	2.35
Branch	9.6	19 822	82.5	17.5	11.2	2.5	7.6	16 349	78.9	21.1	2.66	2.40
Calhoun	4.4	58 691	92.2	7.8	0.9	1.9	11.5	54 100	73.0	27.0	2.57	2.21
Cass	7.9	23 884	82.4	17.6	12.7	1.6	6.6	19 676	81.9	18.1	2.57	2.49
Charlevoix	26.2	15 370	67.7	32.3	28.6	1.3	6.7	10 400	81.1	18.9	2.54	2.22
Cheboygan	32.1	16 583	65.3	34.7	28.8	2.0	7.2	10 835	82.8	17.2	2.43	2.29
Chippewa	16.7	19 430	69.3	30.7	24.6	2.6	9.4	13 474	74.0	26.0	2.48	2.23
Clare	30.8	22 229	57.1	42.9	38.6	2.8	5.9	12 686	82.3	17.7	2.45	2.29
Clinton	17.0	24 630	96.0	4.0	0.4	1.0	6.9	23 653	85.3	14.7	2.77	2.29
Crawford	26.7	10 042	56.0	44.0	40.9	1.7	6.3	5 625	82.8	17.2	2.48	2.33
Delta	9.0	19 223	82.4	17.6	12.1	1.8	8.4	15 836	79.6	20.4	2.51	1.97
Dickinson	7.1	13 702	83.1	16.9	11.5	2.1	8.4	11 386	80.2	19.8	2.47	1.98
Eaton	18.0	42 118	95.4	4.6	0.6	1.3	5.7	40 167	74.2	25.8	2.71	2.04
Emmet	32.2	18 554	67.8	32.2	27.2	1.7	10.9	12 577	75.6	24.4	2.58	2.01
Genesee	5.3	183 630	92.5	7.5	0.5	2.1	10.6	169 825	73.2	26.8	2.62	2.31
Gladwin	26.4	16 828	62.8	37.2	33.2	2.2	6.3	10 561	85.7	14.3	2.45	2.34
Gogebic	-0.3	10 839	68.5	31.5	20.8	3.7	23.4	7 425	78.8	21.2	2.27	1.97
Grand Traverse	26.8	34 842	87.2	12.8	8.7	1.7	5.6	30 396	77.4	22.6	2.60	2.14
Gratiot	6.2	15 516	93.5	6.5	0.8	1.8	7.0	14 501	77.7	22.3	2.63	2.37
Hillsdale	10.9	20 189	85.9	14.1	9.4	1.6	5.8	17 335	79.9	20.1	2.66	2.36
Houghton	4.7	17 748	77.7	22.3	14.9	2.6	7.1	13 793	71.4	28.6	2.52	2.04
Huron	10.0	20 430	71.4	28.6	23.3	2.7	7.4	14 597	83.4	16.6	2.47	2.19
Ingham	5.8	115 056	94.4	5.6	0.5	1.6	6.3	108 593	60.8	39.2	2.59	2.15
Ionia	11.7	22 006	93.6	6.4	1.7	1.1	6.2	20 606	80.0	20.0	2.80	2.33
Iosco	1.2	20 432	57.4	42.6	33.0	11.6	10.0	11 727	82.0	18.0	2.32	2.18
Iron	1.6	8 772	65.5	34.5	27.1	2.8	8.1	5 748	82.4	17.6	2.24	1.95
Isabella	27.5	24 528	91.4	8.6	3.9	1.7	5.2	22 425	63.2	36.8	2.66	2.37
Jackson	8.4	62 906	92.5	7.5	3.0	1.4	6.4	58 168	76.5	23.5	2.64	2.27
Kalamazoo	11.7	99 250	94.2	5.8	0.8	1.6	6.7	93 479	65.7	34.3	2.62	2.08
Kalkaska	30.3	10 822	59.4	40.6	35.4	2.1	9.2	6 428	85.1	14.9	2.56	2.46
Kent	17.1	224 000	95.0	5.0	0.7	1.3	6.0	212 890	70.3	29.7	2.81	2.24
Keweenaw	28.4	2 327	42.9	57.1	50.5	1.2	17.0	998	88.8	11.2	2.18	1.69
Lake	33.0	13 498	34.8	65.2	61.0	3.2	7.7	4 704	83.0	17.0	2.27	2.35
Lapeer	24.6	32 732	93.9	6.1	2.1	1.4	5.3	30 729	84.9	15.1	2.88	2.35

Table B. States and Counties

STATE/County code	MSA/PMSA/NECMA code[1]	County type[2]	STATE County	Population, 2000				Population, 1990				Population and population characteristics, 2000					
												Race (percent)					
												One race					
				Land area, 2000[3] (sq km)	Total persons	Rank	Per square kilometer	Land area, 1990[3] (sq km)	Total persons	Rank	Per square kilometer	White	Black or African American	American Indian or Alaska Native	Asian	Native Hawaiian and other Pacific Islander	Some other race
				1	2	3	4	5	6	7	8	9	10	11	12	13	14
			MICHIGAN—Cont'd														
26 089	...	9	Leelanau	903	21 119	1 731	23.4	903	16 527	1 888	18.3	93.5	0.2	3.7	0.2	0.0	1.3
26 091	0440	1	Lenawee	1 944	98 890	526	50.9	1 944	91 476	503	47.1	92.5	2.1	0.4	0.5	0.0	3.0
26 093	0440	1	Livingston	1 472	156 951	339	106.6	1 472	115 645	398	78.6	97.1	0.5	0.4	0.6	0.0	0.3
26 095	...	9	Luce	2 339	7 024	2 682	3.0	2 339	5 763	2 783	2.5	82.8	7.5	5.5	0.4	0.0	0.5
26 097	...	7	Mackinac	2 646	11 943	2 298	4.5	2 646	10 674	2 319	4.0	80.1	0.2	14.2	0.3	0.0	0.3
26 099	2160	0	Macomb	1 244	788 149	60	633.6	1 244	717 400	57	576.7	92.7	2.7	0.3	2.1	0.0	0.4
26 101	...	7	Manistee	1 408	24 527	1 576	17.4	1 409	21 265	1 617	15.1	94.2	1.6	1.3	0.3	0.0	1.0
26 103	...	5	Marquette	4 717	64 634	752	13.7	4 717	70 887	624	15.0	95.1	1.3	1.5	0.5	0.0	0.2
26 105	...	7	Mason	1 282	28 274	1 438	22.1	1 283	25 537	1 444	19.9	95.8	0.7	0.8	0.3	0.0	0.8
26 107	...	7	Mecosta	1 439	40 553	1 101	28.2	1 439	37 308	1 064	25.9	92.7	3.6	0.6	0.9	0.0	0.4
26 109	...	7	Menominee	2 703	25 326	1 551	9.4	2 703	24 920	1 466	9.2	96.2	0.1	2.3	0.2	0.0	0.2
26 111	6960	2	Midland	1 350	82 874	626	61.4	1 350	75 651	595	56.0	95.5	1.0	0.4	1.5	0.0	0.4
26 113	...	9	Missaukee	1 468	14 478	2 124	9.9	1 468	12 147	2 203	8.3	97.5	0.2	0.5	0.2	0.0	0.4
26 115	2160	1	Monroe	1 427	145 945	375	102.3	1 427	133 600	348	93.6	95.4	1.9	0.3	0.5	0.0	0.6
26 117	...	6	Montcalm	1 834	61 266	795	33.4	1 834	53 059	802	28.9	94.8	2.2	0.6	0.3	0.0	0.6
26 119	...	9	Montmorency	1 418	10 315	2 413	7.3	1 418	8 936	2 476	6.3	98.4	0.2	0.4	0.1	0.0	0.1
26 121	30C0	2	Muskegon	1 319	170 200	318	129.0	1 319	158 983	298	120.5	81.3	14.2	0.8	0.4	0.0	1.3
26 123	...	6	Newaygo	2 182	47 874	955	21.9	2 182	38 206	1 048	17.5	94.8	1.1	0.6	0.3	0.0	1.6
26 125	2160	0	Oakland	2 260	1 194 156	30	528.4	2 260	1 083 592	28	479.5	82.8	10.1	0.3	4.1	0.0	0.8
26 127	...	8	Oceana	1 400	26 873	1 489	19.2	1 400	22 455	1 555	16.0	90.4	0.3	1.0	0.2	0.0	6.1
26 129	...	7	Ogemaw	1 462	21 645	1 711	14.8	1 462	18 681	1 751	12.8	97.5	0.1	0.6	0.4	0.0	0.1
26 131	...	9	Ontonagon	3 397	7 818	2 622	2.3	3 397	8 854	2 484	2.6	97.2	0.0	1.0	0.2	0.0	0.3
26 133	...	9	Osceola	1 466	23 197	1 633	15.8	1 466	20 146	1 668	13.7	97.5	0.3	0.5	0.2	0.0	0.4
26 135	...	9	Oscoda	1 463	9 418	2 495	6.4	1 463	7 842	2 588	5.4	97.8	0.1	0.7	0.1	0.0	0.1
26 137	...	7	Otsego	1 333	23 301	1 629	17.5	1 333	17 957	1 791	13.5	97.5	0.2	0.6	0.3	0.0	0.2
26 139	3000	2	Ottawa	1 465	238 314	243	162.7	1 465	187 768	257	128.2	91.5	1.0	0.4	2.1	0.0	3.5
26 141	...	7	Presque Isle	1 710	14 411	2 130	8.4	1 710	13 743	2 077	8.0	98.1	0.3	0.6	0.2	0.0	0.1
26 143	...	7	Roscommon	1 350	25 469	1 542	18.9	1 350	19 776	1 686	14.6	98.0	0.3	0.6	0.2	0.0	0.1
26 145	6960	2	Saginaw	2 095	210 039	266	100.3	2 095	211 946	236	101.2	75.3	18.6	0.4	0.8	0.0	2.9
26 147	2160	0	St. Clair	1 876	164 235	328	87.5	1 876	145 607	325	77.6	95.0	2.1	0.5	0.4	0.0	0.6
26 149	...	6	St. Joseph	1 305	62 422	777	47.8	1 305	58 913	738	45.1	93.5	2.6	0.4	0.6	0.0	1.5
26 151	...	8	Sanilac	2 496	44 547	1 007	17.8	2 496	39 928	1 004	16.0	96.9	0.3	0.4	0.3	0.0	1.1
26 153	...	7	Schoolcraft	3 051	8 903	2 533	2.9	3 051	8 302	2 535	2.7	88.7	1.6	6.1	0.4	0.0	0.4
26 155	...	4	Shiawassee	1 395	71 687	689	51.4	1 396	69 770	636	50.0	97.4	0.2	0.5	0.3	0.0	0.5
26 157	...	6	Tuscola	2 104	58 266	821	27.7	2 105	55 498	781	26.4	96.0	1.1	0.6	0.3	0.0	0.7
26 159	3720	2	Van Buren	1 582	76 263	658	48.2	1 583	70 060	633	44.3	87.9	5.2	0.9	0.3	0.0	3.4
26 161	0440	0	Washtenaw	1 839	322 895	179	175.6	1 839	282 937	173	153.9	77.4	12.3	0.4	6.3	0.0	1.0
26 163	2160	0	Wayne	1 591	2 061 162	11	1 295.5	1 591	2 111 687	8	1 327.3	51.7	42.2	0.4	1.7	0.0	1.6
26 165	...	7	Wexford	1 465	30 484	1 386	20.8	1 465	26 360	1 410	18.0	97.3	0.2	0.7	0.4	0.0	0.2
27 000	...		MINNESOTA	206 189	4 919 479	X	23.9	206 207	4 375 665	X	21.2	89.4	3.5	1.1	2.9	0.0	1.3
27 001	...	9	Aitkin	4 712	15 301	2 072	3.2	4 712	12 425	2 188	2.6	96.4	0.2	2.3	0.2	0.0	0.2
27 003	5120	0	Anoka	1 097	298 084	189	271.7	1 098	243 641	205	221.9	93.6	1.6	0.7	1.7	0.0	0.6
27 005	...	6	Becker	3 394	30 000	1 396	8.8	3 394	27 881	1 354	8.2	89.4	0.2	7.5	0.4	0.0	0.2
27 007	...	7	Beltrami	6 489	39 650	1 122	6.1	6 489	34 384	1 155	5.3	76.7	0.4	20.4	0.6	0.0	0.2
27 009	6980	3	Benton	1 057	34 226	1 275	32.4	1 057	30 185	1 289	28.6	96.2	0.8	0.5	1.1	0.0	0.4
27 011	...	9	Big Stone	1 287	5 820	2 802	4.5	1 287	6 285	2 723	4.9	98.4	0.2	0.5	0.4	0.0	0.1
27 013	...	5	Blue Earth	1 949	55 941	844	28.7	1 949	54 044	797	27.7	95.0	1.2	0.3	1.8	0.0	0.7
27 015	...	7	Brown	1 582	26 911	1 487	17.0	1 582	26 984	1 392	17.1	97.8	0.1	0.1	0.4	0.0	0.9
27 017	...	6	Carlton	2 228	31 671	1 353	14.2	2 228	29 259	1 321	13.1	91.7	1.0	5.2	0.4	0.0	0.2
27 019	5120	1	Carver	925	70 205	707	75.9	925	47 915	874	51.8	95.9	0.6	0.2	1.6	0.0	0.9
27 021	...	9	Cass	5 226	27 150	1 477	5.2	5 226	21 791	1 590	4.2	86.5	0.1	11.5	0.3	0.0	0.1
27 023	...	7	Chippewa	1 509	13 088	2 223	8.7	1 510	13 228	2 119	8.8	96.8	0.2	1.0	0.3	0.0	0.9
27 025	5120	1	Chisago	1 082	41 101	1 078	38.0	1 082	30 521	1 267	28.2	97.2	0.5	0.5	0.7	0.0	0.3
27 027	2520	3	Clay	2 707	51 229	903	18.9	2 707	50 422	837	18.6	94.0	0.5	1.4	0.9	0.0	1.7
27 029	...	9	Clearwater	2 576	8 423	2 570	3.3	2 576	8 309	2 534	3.2	89.3	0.2	8.6	0.2	0.0	0.3
27 031	...	9	Cook	3 757	5 168	2 839	1.4	3 757	3 868	2 926	1.0	89.5	0.3	7.6	0.3	0.0	0.3
27 033	...	7	Cottonwood	1 658	12 167	2 286	7.3	1 658	12 694	2 166	7.7	95.2	0.3	0.2	1.6	0.1	1.3
27 035	...	7	Crow Wing	2 581	55 099	857	21.3	2 581	44 249	921	17.1	97.6	0.3	0.8	0.3	0.0	0.2
27 037	5120	0	Dakota	1 475	355 904	165	241.3	1 476	275 210	180	186.5	91.4	2.3	0.4	2.9	0.0	1.3
27 039	...	6	Dodge	1 138	17 731	1 915	15.6	1 138	15 731	1 939	13.8	96.6	0.2	0.2	0.4	0.0	1.9
27 041	...	7	Douglas	1 643	32 821	1 324	20.0	1 643	28 674	1 339	17.5	98.5	0.2	0.2	0.4	0.0	0.2
27 043	...	7	Faribault	1 848	16 181	2 010	8.8	1 848	16 937	1 852	9.2	97.1	0.2	0.2	0.4	0.0	1.4
27 045	...	8	Fillmore	2 231	21 122	1 730	9.5	2 231	20 777	1 642	9.3	98.9	0.2	0.1	0.1	0.0	0.2
27 047	...	7	Freeborn	1 833	32 584	1 329	17.8	1 833	33 060	1 189	18.0	95.2	0.2	0.2	0.5	0.0	2.9
27 049	...	6	Goodhue	1 964	44 127	1 014	22.5	1 965	40 690	984	20.7	96.6	0.6	1.0	0.6	0.0	0.5

[1]MSA = Metropolitan Statistical Area. PMSA = Primary MSA. NECMA = New England County Metropolitan Area. See Appendix A for explanation of these concepts. See Appendix B for list of metropolitan areas identified by type, with component counties.
[2]County typology code from the Economic Research Service of USDA. See Appendix A for definition.
[3]Dry land or land partially or temporarily covered by water.

STATE County	Two or more races	White	Black	American Indian or Alaska Native	Asian	Native Hawaiian and other Pacific Islander	Some other race	Hispanic[1]	White	Black or African American	American Indian or Alaska Native	Asian and Pacific Islander	Hispanic[1]
			Race (percent) (cont'd) — Race alone or in combination							Race (percent)			
	15	16	17	18	19	20	21	22	23	24	25	26	27
MICHIGAN—Cont'd													
Leelanau	1.0	94.4	0.4	4.2	0.5	0.1	1.5	3.3	96.6	0.1	2.7	0.3	1.1
Lenawee	1.5	93.9	2.5	0.9	0.6	0.0	3.6	7.0	94.4	1.6	0.3	0.5	6.0
Livingston	1.1	98.1	0.6	1.1	0.8	0.1	0.5	1.2	98.2	0.6	0.6	0.4	0.8
Luce	3.2	85.3	8.1	7.8	0.8	0.1	1.5	1.8	94.0	0.0	5.7	0.1	0.5
Mackinac	4.9	84.9	0.3	18.9	0.4	0.0	0.5	0.9	83.9	0.0	15.8	0.1	0.3
Macomb	1.8	94.3	3.1	0.9	2.5	0.1	1.1	1.6	96.7	1.4	0.4	1.3	1.1
Manistee	1.5	95.5	2.0	2.2	0.6	0.1	1.3	2.6	98.1	0.3	0.9	0.3	1.5
Marquette	1.3	96.4	1.5	2.4	0.7	0.0	0.4	0.7	96.0	1.7	1.3	0.8	0.8
Mason	1.5	97.3	1.0	1.7	0.4	0.0	1.2	3.0	97.7	0.6	0.7	0.3	1.6
Mecosta	1.8	94.3	4.3	1.5	1.1	0.1	0.7	1.3	95.8	2.6	0.7	0.5	1.0
Menominee	1.0	97.2	0.3	3.0	0.3	0.1	0.2	0.8	98.2	0.0	1.5	0.2	0.2
Midland	1.1	96.5	1.3	0.9	1.7	0.1	0.7	1.6	97.1	1.0	0.4	1.1	1.4
Missaukee	1.2	98.7	0.3	1.3	0.3	0.0	0.6	1.2	98.9	0.0	0.6	0.2	0.6
Monroe	1.3	96.7	2.3	0.9	0.6	0.0	0.9	2.1	96.9	1.8	0.4	0.4	1.6
Montcalm	1.5	96.1	2.5	1.4	0.5	0.1	1.0	2.3	96.5	1.8	0.7	0.3	1.7
Montmorency	0.8	99.2	0.3	1.0	0.2	0.0	0.2	0.6	99.2	0.0	0.5	0.1	0.7
Muskegon	2.0	83.0	15.0	1.7	0.7	0.1	1.7	3.5	84.2	13.6	0.8	0.3	2.3
Newaygo	1.5	96.2	1.4	1.4	0.4	0.1	2.1	3.9	96.2	1.2	0.6	0.3	2.5
Oakland	1.9	84.4	10.6	0.8	4.6	0.1	1.5	2.4	89.6	7.2	0.4	2.3	1.8
Oceana	1.9	92.1	0.5	1.9	0.4	0.1	7.0	11.6	94.5	0.3	1.1	0.2	6.2
Ogemaw	1.2	98.7	0.2	1.5	0.5	0.1	0.2	1.2	99.0	0.1	0.7	0.1	0.6
Ontonagon	1.3	98.5	0.1	2.0	0.3	0.0	0.4	0.7	98.5	0.0	1.2	0.2	0.4
Osceola	1.2	98.7	0.6	1.3	0.3	0.0	0.4	1.0	98.8	0.3	0.6	0.2	0.7
Oscoda	1.2	99.0	0.1	1.5	0.2	0.0	0.4	0.9	99.2	0.0	0.5	0.1	0.6
Otsego	1.2	98.6	0.3	1.5	0.4	0.1	0.3	0.8	98.8	0.1	0.6	0.5	0.4
Ottawa	1.5	92.8	1.4	0.8	2.4	0.1	4.1	7.0	95.7	0.5	0.3	1.3	4.2
Presque Isle	0.8	98.8	0.4	1.1	0.2	0.0	0.3	0.5	99.3	0.1	0.3	0.2	0.3
Roscommon	0.7	98.7	0.4	1.1	0.3	0.1	0.2	0.8	99.1	0.2	0.5	0.1	0.5
Saginaw	2.0	76.9	19.4	1.0	1.0	0.1	3.7	6.7	78.1	17.4	0.4	0.6	6.2
St. Clair	1.4	96.3	2.6	1.1	0.6	0.0	1.0	2.2	96.4	2.1	0.5	0.3	1.8
St. Joseph	1.5	94.9	3.0	1.0	0.7	0.0	1.8	4.0	96.2	2.7	0.4	0.4	0.9
Sanilac	1.1	98.0	0.4	1.0	0.4	0.0	1.4	2.8	98.3	0.1	0.5	0.2	2.3
Schoolcraft	2.8	91.4	1.8	8.6	0.6	0.1	0.5	0.9	93.4	0.1	6.3	0.2	0.4
Shiawassee	1.2	98.5	0.4	1.2	0.4	0.0	0.7	1.8	98.4	0.1	0.6	0.3	1.5
Tuscola	1.3	97.2	1.2	1.3	0.4	0.1	1.1	2.3	97.4	0.9	0.6	0.4	2.1
Van Buren	2.2	89.9	5.9	1.9	0.5	0.0	4.1	7.4	90.2	6.7	0.9	0.3	3.2
Washtenaw	2.6	79.6	13.3	1.0	7.0	0.1	1.7	2.7	83.5	11.2	0.4	4.1	2.0
Wayne	2.5	53.7	43.0	1.0	2.1	0.1	2.8	3.7	57.4	40.2	0.4	1.0	2.4
Wexford	1.1	98.3	0.4	1.3	0.6	0.0	0.5	1.0	98.8	0.1	0.7	0.3	0.6
MINNESOTA	1.7	90.8	4.1	1.6	3.3	0.1	1.8	2.9	94.4	2.2	1.1	1.8	1.2
Aitkin	0.7	97.1	0.4	2.8	0.3	0.0	0.2	0.6	98.1	0.1	1.4	0.2	0.3
Anoka	1.7	95.2	2.1	1.3	2.1	0.1	1.0	1.7	97.2	0.5	0.8	1.2	0.9
Becker	2.3	91.6	0.3	9.5	0.5	0.1	0.4	0.8	92.7	0.1	6.7	0.4	0.4
Beltrami	1.8	78.4	0.6	21.8	0.8	0.1	0.4	1.0	82.6	0.3	16.4	0.6	0.4
Benton	0.9	97.1	1.1	0.8	1.4	0.1	0.5	0.9	98.8	0.2	0.4	0.4	0.5
Big Stone	0.3	98.7	0.3	0.7	0.4	0.0	0.2	0.3	99.2	0.1	0.4	0.2	0.4
Blue Earth	1.0	95.8	1.5	0.6	2.1	0.1	1.0	1.8	97.4	0.5	0.2	1.5	0.9
Brown	0.6	98.4	0.2	0.3	0.5	0.0	1.1	2.0	99.3	0.0	0.1	0.4	0.6
Carlton	1.5	93.1	1.2	6.3	0.5	0.1	0.4	0.8	95.1	0.1	4.4	0.3	0.3
Carver	0.8	96.7	0.9	0.4	1.8	0.0	1.1	2.6	98.4	0.2	0.2	0.9	0.5
Cass	1.5	87.9	0.3	12.6	0.4	0.0	0.3	0.8	88.6	0.2	10.9	0.2	0.4
Chippewa	0.8	97.5	0.4	1.5	0.5	0.1	1.0	1.9	99.1	0.0	0.2	0.3	0.7
Chisago	0.8	97.9	0.7	0.8	0.9	0.1	0.4	1.2	98.9	0.2	0.4	0.3	0.4
Clay	1.5	95.4	0.8	2.0	1.3	0.1	2.1	3.7	96.3	0.3	1.1	0.8	2.3
Clearwater	1.5	90.7	0.2	9.7	0.4	0.0	0.4	0.8	92.2	0.0	7.6	0.1	0.2
Cook	2.1	91.5	0.4	9.3	0.5	0.1	0.4	0.8	92.3	0.1	7.0	0.5	0.4
Cottonwood	1.1	95.9	0.4	0.5	2.2	0.1	2.1	2.2	99.0	0.1	0.1	0.7	0.5
Crow Wing	0.8	98.4	0.5	1.2	0.4	0.0	0.3	0.7	98.6	0.2	0.7	0.3	0.4
Dakota	1.8	92.9	2.9	0.8	3.4	0.1	1.8	2.9	96.2	1.2	0.3	1.7	1.5
Dodge	0.7	97.3	0.3	0.4	0.6	0.0	2.1	3.0	98.7	0.1	0.2	0.4	1.0
Douglas	0.5	99.0	0.3	0.5	0.5	0.0	0.2	0.6	99.3	0.0	0.3	0.3	0.3
Faribault	0.7	97.7	0.4	0.4	0.5	0.1	1.5	3.5	98.4	0.1	0.1	0.3	1.9
Fillmore	0.5	99.3	0.3	0.3	0.3	0.0	0.3	0.5	99.4	0.0	0.2	0.2	0.3
Freeborn	0.9	96.0	0.4	0.4	0.7	0.0	3.3	6.3	97.5	0.0	0.2	0.4	3.3
Goodhue	0.7	97.2	0.8	1.3	0.7	0.1	0.6	1.1	98.6	0.2	0.7	0.4	0.4

[1] Hispanic persons may be of any race.

Table B. States and Counties

STATE County	Under 5 years	5 to 17 years	18 to 24 years	25 to 34 years	35 to 44 years	45 to 54 years	55 to 64 years	65 to 74 years	75 years and over	Median age (years)	Percent Female
	28	29	30	31	32	33	34	35	36	37	38
MICHIGAN—Cont'd											
Leelanau	5.1	19.3	5.7	8.7	15.5	16.9	11.4	10.1	7.3	42.6	50.1
Lenawee	6.3	19.6	9.1	12.8	15.8	14.5	9.1	6.6	6.1	36.4	50.0
Livingston	7.2	21.5	6.6	12.4	19.2	15.7	8.9	4.7	3.6	36.2	49.5
Luce	5.0	16.4	8.6	14.5	16.0	13.6	10.5	8.2	7.2	38.6	44.5
Mackinac	4.7	17.5	6.0	10.2	14.9	15.3	13.1	10.5	7.8	42.8	50.1
Macomb	6.5	17.6	8.0	14.7	16.8	13.7	9.1	7.1	6.6	36.9	51.0
Manistee	5.3	17.3	6.7	11.2	15.2	14.9	11.4	9.8	8.3	41.5	49.2
Marquette	5.1	16.3	13.6	11.5	15.4	15.5	9.1	6.8	6.7	37.5	49.8
Mason	5.4	18.8	7.1	10.8	15.4	14.7	11.1	8.3	8.5	40.4	50.6
Mecosta	6.0	16.5	19.8	10.8	12.2	11.7	9.8	7.6	5.6	31.9	49.3
Menominee	5.8	18.1	7.6	10.2	16.0	14.7	10.1	8.7	8.6	40.4	50.3
Midland	6.5	20.4	8.7	12.5	16.7	14.2	9.0	6.4	5.6	36.3	51.0
Missaukee	6.4	20.7	7.5	11.3	15.9	12.8	10.6	8.0	6.8	37.7	50.1
Monroe	6.6	20.8	8.1	12.8	17.0	14.6	8.9	6.2	4.9	36.0	50.4
Montcalm	6.5	20.5	8.3	13.7	16.5	13.0	9.3	6.7	5.5	35.6	48.7
Montmorency	4.4	15.9	5.9	8.0	12.8	14.4	14.7	13.9	10.0	47.0	50.9
Muskegon	6.9	20.7	8.7	13.0	16.0	13.5	8.4	6.6	6.2	35.5	50.4
Newaygo	6.9	22.2	7.4	11.4	16.1	13.2	9.9	7.2	5.6	36.4	50.1
Oakland	6.7	18.5	7.2	14.8	17.7	15.1	8.8	5.9	5.4	36.7	51.0
Oceana	6.4	21.7	7.9	11.1	15.2	13.5	10.0	7.9	6.1	36.9	49.6
Ogemaw	5.2	18.3	6.4	9.7	14.7	13.7	13.3	10.9	7.8	42.3	50.4
Ontonagon	4.4	15.8	4.7	8.7	14.6	15.7	14.4	11.2	10.4	45.9	49.3
Osceola	6.2	21.0	8.0	11.2	15.3	13.4	10.8	8.1	6.0	37.6	50.6
Oscoda	5.2	18.1	5.6	8.6	14.2	13.7	14.3	11.8	8.4	43.7	50.9
Otsego	6.2	20.6	7.0	12.1	16.5	13.7	10.3	8.1	5.7	37.7	50.4
Ottawa	7.7	21.0	11.9	13.4	15.9	12.5	7.5	5.1	5.0	32.3	50.8
Presque Isle	4.8	16.1	6.5	8.4	14.0	14.8	13.0	12.2	10.2	45.1	50.2
Roscommon	4.3	15.7	5.5	8.1	13.3	13.8	15.5	14.0	9.8	47.2	50.8
Saginaw	6.8	19.8	9.0	12.5	15.1	14.0	9.2	6.9	6.6	36.3	51.9
St. Clair	6.7	20.1	7.9	13.1	16.9	14.1	9.1	6.4	5.8	36.4	50.7
St. Joseph	7.2	20.3	8.9	12.7	15.4	13.3	9.3	6.9	6.1	35.6	50.6
Sanilac	6.5	20.4	7.6	11.5	15.6	13.1	10.0	8.1	7.3	37.8	50.4
Schoolcraft	5.6	17.1	6.8	11.2	14.9	14.2	11.6	9.7	8.9	41.4	50.0
Shiawassee	6.8	20.1	8.3	12.6	16.7	14.2	9.4	6.4	5.5	36.4	50.9
Tuscola	6.0	20.7	8.2	12.0	16.1	14.1	10.0	6.6	6.2	37.0	50.1
Van Buren	6.8	21.3	7.9	11.8	16.3	14.4	9.3	6.7	5.6	36.6	50.4
Washtenaw	6.2	15.8	17.1	16.6	15.5	13.5	7.1	4.3	3.8	31.3	50.3
Wayne	7.4	20.6	8.7	14.8	15.5	13.1	7.8	6.3	5.8	34.0	52.0
Wexford	6.4	20.5	7.7	11.8	16.2	13.6	9.8	7.5	6.5	37.3	50.5
MINNESOTA	6.7	19.5	9.6	13.7	16.8	13.5	8.2	6.0	6.1	35.4	50.5
Aitkin	4.5	16.4	5.5	7.9	13.7	14.0	15.1	13.0	10.0	46.5	49.6
Anoka	7.6	21.3	8.3	15.0	19.1	13.7	7.9	4.2	2.8	33.7	49.7
Becker	6.3	20.4	7.1	11.0	14.9	14.4	10.6	8.6	7.8	39.4	50.1
Beltrami	7.1	21.6	13.9	11.3	14.0	12.5	7.9	6.0	5.6	31.5	50.7
Benton	7.2	19.8	12.2	15.4	15.6	12.0	6.7	5.1	5.9	31.9	50.1
Big Stone	4.8	20.1	5.3	7.9	14.1	13.1	10.9	11.0	13.0	43.6	51.5
Blue Earth	5.6	15.8	22.1	12.4	13.2	11.8	7.0	5.5	6.6	29.9	50.2
Brown	5.4	19.9	9.7	10.2	15.4	13.0	8.8	8.3	9.2	38.4	50.5
Carlton	5.9	19.5	7.7	11.6	16.8	14.3	9.2	7.6	7.6	38.4	49.3
Carver	8.8	22.7	6.9	13.9	20.8	13.1	6.4	4.0	3.5	33.9	50.0
Cass	5.1	19.9	6.1	8.8	14.2	14.2	13.7	10.6	7.4	42.2	49.5
Chippewa	5.9	19.5	7.1	9.9	14.7	13.6	9.4	8.4	11.6	40.5	51.3
Chisago	7.6	22.6	7.1	13.9	18.3	12.9	7.9	5.1	4.7	34.3	49.1
Clay	6.2	18.8	17.1	11.0	14.7	12.0	7.3	6.2	6.7	32.3	51.6
Clearwater	5.8	20.2	7.6	10.0	14.6	13.3	11.0	8.1	9.3	39.7	49.7
Cook	4.5	15.9	5.4	9.6	16.2	18.0	13.3	9.4	7.8	44.0	50.1
Cottonwood	5.8	19.2	6.5	9.6	13.6	13.3	9.8	9.6	12.5	41.7	51.4
Crow Wing	6.1	18.8	8.1	10.6	15.0	13.5	10.8	9.2	7.9	39.4	50.8
Dakota	7.8	21.4	7.9	15.2	19.2	13.8	7.3	4.2	3.2	33.7	50.6
Dodge	7.6	22.6	7.6	12.6	17.3	12.4	7.9	5.8	6.3	34.8	50.3
Douglas	5.5	18.5	9.2	10.2	14.8	13.4	10.5	8.8	9.1	39.7	50.3
Faribault	5.2	19.2	6.7	8.7	14.5	13.3	10.2	10.1	12.1	42.4	50.7
Fillmore	5.7	20.4	7.0	10.2	14.9	13.0	9.5	8.8	10.6	39.8	50.7
Freeborn	5.7	18.2	7.5	10.5	15.0	13.6	10.5	8.8	10.1	40.4	50.9
Goodhue	6.1	20.4	7.4	11.1	16.7	14.3	9.0	7.1	7.9	38.1	50.5

Table B. States and Counties

STATE County	Population and population characteristics, 1990										Population—change, 1980–2000				
	Age (percent)										Total persons			Percent change	
	Under 5 years	5 to 17 years	18 to 24 years	25 to 34 years	35 to 44 years	45 to 54 years	55 to 64 years	65 to 74 years	75 years and over	Percent Female	2000	1990	1980	1990–2000	1980–1990
	39	40	41	42	43	44	45	46	47	48	49	50	51	52	53
MICHIGAN—Cont'd															
Leelanau	7.5	18.5	6.7	14.3	17.2	10.4	10.4	8.8	6.1	50.2	21 119	16 527	14 007	27.8	18.0
Lenawee	7.3	20.9	10.4	15.3	15.2	10.4	8.4	7.1	5.0	50.7	98 890	91 476	89 948	8.1	1.7
Livingston	7.5	21.1	8.8	16.4	18.1	12.5	7.3	5.1	3.1	49.5	156 951	115 645	100 289	35.7	15.3
Luce	6.5	20.7	6.7	12.8	14.4	10.8	10.9	9.9	7.3	50.9	7 024	5 763	6 659	21.9	-13.5
Mackinac	6.8	19.1	7.0	14.0	13.5	10.6	11.9	9.9	7.1	50.5	11 943	10 674	10 178	11.9	4.9
Macomb	6.8	17.1	10.3	17.9	15.0	11.1	9.5	7.7	4.6	51.4	788 149	717 400	694 600	9.9	3.3
Manistee	6.2	17.8	7.3	13.9	14.4	10.9	11.2	10.2	8.1	51.6	24 527	21 265	23 019	15.3	-7.6
Marquette	7.1	18.8	14.3	17.1	15.5	8.8	7.1	6.2	5.0	49.2	64 634	70 887	74 101	-8.8	-4.3
Mason	7.0	19.3	7.9	13.9	14.4	10.3	10.1	9.6	7.5	51.3	28 274	25 537	26 365	10.7	-3.1
Mecosta	6.1	15.8	27.3	12.3	11.2	8.2	7.8	6.8	4.5	48.4	40 553	37 308	36 961	8.7	0.9
Menominee	6.3	20.1	7.4	14.8	14.7	9.8	9.6	9.4	7.8	50.7	25 326	24 920	26 201	1.6	-4.9
Midland	7.5	19.8	10.3	16.8	15.8	11.3	8.4	5.9	4.0	50.6	82 874	75 651	73 578	9.5	2.8
Missaukee	7.7	21.9	7.5	15.2	13.0	10.2	9.5	9.0	5.9	50.7	14 478	12 147	10 009	19.2	21.4
Monroe	7.7	21.0	9.8	16.3	15.5	10.8	8.5	6.1	4.3	50.7	145 945	133 600	134 659	9.2	-0.8
Montcalm	7.7	20.9	9.3	16.8	14.3	10.0	8.5	7.3	5.1	49.0	61 266	53 059	47 555	15.5	11.6
Montmorency	5.8	17.7	6.3	11.6	11.9	9.5	14.3	13.9	9.0	51.0	10 315	8 936	7 492	15.4	19.3
Muskegon	8.1	20.0	9.4	16.4	14.7	9.7	8.7	7.7	5.3	51.2	170 200	158 983	157 589	7.1	0.9
Newaygo	8.4	21.2	7.8	15.4	13.8	10.5	9.4	8.1	5.5	50.8	47 874	38 206	34 917	25.3	9.4
Oakland	7.2	17.5	9.2	18.4	16.8	11.4	8.6	6.5	4.4	51.4	1 194 156	1 083 592	1 011 793	10.2	7.1
Oceana	7.9	21.7	7.7	14.9	13.9	10.7	9.5	8.2	5.5	50.9	26 873	22 455	22 002	19.7	2.1
Ogemaw	6.7	19.6	7.3	13.5	12.5	10.1	12.0	11.3	6.9	50.8	21 645	18 681	16 436	15.9	13.7
Ontonagon	6.1	17.8	6.3	12.7	13.9	12.3	11.5	10.6	8.9	49.1	7 818	8 854	9 861	-11.7	-10.2
Osceola	7.6	22.1	8.4	14.2	13.4	10.6	9.9	8.5	5.5	50.5	23 197	20 146	18 928	15.1	6.4
Oscoda	6.8	17.2	6.7	13.2	11.0	10.5	14.0	13.0	7.6	50.7	9 418	7 842	6 858	20.1	14.3
Otsego	7.7	20.8	8.3	15.4	14.8	9.9	9.6	8.1	5.4	50.9	23 301	17 957	14 993	29.8	19.8
Ottawa	8.5	20.8	11.8	17.1	15.1	9.8	7.1	5.6	4.2	50.7	238 314	187 768	157 174	26.9	19.5
Presque Isle	6.2	19.3	7.0	12.6	12.8	9.9	12.5	11.9	7.9	50.6	14 411	13 743	14 267	4.9	-3.7
Roscommon	5.4	15.7	6.0	11.8	11.2	9.7	15.3	16.1	8.8	51.1	25 469	19 776	16 374	28.8	20.8
Saginaw	7.8	20.4	10.0	15.5	14.9	10.8	8.6	6.9	5.1	52.4	210 039	211 946	228 059	-0.9	-7.1
St. Clair	7.6	20.2	9.7	16.2	15.0	10.5	8.5	7.2	5.1	51.3	164 235	145 607	138 802	12.8	4.9
St. Joseph	7.8	21.0	8.9	15.8	14.6	10.1	8.8	7.3	5.8	51.1	62 422	58 913	56 083	6.0	5.0
Sanilac	7.4	20.9	8.2	15.0	13.4	10.0	9.5	9.0	6.6	51.0	44 547	39 928	40 789	11.6	-2.1
Schoolcraft	6.1	19.6	6.5	14.0	13.7	10.4	11.2	10.5	8.0	52.0	8 903	8 302	8 575	7.2	-3.2
Shiawassee	7.4	21.2	9.7	16.0	15.4	11.1	8.1	6.6	4.6	51.2	71 687	69 770	71 140	2.7	-1.9
Tuscola	7.1	21.4	9.2	15.6	15.2	11.1	8.2	7.0	5.0	50.4	58 266	55 498	56 961	5.0	-2.6
Van Buren	7.7	21.4	8.4	15.3	15.4	10.3	8.8	7.1	5.5	51.1	76 263	70 060	66 814	8.9	4.9
Washtenaw	6.8	14.8	19.6	19.9	16.1	9.3	6.1	4.4	3.1	50.5	322 895	282 937	264 740	14.1	6.9
Wayne	8.1	18.9	10.4	17.1	14.7	9.5	8.7	7.6	4.9	52.6	2 061 162	2 111 687	2 337 843	-2.4	-9.7
Wexford	7.8	20.9	8.3	15.8	14.4	9.8	9.2	8.1	5.7	51.3	30 484	26 360	25 102	15.6	5.0
MINNESOTA	7.7	19.0	10.1	17.8	15.2	9.8	7.9	6.7	5.8	51.0	4 919 479	4 375 665	4 075 970	12.4	7.4
Aitkin	5.4	18.4	4.8	11.4	12.6	11.1	12.7	13.9	9.6	50.4	15 301	12 425	13 404	23.1	-7.3
Anoka	8.8	21.7	9.8	20.0	16.9	10.8	6.3	3.5	2.0	49.9	298 084	243 641	195 998	22.3	24.3
Becker	7.4	21.7	7.0	13.9	14.1	10.0	9.4	8.6	7.8	50.4	30 000	27 881	29 336	7.6	-5.0
Beltrami	8.4	21.4	14.2	14.9	13.7	8.5	7.3	6.2	5.4	50.5	39 650	34 384	30 982	15.3	11.0
Benton	8.7	21.2	11.7	18.8	13.3	8.1	6.4	5.7	5.9	50.8	34 226	30 185	25 187	13.4	19.8
Big Stone	7.0	19.1	5.0	11.9	12.1	10.0	11.1	11.3	12.4	52.1	5 820	6 285	7 716	-7.4	-18.5
Blue Earth	6.3	16.6	23.0	14.9	12.4	7.8	6.8	6.3	5.8	50.5	55 941	54 044	52 314	3.5	3.3
Brown	7.3	20.1	8.5	14.9	13.1	9.3	9.2	8.9	8.7	51.6	26 911	26 984	28 645	-0.3	-5.8
Carlton	7.0	21.1	7.3	14.7	14.8	10.3	9.4	8.6	6.8	50.6	31 671	29 259	29 936	8.2	-2.3
Carver	9.5	20.8	8.7	20.3	16.1	9.6	6.6	4.5	3.9	49.7	70 205	47 915	37 046	46.5	29.3
Cass	7.0	20.2	5.7	12.6	13.1	10.7	11.6	11.0	8.2	49.7	27 150	21 791	21 050	24.6	3.5
Chippewa	6.7	20.4	6.1	13.3	13.5	9.6	9.6	10.3	10.6	51.9	13 088	13 228	14 941	-1.1	-11.5
Chisago	8.1	22.7	7.7	16.2	15.6	10.3	7.3	6.4	5.7	49.7	41 101	30 521	25 717	34.7	18.7
Clay	7.0	18.0	19.8	14.1	13.0	8.5	7.7	6.3	5.6	52.0	51 229	50 422	49 327	1.6	2.2
Clearwater	7.0	22.1	6.5	12.5	12.9	10.6	9.0	9.2	10.3	49.7	8 423	8 309	8 761	1.4	-5.2
Cook	6.7	17.5	5.2	14.3	17.7	11.7	10.4	9.4	7.1	50.2	5 168	3 868	4 092	33.6	-5.5
Cottonwood	6.4	19.6	6.0	12.3	12.9	10.1	10.2	10.7	11.8	51.5	12 167	12 694	14 854	-4.2	-14.5
Crow Wing	7.2	19.8	7.9	14.0	13.9	10.0	10.0	9.6	7.7	51.6	55 099	44 249	41 722	24.5	6.1
Dakota	9.3	20.6	9.2	21.4	17.2	10.1	6.0	3.8	2.6	50.6	355 904	275 210	194 279	29.3	41.6
Dodge	8.5	22.9	7.9	16.7	14.0	9.5	7.2	7.1	6.2	50.6	17 731	15 731	14 773	12.7	6.5
Douglas	7.0	20.1	8.4	14.1	13.4	9.7	9.0	9.3	8.8	50.9	32 821	28 674	27 839	14.5	3.0
Faribault	6.2	20.3	5.8	12.5	12.8	10.1	10.7	10.7	11.0	52.1	16 181	16 937	19 714	-4.5	-14.1
Fillmore	7.2	20.6	6.9	13.3	12.7	9.4	9.6	10.0	10.2	50.6	21 122	20 777	21 930	1.7	-5.3
Freeborn	6.8	19.0	7.2	14.0	13.7	10.8	9.9	9.9	8.7	51.1	32 584	33 060	36 329	-1.4	-9.0
Goodhue	7.4	20.8	7.4	15.7	14.6	9.8	8.4	7.6	8.2	50.8	44 127	40 690	38 749	8.4	5.0

Table B. States and Counties

STATE County	Total population	Total in households	House-holder	Spouse	Child Total	Own child under 18 years	Other relatives Total	Under 18 years	Nonrelatives Total	Unmarried partner	Total in group quarters	Correctional institutions	Nursing homes	Other institutions	College dormitories	Military quarters	Other
	54	55	56	57	58	59	60	61	62	63	64	65	66	67	68	69	70
MICHIGAN—Cont'd																	
Leelanau	21 119	99.0	39.9	25.4	28.1	23.0	2.0	0.7	3.5	1.6	1.0	0.1	0.4	0.1	0.0	0.0	0.4
Lenawee	98 890	94.8	36.3	21.3	29.9	23.5	3.2	1.5	4.0	1.9	5.2	2.4	0.5	0.3	1.0	0.0	1.0
Livingston	156 951	98.9	35.3	24.2	33.6	27.1	2.6	1.0	3.3	1.5	1.1	0.3	0.1	0.3	0.0	0.0	0.4
Luce	7 024	84.9	35.3	20.4	23.2	19.4	2.4	1.1	3.6	1.8	15.1	13.3	0.7	0.1	0.0	0.0	0.9
Mackinac	11 943	98.4	42.4	23.6	25.8	20.7	2.3	0.9	4.2	2.6	1.6	0.1	1.0	0.0	0.0	0.0	0.5
Macomb	788 149	98.9	39.2	21.3	30.8	22.5	3.9	1.2	3.7	1.8	1.1	0.3	0.5	0.0	0.0	0.0	0.3
Manistee	24 527	95.3	40.2	22.1	26.1	20.6	2.6	1.1	4.2	2.2	4.7	3.1	0.8	0.1	0.0	0.0	0.8
Marquette	64 634	93.8	39.9	20.5	26.0	20.1	2.1	0.7	5.4	2.2	6.2	1.9	1.0	0.1	3.0	0.0	0.4
Mason	28 274	98.1	40.3	22.7	28.1	22.3	2.8	1.2	4.1	1.9	1.9	0.7	0.7	0.0	0.0	0.0	0.5
Mecosta	40 553	91.7	36.8	19.6	25.5	20.8	2.5	1.0	7.3	2.2	8.3	0.0	0.5	0.0	7.6	0.0	0.2
Menominee	25 326	98.3	41.6	22.3	28.1	22.4	2.3	1.0	3.9	2.1	1.7	0.1	1.1	0.0	0.0	0.0	0.4
Midland	82 874	98.2	38.3	23.0	30.8	25.5	2.0	0.8	4.0	1.8	1.8	0.1	0.6	0.0	0.8	0.0	0.3
Missaukee	14 478	98.6	37.6	23.6	30.5	25.0	2.7	1.3	4.2	2.0	1.4	0.2	0.6	0.0	0.0	0.0	0.7
Monroe	145 945	98.9	36.8	22.1	32.9	25.1	3.5	1.7	3.6	1.9	1.1	0.2	0.3	0.1	0.0	0.0	0.5
Montcalm	61 266	95.6	36.0	21.2	30.5	24.8	3.0	1.4	4.8	2.4	4.4	3.8	0.2	0.1	0.0	0.0	0.4
Montmorency	10 315	98.8	43.2	25.1	23.7	18.4	2.8	1.2	3.9	2.0	1.2	0.0	0.8	0.0	0.0	0.0	0.4
Muskegon	170 200	96.4	37.2	19.2	31.5	24.9	4.0	2.0	4.6	2.1	3.6	2.3	0.6	0.1	0.1	0.0	0.5
Newaygo	47 874	98.6	36.8	22.1	32.1	26.5	3.4	1.6	4.2	2.0	1.4	0.4	0.5	0.1	0.0	0.0	0.4
Oakland	1 194 156	98.8	39.5	21.4	30.3	23.6	3.6	1.2	4.1	1.7	1.2	0.2	0.4	0.0	0.2	0.0	0.4
Oceana	26 873	97.2	36.4	22.0	31.0	25.0	3.6	1.5	4.2	1.9	2.8	0.2	0.5	0.5	0.0	0.0	1.6
Ogemaw	21 645	98.6	40.9	23.4	27.0	21.5	3.1	1.3	4.2	2.2	1.4	0.2	0.9	0.0	0.0	0.0	0.2
Ontonagon	7 818	97.7	44.2	23.7	23.9	19.0	2.1	0.6	3.8	1.9	2.3	0.2	1.5	0.0	0.0	0.0	0.6
Osceola	23 197	98.4	38.2	22.2	30.3	24.6	3.0	1.3	4.7	2.5	1.6	0.4	0.2	0.2	0.0	0.0	0.7
Oscoda	9 418	99.4	41.6	24.2	26.2	21.1	3.1	1.6	4.2	2.3	0.6	0.0	0.6	0.0	0.0	0.0	0.0
Otsego	23 301	99.0	38.6	23.3	30.2	25.1	2.6	1.0	4.2	2.1	1.0	0.2	0.4	0.0	0.0	0.0	0.5
Ottawa	238 314	96.3	34.3	22.1	33.1	27.2	2.6	1.0	4.2	1.3	3.7	0.1	0.7	0.0	2.1	0.0	0.7
Presque Isle	14 411	98.5	42.7	25.1	25.1	19.4	2.3	0.9	3.2	1.6	1.5	0.1	0.6	0.0	0.0	0.0	0.8
Roscommon	25 469	98.7	44.2	25.1	22.5	18.0	2.9	1.2	4.1	2.3	1.3	0.3	0.6	0.2	0.0	0.0	0.2
Saginaw	210 039	97.3	38.3	19.2	31.4	23.9	4.2	2.1	4.2	2.0	2.7	0.9	0.5	0.1	0.4	0.0	0.8
St. Clair	164 235	99.0	37.8	21.7	31.8	24.7	3.4	1.4	4.3	2.2	1.0	0.1	0.4	0.0	0.0	0.0	0.5
St. Joseph	62 422	98.4	37.5	20.9	30.6	24.7	4.0	1.8	5.5	2.5	1.6	0.4	0.7	0.0	0.0	0.0	0.5
Sanilac	44 547	98.3	37.9	22.7	31.2	24.8	3.0	1.2	3.6	1.8	1.7	0.2	0.5	0.3	0.0	0.0	0.7
Schoolcraft	8 903	95.7	40.5	23.3	26.1	21.2	2.2	0.9	3.5	2.1	4.3	2.6	1.1	0.0	0.0	0.0	0.6
Shiawassee	71 687	99.0	37.5	22.2	31.6	24.6	3.2	1.5	4.4	2.2	1.0	0.2	0.4	0.0	0.1	0.0	0.2
Tuscola	58 266	97.5	36.8	22.5	31.1	24.0	3.2	1.5	3.9	1.9	2.5	0.6	0.4	0.8	0.0	0.0	0.7
Van Buren	76 263	97.5	36.7	20.8	30.9	24.6	4.3	2.0	4.8	2.4	2.5	0.1	0.5	0.3	0.0	0.0	1.6
Washtenaw	322 895	93.4	38.8	18.0	25.1	20.5	3.0	1.1	8.5	2.1	6.6	1.0	0.4	0.2	4.6	0.0	0.4
Wayne	2 061 162	98.4	37.3	15.2	32.8	23.7	8.0	3.6	5.1	2.1	1.6	0.3	0.5	0.2	0.1	0.0	0.6
Wexford	30 484	98.8	38.8	21.8	29.9	24.5	3.2	1.4	5.0	2.5	1.2	0.1	0.6	0.0	0.0	0.0	0.5
MINNESOTA	4 919 479	97.2	38.5	20.7	29.9	24.6	2.8	1.0	5.3	2.0	2.8	0.3	0.8	0.1	0.9	0.0	0.6
Aitkin	15 301	98.9	43.4	24.9	23.9	19.1	2.5	1.1	4.1	2.2	1.1	0.1	1.0	0.0	0.0	0.0	0.0
Anoka	298 084	99.0	35.7	21.7	33.8	27.2	3.0	1.1	4.8	2.2	1.0	0.5	0.1	0.1	0.0	0.0	0.2
Becker	30 000	98.4	39.5	22.6	30.2	24.9	2.4	1.2	3.7	2.0	1.6	0.2	1.3	0.0	0.0	0.0	0.1
Beltrami	39 650	95.2	36.2	17.8	30.3	24.8	4.4	2.5	6.6	2.7	4.8	0.2	0.7	0.4	2.9	0.0	0.6
Benton	34 226	97.8	38.2	19.9	31.3	25.8	2.2	0.7	6.2	2.7	2.2	0.2	1.3	0.0	0.0	0.0	0.7
Big Stone	5 820	97.0	40.8	24.3	28.9	24.4	1.2	0.3	1.7	1.0	3.0	0.0	2.7	0.0	0.0	0.0	0.3
Blue Earth	55 941	92.6	37.7	18.3	24.8	20.4	1.8	0.5	10.1	2.1	7.4	0.1	0.9	0.0	5.5	0.0	0.9
Brown	26 911	95.7	39.4	22.6	29.4	24.4	1.3	0.4	2.9	1.4	4.3	0.2	0.2	0.0	2.9	0.0	1.0
Carlton	31 671	95.4	38.1	21.5	29.3	23.6	2.4	1.1	4.1	2.0	4.6	2.8	1.0	0.4	0.1	0.0	0.3
Carver	70 205	98.5	34.7	23.1	35.6	30.5	1.8	0.6	3.4	1.5	1.5	0.1	0.3	0.0	0.7	0.0	0.3
Cass	27 150	98.4	40.1	23.4	27.3	22.4	3.2	1.7	4.3	2.3	1.6	0.2	0.3	0.0	0.0	0.0	1.1
Chippewa	13 088	97.7	41.0	23.3	29.1	24.5	1.5	0.5	2.9	1.5	2.3	0.1	1.6	0.0	0.0	0.0	0.6
Chisago	41 101	98.2	35.2	22.7	33.8	28.4	2.2	0.9	4.3	2.0	1.8	0.7	0.4	0.5	0.0	0.0	0.3
Clay	51 229	92.1	36.4	19.6	28.6	23.9	1.8	0.6	5.7	1.6	7.9	0.2	1.1	0.1	5.9	0.0	0.6
Clearwater	8 423	97.9	39.5	22.4	29.8	24.2	2.7	1.5	3.3	1.7	2.1	0.4	1.6	0.0	0.0	0.0	0.2
Cook	5 168	98.9	45.5	23.6	22.8	19.4	1.7	0.6	5.3	2.6	1.1	0.0	1.1	0.0	0.0	0.0	0.0
Cottonwood	12 167	96.7	40.4	23.5	28.4	23.7	1.5	0.5	2.9	1.4	3.3	0.0	2.0	0.0	0.0	0.0	1.3
Crow Wing	55 099	98.1	40.4	22.9	28.1	23.3	2.1	0.8	4.6	2.1	1.9	0.2	0.7	0.4	0.0	0.0	0.6
Dakota	355 904	99.3	36.9	21.8	33.6	28.0	2.5	0.8	4.6	1.9	0.7	0.0	0.2	0.1	0.0	0.0	0.4
Dodge	17 731	98.9	36.2	23.4	33.8	28.8	1.7	0.7	3.8	1.9	1.1	0.0	0.9	0.0	0.0	0.0	0.2
Douglas	32 821	97.9	40.4	23.9	27.8	23.1	1.5	0.4	4.3	1.6	2.1	0.1	1.4	0.1	0.0	0.0	0.5
Faribault	16 181	97.2	41.1	23.8	27.9	22.8	1.6	0.7	2.8	1.6	2.8	0.1	0.9	1.6	0.0	0.0	0.2
Fillmore	21 122	97.5	39.0	23.6	30.3	25.1	1.7	0.6	3.0	1.6	2.5	0.0	2.2	0.1	0.0	0.0	0.2
Freeborn	32 584	98.2	41.0	23.2	27.4	22.4	2.4	0.9	4.2	2.1	1.8	0.1	1.2	0.0	0.0	0.0	0.5
Goodhue	44 127	97.5	38.5	22.8	30.5	25.1	1.9	0.7	3.9	1.9	2.5	0.1	1.5	0.5	0.0	0.0	0.4

Tablo B. States and Counties

STATE County	Total households	Total	With own children under 18 years	Total	With own children under 18 years	Total	With own children under 18 years	Total	Total	65 years and over	Average household size	Average family size	Total households	Female householder[1]	Householder living alone
	71	72	73	74	75	76	77	78	79	80	81	82	83	84	85
MICHIGAN—Cont'd															
Leelanau	8 436	73.7	29.9	63.6	23.5	7.1	4.6	26.3	22.3	8.8	2.48	2.89	6 274	7.2	20.1
Lenawee	35 930	72.5	34.2	58.7	25.7	10.0	6.2	27.5	22.9	9.7	2.61	3.07	31 635	9.9	20.2
Livingston	55 384	78.6	39.8	68.5	34.0	6.8	4.0	21.4	17.1	5.4	2.80	3.18	38 887	6.9	15.1
Luce	2 481	70.1	29.5	57.9	21.3	8.5	5.6	29.9	26.3	12.1	2.40	2.86	2 154	8.5	25.1
Mackinac	5 067	67.3	26.5	55.6	19.5	8.1	4.8	32.7	28.0	11.9	2.32	2.81	4 240	8.3	25.2
Macomb	309 203	68.2	31.1	54.3	24.4	10.1	5.1	31.8	26.9	10.3	2.52	3.09	264 991	10.1	22.2
Manistee	9 860	68.1	27.4	55.1	19.5	9.1	5.6	31.9	27.3	13.2	2.37	2.86	8 580	8.3	26.2
Marquette	25 767	64.0	28.6	51.3	20.7	8.9	5.9	36.0	28.9	10.5	2.35	2.90	25 435	8.6	23.5
Mason	11 406	69.1	29.7	56.4	21.4	9.2	6.2	30.9	26.5	11.7	2.43	2.92	9 984	9.1	24.6
Mecosta	14 915	66.3	29.1	53.3	20.3	9.3	6.5	33.7	24.5	8.9	2.49	2.95	12 260	8.7	20.8
Menominee	10 529	66.5	28.9	53.8	21.0	8.8	5.7	33.5	29.2	13.2	2.36	2.91	9 766	8.5	26.5
Midland	31 769	71.4	34.9	60.1	27.6	8.1	5.3	28.6	23.5	9.0	2.56	3.04	27 791	7.9	20.4
Missaukee	5 450	74.2	34.0	62.8	26.6	7.4	4.8	25.8	21.5	9.5	2.62	3.03	4 389	6.9	19.3
Monroe	53 772	74.3	36.0	60.0	27.7	10.1	5.9	25.7	21.7	8.5	2.69	3.07	46 508	10.3	18.9
Montcalm	22 079	73.3	35.3	58.8	25.5	9.7	6.5	26.7	21.9	9.2	2.65	3.07	18 563	9.9	20.1
Montmorency	4 455	68.4	22.5	58.1	16.6	7.1	4.0	31.6	27.5	15.4	2.29	2.75	3 600	7.9	23.6
Muskegon	63 330	69.9	34.6	51.6	22.8	13.9	9.1	30.1	25.2	10.4	2.59	3.10	57 798	13.9	23.1
Newaygo	17 599	73.5	35.2	60.2	26.4	9.0	6.0	26.5	22.2	9.0	2.68	3.13	13 776	9.0	19.4
Oakland	471 115	66.9	32.4	54.2	25.7	9.5	5.2	33.1	27.3	8.5	2.51	3.09	410 488	9.6	23.6
Oceana	9 778	74.3	34.0	60.5	25.2	9.2	6.0	25.7	21.6	9.5	2.67	3.09	8 071	8.7	19.8
Ogemaw	8 842	70.0	27.1	57.4	19.5	8.8	5.5	30.0	25.7	12.2	2.41	2.87	7 190	8.9	22.1
Ontonagon	3 456	64.4	23.6	53.6	17.2	6.3	3.9	35.6	31.5	16.0	2.21	2.75	3 641	6.9	27.9
Osceola	8 861	72.4	32.9	58.1	23.2	9.7	6.8	27.6	22.6	9.8	2.58	3.01	7 347	9.2	21.6
Oscoda	3 921	69.3	25.3	58.1	18.1	7.5	4.6	30.7	26.0	12.7	2.39	2.85	3 160	6.8	24.3
Otsego	8 995	72.7	34.1	60.4	26.2	8.3	5.5	27.3	22.5	9.1	2.56	3.00	6 522	7.9	20.1
Ottawa	81 662	75.1	39.3	64.6	32.6	7.5	4.9	24.9	19.6	7.4	2.81	3.25	62 664	6.9	16.7
Presque Isle	6 155	68.3	24.5	58.8	18.9	6.3	3.7	31.7	28.4	14.5	2.31	2.80	5 376	7.3	24.3
Roscommon	11 250	67.7	21.9	56.9	15.0	7.7	4.8	32.3	28.1	14.0	2.23	2.69	8 516	7.2	25.9
Saginaw	80 430	69.4	32.7	50.2	20.8	15.4	10.0	30.6	26.0	10.4	2.54	3.06	78 256	15.3	23.2
St. Clair	62 072	71.9	34.6	57.4	25.8	10.4	6.5	28.1	23.4	9.6	2.62	3.09	52 882	10.9	21.3
St. Joseph	23 381	71.0	34.1	55.9	24.1	10.4	6.9	29.0	23.6	10.1	2.63	3.08	21 579	10.1	21.6
Sanilac	16 871	72.1	32.7	59.8	25.5	8.6	5.0	27.9	24.3	11.6	2.60	3.08	14 658	8.4	22.0
Schoolcraft	3 606	69.3	28.1	57.6	20.2	8.1	5.7	30.7	27.4	13.0	2.36	2.84	3 294	8.4	24.8
Shiawassee	26 896	73.8	35.3	59.1	26.2	10.3	6.3	26.2	21.7	9.1	2.64	3.06	24 864	10.1	19.4
Tuscola	21 454	74.5	34.4	61.2	26.3	9.2	5.5	25.5	21.9	9.4	2.65	3.07	19 469	9.2	19.1
Van Buren	27 982	72.6	35.0	56.7	25.1	11.2	7.0	27.4	22.5	8.9	2.66	3.10	25 402	11.3	20.9
Washtenaw	125 391	58.8	29.2	46.4	22.0	9.3	5.7	41.2	29.5	5.9	2.41	3.02	104 528	9.3	26.3
Wayne	768 440	66.6	32.8	40.7	18.8	20.6	11.7	33.4	28.3	10.0	2.64	3.26	780 535	20.8	26.7
Wexford	11 824	70.9	33.6	56.2	23.7	10.3	6.9	29.1	24.2	10.1	2.55	3.00	9 923	10.5	22.9
MINNESOTA	1 895 127	66.2	33.0	53.7	25.2	8.9	5.9	33.8	26.9	9.3	2.52	3.09	1 647 853	8.6	25.1
Aitkin	6 644	67.1	22.6	57.5	16.9	6.3	3.6	32.9	28.7	14.0	2.28	2.76	5 126	5.2	26.8
Anoka	106 428	74.6	39.9	60.7	31.3	9.8	6.4	25.4	19.3	5.3	2.77	3.19	82 437	9.7	15.6
Becker	11 844	69.1	31.3	57.1	23.3	7.9	5.4	30.9	26.9	12.6	2.49	3.02	10 477	8.3	24.6
Beltrami	14 337	68.0	34.6	49.3	21.8	13.6	9.6	32.0	24.8	9.5	2.63	3.13	11 870	11.6	22.9
Benton	13 065	65.2	35.3	52.1	26.4	8.8	6.2	34.8	25.8	8.9	2.56	3.14	10 935	8.2	23.9
Big Stone	2 377	67.8	29.0	59.6	23.7	5.3	3.9	32.2	30.2	16.9	2.38	2.97	2 463	4.6	29.0
Blue Earth	21 062	59.9	29.1	48.6	22.1	7.8	5.3	40.1	27.1	9.5	2.46	2.99	19 277	7.4	24.3
Brown	10 598	67.6	31.5	57.3	25.1	6.9	4.6	32.4	29.0	14.3	2.43	3.00	10 321	5.9	28.0
Carlton	12 064	69.7	32.6	56.5	23.9	9.0	6.1	30.3	26.1	12.0	2.50	3.00	10 842	8.3	24.6
Carver	24 356	77.1	45.2	66.4	38.2	7.3	5.0	22.9	18.1	6.1	2.84	3.26	16 601	6.8	17.9
Cass	10 893	71.0	27.7	58.4	19.6	8.0	5.4	29.0	25.0	11.9	2.45	2.90	8 302	7.7	23.6
Chippewa	5 361	67.1	31.2	57.0	24.4	6.6	4.6	32.9	29.2	15.7	2.39	2.96	5 245	5.4	27.8
Chisago	14 454	76.7	41.0	64.5	32.3	8.0	5.9	23.3	18.4	7.4	2.79	3.18	10 551	6.9	18.7
Clay	18 670	66.1	33.8	53.9	25.6	8.8	6.4	33.9	26.1	10.6	2.53	3.07	17 490	8.9	23.4
Clearwater	3 330	68.7	30.6	56.8	23.1	7.5	4.8	31.3	27.9	14.5	2.48	3.02	3 064	8.0	25.1
Cook	2 350	61.2	24.4	52.0	17.7	6.1	4.7	38.8	32.5	10.8	2.17	2.73	1 632	5.3	29.2
Cottonwood	4 917	67.9	28.6	58.1	22.5	6.9	4.5	32.1	28.9	15.9	2.39	2.94	5 060	5.3	27.8
Crow Wing	22 250	68.2	30.2	56.7	22.4	8.0	5.5	31.8	26.4	11.7	2.43	2.93	17 204	8.1	25.3
Dakota	131 151	71.7	40.0	56.7	31.9	9.1	6.2	28.3	21.7	5.5	2.70	3.19	98 293	8.9	18.8
Dodge	6 420	75.6	40.7	64.7	33.0	7.2	5.2	24.4	20.2	9.7	2.42	2.93	5 538	5.6	19.9
Douglas	13 276	68.0	29.9	59.0	24.1	6.4	4.3	32.0	26.5	12.3	2.36	2.93	10 988	6.3	24.5
Faribault	6 652	67.3	28.5	57.8	22.5	6.1	3.9	32.7	29.7	16.8	2.36	2.93	6 772	6.2	28.7
Fillmore	8 228	69.5	30.9	60.6	25.4	6.1	4.0	30.5	26.6	14.0	2.50	3.05	7 822	5.4	25.2
Freeborn	13 356	67.5	29.1	56.5	22.1	7.5	5.1	32.5	28.2	14.0	2.40	2.92	13 029	6.7	25.9
Goodhue	16 983	70.1	33.8	59.2	26.7	7.2	5.0	29.9	25.2	11.5	2.53	3.04	15 198	6.5	24.9

[1] No spouse present.

Items 71—85

Table B. States and Counties

STATE County	Percent change of households, 1990–2000	Total housing units	Occupied housing units (percent)	Vacant housing units		Homeowner vacancy rate (percent)	Rental vacancy rate (percent)	Occupied housing units			Average household size of owner-occupied units	Average household size of renter-occupied units
				Total	For seasonal, recreational, or occasional use			Total	Percent owner-occupied housing units	Percent renter-occupied housing units		
	86	87	88	89	90	91	92	93	94	95	96	97
MICHIGAN—Cont'd												
Leelanau	34.5	13 297	63.4	36.6	30.9	1.1	21.8	8 436	84.6	15.4	2.47	2.51
Lenawee	13.6	39 769	90.3	9.7	4.8	1.7	6.8	35 930	78.2	21.8	2.69	2.33
Livingston	42.4	58 919	94.0	6.0	2.0	1.5	5.4	55 384	88.0	12.0	2.89	2.16
Luce	15.2	4 008	61.9	38.1	31.3	4.0	8.4	2 401	80.3	19.7	2.44	2.24
Mackinac	19.5	9 413	53.8	46.2	41.9	1.6	9.4	5 067	79.2	20.8	2.34	2.22
Macomb	16.7	320 276	96.5	3.5	0.4	1.2	4.7	309 203	78.9	21.1	2.66	1.99
Manistee	14.9	14 272	69.1	30.9	24.4	2.2	8.6	9 860	81.3	18.7	2.40	2.22
Marquette	1.3	32 877	78.4	21.6	12.9	2.1	8.7	25 767	69.8	30.2	2.54	1.91
Mason	14.2	16 063	71.0	29.0	23.5	2.1	6.1	11 406	78.4	21.6	2.52	2.13
Mecosta	21.7	19 593	76.1	23.9	18.4	2.3	7.9	14 915	73.7	26.3	2.56	2.31
Menominee	7.8	13 639	77.2	22.8	17.4	1.2	9.4	10 529	79.5	20.5	2.44	2.08
Midland	14.3	33 796	94.0	6.0	1.6	1.3	6.8	31 769	78.4	21.6	2.70	2.08
Missaukee	24.2	8 621	63.2	36.8	32.9	1.7	7.8	5 450	83.7	16.3	2.64	2.53
Monroe	15.6	56 471	95.2	4.8	0.6	1.6	5.9	53 772	81.0	19.0	2.79	2.25
Montcalm	18.9	25 900	85.2	14.8	9.3	2.0	7.6	22 079	81.6	18.4	2.71	2.38
Montmorency	23.8	9 238	48.2	51.8	47.5	2.8	5.6	4 455	86.1	13.9	2.31	2.14
Muskegon	9.6	68 556	92.4	7.6	2.0	1.9	7.7	63 330	77.7	22.3	2.67	2.32
Newaygo	27.8	23 202	75.9	24.1	18.9	1.9	6.4	17 599	84.4	15.6	2.73	2.44
Oakland	14.8	492 006	95.8	4.2	0.8	1.2	5.6	471 115	74.7	25.3	2.68	1.98
Oceana	21.1	15 009	65.1	34.9	27.7	1.7	9.1	9 778	82.7	17.3	2.66	2.73
Ogemaw	23.0	15 404	57.4	42.6	37.8	3.5	5.9	8 842	84.6	15.4	2.43	2.33
Ontonagon	-5.1	5 404	64.0	36.0	27.5	2.3	17.0	3 456	85.0	15.0	2.26	1.94
Osceola	20.6	12 853	68.9	31.1	26.2	2.3	7.1	8 861	81.4	18.6	2.62	2.39
Oscoda	24.1	8 690	45.1	54.9	48.0	2.4	15.9	3 921	85.8	14.2	2.41	2.26
Otsego	37.9	13 375	67.3	32.7	28.4	1.8	8.5	8 995	81.7	18.3	2.65	2.18
Ottawa	30.3	86 856	94.0	6.0	2.4	1.3	5.7	81 662	80.7	19.3	2.91	2.39
Presque Isle	14.5	9 910	62.1	37.9	33.1	1.9	9.7	6 155	85.6	14.4	2.36	2.01
Roscommon	32.1	23 109	48.7	51.3	48.0	2.3	9.9	11 250	85.9	14.1	2.23	2.27
Saginaw	2.8	85 505	94.1	5.9	0.4	1.5	6.6	80 430	73.8	26.2	2.64	2.28
St. Clair	17.4	67 107	92.5	7.5	2.9	1.7	6.9	62 072	79.6	20.4	2.72	2.24
St. Joseph	8.4	26 503	88.2	11.8	6.3	1.8	6.4	23 381	76.9	23.1	2.70	2.39
Sanilac	15.1	21 314	79.2	20.8	15.2	2.7	6.3	16 871	81.9	18.1	2.64	2.37
Schoolcraft	9.5	5 700	63.3	36.7	30.2	2.1	10.5	3 606	82.0	18.0	2.43	2.04
Shiawassee	8.2	29 087	92.5	7.5	3.3	1.3	6.6	26 896	80.1	19.9	2.73	2.28
Tuscola	10.2	23 378	91.8	8.2	3.1	1.6	6.1	21 454	84.1	15.9	2.70	2.39
Van Buren	10.2	33 975	82.4	17.6	11.4	2.1	8.0	27 982	79.6	20.4	2.71	2.46
Washtenaw	19.9	131 069	95.6	4.4	0.8	1.1	4.2	125 327	59.7	40.3	2.65	2.05
Wayne	-1.5	826 145	93.0	7.0	0.3	1.4	7.2	768 440	66.6	33.4	2.73	2.46
Wexford	19.2	14 872	79.5	20.5	14.8	2.2	6.7	11 824	79.3	20.7	2.62	2.28
MINNESOTA	15.0	2 065 946	91.7	8.3	5.1	0.9	4.1	1 895 127	74.6	25.4	2.69	2.03
Aitkin	29.6	14 168	46.9	53.1	47.1	1.2	9.1	6 644	85.4	14.6	2.33	1.97
Anoka	29.1	108 091	98.5	1.5	0.3	0.5	1.7	106 428	83.4	16.6	2.90	2.15
Becker	13.0	16 612	71.3	28.7	24.9	1.4	6.0	11 844	80.5	19.5	2.59	2.08
Beltrami	20.8	16 989	84.4	15.6	11.6	1.1	4.4	14 337	74.5	25.5	2.72	2.38
Benton	19.5	13 460	97.1	2.9	0.6	0.7	3.0	13 065	67.3	32.7	2.88	1.90
Big Stone	-3.5	3 171	75.0	25.0	13.7	5.3	20.4	2 377	85.1	14.9	2.44	1.98
Blue Earth	9.3	21 971	95.9	4.1	1.2	1.1	3.2	21 062	66.4	33.6	2.64	2.11
Brown	2.7	11 163	94.9	5.1	0.3	1.2	8.3	10 598	80.0	20.0	2.57	1.86
Carlton	11.3	13 721	87.9	12.1	8.0	0.8	4.5	12 064	82.1	17.9	2.62	1.97
Carver	46.7	24 883	97.9	2.1	0.5	0.6	2.7	24 356	83.5	16.5	2.99	2.11
Cass	31.2	21 286	51.2	48.8	45.0	2.2	5.0	10 893	85.9	14.1	2.46	2.41
Chippewa	2.2	5 855	91.6	8.4	0.8	2.2	11.6	5 361	76.6	23.4	2.53	1.90
Chisago	37.0	15 533	93.1	6.9	4.4	1.0	2.5	14 454	87.1	12.9	2.90	2.07
Clay	6.7	19 746	94.6	5.4	0.7	1.2	6.7	18 670	71.6	28.4	2.71	2.06
Clearwater	8.7	4 114	80.9	19.1	13.0	2.1	5.0	3 330	81.6	18.4	2.56	2.06
Cook	44.0	4 708	49.9	50.1	47.9	1.0	6.4	2 350	78.3	21.7	2.29	1.77
Cottonwood	-2.8	5 376	91.5	8.5	1.0	2.8	9.3	4 917	80.4	19.6	2.47	2.07
Crow Wing	29.3	33 483	66.5	33.5	30.6	1.1	3.5	22 250	79.7	20.3	2.53	2.02
Dakota	33.4	133 750	98.1	1.9	0.3	0.5	3.2	131 151	78.2	21.8	2.86	2.10
Dodge	15.9	6 642	96.7	3.3	0.3	0.9	3.3	6 420	84.0	16.0	2.83	2.23
Douglas	20.8	16 694	79.5	20.5	16.5	1.5	5.8	13 276	77.2	22.8	2.58	1.87
Faribault	-1.8	7 247	91.8	8.2	1.0	2.1	9.1	6 652	80.7	19.3	2.45	2.01
Fillmore	5.2	8 908	92.4	7.6	2.8	1.6	7.8	8 228	80.9	19.1	2.61	2.06
Freeborn	2.5	13 996	95.4	4.6	0.5	1.1	5.5	13 356	78.7	21.3	2.50	2.03
Goodhue	11.7	17 879	95.0	5.0	1.8	1.2	4.3	16 983	79.0	21.0	2.69	1.94

Table B. States and Counties

STATE/ County code	MSA/ PMSA/ NECMA code[1]	County type[2]	STATE County	Land area, 2000[3] (sq km)	Population, 2000 Total persons	Rank	Per square kilometer	Land area, 1990[3] (sq km)	Population, 1990 Total persons	Rank	Per square kilometer	White	Black or African American	American Indian or Alaska Native	Asian	Native Hawaiian and other Pacific Islander	Some other race
				1	2	3	4	5	6	7	8	9	10	11	12	13	14
			MINNESOTA—Cont'd														
27 051	...	9	Grant	1 415	6 289	2 758	4.4	1 415	6 246	2 729	4.4	98.3	0.2	0.3	0.2	0.0	0.3
27 053	5120	0	Hennepin	1 442	1 116 200	32	774.1	1 442	1 032 431	30	716.0	80.5	9.0	1.0	4.8	0.0	2.1
27 055	3870	3	Houston	1 446	19 718	1 809	13.6	1 446	18 497	1 761	12.8	98.5	0.3	0.2	0.4	0.0	0.1
27 057	...	9	Hubbard	2 389	18 376	1 875	7.7	2 389	14 939	1 991	6.3	96.3	0.2	2.1	0.3	0.0	0.2
27 059	5120	1	Isanti	1 137	31 287	1 367	27.5	1 137	25 921	1 425	22.8	97.6	0.3	0.6	0.4	0.0	0.2
27 061	...	6	Itasca	6 902	43 992	1 016	6.4	6 903	40 844	981	5.9	94.6	0.2	3.4	0.3	0.0	0.2
27 063	...	7	Jackson	1 817	11 268	2 352	6.2	1 818	11 677	2 240	6.4	97.1	0.1	0.1	1.4	0.0	1.0
27 065	...	6	Kanabec	1 360	14 996	2 090	11.0	1 360	12 802	2 156	9.4	97.3	0.2	0.8	0.4	0.0	0.2
27 067	...	7	Kandiyohi	2 062	41 203	1 073	20.0	2 062	38 761	1 033	18.8	93.6	0.5	0.3	0.4	0.1	4.2
27 069	...	9	Kittson	2 841	5 285	2 830	1.9	2 841	5 767	2 782	2.0	98.1	0.2	0.3	0.2	0.0	0.4
27 071	...	7	Koochiching	8 035	14 355	2 136	1.8	8 035	16 299	1 904	2.0	96.1	0.2	2.2	0.2	0.1	0.1
27 073	...	9	Lac qui Parle	1 981	8 067	2 601	4.1	1 981	8 924	2 477	4.5	98.8	0.2	0.2	0.3	0.0	0.1
27 075	...	6	Lake	5 437	11 058	2 361	2.0	5 437	10 415	2 348	1.9	98.0	0.1	0.7	0.2	0.0	0.1
27 077	...	9	Lake of the Woods	3 358	4 522	2 877	1.3	3 358	4 076	2 909	1.2	97.2	0.3	1.1	0.2	0.0	0.1
27 079	...	6	Le Sueur	1 162	25 426	1 546	21.9	1 162	23 239	1 529	20.0	96.6	0.1	0.3	0.3	0.0	2.0
27 081	...	9	Lincoln	1 391	6 429	2 747	4.6	1 391	6 890	2 672	5.0	98.8	0.0	0.3	0.2	0.0	0.4
27 083	...	7	Lyon	1 850	25 425	1 547	13.7	1 850	24 789	1 472	13.4	93.6	1.5	0.3	1.7	0.0	1.9
27 085	...	6	McLeod	1 274	34 898	1 253	27.4	1 274	32 030	1 210	25.1	96.6	0.2	0.2	0.6	0.1	1.8
27 087	...	9	Mahnomen	1 440	5 190	2 837	3.6	1 440	5 044	2 839	3.5	62.9	0.1	28.6	0.1	0.0	0.3
27 089	...	8	Marshall	4 590	10 155	2 431	2.2	4 590	10 993	2 296	2.4	97.2	0.1	0.3	0.2	0.0	1.6
27 091	...	7	Martin	1 837	21 802	1 702	11.9	1 837	22 914	1 537	12.5	97.2	0.3	0.1	0.4	0.0	1.3
27 093	...	6	Meeker	1 576	22 644	1 663	14.4	1 576	20 846	1 637	13.2	97.3	0.2	0.2	0.4	0.0	1.4
27 095	...	6	Mille Lacs	1 488	22 330	1 678	15.0	1 488	18 670	1 753	12.5	93.6	0.3	4.7	0.2	0.0	0.2
27 097	...	6	Morrison	2 912	31 712	1 351	10.9	2 913	29 604	1 313	10.2	98.5	0.2	0.3	0.3	0.0	0.2
27 099	...	4	Mower	1 843	38 603	1 148	20.9	1 843	37 385	1 061	20.3	94.7	0.6	0.2	1.5	0.0	2.2
27 101	...	9	Murray	1 824	9 165	2 517	5.0	1 825	9 660	2 418	5.3	98.3	0.1	0.2	0.2	0.0	0.4
27 103	...	7	Nicollet	1 171	29 771	1 405	25.4	1 172	28 076	1 348	24.0	96.4	0.8	0.3	1.1	0.0	0.7
27 105	...	7	Nobles	1 853	20 832	1 742	11.2	1 853	20 098	1 670	10.8	86.5	1.1	0.3	4.0	0.1	6.6
27 107	...	8	Norman	2 270	7 442	2 645	3.3	2 270	7 975	2 572	3.5	95.3	0.1	1.7	0.3	0.0	1.1
27 109	6820	3	Olmsted	1 691	124 277	434	73.5	1 691	106 470	435	63.0	90.3	2.7	0.3	4.3	0.0	0.9
27 111	...	7	Otter Tail	5 127	57 159	833	11.1	5 128	50 714	831	9.9	97.1	0.3	0.5	0.4	0.0	0.8
27 113	...	7	Pennington	1 597	13 584	2 191	8.5	1 597	13 306	2 114	8.3	97.0	0.2	0.8	0.6	0.0	0.5
27 115	...	6	Pine	3 655	26 530	1 500	7.3	3 655	21 264	1 618	5.8	94.4	1.3	2.7	0.3	0.0	0.3
27 117	...	7	Pipestone	1 207	9 895	2 457	8.2	1 207	10 491	2 336	8.7	96.7	0.2	1.5	0.5	0.0	0.3
27 119	2985	3	Polk	5 103	31 369	1 363	6.1	5 104	32 589	1 200	6.4	94.2	0.3	1.3	0.3	0.0	2.6
27 121	...	6	Pope	1 736	11 236	2 354	6.5	1 736	10 745	2 314	6.2	98.9	0.2	0.2	0.1	0.0	0.2
27 123	5120	0	Ramsey	403	511 035	108	1 268.1	404	485 760	100	1 202.4	77.4	7.6	0.8	8.8	0.1	2.5
27 125	...	9	Red Lake	1 120	4 299	2 896	3.8	1 120	4 525	2 872	4.0	97.4	0.2	1.8	0.1	0.0	0.1
27 127	...	7	Redwood	2 278	16 815	1 966	7.4	2 279	17 254	1 838	7.6	95.0	0.1	3.2	0.3	0.1	0.4
27 129	...	7	Renville	2 546	17 154	1 945	6.7	2 546	17 673	1 807	6.9	95.7	0.1	0.5	0.2	0.0	2.8
27 131	...	4	Rice	1 289	56 665	836	44.0	1 289	49 183	855	38.2	93.6	1.3	0.4	1.5	0.0	1.9
27 133	...	6	Rock	1 250	9 721	2 468	7.8	1 250	9 806	2 403	7.8	97.3	0.5	0.4	0.6	0.0	0.5
27 135	...	9	Roseau	4 306	16 338	2 001	3.8	4 306	15 026	1 985	3.5	95.9	0.1	1.4	1.7	0.0	0.1
27 137	2240	3	St. Louis	16 123	200 528	275	12.4	16 124	198 232	245	12.3	94.9	0.8	2.0	0.7	0.0	0.2
27 139	5120	1	Scott	924	89 498	577	96.9	924	57 846	752	62.6	93.6	0.9	0.8	2.2	0.0	1.2
27 141	5120	1	Sherburne	1 130	64 417	756	57.0	1 131	41 945	957	37.1	96.7	0.9	0.4	0.6	0.0	0.4
27 143	...	8	Sibley	1 525	15 356	2 064	10.1	1 525	14 366	2 025	9.4	95.6	0.1	0.3	0.3	0.0	3.1
27 145	6980	3	Stearns	3 482	133 166	403	38.2	3 482	119 324	388	34.3	96.0	0.8	0.3	1.6	0.0	0.5
27 147	...	7	Steele	1 113	33 680	1 291	30.3	1 113	30 729	1 255	27.6	95.2	1.1	0.1	0.8	0.0	1.6
27 149	...	7	Stevens	1 456	10 053	2 439	6.9	1 456	10 634	2 323	7.3	96.1	0.9	0.7	0.9	0.0	0.4
27 151	...	7	Swift	1 926	11 956	2 297	6.2	1 926	10 724	2 317	5.6	90.7	2.7	0.5	1.4	1.5	1.4
27 153	...	6	Todd	2 440	24 426	1 578	10.0	2 440	23 363	1 523	9.6	97.5	0.1	0.5	0.3	0.0	0.7
27 155	...	9	Traverse	1 487	4 134	2 905	2.8	1 487	4 463	2 877	3.0	96.4	0.0	2.8	0.3	0.1	0.0
27 157	...	6	Wabasha	1 360	21 610	1 712	15.9	1 360	19 744	1 687	14.5	98.0	0.2	0.3	0.4	0.0	0.6
27 159	...	7	Wadena	1 386	13 713	2 182	9.9	1 387	13 154	2 127	9.5	97.9	0.5	0.6	0.2	0.0	0.3
27 161	...	7	Waseca	1 096	19 526	1 816	17.8	1 096	18 079	1 787	16.5	94.7	2.3	0.6	0.5	0.0	1.3
27 163	5120	0	Washington	1 015	201 130	272	198.2	1 015	145 860	324	143.7	93.6	1.8	0.4	2.1	0.0	0.6
27 165	...	7	Watonwan	1 125	11 876	2 300	10.6	1 125	11 682	2 238	10.4	88.5	0.4	0.2	0.9	0.0	8.8
27 167	...	6	Wilkin	1 946	7 138	2 675	3.7	1 946	7 516	2 615	3.9	97.8	0.2	0.4	0.2	0.0	0.5
27 169	...	4	Winona	1 622	49 985	915	30.8	1 622	47 828	878	29.5	95.8	0.8	0.2	1.9	0.0	0.5
27 171	5120	1	Wright	1 711	89 986	573	52.6	1 712	68 710	644	40.1	97.9	0.3	0.3	0.4	0.0	0.4
27 173	...	7	Yellow Medicine	1 963	11 080	2 360	5.6	1 963	11 684	2 237	6.0	96.1	0.1	2.0	0.3	0.0	0.9

[1]MSA = Metropolitan Statistical Area. PMSA = Primary MSA. NECMA = New England County Metropolitan Area. See Appendix A for explanation of these concepts. See Appendix B for list of metropolitan areas identified by type, with component counties.
[2]County typology code from the Economic Research Service of USDA. See Appendix A for definition.
[3]Dry land or land partially or temporarily covered by water.

STATE County	Population and population characteristics, 2000 (cont'd)								Population and population characteristics, 1990				
	Race (percent) (cont'd)								Race (percent)				
	Race alone or in combination												
	Two or more races	White	Black	American Indian or Alaska Native	Asian	Native Hawaiian and other Pacific Islander	Some other race	Hispanic[1]	White	Black or African American	American Indian or Alaska Native	Asian and Pacific Islander	Hispanic[1]
	15	16	17	18	19	20	21	22	23	24	25	26	27
MINNESOTA—Cont'd													
Grant	0.7	99.0	0.3	0.6	0.3	0.0	0.5	0.5	99.5	0.0	0.2	0.2	0.1
Hennepin	2.6	82.4	10.3	1.6	5.4	0.2	2.9	4.1	89.3	5.8	1.4	2.9	1.4
Houston	0.5	99.0	0.5	0.3	0.5	0.1	0.2	0.6	99.3	0.1	0.3	0.3	0.2
Hubbard	0.9	97.2	0.4	2.8	0.3	0.0	0.3	0.7	98.0	0.0	1.9	0.1	0.2
Isanti	0.9	98.5	0.5	1.1	0.6	0.0	0.3	0.8	98.7	0.3	0.5	0.4	0.5
Itasca	1.3	95.9	0.3	4.5	0.4	0.0	0.2	0.6	96.3	0.1	3.3	0.2	0.3
Jackson	0.4	97.4	0.1	0.3	1.5	0.0	1.0	1.9	97.7	0.0	0.1	1.4	1.0
Kanabec	1.1	98.4	0.4	1.4	0.6	0.1	0.3	0.9	98.9	0.2	0.5	0.4	0.5
Kandiyohi	0.9	94.3	0.8	0.5	0.5	0.1	4.7	8.0	97.6	0.2	0.4	0.3	3.5
Kittson	0.9	98.8	0.3	0.6	0.5	0.0	0.6	1.3	99.4	0.0	0.1	0.2	0.8
Koochiching	1.2	97.3	0.3	3.0	0.3	0.1	0.2	0.6	95.9	0.3	2.8	0.3	1.1
Lac qui Parle	0.4	99.2	0.3	0.3	0.4	0.0	0.1	0.3	99.4	0.1	0.1	0.3	0.3
Lake	0.9	98.9	0.2	1.3	0.3	0.0	0.2	0.6	99.2	0.0	0.6	0.2	0.3
Lake of the Woods	1.0	98.2	0.6	1.9	0.4	0.0	0.2	0.6	99.2	0.0	0.5	0.2	0.6
Le Sueur	0.7	97.1	0.3	0.6	0.5	0.1	2.1	3.9	99.3	0.1	0.2	0.3	0.5
Lincoln	0.2	99.0	0.1	0.4	0.2	0.0	0.5	0.9	99.5	0.0	0.1	0.1	0.4
Lyon	1.0	94.4	1.8	0.6	1.9	0.1	2.3	4.0	98.5	0.3	0.3	0.5	0.9
McLeod	0.6	97.2	0.3	0.4	0.7	0.1	1.9	3.6	98.9	0.1	0.2	0.4	0.9
Mahnomen	8.1	70.6	0.3	36.5	0.2	0.0	0.4	0.9	76.0	0.0	23.7	0.1	0.5
Marshall	0.6	97.8	0.2	0.7	0.3	0.0	1.7	2.9	99.1	0.0	0.5	0.1	1.0
Martin	0.7	97.9	0.4	0.3	0.5	0.0	1.6	1.9	99.1	0.0	0.2	0.4	0.6
Meeker	0.5	97.8	0.3	0.3	0.5	0.0	1.5	2.2	98.7	0.1	0.1	0.4	1.1
Mille Lacs	1.1	94.5	0.5	5.2	0.4	0.0	0.4	1.0	96.2	0.1	3.3	0.2	0.5
Morrison	0.5	99.0	0.3	0.6	0.4	0.1	0.2	0.6	99.3	0.1	0.3	0.2	0.3
Mower	0.9	95.5	0.8	0.4	1.7	0.0	2.5	4.3	98.7	0.2	0.1	0.8	0.7
Murray	0.7	99.0	0.2	0.6	0.4	0.1	0.5	1.5	99.7	0.0	0.0	0.2	0.2
Nicollet	0.7	97.0	1.1	0.5	1.3	0.0	0.8	1.8	98.4	0.3	0.2	0.7	0.7
Nobles	1.4	87.6	1.3	0.6	4.5	0.1	7.3	11.2	96.6	0.2	0.4	2.0	1.3
Norman	1.4	96.7	0.2	2.8	0.4	0.0	1.4	3.1	98.6	0.1	0.9	0.2	0.9
Olmsted	1.5	91.4	3.2	0.6	4.8	0.1	1.5	2.4	95.7	0.7	0.3	3.0	0.9
Otter Tail	0.8	97.8	0.4	0.8	0.6	0.1	1.1	1.7	99.0	0.1	0.5	0.4	0.4
Pennington	0.8	97.8	0.4	1.3	0.7	0.1	0.6	1.2	98.5	0.1	0.8	0.4	0.8
Pine	1.0	95.3	1.5	3.2	0.5	0.1	0.4	1.8	95.8	1.7	1.7	0.4	1.6
Pipestone	0.9	97.5	0.3	2.1	0.6	0.1	0.4	0.7	97.7	0.1	1.5	0.7	0.4
Polk	1.3	95.4	0.5	2.0	0.5	0.0	2.9	4.8	96.9	0.2	1.3	0.3	3.5
Pope	0.5	99.2	0.4	0.4	0.1	0.1	0.3	0.5	99.6	0.0	0.2	0.1	0.1
Ramsey	2.9	79.5	8.8	1.5	9.6	0.3	3.4	5.3	88.0	4.7	0.9	5.1	2.9
Red Lake	0.3	97.8	0.3	2.1	0.1	0.0	0.1	0.3	98.9	0.0	0.2	0.1	1.0
Redwood	0.9	95.7	0.3	3.8	0.4	0.1	0.6	1.1	97.8	0.2	1.6	0.2	0.5
Renville	0.7	96.4	0.1	0.8	0.3	0.1	3.1	5.1	98.6	0.0	0.3	0.3	1.2
Rice	1.3	94.7	1.6	0.8	1.8	0.1	2.4	5.5	97.8	0.4	0.2	1.2	1.1
Rock	0.6	97.8	0.7	0.7	0.7	0.0	0.7	1.3	99.2	0.1	0.3	0.2	0.3
Roseau	0.7	96.5	0.2	1.9	1.9	0.0	0.1	0.4	98.3	0.0	1.0	0.6	0.2
St. Louis	1.3	96.1	1.2	2.8	0.9	0.1	0.4	0.8	96.9	0.6	1.9	0.5	0.5
Scott	1.2	94.7	1.2	1.2	2.5	0.1	1.5	2.7	97.8	0.5	0.6	0.9	0.7
Sherburne	0.9	97.6	1.1	0.9	0.8	0.1	0.6	1.1	98.2	0.6	0.5	0.5	0.6
Sibley	0.6	96.2	0.2	0.5	0.5	0.0	3.3	5.4	99.3	0.0	0.1	0.2	0.9
Stearns	0.8	96.7	1.1	0.6	1.8	0.1	0.6	1.4	98.5	0.3	0.3	0.7	0.4
Steele	1.1	95.9	1.6	0.3	1.0	0.0	2.3	3.8	98.5	0.2	0.2	0.5	1.8
Stevens	1.0	97.1	1.1	1.2	0.9	0.0	0.7	0.9	97.5	0.5	0.5	1.1	0.5
Swift	1.8	91.9	2.8	0.8	2.4	2.6	1.6	2.7	99.1	0.0	0.4	0.4	0.7
Todd	0.8	98.4	0.2	0.8	0.5	0.0	1.0	1.9	99.4	0.0	0.2	0.2	0.2
Traverse	0.4	96.8	0.2	2.9	0.3	0.1	0.1	1.2	96.8	0.0	2.8	0.4	0.2
Wabasha	0.4	98.4	0.3	0.5	0.5	0.0	0.7	1.7	99.2	0.1	0.2	0.5	0.4
Wadena	0.6	98.4	0.6	0.9	0.2	0.1	0.3	0.9	99.0	0.1	0.6	0.3	0.4
Waseca	0.7	95.3	2.5	0.9	0.6	0.0	1.5	2.9	98.9	0.1	0.3	0.4	0.7
Washington	1.4	94.9	2.3	0.8	2.5	0.1	0.9	1.9	96.8	1.1	0.5	1.1	1.3
Watonwan	1.2	89.5	0.6	0.4	1.1	0.1	9.6	15.2	95.2	0.1	0.2	0.5	5.1
Wilkin	1.0	98.8	0.3	0.9	0.3	0.1	0.6	1.5	98.8	0.0	0.5	0.3	0.6
Winona	0.8	96.5	0.9	0.5	2.1	0.1	0.8	1.4	98.0	0.4	0.2	1.1	0.7
Wright	0.8	98.6	0.5	0.6	0.6	0.0	0.5	1.1	99.0	0.1	0.3	0.4	0.4
Yellow Medicine	0.7	96.7	0.2	2.5	0.3	0.0	1.0	1.8	98.4	0.0	1.0	0.2	0.7

[1] Hispanic persons may be of any race.

Table B. States and Counties

STATE County	Population and population characteristics, 2000										
	Age (percent)										
	Under 5 years	5 to 17 years	18 to 24 years	25 to 34 years	35 to 44 years	45 to 54 years	55 to 64 years	65 to 74 years	75 years and over	Median age (years)	Percent Female
	28	29	30	31	32	33	34	35	36	37	38
MINNESOTA—Cont'd											
Grant	5.0	19.0	6.9	8.6	14.5	12.9	10.2	10.2	12.7	42.5	51.4
Hennepin	6.6	17.4	9.7	16.5	17.2	14.0	7.7	5.4	5.6	34.9	50.8
Houston	5.8	21.4	6.8	10.4	16.4	14.5	8.6	7.6	8.4	38.8	50.6
Hubbard	5.4	19.1	6.4	9.2	14.9	14.2	12.8	10.1	7.9	41.8	50.0
Isanti	6.6	22.1	7.8	12.4	18.1	13.5	8.7	5.3	5.5	35.7	49.9
Itasca	5.3	19.1	7.6	9.3	15.1	15.6	11.1	8.8	8.0	41.1	50.1
Jackson	5.2	19.3	7.0	10.1	15.2	13.5	9.2	9.1	11.3	40.8	49.8
Kanabec	6.0	21.5	6.9	11.2	16.3	13.7	10.2	7.9	6.2	38.0	49.5
Kandiyohi	6.2	20.4	9.5	11.4	15.1	13.7	8.8	7.1	7.8	36.9	50.5
Kittson	6.4	18.7	5.5	9.0	14.6	14.4	9.8	9.8	11.8	42.4	50.4
Koochiching	5.4	18.4	6.4	10.4	15.4	15.2	10.8	9.5	8.5	41.5	50.4
Lac qui Parle	5.0	19.5	5.7	7.9	14.8	13.7	10.2	10.0	13.2	43.4	50.3
Lake	5.1	17.2	6.6	9.0	15.5	15.3	11.4	11.2	8.8	42.9	50.1
Lake of the Woods	4.2	20.6	5.7	8.9	16.3	15.3	11.9	8.6	8.6	41.6	49.8
Le Sueur	6.2	21.1	7.5	11.5	16.3	13.9	9.3	6.9	7.2	37.3	49.9
Lincoln	5.5	18.2	6.1	9.4	13.6	11.7	11.0	10.2	14.3	43.0	50.7
Lyon	6.6	19.6	13.3	11.9	14.6	11.9	7.7	6.3	8.3	34.0	51.1
McLeod	7.0	20.8	7.8	13.5	15.7	12.9	8.4	6.5	7.4	35.6	50.4
Mahnomen	7.1	22.1	7.2	9.4	14.1	12.9	10.5	8.2	8.5	38.2	49.3
Marshall	5.7	19.7	6.7	9.7	15.1	14.3	10.4	9.0	9.5	40.5	49.2
Martin	5.5	19.4	6.4	9.7	15.2	14.3	9.7	8.9	11.0	41.5	51.2
Meeker	6.4	20.5	7.4	10.9	15.4	13.7	9.3	7.8	8.6	38.3	49.6
Mille Lacs	6.2	20.8	7.5	11.0	15.8	12.7	9.9	8.1	8.1	38.0	50.5
Morrison	6.6	21.4	8.0	11.2	15.5	12.8	8.9	7.8	7.8	36.9	49.7
Mower	6.1	19.0	8.2	11.0	14.7	12.6	8.8	9.0	10.6	38.9	50.6
Murray	5.3	19.7	5.9	9.2	14.0	14.0	10.7	10.3	10.9	42.4	50.4
Nicollet	6.0	18.8	16.4	11.8	15.1	13.6	7.6	5.7	5.2	32.6	50.2
Nobles	6.9	19.6	8.2	11.8	14.8	12.4	8.9	8.1	9.3	37.5	50.1
Norman	6.1	19.6	6.2	9.3	14.8	12.8	10.2	9.8	11.1	40.9	50.3
Olmsted	7.2	19.8	8.5	14.5	17.7	13.3	8.3	5.4	5.4	35.0	50.9
Otter Tail	5.5	19.4	7.2	9.3	14.9	13.8	10.9	9.5	9.5	41.1	49.9
Pennington	6.1	18.4	10.3	11.5	15.0	13.6	9.3	7.0	8.8	37.9	50.6
Pine	5.5	20.0	7.7	11.4	16.5	13.2	10.7	8.4	6.7	38.4	47.9
Pipestone	5.8	20.0	6.8	10.0	14.7	12.3	9.1	9.3	12.0	40.2	51.9
Polk	6.0	20.0	9.7	10.0	14.8	13.2	9.0	7.7	9.7	38.2	50.5
Pope	4.9	19.9	6.7	8.7	14.3	13.7	10.1	9.6	11.9	42.1	50.8
Ramsey	6.8	18.7	11.3	15.0	15.7	13.2	7.6	5.6	6.0	33.7	51.8
Red Lake	5.6	20.0	7.5	9.7	15.0	13.4	9.8	9.0	10.0	40.4	49.8
Redwood	6.1	20.4	6.6	10.5	14.3	12.9	9.8	8.4	10.9	39.5	50.1
Renville	6.0	20.5	6.6	10.3	15.0	12.7	9.0	9.1	10.7	39.7	50.2
Rice	6.1	19.1	15.8	11.7	15.7	12.3	7.8	5.6	5.8	32.9	49.6
Rock	5.9	20.4	7.2	10.0	14.1	13.2	8.9	8.8	11.6	39.9	50.6
Roseau	7.3	22.5	6.8	12.8	17.1	12.4	8.5	5.6	7.0	35.3	48.8
St. Louis	5.2	17.1	11.4	10.8	15.2	15.1	9.2	7.6	8.5	39.0	50.8
Scott	9.3	22.0	6.7	16.7	20.6	12.0	6.5	3.4	2.8	32.7	49.5
Sherburne	8.4	22.5	9.6	15.5	18.4	12.0	6.5	3.6	3.5	31.4	48.9
Sibley	6.6	21.1	7.5	11.3	15.8	12.3	9.0	8.2	8.2	37.3	49.3
Stearns	6.4	19.3	16.1	12.8	15.2	12.0	7.1	5.9	5.1	31.6	49.7
Steele	6.9	21.0	8.2	12.8	16.2	13.3	8.3	6.5	6.8	35.7	50.6
Stevens	5.3	16.3	20.8	8.6	13.0	11.8	7.2	7.7	9.3	33.9	51.6
Swift	5.4	17.7	7.3	12.7	16.9	12.9	8.7	7.8	10.7	39.3	45.3
Todd	5.9	21.4	8.1	9.6	15.1	13.5	10.3	8.3	7.9	38.5	49.5
Traverse	5.4	19.9	5.6	8.5	13.2	11.4	9.8	12.0	14.2	42.9	50.8
Wabasha	5.7	21.4	7.2	11.1	15.9	14.0	9.8	7.2	7.8	38.0	50.0
Wadena	6.4	19.5	8.1	9.5	14.1	12.5	10.0	9.5	10.4	39.9	50.5
Waseca	6.7	19.1	8.7	13.3	16.6	13.6	7.7	6.6	7.5	36.3	47.8
Washington	7.6	21.8	6.8	13.6	19.3	15.0	8.2	4.4	3.2	35.1	50.3
Watonwan	7.2	20.4	7.8	10.4	13.9	12.3	9.4	8.9	9.7	38.6	51.2
Wilkin	6.3	21.5	7.0	10.6	17.1	12.5	8.9	7.7	8.4	38.1	51.2
Winona	5.6	17.2	18.6	11.1	13.9	12.7	7.8	6.1	6.9	32.8	51.2
Wright	8.3	22.8	7.6	14.5	18.1	12.3	7.5	4.6	4.2	33.1	49.6
Yellow Medicine	5.7	20.0	7.4	9.1	15.1	12.3	9.8	8.9	11.6	40.4	50.5

Table B. States and Counties

STATE County	Under 5 years	5 to 17 years	18 to 24 years	25 to 34 years	35 to 44 years	45 to 54 years	55 to 64 years	65 to 74 years	75 years and over	Percent Female	2000	1990	1980	1990–2000	1980–1990
	39	40	41	42	43	44	45	46	47	48	49	50	51	52	53
MINNESOTA—Cont'd															
Grant	6.4	19.5	4.6	12.3	12.3	9.9	11.0	11.6	12.4	51.7	6 289	6 246	7 171	0.7	-12.9
Hennepin	7.5	15.7	10.6	21.0	16.5	9.9	7.6	6.2	5.1	51.6	1 116 200	1 032 431	941 411	8.1	9.7
Houston	7.9	20.8	7.1	15.4	14.7	9.2	9.0	8.2	7.7	50.5	19 718	18 497	18 382	6.6	0.6
Hubbard	6.9	20.5	5.8	13.0	13.9	11.2	10.9	9.9	7.9	50.7	18 376	14 939	14 098	23.0	6.0
Isanti	7.9	23.4	7.6	16.3	15.8	11.0	6.9	5.5	5.6	50.0	31 287	25 921	23 600	20.7	9.8
Itasca	6.6	21.7	7.0	13.2	15.5	10.6	9.6	9.1	6.8	50.6	43 992	40 844	43 069	7.7	-5.1
Jackson	6.8	20.0	6.7	13.7	13.2	9.2	10.4	10.1	9.8	50.5	11 268	11 677	13 690	-3.5	-14.7
Kanabec	7.6	22.7	7.0	15.1	13.7	10.3	8.8	8.2	6.4	50.2	14 996	12 802	12 161	17.1	5.3
Kandiyohi	7.7	20.8	9.5	15.3	14.1	9.5	8.1	7.9	7.1	50.8	41 203	38 761	36 763	6.3	5.4
Kittson	7.1	19.0	5.4	13.1	13.7	9.7	10.3	10.8	10.9	50.9	5 285	5 767	6 672	-8.4	-13.6
Koochiching	6.3	19.1	8.4	15.2	15.0	11.0	9.9	8.5	6.5	48.2	14 355	16 299	17 571	-11.9	-7.2
Lac qui Parle	6.8	19.7	4.5	12.7	12.7	9.6	10.9	11.6	11.5	50.6	8 067	8 924	10 592	-9.6	-15.7
Lake	6.0	18.3	5.6	13.5	14.2	11.6	13.3	10.0	7.5	50.2	11 058	10 415	13 043	6.2	-20.1
Lake of the Woods	8.3	19.4	6.4	15.2	13.9	10.6	9.2	9.8	7.2	50.0	4 522	4 076	3 764	10.9	8.3
Le Sueur	7.7	21.8	7.7	15.1	14.0	10.1	8.5	8.0	7.1	50.3	25 426	23 239	23 434	9.4	-0.8
Lincoln	5.3	20.9	5.0	11.0	11.5	10.4	10.8	12.3	12.9	51.2	6 429	6 890	8 207	-6.7	-16.0
Lyon	7.0	20.1	13.3	14.7	12.9	8.8	7.6	7.9	7.6	51.0	25 425	24 789	25 207	2.6	-1.7
McLeod	8.1	20.9	8.4	16.1	14.2	9.7	7.9	7.5	7.3	50.5	34 898	32 030	29 657	9.0	8.0
Mahnomen	6.8	24.4	6.2	12.6	11.7	10.3	9.7	9.7	8.6	49.6	5 190	5 044	5 535	2.9	-8.9
Marshall	6.3	22.5	6.0	12.9	13.4	10.5	10.0	9.9	8.4	49.4	10 155	10 993	13 027	-7.6	-15.6
Martin	6.9	19.9	5.9	14.2	13.9	9.9	9.4	10.0	9.8	51.3	21 802	22 914	24 687	-4.9	-7.2
Meeker	7.6	21.8	6.8	13.9	13.7	9.7	9.3	9.1	8.0	50.7	22 644	20 846	20 594	8.6	1.2
Mille Lacs	7.6	21.5	7.3	13.9	13.5	10.0	9.1	8.6	8.5	50.9	22 330	18 670	18 430	19.6	1.3
Morrison	7.9	23.4	7.6	14.7	13.0	8.9	8.9	8.5	7.1	50.1	31 712	29 604	29 311	7.1	1.0
Mower	6.5	19.0	7.4	13.8	12.9	9.5	10.8	10.8	9.4	51.5	38 603	37 385	40 390	3.3	-7.4
Murray	6.6	20.5	6.1	12.0	13.2	9.6	11.3	11.3	9.3	50.6	9 165	9 660	11 507	-5.1	-16.1
Nicollet	7.2	19.0	16.1	15.7	14.8	8.9	7.3	5.7	5.3	50.5	29 771	28 076	26 929	6.0	4.3
Nobles	6.7	19.8	8.1	14.2	12.8	9.9	9.9	9.3	9.2	51.0	20 832	20 098	21 840	3.7	-8.0
Norman	6.1	20.9	5.1	12.6	12.5	9.8	10.7	10.6	11.7	50.4	7 442	7 975	9 379	-6.7	-15.0
Olmsted	8.6	19.1	9.2	20.1	15.4	10.5	7.1	5.3	4.7	51.5	124 277	106 470	92 006	16.7	15.7
Otter Tail	6.8	19.7	6.8	13.4	13.4	10.1	10.5	9.9	9.5	50.5	57 159	50 714	51 937	12.7	-2.4
Pennington	6.8	20.0	10.3	14.1	13.7	9.9	8.3	8.0	8.9	50.4	13 584	13 306	15 258	2.1	-12.8
Pine	6.8	21.6	7.0	15.4	13.4	10.2	9.8	8.7	7.1	47.8	26 530	21 264	19 871	24.8	7.0
Pipestone	7.6	20.5	7.1	13.5	12.0	8.6	9.7	10.7	10.2	52.2	9 895	10 491	11 690	-5.7	-10.3
Polk	7.2	20.9	8.4	13.8	13.5	9.5	8.9	9.0	8.8	50.8	31 369	32 589	34 844	-3.7	-6.5
Pope	6.9	20.6	5.3	12.3	12.9	9.4	10.2	11.5	10.7	50.9	11 236	10 745	11 657	4.6	-7.8
Ramsey	8.0	16.7	11.6	19.4	15.1	9.2	7.7	6.6	5.6	52.2	511 035	485 760	459 784	5.2	5.7
Red Lake	7.2	22.8	5.8	13.6	13.1	9.7	9.4	9.6	8.9	49.5	4 299	4 525	5 471	-5.0	-17.3
Redwood	7.4	20.7	6.2	13.5	12.5	9.8	9.3	10.5	10.1	50.8	16 815	17 254	19 341	-2.5	-10.8
Renville	7.3	20.6	6.0	13.7	12.6	9.1	10.4	10.4	9.9	50.6	17 154	17 673	20 401	-2.9	-13.4
Rice	6.9	19.3	16.5	15.2	13.6	9.5	7.1	6.1	5.7	50.9	56 665	49 183	46 087	15.2	6.7
Rock	6.9	21.5	6.2	13.1	13.2	9.4	9.8	10.4	9.4	51.5	9 721	9 806	10 703	-0.9	-8.4
Roseau	9.6	21.6	8.6	17.7	12.8	9.2	7.0	6.9	6.6	48.8	16 338	15 026	12 574	8.7	19.5
St. Louis	6.1	18.2	10.2	14.2	15.3	9.9	9.2	9.1	7.8	51.3	200 528	198 232	222 229	1.2	-10.8
Scott	9.5	21.6	8.7	20.7	16.3	10.0	5.9	4.0	3.3	49.4	89 498	57 846	43 784	54.7	32.1
Sherburne	8.7	23.1	11.7	18.3	16.1	9.5	5.6	3.9	3.2	48.9	64 417	41 945	29 908	53.6	40.2
Sibley	7.4	21.0	6.7	14.2	12.9	9.8	10.3	9.0	8.7	50.2	15 356	14 366	15 448	6.9	-7.0
Stearns	7.6	20.2	17.4	16.2	12.9	8.1	7.1	5.8	4.7	49.9	133 166	119 324	108 161	11.6	10.3
Steele	7.8	20.8	8.8	16.3	14.5	9.7	8.2	7.4	6.6	51.1	33 680	30 729	30 328	9.6	1.3
Stevens	5.8	17.7	21.1	11.3	11.7	7.6	8.9	8.2	7.8	51.7	10 053	10 634	11 322	-5.5	-6.1
Swift	6.3	20.6	5.6	13.4	12.4	9.5	10.0	11.3	10.8	50.8	11 956	10 724	12 920	11.5	-17.0
Todd	7.0	22.5	7.0	13.0	13.2	9.9	9.3	9.0	8.0	50.3	24 426	23 363	24 991	4.5	-6.5
Traverse	6.9	19.4	4.7	11.6	11.2	9.6	12.2	11.6	12.8	51.5	4 134	4 463	5 542	-7.4	-19.5
Wabasha	7.8	21.1	7.4	14.9	14.3	10.1	8.5	8.5	7.5	50.4	21 610	19 744	19 335	9.5	2.1
Wadena	7.3	20.9	7.2	13.3	12.2	10.2	9.7	9.6	9.6	51.2	13 713	13 154	14 192	4.2	-7.3
Waseca	7.5	21.2	9.1	15.1	14.5	8.7	8.2	8.2	7.4	50.6	19 526	18 079	18 448	8.0	-2.0
Washington	8.3	22.1	8.1	18.4	18.4	11.6	6.7	3.9	2.7	49.8	201 130	145 860	113 571	37.9	28.4
Watonwan	7.5	20.6	6.8	14.1	12.5	9.7	10.5	9.2	9.1	50.9	11 876	11 682	12 361	1.7	-5.5
Wilkin	7.8	20.5	7.4	15.2	12.8	9.1	10.0	8.6	8.6	50.5	7 138	7 516	8 454	-5.0	-11.1
Winona	6.7	17.9	18.1	14.3	13.3	8.6	7.4	6.8	6.9	51.3	49 985	47 828	46 256	4.5	3.4
Wright	9.0	23.5	8.7	17.8	15.1	9.7	6.3	5.2	4.5	49.6	89 986	68 710	58 681	31.0	17.1
Yellow Medicine	6.7	20.3	6.3	13.2	11.9	10.0	10.2	10.5	10.9	50.5	11 080	11 684	13 653	-5.2	-14.4

Table B. States and Counties

STATE County	Total population	Total in households	House-holder	Spouse	Child Total	Child Own child under 18 years	Other relatives Total	Other relatives Under 18 years	Nonrelatives Total	Nonrelatives Unmarried partner	Total in group quarters	Institutionalized Correctional institutions	Institutionalized Nursing homes	Institutionalized Other institutions	Noninstitutionalized College dormitories	Noninstitutionalized Military quarters	Other
	54	55	56	57	58	59	60	61	62	63	64	65	66	67	68	69	70
MINNESOTA—Cont'd																	
Grant	6 289	96.8	40.3	23.8	28.1	22.8	1.9	0.7	2.8	1.5	3.2	0.0	2.5	0.0	0.0	0.0	0.7
Hennepin	1 116 200	97.5	40.9	18.5	27.2	22.2	3.8	1.2	7.1	2.3	2.5	0.1	0.8	0.1	0.7	0.0	0.8
Houston	19 718	98.1	38.7	23.2	31.5	26.1	1.6	0.5	3.1	1.7	1.9	0.1	1.4	0.1	0.0	0.0	0.4
Hubbard	18 376	99.1	40.5	24.7	27.6	22.8	2.4	1.1	3.9	1.9	0.9	0.1	0.7	0.0	0.0	0.0	0.1
Isanti	31 287	98.5	35.9	22.3	33.0	26.7	2.6	1.2	4.6	2.2	1.5	0.2	0.9	0.1	0.0	0.0	0.3
Itasca	43 992	98.4	40.4	23.6	27.9	22.4	2.3	1.0	4.2	2.0	1.6	0.2	0.8	0.2	0.0	0.0	0.5
Jackson	11 268	97.2	40.4	24.3	28.5	23.5	1.3	0.4	2.8	1.3	2.8	0.1	1.8	0.0	0.0	0.0	0.9
Kanabec	14 996	99.2	38.4	22.6	31.1	25.7	2.4	1.0	4.7	2.4	0.8	0.1	0.6	0.0	0.0	0.0	0.1
Kandiyohi	41 203	97.9	38.7	22.3	30.1	25.1	2.3	0.8	4.6	1.7	2.1	0.1	1.2	0.4	0.0	0.0	0.4
Kittson	5 285	97.2	41.0	23.5	28.8	24.1	1.4	0.4	2.5	1.3	2.8	0.1	2.5	0.0	0.0	0.0	0.2
Koochiching	14 355	98.0	42.1	22.4	27.7	22.5	1.9	0.8	3.9	2.1	2.0	0.1	1.4	0.0	0.3	0.0	0.3
Lac qui Parle	8 067	97.4	41.1	24.6	27.9	23.7	1.5	0.4	2.3	1.2	2.6	0.1	2.5	0.0	0.0	0.0	0.1
Lake	11 058	97.6	42.0	24.3	26.2	21.4	1.6	0.5	3.4	2.0	2.4	0.0	1.9	0.0	0.1	0.0	0.4
Lake of the Woods	4 522	99.0	42.1	24.2	28.1	23.8	1.7	0.5	2.9	1.8	1.0	0.0	1.0	0.0	0.0	0.0	0.0
Le Sueur	25 426	98.8	37.9	23.3	31.6	25.9	2.3	0.9	3.8	1.8	1.2	0.1	0.5	0.4	0.0	0.0	0.3
Lincoln	6 429	96.8	41.3	24.7	27.5	23.1	1.4	0.3	2.0	1.0	3.2	0.1	1.3	1.4	0.0	0.0	0.4
Lyon	25 425	95.1	38.2	21.1	29.1	25.0	1.8	0.7	4.9	1.5	4.9	0.1	1.2	0.1	3.1	0.0	0.4
McLeod	34 898	98.6	38.5	22.8	31.5	26.4	2.1	0.7	3.8	1.8	1.4	0.1	0.9	0.0	0.0	0.0	0.4
Mahnomen	5 190	98.6	37.9	19.6	32.3	25.4	4.4	2.8	4.4	2.5	1.4	0.0	0.8	0.0	0.0	0.0	0.6
Marshall	10 155	98.8	40.4	24.3	30.1	24.5	1.6	0.4	2.4	1.1	1.2	0.1	0.9	0.1	0.0	0.0	0.1
Martin	21 802	97.8	41.6	23.6	28.3	23.7	1.3	0.5	3.1	1.7	2.2	0.1	1.3	0.3	0.0	0.0	0.5
Meeker	22 644	97.7	37.9	23.3	30.9	25.8	1.9	0.7	3.7	1.8	2.3	0.3	1.8	0.0	0.0	0.0	0.2
Mille Lacs	22 330	97.7	38.7	21.5	30.3	24.7	2.8	1.3	4.5	2.4	2.3	0.6	1.4	0.0	0.0	0.0	0.3
Morrison	31 712	98.2	37.3	22.1	33.2	26.8	2.0	0.7	3.6	1.9	1.8	0.1	0.5	0.0	0.0	0.0	1.1
Mower	38 603	97.8	40.4	22.1	28.5	23.4	2.2	0.8	4.6	2.0	2.2	0.1	1.2	0.2	0.0	0.0	0.7
Murray	9 165	98.2	40.6	25.4	28.1	24.0	1.5	0.6	2.7	1.3	1.8	0.0	1.3	0.0	0.0	0.0	0.4
Nicollet	29 771	91.4	35.7	20.6	28.3	23.7	1.5	0.5	5.3	1.9	8.6	0.1	0.6	1.4	6.3	0.0	0.1
Nobles	20 832	98.1	38.1	22.4	30.3	25.0	3.2	1.1	4.1	1.4	1.9	0.1	1.1	0.0	0.0	0.0	0.6
Norman	7 442	97.5	40.4	23.4	29.7	24.8	1.9	0.7	2.1	1.0	2.5	0.0	2.2	0.0	0.0	0.0	0.3
Olmsted	124 277	97.5	38.5	21.8	30.3	25.8	2.2	0.7	4.8	1.8	2.5	0.8	0.5	0.1	0.1	0.0	1.0
Otter Tail	57 159	97.6	39.7	23.9	28.9	23.8	1.8	0.6	3.4	1.5	2.4	0.1	1.6	0.3	0.0	0.0	0.4
Pennington	13 584	96.8	40.7	21.0	28.1	23.1	1.8	0.6	5.1	2.2	3.2	0.4	1.2	0.0	0.5	0.0	1.1
Pine	26 530	95.0	37.5	21.2	28.6	23.0	2.9	1.2	4.8	2.4	5.0	3.6	0.8	0.3	0.0	0.0	0.3
Pipestone	9 895	97.7	41.1	23.7	29.1	25.0	1.4	0.5	2.4	1.3	2.3	0.1	2.1	0.0	0.0	0.0	0.2
Polk	31 369	95.2	38.5	21.1	30.1	24.5	1.9	0.8	3.6	1.5	4.8	0.2	2.1	0.1	1.4	0.0	1.1
Pope	11 236	97.2	40.2	23.7	29.0	23.9	1.4	0.4	2.9	1.4	2.8	0.0	2.3	0.3	0.0	0.0	0.2
Ramsey	511 035	96.6	39.4	17.3	29.3	23.5	4.1	1.5	6.5	2.3	3.4	0.1	0.8	0.1	1.6	0.0	0.8
Red Lake	4 299	96.2	40.2	22.3	29.4	24.3	1.5	0.4	2.9	1.5	3.8	0.0	2.2	0.0	0.0	0.0	1.6
Redwood	16 815	97.0	39.7	22.7	30.1	25.5	1.6	0.6	2.9	1.5	3.0	0.2	2.0	0.0	0.0	0.0	0.7
Renville	17 154	97.8	39.5	23.4	30.2	25.4	1.7	0.6	3.1	1.6	2.2	0.0	1.7	0.0	0.0	0.0	0.5
Rice	56 665	88.2	33.3	19.4	28.7	23.6	2.3	0.8	4.5	1.9	11.8	2.0	1.2	0.3	7.4	0.0	0.9
Rock	9 721	97.6	39.5	24.5	30.0	25.2	1.5	0.6	2.1	1.1	2.4	0.0	2.0	0.0	0.0	0.0	0.4
Roseau	16 338	98.5	37.9	22.8	33.1	28.8	1.6	0.5	3.2	1.7	1.5	0.1	1.2	0.0	0.0	0.0	0.2
St. Louis	200 528	95.5	41.2	20.3	26.2	20.8	2.1	0.8	5.7	2.2	4.5	0.5	1.2	0.2	1.8	0.0	0.8
Scott	89 498	99.0	34.3	22.9	35.1	30.1	2.3	0.7	4.3	1.8	1.0	0.5	0.4	0.0	0.0	0.0	0.1
Sherburne	64 417	97.5	33.5	22.2	34.9	29.5	2.0	0.8	4.9	2.1	2.5	1.5	0.7	0.0	0.0	0.0	0.3
Sibley	15 356	97.9	37.6	23.0	31.7	25.8	2.3	0.9	3.4	1.6	2.1	0.1	1.0	0.0	0.0	0.0	1.0
Stearns	133 166	94.5	35.7	20.1	29.9	24.6	1.9	0.5	6.8	1.8	5.5	0.1	0.6	0.2	4.0	0.0	0.7
Steele	33 680	98.1	38.1	22.7	31.6	26.6	1.8	0.8	3.8	1.9	1.9	0.1	0.8	0.0	0.5	0.0	0.5
Stevens	10 053	90.5	37.3	20.7	24.8	20.8	1.4	0.4	6.3	1.0	9.5	0.0	1.0	0.0	7.6	0.0	0.9
Swift	11 956	87.1	36.4	20.7	26.1	21.9	1.4	0.4	2.5	1.3	12.9	11.1	1.3	0.0	0.0	0.0	0.4
Todd	24 426	98.8	38.2	22.9	31.9	26.0	2.2	0.9	3.5	1.6	1.2	0.1	0.8	0.0	0.0	0.0	0.3
Traverse	4 134	97.4	41.5	23.7	28.9	24.8	1.3	0.3	2.0	1.0	2.6	0.0	2.6	0.0	0.0	0.0	0.0
Wabasha	21 610	98.3	38.3	23.3	31.0	25.8	1.9	0.7	3.7	2.0	1.7	0.0	1.2	0.0	0.0	0.0	0.5
Wadena	13 713	96.8	39.6	21.9	29.4	24.4	1.9	0.7	4.1	1.8	3.2	0.2	2.4	0.0	0.0	0.0	0.7
Waseca	19 526	92.6	36.2	21.3	29.7	24.5	2.0	0.7	3.4	1.7	7.4	5.8	1.3	0.0	0.0	0.0	0.3
Washington	201 130	98.4	35.5	23.0	34.2	28.3	2.2	0.8	3.4	1.6	1.6	1.0	0.3	0.0	0.0	0.0	0.3
Watonwan	11 876	98.6	39.0	22.1	30.5	25.7	3.1	1.1	3.9	1.7	1.4	0.0	1.3	0.0	0.0	0.0	0.1
Wilkin	7 138	97.9	38.6	22.9	31.8	26.4	1.6	0.6	3.0	1.4	2.1	0.0	1.6	0.2	0.0	0.0	0.3
Winona	49 985	92.4	37.5	19.3	26.7	21.7	1.7	0.6	7.2	2.0	7.6	0.0	1.3	0.0	5.6	0.0	0.7
Wright	89 986	99.0	35.0	22.5	35.6	29.8	2.1	0.7	3.8	1.9	1.0	0.1	0.6	0.0	0.0	0.0	0.3
Yellow Medicine	11 080	97.0	40.1	23.5	29.2	24.9	1.2	0.5	3.0	1.6	3.0	0.0	2.3	0.0	0.0	0.0	0.7

Table B. States and Counties

STATE County	Households by type, 2000												Households, 1990		
	Family households							Nonfamily households							
				Married couple		Female householder[1]			Householder living alone						Householder living alone
	Total households	Total	With own children under 18 years	Total	With own children under 18 years	Total	With own children under 18 years	Total	Total	65 years and over	Average household size	Average family size	Total households	Female householder[1]	
	71	72	73	74	75	76	77	78	79	80	81	82	83	84	85
MINNESOTA—Cont'd															
Grant	2 534	68.7	29.2	59.0	23.3	6.5	4.2	31.3	28.0	16.5	2.40	2.94	2 454	5.3	27.3
Hennepin	456 129	58.6	28.8	45.3	20.9	9.9	6.2	41.4	31.8	8.4	2.39	3.07	419 060	10.0	29.0
Houston	7 633	70.9	34.4	60.0	27.1	7.4	5.3	29.1	25.4	12.0	2.53	3.05	6 844	7.2	23.4
Hubbard	7 435	71.9	29.3	61.1	22.2	7.1	4.7	28.1	24.2	11.3	2.45	2.88	5 781	6.0	23.5
Isanti	11 236	74.9	38.1	62.1	29.5	8.4	5.8	25.1	20.1	8.2	2.74	3.15	8 810	7.1	19.0
Itasca	17 789	69.6	29.2	58.3	21.8	7.6	5.0	30.4	26.0	12.2	2.43	2.91	15 461	7.9	23.1
Jackson	4 556	68.4	29.8	60.0	24.2	5.4	3.6	31.6	28.5	13.4	2.40	2.95	4 560	5.3	25.7
Kanabec	5 759	72.0	34.1	58.8	25.0	8.4	6.0	28.0	23.8	10.3	2.58	3.03	4 753	7.4	24.0
Kandiyohi	15 936	68.9	33.1	57.7	25.6	7.5	5.5	31.1	25.7	10.8	2.53	3.05	14 298	6.8	23.9
Kittson	2 167	66.8	29.2	57.4	24.1	6.0	3.3	33.2	30.5	16.3	2.37	2.96	2 274	5.3	28.7
Koochiching	6 040	65.6	28.4	53.3	20.6	8.5	5.5	34.4	30.4	14.5	2.33	2.88	6 025	8.5	24.8
Lac qui Parle	3 316	67.1	27.9	59.8	23.6	4.1	2.5	32.9	30.2	17.9	2.37	2.96	3 505	3.6	27.7
Lake	4 646	67.6	27.1	57.8	20.7	6.6	4.5	32.4	28.0	12.7	2.32	2.83	4 242	6.2	25.4
Lake of the Woods	1 903	66.6	29.2	57.4	23.5	5.3	3.3	33.4	29.7	12.9	2.35	2.93	1 576	5.9	23.4
Le Sueur	9 630	71.9	34.4	61.4	28.0	6.8	4.4	28.1	23.7	10.9	2.61	3.10	8 468	6.2	23.1
Lincoln	2 653	67.3	27.0	59.7	22.9	4.6	2.5	32.7	30.5	16.8	2.35	2.93	2 704	4.3	28.0
Lyon	9 715	65.2	33.0	55.1	26.4	7.1	5.0	34.8	27.9	12.4	2.49	3.09	9 073	6.3	26.1
McLeod	13 449	70.1	34.9	59.2	27.7	7.3	5.0	29.9	25.0	10.8	2.56	3.08	11 815	6.2	23.4
Mahnomen	1 969	69.4	32.4	51.6	21.0	11.6	7.6	30.6	27.0	14.9	2.60	3.14	1 805	8.2	24.3
Marshall	4 101	69.2	30.2	60.2	24.9	5.4	3.4	30.8	28.7	15.1	2.45	3.01	4 194	4.9	26.3
Martin	9 067	66.7	29.8	56.6	23.1	7.2	5.0	33.3	30.0	15.2	2.35	2.92	9 129	6.4	27.8
Meeker	8 590	71.4	33.7	61.5	27.1	6.3	4.2	28.6	24.4	12.0	2.58	3.07	7 651	5.4	24.0
Mille Lacs	8 638	69.5	32.2	55.5	22.9	9.5	6.4	30.5	25.9	12.0	2.53	3.03	6 911	7.7	23.9
Morrison	11 816	71.6	34.5	59.4	26.8	7.8	5.1	28.4	24.9	11.8	2.64	3.15	10 399	7.1	23.2
Mower	15 582	66.2	29.7	54.7	22.3	8.0	5.4	33.8	29.1	14.8	2.42	2.98	15 028	7.2	27.8
Murray	3 722	69.9	29.0	62.5	24.3	4.6	3.0	30.1	27.1	15.3	2.42	2.94	3 758	4.1	26.2
Nicollet	10 642	68.7	35.3	57.5	27.7	7.9	5.7	31.3	24.0	8.8	2.56	3.05	9 478	7.1	22.1
Nobles	7 939	69.5	32.1	58.8	25.7	6.9	4.4	30.5	26.5	14.1	2.58	3.11	7 683	5.9	25.1
Norman	3 010	66.7	30.1	57.8	25.0	5.9	3.7	33.3	31.3	17.0	2.41	3.04	3 118	4.5	29.3
Olmsted	47 807	67.6	35.2	56.7	28.0	8.0	5.4	32.4	25.8	7.6	2.53	3.09	40 058	7.5	24.6
Otter Tail	22 671	69.6	30.3	60.1	24.4	6.1	4.0	30.4	26.6	13.3	2.46	2.98	19 510	5.8	25.8
Pennington	5 525	64.3	30.6	51.7	22.4	9.1	6.2	35.7	29.5	12.6	2.38	2.95	5 173	8.1	28.1
Pine	9 939	69.6	31.2	56.5	22.8	8.7	5.7	30.4	25.1	10.9	2.53	3.02	7 577	7.2	24.2
Pipestone	4 069	67.0	31.0	57.6	24.5	6.5	4.6	33.0	30.1	17.2	2.38	2.96	4 078	5.6	28.7
Polk	12 070	66.7	32.3	54.9	24.7	8.5	5.7	33.3	28.9	13.8	2.47	3.07	11 984	7.9	26.0
Pope	4 513	67.9	29.7	59.0	24.5	5.9	3.8	32.1	28.7	16.1	2.42	2.99	4 135	4.9	26.3
Ramsey	201 236	59.6	29.8	44.0	20.3	11.9	7.7	40.4	32.0	9.5	2.45	3.16	190 500	11.3	29.3
Red Lake	1 727	65.5	30.7	55.4	24.3	6.8	5.0	34.5	30.5	15.5	2.39	3.02	1 730	5.1	30.5
Redwood	6 674	67.8	31.5	57.3	24.4	7.1	5.0	32.2	28.8	14.7	2.44	3.02	6 554	5.2	27.0
Renville	6 779	68.2	31.5	59.1	25.8	5.6	3.7	31.8	28.5	15.1	2.48	3.05	6 790	4.7	26.6
Rice	18 888	70.7	36.5	58.1	28.1	8.6	5.8	29.3	23.9	9.1	2.65	3.14	16 347	7.8	24.1
Rock	3 843	70.4	31.3	62.1	26.1	5.5	3.6	29.6	27.0	15.7	2.47	3.01	3 754	5.1	25.6
Roseau	6 190	71.7	38.4	60.0	30.2	6.8	5.0	28.3	24.6	9.9	2.60	3.11	5 415	6.2	22.0
St. Louis	82 619	62.2	27.6	49.3	19.5	9.4	6.2	37.8	31.2	13.0	2.32	2.90	78 901	9.2	28.8
Scott	30 692	78.1	45.4	66.9	37.9	7.4	5.2	21.9	16.0	4.5	2.89	3.25	19 367	7.2	15.5
Sherburne	21 581	77.6	44.9	66.2	36.8	7.5	5.5	22.4	15.7	5.2	2.91	3.27	13 643	6.8	15.2
Sibley	5 772	70.8	33.6	61.1	27.9	5.8	3.6	29.2	25.4	13.0	2.60	3.14	5 323	4.6	23.8
Stearns	47 604	67.5	35.0	56.3	28.0	7.5	5.0	32.5	23.6	8.4	2.64	3.15	39 776	7.3	21.5
Steele	12 846	70.7	35.5	59.5	27.9	7.4	5.2	29.3	24.6	10.3	2.57	3.08	11 342	6.3	23.1
Stevens	3 751	63.1	28.6	55.4	24.1	5.1	3.2	36.9	29.1	14.2	2.43	2.99	3 823	5.4	25.5
Swift	4 353	66.2	30.0	56.9	24.3	6.1	4.0	33.8	30.9	17.6	2.39	3.00	4 268	5.3	29.5
Todd	9 342	69.7	31.8	59.8	25.8	6.1	4.0	30.3	26.3	13.0	2.58	3.14	8 589	5.4	24.7
Traverse	1 717	65.8	28.3	57.0	22.4	6.0	4.3	34.2	32.0	19.2	2.34	2.97	1 778	5.1	28.2
Wabasha	8 277	71.0	33.8	60.8	27.0	6.5	4.6	29.0	24.3	10.8	2.57	3.07	7 286	5.7	23.0
Wadena	5 426	66.5	30.0	55.3	22.8	7.6	5.0	33.5	29.2	15.1	2.45	3.02	4 978	7.3	27.3
Waseca	7 059	70.7	34.7	59.0	27.3	7.8	5.1	29.3	25.1	10.7	2.56	3.07	6 649	6.9	24.6
Washington	71 462	76.5	41.6	64.8	34.0	8.5	5.7	23.5	18.7	5.4	2.77	3.19	49 246	8.5	16.1
Watonwan	4 627	67.9	32.5	56.6	24.7	7.3	5.3	32.1	28.7	15.4	2.53	3.10	4 530	5.5	27.9
Wilkin	2 752	70.0	35.2	59.5	29.2	7.0	4.3	30.0	25.9	13.4	2.54	3.09	2 805	6.0	25.3
Winona	18 744	62.4	30.2	51.3	23.2	7.8	5.1	37.6	28.2	10.5	2.46	3.04	16 930	7.1	25.5
Wright	31 465	76.0	42.1	64.5	34.3	7.7	5.4	24.0	18.8	6.8	2.83	3.26	23 013	6.9	17.5
Yellow Medicine	4 439	67.0	30.3	58.6	24.8	5.7	4.1	33.0	29.3	15.2	2.42	3.01	4 607	4.4	28.6

[1] No spouse present.

Table B. States and Counties

STATE County	Percent change of households, 1990–2000	Total housing units	Occupied housing units (percent)	Vacant housing units				Occupied housing units				
				Total	For seasonal, recreational, or occasional use	Homeowner vacancy rate (percent)	Rental vacancy rate (percent)	Total	Percent owner-occupied housing units	Percent renter-occupied housing units	Average household size of owner-occupied units	Average household size of renter-occupied units
	86	87	88	89	90	91	92	93	94	95	96	97
MINNESOTA—Cont'd												
Grant	3.3	3 098	81.8	18.2	10.0	2.3	11.4	2 534	82.1	17.9	2.49	1.99
Hennepin	8.8	468 824	97.3	2.7	0.5	0.5	2.7	456 129	66.2	33.8	2.59	1.98
Houston	11.5	8 168	93.5	6.5	3.2	1.2	4.8	7 633	81.0	19.0	2.67	1.97
Hubbard	28.6	12 229	60.8	39.2	35.8	1.2	7.1	7 435	83.3	16.7	2.52	2.08
Isanti	27.5	12 062	93.2	6.8	3.5	0.8	8.1	11 236	85.7	14.3	2.86	2.03
Itasca	15.1	24 528	72.5	27.5	23.4	1.5	4.5	17 789	83.0	17.0	2.52	1.99
Jackson	-0.1	5 092	89.5	10.5	2.0	2.4	12.2	4 556	79.0	21.0	2.47	2.15
Kanabec	21.2	6 846	84.1	15.9	11.8	1.2	5.0	5 759	84.6	15.4	2.66	2.14
Kandiyohi	11.5	18 415	86.5	13.5	9.0	1.5	7.9	15 936	75.6	24.4	2.67	2.11
Kittson	-4.7	2 719	79.7	20.3	5.9	3.3	16.2	2 167	82.8	17.2	2.43	2.09
Koochiching	0.2	7 719	78.2	21.8	14.5	2.5	10.8	6 040	80.4	19.6	2.44	1.86
Lac qui Parle	-5.4	3 774	87.9	12.1	3.1	3.6	9.7	3 316	80.9	19.1	2.49	1.85
Lake	9.5	6 840	67.9	32.1	26.8	1.4	10.3	4 646	84.0	16.0	2.39	1.95
Lake of the Woods	20.7	3 238	58.8	41.2	34.7	2.7	10.3	1 903	85.3	14.7	2.45	1.80
Le Sueur	13.7	10 858	88.7	11.3	9.0	0.9	3.8	9 630	83.3	16.7	2.70	2.17
Lincoln	-1.9	3 043	87.2	12.8	5.2	2.7	7.1	2 653	80.3	19.7	2.45	1.93
Lyon	7.1	10 298	94.3	5.7	0.5	1.8	7.7	9 715	68.4	31.6	2.70	2.03
McLeod	13.8	14 087	95.5	4.5	0.3	1.4	7.7	13 449	78.2	21.8	2.73	1.93
Mahnomen	9.1	2 700	72.9	27.1	21.6	0.9	7.1	1 969	77.2	22.8	2.60	2.58
Marshall	-2.2	4 791	85.6	14.4	5.2	2.4	10.5	4 101	83.6	16.4	2.57	1.83
Martin	-0.7	9 800	92.5	7.5	1.1	1.9	8.2	9 067	77.4	22.6	2.44	2.05
Meeker	12.3	9 821	87.5	12.5	8.8	1.4	5.0	8 590	81.7	18.3	2.71	1.97
Mille Lacs	25.0	10 467	82.5	17.5	13.9	0.8	4.2	8 638	80.1	19.9	2.63	2.09
Morrison	13.6	13 870	85.2	14.8	12.0	0.8	3.5	11 816	81.9	18.1	2.76	2.08
Mower	3.7	16 251	95.9	4.1	0.3	1.2	5.0	15 582	78.2	21.8	2.53	2.05
Murray	-1.0	4 357	85.4	14.6	7.2	1.8	11.9	3 722	84.2	15.8	2.48	2.12
Nicollet	12.3	11 240	94.7	5.3	0.3	1.2	8.7	10 642	75.8	24.2	2.72	2.05
Nobles	3.3	8 465	93.8	6.2	0.3	2.1	7.3	7 939	75.0	25.0	2.61	2.48
Norman	-3.5	3 455	87.1	12.9	1.5	4.0	13.3	3 010	81.0	19.0	2.53	1.90
Olmsted	19.3	49 422	96.7	3.3	0.5	0.7	3.9	47 807	75.9	24.1	2.71	1.98
Otter Tail	16.2	33 862	67.0	33.0	28.8	1.6	7.7	22 671	80.0	20.0	2.60	1.91
Pennington	6.8	6 033	91.6	8.4	1.0	1.9	10.7	5 525	74.4	25.6	2.55	1.87
Pine	31.2	15 353	64.7	35.3	29.8	1.8	4.5	9 939	83.7	16.3	2.61	2.17
Pipestone	-0.2	4 434	91.8	8.2	0.2	2.7	13.1	4 069	78.0	22.0	2.49	1.96
Polk	0.7	14 008	86.2	13.8	6.6	2.5	9.1	12 070	74.1	25.9	2.64	1.99
Pope	9.1	5 827	77.4	22.6	17.6	1.8	3.4	4 513	81.0	19.0	2.54	1.93
Ramsey	5.6	206 448	97.5	2.5	0.4	0.5	2.5	201 236	63.5	36.5	2.67	2.07
Red Lake	-0.2	1 883	91.7	8.3	2.0	1.7	10.2	1 727	80.1	19.9	2.56	1.74
Redwood	1.8	7 230	92.3	7.7	0.9	2.6	9.4	6 674	79.8	20.2	2.55	2.02
Renville	-0.2	7 413	91.4	8.6	1.0	1.4	11.9	6 779	80.9	19.1	2.55	2.18
Rice	15.5	20 061	94.2	5.8	3.1	0.9	4.4	18 888	77.9	22.1	2.79	2.12
Rock	2.4	4 137	92.9	7.1	0.6	1.4	12.5	3 843	77.9	22.1	2.59	2.05
Roseau	14.3	7 101	87.2	12.8	5.0	2.8	11.1	6 190	83.8	16.2	2.74	1.89
St. Louis	4.7	95 800	86.2	13.8	9.3	1.1	6.0	82 619	74.7	25.3	2.47	1.88
Scott	58.5	31 609	97.1	2.9	0.5	1.1	4.3	30 692	86.5	13.5	2.99	2.24
Sherburne	58.2	22 827	94.5	5.5	3.7	0.8	2.5	21 581	84.1	15.9	3.05	2.16
Sibley	8.4	6 024	95.8	4.2	0.4	1.3	4.6	5 772	80.9	19.1	2.69	2.23
Stearns	19.7	50 291	94.7	5.3	2.7	0.7	3.6	47 604	73.8	26.2	2.83	2.11
Steele	13.3	13 306	96.5	3.5	0.8	0.9	2.7	12 846	80.1	19.9	2.69	2.09
Stevens	-1.9	4 074	92.1	7.9	1.5	2.0	7.2	3 751	70.4	29.6	2.61	2.00
Swift	2.0	4 821	90.3	9.7	1.2	2.6	13.1	4 353	77.0	23.0	2.54	1.90
Todd	8.8	11 900	78.5	21.5	15.7	2.4	9.3	9 342	83.2	16.8	2.70	2.01
Traverse	-3.4	2 199	78.1	21.9	10.3	4.5	17.5	1 717	80.5	19.5	2.42	2.02
Wabasha	13.6	9 066	91.3	8.7	2.6	1.5	5.5	8 277	82.4	17.6	2.67	2.09
Wadena	9.0	6 334	85.7	14.3	8.3	2.4	6.0	5 426	77.6	22.4	2.58	2.00
Waseca	6.2	7 427	95.0	5.0	1.1	1.3	7.1	7 059	80.1	19.9	2.68	2.10
Washington	45.1	73 635	97.0	3.0	0.8	0.7	5.4	71 462	85.7	14.3	2.88	2.10
Watonwan	2.1	5 036	91.9	8.1	1.0	1.6	12.4	4 627	77.1	22.9	2.63	2.19
Wilkin	-1.9	3 105	88.6	11.4	0.7	3.1	15.1	2 752	80.8	19.2	2.71	1.83
Winona	10.7	19 551	95.9	4.1	0.8	0.8	4.5	18 744	70.8	29.2	2.63	2.06
Wright	36.7	34 355	91.6	8.4	6.0	1.1	3.1	31 465	84.4	15.6	2.98	2.04
Yellow Medicine	-3.6	4 873	91.1	8.9	0.6	2.7	10.1	4 439	79.5	20.5	2.53	2.00

Table B. States and Counties

STATE/County code	MSA/PMSA/NECMA code[1]	County type[2]	STATE County	Population, 2000				Population, 1990				Population and population characteristics, 2000					
												Race (percent)					
												One race					
				Land area, 2000[3] (sq km)	Total persons	Rank	Per square kilometer	Land area, 1990[3] (sq km)	Total persons	Rank	Per square kilometer	White	Black or African American	American Indian or Alaska Native	Asian	Native Hawaiian and other Pacific Islander	Some other race
				1	2	3	4	5	6	7	8	9	10	11	12	13	14
28 000	...		MISSISSIPPI	121 488	2 844 658	X	23.4	121 506	2 575 475	X	21.2	61.4	36.3	0.4	0.7	0.0	0.5
28 001	...	7	Adams	1 192	34 340	1 260	28.8	1 192	35 356	1 119	29.7	46.0	52.8	0.1	0.2	0.0	0.2
28 003	...	7	Alcorn	1 036	34 558	1 263	33.4	1 036	31 722	1 220	30.6	87.4	11.1	0.1	0.2	0.1	0.6
28 005	...	9	Amite	1 890	13 599	2 190	7.2	1 890	13 328	2 111	7.1	56.4	42.7	0.1	0.1	0.0	0.2
28 007	...	6	Attala	1 904	19 661	1 814	10.3	1 904	18 481	1 764	9.7	58.3	40.0	0.2	0.3	0.0	0.6
28 009	...	8	Benton	1 054	8 026	2 602	7.6	1 054	8 046	2 560	7.6	61.7	36.8	0.6	0.0	0.0	0.3
28 011	...	5	Bolivar	2 270	40 633	1 096	17.9	2 270	41 875	958	18.4	33.2	65.1	0.1	0.5	0.0	0.5
28 013	...	9	Calhoun	1 519	15 069	2 086	9.9	1 519	14 908	1 993	9.8	69.4	28.7	0.1	0.1	0.0	1.1
28 015	...	9	Carroll	1 626	10 769	2 378	6.6	1 626	9 237	2 451	5.7	62.7	36.6	0.1	0.2	0.0	0.1
28 017	...	7	Chickasaw	1 299	19 440	1 821	15.0	1 299	18 085	1 786	13.9	56.9	41.3	0.2	0.2	0.0	1.0
28 019	...	9	Choctaw	1 085	9 758	2 465	9.0	1 086	9 071	2 462	8.4	68.0	30.7	0.3	0.1	0.0	0.4
28 021	...	8	Claiborne	1 261	11 831	2 302	9.4	1 261	11 370	2 262	9.0	15.2	84.1	0.1	0.1	0.0	0.1
28 023	...	7	Clarke	1 790	17 955	1 899	10.0	1 791	17 313	1 832	9.7	64.5	34.8	0.1	0.1	0.0	0.2
28 025	...	7	Clay	1 058	21 979	1 694	20.8	1 058	21 120	1 624	20.0	42.8	56.3	0.1	0.2	0.0	0.2
28 027	...	7	Coahoma	1 435	30 622	1 384	21.3	1 435	31 665	1 225	22.1	29.3	69.2	0.1	0.5	0.0	0.3
28 029	...	6	Copiah	2 011	28 757	1 429	14.3	2 012	27 592	1 370	13.7	47.8	51.0	0.1	0.2	0.0	0.5
28 031	...	7	Covington	1 072	19 407	1 823	18.1	1 072	16 527	1 888	15.4	63.4	35.6	0.1	0.1	0.0	0.2
28 033	4920	1	De Soto	1 238	107 199	498	86.6	1 239	67 910	652	54.8	85.8	11.4	0.3	0.6	0.0	1.1
28 035	3285	5	Forrest	1 208	72 604	686	60.1	1 209	68 314	646	56.5	64.3	33.6	0.2	0.7	0.0	0.4
28 037	...	9	Franklin	1 462	8 448	2 568	5.8	1 462	8 377	2 525	5.7	62.8	36.3	0.2	0.1	0.0	0.8
28 039	...	6	George	1 239	19 144	1 840	15.5	1 239	16 673	1 870	13.5	89.4	8.8	0.2	0.2	0.0	0.8
28 041	...	8	Greene	1 846	13 299	2 204	7.2	1 847	10 220	2 370	5.5	72.8	26.2	0.2	0.1	0.0	0.3
28 043	...	7	Grenada	1 092	23 263	1 630	21.3	1 093	21 555	1 600	19.7	57.9	40.9	0.1	0.3	0.0	0.1
28 045	0920	2	Hancock	1 235	42 967	1 037	34.8	1 235	31 760	1 219	25.7	90.2	6.8	0.6	0.9	0.0	0.3
28 047	0920	2	Harrison	1 505	189 601	290	126.0	1 505	165 365	288	109.9	73.1	21.1	0.5	2.6	0.1	0.9
28 049	3560	2	Hinds	2 251	250 800	229	111.4	2 251	254 441	197	113.0	37.3	61.1	0.1	0.6	0.0	0.2
28 051	...	6	Holmes	1 958	21 609	1 713	11.0	1 958	21 604	1 598	11.0	20.5	78.7	0.1	0.2	0.0	0.2
28 053	...	7	Humphreys	1 083	11 206	2 356	10.3	1 083	12 134	2 204	11.2	27.2	71.5	0.1	0.3	0.0	0.6
28 055	...	9	Issaquena	1 070	2 274	3 043	2.1	1 070	1 909	3 074	1.8	36.3	62.8	0.1	0.0	0.0	0.2
28 057	...	7	Itawamba	1 379	22 770	1 657	16.5	1 379	20 017	1 676	14.5	92.5	6.5	0.1	0.2	0.0	0.3
28 059	0920	2	Jackson	1 883	131 420	407	69.8	1 882	115 243	400	61.2	75.4	20.9	0.3	1.6	0.0	0.7
28 061	...	9	Jasper	1 751	18 149	1 890	10.4	1 751	17 114	1 843	9.8	46.5	52.9	0.1	0.1	0.0	0.1
28 063	...	9	Jefferson	1 345	9 740	2 467	7.2	1 345	8 653	2 495	6.4	13.1	86.5	0.1	0.1	0.0	0.0
28 065	...	9	Jefferson Davis	1 058	13 962	2 163	13.2	1 058	14 051	2 053	13.3	41.7	57.4	0.1	0.2	0.0	0.1
28 067	...	5	Jones	1 797	64 958	748	36.1	1 797	62 031	702	34.5	71.1	26.3	0.4	0.3	0.0	1.4
28 069	...	9	Kemper	1 984	10 453	2 401	5.3	1 984	10 356	2 354	5.2	39.0	58.1	2.1	0.1	0.0	0.1
28 071	...	7	Lafayette	1 635	38 744	1 146	23.7	1 635	31 826	1 217	19.5	71.9	25.0	0.2	1.7	0.0	0.4
28 073	3285	7	Lamar	1 287	39 070	1 136	30.4	1 288	30 424	1 272	23.6	85.3	12.9	0.2	0.7	0.0	0.3
28 075	...	5	Lauderdale	1 822	78 161	650	42.9	1 822	75 555	596	41.5	60.1	38.2	0.2	0.5	0.0	0.3
28 077	...	9	Lawrence	1 115	13 258	2 207	11.9	1 115	12 458	2 185	11.2	66.9	32.1	0.2	0.3	0.0	0.1
28 079	...	6	Leake	1 509	20 940	1 740	13.9	1 509	18 436	1 766	12.2	56.1	37.4	4.6	0.1	0.0	1.1
28 081	...	5	Lee	1 164	75 755	661	65.1	1 165	65 579	668	56.3	73.7	24.5	0.1	0.5	0.0	0.4
28 083	...	7	Leflore	1 533	37 947	1 167	24.8	1 533	37 341	1 063	24.4	30.0	67.7	0.1	0.6	0.0	1.0
28 085	...	7	Lincoln	1 517	33 166	1 310	21.9	1 517	30 278	1 281	20.0	69.4	29.7	0.2	0.2	0.0	0.2
28 087	...	5	Lowndes	1 301	61 586	790	47.3	1 301	59 308	732	45.6	56.5	41.6	0.2	0.5	0.0	0.4
28 089	3560	2	Madison	1 857	74 674	670	40.2	1 863	53 794	799	28.9	60.3	37.5	0.1	1.3	0.0	0.3
28 091	...	7	Marion	1 405	25 595	1 532	18.2	1 405	25 544	1 443	18.2	67.0	31.9	0.2	0.2	0.0	0.1
28 093	...	6	Marshall	1 829	34 993	1 249	19.1	1 830	30 361	1 275	16.6	48.4	50.4	0.2	0.1	0.0	0.1
28 095	...	7	Monroe	1 979	38 014	1 165	19.2	1 979	36 582	1 087	18.5	68.4	30.8	0.1	0.2	0.0	0.1
28 097	...	7	Montgomery	1 054	12 189	2 283	11.6	1 054	12 387	2 190	11.8	54.3	45.0	0.1	0.3	0.0	0.3
28 099	...	7	Neshoba	1 476	28 684	1 430	19.4	1 476	24 800	1 470	16.8	65.5	19.3	13.8	0.2	0.0	0.3
28 101	...	7	Newton	1 497	21 838	1 698	14.6	1 497	20 291	1 661	13.6	65.0	30.4	3.7	0.2	0.0	0.3
28 103	...	9	Noxubee	1 799	12 548	2 260	7.0	1 800	12 604	2 177	7.0	29.5	69.3	0.2	0.1	0.0	0.4
28 105	...	7	Oktibbeha	1 185	42 902	1 040	36.2	1 186	38 375	1 043	32.4	58.7	37.4	0.2	2.5	0.0	0.5
28 107	...	7	Panola	1 772	34 274	1 271	19.3	1 772	29 996	1 297	16.9	50.5	48.4	0.2	0.2	0.0	0.4
28 109	...	6	Pearl River	2 101	48 621	936	23.1	2 102	38 714	1 035	18.4	85.6	12.2	0.5	0.3	0.0	0.3
28 111	...	9	Perry	1 676	12 138	2 288	7.2	1 676	10 865	2 307	6.5	76.2	22.6	0.3	0.1	0.0	0.3
28 113	...	7	Pike	1 059	38 940	1 143	36.8	1 059	36 882	1 078	34.8	51.2	47.5	0.2	0.3	0.0	0.2
28 115	...	7	Pontotoc	1 288	26 726	1 494	20.8	1 288	22 237	1 568	17.3	84.4	14.0	0.3	0.1	0.0	0.7
28 117	...	7	Prentiss	1 075	25 556	1 537	23.8	1 075	23 278	1 526	21.7	85.9	12.9	0.2	0.2	0.0	0.2
28 119	...	9	Quitman	1 049	10 117	2 435	9.6	1 049	10 490	2 337	10.0	30.5	68.6	0.1	0.2	0.0	0.1
28 121	3560	2	Rankin	2 006	115 327	467	57.5	2 006	87 161	523	43.5	81.0	17.1	0.2	0.7	0.0	0.4
28 123	...	6	Scott	1 578	28 423	1 434	18.0	1 578	24 137	1 489	15.3	57.2	38.9	0.3	0.2	0.0	2.5
28 125	...	9	Sharkey	1 108	6 580	2 730	5.9	1 108	7 066	2 651	6.4	29.4	69.3	0.2	0.3	0.0	0.3
28 127	...	6	Simpson	1 525	27 639	1 460	18.1	1 525	23 953	1 495	15.7	64.4	34.3	0.1	0.1	0.0	0.5
28 129	...	8	Smith	1 647	16 182	2 009	9.8	1 647	14 798	2 001	9.0	76.1	23.1	0.1	0.1	0.0	0.2
28 131	...	6	Stone	1 153	13 622	2 189	11.8	1 154	10 750	2 312	9.3	79.4	19.2	0.3	0.2	0.0	0.2

[1]MSA = Metropolitan Statistical Area. PMSA = Primary MSA. NECMA = New England County Metropolitan Area. See **Appendix A** for explanation of these concepts. See Appendix B for list of metropolitan areas identified by type, with component counties.
[2]County typology code from the Economic Research Service of USDA. See Appendix A for definition.
[3]Dry land or land partially or temporarily covered by water.

Table B. States and Counties

STATE County	Population and population characteristics, 2000 (cont'd)								Population and population characteristics, 1990				
	Race (percent) (cont'd)								Race (percent)				
		Race alone or in combination											
	Two or more races	White	Black	American Indian or Alaska Native	Asian	Native Hawaiian and other Pacific Islander	Some other race	Hispanic[1]	White	Black or African American	American Indian or Alaska Native	Asian and Pacific Islander	Hispanic[1]
	15	16	17	18	19	20	21	22	23	24	25	26	27
MISSISSIPPI	0.7	61.9	36.6	0.7	0.8	0.1	0.7	1.4	63.5	35.6	0.3	0.5	0.6
Adams	0.6	46.4	53.1	0.4	0.4	0.1	0.3	0.8	51.0	48.7	0.1	0.2	0.4
Alcorn	0.6	87.9	11.3	0.4	0.3	0.1	0.7	1.3	88.5	11.2	0.1	0.2	0.4
Amite	0.5	56.8	42.8	0.5	0.1	0.0	0.3	0.8	54.6	45.3	0.1	0.0	0.2
Attala	0.6	58.8	40.2	0.5	0.3	0.0	0.8	1.4	60.1	39.5	0.2	0.2	0.3
Benton	0.6	62.2	36.9	0.9	0.1	0.0	0.5	1.0	60.5	39.4	0.1	0.0	0.5
Bolivar	0.6	33.6	65.4	0.2	0.6	0.1	0.7	1.2	36.4	62.9	0.1	0.3	0.9
Calhoun	0.6	69.9	28.9	0.4	0.2	0.1	1.2	2.1	72.6	27.0	0.1	0.0	0.5
Carroll	0.4	62.9	36.8	0.2	0.2	0.0	0.2	0.7	60.2	39.6	0.1	0.1	0.5
Chickasaw	0.5	57.3	41.4	0.4	0.3	0.1	1.1	2.3	61.2	38.6	0.1	0.1	0.5
Choctaw	0.4	68.3	30.9	0.5	0.3	0.0	0.5	0.8	69.7	30.1	0.1	0.1	0.3
Claiborne	0.4	15.4	84.4	0.2	0.2	0.0	0.2	0.8	17.5	82.1	0.2	0.1	0.5
Clarke	0.3	64.7	34.9	0.3	0.1	0.0	0.2	0.7	65.3	34.5	0.0	0.0	0.4
Clay	0.4	43.2	56.6	0.2	0.3	0.1	0.3	0.9	46.3	53.3	0.1	0.2	0.4
Coahoma	0.6	29.6	69.6	0.3	0.7	0.1	0.5	0.9	34.7	64.6	0.1	0.4	0.9
Copiah	0.5	48.2	51.2	0.3	0.3	0.0	0.6	1.2	49.3	50.4	0.1	0.1	0.4
Covington	0.6	63.8	35.9	0.4	0.3	0.1	0.3	0.8	64.7	35.1	0.1	0.1	0.3
De Soto	0.8	86.4	11.6	0.5	0.8	0.1	1.4	2.3	86.7	12.8	0.2	0.2	0.5
Forrest	0.8	65.0	33.9	0.5	0.9	0.1	0.6	1.3	68.3	30.7	0.1	0.7	0.7
Franklin	0.6	63.2	36.5	0.7	0.1	0.0	0.1	0.5	63.1	36.8	0.0	0.0	0.3
George	0.6	89.9	8.9	0.6	0.2	0.1	1.0	1.6	90.1	9.5	0.2	0.1	0.3
Greene	0.4	73.1	26.3	0.4	0.1	0.1	0.4	0.8	78.3	21.5	0.1	0.1	0.6
Grenada	0.5	58.3	41.1	0.3	0.5	0.1	0.3	0.6	58.3	41.4	0.1	0.1	0.4
Hancock	1.1	91.2	7.1	1.2	1.1	0.1	0.6	1.8	90.1	8.7	0.4	0.5	1.7
Harrison	1.7	74.6	21.6	1.0	3.1	0.2	1.3	2.6	77.2	19.5	0.3	2.6	1.8
Hinds	0.6	37.7	61.5	0.3	0.7	0.1	0.3	0.8	48.4	50.9	0.1	0.5	0.5
Holmes	0.5	20.7	79.0	0.3	0.3	0.0	0.2	0.9	24.0	75.8	0.1	0.1	0.3
Humphreys	0.3	27.3	71.8	0.2	0.3	0.0	0.7	1.5	31.8	67.8	0.1	0.4	0.6
Issaquena	0.6	36.8	63.1	0.5	0.0	0.0	0.3	0.4	43.6	56.2	0.1	0.2	0.3
Itawamba	0.4	92.9	6.6	0.4	0.3	0.0	0.4	1.0	92.9	6.8	0.1	0.2	0.5
Jackson	1.1	76.3	21.2	0.7	1.9	0.1	1.0	2.1	78.2	20.5	0.2	1.0	0.9
Jasper	0.4	46.8	53.1	0.3	0.2	0.0	0.1	0.6	49.1	50.8	0.0	0.0	0.2
Jefferson	0.2	13.2	86.7	0.2	0.2	0.0	0.0	0.7	13.7	86.2	0.0	0.0	0.5
Jefferson Davis	0.6	42.1	57.7	0.4	0.2	0.0	0.2	0.8	45.1	54.6	0.2	0.2	0.3
Jones	0.5	71.5	26.5	0.6	0.3	0.0	1.5	2.0	74.5	25.0	0.3	0.2	0.3
Kemper	0.6	39.4	58.5	2.3	0.2	0.1	0.2	0.7	42.6	55.4	1.9	0.1	0.3
Lafayette	0.8	72.5	25.2	0.4	2.0	0.1	0.7	1.1	72.7	25.1	0.1	2.0	0.6
Lamar	0.6	85.9	13.1	0.5	0.8	0.0	0.5	1.1	87.4	12.0	0.1	0.4	0.6
Lauderdale	0.6	60.6	38.5	0.4	0.7	0.1	0.5	1.1	64.5	34.8	0.1	0.5	0.7
Lawrence	0.4	67.3	32.3	0.3	0.3	0.0	0.3	0.7	66.6	33.2	0.1	0.1	0.4
Leake	0.6	56.5	37.7	4.8	0.2	0.1	1.3	2.1	60.1	35.6	4.2	0.0	0.3
Lee	0.7	74.3	24.8	0.4	0.7	0.0	0.6	1.2	78.2	21.4	0.1	0.2	0.5
Leflore	0.5	30.2	68.0	0.3	0.8	0.1	1.1	1.9	38.9	60.6	0.1	0.3	0.4
Lincoln	0.4	69.7	29.8	0.4	0.3	0.0	0.2	0.7	69.9	29.9	0.1	0.2	0.2
Lowndes	0.9	57.1	41.9	0.5	0.8	0.1	0.6	1.1	61.9	37.2	0.1	0.5	0.8
Madison	0.5	60.7	37.7	0.3	1.5	0.0	0.4	1.0	55.4	44.1	0.1	0.4	0.5
Marion	0.6	67.4	32.2	0.5	0.3	0.0	0.2	0.6	69.4	30.2	0.1	0.2	0.5
Marshall	0.6	48.8	50.6	0.4	0.2	0.0	0.5	1.2	48.9	50.7	0.2	0.1	0.4
Monroe	0.5	68.7	31.0	0.3	0.2	0.0	0.2	0.7	69.4	30.3	0.1	0.1	0.5
Montgomery	0.4	54.5	45.2	0.3	0.4	0.1	0.2	0.8	55.8	43.9	0.1	0.1	0.4
Neshoba	0.8	66.0	19.7	14.3	0.3	0.1	0.5	1.2	68.3	18.6	12.9	0.1	0.4
Newton	0.4	65.4	30.6	3.8	0.2	0.0	0.4	0.9	67.5	28.7	3.6	0.0	0.4
Noxubee	0.6	29.8	69.6	0.5	0.2	0.0	0.5	1.1	31.4	68.1	0.3	0.1	0.2
Oktibbeha	0.7	59.2	37.7	0.3	2.8	0.1	0.7	1.1	62.7	34.3	0.1	2.7	0.9
Panola	0.4	50.8	48.5	0.3	0.2	0.0	0.5	1.1	51.3	48.4	0.1	0.1	0.5
Pearl River	1.1	86.6	12.4	1.2	0.4	0.1	0.5	1.4	85.0	14.3	0.4	0.2	0.8
Perry	0.5	76.6	22.7	0.6	0.1	0.1	0.4	1.0	76.7	22.5	0.7	0.0	0.4
Pike	0.5	51.5	47.8	0.4	0.5	0.1	0.3	0.7	54.0	45.7	0.1	0.1	0.5
Pontotoc	0.5	84.8	14.1	0.5	0.2	0.0	0.9	1.8	85.1	14.6	0.1	0.1	0.3
Prentiss	0.7	86.5	13.2	0.6	0.2	0.1	0.3	0.7	88.0	11.8	0.1	0.1	0.4
Quitman	0.5	30.8	69.0	0.3	0.3	0.0	0.2	0.5	40.5	59.0	0.2	0.2	0.5
Rankin	0.6	81.6	17.3	0.4	0.8	0.0	0.6	1.3	82.6	16.8	0.1	0.4	0.6
Scott	0.9	57.9	39.3	0.6	0.3	0.1	2.9	5.8	61.4	38.0	0.2	0.1	0.6
Sharkey	0.6	29.8	69.6	0.5	0.3	0.0	0.4	1.3	33.1	66.3	0.1	0.3	0.7
Simpson	0.6	64.9	34.5	0.4	0.2	0.0	0.6	1.2	67.3	32.3	0.2	0.1	0.3
Smith	0.4	76.4	23.3	0.3	0.1	0.1	0.3	0.6	77.8	21.9	0.1	0.0	0.5
Stone	0.7	80.1	19.3	0.6	0.2	0.0	0.4	1.2	77.8	21.8	0.2	0.1	0.5

[1] Hispanic persons may be of any race.

Table B. States and Counties

STATE County	Population and population characteristics, 2000										
	Age (percent)									Median age (years)	Percent Female
	Under 5 years	5 to 17 years	18 to 24 years	25 to 34 years	35 to 44 years	45 to 54 years	55 to 64 years	65 to 74 years	75 years and over		
	28	29	30	31	32	33	34	35	36	37	38
MISSISSIPPI	7.2	20.1	10.9	13.4	15.0	12.7	8.6	6.5	5.5	33.8	51.7
Adams	6.8	20.0	8.6	10.6	15.0	13.9	9.6	8.5	7.0	38.1	53.7
Alcorn	6.5	17.4	9.1	13.4	14.5	13.6	10.7	7.8	7.1	37.6	51.6
Amite	5.9	20.1	8.5	11.2	14.3	13.7	10.9	8.4	7.0	38.3	51.7
Attala	6.4	19.5	9.2	12.1	13.1	12.5	9.9	9.0	8.3	37.3	52.2
Benton	7.4	19.5	10.0	12.2	13.6	12.1	9.9	8.5	6.8	35.6	51.4
Bolivar	7.4	22.2	14.0	12.9	12.8	12.2	7.4	5.5	5.6	29.8	53.2
Calhoun	6.5	18.7	8.4	13.4	13.6	13.0	9.7	8.4	8.2	37.4	52.4
Carroll	5.5	18.9	9.6	11.6	15.1	14.4	11.3	7.3	6.2	38.1	50.2
Chickasaw	7.6	21.0	9.3	12.9	14.7	12.0	9.0	6.9	6.6	34.4	51.9
Choctaw	6.8	21.0	8.8	10.7	14.2	13.7	9.8	7.8	7.1	36.9	52.1
Claiborne	6.8	19.5	23.1	9.9	12.3	11.1	6.8	5.0	5.5	25.6	53.9
Clarke	6.8	20.0	8.6	12.1	14.6	13.1	9.6	8.2	7.0	36.8	52.3
Clay	7.5	21.4	10.4	12.1	14.4	13.1	8.1	6.7	6.4	33.9	52.9
Coahoma	8.9	24.1	10.3	11.7	13.6	11.6	7.6	6.3	6.0	30.5	54.1
Copiah	6.6	20.3	12.5	11.6	15.1	12.7	8.4	6.8	5.9	34.0	51.8
Covington	7.5	21.3	9.6	13.2	14.2	11.9	9.3	6.9	6.1	33.8	51.9
De Soto	7.8	20.4	8.2	15.8	16.9	13.1	9.0	5.5	3.4	33.7	50.5
Forrest	6.9	17.6	18.2	14.3	13.4	11.0	7.3	5.9	5.4	29.7	52.8
Franklin	6.5	20.8	8.8	11.2	15.0	13.2	9.4	8.2	7.0	37.0	52.0
George	7.8	21.4	9.4	14.0	14.7	12.3	9.6	6.2	4.7	33.3	49.8
Greene	7.0	17.1	13.1	16.6	15.5	12.0	8.6	5.5	4.6	32.4	43.5
Grenada	6.9	20.3	9.0	12.8	14.7	12.8	9.1	7.4	7.0	35.7	53.2
Hancock	6.3	18.8	7.3	12.2	15.8	14.4	11.2	8.3	5.7	38.5	50.4
Harrison	7.1	18.9	11.1	14.5	16.1	12.8	8.5	6.5	4.6	33.9	50.2
Hinds	7.4	20.5	12.1	13.9	15.0	12.6	7.5	5.7	5.3	31.9	53.0
Holmes	7.7	24.4	12.4	11.2	13.6	10.6	7.7	6.4	6.0	29.7	53.4
Humphreys	7.8	24.9	10.7	12.3	13.5	11.5	7.4	6.0	6.0	30.5	53.3
Issaquena	5.7	21.9	10.9	14.8	16.1	10.6	9.3	6.2	4.5	33.1	46.8
Itawamba	6.1	18.1	10.6	13.5	14.3	12.7	10.6	7.6	6.6	36.2	51.5
Jackson	7.0	20.6	9.3	13.5	16.3	13.5	9.4	6.1	4.2	34.7	50.4
Jasper	6.9	21.0	9.6	12.3	14.4	12.6	9.2	7.2	6.7	35.1	52.3
Jefferson	7.3	21.5	12.1	12.3	16.2	12.0	7.6	5.6	5.3	32.4	52.7
Jefferson Davis	7.2	21.2	9.9	11.7	13.6	12.9	9.6	7.1	6.7	35.0	52.7
Jones	7.0	18.8	10.5	12.6	14.7	13.0	9.2	7.9	6.3	35.8	51.6
Kemper	6.7	18.8	12.5	11.8	13.4	12.6	9.2	7.4	7.7	35.2	52.0
Lafayette	5.4	14.2	27.1	13.8	12.5	10.2	6.9	5.1	4.7	26.9	50.8
Lamar	7.4	20.6	10.9	14.5	15.9	12.9	8.1	5.7	4.1	32.6	51.7
Lauderdale	7.1	19.5	9.8	13.5	14.5	12.8	8.6	7.1	7.0	35.0	52.5
Lawrence	6.8	20.5	9.4	12.2	15.3	13.0	9.6	7.5	5.8	35.8	52.0
Leake	7.3	19.6	10.1	13.2	13.8	12.8	8.9	7.8	6.5	34.8	50.5
Lee	7.5	20.2	8.5	14.4	16.1	13.0	8.8	6.0	5.4	34.6	52.0
Leflore	7.8	21.9	13.1	13.4	13.6	11.1	7.1	5.8	6.1	30.1	52.0
Lincoln	7.1	19.6	9.5	12.7	14.9	13.3	9.0	7.6	6.4	35.8	52.0
Lowndes	7.7	20.9	10.6	13.9	15.3	12.4	7.9	5.9	5.3	32.7	52.7
Madison	7.8	20.8	8.9	15.0	17.4	13.3	7.0	4.9	4.8	33.4	52.6
Marion	6.9	20.9	9.5	12.5	14.4	12.9	8.6	7.6	6.6	35.1	51.6
Marshall	7.0	19.5	11.8	13.2	15.4	12.9	9.1	6.5	4.6	33.9	50.5
Monroe	6.6	20.6	8.7	13.1	14.5	12.8	9.7	7.2	6.8	35.7	52.7
Montgomery	6.6	20.1	8.9	11.2	14.0	12.7	9.7	8.6	8.0	37.3	53.6
Neshoba	7.8	20.5	9.0	13.1	13.9	12.7	8.9	7.5	6.6	34.7	52.3
Newton	7.1	19.0	11.2	12.5	13.5	12.5	9.2	7.8	7.2	35.1	52.0
Noxubee	8.1	22.6	10.3	12.1	14.6	11.7	7.7	6.8	6.1	32.3	52.5
Oktibbeha	6.0	15.1	29.6	13.1	11.8	9.6	6.5	4.6	4.0	24.8	50.0
Panola	7.7	21.7	10.4	12.8	14.5	12.3	8.5	6.6	5.5	33.0	52.1
Pearl River	7.0	19.9	9.4	12.3	14.8	13.7	10.2	7.5	5.1	35.9	51.4
Perry	7.7	21.0	10.0	13.1	14.9	12.7	9.5	6.4	4.6	33.5	51.1
Pike	7.4	20.3	10.1	11.9	14.1	13.3	8.8	7.3	6.8	35.2	53.2
Pontotoc	7.2	20.4	8.7	14.0	15.5	12.8	8.5	6.8	6.1	34.8	51.4
Prentiss	6.8	18.2	11.6	13.4	13.8	12.5	9.9	7.3	6.6	35.0	51.5
Quitman	8.1	23.9	9.6	12.4	13.3	11.1	8.4	6.7	6.5	31.8	53.6
Rankin	7.0	18.9	9.1	15.6	16.8	14.2	8.9	5.8	3.7	34.6	51.1
Scott	7.4	21.2	9.6	13.2	14.7	12.7	8.7	6.7	5.7	33.8	51.4
Sharkey	8.6	24.4	10.4	10.9	13.9	13.0	7.4	5.5	5.8	30.8	53.0
Simpson	7.1	20.8	9.4	12.7	14.8	13.0	9.1	7.2	5.9	35.0	51.4
Smith	7.0	20.5	8.7	12.9	14.4	12.6	10.0	7.8	6.1	35.6	51.1
Stone	6.9	19.9	12.2	12.6	14.8	13.0	9.4	6.3	4.8	33.6	50.4

Table B. States and Counties

STATE County	Population and population characteristics, 1990										Population—change, 1980–2000				
	Age (percent)										Total persons			Percent change	
	Under 5 years	5 to 17 years	18 to 24 years	25 to 34 years	35 to 44 years	45 to 54 years	55 to 64 years	65 to 74 years	75 years and over	Percent Female	2000	1990	1980	1990–2000	1980–1990
	39	40	41	42	43	44	45	46	47	48	49	50	51	52	53
MISSISSIPPI	7.6	21.4	11.4	15.5	13.6	9.6	8.3	7.0	5.5	52.2	2 844 658	2 575 475	2 520 770	10.5	2.2
Adams	7.5	21.5	8.5	14.6	13.8	9.8	9.9	8.3	6.1	54.0	34 340	35 356	38 071	-2.9	-7.1
Alcorn	6.3	19.2	9.4	14.5	14.5	11.5	9.2	8.4	7.0	52.1	34 558	31 722	33 036	8.9	-4.0
Amite	7.2	22.1	9.2	14.1	12.3	10.2	9.4	8.8	6.6	51.7	13 599	13 328	13 369	2.0	-0.3
Attala	6.9	20.4	9.5	13.1	12.1	9.8	9.8	9.8	8.6	53.1	19 661	18 481	19 865	6.4	-7.0
Benton	7.4	22.4	10.1	15.1	11.4	9.3	9.5	8.4	6.3	51.8	8 026	8 046	8 153	-0.2	-1.3
Bolivar	8.7	25.1	14.3	12.9	12.0	8.0	6.5	6.6	5.8	54.0	40 633	41 875	45 965	-3.0	-8.9
Calhoun	6.8	19.5	10.3	13.7	13.0	10.4	9.4	8.8	8.1	52.2	15 069	14 908	15 664	1.1	-4.8
Carroll	7.1	21.6	8.9	13.9	12.9	11.3	9.1	8.5	6.7	52.1	10 769	9 237	9 776	16.6	-5.5
Chickasaw	8.1	21.8	10.4	15.1	12.7	9.6	8.5	7.4	6.4	52.3	19 440	18 085	17 851	7.5	1.3
Choctaw	7.0	23.2	8.8	14.2	12.7	10.4	9.0	7.5	7.2	52.6	9 758	9 071	8 996	7.6	0.8
Claiborne	7.0	21.0	24.2	12.3	10.6	7.0	6.3	6.3	5.4	53.7	11 831	11 370	12 279	4.1	-7.4
Clarke	6.9	22.1	9.8	14.0	13.5	9.7	9.1	7.8	7.1	52.6	17 955	17 313	16 945	3.7	2.2
Clay	7.8	23.2	11.1	14.5	13.3	8.7	8.0	7.2	6.1	52.7	21 979	21 120	21 082	4.1	0.2
Coahoma	9.0	25.2	10.6	13.5	11.4	8.3	7.9	7.4	6.8	54.5	30 622	31 665	36 918	-3.3	-14.2
Copiah	7.7	22.2	12.5	14.5	12.4	9.1	8.1	7.2	6.2	52.3	28 757	27 592	26 503	4.2	4.1
Covington	7.9	23.0	10.3	14.5	12.8	10.3	8.3	7.2	5.7	51.7	19 407	16 527	15 927	17.4	3.8
De Soto	7.9	21.0	10.1	17.0	15.8	12.2	7.8	5.3	3.0	50.8	107 199	67 910	53 930	57.9	25.9
Forrest	7.3	18.6	17.5	16.1	12.4	8.5	7.5	6.8	5.3	53.4	72 604	68 314	66 018	6.3	3.5
Franklin	7.5	22.1	8.3	14.3	12.8	8.8	10.0	8.9	7.3	52.4	8 448	8 377	8 208	0.8	2.1
George	7.6	22.7	10.6	15.2	13.5	10.9	8.2	6.4	4.9	50.8	19 144	16 673	15 297	14.8	9.0
Greene	7.1	22.9	10.3	16.6	13.5	10.2	7.7	6.7	5.0	48.5	13 299	10 220	9 827	30.1	4.0
Grenada	7.9	21.3	9.8	14.9	13.9	9.6	8.5	7.9	6.2	53.4	23 263	21 555	21 115	7.9	2.1
Hancock	7.2	20.1	8.8	14.6	13.7	10.8	10.5	9.4	4.8	50.2	42 967	31 760	24 496	35.3	29.7
Harrison	8.0	19.5	12.1	17.9	13.8	9.4	8.4	6.7	4.1	50.2	189 601	165 365	157 665	14.7	4.9
Hinds	7.7	20.2	12.2	17.3	14.5	9.1	7.8	6.4	4.8	53.2	250 800	254 441	250 998	-1.4	1.4
Holmes	8.9	26.1	11.6	13.1	10.9	7.6	7.4	7.4	6.9	53.8	21 609	21 604	22 970	0.0	-5.9
Humphreys	9.0	26.8	10.5	14.4	11.0	8.1	7.4	6.4	6.3	53.4	11 206	12 134	13 931	-7.6	-12.9
Issaquena	8.9	23.7	9.9	15.0	10.5	11.5	7.6	7.1	5.9	51.4	2 274	1 909	2 513	19.1	-24.0
Itawamba	6.1	18.2	11.8	13.9	13.5	11.4	9.8	8.5	6.9	51.1	22 770	20 017	20 518	13.8	-2.4
Jackson	7.6	22.1	9.7	16.1	15.1	11.4	8.7	5.9	3.5	50.9	131 420	115 243	118 015	14.0	-2.3
Jasper	7.0	23.6	9.9	14.3	12.6	9.3	8.5	7.8	7.0	52.3	18 149	17 114	17 265	6.0	-0.9
Jefferson	8.8	26.6	10.4	14.7	11.8	8.5	7.5	6.4	5.5	52.9	9 740	8 653	9 181	12.6	-5.8
Jefferson Davis	7.3	23.7	10.7	13.6	12.5	9.6	8.2	8.1	6.3	52.7	13 962	14 051	13 846	-0.6	1.5
Jones	6.9	20.5	10.0	14.8	13.9	10.1	9.6	8.0	6.3	52.3	64 958	62 031	61 912	4.7	0.2
Kemper	7.3	22.4	11.3	13.3	12.0	9.2	8.7	8.0	7.8	52.0	10 453	10 356	10 148	0.9	2.0
Lafayette	5.4	15.3	27.9	15.1	11.5	8.2	6.5	5.4	4.7	51.3	38 744	31 826	31 030	21.7	2.6
Lamar	7.9	22.0	10.7	17.6	15.1	9.8	7.5	5.5	3.9	51.3	39 070	30 424	23 821	28.4	27.7
Lauderdale	7.5	20.5	10.8	15.8	13.9	9.5	8.5	7.5	6.0	52.6	78 161	75 555	77 285	3.4	-2.2
Lawrence	7.0	23.1	9.3	14.8	12.7	10.2	9.3	7.6	5.9	52.0	13 258	12 458	12 518	6.4	-0.5
Leake	7.0	21.5	9.5	13.8	12.8	9.5	9.8	8.2	7.9	52.2	20 940	18 436	18 790	13.6	-1.9
Lee	8.0	20.2	9.8	17.1	14.7	10.4	8.2	6.5	5.1	52.3	75 755	65 579	57 061	15.5	14.9
Leflore	8.3	23.9	11.9	14.0	12.0	8.3	7.7	7.5	6.4	53.7	37 947	37 341	41 525	1.6	-10.1
Lincoln	6.4	21.9	9.3	14.3	14.1	9.9	9.2	8.1	6.6	52.5	33 166	30 278	30 174	9.5	0.3
Lowndes	8.5	21.2	12.1	17.4	14.0	9.2	7.5	5.7	4.4	52.3	61 586	59 308	57 304	3.8	3.5
Madison	8.8	20.8	10.8	20.1	14.7	8.3	6.9	5.1	4.4	52.6	74 674	53 794	41 613	38.8	29.3
Marion	7.1	23.4	9.4	14.5	13.0	9.2	9.0	8.1	6.3	51.8	25 595	25 544	25 708	0.2	-0.6
Marshall	8.1	21.9	12.3	15.4	12.9	9.7	8.3	6.7	4.8	52.2	34 993	30 361	29 296	15.3	3.6
Monroe	7.3	21.3	10.1	14.5	13.5	10.2	8.7	7.8	6.5	52.9	38 014	36 582	36 404	3.9	0.5
Montgomery	6.9	21.6	9.7	13.2	12.3	10.0	9.5	8.8	8.0	53.4	12 189	12 387	13 366	-1.6	-7.3
Neshoba	7.3	22.5	9.7	14.0	13.6	9.5	9.1	7.7	6.6	52.1	28 684	24 800	23 789	15.7	4.2
Newton	7.0	20.5	11.6	13.5	12.7	9.6	9.4	8.3	7.3	52.1	21 838	20 291	19 967	7.6	1.6
Noxubee	9.2	24.6	10.3	15.1	11.3	8.2	8.0	6.9	6.5	53.0	12 548	12 604	13 212	-0.4	-4.6
Oktibbeha	6.3	16.3	28.7	14.9	11.2	7.7	6.0	4.8	4.1	50.1	42 902	38 375	36 018	11.8	6.5
Panola	8.2	23.7	10.8	14.7	12.3	8.8	8.4	7.2	6.0	52.6	34 274	29 996	28 164	14.3	6.5
Pearl River	7.4	21.6	10.3	14.3	14.0	11.2	9.6	7.2	4.4	51.6	48 621	38 714	33 795	25.6	14.6
Perry	7.7	23.6	10.3	15.4	13.4	10.2	8.1	6.5	4.9	51.6	12 138	10 865	9 864	11.7	10.1
Pike	7.0	23.1	10.1	13.8	13.4	9.2	8.8	8.1	6.5	53.3	38 940	36 882	36 173	5.6	2.0
Pontotoc	7.2	19.9	10.2	15.6	13.9	9.9	9.0	8.0	6.3	51.6	26 726	22 237	20 918	20.2	6.3
Prentiss	7.0	18.8	12.6	14.3	13.2	10.7	9.1	8.1	6.2	52.0	25 556	23 278	24 025	9.8	-3.1
Quitman	8.6	24.5	10.4	13.3	11.4	8.1	7.9	8.5	7.2	53.5	10 117	10 490	12 636	-3.6	-17.0
Rankin	6.9	20.7	9.4	17.1	17.0	11.3	8.4	5.5	3.7	51.3	115 327	87 161	69 427	32.3	25.5
Scott	8.2	22.0	10.2	14.8	13.0	9.6	8.9	7.1	6.2	52.0	28 423	24 137	24 556	17.8	-1.7
Sharkey	8.6	28.2	11.0	13.1	12.5	7.6	6.9	6.5	5.6	53.8	6 580	7 066	7 964	-6.9	-11.3
Simpson	7.5	22.1	9.4	15.5	13.7	9.9	9.0	6.9	5.9	51.2	27 639	23 953	23 441	15.4	2.2
Smith	7.2	21.2	9.8	14.5	13.0	10.4	9.5	7.8	6.6	51.1	16 182	14 798	15 077	9.4	-1.9
Stone	7.6	20.9	13.1	14.7	13.5	9.8	8.3	7.3	4.9	50.7	13 622	10 750	9 716	26.7	10.6

Items 39—53

Table B. States and Counties

STATE County	Total population	Total in households	House-holder	Spouse	Child Total	Child Own child under 18 years	Other relatives Total	Other relatives Under 18 years	Nonrelatives Total	Nonrelatives Unmarried partner	Total in group quarters	Correctional institutions	Nursing homes	Other institutions	College dormitories	Military quarters	Other
	54	55	56	57	58	59	60	61	62	63	64	65	66	67	68	69	70
MISSISSIPPI	2 844 658	96.6	36.8	18.3	31.1	23.1	6.8	3.6	3.7	1.6	3.4	0.9	0.6	0.2	1.0	0.2	0.3
Adams	34 340	98.6	39.8	17.1	31.1	22.0	7.4	3.8	3.2	1.8	1.4	0.4	0.8	0.0	0.0	0.0	0.2
Alcorn	34 558	98.5	41.2	22.4	28.3	21.5	4.0	1.9	2.6	1.4	1.5	0.4	0.7	0.2	0.0	0.0	0.2
Amite	13 599	99.8	38.8	20.6	30.8	21.7	7.4	4.0	2.3	1.3	0.2	0.2	0.0	0.0	0.0	0.0	0.0
Attala	19 661	98.1	38.5	19.3	30.3	21.9	7.0	3.5	2.9	1.4	1.9	0.2	1.5	0.1	0.0	0.0	0.2
Benton	8 026	98.6	37.4	20.3	31.5	22.8	6.7	3.7	2.7	1.5	1.4	0.2	1.2	0.0	0.0	0.0	0.0
Bolivar	40 633	94.6	33.9	12.9	32.5	22.7	11.0	6.5	4.3	2.0	5.4	1.1	0.4	0.1	3.3	0.0	0.5
Calhoun	15 069	98.4	39.9	20.4	29.0	21.3	6.4	3.5	2.6	1.4	1.6	0.2	1.1	0.0	0.0	0.0	0.3
Carroll	10 769	97.2	37.8	21.2	29.4	20.8	6.4	3.4	2.3	1.3	2.8	2.8	0.0	0.0	0.0	0.0	0.0
Chickasaw	19 440	98.9	37.3	19.0	33.0	24.5	7.0	3.8	2.7	1.4	1.1	0.3	0.7	0.0	0.0	0.0	0.1
Choctaw	9 758	96.8	37.8	20.1	29.7	22.5	6.5	3.4	2.7	1.3	3.2	0.1	0.8	0.0	0.0	0.0	2.4
Claiborne	11 831	84.8	31.1	11.4	29.9	20.4	9.0	5.4	3.3	2.0	15.2	0.1	0.6	0.1	14.5	0.0	0.0
Clarke	17 955	99.0	38.9	20.2	31.6	23.4	5.7	3.0	2.6	1.5	1.0	0.0	0.8	0.2	0.0	0.0	0.0
Clay	21 979	98.1	37.1	17.0	34.3	24.5	7.3	4.1	2.3	1.3	1.9	0.4	0.8	0.0	0.5	0.0	0.2
Coahoma	30 622	97.5	34.5	12.8	34.9	25.5	11.5	7.0	3.8	2.2	2.5	0.4	0.6	0.5	0.5	0.0	0.5
Copiah	28 757	95.7	35.3	17.2	31.3	21.6	8.9	4.6	3.0	1.5	4.3	0.2	0.4	0.0	2.8	0.0	0.9
Covington	19 407	98.5	36.7	18.9	32.9	24.5	7.0	3.9	3.0	1.7	1.5	0.1	1.1	0.3	0.0	0.0	0.0
De Soto	107 199	99.5	36.2	22.3	31.8	25.4	5.2	2.2	4.0	1.6	0.5	0.2	0.2	0.1	0.0	0.0	0.1
Forrest	72 604	92.5	37.4	15.9	27.4	20.8	6.1	3.0	5.7	1.7	7.5	0.6	1.0	0.5	4.7	0.3	0.3
Franklin	8 448	98.9	38.0	20.6	31.9	23.5	6.3	3.5	2.1	1.1	1.1	0.0	0.8	0.1	0.0	0.0	0.2
George	19 144	97.9	35.2	22.5	32.5	25.6	5.0	2.6	2.6	1.2	2.1	0.6	0.5	0.1	0.0	0.0	0.9
Greene	13 299	83.2	31.2	19.1	27.4	21.4	3.8	2.2	1.7	0.9	16.8	15.5	0.8	0.0	0.0	0.0	0.4
Grenada	23 263	97.7	37.9	18.5	30.8	22.7	7.3	4.0	3.2	1.6	2.3	0.6	1.3	0.0	0.0	0.0	0.3
Hancock	42 967	98.9	39.3	21.2	28.3	22.0	5.3	2.5	4.8	2.4	1.1	0.3	0.5	0.0	0.0	0.0	0.2
Harrison	189 601	96.2	37.7	18.1	29.4	22.7	5.5	2.7	5.4	2.3	3.8	0.6	0.4	0.4	0.1	2.0	0.4
Hinds	250 800	95.9	36.3	14.9	32.1	23.0	8.1	4.2	4.5	1.9	4.1	0.4	0.5	0.4	2.0	0.0	0.7
Holmes	21 609	96.9	33.8	11.8	36.5	24.8	11.8	6.9	3.0	1.7	3.1	0.3	0.6	0.0	2.2	0.0	0.0
Humphreys	11 206	99.2	33.6	12.9	36.0	24.1	12.3	7.7	4.4	2.1	0.8	0.2	0.7	0.0	0.0	0.0	0.0
Issaquena	2 274	88.4	31.9	14.6	29.9	22.2	8.8	5.1	3.3	2.1	11.6	11.6	0.0	0.0	0.0	0.0	0.0
Itawamba	22 770	96.6	38.5	23.2	28.4	21.9	4.1	1.9	2.4	1.3	3.4	0.1	0.8	0.0	2.4	0.0	0.2
Jackson	131 420	98.5	36.3	20.2	32.0	24.1	5.8	3.0	4.1	1.7	1.5	0.3	0.3	0.0	0.0	0.7	0.3
Jasper	18 149	99.1	37.0	18.8	32.7	23.0	8.3	4.5	2.3	1.2	0.9	0.2	0.6	0.0	0.0	0.0	0.1
Jefferson	9 740	93.5	34.0	12.2	34.7	22.9	9.7	5.6	2.9	2.0	6.5	6.0	0.6	0.0	0.0	0.0	0.0
Jefferson Davis	13 962	99.3	37.1	16.9	32.4	22.1	10.0	5.8	2.8	1.6	0.7	0.3	0.4	0.1	0.0	0.0	0.0
Jones	64 958	97.4	37.4	19.8	29.8	21.8	6.7	3.4	3.8	1.4	2.6	0.2	0.4	0.0	0.8	0.0	1.2
Kemper	10 453	96.2	37.4	17.5	32.1	21.8	6.8	3.3	2.5	1.4	3.8	0.1	0.8	0.0	3.0	0.0	0.0
Lafayette	38 744	87.6	37.1	16.0	22.3	17.3	4.0	1.8	8.2	1.2	12.4	0.3	0.8	0.0	10.2	0.0	1.0
Lamar	39 070	98.8	36.8	22.0	32.0	25.5	4.1	1.9	3.9	1.3	1.2	0.2	0.3	0.3	0.0	0.0	0.4
Lauderdale	78 161	95.6	38.4	17.9	30.9	23.5	5.3	2.5	3.2	1.4	4.4	0.9	1.1	1.0	0.4	0.8	0.3
Lawrence	13 258	99.3	38.0	21.3	32.1	23.9	6.0	3.2	1.9	1.1	0.7	0.3	0.4	0.0	0.0	0.0	0.0
Leake	20 940	96.4	36.3	19.0	30.5	22.4	7.1	3.8	3.5	1.5	3.6	2.7	0.9	0.0	0.0	0.0	0.0
Lee	75 755	98.2	38.5	20.3	31.1	24.6	4.9	2.5	3.4	1.7	1.8	0.2	0.9	0.2	0.0	0.0	0.4
Leflore	37 947	92.2	34.1	12.3	32.6	23.5	9.7	5.8	3.5	1.8	7.8	3.3	1.0	0.1	2.6	0.0	0.8
Lincoln	33 166	98.1	37.8	20.7	31.2	23.2	5.8	3.0	2.5	1.2	1.9	0.2	1.0	0.5	0.0	0.0	0.3
Lowndes	61 586	96.9	37.1	18.2	32.5	24.9	5.9	3.2	3.1	1.5	3.1	0.3	0.9	0.4	1.0	0.4	0.1
Madison	74 674	97.2	36.5	18.9	32.1	24.9	6.6	3.4	3.2	1.3	2.8	0.5	1.2	0.3	0.7	0.0	0.1
Marion	25 595	96.4	36.5	19.7	30.8	22.6	6.9	3.7	2.5	1.3	3.6	1.5	1.0	1.1	0.0	0.0	0.0
Marshall	34 993	95.1	34.8	17.3	31.2	21.3	8.6	4.7	3.4	1.7	4.9	3.0	0.3	0.0	1.5	0.0	0.1
Monroe	38 014	98.9	38.4	20.0	31.8	23.5	6.2	3.3	2.5	1.3	1.1	0.2	0.6	0.2	0.0	0.0	0.0
Montgomery	12 189	98.8	38.5	18.7	31.4	22.4	7.9	4.3	2.3	1.3	1.2	0.0	1.0	0.2	0.0	0.0	0.2
Neshoba	28 684	97.9	37.3	19.6	31.4	23.8	6.1	3.4	3.5	1.8	2.1	0.2	1.4	0.2	0.0	0.0	0.2
Newton	21 838	96.6	37.6	20.0	30.2	22.4	5.9	3.2	2.9	1.3	3.4	0.0	0.8	0.2	2.2	0.0	0.2
Noxubee	12 548	98.6	35.6	15.3	35.9	25.1	9.4	5.3	2.4	1.3	1.4	0.9	0.5	0.0	0.0	0.0	0.0
Oktibbeha	42 902	89.8	37.2	14.8	24.3	18.4	4.7	2.3	8.8	1.3	10.2	0.2	0.6	0.0	9.2	0.0	0.1
Panola	34 274	98.3	35.7	17.5	32.9	23.8	8.9	4.9	3.4	1.8	1.7	0.3	0.5	0.1	0.0	0.0	0.8
Pearl River	48 621	98.4	37.2	21.7	30.5	23.4	5.8	3.0	3.2	1.6	1.6	0.2	0.6	0.0	0.7	0.0	0.1
Perry	12 138	99.0	36.4	21.2	32.4	24.3	6.2	3.6	2.9	1.3	1.0	0.2	0.6	0.0	0.0	0.0	0.2
Pike	38 940	97.8	38.0	17.8	32.0	23.4	7.4	3.9	2.7	1.4	2.2	0.4	1.0	0.0	0.7	0.0	0.1
Pontotoc	26 726	99.1	37.8	22.4	31.6	24.8	4.8	2.3	2.6	1.3	0.9	0.1	0.6	0.0	0.0	0.0	0.2
Prentiss	25 556	96.7	38.4	21.7	29.6	22.3	4.8	2.3	2.2	1.1	3.3	0.2	0.5	0.1	2.6	0.0	0.0
Quitman	10 117	98.7	35.2	13.2	34.2	23.9	12.5	7.6	3.6	2.2	1.3	0.7	0.6	0.0	0.0	0.0	0.0
Rankin	115 327	95.8	36.5	21.2	30.1	23.2	4.7	2.2	3.3	1.3	4.2	2.3	0.2	1.2	0.0	0.0	0.4
Scott	28 423	98.9	35.8	17.8	32.4	23.7	8.3	4.3	4.5	1.9	1.1	0.3	0.5	0.1	0.0	0.0	0.1
Sharkey	6 580	98.4	32.9	13.1	34.4	23.1	14.3	9.4	3.6	2.2	1.6	0.2	0.9	0.1	0.0	0.0	0.4
Simpson	27 639	96.5	36.5	19.7	30.8	23.1	6.6	3.6	2.9	1.5	3.5	0.4	0.8	1.1	0.0	0.0	1.2
Smith	16 182	99.2	37.4	22.3	32.0	24.0	5.8	3.2	1.8	1.0	0.8	0.1	0.0	0.0	0.0	0.0	0.7
Stone	13 622	94.8	34.8	20.5	30.4	22.9	5.9	3.2	3.3	1.7	5.2	0.2	0.9	0.0	3.7	0.0	0.4

Table B. States and Counties

STATE County	Households by type, 2000												Households, 1990		
		Family households						Nonfamily households							
				Married couple		Female householder[1]			Householder living alone						
	Total households	Total	With own children under 18 years	Total	With own children under 18 years	Total	With own children under 18 years	Total	Total	65 years and over	Average household size	Average family size	Total households	Female householder[1]	Householder living alone
	71	72	73	74	75	76	77	78	79	80	81	82	83	84	85
MISSISSIPPI	1 046 434	71.4	34.7	49.8	22.4	17.3	10.1	28.6	24.6	9.6	2.63	3.14	911 374	15.9	23.4
Adams	13 677	68.8	31.8	42.8	17.2	21.5	12.5	31.2	28.0	11.9	2.48	3.03	13 262	19.8	25.1
Alcorn	14 224	69.7	30.9	54.5	22.4	11.5	6.6	30.3	27.6	11.9	2.39	2.91	12 449	10.5	25.0
Amite	5 271	73.6	31.2	53.1	21.4	16.3	8.3	26.4	24.5	12.0	2.58	3.06	4 830	14.4	24.3
Attala	7 567	71.1	32.1	50.3	21.1	16.7	9.1	28.9	26.4	14.5	2.55	3.07	6 945	13.7	26.3
Benton	2 999	73.9	33.4	54.2	23.3	14.8	7.8	26.1	23.8	11.7	2.64	3.12	2 842	13.9	21.7
Bolivar	13 776	70.6	35.2	38.2	16.6	27.3	16.2	29.4	25.3	9.9	2.79	3.36	13 292	26.3	24.0
Calhoun	6 019	70.7	31.6	51.0	20.6	15.4	8.8	29.3	27.1	13.9	2.46	2.97	5 662	12.7	24.9
Carroll	4 071	75.4	32.1	56.2	22.5	15.2	7.8	24.6	22.4	10.8	2.57	3.01	3 352	14.6	22.3
Chickasaw	7 253	72.9	36.3	50.8	23.7	18.0	10.4	27.1	24.9	11.9	2.65	3.17	6 480	15.3	22.7
Choctaw	3 686	72.4	32.6	53.3	22.5	14.6	8.2	27.6	25.0	12.2	2.56	3.06	3 217	13.6	23.1
Claiborne	3 685	68.7	34.8	36.5	16.1	26.9	15.7	31.3	28.0	10.9	2.72	3.35	3 342	25.1	27.6
Clarke	6 978	72.0	33.2	52.0	22.0	15.9	9.2	28.0	25.5	11.8	2.55	3.06	6 334	15.5	23.2
Clay	8 152	72.2	35.7	45.8	20.3	22.4	13.7	27.8	25.5	11.0	2.64	3.19	7 251	19.4	23.0
Coahoma	10 553	70.9	36.8	37.2	16.9	28.7	17.4	29.1	26.2	11.5	2.83	3.42	10 530	25.1	26.4
Copiah	10 142	73.9	34.4	48.7	21.5	20.1	10.7	26.1	23.6	10.3	2.71	3.20	9 304	18.6	23.1
Covington	7 126	74.1	36.6	51.5	23.7	17.2	10.0	25.9	23.6	10.7	2.68	3.16	5 786	14.4	22.1
De Soto	38 792	77.6	39.4	61.7	29.8	11.6	7.1	22.4	18.1	5.6	2.75	3.11	23 273	11.1	14.8
Forrest	27 183	63.7	31.0	42.6	18.9	17.2	10.3	36.3	28.5	8.8	2.47	3.07	25 150	16.8	27.6
Franklin	3 211	72.8	34.6	54.2	24.8	14.6	8.0	27.2	25.6	13.3	2.60	3.13	3 086	14.2	24.7
George	6 742	78.7	38.7	64.0	30.5	10.4	5.8	21.3	19.1	8.2	2.78	3.17	5 779	10.4	18.9
Greene	4 148	76.0	37.2	61.2	28.7	11.9	6.9	24.0	22.0	9.3	2.67	3.12	3 327	12.9	19.6
Grenada	8 820	71.4	33.9	48.9	20.8	18.6	11.2	28.6	25.3	10.6	2.58	3.09	7 701	17.0	23.6
Hancock	16 897	70.0	31.5	53.9	22.3	11.3	6.5	30.0	24.7	9.2	2.52	2.99	11 817	11.3	23.3
Harrison	71 538	67.9	33.5	48.1	21.6	15.1	9.4	32.1	25.8	8.3	2.55	3.07	59 557	13.9	24.2
Hinds	91 030	68.5	34.4	41.1	18.8	22.7	13.4	31.5	26.7	8.7	2.64	3.22	91 023	19.2	25.6
Holmes	7 314	71.5	36.0	34.9	15.7	31.2	18.1	28.5	26.3	12.1	2.86	3.48	7 139	28.3	25.5
Humphreys	3 765	71.6	36.6	38.3	18.1	27.7	15.6	28.4	24.9	10.9	2.95	3.54	3 926	24.2	23.7
Issaquena	726	70.2	34.2	45.6	21.2	16.0	8.7	29.8	26.2	12.3	2.77	3.37	633	14.8	23.2
Itawamba	8 773	74.1	33.2	60.3	25.8	9.9	5.2	25.9	23.4	11.1	2.51	2.95	7 497	8.1	21.9
Jackson	47 676	74.9	37.0	55.7	25.6	14.5	8.9	25.1	20.8	7.1	2.72	3.14	40 454	13.5	19.3
Jasper	6 708	73.9	35.0	50.9	22.9	18.2	9.9	26.1	24.2	11.3	2.68	3.19	5 956	16.0	21.6
Jefferson	3 308	70.7	36.6	36.0	17.0	28.5	16.7	29.3	27.1	10.1	2.75	3.36	2 814	27.9	23.1
Jefferson Davis	5 177	72.8	32.9	45.7	18.8	21.6	11.7	27.2	25.0	11.9	2.68	3.20	4 787	18.2	22.0
Jones	24 275	72.3	32.6	53.0	22.2	15.1	8.3	27.7	24.4	11.0	2.61	3.08	22 506	13.7	22.9
Kemper	3 909	71.3	32.2	46.7	18.9	20.2	11.4	28.7	26.4	12.6	2.57	3.11	3 626	17.1	25.7
Lafayette	14 373	57.9	26.9	43.2	18.8	11.4	6.8	42.1	29.1	7.8	2.36	2.97	11 090	11.2	26.8
Lamar	14 396	74.5	38.4	59.6	29.6	11.5	7.0	25.5	20.4	7.1	2.68	3.11	10 883	11.6	19.1
Lauderdale	29 990	68.6	33.9	46.7	20.8	18.3	11.3	31.4	28.0	11.7	2.49	3.06	28 232	17.1	26.4
Lawrence	5 040	74.4	35.4	55.9	25.4	14.4	7.9	25.6	24.1	11.4	2.61	3.10	4 506	13.6	23.4
Leake	7 611	73.1	34.3	52.2	23.2	16.5	9.0	26.9	24.3	11.7	2.65	3.13	6 788	13.3	24.3
Lee	29 200	71.3	36.1	52.6	24.7	14.6	9.2	28.7	25.0	8.5	2.55	3.05	24 450	13.1	23.4
Leflore	12 956	68.6	35.4	36.0	16.0	27.6	17.0	31.4	28.2	11.6	2.70	3.33	12 749	23.6	27.1
Lincoln	12 538	73.3	34.9	54.9	25.0	14.7	8.3	26.7	24.4	11.5	2.59	3.08	11 089	14.4	23.8
Lowndes	22 849	71.8	36.5	49.2	22.6	18.7	11.9	28.2	24.6	8.9	2.61	3.13	21 402	16.7	23.5
Madison	27 219	71.0	37.4	51.9	26.6	15.6	9.2	29.0	25.0	6.7	2.67	3.23	19 276	16.7	25.1
Marion	9 336	73.7	34.8	54.0	24.3	15.6	8.8	26.3	24.2	12.6	2.64	3.13	9 110	13.7	23.0
Marshall	12 163	74.9	34.3	49.6	20.8	20.1	11.0	25.1	22.0	7.9	2.74	3.19	10 077	17.9	20.8
Monroe	14 603	73.0	34.7	52.0	22.9	17.2	9.9	27.0	24.7	11.8	2.57	3.07	13 348	15.1	22.9
Montgomery	4 690	71.8	32.6	48.5	20.2	18.8	10.5	28.2	26.1	13.6	2.57	3.10	4 532	17.1	25.0
Neshoba	10 694	72.4	34.9	52.5	23.2	15.6	9.3	27.6	24.7	11.5	2.63	3.11	8 848	13.7	21.9
Newton	8 221	73.0	33.5	53.0	22.7	16.0	8.9	27.0	24.6	11.6	2.57	3.04	7 358	13.5	23.0
Noxubee	4 470	72.1	35.8	43.0	19.9	24.7	14.0	27.9	25.9	11.5	2.77	3.36	4 140	22.6	24.2
Oktibbeha	15 945	58.1	28.2	39.9	17.5	14.8	9.2	41.9	27.7	6.7	2.42	3.03	12 916	14.3	25.7
Panola	12 232	73.7	36.1	48.9	22.0	19.9	11.7	26.3	23.2	10.1	2.75	3.25	10 130	18.0	22.6
Pearl River	18 078	75.1	34.8	58.3	25.3	12.5	7.1	24.9	21.7	9.0	2.65	3.08	13 760	12.2	20.3
Perry	4 420	75.4	37.6	58.1	27.9	13.2	7.5	24.6	21.9	8.7	2.72	3.18	3 802	13.1	21.2
Pike	14 792	71.0	34.2	46.8	20.3	19.9	12.0	29.0	26.5	12.0	2.57	3.12	13 408	18.4	25.7
Pontotoc	10 097	74.9	37.1	59.2	28.2	11.9	6.9	25.1	22.7	10.4	2.62	3.08	8 346	10.6	22.3
Prentiss	9 821	73.0	33.7	56.3	25.0	12.6	6.8	27.0	24.9	12.0	2.52	3.00	8 647	11.6	22.4
Quitman	3 565	70.3	34.4	37.6	16.2	26.8	15.3	29.7	26.9	12.3	2.80	3.42	3 521	19.7	25.1
Rankin	42 089	74.0	36.7	58.1	27.6	12.2	7.0	26.0	21.9	6.2	2.62	3.07	29 858	11.2	17.7
Scott	10 183	74.0	36.2	49.8	22.9	18.8	10.9	26.0	22.2	10.0	2.76	3.21	8 511	15.9	22.0
Sharkey	2 163	73.5	36.1	40.0	18.1	26.8	14.2	26.5	23.5	9.9	2.99	3.56	2 084	25.3	20.3
Simpson	10 076	73.3	34.8	54.2	24.3	14.8	8.3	26.7	24.0	11.1	2.65	3.14	8 357	13.4	22.6
Smith	6 046	75.4	35.9	59.6	27.7	11.9	6.2	24.6	23.0	11.6	2.65	3.13	5 276	9.4	21.2
Stone	4 747	76.4	37.3	58.8	27.1	13.3	7.7	23.6	20.6	8.9	2.72	3.13	3 685	12.4	22.0

[1] No spouse present.

Table B. States and Counties

STATE County	Housing occupancy, 2000							Housing tenure, 2000				
			Vacant housing units					Occupied housing units				
	Percent change of households, 1990–2000	Total housing units	Occupied housing units (percent)	Total	For seasonal, recreational, or occasional use	Homeowner vacancy rate (percent)	Rental vacancy rate (percent)	Total	Percent owner-occupied housing units	Percent renter-occupied housing units	Average household size of owner-occupied units	Average household size of renter-occupied units
	86	87	88	89	90	91	92	93	94	95	96	97
MISSISSIPPI	14.8	1 161 953	90.1	9.9	1.9	1.6	9.2	1 046 434	72.3	27.7	2.67	2.52
Adams	3.1	15 175	90.1	9.9	1.2	1.3	7.4	13 677	70.3	29.7	2.49	2.45
Alcorn	14.3	15 818	89.9	10.1	0.7	2.3	12.4	14 224	73.5	26.5	2.45	2.23
Amite	9.1	6 446	81.8	18.2	7.6	1.3	4.8	5 271	86.0	14.0	2.59	2.46
Attala	9.0	8 639	87.6	12.4	2.2	1.7	6.6	7 567	77.7	22.3	2.54	2.59
Benton	5.5	3 456	86.8	13.2	6.8	2.2	10.1	2 999	84.3	15.7	2.63	2.67
Bolivar	3.6	14 939	92.2	7.8	2.4	0.9	4.9	13 776	61.1	38.9	2.79	2.79
Calhoun	6.3	6 902	87.2	12.8	1.5	2.7	7.0	6 019	76.3	23.7	2.47	2.44
Carroll	21.4	4 888	83.3	16.7	9.0	1.1	12.7	4 071	84.8	15.2	2.59	2.49
Chickasaw	11.9	7 981	90.9	9.1	0.8	1.7	9.3	7 253	77.9	22.1	2.69	2.51
Choctaw	14.6	4 249	86.7	13.3	4.0	1.5	12.2	3 686	81.3	18.7	2.59	2.42
Claiborne	10.3	4 252	86.7	13.3	3.5	1.1	8.5	3 685	80.2	19.8	2.73	2.70
Clarke	10.2	8 100	86.1	13.9	2.0	3.6	7.9	6 978	84.3	15.7	2.55	2.56
Clay	12.4	8 810	92.5	7.5	2.1	1.2	7.7	8 152	73.6	26.4	2.68	2.55
Coahoma	0.2	11 490	91.8	8.2	1.3	1.8	4.9	10 553	57.3	42.7	2.81	2.85
Copiah	9.0	11 101	91.4	8.6	1.6	1.4	8.6	10 142	79.9	20.1	2.73	2.65
Covington	23.2	8 083	88.2	11.8	1.5	0.9	10.4	7 126	84.9	15.1	2.70	2.61
De Soto	66.7	40 795	95.1	4.9	0.6	1.9	6.3	38 792	79.2	20.8	2.78	2.63
Forrest	8.1	29 913	90.9	9.1	0.6	1.8	10.0	27 183	60.2	39.8	2.61	2.26
Franklin	4.1	4 119	78.0	22.0	10.5	2.0	8.8	3 211	86.1	13.9	2.60	2.60
George	16.7	7 513	89.7	10.3	2.5	1.4	11.3	6 742	86.2	13.8	2.79	2.70
Greene	24.7	4 947	83.8	16.2	5.4	2.9	11.6	4 148	87.1	12.9	2.69	2.51
Grenada	14.5	9 973	88.4	11.6	3.5	1.5	8.2	8 820	69.2	30.8	2.59	2.54
Hancock	43.0	21 072	80.2	19.8	11.3	2.1	15.3	16 897	79.6	20.4	2.55	2.39
Harrison	20.1	79 636	89.8	10.2	2.1	1.9	10.6	71 538	62.7	37.3	2.63	2.42
Hinds	0.0	100 287	90.8	9.2	0.4	1.9	11.2	91 030	63.9	36.1	2.72	2.50
Holmes	2.5	8 439	86.7	13.3	4.2	1.5	3.5	7 314	73.3	26.7	2.84	2.92
Humphreys	-4.1	4 138	91.0	9.0	1.4	0.7	6.0	3 765	61.4	38.6	2.89	3.04
Issaquena	14.7	877	82.8	17.2	4.6	1.8	9.8	726	66.9	33.1	2.74	2.83
Itawamba	17.0	9 804	89.5	10.5	1.7	2.1	10.7	8 773	82.4	17.6	2.52	2.45
Jackson	17.9	51 678	92.3	7.7	1.2	1.5	10.1	47 676	74.6	25.4	2.76	2.59
Jasper	12.6	7 671	87.4	12.6	2.8	0.9	6.4	6 708	86.7	13.3	2.69	2.61
Jefferson	17.6	3 819	86.6	13.4	4.4	0.8	6.2	3 308	80.4	19.6	2.78	2.65
Jefferson Davis	8.1	5 891	87.9	12.1	2.1	1.6	8.9	5 177	84.5	15.5	2.70	2.57
Jones	7.9	26 921	90.2	9.8	0.9	1.1	9.8	24 275	76.8	23.2	2.59	2.66
Kemper	7.8	4 533	86.2	13.8	1.9	1.3	5.2	3 909	83.8	16.2	2.59	2.49
Lafayette	29.6	16 587	86.7	13.3	4.2	2.1	10.5	14 373	60.6	39.4	2.52	2.11
Lamar	32.3	15 433	93.3	6.7	0.6	1.5	8.4	14 396	75.8	24.2	2.78	2.36
Lauderdale	6.2	33 418	89.7	10.3	0.7	2.1	10.2	29 990	67.8	32.2	2.54	2.38
Lawrence	11.9	5 688	88.6	11.4	4.2	1.2	8.3	5 040	84.2	15.8	2.60	2.66
Leake	12.1	8 585	88.7	11.3	1.9	1.1	7.9	7 611	82.0	18.0	2.63	2.76
Lee	19.4	31 887	91.6	8.4	0.6	1.5	11.5	29 200	69.2	30.8	2.63	2.37
Leflore	1.6	14 097	91.9	8.1	1.0	1.7	6.7	12 956	53.4	46.6	2.69	2.71
Lincoln	13.1	14 052	89.2	10.8	1.5	1.4	8.3	12 538	78.1	21.9	2.63	2.46
Lowndes	6.8	25 104	91.0	9.0	0.9	1.5	9.4	22 849	66.5	33.5	2.67	2.50
Madison	41.2	28 781	94.6	5.4	0.7	1.4	4.5	27 219	70.9	29.1	2.81	2.31
Marion	2.5	10 395	89.8	10.2	1.0	1.6	11.3	9 336	80.4	19.6	2.66	2.57
Marshall	20.7	13 252	91.8	8.2	1.6	1.1	7.1	12 163	80.5	19.5	2.76	2.65
Monroe	9.4	16 236	89.9	10.1	1.5	1.7	12.3	14 603	79.0	21.0	2.59	2.50
Montgomery	3.5	5 402	86.8	13.2	3.1	1.4	9.0	4 690	77.0	23.0	2.55	2.63
Neshoba	20.9	11 980	89.3	10.7	1.7	0.8	9.1	10 694	79.5	20.5	2.65	2.54
Newton	11.7	9 259	88.8	11.2	1.2	2.0	9.9	8 221	81.9	18.1	2.58	2.49
Noxubee	8.0	5 228	85.5	14.5	4.1	1.6	7.0	4 470	79.5	20.5	2.79	2.66
Oktibbeha	23.5	17 344	91.9	8.1	0.8	1.4	8.3	15 945	55.6	44.4	2.62	2.16
Panola	20.8	13 736	89.1	10.9	4.7	1.4	7.3	12 232	77.9	22.1	2.75	2.78
Pearl River	31.4	20 610	87.7	12.3	4.1	1.7	11.5	18 078	79.8	20.2	2.66	2.58
Perry	16.3	5 107	86.5	13.5	2.8	1.0	13.8	4 420	84.5	15.5	2.75	2.53
Pike	10.3	16 720	88.5	11.5	1.7	1.8	9.7	14 792	74.4	25.6	2.58	2.57
Pontotoc	21.0	10 816	93.4	6.6	0.5	1.3	8.0	10 097	77.9	22.1	2.66	2.50
Prentiss	13.6	10 681	91.9	8.1	0.7	1.2	9.9	9 821	77.9	22.1	2.57	2.33
Quitman	1.2	3 923	90.9	9.1	1.5	1.6	3.4	3 565	68.5	31.5	2.82	2.76
Rankin	41.0	45 070	93.4	6.6	0.9	1.5	9.9	42 089	77.1	22.9	2.70	2.37
Scott	19.6	11 116	91.6	8.4	0.8	1.0	6.8	10 183	78.3	21.7	2.73	2.87
Sharkey	3.8	2 416	89.5	10.5	2.0	1.0	6.4	2 163	65.5	34.5	2.92	3.13
Simpson	20.6	11 307	89.1	10.9	1.8	1.5	7.8	10 076	81.1	18.9	2.66	2.58
Smith	14.6	7 005	86.3	13.7	2.4	1.2	7.9	6 046	86.9	13.1	2.67	2.57
Stone	28.8	5 343	88.8	11.2	2.2	1.8	11.8	4 747	81.2	18.8	2.72	2.73

Table B. States and Counties

STATE/County code	MSA/PMSA/NECMA code[1]	County type[2]	STATE County	Population, 2000				Population, 1990				Population and population characteristics, 2000					
												Race (percent)					
												One race					
				Land area, 2000[3] (sq km)	Total persons	Rank	Per square kilometer	Land area, 1990[3] (sq km)	Total persons	Rank	Per square kilometer	White	Black or African American	American Indian or Alaska Native	Asian	Native Hawaiian and other Pacific Islander	Some other race
				1	2	3	4	5	6	7	8	9	10	11	12	13	14
			MISSISSIPPI—Cont'd														
28 133	...	7	Sunflower	1 797	34 369	1 268	19.1	1 797	35 129	1 127	19.5	28.9	69.9	0.1	0.4	0.0	0.5
28 135	...	9	Tallahatchie	1 668	14 903	2 098	8.9	1 668	15 210	1 975	9.1	39.6	59.4	0.1	0.4	0.0	0.0
28 137	...	6	Tate	1 048	25 370	1 548	24.2	1 048	21 432	1 607	20.5	67.8	31.0	0.2	0.1	0.0	0.2
28 139	...	7	Tippah	1 186	20 826	1 743	17.6	1 186	19 523	1 699	16.5	81.8	15.9	0.2	0.1	0.0	1.3
28 141	...	6	Tishomingo	1 098	19 163	1 837	17.5	1 099	17 683	1 806	16.1	94.9	3.1	0.2	0.1	0.0	1.1
28 143	...	8	Tunica	1 178	9 227	2 510	7.8	1 178	8 164	2 549	6.9	27.5	70.2	0.1	0.4	0.1	1.0
28 145	...	7	Union	1 076	25 362	1 549	23.6	1 076	22 085	1 572	20.5	83.4	14.9	0.1	0.2	0.0	0.7
28 147	...	9	Walthall	1 046	15 156	2 080	14.5	1 046	14 352	2 027	13.7	54.6	44.1	0.1	0.2	0.0	0.3
28 149	...	4	Warren	1 519	49 644	923	32.7	1 519	47 880	876	31.5	55.0	43.2	0.2	0.6	0.0	0.3
28 151	...	5	Washington	1 875	62 977	771	33.6	1 875	67 935	651	36.2	34.0	64.6	0.1	0.5	0.0	0.2
28 153	...	7	Wayne	2 099	21 216	1 724	10.1	2 099	19 517	1 700	9.3	61.3	38.0	0.1	0.2	0.0	0.1
28 155	...	9	Webster	1 094	10 294	2 416	9.4	1 095	10 222	2 369	9.3	77.6	20.9	0.1	0.2	0.0	0.8
28 157	...	9	Wilkinson	1 753	10 312	2 414	5.9	1 753	9 678	2 414	5.5	31.2	68.2	0.1	0.0	0.0	0.1
28 159	...	7	Winston	1 572	20 160	1 784	12.8	1 572	19 433	1 708	12.4	55.3	43.2	0.7	0.1	0.0	0.3
28 161	...	7	Yalobusha	1 210	13 051	2 227	10.8	1 210	12 033	2 215	9.9	60.5	38.7	0.2	0.1	0.1	0.1
28 163	...	6	Yazoo	2 381	28 149	1 446	11.8	2 382	25 506	1 448	10.7	44.7	54.0	0.2	0.4	0.0	0.2
29 000	...		**MISSOURI**	178 414	5 595 211	X	31.4	178 446	5 116 901	X	28.7	84.9	11.2	0.4	1.1	0.1	0.8
29 001	...	7	Adair	1 469	24 977	1 560	17.0	1 470	24 577	1 478	16.7	95.8	1.2	0.3	1.4	0.0	0.4
29 003	7000	3	Andrew	1 127	16 492	1 989	14.6	1 127	14 632	2 009	13.0	98.4	0.4	0.3	0.2	0.0	0.2
29 005	...	9	Atchison	1 411	6 430	2 745	4.6	1 411	7 457	2 617	5.3	97.0	2.1	0.2	0.1	0.0	0.3
29 007	...	6	Audrain	1 795	25 853	1 523	14.4	1 796	23 599	1 509	13.1	91.1	7.2	0.3	0.3	0.0	0.2
29 009	...	7	Barry	2 018	34 010	1 280	16.9	2 018	27 547	1 371	13.7	94.1	0.1	0.9	0.3	0.0	3.3
29 011	...	6	Barton	1 539	12 541	2 261	8.1	1 539	11 312	2 274	7.4	96.9	0.3	0.8	0.3	0.1	0.1
29 013	...	6	Bates	2 198	16 653	1 981	7.6	2 198	15 025	1 986	6.8	97.3	0.6	0.6	0.2	0.0	0.4
29 015	...	9	Benton	1 827	17 180	1 942	9.4	1 827	13 859	2 066	7.6	98.0	0.1	0.5	0.1	0.0	0.1
29 017	...	9	Bollinger	1 608	12 029	2 293	7.5	1 608	10 619	2 325	6.6	97.8	0.2	0.7	0.2	0.0	0.1
29 019	1740	3	Boone	1 775	135 454	398	76.3	1 775	112 379	409	63.3	85.4	8.5	0.4	3.0	0.0	0.7
29 021	7000	3	Buchanan	1 061	85 998	606	81.1	1 061	83 083	548	78.3	92.7	4.4	0.4	0.4	0.0	0.6
29 023	...	7	Butler	1 807	40 867	1 087	22.6	1 807	38 765	1 032	21.5	92.2	5.2	0.6	0.4	0.0	0.3
29 025	...	8	Caldwell	1 112	8 969	2 529	8.1	1 112	8 380	2 524	7.5	98.6	0.1	0.3	0.1	0.0	0.2
29 027	...	6	Callaway	2 173	40 766	1 089	18.8	2 173	32 809	1 195	15.1	91.8	5.7	0.5	0.5	0.0	0.3
29 029	...	7	Camden	1 697	37 051	1 188	21.8	1 697	27 495	1 375	16.2	97.7	0.3	0.5	0.3	0.0	0.3
29 031	...	5	Cape Girardeau	1 499	68 693	717	45.8	1 499	61 633	708	41.1	92.1	5.3	0.4	0.7	0.0	0.3
29 033	...	6	Carroll	1 799	10 285	2 418	5.7	1 799	10 748	2 313	6.0	96.9	1.7	0.3	0.1	0.0	0.1
29 035	...	9	Carter	1 315	5 941	2 789	4.5	1 315	5 515	2 801	4.2	96.6	0.1	1.3	0.1	0.0	0.0
29 037	3760	1	Cass	1 810	82 092	632	45.4	1 811	63 808	686	35.2	95.6	1.4	0.6	0.5	0.0	0.5
29 039	...	7	Cedar	1 233	13 733	2 178	11.1	1 233	12 093	2 209	9.8	96.6	0.3	0.7	0.5	0.0	0.5
29 041	...	9	Chariton	1 958	8 438	2 569	4.3	1 958	9 202	2 453	4.7	96.0	3.2	0.2	0.1	0.0	0.1
29 043	7920	2	Christian	1 459	54 285	867	37.2	1 459	32 644	1 199	22.4	97.3	0.3	0.6	0.3	0.0	0.4
29 045	...	9	Clark	1 314	7 416	2 647	5.6	1 314	7 547	2 612	5.7	98.8	0.1	0.2	0.1	0.0	0.2
29 047	3760	0	Clay	1 027	184 006	296	179.2	1 027	153 411	302	149.4	92.5	2.7	0.5	1.3	0.1	1.2
29 049	3760	1	Clinton	1 085	18 979	1 847	17.5	1 085	16 595	1 879	15.3	96.6	1.5	0.3	0.2	0.0	0.5
29 051	...	4	Cole	1 014	71 397	693	70.4	1 014	63 579	688	62.7	87.1	9.9	0.3	0.9	0.0	0.5
29 053	...	6	Cooper	1 463	16 670	1 978	11.4	1 463	14 835	1 998	10.1	89.0	9.0	0.4	0.2	0.0	0.3
29 055	...	6	Crawford	1 923	22 804	1 653	11.9	1 923	19 173	1 722	10.0	98.3	0.1	0.4	0.1	0.1	0.1
29 057	...	8	Dade	1 270	7 923	2 612	6.2	1 270	7 449	2 619	5.9	97.5	0.3	0.7	0.1	0.1	0.2
29 059	...	8	Dallas	1 403	15 661	2 043	11.2	1 403	12 646	2 172	9.0	97.5	0.1	0.8	0.1	0.0	0.2
29 061	...	9	Daviess	1 468	8 016	2 603	5.5	1 469	7 865	2 584	5.4	98.7	0.0	0.4	0.1	0.0	0.3
29 063	...	8	De Kalb	1 099	11 597	2 325	10.6	1 099	9 967	2 389	9.1	89.1	8.9	0.7	0.2	0.0	0.3
29 065	...	7	Dent	1 952	14 927	2 097	7.6	1 952	13 702	2 080	7.0	97.1	0.4	0.7	0.2	0.0	0.2
29 067	...	6	Douglas	2 110	13 084	2 224	6.2	2 110	11 876	2 225	5.6	96.9	0.1	0.9	0.2	0.0	0.2
29 069	...	7	Dunklin	1 413	33 155	1 312	23.5	1 413	33 112	1 187	23.4	88.6	8.7	0.3	0.3	0.0	1.0
29 071	7040	1	Franklin	2 390	93 807	546	39.2	2 388	80 603	565	33.8	97.5	0.9	0.2	0.3	0.0	0.2
29 073	...	6	Gasconade	1 349	15 342	2 066	11.4	1 345	14 006	2 056	10.4	98.7	0.1	0.2	0.2	0.0	0.1
29 075	...	8	Gentry	1 273	6 861	2 702	5.4	1 273	6 854	2 673	5.4	98.6	0.1	0.3	0.2	0.2	0.1
29 077	7920	2	Greene	1 748	240 391	239	137.5	1 748	207 949	240	119.0	93.5	2.3	0.7	1.1	0.0	0.5
29 079	...	7	Grundy	1 129	10 432	2 403	9.2	1 129	10 536	2 332	9.3	97.6	0.4	0.3	0.2	0.0	0.5
29 081	...	7	Harrison	1 878	8 850	2 539	4.7	1 878	8 469	2 515	4.5	98.3	0.1	0.2	0.1	0.1	0.1
29 083	...	6	Henry	1 819	21 997	1 692	12.1	1 819	20 044	1 675	11.0	96.6	1.0	0.7	0.2	0.0	0.3
29 085	...	9	Hickory	1 032	8 940	2 531	8.7	1 033	7 335	2 626	7.1	97.5	0.1	0.7	0.1	0.0	0.2
29 087	...	8	Holt	1 196	5 351	2 825	4.5	1 196	6 034	2 753	5.0	98.5	0.1	0.5	0.1	0.0	0.1
29 089	...	6	Howard	1 206	10 212	2 426	8.5	1 206	9 631	2 421	8.0	91.1	6.8	0.3	0.1	0.1	0.4
29 091	...	7	Howell	2 403	37 238	1 184	15.5	2 403	31 447	1 232	13.1	96.4	0.3	1.0	0.4	0.0	0.3
29 093	...	9	Iron	1 428	10 697	2 384	7.5	1 428	10 726	2 316	7.5	96.7	1.6	0.3	0.1	0.0	0.2
29 095	3760	0	Jackson	1 567	654 880	81	417.9	1 566	633 234	74	404.4	70.1	23.3	0.5	1.3	0.2	2.4

[1] MSA = Metropolitan Statistical Area. PMSA = Primary MSA. NECMA = New England County Metropolitan Area. See Appendix A for explanation of these concepts. See Appendix B for list of metropolitan areas identified by type, with component counties.
[2] County typology code from the Economic Research Service of USDA. See Appendix A for definition.
[3] Dry land or land partially or temporarily covered by water.

Table B. States and Counties

STATE County	Population and population characteristics, 2000 (cont'd)								Population and population characteristics, 1990				
	Race (percent) (cont'd)								Race (percent)				
	Race alone or in combination												
	Two or more races	White	Black	American Indian or Alaska Native	Asian	Native Hawaiian and other Pacific Islander	Some other race	Hispanic¹	White	Black or African American	American Indian or Alaska Native	Asian and Pacific Islander	Hispanic¹
	15	16	17	18	19	20	21	22	23	24	25	26	27
MISSISSIPPI—Cont'd													
Sunflower	0.3	29.0	70.0	0.2	0.5	0.0	0.6	1.3	35.3	64.2	0.1	0.3	0.6
Tallahatchie	0.5	39.8	59.7	0.4	0.5	0.0	0.2	0.9	41.1	58.4	0.1	0.3	0.5
Tate	0.6	68.3	31.2	0.5	0.1	0.1	0.3	0.9	65.1	34.6	0.2	0.1	0.6
Tippah	0.6	82.4	16.1	0.5	0.2	0.0	1.4	2.1	83.2	16.6	0.1	0.1	0.3
Tishomingo	0.6	95.4	3.3	0.6	0.1	0.1	1.2	1.8	96.2	3.6	0.1	0.1	0.3
Tunica	0.7	27.9	70.5	0.5	0.7	0.2	1.1	2.5	24.4	75.3	0.1	0.1	1.0
Union	0.6	84.0	15.2	0.3	0.3	0.0	0.8	1.6	85.1	14.5	0.1	0.1	0.5
Walthall	0.7	55.1	44.3	0.4	0.4	0.0	0.5	1.3	57.5	42.2	0.1	0.2	0.3
Warren	0.7	55.4	43.5	0.5	0.8	0.0	0.5	1.0	60.3	39.0	0.1	0.5	0.5
Washington	0.6	34.3	64.9	0.3	0.7	0.1	0.4	0.8	41.7	57.7	0.1	0.4	0.6
Wayne	0.3	61.5	38.2	0.2	0.3	0.0	0.2	0.6	64.1	35.6	0.1	0.2	0.4
Webster	0.4	77.9	21.0	0.3	0.3	0.0	1.0	1.7	77.8	22.1	0.0	0.1	0.6
Wilkinson	0.4	31.5	68.5	0.2	0.1	0.1	0.1	0.4	32.3	67.5	0.2	0.0	0.5
Winston	0.5	55.6	43.5	0.8	0.2	0.0	0.4	1.2	57.4	41.7	0.9	0.1	0.4
Yalobusha	0.4	60.8	38.7	0.4	0.1	0.0	0.2	1.0	62.2	37.6	0.1	0.1	0.4
Yazoo	0.5	45.0	54.3	0.4	0.5	0.0	0.3	4.4	46.9	52.7	0.1	0.2	0.4
MISSOURI	1.5	86.1	11.7	1.1	1.4	0.1	1.2	2.1	87.7	10.7	0.4	0.8	1.2
Adair	0.9	96.6	1.4	0.6	1.7	0.1	0.6	1.3	97.8	0.9	0.2	0.9	0.7
Andrew	0.5	98.8	0.5	0.7	0.2	0.0	0.2	0.8	99.2	0.2	0.3	0.2	0.7
Atchison	0.3	97.3	2.2	0.3	0.2	0.0	0.3	0.7	97.6	1.1	0.2	0.2	1.4
Audrain	0.9	91.9	7.6	0.6	0.5	0.1	0.4	0.7	93.4	6.0	0.1	0.4	0.3
Barry	1.4	95.5	0.2	1.9	0.3	0.1	3.5	5.0	98.5	0.1	1.0	0.3	0.6
Barton	1.4	98.3	0.4	1.8	0.4	0.1	0.3	0.9	98.6	0.1	1.0	0.2	0.5
Bates	0.9	98.2	0.7	1.3	0.2	0.0	0.5	1.1	98.6	0.7	0.5	0.1	0.5
Benton	1.1	99.0	0.2	1.3	0.3	0.0	0.2	0.9	99.1	0.1	0.5	0.1	0.6
Bollinger	0.9	98.7	0.3	1.5	0.3	0.0	0.3	0.6	99.3	0.1	0.3	0.3	0.7
Boone	1.9	87.1	9.4	1.0	3.4	0.1	1.1	1.8	89.0	7.5	0.4	2.8	1.1
Buchanan	1.4	94.0	4.9	0.9	0.6	0.1	0.9	2.4	95.5	3.2	0.3	0.3	2.1
Butler	1.4	93.4	5.6	1.3	0.6	0.0	0.5	1.0	94.1	5.1	0.3	0.3	0.6
Caldwell	0.7	99.2	0.3	0.7	0.2	0.0	0.3	0.7	99.5	0.2	0.3	0.0	0.6
Callaway	1.2	92.9	6.0	1.1	0.7	0.1	0.5	0.9	94.3	4.8	0.3	0.4	0.5
Camden	1.0	98.7	0.3	1.2	0.4	0.1	0.3	0.9	99.1	0.2	0.4	0.2	0.6
Cape Girardeau	1.1	93.2	5.7	0.9	0.9	0.1	0.5	0.9	94.0	4.8	0.2	0.8	0.5
Carroll	0.8	97.7	2.0	0.7	0.2	0.0	0.3	0.7	97.6	2.0	0.1	0.1	0.4
Carter	1.8	98.4	0.1	2.9	0.2	0.1	0.3	1.2	99.1	0.0	0.7	0.1	0.6
Cass	1.4	96.9	1.7	1.3	0.7	0.1	0.7	2.2	97.5	1.1	0.6	0.4	1.3
Cedar	1.4	98.0	0.5	1.6	0.6	0.1	0.8	1.1	99.0	0.0	0.6	0.2	0.5
Chariton	0.4	96.4	3.3	0.4	0.2	0.0	0.1	0.6	96.0	3.7	0.2	0.1	0.2
Christian	1.1	98.4	0.4	1.3	0.5	0.1	0.5	1.3	98.9	0.1	0.6	0.2	0.7
Clark	0.6	99.4	0.2	0.5	0.1	0.0	0.4	0.7	99.7	0.0	0.1	0.1	0.3
Clay	1.8	94.1	3.1	1.1	1.7	0.2	1.7	3.6	96.3	1.8	0.5	0.7	2.3
Clinton	1.1	97.7	1.8	1.0	0.2	0.0	0.4	1.1	97.1	2.0	0.4	0.1	0.8
Cole	1.2	88.0	10.5	0.8	1.2	0.1	0.8	1.3	91.4	7.6	0.4	0.4	0.7
Cooper	1.1	90.0	9.5	0.9	0.4	0.1	0.4	0.9	91.4	7.7	0.4	0.3	0.6
Crawford	0.8	99.1	0.2	1.1	0.2	0.1	0.2	0.8	99.6	0.0	0.2	0.2	0.6
Dade	1.2	98.6	0.3	1.7	0.3	0.1	0.3	0.8	98.5	0.3	0.9	0.2	1.0
Dallas	1.4	98.8	0.2	1.8	0.2	0.1	0.3	0.9	99.0	0.1	0.7	0.1	0.5
Daviess	0.4	99.1	0.2	0.5	0.1	0.2	0.3	0.7	99.3	0.0	0.4	0.2	0.6
De Kalb	0.9	89.9	9.0	1.2	0.4	0.1	0.4	1.1	90.4	7.4	0.8	0.3	2.0
Dent	1.4	98.4	0.5	1.8	0.3	0.1	0.4	0.8	99.0	0.1	0.5	0.2	0.6
Douglas	1.7	98.5	0.2	2.3	0.3	0.1	0.3	0.8	99.0	0.0	0.7	0.1	0.8
Dunklin	1.1	89.6	9.0	0.9	0.4	0.0	1.2	2.5	91.4	7.9	0.3	0.2	0.5
Franklin	0.9	98.3	1.1	0.7	0.4	0.0	0.3	0.7	98.5	0.9	0.2	0.2	0.5
Gasconade	0.7	99.4	0.2	0.7	0.3	0.0	0.2	0.4	99.6	0.1	0.2	0.1	0.2
Gentry	0.6	99.1	0.3	0.7	0.3	0.2	0.1	0.6	99.3	0.1	0.4	0.1	0.4
Greene	1.7	95.1	2.7	1.5	1.4	0.1	1.0	1.8	96.6	1.8	0.6	0.7	0.9
Grundy	1.0	98.5	0.5	0.9	0.3	0.0	0.8	1.6	99.2	0.1	0.4	0.2	0.7
Harrison	1.0	99.3	0.4	0.9	0.4	0.3	0.3	1.0	99.2	0.1	0.4	0.3	0.4
Henry	1.1	97.6	1.2	1.4	0.4	0.1	0.5	0.9	98.1	1.1	0.4	0.2	0.7
Hickory	1.4	98.9	0.3	1.7	0.2	0.0	0.4	0.8	99.0	0.1	0.7	0.1	0.4
Holt	0.7	99.1	0.3	1.1	0.1	0.0	0.1	0.4	99.3	0.1	0.4	0.1	0.3
Howard	1.1	92.2	7.2	0.9	0.2	0.1	0.6	0.9	91.8	7.6	0.3	0.2	0.5
Howell	1.6	98.0	0.4	2.1	0.6	0.1	0.5	1.2	98.9	0.2	0.5	0.2	0.5
Iron	1.0	97.7	1.7	1.1	0.2	0.1	0.3	0.6	99.1	0.5	0.1	0.1	0.4
Jackson	2.3	71.9	24.2	1.3	1.6	0.3	3.2	5.4	75.6	21.4	0.5	1.0	3.0

¹Hispanic persons may be of any race.

Table B. States and Counties

STATE County	Population and population characteristics, 2000										
	Age (percent)									Median age (years)	Percent Female
	Under 5 years	5 to 17 years	18 to 24 years	25 to 34 years	35 to 44 years	45 to 54 years	55 to 64 years	65 to 74 years	75 years and over		
	28	29	30	31	32	33	34	35	36	37	38
MISSISSIPPI—Cont'd											
Sunflower	7.0	20.9	14.0	15.2	15.1	11.6	6.5	4.9	4.8	30.2	46.3
Tallahatchie	7.0	23.1	10.0	12.0	13.9	12.0	8.8	6.8	6.4	33.3	53.3
Tate	6.9	20.2	11.7	12.3	15.1	13.2	9.1	6.1	5.3	34.2	51.6
Tippah	6.3	18.6	10.1	13.6	14.4	12.6	9.9	7.4	7.1	35.9	51.6
Tishomingo	5.9	17.3	7.8	12.8	14.7	13.3	11.4	9.1	7.7	39.1	51.9
Tunica	8.4	23.1	10.9	13.0	14.4	12.4	7.8	5.4	4.7	30.6	52.3
Union	7.4	18.6	9.2	13.9	14.6	12.9	9.4	7.5	6.6	35.6	51.6
Walthall	7.1	21.3	9.9	11.6	13.8	12.6	9.7	7.4	6.7	35.1	52.2
Warren	7.6	21.0	9.1	12.7	15.7	13.7	8.6	6.0	5.6	34.8	53.1
Washington	8.4	23.1	10.1	12.6	13.9	12.6	7.8	6.0	5.5	31.5	53.3
Wayne	7.6	21.6	9.7	12.7	14.9	12.4	9.3	6.5	5.3	33.8	52.2
Webster	6.7	19.4	9.0	11.6	15.0	12.2	9.6	8.3	8.2	37.3	51.7
Wilkinson	5.8	20.0	10.7	13.5	15.5	12.2	8.4	6.9	6.9	35.0	48.1
Winston	6.7	20.0	9.2	12.2	13.8	13.2	9.3	8.3	7.2	36.3	51.6
Yalobusha	6.4	19.1	8.9	12.1	14.0	13.4	10.4	8.2	7.5	37.7	52.3
Yazoo	7.4	21.0	9.8	13.6	15.6	12.2	7.9	6.5	5.9	33.7	49.1
MISSOURI	6.6	18.9	9.6	13.2	15.9	13.3	9.1	7.0	6.5	36.1	51.4
Adair	5.3	13.9	27.4	10.9	11.9	10.8	7.6	5.8	6.5	27.9	53.1
Andrew	6.3	20.0	7.9	11.6	16.1	14.4	9.3	6.9	7.5	37.8	51.3
Atchison	4.5	19.6	6.5	10.1	14.1	13.8	10.3	9.4	11.6	41.7	50.2
Audrain	6.4	18.2	7.9	12.7	15.5	13.3	9.2	7.8	9.1	38.0	54.3
Barry	6.7	19.4	7.8	11.3	14.8	12.7	11.2	8.8	7.3	38.2	50.4
Barton	7.7	19.8	8.3	11.1	15.0	12.9	8.8	8.1	8.3	37.3	51.0
Bates	6.1	20.4	7.5	11.0	15.0	12.6	9.9	8.6	8.8	38.4	51.2
Benton	4.8	15.7	5.7	8.3	13.5	14.1	15.6	13.5	8.8	46.3	50.5
Bollinger	6.1	20.1	7.8	11.9	14.9	13.8	10.7	8.3	6.5	37.9	50.5
Boone	6.2	16.6	19.9	15.2	14.7	12.1	6.6	4.4	4.2	29.5	51.7
Buchanan	6.3	18.1	11.0	13.1	15.5	12.6	8.6	7.3	7.7	36.1	50.8
Butler	6.4	17.8	8.4	12.1	14.5	13.6	10.5	8.9	7.8	38.7	52.1
Caldwell	6.3	20.8	7.1	10.5	14.6	13.3	10.4	8.4	8.7	38.8	50.6
Callaway	6.2	19.2	11.1	14.0	17.1	13.3	8.2	6.0	5.0	34.7	48.2
Camden	4.6	15.6	6.1	9.3	14.0	15.1	16.2	12.2	6.8	45.2	50.0
Cape Girardeau	6.0	17.5	13.4	12.9	14.8	13.2	8.5	6.8	7.0	35.2	51.8
Carroll	6.4	18.8	7.4	10.7	13.8	13.0	9.9	9.0	11.0	40.0	51.5
Carter	6.2	18.9	8.0	11.1	14.8	13.6	11.4	9.4	6.5	38.9	50.9
Cass	7.4	21.0	7.3	12.9	17.3	13.1	9.2	6.4	5.4	35.8	51.0
Cedar	5.7	19.0	6.4	9.5	13.3	12.9	12.5	11.0	9.8	42.2	51.1
Chariton	5.1	18.6	6.5	9.1	14.6	13.2	10.5	10.6	11.7	42.5	52.1
Christian	7.7	20.2	8.1	14.9	16.8	13.2	8.6	5.9	4.7	34.5	51.4
Clark	6.1	18.8	7.8	11.0	14.5	14.2	10.8	8.2	8.5	39.2	50.6
Clay	7.2	18.6	8.7	15.4	17.0	13.7	8.6	5.9	4.9	35.0	51.4
Clinton	6.6	20.2	7.4	11.6	16.6	13.5	10.0	6.8	7.3	37.7	51.0
Cole	6.5	17.7	9.8	15.2	17.1	14.4	8.0	5.8	5.5	35.5	48.6
Cooper	5.8	17.0	14.0	13.0	14.4	12.1	8.5	7.0	8.2	35.2	46.0
Crawford	6.5	19.8	7.9	11.4	15.6	12.7	10.4	8.6	7.2	37.9	50.7
Dade	5.8	18.5	6.8	9.6	14.6	13.0	11.4	10.2	10.1	41.7	51.0
Dallas	6.7	20.8	7.4	10.9	15.6	12.8	10.7	8.3	6.8	37.9	50.4
Daviess	7.0	20.0	7.6	10.7	13.4	12.9	10.8	9.5	8.1	38.9	51.8
De Kalb	5.2	15.5	8.2	15.4	20.8	12.3	8.6	7.0	6.9	37.7	39.6
Dent	6.4	18.5	7.6	10.8	14.8	12.9	11.2	9.2	8.6	39.6	51.5
Douglas	6.0	19.8	7.0	10.1	14.4	13.5	12.0	9.5	7.6	40.1	50.9
Dunklin	7.1	18.8	8.1	12.1	13.8	12.6	10.9	8.1	8.4	37.8	52.7
Franklin	6.9	20.4	8.2	13.2	16.8	13.2	9.2	6.6	5.5	35.8	50.4
Gasconade	5.8	18.9	6.9	10.2	15.6	13.1	10.6	9.1	9.7	40.3	51.4
Gentry	6.2	19.8	7.0	9.7	14.0	11.2	10.4	9.7	11.9	40.2	51.2
Greene	6.1	16.1	13.8	13.8	14.8	13.2	8.6	6.8	6.8	35.1	51.5
Grundy	6.1	17.1	8.3	10.2	13.5	12.9	11.3	9.7	10.9	41.3	52.5
Harrison	6.4	17.3	7.2	10.3	13.5	11.5	11.6	10.4	11.6	41.7	51.5
Henry	6.0	17.8	7.8	11.2	14.6	13.2	11.2	9.0	9.2	40.0	51.2
Hickory	4.3	15.6	5.3	7.5	11.5	13.7	15.9	15.4	10.7	49.7	51.0
Holt	4.8	19.0	6.5	10.0	14.3	13.8	10.1	9.5	12.0	41.8	50.6
Howard	5.6	18.4	13.3	10.6	14.6	12.5	8.9	7.3	8.8	36.7	51.6
Howell	6.7	19.3	7.8	11.8	14.4	12.7	10.5	8.8	7.9	38.2	51.7
Iron	5.9	19.1	7.8	10.9	14.4	13.5	11.3	8.9	8.2	39.7	51.3
Jackson	7.0	18.8	9.1	14.8	16.2	13.2	8.3	6.5	6.0	35.2	51.8

Table B. States and Counties

STATE County	Population and population characteristics, 1990										Population—change, 1980–2000				
	Age (percent)										Total persons			Percent change	
	Under 5 years	5 to 17 years	18 to 24 years	25 to 34 years	35 to 44 years	45 to 54 years	55 to 64 years	65 to 74 years	75 years and over	Percent Female	2000	1990	1980	1990–2000	1980–1990
	39	40	41	42	43	44	45	46	47	48	49	50	51	52	53
MISSISSIPPI—Cont'd															
Sunflower	7.8	24.0	12.3	16.3	12.5	7.7	6.9	6.5	6.0	49.9	34 369	35 129	34 844	-2.2	0.8
Tallahatchie	8.7	24.5	10.6	13.8	11.5	8.6	8.0	7.9	6.5	52.9	14 903	15 210	17 157	-2.0	-11.3
Tate	7.6	21.8	12.5	14.8	13.4	10.0	7.8	6.6	5.5	51.8	25 370	21 432	20 119	18.4	6.5
Tippah	6.9	20.1	10.7	14.6	12.9	10.3	9.1	7.9	7.5	52.0	20 826	19 523	18 739	6.7	4.2
Tishomingo	6.3	17.3	9.8	13.9	13.7	11.5	10.6	9.4	7.5	52.3	19 163	17 683	18 434	8.4	-4.1
Tunica	9.7	28.1	11.4	13.2	11.1	7.8	6.7	6.9	5.1	53.3	9 227	8 164	9 652	13.0	-15.4
Union	6.7	19.7	10.0	14.4	14.0	10.3	9.4	8.1	7.3	51.8	25 362	22 085	21 741	14.8	1.6
Walthall	7.5	24.1	9.6	14.0	11.9	9.4	9.0	7.7	6.8	51.7	15 156	14 352	13 761	5.6	4.3
Warren	7.2	22.7	9.1	15.3	14.7	10.2	7.8	7.2	5.9	52.8	49 644	47 880	51 627	3.7	-7.3
Washington	8.7	25.2	10.3	14.8	12.8	8.5	7.7	6.6	5.4	53.3	62 977	67 935	72 344	-7.3	-6.1
Wayne	7.7	23.6	9.9	15.9	13.2	9.8	8.2	6.6	5.1	52.1	21 216	19 517	19 135	8.7	2.0
Webster	6.5	20.4	9.7	13.7	12.7	10.1	9.4	9.3	8.3	52.1	10 294	10 222	10 300	0.7	-0.8
Wilkinson	8.1	22.3	9.9	14.9	12.6	9.1	8.3	8.1	6.8	53.1	10 312	9 678	10 021	6.6	-3.4
Winston	7.1	22.3	9.2	12.9	13.7	9.5	9.9	8.1	7.2	52.9	20 160	19 433	19 474	3.7	-0.2
Yalobusha	7.0	21.0	9.0	13.4	13.0	9.7	9.4	9.9	7.8	53.3	13 051	12 033	13 183	8.5	-8.7
Yazoo	8.3	24.1	9.2	14.1	11.8	8.8	8.9	7.8	6.9	53.2	28 149	25 506	27 349	10.4	-6.7
MISSOURI	7.2	18.5	10.1	16.7	14.4	10.2	8.9	7.7	6.3	51.8	5 595 211	5 116 901	4 916 766	9.3	4.1
Adair	5.6	14.6	26.6	13.6	11.8	8.0	6.7	6.8	6.5	53.2	24 977	24 577	24 870	1.6	-1.2
Andrew	6.7	20.3	8.1	14.6	14.9	10.7	8.9	8.2	7.6	51.4	16 492	14 632	13 980	12.7	4.7
Atchison	5.3	17.2	11.5	12.3	13.1	9.4	10.1	10.9	10.2	51.1	6 430	7 457	8 605	-13.8	-13.3
Audrain	6.7	19.7	7.2	13.5	13.6	10.1	9.9	10.4	8.9	51.8	25 853	23 599	26 458	9.6	-10.8
Barry	6.6	18.7	7.8	14.0	12.3	11.1	10.9	10.5	8.2	51.0	34 010	27 547	24 408	23.5	12.9
Barton	6.8	19.6	7.3	14.7	12.9	9.3	9.8	9.9	9.8	51.8	12 541	11 312	11 292	10.9	0.2
Bates	6.5	19.6	7.0	13.2	12.8	10.2	10.8	10.0	9.7	51.8	16 653	15 025	15 873	10.8	-5.3
Benton	5.1	16.4	6.3	10.8	11.7	12.1	14.9	13.5	9.1	51.1	17 180	13 859	12 183	24.0	13.8
Bollinger	7.0	19.2	8.5	14.0	13.1	10.8	10.3	9.6	7.4	50.4	12 029	10 619	10 301	13.3	3.1
Boone	7.1	15.5	22.1	18.9	14.2	8.1	5.8	4.6	3.8	51.6	135 454	112 379	100 376	20.5	12.0
Buchanan	7.2	18.6	9.8	15.8	13.5	9.5	9.2	8.7	7.7	52.6	85 998	83 083	87 888	3.5	-5.5
Butler	6.5	19.2	8.6	14.4	13.5	10.5	10.6	9.4	7.1	52.4	40 867	38 765	37 693	5.4	2.8
Caldwell	7.0	19.3	7.2	13.1	12.5	10.5	9.8	10.4	10.4	52.4	8 969	8 380	8 660	7.0	-3.2
Callaway	7.3	18.9	11.6	16.3	14.9	10.1	8.4	6.6	5.8	51.5	40 766	32 809	32 252	24.3	1.7
Camden	5.8	16.0	6.5	12.8	13.3	12.3	14.8	12.4	6.0	50.1	37 051	27 495	20 017	34.8	37.4
Cape Girardeau	6.7	17.1	14.9	15.7	14.2	9.6	8.1	7.4	6.4	52.0	68 693	61 633	58 837	11.5	4.8
Carroll	6.5	19.8	7.0	12.6	12.5	10.2	10.0	10.6	10.8	52.4	10 285	10 748	12 131	-4.3	-11.4
Carter	7.1	20.5	8.1	13.3	12.9	11.2	11.0	8.7	7.1	50.6	5 941	5 515	5 428	7.7	1.6
Cass	8.0	21.0	8.6	17.1	15.1	11.3	8.1	5.7	5.0	51.3	82 092	63 808	51 029	28.7	25.0
Cedar	5.9	17.3	6.7	11.5	11.5	10.6	12.4	12.6	11.5	52.6	13 733	12 093	11 894	13.6	1.7
Chariton	6.8	19.0	6.6	12.9	12.2	9.9	10.9	10.8	10.9	52.1	8 438	9 202	10 489	-8.3	-12.3
Christian	7.4	21.1	8.7	17.1	15.9	10.6	8.0	6.2	4.9	51.2	54 285	32 644	22 402	66.3	45.7
Clark	6.6	20.6	8.3	13.2	13.9	10.7	9.5	8.8	8.3	50.3	7 416	7 547	8 493	-1.7	-11.1
Clay	7.4	18.3	9.9	18.5	16.0	11.1	8.5	6.4	4.0	51.7	184 006	153 411	136 488	19.9	12.4
Clinton	7.2	20.6	7.5	14.6	14.2	11.9	9.0	7.4	7.7	51.6	18 979	16 595	15 916	14.4	4.3
Cole	6.9	18.2	10.1	19.0	16.2	9.7	7.7	6.5	5.7	49.0	71 397	63 579	56 663	12.3	12.2
Cooper	6.4	18.0	13.4	13.5	12.7	9.3	8.6	9.6	8.4	48.4	16 670	14 835	14 643	12.4	1.3
Crawford	6.8	20.2	7.8	14.6	12.7	10.6	10.3	9.4	7.8	51.3	22 804	19 173	18 300	18.9	4.8
Dade	7.0	18.3	6.6	13.0	12.0	9.9	11.0	10.7	11.5	52.4	7 923	7 449	7 383	6.4	0.9
Dallas	7.1	19.7	7.3	13.8	12.5	10.6	10.7	9.9	8.4	51.0	15 661	12 646	12 096	23.8	4.5
Daviess	6.9	20.0	7.0	12.6	11.9	10.8	10.5	10.4	9.9	52.5	8 016	7 865	8 905	1.9	-11.7
De Kalb	5.6	15.7	10.4	21.0	13.6	9.2	8.2	7.9	8.5	41.6	11 597	9 967	8 222	16.4	21.2
Dent	6.2	20.1	7.5	13.2	12.9	10.9	10.4	10.0	8.7	52.0	14 927	13 702	14 517	8.9	-5.6
Douglas	6.9	19.9	7.2	13.3	12.6	11.8	11.0	9.2	8.1	51.5	13 084	11 876	11 594	10.2	2.4
Dunklin	6.7	19.7	8.6	13.5	12.8	11.1	9.6	9.9	8.2	53.6	33 155	33 112	36 324	0.1	-8.8
Franklin	7.8	20.7	9.6	16.6	14.0	10.6	8.5	6.8	5.3	50.6	93 807	80 603	71 233	16.4	13.2
Gasconade	6.8	18.1	7.2	14.6	12.5	9.5	10.3	11.2	9.9	51.7	15 342	14 006	13 181	9.5	6.3
Gentry	6.5	18.2	6.7	12.9	10.3	10.1	10.2	11.9	13.3	52.9	6 861	6 854	7 887	0.1	-13.1
Greene	6.4	16.5	14.8	16.3	14.5	9.9	8.3	7.3	6.0	52.1	240 391	207 949	185 302	15.6	12.2
Grundy	6.2	17.5	7.2	12.8	12.7	10.9	10.6	11.0	11.1	53.6	10 432	10 536	11 959	-1.0	-11.9
Harrison	5.8	17.1	6.4	13.2	11.0	10.7	11.7	11.4	12.7	52.1	8 850	8 469	9 890	4.5	-14.4
Henry	6.4	18.2	7.6	13.4	12.9	10.7	10.2	10.4	10.1	52.1	21 997	20 044	19 672	9.7	1.9
Hickory	4.6	14.7	5.1	9.4	10.6	10.5	16.9	17.7	10.6	50.9	8 940	7 335	6 367	21.9	15.2
Holt	6.6	19.0	6.9	12.8	12.8	9.3	9.8	10.9	11.9	51.2	5 351	6 034	6 882	-11.3	-12.3
Howard	6.3	18.4	11.6	13.8	12.4	9.3	9.3	9.3	9.7	51.6	10 212	9 631	10 008	6.0	-3.8
Howell	6.8	19.5	8.2	13.6	13.3	10.9	10.3	9.4	8.0	51.9	37 238	31 447	28 807	18.4	9.2
Iron	6.3	20.4	7.7	12.9	12.7	10.7	10.4	9.6	9.3	52.9	10 697	10 726	11 084	-0.3	-3.2
Jackson	7.6	17.8	9.7	18.4	14.8	10.0	8.7	7.3	5.8	52.4	654 880	633 234	629 266	3.4	0.6

Table B. States and Counties

STATE County	Total population	Total in house-holds	House-holder	Spouse	Child Total	Child Own child under 18 years	Other relatives Total	Other relatives Under 18 years	Nonrelatives Total	Nonrelatives Unmarried partner	Total in group quarters	Institutionalized Correctional institutions	Institutionalized Nursing homes	Institutionalized Other institutions	Noninstitutionalized College dormitories	Noninstitutionalized Military quarters	Other
	54	55	56	57	58	59	60	61	62	63	64	65	66	67	68	69	70
MISSISSIPPI—Cont'd																	
Sunflower	34 369	84.5	28.0	11.9	29.9	20.1	11.5	7.1	3.2	1.7	15.5	13.7	0.6	0.0	1.2	0.0	0.1
Tallahatchie	14 903	99.3	35.3	15.3	33.1	22.6	12.1	7.1	3.4	2.1	0.7	0.2	0.4	0.0	0.0	0.0	0.0
Tate	25 370	95.5	34.9	19.5	31.2	22.8	7.0	3.6	2.9	1.4	4.5	0.2	0.5	0.0	3.1	0.0	0.7
Tippah	20 826	98.2	38.9	22.3	29.8	22.3	4.6	2.1	2.6	1.2	1.8	0.1	0.8	0.3	0.6	0.0	0.0
Tishomingo	19 163	98.6	41.3	23.6	27.3	21.1	4.1	1.7	2.3	1.1	1.4	0.1	1.3	0.0	0.0	0.0	0.0
Tunica	9 227	98.8	35.3	12.0	33.7	23.5	12.3	7.2	5.6	2.9	1.2	0.6	0.6	0.0	0.0	0.0	0.1
Union	25 362	99.0	38.6	22.7	30.1	23.2	4.8	2.2	2.7	1.3	1.0	0.2	0.5	0.0	0.0	0.0	0.3
Walthall	15 156	98.8	36.8	19.5	32.4	23.7	7.7	4.2	2.5	1.3	1.2	0.2	0.9	0.0	0.0	0.0	0.1
Warren	49 644	98.8	37.8	17.7	32.6	24.4	6.7	3.5	4.0	2.1	1.2	0.2	0.8	0.0	0.0	0.0	0.2
Washington	62 977	98.6	35.2	14.3	34.2	24.5	10.9	6.5	4.0	2.2	1.4	0.4	0.6	0.1	0.0	0.0	0.3
Wayne	21 216	99.1	37.0	19.6	33.5	25.3	6.2	3.4	2.8	1.5	0.9	0.2	0.6	0.0	0.0	0.0	0.2
Webster	10 294	98.1	37.9	21.3	31.0	23.1	5.5	2.6	2.3	1.3	1.9	0.1	1.4	0.0	0.2	0.0	0.1
Wilkinson	10 312	89.9	34.7	14.0	29.5	20.1	9.0	5.2	2.7	1.6	10.1	9.2	0.9	0.0	0.0	0.0	0.0
Winston	20 160	97.2	37.6	18.8	31.0	22.6	6.9	3.7	2.9	1.5	2.8	1.4	1.0	0.0	0.0	0.0	0.4
Yalobusha	13 051	99.2	40.3	18.8	29.9	21.1	7.1	3.8	3.2	1.8	0.8	0.1	0.5	0.1	0.0	0.0	0.1
Yazoo	28 149	91.6	32.6	14.1	31.9	22.6	9.4	5.4	3.5	1.8	8.4	7.5	0.7	0.1	0.0	0.0	0.2
MISSOURI	5 595 211	97.1	39.2	20.4	29.2	23.1	3.8	1.7	4.5	2.0	2.9	0.6	0.9	0.1	0.8	0.1	0.4
Adair	24 977	88.8	38.7	17.6	21.2	17.8	1.8	0.7	9.5	1.5	11.2	0.1	0.9	0.2	9.4	0.0	0.6
Andrew	16 492	98.4	38.0	23.8	30.5	24.4	2.8	1.4	3.3	1.8	1.6	0.1	1.4	0.0	0.0	0.0	0.1
Atchison	6 430	95.4	42.3	23.6	24.7	20.6	1.9	0.9	2.8	1.5	4.6	0.0	1.5	3.0	0.0	0.0	0.1
Audrain	25 853	92.5	38.1	21.0	27.6	22.8	2.6	1.1	3.3	1.8	7.5	5.4	1.7	0.1	0.0	0.0	0.4
Barry	34 010	99.0	39.4	23.4	28.7	23.6	3.7	1.8	3.8	1.9	1.0	0.1	0.9	0.0	0.0	0.0	0.1
Barton	12 541	98.6	39.0	22.7	30.2	25.1	3.1	1.5	3.6	1.7	1.4	0.1	0.9	0.1	0.0	0.0	0.2
Bates	16 653	98.3	39.1	23.0	29.3	24.4	3.0	1.4	3.9	1.9	1.7	0.1	1.6	0.0	0.0	0.0	0.0
Benton	17 180	98.6	43.2	25.8	22.7	18.3	3.3	1.5	3.6	2.0	1.4	0.1	1.0	0.0	0.0	0.0	0.3
Bollinger	12 029	98.6	38.0	24.3	30.4	24.3	3.0	1.3	2.9	1.6	1.4	0.1	0.5	0.0	0.0	0.0	0.7
Boone	135 454	93.4	39.2	17.8	25.1	21.3	2.6	0.9	8.7	2.3	6.6	0.2	0.5	0.0	5.5	0.0	0.4
Buchanan	85 998	94.6	39.0	19.3	27.7	21.9	3.6	1.7	5.0	2.4	5.4	2.5	0.9	0.4	1.1	0.0	0.6
Butler	40 867	97.7	40.9	21.5	27.3	21.5	4.0	1.9	4.0	2.0	2.3	0.4	1.3	0.0	0.0	0.0	0.5
Caldwell	8 969	98.7	39.3	23.2	30.9	25.3	2.7	1.5	2.6	1.5	1.3	0.0	1.3	0.0	0.0	0.0	0.0
Callaway	40 766	90.6	35.4	20.2	27.8	23.1	2.8	1.3	4.5	2.3	9.4	6.0	0.8	0.2	2.2	0.0	0.2
Camden	37 051	98.3	42.6	26.3	22.2	18.2	2.9	1.2	4.4	2.3	1.7	0.1	0.5	0.4	0.0	0.0	0.6
Cape Girardeau	68 693	95.0	39.3	21.1	27.3	21.7	2.9	1.1	4.5	1.7	5.0	0.1	1.6	0.0	2.8	0.0	0.5
Carroll	10 285	98.1	40.5	23.3	28.7	23.5	2.9	1.3	2.8	1.5	1.9	0.3	1.5	0.0	0.0	0.0	0.1
Carter	5 941	98.6	40.0	23.0	28.8	23.0	3.6	1.6	3.2	1.7	1.4	0.0	0.8	0.0	0.0	0.0	0.7
Cass	82 092	98.8	36.7	23.4	32.0	26.3	3.2	1.4	3.5	1.6	1.2	0.1	1.0	0.0	0.0	0.0	0.1
Cedar	13 733	97.5	41.4	23.8	26.2	21.8	2.6	1.3	3.5	1.7	2.5	0.1	1.2	0.2	0.9	0.0	0.1
Chariton	8 438	97.7	41.1	24.0	27.6	22.2	2.3	1.0	2.7	1.5	2.3	0.1	2.1	0.0	0.0	0.0	0.1
Christian	54 285	98.9	37.6	24.1	31.0	26.0	2.7	1.2	3.5	1.6	1.1	0.0	0.7	0.0	0.0	0.0	0.4
Clark	7 416	98.4	40.0	23.5	28.7	22.8	2.5	1.4	3.7	2.3	1.6	0.1	1.5	0.1	0.0	0.0	0.0
Clay	184 006	98.4	39.4	21.8	29.4	23.9	3.3	1.3	4.4	2.1	1.6	0.1	0.7	0.1	0.4	0.0	0.4
Clinton	18 979	97.7	37.7	23.2	30.4	24.8	3.0	1.5	3.4	1.7	2.3	0.1	1.7	0.1	0.0	0.0	0.4
Cole	71 397	92.0	37.9	20.1	27.8	22.7	2.4	0.9	3.8	1.7	8.0	6.3	0.6	0.0	0.7	0.0	0.3
Cooper	16 670	87.6	35.6	20.4	25.9	21.1	2.5	1.2	3.1	1.7	12.4	10.2	1.3	0.1	0.5	0.0	0.3
Crawford	22 804	98.3	38.8	22.8	29.5	23.9	3.3	1.7	3.9	2.1	1.7	0.1	1.1	0.0	0.0	0.0	0.4
Dade	7 923	98.5	40.4	24.8	28.3	22.8	2.5	1.2	2.5	1.4	1.5	0.1	1.5	0.0	0.0	0.0	0.0
Dallas	15 661	99.1	38.5	23.4	30.1	24.9	3.6	1.8	3.5	1.9	0.9	0.1	0.6	0.0	0.1	0.0	0.1
Daviess	8 016	99.3	39.6	24.1	30.2	25.3	2.6	1.2	2.7	1.6	0.7	0.0	0.7	0.0	0.0	0.0	0.0
De Kalb	11 597	76.1	30.4	18.1	23.6	19.4	1.8	0.9	2.2	1.1	23.9	22.7	1.1	0.0	0.0	0.0	0.1
Dent	14 927	98.2	40.1	23.7	27.6	22.5	3.0	1.4	3.8	1.8	1.8	0.1	0.7	0.4	0.0	0.0	0.6
Douglas	13 084	99.0	39.8	23.8	28.6	23.5	3.5	1.5	3.3	1.6	1.0	0.0	0.4	0.0	0.0	0.0	0.5
Dunklin	33 155	97.9	40.4	20.9	28.5	22.8	4.4	2.4	3.6	2.0	2.1	0.2	1.6	0.0	0.0	0.0	0.3
Franklin	93 807	98.9	37.3	22.5	32.0	25.2	3.3	1.5	3.9	2.0	1.1	0.1	0.8	0.0	0.0	0.0	0.1
Gasconade	15 342	98.0	40.2	23.3	28.3	23.0	2.8	1.1	3.3	1.8	2.0	0.0	1.9	0.0	0.0	0.0	0.1
Gentry	6 861	97.1	40.0	23.2	29.8	24.8	1.8	0.8	2.2	1.2	2.9	0.1	2.0	0.0	0.0	0.0	0.9
Greene	240 391	95.1	40.7	20.4	25.4	20.4	3.0	1.1	5.7	2.1	4.9	0.6	0.8	0.1	2.8	0.0	0.6
Grundy	10 432	96.6	42.0	23.0	26.2	21.4	2.1	1.0	3.3	1.6	3.4	0.0	1.7	0.0	1.1	0.0	0.5
Harrison	8 850	97.4	41.3	23.5	26.8	22.1	2.6	1.1	3.2	1.9	2.6	0.1	2.1	0.0	0.0	0.0	0.4
Henry	21 997	98.4	41.5	23.0	26.7	21.5	3.0	1.4	4.1	2.2	1.6	0.2	1.0	0.0	0.0	0.0	0.4
Hickory	8 940	98.8	43.7	26.2	22.1	17.8	3.6	1.7	3.2	1.7	1.2	0.1	1.0	0.0	0.0	0.0	0.1
Holt	5 351	98.1	41.8	24.0	27.7	22.4	2.0	0.8	2.7	1.5	1.9	0.1	1.8	0.0	0.0	0.0	0.0
Howard	10 212	92.2	37.6	20.8	27.7	22.2	2.7	1.1	3.5	1.8	7.8	0.1	0.9	0.0	5.4	0.0	1.4
Howell	37 238	98.0	39.6	23.3	28.9	24.0	3.0	1.4	3.2	1.5	2.0	0.2	1.3	0.0	0.1	0.0	0.4
Iron	10 697	96.4	39.2	22.3	28.5	22.9	2.9	1.4	3.5	1.9	3.6	0.1	2.5	0.1	0.0	0.0	0.9
Jackson	654 880	98.2	40.7	17.7	29.1	22.6	5.4	2.4	5.4	2.3	1.8	0.2	0.6	0.2	0.2	0.0	0.5

Table B. States and Counties

	Households by type, 2000												Households, 1990		
	Family households						Nonfamily households								
			Married couple		Female householder[1]			Householder living alone							
STATE County	Total households	Total	With own children under 18 years	Total	With own children under 18 years	Total	With own children under 18 years	Total	Total	65 years and over	Average house-hold size	Average family size	Total house-holds	Female house-holder[1]	House-holder living alone
	71	72	73	74	75	76	77	78	79	80	81	82	83	84	85
MISSISSIPPI—Cont'd															
Sunflower	9 637	75.9	38.4	42.3	19.7	28.4	16.3	24.1	21.2	9.7	3.01	3.50	9 650	23.4	25.3
Tallahatchie	5 263	72.7	34.0	43.5	18.5	23.5	12.7	27.3	24.6	11.6	2.81	3.36	5 034	20.2	24.4
Tate	8 850	75.9	36.1	56.0	25.5	15.5	8.6	24.1	21.3	9.1	2.74	3.18	7 024	14.0	18.7
Tippah	8 108	72.9	33.7	57.2	25.1	11.8	6.8	27.1	24.9	11.4	2.52	3.00	7 158	10.5	21.9
Tishomingo	7 917	70.4	30.2	57.1	23.3	10.1	5.5	29.6	27.5	12.8	2.39	2.89	7 059	9.0	23.5
Tunica	3 258	67.3	33.3	33.9	14.7	26.9	15.5	32.7	26.9	9.9	2.80	3.44	2 526	26.4	23.0
Union	9 786	74.0	34.7	58.9	26.1	11.1	6.5	26.0	23.4	11.3	2.57	3.02	8 367	9.7	23.0
Walthall	5 571	73.8	34.0	53.0	22.7	16.9	9.6	26.2	24.0	11.5	2.69	3.19	4 929	14.7	22.2
Warren	18 756	70.5	35.6	46.8	21.6	19.1	11.6	29.5	25.8	9.7	2.61	3.14	17 407	16.5	24.9
Washington	22 158	71.9	36.3	40.6	18.1	26.0	15.6	28.1	24.6	10.0	2.80	3.35	22 593	23.7	23.2
Wayne	7 857	74.5	37.7	53.0	25.1	17.2	10.5	25.5	23.1	9.7	2.67	3.15	6 858	15.8	21.1
Webster	3 905	73.7	33.9	56.2	24.8	13.1	7.2	26.3	24.0	12.2	2.59	3.07	3 826	13.3	25.5
Wilkinson	3 578	70.2	32.9	40.4	17.0	24.5	13.4	29.8	27.9	12.0	2.59	3.16	3 347	24.3	23.4
Winston	7 578	72.2	33.5	49.9	21.1	18.1	10.4	27.8	25.2	12.5	2.59	3.09	7 061	15.8	24.5
Yalobusha	5 260	68.4	29.7	46.6	18.4	17.6	9.4	31.6	28.7	14.0	2.46	3.02	4 614	15.6	28.1
Yazoo	9 178	72.4	35.6	43.2	18.8	23.7	13.9	27.6	24.5	11.7	2.81	3.35	8 813	20.3	25.0
MISSOURI	2 194 594	67.3	31.9	52.0	22.7	11.6	7.1	32.7	27.3	10.3	2.48	3.02	1 961 206	10.6	26.0
Adair	9 669	55.3	25.2	45.5	19.3	7.2	4.6	44.7	31.5	10.5	2.29	2.90	9 060	7.5	30.2
Andrew	6 273	73.9	34.5	62.7	27.3	7.4	4.7	26.1	22.3	10.5	2.59	3.03	5 429	6.8	20.6
Atchison	2 722	65.3	26.6	55.8	20.7	6.1	3.8	34.7	31.5	17.6	2.25	2.82	2 961	6.8	28.0
Audrain	9 844	68.7	31.4	55.2	22.5	9.9	6.7	31.3	27.8	13.4	2.43	2.96	9 205	8.5	25.5
Barry	13 398	71.5	31.2	59.3	23.7	8.4	5.2	28.5	24.7	11.6	2.51	2.98	10 858	7.0	23.5
Barton	4 895	70.3	34.0	58.1	26.3	8.5	5.4	29.7	26.4	13.3	2.53	3.04	4 524	7.1	27.7
Bates	6 511	70.0	32.3	58.8	25.1	7.6	4.9	30.0	26.1	13.9	2.51	3.02	5 918	7.3	25.4
Benton	7 420	69.8	23.2	59.6	17.1	6.8	4.2	30.2	26.3	13.8	2.28	2.72	5 764	6.2	24.7
Bollinger	4 576	75.7	34.3	63.8	27.2	8.4	5.2	24.3	21.6	10.5	2.59	3.00	3 946	7.2	20.6
Boone	53 094	59.1	30.3	45.5	21.3	10.4	7.2	40.9	28.7	6.2	2.38	2.97	41 937	9.5	27.5
Buchanan	33 557	65.3	30.6	49.3	20.8	12.0	7.4	34.7	28.9	12.5	2.42	2.98	32 486	11.4	27.7
Butler	16 718	67.7	29.7	52.5	20.5	11.6	7.1	32.3	28.0	12.7	2.39	2.91	15 334	11.3	25.6
Caldwell	3 523	71.0	32.3	59.2	24.6	8.0	5.5	29.0	25.5	13.0	2.51	3.04	3 222	6.7	24.8
Callaway	14 416	71.7	35.8	57.1	25.7	10.4	7.1	28.3	23.0	8.8	2.56	3.00	11 552	8.8	21.8
Camden	15 779	71.6	23.8	61.8	17.5	6.6	4.3	28.4	23.3	9.5	2.31	2.68	11 305	5.7	20.6
Cape Girardeau	26 980	66.5	31.2	53.8	23.5	9.8	6.1	33.5	27.3	10.1	2.42	2.96	23 390	8.9	25.4
Carroll	4 169	69.1	30.2	57.4	23.2	8.0	4.7	30.9	27.8	15.5	2.42	2.96	4 332	7.4	28.5
Carter	2 378	70.4	30.8	57.4	23.3	8.9	5.3	29.6	26.7	12.6	2.46	2.97	2 128	8.8	26.5
Cass	30 168	76.2	38.1	63.6	29.9	9.1	6.0	23.8	20.0	8.5	2.69	3.09	22 892	8.2	19.1
Cedar	5 685	68.5	27.8	57.5	20.7	7.9	5.0	31.5	28.1	15.3	2.35	2.86	5 003	6.8	27.4
Chariton	3 469	67.6	28.4	58.3	23.3	6.5	3.8	32.4	29.8	17.3	2.38	2.94	3 661	5.8	27.6
Christian	20 425	76.6	38.6	64.0	30.0	9.3	6.4	23.4	19.1	7.0	2.63	3.00	11 937	8.0	17.8
Clark	2 966	70.1	30.3	58.7	23.1	7.0	4.6	29.9	26.4	13.6	2.46	2.95	2 859	6.9	24.5
Clay	72 558	69.1	33.8	55.4	25.4	10.2	6.4	30.9	25.2	7.4	2.50	3.00	58 915	9.0	23.5
Clinton	7 152	74.1	34.9	61.4	26.8	8.8	5.6	25.9	22.0	10.5	2.59	3.03	6 112	7.2	21.7
Cole	27 040	66.3	33.6	53.0	24.8	10.0	6.8	33.7	28.7	9.3	2.43	3.00	22 976	8.8	27.4
Cooper	5 932	69.8	31.8	57.4	24.1	9.0	5.7	30.2	26.1	12.6	2.46	2.97	5 359	7.8	25.0
Crawford	8 858	71.7	32.8	58.7	24.3	9.0	5.9	28.3	24.3	11.3	2.53	3.00	7 299	7.4	23.0
Dade	3 202	71.1	29.1	61.3	23.5	6.5	3.5	28.9	26.5	14.7	2.44	2.93	2 976	6.1	27.7
Dallas	6 030	72.7	32.9	60.8	25.4	8.4	5.4	27.3	23.7	11.6	2.57	3.04	4 899	7.2	23.6
Daviess	3 178	71.3	31.5	60.8	24.7	7.5	4.9	28.7	25.7	13.2	2.50	3.02	3 040	5.7	25.5
De Kalb	3 528	70.1	32.4	59.6	25.5	7.4	5.0	29.9	26.9	14.7	2.50	3.04	3 054	5.8	25.0
Dent	5 982	71.5	30.6	59.0	22.8	9.1	5.7	28.5	25.0	13.1	2.45	2.90	5 327	8.2	23.8
Douglas	5 201	70.6	30.1	60.0	23.3	7.2	4.5	29.4	26.1	13.0	2.49	2.99	4 587	6.3	23.3
Dunklin	13 411	68.3	31.3	51.6	20.9	13.2	8.2	31.7	28.1	14.0	2.42	2.94	13 128	12.3	27.2
Franklin	34 945	73.5	36.1	60.4	28.1	9.0	5.5	26.5	22.1	8.9	2.66	3.11	28 856	8.4	20.0
Gasconade	6 171	69.5	31.0	58.0	23.8	7.6	4.8	30.5	27.0	14.6	2.44	2.95	5 543	6.2	25.8
Gentry	2 747	68.6	31.1	58.0	24.2	7.2	4.9	31.4	29.3	16.9	2.42	3.00	2 756	6.2	29.3
Greene	97 859	63.2	28.3	50.0	20.3	9.8	6.1	36.8	29.1	9.7	2.34	2.89	81 463	9.2	26.6
Grundy	4 382	65.9	27.1	54.8	19.8	8.0	5.3	34.1	30.8	16.3	2.30	2.85	4 346	7.2	29.1
Harrison	3 658	68.0	28.3	56.9	21.6	7.7	4.8	32.0	28.8	15.9	2.36	2.98	3 574	5.8	29.7
Henry	9 133	68.4	28.4	55.3	20.1	9.3	6.1	31.6	27.7	13.3	2.37	2.86	8 189	7.8	28.0
Hickory	3 911	70.0	22.0	59.9	16.1	6.7	3.8	30.0	26.5	15.1	2.26	2.70	3 183	5.2	24.4
Holt	2 237	67.2	28.2	57.3	22.1	6.1	4.1	32.8	29.7	16.7	2.35	2.91	2 440	5.2	28.8
Howard	3 836	68.6	31.5	55.3	23.4	9.5	6.1	31.4	27.3	13.3	2.46	2.98	3 571	8.5	26.9
Howell	14 762	71.9	32.7	58.8	24.3	9.9	6.4	28.1	25.0	12.3	2.47	2.94	12 283	8.4	24.4
Iron	4 197	70.6	32.0	56.8	22.4	9.4	6.7	29.4	25.8	11.4	2.46	2.94	3 995	8.7	23.5
Jackson	266 294	62.4	29.9	43.4	18.7	14.7	9.0	37.6	31.2	9.9	2.42	3.05	252 582	13.6	29.6

[1]No spouse present.

Table B. States and Counties

STATE County	Percent change of households, 1990–2000	Total housing units	Occupied housing units (percent)	Vacant housing units — Total	For seasonal, recreational, or occasional use	Homeowner vacancy rate (percent)	Rental vacancy rate (percent)	Occupied housing units — Total	Percent owner-occupied housing units	Percent renter-occupied housing units	Average household size of owner-occupied units	Average household size of renter-occupied units
	86	87	88	89	90	91	92	93	94	95	96	97
MISSISSIPPI—Cont'd												
Sunflower	-0.1	10 338	93.2	6.8	0.4	1.6	5.2	9 637	61.8	38.2	2.97	3.08
Tallahatchie	4.5	5 711	92.2	7.8	0.8	1.3	4.3	5 263	76.2	23.8	2.82	2.78
Tate	26.0	9 354	94.6	5.4	0.6	1.1	3.8	8 850	78.3	21.7	2.75	2.70
Tippah	13.3	8 868	91.4	8.6	1.3	1.4	9.5	8 108	78.2	21.8	2.55	2.44
Tishomingo	12.2	9 553	82.9	17.1	5.5	2.6	13.0	7 917	78.9	21.1	2.40	2.32
Tunica	29.0	3 705	87.9	12.1	5.3	1.3	5.8	3 258	51.7	48.3	2.97	2.62
Union	17.0	10 693	91.5	8.5	1.0	1.5	7.8	9 786	77.6	22.4	2.59	2.47
Walthall	13.0	6 418	86.8	13.2	3.8	1.8	7.6	5 571	83.3	16.7	2.69	2.67
Warren	7.7	20 789	90.2	9.8	1.0	1.5	12.1	18 756	68.2	31.8	2.65	2.53
Washington	-1.9	24 381	90.9	9.1	0.5	1.6	8.1	22 158	59.5	40.5	2.76	2.87
Wayne	14.6	9 049	86.8	13.2	2.1	1.2	13.7	7 857	85.0	15.0	2.70	2.55
Webster	2.1	4 344	89.9	10.1	1.8	1.5	5.4	3 905	78.4	21.6	2.59	2.56
Wilkinson	6.9	5 106	70.1	29.9	18.4	1.3	5.2	3 578	83.3	16.7	2.60	2.53
Winston	7.3	8 472	89.4	10.6	1.7	1.7	4.6	7 578	79.7	20.3	2.54	2.76
Yalobusha	14.0	6 224	84.5	15.5	6.4	2.5	11.5	5 260	79.0	21.0	2.48	2.41
Yazoo	4.1	10 015	91.6	8.4	0.7	1.3	7.1	9 178	68.8	31.2	2.75	2.93
MISSOURI	11.9	2 442 017	89.9	10.1	2.7	2.1	9.0	2 194 594	70.3	29.7	2.59	2.20
Adair	6.7	10 826	89.3	10.7	1.5	2.9	8.3	9 669	60.3	39.7	2.43	2.08
Andrew	15.5	6 662	94.2	5.8	0.9	1.7	5.8	6 273	80.0	20.0	2.66	2.29
Atchison	-8.1	3 103	87.7	12.3	1.2	3.5	12.5	2 722	69.0	31.0	2.31	2.14
Audrain	6.9	10 881	90.5	9.5	0.6	2.4	10.5	9 844	74.1	25.9	2.49	2.27
Barry	23.4	15 964	83.9	16.1	8.2	4.4	9.6	13 398	75.7	24.3	2.52	2.49
Barton	8.2	5 409	90.5	9.5	0.9	2.9	9.5	4 895	73.5	26.5	2.57	2.42
Bates	10.0	7 247	89.8	10.2	1.9	3.1	7.1	6 511	75.1	24.9	2.54	2.43
Benton	28.7	12 691	58.5	41.5	33.4	4.7	6.6	7 420	82.2	17.8	2.28	2.28
Bollinger	16.0	5 522	82.9	17.1	6.6	3.4	7.2	4 576	81.3	18.7	2.63	2.43
Boone	26.6	56 678	93.7	6.3	0.4	2.2	7.3	53 094	57.5	42.5	2.58	2.12
Buchanan	3.3	36 574	91.8	8.2	0.5	1.8	7.4	33 557	67.6	32.4	2.52	2.23
Butler	9.0	18 707	89.4	10.6	1.7	2.3	9.2	16 718	68.9	31.1	2.43	2.30
Caldwell	9.3	4 493	78.4	21.6	12.7	4.2	6.3	3 523	77.3	22.7	2.56	2.33
Callaway	24.8	16 167	89.2	10.8	2.3	2.1	12.0	14 416	76.8	23.2	2.64	2.30
Camden	39.6	33 470	47.1	52.9	46.1	3.9	24.2	15 779	82.2	17.8	2.30	2.33
Cape Girardeau	15.3	29 434	91.7	8.3	0.9	2.4	10.3	26 980	68.4	31.6	2.58	2.08
Carroll	-3.8	4 897	85.1	14.9	1.8	4.3	10.8	4 169	74.0	26.0	2.48	2.26
Carter	11.7	3 028	78.5	21.5	9.2	4.7	9.2	2 378	76.8	23.2	2.51	2.30
Cass	31.8	31 677	95.2	4.8	0.3	2.0	6.3	30 168	79.5	20.5	2.76	2.41
Cedar	13.6	6 813	83.4	16.6	5.8	3.7	11.5	5 685	78.3	21.7	2.39	2.23
Chariton	-5.2	4 250	81.6	18.4	6.6	2.0	17.7	3 469	80.6	19.4	2.41	2.21
Christian	71.1	21 827	93.6	6.4	0.7	2.8	8.5	20 425	75.9	24.1	2.69	2.42
Clark	3.7	3 483	85.2	14.8	4.7	2.3	7.3	2 966	78.5	21.5	2.54	2.18
Clay	23.2	76 230	95.2	4.8	0.3	1.5	7.4	72 558	70.7	29.3	2.65	2.13
Clinton	17.0	7 877	90.8	9.2	2.0	2.3	7.4	7 152	78.9	21.1	2.66	2.34
Cole	17.7	28 915	93.5	6.5	1.0	1.7	7.0	27 040	67.8	32.2	2.62	2.02
Cooper	10.7	6 676	88.9	11.1	0.8	2.6	12.9	5 932	74.1	25.9	2.52	2.30
Crawford	21.4	10 850	81.6	18.4	9.6	2.5	8.5	8 858	76.6	23.4	2.57	2.40
Dade	7.6	3 758	85.2	14.8	4.5	3.1	9.5	3 202	78.5	21.5	2.43	2.45
Dallas	23.1	6 914	87.2	12.8	2.5	3.3	8.4	6 030	79.2	20.8	2.61	2.43
Daviess	4.5	3 853	82.5	17.5	6.4	3.0	9.8	3 178	76.6	23.4	2.54	2.40
De Kalb	15.5	3 839	91.9	8.1	0.7	1.8	7.3	3 528	73.6	26.4	2.65	2.09
Dent	12.3	6 994	85.5	14.5	4.2	3.4	9.3	5 982	74.2	25.8	2.50	2.32
Douglas	13.4	5 919	87.9	12.1	2.4	2.8	6.8	5 201	79.0	21.0	2.51	2.41
Dunklin	2.2	14 682	91.3	8.7	0.4	2.2	9.4	13 411	66.0	34.0	2.40	2.46
Franklin	21.1	38 295	91.3	8.7	3.1	1.7	8.8	34 945	78.1	21.9	2.74	2.34
Gasconade	11.3	7 813	79.0	21.0	13.8	2.3	9.6	6 171	80.4	19.6	2.48	2.24
Gentry	-0.3	3 214	85.5	14.5	1.9	4.0	8.3	2 747	75.5	24.5	2.52	2.14
Greene	20.1	104 517	93.6	6.4	0.4	2.3	7.2	97 859	63.6	36.4	2.46	2.12
Grundy	0.8	5 102	85.9	14.1	3.2	2.6	10.6	4 382	71.8	28.2	2.37	2.12
Harrison	2.4	4 316	84.8	15.2	2.5	3.0	9.0	3 658	74.8	25.2	2.44	2.12
Henry	11.5	10 261	89.0	11.0	3.0	2.6	8.8	9 133	72.9	27.1	2.43	2.20
Hickory	22.9	6 184	63.2	36.8	25.5	5.4	9.9	3 911	84.5	15.5	2.25	2.28
Holt	-8.3	2 931	76.3	23.7	13.3	2.8	9.1	2 237	74.5	25.5	2.40	2.19
Howard	7.4	4 346	88.3	11.7	2.0	2.7	12.9	3 836	75.3	24.7	2.54	2.19
Howell	20.2	16 340	90.3	9.7	0.7	2.3	12.9	14 762	73.6	26.4	2.52	2.34
Iron	5.1	4 907	85.5	14.5	4.7	4.0	6.2	4 197	75.9	24.1	2.49	2.35
Jackson	5.4	288 231	92.4	7.6	0.3	1.7	8.8	266 294	62.9	37.1	2.58	2.14

Table B. States and Counties

STATE/ County code	MSA/ PMSA/ NECMA code[1]	County type[2]	STATE County	Land area, 2000[3] (sq km)	Total persons	Rank	Per square kilometer	Land area, 1990[3] (sq km)	Total persons	Rank	Per square kilometer	White	Black or African American	American Indian or Alaska Native	Asian	Native Hawaiian and other Pacific Islander	Some other race
												Population and population characteristics, 2000 — Race (percent) — One race					
				1	2	3	4	5	6	7	8	9	10	11	12	13	14
			MISSOURI—Cont'd														
29 097	3710	3	Jasper	1 657	104 686	504	63.2	1 657	90 465	506	54.6	92.6	1.5	1.3	0.7	0.1	1.6
29 099	7040	1	Jefferson	1 701	198 099	279	116.5	I 701	171 380	282	100.8	97.5	0.7	0.3	0.4	0.0	0.2
29 101	...	6	Johnson	2 151	48 258	943	22.4	2 151	42 514	944	19.8	90.1	4.3	0.7	1.4	0.1	1.3
29 103	...	9	Knox	1 310	4 361	2 890	3.3	1 310	4 482	2 876	3.4	98.5	0.1	0.0	0.1	0.0	0.2
29 105	...	6	Laclede	1 984	32 513	1 330	16.4	1 984	27 158	1 384	13.7	97.0	0.4	0.5	0.3	0.0	0.3
29 107	3760	1	Lafayette	1 630	32 960	1 321	20.2	1 630	31 107	1 241	19.1	95.5	2.3	0.3	0.2	0.0	0.5
29 109	...	6	Lawrence	1 588	35 204	1 242	22.2	1 588	30 236	1 283	19.0	95.7	0.3	0.8	0.2	0.0	1.7
29 111	...	7	Lewis	1 308	10 494	2 399	8.0	1 308	10 233	2 365	7.8	95.9	2.5	0.2	0.2	0.0	0.4
29 113	7040	1	Lincoln	1 633	38 944	1 141	23.8	1 633	28 892	1 333	17.7	96.1	1.7	0.4	0.2	0.0	0.4
29 115	...	7	Linn	1 607	13 754	2 177	8.6	1 607	13 885	2 065	8.6	98.0	0.6	0.4	0.1	0.0	0.2
29 117	...	7	Livingston	1 384	14 558	2 117	10.5	1 385	14 592	2 013	10.5	95.9	2.3	0.3	0.3	0.0	0.2
29 119	...	8	McDonald	1 397	21 681	1 708	15.5	1 397	16 938	1 851	12.1	89.7	0.2	2.9	0.1	0.1	3.7
29 121	...	7	Macon	2 082	15 762	2 034	7.6	2 082	15 345	1 968	7.4	96.2	2.2	0.4	0.2	0.0	0.2
29 123	...	9	Madison	1 287	11 800	2 305	9.2	1 287	11 127	2 283	8.6	98.3	0.1	0.3	0.3	0.0	0.2
29 125	...	9	Maries	1 367	8 903	2 533	6.5	1 367	7 976	2 570	5.8	97.4	0.3	0.6	0.1	0.0	0.3
29 127	...	5	Marion	1 135	28 289	1 437	24.9	1 135	27 682	1 363	24.4	93.3	4.6	0.3	0.3	0.1	0.2
29 129	...	9	Mercer	1 176	3 757	2 934	3.2	1 177	3 723	2 936	3.2	98.7	0.2	0.6	0.0	0.1	0.0
29 131	...	7	Miller	1 534	23 564	1 610	15.4	1 534	20 700	1 644	13.5	98.0	0.1	0.5	0.1	0.0	0.3
29 133	...	7	Mississippi	1 070	13 427	2 198	12.5	1 070	14 442	2 021	13.5	77.9	20.5	0.2	0.1	0.0	0.3
29 135	...	6	Moniteau	1 079	14 827	2 102	13.7	1 079	12 298	2 196	11.4	92.7	3.8	0.4	0.3	0.0	1.5
29 137	...	9	Monroe	1 673	9 311	2 505	5.6	1 673	9 104	2 460	5.4	94.7	3.8	0.4	0.1	0.0	0.2
29 139	...	8	Montgomery	1 392	12 136	2 289	8.7	1 395	11 355	2 267	8.1	96.0	2.0	0.2	0.3	0.0	0.2
29 141	...	9	Morgan	1 547	19 309	1 827	12.5	1 547	15 574	1 949	10.1	97.3	0.5	0.6	0.1	0.0	0.3
29 143	...	7	New Madrid	1 756	19 760	1 805	11.3	1 756	20 928	1 633	11.9	83.2	15.4	0.2	0.1	0.0	0.3
29 145	3710	3	Newton	1 622	52 636	886	32.5	1 623	44 445	920	27.4	93.3	0.6	2.2	0.3	0.3	1.1
29 147	...	6	Nodaway	2 270	21 912	1 696	9.7	2 271	21 709	1 592	9.6	96.6	1.3	0.2	0.9	0.0	0.3
29 149	...	9	Oregon	2 050	10 344	2 409	5.0	2 050	9 470	2 437	4.6	94.6	0.1	2.9	0.1	0.0	0.1
29 151	...	9	Osage	1 570	13 062	2 225	8.3	1 570	12 018	2 218	7.7	98.6	0.2	0.2	0.1	0.0	0.1
29 153	...	9	Ozark	1 922	9 542	2 485	5.0	1 934	8 598	2 503	4.4	97.6	0.1	0.6	0.1	0.0	0.2
29 155	...	7	Pemiscot	1 277	20 047	1 791	15.7	1 277	21 921	1 582	17.2	71.8	26.2	0.3	0.3	0.0	0.6
29 157	...	7	Perry	1 229	18 132	1 891	14.8	1 229	16 648	1 874	13.5	98.2	0.2	0.2	0.6	0.0	0.1
29 159	...	7	Pettis	1 774	39 403	1 127	22.2	1 774	35 437	1 115	20.0	92.1	3.0	0.4	0.4	0.1	2.5
29 161	...	7	Phelps	1 743	39 825	1 117	22.8	1 743	35 248	1 123	20.2	93.2	1.5	0.6	2.4	0.1	0.5
29 163	...	6	Pike	1 743	18 351	1 876	10.5	1 743	15 969	1 926	9.2	88.4	9.2	0.2	0.2	0.0	0.9
29 165	3760	0	Platte	1 089	73 781	680	67.8	1 089	57 867	750	53.1	91.5	3.5	0.5	1.5	0.2	1.0
29 167	...	6	Polk	1 650	26 992	1 483	16.4	1 650	21 826	1 588	13.2	97.3	0.5	0.7	0.2	0.0	0.3
29 169	...	7	Pulaski	1 417	41 165	1 076	29.1	1 417	41 307	975	29.2	78.4	12.0	1.0	2.3	0.3	2.5
29 171	...	9	Putnam	1 341	5 223	2 836	3.9	1 342	5 079	2 833	3.8	99.1	0.1	0.1	0.1	0.0	0.1
29 173	...	9	Ralls	1 220	9 626	2 476	7.9	1 220	8 476	2 514	6.9	97.9	1.1	0.2	0.1	0.0	0.0
29 175	...	6	Randolph	1 249	24 663	1 568	19.7	1 249	24 370	1 482	19.5	90.6	7.0	0.5	0.4	0.0	0.2
29 177	3760	1	Ray	1 475	23 354	1 626	15.8	1 475	21 968	1 577	14.9	96.5	1.5	0.4	0.2	0.0	0.4
29 179	...	9	Reynolds	2 101	6 689	2 718	3.2	2 101	6 661	2 688	3.2	95.6	0.5	1.3	0.2	0.0	0.2
29 181	...	9	Ripley	1 630	13 509	2 193	8.3	1 630	12 303	2 194	7.5	97.2	0.0	1.3	0.2	0.0	0.1
29 183	7040	0	St. Charles	1 451	283 883	198	195.6	1 454	212 751	234	146.3	94.7	2.7	0.2	0.9	0.0	0.5
29 185	...	9	St. Clair	1 753	9 652	2 473	5.5	1 753	8 457	2 516	4.8	97.4	0.2	0.7	0.1	0.0	0.3
29 186	...	6	Ste. Genevieve	1 301	17 842	1 908	13.7	1 301	16 037	1 921	12.3	98.0	0.7	0.3	0.2	0.0	0.1
29 187	...	6	St. Francois	1 164	55 641	848	47.8	1 164	48 904	858	42.0	96.1	2.0	0.4	0.3	0.0	0.2
29 189	7040	0	St. Louis	1 315	1 016 315	34	772.9	1 315	993 508	31	755.5	76.8	19.0	0.2	2.2	0.0	0.5
29 195	...	7	Saline	1 957	23 756	1 600	12.1	1 957	23 523	1 512	12.0	90.0	5.4	0.3	0.4	0.2	2.1
29 197	...	9	Schuyler	797	4 170	2 901	5.2	797	4 236	2 896	5.3	98.4	0.0	0.3	0.2	0.0	0.2
29 199	...	9	Scotland	1 136	4 983	2 850	4.4	1 136	4 822	2 854	4.2	98.8	0.2	0.1	0.1	0.0	0.2
29 201	...	5	Scott	1 090	40 422	1 107	37.1	1 091	39 376	1 015	36.1	87.7	10.5	0.3	0.2	0.0	0.4
29 203	...	9	Shannon	2 600	8 324	2 579	3.2	2 600	7 613	2 609	2.9	95.1	0.2	1.8	0.0	0.0	0.2
29 205	...	9	Shelby	1 297	6 799	2 712	5.2	1 297	6 942	2 665	5.4	97.9	1.0	0.3	0.1	0.0	0.2
29 207	...	7	Stoddard	2 142	29 705	1 408	13.9	2 142	28 895	1 332	13.5	97.3	0.9	0.4	0.1	0.0	0.2
29 209	...	8	Stone	1 200	28 658	1 431	23.9	1 200	19 078	1 729	15.9	97.6	0.1	0.6	0.2	0.0	0.3
29 211	...	9	Sullivan	1 686	7 219	2 664	4.3	1 686	6 326	2 719	3.8	95.0	0.1	0.2	0.1	0.1	3.5
29 213	...	6	Taney	1 638	39 703	1 118	24.2	1 638	25 561	1 441	15.6	96.2	0.3	0.9	0.3	0.1	0.7
29 215	...	9	Texas	3 052	23 003	1 641	7.5	3 053	21 476	1 604	7.0	96.5	0.2	1.0	0.3	0.0	0.2
29 217	...	7	Vernon	2 160	20 454	1 762	9.5	2 160	19 041	1 732	8.8	97.0	0.6	0.8	0.3	0.0	0.3
29 219	7040	1	Warren	1 117	24 525	1 577	22.0	1 118	19 534	1 697	17.5	95.9	1.9	0.4	0.2	0.0	0.4
29 221	...	6	Washington	1 967	23 344	1 627	11.9	1 968	20 380	1 657	10.4	95.5	2.5	0.7	0.1	0.0	0.2
29 223	...	9	Wayne	1 971	13 259	2 206	6.7	1 971	11 543	2 253	5.9	97.7	0.2	0.6	0.1	0.0	0.1
29 225	7920	2	Webster	1 537	31 045	1 376	20.2	1 537	23 753	1 501	15.5	96.2	1.2	0.7	0.3	0.0	0.3
29 227	...	9	Worth	690	2 382	3 034	3.5	690	2 440	3 026	3.5	99.0	0.2	0.3	0.1	0.0	0.0
29 229	...	6	Wright	1 767	17 955	1 899	10.2	1 767	16 758	1 864	9.5	97.6	0.3	0.7	0.1	0.0	0.3

[1]MSA = Metropolitan Statistical Area. PMSA = Primary MSA. NECMA = New England County Metropolitan Area. See Appendix A for explanation of these concepts. See Appendix B for list of metropolitan areas identified by type, with component counties.
[2]County typology code from the Economic Research Service of USDA. See Appendix A for definition.
[3]Dry land or land partially or temporarily covered by water.

Table B. States and Counties

STATE County	Two or more races	White	Black	American Indian or Alaska Native	Asian	Native Hawaiian and other Pacific Islander	Some other race	Hispanic[1]	White	Black or African American	American Indian or Alaska Native	Asian and Pacific Islander	Hispanic[1]
	15	16	17	18	19	20	21	22	23	24	25	26	27
MISSOURI—Cont'd													
Jasper	2.2	94.7	1.9	2.7	0.9	0.1	2.0	3.5	96.3	1.3	1.7	0.6	0.9
Jefferson	0.9	98.4	0.9	0.8	0.5	0.0	0.4	1.0	98.6	0.7	0.2	0.3	0.7
Johnson	2.0	91.9	4.9	1.4	2.0	0.2	1.7	2.9	91.7	5.8	0.5	1.4	1.7
Knox	1.1	99.6	0.4	0.7	0.3	0.0	0.2	0.6	99.5	0.1	0.2	0.1	0.2
Laclede	1.4	98.4	0.6	1.3	0.5	0.1	0.5	1.2	98.7	0.4	0.5	0.3	0.5
Lafayette	1.1	96.6	2.6	0.9	0.4	0.1	0.6	1.2	96.4	2.8	0.3	0.2	0.7
Lawrence	1.4	97.0	0.4	1.6	0.3	0.0	2.0	3.4	98.6	0.1	0.9	0.2	0.7
Lewis	0.7	96.6	2.9	0.3	0.4	0.0	0.5	0.7	96.2	3.3	0.2	0.2	0.3
Lincoln	1.1	97.2	2.1	1.0	0.3	0.1	0.6	1.1	97.2	2.0	0.4	0.2	0.8
Linn	0.8	98.7	0.9	0.7	0.3	0.0	0.3	0.8	98.8	0.8	0.2	0.1	0.7
Livingston	0.9	96.7	2.7	0.7	0.5	0.0	0.4	0.6	97.3	2.2	0.3	0.2	0.4
McDonald	3.3	92.9	0.3	5.5	0.3	0.2	4.3	9.4	96.3	0.0	3.2	0.2	0.7
Macon	0.8	97.0	2.5	0.8	0.2	0.0	0.3	0.8	97.1	2.4	0.3	0.1	0.4
Madison	0.8	99.1	0.2	0.8	0.4	0.0	0.3	0.6	99.2	0.1	0.3	0.3	0.6
Maries	1.2	98.7	0.5	1.5	0.2	0.0	0.5	1.2	99.2	0.3	0.2	0.1	0.5
Marion	1.3	94.5	5.2	0.8	0.4	0.1	0.4	0.9	94.7	4.5	0.3	0.4	0.4
Mercer	0.5	99.2	0.2	1.0	0.0	0.1	0.1	0.3	99.7	0.1	0.2	0.0	0.2
Miller	0.8	98.0	0.4	1.1	0.2	0.0	0.4	1.0	99.3	0.1	0.4	0.1	0.5
Mississippi	0.9	78.7	20.8	0.7	0.2	0.0	0.5	1.0	80.3	19.4	0.2	0.1	0.3
Moniteau	1.3	93.8	4.0	1.2	0.5	0.1	1.7	2.9	97.9	1.3	0.4	0.3	0.4
Monroe	0.8	95.4	4.1	0.8	0.2	0.0	0.2	0.6	95.7	3.9	0.2	0.2	0.5
Montgomery	1.3	97.2	2.4	0.9	0.4	0.1	0.4	0.8	97.0	2.5	0.1	0.2	0.4
Morgan	1.2	98.5	0.6	1.4	0.2	0.1	0.5	0.8	98.7	0.6	0.4	0.2	0.4
New Madrid	0.8	83.9	15.6	0.6	0.3	0.0	0.4	0.9	83.9	15.7	0.2	0.2	0.4
Newton	2.2	95.3	0.8	3.9	0.5	0.4	1.4	2.2	96.7	0.4	2.1	0.5	0.8
Nodaway	0.7	97.3	1.5	0.6	1.0	0.1	0.4	0.7	98.0	0.8	0.2	0.8	0.6
Oregon	2.2	96.7	0.1	4.9	0.2	0.0	0.3	1.1	99.3	0.0	0.4	0.1	0.3
Osage	0.8	99.4	0.3	0.9	0.1	0.1	0.1	0.6	99.4	0.3	0.2	0.0	0.5
Ozark	1.4	98.9	0.3	1.7	0.3	0.1	0.3	0.9	99.2	0.0	0.5	0.1	0.7
Pemiscot	0.8	72.5	26.6	0.6	0.4	0.0	0.9	1.6	74.0	25.5	0.2	0.2	0.4
Perry	0.6	98.8	0.2	0.6	0.7	0.1	0.2	0.5	99.3	0.1	0.2	0.4	0.4
Pettis	1.6	93.6	3.5	1.0	0.7	0.1	2.8	3.9	95.8	3.3	0.3	0.3	0.8
Phelps	1.8	94.9	1.8	1.4	2.7	0.1	1.0	1.2	95.9	1.1	0.4	2.2	0.9
Pike	1.0	89.3	9.7	0.6	0.3	0.1	1.1	1.6	94.1	5.3	0.3	0.2	0.7
Platte	1.9	93.1	4.0	1.1	1.9	0.3	1.7	3.0	95.3	2.1	0.5	1.4	2.0
Polk	1.1	98.3	0.6	1.3	0.3	0.1	0.5	1.3	98.5	0.3	0.6	0.3	0.8
Pulaski	3.6	81.3	13.0	2.0	3.3	0.7	3.6	5.8	80.2	13.6	0.6	2.9	4.7
Putnam	0.5	99.6	0.1	0.4	0.2	0.0	0.2	0.6	99.6	0.0	0.2	0.1	0.5
Ralls	0.6	98.6	1.2	0.5	0.2	0.0	0.1	0.4	98.1	1.6	0.2	0.1	0.2
Randolph	1.3	91.7	7.4	1.1	0.6	0.1	0.4	1.1	91.6	7.5	0.3	0.3	0.7
Ray	1.1	97.6	1.8	1.0	0.3	0.1	0.5	1.1	97.8	1.4	0.5	0.2	0.5
Reynolds	2.1	97.7	0.7	2.9	0.5	0.1	0.3	0.8	99.6	0.0	0.2	0.1	0.4
Ripley	1.2	98.3	0.1	2.2	0.3	0.0	0.2	1.0	99.3	0.0	0.4	0.2	0.6
St. Charles	1.1	95.7	3.0	0.6	1.1	0.1	0.7	1.5	96.5	2.3	0.2	0.7	1.1
St. Clair	1.2	98.5	0.4	1.6	0.2	0.0	0.5	1.0	99.1	0.3	0.5	0.1	0.4
Ste. Genevieve	0.7	98.7	0.8	0.7	0.2	0.0	0.3	0.7	99.3	0.3	0.2	0.1	0.3
St. Francois	0.9	96.9	2.2	0.9	0.5	0.1	0.4	0.8	97.4	2.0	0.2	0.3	0.5
St. Louis	1.3	77.8	19.6	0.5	2.6	0.1	0.8	1.4	84.2	14.0	0.1	1.4	1.0
Saline	1.6	91.5	6.1	0.8	0.5	0.3	2.4	4.4	93.4	5.7	0.2	0.3	0.9
Schuyler	0.8	99.3	0.2	0.9	0.2	0.0	0.2	0.6	99.6	0.0	0.2	0.1	0.4
Scotland	0.6	99.4	0.3	0.6	0.1	0.0	0.3	0.8	99.7	0.1	0.2	0.0	0.2
Scott	0.9	88.5	10.8	0.8	0.3	0.0	0.6	1.1	90.6	8.9	0.2	0.2	0.5
Shannon	2.7	97.6	0.3	4.2	0.2	0.1	0.5	0.9	99.5	0.0	0.4	0.1	0.3
Shelby	0.6	98.4	1.1	0.5	0.2	0.0	0.3	0.6	98.8	0.8	0.3	0.0	0.3
Stoddard	1.0	98.3	1.0	1.1	0.2	0.1	0.4	0.8	98.1	1.4	0.2	0.2	0.5
Stone	1.2	98.8	0.1	1.5	0.3	0.1	0.4	1.0	99.0	0.0	0.7	0.2	0.6
Sullivan	0.9	95.8	0.3	0.6	0.2	0.1	3.9	8.8	99.7	0.0	0.2	0.0	0.4
Taney	1.4	97.6	0.4	1.7	0.6	0.1	1.1	2.4	98.8	0.1	0.6	0.3	0.8
Texas	1.8	98.2	0.4	2.3	0.6	0.1	0.4	1.0	99.2	0.1	0.4	0.3	0.5
Vernon	1.0	97.9	0.7	1.4	0.4	0.1	0.5	0.8	98.7	0.3	0.6	0.3	0.5
Warren	1.0	96.8	2.2	1.0	0.4	0.1	0.6	1.3	96.8	2.6	0.2	0.2	0.8
Washington	1.1	96.5	2.6	1.4	0.2	0.0	0.3	0.7	97.7	1.9	0.2	0.1	0.4
Wayne	1.4	99.0	0.2	1.7	0.2	0.0	0.2	0.5	99.4	0.1	0.4	0.1	0.4
Webster	1.4	97.5	1.3	1.5	0.4	0.1	0.6	1.3	98.2	0.8	0.6	0.2	0.6
Worth	0.4	99.4	0.2	0.5	0.2	0.3	0.0	0.3	99.4	0.0	0.0	0.2	0.4
Wright	1.0	98.6	0.4	1.4	0.2	0.0	0.5	0.8	98.9	0.2	0.7	0.1	0.4

[1] Hispanic persons may be of any race.

Table B. States and Counties

STATE County	Under 5 years	5 to 17 years	18 to 24 years	25 to 34 years	35 to 44 years	45 to 54 years	55 to 64 years	65 to 74 years	75 years and over	Median age (years)	Percent Female
	28	29	30	31	32	33	34	35	36	37	38
MISSOURI—Cont'd											
Jasper	7.3	18.5	11.0	13.4	14.7	12.7	8.7	7.0	6.7	34.9	51.5
Jefferson	7.2	20.7	8.5	13.8	18.1	13.8	8.7	5.4	3.8	34.9	50.3
Johnson	6.7	18.4	20.2	13.0	14.6	10.6	7.2	5.1	4.2	28.5	49.5
Knox	6.1	18.8	6.2	9.1	14.6	12.7	11.2	10.9	10.4	41.6	51.8
Laclede	6.9	19.8	8.4	12.3	15.5	13.0	10.0	7.6	6.5	36.6	50.9
Lafayette	6.1	20.1	7.6	11.8	15.7	13.2	10.1	7.6	7.8	37.9	51.1
Lawrence	7.1	20.1	7.9	12.1	14.8	12.5	9.9	7.7	7.9	36.9	50.8
Lewis	7.2	17.8	12.9	10.7	13.9	11.7	9.7	7.7	8.4	36.0	51.0
Lincoln	7.3	22.7	8.1	12.6	17.6	12.4	8.5	5.8	5.0	34.5	50.4
Linn	6.1	19.3	7.0	10.5	13.9	12.5	10.2	9.2	11.4	40.3	52.8
Livingston	6.1	18.3	7.4	11.4	14.9	13.4	9.7	8.5	10.5	39.7	54.1
McDonald	7.8	21.1	8.7	13.4	15.1	12.6	10.0	6.4	4.8	34.3	49.4
Macon	6.4	17.8	7.5	11.2	14.0	13.5	10.5	8.6	10.4	40.1	51.2
Madison	5.9	18.7	7.9	11.3	15.0	13.0	10.3	9.1	8.9	39.1	52.1
Maries	6.6	19.4	7.3	11.4	15.2	13.0	11.5	8.9	6.7	38.5	49.7
Marion	6.8	18.9	9.5	11.8	14.6	13.4	8.3	7.7	9.0	37.1	52.8
Mercer	5.6	17.4	6.7	9.3	15.0	12.7	11.3	10.9	11.2	42.4	51.1
Miller	6.8	19.5	8.4	12.2	15.2	12.8	9.9	8.1	7.2	37.2	50.7
Mississippi	7.2	19.2	8.8	11.8	13.6	12.9	10.7	8.0	7.9	37.3	53.3
Moniteau	6.7	19.2	8.2	14.3	16.8	12.7	8.2	6.5	7.4	35.9	46.9
Monroe	6.5	19.4	7.3	10.5	14.6	13.0	11.2	8.5	9.1	39.4	50.9
Montgomery	5.7	19.7	7.4	10.7	15.4	13.3	10.6	8.0	9.2	39.4	50.5
Morgan	6.0	17.8	6.2	9.9	13.2	13.4	13.8	11.8	7.8	42.6	50.7
New Madrid	6.6	19.8	8.5	11.9	14.5	13.0	10.2	8.1	7.4	37.4	52.0
Newton	7.0	19.2	8.7	12.0	15.1	13.5	10.3	7.6	6.5	37.1	51.1
Nodaway	4.7	14.7	25.1	10.5	12.6	10.9	7.7	6.5	7.4	30.2	50.1
Oregon	5.9	18.4	7.0	10.5	13.6	14.0	12.5	9.6	8.4	41.0	50.9
Osage	6.7	19.6	9.5	12.5	15.2	12.3	9.4	7.4	7.3	36.1	49.3
Ozark	5.4	16.7	6.9	9.2	13.6	14.1	14.6	11.5	8.0	43.6	50.5
Pemiscot	8.1	21.9	9.1	11.7	13.3	12.2	8.9	7.6	7.2	34.4	53.1
Perry	6.8	19.3	8.6	12.5	15.4	12.9	8.9	7.5	8.2	36.8	50.2
Pettis	7.0	19.3	9.3	12.3	15.0	12.2	8.9	7.8	7.6	36.4	51.4
Phelps	5.7	18.0	14.5	11.9	14.2	12.4	9.3	7.1	6.8	34.9	49.2
Pike	5.4	18.0	9.1	13.3	16.5	13.0	9.8	7.4	7.5	37.7	45.6
Platte	6.8	18.9	8.3	14.4	18.2	15.4	9.1	4.7	4.2	35.9	50.5
Polk	6.8	19.0	12.6	11.6	13.9	11.6	9.2	8.0	7.3	35.0	51.3
Pulaski	7.7	19.9	16.6	16.8	15.2	9.7	6.2	4.7	3.2	28.5	47.2
Putnam	6.5	17.5	6.2	10.4	13.6	12.8	12.3	10.3	10.4	41.9	51.0
Ralls	5.7	19.6	7.1	10.9	16.0	15.2	11.3	7.5	6.8	39.3	49.8
Randolph	6.4	17.5	9.6	13.4	15.9	13.7	8.7	7.4	7.5	37.2	48.2
Ray	6.6	20.9	7.4	11.9	16.4	13.7	10.2	7.0	5.9	37.1	50.0
Reynolds	5.8	18.2	6.8	11.4	13.6	14.2	13.7	9.6	6.6	40.7	49.6
Ripley	6.0	18.8	7.9	11.0	14.2	13.0	11.8	9.6	7.7	39.4	51.5
St. Charles	7.6	21.3	8.2	14.0	18.6	13.6	8.0	5.1	3.7	34.3	50.7
St. Clair	5.5	17.5	5.6	9.3	13.6	13.4	13.9	11.2	10.1	43.9	50.4
Ste. Genevieve	6.0	20.6	7.6	11.1	16.8	13.5	9.8	7.9	6.6	37.7	49.7
St. Francois	6.0	17.9	9.2	13.3	16.1	12.9	9.6	7.9	7.0	37.2	49.2
St. Louis	6.3	18.9	8.3	12.6	16.3	14.4	9.1	7.2	6.8	37.5	52.6
Saline	6.1	18.2	12.0	10.8	14.4	13.0	9.3	7.4	8.8	37.2	51.0
Schuyler	6.0	18.6	6.7	10.5	14.3	12.3	11.7	9.2	10.6	40.8	51.8
Scotland	7.2	21.4	7.6	10.2	13.9	10.9	9.9	8.1	10.9	37.4	51.5
Scott	7.0	20.4	8.5	12.7	14.8	13.4	9.4	7.0	6.7	36.0	52.2
Shannon	6.2	20.3	7.2	11.1	15.0	13.4	11.9	8.5	6.5	38.8	51.2
Shelby	5.7	19.7	7.2	9.7	14.6	13.2	10.1	8.7	11.0	40.4	52.2
Stoddard	5.7	18.2	8.5	11.6	14.7	13.2	10.9	8.6	8.7	39.1	51.9
Stone	5.5	16.0	6.2	10.1	13.7	14.3	15.4	12.1	6.8	44.1	51.0
Sullivan	7.1	17.9	7.5	12.4	13.9	12.6	10.1	8.3	10.2	38.9	50.0
Taney	6.1	16.3	10.2	12.2	14.0	13.4	11.5	9.3	6.9	38.8	51.6
Texas	5.8	19.2	7.1	9.9	15.0	13.8	11.5	9.7	8.1	40.4	51.7
Vernon	6.7	19.9	9.2	11.4	14.0	13.2	9.3	8.4	8.0	37.1	51.7
Warren	6.5	20.3	7.6	11.4	17.4	13.1	10.6	7.5	5.5	37.4	50.3
Washington	6.6	20.0	9.8	13.4	15.9	12.9	9.8	7.0	4.7	35.2	48.4
Wayne	5.3	17.9	6.7	9.7	13.8	13.1	13.7	11.7	8.1	42.5	50.4
Webster	7.5	21.3	8.3	13.5	16.2	12.5	9.1	6.2	5.3	34.6	49.7
Worth	5.5	18.8	6.8	8.4	15.1	11.9	11.3	10.5	11.8	41.9	51.0
Wright	7.0	20.2	8.2	10.9	14.3	12.3	10.5	8.8	7.7	37.7	51.5

Table B. States and Counties

| | Population and population characteristics, 1990 | | | | | | | | | | Population—change, 1980–2000 | | | | |
| | Age (percent) | | | | | | | | | | Total persons | | | Percent change | |
STATE County	Under 5 years	5 to 17 years	18 to 24 years	25 to 34 years	35 to 44 years	45 to 54 years	55 to 64 years	65 to 74 years	75 years and over	Percent Female	2000	1990	1980	1990–2000	1980–1990
	39	40	41	42	43	44	45	46	47	48	49	50	51	52	53
MISSOURI—Cont'd															
Jasper	6.8	18.8	10.2	15.7	14.0	9.9	9.0	8.4	7.1	52.4	104 686	90 465	86 958	15.7	4.0
Jefferson	8.4	21.4	9.4	19.0	15.6	10.6	7.3	5.0	3.3	50.4	198 099	171 380	146 183	15.6	17.2
Johnson	7.6	16.8	23.4	16.7	11.5	8.2	6.5	5.0	4.3	49.4	48 258	42 514	39 059	13.5	8.8
Knox	6.4	17.5	7.1	12.9	11.6	11.2	11.8	10.8	10.9	52.0	4 361	4 482	5 508	-2.7	-18.6
Laclede	7.2	19.6	8.9	15.5	13.5	10.8	9.2	8.4	6.9	51.3	32 513	27 158	24 323	19.7	11.7
Lafayette	7.0	19.5	8.7	14.5	13.8	10.7	9.3	8.2	8.4	51.1	32 960	31 107	29 931	6.0	3.9
Lawrence	7.1	19.7	8.2	14.2	12.9	10.8	9.3	9.4	8.4	51.6	35 204	30 236	28 973	16.4	4.4
Lewis	6.0	17.5	14.5	13.1	11.6	10.5	9.0	8.7	9.0	52.2	10 494	10 233	10 901	2.6	-6.1
Lincoln	8.5	21.6	8.0	17.5	14.2	10.5	8.2	6.3	5.2	50.1	38 944	28 892	22 193	34.8	30.2
Linn	6.3	18.6	6.5	13.1	12.3	9.5	10.4	11.6	11.8	53.4	13 754	13 885	15 495	-0.9	-10.4
Livingston	6.5	18.8	7.7	14.3	13.3	10.2	9.8	9.8	9.7	54.2	14 558	14 592	15 739	-0.2	-7.3
McDonald	7.8	19.8	8.8	15.0	12.9	11.2	10.1	8.1	6.3	50.4	21 681	16 938	14 917	28.0	13.5
Macon	5.8	18.8	7.7	13.1	13.2	10.2	9.8	10.9	10.6	52.5	15 762	15 345	16 313	2.7	-5.9
Madison	6.7	19.0	8.0	14.2	12.5	10.0	10.6	10.1	9.0	51.7	11 800	11 127	10 725	6.0	3.7
Maries	6.8	19.1	8.4	13.8	12.1	12.0	10.8	9.4	7.5	50.5	8 903	7 976	7 551	11.6	5.6
Marion	7.1	20.2	8.3	14.9	13.7	9.0	8.9	8.9	9.0	52.9	28 289	27 682	28 638	2.2	-3.3
Mercer	4.9	17.6	5.5	12.0	11.8	9.4	13.2	12.7	13.0	51.4	3 757	3 723	4 685	0.9	-20.5
Miller	7.4	20.5	8.4	15.2	13.3	10.0	9.6	8.2	7.3	51.3	23 564	20 700	18 539	13.8	11.7
Mississippi	7.3	21.6	8.6	14.1	12.5	10.4	9.1	8.9	7.5	53.3	13 427	14 442	15 726	-7.0	-8.2
Moniteau	6.9	20.6	8.5	15.1	13.8	9.6	8.4	8.8	8.1	50.8	14 827	12 298	12 068	20.6	1.9
Monroe	7.2	20.3	7.1	14.0	12.7	10.5	9.3	9.1	9.8	51.1	9 311	9 104	9 716	2.3	-6.3
Montgomery	6.9	19.3	7.3	13.9	12.4	10.7	9.8	9.5	10.3	51.7	12 136	11 355	11 537	6.9	-1.6
Morgan	6.6	16.6	7.1	12.0	11.7	11.7	13.8	11.9	8.8	51.1	19 309	15 574	13 807	24.0	12.8
New Madrid	7.2	22.1	9.0	14.4	13.0	10.2	9.1	8.5	6.4	52.4	19 760	20 928	22 945	-5.6	-8.8
Newton	7.2	19.3	9.3	14.8	14.1	11.3	9.5	8.1	6.4	51.3	52 636	44 445	40 555	18.4	9.6
Nodaway	5.7	16.7	23.2	13.0	10.7	8.0	7.4	7.4	7.7	51.7	21 912	21 709	21 996	0.9	-1.3
Oregon	5.6	18.2	7.6	11.9	13.3	11.7	11.8	10.7	9.2	51.8	10 344	9 470	10 238	9.2	-7.5
Osage	7.1	20.7	10.8	15.2	12.6	9.8	8.7	8.4	6.7	48.5	13 062	12 018	12 014	8.7	0.0
Ozark	5.0	18.1	6.3	11.8	12.7	11.5	13.5	12.5	8.6	50.5	9 542	8 598	7 961	11.0	8.0
Pemiscot	8.3	22.5	9.1	13.4	12.1	9.1	9.0	8.9	7.6	53.3	20 047	21 921	24 987	-8.5	-12.3
Perry	7.2	20.8	8.4	14.4	13.3	9.2	8.9	8.9	8.8	50.5	18 132	16 648	16 784	8.9	-0.8
Pettis	7.2	18.8	8.8	15.7	13.3	10.0	9.8	8.8	7.5	51.9	39 403	35 437	36 378	11.2	-2.6
Phelps	6.5	17.4	15.7	15.0	12.9	10.2	8.6	7.7	6.0	48.7	39 825	35 248	33 633	13.0	4.8
Pike	7.1	20.2	7.7	13.7	12.9	11.0	10.2	9.3	8.0	51.7	18 351	15 969	17 568	14.9	-9.1
Platte	7.3	18.9	9.5	18.6	17.7	12.4	7.3	5.0	3.3	50.4	73 781	57 867	46 341	27.5	24.9
Polk	6.5	18.1	14.1	13.5	12.0	9.7	9.2	9.0	7.9	51.2	26 992	21 826	18 822	23.7	16.0
Pulaski	8.8	20.0	17.2	20.9	13.8	7.0	5.6	3.9	2.9	44.6	41 165	41 307	42 011	-0.3	-1.7
Putnam	5.5	17.1	6.9	12.0	12.1	10.3	12.0	12.2	11.8	51.8	5 223	5 079	6 092	2.8	-16.6
Ralls	6.3	20.2	7.3	13.8	15.0	11.0	9.6	9.3	7.4	51.3	9 626	8 476	8 984	13.6	-5.7
Randolph	6.4	18.6	9.6	16.4	14.5	9.7	8.4	8.0	8.4	49.6	24 663	24 370	25 460	1.2	-4.3
Ray	7.4	21.2	7.7	15.2	14.2	11.9	9.2	7.2	6.1	51.0	23 354	21 968	21 378	6.3	2.8
Reynolds	6.3	20.1	7.4	13.7	12.8	11.8	11.4	9.4	7.2	50.8	6 689	6 661	7 230	0.4	-7.9
Ripley	6.8	20.1	7.8	12.7	11.8	10.9	11.4	10.1	8.4	52.6	13 509	12 303	12 458	9.8	-1.2
St. Charles	8.9	21.2	9.0	20.0	17.0	10.4	6.6	4.2	2.7	50.5	283 883	212 751	144 107	33.4	47.6
St. Clair	6.1	17.3	6.6	11.7	11.6	10.4	13.1	12.1	11.1	52.4	9 652	8 457	8 622	14.1	-1.9
Ste. Genevieve	7.2	20.8	8.1	15.6	14.0	10.3	9.8	7.8	6.4	50.3	17 842	16 037	15 180	11.3	5.6
St. Francois	6.5	19.0	9.4	16.2	13.6	10.1	9.6	9.0	6.8	50.1	55 641	48 904	42 600	13.8	14.8
St. Louis	7.0	17.6	9.0	17.1	15.7	11.1	9.5	7.5	5.6	52.3	1 016 315	993 508	974 180	2.3	2.0
Saline	6.2	18.9	10.4	14.3	13.3	9.7	9.0	9.4	8.9	51.8	23 756	23 523	24 913	1.0	-5.6
Schuyler	7.1	17.4	7.4	13.0	12.1	10.4	9.7	11.2	11.7	52.1	4 170	4 236	4 979	-1.6	-14.9
Scotland	7.3	18.1	7.1	13.0	11.6	10.3	9.8	11.1	11.6	51.9	4 983	4 822	5 415	3.3	-11.0
Scott	7.7	20.7	9.2	15.3	14.2	10.4	8.2	8.0	6.3	52.7	40 422	39 376	39 647	2.7	-0.7
Shannon	7.3	19.4	7.8	14.7	13.0	11.3	10.2	9.3	6.9	51.2	8 324	7 613	7 885	9.3	-3.4
Shelby	6.8	19.1	6.0	13.5	11.7	10.0	9.6	10.6	12.7	53.1	6 799	6 942	7 826	-2.1	-11.3
Stoddard	6.1	18.9	8.7	13.9	13.5	11.3	10.0	9.5	8.1	52.2	29 705	28 895	29 009	2.8	-0.4
Stone	5.3	16.2	7.0	11.9	12.2	12.0	14.3	13.2	7.8	51.3	28 658	19 078	15 587	50.2	22.4
Sullivan	5.3	16.6	7.8	11.7	12.1	10.9	10.8	12.3	12.6	52.1	7 219	6 326	7 434	14.1	-14.9
Taney	5.3	15.4	10.1	12.5	12.1	10.8	12.5	12.4	8.9	51.8	39 703	25 561	20 467	55.3	24.9
Texas	6.8	20.2	7.4	13.6	13.3	11.0	10.8	9.3	7.6	51.8	23 003	21 476	21 070	7.1	1.9
Vernon	6.7	19.3	9.3	13.7	13.8	10.1	9.8	9.3	7.9	53.0	20 454	19 806	19 806	7.4	-3.9
Warren	8.2	19.9	8.0	16.2	14.1	10.9	8.9	8.0	5.9	50.4	24 525	19 534	14 900	25.6	31.1
Washington	7.6	22.3	9.7	16.0	13.7	10.5	8.7	6.7	4.9	49.2	23 344	20 380	17 983	14.5	13.3
Wayne	6.0	17.6	8.1	12.6	11.3	11.8	12.8	11.0	8.9	51.1	13 259	11 543	11 277	14.9	2.4
Webster	7.6	21.1	9.4	15.6	14.0	11.1	8.4	7.0	6.0	49.6	31 045	23 753	20 414	30.7	16.4
Worth	6.6	17.4	6.2	11.9	10.0	10.4	11.8	11.4	14.2	52.4	2 382	2 440	3 008	-2.4	-18.9
Wright	7.2	20.9	7.8	14.0	12.3	10.3	10.4	9.1	8.0	51.7	17 955	16 758	16 188	7.1	3.5

Table B. States and Counties

STATE County	Total population	Household relationship, 2000																
		In households (percent)										In group quarters (percent)						
					Child		Other relatives		Nonrelatives				Institutionalized population			Noninstitutionalized population		
		Total in house-holds	House-holder	Spouse	Total	Own child under 18 years	Total	Under 18 years	Total	Unmar-ried partner	Total in group quarters	Correc-tional institu-tions	Nurs-ing homes	Other institu-tions	Col-lege dormi-tories	Mili-tary quar-ters	Other
	54	55	56	57	58	59	60	61	62	63	64	65	66	67	68	69	70
MISSOURI—Cont'd																	
Jasper	104 686	97.5	39.6	20.8	28.5	23.1	3.6	1.6	5.0	2.1	2.5	0.2	0.7	0.1	0.9	0.0	0.6
Jefferson	198 099	99.0	36.1	22.0	32.7	25.4	3.7	1.7	4.4	2.3	1.0	0.1	0.6	0.0	0.0	0.0	0.3
Johnson	48 258	93.1	36.1	20.2	27.8	23.5	2.6	1.1	6.4	1.8	6.9	0.1	0.6	0.0	5.0	1.1	0.2
Knox	4 361	97.9	41.1	23.6	28.1	23.2	2.0	0.8	3.1	1.6	2.1	0.0	1.4	0.0	0.0	0.0	0.6
Laclede	32 513	98.8	39.2	23.1	29.0	24.2	3.4	1.7	4.0	2.1	1.2	0.3	0.8	0.0	0.0	0.0	0.1
Lafayette	32 960	97.2	38.1	22.6	29.9	24.2	3.0	1.4	3.5	1.8	2.8	0.1	1.9	0.7	0.0	0.0	0.1
Lawrence	35 204	98.2	38.5	22.7	30.0	24.9	3.4	1.5	3.6	1.7	1.8	0.1	1.3	0.3	0.0	0.0	0.1
Lewis	10 494	92.9	37.7	21.4	27.9	23.1	2.2	1.1	3.6	1.9	7.1	0.1	1.7	0.0	5.2	0.0	0.2
Lincoln	38 944	98.5	35.6	21.9	33.5	27.5	3.4	1.6	4.2	2.2	1.5	0.2	0.8	0.1	0.0	0.0	0.4
Linn	13 754	98.3	41.4	22.2	28.6	23.7	2.4	1.0	3.7	2.0	1.7	0.0	1.6	0.0	0.0	0.0	0.2
Livingston	14 558	93.6	39.4	21.5	27.7	23.0	2.0	0.9	3.0	1.8	6.4	3.7	2.7	0.0	0.0	0.0	0.0
McDonald	21 681	99.2	37.4	21.6	30.9	26.0	4.7	2.0	4.7	2.2	0.8	0.1	0.4	0.0	0.0	0.0	0.2
Macon	15 762	98.0	41.2	23.0	27.8	22.2	2.5	1.3	3.5	1.8	2.0	0.0	1.8	0.0	0.0	0.0	0.1
Madison	11 800	98.1	39.9	22.9	28.3	22.5	3.3	1.5	3.6	2.0	1.9	0.2	0.8	0.9	0.0	0.0	0.1
Maries	8 903	99.0	39.5	23.3	29.8	23.9	3.2	1.4	3.3	1.8	1.0	0.1	0.9	0.0	0.0	0.0	0.0
Marion	28 289	95.6	39.1	20.9	29.1	23.7	2.6	1.3	3.8	2.0	4.4	0.4	2.0	0.1	1.2	0.0	0.8
Mercer	3 757	98.4	42.6	24.5	26.5	21.8	1.9	0.7	2.8	1.4	1.6	0.1	1.0	0.0	0.0	0.0	0.6
Miller	23 564	98.3	39.4	22.1	29.4	23.9	3.1	1.4	4.4	2.4	1.7	0.6	0.6	0.1	0.0	0.0	0.4
Mississippi	13 427	98.0	40.1	19.1	29.1	22.1	6.1	3.5	3.6	1.9	2.0	0.6	1.3	0.1	0.0	0.0	0.0
Moniteau	14 827	90.9	35.5	20.6	29.0	24.1	2.4	1.2	3.4	1.9	9.1	7.8	0.9	0.0	0.0	0.0	0.4
Monroe	9 311	98.0	39.3	23.2	29.5	24.2	3.0	1.2	3.1	1.6	2.0	0.1	1.6	0.1	0.0	0.0	0.2
Montgomery	12 136	97.3	39.3	22.4	28.6	23.0	3.1	1.4	4.0	2.1	2.7	0.2	2.2	0.3	0.0	0.0	0.0
Morgan	19 309	98.5	40.7	24.6	26.5	21.8	3.0	1.3	3.8	2.2	1.5	0.1	0.7	0.0	0.0	0.0	0.7
New Madrid	19 760	98.2	39.6	20.6	29.8	23.2	4.9	2.7	3.3	1.8	1.8	0.2	1.6	0.0	0.0	0.0	0.0
Newton	52 636	98.2	38.3	23.2	29.3	23.9	3.4	1.5	4.0	1.9	1.8	0.1	1.1	0.0	0.4	0.0	0.3
Nodaway	21 912	86.7	37.1	18.6	22.6	18.6	1.4	0.5	6.9	1.4	13.3	2.5	1.1	0.0	9.0	0.0	0.7
Oregon	10 344	98.9	41.2	24.2	27.0	22.0	3.1	1.4	3.4	1.6	1.1	0.0	0.9	0.0	0.0	0.0	0.1
Osage	13 062	98.5	37.7	23.3	32.1	25.0	2.3	0.9	3.1	1.3	1.5	0.0	1.2	0.0	0.0	0.0	0.3
Ozark	9 542	99.2	41.4	25.7	25.2	19.8	3.2	1.7	3.7	1.7	0.8	0.0	0.8	0.0	0.0	0.0	0.0
Pemiscot	20 047	98.6	39.2	17.6	32.5	26.0	5.6	3.4	3.7	2.1	1.4	0.2	1.0	0.0	0.0	0.0	0.2
Perry	18 132	97.9	38.1	23.0	31.0	24.3	2.4	1.1	3.4	1.8	2.1	0.2	1.5	0.0	0.0	0.0	0.4
Pettis	39 403	98.3	39.5	21.1	29.1	23.7	3.6	1.5	5.0	2.2	1.7	0.1	1.0	0.0	0.1	0.0	0.5
Phelps	39 825	93.9	39.4	20.7	26.1	21.4	2.6	1.2	5.0	1.7	6.1	0.1	1.0	0.4	4.2	0.0	0.4
Pike	18 351	87.7	35.2	19.6	26.7	21.5	2.8	1.3	3.4	1.8	12.3	10.4	1.3	0.0	0.0	0.0	0.6
Platte	73 781	98.9	39.7	22.6	29.5	24.3	2.8	1.0	4.3	2.0	1.1	0.1	0.5	0.1	0.2	0.0	0.2
Polk	26 992	94.1	36.7	22.2	28.2	23.5	3.0	1.4	4.0	1.4	5.9	0.0	1.4	0.5	3.6	0.0	0.4
Pulaski	41 165	87.3	32.6	19.8	29.2	25.4	2.6	1.3	3.2	1.3	12.7	0.1	0.5	0.1	0.0	11.9	0.1
Putnam	5 223	98.9	42.7	24.4	26.3	22.3	2.4	1.0	3.2	1.7	1.1	0.2	0.8	0.0	0.0	0.0	0.1
Ralls	9 626	98.9	38.8	24.9	29.2	23.7	2.3	0.9	3.7	2.2	1.1	0.0	0.8	0.0	0.0	0.0	0.2
Randolph	24 663	90.7	37.3	19.7	26.3	21.4	3.2	1.5	4.3	2.1	9.3	7.4	1.3	0.0	0.5	0.0	0.0
Ray	23 354	98.6	37.4	23.6	31.1	25.3	3.3	1.7	3.1	1.6	1.4	0.6	0.8	0.0	0.0	0.0	0.0
Reynolds	6 689	97.7	40.7	24.1	25.5	20.4	3.5	1.5	3.9	1.8	2.3	0.1	0.6	0.0	0.0	0.0	1.7
Ripley	13 509	98.8	40.1	23.0	28.0	22.1	4.4	2.1	3.3	1.7	1.2	0.1	0.9	0.0	0.0	0.0	0.1
St. Charles	283 883	98.7	35.8	22.6	33.8	27.3	2.9	1.2	3.6	1.7	1.3	0.1	0.3	0.1	0.6	0.0	0.3
St. Clair	9 652	98.1	41.9	24.1	24.9	20.4	3.7	1.9	3.5	2.1	1.9	0.4	1.5	0.0	0.0	0.0	0.1
Ste. Genevieve	17 842	98.0	36.9	23.5	31.6	24.7	2.7	1.2	3.3	1.9	2.0	0.5	1.2	0.0	0.0	0.0	0.3
St. Francois	55 641	92.8	37.4	20.5	27.3	21.5	3.4	1.6	4.2	2.3	7.2	4.9	1.6	0.2	0.0	0.0	0.5
St. Louis	1 016 315	98.1	39.8	20.3	30.3	23.1	3.9	1.7	3.8	1.7	1.9	0.2	0.9	0.1	0.5	0.0	0.3
Saline	23 756	93.0	37.9	19.7	26.4	21.1	3.9	1.8	5.1	2.4	7.0	0.1	1.3	1.6	3.5	0.0	0.5
Schuyler	4 170	98.7	41.4	24.5	28.3	23.3	1.7	0.8	2.9	1.8	1.3	0.0	1.3	0.0	0.0	0.0	0.0
Scotland	4 983	97.5	38.2	22.2	32.1	27.2	2.0	0.7	3.0	1.4	2.5	0.1	2.4	0.0	0.0	0.0	0.0
Scott	40 422	98.6	38.7	21.1	31.1	24.6	4.1	2.0	3.6	1.8	1.4	0.1	1.0	0.0	0.0	0.0	0.3
Shannon	8 324	99.2	39.9	23.5	29.2	24.0	3.2	1.7	3.4	1.8	0.8	0.2	0.6	0.0	0.0	0.0	0.1
Shelby	6 799	96.2	40.4	23.0	28.9	23.4	2.0	0.9	2.0	1.1	3.8	0.0	1.5	0.4	0.0	0.0	1.9
Stoddard	29 705	97.3	40.6	23.3	26.8	21.2	3.4	1.6	3.1	1.7	2.7	0.2	1.0	0.0	0.0	0.0	1.5
Stone	28 658	99.1	41.3	26.7	24.2	19.2	3.4	1.5	3.6	1.8	0.9	0.1	0.6	0.0	0.0	0.0	0.2
Sullivan	7 219	97.9	40.5	21.6	27.8	23.0	3.5	1.4	4.5	1.9	2.1	0.1	1.5	0.0	0.0	0.0	0.5
Taney	39 703	96.3	40.7	23.0	24.6	20.3	3.3	1.4	4.7	2.1	3.7	0.1	0.7	0.1	2.5	0.0	0.2
Texas	23 003	98.5	40.8	23.7	27.9	22.9	2.9	1.3	3.2	1.7	1.5	0.0	1.1	0.1	0.0	0.0	0.3
Vernon	20 454	94.8	38.9	21.5	28.3	23.6	2.5	1.2	3.5	1.8	5.2	0.1	1.8	1.9	1.2	0.0	0.2
Warren	24 525	98.9	37.5	23.3	31.0	24.8	3.2	1.4	4.0	2.1	1.1	0.2	0.3	0.0	0.0	0.0	0.6
Washington	23 344	95.0	36.0	21.1	29.7	23.6	3.8	2.0	4.3	2.4	5.0	4.1	0.7	0.0	0.0	0.0	0.2
Wayne	13 259	98.9	41.9	23.5	25.3	20.2	4.3	2.2	3.9	1.9	1.1	0.0	0.9	0.0	0.0	0.0	0.1
Webster	31 045	96.9	35.7	22.8	32.4	26.9	2.8	1.3	3.2	1.6	3.1	2.2	0.8	0.0	0.0	0.0	0.1
Worth	2 382	97.9	42.4	23.9	27.2	23.1	1.6	0.7	2.9	1.3	2.1	0.0	1.6	0.0	0.0	0.0	0.5
Wright	17 955	98.8	39.4	23.1	30.3	25.0	2.9	1.3	3.1	1.6	1.2	0.1	1.0	0.1	0.0	0.0	0.1

Table B. States and Counties

	Households by type, 2000												Households, 1990		
	Family households						Nonfamily households								
				Married couple		Female householder[1]			Householder living alone						
STATE County	Total households	Total	With own children under 18 years	Total	With own children under 18 years	Total	With own children under 18 years	Total	Total	65 years and over	Average house-hold size	Average family size	Total house-holds	Female house-holder[1]	House-holder living alone
	71	72	73	74	75	76	77	78	79	80	81	82	83	84	85

MISSOURI—Cont'd

STATE County	71	72	73	74	75	76	77	78	79	80	81	82	83	84	85
Jasper	41 412	67.5	32.0	52.5	22.4	11.1	7.2	32.5	27.2	11.3	2.46	2.98	36 134	9.8	27.4
Jefferson	71 499	76.3	38.9	61.0	29.5	10.4	6.5	23.7	18.9	6.1	2.74	3.12	59 199	9.2	16.7
Johnson	17 410	67.9	35.1	55.9	27.1	8.5	6.0	32.1	22.7	7.1	2.58	3.07	14 579	6.9	21.6
Knox	1 791	68.0	27.9	57.5	22.3	6.9	3.4	32.0	29.3	16.0	2.38	2.93	1 819	6.3	28.1
Laclede	12 760	72.0	33.9	58.9	25.3	9.4	6.2	28.0	24.0	11.0	2.52	2.97	10 420	8.0	23.2
Lafayette	12 569	72.4	33.9	59.3	25.6	9.4	5.9	27.6	24.0	11.2	2.55	3.01	11 732	7.9	24.8
Lawrence	13 568	71.7	33.6	58.9	25.8	9.0	5.5	28.3	24.5	11.9	2.55	3.03	11 724	7.9	25.2
Lewis	3 956	68.5	32.0	56.7	24.1	8.3	5.8	31.5	27.4	13.3	2.46	3.00	3 745	7.0	26.4
Lincoln	13 851	76.2	40.0	61.5	29.9	10.1	7.1	23.8	19.7	7.7	2.77	3.17	10 316	7.3	20.7
Linn	5 697	66.0	29.6	53.6	21.7	8.9	5.7	34.0	30.3	16.8	2.37	2.94	5 704	6.5	30.6
Livingston	5 736	66.2	30.4	54.5	22.8	8.4	5.4	33.8	30.5	15.6	2.38	2.96	5 645	7.7	28.7
McDonald	8 113	72.3	35.7	57.6	26.1	9.6	6.3	27.7	23.3	9.1	2.65	3.11	6 386	7.9	22.5
Macon	6 501	67.4	29.1	55.7	21.7	8.4	5.4	32.6	29.0	15.0	2.38	2.92	6 160	6.6	27.0
Madison	4 711	70.7	31.2	57.4	23.4	10.1	6.1	29.3	25.9	14.3	2.46	2.93	4 344	8.9	24.0
Maries	3 519	71.1	31.6	59.0	24.2	7.7	4.5	28.9	25.7	12.3	2.51	3.00	3 028	6.8	23.5
Marion	11 066	68.0	33.3	53.5	23.6	11.4	7.7	32.0	28.1	13.8	2.44	2.98	10 728	9.4	28.4
Mercer	1 600	68.1	28.3	57.6	21.6	6.7	4.6	31.9	29.3	17.6	2.31	2.83	1 577	4.2	29.8
Miller	9 284	69.4	32.6	56.0	24.1	9.2	5.8	30.6	26.1	11.9	2.50	3.00	7 977	8.5	25.1
Mississippi	5 383	68.2	31.2	47.7	18.5	17.3	10.8	31.8	28.5	14.4	2.44	2.98	5 411	16.1	24.7
Moniteau	5 259	70.9	35.3	58.0	26.6	8.6	5.9	29.1	25.6	13.0	2.56	3.07	4 583	7.1	25.5
Monroe	3 656	70.2	31.6	59.1	25.1	7.7	4.5	29.8	26.5	12.9	2.50	3.02	3 471	6.3	26.9
Montgomery	4 775	69.9	31.3	56.9	23.6	8.6	5.1	30.1	26.3	13.2	2.47	2.97	4 341	7.5	26.1
Morgan	7 850	70.7	26.6	60.5	20.4	7.1	4.3	29.3	25.1	11.9	2.42	2.88	6 269	6.0	24.3
New Madrid	7 824	70.4	32.8	52.0	21.4	14.6	9.1	29.6	26.5	13.2	2.48	2.99	7 795	13.7	24.3
Newton	20 140	73.2	33.1	60.5	25.3	8.8	5.5	26.8	22.7	9.7	2.57	3.00	16 886	7.5	22.1
Nodaway	8 138	59.2	27.3	50.0	21.7	6.2	4.0	40.8	30.0	11.6	2.33	2.94	7 620	6.5	27.1
Oregon	4 263	70.8	29.3	58.8	22.3	8.4	4.9	29.2	26.2	13.9	2.40	2.86	3 851	7.4	25.2
Osage	4 922	72.7	34.9	61.7	28.6	6.7	4.0	27.3	23.8	10.8	2.61	3.10	4 262	5.9	22.3
Ozark	3 950	72.3	26.2	62.2	20.7	6.9	3.6	27.7	24.4	12.2	2.40	2.81	3 486	6.0	22.9
Pemiscot	7 855	67.7	33.6	45.0	18.7	18.5	12.5	32.3	28.8	14.3	2.52	3.10	8 210	17.2	27.6
Perry	6 904	71.8	34.2	60.5	27.2	7.9	5.1	28.2	24.5	11.6	2.57	3.07	6 111	7.0	23.5
Pettis	15 568	67.9	32.5	53.3	23.4	10.5	6.7	32.1	27.0	11.7	2.49	3.01	14 056	9.0	25.9
Phelps	15 683	65.3	30.3	52.7	22.2	9.5	6.2	34.7	28.6	10.7	2.38	2.92	13 277	8.3	26.1
Pike	6 451	69.4	31.3	55.7	22.7	9.6	6.0	30.6	26.7	12.9	2.50	3.01	6 083	8.4	25.7
Platte	29 278	69.1	34.1	57.0	26.2	8.8	5.8	30.9	24.9	6.0	2.49	3.00	22 142	7.9	22.9
Polk	9 917	72.0	33.0	60.5	25.5	8.2	5.4	28.0	23.2	10.7	2.56	3.02	8 031	6.5	22.9
Pulaski	13 433	74.1	42.3	60.6	32.7	9.7	7.0	25.9	21.6	7.2	2.68	3.13	12 397	9.0	18.0
Putnam	2 228	68.1	27.9	57.2	21.1	7.2	4.3	31.9	28.7	15.9	2.32	2.83	2 166	6.1	30.3
Ralls	3 736	74.5	34.0	64.2	27.2	6.5	4.1	25.5	21.2	10.0	2.55	2.95	3 226	6.1	21.5
Randolph	9 199	67.8	31.4	52.7	21.6	11.1	7.4	32.2	27.9	13.1	2.43	2.94	8 943	8.8	26.9
Ray	8 743	74.8	35.2	63.1	27.5	8.0	5.2	25.2	22.1	9.9	2.63	3.07	8 020	7.4	20.4
Reynolds	2 721	70.4	27.8	59.2	21.4	7.8	4.7	29.6	26.0	11.1	2.40	2.85	2 542	7.5	21.0
Ripley	5 416	71.0	30.3	57.4	22.8	9.6	5.2	29.0	25.9	13.3	2.46	2.95	4 788	9.6	24.7
St. Charles	101 663	75.8	40.5	63.2	32.5	9.2	6.0	24.2	19.4	5.9	2.76	3.18	74 331	8.0	18.0
St. Clair	4 040	69.1	26.3	57.6	19.4	7.7	4.5	30.9	27.4	14.8	2.34	2.83	3 499	6.3	28.2
Ste. Genevieve	6 586	74.8	35.1	63.6	27.9	7.6	4.7	25.2	21.8	10.4	2.66	3.09	5 707	6.6	20.2
St. Francois	20 793	70.5	32.6	54.9	22.8	11.3	7.2	29.5	24.9	11.2	2.48	2.94	17 670	10.1	23.1
St. Louis	404 312	67.0	31.6	51.0	22.7	12.7	7.4	33.0	28.0	10.1	2.47	3.05	380 110	10.7	24.6
Saline	9 015	66.7	30.6	51.9	21.3	10.3	6.5	33.3	28.2	14.6	2.45	2.97	8 903	9.5	28.1
Schuyler	1 725	69.2	29.6	59.1	23.0	7.2	4.8	30.8	28.2	15.2	2.39	2.90	1 729	6.8	27.0
Scotland	1 902	68.5	32.4	58.2	26.2	7.0	4.6	31.5	28.2	15.3	2.55	3.16	1 956	6.3	30.0
Scott	15 626	71.8	35.4	54.6	24.4	13.4	8.9	28.2	25.0	11.8	2.55	3.03	14 761	12.3	23.6
Shannon	3 319	71.0	32.5	58.8	24.9	8.2	5.1	29.0	26.3	12.6	2.49	2.97	2 917	7.0	22.8
Shelby	2 745	67.3	30.6	56.9	23.7	7.3	5.0	32.7	30.3	16.6	2.38	2.98	2 809	6.6	29.8
Stoddard	12 064	70.3	30.5	57.4	22.7	9.4	5.8	29.7	26.6	13.7	2.39	2.88	11 383	9.2	24.6
Stone	11 822	74.8	25.6	64.7	19.5	7.2	4.3	25.2	21.4	10.3	2.40	2.76	7 885	5.8	21.5
Sullivan	2 925	67.0	29.6	53.3	21.4	9.1	5.6	33.0	29.1	15.0	2.42	2.95	2 615	6.2	28.8
Taney	16 158	68.4	27.8	56.6	20.4	8.6	5.5	31.6	25.7	10.0	2.37	2.83	10 321	6.8	24.2
Texas	9 378	70.9	30.8	58.1	22.7	8.9	5.8	29.1	26.0	13.2	2.42	2.89	8 441	7.9	24.7
Vernon	7 966	68.2	32.2	55.3	23.6	9.6	6.5	31.8	28.1	13.0	2.44	2.97	7 301	9.0	28.0
Warren	9 185	75.0	34.7	62.2	26.6	8.9	5.8	25.0	20.8	8.8	2.64	3.05	7 070	6.6	20.1
Washington	8 406	74.2	36.4	58.6	26.4	10.6	6.9	25.8	22.0	9.4	2.64	3.05	6 982	10.4	19.7
Wayne	5 551	69.2	27.4	56.2	19.4	9.2	5.6	30.8	27.2	14.4	2.36	2.84	4 607	8.9	23.2
Webster	11 073	76.2	37.9	64.0	29.9	8.3	5.5	23.8	20.4	9.5	2.72	3.14	8 391	7.5	19.9
Worth	1 009	67.1	28.9	56.4	22.0	7.7	5.2	32.9	30.0	16.7	2.31	2.85	1 037	5.2	32.4
Wright	7 081	70.9	33.1	58.5	24.8	8.8	5.8	29.1	26.3	13.3	2.50	3.01	6 510	8.0	25.8

[1] No spouse present.

STATE County	Percent change of households, 1990–2000	Housing occupancy, 2000						Housing tenure, 2000				
		Total housing units	Occupied housing units (percent)	Vacant housing units		Homeowner vacancy rate (percent)	Rental vacancy rate (percent)	Occupied housing units			Average household size of owner-occupied units	Average household size of renter-occupied units
				Total	For seasonal, recreational, or occasional use			Total	Percent owner-occupied housing units	Percent renter-occupied housing units		
	86	87	88	89	90	91	92	93	94	95	96	97
MISSOURI—Cont'd												
Jasper	14.6	45 571	90.9	9.1	0.3	2.9	10.1	41 412	67.0	33.0	2.53	2.34
Jefferson	20.8	75 586	94.6	5.4	0.9	1.3	8.2	71 499	83.4	16.6	2.81	2.42
Johnson	19.4	18 886	92.2	7.8	0.5	2.8	7.8	17 410	61.7	38.3	2.68	2.42
Knox	-1.5	2 317	77.3	22.7	7.8	3.3	12.9	1 791	77.4	22.6	2.42	2.26
Laclede	22.5	14 320	89.1	10.9	1.9	3.0	11.5	12 760	72.8	27.2	2.58	2.37
Lafayette	7.1	13 707	91.7	8.3	0.6	2.3	7.8	12 569	75.4	24.6	2.61	2.37
Lawrence	15.7	14 789	91.7	8.3	0.6	2.7	8.6	13 568	74.3	25.7	2.58	2.46
Lewis	5.6	4 602	86.0	14.0	1.9	2.9	13.5	3 956	76.5	23.5	2.58	2.08
Lincoln	34.3	15 511	89.3	10.7	3.2	1.7	11.2	13 851	80.7	19.3	2.84	2.49
Linn	-0.1	6 554	86.9	13.1	2.0	2.4	9.9	5 697	76.9	23.1	2.44	2.14
Livingston	1.6	6 467	88.7	11.3	1.4	2.9	10.8	5 736	70.7	29.3	2.47	2.14
McDonald	27.0	9 287	87.4	12.6	2.5	4.2	8.7	8 113	71.4	28.6	2.63	2.72
Macon	5.5	7 502	86.7	13.3	2.7	2.9	8.4	6 501	76.2	23.8	2.47	2.09
Madison	8.4	5 656	83.3	16.7	7.0	3.6	8.7	4 711	76.2	23.8	2.48	2.37
Maries	16.2	4 149	84.8	15.2	7.5	2.1	9.3	3 519	81.7	18.3	2.55	2.31
Marion	3.2	12 443	88.9	11.1	1.3	2.7	13.3	11 066	70.3	29.7	2.54	2.22
Mercer	1.5	2 125	75.3	24.7	12.4	2.9	10.1	1 600	76.8	23.3	2.37	2.10
Miller	16.4	11 263	82.4	17.6	9.7	2.3	11.7	9 284	75.0	25.0	2.59	2.23
Mississippi	-0.5	5 840	92.2	7.8	0.7	2.3	7.5	5 383	63.6	36.4	2.41	2.50
Moniteau	14.8	5 742	91.6	8.4	0.9	2.1	9.9	5 259	77.7	22.3	2.63	2.34
Monroe	5.3	4 565	80.1	19.9	10.3	2.4	8.9	3 656	78.7	21.3	2.55	2.31
Montgomery	10.0	5 726	83.4	16.6	6.1	2.2	10.5	4 775	78.5	21.5	2.50	2.38
Morgan	25.2	13 898	56.5	43.5	37.2	3.8	12.4	7 850	82.8	17.2	2.45	2.28
New Madrid	0.4	8 600	91.0	9.0	0.7	2.5	9.1	7 824	66.0	34.0	2.50	2.45
Newton	19.3	21 897	92.0	8.0	0.6	2.7	9.3	20 140	76.6	23.4	2.60	2.47
Nodaway	6.8	8 909	91.3	8.7	0.7	2.5	7.9	8 138	63.7	36.3	2.50	2.04
Oregon	10.7	4 997	85.3	14.7	3.2	4.3	10.4	4 263	78.2	21.8	2.40	2.41
Osage	15.5	5 904	83.4	16.6	7.5	2.7	12.6	4 922	82.9	17.1	2.71	2.16
Ozark	13.3	5 114	77.2	22.8	10.3	3.3	11.3	3 950	81.3	18.7	2.40	2.40
Pemiscot	-4.3	8 793	89.3	10.7	0.8	1.9	11.5	7 855	58.3	41.7	2.49	2.55
Perry	13.0	7 815	88.3	11.7	5.1	1.7	9.5	6 904	80.1	19.9	2.63	2.35
Pettis	10.8	16 963	91.8	8.2	0.4	2.1	9.0	15 568	72.5	27.5	2.53	2.38
Phelps	18.1	17 501	89.6	10.4	1.7	2.2	11.9	15 683	65.5	34.5	2.50	2.16
Pike	6.0	7 493	86.1	13.9	4.2	3.2	12.4	6 451	74.0	26.0	2.57	2.29
Platte	32.2	30 902	94.7	5.3	0.8	1.2	8.2	29 278	67.5	32.5	2.70	2.06
Polk	23.5	11 183	88.7	11.3	2.2	3.7	11.4	9 917	72.8	27.2	2.61	2.42
Pulaski	8.4	15 408	87.2	12.8	3.1	3.9	9.1	13 433	58.1	41.9	2.60	2.79
Putnam	2.9	2 914	76.5	23.5	12.0	2.8	8.6	2 228	77.0	23.0	2.35	2.22
Ralls	15.8	4 564	81.9	18.1	9.6	2.8	16.3	3 736	82.2	17.8	2.59	2.35
Randolph	2.9	10 740	85.7	14.3	1.9	3.3	18.3	9 199	72.1	27.9	2.50	2.26
Ray	9.0	9 371	93.3	6.7	0.7	2.8	6.1	8 743	79.5	20.5	2.71	2.32
Reynolds	7.0	3 759	72.4	27.6	14.8	1.9	13.8	2 721	77.3	22.7	2.44	2.28
Ripley	13.1	6 392	84.7	15.3	5.6	2.8	11.8	5 416	77.9	22.1	2.49	2.38
St. Charles	36.8	105 514	96.4	3.6	0.5	1.3	6.1	101 663	82.0	18.0	2.88	2.18
St. Clair	15.5	5 205	77.6	22.4	12.2	3.4	12.9	4 040	79.4	20.6	2.37	2.26
Ste. Genevieve	15.4	8 018	82.1	17.9	12.1	1.5	7.0	6 586	82.3	17.7	2.73	2.30
St. Francois	17.7	24 449	85.0	15.0	7.5	2.5	8.5	20 793	73.1	26.9	2.56	2.29
St. Louis	6.4	423 749	95.4	4.6	0.4	1.3	6.7	404 312	74.1	25.9	2.62	2.03
Saline	1.3	10 019	90.0	10.0	0.8	2.1	7.7	9 015	69.1	30.9	2.47	2.41
Schuyler	-0.2	2 027	85.1	14.9	2.8	5.7	10.8	1 725	75.5	24.5	2.48	2.10
Scotland	-2.8	2 292	83.0	17.0	2.9	3.4	12.9	1 902	76.6	23.4	2.60	2.41
Scott	5.9	16 951	92.2	7.8	0.6	2.5	8.1	15 626	69.4	30.6	2.60	2.44
Shannon	13.8	3 862	85.9	14.1	4.4	3.5	10.8	3 319	79.2	20.8	2.53	2.39
Shelby	-2.3	3 245	84.6	15.4	3.1	4.5	9.0	2 745	74.7	25.3	2.45	2.19
Stoddard	6.0	13 221	91.2	8.8	1.0	2.6	8.1	12 064	72.4	27.6	2.42	2.33
Stone	49.9	16 241	72.8	27.2	17.7	3.5	18.3	11 822	81.2	18.8	2.38	2.49
Sullivan	11.9	3 364	87.0	13.0	2.6	2.6	9.6	2 925	71.5	28.5	2.41	2.44
Taney	56.6	19 688	82.1	17.9	8.9	4.1	12.0	16 158	68.9	31.1	2.41	2.27
Texas	11.1	10 764	87.1	12.9	2.7	3.0	11.9	9 378	76.6	23.4	2.46	2.28
Vernon	9.1	8 872	89.8	10.2	1.3	2.6	8.9	7 966	72.2	27.8	2.51	2.24
Warren	29.9	11 046	83.2	16.8	4.8	1.7	6.7	9 185	83.1	16.9	2.68	2.44
Washington	20.4	9 894	85.0	15.0	5.6	1.7	8.6	8 406	80.0	20.0	2.67	2.50
Wayne	20.5	7 496	74.1	25.9	12.4	3.2	9.4	5 551	78.2	21.8	2.36	2.38
Webster	32.0	12 052	91.9	8.1	0.8	3.1	8.2	11 073	77.9	22.1	2.76	2.56
Worth	-2.7	1 245	81.0	19.0	3.9	4.1	6.7	1 009	76.6	23.4	2.35	2.20
Wright	8.8	7 957	89.0	11.0	1.0	2.5	10.7	7 081	73.1	26.9	2.55	2.39

Table B. States and Counties

STATE/ County code	MSA/ PMSA/ NECMA code[1]	County type[2]	STATE County	Population, 2000				Population, 1990				Population and population characteristics, 2000					
												Race (percent)					
												One race					
				Land area, 2000[3] (sq km)	Total persons	Rank	Per square kilometer	Land area, 1990[3] (sq km)	Total persons	Rank	Per square kilometer	White	Black or African American	American Indian or Alaska Native	Asian	Native Hawaiian and other Pacific Islander	Some other race
				1	2	3	4	5	6	7	8	9	10	11	12	13	14
			MISSOURI—Cont'd														
29 510	7040	0	St. Louis city	160	348 189	168	2 176.2	160	396 685	126	2 479.3	43.8	51.2	0.3	2.0	0.0	0.8
30 000	...		MONTANA	376 979	902 195	X	2.4	376 991	799 065	X	2.1	90.6	0.3	6.2	0.5	0.1	0.6
30 001	...	7	Beaverhead	14 355	9 202	2 513	0.6	14 355	8 424	2 518	0.6	95.9	0.2	1.5	0.2	0.0	1.1
30 003	...	6	Big Horn	12 936	12 671	2 249	1.0	12 937	11 337	2 270	0.9	36.6	0.0	59.7	0.2	0.0	0.7
30 005	...	9	Blaine	10 946	7 009	2 685	0.6	10 946	6 728	2 684	0.6	52.6	0.2	45.4	0.1	0.0	0.2
30 007	...	9	Broadwater	3 086	4 385	2 887	1.4	3 086	3 318	2 970	1.1	97.0	0.3	1.2	0.1	0.1	0.3
30 009	...	8	Carbon	5 304	9 552	2 484	1.8	5 304	8 080	2 556	1.5	97.1	0.3	0.7	0.4	0.0	0.6
30 011	...	9	Carter	8 649	1 360	3 099	0.2	8 650	1 503	3 097	0.2	98.6	0.1	0.4	0.1	0.0	0.3
30 013	3040	3	Cascade	6 988	80 357	638	11.5	6 988	77 691	585	11.1	90.7	1.1	4.2	0.8	0.1	0.7
30 015	...	8	Chouteau	10 291	5 970	2 787	0.6	10 291	5 452	2 804	0.5	84.0	0.1	14.6	0.2	0.1	0.2
30 017	...	7	Custer	9 798	11 696	2 319	1.2	9 799	11 697	2 234	1.2	97.0	0.1	1.3	0.3	0.1	0.3
30 019	...	9	Daniels	3 694	2 017	3 064	0.5	3 694	2 266	3 044	0.6	96.0	0.0	1.3	0.2	0.1	0.6
30 021	...	7	Dawson	6 146	9 059	2 525	1.5	6 147	9 505	2 433	1.5	97.4	0.3	1.2	0.1	0.0	0.3
30 023	...	7	Deer Lodge	1 909	9 417	2 496	4.9	1 909	10 356	2 354	5.4	95.9	0.2	1.8	0.4	0.0	0.2
30 025	...	9	Fallon	2 837	3 003	0.7		4 197	3 103	2 992	0.7	98.6	0.1	0.3	0.4	0.0	0.1
30 027	...	7	Fergus	11 238	11 893	2 299	1.1	11 239	12 083	2 211	1.1	97.1	0.1	1.2	0.2	0.0	0.3
30 029	...	5	Flathead	13 205	74 471	672	5.6	13 205	59 218	735	4.5	96.3	0.2	1.1	0.5	0.1	0.4
30 031	...	5	Gallatin	6 749	67 831	723	10.1	6 493	50 484	834	7.8	96.2	0.2	0.9	0.9	0.1	0.5
30 033	...	9	Garfield	12 090	1 279	3 101	0.1	12 091	1 589	3 091	0.1	99.1	0.1	0.4	0.1	0.0	0.0
30 035	...	7	Glacier	7 756	13 247	2 209	1.7	7 756	12 121	2 207	1.6	35.4	0.1	61.8	0.1	0.1	0.2
30 037	...	8	Golden Valley	3 044	1 042	3 109	0.3	3 044	912	3 116	0.3	99.1	0.0	0.6	0.1	0.0	0.0
30 039	...	9	Granite	4 474	2 830	3 004	0.6	4 474	2 548	3 020	0.6	96.3	0.0	1.3	0.1	0.0	0.5
30 041	...	7	Hill	7 502	16 673	1 977	2.2	7 502	17 654	1 808	2.4	79.5	0.1	17.3	0.4	0.0	0.4
30 043	...	9	Jefferson	4 291	10 049	2 440	2.3	4 291	7 939	2 578	1.9	96.1	0.1	1.3	0.4	0.1	0.4
30 045	...	8	Judith Basin	4 843	2 329	3 036	0.5	4 843	2 282	3 041	0.5	98.6	0.0	0.3	0.1	0.0	0.0
30 047	...	5	Lake	3 869	26 507	1 502	6.9	3 869	21 041	1 628	5.4	71.4	0.1	23.8	0.3	0.0	0.7
30 049	...	7	Lewis and Clark	8 964	55 716	847	6.2	8 964	47 495	884	5.3	95.2	0.2	2.0	0.5	0.1	0.4
30 051	...	9	Liberty	3 703	2 158	3 054	0.6	3 703	2 295	3 039	0.6	99.2	0.0	0.1	0.3	0.0	0.1
30 053	...	7	Lincoln	9 357	18 837	1 851	2.0	9 357	17 481	1 821	1.9	96.1	0.1	1.2	0.3	0.0	0.4
30 055	...	9	McCone	6 844	1 977	3 065	0.3	6 844	2 276	3 043	0.3	97.0	0.3	1.1	0.3	0.0	0.0
30 057	...	9	Madison	9 289	6 851	2 705	0.7	9 289	5 989	2 759	0.6	97.0	0.0	0.5	0.3	0.0	0.8
30 059	...	8	Meagher	6 195	1 932	3 069	0.3	6 195	1 819	3 077	0.3	97.2	0.0	1.0	0.2	0.1	0.6
30 061	...	9	Mineral	3 159	3 884	2 924	1.2	3 159	3 315	2 974	1.0	94.6	0.2	1.9	0.5	0.0	0.3
30 063	5140	5	Missoula	6 729	95 802	540	14.2	6 729	78 687	575	11.7	94.0	0.3	2.3	1.0	0.1	0.4
30 065	...	8	Musselshell	4 836	4 497	2 880	0.9	4 836	4 106	2 907	0.8	96.9	0.1	1.3	0.2	0.0	0.4
30 067	...	7	Park	7 258	15 694	2 038	2.2	6 879	14 515	2 018	2.1	96.6	0.4	0.9	0.4	0.0	0.5
30 069	...	9	Petroleum	4 284	493	3 136	0.1	4 284	519	3 135	0.1	99.2	0.0	0.2	0.0	0.0	0.2
30 071	...	9	Phillips	13 311	4 601	2 872	0.3	13 312	5 163	2 829	0.4	89.4	0.2	7.6	0.3	0.0	0.4
30 073	...	7	Pondera	4 208	6 424	2 748	1.5	4 208	6 433	2 714	1.5	83.7	0.1	14.5	0.1	0.0	0.1
30 075	...	9	Powder River	8 540	1 858	3 075	0.2	8 540	2 090	3 063	0.2	97.4	0.0	1.8	0.1	0.0	0.2
30 077	...	7	Powell	6 024	7 180	2 668	1.2	6 024	6 620	2 695	1.1	92.5	0.5	3.5	0.4	0.0	0.7
30 079	...	9	Prairie	4 498	1 199	3 104	0.3	4 498	1 383	3 103	0.3	98.0	0.0	0.5	0.2	0.0	0.2
30 081	...	7	Ravalli	6 201	36 070	1 213	5.8	6 201	25 010	1 462	4.0	96.7	0.1	0.9	0.3	0.1	0.4
30 083	...	7	Richland	5 398	9 667	2 472	1.8	5 398	10 716	2 318	2.0	96.6	0.1	1.5	0.2	0.0	0.8
30 085	...	7	Roosevelt	6 101	10 620	2 389	1.7	6 101	10 999	2 294	1.8	40.9	0.0	55.8	0.4	0.0	0.3
30 087	...	7	Rosebud	12 982	9 383	2 499	0.7	12 982	10 505	2 335	0.8	64.4	0.2	32.4	0.3	0.0	0.7
30 089	...	9	Sanders	7 154	10 227	2 423	1.4	7 154	8 669	2 494	1.2	91.9	0.1	4.7	0.3	0.0	0.3
30 091	...	9	Sheridan	4 342	4 105	2 907	0.9	4 343	4 732	2 860	1.1	97.0	0.1	1.2	0.3	0.0	0.3
30 093	...	5	Silver Bow	1 860	34 606	1 262	18.6	1 860	33 941	1 166	18.2	95.4	0.2	2.0	0.4	0.1	0.6
30 095	...	8	Stillwater	4 649	8 195	2 594	1.8	4 648	6 536	2 703	1.4	96.8	0.1	0.7	0.2	0.0	0.9
30 097	...	9	Sweet Grass	4 805	3 609	2 943	0.8	4 805	3 154	2 988	0.7	97.0	0.1	0.6	0.3	0.0	0.7
30 099	...	8	Teton	5 886	6 445	2 743	1.1	5 886	6 271	2 727	1.1	96.3	0.2	1.5	0.1	0.0	0.4
30 101	...	7	Toole	4 949	5 267	2 833	1.1	4 949	5 046	2 838	1.0	93.9	0.2	3.2	0.3	0.0	0.3
30 103	...	8	Treasure	2 535	861	3 118	0.3	2 535	874	3 119	0.3	96.4	0.1	1.6	0.3	0.0	0.9
30 105	...	7	Valley	12 745	7 675	2 631	0.6	12 745	8 239	2 545	0.6	88.1	0.1	9.4	0.2	0.0	0.3
30 107	...	9	Wheatland	3 686	2 259	3 045	0.6	3 686	2 246	3 051	0.6	97.0	0.1	0.6	0.2	0.2	0.3
30 109	...	9	Wibaux	2 303	1 068	3 107	0.5	2 303	1 191	3 108	0.5	98.0	0.2	0.5	0.2	0.0	0.3
30 111	0880	3	Yellowstone	6 825	129 352	415	19.0	6 825	113 419	404	16.6	92.8	0.4	3.1	0.5	0.0	1.3
31 000	...		NEBRASKA...............	199 099	1 711 263	X	8.6	199 113	1 578 417	X	7.9	89.6	4.0	0.9	1.3	0.0	2.8
31 001	...	5	Adams	1 459	31 151	1 373	21.4	1 459	29 625	1 312	20.3	94.5	0.6	0.4	1.6	0.0	2.0
31 003	...	9	Antelope	2 220	7 452	2 644	3.4	2 220	7 965	2 576	3.6	98.8	0.1	0.3	0.1	0.0	0.3
31 005	...	9	Arthur	1 853	444	3 137	0.2	1 853	462	3 137	0.2	96.4	0.0	0.2	0.7	0.2	0.9
31 007	...	9	Banner	1 933	819	3 122	0.4	1 933	852	3 120	0.4	95.8	0.1	0.2	0.1	0.0	3.1

[1]MSA = Metropolitan Statistical Area. PMSA = Primary MSA. NECMA = New England County Metropolitan Area. See Appendix A for explanation of these concepts. See Appendix B for list of metropolitan areas identified by type, with component counties.
[2]County typology code from the Economic Research Service of USDA. See Appendix A for definition.
[3]Dry land or land partially or temporarily covered by water.

Table B. States and Counties

STATE County	Population and population characteristics, 2000 (cont'd)								Population and population characteristics, 1990				
	Race (percent) (cont'd)								Race (percent)				
	Race alone or in combination												
	Two or more races	White	Black	American Indian or Alaska Native	Asian	Native Hawaiian and other Pacific Islander	Some other race	Hispanic[1]	White	Black or African American	American Indian or Alaska Native	Asian and Pacific Islander	Hispanic[1]
	15	16	17	18	19	20	21	22	23	24	25	26	27
MISSOURI—Cont'd													
St. Louis city	1.9	45.2	52.1	0.8	2.3	0.1	1.5	2.0	50.0	47.5	0.2	0.9	1.3
MONTANA	1.7	92.2	0.5	7.4	0.8	0.1	0.9	2.0	92.7	0.3	6.0	0.5	1.5
Beaverhead	1.2	97.0	0.2	2.2	0.5	0.1	1.3	2.7	97.3	0.1	1.4	0.3	1.6
Big Horn.............................	2.8	39.1	0.2	62.0	0.5	0.0	1.0	3.7	43.4	0.2	55.5	0.4	2.6
Blaine.................................	1.5	53.9	0.3	46.7	0.1	0.1	0.4	1.0	60.0	0.1	39.6	0.1	0.8
Broadwater.........................	1.0	98.0	0.3	2.0	0.1	0.1	0.4	1.3	98.1	0.0	1.4	0.2	1.0
Carbon................................	1.0	98.1	0.3	1.3	0.4	0.0	0.8	1.8	98.7	0.00	0.5	0.2	1.1
Carter.................................	0.5	99.1	0.1	0.5	0.1	0.1	0.6	0.6	98.9	0.0	0.6	0.1	0.8
Cascade..............................	2.4	92.9	1.5	5.7	1.3	0.2	1.0	2.4	93.1	1.4	4.0	1.0	1.8
Chouteau............................	0.7	84.7	0.1	15.1	0.4	0.1	0.4	0.7	95.8	0.1	3.9	0.2	0.5
Custer.................................	1.0	98.0	0.2	1.9	0.4	0.1	0.5	1.5	97.4	0.1	1.7	0.2	1.4
Daniels...............................	1.7	97.7	0.3	2.6	0.2	0.1	0.8	1.6	98.9	0.0	0.3	0.8	0.5
Dawson...............................	0.6	98.0	0.3	1.6	0.2	0.0	0.4	0.9	98.6	0.0	0.9	0.3	0.7
Deer Lodge.........................	1.6	97.5	0.3	3.0	0.5	0.1	0.4	1.6	96.4	0.0	2.5	0.2	1.5
Fallon.................................	0.5	99.0	0.2	0.6	0.5	0.0	0.1	0.4	99.2	0.0	0.3	0.4	0.2
Fergus................................	1.2	98.2	0.2	2.0	0.4	0.0	0.5	0.8	98.7	0.1	1.0	0.1	0.6
Flathead..............................	1.5	97.7	0.3	2.1	0.7	0.2	0.6	1.4	97.8	0.1	1.5	0.4	1.0
Gallatin...............................	1.2	97.3	0.4	1.4	1.2	0.2	0.8	1.5	97.5	0.2	1.2	0.9	1.2
Garfield..............................	0.2	99.4	0.1	0.5	0.1	0.1	0.2	0.4	99.6	0.0	0.3	0.1	0.0
Glacier................................	2.4	37.2	0.7	63.9	0.2	0.1	0.3	1.2	43.4	0.1	56.3	0.1	0.6
Golden Valley	0.2	99.3	0.0	0.7	0.2	0.0	0.0	1.2	98.1	0.0	1.1	0.4	0.9
Granite...............................	1.8	98.1	0.1	2.6	0.4	0.0	0.7	1.3	98.9	0.0	0.8	0.2	0.4
Hill......................................	2.3	81.8	0.2	19.0	0.6	0.0	0.7	1.2	83.4	0.1	15.7	0.5	1.0
Jefferson............................	1.7	97.7	0.2	2.4	0.6	0.2	0.6	1.5	98.0	0.1	1.5	0.2	1.0
Judith Basin........................	0.9	99.5	0.0	1.0	0.3	0.0	0.0	0.6	99.4	0.0	0.3	0.3	0.4
Lake....................................	3.7	74.9	0.2	26.8	0.5	0.1	1.3	2.5	78.0	0.1	21.4	0.2	1.9
Lewis and Clark..................	1.6	96.8	0.3	3.1	0.8	0.1	0.6	1.5	96.8	0.1	2.2	0.5	1.2
Liberty................................	0.3	99.5	0.1	0.2	0.4	0.0	0.1	0.2	99.3	0.1	0.5	0.1	0.2
Lincoln	1.9	97.9	0.3	2.5	0.5	0.1	0.6	1.4	97.8	0.1	1.6	0.3	1.1
McCone...............................	1.4	98.3	0.5	2.0	0.5	0.0	0.2	1.0	99.1	0.0	0.7	0.1	0.4
Madison..............................	1.4	98.3	0.1	1.6	0.4	0.0	1.0	1.9	98.6	0.0	0.7	0.2	1.5
Meagher..............................	1.0	98.2	0.1	1.7	0.3	0.1	0.9	1.5	98.1	0.0	1.0	0.1	1.4
Mineral...............................	2.5	97.0	0.5	3.6	0.8	0.1	0.6	1.6	96.7	0.1	2.4	0.7	1.2
Missoula.............................	1.9	95.8	0.5	3.4	1.4	0.2	0.8	1.6	96.1	0.2	2.3	1.1	1.2
Musselshell.........................	1.2	98.0	0.2	2.1	0.3	0.2	0.5	1.6	98.8	0.0	0.6	0.2	0.9
Park....................................	1.2	97.7	0.5	1.7	0.6	0.1	0.7	1.8	97.7	0.5	0.8	0.5	1.6
Petroleum	0.4	99.6	0.0	0.4	0.0	0.0	0.4	1.2	99.4	0.0	0.6	0.0	0.0
Phillips...............................	2.1	91.4	0.2	9.6	0.3	0.0	0.5	1.2	91.8	0.0	7.6	0.3	0.9
Pondera..............................	1.5	85.1	0.2	15.6	0.2	0.1	0.3	0.8	88.5	0.1	10.9	0.3	0.5
Powder River.......................	0.5	97.9	0.0	2.2	0.2	0.0	0.3	0.6	97.8	0.0	1.8	0.1	1.0
Powell.................................	2.3	94.7	0.6	5.3	0.8	0.1	0.9	1.9	94.7	0.3	3.8	0.4	1.2
Prairie................................	1.2	99.2	0.0	1.3	0.4	0.0	0.3	0.7	98.4	0.0	1.1	0.3	1.2
Ravalli................................	1.4	98.1	0.3	1.8	0.5	0.2	0.7	1.9	98.1	0.1	1.1	0.3	1.5
Richland..............................	0.8	97.4	0.1	2.0	0.2	0.1	1.1	2.2	97.5	0.0	1.3	0.2	2.2
Roosevelt............................	2.5	43.3	0.1	57.8	0.6	0.1	0.7	1.2	50.6	0.2	48.7	0.4	0.9
Rosebud..............................	2.0	66.2	0.4	34.1	0.5	0.0	0.9	2.3	71.8	0.3	26.7	0.5	2.1
Sanders..............................	2.6	94.5	0.3	6.8	0.5	0.1	0.7	1.6	93.8	0.1	5.4	0.4	1.2
Sheridan.............................	1.2	98.2	0.1	2.2	0.4	0.1	0.3	1.1	98.3	0.0	1.1	0.3	0.8
Silver Bow...........................	1.4	96.7	0.3	3.0	0.7	0.1	0.4	2.7	97.3	0.1	1.5	0.4	2.4
Stillwater............................	1.2	97.9	0.3	1.4	0.5	0.1	1.2	2.0	98.4	0.1	0.8	0.2	1.4
Sweet Grass........................	1.3	98.3	0.1	1.4	0.5	0.1	1.0	1.5	99.1	0.1	0.5	0.2	0.2
Teton..................................	1.5	97.7	0.3	2.7	0.2	0.0	0.7	1.1	98.1	0.0	1.5	0.1	0.6
Toole...................................	2.1	95.8	0.3	4.9	0.6	0.1	0.4	1.2	97.1	0.1	2.3	0.3	0.7
Treasure.............................	0.6	97.0	0.1	2.0	0.6	0.0	0.9	1.5	97.7	0.0	1.0	0.2	3.0
Valley.................................	1.8	89.9	0.3	10.7	0.4	0.1	0.5	0.8	90.1	0.1	9.3	0.2	0.8
Wheatland...........................	1.6	98.5	0.4	1.4	0.4	0.2	0.7	1.1	98.1	0.0	0.8	0.4	1.0
Wibaux................................	0.8	98.9	0.5	0.7	0.5	0.1	0.3	0.4	99.7	0.0	0.2	0.2	0.2
Yellowstone.........................	1.9	94.5	0.8	4.1	0.8	0.1	1.7	3.7	95.2	0.5	2.9	0.5	2.8
NEBRASKA	1.4	90.8	4.4	1.3	1.6	0.1	3.3	5.5	93.8	3.6	0.8	0.8	2.3
Adams.................................	0.8	95.3	0.8	0.7	1.8	0.0	2.3	4.6	98.2	0.6	0.4	0.4	1.0
Antelope..............................	0.5	99.3	0.1	0.5	0.1	0.0	0.4	0.7	99.6	0.0	0.3	0.1	0.1
Arthur..................................	1.6	98.0	0.0	1.1	0.9	0.2	1.4	1.4	99.4	0.0	0.4	0.0	0.0
Banner................................	0.6	96.5	0.1	0.6	0.4	0.0	3.1	5.6	97.7	0.1	0.4	0.0	2.2

[1] Hispanic persons may be of any race.

Table B. States and Counties

STATE County	Population and population characteristics, 2000										
	Age (percent)										
	Under 5 years	5 to 17 years	18 to 24 years	25 to 34 years	35 to 44 years	45 to 54 years	55 to 64 years	65 to 74 years	75 years and over	Median age (years)	Percent Female
	28	29	30	31	32	33	34	35	36	37	38
MISSOURI—Cont'd											
St. Louis city	6.7	19.0	10.6	15.6	15.3	11.8	7.2	6.6	7.1	33.7	53.0
MONTANA	6.1	19.4	9.5	11.4	15.7	15.0	9.4	6.9	6.5	37.5	50.2
Beaverhead	5.7	18.8	11.9	10.1	15.0	14.9	10.0	7.2	6.4	37.6	48.8
Big Horn	9.3	26.5	8.6	12.1	14.4	12.6	7.9	4.6	4.0	29.8	50.7
Blaine	8.1	24.5	8.0	10.2	14.6	12.9	8.7	6.9	6.0	34.4	50.6
Broadwater	5.3	19.9	4.8	9.3	16.9	15.9	11.5	9.0	7.4	41.3	49.0
Carbon	5.2	18.8	5.7	9.3	16.9	16.8	10.5	8.7	8.1	41.9	49.9
Carter	4.0	22.5	4.1	9.1	15.8	14.6	11.9	8.5	9.4	41.8	51.3
Cascade	6.6	19.4	9.1	12.3	15.8	13.3	9.4	7.2	6.7	36.7	50.5
Chouteau	6.5	22.4	6.5	8.9	15.2	14.0	9.2	8.5	9.0	39.3	49.8
Custer	5.9	19.2	8.4	10.3	15.3	14.4	9.3	8.5	8.6	39.3	51.1
Daniels	4.3	17.8	4.9	6.8	13.1	16.6	12.9	10.9	12.6	47.0	51.0
Dawson	5.1	18.0	8.8	9.9	15.1	15.3	10.1	9.0	8.7	41.0	50.4
Deer Lodge	4.6	17.9	7.9	9.5	14.5	15.7	11.0	9.6	9.3	42.3	50.1
Fallon	4.9	20.7	6.2	9.3	16.2	15.3	9.6	9.9	8.0	41.1	49.5
Fergus	5.2	19.4	6.1	8.8	14.8	15.0	10.9	9.5	10.4	42.4	51.3
Flathead	5.9	20.0	7.4	10.8	16.6	16.5	9.9	6.9	6.1	39.0	50.4
Gallatin	5.8	16.2	18.5	14.8	15.6	13.7	8.3	4.4	4.1	30.7	48.0
Garfield	6.7	17.7	7.1	9.7	13.6	16.2	9.6	8.4	10.9	41.6	48.4
Glacier	8.1	26.8	9.1	11.0	15.9	12.1	7.8	5.1	4.1	30.6	50.5
Golden Valley	5.2	22.5	5.9	8.3	14.8	14.6	12.4	10.6	6.0	41.5	48.3
Granite	4.8	19.4	5.7	8.4	14.9	17.0	13.9	8.5	7.4	42.8	48.8
Hill	7.1	21.1	11.6	10.7	15.3	13.7	7.7	6.6	6.2	34.5	50.2
Jefferson	5.2	22.6	5.2	8.4	18.4	18.9	10.9	6.1	4.2	40.2	49.8
Judith Basin	5.2	21.6	4.6	7.5	15.8	16.2	12.0	9.1	8.1	42.0	48.1
Lake	6.7	21.4	8.0	9.9	14.6	14.6	10.4	7.9	6.6	38.2	50.9
Lewis and Clark	6.2	19.4	8.5	11.2	16.7	16.8	9.5	6.2	5.6	38.0	50.9
Liberty	5.1	20.8	5.8	8.9	15.8	14.3	9.8	9.1	10.6	41.5	50.7
Lincoln	5.0	20.4	5.5	8.7	15.5	16.7	13.1	8.9	6.3	42.1	49.3
McCone	5.4	19.4	5.4	8.0	16.3	15.5	11.0	10.2	8.8	42.4	50.1
Madison	4.7	18.2	4.9	9.2	15.8	17.0	13.0	9.6	7.6	43.4	49.4
Meagher	5.0	20.0	6.1	7.6	15.1	16.7	11.3	9.7	8.5	42.8	49.9
Mineral	5.0	19.3	6.4	9.8	15.6	16.3	13.5	8.6	5.5	41.1	48.5
Missoula	5.7	17.2	15.4	14.0	15.1	14.6	7.9	5.0	5.0	33.2	50.0
Musselshell	4.9	18.4	5.7	8.8	15.2	18.4	11.1	8.5	9.0	43.2	51.2
Park	5.8	17.8	6.5	11.1	16.8	17.6	9.5	7.4	7.4	40.6	50.6
Petroleum	7.1	18.9	6.1	9.9	12.8	16.6	11.6	9.3	7.7	41.1	47.5
Phillips	4.9	22.4	5.5	8.0	16.5	14.5	10.6	8.2	9.4	40.8	49.9
Pondera	6.2	23.4	6.4	9.3	15.5	13.5	9.5	8.3	7.9	38.6	50.7
Powder River	5.9	20.7	4.8	8.1	15.2	16.4	10.4	10.1	8.4	42.1	50.7
Powell	4.6	16.6	7.8	12.4	18.4	15.7	10.5	7.2	6.7	39.7	41.1
Prairie	4.2	14.5	4.3	7.3	12.7	19.7	13.2	10.7	13.4	48.9	48.4
Ravalli	5.7	19.8	6.2	9.9	14.8	16.2	11.8	8.3	7.2	41.1	50.3
Richland	5.8	21.8	6.4	10.1	16.6	14.7	9.1	7.8	7.8	39.2	50.3
Roosevelt	8.1	26.5	7.9	10.4	15.4	12.8	7.4	5.8	5.8	32.3	50.4
Rosebud	7.7	25.8	7.2	9.9	15.8	15.9	8.8	5.1	3.8	34.5	49.8
Sanders	4.7	19.1	5.5	8.2	13.8	17.7	14.1	9.7	7.1	44.2	49.5
Sheridan	4.5	18.5	4.8	6.9	15.2	15.7	10.8	11.3	12.3	45.1	50.3
Silver Bow	5.8	17.9	9.6	11.2	15.4	14.2	9.8	7.7	8.3	38.9	50.6
Stillwater	5.5	19.8	5.7	10.1	16.8	16.7	10.9	7.9	6.6	40.8	49.0
Sweet Grass	5.8	20.1	5.3	10.4	14.3	15.5	10.9	8.1	9.4	41.2	50.1
Teton	6.2	21.1	6.1	9.2	15.4	14.3	11.1	7.8	8.8	40.0	50.8
Toole	5.4	20.2	6.8	11.3	16.9	14.7	8.9	7.8	8.1	39.1	48.4
Treasure	5.3	22.4	5.0	7.8	15.4	14.6	12.7	7.5	9.2	41.8	49.0
Valley	5.5	19.6	6.0	8.8	15.5	14.8	10.8	9.5	9.5	41.7	50.5
Wheatland	6.0	20.8	6.4	9.7	12.3	14.2	11.3	8.9	10.4	41.4	50.5
Wibaux	5.2	20.6	5.8	8.3	14.1	15.7	8.6	10.6	11.0	42.3	52.0
Yellowstone	6.6	18.9	9.3	12.6	16.2	14.4	8.8	6.8	6.5	36.9	51.2
NEBRASKA	6.8	19.5	10.2	13.0	15.4	13.2	8.3	6.8	6.8	35.3	50.7
Adams	6.4	18.1	11.9	11.7	14.5	13.3	8.4	7.2	8.7	36.5	51.0
Antelope	6.0	21.5	6.2	8.2	15.1	13.5	9.6	9.1	10.8	40.6	50.8
Arthur	5.2	18.7	5.4	12.6	16.9	10.8	14.0	9.7	6.8	40.3	49.5
Banner	4.8	24.1	3.7	8.2	16.1	15.9	11.4	10.9	5.1	39.9	48.0

Table B. States and Counties

STATE County	Under 5 years	5 to 17 years	18 to 24 years	25 to 34 years	35 to 44 years	45 to 54 years	55 to 64 years	65 to 74 years	75 years and over	Percent Female	Total persons 2000	Total persons 1990	Total persons 1980	Percent change 1990–2000	Percent change 1980–1990
	Population and population characteristics, 1990 — Age (percent)										**Population—change, 1980–2000**				
	39	40	41	42	43	44	45	46	47	48	49	50	51	52	53
MISSOURI—Cont'd															
St. Louis city	7.9	17.3	10.4	18.3	12.8	8.0	8.5	8.4	8.2	54.5	348 189	396 685	452 801	-12.2	-12.4
MONTANA	7.4	20.4	8.8	15.4	15.9	10.3	8.6	7.6	5.7	50.5	902 195	799 065	786 690	12.9	1.6
Beaverhead	7.3	20.5	11.3	14.9	14.6	10.5	8.0	6.8	6.1	49.4	9 202	8 424	8 186	9.2	2.9
Big Horn	10.7	25.9	8.8	15.2	14.1	9.7	6.7	5.2	3.8	50.7	12 671	11 337	11 096	11.8	2.2
Blaine	9.5	23.7	7.7	14.1	13.9	9.3	8.6	7.0	6.2	50.1	7 009	6 728	6 999	4.2	-3.9
Broadwater	6.7	22.1	5.2	13.8	14.6	11.4	9.8	10.1	6.3	49.1	4 385	3 318	3 267	32.2	1.6
Carbon	5.8	21.1	4.4	12.5	16.4	10.0	10.2	10.8	8.9	51.8	9 552	8 080	8 099	18.2	-0.2
Carter	7.0	18.7	5.7	14.0	13.4	12.0	10.5	10.2	8.6	48.8	1 360	1 503	1 799	-9.5	-16.5
Cascade	8.2	19.5	9.1	17.0	14.6	10.3	8.6	7.2	5.4	50.7	80 357	77 691	80 696	3.4	-3.7
Chouteau	7.1	21.1	5.2	13.6	15.1	9.8	10.6	10.2	7.3	49.0	5 970	5 452	6 092	9.5	-10.5
Custer	6.5	21.0	7.6	14.1	14.6	9.7	9.5	9.5	7.5	51.1	11 696	11 697	13 109	0.0	-10.8
Daniels	4.5	21.0	4.2	10.6	14.8	10.8	11.9	12.6	9.6	50.8	2 017	2 266	2 835	-11.0	-20.1
Dawson	6.7	21.0	7.3	14.2	15.3	10.5	10.0	8.3	6.8	50.4	9 059	9 505	11 805	-4.7	-19.5
Deer Lodge	5.6	17.7	8.8	12.6	14.6	10.2	10.6	11.7	8.2	50.6	9 417	10 356	12 518	-9.1	-17.3
Fallon	7.6	23.0	4.5	14.6	14.1	10.0	11.3	8.1	6.8	50.3	2 837	3 103	3 763	-8.6	-17.5
Fergus	6.5	20.2	5.9	13.1	14.1	10.0	10.4	10.4	9.5	51.0	11 893	12 083	13 076	-1.6	-7.6
Flathead	7.1	21.2	6.5	14.7	17.9	11.0	8.6	7.7	5.3	50.5	74 471	59 218	51 966	25.8	14.0
Gallatin	7.0	17.4	17.7	17.7	16.4	8.8	6.2	5.3	3.5	48.9	67 831	50 484	42 865	34.4	17.7
Garfield	6.8	23.5	5.2	13.7	14.2	9.9	9.9	9.6	7.2	48.6	1 279	1 589	1 656	-19.5	-4.0
Glacier	11.0	26.1	8.2	15.9	13.0	9.2	7.0	5.5	4.1	50.6	13 247	12 121	10 628	9.3	14.0
Golden Valley	7.0	20.7	6.6	12.4	13.5	9.6	12.0	10.1	8.1	48.8	1 042	912	1 026	14.3	-11.1
Granite	6.6	20.0	5.6	12.7	15.0	12.3	9.3	10.9	7.5	48.0	2 830	2 548	2 700	11.1	-5.6
Hill	8.5	22.2	9.2	16.0	14.9	9.0	8.2	7.0	5.1	50.2	16 673	17 654	17 985	-5.6	-1.8
Jefferson	7.1	22.3	5.7	14.6	19.5	12.7	7.5	6.2	4.3	49.3	10 049	7 939	7 029	26.6	12.9
Judith Basin	6.1	19.3	5.2	14.0	15.4	11.7	10.6	10.3	7.5	48.9	2 329	2 282	2 646	2.1	-13.8
Lake	8.0	22.2	7.6	12.7	14.3	10.1	9.4	8.8	6.9	50.1	26 507	21 041	19 056	26.0	10.4
Lewis and Clark	7.3	20.3	8.2	15.7	17.9	11.0	8.0	6.7	4.9	51.2	55 716	47 495	43 039	17.3	10.4
Liberty	8.2	23.7	4.9	15.0	14.2	9.1	9.5	8.5	7.0	51.2	2 158	2 295	2 329	-6.0	-1.5
Lincoln	7.2	22.8	6.3	14.2	16.4	11.9	9.1	7.7	4.6	49.8	18 837	17 481	17 752	7.8	-1.5
McCone	6.5	22.4	5.9	13.6	14.9	9.4	10.9	10.2	6.3	48.9	1 977	2 276	2 702	-13.1	-15.8
Madison	6.0	19.5	6.2	13.6	16.0	11.1	10.7	9.0	7.8	48.5	6 851	5 989	5 448	14.4	9.9
Meagher	6.5	20.1	5.4	14.0	15.2	10.3	11.1	10.8	6.5	48.2	1 932	1 819	2 154	6.2	-15.6
Mineral	6.8	22.8	5.4	14.3	15.6	11.9	10.6	8.1	4.5	49.7	3 884	3 315	3 675	17.2	-9.8
Missoula	7.3	18.4	13.0	17.1	17.1	9.8	6.9	5.8	4.5	50.8	95 802	78 687	76 016	21.8	3.5
Musselshell	4.8	20.6	5.9	10.9	15.9	10.6	11.3	11.2	8.8	50.1	4 497	4 106	4 428	9.5	-7.3
Park	7.0	18.3	5.5	15.1	18.8	10.4	9.1	9.0	6.8	51.2	15 694	14 515	12 869	8.1	12.5
Petroleum	8.3	18.9	6.0	15.6	15.0	11.8	10.8	9.4	4.2	46.8	493	519	655	-5.0	-20.8
Phillips	7.5	22.8	6.4	14.9	13.6	10.4	9.0	8.5	6.9	50.9	4 601	5 163	5 367	-10.9	-3.8
Pondera	8.2	22.5	6.2	14.4	13.2	9.7	9.6	8.6	7.6	50.3	6 424	6 433	6 731	-0.1	-4.4
Powder River	7.5	20.1	6.5	13.1	15.3	10.5	11.3	9.3	6.4	49.2	1 858	2 090	2 520	-11.1	-17.1
Powell	6.0	16.4	7.4	18.5	17.3	11.7	8.5	7.9	6.1	41.7	7 180	6 620	6 958	8.5	-4.9
Prairie	5.0	18.7	4.6	9.5	14.8	10.6	11.6	13.9	11.4	48.3	1 199	1 383	1 836	-13.3	-24.7
Ravalli	6.6	20.8	6.2	11.8	16.0	12.0	10.1	9.6	7.0	50.7	36 070	25 010	22 493	44.2	11.2
Richland	8.1	23.5	6.3	15.8	14.9	9.5	8.5	7.7	5.7	50.4	9 667	10 716	12 243	-9.8	-12.5
Roosevelt	10.8	24.4	7.8	16.2	13.9	8.7	7.3	6.1	4.8	51.1	10 620	10 999	10 467	-3.4	5.1
Rosebud	9.3	27.2	7.4	15.9	17.4	9.5	6.3	4.4	2.7	48.7	9 383	10 505	9 899	-10.7	6.1
Sanders	6.9	21.7	5.6	12.4	15.9	11.2	10.1	9.1	7.0	49.5	10 227	8 669	8 675	18.0	0.0
Sheridan	5.9	20.5	3.9	12.7	14.4	9.9	11.1	11.7	9.9	50.7	4 105	4 732	5 414	-13.3	-12.6
Silver Bow	6.8	18.1	9.1	14.6	14.4	10.5	9.5	9.3	7.7	50.9	34 606	33 941	38 092	2.0	-10.9
Stillwater	7.3	20.6	5.7	13.8	16.2	10.6	9.1	9.1	7.5	50.1	8 195	6 536	5 598	25.4	16.8
Sweet Grass	6.6	20.0	4.6	11.4	15.7	10.7	9.9	11.0	10.1	51.1	3 609	3 154	3 216	14.4	-1.9
Teton	6.6	22.5	6.0	12.8	13.8	11.1	9.4	9.4	8.4	50.4	6 445	6 271	6 491	2.8	-3.4
Toole	7.3	22.0	5.5	14.6	14.9	10.5	8.9	9.9	6.3	50.7	5 267	5 046	5 559	4.4	-9.2
Treasure	6.5	21.5	6.9	13.2	14.0	12.0	10.3	8.1	7.6	50.2	861	874	981	-1.5	-10.9
Valley	6.6	20.7	6.1	13.4	15.0	10.7	10.6	9.3	7.5	50.1	7 675	8 239	10 250	-6.8	-19.6
Wheatland	6.7	20.4	6.5	11.9	13.4	10.0	10.5	11.8	8.7	49.6	2 259	2 246	2 359	0.6	-4.8
Wibaux	6.1	21.6	5.0	13.8	13.5	9.4	10.7	10.2	9.7	49.5	1 068	1 191	1 476	-10.3	-19.3
Yellowstone	7.4	19.8	8.9	16.7	16.0	10.3	8.6	7.2	5.2	51.5	129 352	113 419	108 035	14.0	5.0
NEBRASKA	7.6	19.6	9.9	16.3	14.5	9.5	8.6	7.5	6.7	51.3	1 711 263	1 578 417	1 569 825	8.4	0.5
Adams	7.1	17.7	10.7	15.6	14.1	9.4	8.7	8.4	8.3	51.7	31 151	29 625	30 656	5.2	-3.4
Antelope	8.2	22.3	5.2	13.5	12.7	9.0	9.5	9.7	9.7	50.9	7 452	7 965	8 675	-6.4	-8.2
Arthur	7.8	18.0	5.0	15.2	11.5	14.1	10.2	10.8	7.6	49.6	444	462	513	-3.9	-9.9
Banner	7.7	21.9	5.4	12.8	14.4	12.0	10.7	8.9	6.1	49.6	819	852	918	-3.9	-7.2

Table B. States and Counties

STATE County	Total population	Total in house-holds	House-holder	Spouse	Child Total	Child Own child under 18 years	Other relatives Total	Other relatives Under 18 years	Nonrelatives Total	Nonrelatives Unmar-ried partner	Total in group quarters	Correc-tional institu-tions	Nurs-ing homes	Other institu-tions	Col-lege dormi-tories	Mili-tary quar-ters	Other
	54	55	56	57	58	59	60	61	62	63	64	65	66	67	68	69	70
MISSOURI—Cont'd																	
St. Louis city	348 189	96.9	42.2	11.0	29.1	21.0	8.2	3.9	6.4	2.8	3.1	0.3	0.8	0.2	0.8	0.0	0.9
MONTANA........................	902 195	97.3	39.8	21.3	28.2	23.5	2.9	1.3	5.1	2.0	2.7	0.5	0.7	0.2	0.8	0.0	0.6
Beaverhead	9 202	94.6	40.0	21.9	26.1	22.4	2.0	0.7	4.6	1.5	5.4	0.1	0.7	0.0	4.1	0.0	0.4
Big Horn................................	12 671	98.3	31.0	16.7	35.1	27.4	12.0	7.5	3.6	1.9	1.7	0.3	0.5	0.2	0.0	0.0	0.7
Blaine....................................	7 009	99.1	35.7	18.7	34.1	26.9	7.7	5.1	3.0	1.6	0.9	0.1	0.5	0.0	0.0	0.0	0.3
Broadwater............................	4 385	98.6	40.0	24.5	28.5	23.6	2.3	1.1	3.3	1.5	1.4	0.0	1.3	0.0	0.0	0.0	0.1
Carbon..................................	9 552	98.9	42.6	24.1	26.9	22.7	1.8	0.7	3.6	1.9	1.1	0.1	0.7	0.0	0.0	0.0	0.2
Carter....................................	1 360	98.8	39.9	24.2	29.6	25.2	2.4	0.8	2.6	0.9	1.3	0.0	1.3	0.0	0.0	0.0	0.0
Cascade................................	80 357	97.6	40.5	21.2	28.9	24.3	2.6	1.1	4.4	1.9	2.4	0.6	0.6	0.5	0.0	0.5	0.3
Chouteau	5 970	96.7	37.3	22.7	30.9	26.2	3.4	2.0	2.4	1.3	3.3	0.1	1.7	0.7	0.0	0.0	0.8
Custer	11 696	96.4	40.8	20.8	27.7	22.9	2.8	1.2	4.4	2.0	3.6	0.1	2.0	0.4	0.5	0.0	0.6
Daniels..................................	2 017	98.2	44.2	24.3	25.5	21.1	1.4	0.5	2.7	1.0	1.8	0.0	1.7	0.0	0.0	0.0	0.0
Dawson	9 059	94.7	40.0	23.4	27.1	22.2	1.4	0.4	2.8	1.4	5.3	1.6	1.5	0.5	1.0	0.0	0.7
Deer Lodge...........................	9 417	96.1	42.4	21.2	25.8	20.4	2.3	0.8	4.3	1.7	3.9	0.0	0.6	1.8	0.0	0.0	1.6
Fallon	2 837	98.4	40.2	24.3	29.4	24.5	1.8	0.6	2.7	1.2	1.6	0.1	1.3	0.1	0.0	0.0	0.1
Fergus...................................	11 893	95.3	40.9	22.9	26.6	22.4	1.8	0.8	3.1	1.5	4.7	0.1	1.2	1.2	0.0	0.0	2.2
Flathead................................	74 471	98.5	39.7	22.6	28.9	24.2	2.6	1.0	4.6	2.0	1.5	0.1	0.9	0.0	0.1	0.0	0.4
Gallatin	67 831	95.4	38.8	20.1	24.4	21.1	1.9	0.5	10.2	2.3	4.6	0.1	0.4	0.0	3.8	0.0	0.3
Garfield	1 279	99.1	41.6	25.1	28.7	23.8	1.5	0.5	2.2	1.0	0.9	0.0	0.9	0.0	0.0	0.0	0.1
Glacier	13 247	98.6	32.5	17.3	36.7	28.9	8.7	5.4	3.3	1.8	1.4	0.4	0.5	0.2	0.0	0.0	0.3
Golden Valley	1 042	84.5	35.0	23.4	22.1	18.7	1.2	0.1	2.7	1.1	15.5	0.0	0.0	0.0	0.0	0.0	15.5
Granite	2 830	98.9	42.4	23.2	27.3	22.8	2.4	1.1	3.5	1.9	1.1	0.0	0.7	0.0	0.0	0.0	0.4
Hill..	16 673	97.9	38.7	19.6	35.1	25.4	4.1	2.2	4.4	1.9	2.1	0.1	0.1	0.7	1.0	0.0	0.2
Jefferson...............................	10 049	97.8	37.3	25.0	30.5	25.8	2.0	0.9	3.0	1.4	2.2	0.2	0.3	1.4	0.0	0.0	0.2
Judith Basin	2 329	100.0	40.8	25.6	30.4	26.1	1.5	0.5	1.7	1.1	0.0	0.0	0.0	0.0	0.0	0.0	0.0
Lake......................................	26 507	97.7	38.5	21.1	29.9	24.9	4.0	2.1	4.3	2.2	2.3	0.2	0.7	0.0	0.4	0.0	1.0
Lewis and Clark....................	55 716	97.8	41.0	21.5	28.4	24.1	2.4	0.9	4.4	2.0	2.2	0.1	0.4	0.0	0.9	0.0	0.7
Liberty	2 158	97.0	38.6	24.2	31.7	24.9	1.3	0.6	1.3	0.7	3.0	0.0	2.8	0.0	0.0	0.0	0.2
Lincoln	18 837	99.0	41.2	23.5	27.4	23.2	2.8	1.3	4.1	2.0	1.0	0.1	0.7	0.1	0.0	0.0	0.1
McCone	1 977	100.0	41.0	27.4	27.6	23.5	2.0	0.8	2.0	0.8	0.0	0.0	0.0	0.0	0.0	0.0	0.0
Madison	6 851	98.9	43.1	24.9	25.0	21.8	1.9	0.7	3.9	2.1	1.1	0.0	0.9	0.0	0.0	0.0	0.1
Meagher	1 932	98.7	41.6	23.6	28.7	23.7	2.4	1.1	2.4	1.6	1.3	0.2	1.1	0.0	0.0	0.0	0.0
Mineral	3 884	98.4	40.8	23.5	25.8	21.5	2.8	1.5	5.4	2.0	1.6	0.7	0.9	0.0	0.0	0.0	0.0
Missoula................................	95 802	96.2	40.1	19.0	25.9	21.3	2.5	0.9	8.7	2.7	3.8	0.4	0.4	0.0	2.1	0.0	0.8
Musselshell...........................	4 497	97.4	41.8	23.2	26.4	21.3	2.6	1.0	3.4	1.7	2.6	0.1	0.7	0.0	0.0	0.0	1.8
Park	15 694	98.6	43.5	22.2	26.3	22.4	2.1	0.7	4.5	2.2	1.4	0.1	0.5	0.0	0.0	0.0	0.7
Petroleum	493	100.0	42.8	23.9	28.8	25.4	1.4	0.4	3.0	2.0	0.0	0.0	0.0	0.0	0.0	0.0	0.0
Phillips..................................	4 601	98.3	40.2	23.0	29.1	24.7	2.6	1.7	3.4	1.5	1.7	0.1	1.0	0.0	0.0	0.0	0.6
Pondera.................................	6 424	98.8	37.5	22.5	32.9	27.3	3.6	2.0	2.3	1.0	1.2	0.1	0.8	0.0	0.0	0.0	0.3
Powder River	1 858	98.2	39.7	25.7	28.7	25.4	1.8	0.9	2.4	1.7	1.8	0.0	1.8	0.0	0.0	0.0	0.0
Powell	7 180	80.5	33.7	18.7	23.3	19.5	1.8	0.8	2.9	1.5	19.5	18.6	0.7	0.2	0.0	0.0	0.0
Prairie	1 199	98.0	44.8	27.4	21.5	17.8	2.5	0.8	1.8	1.1	2.0	0.0	1.6	0.0	0.0	0.0	0.4
Ravalli...................................	36 070	98.4	39.6	23.9	28.0	23.7	2.9	1.2	3.9	1.9	1.6	0.2	0.7	0.0	0.0	0.0	0.7
Richland................................	9 667	98.8	40.1	23.0	31.1	26.2	1.8	0.8	2.7	1.4	1.2	0.0	0.9	0.0	0.0	0.0	0.3
Roosevelt..............................	10 620	97.5	33.7	15.9	34.6	27.8	8.7	5.6	4.5	2.7	2.5	0.2	0.8	0.5	0.0	0.0	0.9
Rosebud	9 383	99.0	35.2	19.7	33.5	27.8	7.0	4.7	3.5	1.7	1.0	0.6	0.4	0.0	0.0	0.0	0.0
Sanders	10 227	98.1	41.8	24.0	25.8	21.6	2.8	1.3	3.8	1.9	1.9	0.2	0.5	0.0	0.4	0.0	0.7
Sheridan	4 105	97.1	42.4	24.4	26.0	21.7	1.7	0.6	2.6	1.0	2.9	0.0	2.1	0.0	0.0	0.0	0.8
Silver Bow.............................	34 606	96.8	41.7	19.9	28.0	21.8	2.8	1.2	4.4	1.9	3.2	0.8	1.1	0.2	0.6	0.0	0.5
Stillwater	8 195	97.9	39.5	25.5	28.1	23.9	2.1	0.9	2.8	1.4	2.1	0.0	0.9	0.0	0.0	0.0	1.2
Sweet Grass	3 609	98.4	40.9	24.5	28.5	25.0	1.8	0.7	2.7	1.2	1.6	0.0	1.4	0.0	0.0	0.0	0.1
Teton	6 445	99.0	39.4	24.0	31.3	26.1	1.7	0.8	2.5	1.1	1.0	0.0	0.8	0.0	0.0	0.0	0.2
Toole	5 267	92.0	37.3	21.2	29.1	24.3	1.8	0.8	2.7	1.4	8.0	6.3	1.5	0.0	0.0	0.0	0.3
Treasure	861	100.0	41.5	24.5	28.8	25.2	2.3	1.3	2.9	1.2	0.0	0.0	0.0	0.0	0.0	0.0	0.0
Valley	7 675	97.6	41.0	22.8	28.0	23.2	2.8	1.3	3.0	1.7	2.4	0.0	0.8	0.1	0.1	0.0	1.4
Wheatland	2 259	84.4	37.8	20.3	22.5	18.5	1.7	0.9	2.1	1.0	15.6	0.2	1.5	1.9	0.0	0.0	12.0
Wibaux	1 068	96.5	39.4	22.9	30.1	24.8	1.1	0.1	2.9	1.1	3.5	0.0	3.5	0.0	0.0	0.0	0.0
Yellowstone	129 352	97.7	40.3	20.9	28.7	23.6	2.8	1.2	5.1	2.1	2.3	0.4	0.8	0.1	0.6	0.0	0.4
NEBRASKA	1 711 263	97.0	38.9	21.1	29.6	24.6	2.8	1.1	4.7	1.7	3.0	0.4	0.9	0.2	1.1	0.0	0.3
Adams..................................	31 151	94.7	39.0	21.2	27.5	23.0	2.4	0.9	4.7	1.5	5.3	0.7	1.0	0.5	2.6	0.0	0.4
Antelope	7 452	98.6	39.6	24.8	31.0	26.7	1.1	0.4	2.1	1.0	1.4	0.0	1.2	0.1	0.0	0.0	0.1
Arthur	444	100.0	41.7	26.4	27.3	22.7	2.3	0.7	2.5	1.1	0.0	0.0	0.0	0.0	0.0	0.0	0.0
Banner	819	100.0	38.0	26.6	30.5	26.7	2.8	1.5	2.1	0.9	0.0	0.0	0.0	0.0	0.0	0.0	0.0

	Households by type, 2000											Households, 1990		
	Family households						Nonfamily households							
			Married couple		Female householder[1]			Householder living alone						
STATE County	Total households	Total	With own children under 18 years	Total	With own children under 18 years	Total	With own children under 18 years	Total	Total	65 years and over	Average household size	Average family size	Total households	Female householder[1]	Householder living alone
	71	72	73	74	75	76	77	78	79	80	81	82	83	84	85
MISSOURI—Cont'd															
St. Louis city	147 076	52.3	25.4	20.2	10.8	21.3	12.4	47.7	40.3	12.9	2.30	3.19	164 931	20.5	39.2
MONTANA	358 667	66.2	31.2	53.6	23.0	8.9	5.9	33.8	27.4	10.0	2.45	2.99	306 163	8.6	26.3
Beaverhead	3 684	63.9	30.1	54.8	24.6	6.2	3.7	36.1	29.7	11.0	2.36	2.95	3 211	7.7	27.6
Big Horn	3 924	77.3	42.4	54.0	28.6	17.6	10.4	22.7	19.3	6.7	3.17	3.66	3 448	15.5	18.4
Blaine	2 501	71.7	36.0	52.3	25.0	14.4	8.7	28.3	26.0	10.8	2.78	3.36	2 379	12.7	26.4
Broadwater	1 752	72.5	30.1	61.4	23.9	6.9	3.8	27.5	24.1	9.9	2.47	2.91	1 280	7.0	24.6
Carbon	4 065	66.6	28.4	56.7	22.5	6.7	4.1	33.4	28.8	12.1	2.32	2.86	3 269	7.0	27.4
Carter	543	70.5	30.6	60.6	25.0	7.0	3.5	29.5	27.1	14.9	2.47	2.99	589	4.4	28.7
Cascade	32 547	65.9	32.2	52.3	23.0	9.9	6.8	34.1	28.8	10.9	2.41	2.97	30 133	9.3	26.2
Chouteau	2 226	72.5	34.0	60.9	26.7	8.4	5.4	27.5	24.9	10.6	2.59	3.11	2 064	5.9	24.7
Custer	4 768	64.8	30.4	51.1	21.0	10.0	7.0	35.2	29.9	12.3	2.36	2.94	4 631	9.1	29.3
Daniels	892	62.9	23.7	54.9	18.7	5.5	3.5	37.1	33.6	17.5	2.22	2.84	919	5.1	29.2
Dawson	3 625	68.3	29.7	58.5	23.2	6.8	4.6	31.7	28.4	12.2	2.37	2.90	3 691	6.5	26.6
Deer Lodge	3 995	63.2	25.8	50.0	17.8	9.4	5.6	36.8	33.4	16.7	2.26	2.84	4 060	9.3	32.5
Fallon	1 140	70.5	32.1	60.5	26.2	6.0	3.5	29.5	26.6	13.2	2.45	2.96	1 166	4.9	23.8
Fergus	4 860	65.8	28.7	56.1	22.6	6.7	4.1	34.2	30.5	13.9	2.33	2.91	4 603	6.2	27.6
Flathead	29 588	69.0	32.5	56.9	24.2	8.3	5.7	31.0	25.2	8.9	2.48	2.97	22 834	8.0	24.1
Gallatin	26 323	61.5	29.7	51.8	23.6	6.6	4.5	38.5	24.1	5.7	2.46	2.94	19 015	6.8	24.2
Garfield	532	68.8	28.8	60.3	23.9	4.5	3.2	31.2	28.2	13.5	2.38	2.93	577	4.3	24.1
Glacier	4 304	75.4	42.9	53.3	29.4	16.2	10.0	24.6	21.6	7.7	3.03	3.56	3 816	15.7	21.7
Golden Valley	365	72.1	26.8	66.8	24.1	3.3	1.9	27.9	24.4	11.0	2.41	2.85	330	3.6	27.9
Granite	1 200	65.4	27.1	54.7	20.7	7.4	4.6	34.6	30.1	12.3	2.33	2.91	1 051	5.8	29.7
Hill	6 457	65.9	34.3	50.5	24.1	10.9	7.6	34.1	28.6	11.4	2.53	3.15	6 426	9.9	26.2
Jefferson	3 747	76.0	35.6	67.1	29.9	5.9	3.7	24.0	20.2	7.3	2.62	3.03	2 867	6.5	21.4
Judith Basin	951	69.6	30.0	62.7	26.4	4.3	2.4	30.4	27.5	12.3	2.45	3.02	908	3.6	26.5
Lake	10 192	70.8	33.0	54.8	22.2	11.5	7.9	29.2	24.5	9.9	2.54	3.02	7 814	11.0	24.1
Lewis and Clark	22 850	65.5	32.2	52.4	23.3	9.2	6.5	34.5	29.1	8.9	2.38	2.95	18 649	9.8	28.0
Liberty	833	70.1	30.4	62.7	25.8	5.6	3.8	29.9	27.9	14.0	2.51	3.11	788	5.8	28.2
Lincoln	7 764	68.7	29.1	57.1	21.2	7.8	5.3	31.3	26.7	10.0	2.40	2.90	6 668	7.2	23.3
McCone	810	73.7	30.2	66.9	26.9	3.8	1.7	26.3	24.6	11.4	2.44	2.89	844	3.3	22.6
Madison	2 956	65.0	26.1	57.8	21.7	4.4	2.9	35.0	29.3	10.9	2.29	2.85	2 387	5.1	28.2
Meagher	803	65.9	27.3	56.8	21.4	6.1	3.7	34.1	31.0	13.7	2.37	3.00	709	4.4	29.2
Mineral	1 584	67.4	27.7	57.7	20.7	6.0	4.4	32.6	26.6	8.2	2.41	2.90	1 282	7.6	25.5
Missoula	38 439	60.2	29.2	47.4	21.0	9.2	6.1	39.8	28.0	7.5	2.40	2.96	30 782	9.5	27.3
Musselshell	1 878	65.8	27.2	55.6	20.9	6.6	4.0	34.2	30.1	13.8	2.33	2.91	1 661	5.2	30.8
Park	6 828	61.8	28.1	51.0	21.0	7.3	4.7	38.2	32.4	11.7	2.27	2.88	5 619	7.2	28.0
Petroleum	211	64.9	31.3	55.9	25.1	5.7	4.3	35.1	31.3	17.5	2.34	2.95	209	4.3	23.0
Phillips	1 848	67.2	31.9	57.2	25.6	6.8	4.5	32.8	29.1	14.6	2.45	3.03	1 931	7.6	26.8
Pondera	2 410	72.2	35.3	60.0	27.3	8.4	5.5	27.8	25.5	12.3	2.63	3.18	2 246	6.6	25.4
Powder River	737	71.2	30.7	64.9	26.7	4.1	2.4	28.8	24.8	9.9	2.48	2.99	805	4.7	25.8
Powell	2 422	67.5	29.5	55.5	21.4	7.7	5.5	32.5	28.6	13.3	2.39	2.93	2 234	6.5	28.6
Prairie	537	66.1	22.3	61.1	19.7	2.4	1.5	33.9	31.3	17.3	2.19	2.74	568	3.2	26.9
Ravalli	14 289	71.3	30.2	60.3	22.8	7.5	5.1	28.7	24.1	9.8	2.48	2.94	9 698	6.5	23.9
Richland	3 878	68.4	33.6	57.3	25.9	7.4	5.2	31.6	28.8	12.9	2.46	3.04	3 956	6.8	24.3
Roosevelt	3 581	73.0	40.5	47.2	23.6	18.9	12.2	27.0	23.6	10.3	2.89	3.40	3 694	15.3	22.8
Rosebud	3 307	73.1	38.7	56.0	26.7	11.8	8.2	26.9	24.3	8.4	2.81	3.34	3 479	10.6	21.4
Sanders	4 273	67.8	26.2	57.3	19.4	7.1	4.8	32.2	28.0	11.6	2.35	2.86	3 397	5.5	27.1
Sheridan	1 741	65.5	27.0	57.5	22.6	4.8	2.6	34.5	32.3	16.6	2.29	2.87	1 899	5.6	27.4
Silver Bow	14 432	61.9	28.0	47.8	19.7	10.5	6.2	38.1	32.8	13.7	2.32	2.97	13 899	9.5	31.9
Stillwater	3 234	72.6	32.6	64.6	27.4	5.0	3.4	27.4	24.1	9.6	2.48	2.94	2 523	5.8	24.1
Sweet Grass	1 476	66.9	30.8	60.0	26.9	4.5	2.6	33.1	28.9	14.2	2.41	3.00	1 281	4.1	29.7
Teton	2 538	69.4	31.6	61.1	26.0	5.9	4.0	30.6	27.3	13.9	2.51	3.09	2 329	4.7	26.6
Toole	1 962	66.7	32.3	56.8	26.0	6.5	4.1	33.3	30.2	13.7	2.47	3.09	1 922	6.7	29.4
Treasure	357	67.8	30.8	59.1	26.6	4.2	1.7	32.2	30.0	15.1	2.41	2.98	339	5.3	23.6
Valley	3 150	67.6	29.7	55.5	22.0	8.2	5.2	32.4	29.3	12.0	2.38	2.93	3 268	7.4	27.9
Wheatland	853	63.4	25.8	53.8	20.4	4.9	3.0	36.6	34.5	16.4	2.24	2.86	849	4.8	32.9
Wibaux	421	68.2	29.2	58.2	24.0	5.9	3.1	31.8	29.0	15.9	2.45	3.02	454	6.4	28.4
Yellowstone	52 084	65.7	31.6	51.8	22.6	10.1	6.6	34.3	27.9	10.1	2.43	2.98	44 689	9.7	26.5
NEBRASKA	666 184	66.6	32.7	54.2	24.9	9.1	6.0	33.4	27.6	10.7	2.49	3.06	602 363	8.3	26.5
Adams	12 141	65.6	30.9	54.4	23.7	8.3	5.4	34.4	28.6	13.0	2.43	3.00	11 593	7.6	28.8
Antelope	2 953	70.2	32.2	62.5	27.2	5.5	3.6	29.8	27.8	16.2	2.49	3.05	3 045	5.1	26.8
Arthur	185	74.6	27.6	63.2	22.7	7.6	2.2	25.4	21.6	10.8	2.40	2.80	187	5.3	24.1
Banner	311	76.5	30.2	70.1	27.0	4.2	1.9	23.5	19.9	9.6	2.63	3.06	305	4.3	13.8

[1] No spouse present.

Table B. States and Counties

STATE County	Percent change of households, 1990–2000	Total housing units	Occupied housing units (percent)	Vacant housing units Total	For seasonal, recreational, or occasional use	Homeowner vacancy rate (percent)	Rental vacancy rate (percent)	Occupied housing units Total	Percent owner-occupied housing units	Percent renter-occupied housing units	Average household size of owner-occupied units	Average household size of renter-occupied units
	86	87	88	89	90	91	92	93	94	95	96	97
MISSOURI—Cont'd												
St. Louis city	-10.8	176 354	83.4	16.6	0.3	3.5	11.8	147 076	46.9	53.1	2.49	2.12
MONTANA	17.1	412 633	86.9	13.1	5.9	2.2	7.6	358 667	69.1	30.9	2.55	2.22
Beaverhead	14.7	4 571	80.6	19.4	10.9	2.5	9.3	3 684	63.4	36.6	2.49	2.15
Big Horn	13.8	4 655	84.3	15.7	6.4	2.2	6.3	3 924	64.6	35.4	3.13	3.25
Blaine	5.1	2 947	84.9	15.1	3.5	2.7	7.6	2 501	61.1	38.9	2.76	2.80
Broadwater	36.9	2 002	87.5	12.5	5.9	1.8	9.1	1 752	79.4	20.6	2.51	2.30
Carbon	24.3	5 494	74.0	26.0	18.5	3.0	8.1	4 065	74.4	25.6	2.36	2.21
Carter	-7.8	811	67.0	33.0	14.7	6.9	8.1	543	74.8	25.2	2.47	2.48
Cascade	8.0	35 225	92.4	7.6	1.3	1.7	6.6	32 547	64.9	35.1	2.53	2.19
Chouteau	7.8	2 776	80.2	19.8	4.6	3.8	8.3	2 226	68.8	31.2	2.49	2.83
Custer	3.0	5 360	89.0	11.0	1.6	2.6	11.6	4 768	70.2	29.8	2.48	2.09
Daniels	-2.9	1 154	77.3	22.7	4.9	3.9	11.9	892	78.4	21.6	2.32	1.87
Dawson	-1.8	4 168	87.0	13.0	2.2	3.6	12.5	3 625	74.0	26.0	2.48	2.05
Deer Lodge	-1.6	4 958	80.6	19.4	5.4	4.0	17.0	3 995	73.6	26.4	2.30	2.16
Fallon	-2.2	1 410	80.9	19.1	3.7	6.3	22.5	1 140	77.4	22.6	2.52	2.21
Fergus	5.6	5 558	87.4	12.6	3.4	2.4	13.0	4 860	73.5	26.5	2.42	2.10
Flathead	29.6	34 773	85.1	14.9	10.3	1.7	7.0	29 588	73.3	26.7	2.57	2.23
Gallatin	38.4	29 489	89.3	10.7	5.8	1.8	5.7	26 323	62.4	37.6	2.60	2.23
Garfield	-7.8	961	55.4	44.6	30.5	4.6	14.6	532	73.7	26.3	2.43	2.24
Glacier	12.8	5 243	82.1	17.9	7.4	1.6	11.6	4 304	62.0	38.0	2.99	3.10
Golden Valley	10.6	450	81.1	18.9	6.2	6.3	8.8	365	77.3	22.7	2.45	2.27
Granite	14.2	2 074	57.9	42.1	32.9	4.5	12.8	1 200	74.4	25.6	2.37	2.21
Hill	0.5	7 453	86.6	13.4	3.7	2.8	8.9	6 457	64.3	35.7	2.62	2.37
Jefferson	30.7	4 199	89.2	10.8	4.5	1.3	12.5	3 747	83.2	16.8	2.68	2.36
Judith Basin	4.7	1 325	71.8	28.2	14.3	3.2	7.2	951	77.1	22.9	2.44	2.48
Lake	30.4	13 605	74.9	25.1	19.8	1.9	6.9	10 192	71.4	28.6	2.56	2.48
Lewis and Clark	22.5	25 672	89.0	11.0	6.5	1.5	5.8	22 850	70.1	29.9	2.54	2.02
Liberty	5.7	1 070	77.9	22.1	7.1	6.3	10.2	833	71.3	28.7	2.54	2.45
Lincoln	16.4	9 319	83.3	16.7	8.8	2.9	12.3	7 764	76.6	23.4	2.45	2.24
McCone	-4.0	1 087	74.5	25.5	9.8	3.1	25.8	810	78.0	22.0	2.50	2.24
Madison	23.8	4 671	63.3	36.7	24.5	4.5	10.8	2 956	70.4	29.6	2.34	2.17
Meagher	13.3	1 363	58.9	41.1	27.0	8.0	19.8	803	73.2	26.8	2.35	2.45
Mineral	23.6	1 961	80.8	19.2	10.4	4.0	11.3	1 584	73.4	26.6	2.45	2.30
Missoula	24.9	41 319	93.0	7.0	3.2	1.1	4.0	38 439	61.9	38.1	2.60	2.08
Musselshell	13.1	2 317	81.1	18.9	3.5	6.8	8.4	1 878	76.9	23.1	2.39	2.14
Park	21.5	8 247	82.8	17.2	9.6	2.3	7.4	6 828	66.4	33.6	2.39	2.03
Petroleum	1.0	292	72.3	27.7	9.6	7.6	8.5	211	74.4	25.6	2.34	2.31
Phillips	-4.3	2 502	73.9	26.1	10.6	7.2	14.1	1 848	70.6	29.4	2.51	2.29
Pondera	7.3	2 834	85.0	15.0	1.6	4.8	12.8	2 410	70.5	29.5	2.70	2.47
Powder River	-8.4	1 007	73.2	26.8	10.9	3.0	13.1	737	73.8	26.2	2.49	2.44
Powell	8.4	2 930	82.7	17.3	7.4	2.6	13.0	2 422	71.3	28.7	2.44	2.25
Prairie	-5.5	718	74.8	25.2	5.2	5.5	15.4	537	77.5	22.5	2.21	2.12
Ravalli	47.3	15 946	89.6	10.4	4.8	2.5	6.1	14 289	75.7	24.3	2.53	2.33
Richland	-2.0	4 557	85.1	14.9	1.7	2.7	14.2	3 878	72.4	27.6	2.58	2.17
Roosevelt	-3.1	4 044	88.6	11.4	1.8	1.2	9.2	3 581	65.1	34.9	2.76	3.14
Rosebud	-4.9	3 912	84.5	15.5	4.8	1.9	11.7	3 307	67.1	32.9	2.79	2.85
Sanders	25.8	5 271	81.1	18.9	8.4	3.4	12.8	4 273	76.4	23.6	2.38	2.23
Sheridan	-8.3	2 167	80.3	19.7	4.0	3.2	19.8	1 741	80.2	19.8	2.32	2.14
Silver Bow	3.8	16 176	89.2	10.8	1.1	3.1	12.6	14 432	70.4	29.6	2.46	1.99
Stillwater	28.2	3 947	81.9	18.1	12.0	2.7	6.1	3 234	76.0	24.0	2.53	2.34
Sweet Grass	15.2	1 860	79.4	20.6	10.9	2.1	10.3	1 476	74.1	25.9	2.48	2.20
Teton	9.0	2 910	87.2	12.8	5.0	2.2	7.3	2 538	75.4	24.6	2.62	2.20
Toole	2.1	2 300	85.3	14.7	2.0	4.6	11.0	1 962	71.2	28.8	2.62	2.10
Treasure	5.3	422	84.6	15.4	5.2	2.3	6.4	357	71.4	28.6	2.38	2.50
Valley	-3.6	4 847	65.0	35.0	7.8	6.5	7.9	3 150	75.8	24.2	2.41	2.27
Wheatland	0.5	1 154	73.9	26.1	8.4	6.4	18.2	853	72.6	27.4	2.28	2.11
Wibaux	-7.3	587	71.7	28.3	1.9	6.4	18.8	421	73.4	26.6	2.54	2.21
Yellowstone	16.5	54 563	95.5	4.5	0.5	1.2	5.4	52 084	69.2	30.8	2.58	2.10
NEBRASKA	10.6	722 668	92.2	7.8	1.6	1.8	7.6	666 184	67.4	32.6	2.63	2.20
Adams	4.7	13 014	93.3	6.7	0.3	1.7	8.6	12 141	66.8	33.2	2.58	2.12
Antelope	-3.0	3 346	88.3	11.7	1.6	3.1	8.6	2 953	76.4	23.6	2.49	2.47
Arthur	-1.1	273	67.8	32.2	12.8	11.4	8.1	185	63.2	36.8	2.22	2.71
Banner	2.0	375	82.9	17.1	2.9	6.9	0.0	311	64.6	35.4	2.53	2.82

Table B. States and Counties

STATE/ County code	MSA/ PMSA/ NECMA code[1]	County type[2]	STATE County	Population, 2000				Population, 1990				Population and population characteristics, 2000					
												Race (percent)					
												One race					
				Land area, 2000[3] (sq km)	Total persons	Rank	Per square kilometer	Land area, 1990[3] (sq km)	Total persons	Rank	Per square kilometer	White	Black or African American	American Indian or Alaska Native	Asian	Native Hawaiian and other Pacific Islander	Some other race
				1	2	3	4	5	6	7	8	9	10	11	12	13	14
			NEBRASKA—Cont'd														
31 009	...	9	Blaine	1 841	583	3 133	0.3	1 841	675	3 132	0.4	99.0	0.0	0.5	0.0	0.0	0.0
31 011	...	9	Boone	1 779	6 259	2 760	3.5	1 779	6 667	2 687	3.7	99.2	0.0	0.0	0.0	0.0	0.3
31 013	...	7	Box Butte	2 785	12 158	2 287	4.4	2 785	13 130	2 128	4.7	90.8	0.4	2.7	0.5	0.0	3.6
31 015	...	9	Boyd	1 399	2 438	3 027	1.7	1 399	2 835	3 009	2.0	98.6	0.0	0.6	0.2	0.0	0.0
31 017	...	9	Brown	3 163	3 525	2 952	1.1	3 163	3 657	2 943	1.2	98.6	0.0	0.2	0.3	0.0	0.2
31 019	...	5	Buffalo	2 507	42 259	1 052	16.9	2 507	37 447	1 060	14.9	95.2	0.5	0.3	0.7	0.0	2.2
31 021	...	8	Burt	1 276	7 791	2 626	6.1	1 276	7 868	2 583	6.2	97.6	0.2	1.1	0.2	0.0	0.2
31 023	...	6	Butler	1 511	8 767	2 548	5.8	1 512	8 601	2 502	5.7	98.4	0.1	0.1	0.1	0.1	0.8
31 025	5920	2	Cass	1 448	24 334	1 581	16.8	1 449	21 318	1 616	14.7	97.9	0.2	0.3	0.3	0.0	0.4
31 027	...	9	Cedar	1 917	9 615	2 478	5.0	1 917	10 131	2 375	5.3	99.1	0.1	0.2	0.0	0.0	0.2
31 029	...	9	Chase	2 317	4 068	2 914	1.8	2 317	4 381	2 883	1.9	97.8	0.2	0.1	0.2	0.0	1.5
31 031	...	7	Cherry	15 438	6 148	2 767	0.4	15 438	6 307	2 720	0.4	94.2	0.1	3.3	0.4	0.0	0.3
31 033	...	7	Cheyenne	3 099	9 830	2 463	3.2	3 099	9 494	2 434	3.1	96.3	0.1	0.7	0.4	0.0	1.5
31 035	...	9	Clay	1 484	7 039	2 680	4.7	1 484	7 123	2 642	4.8	97.6	0.2	0.3	0.3	0.0	1.2
31 037	...	7	Colfax	1 070	10 441	2 402	9.8	1 070	9 139	2 456	8.5	81.7	0.1	0.2	0.2	0.1	15.9
31 039	...	7	Cuming	1 481	10 203	2 428	6.9	1 482	10 117	2 376	6.8	95.9	0.1	0.3	0.2	0.0	2.6
31 041	...	7	Custer	6 671	11 793	2 307	1.8	6 671	12 270	2 198	1.8	98.6	0.0	0.4	0.2	0.0	0.2
31 043	7720	3	Dakota	683	20 253	1 776	29.7	684	16 742	1 866	24.5	78.8	0.6	1.9	3.1	0.1	12.9
31 045	...	7	Dawes	3 616	9 060	2 524	2.5	3 616	9 021	2 467	2.5	93.3	0.8	2.9	0.3	0.1	1.0
31 047	...	7	Dawson	2 623	24 365	1 580	9.3	2 624	19 940	1 683	7.6	82.3	0.3	0.7	0.7	0.0	14.5
31 049	...	9	Deuel	1 139	2 098	3 058	1.8	1 139	2 237	3 052	2.0	97.3	0.0	0.4	0.4	0.0	1.1
31 051	...	8	Dixon	1 234	6 339	2 752	5.1	1 234	6 143	2 740	5.0	94.6	0.0	0.5	0.3	0.0	3.8
31 053	...	4	Dodge	1 384	36 160	1 209	26.1	1 384	34 500	1 150	24.9	95.9	0.4	0.3	0.5	0.1	2.1
31 055	5920	2	Douglas	857	463 585	124	540.9	857	416 444	121	485.9	81.0	11.5	0.6	1.7	0.1	3.4
31 057	...	9	Dundy	2 382	2 292	3 040	1.0	2 383	2 582	3 017	1.1	96.9	0.0	0.8	0.5	0.0	0.9
31 059	...	9	Fillmore	1 493	6 634	2 722	4.4	1 493	7 103	2 645	4.8	97.8	0.2	0.4	0.1	0.0	0.8
31 061	...	9	Franklin	1 492	3 574	2 946	2.4	1 492	3 938	2 922	2.6	99.2	0.0	0.3	0.1	0.0	0.1
31 063	...	9	Frontier	2 524	3 099	2 985	1.2	2 524	3 101	2 993	1.2	98.3	0.1	0.3	0.3	0.0	0.4
31 065	...	9	Furnas	1 860	5 324	2 828	2.9	1 860	5 553	2 796	3.0	98.2	0.1	0.4	0.2	0.0	0.3
31 067	...	6	Gage	2 215	22 993	1 643	10.4	2 215	22 794	1 544	10.3	97.7	0.3	0.6	0.3	0.0	0.3
31 069	...	9	Garden	4 414	2 292	3 040	0.5	4 415	2 460	3 024	0.6	98.3	0.1	0.3	0.3	0.0	0.5
31 071	...	9	Garfield	1 476	1 902	3 073	1.3	1 476	2 141	3 058	1.5	98.8	0.0	0.2	0.1	0.1	0.4
31 073	...	9	Gosper	1 187	2 143	3 057	1.8	1 187	1 928	3 070	1.6	98.8	0.0	0.1	0.2	0.0	0.4
31 075	...	9	Grant	2 010	747	3 129	0.4	2 011	769	3 125	0.4	98.8	0.0	0.1	0.3	0.0	0.8
31 077	...	9	Greeley	1 476	2 714	3 013	1.8	1 476	3 006	2 999	2.0	97.9	0.7	0.1	0.1	0.0	0.8
31 079	...	5	Hall	1 415	53 534	874	37.8	1 415	48 925	857	34.6	88.7	0.4	0.3	1.1	0.1	8.2
31 081	...	7	Hamilton	1 408	9 403	2 497	6.7	1 408	8 862	2 483	6.3	98.4	0.2	0.1	0.2	0.0	0.5
31 083	...	9	Harlan	1 432	3 786	2 930	2.6	1 432	3 810	2 929	2.7	98.9	0.1	0.1	0.1	0.0	0.3
31 085	...	9	Hayes	1 847	1 068	3 107	0.6	1 847	1 222	3 107	0.7	97.2	0.2	0.0	0.3	0.0	1.8
31 087	...	9	Hitchcock	1 839	3 111	2 984	1.7	1 839	3 750	2 934	2.0	98.4	0.1	0.3	0.1	0.0	0.3
31 089	...	7	Holt	6 249	11 551	2 329	1.8	6 249	12 599	2 178	2.0	98.9	0.0	0.3	0.2	0.1	0.3
31 091	...	9	Hooker	1 868	783	3 126	0.4	1 868	793	3 124	0.4	98.7	0.0	0.4	0.1	0.0	0.1
31 093	...	9	Howard	1 475	6 567	2 731	4.5	1 475	6 057	2 750	4.1	98.7	0.3	0.2	0.1	0.0	0.3
31 095	...	7	Jefferson	1 484	8 333	2 578	5.6	1 484	8 759	2 489	5.9	98.4	0.1	0.4	0.2	0.0	0.5
31 097	...	8	Johnson	974	4 488	2 881	4.6	974	4 673	2 863	4.8	93.5	0.1	0.4	2.7	0.0	2.0
31 099	...	7	Kearney	1 337	6 882	2 698	5.1	1 337	6 629	2 692	5.0	97.8	0.2	0.2	0.2	0.0	1.0
31 101	...	7	Keith	2 749	8 875	2 535	3.2	2 749	8 584	2 505	3.1	96.8	0.1	0.7	0.2	0.0	1.5
31 103	...	9	Keya Paha	2 003	983	3 112	0.5	2 003	1 029	3 111	0.5	99.4	0.0	0.2	0.0	0.0	0.0
31 105	...	6	Kimball	2 465	4 089	2 910	1.7	2 465	4 108	2 906	1.7	97.0	0.2	0.7	0.1	0.0	0.7
31 107	...	9	Knox	2 870	9 374	2 500	3.3	2 870	9 564	2 427	3.3	91.6	0.1	7.1	0.2	0.0	0.3
31 109	4360	3	Lancaster	2 173	250 291	230	115.2	2 173	213 641	233	98.3	90.1	2.8	0.6	2.9	0.1	1.7
31 111	...	5	Lincoln	6 641	34 632	1 261	5.2	6 641	32 508	1 201	4.9	94.7	0.5	0.5	0.4	0.0	2.7
31 113	...	9	Logan	1 478	774	3 127	0.5	1 478	878	3 118	0.6	98.6	0.1	1.0	0.0	0.0	0.0
31 115	...	9	Loup	1 476	712	3 132	0.5	1 476	683	3 131	0.5	98.9	0.0	0.3	0.1	0.0	0.4
31 117	...	9	McPherson	2 225	533	3 135	0.2	2 225	546	3 134	0.2	97.9	0.0	0.0	0.4	0.0	1.7
31 119	...	5	Madison	1 483	35 226	1 240	23.8	1 483	32 655	1 197	22.0	91.4	0.9	1.2	0.4	0.0	5.1
31 121	...	7	Merrick	1 256	8 204	2 592	6.5	1 255	8 062	2 557	6.4	98.3	0.2	0.1	0.2	0.0	0.7
31 123	...	9	Morrill	3 687	5 440	2 821	1.5	3 688	5 423	2 805	1.5	93.7	0.1	0.7	0.2	0.0	4.1
31 125	...	9	Nance	1 143	4 038	2 919	3.5	1 143	4 275	2 890	3.7	98.4	0.0	0.4	0.0	0.0	0.4
31 127	...	7	Nemaha	1 060	7 576	2 638	7.1	1 060	7 980	2 569	7.5	97.6	0.4	0.3	0.6	0.0	0.4
31 129	...	9	Nuckolls	1 490	5 057	2 848	3.4	1 490	5 786	2 780	3.9	98.4	0.0	0.1	0.2	0.0	0.5
31 131	...	6	Otoe	1 595	15 396	2 060	9.7	1 595	14 252	2 034	8.9	97.4	0.3	0.2	0.2	0.0	1.1
31 133	...	9	Pawnee	1 118	3 087	2 986	2.8	1 118	3 317	2 972	3.0	98.9	0.0	0.2	0.3	0.0	0.0
31 135	...	9	Perkins	2 287	3 200	2 979	1.4	2 287	3 367	2 965	1.5	97.7	0.0	0.3	0.2	0.0	1.3
31 137	...	7	Phelps	1 399	9 747	2 466	7.0	1 399	9 715	2 409	6.9	97.8	0.1	0.3	0.3	0.0	0.8
31 139	...	9	Pierce	1 486	7 857	2 618	5.3	1 487	7 827	2 592	5.3	98.7	0.1	0.4	0.2	0.0	0.4

[1] MSA = Metropolitan Statistical Area. PMSA = Primary MSA. NECMA = New England County Metropolitan Area. See Appendix A for explanation of these concepts. See Appendix B for list of metropolitan areas identified by type, with component counties.
[2] County typology code from the Economic Research Service of USDA. See Appendix A for definition.
[3] Dry land or land partially or temporarily covered by water.

STATE County	Population and population characteristics, 2000 (cont'd)								Population and population characteristics, 1990				
	Race (percent) (cont'd)								Race (percent)				
		Race alone or in combination											
	Two or more races	White	Black	American Indian or Alaska Native	Asian	Native Hawaiian and other Pacific Islander	Some other race	Hispanic[1]	White	Black or African American	American Indian or Alaska Native	Asian and Pacific Islander	Hispanic[1]
	15	16	17	18	19	20	21	22	23	24	25	26	27
NEBRASKA—Cont'd													
Blaine	0.5	99.5	0.0	1.0	0.0	0.0	0.0	0.2	99.4	0.1	0.1	0.0	0.0
Boone	0.3	99.5	0.1	0.2	0.0	0.0	0.4	0.9	99.7	0.0	0.2	0.0	0.3
Box Butte	2.0	92.6	0.6	3.8	0.8	0.0	4.2	7.6	95.2	0.4	2.3	0.4	5.5
Boyd	0.4	99.3	0.0	0.9	0.2	0.0	0.0	0.1	99.1	0.0	0.8	0.0	0.2
Brown	0.6	99.2	0.2	0.5	0.5	0.0	0.3	0.8	99.4	0.0	0.3	0.2	0.6
Buffalo	1.0	96.1	0.8	0.6	0.9	0.1	2.6	4.7	97.3	0.4	0.3	0.4	2.7
Burt	0.7	98.3	0.2	1.5	0.3	0.1	0.3	1.3	98.5	0.1	0.9	0.2	0.9
Butler	0.4	98.7	0.2	0.4	0.1	0.1	0.9	1.7	99.5	0.1	0.2	0.2	0.2
Cass	0.9	98.8	0.3	0.7	0.5	0.1	0.6	1.5	98.7	0.2	0.5	0.3	0.9
Cedar	0.4	99.5	0.1	0.4	0.2	0.1	0.3	0.4	99.7	0.1	0.1	0.1	0.2
Chase	0.2	98.1	0.2	0.2	0.2	0.0	1.5	3.4	99.3	0.0	0.1	0.0	2.0
Cherry	1.7	95.7	0.2	4.5	0.5	0.3	0.7	0.9	96.8	0.0	2.8	0.2	0.4
Cheyenne	1.0	97.3	0.2	0.9	0.5	0.1	2.0	4.5	97.4	0.1	0.8	0.2	3.3
Clay	0.4	98.0	0.2	0.5	0.3	0.0	1.4	3.5	99.2	0.0	0.2	0.2	0.6
Colfax	1.7	83.3	0.2	0.4	0.3	0.3	17.2	26.2	98.5	0.0	0.4	0.1	2.5
Cuming	0.9	96.7	0.2	0.4	0.3	0.1	3.2	5.5	99.6	0.1	0.1	0.2	0.1
Custer	0.6	99.2	0.1	0.7	0.2	0.0	0.3	0.9	99.0	0.0	0.6	0.1	0.7
Dakota	2.6	81.1	1.0	2.6	3.5	0.1	14.6	22.6	92.5	0.5	1.8	2.1	6.1
Dawes	1.6	94.8	1.0	3.7	0.6	0.2	1.4	2.4	94.1	0.6	3.9	0.8	1.6
Dawson	1.5	83.7	0.4	1.1	0.8	0.0	15.6	25.4	97.9	0.1	0.3	0.2	3.3
Deuel	0.7	98.0	0.0	0.7	0.6	0.0	1.4	2.7	97.7	0.0	0.4	0.3	4.6
Dixon	0.8	95.4	0.1	0.7	0.4	0.0	4.2	5.5	99.7	0.1	0.2	0.0	0.1
Dodge	0.7	96.5	0.6	0.6	0.7	0.2	2.3	3.9	98.9	0.2	0.3	0.3	0.6
Douglas	1.8	82.4	12.3	1.1	2.1	0.1	3.9	6.7	86.3	10.9	0.6	1.0	2.7
Dundy	0.8	97.8	0.2	1.4	0.5	0.1	1.0	3.2	99.5	0.0	0.2	0.2	0.6
Fillmore	0.7	98.4	0.3	1.0	0.1	0.0	1.0	1.7	99.1	0.2	0.5	0.1	0.5
Franklin	0.3	99.6	0.0	0.5	0.1	0.0	0.1	0.6	99.4	0.2	0.3	0.2	0.2
Frontier	0.7	99.0	0.1	0.7	0.5	0.0	0.5	1.0	99.1	0.0	0.1	0.3	0.6
Furnas	0.8	99.0	0.1	0.9	0.2	0.0	0.5	1.1	99.3	0.1	0.3	0.1	0.7
Gage	0.8	98.5	0.5	1.1	0.4	0.1	0.4	0.9	98.8	0.2	0.4	0.3	0.5
Garden	0.5	98.8	0.1	0.7	0.3	0.0	0.5	1.4	99.8	0.0	0.0	0.0	0.6
Garfield	0.5	99.3	0.1	0.6	0.1	0.1	0.4	1.0	99.6	0.0	0.1	0.2	0.1
Gosper	0.4	99.2	0.0	0.4	0.3	0.0	0.6	1.3	99.9	0.0	0.0	0.1	0.5
Grant	0.0	98.8	0.0	0.1	0.3	0.0	0.8	1.3	98.8	0.0	0.7	0.4	0.3
Greeley	0.5	98.4	0.8	0.3	0.1	0.0	0.8	0.8	99.8	0.0	0.1	0.1	0.1
Hall	1.2	89.8	0.5	0.6	1.3	0.2	8.9	14.0	96.6	0.3	0.3	1.1	4.3
Hamilton	0.6	99.0	0.3	0.3	0.3	0.0	0.7	1.1	99.4	0.1	0.1	0.3	0.6
Harlan	0.6	99.5	0.2	0.4	0.1	0.0	0.4	0.8	99.8	0.1	0.1	0.0	0.1
Hayes	0.6	97.8	0.4	0.2	0.5	0.0	1.8	2.5	99.7	0.0	0.2	0.2	0.5
Hitchcock	0.8	99.2	0.2	0.9	0.1	0.0	0.4	1.4	99.5	0.0	0.2	0.1	0.6
Holt	0.4	99.2	0.1	0.5	0.2	0.1	0.3	0.7	99.5	0.0	0.2	0.1	0.2
Hooker	0.6	99.4	0.0	1.0	0.1	0.0	0.1	1.0	99.9	0.0	0.0	0.0	1.8
Howard	0.3	99.0	0.3	0.4	0.1	0.0	0.4	1.0	99.4	0.0	0.2	0.0	0.7
Jefferson	0.4	98.8	0.1	0.7	0.3	0.0	0.6	1.3	99.4	0.0	0.3	0.1	0.9
Johnson	1.3	94.1	0.2	0.9	3.4	0.0	2.7	2.9	97.2	0.0	0.0	2.3	1.0
Kearney	0.6	98.4	0.2	0.5	0.3	0.0	1.2	2.3	99.2	0.0	0.0	0.1	1.7
Keith	0.8	97.5	0.2	1.0	0.4	0.0	1.8	4.2	97.9	0.1	0.6	0.2	3.9
Keya Paha	0.4	99.8	0.0	0.4	0.0	0.0	0.2	3.9	99.9	0.0	0.1	0.0	0.1
Kimball	1.3	98.3	0.4	1.4	0.1	0.0	1.1	3.3	99.2	0.0	0.2	0.1	3.6
Knox	0.6	92.2	0.1	7.5	0.2	0.1	0.5	0.9	94.7	0.0	5.1	0.2	0.1
Lancaster	1.9	91.7	3.5	1.1	3.3	0.1	2.3	3.4	94.9	2.2	0.6	1.6	1.8
Lincoln	1.2	95.8	0.8	0.8	0.5	0.0	3.3	5.4	96.5	0.3	0.4	0.4	5.0
Logan	0.3	98.8	0.1	1.3	0.0	0.0	0.0	0.9	99.4	0.3	0.0	0.0	0.3
Loup	0.3	99.2	0.0	0.4	0.1	0.0	0.6	1.7	99.9	0.0	0.0	0.1	0.1
McPherson	0.0	97.9	0.0	0.0	0.4	0.0	1.7	1.5	99.8	0.2	0.0	0.0	0.0
Madison	1.0	92.3	1.2	1.5	0.5	0.1	5.5	8.6	97.2	0.7	0.7	0.3	1.7
Merrick	0.5	98.7	0.3	0.3	0.3	0.0	0.9	2.0	99.4	0.0	0.2	0.3	0.9
Morrill	1.2	94.9	0.2	1.0	0.2	0.0	4.9	10.1	95.9	0.0	0.6	0.1	8.0
Nance	0.7	99.1	0.0	0.8	0.1	0.0	0.7	1.1	99.4	0.0	0.1	0.2	0.9
Nemaha	0.7	98.2	0.5	0.7	0.7	0.1	0.6	1.0	98.7	0.9	0.2	0.2	0.3
Nuckolls	0.3	99.2	0.1	0.3	0.2	0.0	0.6	1.0	99.8	0.0	0.1	0.0	0.3
Otoe	0.6	98.1	0.3	0.6	0.4	0.0	1.3	2.4	99.2	0.2	0.2	0.2	0.7
Pawnee	0.6	99.5	0.0	0.5	0.3	0.0	0.3	0.7	99.6	0.1	0.0	0.1	0.5
Perkins	0.4	98.1	0.2	0.5	0.3	0.0	1.4	2.3	98.6	0.0	0.2	0.2	1.6
Phelps	0.7	98.4	0.3	0.5	0.5	0.1	1.0	2.3	99.4	0.1	0.2	0.2	0.9
Pierce	0.5	99.1	0.1	0.6	0.3	0.0	0.3	0.7	99.4	0.0	0.3	0.1	0.2

[1] Hispanic persons may be of any race.

Table B. States and Counties

STATE County	Population and population characteristics, 2000										
	Age (percent)										
	Under 5 years	5 to 17 years	18 to 24 years	25 to 34 years	35 to 44 years	45 to 54 years	55 to 64 years	65 to 74 years	75 years and over	Median age (years)	Percent Female
	28	29	30	31	32	33	34	35	36	37	38
NEBRASKA—Cont'd											
Blaine	5.5	20.8	3.9	11.1	15.4	13.6	12.9	10.1	6.7	39.8	49.6
Boone	5.9	23.2	5.0	8.9	15.2	12.3	9.1	9.5	10.9	39.9	50.2
Box Butte	6.6	21.6	7.4	10.8	16.0	15.2	7.9	7.2	7.3	38.2	50.2
Boyd	5.0	19.9	5.4	6.8	14.4	13.5	10.6	11.0	13.3	43.8	51.7
Brown	5.3	19.5	5.2	9.0	13.9	13.8	10.8	10.2	12.3	43.1	50.9
Buffalo	6.6	18.4	17.8	13.1	13.6	12.1	6.9	5.4	6.1	30.0	51.0
Burt	5.7	20.0	5.4	8.5	14.9	13.5	10.2	11.0	10.8	42.2	51.6
Butler	6.8	21.0	6.6	10.3	15.1	13.1	9.4	8.9	8.8	38.8	49.0
Cass	7.0	20.9	7.0	11.9	17.1	14.4	9.4	6.6	5.7	36.9	50.6
Cedar	6.1	23.4	6.0	9.7	14.6	12.0	8.4	9.3	10.8	38.8	50.0
Chase	5.6	19.6	5.9	9.3	14.6	13.9	10.1	10.1	11.0	42.1	50.9
Cherry	6.2	20.8	6.2	11.1	14.4	13.6	10.4	8.7	8.6	39.4	50.3
Cheyenne	6.4	19.9	7.0	11.4	15.3	13.8	9.0	8.8	8.5	38.7	51.0
Clay	5.8	21.5	5.9	9.7	15.6	13.8	9.7	8.9	9.1	39.9	51.3
Colfax	7.2	21.7	8.5	12.6	15.3	10.9	7.7	7.5	8.5	35.0	48.5
Cuming	6.5	20.7	6.5	10.5	14.7	12.2	8.7	9.3	10.9	39.2	49.5
Custer	5.7	20.6	5.5	9.2	14.3	13.5	10.2	9.7	11.3	41.3	51.0
Dakota	8.7	21.7	10.1	14.4	15.0	12.3	7.8	5.1	4.9	31.4	50.1
Dawes	5.0	16.2	23.4	9.3	11.1	11.7	8.6	7.0	7.8	30.6	51.1
Dawson	8.4	20.8	8.4	13.4	14.2	12.6	8.1	6.8	7.3	34.3	49.6
Deuel	4.3	19.0	4.9	8.2	16.2	13.7	10.8	10.0	12.9	43.5	51.3
Dixon	6.4	21.1	7.1	10.7	14.2	13.7	8.7	8.3	9.8	38.7	50.4
Dodge	6.2	18.5	9.6	11.3	14.9	12.7	9.2	8.6	9.0	37.9	51.8
Douglas	7.4	19.2	10.3	15.2	16.0	13.3	7.7	5.7	5.2	33.6	51.1
Dundy	5.3	18.0	5.7	9.1	14.4	15.7	9.4	10.2	12.2	43.5	50.8
Fillmore	5.8	20.5	5.1	9.6	14.4	13.3	10.0	9.2	12.0	41.4	51.7
Franklin	5.2	19.3	4.5	9.3	14.3	13.0	10.5	10.9	13.0	42.8	51.9
Frontier	5.5	20.5	11.3	8.6	14.2	12.9	10.1	8.6	8.3	38.5	49.9
Furnas	5.6	18.5	5.3	9.0	13.9	13.6	10.3	10.9	12.8	43.5	52.0
Gage	5.9	18.1	7.7	11.0	15.3	13.4	9.5	8.9	10.3	39.9	51.5
Garden	3.6	18.2	4.6	7.2	15.4	13.7	13.3	11.8	12.2	45.6	51.3
Garfield	4.8	18.7	4.4	7.0	13.5	14.1	12.7	9.5	15.3	45.9	52.1
Gosper	5.2	18.6	5.4	8.4	15.6	13.8	12.3	10.1	10.7	43.4	49.5
Grant	5.0	24.2	5.2	7.9	16.5	15.8	11.8	8.6	5.1	39.9	46.7
Greeley	5.7	21.3	5.9	8.7	13.0	12.8	9.6	11.1	12.1	41.7	50.7
Hall	7.6	19.5	8.9	13.2	15.2	13.3	8.4	6.9	7.0	35.6	50.4
Hamilton	6.7	22.4	5.9	10.6	15.9	14.2	9.0	7.6	7.7	38.1	50.2
Harlan	4.8	19.4	5.0	7.9	13.7	14.8	11.4	11.2	11.8	44.5	50.5
Hayes	4.4	22.2	5.5	6.3	15.3	15.8	10.7	11.7	8.1	42.5	49.9
Hitchcock	4.3	19.4	5.9	7.6	15.0	13.9	11.5	10.7	11.6	43.6	51.3
Holt	5.8	21.4	5.7	8.9	15.6	13.3	9.4	9.4	10.4	40.5	50.8
Hooker	4.1	19.9	4.1	7.0	14.6	13.8	9.6	10.3	16.6	45.3	54.5
Howard	6.0	22.3	6.6	10.5	14.8	13.1	9.5	8.5	8.6	38.1	49.7
Jefferson	5.3	18.0	6.1	9.6	14.1	14.3	10.0	9.7	13.0	42.9	51.1
Johnson	5.5	18.7	5.7	8.8	15.6	13.3	10.2	9.8	12.3	42.4	52.1
Kearney	6.2	20.6	6.4	11.2	16.3	13.4	9.3	7.9	8.8	38.7	50.4
Keith	5.7	19.5	5.7	9.9	15.4	13.8	11.6	9.9	8.4	41.1	50.9
Keya Paha	6.1	17.7	6.7	9.8	13.6	13.1	12.3	10.5	10.2	41.9	49.6
Kimball	5.4	19.3	5.9	8.4	14.7	13.5	11.8	10.4	10.6	42.8	51.1
Knox	5.7	19.8	5.5	8.1	13.8	13.6	10.3	10.5	12.6	43.0	50.8
Lancaster	6.7	16.8	15.4	15.3	15.1	13.1	7.2	5.3	5.1	32.0	50.9
Lincoln	6.6	19.6	8.3	11.8	14.7	14.5	9.2	7.7	7.4	37.8	50.9
Logan	5.2	22.1	4.4	8.5	15.5	16.3	10.5	9.9	7.6	41.8	50.3
Loup	6.3	20.4	4.5	7.7	14.6	14.7	12.2	10.7	8.8	42.9	47.9
McPherson	7.3	20.3	5.3	10.5	15.6	13.7	9.2	8.8	9.4	40.6	50.1
Madison	6.9	19.9	11.6	11.6	15.5	12.4	7.7	6.6	7.8	35.0	50.4
Merrick	6.4	21.2	6.4	10.0	14.7	13.5	10.3	8.5	9.0	39.2	51.0
Morrill	5.9	21.3	7.2	9.6	14.8	13.5	10.7	8.8	8.2	39.5	50.5
Nance	6.2	21.7	6.8	7.9	15.7	13.3	8.6	10.3	9.4	40.1	49.0
Nemaha	4.6	18.5	11.9	8.8	15.1	14.0	8.8	8.1	10.3	39.4	51.7
Nuckolls	4.9	18.5	5.4	8.2	14.3	12.9	11.4	11.5	12.8	44.1	51.9
Otoe	6.4	19.9	6.4	10.6	15.5	13.2	9.6	8.4	10.0	39.5	51.0
Pawnee	4.9	17.8	5.1	8.0	13.0	13.0	11.1	12.0	15.1	45.9	52.0
Perkins	5.4	21.2	6.0	9.5	13.9	14.7	9.9	7.7	11.6	40.7	49.8
Phelps	6.2	20.3	6.1	10.7	15.1	13.9	9.6	8.6	9.5	39.4	51.0
Pierce	6.0	23.0	7.0	9.9	16.1	12.0	8.9	7.7	9.4	37.9	50.0

Table B. States and Counties

STATE County	Population and population characteristics, 1990										Population—change, 1980–2000				
	Age (percent)									Percent Female	Total persons			Percent change	
	Under 5 years	5 to 17 years	18 to 24 years	25 to 34 years	35 to 44 years	45 to 54 years	55 to 64 years	65 to 74 years	75 years and over		2000	1990	1980	1990–2000	1980–1990
	39	40	41	42	43	44	45	46	47	48	49	50	51	52	53
NEBRASKA—Cont'd															
Blaine	6.1	21.8	5.2	14.1	12.0	12.9	11.3	8.0	8.7	51.3	583	675	867	-13.6	-22.1
Boone	8.0	21.2	5.3	13.9	11.9	9.1	10.6	10.3	9.7	50.1	6 259	6 667	7 391	-6.1	-9.8
Box Butte	8.1	24.2	6.0	16.2	16.0	8.7	7.5	6.7	6.6	50.7	12 158	13 130	13 696	-7.4	-4.1
Boyd	6.2	20.9	3.5	11.5	12.6	9.2	11.1	11.8	13.3	50.6	2 438	2 835	3 331	-14.0	-14.9
Brown	7.0	19.8	5.2	12.7	12.6	10.8	10.5	10.7	10.8	51.8	3 525	3 657	4 377	-3.6	-16.4
Buffalo	7.2	18.5	19.0	15.2	13.2	7.7	7.0	6.1	6.0	51.3	42 259	37 447	34 797	12.9	7.6
Burt	6.6	20.3	5.1	12.3	13.3	9.6	11.2	10.1	11.5	51.5	7 791	7 868	8 813	-1.0	-10.7
Butler	7.0	21.0	6.0	13.3	12.7	9.5	10.1	9.9	10.5	50.3	8 767	8 601	9 330	1.9	-7.8
Cass	7.9	20.9	7.9	16.0	14.9	10.5	8.9	7.1	5.9	50.1	24 334	21 318	20 297	14.1	5.0
Cedar	8.3	22.7	6.3	13.4	11.9	8.6	9.8	9.2	9.7	50.1	9 615	10 131	11 375	-5.1	-10.9
Chase	7.5	21.4	4.8	13.4	14.0	9.9	10.4	9.6	9.1	51.1	4 068	4 381	4 758	-7.1	-7.9
Cherry	8.2	20.0	5.8	14.5	13.5	11.1	10.1	8.4	8.6	50.4	6 148	6 307	6 758	-2.5	-6.7
Cheyenne	7.3	20.3	6.8	14.3	13.6	9.4	10.5	9.6	8.3	51.7	9 830	9 494	10 057	3.5	-5.6
Clay	6.6	20.6	5.9	13.6	13.3	10.6	9.8	10.1	9.5	51.5	7 039	7 123	8 106	-1.2	-12.1
Colfax	7.7	20.0	7.0	15.0	11.6	8.8	9.4	9.4	11.2	50.6	10 441	9 139	9 890	14.2	-7.6
Cuming	7.2	20.7	6.4	13.3	12.1	9.5	10.4	10.2	10.1	50.5	10 203	10 117	11 664	0.9	-13.3
Custer	6.9	20.2	5.2	12.2	12.9	9.9	10.8	10.6	11.3	51.7	11 793	12 270	13 877	-3.9	-11.6
Dakota	8.6	21.7	9.1	17.1	14.4	9.7	7.7	6.3	5.4	50.5	20 253	16 742	16 573	21.0	1.0
Dawes	6.6	18.7	18.1	12.2	12.0	8.5	8.1	7.9	7.7	50.9	9 060	9 021	9 609	0.4	-6.1
Dawson	7.1	20.9	6.7	13.7	14.5	10.3	9.5	9.1	8.2	51.4	24 365	19 940	22 304	22.2	-10.6
Deuel	6.1	20.2	5.5	13.9	11.4	9.9	10.2	11.5	11.4	50.4	2 098	2 237	2 462	-6.2	-9.1
Dixon	7.5	20.7	6.3	12.7	13.4	9.3	9.9	9.9	10.7	50.9	6 339	6 143	7 137	3.2	-13.9
Dodge	6.9	19.2	9.0	14.2	13.4	10.0	10.0	8.8	8.5	52.2	36 160	34 500	35 847	4.8	-3.8
Douglas	8.0	18.9	10.4	18.5	15.3	9.5	8.0	6.5	4.9	51.8	463 585	416 444	397 038	11.3	4.9
Dundy	5.0	19.9	6.1	12.7	13.6	9.1	10.5	12.1	11.0	51.7	2 292	2 582	2 861	-11.2	-9.8
Fillmore	6.9	19.6	5.6	13.1	13.3	9.6	10.2	10.3	11.4	51.5	6 634	7 103	7 920	-6.6	-10.3
Franklin	6.6	16.9	4.6	12.2	12.2	10.2	10.8	12.6	13.9	51.8	3 574	3 938	4 377	-9.2	-10.0
Frontier	6.3	21.5	5.7	13.0	14.0	11.1	10.7	8.8	8.9	50.4	3 099	3 101	3 647	-0.1	-15.0
Furnas	5.2	18.5	4.9	11.8	12.8	9.1	10.4	11.9	15.5	51.9	5 324	5 553	6 486	-4.1	-14.4
Gage	6.7	17.8	7.3	14.8	13.7	9.8	10.3	9.8	9.9	52.1	22 993	22 794	24 456	0.9	-6.8
Garden	6.5	16.7	5.4	12.3	12.3	11.1	11.7	11.9	12.1	51.9	2 292	2 460	2 802	-6.8	-12.2
Garfield	6.3	19.6	4.9	11.3	12.2	11.9	9.8	11.3	12.8	52.1	1 902	2 141	2 363	-11.2	-9.4
Gosper	5.4	19.0	4.7	12.6	13.4	11.6	12.1	11.5	9.8	49.3	2 143	1 928	2 140	11.2	-9.9
Grant	8.3	20.9	4.4	16.1	14.3	10.3	10.3	9.5	5.9	49.2	747	769	877	-2.9	-12.3
Greeley	7.0	23.8	4.7	12.3	12.3	8.9	10.1	9.8	11.0	50.8	2 714	3 006	3 462	-9.7	-13.2
Hall	7.8	20.5	8.5	16.0	14.8	9.4	8.7	7.7	6.6	51.5	53 534	48 925	47 690	9.4	2.6
Hamilton	7.7	21.4	6.1	14.6	14.7	9.8	9.7	8.0	8.1	51.1	9 403	8 862	9 301	6.1	-4.7
Harlan	6.4	18.2	4.3	12.5	13.8	9.6	11.2	12.7	11.3	52.0	3 786	3 810	4 292	-0.6	-11.2
Hayes	7.4	19.6	4.8	13.6	13.0	11.3	12.2	10.8	7.2	48.8	1 068	1 222	1 356	-12.6	-9.9
Hitchcock	6.7	22.2	4.8	12.7	13.2	8.7	10.3	10.5	10.9	50.9	3 111	3 750	4 079	-17.0	-8.1
Holt	8.4	21.8	6.1	14.6	13.0	8.9	9.8	9.0	8.4	50.2	11 551	12 599	13 552	-8.3	-7.0
Hooker	6.2	18.4	5.5	10.2	12.9	9.5	9.6	12.9	14.9	51.1	783	793	990	-1.3	-19.9
Howard	7.1	21.4	6.3	12.6	12.7	10.0	11.0	9.6	9.3	51.1	6 567	6 057	6 773	8.4	-10.6
Jefferson	6.5	18.1	6.1	12.6	13.0	9.4	10.6	11.8	11.8	51.7	8 333	8 759	9 817	-4.9	-10.8
Johnson	5.7	18.8	5.0	13.6	11.6	10.8	10.8	11.4	12.2	51.8	4 488	4 673	5 285	-4.0	-11.6
Kearney	7.6	19.4	6.7	15.2	14.0	10.2	9.4	8.7	8.8	50.5	6 882	6 629	7 053	3.8	-6.0
Keith	7.0	20.8	5.8	14.2	13.2	11.1	11.0	9.4	7.5	51.4	8 875	8 584	9 364	3.4	-8.3
Keya Paha	4.9	21.3	4.3	13.2	13.5	10.5	11.3	11.8	9.3	47.7	983	1 029	1 301	-4.5	-20.9
Kimball	6.9	19.7	4.7	14.2	13.0	11.4	11.0	10.6	8.4	50.9	4 089	4 108	4 882	-0.5	-15.9
Knox	6.4	19.9	4.9	11.6	12.5	9.6	11.3	11.9	11.9	51.2	9 374	9 564	11 457	-2.0	-16.5
Lancaster	7.1	16.8	15.6	18.3	15.3	8.8	7.2	5.9	4.9	51.1	250 291	213 641	192 884	17.2	10.8
Lincoln	7.3	21.6	7.6	14.2	14.9	10.0	9.3	8.2	7.1	51.5	34 632	32 508	36 455	6.5	-10.8
Logan	8.1	25.3	4.8	14.1	14.0	7.7	10.7	8.2	7.1	49.8	774	878	983	-11.8	-10.7
Loup	7.2	20.4	3.7	13.5	13.6	12.4	10.5	10.5	8.2	50.7	712	683	859	4.2	-20.5
McPherson	7.3	22.0	3.5	14.8	11.7	9.9	11.0	10.3	9.5	49.5	533	546	593	-2.4	-7.9
Madison	8.2	20.3	9.3	17.1	13.9	8.5	8.0	7.4	7.4	51.1	35 226	32 655	31 382	7.9	4.1
Merrick	7.2	20.7	6.7	13.8	13.1	11.0	9.9	8.8	8.9	50.5	8 204	8 062	8 945	1.8	-10.0
Morrill	7.4	20.6	5.3	13.0	13.6	10.8	10.4	9.2	9.6	50.5	5 440	5 423	6 085	0.3	-10.9
Nance	7.8	20.9	5.2	14.2	12.6	8.7	10.9	9.6	10.0	50.6	4 038	4 275	4 740	-5.5	-9.8
Nemaha	6.4	18.1	12.3	13.2	13.2	9.3	8.9	9.1	9.6	50.4	7 576	7 980	8 367	-5.1	-4.6
Nuckolls	5.9	20.0	4.3	12.7	12.3	9.9	11.4	11.5	12.0	51.9	5 057	5 786	6 726	-12.6	-14.0
Otoe	6.7	19.5	6.3	13.3	13.3	10.1	10.2	10.3	10.4	52.1	15 396	14 252	15 183	8.0	-6.1
Pawnee	6.4	16.7	5.5	10.2	12.2	9.0	11.4	14.8	13.8	51.9	3 087	3 317	3 937	-6.9	-15.7
Perkins	6.7	23.0	4.8	11.4	14.0	10.3	9.1	10.3	10.2	50.4	3 200	3 367	3 637	-5.0	-7.4
Phelps	7.3	20.1	6.6	14.5	14.1	9.9	9.6	8.3	9.5	51.8	9 747	9 715	9 769	0.3	-0.6
Pierce	7.9	21.3	6.2	14.0	12.2	9.6	9.5	9.7	9.5	51.0	7 857	7 827	8 481	0.4	-7.7

STATE County	Total population	In households (percent) Total in house-holds	House-holder	Spouse	Child Total	Own child under 18 years	Other relatives Total	Under 18 years	Nonrelatives Total	Unmarried partner	Total in group quarters	Institutionalized population Correctional institutions	Nursing homes	Other institutions	Noninstitutionalized population College dormitories	Military quarters	Other
	54	55	56	57	58	59	60	61	62	63	64	65	66	67	68	69	70
NEBRASKA—Cont'd																	
Blaine	583	100.0	40.8	26.9	28.8	26.1	1.7	0.2	1.7	0.7	0.0	0.0	0.0	0.0	0.0	0.0	0.0
Boone	6 259	98.2	39.2	23.8	32.2	28.4	1.4	0.4	1.6	0.8	1.8	0.1	1.7	0.0	0.0	0.0	0.0
Box Butte	12 158	98.1	39.3	22.7	30.9	26.4	2.1	1.0	3.1	1.8	1.9	0.1	1.4	0.0	0.0	0.0	0.4
Boyd	2 438	98.1	41.6	24.7	28.6	23.7	1.2	0.5	2.0	0.8	1.9	0.0	1.9	0.0	0.0	0.0	0.0
Brown	3 525	98.6	43.4	24.7	26.4	23.7	1.5	0.7	2.6	1.2	1.4	0.0	1.4	0.0	0.0	0.0	0.2
Buffalo	42 259	93.4	37.7	19.9	27.0	23.2	1.9	0.6	6.8	1.8	6.6	0.1	0.9	0.7	4.6	0.0	0.1
Burt	7 791	98.5	40.5	24.8	28.6	24.2	2.0	0.9	2.6	1.4	1.5	0.0	1.3	0.0	0.0	0.0	0.1
Butler	8 767	98.8	39.1	23.4	31.9	26.9	1.7	0.6	2.7	1.3	1.2	0.0	0.7	0.1	0.0	0.0	0.3
Cass	24 334	99.0	37.6	23.8	31.7	26.2	2.3	1.0	3.5	1.7	1.0	0.0	1.0	0.0	0.0	0.0	0.0
Cedar	9 615	98.1	37.7	24.0	33.1	28.7	1.6	0.5	1.7	0.9	1.9	0.1	1.9	0.0	0.0	0.0	0.0
Chase	4 068	97.5	40.9	25.4	27.8	24.4	1.5	0.6	2.1	1.1	2.5	0.0	2.5	0.0	0.0	0.0	0.1
Cherry	6 148	98.7	40.8	23.6	29.7	25.6	1.9	0.8	2.7	1.2	1.3	0.1	1.1	0.0	0.0	0.0	0.1
Cheyenne	9 830	98.7	41.4	22.7	29.2	24.9	1.8	0.7	3.6	1.7	1.3	0.1	1.1	0.0	0.0	0.0	0.1
Clay	7 039	98.6	39.2	24.9	30.2	25.9	1.8	0.8	2.4	1.3	1.4	0.1	1.1	0.0	0.0	0.0	0.1
Colfax	10 441	98.7	35.3	20.8	31.2	26.4	5.4	1.8	6.1	1.3	1.3	0.0	1.1	0.0	0.0	0.0	0.1
Cuming	10 203	97.6	38.7	23.9	30.5	26.4	2.0	0.5	2.7	1.2	2.4	0.0	2.2	0.1	0.0	0.0	0.0
Custer	11 793	98.0	40.9	24.9	28.5	25.0	1.6	0.7	2.1	0.9	2.0	0.1	1.8	0.0	0.0	0.0	0.2
Dakota	20 253	98.6	35.0	19.1	33.4	27.5	5.3	2.0	5.7	2.4	1.4	0.1	1.0	0.0	0.0	0.0	0.3
Dawes	9 060	88.5	38.8	18.8	22.2	18.8	2.1	0.8	6.6	1.8	11.5	0.1	0.9	0.0	8.4	0.0	2.2
Dawson	24 365	98.1	36.2	21.3	31.2	26.9	4.4	1.6	4.9	1.6	1.9	0.5	0.9	0.0	0.0	0.0	0.6
Deuel	2 098	98.9	43.3	24.9	26.6	22.2	1.9	0.8	2.2	1.1	1.1	0.0	1.1	0.0	0.0	0.0	0.0
Dixon	6 339	98.2	38.1	23.4	31.4	26.0	2.3	0.9	3.0	1.2	1.8	0.1	1.6	0.0	1.4	0.0	0.2
Dodge	36 160	96.8	39.9	22.3	28.0	23.2	2.2	0.9	4.3	1.9	3.2	0.1	0.7	0.4	0.6	0.0	0.5
Douglas	463 585	97.5	39.3	18.6	30.1	24.2	3.9	1.5	5.5	2.0	2.5	0.4	2.4	0.0	0.0	0.0	1.4
Dundy	2 292	96.2	41.9	25.1	25.1	21.8	1.8	0.8	2.2	0.8	3.8	0.0	2.6	1.3	0.0	0.0	0.0
Fillmore	6 634	96.0	40.5	23.9	27.5	24.0	1.5	0.7	2.5	1.3	4.0	0.1	2.3	0.0	0.0	0.0	0.7
Franklin	3 574	97.0	41.6	24.7	27.3	23.6	1.5	0.5	2.0	1.1	3.0	0.0	2.3	0.0	0.0	0.0	0.7
Frontier	3 099	95.4	38.5	24.0	28.6	25.1	1.4	0.6	2.9	0.9	4.6	0.1	1.2	0.0	3.3	0.0	0.2
Furnas	5 324	97.5	42.8	24.5	26.6	22.8	1.4	0.7	2.2	1.0	2.5	0.0	2.3	0.0	0.0	0.0	0.2
Gage	22 993	95.5	44.5	23.0	26.9	22.8	1.6	0.7	3.5	1.8	4.5	0.0	1.5	2.3	0.5	0.0	0.1
Garden	2 292	97.4	44.5	24.9	24.3	20.9	1.8	0.7	1.9	1.1	2.6	0.0	2.6	0.0	0.0	0.0	0.0
Garfield	1 902	97.0	42.7	25.5	25.7	22.3	1.2	0.6	1.9	0.7	3.0	0.0	3.0	0.0	0.0	0.0	0.0
Gosper	2 143	97.6	40.3	27.8	27.0	23.2	1.1	0.2	1.4	0.8	2.4	0.0	2.4	0.0	0.0	0.0	0.0
Grant	747	100.0	39.1	26.4	32.7	28.2	0.9	0.8	0.9	0.7	0.0	0.0	0.0	0.0	0.0	0.0	0.0
Greeley	2 714	97.7	39.7	23.4	30.9	25.4	2.0	0.8	1.7	0.6	2.3	0.0	2.3	0.0	0.0	0.0	0.0
Hall	53 534	97.7	38.0	21.2	29.7	25.0	3.8	1.4	5.0	1.9	2.3	0.2	1.4	0.1	0.0	0.0	0.6
Hamilton	9 403	98.4	37.3	25.1	32.3	27.7	1.6	0.8	2.3	1.1	1.6	0.1	1.5	0.0	0.0	0.0	0.1
Harlan	3 786	98.5	42.2	24.9	27.0	22.7	1.5	0.9	3.0	1.6	1.5	0.0	1.1	0.3	0.0	0.0	0.1
Hayes	1 068	100.0	40.3	27.0	30.1	25.7	1.9	0.5	0.8	0.5	0.0	0.0	0.0	0.0	0.0	0.0	0.0
Hitchcock	3 111	98.0	41.4	25.3	27.5	22.7	1.8	0.8	2.1	1.2	2.0	0.2	1.7	0.0	0.0	0.0	0.0
Holt	11 551	98.1	39.9	24.2	30.7	26.3	1.5	0.6	1.7	0.8	1.9	0.1	1.6	0.2	0.0	0.0	0.0
Hooker	783	96.7	42.8	25.8	26.4	23.6	1.0	0.4	0.6	0.4	3.3	0.0	3.3	0.0	0.0	0.0	0.0
Howard	6 567	99.4	38.8	23.6	31.7	27.0	1.9	0.8	3.4	1.5	0.6	0.0	0.6	0.0	0.0	0.0	0.0
Jefferson	8 333	98.0	42.3	24.5	26.4	22.2	1.5	0.5	3.3	1.5	2.0	0.1	1.5	0.0	0.0	0.0	0.3
Johnson	4 488	98.6	42.0	24.4	27.4	23.1	2.0	0.7	2.8	1.3	1.4	0.0	1.4	0.0	0.0	0.0	0.0
Kearney	6 882	96.2	38.4	24.2	29.0	25.4	1.5	0.8	3.1	1.5	3.8	0.1	1.5	0.6	0.0	0.0	1.7
Keith	8 875	98.9	41.8	24.5	27.4	23.8	2.0	0.8	3.2	1.5	1.1	0.2	0.7	0.0	0.0	0.0	0.0
Keya Paha	983	100.0	41.6	26.8	27.7	22.8	2.2	1.0	1.7	0.9	0.0	0.0	0.0	0.0	0.0	0.0	0.0
Kimball	4 089	98.5	42.2	23.7	26.8	22.7	2.2	0.9	3.7	1.6	1.5	0.1	1.4	0.0	0.0	0.0	0.2
Knox	9 374	97.4	40.7	24.0	28.7	24.2	2.1	0.9	2.0	1.0	2.6	0.1	2.3	0.0	2.8	0.0	0.4
Lancaster	250 291	95.1	39.6	19.3	26.7	22.2	2.5	0.8	6.9	2.1	4.9	1.1	0.4	0.1	0.2	0.0	0.6
Lincoln	34 632	98.1	40.6	22.7	28.7	24.5	2.3	1.0	3.7	1.8	1.9	0.2	0.9	0.0	0.0	0.0	0.0
Logan	774	100.0	40.8	27.1	28.4	26.0	2.1	0.9	1.6	0.5	0.0	0.0	0.0	0.0	0.0	0.0	0.0
Loup	712	100.0	40.6	26.3	29.5	25.4	2.1	0.8	1.5	0.1	0.0	0.0	0.0	0.0	0.0	0.0	0.0
McPherson	533	100.0	37.9	28.0	30.8	26.3	0.9	0.4	2.4	0.9	0.0	0.0	0.0	0.0	0.8	0.0	0.7
Madison	35 226	96.2	38.1	20.9	30.0	25.2	2.7	1.1	4.5	1.6	3.8	0.3	1.4	0.5	0.0	0.0	0.2
Merrick	8 204	98.4	39.1	23.9	30.2	25.8	1.9	0.8	3.3	1.5	1.6	0.1	1.4	0.0	0.0	0.0	0.5
Morrill	5 440	98.0	39.3	23.4	29.5	24.8	2.7	1.3	3.1	1.7	2.0	0.1	1.8	0.0	0.0	0.0	1.0
Nance	4 038	97.2	39.1	23.6	30.9	26.8	1.6	0.6	2.1	1.0	2.8	0.0	1.4	0.0	4.7	0.0	0.4
Nemaha	7 576	93.5	40.2	22.1	26.4	22.3	1.4	0.6	3.4	1.6	6.5	0.1	1.4	0.0	0.0	0.0	0.0
Nuckolls	5 057	99.1	43.9	25.8	26.1	22.4	1.4	0.6	2.1	1.0	0.9	0.0	0.9	0.0	0.0	0.0	0.0
Otoe	15 396	97.7	39.4	23.5	29.5	24.8	2.2	1.0	3.1	1.6	2.3	0.1	1.9	0.1	0.0	0.0	0.3
Pawnee	3 087	98.3	43.4	23.8	25.6	21.1	1.7	0.4	3.8	1.7	1.7	0.0	1.7	0.0	0.0	0.0	0.0
Perkins	3 200	98.3	39.8	25.3	29.5	25.4	1.7	0.8	2.3	1.1	1.7	0.0	1.7	0.0	0.0	0.0	0.0
Phelps	9 747	97.3	39.4	24.3	29.5	25.6	1.3	0.5	2.9	1.4	2.7	0.0	2.6	0.0	0.0	0.0	0.0
Pierce	7 857	98.3	37.9	24.0	33.0	28.0	1.4	0.6	2.0	1.1	1.7	0.1	1.5	0.0	0.0	0.0	0.0

Table B. States and Counties

STATE County	Households by type, 2000												Households, 1990		
		Family households						Nonfamily households							
				Married couple		Female householder[1]			Householder living alone						House-holder living alone
	Total households	Total	With own children under 18 years	Total	With own children under 18 years	Total	With own children under 18 years	Total	Total	65 years and over	Average house-hold size	Average family size	Total house-holds	Female house-holder[1]	
	71	72	73	74	75	76	77	78	79	80	81	82	83	84	85
NEBRASKA—Cont'd															
Blaine	238	71.0	30.3	66.0	27.3	2.5	2.1	29.0	26.9	13.9	2.45	2.98	268	2.6	28.0
Boone	2 454	69.3	33.9	60.8	28.8	5.5	3.5	30.7	29.1	16.5	2.50	3.11	2 560	3.9	27.7
Box Butte	4 780	69.0	35.6	57.7	27.4	8.3	6.3	31.0	27.5	11.1	2.50	3.05	4 898	7.6	26.4
Boyd	1 014	66.1	29.0	59.4	25.0	3.7	2.4	33.9	32.0	19.6	2.36	2.98	1 148	4.2	30.7
Brown	1 530	65.1	26.6	57.0	21.4	5.9	4.0	34.9	31.6	16.9	2.27	2.86	1 499	5.9	29.4
Buffalo	15 930	64.2	32.7	52.9	25.1	8.3	5.8	35.8	26.1	9.6	2.48	3.02	13 736	7.2	26.0
Burt	3 155	71.0	29.5	61.3	23.5	6.2	3.9	29.0	26.5	15.6	2.43	2.93	3 139	5.5	29.1
Butler	3 426	68.6	33.0	59.9	27.9	5.7	3.5	31.4	28.3	14.4	2.53	3.13	3 253	4.9	27.4
Cass	9 161	74.3	35.8	63.3	28.5	7.6	5.2	25.7	21.6	9.4	2.63	3.07	7 797	6.5	21.0
Cedar	3 623	70.8	34.8	63.6	30.8	4.3	2.5	29.2	27.0	15.7	2.60	3.20	3 652	3.9	26.4
Chase	1 662	70.0	30.6	62.1	25.0	5.5	3.9	30.0	27.3	13.8	2.39	2.91	1 704	5.5	26.8
Cherry	2 508	68.2	31.7	57.9	24.9	6.9	4.6	31.8	28.9	12.7	2.42	2.98	2 438	5.3	25.8
Cheyenne	4 071	66.0	31.1	54.8	23.3	8.0	5.5	34.0	30.1	13.3	2.38	2.96	3 851	7.5	28.7
Clay	2 756	71.9	32.9	63.7	27.4	5.5	4.0	28.1	25.7	13.1	2.52	3.03	2 741	4.5	24.8
Colfax	3 682	70.4	35.6	58.9	29.0	7.1	4.4	29.6	25.7	15.4	2.80	3.31	3 562	5.3	28.9
Cuming	3 945	69.9	32.6	61.7	27.7	5.3	3.5	30.1	27.1	14.9	2.53	3.08	3 851	3.5	27.0
Custer	4 826	68.8	30.3	60.9	25.3	5.4	3.3	31.2	28.9	15.0	2.39	2.95	4 953	5.2	28.9
Dakota	7 095	71.7	39.9	54.6	28.5	11.9	8.5	28.3	22.9	9.0	2.81	3.30	6 035	10.5	22.9
Dawes	3 512	59.4	26.2	48.5	19.0	7.9	5.4	40.6	31.0	12.9	2.28	2.87	3 327	8.5	29.8
Dawson	8 824	71.1	35.8	58.8	27.5	7.9	5.6	28.9	24.6	12.0	2.71	3.21	7 829	6.3	25.6
Deuel	908	66.2	25.6	57.6	20.5	5.9	3.5	33.8	31.2	16.5	2.29	2.87	915	4.8	29.3
Dixon	2 413	70.7	33.3	61.5	27.5	6.5	4.4	29.3	25.9	14.4	2.58	3.12	2 338	5.8	26.3
Dodge	14 433	67.6	31.1	55.8	23.4	8.5	5.7	32.4	27.6	13.4	2.42	2.95	13 445	6.8	26.8
Douglas	182 194	63.2	32.0	47.5	22.6	12.1	7.6	36.8	29.8	8.7	2.48	3.12	161 113	12.2	28.1
Dundy	961	66.3	27.8	59.9	24.1	3.9	2.5	33.7	30.9	17.6	2.29	2.87	1 085	5.0	31.5
Fillmore	2 689	67.0	30.2	59.1	25.1	5.0	3.1	33.0	30.2	16.3	2.37	2.95	2 829	4.2	29.3
Franklin	1 485	68.8	28.6	59.4	22.7	6.0	4.0	31.2	29.2	16.0	2.34	2.87	1 655	3.7	30.3
Frontier	1 192	69.5	31.4	62.5	26.1	4.8	3.9	30.5	26.3	12.3	2.48	3.02	1 206	3.6	27.1
Furnas	2 278	65.4	28.0	57.2	22.6	5.9	3.7	34.6	32.5	19.8	2.28	2.88	2 334	4.4	33.8
Gage	9 316	66.6	30.3	56.7	23.6	7.1	4.9	33.4	29.2	15.0	2.36	2.91	9 019	6.7	28.2
Garden	1 020	64.6	24.8	55.9	19.5	6.0	3.6	35.4	32.5	16.2	2.19	2.77	1 040	4.9	30.3
Garfield	813	65.1	26.1	59.7	22.3	3.6	2.5	34.9	32.7	20.0	2.27	2.88	864	4.7	28.7
Gosper	863	75.9	29.9	69.1	25.7	3.9	2.4	24.1	22.8	10.5	2.42	2.83	764	3.7	21.2
Grant	292	77.4	37.0	67.5	29.8	6.5	3.8	22.6	22.3	8.9	2.56	2.98	303	6.6	24.1
Greeley	1 077	68.2	29.3	59.0	25.2	6.4	3.2	31.8	30.5	18.8	2.46	3.08	1 133	6.4	30.1
Hall	20 356	69.2	34.8	55.9	25.9	9.7	6.8	30.8	25.5	10.5	2.57	3.08	18 678	8.5	26.0
Hamilton	3 503	76.4	37.3	67.4	30.9	5.9	4.1	23.6	21.1	10.1	2.64	3.07	3 235	4.3	21.7
Harlan	1 597	65.7	25.7	59.0	21.5	4.3	2.9	34.3	30.8	16.7	2.34	2.93	1 585	3.7	29.2
Hayes	430	72.6	28.1	67.0	27.4	2.6	0.7	27.4	26.5	15.6	2.48	3.02	480	3.3	22.7
Hitchcock	1 287	69.9	28.0	61.1	22.3	6.4	4.3	30.1	27.4	15.5	2.37	2.89	1 467	4.3	28.6
Holt	4 608	68.8	31.6	60.7	27.0	5.6	3.3	31.2	28.7	15.1	2.46	3.06	4 744	5.1	27.3
Hooker	335	65.7	26.9	60.3	24.2	3.9	2.1	34.3	33.1	19.1	2.26	2.90	332	4.5	33.7
Howard	2 546	70.6	33.8	61.0	27.1	6.2	4.1	29.4	26.0	15.0	2.56	3.09	2 309	4.8	25.2
Jefferson	3 527	66.7	28.0	57.9	22.8	5.8	3.6	33.3	29.6	17.2	2.32	2.85	3 634	5.1	28.8
Johnson	1 887	66.5	29.6	58.1	24.5	5.5	3.4	33.5	29.9	17.7	2.35	2.92	1 940	5.2	30.8
Kearney	2 643	72.0	34.4	62.9	27.8	6.4	4.7	28.0	24.3	10.9	2.50	2.98	2 523	4.8	24.1
Keith	3 707	68.4	30.2	58.6	23.7	7.0	4.7	31.6	27.9	13.5	2.37	2.89	3 430	6.7	27.3
Keya Paha	409	71.4	24.9	64.3	21.5	4.4	2.0	28.6	26.2	13.9	2.40	2.91	419	2.1	24.8
Kimball	1 727	65.8	26.3	56.1	20.6	6.7	4.2	34.2	30.5	15.4	2.33	2.89	1 650	6.8	26.7
Knox	3 811	68.1	29.3	59.0	23.8	6.0	3.8	31.9	29.9	17.4	2.40	2.98	3 817	5.1	29.7
Lancaster	99 187	61.2	30.3	48.8	22.5	9.1	6.0	38.8	29.1	8.3	2.40	3.00	82 759	8.7	27.5
Lincoln	14 076	67.1	32.0	55.9	24.4	8.0	5.6	32.9	28.3	11.6	2.41	2.97	12 676	8.0	27.0
Logan	316	72.5	29.7	66.5	25.6	3.8	2.8	27.5	25.0	12.7	2.45	2.95	320	4.4	21.9
Loup	289	71.6	31.8	64.7	28.4	4.2	2.1	28.4	27.0	17.0	2.46	2.99	276	4.0	27.2
McPherson	202	78.2	34.2	73.8	31.2	3.5	2.5	21.8	19.8	14.4	2.64	3.01	212	2.8	23.6
Madison	13 436	66.2	33.2	54.7	25.6	8.4	6.0	33.8	27.9	12.4	2.52	3.12	12 283	7.0	26.7
Merrick	3 209	71.9	33.3	61.1	26.3	6.5	4.3	28.1	25.0	13.1	2.51	2.99	3 061	4.3	25.3
Morrill	2 138	69.9	32.1	59.5	25.5	6.5	4.0	30.1	26.9	13.0	2.49	3.03	2 083	3.8	25.7
Nance	1 577	70.2	32.8	60.5	26.6	5.6	3.9	29.8	27.6	13.8	2.49	3.05	1 585	4.3	27.3
Nemaha	3 047	65.0	29.5	55.0	23.1	7.2	4.8	35.0	30.5	16.2	2.32	2.91	3 079	5.7	28.9
Nuckolls	2 218	65.1	26.5	58.8	22.1	4.6	3.3	34.9	32.3	18.0	2.26	2.86	2 359	4.3	29.0
Otoe	6 060	69.8	32.5	59.7	26.2	7.2	4.5	30.2	26.4	14.1	2.48	3.01	5 657	6.5	28.0
Pawnee	1 339	63.5	24.4	54.8	19.6	5.6	3.0	36.5	32.9	20.2	2.27	2.86	1 408	3.9	31.0
Perkins	1 275	70.1	32.5	62.9	27.3	4.6	3.5	29.9	27.5	15.7	2.47	3.01	1 283	4.8	25.8
Phelps	3 844	69.8	33.1	61.6	27.5	5.8	4.0	30.2	26.7	13.0	2.47	3.00	3 769	5.3	26.2
Pierce	2 979	71.9	35.3	63.4	30.0	5.7	3.5	28.1	25.7	13.7	2.59	3.14	2 929	4.5	25.2

[1] No spouse present.

Table B. States and Counties

STATE County	Percent change of households, 1990–2000	Total housing units	Occupied housing units (percent)	Vacant housing units — Total	For seasonal, recreational, or occasional use	Homeowner vacancy rate (percent)	Rental vacancy rate (percent)	Occupied housing units — Total	Percent owner-occupied housing units	Percent renter-occupied housing units	Average household size of owner-occupied units	Average household size of renter-occupied units
	86	87	88	89	90	91	92	93	94	95	96	97
NEBRASKA—Cont'd												
Blaine	-11.2	333	71.5	28.5	9.6	3.1	10.9	238	65.5	34.5	2.25	2.83
Boone	-4.1	2 733	89.8	10.2	1.1	3.1	9.8	2 454	75.1	24.9	2.55	2.37
Box Butte	-2.4	5 488	87.1	12.9	0.8	2.2	15.4	4 780	70.1	29.0	2.62	2.20
Boyd	-11.7	1 406	72.1	27.9	12.8	3.3	14.1	1 014	80.2	19.8	2.36	2.34
Brown	2.1	1 916	79.9	20.1	6.6	4.4	10.6	1 530	74.2	25.8	2.31	2.16
Buffalo	16.0	16 830	94.7	5.3	0.4	2.0	5.7	15 930	63.6	36.4	2.64	2.19
Burt	0.5	3 723	84.7	15.3	7.4	3.2	7.2	3 155	75.8	24.2	2.51	2.19
Butler	5.3	3 901	87.8	12.2	3.9	1.5	9.7	3 426	75.8	24.2	2.61	2.28
Cass	17.5	10 179	90.0	10.0	5.3	1.9	7.8	9 161	79.5	20.5	2.68	2.43
Cedar	-0.8	4 200	86.3	13.7	6.2	2.3	13.4	3 623	80.6	19.4	2.68	2.28
Chase	-2.5	1 927	86.2	13.8	3.6	4.2	6.8	1 662	76.9	23.1	2.38	2.42
Cherry	2.9	3 220	77.9	22.1	7.0	5.4	9.3	2 508	62.4	37.6	2.44	2.39
Cheyenne	5.7	4 569	89.1	10.9	1.2	2.1	15.0	4 071	72.8	27.2	2.44	2.23
Clay	0.5	3 066	89.9	10.1	0.7	3.6	11.4	2 756	77.8	22.2	2.59	2.27
Colfax	3.4	4 088	90.1	9.9	2.1	1.8	8.6	3 682	75.2	24.8	2.77	2.89
Cuming	2.4	4 283	92.1	7.9	0.8	2.5	5.6	3 945	71.4	28.6	2.56	2.44
Custer	-2.6	5 585	86.4	13.6	1.3	5.2	11.2	4 826	73.0	27.0	2.42	2.32
Dakota	17.6	7 528	94.2	5.8	0.5	1.3	9.3	7 095	67.4	32.6	2.99	2.46
Dawes	5.6	4 004	87.7	12.3	2.0	3.0	11.8	3 512	62.7	37.3	2.42	2.05
Dawson	12.7	9 805	90.0	10.0	3.6	1.6	9.8	8 824	69.2	30.8	2.74	2.63
Deuel	-0.8	1 032	88.0	12.0	2.4	3.5	7.4	908	78.0	22.0	2.26	2.36
Dixon	3.2	2 673	90.3	9.7	2.5	2.8	7.1	2 413	76.3	23.7	2.60	2.53
Dodge	7.3	15 468	93.3	6.7	2.5	1.1	5.0	14 433	67.8	32.2	2.52	2.23
Douglas	13.1	192 672	94.6	5.4	0.5	1.0	7.5	182 194	63.3	36.7	2.70	2.10
Dundy	-11.4	1 196	80.4	19.6	4.9	4.8	20.1	961	72.7	27.3	2.26	2.38
Fillmore	-4.9	2 990	89.9	10.1	1.1	3.4	7.5	2 689	74.5	25.5	2.43	2.20
Franklin	-10.3	1 746	85.1	14.9	2.9	3.4	5.5	1 485	81.3	18.7	2.30	2.49
Frontier	-1.2	1 543	77.3	22.7	12.9	4.1	9.6	1 192	72.5	27.5	2.49	2.46
Furnas	-2.4	2 730	83.4	16.6	1.8	5.7	9.7	2 278	76.6	23.4	2.33	2.10
Gage	3.3	10 030	92.9	7.1	0.6	2.3	8.7	9 316	71.2	28.8	2.45	2.12
Garden	-1.9	1 298	78.6	21.4	5.2	4.5	5.0	1 020	70.1	29.9	2.12	2.34
Garfield	-5.9	1 021	79.6	20.4	7.1	4.5	13.2	813	72.6	27.4	2.35	2.05
Gosper	13.0	1 281	67.4	32.6	25.9	4.5	5.5	863	75.9	24.1	2.40	2.51
Grant	-3.6	449	65.0	35.0	11.8	9.9	22.2	292	68.8	31.2	2.48	2.74
Greeley	-4.9	1 199	89.8	10.2	1.0	1.6	5.3	1 077	78.6	21.4	2.48	2.41
Hall	9.0	21 574	94.4	5.6	0.3	1.9	7.2	20 356	65.9	34.1	2.70	2.30
Hamilton	8.3	3 850	91.0	9.0	2.5	2.5	8.8	3 503	75.1	24.9	2.71	2.45
Harlan	0.8	2 327	68.6	31.4	23.6	1.9	8.2	1 597	80.3	19.7	2.32	2.41
Hayes	-10.4	526	81.7	18.3	6.7	2.8	12.9	430	71.9	28.1	2.31	2.92
Hitchcock	-12.3	1 675	76.8	23.2	12.9	5.7	15.6	1 287	78.2	21.8	2.35	2.46
Holt	-2.9	5 281	87.3	12.7	2.2	2.4	11.6	4 608	73.6	26.4	2.51	2.32
Hooker	0.9	440	76.1	23.9	5.2	6.7	21.1	335	74.3	25.7	2.25	2.28
Howard	10.3	2 782	91.5	8.5	1.5	1.6	9.0	2 546	76.9	23.1	2.58	2.50
Jefferson	-2.9	3 942	89.5	10.5	0.8	2.5	9.4	3 527	76.1	23.9	2.38	2.11
Johnson	-2.7	2 116	89.2	10.8	0.7	3.5	13.5	1 887	75.3	24.7	2.38	2.24
Kearney	4.8	2 846	92.9	7.1	1.5	2.1	7.4	2 643	74.3	25.7	2.54	2.40
Keith	8.1	5 178	71.6	28.4	21.0	2.3	12.0	3 707	72.9	27.1	2.40	2.28
Keya Paha	-2.4	548	74.6	25.4	11.7	8.7	8.1	409	72.1	27.9	2.32	2.63
Kimball	4.7	1 972	87.6	12.4	0.9	2.7	14.4	1 727	76.3	23.7	2.35	2.28
Knox	-0.2	4 773	79.8	20.2	10.3	3.3	9.3	3 811	75.0	25.0	2.40	2.39
Lancaster	19.9	104 217	95.2	4.8	0.3	1.2	6.2	99 187	60.5	39.5	2.62	2.06
Lincoln	11.0	15 438	91.2	8.8	2.5	2.1	8.2	14 076	69.2	30.8	2.53	2.16
Logan	-1.3	386	81.9	18.1	1.8	5.0	4.3	316	71.5	28.5	2.32	2.77
Loup	4.7	377	76.7	23.3	11.4	3.4	0.0	289	78.2	21.8	2.39	2.73
McPherson	-4.7	283	71.4	28.6	7.1	15.0	1.5	202	67.3	32.7	2.43	3.08
Madison	9.4	14 432	93.1	6.9	0.5	1.9	9.5	13 436	65.6	34.4	2.70	2.18
Merrick	4.8	3 649	87.9	12.1	5.1	2.2	7.4	3 209	74.1	25.9	2.57	2.35
Morrill	2.6	2 460	86.9	13.1	2.0	4.3	7.8	2 138	71.4	28.6	2.48	2.53
Nance	-0.5	1 787	88.2	11.8	2.0	3.2	9.3	1 577	74.7	25.3	2.53	2.38
Nemaha	-1.0	3 439	88.6	11.4	1.6	3.1	12.6	3 047	72.5	27.5	2.38	2.18
Nuckolls	-6.0	2 530	87.7	12.3	1.1	2.6	12.3	2 218	80.0	20.0	2.32	2.01
Otoe	7.1	6 567	92.3	7.7	0.6	2.3	9.5	6 060	74.0	26.0	2.56	2.27
Pawnee	-4.9	1 587	84.4	15.6	4.9	3.5	6.9	1 339	80.7	19.3	2.30	2.13
Perkins	-0.6	1 444	88.3	11.7	1.2	2.5	9.4	1 275	75.7	24.3	2.51	2.34
Phelps	2.0	4 191	91.7	8.3	0.8	3.1	8.6	3 844	73.4	26.6	2.58	2.17
Pierce	1.7	3 247	91.7	8.3	0.3	3.1	8.6	2 979	77.6	22.4	2.62	2.50

Table B. States and Counties

STATE/ County code	MSA/ PMSA/ NECMA code[1]	County type[2]	STATE County	Population, 2000				Population, 1990				Population and population characteristics, 2000					
												Race (percent)					
												One race					
				Land area, 2000[3] (sq km)	Total persons	Rank	Per square kilometer	Land area, 1990[3] (sq km)	Total persons	Rank	Per square kilometer	White	Black or African American	American Indian or Alaska Native	Asian	Native Hawaiian and other Pacific Islander	Some other race
				1	2	3	4	5	6	7	8	9	10	11	12	13	14
			NEBRASKA—Cont'd														
31 141	...	7	Platte	1 756	31 662	1 354	18.0	1 756	29 820	1 303	17.0	94.3	0.4	0.3	0.4	0.0	3.5
31 143	...	9	Polk	1 137	5 639	2 811	5.0	1 137	5 655	2 787	5.0	98.9	0.0	0.3	0.1	0.0	0.3
31 145	...	7	Red Willow	1 856	11 448	2 338	6.2	1 856	11 705	2 232	6.3	97.5	0.2	0.4	0.2	0.0	0.9
31 147	...	7	Richardson	1 433	9 531	2 487	6.7	1 434	9 937	2 391	6.9	95.6	0.2	2.3	0.1	0.0	0.2
31 149	...	9	Rock	2 612	1 756	3 082	0.7	2 612	2 019	3 065	0.8	99.0	0.0	0.5	0.2	0.0	0.1
31 151	...	6	Saline	1 490	13 843	2 170	9.3	1 490	12 715	2 165	8.5	93.0	0.4	0.4	1.7	0.0	3.4
31 153	5920	2	Sarpy	623	122 595	443	196.8	623	102 583	448	164.7	89.2	4.4	0.4	1.9	0.1	1.9
31 155	...	6	Saunders	1 953	19 830	1 799	10.2	1 953	18 285	1 774	9.4	98.5	0.1	0.3	0.2	0.0	0.3
31 157	...	5	Scotts Bluff	1 915	36 951	1 191	19.3	1 915	36 025	1 100	18.8	87.6	0.3	1.9	0.6	0.0	8.0
31 159	...	6	Seward	1 489	16 496	1 988	11.1	1 489	15 450	1 957	10.4	98.0	0.3	0.2	0.3	0.0	0.4
31 161	...	9	Sheridan	6 322	6 198	2 762	1.0	6 323	6 750	2 681	1.1	88.1	0.1	9.2	0.1	0.0	0.3
31 163	...	9	Sherman	1 466	3 318	2 972	2.3	1 466	3 718	2 938	2.5	98.5	0.1	0.2	0.2	0.0	0.4
31 165	...	9	Sioux	5 352	1 475	3 094	0.3	5 353	1 549	3 093	0.3	97.6	0.0	0.1	0.2	0.0	1.2
31 167	...	9	Stanton	1 113	6 455	2 742	5.8	1 113	6 244	2 730	5.6	96.7	0.4	0.5	0.1	0.0	1.4
31 169	...	9	Thayer	1 488	6 055	2 775	4.1	1 488	6 635	2 691	4.5	98.7	0.0	0.3	0.1	0.0	0.3
31 171	...	9	Thomas	1 846	729	3 130	0.4	1 846	851	3 121	0.5	99.5	0.0	0.3	0.0	0.0	0.0
31 173	...	8	Thurston	1 020	7 171	2 670	7.0	1 020	6 936	2 666	6.8	45.8	0.2	52.0	0.1	0.0	0.8
31 175	...	9	Valley	1 471	4 647	2 870	3.2	1 471	5 169	2 827	3.5	98.1	0.2	0.3	0.1	0.1	0.8
31 177	5920	2	Washington	1 011	18 780	1 856	18.6	1 011	16 607	1 877	16.4	98.1	0.3	0.2	0.3	0.1	0.3
31 179	...	7	Wayne	1 148	9 851	2 461	8.6	1 149	9 364	2 441	8.1	96.8	0.9	0.3	0.3	0.0	0.9
31 181	...	9	Webster	1 489	4 061	2 916	2.7	1 489	4 279	2 889	2.9	98.1	0.1	0.3	0.5	0.1	0.2
31 183	...	9	Wheeler	1 490	886	3 117	0.6	1 490	948	3 115	0.6	99.1	0.0	0.2	0.0	0.0	0.6
31 185	...	7	York	1 491	14 598	2 112	9.8	1 491	14 428	2 024	9.7	96.8	1.0	0.3	0.5	0.1	0.6
32 000	...		NEVADA	284 448	1 998 257	X	7.0	284 397	1 201 675	X	4.2	75.2	6.8	1.3	4.5	0.4	8.0
32 001	...	6	Churchill	12 766	23 982	1 594	1.9	12 767	17 938	1 792	1.4	84.2	1.6	4.8	2.7	0.2	3.2
32 003	4120	2	Clark	20 488	1 375 765	25	67.1	20 489	741 368	52	36.2	71.6	9.1	0.8	5.3	0.5	8.6
32 005	...	7	Douglas	1 839	41 259	1 072	22.4	1 839	27 637	1 366	15.0	91.9	0.3	1.7	1.3	0.2	2.5
32 007	...	5	Elko	44 493	45 291	993	1.0	44 500	33 463	1 178	0.8	82.0	0.6	5.3	0.7	0.1	8.5
32 009	...	9	Esmeralda	9 294	971	3 113	0.1	9 295	1 344	3 104	0.1	82.0	0.1	5.1	0.0	0.2	7.6
32 011	...	9	Eureka	10 815	1 651	3 087	0.2	10 816	1 547	3 094	0.1	89.3	0.4	1.6	0.8	0.1	4.4
32 013	...	7	Humboldt	24 988	16 106	2 015	0.6	24 989	12 844	2 152	0.5	83.2	0.5	4.0	0.6	0.1	8.5
32 015	...	7	Lander	14 228	5 794	2 804	0.4	14 229	6 266	2 728	0.4	84.4	0.2	4.0	0.3	0.0	8.7
32 017	...	8	Lincoln	27 541	4 165	2 902	0.2	27 544	3 775	2 932	0.1	91.5	1.8	1.8	0.3	0.0	2.7
32 019	...	6	Lyon	5 164	34 501	1 264	6.7	5 164	20 001	1 678	3.9	88.6	0.7	2.4	0.6	0.1	4.6
32 021	...	7	Mineral	9 729	5 071	2 847	0.5	9 730	6 475	2 712	0.7	73.9	4.8	15.4	0.8	0.1	2.7
32 023	4120	2	Nye	47 000	32 485	1 333	0.7	47 001	17 781	1 799	0.4	89.6	1.2	2.0	0.8	0.3	3.0
32 027	...	9	Pershing	15 635	6 693	2 717	0.4	15 564	4 336	2 888	0.3	77.7	5.3	3.4	0.6	0.2	9.4
32 029	...	8	Storey	682	3 399	2 963	5.0	682	2 526	3 021	3.7	93.0	0.3	1.4	1.0	0.1	1.7
32 031	6720	2	Washoe	16 426	339 486	172	20.7	16 427	254 667	196	15.5	80.4	2.1	1.8	4.3	0.5	7.7
32 033	...	7	White Pine	22 989	9 181	2 515	0.4	22 990	9 264	2 447	0.4	86.4	4.1	3.3	0.8	0.2	3.1
32 510	...	4	Carson City city	371	52 457	891	141.4	372	40 443	988	108.7	85.3	1.8	2.4	1.8	0.1	6.5
33 000	...		NEW HAMPSHIRE	23 227	1 235 786	X	53.2	23 231	1 109 252	X	47.7	96.0	0.7	0.2	1.3	0.0	0.6
33 001	...	6	Belknap	1 039	56 325	839	54.2	1 039	49 216	853	47.4	97.6	0.3	0.3	0.6	0.0	0.2
33 003	...	6	Carroll	2 419	43 666	1 023	18.1	2 419	35 410	1 118	14.6	98.2	0.2	0.3	0.4	0.0	0.2
33 005	...	4	Cheshire	1 832	73 825	678	40.3	1 832	70 121	631	38.3	97.8	0.4	0.3	0.5	0.0	0.2
33 007	...	7	Coos	4 663	33 111	1 315	7.1	4 664	34 828	1 139	7.5	98.1	0.1	0.3	0.4	0.0	0.2
33 009	...	5	Grafton	4 438	81 743	635	18.4	4 438	74 929	601	16.9	95.8	0.5	0.3	1.7	0.0	0.3
33 011	1123	2	Hillsborough	2 270	380 841	153	167.8	2 270	335 838	152	147.9	93.9	1.3	0.2	2.0	0.0	1.3
33 013	...	4	Merrimack	2 420	136 225	396	56.3	2 420	120 240	385	49.7	97.1	0.5	0.2	0.9	0.0	0.2
33 015	1123	2	Rockingham	1 800	277 359	204	154.1	1 801	245 845	204	136.5	96.8	0.6	0.2	1.1	0.0	0.4
33 017	1123	2	Strafford	955	112 233	479	117.5	955	104 233	442	109.1	96.3	0.6	0.2	1.4	0.0	0.3
33 019	...	7	Sullivan	1 392	40 458	1 105	29.1	1 392	38 592	1 037	27.7	98.0	0.2	0.3	0.4	0.0	0.1
34 000	...		NEW JERSEY	19 211	8 414 350	X	438.0	19 215	7 747 750	X	403.2	72.6	13.6	0.2	5.7	0.0	5.4
34 001	0560	2	Atlantic	1 453	252 552	223	173.8	1 453	224 327	222	154.4	68.4	17.6	0.3	5.1	0.0	6.1
34 003	0875	0	Bergen	607	884 118	46	1 456.5	607	825 380	44	1 359.8	78.4	5.3	0.2	10.7	0.0	3.2
34 005	6160	0	Burlington	2 084	423 394	142	203.2	2 084	395 066	127	189.6	78.4	15.1	0.2	2.7	0.0	1.5
34 007	6160	0	Camden	576	508 932	110	883.6	576	502 824	96	873.0	70.9	18.1	0.3	3.7	0.0	5.1
34 009	0560	2	Cape May	661	102 326	519	154.8	661	95 089	488	143.9	91.6	5.1	0.2	0.6	0.0	1.3
34 011	8760	3	Cumberland	1 267	146 438	373	115.6	1 267	138 053	343	109.0	65.9	20.2	1.0	1.0	0.1	9.1
34 013	5640	0	Essex	327	793 633	59	2 427.0	327	777 964	50	2 379.1	44.5	41.2	0.2	3.7	0.1	6.9
34 015	6160	0	Gloucester	841	254 673	221	302.8	841	230 082	213	273.6	87.1	9.1	0.2	1.5	0.0	0.9
34 017	3640	0	Hudson	121	608 975	88	5 032.9	121	553 099	85	4 571.1	55.6	13.5	0.4	9.4	0.1	15.5
34 019	5015	1	Hunterdon	1 114	121 989	445	109.5	1 114	107 852	427	96.8	93.3	2.2	0.1	1.9	0.0	0.8

[1]MSA = Metropolitan Statistical Area. PMSA = Primary MSA. NECMA = New England County Metropolitan Area. See Appendix A for explanation of these concepts. See Appendix B for list of metropolitan areas identified by type, with component counties.
[2]County typology code from the Economic Research Service of USDA. See Appendix A for definition.
[3]Dry land or land partially or temporarily covered by water.

Table B. States and Counties

	Population and population characteristics, 2000 (cont'd)								Population and population characteristics, 1990				
	Race (percent) (cont'd)								Race (percent)				
	Race alone or in combination												
STATE County	Two or more races	White	Black	American Indian or Alaska Native	Asian	Native Hawaiian and other Pacific Islander	Some other race	Hispanic[1]	White	Black or African American	American Indian or Alaska Native	Asian and Pacific Islander	Hispanic[1]
	15	16	17	18	19	20	21	22	23	24	25	26	27
NEBRASKA—Cont'd													
Platte	1.2	95.4	0.5	0.7	0.5	0.1	4.1	6.5	99.0	0.2	0.2	0.2	0.9
Polk	0.4	99.3	0.1	0.4	0.3	0.0	0.3	1.1	99.2	0.0	0.2	0.2	0.5
Red Willow	0.8	98.3	0.3	0.8	0.2	0.0	1.2	2.5	98.8	0.1	0.2	0.2	1.8
Richardson	1.5	97.1	0.4	3.3	0.2	0.0	0.5	1.0	98.0	0.1	1.8	0.1	0.4
Rock	0.3	99.2	0.0	0.7	0.3	0.0	0.1	0.5	99.9	0.0	0.0	0.0	0.3
Saline	1.1	94.1	0.6	0.6	1.9	0.1	3.9	6.6	98.6	0.1	0.2	0.9	0.6
Sarpy	2.2	91.1	5.1	0.9	2.7	0.2	2.4	4.4	91.4	5.2	0.4	1.9	3.3
Saunders	0.5	99.0	0.2	0.6	0.3	0.0	0.4	1.0	99.3	0.1	0.3	0.2	0.6
Scotts Bluff	1.6	89.0	0.4	2.4	0.7	0.1	9.0	17.2	91.1	0.2	1.8	0.5	14.5
Seward	0.7	98.8	0.4	0.5	0.4	0.1	0.5	1.1	99.2	0.1	0.2	0.2	0.5
Sheridan	2.1	90.0	0.3	10.7	0.3	0.0	0.6	1.5	91.9	0.0	7.8	0.2	1.0
Sherman	0.5	98.9	0.1	0.6	0.4	0.1	0.6	1.0	99.5	0.0	0.1	0.3	0.2
Sioux	0.9	98.5	0.0	0.5	0.3	0.0	1.6	2.3	97.5	0.0	0.1	0.1	2.8
Stanton	0.9	97.6	0.6	0.9	0.2	0.0	1.6	2.3	98.8	0.4	0.6	0.1	0.4
Thayer	0.6	99.3	0.1	0.5	0.2	0.0	0.4	1.0	99.4	0.1	0.3	0.1	0.9
Thomas	0.3	99.7	0.0	0.4	0.0	0.0	0.1	0.8	99.5	0.0	0.5	0.0	1.3
Thurston	1.2	46.8	0.4	53.2	0.1	0.0	0.9	2.4	55.7	0.1	43.9	0.1	0.9
Valley	0.4	98.6	0.3	0.4	0.2	0.1	0.9	1.6	99.2	0.1	0.2	0.2	0.3
Washington	0.6	98.7	0.5	0.5	0.4	0.1	0.4	1.1	98.8	0.5	0.2	0.2	0.6
Wayne	0.7	97.4	1.2	0.6	0.6	0.1	0.2	0.5	99.5	0.0	0.1	0.3	0.2
Webster	0.7	98.8	0.2	0.7	0.6	0.2	0.7	0.6	99.7	0.0	0.0	0.3	0.0
Wheeler	0.1	99.2	0.0	0.2	0.0	0.0	0.7	0.6	98.5	0.0	0.0	0.3	0.8
York	0.8	97.5	1.2	0.7	0.6	0.1	0.8	1.4	98.5	0.6	0.3	0.3	0.8
NEVADA	3.8	78.4	7.5	2.1	5.6	0.8	9.7	19.7	84.3	6.6	1.6	3.2	10.4
Churchill	3.3	87.1	1.9	6.0	3.7	0.5	4.2	8.7	89.4	1.1	5.0	2.6	5.6
Clark	4.2	75.0	10.0	1.5	6.6	0.9	10.5	22.0	81.3	9.5	0.9	3.5	11.2
Douglas	2.2	93.9	0.5	2.5	1.9	0.4	3.2	7.4	94.5	0.3	2.1	1.3	6.0
Elko	2.8	84.6	0.8	6.3	1.0	0.2	10.1	19.7	86.4	0.8	6.3	0.8	12.9
Esmeralda	4.9	86.8	0.1	8.3	0.0	0.2	9.5	10.2	87.1	0.5	5.5	0.6	9.3
Eureka	3.5	92.7	0.5	4.1	0.8	0.1	5.2	9.6	93.2	0.3	2.7	0.7	8.9
Humboldt	3.1	86.1	0.7	5.1	0.9	0.1	10.4	18.9	83.8	0.6	5.6	0.5	18.2
Lander	2.3	86.7	0.4	4.8	0.4	0.1	10.0	18.5	90.4	0.1	4.7	0.3	12.6
Lincoln	1.9	93.3	2.1	2.6	0.6	0.2	3.5	5.3	94.2	2.1	1.5	0.4	4.1
Lyon	2.9	91.4	1.0	3.7	1.1	0.3	5.7	11.0	91.9	0.3	3.1	0.8	7.6
Mineral	2.4	76.1	5.3	16.5	1.0	0.1	3.4	8.4	79.4	5.4	11.6	1.1	8.4
Nye	3.1	92.5	1.5	3.4	1.2	0.5	4.2	8.4	92.2	1.6	2.8	0.9	7.0
Pershing	3.3	80.7	5.6	4.9	0.9	0.5	11.0	19.3	86.8	0.3	4.7	0.6	15.3
Storey	2.4	95.3	0.4	2.8	1.4	0.4	2.3	5.1	94.6	0.3	2.0	1.1	3.8
Washoe	3.3	83.2	2.6	2.7	5.2	0.7	9.1	16.6	88.4	2.2	1.9	3.9	9.0
White Pine	2.1	88.1	4.2	4.3	1.1	0.4	4.1	11.0	91.3	2.0	3.2	0.4	9.2
Carson City city	2.1	87.2	2.1	3.3	2.2	0.3	7.2	14.2	90.7	1.7	2.7	1.4	7.7
NEW HAMPSHIRE	1.1	97.0	1.0	0.6	1.6	0.1	0.9	1.7	98.0	0.6	0.2	0.8	1.0
Belknap	1.1	98.6	0.4	0.9	0.7	0.1	0.4	0.7	99.1	0.1	0.2	0.4	0.5
Carroll	0.8	99.0	0.3	0.7	0.5	0.0	0.3	0.5	99.3	0.2	0.2	0.3	0.4
Cheshire	0.9	98.6	0.6	0.7	0.7	0.1	0.3	0.7	99.0	0.3	0.2	0.4	0.5
Coos	1.0	99.0	0.2	0.8	0.5	0.0	0.4	0.6	99.2	0.1	0.2	0.4	0.8
Grafton	1.3	96.9	0.8	0.9	2.1	0.1	0.6	1.1	98.0	0.5	0.2	1.1	0.8
Hillsborough	1.2	95.0	1.6	0.6	2.3	0.1	1.7	3.2	97.2	0.9	0.2	1.1	1.7
Merrimack	1.0	98.1	0.8	0.7	1.1	0.0	0.4	1.0	98.8	0.4	0.2	0.5	0.6
Rockingham	0.9	97.6	0.8	0.5	1.4	0.1	0.6	1.2	97.7	0.9	0.2	0.9	1.0
Strafford	1.1	97.3	0.9	0.6	1.7	0.1	0.5	1.0	98.2	0.6	0.2	0.9	0.8
Sullivan	0.9	98.9	0.4	0.9	0.5	0.0	0.3	0.5	99.0	0.2	0.3	0.4	0.4
NEW JERSEY	2.5	74.4	14.4	0.6	6.2	0.1	6.9	13.3	79.3	13.4	0.2	3.5	9.6
Atlantic	2.6	70.2	18.6	0.8	5.6	0.1	7.5	12.2	76.7	17.4	0.3	2.1	7.2
Bergen	2.3	80.2	5.8	0.4	11.3	0.1	4.6	10.3	87.0	4.9	0.1	6.6	6.0
Burlington	2.1	80.0	16.2	0.7	3.3	0.1	2.1	4.2	82.2	14.3	0.2	2.1	3.2
Camden	1.9	72.2	19.0	0.7	4.2	0.1	6.0	9.7	76.6	16.2	0.2	2.3	7.2
Cape May	1.2	92.5	5.6	0.5	0.8	0.1	1.7	3.3	92.6	5.6	0.2	0.6	2.0
Cumberland	2.9	67.9	21.5	1.7	1.2	0.2	10.6	19.0	73.5	16.9	0.9	0.8	13.3
Essex	3.4	46.4	42.9	0.6	4.2	0.2	9.3	15.4	51.1	40.6	0.2	2.7	12.6
Gloucester	1.3	88.1	9.7	0.5	1.8	0.1	1.2	2.6	89.3	8.7	0.2	1.2	1.8
Hudson	5.6	59.9	14.7	0.8	10.3	0.2	19.9	39.8	68.8	14.4	0.2	6.6	33.2
Hunterdon	1.0	94.8	2.5	0.4	2.2	0.1	1.1	2.8	96.3	2.1	0.1	1.3	1.6

[1] Hispanic persons may be of any race.

Table B. States and Counties

STATE County	Population and population characteristics, 2000 Age (percent)										
	Under 5 years	5 to 17 years	18 to 24 years	25 to 34 years	35 to 44 years	45 to 54 years	55 to 64 years	65 to 74 years	75 years and over	Median age (years)	Percent Female
	28	29	30	31	32	33	34	35	36	37	38
NEBRASKA—Cont'd											
Platte	7.3	21.8	8.1	11.8	15.7	13.1	8.4	6.9	7.0	35.8	50.4
Polk	5.8	19.4	6.0	10.0	14.3	14.0	9.2	9.2	12.2	41.6	49.9
Red Willow	6.2	18.6	8.8	9.9	14.7	12.8	9.8	9.4	9.6	39.9	51.6
Richardson	5.2	20.3	5.9	8.9	14.8	12.9	10.4	9.5	12.0	41.4	51.7
Rock	5.5	17.5	6.5	8.3	15.3	14.7	9.9	10.6	11.7	43.5	52.0
Saline	6.2	18.9	12.3	10.7	14.3	12.2	8.2	7.4	9.8	36.4	50.6
Sarpy	8.2	22.2	9.4	15.9	17.8	12.6	7.1	4.1	2.5	31.5	50.3
Saunders	6.4	21.5	6.3	10.8	16.8	13.7	9.2	8.0	7.3	38.0	50.2
Scotts Bluff	6.5	19.4	8.4	11.1	14.3	13.8	9.2	8.7	8.5	38.4	52.3
Seward	5.6	19.1	14.3	10.0	14.6	12.7	8.5	7.1	8.1	35.7	49.2
Sheridan	5.8	19.8	6.2	9.4	13.5	13.8	9.8	9.9	11.7	42.0	51.0
Sherman	5.2	19.3	4.5	9.9	13.8	13.4	10.7	11.3	11.8	43.3	50.8
Sioux	5.4	19.0	7.2	8.6	16.1	15.7	11.9	10.4	5.8	41.5	47.4
Stanton	6.7	23.1	7.6	11.3	16.1	12.8	9.0	6.7	6.8	35.9	50.4
Thayer	5.7	18.4	4.9	8.8	13.5	13.8	10.4	10.7	13.9	44.1	51.1
Thomas	5.9	17.7	4.4	10.3	13.6	17.4	10.4	9.9	10.4	44.2	50.1
Thurston	9.6	27.2	8.3	11.3	12.6	10.1	7.6	7.4	5.8	29.8	50.1
Valley	5.6	19.1	4.8	9.3	13.3	13.6	10.3	11.3	12.7	43.5	52.2
Washington	6.4	20.7	9.3	10.4	16.3	15.2	8.9	6.7	6.2	37.1	50.3
Wayne	5.3	16.3	25.4	9.1	12.1	10.8	7.2	6.9	6.8	27.9	52.0
Webster	5.2	18.4	4.6	8.3	14.6	13.2	11.4	10.6	13.7	44.2	51.9
Wheeler	7.8	21.3	6.4	7.7	14.2	15.0	10.7	10.0	6.8	40.4	51.0
York	5.6	19.7	9.0	10.4	15.0	13.7	9.3	8.2	9.2	38.8	52.2
NEVADA	7.3	18.3	9.0	15.3	16.1	13.5	9.5	6.6	4.4	35.0	49.1
Churchill	8.0	20.9	8.1	13.4	15.3	12.9	9.4	6.7	5.3	34.7	49.8
Clark	7.5	18.1	9.2	16.2	16.0	12.9	9.4	6.6	4.1	34.4	49.1
Douglas	5.2	18.9	5.5	9.6	16.8	16.8	12.1	9.3	5.9	41.7	49.5
Elko	8.5	24.0	8.8	14.5	17.1	13.5	7.8	3.5	2.4	31.2	47.9
Esmeralda	4.3	16.2	6.0	9.6	13.8	16.1	16.9	10.3	6.9	45.1	44.7
Eureka	5.9	21.9	5.2	11.3	17.3	14.5	11.4	8.1	4.3	38.3	48.4
Humboldt	8.0	23.4	7.5	13.3	17.8	14.2	8.1	4.4	3.1	33.4	47.6
Lander	7.5	24.7	6.8	12.3	16.7	15.1	9.9	4.1	2.8	34.1	48.7
Lincoln	6.3	23.8	6.0	9.1	12.8	12.9	13.0	9.0	7.2	38.8	48.1
Lyon	6.5	20.6	6.6	11.3	16.0	14.0	11.2	8.5	5.3	38.2	49.4
Mineral	5.3	19.1	6.2	9.2	13.2	14.9	12.2	11.0	8.8	42.9	49.6
Nye	6.0	17.8	5.4	9.5	14.5	14.1	14.4	12.2	6.2	42.9	48.7
Pershing	6.5	19.2	8.5	17.0	19.0	12.5	9.5	4.3	3.5	34.4	38.6
Storey	4.4	15.3	4.7	8.6	18.2	20.6	15.1	8.4	4.7	44.5	48.2
Washoe	7.0	17.9	9.8	14.5	16.5	14.7	9.1	6.0	4.6	35.6	49.3
White Pine	6.0	18.2	7.6	13.8	16.1	14.9	9.9	7.4	6.1	37.7	43.8
Carson City city	6.3	17.1	7.9	12.9	16.0	14.7	10.2	7.8	7.1	38.7	48.3
NEW HAMPSHIRE	6.1	18.9	8.4	13.0	17.9	14.9	8.9	6.3	5.6	37.1	50.8
Belknap	5.3	18.3	6.7	11.3	16.8	16.0	10.5	8.0	7.1	40.1	50.7
Carroll	4.8	17.8	5.3	10.2	16.3	16.1	11.6	9.9	7.9	42.5	50.9
Cheshire	5.2	18.1	11.7	11.1	15.9	14.9	9.4	7.2	6.5	37.6	51.3
Coos	5.1	17.8	6.3	10.9	15.8	15.1	10.6	9.4	9.0	41.5	51.1
Grafton	5.2	16.7	13.5	11.9	15.1	14.8	9.4	7.0	6.4	37.0	50.8
Hillsborough	6.8	19.6	7.7	14.3	18.4	14.4	8.2	5.5	5.1	35.9	50.7
Merrimack	6.0	19.0	8.1	12.4	18.2	15.3	8.7	6.3	6.1	37.7	50.8
Rockingham	6.5	19.9	6.2	13.1	19.7	15.6	8.8	5.6	4.5	37.2	50.7
Strafford	5.9	17.7	13.6	13.6	17.0	13.1	7.8	6.0	5.2	34.4	51.5
Sullivan	5.6	18.3	6.4	11.9	16.2	15.6	10.3	8.5	7.3	40.0	50.7
NEW JERSEY	6.7	18.1	8.0	14.1	17.1	13.8	9.0	6.8	6.4	36.7	51.5
Atlantic	6.5	18.8	8.1	13.3	17.3	13.4	9.0	7.2	6.4	37.0	51.7
Bergen	6.3	16.7	6.6	13.3	17.3	14.6	9.9	7.8	7.5	39.1	51.9
Burlington	6.4	18.7	7.5	13.6	17.9	14.2	9.1	6.9	5.7	37.1	50.5
Camden	6.8	20.0	8.1	13.9	16.7	13.6	8.5	6.5	6.1	35.8	51.7
Cape May	5.1	17.2	6.4	10.2	15.3	14.0	11.5	10.4	9.8	42.3	51.9
Cumberland	6.3	19.1	8.5	15.1	16.1	13.2	8.7	6.6	6.4	35.6	49.0
Essex	7.3	18.8	9.4	15.0	16.1	13.0	8.6	6.2	5.7	34.7	52.4
Gloucester	6.6	19.8	8.9	12.8	17.6	14.1	8.5	6.3	5.3	36.1	51.6
Hudson	6.4	16.2	10.4	19.6	16.0	11.9	8.2	6.0	5.3	33.6	50.9
Hunterdon	6.6	19.1	5.8	11.4	19.9	17.3	9.8	5.6	4.5	38.8	50.6

Table B. States and Counties

STATE County	Age (percent) Under 5 years	5 to 17 years	18 to 24 years	25 to 34 years	35 to 44 years	45 to 54 years	55 to 64 years	65 to 74 years	75 years and over	Percent Female	Total persons 2000	1990	1980	1990–2000	1980–1990
	39	40	41	42	43	44	45	46	47	48	49	50	51	52	53
NEBRASKA—Cont'd															
Platte	8.6	22.4	7.9	15.9	14.1	9.3	8.5	7.3	6.0	50.9	31 662	29 820	28 852	6.2	3.4
Polk	6.1	20.6	5.0	11.9	13.5	9.7	10.3	10.9	12.1	50.9	5 639	5 655	6 320	-0.3	-10.3
Red Willow	7.2	20.0	8.3	14.5	13.2	9.3	10.3	9.1	8.1	52.5	11 448	11 705	12 615	-2.2	-7.2
Richardson	7.0	17.9	6.1	13.0	12.2	10.0	10.0	11.8	12.0	52.0	9 531	9 937	11 315	-4.1	-12.2
Rock	7.1	21.7	5.2	13.1	14.6	9.5	10.6	8.6	9.6	50.7	1 756	2 019	2 383	-13.0	-15.3
Saline	6.5	18.4	10.8	13.3	12.7	8.8	9.0	9.6	10.9	51.7	13 843	12 715	13 131	8.9	-3.2
Sarpy	9.3	22.9	10.4	20.1	17.1	9.6	5.8	3.0	1.8	49.6	122 595	102 583	86 015	19.5	19.3
Saunders	7.5	21.1	6.5	14.8	14.1	10.0	10.1	7.9	8.0	49.9	19 830	18 285	18 716	8.4	-2.3
Scotts Bluff	7.1	20.9	7.8	14.1	14.6	9.6	9.9	8.7	7.4	52.0	36 951	36 025	38 344	2.6	-6.0
Seward	6.9	19.7	12.9	13.3	13.4	9.2	8.6	8.0	7.9	49.8	16 496	15 450	15 789	6.8	-2.1
Sheridan	6.0	21.9	5.9	11.8	13.6	9.3	10.8	10.9	9.9	51.3	6 198	6 750	7 544	-8.2	-10.5
Sherman	6.5	21.7	6.2	11.0	12.3	10.0	11.0	11.0	10.3	49.3	3 318	3 718	4 226	-10.8	-12.0
Sioux	6.5	19.8	5.2	13.0	14.2	12.9	12.2	9.0	7.2	49.8	1 475	1 549	1 845	-4.8	-16.0
Stanton	9.2	23.9	6.6	16.3	13.4	10.0	8.5	6.0	6.2	50.3	6 455	6 244	6 549	3.4	-4.7
Thayer	5.8	18.9	5.2	11.6	12.3	9.7	10.4	12.4	13.6	51.6	6 055	6 635	7 582	-8.7	-12.5
Thomas	6.1	25.5	4.9	11.9	15.5	10.7	10.6	8.6	6.2	51.7	729	851	973	-14.3	-12.5
Thurston	10.9	24.2	8.3	13.7	11.2	8.8	9.2	7.7	6.0	50.6	7 171	6 936	7 186	3.4	-3.5
Valley	6.2	19.7	5.6	11.9	13.0	9.9	10.5	11.0	12.0	52.0	4 647	5 169	5 633	-10.1	-8.2
Washington	6.4	21.0	8.8	14.1	16.0	10.9	9.2	7.0	6.6	51.0	18 780	16 607	15 508	13.1	7.1
Wayne	6.9	17.2	21.2	13.4	11.0	7.9	8.4	6.7	7.3	51.7	9 851	9 364	9 858	5.2	-5.0
Webster	6.1	17.6	4.5	11.9	11.3	10.2	11.7	12.9	13.8	51.8	4 061	4 279	4 858	-5.1	-11.9
Wheeler	9.4	23.3	4.6	15.4	12.1	9.9	10.4	7.9	6.9	49.8	886	948	1 060	-6.5	-10.6
York	7.9	19.5	8.3	14.5	14.0	9.7	9.1	8.7	8.3	51.7	14 598	14 428	14 798	1.2	-2.5
NEVADA	7.7	17.0	9.9	18.5	16.0	11.3	9.0	7.1	3.5	49.1	1 998 257	1 201 675	800 508	66.3	50.1
Churchill	8.4	19.8	9.0	16.0	15.1	10.1	8.9	7.9	4.9	49.6	23 982	17 938	13 917	33.7	28.9
Clark	7.7	16.8	10.2	18.8	15.6	11.3	9.1	7.2	3.3	49.3	1 375 765	741 368	463 087	85.6	60.1
Douglas	7.4	18.2	6.2	15.9	18.9	11.7	9.6	8.6	3.5	49.7	41 259	27 637	19 421	49.3	42.3
Elko	9.6	22.6	9.6	19.4	16.2	10.6	6.0	3.7	2.4	46.8	45 291	33 463	17 269	35.3	93.8
Esmeralda	6.3	17.7	8.0	16.8	16.7	13.2	10.3	7.2	3.8	44.3	971	1 344	777	-27.8	73.0
Eureka	8.8	18.7	7.7	17.7	16.1	13.1	9.7	5.8	2.5	45.4	1 651	1 547	1 198	6.7	29.1
Humboldt	8.6	21.8	9.4	19.1	16.1	10.4	7.4	4.9	2.4	46.3	16 106	12 844	9 449	25.4	35.9
Lander	9.8	24.3	9.4	18.3	15.8	10.7	5.7	3.8	2.1	48.1	5 794	6 266	4 076	-7.5	53.7
Lincoln	8.1	25.9	5.6	12.6	11.7	10.6	9.8	9.4	6.5	48.0	4 165	3 775	3 732	10.3	1.2
Lyon	7.9	19.4	6.2	14.3	14.7	11.6	10.8	10.3	4.8	49.0	34 501	20 001	13 594	72.5	47.1
Mineral	8.8	20.2	7.7	15.1	13.8	10.4	10.9	8.6	4.5	49.0	5 071	6 475	6 217	-21.7	4.1
Nye	7.3	17.6	6.7	16.2	14.5	13.4	12.1	9.0	3.3	46.6	32 485	17 781	9 048	82.7	96.5
Pershing	9.9	20.5	8.7	16.8	12.8	10.8	8.8	7.1	4.5	48.7	6 693	4 336	3 408	54.4	27.2
Storey	6.6	16.6	6.1	15.5	19.3	15.5	10.1	6.4	4.0	50.5	3 399	2 526	1 503	34.6	68.1
Washoe	7.4	15.8	10.5	19.0	17.3	11.2	8.5	6.7	3.6	49.3	339 486	254 667	193 623	33.3	31.5
White Pine	7.6	20.1	7.8	16.5	15.5	11.2	9.5	7.3	4.5	45.5	9 181	9 264	8 167	-0.9	13.4
Carson City city	6.7	15.6	8.5	16.5	16.5	11.4	9.7	9.6	5.4	48.9	52 457	40 443	32 022	29.7	26.3
NEW HAMPSHIRE	7.6	17.5	10.6	18.5	16.5	10.1	8.0	6.4	4.8	51.0	1 235 786	1 109 252	920 610	11.4	20.5
Belknap	7.0	18.6	7.9	16.5	16.6	10.5	9.2	8.1	5.6	51.1	56 325	49 216	42 884	14.4	14.8
Carroll	6.9	17.1	6.7	16.0	16.8	10.3	10.2	9.5	6.6	51.3	43 666	35 410	27 931	23.3	26.8
Cheshire	7.1	17.3	12.7	15.6	15.5	10.2	8.5	7.4	5.7	51.7	73 825	70 121	62 116	5.3	12.9
Coos	6.4	18.2	8.2	15.2	14.7	10.3	10.5	9.4	7.1	51.5	33 111	34 828	35 147	-4.9	-0.9
Grafton	6.6	16.4	15.8	15.8	15.4	9.5	8.2	6.9	5.5	50.7	81 743	74 929	65 806	9.1	13.9
Hillsborough	8.1	17.6	10.2	19.7	16.5	10.1	7.5	5.9	4.4	51.1	380 841	335 838	276 608	13.4	21.4
Merrimack	7.5	17.8	9.3	18.4	16.9	10.0	8.0	6.4	5.7	51.0	136 225	120 240	98 302	13.3	22.3
Rockingham	8.1	17.9	9.0	20.0	17.9	10.6	7.2	5.4	3.8	50.4	277 359	245 845	190 345	12.8	29.2
Strafford	7.4	16.1	16.2	18.6	14.3	9.1	7.7	6.2	4.5	51.6	112 233	104 233	85 408	7.7	22.0
Sullivan	7.4	18.2	8.3	15.6	16.1	10.4	9.3	8.6	6.1	51.0	40 458	38 592	36 063	4.8	7.0
NEW JERSEY	6.9	16.4	10.1	17.6	15.5	10.9	9.3	7.9	5.5	51.7	8 414 350	7 747 750	7 365 011	8.6	5.0
Atlantic	7.2	15.8	10.4	18.5	14.6	9.8	9.1	8.3	6.2	51.9	252 552	224 327	194 119	12.6	15.6
Bergen	5.9	14.5	9.0	16.5	15.7	12.1	11.1	9.1	6.2	52.0	884 118	825 380	845 385	7.1	-2.4
Burlington	7.2	17.7	10.7	18.1	15.8	10.9	9.0	6.7	4.0	50.6	423 394	395 066	362 542	7.2	9.0
Camden	7.9	18.6	9.8	17.8	15.1	10.1	8.6	7.4	4.8	51.9	508 932	502 824	471 650	1.2	6.6
Cape May	6.7	15.4	8.6	15.5	13.5	9.5	10.7	11.6	8.5	52.0	102 326	95 089	82 266	7.6	15.6
Cumberland	7.3	18.7	10.2	16.6	14.5	10.3	8.9	7.9	5.6	51.2	146 438	138 053	132 866	6.1	3.9
Essex	7.0	17.2	10.9	17.6	15.0	10.6	9.0	7.3	5.4	52.7	793 633	777 964	851 304	2.0	-8.6
Gloucester	7.6	19.2	10.3	17.7	16.0	10.2	8.4	6.8	4.0	51.3	254 673	230 082	199 917	10.7	15.1
Hudson	6.7	15.5	11.1	20.4	14.4	10.1	9.1	7.5	5.2	51.5	608 975	553 099	556 972	10.1	-0.7
Hunterdon	7.1	17.0	8.5	17.1	19.1	13.3	8.4	5.6	3.9	50.1	121 989	107 852	87 361	13.1	23.4

Table B. States and Counties

STATE County	Total population	In households (percent) Total in house-holds	House-holder	Spouse	Child Total	Child Own child under 18 years	Other relatives Total	Other relatives Under 18 years	Nonrelatives Total	Unmar-ried partner	In group quarters (percent) Total in group quarters	Institutionalized population Correc-tional institu-tions	Nurs-ing homes	Other institu-tions	Noninstitutionalized population Col-lege dormi-tories	Mili-tary quar-ters	Other
	54	55	56	57	58	59	60	61	62	63	64	65	66	67	68	69	70
NEBRASKA—Cont'd																	
Platte	31 662	99.0	38.1	22.6	32.6	27.8	2.2	0.7	3.5	1.5	1.0	0.1	0.6	0.0	0.3	0.0	0.0
Polk	5 639	97.2	40.1	25.2	28.2	24.1	1.3	0.5	2.4	1.1	2.8	0.1	2.8	0.0	0.0	0.0	0.0
Red Willow	11 448	97.7	41.1	23.6	28.4	24.0	1.5	0.6	3.0	1.5	2.3	0.0	1.2	0.0	0.7	0.0	0.4
Richardson	9 531	97.9	41.9	22.4	28.1	23.9	2.0	0.8	3.5	1.8	2.1	0.1	2.0	0.0	0.0	0.0	0.0
Rock	1 756	98.3	43.5	24.9	26.5	22.3	1.1	0.5	2.2	1.3	1.7	0.0	1.7	0.0	0.0	0.0	0.0
Saline	13 843	93.6	37.5	21.2	28.2	23.8	2.4	0.9	4.3	1.6	6.4	0.0	1.2	0.6	4.4	0.0	0.1
Sarpy	122 595	98.9	35.4	22.6	34.7	28.9	2.5	1.0	3.7	1.5	1.1	0.1	0.3	0.1	0.0	0.5	0.1
Saunders	19 830	98.7	37.8	23.7	32.1	26.5	2.0	0.8	3.1	1.4	1.3	0.1	1.1	0.0	0.0	0.0	0.1
Scotts Bluff	36 951	98.2	40.3	21.8	29.2	23.7	3.2	1.6	3.8	1.9	1.8	0.1	1.1	0.1	0.2	0.0	0.2
Seward	16 496	92.2	36.5	22.4	28.3	23.8	1.5	0.6	3.5	1.1	7.8	0.1	1.4	0.1	6.0	0.0	0.2
Sheridan	6 198	97.8	41.1	23.3	28.5	24.1	2.4	1.1	2.4	1.1	2.2	0.3	1.7	0.1	0.0	0.0	0.1
Sherman	3 318	98.3	42.0	24.9	27.6	23.2	1.4	0.6	2.4	1.3	1.7	0.0	1.7	0.0	0.0	0.0	0.0
Sioux	1 475	100.0	41.0	26.8	27.1	22.4	2.2	0.9	2.8	1.0	0.0	0.0	0.0	0.0	0.0	0.0	0.0
Stanton	6 455	98.1	35.6	24.0	33.7	28.3	2.0	0.9	2.8	1.2	1.9	0.0	1.8	0.0	0.0	0.0	0.0
Thayer	6 055	97.0	42.0	24.7	26.8	23.2	1.5	0.5	2.0	1.1	3.0	0.0	3.0	0.0	0.0	0.0	0.0
Thomas	729	100.0	44.6	27.0	26.3	23.5	1.1	0.1	1.0	0.7	0.0	0.0	0.0	0.0	0.0	0.0	0.0
Thurston	7 171	98.6	31.4	15.9	36.5	28.9	11.1	7.4	3.7	2.0	1.4	0.2	0.8	0.2	0.0	0.0	0.2
Valley	4 647	98.2	42.3	24.8	27.5	24.0	1.6	0.4	2.0	0.8	1.8	0.1	1.4	0.0	0.0	0.0	0.3
Washington	18 780	97.1	37.0	23.7	31.5	25.9	2.0	0.9	2.9	1.4	2.9	0.2	1.0	0.0	1.7	0.0	0.0
Wayne	9 851	87.6	34.9	19.6	24.2	20.8	1.4	0.5	7.5	1.1	12.4	0.0	0.6	0.0	10.9	0.0	1.0
Webster	4 061	96.0	42.1	24.3	26.3	22.6	1.6	0.7	1.8	0.9	4.0	0.0	2.9	0.0	0.0	0.0	1.0
Wheeler	886	100.0	39.7	24.9	31.8	27.8	1.0	0.5	2.5	1.5	0.0	0.0	0.0	0.0	0.0	0.0	0.0
York	14 598	95.0	39.2	23.6	28.0	24.1	1.2	0.4	3.0	1.1	5.0	1.4	1.2	0.3	1.9	0.0	0.2
NEVADA	1 998 257	98.3	37.6	18.7	28.0	22.6	6.7	2.2	7.4	2.7	1.7	0.8	0.2	0.1	0.1	0.1	0.4
Churchill	23 982	98.3	37.2	21.4	30.9	26.5	4.1	1.8	4.7	2.0	1.7	0.2	0.5	0.0	0.0	1.0	0.1
Clark	1 375 765	98.6	37.2	18.2	28.0	22.4	7.4	2.4	7.7	2.7	1.4	0.6	0.2	0.1	0.1	0.1	0.4
Douglas	41 259	99.4	39.8	24.1	26.5	22.1	3.7	1.3	5.4	2.3	0.6	0.2	0.2	0.0	0.0	0.0	0.2
Elko	45 291	98.2	34.5	20.5	34.5	29.8	4.1	1.7	4.6	2.2	1.8	0.9	0.2	0.4	0.0	0.0	0.3
Esmeralda	971	99.4	46.9	21.7	22.6	18.5	3.7	1.4	4.5	3.0	0.6	0.6	0.0	0.0	0.0	0.0	0.0
Eureka	1 651	99.5	40.3	22.8	30.5	26.7	2.2	0.7	3.7	1.6	0.5	0.5	0.0	0.0	0.0	0.0	0.0
Humboldt	16 106	98.6	35.6	21.2	33.3	28.9	4.1	1.8	4.4	1.9	1.4	1.0	0.2	0.0	0.0	0.0	0.2
Lander	5 794	98.5	36.1	21.6	33.7	30.1	3.2	1.3	3.9	1.8	1.5	0.0	0.3	0.1	0.0	0.0	1.0
Lincoln	4 165	91.6	37.0	20.8	28.4	24.2	2.9	1.8	2.5	0.9	8.4	4.4	0.4	3.7	0.0	0.0	0.0
Lyon	34 501	98.5	37.7	22.0	28.5	23.9	4.8	1.9	5.5	2.5	1.5	1.1	0.2	0.0	0.0	0.0	0.2
Mineral	5 071	97.9	43.3	19.6	24.5	20.2	4.5	2.3	6.0	3.5	2.1	0.4	0.5	0.0	0.0	0.0	1.3
Nye	32 485	99.3	41.0	23.1	25.3	21.2	4.6	1.9	5.4	2.3	0.7	0.5	0.1	0.0	0.0	0.0	0.1
Pershing	6 693	78.9	29.3	16.8	26.1	23.2	3.0	1.6	3.7	1.8	21.1	20.6	0.4	0.0	0.0	0.0	0.2
Storey	3 399	99.9	43.0	23.5	20.8	16.4	5.3	2.2	7.3	3.0	0.1	0.1	0.0	0.0	0.0	0.0	0.0
Washoe	339 486	98.4	36.3	18.6	27.3	22.3	5.7	1.9	7.9	2.9	1.6	0.3	0.3	0.1	0.4	0.0	0.5
White Pine	9 181	86.5	35.7	18.5	26.1	22.3	2.7	1.3	3.4	1.9	13.5	12.6	0.8	0.0	0.1	0.0	0.0
Carson City city	52 457	93.9	38.5	19.2	25.5	20.9	5.1	1.8	5.6	2.4	6.1	5.4	0.5	0.0	0.0	0.0	0.2
NEW HAMPSHIRE	1 235 786	97.1	38.4	21.2	28.8	23.4	3.0	1.0	5.6	2.6	2.9	0.3	0.8	0.1	1.4	0.0	0.3
Belknap	56 325	97.8	39.9	22.2	27.3	22.0	3.0	1.0	5.5	2.9	2.2	0.8	1.1	0.0	0.1	0.0	0.2
Carroll	43 666	98.7	42.0	23.2	25.5	20.9	2.7	1.0	5.2	2.6	1.3	0.1	0.7	0.0	0.0	0.0	0.5
Cheshire	73 825	94.5	38.3	20.5	26.7	21.6	2.8	1.0	6.2	2.7	5.5	0.1	0.9	0.1	4.0	0.0	0.4
Coos	33 111	98.0	42.2	22.1	25.9	21.1	2.5	0.8	5.4	3.1	2.0	0.0	1.4	0.0	0.0	0.0	0.5
Grafton	81 743	92.2	38.7	20.2	24.7	20.4	2.2	0.8	6.4	2.8	7.8	0.1	1.0	0.0	6.2	0.0	0.5
Hillsborough	380 841	98.0	37.9	20.9	30.4	24.7	3.3	1.0	5.5	2.6	2.0	0.2	0.7	0.1	0.7	0.0	0.4
Merrimack	136 225	95.4	38.1	20.9	28.3	23.2	2.8	1.0	5.3	2.8	4.6	1.3	1.0	0.4	1.6	0.0	0.3
Rockingham	277 359	99.1	37.7	22.4	31.0	24.9	3.3	1.1	4.8	2.3	0.9	0.1	0.5	0.0	0.0	0.0	0.2
Strafford	112 233	94.9	37.9	19.4	26.9	22.1	2.7	1.0	7.9	3.0	5.1	0.1	0.6	0.0	4.1	0.0	0.3
Sullivan	40 458	98.6	40.9	22.3	26.5	21.8	3.1	1.1	5.8	3.0	1.4	0.1	0.8	0.0	0.1	0.0	0.4
NEW JERSEY	8 414 350	97.7	36.4	19.5	30.8	22.3	6.5	2.0	4.6	1.8	2.3	0.6	0.6	0.1	0.5	0.0	0.4
Atlantic	252 552	97.4	37.6	17.5	29.4	22.1	7.1	2.6	5.9	2.6	2.6	0.4	0.6	0.0	0.8	0.0	0.7
Bergen	884 118	98.7	37.4	21.7	30.4	21.5	5.7	1.2	3.5	1.3	1.3	0.1	0.5	0.1	0.3	0.0	0.4
Burlington	423 394	96.7	36.5	21.0	30.7	22.8	4.7	1.9	3.7	1.8	3.3	2.0	0.7	0.1	0.0	0.3	0.3
Camden	508 932	98.0	36.0	18.2	32.5	23.6	6.3	2.6	4.5	2.2	2.0	0.7	0.6	0.2	0.1	0.0	0.5
Cape May	102 326	97.4	41.2	20.8	26.8	20.3	4.4	1.6	4.2	2.2	2.6	0.1	1.0	0.6	0.0	0.3	0.5
Cumberland	146 438	91.6	33.6	16.3	29.5	21.4	6.9	3.2	5.4	2.6	8.4	6.3	0.8	0.0	0.0	0.0	1.2
Essex	793 633	97.1	35.8	15.1	31.4	22.0	9.5	3.5	5.3	2.0	2.9	0.7	0.8	0.2	0.8	0.0	0.5
Gloucester	254 673	98.0	35.6	20.8	33.1	24.1	4.7	1.8	3.8	1.9	2.0	0.1	0.5	0.0	0.9	0.0	0.5
Hudson	608 975	98.4	37.9	15.1	29.0	19.6	9.5	2.6	7.0	2.3	1.6	0.4	0.4	0.1	0.3	0.0	0.3
Hunterdon	121 989	96.4	35.8	23.7	30.9	24.7	2.9	0.7	3.1	1.5	3.6	2.1	0.4	0.8	0.0	0.0	0.3

STATE County	Households by type, 2000												Households, 1990		
		Family households						Nonfamily households							
				Married couple		Female householder[1]			Householder living alone						Householder
	Total households	Total	With own children under 18 years	Total	With own children under 18 years	Total	With own children under 18 years	Total	Total	65 years and over	Average household size	Average family size	Total households	Female householder[1]	living alone
	71	72	73	74	75	76	77	78	79	80	81	82	83	84	85
NEBRASKA—Cont'd															
Platte	12 076	70.1	36.1	59.2	28.9	7.6	5.4	29.9	25.9	11.4	2.59	3.14	10 954	6.1	24.7
Polk	2 259	69.5	29.9	62.9	26.0	4.1	2.5	30.5	27.6	15.4	2.43	2.07	2 223	4 7	27.1
Red Willow	4 710	67.7	30.2	57.5	23.6	7.2	4.8	32.3	28.6	13.5	2.37	2.92	4 723	7.1	28.5
Richardson	3 993	64.3	29.5	53.4	22.0	7.4	5.1	35.7	32.2	17.7	2.34	2.95	4 120	6.0	31.1
Rock	763	65.7	26.9	57.4	22.3	6.4	3.7	34.3	31.3	15.9	2.26	2.84	798	5.8	26.9
Saline	5 188	67.6	32.8	56.5	25.1	7.2	5.2	32.4	27.5	14.3	2.50	3.04	4 829	4.9	28.8
Sarpy	43 426	76.5	43.0	63.8	34.4	9.6	6.6	23.5	18.4	4.7	2.79	3.21	33 960	8.4	15.1
Saunders	7 498	72.6	34.2	62.6	28.5	6.7	4.0	27.4	23.6	11.9	2.61	3.11	6 809	5.6	23.6
Scotts Bluff	14 887	68.3	31.5	54.2	22.1	10.7	7.2	31.7	27.8	12.8	2.44	2.97	14 056	9.0	27.1
Seward	6 013	70.1	32.8	61.5	27.2	5.6	3.8	29.9	24.9	12.1	2.53	3.04	5 432	5.0	22.5
Sheridan	2 549	67.8	30.0	56.8	22.8	8.0	5.5	32.2	29.6	16.3	2.38	2.95	2 618	6.6	27.8
Sherman	1 394	67.1	27.6	59.2	23.2	5.7	3.2	32.9	30.4	16.7	2.34	2.91	1 431	3.9	28.0
Sioux	605	73.4	28.1	65.3	24.3	5.1	3.0	26.6	23.6	9.4	2.44	2.86	612	5.6	22.7
Stanton	2 297	77.7	38.9	67.5	32.6	7.2	4.7	22.3	19.2	8.1	2.76	3.16	2 167	5.9	19.5
Thayer	2 541	66.5	27.7	58.8	22.7	5.0	3.4	33.5	31.5	18.2	2.31	2.90	2 669	4.1	28.3
Thomas	325	66.5	26.8	60.6	22.5	4.3	3.4	33.5	31.4	16.6	2.24	2.84	316	5.7	21.2
Thurston	2 255	76.5	40.0	50.6	24.3	19.1	12.3	23.5	21.3	10.1	3.14	3.64	2 288	16.3	23.3
Valley	1 965	66.1	28.0	58.7	23.4	5.1	3.6	33.9	31.0	17.9	2.32	2.93	2 141	4.1	31.2
Washington	6 940	74.2	36.4	64.0	30.1	7.0	4.6	25.8	21.8	10.1	2.63	3.09	6 017	5.5	21.3
Wayne	3 437	64.2	30.5	56.2	25.3	5.4	3.7	35.8	25.1	10.6	2.51	3.02	3 232	4.9	25.6
Webster	1 708	65.5	26.8	57.7	21.7	5.0	3.6	34.5	32.6	17.9	2.28	2.89	1 755	4.0	29.8
Wheeler	352	69.3	31.8	62.8	27.6	3.1	1.4	30.7	29.0	14.8	2.52	3.10	350	4.6	23.7
York	5 722	68.7	31.1	60.2	25.4	6.0	4.1	31.3	27.5	14.0	2.42	2.96	5 467	5.1	26.1
NEVADA	751 165	66.3	31.8	49.7	22.1	11.1	6.7	33.7	24.9	7.1	2.62	3.14	466 297	10.2	25.7
Churchill	8 912	72.5	37.2	57.7	27.1	10.4	7.2	27.5	22.5	8.5	2.64	3.09	6 666	7.9	23.0
Clark	512 253	66.3	31.7	48.7	21.7	11.8	7.0	33.7	24.5	6.7	2.65	3.17	287 025	11.2	25.5
Douglas	16 401	72.5	30.7	60.5	23.0	8.0	5.3	27.5	20.7	6.6	2.50	2.88	10 571	7.4	18.2
Elko	15 638	73.5	43.0	59.3	33.3	8.4	5.9	26.5	20.9	4.8	2.85	3.33	11 777	7.7	22.4
Esmeralda	455	57.1	21.1	46.4	15.2	6.4	4.2	42.9	36.0	13.2	2.12	2.79	588	4.8	34.0
Eureka	666	66.1	33.0	56.5	27.9	5.0	3.0	33.9	29.1	9.9	2.47	3.08	617	3.2	30.6
Humboldt	5 733	72.1	40.9	59.6	32.4	7.6	5.5	27.9	22.8	6.3	2.77	3.28	4 538	7.4	23.2
Lander	2 093	72.8	39.7	59.7	30.4	8.1	5.8	27.2	22.3	5.0	2.73	3.23	2 212	6.2	21.6
Lincoln	1 540	65.6	29.0	56.2	23.6	7.9	4.6	34.4	31.3	16.1	2.48	3.15	1 325	8.1	29.3
Lyon	13 007	72.6	33.2	58.4	24.6	9.1	5.5	27.4	21.4	8.3	2.61	3.02	7 680	7.2	22.1
Mineral	2 197	62.8	25.4	45.2	14.4	11.5	7.1	37.2	31.6	15.1	2.26	2.78	2 529	9.1	26.7
Nye	13 309	68.1	26.4	56.3	19.2	7.4	4.6	31.9	25.7	10.3	2.42	2.90	6 664	5.1	25.0
Pershing	1 962	70.5	38.4	57.2	29.0	7.3	5.5	29.5	24.3	8.6	2.69	3.22	1 614	5.8	25.2
Storey	1 462	66.3	21.8	54.6	15.6	7.5	3.8	33.7	25.6	6.9	2.32	2.74	1 006	6.8	25.0
Washoe	132 084	63.4	31.1	47.9	21.8	10.3	6.4	36.6	27.0	7.7	2.53	3.09	102 294	9.4	27.6
White Pine	3 282	65.8	31.2	51.8	21.6	9.3	6.3	34.2	29.6	11.5	2.42	3.01	3 296	7.0	26.6
Carson City city	20 171	65.7	29.8	50.0	20.3	11.0	6.7	34.3	27.8	11.0	2.44	2.97	15 895	9.6	27.2
NEW HAMPSHIRE	474 606	68.2	33.4	55.3	25.4	9.1	5.7	31.8	24.4	8.5	2.53	3.03	411 186	8.5	22.0
Belknap	22 459	69.0	30.4	55.7	21.9	9.2	6.0	31.0	24.4	9.7	2.45	2.91	18 839	8.5	22.8
Carroll	18 351	67.1	27.4	55.3	20.0	7.8	5.0	32.9	26.6	11.1	2.35	2.82	14 253	7.6	24.3
Cheshire	28 299	66.4	30.6	53.5	22.6	9.0	5.6	33.6	25.5	9.6	2.47	2.96	25 856	8.7	22.8
Coos	13 961	65.6	28.1	52.3	19.6	8.8	5.7	34.4	28.8	14.1	2.33	2.82	13 799	8.2	25.6
Grafton	31 598	64.1	29.5	52.4	21.8	8.3	5.4	35.9	27.4	9.5	2.38	2.90	27 542	8.2	24.4
Hillsborough	144 455	68.4	35.1	55.0	26.9	9.5	6.0	31.6	24.3	7.8	2.58	3.10	124 567	8.9	22.1
Merrimack	51 843	68.4	33.9	54.9	25.0	9.8	6.5	31.6	24.6	9.0	2.51	3.00	44 595	8.6	22.5
Rockingham	104 529	71.1	35.9	59.5	29.2	8.2	4.8	28.9	22.0	7.0	2.63	3.11	89 118	7.7	19.3
Strafford	42 581	65.2	32.6	51.1	23.3	10.0	6.8	34.8	24.8	8.2	2.50	2.98	37 744	9.1	21.9
Sullivan	16 530	67.6	29.4	54.7	21.0	8.6	5.6	32.4	25.7	10.9	2.41	2.88	14 873	8.6	22.9
NEW JERSEY	3 064 645	70.3	33.5	53.5	25.3	12.6	6.4	29.7	24.5	9.8	2.68	3.21	2 794 711	12.1	23.1
Atlantic	95 024	66.5	31.7	46.5	20.9	14.8	8.3	33.5	27.0	10.7	2.59	3.16	85 123	13.7	26.6
Bergen	330 817	71.1	32.1	57.9	27.1	9.7	3.9	28.9	24.7	10.2	2.64	3.17	308 880	9.4	23.2
Burlington	154 371	72.3	34.3	57.7	27.0	10.9	5.6	27.7	22.9	8.5	2.65	3.14	136 554	10.3	19.6
Camden	185 744	69.9	34.6	49.8	23.8	15.4	8.6	30.1	25.1	9.7	2.68	3.23	178 758	14.7	23.1
Cape May	42 148	64.9	26.1	50.5	18.5	10.9	5.8	35.1	30.2	14.7	2.36	2.94	37 856	10.3	27.5
Cumberland	49 143	71.6	34.1	48.7	21.0	17.3	10.1	28.4	23.6	11.1	2.73	3.19	47 118	15.8	21.6
Essex	283 736	68.2	33.8	42.3	20.5	20.4	11.1	31.8	26.7	9.6	2.72	3.30	278 752	19.2	27.1
Gloucester	90 717	74.1	36.7	58.3	28.5	11.6	6.1	25.9	21.2	8.4	2.75	3.22	78 845	10.7	18.9
Hudson	230 546	62.3	29.6	39.8	18.7	16.6	8.8	37.7	29.5	9.6	2.60	3.27	208 739	16.5	28.7
Hunterdon	43 678	75.2	37.1	66.3	32.7	6.3	3.3	24.8	20.0	6.5	2.69	3.14	37 906	6.3	17.9

[1] No spouse present.

Table B. States and Counties

STATE County	Percent change of households, 1990–2000	Housing occupancy, 2000 — Total housing units	Occupied housing units (percent)	Vacant housing units — Total	Vacant housing units — For seasonal, recreational, or occasional use	Homeowner vacancy rate (percent)	Rental vacancy rate (percent)	Housing tenure, 2000 — Occupied housing units — Total	Percent owner-occupied housing units	Percent renter-occupied housing units	Average household size of owner-occupied units	Average household size of renter-occupied units
	86	87	88	89	90	91	92	93	94	95	96	97
NEBRASKA—Cont'd												
Platte	10.2	12 916	93.5	6.5	1.5	1.5	8.8	12 076	73.3	26.7	2.73	2.23
Polk	1.6	2 717	83.1	16.9	10.2	3.4	9.3	2 259	77.2	22.8	2.42	2.44
Red Willow	-0.3	5 278	89.2	10.8	0.8	2.1	11.4	4 710	70.6	29.4	2.49	2.09
Richardson	-3.1	4 560	87.6	12.4	1.3	3.4	10.1	3 993	74.9	25.1	2.40	2.16
Rock	-4.4	935	81.6	18.4	3.3	5.6	4.6	763	73.0	27.0	2.25	2.30
Saline	7.4	5 611	92.5	7.5	1.3	2.6	4.8	5 188	70.7	29.3	2.53	2.42
Sarpy	27.9	44 981	96.5	3.5	0.5	0.9	4.7	43 426	69.2	30.8	2.92	2.50
Saunders	10.1	8 266	90.7	9.3	4.8	1.4	5.8	7 498	79.7	20.3	2.70	2.25
Scotts Bluff	5.9	16 119	92.4	7.6	1.2	2.1	7.8	14 887	66.2	33.8	2.51	2.30
Seward	10.7	6 428	93.5	6.5	1.3	1.4	6.2	6 013	72.0	28.0	2.65	2.23
Sheridan	-2.6	3 013	84.6	15.4	3.0	4.8	13.2	2 549	70.2	29.8	2.34	2.47
Sherman	-2.6	1 839	75.8	24.2	12.8	4.4	14.2	1 394	80.0	20.0	2.36	2.27
Sioux	-1.1	780	77.6	22.4	8.7	4.3	4.3	605	66.6	33.4	2.36	2.59
Stanton	6.0	2 452	93.7	6.3	0.5	2.4	5.0	2 297	80.0	20.0	2.78	2.67
Thayer	-4.8	2 828	89.9	10.1	1.0	4.4	7.7	2 541	80.0	20.0	2.33	2.24
Thomas	2.8	446	72.9	27.1	7.2	8.1	11.2	325	73.2	26.8	2.11	2.61
Thurston	-1.4	2 467	91.4	8.6	0.8	2.9	5.3	2 255	60.8	39.2	2.92	3.47
Valley	-8.2	2 273	86.4	13.6	1.1	3.4	17.2	1 965	75.7	24.3	2.34	2.25
Washington	15.3	7 408	93.7	6.3	1.7	1.0	8.5	6 940	77.2	22.8	2.75	2.22
Wayne	6.3	3 662	93.9	6.1	0.4	2.2	5.5	3 437	64.9	35.1	2.59	2.36
Webster	-2.7	1 972	86.6	13.4	1.6	3.6	15.9	1 708	78.6	21.4	2.33	2.11
Wheeler	0.6	561	62.7	37.3	26.6	2.8	7.7	352	69.3	30.7	2.29	3.03
York	4.7	6 172	92.7	7.3	1.0	1.8	8.3	5 722	69.5	30.5	2.54	2.16
NEVADA	61.1	827 457	90.8	9.2	2.0	2.6	9.7	751 165	60.9	39.1	2.71	2.47
Churchill	33.7	9 732	91.6	8.4	0.7	2.6	8.5	8 912	65.8	34.2	2.64	2.66
Clark	78.5	559 799	91.5	8.5	1.5	2.6	9.7	512 253	59.1	40.9	2.75	2.50
Douglas	55.2	19 006	86.3	13.7	9.3	1.9	6.0	16 401	74.3	25.7	2.49	2.53
Elko	32.8	18 456	84.7	15.3	3.9	3.2	16.9	15 638	69.9	30.1	2.97	2.55
Esmeralda	-22.6	833	54.6	45.4	9.5	4.4	40.5	455	67.0	33.0	2.10	2.17
Eureka	7.9	1 025	65.0	35.0	6.2	5.4	37.9	666	73.7	26.3	2.48	2.43
Humboldt	26.3	6 954	82.4	17.6	3.2	3.9	19.7	5 733	72.9	27.1	2.87	2.51
Lander	-5.4	2 780	75.3	24.7	2.8	4.0	32.4	2 093	77.2	22.8	2.81	2.44
Lincoln	16.2	2 178	70.7	29.3	14.0	4.0	9.2	1 540	75.1	24.9	2.55	2.24
Lyon	69.4	14 279	91.1	8.9	1.3	3.1	10.0	13 007	75.8	24.2	2.58	2.71
Mineral	-13.1	2 866	76.7	23.3	3.2	3.6	27.9	2 197	72.5	27.5	2.26	2.26
Nye	99.7	15 934	83.5	16.5	3.5	3.4	17.9	13 309	76.4	23.6	2.42	2.43
Pershing	21.6	2 389	82.1	17.9	1.8	3.5	25.7	1 962	69.5	30.5	2.73	2.61
Storey	45.3	1 596	91.6	8.4	1.9	4.1	6.6	1 462	79.8	20.2	2.38	2.08
Washoe	29.1	143 908	91.8	8.2	2.5	2.0	7.8	132 084	59.3	40.7	2.65	2.35
White Pine	-0.4	4 439	73.9	26.1	4.5	6.7	23.8	3 282	76.6	23.4	2.45	2.30
Carson City city	26.9	21 283	94.8	5.2	0.5	1.5	6.8	20 171	63.1	36.9	2.46	2.41
NEW HAMPSHIRE	15.4	547 024	86.8	13.2	10.3	1.0	3.5	474 606	69.7	30.3	2.70	2.14
Belknap	19.2	32 121	69.9	30.1	26.7	1.4	6.5	22 459	74.1	25.9	2.55	2.19
Carroll	28.8	34 750	52.8	47.2	42.8	2.3	7.6	18 351	77.8	22.2	2.41	2.15
Cheshire	9.4	31 876	88.8	11.2	7.9	1.2	3.5	28 299	70.8	29.2	2.62	2.09
Coos	1.2	19 623	71.1	28.9	21.4	2.7	11.2	13 961	71.2	28.8	2.45	2.01
Grafton	14.7	43 729	72.3	27.7	23.8	2.0	3.7	31 598	68.6	31.4	2.51	2.11
Hillsborough	16.0	149 961	96.3	3.7	1.5	0.5	2.5	144 455	64.9	35.1	2.80	2.19
Merrimack	16.3	56 244	92.2	7.8	5.1	0.9	2.8	51 843	69.5	30.5	2.69	2.08
Rockingham	17.3	113 023	92.5	7.5	5.3	0.6	3.3	104 529	75.6	24.4	2.81	2.08
Strafford	12.8	45 539	93.5	6.5	4.0	0.7	2.4	42 581	64.5	35.5	2.66	2.21
Sullivan	11.1	20 158	82.0	18.0	13.7	1.6	5.4	16 530	72.0	28.0	2.51	2.16
NEW JERSEY	9.7	3 310 275	92.6	7.4	3.3	1.2	4.5	3 064 645	65.6	34.4	2.81	2.43
Atlantic	11.6	114 090	83.3	16.7	10.3	2.2	8.0	95 024	66.4	33.6	2.69	2.38
Bergen	7.1	339 820	97.4	2.6	0.4	0.7	2.6	330 817	67.2	32.8	2.82	2.26
Burlington	13.0	161 311	95.7	4.3	0.3	1.4	5.8	154 371	77.4	22.6	2.77	2.24
Camden	3.9	199 679	93.0	7.0	0.2	1.8	6.8	185 744	70.0	30.0	2.85	2.29
Cape May	11.3	91 047	46.3	53.7	47.4	2.5	22.5	42 148	74.2	25.8	2.42	2.21
Cumberland	4.3	52 863	93.0	7.0	1.6	1.9	5.5	49 143	67.9	32.1	2.73	2.74
Essex	1.8	301 011	94.3	5.7	0.2	1.2	4.8	283 736	45.6	54.4	2.99	2.49
Gloucester	15.1	95 054	95.4	4.6	0.3	1.3	5.7	90 717	79.9	20.1	2.88	2.24
Hudson	10.4	240 618	95.8	4.2	0.3	1.2	2.7	230 546	30.7	69.3	2.81	2.51
Hunterdon	15.2	45 032	97.0	3.0	0.6	0.7	3.2	43 678	83.6	16.4	2.81	2.11

Table B. States and Counties

STATE/ County code	MSA/ PMSA/ NECMA code[1]	County type[2]	STATE County	Population, 2000 Land area, 2000[3] (sq km)	Total persons	Rank	Per square kilometer	Population, 1990 Land area, 1990[3] (sq km)	Total persons	Rank	Per square kilometer	Race (percent) One race White	Black or African American	American Indian or Alaska Native	Asian	Native Hawaiian and other Pacific Islander	Some other race
				1	2	3	4	5	6	7	8	9	10	11	12	13	14
			NEW JERSEY—Cont'd														
34 021	8480	2	Mercer	585	350 761	167	599.6	585	325 759	157	556.9	68.5	19.0	0.2	4.9	0.1	4.3
34 023	5015	0	Middlesex	802	750 162	66	935.4	805	671 712	64	834.4	68.4	9.1	0.2	13.9	0.0	5.7
34 025	5190	0	Monmouth	1 222	615 301	87	503.5	1 222	553 192	84	452.7	84.4	8.1	0.1	4.0	0.0	1.7
34 027	5640	0	Morris	1 215	470 212	123	387.0	1 215	421 330	120	346.8	87.2	2.8	0.1	6.3	0.0	2.0
34 029	5190	0	Ocean	1 648	510 916	109	310.0	1 648	433 203	115	262.9	93.0	3.0	0.1	1.3	0.0	1.2
34 031	0875	0	Passaic	480	489 049	115	1 018.9	479	470 872	104	983.0	62.3	13.2	0.4	3.7	0.0	16.2
34 033	6160	1	Salem	875	64 285	758	73.5	875	65 294	671	74.6	81.2	14.8	0.4	0.6	0.0	1.6
34 035	5015	0	Somerset	789	297 490	190	377.0	789	240 222	207	304.5	79.3	7.5	0.1	8.4	0.0	2.7
34 037	5640	1	Sussex	1 350	144 166	379	106.8	1 350	130 936	354	97.0	95.7	1.0	0.1	1.2	0.0	0.7
34 039	5640	0	Union	268	522 541	106	1 949.8	268	493 819	99	1 842.6	65.5	20.8	0.2	3.8	0.0	6.4
34 041	5640	1	Warren	927	102 437	518	110.5	927	91 675	501	98.9	94.5	1.9	0.1	1.2	0.0	1.0
35 000	...		NEW MEXICO	314 309	1 819 046	X	5.8	314 334	1 515 069	X	4.8	66.8	1.9	9.5	1.1	0.1	17.0
35 001	0200	2	Bernalillo	3 020	556 678	100	184.3	3 020	480 577	102	159.1	70.8	2.8	4.2	1.9	0.1	16.1
35 003	...	9	Catron	17 943	3 543	2 951	0.2	17 944	2 563	3 019	0.1	87.8	0.3	2.2	0.7	0.1	5.4
35 005	...	5	Chaves	15 723	61 382	792	3.9	15 725	57 849	751	3.7	72.0	2.0	1.1	0.5	0.1	21.2
35 006	...	6	Cibola	11 757	25 595	1 532	2.2	11 757	23 794	1 500	2.0	39.6	1.0	40.3	0.4	0.1	15.4
35 007	...	7	Colfax	9 730	14 189	2 148	1.5	9 730	12 925	2 143	1.3	81.5	0.3	1.5	0.3	0.0	12.8
35 009	...	5	Curry	3 641	45 044	998	12.4	3 642	42 207	954	11.6	72.4	6.9	1.0	1.8	0.1	14.1
35 011	...	9	De Baca	6 021	2 240	3 048	0.4	6 022	2 252	3 047	0.4	84.0	0.0	0.9	0.2	0.0	12.5
35 013	4100	3	Dona Ana	9 861	174 682	313	17.7	9 861	135 510	346	13.7	67.8	1.6	1.5	0.8	0.1	24.7
35 015	...	5	Eddy	10 831	51 658	898	4.8	10 832	48 605	861	4.5	76.3	1.6	1.3	0.4	0.1	17.7
35 017	...	7	Grant	10 272	31 002	1 378	3.0	10 272	27 676	1 364	2.7	75.7	0.5	1.4	0.3	0.0	19.0
35 019	...	9	Guadalupe	7 849	4 680	2 868	0.6	7 849	4 156	2 899	0.5	54.1	1.3	1.1	0.5	0.0	39.1
35 021	...	9	Harding	5 505	810	3 123	0.1	5 505	987	3 114	0.2	84.3	0.4	1.4	0.0	0.0	10.6
35 023	...	7	Hidalgo	8 924	5 932	2 790	0.7	8 925	5 958	2 763	0.7	83.8	0.4	0.8	0.3	0.0	11.9
35 025	...	5	Lea	11 378	55 511	850	4.9	11 379	55 765	777	4.9	67.1	4.4	1.0	0.4	0.0	23.8
35 027	...	7	Lincoln	12 512	19 411	1 822	1.6	12 513	12 219	2 200	1.0	83.6	0.4	2.0	0.3	0.1	11.3
35 028	7490	3	Los Alamos	283	18 343	1 877	64.8	283	18 115	1 783	64.0	90.3	0.4	0.6	3.8	0.0	2.7
35 029	...	6	Luna	7 680	25 016	1 559	3.3	7 680	18 110	1 784	2.4	74.3	0.9	1.1	0.3	0.0	20.2
35 031	...	5	McKinley	14 112	74 798	667	5.3	14 113	60 686	716	4.3	16.4	0.4	74.7	0.5	0.0	5.5
35 033	...	8	Mora	5 002	5 180	2 838	1.0	5 002	4 264	2 892	0.9	58.9	0.1	1.1	0.1	0.0	37.0
35 035	...	4	Otero	17 163	62 298	781	3.6	17 164	51 928	814	3.0	73.7	3.9	5.8	1.2	0.1	11.7
35 037	...	7	Quay	7 446	10 155	2 431	1.4	7 447	10 823	2 309	1.5	82.1	0.8	1.3	0.8	0.1	12.1
35 039	...	6	Rio Arriba	15 171	41 190	1 074	2.7	15 172	34 365	1 158	2.3	56.6	0.3	13.9	0.1	0.1	25.6
35 041	...	7	Roosevelt	6 342	18 018	1 896	2.8	6 342	16 702	1 868	2.6	74.1	1.7	1.1	0.6	0.1	19.8
35 043	0200	2	Sandoval	9 607	89 908	575	9.4	9 608	63 319	689	6.6	65.1	1.7	16.3	1.0	0.1	12.4
35 045	...	5	San Juan	14 281	113 801	473	8.0	14 282	91 605	502	6.4	52.8	0.4	36.9	0.3	0.0	6.8
35 047	...	6	San Miguel	12 217	30 126	1 392	2.5	12 218	25 743	1 430	2.1	56.2	0.8	1.8	0.5	0.1	36.2
35 049	7490	3	Santa Fe	4 945	129 292	417	26.1	4 945	98 928	465	20.0	73.5	0.6	3.1	0.9	0.1	17.7
35 051	...	6	Sierra	10 827	13 270	2 205	1.2	10 828	9 912	2 395	0.9	87.0	0.5	1.5	0.2	0.1	8.3
35 053	...	7	Socorro	17 214	18 078	1 895	1.1	17 216	14 764	2 002	0.9	62.9	0.6	10.9	1.1	0.1	20.1
35 055	...	7	Taos	5 706	29 979	1 397	5.3	5 707	23 118	1 532	4.1	63.8	0.4	6.6	0.4	0.1	24.8
35 057	...	8	Torrance	8 663	16 911	1 958	2.0	8 664	10 285	2 361	1.2	73.9	1.7	2.1	0.3	0.1	17.9
35 059	...	9	Union	9 920	4 174	2 900	0.4	9 920	4 124	2 903	0.4	80.4	0.0	1.0	0.3	0.1	16.0
35 061	0200	2	Valencia	2 765	66 152	739	23.9	2 765	45 235	910	16.4	66.5	1.3	3.3	0.4	0.1	23.9
36 000	...		NEW YORK	122 283	18 976 457	X	155.2	122 310	17 990 778	X	147.1	67.9	15.9	0.4	5.5	0.0	7.1
36 001	0160	2	Albany	1 356	294 565	191	217.2	1 357	292 812	166	215.8	83.2	11.1	0.2	2.7	0.0	1.1
36 003	...	7	Allegany	2 668	49 927	917	18.7	2 668	50 470	836	18.9	97.0	0.7	0.3	0.7	0.0	0.4
36 005	5600	0	Bronx	109	1 332 650	27	12 226.1	109	1 203 789	24	11 043.9	29.9	35.6	0.9	3.0	0.1	24.7
36 007	0960	2	Broome	1 831	200 536	274	109.5	1 831	212 160	235	115.9	91.3	3.3	0.2	2.8	0.0	0.8
36 009	...	4	Cattaraugus	3 393	83 955	619	24.7	3 393	84 234	542	24.8	94.6	1.1	2.6	0.5	0.0	0.2
36 011	8160	2	Cayuga	1 795	81 963	633	45.7	1 796	82 313	551	45.8	93.3	4.0	0.3	0.4	0.0	0.9
36 013	3610	3	Chautauqua	2 751	139 750	391	50.8	2 751	141 895	336	51.6	94.0	2.2	0.4	0.4	0.0	1.7
36 015	2335	3	Chemung	1 057	91 070	565	86.2	1 057	95 195	486	90.1	91.0	5.8	0.2	0.8	0.0	0.7
36 017	...	6	Chenango	2 316	51 401	900	22.2	2 317	51 768	816	22.3	97.6	0.8	0.3	0.3	0.0	0.2
36 019	...	5	Clinton	2 691	79 894	643	29.7	2 692	85 969	533	31.9	93.3	3.6	0.4	0.7	0.0	1.1
36 021	...	6	Columbia	1 647	63 094	769	38.3	1 647	62 982	692	38.2	92.1	4.5	0.2	0.8	0.0	0.9
36 023	...	4	Cortland	1 294	48 599	937	37.6	1 294	48 963	856	37.8	96.9	0.9	0.3	0.4	0.0	0.5
36 025	...	6	Delaware	3 746	48 055	952	12.8	3 746	47 352	886	12.6	96.4	1.2	0.3	0.5	0.0	0.5
36 027	2281	2	Dutchess	2 076	280 150	201	134.9	2 076	259 462	194	125.0	83.7	9.3	0.2	2.5	0.0	2.4
36 029	1280	0	Erie	2 704	950 265	37	351.4	2 706	968 584	32	357.9	82.2	13.0	0.6	1.5	0.0	1.4
36 031	...	6	Essex	4 654	38 851	1 145	8.3	4 654	37 152	1 069	8.0	94.8	2.8	0.3	0.4	0.1	0.4
36 033	...	7	Franklin	4 226	51 134	904	12.1	4 226	46 540	896	11.0	84.0	6.6	6.2	0.4	0.0	2.1
36 035	...	4	Fulton	1 285	55 073	858	42.9	1 285	54 191	793	42.2	96.0	1.8	0.2	0.5	0.0	0.6

[1]MSA = Metropolitan Statistical Area. PMSA = Primary MSA. NECMA = New England County Metropolitan Area. See Appendix A for explanation of these concepts. See Appendix B for list of metropolitan areas identified by type, with component counties.
[2]County typology code from the Economic Research Service of USDA. See Appendix A for definition.
[3]Dry land or land partially or temporarily covered by water.

Table B. States and Counties

STATE County	Population and population characteristics, 2000 (cont'd)								Population and population characteristics, 1990				
	Race (percent) (cont'd)								Race (percent)				
	Two or more races	Race alone or in combination						Hispanic[1]	White	Black or African American	American Indian or Alaska Native	Asian and Pacific Islander	Hispanic[1]
		White	Black	American Indian or Alaska Native	Asian	Native Hawaiian and other Pacific Islander	Some other race						
	15	16	17	18	19	20	21	22	23	24	25	26	27
NEW JERSEY—Cont'd													
Mercer	2.2	70.0	20.7	0.5	5.5	0.2	5.4	9.7	75.1	18.9	0.2	3.1	6.0
Middlesex	2.6	70.3	9.8	0.6	14.6	0.1	7.3	13.6	81.9	8.0	0.2	6.7	8.9
Monmouth	1.7	85.7	8.7	0.5	4.4	0.1	2.5	6.2	87.4	8.5	0.1	2.8	4.1
Morris	1.6	88.5	3.1	0.4	6.8	0.1	2.8	7.8	91.8	3.0	0.1	4.0	4.7
Ocean	1.3	94.2	3.3	0.4	1.5	0.1	1.8	5.0	95.3	2.8	0.1	0.9	3.2
Passaic	4.0	65.4	14.1	0.8	4.3	0.2	19.4	30.0	71.9	14.6	0.3	2.6	21.7
Salem	1.5	82.3	15.5	0.9	0.7	0.1	2.0	3.9	83.3	14.7	0.3	0.6	2.2
Somerset	1.8	80.8	8.0	0.4	9.0	0.1	3.7	8.7	88.0	6.2	0.1	4.4	4.2
Sussex	1.1	96.8	1.3	0.4	1.5	0.1	1.2	3.3	97.6	0.9	0.1	0.9	2.2
Union	3.2	67.8	21.9	0.6	4.2	0.1	8.7	19.7	74.4	18.8	0.2	2.8	13.7
Warren	1.2	95.6	2.2	0.4	1.5	0.0	1.5	3.7	97.2	1.4	0.1	0.8	1.9
NEW MEXICO	3.6	69.9	2.3	10.5	1.5	0.2	19.4	42.1	75.6	2.0	8.9	0.9	38.2
Bernalillo	4.2	74.4	3.4	5.2	2.5	0.2	18.7	42.0	76.9	2.7	3.4	1.5	37.1
Catron	3.6	91.1	0.5	3.7	0.9	0.1	7.7	19.2	97.9	0.3	0.8	0.1	28.4
Chaves	3.1	74.8	2.3	1.9	0.8	0.1	23.4	43.8	82.6	2.1	0.6	0.5	36.8
Cibola	3.2	42.2	1.3	41.8	0.5	0.1	17.5	33.4	58.4	0.8	38.5	0.3	34.1
Colfax	3.6	84.9	0.4	2.5	0.4	0.1	15.4	47.5	82.8	0.3	0.7	0.2	47.9
Curry	3.7	75.5	7.9	1.8	2.5	0.3	16.0	30.4	75.6	6.9	0.7	1.9	23.7
De Baca	2.2	86.2	0.1	1.7	0.4	0.0	13.9	35.3	93.6	0.1	1.9	0.0	32.7
Dona Ana	3.6	71.0	2.0	2.2	1.1	0.2	27.3	63.4	91.1	1.6	0.7	0.9	56.4
Eddy	2.6	78.7	1.9	1.9	0.6	0.1	19.4	38.8	81.5	1.7	0.5	0.4	35.3
Grant	3.1	78.5	0.8	2.3	0.5	0.1	21.1	48.8	93.0	0.5	0.8	0.2	50.8
Guadalupe	3.8	57.6	1.3	1.5	0.8	0.1	42.6	81.2	74.0	0.3	0.5	0.7	84.3
Harding	3.3	87.3	0.4	3.1	0.0	0.0	13.0	44.9	79.7	0.2	0.5	0.1	46.7
Hidalgo	2.9	86.5	0.6	1.2	0.5	0.0	14.2	56.0	91.6	0.2	0.3	0.6	50.1
Lea	3.3	70.1	4.8	1.7	0.5	0.1	26.2	39.6	82.2	4.7	0.6	0.4	29.8
Lincoln	2.5	85.8	0.6	2.9	0.4	0.1	12.8	25.6	91.5	0.5	1.1	0.2	28.0
Los Alamos	2.3	92.4	0.6	1.2	4.4	0.1	3.6	11.7	94.2	0.5	0.7	2.4	11.1
Luna	3.1	77.1	1.2	1.9	0.5	0.0	22.4	57.7	90.0	1.4	0.6	0.3	47.6
McKinley	2.5	18.2	0.7	76.4	0.6	0.1	6.7	12.4	21.9	0.5	71.8	0.4	12.8
Mora	2.8	61.3	0.3	1.6	0.2	0.0	39.3	81.6	56.8	0.0	0.5	0.1	85.0
Otero	3.6	76.9	4.5	6.6	1.8	0.3	13.7	32.2	79.6	5.3	5.7	1.9	23.8
Quay	2.7	84.4	1.0	2.1	1.0	0.2	14.0	38.0	74.2	1.4	1.0	0.4	37.5
Rio Arriba	3.3	59.5	0.5	14.7	0.3	0.2	28.2	72.9	70.8	0.4	15.2	0.2	72.6
Roosevelt	2.7	76.5	2.0	1.8	0.8	0.1	21.6	33.3	79.7	1.3	0.8	0.6	27.2
Sandoval	3.5	68.1	2.2	17.2	1.5	0.2	14.4	29.4	68.6	1.5	19.7	0.8	27.4
San Juan	2.8	55.2	0.7	38.2	0.5	0.1	8.1	15.0	56.6	0.5	36.7	0.2	13.1
San Miguel	4.3	60.1	1.1	2.8	0.8	0.2	39.6	78.0	63.7	0.7	0.9	0.6	79.6
Santa Fe	4.1	77.1	0.9	4.1	1.3	0.2	20.6	49.0	80.3	0.6	2.9	0.5	49.5
Sierra	2.5	89.4	0.6	2.5	0.4	0.2	9.8	26.3	93.4	0.4	0.8	0.1	24.0
Socorro	4.3	66.6	1.0	12.2	1.6	0.1	23.2	48.7	77.4	0.8	10.1	1.4	47.8
Taos	4.0	67.3	0.6	7.6	0.6	0.2	27.8	57.9	73.0	0.3	6.8	0.4	64.9
Torrance	4.0	77.6	2.0	3.4	0.6	0.2	20.3	37.2	87.0	0.4	1.2	0.2	37.8
Union	2.2	82.4	0.1	1.8	0.5	0.1	17.3	35.1	96.2	0.0	0.3	0.1	33.7
Valencia	4.6	70.6	1.6	4.5	0.7	0.1	27.2	55.0	77.5	1.1	2.9	0.4	50.3
NEW YORK	3.1	70.0	17.0	0.9	6.2	0.2	9.1	15.1	74.4	15.9	0.3	3.9	12.3
Albany	1.7	84.5	11.9	0.6	3.2	0.1	1.6	3.1	89.1	8.4	0.2	1.7	1.8
Allegany	0.9	97.8	1.0	0.7	0.9	0.0	0.5	0.9	98.4	0.6	0.2	0.6	0.6
Bronx	5.8	33.1	38.3	1.5	3.6	0.3	29.2	48.4	35.7	37.3	0.5	3.0	43.5
Broome	1.6	92.7	4.0	0.6	3.1	0.1	1.3	2.0	95.7	2.0	0.2	1.7	1.2
Cattaraugus	1.0	95.6	1.4	3.1	0.6	0.1	0.4	0.9	96.3	0.9	2.2	0.4	0.6
Cayuga	1.0	94.3	4.5	0.7	0.6	0.1	1.1	2.0	95.1	3.6	0.3	0.4	1.5
Chautauqua	1.2	95.2	2.6	0.8	0.5	0.1	2.2	4.2	96.1	1.7	0.4	0.4	2.9
Chemung	1.4	92.3	6.7	0.6	1.0	0.0	1.0	1.8	92.8	5.5	0.2	0.7	1.5
Chenango	0.7	98.4	1.0	0.7	0.4	0.0	0.4	1.1	98.5	0.6	0.3	0.3	0.9
Clinton	0.9	94.2	3.9	0.7	0.9	0.1	1.3	2.5	93.7	4.4	0.2	0.8	2.4
Columbia	1.4	93.3	5.3	0.6	1.1	0.1	1.3	2.5	95.1	3.9	0.2	0.4	1.6
Cortland	1.2	98.1	1.2	0.8	0.6	0.1	0.5	1.2	98.3	0.7	0.3	0.5	0.9
Delaware	1.0	97.3	1.5	0.8	0.7	0.0	0.8	2.0	98.1	1.0	0.2	0.4	1.1
Dutchess	1.9	85.1	10.2	0.7	2.9	0.1	3.1	6.4	88.3	8.4	0.1	2.2	3.8
Erie	1.3	83.2	13.6	0.9	1.7	0.1	1.9	3.3	85.9	11.3	0.6	1.1	2.3
Essex	0.9	95.7	2.9	0.8	0.5	0.1	0.9	2.2	96.0	2.8	0.3	0.4	2.0
Franklin	0.7	84.7	6.8	6.6	0.5	0.0	2.2	4.0	90.0	3.7	5.0	0.3	2.4
Fulton	0.9	96.8	2.1	0.5	0.7	0.1	0.8	1.6	98.0	1.2	0.2	0.4	0.8

[1] Hispanic persons may be of any race.

Table B. States and Counties

STATE County	Population and population characteristics, 2000 — Age (percent)										
	Under 5 years	5 to 17 years	18 to 24 years	25 to 34 years	35 to 44 years	45 to 54 years	55 to 64 years	65 to 74 years	75 years and over	Median age (years)	Percent Female
	28	29	30	31	32	33	34	35	36	37	38
NEW JERSEY—Cont'd											
Mercer	6.3	17.7	10.2	14.0	16.5	14.0	8.6	6.4	6.1	36.0	51.3
Middlesex	6.6	17.1	9.5	15.6	17.2	13.4	8.3	6.5	5.8	35.7	50.9
Monmouth	6.9	19.2	6.9	12.2	18.2	15.0	9.1	6.5	6.0	37.7	51.4
Morris	7.0	17.8	6.4	13.5	18.4	15.3	10.0	6.3	5.3	37.8	51.1
Ocean	6.3	17.0	6.6	11.2	14.9	12.4	9.5	10.6	11.5	41.0	52.5
Passaic	7.4	18.7	9.3	15.0	16.3	12.8	8.5	6.2	5.9	34.8	51.5
Salem	6.1	19.5	7.8	11.9	16.0	14.6	9.6	7.3	7.2	38.0	51.7
Somerset	7.5	18.1	5.9	14.2	19.6	14.7	8.8	6.0	5.2	37.2	51.2
Sussex	6.8	21.1	6.2	12.1	19.3	16.2	9.0	4.9	4.2	37.1	50.5
Union	7.0	17.9	7.9	14.4	16.9	13.3	8.8	6.8	7.0	36.6	51.9
Warren	6.9	19.2	6.3	12.8	18.5	14.6	8.9	6.6	6.3	37.6	51.3
NEW MEXICO	7.2	20.8	9.8	12.9	15.5	13.5	8.7	6.5	5.2	34.6	50.8
Bernalillo	6.9	18.4	10.3	14.3	16.1	14.0	8.4	6.1	5.4	35.0	51.2
Catron	4.2	16.9	4.2	6.7	12.8	18.6	17.8	11.8	7.0	47.8	48.9
Chaves	7.2	21.9	9.4	11.2	14.1	12.7	8.7	7.6	7.1	35.2	51.0
Cibola	7.9	22.7	9.6	12.1	15.4	12.6	8.9	6.7	4.0	33.1	51.1
Colfax	5.4	19.7	6.9	9.8	14.7	14.7	11.8	8.9	8.0	40.8	49.3
Curry	8.6	21.5	11.5	13.9	14.9	10.7	7.5	6.1	5.3	30.8	50.6
De Baca	5.1	19.0	5.7	8.6	13.1	12.6	10.6	12.6	12.8	43.8	51.0
Dona Ana	7.8	21.9	13.3	12.9	14.1	11.5	7.7	6.2	4.4	30.2	50.9
Eddy	7.3	21.5	8.4	10.9	14.8	13.5	8.9	7.6	7.1	36.4	51.0
Grant	6.9	19.4	8.5	10.4	13.3	14.0	11.0	9.1	7.3	38.8	51.3
Guadalupe	5.3	19.0	9.2	11.8	12.5	12.5	9.4	7.8	6.0	37.5	45.1
Harding	3.1	17.2	4.6	7.4	11.4	17.3	10.9	15.9	12.3	48.7	49.4
Hidalgo	7.7	24.1	7.8	10.7	14.4	12.5	9.3	7.3	6.4	34.8	50.1
Lea	7.7	22.4	10.1	12.3	15.0	12.2	8.1	7.0	5.2	33.1	49.9
Lincoln	5.1	17.7	6.0	8.9	14.3	16.2	13.9	11.4	6.4	43.8	51.0
Los Alamos	5.6	20.2	4.4	10.2	17.5	17.6	12.4	6.7	5.4	40.8	49.6
Luna	7.7	22.3	7.6	10.4	12.3	11.1	10.4	10.7	7.5	36.7	51.2
McKinley	9.1	28.8	9.7	13.1	14.7	10.9	6.7	4.1	2.8	26.9	51.7
Mora	6.1	20.6	7.5	9.5	14.8	15.0	11.1	9.0	6.4	39.6	49.5
Otero	7.4	22.0	9.3	12.9	15.7	12.0	9.0	7.2	4.5	33.8	50.2
Quay	5.5	19.5	6.7	9.6	13.7	14.1	12.0	10.1	8.9	41.5	51.6
Rio Arriba	7.0	21.6	8.9	13.2	15.6	13.9	8.9	6.4	4.5	34.5	50.5
Roosevelt	7.5	20.6	16.0	12.5	13.0	10.7	7.7	6.3	5.8	29.5	50.9
Sandoval	7.3	22.2	7.5	12.7	17.4	14.1	8.1	5.7	5.0	35.1	51.2
San Juan	8.0	24.6	10.0	12.3	15.8	12.5	7.7	5.3	3.8	31.0	50.4
San Miguel	6.5	20.9	10.9	11.6	15.4	13.6	9.4	6.4	5.3	35.1	50.8
Santa Fe	6.2	17.9	8.1	13.1	16.6	17.3	10.0	6.1	4.6	37.9	51.1
Sierra	4.8	15.3	5.4	7.6	11.9	13.4	13.9	14.9	12.8	48.9	50.0
Socorro	7.0	21.4	12.6	12.0	14.2	12.7	9.3	6.2	4.7	32.4	49.2
Taos	5.8	18.7	6.9	11.8	15.6	17.7	11.1	7.0	5.4	39.5	51.0
Torrance	6.9	23.4	7.5	12.5	16.7	14.1	9.1	5.8	4.0	34.8	48.7
Union	6.0	21.3	6.3	10.1	14.5	13.2	10.9	9.7	8.1	39.9	50.8
Valencia	7.6	22.5	8.4	13.3	16.4	13.2	8.6	5.9	4.2	33.8	49.8
NEW YORK	6.5	18.2	9.3	14.5	16.2	13.5	8.9	6.7	6.2	35.9	51.8
Albany	5.7	16.9	11.3	13.4	15.5	14.3	8.5	7.1	7.4	36.8	52.2
Allegany	5.6	18.8	15.5	10.1	13.8	13.0	9.1	7.5	6.5	35.0	50.0
Bronx	8.2	21.6	10.6	15.6	15.0	11.2	7.7	5.3	4.7	31.2	53.5
Broome	5.6	17.4	11.0	11.3	15.5	13.4	9.3	8.0	8.4	38.2	51.8
Cattaraugus	6.2	20.0	9.3	11.3	15.2	14.0	9.4	7.7	6.9	37.4	51.0
Cayuga	5.9	19.2	8.2	12.9	16.8	13.9	8.8	7.1	7.3	37.3	49.5
Chautauqua	5.8	18.7	10.3	11.3	15.0	13.6	9.3	8.0	8.0	37.9	51.2
Chemung	6.0	18.4	8.8	12.3	16.0	13.3	9.0	7.8	7.8	37.9	50.6
Chenango	5.9	20.2	7.0	11.4	16.1	14.1	10.3	7.5	7.4	38.4	50.8
Clinton	5.1	17.8	12.4	13.4	17.1	13.4	8.8	6.8	5.1	35.7	48.8
Columbia	5.3	18.7	6.4	11.1	15.8	15.3	11.0	8.3	8.1	40.5	50.2
Cortland	5.9	17.8	15.5	11.8	14.7	13.0	8.7	6.2	6.3	34.2	51.7
Delaware	5.1	17.9	8.2	9.8	14.1	14.4	11.7	9.7	8.9	41.4	50.8
Dutchess	6.2	18.8	9.4	12.5	17.7	14.2	9.0	6.5	5.5	36.7	50.0
Erie	6.1	18.2	8.7	12.5	15.8	13.7	9.1	8.0	7.9	38.0	52.2
Essex	5.0	17.8	6.9	13.1	16.7	14.4	10.2	8.5	7.5	39.4	48.2
Franklin	4.9	17.8	9.5	15.2	17.9	13.3	8.4	6.8	6.1	36.3	45.1
Fulton	5.7	19.2	7.2	12.3	15.8	14.1	9.5	7.9	8.4	38.6	50.7

Table B. States and Counties

STATE County	Under 5 years	5 to 17 years	18 to 24 years	25 to 34 years	35 to 44 years	45 to 54 years	55 to 64 years	65 to 74 years	75 years and over	Percent Female	2000	1990	1980	1990–2000	1980–1990
	39	40	41	42	43	44	45	46	47	48	49	50	51	52	53
NEW JERSEY—Cont'd															
Mercer	6.7	15.8	11.9	17.3	15.7	10.7	9.0	7.8	5.2	51.6	350 761	325 759	307 863	7.7	5.8
Middlesex	6.7	14.8	12.0	19.6	15.5	10.5	9.1	7.6	4.2	50.8	750 162	671 712	595 893	11.7	12.7
Monmouth	7.0	17.3	9.1	16.5	16.7	11.5	9.1	7.3	5.4	51.5	615 301	553 192	503 173	11.2	9.9
Morris	6.6	16.3	9.8	17.0	17.1	13.3	9.5	6.2	4.4	51.2	470 212	421 330	407 630	11.6	3.4
Ocean	6.7	16.0	7.9	14.5	13.6	9.0	9.1	12.9	10.3	52.9	510 916	433 203	346 038	17.9	25.2
Passaic	7.3	16.7	11.2	17.7	14.7	10.6	9.0	7.4	5.5	51.8	489 049	470 872	447 585	3.9	1.3
Salem	6.6	19.0	9.0	15.2	15.2	10.9	9.4	8.6	6.0	51.8	64 285	65 294	64 676	-1.5	1.0
Somerset	7.0	15.0	8.5	20.0	17.0	12.0	9.7	6.6	4.2	50.9	297 490	240 222	203 129	23.8	18.3
Sussex	8.3	19.5	8.4	17.9	18.6	11.6	6.7	5.0	3.9	50.4	144 166	130 936	116 119	10.1	12.8
Union	6.6	15.3	9.6	17.2	14.9	11.1	10.2	8.9	6.1	52.1	522 541	493 819	504 094	5.8	-2.0
Warren	7.6	17.2	8.9	17.4	16.1	10.8	8.8	7.7	5.6	51.7	102 437	91 675	84 429	11.7	8.5
NEW MEXICO	8.3	21.2	10.0	16.9	15.0	9.7	8.0	6.4	4.3	50.8	1 819 046	1 515 069	1 303 302	20.1	16.2
Bernalillo	7.7	18.4	10.5	18.7	16.2	10.1	7.9	6.4	4.1	51.2	556 678	480 577	420 261	15.8	14.4
Catron	6.2	20.4	5.9	12.5	16.0	12.4	11.3	9.4	5.9	47.4	3 543	2 563	2 720	38.2	-5.8
Chaves	8.2	22.4	9.6	14.6	13.1	8.9	8.7	8.2	6.4	50.8	61 382	57 849	51 103	6.1	13.2
Cibola	8.9	25.1	9.4	16.2	13.9	9.8	8.3	5.2	3.2	51.0	25 595	23 794	30 346	7.6	-21.6
Colfax	7.0	21.6	7.1	13.5	14.2	10.4	9.9	9.1	7.2	49.9	14 189	12 925	13 667	9.8	-5.4
Curry	9.1	21.6	11.5	18.3	12.8	8.5	7.3	6.0	4.8	50.9	45 044	42 207	42 019	6.7	0.4
De Baca	6.3	19.0	5.6	12.4	11.4	10.8	12.0	11.4	11.1	51.0	2 240	2 252	2 454	-0.5	-8.2
Dona Ana	8.6	21.8	14.5	16.9	13.3	8.6	7.5	5.5	3.3	50.3	174 682	135 510	96 340	28.9	40.7
Eddy	7.8	22.4	8.0	14.4	13.9	9.2	9.1	8.4	6.8	51.0	51 658	48 605	47 855	6.3	1.6
Grant	7.5	22.8	9.3	12.8	13.8	10.2	9.4	8.4	5.7	50.9	31 002	27 676	26 204	12.0	5.6
Guadalupe	7.6	23.1	8.1	15.8	12.3	10.4	9.1	6.8	6.9	49.8	4 680	4 156	4 496	12.6	-7.6
Harding	6.7	21.5	6.4	10.5	13.8	9.1	11.1	11.1	9.7	48.5	810	987	1 090	-17.9	-9.4
Hidalgo	8.0	25.1	8.8	14.9	13.3	9.9	8.5	6.5	5.0	49.3	5 932	5 958	6 049	-0.4	-1.5
Lea	8.7	24.5	8.9	16.0	13.6	9.0	8.7	6.4	4.2	50.6	55 511	55 765	55 993	-0.5	-0.4
Lincoln	6.6	18.8	6.7	14.3	15.4	11.4	11.1	9.8	5.8	50.7	19 411	12 219	10 997	58.9	11.1
Los Alamos	6.2	19.8	5.0	14.1	18.1	16.7	10.9	6.8	2.4	49.3	18 343	18 115	17 599	1.3	2.9
Luna	7.2	21.9	7.3	11.7	11.2	9.4	11.2	12.2	8.0	51.9	25 016	18 110	15 585	38.1	16.2
McKinley	11.7	27.1	10.6	16.8	13.1	8.3	6.0	3.7	2.6	51.7	74 798	60 686	56 536	23.3	7.3
Mora	6.9	22.3	8.6	14.0	13.8	9.7	10.0	8.0	6.7	50.0	5 180	4 264	4 205	21.5	1.4
Otero	9.5	21.0	11.3	18.5	13.5	8.9	8.0	5.8	3.3	49.4	62 298	51 928	44 665	20.0	16.3
Quay	6.8	20.8	7.0	12.7	14.1	11.5	10.4	9.3	7.4	51.8	10 155	10 823	10 577	-6.2	2.3
Rio Arriba	9.2	23.2	9.6	16.3	14.5	9.6	7.8	5.7	4.0	50.4	41 190	34 365	29 282	19.9	17.4
Roosevelt	7.4	19.8	17.3	14.0	11.5	8.6	7.9	7.5	6.1	51.3	18 018	16 702	15 695	7.9	6.4
Sandoval	9.9	22.1	7.7	18.8	16.1	8.6	6.7	6.4	3.7	50.9	89 908	63 319	34 400	42.0	84.1
San Juan	9.7	26.7	8.7	16.7	14.6	9.0	7.0	4.8	2.9	50.9	113 801	91 605	81 433	24.2	12.5
San Miguel	8.1	22.1	11.1	16.0	13.9	9.7	7.5	6.4	5.2	50.4	30 126	25 743	22 751	17.0	13.2
Santa Fe	7.3	18.7	8.7	16.5	19.1	11.5	8.0	6.1	4.0	51.0	129 292	98 928	75 519	30.7	31.0
Sierra	5.6	14.1	5.3	9.7	9.4	9.8	14.5	17.4	14.1	50.9	13 270	9 912	8 454	33.9	17.2
Socorro	8.2	22.2	11.6	16.1	13.9	9.9	7.7	6.2	4.2	49.2	18 078	14 764	12 566	22.4	17.5
Taos	7.6	21.5	8.0	14.6	17.3	11.2	8.6	6.3	4.7	51.0	29 979	23 118	19 456	29.7	18.8
Torrance	7.8	24.3	6.6	15.0	15.9	10.5	8.5	6.8	4.6	49.8	16 911	10 285	7 491	64.4	37.3
Union	7.5	20.7	6.0	13.1	12.9	11.1	10.7	9.5	8.5	51.2	4 174	4 124	4 725	1.2	-12.7
Valencia	8.4	22.4	8.4	17.1	15.5	10.0	8.1	6.3	3.8	49.8	66 152	45 235	30 769	46.2	47.0
NEW YORK	7.0	16.7	10.9	17.4	15.1	10.6	9.1	7.5	5.6	52.1	18 976 457	17 990 778	17 558 165	5.5	2.5
Albany	6.3	15.1	13.5	16.9	15.3	9.5	8.8	8.1	6.6	52.6	294 565	292 812	285 909	0.6	2.4
Allegany	6.9	18.9	16.6	12.9	13.0	9.5	8.9	7.2	6.2	50.4	49 927	50 470	51 742	-1.1	-2.5
Bronx	8.5	19.0	11.7	17.7	13.7	9.8	7.9	6.2	5.4	53.9	1 332 650	1 203 789	1 168 972	10.7	3.0
Broome	6.8	16.1	11.9	16.7	14.0	10.1	9.4	8.5	6.5	51.8	200 536	212 160	213 648	-5.5	-0.7
Cattaraugus	7.5	20.1	10.8	14.4	14.2	9.7	9.3	8.1	6.0	51.5	83 955	84 234	85 697	-0.3	-1.7
Cayuga	7.4	18.8	9.9	17.1	14.7	9.4	8.4	8.0	6.0	50.0	81 963	82 313	79 894	-0.4	3.0
Chautauqua	6.9	18.4	11.0	14.7	13.9	9.8	9.5	8.5	7.2	51.8	139 750	141 895	146 925	-1.5	-3.4
Chemung	7.1	18.2	10.2	15.6	14.5	10.0	9.3	8.8	6.3	51.4	91 070	95 195	97 656	-4.3	-2.5
Chenango	7.5	20.1	8.5	15.7	14.8	10.7	8.7	7.8	6.1	51.0	51 401	51 768	49 344	-0.7	4.9
Clinton	7.5	17.4	15.0	19.6	14.1	9.1	7.6	5.4	4.2	48.8	79 894	85 969	80 750	-7.1	6.5
Columbia	7.0	17.5	8.3	14.8	15.6	11.1	9.4	9.0	7.4	50.8	63 094	62 982	59 487	0.2	5.9
Cortland	7.1	17.7	17.0	15.2	13.7	9.4	7.7	6.7	5.4	52.4	48 599	48 963	48 820	-0.7	0.3
Delaware	6.8	18.4	10.7	13.3	13.9	10.7	10.0	9.3	7.1	50.8	48 055	47 352	46 824	1.5	0.9
Dutchess	7.1	16.8	11.1	17.9	16.1	11.1	8.5	6.4	5.0	49.7	280 150	259 462	245 055	8.0	5.9
Erie	6.9	16.4	10.7	16.5	14.3	10.0	9.9	9.0	6.2	52.4	950 265	968 584	1 015 472	-1.9	-4.6
Essex	6.9	17.4	8.9	16.8	15.1	10.7	9.5	8.3	6.4	48.7	38 851	37 152	36 176	4.6	2.7
Franklin	6.9	18.7	10.7	17.9	14.6	9.8	8.7	7.4	5.5	48.4	51 134	46 540	44 929	9.9	3.6
Fulton	6.7	19.2	8.9	14.8	14.4	10.1	9.3	9.2	7.3	51.9	55 073	54 191	55 153	1.6	-1.7

Table B. States and Counties

STATE County	Household relationship, 2000																
	In households (percent)										In group quarters (percent)						
					Child		Other relatives		Nonrelatives			Institutionalized population			Noninstitutionalized population		
	Total population	Total in house-holds	House-holder	Spouse	Total	Own child under 18 years	Total	Under 18 years	Total	Unmar-ried partner	Total in group quarters	Correc-tional institu-tions	Nurs-ing homes	Other institu-tions	Col-lege dormi-tories	Mili-tary quar-ters	Other
	54	55	56	57	58	59	60	61	62	63	64	65	66	67	68	69	70
NEW JERSEY—Cont'd																	
Mercer	350 761	94.0	35.9	18.1	28.8	21.4	6.1	2.2	5.1	1.9	6.0	1.2	0.6	0.2	3.5	0.0	0.5
Middlesex	750 162	97.2	35.4	20.2	30.0	21.5	6.7	1.7	5.0	1.8	2.0	0.5	0.4	0.1	1.3	0.0	0.5
Monmouth	615 301	98.4	36.4	21.2	32.1	24.2	4.8	1.5	3.7	1.5	1.6	0.2	0.6	0.0	0.2	0.2	0.4
Morris	470 212	98.0	36.1	22.7	30.9	23.5	4.5	1.0	3.9	1.3	2.0	0.1	0.7	0.2	0.6	0.0	0.4
Ocean	510 916	98.5	39.2	22.1	29.0	21.5	4.4	1.4	3.8	1.7	1.5	0.1	0.9	0.2	0.2	0.0	0.2
Passaic	489 049	98.0	33.5	17.3	32.5	22.5	9.5	3.1	5.1	2.0	2.0	0.4	0.5	0.0	0.4	0.0	0.7
Salem	64 285	98.1	37.8	20.3	30.9	22.6	5.1	2.4	4.0	2.1	1.9	0.4	0.8	0.0	0.0	0.0	0.7
Somerset	297 490	98.5	36.6	22.2	30.8	24.1	4.7	1.2	4.2	1.5	1.5	0.1	0.7	0.3	0.0	0.0	0.4
Sussex	144 166	98.8	35.3	22.9	33.9	26.4	3.5	1.0	3.3	1.8	1.2	0.1	0.7	0.0	0.0	0.0	0.3
Union	522 541	98.5	35.6	18.7	31.3	22.0	8.0	2.5	4.8	1.7	1.5	0.3	0.5	0.1	0.2	0.0	0.3
Warren	102 437	98.6	37.7	21.9	31.4	24.5	3.7	1.2	3.8	2.0	1.4	0.1	0.7	0.0	0.3	0.0	0.3
NEW MEXICO	1 819 046	98.0	37.3	18.8	31.2	24.5	5.8	2.8	4.9	2.4	2.0	0.6	0.4	0.1	0.4	0.1	0.4
Bernalillo	556 678	98.1	39.7	18.2	28.6	22.3	5.4	2.3	6.1	2.7	1.9	0.3	0.3	0.1	0.4	0.1	0.6
Catron	3 543	99.7	44.7	24.8	22.8	19.0	3.9	1.5	3.6	1.6	0.3	0.3	0.0	0.0	0.0	0.0	0.0
Chaves	61 382	97.9	36.8	19.4	31.8	25.3	5.7	2.9	4.3	2.1	2.1	0.5	0.5	0.1	0.6	0.0	0.5
Cibola	25 595	95.8	32.5	16.5	33.5	24.4	9.2	5.6	4.1	2.4	4.2	3.2	0.5	0.2	0.0	0.0	0.3
Colfax	14 189	97.0	41.0	21.7	27.1	21.9	3.4	1.7	3.9	2.4	3.0	0.2	1.0	1.6	0.0	0.0	0.2
Curry	45 044	97.4	37.2	20.1	32.2	27.2	4.3	2.3	3.6	1.6	2.6	0.4	0.7	0.0	0.0	1.2	0.3
De Baca	2 240	96.8	41.2	23.3	26.5	21.7	3.9	2.0	1.9	1.3	3.2	0.2	2.9	0.0	0.0	0.0	0.0
Dona Ana	174 682	97.1	34.1	17.9	33.4	25.9	6.7	3.3	5.1	2.2	2.9	0.9	0.2	0.0	1.3	0.0	0.3
Eddy	51 658	98.5	37.5	21.0	31.6	25.4	5.0	2.8	3.4	1.8	1.5	0.3	0.8	0.0	0.0	0.0	0.3
Grant	31 002	98.1	39.2	20.6	29.9	23.4	4.7	2.4	3.7	2.1	1.9	0.2	1.0	0.0	0.6	0.0	0.2
Guadalupe	4 680	88.8	35.4	17.5	28.7	22.1	4.0	2.0	3.3	2.1	11.2	10.4	0.4	0.0	0.0	0.0	0.4
Harding	810	100.0	45.8	24.1	24.9	18.6	3.8	1.6	1.4	0.9	0.0	0.0	0.0	0.0	0.0	0.0	0.0
Hidalgo	5 932	98.6	36.3	19.5	35.0	28.6	4.9	2.8	2.8	1.5	1.4	0.5	0.9	0.0	0.0	0.0	0.0
Lea	55 511	96.8	35.5	20.5	33.0	27.0	4.8	2.5	3.0	1.6	3.2	2.3	0.5	0.0	0.3	0.0	0.1
Lincoln	19 411	98.9	42.3	23.5	25.0	20.2	3.8	1.8	4.3	2.0	1.1	0.4	0.4	0.3	0.0	0.0	0.1
Los Alamos	18 343	99.5	40.9	25.6	28.8	25.0	1.6	0.5	2.6	1.2	0.5	0.1	0.3	0.0	0.0	0.0	0.1
Luna	25 016	99.0	37.6	20.1	32.1	26.2	5.8	3.2	3.4	1.7	1.0	0.5	0.4	0.1	0.0	0.0	0.0
McKinley	74 798	98.9	28.7	13.7	41.2	30.6	11.9	6.9	3.4	2.2	1.1	0.3	0.2	0.2	0.0	0.0	0.4
Mora	5 180	98.9	38.9	19.7	31.2	22.7	5.3	2.6	3.8	2.6	1.1	0.0	0.0	0.0	0.0	0.0	1.1
Otero	62 298	98.0	36.9	21.2	31.8	26.5	4.6	2.4	3.5	1.6	2.0	0.3	0.3	0.0	0.0	1.3	0.1
Quay	10 155	98.1	41.4	21.5	27.1	21.7	4.5	2.4	3.6	1.9	1.9	0.7	1.0	0.0	0.0	0.0	0.1
Rio Arriba	41 190	98.9	36.5	17.8	33.6	25.0	6.1	3.2	4.8	3.1	1.1	0.3	0.2	0.0	0.0	0.0	0.6
Roosevelt	18 018	95.8	36.8	19.5	30.1	25.2	4.3	2.1	5.0	1.9	4.2	0.3	0.4	0.1	3.0	0.0	0.5
Sandoval	89 908	99.2	34.9	20.2	33.3	25.5	6.8	3.6	4.1	2.2	0.8	0.0	0.3	0.0	0.0	0.0	0.5
San Juan	113 801	98.9	33.1	18.5	36.3	28.3	6.9	3.7	4.1	2.2	1.1	0.5	0.4	0.0	0.0	0.0	0.2
San Miguel	30 126	95.4	37.0	16.4	30.5	23.5	5.6	2.7	5.9	3.3	4.6	0.4	0.4	0.0	2.4	0.0	1.5
Santa Fe	129 292	98.2	40.6	18.5	27.4	21.6	5.1	2.0	6.6	3.1	1.8	0.6	0.3	0.0	0.6	0.0	0.3
Sierra	13 270	98.0	46.1	21.9	22.0	17.9	3.8	1.7	4.2	2.2	2.0	0.2	1.7	0.0	0.0	0.0	0.1
Socorro	18 078	96.8	36.9	17.9	30.6	24.2	6.1	3.3	5.3	2.5	3.2	0.2	0.3	0.0	2.5	0.0	0.2
Taos	29 979	99.0	42.3	18.1	28.7	22.0	4.4	2.0	5.6	3.4	1.0	0.1	0.5	0.0	0.0	0.0	0.4
Torrance	16 911	96.9	35.6	19.7	32.7	27.1	4.9	2.6	4.0	2.0	3.1	3.1	0.0	0.0	0.0	0.0	0.0
Union	4 174	99.6	41.5	22.7	30.3	25.3	3.0	1.7	2.0	1.2	0.4	0.2	0.0	0.0	0.0	0.0	0.2
Valencia	66 152	97.9	34.3	19.6	33.1	26.4	6.1	2.9	4.7	2.4	2.1	1.7	0.2	0.1	0.0	0.0	0.1
NEW YORK	18 976 457	96.9	37.2	17.3	30.2	21.9	6.7	2.2	5.5	2.0	3.1	0.6	0.7	0.2	0.9	0.0	0.7
Albany	294 565	94.7	40.9	17.7	26.8	20.8	3.5	1.2	5.9	2.5	5.3	0.2	1.0	0.2	3.1	0.0	0.7
Allegany	49 927	91.4	36.1	19.6	27.8	22.5	2.6	1.1	5.4	2.4	8.6	0.1	0.7	0.0	7.4	0.0	0.4
Bronx	1 332 650	96.5	34.8	10.9	34.8	24.8	10.2	3.9	5.7	2.3	3.5	1.0	0.9	0.2	0.4	0.0	1.0
Broome	200 536	95.5	40.3	19.2	27.2	21.2	3.1	1.1	5.8	2.4	4.5	0.2	1.1	0.3	2.5	0.0	0.3
Cattaraugus	83 955	96.1	38.1	19.9	30.0	23.9	3.0	1.3	5.1	2.6	3.9	0.1	0.9	0.2	1.9	0.0	0.8
Cayuga	81 963	94.1	37.3	19.4	29.4	23.0	3.1	1.2	5.0	2.7	5.9	4.0	0.7	0.0	0.4	0.0	0.6
Chautauqua	139 750	95.4	39.0	19.9	28.5	22.4	2.8	1.2	5.2	2.5	4.6	1.0	0.9	0.2	1.6	0.0	0.9
Chemung	91 070	93.9	38.5	19.2	28.0	22.1	3.3	1.5	5.0	2.7	6.1	3.3	1.1	0.2	1.2	0.0	0.4
Chenango	51 401	97.6	38.8	20.6	29.4	23.9	2.9	1.2	5.9	3.2	2.4	0.6	1.3	0.0	0.0	0.0	0.6
Clinton	79 894	91.1	36.8	18.8	26.4	21.1	2.5	1.0	6.6	3.1	8.9	4.9	0.7	0.1	2.9	0.0	0.4
Columbia	63 094	95.7	39.3	20.5	27.4	21.5	3.4	1.2	5.1	2.8	4.3	1.0	1.4	1.1	0.0	0.0	0.8
Cortland	48 599	93.6	37.5	18.4	26.8	21.7	2.6	1.1	8.2	3.1	6.4	0.1	0.7	0.1	5.0	0.0	0.4
Delaware	48 055	95.8	40.1	21.2	26.3	21.0	2.9	1.1	5.3	2.8	4.2	0.0	1.1	0.3	2.0	0.0	0.8
Dutchess	280 150	93.5	35.5	19.7	29.5	22.9	4.2	1.4	4.5	2.0	6.5	2.3	0.6	0.3	2.3	0.0	0.9
Erie	950 265	96.8	40.1	18.6	30.0	22.4	3.6	1.4	4.4	2.0	3.2	0.7	0.9	0.1	0.9	0.0	0.6
Essex	38 851	92.5	38.7	20.2	26.1	21.2	2.6	1.0	5.0	2.7	7.5	5.7	0.9	0.0	0.2	0.0	0.7
Franklin	51 134	86.4	35.1	17.4	26.3	21.0	2.4	0.9	5.2	2.9	13.6	10.8	0.5	0.2	1.0	0.0	1.1
Fulton	55 073	96.5	39.7	19.9	28.0	22.0	3.3	1.4	5.6	3.3	3.5	1.1	0.9	0.7	0.0	0.0	0.8

Table B. States and Counties

STATE County	Households by type, 2000										Average house-hold size	Average family size	Households, 1990		
	Family households						Nonfamily households								
			Married couple		Female householder[1]			Householder living alone							
	Total households	Total	With own children under 18 years	Total	With own children under 18 years	Total	With own children under 18 years	Total	Total	65 years and over	Average house-hold size	Average family size	Total house-holds	Female house-holder[1]	House-holder living alone
	71	72	73	74	75	76	77	78	79	80	81	82	83	84	85
NEW JERSEY—Cont'd															
Mercer	125 807	68.6	32.8	50.6	23.7	13.8	7.4	31.4	25.6	9.9	2.62	3.16	116 941	13.2	24.2
Middlesex	265 815	71.8	34.2	57.0	27.6	10.8	5.1	28.2	22.4	8.7	2.74	3.23	238 833	10.0	21.3
Monmouth	224 236	71.5	35.5	58.2	29.2	10.0	5.0	28.5	23.8	9.6	2.70	3.24	197 570	9.8	22.0
Morris	169 711	73.6	35.4	62.8	30.7	7.9	3.6	26.4	21.5	7.3	2.72	3.18	148 751	8.0	19.0
Ocean	200 402	68.8	28.1	56.4	22.4	9.2	4.3	31.2	27.0	16.5	2.51	3.06	168 147	8.6	24.9
Passaic	163 856	73.0	35.6	51.5	25.1	16.0	8.2	27.0	22.2	9.5	2.92	3.42	155 269	14.7	21.7
Salem	24 295	71.5	32.4	53.8	22.5	13.3	7.7	28.5	24.3	10.6	2.60	3.08	23 794	12.7	22.4
Somerset	108 984	71.9	36.2	60.6	30.9	8.2	4.1	28.1	22.8	7.0	2.69	3.19	88 346	8.2	20.6
Sussex	50 831	76.3	39.9	65.0	33.9	8.0	4.2	23.7	18.9	6.3	2.80	3.24	44 456	7.6	16.2
Union	186 124	71.6	34.0	52.6	25.4	14.2	6.8	28.4	23.6	10.2	2.77	3.28	180 076	12.7	23.0
Warren	38 660	71.1	34.7	58.2	27.9	9.2	5.0	28.9	24.0	10.0	2.61	3.12	33 997	9.1	22.2
NEW MEXICO	677 971	68.8	34.7	50.4	23.3	13.2	8.3	31.2	25.4	8.2	2.63	3.18	542 709	11.9	23.0
Bernalillo	220 936	63.9	31.4	46.0	20.6	12.9	7.9	36.1	28.5	7.9	2.47	3.06	185 582	11.9	26.1
Catron	1 584	65.7	22.3	55.4	16.5	7.6	4.5	34.3	30.1	11.4	2.23	2.75	1 010	5.8	27.1
Chaves	22 561	71.3	35.6	52.7	23.7	13.7	8.9	28.7	24.8	11.6	2.66	3.17	20 589	11.7	23.3
Cibola	8 327	75.4	38.0	50.6	23.2	18.3	10.8	24.6	21.1	7.3	2.95	3.41	7 292	16.0	17.8
Colfax	5 821	68.3	30.3	52.8	20.0	10.3	6.8	31.7	27.7	11.9	2.37	2.86	4 959	10.9	25.3
Curry	16 766	70.8	38.0	54.0	26.5	12.8	8.9	29.2	25.5	9.0	2.62	3.15	15 113	11.1	21.2
De Baca	922	66.7	27.2	56.6	21.9	7.3	3.9	33.3	30.8	18.0	2.35	2.96	913	7.9	28.5
Dona Ana	59 556	72.1	38.4	52.4	25.9	14.7	9.7	27.9	21.3	6.9	2.85	3.36	45 043	12.0	19.6
Eddy	19 379	72.6	35.6	56.1	25.0	11.9	7.7	27.4	24.2	10.7	2.63	3.12	17 472	9.9	21.8
Grant	12 146	70.1	31.3	52.7	20.3	12.9	8.2	29.9	25.7	10.7	2.50	3.01	9 773	11.3	21.2
Guadalupe	1 655	69.2	33.8	49.5	21.9	14.3	8.5	30.8	27.9	11.5	2.51	3.05	1 520	16.2	23.2
Harding	371	62.5	22.1	52.6	18.6	7.5	2.7	37.5	35.3	21.0	2.18	2.84	396	7.1	29.5
Hidalgo	2 152	71.7	37.5	53.8	26.1	13.6	9.1	28.3	25.3	10.7	2.72	3.29	2 004	10.5	20.5
Lea	19 699	74.7	39.3	57.8	28.2	12.2	8.2	25.3	22.5	9.9	2.73	3.20	19 306	10.5	20.3
Lincoln	8 202	68.7	26.2	55.6	17.9	9.3	6.1	31.3	26.7	10.0	2.34	2.80	4 789	9.6	24.9
Los Alamos	7 497	71.2	33.5	62.7	27.3	5.7	4.2	28.8	24.9	6.7	2.43	2.92	7 213	5.0	22.9
Luna	9 397	70.2	33.9	53.6	23.1	12.4	8.3	29.8	26.4	14.0	2.64	3.20	6 797	11.8	25.4
McKinley	21 476	77.7	46.0	47.7	28.5	22.7	13.1	22.3	19.5	5.3	3.44	3.99	16 588	20.1	17.0
Mora	2 017	69.3	31.2	55.4	20.5	11.9	6.7	30.7	26.9	10.6	2.54	3.08	1 519	12.4	22.8
Otero	22 984	73.1	37.1	57.5	26.5	11.8	8.1	26.9	23.3	8.1	2.66	3.14	18 155	9.8	20.1
Quay	4 201	67.7	28.9	52.1	19.2	12.0	7.5	32.3	28.9	13.8	2.37	2.90	4 238	10.1	25.6
Rio Arriba	15 044	71.9	36.9	48.8	23.0	15.9	9.3	28.1	23.5	7.8	2.71	3.19	11 461	14.3	19.9
Roosevelt	6 639	68.4	35.5	53.0	25.7	11.7	7.5	31.6	24.7	9.1	2.60	3.14	5 991	10.5	25.5
Sandoval	31 411	75.2	38.6	57.7	28.3	12.2	7.2	24.8	19.9	6.9	2.84	3.29	20 867	11.5	16.8
San Juan	37 711	76.7	42.0	55.7	28.8	14.7	9.1	23.3	19.3	6.4	2.99	3.43	28 740	13.0	17.7
San Miguel	11 134	67.7	34.6	44.5	20.1	16.4	10.1	32.3	26.6	8.2	2.58	3.10	8 701	16.2	22.8
Santa Fe	52 482	62.5	30.4	45.5	19.9	11.7	7.4	37.5	29.4	7.4	2.42	3.01	37 840	11.5	26.9
Sierra	6 113	59.2	20.4	47.5	13.6	8.6	4.9	40.8	35.9	19.3	2.13	2.75	4 428	7.6	33.0
Socorro	6 675	67.3	33.8	48.4	21.7	13.3	8.6	32.7	26.8	8.2	2.62	3.20	5 217	10.6	24.0
Taos	12 675	61.2	29.9	42.7	18.0	12.7	8.1	38.8	32.1	8.9	2.34	2.98	8 752	13.2	25.6
Torrance	6 024	72.9	37.8	55.4	26.7	12.3	7.7	27.1	23.2	7.9	2.72	3.20	3 670	9.0	21.0
Union	1 733	67.9	31.1	54.7	23.5	9.1	5.3	32.1	30.0	14.9	2.40	2.99	1 615	9.0	27.2
Valencia	22 681	76.5	39.6	57.2	27.5	13.1	8.2	23.5	18.8	6.4	2.86	3.25	15 170	11.1	17.3
NEW YORK	7 056 860	65.7	31.6	46.6	21.6	14.7	8.1	34.3	28.1	10.1	2.61	3.22	6 639 322	13.8	27.2
Albany	120 512	58.9	27.9	43.2	18.8	12.2	7.4	41.1	33.0	11.3	2.32	2.99	115 824	11.5	30.3
Allegany	18 009	67.7	31.5	54.2	23.0	9.0	5.8	32.3	26.0	11.3	2.53	3.04	17 011	8.6	23.2
Bronx	463 212	68.0	38.1	31.4	16.2	30.4	19.2	32.0	27.4	9.4	2.78	3.37	424 112	28.0	28.1
Broome	80 749	62.2	28.2	47.6	19.6	10.8	6.5	37.8	31.0	12.4	2.37	2.97	81 843	10.0	26.9
Cattaraugus	32 023	67.6	32.1	52.3	22.5	10.8	6.8	32.4	26.8	11.6	2.52	3.05	30 456	10.6	24.8
Cayuga	30 558	68.2	32.6	52.0	22.7	11.0	6.9	31.8	26.2	11.9	2.53	3.04	29 075	10.8	23.6
Chautauqua	54 515	66.0	30.5	50.9	21.0	10.8	7.0	34.0	28.1	12.6	2.45	2.99	53 696	10.3	26.1
Chemung	35 049	66.4	31.0	49.8	20.5	12.4	8.1	33.6	27.9	12.2	2.44	2.97	35 275	11.5	25.5
Chenango	19 926	68.0	32.5	53.1	22.5	9.8	6.6	32.0	26.1	11.4	2.52	3.01	19 141	8.7	23.3
Clinton	29 423	65.5	32.0	51.0	22.5	10.2	6.6	34.5	26.3	10.0	2.47	2.98	29 123	8.9	22.1
Columbia	24 796	66.9	29.9	52.2	21.1	10.3	6.3	33.1	27.1	11.5	2.43	2.95	23 696	9.9	24.0
Cortland	18 210	63.8	31.0	49.2	21.5	10.3	6.7	36.2	26.5	10.4	2.50	3.00	17 247	9.7	23.6
Delaware	19 270	66.1	28.1	52.8	19.9	9.0	5.4	33.9	28.3	13.6	2.39	2.90	17 646	8.8	25.3
Dutchess	99 536	69.5	34.5	55.5	26.6	10.3	6.0	30.5	24.6	9.0	2.63	3.16	89 567	9.3	22.2
Erie	380 873	63.9	29.6	46.5	20.0	13.7	8.0	36.1	30.5	12.5	2.41	3.04	376 994	13.3	27.9
Essex	15 028	65.4	29.2	52.2	21.1	8.9	5.4	34.6	28.3	12.6	2.39	2.93	13 721	8.8	25.7
Franklin	17 931	65.8	32.2	49.5	21.6	11.1	7.3	34.2	28.2	12.0	2.46	3.00	16 284	10.3	25.8
Fulton	21 884	66.3	30.5	50.0	20.2	11.3	7.1	33.7	27.7	12.9	2.43	2.94	20 995	10.7	25.8

[1] No spouse present.

Table B. States and Counties

STATE County	Percent change of households, 1990–2000	Total housing units	Occupied housing units (percent)	Vacant housing units				Occupied housing units				
				Total	For seasonal, recreational, or occasional use	Homeowner vacancy rate (percent)	Rental vacancy rate (percent)	Total	Percent owner-occupied housing units	Percent renter-occupied housing units	Average household size of owner-occupied units	Average household size of renter-occupied units
	86	87	88	89	90	91	92	93	94	95	96	97
NEW JERSEY—Cont'd												
Mercer	7.6	133 280	94.4	5.6	0.3	1.6	5.4	125 807	67.0	33.0	2.75	2.37
Middlesex	11.3	273 637	97.1	2.9	0.3	0.8	2.7	265 815	66.7	33.3	2.86	2.50
Monmouth	13.5	240 884	93.1	6.9	3.2	1.1	4.6	224 236	74.6	25.4	2.87	2.21
Morris	14.1	174 379	97.3	2.7	0.7	0.6	2.9	169 711	76.0	24.0	2.88	2.21
Ocean	19.2	248 711	80.6	19.4	13.3	1.8	11.7	200 402	83.2	16.8	2.49	2.59
Passaic	5.5	170 048	96.4	3.6	0.5	1.0	2.9	163 856	55.6	44.4	2.99	2.84
Salem	2.1	26 158	92.9	7.1	0.5	2.0	7.1	24 295	73.0	27.0	2.69	2.34
Somerset	23.4	112 023	97.3	2.7	0.4	0.7	3.1	108 984	77.2	22.8	2.78	2.36
Sussex	14.3	56 528	89.9	10.1	6.3	1.5	5.0	50 831	82.7	17.3	2.92	2.27
Union	3.4	192 945	96.5	3.5	0.2	0.9	3.3	186 124	61.6	38.4	2.92	2.52
Warren	13.7	41 157	93.9	6.1	0.9	2.2	6.0	38 660	72.7	27.3	2.77	2.19
NEW MEXICO	24.9	780 579	86.9	13.1	4.1	2.2	11.6	677 971	70.0	30.0	2.72	2.41
Bernalillo	19.1	239 074	92.4	7.6	0.5	1.8	11.5	220 936	63.7	36.3	2.61	2.22
Catron	56.8	2 548	62.2	37.8	25.0	4.2	5.2	1 584	80.6	19.4	2.21	2.32
Chaves	9.6	25 647	88.0	12.0	1.0	3.0	13.5	22 561	70.9	29.1	2.71	2.55
Cibola	14.2	10 328	80.6	19.4	7.8	1.9	10.9	8 327	77.0	23.0	2.98	2.85
Colfax	17.4	8 959	65.0	35.0	25.3	3.8	13.4	5 821	72.6	27.4	2.40	2.29
Curry	10.9	19 212	87.3	12.7	0.6	4.6	10.0	16 766	59.4	40.6	2.62	2.62
De Baca	1.0	1 307	70.5	29.5	13.1	3.7	14.3	922	78.0	22.0	2.32	2.47
Dona Ana	32.2	65 210	91.3	8.7	0.8	1.8	10.3	59 556	67.5	32.5	2.98	2.58
Eddy	10.9	22 249	87.1	12.9	1.3	2.9	18.1	19 379	74.3	25.7	2.67	2.50
Grant	24.3	14 066	86.4	13.6	3.3	2.6	14.7	12 146	74.4	25.6	2.54	2.39
Guadalupe	8.9	2 160	76.6	23.4	5.5	3.7	12.3	1 655	73.8	26.2	2.58	2.31
Harding	-6.3	545	68.1	31.9	14.3	1.4	7.1	371	75.2	24.8	2.24	2.02
Hidalgo	7.4	2 848	75.6	24.4	3.0	3.3	19.5	2 152	67.9	32.1	2.73	2.68
Lea	2.0	23 405	84.2	15.8	0.5	3.6	18.7	19 699	72.6	27.4	2.76	2.65
Lincoln	71.3	15 298	53.6	46.4	39.4	4.1	15.4	8 202	77.2	22.8	2.33	2.36
Los Alamos	3.9	7 937	94.5	5.5	0.9	1.1	11.3	7 497	78.6	21.4	2.56	1.98
Luna	38.3	11 291	83.2	16.8	3.3	3.4	16.6	9 397	74.9	25.1	2.65	2.58
McKinley	29.5	26 718	80.4	19.6	7.0	1.4	6.8	21 476	72.4	27.6	3.53	3.21
Mora	32.8	2 973	67.8	32.2	14.4	0.9	5.1	2 017	82.4	17.6	2.59	2.32
Otero	26.6	29 272	78.5	21.5	8.4	3.5	16.4	22 984	66.9	33.1	2.68	2.62
Quay	-0.9	5 664	74.2	25.8	9.1	4.4	18.9	4 201	70.6	29.4	2.38	2.35
Rio Arriba	31.3	18 016	83.5	16.5	5.8	1.2	8.0	15 044	81.6	18.4	2.74	2.57
Roosevelt	10.8	7 746	85.7	14.3	0.3	3.6	11.7	6 639	62.7	37.3	2.61	2.58
Sandoval	50.5	34 866	90.1	9.9	3.6	2.1	11.4	31 411	83.6	16.4	2.90	2.54
San Juan	31.2	43 221	87.3	12.7	4.0	1.2	9.3	37 711	75.4	24.6	3.03	2.85
San Miguel	28.0	14 254	78.1	21.9	10.8	1.7	12.2	11 134	73.1	26.9	2.71	2.23
Santa Fe	38.7	57 701	91.0	9.0	4.0	1.5	5.6	52 482	68.6	31.4	2.55	2.14
Sierra	38.1	8 727	70.0	30.0	17.7	5.5	17.4	6 113	74.9	25.1	2.13	2.12
Socorro	27.9	7 808	85.5	14.5	3.1	2.5	11.8	6 675	71.1	28.9	2.72	2.38
Taos	44.8	17 404	72.8	27.2	17.1	1.7	16.0	12 675	75.5	24.5	2.42	2.10
Torrance	64.1	7 257	83.0	17.0	2.9	4.3	9.3	6 024	83.9	16.1	2.73	2.69
Union	7.3	2 225	77.9	22.1	5.8	2.4	7.3	1 733	73.0	27.0	2.39	2.43
Valencia	49.5	24 643	92.0	8.0	0.6	2.8	11.8	22 681	83.9	16.1	2.87	2.77
NEW YORK	6.3	7 679 307	91.9	8.1	3.1	1.6	4.6	7 056 860	53.0	47.0	2.78	2.41
Albany	4.0	129 972	92.7	7.3	0.9	1.8	6.5	120 512	57.7	42.3	2.56	1.98
Allegany	5.9	24 505	73.5	26.5	19.9	2.9	9.4	18 009	73.8	26.2	2.63	2.26
Bronx	9.2	490 659	94.4	5.6	0.2	2.0	4.2	463 212	19.6	80.4	2.83	2.76
Broome	-1.3	88 817	90.9	9.1	1.4	2.2	10.1	80 749	65.1	34.9	2.53	2.07
Cattaraugus	5.1	39 839	80.4	19.6	12.2	2.5	10.9	32 023	74.4	25.6	2.62	2.24
Cayuga	5.1	35 477	86.1	13.9	7.2	2.0	10.2	30 558	72.1	27.9	2.65	2.20
Chautauqua	1.5	64 900	84.0	16.0	9.0	1.9	9.6	54 515	69.2	30.8	2.56	2.18
Chemung	-0.6	37 745	92.9	7.1	0.7	1.8	9.2	35 049	68.9	31.1	2.54	2.22
Chenango	4.1	23 890	83.4	16.6	8.2	3.2	11.0	19 926	75.3	24.7	2.62	2.19
Clinton	1.0	33 091	88.9	11.1	5.3	1.7	6.8	29 423	68.5	31.5	2.65	2.09
Columbia	4.6	30 207	82.1	17.9	11.3	2.6	6.1	24 796	70.6	29.4	2.51	2.26
Cortland	5.6	20 116	90.5	9.5	2.9	2.3	8.1	18 210	64.3	35.7	2.64	2.24
Delaware	9.2	28 952	66.6	33.4	26.6	3.1	11.0	19 270	75.7	24.3	2.45	2.20
Dutchess	11.1	106 103	93.8	6.2	2.3	1.3	4.5	99 536	69.0	31.0	2.81	2.23
Erie	1.0	415 868	91.6	8.4	0.5	1.8	8.8	380 873	65.3	34.7	2.60	2.07
Essex	9.5	23 115	65.0	35.0	26.5	3.1	13.3	15 028	73.8	26.2	2.49	2.10
Franklin	10.1	23 936	74.9	25.1	18.0	2.6	9.6	17 931	70.5	29.5	2.60	2.13
Fulton	4.2	27 787	78.8	21.2	13.1	3.3	9.2	21 884	72.1	27.9	2.53	2.16

Table B. States and Counties

STATE/ County code	MSA/ PMSA/ NECMA code[1]	County type[2]	STATE County	Population, 2000				Population, 1990				Population and population characteristics, 2000					
												Race (percent)					
												One race					
				Land area, 2000[3] (sq km)	Total persons	Rank	Per square kilometer	Land area, 1990[3] (sq km)	Total persons	Rank	Per square kilometer	White	Black or African American	American Indian or Alaska Native	Asian	Native Hawaiian and other Pacific Islander	Some other race
				1	2	3	4	5	6	7	8	9	10	11	12	13	14
			NEW YORK—Cont'd														
36 037	6840	1	Genesee	1 280	60 370	802	47.2	1 280	60 060	723	46.9	94.7	2.1	0.8	0.5	0.0	0.7
36 039	...	6	Greene	1 678	48 195	944	28.7	1 678	44 739	915	26.7	90.8	5.5	0.3	0.5	0.0	1.5
36 041	...	8	Hamilton	4 456	5 379	2 822	1.2	4 457	5 279	2 822	1.2	97.7	0.4	0.3	0.1	0.1	0.7
36 043	8680	2	Herkimer	3 655	64 427	755	17.6	3 657	65 809	666	18.0	97.8	0.5	0.2	0.4	0.0	0.2
36 045	...	5	Jefferson	3 295	111 738	482	33.9	3 295	110 943	416	33.7	88.7	5.8	0.5	0.9	0.1	2.1
36 047	5600	0	Kings	183	2 465 326	7	13 471.7	183	2 300 664	6	12 571.9	41.2	36.4	0.4	7.5	0.1	10.1
36 049	...	6	Lewis	3 303	26 944	1 485	8.2	3 304	26 796	1 396	8.1	98.2	0.4	0.3	0.2	0.1	0.3
36 051	6840	1	Livingston	1 637	64 328	757	39.3	1 637	62 372	698	38.1	94.0	3.0	0.3	0.8	0.0	0.8
36 053	8160	2	Madison	1 699	69 441	713	40.9	1 699	69 166	641	40.7	96.5	1.3	0.5	0.6	0.0	0.3
36 055	6840	0	Monroe	1 708	735 343	68	430.5	1 708	713 968	58	418.0	79.1	13.7	0.3	2.4	0.0	2.4
36 057	0160	2	Montgomery	1 048	49 708	921	47.4	1 048	51 981	813	49.6	94.9	1.2	0.2	0.5	0.0	1.9
36 059	5380	0	Nassau	743	1 334 544	26	1 796.2	743	1 287 873	22	1 733.3	79.3	10.1	0.2	4.7	0.0	3.6
36 061	5600	0	New York	59	1 537 195	17	26 054.2	73	1 487 536	15	20 377.2	54.4	17.4	0.5	9.4	0.1	14.1
36 063	1280	0	Niagara	1 354	219 846	257	162.4	1 354	220 756	225	163.0	90.7	6.1	0.9	0.6	0.0	0.4
36 065	8680	2	Oneida	3 141	235 469	246	75.0	3 141	250 836	199	79.9	90.2	5.7	0.2	1.2	0.0	1.1
36 067	8160	2	Onondaga	2 021	458 336	126	226.8	2 021	468 973	105	232.0	84.8	9.4	0.9	2.1	0.0	0.9
36 069	6840	1	Ontario	1 669	100 224	524	60.1	1 669	95 101	487	57.0	95.0	2.1	0.2	0.7	0.0	0.7
36 071	5660	2	Orange	2 114	341 367	171	161.5	2 114	307 571	162	145.5	83.7	8.1	0.4	1.5	0.0	4.1
36 073	6840	1	Orleans	1 014	44 171	1 013	43.6	1 014	41 846	959	41.3	89.1	7.3	0.5	0.3	0.0	1.5
36 075	8160	2	Oswego	2 469	122 377	444	49.6	2 469	121 785	378	49.3	97.2	0.6	0.4	0.4	0.0	0.5
36 077	...	6	Otsego	2 597	61 676	788	23.7	2 598	60 390	718	23.2	95.8	1.7	0.2	0.6	0.1	0.5
36 079	5600	1	Putnam	599	95 745	541	159.8	600	83 941	545	139.9	93.9	1.6	0.1	1.2	0.0	1.7
36 081	5600	0	Queens	283	2 229 379	9	7 877.7	283	1 951 598	9	6 896.1	44.1	20.0	0.5	17.6	0.1	11.7
36 083	0160	2	Rensselaer	1 694	152 538	349	90.0	1 694	154 429	301	91.2	91.1	4.7	0.2	1.7	0.0	0.9
36 085	5600	0	Richmond	151	443 728	134	2 938.6	152	378 977	133	2 493.3	77.6	9.7	0.2	5.7	0.0	4.1
36 087	5600	0	Rockland	451	286 753	195	635.8	451	265 475	185	588.6	76.9	11.0	0.2	5.5	0.1	3.8
36 089	...	5	St. Lawrence	6 956	111 931	481	16.1	6 956	111 974	410	16.1	94.5	2.4	0.9	0.7	0.0	0.7
36 091	0160	2	Saratoga	2 103	200 635	273	95.4	2 103	181 276	270	86.2	96.0	1.4	0.2	1.0	0.0	0.4
36 093	0160	2	Schenectady	534	146 555	372	274.4	534	149 285	317	279.6	87.8	6.8	0.2	2.0	0.0	1.2
36 095	0160	2	Schoharie	1 611	31 582	1 359	19.6	1 611	31 840	1 216	19.8	96.6	1.3	0.3	0.4	0.0	0.5
36 097	...	8	Schuyler	851	19 224	1 831	22.6	851	18 662	1 754	21.9	96.5	1.5	0.4	0.3	0.0	0.4
36 099	...	6	Seneca	842	33 342	1 303	39.6	842	33 683	1 174	40.0	95.0	2.3	0.2	0.7	0.0	0.7
36 101	...	4	Steuben	3 607	98 726	528	27.4	3 607	99 088	463	27.5	96.4	1.4	0.3	0.9	0.0	0.2
36 103	5380	0	Suffolk	2 363	1 419 369	22	600.7	2 360	1 321 339	20	559.9	84.6	6.9	0.3	2.4	0.0	3.7
36 105	...	6	Sullivan	2 512	73 966	675	29.4	2 512	69 277	640	27.6	85.3	8.5	0.3	1.1	0.0	2.9
36 107	0960	2	Tioga	1 343	51 784	896	38.6	1 343	52 337	809	39.0	97.5	0.5	0.2	0.6	0.0	0.2
36 109	...	5	Tompkins	1 233	96 501	535	78.3	1 233	94 097	491	76.3	85.5	3.6	0.3	7.2	0.0	1.1
36 111	...	4	Ulster	2 918	177 749	310	60.9	2 918	165 380	287	56.7	88.9	5.4	0.3	1.2	0.0	2.2
36 113	2975	3	Warren	2 251	63 303	766	28.1	2 253	59 209	736	26.3	97.5	0.6	0.2	0.5	0.0	0.2
36 115	2975	3	Washington	2 164	61 042	798	28.2	2 164	59 330	731	27.4	95.0	2.9	0.2	0.3	0.0	0.8
36 117	6840	1	Wayne	1 565	93 765	547	59.9	1 565	89 123	515	56.9	93.8	3.2	0.3	0.5	0.0	0.9
36 119	5600	0	Westchester	1 121	923 459	40	823.8	1 121	874 866	35	780.4	71.3	14.2	0.3	4.5	0.0	6.6
36 121	...	6	Wyoming	1 536	43 424	1 030	28.3	1 536	42 507	945	27.7	91.8	5.5	0.3	0.4	0.0	1.3
36 123	...	6	Yates	876	24 621	1 570	28.1	876	22 810	1 542	26.0	97.9	0.6	0.1	0.3	0.0	0.4
37 000	...		NORTH CAROLINA	126 161	8 049 313	X	63.8	126 180	6 632 448	X	52.6	72.1	21.6	1.2	1.4	0.0	2.3
37 001	3120	3	Alamance	1 114	130 800	410	117.4	1 115	108 213	426	97.1	75.6	18.8	0.4	0.9	0.0	3.2
37 003	3290	2	Alexander	674	33 603	1 297	49.9	674	27 544	1 372	40.9	92.0	4.6	0.1	1.0	0.0	1.3
37 005	...	9	Alleghany	608	10 677	2 387	17.6	608	9 590	2 424	15.8	95.7	1.2	0.3	0.2	0.0	1.8
37 007	...	6	Anson	1 377	25 275	1 555	18.4	1 377	23 474	1 515	17.0	49.5	48.6	0.4	0.6	0.0	0.3
37 009	...	9	Ashe	1 104	24 384	1 572	22.1	1 104	22 209	1 571	20.1	97.2	0.7	0.3	0.2	0.0	1.1
37 011	...	9	Avery	640	17 167	1 943	26.8	640	14 867	1 997	23.2	94.0	3.5	0.3	0.2	0.0	1.3
37 013	...	6	Beaufort	2 144	44 958	1 000	21.0	2 144	42 283	953	19.7	68.4	29.0	0.2	0.2	0.0	1.4
37 015	...	9	Bertie	1 811	19 773	1 803	10.9	1 811	20 388	1 656	11.3	36.3	62.3	0.4	0.1	0.0	0.3
37 017	...	6	Bladen	2 266	32 278	1 340	14.2	2 266	28 663	1 341	12.6	57.2	37.9	2.0	0.1	0.0	2.0
37 019	9200	3	Brunswick	2 214	73 143	685	33.0	2 214	50 985	828	23.0	82.3	14.4	0.7	0.3	0.0	1.3
37 021	0480	3	Buncombe	1 699	206 330	269	121.4	1 700	174 357	276	102.6	89.1	7.5	0.4	0.7	0.0	1.1
37 023	3290	2	Burke	1 312	89 148	582	67.9	1 312	75 740	593	57.7	86.0	6.7	0.3	3.5	0.0	2.2
37 025	1520	0	Cabarrus	944	131 063	408	138.8	944	98 935	464	104.8	83.3	12.2	0.3	0.9	0.0	2.3
37 027	3290	2	Caldwell	1 221	77 415	655	63.4	1 222	70 709	627	57.9	91.7	5.5	0.2	0.4	0.0	1.4
37 029	...	8	Camden	623	6 885	2 696	11.1	623	5 904	2 771	9.5	80.6	17.3	0.4	0.6	0.0	0.1
37 031	...	6	Carteret	1 346	59 383	809	44.1	1 376	52 407	807	38.1	90.3	7.0	0.4	0.5	0.1	0.6
37 033	...	8	Caswell	1 100	23 501	1 615	21.4	1 103	20 662	1 646	18.7	61.1	36.5	0.2	0.2	0.0	1.2
37 035	3290	2	Catawba	1 036	141 685	386	136.8	1 036	118 412	393	114.3	85.0	8.4	0.3	2.9	0.1	2.3
37 037	6640	2	Chatham	1 769	49 329	927	27.9	1 769	38 979	1 023	22.0	74.9	17.1	0.4	0.6	0.0	5.8
37 039	...	7	Cherokee	1 179	24 298	1 584	20.6	1 179	20 170	1 666	17.1	94.8	1.6	1.6	0.3	0.0	0.4

[1] MSA = Metropolitan Statistical Area. PMSA = Primary MSA. NECMA = New England County Metropolitan Area. See Appendix A for explanation of these concepts. See Appendix B for list of metropolitan areas identified by type, with component counties.
[2] County typology code from the Economic Research Service of USDA. See Appendix A for definition.
[3] Dry land or land partially or temporarily covered by water.

Table B. States and Counties

STATE County	Two or more races	White	Black	American Indian or Alaska Native	Asian	Native Hawaiian and other Pacific Islander	Some other race	Hispanic[1]	White	Black or African American	American Indian or Alaska Native	Asian and Pacific Islander	Hispanic[1]
	15	16	17	18	19	20	21	22	23	24	25	26	27
NEW YORK—Cont'd													
Genesee	1.2	95.7	2.7	1.2	0.6	0.0	1.0	1.5	96.5	1.8	1.1	0.4	0.8
Greene	1.4	92.0	6.0	0.7	0.8	0.1	1.9	4.3	93.0	4.9	0.3	0.4	3.4
Hamilton	0.7	98.4	0.6	0.7	0.2	0.1	0.8	1.1	99.4	0.2	0.2	0.1	0.6
Herkimer	0.8	98.6	0.7	0.6	0.5	0.0	0.4	0.9	99.2	0.3	0.2	0.2	0.6
Jefferson	1.8	90.2	6.6	1.1	1.3	0.3	2.5	4.2	91.2	5.9	0.4	0.9	2.8
Kings	4.3	43.7	38.1	0.8	8.4	0.2	13.2	19.8	46.9	37.9	0.3	4.8	20.1
Lewis	0.6	98.7	0.5	0.6	0.3	0.1	0.5	0.6	98.8	0.4	0.2	0.3	0.5
Livingston	1.0	95.0	3.4	0.7	0.9	0.1	1.0	2.3	96.2	2.4	0.3	0.5	1.6
Madison	0.8	97.2	1.6	0.9	0.7	0.0	0.4	1.1	97.6	1.1	0.4	0.6	0.8
Monroe	1.9	80.6	14.7	0.7	2.8	0.1	3.2	5.3	84.1	11.9	0.3	1.8	3.7
Montgomery	1.3	96.0	1.5	0.6	0.7	0.0	2.5	6.9	96.5	0.9	0.2	0.4	5.2
Nassau	2.1	80.8	10.8	0.4	5.3	0.1	4.9	10.0	86.6	8.6	0.1	3.1	6.0
New York	4.1	57.1	19.0	1.0	10.2	0.2	16.9	27.2	58.3	22.0	0.4	7.4	26.0
Niagara	1.2	91.8	6.7	1.4	0.7	0.0	0.6	1.3	93.0	5.5	0.9	0.4	1.0
Oneida	1.5	91.6	6.3	0.5	1.4	0.1	1.8	3.2	92.7	5.4	0.2	0.9	2.3
Onondaga	2.0	86.4	10.3	1.5	2.4	0.1	1.3	2.4	89.2	8.0	0.7	1.5	1.5
Ontario	1.3	96.2	2.6	0.6	0.9	0.1	1.0	2.1	97.0	1.8	0.2	0.5	1.3
Orange	2.2	85.5	9.1	0.8	1.9	0.1	5.0	11.6	88.9	7.2	0.3	1.2	7.0
Orleans	1.2	90.2	7.9	0.9	0.5	0.1	1.8	3.9	91.5	6.6	0.5	0.4	2.5
Oswego	0.9	98.0	0.8	0.8	0.6	0.0	0.7	1.3	98.5	0.5	0.4	0.4	1.0
Otsego	1.0	96.7	2.1	0.6	0.8	0.1	0.8	1.9	97.7	1.3	0.2	0.5	1.2
Putnam	1.4	95.2	2.0	0.5	1.5	0.1	2.3	6.2	97.5	1.0	0.1	0.9	2.7
Queens	6.1	47.4	21.8	1.2	19.4	0.2	16.3	25.0	57.9	21.7	0.4	12.2	19.5
Rensselaer	1.3	92.3	5.3	0.6	1.9	0.1	1.3	2.1	94.7	3.3	0.2	1.4	1.2
Richmond	2.7	79.5	10.5	0.6	6.3	0.1	5.8	12.1	85.0	8.1	0.2	4.5	8.0
Rockland	2.5	78.4	12.2	0.6	6.0	0.2	5.3	10.2	83.9	10.0	0.2	4.1	6.7
St. Lawrence	0.8	95.2	2.6	1.3	0.9	0.1	0.9	1.8	96.7	1.4	0.7	0.7	1.1
Saratoga	1.0	96.9	1.7	0.6	1.3	0.0	0.6	1.4	97.6	1.3	0.1	0.8	1.1
Schenectady	2.0	89.4	7.8	0.7	2.4	0.1	1.8	3.2	93.7	4.3	0.2	1.2	1.7
Schoharie	0.9	97.5	1.6	0.8	0.5	0.0	0.7	1.9	97.6	1.3	0.2	0.3	1.7
Schuyler	1.0	97.4	1.7	1.0	0.3	0.0	0.6	1.2	98.3	0.8	0.3	0.2	0.9
Seneca	1.1	96.0	2.6	0.7	0.9	0.1	0.9	2.0	97.2	1.6	0.2	0.6	1.1
Steuben	0.8	97.2	1.6	0.6	1.0	0.0	0.4	0.8	97.9	1.2	0.2	0.6	0.5
Suffolk	2.1	86.1	7.7	0.6	2.9	0.1	4.8	10.5	90.0	6.3	0.2	1.7	6.6
Sullivan	1.9	86.8	9.3	0.7	1.4	0.1	3.7	9.2	88.4	8.5	0.2	0.8	6.9
Tioga	0.9	98.3	0.8	0.7	0.7	0.0	0.4	1.0	98.4	0.6	0.2	0.6	0.7
Tompkins	2.3	87.3	4.4	0.8	8.0	0.3	1.7	3.1	90.2	3.3	0.3	5.5	2.2
Ulster	2.0	90.6	6.3	0.9	1.5	0.1	2.8	6.2	92.6	4.9	0.3	1.2	4.1
Warren	0.9	98.3	0.9	0.6	0.7	0.0	0.4	1.0	98.7	0.5	0.2	0.5	0.8
Washington	0.8	95.7	3.1	0.6	0.4	0.1	0.9	2.0	95.6	3.5	0.2	0.2	2.2
Wayne	1.3	95.0	3.8	0.8	0.6	0.0	1.1	2.4	95.4	3.1	0.3	0.4	1.7
Westchester	3.0	73.6	15.2	0.6	5.1	0.1	8.7	15.6	79.4	13.7	0.3	3.7	9.9
Wyoming	0.7	92.4	5.6	0.5	0.6	0.0	1.5	2.9	93.5	4.9	0.2	0.3	2.4
Yates	0.7	98.6	0.8	0.5	0.4	0.1	0.5	0.9	98.6	0.6	0.2	0.3	1.0
NORTH CAROLINA	1.3	73.1	22.1	1.6	1.7	0.1	2.8	4.7	75.6	22.0	1.2	0.8	1.2
Alamance	1.2	76.5	19.2	0.7	1.1	0.1	3.6	6.8	79.8	19.2	0.3	0.5	0.7
Alexander	0.8	92.7	4.9	0.5	1.2	0.0	1.5	2.5	93.2	6.1	0.2	0.2	0.7
Alleghany	0.9	96.5	1.4	0.8	0.2	0.0	2.0	5.0	97.4	1.8	0.1	0.1	0.9
Anson	0.5	49.9	48.8	0.7	0.7	0.0	0.4	0.8	52.2	47.3	0.3	0.1	0.3
Ashe	0.6	97.7	0.8	0.6	0.3	0.0	1.2	2.4	98.9	0.6	0.1	0.1	0.5
Avery	0.7	94.6	3.6	0.8	0.3	0.1	1.4	2.4	98.2	1.1	0.2	0.2	0.8
Beaufort	0.7	69.0	29.3	0.4	0.3	0.0	1.7	3.2	68.5	31.2	0.1	0.1	0.5
Bertie	0.5	36.6	62.6	0.5	0.2	0.0	0.5	1.0	38.2	61.5	0.2	0.1	0.2
Bladen	0.7	57.8	38.2	2.4	0.2	0.1	2.2	3.7	59.1	39.1	1.6	0.1	0.5
Brunswick	1.0	83.2	14.7	1.2	0.4	0.1	1.6	2.7	81.1	18.1	0.5	0.2	0.7
Buncombe	1.2	90.2	7.9	0.9	0.9	0.1	1.5	2.8	90.9	8.2	0.3	0.4	0.7
Burke	1.1	86.7	7.0	0.7	3.9	0.3	2.6	3.6	91.8	6.8	0.2	1.0	0.5
Cabarrus	1.0	84.1	12.5	0.6	1.1	0.1	2.7	5.1	86.2	13.0	0.3	0.4	0.5
Caldwell	0.8	92.4	5.7	0.5	0.5	0.0	1.7	2.5	94.1	5.5	0.1	0.2	0.4
Camden	1.0	81.6	17.5	1.0	0.7	0.0	0.3	0.7	74.3	25.1	0.4	0.2	0.4
Carteret	1.1	91.2	7.3	0.9	0.8	0.2	0.8	1.7	90.3	8.3	0.5	0.6	0.9
Caswell	0.9	61.7	37.0	0.5	0.3	0.1	1.4	1.8	58.7	40.8	0.1	0.1	0.7
Catawba	1.1	85.9	8.7	0.5	3.2	0.1	2.7	5.6	89.8	9.0	0.2	0.7	0.8
Chatham	1.1	75.9	17.5	0.8	0.7	0.1	6.3	9.6	75.9	22.8	0.3	0.2	1.5
Cherokee	1.2	96.0	1.8	2.5	0.4	0.0	0.6	1.2	95.8	1.8	2.0	0.2	0.6

[1] Hispanic persons may be of any race.

Table B. States and Counties

STATE County	Population and population characteristics, 2000 Age (percent)									Median age (years)	Percent Female
	Under 5 years	5 to 17 years	18 to 24 years	25 to 34 years	35 to 44 years	45 to 54 years	55 to 64 years	65 to 74 years	75 years and over		
	28	29	30	31	32	33	34	35	36	37	38
NEW YORK—Cont'd											
Genesee	6.1	20.0	7.5	12.5	17.0	13.4	9.1	7.1	7.3	37.4	50.8
Greene	5.4	17.6	9.5	11.4	15.6	14.2	10.6	8.4	7.3	39.1	48.4
Hamilton	4.3	15.4	5.2	9.8	14.4	16.4	14.5	11.1	8.9	45.4	50.0
Herkimer	5.6	18.8	8.3	11.3	15.2	14.0	9.9	7.9	8.9	39.0	51.5
Jefferson	7.3	19.1	11.8	15.5	15.9	11.7	7.4	5.8	5.5	32.5	48.2
Kings	7.4	19.5	10.3	15.8	15.0	12.5	8.2	6.1	5.4	33.1	53.1
Lewis	6.1	21.7	7.7	11.6	16.5	13.4	9.2	7.7	6.1	36.8	50.3
Livingston	5.4	18.0	14.2	12.0	16.9	13.9	8.3	6.1	5.3	35.3	49.8
Madison	5.9	19.0	12.0	11.5	16.1	13.7	9.4	6.6	5.8	36.1	50.9
Monroe	6.4	19.2	9.5	13.3	16.1	14.0	8.6	6.3	6.7	36.1	51.8
Montgomery	5.9	18.6	7.2	11.6	14.7	13.8	9.0	8.5	10.7	39.7	52.2
Nassau	6.5	18.2	7.3	12.2	16.7	14.6	9.4	7.9	7.1	38.5	51.9
New York	4.9	11.8	10.2	21.5	16.7	13.4	9.2	6.4	5.7	35.7	52.5
Niagara	6.0	18.7	8.5	11.9	16.5	14.0	9.1	7.8	7.6	38.2	51.7
Oneida	5.7	18.2	8.6	12.5	15.6	13.6	9.2	7.8	8.7	38.2	50.3
Onondaga	6.5	19.2	9.5	12.8	16.1	13.6	8.4	7.0	6.8	36.3	52.2
Ontario	6.0	19.4	8.3	11.6	16.8	15.2	9.5	6.6	6.5	37.9	51.1
Orange	7.6	21.4	8.7	12.7	17.3	13.8	8.1	5.3	5.0	34.7	49.9
Orleans	6.2	19.9	8.2	13.6	17.8	13.3	8.6	6.2	6.2	36.2	50.4
Oswego	6.2	20.6	10.9	12.3	16.6	13.5	8.6	6.0	5.3	35.0	50.6
Otsego	4.8	17.9	14.4	10.2	14.1	13.9	9.7	7.5	7.5	37.1	51.8
Putnam	6.9	19.6	6.3	12.4	19.7	16.0	9.5	5.4	4.1	37.4	50.1
Queens	6.4	16.4	9.6	16.8	16.3	12.9	8.8	6.6	6.1	35.4	51.8
Rensselaer	6.1	18.2	10.1	12.9	16.2	14.2	8.8	6.9	6.6	36.7	51.0
Richmond	6.7	18.8	8.5	14.3	16.6	14.3	9.2	6.3	5.3	35.9	51.7
Rockland	7.6	20.4	7.9	12.2	15.8	14.3	10.1	6.7	5.1	36.2	51.2
St. Lawrence	5.4	18.0	13.8	12.2	15.2	13.4	9.0	7.1	5.9	35.4	49.2
Saratoga	6.5	18.6	7.8	13.8	17.7	15.0	9.2	6.1	5.3	36.9	50.7
Schenectady	6.1	18.2	7.9	12.1	16.1	14.1	8.9	7.8	8.9	38.6	51.9
Schoharie	5.6	18.4	10.6	11.0	15.2	14.6	9.8	7.9	7.0	38.0	50.2
Schuyler	5.8	19.5	7.9	11.2	15.4	15.2	10.3	7.6	7.0	38.8	49.9
Seneca	5.6	19.2	7.5	12.9	15.8	14.2	9.6	7.9	7.2	38.2	50.0
Steuben	6.1	19.9	7.4	11.6	15.5	14.4	9.8	7.9	7.2	38.2	51.0
Suffolk	7.1	19.0	7.6	13.5	17.7	13.9	9.4	6.5	5.3	36.5	51.0
Sullivan	5.9	19.1	7.3	11.7	16.4	14.8	10.6	7.9	6.4	38.8	49.1
Tioga	6.3	20.7	7.0	11.0	17.8	14.1	9.9	7.4	5.7	38.0	50.6
Tompkins	4.4	14.5	26.0	13.4	12.8	12.5	6.9	4.8	4.8	28.6	50.6
Ulster	5.5	18.0	8.7	12.4	17.3	15.2	9.5	7.1	6.3	38.2	50.2
Warren	5.4	18.6	7.5	12.0	16.3	14.8	10.2	8.1	7.1	39.0	51.5
Washington	5.6	19.0	8.3	13.0	16.3	14.0	9.7	7.5	6.5	37.5	48.7
Wayne	6.6	20.8	6.8	12.6	17.5	14.3	9.2	6.5	5.7	36.9	50.5
Westchester	7.0	18.0	7.2	13.4	17.0	14.1	9.4	7.2	6.7	37.6	52.2
Wyoming	5.3	18.8	8.2	14.6	18.2	14.1	8.7	6.2	6.0	36.7	45.8
Yates	6.6	20.0	9.3	10.0	14.6	13.5	10.4	8.3	7.2	37.9	51.2
NORTH CAROLINA	6.7	17.7	10.0	15.1	16.0	13.5	9.0	6.6	5.4	35.3	51.0
Alamance	6.4	17.4	9.9	14.3	15.6	13.2	9.1	7.4	6.7	36.3	52.0
Alexander	6.9	17.6	7.9	14.9	16.1	14.2	10.5	7.0	4.9	36.6	50.2
Alleghany	5.2	14.2	7.4	12.2	14.0	14.7	13.0	10.8	8.4	43.0	50.7
Anson	6.5	18.7	8.6	13.8	15.2	13.5	9.3	7.2	7.2	36.6	50.9
Ashe	5.3	14.5	7.5	12.1	14.9	15.3	12.4	9.5	8.4	42.1	50.7
Avery	4.8	14.6	10.3	14.8	15.3	13.7	10.7	8.7	7.1	38.4	47.2
Beaufort	6.0	17.4	7.7	11.7	14.4	15.4	11.6	8.9	6.9	40.2	52.3
Bertie	6.4	19.7	7.7	11.1	15.3	13.8	10.0	8.7	7.3	38.6	53.3
Bladen	6.6	18.0	8.7	12.6	14.6	14.7	10.5	8.0	6.3	37.9	51.9
Brunswick	5.5	15.7	7.0	11.6	14.1	14.5	14.7	11.1	5.8	42.2	50.8
Buncombe	5.6	16.2	8.6	13.6	15.7	14.9	9.9	7.9	7.5	38.9	52.0
Burke	6.2	17.8	8.9	14.1	15.6	13.8	10.2	7.5	5.9	36.9	50.0
Cabarrus	7.1	18.7	8.1	15.5	17.0	13.4	8.7	6.2	5.4	35.4	50.8
Caldwell	6.4	17.0	7.8	14.7	15.8	14.4	10.7	7.5	5.8	37.5	50.6
Camden	5.6	18.9	6.3	12.2	18.3	13.9	11.3	8.0	5.5	39.1	50.4
Carteret	4.9	15.8	6.4	11.5	15.7	15.7	12.7	10.1	7.1	42.3	50.9
Caswell	5.7	17.5	7.7	13.8	16.4	15.2	10.7	7.1	5.9	38.2	49.4
Catawba	6.5	17.7	8.8	15.1	16.0	14.0	9.5	6.8	5.5	36.1	50.7
Chatham	6.3	16.2	7.3	14.3	16.1	14.9	9.8	8.0	7.3	38.8	50.8
Cherokee	5.4	15.1	6.5	11.4	13.0	14.9	13.9	10.7	9.0	44.0	51.5

Table B. States and Counties

STATE County	| Age (percent) Under 5 years	5 to 17 years	18 to 24 years	25 to 34 years	35 to 44 years	45 to 54 years	55 to 64 years	65 to 74 years	75 years and over	Percent Female	Total persons 2000	1990	1980	Percent change 1990–2000	1980–1990
	39	40	41	42	43	44	45	46	47	48	49	50	51	52	53
NEW YORK—Cont'd															
Genesee	7.5	18.9	9.8	16.5	14.3	10.3	8.9	7.7	5.9	51.3	60 370	60 060	59 400	0.5	1.1
Greene	6.5	16.7	9.7	16.2	14.7	10.5	9.7	8.7	7.2	49.2	48 195	44 739	40 861	7.7	9.5
Hamilton	4.8	16.8	7.3	13.4	14.7	12.5	13.4	10.7	6.4	49.7	5 379	5 279	5 034	1.9	4.9
Herkimer	6.8	18.8	9.6	14.4	14.2	10.3	9.1	9.8	7.1	51.7	64 427	65 809	66 714	-2.1	-1.4
Jefferson	8.6	19.0	14.1	18.6	13.4	8.2	7.1	6.1	4.8	48.7	111 738	110 943	88 151	0.7	25.9
Kings	7.8	18.6	10.8	17.6	14.7	9.9	8.3	7.0	5.4	53.4	2 465 326	2 300 664	2 231 028	7.2	3.1
Lewis	8.4	22.1	8.9	16.6	13.8	9.5	8.8	6.8	5.2	50.1	26 944	26 796	25 035	0.6	7.0
Livingston	6.8	17.5	15.4	16.6	14.6	9.7	8.2	6.3	4.9	51.8	64 328	62 372	57 006	3.1	9.4
Madison	7.1	18.2	16.0	15.1	14.1	10.2	7.9	6.7	4.8	50.8	69 441	69 166	65 150	0.4	6.2
Monroe	7.6	16.9	11.4	17.7	15.4	10.3	8.2	7.1	5.4	52.0	735 343	713 968	702 238	3.0	1.7
Montgomery	6.9	17.8	8.5	14.4	13.9	9.3	9.6	10.8	8.6	52.4	49 708	51 981	53 439	-4.4	-2.7
Nassau	6.1	15.7	10.0	15.7	15.3	11.5	11.4	9.0	5.2	51.7	1 334 544	1 287 873	1 321 582	3.6	-2.6
New York	5.3	11.3	10.1	21.6	17.6	11.7	9.1	7.2	6.1	52.9	1 537 195	1 487 536	1 428 285	3.3	4.1
Niagara	7.1	17.8	9.7	16.1	14.4	10.0	9.7	9.0	6.1	52.1	219 846	220 756	227 354	-0.4	-2.9
Oneida	7.0	17.2	11.3	16.4	13.8	9.8	9.0	8.9	6.6	50.5	235 469	250 836	253 466	-6.1	-1.0
Onondaga	7.5	17.0	12.0	17.4	14.7	9.7	8.7	7.5	5.5	52.1	458 336	468 973	463 920	-2.3	1.1
Ontario	7.3	17.8	10.4	16.1	16.1	10.5	8.6	7.5	5.6	50.9	100 224	95 101	88 909	5.4	7.0
Orange	8.3	19.3	10.7	17.3	16.1	10.3	7.4	5.9	4.5	49.7	341 367	307 571	259 603	11.0	18.5
Orleans	7.4	19.5	10.1	17.4	14.8	10.0	8.1	7.2	5.4	49.9	44 171	41 846	38 496	5.6	8.7
Oswego	7.8	20.1	13.2	16.6	14.4	9.6	7.7	6.3	4.4	50.9	122 377	121 785	113 901	0.5	6.9
Otsego	6.3	16.9	16.3	13.1	13.7	10.0	8.7	8.2	6.9	52.3	61 676	60 390	59 075	2.1	2.4
Putnam	7.7	18.1	9.2	17.4	18.0	12.7	7.8	5.0	4.0	50.1	95 745	83 941	77 193	14.1	8.7
Queens	6.2	14.7	10.2	18.6	14.9	10.9	9.7	8.3	6.4	52.5	2 229 379	1 951 598	1 891 325	14.2	3.2
Rensselaer	7.0	16.8	13.0	16.8	14.8	9.7	8.6	7.5	5.7	50.9	152 538	154 429	151 966	-1.2	1.6
Richmond	7.4	17.4	10.6	17.5	16.1	11.3	8.5	6.6	4.6	51.7	443 728	378 977	352 029	17.1	7.7
Rockland	7.2	18.8	10.2	15.3	15.5	12.9	10.0	5.7	4.4	51.4	286 753	265 475	259 530	8.0	2.3
St. Lawrence	6.6	18.6	16.4	14.7	13.4	9.5	8.6	6.9	5.2	49.7	111 931	111 974	114 347	0.0	-2.1
Saratoga	7.4	18.3	10.5	17.9	16.6	11.0	8.0	6.2	4.1	50.6	200 635	181 276	153 759	10.7	17.9
Schenectady	7.0	16.0	9.8	16.3	14.8	9.9	9.6	9.2	7.3	52.3	146 555	149 285	149 946	-1.8	-0.4
Schoharie	6.3	18.1	13.9	14.0	14.4	10.1	9.1	8.1	6.1	51.2	31 582	31 840	29 710	-0.8	7.2
Schuyler	7.1	19.9	8.6	14.8	15.3	11.0	9.0	8.1	6.1	50.4	19 224	18 662	17 686	3.0	5.5
Seneca	7.4	18.5	8.9	15.7	15.1	10.2	9.4	8.4	6.4	50.8	33 342	33 683	33 733	-1.0	-0.1
Steuben	7.4	19.8	8.7	15.0	14.4	10.5	9.6	8.4	6.1	50.9	98 726	99 088	99 217	-0.4	-0.1
Suffolk	7.0	17.7	10.7	17.2	15.7	11.9	9.1	6.3	4.5	51.1	1 419 369	1 321 339	1 284 231	7.4	2.9
Sullivan	7.2	17.6	9.2	16.4	15.4	10.4	9.2	8.6	6.1	48.7	73 966	69 277	65 155	6.8	6.3
Tioga	7.9	20.5	8.3	17.0	15.0	11.3	9.1	6.4	4.5	50.7	51 784	52 337	49 812	-1.1	5.1
Tompkins	5.6	13.8	26.7	16.9	13.9	8.1	6.1	5.0	4.0	50.4	96 501	94 097	87 085	2.6	8.1
Ulster	6.9	16.5	10.3	17.5	16.1	10.7	9.0	7.3	5.7	50.4	177 749	165 380	158 158	7.5	4.5
Warren	6.8	18.1	10.0	16.0	15.2	10.4	9.0	8.1	6.3	51.8	63 303	59 209	54 854	6.9	7.9
Washington	7.3	18.5	10.2	17.4	14.6	10.1	8.8	7.6	5.5	48.7	61 042	59 330	54 795	2.9	8.3
Wayne	8.1	19.9	8.8	17.1	15.7	10.7	8.3	6.5	5.0	50.7	93 765	89 123	84 581	5.2	5.4
Westchester	6.6	15.2	9.6	16.7	15.5	11.7	10.3	8.0	6.4	52.5	923 459	874 866	866 599	5.6	1.0
Wyoming	7.0	19.4	9.7	18.8	15.3	10.1	7.6	6.9	5.2	46.7	43 424	42 507	39 895	2.2	6.5
Yates	7.4	19.2	9.1	14.6	14.6	10.1	9.7	8.3	7.0	51.6	24 621	22 810	21 459	7.9	6.3
NORTH CAROLINA	6.9	17.3	11.8	17.3	15.2	10.5	8.9	7.3	4.8	51.5	8 049 313	6 632 448	5 880 095	21.4	12.8
Alamance	6.3	15.6	11.4	15.8	14.8	11.1	10.1	8.9	5.9	52.6	130 800	108 213	99 319	20.9	9.0
Alexander	6.3	18.3	10.4	16.9	15.6	12.3	9.2	6.6	4.5	50.2	33 603	27 544	24 999	22.0	10.2
Alleghany	4.9	16.5	8.0	14.2	13.9	12.1	11.8	10.4	8.2	51.8	10 677	9 590	9 587	11.3	0.0
Anson	6.7	20.4	9.6	14.5	14.4	9.6	9.1	9.0	6.7	53.2	25 275	23 474	25 649	7.7	-8.5
Ashe	5.1	16.6	8.7	14.4	14.7	12.3	11.1	9.5	7.7	51.6	24 384	22 209	22 325	9.8	-0.5
Avery	5.7	16.8	13.5	14.0	14.7	11.1	9.6	8.6	6.0	49.9	17 167	14 867	14 409	15.5	3.2
Beaufort	6.5	19.4	8.6	14.3	14.9	10.9	10.3	8.7	6.2	52.8	44 958	42 283	40 355	6.3	4.8
Bertie	7.4	21.3	8.7	15.2	13.1	9.6	10.1	8.7	5.9	53.9	19 773	20 388	21 024	-3.0	-3.0
Biaden	6.3	20.2	9.3	14.3	15.0	11.0	9.6	8.5	5.7	53.0	32 278	28 663	30 491	12.6	-6.0
Brunswick	6.5	17.1	8.6	14.8	14.1	11.8	12.5	10.3	4.4	51.1	73 143	50 985	35 777	43.5	42.5
Buncombe	6.3	16.0	9.4	15.4	15.7	11.2	9.9	9.2	6.9	52.5	206 330	174 357	160 934	18.3	8.6
Burke	6.3	17.2	10.3	16.0	15.3	12.1	9.8	7.8	5.2	51.1	89 148	75 740	72 504	17.7	4.5
Cabarrus	6.9	17.3	10.1	16.4	15.5	11.3	9.3	7.8	5.4	51.6	131 063	98 935	85 895	32.5	15.2
Caldwell	6.4	17.2	10.6	16.5	15.4	12.2	9.7	7.3	4.8	51.0	77 415	70 709	67 746	9.5	4.4
Camden	6.5	17.8	8.6	15.9	14.5	12.0	10.7	8.8	5.3	49.9	6 885	5 904	5 829	16.6	1.3
Carteret	6.3	16.2	9.3	16.8	15.0	11.1	11.0	9.2	5.1	50.6	59 383	52 407	41 092	13.3	27.9
Caswell	6.0	17.8	9.2	15.7	15.6	11.9	9.4	8.5	5.8	51.2	23 501	20 662	20 705	13.7	0.0
Catawba	6.5	17.4	10.5	16.8	15.9	11.5	9.4	7.3	4.6	51.4	141 685	118 412	105 208	19.7	12.6
Chatham	6.9	15.5	8.7	16.8	17.1	10.8	9.8	8.7	5.7	51.5	49 329	38 979	33 415	26.6	16.0
Cherokee	5.3	17.4	8.8	12.8	14.1	11.5	11.2	11.3	7.6	52.0	24 298	20 170	18 933	20.5	6.5

STATE County	Total population	Total in house-holds	House-holder	Spouse	Child Total	Child Own child under 18 years	Other relatives Total	Other relatives Under 18 years	Nonrelatives Total	Nonrelatives Unmar-ried partner	Total in group quarters	Correc-tional institu-tions	Nurs-ing homes	Other institu-tions	Col-lege dormi-tories	Mili-tary quar-ters	Other
	54	55	56	57	58	59	60	61	62	63	64	65	66	67	68	69	70
NEW YORK—Cont'd																	
Genesee	60 370	97.6	37.7	20.9	31.0	24.0	3.2	1.3	4.8	2.4	2.4	0.8	1.1	0.0	0.0	0.0	0.4
Greene	48 195	91.8	37.9	19.4	26.5	20.8	3.3	1.1	4.7	2.6	8.2	6.0	0.8	0.0	0.0	0.0	1.4
Hamilton	5 379	98.2	43.9	24.4	23.4	18.4	2.6	0.9	3.9	2.0	1.8	0.1	0.0	0.0	0.0	0.0	1.7
Herkimer	64 427	98.3	39.9	20.5	29.2	22.5	3.1	1.1	5.5	2.7	1.7	0.1	0.9	0.1	0.3	0.0	0.4
Jefferson	111 738	92.7	35.9	19.9	29.6	24.6	2.6	1.0	4.6	2.4	7.3	2.0	0.7	0.0	0.0	4.1	0.4
Kings	2 465 326	98.4	35.7	13.8	33.2	22.8	10.1	3.4	5.6	1.8	1.6	0.1	0.4	0.2	0.1	0.0	0.8
Lewis	26 944	99.0	37.3	22.1	32.8	26.1	2.5	0.9	4.3	2.2	1.0	0.1	0.6	0.0	0.0	0.0	0.3
Livingston	64 328	89.5	34.4	18.9	27.3	21.8	2.6	1.0	6.3	2.5	10.5	3.8	0.7	0.0	5.1	0.0	0.9
Madison	69 441	93.3	36.5	20.1	28.9	23.1	2.6	1.0	5.1	2.7	6.7	0.5	0.5	0.2	5.3	0.0	0.2
Monroe	735 343	96.4	39.0	18.5	29.8	23.5	3.9	1.6	5.3	2.3	3.6	0.2	0.8	0.1	1.8	0.0	0.7
Montgomery	49 708	97.6	40.3	19.8	28.9	22.5	3.5	1.2	5.1	2.9	2.4	0.3	1.2	0.6	0.0	0.0	0.4
Nassau	1 334 544	98.4	33.5	21.1	32.6	22.3	7.2	2.0	4.0	1.0	1.6	0.1	0.6	0.0	0.5	0.0	0.4
New York	1 537 195	96.1	48.1	12.1	20.3	13.9	6.7	2.3	8.9	2.7	3.9	0.2	0.4	0.2	1.8	0.0	1.3
Niagara	219 846	98.1	40.0	20.1	30.5	22.8	3.4	1.3	4.1	2.2	1.9	0.2	0.8	0.0	0.6	0.0	0.3
Oneida	235 469	93.5	38.4	18.9	28.7	22.0	3.2	1.2	4.3	2.3	6.5	2.8	1.2	0.7	1.3	0.0	0.6
Onondaga	458 336	97.1	39.5	18.6	30.0	23.8	3.5	1.4	5.5	2.4	2.9	0.2	0.7	0.0	1.5	0.0	0.5
Ontario	100 224	96.9	38.3	21.1	29.4	23.6	2.9	1.1	5.2	2.6	3.1	0.2	0.6	0.3	1.6	0.0	0.5
Orange	341 367	96.0	33.6	19.5	33.9	26.7	4.9	1.7	4.1	1.9	4.0	1.0	0.6	0.3	0.4	1.1	0.8
Orleans	44 171	92.1	34.8	18.9	29.6	23.5	3.7	1.7	5.1	2.8	7.9	6.6	0.8	0.0	0.0	0.0	0.5
Oswego	122 377	96.7	37.2	19.7	30.5	24.7	3.0	1.2	6.4	3.1	3.3	0.1	0.6	0.0	2.4	0.0	0.2
Otsego	61 676	91.9	37.8	19.3	25.6	20.5	2.6	1.0	6.6	2.8	8.1	0.1	0.4	0.5	5.7	0.0	1.4
Putnam	95 745	97.7	34.2	22.3	32.8	24.8	4.6	1.3	3.8	1.5	2.3	0.1	0.2	0.3	1.1	0.0	0.6
Queens	2 229 379	98.8	35.1	16.5	29.8	19.4	11.3	2.8	6.1	1.5	1.2	0.0	0.5	0.1	0.0	0.0	0.5
Rensselaer	152 538	96.6	39.3	19.2	29.1	22.4	3.4	1.2	5.6	2.7	3.4	0.2	1.0	0.1	1.8	0.0	0.4
Richmond	443 728	97.9	35.2	19.4	33.8	23.4	6.2	1.7	3.3	1.4	2.1	0.2	0.7	0.2	0.2	0.0	0.7
Rockland	286 753	97.3	32.3	20.3	34.7	25.8	6.1	1.7	3.9	1.1	2.7	0.1	0.7	0.4	0.5	0.0	1.0
St. Lawrence	111 931	90.0	36.2	18.6	26.8	21.6	2.5	1.0	5.9	2.9	10.0	2.9	0.9	0.2	5.6	0.0	0.5
Saratoga	200 635	97.9	39.0	21.9	29.3	23.5	2.7	1.0	5.0	2.6	2.1	0.5	0.4	0.0	0.8	0.0	0.3
Schenectady	146 555	96.8	40.7	19.3	28.6	22.6	3.3	1.1	4.9	2.5	3.2	0.2	1.2	0.1	1.0	0.0	0.7
Schoharie	31 582	94.5	38.0	20.6	27.5	21.9	3.2	1.1	5.3	2.7	5.5	0.9	0.5	0.1	3.7	0.0	0.3
Schuyler	19 224	96.8	38.4	21.4	28.4	22.8	3.1	1.4	5.5	3.1	3.2	0.1	1.1	1.6	0.0	0.0	0.4
Seneca	33 342	95.1	37.9	20.3	28.4	22.8	2.9	1.2	5.6	2.9	4.9	2.6	0.9	0.1	0.7	0.0	0.6
Steuben	98 726	98.5	39.6	20.4	29.9	23.8	3.0	1.3	5.6	2.9	1.5	0.1	0.6	0.5	0.0	0.0	0.4
Suffolk	1 419 369	98.0	33.1	20.5	32.7	23.4	6.7	2.1	5.0	1.5	2.0	0.1	0.6	0.1	0.6	0.0	0.6
Sullivan	73 966	93.5	37.4	18.7	28.1	22.3	4.0	1.7	5.3	2.7	6.5	2.6	0.5	0.5	0.2	0.0	2.6
Tioga	51 784	99.0	38.1	22.4	31.2	25.1	2.8	1.2	4.5	2.4	1.0	0.0	0.6	0.0	0.0	0.0	0.4
Tompkins	96 501	87.6	37.7	15.6	20.6	17.2	2.0	0.7	11.7	2.6	12.4	0.1	0.5	0.5	11.1	0.0	0.3
Ulster	177 749	93.6	38.0	18.7	27.4	21.2	3.7	1.4	5.9	2.9	6.4	2.0	0.6	0.2	1.2	0.0	2.3
Warren	63 303	98.0	40.6	21.1	28.1	22.4	2.9	1.0	5.2	2.9	2.0	0.1	0.7	0.1	0.8	0.0	0.4
Washington	61 042	93.9	36.8	20.3	28.3	22.3	3.4	1.4	5.1	2.8	6.1	4.5	0.9	0.0	0.0	0.0	0.7
Wayne	93 765	98.2	37.2	21.1	31.4	25.3	3.2	1.4	5.3	2.9	1.8	0.7	0.6	0.0	0.0	0.0	0.5
Westchester	923 459	97.4	36.5	19.7	30.7	22.8	6.1	1.6	4.5	1.4	2.6	0.5	0.7	0.2	0.6	0.0	0.5
Wyoming	43 424	89.8	34.3	20.0	28.8	22.4	2.5	0.9	4.2	2.1	10.2	9.2	0.7	0.0	0.0	0.0	0.3
Yates	24 621	95.2	36.7	20.5	29.6	24.2	2.9	1.2	5.4	2.8	4.8	0.3	1.2	0.5	2.3	0.0	0.6
NORTH CAROLINA	8 049 313	96.8	38.9	20.4	27.6	21.7	5.1	2.2	4.8	1.8	3.2	0.6	0.6	0.1	0.9	0.5	0.4
Alamance	130 800	97.1	39.4	20.5	27.2	21.3	5.2	2.0	4.8	1.9	2.9	0.1	0.8	0.0	1.4	0.0	0.6
Alexander	33 603	99.3	39.1	23.6	28.7	22.2	4.3	1.7	3.6	2.0	0.7	0.0	0.5	0.0	0.0	0.0	0.1
Alleghany	10 677	98.0	43.0	25.1	23.5	17.9	3.4	1.1	3.1	1.3	2.0	0.2	1.1	0.0	0.0	0.0	0.6
Anson	25 275	94.4	36.4	17.4	29.5	20.3	8.3	4.6	2.7	1.6	5.6	4.6	0.9	0.0	0.0	0.0	0.1
Ashe	24 384	98.8	42.7	25.4	24.5	18.2	3.5	1.2	2.8	1.3	1.2	0.0	0.9	0.0	0.0	0.0	0.3
Avery	17 167	89.1	38.0	21.7	23.1	17.6	3.3	1.4	2.9	1.3	10.9	7.2	0.9	0.1	2.0	0.0	0.8
Beaufort	44 958	98.7	40.7	21.8	27.2	20.4	5.4	2.5	3.5	1.7	1.3	0.1	0.9	0.0	0.0	0.0	0.3
Bertie	19 773	99.0	39.2	18.0	29.6	20.8	9.0	4.9	3.2	1.6	1.0	0.3	0.4	0.0	0.0	0.0	0.2
Bladen	32 278	97.8	40.0	19.5	28.3	20.7	6.6	3.2	3.4	1.6	2.2	0.5	1.1	0.0	0.0	0.0	0.6
Brunswick	73 143	99.0	41.6	24.2	23.9	18.4	4.9	2.2	4.4	2.1	1.0	0.1	0.5	0.0	0.0	0.3	0.3
Buncombe	206 330	96.7	41.6	21.0	25.1	19.6	4.1	1.6	5.0	2.0	3.3	0.6	0.8	0.3	0.8	0.0	0.8
Burke	89 148	96.0	38.7	21.2	27.2	21.2	4.6	1.9	4.2	1.8	4.0	1.7	0.6	1.0	0.0	0.0	0.6
Cabarrus	131 063	98.3	37.8	22.4	29.2	23.2	5.1	2.0	3.9	1.6	1.7	0.3	0.6	0.2	0.2	0.0	0.3
Caldwell	77 415	98.5	39.7	22.8	27.0	20.6	4.9	2.2	4.1	2.0	1.5	0.5	0.7	0.0	0.0	0.0	0.3
Camden	6 885	99.9	38.7	24.1	28.9	21.5	5.1	2.5	3.3	1.7	0.1	0.0	0.1	0.0	0.0	0.0	0.0
Carteret	59 383	98.2	42.4	23.8	24.0	18.8	3.7	1.5	4.2	1.9	1.8	0.5	0.6	0.0	0.0	0.0	0.6
Caswell	23 501	94.5	36.9	20.4	28.1	19.9	6.3	2.8	2.8	1.4	5.5	4.3	0.6	0.0	0.0	0.0	0.6
Catawba	141 685	98.5	39.2	21.6	27.9	21.7	5.3	2.0	4.6	2.0	1.5	0.2	0.4	0.0	0.4	0.0	0.4
Chatham	49 329	98.8	40.0	22.5	25.6	19.8	5.6	2.0	5.0	1.8	1.2	0.0	1.0	0.2	0.0	0.0	0.1
Cherokee	24 298	98.8	42.5	25.0	24.6	18.6	3.9	1.5	2.8	1.3	1.2	0.1	0.9	0.0	0.0	0.0	0.2

Table B. States and Counties

STATE County	Households by type, 2000										Average house-hold size	Average family size	Households, 1990		
	Family households						Nonfamily households								
			Married couple		Female householder¹			Householder living alone							
	Total households	Total	With own children under 18 years	Total	With own children under 18 years	Total	With own children under 18 years	Total	Total	65 years and over			Total house-holds	Female house-holder¹	House-holder living alone
	71	72	73	74	75	76	77	78	79	80	81	82	83	84	85
NEW YORK—Cont'd															
Genesee	22 770	69.5	33.3	55.4	25.0	9.8	6.0	30.5	24.8	11.1	2.59	3.10	21 614	9.5	21.6
Greene	18 256	66.1	29.2	51.2	20.4	10.3	6.3	33.9	27.9	12.2	2.42	2.97	16 596	9.7	25.6
Hamilton	2 362	66.0	23.6	55.7	17.9	6.7	3.7	34.0	29.6	13.7	2.24	2.74	2 153	7.9	25.5
Herkimer	25 734	66.5	30.6	51.2	21.4	10.3	6.2	33.5	27.6	13.7	2.46	2.99	24 936	9.5	25.0
Jefferson	40 068	70.2	37.2	55.6	27.4	10.4	7.0	29.8	24.4	10.1	2.58	3.07	37 851	9.7	21.1
Kings	880 727	66.3	33.3	38.6	19.1	22.3	12.2	33.7	27.8	9.8	2.75	3.41	828 199	21.5	28.6
Lewis	10 040	72.8	35.3	59.4	27.4	8.4	5.1	27.2	22.6	10.8	2.66	3.12	9 253	8.0	20.4
Livingston	22 150	69.3	34.0	54.8	24.8	10.0	6.4	30.7	23.1	9.4	2.60	3.05	21 197	8.9	21.9
Madison	25 368	69.3	33.6	55.1	24.7	9.7	6.1	30.7	24.5	10.3	2.55	3.04	23 567	9.2	21.4
Monroe	286 512	64.4	31.8	47.4	21.4	13.4	8.6	35.6	28.6	9.9	2.47	3.08	271 944	12.5	26.2
Montgomery	20 038	65.4	29.4	49.0	19.7	11.6	7.0	34.6	29.5	14.9	2.42	2.98	20 185	10.9	26.9
Nassau	447 387	77.6	35.3	63.1	29.9	10.9	4.3	22.4	18.8	9.4	2.93	3.34	431 515	10.2	17.1
New York	738 644	40.9	17.1	25.2	9.6	12.6	6.5	59.1	48.0	10.9	2.00	2.99	716 422	12.8	48.6
Niagara	87 846	66.7	30.9	50.3	21.4	12.3	7.4	33.3	28.6	12.0	2.45	3.03	84 809	11.6	26.1
Oneida	90 496	65.4	30.4	49.1	20.8	12.0	7.4	34.6	29.5	13.1	2.43	3.02	92 562	11.2	27.0
Onondaga	181 153	63.7	31.9	46.9	21.5	12.9	8.3	36.3	29.4	10.8	2.46	3.07	177 898	11.9	26.4
Ontario	38 370	68.7	32.8	55.0	24.3	9.9	6.2	31.3	24.7	10.1	2.53	3.03	34 929	9.2	22.1
Orange	114 788	73.6	39.6	57.9	30.7	11.4	6.7	26.4	21.5	8.5	2.85	3.35	101 506	10.2	19.7
Orleans	15 363	70.6	35.0	54.3	24.5	11.2	7.2	29.4	23.7	10.7	2.65	3.13	14 428	10.3	21.6
Oswego	45 522	68.6	35.0	52.8	24.5	10.8	7.2	31.4	24.3	9.7	2.60	3.08	42 434	10.0	21.6
Otsego	23 291	64.9	29.6	51.1	21.0	9.5	5.8	35.1	27.0	11.6	2.43	2.94	21 725	8.3	24.9
Putnam	32 703	77.0	38.9	65.4	33.5	8.3	4.2	23.0	18.1	5.9	2.86	3.27	28 094	7.2	15.7
Queens	782 664	68.7	31.5	46.9	22.4	16.0	7.3	31.3	25.6	9.7	2.81	3.39	720 149	14.3	27.2
Rensselaer	59 894	65.2	31.3	48.8	21.5	12.0	7.3	34.8	27.9	10.3	2.46	3.02	57 612	11.2	25.5
Richmond	156 341	73.0	35.8	55.0	27.3	13.9	7.1	27.0	23.2	8.4	2.78	3.31	130 519	12.4	20.9
Rockland	92 675	76.6	37.6	62.8	31.4	10.3	5.0	23.4	19.3	7.8	3.01	3.47	84 874	9.8	17.8
St. Lawrence	40 506	66.5	31.8	51.5	21.9	10.3	6.8	33.5	26.5	11.2	2.49	2.99	37 964	9.6	23.5
Saratoga	78 165	68.7	33.6	56.2	26.0	9.0	5.5	31.3	24.5	8.5	2.51	3.01	66 425	8.4	21.4
Schenectady	59 684	63.7	30.0	47.5	20.2	12.3	7.7	36.3	30.6	12.6	2.38	2.97	59 181	11.1	28.1
Schoharie	11 991	68.2	31.2	54.2	22.7	9.3	5.8	31.8	25.8	11.7	2.49	2.98	11 257	9.0	22.4
Schuyler	7 374	70.4	32.3	55.7	22.8	9.7	6.3	29.6	23.6	10.7	2.52	2.96	6 818	9.1	21.6
Seneca	12 630	68.3	31.9	53.6	22.4	10.3	6.6	31.7	25.3	11.6	2.51	2.99	12 285	9.4	22.0
Steuben	39 071	67.1	31.8	51.7	21.9	10.6	6.8	32.9	27.2	11.9	2.49	3.01	37 299	9.7	24.6
Suffolk	469 299	76.8	37.0	62.0	30.5	10.8	5.0	23.2	18.3	7.8	2.96	3.36	424 719	10.4	16.0
Sullivan	27 661	66.2	31.3	50.1	21.2	11.4	7.2	33.8	27.9	11.4	2.50	3.05	24 576	9.5	25.3
Tioga	19 725	72.6	34.7	58.7	25.8	9.8	6.3	27.4	22.4	9.4	2.60	3.04	18 838	8.7	19.5
Tompkins	36 420	52.5	25.8	41.2	18.3	8.2	5.6	47.5	32.5	8.1	2.32	2.93	33 338	8.0	27.2
Ulster	67 499	64.5	30.7	49.2	21.8	10.9	6.5	35.5	27.9	10.2	2.47	3.03	60 807	10.2	24.3
Warren	25 726	66.3	30.7	51.9	21.9	10.4	6.4	33.7	27.3	11.3	2.41	2.93	22 559	10.0	24.5
Washington	22 458	70.3	33.2	55.2	23.9	10.4	6.4	29.7	24.0	10.8	2.55	3.01	20 256	10.0	21.2
Wayne	34 908	71.8	36.1	56.7	26.1	10.3	6.8	28.2	22.4	9.3	2.64	3.08	31 977	9.5	20.1
Westchester	337 142	69.8	34.0	53.9	26.4	12.2	6.3	30.2	25.7	10.3	2.67	3.21	320 030	11.6	24.8
Wyoming	14 906	71.9	34.2	58.3	25.8	9.2	5.6	28.1	23.2	10.2	2.62	3.08	13 897	8.5	20.5
Yates	9 029	69.6	31.5	56.0	22.7	9.4	6.0	30.4	24.6	11.6	2.59	3.08	8 419	8.3	22.7
NORTH CAROLINA	3 132 013	68.9	31.8	52.5	22.6	12.5	7.3	31.1	25.4	8.6	2.49	2.98	2 517 026	12.3	23.7
Alamance	51 584	68.9	31.1	52.1	21.7	12.7	7.3	31.1	26.0	10.1	2.46	2.95	42 652	12.0	24.5
Alexander	13 137	74.2	32.8	60.5	25.2	9.4	5.4	25.8	21.9	8.4	2.54	2.95	10 331	9.2	19.6
Alleghany	4 593	69.0	24.8	58.3	19.6	7.5	3.7	31.0	27.8	14.0	2.28	2.75	3 894	7.8	25.4
Anson	9 204	72.4	31.0	47.8	18.5	19.8	10.1	27.6	25.1	11.0	2.59	3.09	8 531	17.3	23.9
Ashe	10 411	71.3	26.2	59.4	20.3	8.4	4.1	28.7	25.8	12.1	2.31	2.75	8 848	9.2	21.9
Avery	6 532	69.6	27.1	57.1	21.1	9.1	4.4	30.4	26.6	11.0	2.34	2.82	5 520	8.7	22.3
Beaufort	18 319	70.7	28.8	53.6	19.5	13.3	7.6	29.3	25.7	11.5	2.42	2.89	16 157	13.5	24.2
Bertie	7 743	70.1	29.7	46.0	17.9	20.1	10.1	29.9	27.0	13.1	2.53	3.07	7 412	19.1	24.2
Bladen	12 897	69.3	30.4	48.9	19.8	15.7	8.4	30.7	27.7	11.5	2.45	2.97	10 760	16.4	24.0
Brunswick	30 438	72.4	25.7	58.1	17.7	10.2	5.8	27.6	22.9	8.6	2.38	2.76	20 069	10.1	21.1
Buncombe	85 776	64.9	27.5	50.5	19.6	10.8	6.1	35.1	28.9	10.6	2.33	2.86	70 802	10.9	26.6
Burke	34 528	70.5	31.0	54.9	22.5	11.0	6.0	29.5	25.5	9.9	2.48	2.94	29 184	10.8	22.6
Cabarrus	49 519	73.8	34.9	59.2	26.8	10.5	6.0	26.2	21.8	8.0	2.60	3.03	37 515	10.6	21.4
Caldwell	30 768	72.8	31.1	57.3	22.6	11.0	6.0	27.2	23.1	9.0	2.48	2.89	27 172	10.8	20.8
Camden	2 662	76.0	31.6	62.2	25.5	9.4	4.0	24.0	20.7	9.5	2.58	2.97	2 180	10.3	20.0
Carteret	25 204	68.9	26.5	56.0	19.1	9.6	5.6	31.1	26.1	10.1	2.31	2.76	21 238	9.5	23.9
Caswell	8 670	73.8	31.0	55.2	22.3	14.2	7.0	26.2	23.2	10.2	2.56	3.01	7 468	13.7	21.3
Catawba	55 533	70.4	31.5	55.1	23.2	10.9	6.1	29.6	24.6	9.1	2.51	2.98	45 700	10.6	22.5
Chatham	19 741	70.2	28.8	56.3	22.0	10.0	5.1	29.8	24.5	10.0	2.47	2.91	15 293	10.5	22.5
Cherokee	10 336	71.3	25.6	58.8	19.5	9.3	4.6	28.7	25.7	12.5	2.32	2.76	7 966	9.6	22.1

¹No spouse present.

Table B. States and Counties

STATE County	Percent change of households, 1990–2000	Total housing units	Occupied housing units (percent)	Vacant housing units — Total	Vacant housing units — For seasonal, recreational, or occasional use	Homeowner vacancy rate (percent)	Rental vacancy rate (percent)	Occupied housing units — Total	Occupied — Percent owner-occupied housing units	Occupied — Percent renter-occupied housing units	Average household size of owner-occupied units	Average household size of renter-occupied units
	86	87	88	89	90	91	92	93	94	95	96	97
NEW YORK—Cont'd												
Genesee	5.3	24 190	94.1	5.9	0.8	1.1	8.1	22 770	73.0	27.0	2.74	2.18
Greene	10.0	26 544	68.8	31.2	22.4	3.4	12.2	18 256	72.1	27.9	2.52	2.18
Hamilton	9.7	7 965	29.7	70.3	65.4	4.5	24.8	2 362	79.3	20.7	2.28	2.09
Herkimer	3.2	32 026	80.4	19.6	13.0	2.1	8.4	25 734	71.2	28.8	2.60	2.12
Jefferson	5.9	54 070	74.1	25.9	18.4	3.1	9.5	40 068	59.7	40.3	2.65	2.49
Kings	6.3	930 866	94.6	5.4	0.3	1.6	3.1	880 727	27.1	72.9	3.04	2.65
Lewis	8.5	15 134	66.3	33.7	24.6	3.4	13.3	10 040	77.2	22.8	2.77	2.29
Livingston	4.5	24 023	92.2	7.8	2.9	1.2	7.5	22 150	74.5	25.5	2.69	2.32
Madison	7.6	28 646	88.6	11.4	6.0	1.9	6.9	25 368	75.0	25.0	2.68	2.18
Monroe	5.4	304 388	94.1	5.9	0.4	1.4	7.6	286 512	65.1	34.9	2.67	2.11
Montgomery	-0.7	22 522	89.0	11.0	1.1	3.5	10.0	20 038	67.3	32.7	2.53	2.20
Nassau	3.7	458 151	97.7	2.3	0.7	0.5	2.1	447 387	80.3	19.7	3.03	2.53
New York	3.1	798 144	92.5	7.5	2.4	2.7	3.4	738 644	20.1	79.9	1.88	2.03
Niagara	3.6	95 715	91.8	8.2	0.7	1.8	11.2	87 846	69.9	30.1	2.62	2.07
Oneida	-2.2	102 803	88.0	12.0	2.7	2.3	11.5	90 496	67.2	32.8	2.58	2.13
Onondaga	1.8	196 633	92.1	7.9	1.0	2.0	9.4	181 153	64.5	35.5	2.65	2.10
Ontario	9.9	42 647	90.0	10.0	5.0	1.7	8.1	38 370	73.6	26.4	2.67	2.15
Orange	13.1	122 754	93.5	6.5	1.8	1.5	4.3	114 788	67.0	33.0	2.96	2.64
Orleans	6.5	17 347	88.6	11.4	5.1	2.1	8.5	15 363	75.6	24.4	2.71	2.45
Oswego	7.3	52 831	86.2	13.8	6.6	2.2	9.6	45 522	72.8	27.2	2.71	2.31
Otsego	7.2	28 481	81.8	18.2	9.9	2.9	9.3	23 291	73.0	27.0	2.54	2.15
Putnam	16.4	35 030	93.4	6.6	4.0	0.9	3.2	32 703	82.2	17.8	2.97	2.36
Queens	8.7	817 250	95.8	4.2	0.6	1.3	2.3	782 664	42.8	57.2	2.99	2.68
Rensselaer	4.0	66 120	90.6	9.4	2.0	1.8	7.9	59 894	64.9	35.1	2.63	2.14
Richmond	19.8	163 993	95.3	4.7	0.3	1.4	4.1	156 341	63.8	36.2	3.00	2.40
Rockland	9.2	94 973	97.6	2.4	0.4	0.6	2.8	92 675	71.7	28.3	3.09	2.81
St. Lawrence	6.7	49 721	81.5	18.5	12.3	2.4	7.3	40 506	70.6	29.4	2.61	2.19
Saratoga	17.7	86 701	90.2	9.8	5.3	1.4	6.1	78 165	72.0	28.0	2.69	2.04
Schenectady	0.8	65 032	91.8	8.2	0.5	2.2	8.0	59 684	65.4	34.6	2.55	2.06
Schoharie	6.5	15 915	75.3	24.7	18.0	2.9	9.5	11 991	75.2	24.8	2.60	2.16
Schuyler	8.2	9 181	80.3	19.7	13.7	2.3	8.5	7 374	77.1	22.9	2.59	2.31
Seneca	2.8	14 794	85.4	14.6	8.1	2.3	11.4	12 630	73.8	26.2	2.60	2.25
Steuben	4.8	46 132	84.7	15.3	8.3	2.5	9.3	39 071	73.2	26.8	2.59	2.20
Suffolk	10.5	522 323	89.8	10.2	7.3	0.9	3.4	469 299	79.8	20.2	3.07	2.55
Sullivan	12.6	44 730	61.8	38.2	29.8	3.8	12.3	27 661	68.1	31.9	2.53	2.44
Tioga	4.7	21 410	92.1	7.9	1.7	1.8	8.6	19 725	77.8	22.2	2.68	2.31
Tompkins	9.2	38 625	94.3	5.7	1.1	1.6	4.6	36 420	53.7	46.3	2.56	2.05
Ulster	11.0	77 656	86.9	13.1	6.7	1.9	5.6	67 499	68.0	32.0	2.60	2.18
Warren	14.0	34 852	73.8	26.2	20.8	2.6	7.8	25 726	69.8	30.2	2.55	2.09
Washington	10.9	26 794	83.8	16.2	9.7	2.3	7.5	22 458	74.4	25.6	2.62	2.36
Wayne	9.2	38 767	90.0	10.0	4.4	1.6	8.5	34 908	77.6	22.4	2.75	2.24
Westchester	5.3	349 445	96.5	3.5	0.8	0.9	3.0	337 142	60.1	39.9	2.80	2.47
Wyoming	7.3	16 940	88.0	12.0	7.4	1.6	7.1	14 906	76.7	23.3	2.73	2.26
Yates	7.2	12 064	74.8	25.2	19.9	2.1	8.6	9 029	77.1	22.9	2.69	2.28
NORTH CAROLINA	24.4	3 523 944	88.9	11.1	3.8	2.0	8.8	3 132 013	69.4	30.6	2.54	2.37
Alamance	20.9	55 463	93.0	7.0	0.3	1.9	9.0	51 584	70.1	29.9	2.49	2.41
Alexander	27.2	14 098	93.2	6.8	1.2	1.0	8.2	13 137	80.5	19.5	2.55	2.50
Alleghany	18.0	6 412	71.6	28.4	20.5	2.2	5.8	4 593	78.9	21.1	2.28	2.27
Anson	7.9	10 221	90.0	10.0	1.0	1.1	8.2	9 204	75.9	24.1	2.59	2.60
Ashe	17.7	13 268	78.5	21.5	14.9	1.7	9.8	10 411	81.0	19.0	2.32	2.30
Avery	18.3	11 911	54.8	45.2	39.9	1.4	11.1	6 532	80.6	19.4	2.37	2.21
Beaufort	13.4	22 139	82.7	17.3	8.5	1.6	9.0	18 319	75.0	25.0	2.44	2.36
Bertie	4.5	9 050	85.6	14.4	3.9	2.7	7.6	7 743	74.9	25.1	2.57	2.41
Bladen	19.9	15 316	84.2	15.8	7.0	1.4	10.2	12 897	77.8	22.2	2.49	2.31
Brunswick	51.7	51 431	59.2	40.8	30.2	3.8	28.2	30 438	82.2	17.8	2.37	2.43
Buncombe	21.1	93 973	91.3	8.7	2.2	1.8	8.5	85 776	70.3	29.7	2.41	2.13
Burke	18.3	37 427	92.3	7.7	1.6	1.3	7.3	34 528	74.1	25.9	2.51	2.39
Cabarrus	32.0	52 848	93.7	6.3	0.2	1.8	8.2	49 519	74.7	25.3	2.64	2.50
Caldwell	13.2	33 430	92.0	8.0	2.4	1.2	6.9	30 768	74.9	25.1	2.52	2.37
Camden	22.1	2 973	89.5	10.5	1.5	1.9	7.9	2 662	83.4	16.6	2.60	2.51
Carteret	18.7	40 947	61.6	38.4	32.6	2.3	12.8	25 204	76.6	23.4	2.34	2.23
Caswell	16.1	9 601	90.3	9.7	1.9	1.1	8.3	8 670	79.3	20.7	2.59	2.46
Catawba	21.5	59 919	92.7	7.3	1.7	1.9	7.4	55 533	72.5	27.5	2.54	2.44
Chatham	29.1	21 358	92.4	7.6	0.8	1.4	7.0	19 741	77.2	22.8	2.47	2.47
Cherokee	29.8	13 499	76.6	23.4	14.1	2.7	9.7	10 336	82.2	17.8	2.34	2.23

Table B. States and Counties

STATE/ County code	MSA/ PMSA/ NECMA code¹	County type²	STATE County	Population, 2000				Population, 1990				Population and population characteristics, 2000					
												Race (percent)					
												One race					
				Land area, 2000³ (sq km)	Total persons	Rank	Per square kilometer	Land area, 1990³ (sq km)	Total persons	Rank	Per square kilometer	White	Black or African American	American Indian or Alaska Native	Asian	Native Hawaiian and other Pacific Islander	Some other race
				1	2	3	4	5	6	7	8	9	10	11	12	13	14
			NORTH CAROLINA —Cont'd														
37 041	...	7	Chowan	447	14 526	2 120	32.5	447	13 506	2 101	30.2	60.5	37.5	0.3	0.3	0.0	0.6
37 043	...	9	Clay	556	8 775	2 547	15.8	556	7 155	2 638	12.9	98.0	0.8	0.3	0.1	0.1	0.1
37 045	...	4	Cleveland	1 203	96 287	538	80.0	1 203	84 958	540	70.6	76.8	20.9	0.2	0.7	0.0	0.7
37 047	...	6	Columbus	2 426	54 749	861	22.6	2 426	49 587	847	20.4	63.4	30.9	3.1	0.2	0.0	1.5
37 049	...	5	Craven	1 835	91 436	561	49.8	1 801	81 812	555	45.4	69.9	25.1	0.4	1.0	0.1	1.8
37 051	2560	2	Cumberland	1 691	302 963	187	179.2	1 692	274 713	181	162.4	55.2	34.9	1.5	1.9	0.3	3.1
37 053	5720	1	Currituck	678	18 190	1 888	26.8	678	13 736	2 079	20.3	90.4	7.2	0.5	0.4	0.0	0.5
37 055	...	7	Dare	993	29 967	1 398	30.2	989	22 746	1 547	23.0	94.7	2.7	0.3	0.4	0.0	0.9
37 057	3120	2	Davidson	1 430	147 246	369	103.0	1 430	126 688	366	88.6	87.1	9.1	0.4	0.8	0.0	1.7
37 059	3120	2	Davie	687	34 835	1 257	50.7	687	27 859	1 355	40.6	90.4	6.8	0.2	0.3	0.0	1.3
37 061	...	6	Duplin	2 118	49 063	929	23.2	2 118	39 995	999	18.9	58.7	28.9	0.2	0.2	0.1	10.9
37 063	6640	2	Durham	752	223 314	254	297.0	753	181 844	267	241.5	50.9	39.5	0.3	3.3	0.0	4.2
37 065	6895	3	Edgecombe	1 308	55 606	849	42.5	1 308	56 692	769	43.3	40.1	57.5	0.2	0.1	0.0	1.6
37 067	3120	2	Forsyth	1 061	306 067	186	288.5	1 061	265 855	184	250.6	68.5	25.6	0.3	1.0	0.0	3.3
37 069	6640	2	Franklin	1 274	47 260	963	37.1	1 273	36 414	1 092	28.6	66.0	30.0	0.4	0.3	0.0	2.3
37 071	1520	0	Gaston	923	190 365	289	206.2	923	174 769	275	189.3	83.0	13.9	0.3	1.0	0.0	1.0
37 073	...	8	Gates	882	10 516	2 396	11.9	882	9 305	2 443	10.5	59.1	39.2	0.4	0.2	0.0	0.1
37 075	...	9	Graham	756	7 993	2 607	10.6	756	7 196	2 634	9.5	91.9	0.2	6.8	0.2	0.0	0.1
37 077	...	6	Granville	1 376	48 498	941	35.2	1 376	38 341	1 044	27.9	60.7	34.9	0.5	0.4	0.0	2.4
37 079	...	8	Greene	687	18 974	1 848	27.6	688	15 384	1 965	22.4	51.8	41.2	0.3	0.1	0.0	5.7
37 081	3120	2	Guilford	1 682	421 048	143	250.3	1 684	347 431	148	206.3	64.5	29.3	0.5	2.4	0.0	1.8
37 083	...	4	Halifax	1 879	57 370	832	30.5	1 879	55 516	780	29.5	42.6	52.6	3.1	0.5	0.0	0.5
37 085	...	6	Harnett	1 541	91 025	566	59.1	1 541	67 833	653	44.0	71.1	22.5	0.9	0.6	0.1	3.2
37 087	...	6	Haywood	1 434	54 033	868	37.7	1 435	46 948	891	32.7	96.8	1.3	0.5	0.2	0.0	0.4
37 089	...	6	Henderson	969	89 173	581	92.0	968	69 747	637	72.1	92.5	1.3	0.3	0.6	0.0	2.5
37 091	...	6	Hertford	915	22 601	1 666	24.7	916	22 317	1 562	24.4	37.4	59.6	1.2	0.3	0.0	0.7
37 093	...	6	Hoke	1 013	33 646	1 293	33.2	1 013	22 856	1 539	22.6	44.5	37.6	11.4	0.8	0.2	3.3
37 095	...	9	Hyde	1 587	5 826	2 801	3.7	1 587	5 411	2 807	3.4	62.7	35.1	0.3	0.4	0.0	0.8
37 097	...	4	Iredell	1 491	122 660	442	82.3	1 488	93 205	496	62.6	82.2	15.7	0.3	0.4	0.0	1.7
37 099	...	7	Jackson	1 271	33 121	1 314	26.1	1 271	26 835	1 394	21.1	85.7	1.7	10.2	0.5	0.0	0.5
37 101	6640	2	Johnston	2 051	121 965	446	59.5	2 051	81 306	560	39.6	78.1	15.7	0.4	0.3	0.0	4.5
37 103	...	8	Jones	1 222	10 381	2 404	8.5	1 226	9 361	2 442	7.6	61.0	35.9	0.4	0.2	0.0	1.7
37 105	...	6	Lee	666	49 040	930	73.6	666	41 370	973	62.1	70.0	20.5	0.4	0.7	0.0	7.3
37 107	...	4	Lenoir	1 036	59 648	805	57.6	1 036	57 274	762	55.3	56.5	40.4	0.2	0.3	0.1	1.9
37 109	1520	1	Lincoln	774	63 780	761	82.4	774	50 319	838	65.0	90.2	6.4	0.3	0.3	0.0	1.7
37 111	...	6	McDowell	1 144	42 151	1 055	36.8	1 144	35 681	1 108	31.2	92.2	4.2	0.3	0.9	0.0	1.6
37 113	...	7	Macon	1 338	29 811	1 403	22.3	1 338	23 504	1 513	17.6	97.2	1.2	0.3	0.4	0.0	0.3
37 115	0480	3	Madison	1 164	19 635	1 815	16.9	1 164	16 953	1 850	14.6	97.6	0.8	0.3	0.2	0.0	0.4
37 117	...	6	Martin	1 194	25 593	1 534	21.4	1 198	25 078	1 458	20.9	52.5	45.4	0.3	0.2	0.0	0.9
37 119	1520	0	Mecklenburg	1 363	695 454	72	510.2	1 366	511 211	92	374.2	64.0	27.9	0.4	3.1	0.0	3.0
37 121	...	9	Mitchell	573	15 687	2 039	27.4	574	14 433	2 022	25.1	97.9	0.2	0.4	0.2	0.0	0.7
37 123	...	7	Montgomery	1 273	26 822	1 490	21.1	1 272	23 359	1 524	18.4	69.1	21.8	0.4	1.6	0.0	5.7
37 125	...	6	Moore	1 807	74 769	668	41.4	1 810	59 000	737	32.6	80.2	15.5	0.7	0.4	0.1	2.2
37 127	6895	3	Nash	1 399	87 420	599	62.5	1 399	76 677	589	54.8	61.9	33.9	0.5	0.6	0.0	2.1
37 129	9200	3	New Hanover	515	160 307	332	311.3	515	120 284	384	233.6	79.9	17.0	0.4	0.8	0.1	0.8
37 131	...	9	Northampton	1 389	22 086	1 689	15.9	1 389	21 004	1 629	15.1	39.1	59.4	0.3	0.1	0.0	0.4
37 133	3605	3	Onslow	1 986	150 355	358	75.7	1 986	149 838	315	75.4	72.1	18.5	0.7	1.7	0.2	3.6
37 135	6640	2	Orange	1 036	118 227	457	114.1	1 035	93 662	439	90.5	78.0	13.8	0.4	4.1	0.0	2.0
37 137	...	9	Pamlico	873	12 934	2 238	14.8	873	11 368	2 263	13.0	73.2	24.6	0.5	0.4	0.0	0.6
37 139	...	7	Pasquotank	588	34 897	1 254	59.3	588	31 298	1 236	53.2	56.9	40.0	0.4	0.9	0.0	0.5
37 141	...	8	Pender	2 255	41 082	1 080	18.2	2 255	28 855	1 334	12.8	72.7	23.6	0.5	0.2	0.0	2.0
37 143	...	9	Perquimans	640	11 368	2 344	17.8	640	10 447	2 342	16.3	70.8	28.0	0.2	0.2	0.0	0.1
37 145	...	6	Person	1 016	35 623	1 228	35.1	1 016	30 180	1 290	29.7	68.8	28.2	0.6	0.1	0.0	1.4
37 147	3150	3	Pitt	1 688	133 798	401	79.3	1 688	108 480	424	64.3	62.1	33.6	0.3	1.1	0.0	1.8
37 149	...	8	Polk	616	18 324	1 879	29.7	616	14 458	2 020	23.5	92.3	5.9	0.2	0.2	0.0	0.6
37 151	3120	2	Randolph	2 039	130 454	411	64.0	2 040	106 546	434	52.2	89.2	5.6	0.4	0.6	0.0	3.0
37 153	...	7	Richmond	1 228	46 564	969	37.9	1 228	44 511	918	36.2	64.8	30.5	1.7	0.7	0.0	1.1
37 155	...	4	Robeson	2 457	123 339	437	50.2	2 458	105 170	493	42.8	32.8	25.1	38.0	0.3	0.1	2.3
37 157	...	4	Rockingham	1 467	91 928	556	62.7	1 467	86 064	532	58.7	77.3	19.6	0.3	0.3	0.0	1.7
37 159	1520	1	Rowan	1 324	130 340	413	98.4	1 325	110 605	418	83.5	80.0	15.8	0.3	0.8	0.0	2.0
37 161	...	6	Rutherford	1 461	62 899	773	43.1	1 461	56 956	765	39.0	86.8	11.2	0.2	0.3	0.0	0.7
37 163	...	6	Sampson	2 449	60 161	804	24.6	2 449	47 297	887	19.3	59.8	29.9	1.8	0.3	0.1	7.0
37 165	...	7	Scotland	827	35 998	1 218	43.5	827	33 763	1 171	40.8	51.5	37.3	8.9	0.5	0.0	0.5
37 167	...	6	Stanly	1 023	58 100	823	56.8	1 023	51 765	817	50.6	84.7	11.5	0.2	1.8	0.0	1.0
37 169	3120	2	Stokes	1 170	44 711	1 004	38.2	1 170	37 224	1 066	31.8	93.4	4.7	0.2	0.2	0.1	0.9
37 171	...	6	Surry	1 390	71 219	697	51.2	1 390	61 704	707	44.4	90.4	4.2	0.2	0.6	0.0	3.5

¹MSA = Metropolitan Statistical Area. PMSA = Primary MSA. NECMA = New England County Metropolitan Area. See Appendix A for explanation of these concepts. See Appendix B for list of metropolitan areas identified by type, with component counties.
²County typology code from the Economic Research Service of USDA. See Appendix A for definition.
³Dry land or land partially or temporarily covered by water.

Table B. States and Counties

STATE County	Population and population characteristics, 2000 (cont'd)								Population and population characteristics, 1990				
	Race (percent) (cont'd)								Race (percent)				
	Race alone or in combination												
	Two or more races	White	Black	American Indian or Alaska Native	Asian	Native Hawaiian and other Pacific Islander	Some other race	Hispanic[1]	White	Black or African American	American Indian or Alaska Native	Asian and Pacific Islander	Hispanic[1]
	15	16	17	18	19	20	21	22	23	24	25	26	27
NORTH CAROLINA— Cont'd													
Chowan	0.7	61.1	37.9	0.6	0.4	0.0	0.7	1.5	61.8	37.7	0.2	0.2	0.7
Clay	0.6	98.6	0.9	0.7	0.2	0.1	0.2	0.8	98.7	0.6	0.5	0.1	0.6
Cleveland	0.7	77.4	21.2	0.4	0.8	0.1	0.9	1.5	78.3	20.9	0.1	0.5	0.4
Columbus	0.8	64.0	31.3	3.5	0.3	0.1	1.7	2.3	66.3	30.6	2.8	0.1	0.5
Craven	1.7	71.2	25.8	0.9	1.5	0.1	2.3	4.0	71.9	25.9	0.4	0.9	2.2
Cumberland	3.1	57.4	36.3	2.4	2.7	0.5	4.1	6.9	61.9	31.9	1.6	2.1	4.8
Currituck	1.0	91.3	7.5	0.9	0.6	0.1	0.7	1.4	87.7	11.2	0.5	0.4	0.8
Dare	1.0	95.7	2.9	0.7	0.5	0.1	1.1	2.2	95.7	3.6	0.2	0.3	0.9
Davidson	0.9	87.8	9.4	0.7	1.0	0.0	2.0	3.2	89.4	9.7	0.3	0.4	0.5
Davie	0.9	91.2	7.2	0.5	0.5	0.1	1.6	3.5	90.4	8.9	0.3	0.2	0.5
Duplin	1.1	59.4	29.3	0.5	0.2	0.1	11.5	15.1	64.8	33.2	0.3	0.1	2.5
Durham	1.8	52.2	40.2	0.8	3.7	0.1	5.0	7.6	60.4	37.2	0.2	1.8	1.1
Edgecombe	0.6	40.4	57.8	0.4	0.2	0.0	1.8	2.8	43.6	56.0	0.1	0.1	0.5
Forsyth	1.3	69.5	26.2	0.6	1.3	0.1	3.7	6.4	74.1	24.9	0.2	0.6	0.8
Franklin	0.9	66.7	30.4	0.8	0.5	0.1	2.6	4.4	64.0	35.3	0.2	0.2	0.8
Gaston	0.9	83.7	14.2	0.6	1.1	0.1	1.3	3.0	86.2	13.0	0.2	0.5	0.5
Gates	0.9	59.8	39.5	0.8	0.5	0.1	0.3	0.8	54.8	44.9	0.1	0.1	0.2
Graham	0.8	92.6	0.3	7.5	0.2	0.1	0.2	0.8	93.5	0.0	6.3	0.1	0.4
Granville	1.1	61.5	35.5	0.9	0.6	0.1	2.8	4.0	60.2	38.9	0.3	0.3	0.9
Greene	0.8	52.5	41.5	0.5	0.3	0.0	6.1	8.0	56.9	42.4	0.1	0.0	1.1
Guilford	1.5	65.5	29.9	0.8	2.8	0.1	2.4	3.8	71.8	26.4	0.5	1.1	0.8
Halifax	0.7	43.0	53.0	3.5	0.6	0.1	0.6	1.0	46.8	49.7	3.1	0.3	0.4
Harnett	1.6	72.3	23.1	1.4	0.9	0.2	3.7	5.9	75.4	22.6	0.9	0.4	1.7
Haywood	0.7	97.5	1.4	0.9	0.3	0.1	0.6	1.4	98.0	1.4	0.4	0.1	0.5
Henderson	1.0	93.4	3.3	0.7	0.8	0.1	2.8	5.5	95.5	3.4	0.3	0.4	1.2
Hertford	0.8	38.0	60.1	1.5	0.5	0.1	0.9	1.6	40.9	57.6	1.0	0.4	0.4
Hoke	2.1	46.1	38.4	12.3	1.3	0.3	3.9	7.2	42.2	43.2	13.9	0.4	1.0
Hyde	0.8	63.2	35.4	0.6	0.5	0.0	1.1	2.2	66.5	32.9	0.1	0.1	0.8
Iredell	0.9	82.9	14.0	0.5	1.4	0.1	2.0	3.4	83.1	16.0	0.2	0.4	0.7
Jackson	1.4	86.9	1.8	11.2	0.6	0.0	0.8	1.7	87.9	1.6	9.9	0.4	0.6
Johnston	1.0	78.9	15.9	0.7	0.4	0.1	5.0	7.7	80.9	17.7	0.2	0.2	1.6
Jones	0.9	61.6	36.3	0.7	0.4	0.2	1.9	2.7	60.4	39.1	0.1	0.2	0.6
Lee	1.1	70.8	20.8	0.7	0.9	0.1	7.8	11.7	75.4	22.7	0.4	0.5	1.9
Lenoir	0.7	57.0	40.7	0.4	0.5	0.1	2.1	3.2	59.9	39.4	0.1	0.3	0.8
Lincoln	1.0	91.2	6.7	0.5	0.4	0.0	2.2	5.7	90.8	8.2	0.2	0.3	1.1
McDowell	0.8	92.9	4.4	0.6	1.1	0.0	1.8	2.9	95.0	4.1	0.2	0.6	0.3
Macon	0.6	97.7	1.3	0.7	0.5	0.0	0.4	1.5	97.5	1.6	0.3	0.3	0.7
Madison	0.6	98.2	0.9	0.6	0.3	0.0	0.6	1.4	98.8	0.8	0.1	0.2	0.5
Martin	0.6	52.9	45.7	0.5	0.3	0.1	1.1	2.1	55.0	44.6	0.1	0.2	0.4
Mecklenburg	1.5	65.2	28.4	0.7	3.5	0.1	3.8	6.5	71.3	26.3	0.4	1.7	1.3
Mitchell	0.6	98.4	0.3	0.9	0.3	0.0	0.8	2.0	99.5	0.2	0.1	0.1	0.3
Montgomery	1.3	70.1	22.1	0.9	1.9	0.1	6.4	10.4	71.8	25.7	0.4	0.6	2.4
Moore	0.9	81.0	15.8	1.0	0.6	0.1	2.4	4.0	80.4	18.4	0.5	0.3	0.8
Nash	1.0	62.7	34.4	0.8	0.8	0.1	2.4	3.4	67.7	31.5	0.3	0.3	0.8
New Hanover	1.1	80.8	17.3	0.7	1.0	0.1	1.1	2.0	78.9	20.0	0.4	0.5	0.8
Northampton	0.6	39.5	59.8	0.7	0.1	0.1	0.6	0.7	40.4	59.3	0.2	0.1	0.6
Onslow	3.2	74.6	19.7	1.6	2.6	0.4	4.6	7.2	74.7	19.9	0.6	2.0	5.4
Orange	1.7	79.4	14.4	0.9	4.6	0.1	2.4	4.5	80.8	15.9	0.3	2.5	1.4
Pamlico	0.7	73.8	24.8	0.9	0.5	0.0	0.7	1.3	73.5	25.9	0.3	0.2	0.5
Pasquotank	1.3	57.9	40.6	0.9	1.1	0.1	0.7	1.2	62.0	37.0	0.2	0.6	0.8
Pender	0.9	73.5	23.9	0.9	0.3	0.0	2.3	3.6	68.7	30.4	0.3	0.2	0.9
Perquimans	0.6	71.4	28.3	0.5	0.3	0.0	0.2	0.6	66.8	32.8	0.2	0.2	0.3
Person	0.9	69.5	28.7	0.9	0.2	0.0	1.6	2.1	68.7	30.2	0.6	0.0	0.8
Pitt	1.1	62.9	34.1	0.5	1.3	0.1	2.2	3.2	65.5	33.3	0.2	0.7	0.9
Polk	0.8	93.0	6.1	0.5	0.3	0.0	0.9	3.0	92.1	7.3	0.1	0.2	0.8
Randolph	1.1	90.1	5.9	0.8	0.8	0.1	3.4	6.6	93.0	6.0	0.4	0.3	0.7
Richmond	1.2	65.7	31.0	2.3	0.8	0.1	1.3	2.8	69.2	28.9	1.1	0.4	0.7
Robeson	1.4	33.7	25.5	39.0	0.5	0.1	2.7	4.9	36.1	24.9	38.5	0.2	0.7
Rockingham	0.8	78.0	19.9	0.6	0.4	0.1	2.0	3.1	78.9	20.4	0.2	0.2	0.7
Rowan	1.0	80.8	16.1	0.7	1.0	0.1	2.3	4.1	83.0	16.1	0.2	0.4	0.6
Rutherford	0.7	87.5	11.5	0.5	0.4	0.1	0.8	1.8	88.1	11.4	0.2	0.2	0.6
Sampson	1.1	60.5	30.4	2.1	0.5	0.2	7.5	10.8	64.0	33.2	1.9	0.2	1.5
Scotland	1.3	52.5	37.7	9.8	0.6	0.0	0.6	1.2	56.4	36.1	7.2	0.2	0.9
Stanly	0.8	85.3	11.7	0.5	2.0	0.0	1.2	2.1	87.5	11.5	0.3	0.5	0.6
Stokes	0.5	93.9	4.8	0.5	0.2	0.1	1.0	1.9	93.8	5.6	0.1	0.2	0.7
Surry	1.1	91.4	4.4	0.5	0.7	0.0	4.2	6.5	94.6	4.5	0.1	0.1	1.0

[1] Hispanic persons may be of any race.

Table B. States and Counties

	Population and population characteristics, 2000										
	Age (percent)										
STATE County	Under 5 years	5 to 17 years	18 to 24 years	25 to 34 years	35 to 44 years	45 to 54 years	55 to 64 years	65 to 74 years	75 years and over	Median age (years)	Percent Female
	28	29	30	31	32	33	34	35	36	37	38
NORTH CAROLINA— Cont'd											
Chowan	5.9	18.1	9.6	9.9	14.3	13.7	10.7	9.4	8.5	39.8	53.2
Clay	4.2	14.3	6.2	9.4	13.4	16.3	13.5	12.1	10.6	46.7	51.3
Cleveland	6.7	18.5	8.8	13.6	15.2	13.8	9.9	7.3	6.2	36.5	51.9
Columbus	6.6	19.1	8.7	12.6	14.8	14.1	10.3	7.8	6.0	36.9	51.9
Craven	7.3	17.3	12.8	13.3	14.6	12.4	8.8	8.0	5.4	34.4	49.5
Cumberland	8.2	19.7	13.7	17.3	15.6	10.9	6.8	4.8	2.9	29.6	49.4
Currituck	6.1	19.3	6.7	12.3	18.3	14.4	11.0	7.2	4.8	38.3	50.3
Dare	5.2	16.2	6.3	12.9	17.8	16.1	11.7	8.7	5.1	40.4	49.6
Davidson	6.5	17.8	7.6	14.6	16.6	14.1	10.0	7.1	5.6	37.1	51.0
Davie	6.5	17.8	7.1	13.2	16.2	14.9	10.5	7.4	6.4	38.4	50.8
Duplin	7.4	18.7	9.6	14.4	14.9	12.8	9.3	7.1	5.7	34.9	50.4
Durham	6.9	16.0	12.8	19.0	15.8	12.7	7.1	4.9	4.8	32.2	51.8
Edgecombe	6.8	20.3	8.6	12.6	15.8	14.3	9.1	6.9	5.6	36.2	53.5
Forsyth	6.7	17.2	9.6	14.9	16.2	13.9	8.9	6.9	5.7	36.0	52.2
Franklin	7.0	18.3	8.4	14.9	17.5	13.9	8.9	6.0	5.0	35.8	50.7
Gaston	6.7	18.0	8.2	15.2	15.9	14.2	9.3	7.1	5.5	36.2	51.6
Gates	5.8	20.9	6.1	11.7	17.4	13.2	10.5	7.8	6.6	38.1	51.0
Graham	5.8	16.1	7.3	11.7	13.5	14.7	12.8	9.9	8.0	41.5	51.2
Granville	6.2	17.7	8.5	15.5	17.8	13.7	9.1	6.5	4.9	36.2	47.5
Greene	7.0	18.3	9.4	14.6	16.3	13.4	9.0	6.6	5.4	35.5	48.6
Guilford	6.6	17.1	11.0	15.5	15.9	13.6	8.5	6.3	5.4	34.9	52.1
Halifax	6.2	19.9	8.0	12.5	15.2	13.6	9.6	8.1	6.8	37.2	52.4
Harnett	7.6	19.3	10.6	16.6	15.5	12.0	8.0	5.9	4.5	32.5	50.6
Haywood	5.3	15.5	6.2	12.4	14.5	14.4	12.7	10.4	8.6	42.3	52.1
Henderson	5.6	15.2	6.4	12.0	14.1	13.5	11.6	11.2	10.5	42.7	51.6
Hertford	5.5	19.9	7.8	11.0	15.3	14.5	10.3	8.5	7.3	39.2	54.1
Hoke	9.2	20.6	10.7	18.2	15.9	10.9	6.7	4.7	3.0	30.0	49.5
Hyde	4.5	15.9	7.9	14.2	16.6	14.2	10.4	8.5	7.9	39.7	47.1
Iredell	6.9	18.7	7.5	14.4	16.9	13.8	9.5	6.8	5.5	36.5	51.0
Jackson	5.1	13.9	17.9	11.6	12.8	13.9	11.0	7.9	5.9	36.2	51.2
Johnston	7.8	18.2	8.1	17.2	17.0	13.1	8.6	5.5	4.3	34.2	50.3
Jones	6.0	19.6	6.8	11.1	15.8	14.8	10.4	8.4	7.1	39.1	51.8
Lee	6.9	18.7	9.0	13.9	15.8	13.5	9.2	7.2	5.7	35.9	50.6
Lenoir	6.6	18.7	7.9	12.2	15.4	14.5	10.1	8.2	6.4	38.1	52.5
Lincoln	6.4	18.5	7.7	14.9	16.8	14.3	10.0	6.5	5.0	36.4	50.3
McDowell	6.1	16.7	8.2	14.6	15.3	14.1	10.7	7.9	6.4	38.0	50.2
Macon	5.0	15.4	6.1	9.9	13.3	14.5	13.4	12.1	10.2	45.2	52.1
Madison	5.9	15.4	10.3	12.4	14.1	14.8	11.2	8.3	7.7	39.3	50.7
Martin	6.2	19.3	7.5	11.7	15.0	14.7	10.3	8.2	7.0	38.7	53.6
Mecklenburg	7.3	17.8	9.7	18.7	17.6	13.1	7.2	4.7	3.9	33.1	50.9
Mitchell	5.1	16.1	6.8	12.0	14.4	14.6	12.4	10.3	8.3	42.0	51.1
Montgomery	6.8	18.1	9.0	13.8	14.7	13.7	10.0	7.5	6.5	36.7	49.4
Moore	5.6	16.5	6.6	11.6	14.2	12.5	11.2	11.5	10.3	41.8	51.8
Nash	6.6	18.8	8.5	13.8	16.3	14.6	8.9	6.8	5.6	36.5	51.9
New Hanover	5.7	15.2	12.0	15.1	15.3	14.1	9.6	7.2	5.7	36.3	51.7
Northampton	5.7	18.6	6.9	11.4	15.1	13.8	11.1	9.2	8.2	40.0	52.1
Onslow	8.8	17.3	23.8	15.8	13.4	8.6	5.8	4.0	2.3	25.0	44.8
Orange	5.0	15.3	21.0	15.1	14.8	13.5	6.9	4.5	3.9	30.4	52.6
Pamlico	5.0	16.1	6.4	10.8	15.0	15.2	12.8	11.2	7.5	42.9	49.6
Pasquotank	6.2	18.6	11.3	12.4	16.0	12.6	8.8	7.3	6.8	35.9	51.6
Pender	5.9	17.3	7.4	13.1	16.4	14.5	11.4	8.5	5.5	38.8	49.7
Perquimans	5.2	17.8	6.8	10.2	14.2	13.6	13.0	10.6	8.7	42.2	52.3
Person	6.3	17.7	7.4	13.6	17.0	14.4	9.8	7.5	6.2	38.0	51.8
Pitt	6.5	17.1	17.5	15.4	14.5	12.3	7.1	5.2	4.3	30.4	52.6
Polk	5.2	14.9	5.8	10.7	13.5	14.6	11.7	10.7	12.9	44.9	52.6
Randolph	6.8	18.2	8.0	15.0	16.3	13.9	9.7	6.7	5.4	36.2	50.6
Richmond	6.8	19.0	10.1	13.3	14.4	13.3	9.5	7.4	6.2	35.5	50.9
Robeson	8.0	21.1	10.6	14.5	14.8	12.8	8.2	5.6	4.3	32.0	51.4
Rockingham	6.2	17.2	7.6	13.7	15.7	14.6	10.2	7.9	6.9	38.5	51.7
Rowan	6.6	18.1	9.1	13.8	15.9	13.3	9.1	7.2	6.8	36.4	50.6
Rutherford	6.2	17.6	8.0	13.3	14.6	13.8	10.5	8.4	7.7	38.3	51.8
Sampson	7.3	18.5	9.4	14.8	14.9	12.9	9.4	7.0	5.8	35.0	50.5
Scotland	7.3	20.8	9.5	12.8	14.8	14.2	9.2	6.3	5.1	34.6	53.1
Stanly	6.2	18.8	8.4	13.5	15.5	13.7	9.7	7.6	6.6	36.9	50.7
Stokes	6.6	17.9	7.3	14.3	17.0	14.6	10.4	6.5	5.3	37.2	51.0
Surry	6.3	17.2	7.9	14.0	15.1	13.6	10.5	8.1	7.3	38.0	51.1

Table B. States and Counties

STATE County	Population and population characteristics, 1990										Population—change, 1980–2000				
	Age (percent)										Total persons			Percent change	
	Under 5 years	5 to 17 years	18 to 24 years	25 to 34 years	35 to 44 years	45 to 54 years	55 to 64 years	65 to 74 years	75 years and over	Percent Female	2000	1990	1980	1990–2000	1980–1990
	39	40	41	42	43	44	45	46	47	48	49	50	51	52	53
NORTH CAROLINA—Cont'd															
Chowan	6.9	19.3	7.7	14.0	14.1	10.0	10.5	10.3	7.3	53.5	14 526	13 506	12 558	7.6	7.5
Clay	4.8	17.8	7.5	12.5	14.5	11.3	11.3	12.5	7.8	51.3	8 775	7 155	6 619	22.6	8.1
Cleveland	6.8	17.8	10.5	15.4	15.0	11.4	9.5	8.1	5.5	52.0	96 287	84 958	83 435	13.3	1.5
Columbus	6.8	20.7	8.9	14.7	14.5	11.1	9.8	8.2	5.2	52.9	54 749	49 587	51 037	10.4	-2.8
Craven	8.5	18.5	13.2	17.9	13.6	8.7	8.4	7.3	3.9	50.2	91 436	81 812	71 043	11.8	14.9
Cumberland	9.1	18.9	17.1	20.3	13.6	8.4	6.5	4.1	2.1	48.3	302 963	274 713	247 160	10.3	11.1
Currituck	7.3	18.1	8.2	17.6	14.9	11.2	10.1	7.8	4.7	49.6	18 190	13 736	11 089	32.4	23.9
Dare	6.8	15.5	8.1	19.2	17.0	10.5	10.3	8.3	4.1	50.3	29 967	22 746	13 377	31.7	70.0
Davidson	6.5	17.4	10.1	16.8	15.6	12.0	9.6	7.3	4.7	51.0	147 246	126 688	113 162	16.2	11.9
Davie	5.8	17.6	9.1	15.2	16.5	12.0	9.9	8.3	5.5	50.9	34 835	27 859	24 599	25.0	13.3
Duplin	6.9	19.5	9.5	15.2	14.5	10.7	9.7	8.3	5.7	52.0	49 063	39 995	40 952	22.7	-2.3
Durham	7.1	15.6	13.5	20.2	16.5	9.2	7.1	6.1	4.6	52.8	223 314	181 844	152 235	22.8	19.5
Edgecombe	7.5	20.8	9.7	16.1	15.1	9.8	8.7	7.5	4.8	54.3	55 606	56 692	55 988	-1.9	1.3
Forsyth	6.8	15.9	11.1	18.1	15.8	10.9	9.2	7.1	5.2	52.8	306 067	265 855	243 704	15.1	9.1
Franklin	6.7	17.6	10.9	16.9	15.1	10.6	8.8	7.8	5.6	52.0	47 260	36 414	30 055	29.8	21.2
Gaston	7.1	18.1	10.8	16.5	15.2	10.9	9.3	7.2	4.9	52.0	190 365	174 769	162 568	8.9	7.7
Gates	7.3	18.2	9.1	16.6	13.9	10.3	9.9	8.7	5.9	50.6	10 516	9 305	8 875	13.0	4.8
Graham	5.7	17.9	10.2	13.4	14.3	12.0	10.5	9.7	6.4	50.3	7 993	7 196	7 217	11.1	-0.3
Granville	6.6	17.5	9.7	18.0	15.4	11.3	9.2	7.3	5.1	50.5	48 498	38 341	34 043	26.5	12.6
Greene	6.5	19.5	9.1	17.6	15.2	10.3	9.5	7.5	4.8	50.2	18 974	15 384	16 117	23.3	-4.5
Guilford	6.5	15.8	12.9	17.5	15.6	10.7	9.0	7.0	4.9	52.7	421 048	347 431	317 154	21.2	9.5
Halifax	7.2	20.4	9.2	15.3	14.0	9.9	9.6	8.4	5.8	52.5	57 370	55 516	55 076	3.3	0.8
Harnett	7.7	17.8	13.5	16.8	13.8	10.0	8.7	7.0	4.7	51.4	91 025	67 833	59 570	34.2	13.9
Haywood	5.5	15.2	8.8	13.7	14.3	12.7	11.7	10.7	7.5	52.3	54 033	46 948	46 495	15.1	1.0
Henderson	5.5	15.5	7.6	13.4	14.0	10.8	11.2	12.9	9.0	52.2	89 173	69 747	58 580	27.9	18.3
Hertford	7.1	20.0	10.7	14.3	13.6	10.1	9.6	8.4	6.2	53.6	22 601	22 317	23 368	1.3	-3.6
Hoke	8.3	22.2	11.5	17.5	14.2	9.2	7.8	5.8	3.5	49.9	33 646	22 856	20 383	47.2	12.1
Hyde	6.3	18.8	9.0	14.6	14.2	10.5	10.1	9.1	7.5	51.0	5 826	5 411	5 873	7.7	-7.9
Iredell	6.7	17.4	9.9	16.3	14.9	11.6	9.9	7.8	5.4	51.7	122 660	93 205	82 538	31.6	12.6
Jackson	5.0	15.2	19.7	12.6	13.7	11.1	9.0	7.9	5.9	51.8	33 121	26 835	25 811	23.4	4.0
Johnston	6.8	17.9	9.7	16.7	15.6	11.5	9.1	7.8	4.9	51.7	121 965	81 306	70 599	50.0	15.2
Jones	7.7	18.9	8.6	16.1	13.8	10.6	9.9	9.0	5.3	53.0	10 381	9 361	9 705	10.9	-3.0
Lee	7.2	18.8	9.2	16.2	15.1	10.7	9.7	8.3	4.8	51.8	49 040	41 370	36 718	18.5	12.7
Lenoir	6.4	19.6	9.2	15.3	15.0	11.0	9.8	8.4	5.3	53.3	59 648	57 274	59 819	4.1	-4.3
Lincoln	7.0	17.9	10.3	16.7	15.6	11.8	9.1	7.2	4.4	50.8	63 780	50 319	42 372	26.8	18.8
McDowell	6.2	17.7	9.8	15.2	14.9	11.6	10.1	8.5	6.0	51.3	42 151	35 681	35 135	18.1	1.6
Macon	5.1	14.7	7.4	12.2	13.7	11.6	12.7	12.9	9.6	52.0	29 811	23 504	20 178	26.8	16.5
Madison	5.5	16.3	12.3	13.2	14.5	11.5	10.0	9.2	7.5	50.9	19 635	16 953	16 827	15.8	0.7
Martin	7.0	19.7	9.2	14.6	14.6	10.7	9.8	8.8	5.7	53.0	25 593	25 078	25 948	2.1	-3.4
Mecklenburg	7.5	16.6	11.4	20.5	16.6	10.3	7.7	5.7	3.7	52.0	695 454	511 211	404 270	36.0	26.5
Mitchell	5.7	15.9	8.3	14.1	14.5	11.9	11.8	9.8	7.9	52.0	15 687	14 433	14 428	8.7	0.0
Montgomery	6.7	19.1	10.4	16.0	14.7	10.4	9.0	8.3	5.3	49.6	26 822	23 359	22 469	14.8	3.9
Moore	6.1	16.5	8.1	14.4	13.1	9.6	11.5	13.3	7.5	52.3	74 769	59 000	50 505	26.7	16.8
Nash	6.9	18.7	9.8	16.7	16.1	10.6	8.9	7.6	4.8	52.6	87 420	76 677	67 153	14.0	14.2
New Hanover	6.2	16.6	12.5	16.5	16.0	10.7	9.0	7.8	4.7	52.6	160 307	120 284	103 471	33.3	16.2
Northampton	6.3	18.8	8.5	14.6	13.6	10.5	10.9	10.4	6.5	51.6	22 086	21 004	22 195	5.2	-6.3
Onslow	9.1	15.2	27.4	22.3	11.3	5.8	4.5	2.9	1.5	40.2	150 355	149 838	112 784	0.3	32.9
Orange	5.7	13.2	22.7	19.4	15.3	8.7	6.3	5.1	3.6	52.6	118 227	93 662	77 055	26.2	21.8
Pamlico	6.3	17.5	7.6	13.8	14.2	11.3	12.5	10.2	6.6	52.0	12 934	11 368	10 398	13.8	9.3
Pasquotank	7.9	19.2	11.4	16.3	13.5	9.2	8.7	8.2	5.7	53.1	34 897	31 298	28 462	11.5	10.0
Pender	6.8	17.9	8.8	15.1	14.9	11.6	10.7	9.3	5.0	51.4	41 082	28 855	22 262	42.4	29.6
Perquimans	6.6	18.0	7.9	14.0	12.8	10.7	11.7	10.9	7.3	52.1	11 368	10 447	9 486	8.8	10.1
Person	6.8	17.7	9.1	16.7	15.0	10.9	9.6	8.3	5.9	52.2	35 623	30 180	29 164	18.0	3.5
Pitt	7.1	17.0	17.9	17.4	14.5	8.8	7.4	6.0	3.9	52.5	133 798	108 480	90 146	23.3	20.3
Polk	5.3	14.1	7.2	12.4	13.2	10.9	12.2	13.7	10.9	53.1	18 324	14 458	12 984	26.7	11.0
Randolph	6.9	17.2	10.0	17.1	15.6	11.7	9.3	7.4	4.8	51.1	130 454	106 546	91 300	22.4	16.7
Richmond	6.7	19.7	10.3	14.6	14.2	10.6	9.6	8.8	5.4	52.2	46 564	44 511	45 161	4.6	-1.4
Robeson	8.1	22.6	11.3	15.5	14.4	9.6	7.8	6.6	4.1	52.7	123 339	105 170	101 610	17.3	3.5
Rockingham	6.5	17.2	9.7	15.8	15.2	11.4	9.8	8.4	5.9	52.4	91 928	86 064	83 426	6.8	3.2
Rowan	6.7	16.9	10.0	16.0	14.5	10.7	9.9	8.9	6.3	51.5	130 340	110 605	99 186	17.8	11.5
Rutherford	6.5	17.9	10.0	14.7	14.2	11.1	10.1	8.9	6.6	51.9	62 899	56 956	53 787	10.4	5.8
Sampson	6.5	19.8	9.4	14.8	14.5	11.0	9.8	8.5	5.8	52.5	60 161	47 297	49 687	27.2	-4.8
Scotland	7.2	22.2	11.5	14.4	15.5	10.3	7.8	6.8	4.3	53.3	35 998	33 763	32 273	6.6	4.6
Stanly	7.1	17.4	10.5	15.2	14.5	10.8	9.8	8.7	5.9	51.8	58 100	51 765	48 517	12.2	6.7
Stokes	6.4	18.0	10.1	16.8	16.2	12.3	8.7	6.7	4.8	50.9	44 711	37 224	33 086	20.1	12.5
Surry	6.0	16.9	10.0	15.2	14.8	12.0	10.4	8.6	6.2	52.1	71 219	61 704	59 449	15.4	3.8

Table B. States and Counties

STATE County	Total population	Total in house-holds	House-holder	Spouse	Child Total	Child Own child under 18 years	Other relatives Total	Other relatives Under 18 years	Nonrelatives Total	Nonrelatives Unmar-ried partner	Total in group quarters	Correc-tional institu-tions	Nurs-ing homes	Other institu-tions	Col-lege dormi-tories	Mili-tary quar-ters	Other
	54	55	56	57	58	59	60	61	62	63	64	65	66	67	68	69	70
NORTH CAROLINA—Cont'd																	
Chowan	14 526	95.2	38.4	20.3	27.6	20.6	5.6	2.9	3.2	1.6	4.8	0.1	1.9	0.1	2.6	0.0	0.2
Clay	8 775	98.6	43.8	26.2	22.6	17.1	3.6	1.3	2.4	1.3	1.4	0.0	1.1	0.0	0.0	0.0	0.2
Cleveland	96 287	97.4	38.5	21.1	28.5	21.8	5.8	2.8	3.5	1.8	2.6	0.2	0.8	0.1	1.1	0.0	0.4
Columbus	54 749	97.5	38.9	19.8	29.1	21.5	6.5	3.5	3.2	1.6	2.5	1.4	0.0	0.1	0.0	0.0	1.0
Craven	91 436	94.4	37.8	21.5	27.2	22.0	4.2	2.1	3.7	1.5	5.6	0.7	0.4	0.5	0.0	3.7	0.3
Cumberland	302 963	93.9	35.4	18.7	30.5	24.8	4.8	2.4	4.5	1.6	6.1	0.1	0.4	0.0	0.6	4.6	0.3
Currituck	18 190	99.1	37.9	23.4	28.5	22.4	4.7	2.1	4.6	2.0	0.9	0.4	0.5	0.0	0.0	0.0	0.0
Dare	29 967	99.2	42.3	23.3	24.1	19.8	3.1	1.1	6.5	2.8	0.8	0.1	0.0	0.4	0.0	0.1	0.1
Davidson	147 246	98.7	39.5	22.9	28.1	21.8	4.4	1.8	3.8	1.9	1.3	0.4	0.5	0.1	0.0	0.0	0.3
Davie	34 835	98.9	39.5	24.2	28.3	22.3	3.8	1.5	3.2	1.5	1.1	0.1	0.8	0.0	0.0	0.0	0.2
Duplin	49 063	98.0	37.2	19.5	29.1	22.3	7.2	3.1	5.0	1.8	2.0	0.7	0.0	0.0	0.0	0.0	1.3
Durham	223 314	95.6	39.9	16.8	25.3	20.1	6.2	2.3	7.5	2.1	4.4	0.3	0.9	0.0	2.8	0.0	0.4
Edgecombe	55 606	98.0	36.7	16.9	30.6	21.5	9.9	5.0	3.9	1.7	2.0	1.1	0.5	0.0	0.0	0.0	0.4
Forsyth	306 067	96.7	40.5	19.8	26.9	21.4	5.0	2.0	4.5	1.7	3.3	0.4	0.9	0.0	1.6	0.0	0.4
Franklin	47 260	97.4	37.8	20.6	28.7	22.1	6.0	2.6	4.3	2.0	2.6	1.0	0.8	0.0	0.6	0.0	0.2
Gaston	190 365	98.4	38.8	21.0	28.2	21.4	6.0	2.6	4.3	1.9	1.6	0.3	0.8	0.0	0.2	0.0	0.3
Gates	10 516	98.5	37.1	21.2	30.7	22.9	6.4	3.4	3.1	1.6	1.5	0.8	0.0	0.0	0.0	0.0	0.7
Graham	7 993	98.5	42.0	25.5	25.2	19.5	4.1	2.0	1.8	1.0	1.5	0.1	1.0	0.0	0.0	0.0	0.4
Granville	48 498	88.7	34.3	18.2	26.3	19.7	6.3	2.9	3.5	1.6	11.3	7.3	0.6	3.2	0.0	0.0	0.2
Greene	18 974	93.6	35.3	18.4	28.9	21.3	7.4	3.5	3.6	1.6	6.4	5.5	0.7	0.0	0.0	0.0	0.2
Guilford	421 048	96.7	40.1	19.2	27.0	21.3	4.9	1.9	5.4	1.8	3.3	0.1	0.6	0.0	2.1	0.0	0.5
Halifax	57 370	96.9	38.6	17.0	30.0	21.6	8.0	4.1	3.4	1.8	3.1	1.9	0.8	0.0	0.0	0.0	0.3
Harnett	91 025	96.8	37.1	19.8	29.7	23.8	5.4	2.5	4.8	2.0	3.2	1.0	0.6	0.0	1.2	0.0	0.5
Haywood	54 033	98.2	42.8	24.2	24.1	18.7	3.8	1.5	3.3	1.7	1.8	0.3	0.8	0.1	0.2	0.0	0.6
Henderson	89 173	97.9	42.0	24.6	24.1	19.0	3.9	1.4	3.4	1.5	2.1	0.2	1.2	0.0	0.0	0.0	0.6
Hertford	22 601	98.1	39.6	18.2	29.0	20.9	7.7	4.0	3.7	1.7	1.9	0.3	0.8	0.3	0.0	0.0	0.5
Hoke	33 646	96.7	33.8	17.8	32.2	25.2	7.9	4.0	5.0	2.0	3.3	2.8	0.3	0.0	0.0	0.0	0.2
Hyde	5 826	88.6	37.5	18.3	23.5	17.0	6.0	3.1	3.3	1.5	11.4	9.9	1.4	0.0	0.0	0.0	0.1
Iredell	122 660	98.7	38.6	22.3	29.2	23.0	4.9	2.0	3.7	1.7	1.3	0.2	0.7	0.0	0.0	0.0	0.4
Jackson	33 121	91.7	39.8	20.5	22.3	17.0	3.7	1.6	5.4	1.9	8.3	0.1	0.5	0.0	7.4	0.0	0.3
Johnston	121 965	98.6	38.2	22.1	29.0	23.5	4.9	1.9	4.5	1.8	1.4	0.7	0.5	0.0	0.0	0.0	0.2
Jones	10 381	98.9	39.1	20.4	29.1	22.1	6.7	3.0	3.5	1.7	1.1	0.0	1.0	0.0	0.0	0.0	0.2
Lee	49 040	98.2	37.7	20.4	29.0	22.3	6.5	2.8	4.6	1.7	1.8	0.7	0.9	0.0	0.0	0.0	0.3
Lenoir	59 648	97.0	40.0	18.6	28.2	21.4	6.3	2.9	4.0	1.8	3.0	0.2	0.5	1.6	0.0	0.0	0.7
Lincoln	63 780	98.6	37.7	23.1	28.8	22.3	5.0	2.0	4.0	1.9	1.4	0.4	0.7	0.0	0.0	0.0	0.3
McDowell	42 151	96.7	39.4	22.7	26.5	20.2	4.8	2.0	3.4	1.7	3.3	2.0	0.9	0.0	0.0	0.0	0.3
Macon	29 811	98.2	43.0	25.2	23.3	18.2	3.6	1.4	3.1	1.4	1.8	0.1	0.5	0.2	0.0	0.0	0.9
Madison	19 635	95.4	40.7	23.4	24.6	19.5	3.4	1.3	3.2	1.5	4.6	0.1	0.5	0.5	3.2	0.0	0.3
Martin	25 593	98.9	39.2	19.7	30.3	21.9	6.8	3.3	3.0	1.5	1.1	0.0	0.0	0.0	0.0	0.0	1.1
Mecklenburg	695 454	97.8	39.3	18.8	27.7	22.5	5.5	2.1	6.5	2.0	2.2	0.3	0.5	0.1	0.9	0.0	0.4
Mitchell	15 687	98.8	41.8	25.4	25.7	19.6	3.9	1.3	2.0	1.0	1.2	0.1	0.8	0.0	0.1	0.0	0.2
Montgomery	26 822	96.0	36.7	20.4	28.0	21.2	7.3	3.2	3.5	1.5	4.0	2.9	0.8	0.0	0.0	0.0	0.3
Moore	74 769	97.8	41.1	23.9	24.8	19.4	4.4	2.0	3.6	1.6	2.2	0.2	0.9	0.3	0.0	0.0	0.8
Nash	87 420	97.6	38.5	20.3	29.2	22.2	5.9	2.7	3.7	1.7	2.4	0.9	0.7	0.0	0.5	0.0	0.4
New Hanover	160 307	97.3	42.5	19.8	23.9	18.9	3.9	1.5	7.2	2.1	2.7	0.4	0.3	0.0	1.2	0.0	0.7
Northampton	22 086	96.0	39.4	17.9	27.4	19.6	8.2	4.3	3.2	1.8	4.0	2.5	1.3	0.0	0.0	0.0	0.2
Onslow	150 355	87.1	32.0	19.5	28.2	24.2	3.1	1.4	4.2	1.4	12.9	0.1	0.1	0.0	0.0	12.3	0.3
Orange	118 227	91.6	38.8	17.3	22.6	18.8	3.3	1.1	9.7	1.8	8.4	0.2	0.6	0.0	7.3	0.0	0.3
Pamlico	12 934	95.1	40.0	22.7	23.9	17.6	5.6	3.0	3.0	1.5	4.9	4.1	0.7	0.0	0.0	0.0	0.1
Pasquotank	34 897	93.0	37.0	18.6	28.5	21.8	5.3	2.6	3.7	1.5	7.0	2.7	0.9	0.0	2.8	0.1	0.5
Pender	41 082	97.2	39.1	22.6	26.2	20.2	5.3	2.4	3.9	1.7	2.8	1.9	0.6	0.0	0.0	0.0	0.4
Perquimans	11 368	98.9	40.9	23.1	27.0	20.1	5.1	2.4	2.9	1.4	1.1	0.0	1.0	0.0	0.0	0.0	0.1
Person	35 623	98.9	39.5	21.3	28.5	21.0	5.7	2.5	3.9	1.9	1.1	0.2	0.8	0.0	0.0	0.0	0.1
Pitt	133 798	95.3	39.3	17.0	26.2	20.6	5.5	2.4	7.3	2.0	4.7	0.2	0.4	0.1	3.5	0.0	0.5
Polk	18 324	98.2	43.2	24.3	23.5	18.0	4.2	1.7	3.1	1.3	1.8	0.1	1.3	0.3	0.0	0.0	0.1
Randolph	130 454	99.0	38.8	23.0	28.6	22.6	4.7	1.8	3.8	1.8	1.0	0.2	0.5	0.0	0.0	0.0	0.3
Richmond	46 564	96.3	38.4	18.5	29.1	21.7	6.5	3.2	3.8	1.6	3.7	1.7	0.8	0.1	0.0	0.8	0.3
Robeson	123 339	97.3	35.4	16.5	32.1	23.8	8.4	4.4	4.8	2.2	2.7	1.1	0.7	0.2	0.6	0.0	0.2
Rockingham	91 928	98.7	40.2	21.6	27.6	20.3	5.8	2.5	3.5	1.7	1.3	0.1	0.7	0.0	0.0	0.0	0.5
Rowan	130 340	96.4	38.3	21.0	28.0	21.8	5.1	2.2	4.1	1.8	3.6	0.9	1.2	0.1	0.9	0.0	0.6
Rutherford	62 899	97.6	40.0	22.2	27.4	21.0	4.6	2.1	3.3	1.6	2.4	0.6	1.5	0.1	0.0	0.0	0.3
Sampson	60 161	97.8	37.0	19.8	29.2	22.0	7.4	3.3	4.3	1.6	2.2	0.8	0.1	0.0	0.0	0.0	1.3
Scotland	35 998	97.3	37.2	17.5	31.5	23.5	7.4	4.0	3.7	1.8	2.7	0.3	0.8	0.0	1.1	0.0	0.6
Stanly	58 100	96.9	38.2	22.3	29.0	22.5	4.3	2.0	3.1	1.4	3.1	1.2	0.9	0.0	0.7	0.0	0.3
Stokes	44 711	98.7	39.3	23.8	28.7	22.3	3.9	1.7	2.9	1.6	1.3	0.1	0.7	0.1	0.0	0.0	0.4
Surry	71 219	98.2	39.9	23.3	27.6	21.3	4.5	1.6	3.0	1.3	1.8	0.1	1.2	0.1	0.0	0.0	0.3

Table B. States and Counties

STATE County	Households by type, 2000												Households, 1990		
		Family households						Nonfamily households							
				Married couple		Female householder[1]			Householder living alone						House-holder
	Total households	Total	With own children under 18 years	Total	With own children under 18 years	Total	With own children under 18 years	Total	Total	65 years and over	Average house-hold size	Average family size	Total house-holds	Female house-holder[1]	living alone
	71	72	73	74	75	76	77	78	79	80	81	82	83	84	85
NORTH CAROLINA— Cont'd															
Chowan	5 580	71.8	30.3	53.0	19.5	15.7	9.4	28.2	25.3	12.1	2.48	2.94	5 113	15.0	24.2
Clay	3 847	70.9	23.5	59.8	18.0	7.5	4.0	29.1	26.3	14.4	2.25	2.68	2 928	6.9	23.9
Cleveland	37 046	72.9	32.2	55.0	22.3	13.7	7.6	27.1	23.6	9.6	2.53	2.98	32 037	13.0	21.9
Columbus	21 308	70.6	31.5	50.8	20.9	15.8	8.6	29.4	26.5	11.7	2.50	3.01	18 459	14.9	23.6
Craven	34 582	72.5	33.3	56.8	23.7	12.5	7.8	27.5	23.4	8.9	2.50	2.93	29 542	11.9	20.7
Cumberland	107 358	72.3	39.4	52.9	27.0	15.5	10.1	27.7	22.4	5.9	2.65	3.11	91 500	14.1	19.4
Currituck	6 902	75.4	33.6	61.6	25.7	9.2	5.3	24.6	19.4	7.6	2.61	2.98	5 038	8.1	19.5
Dare	12 690	66.6	27.3	55.0	20.2	8.1	5.0	33.4	25.0	7.9	2.34	2.79	9 349	7.3	24.2
Davidson	58 156	73.1	32.7	58.0	24.3	10.8	6.1	26.9	22.9	8.8	2.50	2.92	48 944	10.5	21.0
Davie	13 750	74.6	32.7	61.4	25.5	9.2	4.9	25.4	22.2	9.7	2.51	2.91	10 785	8.8	20.8
Duplin	18 267	71.5	33.2	52.2	23.2	14.2	7.7	28.5	24.5	11.1	2.63	3.10	14 925	14.1	23.8
Durham	89 015	60.7	29.1	42.0	18.5	14.8	9.0	39.3	30.0	7.0	2.40	2.99	72 297	14.3	28.9
Edgecombe	20 392	72.6	32.8	46.2	19.1	21.5	11.6	27.4	24.0	10.1	2.67	3.16	20 319	21.1	23.1
Forsyth	123 851	66.0	30.5	48.9	20.6	13.5	8.2	34.0	28.9	9.3	2.39	2.94	107 419	13.1	27.8
Franklin	17 843	72.2	33.5	54.5	24.3	13.1	6.9	27.8	23.5	8.4	2.58	3.03	13 503	13.8	23.1
Gaston	73 936	72.1	32.0	54.2	22.5	13.2	7.1	27.9	23.3	8.8	2.53	2.97	65 347	12.9	20.8
Gates	3 901	75.2	34.2	57.2	25.1	13.3	6.9	24.8	21.7	11.3	2.66	3.09	3 352	12.1	21.0
Graham	3 354	71.9	27.1	60.8	21.7	8.4	4.1	28.1	26.0	12.3	2.35	2.82	2 772	8.9	20.3
Granville	16 654	72.3	33.3	53.1	23.4	15.0	8.0	27.7	23.9	9.0	2.58	3.05	13 134	14.1	22.0
Greene	6 696	74.0	34.3	52.1	22.9	17.3	9.2	26.0	22.6	10.0	2.65	3.09	5 395	16.2	22.0
Guilford	168 667	65.1	30.4	48.0	20.7	13.4	8.0	34.9	27.9	8.3	2.41	2.96	137 706	12.8	26.6
Halifax	22 122	69.2	31.2	44.1	17.9	20.4	11.4	30.8	27.7	12.0	2.51	3.06	20 335	19.8	24.6
Harnett	33 800	71.3	36.0	53.2	25.1	13.5	8.4	28.7	23.3	8.5	2.61	3.07	25 150	12.5	23.0
Haywood	23 100	69.5	26.2	56.7	19.4	9.5	5.1	30.5	26.7	12.3	2.30	2.76	19 211	9.2	23.9
Henderson	37 414	70.4	26.0	58.6	19.8	8.4	4.6	29.6	25.7	12.4	2.33	2.78	28 709	8.2	23.8
Hertford	8 953	69.7	30.0	45.8	17.4	19.5	10.6	30.3	26.9	12.1	2.48	2.99	8 150	18.1	25.3
Hoke	11 373	76.9	41.4	52.7	27.2	18.2	11.2	23.1	19.0	5.8	2.86	3.22	7 405	21.7	19.2
Hyde	2 185	65.6	26.4	48.7	19.4	13.1	5.5	34.4	30.6	13.9	2.36	2.94	2 094	15.3	24.6
Iredell	47 360	73.2	33.5	57.8	24.9	11.3	6.5	26.8	22.7	8.4	2.56	3.00	35 573	11.3	21.5
Jackson	13 191	65.1	25.5	51.4	18.0	10.0	5.6	34.9	27.0	9.8	2.30	2.79	9 683	10.1	23.2
Johnston	46 595	73.2	35.4	57.8	26.9	10.6	6.5	27.7	23.1	8.6	2.58	3.02	31 566	11.5	23.6
Jones	4 061	72.3	31.7	52.2	21.0	15.2	8.4	27.7	24.5	11.4	2.53	2.99	3 492	13.8	22.2
Lee	18 466	72.4	33.3	54.3	23.0	13.4	7.9	27.6	23.5	8.8	2.61	3.05	15 689	13.6	22.2
Lenoir	23 862	67.8	31.3	46.4	18.9	17.3	10.4	32.2	28.4	11.8	2.43	2.96	21 938	17.3	26.0
Lincoln	24 041	75.6	34.1	61.2	26.4	10.0	5.4	24.4	20.1	7.8	2.62	3.00	18 764	9.7	19.1
McDowell	16 604	72.0	30.3	57.5	22.6	10.2	5.3	28.0	24.3	10.3	2.45	2.90	13 680	10.0	21.9
Macon	12 828	69.4	24.8	58.5	18.9	8.0	4.3	30.6	27.0	13.6	2.28	2.74	9 834	7.9	24.3
Madison	8 000	69.9	28.4	57.5	21.7	8.9	4.9	30.1	26.3	11.8	2.34	2.81	6 488	8.0	23.3
Martin	10 020	71.8	31.6	50.3	20.4	17.6	9.5	28.2	25.7	11.9	2.53	3.02	9 317	16.3	23.8
Mecklenburg	273 416	64.0	32.1	47.7	22.8	12.4	7.6	36.0	27.6	5.9	2.49	3.06	200 219	12.5	26.0
Mitchell	6 551	72.3	27.4	60.9	21.7	8.1	4.0	27.7	25.2	12.0	2.37	2.82	5 779	8.3	21.9
Montgomery	9 848	73.0	31.0	55.6	22.4	12.4	6.3	27.0	24.1	10.7	2.61	3.08	8 290	13.5	22.2
Moore	30 713	71.5	26.7	58.1	19.2	10.2	5.8	28.5	24.9	11.3	2.38	2.81	23 827	10.4	23.8
Nash	33 644	71.1	32.7	52.7	22.8	14.5	8.1	28.9	25.0	9.6	2.54	3.02	29 041	13.7	23.8
New Hanover	68 183	61.0	26.1	46.5	17.8	11.5	6.9	39.0	28.9	8.5	2.29	2.83	48 139	13.3	25.8
Northampton	8 691	68.5	27.7	45.5	16.2	18.3	9.4	31.5	28.4	13.2	2.44	2.99	7 591	18.9	23.9
Onslow	48 122	76.0	42.6	61.0	32.5	11.6	8.0	24.0	18.6	5.2	2.72	3.09	40 658	9.5	15.4
Orange	45 863	57.0	28.3	44.6	21.1	9.4	5.8	43.0	28.1	6.1	2.36	2.95	36 104	9.4	28.0
Pamlico	5 178	71.8	25.2	56.6	18.3	11.5	5.3	28.2	25.0	12.1	2.38	2.81	4 523	12.1	23.3
Pasquotank	12 907	70.5	33.4	50.4	21.2	16.3	10.3	29.5	25.4	11.4	2.52	3.01	11 384	14.8	23.9
Pender	16 054	73.0	29.4	57.9	21.4	11.2	6.0	27.0	22.9	8.5	2.49	2.90	11 112	12.3	21.5
Perquimans	4 645	72.7	28.2	56.5	19.8	12.6	6.6	27.3	24.1	11.9	2.42	2.86	3 988	11.7	21.6
Person	14 085	71.8	31.5	53.8	22.0	13.8	7.5	28.2	24.2	10.1	2.50	2.95	11 423	13.5	22.8
Pitt	52 539	61.4	29.9	43.4	19.5	14.4	8.7	38.6	28.3	7.3	2.43	3.02	40 491	14.5	25.7
Polk	7 908	67.5	23.5	56.3	18.0	7.9	3.9	32.5	28.9	15.0	2.28	2.78	6 110	8.4	26.2
Randolph	50 659	73.7	33.7	59.1	25.5	10.2	5.9	26.3	22.5	8.6	2.55	2.97	41 096	9.6	20.9
Richmond	17 873	70.4	32.1	48.3	19.7	17.0	9.9	29.6	26.3	11.2	2.51	3.01	16 793	15.2	24.9
Robeson	43 677	73.3	37.0	46.6	21.6	20.6	12.2	26.7	22.7	8.3	2.75	3.20	36 154	20.3	21.8
Rockingham	36 989	70.8	30.1	53.6	21.4	12.8	6.6	29.2	25.7	10.8	2.45	2.93	33 446	12.5	23.8
Rowan	49 940	71.1	32.4	54.8	23.1	11.9	7.0	28.9	24.7	10.2	2.52	2.98	42 512	10.9	24.1
Rutherford	25 191	71.2	30.0	55.4	21.5	11.7	6.5	28.8	25.5	11.1	2.44	2.90	22 198	11.5	23.7
Sampson	22 273	72.8	33.4	53.6	23.5	14.3	7.7	27.2	23.7	10.2	2.64	3.09	17 526	14.4	22.7
Scotland	13 399	72.2	34.4	47.1	19.8	20.4	12.2	27.8	24.4	8.9	2.61	3.10	11 837	19.8	22.1
Stanly	22 223	72.7	32.6	58.3	24.6	10.5	6.0	27.3	24.3	10.8	2.53	3.00	19 747	10.0	22.3
Stokes	17 579	74.2	33.8	60.6	26.2	9.7	5.5	25.8	22.8	8.9	2.51	2.94	14 123	9.0	20.0
Surry	28 408	72.1	30.8	58.4	23.9	9.7	5.1	27.9	25.0	11.7	2.46	2.92	24 252	9.7	22.6

[1] No spouse present.

Table B. States and Counties

STATE County	Percent change of households, 1990–2000	Total housing units	Occupied housing units (percent)	Vacant housing units Total	For seasonal, recreational, or occasional use	Homeowner vacancy rate (percent)	Rental vacancy rate (percent)	Occupied housing units Total	Percent owner-occupied housing units	Percent renter-occupied housing units	Average household size of owner-occupied units	Average household size of renter-occupied units
	86	87	88	89	90	91	92	93	94	95	96	97
NORTH CAROLINA— Cont'd												
Chowan	9.1	6 443	86.6	13.4	5.2	2.8	7.1	5 580	72.2	27.8	2.48	2.46
Clay	31.4	5 425	70.9	29.1	21.9	3.0	8.2	3 847	84.5	15.5	2.27	2.14
Cleveland	15.6	40 317	91.9	8.1	0.5	1.9	10.9	37 046	72.8	27.2	2.56	2.47
Columbus	15.4	24 060	88.6	11.4	2.1	1.7	11.0	21 308	76.4	23.6	2.55	2.36
Craven	17.1	38 150	90.6	9.4	1.1	2.1	10.1	34 582	66.7	33.3	2.48	2.52
Cumberland	17.3	118 425	90.7	9.3	0.3	2.7	10.1	107 358	59.4	40.6	2.68	2.61
Currituck	37.0	10 687	64.6	35.4	30.9	1.5	7.0	6 902	81.6	18.4	2.60	2.66
Dare	35.7	26 671	47.6	52.4	50.1	1.2	7.9	12 690	74.5	25.5	2.37	2.27
Davidson	18.8	62 432	93.2	6.8	1.7	1.4	6.4	58 156	74.2	25.8	2.52	2.44
Davie	27.5	14 953	92.0	8.0	0.7	2.5	8.1	13 750	83.3	16.7	2.51	2.48
Duplin	22.4	20 520	89.0	11.0	0.8	1.0	8.2	18 267	74.9	25.1	2.57	2.81
Durham	23.1	95 452	93.3	6.7	0.5	2.3	6.7	89 015	54.3	45.7	2.48	2.31
Edgecombe	0.4	24 002	85.0	15.0	0.5	1.5	5.7	20 392	64.1	35.9	2.65	2.70
Forsyth	15.3	133 093	93.1	6.9	0.3	2.1	9.6	123 851	65.6	34.4	2.45	2.27
Franklin	32.1	20 364	87.6	12.4	3.7	2.9	8.6	17 843	77.8	22.2	2.58	2.57
Gaston	13.1	78 842	93.8	6.2	0.3	1.6	7.4	73 936	68.8	31.2	2.57	2.46
Gates	16.4	4 389	88.9	11.1	1.6	2.0	7.9	3 901	82.1	17.9	2.64	2.74
Graham	21.0	5 084	66.0	34.0	26.6	1.7	13.0	3 354	82.7	17.3	2.39	2.16
Granville	26.8	17 896	93.1	6.9	1.1	1.1	6.7	16 654	75.0	25.0	2.60	2.52
Greene	24.1	7 368	90.9	9.1	0.5	1.0	7.4	6 696	74.7	25.3	2.62	2.73
Guilford	22.5	180 391	93.5	6.5	0.4	1.8	7.2	168 667	62.7	37.3	2.51	2.26
Halifax	8.8	25 309	87.4	12.6	2.8	1.7	7.4	22 122	67.0	33.0	2.53	2.47
Harnett	34.4	38 605	87.6	12.4	0.5	3.3	15.8	33 800	70.3	29.7	2.65	2.51
Haywood	20.2	28 640	80.7	19.3	8.7	2.0	11.2	23 100	77.4	22.6	2.31	2.24
Henderson	30.3	42 996	87.0	13.0	6.3	1.9	8.3	37 414	78.8	21.2	2.33	2.33
Hertford	9.9	9 724	92.1	7.9	0.8	1.4	5.7	8 953	70.0	30.0	2.50	2.43
Hoke	53.6	12 518	90.9	9.1	0.5	2.4	8.8	11 373	75.0	25.0	2.86	2.87
Hyde	4.3	3 302	66.2	33.8	20.2	2.1	16.0	2 185	78.4	21.6	2.39	2.24
Iredell	33.1	51 918	91.2	8.8	2.5	1.8	9.3	47 360	75.4	24.6	2.59	2.47
Jackson	36.2	19 291	68.4	31.6	23.9	2.2	10.6	13 191	72.5	27.5	2.39	2.08
Johnston	47.6	50 196	92.8	7.2	0.5	2.2	8.0	46 595	73.4	26.6	2.59	2.56
Jones	16.3	4 679	86.8	13.2	1.1	1.3	16.5	4 061	79.8	20.2	2.56	2.40
Lee	17.7	19 909	92.8	7.2	0.7	1.4	10.0	18 466	71.7	28.3	2.62	2.56
Lenoir	8.8	27 184	87.8	12.2	0.3	1.3	6.7	23 862	67.0	33.0	2.47	2.34
Lincoln	28.1	25 717	93.5	6.5	1.3	1.4	5.7	24 041	78.5	21.5	2.62	2.60
McDowell	21.4	18 377	90.4	9.6	3.1	1.2	6.7	16 604	77.2	22.8	2.49	2.33
Macon	30.4	20 746	61.8	38.2	30.4	2.7	9.6	12 828	81.3	18.7	2.30	2.20
Madison	23.3	9 722	82.3	17.7	7.0	2.1	10.1	8 000	76.6	23.4	2.36	2.29
Martin	7.5	10 930	91.7	8.3	0.8	1.1	5.3	10 020	71.8	28.2	2.53	2.51
Mecklenburg	36.6	292 780	93.4	6.6	0.5	2.4	8.7	273 416	62.3	37.7	2.60	2.29
Mitchell	13.4	7 919	82.7	17.3	6.0	2.6	7.3	6 551	80.8	19.2	2.39	2.26
Montgomery	18.8	14 145	69.6	30.4	24.1	1.6	6.5	9 848	76.7	23.3	2.59	2.70
Moore	28.9	35 151	87.4	12.6	3.6	2.8	13.2	30 713	78.7	21.3	2.40	2.31
Nash	15.9	37 051	90.8	9.2	0.5	1.5	6.2	33 644	67.7	32.3	2.59	2.42
New Hanover	41.6	79 616	85.6	14.4	5.5	3.2	14.1	68 183	64.7	35.3	2.39	2.11
Northampton	14.5	10 455	83.1	16.9	7.6	0.9	5.1	8 691	77.0	23.0	2.43	2.47
Onslow	18.4	55 726	86.4	13.6	5.2	2.9	10.3	48 122	58.1	41.9	2.70	2.75
Orange	27.0	49 289	93.0	7.0	0.6	1.6	7.5	45 863	57.6	42.4	2.56	2.09
Pamlico	14.5	6 781	76.4	23.6	13.3	1.7	13.8	5 178	82.2	17.8	2.38	2.36
Pasquotank	13.4	14 289	90.3	9.7	1.1	3.3	10.3	12 907	65.7	34.3	2.53	2.49
Pender	44.5	20 798	77.2	22.8	13.9	2.4	13.6	16 054	82.6	17.4	2.49	2.48
Perquimans	16.5	6 043	76.9	23.1	10.2	2.3	5.8	4 645	78.6	21.4	2.41	2.45
Person	23.3	15 504	90.8	9.2	3.2	1.2	6.6	14 085	74.6	25.4	2.52	2.44
Pitt	29.8	58 408	90.0	10.0	0.4	2.1	6.0	52 539	58.1	41.9	2.60	2.18
Polk	29.4	9 192	86.0	14.0	7.2	1.3	9.3	7 908	78.7	21.3	2.32	2.11
Randolph	23.3	54 422	93.1	6.9	0.4	1.4	8.4	50 659	76.6	23.4	2.57	2.49
Richmond	6.4	19 886	89.9	10.1	0.7	1.6	13.2	17 873	71.9	28.1	2.51	2.51
Robeson	20.8	47 779	91.4	8.6	0.5	1.3	10.6	43 677	72.8	27.2	2.79	2.64
Rockingham	10.6	40 208	92.0	8.0	0.6	1.6	8.3	36 989	73.7	26.3	2.48	2.37
Rowan	17.5	53 980	92.5	7.5	1.0	1.6	7.0	49 940	73.6	26.4	2.55	2.43
Rutherford	13.5	29 535	85.3	14.7	5.1	2.4	17.6	25 191	74.5	25.5	2.47	2.33
Sampson	27.1	25 142	88.6	11.4	0.9	1.4	10.9	22 273	73.5	26.5	2.63	2.66
Scotland	13.2	14 693	91.2	8.8	0.8	1.5	8.8	13 399	69.2	30.8	2.68	2.46
Stanly	12.5	24 582	90.4	9.6	2.5	1.6	7.2	22 223	76.3	23.7	2.53	2.56
Stokes	24.5	19 262	91.3	8.7	1.5	1.4	8.4	17 579	82.1	17.9	2.55	2.31
Surry	17.1	31 033	91.5	8.5	1.1	1.3	9.2	28 408	76.3	23.7	2.49	2.37

Table B. States and Counties

STATE/ County code	MSA/ PMSA/ NECMA code[1]	County type[2]	STATE County	Population, 2000				Population, 1990				Population and population characteristics, 2000 — Race (percent) — One race					
				Land area, 2000[3] (sq km)	Total persons	Rank	Per square kilometer	Land area, 1990[3] (sq km)	Total persons	Rank	Per square kilometer	White	Black or African American	American Indian or Alaska Native	Asian	Native Hawaiian and other Pacific Islander	Some other race
				1	2	3	4	5	6	7	8	9	10	11	12	13	14
			NORTH CAROLINA —Cont'd														
37 173	...	9	Swain	1 368	12 968	2 235	9.5	1 368	11 268	2 277	8.2	66.3	1.7	29.0	0.2	0.0	0.5
37 175	...	6	Transylvania	980	29 334	1 418	29.9	980	25 520	1 440	26.0	93.7	4.2	0.3	0.4	0.0	0.3
37 177	...	9	Tyrrell	1 010	4 149	2 903	4.1	1 010	3 856	2 927	3.8	56.5	39.4	0.2	0.7	0.0	2.0
37 179	1520	1	Union	1 651	123 677	435	74.9	1 651	84 210	543	51.0	82.8	12.5	0.4	0.6	0.0	2.6
37 181	...	6	Vance	657	42 954	1 038	65.4	657	38 892	1 025	59.2	48.2	48.3	0.2	0.4	0.0	2.5
37 183	6640	2	Wake	2 155	627 846	85	291.3	2 160	426 311	118	197.4	72.4	19.7	0.3	3.4	0.0	2.5
37 185	...	8	Warren	1 110	19 972	1 794	18.0	1 110	17 265	1 837	15.6	38.9	54.5	4.8	0.1	0.0	0.8
37 187	...	7	Washington	903	13 723	2 180	15.2	901	13 997	2 058	15.5	48.3	48.9	0.1	0.3	0.0	1.7
37 189	...	7	Watauga	809	42 695	1 044	52.8	810	36 952	1 074	45.6	96.5	1.6	0.3	0.6	0.0	0.5
37 191	2980	3	Wayne	1 431	113 329	475	79.2	1 431	104 666	441	73.1	61.3	33.0	0.4	1.0	0.0	3.1
37 193	...	7	Wilkes	1 961	65 632	743	33.5	1 961	59 393	728	30.3	93.0	4.2	0.1	0.3	0.0	1.7
37 195	...	4	Wilson	961	73 814	679	76.8	961	66 061	663	68.7	55.8	39.3	0.3	0.4	0.0	3.2
37 197	3120	2	Yadkin	869	36 348	1 204	41.8	869	30 488	1 269	35.1	92.5	3.4	0.2	0.2	0.0	2.9
37 199	...	8	Yancey	809	17 774	1 911	22.0	809	15 419	1 962	19.1	98.0	0.6	0.3	0.1	0.0	0.4
38 000	...		**NORTH DAKOTA**	178 647	642 200	X	3.6	178 695	638 800	X	3.6	92.4	0.6	4.9	0.6	0.0	0.4
38 001	...	9	Adams	2 559	2 593	3 021	1.0	2 559	3 174	2 986	1.2	98.5	0.5	0.3	0.2	0.0	0.1
38 003	...	7	Barnes	3 863	11 775	2 309	3.0	3 864	12 545	2 179	3.2	97.9	0.5	0.8	0.2	0.0	0.1
38 005	...	9	Benson	3 576	6 964	2 689	1.9	3 596	7 198	2 633	2.0	50.8	0.1	48.0	0.0	0.0	0.2
38 007	...	9	Billings	2 982	888	3 115	0.3	2 982	1 108	3 110	0.4	98.8	0.0	0.1	0.0	0.1	0.1
38 009	...	7	Bottineau	4 322	7 149	2 672	1.7	4 322	8 011	2 564	1.9	97.2	0.2	1.5	0.2	0.0	0.1
38 011	...	9	Bowman	3 010	3 242	2 977	1.1	3 010	3 596	2 950	1.2	99.0	0.0	0.2	0.0	0.0	0.2
38 013	...	9	Burke	2 858	2 242	3 047	0.8	2 858	3 002	3 000	1.1	99.2	0.1	0.2	0.1	0.0	0.0
38 015	1010	3	Burleigh	4 230	69 416	715	16.4	4 230	60 131	722	14.2	95.0	0.3	3.3	0.4	0.0	0.2
38 017	2520	3	Cass	4 572	123 138	438	26.9	4 573	102 874	447	22.5	95.1	0.8	1.1	1.3	0.0	0.4
38 019	...	9	Cavalier	3 855	4 831	2 858	1.3	3 857	6 064	2 749	1.6	98.1	0.1	0.5	0.1	0.0	0.1
38 021	...	9	Dickey	2 929	5 757	2 805	2.0	2 930	6 107	2 742	2.1	97.8	0.1	0.3	0.5	0.0	0.6
38 023	...	9	Divide	3 262	2 283	3 042	0.7	3 262	2 899	3 006	0.9	99.0	0.0	0.1	0.5	0.0	0.2
38 025	...	9	Dunn	5 205	3 600	2 944	0.7	5 206	4 005	2 918	0.8	86.6	0.0	12.4	0.1	0.0	0.3
38 027	...	9	Eddy	1 632	2 757	3 008	1.7	1 637	2 951	3 003	1.8	96.4	0.1	2.4	0.1	0.1	0.3
38 029	...	8	Emmons	3 911	4 331	2 894	1.1	3 911	4 830	2 853	1.2	99.1	0.0	0.1	0.2	0.2	0.3
38 031	...	9	Foster	1 645	3 759	2 933	2.3	1 645	3 983	2 919	2.4	99.0	0.1	0.4	0.0	0.0	0.1
38 033	...	9	Golden Valley	2 595	1 924	3 070	0.7	2 595	2 108	3 062	0.8	97.8	0.0	0.7	0.1	0.0	0.3
38 035	2985	3	Grand Forks	3 724	66 109	740	17.8	3 724	70 683	628	19.0	93.0	1.4	2.3	1.0	0.1	0.7
38 037	...	8	Grant	4 298	2 841	3 002	0.7	4 298	3 549	2 953	0.8	96.9	0.0	1.7	0.4	0.0	0.4
38 039	...	9	Griggs	1 835	2 754	3 009	1.5	1 835	3 303	2 976	1.8	99.3	0.0	0.2	0.1	0.0	0.1
38 041	...	9	Hettinger	2 933	2 715	3 012	0.9	2 933	3 445	2 959	1.2	98.9	0.1	0.4	0.1	0.1	0.0
38 043	...	8	Kidder	3 499	2 753	3 010	0.8	3 501	3 332	2 967	1.0	99.5	0.2	0.1	0.1	0.0	0.1
38 045	...	9	La Moure	2 971	4 701	2 867	1.6	2 971	5 383	2 811	1.8	99.2	0.0	0.2	0.1	0.0	0.1
38 047	...	9	Logan	2 571	2 308	3 037	0.9	2 571	2 847	3 008	1.1	99.2	0.1	0.1	0.2	0.0	0.1
38 049	...	9	McHenry	4 854	5 987	2 782	1.2	4 854	6 528	2 705	1.3	98.7	0.1	0.4	0.0	0.0	0.1
38 051	...	9	McIntosh	2 526	3 390	2 964	1.3	2 526	4 021	2 915	1.6	98.9	0.0	0.1	0.3	0.0	0.1
38 053	...	9	McKenzie	7 102	5 737	2 808	0.8	7 102	6 383	2 718	0.9	77.4	0.1	21.2	0.1	0.0	0.1
38 055	...	8	McLean	5 465	9 311	2 505	1.7	5 466	10 457	2 341	1.9	92.5	0.0	5.9	0.1	0.0	0.2
38 057	...	7	Mercer	2 708	8 644	2 555	3.2	2 708	9 808	2 402	3.6	96.0	0.0	2.0	0.3	0.4	0.1
38 059	1010	3	Morton	4 989	25 303	1 553	5.1	4 989	23 700	1 503	4.8	95.8	0.2	2.4	0.3	0.0	0.2
38 061	...	9	Mountrail	4 724	6 631	2 723	1.4	4 724	7 021	2 655	1.5	66.0	0.1	30.0	0.2	0.0	0.3
38 063	...	8	Nelson	2 542	3 715	2 941	1.5	2 543	4 410	2 879	1.7	98.6	0.1	0.3	0.3	0.0	0.1
38 065	...	8	Oliver	1 874	2 065	3 062	1.1	1 874	2 381	3 033	1.3	97.6	0.1	1.3	0.1	0.0	0.0
38 067	...	9	Pembina	2 898	8 585	2 558	3.0	2 898	9 238	2 450	3.2	95.5	0.2	1.4	0.2	0.0	1.3
38 069	...	7	Pierce	2 636	4 675	2 869	1.8	2 636	5 052	2 835	1.9	98.5	0.1	0.7	0.3	0.0	0.0
38 071	...	7	Ramsey	3 069	12 066	2 291	3.9	3 072	12 681	2 168	4.1	92.3	0.2	5.4	0.3	0.0	0.2
38 073	...	8	Ransom	2 235	5 890	2 794	2.6	2 235	5 921	2 768	2.6	97.9	0.2	0.3	0.3	0.0	0.4
38 075	...	9	Renville	2 266	2 610	3 019	1.2	2 266	3 160	2 987	1.4	97.7	0.2	0.7	0.5	0.0	0.1
38 077	...	6	Richland	3 721	17 998	1 897	4.8	3 722	18 148	1 780	4.9	96.8	0.3	1.7	0.2	0.0	0.1
38 079	...	9	Rolette	2 337	13 674	2 186	5.9	2 338	12 772	2 160	5.5	25.1	0.1	73.0	0.1	0.0	0.5
38 081	...	9	Sargent	2 224	4 366	2 889	2.0	2 224	4 549	2 868	2.0	98.2	0.0	0.5	0.0	0.0	0.5
38 083	...	9	Sheridan	2 517	1 710	3 084	0.7	2 517	2 148	3 057	0.9	99.2	0.1	0.4	0.0	0.0	0.1
38 085	...	9	Sioux	2 834	4 044	2 917	1.4	2 834	3 761	2 933	1.3	14.3	0.0	84.6	0.0	0.0	0.1
38 087	...	9	Slope	3 154	767	3 128	0.2	3 155	907	3 117	0.3	99.7	0.0	0.1	0.0	0.0	0.0
38 089	...	7	Stark	3 466	22 636	1 664	6.5	3 466	22 832	1 540	6.6	97.5	0.2	0.9	0.2	0.0	0.3
38 091	...	8	Steele	1 845	2 258	3 046	1.2	1 845	2 420	3 028	1.3	98.3	0.0	0.6	0.0	0.0	0.2
38 093	...	7	Stutsman	5 753	21 908	1 697	3.8	5 754	22 241	1 567	3.9	97.5	0.3	0.9	0.4	0.0	0.2
38 095	...	9	Towner	2 654	2 876	3 001	1.1	2 656	3 627	2 948	1.4	97.3	0.1	2.1	0.1	0.0	0.0
38 097	...	8	Traill	2 232	8 477	2 567	3.8	2 232	8 752	2 490	3.9	97.3	0.1	0.9	0.2	0.0	1.0
38 099	...	6	Walsh	3 320	12 389	2 273	3.7	3 320	13 840	2 070	4.2	94.9	0.3	1.0	0.2	0.0	2.5

[1]MSA = Metropolitan Statistical Area. PMSA = Primary MSA. NECMA = New England County Metropolitan Area. See Appendix A for explanation of these concepts. See Appendix B for list of metropolitan areas identified by type, with component counties.
[2]County typology code from the Economic Research Service of USDA. See Appendix A for definition.
[3]Dry land or land partially or temporarily covered by water.

Table B. States and Counties

STATE County	Population and population characteristics, 2000 (cont'd)								Population and population characteristics, 1990				
	Race (percent) (cont'd)								Race (percent)				
	Race alone or in combination												
	Two or more races	White	Black	American Indian or Alaska Native	Asian	Native Hawaiian and other Pacific Islander	Some other race	Hispanic¹	White	Black or African American	American Indian or Alaska Native	Asian and Pacific Islander	Hispanic¹
	15	16	17	18	19	20	21	22	23	24	25	26	27
NORTH CAROLINA —Cont'd													
Swain	2.3	68.4	1.8	31.0	0.3	0.0	0.8	1.5	70.6	1.7	27.3	0.3	0.7
Transylvania	1.1	94.7	4.7	0.8	0.5	0.1	0.5	1.0	94.5	4.7	0.3	0.4	0.6
Tyrrell	1.1	57.0	39.8	0.5	1.2	0.1	2.6	3.6	59.6	40.0	0.1	0.1	0.3
Union	1.0	83.7	12.8	0.7	0.8	0.0	3.0	6.2	83.2	15.9	0.3	0.3	0.8
Vance	0.8	48.8	48.7	0.4	0.5	0.1	2.4	4.6	54.4	45.0	0.2	0.2	0.7
Wake	1.6	73.7	20.3	0.7	3.8	0.1	3.1	5.4	76.5	20.8	0.3	1.9	1.3
Warren	0.9	39.3	55.1	5.4	0.2	0.1	1.0	1.6	38.2	57.0	4.4	0.1	0.6
Washington	0.7	48.8	49.3	0.3	0.5	0.1	1.8	2.3	54.0	45.5	0.1	0.3	0.5
Watauga	0.6	97.0	1.7	0.5	0.7	0.1	0.6	1.5	97.2	2.1	0.2	0.4	0.7
Wayne	1.3	62.2	33.6	0.7	1.3	0.1	3.4	4.9	66.1	32.3	0.3	0.8	1.3
Wilkes	0.7	93.6	4.4	0.4	0.4	0.1	1.9	3.4	94.7	4.8	0.1	0.2	0.6
Wilson	0.9	56.5	39.7	0.5	0.6	0.1	3.6	6.0	61.5	37.7	0.1	0.3	0.8
Yadkin	0.8	93.2	3.6	0.5	0.3	0.1	3.2	6.5	94.7	4.2	0.1	0.1	1.3
Yancey	0.6	98.5	0.7	0.6	0.2	0.0	0.5	2.7	98.7	1.0	0.2	0.1	0.3
NORTH DAKOTA	1.2	93.4	0.8	5.5	0.8	0.1	0.6	1.2	94.6	0.6	4.1	0.5	0.7
Adams	0.3	98.8	0.5	0.6	0.2	0.0	0.2	0.3	99.6	0.1	0.3	0.0	0.0
Barnes	0.6	98.5	0.6	1.1	0.3	0.0	0.2	0.5	98.9	0.2	0.5	0.3	0.3
Benson	0.8	51.6	0.2	48.8	0.0	0.0	0.2	0.8	61.4	0.0	38.5	0.0	0.3
Billings	0.9	99.7	0.0	0.9	0.0	0.2	0.1	0.3	99.7	0.0	0.3	0.0	0.0
Bottineau	0.8	98.0	0.3	2.0	0.3	0.0	0.2	0.5	99.0	0.1	0.7	0.2	0.2
Bowman	0.6	99.6	0.1	0.4	0.2	0.0	0.3	0.7	99.7	0.0	0.1	0.1	0.2
Burke	0.2	99.4	0.2	0.2	0.3	0.0	0.1	0.4	99.3	0.0	0.4	0.2	0.5
Burleigh	0.8	95.8	0.4	3.8	0.5	0.1	0.3	0.7	96.6	0.1	2.7	0.4	0.6
Cass	1.3	96.2	1.1	1.5	1.6	0.1	0.8	1.2	97.6	0.3	0.9	1.0	0.7
Cavalier	1.0	99.1	0.4	1.2	0.2	0.0	0.2	0.6	99.1	0.1	0.7	0.1	0.1
Dickey	0.7	98.5	0.3	0.7	0.7	0.1	0.6	1.4	99.1	0.1	0.3	0.2	0.5
Divide	0.2	99.2	0.1	0.2	0.5	0.0	0.2	0.6	99.3	0.0	0.3	0.2	0.2
Dunn	0.9	87.4	0.1	13.1	0.1	0.0	0.2	0.8	90.0	0.0	9.5	0.1	0.6
Eddy	0.7	97.1	0.2	3.0	0.1	0.1	0.3	0.6	98.3	0.0	1.7	0.0	0.1
Emmons	0.1	99.1	0.1	0.2	0.2	0.2	0.3	1.2	99.8	0.0	0.1	0.1	0.1
Foster	0.4	99.4	0.3	0.5	0.0	0.0	0.2	0.2	99.3	0.0	0.6	0.1	0.3
Golden Valley	1.1	98.7	0.2	1.7	0.2	0.0	0.4	1.0	99.0	0.0	0.6	0.4	0.0
Grand Forks	1.6	94.4	1.8	3.0	1.4	0.1	1.0	2.1	94.5	2.0	1.8	1.2	1.5
Grant	0.7	97.6	0.0	2.2	0.4	0.1	0.4	0.6	98.9	0.0	0.9	0.1	0.3
Griggs	0.2	99.5	0.1	0.3	0.1	0.0	0.1	0.4	99.6	0.0	0.2	0.2	0.1
Hettinger	0.4	99.3	0.1	0.6	0.1	0.1	0.1	0.2	99.6	0.0	0.2	0.2	0.1
Kidder	0.1	99.6	0.2	0.1	0.2	0.0	0.0	0.6	99.9	0.0	0.0	0.1	0.2
La Moure	0.3	99.6	0.2	0.3	0.1	0.0	0.2	0.6	99.8	0.0	0.1	0.0	0.1
Logan	0.3	99.5	0.1	0.2	0.3	0.0	0.1	0.7	99.7	0.0	0.2	0.0	0.3
McHenry	0.7	99.4	0.2	0.9	0.2	0.0	0.2	0.4	99.5	0.1	0.2	0.2	0.2
McIntosh	0.6	99.4	0.0	0.5	0.4	0.0	0.1	0.8	99.7	0.0	0.1	0.1	0.1
McKenzie	1.2	78.5	0.2	22.0	0.1	0.1	0.3	1.0	85.3	0.0	14.4	0.0	0.8
McLean	1.2	93.6	0.1	6.9	0.2	0.0	0.3	0.9	94.4	0.0	5.4	0.1	0.4
Mercer	1.2	97.2	0.1	2.6	0.3	0.5	0.5	0.4	97.1	0.1	2.3	0.4	0.4
Morton	1.2	96.9	0.3	3.1	0.5	0.0	0.3	0.6	97.9	0.1	1.8	0.2	0.3
Mountrail	3.4	69.3	0.1	31.0	0.2	0.1	2.6	1.3	79.8	0.1	19.9	0.2	0.4
Nelson	0.6	99.2	0.1	0.6	0.4	0.0	0.3	0.2	99.7	0.0	0.2	0.1	0.2
Oliver	0.9	98.4	0.2	2.1	0.1	0.0	0.3	0.6	98.3	0.0	1.7	0.0	0.2
Pembina	1.4	96.9	0.2	2.6	0.3	0.0	1.5	3.1	97.4	0.2	1.6	0.1	0.9
Pierce	0.4	98.9	0.1	0.9	0.4	0.0	0.1	0.6	99.2	0.0	0.5	0.3	0.0
Ramsey	1.6	93.9	0.3	6.8	0.3	0.0	0.3	0.5	94.8	0.2	4.7	0.2	0.4
Ransom	0.9	98.9	0.4	0.8	0.4	0.0	0.5	0.8	99.5	0.1	0.2	0.1	0.4
Renville	0.8	98.5	0.3	1.2	0.6	0.0	0.2	0.7	98.3	0.4	0.7	0.3	0.2
Richland	0.7	97.5	0.4	2.1	0.4	0.1	0.2	0.7	97.1	0.1	2.3	0.5	0.3
Rolette	1.6	26.6	0.2	74.5	0.1	0.0	0.2	0.8	33.0	0.2	66.5	0.1	0.5
Sargent	0.7	98.9	0.1	0.9	0.2	0.0	0.6	0.7	99.5	0.0	0.2	0.1	0.2
Sheridan	0.2	99.4	0.1	0.5	0.1	0.0	0.1	0.4	99.5	0.0	0.4	0.0	0.0
Sioux	0.9	15.0	0.1	85.3	0.0	0.2	0.3	1.6	24.1	0.1	75.4	0.3	0.8
Slope	0.1	99.9	0.0	0.3	0.0	0.0	0.0	0.1	99.6	0.0	0.3	0.0	0.1
Stark	0.8	98.3	0.4	1.4	0.3	0.1	0.4	1.0	98.8	0.1	0.6	0.3	0.6
Steele	0.8	99.1	0.3	1.2	0.0	0.0	0.3	0.2	99.8	0.0	0.1	0.1	0.2
Stutsman	0.6	98.1	0.4	1.3	0.5	0.1	0.3	0.9	98.6	0.2	0.6	0.4	0.4
Towner	0.5	97.8	0.1	2.5	0.1	0.0	0.1	0.2	98.3	0.1	1.5	0.1	0.1
Traill	0.5	97.7	0.2	1.2	0.2	0.0	1.2	2.2	98.5	0.1	0.5	0.3	1.2
Walsh	1.1	95.8	0.5	1.5	0.4	0.1	3.0	5.7	97.2	0.1	0.7	0.4	3.2

¹Hispanic persons may be of any race.

Table B. States and Counties

STATE County	Population and population characteristics, 2000										
	Age (percent)										
	Under 5 years	5 to 17 years	18 to 24 years	25 to 34 years	35 to 44 years	45 to 54 years	55 to 64 years	65 to 74 years	75 years and over	Median age (years)	Percent Female
	28	29	30	31	32	33	34	35	36	37	38
NORTH CAROLINA —Cont'd											
Swain	6.1	18.1	8.3	12.2	14.5	14.1	11.3	8.4	6.9	38.8	51.4
Transylvania	4.9	15.5	8.2	9.9	13.2	13.6	13.3	11.7	9.7	43.9	51.9
Tyrrell	4.9	17.7	8.2	13.0	17.3	13.3	9.5	8.3	7.8	38.7	46.7
Union	8.1	20.0	8.2	15.5	17.7	13.1	8.4	5.3	3.7	34.0	50.1
Vance	7.0	20.0	8.9	14.1	14.7	13.6	9.0	7.0	5.6	35.0	52.7
Wake	7.2	17.9	10.7	18.1	18.4	13.4	7.0	4.1	3.2	32.9	50.4
Warren	5.4	18.2	8.0	11.4	14.9	13.9	10.9	9.6	7.8	39.7	50.9
Washington	6.6	19.4	7.7	11.0	14.0	14.8	11.0	8.3	7.2	39.2	52.7
Watauga	3.9	12.4	27.8	11.0	12.4	12.8	8.7	6.1	4.9	29.9	50.2
Wayne	7.0	19.2	9.9	14.2	16.3	13.0	8.9	6.8	4.8	34.8	50.7
Wilkes	6.2	16.4	7.9	14.0	15.7	14.6	11.1	7.9	6.2	38.5	50.7
Wilson	6.9	18.7	9.1	13.5	15.3	14.2	9.4	7.1	5.8	36.2	52.3
Yadkin	6.6	17.3	7.5	14.1	16.0	13.7	10.6	7.9	6.3	37.6	50.9
Yancey	5.5	15.7	7.0	12.2	14.2	15.3	11.8	9.7	8.5	41.9	51.1
NORTH DAKOTA	6.1	18.9	11.4	12.0	15.3	13.3	8.3	7.1	7.6	36.2	50.1
Adams	4.5	18.7	4.1	7.6	14.0	15.7	11.3	10.8	13.3	45.6	52.2
Barnes	5.3	17.0	11.3	9.3	13.7	13.9	9.8	8.5	11.3	40.6	50.8
Benson	8.9	27.2	7.8	10.4	12.9	11.1	8.3	7.0	6.5	31.4	49.5
Billings	3.5	21.4	4.5	7.5	19.0	17.7	10.4	8.2	7.8	41.9	47.0
Bottineau	3.9	18.3	8.0	7.9	14.4	15.5	10.7	9.7	11.6	43.4	49.6
Bowman	4.6	19.5	5.3	8.7	15.9	14.4	9.8	10.4	11.4	43.0	51.4
Burke	3.7	17.2	3.5	7.5	14.8	16.7	11.6	13.4	11.7	47.5	49.6
Burleigh	6.2	18.5	11.0	13.0	16.3	14.3	8.2	6.5	5.9	35.9	51.1
Cass	6.6	16.8	16.0	15.9	15.4	12.9	6.7	4.9	4.7	31.3	49.9
Cavalier	4.3	20.3	3.7	7.0	14.3	15.4	12.1	11.3	11.7	45.2	50.3
Dickey	5.7	18.1	10.2	9.5	12.9	12.1	10.1	9.3	12.0	40.7	50.7
Divide	3.1	17.2	3.6	6.0	14.1	14.7	11.9	12.2	17.3	49.0	49.8
Dunn	5.7	21.7	5.8	8.5	15.0	15.4	10.6	8.4	8.9	40.9	49.0
Eddy	5.0	18.6	6.1	7.6	14.8	13.5	9.6	11.3	13.4	43.8	51.1
Emmons	5.3	19.5	3.7	7.8	14.5	12.2	11.4	12.7	12.8	44.5	49.6
Foster	5.3	20.9	5.5	9.9	16.0	11.8	9.2	10.9	10.5	40.5	50.3
Golden Valley	5.5	22.9	5.1	8.3	13.9	13.3	9.7	9.0	12.3	41.2	51.9
Grand Forks	6.4	17.4	19.6	14.2	14.5	11.7	6.4	4.7	4.9	29.2	49.1
Grant	4.3	19.1	4.3	7.9	12.6	15.0	12.1	11.6	13.2	46.5	49.0
Griggs	4.7	17.8	4.9	7.7	13.3	16.3	9.5	10.9	14.8	45.8	50.1
Hettinger	4.4	18.9	3.9	7.3	13.3	15.1	11.9	12.3	12.9	46.2	49.9
Kidder	5.0	18.2	5.0	7.5	15.4	14.1	10.9	12.1	12.0	44.5	49.2
La Moure	4.4	19.8	5.4	7.8	15.1	13.3	10.7	11.5	11.9	43.3	49.4
Logan	5.5	17.1	3.6	8.1	13.6	11.7	13.3	13.6	13.4	46.4	50.4
McHenry	4.9	19.0	5.9	8.8	14.4	14.3	10.8	10.8	11.0	43.0	49.0
McIntosh	4.2	15.2	4.6	6.5	12.9	10.6	11.8	14.9	19.4	51.0	52.2
McKenzie	6.3	24.4	5.5	7.8	15.5	14.9	10.0	7.4	8.3	39.5	49.8
McLean	4.7	19.1	5.1	8.1	14.6	16.5	11.5	9.4	11.0	44.1	50.4
Mercer	4.6	24.5	4.2	7.6	20.0	16.0	8.8	6.9	7.4	40.1	49.7
Morton	6.5	20.5	7.8	11.7	16.5	14.1	8.3	7.6	7.0	37.4	50.2
Mountrail	6.5	21.6	6.8	9.5	13.7	14.5	9.7	8.0	9.7	39.6	50.8
Nelson	3.7	18.4	4.0	7.0	13.4	14.5	11.7	12.1	15.4	47.2	51.1
Oliver	4.5	22.9	4.7	7.9	15.6	19.8	10.4	7.8	6.4	42.0	48.2
Pembina	5.0	19.9	6.2	9.2	15.4	15.3	9.4	9.2	10.3	41.6	49.9
Pierce	5.3	18.6	5.5	9.1	14.8	12.5	10.2	10.7	13.5	42.9	50.9
Ramsey	5.7	19.4	8.0	10.2	15.7	13.2	9.1	8.4	10.4	39.5	50.7
Ransom	5.9	19.1	5.9	10.8	14.6	13.3	9.2	9.8	11.4	40.7	48.5
Renville	4.3	19.0	4.9	9.2	15.3	14.8	10.5	10.5	11.6	43.6	49.9
Richland	6.0	18.7	14.5	10.4	15.3	12.4	7.6	7.0	8.2	35.4	48.1
Rolette	8.8	27.6	9.5	11.2	14.6	10.9	7.6	5.2	4.5	28.9	50.7
Sargent	5.7	20.8	5.3	10.7	15.0	14.7	11.0	8.1	8.8	40.3	47.5
Sheridan	3.2	18.2	3.8	6.4	13.5	14.8	13.5	13.7	12.9	48.1	48.6
Sioux	10.5	29.8	11.1	13.5	13.4	9.8	6.4	3.7	1.9	23.9	49.0
Slope	4.7	20.6	4.2	8.1	16.9	17.6	10.0	11.3	6.5	42.5	46.2
Stark	5.8	19.8	11.6	10.4	15.6	13.1	8.3	7.5	8.0	36.9	50.8
Steele	5.6	22.0	4.7	8.2	14.8	13.7	11.3	10.8	8.8	41.4	48.3
Stutsman	5.4	17.5	10.5	10.1	15.7	14.1	9.1	8.6	9.1	39.6	50.9
Towner	4.8	19.9	3.6	7.6	16.4	14.6	9.9	9.8	13.5	44.0	50.8
Traill	6.0	18.8	9.7	9.9	14.9	12.7	8.8	8.4	10.7	39.0	49.8
Walsh	5.7	19.2	6.5	9.6	15.4	14.4	9.8	8.9	10.3	40.9	50.0

Table B. States and Counties

STATE County	Under 5 years	5 to 17 years	18 to 24 years	25 to 34 years	35 to 44 years	45 to 54 years	55 to 64 years	65 to 74 years	75 years and over	Percent Female	2000	1990	1980	1990–2000	1980–1990
	Population and population characteristics, 1990 — Age (percent)										Population—change, 1980–2000 — Total persons			Percent change	
	39	40	41	42	43	44	45	46	47	48	49	50	51	52	53
NORTH CAROLINA —Cont'd															
Swain	6.6	18.7	9.8	14.4	13.8	11.0	10.3	8.0	6.7	50.2	12 968	11 268	10 283	15.1	9.6
Transylvania	5.6	16.2	10.6	13.6	13.0	11.2	11.3	11.4	7.1	51.1	29 334	25 520	23 417	14.0	9.0
Tyrrell	6.5	21.1	7.5	14.3	13.0	10.0	9.9	9.8	7.8	52.2	4 149	3 856	3 975	7.6	-3.0
Union	7.7	19.6	11.1	16.7	15.6	11.5	8.0	5.9	3.7	51.0	123 677	84 210	70 436	46.9	19.6
Vance	7.4	19.3	10.7	15.7	14.9	9.9	9.0	7.7	5.3	52.8	42 954	38 892	36 748	10.4	5.8
Wake	7.1	16.0	13.0	21.5	17.4	10.4	6.8	4.7	3.1	51.1	627 846	426 311	301 429	47.3	41.4
Warren	6.6	18.6	8.2	13.4	13.7	9.9	11.7	10.6	7.3	52.1	19 972	17 265	16 232	15.7	6.4
Washington	7.4	20.4	9.6	14.3	14.8	10.3	9.4	8.3	5.5	52.5	13 723	13 997	14 801	-2.0	-5.4
Watauga	4.6	12.5	29.2	13.4	12.6	9.5	7.6	6.3	4.3	51.1	42 695	36 952	31 666	15.5	16.7
Wayne	7.6	18.6	10.8	18.9	15.0	10.3	8.7	6.4	3.8	50.2	113 329	104 666	97 054	8.3	7.8
Wilkes	5.9	17.6	9.9	16.2	15.5	12.1	9.5	7.8	5.4	51.1	65 632	59 393	58 657	10.5	1.3
Wilson	6.6	19.5	10.5	15.3	15.5	10.7	9.2	7.8	5.0	53.3	73 814	66 061	63 132	11.7	4.6
Yadkin	6.0	16.4	9.3	15.8	15.0	12.3	10.3	8.6	6.3	51.5	36 348	30 488	28 439	19.2	7.2
Yancey	5.8	16.4	9.1	14.2	15.2	11.4	10.7	9.9	7.3	51.6	17 774	15 419	14 934	15.3	3.2
NORTH DAKOTA	7.5	20.0	10.6	16.3	14.1	8.9	8.4	7.4	6.8	50.2	642 200	638 800	652 717	0.5	-2.1
Adams	6.7	19.3	5.3	12.3	15.0	9.6	10.3	10.9	10.6	50.6	2 593	3 174	3 584	-18.3	-11.4
Barnes	6.4	18.2	10.4	12.7	12.9	9.3	9.0	10.6	10.5	51.2	11 775	12 545	13 960	-6.1	-10.1
Benson	9.9	24.8	7.8	12.7	12.0	8.6	8.5	8.0	7.6	49.6	6 964	7 198	7 944	-3.3	-9.4
Billings	7.6	25.3	5.3	15.2	14.9	9.9	10.5	6.4	5.0	47.7	888	1 108	1 138	-19.9	-2.6
Bottineau	6.1	19.7	7.8	12.4	13.8	9.5	9.8	10.0	10.9	49.7	7 149	8 011	9 239	-10.8	-13.3
Bowman	6.5	21.6	5.3	13.1	14.5	9.8	10.8	9.7	8.8	51.0	3 242	3 596	4 229	-9.8	-15.0
Burke	4.6	20.1	4.2	11.3	12.9	10.0	13.4	11.5	12.0	49.8	2 242	3 002	3 822	-25.3	-21.5
Burleigh	7.5	20.3	9.9	17.8	16.1	9.7	8.0	5.9	4.8	51.5	69 416	60 131	54 811	15.4	9.7
Cass	7.4	17.6	15.3	19.1	15.5	8.5	6.8	5.2	4.6	50.2	123 138	102 874	88 247	19.7	16.6
Cavalier	7.0	19.9	5.3	12.3	13.3	10.7	11.9	9.9	9.7	50.0	4 831	6 064	7 636	-20.3	-20.6
Dickey	5.8	19.2	9.9	12.1	12.1	9.4	10.0	10.5	11.1	50.5	5 757	6 107	7 207	-5.7	-15.3
Divide	5.5	18.4	3.8	11.2	12.7	10.9	10.8	13.6	13.2	50.1	2 283	2 899	3 494	-21.2	-17.0
Dunn	8.2	22.6	5.6	13.3	14.5	9.6	9.5	9.8	6.8	48.4	3 600	4 005	4 627	-10.1	-13.4
Eddy	5.8	19.2	4.9	12.7	12.3	8.4	12.1	12.0	12.5	50.6	2 757	2 951	3 554	-6.6	-17.0
Emmons	6.5	19.2	5.8	11.8	11.8	10.7	12.9	11.4	10.0	49.0	4 331	4 830	5 877	-10.3	-17.8
Foster	6.9	20.5	5.6	13.8	12.0	9.4	11.3	9.7	11.0	51.1	3 759	3 983	4 611	-5.6	-13.6
Golden Valley	6.4	24.5	5.9	12.0	12.3	8.5	9.8	10.8	9.8	49.1	1 924	2 108	2 391	-8.7	-11.8
Grand Forks	8.4	17.6	19.1	20.0	13.3	7.1	5.7	4.7	4.1	48.9	66 109	70 683	66 100	-6.5	6.9
Grant	6.4	20.1	5.2	11.2	13.6	10.3	11.9	10.5	10.8	49.3	2 841	3 549	4 274	-19.9	-17.0
Griggs	6.1	19.8	4.9	10.1	14.8	9.2	11.0	12.0	12.1	50.3	2 754	3 303	3 714	-16.6	-11.1
Hettinger	7.1	19.0	5.0	11.8	12.2	10.4	12.0	12.2	10.2	50.4	2 715	3 445	4 275	-21.2	-19.4
Kidder	6.1	21.4	5.5	12.0	12.4	10.4	12.2	10.7	9.2	48.5	2 753	3 332	3 833	-17.4	-13.1
La Moure	6.2	21.0	4.9	12.3	11.9	10.0	11.4	11.4	10.9	49.4	4 701	5 383	6 473	-12.7	-16.8
Logan	6.1	18.7	4.7	12.6	10.6	10.7	13.8	12.2	10.7	49.5	2 308	2 847	3 493	-18.9	-18.5
McHenry	6.0	21.1	5.0	11.4	13.7	10.7	11.2	10.3	10.5	49.3	5 987	6 528	7 858	-8.3	-16.9
McIntosh	5.6	16.1	3.8	11.3	9.8	9.8	14.2	13.9	15.4	51.7	3 390	4 021	4 800	-15.7	-16.2
McKenzie	9.0	24.0	5.7	14.6	14.8	9.7	8.4	8.2	5.6	49.4	5 737	6 383	7 132	-10.1	-10.5
McLean	6.5	22.7	4.8	12.3	15.2	9.7	9.6	10.4	8.9	49.5	9 311	10 457	12 383	-11.0	-15.6
Mercer	8.8	23.6	4.8	18.2	16.0	9.1	6.8	7.0	5.7	49.6	8 644	9 808	9 404	-11.9	4.3
Morton	7.2	23.0	7.5	15.4	14.8	9.4	9.1	7.4	6.1	50.5	25 303	23 700	25 177	6.8	-5.9
Mountrail	7.2	22.8	6.1	12.6	13.7	10.0	9.2	9.8	8.6	50.6	6 631	7 021	7 679	-5.6	-8.6
Nelson	5.4	17.9	3.9	11.4	12.2	10.4	12.2	12.7	13.9	50.5	3 715	4 410	5 233	-15.8	-15.7
Oliver	7.9	25.7	5.2	14.1	17.4	9.4	8.9	6.7	4.7	48.0	2 065	2 381	2 495	-13.3	-4.6
Pembina	6.7	21.3	5.6	13.6	14.8	9.4	10.1	9.4	9.1	50.5	8 585	9 238	10 399	-7.1	-11.2
Pierce	5.4	20.1	5.8	12.1	11.8	9.8	10.8	10.9	13.3	50.6	4 675	5 052	6 166	-7.5	-18.1
Ramsey	7.0	19.4	8.3	15.1	13.3	9.4	9.3	8.9	9.4	50.9	12 066	12 681	13 048	-4.8	-2.8
Ransom	6.2	19.6	5.3	13.4	13.7	9.1	11.0	10.2	11.5	48.9	5 890	5 921	6 698	-0.5	-11.6
Renville	5.6	22.0	5.4	13.6	13.6	9.9	10.3	9.1	10.5	50.6	2 610	3 160	3 608	-17.4	-12.4
Richland	7.2	19.9	12.2	14.9	12.9	8.2	8.5	8.0	8.1	48.7	17 998	18 148	19 207	-0.8	-5.5
Rolette	11.1	27.1	9.2	15.0	11.7	8.5	6.9	5.8	4.6	51.0	13 674	12 772	12 177	7.1	4.9
Sargent	6.5	20.4	6.2	12.9	14.6	11.7	9.8	10.0	7.9	48.7	4 366	4 549	5 512	-4.0	-17.5
Sheridan	6.3	17.7	4.4	11.5	12.7	11.0	13.2	13.0	10.2	48.1	1 710	2 148	2 819	-20.4	-23.8
Sioux	12.2	30.9	9.5	14.7	12.3	8.1	6.0	4.5	1.7	48.3	4 044	3 761	3 620	7.5	3.9
Slope	6.9	23.0	6.8	13.7	14.9	9.2	13.0	8.8	3.6	47.3	767	907	1 157	-15.4	-21.6
Stark	7.8	21.8	9.5	17.1	13.9	8.7	8.0	7.2	6.0	50.8	22 636	22 832	23 697	-0.9	-3.7
Steele	6.6	19.5	4.5	12.9	12.3	11.5	12.3	11.9	8.4	49.8	2 258	2 420	3 106	-6.7	-22.1
Stutsman	6.7	19.3	8.7	15.4	14.4	9.5	9.9	8.5	7.7	51.2	21 908	22 241	24 154	-1.5	-7.9
Towner	7.9	19.0	5.7	13.6	12.3	8.5	10.4	10.9	11.7	49.9	2 876	3 627	4 052	-20.7	-10.5
Traill	6.3	19.3	10.1	13.3	12.4	9.3	9.0	9.7	10.6	51.0	8 477	8 752	9 624	-3.1	-9.1
Walsh	7.0	20.5	6.4	14.4	13.7	9.6	9.6	9.9	8.9	50.2	12 389	13 840	15 371	-10.5	-10.0

Table B. States and Counties

STATE County	Total population	Total in house-holds	House-holder	Spouse	Child Total	Own child under 18 years	Other relatives Total	Under 18 years	Nonrelatives Total	Unmar-ried partner	Total in group quarters	Correc-tional institu-tions	Nurs-ing homes	Other institu-tions	Col-lege dormi-tories	Mili-tary quar-ters	Other
	54	55	56	57	58	59	60	61	62	63	64	65	66	67	68	69	70
NORTH CAROLINA —Cont'd																	
Swain	12 968	96.8	39.6	20.7	27.4	20.6	5.3	2.6	3.8	1.9	3.2	0.3	1.4	0.0	0.0	0.0	1.5
Transylvania	29 334	96.4	42.0	24.6	23.7	18.4	3.2	1.3	2.9	1.4	3.6	0.1	0.9	0.0	1.3	0.0	1.3
Tyrrell	4 149	89.5	37.0	17.6	25.5	18.8	6.5	3.4	2.9	1.3	10.5	10.3	0.0	0.0	0.0	0.0	0.2
Union	123 677	98.7	35.1	22.9	31.5	25.5	5.3	2.1	3.9	1.4	1.3	0.2	0.5	0.0	0.4	0.0	0.1
Vance	42 954	98.1	37.7	17.7	30.4	22.6	7.7	3.7	4.6	2.0	1.9	0.2	1.0	0.0	0.0	0.0	0.8
Wake	627 846	96.9	38.6	20.2	27.7	23.3	4.1	1.4	6.3	1.8	3.1	0.5	0.4	0.1	1.7	0.0	0.3
Warren	19 972	95.7	38.6	19.0	27.6	19.7	7.1	3.4	3.4	1.7	4.3	3.0	0.8	0.0	0.0	0.0	0.4
Washington	13 723	98.7	39.1	19.6	30.4	22.2	6.8	3.4	2.9	1.4	1.3	0.2	0.9	0.1	0.0	0.0	0.2
Watauga	42 695	87.4	38.7	18.4	19.2	15.4	2.1	0.7	8.9	1.5	12.6	0.1	0.4	0.0	11.0	0.0	1.2
Wayne	113 329	95.9	37.6	19.4	29.4	23.0	5.4	2.5	4.2	1.7	4.1	1.5	0.7	0.5	0.2	0.5	0.7
Wilkes	65 632	98.6	40.6	24.0	27.0	20.5	4.0	1.6	3.0	1.6	1.4	0.5	0.7	0.0	0.0	0.0	0.2
Wilson	73 814	97.5	38.8	18.7	28.7	21.7	7.0	3.2	4.4	1.8	2.5	0.3	1.1	0.2	0.5	0.0	0.5
Yadkin	36 348	98.7	39.9	24.0	27.7	21.8	4.2	1.7	3.0	1.5	1.3	0.1	0.7	0.1	0.0	0.0	0.4
Yancey	17 774	99.2	42.0	25.7	25.7	19.7	3.3	1.2	2.5	1.2	0.8	0.1	0.6	0.0	0.0	0.0	0.2
NORTH DAKOTA	642 200	96.3	40.0	21.4	28.4	23.8	2.0	0.8	4.5	1.8	3.7	0.2	1.1	0.1	1.6	0.2	0.4
Adams	2 593	97.0	43.2	24.5	26.1	22.4	1.0	0.4	2.1	1.2	3.0	0.1	2.4	0.2	0.0	0.0	0.3
Barnes	11 775	95.2	41.5	22.3	26.0	21.4	1.8	0.5	3.5	1.5	4.8	0.2	1.5	0.1	2.8	0.0	0.3
Benson	6 964	99.3	33.4	16.2	36.3	29.2	8.1	5.4	5.3	2.6	0.7	0.0	0.6	0.0	0.0	0.0	0.1
Billings	888	100.0	41.2	25.8	28.5	24.0	2.0	0.3	2.5	1.4	0.0	0.0	0.0	0.0	0.0	0.0	0.0
Bottineau	7 149	95.4	41.4	24.3	26.3	21.4	1.5	0.6	1.9	1.2	4.6	0.0	1.9	0.0	2.7	0.0	0.0
Bowman	3 242	97.2	41.9	24.9	27.5	23.3	1.1	0.5	1.9	0.8	2.8	0.0	2.5	0.0	0.0	0.0	0.2
Burke	2 242	100.0	45.2	26.3	25.6	20.4	1.9	0.4	0.9	0.5	0.0	0.0	0.0	0.0	0.0	0.0	0.0
Burleigh	69 416	96.4	39.9	21.5	28.8	23.7	1.8	0.6	4.3	1.8	3.6	1.1	1.0	0.0	1.3	0.0	0.4
Cass	123 138	96.7	41.7	19.7	26.4	22.5	1.8	0.4	7.1	2.4	3.3	0.1	0.6	0.0	2.1	0.0	0.4
Cavalier	4 831	97.5	41.8	25.4	27.8	24.1	1.2	0.2	1.4	0.6	2.5	0.0	2.0	0.0	0.0	0.0	0.4
Dickey	5 757	93.5	39.7	23.0	27.0	22.8	1.8	0.6	2.0	0.9	6.5	0.0	3.2	0.0	3.3	0.0	0.0
Divide	2 283	96.1	44.0	25.0	24.4	19.6	1.4	0.5	1.2	0.7	3.9	0.0	3.7	0.3	0.0	0.0	0.0
Dunn	3 600	98.5	38.3	23.1	32.1	26.0	2.6	1.0	2.5	1.5	1.5	0.0	1.5	0.0	0.0	0.0	0.0
Eddy	2 757	97.2	42.2	23.8	27.7	23.0	1.3	0.4	2.1	0.9	2.8	0.0	2.8	0.0	0.0	0.0	0.0
Emmons	4 331	98.0	41.2	25.2	28.1	23.9	1.9	0.6	1.7	0.9	2.0	0.0	1.6	0.0	0.0	0.0	0.3
Foster	3 759	97.8	41.0	23.5	29.7	25.4	1.5	0.5	2.1	1.1	2.2	0.0	2.0	0.1	0.0	0.0	0.2
Golden Valley	1 924	94.0	39.6	23.1	28.0	23.9	1.8	0.7	1.6	0.9	6.0	0.0	2.0	3.9	0.0	0.0	0.1
Grand Forks	66 109	93.3	38.5	19.0	27.5	23.0	1.6	0.5	6.8	2.0	6.7	0.1	0.9	0.0	4.7	0.7	0.2
Grant	2 841	96.9	42.1	25.6	26.2	21.3	1.8	0.8	1.3	0.6	3.1	0.0	1.9	0.0	0.0	0.0	1.2
Griggs	2 754	97.9	42.8	25.4	26.5	21.9	1.5	0.2	1.8	0.7	2.1	0.0	2.1	0.0	0.0	0.0	0.0
Hettinger	2 715	97.6	42.4	26.0	26.9	22.6	1.3	0.6	1.0	0.5	2.4	0.0	2.2	0.0	0.0	0.0	0.2
Kidder	2 753	98.4	42.1	25.5	27.4	22.4	1.7	0.6	1.7	1.2	1.6	0.0	1.6	0.0	0.0	0.0	0.0
La Moure	4 701	98.3	41.3	25.0	28.8	23.3	1.5	0.5	1.7	0.8	1.7	0.0	1.6	0.0	0.0	0.0	0.1
Logan	2 308	96.9	41.7	26.3	26.0	22.3	1.4	0.3	1.5	1.0	3.1	0.0	1.6	0.0	0.0	0.0	1.6
McHenry	5 987	98.9	42.2	24.5	28.0	22.9	2.1	0.8	2.2	1.2	1.1	0.0	0.9	0.0	0.0	0.0	0.3
McIntosh	3 390	94.9	43.3	26.1	22.9	19.1	1.3	0.1	1.4	0.8	5.1	0.0	4.8	0.0	0.0	0.0	0.4
McKenzie	5 737	98.9	37.5	21.7	32.6	27.7	4.4	2.4	2.8	1.8	1.1	0.0	1.0	0.0	0.0	0.0	0.0
McLean	9 311	98.2	41.0	25.5	27.2	22.4	2.0	0.9	2.6	1.4	1.8	0.0	1.5	0.1	0.0	0.0	0.2
Mercer	8 644	98.6	38.7	25.2	31.6	28.0	1.0	0.6	2.0	1.0	1.4	0.1	0.9	0.0	0.0	0.0	0.4
Morton	25 303	98.1	39.1	22.8	31.1	25.6	1.8	0.6	3.3	1.7	1.9	0.1	1.1	0.4	0.0	0.0	0.2
Mountrail	6 631	97.5	38.6	20.0	30.6	24.9	4.7	2.8	3.6	2.2	2.5	0.2	2.1	0.0	0.0	0.0	0.2
Nelson	3 715	95.7	43.8	23.6	24.9	20.9	1.4	0.3	2.0	0.9	4.3	0.0	3.7	0.2	0.0	0.0	0.4
Oliver	2 065	100.0	38.3	26.5	32.2	26.8	1.2	0.4	1.8	1.2	0.0	0.0	0.0	0.0	0.0	0.0	0.0
Pembina	8 585	97.8	41.2	24.0	29.0	24.0	1.4	0.5	2.2	1.3	2.2	0.1	1.7	0.0	0.0	0.4	0.0
Pierce	4 675	97.1	42.0	23.7	28.0	23.2	1.4	0.5	2.0	1.4	2.9	0.1	1.9	0.0	0.0	0.0	0.9
Ramsey	12 066	96.3	41.1	21.3	28.2	23.7	1.7	0.7	4.1	2.1	3.7	0.3	2.1	0.0	0.9	0.0	0.3
Ransom	5 890	95.5	39.9	23.2	28.7	24.4	1.3	0.3	2.4	1.2	4.5	0.0	4.5	0.0	0.0	0.0	0.0
Renville	2 610	97.8	41.6	25.1	27.7	22.8	1.6	0.3	1.8	0.7	2.2	0.0	2.2	0.0	0.0	0.0	0.0
Richland	17 998	92.8	38.3	20.7	28.1	23.7	1.7	0.5	4.0	1.6	7.2	0.1	1.6	0.1	5.0	0.0	0.5
Rolette	13 674	98.8	33.3	14.6	38.7	31.1	6.9	4.5	5.2	3.4	1.2	0.2	0.6	0.0	0.0	0.0	0.3
Sargent	4 366	99.3	40.9	24.9	29.8	25.7	1.8	0.6	1.9	1.1	0.7	0.0	0.7	0.0	0.0	0.0	0.0
Sheridan	1 710	98.8	42.7	26.8	25.1	20.4	2.2	0.6	1.9	0.9	1.2	0.0	1.2	0.0	0.0	0.0	0.0
Sioux	4 044	98.4	27.1	10.6	39.0	28.8	14.7	9.8	7.0	3.5	1.6	1.0	0.0	0.0	0.0	0.0	0.5
Slope	767	100.0	40.8	26.3	29.6	24.6	1.0	0.4	2.2	1.4	0.0	0.0	0.0	0.0	0.0	0.0	0.0
Stark	22 636	96.2	39.5	21.6	29.6	24.4	1.7	0.6	3.8	1.6	3.8	0.0	1.1	0.3	1.8	0.0	0.6
Steele	2 258	100.0	40.9	25.5	30.1	26.3	1.0	0.6	2.6	1.2	0.0	0.0	0.0	0.0	0.0	0.0	0.0
Stutsman	21 908	93.0	40.9	21.4	25.8	21.7	1.4	0.5	3.5	1.7	7.0	1.2	1.6	0.8	2.9	0.0	0.5
Towner	2 876	97.6	42.4	24.1	27.3	23.5	1.5	0.6	2.4	1.2	2.4	0.0	0.0	2.4	0.0	0.0	0.0
Traill	8 477	94.9	39.4	22.9	28.2	24.0	1.5	0.5	3.0	1.1	5.1	0.0	2.3	0.0	2.7	0.0	0.0
Walsh	12 389	96.9	40.6	22.4	29.2	23.8	2.0	0.6	2.8	1.4	3.1	0.0	1.6	0.0	0.0	0.0	1.5

Table B. States and Counties

	Households by type, 2000												Households, 1990		
	Family households						Nonfamily households								
			Married couple		Female householder[1]			Householder living alone							
STATE County	Total households	Total	With own children under 18 years	Total	With own children under 18 years	Total	With own children under 18 years	Total	Total	65 years and over	Average household size	Average family size	Total households	Female householder[1]	Householder living alone
	71	72	73	74	75	76	77	78	79	80	81	82	83	84	85
NORTH CAROLINA —Cont'd															
Swain	5 137	70.7	30.0	52.3	19.5	13.9	7.6	29.3	25.8	11.1	2.44	2.91	4 173	13.2	23.6
Transylvania	12 320	70.3	25.1	58.6	18.4	8.7	4.9	29.7	26.1	12.4	2.30	2.74	9 924	8.0	22.4
Tyrrell	1 537	68.7	28.6	47.4	17.8	16.6	8.8	31.3	28.2	14.4	2.42	2.95	1 471	14.5	24.4
Union	43 390	79.0	39.5	65.3	32.1	9.8	5.4	21.0	17.0	6.1	2.81	3.15	29 307	10.5	17.1
Vance	16 199	71.9	33.5	47.0	19.6	20.4	11.7	28.1	24.2	9.9	2.60	3.06	14 166	18.2	22.9
Wake	242 040	65.6	34.0	52.5	26.4	9.8	6.1	34.4	25.7	5.1	2.51	3.06	165 743	10.0	25.7
Warren	7 708	70.7	28.2	49.2	17.6	17.3	8.8	29.3	26.2	12.2	2.48	2.97	6 305	17.9	22.6
Washington	5 367	72.8	31.7	50.1	19.0	18.8	11.2	27.2	24.7	11.7	2.52	2.99	5 052	16.5	22.8
Watauga	16 540	56.9	23.2	47.4	18.1	6.8	3.8	43.1	28.6	8.0	2.26	2.80	13 693	7.1	25.1
Wayne	42 612	71.0	34.7	51.6	23.2	15.4	9.3	29.0	24.5	9.0	2.43	2.87	23 021	9.9	21.1
Wilkes	26 650	72.5	30.2	59.1	23.2	9.4	5.0	27.5	24.5	10.0	2.43	3.03	25 093	16.7	25.0
Wilson	28 613	69.1	31.9	48.1	20.4	16.5	9.6	30.9	26.4	10.2	2.51	2.92	12 068	9.3	22.1
Yadkin	14 505	73.0	32.1	60.0	25.1	9.0	4.9	27.0	24.0	10.5	2.47	2.92	6 124	8.3	22.1
Yancey	7 472	71.9	27.3	61.2	22.3	7.8	3.7	28.1	25.4	12.5	2.36	2.81			
NORTH DAKOTA	257 152	64.6	31.3	53.4	24.1	7.8	5.3	35.4	29.3	11.5	2.41	3.00	240 878	7.3	26.5
Adams	1 121	64.7	26.6	56.6	21.0	5.5	4.0	35.3	32.6	17.9	2.24	2.85	1 266	4.0	29.9
Barnes	4 884	63.8	27.4	53.9	21.5	6.8	4.3	36.2	31.5	15.9	2.29	2.89	4 975	6.2	29.6
Benson	2 328	73.1	38.0	48.5	21.9	16.6	11.0	26.9	24.5	12.5	2.97	3.48	2 415	13.9	22.7
Billings	366	69.9	29.2	62.6	27.3	4.4	1.4	30.1	26.8	7.7	2.43	2.95	387	1.8	19.1
Bottineau	2 962	66.0	27.3	58.7	23.2	4.3	2.6	34.0	31.5	16.4	2.30	2.90	3 105	5.4	28.3
Bowman	1 358	65.6	29.5	59.5	25.8	4.1	2.5	34.4	31.5	17.2	2.32	2.95	1 420	5.3	29.0
Burke	1 013	67.2	23.0	58.2	18.8	5.3	2.9	32.8	31.6	17.6	2.21	2.77	1 252	4.3	29.5
Burleigh	27 670	65.8	32.6	54.0	25.1	8.7	5.9	34.2	28.1	9.5	2.42	2.99	22 684	8.8	25.4
Cass	51 315	58.1	29.9	47.3	22.9	7.6	5.3	41.9	31.2	7.6	2.32	2.98	40 281	7.4	28.2
Cavalier	2 017	67.5	27.5	60.8	24.1	3.8	2.0	32.5	30.8	17.0	2.34	2.93	2 375	3.3	27.9
Dickey	2 283	65.7	27.9	58.0	23.1	4.9	3.2	34.3	32.0	17.6	2.36	2.99	2 299	4.8	28.3
Divide	1 005	64.6	22.5	56.8	18.7	4.2	2.3	35.4	33.4	19.9	2.18	2.79	1 193	5.0	29.2
Dunn	1 378	71.6	32.0	60.3	26.0	7.2	3.8	28.4	25.3	12.3	2.57	3.11	1 433	5.9	23.2
Eddy	1 164	63.9	27.7	56.4	22.9	5.0	3.4	36.1	34.2	20.4	2.30	2.96	1 194	4.8	31.7
Emmons	1 786	69.5	27.2	61.0	22.8	4.4	2.4	30.5	28.4	16.4	2.38	2.92	1 849	3.9	24.3
Foster	1 540	67.0	31.0	58.2	25.5	6.4	3.8	33.0	30.6	16.0	2.39	2.99	1 541	4.7	26.9
Golden Valley	761	66.6	29.2	58.3	23.4	4.9	3.7	33.4	31.5	15.8	2.38	3.01	811	4.2	30.9
Grand Forks	25 435	61.4	32.4	49.5	24.3	8.8	6.3	38.6	28.3	8.2	2.43	3.03	25 340	8.0	25.6
Grant	1 195	67.0	25.1	60.8	22.2	3.8	2.2	33.0	31.8	17.9	2.30	2.90	1 374	3.6	26.4
Griggs	1 178	66.3	26.7	59.3	23.9	4.7	2.1	33.7	31.6	18.6	2.29	2.88	1 294	4.8	25.4
Hettinger	1 152	67.6	26.4	61.2	22.7	3.8	2.4	32.4	31.2	18.2	2.30	2.89	1 341	3.3	25.8
Kidder	1 158	68.0	27.2	60.7	23.2	4.1	2.2	32.0	29.9	17.7	2.34	2.91	1 247	3.4	22.0
La Moure	1 942	67.4	27.5	60.5	23.5	4.0	2.4	32.6	30.8	16.6	2.38	2.99	2 075	3.3	27.5
Logan	963	68.5	25.8	63.1	23.4	3.1	1.8	31.5	29.2	16.0	2.32	2.88	1 096	2.4	24.5
McHenry	2 526	67.3	28.3	58.2	23.1	5.6	3.4	32.7	29.8	15.4	2.35	2.92	2 551	5.3	26.4
McIntosh	1 467	66.5	22.3	60.3	19.1	3.5	2.2	33.5	32.0	19.9	2.19	2.75	1 687	3.1	28.4
McKenzie	2 151	72.0	34.5	57.9	25.4	9.3	5.8	28.0	25.8	13.1	2.64	3.17	2 301	7.3	25.2
McLean	3 815	71.1	29.3	62.3	24.0	5.6	3.7	28.9	26.6	14.3	2.40	2.88	3 933	5.1	25.4
Mercer	3 346	73.1	37.1	65.2	31.5	5.1	3.6	26.9	24.8	11.1	2.55	3.05	3 560	4.6	22.2
Morton	9 889	70.1	34.9	58.2	26.6	8.5	6.4	29.9	25.7	10.9	2.51	3.03	8 677	7.5	23.6
Mountrail	2 560	68.5	31.8	51.8	21.6	11.8	7.1	31.5	28.5	14.6	2.53	3.09	2 587	9.9	26.6
Nelson	1 628	61.7	24.2	53.8	20.2	5.2	2.8	38.3	36.3	21.9	2.18	2.84	1 831	5.2	31.9
Oliver	791	76.4	35.5	69.2	30.7	3.9	2.5	23.6	21.0	10.7	2.61	3.05	809	3.0	18.7
Pembina	3 535	66.9	29.8	58.2	24.5	5.3	3.3	33.1	30.5	15.7	2.38	2.98	3 555	5.7	27.6
Pierce	1 964	65.0	28.2	56.4	22.4	6.3	4.7	35.0	32.0	17.1	2.31	2.94	1 974	5.3	29.7
Ramsey	4 957	64.3	29.9	51.8	21.7	8.5	5.9	35.7	31.1	14.6	2.34	2.94	4 977	9.0	29.4
Ransom	2 350	66.4	31.0	58.1	26.1	5.1	3.3	33.6	30.7	15.5	2.39	3.01	2 284	4.6	24.8
Renville	1 085	69.0	28.7	60.4	23.7	5.6	3.1	31.0	28.5	14.7	2.35	2.90	1 209	6.1	24.8
Richland	6 885	64.3	32.4	54.2	26.2	6.6	4.3	35.7	29.4	11.6	2.43	3.06	6 518	5.9	27.0
Rolette	4 556	73.9	43.8	44.0	22.8	22.7	16.1	26.1	22.6	9.5	2.97	3.45	4 150	21.3	22.3
Sargent	1 786	69.6	30.3	61.0	25.6	3.9	2.4	30.4	27.7	14.1	2.43	2.99	1 763	4.0	26.5
Sheridan	731	70.5	25.0	62.8	21.3	4.4	2.7	29.5	27.5	16.7	2.31	2.80	858	2.8	23.5
Sioux	1 095	79.6	48.9	39.1	23.0	29.1	18.9	20.4	16.6	4.4	3.63	3.98	1 022	23.5	16.8
Slope	313	71.2	30.0	64.5	26.5	3.8	1.6	28.8	27.2	10.5	2.96		333	4.2	24.0
Stark	8 932	65.8	32.1	54.9	25.3	7.9	5.2	34.2	29.1	11.9	2.44	3.04	8 479	7.9	26.1
Steele	923	68.8	29.7	62.3	25.4	4.4	3.1	31.2	28.3	13.1	2.45	3.01	991	2.1	27.9
Stutsman	8 954	63.1	28.8	52.5	22.0	7.5	5.0	36.9	32.7	14.6	2.28	2.89	8 661	7.1	29.3
Towner	1 218	64.5	27.3	56.9	22.6	4.6	3.0	35.5	33.6	18.7	2.31	2.93	1 433	5.7	30.6
Traill	3 341	66.8	30.9	58.0	25.8	5.4	3.5	33.2	29.3	15.1	2.41	3.00	3 327	5.2	27.1
Walsh	5 029	66.0	30.6	55.1	23.8	7.5	4.8	34.0	31.3	15.2	2.39	3.00	5 229	6.4	27.4

[1] No spouse present.

Table B. States and Counties

STATE County	Housing occupancy, 2000							Housing tenure, 2000				
				Vacant housing units				Occupied housing units				
	Percent change of households, 1990–2000	Total housing units	Occupied housing units (percent)	Total	For seasonal, recreational, or occasional use	Homeowner vacancy rate (percent)	Rental vacancy rate (percent)	Total	Percent owner-occupied housing units	Percent renter-occupied housing units	Average household size of owner-occupied units	Average household size of renter-occupied units
	86	87	88	89	90	91	92	93	94	95	96	97
NORTH CAROLINA —Cont'd												
Swain	23.1	7 105	72.3	27.7	18.0	2.3	11.7	5 137	76.8	23.2	2.48	2.32
Transylvania	24.1	15 553	79.2	20.8	14.9	1.2	5.7	12 320	79.4	20.6	2.33	2.19
Tyrrell	4.5	2 032	75.6	24.4	12.1	3.7	7.4	1 537	74.9	25.1	2.42	2.39
Union	48.1	45 695	95.0	5.0	0.4	2.0	4.6	43 390	80.5	19.5	2.80	2.87
Vance	14.4	18 196	89.0	11.0	3.3	1.7	6.6	16 199	66.3	33.7	2.61	2.57
Wake	46.0	258 953	93.5	6.5	0.4	2.5	8.8	242 040	65.9	34.1	2.66	2.24
Warren	22.3	10 548	73.1	26.9	18.1	1.2	6.4	7 708	77.4	22.6	2.49	2.44
Washington	6.2	6 174	86.9	13.1	3.4	2.2	7.5	5 367	73.6	26.4	2.51	2.55
Watauga	20.8	23 155	71.4	28.6	22.0	1.6	7.7	16 540	62.9	37.1	2.38	2.04
Wayne	15.5	47 313	90.1	9.9	0.4	1.7	8.0	42 612	65.4	34.6	2.58	2.50
Wilkes	15.8	29 261	91.1	8.9	1.9	1.1	9.1	26 650	77.9	22.1	2.46	2.32
Wilson	14.0	30 729	93.1	6.9	0.4	1.8	5.0	28 613	61.2	38.8	2.54	2.47
Yadkin	20.2	15 821	91.7	8.3	0.9	1.3	8.2	14 505	80.3	19.7	2.47	2.47
Yancey	22.0	9 729	76.8	23.2	12.6	1.6	8.0	7 472	80.2	19.8	2.37	2.33
NORTH DAKOTA	6.8	289 677	88.8	11.2	2.9	2.7	8.2	257 152	66.6	33.4	2.60	2.02
Adams	-11.5	1 416	79.2	20.8	3.8	5.8	16.9	1 121	71.1	28.9	2.36	1.95
Barnes	-1.8	5 599	87.2	12.8	4.6	2.7	10.5	4 884	71.2	28.8	2.48	1.83
Benson	-3.6	2 932	79.4	20.6	4.8	6.3	9.4	2 328	68.3	31.7	2.78	3.37
Billings	-5.4	529	69.2	30.8	19.3	1.4	14.1	366	76.8	23.2	2.48	2.26
Bottineau	-4.6	4 409	67.2	32.8	19.3	3.9	13.1	2 962	80.0	20.0	2.40	1.91
Bowman	-4.4	1 596	85.1	14.9	2.6	4.0	15.4	1 358	79.4	20.6	2.40	2.01
Burke	-19.1	1 412	71.7	28.3	7.7	7.2	19.4	1 013	84.4	15.6	2.24	2.08
Burleigh	22.0	29 003	95.4	4.6	0.5	1.1	5.7	27 670	68.0	32.0	2.66	1.89
Cass	27.4	53 790	95.4	4.6	0.5	1.7	5.0	51 315	54.3	45.7	2.70	1.87
Cavalier	-15.1	2 725	74.0	26.0	4.1	3.8	17.8	2 017	81.5	18.5	2.41	2.01
Dickey	-0.7	2 656	86.0	14.0	2.3	3.8	16.4	2 283	71.5	28.5	2.47	2.07
Divide	-15.8	1 469	68.4	31.6	9.5	8.5	20.7	1 005	82.1	17.9	2.24	1.93
Dunn	-3.8	1 965	70.1	29.9	13.4	2.4	11.3	1 378	80.0	20.0	2.59	2.53
Eddy	-2.5	1 418	82.1	17.9	2.5	4.8	18.5	1 164	75.4	24.6	2.44	1.88
Emmons	-3.4	2 168	82.4	17.6	6.0	4.4	10.3	1 786	83.4	16.6	2.43	2.13
Foster	-0.1	1 793	85.9	14.1	5.0	3.2	9.4	1 540	74.4	25.6	2.56	1.89
Golden Valley	-6.2	973	78.2	21.8	3.3	5.7	13.5	761	78.1	21.9	2.43	2.20
Grand Forks	0.4	27 373	92.9	7.1	0.4	2.6	6.6	25 435	53.9	46.1	2.70	2.11
Grant	-13.0	1 722	69.4	30.6	16.3	5.7	13.6	1 195	79.3	20.7	2.38	2.02
Griggs	-9.0	1 521	77.4	22.6	8.2	5.5	15.0	1 178	78.3	21.7	2.35	2.06
Hettinger	-14.1	1 419	81.2	18.8	5.8	3.0	15.2	1 152	83.6	16.4	2.37	1.94
Kidder	-7.1	1 610	71.9	28.1	14.7	5.8	3.6	1 158	81.7	18.3	2.38	2.15
La Moure	-6.4	2 271	85.5	14.5	1.9	4.9	13.7	1 942	80.6	19.4	2.48	1.98
Logan	-12.1	1 193	80.7	19.3	6.0	3.3	12.2	963	85.8	14.2	2.38	1.97
McHenry	-1.0	2 983	84.7	15.3	2.3	3.5	9.3	2 526	81.4	18.6	2.43	1.98
McIntosh	-13.0	1 853	79.2	20.8	6.2	5.4	14.8	1 467	83.1	16.9	2.28	1.77
McKenzie	-6.5	2 719	79.1	20.9	6.0	3.7	15.0	2 151	73.9	26.1	2.57	2.82
McLean	-3.0	5 264	72.5	27.5	17.5	3.2	12.4	3 815	82.2	17.8	2.44	2.20
Mercer	-6.0	4 402	76.0	24.0	9.6	3.5	29.8	3 346	84.5	15.5	2.65	2.00
Morton	14.0	10 587	93.4	6.6	0.8	1.6	7.3	9 889	75.5	24.5	2.66	2.05
Mountrail	-1.0	3 438	74.5	25.5	15.2	2.8	7.9	2 560	72.6	27.4	2.51	2.58
Nelson	-11.1	2 014	80.8	19.2	3.4	4.5	13.7	1 628	80.2	19.8	2.28	1.79
Oliver	-2.2	903	87.6	12.4	1.2	2.4	8.1	791	85.7	14.3	2.69	2.13
Pembina	-0.6	4 115	85.9	14.1	1.5	4.2	15.3	3 535	78.4	21.6	2.51	1.89
Pierce	-0.5	2 269	86.6	13.4	2.2	3.2	9.7	1 964	72.9	27.1	2.50	1.81
Ramsey	-0.4	5 729	86.5	13.5	2.4	4.1	13.8	4 957	65.0	35.0	2.60	1.87
Ransom	2.9	2 604	90.2	9.8	1.7	3.0	9.5	2 350	75.3	24.7	2.57	1.86
Renville	-10.3	1 413	76.8	23.2	10.0	6.6	13.0	1 085	77.8	22.2	2.43	2.09
Richland	5.6	7 575	90.9	9.1	1.1	2.9	9.9	6 885	69.6	30.4	2.64	1.93
Rolette	9.8	5 027	90.6	9.4	2.5	1.1	7.1	4 556	67.4	32.6	3.04	2.80
Sargent	1.3	2 016	88.6	11.4	1.0	3.7	13.0	1 786	79.8	20.2	2.57	1.89
Sheridan	-14.8	924	79.1	20.9	3.8	6.9	11.0	731	84.5	15.5	2.34	2.17
Sioux	7.1	1 216	90.0	10.0	2.1	1.4	3.3	1 095	46.3	53.7	3.35	3.88
Slope	-6.0	451	69.4	30.6	9.8	3.9	6.8	313	86.9	13.1	2.52	1.98
Stark	5.3	9 722	91.9	8.1	0.7	1.5	10.9	8 932	70.3	29.7	2.67	1.89
Steele	-6.9	1 231	75.0	25.0	14.2	3.9	7.9	923	77.2	22.8	2.55	2.09
Stutsman	3.4	9 817	91.2	8.8	1.7	2.0	8.5	8 954	67.2	32.8	2.50	1.82
Towner	-15.0	1 558	78.2	21.8	4.4	5.0	21.9	1 218	73.9	26.1	2.43	1.94
Traill	0.4	3 708	90.1	9.9	0.8	3.8	11.9	3 341	72.6	27.4	2.59	1.92
Walsh	-3.8	5 757	87.4	12.6	1.2	3.9	12.5	5 029	76.8	23.2	2.49	2.04

Table B. States and Counties

STATE/ County code	MSA/ PMSA/ NECMA code[1]	County type[2]	STATE County	Population, 2000				Population, 1990				Population and population characteristics, 2000					
												Race (percent)					
												One race					
				Land area, 2000[3] (sq km)	Total persons	Rank	Per square kilometer	Land area, 1990[3] (sq km)	Total persons	Rank	Per square kilometer	White	Black or African American	American Indian or Alaska Native	Asian	Native Hawaiian and other Pacific Islander	Some other race
				1	2	3	4	5	6	7	8	9	10	11	12	13	14
			NORTH DAKOTA— Cont'd														
38 101	...	5	Ward	5 213	58 795	815	11.3	5 214	57 921	748	11.1	92.4	2.2	2.1	0.8	0.1	0.7
38 103	...	9	Wells	3 293	5 102	2 843	1.5	3 293	5 864	2 774	1.8	99.1	0.1	0.2	0.2	0.0	0.0
38 105	...	7	Williams	5 362	19 761	1 804	3.7	5 363	21 129	1 623	3.9	92.9	0.1	4.4	0.2	0.0	0.1
39 000	...		OHIO	106 056	11 353 140	X	107.0	106 067	10 847 115	X	102.3	85.0	11.5	0.2	1.2	0.0	0.8
39 001	...	6	Adams	1 512	27 330	1 472	18.1	1 512	25 371	1 452	16.8	97.8	0.2	0.7	0.1	0.0	0.1
39 003	4320	3	Allen	1 047	108 473	497	103.6	1 048	109 755	420	104.7	84.9	12.2	0.2	0.6	0.0	0.6
39 005	...	4	Ashland	1 099	52 523	889	47.8	1 099	47 507	882	43.2	97.5	0.8	0.1	0.5	0.0	0.2
39 007	1680	1	Ashtabula	1 819	102 728	517	56.5	1 820	99 880	459	54.9	94.1	3.2	0.2	0.3	0.0	0.9
39 009	...	4	Athens	1 312	62 223	782	47.4	1 313	59 549	727	45.4	93.5	2.4	0.3	1.9	0.0	0.4
39 011	4320	3	Auglaize	1 039	46 611	968	44.9	1 039	44 585	916	42.9	98.1	0.2	0.2	0.4	0.0	0.2
39 013	9000	3	Belmont	1 392	70 226	706	50.4	1 392	71 074	623	51.1	95.0	3.6	0.1	0.3	0.0	0.2
39 015	1640	1	Brown	1 274	42 285	1 050	33.2	1 274	34 966	1 134	27.4	98.1	0.9	0.2	0.1	0.0	0.1
39 017	3200	0	Butler	1 210	332 807	175	275.0	1 210	291 479	167	240.9	91.2	5.3	0.2	1.5	0.0	0.6
39 019	1320	2	Carroll	1 022	28 836	1 425	28.2	1 022	26 521	1 407	26.0	98.2	0.5	0.3	0.1	0.0	0.1
39 021	...	6	Champaign	1 110	38 890	1 144	35.0	1 110	36 019	1 101	32.4	95.7	2.3	0.3	0.3	0.0	0.5
39 023	2000	2	Clark	1 036	144 742	378	139.7	1 036	147 538	319	142.4	88.1	8.9	0.3	0.5	0.0	0.5
39 025	1640	0	Clermont	1 171	177 977	309	152.0	1 171	150 094	314	128.2	97.1	0.9	0.2	0.6	0.0	0.3
39 027	...	6	Clinton	1 064	40 543	1 102	38.1	1 064	35 444	1 114	33.3	96.0	2.2	0.3	0.4	0.0	0.2
39 029	9320	2	Columbiana	1 379	112 075	480	81.3	1 379	108 276	425	78.5	96.4	2.2	0.2	0.2	0.0	0.1
39 031	...	6	Coshocton	1 461	36 655	1 197	25.1	1 461	35 427	1 116	24.2	97.4	1.1	0.2	0.3	0.0	0.2
39 033	4800	3	Crawford	1 041	46 966	964	45.1	1 042	47 870	877	45.9	98.0	0.6	0.2	0.3	0.0	0.2
39 035	1680	0	Cuyahoga	1 187	1 393 978	23	1 174.4	1 187	1 412 140	17	1 189.7	67.4	27.4	0.2	1.8	0.0	1.5
39 037	...	6	Darke	1 553	53 309	877	34.3	1 554	53 617	800	34.5	98.1	0.4	0.2	0.2	0.0	0.4
39 039	...	4	Defiance	1 065	39 500	1 126	37.1	1 065	39 350	1 016	36.9	92.6	1.8	0.3	0.4	0.0	3.6
39 041	1840	1	Delaware	1 146	109 989	494	96.0	1 146	66 929	659	58.4	94.2	2.5	0.1	1.5	0.0	0.4
39 043	...	4	Erie	660	79 551	645	120.5	659	76 781	588	116.5	88.6	8.6	0.2	0.4	0.0	0.5
39 045	1840	1	Fairfield	1 308	122 759	441	93.9	1 310	103 468	445	79.0	95.1	2.7	0.2	0.7	0.0	0.2
39 047	...	6	Fayette	1 053	28 433	1 433	27.0	1 053	27 466	1 376	26.1	95.6	2.1	0.2	0.5	0.0	0.6
39 049	1840	0	Franklin	1 398	1 068 978	33	764.6	1 399	961 437	33	687.2	75.5	17.9	0.3	3.1	0.0	1.0
39 051	8400	2	Fulton	1 054	42 084	1 056	39.9	1 054	38 498	1 040	36.5	95.7	0.2	0.3	0.4	0.0	2.3
39 053	...	6	Gallia	1 214	31 069	1 375	25.6	1 214	30 954	1 247	25.5	95.3	2.7	0.4	0.4	0.0	0.1
39 055	1680	1	Geauga	1 045	90 895	568	87.0	1 047	81 087	562	77.4	97.4	1.2	0.1	0.4	0.0	0.1
39 057	2000	2	Greene	1 075	147 886	367	137.6	1 075	136 731	344	127.2	89.2	6.4	0.3	2.0	0.0	0.4
39 059	...	7	Guernsey	1 352	40 792	1 088	30.2	1 352	39 024	1 021	28.9	96.3	1.5	0.3	0.3	0.0	0.2
39 061	1640	0	Hamilton	1 055	845 303	52	801.2	1 055	866 228	36	821.1	72.9	23.4	0.2	1.6	0.0	0.5
39 063	...	4	Hancock	1 376	71 295	696	51.8	1 376	65 536	670	47.6	95.1	1.1	0.2	1.2	0.0	1.2
39 065	...	6	Hardin	1 218	31 945	1 347	26.2	1 218	31 111	1 240	25.5	97.5	0.7	0.3	0.4	0.0	0.2
39 067	...	6	Harrison	1 045	15 856	2 029	15.2	1 045	16 085	1 917	15.4	96.5	2.2	0.1	0.1	0.0	0.1
39 069	...	6	Henry	1 079	29 210	1 422	27.1	1 079	29 108	1 326	27.0	95.3	0.6	0.3	0.4	0.0	2.6
39 071	...	6	Highland	1 433	40 875	1 086	28.5	1 433	35 728	1 105	24.9	96.9	1.5	0.2	0.3	0.0	0.2
39 073	...	6	Hocking	1 095	28 241	1 441	25.8	1 095	25 533	1 445	23.3	97.5	0.9	0.3	0.1	0.0	0.1
39 075	...	7	Holmes	1 096	38 943	1 142	35.5	1 096	32 849	1 194	30.0	99.0	0.3	0.1	0.1	0.0	0.1
39 077	...	4	Huron	1 276	59 487	807	46.6	1 277	56 238	771	44.0	96.0	1.0	0.2	0.3	0.0	1.6
39 079	...	7	Jackson	1 089	32 641	1 327	30.0	1 089	30 230	1 286	27.8	97.9	0.6	0.3	0.2	0.0	0.2
39 081	8080	3	Jefferson	1 061	73 894	677	69.6	1 061	80 298	571	75.7	92.5	5.7	0.2	0.3	0.0	0.2
39 083	...	6	Knox	1 365	54 500	864	39.9	1 365	47 473	885	34.8	97.7	0.7	0.2	0.3	0.0	0.2
39 085	1680	0	Lake	591	227 511	250	385.0	591	215 500	231	364.6	95.4	2.0	0.1	0.9	0.0	0.5
39 087	3400	2	Lawrence	1 178	62 319	779	52.9	1 180	61 834	706	52.4	96.6	2.1	0.2	0.2	0.0	0.1
39 089	1840	0	Licking	1 778	145 491	376	81.8	1 778	128 300	362	72.2	95.6	2.1	0.3	0.6	0.0	0.3
39 091	...	6	Logan	1 187	46 005	983	38.8	1 187	42 310	951	35.6	96.1	1.7	0.2	0.4	0.0	0.3
39 093	1680	0	Lorain	1 276	284 664	197	223.1	1 276	271 126	183	212.5	85.5	8.5	0.3	0.6	0.0	2.9
39 095	8400	2	Lucas	882	455 054	129	515.9	882	462 361	108	524.2	77.5	17.0	0.3	1.2	0.0	1.9
39 097	1840	1	Madison	1 205	40 213	1 110	33.4	1 205	37 078	1 070	30.8	91.8	6.2	0.2	0.4	0.0	0.3
39 099	9320	2	Mahoning	1 075	257 555	218	239.6	1 076	264 806	187	246.1	81.0	15.9	0.2	0.5	0.0	1.0
39 101	...	4	Marion	1 046	66 217	737	63.3	1 046	64 274	681	61.4	92.1	5.7	0.2	0.5	0.0	0.5
39 103	1680	1	Medina	1 092	151 095	355	138.4	1 092	122 354	376	112.0	97.3	0.9	0.2	0.6	0.0	0.2
39 105	...	6	Meigs	1 112	23 072	1 640	20.7	1 112	22 987	1 535	20.7	97.7	0.7	0.3	0.1	0.0	0.2
39 107	...	7	Mercer	1 200	40 924	1 083	34.1	1 200	39 443	1 013	32.9	98.4	0.1	0.3	0.3	0.0	0.3
39 109	2000	2	Miami	1 054	98 868	527	93.8	1 054	93 184	497	88.4	95.8	2.0	0.2	0.8	0.0	0.3
39 111	...	6	Monroe	1 180	15 180	2 078	12.9	1 180	15 497	1 954	13.1	98.7	0.3	0.2	0.1	0.0	0.1
39 113	2000	2	Montgomery	1 196	559 062	99	467.4	1 196	573 809	83	479.8	76.6	19.9	0.2	1.3	0.0	0.5
39 115	...	8	Morgan	1 082	14 897	2 099	13.8	1 082	14 194	2 038	13.1	93.7	3.4	0.3	0.1	0.0	0.3
39 117	...	6	Morrow	1 052	31 628	1 355	30.1	1 050	27 749	1 362	26.4	98.4	0.3	0.3	0.1	0.0	0.2
39 119	...	4	Muskingum	1 721	84 585	616	49.1	1 721	82 068	553	47.7	93.9	4.0	0.2	0.3	0.0	0.2
39 121	...	8	Noble	1 033	14 058	2 159	13.6	1 033	11 336	2 271	11.0	92.5	6.7	0.3	0.1	0.0	0.0

[1]MSA = Metropolitan Statistical Area. PMSA = Primary MSA. NECMA = New England County Metropolitan Area. See Appendix A for explanation of these concepts. See Appendix B for list of metropolitan areas identified by type, with component counties.
[2]County typology code from the Economic Research Service of USDA. See Appendix A for definition.
[3]Dry land or land partially or temporarily covered by water.

Table B. States and Counties

STATE County	Population and population characteristics, 2000 (cont'd)								Population and population characteristics, 1990				
	Race (percent) (cont'd)								Race (percent)				
		Race alone or in combination											
	Two or more races	White	Black	American Indian or Alaska Native	Asian	Native Hawaiian and other Pacific Islander	Some other race	Hispanic[1]	White	Black or African American	American Indian or Alaska Native	Asian and Pacific Islander	Hispanic[1]
	15	16	17	18	19	20	21	22	23	24	25	26	27
NORTH DAKOTA— Cont'd													
Ward	1.7	93.9	2.8	2.8	1.3	0.1	1.0	1.9	94.2	2.4	1.7	1.0	1.5
Wells	0.3	99.4	0.2	0.4	0.3	0.0	0.1	0.3	99.7	0.0	0.1	0.1	0.1
Williams	2.2	95.1	0.3	6.3	0.3	0.0	0.3	0.9	94.8	0.1	4.8	0.2	0.5
OHIO	1.4	86.1	12.1	0.7	1.4	0.1	1.1	1.9	87.8	10.6	0.2	0.8	1.3
Adams	1.1	98.8	0.3	1.6	0.2	0.0	0.2	0.6	99.4	0.2	0.3	0.1	0.4
Allen	1.5	86.3	13.0	0.6	0.7	0.0	0.9	1.4	87.6	11.2	0.2	0.5	1.1
Ashland	0.8	98.3	1.0	0.5	0.7	0.1	0.3	0.6	98.3	1.0	0.1	0.6	0.4
Ashtabula	1.4	95.4	3.7	0.7	0.5	0.1	1.2	2.2	95.6	3.1	0.2	0.4	1.5
Athens	1.6	94.9	2.9	1.0	2.2	0.1	0.7	1.0	94.3	2.8	0.3	2.3	0.7
Auglaize	0.8	98.9	0.5	0.6	0.5	0.0	0.3	0.7	99.2	0.1	0.1	0.4	0.5
Belmont	0.8	95.7	4.0	0.4	0.4	0.0	0.3	0.4	97.8	1.8	0.1	0.2	0.3
Brown	0.6	98.7	1.1	0.5	0.2	0.0	0.2	0.4	98.6	1.2	0.1	0.1	0.1
Butler	1.1	92.2	5.7	0.6	1.8	0.1	0.8	1.4	94.3	4.5	0.1	0.9	0.5
Carroll	0.7	98.9	0.7	0.7	0.2	0.0	0.2	0.5	99.0	0.5	0.2	0.1	0.4
Champaign	1.1	96.7	2.0	0.8	0.4	0.0	0.4	0.7	96.3	2.8	0.2	0.3	0.7
Clark	1.6	89.5	9.7	0.9	0.7	0.1	0.7	1.2	90.3	8.8	0.2	0.4	0.7
Clermont	0.9	97.9	1.1	0.6	0.8	0.0	0.4	0.9	98.6	0.9	0.1	0.3	0.5
Clinton	1.0	96.9	2.6	0.7	0.5	0.0	0.3	0.7	97.3	2.0	0.2	0.4	0.3
Columbiana	0.8	97.2	2.5	0.5	0.3	0.0	0.3	1.2	98.2	1.3	0.2	0.2	0.4
Coshocton	0.8	98.2	1.4	0.6	0.4	0.0	0.3	0.6	98.3	1.2	0.2	0.3	0.3
Crawford	0.6	98.6	0.8	0.5	0.4	0.0	0.4	0.8	98.9	0.5	0.1	0.2	0.5
Cuyahoga	1.7	68.7	28.2	0.6	2.1	0.1	2.2	3.4	72.6	24.8	0.2	1.3	2.2
Darke	0.7	98.8	0.7	0.5	0.4	0.0	0.4	0.9	99.0	0.3	0.2	0.2	0.6
Defiance	1.4	93.9	2.1	0.6	0.4	0.0	4.3	7.2	93.9	1.3	0.2	0.3	6.8
Delaware	1.1	95.3	2.9	0.6	1.8	0.1	0.6	1.0	97.0	2.1	0.2	0.6	0.5
Erie	1.6	90.1	9.5	0.7	0.5	0.0	0.9	2.1	90.7	8.2	0.2	0.3	1.5
Fairfield	1.0	96.1	3.0	0.7	0.9	0.1	0.4	0.8	98.2	1.1	0.2	0.4	0.5
Fayette	1.2	96.7	2.6	0.6	0.6	0.1	0.7	1.2	96.8	2.4	0.2	0.4	0.3
Franklin	2.2	77.1	19.1	0.9	3.5	0.1	1.7	2.3	81.5	15.9	0.2	2.0	1.0
Fulton	1.1	96.6	0.4	0.6	0.5	0.1	2.8	5.8	96.4	0.2	0.2	0.4	4.8
Gallia	1.1	96.3	3.1	1.0	0.4	0.0	0.3	0.6	96.4	2.8	0.3	0.4	0.5
Geauga	0.7	98.1	1.4	0.4	0.6	0.1	0.2	0.6	98.2	1.3	0.1	0.4	0.4
Greene	1.7	90.7	7.1	0.9	2.5	0.1	0.6	1.2	90.7	7.0	0.3	1.6	1.0
Guernsey	1.4	97.6	2.1	1.0	0.4	0.0	0.4	0.6	97.8	1.6	0.2	0.4	0.3
Hamilton	1.3	74.0	24.1	0.6	1.9	0.1	0.8	1.1	77.7	20.9	0.1	1.1	0.6
Hancock	1.1	96.2	1.4	0.5	1.4	0.0	1.6	3.1	97.0	0.9	0.1	0.6	2.6
Hardin	0.8	98.4	0.9	0.7	0.6	0.0	0.3	0.8	98.6	0.8	0.2	0.4	0.5
Harrison	1.0	97.5	2.8	0.4	0.2	0.0	0.2	0.4	97.3	2.4	0.1	0.1	0.3
Henry	0.8	96.1	0.7	0.5	0.5	0.0	3.0	5.4	96.0	0.5	0.2	0.3	4.6
Highland	0.9	97.7	1.8	0.7	0.4	0.1	0.3	0.5	97.6	1.9	0.2	0.2	0.3
Hocking	1.1	98.6	1.1	1.0	0.2	0.0	0.1	0.4	98.7	0.9	0.2	0.1	0.4
Holmes	0.4	99.4	0.4	0.3	0.1	0.0	0.2	0.7	99.6	0.2	0.1	0.1	0.4
Huron	1.0	96.9	1.3	0.5	0.3	0.0	1.9	3.6	97.8	1.1	0.2	0.3	1.8
Jackson	0.8	98.7	0.8	0.8	0.3	0.0	0.2	0.6	98.9	0.7	0.2	0.1	0.3
Jefferson	1.0	93.4	6.2	0.6	0.5	0.0	0.4	0.6	93.7	5.6	0.2	0.3	0.5
Knox	0.9	98.5	0.9	0.7	0.4	0.0	0.3	0.7	98.5	0.8	0.2	0.4	0.4
Lake	0.9	96.3	2.3	0.4	1.1	0.0	0.9	1.7	97.4	1.6	0.1	0.7	0.7
Lawrence	0.9	97.4	2.5	0.6	0.3	0.0	0.2	0.6	97.2	2.5	0.1	0.1	0.2
Licking	1.1	96.7	2.5	0.7	0.8	0.1	0.4	0.8	97.6	1.7	0.2	0.4	0.5
Logan	1.2	97.3	2.3	0.6	0.6	0.1	0.4	0.7	97.3	1.9	0.1	0.6	0.4
Lorain	2.2	87.5	9.4	0.9	0.8	0.1	3.6	6.9	89.1	7.8	0.3	0.5	5.6
Lucas	2.2	79.4	17.9	0.8	1.5	0.1	2.6	4.5	82.2	14.8	0.3	1.1	3.4
Madison	1.0	92.7	6.7	0.5	0.6	0.1	0.5	0.7	91.6	7.5	0.3	0.4	0.6
Mahoning	1.4	82.2	16.6	0.6	0.6	0.0	1.5	3.0	83.5	15.0	0.2	0.4	2.2
Marion	0.9	92.9	6.1	0.6	0.7	0.0	0.7	1.1	94.8	4.2	0.2	0.4	0.8
Medina	0.8	98.0	1.1	0.5	0.8	0.0	0.4	0.9	98.5	0.7	0.1	0.6	0.6
Meigs	1.0	98.7	1.0	0.9	0.2	0.0	0.3	0.6	98.9	0.8	0.2	0.1	0.3
Mercer	0.6	99.0	0.2	0.6	0.3	0.0	0.4	1.1	99.2	0.0	0.2	0.3	0.7
Miami	1.0	96.7	2.4	0.5	0.9	0.0	0.4	0.7	97.1	1.9	0.2	0.7	0.4
Monroe	0.7	99.3	0.3	0.6	0.2	0.0	0.2	0.4	99.6	0.1	0.2	0.1	0.2
Montgomery	1.5	77.8	20.6	0.7	1.7	0.1	0.8	1.3	80.8	17.7	0.2	1.0	0.8
Morgan	2.2	95.6	5.0	1.7	0.2	0.0	0.3	0.4	95.3	4.0	0.5	0.1	0.3
Morrow	0.7	99.1	0.4	0.8	0.2	0.0	0.3	0.6	99.4	0.2	0.2	0.1	0.3
Muskingum	1.4	95.2	4.9	0.7	0.4	0.0	0.3	0.5	95.2	4.2	0.3	0.2	0.3
Noble	0.4	92.9	6.8	0.5	0.1	0.0	0.1	0.4	99.7	0.1	0.1	0.1	0.2

[1] Hispanic persons may be of any race.

Table B. States and Counties

STATE County	Population and population characteristics, 2000										
	Age (percent)										
	Under 5 years	5 to 17 years	18 to 24 years	25 to 34 years	35 to 44 years	45 to 54 years	55 to 64 years	65 to 74 years	75 years and over	Median age (years)	Percent Female
	28	29	30	31	32	33	34	35	36	37	38
NORTH DAKOTA— Cont'd											
Ward	7.4	18.8	13.0	14.1	15.0	11.7	7.4	6.2	6.3	32.4	50.2
Wells	4.4	18.1	4.6	7.5	15.2	13.1	11.2	12.2	13.8	45.2	50.9
Williams	5.7	20.4	7.8	9.4	16.2	14.7	9.3	7.9	8.6	39.8	51.0
OHIO	6.6	18.8	9.3	13.4	15.9	13.8	8.9	7.0	6.3	36.2	51.4
Adams	6.4	19.9	8.7	13.1	15.1	13.2	10.2	7.4	5.9	36.3	51.0
Allen	6.7	19.2	9.9	12.3	15.3	13.7	8.7	7.3	6.9	36.3	50.0
Ashland	6.6	19.1	10.8	11.8	14.7	13.5	9.5	7.1	6.8	36.3	50.9
Ashtabula	6.5	19.6	7.6	12.4	15.6	14.0	9.6	7.6	7.0	37.6	51.3
Athens	4.8	13.6	30.7	12.0	11.6	11.0	7.0	4.9	4.4	25.7	51.1
Auglaize	6.8	20.8	7.8	12.4	15.8	13.6	8.4	7.0	7.4	36.5	50.9
Belmont	5.0	16.7	7.7	11.9	15.5	15.0	9.9	9.0	9.2	40.9	50.9
Brown	7.0	20.5	8.1	13.7	16.6	13.2	9.3	6.6	5.0	35.4	50.8
Butler	6.9	19.0	11.9	13.4	16.4	13.6	8.1	6.1	4.6	34.2	51.2
Carroll	6.0	19.1	7.5	11.6	15.9	15.1	10.6	8.0	6.2	38.8	50.5
Champaign	6.5	19.6	7.9	13.0	15.8	14.2	10.4	6.5	6.1	37.0	51.0
Clark	6.5	18.6	9.1	12.2	14.6	14.3	10.1	7.5	7.2	37.6	51.9
Clermont	7.6	20.3	8.4	14.1	17.6	14.2	8.4	5.4	4.0	34.8	50.9
Clinton	7.1	19.3	10.2	12.9	16.2	13.5	8.6	6.4	5.8	35.3	51.0
Columbiana	5.9	18.4	7.8	12.7	15.9	14.5	9.7	8.0	7.1	38.5	50.3
Coshocton	6.4	19.8	7.8	11.9	15.4	13.8	10.2	7.8	6.9	37.8	51.2
Crawford	6.6	18.4	8.0	12.5	15.1	13.9	10.4	7.9	7.3	38.2	51.7
Cuyahoga	6.5	18.4	8.0	13.5	15.7	13.5	8.7	7.7	7.9	37.3	52.8
Darke	6.7	19.6	7.8	12.3	15.2	13.4	9.8	7.5	7.8	37.4	51.0
Defiance	7.0	19.6	9.2	12.2	15.2	14.6	9.4	6.8	6.1	36.5	50.7
Delaware	7.9	20.3	7.6	13.6	19.0	15.2	8.1	4.8	3.4	35.3	50.5
Erie	6.0	18.7	7.2	11.4	15.6	15.2	10.3	8.1	7.5	39.5	51.3
Fairfield	7.0	19.8	8.0	13.3	16.9	14.6	9.2	6.1	5.0	36.2	50.2
Fayette	6.7	18.6	8.0	13.1	15.3	14.2	9.8	7.6	6.8	37.5	50.7
Franklin	7.2	17.9	11.7	17.1	16.2	12.8	7.3	5.3	4.5	32.5	51.4
Fulton	7.2	21.1	7.7	12.4	16.3	14.0	8.6	6.4	6.3	36.1	51.1
Gallia	6.3	18.7	9.7	11.8	15.7	13.7	10.5	7.6	5.9	37.4	51.2
Geauga	6.8	21.6	6.4	9.9	16.7	16.1	10.6	6.5	5.5	38.7	50.8
Greene	5.9	18.0	13.7	11.6	15.5	14.4	9.2	6.7	5.2	35.6	51.3
Guernsey	6.7	19.4	7.9	12.1	15.3	13.8	10.2	7.9	6.5	37.7	51.4
Hamilton	6.7	19.1	9.6	13.9	15.7	13.3	8.2	6.9	6.6	35.5	52.3
Hancock	6.8	19.0	9.7	13.0	15.7	13.7	8.9	6.5	6.7	36.0	51.5
Hardin	6.4	17.9	15.4	12.3	13.7	12.5	8.8	6.6	6.3	33.3	51.0
Harrison	5.8	17.2	6.9	11.1	15.5	14.9	10.9	9.1	8.6	41.1	51.5
Henry	6.7	20.9	8.2	12.1	15.9	13.2	8.9	7.0	7.0	36.5	50.6
Highland	7.1	19.9	8.5	13.0	14.9	13.2	9.7	7.5	6.3	36.1	51.2
Hocking	6.7	18.8	8.1	12.3	16.0	14.3	10.7	7.5	5.6	37.7	50.2
Holmes	10.3	25.3	10.4	12.7	12.9	10.6	7.2	5.6	4.9	28.0	50.1
Huron	7.5	20.8	8.5	13.3	15.6	13.3	8.6	6.7	5.6	34.9	51.0
Jackson	6.6	19.4	8.7	13.4	15.3	13.7	9.3	7.2	6.4	36.3	51.7
Jefferson	5.2	16.2	8.5	10.9	14.6	15.2	10.7	9.6	9.0	41.6	52.3
Knox	6.2	18.6	11.7	11.4	15.3	13.5	9.5	7.3	6.5	36.5	51.4
Lake	6.1	18.1	7.3	12.9	16.9	14.8	9.9	7.5	6.6	38.6	51.4
Lawrence	6.2	18.3	8.6	13.1	14.9	13.9	10.6	8.1	6.3	37.6	52.0
Licking	6.9	19.1	8.8	12.6	16.8	14.2	9.7	6.6	5.3	36.6	51.3
Logan	6.9	19.8	8.2	12.3	15.6	13.8	9.5	7.6	6.3	36.9	51.0
Lorain	6.9	19.3	8.7	12.8	16.6	14.3	9.0	6.6	5.9	36.5	50.9
Lucas	6.9	19.4	9.8	13.9	15.3	13.5	8.2	6.7	6.4	35.0	51.9
Madison	6.2	18.4	9.1	14.8	18.0	13.7	8.8	6.0	4.9	35.8	46.1
Mahoning	6.0	17.8	8.4	11.5	14.9	14.4	9.3	8.8	8.9	39.7	52.2
Marion	6.0	18.4	8.3	13.7	16.6	14.3	9.2	7.2	6.2	37.2	48.3
Medina	7.0	20.5	7.0	12.7	17.9	15.2	9.2	5.7	4.8	36.6	50.7
Meigs	5.7	18.2	8.4	12.4	15.3	14.6	10.6	7.9	6.8	38.6	51.4
Mercer	7.3	22.3	7.9	11.5	15.2	13.0	8.2	7.5	7.0	35.7	50.1
Miami	6.4	19.5	7.6	12.5	15.9	14.6	10.2	7.1	6.2	37.7	51.0
Monroe	5.3	18.3	7.1	11.3	14.7	15.1	12.0	8.8	7.5	40.8	50.6
Montgomery	6.6	18.1	9.7	13.6	15.4	13.7	9.2	7.3	6.4	36.4	52.0
Morgan	6.1	19.2	7.8	11.2	15.1	14.1	10.9	8.6	7.0	38.9	50.9
Morrow	6.5	20.8	7.6	12.8	16.5	14.4	9.8	6.6	4.9	36.5	50.2
Muskingum	6.7	19.3	9.4	12.5	15.2	13.3	9.3	7.5	6.8	36.5	52.1
Noble	5.0	17.6	11.7	14.9	16.9	12.2	8.6	7.3	5.7	35.5	43.3

Table B. States and Counties

STATE County	Under 5 years	5 to 17 years	18 to 24 years	25 to 34 years	35 to 44 years	45 to 54 years	55 to 64 years	65 to 74 years	75 years and over	Percent Female	2000	1990	1980	1990–2000	1980–1990
	39	40	41	42	43	44	45	46	47	48	49	50	51	52	53
NORTH DAKOTA— Cont'd															
Ward	8.7	19.4	13.4	18.6	13.6	8.0	7.0	5.9	5.3	50.2	58 795	57 921	58 392	1.5	-0.8
Wells	6.3	18.2	4.7	12.6	11.6	10.7	11.9	11.1	13.0	51.7	5 102	5 864	6 979	-13.0	-16.0
Williams	7.5	22.4	6.8	16.2	15.0	9.4	8.5	7.6	6.6	50.8	19 761	21 129	22 237	-6.5	-5.0
OHIO	7.2	18.6	10.5	16.5	14.9	10.3	9.0	7.6	5.3	51.8	11 353 140	10 847 115	10 797 603	4.7	0.5
Adams	7.3	21.7	9.6	14.4	13.8	10.5	9.1	7.8	5.8	50.9	27 330	25 371	24 328	7.7	4.3
Allen	7.6	19.8	10.0	16.1	14.5	9.8	8.9	7.7	5.7	50.5	108 473	109 755	112 241	-1.2	-2.2
Ashland	7.0	20.3	10.8	14.6	14.1	10.5	8.9	7.7	6.0	51.2	52 523	47 507	46 178	10.6	2.9
Ashtabula	7.3	20.0	8.8	14.8	14.6	10.3	9.5	8.5	6.2	51.7	102 728	99 880	104 215	2.9	-4.2
Athens	5.4	15.0	29.0	14.3	12.0	8.0	6.5	5.6	4.2	50.9	62 223	59 549	56 399	4.5	5.6
Auglaize	8.0	21.3	8.7	15.7	14.7	9.5	8.7	7.6	5.9	51.3	46 611	44 585	42 554	4.5	4.8
Belmont	5.9	17.8	8.0	13.8	14.7	10.3	10.7	10.7	8.0	53.0	70 226	71 074	82 569	-1.2	-13.9
Brown	7.5	21.1	9.2	16.0	14.1	10.4	8.9	7.2	5.6	50.9	42 285	34 966	31 920	20.9	9.5
Butler	7.4	18.8	13.2	16.7	15.2	10.1	8.5	6.1	4.1	51.6	332 807	291 479	258 787	14.2	12.6
Carroll	7.0	20.4	8.3	15.5	15.0	10.9	9.4	8.3	5.4	50.9	28 836	26 521	25 598	8.7	3.6
Champaign	6.8	19.7	9.5	15.0	14.9	12.6	8.5	7.3	5.5	50.8	38 890	36 019	33 649	8.0	7.0
Clark	6.9	18.8	10.7	14.6	14.6	11.4	9.2	8.0	5.8	52.1	144 742	147 538	150 236	-1.9	-1.8
Clermont	8.2	21.2	9.8	18.3	16.0	10.4	7.5	5.3	3.4	51.0	177 977	150 094	128 483	18.6	16.9
Clinton	7.2	20.1	10.7	15.8	14.6	10.0	8.5	7.5	5.6	51.4	40 543	35 444	34 603	14.4	2.4
Columbiana	7.0	19.6	8.6	14.8	14.8	10.5	9.9	9.0	5.9	51.8	112 075	108 276	113 572	3.5	-4.7
Coshocton	7.2	20.1	8.2	14.9	14.6	10.8	9.8	8.3	6.1	51.7	36 655	35 427	36 024	3.5	-1.7
Crawford	7.2	19.5	9.0	15.1	14.2	11.2	9.4	8.2	6.3	51.7	46 966	47 870	50 075	-1.9	-4.4
Cuyahoga	7.1	16.8	9.4	16.9	14.4	10.0	9.8	9.2	6.4	53.0	1 393 978	1 412 140	1 498 400	-1.3	-5.8
Darke	7.2	20.4	9.0	15.1	14.0	10.8	8.8	8.1	6.6	51.6	53 309	53 617	55 096	-0.6	-2.7
Defiance	7.3	21.4	10.0	15.3	15.2	10.8	8.3	6.8	4.9	50.7	39 500	39 350	39 987	0.4	-1.6
Delaware	7.4	20.1	10.0	15.4	18.0	11.7	8.2	5.3	3.8	50.5	109 989	66 929	53 840	64.3	24.3
Erie	7.0	19.1	8.6	15.3	15.2	11.3	9.8	8.4	5.2	51.4	79 551	76 781	79 655	3.6	-3.6
Fairfield	6.9	20.2	9.9	15.3	16.3	11.6	8.6	6.5	4.8	50.4	122 759	103 468	93 678	18.6	10.5
Fayette	6.9	19.5	9.1	14.8	14.7	10.8	9.5	8.2	6.6	51.5	28 433	27 466	27 467	3.5	0.0
Franklin	7.6	17.0	13.4	20.1	15.3	9.3	7.6	5.7	3.9	51.8	1 068 978	961 437	869 126	11.2	10.6
Fulton	7.7	21.8	8.7	16.1	15.0	10.0	8.1	7.1	5.6	51.1	42 084	38 498	37 751	9.3	2.0
Gallia	6.8	19.9	10.1	15.8	14.1	11.2	9.3	7.2	5.6	51.1	31 069	30 954	30 098	0.4	2.8
Geauga	7.9	20.8	8.2	13.9	16.9	12.7	8.9	6.5	4.1	50.5	90 895	81 087	74 474	12.1	8.9
Greene	6.7	19.0	13.2	15.3	15.9	11.3	8.8	6.2	3.6	51.0	147 886	136 731	129 769	8.2	5.4
Guernsey	7.0	19.9	8.6	15.0	14.5	10.6	9.5	8.5	6.4	52.3	40 792	39 024	42 024	4.5	-7.1
Hamilton	7.8	18.2	10.5	17.4	14.3	9.6	8.9	7.4	5.9	52.7	845 303	866 228	873 203	-2.4	-0.8
Hancock	7.4	19.5	9.9	16.6	14.9	10.4	8.3	7.4	5.6	51.6	71 295	65 536	64 581	8.8	1.5
Hardin	6.7	19.0	14.7	14.6	13.1	9.9	8.5	7.5	6.1	51.0	31 945	31 111	32 719	2.7	-4.9
Harrison	5.8	19.5	8.1	13.8	14.5	10.5	10.4	9.9	7.5	51.7	15 856	16 085	18 152	-1.4	-11.4
Henry	7.7	21.4	8.7	15.6	13.9	10.1	9.0	7.5	6.1	50.8	29 210	29 108	28 383	0.4	2.6
Highland	7.3	20.1	9.0	14.8	13.7	10.5	9.6	8.5	6.5	51.4	40 875	35 728	33 477	14.4	6.7
Hocking	7.0	19.6	9.3	15.2	14.4	11.7	9.5	7.7	5.7	50.0	28 241	25 533	24 304	10.6	5.1
Holmes	10.8	25.1	10.0	14.7	12.4	8.7	7.5	5.8	4.9	50.8	38 943	32 849	29 416	18.6	11.7
Huron	8.1	21.2	9.5	16.1	14.6	10.0	8.6	7.0	4.9	51.3	59 487	56 238	54 608	5.8	3.0
Jackson	7.0	20.5	9.2	15.1	14.5	10.1	9.6	8.0	6.0	52.3	32 641	30 230	30 592	8.0	-1.2
Jefferson	5.7	17.9	8.9	13.4	14.6	11.0	11.3	10.4	6.8	52.7	73 894	80 298	91 564	-8.0	-12.3
Knox	6.4	18.6	12.0	14.4	14.3	10.5	9.3	8.4	6.4	51.8	54 500	47 473	46 304	14.8	2.5
Lake	6.9	18.0	9.1	17.3	15.9	11.4	9.4	7.5	4.5	51.4	227 511	215 500	212 801	5.6	1.3
Lawrence	6.7	20.4	9.6	14.6	14.2	11.4	9.9	8.0	5.3	52.4	62 319	61 834	63 849	0.8	-3.2
Licking	7.2	19.1	10.2	16.0	15.1	11.5	9.1	6.9	4.9	51.6	145 491	128 300	120 981	13.4	6.0
Logan	7.4	20.2	9.3	15.2	14.2	10.0	9.3	8.4	6.0	51.6	46 005	42 310	39 155	8.7	8.1
Lorain	7.4	20.1	10.2	16.2	15.5	10.4	8.7	7.1	4.5	51.3	284 664	271 126	274 909	5.0	-1.4
Lucas	7.8	18.6	11.0	16.9	14.6	9.5	8.6	7.5	5.5	52.3	455 054	462 361	471 741	-1.6	-2.0
Madison	6.8	17.9	10.8	20.0	16.2	10.6	7.6	6.1	4.0	45.8	40 213	37 078	33 004	8.5	12.3
Mahoning	6.5	18.0	8.9	14.6	14.4	9.9	10.6	10.5	6.6	52.8	257 555	264 806	289 487	-2.7	-8.5
Marion	7.5	19.2	9.1	16.7	15.4	10.5	8.9	7.5	5.2	50.2	66 217	64 274	67 974	3.0	-5.4
Medina	7.3	21.2	8.7	15.8	17.5	11.9	7.9	5.8	3.9	50.8	151 095	122 354	113 150	23.5	8.1
Meigs	6.6	20.3	8.9	14.1	14.6	10.9	9.6	8.7	6.3	51.6	23 072	22 987	23 641	0.4	-2.8
Mercer	8.7	22.3	8.7	15.4	13.6	8.9	8.9	7.8	5.7	50.1	40 924	39 443	38 334	3.8	2.9
Miami	7.0	19.8	9.0	15.4	15.3	11.8	9.1	7.5	5.1	51.4	98 868	93 184	90 381	6.1	3.1
Monroe	6.2	19.5	8.5	13.6	14.5	12.0	10.0	8.5	7.1	50.9	15 180	15 497	17 382	-2.0	-10.8
Montgomery	7.4	17.5	10.6	17.5	14.8	10.5	9.3	7.6	5.0	52.1	559 062	573 809	571 697	-2.6	0.4
Morgan	7.2	21.5	8.2	14.5	13.6	10.4	9.6	8.5	6.5	51.5	14 897	14 194	14 241	5.0	-0.3
Morrow	7.3	21.7	9.1	15.2	15.3	11.7	8.6	6.3	4.7	50.4	31 628	27 749	26 480	14.0	4.8
Muskingum	7.2	19.5	10.3	15.4	14.0	10.3	9.4	7.8	6.0	52.4	84 585	82 068	83 340	3.1	-1.5
Noble	7.5	21.4	8.0	15.2	13.4	9.7	9.7	8.0	7.0	51.1	14 058	11 336	11 310	24.0	0.2

Table B. States and Counties

STATE County	Household relationship, 2000																
		In households (percent)									In group quarters (percent)						
					Child		Other relatives		Nonrelatives			Institutionalized population			Noninstitutionalized population		
	Total population	Total in house-holds	House-holder	Spouse	Total	Own child under 18 years	Total	Under 18 years	Total	Unmar-ried partner	Total in group quarters	Correc-tional institu-tions	Nurs-ing homes	Other institu-tions	Col-lege dormi-tories	Mili-tary quar-ters	Other
	54	55	56	57	58	59	60	61	62	63	64	65	66	67	68	69	70
NORTH DAKOTA—Cont'd																	
Ward	58 795	96.3	39.2	21.6	29.2	24.9	1.8	0.6	4.5	1.7	3.7	0.1	0.7	0.3	0.8	1.2	0.6
Wells	5 102	97.7	43.4	25.4	25.8	21.7	1.4	0.5	1.6	0.8	2.3	0.0	0.0	1.9	0.0	0.0	0.4
Williams	19 761	97.6	41.0	21.8	29.4	24.7	1.8	0.9	3.5	1.7	2.4	0.1	0.4	0.3	0.3	0.0	1.3
OHIO	11 353 140	97.4	39.2	20.1	29.7	23.2	3.9	1.7	4.4	2.0	2.6	0.6	0.8	0.1	0.8	0.0	0.3
Adams	27 330	98.7	38.4	22.0	30.7	24.0	4.0	1.8	3.7	2.3	1.3	0.0	0.8	0.0	0.0	0.0	0.5
Allen	108 473	94.4	37.5	19.9	29.9	23.6	3.5	1.7	3.7	1.8	5.6	3.1	1.1	0.1	1.1	0.0	0.4
Ashland	52 523	95.8	37.2	22.1	29.8	23.6	3.0	1.4	3.7	1.7	4.2	0.1	1.0	0.3	2.6	0.0	0.3
Ashtabula	102 728	98.3	38.4	21.0	30.3	23.7	4.1	1.8	4.5	2.4	1.7	0.1	1.2	0.0	0.0	0.0	0.4
Athens	62 223	86.8	36.2	15.7	21.1	16.8	2.4	0.9	11.4	2.3	13.2	0.4	0.5	0.2	12.0	0.0	0.1
Auglaize	46 611	97.6	37.3	23.2	32.4	26.1	2.2	1.0	2.7	1.5	2.4	0.1	1.4	0.0	0.0	0.0	0.8
Belmont	70 226	95.5	40.3	21.4	27.2	19.9	3.5	1.3	3.2	1.8	4.5	3.1	1.0	0.2	0.0	0.0	0.2
Brown	42 285	98.9	36.8	22.5	31.5	25.0	4.1	1.9	3.9	2.2	1.1	0.1	0.8	0.0	0.0	0.0	0.2
Butler	332 807	96.6	37.0	21.1	30.0	23.9	3.7	1.6	4.9	1.9	3.4	0.2	0.7	0.0	2.3	0.0	0.2
Carroll	28 836	98.7	38.6	23.9	29.6	23.0	3.1	1.5	3.6	2.0	1.3	0.0	0.9	0.0	0.0	0.0	0.4
Champaign	38 890	98.3	38.4	22.9	30.1	24.2	3.2	1.4	3.6	1.7	1.7	0.1	1.0	0.0	0.5	0.0	0.1
Clark	144 742	97.3	39.1	20.6	29.0	22.5	4.2	1.9	4.4	2.2	2.7	0.1	1.2	0.1	0.9	0.0	0.4
Clermont	177 977	99.2	37.1	22.4	32.3	25.9	3.6	1.5	3.8	2.1	0.8	0.1	0.5	0.0	0.0	0.0	0.2
Clinton	40 543	97.5	38.0	21.8	30.2	24.3	3.4	1.6	4.1	2.1	2.5	0.0	0.7	0.0	1.7	0.0	0.1
Columbiana	112 075	96.6	38.3	21.9	29.4	22.2	3.4	1.5	3.5	1.9	3.4	2.3	0.6	0.1	0.0	0.0	0.4
Coshocton	36 655	98.7	39.2	22.6	30.5	24.5	2.7	1.1	3.7	2.2	1.3	0.1	0.6	0.1	0.0	0.0	0.4
Crawford	46 966	98.7	40.4	22.2	29.1	22.9	3.0	1.4	3.9	2.2	1.3	0.2	0.7	0.0	0.0	0.0	0.3
Cuyahoga	1 393 978	97.8	41.0	17.4	29.8	22.1	5.4	2.3	4.3	2.0	2.2	0.2	0.9	0.1	0.5	0.0	0.5
Darke	53 309	98.2	38.3	23.4	30.7	24.5	2.6	1.2	3.3	1.7	1.8	0.0	0.7	0.1	0.0	0.0	0.9
Defiance	39 500	98.5	38.3	22.6	31.0	24.6	2.8	1.4	3.7	2.0	1.5	0.0	0.8	0.0	0.7	0.0	0.1
Delaware	109 989	97.5	36.1	24.4	31.5	26.8	2.4	0.8	3.1	1.5	2.5	0.1	0.5	0.4	1.4	0.0	0.0
Erie	79 551	97.7	39.9	21.4	28.9	22.4	3.6	1.8	3.8	2.1	2.3	0.1	1.8	0.0	0.0	0.0	0.4
Fairfield	122 759	97.9	37.0	23.2	31.0	24.9	3.1	1.3	3.6	1.8	2.1	1.4	0.6	0.0	0.0	0.0	0.1
Fayette	28 433	97.7	38.9	21.3	28.8	22.5	3.9	2.0	4.8	2.6	2.3	0.1	1.5	0.0	0.0	0.0	0.7
Franklin	1 068 978	97.9	41.0	17.7	28.0	22.8	4.3	1.8	6.9	2.5	2.1	0.1	0.5	0.1	1.1	0.0	0.3
Fulton	42 084	99.0	36.8	23.2	33.1	26.5	2.8	1.3	3.1	1.7	1.0	0.0	0.9	0.0	0.0	0.0	0.1
Gallia	31 069	97.0	38.8	21.9	29.3	22.8	3.6	1.6	3.3	1.9	3.0	0.0	0.7	0.8	1.2	0.0	0.3
Geauga	90 895	98.8	34.8	24.0	34.6	27.1	3.0	1.0	2.4	1.1	1.2	0.1	0.6	0.2	0.0	0.0	0.3
Greene	147 886	94.7	37.4	21.7	28.3	22.4	2.9	1.1	4.5	1.5	5.3	0.1	0.8	0.0	3.8	0.2	0.3
Guernsey	40 792	98.8	39.5	21.3	30.0	23.7	3.7	1.8	4.3	2.4	1.2	0.2	0.7	0.1	0.0	0.0	0.2
Hamilton	845 303	97.8	41.0	17.8	30.0	23.4	4.2	1.9	4.7	2.0	2.2	0.3	0.9	0.1	0.6	0.0	0.4
Hancock	71 295	97.6	39.1	22.1	29.3	23.9	2.6	1.2	4.5	1.9	2.4	0.2	1.1	0.0	1.0	0.0	0.3
Hardin	31 945	94.0	37.4	20.6	28.0	22.2	3.0	1.5	5.0	1.9	6.0	0.0	0.7	0.0	5.1	0.0	0.2
Harrison	15 856	98.3	40.4	23.6	27.9	21.2	3.2	1.4	3.3	2.1	1.7	0.0	1.7	0.0	0.0	0.0	0.0
Henry	29 210	98.0	37.4	22.9	32.1	25.5	2.4	1.1	3.2	1.8	2.0	0.0	1.0	0.4	0.0	0.0	0.6
Highland	40 875	99.0	38.1	22.3	30.8	24.2	3.8	1.9	4.0	2.1	1.0	0.1	0.7	0.0	0.0	0.0	0.2
Hocking	28 241	97.4	38.4	22.4	29.2	23.2	3.5	1.6	4.1	2.3	2.6	1.6	0.7	0.1	0.0	0.0	0.2
Holmes	38 943	97.7	29.1	20.8	43.1	34.4	2.6	0.9	2.0	1.0	2.3	0.1	2.2	0.0	0.0	0.0	0.1
Huron	59 487	99.0	37.5	21.9	32.4	26.1	3.2	1.5	3.9	2.1	1.0	0.2	0.7	0.0	0.0	0.0	0.1
Jackson	32 641	98.7	38.7	21.4	30.2	23.2	4.3	2.1	4.1	2.4	1.3	0.0	1.2	0.1	0.0	0.0	0.1
Jefferson	73 894	97.2	41.2	21.5	26.9	19.4	3.9	1.5	3.6	1.9	2.8	0.3	0.8	0.0	1.2	0.0	0.5
Knox	54 500	93.6	36.7	21.9	28.8	23.1	2.8	1.1	3.5	1.8	6.4	0.1	1.0	0.6	4.4	0.0	0.2
Lake	227 511	98.7	39.4	22.1	30.1	22.6	3.5	1.2	3.6	1.7	1.3	0.1	0.7	0.0	0.1	0.0	0.3
Lawrence	62 319	99.0	39.7	22.2	29.5	22.0	4.3	1.9	3.3	1.8	1.0	0.0	0.8	0.0	0.0	0.0	0.1
Licking	145 491	97.8	38.2	22.4	29.8	23.9	3.2	1.4	4.2	2.1	2.2	0.1	0.7	0.0	1.3	0.0	0.1
Logan	46 005	98.7	39.0	22.3	30.2	24.5	3.2	1.4	4.1	2.2	1.3	0.1	1.1	0.0	0.0	0.0	0.1
Lorain	284 664	97.0	37.2	20.5	31.0	23.6	4.2	2.0	4.1	2.0	3.0	1.4	0.7	0.0	0.6	0.0	0.2
Lucas	455 054	98.0	40.2	18.0	30.3	23.7	4.2	2.0	5.3	2.4	2.0	0.1	0.8	0.0	0.6	0.0	0.5
Madison	40 213	89.0	34.0	20.1	28.1	22.4	3.3	1.5	3.5	1.8	11.0	10.0	0.6	0.0	0.3	0.0	0.1
Mahoning	257 555	97.2	39.8	19.5	29.6	21.2	4.8	2.0	3.4	1.7	2.8	1.0	1.0	0.1	0.3	0.0	0.4
Marion	66 217	93.0	37.1	20.2	27.6	22.0	3.7	1.7	4.3	2.2	7.0	6.2	0.5	0.1	0.0	0.0	0.2
Medina	151 095	99.0	36.1	24.0	33.0	26.0	3.1	1.1	2.8	1.4	1.0	0.2	0.7	0.0	0.0	0.0	0.2
Meigs	23 072	99.0	40.0	22.8	28.8	21.8	3.7	1.6	3.7	2.2	1.0	0.0	0.8	0.1	0.0	0.0	0.1
Mercer	40 924	98.7	36.1	23.1	35.2	28.3	2.1	0.8	2.3	1.2	1.3	0.0	1.0	0.0	0.0	0.0	0.3
Miami	98 868	98.6	38.9	23.1	30.0	24.0	3.0	1.3	3.6	1.8	1.4	0.3	0.9	0.1	0.0	0.0	0.1
Monroe	15 180	99.1	39.7	24.5	29.2	21.8	3.2	1.4	2.5	1.4	0.9	0.0	0.8	0.0	0.0	0.0	0.1
Montgomery	559 062	97.2	41.0	19.0	28.3	22.2	4.2	1.9	4.7	2.2	2.8	0.4	0.9	0.1	1.1	0.0	0.3
Morgan	14 897	98.8	39.5	22.5	29.9	23.2	3.3	1.5	3.6	2.0	1.2	0.0	1.2	0.0	0.0	0.0	0.0
Morrow	31 628	98.8	36.4	23.5	31.1	24.6	4.0	2.0	3.8	2.0	1.2	0.4	0.6	0.0	0.0	0.0	0.1
Muskingum	84 585	97.1	38.4	20.9	29.8	23.5	3.6	1.7	4.4	2.4	2.9	0.2	1.2	0.1	1.2	0.0	0.2
Noble	14 058	84.3	32.3	19.9	27.0	21.0	2.6	1.2	2.5	1.4	15.7	14.8	1.0	0.0	0.0	0.0	0.0

Table B. States and Counties

STATE County	Households by type, 2000												Households, 1990		
		Family households						Nonfamily households							
				Married couple		Female householder[1]			Householder living alone						House-holder living alone
	Total households	Total	With own children under 18 years	Total	With own children under 18 years	Total	With own children under 18 years	Total	Total	65 years and over	Average house-hold size	Average family size	Total house-holds	Female house-holder[1]	
	71	72	73	74	75	76	77	78	79	80	81	82	83	84	85
NORTH DAKOTA— Cont'd															
Ward	23 041	66.7	34.3	55.2	26.6	8.4	5.8	33.3	27.2	9.8	2.46	3.01	21 485	8.0	24.9
Wells	2 215	65.6	25.4	58.6	21.7	4.8	2.8	34.4	32.6	18.6	2.25	2.85	2 406	5.0	29.1
Williams	8 095	65.0	31.2	53.3	23.1	8.8	6.3	35.0	30.9	13.1	2.38	2.99	8 041	7.4	26.8
OHIO	4 445 773	67.3	31.7	51.4	22.4	12.1	7.3	32.7	27.3	10.0	2.49	3.04	4 087 546	11.7	25.0
Adams	10 501	72.5	34.0	57.1	24.9	10.4	6.3	27.5	24.0	11.0	2.57	3.03	9 192	11.2	21.4
Allen	40 646	69.4	32.9	53.0	22.6	12.4	8.1	30.6	26.3	11.2	2.52	3.05	39 408	11.7	23.6
Ashland	19 524	71.8	32.5	59.5	24.9	8.5	5.3	28.2	24.0	10.3	2.58	3.06	17 101	8.0	22.6
Ashtabula	39 397	70.5	32.4	54.8	23.0	11.4	6.9	29.5	24.8	10.7	2.56	3.05	36 760	11.0	22.8
Athens	22 501	56.5	26.4	43.5	18.4	9.2	5.7	43.5	28.3	8.3	2.40	2.92	20 139	9.8	25.8
Auglaize	17 376	73.5	35.3	62.1	28.2	7.8	4.9	26.5	23.3	10.5	2.62	3.11	15 976	7.6	21.0
Belmont	28 309	68.0	28.3	53.1	20.4	11.2	6.1	32.0	28.7	15.1	2.37	2.90	28 161	10.8	26.1
Brown	15 555	75.8	37.1	61.3	28.1	10.0	6.1	24.2	20.2	8.5	2.69	3.09	12 379	9.6	19.1
Butler	123 082	71.4	35.5	57.0	26.8	10.7	6.6	28.6	22.7	7.6	2.61	3.07	104 535	10.4	20.8
Carroll	11 126	73.3	31.9	61.9	25.2	7.7	4.6	26.7	22.9	10.4	2.56	3.00	9 667	7.8	20.6
Champaign	14 952	72.7	34.0	59.7	26.0	9.2	5.5	27.3	23.5	9.4	2.56	3.01	13 253	8.3	21.2
Clark	56 648	69.5	31.4	52.6	21.2	12.8	7.9	30.5	26.0	11.1	2.49	2.97	55 198	11.9	23.3
Clermont	66 013	74.3	38.1	60.4	29.4	10.0	6.2	25.7	21.0	7.0	2.67	3.11	52 726	10.0	18.2
Clinton	15 416	71.8	34.7	57.4	25.4	10.1	6.6	28.2	23.7	9.9	2.56	3.03	13 038	9.5	22.3
Columbiana	42 973	71.4	31.7	57.1	23.7	10.3	5.9	28.6	24.8	11.9	2.52	3.00	40 775	10.3	22.9
Coshocton	14 356	70.8	32.6	57.8	24.3	9.2	5.9	29.2	25.4	11.9	2.52	3.01	13 433	8.7	23.7
Crawford	18 957	69.5	31.2	55.1	22.2	10.5	6.7	30.5	26.3	11.5	2.45	2.94	18 383	9.9	23.8
Cuyahoga	571 457	62.1	28.5	42.4	17.9	15.7	8.9	37.9	32.8	12.1	2.39	3.06	563 243	14.9	30.2
Darke	20 419	73.0	33.3	61.0	25.9	8.0	4.8	27.0	23.5	11.0	2.56	3.03	19 459	7.9	21.0
Defiance	15 138	72.8	34.3	58.9	25.2	9.6	6.4	27.2	23.0	9.5	2.57	3.02	14 070	8.1	21.5
Delaware	39 674	77.3	40.1	67.7	34.2	6.7	4.2	22.7	18.1	5.3	2.70	3.09	23 116	7.2	17.0
Erie	31 727	68.6	30.4	53.7	21.5	11.2	6.9	31.4	27.0	10.8	2.45	2.97	28 932	10.4	24.1
Fairfield	45 425	75.2	36.8	62.7	29.2	9.1	5.6	24.8	20.7	8.2	2.65	3.06	36 813	8.8	19.0
Fayette	11 054	70.9	32.4	54.8	22.4	11.5	7.1	29.1	24.5	11.2	2.51	2.96	10 221	10.5	21.8
Franklin	438 778	60.1	30.4	43.0	20.0	13.0	8.3	39.9	30.9	7.4	2.39	3.03	378 723	12.6	28.0
Fulton	15 480	75.5	37.1	63.2	29.4	8.2	5.2	24.5	21.1	9.4	2.69	3.13	13 504	7.2	19.5
Gallia	12 060	71.2	33.0	56.5	24.1	11.0	6.7	28.8	25.2	10.4	2.50	2.98	11 367	10.2	22.4
Geauga	31 630	79.0	37.1	68.9	32.0	7.2	3.8	21.0	17.6	6.9	2.84	3.24	26 906	7.1	14.9
Greene	55 312	70.8	32.8	58.0	25.1	9.6	6.0	29.2	23.0	7.7	2.53	3.00	48 351	9.2	19.3
Guernsey	16 094	69.8	32.4	53.9	22.6	11.4	7.0	30.2	26.1	11.2	2.50	3.00	14 894	11.4	25.1
Hamilton	346 790	61.3	30.2	43.4	19.4	14.3	9.0	38.7	32.9	10.6	2.38	3.07	338 881	14.0	29.9
Hancock	27 898	68.6	32.6	56.4	24.8	8.7	5.7	31.4	26.0	9.8	2.49	3.01	24 642	8.0	23.5
Hardin	11 963	68.0	31.4	55.0	23.3	8.9	5.7	32.0	26.5	10.8	2.51	3.03	11 250	8.6	24.7
Harrison	6 398	70.6	29.1	58.5	22.2	8.8	5.1	29.4	25.6	13.0	2.44	2.92	6 111	9.0	23.4
Henry	10 935	72.8	35.2	61.1	27.8	8.1	5.1	27.2	23.5	10.4	2.62	3.10	10 401	7.2	21.3
Highland	15 587	73.1	34.0	58.4	25.3	10.3	6.0	26.9	23.2	10.6	2.60	3.04	13 230	10.0	22.4
Hocking	10 843	72.2	33.5	58.3	24.8	9.5	5.9	27.8	23.7	10.0	2.54	2.98	9 351	9.1	21.2
Holmes	11 337	81.1	44.3	71.5	39.3	6.5	3.4	18.9	16.1	6.9	3.35	3.82	9 315	6.1	15.8
Huron	22 307	72.7	36.3	58.5	27.2	10.4	6.8	27.3	23.1	9.7	2.64	3.11	20 239	9.2	21.2
Jackson	12 619	72.4	34.5	55.4	24.7	12.0	7.1	27.6	24.0	10.5	2.55	3.00	11 260	12.0	22.6
Jefferson	30 417	67.7	26.7	52.3	18.8	11.6	6.1	32.3	28.5	14.4	2.36	2.88	31 311	11.7	25.5
Knox	19 975	71.9	32.5	59.6	25.1	8.5	5.2	28.1	23.9	10.6	2.56	3.03	17 230	8.7	22.8
Lake	89 700	69.7	31.1	56.1	24.0	10.0	5.2	30.3	25.6	9.8	2.50	3.03	80 421	9.6	22.0
Lawrence	24 732	72.0	32.0	56.0	22.9	11.9	6.8	28.0	24.9	11.2	2.49	2.96	22 899	12.2	21.6
Licking	55 609	72.2	34.4	58.5	25.8	10.0	6.4	27.8	23.1	9.1	2.56	3.01	47 254	9.5	21.3
Logan	17 956	70.9	33.3	57.0	24.3	9.5	6.2	29.1	24.8	10.3	2.53	3.01	15 952	8.7	23.0
Lorain	105 836	72.0	33.6	55.2	23.8	12.6	7.7	28.0	23.6	9.2	2.61	3.08	96 064	11.7	20.8
Lucas	182 847	63.6	31.1	44.7	19.6	14.7	9.3	36.4	30.1	10.5	2.44	3.06	177 500	13.9	27.3
Madison	13 672	73.4	35.2	59.2	26.6	9.9	6.0	26.6	22.3	9.5	2.62	3.06	11 990	9.2	19.8
Mahoning	102 587	67.1	28.4	49.0	19.2	14.1	7.6	32.9	29.1	13.1	2.44	3.02	101 136	13.9	25.5
Marion	24 578	70.2	32.3	54.5	22.5	11.4	7.1	29.8	25.1	10.9	2.50	2.98	23 484	10.7	22.8
Medina	54 542	77.4	37.7	66.5	31.6	7.8	4.5	22.6	18.9	6.9	2.74	3.15	41 792	7.7	16.3
Meigs	9 234	71.2	31.2	56.9	22.9	10.0	5.8	28.8	25.0	11.7	2.47	2.94	8 662	10.1	22.7
Mercer	14 756	74.7	37.1	64.1	30.9	7.4	4.5	25.3	22.7	10.8	2.74	3.24	13 398	6.7	20.4
Miami	38 437	72.7	33.3	59.5	25.1	9.7	6.1	27.3	23.2	9.5	2.54	2.99	34 559	8.7	21.0
Monroe	6 021	73.3	29.5	61.7	24.0	8.1	4.0	26.7	24.0	11.5	2.50	2.96	5 754	8.1	21.7
Montgomery	229 229	64.1	29.6	46.3	19.1	13.8	8.4	35.9	30.4	10.1	2.37	2.96	226 192	13.2	27.0
Morgan	5 890	70.9	30.9	56.9	22.4	9.9	6.0	29.1	25.5	12.0	2.50	2.98	5 170	9.4	21.9
Morrow	11 499	77.0	35.6	64.6	28.1	8.1	4.8	23.0	19.0	7.9	2.72	3.09	9 656	8.1	16.7
Muskingum	32 518	70.3	33.3	54.3	23.2	12.0	7.6	29.7	24.9	10.9	2.53	3.01	30 753	11.5	23.8
Noble	4 546	73.0	33.5	61.5	27.0	7.7	4.6	27.0	24.3	12.6	2.61	3.10	4 137	7.6	22.7

[1]No spouse present.

Table B. States and Counties

| STATE County | Percent change of households, 1990–2000 | Total housing units | Occupied housing units (percent) | Vacant housing units | | Homeowner vacancy rate (percent) | Rental vacancy rate (percent) | Occupied housing units | | | Average household size of owner-occupied units | Average household size of renter-occupied units |
				Total	For seasonal, recreational, or occasional use			Total	Percent owner-occupied housing units	Percent renter-occupied housing units		
	86	87	88	89	90	91	92	93	94	95	96	97
NORTH DAKOTA— Cont'd												
Ward	7.2	25 097	91.8	8.2	1.3	2.0	5.9	23 041	62.6	37 4	2.59	2.24
Wells	-7.9	2 643	83.8	16.2	2.4	5.0	13.5	2 215	76.5	23.5	2.36	1.90
Williams	0.7	9 680	83.6	16.4	4.4	2.9	15.8	8 095	71.4	28.6	2.55	1.97
OHIO	8.8	4 783 051	92.9	7.1	1.0	1.6	8.3	4 445 773	69.1	30.9	2.62	2.19
Adams	14.2	11 822	88.8	11.2	3.6	2.0	9.2	10 501	73.9	26.1	2.59	2.52
Allen	3.1	44 245	91.9	8.1	0.4	1.6	11.3	40 646	72.1	27.9	2.60	2.30
Ashland	14.2	20 832	93.7	6.3	1.5	1.6	6.2	19 524	75.6	24.4	2.68	2.27
Ashtabula	7.2	43 792	90.0	10.0	4.4	1.8	7.6	39 397	74.1	25.9	2.62	2.40
Athens	11.7	24 901	90.4	9.6	1.6	2.6	8.4	22 501	60.5	39.5	2.49	2.26
Auglaize	8.8	18 470	94.1	5.9	0.9	1.5	8.3	17 376	77.9	22.1	2.72	2.26
Belmont	0.5	31 236	90.6	9.4	1.2	1.8	8.5	28 309	75.0	25.0	2.44	2.15
Brown	25.7	17 193	90.5	9.5	1.7	1.9	6.8	15 555	79.6	20.4	2.73	2.54
Butler	17.7	129 793	94.8	5.2	0.3	1.6	7.3	123 082	71.6	28.4	2.72	2.34
Carroll	15.1	13 016	85.5	14.5	9.3	1.2	5.2	11 126	80.0	20.0	2.60	2.40
Champaign	12.8	15 890	94.1	5.9	0.6	1.8	6.7	14 952	75.9	24.1	2.63	2.32
Clark	2.6	61 056	92.8	7.2	0.4	1.8	9.3	56 648	71.5	28.5	2.53	2.37
Clermont	25.2	69 226	95.4	4.6	0.4	1.3	7.0	66 013	74.7	25.3	2.81	2.27
Clinton	18.2	16 577	93.0	7.0	0.9	1.9	8.1	15 416	68.9	31.1	2.65	2.37
Columbiana	5.4	46 083	93.3	6.7	1.1	1.4	6.4	42 973	76.0	24.0	2.60	2.27
Coshocton	6.9	16 107	89.1	10.9	4.1	1.3	11.0	14 356	76.0	24.0	2.59	2.29
Crawford	3.1	20 178	93.9	6.1	0.5	1.4	7.6	18 957	72.6	27.4	2.50	2.31
Cuyahoga	1.5	616 903	92.6	7.4	0.4	1.4	9.4	571 457	63.2	36.8	2.56	2.09
Darke	4.9	21 583	94.6	5.4	0.5	1.6	6.0	20 419	76.6	23.4	2.62	2.39
Defiance	7.6	16 040	94.4	5.6	0.4	1.7	8.2	15 138	79.6	20.4	2.63	2.35
Delaware	71.6	42 374	93.6	6.4	0.5	2.3	10.2	39 674	80.4	19.6	2.83	2.17
Erie	9.7	35 909	88.4	11.6	6.0	1.6	9.3	31 727	72.0	28.0	2.55	2.18
Fairfield	23.4	47 922	94.8	5.2	1.0	1.4	6.2	45 425	76.3	23.7	2.75	2.31
Fayette	8.1	11 904	92.9	7.1	0.3	1.6	7.2	11 054	66.6	33.4	2.55	2.45
Franklin	15.9	471 016	93.2	6.8	0.4	1.7	8.2	438 778	56.9	43.1	2.56	2.15
Fulton	14.6	16 232	95.4	4.6	0.5	1.4	4.9	15 480	80.1	19.9	2.77	2.39
Gallia	6.1	13 498	89.3	10.7	2.4	1.7	8.5	12 060	74.9	25.1	2.54	2.36
Geauga	17.6	32 805	96.4	3.6	0.7	1.1	4.5	31 630	87.2	12.8	2.91	2.34
Greene	14.4	58 224	95.0	5.0	0.5	1.4	7.0	55 312	69.7	30.3	2.63	2.30
Guernsey	8.1	18 771	85.7	14.3	5.8	2.2	8.9	16 094	73.4	26.6	2.57	2.31
Hamilton	2.3	373 393	92.9	7.1	0.3	1.4	8.9	346 790	59.9	40.1	2.62	2.02
Hancock	13.2	29 785	93.7	6.3	0.6	1.8	7.9	27 898	73.1	26.9	2.61	2.19
Hardin	6.3	12 907	92.7	7.3	0.7	1.8	9.0	11 963	73.0	27.0	2.60	2.27
Harrison	4.7	7 680	83.3	16.7	9.1	2.1	7.7	6 398	77.6	22.4	2.47	2.33
Henry	5.1	11 622	94.1	5.9	0.5	1.9	6.4	10 935	80.5	19.5	2.67	2.39
Highland	17.8	17 583	88.6	11.4	4.4	1.8	7.9	15 587	75.3	24.7	2.64	2.47
Hocking	16.0	12 141	89.3	10.7	5.1	1.2	4.5	10 843	75.7	24.3	2.56	2.46
Holmes	21.7	12 280	92.3	7.7	3.2	1.0	5.7	11 337	77.0	23.0	3.51	2.83
Huron	10.2	23 594	94.5	5.5	0.8	1.4	5.9	22 307	72.2	27.8	2.73	2.41
Jackson	12.1	13 909	90.7	9.3	1.4	1.7	8.6	12 619	73.9	26.1	2.59	2.43
Jefferson	-2.9	33 291	91.4	8.6	0.5	1.5	8.9	30 417	74.3	25.7	2.43	2.15
Knox	15.9	21 793	91.7	8.3	2.7	1.7	7.3	19 975	75.7	24.3	2.63	2.31
Lake	11.5	93 487	95.9	4.1	0.6	1.1	6.1	89 700	77.5	22.5	2.61	2.12
Lawrence	8.0	27 189	91.0	9.0	0.9	1.7	10.2	24 732	74.8	25.2	2.53	2.40
Licking	17.7	58 760	94.6	5.4	0.7	1.6	6.2	55 609	74.4	25.6	2.66	2.27
Logan	12.6	21 571	83.2	16.8	10.8	2.3	7.6	17 956	75.6	24.4	2.57	2.39
Lorain	10.2	111 368	95.0	5.0	0.4	1.4	7.5	105 836	74.2	25.8	2.69	2.37
Lucas	3.0	196 259	93.2	6.8	0.3	1.4	8.3	182 847	65.4	34.6	2.59	2.15
Madison	14.0	14 399	95.0	5.0	0.5	1.5	6.3	13 672	72.3	27.7	2.68	2.45
Mahoning	1.4	111 762	91.8	8.2	0.6	1.9	9.7	102 587	72.8	27.2	2.56	2.13
Marion	4.7	26 298	93.5	6.5	0.2	1.9	8.1	24 578	72.9	27.1	2.57	2.33
Medina	30.5	56 793	96.0	4.0	0.5	1.1	6.7	54 542	81.3	18.7	2.87	2.19
Meigs	6.6	10 782	85.6	14.4	4.0	2.6	7.3	9 234	79.4	20.6	2.50	2.37
Mercer	10.1	15 875	93.0	7.0	2.9	1.3	7.0	14 756	80.1	19.9	2.86	2.24
Miami	11.2	40 554	94.8	5.2	0.3	1.5	6.9	38 437	72.3	27.7	2.62	2.32
Monroe	4.6	7 212	83.5	16.5	1.9	2.7	7.1	6 021	80.8	19.2	2.55	2.26
Montgomery	1.3	248 443	92.3	7.7	0.4	1.8	9.7	229 229	64.7	35.3	2.48	2.18
Morgan	13.9	7 771	75.8	24.2	17.2	1.9	9.5	5 890	78.3	21.7	2.51	2.45
Morrow	19.1	12 132	94.8	5.2	1.0	1.1	5.1	11 499	82.2	17.8	2.74	2.60
Muskingum	5.7	35 163	92.5	7.5	1.0	1.8	7.9	32 518	73.5	26.5	2.61	2.29
Noble	9.9	5 480	83.0	17.0	9.8	1.2	5.7	4 546	79.8	20.2	2.68	2.30

Table B. States and Counties

STATE/ County code	MSA/ PMSA/ NECMA code[1]	County type[2]	STATE County	Land area, 2000[3] (sq km)	Total persons	Rank	Per square kilometer	Land area, 1990[3] (sq km)	Total persons	Rank	Per square kilometer	White	Black or African American	American Indian or Alaska Native	Asian	Native Hawaiian and other Pacific Islander	Some other race
				1	2	3	4	5	6	7	8	9	10	11	12	13	14
			OHIO—Cont'd														
39 123	...	6	Ottawa	660	40 985	1 081	62.1	661	40 029	997	60.6	96.6	0.6	0.2	0.2	0.0	1.4
39 125	...	6	Paulding	1 078	20 293	1 774	18.8	1 078	20 488	1 654	19.0	95.9	1.0	0.3	0.2	0.0	1.4
39 127	...	6	Perry	1 061	34 078	1 278	32.1	1 062	31 557	1 229	29.7	98.5	0.2	0.3	0.1	0.0	0.1
39 129	1840	1	Pickaway	1 300	52 727	883	40.6	1 301	48 248	865	37.1	91.9	6.4	0.3	0.2	0.0	0.2
39 131	...	7	Pike	1 143	27 695	1 459	24.2	1 144	24 249	1 486	21.2	96.7	0.9	0.7	0.2	0.0	0.1
39 133	0080	2	Portage	1 275	152 061	353	119.3	1 275	142 585	333	111.8	94.4	3.2	0.2	0.8	0.0	0.2
39 135	...	6	Preble	1 100	42 337	1 049	38.5	1 100	40 113	996	36.5	98.5	0.3	0.2	0.3	0.0	0.1
39 137	...	6	Putnam	1 253	34 726	1 260	27.7	1 253	33 819	1 169	27.0	96.3	0.2	0.2	0.2	0.0	2.5
39 139	4800	3	Richland	1 287	128 852	419	100.1	1 287	126 137	367	98.0	88.2	9.4	0.2	0.5	0.0	0.4
39 141	...	4	Ross	1 783	73 345	682	41.1	1 783	69 330	639	38.9	91.7	6.2	0.3	0.4	0.0	0.2
39 143	...	4	Sandusky	1 060	61 792	785	58.3	1 060	61 963	703	58.5	92.2	2.7	0.1	0.3	0.0	3.1
39 145	...	4	Scioto	1 586	79 195	648	49.9	1 586	80 327	569	50.6	94.9	2.7	0.6	0.2	0.0	0.2
39 147	...	5	Seneca	1 426	58 683	817	41.2	1 426	59 733	725	41.9	95.0	1.8	0.2	0.4	0.0	1.4
39 149	...	6	Shelby	1 060	47 910	954	45.2	1 060	44 915	914	42.4	96.0	1.5	0.2	1.0	0.1	0.2
39 151	1320	2	Stark	1 492	378 098	155	253.4	1 492	367 585	140	246.4	90.3	7.2	0.2	0.5	0.0	0.3
39 153	0080	2	Summit	1 069	542 899	103	507.9	1 069	514 990	91	481.7	83.5	13.2	0.2	1.4	0.0	0.3
39 155	9320	2	Trumbull	1 597	225 116	252	141.0	1 595	227 795	216	142.8	90.2	7.9	0.1	0.5	0.0	0.2
39 157	...	4	Tuscarawas	1 470	90 914	567	61.8	1 470	84 090	544	57.2	97.9	0.7	0.2	0.2	0.0	0.2
39 159	...	6	Union	1 131	40 909	1 084	36.2	1 131	31 969	1 213	28.3	95.2	2.8	0.2	0.5	0.0	0.2
39 161	...	6	Van Wert	1 062	29 659	1 410	27.9	1 062	30 464	1 270	28.7	97.4	0.7	0.1	0.2	0.0	0.8
39 163	...	9	Vinton	1 072	12 806	2 246	11.9	1 073	11 098	2 284	10.3	98.1	0.4	0.5	0.1	0.0	0.1
39 165	1640	1	Warren	1 035	158 383	336	153.0	1 036	113 973	402	110.0	94.7	2.7	0.2	1.3	0.0	0.3
39 167	6020	3	Washington	1 645	63 251	767	38.5	1 645	62 254	700	37.8	97.3	0.9	0.2	0.4	0.0	0.1
39 169	...	4	Wayne	1 438	111 564	483	77.6	1 438	101 461	451	70.6	96.5	1.6	0.2	0.7	0.0	0.2
39 171	...	7	Williams	1 092	39 188	1 133	35.9	1 092	36 956	1 073	33.8	96.5	0.7	0.2	0.2	0.0	1.2
39 173	8400	2	Wood	1 599	121 065	448	75.7	1 599	113 269	406	70.8	94.8	1.3	0.2	1.0	0.0	1.5
39 175	...	7	Wyandot	1 051	22 908	1 648	21.8	1 051	22 254	1 566	21.2	97.9	0.1	0.1	0.5	0.0	0.7
40 000	...		OKLAHOMA	177 847	3 450 654	X	19.4	177 878	3 145 576	X	17.7	76.2	7.6	7.9	1.4	0.1	2.4
40 001	...	6	Adair	1 491	21 038	1 733	14.1	1 491	18 421	1 768	12.4	48.5	0.2	42.5	0.1	0.0	1.2
40 003	...	8	Alfalfa	2 245	6 105	2 769	2.7	2 245	6 416	2 715	2.9	89.4	4.2	2.7	0.1	0.0	1.4
40 005	...	7	Atoka	2 534	13 879	2 168	5.5	2 534	12 778	2 158	5.0	75.9	5.9	11.4	0.2	0.0	0.6
40 007	...	9	Beaver	4 699	5 857	2 798	1.2	4 699	6 023	2 754	1.3	92.7	0.3	1.2	0.1	0.0	3.8
40 009	...	7	Beckham	2 336	19 799	1 800	8.5	2 336	18 812	1 746	8.1	87.1	5.5	2.6	0.4	0.0	2.2
40 011	...	6	Blaine	2 405	11 976	2 295	5.0	2 405	11 470	2 257	4.8	76.3	6.7	8.7	0.7	0.8	2.9
40 013	...	6	Bryan	2 354	36 534	1 201	15.5	2 354	32 089	1 209	13.6	80.0	1.4	12.2	0.4	0.0	1.1
40 015	...	6	Caddo	3 311	30 150	1 391	9.1	3 311	29 550	1 315	8.9	65.5	2.9	24.3	0.2	0.0	2.7
40 017	5880	2	Canadian	2 330	87 697	598	37.6	2 331	74 409	603	31.9	87.0	2.2	4.3	2.4	0.0	1.4
40 019	...	5	Carter	2 134	45 621	989	21.4	2 134	42 919	939	20.1	77.9	7.6	8.3	0.6	0.0	1.1
40 021	...	6	Cherokee	1 945	42 521	1 045	21.9	1 945	34 049	1 162	17.5	56.4	1.2	32.4	0.3	0.0	2.1
40 023	...	7	Choctaw	2 004	15 342	2 066	7.7	2 005	15 302	1 973	7.6	68.6	10.9	15.0	0.2	0.0	0.5
40 025	...	9	Cimarron	4 753	3 148	2 982	0.7	4 753	3 301	2 977	0.7	85.8	0.6	1.0	0.2	0.0	9.9
40 027	5880	2	Cleveland	1 389	208 016	267	149.8	1 389	174 253	277	125.5	83.6	3.6	4.4	2.8	0.0	1.4
40 029	...	9	Coal	1 342	6 031	2 777	4.5	1 342	5 780	2 781	4.3	75.2	0.4	17.3	0.3	0.0	0.7
40 031	4200	3	Comanche	2 770	114 996	471	41.5	2 770	111 486	412	40.2	65.2	19.0	5.1	2.1	0.4	3.5
40 033	...	6	Cotton	1 649	6 614	2 726	4.0	1 649	6 651	2 689	4.0	84.7	2.9	7.4	0.1	0.0	1.8
40 035	...	6	Craig	1 971	14 950	2 095	7.6	1 971	14 104	2 047	7.2	68.5	3.1	16.3	0.2	0.0	0.5
40 037	8560	2	Creek	2 475	67 367	727	27.2	2 475	60 915	715	24.6	82.3	2.6	9.1	0.3	0.0	0.6
40 039	...	7	Custer	2 555	26 142	1 511	10.2	2 555	26 897	1 393	10.5	81.4	2.9	5.8	0.9	0.0	5.8
40 041	...	6	Delaware	1 918	37 077	1 187	19.3	1 919	28 070	1 350	14.6	70.2	0.1	22.3	0.2	0.0	0.6
40 043	...	9	Dewey	2 590	4 743	2 864	1.8	2 591	5 551	2 797	2.1	92.2	0.1	4.6	0.1	0.0	0.7
40 045	...	9	Ellis	3 183	4 075	2 912	1.3	3 184	4 497	2 875	1.4	96.3	0.0	1.2	0.1	0.0	0.7
40 047	2340	3	Garfield	2 741	57 813	826	21.1	2 742	56 735	768	20.7	88.7	3.3	2.1	0.8	0.5	2.0
40 049	...	6	Garvin	2 091	27 210	1 475	13.0	2 096	26 605	1 403	12.7	84.9	2.6	7.4	0.2	0.0	1.5
40 051	...	6	Grady	2 851	45 516	991	16.0	2 852	41 747	962	14.6	87.3	3.1	4.8	0.3	0.0	1.1
40 053	...	8	Grant	2 591	5 144	2 841	2.0	2 592	5 689	2 785	2.2	95.3	0.1	2.4	0.1	0.0	0.7
40 055	...	7	Greer	1 656	6 061	2 774	3.7	1 656	6 559	2 702	4.0	81.5	8.8	2.5	0.3	0.0	4.0
40 057	...	7	Harmon	1 393	3 283	2 974	2.4	1 393	3 793	2 930	2.7	72.6	9.8	1.1	0.2	0.0	14.3
40 059	...	9	Harper	2 691	3 562	2 948	1.3	2 691	4 063	2 911	1.5	95.9	0.0	0.9	0.1	0.0	2.4
40 061	...	6	Haskell	1 495	11 792	2 308	7.9	1 495	10 940	2 298	7.3	78.2	0.6	14.6	0.3	0.0	0.4
40 063	...	7	Hughes	2 089	14 154	2 150	6.8	2 090	13 014	2 140	6.2	72.8	4.5	16.2	0.2	0.0	1.0
40 065	...	5	Jackson	2 079	28 439	1 432	13.7	2 079	28 764	1 337	13.8	76.1	8.0	1.7	1.2	0.2	9.3
40 067	...	9	Jefferson	1 965	6 818	2 709	3.5	1 965	7 010	2 657	3.6	87.1	0.7	5.2	1.1	0.0	2.9
40 069	...	7	Johnston	1 669	10 513	2 397	6.3	1 669	10 032	2 384	6.0	76.1	1.7	15.3	0.3	0.0	1.2
40 071	...	5	Kay	2 379	48 080	949	20.2	2 380	48 056	869	20.2	84.2	1.8	7.5	0.5	0.0	2.0
40 073	...	6	Kingfisher	2 339	13 926	2 166	6.0	2 339	13 212	2 121	5.6	88.1	1.6	3.0	0.2	0.0	4.3

[1] MSA = Metropolitan Statistical Area. PMSA = Primary MSA. NECMA = New England County Metropolitan Area. See Appendix A for explanation of these concepts. See Appendix B for list of metropolitan areas identified by type, with component counties.
[2] County typology code from the Economic Research Service of USDA. See Appendix A for definition.
[3] Dry land or land partially or temporarily covered by water.

Table B. States and Counties

STATE County	Population and population characteristics, 2000 (cont'd)								Population and population characteristics, 1990				
	Race (percent) (cont'd)								Race (percent)				
	Race alone or in combination												
	Two or more races	White	Black	American Indian or Alaska Native	Asian	Native Hawaiian and other Pacific Islander	Some other race	Hispanic[1]	White	Black or African American	American Indian or Alaska Native	Asian and Pacific Islander	Hispanic[1]
	15	16	17	18	19	20	21	22	23	24	25	26	27
OHIO—Cont'd													
Ottawa	0.9	97.4	0.9	0.5	0.3	0.1	1.8	3.7	97.5	0.7	0.1	0.2	3.7
Paulding	1.3	97.1	1.3	0.8	0.2	0.0	1.9	3.0	97.2	1.2	0.3	0.1	3.1
Perry	0.8	99.3	0.4	0.7	0.2	0.1	0.3	0.4	99.5	0.2	0.1	0.1	0.3
Pickaway	0.9	92.8	6.7	0.8	0.3	0.1	0.2	0.6	93.0	6.3	0.3	0.2	0.7
Pike	1.4	98.1	1.2	1.7	0.3	0.1	0.2	0.6	98.2	1.3	0.3	0.2	0.3
Portage	1.2	95.5	3.6	0.7	1.0	0.0	0.4	0.7	96.1	2.7	0.2	0.8	0.6
Preble	0.6	99.1	0.5	0.6	0.3	0.0	0.2	0.4	99.3	0.4	0.1	0.2	0.3
Putnam	0.7	97.0	0.3	0.3	0.2	0.0	2.9	4.4	98.2	0.1	0.1	0.1	4.2
Richland	1.3	89.3	10.1	0.7	0.7	0.1	0.6	0.9	91.2	7.9	0.2	0.5	0.7
Ross	1.2	92.9	6.7	0.9	0.5	0.1	0.3	0.6	92.8	6.4	0.2	0.4	0.5
Sandusky	1.6	93.7	3.3	0.4	0.4	0.0	3.8	7.0	94.1	2.5	0.2	0.2	5.7
Scioto	1.3	96.1	3.0	1.5	0.4	0.1	0.3	0.6	96.2	3.1	0.5	0.2	0.3
Seneca	1.2	96.2	2.3	0.5	0.5	0.0	1.8	3.4	96.2	2.0	0.2	0.4	2.8
Shelby	1.0	97.0	2.0	0.5	1.2	0.1	0.4	0.8	97.5	1.4	0.1	0.9	0.4
Stark	1.4	91.6	8.0	0.7	0.7	0.0	0.5	0.9	92.3	6.8	0.3	0.4	0.7
Summit	1.4	84.7	13.9	0.7	1.7	0.1	0.6	0.9	86.8	11.9	0.2	1.0	0.6
Trumbull	1.1	91.2	8.4	0.5	0.6	0.0	0.4	0.8	92.6	6.7	0.1	0.4	0.6
Tuscarawas	0.7	98.6	1.0	0.5	0.3	0.1	0.3	0.7	98.8	0.7	0.2	0.2	0.3
Union	1.0	96.2	3.1	0.6	0.7	0.0	0.4	0.8	95.6	3.7	0.2	0.4	0.5
Van Wert	0.8	98.2	1.0	0.3	0.3	0.0	1.0	1.6	98.1	0.6	0.1	0.3	1.6
Vinton	1.0	99.0	0.4	1.2	0.2	0.0	0.1	0.5	99.8	0.0	0.1	0.0	0.3
Warren	0.8	95.4	3.0	0.5	1.5	0.1	0.5	1.0	97.0	2.1	0.2	0.6	0.5
Washington	0.9	98.2	1.3	0.7	0.6	0.1	0.2	0.5	98.2	1.2	0.2	0.3	0.4
Wayne	0.8	97.3	1.9	0.5	0.8	0.0	0.4	0.8	97.7	1.5	0.1	0.5	0.4
Williams	0.8	97.3	0.9	0.6	0.6	0.0	1.5	2.7	98.4	0.1	0.1	0.3	2.2
Wood	1.2	95.9	1.5	0.6	1.3	0.1	1.9	3.3	96.5	1.0	0.2	0.9	2.5
Wyandot	0.6	98.5	0.2	0.3	0.7	0.0	1.0	1.5	99.2	0.1	0.1	0.3	0.7
OKLAHOMA	4.5	80.3	8.3	11.4	1.7	0.1	3.0	5.2	82.1	7.4	8.0	1.1	2.7
Adair	7.5	55.6	0.3	49.6	0.2	0.1	1.8	3.1	55.6	0.0	43.8	0.1	1.3
Alfalfa	2.1	91.3	4.5	4.5	0.2	0.1	1.7	2.9	93.1	3.2	2.6	0.1	1.6
Atoka	6.1	81.7	6.2	16.9	0.4	0.0	1.0	1.4	81.1	5.9	12.4	0.1	0.9
Beaver	1.9	94.5	0.4	2.4	0.2	0.0	4.4	10.8	95.3	0.0	1.0	0.0	5.0
Beckham	2.2	89.1	5.9	4.1	0.5	0.1	2.7	5.4	93.4	2.0	1.9	0.2	4.2
Blaine	4.0	79.1	7.5	11.0	1.5	1.8	3.4	6.6	85.2	4.4	8.7	0.2	2.5
Bryan	4.8	84.7	1.7	16.5	0.6	0.1	1.4	2.6	83.5	1.3	14.2	0.4	1.4
Caddo	4.4	69.2	3.8	27.8	0.4	0.1	3.3	6.3	72.0	2.5	22.6	0.2	4.8
Canadian	2.7	89.6	2.5	6.2	2.7	0.1	1.8	3.9	90.7	2.4	4.2	1.6	2.6
Carter	4.4	81.7	8.5	12.1	0.8	0.1	1.5	2.8	82.0	8.3	8.5	0.4	1.8
Cherokee	7.6	63.6	1.6	39.4	0.5	0.1	2.6	4.1	64.8	1.1	33.4	0.2	1.4
Choctaw	4.9	72.7	11.7	19.4	0.3	0.1	0.9	1.6	71.4	12.8	15.2	0.2	1.3
Cimarron	2.5	88.3	0.7	2.1	0.2	0.0	11.2	15.4	92.6	0.0	1.0	0.4	12.5
Cleveland	4.2	87.5	4.2	7.2	3.4	0.1	1.9	4.0	88.5	3.0	5.1	2.3	2.7
Coal	6.1	81.0	0.6	22.9	0.5	0.0	1.1	2.1	82.3	0.8	16.5	0.0	0.7
Comanche	4.7	69.0	20.6	7.0	3.2	0.7	4.6	8.4	71.5	17.9	4.6	2.7	6.2
Cotton	3.1	87.4	3.1	9.7	0.3	0.2	2.5	4.9	87.4	2.1	7.9	0.1	3.5
Craig	11.4	79.4	3.9	27.0	0.4	0.1	0.8	1.2	77.0	3.4	19.1	0.2	0.7
Creek	5.2	87.2	3.0	13.6	0.4	0.1	0.9	1.9	87.9	3.1	8.4	0.2	1.1
Custer	3.2	84.1	3.5	7.8	1.1	0.1	6.7	9.0	85.1	3.5	6.2	0.6	6.0
Delaware	6.5	76.6	0.3	28.5	0.3	0.1	0.9	1.8	74.3	0.1	25.3	0.2	0.8
Dewey	2.3	94.3	0.3	6.5	0.1	0.0	1.0	2.7	93.4	0.1	5.7	0.1	1.3
Ellis	1.6	97.9	0.3	2.2	0.1	0.1	1.0	2.6	96.8	0.1	1.5	0.2	3.1
Garfield	2.6	91.0	3.8	3.6	1.2	0.6	2.5	4.1	92.4	3.6	2.2	1.0	1.9
Garvin	3.3	88.0	2.9	10.2	0.4	0.1	1.8	3.4	89.4	2.7	7.1	0.2	1.2
Grady	3.3	90.4	3.4	7.4	0.6	0.1	1.5	2.9	90.1	3.7	5.2	0.3	1.7
Grant	1.3	96.5	0.2	3.4	0.3	0.1	0.9	1.8	97.8	0.1	1.3	0.2	1.0
Greer	3.0	84.0	9.4	4.5	0.4	0.0	4.8	7.4	87.1	6.9	2.2	0.2	5.1
Harmon	1.9	74.4	10.0	1.9	0.3	0.1	15.3	22.8	75.2	7.6	1.0	0.2	17.3
Harper	0.7	96.5	0.0	1.3	0.1	0.1	2.6	5.6	97.8	0.1	0.7	0.1	1.8
Haskell	5.8	83.7	1.0	20.1	0.5	0.1	0.8	1.5	84.2	0.9	14.6	0.1	0.7
Hughes	5.4	77.8	4.8	21.2	0.4	0.1	1.2	2.5	79.5	2.9	17.1	0.1	1.0
Jackson	3.4	79.0	8.8	3.0	1.7	0.3	10.8	15.6	80.2	9.4	1.8	1.4	11.6
Jefferson	2.9	89.8	0.8	7.7	1.2	0.1	3.3	7.0	90.4	0.6	4.9	0.3	4.4
Johnston	5.4	81.3	2.1	20.1	0.4	0.1	1.5	2.5	81.5	2.1	15.8	0.1	1.2
Kay	4.0	87.9	2.1	10.8	0.8	0.1	2.5	4.3	89.4	1.8	7.6	0.5	1.8
Kingfisher	2.7	90.7	1.9	5.1	0.3	0.0	4.9	6.9	92.3	2.3	2.7	0.1	3.1

[1] Hispanic persons may be of any race.

Table B. States and Counties

| STATE County | Population and population characteristics, 2000 Age (percent) | | | | | | | | | | |
	Under 5 years	5 to 17 years	18 to 24 years	25 to 34 years	35 to 44 years	45 to 54 years	55 to 64 years	65 to 74 years	75 years and over	Median age (years)	Percent Female
	28	29	30	31	32	33	34	35	36	37	38
OHIO—Cont'd											
Ottawa	5.2	18.0	6.7	10.8	16.1	15.4	11.4	8.8	7.6	41.0	50.6
Paulding	6.6	20.2	8.6	12.3	15.7	14.2	9.8	6.7	5.9	36.5	50.8
Perry	7.4	20.8	8.5	13.4	15.7	13.5	8.9	6.6	5.5	35.0	50.3
Pickaway	5.9	18.3	9.0	14.9	17.7	13.9	9.5	6.2	4.7	36.0	45.0
Pike	6.9	20.3	8.9	13.5	15.4	12.3	9.2	7.1	6.4	35.3	51.2
Portage	6.1	17.6	14.3	12.7	15.9	13.7	8.7	6.2	4.7	34.4	51.2
Preble	6.3	19.7	7.7	12.4	16.3	14.5	10.0	7.2	5.9	37.5	50.2
Putnam	7.3	22.4	8.3	11.9	16.2	12.6	8.0	6.7	6.6	35.0	50.4
Richland	6.4	18.4	8.4	12.9	15.7	14.2	9.9	7.7	6.4	37.7	49.7
Ross	6.2	17.8	8.6	14.4	17.2	14.1	9.5	6.7	5.5	36.9	48.0
Sandusky	6.5	19.7	8.1	12.4	15.9	13.9	9.1	7.4	7.0	37.3	51.1
Scioto	6.3	18.1	9.6	13.6	14.7	13.0	9.7	8.0	6.9	36.7	51.2
Seneca	6.2	19.7	10.4	11.7	15.5	13.9	8.5	7.5	6.6	36.3	50.5
Shelby	7.6	21.0	8.2	13.5	15.8	13.2	8.5	6.2	6.0	34.8	50.4
Stark	6.4	18.5	8.3	12.2	15.6	14.4	9.5	7.7	7.4	38.2	52.0
Summit	6.6	18.4	8.2	13.4	16.2	14.3	8.7	7.3	6.8	37.2	51.8
Trumbull	6.1	18.2	7.7	12.2	15.1	14.7	10.1	8.2	7.6	39.0	51.6
Tuscarawas	6.6	18.8	8.0	12.4	15.7	14.1	9.5	7.7	7.2	37.9	51.3
Union	7.6	20.0	7.5	15.7	18.3	13.3	7.9	5.3	4.3	34.5	52.2
Van Wert	6.4	19.7	8.3	11.9	15.3	13.6	9.3	7.8	7.7	37.6	51.2
Vinton	7.2	19.7	8.8	13.5	15.5	13.4	9.7	7.1	5.0	35.5	50.2
Warren	7.8	19.9	7.1	14.8	19.2	13.8	8.0	5.4	4.0	35.2	49.4
Washington	5.8	17.7	8.8	11.7	15.8	14.7	10.5	8.0	6.9	39.1	51.4
Wayne	7.0	20.4	9.8	12.2	15.7	13.7	9.0	6.5	5.7	35.4	50.6
Williams	6.4	19.8	8.3	12.6	16.1	13.4	9.5	6.8	7.0	36.9	50.3
Wood	5.8	17.9	17.2	12.0	14.9	13.5	7.7	5.8	5.3	32.6	51.6
Wyandot	6.5	19.4	8.2	12.5	15.4	13.4	9.3	7.9	7.6	37.4	51.3
OKLAHOMA	6.8	19.0	10.3	13.1	15.2	13.1	9.2	7.0	6.2	35.5	50.9
Adair	7.5	22.7	8.9	13.3	13.9	12.3	9.3	6.7	5.3	33.2	50.7
Alfalfa	4.5	14.9	6.4	10.9	17.8	13.3	11.8	9.9	10.5	42.3	43.3
Atoka	5.9	17.7	8.2	13.1	16.0	13.8	10.5	7.8	6.9	38.3	45.9
Beaver	5.7	21.1	6.5	10.2	15.5	13.7	10.4	8.7	8.2	39.3	49.5
Beckham	6.2	17.9	9.8	13.7	15.9	12.7	8.3	7.6	7.8	36.6	47.7
Blaine	5.7	18.3	9.1	13.1	15.5	12.2	9.2	8.0	8.8	37.6	45.6
Bryan	6.5	18.3	11.7	12.4	13.2	12.6	9.7	8.0	7.4	35.8	51.3
Caddo	6.6	21.9	8.5	11.5	14.5	12.4	9.6	7.8	7.2	36.0	50.4
Canadian	6.8	21.3	8.2	13.1	17.6	14.6	8.9	5.5	4.1	35.4	50.1
Carter	6.9	19.3	7.9	11.7	15.1	13.6	9.6	8.4	7.6	38.0	51.9
Cherokee	7.0	19.3	14.6	12.2	13.6	12.2	9.3	6.8	5.2	32.3	50.9
Choctaw	6.4	19.6	7.8	11.4	13.3	13.1	11.0	8.7	8.7	38.7	52.5
Cimarron	6.6	21.0	6.4	10.1	13.3	13.2	10.8	8.4	10.2	39.3	50.7
Cleveland	6.3	18.2	14.7	14.6	16.2	13.6	8.1	4.9	3.5	32.2	49.8
Coal	6.6	20.0	7.7	11.5	13.8	12.7	9.8	9.5	8.4	38.1	50.9
Comanche	7.9	19.8	13.9	15.5	15.2	10.7	7.2	5.6	4.1	30.1	48.2
Cotton	6.6	18.8	7.4	12.1	14.6	12.3	10.5	8.3	9.4	38.6	50.4
Craig	6.0	17.9	7.8	11.6	16.3	13.3	11.0	8.5	7.7	39.3	49.7
Creek	6.8	20.6	8.0	12.0	15.3	14.1	10.4	7.2	5.7	36.9	51.0
Custer	6.1	18.2	17.4	10.8	13.7	11.7	8.4	6.8	7.0	32.7	51.3
Delaware	6.1	18.3	6.9	10.8	13.5	13.5	13.2	10.1	7.4	40.8	50.9
Dewey	4.8	18.5	7.1	8.5	14.5	13.6	12.1	8.9	12.1	43.0	51.3
Ellis	4.9	16.8	6.0	8.8	12.9	16.6	12.0	9.7	12.3	45.3	50.6
Garfield	6.7	18.3	9.1	12.1	15.3	13.0	9.4	7.9	8.1	37.7	51.6
Garvin	6.5	18.4	8.1	11.7	14.3	12.6	10.5	8.9	9.0	39.0	51.9
Grady	6.8	19.8	9.3	11.8	15.9	13.3	9.9	7.0	6.1	36.5	51.2
Grant	5.1	20.1	6.5	9.3	14.8	12.7	10.1	10.8	10.7	41.4	51.4
Greer	4.7	15.3	9.1	13.5	15.0	12.8	9.6	9.3	10.8	40.0	44.7
Harmon	6.1	19.8	7.9	10.1	14.0	12.3	8.8	8.9	12.1	39.9	51.5
Harper	4.7	18.6	6.4	8.5	14.9	14.3	10.9	11.5	10.2	43.1	50.9
Haskell	6.8	19.2	8.1	11.3	13.1	13.0	11.3	9.0	8.2	38.6	51.1
Hughes	5.8	17.4	8.0	12.6	14.5	13.1	10.1	9.3	9.3	39.3	48.6
Jackson	8.2	21.0	10.3	13.7	15.3	11.6	8.0	6.2	5.7	33.0	50.2
Jefferson	6.1	17.8	7.2	11.7	13.7	12.7	10.6	10.0	10.2	40.4	51.4
Johnston	6.3	19.2	9.7	10.9	14.2	13.6	10.7	8.2	7.2	38.0	50.8
Kay	6.8	19.6	8.8	10.6	14.4	13.3	9.5	8.4	8.6	38.1	51.6
Kingfisher	6.2	21.0	8.2	10.4	16.5	13.1	9.3	7.8	7.5	38.0	51.3

Table B. States and Counties

STATE County	Under 5 years	5 to 17 years	18 to 24 years	25 to 34 years	35 to 44 years	45 to 54 years	55 to 64 years	65 to 74 years	75 years and over	Percent Female	2000	1990	1980	1990–2000	1980–1990
	39	40	41	42	43	44	45	46	47	48	49	50	51	52	53
OHIO—Cont'd															
Ottawa	6.2	18.7	8.1	14.9	15.0	11.1	10.5	9.5	6.0	51.1	40 985	40 029	40 076	2.4	-0.1
Paulding	7.7	22.1	9.3	15.5	14.5	10.7	8.2	7.0	4.9	50.8	20 293	20 488	21 302	-1.0	-3.8
Perry	7.5	21.5	9.4	15.9	14.1	10.0	8.6	7.4	5.5	51.2	34 078	31 557	31 032	8.0	1.7
Pickaway	6.6	17.6	10.7	19.1	16.2	11.4	8.4	6.1	3.9	45.2	52 727	48 248	43 662	9.3	10.5
Pike	7.2	21.6	9.3	15.2	13.8	10.3	9.0	7.5	6.0	51.3	27 695	24 249	22 802	14.2	6.3
Portage	6.6	18.0	17.5	16.1	14.5	9.9	8.1	5.8	3.6	51.3	152 061	142 585	135 856	6.6	5.0
Preble	7.1	20.5	8.9	15.6	15.3	11.1	9.2	7.5	4.8	50.7	42 337	40 113	38 223	5.5	4.9
Putnam	8.7	22.9	9.1	16.3	13.5	9.1	8.2	6.7	5.5	50.2	34 726	33 819	32 991	2.7	2.5
Richland	6.9	19.2	9.4	15.5	14.8	11.3	9.8	7.7	5.2	51.0	128 852	126 137	131 205	2.2	-3.9
Ross	6.4	18.6	9.4	17.9	15.5	11.0	8.9	7.4	5.0	47.9	73 345	69 330	65 004	5.8	6.7
Sandusky	7.3	20.7	9.1	16.0	14.5	9.8	9.2	7.7	5.7	51.0	61 792	61 963	63 267	-0.3	-2.1
Scioto	6.6	20.1	9.2	15.3	13.8	10.3	9.8	8.3	6.6	51.5	79 195	80 327	84 545	-1.4	-5.0
Seneca	7.2	21.3	10.3	15.3	14.3	9.4	8.9	7.6	5.8	51.3	58 683	59 733	61 901	-1.8	-3.5
Shelby	8.0	21.9	9.2	16.6	14.5	9.9	8.3	6.6	5.0	50.1	47 910	44 915	43 089	6.7	4.2
Stark	6.9	18.3	9.4	15.5	15.2	10.7	9.6	8.6	5.8	52.1	378 098	367 585	378 823	2.9	-3.0
Summit	7.0	17.4	10.2	16.6	15.4	10.1	9.5	8.3	5.5	52.1	542 899	514 990	524 472	5.4	-1.8
Trumbull	6.7	18.5	9.2	14.7	15.2	11.2	10.1	9.0	5.4	52.1	225 116	227 795	241 863	-1.2	-5.8
Tuscarawas	7.0	19.3	8.3	15.4	14.8	10.5	9.7	8.5	6.4	52.2	90 914	84 090	84 614	8.1	-0.6
Union	7.3	19.4	9.2	18.2	16.1	10.6	8.1	6.3	4.8	53.4	40 909	31 969	29 536	28.0	8.2
Van Wert	7.2	20.5	8.4	15.6	14.4	9.8	9.2	8.2	6.8	51.4	29 659	30 464	30 458	-2.6	0.0
Vinton	7.1	20.6	9.5	15.0	14.1	10.5	9.3	7.8	6.0	50.9	12 806	11 098	11 584	15.4	-4.2
Warren	7.7	19.2	8.9	18.7	16.9	11.2	8.3	5.4	3.6	49.5	158 383	113 973	99 276	39.0	14.8
Washington	6.5	19.2	9.8	15.2	15.0	11.1	9.6	7.8	5.9	51.8	63 251	62 254	64 266	1.6	-3.1
Wayne	7.9	20.5	10.4	15.9	15.0	10.3	8.4	6.6	5.0	51.0	111 564	101 461	97 408	10.0	4.2
Williams	7.5	20.8	8.6	16.3	14.4	10.3	8.4	7.7	6.0	50.9	39 188	36 956	36 369	6.0	1.6
Wood	6.4	17.9	19.2	15.3	14.4	9.2	7.5	5.9	4.3	52.0	121 065	113 269	107 372	6.9	5.5
Wyandot	7.2	20.3	8.6	15.4	13.8	10.4	9.6	7.8	6.9	51.9	22 908	22 254	22 651	2.9	-1.8
OKLAHOMA	7.2	19.4	10.2	16.2	14.4	10.3	8.9	7.5	6.0	51.3	3 450 654	3 145 576	3 025 487	9.7	4.0
Adair	7.8	22.9	9.7	14.4	12.9	10.2	8.6	7.7	5.9	50.9	21 038	18 421	18 575	14.2	-0.8
Alfalfa	5.2	15.9	7.4	14.9	12.0	11.0	10.9	10.8	12.0	47.4	6 105	6 416	7 077	-4.8	-9.3
Atoka	6.3	19.7	8.7	15.7	13.7	10.5	10.0	8.6	6.8	47.5	13 879	12 778	12 748	8.6	0.2
Beaver	6.2	21.5	6.2	13.8	14.0	11.1	10.3	9.0	7.9	50.8	5 857	6 023	6 806	-2.8	-11.5
Beckham	7.4	20.7	7.6	15.2	12.9	9.2	9.0	8.6	9.4	52.2	19 799	18 812	19 243	5.2	-2.2
Blaine	7.2	20.4	7.5	13.7	12.3	10.0	9.5	9.6	9.7	52.0	11 976	11 470	13 443	4.4	-14.7
Bryan	6.7	18.5	12.0	13.4	12.8	10.2	9.4	9.1	8.0	52.0	36 534	32 089	30 535	13.9	5.1
Caddo	7.5	21.0	8.3	14.1	12.8	10.2	9.5	8.4	8.3	51.6	30 150	29 550	30 905	2.0	-4.4
Canadian	7.7	22.5	7.9	17.7	17.5	11.2	7.2	4.6	3.7	49.9	87 697	74 409	56 452	17.9	31.8
Carter	7.0	20.3	7.5	14.8	14.1	10.0	9.8	8.6	7.9	52.1	45 621	42 919	43 610	6.3	-1.6
Cherokee	7.2	19.9	12.7	14.6	12.9	9.9	9.0	7.8	5.9	51.5	42 521	34 049	30 684	24.9	11.0
Choctaw	7.2	20.9	7.9	12.9	12.4	10.0	10.2	10.0	8.6	52.5	15 342	15 302	17 203	0.3	-11.1
Cimarron	6.7	20.8	6.8	12.2	14.0	10.1	10.1	10.4	8.8	50.3	3 148	3 301	3 648	-4.6	-9.5
Cleveland	7.1	19.3	14.8	19.1	16.3	10.2	6.5	4.1	2.6	49.7	208 016	174 253	133 173	19.4	30.8
Coal	6.2	20.4	8.0	13.5	13.0	10.0	10.2	9.3	9.5	52.1	6 031	5 780	6 041	4.3	-4.3
Comanche	8.5	19.8	15.5	19.0	13.1	8.4	7.1	5.2	3.5	48.1	114 996	111 486	112 456	3.1	-0.9
Cotton	6.1	19.4	8.0	13.8	12.1	10.8	9.8	10.0	10.0	52.7	6 614	6 651	7 338	-0.6	-9.4
Craig	5.9	17.5	7.8	14.4	14.1	12.1	10.5	9.5	8.1	51.3	14 950	14 104	15 014	6.0	-6.1
Creek	7.3	20.8	8.6	14.6	15.0	11.6	9.1	7.2	5.7	51.4	67 367	60 915	59 016	10.6	3.2
Custer	7.2	19.3	16.3	15.3	12.4	8.7	7.5	6.7	6.6	51.2	26 142	26 897	25 995	-2.8	3.5
Delaware	6.2	18.0	7.8	12.0	12.0	11.4	12.5	12.2	7.9	51.4	37 077	28 070	23 946	32.1	17.2
Dewey	6.3	20.0	5.8	14.0	12.2	10.4	9.6	10.2	11.5	51.6	4 743	5 551	5 922	-14.6	-6.3
Ellis	5.5	20.7	4.8	11.5	14.8	10.4	9.6	11.2	11.6	51.2	4 075	4 497	5 596	-9.4	-19.6
Garfield	6.9	19.3	8.7	16.3	13.9	10.1	9.3	8.1	7.3	52.0	57 813	56 735	62 820	1.9	-9.7
Garvin	6.1	19.3	7.8	14.1	12.5	10.1	10.3	9.9	9.9	52.5	27 210	26 605	27 856	2.3	-4.5
Grady	7.1	21.2	8.6	15.6	14.2	11.1	8.6	7.0	6.5	51.9	45 516	41 747	39 490	9.0	5.7
Grant	6.8	18.4	5.4	13.5	12.7	9.3	11.1	11.0	11.8	52.5	5 144	5 689	6 518	-9.6	-12.7
Greer	5.0	15.0	8.8	14.9	12.0	9.8	10.2	11.4	13.0	47.8	6 061	6 559	7 028	-7.6	-6.7
Harmon	6.8	20.6	7.5	11.9	10.6	8.7	9.9	11.3	12.6	52.3	3 283	3 793	4 519	-13.4	-16.1
Harper	5.6	19.8	4.8	13.2	13.5	10.5	11.9	9.9	10.8	50.8	3 562	4 063	4 715	-12.3	-13.8
Haskell	6.1	19.8	7.8	12.5	13.0	10.9	10.9	10.6	8.3	51.7	11 792	10 940	11 010	7.8	-0.6
Hughes	5.6	18.9	7.1	11.7	12.2	10.6	11.2	11.1	11.6	53.0	14 154	13 014	14 338	8.8	-9.2
Jackson	9.1	20.4	12.0	17.6	12.9	8.7	7.2	6.4	5.7	50.4	28 439	28 764	30 356	-1.1	-5.2
Jefferson	5.9	18.8	7.6	12.8	12.9	9.7	10.4	10.4	11.5	52.5	6 818	7 010	8 294	-2.7	-15.5
Johnston	6.2	20.5	10.0	13.0	13.0	10.5	9.5	9.2	8.2	51.3	10 513	10 032	10 356	4.8	-3.1
Kay	7.1	19.5	8.0	14.5	14.0	10.0	9.4	9.2	8.3	51.8	48 080	48 056	49 852	0.0	-3.6
Kingfisher	7.2	21.5	6.8	16.1	13.2	10.2	9.2	8.1	7.8	51.5	13 926	13 212	14 187	5.4	-6.9

Table B. States and Counties

STATE County	Total population	Total in households	House-holder	Spouse	Child Total	Child Own child under 18 years	Other relatives Total	Other relatives Under 18 years	Nonrelatives Total	Nonrelatives Unmarried partner	Total in group quarters	Institutionalized population Correctional institutions	Institutionalized population Nursing homes	Institutionalized population Other institutions	Noninstitutionalized population College dormitories	Noninstitutionalized population Military quarters	Other
	54	55	56	57	58	59	60	61	62	63	64	65	66	67	68	69	70
OHIO—Cont'd																	
Ottawa	40 985	98.4	40.2	23.7	28.3	21.6	3.0	1.3	3.3	1.8	1.6	0.2	0.9	0.3	0.0	0.0	0.1
Paulding	20 293	99.4	38.3	23.3	31.6	24.8	2.8	1.4	3.4	1.8	0.6	0.0	0.4	0.0	0.0	0.0	0.2
Perry	34 078	99.1	36.7	22.1	32.7	25.7	3.6	1.7	4.1	2.3	0.9	0.0	0.5	0.0	0.0	0.0	0.3
Pickaway	52 727	87.7	33.4	20.5	27.1	21.7	3.1	1.5	3.5	2.0	12.3	11.0	0.6	0.3	0.1	0.0	0.4
Pike	27 695	98.3	37.7	21.4	31.1	24.6	4.0	1.9	4.0	2.3	1.7	0.0	1.3	0.2	0.0	0.0	0.2
Portage	152 061	95.0	37.1	20.6	28.4	21.9	3.4	1.3	5.5	2.0	5.0	0.1	0.5	0.1	4.1	0.0	0.2
Preble	42 337	98.8	37.8	24.0	30.4	23.9	3.4	1.5	3.3	1.7	1.2	0.1	0.7	0.0	0.0	0.0	0.2
Putnam	34 726	98.7	35.1	22.8	36.5	28.5	2.1	0.9	2.2	1.1	1.3	0.0	0.9	0.0	0.0	0.0	0.4
Richland	128 852	95.0	38.4	20.9	28.4	22.3	3.5	1.7	3.8	1.9	5.0	3.8	0.6	0.1	0.0	0.0	0.5
Ross	73 345	92.6	37.0	20.4	27.6	21.7	3.6	1.6	4.0	2.3	7.4	6.3	0.6	0.1	0.0	0.0	0.3
Sandusky	61 792	98.4	38.4	21.7	30.8	23.9	3.3	1.6	4.1	2.2	1.6	0.1	1.0	0.0	0.0	0.0	0.5
Scioto	79 195	95.7	39.0	20.4	28.6	21.7	4.0	2.0	3.7	1.9	4.3	2.1	1.3	0.4	0.2	0.0	0.3
Seneca	58 683	97.2	38.0	21.3	30.6	23.9	2.9	1.3	4.4	2.2	2.8	0.0	0.6	0.0	1.3	0.0	0.9
Shelby	47 910	98.6	36.8	22.3	33.0	26.6	2.8	1.2	3.7	1.9	1.4	0.3	1.1	0.0	0.0	0.0	0.1
Stark	378 098	97.6	39.2	21.2	29.4	22.5	3.7	1.6	4.0	2.0	2.4	0.1	1.1	0.1	0.7	0.0	0.3
Summit	542 899	98.3	40.1	20.1	29.7	22.9	3.9	1.6	4.5	2.0	1.7	0.2	0.8	0.1	0.3	0.0	0.3
Trumbull	225 116	98.2	39.5	20.9	30.0	22.0	4.3	1.9	3.4	1.8	1.8	0.8	0.9	0.0	0.0	0.0	0.1
Tuscarawas	90 914	98.7	39.2	22.8	30.1	23.5	3.0	1.3	3.7	2.0	1.3	0.1	1.0	0.0	0.0	0.0	0.2
Union	40 909	94.7	35.1	22.6	30.8	25.7	2.8	1.2	3.5	1.8	5.3	4.5	0.4	0.4	0.0	0.0	0.0
Van Wert	29 659	98.4	39.1	23.5	30.6	24.3	2.3	1.0	3.0	1.6	1.6	0.2	1.0	0.1	0.0	0.0	0.3
Vinton	12 806	98.9	38.2	21.8	30.4	23.8	4.4	2.3	4.1	2.5	1.1	0.0	0.7	0.0	0.0	0.0	0.4
Warren	158 383	96.0	35.3	23.4	31.6	26.1	2.9	1.2	2.8	1.4	4.0	3.1	0.7	0.0	0.0	0.0	0.1
Washington	63 251	97.3	39.7	23.0	28.0	21.8	2.9	1.3	3.6	2.0	2.7	0.1	1.2	0.0	1.4	0.0	0.1
Wayne	111 564	97.1	36.3	22.1	32.5	25.8	2.9	1.1	3.4	1.6	2.9	0.1	0.9	0.1	1.3	0.0	0.4
Williams	39 188	97.2	38.5	22.1	29.6	24.1	2.8	1.3	4.2	2.2	2.8	1.6	1.0	0.0	0.0	0.0	0.2
Wood	121 065	93.6	37.3	20.1	27.7	22.2	2.3	1.0	6.2	1.9	6.4	0.1	0.6	0.1	5.3	0.0	0.3
Wyandot	22 908	98.1	38.8	22.4	30.3	23.9	2.9	1.3	3.7	2.0	1.9	0.1	1.7	0.0	0.0	0.0	0.2
OKLAHOMA	3 450 654	96.7	38.9	20.8	28.7	23.1	4.4	2.1	3.9	1.5	3.3	1.0	0.8	0.1	0.8	0.2	0.3
Adair	21 038	98.2	35.5	20.3	32.8	25.4	6.4	3.6	3.1	1.4	1.8	0.1	0.8	0.6	0.0	0.0	0.3
Alfalfa	6 105	82.6	36.0	21.4	22.2	18.3	1.6	0.9	1.3	0.7	17.4	16.1	1.3	0.0	0.0	0.0	0.0
Atoka	13 879	88.8	35.8	20.4	26.2	20.7	4.2	2.3	2.3	1.1	11.2	10.3	0.9	0.0	0.0	0.0	0.0
Beaver	5 857	98.4	38.3	25.4	29.6	24.8	2.9	1.3	2.1	0.8	1.6	0.8	0.8	0.1	0.0	0.0	0.0
Beckham	19 799	90.5	37.2	20.0	26.8	21.9	3.3	1.6	3.2	1.6	9.5	8.1	1.3	0.0	0.0	0.0	0.0
Blaine	11 976	86.7	34.7	19.5	25.8	21.0	4.4	2.4	2.3	1.0	13.3	11.3	1.6	0.3	0.0	0.0	0.1
Bryan	36 534	97.4	39.5	21.3	27.5	21.8	4.9	2.4	4.1	1.5	2.6	0.2	0.8	0.0	1.2	0.0	0.4
Caddo	30 150	95.3	36.3	20.0	29.6	23.2	6.5	3.7	2.8	1.4	4.7	2.6	0.8	0.0	0.0	0.0	1.3
Canadian	87 697	97.2	35.9	23.1	31.9	25.8	3.5	1.7	2.8	1.2	2.8	2.0	0.5	0.1	0.0	0.0	0.2
Carter	45 621	97.6	39.4	21.5	28.8	23.1	4.7	2.5	3.2	1.5	2.4	0.6	1.5	0.1	0.0	0.0	0.2
Cherokee	42 521	96.0	38.0	20.0	28.4	22.9	4.9	2.5	4.7	1.7	4.0	0.1	0.6	0.1	2.6	0.0	0.6
Choctaw	15 342	98.5	40.5	20.8	28.0	22.1	6.0	3.1	3.1	1.4	1.5	0.3	1.0	0.1	0.0	0.0	0.1
Cimarron	3 148	98.7	39.9	24.1	29.9	25.7	2.9	1.5	1.8	0.7	1.3	0.3	1.0	0.0	0.0	0.0	0.0
Cleveland	208 016	95.4	38.1	20.7	27.9	22.5	3.5	1.5	5.2	1.6	4.6	1.3	0.6	0.1	2.4	0.0	0.2
Coal	6 031	98.7	39.3	21.7	30.0	23.4	4.4	2.4	3.2	1.4	1.3	0.2	1.0	0.0	0.0	0.0	0.0
Comanche	114 996	91.0	34.6	18.9	29.9	24.7	4.0	2.1	3.6	1.4	9.0	1.9	0.7	0.1	0.2	5.7	0.3
Cotton	6 614	97.4	39.5	22.8	28.5	22.6	4.3	2.4	2.3	1.1	2.6	1.6	1.1	0.0	0.0	0.0	0.0
Craig	14 950	92.4	37.6	21.5	26.5	21.2	4.0	2.1	2.7	1.3	7.6	3.0	1.0	2.1	0.0	0.0	1.6
Creek	67 367	99.0	37.5	22.6	30.7	24.2	5.0	2.5	3.2	1.5	1.0	0.0	0.9	0.1	0.0	0.0	0.0
Custer	26 142	95.2	38.8	20.0	27.0	21.7	4.5	2.2	4.9	1.4	4.8	0.2	1.7	0.0	2.8	0.0	0.0
Delaware	37 077	98.6	40.0	23.8	26.6	21.4	4.5	2.3	3.6	1.8	1.4	0.1	0.5	0.1	0.0	0.0	0.7
Dewey	4 743	97.2	41.4	24.7	26.2	21.2	3.3	1.5	1.6	0.7	2.8	0.3	2.5	0.0	0.0	0.0	0.0
Ellis	4 075	98.5	43.4	26.0	24.5	20.1	3.0	1.3	1.6	0.7	1.5	0.3	1.2	0.0	0.0	0.0	0.0
Garfield	57 813	97.0	40.1	21.7	27.9	22.8	3.6	1.7	3.7	1.6	3.0	0.4	1.6	0.1	0.0	0.4	0.5
Garvin	27 210	97.9	39.9	22.5	28.2	22.3	4.0	1.9	3.2	1.4	2.1	0.2	1.1	0.0	0.0	0.0	0.8
Grady	45 516	98.2	38.1	23.0	29.8	24.0	4.0	2.0	3.2	1.4	1.8	0.2	0.8	0.0	0.7	0.0	0.1
Grant	5 144	98.1	40.6	24.5	28.5	23.6	2.2	1.0	2.2	1.0	1.9	0.1	1.9	0.0	0.0	0.0	0.0
Greer	6 061	83.8	36.9	18.8	21.7	17.3	4.0	2.0	2.3	1.1	16.2	15.1	1.0	0.0	0.0	0.0	0.2
Harmon	3 283	95.3	38.6	21.5	27.9	22.6	4.1	2.1	3.3	1.5	4.7	0.2	2.7	0.6	0.0	0.0	1.2
Harper	3 562	98.7	42.4	24.8	26.6	21.9	2.8	1.1	2.2	0.9	1.3	0.1	1.2	0.0	0.0	0.0	0.0
Haskell	11 792	98.8	39.2	23.8	28.4	22.8	5.1	2.5	2.3	1.0	1.2	0.2	1.0	0.0	0.0	0.0	0.0
Hughes	14 154	90.8	37.6	20.1	25.4	19.8	5.2	2.7	2.4	1.4	9.2	7.1	1.5	0.0	0.0	0.0	0.6
Jackson	28 439	97.3	37.2	21.5	31.3	26.6	3.9	2.0	3.3	1.4	2.7	0.4	1.0	0.0	0.1	1.0	0.1
Jefferson	6 818	95.0	39.8	22.2	26.8	21.5	3.5	1.7	2.7	1.4	5.0	2.8	2.2	0.0	0.0	0.0	0.0
Johnston	10 513	97.6	38.6	21.8	28.3	22.1	5.6	2.8	3.3	1.5	2.4	0.3	1.0	0.0	1.1	0.0	0.0
Kay	48 080	97.6	39.8	21.8	28.8	23.9	3.6	1.8	3.5	1.7	2.4	0.1	1.0	0.1	0.6	0.0	0.5
Kingfisher	13 926	98.0	37.7	23.4	31.1	25.2	3.6	1.7	2.2	1.0	2.0	0.1	1.3	0.6	0.0	0.0	0.0

Table B. States and Counties

STATE County	Total households	Family households Total	With own children under 18 years	Married couple Total	With own children under 18 years	Female householder[1] Total	With own children under 18 years	Nonfamily households Total	Householder living alone Total	65 years and over	Average household size	Average family size	Households, 1990 Total households	Female householder[1]	Householder living alone
	71	72	73	74	75	76	77	78	79	80	81	82	83	84	85
OHIO—Cont'd															
Ottawa	16 474	71.2	29.1	58.9	22.4	8.5	4.7	28.8	25.0	11.2	2.45	2.92	15 170	7.7	21.9
Paulding	7 773	73.2	34.1	60.9	26.5	8.1	5.0	26.8	23.0	10.3	2.59	3.06	7 252	7.5	19.8
Perry	12 500	74.8	36.7	60.1	27.7	9.8	6.0	25.2	21.4	9.9	2.70	3.13	11 264	10.2	20.8
Pickaway	17 599	75.5	35.4	61.5	26.7	9.8	6.1	24.5	20.6	9.1	2.63	3.02	15 602	9.3	18.8
Pike	10 444	73.4	35.5	56.8	25.2	11.9	7.4	26.6	22.8	10.4	2.61	3.04	8 805	12.4	21.5
Portage	56 449	69.4	32.3	55.6	24.2	10.1	6.1	30.6	23.3	7.4	2.56	3.03	49 229	9.5	20.3
Preble	16 001	75.9	34.2	63.5	26.9	8.5	4.9	24.1	20.6	8.9	2.62	3.02	14 347	8.1	18.1
Putnam	12 200	76.3	39.2	64.9	33.0	7.4	4.1	23.7	21.3	10.5	2.81	3.29	11 082	6.7	18.2
Richland	49 534	69.2	30.9	54.3	21.8	11.4	7.0	30.8	26.5	10.9	2.47	2.98	47 573	10.4	24.1
Ross	27 136	70.7	32.7	55.2	23.4	11.1	6.7	29.3	24.9	10.3	2.50	2.97	24 325	11.2	22.6
Sandusky	23 717	71.5	33.3	56.5	24.3	10.5	6.4	28.5	24.1	10.6	2.56	3.04	22 464	9.9	21.7
Scioto	30 871	69.2	31.8	52.3	22.2	13.1	7.5	30.8	26.9	12.5	2.45	2.96	29 786	12.9	25.2
Seneca	22 292	70.6	33.4	56.1	24.3	10.2	6.4	29.4	24.7	10.6	2.56	3.04	21 277	9.4	22.9
Shelby	17 636	74.2	36.9	60.7	28.4	9.3	6.1	25.8	22.0	8.9	2.68	3.13	15 626	8.0	19.7
Stark	148 316	69.3	31.0	54.2	22.4	11.5	6.7	30.7	26.1	10.9	2.49	3.00	139 573	10.9	23.9
Summit	217 788	66.4	30.7	50.1	21.4	12.6	7.4	33.6	28.0	10.3	2.45	3.02	199 998	12.3	25.7
Trumbull	89 020	69.3	29.9	52.9	21.0	12.5	7.0	30.7	26.9	11.4	2.48	3.02	86 056	11.6	23.5
Tuscarawas	35 653	71.0	32.3	58.1	24.7	9.3	5.5	29.0	24.9	11.5	2.52	3.01	31 971	8.6	23.4
Union	14 346	75.9	38.5	64.4	31.3	8.0	5.0	24.1	19.9	7.3	2.70	3.11	11 037	8.2	19.6
Van Wert	11 587	72.1	32.9	60.2	25.6	8.5	5.1	27.9	24.7	11.4	2.52	3.00	11 266	7.4	21.6
Vinton	4 892	72.6	34.0	57.2	24.4	10.2	6.1	27.4	23.6	9.4	2.59	3.04	4 069	9.2	20.9
Warren	55 966	77.3	39.7	66.2	33.0	8.0	4.9	22.7	18.9	6.4	2.72	3.12	39 150	8.7	16.3
Washington	25 137	70.3	30.9	57.9	23.6	9.1	5.3	29.7	25.4	11.2	2.45	2.93	23 636	9.2	23.4
Wayne	40 445	72.9	35.0	60.8	27.8	8.7	5.2	27.1	22.7	8.7	2.68	3.17	35 619	8.4	21.0
Williams	15 105	70.6	33.3	57.5	24.7	9.0	5.9	29.4	24.9	10.5	2.52	3.00	13 807	7.7	22.4
Wood	45 172	65.7	32.0	53.9	24.6	8.5	5.4	34.3	25.8	9.1	2.51	3.04	39 677	7.9	22.8
Wyandot	8 882	70.6	33.1	57.9	25.0	9.2	5.6	29.4	25.4	11.7	2.53	3.03	8 168	8.7	22.2
OKLAHOMA	1 342 293	68.7	32.4	53.5	23.2	11.4	7.0	31.3	26.7	10.1	2.49	3.02	1 206 135	10.4	25.6
Adair	7 471	74.5	37.3	57.1	27.6	12.9	7.1	25.5	22.8	9.8	2.76	3.25	6 386	12.3	21.1
Alfalfa	2 199	67.4	26.9	59.3	22.2	5.7	3.4	32.6	31.0	17.6	2.29	2.86	2 469	5.2	28.5
Atoka	4 964	70.6	31.3	56.9	23.6	10.2	5.7	29.4	27.1	13.9	2.48	3.01	4 495	10.0	23.8
Beaver	2 245	76.0	33.5	66.3	27.7	6.1	4.1	24.0	22.0	12.3	2.57	2.99	2 327	5.0	22.7
Beckham	7 356	68.0	32.3	53.8	23.3	10.4	6.5	32.0	28.5	13.5	2.44	2.99	7 351	9.4	27.2
Blaine	4 159	68.9	30.8	56.2	23.6	8.6	4.8	31.1	29.0	15.5	2.50	3.08	4 418	7.5	27.3
Bryan	14 422	68.9	30.4	54.0	22.0	10.8	6.3	31.1	26.6	11.5	2.47	2.98	12 524	10.5	26.1
Caddo	10 957	72.7	33.3	55.2	23.5	13.0	7.5	27.3	24.8	12.5	2.62	3.13	10 879	11.8	24.0
Canadian	31 484	77.6	39.8	64.3	31.1	9.7	6.4	22.4	19.2	7.1	2.71	3.10	25 597	8.8	18.1
Carter	17 992	70.3	32.5	54.5	23.1	12.0	7.2	29.7	26.6	12.2	2.47	2.98	16 601	11.1	25.3
Cherokee	16 175	68.5	32.7	52.5	22.9	11.9	7.5	31.5	25.3	9.0	2.52	3.04	12 657	11.7	23.2
Choctaw	6 220	68.9	30.0	51.3	20.0	14.4	8.3	31.1	28.3	14.9	2.43	2.96	5 952	13.1	27.2
Cimarron	1 257	69.1	31.3	60.4	26.5	6.0	2.9	30.9	29.3	15.5	2.47	3.07	1 300	5.8	26.3
Cleveland	79 186	68.0	33.6	54.4	25.3	10.0	6.2	32.0	24.4	5.8	2.51	3.02	63 991	9.2	23.2
Coal	2 373	69.7	30.7	55.2	22.9	10.6	5.6	30.3	27.3	14.3	2.51	3.05	2 279	10.3	28.5
Comanche	39 808	72.5	39.0	54.6	27.2	14.1	9.4	27.5	23.4	7.9	2.63	3.10	37 569	12.1	20.4
Cotton	2 614	70.4	31.3	57.6	23.8	9.7	5.8	29.6	27.3	14.9	2.46	3.00	2 609	9.2	25.3
Craig	5 620	70.2	30.9	57.3	23.1	9.7	5.8	29.8	27.0	13.9	2.46	2.97	5 272	8.6	27.5
Creek	25 289	75.2	34.8	60.1	26.0	10.9	6.3	24.8	21.6	9.4	2.64	3.06	22 470	9.4	20.7
Custer	10 136	64.9	30.2	51.6	22.6	9.5	5.7	35.1	27.8	10.8	2.45	3.05	9 918	8.9	25.4
Delaware	14 838	72.6	29.0	59.5	21.1	8.9	5.3	27.4	24.0	11.2	2.46	2.89	11 003	8.0	22.4
Dewey	1 962	68.1	26.7	59.8	22.9	5.0	2.5	31.9	30.0	16.4	2.35	2.93	2 221	5.9	27.6
Ellis	1 769	68.9	25.3	59.9	20.4	6.0	3.6	31.1	29.2	15.7	2.27	2.79	1 826	6.4	27.1
Garfield	23 175	68.2	31.4	54.2	22.6	10.5	6.7	31.8	27.7	12.1	2.42	2.95	22 460	9.1	26.9
Garvin	10 865	70.0	30.7	56.4	23.1	10.1	5.8	30.0	26.9	14.3	2.45	2.96	10 417	9.1	26.0
Grady	17 341	73.8	34.7	60.5	26.5	9.7	6.1	26.2	22.9	10.5	2.58	3.02	15 544	9.5	21.6
Grant	2 089	69.7	30.7	60.4	24.5	6.3	4.2	30.3	28.4	15.8	2.42	2.95	2 327	5.5	27.8
Greer	2 237	64.5	25.6	51.0	17.8	9.6	5.7	35.5	33.4	19.8	2.27	2.87	2 551	8.4	33.5
Harmon	1 266	68.2	30.2	55.7	22.0	9.2	6.1	31.8	29.0	17.5	2.47	3.03	1 486	8.1	31.0
Harper	1 509	68.3	28.0	58.6	22.6	6.5	3.5	31.7	29.2	15.6	2.33	2.87	1 645	5.4	27.5
Haskell	4 624	73.1	31.7	60.6	25.1	9.1	4.8	26.9	24.7	13.0	2.52	3.00	4 319	8.5	25.4
Hughes	5 319	69.1	28.8	53.5	20.8	11.3	5.9	30.9	28.6	16.0	2.42	2.96	5 224	11.5	27.2
Jackson	10 590	72.4	38.1	57.8	28.1	10.7	7.4	27.6	24.2	9.7	2.61	3.11	10 455	10.3	22.4
Jefferson	2 716	68.6	29.2	55.6	21.5	9.2	5.5	31.4	28.8	15.4	2.38	2.92	2 843	8.1	29.7
Johnston	4 057	71.5	31.3	56.6	23.8	10.7	5.5	28.5	25.2	12.2	2.53	3.02	3 783	11.3	25.2
Kay	19 157	68.6	31.9	54.7	23.0	10.2	6.6	31.4	27.9	13.1	2.45	2.99	19 083	7.8	27.2
Kingfisher	5 247	74.2	35.4	62.2	28.5	8.0	4.7	25.8	23.5	12.0	2.60	3.08	4 932	7.0	23.8

[1] No spouse present.

Table B. States and Counties

STATE County	Percent change of households, 1990–2000	Total housing units	Occupied housing units (percent)	Vacant housing units		Homeowner vacancy rate (percent)	Rental vacancy rate (percent)	Occupied housing units			Average household size of owner-occupied units	Average household size of renter-occupied units
				Total	For seasonal, recreational, or occasional use			Total	Percent owner-occupied housing units	Percent renter-occupied housing units		
	86	87	88	89	90	91	92	93	94	95	96	97
OHIO—Cont'd												
Ottawa	8.6	25 532	64.5	35.5	30.7	1.9	11.2	16 474	80.6	19.4	2.50	2.24
Paulding	7.2	8 478	91.7	8.3	2.7	1.9	7.4	7 773	83.8	16.2	2.63	2.40
Perry	11.0	13 655	91.5	8.5	2.1	1.5	6.4	12 500	79.4	20.6	2.74	2.57
Pickaway	12.8	18 596	94.6	5.4	0.3	1.3	6.5	17 599	74.6	25.4	2.68	2.48
Pike	18.6	11 602	90.0	10.0	2.3	2.0	8.5	10 444	70.0	30.0	2.67	2.46
Portage	14.7	60 096	93.9	6.1	1.1	1.6	6.9	56 449	71.3	28.7	2.71	2.18
Preble	11.5	17 186	93.1	6.9	2.5	1.5	5.6	16 001	78.9	21.1	2.65	2.49
Putnam	10.1	12 753	95.7	4.3	0.3	0.9	6.6	12 200	84.1	15.9	2.91	2.29
Richland	4.1	53 062	93.4	6.6	0.6	1.4	8.9	49 534	71.5	28.5	2.57	2.23
Ross	11.6	29 461	92.1	7.9	0.7	1.8	7.5	27 136	73.5	26.5	2.57	2.31
Sandusky	5.6	25 253	93.9	6.1	1.1	1.2	8.3	23 717	75.3	24.7	2.63	2.35
Scioto	3.6	34 054	90.7	9.3	0.8	1.9	9.5	30 871	70.1	29.9	2.53	2.27
Seneca	4.8	23 692	94.1	5.9	0.4	1.4	7.5	22 292	75.1	24.9	2.64	2.31
Shelby	12.9	18 682	94.4	5.6	0.9	1.6	6.3	17 636	74.3	25.7	2.76	2.46
Stark	6.3	157 024	94.5	5.5	0.3	1.4	8.2	148 316	72.4	27.6	2.61	2.18
Summit	8.9	230 880	94.3	5.7	0.4	1.4	8.1	217 788	70.2	29.8	2.58	2.14
Trumbull	3.4	95 117	93.6	6.4	0.4	1.6	10.5	89 020	74.3	25.7	2.57	2.22
Tuscarawas	11.5	38 113	93.5	6.5	1.0	1.4	7.2	35 653	74.9	25.1	2.60	2.28
Union	30.0	15 217	94.3	5.7	0.5	1.8	8.1	14 346	77.5	22.5	2.79	2.40
Van Wert	2.8	12 363	93.7	6.3	0.4	1.9	8.1	11 587	81.7	18.3	2.57	2.27
Vinton	20.2	5 653	86.5	13.5	5.5	1.5	6.6	4 892	77.8	22.2	2.61	2.51
Warren	43.0	58 692	95.4	4.6	0.3	1.5	7.5	55 966	78.5	21.5	2.84	2.28
Washington	6.4	27 760	90.6	9.4	2.0	2.2	9.2	25 137	76.3	23.7	2.53	2.19
Wayne	13.5	42 324	95.6	4.4	0.3	1.2	6.2	40 445	73.3	26.7	2.80	2.34
Williams	9.4	16 140	93.6	6.4	1.7	1.5	6.0	15 105	76.8	23.2	2.59	2.30
Wood	13.8	47 468	95.2	4.8	0.4	1.7	5.5	45 172	70.7	29.3	2.68	2.10
Wyandot	8.7	9 324	95.3	4.7	0.4	0.9	5.8	8 882	74.7	25.3	2.61	2.30
OKLAHOMA	11.3	1 514 400	88.6	11.4	2.1	2.5	10.6	1 342 293	68.4	31.6	2.55	2.36
Adair	17.0	8 348	89.5	10.5	1.3	2.4	10.7	7 471	73.4	26.6	2.75	2.81
Alfalfa	-10.9	2 832	77.6	22.4	4.0	7.9	13.9	2 199	81.6	18.4	2.26	2.43
Atoka	10.4	5 673	87.5	12.5	2.5	2.2	12.9	4 964	76.2	23.8	2.52	2.36
Beaver	-3.5	2 719	82.6	17.4	1.4	6.1	14.6	2 245	79.1	20.9	2.49	2.86
Beckham	0.1	8 796	83.6	16.4	0.9	4.5	20.4	7 356	71.0	29.0	2.46	2.37
Blaine	-5.9	5 208	79.9	20.1	2.6	6.3	14.9	4 159	76.8	23.2	2.48	2.56
Bryan	15.2	16 715	86.3	13.7	3.9	2.7	9.7	14 422	69.4	30.6	2.51	2.36
Caddo	0.7	13 096	83.7	16.3	3.2	3.4	11.5	10 957	73.4	26.6	2.59	2.71
Canadian	23.0	33 969	92.7	7.3	1.2	2.0	9.3	31 484	79.0	21.0	2.76	2.49
Carter	8.4	20 577	87.4	12.6	1.0	3.2	14.3	17 992	71.2	28.8	2.48	2.46
Cherokee	27.8	19 499	83.0	17.0	9.0	2.5	9.3	16 175	66.8	33.2	2.60	2.38
Choctaw	4.5	7 539	82.5	17.5	2.9	4.2	15.6	6 220	70.9	29.1	2.43	2.43
Cimarron	-3.3	1 583	79.4	20.6	1.6	9.2	11.4	1 257	72.2	27.8	2.41	2.64
Cleveland	23.7	84 844	93.3	6.7	0.5	1.8	8.9	79 186	67.0	33.0	2.67	2.17
Coal	4.1	2 744	86.5	13.5	2.0	4.7	9.6	2 373	75.1	24.9	2.54	2.41
Comanche	6.0	45 416	87.7	12.3	0.6	4.3	13.2	39 808	60.3	39.7	2.62	2.65
Cotton	0.2	3 085	84.7	15.3	0.8	7.5	10.3	2 614	76.6	23.4	2.46	2.47
Craig	6.6	6 459	87.0	13.0	1.9	3.8	9.5	5 620	75.1	24.9	2.47	2.41
Creek	12.5	27 986	90.4	9.6	0.8	1.6	10.1	25 289	78.0	22.0	2.66	2.55
Custer	2.2	11 675	86.8	13.2	1.5	2.9	11.3	10 136	63.6	36.4	2.57	2.25
Delaware	34.9	22 290	66.6	33.4	24.4	3.2	8.8	14 838	79.2	20.8	2.44	2.54
Dewey	-11.7	2 425	80.9	19.1	3.5	2.5	9.3	1 962	79.2	20.8	2.36	2.32
Ellis	-3.1	2 146	82.4	17.6	1.6	7.4	7.1	1 769	80.7	19.3	2.23	2.41
Garfield	3.2	26 047	89.0	11.0	0.5	3.1	11.0	23 175	70.3	29.7	2.43	2.40
Garvin	4.3	12 641	86.0	14.0	0.6	3.4	15.9	10 865	73.8	26.2	2.44	2.49
Grady	11.6	19 444	89.2	10.8	0.5	2.6	12.2	17 341	75.7	24.3	2.61	2.46
Grant	-10.2	2 622	79.7	20.3	1.1	7.6	12.7	2 089	78.7	21.3	2.44	2.32
Greer	-12.3	2 788	80.2	19.8	2.2	5.5	16.9	2 237	75.0	25.0	2.25	2.34
Harmon	-14.8	1 647	76.9	23.1	2.6	6.3	19.6	1 266	77.0	23.0	2.40	2.71
Harper	-8.3	1 863	81.0	19.0	2.5	9.5	16.3	1 509	79.2	20.8	2.30	2.43
Haskell	7.1	5 573	83.0	17.0	6.6	2.3	7.4	4 624	77.5	22.5	2.53	2.49
Hughes	1.8	6 237	85.3	14.7	2.5	3.0	8.2	5 319	75.8	24.2	2.40	2.46
Jackson	1.3	12 377	85.6	14.4	0.6	4.3	14.5	10 590	60.2	39.8	2.55	2.70
Jefferson	-4.5	3 373	80.5	19.5	3.1	3.7	16.4	2 716	74.2	25.8	2.37	2.42
Johnston	7.2	4 782	84.8	15.2	3.6	3.3	10.3	4 057	73.9	26.1	2.52	2.54
Kay	0.4	21 804	87.9	12.1	1.9	3.1	11.4	19 157	71.7	28.3	2.48	2.37
Kingfisher	6.4	5 879	89.2	10.8	0.7	3.3	11.0	5 247	78.2	21.8	2.61	2.56

Table B. States and Counties

STATE/ County code	MSA/ PMSA/ NECMA code[1]	County type[2]	STATE County	Population, 2000				Population, 1990				Population and population characteristics, 2000 — Race (percent) — One race					
				Land area, 2000[3] (sq km)	Total persons	Rank	Per square kilometer	Land area, 1990[3] (sq km)	Total persons	Rank	Per square kilometer	White	Black or African American	American Indian or Alaska Native	Asian	Native Hawaiian and other Pacific Islander	Some other race
				1	2	3	4	5	6	7	8	9	10	11	12	13	14
			OKLAHOMA—Cont'd														
40 075	...	6	Kiowa	2 628	10 227	2 423	3.9	2 628	11 347	2 268	4.3	83.5	4.7	6.3	0.3	0.1	2.7
40 077	...	7	Latimer	1 870	10 692	2 385	5.7	1 871	10 333	2 356	5.5	73.0	1.0	19.4	0.2	0.0	0.5
40 079	...	6	Le Flore	4 107	48 109	947	11.7	4 108	43 270	934	10.5	80.4	2.2	10.7	0.2	0.0	1.4
40 081	...	6	Lincoln	2 481	32 080	1 343	12.9	2 483	29 216	1 323	11.8	86.4	2.5	6.6	0.2	0.0	0.4
40 083	5880	2	Logan	1 928	33 924	1 283	17.6	1 929	29 011	1 328	15.0	81.6	11.0	2.9	0.3	0.0	1.2
40 085	...	9	Love	1 335	8 831	2 542	6.6	1 335	7 788	2 596	5.8	84.1	2.2	6.4	0.3	0.0	3.6
40 087	5880	2	McClain	1 475	27 740	1 457	18.8	1 475	22 795	1 543	15.5	87.3	0.7	5.6	0.2	0.0	2.2
40 089	...	7	McCurtain	4 797	34 402	1 267	7.2	4 798	33 433	1 179	7.0	70.5	9.3	13.6	0.2	0.0	1.3
40 091	...	7	McIntosh	1 606	19 456	1 820	12.1	1 606	16 779	1 861	10.4	72.6	4.1	16.2	0.1	0.0	0.3
40 093	...	6	Major	2 478	7 545	2 639	3.0	2 478	8 055	2 558	3.3	95.0	0.2	0.9	0.1	0.0	2.4
40 095	...	6	Marshall	961	13 184	2 211	13.7	961	10 829	2 308	11.3	78.0	1.8	9.1	0.2	0.0	6.2
40 097	...	6	Mayes	1 699	38 369	1 155	22.6	1 700	33 366	1 180	19.6	72.1	0.3	19.1	0.3	0.0	0.6
40 099	...	7	Murray	1 083	12 623	2 254	11.7	1 083	12 042	2 214	11.1	80.8	1.9	11.6	0.3	0.0	1.2
40 101	...	4	Muskogee	2 108	69 451	712	32.9	2 108	68 078	650	32.3	63.7	13.2	14.9	0.6	0.0	1.2
40 103	...	7	Noble	1 896	11 411	2 340	6.0	1 896	11 045	2 288	5.8	86.4	1.6	7.6	0.3	0.0	0.6
40 105	...	6	Nowata	1 463	10 569	2 392	7.2	1 463	9 992	2 386	6.8	72.4	2.5	16.6	0.1	0.0	0.3
40 107	...	6	Okfuskee	1 618	11 814	2 304	7.3	1 618	11 551	2 252	7.1	65.5	10.4	18.2	0.1	0.0	0.6
40 109	5880	2	Oklahoma	1 837	660 448	80	359.5	1 837	599 611	77	326.4	70.4	15.0	3.4	2.8	0.1	4.4
40 111	...	6	Okmulgee	1 805	39 685	1 119	22.0	1 805	36 490	1 089	20.2	69.7	10.2	12.8	0.2	0.0	0.6
40 113	8560	2	Osage	5 830	44 437	1 009	7.6	5 830	41 645	965	7.1	67.0	10.8	14.4	0.2	0.0	0.6
40 115	...	6	Ottawa	1 221	33 194	1 309	27.2	1 221	30 561	1 263	25.0	74.1	0.6	16.5	0.3	0.1	1.5
40 117	...	6	Pawnee	1 475	16 612	1 983	11.3	1 475	15 575	1 948	10.6	82.3	0.7	12.1	0.2	0.0	0.2
40 119	...	4	Payne	1 778	68 190	722	38.4	1 778	61 507	710	34.6	84.3	3.6	4.6	3.0	0.0	0.8
40 121	...	7	Pittsburg	3 382	43 953	1 017	13.0	3 383	40 950	980	12.1	77.2	4.0	12.5	0.3	0.0	0.8
40 123	...	6	Pontotoc	1 864	35 143	1 243	18.9	1 864	34 119	1 161	18.3	75.8	2.1	15.5	0.5	0.0	0.8
40 125	5880	2	Pottawatomie	2 040	65 521	745	32.1	2 041	58 760	739	28.8	79.9	2.9	11.2	0.6	0.1	0.6
40 127	...	7	Pushmataha	3 619	11 667	2 320	3.2	3 619	10 997	2 295	3.0	78.0	0.8	15.6	0.1	0.1	0.3
40 129	...	9	Roger Mills	2 957	3 436	2 960	1.2	2 958	4 147	2 900	1.4	91.8	0.3	5.5	0.1	0.0	0.5
40 131	8560	2	Rogers	1 748	70 641	703	40.4	1 748	55 170	782	31.6	79.9	0.7	12.1	0.3	0.0	0.6
40 133	...	6	Seminole	1 638	24 894	1 561	15.2	1 638	25 412	1 451	15.5	70.7	5.6	17.4	0.2	0.0	0.7
40 135	2720	3	Sequoyah	1 745	38 972	1 139	22.3	1 745	33 828	1 168	19.4	68.1	1.9	19.6	0.2	0.0	0.7
40 137	...	4	Stephens	2 264	43 182	1 033	19.1	2 272	42 299	952	18.6	88.4	2.2	4.9	0.3	0.0	1.4
40 139	...	7	Texas	5 276	20 107	1 789	3.8	5 277	16 419	1 898	3.1	76.7	0.7	1.2	0.6	0.1	18.1
40 141	...	6	Tillman	2 258	9 287	2 507	4.1	2 259	10 384	2 349	4.6	74.2	9.0	2.7	0.3	0.0	10.6
40 143	8560	2	Tulsa	1 477	563 299	98	381.4	1 477	503 341	95	340.8	75.0	10.9	5.2	1.6	0.0	2.8
40 145	8560	2	Wagoner	1 458	57 491	830	39.4	1 458	47 883	875	32.8	80.1	3.8	9.4	0.5	0.0	0.9
40 147	...	4	Washington	1 080	48 996	933	45.4	1 080	48 066	868	44.5	81.2	2.5	8.6	0.7	0.0	0.9
40 149	...	7	Washita	2 599	11 508	2 334	4.4	2 599	11 441	2 259	4.4	92.3	0.4	3.0	0.3	0.0	2.2
40 151	...	7	Woods	3 332	9 089	2 522	2.7	3 332	9 103	2 461	2.7	93.4	2.4	1.6	0.5	0.0	0.6
40 153	...	7	Woodward	3 218	18 486	1 870	5.7	3 218	18 976	1 736	5.9	92.2	1.1	2.1	0.5	0.0	2.5
41 000	...		**OREGON**	248 631	3 421 399	X	13.8	248 647	2 842 337	X	11.4	86.6	1.6	1.3	3.0	0.2	4.2
41 001	...	7	Baker	7 946	16 741	1 973	2.1	7 947	15 317	1 971	1.9	95.7	0.2	1.1	0.4	0.0	0.9
41 003	1890	4	Benton	1 752	78 153	651	44.6	1 752	70 811	626	40.4	89.2	0.8	0.8	4.5	0.2	1.9
41 005	6440	0	Clackamas	4 839	338 391	173	69.9	4 839	278 850	177	57.6	91.3	0.7	0.7	2.5	0.2	2.3
41 007	...	6	Clatsop	2 143	35 630	1 227	16.6	2 143	33 301	1 183	15.5	93.1	0.5	1.0	1.2	0.2	1.6
41 009	6440	1	Columbia	1 701	43 560	1 028	25.6	1 701	37 557	1 058	22.1	94.4	0.2	1.3	0.6	0.1	0.8
41 011	...	5	Coos	4 145	62 779	775	15.1	4 145	60 273	719	14.5	92.0	0.3	2.4	0.9	0.2	1.1
41 013	...	7	Crook	7 717	19 182	1 834	2.5	7 717	14 111	2 045	1.8	93.0	0.0	1.3	0.4	0.0	3.8
41 015	...	7	Curry	4 215	21 137	1 728	5.0	4 215	19 327	1 713	4.6	92.9	0.2	2.1	0.7	0.1	1.1
41 017	...	5	Deschutes	7 817	115 367	466	14.8	7 817	74 976	599	9.6	94.8	0.2	0.8	0.7	0.1	1.4
41 019	...	4	Douglas	13 045	100 399	523	7.7	13 045	94 649	490	7.3	93.9	0.2	1.5	0.6	0.1	1.0
41 021	...	9	Gilliam	3 119	1 915	3 071	0.6	3 119	1 717	3 082	0.6	96.8	0.2	0.8	0.2	0.0	1.1
41 023	...	9	Grant	11 729	7 935	2 611	0.7	11 730	7 853	2 586	0.7	95.7	0.1	1.6	0.2	0.0	0.7
41 025	...	7	Harney	26 248	7 609	2 635	0.3	26 249	7 060	2 653	0.3	91.9	0.1	4.0	0.5	0.1	1.3
41 027	...	6	Hood River	1 353	20 411	1 765	15.1	1 353	16 903	1 856	12.5	78.9	0.6	1.1	1.5	0.1	15.4
41 029	4890	3	Jackson	7 214	181 269	304	25.1	7 214	146 387	323	20.3	91.6	0.4	1.1	0.9	0.2	2.9
41 031	...	7	Jefferson	4 612	19 009	1 845	4.1	4 613	13 676	2 083	3.0	69.0	0.3	15.7	0.3	0.2	11.3
41 033	...	4	Josephine	4 247	75 726	662	17.8	4 247	62 649	694	14.8	93.9	0.3	1.3	0.6	0.1	1.2
41 035	...	5	Klamath	15 395	63 775	762	4.1	15 397	57 702	754	3.7	87.3	0.6	4.2	0.8	0.1	3.4
41 037	...	7	Lake	21 072	7 422	2 646	0.4	21 073	7 186	2 635	0.3	91.0	0.1	2.4	0.7	0.1	3.2
41 039	2400	2	Lane	11 795	322 959	178	27.4	11 795	282 912	174	24.0	90.6	0.8	1.1	2.0	0.2	1.9
41 041	...	7	Lincoln	2 537	44 479	1 008	17.5	2 537	38 889	1 026	15.3	90.6	0.3	3.1	0.9	0.2	1.7
41 043	...	4	Linn	5 937	103 069	515	17.4	5 935	91 227	504	15.4	93.2	0.3	1.3	0.8	0.1	1.8
41 045	...	7	Malheur	25 607	31 615	1 356	1.2	25 609	26 038	1 419	1.0	75.8	1.2	1.0	2.0	0.1	17.4
41 047	7080	2	Marion	3 066	284 834	196	92.9	3 069	228 483	215	74.4	81.6	0.9	1.4	1.8	0.4	10.6

[1] MSA = Metropolitan Statistical Area. PMSA = Primary MSA. NECMA = New England County Metropolitan Area. See Appendix A for explanation of these concepts. See Appendix B for list of metropolitan areas identified by type, with component counties.
[2] County typology code from the Economic Research Service of USDA. See Appendix A for definition.
[3] Dry land or land partially or temporarily covered by water.

STATE County	Population and population characteristics, 2000 (cont'd)								Population and population characteristics, 1990				
	Race (percent) (cont'd)								Race (percent)				
	Race alone or in combination												
	Two or more races	White	Black	American Indian or Alaska Native	Asian	Native Hawaiian and other Pacific Islander	Some other race	Hispanic[1]	White	Black or African American	American Indian or Alaska Native	Asian and Pacific Islander	Hispanic[1]
	15	16	17	18	19	20	21	22	23	24	25	26	27
OKLAHOMA—Cont'd													
Kiowa	2.4	85.8	5.1	7.9	0.5	0.2	3.1	6.7	84.0	5.4	6.7	0.3	5.3
Latimer	5.9	78.7	1.3	25.0	0.3	0.0	0.8	1.5	82.5	1.5	15.2	0.2	1.1
Le Flore	5.0	85.2	2.5	15.2	0.4	0.1	1.8	3.8	85.3	2.4	11.8	0.2	1.0
Lincoln	3.8	90.1	2.8	9.8	0.4	0.1	0.7	1.5	90.3	2.7	6.3	0.2	1.1
Logan	2.9	84.2	11.6	5.0	0.5	0.1	1.5	2.9	81.5	13.9	3.2	0.3	1.9
Love	3.4	87.5	2.5	8.8	0.5	0.1	4.2	7.0	85.7	4.4	6.9	0.1	4.1
McClain	4.0	91.1	0.9	8.9	0.4	0.1	2.7	4.9	91.1	1.0	6.6	0.2	2.5
McCurtain	5.0	75.1	10.0	18.0	0.3	0.0	1.7	3.1	74.2	10.3	14.6	0.3	1.4
McIntosh	6.6	78.5	5.0	22.3	0.3	0.1	0.6	1.3	76.0	5.3	18.3	0.2	0.9
Major	1.4	96.3	0.3	2.0	0.2	0.0	2.7	4.0	97.3	0.0	1.7	0.1	1.6
Marshall	4.7	82.4	2.1	13.0	0.4	0.0	6.8	8.6	86.9	1.7	10.0	0.1	2.5
Mayes	7.5	79.6	0.5	26.3	0.4	0.1	0.9	1.9	81.3	0.2	18.0	0.2	0.9
Murray	4.3	84.9	2.2	15.4	0.3	0.1	1.4	3.1	86.5	1.7	11.1	0.1	1.4
Muskogee	6.4	69.4	14.3	20.7	0.8	0.1	1.5	2.7	71.8	14.0	13.3	0.4	1.3
Noble	3.4	89.7	1.8	10.5	0.4	0.0	1.0	1.8	89.0	1.8	8.5	0.2	1.1
Nowata	8.2	80.3	3.0	24.1	0.4	0.0	0.6	1.2	79.8	3.6	16.4	0.1	0.7
Okfuskee	5.3	70.3	11.1	23.0	0.2	0.0	0.8	1.6	67.8	11.5	20.2	0.1	1.2
Oklahoma	3.9	73.7	16.1	5.7	3.3	0.2	5.2	8.7	77.0	14.7	4.1	2.0	4.2
Okmulgee	6.4	75.4	11.2	18.5	0.4	0.1	1.1	1.9	75.0	12.1	12.2	0.2	1.3
Osage	6.8	73.4	11.6	20.7	0.4	0.1	0.9	2.1	74.4	10.1	14.8	0.2	1.6
Ottawa	6.8	80.8	0.8	22.8	0.5	0.2	1.8	3.2	80.2	0.6	18.2	0.3	1.2
Pawnee	4.4	86.6	1.0	16.2	0.2	0.1	0.5	1.2	88.4	0.8	10.5	0.2	0.7
Payne	3.6	87.7	4.2	7.1	3.5	0.1	1.2	2.1	89.4	2.9	4.3	2.8	1.5
Pittsburg	5.2	82.0	4.6	17.0	0.4	0.1	1.2	2.1	83.2	3.7	12.3	0.3	1.2
Pontotoc	5.4	80.6	2.9	20.3	0.6	0.0	1.1	2.3	82.8	2.5	13.9	0.3	1.2
Pottawatomie	4.7	84.2	3.5	15.1	0.9	0.2	1.1	2.4	85.0	2.3	11.7	0.6	1.7
Pushmataha	5.2	82.9	1.1	20.4	0.2	0.1	0.5	1.6	83.3	1.0	15.2	0.1	1.2
Roger Mills	1.9	93.4	0.4	7.1	0.1	0.0	1.0	2.6	95.2	0.1	4.0	0.1	1.8
Rogers	6.4	86.2	0.9	17.9	0.5	0.1	0.9	1.8	85.6	0.8	12.9	0.3	1.1
Seminole	5.3	75.3	6.6	22.0	0.4	0.1	1.1	2.2	74.9	7.6	16.9	0.2	1.3
Sequoyah	9.4	77.2	2.3	28.5	0.4	0.1	1.1	2.0	76.5	2.3	20.7	0.2	0.9
Stephens	2.7	91.0	2.4	7.1	0.5	0.1	4.0	4.0	91.8	2.2	4.1	0.4	2.2
Texas	2.6	79.1	0.9	2.1	0.7	0.1	19.6	29.9	92.2	0.4	1.1	0.2	10.0
Tillman	3.1	76.9	9.8	4.2	0.5	0.1	11.8	17.7	75.7	10.0	3.4	0.3	14.1
Tulsa	4.4	78.9	11.8	8.3	2.0	0.1	3.4	6.0	83.0	9.9	5.0	1.2	2.4
Wagoner	5.4	85.2	4.3	14.1	0.7	0.1	1.2	2.5	85.9	4.1	9.2	0.4	1.3
Washington	6.1	87.1	3.0	13.9	1.0	0.0	1.3	2.6	88.1	2.7	7.9	0.9	1.6
Washita	1.8	94.1	0.6	4.2	0.3	0.1	2.6	4.5	95.7	0.2	2.3	0.2	3.5
Woods	1.5	94.8	2.6	2.6	0.6	0.1	0.8	2.4	96.8	0.5	1.5	0.3	1.5
Woodward	1.6	93.6	1.2	3.2	0.6	0.0	2.9	4.8	94.8	0.7	2.5	0.4	3.0
OREGON	3.1	89.3	2.1	2.5	3.7	0.5	5.2	8.0	92.8	1.6	1.4	2.4	4.0
Baker	1.7	97.3	0.4	2.0	0.6	0.1	1.4	2.3	98.1	0.2	1.0	0.3	1.8
Benton	2.6	91.5	1.2	1.7	5.4	0.5	2.6	4.7	92.0	0.9	0.8	5.5	2.5
Clackamas	2.5	93.5	1.0	1.6	3.2	0.4	2.9	4.9	96.3	0.4	0.7	1.7	2.6
Clatsop	2.3	95.2	0.7	2.2	1.8	0.4	2.2	4.5	96.4	0.3	1.1	1.3	1.9
Columbia	2.5	96.9	0.4	2.8	1.1	0.2	1.3	2.5	97.3	0.1	1.4	0.8	1.8
Coos	3.2	95.0	0.6	4.7	1.3	0.3	1.4	3.4	95.9	0.2	2.3	1.0	2.2
Crook	1.4	94.4	0.1	2.1	0.7	0.1	4.1	5.6	96.6	0.1	1.6	0.3	2.7
Curry	2.9	95.7	0.3	4.1	0.9	0.2	1.8	3.6	96.4	0.2	2.4	0.6	1.8
Deschutes	2.0	96.7	0.4	1.8	1.2	0.2	1.8	3.7	97.8	0.1	0.9	0.6	2.0
Douglas	2.7	96.5	0.4	3.4	1.0	0.2	1.4	3.3	96.9	0.2	1.6	0.7	2.4
Gilliam	0.9	97.7	0.2	1.6	0.3	0.0	1.2	1.8	98.6	0.0	0.6	0.5	1.7
Grant	1.7	97.4	0.2	2.7	0.3	0.1	1.1	2.1	97.9	0.1	1.1	0.2	1.9
Harney	2.1	94.0	0.2	5.1	0.9	0.1	1.8	4.2	94.8	0.0	3.7	0.6	3.1
Hood River	2.5	81.2	0.8	1.7	1.9	0.3	16.6	25.0	90.8	0.3	1.2	1.8	16.3
Jackson	2.9	94.4	0.7	2.4	1.4	0.4	3.8	6.7	95.8	0.2	1.3	1.0	4.1
Jefferson	3.2	71.7	0.5	17.5	0.6	0.4	12.7	17.7	74.2	0.2	19.6	0.5	10.6
Josephine	2.7	96.5	0.5	2.9	1.0	0.3	1.7	4.3	97.0	0.2	1.4	0.7	2.8
Klamath	3.5	90.6	1.0	6.1	1.3	0.3	4.4	7.8	92.2	0.7	4.1	0.8	5.2
Lake	2.5	93.4	0.3	4.0	0.9	0.1	3.8	5.4	95.0	0.1	2.8	0.6	3.8
Lane	3.3	93.7	1.3	2.6	2.8	0.4	2.8	4.6	95.4	0.7	1.1	2.0	2.4
Lincoln	3.2	93.6	0.6	5.3	1.4	0.4	2.3	4.8	96.1	0.2	2.4	0.9	1.5
Linn	2.5	95.5	0.5	2.6	1.2	0.3	2.5	4.4	96.9	0.2	1.2	0.9	2.4
Malheur	2.6	78.1	1.4	1.9	2.4	0.2	18.6	25.6	81.6	0.2	0.9	3.1	19.8
Marion	3.4	84.6	1.3	2.6	2.4	0.6	12.1	17.1	91.5	0.9	1.4	1.8	8.0

[1] Hispanic persons may be of any race.

Table B. States and Counties

STATE County	Population and population characteristics, 2000										
	Age (percent)										
	Under 5 years	5 to 17 years	18 to 24 years	25 to 34 years	35 to 44 years	45 to 54 years	55 to 64 years	65 to 74 years	75 years and over	Median age (years)	Percent Female
	28	29	30	31	32	33	34	35	36	37	38
OKLAHOMA—Cont'd											
Kiowa	5.6	18.5	7.5	9.7	14.9	12.7	10.7	9.7	10.6	40.9	51.1
Latimer	6.8	19.0	11.4	10.4	13.8	11.8	10.7	8.6	7.5	36.8	50.6
Le Flore	6.8	19.3	9.7	12.6	14.4	13.2	10.2	7.3	6.4	36.1	50.2
Lincoln	6.5	20.9	7.8	11.2	15.5	13.6	10.6	7.6	6.3	37.5	50.7
Logan	6.1	19.3	12.0	11.0	15.5	14.1	9.6	6.7	5.6	36.1	50.6
Love	6.1	19.6	7.0	11.2	14.3	13.8	11.9	8.6	7.6	39.4	50.5
McClain	6.6	20.2	8.1	12.1	17.0	13.4	10.6	6.9	5.1	36.9	50.3
McCurtain	7.3	20.9	8.3	12.2	14.0	13.1	10.3	7.6	6.4	36.0	51.9
McIntosh	5.4	17.2	6.4	9.3	13.0	13.2	13.7	12.3	9.5	44.1	52.2
Major	5.7	18.9	6.7	9.2	15.2	13.4	11.5	9.5	9.9	41.6	51.2
Marshall	6.2	17.3	7.5	10.5	13.6	13.0	12.5	10.8	8.7	41.3	50.9
Mayes	6.8	19.8	8.6	11.8	14.4	13.3	10.5	8.2	6.7	37.2	50.4
Murray	6.6	17.6	8.0	11.2	13.9	13.3	11.0	9.5	9.0	39.8	50.7
Muskogee	7.0	18.9	9.5	11.9	14.8	13.2	9.4	7.6	7.7	37.0	51.7
Noble	6.4	19.1	7.9	11.9	15.6	13.2	10.7	8.1	7.1	38.3	50.7
Nowata	6.5	19.6	7.6	10.6	14.7	13.1	10.6	9.1	8.2	39.0	50.8
Okfuskee	6.2	18.5	8.2	11.6	15.0	13.1	11.1	8.3	8.0	38.6	48.4
Oklahoma	7.3	18.3	10.9	14.6	15.3	13.1	8.3	6.5	5.8	34.2	51.5
Okmulgee	6.8	20.1	9.5	11.1	14.1	13.0	10.2	7.8	7.3	36.9	51.2
Osage	6.2	20.2	7.7	11.1	16.4	14.9	10.6	7.5	5.6	38.1	49.5
Ottawa	6.6	19.1	9.7	11.7	13.1	12.6	10.3	8.9	8.0	37.3	51.5
Pawnee	6.3	20.3	7.3	11.3	14.9	14.0	11.2	7.9	6.9	38.5	50.7
Payne	5.4	14.1	25.9	13.5	12.6	10.6	7.0	5.2	5.5	27.6	49.2
Pittsburg	5.6	17.9	7.8	12.1	14.9	13.7	10.9	9.0	8.2	39.4	49.6
Pontotoc	6.3	18.4	12.5	12.0	14.0	12.2	9.7	7.7	7.2	35.7	51.7
Pottawatomie	6.8	19.0	11.2	12.2	14.7	12.9	9.5	7.5	6.3	35.5	51.7
Pushmataha	6.2	19.7	6.6	10.4	13.6	13.0	12.2	9.9	8.4	40.1	51.9
Roger Mills	5.5	18.3	6.7	9.3	15.4	13.9	12.1	9.4	9.3	41.7	49.9
Rogers	6.9	21.7	7.4	12.0	16.6	14.0	10.0	6.6	4.7	36.2	50.8
Seminole	6.7	19.6	9.0	10.6	13.8	13.0	10.4	8.7	8.1	38.1	51.8
Sequoyah	7.1	20.4	8.2	12.3	14.6	13.2	10.8	7.8	5.7	36.4	50.7
Stephens	6.3	18.3	7.8	10.3	14.9	13.8	10.2	9.8	8.6	40.1	51.6
Texas	8.5	20.3	12.7	14.7	14.4	11.5	7.7	5.5	4.7	30.4	48.6
Tillman	6.2	20.5	7.2	10.8	13.2	12.0	10.8	9.0	10.4	38.9	51.0
Tulsa	7.4	18.9	10.0	14.7	15.7	13.4	8.1	6.2	5.6	34.4	51.5
Wagoner	7.1	21.1	7.9	12.3	16.2	14.8	10.6	6.2	3.9	36.2	50.6
Washington	6.0	19.1	7.7	10.6	14.4	14.1	10.4	9.1	8.6	40.1	52.0
Washita	6.1	20.1	7.6	10.3	15.0	12.3	9.8	8.9	9.9	39.2	51.6
Woods	4.4	14.7	16.8	10.8	12.4	11.2	9.7	8.8	11.1	37.8	49.0
Woodward	6.6	19.2	9.3	11.5	16.1	13.2	9.9	7.5	6.7	37.4	50.0
OREGON	6.5	18.2	9.6	13.8	15.4	14.8	8.9	6.4	6.4	36.3	50.4
Baker	5.3	18.9	5.8	9.1	14.6	15.2	12.1	9.7	9.3	42.7	50.5
Benton	5.1	16.2	20.2	12.9	13.8	14.2	7.2	5.1	5.2	31.1	50.2
Clackamas	6.5	19.7	8.0	12.1	16.6	16.6	9.5	5.6	5.5	37.5	50.6
Clatsop	5.6	18.0	8.9	10.5	14.7	16.4	10.3	8.0	7.6	40.0	50.5
Columbia	6.4	20.9	7.0	11.6	16.4	16.0	10.0	6.2	5.4	37.7	50.0
Coos	4.9	17.1	7.1	9.6	14.4	15.8	12.1	10.0	9.1	43.1	51.0
Crook	6.5	20.1	7.5	11.3	14.2	14.6	11.1	8.2	6.5	38.6	50.1
Curry	4.1	15.1	4.8	7.3	12.7	15.2	14.2	14.2	12.4	48.8	50.9
Deschutes	6.1	18.6	7.8	12.7	15.9	15.7	10.0	7.2	5.9	38.3	50.3
Douglas	5.6	18.4	7.5	10.1	14.1	15.2	11.2	9.6	8.2	41.2	50.8
Gilliam	4.5	18.7	5.4	9.6	16.0	15.4	11.3	9.6	9.5	42.8	49.5
Grant	5.7	20.1	5.6	9.3	14.7	15.9	12.0	8.6	8.1	41.7	50.2
Harney	5.7	20.3	6.4	10.3	16.2	15.1	11.0	8.3	6.7	39.8	49.3
Hood River	7.4	20.6	8.2	13.4	16.1	13.7	7.8	6.3	6.6	35.3	50.3
Jackson	6.0	18.4	8.7	11.2	14.3	15.4	10.0	7.9	8.1	39.2	51.4
Jefferson	7.7	22.1	7.7	12.8	14.1	12.8	10.4	7.6	4.9	34.8	49.5
Josephine	5.3	17.7	6.5	9.6	13.6	15.3	11.9	10.2	9.9	43.1	51.4
Klamath	6.4	19.4	8.6	11.4	14.1	15.0	10.2	8.1	6.8	38.2	50.0
Lake	5.0	19.9	5.1	9.5	14.7	16.0	12.1	9.8	7.9	42.7	49.9
Lane	5.8	17.1	12.0	13.0	14.5	15.3	9.0	6.6	6.7	36.6	50.8
Lincoln	4.9	16.6	6.5	9.4	14.1	16.7	12.3	10.7	8.8	44.1	51.5
Linn	6.8	19.2	8.4	12.3	14.7	14.3	9.8	7.2	7.3	37.4	50.6
Malheur	7.6	20.1	10.6	13.1	14.1	12.5	8.5	6.8	6.9	34.0	46.3
Marion	7.7	19.7	10.3	14.1	14.6	13.2	8.1	6.0	6.3	33.7	49.7

	Population and population characteristics, 1990										Population—change, 1980–2000				
	Age (percent)										Total persons			Percent change	
STATE County	Under 5 years	5 to 17 years	18 to 24 years	25 to 34 years	35 to 44 years	45 to 54 years	55 to 64 years	65 to 74 years	75 years and over	Percent Female	2000	1990	1980	1990–2000	1980–1990
	39	40	41	42	43	44	45	46	47	48	49	50	51	52	53
OKLAHOMA—Cont'd															
Kiowa	6.9	19.8	7.0	12.9	11.5	9.4	10.1	10.3	12.0	52.9	10 227	11 347	12 711	-9.9	-10.7
Latimer	6.7	20.3	11.0	13.5	12.1	9.7	9.4	9.7	7.6	50.2	10 692	10 333	9 840	3.5	5.0
Le Flore	7.1	20.5	9.1	14.5	13.5	11.2	9.0	8.0	7.1	50.9	48 109	43 270	40 698	11.2	6.3
Lincoln	6.8	21.4	7.7	14.4	13.9	11.3	9.7	8.0	6.9	51.0	32 080	29 216	20 601	9.8	9.8
Logan	6.7	20.4	12.2	14.2	14.2	10.4	8.5	6.8	6.0	51.1	33 924	29 011	26 881	16.9	7.9
Love	5.9	19.2	8.9	14.4	14.4	11.1	9.7	8.9	7.5	48.7	8 831	7 788	7 469	13.4	9.2
McClain	6.4	21.2	8.4	15.1	14.7	12.6	9.5	6.7	5.4	50.1	27 740	22 795	20 291	21.7	12.3
McCurtain	7.7	21.9	9.1	14.0	13.3	10.7	9.2	7.7	6.5	52.1	34 402	33 433	36 151	2.9	-7.5
McIntosh	5.6	17.8	7.1	11.3	11.4	11.6	13.7	12.7	8.9	51.8	19 456	16 779	15 562	16.0	7.8
Major	6.3	20.7	6.4	13.4	13.4	10.8	9.8	9.5	9.8	51.5	7 545	8 055	8 772	-6.3	-8.2
Marshall	5.8	16.9	7.6	12.9	11.6	10.8	11.5	13.0	9.9	52.0	13 184	10 829	10 550	21.7	2.6
Mayes	7.0	20.2	8.2	13.8	13.4	11.5	10.3	9.2	6.4	51.0	38 369	33 366	32 261	15.0	3.4
Murray	6.0	19.5	7.4	12.7	14.0	10.4	10.8	10.2	9.1	51.3	12 623	12 042	12 147	4.8	-0.9
Muskogee	7.0	20.4	8.9	14.9	13.9	9.9	9.3	8.7	7.1	52.1	69 451	68 078	67 033	2.0	1.6
Noble	7.0	20.0	7.6	15.2	13.5	11.1	9.3	7.9	8.4	51.4	11 411	11 045	11 573	3.3	-4.6
Nowata	6.3	19.0	7.4	12.8	13.1	11.1	11.2	9.9	9.3	51.2	10 569	9 992	11 486	5.8	-13.0
Okfuskee	6.5	19.7	8.2	14.1	12.7	11.0	9.9	9.3	8.6	49.2	11 814	11 551	11 125	2.3	3.8
Oklahoma	7.6	18.5	10.4	18.1	14.8	9.9	8.6	7.0	5.1	52.0	660 448	599 611	568 933	10.1	5.4
Okmulgee	7.1	19.6	9.4	13.2	13.1	10.8	9.5	9.2	8.0	51.7	39 685	36 490	39 169	8.8	-6.8
Osage	7.0	20.7	7.5	14.9	15.3	11.4	9.4	7.9	5.8	50.3	44 437	41 645	39 327	6.7	5.9
Ottawa	6.2	17.8	10.9	12.5	12.8	10.5	10.8	10.9	7.6	52.6	33 194	30 561	32 870	8.6	-7.0
Pawnee	6.8	20.1	7.5	13.8	14.4	11.4	9.7	9.1	7.1	50.5	16 612	15 575	15 310	6.7	1.7
Payne	5.8	15.3	25.4	16.7	11.7	7.8	6.3	5.7	5.2	50.0	68 190	61 507	62 435	10.9	-1.5
Pittsburg	5.9	18.9	7.7	14.0	13.5	11.0	10.8	9.9	8.3	51.0	43 953	40 950	40 524	7.3	0.1
Pontotoc	6.4	18.6	12.3	13.9	13.1	9.8	9.2	8.7	8.1	52.7	35 143	34 119	32 598	3.0	4.7
Pottawatomie	6.7	20.3	11.0	14.3	13.7	10.5	9.1	7.6	6.8	52.2	65 521	58 760	55 239	11.5	6.4
Pushmataha	6.3	19.2	7.6	12.1	12.6	11.8	11.6	10.0	8.8	50.9	11 667	10 997	11 773	6.1	-6.6
Roger Mills	6.4	21.4	6.9	13.6	13.6	10.5	9.3	9.6	8.6	50.7	3 436	4 147	4 799	-17.1	-13.6
Rogers	7.3	21.1	8.5	14.8	16.1	12.7	9.2	6.1	4.1	50.6	70 641	55 170	46 436	28.0	18.8
Seminole	6.5	20.1	8.4	13.2	12.7	10.4	10.0	9.8	8.8	52.4	24 894	25 412	27 465	-2.0	-7.5
Sequoyah	7.3	21.2	9.5	14.4	13.7	11.4	9.4	7.4	5.8	51.2	38 972	33 828	30 749	15.2	10.0
Stephens	6.4	19.6	7.1	14.0	14.1	9.8	10.8	9.8	8.4	52.3	43 182	42 299	43 419	2.1	-2.6
Texas	6.9	21.2	10.2	14.9	14.0	10.3	9.4	7.3	5.7	50.4	20 107	16 419	17 727	22.5	-7.4
Tillman	7.0	20.9	8.3	12.5	11.5	10.0	9.4	10.1	10.2	52.1	9 287	10 384	12 398	-10.6	-16.2
Tulsa	7.7	18.4	10.1	18.1	15.7	10.1	8.4	6.7	4.8	51.8	563 299	503 341	470 593	11.9	7.0
Wagoner	7.2	22.5	8.5	15.2	16.5	12.2	8.1	5.8	3.9	50.7	57 491	47 883	41 801	20.1	14.5
Washington	6.8	19.1	7.4	14.1	14.9	11.3	10.3	9.4	6.8	52.2	48 996	48 066	48 113	1.9	0.0
Washita	6.7	20.3	6.7	13.9	12.5	10.1	10.0	10.2	9.6	51.7	11 508	11 441	13 798	0.6	-17.1
Woods	5.6	16.0	13.1	12.4	11.3	9.7	9.6	10.8	11.5	52.1	9 089	9 103	10 923	-0.2	-16.7
Woodward	6.9	21.3	8.1	16.8	14.2	10.4	9.1	7.1	6.2	50.0	18 486	18 976	21 172	-2.6	-10.4
OREGON	7.1	18.4	9.4	15.9	16.7	10.4	8.3	7.9	5.9	50.8	3 421 399	2 842 337	2 633 156	20.4	7.9
Baker	6.7	19.5	5.9	13.3	14.0	11.2	10.5	10.2	8.6	50.2	16 741	15 317	16 134	9.3	-5.1
Benton	6.2	16.1	21.1	16.0	15.7	8.8	6.5	5.7	4.0	49.4	78 153	70 811	68 211	10.4	3.8
Clackamas	7.0	19.7	8.0	15.1	18.4	12.2	8.1	6.7	4.8	50.9	338 391	278 850	241 911	21.4	15.3
Clatsop	6.9	18.8	8.2	14.5	16.0	10.2	9.2	9.2	7.0	50.3	35 630	33 301	32 489	7.0	2.5
Columbia	7.4	21.3	7.4	14.3	17.0	11.7	8.4	7.5	5.1	50.0	43 560	37 557	35 646	16.0	5.4
Coos	6.4	18.7	7.0	13.7	14.9	11.3	10.6	10.3	7.0	50.6	62 779	60 273	64 047	4.2	-5.9
Crook	7.3	20.1	7.7	13.7	15.1	10.5	9.7	9.5	6.4	49.9	19 182	14 111	13 091	35.9	7.8
Curry	5.6	15.0	5.2	11.4	14.0	10.8	13.5	15.7	8.7	50.6	21 137	19 327	16 992	9.4	13.7
Deschutes	6.9	18.9	7.4	15.1	17.9	10.8	9.1	8.7	5.2	50.2	115 367	74 976	62 142	53.9	20.7
Douglas	7.1	19.8	7.7	13.8	15.2	10.9	10.2	9.2	6.2	50.5	100 399	94 649	93 748	6.1	1.0
Gilliam	6.6	20.2	4.9	14.2	14.0	9.5	11.2	11.3	8.0	50.1	1 915	1 717	2 057	11.5	-16.5
Grant	6.9	20.2	6.4	14.2	15.9	11.6	10.3	8.3	6.2	49.7	7 935	7 853	8 210	1.0	-4.3
Harney	7.7	20.3	6.4	14.6	15.0	12.1	10.1	8.0	5.9	49.7	7 609	7 060	8 314	7.8	-15.1
Hood River	7.6	19.7	7.9	16.4	15.9	10.2	8.4	8.0	6.0	49.0	20 411	16 903	15 835	20.8	6.7
Jackson	6.7	18.4	8.5	13.7	16.3	10.9	9.4	9.5	6.7	51.2	181 269	146 387	132 456	23.8	10.5
Jefferson	10.2	21.1	8.6	15.5	13.7	9.5	9.0	7.7	4.8	49.8	19 009	13 676	11 599	39.0	17.9
Josephine	6.3	17.9	6.5	12.1	14.8	11.1	10.7	12.2	8.3	51.4	75 726	62 649	58 855	20.9	6.4
Klamath	7.1	19.5	9.5	14.1	15.4	10.5	9.6	8.6	5.7	49.6	63 775	57 702	59 117	10.5	-2.4
Lake	7.4	20.7	6.3	13.6	15.3	11.5	10.8	8.6	5.8	49.7	7 422	7 186	7 532	3.3	-4.6
Lane	6.7	17.8	11.8	15.6	16.9	10.3	7.9	7.6	5.5	51.3	322 959	282 912	275 226	14.2	2.8
Lincoln	6.1	17.3	5.8	12.9	16.0	10.3	11.5	12.7	7.3	51.8	44 479	38 889	35 264	14.4	10.3
Linn	7.2	19.5	8.8	14.8	15.3	10.9	8.7	8.7	6.2	50.8	103 069	91 227	89 495	13.0	1.9
Malheur	8.2	22.4	8.4	12.8	13.0	10.0	9.6	8.9	6.7	51.0	31 615	26 038	26 896	21.4	-3.2
Marion	7.4	19.0	9.6	16.1	15.6	10.0	7.9	7.8	6.5	50.4	284 834	228 483	204 692	24.7	11.6

STATE County	Total population	Total in households	House-holder	Spouse	Child Total	Child Own child under 18 years	Other relatives Total	Other relatives Under 18 years	Nonrelatives Total	Nonrelatives Unmarried partner	Total in group quarters	Correctional institutions	Nursing homes	Other institutions	College dormitories	Military quarters	Other
	54	55	56	57	58	59	60	61	62	63	64	65	66	67	68	69	70
OKLAHOMA—Cont'd																	
Kiowa	10 227	96.7	41.1	21.4	26.9	21.2	4.4	2.2	2.9	1.4	3.3	1.1	2.0	0.2	0.0	0.0	0.1
Latimer	10 692	93.8	37.0	21.0	28.1	22.3	4.6	2.6	3.1	1.4	6.2	0.1	2.5	0.0	3.5	0.0	0.1
Le Flore	48 109	96.9	37.1	21.7	29.0	22.7	5.6	2.8	3.4	1.5	3.1	1.6	0.9	0.0	0.4	0.0	0.2
Lincoln	32 080	98.5	38.0	23.4	30.1	24.4	4.3	2.2	2.8	1.3	1.5	0.1	0.7	0.0	0.0	0.0	0.7
Logan	33 924	93.9	36.5	21.6	28.6	22.8	3.9	1.9	3.3	1.4	6.1	0.0	0.3	0.0	3.6	0.0	2.2
Love	8 831	98.9	39.0	23.5	28.8	22.9	4.6	2.1	3.0	1.3	1.1	0.2	0.8	0.0	0.0	0.0	0.1
McClain	27 740	99.2	37.2	24.3	30.8	24.5	4.1	1.9	2.7	1.3	0.8	0.2	0.5	0.0	0.0	0.0	0.1
McCurtain	34 402	98.5	38.4	20.5	30.7	24.3	6.0	3.3	3.0	1.4	1.5	0.4	1.1	0.0	0.0	0.0	0.0
McIntosh	19 456	98.3	41.6	23.5	25.2	19.5	5.0	2.5	3.1	1.4	1.7	0.1	1.2	0.3	0.0	0.0	0.0
Major	7 545	98.4	40.4	25.7	27.9	23.1	2.5	1.2	1.9	1.0	1.6	0.1	1.5	0.0	0.0	0.0	0.0
Marshall	13 184	97.9	40.7	23.7	25.5	20.3	4.8	2.3	3.2	1.3	2.1	0.6	1.1	0.0	0.0	0.0	0.4
Mayes	38 369	98.6	38.6	23.3	29.4	23.5	4.4	2.2	2.9	1.3	1.4	0.1	0.6	0.5	0.0	0.0	0.2
Murray	12 623	97.2	39.6	22.9	27.6	21.8	4.0	2.0	3.0	1.5	2.8	0.3	2.4	0.0	0.0	0.0	0.1
Muskogee	69 451	95.4	38.1	20.1	28.5	22.4	5.3	2.6	3.5	1.5	4.6	2.6	1.1	0.0	0.4	0.0	0.4
Noble	11 411	97.6	39.5	23.3	28.5	23.1	3.7	2.0	2.7	1.4	2.4	0.2	1.0	1.3	0.0	0.0	0.0
Nowata	10 569	98.1	39.2	23.1	29.1	23.3	3.7	2.0	3.0	1.5	1.9	0.5	1.4	0.0	0.0	0.0	0.0
Okfuskee	11 814	91.0	36.1	19.5	26.8	20.8	5.5	3.1	3.0	1.3	9.0	5.9	1.3	0.0	0.0	0.0	1.9
Oklahoma	660 448	97.4	40.4	18.7	28.4	22.7	5.0	2.2	4.9	1.8	2.6	0.8	0.6	0.1	0.6	0.1	0.4
Okmulgee	39 685	97.4	38.6	20.4	29.6	23.2	5.7	3.0	3.2	1.5	2.6	0.2	1.1	0.1	1.0	0.0	0.2
Osage	44 437	96.5	37.4	22.2	29.4	23.2	4.5	2.5	3.0	1.5	3.5	2.9	0.4	0.0	0.0	0.0	0.0
Ottawa	33 194	97.0	39.1	21.8	28.3	22.5	4.4	2.2	3.4	1.7	3.0	0.1	0.9	0.4	1.5	0.0	0.2
Pawnee	16 612	99.0	38.4	23.7	29.9	23.9	4.3	2.1	2.8	1.3	1.0	0.2	0.8	0.0	0.0	0.0	0.0
Payne	68 190	89.7	39.1	17.9	22.0	18.1	2.9	1.1	7.8	1.6	10.3	1.4	0.5	0.0	7.8	0.0	0.5
Pittsburg	43 953	93.6	39.0	21.4	25.5	20.0	4.7	2.4	2.9	1.3	6.4	4.7	1.3	0.3	0.0	0.0	0.1
Pontotoc	35 143	96.9	39.8	21.0	27.7	22.0	4.5	2.1	3.9	1.5	3.1	0.2	0.9	0.6	1.4	0.0	0.0
Pottawatomie	65 521	95.5	37.5	21.2	28.5	22.5	4.9	2.5	3.5	1.4	4.5	1.4	0.9	0.1	2.0	0.0	0.1
Pushmataha	11 667	98.4	40.6	22.5	27.7	22.6	4.5	2.4	3.1	1.4	1.6	0.2	1.3	0.0	0.0	0.0	0.0
Roger Mills	3 436	98.9	41.6	24.4	27.1	21.6	3.3	1.9	2.4	1.5	1.1	0.3	0.8	0.0	0.0	0.0	0.0
Rogers	70 641	98.8	36.4	23.9	32.1	26.4	3.7	1.8	2.7	1.2	1.2	0.1	0.9	0.0	0.1	0.0	0.1
Seminole	24 894	97.8	38.5	20.5	28.8	22.0	6.6	3.7	3.4	1.5	2.2	0.2	1.7	0.0	0.1	0.0	0.1
Sequoyah	38 972	98.7	37.9	22.1	30.2	23.9	5.4	2.8	3.2	1.5	1.3	0.1	0.8	0.0	0.0	0.0	0.3
Stephens	43 182	98.6	40.4	24.1	27.6	22.1	4.0	2.0	2.4	1.1	1.4	0.2	1.1	0.0	0.0	0.0	0.2
Texas	20 107	97.8	35.6	21.9	30.8	26.4	4.5	1.7	5.1	1.4	2.2	0.3	0.3	0.0	1.2	0.0	0.3
Tillman	9 287	95.8	38.7	21.3	28.5	22.5	5.0	2.6	2.3	1.2	4.2	1.4	1.4	0.7	0.0	0.0	0.6
Tulsa	563 299	97.9	40.3	19.8	29.1	23.8	4.3	1.9	4.4	1.7	2.1	0.2	0.6	0.2	0.7	0.0	0.4
Wagoner	57 491	99.6	36.5	24.1	31.9	25.5	4.3	2.1	2.8	1.3	0.4	0.1	0.2	0.0	0.0	0.0	0.1
Washington	48 996	98.7	41.2	23.6	27.9	23.1	3.2	1.5	2.9	1.3	1.3	0.1	0.7	0.0	0.4	0.0	0.1
Washita	11 508	98.0	39.2	23.9	29.6	24.3	3.1	1.6	2.2	1.1	2.0	0.2	1.8	0.0	0.0	0.0	0.0
Woods	9 089	89.0	40.5	20.6	21.8	17.7	2.3	0.8	3.9	1.3	11.0	4.7	1.2	0.7	4.0	0.0	0.3
Woodward	18 486	95.6	38.6	22.8	28.0	23.4	3.0	1.6	3.2	1.6	4.4	2.9	0.8	0.2	0.0	0.0	0.4
OREGON	3 421 399	97.7	39.0	20.2	27.4	22.4	4.2	1.5	6.9	2.5	2.3	0.6	0.4	0.1	0.6	0.0	0.6
Baker	16 741	97.5	41.1	23.1	26.4	22.2	2.9	1.3	4.0	1.8	2.5	1.2	0.4	0.0	0.0	0.0	0.9
Benton	78 153	93.6	38.6	19.4	23.7	20.0	2.5	0.7	9.4	2.2	6.4	0.0	0.3	0.1	5.5	0.0	0.4
Clackamas	338 391	99.1	37.9	22.2	29.9	24.1	3.9	1.4	5.3	2.1	0.9	0.2	0.4	0.0	0.0	0.0	0.3
Clatsop	35 630	96.9	41.3	20.9	25.9	21.2	3.2	1.3	5.6	2.6	3.1	0.2	0.6	0.2	0.2	0.1	1.8
Columbia	43 560	99.4	37.6	22.8	30.5	25.0	3.5	1.4	5.0	2.2	0.6	0.1	0.2	0.0	0.0	0.0	0.2
Coos	62 779	97.7	41.8	22.1	24.3	19.5	3.7	1.5	5.8	2.4	2.3	0.7	0.4	0.1	0.3	0.0	0.7
Crook	19 182	98.6	38.3	23.6	28.1	23.6	3.9	1.7	4.7	2.1	1.4	0.1	0.2	0.7	0.0	0.0	0.4
Curry	21 137	98.7	45.1	24.6	20.9	17.4	3.2	1.2	4.9	2.4	1.3	0.2	0.3	0.0	0.0	0.0	0.7
Deschutes	115 367	98.9	39.5	22.9	27.1	23.0	2.9	1.1	6.6	2.5	1.1	0.2	0.2	0.0	0.1	0.0	0.5
Douglas	100 399	98.5	39.7	22.7	26.6	21.3	4.2	1.8	5.3	2.3	1.5	0.2	0.6	0.1	0.0	0.0	0.6
Gilliam	1 915	98.6	42.8	24.8	25.3	21.6	2.6	1.3	3.2	1.8	1.4	0.0	0.0	0.0	0.0	0.0	1.4
Grant	7 935	97.8	40.9	23.7	27.0	23.5	2.5	1.3	3.8	1.9	2.2	0.4	0.6	0.0	0.0	0.0	1.2
Harney	7 609	97.8	39.9	23.1	27.2	23.4	3.0	1.2	4.5	2.2	2.2	0.2	0.8	0.8	0.0	0.0	0.4
Hood River	20 411	95.7	35.5	20.8	29.4	24.5	4.2	1.5	5.8	1.9	4.3	0.0	0.9	0.7	0.0	0.0	2.7
Jackson	181 269	98.0	39.5	21.0	27.1	22.1	4.0	1.5	6.4	2.4	2.0	0.2	0.6	0.0	0.5	0.0	0.7
Jefferson	19 009	99.2	35.4	21.4	30.5	25.9	6.8	3.0	5.2	2.4	0.8	0.4	0.2	0.0	0.0	0.0	0.2
Josephine	75 726	98.7	40.9	22.3	25.8	20.5	4.2	1.7	5.5	2.3	1.3	0.1	0.7	0.2	0.0	0.0	0.4
Klamath	63 775	98.4	39.5	21.4	27.7	23.1	3.9	1.7	5.9	2.5	1.6	0.2	0.3	0.1	0.6	0.0	0.4
Lake	7 422	99.3	41.6	24.4	26.3	22.9	2.8	1.2	4.3	1.7	0.7	0.1	0.0	0.5	0.0	0.0	0.2
Lane	322 959	97.7	40.4	19.8	25.5	20.7	3.5	1.3	8.5	2.8	2.3	0.2	0.3	0.1	1.0	0.0	0.7
Lincoln	44 479	98.6	43.4	21.5	22.9	18.8	3.8	1.5	7.0	3.2	1.4	0.2	0.4	0.0	0.0	0.0	0.8
Linn	103 069	99.0	38.4	21.8	29.0	23.4	4.3	1.8	5.6	2.2	1.0	0.2	0.4	0.1	0.0	0.0	0.2
Malheur	31 615	89.5	32.3	18.5	29.9	24.9	4.5	2.0	4.2	1.6	10.5	9.4	0.5	0.0	0.2	0.0	0.4
Marion	284 834	96.3	35.7	19.2	29.7	24.5	5.3	1.9	6.4	2.2	3.7	1.6	0.5	0.5	0.5	0.0	0.7

Table B. States and Counties

STATE County	Total households	Family households — Total	With own children under 18 years	Married couple — Total	With own children under 18 years	Female householder[1] — Total	With own children under 18 years	Nonfamily households — Total	Householder living alone — Total	65 years and over	Average household size	Average family size	Total households (1990)	Female householder[1] (1990)	Householder living alone (1990)
	71	72	73	74	75	76	77	78	79	80	81	82	83	84	85
OKLAHOMA—Cont'd															
Kiowa	4 208	66.9	27.9	52.0	19.7	10.4	5.6	33.1	30.6	16.3	2.35	2.92	4 551	11.0	28.8
Latimer	3 951	72.6	32.2	56.9	22.8	11.5	6.9	27.4	24.9	12.3	2.54	3.00	3 693	10.0	22.8
Le Flore	17 861	73.9	33.4	58.5	25.2	11.0	6.0	26.1	23.1	10.9	2.61	3.05	15 938	10.3	22.4
Lincoln	12 178	74.9	34.1	61.5	26.0	9.2	5.6	25.1	22.4	10.5	2.59	3.03	10 839	7.8	21.4
Logan	12 389	72.6	33.7	59.2	25.8	9.8	5.8	27.4	23.7	9.7	2.57	3.04	10 180	10.0	22.6
Love	3 442	74.3	31.7	60.4	24.0	10.0	5.4	25.7	22.9	12.0	2.54	2.97	2 992	8.4	23.3
McClain	10 331	77.8	36.0	65.3	28.4	9.0	5.6	22.2	19.4	8.4	2.66	3.04	8 332	7.2	18.5
McCurtain	13 216	72.2	34.0	53.3	22.9	14.6	8.9	27.8	25.4	11.0	2.56	3.06	12 234	13.4	23.0
McIntosh	8 085	70.3	25.6	56.6	17.8	10.4	5.9	29.7	26.7	14.5	2.37	2.84	6 786	9.4	24.3
Major	3 046	72.5	31.0	63.7	25.0	6.0	4.1	27.5	25.2	13.5	2.44	2.92	3 121	6.0	23.6
Marshall	5 371	70.8	27.3	58.1	20.6	8.8	4.8	29.2	26.4	14.5	2.40	2.87	4 350	8.2	25.2
Mayes	14 823	73.0	32.6	60.2	24.9	9.0	5.5	27.0	23.8	11.1	2.55	3.02	12 672	8.4	21.7
Murray	5 003	71.7	30.9	57.7	22.8	10.2	5.9	28.3	25.2	12.7	2.45	2.92	4 651	9.2	26.3
Muskogee	26 458	69.8	31.8	52.8	22.0	13.3	7.8	30.2	26.7	12.3	2.51	3.03	25 174	12.5	25.5
Noble	4 504	71.3	32.0	59.0	25.0	8.4	4.8	28.7	25.5	11.2	2.47	2.97	4 225	7.7	26.0
Nowata	4 147	72.1	31.8	58.8	23.4	9.8	6.1	27.9	25.5	13.3	2.50	2.97	3 994	8.6	26.4
Okfuskee	4 270	69.6	29.2	54.1	21.2	11.2	5.8	30.4	27.8	14.5	2.52	3.06	4 164	10.8	25.8
Oklahoma	266 834	64.0	30.9	46.3	20.2	13.5	8.5	36.0	30.2	9.2	2.41	3.02	237 879	12.6	28.6
Okmulgee	15 300	69.9	32.0	52.8	22.2	13.1	7.6	30.1	27.1	12.6	2.53	3.06	14 044	12.4	26.5
Osage	16 617	73.5	33.2	59.4	24.8	10.3	5.9	26.5	23.3	10.1	2.58	3.04	15 383	9.2	23.3
Ottawa	12 984	70.2	30.9	55.6	22.3	10.7	6.3	29.8	26.6	13.6	2.48	2.98	12 124	9.7	27.3
Pawnee	6 383	74.4	32.6	61.6	25.5	9.0	5.1	25.6	22.8	11.0	2.58	3.02	6 006	7.2	23.1
Payne	26 680	57.4	25.9	45.6	19.1	8.3	5.0	42.6	30.1	8.1	2.29	2.90	23 834	7.6	29.1
Pittsburg	17 157	69.6	29.0	54.9	20.6	11.2	6.4	30.4	27.7	13.3	2.40	2.90	15 911	10.2	26.5
Pontotoc	13 978	67.4	30.8	52.9	22.2	10.8	6.5	32.6	28.1	12.3	2.44	2.98	13 310	10.3	27.1
Pottawatomie	24 540	72.2	32.7	56.5	23.4	11.8	7.1	27.8	24.0	10.5	2.55	3.02	21 796	10.2	24.0
Pushmataha	4 739	69.4	30.2	55.3	21.7	10.8	6.5	30.6	27.9	14.2	2.42	2.94	4 370	8.4	26.5
Roger Mills	1 428	69.2	29.4	58.8	23.6	6.8	3.6	30.8	28.6	16.9	2.38	2.91	1 586	6.3	23.8
Rogers	25 724	78.1	38.4	65.6	30.5	8.9	5.7	21.9	19.0	7.5	2.71	3.10	19 866	7.7	17.8
Seminole	9 575	70.9	30.7	53.3	21.3	13.3	7.2	29.1	25.9	13.1	2.54	3.05	9 665	11.9	25.7
Sequoyah	14 761	74.4	34.2	58.2	24.8	11.9	7.0	25.6	22.4	10.2	2.61	3.05	12 335	11.3	20.8
Stephens	17 463	72.1	30.4	59.5	23.2	9.2	5.5	27.9	25.3	12.8	2.44	2.91	16 764	8.2	24.5
Texas	7 153	73.4	39.0	61.5	31.2	7.5	5.1	26.6	21.2	8.2	2.75	3.19	6 214	7.4	23.4
Tillman	3 594	69.2	30.5	55.1	22.8	10.7	5.8	30.8	28.8	16.8	2.48	3.05	3 933	10.2	26.4
Tulsa	226 892	64.9	32.2	49.1	22.4	12.1	7.8	35.1	29.6	8.9	2.43	3.03	202 537	11.0	28.8
Wagoner	21 010	79.5	37.4	65.9	29.2	9.8	6.0	20.5	17.7	6.7	2.73	3.08	16 946	8.6	17.2
Washington	20 179	69.5	30.5	57.2	22.8	9.3	5.9	30.5	27.5	13.0	2.40	2.91	19 242	7.9	24.8
Washita	4 506	72.5	33.6	61.0	26.3	8.5	5.5	27.5	25.3	13.4	2.50	3.00	4 421	6.4	24.1
Woods	3 684	60.9	24.1	50.9	18.3	7.3	4.2	39.1	33.4	16.4	2.20	2.81	3 803	6.2	32.4
Woodward	7 141	71.1	33.1	59.1	25.1	8.4	5.7	28.9	25.4	11.2	2.48	2.96	7 087	8.1	24.2
OREGON	1 333 723	65.8	30.8	51.9	22.2	9.8	6.2	34.2	26.1	9.1	2.51	3.02	1 103 313	9.2	25.3
Baker	6 883	68.0	28.0	56.2	20.1	8.6	5.7	32.0	27.8	13.4	2.37	2.87	6 118	7.2	26.0
Benton	30 145	60.5	28.4	50.4	22.2	7.2	4.7	39.5	26.1	6.7	2.43	2.95	26 126	7.1	25.2
Clackamas	128 201	71.5	34.2	58.6	26.5	9.0	5.5	28.5	22.0	7.8	2.62	3.07	103 530	8.2	20.5
Clatsop	14 703	64.3	28.5	50.6	19.5	9.7	6.4	35.7	29.5	11.7	2.35	2.88	13 374	8.3	28.0
Columbia	16 375	73.5	34.4	60.5	25.8	8.7	5.7	26.5	21.1	8.1	2.65	3.06	13 910	7.6	21.3
Coos	26 213	66.6	26.0	52.9	17.7	9.9	6.0	33.4	27.2	12.3	2.34	2.80	24 134	9.1	24.6
Crook	7 354	73.8	32.3	61.5	24.3	8.2	5.3	26.2	21.3	9.5	2.57	2.96	5 455	6.4	22.7
Curry	9 543	64.8	20.9	54.5	14.5	7.2	4.5	35.2	29.7	14.7	2.19	2.66	8 311	5.9	24.4
Deschutes	45 595	70.1	32.1	58.0	23.7	8.5	6.0	29.9	22.0	7.7	2.50	2.91	29 217	7.6	21.0
Douglas	39 821	70.9	29.1	57.2	20.5	9.6	6.1	29.1	23.9	11.0	2.48	2.90	35 872	8.8	21.5
Gilliam	819	66.4	27.6	57.9	22.5	5.9	3.9	33.6	29.5	12.1	2.31	2.85	696	5.0	25.3
Grant	3 246	68.8	30.1	57.9	22.2	7.9	5.9	31.2	27.1	10.9	2.39	2.89	3 092	5.9	24.6
Harney	3 036	69.0	29.4	58.0	22.7	6.8	4.1	31.0	25.9	10.2	2.45	2.94	2 760	7.2	24.6
Hood River	7 248	71.4	35.7	58.6	27.8	8.8	5.6	28.6	22.7	9.9	2.70	3.15	6 425	7.5	24.2
Jackson	71 532	67.7	30.3	53.2	21.0	10.5	6.8	32.3	25.1	11.0	2.48	2.95	57 238	9.1	24.0
Jefferson	6 727	76.8	35.6	60.5	25.0	10.5	6.9	23.2	18.6	6.9	2.80	3.16	4 744	9.8	18.8
Josephine	31 000	68.9	26.9	54.4	18.2	10.4	6.4	31.1	25.4	12.1	2.41	2.85	25 081	9.3	23.7
Klamath	25 205	68.6	30.3	54.2	20.7	10.0	6.7	31.4	25.3	10.4	2.49	2.95	22 341	8.4	24.2
Lake	3 084	69.8	29.0	58.6	21.2	7.5	5.1	30.2	26.2	11.1	2.39	2.84	2 765	6.3	22.5
Lane	130 453	63.0	28.5	48.9	19.6	10.0	6.5	37.0	26.6	9.1	2.42	2.92	110 799	9.4	25.1
Lincoln	19 296	63.5	24.4	49.5	15.3	10.0	6.6	36.5	29.3	12.7	2.27	2.75	16 455	7.7	26.5
Linn	39 541	71.4	32.0	56.9	23.0	10.0	6.3	28.6	23.0	10.1	2.58	3.01	34 716	9.0	22.2
Malheur	10 221	71.9	36.2	57.3	26.6	10.4	7.1	28.1	23.7	12.0	2.77	3.28	9 457	8.8	24.1
Marion	101 641	69.3	34.5	53.7	24.7	11.0	7.2	30.7	24.0	9.5	2.70	3.19	83 494	10.3	24.6

[1] No spouse present.

Table B. States and Counties

STATE County	Housing occupancy, 2000							Housing tenure, 2000				
				Vacant housing units				Occupied housing units				
	Percent change of households, 1990–2000	Total housing units	Occupied housing units (percent)	Total	For seasonal, recreational, or occasional use	Homeowner vacancy rate (percent)	Rental vacancy rate (percent)	Total	Percent owner-occupied housing units	Percent renter-occupied housing units	Average household size of owner-occupied units	Average household size of renter-occupied units
	86	87	88	89	90	91	92	93	94	95	96	97
OKLAHOMA—Cont'd												
Kiowa	-7.5	5 304	79.3	20.7	3.0	5.5	19.4	4 208	75.3	24.7	2.35	2.35
Latimer	7.0	4 709	83.9	16.1	2.6	2.7	16.1	3 951	74.6	25.4	2.56	2.47
Le Flore	12.1	20 142	88.7	11.3	1.8	3.2	10.6	17 861	75.2	24.8	2.59	2.65
Lincoln	12.4	13 712	88.8	11.2	1.1	2.6	10.9	12 170	80.0	20.0	2.62	2.51
Logan	21.7	13 906	89.1	10.9	1.4	2.6	8.7	12 389	78.4	21.6	2.61	2.43
Love	15.0	4 066	84.7	15.3	4.9	2.8	10.3	3 442	81.6	18.4	2.53	2.58
McClain	24.0	11 189	92.3	7.7	0.7	1.9	10.8	10 331	81.4	18.6	2.67	2.63
McCurtain	8.0	15 427	85.7	14.3	3.5	2.4	11.8	13 216	73.3	26.7	2.56	2.57
McIntosh	19.1	12 640	64.0	36.0	27.1	3.4	11.7	8 085	79.0	21.0	2.35	2.42
Major	-2.4	3 540	86.0	14.0	1.7	3.8	7.6	3 046	81.1	18.9	2.42	2.49
Marshall	23.5	8 517	63.1	36.9	28.4	3.9	10.9	5 371	79.3	20.7	2.40	2.40
Mayes	17.0	17 423	85.1	14.9	6.8	3.2	9.3	14 823	77.0	23.0	2.57	2.49
Murray	7.6	6 479	77.2	22.8	11.2	3.3	15.7	5 003	74.2	25.8	2.44	2.49
Muskogee	5.1	29 575	89.5	10.5	0.8	2.4	10.2	26 458	69.6	30.4	2.57	2.36
Noble	6.6	5 082	88.6	11.4	1.5	1.9	12.2	4 504	75.3	24.7	2.51	2.36
Nowata	3.8	4 705	88.1	11.9	0.4	3.2	7.9	4 147	77.8	22.2	2.50	2.49
Okfuskee	2.5	5 114	83.5	16.5	2.6	4.0	10.6	4 270	76.2	23.8	2.52	2.52
Oklahoma	12.2	295 020	90.4	9.6	0.5	2.1	11.4	266 834	60.4	39.6	2.49	2.30
Okmulgee	8.9	17 316	88.4	11.6	0.8	1.9	11.6	15 300	72.5	27.5	2.55	2.46
Osage	8.0	18 826	88.3	11.7	1.8	3.2	9.6	16 617	80.6	19.4	2.62	2.43
Ottawa	7.1	14 842	87.5	12.5	3.3	2.3	8.4	12 984	73.9	26.1	2.50	2.41
Pawnee	6.3	7 464	85.5	14.5	1.8	3.2	14.6	6 383	80.1	19.9	2.59	2.53
Payne	11.9	29 326	91.0	9.0	0.8	2.4	7.3	26 680	55.9	44.1	2.48	2.05
Pittsburg	7.8	21 520	79.7	20.3	8.8	2.5	11.8	17 157	76.0	24.0	2.41	2.35
Pontotoc	5.0	15 575	89.7	10.3	0.6	1.9	10.1	13 978	67.0	33.0	2.51	2.29
Pottawatomie	12.6	27 302	89.9	10.1	0.9	2.0	10.9	24 540	72.1	27.9	2.59	2.45
Pushmataha	8.4	5 795	81.8	18.2	7.6	3.0	9.3	4 739	77.7	22.3	2.44	2.36
Roger Mills	-10.0	1 749	81.6	18.4	5.3	5.2	7.9	1 428	78.7	21.3	2.39	2.34
Rogers	29.5	27 476	93.6	6.4	0.5	1.9	8.2	25 724	81.1	18.9	2.78	2.44
Seminole	-0.9	11 146	85.9	14.1	1.4	2.6	12.0	9 575	72.5	27.5	2.52	2.60
Sequoyah	19.7	16 940	87.1	12.9	4.5	2.6	8.9	14 761	75.2	24.8	2.61	2.61
Stephens	4.2	19 854	88.0	12.0	1.5	3.3	12.4	17 463	75.5	24.5	2.44	2.43
Texas	15.1	8 014	89.3	10.7	0.8	2.4	10.5	7 153	66.8	33.2	2.68	2.89
Tillman	-8.6	4 342	82.8	17.2	0.8	2.4	14.2	3 594	77.3	22.7	2.47	2.51
Tulsa	12.0	243 953	93.0	7.0	0.4	1.6	8.6	226 892	61.8	38.2	2.55	2.24
Wagoner	24.0	23 174	90.7	9.3	3.4	1.4	10.0	21 010	81.1	18.9	2.74	2.67
Washington	4.9	22 250	90.7	9.3	0.7	1.7	8.0	20 179	74.0	26.0	2.44	2.27
Washita	1.9	5 452	82.6	17.4	1.1	7.7	13.0	4 506	74.7	25.3	2.47	2.59
Woods	-3.1	4 492	82.0	18.0	2.3	5.3	11.6	3 684	69.8	30.2	2.23	2.12
Woodward	0.8	8 341	85.6	14.4	1.0	3.5	17.8	7 141	72.0	28.0	2.50	2.42
OREGON	20.9	1 452 709	91.8	8.2	2.5	2.3	7.3	1 333 723	64.3	35.7	2.59	2.36
Baker	12.5	8 402	81.9	18.1	8.4	3.2	11.7	6 883	70.1	29.9	2.37	2.38
Benton	15.4	31 980	94.3	5.7	0.4	1.9	7.2	30 145	57.3	42.7	2.62	2.16
Clackamas	23.8	136 954	93.6	6.4	1.4	2.0	8.1	128 201	71.1	28.9	2.73	2.34
Clatsop	9.9	19 685	74.7	25.3	15.7	3.8	14.8	14 703	64.2	35.8	2.40	2.24
Columbia	17.7	17 572	93.2	6.8	0.8	2.4	8.3	16 375	76.1	23.9	2.69	2.49
Coos	8.6	29 247	89.6	10.4	2.9	2.3	10.2	26 213	68.1	31.9	2.34	2.34
Crook	34.8	8 264	89.0	11.0	5.7	2.0	7.0	7 354	74.3	25.7	2.54	2.66
Curry	14.8	11 406	83.7	16.3	7.2	3.5	13.5	9 543	73.0	27.0	2.15	2.27
Deschutes	56.1	54 583	83.5	16.5	10.7	2.3	10.4	45 595	72.3	27.7	2.54	2.41
Douglas	11.0	43 284	92.0	8.0	1.7	2.3	8.6	39 821	71.7	28.3	2.50	2.45
Gilliam	17.7	1 043	78.5	21.5	2.9	10.4	15.6	819	70.2	29.8	2.30	2.32
Grant	5.0	4 004	81.1	18.9	7.6	2.1	14.1	3 246	73.5	26.5	2.41	2.33
Harney	10.0	3 533	85.9	14.1	3.6	2.3	15.8	3 036	72.7	27.3	2.45	2.45
Hood River	12.8	7 818	92.7	7.3	2.9	1.4	3.7	7 248	64.9	35.1	2.67	2.75
Jackson	25.0	75 737	94.4	5.6	1.1	1.8	5.0	71 532	66.5	33.5	2.52	2.40
Jefferson	41.8	8 319	80.9	19.1	14.1	2.2	7.0	6 727	71.3	28.7	2.75	2.94
Josephine	23.6	33 239	93.3	6.7	1.3	1.8	5.9	31 000	70.1	29.9	2.40	2.43
Klamath	12.8	28 883	87.3	12.7	5.1	3.0	8.5	25 205	68.0	32.0	2.51	2.44
Lake	11.5	3 999	77.1	22.9	9.3	5.3	12.6	3 084	68.9	31.1	2.38	2.42
Lane	17.7	138 946	93.9	6.1	1.2	1.8	6.3	130 453	62.3	37.7	2.52	2.25
Lincoln	17.3	26 889	71.8	28.2	19.1	5.4	13.6	19 296	65.7	34.3	2.24	2.34
Linn	13.9	42 521	93.0	7.0	0.7	2.2	9.2	39 541	67.9	32.1	2.62	2.50
Malheur	8.1	11 233	91.0	9.0	1.1	2.1	8.5	10 221	63.8	36.2	2.77	2.77
Marion	21.7	108 174	94.0	6.0	0.7	2.5	6.8	101 641	62.9	37.1	2.72	2.67

Table B. States and Counties

STATE/ County code	MSA/ PMSA/ NECMA code[1]	County type[2]	STATE County	Land area, 2000[3] (sq km)	Total persons	Rank	Per square kilometer	Land area, 1990[3] (sq km)	Total persons	Rank	Per square kilometer	White	Black or African American	American Indian or Alaska Native	Asian	Native Hawaiian and other Pacific Islander	Some other race
								Population, 2000				**Population, 1990**		**Population and population characteristics, 2000 — Race (percent) — One race**			
				1	2	3	4	5	6	7	8	9	10	11	12	13	14
			OREGON—Cont'd														
41 049	...	9	Morrow	5 264	10 995	2 367	2.1	5 265	7 625	2 607	1.4	76.3	0.1	1.4	0.4	0.1	19.5
41 051	6440	0	Multnomah	1 127	660 486	79	586.1	1 127	583 887	81	518.1	79.2	5.7	1.0	5.7	0.4	4.0
41 053	7080	2	Polk	1 919	62 380	778	32.5	1 919	49 541	848	25.8	89.2	0.4	1.8	1.1	0.2	4.5
41 055	...	9	Sherman	2 132	1 934	3 068	0.9	2 132	1 918	3 072	0.9	93.6	0.2	1.4	0.5	0.0	2.8
41 057	...	6	Tillamook	2 855	24 262	1 585	8.5	2 855	21 570	1 599	7.6	93.9	0.2	1.2	0.6	0.2	1.9
41 059	...	4	Umatilla	8 327	70 548	704	8.5	8 328	59 249	734	7.1	82.0	0.8	3.4	0.8	0.2	10.7
41 061	...	7	Union	5 275	24 530	1 575	4.7	5 275	23 598	1 510	4.5	94.3	0.5	0.8	0.9	0.6	1.2
41 063	...	9	Wallowa	8 146	7 226	2 663	0.9	8 147	6 911	2 669	0.8	96.5	0.0	0.7	0.2	0.0	1.0
41 065	...	7	Wasco	6 167	23 791	1 599	3.9	6 167	21 683	1 594	3.5	86.6	0.3	3.8	0.8	0.5	5.6
41 067	6440	0	Washington	1 874	445 342	133	237.6	1 875	311 554	161	166.2	82.2	1.1	0.7	6.7	0.3	5.9
41 069	...	9	Wheeler	4 442	1 547	3 092	0.3	4 442	1 396	3 102	0.3	93.3	0.1	0.8	0.3	0.1	3.5
41 071	6440	1	Yamhill	1 853	84 992	612	45.9	1 853	65 551	669	35.4	89.0	0.8	1.5	1.1	0.1	5.1
42 000	...		PENNSYLVANIA	116 074	12 281 054	X	105.8	116 083	11 882 842	X	102.4	85.4	10.0	0.1	1.8	0.0	1.5
42 001	...	6	Adams	1 347	91 292	563	67.8	1 347	78 274	577	58.1	95.4	1.2	0.2	0.5	0.0	1.7
42 003	6280	0	Allegheny	1 891	1 281 666	28	677.8	1 891	1 336 449	19	706.7	84.3	12.4	0.1	1.7	0.0	0.3
42 005	...	6	Armstrong	1 694	72 392	687	42.7	1 694	73 478	612	43.4	98.3	0.8	0.1	0.1	0.0	0.1
42 007	6280	0	Beaver	1 125	181 412	303	161.3	1 127	186 093	261	165.1	92.5	6.0	0.1	0.3	0.0	0.2
42 009	...	6	Bedford	2 628	49 984	916	19.0	2 628	47 919	873	18.2	98.5	0.4	0.1	0.3	0.0	0.2
42 011	6680	2	Berks	2 224	373 638	157	168.0	2 225	336 523	151	151.2	88.2	3.7	0.2	1.0	0.0	5.4
42 013	0280	3	Blair	1 362	129 144	418	94.8	1 362	130 542	357	95.8	97.6	1.2	0.1	0.4	0.0	0.1
42 015	...	6	Bradford	2 980	62 761	776	21.1	2 980	60 967	714	20.5	97.9	0.4	0.3	0.5	0.0	0.2
42 017	6160	0	Bucks	1 573	597 635	91	379.9	1 574	541 174	89	343.8	92.5	3.3	0.1	2.3	0.0	0.8
42 019	6280	1	Butler	2 042	174 083	314	85.3	2 042	152 013	306	74.4	97.8	0.8	0.1	0.6	0.0	0.2
42 021	3680	3	Cambria	1 782	152 598	348	85.6	1 782	163 062	292	91.5	95.8	2.8	0.1	0.4	0.0	0.2
42 023	...	7	Cameron	1 029	5 974	2 784	5.8	1 029	5 913	2 770	5.7	98.8	0.4	0.1	0.1	0.1	0.1
42 025	0240	2	Carbon	987	58 802	814	59.6	991	56 803	767	57.3	97.8	0.6	0.2	0.3	0.0	0.3
42 027	8050	3	Centre	2 868	135 758	397	47.3	2 869	124 812	369	43.5	91.4	2.6	0.1	4.0	0.1	0.7
42 029	6160	0	Chester	1 958	433 501	138	221.4	1 958	376 389	135	192.2	89.2	6.2	0.1	2.0	0.0	1.3
42 031	...	7	Clarion	1 560	41 765	1 060	26.8	1 560	41 699	964	26.7	98.2	0.8	0.1	0.3	0.0	0.1
42 033	...	6	Clearfield	2 972	83 382	624	28.1	2 972	78 097	579	26.3	97.4	1.5	0.1	0.3	0.0	0.3
42 035	...	6	Clinton	2 307	37 914	1 168	16.4	2 307	37 182	1 067	16.1	98.3	0.5	0.1	0.4	0.0	0.1
42 037	7560	2	Columbia	1 258	64 151	760	51.0	1 258	63 202	691	50.2	97.6	0.8	0.1	0.5	0.0	0.3
42 039	...	4	Crawford	2 623	90 366	571	34.5	2 623	86 166	530	32.9	97.0	1.6	0.2	0.3	0.0	0.1
42 041	3240	2	Cumberland	1 425	213 674	261	149.9	1 425	195 257	246	137.0	94.4	2.4	0.1	1.7	0.0	0.4
42 043	3240	2	Dauphin	1 360	251 798	226	185.1	1 361	237 813	211	174.7	77.1	16.9	0.2	2.0	0.0	2.0
42 045	6160	0	Delaware	477	550 864	102	1 154.9	477	547 658	86	1 148.1	80.3	14.5	0.1	3.3	0.0	0.6
42 047	...	7	Elk	2 146	35 112	1 246	16.4	2 146	34 878	1 137	16.3	99.0	0.1	0.1	0.3	0.0	0.1
42 049	2360	2	Erie	2 077	280 843	199	135.2	2 077	275 575	179	132.7	90.9	6.1	0.2	0.7	0.0	0.9
42 051	6280	1	Fayette	2 046	148 644	364	72.7	2 046	145 351	326	71.0	95.3	3.5	0.1	0.2	0.0	0.1
42 053	...	9	Forest	1 109	4 946	2 851	4.5	1 109	4 802	2 857	4.3	95.9	2.2	0.4	0.1	0.0	0.7
42 055	...	4	Franklin	1 999	129 313	416	64.7	1 999	121 082	380	60.6	95.3	2.3	0.1	0.6	0.0	0.7
42 057	...	8	Fulton	1 133	14 261	2 144	12.6	1 133	13 837	2 071	12.2	98.3	0.7	0.2	0.1	0.0	0.0
42 059	...	6	Greene	1 491	40 672	1 093	27.3	1 492	39 550	1 010	26.5	95.1	3.9	0.1	0.2	0.0	0.1
42 061	...	6	Huntingdon	2 264	45 586	990	20.1	2 267	44 164	922	19.5	93.3	5.1	0.1	0.2	0.0	0.4
42 063	...	6	Indiana	2 148	89 605	576	41.7	2 148	89 994	511	41.9	96.9	1.6	0.1	0.7	0.0	0.2
42 065	...	7	Jefferson	1 698	45 932	985	27.1	1 698	46 083	902	27.1	99.0	0.1	0.2	0.2	0.0	0.1
42 067	...	8	Juniata	1 014	22 821	1 652	22.5	1 014	20 625	1 649	20.3	98.1	0.4	0.1	0.2	0.2	0.5
42 069	7560	2	Lackawanna	1 188	213 295	263	179.5	1 188	219 097	226	184.4	96.7	1.3	0.1	0.8	0.0	0.5
42 071	4000	2	Lancaster	2 458	470 658	122	191.5	2 458	422 822	119	172.0	91.5	2.8	0.1	1.4	0.0	2.9
42 073	...	4	Lawrence	934	94 643	543	101.3	934	96 246	481	103.0	95.0	3.6	0.1	0.3	0.0	0.2
42 075	3240	2	Lebanon	937	120 327	452	128.4	937	113 744	403	121.4	94.5	1.3	0.1	0.9	0.0	2.3
42 077	0240	2	Lehigh	898	312 090	183	347.5	898	291 130	169	324.2	87.0	3.6	0.2	2.1	0.0	5.3
42 079	7560	2	Luzerne	2 307	319 250	181	138.4	2 308	328 149	155	142.2	96.6	1.7	0.1	0.6	0.0	0.4
42 081	9140	3	Lycoming	3 198	120 044	454	37.5	3 198	118 710	391	37.1	93.9	4.3	0.2	0.4	0.0	0.3
42 083	...	7	McKean	2 542	45 936	984	18.1	2 542	47 131	889	18.5	96.5	1.9	0.3	0.3	0.0	0.4
42 085	7610	3	Mercer	1 740	120 293	453	69.1	1 740	121 003	381	69.5	93.1	5.3	0.1	0.4	0.0	0.2
42 087	...	6	Mifflin	1 067	46 486	973	43.6	1 064	46 197	899	43.4	98.5	0.5	0.1	0.3	0.0	0.2
42 089	...	6	Monroe	1 576	138 687	393	88.0	1 573	95 681	483	60.8	88.2	6.0	0.2	1.1	0.0	2.4
42 091	6160	0	Montgomery	1 251	750 097	67	599.6	1 251	678 193	61	542.1	86.5	7.5	0.1	4.0	0.0	0.7
42 093	...	6	Montour	339	18 236	1 884	53.8	339	17 735	1 801	52.3	96.7	1.0	0.1	1.3	0.0	0.4
42 095	0240	2	Northampton	968	267 066	206	275.9	968	247 110	202	255.3	91.2	2.8	0.2	1.4	0.0	3.1
42 097	...	4	Northumberland	1 191	94 556	544	79.4	1 191	96 771	476	81.3	97.1	1.5	0.1	0.2	0.0	0.5
42 099	3240	2	Perry	1 434	43 602	1 027	30.4	1 434	41 172	976	28.7	98.5	0.4	0.1	0.1	0.0	0.2
42 101	6160	0	Philadelphia	350	1 517 550	18	4 335.9	350	1 585 577	12	4 530.2	45.0	43.2	0.3	4.5	0.0	4.8
42 103	5660	1	Pike	1 416	46 302	976	32.7	1 417	28 032	1 351	19.8	93.1	3.3	0.2	0.6	0.0	1.3

[1]MSA = Metropolitan Statistical Area. PMSA = Primary MSA. NECMA = New England County Metropolitan Area. See Appendix A for explanation of these concepts. See Appendix B for list of metropolitan areas identified by type, with component counties.
[2]County typology code from the Economic Research Service of USDA. See Appendix A for definition.
[3]Dry land or land partially or temporarily covered by water.

Table B. States and Counties

STATE County	Population and population characteristics, 2000 (cont'd)								Population and population characteristics, 1990				
	Race (percent) (cont'd)								Race (percent)				
	Two or more races	Race alone or in combination						Hispanic¹	White	Black or African American	American Indian or Alaska Native	Asian and Pacific Islander	Hispanic¹
		White	Black	American Indian or Alaska Native	Asian	Native Hawaiian and other Pacific Islander	Some other race						
	15	16	17	18	19	20	21	22	23	24	25	26	27
OREGON—Cont'd													
Morrow	2.1	78.0	0.3	2.4	0.7	0.2	20.5	24.4	89.6	0.1	1.0	0.4	10.8
Multnomah	4.1	82.6	6.8	2.2	6.8	0.7	5.4	7.5	87.0	6.0	1.2	4.7	3.1
Polk	2.7	91.8	0.7	3.1	1.6	0.4	5.2	8.8	93.3	0.4	1.5	1.4	5.7
Sherman	1.6	95.1	0.5	2.2	0.8	0.0	3.1	4.9	97.2	0.0	1.3	0.7	1.5
Tillamook	2.0	95.8	0.4	2.4	0.9	0.4	2.2	5.1	97.4	0.2	1.1	0.8	1.7
Umatilla	2.2	84.0	1.1	4.2	1.1	0.3	11.7	16.1	89.0	0.6	3.1	0.9	9.0
Union	1.7	95.9	0.7	1.6	1.2	0.8	1.7	2.4	96.7	0.4	1.1	1.2	1.6
Wallowa	1.5	98.0	0.2	1.7	0.4	0.1	1.2	1.7	98.8	0.1	0.5	0.4	1.6
Wasco	2.4	88.8	0.6	4.7	1.2	0.7	6.5	9.3	91.8	0.3	4.1	1.1	4.9
Washington	3.2	84.9	1.6	1.4	7.9	0.6	6.9	11.2	91.9	0.7	0.6	4.3	4.6
Wheeler	1.9	95.3	0.3	2.3	0.4	0.2	3.9	5.1	99.0	0.1	0.8	0.1	0.9
Yamhill	2.4	91.2	1.1	2.5	1.6	0.3	5.8	10.6	94.8	0.6	1.3	1.2	6.3
PENNSYLVANIA	1.2	86.3	10.5	0.4	2.0	0.1	1.9	3.2	88.5	9.2	0.1	1.2	2.0
Adams	1.0	96.3	1.5	0.4	0.7	0.0	2.0	3.6	97.5	1.2	0.1	0.5	1.6
Allegheny	1.1	85.2	13.0	0.4	1.9	0.1	0.6	0.9	87.5	11.2	0.1	1.0	0.7
Armstrong	0.5	98.8	1.0	0.3	0.2	0.0	0.2	0.4	99.0	0.8	0.1	0.1	0.2
Beaver	0.9	93.4	6.5	0.4	0.3	0.0	0.3	0.7	93.9	5.6	0.1	0.2	0.6
Bedford	0.5	99.1	0.5	0.4	0.4	0.0	0.2	0.5	99.3	0.3	0.1	0.2	0.2
Berks	1.5	89.4	4.3	0.4	1.2	0.1	6.2	9.7	93.5	3.0	0.1	0.8	5.1
Blair	0.6	98.2	1.4	0.3	0.5	0.0	0.2	0.5	98.7	0.8	0.1	0.3	0.3
Bradford	0.7	98.6	0.5	0.7	0.6	0.0	0.3	0.6	99.1	0.2	0.2	0.4	0.4
Bucks	1.0	93.3	3.6	0.4	2.6	0.1	1.1	2.3	95.0	2.8	0.1	1.6	1.6
Butler	0.5	98.3	1.0	0.3	0.7	0.1	0.3	0.6	98.9	0.5	0.1	0.4	0.4
Cambria	0.6	96.4	3.2	0.3	0.5	0.1	0.3	0.9	97.3	2.3	0.1	0.2	0.6
Cameron	0.5	99.2	0.5	0.4	0.1	0.1	0.2	0.6	99.4	0.1	0.3	0.1	0.1
Carbon	0.8	98.5	0.8	0.5	0.4	0.0	0.6	1.5	99.2	0.2	0.1	0.3	0.9
Centre	1.1	92.3	2.9	0.4	4.4	0.2	1.0	1.7	94.2	2.3	0.1	3.1	1.1
Chester	1.1	90.1	6.7	0.4	2.2	0.1	1.7	3.7	91.6	6.4	0.1	1.1	2.3
Clarion	0.5	98.6	0.9	0.3	0.5	0.0	0.1	0.4	98.8	0.5	0.2	0.5	0.3
Clearfield	0.5	97.8	1.6	0.3	0.3	0.0	0.4	0.6	99.4	0.2	0.1	0.2	0.3
Clinton	0.5	98.8	0.6	0.3	0.5	0.1	0.2	0.5	99.1	0.4	0.1	0.3	0.2
Columbia	0.6	98.1	1.0	0.4	0.6	0.1	0.4	0.9	99.0	0.4	0.1	0.4	0.5
Crawford	0.8	97.7	1.9	0.5	0.4	0.0	0.3	0.6	98.2	1.2	0.1	0.3	0.4
Cumberland	1.0	95.3	2.7	0.4	2.0	0.1	0.7	1.3	96.8	1.6	0.1	1.3	0.7
Dauphin	1.9	78.6	18.1	0.5	2.3	0.1	2.5	4.1	82.4	15.0	0.1	1.2	2.5
Delaware	1.2	81.2	15.1	0.4	3.6	0.1	0.9	1.5	86.5	11.2	0.1	1.8	1.1
Elk	0.3	99.2	0.2	0.3	0.4	0.1	0.1	0.4	99.5	0.0	0.1	0.3	0.2
Erie	1.2	92.0	6.7	0.5	0.9	0.1	1.2	2.2	93.6	5.2	0.2	0.5	1.2
Fayette	0.7	96.0	3.9	0.3	0.3	0.0	0.2	0.4	96.2	3.5	0.1	0.2	0.3
Forest	0.6	96.5	2.3	0.8	0.2	0.0	0.7	1.2	98.5	0.9	0.2	0.1	0.5
Franklin	0.9	96.1	2.7	0.4	0.7	0.1	0.9	1.8	96.7	2.3	0.1	0.5	0.9
Fulton	0.7	98.9	0.8	0.6	0.2	0.1	0.1	0.4	98.8	0.9	0.2	0.1	0.2
Greene	0.6	95.6	4.0	0.5	0.3	0.1	0.1	0.9	98.5	1.0	0.2	0.3	0.5
Huntingdon	0.8	94.1	5.4	0.3	0.3	0.0	0.7	1.1	95.1	4.5	0.1	0.2	0.4
Indiana	0.6	97.4	1.8	0.3	0.9	0.0	0.3	0.5	97.8	1.3	0.1	0.6	0.4
Jefferson	0.5	99.4	0.2	0.4	0.3	0.0	0.1	0.4	99.6	0.1	0.1	0.2	0.2
Juniata	0.5	98.5	0.5	0.3	0.4	0.2	0.7	1.6	99.5	0.1	0.1	0.2	0.2
Lackawanna	0.7	97.2	1.6	0.2	0.9	0.0	0.7	1.4	98.4	0.7	0.1	0.6	0.5
Lancaster	1.3	92.5	3.3	0.4	1.6	0.1	3.4	5.7	94.1	2.4	0.1	1.1	3.7
Lawrence	0.8	95.8	4.1	0.3	0.4	0.0	0.3	0.6	96.5	3.0	0.1	0.3	0.4
Lebanon	0.9	95.3	1.6	0.3	1.0	0.1	2.7	5.0	97.5	0.6	0.1	0.8	2.3
Lehigh	1.8	88.6	4.2	0.4	2.4	0.1	6.2	10.2	93.3	2.3	0.1	1.3	5.2
Luzerne	0.6	97.1	1.9	0.2	0.7	0.0	0.6	1.2	98.1	1.2	0.1	0.5	0.6
Lycoming	0.9	94.7	4.8	0.5	0.5	0.0	0.4	0.7	96.9	2.4	0.2	0.4	0.5
McKean	0.6	97.0	2.0	0.6	0.4	0.1	0.5	1.1	97.9	1.1	0.2	0.3	1.1
Mercer	0.9	94.0	5.7	0.4	0.5	0.0	0.3	0.7	94.6	4.9	0.1	0.3	0.4
Mifflin	0.4	98.9	0.6	0.2	0.4	0.0	0.2	0.6	99.4	0.2	0.1	0.2	0.3
Monroe	2.0	89.7	6.9	0.7	1.4	0.1	3.3	6.6	96.9	1.8	0.1	0.7	2.1
Montgomery	1.2	87.4	8.0	0.4	4.4	0.1	1.1	2.0	91.4	5.8	0.1	2.4	1.2
Montour	0.6	97.2	1.2	0.2	1.4	0.0	0.5	0.9	98.5	0.4	0.0	0.8	0.7
Northampton	1.4	92.4	3.3	0.4	1.6	0.1	3.7	6.7	94.2	2.1	0.1	1.1	4.7
Northumberland	0.6	97.6	1.7	0.3	0.3	0.0	0.6	1.1	99.2	0.3	0.1	0.2	0.5
Perry	0.5	99.1	0.6	0.3	0.2	0.0	0.3	0.7	99.4	0.2	0.1	0.2	0.5
Philadelphia	2.2	46.4	44.3	0.7	4.9	0.2	6.0	8.5	53.5	39.9	0.2	2.7	5.6
Pike	1.5	94.4	3.7	0.8	0.8	0.0	1.9	5.0	98.0	0.9	0.2	0.5	2.3

¹Hispanic persons may be of any race.

Table B. States and Counties

STATE County	Population and population characteristics, 2000										
	Age (percent)										
	Under 5 years	5 to 17 years	18 to 24 years	25 to 34 years	35 to 44 years	45 to 54 years	55 to 64 years	65 to 74 years	75 years and over	Median age (years)	Percent Female
	28	29	30	31	32	33	34	35	36	37	38
OREGON—Cont'd											
Morrow	8.5	22.2	8.9	12.3	15.0	13.4	9.0	6.3	4.3	33.3	48.4
Multnomah	6.4	15.9	10.3	17.5	16.3	14.8	7.6	5.2	5.9	34.9	50.5
Polk	6.3	19.1	11.7	11.0	13.7	14.6	8.9	6.8	8.0	36.5	51.5
Sherman	5.1	21.4	5.8	7.6	15.8	15.0	11.1	10.1	8.1	41.8	49.3
Tillamook	4.8	17.4	6.5	9.5	14.0	15.7	12.3	11.2	8.5	43.5	49.9
Umatilla	7.5	20.3	9.4	13.3	14.9	13.6	8.6	6.2	6.1	34.6	48.8
Union	5.9	18.7	12.1	10.2	13.3	15.4	9.7	7.3	7.4	37.7	51.3
Wallowa	4.9	19.4	4.9	7.5	14.4	18.0	12.1	10.0	8.8	44.4	50.0
Wasco	6.5	18.8	7.4	10.7	14.5	15.2	10.2	8.2	8.5	39.9	50.5
Washington	7.9	19.0	9.3	17.1	16.9	13.8	7.2	4.3	4.5	33.0	50.2
Wheeler	4.7	18.0	3.4	8.0	11.3	14.8	16.5	13.8	9.4	48.1	49.5
Yamhill	7.0	19.9	11.4	12.9	15.6	13.4	8.0	5.8	6.0	34.1	49.5
PENNSYLVANIA	5.9	17.9	8.9	12.7	15.9	13.9	9.2	7.9	7.7	38.0	51.7
Adams	5.9	19.0	9.2	12.5	16.4	13.8	9.2	7.3	6.6	37.0	50.9
Allegheny	5.5	16.4	8.5	12.6	15.8	14.2	9.2	8.8	9.0	39.6	52.6
Armstrong	5.4	17.5	7.2	11.6	16.1	14.4	9.8	9.1	8.9	40.4	51.4
Beaver	5.4	17.2	7.4	11.1	16.2	14.3	9.9	9.6	8.8	40.7	52.1
Bedford	6.0	17.5	7.2	12.6	15.5	13.6	11.0	9.1	7.4	39.5	50.7
Berks	6.2	18.4	8.8	12.7	16.2	13.7	8.9	7.7	7.3	37.4	51.0
Blair	5.6	17.1	8.9	12.0	15.0	14.3	9.7	8.6	8.8	39.5	52.1
Bradford	6.1	19.5	6.8	11.8	15.4	14.2	10.5	8.1	7.6	38.9	51.3
Bucks	6.4	19.3	7.0	12.6	18.0	15.1	9.2	6.7	5.7	37.7	50.9
Butler	6.4	18.2	8.8	12.4	16.9	14.2	8.8	6.9	7.3	37.6	51.2
Cambria	5.0	16.0	9.0	11.4	14.7	14.5	9.6	9.6	10.1	41.2	51.5
Cameron	4.8	19.7	6.0	10.9	14.0	14.2	10.6	9.5	10.2	41.3	50.9
Carbon	5.1	17.0	6.9	12.2	16.1	14.0	10.2	9.6	8.9	40.6	51.3
Centre	4.6	13.4	26.8	13.4	13.1	11.1	7.2	5.6	4.8	28.7	48.9
Chester	6.8	19.4	7.9	12.6	17.7	14.9	8.9	6.3	5.4	36.9	50.9
Clarion	5.4	16.2	15.4	11.4	13.8	12.9	9.8	8.0	7.2	36.3	51.7
Clearfield	5.5	17.2	7.7	12.9	15.9	13.8	10.1	8.5	8.4	39.3	50.1
Clinton	5.4	16.1	13.6	11.4	14.1	12.9	9.8	8.8	8.0	37.8	51.5
Columbia	4.9	15.9	14.3	11.5	14.4	13.5	9.6	8.0	7.9	37.5	52.4
Crawford	5.9	18.8	9.2	11.8	14.8	14.1	9.8	7.9	7.6	38.1	51.3
Cumberland	5.5	16.5	10.6	12.6	15.9	14.7	9.4	7.6	7.2	38.1	51.2
Dauphin	6.2	18.1	7.6	13.6	16.5	14.9	9.0	7.4	6.8	37.9	52.0
Delaware	6.2	18.6	8.9	12.5	16.2	13.4	8.5	7.6	7.9	37.4	52.3
Elk	5.7	18.3	6.8	12.5	16.1	13.6	9.7	9.1	8.2	39.4	50.5
Erie	6.2	18.8	10.8	12.5	15.1	13.6	8.6	7.1	7.2	36.2	51.2
Fayette	5.7	17.0	7.7	12.2	15.0	14.4	9.8	9.0	9.1	40.2	52.1
Forest	3.6	19.1	5.9	9.0	13.7	13.9	14.9	11.0	8.9	44.2	47.4
Franklin	6.3	17.8	7.9	13.0	15.2	13.7	10.0	8.3	7.7	38.3	51.3
Fulton	6.3	18.3	7.6	13.1	15.3	13.4	11.6	8.4	6.1	38.2	50.0
Greene	5.2	16.9	9.7	13.8	15.2	15.0	9.0	7.5	7.7	38.2	48.5
Huntingdon	5.4	16.3	10.1	13.9	15.5	14.0	10.0	8.3	6.5	37.7	47.7
Indiana	4.9	16.1	16.6	10.9	14.0	13.6	9.1	7.4	7.5	36.2	51.5
Jefferson	5.5	18.0	7.7	11.6	15.6	13.6	10.0	8.9	9.0	39.8	51.1
Juniata	6.5	18.5	8.0	12.8	15.2	13.6	10.2	8.2	7.0	37.7	50.3
Lackawanna	5.3	16.5	8.9	11.7	14.7	13.8	9.7	9.3	10.2	40.3	52.8
Lancaster	6.9	19.7	9.2	12.6	15.7	13.2	8.6	6.9	7.1	36.1	51.2
Lawrence	5.6	17.5	8.3	10.9	14.8	14.0	9.6	9.3	9.9	40.5	52.5
Lebanon	6.1	17.6	8.2	12.4	15.6	14.1	9.7	8.3	8.1	38.7	51.3
Lehigh	6.0	17.9	8.1	12.7	16.4	14.0	9.0	7.8	8.0	38.3	51.8
Luzerne	5.0	16.1	8.1	12.2	15.0	14.0	10.0	9.4	10.2	40.8	51.8
Lycoming	5.5	17.8	9.7	12.0	15.6	14.1	9.4	8.2	7.8	38.4	51.1
McKean	5.7	18.0	7.9	13.1	15.4	13.5	9.7	8.4	8.3	38.7	49.9
Mercer	5.7	17.7	8.9	11.2	14.8	13.7	9.7	9.1	9.0	39.6	51.3
Mifflin	6.3	18.3	7.0	12.7	14.7	13.3	10.6	8.8	8.2	38.8	51.8
Monroe	6.0	20.8	8.6	10.9	17.9	14.3	9.2	7.1	5.1	37.2	50.6
Montgomery	6.3	17.8	7.1	13.5	17.1	14.2	9.1	7.4	7.5	38.2	51.7
Montour	5.7	18.7	6.4	11.8	16.3	14.1	9.8	8.2	8.9	39.8	52.5
Northampton	5.6	17.8	9.2	12.0	16.3	14.2	9.1	7.8	7.9	38.5	51.3
Northumberland	5.1	16.8	7.0	12.3	15.3	14.1	10.3	9.3	9.7	40.8	51.0
Perry	6.1	19.4	7.4	13.1	16.7	15.5	9.5	6.9	5.3	37.5	50.4
Philadelphia	6.5	18.8	11.1	14.8	14.5	12.0	8.3	7.1	7.0	34.2	53.5
Pike	5.9	20.8	5.3	10.0	17.7	14.2	11.0	9.6	5.6	39.6	50.2

Table B. States and Counties

STATE County	Population and population characteristics, 1990										Population—change, 1980–2000				
	Age (percent)										Total persons			Percent change	
	Under 5 years	5 to 17 years	18 to 24 years	25 to 34 years	35 to 44 years	45 to 54 years	55 to 64 years	65 to 74 years	75 years and over	Percent Female	2000	1990	1980	1990–2000	1980–1990
	39	40	41	42	43	44	45	46	47	48	49	50	51	52	53
OREGON—Cont'd															
Morrow	7.8	22.5	7.6	14.4	15.6	10.6	9.9	6.6	5.2	49.4	10 995	7 625	7 519	44.2	1.4
Multnomah	7.1	16.0	10.0	18.4	17.6	9.6	7.6	7.4	6.2	51.4	660 486	503 007	562 647	13.1	3.8
Polk	6.9	19.6	11.5	13.2	15.7	9.9	8.3	8.4	6.6	51.8	62 380	49 541	45 203	25.9	9.6
Sherman	8.0	19.8	3.9	14.1	15.5	9.2	12.7	11.0	5.8	48.7	1 934	1 918	2 172	0.8	-11.7
Tillamook	6.1	17.4	5.9	12.5	14.3	10.3	12.6	13.0	7.9	50.8	24 262	21 570	21 164	12.5	1.9
Umatilla	7.5	20.3	9.5	15.5	15.0	10.0	8.4	8.0	5.9	49.4	70 548	59 249	58 861	19.1	0.7
Union	6.9	20.8	10.5	13.2	15.8	10.2	8.4	7.5	6.6	50.7	24 530	23 598	23 921	3.9	-1.4
Wallowa	6.8	19.8	5.3	12.9	15.5	10.9	10.8	10.1	7.8	50.4	7 226	6 911	7 273	4.6	-5.0
Wasco	6.9	20.1	6.5	13.4	15.6	10.6	9.4	9.7	7.8	51.5	23 791	21 683	21 732	9.7	-0.2
Washington	7.8	19.0	9.0	18.6	18.2	10.5	6.8	5.7	4.4	51.1	445 342	311 554	245 860	42.9	26.7
Wheeler	5.4	16.7	5.9	9.2	14.0	13.3	14.0	13.0	8.4	50.2	1 547	1 396	1 513	10.8	-7.7
Yamhill	7.5	20.8	10.1	15.1	15.7	9.8	7.7	7.4	5.8	49.9	84 992	65 551	55 332	29.7	18.5
PENNSYLVANIA	6.7	16.8	10.3	16.1	14.7	10.2	9.8	9.0	6.4	52.1	12 281 054	11 882 842	11 864 720	3.4	0.2
Adams	7.0	18.0	11.3	16.2	14.8	10.2	8.8	7.7	5.8	51.2	91 292	78 274	68 292	16.6	14.6
Allegheny	6.3	14.8	9.7	16.5	14.7	10.0	10.6	10.3	7.1	53.1	1 281 666	1 336 449	1 450 195	-4.1	-7.8
Armstrong	6.0	18.0	8.5	15.0	14.4	10.2	10.3	10.2	7.4	51.9	72 392	73 478	77 768	-1.5	-5.5
Beaver	6.3	17.0	8.5	15.1	14.2	10.5	11.4	10.5	6.4	52.4	181 412	186 093	204 441	-2.5	-9.0
Bedford	6.4	18.7	9.1	14.9	13.7	11.4	10.5	9.2	6.2	51.1	49 984	47 919	46 784	4.3	2.4
Berks	6.7	16.6	10.0	16.1	14.8	10.3	9.9	8.8	6.8	51.7	373 638	336 523	312 509	11.0	7.7
Blair	6.3	18.1	9.2	14.5	14.5	10.2	10.2	9.8	7.2	52.9	129 144	130 542	136 621	-1.1	-4.4
Bradford	7.1	20.0	8.5	15.0	14.5	11.0	9.3	8.4	6.3	51.4	62 761	60 967	62 919	2.9	-3.1
Bucks	7.3	18.3	9.1	17.5	16.7	11.1	9.0	6.7	4.2	50.8	597 635	541 174	479 180	10.4	12.9
Butler	6.8	18.0	11.0	16.0	15.5	10.3	9.0	7.8	5.7	51.2	174 083	152 013	147 912	14.5	2.8
Cambria	5.7	17.6	9.3	13.7	14.4	9.7	10.8	11.2	7.5	52.1	152 598	163 062	183 263	-6.4	-11.0
Cameron	7.2	18.4	7.7	13.4	14.0	10.1	10.8	11.1	7.4	51.1	5 974	5 913	6 674	1.0	-11.4
Carbon	6.2	16.7	8.4	15.1	14.0	10.1	11.1	11.0	7.4	51.7	58 802	56 803	53 285	3.5	6.9
Centre	5.6	12.7	28.2	16.8	12.5	8.4	6.9	5.3	3.7	48.2	135 758	124 812	112 760	8.8	10.7
Chester	7.4	17.5	10.0	17.1	16.9	11.4	8.7	6.6	4.3	51.0	433 501	376 389	316 660	15.2	18.9
Clarion	5.8	17.4	17.0	13.8	12.9	10.1	9.2	7.9	6.0	51.7	41 765	41 699	43 362	0.2	-3.8
Clearfield	6.5	18.6	8.9	15.0	13.9	10.5	9.9	9.8	6.8	51.8	83 382	78 097	83 578	6.8	-6.6
Clinton	5.8	17.4	13.6	13.4	13.3	10.1	10.3	9.5	6.4	52.1	37 914	37 182	38 971	2.0	-4.6
Columbia	5.9	15.9	15.5	14.0	13.6	9.9	9.4	9.3	6.5	52.7	64 151	63 202	61 967	1.5	2.0
Crawford	6.8	19.1	10.6	14.0	14.3	10.3	9.3	8.8	6.6	51.5	90 366	86 166	88 869	4.9	-3.0
Cumberland	5.9	16.0	12.8	15.8	15.6	10.9	9.5	7.9	5.5	51.7	213 674	195 257	179 625	9.4	8.7
Dauphin	7.0	16.4	9.3	17.4	15.9	10.3	9.5	8.3	6.0	52.2	251 798	237 813	232 317	5.9	2.4
Delaware	7.0	16.1	10.7	16.9	14.2	9.7	9.8	9.2	6.3	52.3	550 864	547 658	555 029	0.6	-1.3
Elk	6.8	18.8	8.4	15.3	13.6	10.4	10.6	9.6	6.4	50.9	35 112	34 878	38 338	0.7	-9.0
Erie	7.2	18.7	12.0	15.5	14.4	9.6	8.9	8.4	5.4	51.7	280 843	275 575	279 780	1.9	-1.5
Fayette	6.1	18.1	8.8	14.1	14.4	10.0	10.6	10.7	7.3	52.5	148 644	145 351	159 417	2.3	-8.8
Forest	5.4	17.8	7.5	11.8	12.9	12.1	12.3	12.3	7.9	48.5	4 946	4 802	5 072	3.0	-5.3
Franklin	6.6	17.8	9.9	15.6	14.8	11.0	9.7	8.4	6.0	51.5	129 313	121 082	113 629	6.8	6.6
Fulton	7.1	19.7	9.5	15.2	14.1	11.5	10.0	7.8	5.2	50.4	14 261	13 837	12 842	3.1	7.7
Greene	6.4	19.3	10.0	14.1	15.2	9.6	9.0	9.3	7.1	52.5	40 672	39 550	40 476	2.8	-2.3
Huntingdon	6.3	17.2	11.8	15.8	15.2	10.4	9.8	7.7	5.8	48.3	45 586	44 164	42 253	3.2	4.5
Indiana	5.8	17.5	17.4	13.9	13.7	9.4	8.4	8.1	5.7	51.8	89 605	89 994	92 281	-0.4	-2.5
Jefferson	6.5	18.9	8.6	14.9	13.9	10.0	10.0	9.7	7.6	51.7	45 932	46 083	48 303	-0.3	-4.6
Juniata	6.8	19.1	9.1	15.7	14.5	10.8	9.6	8.1	6.3	50.8	22 821	20 625	19 188	10.6	7.5
Lackawanna	6.0	15.9	10.2	14.1	13.6	9.9	10.5	11.2	8.6	53.3	213 295	219 097	227 908	-2.6	-3.9
Lancaster	7.9	18.6	10.6	16.6	14.7	9.9	8.6	7.4	5.7	51.4	470 658	422 822	362 346	11.3	16.7
Lawrence	6.2	17.3	9.3	13.8	14.0	10.1	10.9	11.1	7.4	52.6	94 643	96 246	107 150	-1.7	-10.2
Lebanon	6.7	17.7	9.5	15.8	14.9	10.6	9.8	8.5	6.5	51.2	120 327	113 744	108 582	5.8	4.8
Lehigh	6.6	16.0	9.4	16.9	15.4	10.4	9.9	8.9	6.5	51.9	312 090	291 130	272 349	7.2	6.9
Luzerne	5.9	15.5	9.6	14.4	13.8	10.2	10.9	11.2	8.5	52.7	319 250	328 149	343 079	-2.7	-4.4
Lycoming	6.9	18.0	9.9	15.5	14.7	10.1	9.7	8.7	6.4	51.8	120 044	118 710	118 416	1.1	0.2
McKean	6.5	18.3	9.1	14.8	14.1	10.3	10.2	9.0	7.7	50.7	45 936	47 131	50 635	-2.5	-6.9
Mercer	6.2	17.2	10.3	14.2	13.8	10.3	10.7	10.0	7.2	51.5	120 293	121 003	128 299	-0.6	-5.7
Mifflin	7.0	17.9	9.4	14.7	13.7	11.2	10.0	9.2	6.8	52.1	46 486	46 197	46 908	0.6	-1.5
Monroe	7.4	17.5	10.3	16.6	16.0	10.1	9.2	8.1	5.0	50.8	138 687	95 681	69 409	44.9	37.7
Montgomery	6.8	15.8	8.9	17.2	15.5	10.9	9.9	8.6	6.4	51.9	750 097	678 193	643 371	10.6	5.4
Montour	7.1	17.3	8.5	16.8	14.2	10.4	9.3	8.6	7.9	53.2	18 236	17 735	16 675	2.8	6.4
Northampton	6.7	16.5	11.1	15.8	15.2	10.2	9.5	9.0	6.0	51.4	267 066	247 110	225 418	8.1	9.6
Northumberland	6.2	17.0	8.4	14.3	13.9	10.5	10.7	10.7	8.2	52.6	94 556	96 771	100 381	-2.3	-3.6
Perry	7.3	19.7	9.1	16.8	16.7	10.6	8.7	6.9	4.2	50.2	43 602	41 172	35 718	5.9	15.3
Philadelphia	7.3	16.6	11.6	17.5	13.5	9.3	9.0	8.7	6.5	53.5	1 517 550	1 585 577	1 688 210	-4.3	-6.1
Pike	8.1	17.2	6.5	16.8	15.0	9.8	11.1	10.1	5.4	50.4	46 302	28 032	18 271	65.2	53.1

Table B. States and Counties

	Household relationship, 2000																
	In households (percent)										In group quarters (percent)						
					Child		Other relatives		Nonrelatives			Institutionalized population			Noninstitutionalized population		
STATE County	Total population	Total in households	House-holder	Spouse	Total	Own child under 18 years	Total	Under 18 years	Total	Unmarried partner	Total in group quarters	Correctional institutions	Nursing homes	Other institutions	College dormitories	Military quarters	Other
	54	55	56	57	58	59	60	61	62	63	64	65	66	67	68	69	70
OREGON—Cont'd																	
Morrow	10 995	99.6	34.3	21.5	33.4	27.6	5.7	2.3	4.7	2.2	0.4	0.0	0.0	0.2	0.0	0.0	0.2
Multnomah	660 486	97.5	41.2	16.9	25.0	19.8	4.9	1.6	9.5	3.2	2.5	0.4	0.5	0.1	0.7	0.0	0.8
Polk	62 380	96.7	37.0	21.1	28.4	23.2	3.9	1.5	6.4	1.9	3.3	0.1	1.2	0.0	1.2	0.0	0.7
Sherman	1 934	100.0	41.2	24.1	28.6	24.7	2.7	0.9	3.3	1.1	0.0	0.0	0.0	0.0	0.0	0.0	0.0
Tillamook	24 262	98.1	42.0	23.0	24.2	19.9	3.7	1.4	5.2	2.3	1.9	1.0	0.3	0.2	0.0	0.0	0.3
Umatilla	70 548	95.3	35.7	19.7	29.8	24.7	4.8	1.9	5.4	2.3	4.7	3.4	0.3	0.2	0.0	0.0	0.7
Union	24 530	97.3	39.7	21.9	26.9	22.4	2.9	1.2	6.0	2.2	2.7	0.2	0.6	0.1	1.4	0.0	0.5
Wallowa	7 226	98.5	41.9	24.6	26.3	22.8	2.4	0.9	3.3	1.8	1.5	0.0	0.9	0.0	0.0	0.0	0.6
Wasco	23 791	97.8	39.5	21.6	27.6	22.5	4.3	2.0	4.8	2.1	2.2	0.6	0.9	0.1	0.0	0.0	0.6
Washington	445 342	99.1	38.0	20.7	29.6	25.0	4.4	1.3	6.4	2.2	0.9	0.1	0.2	0.0	0.1	0.0	0.4
Wheeler	1 547	98.0	42.2	26.2	21.6	18.7	2.7	1.3	5.3	1.7	2.0	0.0	0.0	0.0	0.4	0.0	1.6
Yamhill	84 992	94.1	33.8	20.3	29.8	24.5	4.6	1.7	5.6	1.8	5.9	2.6	0.8	0.0	2.2	0.0	0.3
PENNSYLVANIA	12 281 054	96.5	38.9	20.1	28.9	21.6	4.3	1.6	4.3	1.9	3.5	0.6	0.9	0.2	1.2	0.0	0.6
Adams	91 292	96.0	36.9	22.5	29.1	23.0	3.2	1.2	4.3	2.2	4.0	0.2	1.1	0.2	2.1	0.0	0.4
Allegheny	1 281 666	96.8	41.9	19.3	27.6	20.2	3.9	1.4	4.1	1.8	3.2	0.4	0.9	0.2	1.1	0.0	0.6
Armstrong	72 392	98.4	40.1	23.2	29.0	21.3	3.0	1.1	3.1	1.8	1.6	0.1	0.6	0.0	0.1	0.0	0.9
Beaver	181 412	97.6	40.0	21.8	28.8	20.8	3.9	1.5	3.0	1.7	2.4	0.2	0.9	0.1	0.6	0.0	0.6
Bedford	49 984	99.1	39.5	24.4	29.0	21.9	3.1	1.2	3.1	1.6	0.9	0.2	0.5	0.0	0.0	0.0	0.2
Berks	373 638	96.7	37.9	21.0	28.9	22.4	4.0	1.5	4.9	2.5	3.3	0.3	0.9	0.2	1.2	0.0	0.7
Blair	129 144	96.8	39.9	21.0	28.4	20.8	3.5	1.4	4.1	2.0	3.2	0.2	1.7	0.1	0.7	0.0	0.6
Bradford	62 761	98.3	39.0	22.4	29.4	23.5	3.1	1.3	4.5	2.4	1.7	0.2	0.9	0.0	0.0	0.0	0.6
Bucks	597 635	98.5	36.6	22.4	32.0	24.0	3.9	1.3	3.5	1.7	1.5	0.1	0.7	0.1	0.2	0.0	0.3
Butler	174 083	96.3	37.8	22.6	29.8	23.1	2.6	0.9	3.5	1.6	3.7	0.1	1.3	0.4	1.5	0.0	0.5
Cambria	152 598	94.6	39.7	20.9	27.6	19.4	3.5	1.2	2.8	1.6	5.4	1.6	0.9	0.5	1.7	0.0	0.8
Cameron	5 974	98.6	41.3	21.6	28.5	22.6	3.1	1.3	4.2	2.3	1.4	0.1	0.7	0.0	0.0	0.0	0.6
Carbon	58 802	98.4	40.3	22.1	28.0	20.2	3.8	1.2	4.2	2.5	1.6	0.2	0.7	0.3	0.0	0.0	0.4
Centre	135 758	89.1	36.3	17.8	21.3	17.0	1.9	0.6	11.8	1.6	10.9	1.5	0.6	0.1	8.4	0.0	0.3
Chester	433 501	96.6	36.4	22.0	30.7	24.5	3.4	1.2	4.0	1.6	3.4	0.2	0.9	0.4	1.3	0.0	0.7
Clarion	41 765	94.5	38.4	21.1	26.6	20.2	2.4	0.8	5.9	1.9	5.5	0.2	0.9	0.1	4.2	0.0	0.1
Clearfield	83 382	96.1	39.3	22.3	28.0	21.0	3.1	1.2	3.5	1.9	3.9	2.6	0.9	0.0	0.0	0.0	0.3
Clinton	37 914	94.2	39.0	21.0	25.8	19.6	3.0	1.2	5.4	2.2	5.8	0.4	0.7	0.4	4.1	0.0	0.2
Columbia	64 151	94.1	38.8	20.9	25.4	19.2	2.9	1.1	6.2	2.1	5.9	0.2	1.2	0.0	4.2	0.0	0.2
Crawford	90 366	95.9	38.4	21.3	28.7	22.7	3.0	1.2	4.5	2.1	4.1	0.9	1.1	0.1	1.7	0.0	0.3
Cumberland	213 674	93.5	38.9	22.0	26.1	20.7	2.4	0.9	4.1	1.8	6.5	1.7	1.6	0.0	2.9	0.0	0.2
Dauphin	251 798	97.3	40.8	19.4	28.3	21.9	4.2	1.8	4.6	2.3	2.7	0.5	1.1	0.3	0.2	0.0	0.5
Delaware	550 864	96.1	37.5	19.0	31.0	22.5	4.9	1.8	3.6	1.6	3.9	0.4	1.0	0.2	1.7	0.0	0.6
Elk	35 112	98.7	40.2	22.5	30.0	22.7	2.8	0.9	3.1	1.8	1.3	0.2	0.8	0.0	0.0	0.0	0.4
Erie	280 843	95.0	37.9	19.2	29.7	22.8	3.5	1.5	4.8	2.1	5.0	0.9	1.1	0.3	2.1	0.0	0.6
Fayette	148 644	98.0	40.3	20.9	29.0	20.3	4.4	1.7	3.4	1.9	2.0	0.1	0.6	0.0	0.0	0.0	1.3
Forest	4 946	92.4	40.4	22.5	22.9	16.9	3.2	1.4	3.4	1.9	7.6	0.0	1.9	0.0	0.0	0.0	5.7
Franklin	129 313	97.7	39.2	23.5	28.2	22.1	3.0	1.2	3.8	2.1	2.3	0.2	1.2	0.2	0.5	0.0	0.2
Fulton	14 261	99.3	39.7	23.6	29.2	22.6	3.1	1.3	3.6	2.0	0.7	0.0	0.4	0.0	0.0	0.0	0.3
Greene	40 672	92.0	37.0	20.5	27.3	20.1	3.5	1.4	3.7	1.8	8.0	5.4	0.7	0.0	1.3	0.0	0.5
Huntingdon	45 586	89.7	36.8	21.4	25.6	19.9	2.8	1.1	3.2	1.8	10.3	7.0	0.7	0.2	2.2	0.0	0.2
Indiana	89 605	94.1	38.1	20.7	26.6	19.7	2.6	1.0	6.1	1.5	5.9	0.1	0.6	0.0	4.2	0.0	1.0
Jefferson	45 932	98.0	40.0	22.7	29.2	22.1	2.8	1.0	3.2	1.7	2.0	0.1	1.1	0.0	0.2	0.0	0.6
Juniata	22 821	97.9	37.6	24.3	30.0	23.5	2.7	1.0	3.3	1.9	2.1	0.1	1.9	0.0	0.0	0.0	0.2
Lackawanna	213 295	96.3	40.4	19.8	28.6	20.2	4.0	1.1	3.5	1.6	3.7	0.3	1.1	0.2	1.3	0.0	0.8
Lancaster	470 658	96.9	36.7	22.0	31.2	24.9	3.2	1.2	3.9	1.9	3.1	0.2	1.2	0.0	1.1	0.0	0.4
Lawrence	94 643	96.9	39.2	21.3	29.4	21.1	4.0	1.5	2.9	1.6	3.1	0.2	1.0	0.4	1.0	0.0	0.5
Lebanon	120 327	96.4	38.7	22.2	28.5	21.9	3.2	1.2	3.8	2.1	3.6	0.4	1.3	0.3	1.0	0.0	0.6
Lehigh	312 090	96.7	39.1	20.7	28.4	21.9	4.0	1.4	4.6	2.4	3.3	0.4	1.2	0.2	0.9	0.0	0.4
Luzerne	319 250	96.0	40.9	20.0	27.6	19.3	4.0	1.1	3.5	1.9	4.0	1.2	1.2	0.3	0.6	0.0	0.7
Lycoming	120 044	95.4	39.2	20.8	27.6	21.4	3.0	1.2	4.9	2.2	4.6	1.7	0.9	0.0	1.5	0.0	0.4
McKean	45 936	94.3	39.2	20.6	27.4	21.7	2.8	1.2	4.2	2.3	5.7	3.1	1.3	0.0	0.9	0.0	0.5
Mercer	120 293	94.7	38.8	21.3	28.0	21.1	3.4	1.4	3.2	1.7	5.3	0.9	1.1	0.6	2.2	0.0	0.5
Mifflin	46 486	98.5	39.6	22.8	29.2	22.8	3.2	1.3	3.7	2.1	1.5	0.1	1.2	0.0	0.0	0.0	0.1
Monroe	138 687	97.2	35.7	21.6	31.1	24.8	4.2	1.4	4.7	2.2	2.8	0.2	0.5	0.1	1.5	0.0	0.6
Montgomery	750 097	96.9	38.1	21.8	29.6	22.6	3.6	1.1	3.7	1.6	3.1	0.7	1.0	0.2	0.8	0.0	0.5
Montour	18 236	94.5	38.9	21.9	28.2	22.3	2.8	0.9	3.3	1.8	5.5	0.1	1.6	2.3	0.0	0.0	1.5
Northampton	267 066	96.1	38.0	21.5	28.4	21.5	3.9	1.3	4.3	2.1	3.9	0.2	1.0	0.1	2.2	0.0	0.5
Northumberland	94 556	96.1	41.1	21.5	26.6	20.0	3.2	1.1	3.7	2.1	3.9	1.9	1.2	0.2	0.1	0.0	0.6
Perry	43 602	98.8	38.3	23.6	30.1	23.4	3.0	1.3	3.8	2.2	1.2	0.2	0.6	0.3	0.0	0.0	0.1
Philadelphia	1 517 550	96.4	38.9	12.5	29.9	20.4	9.2	4.2	6.0	2.3	3.6	0.5	0.7	0.2	1.4	0.0	0.8
Pike	46 302	99.2	37.7	23.9	30.6	25.1	3.4	1.2	3.6	2.0	0.8	0.4	0.1	0.0	0.1	0.0	0.2

Table B. States and Counties

STATE County	Total households	Family households Total	With own children under 18 years	Married couple Total	With own children under 18 years	Female householder[1] Total	With own children under 18 years	Nonfamily households Total	Householder living alone Total	65 years and over	Average household size	Average family size	Households, 1990 Total households	Female householder[1]	Householder living alone
	71	72	73	74	75	76	77	78	79	80	81	82	83	84	85
OREGON—Cont'd															
Morrow	3 776	77.3	38.9	62.6	28.9	8.8	6.4	22.7	18.1	7.4	2.90	3.28	2 803	7.5	21.5
Multnomah	272 098	55.9	26.5	40.9	17.9	10.8	6.5	44.1	32.5	8.6	2.37	3.03	242 140	10.9	31.0
Polk	23 058	70.0	32.1	57.1	24.0	9.2	6.0	30.0	22.3	9.9	2.62	3.07	18 167	9.1	21.9
Sherman	797	68.5	29.9	58.5	23.8	6.5	3.6	31.5	28.7	14.1	2.43	2.97	784	5.6	26.1
Tillamook	10 200	66.6	24.6	54.8	17.5	7.7	4.8	33.4	27.9	12.6	2.33	2.82	8 846	7.1	25.7
Umatilla	25 195	70.8	35.0	55.1	24.8	10.6	7.1	29.2	23.7	9.7	2.67	3.14	22 020	9.5	24.3
Union	9 740	66.9	30.0	55.1	22.0	8.5	5.9	33.1	26.1	10.8	2.45	2.94	9 035	7.6	24.0
Wallowa	3 029	68.8	28.5	58.7	21.5	6.9	5.1	31.2	27.1	11.9	2.35	2.85	2 796	6.2	25.9
Wasco	9 401	69.2	30.2	54.8	21.1	9.9	6.3	30.8	26.1	11.5	2.47	2.96	8 607	9.5	25.9
Washington	169 162	67.4	35.6	54.5	27.6	9.0	5.8	32.6	24.7	6.7	2.61	3.14	118 997	8.7	23.3
Wheeler	653	68.1	21.3	62.2	17.5	4.0	2.8	31.9	27.4	13.3	2.32	2.76	584	4.1	24.5
Yamhill	28 732	74.4	37.4	60.0	28.2	9.9	6.5	25.6	19.7	8.4	2.78	3.17	22 424	9.0	19.6
PENNSYLVANIA	4 777 003	67.2	30.0	51.7	21.8	11.6	6.2	32.8	27.7	11.6	2.48	3.04	4 495 966	11.3	25.6
Adams	33 652	73.6	33.7	61.1	26.2	8.5	5.1	26.4	21.3	9.2	2.61	3.02	28 067	8.1	19.9
Allegheny	537 150	61.9	26.4	46.1	18.6	12.4	6.4	38.1	32.7	13.2	2.31	2.96	541 261	12.5	29.7
Armstrong	29 050	70.8	29.5	57.9	22.7	9.0	4.7	29.2	25.9	13.7	2.44	2.95	28 309	8.6	24.1
Beaver	72 576	69.6	28.6	54.5	21.1	11.4	5.9	30.4	26.9	13.1	2.44	2.96	71 939	11.2	24.4
Bedford	19 768	73.3	30.7	61.7	24.7	7.7	3.9	26.7	23.5	11.5	2.50	2.95	18 038	7.7	21.6
Berks	141 570	69.6	31.7	55.5	23.6	9.9	5.8	30.4	24.6	10.7	2.55	3.05	127 649	9.1	23.5
Blair	51 518	67.7	29.3	52.6	21.0	11.2	6.0	32.3	27.8	13.3	2.43	2.96	50 332	11.4	25.9
Bradford	24 453	70.8	31.8	57.4	23.7	8.9	5.4	29.2	24.7	11.5	2.52	2.99	22 492	8.7	22.3
Bucks	218 725	73.6	35.3	61.2	29.2	8.8	4.5	26.4	21.5	8.1	2.69	3.17	190 507	8.4	19.2
Butler	65 862	71.1	32.9	59.8	26.7	8.1	4.5	28.9	24.2	10.4	2.55	3.04	55 325	8.3	22.4
Cambria	60 531	67.1	27.0	52.8	20.3	10.4	5.0	32.9	29.8	15.6	2.38	2.96	62 004	10.4	26.9
Cameron	2 465	65.9	27.7	52.4	20.0	9.2	5.2	34.1	30.1	15.4	2.39	2.96	2 395	9.7	29.4
Carbon	23 701	69.3	28.7	54.8	21.2	9.9	5.2	30.7	26.0	13.5	2.44	2.93	21 989	9.2	24.1
Centre	49 323	57.8	25.5	48.9	20.7	6.1	3.4	42.2	26.6	7.6	2.45	2.95	42 683	6.2	23.6
Chester	157 905	71.8	35.1	60.5	29.2	8.1	4.4	28.2	22.6	7.6	2.65	3.15	133 257	8.3	20.2
Clarion	16 052	66.9	28.6	54.9	21.9	8.4	4.9	33.1	26.0	11.3	2.46	2.95	14 990	8.0	24.0
Clearfield	32 785	69.9	29.7	56.6	22.6	9.3	4.9	30.1	26.3	13.1	2.44	2.94	29 808	9.3	24.4
Clinton	14 773	67.2	27.7	54.0	19.8	9.4	5.7	32.8	26.6	13.6	2.42	2.90	13 844	9.6	24.8
Columbia	24 915	66.5	27.7	53.8	20.7	8.7	4.9	33.5	26.6	11.8	2.42	2.90	23 478	8.6	24.1
Crawford	34 678	68.8	30.4	55.6	22.7	9.2	5.4	31.2	26.2	11.6	2.50	3.01	32 185	9.3	24.6
Cumberland	83 015	67.6	29.5	56.5	23.0	8.0	4.7	32.4	26.7	10.3	2.41	2.92	73 452	7.6	24.2
Dauphin	102 670	64.4	29.7	47.6	19.7	12.9	7.9	35.6	30.0	10.3	2.39	2.98	95 264	11.7	28.4
Delaware	206 320	67.6	31.5	50.8	23.5	12.9	6.4	32.4	27.6	11.6	2.56	3.17	201 374	11.9	25.1
Elk	14 124	69.0	31.0	56.0	24.2	8.7	4.8	31.0	27.3	13.6	2.45	2.99	13 131	8.4	24.2
Erie	106 507	66.7	31.6	50.5	22.0	12.1	7.4	33.3	27.6	11.2	2.51	3.07	101 564	11.5	25.4
Fayette	59 969	68.7	28.7	51.8	20.2	12.4	6.4	31.3	28.0	14.5	2.43	2.96	56 110	12.3	25.0
Forest	2 000	66.4	23.2	55.7	18.3	6.7	3.1	33.6	29.1	15.1	2.29	2.81	1 908	7.1	26.3
Franklin	50 633	71.9	30.8	60.0	23.7	8.2	4.8	28.1	23.7	10.7	2.49	2.94	45 675	7.8	21.8
Fulton	5 660	72.4	31.7	59.5	23.9	8.2	4.7	27.6	24.0	10.6	2.50	2.95	5 139	8.0	20.7
Greene	15 060	70.3	30.6	55.4	22.7	10.9	5.7	29.7	25.7	12.7	2.48	2.97	14 624	10.6	24.3
Huntingdon	16 759	70.4	30.1	58.1	22.9	8.3	4.8	29.6	25.8	12.3	2.44	2.92	15 527	8.5	24.3
Indiana	34 123	66.0	27.9	54.3	21.9	8.2	4.2	34.0	26.5	11.8	2.47	2.99	31 710	8.2	23.2
Jefferson	18 375	70.0	30.3	56.8	23.2	9.1	5.0	30.0	26.6	13.8	2.45	2.96	17 608	9.0	24.7
Juniata	8 584	75.3	33.0	64.6	26.8	6.3	3.5	24.7	21.1	10.5	2.60	3.01	7 598	6.6	20.4
Lackawanna	86 218	64.7	27.2	48.9	20.1	11.8	5.6	35.3	31.3	15.7	2.38	3.00	84 528	11.9	28.4
Lancaster	172 560	71.9	33.7	59.9	26.6	8.6	5.2	28.1	23.1	9.3	2.64	3.14	150 956	7.9	20.9
Lawrence	37 091	69.8	28.8	54.5	21.1	11.5	5.9	30.2	27.0	14.4	2.47	3.00	36 350	10.8	24.2
Lebanon	46 551	70.4	30.4	57.4	23.0	9.2	5.3	29.6	25.2	11.1	2.49	2.98	42 688	8.7	22.9
Lehigh	121 906	67.4	30.6	53.0	22.3	10.5	6.1	32.6	27.1	11.2	2.48	3.02	112 887	9.4	25.0
Luzerne	130 687	64.5	26.5	48.8	19.3	11.5	5.4	35.5	31.3	16.0	2.34	2.95	128 483	11.9	28.6
Lycoming	47 003	67.4	29.9	53.1	21.1	10.3	6.3	32.6	26.9	11.9	2.44	2.95	44 949	9.9	24.1
McKean	18 024	67.1	30.5	52.5	21.5	10.1	6.1	32.9	28.3	13.3	2.40	2.93	17 837	9.9	26.4
Mercer	46 712	69.3	29.3	54.8	21.4	10.9	6.1	30.7	27.0	13.2	2.44	2.96	45 591	10.3	24.6
Mifflin	18 413	70.1	30.2	57.6	23.2	8.5	4.7	29.9	26.0	13.2	2.49	2.99	17 697	8.7	24.5
Monroe	49 454	73.7	36.2	60.7	28.6	8.8	5.3	26.3	20.2	7.8	2.73	3.16	34 206	7.5	19.2
Montgomery	286 098	69.1	32.0	57.2	26.3	8.8	4.4	30.9	25.6	9.9	2.54	3.09	254 995	8.3	24.6
Montour	7 085	68.0	30.0	56.3	23.1	8.9	5.4	32.0	28.0	12.0	2.43	2.98	6 543	7.7	26.3
Northampton	101 541	70.0	31.2	56.4	23.9	9.8	5.4	30.0	24.7	11.2	2.53	3.02	90 955	9.1	21.8
Northumberland	38 835	65.9	27.3	52.4	20.0	9.6	5.3	34.1	30.2	15.5	2.34	2.89	38 736	9.5	27.4
Perry	16 695	73.8	33.2	61.6	26.2	7.8	4.5	26.2	21.7	9.3	2.58	3.01	14 949	7.7	18.4
Philadelphia	590 071	59.7	27.6	32.1	13.5	22.3	11.8	40.3	33.8	11.9	2.48	3.22	603 075	20.3	31.6
Pike	17 433	74.7	34.4	63.5	27.7	7.6	4.8	25.3	20.7	8.4	2.63	3.06	10 536	6.1	20.0

[1] No spouse present.

Table B. States and Counties

STATE County	Percent change of households, 1990–2000	Total housing units	Occupied housing units (percent)	Vacant housing units Total	For seasonal, recreational, or occasional use	Homeowner vacancy rate (percent)	Rental vacancy rate (percent)	Occupied housing units Total	Percent owner-occupied housing units	Percent renter-occupied housing units	Average household size of owner-occupied units	Average household size of renter-occupied units
	86	87	88	89	90	91	92	93	94	95	96	97
OREGON—Cont'd												
Morrow	34.7	4 276	88.3	11.7	4.7	2.0	11.2	3 776	73.1	26.9	2.87	2.98
Multnomah	12.4	288 561	94.3	5.7	0.4	2.3	6.3	272 098	56.9	43.1	2.52	2.16
Polk	26.9	24 461	94.3	5.7	0.4	2.1	6.8	23 058	68.4	31.6	2.67	2.50
Sherman	1.7	935	85.2	14.8	2.6	1.7	8.6	797	70.5	29.5	2.30	2.72
Tillamook	15.3	15 906	64.1	35.9	28.9	4.8	11.7	10 200	71.8	28.2	2.30	2.41
Umatilla	14.4	27 676	91.0	9.0	2.5	2.5	8.3	25 195	64.9	35.1	2.72	2.58
Union	7.8	10 603	91.9	8.1	1.5	1.8	9.5	9 740	66.5	33.5	2.54	2.28
Wallowa	8.3	3 900	77.7	22.3	12.6	3.2	10.6	3 029	71.8	28.2	2.37	2.29
Wasco	9.2	10 651	88.3	11.7	5.7	2.6	7.2	9 401	68.4	31.6	2.50	2.42
Washington	42.2	178 913	94.5	5.5	0.4	2.4	6.5	169 162	60.6	39.4	2.75	2.39
Wheeler	11.8	842	77.6	22.4	12.9	3.9	4.7	653	72.1	27.9	2.21	2.62
Yamhill	28.1	30 270	94.9	5.1	0.5	2.0	6.1	28 732	69.6	30.4	2.81	2.73
PENNSYLVANIA	6.3	5 249 750	91.0	9.0	2.8	1.6	7.2	4 777 003	71.3	28.7	2.62	2.12
Adams	19.9	35 831	93.9	6.1	1.9	1.4	4.6	33 652	76.8	23.2	2.67	2.38
Allegheny	-0.8	583 646	92.0	8.0	0.4	1.9	8.9	537 150	67.0	33.0	2.51	1.91
Armstrong	2.5	32 387	89.6	10.4	4.4	1.7	7.1	29 005	77.3	22.7	2.55	2.12
Beaver	0.9	77 765	93.3	6.7	0.4	1.6	7.6	72 576	74.9	25.1	2.55	2.09
Bedford	9.6	23 529	84.0	16.0	10.1	1.5	6.4	19 768	80.1	19.9	2.58	2.22
Berks	10.9	150 222	94.2	5.8	0.5	1.7	6.3	141 570	74.0	26.0	2.65	2.27
Blair	2.4	55 061	93.6	6.4	0.6	1.2	7.5	51 518	72.9	27.1	2.55	2.09
Bradford	8.7	28 664	85.3	14.7	9.1	1.8	7.7	24 453	75.5	24.5	2.62	2.23
Bucks	14.8	225 498	97.0	3.0	0.4	0.8	4.2	218 725	77.4	22.6	2.87	2.09
Butler	19.0	69 868	94.3	5.7	1.2	1.5	7.2	65 862	77.9	22.1	2.70	2.00
Cambria	-2.4	65 796	92.0	8.0	1.0	1.6	9.7	60 531	74.8	25.2	2.52	1.99
Cameron	2.9	4 592	53.7	46.3	42.1	1.2	12.0	2 465	74.8	25.2	2.53	1.98
Carbon	7.8	30 492	77.7	22.3	15.6	2.5	10.2	23 701	78.2	21.8	2.51	2.21
Centre	15.6	53 161	92.8	7.2	2.9	1.2	3.7	49 323	60.2	39.8	2.61	2.22
Chester	18.5	163 773	96.4	3.6	0.3	1.0	4.8	157 905	76.3	23.7	2.80	2.16
Clarion	7.1	19 426	82.6	17.4	12.0	1.4	7.0	16 052	72.3	27.7	2.55	2.21
Clearfield	10.0	37 855	86.6	13.4	7.3	1.9	6.8	32 785	79.2	20.8	2.53	2.12
Clinton	6.7	18 166	81.3	18.7	14.1	2.1	5.7	14 773	72.9	27.1	2.52	2.14
Columbia	6.1	27 733	89.8	10.2	4.7	1.8	6.9	24 915	72.4	27.6	2.49	2.24
Crawford	7.7	42 416	81.8	18.2	11.7	2.0	8.3	34 678	75.5	24.5	2.61	2.17
Cumberland	13.0	86 951	95.5	4.5	0.4	1.5	6.0	83 015	73.1	26.9	2.53	2.06
Dauphin	7.8	111 133	92.4	7.6	0.5	2.1	9.2	102 670	65.4	34.6	2.54	2.09
Delaware	2.5	216 978	95.1	4.9	0.2	1.4	6.0	206 320	71.9	28.1	2.75	2.08
Elk	7.6	18 115	78.0	22.0	16.8	1.9	9.9	14 124	79.4	20.6	2.59	1.92
Erie	4.9	114 322	93.2	6.8	1.0	1.9	7.9	106 507	69.2	30.8	2.65	2.17
Fayette	6.9	66 490	90.2	9.8	2.2	1.5	9.4	59 969	73.2	26.8	2.50	2.24
Forest	4.8	8 701	23.0	77.0	75.4	2.2	6.5	2 000	82.7	17.3	2.34	2.03
Franklin	10.9	53 803	94.1	5.9	1.1	1.4	6.7	50 633	74.0	26.0	2.57	2.27
Fulton	10.1	6 790	83.4	16.6	9.2	1.1	7.7	5 660	78.8	21.2	2.54	2.34
Greene	3.0	16 678	90.3	9.7	2.5	1.8	7.7	15 060	74.1	25.9	2.55	2.31
Huntingdon	7.9	21 058	79.6	20.4	15.1	1.7	7.1	16 759	77.5	22.5	2.53	2.12
Indiana	7.6	37 250	91.6	8.4	1.7	1.6	7.4	34 123	71.7	28.3	2.58	2.20
Jefferson	4.4	22 104	83.1	16.9	10.9	2.0	6.7	18 375	77.1	22.9	2.55	2.12
Juniata	13.0	10 031	85.6	14.4	9.4	1.4	5.4	8 584	77.7	22.3	2.68	2.33
Lackawanna	2.0	95 362	90.4	9.6	2.0	1.9	8.7	86 218	67.6	32.4	2.56	2.01
Lancaster	14.3	179 990	95.9	4.1	0.4	1.4	4.9	172 560	70.8	29.2	2.78	2.31
Lawrence	2.0	39 635	93.6	6.4	0.8	1.6	7.4	37 091	77.3	22.7	2.58	2.12
Lebanon	9.0	49 320	94.4	5.6	0.9	1.7	6.5	46 551	72.7	27.3	2.60	2.21
Lehigh	8.0	128 910	94.6	5.4	0.3	1.5	6.6	121 906	68.8	31.2	2.63	2.13
Luzerne	1.7	144 686	90.3	9.7	1.7	1.9	8.8	130 687	70.3	29.7	2.49	1.99
Lycoming	4.6	52 464	89.6	10.4	4.8	1.6	7.6	47 003	69.4	30.6	2.57	2.14
McKean	1.0	21 644	83.3	16.7	10.3	1.7	8.0	18 024	74.7	25.3	2.50	2.11
Mercer	2.5	49 859	93.7	6.3	1.0	1.5	6.7	46 712	76.3	23.7	2.54	2.12
Mifflin	4.0	20 745	88.8	11.2	5.2	1.5	8.4	18 413	74.0	26.0	2.58	2.23
Monroe	44.6	67 581	73.2	26.8	21.8	2.4	5.5	49 454	78.3	21.7	2.79	2.48
Montgomery	12.2	297 434	96.2	3.8	0.3	1.0	5.6	286 098	73.5	26.5	2.74	1.99
Montour	8.3	7 627	92.9	7.1	1.1	1.7	8.0	7 085	73.0	27.0	2.59	2.00
Northampton	11.6	106 710	95.2	4.8	0.5	1.5	6.0	101 541	73.3	26.7	2.64	2.20
Northumberland	0.3	43 164	90.0	10.0	0.6	2.4	8.9	38 835	73.5	26.5	2.45	2.04
Perry	11.7	18 941	88.1	11.9	6.7	1.3	6.9	16 695	79.8	20.2	2.66	2.29
Philadelphia	-2.2	661 958	89.1	10.9	0.3	1.9	7.0	590 071	59.3	40.7	2.65	2.23
Pike	65.5	34 681	50.3	49.7	44.3	3.6	5.7	17 433	84.8	15.2	2.64	2.57

Table B. States and Counties

				Population, 2000				Population, 1990				Population and population characteristics, 2000					
												Race (percent)					
												One race					
STATE/County code	MSA/PMSA/NECMA code[1]	County type[2]	STATE County	Land area, 2000[3] (sq km)	Total persons	Rank	Per square kilometer	Land area, 1990[3] (sq km)	Total persons	Rank	Per square kilometer	White	Black or African American	American Indian or Alaska Native	Asian	Native Hawaiian and other Pacific Islander	Some other race
				1	2	3	4	5	6	7	8	9	10	11	12	13	14
			PENNSYLVANIA—Cont'd														
42 105	...	7	Potter	2 800	18 080	1 894	6.5	2 800	16 717	1 867	6.0	98.1	0.3	0.2	0.5	0.0	0.2
42 107	...	4	Schuylkill	2 016	150 336	359	74.6	2 017	152 585	303	75.6	96.6	2.1	0.1	0.4	0.0	0.4
42 109	...	7	Snyder	858	37 546	1 175	43.8	858	36 680	1 083	42.8	97.9	0.8	0.0	0.4	0.0	0.3
42 111	3680	3	Somerset	2 783	80 023	641	28.8	2 784	78 218	578	28.1	97.4	1.6	0.1	0.2	0.0	0.3
42 113	...	8	Sullivan	1 165	6 556	2 732	5.6	1 165	6 104	2 744	5.2	95.6	2.2	0.8	0.2	0.0	0.5
42 115	...	8	Susquehanna	2 131	42 238	1 053	19.8	2 132	40 380	989	18.9	98.5	0.3	0.1	0.2	0.0	0.2
42 117	...	6	Tioga	2 936	41 373	1 069	14.1	2 936	41 126	977	14.0	98.1	0.6	0.2	0.3	0.0	0.1
42 119	...	6	Union	820	41 624	1 065	50.8	820	36 176	1 097	44.1	90.1	6.9	0.2	1.1	0.0	0.4
42 121	...	4	Venango	1 748	57 565	829	32.9	1 749	59 381	729	34.0	97.6	1.1	0.2	0.2	0.0	0.2
42 123	...	6	Warren	2 288	43 863	1 020	19.2	2 288	45 050	912	19.7	98.7	0.2	0.2	0.3	0.0	0.1
42 125	6280	0	Washington	2 220	202 897	271	91.4	2 220	204 584	243	92.2	95.3	3.3	0.1	0.4	0.0	0.1
42 127	...	6	Wayne	1 889	47 722	956	25.3	1 889	39 944	1 003	21.1	96.7	1.6	0.1	0.4	0.0	0.5
42 129	6280	0	Westmoreland	2 656	369 993	158	139.3	2 648	370 321	138	139.8	96.6	2.0	0.1	0.5	0.0	0.1
42 131	7560	2	Wyoming	1 029	28 080	1 449	27.3	1 029	28 076	1 348	27.3	98.3	0.5	0.2	0.3	0.0	0.1
42 133	9280	2	York	2 343	381 751	152	162.9	2 343	339 574	149	144.9	92.8	3.7	0.2	0.9	0.0	1.4
44 000	...		RHODE ISLAND	2 706	1 048 319	X	387.4	2 707	1 003 464	X	370.7	85.0	4.5	0.5	2.3	0.1	5.0
44 001	6483	2	Bristol	64	50 648	913	791.4	64	48 859	859	763.4	96.8	0.7	0.2	1.0	0.0	0.3
44 003	6483	2	Kent	441	167 090	323	378.9	440	161 143	296	366.2	95.5	0.9	0.2	1.3	0.0	0.6
44 005	...	4	Newport	269	85 433	611	317.6	269	87 194	521	324.1	91.5	3.7	0.4	1.2	0.1	1.1
44 007	6483	2	Providence	1 070	621 602	86	580.9	1 070	596 270	78	557.3	78.4	6.5	0.5	2.9	0.1	8.0
44 009	6483	2	Washington	862	123 546	436	143.3	862	109 998	419	127.6	94.8	0.9	0.9	1.5	0.0	0.5
45 000	...		SOUTH CAROLINA	77 983	4 012 012	X	51.4	77 988	3 486 310	X	44.7	67.2	29.5	0.3	0.9	0.0	1.0
45 001	...	6	Abbeville	1 316	26 167	1 510	19.9	1 316	23 862	1 498	18.1	68.3	30.3	0.1	0.2	0.0	0.3
45 003	0600	2	Aiken	2 778	142 552	382	51.3	2 779	120 991	382	43.5	71.4	25.6	0.4	0.6	0.0	0.8
45 005	...	7	Allendale	1 057	11 211	2 355	10.6	1 057	11 727	2 231	11.1	27.4	71.0	0.1	0.1	0.1	0.8
45 007	3160	2	Anderson	1 860	165 740	325	89.1	1 860	145 177	327	78.1	81.6	16.6	0.2	0.4	0.0	0.4
45 009	...	7	Bamberg	1 019	16 658	1 979	16.3	1 019	16 902	1 857	16.6	36.5	62.5	0.2	0.2	0.0	0.1
45 011	...	6	Barnwell	1 420	23 478	1 616	16.5	1 421	20 293	1 660	14.3	55.2	42.6	0.3	0.4	0.0	0.8
45 013	1440	2	Beaufort	1 520	120 937	449	79.6	1 520	86 425	527	56.9	70.7	24.0	0.3	0.8	0.1	2.8
45 015	1440	2	Berkeley	2 843	142 651	381	50.2	2 848	128 658	361	45.2	68.0	26.6	0.5	1.9	0.1	1.2
45 017	...	8	Calhoun	985	15 185	2 076	15.4	985	12 753	2 162	12.9	50.0	48.7	0.2	0.1	0.0	0.2
45 019	1440	2	Charleston	2 379	309 969	184	130.3	2 376	295 159	165	124.2	61.9	34.5	0.3	1.1	0.1	1.0
45 021	3160	2	Cherokee	1 017	52 537	887	51.7	1 017	44 506	919	43.8	76.9	20.6	0.2	0.3	0.0	1.2
45 023	...	6	Chester	1 504	34 068	1 279	22.7	1 504	32 170	1 208	21.4	59.9	38.7	0.3	0.3	0.0	0.6
45 025	...	6	Chesterfield	2 068	42 768	1 041	20.7	2 069	38 575	1 039	18.6	64.3	33.2	0.3	0.3	0.0	1.0
45 027	...	6	Clarendon	1 573	32 502	1 331	20.7	1 573	28 450	1 344	18.1	44.9	53.1	0.2	0.3	0.0	0.6
45 029	...	6	Colleton	2 736	38 264	1 158	14.0	2 736	34 377	1 156	12.6	55.5	42.2	0.6	0.3	0.0	0.6
45 031	...	4	Darlington	1 453	67 394	726	46.4	1 456	61 851	705	42.5	57.0	41.7	0.2	0.2	0.0	0.4
45 033	...	6	Dillon	1 049	30 722	1 379	29.3	1 049	29 114	1 325	27.8	50.4	45.3	2.2	0.3	0.0	1.0
45 035	1440	2	Dorchester	1 489	96 413	537	64.8	1 489	83 060	549	55.8	71.0	25.1	0.7	1.1	0.1	0.6
45 037	0600	2	Edgefield	1 300	24 595	1 571	18.9	1 300	18 360	1 771	14.1	56.8	41.5	0.3	0.2	0.0	0.4
45 039	...	6	Fairfield	1 778	23 454	1 619	13.2	1 778	22 295	1 563	12.5	39.6	59.1	0.2	0.2	0.0	0.4
45 041	2655	3	Florence	2 072	125 761	432	60.7	2 070	114 344	401	55.2	58.7	39.3	0.2	0.7	0.0	0.4
45 043	...	6	Georgetown	2 110	55 797	846	26.4	2 110	46 302	898	21.9	59.7	38.6	0.1	0.2	0.0	0.8
45 045	3160	2	Greenville	2 046	379 616	154	185.5	2 052	320 127	158	156.0	77.5	18.3	0.2	1.4	0.0	1.4
45 047	...	5	Greenwood	1 180	66 271	736	56.2	1 180	59 567	726	50.5	65.6	31.7	0.2	0.7	0.0	1.0
45 049	...	7	Hampton	1 450	21 386	1 719	14.7	1 450	18 186	1 778	12.5	42.9	55.7	0.2	0.2	0.0	0.6
45 051	5330	3	Horry	2 936	196 629	281	67.0	2 936	144 053	329	49.1	81.0	15.5	0.4	0.8	0.1	1.2
45 053	...	8	Jasper	1 699	20 678	1 752	12.2	1 695	15 487	1 955	9.1	42.4	52.7	0.4	0.4	0.0	3.4
45 055	...	6	Kershaw	1 881	52 647	885	28.0	1 881	43 599	929	23.2	71.6	26.3	0.3	0.3	0.0	0.6
45 057	...	6	Lancaster	1 422	61 351	793	43.1	1 422	54 516	791	38.3	71.0	26.9	0.2	0.3	0.0	0.9
45 059	...	6	Laurens	1 852	69 567	710	37.6	1 847	58 132	746	31.5	71.6	26.2	0.3	0.1	0.1	1.0
45 061	...	6	Lee	1 063	20 119	1 787	18.9	1 063	18 437	1 765	17.3	35.0	63.6	0.1	0.2	0.0	0.6
45 063	1760	2	Lexington	1 811	216 014	260	119.3	1 815	167 526	286	92.3	84.2	12.6	0.3	1.0	0.0	0.8
45 065	...	8	McCormick	931	9 958	2 450	10.7	931	8 868	2 480	9.5	44.8	53.9	0.1	0.3	0.0	0.4
45 067	...	6	Marion	1 267	35 466	1 235	28.0	1 267	33 899	1 167	26.8	41.7	56.3	0.3	0.3	0.0	0.9
45 069	...	7	Marlboro	1 242	28 818	1 426	23.2	1 242	29 716	1 307	23.9	44.5	50.7	3.4	0.2	0.0	0.2
45 071	...	6	Newberry	1 634	36 108	1 210	22.1	1 634	33 172	1 186	20.3	64.0	33.1	0.3	0.3	0.1	1.3
45 073	...	6	Oconee	1 620	66 215	738	40.9	1 619	57 494	758	35.5	89.1	8.4	0.2	0.4	0.0	1.1
45 075	...	4	Orangeburg	2 865	91 582	559	32.0	2 865	84 804	541	29.6	37.2	60.9	0.5	0.4	0.0	0.4
45 077	3160	2	Pickens	1 287	110 757	490	86.1	1 287	93 896	492	73.0	90.3	6.8	0.2	1.2	0.0	0.7
45 079	1760	2	Richland	1 959	320 677	180	163.7	1 959	286 321	171	146.2	50.3	45.2	0.2	1.7	0.1	1.2
45 081	...	6	Saluda	1 172	19 181	1 835	16.4	1 169	16 441	1 896	14.1	65.8	30.0	0.2	0.0	0.0	3.3
45 083	3160	2	Spartanburg	2 100	253 791	222	120.9	2 100	226 793	217	108.0	75.1	20.8	0.2	1.5	0.0	1.4

[1] MSA = Metropolitan Statistical Area. PMSA = Primary MSA. NECMA = New England County Metropolitan Area. See Appendix A for explanation of these concepts. See Appendix B for list of metropolitan areas identified by type, with component counties.
[2] County typology code from the Economic Research Service of USDA. See Appendix A for definition.
[3] Dry land or land partially or temporarily covered by water.

Table B. States and Counties

	Population and population characteristics, 2000 (cont'd)								Population and population characteristics, 1990				
	Race (percent) (cont'd)								Race (percent)				
	Race alone or in combination												
STATE County	Two or more races	White	Black	American Indian or Alaska Native	Asian	Native Hawaiian and other Pacific Islander	Some other race	Hispanic[1]	White	Black or African American	American Indian or Alaska Native	Asian and Pacific Islander	Hispanic[1]
	15	16	17	18	19	20	21	22	23	24	25	26	27
PENNSYLVANIA—Cont'd													
Potter	0.7	98.7	0.4	0.6	0.6	0.0	0.3	0.6	99.5	0.1	0.2	0.2	0.4
Schuylkill	0.4	97.0	2.2	0.2	0.5	0.0	0.5	1.1	99.0	0.6	0.1	0.3	0.4
Snyder	0.5	98.4	0.9	0.2	0.6	0.0	0.4	1.0	99.1	0.4	0.1	0.3	0.4
Somerset	0.4	97.8	1.7	0.2	0.3	0.0	0.4	0.7	99.6	0.1	0.1	0.2	0.3
Sullivan	0.9	96.3	2.4	1.2	0.3	0.0	0.7	1.1	98.3	1.0	0.5	0.1	0.4
Susquehanna	0.6	99.1	0.4	0.5	0.3	0.0	0.3	0.7	99.3	0.2	0.2	0.2	0.4
Tioga	0.6	98.7	0.8	0.6	0.4	0.0	0.2	0.5	98.8	0.6	0.3	0.3	0.3
Union	1.4	91.2	7.3	0.5	1.4	0.2	0.9	3.9	96.2	2.7	0.2	0.7	1.8
Venango	0.7	98.3	1.4	0.5	0.3	0.0	0.3	0.5	98.7	0.8	0.1	0.2	0.3
Warren	0.5	99.2	0.3	0.5	0.4	0.0	0.2	0.3	99.4	0.1	0.2	0.2	0.3
Washington	0.8	96.0	3.7	0.3	0.5	0.1	0.3	0.6	96.2	3.3	0.1	0.3	0.6
Wayne	0.6	97.3	1.8	0.5	0.4	0.0	0.7	1.7	98.8	0.7	0.1	0.2	0.9
Westmoreland	0.6	97.2	2.3	0.3	0.6	0.0	0.2	0.5	97.5	1.9	0.1	0.4	0.4
Wyoming	0.6	98.9	0.7	0.4	0.4	0.0	0.2	0.7	99.0	0.5	0.1	0.3	0.5
York	1.1	93.7	4.2	0.4	1.0	0.1	1.7	3.0	95.2	3.2	0.1	0.6	1.5
RHODE ISLAND	2.7	86.9	5.5	1.0	2.7	0.2	6.6	8.7	91.4	3.9	0.4	1.8	4.6
Bristol	1.0	97.7	1.0	0.4	1.3	0.1	0.6	1.1	98.8	0.4	0.1	0.6	1.4
Kent	1.3	96.7	1.3	0.7	1.6	0.1	1.1	1.7	98.1	0.7	0.2	0.8	1.1
Newport	2.0	93.0	4.7	1.0	1.7	0.2	1.6	2.8	93.9	3.9	0.4	1.2	2.0
Providence	3.6	80.7	8.0	1.1	3.4	0.2	10.4	13.4	87.7	5.6	0.4	2.4	6.8
Washington	1.4	95.9	1.5	1.5	1.8	0.1	0.8	1.4	96.6	1.0	0.9	1.3	1.0
SOUTH CAROLINA	1.0	68.0	29.9	0.7	1.1	0.1	1.3	2.4	69.0	29.8	0.2	0.6	0.9
Abbeville	0.7	68.9	30.6	0.4	0.3	0.0	0.5	0.8	68.1	31.6	0.1	0.2	0.4
Aiken	1.2	72.3	26.0	0.9	0.8	0.1	1.1	2.1	75.0	24.2	0.2	0.5	0.7
Allendale	0.5	27.6	71.3	0.3	0.3	0.1	1.0	1.6	31.1	68.0	0.1	0.1	1.4
Anderson	0.8	82.3	16.9	0.5	0.6	0.1	0.6	1.1	82.9	16.6	0.1	0.2	0.4
Bamberg	0.5	36.8	62.8	0.4	0.3	0.1	0.2	0.7	38.3	61.4	0.1	0.1	0.4
Barnwell	0.7	55.8	43.0	0.7	0.5	0.1	0.9	1.4	56.7	42.8	0.2	0.1	0.7
Beaufort	1.4	71.8	24.5	0.6	1.1	0.2	3.4	6.8	69.2	28.4	0.3	0.9	2.5
Berkeley	1.7	69.4	27.2	1.0	2.4	0.2	1.6	2.8	72.9	24.2	0.3	2.0	2.0
Calhoun	0.7	50.6	48.9	0.4	0.3	0.1	0.5	1.4	48.2	51.6	0.1	0.1	0.3
Charleston	1.2	62.8	35.0	0.6	1.4	0.1	1.3	2.4	63.6	34.9	0.2	0.9	1.3
Cherokee	0.8	77.6	20.8	0.5	0.5	0.1	1.4	2.1	78.6	20.6	0.1	0.4	0.6
Chester	0.6	60.4	38.9	0.6	0.4	0.0	0.3	0.7	59.6	40.0	0.2	0.1	0.2
Chesterfield	0.8	65.0	33.6	0.7	0.4	0.1	1.2	2.3	66.2	33.4	0.2	0.1	0.4
Clarendon	0.5	45.2	53.4	0.4	0.4	0.1	1.0	1.7	43.1	56.5	0.1	0.1	0.5
Colleton	0.8	56.1	42.5	1.0	0.4	0.1	0.8	1.4	54.3	45.0	0.5	0.1	0.5
Darlington	0.5	57.4	42.0	0.4	0.3	0.0	0.5	1.0	59.6	40.1	0.1	0.1	0.3
Dillon	0.7	50.9	45.7	2.6	0.5	0.1	1.1	1.8	54.5	43.7	1.5	0.2	0.3
Dorchester	1.4	72.1	25.6	1.2	1.5	0.2	0.9	1.8	75.0	23.0	0.7	0.9	1.3
Edgefield	0.7	57.3	41.8	0.6	0.4	0.1	0.6	2.0	53.3	46.3	0.1	0.2	0.4
Fairfield	0.6	40.0	59.4	0.4	0.3	0.0	0.6	1.1	41.5	58.3	0.1	0.1	0.5
Florence	0.7	59.2	39.6	0.5	0.9	0.1	0.6	1.1	60.8	38.7	0.1	0.3	0.4
Georgetown	0.5	60.0	38.8	0.3	0.4	0.1	0.9	1.6	56.5	43.2	0.1	0.1	0.4
Greenville	1.1	78.5	18.7	0.5	1.6	0.1	1.8	3.8	80.9	18.0	0.1	0.7	0.9
Greenwood	0.7	66.1	32.0	0.4	0.9	0.1	1.3	2.9	69.2	30.2	0.1	0.4	0.4
Hampton	0.4	43.2	55.9	0.4	0.2	0.0	0.7	2.6	45.5	54.3	0.0	0.1	0.4
Horry	1.1	82.0	15.9	0.8	1.0	0.1	1.4	2.6	81.3	17.5	0.2	0.8	0.9
Jasper	0.7	42.8	53.0	0.6	0.6	0.1	3.7	5.8	42.2	57.4	0.1	0.2	0.4
Kershaw	0.8	72.3	26.6	0.7	0.4	0.1	0.8	1.7	71.2	28.3	0.2	0.2	0.6
Lancaster	0.7	71.6	27.2	0.5	0.4	0.1	1.0	1.6	74.4	25.4	0.1	0.1	0.4
Laurens	0.8	72.2	26.4	0.6	0.3	0.1	1.2	1.9	71.4	28.2	0.1	0.2	0.4
Lee	0.5	35.3	63.8	0.4	0.4	0.0	0.7	1.3	37.2	62.5	0.1	0.2	0.4
Lexington	1.0	85.0	12.9	0.7	1.2	0.1	1.1	1.9	87.9	11.0	0.2	0.6	0.8
McCormick	0.6	45.1	54.3	0.4	0.5	0.2	0.5	0.9	41.1	58.5	0.1	0.1	0.3
Marion	0.5	42.0	56.7	0.5	0.4	0.0	1.0	1.8	44.7	54.6	0.4	0.1	0.3
Marlboro	0.9	45.2	51.1	3.9	0.3	0.1	0.4	0.7	48.7	48.5	2.5	0.1	0.3
Newberry	0.9	64.7	33.4	0.6	0.4	0.1	1.7	4.2	64.8	34.7	0.1	0.3	0.4
Oconee	0.8	89.9	8.6	0.6	0.5	0.1	1.3	2.4	90.5	8.8	0.1	0.3	0.9
Orangeburg	0.7	37.6	61.3	0.8	0.5	0.1	0.5	1.0	41.2	58.1	0.3	0.4	0.4
Pickens	0.9	91.0	7.1	0.5	1.4	0.0	0.9	1.7	91.6	7.3	0.2	0.8	0.6
Richland	1.3	51.2	45.8	0.6	2.1	0.2	1.6	2.7	56.0	41.8	0.2	1.3	1.6
Saluda	0.6	66.3	30.3	0.4	0.1	0.0	3.6	7.3	66.5	33.1	0.1	0.1	0.5
Spartanburg	1.0	75.9	21.1	0.6	1.7	0.1	1.7	2.8	78.2	20.7	0.1	0.8	0.7

[1] Hispanic persons may be of any race.

Table B. States and Counties

STATE County	Population and population characteristics, 2000										
	Age (percent)										
	Under 5 years	5 to 17 years	18 to 24 years	25 to 34 years	35 to 44 years	45 to 54 years	55 to 64 years	65 to 74 years	75 years and over	Median age (years)	Percent Female
	28	29	30	31	32	33	34	35	36	37	38
PENNSYLVANIA—Cont'd											
Potter	6.2	19.8	6.9	11.4	14.7	13.8	10.6	8.6	8.1	39.1	50.7
Schuylkill	4.9	16.0	7.2	13.0	15.3	14.1	9.7	9.7	10.2	40.9	50.2
Snyder	5.6	18.4	11.2	12.2	15.2	13.5	9.8	7.7	6.4	36.7	51.1
Somerset	5.2	17.0	7.6	12.4	15.4	14.3	10.0	8.9	9.1	40.2	50.1
Sullivan	4.3	16.5	7.9	9.4	14.7	13.1	12.2	11.3	10.6	43.0	49.5
Susquehanna	5.7	19.8	6.7	10.9	16.2	14.3	11.0	8.2	7.3	39.5	50.3
Tioga	5.4	18.3	10.6	10.9	14.5	13.4	10.9	8.4	7.5	38.5	51.0
Union	4.8	15.3	13.9	14.7	16.2	12.9	8.7	6.6	6.8	35.8	44.7
Venango	5.7	18.6	7.2	11.0	15.6	14.9	10.3	9.2	7.6	40.2	51.2
Warren	5.7	18.5	6.4	11.3	15.7	14.8	11.0	8.8	7.8	40.5	51.0
Washington	5.5	16.6	7.7	11.4	15.7	15.0	10.0	8.9	9.1	40.8	52.0
Wayne	5.6	18.4	6.1	11.0	15.9	14.4	11.1	9.5	8.0	40.8	49.8
Westmoreland	5.2	16.8	6.8	11.4	16.1	15.1	10.3	9.3	9.0	41.3	51.8
Wyoming	5.8	19.7	8.0	12.3	15.7	15.0	10.3	7.0	6.2	37.8	50.4
York	6.1	18.5	7.5	13.1	17.2	14.6	9.4	7.1	6.4	37.8	50.8
RHODE ISLAND	6.1	17.5	10.2	13.4	16.2	13.5	8.5	7.0	7.5	36.7	52.0
Bristol	5.4	17.5	9.5	10.7	16.7	14.3	9.1	8.1	8.6	39.3	51.8
Kent	5.9	17.3	7.0	13.0	17.5	14.9	9.2	7.5	7.5	38.9	52.0
Newport	5.8	16.7	8.4	12.9	17.0	15.2	9.6	7.3	7.1	38.6	51.4
Providence	6.3	17.7	11.1	14.1	15.6	12.5	7.9	6.9	7.7	35.4	52.1
Washington	5.9	17.5	11.2	11.5	16.9	15.1	9.2	6.5	6.2	37.4	51.5
SOUTH CAROLINA	6.6	18.6	10.2	14.0	15.6	13.7	9.3	6.7	5.4	35.4	51.4
Abbeville	6.7	18.6	9.5	12.3	14.4	14.1	9.6	7.9	6.8	36.9	52.1
Aiken	6.7	19.5	8.8	12.8	16.1	14.0	9.4	7.3	5.6	36.4	51.8
Allendale	6.9	19.7	9.8	13.5	14.7	14.3	8.5	6.4	6.3	35.1	47.9
Anderson	6.7	17.9	8.4	13.5	15.5	14.0	10.3	7.4	6.2	37.3	51.7
Bamberg	6.2	19.2	12.9	11.5	13.1	13.8	9.4	7.3	6.6	35.2	53.0
Barnwell	7.1	21.0	8.7	12.4	15.5	13.9	8.8	6.9	5.7	35.5	51.9
Beaufort	6.7	16.6	12.0	13.6	13.6	11.6	10.5	9.4	6.1	35.8	49.4
Berkeley	7.2	20.8	11.7	14.7	16.5	12.9	8.2	4.9	3.0	32.0	49.2
Calhoun	6.3	18.7	7.4	11.9	15.1	15.8	11.0	7.6	6.2	38.9	52.6
Charleston	6.4	17.3	12.0	14.9	15.4	13.3	8.7	6.5	5.4	34.5	51.7
Cherokee	7.2	18.7	9.0	14.6	14.9	13.8	9.4	6.8	5.6	35.3	51.6
Chester	6.7	20.2	8.4	13.1	15.1	14.0	9.8	6.9	5.7	36.0	52.0
Chesterfield	6.8	19.9	8.5	13.7	15.3	14.3	9.6	6.8	5.2	35.7	51.8
Clarendon	6.1	19.7	10.5	11.2	14.0	14.0	10.7	8.2	5.8	37.0	50.9
Colleton	6.9	20.6	8.0	12.2	14.7	14.3	10.4	7.3	5.6	36.5	52.1
Darlington	6.9	19.4	9.0	13.2	15.0	14.7	9.7	6.6	5.5	36.0	52.7
Dillon	7.4	21.7	9.5	12.6	14.9	13.6	8.8	6.3	5.2	34.2	53.4
Dorchester	6.7	22.2	7.7	14.0	17.7	14.0	8.6	5.2	3.9	34.7	51.1
Edgefield	6.0	18.1	9.8	15.0	17.1	14.4	8.8	6.0	4.9	35.6	47.0
Fairfield	6.7	19.4	8.6	12.6	15.2	14.9	9.4	7.2	6.0	36.9	52.4
Florence	6.5	19.4	9.7	13.6	15.3	14.4	9.2	6.3	5.5	35.5	53.0
Georgetown	6.2	18.9	7.7	11.6	14.3	14.5	11.7	8.7	6.2	39.1	52.1
Greenville	6.8	17.8	9.6	15.0	16.2	13.8	9.1	6.3	5.5	35.5	51.3
Greenwood	6.9	18.6	10.4	13.8	14.4	13.0	9.2	7.3	6.4	35.2	53.1
Hampton	6.7	20.9	8.5	14.3	15.4	13.7	8.4	6.8	5.4	34.8	49.1
Horry	5.7	15.6	9.4	14.2	15.1	13.7	11.3	9.4	5.6	38.3	50.9
Jasper	7.2	19.5	10.3	14.8	15.9	12.3	9.0	6.2	4.8	33.8	47.4
Kershaw	6.6	19.6	7.6	12.5	16.3	14.7	9.8	7.3	5.6	37.4	51.7
Lancaster	6.5	18.9	8.6	14.5	15.7	13.9	9.7	6.7	5.3	35.9	50.5
Laurens	6.6	18.7	9.2	13.6	14.9	13.8	10.0	7.1	6.0	36.2	51.6
Lee	6.3	19.4	10.0	13.2	16.0	14.4	8.2	6.6	5.8	35.7	49.7
Lexington	6.8	19.2	8.3	14.4	17.2	14.7	9.1	5.7	4.5	35.7	51.4
McCormick	4.2	15.3	8.3	12.9	14.7	14.6	13.5	9.7	6.8	41.1	46.8
Marion	7.0	20.7	9.7	12.6	14.2	14.6	9.2	6.6	5.5	35.1	53.8
Marlboro	6.6	19.5	9.3	13.9	15.5	13.8	9.0	6.8	5.5	35.4	50.9
Newberry	6.4	17.7	9.8	12.9	14.7	13.8	9.9	7.4	7.4	37.1	51.8
Oconee	6.0	16.8	8.0	12.8	14.5	14.1	12.2	9.4	6.2	39.5	50.8
Orangeburg	6.5	19.4	11.9	11.7	14.4	13.4	9.5	7.2	6.0	35.3	53.5
Pickens	6.1	16.2	17.5	13.3	14.3	12.4	8.8	6.1	5.3	32.7	50.1
Richland	6.3	17.9	13.8	15.6	16.0	13.2	7.3	5.3	4.5	32.6	51.7
Saluda	6.5	18.4	9.2	13.0	14.6	13.5	10.3	7.7	6.8	37.0	50.4
Spartanburg	6.6	18.2	9.2	14.3	15.6	14.0	9.5	6.7	5.8	36.1	51.4

Table B. States and Counties

STATE County	Under 5 years	5 to 17 years	18 to 24 years	25 to 34 years	35 to 44 years	45 to 54 years	55 to 64 years	65 to 74 years	75 years and over	Percent Female	2000	1990	1980	1990–2000	1980–1990
	39	40	41	42	43	44	45	46	47	48	49	50	51	52	53
PENNSYLVANIA—Cont'd															
Potter	7.1	20.4	7.8	13.7	14.0	10.6	10.1	9.6	6.9	51.4	18 080	16 717	17 726	8.2	-5.7
Schuylkill	5.7	16.3	8.7	14.2	13.8	9.9	11.3	11.6	8.4	51.8	150 336	152 585	160 630	-1.5	-5.0
Snyder	7.3	18.1	12.9	15.5	14.4	10.3	8.9	7.5	5.1	51.2	37 546	36 680	33 584	2.4	9.2
Somerset	6.4	18.6	8.3	14.7	14.5	10.2	10.4	10.0	6.9	51.8	80 023	78 218	81 243	2.3	-3.7
Sullivan	5.3	17.8	9.7	13.4	12.2	9.5	11.3	10.9	10.0	49.9	6 556	6 104	6 349	7.4	-3.9
Susquehanna	7.2	19.6	8.0	15.3	14.2	11.1	9.2	8.8	6.5	50.6	42 238	40 380	37 876	4.6	6.6
Tioga	6.5	18.7	12.1	13.8	13.3	11.0	9.5	8.7	6.3	51.3	41 373	41 126	40 973	0.6	0.4
Union	6.6	16.4	16.4	14.6	14.8	10.2	8.4	6.8	5.7	48.4	41 624	36 176	32 870	15.1	10.1
Venango	6.6	19.3	7.9	14.9	15.1	10.5	10.7	8.8	6.2	51.5	57 565	59 381	64 444	-3.1	-7.9
Warren	6.7	18.5	7.9	14.9	14.7	11.3	10.4	8.9	6.7	51.3	43 863	45 050	47 449	-2.6	-5.1
Washington	5.8	16.7	9.4	14.3	15.0	10.7	10.7	10.6	6.9	52.1	202 897	204 584	217 074	-0.8	-5.8
Wayne	6.7	18.5	8.1	14.8	14.5	10.3	10.2	9.7	7.2	50.4	47 722	39 944	35 237	19.5	13.4
Westmoreland	6.0	16.5	8.6	14.7	15.2	11.0	10.9	10.4	6.7	52.2	369 993	370 321	392 184	-0.1	-5.6
Wyoming	7.1	20.4	10.6	14.9	15.5	10.5	8.3	7.4	5.2	50.6	28 080	28 076	26 433	0.0	6.2
York	7.0	17.2	9.6	17.1	16.0	10.9	9.1	7.7	5.4	51.1	381 751	339 574	312 963	12.4	8.5
RHODE ISLAND	6.7	15.8	12.0	17.3	14.7	9.6	8.9	8.5	6.5	52.0	1 048 319	1 003 464	947 154	4.5	5.9
Bristol	6.5	15.5	11.2	15.6	14.7	10.6	10.1	9.4	6.4	51.4	50 648	48 859	46 942	3.7	4.1
Kent	6.3	16.2	9.1	17.1	16.0	10.7	9.6	9.0	6.1	52.1	167 090	161 143	154 163	3.7	4.5
Newport	6.6	16.0	12.0	17.8	16.3	10.0	8.4	7.5	5.5	50.2	85 433	87 194	81 383	-2.0	7.1
Providence	6.8	15.6	12.4	17.6	13.9	9.1	8.9	8.8	7.0	52.5	621 602	596 270	571 349	4.2	4.4
Washington	6.6	16.5	14.6	16.4	15.9	9.8	7.9	7.2	5.1	51.2	123 546	109 998	93 317	12.3	17.9
SOUTH CAROLINA	7.4	19.0	11.7	17.0	15.0	10.2	8.4	7.1	4.3	51.6	4 012 012	3 486 310	3 120 729	15.1	11.7
Abbeville	7.0	18.8	11.4	14.0	14.2	10.3	9.6	8.3	6.5	52.6	26 167	23 862	22 627	9.7	5.5
Aiken	7.5	19.8	9.9	16.8	15.1	10.3	9.2	7.2	4.2	51.5	142 552	120 991	105 630	17.8	14.5
Allendale	7.6	21.9	12.2	15.7	14.1	8.5	7.3	7.5	5.2	49.4	11 211	11 727	10 700	-4.4	9.6
Anderson	6.6	18.3	9.9	15.6	15.0	11.6	9.6	8.3	5.3	52.2	165 740	145 177	133 235	14.2	9.0
Bamberg	7.2	21.8	14.6	13.3	13.3	8.8	8.2	7.8	5.0	53.1	16 658	16 902	18 118	-1.4	-6.7
Barnwell	8.1	22.3	9.6	15.6	14.4	9.4	8.3	7.4	4.9	52.0	23 478	20 293	19 868	15.7	2.1
Beaufort	8.5	16.7	14.7	18.5	12.8	7.8	8.5	8.4	3.9	49.3	120 937	86 425	65 364	39.9	32.2
Berkeley	9.8	22.6	11.0	20.3	15.4	9.1	6.0	3.9	1.9	49.5	142 651	128 658	94 745	10.9	35.9
Calhoun	7.2	20.0	9.2	14.8	15.3	10.8	8.8	7.9	5.9	52.6	15 185	12 753	12 206	19.1	4.5
Charleston	8.0	16.9	14.5	19.5	14.4	9.0	7.5	6.4	3.7	50.3	309 969	295 159	276 556	5.0	6.7
Cherokee	7.0	19.3	10.6	15.1	14.8	11.0	9.2	7.8	5.2	52.1	52 537	44 506	40 983	18.0	8.6
Chester	7.5	20.4	10.0	15.0	14.3	10.5	9.0	7.9	5.4	52.7	34 068	32 170	30 148	5.9	6.7
Chesterfield	7.1	20.4	10.1	14.9	14.8	10.7	9.2	7.7	5.0	52.2	42 768	38 575	38 161	10.9	1.1
Clarendon	7.8	21.9	9.5	14.3	14.2	10.2	8.8	8.4	4.9	52.3	32 502	28 450	27 464	14.2	3.6
Colleton	7.6	21.8	9.3	14.6	14.4	10.4	9.2	7.8	5.0	52.3	38 264	34 377	31 776	11.3	8.2
Darlington	7.0	21.2	10.1	14.9	15.6	10.6	8.6	7.3	4.7	53.0	67 394	61 851	62 717	9.0	-1.4
Dillon	8.0	23.5	10.0	14.5	14.0	9.6	8.1	7.6	4.7	53.6	30 722	29 114	31 083	5.5	-6.3
Dorchester	8.8	20.8	10.9	19.7	16.3	9.8	6.3	4.7	2.7	50.1	96 413	83 060	59 045	16.1	40.7
Edgefield	7.8	21.0	9.3	16.0	15.3	9.9	8.5	7.4	4.8	51.6	24 595	18 360	17 528	34.0	4.7
Fairfield	7.2	21.2	10.6	15.0	14.2	9.5	8.7	8.0	5.6	52.1	23 454	22 295	20 700	5.2	7.7
Florence	7.3	21.1	10.6	15.6	15.5	10.5	8.3	7.0	4.2	52.9	125 761	114 344	110 163	10.0	3.8
Georgetown	7.7	22.1	9.1	14.9	14.7	9.6	9.1	8.6	4.3	52.5	55 797	46 302	42 461	20.5	9.0
Greenville	7.1	17.6	11.0	17.2	15.5	11.1	8.7	7.2	4.7	51.9	379 616	320 127	287 895	18.6	11.2
Greenwood	6.9	18.6	11.2	15.2	14.4	10.5	9.3	8.1	5.7	53.1	66 271	59 567	55 859	11.3	6.6
Hampton	8.4	23.5	9.7	14.1	14.3	9.6	8.0	7.5	4.8	53.1	21 386	18 186	18 159	17.6	0.2
Horry	6.6	17.2	10.4	17.8	14.7	10.3	10.3	8.8	3.9	51.0	196 629	144 053	101 419	36.5	42.0
Jasper	8.8	22.8	9.7	15.0	13.1	9.5	8.4	7.4	5.2	52.1	20 678	15 487	14 504	33.5	6.8
Kershaw	6.7	20.4	8.9	15.7	15.7	11.0	9.4	7.6	4.5	51.9	52 647	43 599	39 015	20.8	11.7
Lancaster	7.4	19.5	10.1	15.5	15.1	11.2	9.0	7.6	4.7	52.2	61 351	54 516	53 361	12.5	2.2
Laurens	6.8	18.6	11.3	14.8	14.6	11.0	9.5	7.8	5.6	52.1	69 567	58 132	52 214	19.7	11.3
Lee	7.5	23.2	9.8	16.0	14.2	8.9	8.1	7.3	5.0	53.3	20 119	18 437	18 929	9.1	-2.6
Lexington	7.3	19.3	10.0	17.8	17.1	11.7	7.9	5.7	3.2	51.3	216 014	167 526	140 353	28.9	19.4
McCormick	5.2	18.9	12.3	17.8	14.7	9.5	8.5	7.7	5.4	46.0	9 958	8 868	7 797	12.3	13.7
Marion	7.4	23.8	9.1	14.2	14.8	9.7	8.4	7.7	4.8	54.6	35 466	33 899	34 179	4.6	-0.8
Marlboro	7.3	21.7	10.4	15.3	14.1	9.9	8.4	7.8	5.0	52.7	28 818	29 716	31 634	-3.0	-6.1
Newberry	6.8	18.5	11.1	14.8	14.1	10.4	8.9	9.0	6.5	52.3	36 108	33 172	31 242	8.9	6.2
Oconee	6.2	18.2	9.4	15.4	14.6	11.9	10.5	8.6	5.1	50.9	66 215	57 494	48 611	15.2	18.3
Orangeburg	7.3	20.9	12.9	14.7	13.9	9.6	8.3	7.7	4.8	53.4	91 582	84 804	82 276	8.0	3.1
Pickens	6.1	16.1	19.6	15.0	13.9	10.1	8.1	6.6	4.6	50.3	110 757	93 896	79 292	18.0	18.4
Richland	7.0	17.1	15.0	19.7	15.6	8.9	7.2	5.9	3.6	51.4	320 677	286 321	269 600	12.0	6.2
Saluda	6.5	19.9	9.4	14.8	14.3	11.0	9.7	8.4	5.9	51.3	19 181	16 441	16 136	16.7	1.4
Spartanburg	6.7	17.9	11.0	16.0	15.4	11.2	9.0	7.6	5.0	51.8	253 791	226 793	203 023	11.9	11.7

STATE County	Total population	Total in households	House-holder	Spouse	Child Total	Child Own child under 18 years	Other relatives Total	Other relatives Under 18 years	Nonrelatives Total	Nonrelatives Unmar-ried partner	Total in group quarters	Institutionalized Correc-tional institu-tions	Institutionalized Nurs-ing homes	Institutionalized Other institu-tions	Noninstitutionalized College dormi-tories	Noninstitutionalized Mili-tary quar-ters	Other
	54	55	56	57	58	59	60	61	62	63	64	65	66	67	68	69	70
PENNSYLVANIA—Cont'd																	
Potter	18 080	98.3	38.7	23.0	29.8	24.0	3.0	1.3	3.7	2.0	1.7	0.1	0.9	0.3	0.0	0.0	0.4
Schuylkill	150 336	95.2	40.3	20.7	27.0	19.1	3.9	1.2	3.4	2.0	4.8	3.0	1.4	0.0	0.1	0.0	0.2
Snyder	37 546	93.9	36.4	22.5	28.8	22.6	2.5	0.9	3.7	1.8	6.1	0.4	0.6	1.4	3.7	0.0	0.1
Somerset	80 023	95.6	39.0	22.8	28.0	20.8	3.0	1.1	2.8	1.6	4.4	2.8	1.0	0.0	0.0	0.0	0.5
Sullivan	6 556	93.2	40.6	22.2	23.2	17.1	3.1	1.2	4.2	2.2	6.8	0.0	2.2	0.0	0.0	0.0	4.5
Susquehanna	42 238	99.0	39.1	22.6	29.8	23.5	3.2	1.2	4.3	2.4	1.0	0.1	0.7	0.0	0.0	0.0	0.2
Tioga	41 373	95.4	38.5	22.3	27.0	21.6	3.0	1.2	4.6	2.2	4.6	0.1	0.7	0.1	3.1	0.0	0.6
Union	41 624	79.1	31.7	19.0	23.6	19.0	1.7	0.6	3.2	1.4	20.9	12.8	1.1	0.0	6.4	0.0	0.5
Venango	57 565	96.8	39.5	22.0	28.4	21.9	3.1	1.2	3.8	2.1	3.2	0.3	1.0	0.7	0.0	0.0	1.2
Warren	43 863	97.6	40.3	22.6	28.1	22.3	2.7	1.2	3.8	2.1	2.4	0.1	1.3	0.6	0.0	0.0	0.4
Washington	202 897	97.4	40.0	22.1	28.2	20.4	3.8	1.4	3.3	1.7	2.6	0.1	0.8	0.1	1.0	0.0	0.6
Wayne	47 722	96.0	38.5	22.0	28.2	21.9	3.7	1.4	3.7	1.9	4.0	2.4	1.0	0.0	0.1	0.0	0.5
Westmoreland	369 993	97.7	40.5	23.1	28.3	20.5	3.1	1.0	2.7	1.5	2.3	0.4	0.8	0.1	0.5	0.0	0.5
Wyoming	28 080	97.5	38.3	22.3	30.2	23.4	3.1	1.2	3.7	2.0	2.5	0.2	0.7	0.3	1.0	0.0	0.3
York	381 751	97.9	38.8	22.6	28.7	22.7	3.3	1.3	4.5	2.4	2.1	0.4	0.8	0.0	0.4	0.0	0.6
RHODE ISLAND	1 048 319	96.3	39.0	18.8	29.0	21.8	4.5	1.4	5.1	2.2	3.7	0.3	0.9	0.1	2.0	0.1	0.3
Bristol	50 648	94.5	37.6	21.5	28.6	21.7	3.6	1.0	3.2	1.5	5.5	0.0	1.5	0.0	3.7	0.0	0.2
Kent	167 090	98.9	40.3	21.2	29.2	21.6	3.8	1.2	4.3	2.3	1.1	0.0	0.7	0.0	0.1	0.0	0.3
Newport	85 433	97.1	41.2	20.6	27.1	21.3	2.9	0.9	5.2	2.0	2.9	0.0	0.6	0.0	1.0	1.0	0.2
Providence	621 602	95.7	38.6	17.2	29.4	21.9	5.3	1.6	5.3	2.3	4.3	0.6	0.9	0.1	2.2	0.0	0.4
Washington	123 546	95.8	38.0	21.1	28.0	22.0	3.1	1.0	5.6	2.1	4.2	0.0	0.7	0.0	3.2	0.0	0.4
SOUTH CAROLINA	4 012 012	96.6	38.2	19.5	28.8	21.8	5.9	2.8	4.3	1.8	3.4	0.9	0.5	0.1	1.0	0.4	0.4
Abbeville	26 167	97.3	38.7	20.2	29.1	21.6	6.4	3.2	2.9	1.5	2.7	0.2	0.7	0.0	1.6	0.0	0.2
Aiken	142 552	98.5	39.0	20.8	30.0	23.2	5.2	2.5	3.5	1.6	1.5	0.3	0.6	0.1	0.2	0.0	0.3
Allendale	11 211	89.5	34.9	12.5	28.9	20.4	10.2	5.9	3.0	1.8	10.5	9.7	0.5	0.1	0.0	0.0	0.1
Anderson	165 740	98.4	39.6	21.8	28.5	21.7	5.2	2.4	3.3	1.7	1.6	0.2	0.7	0.1	0.4	0.0	0.3
Bamberg	16 658	93.6	36.8	16.0	29.7	20.7	7.9	4.0	3.2	1.7	6.4	0.2	0.5	0.1	3.8	0.0	1.8
Barnwell	23 478	98.8	38.4	18.2	32.4	24.5	6.3	3.1	3.5	1.7	1.2	0.3	0.7	0.0	0.0	0.0	0.2
Beaufort	120 937	94.5	37.6	21.9	25.2	20.7	4.7	2.1	5.1	1.7	5.5	0.1	0.3	0.0	0.0	4.8	0.2
Berkeley	142 651	96.2	35.0	19.8	31.5	24.6	5.5	2.8	4.3	1.8	3.8	1.5	0.2	0.0	0.0	2.0	0.2
Calhoun	15 185	98.9	39.0	20.3	29.2	20.8	7.6	4.0	2.9	1.8	1.1	0.0	0.8	0.0	0.0	0.0	0.3
Charleston	309 969	96.3	39.8	17.2	27.0	20.4	6.1	2.9	6.3	2.0	3.7	0.5	0.4	0.1	1.6	0.2	0.8
Cherokee	52 537	98.6	39.0	20.0	29.6	22.3	6.3	3.1	3.6	1.8	1.4	0.1	0.5	0.0	0.4	0.0	0.3
Chester	34 068	99.1	37.8	18.4	31.5	22.4	7.8	3.9	3.5	1.9	0.9	0.2	0.6	0.0	0.0	0.0	0.1
Chesterfield	42 768	98.5	38.7	19.2	30.3	22.5	6.7	3.5	3.5	1.8	1.5	0.1	0.8	0.1	0.0	0.0	0.5
Clarendon	32 502	95.3	36.3	17.6	29.9	20.6	8.7	4.4	2.8	1.3	4.7	3.7	0.5	0.1	0.0	0.0	0.4
Colleton	38 264	99.1	37.8	19.3	31.0	22.7	7.5	4.2	3.5	1.7	0.9	0.2	0.3	0.0	0.0	0.0	0.4
Darlington	67 394	98.2	38.3	18.5	30.2	21.7	7.9	4.1	3.4	1.7	1.8	0.2	0.7	0.2	0.4	0.0	0.3
Dillon	30 722	98.6	36.5	16.3	32.8	23.4	9.7	5.3	3.3	1.9	1.4	0.3	0.8	0.0	0.0	0.0	0.3
Dorchester	96 413	97.8	36.0	20.6	32.7	25.9	4.9	2.4	3.6	1.7	2.2	1.3	0.5	0.0	0.0	0.0	0.4
Edgefield	24 595	89.5	33.6	18.7	28.6	20.7	6.2	3.0	2.4	1.1	10.5	9.8	0.4	0.1	0.0	0.0	0.3
Fairfield	23 454	98.2	37.4	17.9	31.5	21.3	8.2	4.3	3.2	1.9	1.8	0.2	1.2	0.0	0.0	0.0	0.3
Florence	125 761	96.9	37.5	18.6	30.5	22.1	6.9	3.3	3.4	1.5	3.1	0.4	0.9	0.3	0.8	0.0	0.6
Georgetown	55 797	99.0	38.8	21.0	28.9	21.0	7.1	3.7	3.1	1.4	1.0	0.2	0.4	0.1	0.0	0.0	0.3
Greenville	379 616	97.1	39.4	20.6	28.3	22.2	4.8	1.9	4.1	1.7	2.9	0.5	0.5	0.1	1.5	0.0	0.3
Greenwood	66 271	96.5	38.8	18.9	28.5	21.8	6.2	3.0	4.1	1.8	3.5	1.0	0.5	0.1	1.3	0.0	0.6
Hampton	21 386	92.0	34.8	16.7	30.7	23.1	6.9	3.9	2.9	1.5	8.0	7.4	0.5	0.0	0.0	0.0	0.2
Horry	196 629	98.7	41.6	21.4	24.6	18.7	5.0	2.1	6.2	2.4	1.3	0.2	0.4	0.0	0.4	0.0	0.2
Jasper	20 678	93.5	34.1	16.4	29.3	21.6	9.0	4.6	4.8	1.7	6.5	6.0	0.4	0.0	0.0	0.0	0.1
Kershaw	52 647	99.0	38.3	21.4	29.9	22.6	6.0	3.0	3.3	1.7	1.0	0.2	0.6	0.0	0.0	0.0	0.3
Lancaster	61 351	96.8	37.8	19.9	29.4	21.9	5.9	2.9	3.8	1.9	3.2	2.4	0.4	0.0	0.0	0.0	0.3
Laurens	69 567	96.2	37.8	19.3	28.8	21.4	6.6	3.2	3.8	2.0	3.8	0.2	0.8	0.6	1.3	0.0	0.9
Lee	20 119	91.6	34.2	14.7	30.0	20.1	9.8	5.3	2.9	1.5	8.4	7.3	0.8	0.0	0.0	0.0	0.3
Lexington	216 014	98.7	38.5	21.8	29.8	23.9	4.1	1.7	4.5	1.8	1.3	0.2	0.5	0.2	0.0	0.0	0.5
McCormick	9 958	85.5	35.7	18.5	22.4	14.7	6.7	3.1	2.1	1.1	14.5	11.9	1.1	0.1	0.0	0.0	1.4
Marion	35 466	99.1	37.5	16.2	32.0	21.9	9.8	5.2	3.5	1.6	0.9	0.3	0.6	0.0	0.0	0.0	0.1
Marlboro	28 818	94.3	36.4	15.5	29.8	20.5	9.3	5.0	3.4	2.0	5.7	4.8	0.6	0.2	0.0	0.0	0.0
Newberry	36 108	97.2	38.8	19.1	28.4	20.7	6.6	3.0	4.2	1.7	2.8	0.2	0.7	0.0	1.5	0.0	0.4
Oconee	66 215	99.0	41.2	23.8	26.5	20.3	4.2	1.8	3.2	1.6	1.0	0.1	0.3	0.0	0.0	0.0	0.5
Orangeburg	91 582	96.0	37.3	16.8	29.8	21.1	8.4	4.3	3.7	1.7	4.0	0.4	0.8	0.0	2.6	0.0	0.3
Pickens	110 757	93.3	37.3	20.8	25.6	20.3	3.8	1.5	5.9	1.5	6.7	0.1	0.4	0.0	5.7	0.0	0.4
Richland	320 677	91.3	37.5	16.4	27.0	20.7	5.4	2.5	5.1	1.7	8.7	1.9	0.5	0.6	2.8	2.2	0.7
Saluda	19 181	98.6	37.2	20.2	29.1	21.0	7.8	3.3	4.4	1.4	1.4	0.1	1.0	0.0	0.0	0.0	0.2
Spartanburg	253 791	97.1	38.5	20.3	28.6	21.7	5.8	2.6	3.8	1.7	2.9	0.9	0.4	0.0	0.8	0.0	0.7

Table B. States and Counties

STATE County	Households by type, 2000												Households, 1990		
		Family households						Nonfamily households							
				Married couple		Female householder[1]			Householder living alone						
	Total households	Total	With own children under 18 years	Total	With own children under 18 years	Total	With own children under 18 years	Total	Total	65 years and over	Average household size	Average family size	Total households	Female householder[1]	Householder living alone
	71	72	73	74	75	76	77	78	79	80	81	82	83	84	85

PENNSYLVANIA—Cont'd

STATE County	71	72	73	74	75	76	77	78	79	80	81	82	83	84	85
Potter	7 005	71.4	31.5	59.5	24.5	7.6	4.3	28.6	24.7	11.4	2.54	3.02	6 246	8.1	23.1
Schuylkill	60 530	66.3	26.8	51.4	19.9	10.2	4.8	33.7	29.9	16.5	2.36	2.93	60 773	10.0	28.0
Snyder	13 654	73.1	32.1	62.0	25.8	7.4	4.1	26.9	22.4	10.3	2.58	3.02	12 764	6.6	20.2
Somerset	31 222	70.6	29.4	58.3	23.2	8.5	4.3	29.4	26.1	13.6	2.45	2.95	29 574	8.6	23.2
Sullivan	2 660	65.9	24.2	54.7	18.2	6.8	3.6	34.1	29.3	15.2	2.30	2.81	2 280	8.0	26.7
Susquehanna	16 529	71.3	31.9	57.7	23.9	8.6	5.1	28.7	24.3	11.5	2.53	2.99	14 898	8.3	21.5
Tioga	15 925	70.3	30.4	57.8	22.8	8.6	5.4	29.7	24.4	11.3	2.48	2.93	14 974	8.1	22.1
Union	13 178	69.9	31.1	59.9	24.7	6.9	4.6	30.1	25.3	11.8	2.50	3.00	11 689	7.0	22.2
Venango	22 747	70.0	30.4	55.8	21.9	9.9	5.9	30.0	26.2	12.5	2.45	2.93	22 408	9.6	23.9
Warren	17 696	68.5	29.8	56.1	22.3	8.4	5.0	31.5	27.2	12.2	2.42	2.93	17 244	8.2	24.5
Washington	81 130	69.1	28.4	55.2	21.8	10.3	5.0	30.9	27.0	13.2	2.44	2.96	78 533	10.3	24.5
Wayne	18 350	70.5	30.3	57.2	22.9	8.9	5.1	29.5	25.2	12.2	2.50	2.98	14 638	8.3	22.1
Westmoreland	149 813	69.8	28.4	57.0	22.3	9.6	4.7	30.2	26.9	13.3	2.41	2.93	144 080	9.5	24.2
Wyoming	10 762	71.6	33.2	58.1	25.4	9.3	5.4	28.4	24.1	9.9	2.55	3.02	10 002	9.1	22.0
York	148 219	71.2	32.5	58.3	24.6	9.0	5.5	28.8	23.3	9.2	2.52	2.98	128 666	8.4	21.3
RHODE ISLAND	408 424	65.0	30.6	48.2	21.0	12.9	7.8	35.0	28.6	11.4	2.47	3.07	377 977	11.7	26.2
Bristol	19 033	70.2	31.8	57.3	25.3	9.9	5.3	29.8	25.1	11.2	2.52	3.04	17 559	8.9	21.7
Kent	67 320	66.8	29.9	52.7	22.6	10.5	5.6	33.2	27.6	11.4	2.45	3.02	62 058	9.7	25.5
Newport	35 228	63.1	28.6	49.9	21.0	10.3	6.2	36.9	29.9	10.8	2.35	2.95	32 687	10.2	25.4
Providence	239 936	64.2	30.7	44.5	19.5	14.9	9.2	36.3	29.8	11.9	2.48	3.11	226 362	13.2	27.7
Washington	46 907	68.3	31.8	55.5	24.7	9.4	5.5	31.7	24.1	9.2	2.52	3.01	39 311	9.0	21.6
SOUTH CAROLINA	1 533 854	69.9	32.3	51.1	21.8	14.8	8.5	30.1	25.0	8.6	2.53	3.02	1 258 044	14.0	22.4
Abbeville	10 131	71.9	31.7	52.2	21.2	15.3	8.4	28.1	25.3	11.3	2.51	3.00	8 780	14.2	23.6
Aiken	55 587	70.9	33.1	53.3	22.9	13.8	8.2	29.1	25.2	9.2	2.53	3.03	44 883	12.5	22.5
Allendale	3 915	66.8	30.3	35.8	13.5	25.8	14.6	33.2	30.0	12.3	2.56	3.21	3 791	25.7	26.0
Anderson	65 649	72.0	31.6	55.0	22.3	12.8	7.1	28.0	24.3	9.6	2.48	2.94	55 481	11.7	22.7
Bamberg	6 123	69.5	31.1	43.6	17.9	21.3	11.5	30.5	27.8	11.6	2.55	3.10	5 587	20.8	24.3
Barnwell	9 021	71.3	34.8	47.4	20.8	19.3	11.8	28.7	25.6	10.2	2.57	3.08	7 100	17.9	22.3
Beaufort	45 532	72.6	30.4	58.2	21.6	11.0	7.0	27.4	21.5	8.3	2.51	2.90	30 712	11.7	20.5
Berkeley	49 922	75.5	39.2	56.7	27.7	14.2	8.8	24.5	19.4	5.6	2.75	3.15	42 386	10.9	15.7
Calhoun	5 917	72.2	30.2	52.0	20.4	15.8	7.7	27.8	24.5	9.6	2.54	3.03	4 487	15.7	22.4
Charleston	123 326	62.8	28.7	43.2	17.9	15.9	9.2	37.2	28.3	8.1	2.42	3.01	107 069	15.1	24.7
Cherokee	20 495	71.3	32.7	51.3	21.7	15.4	8.9	28.7	25.0	9.4	2.53	3.01	16 456	14.2	22.8
Chester	12 880	72.5	32.9	48.8	20.0	18.6	10.5	27.5	24.2	9.9	2.62	3.11	11 448	17.5	22.5
Chesterfield	16 557	70.7	33.4	49.6	21.8	16.3	9.3	29.3	25.9	10.0	2.54	3.05	14 047	15.9	22.7
Clarendon	11 812	72.8	31.4	48.5	19.0	19.8	10.6	27.2	24.6	10.3	2.62	3.12	9 544	19.9	20.6
Colleton	14 470	72.5	33.1	51.1	21.6	16.8	9.3	27.5	24.0	10.1	2.62	3.11	12 040	16.1	21.5
Darlington	25 793	71.2	32.2	48.3	19.9	18.7	10.3	28.5	25.1	9.2	2.57	3.07	21 999	17.8	22.1
Dillon	11 199	72.0	34.6	44.8	20.6	22.3	11.8	28.0	25.1	9.9	2.71	3.24	9 887	21.1	22.9
Dorchester	34 709	75.8	40.0	57.2	28.4	14.6	9.4	24.2	20.2	6.5	2.72	3.13	28 213	11.5	17.0
Edgefield	8 270	75.1	34.8	55.6	24.3	15.5	8.6	24.9	22.4	9.1	2.66	3.12	6 424	14.4	21.9
Fairfield	8 774	72.8	32.4	47.9	19.1	20.0	10.9	27.2	24.4	9.4	2.63	3.12	7 467	18.7	21.9
Florence	47 147	71.7	33.8	49.7	22.1	18.1	10.0	28.3	24.5	8.2	2.59	3.08	40 217	17.3	21.8
Georgetown	21 659	73.2	30.2	54.1	20.0	15.1	8.4	26.8	23.3	9.2	2.55	3.01	16 275	15.0	20.6
Greenville	149 556	68.2	31.9	52.3	22.9	12.3	7.2	31.8	26.8	8.5	2.47	3.00	122 878	12.1	24.7
Greenwood	25 729	69.0	31.7	48.7	20.3	16.1	9.4	31.0	26.3	10.6	2.49	3.00	22 730	14.0	25.3
Hampton	7 444	71.4	34.6	47.9	21.9	18.8	10.6	28.6	25.8	11.2	2.64	3.19	6 322	17.7	22.7
Horry	81 800	66.6	26.3	51.4	17.7	11.5	6.6	33.4	25.8	8.5	2.37	2.84	55 764	11.2	22.3
Jasper	7 042	72.3	34.5	48.1	21.6	18.2	10.2	27.7	23.2	8.8	2.75	3.22	5 298	19.4	21.7
Kershaw	20 188	73.9	33.7	55.8	24.0	13.6	7.5	26.1	22.6	8.9	2.58	3.02	15 810	12.8	20.4
Lancaster	23 178	72.7	33.4	52.6	22.1	15.5	9.0	27.3	23.7	9.4	2.56	3.01	19 778	13.9	20.1
Laurens	26 290	71.8	32.5	51.1	21.1	15.6	8.8	28.2	24.6	9.8	2.55	3.01	20 660	14.2	22.3
Lee	6 886	71.4	32.7	43.0	18.2	23.8	12.6	28.6	25.9	10.6	2.68	3.23	6 054	22.5	21.1
Lexington	83 240	71.9	35.5	56.6	26.2	11.6	7.3	28.1	22.5	6.9	2.56	3.01	61 633	10.7	18.9
McCormick	3 558	73.2	24.8	51.8	14.0	17.6	9.5	26.8	24.4	10.2	2.39	2.82	2 731	17.2	22.7
Marion	13 301	71.5	32.2	43.3	17.9	23.6	12.6	28.5	25.4	9.7	2.64	3.16	11 766	22.4	22.6
Marlboro	10 478	70.0	32.0	42.6	17.8	22.2	11.7	30.0	26.9	11.0	2.59	3.14	10 163	21.1	24.0
Newberry	14 026	69.9	30.4	49.2	19.0	16.1	9.3	30.1	26.5	12.0	2.50	2.99	12 314	15.0	24.9
Oconee	27 283	71.8	28.5	57.8	20.8	10.1	5.7	28.2	24.7	9.5	2.40	2.85	22 358	10.0	22.0
Orangeburg	34 118	70.0	32.0	45.1	18.9	20.3	11.1	30.0	26.0	10.3	2.58	3.11	28 909	19.3	22.7
Pickens	41 306	68.9	31.2	55.6	23.8	9.4	5.4	31.1	23.3	8.2	2.50	2.95	33 422	8.8	21.5
Richland	120 101	63.6	31.5	43.7	20.0	16.3	9.8	36.4	29.1	7.3	2.44	3.05	101 590	15.2	26.5
Saluda	7 127	74.3	31.8	54.2	21.9	14.5	8.0	25.7	22.5	10.4	2.65	3.07	5 824	12.8	21.1
Spartanburg	97 735	70.9	32.2	52.8	22.3	13.8	7.8	29.1	24.8	9.2	2.52	3.01	84 503	13.1	22.5

[1] No spouse present.

Table B. States and Counties

STATE County	Housing occupancy, 2000							Housing tenure, 2000				
				Vacant housing units				Occupied housing units				
	Percent change of households, 1990–2000	Total housing units	Occupied housing units (percent)	Total	For seasonal, recreational, or occasional use	Homeowner vacancy rate (percent)	Rental vacancy rate (percent)	Total	Percent owner-occupied housing units	Percent renter-occupied housing units	Average household size of owner-occupied units	Average household size of renter-occupied units
	86	87	88	89	90	91	92	93	94	95	96	97
PENNSYLVANIA—Cont'd												
Potter	12.2	12 159	57.6	42.4	38.7	1.6	6.6	7 005	77.3	22.7	2.61	2.28
Schuylkill	-0.4	67 806	89.3	10.7	1.3	2.6	9.5	60 530	78.0	22.0	2.47	2.00
Snyder	7.0	14 890	91.7	8.3	3.3	1.5	5.2	13 654	76.5	23.5	2.67	2.30
Somerset	5.6	37 163	84.0	16.0	10.1	1.5	7.4	31 222	78.1	21.9	2.54	2.13
Sullivan	16.7	6 017	44.2	55.8	51.8	3.0	10.2	2 660	80.8	19.2	2.38	1.94
Susquehanna	10.9	21 829	75.7	24.3	18.0	2.5	7.0	16 529	79.5	20.5	2.59	2.28
Tioga	6.4	19 893	80.1	19.9	14.9	1.6	6.6	15 925	76.2	23.8	2.55	2.26
Union	12.7	14 684	89.7	10.3	6.2	1.3	6.1	13 178	73.3	26.7	2.65	2.09
Venango	1.5	26 904	84.5	15.5	9.6	1.7	6.9	22 747	76.4	23.6	2.54	2.15
Warren	2.6	23 058	76.7	23.3	17.9	1.8	9.8	17 696	78.2	21.8	2.53	2.03
Washington	3.3	87 267	93.0	7.0	0.4	1.7	9.5	81 130	77.1	22.9	2.54	2.07
Wayne	25.4	30 593	60.0	40.0	35.5	2.7	6.8	18 350	80.4	19.6	2.55	2.27
Westmoreland	4.0	161 058	93.0	7.0	1.0	1.5	8.3	149 813	78.0	22.0	2.52	2.02
Wyoming	7.6	12 713	84.7	15.3	10.4	1.6	5.4	10 762	78.9	21.1	2.62	2.26
York	15.2	156 720	94.6	5.4	0.6	1.5	7.4	148 219	76.1	23.9	2.61	2.23
RHODE ISLAND	8.1	439 837	92.9	7.1	3.0	1.0	5.0	408 424	60.0	40.0	2.66	2.19
Bristol	8.4	19 881	95.7	4.3	1.4	0.6	3.8	19 033	71.3	28.7	2.71	2.04
Kent	8.5	70 365	95.7	4.3	1.2	1.0	4.9	67 320	71.5	28.5	2.65	1.95
Newport	7.8	39 561	89.0	11.0	6.4	0.7	5.5	35 228	61.6	38.4	2.49	2.14
Providence	6.0	253 214	94.8	5.2	0.5	1.1	5.1	239 936	53.2	46.8	2.69	2.24
Washington	19.3	56 816	82.6	17.4	14.4	0.9	4.8	46 907	72.8	27.2	2.65	2.17
SOUTH CAROLINA	21.9	1 753 670	87.5	12.5	4.0	1.9	12.0	1 533 854	72.2	27.8	2.59	2.37
Abbeville	15.4	11 656	86.9	13.1	4.9	1.2	10.1	10 131	80.5	19.5	2.56	2.30
Aiken	23.8	61 987	89.7	10.3	0.8	2.5	12.1	55 587	75.6	24.4	2.59	2.34
Allendale	3.3	4 568	85.7	14.3	3.1	2.7	6.1	3 915	72.7	27.3	2.59	2.50
Anderson	18.3	73 213	89.7	10.3	2.2	2.0	12.1	65 649	76.3	23.7	2.54	2.29
Bamberg	9.6	7 130	85.9	14.1	3.1	1.8	7.0	6 123	74.7	25.3	2.61	2.36
Barnwell	27.1	10 191	88.5	11.5	1.5	1.5	10.5	9 021	75.5	24.5	2.61	2.45
Beaufort	48.3	60 509	75.2	24.8	15.9	1.6	19.2	45 532	73.2	26.8	2.44	2.71
Berkeley	17.8	54 717	91.2	8.8	2.4	1.1	8.6	49 922	74.2	25.8	2.77	2.69
Calhoun	31.9	6 864	86.2	13.8	5.1	1.4	6.1	5 917	84.4	15.6	2.57	2.37
Charleston	15.2	141 031	87.4	12.6	4.2	1.5	10.9	123 326	61.0	39.0	2.53	2.25
Cherokee	24.5	22 400	91.5	8.5	0.4	1.8	9.8	20 495	73.9	26.1	2.58	2.37
Chester	12.5	14 374	89.6	10.4	1.4	1.5	9.2	12 880	78.4	21.6	2.64	2.54
Chesterfield	17.9	18 818	88.0	12.0	1.3	1.8	13.3	16 557	76.3	23.7	2.57	2.45
Clarendon	23.8	15 303	77.2	22.8	13.9	2.1	8.0	11 812	79.1	20.9	2.66	2.49
Colleton	20.2	18 129	79.8	20.2	10.5	1.6	10.1	14 470	80.3	19.7	2.65	2.49
Darlington	17.2	28 942	89.1	10.9	1.0	1.6	11.2	25 793	77.0	23.0	2.61	2.41
Dillon	13.3	12 679	88.3	11.7	0.9	2.0	11.3	11 199	72.0	28.0	2.75	2.59
Dorchester	23.0	37 237	93.2	6.8	0.7	1.6	6.4	34 709	75.0	25.0	2.80	2.47
Edgefield	28.7	9 223	89.7	10.3	1.3	2.0	11.0	8 270	80.5	19.5	2.71	2.44
Fairfield	17.5	10 383	84.5	15.5	7.0	1.2	6.8	8 774	77.4	22.6	2.66	2.52
Florence	17.2	51 836	91.0	9.0	0.7	1.4	10.0	47 147	73.0	27.0	2.65	2.40
Georgetown	33.1	28 282	76.6	23.4	12.4	2.0	28.6	21 659	81.4	18.6	2.57	2.46
Greenville	21.7	162 803	91.9	8.1	0.7	2.4	10.2	149 556	68.2	31.8	2.57	2.25
Greenwood	13.2	28 243	91.1	8.9	1.6	1.8	8.3	25 729	69.2	30.8	2.51	2.43
Hampton	17.7	8 582	86.7	13.3	3.5	2.5	7.4	7 444	78.1	21.9	2.69	2.48
Horry	46.7	122 085	67.0	33.0	20.4	3.2	30.2	81 800	73.0	27.0	2.39	2.33
Jasper	32.9	7 928	88.8	11.2	2.9	0.7	7.9	7 042	77.7	22.3	2.74	2.76
Kershaw	27.7	22 683	89.0	11.0	3.8	1.5	8.5	20 188	82.0	18.0	2.62	2.41
Lancaster	17.2	24 962	92.9	7.1	0.4	1.3	10.4	23 178	75.0	25.0	2.58	2.51
Laurens	27.3	30 239	86.9	13.1	3.6	1.9	10.3	26 290	77.5	22.5	2.58	2.44
Lee	13.7	7 670	89.8	10.2	1.1	1.5	9.3	6 886	79.4	20.6	2.72	2.50
Lexington	35.1	90 978	91.5	8.5	1.5	1.9	12.3	83 240	77.2	22.8	2.63	2.33
McCormick	30.3	4 459	79.8	20.2	9.3	1.8	8.8	3 558	81.0	19.0	2.45	2.15
Marion	13.0	15 143	87.8	12.2	2.2	2.0	10.3	13 301	73.5	26.5	2.65	2.60
Marlboro	3.1	11 894	88.1	11.9	1.4	2.3	12.6	10 478	70.8	29.2	2.68	2.40
Newberry	13.9	16 805	83.5	16.5	7.5	1.7	10.2	14 026	76.8	23.2	2.50	2.51
Oconee	22.0	32 383	84.3	15.7	7.2	1.9	13.8	27 283	78.4	21.6	2.44	2.26
Orangeburg	18.0	39 304	86.8	13.2	2.7	1.8	11.3	34 118	75.6	24.4	2.63	2.43
Pickens	23.6	46 000	89.8	10.2	1.6	1.8	13.1	41 306	73.5	26.5	2.57	2.32
Richland	18.2	129 793	92.5	7.5	0.5	1.9	8.7	120 101	61.4	38.6	2.57	2.23
Saluda	22.4	8 543	83.4	16.6	7.5	1.4	6.3	7 127	80.6	19.4	2.58	2.97
Spartanburg	15.7	106 986	91.4	8.6	0.5	2.3	10.4	97 735	72.0	28.0	2.57	2.38

Table B. States and Counties

STATE/ County code	MSA/ PMSA/ NECMA code[1]	County type[2]	STATE County	Population, 2000				Population, 1990				Population and population characteristics, 2000 — Race (percent) — One race					
				Land area, 2000[3] (sq km)	Total persons	Rank	Per square kilometer	Land area, 1990[3] (sq km)	Total persons	Rank	Per square kilometer	White	Black or African American	American Indian or Alaska Native	Asian	Native Hawaiian and other Pacific Islander	Some other race
				1	2	3	4	5	6	7	8	9	10	11	12	13	14
			SOUTH CAROLINA —Cont'd														
45 085	8140	3	Sumter	1 723	104 646	505	60.7	1 724	101 276	452	58.7	50.1	46.7	0.3	0.9	0.1	0.8
45 087	...	6	Union	1 332	29 881	1 399	22.4	1 332	30 337	1 278	22.8	67.8	31.0	0.1	0.2	0.0	0.2
45 089	...	6	Williamsburg	2 419	37 217	1 185	15.4	2 419	36 815	1 000	15.2	32.7	66.3	0.2	0.2	0.0	0.2
45 091	1520	2	York	1 768	164 614	327	93.1	1 768	131 497	353	74.4	77.2	19.2	0.9	0.9	0.0	0.9
46 000	...		**SOUTH DAKOTA**	196 540	754 844	X	3.8	196 575	696 004	X	3.5	88.7	0.6	8.3	0.6	0.0	0.5
46 003	...	9	Aurora	1 834	3 058	2 988	1.7	1 834	3 135	2 990	1.7	95.7	0.3	1.9	0.1	0.0	1.4
46 005	...	7	Beadle	3 260	17 023	1 951	5.2	3 262	18 253	1 776	5.6	96.9	0.7	0.9	0.3	0.0	0.3
46 007	...	9	Bennett	3 070	3 574	2 946	1.2	3 070	3 206	2 983	1.0	40.9	0.3	52.1	0.1	0.1	0.2
46 009	...	9	Bon Homme	1 459	7 260	2 658	5.0	1 459	7 089	2 647	4.9	95.5	0.6	3.0	0.1	0.0	0.2
46 011	...	7	Brookings	2 058	28 220	1 444	13.7	2 058	25 207	1 454	12.2	96.4	0.3	0.9	1.3	0.0	0.3
46 013	...	5	Brown	4 437	35 460	1 236	8.0	4 436	35 580	1 110	8.0	95.5	0.3	2.7	0.4	0.1	0.2
46 015	...	9	Brule	2 121	5 364	2 824	2.5	2 121	5 485	2 802	2.6	89.9	0.3	8.3	0.5	0.0	0.1
46 017	...	9	Buffalo	1 219	2 032	3 063	1.7	1 219	1 759	3 080	1.4	16.3	0.1	81.6	0.0	0.0	0.3
46 019	...	6	Butte	5 824	9 094	2 521	1.6	5 824	7 914	2 580	1.4	95.5	0.1	1.6	0.2	0.0	1.1
46 021	...	9	Campbell	1 906	1 782	3 080	0.9	1 906	1 965	3 068	1.0	99.3	0.0	0.3	0.1	0.0	0.0
46 023	...	9	Charles Mix	2 843	9 350	2 502	3.3	2 845	9 131	2 458	3.2	69.6	0.1	28.3	0.1	0.0	0.5
46 025	...	9	Clark	2 481	4 143	2 904	1.7	2 481	4 403	2 881	1.8	98.6	0.1	0.6	0.1	0.0	0.2
46 027	...	7	Clay	1 066	13 537	2 192	12.7	1 066	13 186	2 124	12.4	92.8	1.0	2.7	2.0	0.0	0.3
46 029	...	7	Codington	1 781	25 897	1 521	14.5	1 781	22 698	1 548	12.7	96.7	0.1	1.4	0.3	0.0	0.6
46 031	...	9	Corson	6 405	4 181	2 899	0.7	6 405	4 195	2 897	0.7	37.2	0.1	60.8	0.0	0.0	0.2
46 033	...	8	Custer	4 034	7 275	2 657	1.8	4 035	6 179	2 734	1.5	94.2	0.3	3.1	0.2	0.0	0.4
46 035	...	7	Davison	1 128	18 741	1 857	16.6	1 128	17 503	1 820	15.5	96.2	0.3	2.0	0.4	0.0	0.3
46 037	...	9	Day	2 664	6 267	2 759	2.4	2 664	6 978	2 661	2.6	91.3	0.1	7.4	0.1	0.0	0.2
46 039	...	9	Deuel	1 615	4 498	2 879	2.8	1 615	4 522	2 873	2.8	98.5	0.1	0.3	0.2	0.0	0.2
46 041	...	9	Dewey	5 964	5 972	2 786	1.0	5 964	5 523	2 800	0.9	24.1	0.1	74.2	0.1	0.1	0.1
46 043	...	9	Douglas	1 123	3 458	2 957	3.1	1 123	3 746	2 935	3.3	98.1	0.1	1.0	0.1	0.0	0.1
46 045	...	9	Edmunds	2 967	4 367	2 888	1.5	2 967	4 356	2 887	1.5	99.2	0.1	0.3	0.1	0.0	0.0
46 047	...	7	Fall River	4 506	7 453	2 643	1.7	4 506	7 353	2 624	1.6	90.5	0.3	6.1	0.2	0.1	0.3
46 049	...	9	Faulk	2 590	2 640	3 018	1.0	2 591	2 744	3 013	1.1	99.5	0.1	0.2	0.0	0.0	0.0
46 051	...	7	Grant	1 768	7 847	2 619	4.4	1 768	8 372	2 526	4.7	98.6	0.0	0.4	0.2	0.0	0.4
46 053	...	9	Gregory	2 631	4 792	2 860	1.8	2 631	5 359	2 814	2.0	93.2	0.0	5.6	0.2	0.0	0.1
46 055	...	9	Haakon	4 696	2 196	3 051	0.5	4 696	2 624	3 016	0.6	96.4	0.0	2.5	0.1	0.0	0.0
46 057	...	9	Hamlin	1 313	5 540	2 813	4.2	1 324	4 974	2 842	3.8	98.5	0.1	0.6	0.2	0.0	0.1
46 059	...	9	Hand	3 721	3 741	2 938	1.0	3 721	4 272	2 891	1.1	99.3	0.0	0.1	0.1	0.0	0.1
46 061	...	9	Hanson	1 126	3 139	2 983	2.8	1 126	2 994	3 001	2.7	99.5	0.0	0.1	0.1	0.0	0.0
46 063	...	9	Harding	6 917	1 353	3 100	0.2	6 917	1 669	3 087	0.2	97.6	0.3	0.7	0.6	0.0	0.4
46 065	...	7	Hughes	1 919	16 481	1 990	8.6	1 919	14 817	1 999	7.7	88.9	0.2	8.7	0.4	0.0	0.3
46 067	...	9	Hutchinson	2 105	8 075	2 600	3.8	2 106	8 262	2 541	3.9	98.8	0.1	0.6	0.1	0.0	0.1
46 069	...	9	Hyde	2 230	1 671	3 086	0.7	2 230	1 696	3 084	0.8	91.1	0.1	8.0	0.0	0.1	0.1
46 071	...	9	Jackson	4 841	2 930	2 997	0.6	4 841	2 811	3 011	0.6	50.1	0.0	47.8	0.0	0.0	0.1
46 073	...	9	Jerauld	1 372	2 295	3 039	1.7	1 373	2 425	3 027	1.8	99.0	0.0	0.6	0.1	0.0	0.0
46 075	...	9	Jones	2 514	1 193	3 105	0.5	2 514	1 324	3 105	0.5	95.8	0.0	2.4	0.0	0.1	0.2
46 077	...	9	Kingsbury	2 171	5 815	2 803	2.7	2 172	5 925	2 766	2.7	98.5	0.1	0.4	0.3	0.0	0.2
46 079	...	6	Lake	1 459	11 276	2 351	7.7	1 459	10 550	2 331	7.2	97.8	0.2	0.7	0.5	0.0	0.3
46 081	...	6	Lawrence	2 072	21 802	1 702	10.5	2 072	20 655	1 647	10.0	95.8	0.2	2.2	0.3	0.1	0.3
46 083	7760	3	Lincoln	1 497	24 131	1 589	16.1	1 497	15 427	1 961	10.3	97.5	0.3	0.5	0.5	0.0	0.3
46 085	...	9	Lyman	4 247	3 895	2 923	0.9	4 248	3 638	2 946	0.9	64.7	0.1	33.3	0.2	0.0	0.1
46 087	...	8	McCook	1 488	5 832	2 800	3.9	1 488	5 688	2 786	3.8	98.9	0.1	0.4	0.2	0.0	0.2
46 089	...	9	McPherson	2 945	2 904	2 998	1.0	2 945	3 228	2 982	1.1	99.3	0.0	0.3	0.1	0.0	0.0
46 091	...	9	Marshall	2 170	4 576	2 873	2.1	2 173	4 844	2 849	2.2	92.6	0.1	6.3	0.1	0.0	0.2
46 093	...	6	Meade	8 989	24 253	1 586	2.7	8 989	21 878	1 585	2.4	92.7	1.5	2.0	0.6	0.1	0.6
46 095	...	9	Mellette	3 384	2 083	3 060	0.6	3 384	2 137	3 059	0.6	44.7	0.0	52.4	0.1	0.0	0.2
46 097	...	9	Miner	1 477	2 884	3 000	2.0	1 477	3 272	2 978	2.2	98.8	0.5	0.3	0.1	0.0	0.1
46 099	7760	3	Minnehaha	2 097	148 281	365	70.7	2 096	123 809	370	59.1	93.0	1.5	1.9	1.0	0.1	1.0
46 101	...	8	Moody	1 346	6 595	2 727	4.9	1 346	6 507	2 709	4.8	84.9	0.3	12.0	0.6	0.0	0.1
46 103	6660	3	Pennington	7 190	88 565	589	12.3	7 191	81 343	558	11.3	86.7	0.9	8.1	0.9	0.1	0.7
46 105	...	9	Perkins	7 437	3 363	2 966	0.5	7 442	3 932	2 923	0.5	96.6	0.1	1.6	0.2	0.0	0.5
46 107	...	9	Potter	2 244	2 693	3 015	1.2	2 244	3 190	2 984	1.4	98.1	0.0	0.8	0.2	0.0	0.1
46 109	...	9	Roberts	2 852	10 016	2 444	3.5	2 852	9 914	2 393	3.5	68.3	0.1	29.9	0.2	0.0	0.0
46 111	...	9	Sanborn	1 474	2 675	3 016	1.8	1 474	2 833	3 010	1.9	98.9	0.0	0.3	0.4	0.0	0.1
46 113	...	7	Shannon	5 423	12 466	2 268	2.3	5 423	9 902	2 397	1.8	4.5	0.1	94.2	0.0	0.0	0.2
46 115	...	7	Spink	3 895	7 454	2 642	1.9	3 895	7 981	2 568	2.0	97.6	0.2	1.5	0.1	0.0	0.1
46 117	...	9	Stanley	3 738	2 772	3 006	0.7	3 738	2 453	3 025	0.7	93.0	0.2	4.9	0.3	0.0	0.1
46 119	...	9	Sully	2 608	1 556	3 091	0.6	2 608	1 589	3 091	0.6	97.8	0.0	0.8	0.1	0.0	0.1
46 121	...	9	Todd	3 595	9 050	2 526	2.5	3 596	8 352	2 528	2.3	12.6	0.1	85.6	0.1	0.0	0.2

[1] MSA = Metropolitan Statistical Area. PMSA = Primary MSA. NECMA = New England County Metropolitan Area. See Appendix A for explanation of these concepts. See Appendix B for list of metropolitan areas identified by type, with component counties.
[2] County typology code from the Economic Research Service of USDA. See Appendix A for definition.
[3] Dry land or land partially or temporarily covered by water.

Table B. States and Counties

	Population and population characteristics, 2000 (cont'd)								Population and population characteristics, 1990				
	Race (percent) (cont'd)								Race (percent)				
	Race alone or in combination												
STATE County	Two or more races	White	Black	American Indian or Alaska Native	Asian	Native Hawaiian and other Pacific Islander	Some other race	Hispanic[1]	White	Black or African American	American Indian or Alaska Native	Asian and Pacific Islander	Hispanic[1]
	15	16	17	18	19	20	21	22	23	24	25	26	27
SOUTH CAROLINA— Cont'd													
Sumter	1.2	51.0	47.2	0.6	1.2	0.1	1.1	1.0	55.3	43.2	0.2	0.9	1.2
Union	0.6	68.3	31.4	0.4	0.3	0.1	0.2	0.7	69.8	29.9	0.1	0.1	0.2
Williamsburg	0.5	33.0	66.6	0.4	0.3	0.0	0.3	0.7	35.6	64.2	0.0	0.1	0.4
York	0.9	78.0	19.4	1.2	1.0	0.1	1.1	2.0	78.7	20.0	0.6	0.5	0.6
SOUTH DAKOTA	1.3	89.9	0.9	9.0	0.8	0.1	0.7	1.4	91.6	0.5	7.3	0.4	0.8
Aurora	0.6	96.2	0.4	2.1	0.3	0.0	1.6	2.1	98.4	0.0	1.3	0.1	0.2
Beadle	0.8	97.8	1.0	1.3	0.4	0.1	0.4	0.9	98.3	0.4	0.9	0.3	0.4
Bennett	6.4	47.1	0.5	58.1	0.1	0.3	0.4	2.0	53.3	0.2	46.2	0.1	1.1
Bon Homme	0.6	96.0	0.9	3.3	0.1	0.0	0.3	0.6	97.3	0.3	2.2	0.1	0.5
Brookings	0.7	97.1	0.5	1.2	1.6	0.0	0.5	0.9	97.8	0.3	0.6	1.2	0.3
Brown	0.9	96.3	0.4	3.3	0.5	0.1	0.3	0.7	96.6	0.1	2.8	0.4	0.3
Brule	1.0	90.9	0.4	9.1	0.6	0.0	0.1	0.5	92.6	0.1	7.0	0.2	0.6
Buffalo	1.7	17.8	0.1	83.3	0.0	0.1	0.3	0.9	22.3	0.0	77.6	0.0	0.2
Butte	1.4	96.9	0.2	2.7	0.4	0.0	1.3	2.9	96.4	0.3	1.5	0.2	2.8
Campbell	0.3	99.6	0.0	0.6	0.1	0.0	0.0	0.2	99.7	0.1	0.2	0.0	0.0
Charles Mix	1.4	70.7	0.3	29.5	0.2	0.1	0.7	1.9	78.0	0.0	21.8	0.0	0.4
Clark	0.4	99.0	0.1	0.7	0.2	0.0	0.2	0.5	99.4	0.1	0.3	0.2	0.3
Clay	1.3	94.0	1.3	3.4	2.2	0.1	0.4	0.9	95.2	0.4	3.0	1.1	0.8
Codington	0.8	97.5	0.3	1.9	0.4	0.0	0.7	1.1	98.4	0.1	1.1	0.3	0.2
Corson	1.7	38.7	0.2	62.3	0.1	0.0	0.4	2.1	51.3	0.0	48.5	0.1	1.1
Custer	1.9	96.0	0.5	4.5	0.5	0.1	0.6	1.5	97.1	0.1	2.5	0.2	0.7
Davison	0.8	96.9	0.4	2.4	0.6	0.1	0.4	0.7	98.1	0.1	1.4	0.4	0.2
Day	0.9	92.1	0.2	8.2	0.1	0.1	0.3	0.4	93.1	0.0	6.7	0.1	0.2
Deuel	0.7	99.2	0.1	0.7	0.3	0.1	0.2	0.8	99.5	0.0	0.2	0.2	0.3
Dewey	1.4	25.5	0.1	75.4	0.2	0.1	0.3	0.9	33.0	0.2	66.6	0.1	0.8
Douglas	0.6	98.6	0.2	1.4	0.1	0.0	0.2	0.4	99.3	0.0	0.6	0.1	0.1
Edmunds	0.3	99.5	0.1	0.3	0.2	0.0	0.2	0.5	99.4	0.0	0.4	0.1	0.1
Fall River	2.5	92.9	0.4	8.1	0.4	0.1	0.5	1.7	92.6	0.4	6.1	0.4	1.6
Faulk	0.3	99.7	0.1	0.4	0.0	0.0	0.0	0.2	99.7	0.0	0.2	0.0	0.1
Grant	0.3	98.9	0.0	0.6	0.3	0.0	0.4	0.5	99.3	0.0	0.4	0.2	0.1
Gregory	0.9	93.9	0.1	6.2	0.5	0.0	0.2	0.9	94.5	0.0	5.3	0.1	0.5
Haakon	1.0	97.4	0.0	3.4	0.2	0.0	0.0	0.6	97.9	0.2	1.4	0.5	0.4
Hamlin	0.5	99.0	0.2	0.9	0.3	0.0	0.1	0.6	99.4	0.1	0.2	0.1	0.3
Hand	0.3	99.6	0.1	0.3	0.2	0.0	0.1	0.3	99.5	0.1	0.1	0.3	0.3
Hanson	0.2	99.7	0.0	0.2	0.3	0.0	0.0	0.1	99.8	0.0	0.2	0.0	0.1
Harding	0.4	98.0	0.3	1.1	0.6	0.0	0.4	1.6	98.6	0.3	1.0	0.0	0.2
Hughes	1.5	90.3	0.3	9.9	0.6	0.0	0.4	1.2	92.6	0.1	6.7	0.3	0.8
Hutchinson	0.4	99.2	0.2	0.8	0.1	0.0	0.1	0.5	99.5	0.0	0.3	0.1	0.2
Hyde	0.6	91.7	0.2	8.4	0.0	0.1	0.1	0.5	96.5	0.1	3.4	0.1	0.4
Jackson	1.8	51.7	0.1	49.6	0.2	0.0	0.2	0.4	57.2	0.1	42.4	0.2	0.5
Jerauld	0.3	99.3	0.1	0.8	0.1	0.0	0.0	0.3	99.5	0.0	0.2	0.3	0.0
Jones	1.5	97.3	0.3	3.9	0.0	0.1	0.2	0.3	99.4	0.0	0.5	0.1	0.1
Kingsbury	0.5	99.0	0.1	0.6	0.5	0.0	0.4	0.7	99.7	0.0	0.2	0.1	0.1
Lake	0.5	98.2	0.3	0.9	0.6	0.0	0.5	0.8	99.2	0.1	0.3	0.2	0.3
Lawrence	1.1	96.8	0.4	2.9	0.5	0.1	0.5	1.8	96.6	0.1	2.6	0.3	1.6
Lincoln	0.8	98.3	0.6	0.8	0.7	0.0	0.4	0.7	99.1	0.1	0.4	0.3	0.1
Lyman	1.6	66.2	0.1	34.7	0.4	0.1	0.1	0.5	70.9	0.1	28.9	0.1	0.5
McCook	0.4	99.2	0.1	0.6	0.3	0.0	0.2	0.8	99.4	0.0	0.5	0.1	0.1
McPherson	0.2	99.6	0.0	0.4	0.2	0.0	0.1	0.2	99.8	0.0	0.1	0.1	0.0
Marshall	0.7	93.2	0.2	6.8	0.2	0.1	0.2	0.8	94.3	0.0	5.6	0.0	0.3
Meade	2.5	95.0	1.9	3.4	1.2	0.1	0.9	2.1	94.4	2.4	1.8	0.8	1.8
Mellette	2.5	47.1	0.0	54.9	0.2	0.0	0.3	1.7	53.0	0.0	46.7	0.1	0.7
Miner	0.2	99.0	0.6	0.4	0.1	0.0	0.1	0.6	99.8	0.0	0.1	0.0	0.2
Minnehaha	1.5	94.3	2.0	2.3	1.3	0.1	1.5	2.1	97.3	0.6	1.4	0.6	0.5
Moody	2.2	87.0	0.5	13.8	0.7	0.1	0.2	0.8	91.5	0.2	8.1	0.2	0.2
Pennington	2.7	89.2	1.4	9.9	1.3	0.1	1.0	2.6	89.5	1.6	7.2	1.1	2.2
Perkins	0.8	97.5	0.3	2.2	0.3	0.0	0.7	0.7	98.1	0.2	1.4	0.1	0.4
Potter	0.8	98.9	0.0	1.2	0.5	0.1	0.1	0.2	99.0	0.0	0.8	0.1	0.2
Roberts	1.5	69.7	0.2	31.2	0.3	0.0	0.1	0.6	76.8	0.0	23.0	0.1	0.3
Sanborn	0.3	99.1	0.1	0.4	0.5	0.0	0.2	1.0	99.9	0.0	0.0	0.1	0.5
Shannon	0.9	5.2	0.1	95.1	0.1	0.1	0.4	1.4	5.0	0.1	94.7	0.1	1.8
Spink	0.5	98.1	0.3	1.8	0.2	0.0	0.2	0.4	99.1	0.0	0.8	0.0	0.2
Stanley	1.4	94.4	0.4	6.2	0.3	0.0	0.1	0.4	93.5	0.1	6.3	0.0	0.4
Sully	1.2	99.0	0.2	1.3	0.3	0.0	0.4	0.8	98.9	0.1	0.9	0.0	0.2
Todd	1.4	13.7	0.2	86.9	0.2	0.0	0.4	1.5	17.1	0.1	82.4	0.1	1.5

[1] Hispanic persons may be of any race.

Table B. States and Counties

STATE County	Population and population characteristics, 2000										
	Age (percent)										
	Under 5 years	5 to 17 years	18 to 24 years	25 to 34 years	35 to 44 years	45 to 54 years	55 to 64 years	65 to 74 years	75 years and over	Median age (years)	Percent Female
	28	29	30	31	32	33	34	35	36	37	38
SOUTH CAROLINA— Cont'd											
Sumter	7.5	20.6	10.5	13.7	15.7	12.4	8.3	6.1	5.1	33.4	51.6
Union	6.3	17.5	8.2	12.8	15.1	14.1	10.3	8.3	7.3	38.6	52.9
Williamsburg	6.9	21.7	9.0	11.7	14.0	14.4	9.2	7.3	5.7	35.5	53.2
York	6.8	19.5	9.5	14.4	16.7	13.9	8.9	5.8	4.6	34.9	51.6
SOUTH DAKOTA	6.8	20.1	10.3	12.1	15.3	12.9	8.3	7.0	7.3	35.6	50.4
Aurora	5.7	21.9	6.5	8.5	13.5	12.6	9.6	10.0	11.6	40.6	49.0
Beadle	5.7	19.0	8.3	9.6	15.1	13.8	9.2	9.1	10.2	40.1	50.9
Bennett	8.9	27.4	9.2	11.0	14.3	10.5	7.6	6.0	5.1	29.2	50.4
Bon Homme	4.9	18.1	7.6	10.9	16.0	12.6	9.0	9.4	11.5	40.3	44.8
Brookings	5.7	15.1	26.8	12.0	12.3	10.7	6.6	4.9	5.9	26.6	49.5
Brown	6.4	17.2	11.6	11.9	14.8	13.2	8.7	7.6	8.6	37.2	51.7
Brule	5.7	24.8	6.8	10.1	14.6	12.4	8.8	7.6	9.3	36.9	51.8
Buffalo	10.6	30.7	11.0	12.2	12.9	9.0	7.1	3.5	3.0	23.4	48.7
Butte	6.1	22.2	7.2	10.1	15.8	14.4	9.0	7.9	7.3	38.0	50.8
Campbell	5.2	21.2	3.5	8.1	16.4	11.7	11.7	11.2	10.9	41.9	49.8
Charles Mix	8.6	23.4	7.1	10.1	13.1	11.1	9.4	8.3	9.0	35.7	50.9
Clark	5.4	21.6	5.8	8.3	13.7	13.3	9.7	10.5	11.7	41.6	50.7
Clay	5.4	13.4	31.5	13.3	10.6	9.9	5.9	4.7	5.4	24.9	51.5
Codington	7.1	19.7	10.4	12.4	15.7	12.8	7.9	6.7	7.4	35.3	50.4
Corson	9.1	27.9	9.8	10.4	13.9	10.7	7.7	6.4	4.1	28.3	49.5
Custer	4.6	19.4	6.3	8.4	14.0	17.4	13.7	8.9	7.1	43.2	48.9
Davison	6.5	18.8	12.0	11.3	14.6	12.5	8.0	7.5	8.7	36.0	51.5
Day	5.5	20.0	5.2	8.3	14.2	13.7	9.7	10.8	12.7	42.9	50.9
Deuel	5.5	19.9	5.9	10.2	15.2	12.5	10.1	10.5	10.1	40.8	50.1
Dewey	9.2	29.7	9.0	12.1	15.1	9.7	6.9	5.2	3.0	26.5	51.1
Douglas	5.8	21.9	4.9	8.6	13.8	13.1	9.3	9.9	12.6	41.8	51.2
Edmunds	5.7	21.0	5.1	8.5	14.8	12.1	10.6	10.6	11.6	41.6	50.7
Fall River	4.8	18.0	5.8	7.2	13.4	16.2	12.1	11.5	11.0	45.5	47.7
Faulk	5.5	21.1	5.4	8.4	14.7	12.0	10.0	11.9	10.9	41.5	50.0
Grant	5.9	20.7	5.7	9.3	15.8	14.0	9.6	8.5	10.6	40.3	50.6
Gregory	4.9	19.4	5.1	7.8	14.3	13.3	10.5	10.3	14.5	44.3	51.4
Haakon	5.3	20.4	7.0	8.7	16.5	14.5	9.6	7.5	10.5	41.3	50.9
Hamlin	6.5	22.9	6.9	10.0	14.1	11.6	8.9	8.3	10.8	38.0	50.3
Hand	5.2	19.4	5.1	7.6	14.8	13.3	10.5	12.2	12.0	43.6	51.0
Hanson	7.5	22.0	7.7	11.7	14.4	12.0	9.8	8.4	6.5	36.0	49.9
Harding	4.2	28.3	4.4	8.8	16.0	16.0	8.8	6.5	6.9	37.6	48.9
Hughes	6.6	21.2	6.2	12.2	16.5	14.9	8.8	6.7	7.0	37.5	51.9
Hutchinson	5.9	18.9	5.6	9.2	12.8	12.1	9.2	11.1	15.2	43.1	51.3
Hyde	7.6	18.0	5.8	8.8	14.7	11.7	11.1	10.4	11.9	42.2	49.5
Jackson	8.3	28.2	8.0	10.4	13.2	12.1	8.2	6.0	5.6	30.6	50.3
Jerauld	3.7	17.7	6.9	7.9	11.9	15.1	11.1	11.0	14.6	46.3	50.4
Jones	4.9	21.4	6.2	9.2	16.3	13.7	10.1	10.1	8.1	41.1	49.0
Kingsbury	5.4	19.1	6.1	8.1	14.8	13.2	9.2	11.0	13.2	42.7	51.0
Lake	5.5	18.2	15.0	9.2	14.2	13.1	8.3	7.7	8.6	36.5	50.1
Lawrence	4.8	18.3	13.7	10.5	14.9	14.4	8.8	7.4	7.3	37.2	50.8
Lincoln	8.0	21.6	7.6	14.4	17.6	13.5	6.9	5.0	5.4	34.0	50.1
Lyman	8.6	23.5	7.6	10.9	14.9	12.0	8.9	7.5	6.1	34.5	48.9
McCook	6.7	21.7	6.2	10.5	15.0	11.7	8.7	8.7	10.8	38.6	50.1
McPherson	5.5	16.7	4.5	8.3	11.7	11.7	11.8	14.0	15.5	47.6	51.6
Marshall	5.9	21.1	5.1	9.1	13.7	13.4	10.4	9.6	11.6	41.6	50.0
Meade	7.7	20.7	10.6	13.2	16.4	13.5	7.5	5.6	4.8	33.4	49.5
Mellette	9.0	26.3	7.5	11.3	13.3	12.0	7.5	7.2	6.0	32.1	49.7
Miner	5.1	20.4	5.6	8.5	14.2	13.1	9.2	10.4	13.5	42.5	50.1
Minnehaha	7.3	18.9	10.8	15.3	16.7	12.8	7.2	5.6	5.4	33.5	50.5
Moody	6.2	22.9	7.2	11.1	15.4	13.5	8.7	6.2	8.7	37.0	50.0
Pennington	7.1	19.5	10.5	12.9	16.3	13.7	8.2	6.4	5.4	35.0	50.4
Perkins	5.8	18.3	5.6	8.7	14.7	13.6	9.6	11.1	12.6	43.1	50.9
Potter	4.5	18.5	3.9	7.2	15.1	14.3	11.5	11.6	13.4	45.8	50.8
Roberts	6.7	23.3	7.2	10.0	13.5	12.7	9.5	8.5	8.5	37.1	50.3
Sanborn	5.8	19.9	7.7	8.6	15.1	14.0	9.5	10.5	9.0	40.8	48.3
Shannon	10.9	34.4	10.6	13.3	12.4	8.5	5.3	3.2	1.6	20.6	50.1
Spink	5.6	19.9	6.7	10.3	15.8	13.5	9.1	9.5	9.5	39.9	48.3
Stanley	5.6	21.5	7.1	11.8	16.5	15.4	11.2	6.5	4.5	37.6	49.6
Sully	5.7	19.9	6.1	10.2	16.4	12.9	11.5	9.8	7.6	40.0	48.7
Todd	12.0	31.9	10.4	12.5	12.6	9.5	5.3	3.8	2.0	21.7	50.5

Table B. States and Counties

| | Population and population characteristics, 1990 | | | | | | | | | | Population—change, 1980–2000 | | | | |
| | Age (percent) | | | | | | | | | | Total persons | | | Percent change | |
STATE County	Under 5 years	5 to 17 years	18 to 24 years	25 to 34 years	35 to 44 years	45 to 54 years	55 to 64 years	65 to 74 years	75 years and over	Percent Female	2000	1990	1980	1990–2000	1980–1990
	39	40	41	42	43	44	45	46	47	48	49	50	51	52	53
SOUTH CAROLINA— Cont'd															
Sumter	8.4	20.3	11.9	19.6	14.5	8.8	7.1	5.8	3.6	50.0	104 646	101 276	88 243	3.3	14.8
Union	6.2	18.7	9.7	15.0	14.5	11.1	10.0	8.7	6.1	50.5	29 881	30 337	30 764	-1.5	-1.4
Williamsburg	7.8	24.7	10.2	13.7	14.1	9.1	8.2	7.5	4.5	53.3	37 217	36 815	38 226	1.1	-0.7
York	7.3	18.6	12.1	16.6	15.3	10.9	8.5	6.6	4.0	52.0	164 614	131 497	106 720	25.2	23.2
SOUTH DAKOTA	7.8	20.7	9.8	15.7	13.7	9.0	8.6	7.8	6.9	50.8	754 844	696 004	690 768	8.5	0.8
Aurora	5.8	23.5	4.9	11.8	11.7	9.3	11.3	10.4	11.3	49.6	3 058	3 135	3 628	-2.5	-13.6
Beadle	7.2	19.6	7.4	15.0	13.4	9.3	9.8	9.8	8.4	51.4	17 023	18 253	19 195	-6.7	-4.9
Bennett	9.5	26.3	8.4	14.5	12.0	9.0	8.5	6.1	5.7	51.1	3 574	3 206	3 044	11.5	5.3
Bon Homme	6.6	18.5	6.7	14.6	12.6	8.5	10.1	10.9	11.6	48.9	7 260	7 089	8 059	2.4	-12.0
Brookings	6.0	16.7	25.2	14.6	11.9	7.3	6.3	6.3	5.6	49.0	28 220	25 207	24 332	12.0	3.6
Brown	6.9	18.8	11.9	15.6	14.0	9.0	8.7	7.9	7.2	52.1	35 460	35 580	36 962	-0.3	-3.7
Brule	7.6	25.5	6.3	14.1	11.9	9.2	8.8	8.9	7.7	50.1	5 364	5 485	5 245	-2.2	4.6
Buffalo	12.6	32.1	9.2	14.3	10.4	8.7	5.2	5.2	2.3	47.5	2 032	1 759	1 795	15.5	-2.0
Butte	8.1	21.1	6.8	15.0	13.9	9.6	9.5	9.2	6.8	50.5	9 094	7 914	8 372	14.9	-5.5
Campbell	7.1	18.4	5.2	14.0	11.3	11.5	12.2	11.4	8.9	49.8	1 782	1 965	2 243	-9.3	-12.4
Charles Mix	8.8	23.2	6.6	12.8	11.8	9.5	9.6	8.7	8.9	50.9	9 350	9 131	9 680	2.4	-5.7
Clark	6.6	21.8	4.9	11.4	12.6	9.4	11.6	11.7	9.9	50.1	4 143	4 403	4 894	-5.9	-10.0
Clay	5.8	14.2	33.1	12.9	10.9	6.5	6.2	5.4	4.9	51.5	13 537	13 186	13 689	2.7	-3.7
Codington	7.4	21.2	9.2	15.6	13.6	9.0	8.0	8.2	7.7	51.5	25 897	22 698	20 885	14.1	8.7
Corson	10.8	27.3	7.7	13.7	10.7	9.7	9.2	6.4	4.4	49.2	4 181	4 195	5 196	-0.3	-19.3
Custer	6.0	21.7	5.6	13.6	16.5	11.3	10.4	8.5	6.4	49.4	7 275	6 179	6 000	17.7	3.0
Davison	7.5	20.0	9.6	15.1	13.1	8.7	8.5	8.6	8.8	52.3	18 741	17 503	17 820	7.1	-1.8
Day	7.2	19.9	6.0	12.3	11.7	9.0	10.8	11.5	11.7	50.8	6 267	6 978	8 133	-10.2	-14.2
Deuel	7.0	19.7	5.6	13.0	12.1	10.6	11.3	10.6	10.1	48.9	4 498	4 522	5 289	-0.5	-14.5
Dewey	12.3	27.9	8.5	16.4	11.3	8.1	7.3	4.9	3.4	50.9	5 972	5 523	5 366	8.1	2.9
Douglas	8.4	22.0	5.5	12.0	11.3	9.5	10.4	9.7	11.2	50.8	3 458	3 746	4 181	-7.7	-10.4
Edmunds	6.8	19.9	4.8	12.4	11.0	10.4	11.8	12.0	10.9	50.3	4 367	4 356	5 159	0.3	-15.6
Fall River	5.1	19.2	4.7	11.7	15.2	11.1	12.1	12.4	8.4	48.2	7 453	7 353	8 439	1.4	-12.9
Faulk	7.1	19.7	5.5	12.5	11.0	10.6	12.8	11.0	9.8	50.2	2 640	2 744	3 327	-3.8	-17.5
Grant	7.0	22.7	5.9	14.6	13.7	8.9	9.2	9.2	8.8	50.4	7 847	8 372	9 013	-6.3	-7.1
Gregory	7.3	21.5	4.4	12.4	12.4	9.4	9.9	11.3	11.3	51.4	4 792	5 359	6 015	-10.6	-10.9
Haakon	7.5	28.0	5.3	14.5	14.1	8.6	7.5	7.7	6.8	51.1	2 196	2 624	2 794	-16.3	-6.1
Hamlin	6.9	22.0	6.1	11.4	12.2	8.6	10.1	11.6	11.0	50.9	5 540	4 974	5 261	11.4	-5.5
Hand	6.8	20.7	5.4	13.1	11.8	9.6	12.2	11.0	9.4	50.8	3 741	4 272	4 948	-12.4	-13.7
Hanson	7.4	23.4	7.1	12.7	12.5	10.2	10.6	9.5	6.7	49.7	3 139	2 994	3 415	4.8	-12.3
Harding	8.8	24.4	6.1	15.8	14.5	8.4	8.3	8.0	5.8	48.2	1 353	1 669	1 700	-18.9	-1.8
Hughes	7.8	22.1	6.6	16.6	16.7	10.2	8.3	6.5	5.4	52.3	16 481	14 817	14 220	11.2	4.2
Hutchinson	6.3	18.9	5.1	11.7	11.5	9.2	11.5	12.9	12.9	50.3	8 075	8 262	9 350	-2.3	-11.6
Hyde	7.0	19.3	4.0	13.4	12.0	8.7	12.1	10.6	12.9	52.7	1 671	1 696	2 069	-1.5	-18.0
Jackson	10.1	25.6	7.7	13.4	12.7	9.3	8.5	6.5	6.1	49.9	2 930	2 811	3 437	4.2	-18.2
Jerauld	5.4	20.8	5.0	11.0	12.7	10.4	10.4	12.6	11.6	50.4	2 295	2 425	2 929	-5.4	-17.2
Jones	7.7	20.4	6.3	13.4	13.4	10.4	11.3	9.8	7.3	48.2	1 193	1 324	1 463	-9.9	-9.5
Kingsbury	6.6	19.4	5.1	12.3	12.4	9.1	11.3	11.5	12.3	51.5	5 815	5 925	6 679	-1.9	-11.3
Lake	6.7	19.9	10.6	14.8	12.7	8.3	9.0	9.2	9.0	51.3	11 276	10 550	10 724	6.9	-1.6
Lawrence	6.9	20.3	11.8	15.4	14.6	8.5	8.2	7.8	6.5	50.8	21 802	20 655	18 339	5.6	12.6
Lincoln	8.0	22.7	6.5	15.9	15.6	9.1	7.8	7.2	7.1	50.3	24 131	15 427	13 942	56.4	10.7
Lyman	9.1	24.3	7.4	14.6	12.4	9.4	9.5	7.7	5.7	49.1	3 895	3 638	3 864	7.1	-5.8
McCook	7.1	20.8	5.6	12.2	12.2	9.0	10.5	11.3	11.4	50.8	5 832	5 688	6 444	2.5	-11.7
McPherson	5.2	17.2	4.6	10.0	11.1	10.4	13.9	14.3	13.2	51.2	2 904	3 228	4 027	-10.0	-19.8
Marshall	7.0	19.8	5.6	12.3	12.5	10.1	11.0	10.7	11.1	49.9	4 576	4 844	5 404	-5.5	-10.4
Meade	8.8	23.6	9.5	18.1	15.3	8.0	6.8	5.6	4.2	48.2	24 253	21 878	20 717	10.9	5.6
Mellette	9.7	26.3	7.4	13.4	12.4	8.8	8.8	7.1	6.0	50.3	2 083	2 137	2 249	-2.5	-5.0
Miner	6.9	20.2	5.4	12.4	11.2	8.2	11.2	11.9	12.6	50.2	2 884	3 272	3 739	-11.9	-12.5
Minnehaha	7.9	19.1	10.6	19.1	15.0	8.9	7.7	6.4	5.2	51.9	148 281	123 809	109 435	19.8	13.1
Moody	8.2	22.6	6.8	13.7	13.4	9.3	8.3	9.7	8.0	49.9	6 595	6 507	6 692	1.4	-2.8
Pennington	9.2	20.0	11.0	18.6	14.7	8.9	7.5	5.7	4.3	50.5	88 565	81 343	70 361	8.9	15.6
Perkins	6.0	20.1	4.8	13.9	13.7	9.6	10.9	11.8	9.3	50.2	3 363	3 932	4 700	-14.5	-16.3
Potter	6.2	21.5	4.8	12.2	12.9	9.9	10.9	10.4	11.0	50.8	2 693	3 190	3 674	-15.6	-13.2
Roberts	8.0	22.2	7.0	12.2	12.1	9.8	9.8	9.1	9.7	49.9	10 016	9 914	10 911	1.0	-9.1
Sanborn	7.5	21.2	5.8	14.0	12.4	8.7	11.4	10.5	8.5	49.1	2 675	2 833	3 213	-5.6	-11.8
Shannon	14.0	30.8	12.1	14.1	10.6	7.7	5.5	3.3	2.0	49.3	12 466	9 902	11 323	25.9	-12.5
Spink	7.4	19.8	6.6	14.5	13.4	9.0	10.8	9.7	8.7	51.4	7 454	7 981	9 201	-6.6	-13.3
Stanley	8.2	23.4	7.5	15.2	14.3	11.9	8.6	6.1	4.7	50.1	2 772	2 453	2 533	13.0	-3.2
Sully	5.8	22.1	6.3	14.9	12.9	12.5	10.3	8.1	7.1	49.2	1 556	1 589	1 990	-2.1	-20.2
Todd	13.8	31.3	10.5	14.5	11.6	6.8	5.9	3.7	1.9	50.5	9 050	8 352	7 328	8.4	14.0

Table B. States and Counties

	Household relationship, 2000																
	In households (percent)										In group quarters (percent)						
					Child		Other relatives		Nonrelatives			Institutionalized population			Noninstitutionalized population		
STATE County	Total population	Total in house-holds	House-holder	Spouse	Total	Own child under 18 years	Total	Under 18 years	Total	Unmar-ried partner	Total in group quarters	Correc-tional institu-tions	Nurs-ing homes	Other institu-tions	Col-lege dormi-tories	Mili-tary quar-ters	Other
	54	55	56	57	58	59	60	61	62	63	64	65	66	67	68	69	70
SOUTH CAROLINA—Cont'd																	
Sumter	104 646	96.7	36.1	18.1	31.8	23.9	7.2	3.7	3.5	1.5	3.3	1.0	0.4	0.0	0.6	0.8	0.5
Union	29 881	98.6	40.5	19.8	28.2	19.6	7.0	3.4	3.2	1.9	1.4	0.1	0.4	0.3	0.0	0.0	0.6
Williamsburg	37 217	99.1	36.8	17.0	33.7	23.1	9.3	5.1	2.2	1.2	0.9	0.2	0.5	0.1	0.0	0.0	0.2
York	164 614	97.4	37.1	20.8	29.8	23.3	5.4	2.4	4.3	1.9	2.6	0.3	0.5	0.1	1.2	0.0	0.4
SOUTH DAKOTA	754 844	96.2	38.5	20.9	29.5	24.6	3.0	1.4	4.5	1.8	3.8	0.6	1.0	0.3	1.2	0.1	0.6
Aurora	3 058	93.4	38.1	23.3	28.0	23.6	2.6	0.7	1.5	0.7	6.6	0.0	3.0	3.4	0.0	0.0	0.2
Beadle	17 023	97.4	42.4	22.3	27.5	23.4	1.8	0.6	3.5	1.6	2.6	0.4	1.1	0.1	0.3	0.0	0.7
Bennett	3 574	98.7	31.4	15.3	36.8	28.7	10.7	6.9	4.5	2.2	1.3	0.3	0.0	1.1	0.0	0.0	0.0
Bon Homme	7 260	86.3	36.3	21.7	24.9	21.0	1.3	0.5	2.0	0.9	13.7	10.6	2.0	1.0	0.0	0.0	0.1
Brookings	28 220	90.0	37.8	18.5	23.5	20.1	1.5	0.3	8.7	1.5	10.0	0.1	0.8	0.1	8.7	0.0	0.3
Brown	35 460	95.9	41.3	21.8	26.8	22.4	1.8	0.6	4.3	1.7	4.1	0.1	1.3	0.0	2.2	0.0	0.5
Brule	5 364	92.9	37.2	20.9	30.4	25.1	1.5	0.7	2.7	1.3	7.1	0.2	0.1	1.4	0.0	0.0	5.5
Buffalo	2 032	99.3	25.9	9.7	40.7	29.4	16.6	10.5	6.3	3.0	0.7	0.0	0.0	0.0	0.0	0.0	0.7
Butte	9 094	98.6	38.7	22.2	31.6	26.6	2.3	1.1	3.8	2.0	1.4	0.0	1.0	0.1	0.0	0.0	0.4
Campbell	1 782	98.9	40.7	26.8	30.0	26.2	0.8	0.3	0.7	0.4	1.1	0.0	0.0	0.0	0.0	0.0	1.1
Charles Mix	9 350	98.0	35.8	19.0	33.9	27.8	6.2	3.8	3.2	1.8	2.0	0.1	1.8	0.0	0.0	0.0	0.1
Clark	4 143	98.0	38.6	23.8	31.9	26.2	1.9	0.4	2.0	0.9	2.0	0.0	1.2	0.0	0.0	0.0	0.8
Clay	13 537	83.6	36.0	16.2	21.5	18.2	1.3	0.3	8.8	1.8	16.4	0.1	0.9	0.4	14.7	0.0	0.3
Codington	25 897	98.4	40.0	21.8	30.4	25.8	1.8	0.6	4.4	2.0	1.6	0.2	0.2	0.0	0.0	0.0	1.2
Corson	4 181	99.9	30.4	14.2	35.6	26.5	14.2	9.2	5.5	2.2	0.1	0.0	0.0	0.0	0.0	0.0	0.1
Custer	7 275	95.9	40.8	24.6	24.3	20.2	2.3	1.0	3.8	1.9	4.1	0.0	0.9	2.6	0.0	0.0	0.6
Davison	18 741	96.4	40.5	20.8	28.4	23.9	1.8	0.7	5.0	1.9	3.6	0.2	1.0	0.6	1.3	0.0	0.5
Day	6 267	97.6	41.3	22.4	27.9	23.2	3.0	1.5	3.0	1.7	2.4	0.1	2.2	0.0	0.0	0.0	0.1
Deuel	4 498	98.5	41.0	24.7	29.1	24.6	1.1	0.3	2.5	1.3	1.5	0.0	0.0	0.0	0.0	0.0	1.5
Dewey	5 972	98.2	31.2	13.4	38.5	30.5	10.0	6.8	5.1	2.8	1.8	0.3	0.0	0.6	0.0	0.0	1.0
Douglas	3 458	96.9	38.2	25.0	30.9	27.0	1.6	0.5	1.1	0.5	3.1	0.0	3.1	0.0	0.0	0.0	0.0
Edmunds	4 367	96.9	38.5	25.0	30.2	25.8	1.5	0.4	1.7	0.8	3.1	0.1	3.0	0.0	0.0	0.0	0.0
Fall River	7 453	93.7	42.0	21.4	23.8	19.5	3.0	1.3	3.6	1.8	6.3	0.2	2.7	2.8	0.3	0.0	0.2
Faulk	2 640	98.2	38.4	24.4	31.9	25.6	2.3	0.8	1.2	0.7	1.8	0.2	1.5	0.0	0.0	0.0	0.2
Grant	7 847	97.0	39.7	24.1	30.1	25.8	1.3	0.4	1.8	1.0	3.0	0.1	1.6	0.0	0.0	0.0	1.3
Gregory	4 792	98.1	42.2	23.3	27.3	22.6	2.7	1.2	2.6	1.1	1.9	0.0	1.6	0.1	0.0	0.0	0.3
Haakon	2 196	97.8	39.6	25.2	29.5	24.5	1.7	1.0	1.8	0.8	2.2	0.0	2.2	0.0	0.0	0.0	0.0
Hamlin	5 540	97.0	37.0	23.5	33.4	28.7	1.3	0.5	1.8	0.9	3.0	0.0	1.1	0.0	0.0	0.0	2.0
Hand	3 741	98.1	41.2	25.1	29.3	24.2	1.0	0.2	1.4	0.8	1.9	0.0	1.8	0.1	0.0	0.0	0.0
Hanson	3 139	100.0	35.5	25.0	35.6	28.8	2.5	0.6	1.4	0.8	0.0	0.0	0.0	0.0	0.0	0.0	0.0
Harding	1 353	96.9	38.8	22.7	32.7	29.1	1.7	0.3	1.0	0.7	3.1	3.1	0.0	0.0	0.0	0.0	0.0
Hughes	16 481	95.3	39.5	21.3	28.9	25.0	2.0	0.9	3.6	1.7	4.7	1.1	2.0	1.2	0.0	0.0	0.4
Hutchinson	8 075	95.9	39.5	24.3	29.1	23.7	1.7	0.5	1.3	0.7	4.1	0.0	3.6	0.4	0.0	0.0	0.0
Hyde	1 671	97.8	40.6	22.6	29.6	24.2	2.3	1.0	2.6	1.5	2.2	0.0	2.2	0.0	0.0	0.0	0.0
Jackson	2 930	99.2	32.3	16.6	36.3	28.9	10.1	6.7	4.0	2.0	0.8	0.0	0.8	0.0	0.0	0.0	0.0
Jerauld	2 295	98.3	43.0	24.3	26.0	20.1	2.4	0.7	2.7	1.5	1.7	0.0	1.7	0.0	0.0	0.0	0.0
Jones	1 193	100.0	42.7	22.7	29.4	24.5	2.3	1.3	2.8	1.7	0.0	0.0	0.0	0.0	0.0	0.0	0.0
Kingsbury	5 815	96.9	41.4	24.4	27.5	23.2	1.4	0.7	2.2	1.0	3.1	0.0	2.9	0.0	0.0	0.0	0.2
Lake	11 276	93.5	38.8	21.7	27.3	22.8	1.3	0.5	4.5	1.6	6.5	0.0	1.2	0.0	5.0	0.0	0.3
Lawrence	21 802	94.7	40.7	20.8	25.5	21.1	1.9	0.8	5.8	2.3	5.3	0.1	0.9	0.1	2.8	0.0	1.4
Lincoln	24 131	98.9	36.4	24.2	33.3	28.6	1.7	0.7	3.3	1.5	1.1	0.0	0.9	0.0	0.0	0.0	0.1
Lyman	3 895	99.6	35.9	18.5	34.3	27.7	6.6	3.9	4.2	2.7	0.4	0.0	0.3	0.0	0.0	0.0	0.1
McCook	5 832	97.4	37.8	23.5	31.9	27.3	2.1	0.8	2.1	1.2	2.6	0.0	2.6	0.0	0.0	0.0	0.0
McPherson	2 904	97.7	42.3	26.2	26.3	21.7	1.6	0.4	1.3	0.7	2.3	0.0	2.0	0.3	0.0	0.0	0.0
Marshall	4 576	98.1	40.3	23.0	30.5	25.6	2.2	1.1	2.1	1.1	1.9	0.1	1.9	0.0	0.0	0.0	0.0
Meade	24 253	96.4	36.3	23.4	31.1	26.7	2.2	1.0	3.5	1.6	3.6	0.1	0.8	0.0	0.0	2.3	0.3
Mellette	2 083	97.8	33.3	15.6	35.9	29.2	8.1	5.2	4.9	3.1	2.2	0.0	2.2	0.0	0.0	0.0	0.0
Miner	2 884	98.1	42.0	23.8	29.0	24.9	1.3	0.5	2.0	1.1	1.9	0.0	1.9	0.0	0.0	0.0	0.0
Minnehaha	148 281	96.4	39.1	20.2	29.0	24.5	2.4	0.8	5.6	2.2	3.6	1.0	0.8	0.2	0.9	0.0	0.6
Moody	6 595	98.8	38.3	21.7	32.4	27.2	2.5	1.3	3.9	2.0	1.2	0.0	0.9	0.0	0.0	0.0	0.3
Pennington	88 565	97.3	39.1	20.1	29.4	24.5	3.1	1.3	5.6	2.4	2.7	0.4	0.6	0.1	0.9	0.0	0.8
Perkins	3 363	98.0	42.5	24.6	27.8	23.5	1.3	0.2	1.8	1.0	2.0	0.0	1.2	0.0	0.0	0.0	0.8
Potter	2 693	97.5	42.5	25.2	26.1	22.2	2.2	0.5	1.5	0.6	2.5	0.0	2.0	0.0	0.0	0.0	0.5
Roberts	10 016	97.9	36.8	19.7	32.4	26.0	6.0	3.5	3.0	1.6	2.1	0.3	1.0	0.0	0.0	0.0	0.8
Sanborn	2 675	98.6	39.0	24.0	30.5	24.2	2.1	0.9	3.1	1.5	1.4	0.0	1.4	0.0	0.0	0.0	0.0
Shannon	12 466	97.5	22.3	7.9	42.2	30.5	20.1	13.0	4.9	2.6	2.5	0.4	0.0	0.1	0.0	0.0	2.0
Spink	7 454	93.5	38.2	22.4	29.2	24.3	1.7	0.7	2.1	1.1	6.5	2.5	1.3	2.6	0.0	0.0	0.1
Stanley	2 772	99.7	40.1	22.3	30.6	25.5	2.6	1.1	4.1	2.3	0.3	0.0	0.0	0.0	0.0	0.0	0.3
Sully	1 556	100.0	40.5	25.3	29.3	24.1	1.9	0.9	3.0	1.6	0.0	0.0	0.0	0.0	0.0	0.0	0.0
Todd	9 050	98.6	27.2	9.6	40.5	31.8	15.5	10.2	5.9	3.3	1.4	0.1	0.0	0.7	0.0	0.0	0.6

Table B. States and Counties

STATE County	Households by type, 2000												Households, 1990		
		Family households						Nonfamily households							
				Married couple		Female householder[1]			Householder living alone						House-holder living alone
	Total households	Total	With own children under 18 years	Total	With own children under 18 years	Total	With own children under 18 years	Total	Total	65 years and over	Average house-hold size	Average family size	Total house-holds	Female house-holder[1]	
	71	72	73	74	75	76	77	78	79	80	81	82	83	84	85
SOUTH CAROLINA— Cont'd															
Sumter	37 728	73.2	36.5	50.2	23.8	18.3	10.5	26.0	23.2	8.5	2.68	3.17	32 723	16.7	19.0
Union	12 087	70.3	29.4	48.8	18.5	16.8	8.7	29.7	26.8	11.9	2.44	2.93	11 407	16.0	23.0
Williamsburg	13 714	73.3	34.5	46.3	20.6	22.4	12.1	26.7	24.9	10.4	2.69	3.22	12 108	20.5	21.1
York	61 051	73.6	35.4	56.1	25.6	13.3	7.7	26.4	21.3	6.9	2.63	3.05	47 006	12.7	19.6
SOUTH DAKOTA	290 245	67.0	32.8	54.2	24.5	9.0	6.1	33.0	27.6	11.1	2.50	3.07	259 034	8.0	26.4
Aurora	1 165	70.1	29.7	61.3	25.1	5.0	2.9	29.9	28.2	14.7	2.45	3.02	1 146	4.8	27.6
Beadle	7 210	62.9	28.3	52.5	7.4	4.8	4.8	37.1	33.1	15.0	2.30	2.94	7 341	6.9	29.3
Bennett	1 123	72.9	39.7	48.6	23.9	17.5	11.3	27.1	23.3	10.2	3.14	3.74	1 030	12.8	24.0
Bon Homme	2 635	67.8	28.7	59.8	24.0	5.1	3.1	32.2	29.5	16.5	2.38	2.95	2 647	4.2	28.3
Brookings	10 665	58.3	28.6	49.0	22.7	6.6	4.5	41.7	29.6	8.6	2.38	2.97	8 910	5.9	27.3
Brown	14 638	63.7	29.6	52.8	22.6	7.9	5.3	36.3	30.8	12.1	2.32	2.91	13 867	7.8	28.4
Brule	1 998	66.5	31.0	56.2	24.7	7.2	4.7	33.5	29.9	13.1	2.49	3.14	1 996	5.3	30.1
Buffalo	526	80.2	47.1	37.6	21.9	31.4	18.4	19.8	16.0	5.9	3.83	4.23	446	25.8	10.8
Butte	3 516	70.2	35.0	57.4	26.6	9.0	6.3	29.8	25.6	11.9	2.55	3.07	3 033	7.4	26.8
Campbell	725	70.1	30.3	65.8	28.7	2.6	1.4	29.9	28.6	15.7	2.43	3.02	767	3.5	23.6
Charles Mix	3 343	69.6	34.2	53.1	24.1	11.7	7.5	30.4	28.3	15.1	2.74	3.37	3 232	8.3	27.6
Clark	1 598	69.5	29.3	61.6	25.2	4.7	2.8	30.5	28.1	16.4	2.54	3.14	1 700	3.4	26.8
Clay	4 878	55.8	28.0	45.0	20.1	8.1	6.3	44.2	31.0	8.0	2.32	2.93	4 433	7.7	29.2
Codington	10 357	66.4	33.6	54.5	25.8	8.1	5.7	33.6	27.9	10.8	2.46	3.04	8 739	7.3	28.1
Corson	1 271	74.7	38.3	46.8	23.5	19.7	10.8	25.3	22.1	10.0	3.29	3.82	1 303	13.3	21.3
Custer	2 970	69.6	26.9	60.2	21.2	6.6	4.0	30.4	25.9	10.3	2.35	2.80	2 352	7.7	24.0
Davison	7 585	62.9	31.1	51.4	23.3	8.2	5.7	37.1	30.8	13.4	2.38	3.00	6 948	7.3	31.6
Day	2 586	65.3	27.3	54.4	21.2	6.8	3.8	34.7	31.8	18.0	2.36	2.98	2 732	5.6	28.4
Deuel	1 843	68.3	29.2	60.4	24.9	4.9	3.0	31.7	28.6	14.4	2.40	2.97	1 767	4.9	25.1
Dewey	1 863	74.4	43.7	42.9	24.6	22.3	13.3	25.6	22.1	8.9	3.15	3.66	1 721	21.2	21.6
Douglas	1 321	71.7	32.2	65.4	28.9	3.6	2.0	28.3	26.8	15.4	2.54	3.10	1 352	2.8	25.7
Edmunds	1 681	72.0	31.5	64.9	27.4	4.8	2.9	28.0	25.6	15.0	2.52	3.04	1 669	3.7	26.1
Fall River	3 127	63.2	23.7	50.9	16.1	8.5	5.2	36.8	32.7	14.6	2.23	2.82	2 864	8.3	31.6
Faulk	1 014	69.9	28.9	63.4	25.8	3.4	1.7	30.1	29.1	16.3	2.56	3.18	1 057	3.1	28.0
Grant	3 116	69.2	33.4	60.6	28.2	5.2	3.3	30.8	28.6	15.0	2.44	3.02	3 154	5.0	26.3
Gregory	2 022	63.8	26.4	55.2	21.9	5.7	3.0	36.2	33.9	20.3	2.32	2.98	2 139	5.4	32.3
Haakon	870	71.3	32.6	63.6	27.7	4.8	3.6	28.7	26.0	13.1	2.47	3.00	926	3.7	27.8
Hamlin	2 048	70.9	33.8	63.5	29.3	4.8	3.0	29.1	27.0	14.5	2.62	3.22	1 854	4.5	27.6
Hand	1 543	68.1	28.1	60.9	24.4	4.4	2.3	31.9	30.2	17.4	2.38	2.97	1 625	4.5	26.1
Hanson	1 115	76.1	34.4	70.4	31.6	3.7	2.1	23.9	21.7	11.6	2.82	3.33	1 072	3.5	23.6
Harding	525	67.2	35.0	58.5	29.9	5.3	3.4	32.8	31.0	14.5	2.50	3.19	592	4.6	23.1
Hughes	6 512	66.2	33.8	54.0	25.1	8.9	6.5	33.8	29.6	10.3	2.41	3.00	5 780	8.6	28.9
Hutchinson	3 190	68.7	28.0	61.5	24.5	4.4	2.2	31.3	29.6	18.5	2.43	3.03	3 221	3.6	28.2
Hyde	679	67.2	29.6	55.7	22.2	6.0	4.6	32.8	30.3	17.1	2.41	3.00	680	3.5	31.3
Jackson	945	71.5	38.6	51.4	25.9	14.7	9.7	28.5	25.2	11.9	3.08	3.73	903	10.5	22.9
Jerauld	987	66.0	24.3	56.4	18.6	6.3	3.9	34.0	31.3	17.7	2.28	2.85	966	4.0	28.5
Jones	509	64.4	29.3	53.2	22.6	7.5	3.9	35.6	33.2	15.1	2.34	2.98	519	5.0	25.0
Kingsbury	2 406	66.2	27.9	59.0	23.1	4.4	2.7	33.8	31.5	17.8	2.34	2.95	2 357	3.6	29.3
Lake	4 372	64.7	29.8	55.9	23.9	5.9	4.2	35.3	29.2	13.3	2.41	3.00	4 030	5.3	28.3
Lawrence	8 881	62.6	28.8	51.0	20.7	8.5	6.0	37.4	29.6	11.5	2.33	2.89	7 926	8.1	28.1
Lincoln	8 782	75.9	41.0	66.5	34.7	6.7	4.7	24.1	19.5	8.0	2.72	3.14	5 461	5.2	20.3
Lyman	1 400	72.1	36.1	51.4	22.5	13.8	9.2	27.9	24.6	10.5	2.77	3.29	1 268	9.9	24.3
McCook	2 204	70.7	34.1	62.1	29.0	5.1	3.4	29.3	26.8	15.6	2.58	3.15	2 145	4.6	26.6
McPherson	1 227	67.0	23.6	62.1	21.5	2.7	1.3	33.0	31.1	19.2	2.31	2.91	1 332	3.5	26.4
Marshall	1 844	67.9	29.8	57.2	24.0	6.5	3.4	32.1	30.1	16.1	2.43	3.04	1 919	5.5	28.2
Meade	8 805	76.1	39.9	64.4	31.8	8.3	5.8	23.9	19.9	7.5	2.66	3.05	7 084	7.4	18.3
Mellette	694	71.9	38.9	46.8	23.3	16.7	9.9	28.1	24.2	10.5	2.94	3.49	681	16.2	22.2
Miner	1 212	65.1	28.2	56.5	22.8	5.4	3.5	34.9	32.3	16.9	2.33	2.98	1 276	4.6	28.4
Minnehaha	57 996	64.8	33.8	51.8	25.1	9.5	6.6	35.2	27.8	8.6	2.46	3.04	47 681	8.8	27.0
Moody	2 526	69.8	35.6	56.7	26.5	8.5	5.7	30.2	26.4	12.2	2.58	3.12	2 398	6.3	24.3
Pennington	34 641	67.2	33.5	51.3	22.7	11.7	8.3	32.8	26.1	8.4	2.49	3.00	30 553	10.2	23.4
Perkins	1 429	65.6	27.3	57.8	22.7	5.2	3.2	34.4	32.9	17.5	2.31	2.93	1 586	5.2	28.6
Potter	1 145	67.0	26.6	59.2	22.4	4.9	2.4	33.0	31.3	17.5	2.29	2.88	1 249	4.8	28.2
Roberts	3 683	71.1	33.8	53.5	23.4	11.8	7.0	28.9	26.8	12.4	2.66	3.22	3 619	9.7	26.8
Sanborn	1 043	70.2	30.3	61.5	25.6	4.9	2.9	29.8	25.4	12.7	2.53	3.07	1 059	3.7	25.2
Shannon	2 785	84.5	51.7	35.4	23.0	36.4	21.4	15.5	13.2	3.0	4.36	4.72	2 205	33.3	12.2
Spink	2 847	67.9	30.6	58.6	24.7	6.1	4.3	32.1	29.3	15.8	2.45	3.05	3 022	5.7	29.4
Stanley	1 111	69.8	33.6	55.6	24.5	10.1	6.8	30.2	25.2	7.9	2.49	2.98	921	10.3	24.1
Sully	630	70.3	31.0	62.5	26.8	4.3	1.7	29.7	25.7	10.6	2.47	2.99	621	3.5	23.8
Todd	2 462	77.9	48.9	35.2	20.6	31.8	20.5	22.1	18.9	5.2	3.62	4.09	2 210	28.7	16.7

[1] No spouse present.

Table B. States and Counties

STATE County	Percent change of households, 1990–2000	Total housing units	Occupied housing units (percent)	Vacant housing units				Occupied housing units				
				Total	For seasonal, recreational, or occasional use	Homeowner vacancy rate (percent)	Rental vacancy rate (percent)	Total	Percent owner-occupied housing units	Percent renter-occupied housing units	Average household size of owner-occupied units	Average household size of renter-occupied units
	86	87	88	89	90	91	92	93	94	95	96	97
SOUTH CAROLINA— Cont'd												
Sumter	15.3	41 751	90.4	9.6	0.6	1.9	10.3	37 728	69.5	30.5	2.72	2.60
Union	6.0	13 351	90.5	9.5	0.7	1.7	9.5	12 087	76.7	23.3	2.50	2.24
Williamsburg	13.3	15 552	88.2	11.8	1.9	1.1	7.0	13 714	80.5	19.5	2.74	2.47
York	29.9	66 061	92.4	7.6	1.0	2.4	8.3	61 051	73.1	26.9	2.69	2.47
SOUTH DAKOTA	12.0	323 208	89.8	10.2	3.0	1.8	8.0	290 245	68.2	31.8	2.64	2.22
Aurora	1.7	1 298	89.8	10.2	1.7	3.1	8.1	1 165	76.7	23.3	2.47	2.39
Beadle	-1.8	8 206	87.9	12.1	2.6	2.2	15.1	7 210	67.8	32.2	2.46	1.95
Bennett	9.0	1 278	87.9	12.1	1.7	2.4	6.5	1 123	59.1	40.9	2.74	3.71
Bon Homme	-0.5	3 007	87.6	12.4	2.2	3.5	10.4	2 635	75.9	24.1	2.47	2.08
Brookings	19.7	11 576	92.1	7.9	2.7	1.6	5.8	10 665	58.2	41.8	2.65	2.00
Brown	5.6	15 861	92.3	7.7	1.1	1.7	9.0	14 638	66.3	33.7	2.56	1.85
Brule	0.1	2 272	87.9	12.1	3.0	1.8	7.1	1 998	71.2	28.8	2.66	2.09
Buffalo	17.9	602	87.4	12.6	5.3	3.0	3.8	526	42.8	57.2	3.57	4.03
Butte	15.9	4 059	86.6	13.4	1.8	2.8	15.9	3 516	73.2	26.8	2.65	2.27
Campbell	-5.5	962	75.4	24.6	9.4	5.8	7.9	725	82.2	17.8	2.51	2.07
Charles Mix	3.4	3 853	86.8	13.2	4.9	2.3	9.1	3 343	68.4	31.6	2.71	2.80
Clark	-6.0	1 880	85.0	15.0	2.5	5.2	11.5	1 598	80.3	19.7	2.61	2.28
Clay	10.0	5 438	89.7	10.3	2.4	2.6	7.6	4 878	54.4	45.6	2.54	2.06
Codington	18.5	11 324	91.5	8.5	1.4	1.9	12.6	10 357	70.2	29.8	2.68	1.94
Corson	-2.5	1 536	82.7	17.3	4.4	1.7	3.9	1 271	59.4	40.6	2.86	3.91
Custer	26.3	3 624	82.0	18.0	10.1	2.3	9.1	2 970	77.0	23.0	2.41	2.15
Davison	9.2	8 093	93.7	6.3	0.4	1.4	8.4	7 585	61.9	38.1	2.66	1.93
Day	-5.3	3 618	71.5	28.5	17.3	3.0	14.5	2 586	76.0	24.0	2.43	2.15
Deuel	4.3	2 172	84.9	15.1	7.4	2.6	8.3	1 843	80.1	19.9	2.51	1.98
Dewey	8.3	2 133	87.3	12.7	2.6	1.1	10.5	1 863	55.2	44.8	3.05	3.27
Douglas	-2.3	1 453	90.9	9.1	1.3	1.7	8.7	1 321	80.8	19.2	2.65	2.04
Edmunds	0.7	2 022	83.1	16.9	6.8	2.5	9.5	1 681	81.9	18.1	2.58	2.24
Fall River	9.2	3 812	82.0	18.0	7.5	4.8	9.6	3 127	69.7	30.3	2.38	1.90
Faulk	-4.1	1 235	82.1	17.9	4.4	4.3	4.2	1 014	81.9	18.1	2.59	2.42
Grant	-1.2	3 456	90.2	9.8	1.4	1.9	16.0	3 116	77.6	22.4	2.61	1.87
Gregory	-5.5	2 405	84.1	15.9	3.1	3.4	14.4	2 022	75.0	25.0	2.42	2.04
Haakon	-6.0	1 002	86.8	13.2	3.1	2.2	13.3	870	76.8	23.2	2.53	2.28
Hamlin	10.5	2 626	78.0	22.0	14.7	2.6	8.8	2 048	81.9	18.1	2.69	2.32
Hand	-5.0	1 840	83.9	16.1	1.6	2.1	6.3	1 543	73.8	26.2	2.47	2.11
Hanson	4.0	1 218	91.5	8.5	2.1	1.9	4.1	1 115	79.1	20.9	2.76	3.04
Harding	-11.3	804	65.3	34.7	9.1	8.3	8.6	525	73.5	26.5	2.47	2.57
Hughes	12.7	7 055	92.3	7.7	1.5	1.0	9.7	6 512	66.1	33.9	2.66	1.93
Hutchinson	-1.0	3 517	90.7	9.3	0.9	2.2	6.5	3 190	78.8	21.2	2.47	2.28
Hyde	-0.1	769	88.3	11.7	1.0	3.0	9.4	679	71.7	28.3	2.41	2.40
Jackson	4.7	1 173	80.6	19.4	4.4	2.0	17.8	945	63.4	36.6	2.81	3.54
Jerauld	2.2	1 167	84.6	15.4	2.7	4.6	5.8	987	72.2	27.8	2.30	2.25
Jones	-1.9	614	82.9	17.1	4.4	1.9	11.9	509	72.5	27.5	2.42	2.15
Kingsbury	2.1	2 724	88.3	11.7	2.3	2.9	10.0	2 406	75.6	24.4	2.47	1.93
Lake	8.5	5 282	82.8	17.2	12.6	1.7	3.7	4 372	70.5	29.5	2.57	2.02
Lawrence	12.0	10 427	85.2	14.8	5.7	1.7	10.3	8 881	64.8	35.2	2.56	1.90
Lincoln	60.8	9 131	96.2	3.8	0.3	1.1	6.3	8 782	79.7	20.3	2.87	2.12
Lyman	10.4	1 636	85.6	14.4	3.2	2.7	10.1	1 400	69.4	30.6	2.65	3.05
McCook	2.8	2 383	92.5	7.5	1.0	1.5	9.4	2 204	78.9	21.1	2.68	2.20
McPherson	-7.9	1 465	83.8	16.2	2.9	2.9	11.5	1 227	83.1	16.9	2.39	1.91
Marshall	-3.9	2 562	72.0	28.0	18.7	2.8	15.1	1 844	77.8	22.2	2.49	2.22
Meade	24.3	10 149	86.8	13.2	1.3	1.5	9.9	8 805	68.2	31.8	2.67	2.62
Mellette	1.9	824	84.2	15.8	5.0	2.0	4.7	694	64.7	35.3	2.72	3.33
Miner	-5.0	1 408	86.1	13.9	3.1	2.3	8.1	1 212	76.7	23.3	2.43	2.03
Minnehaha	21.6	60 237	96.3	3.7	0.2	0.9	5.2	57 996	64.7	35.3	2.71	2.02
Moody	5.3	2 745	92.0	8.0	1.1	2.2	8.6	2 526	72.6	27.4	2.67	2.33
Pennington	13.4	37 249	93.0	7.0	2.6	1.0	6.4	34 641	66.2	33.8	2.60	2.26
Perkins	-9.9	1 854	77.1	22.9	4.4	8.8	15.4	1 429	76.6	23.4	2.43	1.89
Potter	-8.3	1 760	65.1	34.9	20.5	3.3	17.3	1 145	79.5	20.5	2.44	1.71
Roberts	1.8	4 734	77.8	22.2	13.9	2.2	6.3	3 683	69.1	30.9	2.62	2.75
Sanborn	-1.5	1 220	85.5	14.5	4.3	3.7	5.0	1 043	77.9	22.1	2.62	2.21
Shannon	26.3	3 123	89.2	10.8	1.1	0.6	2.7	2 785	49.6	50.4	3.88	4.85
Spink	-5.8	3 352	84.9	15.1	4.1	4.5	12.0	2 847	73.8	26.2	2.58	2.06
Stanley	20.6	1 277	87.0	13.0	4.6	2.3	6.4	1 111	76.4	23.6	2.63	2.03
Sully	1.4	844	74.6	25.4	14.5	2.8	7.9	630	75.9	24.1	2.49	2.41
Todd	11.4	2 766	89.0	11.0	2.2	1.1	4.7	2 462	45.1	54.9	3.29	3.90

Table B. States and Counties

STATE/ County code	MSA/ PMSA/ NECMA code[1]	County type[2]	STATE County	Land area, 2000[3] (sq km)	Population, 2000 Total persons	Rank	Per square kilometer	Land area, 1990[3] (sq km)	Population, 1990 Total persons	Rank	Per square kilometer	White	Black or African American	American Indian or Alaska Native	Asian	Native Hawaiian and other Pacific Islander	Some other race
				1	2	3	4	5	6	7	8	9	10	11	12	13	14
			SOUTH DAKOTA— Cont'd														
46 123	...	7	Tripp	4 179	6 430	2 745	1.5	4 179	6 924	2 000	1.7	87.5	0.0	11.2	0.1	0.0	0.1
46 125	...	8	Turner	1 598	8 849	2 540	5.5	1 598	8 576	2 507	5.4	98.9	0.1	0.3	0.2	0.0	0.1
46 127	...	8	Union	1 192	12 584	2 257	10.6	1 192	10 189	2 372	8.5	96.8	0.3	0.4	1.3	0.0	0.2
46 129	...	7	Walworth	1 833	5 974	2 784	3.3	1 833	6 087	2 746	3.3	86.6	0.0	11.8	0.2	0.0	0.1
46 135	...	7	Yankton	1 351	21 652	1 710	16.0	1 351	19 252	1 715	14.3	95.1	1.2	1.6	0.4	0.0	0.7
46 137	...	9	Ziebach	5 082	2 519	3 025	0.5	5 083	2 220	3 053	0.4	26.4	0.0	72.3	0.1	0.0	0.1
47 000	...		TENNESSEE	106 752	5 689 283	X	53.3	106 759	4 877 203	X	45.7	80.2	16.4	0.3	1.0	0.0	1.0
47 001	3840	2	Anderson	874	71 330	694	81.6	874	68 250	648	78.1	93.4	3.9	0.3	0.8	0.0	0.4
47 003	...	6	Bedford	1 227	37 586	1 174	30.6	1 227	30 411	1 273	24.8	86.8	8.5	0.3	0.5	0.1	2.7
47 005	...	7	Benton	1 023	16 537	1 987	16.2	1 023	14 524	2 017	14.2	96.4	2.1	0.3	0.2	0.0	0.2
47 007	...	8	Bledsoe	1 052	12 367	2 276	11.8	1 052	9 669	2 416	9.2	94.4	3.7	0.4	0.1	0.0	0.2
47 009	3840	2	Blount	1 447	105 823	502	73.1	1 447	85 962	534	59.4	94.7	2.9	0.3	0.7	0.0	0.3
47 011	...	4	Bradley	851	87 965	594	103.4	851	73 712	610	86.6	93.0	4.0	0.3	0.6	0.0	0.9
47 013	...	6	Campbell	1 243	39 854	1 116	32.1	1 243	35 079	1 128	28.2	98.1	0.3	0.3	0.2	0.0	0.2
47 015	...	8	Cannon	688	12 826	2 245	18.6	688	10 467	2 339	15.2	96.9	1.5	0.3	0.1	0.0	0.4
47 017	...	6	Carroll	1 551	29 475	1 414	19.0	1 552	27 514	1 374	17.7	87.7	10.3	0.2	0.2	0.0	0.5
47 019	3660	2	Carter	883	56 742	835	64.3	883	51 505	820	58.3	97.5	1.0	0.2	0.3	0.0	0.3
47 021	5360	2	Cheatham	784	35 912	1 221	45.8	784	27 140	1 387	34.6	96.9	1.5	0.4	0.2	0.0	0.4
47 023	3580	6	Chester	747	15 540	2 051	20.8	747	12 819	2 154	17.2	88.1	10.0	0.2	0.2	0.0	0.3
47 025	...	6	Claiborne	1 125	29 862	1 400	26.5	1 125	26 137	1 417	23.2	97.8	0.8	0.2	0.3	0.0	0.2
47 027	...	9	Clay	612	7 976	2 608	13.0	612	7 238	2 631	11.8	96.8	1.4	0.3	0.1	0.1	0.2
47 029	...	7	Cocke	1 125	33 565	1 298	29.8	1 125	29 141	1 324	25.9	96.2	2.0	0.4	0.2	0.0	0.3
47 031	...	5	Coffee	1 111	48 014	953	43.2	1 111	40 343	990	36.3	93.4	3.6	0.3	0.7	0.0	0.9
47 033	...	8	Crockett	687	14 532	2 119	21.2	687	13 378	2 107	19.5	82.0	14.4	0.2	0.1	0.0	2.8
47 035	...	7	Cumberland	1 765	46 802	965	26.5	1 765	34 736	1 143	19.7	98.1	0.1	0.3	0.2	0.0	0.5
47 037	5360	2	Davidson	1 301	569 891	95	438.0	1 301	510 786	93	392.6	67.0	25.9	0.3	2.3	0.1	2.4
47 039	...	9	Decatur	865	11 731	2 315	13.6	865	10 472	2 338	12.1	94.1	3.5	0.2	0.2	0.0	1.2
47 041	...	6	De Kalb	789	17 423	1 927	22.1	789	14 360	2 026	18.2	95.6	1.4	0.3	0.1	0.0	1.6
47 043	5360	2	Dickson	1 269	43 156	1 034	34.0	1 269	35 061	1 131	27.6	93.3	4.6	0.4	0.3	0.0	0.5
47 045	...	7	Dyer	1 322	37 279	1 183	28.2	1 322	34 854	1 138	26.4	85.4	12.9	0.2	0.3	0.0	0.4
47 047	4920	1	Fayette	1 825	28 806	1 427	15.8	1 825	25 559	1 442	14.0	62.5	35.9	0.2	0.2	0.0	0.4
47 049	...	9	Fentress	1 291	16 625	1 982	12.9	1 292	14 669	2 007	11.4	99.2	0.1	0.2	0.1	0.0	0.0
47 051	...	7	Franklin	1 436	39 270	1 131	27.3	1 433	34 923	1 136	24.4	92.2	5.5	0.2	0.4	0.0	0.6
47 053	...	4	Gibson	1 561	48 152	945	30.8	1 561	46 315	897	29.7	78.7	19.7	0.2	0.1	0.0	0.5
47 055	...	6	Giles	1 582	29 447	1 416	18.6	1 582	25 741	1 431	16.3	86.4	11.8	0.3	0.3	0.0	0.2
47 057	...	8	Grainger	726	20 659	1 754	28.5	726	17 095	1 846	23.5	98.4	0.3	0.2	0.1	0.0	0.4
47 059	...	6	Greene	1 610	62 909	772	39.1	1 611	55 832	776	34.7	96.4	2.1	0.2	0.3	0.0	0.4
47 061	...	6	Grundy	934	14 332	2 138	15.3	934	13 362	2 109	14.3	98.3	0.1	0.3	0.2	0.0	0.3
47 063	...	5	Hamblen	417	58 128	822	139.4	417	50 480	835	121.1	90.7	4.1	0.2	0.6	0.1	3.3
47 065	1560	2	Hamilton	1 405	307 896	185	219.1	1 405	285 536	172	203.2	76.3	20.1	0.3	1.3	0.1	0.8
47 067	...	9	Hancock	576	6 786	2 713	11.8	576	6 739	2 683	11.7	97.9	0.5	0.2	0.1	0.0	0.3
47 069	...	6	Hardeman	1 729	28 105	1 448	16.3	1 729	23 377	1 521	13.5	57.3	41.0	0.3	0.3	0.0	0.3
47 071	...	6	Hardin	1 497	25 578	1 536	17.1	1 497	22 633	1 552	15.1	94.9	3.7	0.2	0.2	0.0	0.3
47 073	3660	2	Hawkins	1 260	53 563	873	42.5	1 261	44 565	917	35.3	97.2	1.5	0.2	0.2	0.0	0.4
47 075	...	6	Haywood	1 381	19 797	1 802	14.3	1 381	19 437	1 707	14.1	46.7	51.0	0.1	0.1	0.1	1.4
47 077	...	6	Henderson	1 347	25 522	1 539	18.9	1 347	21 844	1 586	16.2	90.5	8.0	0.1	0.1	0.0	0.3
47 079	...	7	Henry	1 455	31 115	1 374	21.4	1 455	27 888	1 353	19.2	89.2	9.0	0.2	0.3	0.0	0.4
47 081	...	6	Hickman	1 586	22 295	1 680	14.1	1 587	16 754	1 865	10.6	93.7	4.5	0.5	0.1	0.0	0.3
47 083	...	8	Houston	519	8 088	2 598	15.6	519	7 018	2 656	13.5	94.6	3.3	0.2	0.1	0.1	0.8
47 085	...	6	Humphreys	1 378	17 929	1 904	13.0	1 379	15 813	1 935	11.5	95.5	2.9	0.3	0.3	0.0	0.3
47 087	...	9	Jackson	800	10 984	2 368	13.7	800	9 297	2 444	11.6	98.6	0.1	0.3	0.1	0.0	0.1
47 089	...	6	Jefferson	709	44 294	1 011	62.5	709	33 016	1 191	46.6	95.7	2.3	0.3	0.3	0.0	0.6
47 091	...	8	Johnson	773	17 499	1 923	22.6	773	13 766	2 075	17.8	96.4	2.4	0.3	0.1	0.0	0.2
47 093	3840	2	Knox	1 317	382 032	151	290.1	1 317	335 749	153	254.9	88.1	8.6	0.3	1.3	0.0	0.5
47 095	...	9	Lake	423	7 954	2 610	18.8	423	7 129	2 640	16.9	66.6	31.2	0.4	0.1	0.0	0.6
47 097	...	6	Lauderdale	1 218	27 101	1 478	22.3	1 219	23 491	1 514	19.3	63.8	34.1	0.6	0.2	0.0	0.5
47 099	...	6	Lawrence	1 598	39 926	1 114	25.0	1 599	35 303	1 122	22.1	96.8	1.5	0.3	0.2	0.0	0.4
47 101	...	7	Lewis	731	11 367	2 345	15.5	731	9 247	2 449	12.6	97.1	1.5	0.2	0.2	0.0	0.3
47 103	...	6	Lincoln	1 477	31 340	1 364	21.2	1 477	28 157	1 346	19.1	90.3	7.4	0.5	0.3	0.0	0.3
47 105	3840	2	Loudon	593	39 086	1 134	65.9	592	31 255	1 237	52.8	95.9	1.1	0.3	0.2	0.0	1.4
47 107	...	7	McMinn	1 114	49 015	932	44.0	1 114	42 383	950	38.0	92.7	4.5	0.3	0.7	0.0	0.7
47 109	...	7	McNairy	1 451	24 653	1 569	17.0	1 451	22 422	1 557	15.5	92.2	6.2	0.2	0.1	0.0	0.2
47 111	...	6	Macon	795	20 386	1 769	25.6	796	15 906	1 930	20.0	97.9	0.2	0.4	0.2	0.1	0.8
47 113	3580	3	Madison	1 443	91 837	557	63.6	1 443	77 982	581	54.0	65.2	32.5	0.2	0.6	0.0	0.7
47 115	1560	2	Marion	1 291	27 776	1 456	21.5	1 295	24 683	1 474	19.1	94.3	4.1	0.3	0.2	0.0	0.3

[1] MSA = Metropolitan Statistical Area. PMSA = Primary MSA. NECMA = New England County Metropolitan Area. See Appendix A for explanation of these concepts. See Appendix B for list of metropolitan areas identified by type, with component counties.
[2] County typology code from the Economic Research Service of USDA. See Appendix A for definition.
[3] Dry land or land partially or temporarily covered by water.

Table B. States and Counties

STATE County	Population and population characteristics, 2000 (cont'd)								Population and population characteristics, 1990				
	Race (percent) (cont'd)								Race (percent)				
	Race alone or in combination												
	Two or more races	White	Black	American Indian or Alaska Native	Asian	Native Hawaiian and other Pacific Islander	Some other race	Hispanic[1]	White	Black or African American	American Indian or Alaska Native	Asian and Pacific Islander	Hispanic[1]
	15	16	17	18	19	20	21	22	23	24	25	26	27
SOUTH DAKOTA— Cont'd													
Tripp	1.2	88.6	0.2	12.2	0.1	0.0	0.1	0.9	90.2	0.0	9.7	0.1	0.1
Turner	0.4	99.3	0.3	0.5	0.3	0.0	0.1	0.4	99.6	0.0	0.3	0.0	0.2
Union	0.9	97.7	0.5	0.7	1.5	0.1	0.5	1.3	99.0	0.2	0.3	0.3	0.7
Walworth	1.4	87.9	0.2	13.0	0.2	0.0	0.1	0.6	92.1	0.0	7.7	0.2	0.4
Yankton	0.9	95.9	1.5	2.2	0.6	0.0	0.9	1.8	96.9	0.6	2.1	0.3	0.5
Ziebach	1.1	27.4	0.0	73.2	0.1	0.0	0.4	1.0	35.6	0.1	64.0	0.2	1.3
TENNESSEE	1.1	81.2	16.8	0.7	1.2	0.1	1.3	2.2	83.0	16.0	0.2	0.7	0.7
Anderson	1.2	94.5	4.3	0.9	1.0	0.0	0.5	1.1	94.7	4.0	0.4	0.8	0.6
Bedford	1.2	87.9	8.9	0.7	0.6	0.1	3.2	7.5	89.1	10.1	0.1	0.5	0.6
Benton	0.7	97.1	2.2	0.7	0.4	0.0	0.4	0.9	97.1	2.4	0.2	0.2	0.5
Bledsoe	1.1	95.5	3.9	1.1	0.2	0.1	0.3	1.1	95.6	3.9	0.4	0.0	0.4
Blount	1.0	95.7	3.1	0.8	0.9	0.0	0.5	1.1	96.0	3.2	0.2	0.5	0.4
Bradley	1.3	94.1	4.3	0.9	0.7	0.1	1.2	2.1	95.1	3.9	0.3	0.3	1.0
Campbell	0.9	99.0	0.4	1.0	0.2	0.1	0.2	0.7	99.0	0.4	0.5	0.1	0.3
Cannon	0.8	97.6	1.6	0.9	0.2	0.0	0.5	1.2	97.8	1.8	0.1	0.1	0.4
Carroll	1.1	88.7	10.8	0.7	0.3	0.1	0.6	1.3	88.3	11.4	0.1	0.0	0.5
Carter	0.8	98.2	1.2	0.6	0.4	0.0	0.4	0.9	98.6	0.9	0.2	0.3	0.4
Cheatham	0.7	97.5	1.6	0.8	0.3	0.1	0.5	1.2	97.5	2.0	0.3	0.1	0.5
Chester	1.1	89.1	10.2	0.7	0.4	0.1	0.6	1.0	88.6	11.0	0.2	0.2	0.4
Claiborne	0.7	98.5	0.8	0.6	0.1	0.0	0.3	0.6	98.3	1.0	0.2	0.4	0.3
Clay	1.0	97.5	1.7	0.9	0.2	0.1	0.5	1.4	98.1	1.6	0.2	0.0	0.4
Cocke	1.0	97.1	2.2	1.0	0.2	0.1	0.4	1.1	97.5	2.1	0.3	0.1	0.5
Coffee	1.0	94.4	4.0	0.7	0.9	0.1	1.1	2.2	95.3	3.7	0.2	0.6	0.6
Crockett	0.6	82.6	14.5	0.5	0.1	0.0	2.9	5.5	82.9	16.8	0.1	0.1	0.4
Cumberland	0.8	98.9	0.2	0.8	0.4	0.0	0.6	1.2	99.2	0.1	0.4	0.1	0.4
Davidson	2.0	68.5	26.6	0.7	2.8	0.1	3.3	4.6	74.7	23.4	0.2	1.4	0.9
Decatur	0.8	94.8	3.7	0.7	0.3	0.1	1.3	2.0	95.5	4.0	0.2	0.2	0.5
De Kalb	0.9	96.5	1.6	0.8	0.2	0.1	1.9	3.6	98.0	1.5	0.1	0.1	0.4
Dickson	1.0	94.2	4.9	0.9	0.4	0.0	0.6	1.1	94.5	5.0	0.2	0.2	0.5
Dyer	0.7	86.0	13.2	0.5	0.4	0.0	0.5	1.2	87.6	11.9	0.2	0.2	0.4
Fayette	0.8	63.2	36.1	0.7	0.3	0.0	0.5	1.0	55.6	44.2	0.1	0.1	0.5
Fentress	0.4	99.6	0.1	0.4	0.1	0.0	0.0	0.5	99.8	0.0	0.1	0.1	0.3
Franklin	1.1	93.2	5.8	0.7	0.5	0.1	0.8	1.6	93.4	6.0	0.2	0.3	0.5
Gibson	0.8	79.4	19.9	0.6	0.2	0.0	0.7	1.1	80.4	19.3	0.1	0.1	0.4
Giles	0.9	87.3	12.1	0.7	0.5	0.0	0.3	0.9	86.2	13.2	0.2	0.2	0.4
Grainger	0.6	99.0	0.4	0.6	0.1	0.0	0.5	1.1	99.1	0.6	0.2	0.0	0.2
Greene	0.6	97.0	2.2	0.5	0.3	0.0	0.5	1.0	97.5	2.2	0.2	0.1	0.3
Grundy	0.7	99.0	0.2	0.9	0.2	0.0	0.4	1.0	99.5	0.1	0.2	0.0	0.5
Hamblen	1.0	91.6	4.5	0.6	0.7	0.1	3.6	5.7	94.9	4.6	0.2	0.3	0.3
Hamilton	1.1	77.3	20.6	0.7	1.5	0.1	1.1	1.8	79.6	19.1	0.2	0.9	0.7
Hancock	0.9	98.8	0.6	0.9	0.1	0.0	0.5	0.4	97.9	1.8	0.3	0.0	0.5
Hardeman	0.8	57.9	41.3	0.7	0.4	0.1	0.4	1.0	62.2	37.4	0.1	0.3	0.7
Hardin	0.7	95.5	3.9	0.6	0.2	0.0	0.4	1.0	95.2	4.4	0.2	0.2	0.4
Hawkins	0.6	97.8	1.7	0.5	0.3	0.0	0.3	0.8	98.0	1.7	0.2	0.1	0.3
Haywood	0.6	47.2	51.3	0.3	0.2	0.1	1.6	2.6	49.8	49.7	0.1	0.1	0.8
Henderson	0.9	91.4	8.4	0.6	0.2	0.0	0.4	1.0	91.5	8.3	0.1	0.1	0.5
Henry	0.9	90.1	9.3	0.6	0.4	0.0	0.5	1.0	89.5	10.1	0.2	0.2	0.4
Hickman	0.9	94.6	4.7	1.1	0.2	0.0	0.4	1.0	94.5	5.1	0.2	0.0	0.4
Houston	1.0	95.5	3.6	0.7	0.2	0.1	0.8	1.2	95.8	3.8	0.2	0.1	0.6
Humphreys	0.8	96.3	3.1	0.7	0.4	0.1	0.4	0.8	96.1	3.5	0.2	0.2	0.4
Jackson	0.7	99.3	0.2	0.8	0.1	0.1	0.2	0.8	99.5	0.1	0.2	0.2	0.4
Jefferson	0.8	96.4	2.6	0.7	0.3	0.1	0.7	1.3	96.7	2.8	0.2	0.1	0.3
Johnson	0.5	96.8	2.4	0.6	0.2	0.1	0.3	0.9	99.3	0.4	0.1	0.1	0.2
Knox	1.2	89.2	9.0	0.7	1.5	0.1	0.8	1.3	89.8	8.8	0.2	1.0	0.6
Lake	1.0	67.3	31.6	0.9	0.4	0.1	0.9	1.4	76.0	23.9	0.1	0.0	0.4
Lauderdale	0.8	64.4	34.5	1.0	0.2	0.0	0.7	1.2	68.1	31.1	0.5	0.1	0.8
Lawrence	0.7	97.5	1.7	0.7	0.3	0.1	0.5	1.0	98.2	1.4	0.2	0.2	0.4
Lewis	0.8	97.8	1.6	0.6	0.3	0.0	0.5	1.2	98.2	1.3	0.3	0.1	0.6
Lincoln	1.2	91.4	7.8	1.2	0.4	0.1	0.4	1.0	90.9	8.6	0.1	0.2	0.5
Loudon	1.0	96.8	1.3	0.9	0.4	0.0	1.6	2.3	98.3	1.3	0.2	0.2	0.3
McMinn	1.1	93.7	4.8	0.8	0.8	0.1	0.9	1.8	94.6	4.8	0.2	0.3	0.4
McNairy	1.0	93.1	6.5	0.7	0.2	0.1	0.4	0.9	93.3	6.4	0.1	0.2	0.4
Macon	0.4	98.3	0.3	0.7	0.3	0.1	0.8	1.7	99.4	0.3	0.2	0.1	0.2
Madison	0.9	65.9	32.8	0.5	0.8	0.0	0.9	1.7	68.5	31.0	0.1	0.3	0.5
Marion	0.8	95.1	4.3	0.7	0.3	0.0	0.4	0.7	95.5	4.2	0.1	0.1	0.3

[1] Hispanic persons may be of any race.

Table B. States and Counties

STATE County	Under 5 years	5 to 17 years	18 to 24 years	25 to 34 years	35 to 44 years	45 to 54 years	55 to 64 years	65 to 74 years	75 years and over	Median age (years)	Percent Female
	28	29	30	31	32	33	34	35	36	37	38
SOUTH DAKOTA— Cont'd											
Tripp	6.3	21.4	6.2	9.4	15.0	12.5	9.4	9.2	10.5	39.5	50.7
Turner	5.7	20.1	6.2	9.9	14.9	13.6	9.2	9.1	11.4	40.5	50.7
Union	6.9	20.1	7.3	12.7	15.7	15.0	8.7	6.8	6.7	36.9	50.2
Walworth	6.3	17.8	6.5	9.0	13.4	13.5	11.5	11.0	10.9	42.8	51.5
Yankton	6.3	19.4	8.7	12.5	16.6	13.6	8.4	7.0	7.6	37.0	49.5
Ziebach	10.8	29.9	10.8	11.1	13.6	9.5	6.9	4.7	2.7	23.8	50.8
TENNESSEE	6.6	18.0	9.6	14.3	15.9	13.8	9.4	6.7	5.6	35.9	51.3
Anderson	5.6	17.6	7.5	12.1	15.2	14.9	10.6	8.4	8.2	39.9	52.3
Bedford	7.4	18.4	9.9	14.5	15.2	12.7	9.3	6.8	5.9	34.9	50.4
Benton	5.2	16.8	7.0	11.6	14.6	14.4	12.7	9.7	8.0	41.6	51.6
Bledsoe	5.9	17.2	8.4	14.3	17.0	15.0	10.7	6.8	4.6	37.4	45.2
Blount	5.8	17.0	8.3	13.4	15.9	14.8	10.6	7.4	6.7	38.4	51.6
Bradley	6.6	17.1	11.3	14.2	15.6	13.5	10.1	6.8	5.0	35.5	51.2
Campbell	5.9	17.0	8.5	13.7	14.3	13.9	11.6	8.5	6.6	38.3	51.8
Cannon	6.7	18.7	8.3	13.4	15.5	13.1	10.6	7.7	6.0	36.8	51.0
Carroll	5.9	17.3	8.4	12.5	14.2	13.4	10.9	8.8	8.5	39.0	52.0
Carter	5.6	15.8	9.2	14.1	15.0	14.2	11.2	8.0	7.0	38.5	51.4
Cheatham	7.1	20.5	7.3	14.5	19.0	14.4	8.6	5.1	3.5	35.3	49.9
Chester	6.7	17.5	14.4	12.4	14.0	12.5	8.9	7.2	6.4	34.1	51.4
Claiborne	5.7	17.9	8.9	13.7	15.0	14.6	10.8	7.5	6.0	37.4	51.7
Clay	5.1	16.4	7.9	12.5	14.9	14.6	12.9	8.6	7.0	39.9	51.4
Cocke	5.9	16.9	8.3	13.4	15.4	15.0	11.4	8.1	5.5	38.6	51.4
Coffee	6.6	18.5	8.3	12.8	15.6	13.1	10.4	8.2	6.4	37.5	51.3
Crockett	6.4	18.7	8.1	13.0	15.3	12.4	10.3	7.4	8.4	37.4	51.7
Cumberland	5.5	15.9	6.7	11.5	13.6	12.7	13.5	12.7	7.9	42.5	51.4
Davidson	6.6	15.6	11.6	17.6	16.4	13.2	7.9	5.9	5.3	34.1	51.6
Decatur	5.6	16.1	7.9	12.1	13.8	13.9	12.5	9.6	8.6	41.2	51.4
De Kalb	6.1	17.2	8.5	13.8	15.6	13.9	10.7	7.8	6.5	37.7	50.6
Dickson	6.9	19.7	8.1	14.2	16.5	13.4	9.5	6.5	5.2	35.7	51.0
Dyer	6.6	19.1	8.7	13.3	15.4	13.9	9.6	6.9	6.5	36.5	52.1
Fayette	6.7	19.0	8.2	11.3	16.1	14.9	10.7	7.3	5.7	38.1	50.9
Fentress	6.2	18.0	8.0	13.4	14.7	14.4	11.7	7.6	6.0	38.0	51.0
Franklin	6.0	17.1	10.9	11.6	14.9	13.8	10.6	8.6	6.6	38.1	51.3
Gibson	6.2	17.7	8.1	12.2	14.7	13.3	10.0	8.8	8.9	38.8	52.8
Giles	6.2	18.4	8.3	12.4	15.5	13.9	11.0	7.3	7.1	38.0	51.4
Grainger	6.1	16.8	8.2	14.8	15.7	14.5	11.4	7.6	4.9	37.7	50.2
Greene	5.8	16.5	8.1	13.6	15.1	14.5	11.6	8.5	6.3	38.9	51.3
Grundy	6.8	18.3	9.0	13.5	14.3	13.0	11.1	7.3	6.7	36.6	50.9
Hamblen	6.6	16.7	8.9	14.5	15.1	13.8	11.1	7.7	5.6	37.1	50.7
Hamilton	6.0	17.2	9.6	13.6	15.5	14.8	9.6	7.4	6.5	37.4	52.2
Hancock	5.3	17.8	8.8	12.2	14.8	14.5	11.0	8.6	7.1	39.2	51.3
Hardeman	5.9	18.0	9.8	14.6	16.7	13.6	8.7	6.8	5.8	36.0	46.1
Hardin	5.9	17.2	7.9	12.4	14.2	14.5	11.9	9.0	7.1	39.8	50.8
Hawkins	6.2	17.1	7.5	14.7	15.3	14.5	11.4	7.4	5.8	37.8	51.4
Haywood	7.2	20.0	9.8	12.7	14.6	13.6	8.3	7.2	6.6	35.3	53.3
Henderson	6.5	17.9	8.7	13.3	15.5	13.9	10.0	7.9	6.3	37.3	51.8
Henry	5.7	16.5	7.6	11.6	14.6	13.9	11.8	9.8	8.4	40.9	51.5
Hickman	6.5	18.1	8.5	14.6	16.5	13.8	10.1	6.6	5.4	36.3	47.1
Houston	6.7	17.7	7.3	12.4	13.6	13.8	11.8	9.0	7.7	39.5	50.6
Humphreys	6.0	17.9	7.6	12.5	15.0	14.4	11.8	8.5	6.3	39.0	50.8
Jackson	5.7	16.5	7.8	12.9	15.2	15.0	11.8	8.3	6.6	39.8	50.6
Jefferson	6.1	16.7	10.6	13.9	15.2	13.3	11.2	7.5	5.4	36.5	50.6
Johnson	4.9	14.8	7.4	14.6	16.2	14.7	12.4	8.1	6.9	40.0	46.6
Knox	6.1	16.2	11.6	14.4	15.9	14.1	9.0	6.8	5.9	36.0	51.7
Lake	5.0	12.7	13.7	17.2	16.6	12.5	9.0	6.7	6.6	35.8	39.8
Lauderdale	6.8	18.0	10.3	15.1	16.0	12.8	9.0	6.0	6.0	34.9	48.1
Lawrence	6.7	19.5	8.4	13.5	14.5	12.8	10.2	7.7	6.6	36.2	51.5
Lewis	6.5	19.3	8.3	12.2	15.2	14.3	10.5	7.5	6.1	37.3	50.8
Lincoln	6.1	17.8	8.0	12.1	15.6	14.0	10.9	8.4	7.2	38.9	51.6
Loudon	5.8	16.1	6.7	12.6	14.9	14.6	13.1	9.5	6.7	41.0	51.3
McMinn	6.3	17.6	8.4	13.3	15.3	13.9	10.9	7.8	6.5	37.9	51.7
McNairy	6.2	17.5	8.1	12.3	14.4	13.9	11.6	8.8	7.2	39.1	51.5
Macon	7.1	19.0	8.5	14.6	14.8	13.4	10.0	6.8	5.9	35.5	50.6
Madison	6.9	18.9	11.0	13.5	15.6	13.5	8.3	6.3	6.0	34.7	52.1
Marion	5.9	17.8	8.5	13.0	15.6	15.1	11.2	7.6	5.3	38.2	51.1

Table B. States and Counties

	Population and population characteristics, 1990										Population—change, 1980–2000				
	Age (percent)										Total persons			Percent change	
STATE County	Under 5 years	5 to 17 years	18 to 24 years	25 to 34 years	35 to 44 years	45 to 54 years	55 to 64 years	65 to 74 years	75 years and over	Percent Female	2000	1990	1980	1990–2000	1980–1990
	39	40	41	42	43	44	45	46	47	48	49	50	51	52	53
SOUTH DAKOTA— Cont'd															
Tripp	8.0	22.1	6.3	14.2	12.4	9.8	10.0	9.8	7.4	50.1	6 430	6 924	7 268	-7.1	-4.7
Turner	6.3	20.4	5.3	12.4	13.0	9.3	10.8	10.9	11.6	50.9	8 849	8 576	9 255	3.2	-7.3
Union	7.1	22.1	6.8	13.9	14.8	9.2	9.4	9.0	7.6	50.7	12 584	10 189	10 938	23.5	-6.8
Walworth	6.5	19.4	5.7	12.0	12.7	11.1	11.7	10.6	10.3	51.7	5 974	6 087	7 011	-1.9	-13.2
Yankton	7.4	19.1	9.3	16.9	14.1	9.8	8.5	7.7	7.3	51.0	21 652	19 252	18 952	12.5	1.6
Ziebach	11.9	30.6	8.2	15.5	10.1	8.0	7.9	5.0	2.8	50.0	2 519	2 220	2 308	13.5	-3.8
TENNESSEE	6.8	18.1	10.8	16.7	15.2	10.8	8.9	7.3	5.4	51.8	5 689 283	4 877 203	4 591 023	16.7	6.2
Anderson	6.2	17.8	8.7	15.0	15.3	11.4	10.3	9.4	5.9	52.3	71 330	68 250	67 346	4.5	1.3
Bedford	6.7	18.7	9.6	15.2	14.1	11.1	9.7	8.4	6.5	51.5	37 586	30 411	27 916	23.6	8.9
Benton	5.6	17.4	8.6	13.7	13.8	11.8	11.3	10.1	7.7	52.6	16 537	14 524	14 901	13.9	-2.5
Bledsoe	5.9	18.6	9.9	17.2	16.0	11.3	9.0	7.0	5.0	45.6	12 367	9 669	9 478	27.9	2.0
Blount	6.1	16.7	9.8	15.6	15.9	11.8	9.3	8.7	6.0	52.0	105 823	85 962	77 770	23.1	10.5
Bradley	6.4	18.4	11.8	16.5	15.1	11.8	9.0	6.5	4.5	51.8	87 965	73 712	67 547	19.3	9.1
Campbell	6.3	19.3	10.0	14.3	14.2	11.6	9.6	8.5	6.3	52.3	39 854	35 079	34 923	13.6	0.4
Cannon	6.3	18.9	9.4	14.8	13.6	11.3	10.4	8.4	6.8	51.2	12 826	10 467	10 234	22.5	2.3
Carroll	6.2	17.5	9.5	13.7	13.4	11.2	10.4	9.9	8.1	51.9	29 475	27 514	28 285	7.1	-2.7
Carter	5.7	16.4	11.0	15.1	14.7	11.9	9.9	8.7	6.5	51.7	56 742	51 505	50 205	10.2	2.6
Cheatham	7.7	20.3	8.9	18.6	16.9	11.4	7.8	5.0	3.4	50.0	35 912	27 140	21 616	32.3	25.6
Chester	6.4	17.1	15.9	13.6	13.1	10.0	8.9	8.2	6.8	52.2	15 540	12 819	12 727	21.2	0.7
Claiborne	6.2	19.4	11.1	14.9	15.2	11.2	9.1	7.7	5.3	51.5	29 862	26 137	24 595	14.3	6.3
Clay	5.4	17.7	9.5	14.4	14.0	12.4	10.3	9.2	7.0	50.7	7 976	7 238	7 676	10.2	-5.7
Cocke	5.9	18.1	10.2	15.5	15.1	12.0	10.3	7.3	5.6	51.8	33 565	29 141	28 792	15.2	1.2
Coffee	6.9	18.9	9.0	15.3	14.1	11.5	10.5	8.4	5.5	51.8	48 014	40 343	38 311	19.0	5.3
Crockett	6.3	18.1	8.6	15.2	12.9	11.1	8.8	9.9	9.1	52.4	14 532	13 378	14 941	8.6	-10.5
Cumberland	6.1	17.3	8.9	14.4	13.4	10.9	11.5	10.8	6.8	51.6	46 802	34 736	28 676	34.7	21.1
Davidson	7.0	15.8	11.7	20.4	15.5	9.8	8.2	6.6	5.0	52.5	569 891	510 786	477 811	11.6	6.9
Decatur	5.2	17.7	8.9	13.3	13.5	11.9	10.6	10.4	8.5	51.8	11 731	10 472	10 857	12.0	-3.5
De Kalb	6.1	18.1	9.3	14.3	14.1	11.8	10.4	9.0	6.8	52.3	17 423	14 360	13 589	21.3	5.7
Dickson	7.4	19.9	9.8	16.2	14.4	11.0	8.8	6.9	5.6	51.4	43 156	35 061	30 037	23.1	16.7
Dyer	6.7	18.9	9.9	15.5	14.6	10.9	8.6	8.0	6.9	52.6	37 279	34 854	34 663	7.0	0.6
Fayette	7.8	22.1	9.2	15.2	13.8	10.3	8.7	7.1	5.8	51.3	28 806	25 559	25 305	12.7	1.0
Fentress	6.1	20.0	10.2	14.3	15.1	11.7	9.2	7.9	5.6	51.1	16 625	14 669	14 826	13.3	-1.1
Franklin	6.3	18.3	10.8	14.5	14.3	11.3	10.1	8.3	6.1	50.8	39 270	34 923	31 983	12.4	8.6
Gibson	6.2	17.7	9.1	14.3	13.3	10.7	10.4	10.0	8.3	53.1	48 152	46 315	49 467	4.0	-6.4
Giles	6.7	18.3	9.9	14.3	13.8	11.7	9.2	9.0	7.1	51.7	29 447	25 741	24 625	14.4	4.5
Grainger	6.0	18.4	10.5	15.6	14.6	12.2	9.8	7.3	5.6	50.4	20 659	17 095	16 751	20.8	2.1
Greene	5.7	17.2	9.9	15.1	15.1	12.5	10.7	8.0	5.8	51.6	62 909	55 832	54 422	12.7	2.6
Grundy	6.4	21.4	10.0	14.0	13.5	11.7	8.6	8.2	6.1	51.7	14 332	13 362	13 787	7.3	-3.1
Hamblen	6.2	17.8	10.4	15.5	15.1	13.0	10.1	7.4	4.6	51.8	58 128	50 480	49 300	15.2	2.4
Hamilton	6.6	17.5	10.3	16.0	15.6	10.9	9.6	7.7	5.8	52.8	307 896	285 536	287 643	7.8	-0.7
Hancock	6.1	19.1	9.6	15.0	13.3	11.0	10.1	9.1	6.6	50.7	6 786	6 739	6 887	0.7	-2.1
Hardeman	7.6	20.7	9.6	15.3	13.8	9.6	9.1	7.9	6.4	51.9	28 105	23 377	23 873	20.2	-2.1
Hardin	6.3	18.6	9.3	13.8	14.3	11.5	10.6	8.7	6.9	51.7	25 578	22 633	22 280	13.0	1.6
Hawkins	6.0	17.8	9.9	15.7	15.3	12.5	9.5	7.7	5.5	51.2	53 563	44 565	43 751	20.2	1.9
Haywood	7.0	22.0	9.5	14.8	13.7	8.9	8.6	8.0	7.5	53.2	19 797	19 437	20 318	1.9	-4.3
Henderson	6.2	18.8	9.1	15.0	14.4	11.0	10.4	8.6	6.5	51.9	25 522	21 844	21 390	16.8	2.1
Henry	5.7	17.1	8.1	13.6	13.3	11.2	11.3	11.1	8.5	52.1	31 115	27 888	28 656	11.6	-2.7
Hickman	6.3	17.6	9.2	16.8	15.2	11.4	9.3	8.4	5.5	48.5	22 295	16 754	15 151	33.1	10.6
Houston	6.0	18.1	8.7	13.4	13.6	11.6	10.9	9.9	7.9	51.5	8 088	7 018	6 871	15.2	2.1
Humphreys	6.3	18.9	8.7	14.1	14.5	12.2	10.8	8.7	5.8	50.9	17 929	15 813	15 957	13.4	-0.9
Jackson	5.6	17.2	9.2	14.0	14.7	11.5	10.7	9.6	7.6	51.3	10 984	9 297	9 398	18.1	-1.1
Jefferson	5.4	16.5	13.0	14.5	14.1	12.7	10.4	7.9	5.4	51.1	44 294	33 016	31 284	34.2	5.5
Johnson	5.7	17.5	9.3	13.8	14.6	12.5	10.1	9.1	7.4	50.4	17 499	13 766	13 745	27.1	0.2
Knox	6.4	16.0	12.7	17.3	15.5	10.5	8.9	7.4	5.3	52.2	382 032	335 749	319 694	13.8	5.0
Lake	5.6	16.4	12.3	17.2	14.6	10.2	9.0	7.8	7.0	46.6	7 954	7 129	7 455	11.6	-4.4
Lauderdale	7.2	20.1	9.9	16.4	13.3	10.0	8.1	8.0	7.0	51.6	27 101	23 491	24 555	15.4	-4.3
Lawrence	7.2	18.9	10.0	15.1	13.3	11.2	9.6	8.4	6.3	52.0	39 926	35 303	34 110	13.1	3.5
Lewis	6.7	20.1	9.3	14.5	14.2	10.5	9.6	8.4	6.7	51.1	11 367	9 247	9 700	22.9	-4.7
Lincoln	6.6	18.2	9.4	15.1	13.8	11.4	10.1	8.9	6.6	51.8	31 340	28 157	26 483	11.3	6.3
Loudon	6.2	17.2	9.2	15.2	15.2	12.0	10.4	8.7	5.9	51.8	39 086	31 255	28 553	25.1	9.5
McMinn	6.1	18.4	9.9	15.2	14.4	11.9	9.8	8.3	6.1	52.3	49 015	42 383	41 878	15.6	1.2
McNairy	5.9	18.6	8.4	14.1	14.2	12.1	10.5	8.8	7.3	51.7	24 653	22 422	22 525	10.0	-0.5
Macon	6.8	18.5	10.1	15.4	14.3	11.1	9.4	8.6	5.9	51.4	20 386	15 906	15 700	28.2	1.3
Madison	7.1	19.0	11.1	16.2	14.8	9.6	8.4	7.5	6.3	52.9	91 837	77 982	74 546	17.8	4.6
Marion	6.6	19.6	9.6	15.5	15.1	11.7	9.5	7.0	5.2	51.3	27 776	24 683	24 416	12.5	1.8

Table B. States and Counties

STATE County	Total population	Total in house-holds	House-holder	Spouse	Child Total	Own child under 18 years	Other relatives Total	Under 18 years	Nonrelatives Total	Unmarried partner	Total in group quarters	Correctional institutions	Nursing homes	Other institutions	College dormitories	Military quarters	Other
	Household relationship, 2000																
		In households (percent)			Child		Other relatives		Nonrelatives		In group quarters (percent)	Institutionalized population			Noninstitutionalized population		
	54	55	56	57	58	59	60	61	62	63	64	65	66	67	68	69	70
SOUTH DAKOTA—Cont'd																	
Tripp	6 430	98.5	39.7	22.6	29.4	24.9	3.7	2.0	3.2	1.7	1.5	0.0	1.2	0.2	0.0	0.0	0.1
Turner	8 849	97.7	39.7	24.5	29.4	24.6	1.8	0.7	2.4	1.3	2.3	0.0	2.3	0.0	0.0	0.0	0.0
Union	12 584	99.0	39.2	24.3	30.6	25.9	1.5	0.6	3.5	1.7	1.0	0.2	0.8	0.0	0.0	0.0	0.0
Walworth	5 974	97.1	41.9	22.4	26.7	22.0	2.9	1.5	3.1	1.6	2.9	0.2	2.7	0.0	0.0	0.0	0.1
Yankton	21 652	92.0	37.8	20.6	28.5	24.5	1.7	0.6	3.5	1.7	8.0	4.0	0.9	1.0	1.0	0.0	1.1
Ziebach	2 519	100.0	29.4	14.1	41.3	32.4	10.8	7.8	4.4	2.9	0.0	0.0	0.0	0.0	0.0	0.0	0.0
TENNESSEE	5 689 283	97.4	39.2	20.6	28.3	21.8	5.0	2.2	4.1	1.7	2.6	0.7	0.7	0.1	0.8	0.0	0.3
Anderson	71 330	98.8	41.7	22.5	27.6	21.1	4.0	1.7	3.0	1.5	1.2	0.1	0.9	0.0	0.0	0.0	0.2
Bedford	37 586	98.6	37.0	21.2	29.1	22.5	6.4	2.4	5.0	1.8	1.4	0.3	0.7	0.0	0.0	0.0	0.4
Benton	16 537	98.3	41.5	24.1	25.2	19.4	4.6	2.2	3.0	1.5	1.7	0.3	1.0	0.0	0.0	0.0	0.3
Bledsoe	12 367	90.5	35.8	22.0	25.6	19.7	4.4	2.2	2.7	1.5	9.5	7.9	0.3	1.1	0.0	0.0	0.1
Blount	105 823	98.0	40.3	23.6	27.0	20.6	3.9	1.6	3.2	1.4	2.0	0.3	0.6	0.2	0.6	0.0	0.2
Bradley	87 965	97.5	39.0	22.3	27.6	21.2	4.5	1.9	4.0	1.4	2.5	0.1	0.5	0.1	1.6	0.0	0.2
Campbell	39 854	98.7	40.5	22.4	28.0	20.4	5.0	2.1	2.9	1.6	1.3	0.2	0.9	0.0	0.0	0.0	0.1
Cannon	12 826	98.7	39.0	22.9	29.4	23.0	4.2	1.9	3.2	1.6	1.3	0.4	0.8	0.0	0.0	0.0	0.1
Carroll	29 475	96.9	40.0	22.5	27.3	20.6	4.4	2.1	2.8	1.4	3.1	0.2	1.5	0.0	0.8	0.0	0.6
Carter	56 742	97.4	41.4	22.7	26.1	19.3	4.0	1.5	3.3	1.6	2.6	0.6	0.9	0.0	0.9	0.0	0.1
Cheatham	35 912	98.9	35.9	23.3	31.1	24.9	4.6	2.2	4.0	1.8	1.1	0.3	0.7	0.1	0.0	0.0	0.1
Chester	15 540	92.8	36.4	21.5	27.4	21.5	4.4	2.1	3.1	1.3	7.2	0.2	0.9	0.0	6.0	0.0	0.2
Claiborne	29 862	97.8	39.5	23.2	28.1	21.2	4.2	1.7	2.8	1.6	2.2	0.2	0.7	0.3	0.0	0.0	1.0
Clay	7 976	98.9	42.4	23.2	25.9	19.4	3.7	1.5	3.7	2.1	1.1	0.1	0.8	0.1	0.0	0.0	0.1
Cocke	33 565	98.9	41.0	21.8	27.0	19.8	5.4	2.4	3.8	1.9	1.1	0.4	0.6	0.0	0.0	0.0	0.1
Coffee	48 014	98.4	39.3	22.4	28.6	22.6	4.3	1.9	3.7	1.7	1.6	0.3	0.6	0.0	0.0	0.1	0.6
Crockett	14 532	97.9	38.8	21.9	28.5	22.1	5.9	2.5	3.0	1.4	2.1	0.4	1.7	0.0	0.0	0.0	0.0
Cumberland	46 802	98.8	41.7	25.7	24.6	19.3	3.8	1.7	3.1	1.6	1.2	0.3	0.7	0.0	0.0	0.0	0.2
Davidson	569 891	95.8	41.7	16.6	25.1	19.3	5.7	2.3	6.6	2.2	4.2	1.0	0.4	0.4	2.0	0.0	0.4
Decatur	11 731	98.0	41.8	23.7	25.5	19.5	3.7	1.8	3.2	1.6	2.0	0.1	1.9	0.0	0.0	0.0	0.0
De Kalb	17 423	98.2	40.1	22.5	27.0	20.5	4.9	2.1	3.8	1.6	1.8	0.2	0.7	0.0	0.2	0.0	0.7
Dickson	43 156	98.8	38.2	22.3	30.5	24.0	4.2	1.8	3.6	1.7	1.2	0.4	0.6	0.1	0.0	0.0	0.1
Dyer	37 279	98.4	39.6	21.1	29.0	22.7	5.1	2.5	3.6	1.6	1.6	0.4	0.9	0.0	0.0	0.0	0.3
Fayette	28 806	98.6	36.3	21.2	29.7	20.6	8.7	4.2	2.7	1.3	1.4	0.3	0.5	0.5	0.0	0.0	0.0
Fentress	16 625	99.1	40.3	23.0	29.2	22.1	4.0	1.7	2.5	1.4	0.9	0.1	0.8	0.0	0.0	0.0	0.1
Franklin	39 270	95.8	38.2	22.9	27.3	20.5	4.4	2.1	2.9	1.3	4.2	0.2	0.6	0.0	3.3	0.0	0.2
Gibson	48 152	97.8	40.5	21.2	27.9	21.0	5.2	2.5	2.9	1.5	2.2	0.2	1.9	0.0	0.0	0.0	0.1
Giles	29 447	98.1	39.8	22.2	28.8	21.8	4.5	2.1	2.8	1.5	1.9	0.3	0.9	0.0	0.6	0.0	0.1
Grainger	20 659	99.1	40.0	24.8	27.6	20.6	4.0	1.7	2.8	1.5	0.9	0.1	0.6	0.0	0.0	0.0	0.1
Greene	62 909	97.4	40.9	22.8	26.0	19.8	4.2	1.8	3.5	1.8	2.6	0.3	0.8	0.6	0.5	0.0	0.4
Grundy	14 332	98.6	38.8	22.0	29.6	22.0	5.3	2.6	2.9	1.6	1.4	0.2	0.8	0.0	0.0	0.0	0.4
Hamblen	58 128	98.6	39.9	22.4	26.8	20.4	5.3	2.2	4.2	1.6	1.4	0.3	0.8	0.0	0.0	0.0	0.2
Hamilton	307 896	97.5	40.4	20.3	27.4	20.4	5.3	2.3	4.0	1.6	2.5	0.3	0.6	0.2	1.0	0.0	0.5
Hancock	6 786	97.6	40.8	22.5	28.2	21.2	3.7	1.2	2.4	1.2	2.4	1.7	0.7	0.0	0.0	0.0	0.0
Hardeman	28 105	85.9	33.5	16.7	26.3	19.3	6.6	3.8	2.8	1.3	14.1	12.2	0.7	0.8	0.0	0.0	0.4
Hardin	25 578	98.2	40.8	23.4	27.0	20.6	4.2	1.9	2.9	1.6	1.8	0.1	1.4	0.1	0.0	0.0	0.3
Hawkins	53 563	99.1	41.0	24.3	27.4	21.3	3.7	1.5	2.8	1.5	0.9	0.1	0.8	0.0	0.0	0.0	0.0
Haywood	19 797	98.7	38.2	17.5	31.5	22.4	8.3	4.1	3.3	1.6	1.3	0.3	0.8	0.0	0.0	0.0	0.1
Henderson	25 522	98.6	40.4	23.0	28.2	21.7	4.2	2.1	2.8	1.5	1.4	0.3	0.7	0.1	0.0	0.0	0.3
Henry	31 115	98.3	41.8	22.8	25.8	19.7	4.1	1.9	3.8	1.8	1.7	0.4	1.0	0.0	0.0	0.0	0.3
Hickman	22 295	93.8	36.2	21.5	28.4	22.1	4.0	1.8	3.6	1.9	6.2	5.2	0.7	0.3	0.0	0.0	0.1
Houston	8 088	97.7	39.8	22.7	27.9	21.9	4.0	1.9	3.3	1.7	2.3	0.2	2.0	0.0	0.0	0.0	0.2
Humphreys	17 929	98.7	40.4	23.1	27.4	21.3	4.0	1.8	3.8	2.0	1.3	0.2	0.8	0.0	0.0	0.0	0.3
Jackson	10 984	98.8	40.7	22.5	26.9	19.9	4.8	1.7	4.0	2.2	1.2	0.1	1.1	0.0	0.0	0.0	0.0
Jefferson	44 294	96.2	38.7	23.2	26.5	20.4	4.2	1.7	3.6	1.5	3.8	0.2	0.9	0.3	2.3	0.0	0.0
Johnson	17 499	91.5	39.0	21.6	23.0	17.1	4.7	2.0	3.2	1.7	8.5	7.7	0.7	0.0	0.0	0.0	0.1
Knox	382 032	96.6	41.3	20.6	26.0	20.3	3.9	1.5	4.8	1.6	3.4	0.2	0.6	0.2	2.0	0.0	0.4
Lake	7 954	71.4	30.3	14.3	20.1	14.8	4.7	2.4	2.0	1.1	28.6	26.6	2.1	0.0	0.0	0.0	0.0
Lauderdale	27 101	90.1	35.3	17.5	27.5	20.7	6.6	3.6	3.1	1.6	9.9	9.0	0.8	0.0	0.0	0.0	0.0
Lawrence	39 926	99.1	38.8	22.9	30.7	23.9	3.8	1.8	2.9	1.4	0.9	0.1	0.8	0.0	0.0	0.0	0.0
Lewis	11 367	98.0	38.5	22.7	29.0	22.6	4.3	2.1	3.4	1.8	2.0	0.3	1.1	0.6	0.0	0.0	0.1
Lincoln	31 340	98.5	39.9	23.2	28.4	21.7	4.2	1.8	2.8	1.3	1.5	0.3	0.9	0.0	0.0	0.0	0.3
Loudon	39 086	98.9	40.8	25.2	25.8	19.8	4.2	1.7	3.0	1.3	1.1	0.1	0.9	0.0	0.0	0.0	0.1
McMinn	49 015	98.5	40.2	23.6	27.6	21.4	4.3	2.0	2.8	1.2	1.5	0.2	0.8	0.0	0.3	0.0	0.1
McNairy	24 653	97.9	40.5	23.5	27.0	20.9	4.1	1.9	2.7	1.4	2.1	0.3	1.1	0.0	0.0	0.0	0.7
Macon	20 386	99.0	38.8	23.6	29.5	23.7	3.9	1.8	3.2	1.6	1.0	0.2	0.8	0.0	0.0	0.0	0.0
Madison	91 837	96.4	38.7	19.3	29.4	22.8	5.1	2.4	3.9	1.6	3.6	0.4	1.0	0.0	1.9	0.0	0.3
Marion	27 776	99.1	39.7	23.0	28.2	20.5	5.3	2.6	2.9	1.5	0.9	0.3	0.5	0.0	0.0	0.0	0.1

Table B. States and Counties

STATE County	Total households	Total	With own children under 18 years	Total	With own children under 18 years	Total	With own children under 18 years	Total	Total	65 years and over	Average house-hold size	Average family size	Total house-holds	Female house-holder[1]	House-holder living alone
	71	72	73	74	75	76	77	78	79	80	81	82	83	84	85
SOUTH DAKOTA— Cont'd															
Tripp	2 550	67.5	30.4	56.9	24.5	6.6	3.9	32.5	29.6	15.7	2.48	3.08	2 573	7.0	25.8
Turner	3 510	70.6	31.6	61.9	26.5	5.6	3.6	29.4	26.5	14.8	2 46	2.99	3 332	4.1	26.1
Union	4 927	71.4	34.8	62.0	28.3	6.3	4.3	28.6	24.2	10.3	2.53	3.02	3 859	6.5	24.8
Walworth	2 506	65.6	26.9	53.4	19.1	8.9	5.8	34.4	31.4	16.4	2.31	2.89	2 447	7.0	27.4
Yankton	8 187	66.0	33.0	54.4	25.1	8.3	5.9	34.0	29.3	12.0	2.43	3.03	7 107	7.8	28.3
Ziebach	741	80.2	47.2	47.9	25.1	23.8	17.0	19.8	17.4	5.1	3.40	3.81	630	17.1	20.6
TENNESSEE	2 232 905	69.3	31.7	52.6	22.4	12.9	7.4	30.7	25.8	9.0	2.48	2.99	1 853 725	12.6	23.9
Anderson	29 780	68.9	29.6	53.8	21.2	11.5	6.5	31.1	27.7	12.1	2.37	2.88	27 384	10.8	25.2
Bedford	13 905	74.4	34.0	57.3	24.5	11.9	6.8	25.6	21.5	9.2	2.67	3.06	11 608	11.1	21.8
Benton	6 863	71.2	27.3	58.1	20.3	9.5	5.2	28.8	25.7	12.3	2.37	2.82	5 784	8.0	23.3
Bledsoe	4 430	74.8	31.3	61.5	24.2	9.1	4.7	25.2	22.1	9.2	2.53	2.94	3 261	9.2	20.5
Blount	42 667	71.8	30.5	58.4	23.3	10.0	5.5	28.2	24.4	9.5	2.43	2.88	33 624	9.6	22.0
Bradley	34 281	71.9	32.0	57.3	24.0	10.9	6.2	28.1	23.4	8.2	2.50	2.94	27 604	10.3	20.7
Campbell	16 125	71.8	29.8	55.3	21.6	12.6	6.4	28.2	25.4	11.6	2.44	2.91	13 150	12.9	21.2
Cannon	4 998	72.9	33.3	58.6	25.4	9.9	5.5	27.1	24.3	10.9	2.53	2.99	3 980	8.8	21.9
Carroll	11 779	71.3	30.0	56.3	21.9	11.5	6.4	28.7	25.8	12.7	2.42	2.90	10 727	10.2	23.6
Carter	23 486	69.6	28.5	54.9	21.0	11.0	5.8	30.4	26.5	11.0	2.35	2.83	20 189	10.5	23.7
Cheatham	12 878	78.9	39.6	64.9	31.3	9.6	5.5	21.1	16.9	5.3	2.76	3.08	9 515	8.2	16.0
Chester	5 660	74.2	33.6	59.0	25.1	11.5	6.6	25.8	22.6	10.8	2.55	2.97	4 558	9.8	21.1
Claiborne	11 799	73.6	32.0	58.8	24.5	11.0	5.6	26.4	23.4	10.0	2.48	2.91	9 629	10.5	19.8
Clay	3 379	69.0	27.7	54.7	20.1	9.7	5.2	31.0	27.6	12.0	2.33	2.80	2 855	10.5	22.7
Cocke	13 762	70.6	29.5	53.1	20.7	13.0	6.5	29.4	25.7	10.1	2.41	2.87	11 191	13.4	22.1
Coffee	18 885	72.0	32.4	56.9	23.4	11.1	6.7	28.0	24.3	10.3	2.50	2.96	15 500	10.0	22.1
Crockett	5 632	72.2	32.7	56.4	24.4	11.8	6.2	27.8	25.3	11.5	2.53	3.01	5 183	10.9	24.3
Cumberland	19 508	74.4	26.6	61.8	19.5	9.6	5.4	25.6	22.4	10.2	2.37	2.74	13 426	9.4	20.0
Davidson	237 405	58.2	26.7	39.9	16.5	14.3	8.4	41.8	33.4	8.2	2.30	2.96	207 530	14.2	30.3
Decatur	4 908	69.6	27.3	56.7	20.7	9.0	4.6	30.4	27.6	13.4	2.34	2.82	4 216	9.3	24.5
De Kalb	6 984	71.4	30.1	56.1	22.0	11.1	6.1	28.6	25.5	10.7	2.45	2.90	5 696	10.3	22.7
Dickson	16 473	73.9	35.6	58.3	26.2	11.5	7.1	26.1	22.3	8.9	2.59	3.02	13 019	11.6	20.3
Dyer	14 751	70.9	32.9	53.2	22.6	13.6	8.2	29.1	25.3	10.7	2.49	2.97	13 617	12.1	24.7
Fayette	10 467	76.6	31.0	58.5	22.8	14.0	6.6	23.4	20.5	8.6	2.71	3.14	8 453	15.8	18.6
Fentress	6 693	72.0	31.6	57.3	24.3	11.3	5.6	28.0	25.5	11.1	2.46	2.92	5 511	12.1	21.1
Franklin	15 003	74.4	30.9	60.1	23.5	10.4	5.5	25.6	22.6	10.3	2.51	2.92	12 660	9.0	20.0
Gibson	19 518	69.6	30.2	52.2	20.7	13.6	7.6	30.4	27.4	13.7	2.41	2.93	18 361	12.2	24.9
Giles	11 713	71.4	31.4	55.8	23.2	11.9	6.4	28.6	25.7	11.2	2.47	2.96	9 832	11.4	22.6
Grainger	8 270	74.5	31.4	61.9	25.2	8.8	4.3	25.5	22.5	9.1	2.48	2.89	6 394	9.2	19.0
Greene	25 756	70.4	29.2	55.7	21.2	10.8	5.8	29.6	25.8	10.7	2.38	2.84	21 482	10.7	22.1
Grundy	5 562	72.9	33.4	56.6	24.6	12.0	6.7	27.1	24.0	10.2	2.54	3.01	4 784	11.2	20.4
Hamblen	23 211	71.5	30.5	56.1	22.3	11.3	6.2	28.5	24.7	9.6	2.47	2.91	19 429	11.9	21.3
Hamilton	124 444	67.3	28.9	50.2	19.9	13.5	7.4	32.7	27.9	10.0	2.41	2.95	111 799	13.5	26.0
Hancock	2 769	70.0	31.0	55.1	23.5	11.0	5.6	30.0	27.7	13.5	2.39	2.91	2 484	12.9	21.4
Hardeman	9 412	71.9	32.6	50.0	20.7	17.6	10.0	28.1	25.1	11.4	2.56	3.06	8 276	16.4	22.8
Hardin	10 426	71.4	29.7	57.3	22.3	10.1	5.4	28.6	25.5	11.8	2.41	2.87	8 726	10.1	22.2
Hawkins	21 936	72.6	31.3	59.3	23.9	9.8	5.5	27.4	24.4	9.6	2.42	2.86	17 167	9.5	21.2
Haywood	7 558	71.7	33.4	45.8	19.2	22.0	12.5	28.3	25.4	11.1	2.59	3.09	7 014	18.8	24.4
Henderson	10 306	72.3	32.3	56.9	23.5	11.7	6.8	27.7	24.9	10.7	2.44	2.90	8 527	9.6	22.5
Henry	13 019	69.2	27.5	54.4	19.4	11.2	6.4	30.8	27.0	12.8	2.35	2.82	11 362	9.9	25.5
Hickman	8 081	73.7	33.9	59.4	25.9	9.6	5.3	26.3	22.6	9.9	2.59	3.02	5 976	8.8	20.6
Houston	3 216	71.5	31.1	57.0	23.2	10.4	6.0	28.5	25.3	12.1	2.46	2.92	2 683	9.7	22.5
Humphreys	7 238	71.1	30.3	57.3	22.3	10.2	6.1	28.9	25.0	10.6	2.44	2.90	6 063	9.3	22.6
Jackson	4 466	70.3	28.8	55.3	21.3	10.3	4.9	29.7	25.5	10.2	2.43	2.89	3 642	9.2	22.1
Jefferson	17 155	73.5	31.0	59.9	23.6	9.8	5.3	26.5	22.5	8.2	2.49	2.89	12 329	9.3	20.5
Johnson	6 827	69.6	26.4	55.4	19.7	10.0	4.7	30.4	26.4	11.5	2.35	2.81	5 406	11.1	22.8
Knox	157 872	63.8	28.5	49.8	20.8	10.9	6.2	36.2	29.6	9.1	2.34	2.92	133 639	11.6	27.4
Lake	2 410	67.0	28.8	47.2	18.4	16.3	9.0	33.0	30.0	15.5	2.36	2.92	2 418	13.4	25.8
Lauderdale	9 567	71.2	32.8	49.7	20.8	17.6	10.2	28.8	25.6	11.1	2.55	3.06	8 423	14.9	22.5
Lawrence	15 480	73.4	33.7	59.1	25.6	10.6	6.1	26.6	23.7	11.4	2.56	3.02	13 338	9.7	21.6
Lewis	4 381	73.4	33.2	58.9	25.2	10.7	5.9	26.6	23.5	10.6	2.54	2.98	3 533	9.3	24.3
Lincoln	12 503	72.6	31.6	58.2	23.7	10.9	6.1	27.4	24.6	11.6	2.47	2.93	10 881	10.1	22.6
Loudon	15 944	74.0	28.4	61.7	21.8	8.9	4.7	26.0	22.8	10.1	2.42	2.82	12 155	10.7	21.7
McMinn	19 721	72.6	31.4	58.7	23.6	10.6	6.1	27.4	24.4	10.4	2.45	2.90	16 351	10.7	22.0
McNairy	9 980	71.5	29.9	58.0	22.7	9.9	5.3	28.5	25.9	12.5	2.42	2.89	8 834	9.3	22.8
Macon	7 916	73.3	35.0	60.7	27.8	8.8	5.2	26.7	23.8	10.7	2.55	3.00	6 159	8.5	22.9
Madison	35 552	69.3	33.5	49.8	21.9	15.9	9.9	30.7	26.2	9.3	2.49	3.00	29 609	15.2	25.0
Marion	11 037	73.7	31.1	57.9	23.3	11.6	5.7	26.3	23.6	10.2	2.49	2.93	9 215	11.2	20.3

[1] No spouse present.

Table B. States and Counties

STATE County	Percent change of households, 1990-2000	Total housing units	Occupied housing units (percent)	Vacant housing units Total	For seasonal, recreational, or occasional use	Homeowner vacancy rate (percent)	Rental vacancy rate (percent)	Occupied housing units Total	Percent owner-occupied housing units	Percent renter-occupied housing units	Average household size of owner-occupied units	Average household size of renter-occupied units
	86	87	88	89	90	91	92	93	94	95	96	97
SOUTH DAKOTA— Cont'd												
Tripp	-0.9	3 036	84.0	16.0	3.9	1.9	12.4	2 550	74.7	25.3	2.50	2.45
Turner	5.3	3 852	91.1	8.9	2.3	1.5	6.4	3 510	77.5	22.5	2.54	2.19
Union	27.7	5 345	92.2	7.8	1.3	2.7	9.7	4 927	74.4	25.6	2.67	2.13
Walworth	2.4	3 144	79.7	20.3	8.9	5.2	12.1	2 506	71.3	28.7	2.41	2.08
Yankton	15.2	8 840	92.6	7.4	0.9	1.4	9.7	8 187	69.1	30.9	2.65	1.94
Ziebach	17.6	879	84.3	15.7	2.7	2.0	6.2	741	59.4	40.6	3.31	3.52
TENNESSEE	20.5	2 439 443	91.5	8.5	1.5	2.0	8.8	2 232 905	69.9	30.1	2.57	2.29
Anderson	8.7	32 451	91.8	8.2	0.6	1.9	12.8	29 780	72.5	27.5	2.44	2.17
Bedford	19.8	14 990	92.8	7.2	1.6	1.3	5.9	13 905	73.5	26.5	2.62	2.80
Benton	18.7	8 595	79.8	20.2	9.3	3.2	13.9	6 863	80.5	19.5	2.38	2.33
Bledsoe	35.8	5 142	86.2	13.8	4.6	1.4	9.5	4 430	81.8	18.2	2.56	2.38
Blount	26.9	47 059	90.7	9.3	2.4	2.2	10.1	42 667	75.9	24.1	2.49	2.23
Bradley	24.2	36 820	93.1	6.9	0.4	1.5	9.6	34 281	68.6	31.4	2.59	2.32
Campbell	22.6	18 527	87.0	13.0	5.5	2.4	9.4	16 125	73.4	26.6	2.50	2.26
Cannon	25.6	5 420	92.2	7.8	0.6	1.3	8.1	4 998	78.6	21.4	2.57	2.41
Carroll	9.8	13 057	90.2	9.8	0.9	2.1	10.7	11 779	78.9	21.1	2.42	2.45
Carter	16.3	25 920	90.6	9.4	1.8	1.6	9.9	23 486	74.9	25.1	2.40	2.23
Cheatham	35.3	13 508	95.3	4.7	0.5	1.2	5.8	12 878	83.7	16.3	2.78	2.64
Chester	24.2	6 178	91.6	8.4	1.4	1.4	8.3	5 660	77.3	22.7	2.59	2.39
Claiborne	22.5	13 262	89.0	11.0	1.9	1.8	10.0	11 799	78.6	21.4	2.52	2.31
Clay	18.4	3 959	85.3	14.7	6.5	2.5	10.5	3 379	80.1	19.9	2.36	2.22
Cocke	23.0	15 844	86.9	13.1	3.4	1.6	11.2	13 762	75.5	24.5	2.47	2.24
Coffee	21.8	20 746	91.0	9.0	2.0	1.9	9.1	18 885	71.5	28.5	2.55	2.39
Crockett	8.7	6 138	91.8	8.2	0.6	1.4	9.5	5 632	74.9	25.1	2.47	2.70
Cumberland	45.3	22 442	86.9	13.1	6.3	2.5	11.1	19 508	80.6	19.4	2.38	2.33
Davidson	14.4	252 977	93.8	6.2	0.4	2.0	6.5	237 405	55.3	44.7	2.43	2.13
Decatur	16.4	6 448	76.1	23.9	14.8	1.9	9.4	4 908	80.1	19.9	2.38	2.21
De Kalb	22.6	8 409	83.1	16.9	6.0	3.0	8.6	6 984	74.9	25.1	2.43	2.51
Dickson	26.5	17 614	93.5	6.5	0.7	1.4	7.7	16 473	76.1	23.9	2.63	2.44
Dyer	8.3	16 123	91.5	8.5	0.4	2.4	10.2	14 751	65.7	34.3	2.53	2.40
Fayette	23.8	11 214	93.3	6.7	1.0	1.9	5.5	10 467	80.3	19.7	2.76	2.53
Fentress	21.4	7 598	88.1	11.9	2.2	1.9	9.4	6 693	79.1	20.9	2.50	2.31
Franklin	18.5	16 813	89.2	10.8	3.9	2.1	9.0	15 003	78.5	21.5	2.52	2.46
Gibson	6.3	21 059	92.7	7.3	0.4	1.5	8.1	19 518	72.2	27.8	2.43	2.37
Giles	19.1	13 113	89.3	10.7	2.0	2.2	11.2	11 713	75.3	24.7	2.53	2.28
Grainger	29.3	9 732	85.0	15.0	6.1	1.9	9.7	8 270	83.7	16.3	2.48	2.48
Greene	19.9	28 116	91.6	8.4	0.9	1.7	8.7	25 756	76.6	23.4	2.42	2.25
Grundy	16.3	6 282	88.5	11.5	4.4	3.4	8.3	5 562	82.2	17.8	2.59	2.29
Hamblen	19.5	24 693	94.0	6.0	0.4	1.5	7.8	23 211	72.6	27.4	2.48	2.44
Hamilton	11.3	134 692	92.4	7.6	0.5	2.1	8.6	124 444	65.9	34.1	2.54	2.17
Hancock	11.5	3 280	84.4	15.6	5.0	1.7	5.2	2 769	78.9	21.1	2.44	2.23
Hardeman	13.7	10 694	88.0	12.0	3.5	1.8	10.1	9 412	74.2	25.8	2.60	2.46
Hardin	19.5	12 807	81.4	18.6	9.1	2.7	11.3	10 426	77.2	22.8	2.44	2.32
Hawkins	27.8	24 416	89.8	10.2	1.3	2.4	10.9	21 936	78.8	21.2	2.47	2.24
Haywood	7.8	8 086	93.5	6.5	1.0	1.1	6.6	7 558	65.9	34.1	2.60	2.55
Henderson	20.9	11 446	90.0	10.0	1.1	1.6	11.7	10 306	79.3	20.7	2.49	2.25
Henry	14.6	15 783	82.5	17.5	9.1	3.0	9.9	13 019	77.4	22.6	2.38	2.26
Hickman	35.2	8 904	90.8	9.2	2.0	2.0	8.0	8 081	80.2	19.8	2.60	2.55
Houston	19.9	3 901	82.4	17.6	9.9	2.3	11.8	3 216	77.0	23.0	2.49	2.33
Humphreys	19.4	8 482	85.3	14.7	6.2	1.8	13.2	7 238	77.9	22.1	2.45	2.44
Jackson	22.6	5 163	86.5	13.5	3.8	2.9	10.2	4 466	80.7	19.3	2.47	2.26
Jefferson	39.1	19 319	88.8	11.2	3.3	2.3	10.8	17 155	77.9	22.1	2.53	2.34
Johnson	26.3	7 879	86.6	13.4	4.7	1.8	8.6	6 827	79.7	20.3	2.38	2.23
Knox	18.1	171 439	92.1	7.9	0.3	2.5	10.0	157 872	66.9	33.1	2.49	2.03
Lake	-0.3	2 716	88.7	11.3	3.5	1.8	8.8	2 410	60.0	40.0	2.45	2.21
Lauderdale	13.6	10 563	90.6	9.4	2.4	1.4	8.3	9 567	64.8	35.2	2.60	2.46
Lawrence	16.1	16 821	92.0	8.0	0.6	2.0	10.2	15 480	77.1	22.9	2.60	2.40
Lewis	24.0	4 821	90.9	9.1	1.0	3.0	10.4	4 381	79.6	20.4	2.57	2.41
Lincoln	14.9	13 999	89.3	10.7	1.5	1.8	9.2	12 503	76.3	23.7	2.51	2.34
Loudon	31.2	17 277	92.3	7.7	1.2	1.9	9.0	15 944	79.1	20.9	2.44	2.37
McMinn	20.6	21 626	91.2	8.8	0.6	2.2	10.7	19 721	75.7	24.3	2.50	2.29
McNairy	13.0	11 219	89.0	11.0	1.5	2.3	12.0	9 980	80.0	20.0	2.43	2.35
Macon	28.5	8 894	89.0	11.0	1.3	2.1	12.5	7 916	78.6	21.4	2.58	2.44
Madison	20.1	38 205	93.1	6.9	0.4	1.7	9.0	35 552	67.0	33.0	2.58	2.30
Marion	19.8	12 140	90.9	9.1	1.9	1.6	11.5	11 037	80.7	19.3	2.53	2.35

Table B. States and Counties

STATE/County code	MSA/PMSA/NECMA code[1]	County type[2]	STATE County	Population, 2000 Land area, 2000[3] (sq km)	Total persons	Rank	Per square kilometer	Population, 1990 Land area, 1990[3] (sq km)	Total persons	Rank	Per square kilometer	White	Black or African American	American Indian or Alaska Native	Asian	Native Hawaiian and other Pacific Islander	Some other race
				1	2	3	4	5	6	7	8	9	10	11	12	13	14
			TENNESSEE—Cont'd														
47 117	...	6	Marshall	972	26 767	1 491	27.5	972	21 539	1 601	22.2	89.4	7.8	0.2	0.3	0.0	1.5
47 119	...	4	Maury	1 587	69 498	711	43.8	1 587	54 812	784	34.5	82.4	14.3	0.3	0.3	0.0	1.4
47 121	...	8	Meigs	505	11 086	2 358	22.0	505	8 033	2 561	15.9	97.7	1.2	0.2	0.2	0.0	0.1
47 123	...	6	Monroe	1 644	38 961	1 140	23.7	1 645	30 541	1 265	18.6	94.9	2.3	0.4	0.4	0.0	0.9
47 125	1660	3	Montgomery	1 397	134 768	400	96.5	1 396	100 498	456	72.0	73.2	19.2	0.5	1.8	0.2	2.2
47 127	...	9	Moore	335	5 740	2 807	17.1	335	4 696	2 861	14.0	95.8	2.7	0.2	0.1	0.0	0.5
47 129	...	8	Morgan	1 352	19 757	1 806	14.6	1 352	17 300	1 833	12.8	96.7	2.2	0.2	0.1	0.0	0.1
47 131	...	7	Obion	1 411	32 450	1 335	23.0	1 411	31 717	1 221	22.5	88.2	9.8	0.1	0.2	0.0	0.9
47 133	...	7	Overton	1 122	20 118	1 788	17.9	1 122	17 636	1 809	15.7	98.6	0.3	0.3	0.1	0.0	0.2
47 135	...	9	Perry	1 075	7 631	2 634	7.1	1 075	6 612	2 697	6.2	96.6	1.7	0.3	0.1	0.0	0.3
47 137	...	9	Pickett	422	4 945	2 852	11.7	422	4 548	2 869	10.8	99.2	0.1	0.2	0.0	0.0	0.1
47 139	...	9	Polk	1 127	16 050	2 018	14.2	1 127	13 643	2 086	12.1	98.3	0.1	0.3	0.1	0.0	0.1
47 141	...	5	Putnam	1 039	62 315	780	60.0	1 039	51 373	821	49.4	94.5	1.7	0.2	0.9	0.1	1.6
47 143	...	6	Rhea	818	28 400	1 435	34.7	818	24 344	1 483	29.8	95.4	2.0	0.4	0.3	0.0	0.8
47 145	...	4	Roane	935	51 910	894	55.5	935	47 227	888	50.5	95.2	2.7	0.2	0.4	0.0	0.2
47 147	5360	2	Robertson	1 234	54 433	866	44.1	1 234	41 492	971	33.6	89.1	8.6	0.3	0.3	0.0	0.8
47 149	5360	2	Rutherford	1 603	182 023	302	113.6	1 603	118 570	392	74.0	85.7	9.5	0.3	1.9	0.0	1.3
47 151	...	6	Scott	1 378	21 127	1 729	15.3	1 378	18 358	1 772	13.3	98.5	0.1	0.2	0.1	0.0	0.1
47 153	...	6	Sequatchie	689	11 370	2 343	16.5	689	8 863	2 482	12.9	98.7	0.2	0.3	0.1	0.0	0.2
47 155	3840	2	Sevier	1 534	71 170	698	46.4	1 534	51 050	826	33.3	97.3	0.6	0.3	0.6	0.0	0.4
47 157	4920	0	Shelby	1 954	897 472	44	459.3	1 955	826 330	43	422.7	47.3	48.6	0.2	1.6	0.0	1.2
47 159	...	8	Smith	814	17 712	1 916	21.8	814	14 143	2 042	17.4	95.4	2.5	0.4	0.2	0.0	0.6
47 161	...	8	Stewart	1 187	12 370	2 274	10.4	1 185	9 479	2 435	8.0	95.3	1.3	0.6	1.5	0.0	0.2
47 163	3660	2	Sullivan	1 070	153 048	347	143.0	1 070	143 596	331	134.2	96.6	1.9	0.2	0.4	0.0	0.2
47 165	5360	2	Sumner	1 371	130 449	412	95.1	1 371	103 281	446	75.3	91.5	5.8	0.3	0.7	0.0	0.8
47 167	4920	1	Tipton	1 190	51 271	902	43.1	1 190	37 568	1 057	31.6	77.9	19.9	0.4	0.4	0.1	0.4
47 169	...	6	Trousdale	296	7 259	2 660	24.5	296	5 920	2 769	20.0	86.6	11.4	0.2	0.1	0.0	1.0
47 171	3660	2	Unicoi	482	17 667	1 918	36.7	482	16 549	1 885	34.3	98.0	0.1	0.2	0.1	0.0	0.9
47 173	3840	2	Union	579	17 808	1 909	30.8	579	13 694	2 081	23.7	98.5	0.1	0.2	0.2	0.0	0.2
47 175	...	9	Van Buren	708	5 508	2 817	7.8	708	4 846	2 848	6.8	99.0	0.1	0.1	0.1	0.0	0.1
47 177	...	7	Warren	1 121	38 276	1 157	34.1	1 121	32 992	1 192	29.4	91.7	3.2	0.2	0.4	0.0	3.6
47 179	3660	2	Washington	845	107 198	499	126.9	845	92 336	500	109.3	93.7	3.8	0.2	0.7	0.0	0.5
47 181	...	8	Wayne	1 901	16 842	1 965	8.9	1 901	13 935	2 062	7.3	91.9	6.8	0.2	0.2	0.0	0.2
47 183	...	7	Weakley	1 503	34 895	1 255	23.2	1 503	31 972	1 212	21.3	90.3	6.9	0.1	1.3	0.0	0.5
47 185	...	7	White	975	23 102	1 638	23.7	976	20 090	1 673	20.6	96.6	1.6	0.2	0.2	0.1	0.5
47 187	5360	2	Williamson	1 509	126 638	427	83.9	1 509	81 021	563	53.7	91.6	5.2	0.2	1.3	0.0	1.0
47 189	5360	2	Wilson	1 478	88 809	586	60.1	1 478	67 675	655	45.8	91.5	6.3	0.3	0.5	0.0	0.5
48 000	...		TEXAS	678 051	20 851 820	X	30.8	678 358	16 986 335	X	25.0	71.0	11.5	0.6	2.7	0.1	11.7
48 001	...	6	Anderson	2 773	55 109	856	19.9	2 774	48 024	871	17.3	66.4	23.5	0.6	0.4	0.0	8.0
48 003	...	6	Andrews	3 887	13 004	2 233	3.3	3 887	14 338	2 029	3.7	77.1	1.6	0.9	0.7	0.0	16.8
48 005	...	5	Angelina	2 076	80 130	640	38.6	2 076	69 884	634	33.7	75.1	14.7	0.3	0.7	0.0	7.8
48 007	...	6	Aransas	652	22 497	1 671	34.5	653	17 892	1 794	27.4	87.4	1.4	0.6	2.8	0.0	5.3
48 009	9080	3	Archer	2 356	8 854	2 538	3.8	2 356	7 973	2 573	3.4	95.5	0.1	0.6	0.1	0.0	2.3
48 011	...	8	Armstrong	2 366	2 148	3 056	0.9	2 366	2 021	3 064	0.9	95.4	0.3	0.7	0.0	0.0	2.8
48 013	...	6	Atascosa	3 191	38 628	1 147	12.1	3 191	30 533	1 266	9.6	73.2	0.6	0.8	0.3	0.1	21.5
48 015	...	6	Austin	1 690	23 590	1 606	14.0	1 690	19 832	1 685	11.7	80.2	10.6	0.3	0.3	0.0	7.0
48 017	...	7	Bailey	2 141	6 594	2 728	3.1	2 141	7 064	2 652	3.3	66.7	1.3	0.7	0.1	0.0	28.6
48 019	...	8	Bandera	2 051	17 645	1 920	8.6	2 051	10 562	2 330	5.1	94.0	0.3	0.9	0.3	0.1	2.6
48 021	0640	2	Bastrop	2 301	57 733	827	25.1	2 301	38 263	1 047	16.6	80.2	8.8	0.7	0.5	0.1	7.6
48 023	...	7	Baylor	2 255	4 093	2 909	1.8	2 255	4 385	2 882	1.9	91.0	3.3	0.6	0.5	0.1	3.3
48 025	...	6	Bee	2 280	32 359	1 338	14.2	2 280	25 135	1 457	11.0	67.9	9.9	0.4	0.5	0.0	19.2
48 027	3810	2	Bell	2 745	237 974	244	86.7	2 743	191 073	251	69.7	63.4	20.4	0.7	2.6	0.5	8.5
48 029	7240	0	Bexar	3 229	1 392 931	24	431.4	3 230	1 185 394	25	367.0	68.9	7.2	0.8	1.6	0.1	17.8
48 031	...	8	Blanco	1 842	8 418	2 572	4.6	1 842	5 972	2 762	3.2	91.0	0.7	0.6	0.2	0.0	5.9
48 033	...	9	Borden	2 328	729	3 130	0.3	2 328	799	3 123	0.3	90.5	0.1	0.3	0.0	0.0	6.3
48 035	...	6	Bosque	2 562	17 204	1 940	6.7	2 562	15 125	1 980	5.9	90.8	1.9	0.5	0.1	0.0	5.2
48 037	8360	3	Bowie	2 300	89 306	578	38.8	2 300	81 665	557	35.5	73.3	23.4	0.6	0.4	0.0	1.1
48 039	1145	1	Brazoria	3 591	241 767	238	67.3	3 592	191 707	250	53.4	77.1	8.5	0.5	2.0	0.0	9.6
48 041	1260	3	Brazos	1 517	152 415	350	100.5	1 517	121 862	377	80.3	74.5	10.7	0.4	4.0	0.1	8.4
48 043	...	7	Brewster	16 039	8 866	2 536	0.6	16 040	8 653	2 495	0.5	81.1	1.2	0.8	0.4	0.1	13.4
48 045	...	9	Briscoe	2 332	1 790	3 079	0.8	2 332	1 971	3 067	0.8	83.4	2.3	0.4	0.1	0.0	11.5
48 047	...	7	Brooks	2 443	7 976	2 608	3.3	2 443	8 204	2 547	3.4	75.8	0.2	0.5	0.1	0.1	21.6
48 049	...	7	Brown	2 445	37 674	1 170	15.4	2 445	34 371	1 157	14.1	87.4	4.0	0.5	0.4	0.0	6.1
48 051	...	6	Burleson	1 724	16 470	1 991	9.6	1 724	13 625	2 090	7.9	74.1	15.1	0.5	0.2	0.0	8.3
48 053	...	6	Burnet	2 580	34 147	1 277	13.2	2 578	22 677	1 549	8.8	89.6	1.5	0.7	0.3	0.1	6.2

[1]MSA = Metropolitan Statistical Area. PMSA = Primary MSA. NECMA = New England County Metropolitan Area. See Appendix A for explanation of these concepts. See Appendix B for list of metropolitan areas identified by type, with component counties.
[2]County typology code from the Economic Research Service of USDA. See Appendix A for definition.
[3]Dry land or land partially or temporarily covered by water.

Table B. States and Counties

STATE County	\[2000\] Two or more races	White	Black	American Indian or Alaska Native	Asian	Native Hawaiian and other Pacific Islander	Some other race	Hispanic[1]	\[1990\] White	Black or African American	American Indian or Alaska Native	Asian and Pacific Islander	Hispanic[1]
	15	16	17	18	19	20	21	22	23	24	25	26	27
TENNESSEE—Cont'd													
Marshall	0.8	90.1	8.1	0.6	0.4	0.0	1.6	2.9	90.7	8.9	0.1	0.2	0.4
Maury	1.3	83.5	14.7	0.7	0.5	0.1	1.8	3.3	83.7	15.7	0.1	0.3	0.6
Meigs	0.6	98.2	1.3	0.6	0.3	0.0	0.2	0.6	98.1	1.5	0.3	0.0	0.2
Monroe	1.3	96.1	2.5	1.1	0.5	0.0	1.1	1.8	96.8	2.7	0.2	0.2	0.4
Montgomery	2.9	75.5	20.4	1.2	2.7	0.4	2.9	5.2	78.7	17.8	0.4	1.8	3.2
Moore	0.6	96.4	2.9	0.5	0.2	0.0	0.6	0.8	96.1	3.7	0.2	0.0	0.4
Morgan	0.6	97.3	2.2	0.6	0.2	0.0	0.3	0.6	98.0	1.5	0.3	0.1	0.3
Obion	0.7	88.8	10.1	0.4	0.3	0.1	1.0	1.9	89.3	10.3	0.1	0.2	0.4
Overton	0.5	99.1	0.3	0.7	0.1	0.1	0.3	0.7	99.7	0.2	0.1	0.0	0.4
Perry	0.8	97.4	1.8	1.0	0.1	0.1	0.4	0.8	97.9	1.8	0.1	0.1	0.5
Pickett	0.4	99.6	0.2	0.5	0.0	0.0	0.1	0.8	99.9	0.0	0.1	0.0	0.3
Polk	1.0	99.4	0.2	1.1	0.2	0.0	0.1	0.7	99.5	0.0	0.2	0.3	0.3
Putnam	0.9	95.4	1.9	0.6	1.1	0.1	1.8	3.0	97.1	1.7	0.2	0.9	0.6
Rhea	1.1	96.4	2.3	1.0	0.4	0.1	0.9	1.7	96.8	2.4	0.3	0.2	0.5
Roane	1.2	96.4	3.0	1.0	0.5	0.1	0.3	0.7	96.2	3.1	0.2	0.4	0.4
Robertson	0.8	89.9	8.8	0.7	0.4	0.0	1.0	2.7	88.7	11.0	0.2	0.1	0.4
Rutherford	1.2	86.7	9.9	0.6	2.2	0.1	1.7	2.8	89.2	9.0	0.2	1.4	0.8
Scott	0.9	99.4	0.1	1.0	0.2	0.0	0.2	0.6	99.5	0.0	0.4	0.1	0.2
Sequatchie	0.5	99.1	0.2	0.7	0.2	0.0	0.2	0.8	99.9	0.0	0.0	0.1	0.3
Sevier	0.9	98.1	0.7	0.9	0.7	0.0	0.6	1.2	98.9	0.4	0.3	0.4	0.5
Shelby	1.0	48.1	49.0	0.5	1.9	0.1	1.5	2.6	55.1	43.6	0.2	0.9	0.9
Smith	0.9	96.3	2.7	0.9	0.2	0.1	0.7	1.1	96.3	3.2	0.3	0.1	0.3
Stewart	1.1	96.3	1.4	1.3	1.7	0.1	0.4	1.0	98.0	1.0	0.6	0.3	0.5
Sullivan	0.7	97.2	2.1	0.6	0.5	0.0	0.3	0.7	97.5	1.8	0.3	0.3	0.4
Sumner	1.0	92.4	6.1	0.7	0.8	0.1	1.0	1.8	94.0	5.4	0.2	0.3	0.5
Tipton	1.0	78.8	20.2	0.9	0.6	0.1	0.5	1.2	75.7	23.6	0.3	0.3	0.7
Trousdale	0.7	87.3	11.6	0.6	0.1	0.0	1.1	1.5	85.1	14.4	0.1	0.1	0.5
Unicoi	0.7	98.6	0.2	0.6	0.2	0.0	1.1	1.9	99.6	0.0	0.1	0.1	0.6
Union	0.9	99.3	0.1	0.9	0.2	0.1	0.2	0.8	99.7	0.0	0.2	0.0	0.3
Van Buren	0.5	99.5	0.1	0.6	0.1	0.0	0.2	0.3	99.5	0.1	0.3	0.0	0.2
Warren	0.9	92.5	3.4	0.6	0.5	0.1	3.9	4.9	95.5	3.4	0.2	0.4	0.8
Washington	1.0	94.6	4.2	0.6	0.9	0.0	0.7	1.4	95.8	3.5	0.2	0.4	0.5
Wayne	0.6	92.5	6.9	0.6	0.3	0.0	0.3	0.8	98.8	1.0	0.1	0.1	0.4
Weakley	0.8	91.0	7.2	0.5	1.5	0.0	0.7	1.2	91.9	6.9	0.1	0.9	0.4
White	0.8	97.4	1.8	0.6	0.4	0.1	0.6	1.0	97.8	1.9	0.1	0.1	0.4
Williamson	0.8	92.3	5.4	0.4	1.5	0.0	1.2	2.5	92.4	6.7	0.2	0.6	0.6
Wilson	0.9	92.4	6.6	0.7	0.6	0.1	0.7	1.3	92.4	6.8	0.3	0.4	0.6
TEXAS	2.5	73.1	12.0	1.0	3.1	0.1	13.3	32.0	75.2	11.9	0.4	1.9	25.5
Anderson	1.0	67.3	23.8	1.0	0.6	0.1	8.3	12.2	69.5	23.2	0.3	0.3	8.2
Andrews	2.9	79.8	1.9	1.4	0.8	0.1	19.0	40.0	75.6	1.9	0.6	1.1	31.7
Angelina	1.4	76.4	15.0	0.7	0.8	0.0	8.5	14.3	78.3	15.4	0.2	0.4	8.7
Aransas	2.4	89.6	1.7	1.4	3.1	0.1	6.6	20.3	85.4	1.8	0.6	3.3	20.1
Archer	1.3	96.8	0.2	1.4	0.2	0.1	2.7	4.9	97.7	0.1	0.5	0.1	2.4
Armstrong	0.8	96.3	0.3	1.1	0.0	0.0	3.2	5.4	97.8	0.0	0.5	0.3	2.7
Atascosa	3.5	76.5	0.7	1.2	0.5	0.1	24.5	58.6	81.9	0.5	0.4	0.2	52.6
Austin	1.6	81.6	11.1	0.7	0.4	0.0	7.9	16.1	81.9	13.2	0.2	0.1	10.5
Bailey	2.7	69.1	1.5	1.2	0.2	0.1	30.5	47.3	92.5	1.8	0.1	0.2	38.8
Bandera	1.9	95.8	0.5	1.7	0.5	0.1	3.4	13.5	94.9	0.2	0.6	0.2	11.1
Bastrop	2.2	82.1	9.2	1.4	0.7	0.1	8.7	24.0	77.4	11.8	0.5	0.3	18.1
Baylor	1.1	92.1	3.5	1.0	0.6	0.2	3.9	9.3	90.4	4.1	0.2	0.3	7.6
Bee	2.1	69.7	10.1	0.7	0.8	0.1	20.8	53.9	77.4	2.9	0.4	0.9	51.4
Bell	3.9	66.3	21.9	1.5	3.6	0.8	10.1	16.7	71.2	18.9	0.5	2.9	13.1
Bexar	3.6	72.0	7.7	1.3	2.2	0.2	20.4	54.3	74.1	7.1	0.4	1.3	49.7
Blanco	1.6	92.6	0.9	1.5	0.3	0.0	6.4	15.3	93.7	0.9	0.3	0.4	14.1
Borden	2.7	93.3	0.1	1.2	0.3	0.0	8.0	11.9	96.2	0.3	1.3	0.0	15.0
Bosque	1.5	92.1	2.1	1.3	0.2	0.1	5.8	12.2	93.7	2.1	0.2	0.3	9.5
Bowie	1.1	74.2	23.8	1.2	0.6	0.1	1.3	4.5	77.0	21.8	0.5	0.3	1.6
Brazoria	2.2	79.1	8.8	1.0	2.3	0.1	11.0	22.8	80.8	8.3	0.4	1.0	17.6
Brazos	2.0	76.2	11.0	0.8	4.4	0.1	9.5	17.9	77.8	11.2	0.2	3.5	13.7
Brewster	3.0	83.8	1.6	1.7	0.7	0.1	15.3	43.6	95.6	1.0	0.2	0.6	42.6
Briscoe	2.5	85.7	2.7	0.7	0.4	0.0	13.0	22.7	79.1	3.5	0.3	0.0	18.6
Brooks	1.8	77.4	0.3	0.6	0.1	0.1	23.3	91.6	82.3	0.0	0.2	0.1	89.4
Brown	1.7	88.9	4.3	1.1	0.5	0.1	6.9	15.4	88.1	4.5	0.4	0.3	11.1
Burleson	1.9	75.9	15.4	0.9	0.4	0.0	9.4	14.6	74.7	17.8	0.4	0.1	11.9
Burnet	1.6	91.1	1.7	1.3	0.5	0.1	7.0	14.8	91.7	1.2	0.5	0.3	10.8

[1] Hispanic persons may be of any race.

Table B. States and Counties

| STATE County | Population and population characteristics, 2000 ||||||||||
| | Age (percent) ||||||||| Median age (years) | Percent Female |
	Under 5 years	5 to 17 years	18 to 24 years	25 to 34 years	35 to 44 years	45 to 54 years	55 to 64 years	65 to 74 years	75 years and over	Median age (years)	Percent Female
	28	29	30	31	32	33	34	35	36	37	38
TENNESSEE—Cont'd											
Marshall	6.5	19.0	8.7	13.7	16.3	14.1	9.1	6.5	6.1	36.3	51.2
Maury	6.9	19.4	8.7	12.9	16.9	14.5	8.7	6.5	5.5	36.3	51.4
Meigs	6.9	18.2	8.1	14.1	14.8	14.6	11.7	6.8	4.7	36.7	50.0
Monroe	6.4	18.4	8.7	13.9	14.7	13.7	11.1	7.2	6.0	36.8	50.7
Montgomery	8.5	19.9	12.3	18.0	16.3	10.7	6.5	4.6	3.2	30.0	49.7
Moore	5.8	17.6	8.4	11.9	14.5	14.6	11.8	8.5	7.0	39.7	50.5
Morgan	5.8	17.4	8.8	15.3	16.6	14.5	10.0	6.5	5.0	36.5	46.7
Obion	6.4	17.0	8.4	13.1	14.5	14.6	10.8	7.8	7.4	38.7	51.7
Overton	6.2	16.9	8.4	13.3	14.5	14.1	11.8	8.3	6.7	38.8	51.0
Perry	6.1	18.3	7.5	11.9	13.5	14.5	11.8	9.5	6.9	39.8	50.2
Pickett	5.8	15.6	8.6	11.2	13.4	14.3	13.3	10.2	7.5	41.6	50.8
Polk	6.4	16.2	8.2	13.7	14.8	14.3	12.1	8.2	6.2	38.6	50.4
Putnam	6.0	16.2	14.7	13.8	14.0	12.5	9.4	7.2	6.1	34.4	50.4
Rhea	6.2	17.6	10.0	12.8	14.7	13.9	11.1	7.4	6.4	37.2	51.5
Roane	5.9	16.5	7.5	12.1	14.8	15.5	11.7	8.9	7.2	40.7	51.6
Robertson	6.8	20.0	8.5	14.1	17.3	13.7	8.8	6.2	4.6	35.4	50.3
Rutherford	7.5	18.9	13.2	16.4	17.1	12.4	7.0	4.3	3.2	31.2	50.2
Scott	7.0	19.1	10.3	14.1	14.6	13.6	10.0	6.2	5.1	34.7	50.7
Sequatchie	6.9	17.7	8.4	14.5	15.4	14.0	10.8	7.0	5.2	36.7	50.4
Sevier	6.0	17.0	8.3	13.6	16.2	15.0	11.3	7.5	5.1	38.1	51.0
Shelby	7.6	20.6	9.7	15.1	16.0	13.5	7.5	5.3	4.6	32.9	52.2
Smith	6.5	19.0	8.0	13.2	16.8	13.7	9.4	7.0	6.4	36.8	50.8
Stewart	5.9	18.1	7.5	12.5	15.9	14.1	11.2	8.5	6.4	38.7	50.2
Sullivan	5.6	16.2	7.3	13.1	15.3	14.9	11.7	8.7	7.2	40.1	51.7
Sumner	6.8	19.6	8.0	13.7	17.0	14.5	9.7	5.9	4.8	36.1	51.0
Tipton	7.0	22.3	8.6	13.0	17.4	13.0	8.8	5.6	4.3	34.4	50.8
Trousdale	6.0	18.2	8.5	12.5	15.5	14.3	10.6	7.3	7.0	38.1	50.8
Unicoi	5.5	15.0	7.5	12.5	15.0	14.8	11.7	9.4	8.7	41.5	51.2
Union	6.7	19.0	8.9	14.0	17.0	13.5	10.0	6.5	4.3	35.8	50.3
Van Buren	5.9	17.0	9.2	12.3	15.2	15.1	11.2	8.3	5.7	38.7	50.2
Warren	6.6	17.7	9.1	14.2	15.2	13.6	9.8	7.6	6.3	36.6	50.9
Washington	5.9	15.4	10.8	14.6	15.4	14.0	10.0	7.3	6.6	37.1	51.3
Wayne	5.1	16.3	9.1	15.6	16.1	13.5	10.7	7.5	6.1	37.3	45.1
Weakley	5.8	15.9	15.9	12.8	13.3	12.6	9.3	7.1	7.3	34.8	51.5
White	6.0	17.5	7.9	12.8	15.0	14.0	11.4	8.5	6.8	38.8	51.0
Williamson	7.2	22.3	6.2	12.2	19.4	16.8	8.2	4.5	3.3	36.2	50.8
Wilson	6.8	19.4	7.7	13.7	18.0	14.9	9.8	5.5	4.2	36.3	50.6
TEXAS	7.8	20.4	10.5	15.2	15.9	12.5	7.7	5.5	4.5	32.3	50.4
Anderson	5.5	15.2	9.3	18.5	19.2	12.8	7.8	6.1	5.6	35.8	39.1
Andrews	7.4	24.2	8.1	11.3	16.0	12.0	8.5	7.2	5.3	34.1	50.9
Angelina	7.7	20.0	9.7	13.8	14.8	12.6	8.9	6.7	5.9	34.2	50.9
Aransas	5.5	18.3	6.2	9.5	13.7	14.0	13.1	11.8	7.9	42.7	50.3
Archer	6.3	21.9	7.0	10.0	17.4	13.5	9.9	7.9	6.0	38.1	50.0
Armstrong	5.6	20.4	6.1	10.2	14.6	13.3	10.5	8.8	10.4	40.7	51.8
Atascosa	8.3	23.5	8.9	12.9	14.7	12.6	8.3	6.0	4.8	32.3	50.9
Austin	6.6	20.4	8.1	11.1	15.2	14.1	9.7	7.4	7.4	37.6	50.9
Bailey	8.1	22.2	8.6	11.3	13.5	12.0	9.2	8.2	7.0	34.9	51.0
Bandera	5.5	19.1	5.8	9.6	16.1	15.3	12.3	9.9	6.2	41.3	50.2
Bastrop	7.6	20.4	7.6	13.8	17.5	14.5	8.3	5.8	4.5	35.4	48.7
Baylor	4.9	18.5	5.5	8.3	13.1	13.5	12.1	11.5	12.5	44.8	52.8
Bee	6.1	17.3	13.3	19.6	15.7	10.8	7.0	5.6	4.5	31.8	40.3
Bell	8.9	20.0	13.4	17.1	14.9	10.6	6.4	4.7	4.1	29.2	49.8
Bexar	7.9	20.6	10.7	15.1	15.5	12.4	7.5	5.6	4.8	32.1	51.4
Blanco	6.2	18.2	6.2	10.5	15.1	15.8	11.3	8.2	8.5	41.2	50.6
Borden	3.7	20.9	6.7	9.6	17.8	11.8	13.2	10.7	5.6	40.5	49.2
Bosque	5.7	18.7	6.2	9.9	13.9	13.2	11.8	9.6	10.9	41.7	51.1
Bowie	6.4	18.4	9.4	13.8	15.7	13.5	9.0	7.1	6.7	36.3	49.6
Brazoria	7.7	20.8	8.6	14.4	18.0	13.6	7.9	5.3	3.6	34.0	48.4
Brazos	6.2	15.3	32.0	14.5	11.4	8.6	5.2	3.5	3.2	23.6	49.5
Brewster	5.4	16.7	14.8	11.9	12.6	14.0	9.8	8.1	6.8	36.2	50.2
Briscoe	6.4	20.7	6.8	9.2	12.8	14.1	10.7	10.1	9.2	39.9	51.3
Brooks	8.3	23.3	8.9	10.3	13.1	11.9	9.8	8.3	6.1	34.4	51.5
Brown	6.2	19.6	10.1	11.0	13.7	12.9	10.0	8.4	8.1	37.2	50.7
Burleson	6.7	20.2	8.0	11.2	14.6	13.5	9.7	8.9	7.2	37.9	51.4
Burnet	6.5	18.0	7.0	10.7	15.3	13.3	11.2	10.0	7.9	40.2	51.6

Table B. States and Counties

STATE County	Population and population characteristics, 1990										Population—change, 1980–2000				
	Age (percent)									Percent Female	Total persons			Percent change	
	Under 5 years	5 to 17 years	18 to 24 years	25 to 34 years	35 to 44 years	45 to 54 years	55 to 64 years	65 to 74 years	75 years and over		2000	1990	1980	1990–2000	1980–1990
	39	40	41	42	43	44	45	46	47	48	49	50	51	52	53
TENNESSEE—Cont'd															
Marshall	6.4	18.9	9.5	15.4	14.7	10.8	9.1	8.8	6.4	51.7	26 767	21 539	19 698	24.3	9.3
Maury	7.1	19.0	9.3	16.4	15.3	10.4	9.3	7.5	5.7	52.1	69 498	54 812	51 095	26.8	7.3
Meigs	5.7	19.1	10.6	14.5	16.1	12.4	9.2	7.6	4.6	49.7	11 086	8 033	7 431	38.0	8.1
Monroe	6.4	18.9	10.8	14.4	14.6	11.9	9.2	8.1	5.6	51.4	38 961	30 541	28 700	27.6	6.4
Montgomery	8.6	17.9	15.8	20.0	14.2	8.6	7.0	4.7	3.2	48.8	134 768	100 498	83 342	34.1	20.6
Moore	5.7	19.7	9.1	14.1	15.0	12.9	9.9	8.2	5.4	50.2	5 740	4 696	4 510	22.2	4.7
Morgan	6.2	19.6	10.2	17.1	15.6	10.8	8.8	6.8	5.0	47.3	19 757	17 300	16 604	14.2	4.2
Obion	5.8	18.9	9.6	14.0	14.8	11.6	9.6	8.5	7.0	52.2	32 450	31 717	32 781	2.3	-3.2
Overton	5.8	18.3	9.8	14.0	14.6	12.0	10.2	8.8	6.6	50.8	20 118	17 636	17 575	14.1	0.3
Perry	6.9	18.2	8.1	13.1	13.9	11.4	11.8	9.3	7.3	50.9	7 631	6 612	6 111	15.4	8.2
Pickett	6.5	18.1	8.3	13.2	13.7	11.8	11.5	9.1	7.9	51.1	4 945	4 548	4 358	8.7	4.4
Polk	5.8	18.4	10.0	13.9	14.5	12.8	10.2	8.4	6.0	50.7	16 050	13 643	13 602	17.6	0.3
Putnam	6.0	15.9	16.9	15.3	13.7	10.4	8.8	7.4	5.6	51.0	62 315	51 373	47 690	21.3	7.7
Rhea	6.2	19.1	10.7	14.5	14.4	11.6	9.2	8.1	6.2	51.7	28 400	24 344	24 235	16.7	0.4
Roane	5.6	17.9	8.9	13.8	15.3	12.4	11.2	9.3	5.7	51.8	51 910	47 227	48 425	9.9	-2.5
Robertson	7.6	19.8	8.8	17.1	15.1	10.5	8.8	6.8	5.3	51.0	54 433	41 492	37 021	31.2	12.1
Rutherford	7.5	19.3	14.2	18.9	15.5	9.6	6.6	5.0	3.4	50.8	182 023	118 570	84 058	53.5	41.1
Scott	7.0	22.3	10.3	15.2	14.1	10.8	8.3	6.9	5.1	51.3	21 127	18 358	19 259	15.1	-4.7
Sequatchie	6.5	19.3	10.3	15.6	15.7	11.6	8.7	6.5	5.7	50.5	11 370	8 863	8 605	28.3	3.0
Sevier	6.1	17.8	9.4	16.0	15.8	12.4	9.9	7.7	4.8	51.3	71 170	51 050	41 418	39.4	23.2
Shelby	8.1	19.3	11.3	18.1	15.6	9.5	7.7	6.1	4.3	52.4	897 472	826 330	777 113	8.6	6.3
Smith	6.7	18.4	8.9	15.8	14.1	10.7	9.6	8.7	7.2	51.6	17 712	14 143	14 935	25.2	-5.3
Stewart	5.1	17.1	8.7	13.7	14.3	12.1	11.6	9.9	7.5	50.7	12 370	9 479	8 665	30.5	9.4
Sullivan	5.9	16.6	9.7	14.9	15.3	12.8	10.6	8.8	5.5	52.0	153 048	143 596	143 968	6.6	-0.3
Sumner	7.0	20.5	9.3	16.2	16.7	12.1	8.1	6.0	4.2	51.0	130 449	103 281	85 790	26.3	20.4
Tipton	8.6	22.0	9.6	16.6	14.5	10.1	7.8	6.1	4.7	51.2	51 271	37 568	32 930	36.5	14.1
Trousdale	5.8	18.2	9.1	14.9	14.6	11.0	9.6	9.4	7.4	51.5	7 259	5 920	6 137	22.6	-3.5
Unicoi	5.3	16.5	8.9	15.0	14.5	11.7	11.0	9.9	7.3	52.2	17 667	16 549	16 362	6.8	1.1
Union	7.0	19.8	10.5	17.0	14.7	11.5	8.5	6.2	4.8	50.6	17 808	13 694	11 707	30.0	17.0
Van Buren	6.5	19.7	9.8	15.9	15.2	10.9	9.8	7.2	5.0	50.5	5 508	4 846	4 728	13.7	2.5
Warren	6.4	18.7	9.7	15.2	14.5	11.2	9.8	8.2	6.3	51.8	38 276	32 992	32 653	16.0	1.0
Washington	5.7	16.0	12.8	16.1	15.0	11.0	9.4	8.0	5.9	51.6	107 198	92 336	88 755	16.1	4.0
Wayne	6.6	19.1	9.8	14.7	13.9	11.7	9.4	8.5	6.3	51.0	16 842	13 935	13 946	20.9	0.0
Weakley	5.7	16.3	16.6	14.2	12.5	9.9	8.8	8.5	7.6	52.1	34 895	31 972	32 896	9.1	-2.8
White	6.2	17.7	9.4	14.3	14.3	11.6	10.5	9.2	6.9	51.7	23 102	20 090	19 567	15.0	2.7
Williamson	7.4	21.6	7.4	15.1	20.0	12.6	7.6	4.8	3.4	50.9	126 638	81 021	58 108	56.3	39.4
Wilson	7.2	20.2	8.8	16.6	17.3	12.3	7.8	5.8	4.0	50.6	88 809	67 675	56 064	31.2	20.7
TEXAS	8.2	20.3	11.1	18.2	14.9	9.6	7.6	5.9	4.2	50.7	20 851 820	16 986 335	14 225 513	22.8	19.4
Anderson	6.2	17.3	12.0	21.9	13.9	8.5	7.5	6.7	6.0	42.1	55 109	48 024	38 381	14.8	25.1
Andrews	9.2	25.4	8.9	15.9	13.4	9.2	8.5	5.9	3.6	50.6	13 004	14 338	13 323	-9.3	7.6
Angelina	7.6	21.1	10.2	15.5	13.7	10.2	8.7	7.2	5.8	51.5	80 130	69 884	64 172	14.7	8.9
Aransas	6.7	18.5	7.4	13.4	12.6	10.6	12.4	11.9	6.6	50.4	22 497	17 892	14 260	25.7	25.5
Archer	7.1	20.8	7.4	15.1	14.1	11.3	10.1	8.1	5.9	50.1	8 854	7 973	7 266	11.0	9.7
Armstrong	6.1	21.7	5.3	12.4	12.2	9.3	11.1	11.0	10.7	51.6	2 148	2 021	1 994	6.3	1.4
Atascosa	8.5	24.5	9.1	14.8	13.5	9.7	8.1	6.7	5.1	50.5	38 628	30 533	25 055	26.5	21.9
Austin	6.8	20.0	8.2	14.0	13.7	10.4	9.2	8.9	8.8	51.2	23 590	19 832	17 726	18.9	11.9
Bailey	8.0	23.9	8.4	14.1	12.7	10.0	9.3	7.5	6.2	50.5	6 594	7 064	8 168	-6.7	-13.5
Bandera	6.0	17.7	5.6	12.5	14.9	12.2	13.4	10.9	6.7	50.3	17 645	10 562	7 084	67.1	49.1
Bastrop	8.0	20.8	7.7	16.4	16.2	10.1	8.5	6.8	5.5	49.3	57 733	38 263	24 726	50.9	54.7
Baylor	6.3	16.0	6.7	11.4	12.0	10.3	11.2	12.7	13.3	52.7	4 093	4 385	4 919	-6.7	-10.9
Bee	8.7	22.8	10.7	16.1	13.2	8.8	8.2	6.4	5.0	50.5	32 359	25 135	26 030	28.7	-3.4
Bell	9.6	19.2	15.1	19.6	13.3	8.1	6.5	5.1	3.7	49.1	237 974	191 073	157 820	24.5	21.1
Bexar	8.4	20.8	11.6	17.9	14.6	9.3	7.5	6.0	3.9	51.5	1 392 931	1 185 394	988 971	17.5	19.9
Blanco	6.8	18.2	6.7	13.0	13.8	10.7	10.6	11.8	8.4	52.3	8 418	5 972	4 681	41.0	27.6
Borden	7.1	20.9	5.8	14.6	11.6	14.0	11.8	9.0	5.1	48.7	729	799	859	-8.8	-7.0
Bosque	6.1	17.5	7.1	12.0	12.2	10.4	10.2	12.5	12.1	51.7	17 204	15 125	13 401	13.7	12.9
Bowie	7.0	20.2	8.9	15.5	14.9	10.3	8.8	8.2	6.2	51.7	89 306	81 665	75 301	9.4	8.5
Brazoria	8.1	21.2	9.5	19.2	16.3	10.3	7.6	4.8	3.0	48.1	241 767	191 707	169 587	26.1	13.0
Brazos	6.8	14.7	32.0	17.5	11.0	6.7	4.7	3.7	3.0	48.6	152 415	121 862	93 588	25.1	30.2
Brewster	6.5	17.2	15.9	14.1	13.4	9.6	9.3	8.4	5.6	49.5	8 866	8 653	7 573	2.5	14.3
Briscoe	6.5	21.4	5.1	11.1	13.3	11.1	10.6	11.6	9.1	50.4	1 790	1 971	2 579	-9.2	-23.6
Brooks	9.1	23.9	9.4	13.9	11.9	9.4	9.2	7.5	5.7	51.5	7 976	8 204	8 428	-2.8	-2.7
Brown	6.9	20.0	9.8	13.3	13.1	9.7	9.5	9.3	8.4	51.5	37 674	34 371	33 057	9.6	4.0
Burleson	7.2	20.0	8.2	14.0	12.8	9.4	10.9	9.7	7.7	51.2	16 470	13 625	12 313	20.9	10.7
Burnet	6.4	18.2	6.4	12.5	12.7	9.7	11.6	12.6	9.9	51.8	34 147	22 677	17 803	50.6	27.4

Table B. States and Counties

Items 54—70

STATE County	Total population (54)	Total in households (55)	House-holder (56)	Spouse (57)	Child Total (58)	Child Own child under 18 years (59)	Other relatives Total (60)	Other relatives Under 18 years (61)	Nonrelatives Total (62)	Nonrelatives Unmarried partner (63)	Total in group quarters (64)	Correctional institutions (65)	Nursing homes (66)	Other institutions (67)	College dormitories (68)	Military quarters (69)	Other (70)
TENNESSEE—Cont'd																	
Marshall	26 767	98.7	38.5	21.9	29.6	22.7	4.9	2.3	3.8	1.8	1.3	0.2	0.6	0.0	0.0	0.0	0.4
Maury	69 498	98.2	38.1	21.3	30.2	23.1	4.9	2.3	3.8	1.7	1.8	0.3	1.0	0.3	0.0	0.0	0.2
Meigs	11 086	99.0	38.8	24.0	28.7	22.5	4.4	2.0	3.1	1.7	1.0	0.3	0.7	0.0	0.0	0.0	0.0
Monroe	38 961	98.6	39.3	23.4	28.4	22.1	4.4	2.0	3.1	1.5	1.4	0.2	0.6	0.1	0.4	0.0	0.0
Montgomery	134 768	96.8	35.9	21.1	31.3	26.0	3.9	1.8	4.7	1.6	3.2	0.3	0.4	0.0	0.6	1.7	0.2
Moore	5 740	98.0	38.5	25.1	28.2	20.8	4.0	1.9	2.4	1.2	2.0	0.2	1.4	0.0	0.3	0.0	0.1
Morgan	19 757	91.3	35.4	21.5	27.3	20.3	4.4	2.1	2.7	1.5	8.7	7.8	0.6	0.3	0.0	0.0	0.0
Obion	32 450	98.4	40.6	22.9	27.6	20.9	4.3	2.0	3.0	1.5	1.6	0.2	0.9	0.0	0.0	0.0	0.5
Overton	20 118	99.1	40.3	23.8	27.7	20.5	4.4	1.9	2.9	1.4	0.9	0.1	0.7	0.0	0.0	0.0	0.1
Perry	7 631	98.2	39.6	23.5	28.3	22.1	3.8	1.6	2.9	1.5	1.8	0.1	1.4	0.0	0.0	0.0	0.3
Pickett	4 945	98.6	42.3	24.7	26.7	20.2	2.8	0.9	2.2	1.4	1.4	0.1	1.3	0.0	0.0	0.0	0.0
Polk	16 050	98.8	40.2	24.2	26.4	19.9	5.2	2.1	2.8	1.4	1.2	0.3	0.8	0.1	0.0	0.0	0.0
Putnam	62 315	95.9	39.9	21.0	25.5	20.0	4.0	1.6	5.5	1.5	4.1	0.2	0.7	0.1	2.8	0.0	0.3
Rhea	28 400	97.0	39.4	22.6	27.5	21.2	4.1	1.9	3.4	1.6	3.0	0.2	1.0	0.2	1.4	0.0	0.2
Roane	51 910	98.7	40.8	23.8	26.6	19.8	4.4	2.0	2.9	1.5	1.3	0.1	0.7	0.1	0.0	0.0	0.4
Robertson	54 433	99.1	36.6	22.6	30.8	24.0	4.9	2.2	4.1	1.6	0.9	0.3	0.5	0.0	0.0	0.0	0.1
Rutherford	182 023	96.8	36.5	20.5	29.9	24.2	4.2	1.7	5.7	1.8	3.2	0.3	0.5	0.3	1.8	0.0	0.2
Scott	21 127	99.1	38.8	22.2	31.2	23.6	4.2	1.9	2.7	1.4	0.9	0.2	0.7	0.0	0.0	0.0	0.1
Sequatchie	11 370	98.9	39.3	23.1	28.4	22.0	4.5	2.0	3.7	2.2	1.1	0.1	1.0	0.0	0.0	0.0	0.0
Sevier	71 170	99.1	40.0	23.7	26.9	20.7	4.5	1.8	4.0	1.9	0.9	0.2	0.4	0.0	0.1	0.0	0.2
Shelby	897 472	97.9	37.7	16.1	31.8	24.0	7.5	3.6	4.7	1.8	2.1	0.7	0.5	0.1	0.4	0.0	0.3
Smith	17 712	99.2	38.8	23.4	29.4	23.1	4.6	2.0	3.0	1.5	0.8	0.1	0.6	0.0	0.0	0.0	0.1
Stewart	12 370	99.2	39.9	24.8	27.6	21.7	3.9	1.8	3.0	1.3	0.8	0.1	0.7	0.0	0.2	0.0	0.5
Sullivan	153 048	98.2	41.5	23.7	26.4	19.7	3.9	1.6	2.8	1.3	1.8	0.3	0.7	0.0	0.0	0.0	0.5
Sumner	130 449	98.9	37.5	22.9	30.4	23.9	4.5	2.0	3.5	1.5	1.1	0.2	0.7	0.0	0.0	0.0	0.1
Tipton	51 271	98.3	35.3	21.3	33.1	26.0	5.6	2.8	3.0	1.5	1.7	1.2	0.5	0.0	0.0	0.0	0.0
Trousdale	7 259	97.7	38.3	22.3	28.5	21.4	4.9	2.1	3.7	1.7	2.3	0.4	1.2	0.0	0.0	0.0	0.6
Unicoi	17 667	98.3	42.5	24.0	25.1	18.4	4.3	1.8	2.5	1.2	1.7	0.2	1.3	0.0	0.0	0.0	0.1
Union	17 808	99.2	37.9	23.5	29.8	22.9	4.9	2.1	3.2	1.5	0.8	0.2	0.5	0.0	0.0	0.0	0.1
Van Buren	5 508	98.6	39.6	23.5	28.0	20.3	4.3	2.1	3.2	1.8	1.4	0.3	1.1	0.0	0.0	0.0	0.0
Warren	38 276	98.1	39.7	22.3	27.8	21.8	4.4	1.9	4.0	1.7	1.9	0.4	0.7	0.0	0.0	0.0	0.7
Washington	107 198	96.3	41.2	21.7	25.3	19.4	3.8	1.5	4.1	1.7	3.7	0.4	0.9	0.4	1.8	0.0	0.3
Wayne	16 842	87.1	35.2	20.8	25.1	19.0	3.6	1.7	2.4	1.3	12.9	11.4	0.9	0.1	0.0	0.0	0.4
Weakley	34 895	92.8	39.0	21.1	25.2	19.6	3.3	1.5	4.3	1.4	7.2	0.3	1.2	0.1	5.4	0.0	0.2
White	23 102	98.7	39.9	23.4	27.5	20.9	4.6	1.9	3.2	1.7	1.3	0.4	0.6	0.1	0.0	0.0	0.3
Williamson	126 638	99.2	35.3	24.6	33.6	28.0	3.2	1.2	2.4	0.9	0.8	0.3	0.1	0.1	0.0	0.0	0.3
Wilson	88 809	98.7	36.9	23.7	30.5	23.8	4.2	1.9	3.4	1.5	1.3	0.1	0.2	0.0	0.4	0.0	0.5
TEXAS	20 851 820	97.3	35.5	19.1	31.5	24.8	6.8	2.9	4.4	1.6	2.7	1.2	0.5	0.1	0.4	0.2	0.3
Anderson	55 109	73.5	28.4	15.8	22.5	18.1	4.2	2.1	2.4	1.1	26.5	25.5	0.9	0.0	0.0	0.0	0.1
Andrews	13 004	99.4	35.4	22.5	34.7	28.5	4.6	2.5	2.1	1.2	0.6	0.2	0.4	0.1	0.0	0.0	0.0
Angelina	80 130	96.6	35.8	20.7	30.8	24.0	6.2	3.1	3.1	1.3	3.4	1.4	0.8	0.6	0.1	0.0	0.4
Aransas	22 497	98.8	40.6	23.1	26.0	20.8	4.9	2.4	4.3	1.9	1.2	0.2	0.8	0.0	0.0	0.0	0.2
Archer	8 854	99.4	37.8	24.6	31.4	26.3	3.3	1.4	2.4	1.2	0.6	0.1	0.4	0.0	0.0	0.0	0.2
Armstrong	2 148	96.4	37.3	25.1	28.3	24.0	3.4	1.4	2.3	1.0	3.6	0.3	3.3	0.0	0.0	0.0	0.1
Atascosa	38 628	99.1	33.2	20.0	35.8	27.7	6.8	3.5	3.4	1.8	0.9	0.4	0.5	0.0	0.0	0.0	0.0
Austin	23 590	98.8	37.1	22.5	31.4	24.5	5.0	2.2	3.0	1.5	1.2	0.2	0.8	0.0	0.0	0.0	0.2
Bailey	6 594	99.1	35.6	23.1	33.3	27.2	5.0	2.7	2.1	1.1	0.9	0.2	0.7	0.0	0.0	0.0	0.0
Bandera	17 645	99.0	39.7	24.1	26.8	21.3	4.3	2.1	4.1	2.0	1.0	0.1	0.2	0.0	0.0	0.0	0.7
Bastrop	57 733	96.5	34.8	20.4	30.3	24.1	6.5	3.0	4.6	1.8	3.5	2.8	0.5	0.1	0.0	0.0	0.1
Baylor	4 093	98.8	43.8	23.4	25.4	21.2	3.8	1.9	2.5	1.2	1.2	0.0	1.2	0.0	0.0	0.0	0.0
Bee	32 359	76.6	28.0	14.8	26.2	20.3	4.7	2.4	2.9	1.5	23.4	22.2	0.5	0.0	0.4	2.0	0.2
Bell	237 974	96.2	35.9	20.3	31.1	26.2	4.2	2.0	4.6	1.5	3.8	0.3	0.7	0.2	0.4	0.7	0.4
Bexar	1 392 931	97.5	35.1	17.7	32.7	24.5	7.5	3.4	4.5	1.8	2.5	0.5	0.5	0.1	0.3	0.7	0.4
Blanco	8 418	98.2	39.2	24.1	27.5	22.2	4.1	1.7	3.2	1.4	1.8	0.0	1.6	0.0	0.1	0.0	0.0
Borden	729	100.0	40.1	26.1	28.8	23.6	2.5	0.5	2.6	1.2	0.0	0.0	0.0	0.0	0.0	0.0	0.0
Bosque	17 204	96.9	39.1	23.7	26.9	21.9	4.5	2.1	2.7	1.3	3.1	0.2	2.5	0.0	0.0	0.0	0.4
Bowie	89 306	92.4	37.0	19.3	28.0	21.7	5.1	2.7	3.0	1.4	7.6	6.2	0.9	0.1	0.0	0.0	0.2
Brazoria	241 767	95.5	33.9	21.1	31.8	25.7	5.3	2.3	3.3	1.5	4.5	3.9	0.4	0.0	0.0	0.0	0.2
Brazos	152 415	91.2	36.2	15.0	23.3	19.2	4.7	1.6	12.0	1.3	8.8	1.2	0.4	0.0	7.0	0.0	0.2
Brewster	8 866	95.5	41.4	19.3	25.1	19.8	4.6	1.9	5.2	1.5	4.5	0.5	0.4	0.0	3.7	0.0	0.0
Briscoe	1 790	100.0	40.4	24.0	29.3	24.1	4.7	2.7	1.6	0.9	0.0	0.0	0.0	0.0	0.0	0.0	0.0
Brooks	7 976	99.1	34.0	17.7	36.6	27.0	7.8	4.1	2.9	1.9	0.9	0.1	0.8	0.0	0.0	0.0	0.2
Brown	37 674	94.1	38.0	21.2	26.9	21.9	4.4	2.2	3.5	1.3	5.9	1.5	1.4	1.4	1.3	0.0	0.2
Burleson	16 470	99.4	38.6	21.8	30.0	23.6	5.9	3.0	3.0	1.5	0.6	0.2	0.4	0.0	0.0	0.0	0.3
Burnet	34 147	97.4	38.5	23.7	26.9	22.0	4.4	1.9	3.9	1.7	2.6	1.5	0.8	0.0	0.0	0.0	0.3

Table B. States and Counties

STATE County	Total households	Family households		Married couple		Female householder[1]		Nonfamily households	Householder living alone		Average household size	Average family size	Total households (1990)	Female householder[1] (1990)	Householder living alone (1990)
		Total	With own children under 18 years	Total	With own children under 18 years	Total	With own children under 18 years	Total	Total	65 years and over					
	71	72	73	74	75	76	77	78	79	80	81	82	83	84	85
TENNESSEE—Cont'd															
Marshall	10 307	72.5	33.8	50.8	24.8	11.6	6.8	27.5	23.9	10.0	2.56	3.02	8 268	10.7	23.6
Maury	26 444	72.9	34.8	55.9	25.2	12.9	7.5	27.1	23.2	8.8	2.58	3.03	20 608	12.7	22.1
Meigs	4 304	75.8	32.8	61.7	25.3	9.9	5.3	24.2	20.8	7.8	2.55	2.94	2 996	8.7	19.8
Monroe	15 329	73.3	32.1	59.4	24.4	10.0	5.5	26.7	23.3	9.4	2.51	2.94	11 363	10.2	21.0
Montgomery	48 330	74.4	40.7	58.7	30.4	12.2	8.2	25.6	20.2	5.5	2.70	3.11	34 345	10.8	18.1
Moore	2 211	76.3	30.7	65.1	25.0	7.6	3.7	23.7	21.4	11.1	2.55	2.95	1 734	6.5	18.9
Morgan	6 990	74.9	33.5	60.7	26.3	10.3	5.4	25.1	22.1	9.3	2.58	3.01	5 841	11.6	19.2
Obion	13 182	71.3	31.0	56.4	22.5	11.1	6.4	28.7	25.7	12.1	2.42	2.89	12 412	10.3	23.8
Overton	8 110	73.0	29.2	59.2	22.8	9.9	4.6	27.0	24.1	11.0	2.46	2.90	6 734	9.6	20.3
Perry	3 023	71.6	30.6	59.4	24.0	8.8	4.8	28.4	25.2	12.9	2.48	2.96	2 512	7.4	22.6
Pickett	2 091	69.9	27.4	58.3	21.6	7.8	4.0	30.1	27.2	12.9	2.33	2.83	1 786	9.5	24.1
Polk	6 448	73.7	29.8	60.3	23.9	9.0	4.1	26.3	23.3	9.8	2.46	2.89	5 092	8.9	19.4
Putnam	24 865	66.0	29.0	52.7	21.8	9.8	5.6	34.0	27.1	9.6	2.40	2.92	19 753	9.7	24.1
Rhea	11 184	72.5	31.2	57.4	22.6	11.2	6.6	27.5	23.8	9.9	2.46	2.90	9 185	11.8	22.0
Roane	21 200	71.9	28.6	58.3	21.6	10.1	5.3	28.1	25.0	11.2	2.42	2.87	18 453	9.9	22.4
Robertson	19 906	77.6	37.4	61.9	28.5	11.2	6.7	22.4	18.6	7.5	2.71	3.06	14 801	10.4	17.7
Rutherford	66 443	71.4	37.8	56.3	28.5	11.2	7.2	28.6	20.8	5.1	2.65	3.09	42 118	10.1	20.3
Scott	8 203	73.3	35.7	57.2	26.9	11.8	6.6	26.7	24.3	9.5	2.55	3.02	6 534	11.7	20.1
Sequatchie	4 463	74.2	33.0	58.8	24.0	11.2	6.5	25.8	22.4	8.8	2.52	2.92	3 287	10.7	20.0
Sevier	28 467	73.2	30.7	59.3	23.0	10.1	5.7	26.8	22.0	7.9	2.48	2.88	19 520	9.5	19.8
Shelby	338 366	67.6	34.2	42.8	20.1	20.1	12.0	32.4	27.0	7.7	2.60	3.18	303 571	18.6	25.7
Smith	6 878	73.7	34.1	60.1	26.2	9.8	5.9	26.3	23.4	11.1	2.55	3.00	5 358	8.3	21.0
Stewart	4 930	74.1	31.5	62.3	24.5	8.1	4.9	25.9	23.1	10.8	2.49	2.91	3 678	6.8	21.6
Sullivan	63 556	70.5	28.4	57.1	21.7	10.2	5.3	29.5	26.4	11.1	2.36	2.84	56 729	9.9	23.0
Sumner	48 941	75.7	36.3	61.1	27.9	10.8	6.3	24.3	20.3	7.2	2.64	3.04	36 850	9.6	17.3
Tipton	18 106	78.3	39.6	60.2	28.8	13.9	8.6	21.7	18.7	7.4	2.78	3.17	13 033	13.7	18.5
Trousdale	2 780	73.2	31.9	58.3	24.1	11.3	5.6	26.8	23.0	10.3	2.55	2.99	2 261	10.7	22.6
Unicoi	7 516	69.5	26.6	56.4	20.5	9.5	4.4	30.5	27.5	13.4	2.31	2.80	6 621	9.9	23.6
Union	6 742	77.0	35.4	62.2	27.5	10.5	5.5	23.0	19.8	7.4	2.62	2.99	4 932	10.3	17.1
Van Buren	2 180	74.3	30.5	59.5	22.5	11.0	6.1	25.7	21.9	8.7	2.49	2.90	1 799	10.6	17.9
Warren	15 181	71.3	31.9	56.2	23.4	11.2	6.6	28.7	25.0	10.5	2.47	2.93	12 681	10.8	22.3
Washington	44 195	66.7	28.2	52.6	20.7	10.5	5.9	33.3	27.8	9.7	2.33	2.85	35 823	10.6	25.1
Wayne	5 936	72.8	31.0	59.1	24.1	10.1	5.1	27.2	24.4	10.9	2.47	2.93	5 174	9.3	19.5
Weakley	13 599	67.1	29.4	54.2	22.2	9.5	5.4	32.9	27.0	11.5	2.38	2.89	11 992	9.0	24.4
White	9 229	73.4	30.4	58.5	22.6	10.8	5.7	26.6	23.4	10.8	2.47	2.90	7 722	9.9	21.0
Williamson	44 725	80.0	43.0	69.8	37.2	7.8	4.6	20.0	16.6	4.5	2.81	3.18	27 928	8.0	14.8
Wilson	32 798	78.0	37.2	64.2	29.1	10.1	5.9	22.0	18.1	6.1	2.67	3.03	24 070	9.3	16.2
TEXAS	7 393 354	71.0	36.8	54.0	27.1	12.7	7.6	29.0	23.7	7.3	2.74	3.28	6 070 937	11.6	23.9
Anderson	15 678	72.3	34.1	55.5	24.2	13.2	7.9	27.7	24.8	11.8	2.58	3.07	14 223	11.5	22.6
Andrews	4 601	76.5	40.7	63.7	32.6	9.5	5.9	23.5	21.8	10.0	2.81	3.29	4 758	8.1	18.0
Angelina	28 685	74.1	36.1	57.8	26.8	12.3	7.1	25.9	22.8	9.8	2.70	3.18	25 004	11.1	22.2
Aransas	9 132	70.1	27.0	57.0	19.1	9.4	5.7	29.9	25.3	11.6	2.43	2.90	6 938	8.2	23.0
Archer	3 345	75.2	37.2	65.0	30.9	7.2	4.5	24.8	21.9	10.2	2.63	3.08	2 957	6.0	20.5
Armstrong	802	76.4	33.9	67.2	28.4	6.1	3.7	23.6	21.4	12.0	2.58	2.99	768	4.8	24.9
Atascosa	12 816	78.2	41.7	60.3	30.9	13.0	7.9	21.8	18.9	8.7	2.99	3.41	9 940	11.1	18.7
Austin	8 747	74.1	34.7	60.6	27.1	9.6	5.6	25.9	22.8	11.5	2.67	3.14	7 478	8.7	25.3
Bailey	2 348	75.7	37.1	64.9	30.4	7.5	4.6	24.3	22.3	12.8	2.78	3.28	2 454	6.2	20.6
Bandera	7 010	72.2	29.1	60.8	22.4	7.3	4.4	27.8	23.2	9.9	2.49	2.92	4 180	5.5	23.5
Bastrop	20 097	73.5	35.9	58.5	27.1	10.5	6.2	26.5	21.5	7.5	2.77	3.23	13 379	10.1	21.5
Baylor	1 791	64.6	25.2	53.5	18.7	8.2	4.9	35.4	33.3	19.2	2.26	2.86	1 906	5.9	31.7
Bee	9 061	72.6	37.8	52.9	25.6	14.8	9.4	27.4	23.7	9.9	2.74	3.25	8 592	11.6	21.7
Bell	85 507	72.5	40.1	56.6	29.2	12.3	8.7	27.5	22.3	6.5	2.68	3.14	67 240	10.6	21.4
Bexar	488 942	70.7	36.6	50.5	25.2	15.5	9.1	29.3	24.0	7.4	2.78	3.33	409 043	14.5	23.2
Blanco	3 303	72.4	30.4	61.5	24.0	7.2	4.3	27.6	24.0	10.8	2.50	2.96	2 338	5.9	25.1
Borden	292	74.3	30.1	65.1	24.0	6.2	4.8	25.7	22.6	9.2	2.50	2.93	294	5.1	16.7
Bosque	6 726	72.2	29.5	60.6	22.8	8.2	4.7	27.8	25.4	14.1	2.48	2.95	5 990	6.7	25.7
Bowie	33 058	70.9	33.0	52.0	22.0	15.0	9.1	29.1	26.0	11.1	2.50	3.00	30 595	13.2	24.4
Brazoria	81 954	77.0	40.8	62.2	31.7	10.4	6.5	23.0	19.1	6.4	2.82	3.23	64 019	8.6	18.5
Brazos	55 202	55.1	27.9	41.3	20.4	10.0	6.1	44.9	25.5	5.0	2.52	3.16	43 725	9.1	25.2
Brewster	3 669	60.4	26.6	46.7	18.5	10.0	6.5	39.6	32.8	11.4	2.31	2.96	3 350	9.2	29.2
Briscoe	724	70.6	29.3	59.3	22.8	7.6	4.4	29.4	27.9	16.0	2.47	3.03	789	5.8	26.7
Brooks	2 711	76.7	38.9	52.2	25.5	19.1	11.0	23.3	21.4	11.3	2.92	3.38	2 673	16.1	20.8
Brown	14 306	70.0	31.4	55.9	22.7	10.9	6.7	30.0	26.5	12.4	2.48	2.98	13 097	10.3	25.8
Burleson	6 363	71.9	31.9	56.4	23.4	11.4	6.3	28.1	24.9	12.4	2.57	3.08	5 176	10.3	26.4
Burnet	13 133	73.6	30.1	61.5	22.9	8.6	5.2	26.4	22.5	10.8	2.53	2.94	9 055	7.5	23.9

[1] No spouse present.

Table B. States and Counties

STATE County	Percent change of households, 1990–2000	Total housing units	Occupied housing units (percent)	Vacant housing units — Total	Vacant — For seasonal, recreational, or occasional use	Homeowner vacancy rate (percent)	Rental vacancy rate (percent)	Occupied housing units — Total	Percent owner-occupied housing units	Percent renter-occupied housing units	Average household size of owner-occupied units	Average household size of renter-occupied units
	86	87	88	89	90	91	92	93	94	95	96	97

STATE County	86	87	88	89	90	91	92	93	94	95	96	97
TENNESSEE—Cont'd												
Marshall	24.7	11 181	92.2	7.8	0.7	2.3	7.6	10 307	73.1	26.9	2.61	2.44
Maury	28.3	28 674	92.2	7.8	0.4	2.1	10.8	26 444	72.8	27.2	2.64	2.42
Meigs	43.7	5 188	83.0	17.0	9.6	1.4	7.8	4 304	81.9	18.1	2.57	2.45
Monroe	34.9	17 287	88.7	11.3	3.8	1.9	9.9	15 329	78.3	21.7	2.55	2.34
Montgomery	40.7	52 167	92.6	7.4	0.2	2.7	7.3	48 330	63.5	36.5	2.78	2.56
Moore	27.5	2 515	87.9	12.1	3.1	1.4	7.5	2 211	83.7	16.3	2.56	2.49
Morgan	19.7	7 714	90.6	9.4	1.9	1.4	9.7	6 990	82.9	17.1	2.61	2.46
Obion	6.2	14 489	91.0	9.0	1.2	1.7	11.1	13 182	71.5	28.5	2.46	2.33
Overton	20.4	9 168	88.5	11.5	1.8	1.9	11.0	8 110	80.9	19.1	2.49	2.32
Perry	20.3	4 115	73.5	26.5	16.5	2.0	11.7	3 023	86.0	14.0	2.52	2.21
Pickett	17.1	2 956	70.7	29.3	20.9	1.1	10.9	2 091	84.3	15.7	2.37	2.15
Polk	26.6	7 369	87.5	12.5	3.9	1.4	8.9	6 448	80.8	19.2	2.49	2.34
Putnam	25.9	26 916	92.4	7.6	0.6	2.1	7.8	24 865	65.6	34.4	2.50	2.23
Rhea	21.8	12 565	89.0	11.0	3.3	1.9	9.2	11 184	75.5	24.5	2.48	2.40
Roane	14.9	23 369	90.7	9.3	1.9	1.7	13.1	21 200	77.6	22.4	2.47	2.21
Robertson	34.5	20 995	94.8	5.2	0.3	1.4	4.8	19 906	76.5	23.5	2.74	2.60
Rutherford	57.8	70 616	94.1	5.9	0.3	2.1	8.9	66 443	69.8	30.2	2.79	2.35
Scott	25.5	8 909	92.1	7.9	1.6	1.2	7.2	8 203	76.4	23.6	2.62	2.31
Sequatchie	35.8	4 916	90.8	9.2	1.5	2.4	7.9	4 463	76.4	23.6	2.54	2.44
Sevier	45.8	37 252	76.4	23.6	15.1	2.0	17.2	28 467	73.4	26.6	2.53	2.34
Shelby	11.5	362 954	93.2	6.8	0.3	1.9	8.3	338 366	63.1	36.9	2.71	2.40
Smith	28.4	7 665	89.7	10.3	1.4	2.0	7.0	6 878	78.7	21.3	2.60	2.38
Stewart	34.0	5 977	82.5	17.5	8.7	2.3	9.6	4 930	79.2	20.8	2.53	2.32
Sullivan	12.0	69 052	92.0	8.0	0.7	2.0	11.7	63 556	75.7	24.3	2.43	2.18
Sumner	32.8	51 657	94.7	5.3	0.4	1.7	6.9	48 941	75.6	24.4	2.72	2.37
Tipton	38.9	19 064	95.0	5.0	0.4	2.0	5.4	18 106	76.1	23.9	2.81	2.69
Trousdale	23.0	3 095	89.8	10.2	1.3	1.7	7.6	2 780	76.4	23.6	2.57	2.48
Unicoi	13.5	8 214	91.5	8.5	1.4	1.0	6.5	7 516	76.4	23.6	2.35	2.19
Union	36.7	7 916	85.2	14.8	5.8	1.6	12.2	6 742	81.0	19.0	2.64	2.53
Van Buren	21.2	2 453	88.9	11.1	3.1	1.3	5.0	2 180	85.3	14.7	2.51	2.38
Warren	19.7	16 689	91.0	9.0	0.7	2.6	10.6	15 181	72.8	27.2	2.50	2.41
Washington	23.4	47 779	92.5	7.5	0.5	2.2	8.9	44 195	68.2	31.8	2.46	2.07
Wayne	14.7	6 701	88.6	11.4	1.4	1.3	11.3	5 936	82.9	17.1	2.52	2.26
Weakley	13.4	14 928	91.1	8.9	0.9	1.8	9.6	13 599	69.0	31.0	2.47	2.19
White	19.5	10 191	90.6	9.4	1.2	2.3	10.2	9 229	79.8	20.2	2.48	2.41
Williamson	60.1	47 005	95.1	4.9	0.3	2.3	5.7	44 725	81.5	18.5	2.93	2.30
Wilson	36.3	34 921	93.9	6.1	0.8	2.0	8.2	32 798	81.4	18.6	2.73	2.44
TEXAS	21.8	8 157 575	90.6	9.4	2.1	1.8	8.5	7 393 354	63.8	36.2	2.87	2.53
Anderson	10.2	18 436	85.0	15.0	3.9	2.3	15.0	15 678	74.0	26.0	2.57	2.61
Andrews	-3.3	5 400	85.2	14.8	0.2	3.8	22.0	4 601	79.7	20.3	2.86	2.60
Angelina	14.7	32 435	88.4	11.6	3.2	1.8	10.1	28 685	72.4	27.6	2.73	2.62
Aransas	31.6	12 848	71.1	28.9	19.2	2.5	14.6	9 132	75.2	24.8	2.43	2.46
Archer	13.1	3 871	86.4	13.6	5.6	2.1	6.8	3 345	81.3	18.7	2.66	2.50
Armstrong	4.4	920	87.2	12.8	1.6	2.3	12.0	802	78.9	21.1	2.53	2.76
Atascosa	28.9	14 883	86.1	13.9	2.5	1.6	9.9	12 816	78.4	21.6	3.02	2.85
Austin	17.0	10 205	85.7	14.3	5.5	1.8	7.4	8 747	77.2	22.8	2.68	2.62
Bailey	-4.3	2 738	85.8	14.2	0.9	3.2	10.5	2 348	71.4	28.6	2.74	2.89
Bandera	67.7	9 503	73.8	26.2	12.5	3.0	8.1	7 010	82.9	17.1	2.49	2.50
Bastrop	50.2	22 254	90.3	9.7	2.4	1.3	8.9	20 097	80.4	19.6	2.79	2.71
Baylor	-6.0	2 820	63.5	36.5	24.6	3.9	11.9	1 791	72.4	27.6	2.29	2.18
Bee	5.5	10 939	82.8	17.2	2.0	2.7	16.0	9 061	65.5	34.5	2.73	2.75
Bell	27.2	92 782	92.2	7.8	0.4	2.2	8.5	85 507	55.7	44.3	2.77	2.56
Bexar	19.5	521 359	93.8	6.2	0.5	1.4	6.7	488 942	61.2	38.8	2.94	2.52
Blanco	41.3	4 031	81.9	18.1	10.0	2.5	3.4	3 303	78.8	21.2	2.51	2.46
Borden	-0.7	435	67.1	32.9	8.7	2.3	6.2	292	74.0	26.0	2.32	2.99
Bosque	12.3	8 644	77.8	22.2	11.4	3.0	7.3	6 726	77.7	22.3	2.45	2.59
Bowie	8.1	36 463	90.7	9.3	0.6	1.8	11.9	33 058	71.0	29.0	2.52	2.44
Brazoria	28.0	90 628	90.4	9.6	1.7	1.6	13.0	81 954	74.0	26.0	2.90	2.58
Brazos	26.2	59 023	93.5	6.5	0.7	1.6	6.2	55 202	45.6	54.4	2.80	2.28
Brewster	9.5	4 614	79.5	20.5	6.3	2.0	13.6	3 669	59.5	40.5	2.41	2.16
Briscoe	-8.2	1 006	72.0	28.0	11.1	3.3	10.3	724	77.1	22.9	2.45	2.55
Brooks	1.4	3 203	84.6	15.4	3.5	0.9	10.9	2 711	73.0	27.0	2.84	3.11
Brown	9.2	17 889	80.0	20.0	8.9	3.6	10.2	14 306	72.2	27.8	2.51	2.39
Burleson	22.9	8 197	77.6	22.4	10.9	2.3	8.3	6 363	79.7	20.3	2.53	2.73
Burnet	45.0	15 933	82.4	17.6	10.4	2.2	7.5	13 133	78.3	21.7	2.53	2.53

Table B. States and Counties

STATE/ County code	MSA/ PMSA/ NECMA code[1]	County type[2]	STATE County	Land area, 2000[3] (sq km)	Total persons	Rank	Per square kilometer	Land area, 1990[3] (sq km)	Total persons	Rank	Per square kilometer	White	Black or African American	American Indian or Alaska Native	Asian	Native Hawaiian and other Pacific Islander	Some other race
																Race (percent) One race	
				1	2	3	4	5	6	7	8	9	10	11	12	13	14
			TEXAS—Cont'd														
48 055	0640	2	Caldwell	1 413	32 194	1 342	22.8	1 414	26 392	1 409	18.7	70.1	8.5	0.6	0.3	0.0	17.7
48 057	...	6	Calhoun	1 327	20 647	1 755	15.0	1 327	19 053	1 731	14.4	78.0	2.6	0.5	3.3	0.1	13.2
48 059	...	6	Callahan	2 327	12 905	2 240	5.5	2 328	11 859	2 226	5.1	94.8	0.2	0.6	0.3	0.1	2.7
48 061	1240	2	Cameron	2 346	335 227	174	142.9	2 345	260 120	193	110.9	80.3	0.5	0.4	0.5	0.0	16.0
48 063	...	6	Camp	512	11 549	2 330	22.6	512	9 904	2 396	19.3	69.5	19.2	0.3	0.2	0.1	9.6
48 065	...	8	Carson	2 391	6 516	2 738	2.7	2 391	6 576	2 701	2.8	93.8	0.6	1.0	0.1	0.0	3.0
48 067	...	6	Cass	2 428	30 438	1 387	12.5	2 428	29 982	1 298	12.3	78.2	19.5	0.5	0.1	0.0	0.7
48 069	...	7	Castro	2 327	8 285	2 582	3.6	2 327	9 070	2 463	3.9	75.4	2.3	1.2	0.0	0.0	19.1
48 071	3360	1	Chambers	1 552	26 031	1 515	16.8	1 552	20 088	1 674	12.9	81.9	9.8	0.5	0.7	0.0	6.0
48 073	...	6	Cherokee	2 725	46 659	967	17.1	2 726	41 049	979	15.1	74.3	16.0	0.5	0.4	0.1	7.4
48 075	...	7	Childress	1 840	7 688	2 630	4.2	1 840	5 953	2 764	3.2	67.7	14.1	0.3	0.3	0.1	15.7
48 077	...	6	Clay	2 843	11 006	2 365	3.9	2 843	10 024	2 385	3.5	95.3	0.4	1.0	0.1	0.0	1.7
48 079	...	7	Cochran	2 008	3 730	2 940	1.9	2 008	4 377	2 884	2.2	64.5	4.5	0.8	0.2	0.1	27.3
48 081	...	8	Coke	2 328	3 864	2 925	1.7	2 328	3 424	2 961	1.5	88.8	1.9	0.8	0.1	0.0	6.9
48 083	...	6	Coleman	3 264	9 235	2 509	2.8	3 297	9 710	2 410	2.9	88.5	2.2	0.6	0.2	0.0	6.5
48 085	1920	0	Collin	2 195	491 675	113	224.0	2 196	264 036	188	120.2	81.4	4.8	0.5	6.9	0.0	4.3
48 087	...	9	Collingsworth	2 380	3 206	2 978	1.3	2 380	3 573	2 952	1.5	79.8	5.3	1.6	0.2	0.0	10.9
48 089	...	7	Colorado	2 494	20 390	1 768	8.2	2 494	18 383	1 770	7.4	72.8	14.8	0.4	0.2	0.0	10.0
48 091	7240	1	Comal	1 454	78 021	652	53.7	1 454	51 832	815	35.6	89.1	0.9	0.5	0.5	0.0	7.0
48 093	...	7	Comanche	2 429	14 026	2 161	5.8	2 429	13 381	2 106	5.5	87.3	0.4	0.6	0.1	0.0	9.7
48 095	...	8	Concho	2 568	3 966	2 921	1.5	2 568	3 044	2 996	1.2	88.2	1.0	0.5	0.1	0.1	8.9
48 097	...	6	Cooke	2 263	36 363	1 203	16.1	2 263	30 777	1 253	13.6	88.8	3.1	1.0	0.3	0.0	5.2
48 099	3810	2	Coryell	2 724	74 978	665	27.5	2 724	64 226	683	23.6	65.3	21.8	0.9	1.8	0.5	6.3
48 101	...	9	Cottle	2 334	1 904	3 072	0.8	2 334	2 247	3 050	1.0	81.5	9.9	0.0	0.0	0.0	7.2
48 103	...	6	Crane	2 035	3 996	2 920	2.0	2 035	4 652	2 864	2.3	73.7	2.9	1.0	0.4	0.0	19.5
48 105	...	7	Crockett	7 271	4 099	2 908	0.6	7 272	4 078	2 908	0.6	76.3	0.7	0.6	0.3	0.0	19.7
48 107	...	8	Crosby	2 330	7 072	2 678	3.0	2 330	7 304	2 628	3.1	63.8	3.9	0.5	0.1	0.1	29.9
48 109	...	7	Culberson	9 874	2 975	2 993	0.3	9 875	3 407	2 963	0.3	68.9	0.7	0.5	0.6	0.0	27.1
48 111	...	7	Dallam	3 897	6 222	2 761	1.6	3 897	5 461	2 803	1.4	82.6	1.6	0.9	0.2	0.0	12.4
48 113	1920	0	Dallas	2 278	2 218 899	10	974.1	2 279	1 852 691	11	812.9	58.4	20.3	0.6	4.0	0.1	14.0
48 115	...	7	Dawson	2 336	14 985	2 092	6.4	2 336	14 349	2 028	6.1	72.5	8.7	0.3	0.2	0.0	16.6
48 117	...	6	Deaf Smith	3 878	18 561	1 868	4.8	3 878	19 153	1 723	4.9	72.3	1.5	0.8	0.3	0.1	22.9
48 119	...	8	Delta	718	5 327	2 827	7.4	718	4 857	2 847	6.8	87.9	8.3	0.8	0.1	0.0	1.2
48 121	1920	0	Denton	2 301	432 976	139	188.2	2 301	273 644	182	118.9	81.7	5.9	0.6	4.0	0.1	5.6
48 123	...	6	De Witt	2 355	20 013	1 793	8.5	2 355	18 840	1 744	8.0	76.4	11.0	0.5	0.2	0.0	10.0
48 125	...	9	Dickens	2 342	2 762	3 007	1.2	2 342	2 571	3 018	1.1	77.6	8.2	0.4	0.1	0.3	12.3
48 127	...	7	Dimmit	3 447	10 248	2 422	3.0	3 447	10 433	2 345	3.0	77.0	0.9	0.7	0.7	0.1	18.2
48 129	...	9	Donley	2 408	3 828	2 926	1.6	2 408	3 696	2 939	1.5	91.4	3.9	0.9	0.1	0.0	2.7
48 131	...	7	Duval	4 643	13 120	2 220	2.8	4 643	12 918	2 144	2.8	80.2	0.5	0.5	0.1	0.0	15.5
48 133	...	7	Eastland	2 398	18 297	1 880	7.6	2 399	18 488	1 762	7.7	91.0	2.2	0.5	0.2	0.0	4.8
48 135	5800	3	Ector	2 334	121 123	447	51.9	2 334	118 934	390	51.0	73.7	4.6	0.8	0.6	0.0	17.4
48 137	...	9	Edwards	5 490	2 162	3 053	0.4	5 491	2 266	3 044	0.4	83.3	0.8	0.8	0.1	0.0	12.7
48 139	1920	1	Ellis	2 434	111 360	486	45.8	2 435	85 167	539	35.0	80.6	8.6	0.6	0.4	0.0	7.9
48 141	2320	2	El Paso	2 624	679 622	75	259.0	2 624	591 610	79	225.5	73.9	3.1	0.8	1.0	0.1	17.9
48 143	...	6	Erath	2 814	33 001	1 319	11.7	2 814	27 991	1 352	9.9	89.7	0.8	0.7	0.4	0.0	6.8
48 145	...	6	Falls	1 992	18 576	1 866	9.3	1 992	17 712	1 803	8.9	61.5	27.5	0.5	0.1	0.0	8.8
48 147	...	6	Fannin	2 309	31 242	1 369	13.5	2 309	24 804	1 469	10.7	86.6	8.0	0.9	0.3	0.0	2.8
48 149	...	7	Fayette	2 461	21 804	1 701	8.9	2 461	20 095	1 672	8.2	84.6	7.0	0.4	0.2	0.1	6.7
48 151	...	9	Fisher	2 334	4 344	2 892	1.9	2 334	4 842	2 851	2.1	83.7	2.8	0.4	0.1	0.0	11.6
48 153	...	7	Floyd	2 570	7 771	2 628	3.0	2 570	8 497	2 512	3.3	74.2	3.4	0.8	0.2	0.1	19.7
48 155	...	9	Foard	1 830	1 622	3 088	0.9	1 830	1 794	3 078	1.0	84.2	3.3	0.6	0.2	0.0	10.2
48 157	3360	0	Fort Bend	2 265	354 452	166	156.5	2 266	225 421	219	99.5	57.0	19.8	0.3	11.2	0.0	9.1
48 159	...	9	Franklin	740	9 458	2 490	12.8	740	7 802	2 595	10.5	89.2	3.9	0.6	0.2	0.0	5.1
48 161	...	7	Freestone	2 273	17 867	1 907	7.9	2 293	15 818	1 934	6.9	75.6	18.9	0.4	0.3	0.0	3.9
48 163	...	7	Frio	2 935	16 252	2 004	5.5	2 935	13 472	2 103	4.6	71.9	4.9	0.6	0.4	0.0	19.8
48 165	...	7	Gaines	3 891	14 467	2 125	3.7	3 891	14 123	2 044	3.6	80.3	2.3	0.8	0.2	0.0	14.2
48 167	2920	0	Galveston	1 032	250 158	231	242.4	1 033	217 396	228	210.5	72.7	15.4	0.5	2.1	0.0	7.2
48 169	...	6	Garza	2 319	4 872	2 856	2.1	2 320	5 143	2 830	2.2	74.8	4.8	0.2	0.1	0.0	17.1
48 171	...	7	Gillespie	2 748	20 814	1 747	7.6	2 748	17 204	1 842	6.3	92.8	0.2	0.3	0.2	0.0	5.3
48 173	...	8	Glasscock	2 333	1 406	3 097	0.6	2 333	1 447	3 098	0.6	77.5	0.5	0.1	0.0	0.2	19.1
48 175	...	8	Goliad	2 211	6 928	2 693	3.1	2 211	5 980	2 761	2.7	82.6	4.8	0.5	0.2	0.0	10.0
48 177	...	6	Gonzales	2 765	18 628	1 865	6.7	2 766	17 205	1 841	6.2	72.2	8.4	0.5	0.3	0.1	16.5
48 179	...	7	Gray	2 404	22 744	1 661	9.5	2 404	23 967	1 494	10.0	82.2	5.8	0.9	0.4	0.0	8.2
48 181	7640	3	Grayson	2 418	110 595	491	45.7	2 418	95 019	489	39.3	87.2	5.9	1.3	0.6	0.0	2.9
48 183	4420	3	Gregg	710	111 379	485	156.9	710	104 948	440	147.8	72.9	19.9	0.5	0.7	0.0	4.6
48 185	...	6	Grimes	2 055	23 552	1 612	11.5	2 056	18 843	1 743	9.2	71.8	20.0	0.3	0.3	0.0	5.9

[1] MSA = Metropolitan Statistical Area. PMSA = Primary MSA. NECMA = New England County Metropolitan Area. See Appendix A for explanation of these concepts. See Appendix B for list of metropolitan areas identified by type, with component counties.
[2] County typology code from the Economic Research Service of USDA. See Appendix A for definition.
[3] Dry land or land partially or temporarily covered by water.

Table B. States and Counties

STATE County	Population and population characteristics, 2000 (cont'd)								Population and population characteristics, 1990				
	Race (percent) (cont'd)								Race (percent)				
	Race alone or in combination												
	Two or more races	White	Black	American Indian or Alaska Native	Asian	Native Hawaiian and other Pacific Islander	Some other race	Hispanic¹	White	Black or African American	American Indian or Alaska Native	Asian and Pacific Islander	Hispanic¹
	15	16	17	18	19	20	21	22	23	24	25	26	27
TEXAS—Cont'd													
Caldwell	2.7	72.6	8.9	1.1	0.6	0.1	19.6	40.4	71.7	10.7	0.2	0.3	37.8
Calhoun	2.3	80.1	2.9	0.9	3.5	0.1	14.9	40.9	77.8	2.9	0.2	2.9	36.2
Callahan	1.3	96.0	0.4	1.1	0.6	0.1	3.3	6.3	96.8	0.0	0.4	0.3	4.1
Cameron	2.3	82.4	0.6	0.6	0.6	0.1	18.0	84.3	82.4	0.3	0.2	0.3	81.9
Camp	1.1	70.5	19.5	0.8	0.2	0.1	10.0	14.8	72.0	23.8	0.4	0.1	5.1
Carson	1.4	95.1	0.8	1.6	0.2	0.1	3.7	7.0	96.0	0.2	0.7	0.1	5.4
Cass	1.0	79.1	19.8	1.0	0.2	0.0	0.9	1.7	78.9	20.2	0.4	0.1	1.2
Castro	2.1	77.1	2.6	1.6	0.0	0.0	20.8	51.6	60.9	2.9	0.1	0.2	46.2
Chambers	1.2	82.9	10.0	0.9	0.8	0.0	6.5	10.8	83.3	12.7	0.3	0.6	5.9
Cherokee	1.3	75.5	16.3	0.9	0.5	0.1	8.0	13.2	78.1	16.9	0.3	0.5	6.6
Childress	1.8	69.4	14.5	0.8	0.4	0.1	16.8	20.5	83.5	5.4	0.4	0.3	14.3
Clay	1.4	96.8	0.5	2.0	0.2	0.0	2.1	3.7	97.3	0.3	0.9	0.2	2.4
Cochran	2.5	66.5	5.1	1.0	0.2	0.1	29.6	44.1	68.5	5.3	0.3	0.0	42.4
Coke	1.4	90.1	2.0	1.2	0.2	0.1	7.8	16.9	94.1	0.2	0.5	0.1	12.3
Coleman	1.9	90.2	2.4	1.2	0.4	0.0	7.7	14.0	92.6	2.5	0.3	0.1	11.7
Collin	2.1	83.2	5.2	1.0	7.6	0.1	5.2	10.3	89.1	4.1	0.4	2.8	6.9
Collingsworth	2.2	82.0	5.5	2.6	0.3	0.0	11.8	20.4	83.3	6.4	0.9	0.1	15.7
Colorado	1.8	74.3	15.1	0.7	0.4	0.1	11.3	19.7	72.6	17.0	0.2	0.1	15.4
Comal	2.0	90.9	1.2	1.0	0.7	0.1	8.2	22.6	90.3	0.9	0.3	0.3	22.9
Comanche	1.8	88.9	0.6	1.3	0.2	0.0	10.8	20.9	91.9	0.1	0.4	0.1	16.5
Concho	1.2	89.3	1.1	0.8	0.1	0.1	9.9	41.3	89.3	0.5	0.2	0.2	39.2
Cooke	1.6	90.3	3.3	1.6	0.5	0.1	5.8	10.0	92.2	3.8	0.8	0.4	4.6
Coryell	3.5	68.0	23.2	1.6	2.7	0.8	7.5	12.6	70.2	21.2	0.7	2.6	9.7
Cottle	1.5	82.8	10.5	0.9	0.0	0.0	7.7	18.9	82.5	8.9	0.2	0.1	16.3
Crane	2.6	76.1	3.2	1.1	0.4	0.0	21.8	43.9	66.6	2.8	0.2	0.2	33.9
Crockett	2.4	78.5	0.9	1.0	0.3	0.0	21.6	54.7	98.5	1.0	0.2	0.1	49.6
Crosby	1.8	65.2	4.1	0.9	0.2	0.1	31.3	48.9	79.2	4.4	0.2	0.1	42.6
Culberson	2.2	70.9	0.7	0.8	0.7	0.0	29.0	72.2	70.4	0.1	0.5	0.8	71.0
Dallam	2.2	84.6	1.9	1.6	0.4	0.1	13.9	28.4	84.2	2.1	0.8	0.3	21.1
Dallas	2.7	60.6	20.8	1.0	4.4	0.1	15.8	29.9	67.0	19.9	0.5	2.8	17.0
Dawson	1.8	74.1	8.8	0.6	0.3	0.0	17.9	48.2	68.2	4.3	0.2	0.1	42.7
Deaf Smith	2.1	74.1	1.7	1.1	0.4	0.2	24.8	57.4	75.8	1.6	0.3	0.2	48.8
Delta	1.7	89.4	8.8	1.8	0.2	0.0	1.6	3.1	90.3	8.3	0.8	0.1	1.4
Denton	2.2	83.6	6.3	1.2	4.5	0.1	6.5	12.2	88.5	5.0	0.5	2.5	7.0
De Witt	1.8	77.9	11.3	0.9	0.4	0.0	11.4	27.2	76.2	11.2	0.1	0.1	24.2
Dickens	1.1	78.6	8.4	0.9	0.1	0.3	12.8	23.9	85.3	4.4	0.5	0.0	18.6
Dimmit	2.5	79.2	1.1	0.9	0.8	0.1	20.4	83.3	85.0	0.6	0.2	0.1	83.3
Donley	0.9	92.3	4.4	1.1	0.2	0.0	3.0	6.3	95.3	3.4	0.4	0.1	3.8
Duval	3.1	83.2	0.6	0.8	0.2	0.1	18.3	88.0	78.8	0.1	0.1	0.1	87.2
Eastland	1.3	92.2	2.3	0.9	0.2	0.0	5.5	10.8	94.5	2.1	0.3	0.2	7.6
Ector	2.8	76.3	4.9	1.4	0.8	0.1	19.5	42.4	76.8	4.7	0.5	0.6	31.4
Edwards	2.3	85.0	1.4	1.2	0.2	0.0	14.5	45.1	93.3	0.0	0.2	0.2	52.2
Ellis	1.9	82.3	8.9	1.1	0.5	0.0	9.0	18.4	81.1	10.0	0.4	0.3	13.2
El Paso	3.2	76.8	3.5	1.1	1.3	0.2	20.4	78.2	76.5	3.7	0.4	1.1	69.6
Erath	1.6	91.0	1.0	1.2	0.7	0.1	7.7	15.0	94.4	0.7	0.3	0.4	8.8
Falls	1.6	62.9	27.7	0.8	0.2	0.0	9.9	15.8	64.3	27.2	0.2	0.1	11.7
Fannin	1.5	87.9	8.2	1.8	0.4	0.1	3.2	5.6	91.6	6.6	0.7	0.2	2.0
Fayette	1.1	85.6	7.2	0.6	0.3	0.1	7.4	12.8	86.2	8.4	0.1	0.1	8.5
Fisher	1.4	85.1	2.9	0.8	0.2	0.0	12.4	21.4	91.8	3.9	0.4	0.0	20.6
Floyd	1.8	75.8	3.6	1.1	0.2	0.1	21.0	45.9	65.0	3.8	0.2	0.2	39.8
Foard	1.5	85.6	3.5	1.4	0.2	0.0	10.9	16.3	86.5	4.9	0.6	0.2	13.0
Fort Bend	2.6	58.9	20.4	0.6	12.0	0.1	10.7	21.1	62.6	20.7	0.2	6.4	19.5
Franklin	0.9	90.0	4.1	1.1	0.2	0.0	5.5	8.9	91.5	4.5	0.6	0.2	4.6
Freestone	1.0	76.5	19.1	0.6	0.4	0.0	4.3	8.2	78.3	19.0	0.3	0.2	3.9
Frio	2.5	74.2	5.0	0.8	0.5	0.1	22.0	73.8	67.7	1.4	0.2	0.3	72.4
Gaines	2.4	82.4	2.4	1.3	0.3	0.0	15.9	35.8	73.5	2.4	0.3	0.1	32.6
Galveston	2.1	74.5	15.8	0.9	2.5	0.1	8.4	18.0	75.5	17.6	0.3	1.6	14.2
Garza	3.0	77.3	5.4	1.1	0.1	0.2	19.3	37.2	89.2	6.4	0.2	0.4	28.3
Gillespie	1.2	93.9	0.3	0.7	0.3	0.0	6.0	15.9	94.9	0.2	0.3	0.2	14.1
Glasscock	2.5	80.0	0.6	0.3	0.0	0.2	21.4	29.9	79.9	0.0	0.1	0.0	29.3
Goliad	1.7	84.2	5.0	1.0	0.2	0.0	11.3	35.2	82.8	6.8	0.3	0.1	35.9
Gonzales	2.0	73.9	8.8	0.8	0.4	0.2	18.0	39.6	75.7	10.0	0.3	0.1	35.7
Gray	2.4	84.3	6.2	2.3	0.5	0.1	9.0	13.0	90.0	3.8	0.9	0.5	7.9
Grayson	2.1	89.1	6.3	2.4	0.8	0.1	3.5	6.8	90.0	6.9	1.1	0.4	2.9
Gregg	1.5	74.2	20.3	1.1	0.8	0.1	5.1	9.1	78.0	19.0	0.5	0.5	3.6
Grimes	1.6	73.3	20.2	0.7	0.4	0.1	6.9	16.1	68.4	24.5	0.3	0.2	14.1

¹Hispanic persons may be of any race.

Table B. States and Counties

STATE County	Population and population characteristics, 2000										
	Age (percent)										
	Under 5 years	5 to 17 years	18 to 24 years	25 to 34 years	35 to 44 years	45 to 54 years	55 to 64 years	65 to 74 years	75 years and over	Median age (years)	Percent Female
	28	29	30	31	32	33	34	35	36	37	38
TEXAS Cont'd											
Caldwell	7.4	21.0	8.5	14.1	15.7	13.0	7.8	6.4	6.1	34.4	50.6
Calhoun	7.8	20.7	8.7	12.4	14.9	12.6	9.7	8.3	5.0	35.3	49.8
Callahan	5.5	20.7	6.6	9.8	15.1	13.9	11.4	9.3	7.7	39.8	51.4
Cameron	9.5	24.3	10.5	13.8	12.9	10.7	7.1	6.3	4.8	29.0	52.1
Camp	7.3	19.5	8.5	12.0	13.6	12.7	10.1	8.9	7.3	36.9	51.0
Carson	6.1	21.7	6.2	9.8	16.5	13.6	10.3	8.3	7.4	38.9	51.1
Cass	6.0	18.9	7.6	10.6	13.9	13.9	11.5	8.9	8.6	40.0	52.0
Castro	8.5	24.6	9.0	10.9	13.4	12.4	8.5	7.6	5.1	32.3	49.9
Chambers	6.9	22.0	8.2	12.7	17.2	15.3	8.7	5.4	3.6	35.1	49.8
Cherokee	7.0	19.3	9.3	12.9	14.5	12.5	9.4	7.6	7.5	36.0	49.7
Childress	5.7	16.4	12.1	13.8	16.9	10.8	8.6	8.5	7.3	36.6	41.2
Clay	5.8	19.0	6.8	10.1	16.3	14.3	11.6	9.3	6.8	40.2	51.5
Cochran	6.5	25.0	8.0	10.4	14.5	10.9	10.3	8.0	6.5	35.1	52.1
Coke	4.3	20.1	7.5	8.0	12.5	11.7	11.9	13.3	10.8	43.3	50.0
Coleman	5.8	17.9	6.6	9.4	13.3	12.3	11.7	11.1	12.0	43.0	52.0
Collin	8.6	20.1	7.4	17.8	20.1	13.7	7.0	3.1	2.2	32.9	50.0
Collingsworth	5.9	20.5	6.6	9.4	13.2	12.8	9.6	10.3	11.7	40.6	51.8
Colorado	6.0	19.6	8.9	10.0	13.8	13.0	10.2	9.4	9.2	39.3	51.2
Comal	6.2	19.3	7.0	11.4	16.1	14.9	10.3	8.0	6.9	39.0	51.0
Comanche	6.3	19.0	7.1	10.7	12.6	12.0	12.0	10.0	10.3	40.3	51.1
Concho	3.7	12.4	10.4	21.2	17.0	12.2	9.3	6.4	7.4	36.0	35.6
Cooke	6.7	20.6	8.7	11.6	14.5	13.1	9.9	7.7	7.2	36.7	50.7
Coryell	7.8	18.4	17.9	19.8	16.5	8.6	5.2	3.3	2.4	27.8	48.7
Cottle	5.1	18.9	5.7	7.9	13.6	12.5	10.8	11.1	14.4	43.9	53.4
Crane	7.7	24.2	7.7	11.5	15.3	13.5	9.2	5.7	5.2	34.2	51.3
Crockett	6.7	22.2	7.1	10.8	15.6	14.2	10.5	7.0	5.9	37.2	50.5
Crosby	7.8	22.9	8.5	11.6	12.4	11.1	10.0	8.2	7.5	34.3	52.3
Culberson	7.5	24.6	7.8	12.8	13.0	12.8	10.2	7.5	3.8	32.8	49.3
Dallam	8.6	23.2	8.6	14.7	14.1	12.5	8.0	5.8	4.4	31.4	49.5
Dallas	8.2	19.7	10.7	18.0	16.4	12.0	6.9	4.4	3.6	31.1	50.1
Dawson	6.3	19.3	8.9	14.6	16.2	12.6	7.9	7.3	6.9	35.6	44.6
Deaf Smith	9.0	24.3	9.6	12.5	13.0	11.4	8.1	6.4	5.7	30.6	51.1
Delta	5.6	20.0	7.5	11.2	14.3	12.0	11.8	8.1	9.6	38.8	51.4
Denton	8.2	19.6	11.3	18.0	18.9	12.8	6.2	2.9	2.1	31.0	50.3
De Witt	5.5	18.3	7.0	10.9	16.1	13.6	9.6	9.4	9.5	40.1	48.7
Dickens	4.2	14.3	10.4	14.9	14.8	11.9	10.5	8.3	10.7	39.2	43.3
Dimmit	8.3	24.9	8.8	12.0	12.7	12.5	8.1	6.5	6.2	31.6	51.5
Donley	4.7	17.6	9.8	8.6	12.0	12.5	13.0	11.2	10.5	42.8	51.4
Duval	7.4	22.1	9.5	12.3	14.1	11.7	8.9	7.5	6.5	33.8	49.8
Eastland	5.9	17.4	9.8	9.2	13.1	12.6	11.3	10.4	10.4	41.3	51.5
Ector	8.0	22.4	10.5	12.8	15.2	12.4	7.8	6.4	4.5	32.0	51.4
Edwards	5.8	22.7	6.5	8.4	14.8	13.2	12.4	9.9	6.2	39.0	49.4
Ellis	7.6	22.6	9.3	13.1	16.7	13.5	8.0	5.1	4.2	33.2	50.4
El Paso	8.7	23.3	10.6	14.5	14.8	11.3	7.1	5.7	4.0	30.0	51.8
Erath	6.5	18.1	17.0	12.7	13.2	11.2	7.9	6.6	6.8	31.4	50.6
Falls	6.0	21.7	7.8	12.7	14.3	11.6	9.1	8.3	8.6	36.5	53.8
Fannin	5.8	17.4	8.9	13.0	15.7	13.0	10.2	8.1	8.0	38.0	46.8
Fayette	5.4	17.8	7.0	9.1	14.5	13.8	10.4	9.7	12.3	42.6	51.6
Fisher	5.7	18.2	6.3	9.0	14.0	12.5	11.6	11.6	11.1	42.9	51.8
Floyd	8.2	23.2	7.4	11.5	12.9	11.5	9.2	8.2	8.0	34.8	51.6
Foard	5.7	20.1	5.8	10.0	12.3	11.9	11.0	9.7	13.4	41.7	53.6
Fort Bend	7.7	24.3	7.6	12.9	19.3	15.6	6.8	3.4	2.2	33.3	50.2
Franklin	5.7	18.6	7.3	10.9	13.9	13.3	11.7	10.5	8.0	40.3	51.5
Freestone	5.6	18.1	8.9	13.1	14.9	13.0	10.1	8.3	8.1	37.8	47.5
Frio	7.7	21.0	11.2	16.8	14.0	11.3	7.5	5.9	4.7	30.7	45.2
Gaines	8.4	26.7	9.5	11.7	15.0	10.8	7.6	6.1	4.2	29.7	50.8
Galveston	7.0	19.7	8.7	13.2	17.0	14.4	8.9	6.3	4.8	35.9	51.0
Garza	6.5	21.6	7.9	13.9	14.7	12.0	9.3	6.9	7.2	35.1	47.1
Gillespie	5.0	16.5	5.5	8.5	12.6	13.7	12.6	12.7	12.8	46.3	52.7
Glasscock	8.0	25.5	7.1	11.5	17.0	12.5	9.5	6.0	3.0	33.5	47.9
Goliad	5.8	20.1	6.5	10.0	15.1	14.4	10.8	9.5	8.0	40.2	50.3
Gonzales	7.0	21.0	8.7	11.6	14.0	11.8	9.1	8.5	8.2	36.3	50.4
Gray	5.9	18.2	8.4	12.2	15.0	12.4	9.8	9.1	9.0	38.9	49.0
Grayson	6.5	18.8	9.3	12.1	15.4	13.2	9.5	7.7	7.4	37.2	51.6
Gregg	7.0	19.7	10.3	13.0	15.2	12.9	8.6	7.0	6.2	35.0	51.6
Grimes	6.1	18.6	7.7	12.5	17.3	14.5	9.5	7.6	6.1	38.1	46.0

Table B. States and Counties

STATE County	Under 5 years	5 to 17 years	18 to 24 years	25 to 34 years	35 to 44 years	45 to 54 years	55 to 64 years	65 to 74 years	75 years and over	Percent Female	2000	1990	1980	1990–2000	1980–1990
	39	40	41	42	43	44	45	46	47	48	49	50	51	52	53
TEXAS—Cont'd															
Caldwell	7.8	21.9	11.9	14.7	13.3	8.7	8.1	7.1	6.5	49.8	32 194	26 392	23 637	22.0	11.7
Calhoun	7.5	22.0	8.7	15.6	13.8	10.7	10.7	7.0	4.0	50.5	20 647	19 053	19 574	8.4	-2.7
Callahan	6.6	20.8	6.5	13.4	13.9	10.7	10.7	9.0	8.2	51.6	12 905	11 859	10 992	8.8	7.9
Cameron	8.9	26.4	11.3	14.6	12.8	8.1	7.3	6.4	4.2	52.1	335 227	260 120	209 727	28.9	24.0
Camp	6.7	19.6	8.7	13.5	13.6	9.8	10.4	10.0	7.8	52.0	11 549	9 904	9 275	16.6	6.8
Carson	7.1	22.8	6.5	14.4	13.5	10.3	9.9	9.0	6.4	51.5	6 516	6 576	6 672	-0.9	-1.4
Cass	6.6	20.7	8.2	13.5	13.4	10.7	9.8	9.2	7.9	52.0	30 438	29 982	29 430	1.5	1.9
Castro	9.5	26.8	9.1	13.9	12.5	9.5	8.6	5.8	4.2	50.3	8 285	9 070	10 556	-8.7	-14.1
Chambers	6.9	22.8	8.9	15.3	17.3	11.1	8.2	6.1	3.4	49.7	26 031	20 088	18 538	29.6	8.4
Cherokee	7.1	19.1	9.6	14.3	12.9	10.2	9.4	9.2	8.3	50.8	46 659	41 049	38 127	13.7	7.7
Childress	5.7	20.4	6.7	11.4	12.1	10.0	11.0	10.1	12.5	53.5	7 688	5 953	6 950	29.1	-14.3
Clay	6.3	20.0	6.4	14.0	13.3	11.9	11.0	9.1	7.9	51.3	11 006	10 024	9 582	9.8	4.6
Cochran	8.4	24.9	9.1	15.1	10.7	10.4	8.9	6.9	5.6	50.4	3 730	4 377	4 825	-14.8	-9.3
Coke	5.3	17.8	5.4	11.4	10.9	10.0	13.5	12.6	12.9	52.3	3 864	3 424	3 196	12.9	7.1
Coleman	6.6	17.3	6.6	11.8	11.4	9.8	10.8	12.4	13.3	52.6	9 235	9 710	10 439	-4.9	-7.0
Collin	8.5	20.5	9.0	20.8	19.1	11.6	5.3	3.1	2.2	50.3	491 675	264 036	144 576	86.2	82.6
Collingsworth	6.6	20.0	7.0	11.9	12.0	8.4	10.4	11.5	12.2	51.9	3 206	3 573	4 648	-10.3	-23.1
Colorado	7.0	19.6	7.1	13.0	12.7	10.0	10.7	10.3	9.6	52.1	20 390	18 383	18 823	10.9	-2.3
Comal	7.0	18.6	7.9	13.9	15.2	11.0	10.3	9.5	6.6	51.3	78 021	51 832	36 446	50.5	42.2
Comanche	6.4	17.0	7.4	11.7	11.7	10.9	11.3	11.5	12.1	51.1	14 026	13 381	12 617	4.8	6.1
Concho	5.4	17.6	8.7	17.1	13.1	9.9	8.8	9.8	9.6	45.7	3 966	3 044	2 915	30.3	4.4
Cooke	7.5	20.8	8.3	14.5	13.8	9.9	9.3	9.0	6.9	51.0	36 363	30 777	27 656	18.1	11.3
Coryell	8.4	18.0	22.5	22.4	12.1	6.5	4.6	3.1	2.5	43.6	74 978	64 226	56 767	16.7	13.1
Cottle	5.9	19.8	5.6	11.7	11.2	10.0	11.6	12.7	11.5	51.3	1 904	2 247	2 947	-15.3	-23.8
Crane	8.4	26.3	8.6	15.2	14.8	9.7	7.1	6.1	3.8	50.1	3 996	4 652	4 600	-14.1	1.1
Crockett	8.4	22.4	6.8	15.4	14.8	10.8	9.6	6.8	4.9	49.4	4 099	4 078	4 608	0.5	-11.5
Crosby	8.0	23.2	8.3	13.5	10.6	10.6	9.7	8.0	7.9	51.6	7 072	7 304	8 859	-3.2	-17.6
Culberson	9.6	25.2	9.9	14.0	13.9	9.8	8.8	5.8	2.9	49.3	2 975	3 407	3 315	-12.7	2.8
Dallam	8.4	22.0	7.2	16.0	12.7	9.7	9.5	7.7	6.8	51.3	6 222	5 461	6 531	13.9	-16.4
Dallas	8.4	18.3	11.1	21.5	15.7	9.7	6.9	4.9	3.3	50.8	2 218 899	1 852 691	1 556 419	19.8	19.0
Dawson	8.0	23.7	7.8	13.7	12.4	9.3	9.5	8.4	7.1	51.6	14 985	14 349	16 184	4.4	-11.3
Deaf Smith	9.6	25.8	9.7	15.0	12.6	8.8	7.8	5.9	4.9	50.5	18 561	19 153	21 165	-3.1	-9.5
Delta	6.3	18.0	8.5	12.0	11.2	10.5	10.0	11.5	12.1	52.5	5 327	4 857	4 839	9.7	0.4
Denton	8.6	18.4	13.8	23.1	17.2	9.2	4.7	2.9	2.1	50.6	432 976	273 644	143 126	58.2	91.1
De Witt	6.9	19.9	6.9	13.3	12.4	9.1	10.3	10.5	10.6	52.7	20 013	18 840	18 903	6.2	-0.3
Dickens	5.4	18.4	7.3	10.8	11.6	10.7	10.5	12.2	13.1	52.5	2 762	2 571	3 539	7.4	-27.4
Dimmit	8.8	27.5	10.2	12.3	13.3	8.7	7.5	6.6	5.0	51.2	10 248	10 433	11 367	-1.8	-8.2
Donley	4.9	16.7	10.3	10.6	10.7	10.0	11.1	13.1	12.5	52.2	3 828	3 696	4 075	3.6	-9.3
Duval	8.7	24.0	10.0	14.0	12.1	9.3	8.8	7.4	5.7	51.2	13 120	12 918	12 517	1.6	3.2
Eastland	5.6	17.7	9.7	12.1	11.9	9.5	10.5	11.9	11.0	52.0	18 297	18 488	19 480	-1.0	-5.1
Ector	9.1	22.6	9.6	17.5	14.3	9.3	8.4	5.8	3.5	51.1	121 123	118 934	115 374	1.8	3.1
Edwards	8.1	24.8	7.2	13.8	13.0	10.8	9.4	7.1	5.4	49.8	2 162	2 266	2 033	-4.6	11.5
Ellis	8.4	22.6	9.3	16.8	15.1	10.5	7.3	5.4	4.7	50.7	111 360	85 167	59 743	30.8	42.6
El Paso	9.0	23.6	12.3	17.2	13.7	8.7	7.4	5.1	3.0	51.4	679 622	591 610	479 899	14.9	23.3
Erath	7.0	17.0	17.6	14.5	11.9	8.6	7.8	7.6	8.0	50.8	33 001	27 991	22 560	17.9	24.1
Falls	7.2	18.4	9.5	14.8	11.6	8.8	10.0	9.6	10.2	50.0	18 576	17 712	17 946	4.9	-1.3
Fannin	6.3	17.7	8.0	13.1	12.7	10.6	10.6	10.6	10.4	51.7	31 242	24 804	24 285	26.0	2.1
Fayette	6.0	18.0	6.8	13.2	12.9	9.4	10.5	12.0	11.4	51.4	21 804	20 095	18 832	8.5	6.7
Fisher	6.0	19.8	6.5	12.1	12.1	10.6	11.4	10.3	11.2	51.7	4 344	4 842	5 891	-10.3	-17.8
Floyd	8.7	22.9	8.7	13.0	11.3	9.6	9.3	8.5	7.9	51.5	7 771	8 497	9 834	-8.5	-13.6
Foard	6.2	17.7	7.2	12.2	11.4	9.8	10.2	11.5	13.8	51.5	1 622	1 794	2 158	-9.6	-16.9
Fort Bend	9.4	23.7	8.1	18.7	20.1	9.7	5.3	3.1	1.8	49.8	354 452	225 421	130 962	57.2	72.1
Franklin	6.8	18.7	7.5	13.2	12.7	10.9	11.5	10.2	8.5	51.5	9 458	7 802	6 893	21.2	13.2
Freestone	6.6	20.5	7.2	13.5	13.4	9.8	9.7	9.5	9.8	51.8	17 867	15 818	14 830	13.0	6.7
Frio	9.1	25.7	10.1	15.2	12.4	8.9	7.6	6.4	4.7	50.5	16 252	13 472	13 785	20.6	-2.3
Gaines	10.0	26.4	9.2	16.1	12.2	9.1	7.9	5.3	3.9	50.0	14 467	14 123	13 150	2.4	7.4
Galveston	7.6	19.9	9.2	17.7	15.7	10.5	8.8	6.5	4.0	50.8	250 158	217 396	195 738	15.1	11.1
Garza	7.9	23.8	7.6	13.7	12.4	9.9	8.6	8.5	7.7	52.0	4 872	5 143	5 336	-5.3	-3.6
Gillespie	6.0	17.3	5.9	11.9	12.5	10.1	12.0	13.3	11.1	52.1	20 814	17 204	13 532	21.0	27.1
Glasscock	9.9	25.4	8.8	17.2	12.6	11.3	8.8	3.5	2.5	48.9	1 406	1 447	1 304	-2.8	11.0
Goliad	7.1	20.3	6.8	14.4	13.9	9.8	10.8	9.8	7.2	51.8	6 928	5 980	5 193	15.9	15.2
Gonzales	7.9	20.9	8.6	14.0	11.8	9.3	9.8	9.3	8.4	51.0	18 628	17 205	16 949	8.3	1.5
Gray	6.7	19.7	7.5	14.6	12.9	10.4	10.8	9.2	8.2	52.0	22 744	23 967	26 386	-5.1	-9.2
Grayson	6.8	18.6	9.5	15.1	13.9	10.3	9.5	8.8	7.5	52.3	110 595	95 019	89 796	16.4	5.8
Gregg	7.6	19.7	10.0	16.4	14.3	9.9	8.7	7.3	6.0	52.0	111 379	104 948	99 495	6.1	5.5
Grimes	6.8	19.4	10.9	17.3	14.3	9.0	8.6	7.6	6.1	45.4	23 552	18 843	13 580	25.0	38.6

Table B. States and Counties

STATE County	Total population	Total in house-holds	House-holder	Spouse	Child Total	Own child under 18 years	Other relatives Total	Under 18 years	Nonrelatives Total	Unmar-ried partner	Total in group quarters	Correctional institutions	Nursing homes	Other institutions	College dormitories	Military quarters	Other
	54	55	56	57	58	59	60	61	62	63	64	65	66	67	68	69	70
TEXAS—Cont'd																	
Caldwell	32 194	94.8	33.6	18.8	31.3	23.8	7.1	3.5	4.0	1.8	5.2	3.5	1.3	0.2	0.0	0.0	0.1
Calhoun	20 647	99.2	36.0	21.3	31.5	24.7	6.6	3.1	3.7	1.7	0.8	0.2	0.5	0.0	0.0	0.0	0.1
Callahan	12 905	99.1	39.2	24.1	28.8	23.4	4.4	2.4	2.5	1.0	0.9	0.1	0.9	0.0	0.0	0.0	0.0
Cameron	335 227	98.8	29.0	17.6	38.5	28.0	10.9	5.2	2.7	1.0	1.2	0.4	0.4	0.2	0.1	0.0	0.2
Camp	11 549	98.5	37.5	21.1	29.4	23.0	6.5	3.2	3.9	1.4	1.5	0.2	1.1	0.0	0.0	0.0	0.2
Carson	6 516	98.5	37.9	24.8	30.9	25.7	3.5	1.9	1.5	0.6	1.5	0.3	0.8	0.0	0.0	0.0	0.4
Cass	30 438	98.4	40.0	22.0	28.2	21.6	5.2	2.7	2.9	1.4	1.6	0.2	1.3	0.0	0.0	0.0	0.0
Castro	8 285	99.2	33.3	21.7	35.7	28.9	6.6	3.7	1.9	0.8	0.8	0.1	0.6	0.0	0.0	0.0	0.0
Chambers	26 031	99.1	35.1	23.1	32.8	26.0	5.0	2.4	3.1	1.4	0.9	0.4	0.4	0.0	0.0	0.0	0.0
Cherokee	46 659	93.9	35.7	19.9	29.0	23.0	5.9	2.7	3.5	1.3	6.1	3.1	1.3	0.8	0.6	0.0	0.3
Childress	7 688	77.2	32.2	16.9	22.6	19.3	3.4	1.7	2.2	1.1	22.8	21.7	1.1	0.0	0.0	0.0	0.0
Clay	11 006	99.1	39.3	24.8	28.1	22.0	4.3	2.3	2.7	1.4	0.9	0.2	0.6	0.0	0.0	0.0	0.1
Cochran	3 730	98.0	35.1	22.4	33.8	27.1	5.2	2.9	1.5	0.8	2.0	0.1	0.5	1.4	0.0	0.0	0.0
Coke	3 864	92.4	40.0	23.3	23.6	19.4	3.8	2.1	1.7	0.9	7.6	0.0	2.5	5.1	0.0	0.0	0.0
Coleman	9 235	98.2	42.1	22.6	26.0	21.1	4.3	2.0	3.1	1.6	1.8	0.1	1.6	0.0	0.0	0.0	0.0
Collin	491 675	99.3	37.0	23.0	31.6	27.2	4.0	1.2	3.7	1.4	0.7	0.1	0.2	0.0	0.0	0.0	0.3
Collingsworth	3 206	98.3	40.4	23.2	28.9	23.8	4.2	2.3	1.7	0.8	1.7	0.2	1.4	0.0	0.0	0.0	0.0
Colorado	20 390	95.8	37.5	21.1	28.9	22.3	5.3	2.7	3.1	1.4	4.2	0.4	1.5	0.0	1.9	0.0	0.3
Comal	78 021	98.4	37.3	23.4	29.1	22.9	4.9	2.1	3.7	1.5	1.6	0.3	0.7	0.0	0.0	0.0	0.5
Comanche	14 026	97.6	39.4	23.3	28.0	23.0	4.1	1.8	2.8	1.2	2.4	0.7	1.6	0.1	0.0	0.0	0.1
Concho	3 966	65.5	26.7	15.8	18.3	14.3	3.5	1.6	1.1	0.5	34.5	32.8	1.8	0.0	0.0	0.0	0.0
Cooke	36 363	97.7	37.5	22.4	30.1	24.3	4.4	2.0	3.2	1.3	2.3	0.2	0.9	0.8	0.2	0.0	0.1
Coryell	74 978	77.4	26.6	17.2	27.8	24.3	2.8	1.4	3.0	1.0	22.6	11.9	0.4	0.1	0.1	10.1	0.0
Cottle	1 904	98.1	43.1	23.2	25.9	21.5	4.1	2.0	1.8	1.2	1.9	0.0	1.8	0.0	0.0	0.0	0.1
Crane	3 996	98.9	34.0	23.1	35.9	29.1	4.7	2.8	1.3	0.9	1.1	0.3	0.8	0.0	0.0	0.0	0.1
Crockett	4 099	98.7	37.2	22.4	31.2	25.2	5.9	3.4	2.0	1.3	1.3	0.3	1.0	0.0	0.0	0.0	0.1
Crosby	7 072	98.7	35.5	21.0	32.7	25.9	7.2	4.2	2.4	1.1	1.3	0.1	0.9	0.2	0.0	0.0	0.0
Culberson	2 975	99.7	35.4	20.6	35.7	28.5	5.5	3.1	2.6	1.6	0.3	0.1	0.0	0.0	0.0	0.0	0.2
Dallam	6 222	99.7	37.2	20.5	33.5	28.6	4.7	2.3	3.8	1.8	0.3	0.2	0.0	0.0	0.0	0.0	0.1
Dallas	2 218 899	98.5	36.4	17.1	30.5	24.1	8.7	3.2	5.9	1.8	1.5	0.6	0.4	0.1	0.2	0.0	0.2
Dawson	14 985	84.8	31.5	18.7	27.7	22.1	4.9	2.9	1.9	0.9	15.2	14.6	0.5	0.1	0.0	0.0	0.0
Deaf Smith	18 561	98.6	33.3	20.3	35.4	28.7	7.0	4.1	2.5	1.3	1.4	0.5	0.8	0.0	0.0	0.0	0.1
Delta	5 327	97.8	39.3	22.2	28.1	22.2	5.2	2.4	3.0	1.3	2.2	0.3	1.6	0.0	0.0	0.0	0.2
Denton	432 976	97.9	36.7	21.3	30.4	25.9	4.3	1.4	5.2	1.7	2.1	0.2	0.3	0.2	1.2	0.0	0.2
De Witt	20 013	91.1	36.0	19.8	27.0	20.6	5.3	2.7	2.9	1.2	8.9	6.8	2.0	0.0	0.0	0.0	0.2
Dickens	2 762	81.2	35.5	19.4	19.9	15.5	4.5	2.6	2.0	0.9	18.8	17.3	1.4	0.0	0.0	0.0	0.1
Dimmit	10 248	98.8	32.3	18.5	38.0	28.6	7.5	4.0	2.5	1.8	1.2	0.1	0.7	0.1	0.0	0.0	0.3
Donley	3 828	94.7	41.2	23.4	24.9	20.4	3.1	1.6	2.1	1.0	5.3	0.2	1.1	0.0	4.0	0.0	0.0
Duval	13 120	95.5	33.2	17.6	34.0	24.5	8.2	4.4	2.6	1.5	4.5	3.9	0.4	0.1	0.0	0.0	0.1
Eastland	18 297	95.7	40.0	22.2	26.4	20.6	4.6	2.2	2.6	1.2	4.3	0.1	1.4	0.0	2.5	0.0	0.3
Ector	121 123	98.6	36.2	19.6	33.3	26.6	6.1	3.2	3.4	1.8	1.4	0.8	0.4	0.0	0.2	0.0	0.1
Edwards	2 162	98.7	37.0	22.5	30.9	24.4	6.1	3.8	2.1	1.4	1.3	1.2	0.0	0.0	0.0	0.0	0.0
Ellis	111 360	98.3	33.2	21.5	33.4	26.6	6.6	3.0	3.5	1.2	1.7	0.2	0.6	0.0	0.7	0.0	0.2
El Paso	679 622	98.1	30.9	17.5	37.2	27.1	9.5	4.4	2.9	1.1	1.9	0.9	0.2	0.0	0.0	0.4	0.3
Erath	33 001	94.5	38.1	20.4	26.8	22.4	3.8	1.6	5.4	1.4	5.5	0.2	1.4	0.2	3.2	0.0	0.6
Falls	18 576	88.8	35.0	16.9	27.8	21.4	6.3	3.3	2.9	1.4	11.2	7.1	1.4	2.5	0.0	0.0	0.2
Fannin	31 242	89.2	35.5	20.6	25.8	20.4	4.6	2.2	2.6	1.2	10.8	8.5	1.7	0.6	0.0	0.0	0.0
Fayette	21 804	97.4	40.0	23.2	27.2	21.2	4.3	1.6	2.8	1.2	2.6	0.1	2.2	0.0	0.0	0.0	0.3
Fisher	4 344	98.3	41.1	24.2	27.4	21.7	3.6	1.9	1.9	1.0	1.7	0.3	1.2	0.0	0.0	0.0	0.0
Floyd	7 771	98.2	35.1	22.5	34.0	28.3	4.9	2.8	1.8	1.2	1.8	0.1	1.7	0.0	0.0	0.0	0.0
Foard	1 622	97.4	40.9	22.1	29.4	24.1	2.9	1.5	2.0	0.7	2.6	0.1	2.5	0.0	0.0	0.0	0.1
Fort Bend	354 452	98.2	31.3	21.5	36.5	29.2	6.4	2.4	2.5	1.0	1.8	1.2	0.2	0.0	0.0	0.0	0.4
Franklin	9 458	98.3	39.7	24.6	27.5	22.0	4.3	2.0	2.2	1.1	1.7	0.4	1.3	0.0	0.0	0.0	0.0
Freestone	17 867	91.4	36.9	20.9	26.4	20.9	4.5	2.3	2.7	1.3	8.6	7.6	1.1	0.0	0.0	0.0	0.0
Frio	16 252	86.8	29.2	16.1	31.6	24.3	7.0	3.9	3.0	1.9	13.2	12.1	0.9	0.0	0.0	0.0	0.0
Gaines	14 467	99.3	32.4	21.9	38.7	32.2	5.0	2.6	1.4	0.8	0.7	0.2	0.5	0.0	0.0	0.0	0.0
Galveston	250 158	98.3	37.9	19.9	30.4	23.6	5.9	2.6	4.3	1.9	1.7	0.5	0.6	0.1	0.3	0.0	0.2
Garza	4 872	90.6	34.1	20.0	29.4	24.3	4.4	2.3	2.7	1.1	9.4	7.6	0.9	0.8	0.0	0.0	0.0
Gillespie	20 814	97.3	40.9	25.4	24.6	19.8	3.8	1.5	2.6	1.1	2.7	0.0	2.3	0.0	0.0	0.0	0.3
Glasscock	1 406	100.0	34.4	23.2	37.4	31.9	2.8	1.1	2.3	0.5	0.0	0.0	0.0	0.0	0.0	0.0	0.0
Goliad	6 928	98.2	38.2	23.7	28.8	22.8	5.0	2.5	2.6	1.4	1.8	0.5	1.0	0.0	0.0	0.0	0.2
Gonzales	18 628	98.1	36.4	19.7	31.3	24.2	6.9	3.2	3.7	1.6	1.9	0.3	1.4	0.0	0.0	0.0	0.2
Gray	22 744	92.5	38.7	22.0	25.8	21.5	3.6	1.9	2.3	1.1	7.5	6.3	1.2	0.0	0.0	0.0	0.0
Grayson	110 595	97.3	38.7	21.4	28.3	22.4	4.8	2.2	4.0	1.6	2.7	0.3	1.2	0.2	0.8	0.0	0.1
Gregg	111 379	97.2	38.3	19.9	29.4	23.4	5.6	2.6	3.9	1.6	2.8	0.7	0.9	0.1	0.9	0.0	0.2
Grimes	23 552	88.4	32.9	18.2	28.3	21.7	5.7	2.7	3.3	1.5	11.6	10.6	0.9	0.0	0.0	0.0	0.0

Table B. States and Counties

STATE County	Households by type, 2000												Households, 1990		
	Total households	Family households		Married couple		Female householder[1]		Nonfamily households	Householder living alone		Average household size	Average family size	Total households	Female householder[1]	Householder living alone
		Total	With own children under 18 years	Total	With own children under 18 years	Total	With own children under 18 years	Total	Total	65 years and over					
	71	72	73	74	75	76	77	78	79	80	81	82	83	84	85
TEXAS—Cont'd															
Caldwell	10 816	74.7	37.0	56.0	26.4	13.3	7.7	25.3	21.2	9.4	2.82	3.28	8 745	11.6	22.5
Calhoun	7 442	74.9	35.4	59.2	26.4	11.0	6.6	25.1	21.3	8.9	2.75	3.20	6 777	9.1	21.9
Callahan	5 061	74.1	31.9	61.6	24.5	9.3	5.7	25.9	23.3	12.2	2.53	2.97	4 565	8.1	23.7
Cameron	97 267	82.2	45.8	60.8	34.0	17.4	9.9	17.8	15.4	7.6	3.40	3.81	73 278	16.1	16.0
Camp	4 336	72.8	31.5	56.2	22.3	12.5	7.1	27.2	24.2	11.8	2.62	3.09	3 773	11.6	25.0
Carson	2 470	76.3	35.8	65.3	29.4	8.1	5.0	23.7	22.3	11.3	2.60	3.04	2 402	5.6	20.5
Cass	12 190	71.0	30.2	54.9	21.1	12.2	7.2	29.0	26.4	13.5	2.46	2.95	11 320	11.1	23.5
Castro	2 761	78.2	40.9	65.1	33.1	8.7	5.3	21.8	20.5	10.2	2.98	3.45	2 877	8.0	19.1
Chambers	9 139	79.0	40.6	65.7	33.2	9.0	5.1	21.0	17.8	6.7	2.82	3.20	6 930	9.0	18.5
Cherokee	16 651	72.7	33.4	55.7	24.0	12.8	7.4	27.3	24.2	11.9	2.63	3.11	14 981	11.4	24.9
Childress	2 474	66.7	31.3	52.4	22.1	11.4	7.6	33.3	30.8	16.5	2.40	3.00	2 435	9.7	29.8
Clay	4 323	73.6	30.7	63.2	25.2	7.3	3.9	26.4	23.5	11.8	2.52	2.98	3 808	6.6	21.6
Cochran	1 309	77.7	38.1	63.8	30.7	9.9	5.1	22.3	20.9	11.1	2.79	3.25	1 430	7.9	19.2
Coke	1 544	69.2	27.1	58.4	21.2	8.1	4.5	30.8	29.0	18.3	2.31	2.84	1 374	6.0	25.9
Coleman	3 889	67.1	27.2	53.8	19.8	9.3	5.5	32.9	30.2	17.4	2.33	2.88	4 026	8.0	30.3
Collin	181 970	72.7	40.6	62.1	34.1	7.5	4.8	27.3	22.1	3.1	2.68	3.18	95 805	7.2	20.8
Collingsworth	1 294	70.8	29.8	57.5	22.3	9.8	5.2	29.2	27.8	17.5	2.44	2.97	1 447	7.4	30.1
Colorado	7 641	70.7	31.1	56.3	23.4	10.9	6.0	29.3	26.2	14.4	2.56	3.08	7 024	9.5	26.3
Comal	29 066	75.3	33.3	62.8	26.3	9.0	5.2	24.7	20.6	9.0	2.64	3.05	19 315	7.9	21.2
Comanche	5 522	71.1	29.8	59.2	23.1	8.1	4.8	28.9	26.3	15.2	2.48	2.98	5 318	5.8	26.2
Concho	1 058	71.6	29.8	59.4	23.2	9.7	5.1	28.4	26.6	14.2	2.45	2.97	1 063	7.3	27.5
Cooke	13 643	73.3	33.9	59.6	25.9	9.9	6.0	26.7	23.3	11.1	2.60	3.07	11 545	8.4	23.8
Coryell	19 950	79.1	47.7	64.8	37.3	11.0	8.3	20.9	16.9	5.5	2.91	3.27	16 687	8.2	16.3
Cottle	820	67.1	28.0	53.9	20.0	10.6	6.3	32.9	32.0	20.9	2.28	2.84	915	7.8	30.8
Crane	1 360	79.6	43.4	67.8	35.4	7.9	5.5	20.4	18.8	9.5	2.91	3.35	1 537	6.5	18.6
Crockett	1 524	73.1	36.5	60.3	28.8	9.3	5.6	26.9	24.7	11.8	2.65	3.19	1 449	8.4	22.7
Crosby	2 512	74.3	35.6	59.0	26.8	11.4	6.4	25.7	23.8	13.4	2.78	3.30	2 516	7.3	23.3
Culberson	1 052	75.8	39.1	58.2	29.0	13.5	7.3	24.2	21.5	7.4	2.82	3.30	1 076	12.2	16.8
Dallam	2 317	70.3	39.0	55.1	29.1	9.7	6.6	29.7	26.2	10.0	2.68	3.24	2 122	8.6	27.3
Dallas	807 621	66.1	35.1	46.9	24.3	14.1	8.5	33.9	27.3	5.9	2.71	3.34	701 686	12.7	27.8
Dawson	4 726	74.1	35.1	59.4	27.1	11.0	6.1	25.9	23.9	13.3	2.69	3.20	5 084	8.3	23.7
Deaf Smith	6 180	78.2	41.0	61.0	30.2	12.6	8.3	21.8	19.7	10.0	2.96	3.41	6 182	9.8	18.7
Delta	2 094	69.8	30.2	56.4	22.5	10.0	5.8	30.2	27.5	14.7	2.49	3.02	1 901	8.5	26.5
Denton	158 903	70.1	39.1	57.9	31.5	8.6	5.7	29.9	22.2	3.2	2.67	3.18	101 984	7.4	24.0
De Witt	7 207	71.2	31.0	55.1	22.1	11.8	6.6	28.8	26.4	15.0	2.53	3.04	7 195	10.3	27.7
Dickens	980	65.2	23.1	54.6	18.5	7.9	3.5	34.8	32.4	17.6	2.29	2.89	1 073	6.5	32.6
Dimmit	3 308	80.0	42.0	57.4	29.4	17.2	9.7	20.0	18.0	9.3	3.06	3.48	3 072	14.6	15.5
Donley	1 578	67.0	24.8	56.7	18.8	7.5	4.3	33.0	31.4	17.0	2.30	2.86	1 515	6.0	28.0
Duval	4 350	75.1	36.8	53.2	26.0	16.8	8.1	24.9	22.9	11.7	2.88	3.40	4 159	15.4	20.0
Eastland	7 321	68.8	27.7	55.4	20.3	9.5	5.3	31.2	28.6	16.2	2.39	2.93	7 354	7.3	29.2
Ector	43 846	72.3	38.9	54.1	27.2	13.7	8.9	27.7	24.0	8.9	2.72	3.25	42 322	11.3	22.5
Edwards	801	73.2	31.7	60.8	24.3	8.9	5.1	26.8	24.7	13.5	2.66	3.20	795	7.7	23.3
Ellis	37 020	80.1	42.1	64.8	33.3	11.0	6.5	19.9	16.6	6.5	2.96	3.31	28 588	9.8	17.3
El Paso	210 022	79.1	44.9	56.7	32.2	18.0	10.5	20.9	17.8	6.7	3.18	3.63	178 366	15.8	17.0
Erath	12 568	64.5	31.0	53.7	24.8	7.2	4.3	35.5	27.7	10.1	2.48	3.08	10 877	7.0	28.4
Falls	6 496	67.9	30.6	48.2	20.0	15.6	8.6	32.1	29.4	15.4	2.54	3.15	6 492	13.2	29.3
Fannin	11 105	71.9	31.1	57.9	23.5	10.3	5.7	28.1	25.2	12.7	2.51	2.99	9 691	8.2	26.4
Fayette	8 722	69.3	28.5	58.0	22.6	7.8	4.2	30.7	28.0	16.4	2.44	2.97	8 101	7.3	28.4
Fisher	1 785	69.7	27.6	58.9	21.5	8.1	4.6	30.3	28.3	17.8	2.39	2.93	1 892	6.7	25.8
Floyd	2 730	77.3	39.4	63.9	30.7	9.7	6.4	22.7	21.3	12.3	2.79	3.26	2 982	6.6	22.7
Foard	664	66.0	29.1	54.1	21.5	9.5	5.7	34.0	31.8	19.3	2.38	3.02	739	8.3	31.0
Fort Bend	110 915	83.9	49.8	68.8	40.8	11.4	7.1	16.1	13.5	3.1	3.14	3 46	70 424	10.4	13.6
Franklin	3 754	72.8	30.1	61.9	23.7	8.4	5.2	27.2	24.6	12.8	2.48	2.95	3 017	7.4	23.6
Freestone	6 588	70.8	30.3	56.6	22.3	10.7	6.0	29.2	26.4	13.7	2.48	2.98	6 063	9.9	26.7
Frio	4 743	76.8	40.7	55.2	27.8	16.0	9.6	23.2	20.6	9.3	2.98	3.44	4 129	13.9	18.1
Gaines	4 681	80.2	45.3	67.7	37.7	8.8	5.6	19.8	18.2	8.6	3.07	3.53	4 502	6.9	18.4
Galveston	94 782	69.8	33.8	52.4	24.0	13.1	7.7	30.2	25.1	8.1	2.60	3.12	81 451	12.6	24.3
Garza	1 663	73.2	36.0	58.5	27.9	11.2	5.9	26.8	23.8	12.0	2.65	3.15	1 822	9.6	22.4
Gillespie	8 521	71.4	25.9	62.1	21.0	7.0	3.7	28.6	25.8	14.2	2.38	2.84	6 711	5.6	24.2
Glasscock	483	73.5	42.0	67.5	38.3	2.9	2.1	26.5	23.8	7.0	2.91	3.51	456	3.5	13.4
Goliad	2 644	74.7	33.1	62.1	26.2	8.7	4.9	25.3	22.8	11.9	2.57	3.02	2 208	7.8	22.9
Gonzales	6 782	71.9	34.2	54.0	24.1	12.3	7.2	28.1	25.2	14.3	2.69	3.21	6 231	10.9	25.8
Gray	8 793	68.8	30.0	57.0	22.6	9.0	5.7	31.2	28.7	15.3	2.39	2.93	9 548	8.1	25.8
Grayson	42 849	70.5	32.1	55.2	23.2	11.4	6.7	29.5	25.5	11.4	2.51	3.00	36 847	10.2	25.2
Gregg	42 687	69.5	33.5	52.0	23.1	13.5	8.2	30.5	26.1	10.5	2.54	3.06	40 027	11.7	25.9
Grimes	7 753	72.6	34.6	55.4	25.4	12.6	6.9	27.4	23.8	11.2	2.69	3.18	6 040	12.6	23.7

[1]No spouse present.

Table B. States and Counties

STATE County	Percent change of households, 1990–2000	Total housing units	Occupied housing units (percent)	Vacant housing units — Total	For seasonal, recreational, or occasional use	Homeowner vacancy rate (percent)	Rental vacancy rate (percent)	Occupied housing units — Total	Percent owner-occupied housing units	Percent renter-occupied housing units	Average household size of owner-occupied units	Average household size of renter-occupied units
	86	87	88	89	90	91	92	93	94	95	96	97

TEXAS—Cont'd

STATE County	86	87	88	89	90	91	92	93	94	95	96	97
Caldwell	23.7	11 901	90.9	9.1	2.0	1.9	5.8	10 816	69.7	30.3	2.85	2.76
Calhoun	9.8	10 238	72.7	27.3	17.1	2.1	16.0	7 442	72.8	27.2	2.75	2.75
Callahan	10.9	5 925	85.4	14.6	3.1	3.3	8.9	5 061	80.7	19.3	2.50	2.63
Cameron	32.7	119 654	81.3	18.7	9.8	1.6	14.1	97 267	67.7	32.3	3.45	3.31
Camp	14.9	5 228	82.9	17.1	8.9	1.9	9.9	4 336	74.7	25.3	2.52	2.94
Carson	2.8	2 815	87.7	12.3	0.9	3.5	11.6	2 470	83.7	16.3	2.58	2.70
Cass	7.7	13 890	87.8	12.2	2.1	1.7	10.0	12 190	78.6	21.4	2.45	2.48
Castro	-4.0	3 198	86.3	13.7	0.9	1.9	12.7	2 761	71.1	28.9	2.90	3.18
Chambers	31.9	10 336	88.4	11.6	3.5	1.2	17.0	9 139	83.6	16.4	2.84	2.72
Cherokee	11.1	19 173	86.8	13.2	3.6	1.8	10.0	16 651	73.8	26.2	2.62	2.68
Childress	1.6	3 059	80.9	19.1	3.2	4.2	18.1	2 474	70.5	29.5	2.40	2.39
Clay	13.5	4 992	86.6	13.4	4.1	2.7	8.8	4 323	83.0	17.0	2.52	2.55
Cochran	-8.5	1 587	82.5	17.5	1.1	3.7	16.5	1 309	73.6	26.4	2.74	2.93
Coke	12.4	2 843	54.3	45.7	32.4	7.3	12.6	1 544	78.9	21.1	2.32	2.29
Coleman	-3.4	5 248	74.1	25.9	9.8	5.8	12.0	3 889	74.4	25.6	2.34	2.33
Collin	89.9	194 892	93.4	6.6	0.4	1.7	12.3	181 970	68.6	31.4	2.94	2.12
Collingsworth	-10.6	1 723	75.1	24.9	5.6	4.9	18.5	1 294	78.8	21.2	2.45	2.38
Colorado	8.8	9 431	81.0	19.0	6.7	2.4	7.8	7 641	76.7	23.3	2.57	2.52
Comal	50.5	32 718	88.8	11.2	5.1	1.7	10.5	29 066	77.2	22.8	2.68	2.51
Comanche	3.8	7 105	77.7	22.3	9.5	3.4	9.0	5 522	76.2	23.8	2.45	2.57
Concho	-0.5	1 488	71.1	28.9	13.2	4.5	6.0	1 058	75.0	25.0	2.42	2.55
Cooke	18.2	15 061	90.6	9.4	3.4	1.6	6.1	13 643	72.1	27.9	2.61	2.59
Coryell	19.6	21 776	91.6	8.4	1.1	2.3	6.7	19 950	54.9	45.1	2.77	3.07
Cottle	-10.4	1 088	75.4	24.6	5.9	4.4	8.6	820	71.6	28.4	2.20	2.47
Crane	-11.5	1 596	85.2	14.8	0.6	2.0	14.7	1 360	85.1	14.9	2.92	2.82
Crockett	5.2	2 049	74.4	25.6	3.3	3.7	13.4	1 524	71.3	28.7	2.72	2.49
Crosby	-0.2	3 202	78.5	21.5	9.4	2.7	10.0	2 512	69.3	30.7	2.64	3.08
Culberson	-2.2	1 321	79.6	20.4	6.6	1.7	8.4	1 052	70.8	29.2	2.88	2.67
Dallam	9.2	2 697	85.9	14.1	1.0	3.1	11.2	2 317	63.1	36.9	2.70	2.64
Dallas	15.1	854 119	94.6	5.4	0.3	1.3	6.3	807 621	52.6	47.4	2.86	2.54
Dawson	-7.0	5 500	85.9	14.1	0.3	3.1	24.0	4 726	73.5	26.5	2.69	2.70
Deaf Smith	0.0	6 914	89.4	10.6	0.3	2.0	10.4	6 180	67.4	32.6	2.96	2.97
Delta	10.2	2 410	86.9	13.1	3.7	2.2	5.9	2 094	77.3	22.7	2.51	2.43
Denton	55.8	168 069	94.5	5.5	0.2	2.0	7.7	158 903	64.4	35.6	2.93	2.19
De Witt	0.2	8 756	82.3	17.7	3.6	2.6	6.5	7 207	76.5	23.5	2.52	2.56
Dickens	-8.7	1 368	71.6	28.4	3.8	13.4	15.4	980	77.7	22.3	2.23	2.49
Dimmit	7.7	4 112	80.4	19.6	4.3	2.3	7.0	3 308	73.9	26.1	3.03	3.14
Donley	4.2	2 378	66.4	33.6	20.0	3.6	14.2	1 578	74.7	25.3	2.31	2.25
Duval	4.6	5 543	78.5	21.5	6.9	1.5	11.4	4 350	80.9	19.1	2.89	2.86
Eastland	-0.4	9 547	76.7	23.3	6.1	4.4	11.5	7 321	76.7	23.3	2.41	2.34
Ector	3.6	49 500	88.6	11.4	0.4	1.8	17.5	43 846	68.6	31.4	2.86	2.42
Edwards	0.8	1 217	65.8	34.2	19.7	2.6	2.4	801	79.9	20.1	2.64	2.76
Ellis	29.5	39 071	94.8	5.2	0.6	1.3	6.3	37 020	76.2	23.8	2.99	2.86
El Paso	17.7	224 447	93.6	6.4	0.4	1.5	7.8	210 022	63.6	36.4	3.32	2.92
Erath	15.5	14 422	87.1	12.9	2.0	2.2	11.5	12 568	63.2	36.8	2.58	2.31
Falls	0.1	7 658	84.8	15.2	2.4	4.0	12.1	6 496	71.5	28.5	2.53	2.56
Fannin	14.6	12 887	86.2	13.8	3.0	2.1	11.5	11 105	74.8	25.2	2.54	2.43
Fayette	7.7	11 113	78.5	21.5	7.4	2.2	10.6	8 722	78.3	21.7	2.47	2.31
Fisher	-5.7	2 277	78.4	21.6	2.0	5.7	11.0	1 785	76.8	23.2	2.38	2.42
Floyd	-8.5	3 221	84.8	15.2	0.9	3.6	16.0	2 730	73.9	26.1	2.70	3.07
Foard	-10.1	850	78.1	21.9	2.2	12.6	11.3	664	75.2	24.8	2.36	2.44
Fort Bend	57.5	115 991	95.6	4.4	0.4	2.0	5.6	110 915	80.8	19.2	3.20	2.88
Franklin	24.4	5 132	73.1	26.9	16.8	3.7	13.0	3 754	79.0	21.0	2.49	2.41
Freestone	8.7	8 138	81.0	19.0	7.9	2.4	10.3	6 588	78.8	21.2	2.47	2.52
Frio	14.9	5 660	83.8	16.2	3.9	1.8	10.4	4 743	69.0	31.0	2.98	2.97
Gaines	4.0	5 410	86.5	13.5	1.0	2.7	15.0	4 681	78.6	21.4	3.09	3.01
Galveston	16.4	111 733	84.8	15.2	6.8	2.3	13.3	94 782	66.2	33.8	2.71	2.37
Garza	-8.7	1 928	86.3	13.7	2.2	1.3	10.1	1 663	70.7	29.3	2.63	2.72
Gillespie	27.0	9 902	86.1	13.9	7.0	1.9	4.3	8 521	77.5	22.5	2.39	2.34
Glasscock	5.9	660	73.2	26.8	5.9	0.9	7.1	483	67.3	32.7	2.85	3.04
Goliad	19.7	3 426	77.2	22.8	11.2	3.0	7.2	2 644	80.0	20.0	2.58	2.56
Gonzales	8.8	8 194	82.8	17.2	4.8	1.2	9.1	6 782	69.1	30.9	2.64	2.80
Gray	-7.9	10 567	83.2	16.8	4.0	4.0	17.2	8 793	77.4	22.6	2.43	2.27
Grayson	16.3	48 315	88.7	11.3	3.6	2.0	9.2	42 849	70.6	29.4	2.56	2.39
Gregg	6.6	46 349	92.1	7.9	0.6	1.9	9.6	42 687	64.1	35.9	2.62	2.39
Grimes	28.4	9 490	81.7	18.3	7.7	3.0	9.3	7 753	77.7	22.3	2.69	2.68

Table B. States and Counties

STATE/ County code	MSA/ PMSA/ NECMA code[1]	County type[2]	STATE County	Land area, 2000[3] (sq km)	Total persons	Rank	Per square kilometer	Land area, 1990[3] (sq km)	Total persons	Rank	Per square kilometer	White	Black or African American	American Indian or Alaska Native	Asian	Native Hawaiian and other Pacific Islander	Some other race
				1	2	3	4	5	6	7	8	9	10	11	12	13	14
			TEXAS—Cont'd														
48 187	7240	1	Guadalupe	1 842	89 023	584	48.3	1 842	64 873	675	35.2	77.6	5.0	0.5	0.9	0.1	12.8
48 189	...	4	Hale	2 602	36 602	1 199	14.1	2 602	34 671	1 147	13.3	66.8	5.8	0.9	0.3	0.0	23.8
48 191	...	9	Hall	2 339	3 782	2 931	1.6	2 339	3 905	2 924	1.7	72.0	8.2	0.5	0.2	0.0	17.9
48 193	...	6	Hamilton	2 164	8 229	2 589	3.8	2 165	7 733	2 601	3.6	93.8	0.1	0.4	0.1	0.0	4.4
48 195	...	7	Hansford	2 382	5 369	2 823	2.3	2 382	5 848	2 775	2.5	79.9	0.0	0.7	0.2	0.0	17.5
48 197	...	7	Hardeman	1 801	4 724	2 866	2.6	1 801	5 283	2 821	2.9	85.4	4.8	0.8	0.3	0.0	7.1
48 199	0840	2	Hardin	2 316	48 073	950	20.8	2 316	41 320	974	17.8	90.9	6.9	0.3	0.2	0.0	0.7
48 201	3360	0	Harris	4 478	3 400 578	3	759.4	4 478	2 818 101	3	629.3	58.7	18.5	0.4	5.1	0.1	14.2
48 203	4420	3	Harrison	2 328	62 110	783	26.7	2 328	57 483	759	24.7	71.3	24.0	0.3	0.3	0.0	2.9
48 205	...	7	Hartley	3 787	5 537	2 814	1.5	3 788	3 634	2 947	1.0	81.1	8.1	0.4	0.3	0.1	8.6
48 207	...	7	Haskell	2 339	6 093	2 771	2.6	2 339	6 820	2 674	2.9	82.8	2.8	0.5	0.1	0.0	11.7
48 209	0640	2	Hays	1 756	97 589	531	55.6	1 756	65 614	667	37.4	78.9	3.7	0.7	0.8	0.1	13.4
48 211	...	9	Hemphill	2 356	3 351	2 968	1.4	2 356	3 720	2 937	1.6	87.6	1.6	0.7	0.3	0.0	8.5
48 213	1920	1	Henderson	2 264	73 277	683	32.4	2 265	58 543	742	25.8	88.5	6.6	0.5	0.3	0.0	2.7
48 215	4880	2	Hidalgo	4 066	569 463	96	140.1	4 064	383 545	131	94.4	77.7	0.5	0.4	0.6	0.0	18.6
48 217	...	6	Hill	2 493	32 321	1 339	13.0	2 493	27 146	1 386	10.9	84.2	7.4	0.4	0.3	0.0	6.0
48 219	...	6	Hockley	2 352	22 716	1 662	9.7	2 353	24 199	1 487	10.3	74.4	3.7	0.8	0.1	0.0	18.7
48 221	2800	1	Hood	1 092	41 100	1 079	37.6	1 092	28 981	1 331	26.5	94.8	0.3	0.8	0.3	0.0	2.4
48 223	...	6	Hopkins	2 026	31 960	1 346	15.8	2 033	28 833	1 335	14.2	85.1	8.2	0.7	0.2	0.1	4.6
48 225	...	7	Houston	3 188	23 185	1 634	7.3	3 188	21 375	1 613	6.7	68.6	27.9	0.3	0.2	0.1	2.2
48 227	...	5	Howard	2 338	33 627	1 294	14.4	2 339	32 343	1 204	13.8	80.1	4.1	0.6	0.6	0.0	12.4
48 229	...	8	Hudspeth	11 839	3 344	2 969	0.3	11 840	2 915	3 005	0.2	87.2	0.3	1.4	0.2	0.0	8.8
48 231	1920	1	Hunt	2 179	76 596	657	35.2	2 179	64 343	680	29.5	83.6	9.5	0.7	0.5	0.1	3.9
48 233	...	6	Hutchinson	2 298	23 857	1 596	10.4	2 298	25 689	1 434	11.2	87.0	2.4	1.4	0.3	0.0	6.7
48 235	...	8	Irion	2 723	1 771	3 081	0.7	2 724	1 629	3 089	0.6	90.7	0.4	0.8	0.0	0.0	6.5
48 237	...	6	Jack	2 374	8 763	2 549	3.7	2 376	6 981	2 660	2.9	88.7	5.5	0.7	0.3	0.0	3.8
48 239	...	6	Jackson	2 148	14 391	2 132	6.7	2 148	13 039	2 137	6.1	76.5	7.6	0.4	0.4	0.1	12.6
48 241	...	6	Jasper	2 428	35 604	1 229	14.7	2 428	31 102	1 242	12.8	78.2	17.8	0.4	0.3	0.0	2.0
48 243	...	9	Jeff Davis	5 865	2 207	3 050	0.4	5 865	1 946	3 069	0.3	90.5	0.9	0.3	0.1	0.0	5.2
48 245	0840	2	Jefferson	2 340	252 051	225	107.7	2 340	239 389	208	102.3	57.2	33.7	0.3	2.9	0.0	5.8
48 247	...	6	Jim Hogg	2 943	5 281	2 832	1.8	2 943	5 109	2 831	1.7	80.4	0.5	0.8	0.2	0.0	15.8
48 249	...	4	Jim Wells	2 239	39 326	1 128	17.6	2 239	37 679	1 055	16.8	77.9	0.6	0.6	0.4	0.1	17.9
48 251	2800	1	Johnson	1 889	126 811	424	67.1	1 889	97 165	473	51.4	90.0	2.5	0.6	0.5	0.2	4.5
48 253	...	6	Jones	2 411	20 785	1 749	8.6	2 411	16 490	1 895	6.8	78.8	11.5	0.5	0.5	0.0	7.5
48 255	...	6	Karnes	1 943	15 446	2 056	7.9	1 943	12 455	2 186	6.4	68.5	10.8	0.7	0.4	0.1	17.2
48 257	1920	1	Kaufman	2 036	71 313	695	35.0	2 036	52 220	811	25.6	81.1	10.5	0.6	0.5	0.0	5.7
48 259	...	6	Kendall	1 716	23 743	1 601	13.8	1 716	14 589	2 014	8.5	92.9	0.3	0.6	0.2	0.0	4.4
48 261	...	9	Kenedy	3 773	414	3 138	0.1	3 773	460	3 138	0.1	64.5	0.7	0.7	0.5	0.0	31.9
48 263	...	9	Kent	2 337	859	3 119	0.4	2 337	1 010	3 113	0.4	95.5	0.2	0.3	0.0	0.0	3.7
48 265	...	7	Kerr	2 865	43 653	1 025	15.2	2 865	36 304	1 096	12.7	88.9	1.8	0.6	0.5	0.1	6.6
48 267	...	7	Kimble	3 239	4 468	2 884	1.4	3 240	4 122	2 904	1.3	90.3	0.1	0.3	0.4	0.0	7.5
48 269	...	9	King	2 363	356	3 139	0.2	2 363	354	3 139	0.1	94.1	0.0	1.1	0.0	0.0	3.1
48 271	...	9	Kinney	3 531	3 379	2 965	1.0	3 532	3 119	2 991	0.9	75.8	1.7	0.3	0.1	0.0	18.6
48 273	...	4	Kleberg	2 256	31 549	1 360	14.0	2 256	30 274	1 282	13.4	71.9	3.7	0.6	1.5	0.1	19.0
48 275	...	9	Knox	2 199	4 253	2 898	1.9	2 212	4 837	2 852	2.2	74.3	6.9	1.1	0.2	0.1	14.8
48 277	...	5	Lamar	2 375	48 499	940	20.4	2 375	43 949	926	18.5	82.5	13.5	1.1	0.4	0.0	1.2
48 279	...	6	Lamb	2 632	14 709	2 106	5.6	2 632	15 072	1 984	5.7	76.1	4.3	0.7	0.1	0.0	16.9
48 281	...	6	Lampasas	1 844	17 762	1 914	9.6	1 844	13 521	2 100	7.3	86.8	3.1	0.7	0.8	0.1	6.5
48 283	...	6	La Salle	3 856	5 866	2 797	1.5	3 856	5 254	2 823	1.4	81.5	3.5	0.3	0.3	0.0	12.2
48 285	...	6	Lavaca	2 512	19 210	1 832	7.6	2 512	18 690	1 750	7.4	86.9	6.8	0.2	0.2	0.0	4.8
48 287	...	6	Lee	1 628	15 657	2 044	9.6	1 628	12 854	2 150	7.9	76.6	12.1	0.5	0.2	0.0	8.9
48 289	...	8	Leon	2 777	15 335	2 069	5.5	2 777	12 665	2 169	4.6	83.5	10.4	0.3	0.2	0.0	4.5
48 291	3360	1	Liberty	3 004	70 154	708	23.4	3 004	52 726	805	17.6	78.9	12.8	0.5	0.3	0.0	6.0
48 293	...	6	Limestone	2 354	22 051	1 690	9.4	2 354	20 946	1 632	8.9	70.8	19.1	0.5	0.1	0.0	8.1
48 295	...	9	Lipscomb	2 414	3 057	2 989	1.3	2 414	3 143	2 989	1.3	82.9	0.5	1.4	0.1	0.0	13.0
48 297	...	6	Live Oak	2 684	12 309	2 279	4.6	2 684	9 556	2 428	3.6	87.3	2.4	0.4	0.1	0.0	7.7
48 299	...	7	Llano	2 421	17 044	1 950	7.0	2 421	11 631	2 245	4.8	96.3	0.3	0.4	0.4	0.0	1.8
48 301	...	9	Loving	1 743	67	3 141	0.0	1 743	107	3 141	0.1	89.6	0.0	0.0	0.0	0.0	9.0
48 303	4600	3	Lubbock	2 330	242 628	237	104.1	2 330	222 636	224	95.6	74.3	7.7	0.6	1.3	0.0	14.1
48 305	...	6	Lynn	2 310	6 550	2 735	2.8	2 310	6 758	2 679	2.9	75.5	2.8	1.0	0.2	0.0	18.2
48 307	...	7	McCulloch	2 769	8 205	2 591	3.0	2 770	8 778	2 487	3.2	84.6	1.6	0.3	0.2	0.0	11.7
48 309	8800	3	McLennan	2 698	213 517	262	79.1	2 699	189 123	254	70.1	72.2	15.2	0.5	1.1	0.0	9.2
48 311	...	9	McMullen	2 883	851	3 120	0.3	2 883	817	3 122	0.3	88.4	1.2	0.2	0.0	0.0	8.9
48 313	...	6	Madison	1 216	12 940	2 236	10.6	1 216	10 931	2 302	9.0	66.8	22.9	0.3	0.4	0.0	7.9
48 315	...	8	Marion	987	10 941	2 371	11.1	987	9 984	2 387	10.1	72.7	23.9	0.8	0.2	0.0	0.8
48 317	...	6	Martin	2 369	4 746	2 863	2.0	2 369	4 956	2 843	2.1	79.0	1.6	0.8	0.1	0.0	16.1

[1] MSA = Metropolitan Statistical Area. PMSA = Primary MSA. NECMA = New England County Metropolitan Area. See Appendix A for explanation of these concepts. See Appendix B for list of metropolitan areas identified by type, with component counties.
[2] County typology code from the Economic Research Service of USDA. See Appendix A for definition.
[3] Dry land or land partially or temporarily covered by water.

Table B. States and Counties

STATE County	Population and population characteristics, 2000 (cont'd)								Population and population characteristics, 1990				
	Race (percent) (cont'd)								Race (percent)				
	Race alone or in combination							Hispanic[1]	White	Black or African American	American Indian or Alaska Native	Asian and Pacific Islander	Hispanic[1]
	Two or more races	White	Black	American Indian or Alaska Native	Asian	Native Hawaiian and other Pacific Islander	Some other race						
	15	16	17	18	19	20	21	22	23	24	25	26	27
TEXAS—Cont'd													
Guadalupe	3.1	80.5	5.4	1.1	1.3	0.2	14.8	33.2	81.6	5.6	0.4	0.7	29.7
Hale	2.4	68.9	6.1	1.4	0.4	0.1	25.6	47.9	68.7	5.3	0.4	0.4	41.6
Hall	1.2	73.1	8.5	0.9	0.3	0.0	18.5	27.5	74.5	7.8	0.4	0.2	18.6
Hamilton	1.0	94.8	0.2	1.0	0.3	0.1	4.8	7.4	95.6	0.0	0.3	0.3	5.2
Hansford	1.6	81.3	0.3	1.2	0.4	0.0	18.5	31.5	82.4	0.0	0.4	0.2	20.1
Hardeman	1.6	87.0	5.0	1.4	0.3	0.0	7.9	14.5	83.8	6.1	0.5	0.3	11.1
Hardin	0.9	91.8	7.0	0.8	0.3	0.0	1.1	2.5	90.7	8.4	0.3	0.1	1.6
Harris	3.0	61.2	19.0	0.8	5.7	0.1	16.3	32.9	64.7	19.2	0.3	3.9	22.9
Harrison	1.1	72.2	24.3	0.8	0.5	0.1	3.2	5.3	70.3	27.9	0.3	0.3	2.2
Hartley	1.4	82.4	8.3	0.8	0.5	0.1	9.5	13.7	96.6	0.2	0.8	0.2	5.5
Haskell	2.1	84.7	3.1	1.1	0.2	0.0	13.0	20.5	80.4	3.6	0.2	0.2	19.2
Hays	2.5	81.1	4.0	1.3	1.1	0.2	14.9	29.6	84.4	3.4	0.4	0.7	27.8
Hemphill	1.3	88.9	1.6	1.3	0.3	0.1	9.3	15.6	94.2	0.2	0.6	0.1	11.1
Henderson	1.3	89.7	6.8	1.1	0.4	0.1	3.2	6.9	89.2	8.1	0.3	0.2	4.0
Hidalgo	2.1	79.7	0.6	0.6	0.7	0.0	20.6	88.3	74.8	0.2	0.2	0.3	85.2
Hill	1.7	85.8	7.7	1.2	0.4	0.1	6.7	13.5	87.2	9.3	0.3	0.1	8.2
Hockley	2.2	76.4	4.0	1.3	0.2	0.1	20.3	37.2	78.3	4.2	0.4	0.1	31.6
Hood	1.3	96.0	0.5	1.5	0.4	0.1	2.9	7.2	96.8	0.2	0.5	0.6	4.7
Hopkins	1.4	86.4	8.2	1.2	0.3	0.1	5.2	9.3	88.0	8.6	0.4	0.2	4.9
Houston	0.8	69.2	28.2	0.6	0.3	0.1	2.4	7.5	67.2	29.6	0.1	0.2	4.5
Howard	2.1	82.0	4.4	1.1	0.8	0.1	13.8	37.5	78.2	3.8	0.6	0.5	26.6
Hudspeth	2.1	89.3	0.4	1.9	0.2	0.0	10.3	75.0	80.4	0.5	0.3	0.1	66.4
Hunt	1.7	85.1	9.9	1.5	0.7	0.1	4.6	8.3	86.6	10.6	0.4	0.5	4.5
Hutchinson	2.2	89.1	2.6	2.4	0.5	0.1	7.6	14.7	88.2	2.6	1.4	0.4	9.8
Irion	1.6	92.3	0.4	1.3	0.0	0.0	7.6	24.6	98.8	0.1	0.1	0.0	23.6
Jack	1.0	89.6	5.6	1.1	0.3	0.0	4.3	7.9	96.7	0.7	0.3	0.1	3.3
Jackson	2.4	78.6	8.1	0.8	0.5	0.2	14.5	24.7	83.3	9.3	0.3	0.1	21.3
Jasper	1.2	79.2	18.1	1.0	0.5	0.1	2.3	3.9	79.6	18.9	0.2	0.1	1.9
Jeff Davis	3.0	93.2	1.2	1.0	0.1	0.0	7.6	35.5	85.9	0.4	0.6	0.2	39.6
Jefferson	1.5	58.4	34.2	0.7	3.1	0.1	5.0	10.5	64.4	31.1	0.2	2.1	5.3
Jim Hogg	2.3	82.7	0.5	1.0	0.2	0.0	17.9	90.0	85.6	0.1	0.2	0.1	91.2
Jim Wells	2.4	80.2	0.7	0.9	0.5	0.1	20.0	75.7	75.6	0.6	0.2	0.3	72.2
Johnson	1.6	91.5	2.7	1.3	0.7	0.2	5.2	12.1	93.0	2.6	0.4	0.5	7.7
Jones	1.3	80.0	11.7	0.9	0.5	0.0	8.1	20.9	83.6	4.0	0.3	0.2	16.9
Karnes	2.3	70.5	11.1	1.0	0.6	0.1	19.0	47.4	76.7	2.9	0.3	0.1	47.5
Kaufman	1.6	82.6	10.9	1.2	0.6	0.1	6.4	11.1	82.0	14.0	0.4	0.4	6.4
Kendall	1.5	94.3	0.5	1.2	0.4	0.1	5.3	17.9	93.8	0.4	0.5	0.3	16.4
Kenedy	1.7	65.9	0.7	0.7	0.7	0.0	33.6	79.0	82.2	0.0	0.0	0.0	78.7
Kent	0.2	95.7	0.2	0.5	0.0	0.0	3.8	9.1	89.3	0.6	0.1	0.0	11.9
Kerr	1.6	90.4	1.9	1.2	0.7	0.1	7.4	19.1	90.5	2.2	0.4	0.4	16.5
Kimble	1.3	91.5	0.2	0.9	0.5	0.0	8.3	20.7	88.6	0.0	0.1	0.2	18.7
King	1.7	95.8	0.0	1.7	0.0	0.0	4.2	9.6	89.5	0.0	0.0	0.0	15.0
Kinney	3.4	79.0	2.0	1.1	0.2	0.0	21.1	50.5	88.0	1.8	0.8	0.3	50.3
Kleberg	3.2	74.8	4.0	1.1	1.8	0.2	21.5	65.4	68.2	3.3	0.3	1.4	61.2
Knox	2.6	76.8	7.3	1.4	0.4	0.2	16.5	25.1	77.8	7.0	0.1	0.1	22.5
Lamar	1.4	83.7	13.9	1.8	0.5	0.0	1.5	3.3	83.8	14.6	0.9	0.3	1.1
Lamb	1.9	77.7	4.7	1.1	0.3	0.1	18.2	43.5	86.5	5.5	0.6	0.2	36.6
Lampasas	2.1	88.7	3.5	1.4	1.2	0.2	7.4	15.1	90.0	2.0	0.6	1.0	13.0
La Salle	2.1	83.6	3.6	0.6	0.4	0.0	14.0	77.1	67.9	1.0	0.2	0.2	77.4
Lavaca	1.1	87.9	7.1	0.4	0.2	0.0	5.6	11.4	88.5	7.2	0.1	0.1	8.5
Lee	1.7	78.3	12.4	0.9	0.4	0.1	9.9	18.2	78.2	13.8	0.1	0.1	11.0
Leon	1.1	84.5	10.6	0.7	0.4	0.1	5.0	7.9	84.7	12.8	0.3	0.1	4.0
Liberty	1.4	80.2	13.1	1.0	0.5	0.1	6.7	10.9	83.5	13.1	0.3	0.2	5.5
Limestone	1.5	72.1	19.5	0.9	0.2	0.0	8.8	13.0	74.9	19.8	0.2	0.2	7.0
Lipscomb	2.2	84.9	0.6	2.1	0.1	0.0	14.5	20.7	98.4	0.0	1.1	0.4	12.1
Live Oak	1.9	89.0	2.5	0.8	0.4	0.0	9.1	38.0	87.0	0.1	0.4	0.3	34.8
Llano	0.8	97.1	0.4	1.0	0.4	0.0	2.0	5.1	97.9	0.2	0.3	0.2	3.9
Loving	1.5	91.0	0.0	0.0	0.0	0.0	10.4	10.4	86.9	0.0	0.0	0.0	13.1
Lubbock	2.0	76.0	8.0	1.0	1.6	0.1	15.4	27.5	79.1	7.7	0.3	1.2	22.9
Lynn	2.2	77.6	3.1	1.4	0.3	0.1	19.9	44.6	77.2	3.3	0.3	0.2	41.7
McCulloch	1.6	86.2	1.7	0.6	0.2	0.0	13.0	27.0	89.5	1.9	0.2	0.1	26.4
McLennan	1.8	73.7	15.6	0.9	1.3	0.1	10.2	17.9	77.3	15.6	0.3	0.7	12.5
McMullen	1.3	89.4	1.2	0.2	0.2	0.0	10.2	33.1	87.3	0.0	0.4	0.0	39.2
Madison	1.7	68.4	23.2	0.7	0.4	0.1	9.0	15.8	73.0	23.6	0.6	0.1	10.8
Marion	1.5	74.0	24.4	1.8	0.3	0.1	1.0	2.4	68.0	31.0	0.4	0.1	1.5
Martin	2.4	81.1	1.9	1.3	0.3	0.0	17.8	40.6	63.7	1.8	0.2	0.2	39.5

[1] Hispanic persons may be of any race.

Table B. States and Counties

STATE County	Population and population characteristics, 2000										
	Age (percent)										
	Under 5 years	5 to 17 years	18 to 24 years	25 to 34 years	35 to 44 years	45 to 54 years	55 to 64 years	65 to 74 years	75 years and over	Median age (years)	Percent Female
	28	29	30	31	32	33	34	35	36	37	38
TEXAS—Cont'd											
Guadalupe	7.3	21.2	9.0	12.7	16.4	13.4	8.7	6.3	5.0	34.9	50.8
Hale	8.3	21.9	11.4	12.9	14.3	10.4	7.9	6.9	6.0	31.4	49.4
Hall	7.3	19.9	6.8	9.5	12.6	11.3	11.0	10.3	11.2	40.2	52.2
Hamilton	5.6	18.2	6.0	9.7	13.1	11.8	11.9	11.0	12.6	43.1	51.7
Hansford	6.8	22.5	6.8	11.7	14.6	12.5	9.9	8.0	7.3	36.5	50.9
Hardeman	6.5	18.8	7.5	10.2	12.4	13.5	10.8	9.4	10.8	41.2	52.8
Hardin	6.9	20.8	8.5	12.3	15.9	13.7	9.5	7.0	5.2	36.0	50.8
Harris	8.3	20.7	10.3	16.9	16.5	12.8	7.0	4.3	3.1	31.2	50.2
Harrison	6.5	20.4	10.0	11.5	15.5	13.7	9.3	7.1	6.0	36.1	51.5
Hartley	5.7	15.1	4.7	15.1	20.7	16.4	10.5	6.3	5.6	39.6	39.4
Haskell	5.0	18.8	5.7	8.3	13.9	12.4	10.5	12.7	12.8	43.9	52.9
Hays	6.3	18.2	20.5	13.3	15.0	12.4	6.6	4.2	3.4	28.4	49.7
Hemphill	5.7	22.3	6.5	10.3	15.1	15.1	10.3	7.5	7.2	38.6	49.7
Henderson	6.4	17.9	7.6	11.1	13.9	13.0	11.8	10.5	7.7	40.2	51.0
Hidalgo	10.2	25.1	11.3	14.9	12.8	9.8	6.2	5.5	4.2	27.2	51.4
Hill	6.9	19.0	8.5	11.3	13.6	12.8	10.6	9.0	8.3	38.3	50.8
Hockley	7.2	21.9	11.8	11.1	14.8	12.0	8.6	6.8	5.8	33.3	50.9
Hood	5.8	17.8	6.7	10.2	15.0	13.9	12.7	10.6	7.3	41.5	51.0
Hopkins	6.5	19.6	8.4	12.8	14.4	13.1	9.9	7.6	7.6	36.9	51.0
Houston	5.2	18.0	6.8	11.4	16.3	14.0	10.4	9.0	8.9	40.3	46.7
Howard	5.9	18.3	9.0	14.6	16.3	12.8	8.5	7.9	6.7	36.4	45.9
Hudspeth	8.6	25.5	8.9	13.5	13.2	11.3	9.1	6.7	3.2	30.2	49.3
Hunt	6.7	19.8	10.0	12.7	15.3	12.9	10.0	6.8	5.8	35.5	50.5
Hutchinson	6.9	20.6	8.7	10.6	14.9	13.8	8.9	8.4	7.2	37.5	50.8
Irion	5.7	21.0	4.7	9.9	16.9	14.1	12.1	9.4	6.2	39.9	49.9
Jack	5.7	17.7	10.0	13.1	16.7	12.2	9.4	8.3	6.9	37.0	45.4
Jackson	7.1	20.3	8.2	11.3	14.8	13.4	9.0	8.3	7.7	37.3	50.8
Jasper	6.8	19.7	8.0	12.2	14.6	13.0	10.4	8.7	6.7	37.3	51.4
Jeff Davis	4.1	20.3	5.3	9.0	15.1	16.9	13.0	8.6	7.7	42.5	48.9
Jefferson	6.7	19.2	10.0	13.6	15.8	12.9	8.2	7.1	6.5	35.3	49.7
Jim Hogg	7.9	23.7	8.1	11.8	12.8	11.7	9.4	7.8	6.8	33.9	50.8
Jim Wells	8.2	23.2	9.0	12.3	14.2	12.1	8.6	6.8	5.6	32.8	51.2
Johnson	7.4	21.4	8.8	13.5	16.7	13.5	8.8	5.7	4.2	34.3	50.1
Jones	4.9	17.6	11.1	14.6	16.9	11.9	9.1	7.2	6.7	36.0	40.0
Karnes	5.4	16.4	11.5	18.3	15.9	10.8	7.4	7.1	7.3	34.1	40.6
Kaufman	7.2	22.0	8.2	12.8	16.7	13.5	9.0	5.8	4.8	34.9	50.7
Kendall	6.3	20.9	6.1	10.0	16.4	15.7	10.7	7.2	6.6	39.3	51.3
Kenedy	8.9	20.3	9.7	12.3	14.0	13.3	10.9	7.0	3.6	34.2	47.6
Kent	3.5	17.1	5.4	6.5	15.3	12.6	14.2	12.6	12.9	47.1	52.2
Kerr	5.3	17.3	6.7	9.2	13.0	12.2	11.3	12.3	12.6	43.8	52.1
Kimble	6.1	17.6	6.0	9.7	12.9	14.4	12.4	11.2	9.6	43.1	51.9
King	6.7	27.0	3.7	9.6	19.9	15.2	7.6	7.9	2.5	37.0	51.1
Kinney	6.2	19.5	5.3	10.0	11.6	11.6	11.5	14.7	9.6	43.2	50.0
Kleberg	7.6	19.7	15.7	14.9	12.6	10.9	8.0	5.9	4.7	29.2	49.8
Knox	6.4	21.3	5.6	9.2	13.8	10.9	10.1	10.5	12.1	40.5	52.8
Lamar	7.1	19.1	8.6	12.6	14.2	12.6	10.2	7.6	8.0	36.9	52.3
Lamb	7.4	22.2	8.1	10.8	13.4	11.3	9.5	8.7	8.6	36.2	51.5
Lampasas	6.8	20.8	7.7	12.0	15.2	13.0	10.1	7.7	6.8	36.9	50.9
La Salle	7.3	22.0	10.0	13.9	13.9	12.1	9.2	6.6	5.1	33.0	46.8
Lavaca	5.9	18.3	6.9	9.5	14.0	13.0	10.6	9.5	12.3	41.9	51.8
Lee	6.9	21.9	9.2	11.2	15.1	12.5	8.8	7.5	6.9	35.6	49.6
Leon	5.6	18.7	6.7	9.4	14.1	13.2	12.4	11.9	8.2	42.1	50.9
Liberty	7.1	20.5	9.2	14.7	16.8	13.1	8.3	5.9	4.3	34.0	51.1
Limestone	6.4	18.9	9.1	12.3	14.1	12.9	9.8	8.4	8.0	37.4	49.2
Lipscomb	6.2	21.3	5.9	9.5	15.2	13.1	10.3	9.2	9.2	39.5	51.4
Live Oak	4.9	17.3	9.5	12.2	14.9	14.3	10.9	8.8	7.1	39.2	45.0
Llano	3.8	12.1	4.5	6.9	11.5	14.1	16.4	17.0	13.7	53.0	51.4
Loving	3.0	16.4	1.5	3.0	23.9	22.4	13.4	13.4	3.0	45.8	46.3
Lubbock	7.2	18.5	16.3	13.8	14.0	11.7	7.5	6.0	5.1	30.5	51.1
Lynn	7.3	23.9	7.8	10.7	15.3	11.2	9.8	7.8	6.2	35.2	50.1
McCulloch	6.8	19.9	6.6	10.1	12.8	13.7	10.6	9.7	9.8	40.4	52.6
McLennan	7.1	19.5	14.6	12.4	14.0	11.8	7.8	6.5	6.3	31.9	51.5
McMullen	4.0	19.4	6.3	7.2	16.6	14.6	14.1	10.5	7.4	43.1	49.7
Madison	5.4	15.7	13.0	18.2	13.7	11.0	9.0	6.8	7.1	33.4	41.2
Marion	5.6	16.8	6.4	9.7	13.9	14.6	13.8	10.9	8.3	43.3	51.2
Martin	8.6	25.3	6.7	12.6	13.8	11.0	8.7	7.2	6.1	32.5	51.1

Table B. States and Counties

STATE County	Under 5 years	5 to 17 years	18 to 24 years	25 to 34 years	35 to 44 years	45 to 54 years	55 to 64 years	65 to 74 years	75 years and over	Percent Female	2000	1990	1980	1990–2000	1980–1990
	Age (percent)										Population—change, 1980–2000				
											Total persons			Percent change	
	39	40	41	42	43	44	45	46	47	48	49	50	51	52	53
TEXAS—Cont'd															
Guadalupe	7.9	20.6	9.8	16.1	14.4	10.6	8.6	7.2	4.8	50.6	89 023	64 873	46 708	37.2	38.9
Hale	9.1	23.1	10.4	15.5	11.9	9.1	8.5	6.8	5.6	51.0	36 602	34 671	37 592	5.6	-7.8
Hall	5.8	18.0	6.6	10.4	11.6	9.9	11.4	12.6	13.8	53.1	3 782	3 905	5 594	-3.1	-30.2
Hamilton	5.9	16.4	6.6	11.9	10.9	10.0	11.1	12.3	14.9	52.4	8 229	7 733	8 297	6.4	-6.8
Hansford	7.7	23.4	7.2	15.0	13.8	10.8	9.2	7.1	5.7	50.2	5 369	5 848	6 209	-8.2	-5.8
Hardeman	6.8	19.3	7.0	11.9	11.5	10.1	10.3	11.3	11.8	52.6	4 724	5 283	6 368	-10.6	-17.0
Hardin	7.2	22.1	8.7	15.0	14.9	11.2	9.1	6.9	4.8	50.9	48 073	41 320	40 721	16.3	1.5
Harris	8.6	19.9	10.9	20.4	16.6	9.8	6.7	4.4	2.7	50.3	3 400 578	2 818 101	2 409 547	20.7	17.0
Harrison	7.1	21.7	9.5	15.0	14.3	10.1	8.8	7.5	6.0	51.9	62 110	57 483	52 265	8.0	10.0
Hartley	6.4	22.5	5.5	11.9	15.1	12.6	10.2	8.0	7.6	52.0	5 537	3 634	3 987	52.4	-8.9
Haskell	6.3	18.7	6.2	12.3	11.2	9.0	11.7	12.5	12.1	51.9	6 093	6 820	7 725	-10.7	-11.7
Hays	6.7	17.7	23.2	15.9	14.6	8.3	5.8	4.7	3.3	49.8	97 589	65 614	40 594	48.7	61.6
Hemphill	7.4	23.5	6.4	14.7	15.1	10.9	8.7	6.4	6.8	51.2	3 351	3 720	5 304	-9.9	-29.9
Henderson	6.3	17.7	8.2	12.8	12.3	11.1	12.4	12.1	7.1	51.5	73 277	58 543	42 606	25.2	37.4
Hidalgo	9.3	27.3	11.7	14.6	12.7	7.8	6.6	6.1	4.0	51.7	569 463	383 545	283 323	48.5	35.4
Hill	6.6	18.6	8.4	12.6	12.3	10.0	10.4	11.0	9.9	52.1	32 321	27 146	25 024	19.1	8.5
Hockley	8.5	23.7	11.4	15.8	12.7	9.3	7.8	5.9	4.7	50.7	22 716	24 199	23 230	-6.1	4.2
Hood	6.8	18.7	6.6	14.9	14.3	11.1	11.4	10.6	5.5	50.4	41 100	28 981	17 714	41.8	63.6
Hopkins	7.2	19.3	9.4	14.9	13.7	10.3	8.8	8.5	7.8	51.0	31 960	28 833	25 247	10.8	14.2
Houston	6.4	18.7	7.7	15.7	13.2	9.4	9.6	9.8	9.4	49.3	23 185	21 375	22 299	8.5	-4.1
Howard	7.6	19.4	8.8	15.9	13.2	10.3	10.3	8.5	6.0	49.6	33 627	32 343	33 142	4.0	-2.4
Hudspeth	7.4	24.4	9.8	16.1	12.8	10.2	9.2	5.6	4.5	48.4	3 344	2 915	2 728	14.7	6.9
Hunt	7.4	19.0	10.2	15.4	13.3	11.5	9.1	7.8	6.3	51.1	76 596	64 343	55 248	19.0	16.5
Hutchinson	7.2	21.9	7.8	14.7	13.9	9.3	10.2	9.0	6.0	50.6	23 857	25 689	26 304	-7.1	-2.3
Irion	8.1	20.3	8.3	14.5	13.4	11.7	10.4	7.4	5.8	50.2	1 771	1 629	1 386	8.7	17.5
Jack	7.0	19.8	6.2	14.0	13.0	10.1	11.0	9.5	9.3	51.2	8 763	6 981	7 408	25.5	-5.8
Jackson	7.0	21.2	7.4	13.4	13.6	10.2	10.0	9.5	7.6	51.8	14 391	13 039	13 352	10.4	-2.3
Jasper	6.7	21.6	8.1	13.6	13.0	10.5	10.4	9.3	6.9	52.2	35 604	31 102	30 781	14.5	1.0
Jeff Davis	5.7	20.7	7.0	11.5	13.4	11.8	10.9	11.1	7.9	48.6	2 207	1 946	1 647	13.4	18.2
Jefferson	7.4	19.7	9.5	16.2	14.0	9.6	9.7	8.1	5.9	52.0	252 051	239 389	248 652	5.3	-3.7
Jim Hogg	9.3	23.4	9.7	13.4	12.4	9.5	8.7	7.3	6.3	51.1	5 281	5 109	5 168	3.4	-1.1
Jim Wells	8.7	23.9	9.6	14.5	13.5	9.4	8.8	6.6	5.1	50.8	39 326	37 679	36 498	4.4	3.2
Johnson	7.7	21.5	9.4	16.4	15.5	11.1	8.0	5.8	4.6	50.4	126 811	97 165	67 649	30.5	43.6
Jones	6.7	20.9	7.2	13.3	12.9	10.5	9.7	9.7	9.2	52.2	20 785	16 490	17 268	26.0	-4.5
Karnes	8.2	22.3	7.9	13.6	11.5	8.6	10.0	9.6	8.3	52.3	15 446	12 455	13 593	24.0	-8.4
Kaufman	7.7	21.7	8.6	15.4	15.4	10.9	8.4	6.6	5.3	51.1	71 313	52 220	39 038	36.6	33.8
Kendall	7.0	19.2	7.5	13.7	14.8	12.2	9.4	8.7	7.5	51.3	23 743	14 589	10 635	62.7	37.2
Kenedy	7.8	22.2	8.0	16.1	12.4	12.0	12.6	5.4	3.5	51.1	414	460	543	-10.0	-15.3
Kent	6.6	19.2	4.9	12.3	12.5	11.5	11.6	11.5	10.0	52.0	859	1 010	1 145	-15.0	-11.8
Kerr	6.3	17.0	7.3	12.6	12.1	9.4	10.8	13.8	10.9	52.7	43 653	36 304	28 780	20.2	26.1
Kimble	6.5	19.1	5.7	11.1	13.0	11.3	12.2	11.4	9.9	51.0	4 468	4 122	4 063	8.4	1.5
King	6.8	24.0	7.3	16.7	17.5	12.1	9.3	5.4	0.8	48.3	356	354	425	0.6	-16.7
Kinney	6.3	18.9	7.3	11.9	11.9	8.7	12.9	15.3	6.8	49.3	3 379	3 119	2 279	8.3	36.9
Kleberg	8.4	20.8	15.9	16.2	12.4	9.0	7.6	5.6	4.2	50.2	31 549	30 274	33 358	4.2	-9.2
Knox	7.4	20.1	6.3	12.8	11.6	9.2	10.3	11.4	10.8	51.9	4 253	4 837	5 329	-12.1	-9.2
Lamar	7.1	18.9	9.9	13.9	13.2	10.5	9.0	9.1	8.3	52.6	48 499	43 949	42 156	10.4	4.3
Lamb	7.4	22.5	8.0	13.4	11.4	9.7	9.8	9.3	8.6	51.7	14 709	15 072	18 669	-2.4	-19.3
Lampasas	7.8	19.9	8.3	13.4	13.5	11.3	10.1	8.1	7.6	51.5	17 762	13 521	12 005	31.4	12.6
La Salle	8.6	24.6	9.6	14.0	12.9	9.1	7.8	7.9	5.5	50.4	5 866	5 254	5 514	11.6	-4.7
Lavaca	6.3	18.3	7.1	12.6	12.3	9.8	9.9	12.2	11.5	52.2	19 210	18 690	19 004	2.8	-1.7
Lee	7.2	22.4	7.7	14.8	13.4	9.3	9.4	8.4	7.5	49.5	15 657	12 854	10 952	21.8	17.4
Leon	6.9	19.0	7.4	13.4	12.1	9.8	11.7	11.0	8.8	51.5	15 335	12 665	9 594	21.1	32.0
Liberty	7.4	21.8	9.1	15.7	14.7	10.6	9.0	7.1	4.6	50.1	70 154	52 726	47 088	33.1	12.0
Limestone	7.2	19.1	7.6	14.5	13.3	9.8	9.6	9.6	9.4	52.8	22 051	20 946	20 224	5.3	3.6
Lipscomb	6.9	22.2	5.4	14.4	13.8	11.0	9.9	8.7	7.7	49.7	3 057	3 143	3 766	-2.7	-16.5
Live Oak	6.8	20.6	7.2	13.4	13.2	11.2	11.2	9.4	6.9	50.9	12 309	9 556	9 606	28.8	-0.5
Llano	4.5	11.9	4.5	8.8	10.3	9.5	16.5	19.5	14.5	52.7	17 044	11 631	10 144	46.5	14.7
Loving	5.6	20.6	6.5	16.8	11.2	12.1	14.0	10.3	2.8	44.9	67	107	91	-37.4	17.6
Lubbock	7.7	18.8	16.4	17.7	13.3	8.7	7.5	5.7	4.1	50.7	242 628	222 636	211 651	9.0	5.2
Lynn	8.2	22.1	8.7	14.7	10.7	10.3	9.8	8.2	7.1	50.9	6 550	6 758	8 605	-3.1	-21.5
McCulloch	7.1	19.9	7.5	11.7	12.4	9.4	9.8	10.5	11.7	52.3	8 205	8 778	8 735	-6.5	0.5
McLennan	7.5	18.5	14.6	15.3	13.0	9.1	8.4	7.5	6.1	51.5	213 517	189 123	170 755	12.9	10.8
McMullen	8.0	16.8	7.6	13.7	13.0	13.2	12.9	8.4	6.5	49.8	851	817	789	4.2	3.5
Madison	5.7	15.8	18.0	17.8	10.5	8.6	7.7	7.7	8.3	41.8	12 940	10 931	10 649	18.4	2.6
Marion	6.4	18.4	6.8	12.4	12.5	11.7	12.2	11.3	8.3	50.8	10 941	9 984	10 360	9.6	-3.6
Martin	8.9	25.3	8.4	14.0	13.4	9.8	8.6	6.0	5.7	50.4	4 746	4 956	4 684	-4.2	5.8

Table B. States and Counties

STATE County	Household relationship, 2000																
	In households (percent)										In group quarters (percent)						
					Child		Other relatives		Nonrelatives			Institutionalized population			Noninstitutionalized population		
	Total population	Total in house-holds	House-holder	Spouse	Total	Own child under 18 years	Total	Under 18 years	Total	Unmar-ried partner	Total in group quarters	Correc-tional institu-tions	Nurs-ing homes	Other institu-tions	Col-lege dormi-tories	Mili-tary quar-ters	Other
	54	55	56	57	58	59	60	61	62	63	64	65	66	67	68	69	70
TEXAS—Cont'd																	
Guadalupe	89 023	98.2	34.7	21.4	32.2	25.1	6.1	2.8	3.8	1.6	1.8	0.2	0.6	0.0	0.9	0.0	0.1
Hale	36 602	93.4	32.7	19.7	32.2	26.4	6.1	3.3	2.7	1.4	6.6	4.5	0.9	0.1	1.1	0.0	0.0
Hall	3 782	98.9	40.9	22.0	28.4	23.9	4.9	2.8	2.6	1.2	1.1	0.2	0.9	0.0	0.0	0.0	0.0
Hamilton	8 229	97.1	41.0	23.9	26.0	21.6	3.6	1.6	2.7	1.1	2.9	0.1	2.6	0.1	0.0	0.0	0.0
Hansford	5 369	98.4	37.3	24.3	30.8	26.8	4.2	2.0	1.7	0.9	1.6	0.0	0.0	1.4	0.0	0.0	0.2
Hardeman	4 724	98.6	41.1	22.5	28.6	22.9	4.0	2.1	2.3	1.2	1.4	0.1	1.0	0.1	0.0	0.0	0.3
Hardin	48 073	99.1	37.0	23.2	31.8	25.1	4.5	2.2	2.6	1.3	0.9	0.2	0.7	0.0	0.0	0.0	0.0
Harris	3 400 578	98.8	35.5	17.9	32.5	25.4	8.0	3.0	4.9	1.7	1.2	0.4	0.3	0.1	0.1	0.0	0.4
Harrison	62 110	97.3	37.2	20.8	30.2	23.3	6.0	2.9	3.1	1.4	2.7	0.3	0.6	0.1	1.6	0.0	0.1
Hartley	5 537	74.3	29.0	20.0	22.4	19.8	1.3	0.6	1.6	0.6	25.7	24.3	1.4	0.0	0.0	0.0	0.1
Haskell	6 093	98.3	42.2	24.3	26.6	21.6	3.4	1.8	1.8	0.9	1.7	0.1	1.5	0.0	0.0	0.0	0.1
Hays	97 589	92.2	34.2	18.2	26.7	21.4	5.1	2.1	7.9	1.7	7.8	0.8	0.5	0.2	4.5	0.0	1.8
Hemphill	3 351	95.7	38.2	24.9	28.4	23.7	2.8	1.5	1.3	0.7	4.3	0.0	1.4	2.9	0.0	0.0	0.0
Henderson	73 277	98.4	39.3	23.1	26.8	21.0	5.7	2.8	3.6	1.6	1.6	0.2	0.9	0.0	0.3	0.0	0.1
Hidalgo	569 463	99.0	27.5	17.9	40.5	29.7	10.7	5.1	2.4	0.8	1.0	0.6	0.2	0.1	0.0	0.0	0.1
Hill	32 321	97.5	37.8	21.7	28.2	22.3	6.1	3.0	3.7	1.5	2.5	0.2	1.3	0.0	0.6	0.0	0.3
Hockley	22 716	97.3	35.2	21.3	32.5	25.7	5.7	3.0	2.7	1.3	2.7	0.2	0.7	0.2	1.5	0.0	0.0
Hood	41 100	98.5	39.4	25.0	25.8	20.7	4.7	2.1	3.7	1.5	1.5	0.3	0.4	0.3	0.0	0.0	0.5
Hopkins	31 960	98.5	38.4	22.5	29.0	23.1	5.2	2.4	3.5	1.4	1.5	0.3	1.0	0.0	0.0	0.0	0.1
Houston	23 185	87.1	35.6	18.5	25.0	19.2	5.3	2.7	2.6	1.2	12.9	10.5	1.4	1.0	0.0	0.0	0.0
Howard	33 627	85.8	33.9	18.1	26.2	21.2	4.7	2.6	3.0	1.5	14.2	11.8	0.4	0.9	0.7	0.0	0.4
Hudspeth	3 344	99.0	32.7	20.6	36.9	29.4	7.0	4.1	1.9	0.8	1.0	1.0	0.0	0.0	0.0	0.0	0.0
Hunt	76 596	97.5	37.5	21.1	28.8	23.1	5.7	2.7	4.4	1.6	2.5	0.2	0.7	0.1	1.4	0.0	0.2
Hutchinson	23 857	98.8	38.9	23.9	30.1	24.8	3.7	2.0	2.2	1.1	1.2	0.1	0.3	0.0	0.5	0.0	0.3
Irion	1 771	100.0	39.2	25.4	28.4	23.6	4.3	2.6	2.7	1.2	0.0	0.0	0.0	0.0	0.0	0.0	0.0
Jack	8 763	87.7	34.8	21.0	26.0	21.4	3.6	1.4	2.4	1.1	12.3	11.4	0.9	0.0	0.0	0.0	0.0
Jackson	14 391	98.2	37.1	21.6	31.0	24.2	5.5	2.7	3.0	1.3	1.8	0.4	1.3	0.0	0.0	0.0	0.1
Jasper	35 604	97.4	37.8	22.0	29.2	23.0	5.6	3.0	2.9	1.3	2.6	1.8	0.8	0.0	0.0	0.0	0.0
Jeff Davis	2 207	96.9	40.6	24.7	24.8	19.5	4.5	1.9	2.4	1.0	3.1	0.0	0.0	3.1	0.0	0.0	0.0
Jefferson	252 051	94.0	36.8	17.8	29.9	22.5	6.0	2.8	3.5	1.4	6.0	4.8	0.6	0.0	0.2	0.0	0.3
Jim Hogg	5 281	99.2	34.4	19.0	36.6	27.7	6.9	3.5	2.3	1.5	0.8	0.1	0.6	0.0	0.0	0.0	0.1
Jim Wells	39 326	98.7	33.0	19.1	35.8	26.6	8.0	4.4	2.8	1.5	1.3	0.2	0.9	0.0	0.0	0.0	0.2
Johnson	126 811	98.0	34.4	22.3	31.7	25.4	5.8	2.8	3.8	1.4	2.0	1.0	0.6	0.0	0.2	0.0	0.1
Jones	20 785	76.1	29.5	17.6	23.1	18.7	4.0	2.1	1.8	1.0	23.9	22.5	1.0	0.0	0.0	0.0	0.3
Karnes	15 446	76.6	28.8	15.5	25.1	18.9	4.7	2.4	2.5	1.5	23.4	21.7	1.6	0.0	0.0	0.0	0.0
Kaufman	71 313	98.0	34.2	21.6	32.0	25.4	6.8	3.2	3.4	1.4	2.0	0.3	0.9	0.6	0.2	0.0	0.1
Kendall	23 743	98.0	36.3	24.4	30.7	25.1	4.0	1.5	2.7	1.1	2.0	0.1	1.3	0.0	0.2	0.0	0.4
Kenedy	414	99.0	33.3	19.6	32.6	22.7	8.5	4.6	5.1	1.7	1.0	0.0	0.0	0.0	0.0	0.0	1.0
Kent	859	95.6	41.1	25.1	25.7	19.4	1.9	0.9	1.7	0.6	4.4	0.0	4.4	0.0	0.0	0.0	0.0
Kerr	43 653	95.9	40.8	23.2	24.1	19.5	4.5	2.2	3.3	1.4	4.1	0.3	1.4	1.1	0.8	0.0	0.5
Kimble	4 468	98.9	41.8	23.9	25.7	20.8	4.9	2.4	2.5	1.1	1.1	0.3	0.8	0.0	0.0	0.0	0.0
King	356	84.0	30.3	24.2	28.7	27.0	0.3	0.0	0.6	0.3	16.0	0.0	0.8	4.2	0.0	0.0	11.0
Kinney	3 379	99.3	38.9	24.0	28.2	22.3	6.2	3.3	2.0	1.0	0.7	0.7	0.0	0.0	0.0	0.0	0.0
Kleberg	31 549	95.8	34.5	18.0	31.1	23.5	6.9	3.1	5.3	1.7	4.2	0.4	0.5	0.0	2.8	0.4	0.1
Knox	4 253	96.9	39.7	22.3	28.9	25.1	4.3	2.2	1.6	0.9	3.1	0.3	2.8	0.0	0.0	0.0	0.0
Lamar	48 499	97.7	39.3	21.2	28.7	23.0	5.2	2.7	3.2	1.4	2.3	0.4	1.2	0.1	0.5	0.0	0.2
Lamb	14 709	98.0	36.4	21.7	31.8	25.6	5.8	3.4	2.3	1.2	2.0	0.3	1.6	0.0	0.0	0.0	0.0
Lampasas	17 762	98.0	36.9	22.4	29.8	24.2	5.0	2.3	3.9	1.6	2.0	0.2	1.3	0.1	0.0	0.0	0.4
La Salle	5 866	89.7	31.0	17.0	31.9	24.0	7.6	4.4	2.3	1.7	10.3	9.4	0.0	0.8	0.0	0.0	0.1
Lavaca	19 210	97.5	39.9	23.0	28.9	22.4	3.5	1.5	2.2	1.2	2.5	0.1	2.3	0.0	0.0	0.0	0.1
Lee	15 657	96.0	36.2	21.7	30.9	24.9	4.5	1.9	2.8	1.2	4.0	2.6	1.3	0.0	0.0	0.0	0.1
Leon	15 335	99.3	40.4	24.3	27.0	21.5	5.2	2.4	2.4	1.1	0.7	0.2	0.6	0.0	0.0	0.0	0.0
Liberty	70 154	92.8	33.1	20.1	30.5	24.2	5.9	2.8	3.3	1.4	7.2	6.7	0.4	0.0	0.0	0.0	0.0
Limestone	22 051	91.6	35.9	19.3	27.3	21.9	5.7	2.7	3.4	1.4	8.4	4.1	1.5	2.7	0.0	0.0	0.1
Lipscomb	3 057	98.5	39.4	24.5	29.2	25.5	3.3	1.5	2.1	0.7	1.5	0.0	1.5	0.0	0.0	0.0	0.0
Live Oak	12 309	87.0	34.4	20.7	25.1	19.6	4.1	2.2	2.8	1.4	13.0	11.7	1.1	0.0	0.0	0.0	0.2
Llano	17 044	98.5	46.2	27.5	18.1	14.2	3.6	1.4	3.1	1.6	1.5	0.1	1.3	0.0	0.0	0.0	0.1
Loving	67	100.0	46.3	25.4	20.9	16.4	3.0	3.0	4.5	1.5	0.0	0.0	0.0	0.0	0.0	0.0	0.0
Lubbock	242 628	96.0	38.1	18.4	28.1	22.3	5.6	2.7	5.9	1.7	4.0	0.8	0.5	0.2	2.0	0.0	0.4
Lynn	6 550	99.3	35.9	21.9	34.2	27.5	5.1	3.1	2.3	1.2	0.7	0.2	0.4	0.0	0.0	0.0	0.0
McCulloch	8 205	98.5	39.9	22.1	28.3	23.2	5.2	2.8	3.0	1.5	1.5	0.1	1.4	0.0	0.0	0.0	0.0
McLennan	213 517	95.7	36.9	18.4	29.1	23.1	5.8	2.7	5.6	1.4	4.3	0.4	1.0	0.6	2.0	0.0	0.4
McMullen	851	100.0	41.7	24.9	28.0	21.4	3.5	1.8	1.9	0.5	0.0	0.0	0.0	0.0	0.0	0.0	0.0
Madison	12 940	77.8	30.2	17.3	22.8	18.4	4.9	2.3	2.6	1.0	22.2	20.9	1.2	0.0	0.0	0.0	0.1
Marion	10 941	99.2	42.1	21.8	25.5	18.9	6.4	3.1	3.4	1.8	0.8	0.2	0.6	0.0	0.0	0.0	0.0
Martin	4 746	98.2	34.2	22.0	36.2	30.7	4.4	2.8	1.5	0.8	1.8	0.2	1.2	0.0	0.0	0.0	0.4

Table B. States and Counties

STATE County	Total households (71)	Family households — Total (72)	Family households — With own children under 18 years (73)	Married couple — Total (74)	Married couple — With own children under 18 years (75)	Female householder[1] — Total (76)	Female householder[1] — With own children under 18 years (77)	Nonfamily households — Total (78)	Householder living alone — Total (79)	Householder living alone — 65 years and over (80)	Average household size (81)	Average family size (82)	Households 1990 — Total households (83)	Households 1990 — Female householder[1] (84)	Households 1990 — Householder living alone (85)
TEXAS—Cont'd															
Guadalupe	30 900	77.1	30.3	61.6	29.1	11.2	6.9	22.9	18.9	7.6	2.83	3.23	22 663	10.0	19.2
Hale	11 975	76.3	40.4	60.3	30.1	11.6	7.7	23.7	21.0	10.7	2.00	3.32	11 703	9.2	21.6
Hall	1 548	65.5	28.2	53.7	21.6	9.0	4.8	34.5	32.4	19.6	2.42	3.06	1 669	7.4	33.7
Hamilton	3 374	68.9	27.4	58.2	21.8	7.7	4.3	31.1	28.4	17.4	2.37	2.89	3 250	7.1	30.4
Hansford	2 005	74.3	36.9	65.0	31.1	5.9	3.7	25.7	24.0	12.4	2.63	3.14	2 112	5.5	21.9
Hardeman	1 943	67.9	29.9	54.7	22.6	10.4	5.8	32.1	29.5	18.0	2.40	2.97	2 101	7.8	30.3
Hardin	17 805	76.6	37.2	62.6	28.8	10.2	6.2	23.4	20.7	9.2	2.68	3.09	14 693	9.8	19.2
Harris	1 205 516	69.2	37.7	50.6	27.3	13.7	8.3	30.8	25.1	5.3	2.79	3.38	1 026 448	12.7	26.2
Harrison	23 087	73.4	34.4	56.0	24.9	13.6	7.6	26.6	23.7	10.7	2.62	3.09	20 705	13.1	23.0
Hartley	1 604	76.1	35.5	68.9	30.9	4.7	3.0	23.9	21.6	11.8	2.56	2.98	1 332	4.0	20.4
Haskell	2 569	69.1	27.4	57.6	20.7	8.8	5.2	30.9	29.4	18.3	2.33	2.86	2 753	6.8	27.7
Hays	33 410	66.3	34.0	53.1	26.6	9.0	5.4	33.7	21.0	4.9	2.69	3.21	22 218	7.9	22.3
Hemphill	1 280	74.1	32.7	65.2	27.6	5.9	3.6	25.9	24.4	12.0	2.50	2.98	1 348	6.2	22.0
Henderson	28 804	72.8	29.0	58.7	21.2	10.4	5.8	27.2	23.7	11.8	2.50	2.94	22 947	8.8	22.6
Hidalgo	156 824	84.7	49.7	65.0	38.7	15.7	9.2	15.3	13.1	6.3	3.60	3.96	103 479	15.0	13.4
Hill	12 204	71.5	30.7	57.5	23.1	10.1	5.8	28.5	24.8	12.5	2.58	3.07	10 268	9.0	25.7
Hockley	7 994	76.2	38.1	60.4	28.6	11.5	7.0	23.8	21.2	10.0	2.77	3.22	7 988	8.6	18.9
Hood	16 176	74.8	28.8	63.6	22.3	7.8	4.5	25.2	21.6	10.0	2.50	2.88	11 137	6.3	19.2
Hopkins	12 286	72.3	32.5	58.5	24.9	10.0	5.6	27.7	24.1	11.8	2.56	3.04	10 965	8.5	24.2
Houston	8 259	69.7	28.7	51.9	18.8	14.2	8.2	30.3	27.9	15.1	2.44	2.97	7 792	13.6	26.4
Howard	11 389	69.8	32.8	52.3	22.8	12.2	7.5	30.2	26.8	13.2	2.53	3.07	11 477	11.0	23.7
Hudspeth	1 092	77.1	45.3	63.0	36.5	11.4	7.3	22.9	21.1	8.3	3.03	3.56	946	8.9	22.1
Hunt	28 742	71.4	32.9	56.2	24.0	11.0	6.5	28.6	24.1	9.6	2.60	3.08	24 075	9.7	23.9
Hutchinson	9 283	74.0	34.8	61.4	26.8	9.1	5.8	26.0	23.9	11.9	2.54	3.00	9 642	6.9	22.5
Irion	694	75.5	32.4	64.8	26.4	6.6	3.3	24.5	21.8	11.2	2.55	2.97	601	6.0	19.1
Jack	3 047	73.1	32.7	60.3	25.7	9.2	4.7	26.9	24.5	12.8	2.52	2.99	2 725	6.7	26.1
Jackson	5 336	72.9	34.7	58.2	26.6	10.5	6.1	27.1	24.2	12.5	2.65	3.15	4 833	9.7	23.7
Jasper	13 450	74.1	33.4	58.2	24.3	12.5	7.4	25.9	23.3	11.2	2.58	3.03	11 427	11.0	21.9
Jeff Davis	896	70.6	27.3	60.8	22.5	6.9	3.4	29.4	26.3	10.3	2.39	2.88	779	5.8	28.6
Jefferson	92 880	68.7	33.0	48.4	21.4	16.2	9.7	31.3	27.3	11.0	2.55	3.12	90 520	14.1	26.1
Jim Hogg	1 815	74.9	38.5	55.2	27.8	14.6	8.0	25.1	23.4	12.3	2.89	3.43	1 675	14.4	20.4
Jim Wells	12 961	77.9	40.2	58.0	29.0	15.2	8.6	22.1	19.7	9.5	2.99	3.45	11 979	12.1	18.2
Johnson	43 636	78.9	39.5	64.7	31.2	10.0	5.9	21.1	17.3	6.9	2.85	3.20	33 462	8.8	17.1
Jones	6 140	73.7	33.4	59.6	25.3	10.1	6.0	26.3	24.1	13.4	2.58	3.06	6 180	8.1	24.4
Karnes	4 454	72.9	34.0	53.6	23.4	13.7	7.5	27.1	24.4	13.6	2.66	3.15	4 337	11.5	23.7
Kaufman	24 367	78.9	39.5	63.1	30.6	11.3	6.5	21.1	17.8	7.5	2.87	3.24	17 827	10.2	19.0
Kendall	8 613	77.7	36.3	67.2	30.4	7.9	4.6	22.3	19.2	8.4	2.70	3.09	5 342	8.5	19.7
Kenedy	138	80.4	35.5	58.7	26.1	10.9	2.9	19.6	18.8	6.5	2.97	3.26	145	5.5	16.6
Kent	353	70.0	26.1	61.2	22.1	5.9	2.3	30.0	28.0	14.2	2.33	2.83	399	4.5	26.6
Kerr	17 813	69.1	25.5	56.8	18.5	9.2	5.2	30.9	27.5	15.0	2.35	2.84	14 384	8.6	27.4
Kimble	1 866	68.9	28.2	57.2	21.3	8.6	5.1	31.1	28.6	16.0	2.37	2.90	1 624	8.1	24.4
King	108	82.4	41.7	79.6	39.8	1.9	1.9	17.6	16.7	1.9	2.77	3.12	124	3.2	14.5
Kinney	1 314	71.6	27.2	61.8	22.3	6.4	3.3	28.4	26.6	16.4	2.55	3.10	1 187	6.4	26.7
Kleberg	10 896	70.5	34.9	52.1	24.6	13.9	8.2	29.5	22.3	7.6	2.78	3.30	10 058	12.7	21.8
Knox	1 690	69.0	30.7	56.0	22.8	9.9	6.0	31.0	29.6	17.9	2.44	3.02	1 887	7.4	28.8
Lamar	19 077	70.6	32.3	54.0	22.6	13.2	8.0	29.4	26.1	12.3	2.48	2.99	16 798	11.5	25.0
Lamb	5 360	74.5	35.4	59.5	27.1	10.2	5.7	25.5	23.7	12.8	2.69	3.19	5 488	8.3	24.1
Lampasas	6 554	74.4	35.1	60.7	26.8	9.5	5.8	25.6	21.9	10.5	2.66	3.08	5 058	8.6	23.2
La Salle	1 819	74.3	37.7	54.7	28.3	15.4	7.1	25.7	22.9	12.0	2.89	3.45	1 701	14.2	21.6
Lavaca	7 669	70.3	30.0	57.7	23.1	9.3	5.3	29.7	27.6	16.6	2.44	2.98	7 349	8.0	27.5
Lee	5 663	73.3	35.7	60.0	28.2	8.8	4.9	26.7	23.8	11.7	2.65	3.15	4 706	8.3	24.5
Leon	6 189	72.9	28.2	60.2	21.3	9.2	5.0	27.1	24.8	13.1	2.46	2.92	5 006	8.2	26.2
Liberty	23 242	76.4	38.1	60.5	29.1	11.4	6.5	23.6	20.4	8.9	2.80	3.23	18 538	10.3	21.1
Limestone	7 906	71.5	32.0	54.0	22.2	13.5	7.9	28.5	25.6	13.8	2.55	3.04	7 722	12.1	27.4
Lipscomb	1 205	70.2	32.5	62.1	27.5	5.9	4.1	29.8	28.0	16.2	2.50	3.06	1 230	4.7	25.1
Live Oak	4 230	72.6	30.9	60.1	23.9	8.7	5.0	27.4	23.9	12.4	2.53	3.00	3 550	7.6	22.6
Llano	7 879	68.1	16.9	59.5	13.0	5.9	2.8	31.9	28.3	16.0	2.13	2.56	5 278	4.6	27.7
Loving	31	64.5	16.1	54.8	12.9	6.5	3.2	35.5	32.3	6.5	2.16	2.65	42	0.0	33.3
Lubbock	92 516	65.0	31.7	48.2	22.0	12.6	7.6	35.0	26.9	7.9	2.52	3.10	81 534	10.4	25.5
Lynn	2 354	75.5	38.9	61.0	30.1	11.1	6.3	24.5	23.1	12.1	2.76	3.25	2 383	8.2	21.8
McCulloch	3 277	69.2	30.7	55.3	22.7	10.2	5.9	30.8	28.2	15.8	2.47	3.01	3 409	8.4	28.0
McLennan	78 859	67.1	33.0	49.7	22.8	13.6	8.3	32.9	26.0	9.7	2.59	3.15	70 208	12.1	25.8
McMullen	355	67.3	25.9	59.7	22.8	5.6	2.5	32.7	30.7	14.9	2.40	3.01	319	3.8	24.1
Madison	3 914	72.5	31.5	57.1	23.6	11.7	6.3	27.5	24.5	12.4	2.57	3.05	3 349	11.2	26.6
Marion	4 610	67.7	24.5	51.7	16.8	11.9	6.0	32.3	28.8	13.8	2.35	2.88	4 048	11.9	27.0
Martin	1 624	77.4	42.7	64.3	33.1	9.5	7.1	22.6	21.7	11.8	2.87	3.36	1 632	7.0	19.5

[1] No spouse present.

Table B. States and Counties

STATE County	Percent change of households, 1990–2000	Total housing units	Occupied housing units (percent)	Vacant housing units — Total	For seasonal, recreational, or occasional use	Homeowner vacancy rate (percent)	Rental vacancy rate (percent)	Total	Percent owner-occupied housing units	Percent renter-occupied housing units	Average household size of owner-occupied units	Average household size of renter-occupied units
	86	87	88	89	90	91	92	93	94	95	96	97
TEXAS—Cont'd												
Guadalupe	36.3	33 585	92.0	8.0	2.0	1.8	8.5	30 900	77.0	23.0	2.86	2.72
Hale	2.3	13 526	88.5	11.5	0.3	2.0	13.2	11 975	64.8	35.2	2.82	2.91
Hall	-7.2	1 988	77.9	22.1	2.0	6.2	17.1	1 548	74.1	25.9	2.39	2.49
Hamilton	3.8	4 455	75.7	24.3	7.7	3.2	8.2	3 374	78.1	21.9	2.34	2.47
Hansford	-5.1	2 329	86.1	13.9	1.1	3.2	9.5	2 005	74.7	25.3	2.58	2.79
Hardeman	-7.5	2 358	82.4	17.6	0.9	6.4	8.9	1 943	73.3	26.7	2.37	2.46
Hardin	21.2	19 836	89.8	10.2	1.6	2.0	12.9	17 805	82.7	17.3	2.69	2.60
Harris	17.4	1 298 130	92.9	7.1	0.4	1.5	8.7	1 205 516	55.3	44.7	2.97	2.56
Harrison	11.5	26 271	87.9	12.1	2.6	1.8	11.4	23 087	77.2	22.8	2.62	2.60
Hartley	20.4	1 760	91.1	8.9	0.7	1.3	6.4	1 604	76.4	23.6	2.59	2.48
Haskell	-6.7	3 555	72.3	27.7	13.7	5.6	17.6	2 569	78.9	21.1	2.30	2.46
Hays	50.4	35 643	93.7	6.3	1.7	1.2	4.7	33 410	64.8	35.2	2.91	2.29
Hemphill	-5.0	1 548	82.7	17.3	2.2	4.4	18.7	1 280	77.0	23.0	2.53	2.42
Henderson	25.5	35 935	80.2	19.8	10.8	2.5	8.5	28 804	80.0	20.0	2.50	2.53
Hidalgo	51.6	192 658	81.4	18.6	9.1	1.4	10.7	156 824	73.1	26.9	3.69	3.34
Hill	18.9	14 624	83.5	16.5	7.1	2.9	8.1	12 204	74.9	25.1	2.55	2.67
Hockley	0.1	9 148	87.4	12.6	0.7	2.7	15.1	7 994	74.4	25.6	2.77	2.77
Hood	45.2	19 105	84.7	15.3	8.1	2.3	12.4	16 176	81.2	18.8	2.51	2.48
Hopkins	12.0	14 020	87.6	12.4	2.5	2.1	12.7	12 286	71.3	28.7	2.57	2.56
Houston	6.0	10 730	77.0	23.0	10.0	3.3	7.8	8 259	76.1	23.9	2.43	2.48
Howard	-0.8	13 589	83.8	16.2	0.5	4.2	23.4	11 389	69.4	30.6	2.54	2.51
Hudspeth	15.4	1 471	74.2	25.8	6.4	3.4	18.8	1 092	81.0	19.0	3.05	2.95
Hunt	19.4	32 490	88.5	11.5	2.8	2.4	9.7	28 742	71.5	28.5	2.66	2.44
Hutchinson	-3.7	10 871	85.4	14.6	2.6	3.0	17.6	9 283	78.9	21.1	2.56	2.47
Irion	15.5	914	75.9	24.1	9.8	7.9	11.4	694	77.7	22.3	2.61	2.34
Jack	11.8	3 668	83.1	16.9	5.3	3.4	10.2	3 047	76.7	23.3	2.52	2.54
Jackson	10.4	6 545	81.5	18.5	3.5	1.7	15.5	5 336	73.8	26.2	2.63	2.71
Jasper	17.7	16 576	81.1	18.9	8.2	2.2	16.6	13 450	80.7	19.3	2.58	2.57
Jeff Davis	15.0	1 420	63.1	36.9	18.0	3.7	9.2	896	70.1	29.9	2.34	2.51
Jefferson	2.6	102 080	91.0	9.0	0.5	1.6	9.7	92 880	66.0	34.0	2.63	2.41
Jim Hogg	8.4	2 308	78.6	21.4	6.4	2.2	6.9	1 815	77.6	22.4	2.88	2.89
Jim Wells	8.2	14 819	87.5	12.5	2.5	1.8	9.1	12 961	76.5	23.5	3.04	2.84
Johnson	30.4	46 269	94.3	5.7	0.7	1.5	6.2	43 636	78.9	21.1	2.87	2.77
Jones	-0.6	7 236	84.9	15.1	1.8	2.1	13.6	6 140	79.3	20.7	2.57	2.59
Karnes	2.7	5 479	81.3	18.7	4.7	2.2	12.4	4 454	74.2	25.8	2.65	2.68
Kaufman	36.7	26 133	93.2	6.8	0.8	1.7	7.1	24 367	79.2	20.8	2.89	2.79
Kendall	61.2	9 609	89.6	10.4	4.5	1.5	8.8	8 613	79.5	20.5	2.74	2.55
Kenedy	-4.8	281	49.1	50.9	36.7	4.0	1.1	138	34.8	65.2	2.52	3.21
Kent	-11.5	551	64.1	35.9	11.4	10.3	8.8	353	79.3	20.7	2.31	2.37
Kerr	23.8	20 228	88.1	11.9	4.6	2.1	9.9	17 813	73.3	26.7	2.36	2.33
Kimble	14.9	2 996	62.3	37.7	8.5	5.6	9.3	1 866	73.5	26.5	2.36	2.37
King	-12.9	174	62.1	37.9	7.5	40.3	0.0	108	34.3	65.7	2.57	2.87
Kinney	10.7	1 907	68.9	31.1	17.0	9.1	14.7	1 314	77.4	22.6	2.56	2.54
Kleberg	8.3	12 743	85.5	14.5	1.4	2.1	16.7	10 896	58.6	41.4	2.90	2.60
Knox	-10.4	2 129	79.4	20.6	1.8	9.4	10.0	1 690	75.4	24.6	2.40	2.56
Lamar	13.6	21 113	90.4	9.6	1.1	2.1	9.4	19 077	67.2	32.8	2.51	2.43
Lamb	-2.3	6 294	85.2	14.8	0.6	3.5	13.3	5 360	75.6	24.4	2.65	2.81
Lampasas	29.6	7 601	86.2	13.8	4.7	2.2	9.6	6 554	73.9	26.1	2.65	2.67
La Salle	6.9	2 436	74.7	25.3	5.0	1.9	11.7	1 819	74.7	25.3	2.98	2.65
Lavaca	4.4	9 657	79.4	20.6	3.9	2.7	7.3	7 669	78.5	21.5	2.44	2.44
Lee	20.3	6 851	82.7	17.3	4.8	2.3	7.7	5 663	79.3	20.7	2.67	2.59
Leon	23.6	8 299	74.6	25.4	13.7	2.5	16.4	6 189	82.8	17.2	2.46	2.48
Liberty	25.4	26 359	88.2	11.8	3.3	1.7	9.6	23 242	79.0	21.0	2.84	2.65
Limestone	2.4	9 725	81.3	18.7	2.8	2.1	7.8	7 906	74.9	25.1	2.54	2.61
Lipscomb	-2.0	1 541	78.2	21.8	1.5	7.6	18.8	1 205	77.8	22.2	2.47	2.58
Live Oak	19.2	6 196	68.3	31.7	18.8	2.5	18.0	4 230	81.4	18.6	2.52	2.57
Llano	49.3	11 829	66.6	33.4	23.1	3.9	12.8	7 879	80.9	19.1	2.13	2.13
Loving	-26.2	70	44.3	55.7	15.7	0.0	0.0	31	83.9	16.1	2.00	3.00
Lubbock	13.5	100 595	92.0	8.0	0.3	1.6	10.0	92 516	59.2	40.8	2.67	2.30
Lynn	-1.2	2 671	88.1	11.9	0.9	1.4	6.6	2 354	74.3	25.7	2.68	3.01
McCulloch	-3.9	4 184	78.3	21.7	7.3	4.7	7.1	3 277	72.8	27.2	2.45	2.51
McLennan	12.3	84 795	93.0	7.0	0.5	1.6	6.5	78 859	60.2	39.8	2.69	2.44
McMullen	11.3	587	60.5	39.5	28.1	3.4	12.7	355	80.6	19.4	2.33	2.67
Madison	16.9	4 797	81.6	18.4	8.0	2.5	8.6	3 914	77.0	23.0	2.55	2.66
Marion	13.9	6 384	72.2	27.8	14.4	2.4	10.6	4 610	82.1	17.9	2.34	2.43
Martin	-0.5	1 898	85.6	14.4	0.6	5.9	15.5	1 624	74.1	25.9	2.84	2.96

Table B. States and Counties

STATE/ County code	MSA/ PMSA/ NECMA code[1]	County type[2]	STATE County	Land area, 2000[3] (sq km)	Total persons	Rank	Per square kilometer	Land area, 1990[3] (sq km)	Total persons	Rank	Per square kilometer	White	Black or African American	American Indian or Alaska Native	Asian	Native Hawaiian and other Pacific Islander	Some other race
					Population, 2000				Population, 1990			Population and population characteristics, 2000					
												Race (percent)					
												One race					
					1	2	3	4	5	6	7	8	9	10	11	12	13	14

STATE/ County code	MSA/ PMSA/ NECMA code	County type	STATE County	Land area 2000	Total persons	Rank	Per sq km	Land area 1990	Total persons	Rank	Per sq km	White	Black or African American	American Indian or Alaska Native	Asian	Native Hawaiian and other Pacific Islander	Some other race
			TEXAS—Cont'd														
48 319	...	9	Mason	2 414	3 738	2 939	1.5	2 414	3 423	2 962	1.4	91.6	0.1	0.6	0.1	0.0	5.8
48 321	...	4	Matagorda	2 886	37 957	1 166	13.2	2 887	36 928	1 075	12.8	67.8	12.7	0.7	2.4	0.0	14.0
48 323	...	5	Maverick	3 315	47 297	961	14.3	3 316	36 378	1 094	11.0	70.9	0.3	1.3	0.4	0.0	24.1
48 325	...	6	Medina	3 439	39 304	1 130	11.4	3 439	27 312	1 380	7.9	79.4	2.2	0.7	0.3	0.0	14.5
48 327	...	8	Menard	2 336	2 360	3 035	1.0	2 336	2 252	3 047	1.0	87.5	0.5	0.6	0.3	0.0	9.8
48 329	5800	3	Midland	2 332	116 009	465	49.7	2 332	106 611	433	45.7	77.3	7.0	0.6	0.9	0.0	12.2
48 331	...	6	Milam	2 633	24 238	1 587	9.2	2 633	22 946	1 536	8.7	78.9	11.0	0.5	0.2	0.0	7.7
48 333	...	9	Mills	1 938	5 151	2 840	2.7	1 938	4 531	2 870	2.3	89.2	1.3	0.3	0.1	0.1	7.7
48 335	...	7	Mitchell	2 357	9 698	2 470	4.1	2 357	8 016	2 563	3.4	74.5	12.8	0.4	0.4	0.0	10.2
48 337	...	6	Montague	2 410	19 117	1 841	7.9	2 411	17 274	1 836	7.2	96.0	0.2	0.7	0.3	0.0	1.6
48 339	3360	1	Montgomery	2 704	293 768	193	108.6	2 705	182 201	264	67.4	88.3	3.5	0.5	1.1	0.0	4.9
48 341	...	6	Moore	2 330	20 121	1 785	8.6	2 330	17 865	1 795	7.7	63.9	0.7	0.7	0.9	0.0	31.2
48 343	...	6	Morris	659	13 048	2 228	19.8	659	13 200	2 123	20.0	71.7	24.1	0.5	0.2	0.1	2.3
48 345	...	9	Motley	2 562	1 426	3 096	0.6	2 563	1 532	3 095	0.6	87.4	3.5	0.6	0.1	0.1	6.3
48 347	...	5	Nacogdoches	2 452	59 203	812	24.1	2 452	54 753	786	22.3	75.0	16.7	0.4	0.7	0.1	5.7
48 349	...	4	Navarro	2 610	45 124	995	17.3	2 774	39 926	1 005	14.4	70.8	16.8	0.5	0.5	0.3	9.4
48 351	...	8	Newton	2 416	15 072	2 085	6.2	2 416	13 569	2 094	5.6	75.8	20.7	0.6	0.3	0.0	1.6
48 353	...	6	Nolan	2 362	15 802	2 032	6.7	2 362	16 594	1 880	7.0	78.5	4.7	0.5	0.2	0.1	14.0
48 355	1880	2	Nueces	2 165	313 645	182	144.9	2 165	291 145	168	134.5	72.0	4.2	0.6	1.2	0.1	18.7
48 357	...	7	Ochiltree	2 376	9 006	2 528	3.8	2 377	9 128	2 459	3.8	86.2	0.1	0.9	0.4	0.0	10.3
48 359	...	8	Oldham	3 887	2 185	3 052	0.6	3 887	2 278	3 042	0.6	90.7	1.9	1.3	0.4	0.0	4.6
48 361	0840	2	Orange	923	84 966	613	92.1	923	80 509	566	87.2	88.0	8.4	0.6	0.8	0.0	1.1
48 363	...	6	Palo Pinto	2 468	27 026	1 481	11.0	2 468	25 055	1 459	10.2	88.2	2.3	0.7	0.5	0.0	6.6
48 365	...	6	Panola	2 074	22 756	1 660	11.0	2 075	22 035	1 574	10.6	78.8	17.7	0.4	0.2	0.0	1.9
48 367	2800	1	Parker	2 340	88 495	590	37.8	2 340	64 785	676	27.7	92.6	1.8	0.7	0.3	0.0	3.2
48 369	...	7	Parmer	2 283	10 016	2 444	4.4	2 284	9 863	2 400	4.3	66.0	1.0	0.8	0.3	0.0	29.5
48 371	...	7	Pecos	12 338	16 809	1 967	1.4	12 339	14 675	2 006	1.2	75.8	4.4	0.4	0.5	0.0	16.1
48 373	...	6	Polk	2 738	41 133	1 077	15.0	2 739	30 687	1 259	11.2	79.6	13.2	1.7	0.4	0.0	3.7
48 375	0320	3	Potter	2 355	113 546	474	48.2	2 355	97 841	470	41.5	68.6	10.0	0.9	2.5	0.0	15.4
48 377	...	7	Presidio	9 986	7 304	2 655	0.7	9 987	6 637	2 690	0.7	85.0	0.3	0.3	0.1	0.0	13.5
48 379	...	8	Rains	601	9 139	2 518	15.2	601	6 715	2 686	11.2	91.9	2.9	0.8	0.3	0.0	2.5
48 381	0320	3	Randall	2 368	104 312	507	44.1	2 368	89 673	512	37.9	90.4	1.5	0.6	1.0	0.0	4.7
48 383	...	6	Reagan	3 044	3 326	2 970	1.1	3 044	4 514	2 874	1.5	64.6	3.0	0.5	0.3	0.0	29.6
48 385	...	9	Real	1 813	3 047	2 990	1.7	1 813	2 412	3 030	1.3	91.4	0.2	0.6	0.2	0.0	6.0
48 387	...	6	Red River	2 720	14 314	2 139	5.3	2 720	14 317	2 030	5.3	78.0	17.8	0.6	0.1	0.0	2.3
48 389	...	7	Reeves	6 827	13 137	2 219	1.9	6 827	15 852	1 933	2.3	79.3	2.1	0.5	0.4	0.0	15.0
48 391	...	6	Refugio	1 995	7 828	2 621	3.9	1 995	7 976	2 570	4.0	80.2	6.8	0.6	0.3	0.1	10.4
48 393	...	9	Roberts	2 393	887	3 116	0.4	2 394	1 025	3 112	0.4	96.5	0.3	0.6	0.1	0.0	1.4
48 395	...	6	Robertson	2 213	16 000	2 022	7.2	2 213	15 511	1 952	7.0	66.2	24.2	0.4	0.2	0.1	7.2
48 397	1920	0	Rockwall	334	43 080	1 035	129.0	334	25 604	1 438	76.7	89.2	3.2	0.4	1.3	0.1	4.4
48 399	...	6	Runnels	2 721	11 495	2 336	4.2	2 731	11 294	2 276	4.1	81.4	1.4	0.5	0.3	0.0	14.3
48 401	...	6	Rusk	2 392	47 372	960	19.8	2 392	43 735	928	18.3	74.9	19.2	0.3	0.2	0.0	4.2
48 403	...	9	Sabine	1 270	10 469	2 400	8.2	1 270	9 586	2 425	7.5	87.8	9.9	0.4	0.1	0.0	0.8
48 405	...	9	San Augustine	1 367	8 946	2 530	6.5	1 367	7 999	2 566	5.9	69.3	27.9	0.2	0.2	0.0	1.6
48 407	...	8	San Jacinto	1 478	22 246	1 683	15.1	1 478	16 372	1 899	11.1	83.6	12.6	0.5	0.3	0.1	1.6
48 409	1880	2	San Patricio	1 791	67 138	732	37.5	1 792	58 749	740	32.8	76.8	2.8	0.7	0.6	0.1	15.9
48 411	...	7	San Saba	2 938	6 186	2 763	2.1	2 938	5 401	2 808	1.8	84.5	2.7	1.1	0.1	0.0	10.5
48 413	...	8	Schleicher	3 394	2 935	2 996	0.9	3 395	2 990	3 002	0.9	76.6	1.5	0.1	0.2	0.0	19.0
48 415	...	7	Scurry	2 337	16 361	2 000	7.0	2 338	18 634	1 757	8.0	81.3	6.1	0.5	0.3	0.0	10.5
48 417	...	8	Shackelford	2 367	3 302	2 973	1.4	2 367	3 316	2 973	1.4	94.2	0.5	0.4	0.0	0.0	4.2
48 419	...	7	Shelby	2 057	25 224	1 557	12.3	2 057	22 034	1 575	10.7	72.6	19.4	0.4	0.2	0.0	5.9
48 421	...	9	Sherman	2 391	3 186	2 980	1.3	2 391	2 858	3 007	1.2	82.5	0.5	0.7	0.0	0.0	14.6
48 423	8640	3	Smith	2 405	174 706	312	72.6	2 405	151 309	308	62.9	72.6	19.1	0.4	0.7	0.0	5.7
48 425	...	8	Somervell	485	6 809	2 711	14.0	485	5 360	2 813	11.1	92.2	0.3	0.7	0.3	0.0	5.1
48 427	...	6	Starr	3 168	53 597	871	16.9	3 168	40 518	986	12.8	87.9	0.1	0.2	0.3	0.0	9.9
48 429	...	7	Stephens	2 317	9 674	2 471	4.2	2 317	9 010	2 468	3.9	86.9	2.9	0.4	0.3	0.0	8.1
48 431	...	8	Sterling	2 391	1 393	3 098	0.6	2 392	1 438	3 099	0.6	85.7	0.1	0.3	0.0	0.1	11.8
48 433	...	9	Stonewall	2 379	1 693	3 085	0.7	2 380	2 013	3 066	0.8	88.2	3.0	0.4	0.4	0.0	6.4
48 435	...	7	Sutton	3 765	4 077	2 911	1.1	3 766	4 135	2 901	1.1	75.3	0.2	0.4	0.2	0.0	22.3
48 437	...	6	Swisher	2 332	8 378	2 575	3.6	2 332	8 133	2 552	3.5	71.7	5.8	0.5	0.2	0.0	19.4
48 439	2800	0	Tarrant	2 236	1 446 219	20	646.8	2 236	1 170 103	27	523.3	71.2	12.8	0.6	3.6	0.2	9.1
48 441	0040	3	Taylor	2 371	126 555	428	53.4	2 372	119 655	387	50.4	80.6	6.7	0.6	1.2	0.1	8.3
48 443	...	9	Terrell	6 106	1 081	3 106	0.2	6 107	1 410	3 100	0.2	88.3	0.0	1.7	0.6	0.0	8.3
48 445	...	6	Terry	2 305	12 761	2 247	5.5	2 305	13 218	2 120	5.7	76.6	5.0	0.5	0.2	0.0	14.3
48 447	...	9	Throckmorton	2 363	1 850	3 076	0.8	2 363	1 880	3 075	0.8	92.1	0.1	0.4	0.1	0.0	5.6
48 449	...	7	Titus	1 063	28 118	1 447	26.5	1 063	24 009	1 492	22.6	70.1	10.7	0.6	0.4	0.0	16.4

[1] MSA = Metropolitan Statistical Area. PMSA = Primary MSA. NECMA = New England County Metropolitan Area. See Appendix A for explanation of these concepts. See Appendix B for list of metropolitan areas identified by type, with component counties.
[2] County typology code from the Economic Research Service of USDA. See Appendix A for definition.
[3] Dry land or land partially or temporarily covered by water.

Table B. States and Counties

STATE County	Population and population characteristics, 2000 (cont'd)								Population and population characteristics, 1990				
	Race (percent) (cont'd)								Race (percent)				
	Race alone or in combination												
	Two or more races	White	Black	American Indian or Alaska Native	Asian	Native Hawaiian and other Pacific Islander	Some other race	Hispanic[1]	White	Black or African American	American Indian or Alaska Native	Asian and Pacific Islander	Hispanic[1]
	15	16	17	18	19	20	21	22	23	24	25	26	27
TEXAS—Cont'd													
Mason	1.8	93.3	0.2	1.3	0.1	0.0	6.9	20.9	90.1	0.2	0.4	0.1	19.6
Matagorda	2.4	69.9	13.2	1.2	2.6	0.1	15.6	31.3	72.1	13.8	0.2	2.3	24.6
Maverick	2.9	73.6	0.4	1.5	0.5	0.1	26.8	95.0	65.3	0.1	2.0	0.2	93.5
Medina	2.9	82.0	2.4	1.2	0.5	0.1	16.7	45.5	86.4	0.3	0.4	0.2	44.4
Menard	1.1	88.4	0.7	0.8	0.5	0.1	10.6	31.7	92.2	0.3	0.2	0.0	32.2
Midland	1.9	79.0	7.3	1.0	1.1	0.1	13.4	29.0	81.6	7.8	0.4	0.8	21.4
Milam	1.6	80.3	11.3	1.1	0.3	0.0	8.7	18.6	81.1	12.8	0.3	0.2	15.1
Mills	1.3	90.5	1.4	0.8	0.1	0.1	8.6	13.0	93.5	0.2	0.1	0.0	10.7
Mitchell	1.7	76.1	13.0	0.7	0.4	0.0	11.5	31.0	78.8	4.5	0.2	0.1	29.8
Montague	1.2	97.1	0.3	1.5	0.4	0.1	2.0	5.4	97.5	0.0	0.4	0.1	3.2
Montgomery	1.8	89.9	3.7	1.0	1.4	0.1	5.8	12.6	91.2	4.3	0.4	0.7	7.3
Moore	2.6	66.3	0.8	1.4	1.1	0.1	33.1	47.5	71.6	0.5	0.7	1.6	31.9
Morris	1.1	72.7	24.4	1.1	0.3	0.1	2.6	3.7	74.0	24.4	0.5	0.1	1.8
Motley	1.9	88.7	4.2	1.3	0.1	0.2	7.3	12.1	88.9	4.4	0.3	0.3	8.9
Nacogdoches	1.4	76.3	17.0	0.8	0.9	0.1	6.4	11.2	79.9	16.5	0.3	0.6	5.1
Navarro	1.7	72.2	17.2	0.9	0.7	0.4	10.4	15.8	75.9	19.0	0.3	0.7	7.2
Newton	1.0	76.7	20.9	1.2	0.3	0.1	1.8	3.8	76.7	22.4	0.3	0.1	1.1
Nolan	2.1	80.3	5.1	0.8	0.4	0.1	15.5	28.0	78.0	4.7	0.3	0.1	25.6
Nueces	3.1	74.8	4.6	1.1	1.5	0.2	21.1	55.8	75.6	4.4	0.4	0.9	52.2
Ochiltree	2.0	88.2	0.2	1.6	0.5	0.0	11.6	31.8	87.9	0.0	1.2	0.1	18.0
Oldham	1.2	91.7	2.2	1.5	0.6	0.1	5.1	11.0	92.7	0.4	1.3	0.8	8.8
Orange	1.2	89.0	8.6	1.1	0.9	0.1	1.5	3.6	90.2	8.4	0.2	0.6	2.4
Palo Pinto	1.7	89.8	2.6	1.3	0.7	0.1	7.3	13.6	91.0	3.2	0.3	0.7	9.2
Panola	1.1	79.7	17.9	0.8	0.4	0.1	2.3	3.5	80.3	18.4	0.3	0.1	2.2
Parker	1.4	93.9	1.9	1.3	0.5	0.0	3.7	7.0	96.1	0.9	0.6	0.4	4.2
Parmer	2.3	68.1	1.2	1.1	0.4	0.1	31.4	49.2	91.0	1.2	0.3	0.2	41.5
Pecos	2.7	78.3	4.5	0.9	0.7	0.1	18.3	61.1	64.4	0.4	0.3	0.2	56.8
Polk	1.3	80.8	13.4	2.3	0.5	0.0	4.3	9.4	81.8	12.7	2.2	0.3	5.2
Potter	2.6	70.8	10.6	1.6	2.8	0.1	16.8	28.1	75.5	8.9	0.9	2.6	19.7
Presidio	0.9	85.8	0.4	0.5	0.2	0.0	14.0	84.4	84.7	0.1	0.2	0.2	81.6
Rains	1.4	93.2	3.1	1.4	0.4	0.0	3.4	5.5	94.0	4.3	0.4	0.1	2.4
Randall	1.6	92.0	1.7	1.2	1.2	0.1	5.5	10.3	94.4	1.2	0.5	0.7	6.9
Reagan	2.0	66.4	3.4	0.7	0.4	0.1	31.1	49.5	78.6	2.8	0.2	0.0	43.0
Real	1.5	92.9	0.3	1.4	0.3	0.1	6.6	22.6	85.6	0.0	1.0	0.0	23.8
Red River	1.2	79.1	18.1	1.2	0.2	0.0	2.6	4.7	78.2	20.1	0.5	0.1	1.9
Reeves	2.7	81.8	2.2	0.7	0.5	0.0	17.5	73.4	96.5	2.2	0.2	0.2	72.8
Refugio	1.7	81.7	7.0	0.9	0.4	0.1	11.7	44.6	77.7	8.1	0.3	0.1	39.7
Roberts	1.1	97.5	0.3	0.9	0.5	0.2	1.7	3.2	97.8	0.0	0.1	0.2	3.3
Robertson	1.8	67.9	24.5	1.1	0.2	0.1	8.2	14.7	64.8	27.5	0.2	0.1	12.3
Rockwall	1.4	90.4	3.4	0.8	1.6	0.1	5.1	11.1	93.7	3.3	0.4	0.6	5.9
Runnels	2.0	83.1	1.7	0.9	0.5	0.1	15.7	29.3	92.4	1.6	0.1	0.1	24.3
Rusk	1.1	75.9	19.5	0.7	0.3	0.1	4.7	8.4	77.1	20.5	0.3	0.1	4.0
Sabine	0.9	88.7	10.1	1.0	0.1	0.0	1.0	1.8	87.6	11.7	0.1	0.1	1.2
San Augustine	0.7	69.9	28.1	0.6	0.2	0.0	1.9	3.6	70.8	28.1	0.2	0.1	1.7
San Jacinto	1.3	84.8	12.9	1.2	0.4	0.1	1.9	4.9	82.6	15.5	0.5	0.1	2.6
San Patricio	3.0	79.5	3.2	1.2	0.9	0.2	18.1	49.4	76.3	1.6	0.4	0.3	50.7
San Saba	1.1	85.5	2.8	1.3	0.2	0.0	11.3	21.5	91.5	0.3	0.1	0.0	18.5
Schleicher	2.6	78.8	1.8	0.3	0.3	0.0	21.3	43.5	69.5	0.9	0.1	0.0	35.5
Scurry	1.4	82.6	6.3	0.8	0.3	0.0	11.4	27.8	75.7	4.7	0.3	0.2	23.9
Shackelford	0.6	94.8	0.6	0.8	0.0	0.0	4.4	7.6	94.2	0.4	0.3	0.1	8.2
Shelby	1.4	73.5	19.7	0.7	0.3	0.6	6.8	9.9	77.4	21.5	0.2	0.1	2.4
Sherman	1.7	84.0	0.6	1.0	0.2	0.0	15.8	27.4	98.5	0.1	0.4	0.2	18.8
Smith	1.4	73.9	19.4	0.9	0.9	0.1	6.4	11.2	75.1	20.9	0.3	0.4	5.9
Somervell	1.5	93.5	0.4	1.3	0.4	0.0	5.8	13.4	90.5	0.2	0.6	0.4	14.0
Starr	1.5	89.3	0.2	0.3	0.3	0.1	11.3	97.5	61.9	0.1	0.1	0.1	97.2
Stephens	1.4	88.2	3.1	0.8	0.3	0.0	8.9	14.7	90.9	2.8	0.3	0.3	8.5
Sterling	2.0	87.7	0.1	0.5	0.0	0.1	13.7	31.0	86.5	0.0	0.6	0.0	25.5
Stonewall	1.7	89.7	3.5	1.0	0.5	0.1	6.9	11.8	94.3	4.4	0.1	0.3	11.8
Sutton	1.6	76.7	0.4	0.5	0.4	0.0	23.7	51.7	75.6	0.0	0.4	0.1	45.1
Swisher	2.3	73.9	6.1	1.3	0.2	0.0	21.0	35.2	70.1	4.2	0.3	0.2	30.7
Tarrant	2.5	73.4	13.3	1.1	4.1	0.2	10.4	19.7	78.4	12.0	0.5	2.5	12.0
Taylor	2.4	82.7	7.4	1.2	1.8	0.1	9.4	17.6	83.8	6.3	0.4	1.2	14.6
Terrell	1.0	89.4	0.0	1.9	0.6	0.0	9.1	48.6	84.3	0.1	0.4	0.1	53.3
Terry	3.4	79.7	5.3	0.9	0.3	0.0	17.2	44.1	77.2	3.4	0.3	0.2	39.3
Throckmorton	1.8	93.9	0.1	1.0	0.1	0.0	6.8	9.4	94.6	0.0	0.2	0.4	7.2
Titus	1.7	71.6	11.0	0.9	0.6	0.1	17.6	28.3	77.7	13.4	0.4	0.1	10.6

[1] Hispanic persons may be of any race.

Table B. States and Counties

STATE County	Under 5 years (28)	5 to 17 years (29)	18 to 24 years (30)	25 to 34 years (31)	35 to 44 years (32)	45 to 54 years (33)	55 to 64 years (34)	65 to 74 years (35)	75 years and over (36)	Median age (years) (37)	Percent Female (38)
TEXAS—Cont'd											
Mason	5.1	17.3	4.7	8.9	11.8	15.3	13.5	12.0	11.5	46.7	52.0
Matagorda	7.4	22.6	8.9	11.4	15.5	13.0	8.8	6.9	5.5	34.8	50.4
Maverick	10.0	27.0	9.2	13.6	13.0	10.8	6.9	5.7	3.8	27.8	52.1
Medina	7.2	21.8	8.4	13.6	15.1	12.8	8.7	6.8	5.6	34.4	48.6
Menard	4.7	19.6	5.3	8.3	13.6	14.3	12.2	10.8	11.2	44.1	50.1
Midland	7.5	22.7	8.8	12.1	16.3	13.3	7.6	6.5	5.1	34.1	51.7
Milam	6.8	20.6	7.7	10.8	13.9	12.7	10.2	8.3	8.9	38.0	51.0
Mills	5.4	20.2	4.7	8.5	12.0	14.0	12.2	10.6	12.5	44.4	49.4
Mitchell	4.7	15.1	11.5	14.4	16.3	14.1	8.8	7.6	7.6	38.6	38.6
Montague	6.0	18.0	6.8	10.5	13.8	13.0	12.0	10.4	9.4	41.3	52.0
Montgomery	7.7	21.8	8.0	13.3	17.3	14.4	8.7	5.2	3.4	34.4	50.4
Moore	9.3	24.3	9.2	14.1	14.3	11.0	7.2	6.0	4.5	30.4	49.8
Morris	5.9	19.3	7.8	10.1	14.2	13.8	10.7	10.0	8.3	40.2	51.9
Motley	5.9	18.1	6.0	8.0	13.1	12.8	12.4	12.6	11.1	44.4	49.6
Nacogdoches	6.5	17.5	20.0	12.2	12.5	11.6	7.6	6.3	5.8	29.7	51.8
Navarro	7.2	20.1	9.9	12.6	14.3	12.2	9.3	7.1	7.3	35.2	50.8
Newton	6.5	19.7	9.0	12.2	14.4	13.7	10.4	8.4	5.7	36.9	49.0
Nolan	6.7	20.4	8.5	11.4	14.0	12.9	9.7	8.5	7.9	37.4	51.4
Nueces	7.7	20.7	10.5	13.4	15.5	13.1	7.9	6.2	5.0	33.3	51.1
Ochiltree	8.1	22.5	8.4	12.7	15.9	12.5	8.2	6.7	5.0	33.7	50.1
Oldham	6.5	28.5	7.2	9.6	13.7	14.2	8.9	6.8	4.4	32.9	48.1
Orange	6.7	20.6	8.7	12.4	15.7	13.7	9.5	7.3	5.3	36.1	50.9
Palo Pinto	6.7	19.3	8.2	11.3	14.6	13.1	10.5	8.7	7.7	38.3	50.8
Panola	6.2	19.0	9.2	10.6	14.5	14.4	10.3	8.3	7.5	38.8	52.0
Parker	6.3	21.8	7.9	12.1	17.6	14.7	9.6	6.1	4.4	36.5	49.0
Parmer	8.6	24.3	8.5	12.2	14.0	11.1	8.6	6.1	6.6	32.1	50.5
Pecos	6.6	21.1	13.8	13.0	14.2	12.0	8.5	6.3	4.5	31.2	44.8
Polk	5.9	17.0	8.1	12.8	14.0	12.4	11.8	10.5	7.4	39.3	47.9
Potter	8.3	19.7	11.1	14.8	15.3	11.6	7.5	5.9	5.8	32.1	49.8
Presidio	7.8	24.9	8.3	11.9	13.0	11.2	9.0	7.8	6.2	32.8	51.5
Rains	5.6	18.2	7.4	10.6	14.5	14.3	13.4	9.5	6.6	41.0	50.1
Randall	6.8	19.2	11.2	12.8	15.7	13.7	8.6	6.9	5.0	34.9	51.4
Reagan	8.2	26.0	7.6	12.0	16.1	12.8	7.1	5.8	4.5	32.4	49.9
Real	4.9	18.6	5.4	8.8	12.7	13.3	15.5	12.2	8.6	44.6	50.5
Red River	5.8	18.0	7.8	11.0	13.4	13.2	11.1	9.6	10.1	40.4	51.8
Reeves	7.0	22.9	11.3	11.9	13.2	11.8	9.2	7.2	5.4	32.1	47.2
Refugio	6.0	20.2	7.4	11.2	14.8	13.1	10.8	8.8	7.8	38.6	51.1
Roberts	5.0	20.1	4.8	8.2	16.6	18.5	12.4	8.5	6.0	42.0	49.9
Robertson	7.2	21.0	7.5	11.0	13.2	12.8	10.3	8.4	8.5	37.6	52.4
Rockwall	7.5	22.6	7.0	12.4	18.7	14.7	8.5	4.8	3.7	35.3	49.8
Runnels	6.3	20.6	6.4	10.8	13.4	12.7	10.2	9.3	10.3	39.4	51.8
Rusk	6.1	18.8	8.3	12.0	15.8	13.6	9.7	8.0	7.6	38.1	49.0
Sabine	5.2	15.9	5.6	8.9	12.2	11.9	15.3	14.3	10.7	47.0	51.7
San Augustine	5.7	18.0	6.8	10.3	12.6	12.8	12.3	11.3	10.0	42.1	52.1
San Jacinto	6.0	19.1	7.4	10.4	14.6	13.8	12.7	10.2	5.8	40.0	49.9
San Patricio	8.1	23.0	10.0	13.1	15.1	12.1	8.1	6.2	4.3	32.0	49.9
San Saba	5.3	22.6	8.2	9.0	11.8	12.6	10.2	9.6	10.7	39.4	48.2
Schleicher	6.2	21.8	7.3	9.5	14.4	14.7	9.8	8.1	8.3	38.8	50.3
Scurry	6.3	18.9	10.7	11.4	14.8	13.5	8.9	8.2	7.2	37.0	48.1
Shackelford	5.4	21.3	6.0	9.5	15.3	14.2	10.1	9.5	8.7	40.1	52.6
Shelby	7.0	19.6	8.8	12.1	13.7	12.3	10.0	8.5	8.0	36.9	52.0
Sherman	6.9	24.5	7.0	12.5	14.0	12.6	8.8	7.2	6.4	34.4	49.4
Smith	7.1	19.5	9.8	12.9	14.5	12.9	9.2	7.5	6.6	35.5	52.1
Somervell	6.4	22.0	7.7	11.1	15.7	14.9	8.8	6.6	6.7	36.8	50.1
Starr	10.4	27.0	11.0	14.4	12.7	9.5	6.8	4.9	3.3	26.1	51.5
Stephens	5.6	18.8	9.1	11.2	14.4	12.8	10.5	9.3	8.4	38.9	49.2
Sterling	5.1	23.6	6.1	10.3	19.5	13.1	7.7	7.4	7.3	37.9	50.9
Stonewall	5.1	17.7	6.2	9.5	13.1	13.1	11.4	12.0	11.9	43.7	52.6
Sutton	7.2	21.6	6.7	12.6	15.1	15.3	9.1	7.6	4.8	36.5	50.1
Swisher	7.4	20.5	10.3	12.5	13.0	11.0	9.4	8.7	7.2	34.6	47.8
Tarrant	8.0	20.1	10.0	16.3	17.2	12.9	7.3	4.6	3.7	32.3	50.5
Taylor	7.2	19.4	13.8	13.1	14.7	11.5	7.8	6.5	5.9	32.2	51.5
Terrell	5.6	21.0	5.0	8.7	14.7	14.6	12.9	10.5	7.0	42.0	49.2
Terry	7.3	21.0	9.5	12.2	14.8	11.7	8.9	7.9	6.7	35.0	48.1
Throckmorton	5.5	19.7	5.7	8.4	14.4	11.7	14.0	9.9	10.6	41.8	50.7
Titus	8.6	21.7	9.8	14.2	13.7	11.3	8.2	6.2	6.4	31.8	50.6

Table B. States and Counties

STATE County	Under 5 years	5 to 17 years	18 to 24 years	25 to 34 years	35 to 44 years	45 to 54 years	55 to 64 years	65 to 74 years	75 years and over	Percent Female	2000	1990	1980	1990–2000	1980–1990
	39	40	41	42	43	44	45	46	47	48	49	50	51	52	53
TEXAS—Cont'd															
Mason	5.9	17.6	5.9	11.4	12.6	10.4	11.7	12.2	12.3	52.4	3 738	3 423	3 683	9.2	-7.1
Matagorda	8.5	22.8	8.4	16.4	14.0	9.6	8.5	6.6	5.0	50.5	37 957	36 928	37 828	2.8	-2.4
Maverick	9.6	28.5	11.1	13.6	13.0	8.4	7.4	5.3	3.2	52.5	47 297	36 378	31 398	30.0	15.9
Medina	7.8	21.9	8.9	14.1	14.0	9.8	9.5	8.1	5.9	50.4	39 304	27 312	23 164	43.9	17.9
Menard	6.9	17.5	5.7	12.0	12.4	10.0	11.9	11.6	12.1	50.5	2 360	2 252	2 346	4.8	-4.0
Midland	9.4	22.0	8.5	18.4	15.3	9.1	8.4	5.5	3.5	51.5	116 009	106 611	82 636	8.8	29.0
Milam	7.1	21.1	7.8	12.9	12.9	9.8	9.6	9.7	9.0	51.5	24 238	22 946	22 732	5.6	0.9
Mills	5.7	18.2	5.6	11.0	12.3	9.6	10.9	12.9	13.8	51.4	5 151	4 531	4 477	13.7	1.2
Mitchell	6.5	21.0	7.2	12.4	12.4	8.8	10.7	10.7	10.2	52.3	9 698	8 016	9 088	21.0	-11.8
Montague	6.5	18.1	7.2	12.6	12.1	10.6	10.9	11.3	10.7	52.1	19 117	17 274	17 410	10.7	-0.8
Montgomery	7.9	21.8	8.8	16.7	16.8	11.6	7.8	5.3	3.3	50.3	293 768	182 201	127 222	61.2	43.2
Moore	9.5	23.6	9.7	16.7	13.3	9.1	8.3	6.0	3.9	50.0	20 121	17 865	16 575	12.6	7.8
Morris	6.7	20.7	7.4	14.2	13.3	10.1	10.7	9.0	7.9	51.8	13 048	13 200	14 629	-1.2	-9.8
Motley	5.5	17.8	5.7	10.8	11.6	10.6	11.6	13.4	12.9	51.6	1 426	1 532	1 950	-6.9	-21.4
Nacogdoches	6.4	16.7	23.0	14.3	12.3	8.1	7.3	6.3	5.5	51.6	59 203	54 753	46 786	8.1	17.0
Navarro	7.5	19.5	9.8	14.4	12.6	9.9	9.1	8.4	8.7	51.9	45 124	39 926	35 323	13.0	13.0
Newton	7.0	22.5	8.8	13.8	13.3	11.0	10.2	7.8	5.7	51.2	15 072	13 569	13 254	11.1	2.4
Nolan	7.4	20.4	9.0	14.0	13.4	9.9	9.3	8.5	8.0	51.4	15 802	16 594	17 359	-4.8	-4.4
Nueces	8.3	22.3	10.0	17.4	14.8	9.3	8.0	6.1	4.0	51.1	313 645	291 145	268 215	7.7	8.5
Ochiltree	8.3	22.6	8.0	17.7	14.2	9.4	8.9	6.4	4.5	50.0	9 006	9 128	9 588	-1.3	-4.8
Oldham	6.0	35.3	5.7	12.5	12.6	9.0	8.5	6.2	4.3	43.5	2 185	2 278	2 283	-4.1	-0.2
Orange	7.2	21.4	9.3	15.7	14.6	11.4	9.6	6.9	4.0	51.1	84 966	80 509	83 838	5.5	-4.0
Palo Pinto	7.3	19.1	8.3	14.5	13.1	10.4	10.4	9.3	7.7	51.7	27 026	25 055	24 062	7.9	4.1
Panola	6.9	20.9	8.7	13.9	13.9	10.3	9.5	8.6	7.2	52.2	22 756	22 035	20 724	3.3	6.3
Parker	7.4	20.6	8.7	15.7	16.1	11.8	8.8	6.5	4.4	50.0	88 495	64 785	44 609	36.6	45.2
Parmer	9.1	24.0	8.9	14.9	12.7	10.0	7.9	6.8	5.7	49.7	10 016	9 863	11 038	1.6	-10.6
Pecos	8.7	25.9	9.2	14.2	13.0	10.1	9.2	5.8	4.0	50.5	16 809	14 675	14 618	14.5	0.4
Polk	6.4	18.4	7.3	12.2	11.7	10.5	13.1	12.4	8.0	51.2	41 133	30 687	24 407	34.0	25.7
Potter	8.9	19.8	10.4	17.2	13.2	8.8	8.6	7.2	5.9	51.9	113 546	97 841	98 637	16.1	-0.8
Presidio	8.0	24.3	9.6	12.1	12.5	9.7	9.9	7.9	6.0	51.6	7 304	6 637	5 188	10.0	27.9
Rains	5.9	19.2	7.4	13.6	13.0	11.0	11.8	10.9	7.2	50.9	9 139	6 715	4 839	36.1	38.8
Randall	7.3	20.0	10.4	17.2	16.0	10.3	8.8	6.2	3.7	51.8	104 312	89 673	75 062	16.3	19.5
Reagan	10.0	28.0	8.8	16.7	14.9	7.8	6.2	4.5	3.0	49.3	3 326	4 514	4 135	-26.3	9.2
Real	6.1	17.3	9.3	10.0	11.4	12.7	12.6	11.7	8.9	51.9	3 047	2 412	2 469	26.3	-2.3
Red River	5.8	18.2	8.4	12.4	12.1	10.5	10.7	11.1	10.7	53.0	14 314	14 317	16 101	0.0	-11.1
Reeves	8.8	24.7	10.0	15.8	12.6	9.4	8.4	6.1	4.2	48.5	13 137	15 852	15 801	-17.1	0.3
Refugio	6.5	21.0	8.6	13.8	13.1	10.8	10.0	9.0	7.3	52.1	7 828	7 976	9 289	-1.9	-14.1
Roberts	6.8	23.1	4.6	15.2	15.7	12.7	10.4	5.9	5.6	51.2	887	1 025	1 187	-13.5	-13.6
Robertson	8.1	20.5	8.6	13.9	11.7	9.1	9.8	9.8	8.6	52.2	16 000	15 511	14 653	3.2	5.9
Rockwall	7.6	21.8	7.6	16.6	18.2	12.8	7.7	4.5	3.2	50.3	43 080	25 604	14 528	68.3	76.2
Runnels	6.9	20.4	7.6	12.6	12.3	9.7	9.8	10.2	10.5	51.3	11 495	11 294	11 872	1.8	-4.9
Rusk	7.0	20.9	7.9	14.3	13.7	9.8	9.2	8.9	8.3	52.1	47 372	43 735	41 382	8.3	5.7
Sabine	5.5	15.5	6.6	10.6	9.8	11.2	15.5	15.8	9.7	51.8	10 469	9 586	8 702	0.2	10.2
San Augustine	6.5	17.9	7.8	12.3	10.4	10.3	12.4	11.8	10.5	52.8	8 946	7 999	8 785	11.8	-8.9
San Jacinto	6.3	20.0	7.6	12.9	13.1	11.7	12.9	9.8	5.9	49.9	22 246	16 372	11 434	35.9	43.2
San Patricio	8.2	24.1	9.8	14.7	14.2	10.1	8.6	6.2	4.2	50.5	67 138	58 749	58 013	14.3	1.3
San Saba	6.6	19.3	7.2	11.5	12.1	9.9	10.2	10.9	12.3	51.2	6 186	5 401	5 841	14.5	-7.5
Schleicher	7.9	24.6	6.1	13.7	14.0	9.0	9.2	7.9	7.5	51.6	2 935	2 990	2 820	-1.8	6.0
Scurry	7.2	21.3	9.0	16.7	14.2	9.1	9.2	7.1	6.2	48.9	16 361	18 634	18 192	-12.2	2.4
Shackelford	6.3	20.5	6.0	14.1	13.1	9.2	10.3	9.6	10.9	51.4	3 302	3 316	3 915	-0.4	-15.3
Shelby	7.1	19.1	8.5	13.4	12.0	10.2	10.4	10.2	9.1	52.5	25 224	22 034	23 084	14.5	-4.5
Sherman	7.5	21.7	7.6	14.0	13.9	11.2	10.4	7.8	5.8	50.2	3 186	2 858	3 174	11.5	-10.0
Smith	7.4	19.3	10.2	16.0	14.4	10.0	9.0	7.8	5.9	51.9	174 706	151 309	128 366	15.5	17.9
Somervell	8.4	23.7	8.2	14.9	15.7	9.8	7.4	6.4	5.6	49.4	6 809	5 360	4 154	27.0	29.0
Starr	9.9	29.5	12.4	14.6	11.7	8.6	6.2	4.2	2.8	50.8	53 597	40 518	27 266	32.3	48.6
Stephens	6.8	20.5	6.8	13.1	12.8	10.3	10.5	10.4	8.8	52.1	9 674	9 010	9 926	7.4	-9.2
Sterling	8.8	24.8	6.5	19.0	12.6	8.3	7.7	7.1	5.2	51.2	1 393	1 438	1 206	-3.1	19.2
Stonewall	6.8	18.6	6.6	14.4	10.8	10.7	11.4	9.5	11.2	51.6	1 693	2 013	2 406	-15.9	-16.3
Sutton	7.7	23.0	8.9	14.7	15.6	10.7	9.0	6.4	4.1	51.6	4 077	4 135	5 130	-1.4	-19.4
Swisher	8.3	21.9	7.8	13.1	11.9	9.7	10.7	9.3	7.4	50.8	8 378	8 133	9 723	3.0	-16.4
Tarrant	8.5	18.6	11.1	21.0	15.7	9.8	6.9	5.0	3.3	50.5	1 446 219	1 170 103	860 880	23.6	35.9
Taylor	8.2	19.0	13.4	17.3	13.3	8.8	7.9	6.6	5.4	51.4	126 555	119 655	110 932	5.8	7.9
Terrell	6.4	23.2	5.5	13.3	14.1	12.4	10.9	8.0	6.2	47.7	1 081	1 410	1 595	-23.3	-11.6
Terry	8.6	24.5	8.5	13.8	12.0	9.8	9.2	7.6	6.0	51.5	12 761	13 218	14 581	-3.5	-9.3
Throckmorton	6.5	17.1	6.0	13.7	12.1	11.2	10.9	11.1	11.4	51.8	1 850	1 880	2 053	-1.6	-8.4
Titus	8.4	20.2	9.8	15.1	13.4	9.4	8.2	8.2	7.4	51.3	28 118	24 009	21 442	17.1	12.0

Population and population characteristics, 1990 — Age (percent) — columns 39–48. Population—change, 1980–2000 — Total persons (columns 49–51) and Percent change (columns 52–53).

Table B. States and Counties

STATE County	Total population	In households (percent) Total in households	Householder	Spouse	Child Total	Child Own child under 18 years	Other relatives Total	Other relatives Under 18 years	Nonrelatives Total	Nonrelatives Unmarried partner	In group quarters (percent) Total in group quarters	Institutionalized population Correctional institutions	Institutionalized population Nursing homes	Institutionalized population Other institutions	Noninstitutionalized population College dormitories	Noninstitutionalized population Military quarters	Other
	54	55	56	57	58	59	60	61	62	63	64	65	66	67	68	69	70
TEXAS—Cont'd																	
Mason	3 738	99.1	43.0	25.4	25.8	20.9	3.1	1.2	1.8	0.8	0.9	0.0	0.9	—	0.0	0.0	0.0
Matagorda	37 957	98.7	36.6	19.7	33.3	26.6	5.7	2.8	3.4	1.7	1.3	0.4	0.8	0.0	0.0	0.0	0.1
Maverick	47 297	99.8	27.7	18.4	42.2	31.3	10.2	5.4	1.3	0.5	0.2	0.0	0.1	0.0	0.0	0.0	0.1
Medina	39 304	95.5	32.8	20.7	32.7	25.4	6.0	3.0	3.3	1.5	4.5	3.4	0.7	0.0	0.0	0.0	0.4
Menard	2 360	98.3	41.9	22.7	26.7	21.3	4.3	2.5	2.6	1.5	1.7	0.2	1.6	0.0	0.0	0.0	0.0
Midland	116 009	98.6	36.8	21.2	32.9	27.1	4.9	2.5	2.9	1.4	1.4	0.2	0.8	0.0	0.1	0.0	0.3
Milam	24 238	98.2	38.0	21.4	30.3	23.8	5.7	2.9	2.8	1.3	1.8	0.2	1.3	0.3	0.0	0.0	0.0
Mills	5 151	94.4	38.8	23.4	24.9	20.6	3.4	1.5	3.8	0.9	5.6	0.1	2.6	0.0	0.0	0.0	3.0
Mitchell	9 698	72.5	29.3	16.3	21.6	17.2	3.4	2.0	2.0	1.1	27.5	26.1	1.4	0.0	0.0	0.0	0.0
Montague	19 117	97.9	40.6	23.6	26.7	21.4	4.4	2.1	2.5	1.2	2.1	0.2	1.7	0.0	0.0	0.0	0.2
Montgomery	293 768	99.4	35.2	22.6	32.6	26.8	5.3	2.2	3.8	1.5	0.6	0.2	0.3	0.0	0.0	0.0	0.1
Moore	20 121	99.0	33.7	21.9	35.4	30.5	5.1	2.5	2.9	1.5	1.0	0.2	0.5	0.3	0.0	0.0	0.1
Morris	13 048	98.7	40.0	21.6	28.6	21.7	5.8	3.2	2.8	1.5	1.3	0.2	1.1	0.0	0.0	0.0	0.0
Motley	1 426	100.0	42.5	25.6	25.5	21.2	4.3	2.3	2.1	1.0	0.0	0.0	0.0	0.0	0.0	0.0	0.0
Nacogdoches	59 203	92.4	37.2	18.0	26.3	21.2	5.1	2.3	5.8	1.3	7.6	0.3	1.0	0.1	5.9	0.0	0.2
Navarro	45 124	96.8	36.5	20.4	29.3	23.4	6.7	3.0	3.9	1.5	3.2	0.3	0.7	0.1	1.4	0.0	0.7
Newton	15 072	96.0	37.0	21.5	28.8	22.3	6.0	3.4	2.7	1.5	4.0	3.5	0.5	0.0	0.0	0.0	0.0
Nolan	15 802	96.8	39.0	20.7	29.0	23.6	4.9	2.5	3.3	1.5	3.2	0.8	0.9	0.4	0.7	0.0	0.3
Nueces	313 645	98.2	35.2	18.2	32.6	23.9	7.7	3.8	4.5	2.0	1.8	0.3	0.4	0.1	0.2	0.1	0.7
Ochiltree	9 006	99.2	36.2	23.2	32.7	28.3	4.4	1.8	2.7	1.3	0.8	0.2	0.6	0.0	0.0	0.0	0.0
Oldham	2 185	87.6	33.6	22.4	27.0	23.0	2.7	1.4	1.8	0.6	12.4	0.2	0.0	0.0	0.0	0.0	12.1
Orange	84 966	98.8	37.2	21.9	31.3	24.2	5.2	2.5	3.3	1.5	1.2	0.5	0.5	0.0	0.0	0.0	0.1
Palo Pinto	27 026	98.8	39.2	21.8	28.1	22.3	5.8	3.0	4.0	1.7	1.2	0.4	0.7	0.0	0.0	0.0	0.1
Panola	22 756	98.0	38.8	22.5	29.2	22.4	5.2	2.6	2.4	1.1	2.0	0.2	1.1	0.1	0.6	0.0	0.1
Parker	88 495	96.7	35.2	23.1	30.4	24.7	4.6	2.1	3.5	1.3	3.3	2.6	0.5	0.0	0.2	0.0	0.1
Parmer	10 016	98.5	33.2	22.2	35.6	29.8	5.7	2.8	1.8	1.0	1.5	0.1	1.4	0.0	0.0	0.0	0.0
Pecos	16 809	87.7	30.7	19.0	30.1	23.6	5.8	3.3	2.1	1.1	12.3	11.7	0.5	0.1	0.0	0.0	0.0
Polk	41 133	91.9	36.8	21.3	25.1	19.8	5.5	2.6	3.2	1.4	8.1	7.3	0.7	0.0	0.0	0.0	0.2
Potter	113 546	93.8	35.9	17.0	30.2	24.3	6.2	3.0	4.5	2.0	6.2	4.4	1.1	0.1	0.0	0.0	0.5
Presidio	7 304	98.7	34.6	19.6	36.2	28.9	6.3	3.6	1.9	1.0	1.3	1.2	0.0	0.0	0.0	0.0	0.1
Rains	9 139	99.2	39.6	24.5	26.8	20.8	5.1	2.4	3.3	1.4	0.8	0.1	0.7	0.0	0.0	0.0	0.0
Randall	104 312	98.3	39.5	22.7	29.1	24.0	3.3	1.5	3.6	1.3	1.7	0.2	0.2	0.1	1.1	0.0	0.2
Reagan	3 326	98.6	33.3	22.7	36.1	30.8	4.7	3.0	1.9	1.0	1.4	0.4	1.0	0.0	0.0	0.0	0.0
Real	3 047	97.4	40.9	23.9	26.0	21.0	3.9	1.9	2.8	1.5	2.6	0.0	2.3	0.0	0.0	0.0	0.2
Red River	14 314	98.1	40.7	21.8	27.0	20.3	5.4	2.9	3.2	1.4	1.9	0.3	1.6	0.0	0.0	0.0	0.0
Reeves	13 137	91.2	31.1	18.6	32.1	24.7	7.7	4.5	1.7	0.9	8.8	8.1	0.5	0.1	0.0	0.0	0.0
Refugio	7 828	98.6	38.1	21.0	29.9	22.3	6.6	3.3	3.0	1.5	1.4	0.4	1.0	0.0	0.0	0.0	0.0
Roberts	887	100.0	40.8	28.9	27.2	23.6	2.3	1.0	0.9	0.3	0.0	0.0	0.0	0.0	0.0	0.0	0.0
Robertson	16 000	98.3	38.6	19.7	30.8	24.6	6.3	3.3	2.9	1.5	1.7	0.3	1.4	0.0	0.0	0.0	0.0
Rockwall	43 080	98.6	33.7	24.0	33.8	28.1	4.3	1.6	2.8	1.0	1.4	0.2	1.2	0.0	0.0	0.0	0.0
Runnels	11 495	97.5	38.5	22.1	29.5	23.9	4.9	2.5	2.4	1.3	2.5	0.5	2.0	0.0	0.0	0.0	0.1
Rusk	47 372	94.2	36.7	21.3	28.2	21.7	5.5	2.7	2.5	1.2	5.8	4.7	0.8	0.2	0.0	0.0	0.0
Sabine	10 469	98.8	42.8	25.2	23.9	18.5	4.5	2.4	2.4	1.3	1.2	0.1	1.1	0.0	0.0	0.0	0.1
San Augustine	8 946	97.0	40.0	21.4	26.5	19.8	6.6	3.5	2.6	1.2	3.0	0.0	2.9	0.0	0.0	0.0	0.0
San Jacinto	22 246	99.4	38.9	23.4	28.1	22.0	5.4	2.6	3.6	1.6	0.6	0.2	0.4	0.0	0.0	0.0	0.0
San Patricio	67 138	97.7	32.9	20.0	34.8	26.8	6.8	3.7	3.2	1.5	2.3	0.4	0.4	0.1	0.0	1.2	0.1
San Saba	6 186	90.8	37.0	21.8	25.1	20.5	4.7	2.3	2.2	1.1	9.2	0.1	1.8	6.5	0.0	0.0	0.8
Schleicher	2 935	98.4	38.0	23.8	31.2	25.1	4.1	2.5	1.3	0.8	1.6	0.5	1.1	0.0	0.0	0.0	0.0
Scurry	16 361	89.8	35.2	20.6	27.6	22.2	4.1	2.3	2.5	1.3	10.2	8.2	0.8	0.1	1.0	0.0	0.0
Shackelford	3 302	98.1	39.4	24.0	29.8	24.4	3.7	1.8	1.3	0.6	1.9	0.2	1.3	0.0	0.0	0.0	0.5
Shelby	25 224	98.5	38.0	20.9	29.6	23.0	6.5	3.1	3.4	1.3	1.5	0.2	1.2	0.0	0.0	0.0	0.1
Sherman	3 186	97.5	35.3	24.0	33.6	29.1	3.2	1.8	1.5	0.9	2.5	0.1	1.7	0.0	0.0	0.0	0.7
Smith	174 706	97.3	37.6	20.9	28.6	23.3	5.9	2.7	3.4	1.3	2.7	0.5	0.8	0.1	0.7	0.0	0.7
Somervell	6 809	97.7	35.8	22.1	31.8	25.7	4.7	2.1	3.3	1.1	2.3	0.2	0.8	1.2	0.0	0.0	0.1
Starr	53 597	99.3	26.9	17.9	43.1	31.6	10.1	5.4	1.3	0.4	0.7	0.5	0.2	0.0	0.0	0.0	0.1
Stephens	9 674	93.3	37.8	21.7	26.1	21.7	4.2	2.1	3.0	1.6	6.7	5.5	1.2	0.0	0.0	0.0	0.0
Sterling	1 393	98.2	36.8	23.6	31.9	26.5	4.1	2.2	1.7	0.9	1.8	0.0	1.8	0.0	0.0	0.0	0.0
Stonewall	1 693	97.6	42.1	23.8	24.8	20.4	4.7	2.0	2.1	0.9	2.4	0.2	2.1	0.1	0.0	0.0	0.0
Sutton	4 077	99.2	37.2	23.6	31.9	26.0	4.7	2.5	1.8	1.0	0.8	0.1	0.6	0.0	0.0	0.0	0.1
Swisher	8 378	92.4	34.9	21.0	30.2	25.1	4.0	2.2	2.2	1.2	7.6	7.0	0.5	0.0	0.0	0.0	0.1
Tarrant	1 446 219	98.4	36.9	19.4	31.1	25.2	6.1	2.4	4.8	1.7	1.6	0.5	0.5	0.0	0.3	0.0	0.2
Taylor	126 555	95.0	37.4	20.1	28.8	23.8	4.3	2.1	4.5	1.5	5.0	0.3	0.6	0.0	2.2	0.7	1.1
Terrell	1 081	100.0	41.0	22.3	29.5	24.1	5.4	2.0	1.9	0.7	0.0	0.0	0.0	0.0	0.0	0.0	0.0
Terry	12 761	92.4	33.5	20.0	30.9	24.5	5.8	3.4	2.2	1.2	7.6	6.9	0.7	0.0	0.0	0.0	0.0
Throckmorton	1 850	98.8	41.4	24.3	28.0	23.8	3.2	1.3	1.9	0.6	1.2	0.0	1.2	0.0	0.0	0.0	0.0
Titus	28 118	97.7	34.0	20.1	32.7	26.5	7.4	3.1	3.6	1.2	2.3	0.4	0.9	0.5	0.2	0.0	0.2

Table B. States and Counties

STATE County	Households by type, 2000												Households, 1990		
		Family households						Nonfamily households							
				Married couple		Female householder[1]			Householder living alone						House-holder living alone
	Total households	Total	With own children under 18 years	Total	With own children under 18 years	Total	With own children under 18 years	Total	Total	65 years and over	Average house-hold size	Average family size	Total house-holds	Female house-holder[1]	
	71	72	73	74	75	76	77	78	79	80	81	82	83	84	85

TEXAS—Cont'd

Mason	1 607	69.1	25.9	59.1	19.9	7.7	4.6	30.9	29.2	17.9	2.31	2.83	1 435	5.6	28.7
Matagorda	13 901	71.4	36.7	53.8	26.3	12.7	7.8	28.6	25.1	10.4	2.70	3.25	13 164	11.7	22.9
Maverick	13 089	85.8	51.6	66.5	41.3	16.0	8.8	14.2	12.9	6.6	3.60	3.98	9 756	14.5	14.9
Medina	12 880	78.7	39.1	63.2	30.3	11.1	6.3	21.3	18.2	8.2	2.91	3.30	9 109	9.7	18.4
Menard	990	67.2	28.5	54.0	20.4	8.8	6.1	32.8	30.4	17.5	2.34	2.91	937	7.2	30.8
Midland	42 745	72.4	38.9	57.4	29.4	11.4	7.4	27.6	24.2	8.6	2.68	3.21	38 920	9.8	23.7
Milam	9 199	71.7	32.4	56.5	23.9	11.3	6.4	28.3	25.9	14.1	2.59	3.11	8 686	10.0	27.0
Mills	2 001	69.9	27.5	60.2	21.3	7.0	4.6	30.1	27.8	17.1	2.43	2.90	1 782	5.6	27.5
Mitchell	2 837	70.4	30.6	55.6	22.5	11.4	6.3	29.6	27.5	15.5	2.48	3.00	3 054	8.5	27.2
Montague	7 770	70.6	28.7	58.1	21.6	8.8	5.0	29.4	27.1	14.7	2.41	2.91	6 858	7.2	26.2
Montgomery	103 296	77.6	40.6	64.2	32.5	9.5	5.9	22.4	18.3	6.2	2.83	3.21	63 563	9.1	18.0
Moore	6 774	78.7	44.8	65.1	35.3	9.0	6.5	21.3	18.2	8.3	2.94	3.36	6 101	7.1	18.8
Morris	5 215	71.9	29.5	53.9	19.4	14.1	8.0	28.1	25.8	13.2	2.47	2.95	4 988	13.3	23.3
Motley	606	71.8	26.6	60.2	20.6	8.7	4.5	28.2	25.7	15.3	2.35	2.82	647	7.3	29.8
Nacogdoches	22 006	63.8	30.5	48.3	21.7	11.8	7.1	36.2	27.6	9.3	2.49	3.08	20 124	10.9	26.6
Navarro	16 491	72.2	34.0	55.7	24.6	12.2	7.1	27.8	24.1	12.0	2.65	3.14	14 874	11.9	25.3
Newton	5 583	73.3	32.3	58.1	23.9	11.5	6.4	26.7	24.1	10.5	2.59	3.07	4 910	10.8	21.8
Nolan	6 170	69.5	32.2	53.0	21.5	12.6	8.5	30.5	27.1	13.4	2.48	3.01	6 183	9.3	25.1
Nueces	110 365	72.2	36.3	51.8	24.8	15.3	8.8	27.8	22.6	7.9	2.79	3.30	99 740	13.7	21.9
Ochiltree	3 261	76.3	40.9	64.0	32.7	7.9	5.7	23.7	21.0	9.3	2.74	3.18	3 328	6.9	20.6
Oldham	735	77.0	35.1	66.7	29.1	8.8	5.4	23.0	21.0	10.1	2.61	3.02	681	5.3	20.0
Orange	31 642	75.2	35.3	58.8	25.5	12.1	7.3	24.8	21.7	9.3	2.65	3.08	29 025	10.7	19.5
Palo Pinto	10 594	70.3	30.4	55.6	22.0	10.4	5.8	29.7	26.2	12.9	2.52	3.02	9 531	9.4	24.3
Panola	8 821	72.5	32.0	57.9	24.2	11.3	6.3	27.5	25.1	12.8	2.53	3.02	8 241	10.0	24.3
Parker	31 131	78.1	38.0	65.6	30.4	8.7	5.3	21.9	18.3	7.1	2.75	3.11	23 048	7.3	17.8
Parmer	3 322	78.7	42.9	67.0	35.6	8.3	5.4	21.3	19.3	10.5	2.97	3.43	3 241	7.0	18.6
Pecos	5 153	78.2	41.0	62.1	31.1	11.6	7.3	21.8	19.6	8.1	2.86	3.29	4 712	9.8	18.3
Polk	15 119	72.2	28.8	57.9	20.9	10.8	5.9	27.8	24.6	12.5	2.50	2.95	11 855	8.9	23.5
Potter	40 760	67.4	34.7	47.4	22.5	15.0	9.4	32.6	27.6	10.1	2.61	3.21	37 344	12.8	28.3
Presidio	2 530	73.7	40.4	56.5	29.8	13.6	8.6	26.3	24.2	13.2	2.85	3.43	2 255	12.3	23.5
Rains	3 617	74.1	28.8	61.9	21.7	9.1	5.7	25.9	22.3	11.2	2.51	2.92	2 609	7.2	23.7
Randall	41 240	69.8	33.9	57.5	26.2	9.2	5.9	30.2	25.4	8.5	2.49	3.00	34 553	8.2	23.9
Reagan	1 107	78.8	46.8	68.1	39.9	7.2	4.8	21.2	19.8	7.5	2.96	3.42	1 358	3.8	15.7
Real	1 245	69.8	26.5	58.4	20.2	7.6	4.2	30.2	28.2	14.8	2.38	2.88	924	8.3	23.8
Red River	5 827	69.8	28.0	53.5	19.6	11.8	6.2	30.2	27.7	14.6	2.41	2.91	5 688	11.1	27.9
Reeves	4 091	76.5	38.8	59.6	29.9	12.4	7.0	23.5	21.6	10.1	2.93	3.45	4 838	10.5	19.0
Refugio	2 985	72.9	31.6	55.1	22.9	12.8	6.2	27.1	24.6	11.5	2.59	3.07	2 937	12.6	23.8
Roberts	362	76.0	31.8	70.7	28.5	3.9	2.2	24.0	23.8	10.8	2.45	2.88	391	4.6	22.0
Robertson	6 179	70.5	32.0	51.1	20.7	15.5	9.2	29.5	26.9	14.5	2.55	3.09	5 793	14.1	26.9
Rockwall	14 530	82.4	44.4	71.0	37.5	8.0	5.0	17.6	14.4	4.4	2.92	3.23	8 838	7.1	15.4
Runnels	4 428	71.3	31.4	57.4	23.2	9.6	5.7	28.7	26.7	15.7	2.53	3.06	4 346	8.6	26.2
Rusk	17 364	73.3	32.5	58.2	24.6	11.2	6.0	26.7	24.2	12.9	2.57	3.05	16 327	10.2	24.0
Sabine	4 485	70.4	23.6	58.9	17.3	8.7	4.9	29.6	27.0	15.4	2.31	2.78	3 985	7.5	24.8
San Augustine	3 575	70.5	26.8	53.5	18.5	13.5	6.8	29.5	27.0	14.9	2.43	2.93	3 073	12.9	25.3
San Jacinto	8 651	74.0	30.0	60.2	22.5	9.7	5.3	26.0	22.6	10.1	2.55	2.98	6 247	9.2	21.6
San Patricio	22 093	78.0	41.6	60.6	31.5	12.7	7.3	22.0	18.7	8.0	2.97	3.40	18 776	11.7	17.4
San Saba	2 289	70.6	29.1	58.9	22.8	8.4	4.5	29.4	27.5	15.9	2.45	2.97	2 122	7.8	28.0
Schleicher	1 115	73.3	34.3	62.6	28.3	7.5	4.2	26.7	25.4	12.8	2.59	3.12	1 051	6.9	21.5
Scurry	5 756	72.3	33.9	58.4	25.2	10.4	6.4	27.7	25.1	12.9	2.55	3.05	6 368	7.7	21.9
Shackelford	1 300	72.4	32.8	60.9	26.5	8.7	4.9	27.6	26.2	14.6	2.49	3.02	1 336	6.7	29.6
Shelby	9 595	72.0	32.4	55.1	23.3	12.9	7.0	28.0	25.4	13.6	2.59	3.08	8 476	12.0	25.9
Sherman	1 124	77.0	40.7	68.0	34.3	6.0	4.2	23.0	21.5	10.0	2.76	3.24	1 053	3.6	21.4
Smith	65 692	71.4	33.1	55.5	24.1	12.3	7.2	28.6	24.7	9.8	2.59	3.10	56 800	11.3	24.3
Somervell	2 438	75.5	37.4	61.7	29.7	9.6	5.9	24.5	21.3	9.2	2.73	3.17	1 902	8.3	22.1
Starr	14 410	87.9	54.7	66.5	43.1	17.4	9.9	12.1	11.3	5.9	3.69	4.01	10 331	14.2	10.3
Stephens	3 661	70.8	31.2	57.3	23.0	9.9	6.0	29.2	26.4	13.7	2.47	2.96	3 556	8.8	27.8
Sterling	513	75.2	36.8	64.1	30.2	7.0	4.5	24.8	23.2	11.3	2.67	3.15	494	7.1	18.4
Stonewall	713	69.1	26.4	56.5	20.6	8.8	4.2	30.9	29.0	15.1	2.32	2.83	806	6.7	28.4
Sutton	1 515	75.6	38.2	63.6	31.0	7.7	4.4	24.4	22.6	9.6	2.67	3.15	1 466	6.6	22.0
Swisher	2 925	73.6	35.7	60.2	27.2	9.5	6.3	26.4	24.1	13.8	2.65	3.15	2 993	7.9	24.4
Tarrant	533 864	69.2	36.8	52.6	27.0	12.2	7.6	30.8	24.9	5.9	2.67	3.22	438 634	10.8	24.7
Taylor	47 274	68.8	34.7	53.8	25.0	11.5	7.5	31.2	25.7	9.7	2.54	3.07	43 301	9.3	24.7
Terrell	443	66.6	29.8	54.4	23.0	7.4	4.7	33.4	31.8	16.3	2.44	3.09	524	7.1	24.6
Terry	4 278	75.9	35.8	59.7	26.7	11.9	6.9	24.1	22.1	12.3	2.76	3.23	4 478	9.4	19.7
Throckmorton	765	69.9	29.2	58.8	23.0	8.2	4.1	30.1	28.0	16.6	2.39	2.92	790	5.2	31.6
Titus	9 552	74.9	39.1	59.0	29.8	11.4	7.0	25.1	22.1	11.1	2.88	3.36	8 508	9.7	21.9

[1] No spouse present.

Table B. States and Counties

STATE County	Percent change of households, 1990–2000	Total housing units	Occupied housing units (percent)	Vacant housing units Total	For seasonal, recreational, or occasional use	Homeowner vacancy rate (percent)	Rental vacancy rate (percent)	Occupied housing units Total	Percent owner-occupied housing units	Percent renter-occupied housing units	Average household size of owner-occupied units	Average household size of renter-occupied units
	86	87	88	89	90	91	92	93	94	95	96	97
TEXAS—Cont'd												
Mason	12.0	2 372	67.7	32.3	14.8	3.6	7.3	1 607	80.2	19.8	2.31	2.27
Matagorda	5.6	18 611	74.7	25.3	12.9	2.6	12.9	13 901	66.8	33.2	2.72	2.65
Maverick	34.2	14 889	87.9	12.1	1.7	1.6	8.7	13 089	69.6	30.4	3.77	3.22
Medina	41.4	14 826	86.9	13.1	4.3	1.7	9.5	12 880	79.8	20.2	2.93	2.83
Menard	5.7	1 607	61.6	38.4	13.5	3.4	8.1	990	74.6	25.4	2.37	2.26
Midland	9.8	48 060	88.9	11.1	0.4	2.3	19.6	42 745	69.6	30.4	2.84	2.29
Milam	5.9	10 866	84.7	15.3	2.6	3.0	9.3	9 199	73.0	27.0	2.57	2.64
Mills	12.3	2 691	74.4	25.6	10.7	3.1	10.6	2 001	80.5	19.5	2.41	2.50
Mitchell	-7.1	4 168	68.1	31.9	15.7	4.9	19.0	2 837	75.9	24.1	2.47	2.50
Montague	13.3	9 862	78.8	21.2	10.0	4.0	11.4	7 770	78.8	21.2	2.41	2.38
Montgomery	62.5	112 770	91.6	8.4	2.3	1.9	10.4	103 296	78.1	21.9	2.92	2.48
Moore	11.0	7 478	90.6	9.4	0.6	1.2	14.1	6 774	70.5	29.5	2.94	2.94
Morris	4.6	6 017	86.7	13.3	2.0	2.9	12.3	5 215	77.9	22.1	2.45	2.54
Motley	-6.3	839	72.2	27.8	10.4	10.4	9.6	606	76.7	23.3	2.29	2.55
Nacogdoches	9.4	25 051	87.8	12.2	2.5	1.6	9.4	22 006	61.6	38.4	2.61	2.29
Navarro	10.9	18 449	89.4	10.6	2.6	1.7	8.7	16 491	70.8	29.2	2.63	2.69
Newton	13.7	7 331	76.2	23.8	11.8	2.1	12.1	5 583	84.5	15.5	2.59	2.59
Nolan	-0.2	7 112	86.8	13.2	1.3	2.6	10.5	6 170	67.4	32.6	2.50	2.44
Nueces	10.7	123 041	89.7	10.3	2.6	2.0	9.8	110 365	61.3	38.7	2.91	2.60
Ochiltree	-2.0	3 769	86.5	13.5	1.0	3.1	10.5	3 261	72.5	27.5	2.74	2.73
Oldham	7.9	815	90.2	9.8	1.5	2.2	3.9	735	66.4	33.6	2.43	2.95
Orange	9.0	34 781	91.0	9.0	0.7	1.4	15.4	31 642	77.2	22.8	2.67	2.58
Palo Pinto	11.2	14 102	75.1	24.9	15.9	2.4	10.8	10 594	72.0	28.0	2.51	2.56
Panola	7.0	10 524	83.8	16.2	3.9	2.9	11.8	8 821	80.8	19.2	2.54	2.48
Parker	35.1	34 084	91.3	8.7	1.9	1.9	8.0	31 131	80.6	19.4	2.79	2.58
Parmer	2.5	3 732	89.0	11.0	0.6	2.3	9.6	3 322	72.3	27.7	2.89	3.18
Pecos	9.4	6 338	81.3	18.7	2.6	1.9	14.6	5 153	74.1	25.9	2.93	2.66
Polk	27.5	21 177	71.4	28.6	16.6	4.5	13.9	15 119	81.7	18.3	2.50	2.52
Potter	9.1	44 598	91.4	8.6	0.6	1.9	9.3	40 760	60.1	39.9	2.69	2.50
Presidio	12.2	3 299	76.7	23.3	5.6	3.0	12.4	2 530	70.3	29.7	2.97	2.56
Rains	38.6	4 523	80.0	20.0	10.8	3.1	10.7	3 617	82.8	17.2	2.52	2.45
Randall	19.4	43 261	95.3	4.7	0.3	1.4	6.4	41 240	70.3	29.7	2.65	2.11
Reagan	-18.5	1 452	76.2	23.8	3.4	5.0	18.7	1 107	78.4	21.6	3.06	2.60
Real	34.7	2 007	62.0	38.0	28.9	4.2	11.1	1 245	76.9	23.1	2.31	2.63
Red River	2.4	6 916	84.3	15.7	4.0	2.4	9.0	5 827	74.9	25.1	2.39	2.48
Reeves	-15.4	5 043	81.1	18.9	3.0	1.8	15.3	4 091	77.7	22.3	2.97	2.78
Refugio	1.6	3 669	81.4	18.6	5.1	3.1	6.5	2 985	74.9	25.1	2.55	2.69
Roberts	-7.4	449	80.6	19.4	2.7	3.4	23.2	362	79.0	21.0	2.38	2.72
Robertson	6.7	7 874	78.5	21.5	10.0	2.1	9.8	6 179	71.5	28.5	2.50	2.65
Rockwall	64.4	15 351	94.7	5.3	0.7	2.5	7.0	14 530	82.7	17.3	2.97	2.69
Runnels	1.9	5 400	82.0	18.0	3.9	2.6	12.1	4 428	77.4	22.6	2.52	2.57
Rusk	6.4	19 867	87.4	12.6	2.9	1.8	10.3	17 364	79.9	20.1	2.56	2.60
Sabine	12.5	7 659	58.6	41.4	29.7	4.8	13.3	4 485	86.2	13.8	2.30	2.34
San Augustine	16.3	5 356	66.7	33.3	21.2	2.1	9.5	3 575	81.4	18.6	2.41	2.50
San Jacinto	38.5	11 520	75.1	24.9	14.8	3.5	12.8	8 651	87.7	12.3	2.55	2.59
San Patricio	17.7	24 864	88.9	11.1	2.0	2.4	10.0	22 093	68.2	31.8	2.99	2.92
San Saba	7.9	2 951	77.6	22.4	11.3	2.6	10.9	2 289	75.8	24.2	2.43	2.53
Schleicher	6.1	1 371	81.3	18.7	2.3	3.5	13.7	1 115	75.7	24.3	2.55	2.73
Scurry	-9.6	7 112	80.9	19.1	0.7	3.9	19.3	5 756	73.8	26.2	2.58	2.48
Shackelford	-2.7	1 613	80.6	19.4	7.0	3.5	13.1	1 300	79.0	21.0	2.49	2.51
Shelby	13.2	11 955	80.3	19.7	6.6	2.3	9.0	9 595	78.3	21.7	2.55	2.73
Sherman	6.7	1 275	88.2	11.8	2.0	2.2	8.0	1 124	73.6	26.4	2.71	2.92
Smith	15.7	71 701	91.6	8.4	1.3	1.8	9.8	65 692	69.7	30.3	2.67	2.40
Somervell	28.2	2 750	88.7	11.3	1.6	1.9	6.1	2 438	74.9	25.1	2.76	2.63
Starr	39.5	17 589	81.9	18.1	4.9	1.5	14.0	14 410	79.5	20.5	3.74	3.52
Stephens	3.0	4 893	74.8	25.2	11.0	3.1	19.0	3 661	72.4	27.6	2.50	2.38
Sterling	3.8	633	81.0	19.0	4.7	4.4	18.3	513	75.6	24.4	2.69	2.61
Stonewall	-11.5	936	76.2	23.8	7.1	1.8	5.0	713	78.7	21.3	2.33	2.28
Sutton	3.3	1 998	75.8	24.2	5.4	4.9	14.8	1 515	72.3	27.7	2.68	2.65
Swisher	-2.3	3 315	88.2	11.8	0.7	2.5	12.5	2 925	70.4	29.6	2.55	2.87
Tarrant	21.7	565 830	94.4	5.6	0.3	1.5	7.7	533 864	60.8	39.2	2.85	2.39
Taylor	9.2	52 056	90.8	9.2	0.5	2.3	10.5	47 274	61.6	38.4	2.62	2.41
Terrell	-15.5	991	44.7	55.3	28.5	5.8	24.4	443	77.0	23.0	2.40	2.58
Terry	-4.5	5 087	84.1	15.9	0.5	3.0	18.2	4 278	71.2	28.8	2.72	2.85
Throckmorton	-3.2	1 066	71.8	28.2	14.5	4.5	13.3	765	77.0	23.0	2.32	2.61
Titus	12.3	10 675	89.5	10.5	1.1	2.3	10.8	9 552	72.4	27.6	2.85	2.95

Table B. States and Counties

STATE/County code	MSA/PMSA/NECMA code[1]	County type[2]	STATE County	Population, 2000				Population, 1990				Population and population characteristics, 2000 Race (percent) One race					
				Land area, 2000[3] (sq km)	Total persons	Rank	Per square kilometer	Land area, 1990[3] (sq km)	Total persons	Rank	Per square kilometer	White	Black or African American	American Indian or Alaska Native	Asian	Native Hawaiian and other Pacific Islander	Some other race
				1	2	3	4	5	6	7	8	9	10	11	12	13	14
			TEXAS—Cont'd														
48 451	7200	3	Tom Green	3 942	104 010	509	26.4	3 942	98 458	466	25.0	79.1	4.1	0.7	0.9	0.1	12.8
48 453	0640	2	Travis	2 562	812 280	56	317.0	2 563	576 407	82	224.9	68.2	9.3	0.6	4.5	0.1	14.6
48 455	...	7	Trinity	1 794	13 779	2 174	7.7	1 795	11 445	2 258	6.4	83.8	11.9	0.4	0.2	0.0	2.7
48 457	...	6	Tyler	2 390	20 871	1 741	8.7	2 391	16 646	1 875	7.0	83.8	12.0	0.4	0.2	0.0	2.5
48 459	4420	3	Upshur	1 522	35 291	1 239	23.2	1 522	31 370	1 233	20.6	85.7	10.1	0.6	0.2	0.1	2.1
48 461	...	8	Upton	3 216	3 404	2 962	1.1	3 216	4 447	2 878	1.4	77.8	1.6	1.2	0.0	0.1	17.9
48 463	...	7	Uvalde	4 031	25 926	1 520	6.4	4 032	23 340	1 525	5.8	75.7	0.4	0.7	0.4	0.1	19.7
48 465	...	5	Val Verde	8 211	44 856	1 002	5.5	8 212	38 721	1 034	4.7	76.4	1.5	0.7	0.6	0.1	18.2
48 467	...	6	Van Zandt	2 198	48 140	946	21.9	2 198	37 944	1 051	17.3	92.0	2.9	0.6	0.2	0.0	2.7
48 469	8750	3	Victoria	2 286	84 088	618	36.8	2 286	74 361	604	32.5	74.2	6.3	0.5	0.8	0.0	15.9
48 471	...	4	Walker	2 039	61 758	786	30.3	2 040	50 917	829	25.0	69.1	23.9	0.4	0.8	0.1	4.4
48 473	3360	1	Waller	1 330	32 663	1 326	24.6	1 330	23 374	1 522	17.6	57.8	29.2	0.5	0.4	0.0	10.3
48 475	...	6	Ward	2 164	10 909	2 374	5.0	2 164	13 115	2 129	6.1	79.8	4.6	0.7	0.3	0.0	12.5
48 477	...	6	Washington	1 578	30 373	1 388	19.2	1 578	26 154	1 413	16.6	74.7	18.7	0.3	1.2	0.0	4.0
48 479	4080	3	Webb	8 694	193 117	284	22.2	8 695	133 239	349	15.3	82.2	0.4	0.5	0.4	0.0	14.0
48 481	...	6	Wharton	2 823	41 188	1 075	14.6	2 824	39 955	1 002	14.1	69.0	15.0	0.4	0.3	0.1	13.6
48 483	...	9	Wheeler	2 368	5 284	2 831	2.2	2 368	5 879	2 772	2.5	87.8	2.8	0.8	0.5	0.1	6.6
48 485	9080	3	Wichita	1 626	131 664	405	81.0	1 626	122 378	375	75.3	78.8	10.2	0.9	1.8	0.1	5.5
48 487	...	6	Wilbarger	2 515	14 676	2 109	5.8	2 515	15 121	1 981	6.0	78.2	8.9	0.7	0.6	0.0	9.7
48 489	...	6	Willacy	1 545	20 082	1 790	13.0	1 545	17 705	1 805	11.5	70.4	2.2	0.5	0.1	0.0	24.5
48 491	0640	2	Williamson	2 908	249 967	238	86.0	2 912	139 551	340	47.9	82.4	5.1	0.5	2.6	0.1	7.2
48 493	7240	1	Wilson	2 090	32 408	1 336	15.5	2 091	22 650	1 550	10.8	81.2	1.2	0.6	0.3	0.0	14.2
48 495	...	6	Winkler	2 178	7 173	2 669	3.3	2 178	8 626	2 501	4.0	74.8	1.9	0.4	0.2	0.0	20.4
48 497	...	6	Wise	2 343	48 793	935	20.8	2 343	34 679	1 146	14.8	91.0	1.2	0.8	0.2	0.0	5.0
48 499	...	6	Wood	1 684	36 752	1 196	21.8	1 684	29 380	1 319	17.4	89.1	6.1	0.6	0.2	0.0	2.9
48 501	...	7	Yoakum	2 071	7 322	2 653	3.5	2 071	8 786	2 486	4.2	70.6	1.4	0.7	0.1	0.0	25.5
48 503	...	7	Young	2 389	17 943	1 903	7.5	2 389	18 126	1 782	7.6	91.0	1.2	0.6	0.3	0.0	5.3
48 505	...	6	Zapata	2 582	12 182	2 285	4.7	2 582	9 279	2 446	3.6	84.1	0.4	0.3	0.2	0.0	12.6
48 507	...	7	Zavala	3 363	11 600	2 324	3.4	3 363	12 162	2 202	3.6	65.1	0.5	0.6	0.1	0.0	31.1
49 000	...		UTAH	212 751	2 233 169	X	10.5	212 816	1 722 850	X	8.1	89.2	0.8	1.3	1.7	0.7	4.2
49 001	...	9	Beaver	6 708	6 005	2 778	0.9	6 708	4 765	2 859	0.7	93.2	0.3	0.9	0.6	0.1	3.1
49 003	...	6	Box Elder	14 823	42 745	1 042	2.9	14 824	36 485	1 090	2.5	92.9	0.2	0.9	1.0	0.1	3.4
49 005	...	4	Cache	3 016	91 391	562	30.3	3 016	70 183	630	23.3	92.2	0.4	0.6	2.0	0.2	3.3
49 007	...	7	Carbon	3 829	20 422	1 764	5.3	3 829	20 228	1 664	5.3	91.1	0.3	1.1	0.3	0.0	4.8
49 009	...	9	Daggett	1 809	921	3 114	0.5	1 809	690	3 130	0.4	94.6	0.7	0.8	0.1	0.0	2.4
49 011	7160	0	Davis	789	238 994	241	302.9	789	187 941	256	238.2	92.3	1.1	0.6	1.5	0.3	2.3
49 013	...	7	Duchesne	8 387	14 371	2 132	1.7	8 387	12 645	2 173	1.5	90.2	0.1	5.4	0.2	0.1	1.6
49 015	...	9	Emery	11 530	10 860	2 376	0.9	11 531	10 332	2 357	0.9	95.6	0.2	0.7	0.3	0.1	1.9
49 017	...	9	Garfield	13 401	4 735	2 865	0.4	13 402	3 980	2 920	0.3	95.0	0.2	1.8	0.4	0.0	1.1
49 019	...	7	Grand	9 535	8 485	2 566	0.9	9 536	6 620	2 695	0.7	92.6	0.2	3.9	0.2	0.0	1.7
49 021	...	7	Iron	8 542	33 779	1 288	4.0	8 543	20 789	1 641	2.4	93.0	0.4	2.2	0.7	0.3	1.8
49 023	...	6	Juab	8 785	8 238	2 588	0.9	8 785	5 817	2 778	0.7	96.6	0.1	1.0	0.3	0.0	0.9
49 025	2620	7	Kane	10 339	6 046	2 776	0.6	10 340	5 169	2 827	0.5	96.0	0.0	1.6	0.4	0.0	0.7
49 027	...	7	Millard	17 066	12 405	2 271	0.7	17 067	11 333	2 272	0.7	93.9	0.1	1.3	0.5	0.2	2.8
49 029	...	8	Morgan	1 578	7 129	2 676	4.5	1 578	5 528	2 799	3.5	98.1	0.0	0.2	0.2	0.0	0.4
49 031	...	9	Piute	1 963	1 435	3 095	0.7	1 963	1 277	3 106	0.7	95.6	0.1	1.2	0.2	0.1	1.9
49 033	...	9	Rich	2 664	1 961	3 067	0.7	2 664	1 725	3 081	0.6	98.2	0.0	0.1	0.4	0.0	0.9
49 035	7160	0	Salt Lake	1 910	898 387	43	470.4	1 910	725 956	54	380.1	86.3	1.1	0.9	2.6	1.2	5.4
49 037	...	7	San Juan	20 254	14 413	2 129	0.7	20 256	12 621	2 176	0.6	40.8	0.1	55.7	0.2	0.0	1.7
49 039	...	6	Sanpete	4 113	22 763	1 658	5.5	4 113	16 259	1 908	4.0	92.4	0.3	0.9	0.5	0.4	4.1
49 041	...	7	Sevier	4 948	18 842	1 850	3.8	4 948	15 431	1 960	3.1	95.6	0.3	2.0	0.3	0.1	0.8
49 043	...	6	Summit	4 846	29 736	1 406	6.1	4 846	15 518	1 951	3.2	91.8	0.2	0.3	1.0	0.0	5.4
49 045	...	6	Tooele	17 950	40 735	1 092	2.3	17 990	26 601	1 404	1.5	89.2	1.3	1.7	0.6	0.2	4.5
49 047	...	7	Uintah	11 596	25 224	1 557	2.2	11 596	22 211	1 570	1.9	87.7	0.1	9.4	0.2	0.1	1.0
49 049	6520	2	Utah	5 176	368 536	159	71.2	5 176	263 590	189	50.9	92.4	0.3	0.6	1.1	0.6	3.2
49 051	...	6	Wasatch	3 049	15 215	2 074	5.0	3 059	10 089	2 378	3.3	95.6	0.2	0.4	0.3	0.1	2.0
49 053	...	4	Washington	6 285	90 354	572	14.4	6 286	48 560	862	7.7	93.6	0.2	1.5	0.4	0.4	2.2
49 055	...	9	Wayne	6 372	2 509	3 026	0.4	6 373	2 177	3 055	0.3	97.3	0.2	0.4	0.1	0.2	1.2
49 057	7160	0	Weber	1 491	196 533	282	131.8	1 491	158 330	299	106.2	87.7	1.4	0.8	1.3	0.2	6.6
50 000	...		VERMONT	23 956	608 827	X	25.4	23 956	562 758	X	23.5	96.8	0.5	0.4	0.9	0.0	0.2
50 001	...	6	Addison	1 995	35 974	1 219	18.0	1 994	32 953	1 193	16.5	96.9	0.5	0.3	0.7	0.0	0.3
50 003	...	6	Bennington	1 752	36 994	1 190	21.1	1 752	35 845	1 104	20.5	97.7	0.4	0.2	0.6	0.0	0.2
50 005	...	7	Caledonia	1 685	29 702	1 409	17.6	1 686	27 846	1 356	16.5	97.5	0.3	0.5	0.4	0.0	0.2

[1]MSA = Metropolitan Statistical Area. PMSA = Primary MSA. NECMA = New England County Metropolitan Area. See Appendix A for explanation of these concepts. See Appendix B for list of metropolitan areas identified by type, with component counties.
[2]County typology code from the Economic Research Service of USDA. See Appendix A for definition.
[3]Dry land or land partially or temporarily covered by water.

Table B. States and Counties

STATE County	Population and population characteristics, 2000 (cont'd)								Population and population characteristics, 1990				
	Race (percent) (cont'd)								Race (percent)				
	Race alone or in combination												
	Two or more races	White	Black	American Indian or Alaska Native	Asian	Native Hawaiian and other Pacific Islander	Some other race	Hispanic[1]	White	Black or African American	American Indian or Alaska Native	Asian and Pacific Islander	Hispanic[1]
	15	16	17	18	19	20	21	22	23	24	25	26	27
TEXAS—Cont'd													
Tom Green	2.4	81.1	4.0	1.2	1.2	0.1	14.2	30.7	80.8	4.2	0.4	1.0	25.9
Travis	2.9	70.6	9.8	1.1	5.1	0.2	16.2	28.2	73.3	11.0	0.4	2.9	21.1
Trinity	1.0	84.6	12.1	0.8	0.3	0.1	3.1	4.8	84.0	14.4	0.2	0.2	2.4
Tyler	1.1	84.9	12.2	1.0	0.3	0.1	2.8	3.6	87.4	12.0	0.3	0.1	1.1
Upshur	1.2	86.8	10.4	1.2	0.3	0.1	2.4	4.0	86.3	12.4	0.4	0.1	2.0
Upton	1.4	78.9	1.8	1.6	0.3	0.1	18.6	42.6	78.4	2.1	0.4	0.0	37.5
Uvalde	3.2	78.6	0.5	1.0	0.6	0.1	22.4	65.9	64.6	0.2	0.2	0.3	60.4
Val Verde	2.6	78.8	1.7	1.1	0.8	0.1	20.3	75.5	68.9	2.0	0.3	0.6	70.5
Van Zandt	1.6	93.4	3.1	1.2	0.3	0.0	3.5	6.6	93.2	3.8	0.4	0.1	4.0
Victoria	2.2	76.2	6.7	0.9	0.9	0.1	17.5	39.2	79.7	6.6	0.3	0.3	34.1
Walker	1.4	70.3	24.3	0.7	0.9	0.2	5.1	14.1	68.6	24.2	0.4	0.6	10.8
Waller	1.8	59.3	29.7	0.9	0.6	0.1	11.3	19.4	55.5	37.6	0.1	0.3	11.1
Ward	2.1	81.7	4.9	1.2	0.3	0.0	14.0	42.0	75.5	3.5	0.6	0.2	36.8
Washington	1.2	75.7	19.0	0.5	1.3	0.0	4.7	8.7	75.6	20.9	0.2	0.7	4.4
Webb	2.5	84.5	0.5	0.6	0.6	0.0	16.3	94.3	70.3	0.1	0.2	0.4	93.9
Wharton	1.6	70.4	15.3	0.6	0.5	0.1	14.9	31.3	72.9	15.8	0.1	0.3	25.3
Wheeler	1.3	89.1	2.9	1.3	0.8	0.1	7.3	12.6	92.3	2.6	0.7	0.4	6.4
Wichita	2.7	81.0	10.9	1.7	2.4	0.2	6.6	12.2	83.7	9.2	0.7	1.5	8.6
Wilbarger	1.9	79.9	9.2	1.1	0.9	0.1	10.9	20.5	79.4	8.9	0.5	0.5	14.5
Willacy	2.3	72.6	2.3	0.6	0.2	0.0	26.7	85.7	78.1	0.4	0.2	0.1	84.4
Williamson	2.1	84.3	5.5	0.9	3.1	0.2	8.2	17.2	87.4	4.9	0.4	1.3	14.3
Wilson	2.4	83.5	1.4	1.1	0.5	0.1	16.0	36.5	86.8	1.1	0.2	0.1	35.6
Winkler	2.3	76.9	2.0	0.8	0.3	0.0	22.4	44.0	71.7	1.9	0.6	0.1	36.8
Wise	1.7	92.6	1.4	1.5	0.4	0.1	5.7	10.8	93.9	1.1	0.6	0.2	7.7
Wood	1.1	90.1	6.3	1.0	0.3	0.0	3.3	5.7	89.7	8.2	0.4	0.1	2.7
Yoakum	1.7	72.2	1.4	1.1	0.1	0.0	26.8	45.9	71.7	1.0	0.4	0.1	36.6
Young	1.6	92.5	1.4	1.3	0.3	0.1	6.0	10.6	93.9	1.5	0.3	0.3	6.4
Zapata	2.3	86.3	0.5	0.5	0.3	0.1	14.8	84.8	72.0	0.0	0.1	0.1	81.0
Zavala	2.7	67.6	0.6	0.7	0.2	0.1	33.6	91.2	53.0	2.4	0.1	0.0	89.4
UTAH	2.1	91.1	1.1	1.8	2.2	1.0	5.1	9.0	93.8	0.7	1.4	1.9	4.9
Beaver	1.8	94.7	0.4	1.9	1.0	0.3	3.8	5.5	97.5	0.1	0.8	0.4	2.5
Box Elder	1.6	94.3	0.3	1.4	1.4	0.2	4.2	6.5	95.2	0.1	1.1	1.1	4.4
Cache	1.3	93.4	0.6	0.9	2.3	0.3	3.8	6.3	94.8	0.3	0.8	2.7	2.5
Carbon	2.4	93.4	0.5	1.5	0.5	0.1	6.5	10.3	94.2	0.3	0.7	0.6	11.1
Daggett	1.5	95.7	1.2	1.2	0.8	0.1	2.8	5.1	97.7	0.0	1.3	0.7	2.2
Davis	2.0	94.0	1.4	1.0	2.3	0.5	2.9	5.4	94.9	1.3	0.6	1.7	3.9
Duchesne	2.5	92.4	0.3	7.2	0.4	0.1	2.2	3.5	93.4	0.1	5.3	0.3	2.8
Emery	1.2	96.8	0.3	1.3	0.5	0.2	2.3	5.2	98.0	0.0	0.4	0.3	2.1
Garfield	1.5	96.3	0.2	2.5	0.7	0.1	1.8	2.9	97.7	0.0	1.8	0.2	0.9
Grand	1.3	93.8	0.4	4.7	0.4	0.1	2.0	5.6	95.8	0.1	3.1	0.4	4.4
Iron	1.7	94.5	0.5	2.8	1.0	0.4	2.4	4.1	95.8	0.2	3.1	0.5	1.8
Juab	1.0	97.4	0.2	1.5	0.4	0.2	1.4	2.6	97.6	0.0	1.5	0.2	1.3
Kane	1.4	97.3	0.1	2.4	0.4	0.2	1.1	2.3	97.3	0.1	1.5	0.5	2.0
Millard	1.2	95.0	0.2	1.9	0.7	0.2	3.2	7.2	95.3	0.0	1.6	0.9	3.5
Morgan	1.1	99.2	0.2	0.6	0.5	0.0	0.6	1.4	98.8	0.1	0.1	0.3	1.4
Piute	0.9	96.4	0.1	1.9	0.3	0.1	2.0	4.5	99.2	0.0	0.7	0.1	1.2
Rich	0.5	98.6	0.1	0.3	0.6	0.0	1.0	1.8	98.8	0.1	0.1	0.3	1.2
Salt Lake	2.6	88.6	1.4	1.3	3.2	1.6	6.6	11.9	93.0	0.8	0.8	2.8	6.0
San Juan	1.5	42.1	0.3	56.6	0.3	0.2	2.1	3.7	43.6	0.1	54.3	0.3	3.5
Sanpete	1.5	93.8	0.4	1.5	0.7	0.5	4.7	6.6	95.6	0.1	0.8	1.5	3.4
Sevier	1.0	96.5	0.3	2.6	0.4	0.2	1.0	2.6	97.1	0.0	2.1	0.2	1.9
Summit	1.2	92.9	0.4	0.6	1.3	0.1	5.9	8.1	98.6	0.1	0.4	0.5	2.1
Tooele	2.6	91.5	1.6	2.5	1.1	0.3	5.7	10.3	91.5	0.9	1.5	0.8	11.1
Uintah	1.4	89.1	0.2	10.3	0.4	0.1	1.4	3.5	88.0	0.0	10.5	0.4	3.1
Utah	1.9	94.0	0.5	1.0	1.6	1.0	3.9	7.0	96.2	0.1	0.7	1.5	3.2
Wasatch	1.4	96.9	0.3	1.2	0.6	0.3	2.2	5.1	98.5	0.0	0.7	0.2	2.5
Washington	1.6	95.1	0.4	2.1	0.8	0.7	2.8	5.2	97.2	0.1	1.5	0.6	1.8
Wayne	0.7	98.0	0.3	0.8	0.1	0.3	1.4	2.0	97.5	0.0	1.8	0.1	1.1
Weber	2.1	89.6	1.8	1.3	1.8	0.3	7.5	12.6	92.6	1.5	0.7	1.5	7.0
VERMONT	1.2	97.9	0.7	1.1	1.1	0.1	0.4	0.9	98.6	0.3	0.3	0.6	0.7
Addison	1.3	98.0	0.8	0.9	1.1	0.1	0.5	1.1	98.6	0.4	0.2	0.6	0.6
Bennington	0.8	98.5	0.6	0.6	0.8	0.1	0.3	0.9	98.9	0.3	0.2	0.5	0.6
Caledonia	1.1	98.5	0.5	1.3	0.5	0.0	0.3	0.7	99.1	0.2	0.4	0.3	0.3

[1] Hispanic persons may be of any race.

Table B. States and Counties

STATE County	Population and population characteristics, 2000									
	Age (percent)										
	Under 5 years	5 to 17 years	18 to 24 years	25 to 34 years	35 to 44 years	45 to 54 years	55 to 64 years	65 to 74 years	75 years and over	Median age (years)	Percent Female
	28	29	30	31	32	33	34	35	36	37	38
TEXAS—Cont'd											
Tom Green	6.9	19.2	12.8	12.6	14.5	12.3	8.3	6.9	6.5	33.8	51.6
Travis	7.2	16.5	14.7	19.9	16.7	12.3	5.9	3.7	3.1	30.4	48.8
Trinity	5.9	17.0	7.0	9.9	12.5	12.5	13.3	12.7	9.3	43.3	51.7
Tyler	5.8	17.4	8.0	13.0	14.2	12.3	11.5	10.1	7.7	38.9	48.3
Upshur	6.6	20.4	8.0	11.1	15.5	13.4	10.6	8.0	6.3	37.7	51.1
Upton	5.5	23.8	7.9	9.1	15.8	13.4	10.4	8.0	6.2	38.1	51.1
Uvalde	8.4	23.0	9.8	12.3	13.0	11.6	8.3	7.1	6.5	32.2	51.3
Val Verde	8.9	23.1	9.4	14.7	13.2	11.0	8.6	6.3	4.6	30.8	50.8
Van Zandt	6.3	19.2	7.3	10.9	14.3	13.5	11.4	9.3	7.8	39.5	50.8
Victoria	7.6	21.5	9.2	12.8	15.4	13.2	8.3	6.6	5.4	34.2	51.3
Walker	4.9	13.1	23.0	15.3	15.9	11.9	7.1	5.1	3.8	31.0	39.8
Waller	6.9	18.8	18.1	12.3	14.1	12.5	8.0	5.1	4.2	30.1	50.3
Ward	6.6	24.0	7.8	10.3	14.8	13.0	9.2	8.2	6.1	36.0	50.1
Washington	6.0	18.7	11.1	11.1	14.2	13.1	9.0	8.3	8.5	37.4	51.4
Webb	10.6	25.6	11.4	15.9	13.4	9.6	6.0	4.3	3.3	26.5	51.8
Wharton	7.0	21.7	9.3	11.6	14.9	12.7	8.8	7.1	6.8	35.3	50.8
Wheeler	6.0	18.9	6.5	9.1	13.4	13.5	11.7	10.3	10.5	42.5	52.1
Wichita	7.0	18.2	13.7	13.6	15.4	11.6	7.9	6.9	5.8	33.2	49.1
Wilbarger	6.6	21.3	9.5	11.1	13.7	12.2	9.4	7.4	8.8	36.3	50.5
Willacy	8.2	23.4	11.9	12.9	13.7	10.8	7.5	6.7	4.9	29.8	48.7
Williamson	8.5	21.4	8.1	16.8	18.8	12.6	6.5	4.0	3.3	32.3	50.2
Wilson	6.9	22.3	7.6	11.9	16.7	14.2	9.0	6.3	5.2	35.9	50.1
Winkler	7.0	22.8	8.7	11.2	14.9	12.3	8.7	7.7	6.7	35.2	50.9
Wise	6.8	21.5	7.8	13.1	17.2	13.4	9.6	6.1	4.5	35.5	49.6
Wood	5.2	16.6	7.9	9.8	13.2	13.2	13.2	11.6	9.2	43.0	50.7
Yoakum	7.5	24.6	8.3	10.7	16.1	12.7	8.5	6.5	5.0	34.1	51.4
Young	6.0	19.0	7.0	10.0	14.7	13.4	10.2	9.9	9.7	40.7	52.2
Zapata	9.2	23.9	10.0	12.2	11.9	10.5	8.0	8.0	6.3	30.7	50.8
Zavala	8.9	25.2	10.2	13.6	12.1	11.4	7.3	6.2	5.1	29.0	50.6
UTAH	9.4	22.8	14.2	14.6	13.4	10.6	6.4	4.5	4.0	27.1	49.9
Beaver	9.3	24.2	9.4	11.5	12.5	11.7	7.5	7.2	6.7	30.8	48.5
Box Elder	9.3	26.8	10.5	11.4	13.9	10.4	7.3	5.7	4.7	28.0	49.6
Cache	9.9	21.4	22.2	14.8	11.0	8.6	5.1	3.5	3.7	23.9	50.8
Carbon	7.2	21.5	12.3	10.4	14.0	13.4	7.9	6.6	6.6	33.6	51.1
Daggett	6.6	16.6	8.9	12.7	14.7	15.4	11.6	10.0	3.5	39.2	44.4
Davis	9.8	25.4	12.2	13.9	14.3	10.8	6.3	4.2	3.2	26.8	49.8
Duchesne	9.1	27.7	9.4	11.1	13.6	11.3	8.5	5.7	3.6	28.3	49.3
Emery	8.1	27.2	9.6	9.9	14.2	12.5	8.4	5.5	4.5	30.1	49.8
Garfield	8.6	24.1	7.8	10.7	12.5	13.8	8.6	8.0	6.1	33.8	48.9
Grand	7.0	19.9	8.2	12.3	15.6	15.5	9.0	7.2	5.3	36.9	50.9
Iron	9.4	21.9	20.6	12.5	11.1	9.7	6.4	4.8	3.7	24.2	50.4
Juab	11.2	27.4	9.4	13.1	12.2	10.1	6.8	4.8	5.0	26.5	49.9
Kane	6.6	22.8	6.8	9.0	12.2	14.8	11.1	9.3	7.4	39.1	50.4
Millard	8.1	29.2	8.0	9.3	13.6	11.5	7.9	6.6	5.7	29.9	48.8
Morgan	8.1	28.9	9.7	9.5	14.8	11.7	8.5	5.3	3.4	28.5	49.3
Piute	8.2	22.5	6.6	8.6	11.0	12.8	13.2	9.1	8.0	38.9	48.9
Rich	7.2	27.4	7.2	8.9	13.3	12.5	9.4	7.5	6.6	34.3	49.1
Salt Lake	8.9	21.6	12.9	16.1	14.5	11.5	6.5	4.2	3.9	28.9	49.6
San Juan	9.7	29.6	10.0	12.1	13.1	10.1	7.0	4.8	3.6	25.5	50.1
Sanpete	8.3	24.9	16.4	10.4	11.4	10.5	7.3	5.8	5.0	25.3	49.4
Sevier	8.8	25.7	10.1	9.9	12.9	11.2	8.6	6.7	6.2	30.3	50.2
Summit	7.1	22.7	8.4	14.4	19.6	15.6	7.2	3.1	1.7	33.3	48.0
Tooele	11.0	24.0	11.5	15.6	13.9	10.3	6.3	4.2	3.1	27.1	50.8
Uintah	8.4	26.3	10.7	11.0	14.4	11.7	7.6	5.7	4.2	29.0	50.2
Utah	11.0	23.1	21.0	15.2	10.6	7.9	4.8	3.4	3.0	23.3	50.4
Wasatch	9.2	25.0	9.9	13.8	15.2	11.6	6.9	4.9	3.6	29.5	49.2
Washington	9.1	22.1	11.6	11.3	11.1	9.6	8.3	9.1	7.8	31.0	50.7
Wayne	8.8	23.6	8.1	10.4	12.1	13.4	9.2	7.5	7.0	34.1	49.1
Weber	9.0	22.0	12.6	13.9	14.0	11.3	6.9	5.4	5.0	29.3	49.8
VERMONT	5.6	18.6	9.3	12.2	16.7	15.4	9.3	6.7	6.0	37.7	51.0
Addison	5.7	19.2	12.5	11.0	15.9	15.5	8.8	6.0	5.3	36.1	50.6
Bennington	5.2	18.5	7.7	10.6	15.7	15.1	10.6	8.8	7.9	40.3	52.0
Caledonia	5.5	19.8	8.8	11.0	15.3	16.1	9.2	7.4	7.0	38.5	50.6

Table B. States and Counties

STATE County	Under 5 years	5 to 17 years	18 to 24 years	25 to 34 years	35 to 44 years	45 to 54 years	55 to 64 years	65 to 74 years	75 years and over	Percent Female	2000	1990	1980	1990–2000	1980–1990
	39	40	41	42	43	44	45	46	47	48	49	50	51	52	53
TEXAS—Cont'd															
Tom Green	7.8	19.3	12.9	16.4	13.9	9.0	8.1	7.0	5.7	51.5	104 010	98 458	84 784	5.6	16.1
Travis	7.7	16.3	15.8	22.2	16.4	8.4	5.9	4.3	3.0	50.0	812 280	576 407	419 573	40.9	37.4
Trinity	6.2	17.2	7.0	12.6	11.2	10.6	13.3	12.9	8.9	51.6	13 779	11 445	9 450	20.4	21.1
Tyler	5.9	19.1	7.2	12.1	11.8	11.4	12.3	12.1	8.2	51.4	20 871	16 646	16 223	25.4	2.6
Upshur	7.1	20.5	9.4	14.3	13.6	10.8	9.6	7.9	6.7	51.5	35 291	31 370	28 595	12.5	9.7
Upton	8.7	27.0	7.7	15.4	14.1	9.5	8.2	5.4	4.0	50.5	3 404	4 447	4 619	-23.5	-3.7
Uvalde	8.6	23.5	11.2	13.8	12.4	9.4	8.6	6.7	5.8	51.8	25 926	23 340	22 441	11.1	4.0
Val Verde	9.2	23.7	12.1	15.6	12.2	9.5	7.9	6.0	3.7	50.4	44 856	38 721	35 910	15.8	7.8
Van Zandt	6.4	19.2	7.7	12.8	13.4	11.4	11.2	10.0	7.9	51.2	48 140	37 944	31 426	26.9	20.7
Victoria	8.3	22.0	9.2	16.4	15.0	9.8	8.3	6.4	4.5	51.3	84 088	74 361	68 807	13.1	8.1
Walker	5.3	13.7	20.3	20.2	16.0	8.9	6.7	5.1	3.8	40.4	61 758	50 917	41 789	21.3	21.8
Waller	6.7	18.6	20.4	13.6	12.8	9.4	7.6	6.1	4.9	50.9	32 663	23 374	19 798	39.7	18.1
Ward	8.0	25.1	8.9	15.1	13.9	9.1	8.8	6.5	4.7	50.2	10 909	13 115	13 976	-16.8	-6.2
Washington	6.9	18.5	11.2	14.6	13.1	8.8	9.5	8.9	8.4	51.5	30 373	26 154	21 998	16.1	18.9
Webb	10.1	26.5	12.5	16.0	12.4	8.1	6.5	4.6	3.3	52.0	193 117	133 239	99 258	44.9	34.2
Wharton	7.9	22.0	9.0	14.8	13.6	9.6	8.7	7.6	6.8	51.2	41 188	39 955	40 242	3.1	-0.7
Wheeler	6.0	20.7	6.0	12.4	12.4	10.7	10.1	9.8	12.0	52.5	5 284	5 879	7 137	-10.1	-17.6
Wichita	7.6	18.5	12.3	17.3	13.2	9.3	8.9	7.1	5.7	51.0	131 664	122 378	121 082	7.6	1.1
Wilbarger	7.2	19.2	8.8	14.5	12.7	9.7	9.2	9.2	9.6	50.6	14 676	15 121	15 931	-2.9	-5.1
Willacy	8.9	27.7	9.9	14.0	11.8	8.3	8.4	6.5	4.6	51.7	20 082	17 705	17 495	13.4	1.2
Williamson	8.8	22.2	9.5	19.6	17.4	9.4	5.6	4.1	3.5	50.8	249 967	139 551	76 521	79.1	82.4
Wilson	8.0	23.0	8.6	15.1	14.4	9.9	8.4	6.9	5.7	50.2	32 408	22 650	16 756	43.1	35.2
Winkler	8.2	25.0	7.8	15.4	12.4	9.2	9.2	7.4	5.4	50.6	7 173	8 626	9 944	-16.8	-13.3
Wise	7.6	20.6	8.5	15.8	14.8	11.4	8.7	7.1	5.5	49.6	48 793	34 679	26 575	40.7	30.5
Wood	5.8	18.2	7.9	12.3	12.4	10.7	11.7	11.7	9.3	51.9	36 752	29 380	24 697	25.1	19.0
Yoakum	8.6	26.2	8.2	17.3	13.9	9.7	7.4	5.0	3.7	49.6	7 322	8 786	8 299	-16.7	5.9
Young	7.2	19.4	6.9	14.6	13.3	10.0	10.4	9.1	9.2	52.0	17 943	18 126	19 083	-1.0	-5.0
Zapata	9.5	25.3	9.9	13.2	11.7	7.9	7.7	9.0	5.9	50.9	12 182	9 279	6 628	31.3	40.0
Zavala	9.6	26.1	11.6	14.5	12.1	8.2	7.3	6.2	4.5	49.5	11 600	12 162	11 666	-4.6	4.3
UTAH	9.8	26.6	11.6	16.0	13.0	8.0	6.2	5.1	3.6	50.3	2 233 169	1 722 850	1 461 037	29.6	17.9
Beaver	8.0	28.3	6.4	11.3	12.0	8.3	9.4	9.1	7.1	51.0	6 005	4 765	4 378	26.0	8.8
Box Elder	10.4	30.2	7.1	14.7	11.7	8.6	7.5	5.5	4.3	50.1	42 745	36 485	33 222	17.2	9.8
Cache	10.7	25.8	16.5	16.4	11.0	6.6	4.8	4.2	3.9	49.8	91 391	70 183	57 176	30.2	22.7
Carbon	7.9	26.6	8.4	13.5	14.3	8.2	7.6	7.8	5.6	51.4	20 422	20 228	22 179	1.0	-8.8
Daggett	9.1	25.5	6.5	12.8	14.9	9.6	11.7	4.6	5.2	49.0	921	690	769	33.5	-10.3
Davis	10.6	29.5	10.2	15.9	13.1	8.5	6.1	4.0	2.1	49.7	238 994	187 941	146 540	27.2	28.3
Duchesne	10.7	32.3	7.0	13.9	12.4	9.1	6.2	5.0	3.5	49.5	14 371	12 645	12 565	13.6	0.6
Emery	9.5	33.5	6.4	14.1	13.8	8.7	6.1	4.4	3.5	49.0	10 860	10 332	11 451	5.1	-9.8
Garfield	9.2	26.6	6.7	12.1	12.2	9.1	10.1	8.7	5.3	49.0	4 735	3 980	3 673	19.0	8.4
Grand	7.9	24.0	5.7	14.0	15.5	10.0	10.4	8.2	4.3	51.5	8 485	6 620	8 241	28.2	-19.7
Iron	9.0	26.5	15.5	13.1	11.7	8.0	6.7	5.8	3.8	50.3	33 779	20 789	17 349	62.5	19.8
Juab	8.7	30.2	6.8	11.9	12.4	8.3	7.6	7.4	6.7	50.4	8 238	5 817	5 530	41.6	5.2
Kane	8.8	27.9	6.8	11.3	13.5	9.2	8.7	8.5	5.3	49.6	6 046	5 169	4 024	17.0	28.5
Millard	10.6	32.4	5.7	12.8	11.9	7.7	6.9	6.4	5.6	49.7	12 405	11 333	8 970	9.5	26.3
Morgan	9.3	31.9	7.2	12.8	12.6	10.5	7.5	4.8	3.5	49.7	7 129	5 528	4 917	29.0	12.4
Piute	6.3	26.2	6.6	7.6	9.7	12.5	11.7	11.8	7.6	48.9	1 435	1 277	1 329	12.4	-3.9
Rich	10.8	32.3	4.7	13.6	13.7	7.1	6.6	6.3	4.9	49.0	1 961	1 725	2 100	13.7	-17.9
Salt Lake	9.6	25.2	10.4	17.4	14.4	8.4	6.1	5.0	3.5	50.4	898 387	725 956	619 066	23.8	17.3
San Juan	12.1	31.3	9.5	14.3	11.6	7.9	6.3	4.0	3.0	50.5	14 413	12 621	12 253	14.2	3.0
Sanpete	8.3	29.7	12.7	10.5	11.7	7.3	6.5	7.0	6.2	50.9	22 763	16 259	14 620	40.0	11.2
Sevier	9.0	30.3	6.4	11.9	12.3	8.4	7.9	7.5	6.1	50.5	18 842	15 431	14 727	22.1	4.8
Summit	8.9	24.5	8.0	19.0	18.9	9.5	5.4	3.4	2.4	48.9	29 736	15 518	10 198	91.6	52.2
Tooele	8.7	27.5	9.1	14.8	13.5	10.1	7.7	5.5	3.1	49.5	40 735	26 601	26 033	53.1	2.2
Uintah	10.3	31.1	7.2	15.0	13.3	8.4	6.8	4.9	2.9	50.5	25 224	22 211	20 506	13.6	8.3
Utah	10.7	27.0	18.8	15.1	10.1	6.3	4.9	4.0	3.0	50.6	368 536	263 590	218 106	39.8	20.9
Wasatch	9.7	29.8	7.9	14.0	13.6	8.8	6.8	5.1	4.1	49.9	15 215	10 089	8 523	50.8	18.4
Washington	9.4	26.9	10.0	11.8	10.7	7.0	8.0	9.8	6.5	50.9	90 354	48 560	26 065	86.1	86.3
Wayne	8.3	29.4	5.9	12.4	13.2	7.7	7.6	8.8	6.6	48.4	2 509	2 177	1 911	15.3	13.9
Weber	9.0	24.6	10.4	15.6	13.1	8.6	7.5	6.6	4.5	50.8	196 533	158 330	144 616	24.1	9.5
VERMONT	7.3	18.1	11.2	16.9	16.4	10.2	8.0	6.6	5.2	51.0	608 827	562 758	511 456	8.2	10.0
Addison	7.5	18.6	13.8	15.9	16.8	9.7	7.3	6.1	4.3	50.2	35 974	32 953	29 406	9.2	12.1
Bennington	7.3	17.8	9.7	15.4	15.1	10.5	9.3	7.9	7.0	51.6	36 994	35 845	33 345	3.2	7.5
Caledonia	7.5	20.1	9.8	14.9	16.1	9.8	8.6	7.4	5.7	51.1	29 702	27 846	25 808	6.7	7.9

Table B. States and Counties

STATE County	Total population	Total in households	House-holder	Spouse	Child Total	Child Own child under 18 years	Other relatives Total	Under 18 years	Nonrelatives Total	Unmarried partner	Total in group quarters	Correctional institutions	Nursing homes	Other institutions	College dormitories	Military quarters	Other
	54	55	56	57	58	59	60	61	62	63	64	65	66	67	68	69	70
TEXAS—Cont'd																	
Tom Green	104 010	95.9	38.0	19.8	28.8	23.0	5.2	2.5	4.1	1.7	4.1	0.3	0.8	0.0	1.2	1.4	0.5
Travis	812 280	97.5	39.5	16.8	25.8	21.1	6.2	2.1	9.2	2.4	2.5	0.4	0.3	0.2	1.1	0.0	0.6
Trinity	13 779	98.7	41.5	22.9	25.4	19.6	5.5	2.8	3.4	1.7	1.3	0.4	0.9	0.0	0.0	0.0	0.0
Tyler	20 871	92.4	37.3	22.4	25.6	20.1	4.8	2.4	2.4	1.1	7.6	6.4	1.0	0.1	0.0	0.0	0.0
Upshur	35 291	98.7	37.7	22.9	29.7	23.2	5.7	2.9	2.8	1.2	1.3	0.2	0.7	0.3	0.0	0.0	0.0
Upton	3 404	99.0	36.9	22.5	32.5	26.2	4.9	2.7	2.2	1.5	1.0	0.1	0.8	0.0	0.0	0.0	0.0
Uvalde	25 926	97.6	33.0	19.6	35.5	27.3	6.8	3.6	2.6	1.4	2.4	0.5	1.0	0.0	0.6	0.0	0.2
Val Verde	44 856	98.2	31.5	19.7	36.1	27.3	8.6	4.3	2.3	0.9	1.8	0.6	0.4	0.0	0.0	0.6	0.2
Van Zandt	48 140	98.0	37.8	23.7	28.2	22.5	5.1	2.4	2.2	1.3	2.0	0.2	1.2	0.1	0.0	0.0	0.5
Victoria	84 088	98.2	35.8	20.3	32.3	25.3	6.1	3.0	3.7	1.7	1.8	0.6	0.6	0.3	0.0	0.0	0.4
Walker	61 758	72.3	29.6	13.9	19.4	15.5	3.9	1.6	5.5	1.3	27.7	22.8	0.4	0.0	3.7	0.0	0.8
Waller	32 663	90.2	32.3	18.0	28.6	22.2	6.7	2.9	4.5	1.4	9.8	0.2	0.5	0.4	8.3	0.0	0.3
Ward	10 909	96.6	36.3	21.3	31.4	25.2	5.1	3.1	2.5	1.4	3.4	0.7	0.5	2.1	0.0	0.0	0.1
Washington	30 373	94.3	37.3	20.4	28.2	22.0	4.8	2.1	3.6	1.3	5.7	0.2	1.3	1.6	2.4	0.0	0.2
Webb	193 117	98.4	26.3	16.5	41.6	30.3	11.6	5.3	2.5	0.8	1.6	0.6	0.2	0.2	0.2	0.0	0.4
Wharton	41 188	98.2	35.9	20.0	32.8	24.9	6.3	3.1	3.2	1.5	1.8	0.2	0.6	0.0	0.3	0.0	0.7
Wheeler	5 284	97.5	40.7	23.6	27.2	22.5	3.8	2.0	2.1	1.0	2.5	0.1	2.4	0.0	0.0	0.0	0.0
Wichita	131 664	91.6	36.8	19.2	27.6	22.4	4.1	2.0	3.8	1.5	8.4	3.1	0.7	0.3	0.5	3.6	0.3
Wilbarger	14 676	93.7	37.7	20.0	27.8	22.9	4.9	2.4	3.2	1.7	6.3	0.1	1.0	4.3	0.8	0.0	0.1
Willacy	20 082	94.7	27.8	17.3	37.4	26.0	10.4	5.3	1.8	0.9	5.3	5.3	0.0	0.0	0.0	0.0	0.0
Williamson	249 967	98.0	34.7	22.2	32.9	27.9	4.2	1.6	4.0	1.5	2.0	0.8	0.6	0.0	0.4	0.0	0.2
Wilson	32 408	98.4	34.1	22.7	33.8	26.1	5.1	2.5	2.8	1.3	1.6	0.5	1.0	0.0	0.0	0.0	0.1
Winkler	7 173	98.1	36.0	22.3	32.5	26.7	5.0	2.6	2.3	1.4	1.9	1.4	0.5	0.0	0.0	0.0	0.0
Wise	48 793	97.6	35.2	23.3	31.2	25.6	4.7	2.1	3.3	1.4	2.4	1.6	0.6	0.0	0.0	0.0	0.1
Wood	36 752	96.0	39.7	24.4	24.6	19.5	4.5	2.0	2.8	1.2	4.0	1.6	1.3	0.0	1.0	0.0	0.1
Yoakum	7 322	99.3	33.7	23.2	35.8	29.2	5.1	2.8	1.5	1.0	0.7	0.1	0.6	0.0	0.0	0.0	0.0
Young	17 943	97.8	39.9	23.2	27.5	22.5	4.4	2.1	2.8	1.4	2.2	0.2	1.5	0.0	0.0	0.0	0.6
Zapata	12 182	99.8	32.2	20.7	37.8	29.0	7.1	3.6	2.1	1.0	0.2	0.0	0.2	0.0	0.0	0.0	0.0
Zavala	11 600	96.9	29.6	16.3	40.1	28.7	9.0	5.2	1.9	1.2	3.1	2.9	0.0	0.0	0.0	0.0	0.2
UTAH	2 233 169	98.2	31.4	19.8	37.1	29.7	4.7	1.9	5.1	1.1	1.8	0.4	0.3	0.1	0.4	0.1	0.4
Beaver	6 005	96.6	33.0	22.1	36.6	31.7	2.9	1.4	1.9	0.9	3.4	2.6	0.4	0.3	0.0	0.0	0.0
Box Elder	42 745	99.1	30.7	21.8	41.3	33.9	3.4	1.7	1.9	0.7	0.9	0.3	0.4	0.0	0.0	0.0	0.2
Cache	91 391	97.6	30.1	20.0	36.3	29.8	3.2	1.1	8.0	0.6	2.4	0.1	0.3	0.1	1.8	0.0	0.1
Carbon	20 422	97.4	36.3	21.1	33.2	26.5	3.5	1.6	3.3	1.4	2.6	0.2	0.6	0.1	1.5	0.0	0.2
Daggett	921	91.5	36.9	23.2	25.4	21.3	4.0	2.0	2.0	0.8	8.5	8.4	0.0	0.0	0.0	0.3	0.7
Davis	238 994	98.5	29.8	21.1	41.5	33.1	3.6	1.5	2.5	0.8	1.5	1.2	0.0	0.2	0.0	0.0	0.0
Duchesne	14 371	98.5	31.7	21.5	39.1	33.9	3.4	1.8	2.8	1.2	1.5	0.2	0.7	0.0	0.0	0.0	0.0
Emery	10 860	99.1	31.9	22.3	39.9	33.5	2.9	1.4	2.1	0.8	0.9	0.2	0.7	0.0	0.0	0.0	0.0
Garfield	4 735	97.3	33.3	22.1	36.1	30.2	3.3	1.9	2.4	1.2	2.7	2.0	0.6	0.0	0.0	0.0	0.1
Grand	8 485	98.8	40.5	19.7	29.1	24.0	3.9	2.1	5.7	2.7	1.2	0.4	0.1	0.2	0.0	0.0	0.6
Iron	33 779	97.9	31.5	20.2	35.0	29.3	3.4	1.4	7.8	0.8	2.1	0.3	0.3	0.1	1.1	0.0	0.3
Juab	8 238	98.8	29.8	20.6	42.9	36.2	3.6	1.8	1.9	0.8	1.2	0.2	0.8	0.0	0.0	0.0	0.3
Kane	6 046	98.9	37.0	23.9	32.2	27.3	3.3	1.7	2.5	1.2	1.1	0.1	0.1	0.4	0.0	0.0	0.5
Millard	12 405	98.8	31.0	21.8	41.3	35.2	3.3	1.8	1.4	0.5	1.2	0.7	0.3	0.1	0.0	0.0	0.1
Morgan	7 129	100.0	28.7	22.8	44.4	35.1	3.0	1.7	1.1	0.4	0.0	0.0	0.0	0.0	0.0	0.0	0.0
Piute	1 435	98.9	35.5	24.0	33.2	27.0	4.0	2.3	2.2	0.8	1.1	0.0	0.0	0.0	0.0	0.0	1.1
Rich	1 961	99.1	32.9	24.5	39.1	33.1	1.4	0.8	1.3	0.5	0.9	0.1	0.3	0.6	0.0	0.0	0.0
Salt Lake	898 387	98.4	32.9	19.0	35.5	27.7	5.7	2.2	5.4	1.4	1.6	0.6	0.3	0.1	0.2	0.0	0.4
San Juan	14 413	98.2	28.4	17.1	42.8	34.2	7.8	4.8	2.1	1.2	1.8	0.5	0.6	0.0	0.5	0.0	0.0
Sanpete	22 763	93.9	28.8	19.3	37.1	30.9	3.3	1.6	5.5	0.7	6.1	3.5	0.2	0.0	2.2	0.0	0.0
Sevier	18 842	97.7	32.3	22.6	38.1	31.9	2.9	1.4	1.9	0.8	2.3	1.1	0.6	0.1	0.3	0.0	0.2
Summit	29 736	99.8	34.7	22.1	33.1	28.4	2.9	0.9	7.0	1.5	0.2	0.1	0.0	0.0	0.0	0.0	0.0
Tooele	40 735	96.7	31.1	20.6	37.8	31.6	4.1	2.0	3.1	1.3	3.3	0.2	0.1	0.1	0.0	2.8	0.0
Uintah	25 224	99.0	32.5	21.3	38.2	31.7	4.1	2.1	2.9	1.2	1.0	0.4	0.4	0.1	0.0	0.0	0.1
Utah	368 536	97.4	27.1	18.9	39.1	31.8	4.6	1.7	7.6	0.4	2.6	0.1	0.2	0.3	1.3	0.0	0.6
Wasatch	15 215	99.2	31.2	22.1	39.2	32.3	3.7	1.6	3.1	1.1	0.8	0.5	0.3	0.0	0.0	0.0	0.0
Washington	90 354	98.5	33.1	22.4	34.9	29.1	4.0	1.6	4.1	0.8	1.5	0.4	0.5	0.1	0.2	0.0	0.4
Wayne	2 509	99.7	35.5	23.6	35.5	31.2	2.6	1.0	2.6	0.7	0.3	0.0	0.3	0.0	0.0	0.0	0.0
Weber	196 533	98.5	33.4	20.1	35.9	28.3	4.9	2.1	4.2	1.4	1.5	0.2	0.7	0.1	2.1	0.0	0.4
VERMONT	608 827	96.6	39.5	20.8	27.5	22.7	2.4	0.8	6.4	3.0	3.4	0.2	0.7	0.1	2.1	0.0	0.4
Addison	35 974	92.8	36.3	20.8	27.9	23.1	2.3	0.8	5.4	2.9	7.2	0.0	0.4	0.0	5.8	0.0	1.0
Bennington	36 994	96.6	40.1	21.3	27.1	22.1	2.8	1.0	5.2	3.0	3.4	0.0	1.6	0.0	1.6	0.0	0.2
Caledonia	29 702	96.8	39.3	21.0	28.5	23.6	2.5	0.8	5.5	3.0	3.2	0.8	0.5	0.0	1.5	0.0	0.4

Table B. States and Counties

STATE County	Households by type, 2000												Households, 1990		
	Family households						Nonfamily households								
				Married couple		Female householder¹			Householder living alone						House-holder
	Total households	Total	With own children under 18 years	Total	With own children under 18 years	Total	With own children under 18 years	Total	Total	65 years and over	Average house-hold size	Average family size	Total house-holds	Female house-holder¹	living alone
	71	72	73	74	75	76	77	78	79	80	81	82	83	84	85
TEXAS—Cont'd															
Tom Green	30 503	67.8	33.0	52.1	23.4	11.9	7.4	32.2	27.2	10.8	2.52	3.09	35 408	10.5	24.8
Travis	320 766	57.3	29.3	42.6	21.1	10.4	6.4	42.7	30.1	4.4	2.47	3.15	232 861	10.5	31.5
Trinity	5 723	69.9	25.7	55.1	17.4	11.2	6.5	30.1	26.8	14.6	2.38	2.85	4 647	9.4	25.2
Tyler	7 775	73.0	29.7	60.1	22.7	10.0	5.5	27.0	24.3	12.4	2.48	2.94	6 459	8.9	23.0
Upshur	13 290	75.5	33.5	60.7	25.5	11.0	6.0	24.5	21.8	10.3	2.62	3.05	11 360	9.4	21.1
Upton	1 256	74.4	36.3	61.1	27.5	9.1	5.9	25.6	23.5	12.2	2.68	3.19	1 472	7.0	20.2
Uvalde	8 559	77.6	40.2	59.4	29.8	13.7	8.0	22.4	19.9	9.8	2.96	3.42	7 553	12.2	19.3
Val Verde	14 151	80.0	42.9	62.5	33.0	13.9	8.1	20.0	17.5	7.5	3.11	3.55	11 840	12.5	16.6
Van Zandt	18 195	75.1	31.8	62.6	25.0	8.7	4.7	24.9	22.0	11.6	2.59	3.01	14 349	7.6	21.7
Victoria	30 071	73.8	37.2	56.7	26.8	12.7	8.0	26.2	22.4	9.1	2.75	3.23	26 228	11.1	21.2
Walker	18 303	62.2	28.7	46.8	19.8	11.7	7.1	37.8	27.0	8.0	2.44	3.02	14 918	10.2	26.7
Waller	10 557	73.4	35.1	55.7	25.8	13.0	6.9	26.6	21.0	7.5	2.79	3.25	7 402	12.8	22.5
Ward	3 964	73.9	36.6	58.8	27.3	11.6	7.3	26.1	23.6	12.3	2.66	3.15	4 444	9.1	20.9
Washington	11 322	70.1	31.6	54.8	23.2	11.4	6.7	29.9	25.7	12.9	2.53	3.05	9 619	10.6	26.3
Webb	50 740	85.6	53.2	62.6	41.0	18.3	10.2	14.4	12.4	5.1	3.75	4.10	34 438	17.6	12.7
Wharton	14 799	72.6	35.7	55.5	26.3	12.5	7.1	27.4	24.4	12.4	2.73	3.26	14 210	11.7	23.8
Wheeler	2 152	69.1	29.6	58.0	23.0	7.7	4.8	30.9	29.1	16.9	2.39	2.94	2 350	6.6	28.3
Wichita	48 441	67.9	33.6	52.3	23.9	11.9	7.6	32.1	27.2	10.6	2.49	3.04	45 271	10.8	25.3
Wilbarger	5 537	67.7	32.2	53.1	23.4	10.8	6.6	32.3	29.0	14.9	2.48	3.07	5 741	8.5	28.3
Willacy	5 584	82.1	42.9	62.1	33.3	16.1	7.9	17.9	16.5	9.7	3.40	3.85	5 049	14.2	16.6
Williamson	86 766	77.2	43.9	64.0	35.4	9.6	6.5	22.8	17.6	4.6	2.82	3.21	48 792	9.6	19.2
Wilson	11 038	80.0	40.0	66.5	32.5	9.2	5.2	20.0	17.1	7.8	2.89	3.26	7 481	8.1	16.6
Winkler	2 584	76.2	39.2	61.8	30.5	10.1	6.3	23.8	21.7	11.3	2.72	3.18	2 941	7.4	19.3
Wise	17 178	78.4	38.2	66.1	30.9	8.2	4.8	21.6	18.3	7.1	2.77	3.14	12 175	6.3	19.4
Wood	14 583	73.0	26.7	61.5	20.5	8.2	4.4	27.0	24.1	13.2	2.42	2.85	11 426	7.5	24.3
Yoakum	2 469	81.3	43.4	68.8	35.5	8.5	5.8	18.7	17.3	8.5	2.95	3.34	2 839	6.2	15.4
Young	7 167	70.9	30.8	58.0	23.3	9.4	5.6	29.1	26.3	14.3	2.45	2.94	7 101	7.5	25.0
Zapata	3 921	80.7	43.2	64.2	33.9	13.0	7.5	19.3	17.5	10.3	3.10	3.52	2 862	10.3	16.1
Zavala	3 428	81.9	43.8	55.1	30.2	21.8	11.6	18.1	16.6	9.1	3.28	3.70	3 356	17.3	15.6
UTAH	701 281	76.3	42.7	63.2	35.0	9.4	5.8	23.7	17.8	6.3	3.13	3.57	537 273	9.1	18.9
Beaver	1 982	77.2	41.3	67.1	34.6	7.0	4.7	22.8	20.5	11.4	2.93	3.42	1 594	5.6	21.9
Box Elder	13 144	82.2	47.1	71.0	39.8	7.9	5.2	17.8	16.0	7.4	3.22	3.63	10 954	6.6	16.6
Cache	27 543	76.3	43.6	66.4	37.8	7.2	4.4	23.7	14.5	5.5	3.24	3.59	21 021	6.1	17.0
Carbon	7 413	72.6	36.9	58.2	28.2	10.0	6.2	27.4	23.8	11.0	2.68	3.19	6 907	9.5	21.8
Daggett	340	70.6	27.1	62.9	22.9	4.4	3.2	29.4	25.9	7.4	2.48	3.02	253	4.7	25.7
Davis	71 201	83.2	49.5	70.8	41.7	9.2	6.0	16.8	13.6	4.6	3.31	3.67	53 598	8.9	13.3
Duchesne	4 559	80.5	46.3	67.9	37.5	8.9	6.3	19.5	16.8	7.3	3.11	3.51	3 707	7.7	15.7
Emery	3 468	80.7	45.9	69.8	38.7	7.2	5.0	19.3	17.6	8.1	3.10	3.53	2 998	6.6	15.4
Garfield	1 576	76.1	38.4	66.4	32.2	6.8	4.3	23.9	20.5	10.1	2.92	3.43	1 321	5.1	19.8
Grand	3 434	63.2	29.8	48.6	20.0	10.7	7.5	36.8	29.5	9.5	2.44	3.06	2 489	9.5	26.2
Iron	10 627	76.0	41.0	64.2	34.0	8.5	5.4	24.0	15.9	5.9	3.11	3.45	6 269	7.4	16.5
Juab	2 456	80.7	49.3	69.1	41.4	7.9	5.7	19.3	17.5	9.1	3.31	3.79	1 801	6.6	20.7
Kane	2 237	72.8	32.2	64.6	27.4	6.0	3.8	27.2	23.3	10.2	2.67	3.21	1 724	5.2	20.4
Millard	3 840	80.5	46.1	70.6	40.4	7.1	4.4	19.5	18.3	10.1	3.19	3.66	3 349	5.7	18.7
Morgan	2 046	87.1	49.7	79.6	45.1	5.6	3.6	12.9	11.7	5.8	3.48	3.81	1 555	4.8	11.6
Piute	509	76.6	33.0	67.6	27.5	5.7	4.1	23.4	22.4	11.6	2.79	3.25	449	3.6	20.7
Rich	645	80.9	42.2	74.4	38.3	3.7	2.3	19.1	17.1	7.0	3.01	3.44	521	3.8	18.4
Salt Lake	295 141	72.5	40.1	57.8	31.7	10.4	6.2	27.5	20.8	6.2	3.00	3.53	240 680	10.1	22.2
San Juan	4 089	79.1	47.0	60.4	35.6	14.1	8.4	20.9	18.7	6.7	3.46	4.02	3 375	14.6	15.6
Sanpete	6 547	77.4	43.4	67.0	37.1	7.2	4.5	22.6	17.8	10.1	3.27	3.68	4 859	6.5	20.2
Sevier	6 081	80.7	43.0	70.1	36.1	7.8	5.2	19.3	17.6	9.4	3.03	3.44	4 877	6.5	18.9
Summit	10 332	72.6	40.8	63.5	34.7	6.2	4.4	27.4	18.4	3.2	2.87	3.30	5 271	6.2	19.3
Tooele	12 677	79.9	47.4	66.0	38.6	9.5	6.2	20.1	16.8	6.1	3.11	3.51	8 581	10.0	18.4
Uintah	8 187	79.9	44.5	65.7	35.5	10.6	6.9	20.1	17.2	7.3	3.05	3.45	6 670	9.7	16.4
Utah	99 937	80.8	48.3	69.8	42.5	8.0	4.6	19.2	11.2	4.7	3.59	3.86	70 168	7.8	12.2
Wasatch	4 743	81.6	46.2	71.0	39.8	7.5	4.6	18.4	14.3	5.0	3.18	3.55	3 074	6.8	16.9
Washington	29 939	78.3	37.1	67.6	30.4	8.0	5.2	21.7	17.5	8.9	2.97	3.36	15 256	7.9	17.0
Wayne	890	75.2	36.2	66.5	30.4	5.3	4.2	24.8	21.5	9.6	2.81	3.31	699	3.4	19.5
Weber	65 698	75.4	40.3	60.2	31.2	10.7	6.6	24.6	20.0	7.6	2.95	3.42	53 253	10.4	21.1
VERMONT	240 634	65.6	31.8	52.5	23.2	9.3	6.1	34.4	26.2	9.5	2.44	2.96	210 650	9.2	23.4
Addison	13 068	69.7	34.4	57.4	26.5	8.3	5.4	30.3	23.4	8.9	2.55	3.02	11 410	8.2	20.7
Bennington	14 846	66.8	30.5	53.1	21.8	10.1	6.4	33.2	26.8	11.6	2.41	2.91	13 595	10.2	24.3
Caledonia	11 663	67.7	32.4	53.6	22.8	10.4	7.1	32.3	25.6	11.0	2.46	2.95	10 368	10.1	23.3

¹No spouse present.

Table B. States and Counties

STATE County	Percent change of households, 1990–2000	Total housing units	Occupied housing units (percent)	Vacant housing units: Total	For seasonal, recreational, or occasional use	Homeowner vacancy rate (percent)	Rental vacancy rate (percent)	Occupied housing units: Total	Percent owner-occupied housing units	Percent renter-occupied housing units	Average household size of owner-occupied units	Average household size of renter-occupied units
	86	87	88	89	90	91	92	93	94	95	96	97
TEXAS—Cont'd												
Tom Green	11.6	43 916	90.0	10.0	0.9	2.3	11.4	39 503	64.1	35.9	2.65	2.30
Travis	37.7	335 881	95.5	4.5	0.9	1.1	3.5	320 766	51.4	48.6	2.72	2.20
Trinity	23.2	8 141	70.3	29.7	16.2	4.3	11.5	5 723	80.8	19.2	2.37	2.41
Tyler	20.4	10 419	74.6	25.4	12.9	3.4	17.1	7 775	84.1	15.9	2.48	2.49
Upshur	17.0	14 930	89.0	11.0	2.2	1.8	11.7	13 290	81.8	18.2	2.64	2.55
Upton	-14.7	1 609	78.1	21.9	1.1	4.9	17.7	1 256	75.2	24.8	2.66	2.77
Uvalde	13.3	10 166	84.2	15.8	5.2	1.4	10.8	8 559	72.2	27.8	2.98	2.91
Val Verde	19.5	16 288	86.9	13.1	4.1	1.9	8.8	14 151	66.0	34.0	3.19	2.97
Van Zandt	26.8	20 896	87.1	12.9	4.3	2.1	6.8	18 195	80.8	19.2	2.58	2.67
Victoria	14.7	32 945	91.3	8.7	1.6	1.6	11.2	30 071	67.4	32.6	2.81	2.62
Walker	22.7	21 099	86.7	13.3	3.8	2.3	11.2	18 303	59.8	40.2	2.60	2.21
Waller	42.6	11 955	88.3	11.7	2.3	1.4	9.6	10 557	72.5	27.5	2.81	2.73
Ward	-10.8	4 832	82.0	18.0	0.9	5.4	19.4	3 964	78.1	21.9	2.69	2.53
Washington	17.7	13 241	85.5	14.5	6.7	1.7	6.6	11 322	73.5	26.5	2.57	2.42
Webb	47.3	55 206	91.9	8.1	1.6	1.4	5.9	50 740	65.7	34.3	3.91	3.42
Wharton	4.1	16 606	89.1	10.9	1.8	1.5	8.2	14 799	68.8	31.2	2.76	2.68
Wheeler	-8.4	2 687	80.1	19.9	1.4	5.9	13.7	2 152	78.0	22.0	2.31	2.70
Wichita	7.0	53 304	90.9	9.1	0.4	2.3	11.2	48 441	62.3	37.7	2.56	2.37
Wilbarger	-3.6	6 371	86.9	13.1	0.5	3.3	10.7	5 537	66.3	33.7	2.53	2.40
Willacy	10.6	6 727	83.0	17.0	5.9	1.9	16.6	5 584	77.3	22.7	3.40	3.41
Williamson	77.8	90 325	96.1	3.9	0.4	1.3	3.8	86 766	74.2	25.8	2.93	2.53
Wilson	47.5	12 110	91.1	8.9	2.3	1.4	7.5	11 038	85.0	15.0	2.91	2.76
Winkler	-12.1	3 214	80.4	19.6	0.6	4.2	12.3	2 584	83.2	16.8	2.74	2.62
Wise	41.1	19 242	89.3	10.7	2.8	2.3	6.6	17 178	81.4	18.6	2.79	2.69
Wood	27.6	17 939	81.3	18.7	9.7	2.8	9.7	14 583	81.4	18.6	2.41	2.47
Yoakum	-13.0	2 974	83.0	17.0	1.0	3.6	24.4	2 469	78.1	21.9	2.93	3.01
Young	0.9	8 504	84.3	15.7	2.8	2.6	12.4	7 167	73.9	26.1	2.44	2.45
Zapata	37.0	6 167	63.6	36.4	19.3	3.4	27.7	3 921	81.9	18.1	3.11	3.05
Zavala	2.1	4 075	84.1	15.9	2.5	1.2	6.8	3 428	73.1	26.9	3.23	3.41
UTAH	30.5	768 594	91.2	8.8	3.9	2.1	6.5	701 281	71.5	28.5	3.28	2.75
Beaver	24.3	2 660	74.5	25.5	15.0	4.8	19.5	1 982	79.0	21.0	2.99	2.69
Box Elder	20.0	14 209	92.5	7.5	2.2	2.0	7.5	13 144	80.2	19.8	3.32	2.85
Cache	31.0	29 035	94.9	5.1	1.1	1.8	4.4	27 543	64.6	35.4	3.43	2.89
Carbon	7.3	8 741	84.8	15.2	5.6	3.1	11.2	7 413	77.3	22.7	2.74	2.48
Daggett	34.4	1 084	31.4	68.6	63.8	7.7	2.9	340	70.9	29.1	2.44	2.58
Davis	32.8	74 114	96.1	3.9	0.3	2.0	5.6	71 201	77.5	22.5	3.46	2.77
Duchesne	23.0	6 988	65.2	34.8	26.4	3.2	12.9	4 559	80.8	19.2	3.16	2.88
Emery	15.7	4 093	84.7	15.3	5.4	2.2	15.0	3 468	82.0	18.0	3.15	2.90
Garfield	19.3	2 767	57.0	43.0	34.9	4.6	8.9	1 576	79.1	20.9	2.91	2.99
Grand	38.0	4 062	84.5	15.5	6.8	2.0	13.4	3 434	71.0	29.0	2.46	2.38
Iron	69.5	13 618	78.0	22.0	14.6	4.1	7.0	10 627	66.2	33.8	3.18	2.98
Juab	36.4	2 810	87.4	12.6	3.6	2.3	3.3	2 456	79.8	20.2	3.31	3.34
Kane	29.8	3 767	59.4	40.6	33.3	4.2	11.8	2 237	77.9	22.1	2.74	2.43
Millard	14.7	4 522	84.9	15.1	4.8	2.8	7.7	3 840	79.7	20.3	3.25	2.95
Morgan	31.6	2 158	94.8	5.2	2.5	1.6	4.0	2 046	88.3	11.7	3.55	2.96
Piute	13.4	745	68.3	31.7	22.4	4.5	2.9	509	87.0	13.0	2.78	2.82
Rich	23.8	2 408	26.8	73.2	59.6	7.4	41.2	645	83.9	16.1	2.99	3.11
Salt Lake	22.6	310 988	94.9	5.1	0.7	1.6	6.4	295 141	69.0	31.0	3.20	2.53
San Juan	21.2	5 449	75.0	25.0	13.5	2.1	12.8	4 089	79.3	20.7	3.57	3.07
Sanpete	34.7	7 879	83.1	16.9	10.0	2.5	8.2	6 547	78.8	21.2	3.26	3.31
Sevier	24.7	7 016	86.7	13.3	7.2	2.4	7.5	6 081	82.0	18.0	3.05	2.92
Summit	96.0	17 489	59.1	40.9	35.0	2.9	13.6	10 332	75.6	24.4	2.91	2.77
Tooele	47.7	13 812	91.8	8.2	1.2	2.9	13.2	12 677	78.4	21.6	3.18	2.83
Uintah	22.7	9 040	90.6	9.4	2.6	2.0	7.1	8 187	77.0	23.0	3.13	2.78
Utah	42.4	104 315	95.8	4.2	0.8	1.7	3.2	99 937	66.8	33.2	3.78	3.21
Wasatch	54.3	6 564	72.3	27.7	23.2	2.8	6.3	4 743	80.7	19.3	3.23	2.97
Washington	96.2	36 478	82.1	17.9	12.0	3.8	7.3	29 939	73.9	26.1	2.94	3.05
Wayne	27.3	1 329	67.0	33.0	23.3	3.8	9.2	890	77.8	22.2	2.83	2.76
Weber	23.4	70 454	93.2	6.8	1.4	2.5	8.6	65 698	74.9	25.1	3.05	2.63
VERMONT	14.2	294 382	81.7	18.3	14.6	1.4	4.2	240 634	70.6	29.4	2.58	2.11
Addison	14.5	15 312	85.3	14.7	11.4	1.1	3.3	13 068	74.9	25.1	2.66	2.24
Bennington	9.2	19 403	76.5	23.5	18.9	2.0	4.7	14 846	71.4	28.6	2.52	2.13
Caledonia	12.5	14 504	80.4	19.6	13.8	1.8	7.2	11 663	72.9	27.1	2.58	2.16

Table B. States and Counties

STATE/ County code	MSA/ PMSA/ NECMA code[1]	County type[2]	STATE County	Population, 2000 — Land area, 2000[3] (sq km)	Total persons	Rank	Per square kilometer	Population, 1990 — Land area, 1990[3] (sq km)	Total persons	Rank	Per square kilometer	Race (percent) One race — White	Black or African American	American Indian or Alaska Native	Asian	Native Hawaiian and other Pacific Islander	Some other race
				1	2	3	4	5	6	7	8	9	10	11	12	13	14
			VERMONT—Cont'd														
50 007	1303	3	Chittenden	1 396	146 571	371	105.0	1 396	131 761	351	94.4	95.1	0.9	0.3	2.0	0.0	0.3
50 009	...	9	Essex	1 723	6 459	2 741	3.7	1 723	6 405	2 717	3.7	96.0	0.2	0.6	0.3	0.0	0.2
50 011	1303	3	Franklin	1 650	45 417	992	27.5	1 650	39 980	1 001	24.2	96.1	0.3	1.5	0.3	0.0	0.2
50 013	1303	3	Grand Isle	214	6 901	2 695	32.2	214	5 318	2 817	24.9	97.4	0.1	0.9	0.2	0.0	0.0
50 015	...	8	Lamoille	1 194	23 233	1 631	19.5	1 193	19 735	1 690	16.5	97.3	0.3	0.4	0.4	0.0	0.1
50 017	...	9	Orange	1 783	28 226	1 443	15.8	1 784	26 149	1 414	14.7	98.0	0.2	0.3	0.4	0.0	0.1
50 019	...	7	Orleans	1 807	26 277	1 507	14.5	1 805	24 053	1 491	13.3	97.2	0.4	0.7	0.3	0.0	0.1
50 021	...	7	Rutland	2 415	63 400	764	26.3	2 414	62 142	701	25.7	98.1	0.3	0.2	0.4	0.0	0.2
50 023	...	6	Washington	1 785	58 039	824	32.5	1 786	54 928	783	30.8	97.0	0.5	0.3	0.6	0.0	0.3
50 025	...	7	Windham	2 043	44 216	1 012	21.6	2 043	41 588	968	20.4	96.7	0.5	0.2	0.8	0.0	0.3
50 027	...	7	Windsor	2 515	57 418	831	22.8	2 516	54 055	796	21.5	97.7	0.3	0.2	0.6	0.0	0.1
51 000	...		VIRGINIA	102 548	7 078 515	X	69.0	102 558	6 189 197	X	60.3	72.3	19.6	0.3	3.7	0.1	2.0
51 001	...	7	Accomack	1 179	38 305	1 156	32.5	1 177	31 703	1 223	26.9	63.4	31.6	0.3	0.2	0.1	3.6
51 003	1540	3	Albemarle	1 872	79 236	646	42.3	1 872	68 177	649	36.4	85.2	9.7	0.2	2.9	0.0	0.9
51 005	...	6	Alleghany	1 152	12 926	2 239	11.2	1 155	12 815	2 155	11.1	96.3	2.5	0.2	0.2	0.0	0.2
51 007	...	8	Amelia	924	11 400	2 341	12.3	924	8 787	2 485	9.5	70.6	28.1	0.3	0.2	0.0	0.2
51 009	4640	3	Amherst	1 231	31 894	1 348	25.9	1 231	28 578	1 342	23.2	77.7	19.8	0.8	0.4	0.0	0.4
51 011	...	8	Appomattox	864	13 705	2 183	15.9	864	12 300	2 195	14.2	75.9	22.9	0.1	0.2	0.0	0.3
51 013	8840	0	Arlington	67	189 453	291	2 827.7	67	170 895	283	2 550.7	68.9	9.3	0.3	8.6	0.1	8.3
51 015	...	4	Augusta	2 513	65 615	744	26.1	2 517	54 557	790	21.7	95.0	3.6	0.2	0.3	0.0	0.3
51 017	...	9	Bath	1 378	5 048	2 849	3.7	1 378	4 799	2 858	3.5	92.3	6.3	0.2	0.4	0.1	0.1
51 019	4640	3	Bedford	1 954	60 371	801	30.9	1 955	45 553	908	23.3	92.2	6.2	0.2	0.4	0.0	0.2
51 021	...	9	Bland	929	6 871	2 700	7.4	929	6 514	2 708	7.0	94.8	4.2	0.1	0.1	0.0	0.1
51 023	6800	3	Botetourt	1 405	30 496	1 385	21.7	1 406	24 992	1 463	17.8	94.9	3.5	0.2	0.5	0.0	0.2
51 025	...	8	Brunswick	1 466	18 419	1 872	12.6	1 466	15 987	1 924	10.9	42.0	56.9	0.1	0.2	0.0	0.3
51 027	...	9	Buchanan	1 305	26 978	1 484	20.7	1 305	31 333	1 234	24.0	96.7	2.6	0.1	0.1	0.0	0.1
51 029	...	8	Buckingham	1 504	15 623	2 048	10.4	1 505	12 873	2 149	8.6	59.1	39.1	0.2	0.2	0.0	0.4
51 031	4640	3	Campbell	1 307	51 078	907	39.1	1 307	47 499	883	36.3	83.2	14.7	0.2	0.6	0.0	0.3
51 033	...	8	Caroline	1 379	22 121	1 686	16.0	1 379	19 217	1 719	13.9	62.6	34.4	0.8	0.4	0.0	0.5
51 035	...	7	Carroll	1 234	29 245	1 421	23.7	1 234	26 519	1 408	21.5	98.0	0.4	0.1	0.1	0.0	0.8
51 036	6760	2	Charles City County	473	6 926	2 694	14.6	473	6 282	2 724	13.3	35.7	54.9	7.8	0.1	0.0	0.2
51 037	...	8	Charlotte	1 230	12 472	2 267	10.1	1 230	11 688	2 235	9.5	65.5	32.9	0.1	0.2	0.0	0.7
51 041	6760	2	Chesterfield	1 103	259 903	214	235.6	1 103	209 599	238	190.0	76.7	17.8	0.3	2.4	0.0	1.3
51 043	8840	1	Clarke	457	12 652	2 252	27.7	457	12 101	2 208	26.5	91.1	6.7	0.2	0.5	0.0	0.6
51 045	...	8	Craig	856	5 091	2 844	5.9	855	4 372	2 886	5.1	98.9	0.2	0.2	0.2	0.0	0.1
51 047	8840	1	Culpeper	987	34 262	1 273	34.7	987	27 791	1 359	28.2	78.3	18.2	0.3	0.7	0.0	1.1
51 049	...	8	Cumberland	773	9 017	2 527	11.7	773	7 825	2 593	10.1	60.4	37.4	0.2	0.4	0.0	0.6
51 051	...	9	Dickenson	859	16 395	1 998	19.1	862	17 620	1 810	20.4	99.0	0.4	0.1	0.1	0.0	0.1
51 053	6760	2	Dinwiddie	1 305	24 533	1 574	18.8	1 305	22 279	1 564	17.1	64.6	33.7	0.2	0.3	0.0	0.4
51 057	...	8	Essex	668	9 989	2 447	15.0	668	8 689	2 493	13.0	58.0	39.0	0.6	0.8	0.0	0.3
51 059	8840	0	Fairfax	1 023	969 749	36	947.9	1 025	818 310	45	798.4	69.9	8.6	0.3	13.0	0.1	4.5
51 061	8840	1	Fauquier	1 683	55 139	855	32.8	1 684	48 700	860	28.9	88.4	8.8	0.3	0.6	0.0	0.6
51 063	...	8	Floyd	987	13 874	2 169	14.1	988	11 965	2 221	12.1	96.7	2.0	0.1	0.1	0.0	0.4
51 065	1540	3	Fluvanna	744	20 047	1 791	26.9	744	12 429	2 187	16.7	79.4	18.4	0.2	0.4	0.0	0.3
51 067	...	6	Franklin	1 792	47 286	962	26.4	1 793	39 549	1 011	22.1	89.0	9.3	0.2	0.4	0.0	0.4
51 069	...	4	Frederick	1 074	59 209	811	55.1	1 074	45 723	907	42.6	95.0	2.6	0.2	0.7	0.0	0.6
51 071	...	9	Giles	925	16 657	1 980	18.0	927	16 366	1 900	17.7	97.4	1.6	0.1	0.2	0.0	0.2
51 073	5720	1	Gloucester	561	34 780	1 259	62.0	561	30 131	1 292	53.7	86.7	10.3	0.4	0.7	0.1	0.4
51 075	6760	2	Goochland	737	16 863	1 963	22.9	737	14 163	2 040	19.2	72.7	25.6	0.2	0.5	0.0	0.2
51 077	...	9	Grayson	1 146	17 917	1 906	15.6	1 146	16 278	1 905	14.2	91.7	6.8	0.1	0.1	0.0	0.7
51 079	1540	3	Greene	406	15 244	2 073	37.5	406	10 297	2 339	25.4	91.0	6.4	0.2	0.4	0.0	0.6
51 081	...	6	Greensville County	765	11 560	2 328	15.1	765	8 553	2 508	11.2	38.9	59.7	0.1	0.4	0.0	0.5
51 083	...	6	Halifax	2 122	37 355	1 181	17.6	2 108	36 030	1 099	17.1	60.3	38.0	0.2	0.2	0.0	0.4
51 085	6760	2	Hanover	1 224	86 320	602	70.5	1 224	63 306	690	51.7	88.3	9.3	0.3	0.8	0.0	0.4
51 087	6760	2	Henrico	617	262 300	210	425.1	617	217 878	227	353.1	68.9	24.7	0.4	3.6	0.0	1.0
51 089	...	4	Henry	990	57 930	825	58.5	990	56 942	766	57.5	74.4	22.7	0.2	0.4	0.0	1.4
51 091	...	9	Highland	1 077	2 536	3 023	2.4	1 077	2 635	3 015	2.4	99.3	0.1	0.1	0.1	0.0	0.1
51 093	5720	1	Isle of Wight	818	29 728	1 407	36.3	818	25 053	1 460	30.6	71.1	27.1	0.3	0.3	0.0	0.3
51 095	5720	0	James City County	370	48 102	948	130.0	370	34 779	1 141	94.0	82.0	14.4	0.3	1.5	0.0	0.4
51 097	...	8	King and Queen	819	6 630	2 724	8.1	819	6 289	2 722	7.7	61.2	35.7	1.4	0.3	0.0	0.2
51 099	8840	1	King George	466	16 803	1 968	36.1	466	13 527	2 099	29.0	77.7	18.7	0.5	1.0	0.1	0.3
51 101	...	6	King William	713	13 146	2 216	18.4	713	10 913	2 305	15.3	73.8	22.8	1.5	0.4	0.0	0.3
51 103	...	9	Lancaster	345	11 567	2 326	33.5	345	10 896	2 306	31.6	69.9	28.9	0.1	0.3	0.1	0.1
51 105	...	9	Lee	1 132	23 589	1 607	20.8	1 132	24 496	1 479	21.6	98.4	0.4	0.2	0.2	0.0	0.1
51 107	8840	1	Loudoun	1 346	169 599	320	126.0	1 347	86 185	529	64.0	82.8	6.9	0.2	5.3	0.1	2.3

[1]MSA = Metropolitan Statistical Area. PMSA = Primary MSA. NECMA = New England County Metropolitan Area. See Appendix A for explanation of these concepts. See Appendix B for list of metropolitan areas identified by type, with component counties.
[2]County typology code from the Economic Research Service of USDA. See Appendix A for definition.
[3]Dry land or land partially or temporarily covered by water.

Table B. States and Counties

STATE County	Population and population characteristics, 2000 (cont'd)								Population and population characteristics, 1990				
	Race (percent) (cont'd)								Race (percent)				
	Race alone or in combination												
	Two or more races	White	Black	American Indian or Alaska Native	Asian	Native Hawaiian and other Pacific Islander	Some other race	Hispanic¹	White	Black or African American	American Indian or Alaska Native	Asian and Pacific Islander	Hispanic¹
	15	16	17	18	19	20	21	22	23	24	25	26	27
VERMONT—Cont'd													
Chittenden	1.3	96.3	1.3	0.8	2.4	0.1	0.6	1.1	97.8	0.6	0.2	1.1	0.9
Essex	2.1	98.7	0.2	2.2	0.4	0.0	0.8	0.5	99.2	0.2	0.3	0.2	0.5
Franklin	1.6	97.7	0.5	2.8	0.4	0.0	0.4	0.6	98.1	0.1	1.5	0.2	0.3
Grand Isle	1.3	98.7	0.2	1.9	0.3	0.1	0.1	0.4	99.1	0.3	0.4	0.2	0.4
Lamoille	1.4	98.6	0.6	1.3	0.6	0.1	0.3	0.8	99.1	0.1	0.2	0.4	0.5
Orange	1.0	98.9	0.4	0.8	0.5	0.1	0.3	0.6	99.2	0.2	0.3	0.3	0.4
Orleans	1.4	98.5	0.5	1.7	0.4	0.0	0.4	0.7	99.3	0.2	0.2	0.2	0.4
Rutland	0.7	98.8	0.5	0.6	0.5	0.0	0.3	0.7	99.2	0.2	0.1	0.3	0.4
Washington	1.3	98.3	0.7	1.1	0.8	0.0	0.4	1.3	98.9	0.3	0.2	0.4	1.2
Windham	1.4	98.1	0.8	0.9	1.1	0.1	0.6	1.1	98.6	0.4	0.2	0.6	0.7
Windsor	0.9	98.6	0.5	0.7	0.8	0.1	0.3	0.8	98.9	0.2	0.2	0.5	0.5
VIRGINIA	2.0	73.9	20.4	0.7	4.3	0.1	2.7	4.7	77.4	18.8	0.2	2.6	2.6
Accomack	0.9	64.1	31.9	0.7	0.3	0.1	3.8	5.4	64.7	34.5	0.1	0.2	1.4
Albemarle	1.3	86.3	10.2	0.5	3.2	0.0	1.2	2.6	87.1	10.0	0.1	2.4	1.2
Alleghany	0.5	96.9	2.6	0.5	0.3	0.0	0.3	0.4	97.1	2.5	0.1	0.3	0.4
Amelia	0.7	71.2	28.3	0.7	0.2	0.0	0.4	0.8	67.5	32.1	0.2	0.1	0.5
Amherst	0.9	78.3	20.3	1.2	0.4	0.1	0.6	1.0	79.0	20.1	0.4	0.3	0.8
Appomattox	0.6	76.4	23.3	0.3	0.2	0.0	0.4	0.5	76.9	22.9	0.1	0.0	0.2
Arlington	4.3	72.3	10.3	0.8	9.9	0.2	11.1	18.6	76.6	10.5	0.3	6.8	13.5
Augusta	0.6	95.6	3.7	0.4	0.4	0.1	0.4	0.9	95.9	3.7	0.1	0.2	0.4
Bath	0.7	92.9	6.5	0.5	0.4	0.2	0.1	0.4	94.5	5.2	0.0	0.2	0.5
Bedford	0.7	92.8	6.5	0.5	0.6	0.0	0.3	0.7	91.7	7.9	0.1	0.2	0.4
Bland	0.7	95.5	4.2	0.4	0.2	0.0	0.3	0.5	96.1	3.5	0.0	0.1	0.4
Botetourt	0.7	95.5	3.7	0.5	0.6	0.0	0.3	0.6	95.0	4.5	0.1	0.3	0.6
Brunswick	0.5	42.4	57.1	0.3	0.3	0.0	0.5	1.3	41.3	58.5	0.1	0.1	0.3
Buchanan	0.3	97.1	2.7	0.2	0.2	0.0	0.2	0.5	99.3	0.2	0.1	0.2	0.8
Buckingham	1.1	60.0	39.6	0.8	0.2	0.0	0.6	0.8	58.8	40.9	0.1	0.2	0.3
Campbell	0.9	84.0	15.2	0.5	0.8	0.0	0.4	0.8	85.0	14.5	0.1	0.4	0.5
Caroline	1.4	63.6	35.2	1.4	0.6	0.0	0.7	1.3	60.8	37.7	1.1	0.3	0.5
Carroll	0.5	98.5	0.5	0.4	0.2	0.0	1.0	1.6	99.2	0.4	0.1	0.1	0.6
Charles City County	1.4	36.6	55.7	8.9	0.2	0.0	0.3	0.6	28.7	63.2	7.8	0.2	0.4
Charlotte	0.6	65.9	33.2	0.5	0.2	0.0	0.8	1.7	63.2	36.5	0.2	0.0	0.3
Chesterfield	1.4	77.8	18.4	0.7	2.7	0.1	1.8	2.9	84.6	13.0	0.2	1.8	1.2
Clarke	0.9	91.9	7.1	0.6	0.7	0.2	0.7	1.5	90.8	8.7	0.1	0.2	0.7
Craig	0.4	99.3	0.2	0.4	0.3	0.0	0.2	0.3	99.6	0.2	0.1	0.1	0.1
Culpeper	1.4	79.5	18.9	0.8	0.9	0.1	1.4	2.5	81.2	17.2	0.3	1.1	0.7
Cumberland	1.1	61.4	37.8	0.7	0.5	0.0	0.8	1.7	60.9	38.7	0.1	0.2	0.6
Dickenson	0.4	99.4	0.4	0.3	0.2	0.0	0.1	0.4	99.4	0.4	0.1	0.1	0.3
Dinwiddie	0.8	65.2	34.0	0.6	0.5	0.1	0.5	1.0	63.7	35.6	0.2	0.3	0.6
Essex	1.3	59.0	39.8	1.2	0.9	0.0	0.4	0.7	61.3	37.6	0.5	0.5	0.3
Fairfax	3.7	72.9	9.3	0.7	14.5	0.2	6.3	11.0	81.3	7.7	0.2	8.5	6.3
Fauquier	1.3	89.6	9.4	0.7	0.8	0.1	0.9	2.0	87.5	11.2	0.2	0.6	1.2
Floyd	0.7	97.4	2.2	0.5	0.2	0.0	0.5	1.3	97.2	2.4	0.1	0.2	0.5
Fluvanna	1.2	80.6	19.1	0.6	0.6	0.1	0.4	1.2	76.6	22.9	0.2	0.1	0.6
Franklin	0.7	89.6	9.7	0.4	0.5	0.1	0.6	1.2	88.9	10.7	0.1	0.2	0.3
Frederick	1.0	95.9	3.0	0.5	0.9	0.1	0.7	1.7	97.4	1.8	0.1	0.5	0.6
Giles	0.5	97.9	1.7	0.3	0.3	0.0	0.2	0.6	98.0	1.7	0.0	0.1	0.3
Gloucester	1.4	88.0	10.8	1.0	1.1	0.1	0.6	1.6	87.8	11.1	0.2	0.6	1.0
Goochland	0.8	73.4	26.0	0.5	0.6	0.0	0.3	0.9	69.9	29.7	0.1	0.2	0.2
Grayson	0.6	92.3	6.9	0.5	0.1	0.1	0.8	1.5	96.6	3.0	0.1	0.1	0.5
Greene	1.2	92.1	7.0	0.6	0.6	0.1	0.9	1.3	93.0	6.4	0.1	0.3	0.5
Greensville	0.3	39.2	59.9	0.2	0.5	0.0	0.5	0.9	44.1	55.5	0.1	0.3	0.7
Halifax	0.8	60.9	38.5	0.5	0.3	0.0	0.6	1.2	60.3	39.2	0.1	0.1	0.6
Hanover	0.8	89.0	9.7	0.7	1.0	0.0	0.5	1.0	89.2	10.1	0.2	0.4	0.5
Henrico	1.4	70.0	25.3	0.7	4.0	0.1	1.4	2.3	77.3	20.1	0.3	2.0	1.0
Henry	0.9	75.2	23.1	0.4	0.5	0.1	1.7	3.5	76.4	23.1	0.1	0.2	0.4
Highland	0.4	99.5	0.1	0.3	0.3	0.0	0.2	0.5	99.8	0.1	0.0	0.1	0.2
Isle of Wight	0.9	71.8	27.6	0.7	0.5	0.0	0.4	0.9	67.8	31.6	0.2	0.3	0.7
James City County	1.4	83.2	14.9	0.7	1.9	0.2	0.7	1.7	79.8	18.5	0.2	1.3	1.1
King and Queen	1.3	62.1	36.5	2.2	0.4	0.1	0.3	0.9	56.8	41.9	1.0	0.2	0.4
King George	1.6	79.1	19.4	1.1	1.3	0.1	0.7	1.8	78.3	20.2	0.3	0.9	1.2
King William	1.1	74.8	23.4	2.2	0.5	0.0	0.4	0.9	67.4	30.3	2.0	0.2	0.6
Lancaster	0.5	70.4	29.1	0.4	0.4	0.1	0.2	0.6	69.4	30.2	0.1	0.1	0.7
Lee	0.6	99.1	0.5	0.7	0.3	0.0	0.1	0.5	99.4	0.4	0.1	0.1	0.5
Loudoun	2.4	84.9	7.6	0.6	6.2	0.2	3.2	5.9	89.5	7.2	0.2	2.4	2.5

¹ Hispanic persons may be of any race.

Table B. States and Counties

STATE County	Population and population characteristics, 2000										
	Age (percent)										
	Under 5 years	5 to 17 years	18 to 24 years	25 to 34 years	35 to 44 years	45 to 54 years	55 to 64 years	65 to 74 years	75 years and over	Median age (years)	Percent Female
	28	29	30	31	32	33	34	35	36	37	38
VERMONT—Cont'd											
Chittenden	5.8	17.8	13.1	14.5	17.6	14.2	7.7	5.0	4.4	34.2	51.3
Essex	5.4	20.2	6.5	11.3	15.9	14.5	11.0	8.9	6.3	39.0	50.0
Franklin	7.1	21.0	7.0	13.6	17.8	14.0	8.4	6.1	4.9	35.7	50.4
Grand Isle	5.5	19.3	5.6	10.8	17.9	17.0	11.5	7.5	4.8	40.1	50.0
Lamoille	5.5	18.8	10.0	13.2	16.7	15.0	9.5	6.0	5.4	36.5	50.0
Orange	5.6	20.0	7.8	10.9	17.3	15.8	9.7	7.1	5.7	38.6	50.2
Orleans	5.7	19.5	7.1	11.5	15.3	15.3	10.6	7.7	7.4	39.3	50.4
Rutland	5.2	18.1	8.3	11.4	16.3	15.7	10.1	7.6	7.3	39.5	51.4
Washington	5.4	18.1	8.9	12.1	16.7	16.6	9.4	6.5	6.3	38.5	51.0
Windham	5.3	18.3	7.1	11.3	16.9	17.0	10.2	7.2	6.8	40.0	51.3
Windsor	5.0	18.4	5.9	10.8	16.5	16.7	10.9	8.1	7.7	41.3	51.3
VIRGINIA	6.5	18.0	9.6	14.6	17.0	14.1	8.9	6.1	5.1	35.7	51.0
Accomack	6.1	18.2	8.2	11.3	14.9	13.5	11.2	9.2	7.5	39.4	51.5
Albemarle	6.3	18.6	7.3	14.0	16.9	15.2	9.2	6.7	5.8	37.4	52.0
Alleghany	5.6	17.3	6.2	11.7	15.1	15.8	12.7	8.5	7.1	41.1	50.1
Amelia	6.3	19.1	6.7	12.0	17.3	14.1	11.3	7.2	6.1	38.5	50.7
Amherst	5.7	17.8	9.7	12.2	15.5	14.5	10.9	7.9	5.9	38.0	52.3
Appomattox	6.1	18.5	7.1	12.1	15.7	13.8	11.8	8.2	6.5	39.1	51.3
Arlington	5.5	11.0	10.4	25.2	17.2	13.6	7.7	4.4	5.0	34.0	49.6
Augusta	5.7	18.1	6.9	12.4	17.4	15.7	11.1	7.4	5.4	39.0	49.7
Bath	4.4	16.6	5.5	12.0	16.3	14.9	13.6	10.2	6.5	41.8	49.8
Bedford	5.8	18.2	5.8	12.1	17.8	16.1	11.4	7.8	5.0	39.7	50.1
Bland	4.5	14.9	7.6	14.6	16.1	16.3	11.6	8.2	6.3	40.3	45.5
Botetourt	5.7	17.7	5.8	11.0	17.8	17.2	11.6	8.1	5.0	40.7	50.1
Brunswick	5.0	15.5	9.9	14.6	16.1	14.1	10.2	8.3	6.2	38.1	46.9
Buchanan	4.8	16.6	8.5	13.6	17.6	16.0	11.6	6.9	4.6	38.8	49.3
Buckingham	5.0	17.4	7.5	14.4	17.6	14.6	10.1	7.4	6.1	38.2	45.1
Campbell	5.8	18.1	7.7	13.3	16.0	14.7	10.9	7.9	5.6	38.3	51.2
Caroline	6.2	18.5	7.4	13.2	16.7	14.4	10.6	7.1	5.8	37.7	50.2
Carroll	5.6	15.5	7.2	13.1	14.8	14.9	11.8	9.5	7.5	40.7	50.7
Charles City County	5.6	16.5	7.5	11.3	17.5	17.4	11.4	8.0	4.6	39.9	50.9
Charlotte	5.5	18.8	7.2	11.3	14.9	13.3	11.4	9.3	8.2	40.0	52.1
Chesterfield	6.7	21.5	7.7	13.0	18.2	16.4	8.5	4.8	3.3	35.7	51.3
Clarke	5.2	18.2	5.8	10.7	18.3	15.7	11.4	8.1	6.5	40.6	50.5
Craig	5.7	17.9	6.4	12.4	17.2	15.3	11.5	7.7	5.9	39.6	49.2
Culpeper	6.4	19.3	8.1	13.5	17.6	13.9	9.4	6.7	5.2	36.5	49.2
Cumberland	6.3	18.5	7.3	12.5	15.5	14.2	10.9	8.6	6.2	38.4	52.4
Dickenson	5.3	16.7	8.9	12.0	15.7	15.8	11.1	8.2	6.2	39.7	51.1
Dinwiddie	5.6	18.4	6.7	12.8	18.1	15.1	11.1	7.0	5.2	38.5	50.3
Essex	5.2	17.7	7.0	11.8	15.2	14.9	10.8	9.0	8.3	40.3	52.6
Fairfax	7.0	18.4	7.5	15.5	18.4	16.2	9.1	4.6	3.3	35.9	50.4
Fauquier	6.4	20.4	6.4	11.5	18.8	15.8	10.2	5.9	4.6	37.8	50.6
Floyd	5.6	16.6	6.9	12.8	14.8	15.4	11.9	8.0	7.9	40.5	50.6
Fluvanna	6.5	17.1	6.4	14.0	17.7	13.8	10.6	9.2	4.8	38.3	53.6
Franklin	5.4	16.8	8.1	12.1	16.1	15.3	11.9	8.4	5.9	39.7	50.7
Frederick	6.5	19.9	7.0	13.4	18.4	14.4	9.7	6.2	4.5	36.7	50.0
Giles	5.7	16.4	6.8	13.2	15.2	14.6	11.5	8.7	8.0	40.2	51.1
Gloucester	5.8	20.4	6.8	11.8	18.6	14.6	10.2	6.6	5.2	38.0	50.9
Goochland	5.2	16.1	5.3	12.8	19.3	17.1	11.8	7.7	4.8	40.5	49.6
Grayson	4.8	14.7	7.6	14.1	15.7	14.6	11.6	9.5	7.4	40.5	48.2
Greene	7.5	19.8	6.7	14.9	18.3	13.9	9.1	5.4	4.3	35.5	50.4
Greensville	3.8	14.4	7.4	18.1	20.6	15.2	9.0	6.7	4.8	38.1	38.3
Halifax	5.9	17.5	6.9	11.6	14.8	14.8	11.5	8.7	8.3	40.7	52.4
Hanover	6.5	20.6	6.9	11.8	18.9	15.5	9.3	6.1	4.6	37.4	50.8
Henrico	6.8	17.8	7.8	15.7	17.2	14.2	8.0	6.2	6.2	36.0	53.1
Henry	5.5	16.8	7.5	13.2	15.8	14.2	11.9	8.7	6.3	39.3	51.3
Highland	3.7	16.2	4.1	8.6	15.9	16.6	14.6	10.4	9.9	46.0	50.6
Isle of Wight	6.0	19.4	6.6	11.1	18.6	15.3	10.9	7.2	5.0	38.9	51.1
James City County	5.6	17.7	6.4	11.0	16.4	14.6	11.5	9.5	7.3	40.8	51.6
King and Queen	5.4	17.4	7.0	10.7	16.2	15.2	11.8	8.8	7.6	40.9	51.2
King George	7.6	20.2	8.2	13.8	17.9	13.7	9.0	5.3	4.3	35.1	49.8
King William	6.9	19.2	5.9	14.2	17.3	14.9	9.9	6.6	5.1	37.0	50.8
Lancaster	4.2	14.8	5.0	7.2	12.5	13.6	14.4	14.1	14.4	49.8	53.5
Lee	5.8	16.9	8.0	12.6	14.9	14.9	11.4	8.2	7.3	39.7	51.5
Loudoun	9.7	20.1	5.7	17.6	21.3	13.1	6.8	3.2	2.4	33.6	50.6

Table B. States and Counties

STATE County	Under 5 years (39)	5 to 17 years (40)	18 to 24 years (41)	25 to 34 years (42)	35 to 44 years (43)	45 to 54 years (44)	55 to 64 years (45)	65 to 74 years (46)	75 years and over (47)	Percent Female (48)	Total persons 2000 (49)	Total persons 1990 (50)	Total persons 1980 (51)	Percent change 1990–2000 (52)	Percent change 1980–1990 (53)
VERMONT—Cont'd															
Chittenden	7.3	16.1	16.4	19.3	16.3	9.8	6.7	4.6	3.5	51.5	146 571	131 761	115 534	11.2	14.0
Essex	6.9	19.7	6.8	15.1	15.2	11.4	10.6	8.6	5.6	50.8	6 459	6 405	6 313	0.8	1.5
Franklin	8.4	21.1	8.8	18.0	15.7	9.5	7.7	6.2	4.6	50.7	45 417	39 980	34 788	13.6	14.9
Grand Isle	7.9	18.7	7.4	17.1	17.4	10.9	9.5	7.1	4.0	49.7	6 901	5 318	4 613	29.8	15.3
Lamoille	7.5	18.2	12.0	17.6	16.3	10.0	7.4	6.3	4.7	50.0	23 233	19 735	16 767	17.7	17.7
Orange	7.7	20.0	9.1	16.6	16.5	10.1	8.3	6.7	5.0	49.9	28 226	26 149	22 739	7.9	15.0
Orleans	7.3	21.1	8.3	14.6	15.9	10.5	8.8	8.0	5.5	50.7	26 277	24 053	23 440	9.2	2.6
Rutland	7.0	17.1	10.7	16.3	16.0	10.4	8.7	7.7	6.1	51.5	63 400	62 142	58 347	2.0	6.5
Washington	7.1	18.3	10.1	15.9	17.3	10.6	8.2	6.5	6.0	51.0	58 039	54 928	52 393	5.7	4.8
Windham	7.3	18.2	8.5	16.8	17.6	10.4	8.2	7.0	6.0	51.2	44 216	41 588	36 933	6.3	12.6
Windsor	6.9	17.8	7.2	16.2	17.0	11.0	9.1	8.4	6.3	51.0	57 418	54 055	51 030	6.2	5.9
VIRGINIA	7.2	17.2	11.6	18.4	16.0	10.7	8.1	6.5	4.3	51.0	7 078 515	6 189 197	5 346 797	14.4	15.8
Accomack	6.4	17.3	8.3	14.2	13.6	10.6	11.1	10.5	7.9	52.8	38 305	31 703	31 268	20.8	1.4
Albemarle	6.8	15.6	15.3	18.4	16.3	10.2	7.8	5.9	3.8	51.2	79 236	68 177	55 783	16.2	22.2
Alleghany	5.8	18.4	8.6	13.9	15.9	13.1	10.7	8.5	5.2	50.3	12 926	12 815	14 333	0.9	-8.1
Amelia	7.0	19.1	8.6	16.0	14.5	12.0	9.6	7.5	5.6	50.6	11 400	8 787	8 405	29.7	4.5
Amherst	6.3	17.2	11.1	15.5	15.8	12.0	9.9	7.4	4.9	51.9	31 894	28 578	29 122	11.6	-1.9
Appomattox	6.4	18.5	9.1	14.9	14.1	12.2	10.0	8.3	6.4	51.6	13 705	12 300	11 971	11.4	2.7
Arlington	5.5	9.6	11.8	25.8	18.1	10.7	7.0	6.5	4.8	50.9	189 453	170 895	152 599	10.9	12.0
Augusta	6.4	18.2	8.8	16.8	16.7	12.2	9.5	7.0	4.3	49.5	65 615	54 557	47 578	20.3	14.9
Bath	5.4	15.8	9.6	14.0	13.6	14.0	12.1	8.8	6.8	49.2	5 048	4 799	5 860	5.2	-18.1
Bedford	6.6	17.3	8.1	16.8	16.8	12.3	10.0	7.5	4.7	50.2	60 371	45 553	34 927	32.5	30.7
Bland	5.1	17.0	8.8	16.4	17.0	12.0	10.1	7.8	5.8	46.7	6 871	6 514	6 349	5.5	2.6
Botetourt	5.8	17.5	8.4	15.2	17.5	13.2	10.3	7.7	4.5	49.8	30 496	24 992	23 270	22.0	7.4
Brunswick	6.1	17.8	12.3	14.9	14.3	9.9	10.2	8.7	6.6	50.4	18 419	15 987	15 632	15.2	2.3
Buchanan	5.5	22.0	10.4	17.2	16.1	11.9	8.3	5.4	3.3	50.5	26 978	31 333	37 989	-13.9	-17.5
Buckingham	6.9	16.7	9.1	17.1	15.5	10.7	9.3	8.4	6.2	47.8	15 623	12 873	11 751	21.4	9.5
Campbell	6.7	17.7	10.5	16.7	15.2	12.2	9.5	7.3	4.2	50.7	51 078	47 499	45 424	7.5	4.7
Caroline	7.4	18.7	9.9	17.1	14.6	11.3	9.1	7.2	4.6	50.4	22 121	19 217	17 904	15.1	7.3
Carroll	5.5	16.6	9.2	14.5	14.8	12.0	11.4	9.1	6.9	50.7	29 245	26 519	27 270	10.3	-2.5
Charles City County	6.2	17.7	9.3	16.4	16.2	11.8	11.0	6.9	4.4	51.1	6 926	6 282	6 692	10.3	-6.1
Charlotte	6.9	17.9	9.6	13.6	12.6	10.8	11.3	10.5	6.7	51.1	12 472	11 688	12 266	6.7	-4.7
Chesterfield	8.0	21.1	8.9	18.0	19.8	11.3	6.6	4.1	2.0	51.1	259 903	209 599	141 372	24.0	48.2
Clarke	6.4	16.4	8.5	16.2	16.2	11.9	10.4	7.8	6.2	50.5	12 652	12 101	9 965	4.6	21.4
Craig	6.5	16.6	8.7	16.0	15.7	12.1	10.4	8.4	5.6	49.2	5 091	4 372	3 948	16.4	10.7
Culpeper	7.8	18.7	9.5	17.5	15.3	10.4	8.2	7.0	5.5	51.0	34 262	27 791	22 620	23.3	22.9
Cumberland	7.0	19.2	8.9	14.5	13.5	11.9	9.5	8.7	6.8	51.6	9 017	7 825	7 881	15.2	-0.7
Dickenson	5.9	21.4	9.2	15.2	15.4	11.2	9.4	7.2	5.0	51.0	16 395	17 620	19 806	-7.0	-11.0
Dinwiddie	6.7	17.6	9.7	16.4	14.9	12.6	9.7	8.1	4.3	50.8	24 533	22 279	22 602	10.1	-1.3
Essex	5.9	17.6	8.2	14.6	14.1	11.3	10.5	9.4	8.4	53.0	9 989	8 689	8 864	15.0	-2.0
Fairfax	7.1	17.4	9.8	19.4	19.3	13.2	7.4	4.4	2.1	50.3	969 749	818 310	595 754	18.5	37.4
Fauquier	8.0	18.8	8.8	17.9	17.0	12.2	8.1	5.6	3.7	49.6	55 139	48 700	35 889	13.2	36.1
Floyd	5.6	17.3	8.5	14.2	15.7	12.4	9.8	9.2	7.4	50.6	13 874	11 965	11 563	16.0	3.5
Fluvanna	7.6	17.6	8.6	17.3	15.1	10.7	10.0	8.3	4.7	50.7	20 047	12 429	10 244	61.3	21.3
Franklin	6.2	16.6	11.6	15.4	15.3	11.9	10.0	7.7	5.3	50.6	47 286	39 549	35 740	19.6	10.7
Frederick	7.6	19.1	9.0	18.2	16.4	11.8	8.5	6.1	3.4	50.1	59 209	45 723	34 150	29.5	33.9
Giles	5.8	16.3	9.5	14.1	14.8	12.1	10.7	10.3	6.5	51.3	16 657	16 366	17 810	1.8	-8.1
Gloucester	7.5	19.7	7.9	17.7	16.6	11.1	8.2	6.5	4.6	50.6	34 780	30 131	20 107	15.4	49.9
Goochland	6.5	14.8	8.3	18.8	17.7	12.7	10.2	6.4	4.6	51.1	16 863	14 163	11 761	19.1	20.4
Grayson	5.8	16.8	8.9	14.1	14.6	12.0	11.3	9.7	6.9	51.2	17 917	16 278	16 579	10.1	-1.8
Greene	8.6	18.5	8.5	19.1	17.0	10.8	8.0	6.0	3.4	50.4	15 244	10 297	7 625	48.0	35.0
Greensville	7.0	20.2	9.3	13.6	14.4	11.1	10.6	8.5	5.3	52.3	11 560	8 553	10 903	35.2	-20.8
Halifax	5.8	18.5	8.8	14.0	14.6	11.6	10.0	9.6	6.9	51.9	37 355	36 030	30 599	3.7	-5.1
Hanover	6.9	18.1	9.7	16.3	17.1	12.4	9.0	6.6	4.0	51.1	86 320	63 306	50 398	36.4	25.6
Henrico	6.9	16.1	9.0	19.4	16.5	10.4	8.5	7.3	5.1	53.5	262 300	217 878	180 735	20.4	20.5
Henry	6.4	16.9	10.1	16.3	14.7	12.9	10.3	7.6	4.8	51.5	57 930	56 942	57 654	1.7	-1.2
Highland	5.6	15.7	5.8	14.4	15.3	12.0	11.8	11.3	8.1	50.5	2 536	2 635	2 937	-3.8	-10.3
Isle of Wight	7.6	18.4	8.6	17.9	15.6	11.7	9.1	7.0	4.2	50.9	29 728	25 053	21 603	18.7	16.0
James City County	7.1	17.3	9.1	17.0	16.4	11.1	9.7	7.4	4.1	51.1	48 102	34 779	22 339	38.3	56.5
King and Queen	7.3	17.9	9.2	15.2	13.9	11.1	10.3	9.5	5.6	51.1	6 630	6 289	5 968	5.4	5.4
King George	8.4	19.6	9.7	19.0	15.3	10.9	7.7	5.8	3.6	50.0	16 803	13 527	10 543	24.2	28.3
King William	7.4	19.3	8.5	16.3	16.0	11.3	8.5	7.2	5.4	51.7	13 146	10 913	9 334	20.5	16.9
Lancaster	5.0	15.4	5.9	11.2	11.9	10.6	14.0	14.8	11.1	53.2	11 567	10 896	10 129	6.2	7.6
Lee	6.2	19.7	8.9	14.6	14.3	11.2	9.4	8.8	6.8	52.3	23 589	24 496	25 956	-3.7	-5.6
Loudoun	8.8	18.2	9.1	21.3	18.4	11.8	6.3	3.5	2.5	50.3	169 599	86 185	57 427	96.8	50.0

Table B. States and Counties

STATE County	Total population	Total in house-holds	House-holder	Spouse	Child Total	Child Own child under 18 years	Other relatives Total	Other relatives Under 18 years	Nonrelatives Total	Nonrelatives Unmarried partner	Total in group quarters	Correctional institutions	Nursing homes	Other institutions	College dormitories	Military quarters	Other
	54	55	56	57	58	59	60	61	62	63	64	65	66	67	68	69	70
VERMONT—Cont'd																	
Chittenden	146 571	95.0	38.5	19.4	26.7	22.3	2.3	0.7	8.1	2.9	5.0	0.1	0.4	0.1	4.0	0.0	0.4
Essex	6 459	99.6	40.3	22.6	28.6	24.0	2.6	0.8	5.4	3.0	0.4	0.0	0.0	0.0	0.0	0.0	0.4
Franklin	45 417	98.7	36.9	21.5	31.6	26.1	2.7	1.1	5.9	3.2	1.3	0.5	0.5	0.0	0.0	0.0	0.3
Grand Isle	6 901	100.0	40.0	24.0	27.6	23.0	2.9	1.2	5.4	3.0	0.0	0.0	0.0	0.0	0.0	0.0	0.0
Lamoille	23 233	97.4	39.7	20.4	27.2	22.8	2.3	0.8	7.9	3.7	2.6	0.0	0.5	0.0	1.8	0.0	0.2
Orange	28 226	97.7	38.7	21.7	28.9	23.9	2.6	0.9	5.7	3.1	2.3	0.0	0.3	0.1	1.7	0.0	0.2
Orleans	26 277	97.3	39.8	21.6	28.1	23.5	2.2	0.7	5.7	3.0	2.7	1.1	1.3	0.0	0.2	0.0	0.1
Rutland	63 400	96.8	40.5	20.8	27.0	21.7	2.7	0.9	5.7	2.7	3.2	0.2	0.9	0.1	1.6	0.0	0.4
Washington	58 039	96.4	40.8	20.6	26.8	22.2	2.2	0.7	5.9	3.0	3.6	0.0	0.7	0.3	2.4	0.0	0.2
Windham	44 216	97.5	41.6	20.4	26.6	22.0	2.5	0.9	6.4	3.2	2.5	0.0	0.9	0.0	1.3	0.0	0.4
Windsor	57 418	98.8	42.1	22.2	26.5	21.9	2.4	0.7	5.6	2.8	1.2	0.3	0.6	0.0	0.0	0.0	0.3
VIRGINIA	7 078 515	96.7	38.1	20.1	28.1	22.1	5.0	2.0	5.3	1.8	3.3	0.9	0.5	0.1	0.9	0.5	0.3
Accomack	38 305	97.7	39.9	19.6	26.7	20.1	6.8	3.6	4.6	2.3	2.3	0.3	0.7	0.0	0.0	0.1	1.1
Albemarle	79 236	98.1	40.2	21.8	27.9	23.1	3.3	1.3	4.8	1.9	1.9	0.5	1.0	0.2	0.0	0.0	0.3
Alleghany	12 926	98.1	39.8	25.2	26.7	20.4	3.6	1.6	2.8	1.5	1.9	0.0	0.7	0.3	0.0	0.0	0.9
Amelia	11 400	99.1	37.2	22.0	29.4	21.6	6.4	3.1	4.1	2.0	0.9	0.0	0.9	0.0	0.0	0.0	0.0
Amherst	31 894	93.8	37.4	21.0	27.4	20.4	4.6	2.1	3.4	1.8	6.2	0.2	0.2	2.2	2.5	0.0	1.2
Appomattox	13 705	99.0	38.8	23.2	28.5	21.5	5.2	2.6	3.3	1.9	1.0	0.2	0.5	0.0	0.0	0.0	0.4
Arlington	189 453	97.8	45.6	16.1	14.9	14.9	5.8	1.3	11.5	2.3	2.2	0.3	0.5	0.0	0.3	0.9	0.3
Augusta	65 615	97.0	37.8	24.1	28.1	21.7	3.6	1.5	3.3	1.7	3.0	2.1	0.5	0.3	0.0	0.0	0.2
Bath	5 048	95.4	40.7	23.9	24.2	19.6	3.6	1.0	3.0	1.5	4.6	0.1	1.0	0.0	0.0	0.0	3.5
Bedford	60 371	99.4	39.5	25.8	27.9	22.2	3.3	1.4	2.9	1.6	0.6	0.2	0.1	0.0	0.0	0.0	0.3
Bland	6 871	90.7	37.4	23.3	24.7	17.9	3.2	1.2	2.1	1.1	9.3	8.6	0.7	0.0	0.0	0.0	0.0
Botetourt	30 496	98.3	38.4	26.0	27.9	21.4	3.6	1.5	2.4	1.2	1.7	0.9	0.2	0.2	0.0	0.0	0.5
Brunswick	18 419	84.2	34.1	16.0	23.8	16.6	7.0	3.3	3.4	1.8	15.8	13.3	0.5	0.0	1.9	0.0	0.1
Buchanan	26 978	95.5	38.8	23.6	27.1	18.4	4.0	1.8	2.0	1.0	4.5	3.3	0.4	0.1	0.0	0.0	0.6
Buckingham	15 623	85.9	34.1	17.4	24.7	18.4	5.9	2.8	3.8	2.0	14.1	12.8	0.4	0.7	0.0	0.0	0.2
Campbell	51 078	99.0	40.4	22.6	28.2	21.6	4.3	1.9	3.5	1.7	1.0	0.5	0.4	0.1	0.0	0.0	0.0
Caroline	22 121	97.4	36.3	20.4	28.5	20.2	7.6	3.9	4.5	2.1	2.6	1.9	0.6	0.0	0.0	0.0	0.1
Carroll	29 245	98.3	41.7	24.9	25.5	19.2	3.7	1.4	2.5	1.3	1.7	0.0	0.4	0.0	0.0	0.0	1.4
Charles City County	6 926	100.0	38.6	20.7	28.8	17.6	8.2	4.1	3.8	2.1	0.0	0.0	0.0	0.0	0.0	0.0	0.0
Charlotte	12 472	98.1	39.7	20.8	27.8	20.2	6.6	3.4	3.3	1.6	1.9	0.4	0.7	0.0	0.0	0.0	0.7
Chesterfield	259 903	98.4	36.1	22.5	32.2	26.0	4.0	1.6	3.7	1.5	1.6	0.3	0.3	0.2	0.7	0.0	0.1
Clarke	12 652	97.5	39.1	22.7	27.6	21.2	4.3	1.8	3.9	1.9	2.5	1.2	1.1	0.0	0.0	0.0	0.2
Craig	5 091	99.2	40.5	25.1	27.2	21.3	3.4	1.4	3.0	1.5	0.8	0.0	0.0	0.4	0.0	0.0	0.4
Culpeper	34 262	95.0	35.4	20.7	28.7	22.3	5.4	2.4	4.7	2.2	5.0	3.7	0.5	0.6	0.0	0.0	0.2
Cumberland	9 017	99.6	39.1	20.2	28.5	20.9	7.4	3.3	4.4	2.0	0.4	0.0	0.2	0.0	0.0	0.0	0.2
Dickenson	16 395	99.2	41.1	23.8	28.2	19.8	4.0	1.8	2.0	1.1	0.8	0.3	0.5	0.0	0.0	0.0	0.0
Dinwiddie	24 533	95.9	37.1	20.3	28.3	20.3	6.5	3.2	3.7	2.0	4.1	0.5	0.0	3.4	0.0	0.0	0.2
Essex	9 989	98.4	40.0	20.3	26.9	19.5	6.4	2.8	4.8	2.5	1.6	0.0	1.4	0.0	0.0	0.0	0.2
Fairfax	969 749	98.9	36.2	21.5	29.7	23.8	5.7	1.3	5.9	1.4	1.1	0.4	0.3	0.0	0.3	0.0	0.1
Fauquier	55 139	99.0	36.0	23.0	31.0	24.3	4.9	2.0	4.2	1.8	1.0	0.1	0.6	0.0	0.0	0.0	0.3
Floyd	13 874	99.6	41.7	25.0	26.6	20.7	3.2	1.1	3.1	1.5	0.4	0.0	0.4	0.0	0.0	0.0	0.0
Fluvanna	20 047	95.4	36.8	23.4	27.3	21.1	4.3	2.0	3.4	1.8	4.6	4.3	0.3	0.0	0.0	0.0	0.0
Franklin	47 286	97.8	40.1	24.1	26.2	20.0	3.9	1.7	3.4	1.8	2.2	0.2	0.5	0.0	1.5	0.0	0.1
Frederick	59 209	98.7	37.3	23.3	30.1	24.1	3.7	1.5	4.3	2.2	1.3	0.5	0.5	0.2	0.0	0.0	0.2
Giles	16 657	99.4	42.0	23.6	26.4	19.8	4.2	1.7	3.2	1.9	0.6	0.0	0.4	0.0	0.0	0.0	0.2
Gloucester	34 780	99.0	37.7	23.2	30.0	23.8	4.2	1.9	3.9	1.8	1.0	0.0	0.8	0.0	0.0	0.0	0.2
Goochland	16 863	91.8	36.5	23.6	24.4	18.5	4.5	1.9	2.8	1.4	8.2	6.4	0.5	0.7	0.0	0.0	0.7
Grayson	17 917	93.5	40.5	23.3	23.5	17.8	3.4	1.3	2.8	1.6	6.5	5.8	0.7	0.1	0.0	0.0	0.0
Greene	15 244	99.0	36.6	22.6	31.1	25.1	4.5	1.8	4.2	2.2	1.0	0.0	0.7	0.0	0.0	0.0	0.3
Greensville	11 560	73.4	29.2	14.6	20.4	14.0	6.3	3.5	3.0	1.7	26.6	26.2	0.0	0.0	0.0	0.0	0.4
Halifax	37 355	97.5	40.2	20.6	27.5	19.9	6.6	3.1	2.6	1.3	2.5	1.0	1.1	0.0	0.0	0.0	0.3
Hanover	86 320	97.5	36.1	23.9	31.0	25.0	3.7	1.4	2.8	1.2	2.5	0.6	0.3	0.2	1.1	0.0	0.2
Henrico	262 300	98.5	41.2	19.9	28.2	22.6	4.4	1.6	4.9	1.9	1.5	0.2	1.1	0.0	0.0	0.0	0.1
Henry	57 930	99.2	41.3	22.4	26.5	19.3	5.6	2.6	3.4	1.8	0.8	0.4	0.2	0.0	0.0	0.0	0.1
Highland	2 536	100.0	44.6	25.4	23.8	18.5	3.4	1.2	2.8	1.9	0.0	0.0	0.0	0.0	0.0	0.0	0.0
Isle of Wight	29 728	99.4	38.1	23.0	29.9	22.5	5.3	2.5	3.1	1.4	0.6	0.0	0.4	0.0	0.0	0.0	0.2
James City County	48 102	97.4	39.5	24.4	26.3	21.4	3.4	1.5	3.8	1.5	2.6	1.0	0.1	1.0	0.0	0.0	0.5
King and Queen	6 630	100.0	40.3	21.2	26.8	18.5	7.4	3.6	4.3	2.2	0.0	0.0	0.0	0.0	0.0	0.0	0.0
King George	16 803	97.9	36.2	21.6	31.1	25.1	4.4	1.9	4.6	2.1	2.1	0.0	0.7	0.0	0.0	1.4	0.0
King William	13 146	99.2	36.9	23.6	30.0	23.0	5.8	2.6	3.1	1.5	0.8	0.0	0.4	0.0	0.0	0.0	0.3
Lancaster	11 567	96.4	43.3	23.6	22.0	16.3	4.7	2.3	2.8	1.5	3.6	0.2	2.9	0.0	0.0	0.0	0.5
Lee	23 589	99.0	41.1	22.6	28.2	20.1	4.7	2.1	2.4	1.3	1.0	0.2	0.2	0.0	0.0	0.0	0.6
Loudoun	169 599	99.5	35.3	22.7	32.8	28.2	4.0	1.2	4.7	1.6	0.5	0.1	0.3	0.1	0.0	0.0	0.1

Table B. States and Counties

STATE County	Total households (71)	Family households Total (72)	With own children under 18 years (73)	Married couple Total (74)	With own children under 18 years (75)	Female householder[1] Total (76)	With own children under 18 years (77)	Nonfamily households Total (78)	Householder living alone Total (79)	65 years and over (80)	Average household size (81)	Average family size (82)	Households, 1990 Total households (83)	Female householder[1] (84)	Householder living alone (85)
VERMONT—Cont'd															
Chittenden	56 452	62.3	32.1	50.3	24.3	8.7	5.8	37.7	26.1	7.3	2.47	3.02	48 439	8.9	23.0
Essex	2 602	69.4	31.8	56.1	23.4	8.3	5.3	30.6	24.1	11.5	2.47	2.92	2 344	8.1	21.4
Franklin	16 765	72.7	37.7	58.4	28.0	9.9	6.7	27.3	20.6	8.4	2.67	3.08	14 326	9.8	19.8
Grand Isle	2 761	70.8	31.2	60.1	24.6	7.1	4.1	29.2	22.2	8.2	2.50	2.93	2 018	7.5	19.9
Lamoille	9 221	64.9	32.0	51.4	22.8	8.9	6.0	35.1	25.0	8.1	2.45	2.94	7 397	8.5	23.5
Orange	10 936	69.6	33.4	56.1	24.4	8.9	6.1	30.4	23.4	9.2	2.52	2.97	9 455	8.9	20.1
Orleans	10 446	68.5	32.1	54.4	22.5	9.6	6.7	31.5	25.2	10.9	2.45	2.91	8 873	9.1	21.2
Rutland	25 678	65.2	29.8	51.3	21.4	10.1	6.2	34.8	27.9	11.2	2.39	2.92	23 690	9.6	24.6
Washington	23 659	63.6	31.0	50.6	22.2	9.2	6.4	36.4	28.5	10.2	2.36	2.91	20 948	9.2	26.2
Windham	18 375	62.3	29.9	49.2	20.9	9.6	6.7	37.7	29.7	10.2	2.35	2.91	16 264	9.7	25.7
Windsor	24 162	65.1	29.2	52.7	21.2	9.0	5.8	34.9	28.1	11.1	2.35	2.86	21 523	8.7	25.1
VIRGINIA	2 699 173	68.5	32.7	52.8	23.9	11.9	6.9	31.5	25.1	8.0	2.54	3.04	2 291 830	11.1	22.9
Accomack	15 299	67.9	28.9	49.2	18.4	14.4	8.1	32.1	27.7	12.5	2.45	2.96	12 653	13.1	27.4
Albemarle	31 876	66.1	32.0	54.2	24.8	9.1	5.7	33.9	27.0	8.0	2.44	2.99	24 433	8.6	23.0
Alleghany	5 149	75.1	29.9	63.2	23.7	8.3	4.2	24.9	22.2	10.5	2.46	2.85	4 942	7.9	20.3
Amelia	4 240	74.9	32.8	59.1	25.3	11.4	5.2	25.1	20.7	8.1	2.66	3.07	3 131	10.2	19.9
Amherst	11 941	72.4	31.7	56.0	22.6	12.4	7.0	27.6	24.0	9.9	2.51	2.95	9 827	10.9	19.5
Appomattox	5 322	75.4	32.2	59.7	23.9	11.5	6.2	24.6	21.3	10.0	2.55	2.94	4 531	10.9	19.3
Arlington	86 352	45.5	19.3	35.3	14.8	7.0	3.4	54.5	40.8	7.3	2.15	2.96	78 520	7.6	39.3
Augusta	24 818	76.2	33.0	63.7	26.2	8.6	4.8	23.8	20.1	8.1	2.56	2.94	19 781	8.0	18.2
Bath	2 053	70.7	28.0	58.6	21.5	7.8	4.1	29.3	26.3	12.1	2.34	2.80	1 895	7.9	24.2
Bedford	23 838	76.2	32.5	65.4	26.4	7.5	4.1	23.8	20.2	7.3	2.52	2.89	17 292	6.4	18.2
Bland	2 568	74.3	28.3	62.4	22.8	8.7	4.1	25.7	23.3	10.3	2.43	2.85	2 244	8.5	20.9
Botetourt	11 700	77.9	32.4	67.8	27.6	7.0	3.2	22.1	19.2	7.6	2.56	2.92	9 148	7.3	17.9
Brunswick	6 277	68.7	27.4	46.9	16.9	16.6	8.3	31.3	27.6	13.3	2.47	3.00	5 499	14.6	25.7
Buchanan	10 464	75.5	30.6	60.9	24.4	10.6	4.7	24.5	22.5	9.4	2.46	2.87	11 001	9.3	16.6
Buckingham	5 324	70.6	30.4	51.1	19.9	14.2	8.0	29.4	25.1	11.4	2.52	2.99	4 341	12.7	23.0
Campbell	20 639	71.2	30.8	56.0	22.5	11.4	6.4	28.8	24.6	8.8	2.45	2.91	17 952	10.0	19.9
Caroline	8 021	74.9	31.7	56.3	22.6	13.2	6.4	25.1	20.5	8.2	2.69	3.08	6 631	12.9	18.7
Carroll	12 186	72.1	27.8	59.7	21.6	8.6	4.4	27.9	25.4	12.2	2.36	2.80	10 463	9.1	21.2
Charles City County	2 670	74.0	27.5	53.6	18.8	15.2	6.1	26.0	22.5	8.4	2.59	3.02	2 161	14.7	16.9
Charlotte	4 951	69.4	28.1	52.5	20.2	13.0	6.2	30.6	27.4	13.3	2.47	3.00	4 312	12.3	23.0
Chesterfield	93 772	76.9	40.7	62.2	31.6	11.2	7.1	23.1	18.5	4.8	2.73	3.11	73 441	9.7	16.4
Clarke	4 942	71.1	29.4	58.2	23.0	8.9	4.1	28.9	24.1	9.9	2.50	2.97	4 236	9.7	18.8
Craig	2 060	73.2	30.8	61.9	25.3	7.0	3.2	26.8	23.9	10.5	2.45	2.88	1 676	7.3	19.0
Culpeper	12 141	74.5	35.0	58.5	26.0	11.3	6.2	25.5	20.6	7.9	2.68	3.08	9 757	10.0	19.0
Cumberland	3 528	70.5	30.0	51.6	20.4	14.3	7.7	29.5	24.8	10.7	2.55	3.03	2 813	12.6	22.2
Dickenson	6 732	72.6	30.4	58.0	23.5	10.6	5.2	27.4	25.3	11.3	2.42	2.88	6 457	10.8	19.7
Dinwiddie	9 107	73.8	32.1	54.8	22.5	13.9	7.0	26.2	22.2	8.5	2.58	3.01	7 492	12.9	18.8
Essex	3 995	68.6	28.0	50.7	19.0	14.0	7.1	31.4	26.1	11.3	2.46	2.95	3 258	11.3	24.8
Fairfax	350 714	71.4	36.3	59.4	30.1	8.6	4.8	28.6	21.4	4.8	2.74	3.20	292 345	8.4	18.7
Fauquier	19 842	76.3	36.1	63.8	29.8	8.6	4.4	23.7	18.7	6.2	2.75	3.14	16 509	7.7	15.3
Floyd	5 791	71.8	29.1	59.9	22.7	8.1	4.4	28.2	24.7	10.8	2.39	2.83	4 763	8.1	23.0
Fluvanna	7 387	77.2	32.5	63.6	25.2	9.9	5.4	22.8	18.8	7.0	2.59	2.93	4 518	10.1	18.5
Franklin	18 963	73.4	29.1	60.1	22.0	9.4	5.1	26.6	22.6	8.9	2.44	2.84	14 655	8.9	20.0
Frederick	22 097	75.7	36.6	62.5	28.6	8.8	5.3	24.3	19.2	6.8	2.64	3.02	16 470	7.9	16.6
Giles	6 994	69.9	28.1	56.1	21.4	9.7	4.8	30.1	26.6	12.8	2.37	2.85	6 461	10.4	22.9
Gloucester	13 127	75.3	35.2	61.4	27.3	9.9	5.7	24.7	20.3	8.2	2.62	3.02	10 966	8.2	19.0
Goochland	6 158	76.5	29.9	64.6	24.4	8.4	3.9	23.5	19.9	7.4	2.51	2.88	4 880	9.4	17.1
Grayson	7 259	70.1	26.4	57.6	20.7	8.5	3.8	29.9	26.8	12.9	2.31	2.77	6 468	9.3	22.5
Greene	5 574	77.0	38.3	61.9	29.2	10.4	6.1	23.0	18.0	5.3	2.71	3.07	3 749	9.9	17.5
Greensville	3 375	71.0	29.3	49.8	18.7	16.0	7.9	29.0	25.4	11.3	2.51	2.99	3 150	15.5	20.9
Halifax	15 018	70.0	28.6	51.2	19.6	14.8	7.3	30.0	27.4	13.1	2.43	2.94	10 728	13.3	22.0
Hanover	31 121	78.6	39.5	66.4	32.7	9.3	5.3	21.4	17.7	6.8	2.71	3.07	22 628	8.0	16.5
Henrico	108 121	64.6	31.9	48.3	22.3	13.1	8.1	35.4	28.9	8.5	2.39	2.97	89 138	11.8	26.6
Henry	23 910	70.9	28.6	54.3	19.9	12.2	6.5	29.1	25.8	10.3	2.40	2.87	21 771	11.7	20.7
Highland	1 131	67.6	24.0	56.9	19.5	7.1	3.2	32.4	29.1	15.6	2.24	2.74	1 081	6.4	25.3
Isle of Wight	11 319	76.6	34.0	60.4	25.5	12.2	6.6	23.4	20.0	8.6	2.61	2.99	9 032	12.3	18.6
James City County	19 003	73.6	30.5	61.8	23.4	8.9	5.4	26.4	21.4	9.0	2.47	2.86	12 968	9.4	19.6
King and Queen	2 673	71.0	26.8	52.6	19.5	13.5	5.4	29.0	24.6	11.0	2.48	2.94	2 339	13.5	22.0
King George	6 091	74.3	38.0	59.5	28.9	10.5	6.7	25.7	20.4	6.0	2.70	3.12	4 736	9.3	19.7
King William	4 846	78.1	36.4	63.9	29.2	10.2	5.3	21.9	18.3	7.6	2.69	3.06	3 834	10.5	19.0
Lancaster	5 004	68.2	21.2	54.7	13.9	11.1	6.3	31.8	28.7	16.8	2.23	2.71	4 564	10.3	26.3
Lee	9 706	70.6	29.0	55.0	21.7	11.7	5.4	29.4	27.0	12.1	2.41	2.91	9 231	11.6	22.4
Loudoun	59 900	75.2	43.1	64.3	36.6	7.8	4.9	24.8	18.4	3.7	2.82	3.24	30 490	7.9	16.8

[1] No spouse present.

Table B. States and Counties

STATE County	Percent change of households, 1990–2000	Total housing units	Occupied housing units (percent)	Vacant housing units — Total	For seasonal, recreational, or occasional use	Homeowner vacancy rate (percent)	Rental vacancy rate (percent)	Occupied housing units — Total	Percent owner-occupied housing units	Percent renter-occupied housing units	Average household size of owner-occupied units	Average household size of renter-occupied units
	86	87	88	89	90	91	92	93	94	95	96	97

Housing occupancy, 2000 | Housing tenure, 2000

STATE County	86	87	88	89	90	91	92	93	94	95	96	97
VERMONT—Cont'd												
Chittenden	16.5	50 864	95.9	4.1	2.2	0.5	1.8	56 452	66.1	33.9	2.66	2.08
Essex	11.0	4 762	54.6	45.4	30.7	5.4	10.0	2 602	79.5	20.5	2.51	2.34
Franklin	17.0	19 191	87.4	12.6	10.1	1.1	3.1	16 765	75.0	25.0	2.77	2.37
Grand Isle	36.8	4 663	59.2	40.8	37.1	2.3	6.4	2 761	81.4	18.6	2.55	2.20
Lamoille	24.7	11 009	83.8	16.2	13.0	1.0	3.6	9 221	70.9	29.1	2.60	2.10
Orange	15.7	13 386	81.7	18.3	13.8	1.5	8.0	10 936	78.3	21.7	2.59	2.26
Orleans	17.7	14 673	71.2	28.8	23.2	2.4	9.4	10 446	74.1	25.9	2.53	2.21
Rutland	8.4	32 311	79.5	20.5	16.4	1.6	4.9	25 678	69.7	30.3	2.52	2.09
Washington	12.9	27 644	85.6	14.4	11.2	1.0	3.5	23 659	68.5	31.5	2.55	1.96
Windham	13.0	27 039	68.0	32.0	27.8	2.3	5.1	18 375	67.9	32.1	2.49	2.04
Windsor	12.3	31 621	76.4	23.6	19.7	1.6	5.1	24 162	71.5	28.5	2.46	2.06
VIRGINIA	17.8	2 904 192	92.9	7.1	1.9	1.5	5.2	2 699 173	68.1	31.9	2.62	2.36
Accomack	20.9	19 550	78.3	21.7	13.2	1.8	6.5	15 299	75.1	24.9	2.36	2.72
Albemarle	30.5	33 720	94.5	5.5	1.3	1.2	4.0	31 876	65.9	34.1	2.61	2.10
Alleghany	4.2	5 812	88.6	11.4	3.8	1.1	6.1	5 149	84.9	15.1	2.48	2.37
Amelia	35.4	4 609	92.0	8.0	1.4	0.8	5.7	4 240	81.9	18.1	2.68	2.59
Amherst	21.5	12 958	92.2	7.8	1.4	1.6	4.9	11 941	78.1	21.9	2.57	2.27
Appomattox	17.5	5 828	91.3	8.7	1.8	1.8	8.6	5 322	81.1	18.9	2.56	2.50
Arlington	10.0	90 426	95.5	4.5	1.7	0.7	2.4	86 352	43.3	56.7	2.26	2.06
Augusta	25.5	26 738	92.8	7.2	1.7	1.7	5.9	24 818	83.1	16.9	2.59	2.41
Bath	8.3	2 896	70.9	29.1	23.6	0.7	4.6	2 053	79.9	20.1	2.35	2.31
Bedford	37.9	26 841	88.8	11.2	4.7	1.5	8.0	23 838	86.6	13.4	2.55	2.28
Bland	14.4	3 161	81.2	18.8	9.9	2.0	7.8	2 568	86.1	13.9	2.48	2.11
Botetourt	27.9	12 571	93.1	6.9	2.4	1.2	5.0	11 700	87.8	12.2	2.59	2.32
Brunswick	14.1	7 541	83.2	16.8	5.5	1.7	3.8	6 277	77.6	22.4	2.45	2.55
Buchanan	-5.4	11 887	88.0	12.0	0.7	2.3	13.6	10 464	82.9	17.1	2.50	2.28
Buckingham	22.6	6 290	84.6	15.4	4.4	1.8	5.0	5 324	77.8	22.2	2.55	2.43
Campbell	15.0	22 088	93.4	6.6	0.6	1.6	7.0	20 639	77.3	22.7	2.52	2.22
Caroline	21.0	8 889	90.2	9.8	3.1	2.0	6.0	8 021	81.9	18.1	2.69	2.65
Carroll	16.5	14 680	83.0	17.0	8.8	1.5	8.5	12 186	81.7	18.3	2.37	2.29
Charles City County	23.6	2 895	92.2	7.8	1.9	0.9	3.8	2 670	84.9	15.1	2.61	2.51
Charlotte	14.8	5 734	86.3	13.7	2.9	2.7	6.6	4 951	77.6	22.4	2.50	2.39
Chesterfield	27.7	97 707	96.0	4.0	0.3	1.3	8.3	93 772	80.9	19.1	2.78	2.49
Clarke	16.7	5 388	91.7	8.3	3.2	1.5	3.8	4 942	75.6	24.4	2.58	2.24
Craig	22.9	2 554	80.7	19.3	12.9	1.6	6.1	2 060	81.2	18.8	2.51	2.18
Culpeper	24.4	12 871	94.3	5.7	1.1	1.5	2.9	12 141	70.5	29.5	2.73	2.57
Cumberland	25.4	4 085	86.4	13.6	3.5	1.6	5.1	3 528	77.2	22.8	2.58	2.45
Dickenson	4.3	7 684	87.6	12.4	1.5	1.8	9.7	6 732	82.1	17.9	2.46	2.23
Dinwiddie	21.6	9 707	93.8	6.2	0.6	1.1	6.7	9 107	79.2	20.8	2.59	2.58
Essex	22.6	4 926	81.1	18.9	11.0	1.6	3.4	3 995	77.3	22.7	2.49	2.35
Fairfax	20.0	359 411	97.6	2.4	0.6	0.6	2.3	350 714	70.9	29.1	2.80	2.58
Fauquier	20.2	21 046	94.3	5.7	1.5	1.1	3.8	19 842	76.2	23.8	2.83	2.50
Floyd	21.6	6 763	85.6	14.4	6.2	1.0	6.1	5 791	81.9	18.1	2.42	2.25
Fluvanna	63.5	8 018	92.1	7.9	2.7	1.4	4.0	7 387	85.2	14.8	2.58	2.61
Franklin	29.4	22 717	83.5	16.5	11.4	1.5	6.3	18 963	81.1	18.9	2.47	2.30
Frederick	34.2	23 319	94.8	5.2	1.5	1.6	4.7	22 097	80.3	19.7	2.67	2.54
Giles	8.2	7 732	90.5	9.5	2.9	1.3	6.7	6 994	79.1	20.9	2.41	2.22
Gloucester	19.7	14 494	90.6	9.4	3.2	1.6	5.5	13 127	81.4	18.6	2.66	2.46
Goochland	26.2	6 555	93.9	6.1	1.4	0.9	4.6	6 158	86.6	13.4	2.54	2.33
Grayson	12.2	9 123	79.6	20.4	12.0	1.5	9.2	7 259	81.4	18.6	2.32	2.25
Greene	48.7	5 986	93.1	6.9	3.7	1.0	3.8	5 574	81.4	18.6	2.73	2.62
Greensville	7.1	3 765	89.6	10.4	1.6	0.9	3.9	3 375	78.3	21.7	2.52	2.48
Halifax	40.0	16 953	88.6	11.4	1.8	1.7	7.7	15 018	76.1	23.9	2.46	2.32
Hanover	37.5	32 196	96.7	3.3	0.2	1.0	4.9	31 121	84.3	15.7	2.78	2.32
Henrico	21.3	112 570	96.0	4.0	0.4	1.1	5.1	108 121	65.7	34.3	2.54	2.11
Henry	9.8	25 921	92.2	7.8	0.6	1.7	11.5	23 910	76.9	23.1	2.43	2.32
Highland	4.6	1 822	62.1	37.9	30.2	2.4	9.9	1 131	83.8	16.2	2.28	2.07
Isle of Wight	25.3	12 066	93.8	6.2	0.9	1.4	5.5	11 319	80.8	19.2	2.65	2.46
James City County	46.5	20 772	91.5	8.5	1.7	2.3	11.2	19 003	77.0	23.0	2.56	2.15
King and Queen	14.3	3 010	88.8	11.2	3.0	1.0	2.5	2 673	82.5	17.5	2.47	2.52
King George	28.6	6 820	89.3	10.7	3.4	1.7	6.8	6 091	71.8	28.2	2.72	2.65
King William	26.4	5 189	93.4	6.6	1.6	1.2	4.3	4 846	85.0	15.0	2.73	2.50
Lancaster	9.6	6 498	77.0	23.0	14.5	1.8	6.7	5 004	83.0	17.0	2.22	2.28
Lee	5.1	11 086	87.6	12.4	1.2	2.5	10.2	9 706	74.4	25.6	2.42	2.36
Loudoun	96.5	62 160	96.4	3.6	0.6	1.1	3.4	59 900	79.4	20.6	2.92	2.42

Table B. States and Counties

STATE/County code	MSA/PMSA/NECMA code[1]	County type[2]	STATE County	Population, 2000 Land area, 2000[3] (sq km)	Population, 2000 Total persons	Population, 2000 Rank	Population, 2000 Per square kilometer	Population, 1990 Land area, 1990[3] (sq km)	Population, 1990 Total persons	Population, 1990 Rank	Population, 1990 Per square kilometer	Race (percent) One race White	Race (percent) One race Black or African American	Race (percent) One race American Indian or Alaska Native	Race (percent) One race Asian	Race (percent) One race Native Hawaiian and other Pacific Islander	Race (percent) One race Some other race
				1	2	3	4	5	6	7	8	9	10	11	12	13	14
			VIRGINIA—Cont'd														
51 109	...	8	Louisa	1 288	25 627	1 529	19.9	1 289	20 325	1 659	15.8	76.5	21.6	0.4	0.2	0.0	0.2
51 111	...	9	Lunenburg	1 118	13 146	2 216	11.8	1 118	11 419	2 260	10.2	59.1	38.6	0.2	0.2	0.0	0.7
51 113	...	8	Madison	832	12 520	2 263	15.0	833	11 949	2 224	14.3	86.7	11.4	0.1	0.5	0.0	0.3
51 115	5720	1	Mathews	222	9 207	2 512	41.5	222	8 348	2 529	37.6	87.3	11.3	0.2	0.2	0.0	0.3
51 117	...	7	Mecklenburg	1 616	32 380	1 337	20.0	1 616	29 241	1 322	18.1	59.2	39.1	0.2	0.3	0.0	0.5
51 119	...	8	Middlesex	337	9 932	2 453	29.5	337	8 653	2 495	25.7	78.5	20.1	0.3	0.1	0.0	0.4
51 121	...	4	Montgomery	1 005	83 629	621	83.2	1 006	73 913	609	73.5	90.0	3.7	0.2	4.0	0.0	0.6
51 125	...	8	Nelson	1 223	14 445	2 126	11.8	1 223	12 778	2 158	10.4	82.7	14.9	0.2	0.2	0.1	0.6
51 127	6760	2	New Kent	543	13 462	2 196	24.8	543	10 466	2 340	19.3	80.3	16.2	1.3	0.5	0.0	0.5
51 131	...	9	Northampton	537	13 093	2 222	24.4	537	13 061	2 135	24.3	53.3	43.0	0.2	0.2	0.0	2.1
51 133	...	9	Northumberland	498	12 259	2 281	24.6	498	10 524	2 334	21.1	72.2	26.6	0.1	0.2	0.0	0.3
51 135	...	6	Nottoway	815	15 725	2 037	19.3	815	14 993	1 987	18.4	57.2	40.6	0.1	0.4	0.0	1.0
51 137	...	6	Orange	885	25 881	1 522	29.2	885	21 421	1 609	24.2	84.4	13.8	0.2	0.3	0.0	0.4
51 139	...	6	Page	806	23 177	1 635	28.8	806	21 690	1 593	26.9	96.3	2.2	0.1	0.2	0.0	0.5
51 141	...	9	Patrick	1 251	19 407	1 823	15.5	1 251	17 473	1 822	14.0	91.7	6.2	0.2	0.2	0.0	0.9
51 143	1950	3	Pittsylvania	2 514	61 745	787	24.6	2 515	55 672	778	22.1	75.0	23.7	0.1	0.2	0.0	0.4
51 145	6760	2	Powhatan	677	22 377	1 675	33.1	677	15 328	1 969	22.6	81.5	16.9	0.2	0.2	0.0	0.3
51 147	...	7	Prince Edward	914	19 720	1 808	21.6	914	17 320	1 831	18.9	62.2	35.8	0.2	0.5	0.1	0.2
51 149	6760	2	Prince George	688	33 047	1 318	48.0	688	27 390	1 379	39.8	60.9	32.5	0.4	1.7	0.2	2.2
51 153	8840	0	Prince William	875	280 813	200	320.9	877	214 954	232	245.1	68.9	18.8	0.4	3.8	0.1	4.3
51 155	...	7	Pulaski	830	35 127	1 245	42.3	830	34 496	1 151	41.6	92.6	5.6	0.2	0.3	0.0	0.4
51 157	...	8	Rappahannock	690	6 983	2 687	10.1	690	6 622	2 694	9.6	92.6	5.4	0.2	0.2	0.0	0.4
51 159	...	9	Richmond	496	8 809	2 545	17.8	496	7 273	2 629	14.7	64.8	33.2	0.1	0.3	0.1	0.9
51 161	6800	3	Roanoke	650	85 778	610	132.0	649	79 278	574	122.2	93.6	3.4	0.1	1.6	0.0	0.4
51 163	...	6	Rockbridge	1 553	20 808	1 748	13.4	1 553	18 350	1 773	11.8	95.4	3.0	0.3	0.4	0.0	0.1
51 165	...	5	Rockingham	2 204	67 725	724	30.7	2 205	57 482	760	26.1	96.6	1.4	0.1	0.3	0.0	0.9
51 167	...	6	Russell	1 229	30 308	1 390	24.7	1 229	28 667	1 340	23.3	96.1	3.1	0.1	0.0	0.0	0.3
51 169	3660	2	Scott	1 390	23 403	1 623	16.8	1 390	23 204	1 530	16.7	98.5	0.6	0.1	0.1	0.0	0.1
51 171	...	6	Shenandoah	1 327	35 075	1 248	26.4	1 327	31 636	1 227	23.8	95.6	1.2	0.2	0.3	0.0	1.8
51 173	...	6	Smyth	1 171	33 081	1 316	28.3	1 171	32 370	1 203	27.6	96.9	1.9	0.2	0.2	0.0	0.3
51 175	...	6	Southampton	1 553	17 482	1 925	11.3	1 555	17 022	1 849	10.9	56.0	42.9	0.2	0.2	0.0	0.3
51 177	8840	0	Spotsylvania	1 038	90 395	570	87.1	1 038	57 397	761	55.3	82.9	12.5	0.3	1.4	0.0	1.0
51 179	8840	1	Stafford	700	92 446	552	132.1	699	62 255	699	89.1	82.0	12.1	0.5	1.6	0.1	1.2
51 181	...	8	Surry	723	6 829	2 708	9.4	723	6 145	2 738	8.5	46.9	51.6	0.2	0.1	0.0	0.2
51 183	...	8	Sussex	1 271	12 504	2 264	9.8	1 271	10 248	2 364	8.1	36.4	62.1	0.1	0.1	0.0	0.5
51 185	...	7	Tazewell	1 346	44 598	1 006	33.1	1 346	45 960	903	34.1	96.2	2.3	0.2	0.6	0.0	0.2
51 187	8840	1	Warren	553	31 584	1 358	57.1	554	26 142	1 416	47.2	92.7	4.8	0.3	0.4	0.0	0.5
51 191	3660	2	Washington	1 458	51 103	906	35.1	1 461	45 887	905	31.4	97.6	1.3	0.1	0.3	0.0	0.1
51 193	...	6	Westmoreland	594	16 718	1 974	28.1	594	15 480	1 956	26.1	65.4	30.9	0.3	0.4	0.0	1.7
51 195	...	7	Wise	1 046	40 123	1 111	38.4	1 045	39 573	1 009	37.9	96.9	1.8	0.2	0.3	0.0	0.3
51 197	...	7	Wythe	1 200	27 599	1 463	23.0	1 200	25 471	1 449	21.2	95.8	2.9	0.2	0.4	0.0	0.2
51 199	5720	0	York	274	56 297	840	205.5	274	42 434	949	154.9	80.0	13.4	0.3	3.2	0.1	0.9
			Independent Cities														
51 510	8840	NA	Alexandria City	39	128 283	421	3 289.3	40	111 183	413	2 779.6	59.8	22.5	0.3	5.7	0.1	7.4
51 515	4640	NA	Bedford City	18	6 299	2 757	349.9	18	6 176	2 735	343.1	75.3	22.4	0.2	0.6	0.1	0.2
51 520	3660	NA	Bristol City	33	17 367	1 932	526.3	30	18 426	1 767	614.2	92.5	5.6	0.2	0.4	0.0	0.2
51 530	...	NA	Buena Vista City	18	6 349	2 751	352.7	18	6 406	2 716	355.9	93.6	4.8	0.3	0.4	0.0	0.1
51 540	1540	NA	Charlottesville City	27	45 049	997	1 668.5	27	40 470	987	1 498.9	69.6	22.2	0.1	4.9	0.0	1.0
51 550	5720	NA	Chesapeake City	882	199 184	278	225.8	882	151 982	307	172.3	66.9	28.5	0.4	1.8	0.1	0.7
51 560	...	NA	Clifton Forge City	8	4 289	2 897	536.1	8	4 679	2 862	584.9	83.0	14.6	0.1	0.0	0.0	0.5
51 570	6760	NA	Colonial Heights City	19	16 897	1 960	889.3	19	16 064	1 920	845.5	89.1	6.3	0.2	2.7	0.1	0.6
51 580	...	NA	Covington City	15	6 303	2 756	420.2	11	7 352	2 625	668.4	84.1	13.1	0.3	0.7	0.0	0.2
51 590	1950	NA	Danville City	112	48 411	942	432.2	112	53 056	803	473.7	53.9	44.1	0.2	0.6	0.0	0.5
51 595	...	NA	Emporia City	18	5 665	2 810	314.7	18	5 556	2 795	308.7	42.5	56.2	0.1	0.5	0.1	0.3
51 600	8840	NA	Fairfax City	16	21 498	1 715	1 343.6	16	19 945	1 682	1 246.6	72.9	5.1	0.3	12.2	0.1	6.2
51 610	8840	NA	Falls Church City	5	10 377	2 406	2 075.4	5	9 464	2 438	1 892.8	85.0	3.3	0.2	6.5	0.1	2.5
51 620	...	NA	Franklin City	22	8 346	2 577	379.4	20	8 392	2 521	419.6	45.7	52.3	0.1	0.8	0.0	0.2
51 630	8840	NA	Fredericksburg City	27	19 279	1 829	714.0	27	19 033	1 733	704.9	73.2	20.4	0.3	1.5	0.1	2.6
51 640	...	NA	Galax City	21	6 837	2 706	325.6	21	6 745	2 682	321.2	86.1	6.3	0.5	0.7	0.0	5.5
51 650	5720	NA	Hampton City	134	146 437	374	1 092.8	134	133 773	347	998.3	49.5	44.7	0.4	1.8	0.1	1.0
51 660	...	NA	Harrisonburg City	45	40 468	1 104	899.3	45	30 707	1 258	682.4	84.8	5.9	0.2	3.1	0.0	3.3
51 670	6760	NA	Hopewell City	27	22 354	1 676	827.9	27	23 101	1 533	855.6	62.3	33.5	0.4	0.8	0.1	1.2
51 678	...	NA	Lexington City	6	6 867	2 701	1 144.5	6	6 959	2 664	1 159.8	86.0	10.4	0.3	1.9	0.0	0.5
51 680	4640	NA	Lynchburg City	128	65 269	747	509.9	128	66 120	661	516.6	66.6	29.7	0.3	1.3	0.0	0.6

[1] MSA = Metropolitan Statistical Area. PMSA = Primary MSA. NECMA = New England County Metropolitan Area. See Appendix A for explanation of these concepts. See Appendix B for list of metropolitan areas identified by type, with component counties.
[2] County typology code from the Economic Research Service of USDA. See Appendix A for definition.
[3] Dry land or land partially or temporarily covered by water.

Table B. States and Counties

STATE County	Population and population characteristics, 2000 (cont'd) Race (percent) (cont'd) Race alone or in combination								Population and population characteristics, 1990 Race (percent)				
	Two or more races	White	Black	American Indian or Alaska Native	Asian	Native Hawaiian and other Pacific Islander	Some other race	Hispanic[1]	White	Black or African American	American Indian or Alaska Native	Asian and Pacific Islander	Hispanic[1]
	15	16	17	18	19	20	21	22	23	24	25	26	27
VIRGINIA—Cont'd													
Louisa	1.0	77.4	22.2	0.9	0.3	0.0	0.3	0.7	73.7	25.7	0.3	0.2	0.5
Lunenburg	1.1	60.0	39.2	0.6	0.4	0.1	1.0	1.8	62.0	37.6	0.1	0.2	0.7
Madison	0.9	87.6	11.9	0.4	0.7	0.1	0.4	0.8	85.2	14.2	0.2	0.2	0.3
Mathews	0.7	87.8	11.5	0.6	0.3	0.1	0.4	0.8	85.5	14.1	0.1	0.2	0.6
Mecklenburg	0.7	59.7	39.4	0.5	0.4	0.0	0.6	1.2	61.3	38.4	0.1	0.2	0.4
Middlesex	0.6	79.0	20.4	0.5	0.2	0.0	0.5	0.6	75.2	24.6	0.1	0.1	0.6
Montgomery	1.5	91.3	4.0	0.5	4.5	0.1	1.2	1.6	92.0	3.8	0.1	3.8	1.1
Nelson	1.3	83.7	15.6	1.0	0.4	0.1	0.9	2.1	80.2	18.8	0.1	0.2	0.9
New Kent	1.2	81.2	16.6	1.9	0.7	0.0	0.8	1.3	77.3	20.6	1.3	0.3	0.7
Northampton	1.2	54.2	43.5	0.4	0.3	0.1	2.6	3.5	52.7	46.2	0.1	0.1	2.0
Northumberland	0.6	72.6	27.0	0.4	0.2	0.0	0.4	0.9	70.2	29.4	0.1	0.2	0.5
Nottoway	0.7	57.7	40.9	0.4	0.5	0.1	1.2	1.6	58.3	41.1	0.2	0.3	0.6
Orange	0.9	85.2	14.2	0.5	0.5	0.1	0.5	1.3	85.1	14.4	0.1	0.2	0.7
Page	0.7	96.9	2.3	0.5	0.4	0.0	0.6	1.1	97.5	2.0	0.1	0.3	0.5
Patrick	0.7	92.4	6.5	0.5	0.3	0.1	1.1	1.9	92.3	7.2	0.1	0.1	0.7
Pittsylvania	0.6	75.5	23.9	0.4	0.3	0.0	0.5	1.2	72.9	26.8	0.1	0.1	0.4
Powhatan	0.8	82.2	17.2	0.6	0.3	0.0	0.5	0.8	78.0	21.5	0.2	0.2	0.4
Prince Edward	1.0	62.9	36.3	0.5	0.8	0.2	0.4	0.9	63.1	36.2	0.2	0.4	0.7
Prince George	2.0	62.4	33.5	0.8	2.3	0.3	2.9	4.9	66.7	29.1	0.4	2.2	3.9
Prince William	3.6	71.8	20.1	1.0	4.9	0.3	5.8	9.7	83.3	11.6	0.3	3.0	4.5
Pulaski	0.9	93.5	5.9	0.6	0.4	0.0	0.6	1.0	93.8	5.8	0.1	0.2	0.4
Rappahannock	1.1	93.7	5.9	0.7	0.4	0.0	0.5	1.3	92.0	7.4	0.2	0.2	1.0
Richmond	0.7	65.4	33.4	0.4	0.5	0.1	1.0	2.1	69.1	30.2	0.1	0.3	0.7
Roanoke	0.9	94.4	3.6	0.4	1.8	0.0	0.6	1.0	96.5	2.5	0.1	0.8	0.6
Rockbridge	0.8	96.2	3.2	0.6	0.6	0.0	0.2	0.6	96.3	3.1	0.2	0.3	0.3
Rockingham	0.7	97.3	1.6	0.3	0.4	0.0	1.2	3.3	97.7	1.5	0.1	0.2	0.9
Russell	0.4	96.5	3.2	0.3	0.1	0.0	0.4	0.8	98.8	1.1	0.0	0.1	0.3
Scott	0.5	99.0	0.7	0.5	0.2	0.0	0.2	0.4	99.3	0.6	0.1	0.0	0.3
Shenandoah	0.9	96.4	1.4	0.6	0.5	0.1	2.0	3.4	98.2	1.1	0.1	0.3	0.9
Smyth	0.6	97.4	2.1	0.5	0.3	0.1	0.4	0.9	97.6	2.0	0.1	0.2	0.3
Southampton	0.5	56.3	43.2	0.4	0.3	0.0	0.3	0.7	54.9	44.8	0.1	0.1	0.4
Spotsylvania	1.9	84.4	13.3	0.9	1.9	0.1	1.4	2.8	87.5	10.8	0.3	1.1	1.5
Stafford	2.5	84.1	13.1	1.2	2.3	0.3	1.8	3.6	90.7	7.0	0.4	1.2	2.0
Surry	0.9	47.5	52.2	0.8	0.2	0.0	0.3	0.7	44.3	55.5	0.2	0.0	0.3
Sussex	0.7	36.9	62.4	0.5	0.3	0.1	0.6	0.8	41.5	58.1	0.1	0.2	0.2
Tazewell	0.6	96.7	2.4	0.5	0.8	0.0	0.3	0.5	96.7	2.6	0.1	0.5	0.3
Warren	1.3	93.9	5.3	0.7	0.7	0.1	0.7	1.6	94.3	4.9	0.2	0.3	0.9
Washington	0.6	98.1	1.5	0.4	0.4	0.1	0.2	0.6	98.2	1.5	0.1	0.2	0.3
Westmoreland	1.3	66.4	31.5	0.8	0.5	0.0	2.2	3.5	66.3	33.0	0.2	0.4	0.6
Wise	0.6	97.5	2.0	0.4	0.4	0.0	0.3	0.7	97.7	1.8	0.1	0.3	0.3
Wythe	0.6	96.3	3.1	0.4	0.5	0.0	0.3	0.6	96.1	3.5	0.1	0.3	0.2
York	2.0	81.6	14.1	0.9	4.0	0.2	1.3	2.7	81.3	15.6	0.3	2.3	1.7
Independent Cities													
Alexandria City	4.3	62.7	24.0	0.7	6.7	0.2	10.1	14.7	69.1	21.9	0.3	4.2	9.7
Bedford City	1.2	76.3	23.0	0.8	0.7	0.1	0.5	0.9	77.2	22.0	0.1	0.5	0.9
Bristol City	1.1	93.6	6.0	0.7	0.5	0.0	0.3	1.0	93.6	5.8	0.1	0.5	0.3
Buena Vista City	0.8	94.3	5.2	0.5	0.6	0.1	0.2	1.0	95.1	4.4	0.1	0.3	0.2
Charlottesville City	2.1	71.2	23.2	0.5	5.7	0.2	1.5	2.4	76.1	21.2	0.1	2.3	1.2
Chesapeake City	1.6	68.1	29.2	0.9	2.4	0.1	1.0	2.0	70.7	27.4	0.3	1.2	1.3
Clifton Forge City	1.8	84.4	15.9	0.8	0.2	0.1	0.7	0.9	84.8	14.9	0.0	0.2	0.5
Colonial Heights City	1.0	90.0	6.6	0.4	3.1	0.1	0.9	1.6	96.5	0.8	0.2	2.2	1.0
Covington City	1.6	85.5	13.9	0.8	1.0	0.1	0.4	0.6	85.2	13.9	0.1	0.7	0.4
Danville City	0.8	54.5	44.5	0.4	0.7	0.1	0.7	1.3	62.7	36.6	0.1	0.5	0.5
Emporia City	0.4	42.7	56.4	0.3	0.6	0.1	0.4	1.5	53.7	45.6	0.2	0.5	1.1
Fairfax City	3.3	75.6	5.8	0.8	13.4	0.1	7.7	13.6	85.8	4.9	0.2	7.2	5.9
Falls Church City	2.4	87.2	3.8	0.8	7.6	0.2	3.1	8.4	89.1	3.1	0.4	4.8	6.3
Franklin City	0.8	46.4	52.7	0.4	0.9	0.0	0.5	0.6	46.2	53.4	0.1	0.3	0.2
Fredericksburg City	1.9	74.8	21.3	0.8	1.9	0.1	3.1	4.9	76.0	21.6	0.1	1.1	2.4
Galax City	1.0	87.0	6.6	0.8	0.7	0.0	5.8	11.1	93.2	5.8	0.1	0.2	1.0
Hampton City	2.4	51.1	46.1	1.1	2.5	0.2	1.6	2.8	58.4	38.9	0.3	1.7	2.0
Harrisonburg City	2.6	87.1	6.7	0.5	4.1	0.1	4.3	8.8	91.1	6.6	0.1	1.5	1.6
Hopewell City	1.8	63.7	34.3	0.9	1.3	0.2	1.7	2.9	72.2	25.6	0.3	1.3	1.8
Lexington City	0.9	86.8	10.7	0.5	2.3	0.1	0.6	1.6	86.6	11.7	0.3	1.3	0.9
Lynchburg City	1.5	67.8	30.6	0.7	1.5	0.1	0.9	1.3	72.5	26.4	0.2	0.8	0.7

[1] Hispanic persons may be of any race.

Table B. States and Counties

STATE County	Population and population characteristics, 2000										
	Age (percent)										
	Under 5 years	5 to 17 years	18 to 24 years	25 to 34 years	35 to 44 years	45 to 54 years	55 to 64 years	65 to 74 years	75 years and over	Median age (years)	Percent Female
	28	29	30	31	32	33	34	35	36	37	38
VIRGINIA—Cont'd											
Louisa	5.9	18.5	6.6	12.1	17.8	15.2	10.9	7.5	5.4	38.8	50.8
Lunenburg	4.9	16.4	8.0	12.0	16.1	15.1	10.7	9.2	7.6	40.5	46.8
Madison	5.8	18.3	6.9	11.1	16.5	15.3	11.1	8.2	6.8	40.0	51.3
Mathews	4.6	15.3	5.2	9.2	13.9	15.2	15.0	11.4	10.2	46.2	51.8
Mecklenburg	5.4	16.2	7.2	12.1	15.3	14.2	11.8	10.2	7.6	40.9	50.7
Middlesex	3.8	15.4	5.1	9.0	13.9	15.3	15.0	12.5	9.9	46.8	51.9
Montgomery	4.8	12.4	31.3	14.0	11.6	10.4	6.9	4.7	3.9	25.9	47.6
Nelson	5.3	16.4	6.4	10.2	15.3	17.1	12.5	9.8	7.0	42.8	51.3
New Kent	5.6	19.3	5.9	12.4	19.7	17.3	10.4	5.8	3.6	38.4	49.3
Northampton	5.5	17.7	7.1	9.3	14.4	13.8	11.0	11.5	9.7	42.4	53.2
Northumberland	4.3	14.3	4.8	7.7	12.5	13.1	17.0	15.0	11.1	50.1	52.3
Nottoway	5.6	17.3	8.1	13.3	15.9	12.9	9.8	8.8	8.3	38.6	48.4
Orange	6.0	17.0	6.5	11.6	16.1	13.8	11.8	9.9	7.3	40.4	51.6
Page	5.5	17.4	7.7	12.9	15.4	14.0	11.2	8.7	7.0	39.0	51.0
Patrick	5.7	16.0	7.1	12.9	15.1	14.3	12.4	8.9	7.6	40.5	50.8
Pittsylvania	5.7	17.4	7.2	12.1	16.7	15.4	11.3	8.1	6.2	39.6	51.2
Powhatan	5.8	18.1	7.3	15.2	19.5	15.8	9.8	5.2	3.3	36.8	45.0
Prince Edward	5.0	15.3	23.5	10.1	12.4	11.5	8.1	6.9	7.3	31.5	51.1
Prince George	6.0	19.1	13.6	16.2	17.1	13.0	7.7	4.5	2.7	32.1	46.1
Prince William	8.5	21.9	8.8	16.1	19.1	13.7	7.1	3.0	1.8	31.9	50.1
Pulaski	5.5	15.1	7.3	14.1	15.1	15.9	11.8	8.2	7.0	40.3	50.7
Rappahannock	5.1	17.2	5.6	10.0	16.4	18.4	13.4	8.1	5.7	42.6	50.3
Richmond	4.1	14.3	8.0	14.1	17.8	14.0	10.1	8.6	9.1	40.3	43.9
Roanoke	5.3	17.4	6.6	11.4	16.1	16.6	10.6	8.4	7.5	40.9	52.7
Rockbridge	5.4	16.8	7.9	11.6	15.5	15.1	11.9	9.3	6.3	40.4	49.9
Rockingham	6.3	18.4	8.7	12.6	16.3	14.2	9.7	7.5	6.5	37.5	50.8
Russell	5.4	15.8	8.6	14.6	16.3	15.1	10.9	7.6	5.7	38.7	49.3
Scott	5.1	15.5	7.5	12.6	14.7	14.6	12.2	9.6	8.2	41.4	51.7
Shenandoah	5.6	16.7	6.6	12.1	15.5	14.3	11.9	9.4	7.9	40.9	51.3
Smyth	5.3	16.3	8.0	13.0	15.1	14.5	11.5	8.9	7.4	40.0	51.6
Southampton	5.1	17.6	8.8	12.2	17.0	14.1	10.9	7.4	6.8	38.6	47.2
Spotsylvania	7.6	22.4	7.3	13.9	18.3	14.2	8.0	4.8	3.5	34.3	50.7
Stafford	7.8	23.8	7.8	13.9	19.8	14.0	7.1	3.5	2.4	33.1	49.7
Surry	5.6	19.6	7.2	10.3	17.5	14.3	11.4	7.7	6.3	39.4	51.6
Sussex	4.6	15.0	9.0	16.4	17.9	14.4	9.2	7.1	6.3	37.6	42.5
Tazewell	5.3	16.2	8.4	11.8	15.4	16.2	11.3	8.6	7.0	40.7	52.1
Warren	6.6	18.9	7.6	12.9	17.7	14.1	9.8	6.8	5.6	37.1	50.8
Washington	5.1	15.7	8.7	12.4	15.9	15.2	11.7	8.7	6.6	40.3	51.5
Westmoreland	5.2	17.8	6.3	9.8	14.2	14.4	13.4	10.6	8.3	42.8	52.0
Wise	5.8	17.2	10.2	13.0	15.0	14.9	9.9	7.6	6.4	37.8	51.3
Wythe	5.5	16.4	7.6	13.8	15.0	14.8	11.1	8.7	7.2	39.4	52.3
York	6.3	22.8	6.6	11.4	19.2	15.1	9.4	5.6	3.5	36.5	50.9
Independent Cities											
Alexandria City	6.2	10.6	9.2	25.4	18.1	13.8	7.8	4.4	4.6	34.4	51.7
Bedford City	5.6	16.0	7.2	12.3	15.5	12.0	8.8	9.7	12.9	40.9	52.5
Bristol City	5.3	15.0	8.6	12.5	13.7	13.4	10.9	10.2	10.3	41.3	54.9
Buena Vista City	6.2	16.3	10.6	13.0	13.0	13.7	10.9	8.5	7.7	37.9	53.6
Charlottesville City	4.4	10.8	33.8	14.6	11.2	9.3	5.9	5.1	5.0	25.6	53.3
Chesapeake City	7.2	21.6	8.2	13.5	18.9	13.8	7.9	5.1	3.8	34.7	51.4
Clifton Forge City	5.3	15.8	6.7	11.1	14.3	12.2	10.9	10.6	13.1	42.9	55.9
Colonial Heights City	5.3	17.3	8.3	12.0	14.8	13.3	10.4	9.6	9.0	39.9	53.2
Covington City	6.3	15.2	8.2	13.0	13.3	13.0	10.9	9.9	10.3	40.5	52.2
Danville City	6.0	17.3	8.0	11.5	14.0	13.8	9.8	9.7	9.9	40.5	54.5
Emporia City	6.2	19.0	8.1	11.4	14.2	11.4	9.2	8.9	11.7	38.8	54.5
Fairfax City	6.0	14.5	9.2	16.7	17.0	14.2	9.6	6.8	6.0	37.0	51.2
Falls Church City	5.5	17.9	5.1	13.3	17.8	19.0	9.2	5.1	7.1	39.7	51.3
Franklin City	5.1	20.1	7.7	10.4	14.5	13.7	10.2	8.6	9.8	39.9	55.8
Fredericksburg City	5.8	11.9	23.8	14.8	12.4	11.1	7.3	6.3	6.5	30.3	55.0
Galax City	6.4	16.6	7.9	12.8	13.6	13.2	10.4	9.8	9.4	39.8	52.5
Hampton City	6.3	17.9	12.6	14.8	17.7	12.4	8.0	5.8	4.5	34.0	50.4
Harrisonburg City	4.7	10.7	40.9	11.3	9.9	8.0	5.2	4.3	5.0	22.6	52.6
Hopewell City	7.5	19.2	9.1	14.1	14.5	11.9	9.1	7.8	6.8	35.0	53.3
Lexington City	3.0	8.0	41.4	7.7	6.8	9.0	7.6	7.7	8.7	23.3	44.8
Lynchburg City	5.8	16.3	15.5	12.2	13.1	12.4	8.4	7.5	8.8	35.1	54.3

Table B. States and Counties

STATE County	Under 5 years (39)	5 to 17 years (40)	18 to 24 years (41)	25 to 34 years (42)	35 to 44 years (43)	45 to 54 years (44)	55 to 64 years (45)	65 to 74 years (46)	75 years and over (47)	Percent Female (48)	2000 (49)	1990 (50)	1980 (51)	1990–2000 (52)	1980–1990 (53)
VIRGINIA—Cont'd															
Louisa	6.8	18.4	8.6	16.5	15.2	11.1	9.7	8.3	5.5	50.6	25 627	20 325	17 825	26.1	14.0
Lunenburg	6.6	19.3	7.6	13.1	14.8	10.8	10.7	10.9	6.2	51.5	13 146	11 419	12 124	15.1	-5.8
Madison	6.7	18.5	8.2	15.6	14.9	11.3	9.9	8.1	6.8	50.9	12 520	11 949	10 232	4.8	16.8
Mathews	4.8	15.4	7.2	11.8	13.5	12.0	12.7	12.3	10.4	52.2	9 207	8 348	7 995	10.3	4.4
Mecklenburg	6.0	17.3	8.4	14.7	14.1	10.7	11.6	10.4	6.8	52.0	32 380	29 241	29 444	10.7	-0.7
Middlesex	5.7	14.7	6.3	13.4	12.7	11.9	13.3	12.6	9.4	51.9	9 932	8 653	7 719	14.8	12.1
Montgomery	5.4	12.5	31.0	16.4	12.4	8.2	6.0	4.6	3.5	48.2	83 629	73 913	63 284	13.1	16.8
Nelson	6.4	17.7	7.8	14.7	15.8	11.3	10.5	9.3	6.5	51.1	14 445	12 778	12 204	13.0	4.7
New Kent	7.1	18.1	8.1	17.5	19.3	12.3	8.9	5.7	3.1	49.8	13 462	10 466	8 781	28.6	19.0
Northampton	6.8	18.5	7.1	14.0	12.4	9.3	11.9	11.4	8.5	53.6	13 093	13 061	14 625	0.2	-10.7
Northumberland	5.3	14.7	6.2	12.0	11.4	10.9	14.6	15.6	9.3	52.9	12 259	10 524	9 828	16.5	7.1
Nottoway	5.8	16.6	8.8	16.3	14.1	10.5	9.9	10.3	7.8	49.1	15 725	14 993	14 666	4.9	2.2
Orange	6.5	17.8	8.2	15.4	14.7	11.1	10.4	9.7	6.1	51.5	25 881	21 421	18 063	20.8	18.6
Page	6.3	17.3	9.1	15.5	14.6	11.6	10.6	9.0	6.0	51.0	23 177	21 690	19 401	6.9	11.8
Patrick	5.4	16.7	9.1	14.5	14.3	13.0	10.7	9.1	7.1	50.8	19 407	17 473	17 647	11.1	-1.0
Pittsylvania	6.1	18.2	8.9	16.0	15.6	11.9	10.0	8.2	5.2	51.0	61 745	55 672	66 147	10.9	-15.8
Powhatan	6.2	16.8	9.4	20.4	18.4	12.3	7.8	5.7	3.1	43.8	22 377	15 328	13 062	46.0	17.3
Prince Edward	5.6	15.2	25.0	11.9	11.5	8.1	8.4	7.7	6.7	52.1	19 720	17 320	16 456	13.9	5.3
Prince George	7.7	18.9	13.9	19.4	16.5	10.6	6.8	4.2	2.0	46.9	33 047	27 390	25 733	20.7	6.5
Prince William	9.3	21.2	10.9	21.4	18.5	10.8	4.8	2.0	1.0	48.8	280 813	214 954	144 636	30.6	49.1
Pulaski	5.9	16.4	10.4	14.9	15.8	11.8	10.1	8.6	6.2	51.7	35 127	34 496	35 229	1.8	-2.1
Rappahannock	6.8	16.1	7.9	15.0	17.2	13.8	10.2	8.0	5.0	50.0	6 983	6 622	6 093	5.5	8.7
Richmond	6.0	17.2	8.2	14.5	13.5	10.7	10.6	10.2	9.1	51.1	8 809	7 273	6 952	21.1	4.6
Roanoke	5.4	17.0	9.0	14.6	17.7	12.6	10.1	7.8	5.7	52.8	85 778	79 278	72 945	8.2	8.7
Rockbridge	6.1	16.8	9.4	15.2	14.9	12.2	11.7	9.0	4.8	50.1	20 808	18 350	17 724	13.4	3.5
Rockingham	6.8	17.6	10.2	16.2	15.4	11.1	9.3	7.5	5.7	50.8	67 725	57 482	52 068	17.8	10.4
Russell	5.6	19.4	9.4	16.3	15.8	11.7	9.5	7.2	5.0	51.0	30 308	28 667	31 761	5.7	-9.7
Scott	5.2	16.8	9.5	14.0	14.4	12.5	10.8	9.6	7.2	51.7	23 403	23 204	25 068	0.9	-7.4
Shenandoah	6.1	16.0	9.0	15.2	14.7	11.7	10.6	9.5	7.2	51.7	35 075	31 636	27 559	10.9	14.8
Smyth	5.8	17.2	9.9	14.9	14.4	11.8	10.9	8.8	6.3	52.2	33 081	32 370	33 345	2.2	-2.9
Southampton	6.2	17.2	11.0	17.5	13.6	10.8	9.4	8.8	5.5	47.5	17 482	17 022	18 316	2.7	-4.2
Spotsylvania	8.8	21.6	8.9	18.8	17.8	10.3	6.5	4.7	2.6	50.4	90 395	57 397	31 995	57.5	79.4
Stafford	8.4	21.2	11.2	18.3	17.9	11.1	6.0	3.7	2.2	48.4	92 446	62 255	40 470	48.5	51.3
Surry	7.3	19.1	8.6	16.0	14.6	10.6	9.1	8.9	5.8	51.9	6 829	6 145	6 046	11.1	1.6
Sussex	7.0	17.7	10.0	14.8	13.9	10.4	10.8	8.8	6.5	52.4	12 504	10 248	10 874	22.0	-5.8
Tazewell	5.8	19.5	9.2	14.7	16.0	11.3	9.8	8.3	5.4	51.8	44 598	45 960	50 511	-3.0	-9.0
Warren	7.8	16.9	9.4	17.6	14.9	11.2	9.1	7.8	5.2	50.8	31 584	26 142	21 200	20.8	23.3
Washington	5.4	16.9	10.1	14.7	15.7	12.5	10.4	8.5	5.7	51.5	51 103	45 887	46 487	11.4	-1.3
Westmoreland	6.8	16.5	8.1	13.9	13.0	11.2	11.6	11.7	7.3	51.9	16 718	15 480	14 041	8.0	10.2
Wise	6.1	20.4	10.5	14.7	15.4	10.7	9.1	7.7	5.4	51.7	40 123	39 573	43 863	1.4	-9.8
Wythe	5.9	17.5	9.8	14.9	14.8	11.5	10.2	8.9	6.5	52.6	27 599	25 471	25 522	8.4	-0.2
York	7.0	22.2	8.6	15.9	18.4	12.6	7.8	5.0	2.4	50.2	56 297	42 434	35 463	32.7	19.7
Independent Cities															
Alexandria City	5.6	9.8	11.3	27.0	18.3	10.6	7.1	5.8	4.5	52.6	128 283	111 183	103 217	15.4	7.7
Bedford City	6.1	14.7	7.9	14.9	11.9	9.3	10.4	11.6	13.3	53.0	6 299	6 176	5 991	2.0	1.4
Bristol City	6.0	15.6	10.4	14.4	13.1	10.8	10.9	10.4	8.3	55.4	17 367	18 426	19 042	-5.7	-3.2
Buena Vista City	5.0	16.6	13.1	13.2	14.2	11.1	10.6	8.9	7.2	54.6	6 349	6 406	6 904	-0.9	-7.2
Charlottesville City	6.1	11.9	23.4	19.8	12.3	7.5	6.9	6.5	5.7	53.1	45 049	40 470	39 916	11.3	1.4
Chesapeake City	8.3	20.4	9.6	19.0	16.8	10.3	7.2	5.4	3.0	51.0	199 184	151 982	114 486	31.1	32.8
Clifton Forge City	5.7	15.6	8.0	13.6	12.1	10.0	10.8	11.8	12.7	55.2	4 289	4 679	5 046	-8.3	-7.3
Colonial Heights City	5.6	16.2	9.3	14.0	15.1	12.2	12.1	10.2	5.3	53.2	16 897	16 064	16 509	5.2	-2.7
Covington City	5.8	14.4	9.8	14.4	12.5	10.5	10.4	11.7	10.4	53.3	6 303	7 352	9 063	-14.3	-22.9
Danville City	6.5	16.2	9.4	14.4	13.8	10.2	10.9	10.9	7.8	54.4	48 411	53 056	45 642	-8.8	16.2
Emporia City	7.6	17.1	8.3	14.1	11.9	9.4	10.5	11.8	9.3	53.2	5 665	5 556	4 840	2.0	13.2
Fairfax City	5.6	13.5	13.3	20.1	15.3	11.4	10.0	7.1	3.8	51.2	21 498	19 945	20 537	7.8	-4.4
Falls Church City	5.8	13.7	7.3	17.6	20.0	12.2	8.5	8.3	6.7	52.3	10 377	9 464	9 515	9.6	0.0
Franklin City	7.4	19.4	8.4	15.0	14.1	9.9	9.9	9.0	6.9	54.9	8 346	8 392	7 723	-0.5	1.8
Fredericksburg City	6.6	12.0	23.3	17.8	11.5	7.8	7.4	7.5	6.1	54.3	19 279	19 033	17 762	1.3	7.1
Galax City	6.8	14.6	9.0	13.9	12.9	10.8	11.6	10.6	9.9	54.9	6 837	6 745	6 524	1.4	2.2
Hampton City	7.8	17.1	13.4	19.6	14.4	10.0	8.0	6.3	3.3	51.2	146 437	133 773	122 617	9.5	9.1
Harrisonburg City	4.8	10.8	37.2	14.1	10.2	6.7	5.8	5.4	5.0	53.8	40 468	30 707	24 641	31.8	24.6
Hopewell City	8.2	18.0	10.6	17.4	13.7	10.1	9.0	7.5	5.5	52.6	22 354	23 101	23 397	-3.2	-1.3
Lexington City	2.9	8.8	41.9	7.9	8.3	7.2	8.1	7.8	7.1	41.6	6 867	6 959	7 292	-1.3	-4.6
Lynchburg City	6.8	15.6	15.8	14.6	13.0	9.0	8.8	8.5	7.9	55.0	65 269	66 120	66 743	-1.3	-1.0

Table B. States and Counties

	Household relationship, 2000																
	In households (percent)										In group quarters (percent)						
					Child		Other relatives		Nonrelatives			Institutionalized population			Noninstitutionalized population		
STATE County	Total population	Total in house-holds	House-holder	Spouse	Total	Own child under 18 years	Total	Under 18 years	Total	Unmar-ried partner	Total in group quarters	Correc-tional institu-tions	Nurs-ing homes	Other institu-tions	Col-lege dormi-tories	Mili-tary quar-ters	Other
	54	55	56	57	58	59	60	61	62	63	64	65	66	67	68	69	70
VIRGINIA—Cont'd																	
Louisa	25 627	99.3	38.8	22.2	27.7	20.9	6.0	2.9	4.5	2.5	0.7	0.0	0.4	0.0	0.0	0.0	0.3
Lunenburg	13 146	90.9	38.0	18.8	24.5	17.6	5.8	3.0	3.8	2.0	9.1	8.5	0.0	0.4	0.0	0.0	0.1
Madison	12 520	98.3	37.9	23.2	28.7	21.6	5.0	2.2	3.4	1.7	1.7	0.0	1.1	0.0	0.4	0.0	0.2
Mathews	9 207	99.3	42.7	26.2	23.8	18.1	3.6	1.4	2.9	1.5	0.7	0.0	0.7	0.0	0.0	0.1	0.0
Mecklenburg	32 380	95.2	40.0	20.4	25.1	18.3	6.1	2.8	3.5	1.8	4.8	3.9	0.4	0.0	0.0	0.0	0.4
Middlesex	9 932	97.4	42.8	24.0	22.1	16.5	4.6	2.2	3.9	2.0	2.6	1.4	1.2	0.0	0.0	0.0	0.1
Montgomery	83 629	89.0	37.1	16.6	19.4	16.0	2.5	0.8	13.5	1.8	11.0	0.2	0.4	0.1	10.0	0.0	0.3
Nelson	14 445	98.6	40.8	22.7	25.9	19.1	5.5	2.2	3.7	2.0	1.4	0.0	0.4	0.0	0.0	0.0	1.0
New Kent	13 462	97.1	36.6	24.4	28.2	21.9	4.6	2.1	3.3	1.6	2.9	2.3	0.0	0.6	0.0	0.0	0.0
Northampton	13 093	97.2	40.6	18.4	26.0	18.4	8.2	4.0	3.9	2.0	2.8	0.4	1.0	0.1	0.0	0.0	1.3
Northumberland	12 259	99.9	44.6	25.6	21.7	15.8	5.2	2.5	2.8	1.4	0.1	0.1	0.0	0.0	0.0	0.0	0.0
Nottoway	15 725	89.5	36.0	17.5	25.9	19.2	5.9	3.0	4.1	1.8	10.5	8.2	1.1	0.8	0.0	0.0	0.4
Orange	25 881	98.1	39.2	23.0	26.9	20.4	5.0	2.2	4.0	2.1	1.9	0.9	0.8	0.0	0.0	0.0	0.2
Page	23 177	98.9	40.1	22.4	27.3	20.3	4.8	2.1	4.2	2.5	1.1	0.2	0.4	0.4	0.0	0.0	0.1
Patrick	19 407	98.8	41.9	24.7	25.9	19.9	3.7	1.5	2.5	1.4	1.2	0.1	0.7	0.0	0.0	0.0	0.3
Pittsylvania	61 745	99.4	40.0	23.3	28.2	20.3	5.4	2.5	2.5	1.4	0.6	0.3	0.2	0.0	0.0	0.0	0.1
Powhatan	22 377	88.9	32.4	22.6	27.0	21.3	4.0	1.6	2.9	1.3	11.1	9.6	0.0	1.3	0.0	0.0	0.1
Prince Edward	19 720	81.0	33.3	15.5	22.5	17.0	5.2	2.8	4.6	1.7	19.0	1.7	1.0	0.0	15.7	0.0	0.6
Prince George	33 047	85.0	30.7	19.5	28.3	22.7	3.9	1.8	2.6	1.2	15.0	6.7	0.0	0.2	0.0	8.1	0.0
Prince William	280 813	99.1	33.7	20.6	34.0	27.8	5.6	2.0	5.3	1.8	0.9	0.0	0.2	0.0	0.0	0.5	0.1
Pulaski	35 127	96.8	41.7	22.9	24.7	18.3	4.3	1.9	3.3	1.9	3.2	2.0	0.9	0.0	0.0	0.0	0.3
Rappahannock	6 983	99.9	39.9	24.2	27.0	20.3	4.4	1.4	4.3	2.0	0.1	0.1	0.0	0.0	0.0	0.0	0.0
Richmond	8 809	80.1	33.3	17.4	21.9	15.9	4.6	1.9	2.9	1.3	19.9	16.6	3.0	0.0	0.0	0.0	0.3
Roanoke	85 778	97.4	40.4	24.2	26.9	21.2	3.0	1.1	2.8	1.4	2.6	0.0	1.5	0.1	0.7	0.0	0.4
Rockbridge	20 808	99.0	40.8	23.4	26.2	20.2	4.0	1.6	4.6	2.1	1.0	0.4	0.3	0.3	0.0	0.0	0.0
Rockingham	67 725	97.7	37.4	23.4	28.9	22.4	4.1	1.6	3.9	1.9	2.3	0.0	0.4	0.0	1.3	0.0	0.6
Russell	30 308	95.1	38.9	23.7	26.6	19.2	4.0	1.7	1.9	1.1	4.9	4.0	0.6	0.0	0.0	0.0	0.3
Scott	23 403	98.5	41.9	24.9	26.1	18.8	3.7	1.4	2.0	1.1	1.5	0.1	0.7	0.0	0.0	0.0	0.6
Shenandoah	35 075	98.5	40.8	23.2	26.4	20.2	3.9	1.5	4.3	2.0	1.5	0.2	0.9	0.0	0.0	0.0	0.4
Smyth	33 081	96.7	40.8	22.7	26.2	19.4	4.2	1.6	2.8	1.5	3.3	0.8	0.8	0.5	0.0	0.0	1.2
Southampton	17 482	91.0	35.9	19.4	27.0	19.5	5.6	2.5	3.1	1.4	9.0	8.5	0.5	0.0	0.0	0.0	0.0
Spotsylvania	90 395	99.4	34.6	22.5	33.5	27.4	4.6	2.0	4.2	1.9	0.6	0.0	0.4	0.1	0.0	0.0	0.1
Stafford	92 446	98.4	32.7	22.2	35.0	29.1	4.3	1.8	4.2	1.7	1.6	0.2	0.3	0.0	0.0	1.0	0.1
Surry	6 829	100.0	38.4	21.3	29.8	20.7	7.4	4.0	3.1	1.8	0.0	0.0	0.0	0.0	0.0	0.0	0.0
Sussex	12 504	79.7	33.0	14.9	22.7	16.4	6.0	2.9	3.1	1.6	20.3	19.2	0.9	0.0	0.0	0.0	0.2
Tazewell	44 598	98.2	41.0	23.9	26.9	19.3	4.2	1.8	2.3	1.2	1.8	0.5	0.7	0.0	0.4	0.0	0.2
Warren	31 584	98.3	38.3	21.3	29.0	22.8	4.7	2.0	5.0	2.6	1.7	0.2	0.7	0.0	0.7	0.0	0.1
Washington	51 103	97.4	41.2	24.3	25.5	18.8	3.9	1.6	2.5	1.2	2.6	0.2	0.5	0.1	1.1	0.0	0.7
Westmoreland	16 718	99.4	40.9	20.8	26.1	19.0	6.7	3.4	4.9	2.4	0.6	0.0	0.5	0.0	0.0	0.0	0.1
Wise	40 123	97.2	39.9	22.4	28.1	20.4	4.4	2.0	2.4	1.2	2.8	0.4	0.7	0.0	1.0	0.0	0.7
Wythe	27 599	98.5	41.7	23.5	26.5	19.8	3.8	1.6	3.0	1.8	1.5	0.0	1.2	0.1	0.0	0.0	0.2
York	56 297	98.9	35.5	23.9	33.4	27.4	3.2	1.4	2.8	1.2	1.1	0.0	0.2	0.0	0.0	0.7	0.2
Independent Cities																	
Alexandria City	128 283	98.5	48.2	15.5	18.8	14.8	6.1	1.5	9.9	2.8	1.5	0.3	0.7	0.1	0.0	0.0	0.3
Bedford City	6 299	90.3	40.0	17.2	25.2	19.4	4.8	1.8	3.1	1.7	9.7	3.2	3.2	0.0	0.0	0.0	3.2
Bristol City	17 367	96.4	44.2	20.4	24.6	18.0	4.2	1.7	3.0	1.5	3.6	0.6	0.9	0.3	1.6	0.0	0.4
Buena Vista City	6 349	95.4	40.1	19.9	26.9	20.1	4.6	1.8	3.9	2.1	4.6	0.0	1.4	0.0	3.2	0.0	0.0
Charlottesville City	45 049	84.8	37.4	10.9	16.7	13.2	3.6	1.4	16.1	2.0	15.2	0.0	0.8	0.0	13.8	0.0	0.6
Chesapeake City	199 184	97.9	35.1	20.9	32.7	25.6	5.4	2.5	3.8	1.4	2.1	1.1	0.4	0.2	0.0	0.2	0.3
Clifton Forge City	4 289	95.2	42.9	18.6	25.2	18.6	4.4	1.7	4.1	2.0	4.8	0.3	4.3	0.2	0.0	0.0	0.0
Colonial Heights City	16 897	98.6	41.6	20.9	27.2	20.3	4.3	1.7	4.6	1.9	1.4	0.0	1.1	0.0	0.0	0.0	0.2
Covington City	6 303	99.8	45.0	20.2	24.8	18.2	5.5	2.5	4.3	2.3	0.2	0.0	0.0	0.0	0.0	0.0	0.2
Danville City	48 411	96.5	42.6	16.7	27.0	19.5	6.8	3.3	3.5	1.6	3.5	0.7	1.3	0.2	0.6	0.0	0.7
Emporia City	5 665	95.4	39.3	14.7	28.0	20.8	8.2	3.7	5.3	2.6	4.6	0.0	3.2	0.0	0.0	0.0	1.4
Fairfax City	21 498	97.5	37.4	20.4	24.9	18.3	6.8	1.5	8.1	1.4	2.5	0.0	1.7	0.0	0.2	0.0	0.6
Falls Church City	10 377	99.3	43.1	20.3	27.0	22.2	3.5	1.0	5.5	1.4	0.7	0.0	0.6	0.0	0.0	0.0	0.0
Franklin City	8 346	96.7	40.5	17.0	29.2	21.7	6.6	3.1	3.4	1.7	3.3	0.0	3.3	0.0	0.0	0.0	0.0
Fredericksburg City	19 279	88.0	42.0	13.4	19.2	15.3	4.3	1.7	9.1	2.9	12.0	0.2	0.0	0.2	10.6	0.0	0.9
Galax City	6 837	98.0	43.1	19.8	26.2	20.9	5.2	1.7	3.6	1.5	2.0	0.0	2.0	0.0	0.0	0.0	0.1
Hampton City	146 437	91.5	36.8	17.0	27.4	21.0	5.1	2.6	5.2	1.7	8.5	5.7	0.5	0.2	1.8	0.1	0.2
Harrisonburg City	40 468	82.2	32.5	11.8	17.1	14.0	3.0	1.0	17.9	1.5	17.8	0.8	1.5	0.0	15.2	0.0	0.3
Hopewell City	22 354	98.5	40.5	16.5	30.2	23.2	5.9	2.9	5.4	2.6	1.5	0.3	0.6	0.6	0.0	0.0	0.0
Lexington City	6 867	67.0	32.5	12.0	13.2	10.0	2.5	0.8	6.8	0.7	33.0	0.0	2.1	0.0	30.8	0.0	0.1
Lynchburg City	65 269	90.0	39.0	16.2	25.0	19.4	4.7	2.0	5.0	1.7	10.0	0.7	1.7	0.3	6.8	0.0	0.6

STATE County	Households by type, 2000												Households, 1990		
		Family households						Nonfamily households							
				Married couple		Female householder[1]			Householder living alone						
	Total households	Total	With own children under 18 years	Total	With own children under 18 years	Total	With own children under 18 years	Total	Total	65 years and over	Average household size	Average family size	Total households	Female householder[1]	Householder living alone
	71	72	73	74	75	76	77	78	79	80	81	82	83	84	85
VIRGINIA—Cont'd															
Louisa	9 945	73.0	31.2	57.3	22.8	10.8	5.8	27.0	22.1	9.0	2.66	2.97	7 427	10.4	20.7
Lunenburg	4 998	67.7	27.3	49.5	17.9	13.3	7.0	32.3	28.7	14.7	2.39	2.91	4 423	10.9	25.4
Madison	4 739	74.3	30.9	61.4	25.0	8.8	4.1	25.7	21.8	9.5	2.60	3.03	4 144	8.7	19.2
Mathews	3 932	71.8	24.2	61.2	19.4	7.9	3.5	28.2	24.9	13.5	2.32	2.75	3 530	7.6	27.1
Mecklenburg	12 951	69.2	26.5	51.0	17.2	14.1	7.4	30.8	27.2	13.2	2.38	2.87	11 244	13.0	25.0
Middlesex	4 253	68.5	22.4	56.1	16.4	9.5	4.4	31.5	27.1	14.4	2.27	2.73	3 530	9.0	24.8
Montgomery	30 997	55.5	25.3	44.8	19.3	7.6	4.6	44.5	25.5	6.6	2.40	2.87	26 241	7.7	22.9
Nelson	5 887	70.4	27.1	55.7	20.1	10.7	5.0	29.6	25.0	10.3	2.42	2.88	4 807	10.5	22.3
New Kent	4 925	79.1	34.7	66.6	28.4	9.0	4.6	20.9	16.6	5.6	2.65	2.97	3 718	8.6	14.7
Northampton	5 321	66.6	25.7	45.3	15.5	17.5	8.7	33.4	29.4	15.6	2.39	2.94	5 129	16.1	27.8
Northumberland	5 470	69.2	20.1	57.3	14.6	8.7	4.2	30.8	27.7	15.2	2.24	2.70	4 492	9.1	26.1
Nottoway	5 664	68.6	29.9	48.6	19.2	15.4	8.4	31.4	27.6	14.2	2.48	3.00	5 244	13.9	24.8
Orange	10 150	73.6	29.6	58.7	21.5	10.7	5.6	26.4	22.1	10.1	2.50	2.90	7 930	9.7	20.0
Page	9 305	71.3	29.6	55.8	21.4	10.5	5.5	28.7	24.4	11.1	2.46	2.91	8 055	9.4	20.6
Patrick	8 141	71.4	28.5	58.9	21.6	8.6	5.0	28.6	25.8	11.4	2.36	2.81	6 908	8.5	21.8
Pittsylvania	24 684	73.8	30.4	58.3	22.9	11.7	5.7	26.2	23.4	9.8	2.49	2.93	20 613	10.7	19.4
Powhatan	7 258	81.3	37.5	69.7	31.4	8.1	4.4	18.7	14.6	4.8	2.74	3.03	4 672	8.0	13.5
Prince Edward	6 561	65.1	29.0	46.5	18.9	14.9	8.2	34.9	28.9	12.3	2.43	2.99	5 373	14.5	26.7
Prince George	10 159	79.7	41.9	63.5	31.4	12.2	8.1	20.3	17.2	5.8	2.76	3.11	8 250	10.1	13.5
Prince William	94 570	76.9	44.2	61.3	34.2	11.2	7.5	23.1	17.1	3.0	2.94	3.32	69 709	8.4	13.2
Pulaski	14 643	69.3	26.9	54.9	19.5	10.5	5.4	30.7	27.0	11.1	2.32	2.80	13 349	11.1	22.9
Rappahannock	2 788	71.9	27.4	60.5	22.0	7.1	3.2	28.1	23.4	7.9	2.50	2.94	2 496	7.1	19.7
Richmond	2 937	68.1	27.2	52.3	19.5	11.8	5.7	31.9	28.3	14.2	2.40	2.93	2 645	11.3	23.4
Roanoke	34 686	71.2	30.6	59.9	24.5	8.5	4.6	28.8	25.1	10.1	2.41	2.88	30 355	8.4	21.2
Rockbridge	8 486	71.6	29.2	57.5	21.9	9.5	4.8	28.4	23.9	9.9	2.43	2.84	7 202	9.5	21.3
Rockingham	25 355	74.5	32.9	62.4	26.5	7.9	4.1	25.5	21.2	9.1	2.61	3.02	20 750	7.3	19.0
Russell	11 789	74.8	31.0	60.9	24.6	10.1	4.7	25.2	23.1	10.0	2.44	2.87	10 641	9.6	19.2
Scott	9 795	71.7	27.6	59.4	22.2	9.0	4.1	28.3	26.1	13.1	2.35	2.82	8 966	9.8	21.0
Shenandoah	14 296	70.4	28.1	57.0	20.8	9.3	5.0	29.6	25.1	11.3	2.42	2.86	12 452	8.9	23.2
Smyth	13 493	71.2	29.2	55.7	21.2	11.2	5.7	28.8	26.0	12.5	2.37	2.83	12 234	11.3	21.5
Southampton	6 279	71.7	30.8	54.1	22.0	13.5	7.0	28.3	24.9	11.1	2.53	3.02	6 009	12.0	22.1
Spotsylvania	31 308	78.7	42.4	64.8	33.9	9.9	6.0	21.3	16.4	5.4	2.87	3.22	18 945	7.9	13.2
Stafford	30 187	81.1	46.9	68.0	38.2	9.3	6.3	18.9	13.8	3.4	3.01	3.32	19 415	7.3	12.2
Surry	2 619	73.2	30.5	55.5	22.4	14.1	6.3	26.8	23.7	10.1	2.61	3.09	2 283	13.4	22.6
Sussex	4 126	68.1	28.5	45.0	16.6	18.9	10.0	31.9	28.2	12.4	2.41	2.94	3 795	17.3	24.0
Tazewell	18 277	72.4	28.7	58.2	21.9	10.8	5.3	27.6	25.2	11.9	2.40	2.85	17 309	10.7	21.3
Warren	12 087	70.5	32.8	55.6	24.2	10.0	5.7	29.5	24.0	8.8	2.57	3.04	9 879	8.9	22.1
Washington	21 056	71.0	28.1	59.1	22.5	8.7	4.0	29.0	25.8	10.4	2.36	2.84	17 483	8.8	21.1
Westmoreland	6 846	68.5	25.7	50.7	16.5	13.5	7.0	31.5	26.9	13.6	2.43	2.91	6 057	12.3	23.9
Wise	16 013	71.9	31.0	56.2	23.2	12.0	6.0	28.1	25.5	11.2	2.44	2.91	14 513	12.1	20.9
Wythe	11 511	70.4	28.9	56.2	21.6	10.5	5.3	29.6	26.3	11.7	2.36	2.83	9 852	10.4	22.9
York	20 000	79.4	42.2	67.3	34.7	9.4	5.9	20.6	16.7	5.4	2.78	3.15	14 474	8.8	15.1
Independent Cities															
Alexandria City	61 889	44.8	18.6	32.2	12.4	9.2	5.0	55.2	43.4	6.8	2.04	2.87	53 280	9.1	42.0
Bedford City	2 519	63.2	27.7	43.0	15.4	17.2	10.9	36.8	33.0	15.7	2.26	2.87	2 475	16.2	31.0
Bristol City	7 678	62.5	24.8	46.1	16.3	13.6	7.2	37.5	34.3	17.4	2.18	2.78	7 591	14.2	30.7
Buena Vista City	2 547	68.7	30.0	49.5	19.3	14.3	8.2	31.3	27.6	13.5	2.38	2.87	2 404	14.4	23.7
Charlottesville City	16 851	45.3	20.5	29.2	10.9	13.1	8.3	54.7	34.9	8.2	2.27	2.85	16 009	12.9	30.6
Chesapeake City	69 900	77.5	41.0	59.7	30.3	14.0	8.7	22.5	18.0	5.9	2.79	3.17	51 965	12.7	16.1
Clifton Forge City	1 841	62.3	26.1	43.4	16.0	14.9	8.1	37.7	34.4	19.6	2.22	2.80	1 930	13.8	34.5
Colonial Heights City	7 027	67.2	29.1	50.3	19.4	13.0	7.7	32.8	27.6	12.3	2.37	2.88	6 363	10.9	23.0
Covington City	2 835	61.4	23.7	44.9	15.7	12.5	6.6	38.6	34.0	16.4	2.22	2.83	2 998	12.0	30.4
Danville City	20 607	62.8	26.1	39.2	13.4	19.6	11.1	37.2	33.9	15.3	2.27	2.89	21 712	17.3	30.2
Emporia City	2 226	63.2	29.2	37.5	14.9	21.0	12.5	36.8	32.2	17.4	2.43	3.05	2 031	19.4	27.5
Fairfax City	8 035	67.3	28.0	54.5	22.9	9.3	4.1	32.7	23.4	6.7	2.61	3.07	7 362	10.2	20.1
Falls Church City	4 471	58.6	30.1	47.1	23.6	8.6	5.0	41.4	33.8	10.1	2.31	3.01	4 195	8.4	33.1
Franklin City	3 384	67.3	30.1	41.8	15.9	21.9	13.0	32.7	28.9	12.8	2.39	2.93	3 006	21.2	25.1
Fredericksburg City	8 102	48.4	21.6	31.8	11.5	13.1	8.4	51.6	39.2	12.8	2.09	2.81	7 450	12.3	34.7
Galax City	2 950	62.5	27.6	46.0	18.3	12.7	7.7	37.5	34.2	14.9	2.27	2.90	2 750	14.1	29.8
Hampton City	53 887	66.6	32.5	46.2	20.2	16.4	10.3	33.4	26.6	7.9	2.49	3.02	49 673	13.5	23.7
Harrisonburg City	13 133	49.1	23.3	36.4	15.8	9.3	5.7	50.9	28.3	8.6	2.53	3.00	10 310	10.2	28.2
Hopewell City	9 055	67.1	32.1	40.6	15.3	21.2	13.9	32.9	27.6	11.2	2.43	2.94	9 014	16.3	24.9
Lexington City	2 232	48.4	18.3	36.9	13.4	8.8	3.9	51.6	41.0	17.7	2.06	2.76	2 172	9.5	36.4
Lynchburg City	25 477	61.2	27.8	41.6	16.3	16.0	9.7	38.8	32.7	12.9	2.30	2.92	25 143	15.6	30.5

[1] No spouse present.

Table B. States and Counties

STATE County	Percent change of households, 1990–2000	Total housing units	Occupied housing units (percent)	Vacant housing units Total	For seasonal, recreational, or occasional use	Homeowner vacancy rate (percent)	Rental vacancy rate (percent)	Total	Percent owner-occupied housing units	Percent renter-occupied housing units	Average household size of owner-occupied units	Average household size of renter-occupied units
	86	87	88	89	90	91	92	93	94	95	96	97
VIRGINIA—Cont'd												
Louisa	33.9	11 855	83.9	16.1	10.3	1.5	3.8	9 945	81.5	18.5	2.57	2.49
Lunenburg	13.0	5 736	87.1	12.9	2.9	1.2	5.2	4 998	77.7	22.3	2.38	2.44
Madison	14.4	5 239	90.5	9.5	4.8	0.8	3.0	4 739	76.8	23.2	2.59	2.60
Mathews	11.4	5 333	73.7	26.3	16.7	1.9	5.8	3 932	84.7	15.3	2.33	2.29
Mecklenburg	15.2	17 403	74.4	25.6	15.6	3.2	5.9	12 951	74.4	25.6	2.37	2.42
Middlesex	20.5	6 362	66.9	33.1	25.6	2.5	5.5	4 253	83.1	16.9	2.25	2.41
Montgomery	18.1	32 527	95.3	4.7	0.5	1.2	3.8	30 997	55.1	44.9	2.50	2.28
Nelson	22.5	8 554	68.8	31.2	24.7	1.2	5.7	5 887	80.8	19.2	2.44	2.31
New Kent	32.5	5 203	94.7	5.3	1.0	1.5	5.8	4 925	88.7	11.3	2.67	2.52
Northampton	3.7	6 547	81.3	18.7	7.5	1.8	6.3	5 321	68.6	31.4	2.34	2.51
Northumberland	21.8	8 057	67.9	32.1	23.1	2.3	5.9	5 470	87.4	12.6	2.23	2.33
Nottoway	8.0	6 373	88.9	11.1	1.6	2.0	4.3	5 664	70.9	29.1	2.46	2.54
Orange	28.0	11 354	89.4	10.6	4.3	2.1	4.7	10 150	77.1	22.9	2.51	2.46
Page	15.5	10 557	88.1	11.9	6.2	1.7	5.0	9 305	73.9	26.1	2.47	2.43
Patrick	17.8	9 823	82.9	17.1	7.4	1.9	11.0	8 141	80.3	19.7	2.38	2.25
Pittsylvania	19.7	28 011	88.1	11.9	3.6	1.4	9.2	24 684	80.1	19.9	2.52	2.36
Powhatan	55.4	7 509	96.7	3.3	0.5	0.9	3.8	7 258	88.8	11.2	2.76	2.61
Prince Edward	22.1	7 527	87.2	12.8	2.7	2.1	9.9	6 561	68.4	31.6	2.49	2.31
Prince George	23.1	10 726	94.7	5.3	0.3	1.3	4.3	10 159	73.0	27.0	2.70	2.93
Prince William	35.7	98 052	96.4	3.6	0.2	1.4	3.4	94 570	71.7	28.3	3.02	2.75
Pulaski	9.7	16 325	89.7	10.3	4.5	1.2	7.3	14 643	73.7	26.3	2.38	2.17
Rappahannock	11.7	3 303	84.4	15.6	9.4	1.2	5.6	2 788	75.2	24.8	2.51	2.47
Richmond	11.0	3 512	83.6	16.4	8.0	1.4	3.1	2 937	77.4	22.6	2.44	2.27
Roanoke	14.3	36 121	96.0	4.0	0.4	1.2	5.7	34 686	77.2	22.8	2.53	2.01
Rockbridge	17.8	9 550	88.9	11.1	4.0	1.7	8.3	8 486	77.7	22.3	2.46	2.31
Rockingham	22.2	27 328	92.8	7.2	3.0	1.2	4.9	25 355	78.0	22.0	2.65	2.45
Russell	10.8	13 191	89.4	10.6	0.5	1.7	10.8	11 789	81.1	18.9	2.48	2.28
Scott	9.2	11 355	86.3	13.7	2.6	1.7	8.3	9 795	78.2	21.8	2.39	2.23
Shenandoah	14.8	16 709	85.6	14.4	8.7	1.9	4.2	14 296	73.2	26.8	2.42	2.42
Smyth	10.3	15 111	89.3	10.7	3.1	1.4	9.3	13 493	74.1	25.9	2.40	2.28
Southampton	4.5	7 058	89.0	11.0	1.4	1.5	6.4	6 279	74.3	25.7	2.57	2.44
Spotsylvania	65.3	33 329	93.9	6.1	1.7	1.7	6.1	31 308	82.2	17.8	2.92	2.65
Stafford	55.5	31 405	96.1	3.9	0.4	1.5	5.4	30 187	80.6	19.4	3.07	2.79
Surry	14.7	3 294	79.5	20.5	11.2	2.9	10.4	2 619	77.2	22.8	2.63	2.54
Sussex	8.7	4 653	88.7	11.3	1.8	1.6	4.6	4 126	69.5	30.5	2.38	2.49
Tazewell	5.6	20 390	89.6	10.4	1.0	2.2	12.1	18 277	77.3	22.7	2.44	2.24
Warren	22.4	13 299	90.9	9.1	4.0	1.9	4.4	12 087	74.2	25.8	2.62	2.42
Washington	20.4	22 985	91.6	8.4	2.2	1.4	7.4	21 056	77.2	22.8	2.42	2.18
Westmoreland	13.0	9 286	73.7	26.3	18.0	2.7	5.7	6 846	79.2	20.8	2.39	2.58
Wise	10.3	17 792	90.0	10.0	0.5	2.0	11.8	16 013	75.3	24.7	2.48	2.30
Wythe	16.8	12 744	90.3	9.7	2.1	1.7	7.1	11 511	77.3	22.7	2.41	2.19
York	38.2	20 701	96.6	3.4	0.4	1.3	2.7	20 000	75.8	24.2	2.74	2.92
Independent Cities												
Alexandria City	16.2	64 251	96.3	3.7	0.8	1.0	2.4	61 889	40.0	60.0	2.03	2.05
Bedford City	1.8	2 702	93.2	6.8	0.6	1.8	6.5	2 519	60.3	39.7	2.36	2.11
Bristol City	1.1	8 469	90.7	9.3	0.4	2.2	12.5	7 678	65.1	34.9	2.24	2.06
Buena Vista City	5.9	2 716	93.8	6.2	0.3	1.4	4.4	2 547	70.7	29.3	2.40	2.33
Charlottesville City	5.3	17 591	95.8	4.2	0.4	1.1	2.4	16 851	40.8	59.2	2.27	2.26
Chesapeake City	34.5	72 672	96.2	3.8	0.3	1.4	3.6	69 900	74.9	25.1	2.87	2.56
Clifton Forge City	-4.6	2 069	89.0	11.0	0.3	2.9	6.5	1 841	62.6	37.4	2.34	2.01
Colonial Heights City	10.4	7 340	95.7	4.3	0.3	1.2	6.0	7 027	69.3	30.7	2.42	2.27
Covington City	-5.4	3 195	88.7	11.3	0.5	2.8	10.8	2 835	69.7	30.3	2.22	2.22
Danville City	-5.1	23 108	89.2	10.8	0.4	2.8	11.6	20 607	58.1	41.9	2.28	2.25
Emporia City	9.6	2 412	92.3	7.7	0.5	1.9	6.5	2 226	52.2	47.8	2.38	2.48
Fairfax City	9.1	8 204	97.9	2.1	0.4	0.7	2.0	8 035	69.1	30.9	2.62	2.59
Falls Church City	6.6	4 725	94.6	5.4	1.9	0.6	5.3	4 471	60.6	39.4	2.54	1.95
Franklin City	12.6	3 767	89.8	10.2	0.7	2.9	6.0	3 384	53.7	46.3	2.50	2.25
Fredericksburg City	8.8	8 888	91.2	8.8	0.5	2.1	8.2	8 102	35.6	64.4	2.27	1.99
Galax City	7.3	3 217	91.7	8.3	0.9	2.4	5.9	2 950	66.2	33.8	2.29	2.23
Hampton City	8.5	57 311	94.0	6.0	0.5	2.0	5.6	53 887	58.6	41.4	2.55	2.40
Harrisonburg City	27.4	13 689	95.9	4.1	0.3	1.7	3.3	13 133	39.0	61.0	2.52	2.54
Hopewell City	0.5	9 749	92.9	7.1	0.2	3.5	5.7	9 055	56.0	44.0	2.39	2.48
Lexington City	2.8	2 376	93.9	6.1	0.5	2.1	3.6	2 232	54.9	45.1	2.19	1.91
Lynchburg City	1.3	27 640	92.2	7.8	0.5	2.2	7.1	25 477	58.5	41.5	2.44	2.12

Table B. States and Counties

STATE/County code	MSA/PMSA/NECMA code[1]	County type[2]	STATE County	Population, 2000					Population, 1990				Population and population characteristics, 2000					
													Race (percent)					
													One race					
				Land area, 2000[3] (sq km)	Total persons	Rank	Per square kilometer	Land area, 1990[3] (sq km)	Total persons	Rank	Per square kilometer		White	Black or African American	American Indian or Alaska Native	Asian	Native Hawaiian and other Pacific Islander	Some other race
				1	2	3	4	5	6	7	8		9	10	11	12	13	14
			VIRGINIA—Cont'd															
			Independent Cities—Cont'd															
51 683	8840	NA	Manassas City	26	35 135	1 244	1 351.3	26	27 757	1 361	1 067.6		72.1	12.9	0.4	3.4	0.1	7.9
51 685	8840	NA	Manassas Park City	6	10 290	2 417	1 715.0	5	6 798	2 676	1 359.6		72.8	11.2	0.4	4.1	0.1	8.1
51 690	...	NA	Martinsville City	28	15 416	2 058	550.6	28	16 162	1 914	577.2		55.4	42.5	0.1	0.5	0.0	0.7
51 700	5720	NA	Newport News City	177	180 150	306	1 017.8	177	171 477	281	968.8		53.5	39.1	0.4	2.3	0.1	1.8
51 710	5720	NA	Norfolk City	139	234 403	247	1 686.4	139	261 250	192	1 879.5		48.4	44.1	0.5	2.8	0.1	1.7
51 720	...	NA	Norton City	20	3 904	2 922	195.2	19	4 247	2 894	223.5		91.6	6.1	0.1	1.0	0.1	0.2
51 730	6760	NA	Petersburg City	59	33 740	1 289	571.9	59	37 071	1 071	628.3		18.5	79.0	0.2	0.7	0.0	0.6
51 735	5720	NA	Poquoson City	40	11 566	2 327	289.2	40	11 005	2 292	275.1		96.3	0.7	0.2	1.6	0.0	0.3
51 740	5720	NA	Portsmouth City	86	100 565	522	1 169.4	86	103 910	443	1 208.3		45.8	50.6	0.5	0.8	0.1	0.6
51 750	...	NA	Radford City	25	15 859	2 028	634.4	25	15 940	1 927	637.6		88.2	8.1	0.2	1.4	0.0	0.5
51 760	6760	NA	Richmond City	156	197 790	280	1 267.9	156	202 713	244	1 299.4		38.3	57.2	0.2	1.2	0.1	1.5
51 770	6800	NA	Roanoke City	111	94 911	542	855.1	111	96 487	478	869.3		69.4	26.7	0.2	1.2	0.0	0.7
51 775	6800	NA	Salem City	38	24 747	1 566	651.2	38	23 835	1 499	627.2		91.9	5.9	0.1	1.0	0.0	0.2
51 790	...	NA	Staunton City	51	23 853	1 597	467.7	51	24 581	1 477	482.0		83.3	14.0	0.2	0.5	0.0	0.5
51 800	5720	NA	Suffolk City	1 036	63 677	763	61.5	1 036	52 143	812	50.3		53.8	43.5	0.3	0.8	0.0	0.4
51 810	5720	NA	Virginia Beach City	643	425 257	141	661.4	643	393 089	128	611.3		71.4	19.0	0.4	4.9	0.1	1.5
51 820	...	NA	Waynesboro City	40	19 520	1 819	488.0	36	18 549	1 760	515.3		86.5	10.0	0.3	0.6	0.0	1.1
51 830	5720	NA	Williamsburg City	22	11 998	2 294	545.4	22	11 600	2 248	527.3		79.5	13.3	0.3	4.6	0.0	0.8
51 840	...	NA	Winchester City	24	23 585	1 609	982.7	24	21 947	1 579	914.5		82.1	10.5	0.2	1.6	0.0	3.5
53 000	....		WASHINGTON	172 348	5 894 121	X	34.2	172 447	4 866 669	X	28.2		81.8	3.2	1.6	5.5	0.4	3.9
53 001	...	6	Adams	4 986	16 428	1 995	3.3	4 986	13 603	2 092	2.7		65.0	0.3	0.7	0.6	0.0	30.7
53 003	...	7	Asotin	1 646	20 551	1 758	12.5	1 647	17 605	1 814	10.7		95.6	0.2	1.3	0.5	0.0	0.6
53 005	6740	3	Benton	4 411	142 475	383	32.3	4 411	112 560	408	25.5		86.2	0.9	0.8	2.2	0.1	7.0
53 007	...	5	Chelan	7 566	66 616	734	8.8	7 567	52 250	810	6.9		83.6	0.3	1.0	0.7	0.1	12.2
53 009	...	5	Clallam	4 505	64 525	753	14.3	4 520	56 210	772	12.4		89.1	0.8	5.1	1.1	0.2	1.2
53 011	6440	1	Clark	1 627	345 238	169	212.2	1 626	238 053	210	146.4		88.8	1.7	0.8	3.2	0.4	2.0
53 013	...	9	Columbia	2 250	4 064	2 915	1.8	2 250	4 024	2 914	1.8		93.7	0.2	1.0	0.4	0.0	2.7
53 015	...	4	Cowlitz	2 949	92 948	550	31.5	2 949	82 119	552	27.8		91.8	0.5	1.5	1.3	0.1	2.1
53 017	...	7	Douglas	4 715	32 603	1 328	6.9	4 715	26 205	1 412	5.6		84.7	0.3	1.1	0.5	0.1	10.8
53 019	...	9	Ferry	5 708	7 260	2 658	1.3	5 708	6 295	2 721	1.1		75.5	0.2	18.3	0.3	0.1	2.2
53 021	6740	3	Franklin	3 218	49 347	926	15.3	3 217	37 473	1 059	11.6		61.9	2.5	0.7	1.6	0.1	29.0
53 023	...	9	Garfield	1 840	2 397	3 030	1.3	1 840	2 248	3 049	1.2		96.5	0.0	0.4	0.7	0.0	1.4
53 025	...	5	Grant	6 944	74 698	669	10.8	6 932	54 798	785	7.9		76.5	1.0	1.2	0.9	0.1	17.4
53 027	...	4	Grays Harbor	4 965	67 194	729	13.5	4 966	64 175	685	12.9		88.3	0.3	4.7	1.2	0.1	2.3
53 029	7600	1	Island	540	71 558	690	132.5	540	60 195	720	111.5		87.2	2.4	1.0	4.2	0.4	1.4
53 031	...	6	Jefferson	4 699	25 953	1 518	5.5	4 685	20 406	1 655	4.4		92.2	0.4	2.3	1.2	0.1	1.4
53 033	7600	0	King	5 506	1 737 034	12	315.5	5 507	1 507 305	13	273.7		75.7	5.4	0.9	10.8	0.5	2.6
53 035	1150	3	Kitsap	1 026	231 969	249	226.1	1 026	189 731	252	184.9		84.3	2.9	1.6	4.4	0.8	1.4
53 037	...	6	Kittitas	5 950	33 362	1 302	5.6	5 950	26 725	1 400	4.5		91.8	0.7	0.9	2.2	0.1	2.3
53 039	...	7	Klickitat	4 849	19 161	1 838	4.0	4 850	16 616	1 876	3.4		87.6	0.3	3.5	0.7	0.2	5.0
53 041	...	6	Lewis	6 236	68 600	720	11.0	6 236	59 358	730	9.5		93.0	0.4	1.2	0.7	0.2	2.6
53 043	...	8	Lincoln	5 986	10 184	2 430	1.7	5 986	8 864	2 481	1.5		95.6	0.2	1.6	0.2	0.1	0.6
53 045	...	6	Mason	2 489	49 405	925	19.8	2 489	38 341	1 044	15.4		88.5	1.2	3.7	1.1	0.4	2.1
53 047	...	7	Okanogan	13 644	39 564	1 125	2.9	13 645	33 350	1 181	2.4		75.3	0.3	11.5	0.4	0.1	8.9
53 049	...	7	Pacific	2 416	20 984	1 736	8.7	2 524	18 882	1 741	7.5		90.5	0.2	2.4	2.1	0.1	1.8
53 051	...	8	Pend Oreille	3 627	11 732	2 314	3.2	3 627	8 915	2 478	2.5		93.5	0.1	2.9	0.6	0.2	0.6
53 053	8200	2	Pierce	4 348	700 820	71	161.2	4 340	586 203	80	135.1		78.4	7.0	1.4	5.1	0.8	2.2
53 055	...	8	San Juan	453	14 077	2 156	31.1	453	10 035	2 382	22.2		95.0	0.3	0.8	0.9	0.1	0.9
53 057	...	4	Skagit	4 494	102 979	516	22.9	4 494	79 545	573	17.7		86.5	0.4	1.9	1.5	0.2	7.2
53 059	...	8	Skamania	4 290	9 872	2 458	2.3	4 290	8 289	2 537	1.9		92.1	0.3	2.2	0.5	0.2	2.4
53 061	7600	0	Snohomish	5 411	606 024	90	112.0	5 414	465 628	107	86.0		85.6	1.7	1.4	5.8	0.3	1.9
53 063	7840	2	Spokane	4 568	417 939	144	91.5	4 568	361 333	142	79.1		91.4	1.6	1.4	1.9	0.2	0.8
53 065	...	6	Stevens	6 419	40 066	1 112	6.2	6 419	30 948	1 248	4.8		90.0	0.3	5.7	0.5	0.2	0.7
53 067	5910	3	Thurston	1 883	207 355	268	110.1	1 883	161 238	295	85.6		85.7	2.4	1.5	4.4	0.5	1.7
53 069	...	9	Wahkiakum	684	3 824	2 927	5.6	684	3 327	2 968	4.9		93.5	0.3	1.6	0.5	0.1	1.6
53 071	...	4	Walla Walla	3 291	55 180	854	16.8	3 291	48 439	864	14.7		85.3	1.7	0.8	1.1	0.2	8.2
53 073	0860	3	Whatcom	5 490	166 814	324	30.4	5 491	127 780	364	23.3		88.4	0.7	2.8	2.8	0.1	2.5
53 075	...	5	Whitman	5 593	40 740	1 091	7.3	5 593	38 775	1 031	6.9		88.1	1.5	0.7	5.5	0.3	1.2
53 077	9260	3	Yakima	11 127	222 581	255	20.0	11 127	188 823	255	17.0		65.6	1.0	4.5	1.0	0.1	24.4
54 000	....		WEST VIRGINIA	62 361	1 808 344	X	29.0	62 384	1 793 477	X	28.7		95.0	3.2	0.2	0.5	0.0	0.2
54 001	...	7	Barbour	883	15 557	2 050	17.6	883	15 699	1 944	17.8		97.4	0.5	0.7	0.3	0.0	0.1
54 003	8840	3	Berkeley	832	75 905	660	91.2	832	59 253	733	71.2		92.7	4.7	0.2	0.5	0.0	0.6
54 005	...	6	Boone	1 303	25 535	1 538	19.6	1 303	25 870	1 427	19.9		98.5	0.7	0.1	0.1	0.0	0.1

[1] MSA = Metropolitan Statistical Area. PMSA = Primary MSA. NECMA = New England County Metropolitan Area. See Appendix A for explanation of these concepts. See Appendix B for list of metropolitan areas identified by type, with component counties.
[2] County typology code from the Economic Research Service of USDA. See Appendix A for definition.
[3] Dry land or land partially or temporarily covered by water.

Table B. States and Counties

	Population and population characteristics, 2000 (cont'd)								Population and population characteristics, 1990				
	Race (percent) (cont'd)								Race (percent)				
		Race alone or in combination											
STATE County	Two or more races	White	Black	American Indian or Alaska Native	Asian	Native Hawaiian and other Pacific Islander	Some other race	Hispanic[1]	White	Black or African American	American Indian or Alaska Native	Asian and Pacific Islander	Hispanic[1]
	15	16	17	18	19	20	21	22	23	24	25	26	27
VIRGINIA—Cont'd													
Independent Cities—Cont'd													
Manassas City	3.3	74.8	13.9	0.8	4.0	0.2	9.7	15.1	83.5	10.3	0.3	3.1	5.7
Manassas Park City	3.3	75.7	12.0	0.9	4.9	0.3	9.8	15.0	88.2	7.3	0.1	2.5	4.7
Martinsville City	0.8	56.0	43.0	0.4	0.6	0.0	0.9	2.3	62.7	36.8	0.1	0.2	0.4
Newport News City	2.8	55.4	40.6	1.1	3.1	0.3	2.6	4.2	62.6	33.6	0.3	2.3	2.8
Norfolk City	2.5	50.1	45.3	1.1	3.6	0.3	2.4	3.8	56.7	39.1	0.4	2.6	2.9
Norton City	0.9	92.4	6.6	0.4	1.1	0.2	0.3	0.9	92.4	6.3	0.3	0.8	0.7
Petersburg City	1.0	19.1	79.6	0.5	0.9	0.1	0.8	1.4	26.6	72.1	0.2	0.8	1.2
Poquoson City	1.0	97.2	0.8	0.6	1.9	0.1	0.4	1.1	97.5	0.8	0.2	1.5	0.9
Portsmouth City	1.6	47.0	51.5	1.1	1.1	0.2	0.9	1.7	51.2	47.3	0.3	0.8	1.3
Radford City	1.5	89.4	8.7	0.6	1.9	0.1	0.9	1.2	91.9	6.0	0.1	1.7	1.1
Richmond City	1.5	39.2	58.1	0.7	1.5	0.2	2.0	2.6	43.4	55.2	0.2	0.9	0.9
Roanoke City	1.8	70.8	27.7	0.7	1.4	0.1	1.3	1.5	74.6	24.3	0.2	0.7	0.7
Salem City	0.9	92.6	6.2	0.4	1.1	0.1	0.5	0.8	94.6	4.5	0.1	0.7	0.5
Staunton City	1.6	84.6	14.8	0.6	0.8	0.1	0.8	1.1	86.6	12.6	0.2	0.4	0.7
Suffolk City	1.2	54.7	44.1	0.8	1.1	0.1	0.6	1.3	54.7	44.6	0.2	0.4	0.6
Virginia Beach City	2.7	73.6	20.0	1.0	6.0	0.3	2.2	4.2	80.5	13.9	0.4	4.3	3.1
Waynesboro City	1.6	87.9	10.8	0.8	0.8	0.1	1.4	3.3	89.9	9.4	0.2	0.2	0.8
Williamsburg City	1.5	80.8	13.8	0.6	5.2	0.1	1.0	2.5	81.2	15.2	0.2	2.9	1.3
Winchester City	2.1	83.9	11.5	0.9	1.8	0.1	4.0	6.5	88.6	10.0	0.1	1.0	1.0
WASHINGTON	3.6	84.9	4.0	2.7	6.7	0.7	4.9	7.5	88.5	3.1	1.7	4.3	4.4
Adams	2.7	67.4	0.4	1.3	0.9	0.2	32.6	47.1	66.9	0.2	0.5	0.7	32.8
Asotin	1.8	97.3	0.4	2.4	0.7	0.1	1.0	2.0	97.3	0.2	1.5	0.6	1.6
Benton	2.7	88.7	1.3	1.6	2.8	0.2	8.2	12.5	91.4	1.0	0.8	2.0	7.7
Chelan	2.1	85.6	0.4	1.8	1.1	0.2	13.1	19.3	92.5	0.2	0.9	0.7	9.2
Clallam	2.4	91.4	1.1	6.5	1.7	0.3	1.6	3.4	93.0	0.6	4.8	1.1	2.0
Clark	3.1	91.6	2.3	1.8	4.1	0.7	2.8	4.7	94.6	1.3	1.0	2.4	2.5
Columbia	1.9	95.5	0.3	2.0	0.7	0.1	3.3	6.3	96.3	0.0	0.7	0.4	11.5
Cowlitz	2.6	94.3	0.8	3.0	1.8	0.3	2.6	4.6	95.6	0.4	1.6	1.4	2.0
Douglas	2.5	87.0	0.6	1.9	0.9	0.1	12.1	19.7	92.9	0.2	0.9	0.6	10.4
Ferry	3.5	78.7	0.4	20.9	0.6	0.2	2.9	2.8	80.8	0.3	18.0	0.4	1.4
Franklin	4.1	65.6	2.9	1.3	2.0	0.2	32.2	46.7	71.8	3.5	0.7	2.3	30.2
Garfield	1.1	97.5	0.0	1.0	1.0	0.0	1.5	2.0	98.8	0.0	0.5	0.3	1.0
Grant	3.0	79.2	1.3	2.0	1.3	0.2	19.2	30.1	85.8	1.1	1.0	1.2	17.2
Grays Harbor	3.1	91.2	0.7	6.4	1.8	0.3	3.0	4.8	93.9	0.2	4.2	1.1	1.8
Island	3.4	90.1	3.0	2.1	5.7	0.8	2.0	4.0	91.4	2.4	0.8	4.2	3.3
Jefferson	3.0	95.1	0.7	3.8	1.8	0.3	1.6	2.1	95.6	0.4	2.8	1.0	1.2
King	4.1	78.9	6.5	1.9	12.5	0.9	3.7	5.5	84.8	5.1	1.1	7.9	2.9
Kitsap	4.6	88.3	3.8	3.2	6.3	1.3	2.3	4.1	90.2	2.7	1.7	4.4	3.3
Kittitas	2.0	93.5	1.0	1.8	2.8	0.3	2.7	5.0	95.5	0.6	0.8	1.8	2.6
Klickitat	2.7	90.1	0.5	5.0	1.1	0.4	5.8	7.8	92.6	0.2	3.5	0.8	5.6
Lewis	2.0	94.8	0.6	2.2	1.0	0.3	3.2	5.4	97.1	0.3	1.1	0.6	2.3
Lincoln	1.6	97.1	0.6	2.7	0.4	0.1	0.8	1.9	97.7	0.2	1.5	0.4	0.9
Mason	3.0	91.2	1.5	5.4	1.6	0.7	2.7	4.8	93.3	0.9	3.7	1.2	2.3
Okanogan	2.8	77.9	0.5	13.2	0.8	0.2	10.5	14.4	82.8	0.2	10.8	0.5	8.3
Pacific	2.8	93.2	0.4	4.2	2.5	0.2	2.4	5.0	93.7	0.3	2.7	2.5	2.3
Pend Oreille	2.0	95.4	0.4	4.0	1.0	0.4	1.0	2.1	96.9	0.1	2.3	0.3	1.3
Pierce	5.1	82.7	8.6	2.8	7.0	1.4	3.3	5.5	85.1	7.2	1.4	5.0	3.5
San Juan	2.0	96.9	0.4	1.7	1.4	0.2	1.5	2.4	97.8	0.2	0.8	0.9	1.2
Skagit	2.4	88.7	0.7	2.7	2.0	0.3	8.0	11.2	93.2	0.4	2.2	1.0	5.4
Skamania	2.2	94.3	0.5	3.5	0.9	0.4	2.9	4.0	96.4	0.1	2.4	0.6	2.1
Snohomish	3.4	88.6	2.3	2.4	7.0	0.6	2.8	4.7	93.3	1.0	1.4	3.5	2.3
Spokane	2.8	93.9	2.2	2.4	2.6	0.3	1.4	2.8	94.6	1.4	1.5	1.8	1.9
Stevens	2.7	92.6	0.5	7.4	1.0	0.3	1.1	1.8	92.9	0.2	5.8	0.6	1.6
Thurston	3.9	89.0	3.1	2.8	5.8	0.9	2.5	4.5	91.9	1.8	1.5	3.8	3.0
Wahkiakum	2.5	95.9	0.3	3.5	0.8	0.2	1.8	2.6	96.7	0.1	1.6	0.5	2.1
Walla Walla	2.6	87.7	2.0	1.7	1.7	0.4	9.3	15.7	89.4	1.5	0.7	1.3	9.7
Whatcom	2.7	90.8	1.1	3.8	3.7	0.3	3.2	5.2	93.3	0.5	3.1	1.8	2.9
Whitman	2.6	90.3	2.0	1.5	6.6	0.5	1.9	3.0	91.9	1.3	0.6	5.4	1.8
Yakima	3.5	68.6	1.4	5.6	1.5	0.2	26.4	35.9	73.9	1.0	4.5	1.0	23.9
WEST VIRGINIA	0.9	95.9	3.5	0.6	0.7	0.0	0.3	0.7	96.2	3.1	0.1	0.4	0.5
Barbour	1.0	98.3	0.8	1.4	0.3	0.1	0.3	0.5	97.7	0.9	1.0	0.2	0.6
Berkeley	1.3	93.9	5.3	0.6	0.7	0.1	0.8	1.5	95.4	3.7	0.2	0.5	0.7
Boone	0.5	99.1	0.8	0.4	0.1	0.0	0.1	0.5	98.9	0.8	0.1	0.1	0.2

[1] Hispanic persons may be of any race.

Table B. States and Counties

STATE County	Population and population characteristics, 2000										
	Age (percent)										
	Under 5 years	5 to 17 years	18 to 24 years	25 to 34 years	35 to 44 years	45 to 54 years	55 to 64 years	65 to 74 years	75 years and over	Median age (years)	Percent Female
	28	29	30	31	32	33	34	35	36	37	38
VIRGINIA—Cont'd											
Independent Cities—Cont'd											
Manassas City	8.6	21.0	9.8	17.4	18.4	13.1	6.3	3.1	2.3	31.3	49.1
Manassas Park City	10.0	21.1	8.7	20.7	19.4	10.2	5.7	3.0	1.3	30.3	49.1
Martinsville City	5.6	16.9	7.0	11.5	15.1	13.1	10.0	9.7	10.9	40.8	54.8
Newport News City	7.9	19.6	11.5	15.8	16.4	11.5	7.3	5.4	4.7	32.0	51.6
Norfolk City	7.1	17.0	18.2	15.6	14.3	10.7	6.2	5.5	5.4	29.6	48.9
Norton City	5.1	16.6	10.2	13.0	14.3	14.9	10.6	8.1	7.2	39.0	55.0
Petersburg City	6.4	18.7	8.9	13.0	14.5	13.2	9.7	8.0	7.6	36.9	54.3
Poquoson City	5.1	21.7	6.4	9.0	17.7	16.9	11.8	6.6	4.7	39.5	49.9
Portsmouth City	7.1	18.6	11.1	14.0	15.1	12.3	8.0	6.8	6.9	34.5	51.7
Radford City	3.5	9.4	44.0	10.8	8.8	8.2	6.1	4.9	4.4	22.8	54.5
Richmond City	6.3	15.6	13.1	16.6	15.1	12.6	7.5	6.5	6.7	33.9	53.5
Roanoke City	6.5	16.1	8.2	15.2	15.3	13.8	8.5	7.8	8.6	37.6	53.1
Salem City	4.9	16.0	11.7	11.8	15.0	14.0	10.0	8.8	7.9	39.2	52.8
Staunton City	5.2	14.6	10.2	13.0	14.8	14.0	10.1	8.9	9.2	39.8	52.9
Suffolk City	7.3	20.6	7.1	13.4	17.8	13.4	9.2	6.3	5.2	36.0	52.2
Virginia Beach City	7.2	20.3	10.0	16.4	17.8	12.7	7.1	4.9	3.6	32.7	50.5
Waynesboro City	6.6	17.3	7.9	12.9	14.5	12.9	10.3	8.9	8.7	38.9	53.2
Williamsburg City	2.7	6.9	46.0	9.7	8.1	8.0	7.0	5.9	5.8	22.6	55.1
Winchester City	6.1	15.6	13.1	14.9	14.9	12.8	8.1	7.7	6.8	35.2	51.5
WASHINGTON	6.7	19.0	9.5	14.3	16.5	14.4	8.4	5.7	5.5	35.3	50.2
Adams	9.4	24.7	9.8	13.2	13.1	11.6	7.8	5.7	4.7	29.6	48.9
Asotin	6.8	18.7	8.1	11.3	14.8	13.5	10.5	8.0	8.3	38.8	52.3
Benton	7.6	22.2	8.6	12.5	16.1	14.4	8.5	5.5	4.8	34.4	50.3
Chelan	7.1	20.8	8.3	12.0	15.2	14.0	8.7	6.9	6.9	36.3	50.2
Clallam	5.1	16.8	7.1	9.1	13.6	15.1	11.8	10.8	10.5	43.8	50.3
Clark	7.8	20.9	8.4	14.1	16.7	14.4	8.2	5.0	4.5	34.2	50.4
Columbia	5.3	18.6	7.0	8.9	13.9	15.7	12.0	9.2	9.3	42.4	51.2
Cowlitz	6.7	20.1	8.3	12.3	15.2	14.5	9.6	6.8	6.5	36.9	50.5
Douglas	7.6	21.9	8.2	11.5	15.8	13.6	8.8	6.8	5.9	35.7	50.4
Ferry	5.4	21.4	7.6	9.3	14.1	17.3	12.2	7.7	4.9	40.0	48.2
Franklin	10.0	24.6	10.9	14.5	13.7	11.4	6.5	4.7	3.8	28.0	47.8
Garfield	4.6	21.4	5.4	7.8	14.1	16.0	9.8	10.2	10.7	43.0	50.5
Grant	8.7	23.3	9.8	13.1	13.9	11.8	7.8	6.3	5.3	31.1	48.9
Grays Harbor	6.2	19.4	7.9	11.3	14.7	14.7	10.3	8.0	7.4	38.8	50.3
Island	6.7	18.8	8.5	12.8	15.2	13.5	10.2	7.7	6.5	37.0	49.9
Jefferson	4.1	15.7	5.0	7.6	14.0	18.4	14.1	11.7	9.4	47.1	51.1
King	6.1	16.4	9.3	17.0	17.8	14.9	8.1	5.1	5.3	35.7	50.2
Kitsap	6.7	20.1	9.2	12.9	16.8	15.2	8.6	5.4	5.2	35.8	49.3
Kittitas	5.1	15.5	21.6	11.6	13.0	12.5	9.0	5.9	5.7	31.4	50.3
Klickitat	6.4	20.7	6.5	10.3	15.4	16.1	10.9	7.5	6.3	39.5	50.1
Lewis	6.4	20.1	8.2	10.8	14.5	14.3	10.2	7.9	7.7	38.4	50.4
Lincoln	5.7	19.5	5.2	8.7	14.5	15.1	12.3	9.7	9.3	42.8	50.4
Mason	5.4	18.1	7.7	11.1	15.4	14.6	11.2	9.5	7.0	40.3	48.3
Okanogan	6.3	21.4	7.3	10.9	14.6	15.0	10.5	7.8	6.3	38.2	50.2
Pacific	4.6	16.9	6.0	8.4	12.8	15.1	13.8	12.4	10.1	45.8	50.4
Pend Oreille	5.4	20.9	5.5	8.2	15.6	17.1	12.4	8.9	6.0	41.9	49.9
Pierce	7.1	20.1	9.8	14.4	16.9	13.5	8.0	5.4	4.8	34.1	50.3
San Juan	3.7	15.4	4.5	7.3	14.4	20.5	15.2	10.1	8.9	47.4	51.3
Skagit	6.5	19.8	8.6	12.0	14.9	14.4	9.1	7.3	7.3	37.2	50.5
Skamania	6.4	20.2	6.7	10.7	17.9	16.9	10.3	6.4	4.6	38.7	49.7
Snohomish	7.2	20.2	8.5	14.6	18.3	14.3	7.7	4.7	4.4	34.7	50.0
Spokane	6.6	19.1	10.6	13.1	15.8	14.2	8.2	6.0	6.4	35.4	50.9
Stevens	6.1	22.6	6.4	9.3	15.6	16.1	11.0	7.1	5.8	39.2	50.2
Thurston	6.2	19.1	9.3	13.0	16.3	15.7	8.9	5.8	5.6	36.5	51.0
Wahkiakum	5.3	18.1	5.3	8.4	13.8	16.5	14.2	9.9	8.6	44.4	50.0
Walla Walla	6.3	18.3	13.4	12.2	14.2	12.8	8.0	6.6	8.2	34.9	49.1
Whatcom	6.1	18.0	14.2	12.8	14.6	14.4	8.2	5.9	5.7	34.0	50.7
Whitman	4.8	13.2	32.6	13.1	10.9	9.6	6.4	4.4	4.8	24.7	49.4
Yakima	8.7	23.1	9.8	13.3	14.2	12.0	7.7	5.6	5.6	31.2	50.1
WEST VIRGINIA	5.6	16.6	9.5	12.7	15.1	15.0	10.2	8.2	7.1	38.9	51.4
Barbour	5.3	17.7	9.4	12.3	14.5	14.4	10.8	8.2	7.4	38.7	50.9
Berkeley	6.6	19.1	8.3	14.6	16.7	14.4	9.1	6.6	4.6	35.8	50.2
Boone	6.3	16.9	9.0	12.8	15.2	16.5	9.8	7.5	6.1	38.8	51.2

Table B. States and Counties

STATE County	Age (percent)										Population—change, 1980–2000 Total persons			Percent change	
	Under 5 years	5 to 17 years	18 to 24 years	25 to 34 years	35 to 44 years	45 to 54 years	55 to 64 years	65 to 74 years	75 years and over	Percent Female	2000	1990	1980	1990–2000	1980–1990
	39	40	41	42	43	44	45	46	47	48	49	50	51	52	53
VIRGINIA—Cont'd															
Independent Cities—Cont'd															
Manassas City	9.8	18.8	11.8	23.7	17.1	9.2	4.6	2.8	2.1	49.0	35 135	27 757	15 505	26.6	80.3
Manassas Park City	9.7	21.4	11.5	25.7	13.4	8.4	6.3	2.6	1.1	50.3	10 290	6 798	6 524	51.4	3.2
Martinsville City	6.4	16.0	8.2	14.6	13.7	10.6	11.0	11.2	8.1	55.0	15 416	16 162	18 149	-4.6	-10.9
Newport News City	9.3	18.1	12.3	21.6	13.9	8.6	7.0	5.9	3.4	51.0	180 150	171 477	144 903	5.1	18.3
Norfolk City	8.3	14.7	21.8	19.9	11.8	6.6	6.5	6.4	4.1	46.7	234 403	261 250	266 979	-10.3	-2.1
Norton City	6.2	19.9	10.2	15.4	14.8	9.9	9.5	8.2	5.9	54.0	3 904	4 247	4 757	-8.1	-10.7
Petersburg City	7.5	16.0	11.4	17.2	13.7	9.7	9.6	9.1	5.9	53.8	33 740	37 071	41 055	-9.0	-9.8
Poquoson City	6.1	21.4	8.4	13.7	19.2	14.4	8.4	4.6	3.8	50.2	11 566	11 005	8 726	5.1	26.1
Portsmouth City	8.4	18.4	11.0	17.9	13.2	8.7	8.5	8.7	5.1	52.4	100 565	103 910	104 577	-3.2	-0.6
Radford City	3.5	9.2	48.0	9.9	8.6	6.4	5.8	5.2	3.3	55.7	15 859	15 940	13 457	-0.5	18.5
Richmond City	6.9	13.8	13.4	19.2	14.3	8.6	8.5	8.3	7.0	54.3	197 790	202 713	219 214	-2.4	-7.5
Roanoke City	7.1	14.9	9.9	17.8	14.7	9.1	9.4	9.5	7.6	53.7	94 911	96 487	100 220	-1.6	-3.7
Salem City	5.2	14.5	12.5	14.6	14.9	11.0	10.8	9.7	6.9	52.1	24 747	23 835	23 958	3.8	-0.7
Staunton City	5.6	14.9	10.5	16.1	14.8	10.7	10.4	9.5	7.5	52.9	23 853	24 581	24 777	-3.0	-1.3
Suffolk City	7.6	19.5	8.7	16.5	14.4	11.0	9.3	7.9	5.0	52.6	63 677	52 143	47 621	22.1	9.5
Virginia Beach City	8.9	19.1	12.9	22.4	16.1	8.8	6.0	3.9	2.0	49.2	425 257	393 089	262 199	8.2	49.9
Waynesboro City	6.9	16.2	9.3	15.7	13.3	11.4	10.4	10.1	6.7	52.8	19 520	18 549	18 563	5.2	0.0
Williamsburg City	2.7	6.5	48.3	12.5	7.5	5.4	5.3	6.5	5.4	53.6	11 998	11 600	10 294	3.4	10.8
Winchester City	7.0	14.7	12.4	17.9	14.1	9.5	9.3	8.7	6.6	52.2	23 585	21 947	20 217	7.5	8.6
WASHINGTON	7.5	18.4	10.0	17.6	16.5	10.3	7.8	6.9	4.9	50.4	5 894 121	4 866 669	4 132 353	21.1	17.8
Adams	9.2	24.8	8.1	14.2	14.0	9.9	8.4	6.8	4.5	49.6	16 428	13 603	13 267	20.8	2.5
Asotin	7.4	20.3	7.4	15.1	14.1	9.9	9.3	8.9	7.7	52.4	20 551	17 605	16 823	16.7	4.6
Benton	8.3	21.7	8.5	16.6	16.0	10.7	8.1	6.2	3.9	50.6	142 475	112 560	109 444	26.6	2.8
Chelan	7.7	19.0	8.1	15.1	15.6	9.9	8.9	8.6	7.1	50.7	66 616	52 250	45 061	27.5	16.0
Clallam	6.4	17.9	6.9	13.4	14.9	9.9	10.3	12.2	8.2	50.3	64 525	56 210	51 648	14.8	8.8
Clark	7.8	20.6	8.8	16.5	17.2	10.9	7.5	6.3	4.3	50.6	345 238	238 053	192 227	45.0	23.8
Columbia	5.5	19.3	6.4	12.5	14.9	11.9	10.4	11.1	8.1	50.4	4 064	4 024	4 057	1.0	-0.8
Cowlitz	7.4	19.9	8.7	15.2	15.7	10.8	8.8	7.7	5.8	50.6	92 948	82 119	79 548	13.2	3.2
Douglas	7.8	21.0	8.3	15.3	16.1	10.6	8.7	7.3	4.8	49.7	32 603	26 205	22 144	24.4	18.3
Ferry	7.7	23.8	8.5	13.5	16.9	11.0	8.1	6.7	3.9	47.9	7 260	6 295	5 811	15.3	8.3
Franklin	9.4	25.2	10.0	15.5	14.4	8.2	7.4	6.3	3.6	48.7	49 347	37 473	35 025	31.7	7.0
Garfield	5.2	20.9	3.5	10.9	15.2	10.0	12.1	12.3	10.0	51.0	2 397	2 248	2 468	6.6	-8.9
Grant	8.8	22.6	8.7	14.7	14.1	9.4	8.9	7.9	4.8	49.4	74 698	54 798	48 522	36.3	12.9
Grays Harbor	7.3	19.7	8.0	14.5	15.0	10.5	9.2	9.2	6.7	50.2	67 194	64 175	66 314	4.7	-3.2
Island	8.1	17.5	10.9	18.2	14.5	8.7	8.2	9.1	4.7	47.9	71 558	60 195	44 048	18.9	36.7
Jefferson	5.7	16.9	5.2	11.7	17.3	10.9	11.7	13.6	7.1	50.6	25 953	20 406	15 965	27.2	27.8
King	7.0	15.7	10.0	20.0	17.9	10.8	7.6	6.5	4.6	50.7	1 737 034	1 507 305	1 269 898	15.2	18.7
Kitsap	8.2	19.7	10.6	17.0	16.6	10.1	7.1	6.3	4.4	48.9	231 969	189 731	147 152	22.3	28.9
Kittitas	5.6	15.5	22.0	13.1	13.6	9.7	7.3	7.4	5.8	50.4	33 362	26 725	24 877	24.8	7.4
Klickitat	7.5	21.7	7.0	14.5	16.5	10.6	8.4	7.8	5.8	49.7	19 161	16 616	15 822	15.3	5.0
Lewis	7.3	21.1	8.0	13.8	14.7	10.3	9.1	8.7	7.0	50.8	68 600	59 358	56 025	15.6	5.9
Lincoln	6.2	20.4	4.4	12.2	14.4	11.5	11.2	10.5	9.2	50.1	10 184	8 864	9 604	14.9	-7.7
Mason	6.4	18.7	7.4	14.2	15.3	10.6	10.9	10.8	5.6	48.4	49 405	38 341	31 184	28.9	23.0
Okanogan	7.6	21.1	7.2	14.0	15.5	11.1	9.6	7.8	6.1	49.5	39 564	33 350	30 663	18.6	8.8
Pacific	6.4	17.7	6.2	12.0	13.7	10.2	12.3	12.9	8.7	50.6	20 984	18 882	17 237	11.1	9.5
Pend Oreille	7.4	22.0	5.8	13.0	16.0	11.6	10.3	8.4	5.5	50.4	11 732	8 915	8 580	31.6	3.9
Pierce	8.2	19.0	11.4	18.2	15.4	9.7	7.6	6.2	4.3	50.0	700 820	586 203	485 667	19.6	20.7
San Juan	5.8	14.7	3.8	11.0	19.3	12.4	11.6	13.8	7.7	50.5	14 077	10 035	7 838	40.3	28.0
Skagit	7.1	19.1	8.2	14.6	15.9	10.4	9.1	9.1	6.5	50.7	102 979	79 545	64 138	29.5	24.0
Skamania	7.6	22.1	6.8	15.9	16.9	11.5	8.5	6.3	4.5	49.0	9 872	8 289	7 919	19.1	4.7
Snohomish	8.5	19.3	8.8	19.2	17.4	10.3	7.1	5.7	3.8	50.1	606 024	465 628	337 720	30.2	37.9
Spokane	7.4	19.0	10.6	16.4	15.6	9.8	7.9	7.4	5.8	51.4	417 939	361 333	341 835	15.7	5.7
Stevens	7.3	24.2	6.1	13.2	16.8	11.5	8.4	7.1	5.4	50.1	40 066	30 948	28 979	29.5	6.8
Thurston	7.1	19.8	9.3	16.0	17.6	10.8	7.7	6.8	4.9	51.3	207 355	161 238	124 264	28.6	29.8
Wahkiakum	6.0	18.8	6.3	11.3	15.6	11.9	10.6	11.3	8.2	50.3	3 824	3 327	3 832	14.9	-13.2
Walla Walla	6.8	18.0	12.7	14.8	14.3	9.4	8.3	8.4	7.3	49.7	55 180	48 439	47 435	13.9	2.1
Whatcom	6.9	18.2	13.1	15.7	16.4	9.6	7.6	7.0	5.5	50.8	166 814	127 780	106 701	30.5	19.8
Whitman	5.0	12.7	34.5	14.5	10.7	7.4	5.6	5.2	4.3	48.3	40 740	38 775	40 103	5.1	-3.3
Yakima	8.7	21.6	9.8	15.3	14.1	9.6	7.9	7.1	5.9	50.3	222 581	188 823	172 508	17.9	9.5
WEST VIRGINIA	5.9	18.8	10.0	14.6	15.1	10.7	9.9	8.7	6.3	52.0	1 808 344	1 793 477	1 950 186	0.8	-8.0
Barbour	6.1	19.2	11.0	13.8	14.3	10.4	9.2	8.6	7.4	52.2	15 557	15 699	16 639	-0.9	-5.6
Berkeley	7.4	18.7	9.7	17.3	15.6	10.4	9.1	7.2	4.5	50.4	75 905	59 253	46 775	28.1	26.7
Boone	5.7	21.4	9.0	14.7	16.6	10.7	9.3	7.8	4.7	51.4	25 535	25 870	30 447	-1.3	-15.0

STATE County	Total population	Total in house-holds	House-holder	Spouse	Child Total	Own child under 18 years	Other relatives Total	Under 18 years	Nonrelatives Total	Unmar-ried partner	Total in group quarters	Correc-tional institu-tions	Nurs-ing homes	Other institu-tions	Col-lege dormi-tories	Mili-tary quar-ters	Other
	54	55	56	57	58	59	60	61	62	63	64	65	66	67	68	69	70
VIRGINIA—Cont'd																	
Independent Cities Cont'd																	
Manassas City	35 135	97.5	33.5	18.7	32.6	26.9	6.1	1.9	6.8	2.0	2.5	1.5	0.6	0.0	0.0	0.0	0.3
Manassas Park City	10 290	100.0	31.6	19.0	34.4	27.5	8.0	2.9	7.0	2.4	0.0	0.0	0.0	0.0	0.0	0.0	0.0
Martinsville City	15 416	95.5	42.2	16.4	26.0	18.8	6.9	3.2	4.0	1.8	4.5	0.7	3.1	0.0	0.0	0.0	0.6
Newport News City	180 150	96.8	38.7	17.3	30.4	24.4	4.9	2.4	5.6	2.0	3.2	0.4	0.6	0.1	0.4	1.4	0.3
Norfolk City	234 403	90.1	36.8	13.6	26.2	20.4	6.1	3.0	7.4	2.3	9.9	0.6	0.5	0.2	1.4	7.0	0.3
Norton City	3 904	98.7	44.3	19.1	27.1	19.2	5.3	2.3	3.0	1.6	1.3	0.0	1.3	0.0	0.0	0.0	0.0
Petersburg City	33 740	97.3	40.9	12.3	28.3	19.6	9.2	4.6	6.6	2.8	2.7	0.5	1.0	0.3	0.0	0.0	0.9
Poquoson City	11 566	99.2	36.0	25.0	32.3	25.3	3.2	1.2	2.6	1.1	0.8	0.0	0.5	0.0	0.0	0.0	0.3
Portsmouth City	100 565	95.2	38.0	15.6	28.6	20.8	7.6	3.9	5.4	2.1	4.8	1.2	0.4	0.2	0.0	2.5	0.5
Radford City	15 859	82.3	36.6	12.4	14.8	11.7	2.5	0.8	15.9	1.6	17.7	0.0	0.0	0.1	17.3	0.0	0.3
Richmond City	197 790	94.3	42.7	11.6	23.8	17.5	7.6	3.6	8.6	2.6	5.7	0.8	0.7	0.1	2.9	0.0	1.2
Roanoke City	94 911	97.3	44.3	16.4	25.5	19.5	5.6	2.5	5.6	2.5	2.7	0.7	1.1	0.0	0.1	0.0	0.8
Salem City	24 747	93.1	40.2	20.5	24.8	19.2	3.4	1.2	4.3	1.5	6.9	0.9	1.1	0.8	3.7	0.0	0.4
Staunton City	23 853	88.9	40.6	18.0	22.0	16.9	3.7	1.6	4.7	2.2	11.1	4.1	2.0	1.7	2.8	0.0	0.5
Suffolk City	63 677	98.5	36.6	20.2	31.7	24.2	6.4	3.0	3.6	1.5	1.5	0.7	0.7	0.0	0.0	0.0	0.2
Virginia Beach City	425 257	98.2	36.3	20.2	31.2	25.1	4.5	1.8	6.0	1.9	1.8	0.2	0.4	0.0	0.0	1.0	0.1
Waynesboro City	19 520	98.6	42.7	19.9	26.8	21.3	4.7	2.0	4.5	2.4	1.4	0.0	1.2	0.0	0.0	0.0	0.1
Williamsburg City	11 998	62.5	30.2	11.2	11.2	8.4	2.3	0.8	7.7	1.5	37.5	0.0	1.1	0.0	36.3	0.0	0.1
Winchester City	23 585	96.7	42.4	17.2	24.4	19.1	4.5	1.6	8.1	2.9	3.3	0.0	0.6	0.0	2.5	0.0	0.2
WASHINGTON	5 894 121	97.7	38.5	20.1	28.7	23.5	4.0	1.5	6.4	2.4	2.3	0.5	0.4	0.1	0.5	0.2	0.6
Adams	16 428	98.5	31.8	20.2	36.2	30.7	6.4	2.5	3.9	1.5	1.5	0.1	0.5	0.0	0.0	0.0	0.8
Asotin	20 551	98.3	40.7	20.9	28.1	23.3	3.4	1.5	5.2	2.4	1.7	0.2	0.6	0.1	0.0	0.0	0.8
Benton	142 475	99.4	37.1	21.4	33.0	27.6	3.6	1.5	4.3	1.9	0.6	0.2	0.2	0.1	0.0	0.0	0.1
Chelan	66 616	98.4	37.6	21.2	30.5	25.6	4.2	1.6	5.0	2.1	1.6	0.4	0.5	0.1	0.1	0.0	0.6
Clallam	64 525	97.1	42.1	22.7	24.3	20.0	3.0	1.2	5.0	2.3	2.9	2.0	0.4	0.0	0.1	0.1	0.2
Clark	345 238	99.1	36.8	20.9	31.9	26.5	3.9	1.4	5.6	2.3	0.9	0.3	0.3	0.0	0.0	0.0	0.2
Columbia	4 064	98.1	41.5	23.2	26.9	21.7	3.0	1.6	3.5	1.8	1.9	0.0	0.1	1.0	0.0	0.0	0.7
Cowlitz	92 948	98.5	38.6	21.0	29.4	24.2	3.7	1.7	5.7	2.5	1.5	0.3	0.6	0.1	0.0	0.0	0.5
Douglas	32 603	99.1	36.0	22.2	32.6	27.1	4.0	1.6	4.3	1.7	0.9	0.0	0.5	0.0	0.0	0.0	0.3
Ferry	7 260	97.0	38.9	21.3	27.6	22.7	4.5	2.2	4.8	2.5	3.0	0.2	0.0	0.2	0.0	0.0	2.7
Franklin	49 347	98.1	30.1	18.3	36.8	30.6	7.8	3.0	5.2	1.7	1.9	1.2	0.2	0.1	0.0	0.0	0.2
Garfield	2 397	98.5	41.2	23.5	26.8	23.2	3.6	2.0	3.3	1.7	1.5	0.2	1.4	0.0	0.0	0.0	0.0
Grant	74 698	98.5	33.7	20.0	34.1	28.9	5.5	2.1	5.2	1.9	1.5	0.2	0.5	0.1	0.1	0.0	0.6
Grays Harbor	67 194	99.0	39.9	20.2	28.2	22.6	4.2	2.0	6.5	2.9	1.0	0.2	0.3	0.1	0.0	0.0	0.3
Island	71 558	97.9	38.8	24.2	27.9	24.0	2.6	1.0	4.5	1.7	2.1	0.1	0.3	0.0	0.0	1.7	0.1
Jefferson	25 953	99.3	44.9	24.1	22.3	18.4	2.3	0.8	5.7	2.8	0.7	0.2	0.0	0.0	0.0	0.0	0.5
King	1 737 034	97.8	40.9	19.0	25.8	20.7	4.2	1.2	7.8	2.6	2.2	0.3	0.4	0.1	0.6	0.0	0.8
Kitsap	231 969	96.9	37.3	21.5	29.7	24.8	3.1	1.3	5.3	2.1	3.1	1.0	0.6	0.0	0.0	1.2	0.2
Kittitas	33 362	93.5	40.1	19.2	22.8	19.1	2.3	0.8	9.1	2.4	6.5	0.2	0.4	0.0	5.7	0.0	0.1
Klickitat	19 161	98.9	39.0	22.5	28.7	24.4	3.9	2.0	4.7	2.0	1.1	0.2	0.3	0.0	0.0	0.0	0.5
Lewis	68 600	98.5	38.3	21.4	29.1	23.5	4.3	1.9	5.4	2.4	1.5	0.2	0.6	0.3	0.0	0.0	0.3
Lincoln	10 184	98.8	40.8	24.8	27.7	23.8	2.2	1.0	3.3	1.7	1.2	0.0	0.9	0.0	0.0	0.0	0.3
Mason	49 405	95.3	38.3	21.8	25.5	20.6	4.0	1.9	5.7	2.4	4.7	3.9	0.3	0.1	0.0	0.0	0.4
Okanogan	39 564	97.8	38.0	20.7	29.4	24.5	4.5	2.1	5.3	2.7	2.2	0.2	0.2	0.4	0.0	0.0	1.2
Pacific	20 984	98.4	43.3	23.0	23.0	18.6	3.7	1.7	5.4	2.5	1.6	0.2	0.3	0.6	0.0	0.0	0.4
Pend Oreille	11 732	99.1	39.5	22.7	28.5	23.6	3.8	2.0	4.6	2.2	0.9	0.3	0.3	0.0	0.0	0.0	0.3
Pierce	700 820	96.9	37.2	19.6	30.3	24.8	4.0	1.7	5.8	2.3	3.1	0.7	0.4	0.1	0.4	0.9	0.6
San Juan	14 077	99.2	45.9	23.8	21.2	18.1	1.9	0.6	6.3	3.1	0.8	0.0	0.5	0.0	0.0	0.0	0.3
Skagit	102 979	98.2	37.7	21.4	28.9	23.6	4.4	1.7	5.9	2.3	1.8	0.1	0.6	0.1	0.1	0.0	0.8
Skamania	9 872	99.4	38.0	23.0	29.8	24.4	3.6	1.6	4.9	2.4	0.6	0.3	0.3	0.0	0.0	0.0	0.1
Snohomish	606 024	98.5	37.1	20.8	30.8	25.5	3.9	1.3	5.9	2.3	1.5	0.4	0.1	0.0	0.0	0.4	0.6
Spokane	417 939	96.5	39.1	19.5	28.7	23.7	3.1	1.2	6.0	2.3	3.5	0.8	0.6	0.2	0.9	0.2	0.8
Stevens	40 066	99.1	37.5	22.6	30.9	26.0	3.6	1.9	4.5	2.0	0.9	0.1	0.5	0.0	0.0	0.0	0.3
Thurston	207 355	98.4	39.4	20.9	28.3	23.1	3.4	1.3	6.3	2.5	1.6	0.4	0.4	0.2	0.4	0.0	0.2
Wahkiakum	3 824	98.5	40.6	24.9	25.3	21.3	3.0	1.2	4.7	1.6	1.5	0.3	1.3	0.0	0.0	0.0	0.0
Walla Walla	55 180	90.4	35.6	19.2	26.9	22.0	3.9	1.5	4.8	1.6	9.6	4.4	1.0	0.1	3.0	0.0	1.1
Whatcom	166 814	97.0	38.6	19.8	27.2	22.4	3.1	1.1	8.4	2.3	3.0	0.2	0.4	0.1	1.9	0.0	0.4
Whitman	40 740	86.6	37.4	16.6	19.6	17.3	1.6	0.5	11.3	1.6	13.4	0.1	0.4	0.0	12.5	0.0	0.4
Yakima	222 581	98.3	33.2	18.6	34.1	27.7	7.1	3.1	5.3	2.2	1.7	0.5	0.5	0.1	0.0	0.0	0.6
WEST VIRGINIA	1 808 344	97.6	40.7	22.0	27.2	20.1	3.8	1.6	3.9	1.9	2.4	0.6	0.6	0.1	0.8	0.0	0.3
Barbour	15 557	97.2	39.4	22.5	28.0	20.9	3.9	1.5	3.5	1.7	2.8	0.0	0.7	0.0	1.9	0.0	0.1
Berkeley	75 905	98.4	39.0	21.3	28.9	22.9	3.9	1.8	5.3	2.8	1.6	0.3	0.5	0.5	0.0	0.0	0.3
Boone	25 535	99.6	40.3	23.2	28.7	20.8	4.3	1.9	3.2	1.9	0.4	0.0	0.3	0.0	0.0	0.0	0.1

Table B. States and Counties

STATE County	Total households	Family households Total (72)	With own children under 18 years (73)	Married couple Total (74)	With own children under 18 years (75)	Female householder[1] Total (76)	With own children under 18 years (77)	Nonfamily households Total (78)	Householder living alone Total (79)	65 years and over (80)	Average house-hold size (81)	Average family size (82)	Households, 1990 Total house-holds (83)	Female house-holder[1] (84)	House-holder living alone (85)
	71	72	73	74	75	76	77	78	79	80	81	82	83	84	85
VIRGINIA—Cont'd															
Independent Cities—Cont'd															
Manassas City	11 757	71.8	42.3	55.8	32.4	11.3	7.3	28.2	21.1	3.7	2.92	3.39	9 481	9.2	17.0
Manassas Park City	3 254	78.6	45.4	59.9	34.9	12.1	7.1	21.4	14.4	2.6	3.16	3.47	2 182	13.1	13.1
Martinsville City	6 498	61.9	26.3	39.0	14.1	19.1	10.7	38.1	34.2	15.4	2.27	2.89	6 839	17.4	31.4
Newport News City	69 686	66.5	35.7	44.6	21.4	17.9	12.1	33.5	27.0	8.1	2.50	3.04	63 952	15.1	23.7
Norfolk City	86 210	60.2	30.3	36.9	16.4	18.8	11.7	39.8	30.2	9.6	2.45	3.07	89 478	16.1	26.8
Norton City	1 730	61.7	26.1	43.0	15.9	15.7	8.8	38.3	34.9	14.3	2.23	2.88	1 697	16.4	28.4
Petersburg City	13 799	61.7	27.6	30.1	10.2	26.1	15.0	38.3	32.2	11.7	2.38	2.98	14 730	23.0	30.3
Poquoson City	4 166	80.9	39.1	69.4	32.3	8.4	4.9	19.1	15.9	7.1	2.75	3.08	3 769	7.6	13.2
Portsmouth City	38 170	66.8	30.6	41.1	16.4	20.9	12.0	33.2	27.5	10.8	2.51	3.05	38 741	19.3	24.5
Radford City	5 809	45.5	18.8	33.9	12.6	8.9	5.1	54.5	32.0	8.7	2.25	2.78	5 207	8.8	25.2
Richmond City	84 549	51.6	23.1	27.1	9.6	20.4	11.9	48.4	37.6	10.9	2.21	2.95	85 337	19.8	35.9
Roanoke City	42 003	57.7	25.5	37.1	13.8	16.5	9.7	42.3	35.9	12.8	2.20	2.86	41 030	15.7	32.3
Salem City	9 954	65.7	28.2	50.9	20.0	11.5	6.4	34.3	29.0	12.2	2.32	2.84	9 161	10.6	26.5
Staunton City	9 676	59.6	24.9	44.4	16.1	11.7	6.9	40.4	34.7	14.3	2.19	2.81	9 432	11.3	30.7
Suffolk City	23 283	76.1	36.6	55.1	25.0	16.8	9.6	23.9	20.2	8.1	2.69	3.09	18 516	17.1	20.4
Virginia Beach City	154 455	71.8	38.8	55.7	28.6	12.4	8.0	28.2	20.4	5.5	2.70	3.14	135 566	9.5	17.1
Waynesboro City	8 332	65.2	28.9	46.5	17.4	14.5	9.3	34.8	30.1	11.9	2.31	2.85	7 568	12.4	26.5
Williamsburg City	3 619	49.4	16.5	37.2	10.4	9.6	5.1	50.6	35.9	11.4	2.07	2.66	3 468	8.3	35.0
Winchester City	10 001	56.5	25.6	40.5	16.6	11.7	6.8	43.5	34.4	11.8	2.28	2.93	9 084	10.6	32.6
WASHINGTON	2 271 398	66.0	32.7	52.0	23.8	9.9	6.5	34.0	26.2	8.1	2.53	3.07	1 872 431	9.4	25.4
Adams	5 229	78.3	44.0	63.5	34.2	10.1	7.0	21.7	18.7	7.7	3.09	3.52	4 586	7.3	20.4
Asotin	8 364	67.6	31.0	51.4	19.9	11.9	8.5	32.4	27.0	11.7	2.42	2.91	7 003	12.6	25.9
Benton	52 866	72.0	38.2	57.6	28.1	10.2	7.2	28.0	23.2	7.7	2.68	3.17	42 227	9.3	23.5
Chelan	25 021	69.4	34.5	56.4	25.9	8.7	5.9	30.6	25.1	10.8	2.62	3.14	20 645	8.4	26.8
Clallam	27 164	66.5	25.7	53.9	17.4	9.0	5.9	33.5	28.1	13.4	2.31	2.78	22 837	8.2	25.8
Clark	127 208	71.5	37.2	56.8	27.6	10.3	6.9	28.5	21.8	6.8	2.69	3.15	88 440	9.9	22.1
Columbia	1 687	67.5	27.7	56.0	20.0	8.5	5.8	32.5	29.0	13.0	2.36	2.89	1 582	7.0	28.4
Cowlitz	35 850	69.9	32.8	54.6	22.5	10.7	7.4	30.1	24.3	9.7	2.55	3.01	31 640	9.7	23.9
Douglas	11 726	75.7	38.4	61.6	29.2	9.7	6.6	24.3	20.0	7.8	2.76	3.16	9 687	8.1	20.0
Ferry	2 823	70.4	30.1	54.7	19.7	10.2	7.2	29.6	24.8	9.1	2.49	2.95	2 247	9.1	22.1
Franklin	14 840	78.2	45.0	60.8	33.7	11.4	7.9	21.8	17.8	7.3	3.26	3.67	12 196	11.1	19.4
Garfield	987	67.9	28.8	57.0	22.4	6.7	4.1	32.1	28.3	14.4	2.39	2.93	922	5.0	27.3
Grant	25 204	74.1	39.9	59.3	30.0	9.8	7.0	25.9	21.2	8.9	2.92	3.38	19 745	8.4	22.6
Grays Harbor	26 808	66.8	30.5	50.7	20.1	11.1	7.4	33.2	26.7	11.6	2.48	2.98	25 514	9.8	26.8
Island	27 784	72.9	33.3	62.2	26.0	7.8	5.5	27.1	21.5	8.3	2.52	2.93	21 787	6.2	18.7
Jefferson	11 645	65.1	23.2	53.6	15.4	8.2	5.7	34.9	28.5	11.7	2.21	2.67	8 627	7.9	26.8
King	710 916	59.1	28.4	46.4	21.2	9.0	5.4	40.9	30.5	7.5	2.39	3.03	615 792	9.0	29.2
Kitsap	86 416	71.0	36.0	57.7	27.0	9.5	6.6	29.0	22.6	7.6	2.60	3.05	69 267	8.5	22.1
Kittitas	13 382	58.2	26.2	47.8	19.5	7.2	5.1	41.8	28.4	8.6	2.33	2.90	10 460	7.2	29.1
Klickitat	7 473	71.0	32.3	57.7	22.9	9.1	6.5	29.0	23.8	9.0	2.54	2.99	6 210	8.8	22.7
Lewis	26 306	70.6	31.6	55.9	22.1	9.9	6.4	29.4	24.0	11.2	2.57	3.02	22 478	9.1	23.7
Lincoln	4 151	70.2	29.3	60.9	23.0	6.4	4.1	29.8	26.0	12.3	2.42	2.91	3 605	5.2	26.0
Mason	18 912	70.8	28.9	56.9	19.8	9.2	6.1	29.2	23.3	9.9	2.49	2.89	14 565	7.9	22.1
Okanogan	15 027	70.4	33.2	54.4	22.2	11.0	7.8	29.6	24.5	9.7	2.58	3.04	12 654	9.3	24.0
Pacific	9 096	64.7	23.1	53.1	16.1	7.9	4.9	35.3	29.5	14.3	2.27	2.77	7 896	7.9	27.2
Pend Oreille	4 639	70.3	29.6	57.5	20.9	8.4	5.8	29.7	25.0	10.5	2.51	2.98	3 395	8.3	22.8
Pierce	260 800	69.1	35.9	52.8	25.2	11.8	7.9	30.9	24.3	7.6	2.60	3.10	214 652	10.9	23.4
San Juan	6 466	62.1	22.9	51.8	15.3	6.9	5.0	37.9	30.6	10.7	2.16	2.65	4 392	6.0	27.2
Skagit	38 852	70.4	32.8	56.6	23.9	9.7	6.5	29.6	23.3	10.0	2.60	3.06	30 573	8.6	23.5
Skamania	3 755	73.4	34.0	60.5	25.6	8.2	5.4	26.6	21.1	6.6	2.61	3.02	3 066	7.8	20.2
Snohomish	224 852	70.2	37.3	56.0	28.1	9.8	6.5	29.8	22.6	6.5	2.65	3.13	171 713	9.1	20.9
Spokane	163 611	64.8	32.4	49.9	22.5	11.0	7.4	35.2	28.1	9.6	2.46	3.02	141 619	10.8	27.5
Stevens	15 017	73.4	34.4	60.4	25.6	8.7	5.9	26.6	22.0	8.8	2.64	3.08	11 241	8.0	21.0
Thurston	81 625	67.3	33.0	53.1	23.5	10.3	7.0	32.7	25.1	8.0	2.50	2.99	62 150	9.7	24.0
Wahkiakum	1 553	71.4	26.9	61.4	20.2	6.3	4.3	28.6	24.4	10.6	2.42	2.83	1 321	5.5	23.1
Walla Walla	19 647	67.4	32.1	54.0	23.5	9.5	6.3	32.6	27.1	12.4	2.54	3.08	17 623	9.2	26.9
Whatcom	64 446	63.8	30.4	51.2	22.4	8.8	5.9	36.2	25.6	8.4	2.51	3.03	48 543	8.0	24.9
Whitman	15 257	52.8	24.6	44.2	19.0	6.2	4.3	47.2	29.4	7.1	2.31	2.91	13 546	5.2	26.6
Yakima	73 993	73.8	39.7	55.8	27.9	12.5	8.6	26.2	21.5	9.6	2.96	3.44	65 985	11.3	22.7
WEST VIRGINIA	736 481	68.4	28.9	54.0	21.3	10.7	5.7	31.6	27.1	11.9	2.40	2.90	688 557	10.7	24.5
Barbour	6 123	71.3	30.1	57.2	22.8	10.3	5.2	28.7	25.1	12.6	2.47	2.94	5 835	10.7	24.0
Berkeley	29 569	70.0	33.4	54.6	23.8	10.7	6.6	30.0	24.2	8.2	2.53	2.99	22 350	9.5	23.2
Boone	10 291	72.5	31.1	57.5	23.5	10.5	5.3	27.5	24.6	11.0	2.47	2.92	9 656	11.2	21.2

[1] No spouse present.

Table B. States and Counties

STATE County	Percent change of households, 1990–2000	Total housing units	Occupied housing units (percent)	Vacant housing units		Homeowner vacancy rate (percent)	Rental vacancy rate (percent)	Occupied housing units			Average household size of owner-occupied units	Average household size of renter-occupied units
				Total	For seasonal, recreational, or occasional use			Total	Percent owner-occupied housing units	Percent renter-occupied housing units		
	86	87	88	89	90	91	92	93	94	95	96	97
VIRGINIA—Cont'd												
Independent Cities—Cont'd												
Manassas City	24.0	12 114	97.1	2.9	0.2	1.0	3.6	11 757	69.8	30.2	2.98	2.78
Manassas Park City	49.1	3 365	96.7	3.3	0.1	1.3	2.4	3 254	78.7	21.3	3.10	3.38
Martinsville City	-5.0	7 249	89.6	10.4	0.3	3.7	12.9	6 498	60.2	39.8	2.32	2.18
Newport News City	9.0	74 117	94.0	6.0	0.3	1.9	6.2	69 686	52.4	47.6	2.61	2.39
Norfolk City	-3.7	94 416	91.3	8.7	0.3	3.2	6.9	86 210	45.5	54.5	2.51	2.40
Norton City	1.9	1 946	88.9	11.1	0.1	3.2	9.9	1 730	55.9	44.1	2.36	2.06
Petersburg City	-6.3	15 955	86.5	13.5	0.1	3.4	12.4	13 799	51.5	48.5	2.40	2.36
Poquoson City	10.5	4 300	96.9	3.1	0.5	1.0	2.4	4 166	84.1	15.9	2.76	2.70
Portsmouth City	-1.5	41 605	91.7	8.3	0.3	2.6	6.9	38 170	58.6	41.4	2.52	2.49
Radford City	11.6	6 137	94.7	5.3	0.5	1.0	5.2	5 809	44.6	55.4	2.35	2.16
Richmond City	-0.9	92 282	91.6	8.4	0.3	2.4	6.4	84 549	46.1	53.9	2.30	2.12
Roanoke City	2.4	45 257	92.8	7.2	0.4	2.0	6.4	42 003	56.3	43.7	2.30	2.07
Salem City	8.7	10 403	95.7	4.3	0.4	0.9	5.6	9 954	67.6	32.4	2.41	2.13
Staunton City	2.6	10 427	92.8	7.2	0.4	2.7	7.5	9 676	61.4	38.6	2.28	2.05
Suffolk City	25.7	24 704	94.2	5.8	0.3	1.7	6.2	23 283	72.2	27.8	2.71	2.64
Virginia Beach City	13.9	162 277	95.2	4.8	1.4	1.5	4.0	154 455	65.6	34.4	2.79	2.54
Waynesboro City	10.1	8 863	94.0	6.0	0.2	1.9	6.4	8 332	61.2	38.8	2.35	2.26
Williamsburg City	4.4	3 880	93.3	6.7	1.7	2.1	3.9	3 619	44.3	55.7	2.12	2.03
Winchester City	10.1	10 587	94.5	5.5	0.5	1.7	4.5	10 001	45.7	54.3	2.38	2.20
WASHINGTON	21.3	2 451 075	92.7	7.3	2.5	1.8	5.9	2 271 398	64.6	35.4	2.65	2.32
Adams	14.0	5 773	90.6	9.4	1.0	2.1	10.7	5 229	68.4	31.6	3.02	3.26
Asotin	19.4	9 111	91.8	8.2	2.0	2.3	8.2	8 364	67.1	32.9	2.42	2.40
Benton	25.2	55 963	94.5	5.5	0.3	1.4	7.9	52 866	68.7	31.3	2.78	2.45
Chelan	21.2	30 407	82.3	17.7	9.3	2.9	7.2	25 021	64.7	35.3	2.66	2.55
Clallam	18.9	30 683	88.5	11.5	4.6	2.4	10.0	27 164	72.7	27.3	2.32	2.28
Clark	43.8	134 030	94.9	5.1	0.4	2.0	6.6	127 208	67.3	32.7	2.77	2.53
Columbia	6.6	2 018	83.6	16.4	8.0	2.8	10.4	1 687	69.4	30.6	2.34	2.42
Cowlitz	13.3	38 624	92.8	7.2	1.0	2.2	9.2	35 850	67.6	32.4	2.59	2.47
Douglas	21.0	12 944	90.6	9.4	3.4	2.2	6.2	11 726	70.9	29.1	2.72	2.85
Ferry	25.6	3 775	74.8	25.2	15.5	3.1	10.7	2 823	73.0	27.0	2.47	2.57
Franklin	21.7	16 084	92.3	7.7	0.5	2.1	8.1	14 840	65.6	34.4	3.20	3.39
Garfield	7.0	1 288	76.6	23.4	11.6	4.9	9.8	987	74.0	26.0	2.34	2.53
Grant	27.6	29 081	86.7	13.3	5.4	3.2	10.7	25 204	66.7	33.3	2.86	3.04
Grays Harbor	5.1	32 489	82.5	17.5	8.2	3.6	12.5	26 808	69.0	31.0	2.49	2.47
Island	27.5	32 378	85.8	14.2	9.6	2.2	5.1	27 784	70.1	29.9	2.50	2.57
Jefferson	35.0	14 144	82.3	17.7	11.9	2.7	6.3	11 645	76.2	23.8	2.24	2.13
King	15.4	742 237	95.8	4.2	0.7	1.2	4.2	710 916	59.8	40.2	2.60	2.08
Kitsap	24.8	92 644	93.3	6.7	1.6	1.8	6.4	86 416	67.4	32.6	2.68	2.44
Kittitas	27.9	16 475	81.2	18.8	10.9	3.1	6.8	13 382	58.3	41.7	2.48	2.12
Klickitat	20.3	8 633	86.6	13.4	5.5	2.6	8.1	7 473	68.8	31.2	2.52	2.58
Lewis	17.0	29 585	88.9	11.1	4.4	3.0	8.0	26 306	71.4	28.6	2.59	2.51
Lincoln	15.1	5 298	78.4	21.6	10.8	4.4	6.6	4 151	76.8	23.2	2.41	2.47
Mason	29.8	25 515	74.1	25.9	20.2	3.3	7.3	18 912	79.0	21.0	2.46	2.58
Okanogan	18.8	19 085	78.7	21.3	12.3	3.2	8.5	15 027	68.6	31.4	2.54	2.66
Pacific	15.2	13 991	65.0	35.0	26.7	4.9	11.8	9 096	74.8	25.2	2.24	2.37
Pend Oreille	36.6	6 608	70.2	29.8	20.8	4.1	13.9	4 639	77.4	22.6	2.50	2.53
Pierce	21.5	277 060	94.1	5.9	0.9	1.8	6.1	260 800	63.5	36.5	2.71	2.42
San Juan	47.2	9 752	66.3	33.7	28.5	1.7	7.0	6 466	73.5	26.5	2.20	2.04
Skagit	27.1	42 681	91.0	9.0	4.6	1.9	4.7	38 852	69.7	30.3	2.61	2.60
Skamania	22.5	4 576	82.1	17.9	12.7	2.2	6.8	3 755	73.8	26.2	2.62	2.58
Snohomish	30.9	236 205	95.2	4.8	1.0	1.5	5.5	224 852	67.8	32.2	2.78	2.39
Spokane	15.5	175 005	93.5	6.5	0.6	2.0	8.7	163 611	65.5	34.5	2.61	2.19
Stevens	33.6	17 599	85.3	14.7	8.1	2.7	6.8	15 017	78.1	21.9	2.68	2.52
Thurston	31.3	86 652	94.2	5.8	1.1	2.1	6.0	81 625	66.6	33.4	2.61	2.28
Wahkiakum	17.6	1 792	86.7	13.3	5.6	3.5	5.1	1 553	79.7	20.3	2.45	2.33
Walla Walla	11.5	21 147	92.9	7.1	0.8	2.3	6.8	19 647	65.2	34.8	2.62	2.39
Whatcom	32.8	73 893	87.2	12.8	8.0	2.2	5.7	64 446	63.4	36.6	2.63	2.31
Whitman	12.6	16 676	91.5	8.5	0.7	3.9	6.6	15 257	47.9	52.1	2.48	2.15
Yakima	12.1	79 174	93.5	6.5	1.1	1.6	6.6	73 993	64.4	35.6	2.95	2.96
WEST VIRGINIA	7.0	844 623	87.2	12.8	3.9	2.2	9.1	736 481	75.2	24.8	2.47	2.17
Barbour	4.9	7 348	83.3	16.7	4.8	2.2	6.2	6 123	78.6	21.4	2.51	2.33
Berkeley	32.3	32 913	89.8	10.2	4.0	2.3	7.2	29 569	74.2	25.8	2.61	2.29
Boone	6.6	11 575	88.9	11.1	0.6	2.3	12.3	10 291	78.9	21.1	2.50	2.36

Table B. States and Counties

STATE/ County code	MSA/ PMSA/ NECMA code[1]	County type[2]	STATE County	Population, 2000				Population, 1990				Population and population characteristics, 2000					
												Race (percent)					
												One race					
				Land area, 2000[3] (sq km)	Total persons	Rank	Per square kilometer	Land area, 1990[3] (sq km)	Total persons	Rank	Per square kilometer	White	Black or African American	American Indian or Alaska Native	Asian	Native Hawaiian and other Pacific Islander	Some other race
				1	2	3	4	5	6	7	8	9	10	11	12	13	14
			WEST VIRGINIA—Cont'd														
54 007	...	9	Braxton	1 330	14 702	2 107	11.1	1 330	12 998	2 142	9.8	98.0	0.7	0.3	0.1	0.0	0.1
54 009	8080	3	Brooke	230	25 447	1 543	110.6	230	26 992	1 391	117.4	97.9	0.8	0.1	0.3	0.0	0.1
54 011	3400	2	Cabell	729	96 784	534	132.8	729	96 827	475	132.8	93.4	4.3	0.2	0.8	0.0	0.2
54 013	...	9	Calhoun	727	7 582	2 637	10.4	727	7 885	2 582	10.8	98.9	0.1	0.3	0.1	0.0	0.1
54 015	...	8	Clay	887	10 330	2 412	11.6	887	9 983	2 388	11.3	98.2	0.1	0.7	0.0	0.0	0.1
54 017	...	9	Doddridge	830	7 403	2 648	8.9	830	6 994	2 659	8.4	98.3	0.3	0.3	0.1	0.0	0.1
54 019	...	6	Fayette	1 720	47 579	958	27.7	1 720	47 952	872	27.9	92.7	5.6	0.3	0.3	0.0	0.1
54 021	...	9	Gilmer	881	7 160	2 671	8.1	881	7 669	2 604	8.7	97.3	0.9	0.2	0.6	0.0	0.1
54 023	...	8	Grant	1 236	11 299	2 350	9.1	1 236	10 428	2 347	8.4	98.3	0.7	0.3	0.1	0.0	0.1
54 025	...	7	Greenbrier	2 645	34 453	1 265	13.0	2 645	34 693	1 145	13.1	95.2	3.0	0.3	0.2	0.0	0.2
54 027	...	8	Hampshire	1 662	20 203	1 780	12.2	1 662	16 498	1 893	9.9	98.0	0.8	0.2	0.2	0.0	0.1
54 029	8080	3	Hancock	215	32 667	1 325	151.9	215	35 233	1 125	163.9	96.4	2.3	0.1	0.3	0.0	0.1
54 031	...	9	Hardy	1 511	12 669	2 250	8.4	1 511	10 977	2 297	7.3	96.9	1.9	0.2	0.1	0.0	0.2
54 033	...	5	Harrison	1 078	68 652	719	63.7	1 078	69 371	638	64.4	96.5	1.6	0.1	0.6	0.0	0.2
54 035	...	6	Jackson	1 206	28 000	1 451	23.2	1 206	25 938	1 424	21.5	98.7	0.1	0.2	0.2	0.0	0.1
54 037	8840	1	Jefferson	543	42 190	1 054	77.7	543	35 926	1 102	66.2	91.0	6.1	0.3	0.6	0.0	0.6
54 039	1480	2	Kanawha	2 339	200 073	276	85.5	2 339	207 619	241	88.8	90.5	7.0	0.2	0.8	0.0	0.2
54 041	...	7	Lewis	990	16 919	1 957	17.1	1 007	17 223	1 840	17.1	98.6	0.1	0.2	0.3	0.0	0.1
54 043	...	8	Lincoln	1 133	22 108	1 687	19.5	1 133	21 382	1 612	18.9	99.0	0.1	0.1	0.1	0.0	0.1
54 045	...	7	Logan	1 176	37 710	1 169	32.1	1 176	43 032	938	36.6	96.3	2.6	0.1	0.3	0.0	0.1
54 047	...	7	McDowell	1 385	27 329	1 473	19.7	1 385	35 233	1 125	25.4	87.1	11.9	0.2	0.1	0.0	0.1
54 049	...	5	Marion	802	56 598	837	70.6	802	57 249	763	71.4	95.1	3.2	0.2	0.4	0.0	0.1
54 051	9000	3	Marshall	795	35 519	1 231	44.7	795	37 356	1 062	47.0	98.4	0.4	0.1	0.3	0.0	0.1
54 053	...	6	Mason	1 118	25 957	1 517	23.2	1 119	25 178	1 456	22.5	98.4	0.5	0.2	0.3	0.0	0.1
54 055	...	7	Mercer	1 089	62 980	770	57.8	1 089	64 980	674	59.7	92.6	5.8	0.2	0.5	0.0	0.1
54 057	1900	3	Mineral	849	27 078	1 479	31.9	849	26 697	1 401	31.4	96.2	2.5	0.1	0.2	0.0	0.2
54 059	...	7	Mingo	1 095	28 253	1 440	25.8	1 095	33 739	1 173	30.8	96.4	2.3	0.2	0.2	0.0	0.1
54 061	...	5	Monongalia	935	81 866	634	87.6	935	75 509	597	80.8	92.2	3.4	0.2	2.5	0.0	0.3
54 063	...	9	Monroe	1 226	14 583	2 113	11.9	1 226	12 406	2 189	10.1	92.7	6.0	0.2	0.2	0.0	0.0
54 065	...	8	Morgan	593	14 943	2 096	25.2	593	12 128	2 205	20.5	98.3	0.6	0.2	0.1	0.0	0.2
54 067	...	7	Nicholas	1 680	26 562	1 497	15.8	1 680	26 775	1 398	15.9	98.8	0.1	0.2	0.2	0.0	0.1
54 069	9000	3	Ohio	275	47 427	959	172.5	275	50 871	830	185.0	94.5	3.6	0.1	0.8	0.0	0.1
54 071	...	9	Pendleton	1 807	8 196	2 593	4.5	1 808	8 054	2 559	4.5	96.3	2.1	0.3	0.2	0.0	0.3
54 073	...	8	Pleasants	339	7 514	2 641	22.2	339	7 546	2 613	22.3	98.3	0.5	0.5	0.2	0.0	0.1
54 075	...	9	Pocahontas	2 435	9 131	2 520	3.7	2 435	9 008	2 470	3.7	98.4	0.8	0.1	0.1	0.0	0.1
54 077	...	7	Preston	1 679	29 334	1 418	17.5	1 679	29 037	1 327	17.3	98.8	0.3	0.1	0.1	0.0	0.0
54 079	1480	2	Putnam	897	51 589	899	57.5	897	42 835	941	47.8	98.0	0.6	0.2	0.6	0.0	0.1
54 081	...	5	Raleigh	1 572	79 220	647	50.4	1 572	76 819	587	48.9	89.6	8.5	0.2	0.4	0.0	0.1
54 083	...	7	Randolph	2 693	28 262	1 439	10.5	2 693	27 803	1 358	10.3	97.7	1.1	0.2	0.4	0.0	0.2
54 085	...	8	Ritchie	1 175	10 343	2 410	8.8	1 175	10 233	2 365	8.7	98.7	0.1	0.3	0.1	0.0	0.1
54 087	...	8	Roane	1 252	15 446	2 056	12.3	1 253	15 120	1 982	12.1	98.6	0.2	0.2	0.2	0.0	0.2
54 089	...	7	Summers	935	12 999	2 234	13.9	935	14 204	2 036	15.2	96.6	2.2	0.3	0.1	0.0	0.1
54 091	...	7	Taylor	448	16 089	2 017	35.9	448	15 144	1 977	33.8	98.1	0.8	0.2	0.2	0.0	0.1
54 093	...	9	Tucker	1 085	7 321	2 654	6.7	1 085	7 728	2 602	7.1	98.9	0.1	0.2	0.2	0.1	0.1
54 095	...	9	Tyler	667	9 592	2 479	14.4	667	9 796	2 406	14.7	99.4	0.0	0.1	0.1	0.0	0.0
54 097	...	7	Upshur	919	23 404	1 622	25.5	919	22 867	1 538	24.9	98.2	0.6	0.2	0.3	0.0	0.1
54 099	3400	2	Wayne	1 310	42 903	1 039	32.8	1 310	41 636	966	31.8	98.8	0.1	0.2	0.2	0.0	0.1
54 101	...	9	Webster	1 440	9 719	2 469	6.7	1 440	10 729	2 315	7.5	99.2	0.0	0.1	0.1	0.0	0.0
54 103	...	6	Wetzel	930	17 693	1 917	19.0	930	19 258	1 714	20.7	98.9	0.1	0.1	0.3	0.0	0.1
54 105	...	8	Wirt	603	5 873	2 796	9.7	604	5 192	2 825	8.6	98.6	0.3	0.2	0.1	0.0	0.1
54 107	6020	3	Wood	951	87 986	592	92.5	951	86 915	526	91.4	97.3	1.0	0.2	0.5	0.0	0.1
54 109	...	9	Wyoming	1 297	25 708	1 527	19.8	1 297	28 990	1 330	22.4	98.6	0.6	0.1	0.1	0.0	0.1
55 000	...		WISCONSIN	140 663	5 363 675	X	38.1	140 672	4 891 954	X	34.8	88.9	5.7	0.9	1.7	0.0	1.6
55 001	...	9	Adams	1 678	18 643	1 864	11.1	1 678	15 682	1 945	9.3	97.6	0.3	0.6	0.3	0.0	0.3
55 003	...	7	Ashland	2 703	16 866	1 962	6.2	2 704	16 307	1 903	6.0	87.1	0.2	10.3	0.3	0.0	0.3
55 005	...	7	Barron	2 235	44 963	999	20.1	2 235	40 750	983	18.2	97.7	0.1	0.8	0.3	0.0	0.3
55 007	...	8	Bayfield	3 823	15 013	2 089	3.9	3 824	14 008	2 054	3.7	88.5	0.1	9.4	0.3	0.0	0.3
55 009	3080	3	Brown	1 369	226 778	251	165.7	1 369	194 594	248	142.1	91.1	1.2	2.3	2.2	0.0	1.9
55 011	...	8	Buffalo	1 773	13 804	2 172	7.8	1 773	13 584	2 093	7.7	98.7	0.1	0.3	0.3	0.0	0.1
55 013	...	8	Burnett	2 128	15 674	2 040	7.4	2 128	13 084	2 132	6.1	93.2	0.4	4.5	0.2	0.1	0.2
55 015	0460	2	Calumet	828	40 631	1 097	49.1	828	34 291	1 159	41.4	96.7	0.3	0.3	1.5	0.0	0.4
55 017	2290	3	Chippewa	2 617	55 195	853	21.1	2 617	52 360	808	20.0	97.8	0.2	0.3	0.9	0.0	0.2
55 019	...	6	Clark	3 148	33 557	1 299	10.7	3 149	31 647	1 226	10.0	98.1	0.1	0.5	0.3	0.0	0.6
55 021	...	6	Columbia	2 004	52 468	890	26.2	2 004	45 088	911	22.5	97.2	0.9	0.4	0.3	0.0	0.4
55 023	...	7	Crawford	1 483	17 243	1 937	11.6	1 483	15 940	1 927	10.7	97.3	1.4	0.2	0.3	0.0	0.2

[1]MSA = Metropolitan Statistical Area. PMSA = Primary MSA. NECMA = New England County Metropolitan Area. See Appendix A for explanation of these concepts. See Appendix B for list of metropolitan areas identified by type, with component counties.
[2]County typology code from the Economic Research Service of USDA. See Appendix A for definition.
[3]Dry land or land partially or temporarily covered by water.

Table B. States and Counties

STATE County	Population and population characteristics, 2000 (cont'd)								Population and population characteristics, 1990				
	Race (percent) (cont'd)								Race (percent)				
		Race alone or in combination											
	Two or more races	White	Black	American Indian or Alaska Native	Asian	Native Hawaiian and other Pacific Islander	Some other race	Hispanic[1]	White	Black or African American	American Indian or Alaska Native	Asian and Pacific Islander	Hispanic[1]
	15	16	17	18	19	20	21	22	23	24	25	26	27
WEST VIRGINIA—Cont'd													
Braxton	0.7	98.7	0.8	0.9	0.1	0.1	0.1	0.4	99.3	0.4	0.1	0.2	0.3
Brooke	0.7	98.5	1.1	0.4	0.4	0.1	0.2	0.4	98.8	0.7	0.1	0.2	0.3
Cabell	1.1	94.4	4.7	0.6	1.0	0.1	0.4	0.7	95.1	4.1	0.1	0.6	0.5
Calhoun	0.4	99.3	0.1	0.6	0.1	0.0	0.2	0.6	99.4	0.0	0.2	0.4	0.2
Clay	0.9	99.1	0.2	1.5	0.1	0.0	0.2	0.4	99.8	0.0	0.1	0.1	0.1
Doddridge	0.8	99.1	0.4	0.9	0.3	0.0	0.1	0.6	99.4	0.0	0.4	0.1	0.2
Fayette	0.9	93.6	5.9	0.8	0.4	0.1	0.2	0.7	93.2	6.3	0.1	0.3	0.5
Gilmer	0.9	98.2	1.1	0.7	0.7	0.0	0.2	0.7	99.0	0.4	0.1	0.4	0.3
Grant	0.5	98.8	0.9	0.4	0.1	0.0	0.2	0.5	98.5	1.0	0.2	0.2	0.3
Greenbrier	1.0	96.2	3.4	1.0	0.3	0.0	0.3	0.7	96.0	3.7	0.1	0.2	0.4
Hampshire	0.6	98.6	0.9	0.6	0.3	0.0	0.2	0.6	98.9	0.7	0.1	0.1	0.6
Hancock	0.7	97.0	2.5	0.4	0.5	0.0	0.2	0.7	96.9	2.6	0.1	0.3	0.6
Hardy	0.7	97.5	2.1	0.5	0.2	0.0	0.4	0.7	97.9	1.9	0.1	0.0	0.5
Harrison	0.9	97.4	1.9	0.5	0.7	0.1	0.4	1.0	98.1	1.4	0.1	0.3	1.2
Jackson	0.6	99.4	0.2	0.5	0.3	0.0	0.2	0.3	99.5	0.1	0.2	0.2	0.3
Jefferson	1.4	92.2	6.7	0.8	0.9	0.1	0.8	1.7	91.7	7.4	0.2	0.4	1.2
Kanawha	1.3	91.6	7.6	0.7	1.0	0.0	0.4	0.6	92.5	6.6	0.1	0.6	0.4
Lewis	0.7	99.3	0.2	0.7	0.4	0.0	0.1	0.5	99.2	0.3	0.2	0.3	0.4
Lincoln	0.6	99.6	0.2	0.6	0.2	0.0	0.1	0.5	99.8	0.0	0.1	0.1	0.2
Logan	0.6	96.9	2.8	0.4	0.4	0.0	0.2	0.5	96.2	3.2	0.1	0.4	0.7
McDowell	0.7	87.7	12.2	0.6	0.1	0.0	0.2	0.5	86.3	13.5	0.1	0.1	0.5
Marion	0.9	96.0	3.6	0.6	0.5	0.0	0.3	0.7	96.2	3.2	0.2	0.3	0.5
Marshall	0.7	99.0	0.6	0.4	0.4	0.0	0.2	0.6	99.1	0.5	0.1	0.2	0.6
Mason	0.6	98.9	0.7	0.5	0.3	0.0	0.2	0.5	99.1	0.4	0.1	0.3	0.2
Mercer	0.8	93.4	6.0	0.6	0.6	0.0	0.3	0.5	93.0	6.4	0.1	0.5	0.4
Mineral	0.8	96.9	2.9	0.4	0.3	0.0	0.3	0.6	96.9	2.8	0.0	0.3	0.4
Mingo	0.7	97.1	2.5	0.7	0.3	0.0	0.2	0.5	97.2	2.4	0.1	0.2	0.4
Monongalia	1.4	93.5	3.8	0.6	2.9	0.1	0.6	1.0	95.0	2.4	0.2	2.1	0.8
Monroe	0.9	93.6	6.3	0.7	0.2	0.0	0.2	0.5	98.4	1.3	0.2	0.1	0.3
Morgan	0.6	98.9	0.8	0.4	0.2	0.0	0.3	0.8	98.8	0.8	0.2	0.1	0.4
Nicholas	0.5	99.4	0.1	0.6	0.2	0.1	0.1	0.5	99.6	0.0	0.1	0.2	0.2
Ohio	0.9	95.3	4.0	0.3	1.0	0.1	0.2	0.5	95.9	3.3	0.1	0.6	0.3
Pendleton	0.8	97.0	2.6	0.4	0.3	0.1	0.3	0.9	97.7	2.1	0.0	0.2	0.3
Pleasants	0.5	98.8	0.6	0.8	0.2	0.0	0.1	0.4	99.6	0.2	0.1	0.0	0.1
Pocahontas	0.6	99.0	0.8	0.5	0.2	0.0	0.1	0.4	99.0	0.8	0.1	0.0	0.3
Preston	0.5	99.4	0.4	0.4	0.2	0.1	0.1	0.6	99.5	0.3	0.1	0.1	0.3
Putnam	0.6	98.5	0.7	0.4	0.7	0.0	0.3	0.5	99.2	0.3	0.1	0.3	0.3
Raleigh	0.8	90.3	8.9	0.5	0.9	0.0	0.2	0.9	91.6	7.7	0.1	0.5	0.4
Randolph	0.5	98.2	1.2	0.4	0.4	0.1	0.3	0.7	98.7	0.8	0.1	0.3	0.5
Ritchie	0.7	99.4	0.2	0.8	0.2	0.0	0.2	0.5	99.8	0.1	0.0	0.1	0.1
Roane	0.6	99.1	0.3	0.6	0.3	0.0	0.3	0.7	99.6	0.0	0.2	0.2	0.2
Summers	0.8	97.4	2.4	0.6	0.2	0.1	0.2	0.5	93.9	5.1	0.3	0.2	1.5
Taylor	0.6	98.7	1.0	0.5	0.2	0.1	0.2	0.6	99.0	0.6	0.1	0.2	0.4
Tucker	0.7	99.5	0.3	0.5	0.1	0.2	0.2	0.2	99.7	0.1	0.1	0.2	0.2
Tyler	0.4	99.8	0.1	0.4	0.2	0.0	0.1	0.4	99.6	0.0	0.2	0.1	0.2
Upshur	0.6	98.7	0.8	0.5	0.4	0.0	0.2	0.6	99.0	0.5	0.2	0.2	0.5
Wayne	0.6	99.3	0.2	0.6	0.3	0.0	0.1	0.5	99.6	0.0	0.2	0.1	0.3
Webster	0.7	99.8	0.1	0.5	0.1	0.1	0.0	0.4	99.8	0.0	0.1	0.1	0.3
Wetzel	0.5	99.4	0.2	0.4	0.4	0.0	0.1	0.4	99.6	0.1	0.1	0.2	0.2
Wirt	0.7	99.3	0.3	0.6	0.2	0.0	0.4	0.3	99.8	0.1	0.0	0.1	0.1
Wood	0.8	98.1	1.3	0.6	0.6	0.1	0.2	0.6	98.5	0.9	0.2	0.4	0.3
Wyoming	0.5	99.1	0.8	0.4	0.1	0.0	0.1	0.5	98.9	0.8	0.1	0.1	0.3
WISCONSIN	1.2	90.0	6.1	1.3	1.9	0.1	2.0	3.6	92.2	5.0	0.8	1.1	1.9
Adams	0.8	98.5	0.4	1.1	0.4	0.1	0.5	1.4	95.7	2.4	0.8	0.4	2.0
Ashland	1.7	88.6	0.4	11.7	0.5	0.1	0.4	1.1	90.4	0.1	9.1	0.3	0.7
Barron	0.7	98.3	0.3	1.2	0.4	0.1	0.4	1.0	99.0	0.1	0.5	0.2	0.4
Bayfield	1.5	89.9	0.2	10.6	0.4	0.0	0.4	0.6	90.7	0.2	8.9	0.2	0.4
Brown	1.3	92.2	1.5	2.9	2.4	0.1	2.2	3.8	95.9	0.5	2.0	1.3	0.8
Buffalo	0.5	99.1	0.2	0.5	0.5	0.0	0.2	0.6	99.5	0.0	0.2	0.2	0.3
Burnett	1.4	94.6	0.5	5.6	0.4	0.1	0.4	0.8	95.5	0.2	4.1	0.2	0.3
Calumet	0.7	97.3	0.5	0.6	1.8	0.1	0.5	1.1	98.9	0.1	0.4	0.5	0.4
Chippewa	0.6	98.4	0.3	0.6	1.1	0.0	0.3	0.5	99.0	0.1	0.3	0.5	0.3
Clark	0.5	98.5	0.2	0.8	0.4	0.0	0.7	1.2	99.3	0.1	0.3	0.1	0.4
Columbia	0.8	97.9	1.0	0.7	0.5	0.1	0.6	1.6	98.6	0.5	0.3	0.3	0.8
Crawford	0.7	97.9	1.5	0.5	0.4	0.1	0.3	0.7	99.1	0.3	0.2	0.4	0.4

[1] Hispanic persons may be of any race.

Table B. States and Counties

STATE County	Under 5 years	5 to 17 years	18 to 24 years	25 to 34 years	35 to 44 years	45 to 54 years	55 to 64 years	65 to 74 years	75 years and over	Median age (years)	Percent Female
	28	29	30	31	32	33	34	35	36	37	38
WEST VIRGINIA—Cont'd											
Braxton	5.3	17.5	7.5	13.0	15.1	15.0	10.8	8.2	7.7	39.6	49.4
Brooke	5.0	15.4	9.4	11.4	14.4	15.5	10.5	9.6	8.7	41.2	52.1
Cabell	5.4	14.6	13.5	13.1	13.6	13.8	9.8	8.4	7.7	37.5	52.2
Calhoun	5.1	17.3	8.0	10.3	15.5	15.9	11.2	9.0	7.7	41.3	50.1
Clay	6.1	19.5	9.0	12.7	14.8	14.3	9.9	8.0	5.6	36.8	50.5
Doddridge	5.9	19.1	8.4	10.9	15.7	14.6	10.5	8.4	6.4	38.7	49.5
Fayette	5.6	16.1	9.6	12.4	14.7	15.3	9.8	8.6	7.8	39.6	50.5
Gilmer	4.9	15.4	16.4	10.9	13.5	13.2	10.4	8.2	7.2	36.8	49.7
Grant	6.3	16.4	7.8	13.3	14.2	15.1	11.7	8.2	7.1	39.3	50.6
Greenbrier	5.5	16.1	7.7	11.2	14.9	15.4	11.5	9.5	8.2	41.6	51.9
Hampshire	6.1	19.0	7.1	12.4	15.2	14.6	11.0	8.4	6.2	38.5	50.1
Hancock	5.3	15.5	7.2	11.8	15.3	15.8	10.6	9.9	8.5	41.7	52.0
Hardy	6.0	17.4	7.6	13.0	15.9	14.4	10.9	8.5	6.4	38.9	50.6
Harrison	5.7	17.4	8.3	12.4	15.1	14.4	10.1	8.3	8.3	39.2	52.1
Jackson	6.1	18.1	7.9	12.4	15.4	13.8	11.2	8.9	6.4	38.8	51.3
Jefferson	6.3	17.6	10.0	13.1	16.8	15.5	9.7	6.3	4.9	36.8	50.5
Kanawha	5.7	15.6	8.4	12.7	15.4	15.6	10.1	8.7	7.9	40.2	52.4
Lewis	5.3	16.8	7.7	12.7	15.2	15.0	10.9	8.6	7.8	40.1	51.5
Lincoln	6.0	17.6	9.3	13.7	15.4	14.7	10.2	7.7	5.4	37.4	50.7
Logan	5.7	16.4	9.3	12.9	15.1	16.3	9.7	8.4	6.1	39.3	51.5
McDowell	5.1	18.0	7.9	11.4	15.4	15.8	10.3	8.5	7.6	40.5	52.5
Marion	5.1	15.5	10.5	12.6	13.8	14.4	10.3	8.7	9.1	39.9	52.5
Marshall	5.3	17.5	7.3	12.0	15.1	16.0	10.4	8.8	7.5	40.4	51.3
Mason	5.9	16.9	8.3	12.1	15.6	14.9	11.3	8.7	6.5	39.7	51.0
Mercer	5.8	15.3	9.8	12.5	13.7	15.0	10.5	9.0	8.4	40.2	52.3
Mineral	5.5	17.8	8.6	12.6	14.5	14.7	11.3	8.1	7.0	39.1	51.1
Mingo	5.8	18.4	9.2	13.3	15.9	15.6	9.3	7.2	5.2	37.2	51.6
Monongalia	4.9	13.3	23.4	14.3	13.4	12.5	7.5	5.6	5.1	30.4	49.6
Monroe	5.0	15.2	8.1	14.4	16.0	15.0	11.1	8.4	7.0	39.7	55.6
Morgan	6.1	16.3	6.8	11.9	15.4	15.4	11.5	9.8	6.8	40.7	50.9
Nicholas	5.4	17.9	8.1	12.2	15.4	15.4	10.6	8.3	6.7	39.4	51.1
Ohio	5.2	16.1	10.5	10.8	14.3	14.8	9.6	9.3	9.5	40.6	53.2
Pendleton	5.4	16.5	7.3	12.1	14.8	14.8	11.2	9.5	8.4	41.1	49.7
Pleasants	5.9	17.9	7.8	12.7	16.1	14.7	10.1	7.9	7.0	38.9	50.0
Pocahontas	5.0	15.9	7.0	11.9	15.6	15.3	12.1	9.3	7.9	41.9	48.5
Preston	5.6	18.1	8.0	12.3	15.4	15.1	10.5	8.1	6.8	39.1	50.4
Putnam	6.5	18.4	7.6	13.2	17.2	15.5	10.0	6.7	4.9	37.7	50.8
Raleigh	5.5	16.0	8.7	13.6	15.0	15.8	9.8	8.3	7.1	39.5	50.8
Randolph	5.2	17.1	8.7	13.1	15.4	14.6	10.8	7.6	7.5	38.8	49.7
Ritchie	5.5	17.5	7.7	12.0	15.9	14.9	11.3	8.0	7.2	39.9	51.0
Roane	5.7	17.7	8.7	11.7	14.9	15.2	11.3	8.1	6.7	39.5	50.5
Summers	4.6	15.9	7.5	10.6	14.1	15.7	11.6	10.7	9.2	43.4	51.1
Taylor	5.4	17.5	7.9	12.9	15.6	14.9	10.0	8.3	7.5	39.1	51.1
Tucker	4.8	16.4	6.7	11.5	14.8	15.1	12.6	9.5	8.4	42.0	51.2
Tyler	5.2	18.0	6.5	11.9	15.0	15.3	11.6	9.2	7.2	40.8	51.1
Upshur	5.3	17.2	12.6	11.6	14.1	14.3	10.2	7.6	7.1	37.4	51.5
Wayne	5.8	17.6	8.7	13.2	14.5	14.4	10.9	8.6	6.4	38.4	51.1
Webster	5.1	17.8	8.0	11.8	14.9	16.1	11.0	8.2	7.1	40.4	50.8
Wetzel	5.7	18.1	6.8	11.6	14.9	14.9	12.0	9.0	7.2	40.4	51.5
Wirt	5.6	19.8	7.6	12.1	17.5	13.2	11.2	7.3	5.7	37.9	50.0
Wood	5.8	17.2	8.0	12.5	15.4	14.7	10.9	8.1	7.4	39.3	52.0
Wyoming	5.7	16.7	8.7	11.9	15.6	17.2	10.3	8.4	5.5	40.1	50.8
WISCONSIN	6.4	19.1	9.7	13.2	16.3	13.7	8.5	6.6	6.5	36.0	50.6
Adams	4.8	16.0	5.6	9.3	15.0	13.8	14.5	12.9	8.1	44.5	49.3
Ashland	6.3	19.1	11.2	10.9	14.9	12.9	8.9	7.3	8.6	36.9	50.7
Barron	5.7	19.7	8.1	10.9	15.8	13.7	9.7	8.1	8.3	38.8	50.5
Bayfield	5.3	19.4	5.3	9.3	15.8	16.3	12.1	8.9	7.5	42.1	49.4
Brown	6.9	19.2	10.5	14.8	17.1	13.4	7.6	5.4	5.3	34.2	50.3
Buffalo	5.8	19.3	6.9	11.7	16.0	14.0	9.6	8.9	7.9	39.2	49.8
Burnett	4.9	17.2	6.0	9.1	14.1	14.6	13.9	11.8	8.5	44.1	49.6
Calumet	7.0	21.6	7.2	13.7	18.3	13.5	7.9	5.7	5.1	35.2	50.0
Chippewa	6.3	20.2	7.7	11.7	16.5	14.1	8.9	7.4	7.1	37.6	50.2
Clark	7.6	22.3	7.7	11.3	15.0	12.0	8.2	7.6	8.4	35.9	49.9
Columbia	6.1	19.1	7.1	12.7	17.2	14.2	9.2	7.2	7.2	38.0	49.6
Crawford	5.9	20.2	8.1	10.4	14.6	14.5	10.2	8.1	7.9	38.9	49.4

Table B. States and Counties

STATE County	Population and population characteristics, 1990										Population—change, 1980–2000				
	Age (percent)										Total persons			Percent change	
	Under 5 years	5 to 17 years	18 to 24 years	25 to 34 years	35 to 44 years	45 to 54 years	55 to 64 years	65 to 74 years	75 years and over	Percent Female	2000	1990	1980	1990–2000	1980–1990
	39	40	41	42	43	44	45	46	47	48	49	50	51	52	53
WEST VIRGINIA—Cont'd															
Braxton	6 7	19.2	8.1	13.7	14.9	10.3	9.9	9.3	7.8	51.5	14 702	12 998	13 894	13.1	-6.4
Brooke	4.9	17.7	10.9	12.9	15.4	10.8	11.1	9.0	6.6	52.1	25 447	26 992	31 117	-5.7	-13.3
Cabell	5.5	16.4	12.8	14.1	14.0	10.6	10.3	9.3	7.1	53.2	96 784	96 827	106 835	0.0	-9.4
Calhoun	6.4	20.8	7.7	14.2	15.0	10.3	9.9	8.3	7.4	50.9	7 582	7 885	8 250	-3.8	-4.4
Clay	7.0	22.9	9.1	14.2	14.9	9.7	9.4	7.2	5.7	50.7	10 330	9 983	11 265	3.5	-11.4
Doddridge	5.9	20.9	7.8	14.8	14.2	10.3	9.9	9.4	6.8	50.5	7 403	6 994	7 433	5.8	-5.9
Fayette	5.2	20.0	9.7	13.1	14.9	9.7	10.3	9.8	7.3	52.1	47 579	47 952	57 863	-0.8	-17.1
Gilmer	5.8	17.3	15.8	13.5	12.4	9.6	9.3	7.9	8.4	50.4	7 160	7 669	8 334	-6.6	-8.0
Grant	6.1	19.2	9.2	14.4	15.4	11.5	9.3	8.0	6.8	50.8	11 299	10 428	10 210	8.4	2.1
Greenbrier	5.6	18.2	8.3	14.4	15.0	11.1	10.4	9.1	7.8	52.1	34 453	34 693	37 665	-0.7	-7.9
Hampshire	7.0	19.6	9.5	14.6	14.6	10.8	10.1	8.4	5.3	50.5	20 203	16 498	14 867	22.5	11.0
Hancock	5.2	17.7	8.3	14.2	15.7	11.2	11.7	9.9	6.1	52.1	32 667	35 233	41 053	-7.3	-14.2
Hardy	6.5	17.4	8.9	15.6	14.6	10.8	10.8	9.0	6.3	50.7	12 669	10 977	10 030	15.4	9.4
Harrison	5.9	18.7	8.6	14.1	14.4	10.5	10.2	10.0	7.8	52.6	68 652	69 371	77 710	-1.0	-10.7
Jackson	6.5	19.6	8.4	14.5	14.1	12.4	11.1	7.5	6.0	51.1	28 000	25 938	25 794	7.9	0.6
Jefferson	7.1	18.5	12.3	15.9	15.8	10.7	8.3	7.1	4.3	50.8	42 190	35 926	30 302	17.4	18.6
Kanawha	5.9	17.4	8.6	15.3	15.7	10.9	10.6	9.3	6.4	52.8	200 073	207 619	231 414	-3.6	-10.3
Lewis	5.8	18.3	8.8	14.8	14.6	11.0	10.1	9.0	7.5	51.3	16 919	17 223	18 813	-1.8	-8.5
Lincoln	6.0	21.9	9.6	14.9	14.9	10.9	9.3	7.2	5.3	50.9	22 108	21 382	23 675	3.4	-9.7
Logan	5.7	22.2	9.4	14.5	16.2	9.7	9.7	7.7	4.9	51.8	37 710	43 032	50 679	-12.4	-15.1
McDowell	6.2	22.8	8.5	14.1	14.6	9.5	9.6	8.9	5.8	52.9	27 329	35 233	49 899	-22.4	-29.4
Marion	5.4	17.3	10.9	13.1	14.5	10.5	10.1	10.2	8.0	53.4	56 598	57 249	65 789	-1.1	-13.0
Marshall	6.0	18.5	8.7	14.2	16.1	11.0	10.4	9.2	6.0	51.5	35 519	37 356	41 608	-4.9	-10.2
Mason	5.8	20.0	8.0	14.9	15.1	11.5	10.5	8.2	5.9	51.4	25 957	25 178	27 045	3.1	-6.9
Mercer	5.4	18.6	10.2	13.6	15.1	10.4	10.1	9.7	6.9	53.1	62 980	64 980	73 870	-3.1	-12.0
Mineral	6.3	18.7	10.8	13.6	14.7	11.6	9.5	8.7	6.0	51.6	27 078	26 697	27 234	1.4	-2.0
Mingo	6.6	23.9	10.2	16.0	15.1	9.6	8.3	6.5	3.9	51.2	28 253	33 739	37 336	-16.3	-9.6
Monongalia	5.4	14.5	23.2	16.0	13.9	8.7	7.3	6.3	4.6	50.4	81 866	75 509	75 024	8.4	0.6
Monroe	6.0	18.6	9.0	12.9	14.6	11.2	10.8	9.9	7.0	51.5	14 583	12 406	12 873	17.5	-3.6
Morgan	5.6	17.2	8.4	14.1	14.6	11.4	11.8	10.2	6.6	51.4	14 943	12 128	10 711	23.2	13.2
Nicholas	6.5	21.0	8.7	14.3	15.5	10.5	9.6	8.1	5.8	51.0	26 562	26 775	28 126	-0.8	-4.8
Ohio	5.8	16.1	10.5	13.4	14.5	10.1	10.7	10.8	8.1	53.5	47 427	50 871	61 389	-6.8	-17.1
Pendleton	6.6	17.5	8.6	14.9	14.4	10.4	10.5	9.2	8.1	50.1	8 196	8 054	7 910	1.8	1.8
Pleasants	5.7	19.9	8.8	15.8	14.9	11.1	9.4	8.1	6.5	51.4	7 514	7 546	8 236	-0.4	-8.4
Pocahontas	6.0	17.2	7.5	14.2	14.5	11.2	10.6	9.9	9.0	50.2	9 131	9 008	9 919	1.4	-9.2
Preston	6.4	20.8	8.7	14.9	15.0	10.7	9.5	8.0	6.0	50.7	29 334	29 037	30 460	1.0	-4.7
Putnam	6.8	20.0	8.3	16.4	17.0	11.8	8.8	6.6	4.4	51.0	51 589	42 835	38 181	20.4	12.2
Raleigh	5.7	20.4	8.4	13.6	16.3	10.3	10.0	9.0	6.3	52.9	79 220	76 819	86 821	3.1	-11.5
Randolph	6.0	18.2	10.1	15.1	15.1	11.0	8.8	8.7	7.1	50.6	28 262	27 803	28 734	1.7	-3.2
Ritchie	5.6	18.8	8.8	14.7	14.4	10.9	9.5	8.9	8.4	51.4	10 343	10 233	11 442	1.1	-10.6
Roane	5.7	21.1	8.0	13.5	15.1	11.3	9.7	8.6	7.0	50.8	15 446	15 120	15 952	2.2	-5.2
Summers	5.2	18.2	7.7	15.1	15.3	10.2	10.9	9.9	7.6	55.0	12 999	14 204	15 875	-8.5	-10.5
Taylor	6.5	18.9	8.7	14.9	14.8	10.3	9.7	8.8	7.3	51.6	16 089	15 144	16 584	6.2	-8.7
Tucker	5.6	18.5	8.9	13.6	15.3	11.5	9.8	8.7	8.1	51.4	7 321	7 728	8 675	-5.3	-10.9
Tyler	6.2	19.3	8.6	13.9	14.5	11.7	10.3	8.5	6.9	50.9	9 592	9 796	11 320	-2.1	-13.5
Upshur	6.1	19.3	13.0	13.9	14.5	10.3	8.2	7.8	6.9	51.1	23 404	22 867	23 427	2.3	-2.4
Wayne	5.8	19.9	9.7	14.2	15.0	11.8	10.0	8.3	5.5	51.7	42 903	41 636	46 021	3.0	-9.5
Webster	6.4	21.0	8.8	14.2	14.8	9.9	9.5	8.7	6.7	51.5	9 719	10 729	12 245	-9.4	-12.4
Wetzel	6.2	19.5	9.1	13.5	14.5	11.9	10.4	8.0	6.8	52.0	17 693	19 258	21 874	-8.1	-12.0
Wirt	6.5	20.2	8.2	16.1	13.9	11.8	9.1	8.0	6.4	51.0	5 873	5 192	4 922	13.1	5.5
Wood	6.3	18.3	8.8	15.0	15.2	11.9	9.6	8.3	6.5	52.4	87 986	86 915	93 627	1.2	-7.2
Wyoming	5.8	22.8	9.0	14.8	16.5	10.5	9.7	7.0	3.9	51.4	25 708	28 990	35 993	-11.3	-19.5
WISCONSIN	7.4	19.0	10.5	16.8	14.8	9.8	8.5	7.3	6.0	51.1	5 363 675	4 891 954	4 705 642	9.6	4.0
Adams	5.5	15.6	6.5	15.1	13.5	11.3	13.2	12.4	7.0	46.9	18 643	15 682	13 457	18.9	16.5
Ashland	7.3	19.8	10.1	14.7	13.1	8.8	8.3	9.1	8.8	51.1	16 866	16 307	16 783	3.4	-2.8
Barron	7.1	20.6	8.1	15.0	13.8	9.6	8.9	8.9	8.0	50.6	44 963	40 750	38 730	10.3	5.2
Bayfield	6.7	19.9	6.3	13.6	15.0	10.7	10.1	9.8	7.8	49.4	15 013	14 008	13 822	7.2	1.3
Brown	7.8	19.3	11.1	18.5	15.6	9.6	7.4	5.9	4.9	51.2	226 778	194 594	175 280	16.5	11.0
Buffalo	7.2	19.8	7.4	15.7	13.5	9.9	9.8	8.7	8.0	49.8	13 804	13 584	14 309	1.6	-5.1
Burnett	6.2	18.8	6.1	12.6	13.5	10.5	11.9	11.9	8.4	50.5	15 674	13 084	12 340	19.8	6.0
Calumet	8.3	22.3	8.3	17.9	14.9	9.4	7.9	6.3	4.7	50.2	40 631	34 291	30 867	18.5	11.1
Chippewa	7.4	20.9	8.3	16.0	14.8	9.6	8.7	7.6	6.7	50.7	55 195	52 360	52 127	5.4	0.4
Clark	7.7	22.6	7.5	14.0	12.8	9.3	8.9	8.8	8.4	49.9	33 557	31 647	32 910	6.0	-3.8
Columbia	6.9	19.4	7.9	15.4	15.0	10.3	9.3	8.5	7.1	50.3	52 468	45 088	43 222	16.4	4.3
Crawford	7.3	21.7	7.4	13.8	13.7	9.8	9.5	9.3	7.6	50.5	17 243	15 940	16 556	8.2	-3.7

Table B. States and Counties

STATE County	Total population	Total in house-holds	House-holder	Spouse	Child Total	Child Own child under 18 years	Other relatives Total	Other relatives Under 18 years	Nonrelatives Total	Nonrelatives Unmarried partner	Total in group quarters	Correctional institutions	Nursing homes	Other institutions	College dormitories	Military quarters	Other
	54	55	56	57	58	59	60	61	62	63	64	65	66	67	68	69	70
WEST VIRGINIA—Cont'd																	
Braxton	14 702	96.4	39.3	22.5	26.9	20.6	4.0	1.6	3.7	2.1	3.6	3.2	0.4	0.0	0.0	0.0	0.0
Brooke	25 447	96.6	40.9	22.6	26.6	18.7	3.6	1.4	2.9	1.7	3.4	0.0	0.8	0.0	2.3	0.0	0.2
Cabell	96 784	96.6	42.5	20.0	24.9	18.0	3.8	1.4	5.3	1.9	3.4	0.3	0.7	0.4	1.7	0.0	0.4
Calhoun	7 582	99.6	40.5	23.1	28.0	20.2	4.2	1.6	3.7	1.6	0.4	0.0	0.0	0.3	0.0	0.0	0.1
Clay	10 330	99.3	38.9	22.7	30.8	23.6	3.7	1.4	3.3	1.8	0.7	0.0	0.5	0.1	0.0	0.0	0.0
Doddridge	7 403	98.5	38.4	22.8	29.5	21.7	3.8	1.5	4.0	2.0	1.5	0.0	0.0	1.5	0.0	0.0	0.0
Fayette	47 579	95.8	39.8	20.7	27.0	19.2	4.5	2.0	3.8	2.0	4.2	2.1	0.9	0.1	0.8	0.0	0.3
Gilmer	7 160	93.9	38.7	21.0	25.0	18.5	3.7	1.2	5.4	2.5	6.1	0.0	0.9	0.0	5.2	0.0	0.0
Grant	11 299	98.7	40.6	24.2	27.2	21.0	2.9	1.1	3.8	2.2	1.3	0.0	1.0	0.1	0.0	0.0	0.2
Greenbrier	34 453	98.3	42.3	22.9	26.3	19.5	3.6	1.5	3.2	1.8	1.7	0.3	0.9	0.1	0.0	0.0	0.3
Hampshire	20 203	97.9	39.4	22.3	28.3	22.5	3.6	1.5	4.3	2.4	2.1	0.5	0.5	0.6	0.0	0.0	0.4
Hancock	32 667	98.9	41.9	22.9	26.4	18.7	4.0	1.6	3.8	2.1	1.1	0.0	1.0	0.0	0.0	0.0	0.0
Hardy	12 669	99.4	41.1	23.1	27.3	21.2	3.5	1.4	4.4	2.4	0.6	0.0	0.5	0.0	0.0	0.0	0.1
Harrison	68 652	98.3	40.6	21.6	28.5	21.0	3.9	1.6	3.6	2.0	1.7	0.1	0.8	0.1	0.5	0.0	0.2
Jackson	28 000	98.8	39.5	24.3	29.1	22.3	3.0	1.2	2.9	1.5	1.2	0.0	1.0	0.0	0.0	0.0	0.2
Jefferson	42 190	97.3	38.3	21.4	27.5	21.3	4.6	2.0	5.5	2.8	2.7	0.0	0.4	0.0	2.2	0.0	0.1
Kanawha	200 073	98.4	43.1	21.1	26.4	19.2	4.0	1.7	3.8	2.0	1.6	0.2	0.5	0.0	0.3	0.0	0.5
Lewis	16 919	98.7	41.1	22.4	27.2	20.0	3.8	1.4	4.1	2.1	1.3	0.0	0.5	0.9	0.0	0.0	0.0
Lincoln	22 108	99.7	39.2	23.7	29.8	21.3	4.0	1.7	3.0	1.6	0.3	0.0	0.3	0.0	0.0	0.0	0.1
Logan	37 710	98.5	39.5	22.5	28.6	19.2	5.3	2.4	2.7	1.5	1.5	0.7	0.5	0.2	0.0	0.0	0.1
McDowell	27 329	98.9	40.9	20.9	28.3	19.8	5.8	2.8	3.0	1.7	1.1	0.3	0.6	0.0	0.0	0.0	0.2
Marion	56 598	97.8	41.8	21.5	26.4	18.8	3.8	1.5	4.4	1.9	2.2	0.2	0.9	0.1	0.7	0.0	0.3
Marshall	35 519	97.6	40.0	22.7	28.2	20.7	3.5	1.5	3.2	1.9	2.4	1.0	0.6	0.0	0.0	0.0	0.8
Mason	25 957	98.9	40.8	23.5	28.3	20.9	3.4	1.4	3.0	1.8	1.1	0.1	1.0	0.0	0.1	0.0	0.0
Mercer	62 980	98.0	42.1	22.3	25.9	18.7	4.4	1.9	3.2	1.6	2.0	0.0	0.7	0.0	1.0	0.0	0.2
Mineral	27 078	98.1	39.8	23.1	28.5	21.3	3.3	1.4	3.4	1.9	1.9	0.0	0.7	0.0	1.0	0.0	0.2
Mingo	28 253	99.6	40.0	22.5	30.3	21.7	4.7	2.1	2.1	1.2	0.4	0.0	0.4	0.0	0.0	0.0	0.1
Monongalia	81 866	93.1	40.9	17.9	22.3	17.0	2.9	0.9	9.1	2.1	6.9	1.4	0.4	0.0	4.9	0.0	0.2
Monroe	14 583	89.9	37.4	22.3	25.0	18.7	2.9	1.1	2.4	1.4	10.1	9.5	0.5	0.0	0.0	0.0	0.0
Morgan	14 943	98.9	41.1	23.8	26.4	20.6	3.3	1.3	4.2	2.6	1.1	0.0	1.1	0.0	0.0	0.0	0.1
Nicholas	26 562	99.3	40.4	23.7	28.8	21.4	3.5	1.4	3.0	1.6	0.7	0.0	0.7	0.0	0.0	0.0	0.1
Ohio	47 427	94.4	41.6	19.7	26.0	19.5	3.3	1.3	3.9	1.9	5.6	0.2	1.0	0.1	3.6	0.0	0.8
Pendleton	8 196	98.0	40.9	23.5	26.0	19.9	4.1	1.6	3.5	2.0	2.0	0.0	1.1	0.1	0.0	0.7	0.1
Pleasants	7 514	96.6	38.4	23.1	28.3	21.7	3.6	1.5	3.2	1.8	3.4	2.6	0.8	0.0	0.0	0.0	0.0
Pocahontas	9 131	96.7	42.0	22.6	24.7	18.9	3.5	1.4	4.0	2.3	3.3	2.4	0.7	0.0	0.0	0.0	0.1
Preston	29 334	98.5	39.4	23.4	28.4	21.2	3.5	1.3	4.0	2.2	1.5	0.1	0.9	0.0	0.0	0.0	0.5
Putnam	51 589	99.4	38.8	24.9	30.2	23.4	2.8	1.2	2.6	1.5	0.6	0.0	0.2	0.0	0.0	0.0	0.3
Raleigh	79 220	95.4	40.1	21.8	26.6	19.4	4.0	1.7	2.9	1.6	4.6	3.2	0.7	0.0	0.4	0.0	0.2
Randolph	28 262	94.6	39.2	21.4	26.2	20.0	3.7	1.5	4.1	2.2	5.4	3.1	1.0	0.2	0.9	0.0	0.2
Ritchie	10 343	99.3	40.5	23.6	28.1	20.9	3.8	1.5	3.3	1.9	0.7	0.2	0.5	0.0	0.0	0.0	0.0
Roane	15 446	99.3	39.9	23.6	28.3	21.1	3.6	1.4	4.0	1.9	0.7	0.0	0.6	0.0	0.0	0.0	0.1
Summers	12 999	98.8	42.5	22.9	26.2	18.4	4.2	1.7	3.0	1.6	1.2	0.0	1.2	0.0	0.0	0.0	0.0
Taylor	16 089	97.1	39.3	22.2	28.7	21.3	3.5	1.2	3.4	2.0	2.9	1.7	1.1	0.0	0.0	0.0	0.1
Tucker	7 321	98.2	41.7	24.2	26.0	19.4	3.2	1.1	3.0	1.6	1.8	0.0	1.3	0.6	0.0	0.0	0.0
Tyler	9 592	98.9	40.0	24.5	28.1	21.5	3.2	1.3	3.1	1.7	1.1	0.1	0.7	0.0	0.0	0.0	0.3
Upshur	23 404	94.1	38.3	22.3	26.9	20.7	2.8	1.2	3.8	1.8	5.9	0.0	0.5	0.1	5.1	0.0	0.2
Wayne	42 903	99.5	40.2	23.8	29.0	21.2	3.9	1.5	2.7	1.3	0.5	0.0	0.0	0.1	0.0	0.0	0.3
Webster	9 719	99.4	41.3	22.9	28.2	21.0	3.8	1.5	3.3	2.0	0.6	0.0	0.6	0.0	0.0	0.0	0.0
Wetzel	17 693	99.0	40.5	23.4	28.5	21.9	3.4	1.5	3.3	1.9	1.0	0.0	0.7	0.0	0.0	0.0	0.3
Wirt	5 873	99.6	38.9	23.9	29.7	23.5	3.3	1.2	3.8	2.0	0.4	0.4	0.0	0.0	0.0	0.0	0.0
Wood	87 986	98.5	41.2	22.4	27.4	20.9	3.5	1.5	3.9	2.1	1.5	0.1	0.7	0.1	0.3	0.0	0.3
Wyoming	25 708	99.5	40.7	24.1	28.7	20.2	4.0	1.9	2.1	1.3	0.5	0.0	0.2	0.0	0.0	0.0	0.2
WISCONSIN	5 363 675	97.1	38.9	20.7	29.4	23.7	3.0	1.1	5.2	2.2	2.9	0.6	0.8	0.1	1.0	0.0	0.5
Adams	18 643	98.7	42.4	24.8	23.6	18.8	3.1	1.3	4.8	2.5	1.3	0.4	0.5	0.0	0.0	0.0	0.4
Ashland	16 866	95.3	39.8	19.3	28.8	23.5	2.8	1.2	4.5	2.1	4.7	0.4	1.3	0.1	2.5	0.0	0.4
Barron	44 963	98.5	39.7	22.6	29.1	23.6	2.3	0.9	4.7	2.2	1.5	0.1	1.1	0.0	0.0	0.0	0.3
Bayfield	15 013	99.2	41.3	23.1	27.7	22.9	2.7	1.1	4.4	2.3	0.8	0.2	0.5	0.0	0.0	0.0	0.1
Brown	226 778	96.6	38.5	20.5	29.8	24.7	2.4	0.8	5.4	2.5	3.4	1.0	0.6	0.0	1.2	0.0	0.5
Buffalo	13 804	98.8	39.9	23.5	29.6	23.7	2.0	0.7	3.7	2.0	1.2	0.1	1.0	0.0	0.0	0.0	0.2
Burnett	15 674	98.3	42.2	23.7	25.2	20.1	2.7	1.1	4.5	2.4	1.7	0.3	0.9	0.1	0.0	0.0	0.3
Calumet	40 631	99.1	36.7	23.8	33.6	27.7	1.6	0.5	3.4	1.8	0.9	0.1	0.6	0.0	0.0	0.0	0.1
Chippewa	55 195	98.0	38.7	22.6	30.5	24.9	2.1	0.8	4.2	2.2	2.0	0.1	1.1	0.4	0.0	0.0	0.3
Clark	33 557	98.1	35.9	22.0	34.4	28.4	2.4	0.9	3.4	1.8	1.9	0.2	1.4	0.0	0.0	0.0	0.3
Columbia	52 468	97.0	39.0	22.6	29.0	23.8	2.2	0.8	4.2	2.2	3.0	1.7	0.8	0.2	0.0	0.0	0.3
Crawford	17 243	96.1	38.7	22.0	29.6	24.2	2.0	0.7	3.8	2.1	3.9	1.9	1.0	0.6	0.0	0.0	0.4

Table B. States and Counties

STATE County	Households by type, 2000												Households, 1990		
		Family households						Nonfamily households							
				Married couple		Female householder[1]			Householder living alone						
	Total households	Total	With own children under 18 years	Total	With own children under 18 years	Total	With own children under 18 years	Total	Total	65 years and over	Average household size	Average family size	Total households	Female householder[1]	Householder living alone
	71	72	73	74	75	76	77	78	79	80	81	82	83	84	85
WEST VIRGINIA—Cont'd															
Braxton	5 771	71.0	30.3	57.3	23.0	9.2	5.0	29.0	25.2	12.4	2.46	2.92	4 950	10.1	23.3
Brooke	10 396	68.8	26.9	55.3	20.5	9.9	4.8	31.2	27.9	14.4	2.36	2.88	10 131	9.1	23.6
Cabell	41 180	61.9	25.2	47.1	17.6	11.6	6.2	38.1	31.3	12.5	2.27	2.85	39 146	11.5	29.0
Calhoun	3 071	71.7	28.9	57.0	22.5	10.3	4.6	28.3	24.9	12.3	2.46	2.91	2 978	11.9	22.7
Clay	4 020	73.2	33.5	58.2	25.2	10.4	6.0	26.8	24.3	11.4	2.55	3.01	3 627	11.8	21.7
Doddridge	2 845	73.9	32.5	59.3	24.7	10.3	5.2	26.1	22.5	10.9	2.56	2.98	2 623	8.6	22.8
Fayette	18 945	69.3	29.0	52.1	20.3	13.2	6.7	30.7	26.9	13.4	2.41	2.89	18 292	12.6	25.8
Gilmer	2 768	67.3	28.2	54.4	21.1	8.6	5.0	32.7	25.5	12.3	2.43	2.92	2 717	9.3	22.9
Grant	4 591	71.3	30.2	59.5	23.8	8.2	4.6	28.7	24.5	11.3	2.43	2.87	3 925	8.6	21.4
Greenbrier	14 571	68.1	27.6	54.2	20.4	10.7	5.5	31.9	28.6	13.4	2.32	2.83	13 775	10.6	25.9
Hampshire	7 955	70.9	31.3	56.7	22.8	9.5	5.6	29.1	24.6	10.6	2.49	2.94	6 182	8.5	22.3
Hancock	13 678	69.5	26.4	54.7	19.1	10.7	5.3	30.5	26.6	12.5	2.36	2.83	13 781	10.5	23.6
Hardy	5 204	68.5	29.6	56.1	22.7	8.6	4.8	31.5	27.0	12.2	2.42	2.92	4 286	8.6	22.6
Harrison	27 867	68.5	29.7	53.3	21.6	11.4	6.1	31.5	27.7	13.2	2.42	2.94	27 009	11.0	25.8
Jackson	11 061	74.2	31.9	61.6	24.6	9.4	5.7	25.8	22.7	10.3	2.50	2.92	9 645	9.2	19.4
Jefferson	16 165	70.0	31.9	55.9	23.7	10.0	5.8	30.0	23.2	8.5	2.54	2.99	12 914	9.5	21.5
Kanawha	86 226	64.9	26.5	49.0	18.3	12.3	6.5	35.1	30.8	12.5	2.28	2.84	84 713	11.8	27.4
Lewis	6 946	69.2	28.6	54.6	20.9	10.5	5.7	30.8	26.9	13.0	2.40	2.88	6 615	11.1	25.6
Lincoln	8 664	75.4	33.0	60.4	25.3	10.8	5.7	24.6	22.2	10.4	2.54	2.94	7 647	10.6	18.9
Logan	14 880	73.5	30.5	57.0	23.0	12.6	5.8	26.5	24.0	11.4	2.50	2.95	15 425	13.2	20.0
McDowell	11 169	70.2	29.2	51.1	20.1	14.9	7.2	29.8	27.3	13.1	2.42	2.92	12 880	14.3	22.8
Marion	23 652	65.6	26.0	51.4	19.2	10.7	5.3	34.4	28.9	13.9	2.34	2.88	22 667	10.8	26.7
Marshall	14 207	71.1	29.5	56.8	21.8	10.8	5.9	28.9	25.6	12.9	2.44	2.91	14 051	10.1	23.3
Mason	10 587	71.5	30.6	57.6	22.8	10.1	5.7	28.5	25.5	11.5	2.42	2.89	9 603	9.6	22.6
Mercer	26 509	67.7	26.7	53.0	19.4	11.2	5.7	32.3	28.7	13.6	2.33	2.85	25 390	11.7	25.3
Mineral	10 784	71.5	30.4	57.9	22.7	9.7	5.6	28.5	25.0	11.5	2.46	2.93	9 981	9.2	22.4
Mingo	11 303	72.7	33.5	52.8	25.5	12.7	6.4	27.3	25.2	10.4	2.49	2.98	11 830	13.4	20.0
Monongalia	33 446	55.3	24.2	43.8	18.4	8.3	4.4	44.7	31.3	8.4	2.28	2.91	29 087	8.4	28.7
Monroe	5 447	71.3	29.0	59.8	23.3	7.9	3.9	28.7	25.8	13.1	2.41	2.88	4 749	8.2	23.2
Morgan	6 145	70.7	28.7	57.9	21.1	8.2	4.6	29.3	24.5	10.2	2.40	2.84	4 731	7.5	22.2
Nicholas	10 722	72.4	30.7	58.7	23.8	10.0	5.2	27.6	24.8	11.8	2.46	2.91	9 970	10.3	21.1
Ohio	19 733	61.6	25.9	47.3	18.3	11.2	6.0	38.4	33.7	16.0	2.27	2.91	20 646	11.6	31.9
Pendleton	3 350	70.3	28.0	57.4	21.9	8.1	4.0	29.7	25.8	12.2	2.40	2.87	3 061	8.1	21.7
Pleasants	2 887	74.0	32.7	60.1	24.8	10.4	6.1	26.0	22.9	12.3	2.51	2.93	2 769	9.7	22.9
Pocahontas	3 835	65.9	25.8	53.9	19.6	7.9	4.0	34.1	29.6	14.4	2.30	2.83	3 628	8.1	26.6
Preston	11 544	72.4	31.5	59.4	24.6	9.1	4.7	27.6	23.7	11.7	2.50	2.94	10 619	8.9	21.2
Putnam	20 028	76.3	35.4	64.2	28.6	8.9	5.1	23.7	20.6	7.9	2.56	2.96	15 695	8.5	17.6
Raleigh	31 793	69.5	28.6	54.3	20.8	11.9	6.3	30.5	27.1	12.9	2.38	2.88	29 483	11.9	24.3
Randolph	11 072	69.2	29.8	54.7	21.9	9.8	5.3	30.8	26.3	11.9	2.41	2.89	10 366	9.9	25.0
Ritchie	4 184	71.7	30.2	58.2	23.6	9.7	4.8	28.3	25.0	12.3	2.45	2.91	3 928	9.6	23.1
Roane	6 161	72.7	30.7	59.1	23.5	9.3	5.1	27.3	23.5	11.9	2.49	2.91	5 740	9.1	22.9
Summers	5 530	67.9	25.7	53.8	19.0	10.0	4.7	32.1	29.1	14.4	2.32	2.84	5 240	11.0	25.7
Taylor	6 320	71.0	30.9	56.4	23.2	10.9	5.6	29.0	25.5	12.6	2.47	2.95	5 741	10.6	23.9
Tucker	3 052	69.5	27.0	58.0	21.5	7.8	3.8	30.5	27.2	13.6	2.35	2.84	3 017	8.3	25.5
Tyler	3 836	73.9	30.3	61.4	23.6	8.6	4.8	26.1	23.1	12.1	2.47	2.89	3 709	8.2	21.5
Upshur	8 972	70.8	31.1	58.2	23.7	9.1	5.3	29.2	25.2	11.2	2.45	2.92	8 245	9.2	24.0
Wayne	17 239	73.4	31.2	59.2	23.7	10.8	5.8	26.6	24.1	11.1	2.48	2.92	15 626	10.5	21.2
Webster	4 010	70.2	29.8	55.4	21.6	10.6	6.0	29.8	26.5	12.4	2.41	2.89	3 996	12.1	21.2
Wetzel	7 164	70.9	30.2	57.7	22.9	9.3	5.2	29.1	25.7	12.8	2.45	2.92	7 303	9.8	23.4
Wirt	2 284	74.4	35.2	61.5	27.3	8.9	5.4	25.6	22.2	11.6	2.56	2.97	1 942	8.4	21.9
Wood	36 275	68.6	29.3	54.3	21.2	10.8	6.3	31.4	27.1	11.5	2.39	2.88	34 168	10.2	24.2
Wyoming	10 454	73.7	31.0	59.3	23.8	10.5	5.2	26.3	24.4	11.5	2.45	2.89	10 474	11.0	19.2
WISCONSIN	2 084 544	66.5	31.9	53.2	23.7	9.6	6.2	33.5	26.8	9.9	2.50	3.05	1 822 118	9.6	24.3
Adams	7 900	69.2	23.6	58.5	17.2	6.7	4.0	30.8	25.5	11.5	2.33	2.76	5 972	6.4	23.1
Ashland	6 718	63.7	30.3	48.6	20.9	10.9	7.0	36.3	30.8	14.4	2.39	3.01	6 255	9.7	30.6
Barron	17 851	69.2	31.3	56.9	23.5	8.2	5.4	30.8	25.4	12.2	2.48	2.97	15 435	7.9	24.2
Bayfield	6 207	68.9	28.9	55.9	20.4	7.8	5.3	31.1	26.4	11.5	2.40	2.88	5 515	7.5	25.6
Brown	87 295	65.9	33.9	53.2	25.5	8.9	6.2	34.1	26.5	8.4	2.51	3.08	72 280	9.0	24.1
Buffalo	5 511	68.6	30.8	58.9	25.4	6.2	3.6	31.4	27.1	12.6	2.47	3.01	5 123	6.6	23.9
Burnett	6 613	68.1	25.1	56.2	17.7	7.5	4.6	31.9	26.9	12.2	2.33	2.80	5 242	7.6	25.5
Calumet	14 910	74.9	38.5	65.0	32.2	6.5	4.4	25.1	20.4	7.5	2.70	3.15	11 772	6.7	17.8
Chippewa	21 356	70.3	33.7	58.3	26.0	8.0	5.3	29.7	24.7	11.0	2.53	3.03	19 077	7.7	23.0
Clark	12 047	72.0	35.0	61.2	28.6	6.5	4.0	28.0	23.8	12.6	2.73	3.27	11 209	6.2	23.8
Columbia	20 439	69.3	32.2	58.1	25.3	7.4	4.7	30.7	25.5	11.0	2.49	2.99	16 868	7.1	23.6
Crawford	6 677	69.1	31.6	56.7	23.9	8.4	5.3	30.9	26.7	13.0	2.48	3.00	5 914	7.5	24.9

[1] No spouse present.

Table B. States and Counties

STATE County	Percent change of households, 1990–2000	Total housing units	Occupied housing units (percent)	Vacant housing units Total	For seasonal, recreational, or occasional use	Homeowner vacancy rate (percent)	Rental vacancy rate (percent)	Occupied housing units Total	Percent owner-occupied housing units	Percent renter-occupied housing units	Average household size of owner-occupied units	Average household size of renter-occupied units
	86	87	88	89	90	91	92	93	94	95	96	97
WEST VIRGINIA—Cont'd												
Braxton	16.6	7 374	78.3	21.7	9.9	3.1	7.6	5 771	78.2	21.8	2.49	2.35
Brooke	2.6	11 150	93.2	6.8	0.5	1.6	7.7	10 396	76.7	23.3	2.47	2.00
Cabell	5.2	45 615	90.3	9.7	0.5	2.2	8.5	41 180	64.6	35.4	2.41	2.01
Calhoun	3.1	3 848	79.8	20.2	8.8	2.0	6.9	3 071	78.9	21.1	2.48	2.38
Clay	10.8	4 836	83.1	16.9	7.1	1.7	6.4	4 020	79.2	20.8	2.59	2.39
Doddridge	8.5	3 661	77.7	22.3	12.9	2.3	5.6	2 845	81.2	18.8	2.59	2.47
Fayette	3.6	21 616	87.6	12.4	2.1	2.3	9.1	18 945	77.2	22.8	2.43	2.31
Gilmer	1.9	3 621	76.4	23.6	13.2	3.0	14.3	2 768	72.4	27.6	2.44	2.39
Grant	17.0	6 105	75.2	24.8	11.8	1.8	8.5	4 591	80.9	19.1	2.49	2.19
Greenbrier	5.8	17 644	82.6	17.4	5.7	3.0	9.1	14 571	76.6	23.4	2.39	2.10
Hampshire	28.7	11 185	71.1	28.9	22.6	1.7	7.1	7 955	81.1	18.9	2.51	2.40
Hancock	-0.7	14 728	92.9	7.1	0.3	1.3	9.6	13 678	77.1	22.9	2.42	2.15
Hardy	21.4	7 115	73.1	26.9	18.5	1.6	5.3	5 204	80.5	19.5	2.46	2.26
Harrison	3.2	31 112	89.6	10.4	1.0	2.7	10.7	27 867	74.8	25.2	2.49	2.21
Jackson	14.7	12 245	90.3	9.7	2.4	1.5	8.1	11 061	79.6	20.4	2.55	2.33
Jefferson	25.2	17 623	91.7	8.3	2.8	1.5	4.4	16 165	75.8	24.2	2.62	2.29
Kanawha	1.8	93 788	91.9	8.1	0.6	1.9	8.5	86 226	70.3	29.7	2.38	2.06
Lewis	5.0	7 944	87.4	12.6	3.8	1.8	7.5	6 946	73.0	27.0	2.45	2.28
Lincoln	13.3	9 846	88.0	12.0	1.6	2.0	7.7	8 664	79.1	20.9	2.57	2.46
Logan	-3.5	16 807	88.5	11.5	0.9	2.5	13.4	14 880	76.8	23.2	2.53	2.38
McDowell	-13.3	13 582	82.2	17.8	1.0	4.6	13.1	11 169	80.1	19.9	2.43	2.37
Marion	4.3	26 660	88.7	11.3	1.2	2.9	12.9	23 652	74.8	25.2	2.41	2.13
Marshall	1.1	15 814	89.8	10.2	3.4	1.2	6.3	14 207	77.6	22.4	2.50	2.25
Mason	10.2	12 056	87.8	12.2	4.1	1.6	8.1	10 587	81.0	19.0	2.45	2.31
Mercer	4.4	30 143	87.9	12.1	1.5	2.5	10.6	26 509	76.8	23.2	2.38	2.15
Mineral	8.0	12 094	89.2	10.8	2.8	2.2	7.4	10 784	78.0	22.0	2.52	2.27
Mingo	-4.5	12 898	87.6	12.4	0.8	3.0	13.4	11 303	77.7	22.3	2.54	2.31
Monongalia	15.0	36 695	91.1	8.9	1.1	2.4	7.7	33 446	61.0	39.0	2.49	1.95
Monroe	14.7	7 267	75.0	25.0	13.0	2.3	8.0	5 447	84.5	15.5	2.44	2.24
Morgan	29.9	8 076	76.1	23.9	15.0	3.2	7.6	6 145	83.3	16.7	2.42	2.32
Nicholas	7.5	12 406	86.4	13.6	3.7	2.6	7.8	10 722	82.8	17.2	2.50	2.29
Ohio	-4.4	22 166	89.0	11.0	0.4	2.1	13.4	19 733	68.6	31.4	2.43	1.91
Pendleton	9.4	5 102	65.7	34.3	19.3	2.3	10.5	3 350	79.4	20.6	2.40	2.37
Pleasants	4.3	3 214	89.8	10.2	3.5	1.1	5.0	2 887	80.4	19.6	2.55	2.35
Pocahontas	5.7	7 594	50.5	49.5	39.5	2.3	26.7	3 835	80.3	19.7	2.32	2.25
Preston	8.7	13 444	85.9	14.1	5.1	2.1	9.2	11 544	83.0	17.0	2.56	2.23
Putnam	27.6	21 621	92.6	7.4	1.0	1.9	9.0	20 028	84.0	16.0	2.61	2.30
Raleigh	7.8	35 678	89.1	10.9	1.6	2.5	8.8	31 793	76.5	23.5	2.42	2.25
Randolph	6.8	13 478	82.1	17.9	9.0	2.0	7.9	11 072	75.7	24.3	2.50	2.13
Ritchie	6.5	5 513	75.9	24.1	13.7	2.1	5.0	4 184	81.7	18.3	2.48	2.32
Roane	7.3	7 360	83.7	16.3	5.9	2.2	7.3	6 161	79.6	20.4	2.50	2.45
Summers	5.5	7 331	75.4	24.6	14.0	1.9	8.3	5 530	79.1	20.9	2.35	2.20
Taylor	10.1	7 125	88.7	11.3	2.3	2.4	9.4	6 320	79.6	20.4	2.53	2.24
Tucker	1.2	4 634	65.9	34.1	25.9	2.7	17.1	3 052	82.6	17.4	2.41	2.08
Tyler	3.4	4 780	80.3	19.7	12.6	2.2	6.8	3 836	83.7	16.3	2.49	2.36
Upshur	8.8	10 751	83.5	16.5	8.6	2.0	7.9	8 972	76.7	23.3	2.51	2.28
Wayne	10.3	19 107	90.2	9.8	1.2	1.5	7.8	17 239	78.1	21.9	2.55	2.23
Webster	0.4	5 273	76.0	24.0	14.1	1.9	8.0	4 010	79.0	21.0	2.42	2.37
Wetzel	-1.9	8 313	86.2	13.8	5.1	1.7	9.9	7 164	78.5	21.5	2.49	2.30
Wirt	17.6	3 266	69.9	30.1	22.1	1.3	10.4	2 284	83.1	16.9	2.57	2.50
Wood	6.2	39 785	91.2	8.8	1.3	1.8	9.1	36 275	73.4	26.6	2.47	2.17
Wyoming	-0.2	11 698	89.4	10.6	0.4	1.7	8.2	10 454	83.3	16.7	2.47	2.33
WISCONSIN	14.4	2 321 144	89.8	10.2	6.1	1.2	5.6	2 084 544	68.4	31.6	2.66	2.15
Adams	32.3	14 123	55.9	44.1	39.9	2.4	7.1	7 900	85.3	14.7	2.33	2.33
Ashland	7.4	8 883	75.6	24.4	18.5	1.6	7.2	6 718	70.7	29.3	2.54	2.03
Barron	15.7	20 969	85.1	14.9	11.0	1.0	4.6	17 851	75.8	24.2	2.61	2.06
Bayfield	12.5	11 640	53.3	46.7	42.3	1.3	5.0	6 207	82.6	17.4	2.45	2.18
Brown	20.8	90 199	96.8	3.2	0.5	0.9	3.8	87 295	65.4	34.6	2.72	2.11
Buffalo	7.6	6 098	90.4	9.6	4.1	1.2	5.3	5 511	76.5	23.5	2.60	2.06
Burnett	26.2	12 582	52.6	47.4	45.0	1.5	4.9	6 613	84.5	15.5	2.35	2.25
Calumet	26.7	15 758	94.6	5.4	1.8	1.3	8.0	14 910	80.4	19.6	2.85	2.11
Chippewa	11.9	22 821	93.6	6.4	3.0	0.8	5.0	21 356	75.7	24.3	2.67	2.12
Clark	7.5	13 531	89.0	11.0	6.2	1.3	5.8	12 047	81.2	18.8	2.86	2.20
Columbia	21.2	22 685	90.1	9.9	5.5	1.5	6.1	20 439	74.8	25.2	2.63	2.07
Crawford	12.9	8 480	78.7	21.3	14.2	2.8	8.7	6 677	76.8	23.2	2.59	2.11

Table B. States and Counties

STATE/ County code	MSA/ PMSA/ NECMA code[1]	County type[2]	STATE County	Land area, 2000[3] (sq km)	Total persons	Rank	Per square kilometer	Land area, 1990[3] (sq km)	Total persons	Rank	Per square kilometer	White	Black or African American	American Indian or Alaska Native	Asian	Native Hawaiian and other Pacific Islander	Some other race
				1	2	3	4	5	6	7	8	9	10	11	12	13	14
			WISCONSIN—Cont'd														
55 025	4720	2	Dane	3 113	426 526	140	137.0	3 114	367 085	141	117.0	89.0	4.0	0.3	3.5	0.0	1.4
55 027	...	4	Dodge	2 285	85 897	609	37.6	2 285	76 559	590	33.5	95.3	2.5	0.4	0.3	0.0	0.9
55 029	...	7	Door	1 250	27 961	1 452	22.4	1 250	25 690	1 433	20.6	97.8	0.2	0.7	0.3	0.0	0.3
55 031	2240	3	Douglas	3 391	43 287	1 032	12.8	3 391	41 758	961	12.3	95.3	0.6	1.8	0.6	0.0	0.2
55 033	...	6	Dunn	2 207	39 858	1 115	18.1	2 207	35 909	1 103	16.3	96.1	0.3	0.3	2.1	0.0	0.4
55 035	2290	3	Eau Claire	1 651	93 142	549	56.4	1 652	85 183	538	51.6	95.0	0.5	0.5	2.5	0.0	0.3
55 037	...	9	Florence	1 264	5 088	2 845	4.0	1 264	4 590	2 866	3.6	98.2	0.2	0.4	0.3	0.0	0.1
55 039	...	4	Fond du Lac	1 872	97 296	533	52.0	1 873	90 083	509	48.1	96.2	0.9	0.4	0.9	0.0	0.8
55 041	...	9	Forest	2 626	10 024	2 442	3.8	2 627	8 776	2 488	3.3	85.9	1.2	11.3	0.2	0.0	0.2
55 043	...	6	Grant	2 973	49 597	924	16.7	2 973	49 266	852	16.6	98.2	0.5	0.1	0.5	0.0	0.1
55 045	...	6	Green	1 513	33 647	1 292	22.2	1 513	30 339	1 277	20.1	98.1	0.3	0.2	0.3	0.0	0.4
55 047	...	6	Green Lake	918	19 105	1 843	20.8	918	18 651	1 756	20.3	97.8	0.2	0.2	0.3	0.0	0.9
55 049	...	6	Iowa	1 975	22 780	1 656	11.5	1 976	20 150	1 667	10.2	98.7	0.2	0.1	0.3	0.0	0.1
55 051	...	9	Iron	1 961	6 861	2 702	3.5	1 961	6 153	2 737	3.1	98.3	0.1	0.6	0.1	0.0	0.1
55 053	...	6	Jackson	2 557	19 100	1 844	7.5	2 557	16 588	1 881	6.5	89.6	2.3	6.2	0.2	0.0	1.0
55 055	...	4	Jefferson	1 443	74 021	674	51.3	1 443	67 783	654	47.0	96.3	0.3	0.3	0.4	0.0	1.6
55 057	...	7	Juneau	1 988	24 316	1 583	12.2	1 988	21 650	1 596	10.9	96.6	0.3	1.3	0.4	0.0	0.6
55 059	3800	1	Kenosha	707	149 577	360	211.6	707	128 181	363	181.3	88.4	5.1	0.4	0.9	0.0	3.3
55 061	...	6	Kewaunee	887	20 187	1 781	22.8	887	18 878	1 742	21.3	98.6	0.2	0.3	0.1	0.0	0.3
55 063	3870	3	La Crosse	1 173	107 120	500	91.3	1 173	97 904	469	83.5	94.2	0.9	0.4	3.2	0.0	0.3
55 065	...	9	Lafayette	1 641	16 137	2 014	9.8	1 641	16 074	1 918	9.8	99.0	0.1	0.1	0.2	0.0	0.1
55 067	...	6	Langlade	2 260	20 740	1 751	9.2	2 260	19 505	1 701	8.6	97.9	0.1	0.5	0.3	0.0	0.2
55 069	...	6	Lincoln	2 288	29 641	1 411	13.0	2 287	26 993	1 390	11.8	97.8	0.4	0.4	0.4	0.0	0.3
55 071	...	4	Manitowoc	1 532	82 887	625	54.1	1 532	80 421	567	52.5	95.9	0.3	0.4	2.0	0.0	0.6
55 073	8940	3	Marathon	4 001	125 834	431	31.5	4 002	115 400	399	28.8	93.8	0.3	0.3	4.5	0.0	0.3
55 075	...	7	Marinette	3 631	43 384	1 031	11.9	3 631	40 548	985	11.2	98.1	0.2	0.5	0.3	0.0	0.2
55 077	...	9	Marquette	1 180	15 832	2 030	13.4	1 180	12 321	2 123	10.4	93.7	3.4	1.0	0.3	0.1	0.4
55 078	...	NA	Menominee	927	4 562	2 874	4.9	927	4 075	2 910	4.4	11.6	0.1	87.3	0.0	0.0	0.3
55 079	5080	0	Milwaukee	626	940 164	39	1 501.9	626	959 211	34	1 532.3	65.6	24.6	0.7	2.6	0.0	4.2
55 081	...	6	Monroe	2 333	40 899	1 085	17.5	2 333	36 633	1 085	15.7	96.5	0.5	0.9	0.5	0.0	0.8
55 083	...	6	Oconto	2 585	35 634	1 226	13.8	2 585	30 226	1 287	11.7	97.8	0.1	0.8	0.2	0.0	0.2
55 085	...	7	Oneida	2 912	36 776	1 195	12.6	2 913	31 679	1 224	10.9	97.7	0.3	0.7	0.3	0.0	0.2
55 087	0460	2	Outagamie	1 658	160 971	331	97.1	1 659	140 510	338	84.7	93.9	0.5	1.5	2.2	0.0	0.8
55 089	5080	0	Ozaukee	601	82 317	629	137.0	601	72 894	615	121.3	96.7	0.9	0.2	1.1	0.0	0.3
55 091	...	8	Pepin	602	7 213	2 665	12.0	602	7 107	2 644	11.8	98.9	0.1	0.2	0.2	0.0	0.1
55 093	5120	1	Pierce	1 493	36 804	1 194	24.7	1 493	32 765	1 196	21.9	98.0	0.2	0.3	0.4	0.0	0.3
55 095	...	6	Polk	2 376	41 319	1 071	17.4	2 376	34 773	1 142	14.6	97.6	0.2	1.1	0.3	0.0	0.2
55 097	...	4	Portage	2 088	67 182	730	32.2	2 088	61 405	711	29.4	95.7	0.3	0.4	2.2	0.0	0.4
55 099	...	7	Price	3 244	15 822	2 031	4.9	3 244	15 600	1 947	4.8	98.2	0.1	0.6	0.3	0.0	0.1
55 101	6600	3	Racine	863	188 831	293	218.8	863	175 034	274	202.8	83.0	10.5	0.4	0.7	0.0	3.7
55 103	...	7	Richland	1 518	17 924	1 905	11.8	1 518	17 521	1 819	11.5	98.4	0.2	0.3	0.2	0.0	0.3
55 105	3620	3	Rock	1 866	152 307	351	81.6	1 866	139 510	341	74.8	91.0	4.6	0.3	0.8	0.0	1.8
55 107	...	7	Rusk	2 365	15 347	2 065	6.5	2 365	15 079	1 983	6.4	97.7	0.5	0.4	0.3	0.1	0.4
55 109	5120	1	St. Croix	1 870	63 155	768	33.8	1 870	50 251	839	26.9	97.8	0.3	0.3	0.6	0.0	0.2
55 111	...	6	Sauk	2 169	55 225	852	25.5	2 170	46 975	890	21.6	97.4	0.3	0.9	0.3	0.0	0.6
55 113	...	9	Sawyer	3 254	16 196	2 007	5.0	3 254	14 181	2 039	4.4	81.7	0.3	16.1	0.3	0.0	0.3
55 115	...	6	Shawano	2 312	40 664	1 095	17.6	2 312	37 157	1 068	16.1	91.6	0.2	6.3	0.3	0.0	0.3
55 117	7620	3	Sheboygan	1 330	112 646	477	84.7	1 330	103 877	444	78.1	92.7	1.1	0.4	3.3	0.0	1.5
55 119	...	6	Taylor	2 525	19 680	1 813	7.8	2 525	18 901	1 740	7.5	98.7	0.1	0.2	0.2	0.0	0.2
55 121	...	8	Trempealeau	1 901	27 010	1 482	14.2	1 901	25 263	1 453	13.3	98.8	0.1	0.2	0.1	0.0	0.3
55 123	...	6	Vernon	2 059	28 056	1 443	13.6	2 059	25 617	1 437	12.4	98.8	0.1	0.1	0.2	0.0	0.3
55 125	...	9	Vilas	2 263	21 033	1 734	9.3	2 261	17 707	1 804	7.8	89.7	0.2	9.1	0.2	0.0	0.2
55 127	...	4	Walworth	1 438	93 759	548	65.2	1 438	75 000	598	52.2	94.5	0.8	0.2	0.7	0.0	2.6
55 129	...	9	Washburn	2 097	16 036	2 020	7.6	2 097	13 772	2 073	6.6	97.3	0.1	1.0	0.2	0.0	0.1
55 131	5080	1	Washington	1 116	117 493	461	105.3	1 116	95 328	485	85.4	97.7	0.4	0.3	0.6	0.0	0.4
55 133	5080	0	Waukesha	1 439	360 767	164	250.7	1 439	304 715	163	211.8	95.8	0.7	0.2	1.5	0.0	0.9
55 135	...	6	Waupaca	1 945	51 731	897	26.6	1 945	46 104	901	23.7	97.9	0.2	0.4	0.3	0.0	0.5
55 137	...	8	Waushara	1 621	23 154	1 636	14.3	1 622	19 385	1 711	12.0	96.8	0.3	0.3	0.3	0.0	1.4
55 139	0460	2	Winnebago	1 136	156 763	340	138.0	1 136	140 320	339	123.5	94.9	1.1	0.5	1.8	0.0	0.7
55 141	...	4	Wood	2 053	75 555	664	36.8	2 053	73 605	611	35.9	96.4	0.3	0.7	1.6	0.0	0.3
56 000	...		WYOMING	251 489	493 782	X	2.0	251 501	453 589	X	1.8	92.1	0.8	2.3	0.6	0.1	2.5
56 001	...	5	Albany	11 066	32 014	1 345	2.9	11 069	30 797	1 251	2.8	91.3	1.1	1.0	1.7	0.1	2.6
56 003	...	9	Big Horn	8 125	11 461	2 337	1.4	8 125	10 525	2 333	1.3	94.0	0.1	0.8	0.2	0.1	3.4
56 005	...	7	Campbell	12 424	33 698	1 290	2.7	12 424	29 370	1 320	2.4	96.1	0.2	0.9	0.3	0.1	1.1
56 007	...	7	Carbon	20 451	15 639	2 045	0.8	20 452	16 659	1 872	0.8	90.1	0.7	1.3	0.7	0.1	5.2

[1]MSA = Metropolitan Statistical Area. PMSA = Primary MSA. NECMA = New England County Metropolitan Area. See Appendix A for explanation of these concepts. See Appendix B for list of metropolitan areas identified by type, with component counties.
[2]County typology code from the Economic Research Service of USDA. See Appendix A for definition.
[3]Dry land or land partially or temporarily covered by water.

Table B. States and Counties

STATE County	Two or more races	White	Black	American Indian or Alaska Native	Asian	Native Hawaiian and other Pacific Islander	Some other race	Hispanic[1]	White	Black or African American	American Indian or Alaska Native	Asian and Pacific Islander	Hispanic[1]
	\<2000\> Race (percent) (cont'd) — Race alone or in combination								\<1990\> Race (percent)				
	15	16	17	18	19	20	21	22	23	24	25	26	27
WISCONSIN—Cont'd													
Dane	1.8	90.5	4.7	0.8	3.9	0.1	1.9	3.4	93.9	2.9	0.3	2.4	1.6
Dodge	0.6	95.8	2.6	0.6	0.5	0.1	1.1	2.5	97.6	1.5	0.3	0.3	1.2
Door	0.7	98.5	0.3	1.1	0.4	0.0	0.5	1.0	98.8	0.1	0.7	0.2	0.6
Douglas	1.4	96.7	0.8	2.7	0.9	0.1	0.4	0.7	96.9	0.4	1.9	0.6	0.5
Dunn	0.8	96.8	0.5	0.6	2.4	0.1	0.5	0.8	97.3	0.5	0.3	1.8	0.5
Eau Claire	1.1	95.9	0.8	0.9	2.9	0.1	0.5	0.9	96.5	0.3	0.5	2.5	0.5
Florence	0.8	99.0	0.4	0.9	0.4	0.0	0.2	0.5	99.4	0.1	0.3	0.1	0.2
Fond du Lac	0.8	96.9	1.1	0.7	1.0	0.1	1.0	2.0	98.5	0.3	0.3	0.5	1.0
Forest	1.2	87.0	1.3	12.2	0.2	0.1	0.4	1.1	89.4	1.4	8.9	0.2	0.3
Grant	0.5	98.7	0.6	0.3	0.6	0.0	0.3	0.6	99.1	0.2	0.2	0.5	0.3
Green	0.8	98.8	0.5	0.5	0.4	0.0	0.5	1.0	99.5	0.1	0.2	0.2	0.4
Green Lake	0.6	98.3	0.3	0.4	0.5	0.1	1.0	2.1	98.6	0.1	0.2	0.6	1.0
Iowa	0.6	99.2	0.3	0.4	0.5	0.0	0.2	0.3	99.7	0.0	0.1	0.1	0.2
Iron	0.8	99.1	0.2	1.1	0.3	0.0	0.1	0.7	99.5	0.0	0.4	0.0	0.1
Jackson	0.8	90.3	2.3	6.7	0.3	0.1	1.1	1.9	95.3	0.3	4.1	0.2	0.9
Jefferson	0.9	97.2	0.4	0.7	0.6	0.1	2.0	4.1	98.4	0.3	0.3	0.4	1.7
Juneau	0.7	97.3	0.5	1.7	0.5	0.0	0.7	1.4	98.4	0.1	0.8	0.4	0.7
Kenosha	1.9	90.1	5.8	0.9	1.2	0.1	4.0	7.2	93.0	4.1	0.4	0.5	4.4
Kewaunee	0.6	99.1	0.2	0.6	0.2	0.0	0.4	0.8	99.4	0.1	0.3	0.1	0.3
La Crosse	1.0	95.0	1.3	0.7	3.5	0.1	0.4	0.9	96.3	0.4	0.3	2.7	0.7
Lafayette	0.4	99.4	0.2	0.2	0.3	0.1	0.2	0.6	99.6	0.1	0.1	0.1	0.2
Langlade	0.9	98.8	0.3	1.1	0.4	0.0	0.3	0.8	98.9	0.1	0.7	0.1	0.5
Lincoln	0.7	98.4	0.6	0.8	0.5	0.1	0.4	0.8	99.0	0.3	0.4	0.3	0.4
Manitowoc	0.8	96.6	0.5	0.8	2.2	0.1	0.8	1.6	97.9	0.1	0.4	1.3	0.7
Marathon	0.7	94.4	0.4	0.6	4.8	0.1	0.4	0.8	97.2	0.1	0.4	2.2	0.4
Marinette	0.7	98.7	0.3	0.9	0.4	0.1	0.3	0.7	99.3	0.0	0.4	0.2	0.4
Marquette	1.1	94.6	3.7	1.5	0.4	0.2	0.8	2.7	98.8	0.3	0.4	0.1	1.2
Menominee	0.7	12.1	0.3	87.9	0.0	0.0	0.4	2.7	10.7	0.0	89.2	0.0	1.4
Milwaukee	2.2	67.4	25.5	1.3	3.0	0.1	5.1	8.8	74.9	20.4	0.7	1.6	4.7
Monroe	0.7	97.2	0.6	1.3	0.7	0.1	1.0	1.8	98.2	0.4	0.8	0.4	0.6
Oconto	0.9	98.6	0.2	1.4	0.3	0.0	0.4	0.7	99.0	0.1	0.7	0.1	0.4
Oneida	0.8	98.4	0.4	1.1	0.4	0.1	0.3	0.7	98.9	0.2	0.7	0.2	0.3
Outagamie	1.0	94.7	0.7	2.0	2.5	0.1	1.0	2.0	96.8	0.1	1.4	1.4	0.7
Ozaukee	0.7	97.4	1.1	0.4	1.3	0.0	0.5	1.3	98.4	0.7	0.2	0.6	0.7
Pepin	0.5	99.4	0.1	0.6	0.2	0.1	0.1	0.3	99.5	0.0	0.3	0.1	0.3
Pierce	0.7	98.7	0.4	0.6	0.6	0.0	0.4	0.8	98.8	0.3	0.3	0.5	0.6
Polk	0.7	98.3	0.3	1.4	0.4	0.0	0.3	0.8	98.8	0.1	0.9	0.1	0.4
Portage	0.9	96.4	0.5	0.6	2.6	0.1	0.6	1.4	97.7	0.3	0.4	1.3	0.4
Price	0.6	98.8	0.2	1.0	0.4	0.1	0.2	0.7	99.2	0.0	0.5	0.2	0.4
Racine	1.7	84.5	11.2	0.8	0.9	0.1	4.3	7.9	86.9	9.7	0.3	0.6	5.2
Richland	0.7	99.0	0.4	0.5	0.4	0.0	0.4	0.9	99.4	0.1	0.2	0.2	0.3
Rock	1.5	92.4	5.2	0.7	1.0	0.1	2.2	3.9	93.8	4.8	0.3	0.7	1.3
Rusk	0.7	98.3	0.7	0.8	0.3	0.1	0.5	0.8	98.3	0.2	0.5	0.8	0.6
St. Croix	0.8	98.6	0.5	0.5	0.8	0.0	0.4	0.8	99.3	0.1	0.2	0.3	0.4
Sauk	0.6	98.0	0.4	1.1	0.4	0.1	0.7	1.7	98.9	0.1	0.6	0.2	0.4
Sawyer	1.2	82.9	0.4	17.1	0.4	0.0	0.5	0.9	84.4	0.1	15.3	0.1	0.7
Shawano	1.2	92.8	0.4	7.2	0.4	0.1	0.5	1.0	94.9	0.1	4.7	0.2	0.3
Sheboygan	1.1	93.5	1.3	0.7	3.6	0.1	1.8	3.4	96.6	0.4	0.3	2.0	1.6
Taylor	0.6	99.3	0.2	0.5	0.4	0.0	0.3	0.6	99.5	0.0	0.2	0.2	0.2
Trempealeau	0.5	99.3	0.2	0.4	0.2	0.0	0.4	0.9	99.6	0.0	0.1	0.2	0.2
Vernon	0.5	99.3	0.2	0.4	0.3	0.1	0.4	0.7	99.6	0.0	0.1	0.2	0.2
Vilas	0.7	90.3	0.3	9.6	0.2	0.1	0.3	0.9	91.0	0.1	8.7	0.2	0.3
Walworth	1.1	95.5	1.0	0.5	0.9	0.1	3.1	6.5	97.0	0.6	0.3	0.7	2.7
Washburn	1.2	98.5	0.3	1.9	0.3	0.0	0.2	0.9	98.6	0.2	0.9	0.2	0.2
Washington	0.7	98.3	0.5	0.5	0.7	0.1	0.6	1.3	99.1	0.1	0.2	0.4	0.7
Waukesha	0.9	96.6	1.0	0.5	1.7	0.1	1.1	2.6	97.9	0.4	0.2	0.9	1.8
Waupaca	0.7	98.6	0.3	0.7	0.4	0.0	0.7	1.4	99.1	0.0	0.3	0.2	0.9
Waushara	0.9	97.7	0.3	0.8	0.4	0.1	1.6	3.7	98.5	0.1	0.4	0.2	2.0
Winnebago	0.9	95.7	1.3	0.8	2.1	0.1	0.9	2.0	97.5	0.5	0.5	1.2	0.8
Wood	0.7	97.1	0.4	1.0	1.7	0.0	0.4	0.9	98.0	0.1	0.7	1.0	0.5
WYOMING	1.8	93.7	1.0	3.0	0.8	0.1	3.2	6.4	94.2	0.8	2.1	0.6	5.7
Albany	2.2	93.4	1.4	1.9	2.1	0.1	3.4	7.5	93.6	0.8	0.8	2.1	6.5
Big Horn	1.5	95.5	0.2	1.4	0.3	0.1	4.0	6.2	97.0	0.0	0.6	0.2	5.2
Campbell	1.3	97.3	0.3	1.7	0.5	0.1	1.5	3.5	97.6	0.1	1.1	0.3	3.0
Carbon	2.1	92.0	0.8	1.9	0.9	0.1	6.4	13.8	90.7	0.6	0.8	0.5	13.9

[1] Hispanic persons may be of any race.

Table B. States and Counties

STATE County	Population and population characteristics, 2000 Age (percent)									Median age (years)	Percent Female
	Under 5 years	5 to 17 years	18 to 24 years	25 to 34 years	35 to 44 years	45 to 54 years	55 to 64 years	65 to 74 years	75 years and over		
	28	29	30	31	32	33	34	35	36	37	38
WISCONSIN—Cont'd											
Dane	6.1	16.5	14.3	16.0	16.4	14.1	7.2	4.7	4.6	33.2	50.5
Dodge	5.9	18.8	8.3	13.7	17.5	13.2	8.7	6.8	7.2	37.0	47.7
Door	4.6	17.5	6.1	9.6	15.8	15.6	12.1	9.9	8.9	42.9	50.7
Douglas	5.9	17.7	10.3	12.1	15.9	14.7	9.0	7.0	7.5	37.7	50.7
Dunn	5.7	17.6	19.8	12.1	13.7	12.5	7.3	5.6	5.6	30.6	49.6
Eau Claire	6.0	17.5	17.1	12.6	14.1	13.1	7.4	5.9	6.4	32.4	51.6
Florence	4.5	18.4	5.3	10.2	16.8	14.8	12.5	9.4	8.0	41.9	49.0
Fond du Lac	6.0	19.2	9.4	12.6	16.2	13.9	8.5	7.0	7.4	36.9	51.2
Forest	5.7	19.6	7.8	10.1	13.8	12.3	11.5	10.7	8.5	39.9	50.0
Grant	5.2	18.5	14.6	10.5	14.3	12.6	8.9	7.6	7.7	35.9	49.3
Green	6.4	20.1	6.7	12.1	17.1	14.2	8.7	7.0	7.7	37.9	50.8
Green Lake	5.6	18.5	6.6	10.4	15.9	14.1	10.1	9.3	9.6	40.9	50.8
Iowa	6.4	20.6	6.6	12.7	17.8	14.4	8.1	6.9	6.5	37.1	50.2
Iron	4.0	15.4	5.9	9.0	15.7	14.2	12.5	11.7	11.5	45.0	51.0
Jackson	5.6	18.5	8.8	13.2	16.2	13.1	9.7	7.5	7.4	37.6	46.6
Jefferson	6.3	18.9	8.5	13.6	16.8	14.1	9.1	6.4	6.2	36.6	50.4
Juneau	5.9	19.5	6.9	10.8	15.8	13.5	10.8	8.8	8.0	39.4	50.0
Kenosha	6.9	20.1	9.4	13.9	17.4	12.9	7.9	5.9	5.6	34.8	50.4
Kewaunee	5.9	19.9	8.0	12.1	16.1	13.7	9.0	7.1	8.2	37.5	49.8
La Crosse	5.9	17.6	15.6	12.8	14.7	13.1	7.7	6.2	6.4	33.5	51.5
Lafayette	5.9	21.3	7.6	10.5	16.8	13.0	9.1	8.3	7.5	38.1	50.1
Langlade	5.4	19.0	6.5	10.6	15.4	13.5	10.7	9.4	9.4	40.5	50.4
Lincoln	5.7	19.7	6.9	11.6	16.3	13.0	10.3	8.2	8.2	38.9	50.0
Manitowoc	5.8	19.6	7.6	11.7	16.4	13.9	9.1	7.7	8.0	38.3	50.5
Marathon	6.4	20.4	8.2	13.0	16.5	13.9	8.6	6.4	6.6	36.3	50.1
Marinette	5.1	18.4	8.1	9.9	15.9	14.0	10.9	8.7	8.9	40.5	50.6
Marquette	4.8	16.2	6.7	12.3	16.6	13.7	11.3	10.8	7.5	40.9	45.7
Menominee	9.5	29.4	8.4	11.0	13.7	10.2	9.4	6.0	2.4	27.7	50.7
Milwaukee	7.1	19.2	10.5	15.0	15.3	12.6	7.4	6.4	6.6	33.7	52.1
Monroe	6.7	21.4	7.7	11.5	15.9	14.0	8.9	6.9	7.0	36.8	49.6
Oconto	5.7	20.0	6.4	11.4	17.3	13.7	10.3	8.0	7.2	38.8	49.7
Oneida	4.7	17.6	5.7	10.2	16.2	14.7	12.1	10.7	8.0	42.4	50.2
Outagamie	6.9	20.8	8.9	14.4	17.5	13.0	7.7	5.5	5.4	34.4	50.1
Ozaukee	6.2	20.5	6.8	10.2	17.8	16.0	9.9	6.9	5.7	38.9	50.7
Pepin	5.9	20.6	7.9	10.8	15.2	13.6	9.3	7.8	9.1	38.7	49.7
Pierce	5.7	18.7	17.0	12.1	16.0	13.3	7.5	4.8	4.8	32.1	50.7
Polk	5.9	20.3	6.7	11.2	16.4	14.4	9.9	7.5	7.6	38.7	50.0
Portage	5.9	18.2	16.2	12.4	15.3	13.3	7.8	5.6	5.3	33.0	50.2
Price	4.9	19.0	5.8	10.2	15.6	14.9	10.8	9.2	9.7	41.7	49.8
Racine	7.0	20.0	8.3	13.0	16.9	13.9	8.6	6.4	5.9	36.1	50.5
Richland	5.6	19.6	8.4	10.5	15.0	14.1	9.6	8.4	8.8	39.2	50.4
Rock	6.7	19.8	8.6	13.5	16.3	13.6	8.8	6.7	6.0	35.9	50.8
Rusk	5.4	19.4	7.9	10.2	14.6	13.8	10.3	9.1	9.3	40.0	50.4
St. Croix	7.0	20.9	8.2	14.0	18.2	14.1	7.7	5.0	4.8	35.0	50.0
Sauk	6.5	19.6	7.4	12.9	16.4	13.8	9.0	7.0	7.4	37.3	50.6
Sawyer	5.5	18.6	6.0	9.4	15.2	14.7	12.7	10.2	7.7	42.1	49.6
Shawano	6.1	19.5	6.9	11.9	15.7	12.8	10.3	8.4	8.4	38.5	50.1
Sheboygan	6.4	19.1	8.4	13.0	16.8	13.7	8.5	6.7	7.2	36.8	49.8
Taylor	5.8	21.3	7.6	11.6	16.8	13.0	8.8	7.3	7.9	37.4	49.4
Trempealeau	6.2	19.2	6.9	12.3	15.9	13.7	9.4	7.5	8.9	38.3	49.9
Vernon	6.5	20.9	6.8	10.0	15.2	13.7	9.8	8.2	8.8	39.1	50.6
Vilas	4.3	16.4	5.0	8.8	14.3	14.2	14.3	13.1	9.7	45.8	50.2
Walworth	5.9	18.3	13.8	11.9	15.6	13.1	8.6	6.4	6.3	35.1	50.3
Washburn	5.1	18.7	5.8	9.4	15.3	14.8	12.3	9.7	8.8	42.1	49.7
Washington	6.8	19.9	7.2	13.1	18.4	14.5	8.9	5.9	5.4	36.6	50.1
Waukesha	6.4	19.9	6.8	11.7	18.1	15.7	9.4	6.5	5.5	38.1	50.8
Waupaca	6.0	19.6	7.1	11.6	16.2	13.5	9.2	7.8	8.9	38.5	49.9
Waushara	5.0	18.5	6.0	9.5	15.4	14.2	12.1	10.7	8.5	42.1	49.6
Winnebago	6.0	17.8	11.8	13.7	16.7	13.3	8.2	6.3	6.3	35.4	50.1
Wood	6.1	19.5	7.7	11.9	16.4	13.8	9.1	7.3	8.0	38.0	51.0
WYOMING	6.3	19.8	10.1	12.1	16.0	15.0	9.0	6.3	5.3	36.2	49.7
Albany	5.1	13.3	28.2	14.3	11.7	12.3	6.8	4.4	3.9	26.7	48.4
Big Horn	6.8	21.9	7.3	9.6	13.0	14.0	10.7	8.4	8.4	38.7	50.0
Campbell	7.4	23.7	9.5	12.9	19.4	15.6	6.3	3.2	2.0	32.2	48.6
Carbon	5.7	18.4	8.6	11.4	16.9	16.5	10.2	6.8	5.5	38.9	46.4

Table B. States and Counties

STATE County	Under 5 years	5 to 17 years	18 to 24 years	25 to 34 years	35 to 44 years	45 to 54 years	55 to 64 years	65 to 74 years	75 years and over	Percent Female	2000	1990	1980	1990–2000	1980–1990
	39	40	41	42	43	44	45	46	47	48	49	50	51	52	53
WISCONSIN—Cont'd															
Dane	7.0	15.7	15.7	19.9	16.6	9.2	6.6	5.2	4.1	50.9	426 526	367 085	323 545	16.2	13.5
Dodge	7.1	19.6	8.4	17.0	14.6	9.9	8.5	8.0	6.8	48.8	85 897	76 559	75 064	12.2	2.0
Door	6.7	19.2	6.5	15.2	15.1	10.1	9.4	9.3	8.4	50.9	27 961	25 690	25 029	8.8	2.6
Douglas	6.8	18.8	9.7	15.1	15.0	9.7	8.7	8.6	7.7	51.4	43 287	41 758	44 421	3.7	-6.0
Dunn	6.5	18.1	20.5	14.2	13.3	8.2	7.2	6.1	5.9	50.2	39 858	35 909	34 314	11.0	4.6
Eau Claire	7.1	17.7	17.4	15.0	14.4	8.8	7.3	6.9	5.5	52.1	93 142	85 183	78 805	9.3	8.1
Florence	6.6	20.0	6.8	14.8	14.0	11.3	9.6	9.3	7.5	49.4	5 088	4 590	4 172	10.8	10.0
Fond du Lac	7.1	20.2	9.7	15.6	14.8	9.8	8.7	7.5	6.5	51.5	97 296	90 083	88 964	8.0	1.3
Forest	7.6	19.5	9.0	13.0	12.0	9.5	10.5	10.4	8.5	49.6	10 024	8 776	9 044	14.2	-3.0
Grant	6.9	19.9	14.1	14.2	12.7	9.0	8.5	7.8	6.9	49.5	49 597	49 266	51 736	0.7	-4.8
Green	7.1	20.1	7.8	15.9	15.3	10.0	8.5	8.2	7.1	51.0	33 647	30 339	30 012	10.9	1.1
Green Lake	6.4	19.6	7.3	14.1	13.8	9.6	10.0	10.0	9.1	51.4	19 105	18 651	18 370	2.4	1.5
Iowa	7.8	20.7	8.1	16.4	15.1	8.9	8.7	8.0	6.2	50.3	22 780	20 150	19 802	13.1	1.8
Iron	5.0	16.3	6.4	12.9	13.0	10.4	11.6	13.7	10.7	50.6	6 861	6 153	6 730	11.5	-8.6
Jackson	7.0	20.1	7.9	14.2	14.1	9.9	9.6	9.4	7.7	49.2	19 100	16 588	16 831	15.1	-1.4
Jefferson	6.9	19.0	11.9	15.8	14.7	10.5	8.2	7.2	5.9	50.6	74 021	67 783	66 152	9.2	2.5
Juneau	7.1	20.2	7.1	14.9	12.8	10.2	10.2	10.2	9.9	50.6	24 316	21 650	21 037	12.3	2.9
Kenosha	7.9	18.9	10.3	17.2	14.5	10.2	8.3	7.2	5.4	51.1	149 577	128 181	123 137	16.7	4.1
Kewaunee	7.1	21.1	8.6	15.3	13.9	9.5	8.7	8.5	7.3	49.8	20 187	18 878	19 539	6.9	-3.4
La Crosse	7.1	17.6	15.5	16.2	14.4	8.9	7.6	6.8	6.0	52.0	107 120	97 904	91 056	9.4	7.5
Lafayette	7.4	21.7	7.6	15.6	13.2	9.3	9.6	8.7	6.7	50.6	16 137	16 074	17 412	0.4	-7.7
Langlade	6.7	19.9	7.1	14.1	13.2	9.9	10.1	10.4	8.6	51.4	20 740	19 505	19 978	6.3	-2.4
Lincoln	6.6	20.4	8.0	15.3	13.0	10.8	9.8	8.6	7.6	50.5	29 641	26 993	26 555	9.8	1.6
Manitowoc	7.0	19.5	8.6	15.4	14.3	10.0	9.2	8.5	7.5	51.1	82 887	80 421	82 918	3.1	-3.0
Marathon	7.4	20.7	9.3	16.6	15.1	10.1	8.2	7.1	5.6	50.6	125 834	115 400	111 270	9.0	3.7
Marinette	6.9	20.0	7.5	14.7	13.7	10.2	9.4	9.3	8.3	51.1	43 384	40 548	39 314	7.0	3.1
Marquette	5.9	18.7	6.5	13.1	12.7	9.9	12.8	12.2	8.2	50.4	15 832	12 321	11 672	28.5	5.6
Menominee	12.6	28.6	9.6	15.1	10.0	7.8	7.9	5.7	2.7	51.1	4 562	4 075	3 373	12.0	15.3
Milwaukee	7.9	17.8	10.9	18.5	14.2	8.8	8.5	7.5	6.1	52.6	940 164	959 212	964 988	-2.0	-0.6
Monroe	7.9	21.3	7.9	14.9	14.6	9.8	8.8	8.4	6.3	49.8	40 899	36 633	35 074	11.6	4.4
Oconto	7.2	20.1	7.5	15.3	13.9	10.0	9.7	9.3	7.1	50.0	35 634	30 226	28 947	17.9	4.4
Oneida	6.3	17.4	6.3	14.3	14.3	11.4	11.8	10.4	7.6	50.8	36 776	31 679	31 216	16.1	1.5
Outagamie	8.2	20.3	9.9	18.2	15.1	9.7	7.6	6.1	5.0	50.6	160 971	140 510	128 730	14.6	9.2
Ozaukee	7.3	19.7	8.4	15.3	16.9	12.1	9.2	6.6	4.5	50.5	82 317	72 894	66 981	12.9	8.7
Pepin	7.1	21.7	6.8	14.2	13.7	9.1	8.8	9.0	9.6	50.6	7 213	7 107	7 477	1.5	-4.9
Pierce	7.3	19.7	16.1	16.3	14.4	8.9	6.6	5.9	4.7	50.2	36 804	32 765	31 149	12.3	5.2
Polk	7.3	21.2	6.8	15.2	14.9	10.0	8.6	8.3	7.6	50.2	41 319	34 773	32 351	18.8	7.5
Portage	6.9	18.7	17.4	16.1	14.2	8.9	7.0	5.9	4.9	50.0	67 182	61 405	57 420	9.4	6.9
Price	6.6	19.9	6.8	14.1	13.3	9.5	10.3	10.1	9.4	49.8	15 822	15 600	15 788	1.4	-1.2
Racine	7.8	20.0	9.0	17.1	15.1	10.4	8.6	6.9	5.1	51.5	188 831	175 034	173 132	7.9	1.1
Richland	7.0	20.1	8.3	14.1	13.8	9.6	9.5	9.4	8.0	50.5	17 924	17 521	17 476	2.3	0.3
Rock	7.7	19.4	9.8	16.4	14.6	10.6	8.9	7.0	5.6	51.3	152 307	139 510	139 420	9.2	0.0
Rusk	7.2	20.4	8.1	14.1	13.1	9.4	9.4	10.0	8.2	50.6	15 347	15 079	15 589	1.8	-3.3
St. Croix	8.2	21.8	8.5	17.7	16.4	10.1	7.0	5.2	4.9	50.1	63 155	50 251	43 262	25.7	16.2
Sauk	7.5	19.7	8.2	15.9	14.5	9.8	8.6	8.5	7.3	50.8	55 225	46 975	43 469	17.6	8.1
Sawyer	7.0	19.2	6.2	13.1	13.3	10.1	11.7	10.9	8.4	49.5	16 196	14 181	12 843	14.2	10.4
Shawano	7.0	19.8	7.9	14.8	12.6	10.0	9.8	9.7	8.3	50.3	40 664	37 157	35 928	9.4	3.4
Sheboygan	7.1	19.7	8.7	16.6	14.9	9.9	8.6	7.9	6.7	50.5	112 646	103 877	100 935	8.4	2.9
Taylor	8.0	22.2	8.1	16.2	13.0	9.1	8.2	7.9	7.3	49.6	19 680	18 901	18 817	4.1	0.4
Trempealeau	7.0	19.1	8.1	14.7	13.8	10.1	8.8	9.2	9.1	50.2	27 010	25 263	26 158	6.9	-3.4
Vernon	7.2	20.2	6.8	14.0	13.8	9.9	9.4	9.9	8.8	50.9	28 056	25 617	25 642	9.5	0.0
Vilas	5.9	16.3	5.5	11.8	13.0	11.2	13.3	13.6	9.3	50.4	21 033	17 707	16 535	18.8	7.1
Walworth	6.6	17.4	13.8	15.3	14.3	9.9	8.5	7.6	6.7	50.8	93 759	75 000	71 507	25.0	4.9
Washburn	6.5	19.7	6.2	13.0	14.2	10.5	10.8	11.0	8.1	50.2	16 036	13 772	13 174	16.4	4.5
Washington	7.6	20.8	9.1	17.0	16.1	11.1	7.8	5.8	4.6	50.2	117 493	95 328	84 848	23.3	12.4
Waukesha	7.2	20.1	8.5	15.9	17.4	12.1	9.0	5.8	4.0	50.4	360 767	304 715	280 203	18.4	8.7
Waupaca	7.0	19.9	7.9	15.2	14.0	9.5	8.9	9.0	8.7	50.7	51 731	46 104	42 831	12.2	7.6
Waushara	6.4	18.3	6.6	13.6	13.5	10.3	11.8	11.0	8.4	50.5	23 154	19 385	18 526	19.4	4.6
Winnebago	7.0	17.1	12.7	17.5	14.7	9.8	8.3	6.9	5.9	51.0	156 763	140 320	131 772	11.7	6.5
Wood	7.5	20.4	8.6	16.5	14.4	10.0	8.4	7.7	6.5	51.2	75 555	73 605	72 799	2.6	1.1
WYOMING	7.7	22.2	9.1	16.4	16.4	10.0	7.8	6.1	4.3	50.0	493 782	453 589	469 557	8.9	-3.4
Albany	6.3	15.1	25.7	17.7	13.8	8.0	5.7	4.4	3.2	48.3	32 014	30 797	29 062	4.0	6.0
Big Horn	7.6	22.6	6.6	11.5	13.6	10.7	9.3	9.1	8.4	50.1	11 461	10 525	11 896	8.9	-11.5
Campbell	9.0	26.7	7.4	20.5	18.8	8.8	5.1	2.2	1.5	49.1	33 698	29 370	24 367	14.7	20.5
Carbon	7.0	22.8	7.3	16.9	17.2	10.6	7.9	6.0	4.3	47.4	15 639	16 659	21 896	-6.1	-23.9

Table B. States and Counties

STATE County	Total population	Total in house-holds	House-holder	Spouse	Child Total	Own child under 18 years	Other relatives Total	Under 18 years	Nonrelatives Total	Unmar-ried partner	Total in group quarters	Correc-tional institu-tions	Nurs-ing homes	Other institu-tions	Col-lege dormi-tories	Mili-tary quar-ters	Other
	54	55	56	57	58	59	60	61	62	63	64	65	66	67	68	69	70
WISCONSIN—Cont'd																	
Dane	426 526	96.3	40.7	19.1	25.0	21.4	2.2	0.7	8.9	2.7	3.7	0.4	0.5	0.2	2.1	0.0	0.5
Dodge	85 897	93.5	36.6	21.8	29.3	23.5	2.1	0.7	3.8	1.9	6.5	4.9	1.3	0.0	0.0	0.0	0.3
Door	27 961	98.6	42.3	24.6	26.2	21.1	1.9	0.5	3.6	1.8	1.4	0.1	1.0	0.0	0.0	0.0	0.1
Douglas	43 287	97.0	41.1	20.2	27.6	21.9	2.5	1.0	5.6	2.8	3.0	0.4	0.9	0.1	1.2	0.0	0.5
Dunn	39 858	92.5	36.0	19.5	26.9	22.1	1.7	0.6	8.4	2.1	7.5	0.3	0.8	0.0	6.3	0.0	0.2
Eau Claire	93 142	94.5	38.5	19.4	26.7	22.1	2.0	0.6	7.9	2.3	5.5	0.3	0.7	0.2	3.8	0.0	0.5
Florence	5 088	98.5	41.9	24.6	26.6	21.8	1.7	0.6	3.7	2.1	1.5	0.0	1.4	0.0	0.0	0.0	0.1
Fond du Lac	97 296	95.6	38.0	21.9	29.5	23.7	2.0	0.7	4.2	1.9	4.4	1.2	1.2	0.0	1.0	0.0	1.0
Forest	10 024	96.4	40.3	21.8	27.7	23.0	2.8	1.2	3.7	2.3	3.6	0.4	1.4	0.0	0.0	0.0	1.8
Grant	49 597	93.4	37.2	20.9	28.0	22.6	1.8	0.6	5.5	2.0	6.6	0.4	1.2	0.0	4.4	0.0	0.5
Green	33 647	98.5	39.3	22.9	30.1	25.2	2.0	0.7	4.2	2.3	1.5	0.1	0.8	0.0	0.0	0.0	0.5
Green Lake	19 105	98.1	40.3	23.6	28.7	22.9	2.3	0.8	3.2	1.8	1.9	0.2	1.2	0.0	0.0	0.0	0.5
Iowa	22 780	98.6	38.5	22.9	31.4	25.8	2.0	0.7	3.8	2.0	1.4	0.1	0.6	0.1	0.0	0.0	0.6
Iron	6 861	98.4	44.9	23.8	23.5	18.1	2.4	0.9	3.6	2.1	1.6	0.1	1.5	0.0	0.0	0.0	0.0
Jackson	19 100	92.3	37.0	20.5	27.4	22.0	2.9	1.2	4.6	2.5	7.7	5.0	1.0	0.0	0.0	0.0	1.7
Jefferson	74 021	97.3	38.1	22.3	29.6	23.8	2.6	0.8	4.7	2.2	2.7	0.2	0.5	0.7	0.6	0.0	0.8
Juneau	24 316	98.5	39.9	22.1	28.8	23.4	3.0	1.3	4.6	2.4	1.5	0.1	0.8	0.0	0.0	0.0	0.6
Kenosha	149 577	97.3	37.5	19.8	31.1	24.7	3.9	1.6	5.0	2.4	2.7	0.4	0.6	0.0	1.2	0.0	0.4
Kewaunee	20 187	98.7	37.8	23.5	32.1	24.6	2.2	0.7	3.2	1.7	1.3	0.1	0.7	0.0	0.0	0.0	0.5
La Crosse	107 120	95.0	38.8	19.4	26.9	22.2	2.0	0.7	7.8	2.3	5.0	0.3	1.0	0.1	3.1	0.0	0.5
Lafayette	16 137	99.0	38.5	22.7	32.5	26.0	1.8	0.7	3.5	1.8	1.0	0.1	0.5	0.0	0.0	0.0	0.3
Langlade	20 740	98.8	40.8	23.1	28.3	22.7	2.8	1.0	3.8	2.1	1.2	0.2	0.9	0.0	0.0	0.0	0.2
Lincoln	29 641	97.1	39.5	23.1	28.5	22.9	2.3	0.9	3.8	2.0	2.9	0.2	1.0	1.1	0.0	0.0	0.6
Manitowoc	82 887	98.3	39.5	22.5	30.3	24.2	2.1	0.7	3.8	2.0	1.7	0.2	0.8	0.0	0.0	0.0	0.7
Marathon	125 834	98.6	37.9	22.7	31.6	25.5	2.4	0.8	4.0	2.0	1.4	0.2	0.7	0.0	0.1	0.0	0.4
Marinette	43 384	96.6	40.5	22.9	27.4	22.1	2.1	0.7	3.7	2.0	3.4	0.2	0.9	0.2	1.4	0.0	0.7
Marquette	15 832	90.9	37.8	22.2	24.0	19.4	2.7	1.0	4.2	2.2	9.1	8.3	0.3	0.1	0.0	0.0	0.4
Menominee	4 562	98.9	29.5	12.5	38.8	30.1	10.9	7.4	7.2	4.6	1.1	0.8	0.0	0.0	0.0	0.0	0.4
Milwaukee	940 164	97.4	40.2	15.7	29.7	23.1	5.6	2.5	6.3	2.5	2.6	0.4	0.7	0.1	0.7	0.0	0.5
Monroe	40 899	97.8	37.7	21.4	31.7	26.2	2.7	1.1	4.5	2.2	2.2	0.1	0.9	0.6	0.0	0.1	0.4
Oconto	35 634	99.0	39.2	23.8	29.4	24.1	2.2	0.8	4.2	2.2	1.0	0.1	0.7	0.0	0.0	0.0	0.2
Oneida	36 776	97.5	41.7	24.1	25.3	20.8	2.4	0.8	4.0	2.2	2.5	0.9	0.4	0.8	0.0	0.0	0.3
Outagamie	160 971	98.0	37.6	22.1	32.1	26.5	1.9	0.7	4.2	2.0	2.0	0.3	0.7	0.0	0.6	0.0	0.4
Ozaukee	82 317	97.9	37.5	24.6	31.5	25.6	1.7	0.5	2.5	1.3	2.1	0.3	0.5	0.0	1.1	0.0	0.3
Pepin	7 213	98.4	38.3	22.9	32.4	25.6	2.0	0.6	2.9	1.5	1.6	0.1	1.5	0.0	0.0	0.0	0.1
Pierce	36 804	93.6	35.4	20.6	29.0	23.3	2.0	0.7	6.7	2.1	6.4	0.1	0.7	0.0	5.3	0.0	0.3
Polk	41 319	98.6	39.3	22.9	29.9	24.6	2.3	0.9	4.2	2.3	1.4	0.1	1.2	0.0	0.0	0.0	0.1
Portage	67 182	94.7	37.3	20.6	28.3	22.9	1.9	0.6	6.7	2.1	5.3	0.2	0.4	0.0	4.2	0.0	0.4
Price	15 822	98.3	41.5	23.4	27.6	22.6	2.4	0.8	3.4	2.0	1.7	0.1	1.5	0.0	0.0	0.0	0.1
Racine	188 831	97.1	37.5	20.3	31.0	24.5	4.0	1.8	4.4	2.1	2.9	1.3	0.5	0.1	0.0	0.0	1.0
Richland	17 924	98.3	39.7	22.4	29.8	23.7	2.2	0.9	4.3	2.3	1.7	0.1	0.8	0.0	0.5	0.0	0.3
Rock	152 307	97.7	38.5	20.6	29.9	24.3	3.4	1.4	5.3	2.6	2.3	0.3	0.6	0.2	0.6	0.0	0.5
Rusk	15 347	97.4	39.7	22.2	28.3	22.9	2.8	1.1	4.3	2.0	2.6	0.3	0.9	0.0	1.2	0.0	0.2
St. Croix	63 155	98.5	37.1	22.8	32.3	26.8	1.8	0.6	4.5	2.2	1.5	0.3	0.9	0.0	0.0	0.0	0.2
Sauk	55 225	98.4	39.2	22.2	29.8	24.5	2.5	1.0	4.7	2.3	1.6	0.2	0.9	0.0	0.0	0.0	0.5
Sawyer	16 196	98.2	41.0	22.2	27.0	22.0	3.5	1.7	4.4	2.6	1.8	0.8	0.4	0.5	0.0	0.0	0.2
Shawano	40 664	97.8	38.9	22.7	29.6	23.8	2.6	1.0	4.1	2.3	2.2	0.6	1.1	0.2	0.0	0.0	0.3
Sheboygan	112 646	96.8	38.7	22.4	29.9	24.3	2.2	0.8	3.7	1.9	3.2	1.3	1.1	0.0	0.4	0.0	0.4
Taylor	19 680	98.6	38.3	22.7	31.8	25.8	2.5	0.8	3.3	1.9	1.4	0.0	1.1	0.0	0.0	0.0	0.3
Trempealeau	27 010	97.6	39.8	22.0	29.4	23.9	2.2	0.8	4.3	2.4	2.4	0.1	1.4	0.2	0.0	0.0	0.6
Vernon	28 056	98.3	38.6	22.7	31.6	26.1	2.3	0.9	3.2	1.7	1.7	0.1	1.0	0.2	0.0	0.0	0.4
Vilas	21 033	98.6	43.1	25.2	23.7	19.1	2.9	1.1	3.7	2.2	1.4	0.4	0.6	0.0	0.0	0.0	0.4
Walworth	93 759	94.5	36.8	20.4	27.8	22.6	3.2	1.0	6.2	2.0	5.5	0.3	0.8	0.0	3.7	0.0	0.7
Washburn	16 036	98.5	41.2	23.7	26.9	21.9	2.5	1.0	4.2	2.3	1.5	0.1	1.1	0.1	0.0	0.0	0.2
Washington	117 493	98.9	37.3	24.0	32.0	25.6	2.1	0.7	3.5	1.8	1.1	0.1	0.7	0.0	0.0	0.0	0.3
Waukesha	360 767	98.4	37.5	24.3	31.4	25.2	2.1	0.6	3.1	1.4	1.6	0.2	0.7	0.2	0.3	0.0	0.2
Waupaca	51 731	96.5	38.4	22.4	29.4	24.1	2.2	0.7	4.1	2.2	3.5	0.1	2.9	0.1	0.0	0.0	0.3
Waushara	23 154	98.0	40.3	24.2	26.8	21.8	2.8	1.1	3.9	2.1	2.0	0.4	0.5	0.0	0.0	0.0	1.1
Winnebago	156 763	94.7	39.0	20.7	27.4	22.6	2.0	0.7	5.6	2.3	5.3	1.8	0.5	0.3	2.2	0.0	0.5
Wood	75 555	98.4	39.9	22.6	30.0	24.4	2.0	0.7	3.9	1.9	1.6	0.1	0.8	0.0	0.0	0.0	0.6
WYOMING	493 782	97.1	39.2	21.5	28.6	24.0	2.8	1.3	5.0	2.1	2.9	0.8	0.6	0.2	0.8	0.1	0.4
Albany	32 014	92.5	41.4	17.4	20.4	17.3	2.5	0.7	10.7	2.2	7.5	0.1	0.3	0.0	6.7	0.0	0.4
Big Horn	11 461	97.8	37.6	22.9	31.3	26.3	3.1	1.8	2.8	1.5	2.2	0.0	1.9	0.0	0.0	0.0	0.3
Campbell	33 698	99.0	36.2	21.7	33.7	29.3	2.4	1.0	5.0	2.5	1.0	0.3	0.0	0.0	0.0	0.0	0.6
Carbon	15 639	93.8	39.2	21.6	26.2	22.2	2.6	1.2	4.1	2.2	6.2	5.6	0.6	0.0	0.0	0.0	0.1

Table B. States and Counties

STATE County	Total households	Households by type, 2000 Family households Total	With own children under 18 years	Married couple Total	With own children under 18 years	Female householder[1] Total	With own children under 18 years	Nonfamily households Total	Householder living alone Total	65 years and over	Average household size	Average family size	Households, 1990 Total households	Female householder[1]	Householder living alone
	71	72	73	74	75	76	77	78	79	80	81	82	83	84	85
WISCONSIN—Cont'd															
Dane	173 484	58.1	29.0	47.1	21.9	7.9	5.3	41.9	29.4	7.0	2.37	2.97	142 786	8.0	26.4
Dodge	31 417	71.0	33.9	59.6	26.9	7.5	4.8	29.0	24.1	10.8	2.56	3.05	26 853	6.5	21.7
Door	11 828	67.6	26.9	58.1	21.2	6.5	4.1	32.4	28.1	12.7	2.33	2.84	10 066	6.6	25.1
Douglas	17 808	63.3	29.2	49.1	19.9	10.1	6.8	36.7	29.8	12.0	2.36	2.93	16 374	11.1	27.8
Dunn	14 337	64.6	31.4	54.1	24.6	6.9	4.6	35.4	24.4	9.0	2.57	3.07	12 250	6.3	22.9
Eau Claire	35 822	62.2	30.0	50.6	22.5	8.6	5.7	37.8	27.1	10.1	2.46	3.02	31 282	8.6	24.9
Florence	2 133	67.6	27.5	58.6	22.1	6.0	3.8	32.4	27.9	12.5	2.35	2.87	1 755	7.6	22.9
Fond du Lac	36 931	69.0	32.8	57.7	25.8	7.8	5.0	31.0	25.4	10.8	2.52	3.04	32 644	7.8	23.3
Forest	4 043	68.5	29.2	54.0	19.5	9.8	6.9	31.5	28.2	13.2	2.39	2.89	3 290	9.0	24.6
Grant	18 465	67.1	30.5	56.1	23.9	7.5	4.7	32.9	26.0	12.1	2.51	3.03	17 169	6.8	23.5
Green	13 212	69.7	33.7	58.3	26.1	7.5	5.0	30.3	25.0	11.2	2.51	3.01	11 541	7.2	24.2
Green Lake	7 703	69.1	29.4	58.5	23.6	6.9	3.8	30.9	27.0	13.8	2.43	2.96	7 189	6.7	24.9
Iowa	8 764	70.9	34.6	59.5	27.9	7.6	4.5	29.1	24.3	10.1	2.56	3.06	7 406	7.5	23.2
Iron	3 083	63.6	22.2	53.0	16.8	7.0	3.6	36.4	32.0	16.3	2.19	2.74	2 602	6.5	29.2
Jackson	7 070	68.4	31.0	55.4	23.0	8.6	5.4	31.6	26.2	11.8	2.49	3.00	6 253	8.3	25.5
Jefferson	28 205	70.5	33.2	58.5	25.9	8.2	5.2	29.5	23.6	9.6	2.55	3.02	24 019	7.8	22.1
Juneau	9 696	69.1	30.4	55.5	22.1	8.8	5.6	30.9	26.0	12.3	2.47	2.96	8 265	8.1	24.8
Kenosha	56 057	68.6	34.8	52.7	25.0	11.5	7.4	31.4	25.5	9.1	2.60	3.13	47 029	11.6	23.2
Kewaunee	7 623	72.8	33.5	62.4	27.7	6.6	3.8	27.2	23.5	11.8	2.61	3.10	6 756	6.1	22.4
La Crosse	41 599	61.5	29.9	50.0	22.5	8.4	5.6	38.5	28.4	9.8	2.45	3.02	36 662	8.9	26.1
Lafayette	6 211	70.5	33.3	59.0	26.9	7.6	4.3	29.5	25.4	13.1	2.57	3.10	5 876	6.8	24.3
Langlade	8 452	68.8	29.4	56.7	22.2	8.2	5.1	31.2	26.7	13.6	2.42	2.93	7 563	7.5	26.2
Lincoln	11 721	70.2	31.4	58.4	23.8	8.1	5.1	29.8	25.5	12.1	2.46	2.94	10 159	7.2	23.4
Manitowoc	32 721	68.3	31.5	57.1	24.7	7.5	4.7	31.7	26.8	12.1	2.49	3.04	30 112	7.0	24.9
Marathon	47 702	71.0	34.0	59.9	27.3	7.4	4.7	29.0	23.6	9.5	2.60	3.11	41 547	7.2	21.0
Marinette	17 585	67.3	28.8	56.4	22.1	7.4	4.7	32.7	28.3	13.3	2.38	2.92	15 542	7.6	25.8
Marquette	5 986	69.6	26.9	58.7	20.7	6.7	4.1	30.4	25.4	12.3	2.41	2.86	4 831	5.6	23.4
Menominee	1 345	79.2	42.2	42.5	18.7	26.6	17.0	20.8	16.5	6.4	3.35	3.66	1 079	29.9	12.6
Milwaukee	377 729	59.6	29.5	39.0	17.1	16.3	10.4	40.4	33.0	10.7	2.43	3.13	373 048	15.8	29.4
Monroe	15 399	70.1	34.5	56.7	25.9	8.8	5.9	29.9	25.0	10.7	2.60	3.11	13 144	8.2	23.3
Oconto	13 979	71.9	32.2	60.7	25.1	6.9	4.4	28.1	23.5	10.7	2.52	2.97	11 283	6.1	22.5
Oneida	15 333	68.4	27.0	57.8	20.6	7.1	4.4	31.6	26.4	12.0	2.34	2.82	12 666	7.1	24.7
Outagamie	60 530	69.7	36.0	58.9	29.1	7.6	4.9	30.3	24.2	8.4	2.61	3.14	50 527	7.4	21.4
Ozaukee	30 857	74.6	36.0	65.6	30.7	6.5	3.9	25.4	21.4	8.4	2.61	3.07	25 707	6.4	17.0
Pepin	2 759	70.1	32.4	59.9	26.3	6.8	4.1	29.9	26.1	13.6	2.57	3.13	2 612	6.2	25.0
Pierce	13 015	69.4	35.0	58.1	28.0	7.5	4.9	30.6	21.3	7.5	2.65	3.10	11 011	7.0	20.7
Polk	16 254	69.7	32.1	58.2	24.5	7.4	5.0	30.3	25.2	10.6	2.51	3.01	13 056	7.0	23.3
Portage	25 040	65.9	32.1	55.1	25.6	7.3	4.6	34.1	24.5	8.8	2.54	3.07	21 306	7.7	22.0
Price	6 564	67.3	28.9	56.5	22.6	6.6	3.9	32.7	28.5	14.5	2.37	2.91	6 054	6.2	26.2
Racine	70 819	70.4	34.5	54.0	24.2	12.3	8.0	29.6	24.5	9.2	2.59	3.09	63 736	12.3	22.0
Richland	7 118	67.9	30.5	56.3	23.3	7.7	5.0	32.1	27.2	13.4	2.48	3.01	6 593	6.6	24.0
Rock	58 617	68.9	33.6	53.3	23.6	10.9	7.4	31.1	25.1	9.7	2.54	3.03	52 252	10.6	23.4
Rusk	6 095	68.2	28.6	55.9	21.8	7.9	4.2	31.8	27.0	14.3	2.45	2.97	5 693	7.6	24.6
St. Croix	23 410	72.4	38.0	61.6	30.8	7.0	4.9	27.6	21.2	7.3	2.66	3.12	17 638	6.4	19.7
Sauk	21 644	68.7	32.6	56.8	24.9	8.1	5.4	31.3	25.2	10.6	2.51	3.03	17 703	7.4	23.8
Sawyer	6 640	69.0	27.5	54.2	17.8	10.0	6.7	31.0	26.2	11.7	2.39	2.86	5 569	9.6	25.0
Shawano	15 815	70.5	31.5	58.3	24.1	8.0	4.9	29.5	24.9	12.1	2.51	3.00	13 775	6.6	23.1
Sheboygan	43 545	68.7	32.3	58.0	25.6	7.3	4.8	31.3	26.1	10.4	2.50	3.05	38 592	7.1	23.3
Taylor	7 529	71.0	33.8	59.3	26.9	7.1	4.5	29.0	24.7	11.2	2.58	3.10	6 692	5.7	21.9
Trempealeau	10 747	67.4	31.8	55.2	24.1	7.4	4.7	32.6	27.6	13.5	2.45	3.00	9 495	7.4	25.3
Vernon	10 825	69.3	31.5	58.7	25.2	6.8	4.1	30.7	26.7	13.7	2.55	3.11	9 725	6.8	25.8
Vilas	9 066	69.5	23.4	58.4	17.0	7.5	4.5	30.5	26.0	12.6	2.29	2.73	7 294	7.2	23.6
Walworth	34 522	67.4	31.8	55.4	24.8	8.2	5.0	32.6	24.7	9.2	2.57	3.07	27 620	8.0	23.9
Washburn	6 604	68.6	27.5	57.6	20.6	7.0	4.5	31.4	26.7	12.6	2.39	2.88	5 456	6.9	26.9
Washington	43 842	74.7	36.4	64.2	30.2	7.2	4.5	25.3	20.3	7.6	2.65	3.08	32 977	7.0	17.2
Waukesha	135 229	74.3	35.4	64.8	30.1	6.8	4.0	25.7	20.9	8.1	2.63	3.08	105 990	6.7	16.6
Waupaca	19 863	69.9	32.6	58.4	25.5	7.4	4.8	30.1	25.2	11.7	2.51	3.01	17 037	7.0	23.8
Waushara	9 336	70.5	27.6	60.0	21.3	6.7	4.0	29.5	24.9	11.9	2.43	2.89	7 616	6.7	23.4
Winnebago	61 157	64.7	31.0	53.0	23.5	8.3	5.5	35.3	27.6	9.9	2.43	2.99	53 216	8.1	25.1
Wood	30 135	68.0	32.2	56.7	25.0	8.0	5.3	32.0	27.2	11.4	2.47	3.01	27 473	8.0	23.5
WYOMING	193 608	67.4	32.7	54.8	24.3	8.7	6.0	32.6	26.3	8.8	2.48	3.00	168 839	8.3	24.5
Albany	13 269	52.8	23.9	42.0	17.4	7.5	4.9	47.2	31.4	6.2	2.23	2.84	11 957	8.0	29.3
Big Horn	4 312	71.6	32.5	61.0	25.8	6.8	4.4	28.4	25.0	11.9	2.60	3.13	3 905	5.7	25.0
Campbell	12 207	73.8	43.1	59.8	32.6	8.8	6.8	26.2	20.2	3.9	2.73	3.16	9 968	7.7	19.1
Carbon	6 129	67.4	31.2	55.1	22.8	8.3	6.0	32.6	27.5	9.6	2.39	2.91	6 001	7.6	24.7

[1] No spouse present.

Table B. States and Counties

| STATE County | Percent change of households, 1990–2000 | Total housing units | Occupied housing units (percent) | Vacant housing units | | Homeowner vacancy rate (percent) | Rental vacancy rate (percent) | Occupied housing units | | | Average household size of owner-occupied units | Average household size of renter-occupied units |
				Total	For seasonal, recreational, or occasional use			Total	Percent owner-occupied housing units	Percent renter-occupied housing units		
	86	87	88	89	90	91	92	93	94	95	96	97
WISCONSIN—Cont'd												
Dane	21.5	180 398	96.2	3.8	0.6	1.0	4.2	173 484	57.6	42.4	2.61	2.03
Dodge	17.0	33 672	93.3	6.7	2.4	1.5	6.9	31 417	73.4	26.6	2.70	2.16
Door	17.5	19 587	60.4	39.6	35.6	1.4	9.2	11 828	79.4	20.6	2.42	1.98
Douglas	8.8	20 356	87.5	12.5	8.6	0.8	5.9	17 808	71.3	28.7	2.52	1.96
Dunn	17.0	15 277	93.8	6.2	1.9	1.4	5.6	14 337	69.1	30.9	2.72	2.25
Eau Claire	14.5	37 474	95.6	4.4	1.0	0.9	3.5	35 822	65.0	35.0	2.64	2.11
Florence	21.5	4 239	50.3	49.7	46.2	1.5	8.1	2 133	85.7	14.3	2.41	1.97
Fond du Lac	13.1	39 271	94.0	6.0	1.5	1.3	7.7	36 931	72.9	27.1	2.68	2.08
Forest	22.9	8 322	48.6	51.4	46.3	1.5	9.1	4 043	78.9	21.1	2.45	2.17
Grant	7.5	19 940	92.6	7.4	2.7	1.5	7.0	18 465	72.3	27.7	2.64	2.16
Green	14.5	13 878	95.2	4.8	1.1	1.3	4.9	13 212	73.8	26.2	2.63	2.16
Green Lake	7.1	9 831	78.4	21.6	14.5	2.2	9.5	7 703	77.2	22.8	2.52	2.14
Iowa	18.3	9 579	91.5	8.5	4.3	1.6	7.0	8 764	75.9	24.1	2.68	2.21
Iron	18.5	5 706	54.0	46.0	37.8	2.7	24.1	3 083	80.7	19.3	2.30	1.74
Jackson	13.1	8 029	88.1	11.9	6.5	1.5	6.3	7 070	74.9	25.1	2.59	2.20
Jefferson	17.4	30 092	93.7	6.3	2.6	1.2	5.5	28 205	71.7	28.3	2.68	2.24
Juneau	17.3	12 370	78.4	21.6	16.5	2.0	8.3	9 696	77.0	23.0	2.53	2.25
Kenosha	19.2	59 989	93.4	6.6	2.8	1.2	5.1	56 057	69.1	30.9	2.74	2.29
Kewaunee	12.8	8 221	92.7	7.3	3.3	1.4	5.9	7 623	81.8	18.2	2.73	2.10
La Crosse	13.5	43 479	95.7	4.3	0.6	1.0	4.9	41 599	65.1	34.9	2.63	2.10
Lafayette	5.7	6 674	93.1	6.9	1.6	1.5	9.7	6 211	77.5	22.5	2.64	2.33
Langlade	11.8	11 187	75.6	24.4	19.3	1.6	8.1	8 452	79.0	21.0	2.51	2.08
Lincoln	15.4	14 681	79.8	20.2	13.3	1.6	6.3	11 721	78.2	21.8	2.59	1.99
Manitowoc	8.7	34 651	94.4	5.6	1.5	1.1	7.4	32 721	76.0	24.0	2.65	1.98
Marathon	14.8	50 360	94.7	5.3	1.1	1.3	7.5	47 702	75.7	24.3	2.75	2.14
Marinette	13.1	26 260	67.0	33.0	28.9	1.9	7.7	17 585	79.3	20.7	2.49	1.97
Marquette	23.9	8 664	69.1	30.9	26.2	2.1	6.2	5 986	82.3	17.7	2.44	2.25
Menominee	24.7	2 098	64.1	35.9	32.7	1.0	5.4	1 345	73.8	26.2	3.13	3.99
Milwaukee	1.3	400 093	94.4	5.6	0.2	1.1	5.6	377 729	52.6	47.4	2.59	2.24
Monroe	17.2	16 672	92.4	7.6	2.7	1.4	6.6	15 399	73.7	26.3	2.71	2.29
Oconto	23.9	19 812	70.6	29.4	24.4	1.6	5.5	13 979	83.0	17.0	2.59	2.21
Oneida	21.1	26 627	57.6	42.4	39.2	1.6	7.3	15 333	79.7	20.3	2.42	2.03
Outagamie	19.8	62 614	96.7	3.3	0.4	0.9	4.9	60 530	72.4	27.6	2.81	2.08
Ozaukee	20.0	32 034	96.3	3.7	0.8	0.8	5.7	30 857	76.3	23.7	2.79	2.04
Pepin	5.6	3 036	90.9	9.1	4.4	1.5	5.7	2 759	79.7	20.3	2.74	1.92
Pierce	18.2	13 493	96.5	3.5	1.3	0.8	2.2	13 015	73.1	26.9	2.79	2.26
Polk	24.5	21 129	76.9	23.1	19.9	0.9	5.9	16 254	80.2	19.8	2.62	2.06
Portage	17.5	26 589	94.2	5.8	2.1	1.0	4.5	25 040	70.9	29.1	2.70	2.15
Price	8.4	9 574	68.6	31.4	26.3	2.2	7.9	6 564	80.7	19.3	2.48	1.90
Racine	11.1	74 718	94.8	5.2	1.2	1.0	6.3	70 819	70.6	29.4	2.69	2.35
Richland	8.0	8 164	87.2	12.8	7.8	1.8	5.0	7 118	74.2	25.8	2.57	2.21
Rock	12.2	62 187	94.3	5.7	1.2	1.4	7.3	58 617	71.1	28.9	2.64	2.29
Rusk	7.1	7 609	80.1	19.9	15.1	1.4	6.0	6 095	78.7	21.3	2.55	2.10
St. Croix	32.7	24 265	96.5	3.5	1.2	0.8	2.9	23 410	76.4	23.6	2.85	2.04
Sauk	22.3	24 297	89.1	10.9	6.5	1.5	5.9	21 644	73.3	26.7	2.63	2.18
Sawyer	19.2	13 722	48.4	51.6	48.5	2.2	6.8	6 640	77.1	22.9	2.41	2.36
Shawano	14.8	18 317	86.3	13.7	9.8	1.2	6.6	15 815	78.2	21.8	2.61	2.16
Sheboygan	12.8	45 947	94.8	5.2	1.7	1.1	5.4	43 545	71.4	28.6	2.67	2.10
Taylor	12.5	8 595	87.6	12.4	8.2	1.2	5.4	7 529	80.6	19.4	2.72	1.98
Trempealeau	13.2	11 482	93.6	6.4	1.9	1.4	6.4	10 747	74.1	25.9	2.62	1.98
Vernon	11.3	12 416	87.2	12.8	6.9	2.2	7.0	10 825	79.1	20.9	2.66	2.14
Vilas	24.3	22 397	40.5	59.5	56.2	2.8	8.6	9 066	81.8	18.2	2.31	2.17
Walworth	25.0	43 783	78.8	21.2	17.0	1.8	5.3	34 522	69.1	30.9	2.67	2.34
Washburn	21.0	10 814	61.1	38.9	35.3	1.7	9.2	6 604	80.8	19.2	2.46	2.09
Washington	32.9	45 808	95.7	4.3	1.4	0.9	4.7	43 842	76.0	24.0	2.80	2.16
Waukesha	27.6	140 309	96.4	3.6	1.0	0.8	4.9	135 229	76.4	23.6	2.81	2.02
Waupaca	16.6	22 508	88.2	11.8	7.5	1.5	6.6	19 863	77.0	23.0	2.64	2.09
Waushara	22.6	13 667	68.3	31.7	27.0	1.9	6.3	9 336	83.5	16.5	2.47	2.22
Winnebago	14.9	64 721	94.5	5.5	1.6	1.3	6.1	61 157	68.0	32.0	2.60	2.05
Wood	9.7	31 691	95.1	4.9	0.8	1.1	5.8	30 135	74.3	25.7	2.63	2.00
WYOMING	14.7	223 854	86.5	13.5	5.5	2.1	9.7	193 608	70.0	30.0	2.58	2.25
Albany	11.0	15 215	87.2	12.8	7.2	2.0	5.2	13 269	51.5	48.5	2.44	2.01
Big Horn	10.4	5 105	84.5	15.5	5.2	3.5	12.5	4 312	74.7	25.3	2.64	2.48
Campbell	22.5	13 288	91.9	8.1	1.6	1.2	9.0	12 207	73.6	26.4	2.88	2.33
Carbon	2.1	8 307	73.8	26.2	12.6	4.7	16.9	6 129	71.0	29.0	2.46	2.24

Table B. States and Counties

STATE/ County code	MSA/ PMSA/ NECMA code[1]	County type[2]	STATE County	Population, 2000				Population, 1990				Population and population characteristics, 2000					
												Race (percent)					
												One race					
				Land area, 2000[3] (sq km)	Total persons	Rank	Per square kilometer	Land area, 1990[3] (sq km)	Total persons	Rank	Per square kilometer	White	Black or African American	American Indian or Alaska Native	Asian	Native Hawaiian and other Pacific Islander	Some other race
				1	2	3	4	5	6	7	8	9	10	11	12	13	14
			WYOMING—Cont'd														
56 009	...	6	Converse	11 020	12 052	2 292	1.1	11 020	11 128	2 281	1.0	94.7	0.1	0.9	0.3	0.0	2.5
56 011	...	9	Crook	7 404	5 887	2 795	0.8	7 404	5 294	2 819	0.7	97.9	0.1	1.0	0.1	0.0	0.3
56 013	...	7	Fremont	23 782	35 804	1 225	1.5	23 783	33 662	1 175	1.4	76.5	0.1	19.7	0.3	0.0	1.2
56 015	...	7	Goshen	5 764	12 538	2 262	2.2	5 764	12 373	2 191	2.1	93.8	0.2	0.9	0.2	0.1	3.7
56 017	...	7	Hot Springs	5 190	4 882	2 855	0.9	5 190	4 809	2 856	0.9	96.0	0.3	1.5	0.2	0.0	0.6
56 019	...	7	Johnson	10 791	7 075	2 677	0.7	10 791	6 145	2 738	0.6	97.0	0.1	0.6	0.1	0.0	0.6
56 021	1580	3	Laramie	6 957	81 607	637	11.7	6 957	73 142	614	10.5	88.9	2.6	0.8	1.0	0.1	4.0
56 023	...	7	Lincoln	10 539	14 573	2 114	1.4	10 540	12 625	2 175	1.2	97.1	0.1	0.6	0.2	0.1	0.7
56 025	1350	3	Natrona	13 830	66 533	735	4.8	13 831	61 226	712	4.4	94.2	0.8	1.0	0.4	0.0	1.9
56 027	...	9	Niobrara	6 801	2 407	3 028	0.4	6 801	2 499	3 022	0.4	98.0	0.1	0.5	0.1	0.0	0.5
56 029	...	7	Park	17 981	25 786	1 524	1.4	17 982	23 178	1 531	1.3	96.5	0.1	0.5	0.4	0.1	1.4
56 031	...	7	Platte	5 400	8 807	2 546	1.6	5 400	8 145	2 550	1.5	96.2	0.2	0.5	0.2	0.0	1.7
56 033	...	7	Sheridan	6 535	26 560	1 498	4.1	6 536	23 562	1 511	3.6	95.9	0.2	1.3	0.4	0.1	0.8
56 035	...	9	Sublette	12 646	5 920	2 791	0.5	12 643	4 843	2 850	0.4	97.5	0.2	0.5	0.2	0.1	0.5
56 037	...	5	Sweetwater	27 001	37 613	1 173	1.4	27 003	38 823	1 029	1.4	91.6	0.7	1.0	0.6	0.0	3.6
56 039	...	7	Teton	10 380	18 251	1 883	1.8	10 381	11 173	2 279	1.1	93.6	0.1	0.5	0.5	0.0	3.9
56 041	...	7	Uinta	5 391	19 742	1 807	3.7	5 392	18 705	1 749	3.5	94.3	0.1	0.9	0.3	0.1	2.9
56 043	...	7	Washakie	5 802	8 289	2 580	1.4	5 802	8 388	2 523	1.4	90.2	0.1	0.6	0.7	0.0	6.2
56 045	...	7	Weston	6 210	6 644	2 721	1.1	6 211	6 518	2 707	1.0	95.9	0.1	1.3	0.2	0.0	0.9

[1]MSA = Metropolitan Statistical Area. PMSA = Primary MSA. NECMA = New England County Metropolitan Area. See Appendix A for explanation of these concepts. See Appendix B for list of metropolitan areas identified by type, with component counties.
[2]County typology code from the Economic Research Service of USDA. See Appendix A for definition.
[3]Dry land or land partially or temporarily covered by water.

Items 1—14

STATE County	Population and population characteristics, 2000 (cont'd)								Population and population characteristics, 1990				
	Race (percent) (cont'd)								Race (percent)				
	Race alone or in combination												
	Two or more races	White	Black	American Indian or Alaska Native	Asian	Native Hawaiian and other Pacific Islander	Some other race	Hispanic[1]	White	Black or African American	American Indian or Alaska Native	Asian and Pacific Islander	Hispanic[1]
	15	16	17	18	19	20	21	22	23	24	25	26	27
WYOMING—Cont'd													
Converse	1.5	06.2	0.3	1.8	0.4	0.0	2.9	5.5	96.3	0.1	0.9	0.3	5.1
Crook	0.7	98.6	0.2	1.5	0.2	0.1	0.5	0.9	99.3	0.0	0.5	0.1	0.5
Fremont	2.2	78.6	0.2	20.9	0.5	0.1	2.0	4.4	79.5	0.2	18.5	0.3	4.0
Goshen	1.1	94.9	0.3	1.4	0.2	0.2	4.2	8.8	95.0	0.2	0.8	0.1	8.7
Hot Springs	1.3	97.2	0.3	2.6	0.3	0.0	0.9	2.4	96.9	0.3	2.1	0.0	1.4
Johnson	1.6	98.5	0.2	1.5	0.3	0.0	1.1	2.1	98.6	0.0	1.0	0.1	1.3
Laramie	2.6	91.2	3.2	1.7	1.5	0.2	4.9	10.9	90.6	3.0	0.7	1.1	10.0
Lincoln	1.2	98.3	0.2	1.3	0.4	0.1	1.0	2.2	98.5	0.1	0.5	0.3	2.0
Natrona	1.7	95.7	1.1	1.8	0.6	0.1	2.5	4.9	96.9	0.7	0.7	0.5	3.7
Niobrara	0.7	98.8	0.2	0.9	0.1	0.0	0.7	1.5	98.0	0.3	0.8	0.1	1.4
Park	1.1	97.5	0.2	1.0	0.6	0.1	1.7	3.7	97.4	0.1	0.6	0.5	3.6
Platte	1.3	97.4	0.2	1.2	0.3	0.1	2.1	5.3	98.9	0.1	0.3	0.1	5.0
Sheridan	1.3	97.2	0.3	1.9	0.6	0.2	1.2	2.4	98.0	0.2	0.9	0.4	1.9
Sublette	1.0	98.4	0.4	1.0	0.3	0.2	0.8	1.9	98.1	0.1	1.4	0.3	1.2
Sweetwater	2.4	93.9	1.0	1.8	0.9	0.1	4.8	9.4	94.2	0.7	0.8	0.7	8.9
Teton	1.2	94.7	0.2	1.0	0.9	0.1	4.4	6.5	98.4	0.2	0.9	0.4	1.4
Uinta	1.5	95.7	0.2	1.6	0.5	0.1	3.5	5.3	97.7	0.1	0.7	0.4	4.1
Washakie	2.2	92.2	0.3	1.6	1.0	0.1	7.2	11.5	93.8	0.2	0.7	0.5	9.5
Weston	1.5	97.4	0.2	2.3	0.3	0.0	1.4	2.1	98.0	0.0	1.2	0.2	1.3

[1] Hispanic persons may be of any race.

Table B. States and Counties

STATE County	Population and population characteristics, 2000										
	Age (percent)										
	Under 5 years	5 to 17 years	18 to 24 years	25 to 34 years	35 to 44 years	45 to 54 years	55 to 64 years	65 to 74 years	75 years and over	Median age (years)	Percent Female
	28	29	30	31	32	33	34	35	36	37	38
WYOMING—Cont'd											
Converse	6.4	22.1	7.0	11.0	17.1	16.1	9.2	6.5	4.5	37.5	50.2
Crook	5.2	21.7	6.6	8.4	16.2	15.6	11.6	8.4	6.4	40.2	49.4
Fremont	6.5	20.9	8.3	10.7	15.2	14.8	10.2	7.6	5.7	37.7	50.5
Goshen	5.8	18.4	9.4	9.9	14.4	14.0	10.8	8.4	8.9	40.0	50.3
Hot Springs	4.8	17.2	5.9	8.4	14.9	15.1	13.6	10.1	9.9	44.2	51.9
Johnson	5.2	19.0	5.6	9.7	13.8	16.3	12.4	9.7	8.4	43.0	50.9
Laramie	6.6	19.2	9.6	14.2	16.3	14.1	8.6	6.1	5.3	35.3	49.8
Lincoln	6.8	24.1	7.2	9.8	15.6	14.6	9.6	6.9	5.5	36.8	49.5
Natrona	6.5	19.5	10.1	12.1	15.8	14.7	8.6	7.1	5.6	36.4	50.6
Niobrara	4.8	17.8	6.1	9.4	16.6	14.4	12.3	10.3	8.5	42.8	51.2
Park	5.5	18.9	9.1	9.8	15.5	16.0	10.8	7.6	7.0	39.8	51.3
Platte	5.2	20.2	6.6	9.5	14.7	15.8	11.5	8.5	8.0	41.2	50.7
Sheridan	5.3	18.8	8.0	10.1	15.2	16.7	10.4	7.8	7.7	40.6	51.1
Sublette	5.9	19.9	6.0	10.2	17.2	17.7	11.0	7.2	4.8	39.8	48.9
Sweetwater	6.9	22.0	10.1	12.0	17.3	15.8	7.9	4.3	3.7	34.2	49.4
Teton	5.2	14.7	9.8	20.2	18.1	16.7	8.4	4.4	2.5	35.0	46.7
Uinta	8.2	25.2	9.0	11.9	17.3	14.5	6.9	4.0	2.9	31.4	49.1
Washakie	5.9	21.4	6.4	10.0	15.2	14.8	10.5	8.3	7.6	39.4	50.2
Weston	5.2	18.8	7.4	9.9	16.4	15.9	10.7	7.9	7.6	40.7	49.2

Table B. States and Counties

| STATE County | Population and population characteristics, 1990 | | | | | | | | | | Population—change, 1980–2000 | | | | |
| | Age (percent) | | | | | | | | | | Total persons | | | Percent change | |
	Under 5 years	5 to 17 years	18 to 24 years	25 to 34 years	35 to 44 years	45 to 54 years	55 to 64 years	65 to 74 years	75 years and over	Percent Female	2000	1990	1980	1990–2000	1980–1990
	39	40	41	42	43	44	45	46	47	48	49	50	51	52	53
WYOMING—Cont'd															
Converse	8.0	25.0	6.9	15.7	17.2	10.3	8.0	5.4	3.6	51.1	12 052	11 128	14 069	8.3	-20.9
Crook	8.1	24.0	5.9	14.4	15.4	11.0	9.1	7.7	4.5	50.1	5 887	5 294	5 308	11.2	-0.3
Fremont	7.9	23.5	7.6	14.4	15.5	10.7	8.9	6.9	4.6	50.3	35 804	33 662	38 992	6.4	-13.7
Goshen	6.8	21.5	8.2	14.1	13.8	10.3	9.2	9.0	7.1	51.6	12 538	12 373	12 040	1.3	2.8
Hot Springs	5.2	20.9	5.4	13.0	14.9	11.4	10.5	9.7	9.0	50.8	4 882	4 809	5 710	1.5	-15.8
Johnson	6.7	20.1	6.5	12.2	16.0	11.4	9.7	10.2	7.3	50.9	7 075	6 145	6 700	15.1	-8.3
Laramie	8.0	19.8	9.9	17.8	15.8	10.2	8.1	6.1	4.2	50.2	81 607	73 142	68 649	11.6	6.5
Lincoln	9.1	29.0	6.1	14.2	14.9	9.7	6.9	6.4	3.6	49.1	14 573	12 625	12 177	15.4	3.7
Natrona	7.6	21.5	8.3	16.6	16.5	10.0	8.9	6.7	3.9	50.9	66 533	61 226	71 856	8.7	-14.8
Niobrara	6.2	17.9	6.0	14.4	13.9	11.3	11.1	9.8	9.3	53.9	2 407	2 499	2 924	-3.7	-14.5
Park	7.3	20.8	8.8	14.8	15.9	10.6	8.5	7.5	5.8	50.9	25 786	23 178	21 639	11.3	7.1
Platte	7.2	21.7	6.3	12.6	15.8	11.6	9.2	8.5	7.2	50.5	8 807	8 145	11 975	8.1	-32.0
Sheridan	6.2	20.6	7.1	13.7	17.5	10.8	9.3	8.3	6.7	50.9	26 560	23 562	25 048	12.7	-5.9
Sublette	7.4	20.8	6.4	14.7	18.3	11.7	8.8	6.9	5.0	48.2	5 920	4 843	4 548	22.2	6.5
Sweetwater	8.1	26.0	8.0	17.3	17.8	9.7	6.1	4.3	2.9	49.5	37 613	38 823	41 723	-3.1	-7.0
Teton	7.9	16.4	7.6	22.1	21.8	10.8	7.0	4.2	2.3	47.8	18 251	11 173	9 355	63.3	19.4
Uinta	9.7	30.1	7.1	17.8	17.2	7.7	5.1	3.2	2.1	49.2	19 742	18 705	13 021	5.5	43.7
Washakie	7.0	23.0	6.7	14.0	15.3	10.8	9.3	8.0	5.8	49.8	8 289	8 388	9 496	-1.2	-11.7
Weston	6.5	23.2	6.4	15.1	16.3	10.9	9.0	7.8	4.9	50.2	6 644	6 518	7 106	1.9	-8.3

Table B. States and Counties

| STATE County | Total population | In households (percent) | | | | | | | | | In group quarters (percent) | | | | | | |
		Total in house-holds	House-holder	Spouse	Child Total	Child Own child under 18 years	Other relatives Total	Other relatives Under 18 years	Nonrelatives Total	Nonrelatives Unmar-ried partner	Total in group quarters	Institutionalized population Correc-tional institu-tions	Institutionalized population Nurs-ing homes	Institutionalized population Other institu-tions	Noninstitutionalized population Col-lege dormi-tories	Noninstitutionalized population Mili-tary quar-ters	Other
	54	55	56	57	58	59	60	61	62	63	64	65	66	67	68	69	70
WYOMING—Cont'd																	
Converse	12 052	99.2	38.9	23.6	31.1	26.8	2.2	1.0	3.4	1.6	0.8	0.3	0.4	0.0	0.0	0.0	0.1
Crook	5 887	98.3	39.2	24.4	29.9	25.4	1.8	0.7	2.9	1.6	1.7	0.1	1.3	0.3	0.0	0.0	0.1
Fremont	35 804	97.7	37.8	20.5	29.5	23.5	5.6	3.2	4.2	2.1	2.3	0.7	0.5	0.3	0.3	0.0	0.5
Goshen	12 538	96.1	40.4	22.9	26.4	22.0	2.6	1.3	3.8	1.9	3.9	0.5	0.6	0.4	1.8	0.0	0.6
Hot Springs	4 882	97.0	43.2	23.5	24.6	20.0	2.3	1.3	3.5	1.6	3.0	0.3	2.4	0.2	0.0	0.0	0.0
Johnson	7 075	98.7	41.8	23.9	27.4	22.8	2.3	0.8	3.3	1.6	1.3	0.2	0.7	0.0	0.0	0.0	0.4
Laramie	81 607	96.0	39.1	21.1	28.5	23.7	2.9	1.3	4.3	2.0	4.0	2.2	0.6	0.0	0.1	0.7	0.5
Lincoln	14 573	99.5	36.1	24.1	33.9	29.1	2.4	1.2	2.9	1.5	0.5	0.2	0.3	0.0	0.0	0.0	0.0
Natrona	66 533	97.7	40.3	20.7	28.5	23.7	2.8	1.3	5.3	2.6	2.3	0.5	0.7	0.1	0.5	0.0	0.5
Niobrara	2 407	95.8	42.0	24.2	25.1	21.5	1.9	0.6	2.6	1.3	4.2	4.2	0.0	0.0	0.0	0.0	0.0
Park	25 786	96.6	40.0	23.5	27.2	22.9	2.1	0.8	3.8	1.8	3.4	0.2	0.5	0.5	1.9	0.0	0.4
Platte	8 807	98.9	41.2	24.2	27.9	23.7	2.3	1.1	3.3	1.7	1.1	0.1	0.9	0.0	0.0	0.0	0.1
Sheridan	26 560	97.3	42.0	21.8	26.3	21.9	2.4	1.0	4.7	2.1	2.7	0.1	1.1	0.6	0.6	0.0	0.3
Sublette	5 920	98.8	40.1	25.4	27.9	24.4	1.9	0.8	3.5	1.9	1.2	0.1	1.1	0.0	0.0	0.0	0.0
Sweetwater	37 613	98.4	37.5	21.7	32.0	26.6	2.9	1.5	4.2	2.1	1.6	0.2	0.3	0.0	0.9	0.0	0.2
Teton	18 251	99.3	42.1	19.1	21.4	18.5	2.9	0.7	13.8	3.3	0.7	0.2	0.3	0.0	0.0	0.0	0.3
Uinta	19 742	98.2	34.6	21.1	36.7	31.6	2.5	1.2	3.3	1.8	1.8	0.5	0.4	0.7	0.0	0.0	0.3
Washakie	8 289	97.6	39.5	23.7	29.5	24.9	2.7	1.1	2.3	1.4	2.4	0.4	0.9	1.0	0.0	0.0	0.1
Weston	6 644	95.5	39.5	23.9	26.9	22.6	2.3	0.8	3.0	1.5	4.5	2.9	0.7	0.0	0.0	0.0	0.8

Table B. States and Counties

STATE County	Households by type, 2000												Households, 1990		
	Total households	Family households						Nonfamily households			Average house-hold size	Average family size	Total house-holds	Female house-holder[1]	House-holder living alone
		Total	With own children under 18 years	Married couple		Female householder[1]		Total	Householder living alone						
				Total	With own children under 18 years	Total	With own children under 18 years		Total	65 years and over					
	71	72	73	74	75	76	77	78	79	80	81	82	83	84	85
WYOMING—Cont'd															
Converse	4 694	72.6	36.5	60.6	27.7	8.4	6.3	27.4	23.4	9.0	2.55	3.01	4 046	8.9	21.7
Crook	2 308	71.3	32.3	62.3	26.4	5.4	3.8	28.7	24.9	10.3	2.51	3.01	1 892	5.3	20.6
Fremont	13 545	70.0	32.2	54.3	22.5	10.9	7.0	30.0	25.5	10.0	2.58	3.10	12 002	10.7	22.2
Goshen	5 061	67.7	28.6	56.7	21.6	7.7	5.0	32.3	27.6	13.1	2.38	2.90	4 790	7.9	25.5
Hot Springs	2 108	64.2	25.5	54.3	19.2	7.4	4.7	35.8	31.7	14.8	2.25	2.82	1 943	7.8	29.2
Johnson	2 959	67.8	28.7	57.0	21.7	7.1	4.8	32.2	28.5	12.0	2.36	2.89	2 397	6.4	25.7
Laramie	31 927	67.7	33.2	53.9	24.1	9.9	6.8	32.3	27.2	8.9	2.45	2.98	28 092	9.7	25.3
Lincoln	5 266	75.0	36.5	66.7	31.3	5.1	3.4	25.0	21.0	7.9	2.75	3.23	4 137	5.7	19.3
Natrona	26 819	66.2	32.2	51.4	22.1	10.6	7.4	33.8	27.5	9.4	2.42	2.95	23 837	9.7	25.9
Niobrara	1 011	67.2	27.1	57.6	21.3	6.0	4.2	32.8	29.5	14.1	2.28	2.81	1 032	7.7	31.8
Park	10 312	68.8	30.1	58.9	23.6	7.1	4.9	31.2	26.2	10.0	2.42	2.92	8 757	7.1	24.2
Platte	3 625	68.8	30.0	58.9	23.6	6.8	4.5	31.2	27.3	13.2	2.40	2.92	3 179	6.0	25.8
Sheridan	11 167	63.4	28.4	52.0	20.8	8.2	5.6	36.6	30.9	12.5	2.31	2.90	9 426	8.4	28.3
Sublette	2 371	72.0	32.7	63.3	26.6	5.3	3.8	28.0	23.6	6.5	2.47	2.91	1 834	4.4	23.4
Sweetwater	14 105	71.6	38.2	57.8	28.6	9.2	6.5	28.4	23.6	6.9	2.62	3.11	13 616	7.7	22.2
Teton	7 688	54.3	25.6	45.3	20.1	5.7	3.9	45.7	27.3	3.7	2.36	2.89	4 568	5.4	26.6
Uinta	6 823	75.4	44.7	61.2	33.9	9.9	7.6	24.6	20.9	5.6	2.84	3.31	5 885	7.8	18.7
Washakie	3 278	70.5	32.4	59.9	25.6	7.3	4.6	29.5	26.5	11.9	2.47	3.00	3 156	6.4	24.7
Weston	2 624	71.2	31.1	60.4	24.8	7.3	4.6	28.8	25.0	11.5	2.42	2.88	2 419	7.2	22.1

[1]No spouse present.

Table B. States and Counties

STATE County	Percent change of households, 1990–2000	Housing occupancy, 2000						Housing tenure, 2000				
		Total housing units	Occupied housing units (percent)	Vacant housing units		Homeowner vacancy rate (percent)	Rental vacancy rate (percent)	Occupied housing units			Average household size of owner-occupied units	Average household size of renter-occupied units
				Total	For seasonal, recreational, or occasional use			Total	Percent owner-occupied housing units	Percent renter-occupied housing units		
	86	87	88	89	90	91	92	93	94	95	96	97
WYOMING—Cont'd												
Converse	16.0	5 669	82.8	17.2	5.6	2.3	19.0	4 694	74.0	26.0	2.63	2.33
Crook	22.0	2 935	78.6	21.4	11.7	1.9	14.3	2 308	79.9	20.1	2.55	2.35
Fremont	12.9	15 541	87.2	12.8	4.2	2.0	11.3	13 545	72.9	27.1	2.61	2.50
Goshen	5.7	5 881	86.1	13.9	2.2	2.9	9.5	5 061	70.7	29.3	2.42	2.29
Hot Springs	8.5	2 536	83.1	16.9	5.4	4.3	9.4	2 108	68.4	31.6	2.33	2.08
Johnson	23.4	3 503	84.5	15.5	10.2	1.8	3.8	2 959	73.7	26.3	2.42	2.18
Laramie	13.7	34 213	93.3	6.7	0.7	1.5	7.7	31 927	69.1	30.9	2.54	2.25
Lincoln	27.3	6 831	77.1	22.9	13.4	2.8	21.8	5 266	81.3	18.7	2.81	2.50
Natrona	12.5	29 882	89.7	10.3	3.1	1.5	8.4	26 819	69.9	30.1	2.52	2.19
Niobrara	-2.0	1 338	75.6	24.4	4.7	7.5	18.2	1 011	72.9	27.1	2.33	2.15
Park	17.8	11 869	86.9	13.1	6.8	1.9	7.9	10 312	71.4	28.6	2.50	2.21
Platte	14.0	4 528	80.1	19.9	6.6	4.4	14.4	3 625	76.0	24.0	2.43	2.32
Sheridan	18.5	12 577	88.8	11.2	6.3	1.1	4.7	11 167	68.9	31.1	2.39	2.14
Sublette	29.3	3 552	66.8	33.2	26.2	2.4	7.4	2 371	73.3	26.7	2.52	2.32
Sweetwater	3.6	15 921	88.6	11.4	1.5	2.6	16.2	14 105	75.1	24.9	2.74	2.28
Teton	68.3	10 267	74.9	25.1	20.7	1.3	5.2	7 688	54.8	45.2	2.47	2.22
Uinta	15.9	8 011	85.2	14.8	3.0	3.6	17.7	6 823	75.3	24.7	2.94	2.54
Washakie	3.9	3 654	89.7	10.3	3.0	1.2	10.9	3 278	73.1	26.9	2.52	2.33
Weston	8.5	3 231	81.2	18.8	4.4	4.8	12.0	2 624	77.9	22.1	2.47	2.25

TABLE C:

Metropolitan Areas

(For explanation of symbols, see page xi.)

Page

444   Abilene, TX—Columbia, MO
451   Columbia, SC—Harrisburg-Lebanon-Carlisle, PA
458   Hartford, CT—Memphis, TN-AR-MS
465   Merced, CA—Rapid City, SD
472   Reading, PA—Topeka, KS
479   Tucson, AZ—Yuma, AZ

Table C—Metropolitan Areas

Table C. Metropolitan Areas

CMSA/ MSA/ PMSA/ NECMA code[1]	Area Name	Population, 2000 Land area, 2000[2] (sq km)	Total persons	Rank	Per square kilometer	Population, 1990 Land area, 1990[2] (sq km)	Total persons	Rank	Per square kilometer	Population and population characteristics, 2000 — Race (percent) — One race White	Black or African American	American Indian or Alaska Native	Asian	Native Hawaiian and other Pacific Islander	Some other race
		1	2	3	4	5	6	7	8	9	10	11	12	13	14
0040	Abilene, TX	2 371	126 555	269	53.4	2 372	119 655	264	50.4	80.6	6.7	0.6	1.2	0.1	8.3
0120	Albany, GA	1 775	120 822	277	68.1	1 776	112 571	275	63.4	46.9	51.0	0.2	0.6	0.0	0.5
0160	Albany-Schenectady-Troy, NY	8 345	875 583	69	104.9	8 347	861 623	62	103.2	89.4	6.1	0.2	1.8	0.0	0.9
0200	Albuquerque, NM	15 392	712 738	75	46.3	15 393	589 131	83	38.3	69.6	2.5	5.6	1.7	0.1	16.3
0220	Alexandria, LA	3 425	126 337	270	36.9	3 426	131 556	243	38.4	66.5	30.4	0.7	0.9	0.0	0.4
0240	Allentown-Bethlehem-Easton, PA	2 853	637 958	81	223.6	2 857	595 043	81	208.3	89.8	3.0	0.2	1.6	0.0	3.9
0280	Altoona, PA	1 362	129 144	265	94.8	1 362	130 542	248	95.8	97.6	1.2	0.1	0.4	0.0	0.1
0320	Amarillo, TX	4 723	217 858	192	46.1	4 723	187 514	191	39.7	79.1	5.9	0.8	1.8	0.0	10.3
0380	Anchorage, AK	4 396	260 283	168	59.2	4 397	226 338	172	51.5	72.2	5.8	7.3	5.5	0.9	2.2
0450	Anniston, AL	1 576	112 249	288	71.2	1 576	116 032	270	73.6	78.9	18.5	0.4	0.6	0.1	0.6
0460	Appleton-Oshkosh-Neenah, WI	3 623	358 365	139	98.9	3 623	315 121	139	87.0	94.6	0.8	0.9	2.0	0.0	0.7
0480	Asheville, NC	2 863	225 965	188	78.9	2 864	191 310	186	66.8	89.8	6.9	0.4	0.6	0.0	1.1
0500	Athens, GA	1 529	153 444	233	100.4	1 531	126 262	254	82.5	73.2	20.5	0.2	2.4	0.0	2.5
0520	Atlanta, GA	15 861	4 112 198	9	259.3	15 867	2 959 500	9	186.5	63.0	28.9	0.3	3.3	0.0	2.8
0580	Auburn-Opalika, AL	1 577	115 092	283	73.0	1 577	87 146	304	55.3	74.1	22.7	0.2	1.6	0.0	0.5
0600	Augusta-Aiken, GA-SC	6 341	477 441	107	75.3	6 342	415 220	107	65.5	61.5	34.4	0.3	1.5	0.1	0.9
0640	Austin-San Marcos, TX	10 940	1 249 763	48	114.2	10 946	846 227	65	77.3	72.5	8.0	0.6	3.5	0.1	12.8
0680	Bakersfield, CA	21 085	661 645	80	31.4	21 087	544 981	88	25.8	61.6	6.0	1.5	3.4	0.1	23.2
0733	Bangor, ME	8 795	144 919	248	16.5	8 796	146 601	225	16.7	96.6	0.5	1.0	0.7	0.0	0.2
0743	Barnstable-Yarmouth, MA	1 024	222 230	190	216.9	1 025	186 605	192	182.1	94.2	1.8	0.6	0.6	0.0	1.1
0760	Baton Rouge, LA	4 108	602 894	88	146.8	4 108	528 261	89	128.6	64.9	31.9	0.2	1.5	0.0	0.5
0840	Beaumont-Port Arthur, TX	5 580	385 090	130	69.0	5 579	361 218	124	64.7	68.2	24.8	0.4	2.1	0.0	3.1
0860	Bellingham, WA	5 490	166 814	224	30.4	5 491	127 780	252	23.3	88.4	0.7	2.8	2.8	0.1	2.5
0870	Benton Harbor, MI	1 479	162 453	227	109.8	1 479	161 378	208	109.1	79.7	15.9	0.4	1.1	0.0	1.1
0880	Billings, MT	6 825	129 352	264	19.0	6 825	113 419	274	16.6	92.8	0.4	3.1	0.5	0.0	1.3
0920	Biloxi-Gulfport-Pascagoula, MS	4 623	363 988	137	78.7	4 622	312 368	141	67.6	76.0	19.3	0.4	2.0	0.1	0.8
0960	Binghamton, NY	3 174	252 320	172	79.5	3 174	264 497	154	83.3	92.6	2.7	0.2	2.3	0.0	0.7
1000	Birmingham, AL	8 253	921 106	67	111.6	8 255	839 942	66	101.7	67.3	30.1	0.3	0.8	0.0	0.7
1010	Bismarck, ND	9 219	94 719	305	10.3	9 219	83 831	307	9.1	95.2	0.2	3.0	0.4	0.0	0.2
1020	Bloomington, IN	1 021	120 563	278	118.0	1 021	108 978	280	106.7	90.8	3.0	0.3	3.4	0.0	0.9
1040	Bloomington-Normal, IL	3 065	150 433	238	49.1	3 066	129 180	250	42.1	89.2	6.2	0.2	2.1	0.0	1.0
1080	Boise City, ID	4 260	432 345	119	101.5	4 260	295 851	143	69.4	89.9	0.5	0.7	1.5	0.1	4.9
1123	Boston-Worcester-Lawrence-Lowell-Brockton, MA-NH	16 711	6 057 826	4	362.5	16 706	5 685 769	4	340.3	85.4	5.0	0.2	3.9	0.0	3.2
1240	Brownsville-Harlingen-San Benito, TX	2 346	335 227	147	142.9	2 345	260 120	158	110.9	80.3	0.5	0.4	0.5	0.0	16.0
1260	Bryan-College Station, TX	1 517	152 415	235	100.5	1 517	121 862	259	80.3	74.5	10.7	0.4	4.0	0.1	8.4
1280	Buffalo-Niagara Falls, NY	4 059	1 170 111	51	288.3	4 060	1 189 340	44	292.9	83.8	11.7	0.7	1.3	0.0	1.2
1303	Burlington, VT	3 260	198 889	202	61.0	3 260	177 059	198	54.3	95.4	0.7	0.6	1.5	0.0	0.3
1320	Canton-Massillon, OH	2 514	406 934	123	161.8	2 514	394 106	115	156.8	90.8	6.7	0.2	0.5	0.0	0.3
1350	Casper, WY	13 830	66 533	317	4.8	13 831	61 226	317	4.4	94.2	0.8	1.0	0.4	0.0	1.9
1360	Cedar Rapids, IA	1 858	191 701	207	103.2	1 858	168 767	205	90.8	93.9	2.6	0.2	1.4	0.0	0.5
1400	Champaign-Urbana, IL	2 582	179 669	214	69.6	2 583	173 025	202	67.0	78.8	11.2	0.2	6.5	0.0	1.3
1480	Charleston, WV	3 236	251 662	173	77.8	3 236	250 454	165	77.4	92.0	5.7	0.2	0.8	0.0	0.2
1440	Charleston-North Charleston, SC	6 711	549 033	96	81.8	6 713	506 877	92	75.5	65.1	30.8	0.4	1.3	0.1	1.0
1520	Charlotte-Gastonia-Rock Hill, NC-SC	8 746	1 499 293	43	171.4	8 751	1 161 546	45	132.7	73.6	20.5	0.4	1.9	0.0	2.3
1540	Charlottesville, VA	3 048	159 576	229	52.4	3 049	131 373	245	43.1	80.6	14.0	0.2	2.9	0.0	0.8
1560	Chattanooga, TN-GA	4 723	465 161	110	98.5	4 726	424 176	105	89.8	82.8	14.2	0.3	1.0	0.0	0.6
1580	Cheyenne, WY	6 957	81 607	313	11.7	6 957	73 142	313	10.5	88.9	2.6	0.8	1.0	0.1	4.0
14	Chicago-Gary-Kenosha, IL-IN-WI	17 941	9 157 540	X	510.4	17 951	8 239 820	X	459.0	66.8	18.6	0.3	4.2	0.0	7.7
1600	Chicago, IL	13 111	8 272 768	3	631.0	13 119	7 410 858	3	564.9	65.8	18.9	0.3	4.6	0.0	8.2
2960	Gary, IN	2 370	631 362	82	266.4	2 370	604 526	78	255.1	73.4	19.7	0.3	0.8	0.0	4.1
3740	Kankakee, IL	1 753	103 833	296	59.2	1 755	96 255	297	54.8	79.9	15.5	0.2	0.7	0.0	2.4
3800	Kenosha, WI	707	149 577	240	211.7	707	128 181	251	181.3	88.4	5.1	0.4	0.9	0.0	3.3
1620	Chico-Paradise, CA	4 246	203 171	200	47.8	4 247	182 120	195	42.9	84.5	1.4	1.9	3.3	0.1	4.8
21	Cincinnati-Hamilton, OH-KY-IN	9 865	1 979 202	X	200.6	9 868	1 817 542	X	184.2	85.3	11.7	0.2	1.2	0.0	0.5
1640	Cincinnati, OH-KY-IN	8 655	1 646 395	33	190.2	8 658	1 526 063	30	176.3	84.1	13.0	0.2	1.2	0.0	0.4
3200	Hamilton-Middletown, OH	1 210	332 807	149	275.0	1 210	291 479	147	240.9	91.2	5.3	0.2	1.5	0.0	0.4
1660	Clarksville-Hopkinsville, TN-KY	3 265	207 033	199	63.4	3 264	169 439	204	51.9	72.0	20.8	0.5	1.5	0.2	2.2
28	Cleveland-Akron, OH	9 355	2 945 831	X	314.9	9 357	2 859 662	X	305.6	79.0	16.8	0.2	1.3	0.0	1.2
0080	Akron, OH	2 344	694 960	77	296.5	2 344	657 575	74	280.5	85.9	11.0	0.2	1.3	0.0	0.3
1680	Cleveland-Lorain-Elyria, OH	7 011	2 250 871	24	321.1	7 013	2 202 087	20	314.0	76.9	18.5	0.2	1.4	0.0	1.4
1720	Colorado Springs, CO	5 507	516 929	101	93.9	5 508	397 014	113	72.1	81.2	6.5	0.9	2.5	0.2	4.7
1740	Columbia, MO	1 775	135 454	258	76.3	1 775	112 379	276	63.3	85.4	8.5	0.4	3.0	0.0	0.7

[1]MSA = Metropolitan Statistical Area. PMSA = Primary MSA. NECMA = New England County Metropolitan Area. See Appendix A for explanation of these concepts. See Appendix B for list of metropolitan areas identified by type, with component counties.
[2]Dry land or land partially or temporarily covered by water.

Table C. Metropolitan Areas

Area Name	Population and population characteristics, 2000 (cont'd) Race (percent) (cont'd) — Race alone or in combination								Population and population characteristics, 1990 Race (percent)				
	Two or more races	White	Black	American Indian or Alaska Native	Asian	Native Hawaiian and other Pacific Islander	Some other race	Hispanic[1]	White	Black or African American	American Indian or Alaska Native	Asian and Pacific Islander	Hispanic[1]
	15	16	17	18	19	20	21	22	23	24	25	26	27
Abilene, TX	2.4	82.7	7.4	1.2	1.8	0.1	9.4	17.6	83.8	6.3	0.4	1.2	14.6
Albany, GA	0.7	47.4	51.4	0.5	0.8	0.1	0.7	1.3	53.3	45.8	0.2	0.4	0.8
Albany-Schenectady-Troy, NY	1.5	90.6	6.8	0.6	2.1	0.1	1.4	2.7	93.3	4.7	0.2	1.2	1.8
Albuquerque, NM	4.2	73.2	3.1	6.6	2.2	0.2	19.0	41.6	76.9	2.7	3.4	1.5	37.1
Alexandria, LA	1.0	67.3	30.8	1.2	1.0	0.1	0.7	1.4	70.7	28.0	0.4	0.7	1.2
Allentown-Bethlehem-Easton, PA	1.5	91.1	3.5	0.4	1.9	0.1	4.7	7.9	94.6	2.0	0.1	1.1	4.2
Altoona, PA	0.6	98.2	1.4	0.3	0.5	0.0	0.2	0.5	98.7	0.8	0.1	0.3	0.3
Amarillo, TX	2.1	80.9	6.3	1.4	2.1	0.1	11.4	19.6	84.5	5.2	0.7	1.7	13.5
Anchorage, AK	6.0	77.2	7.2	10.4	7.1	1.4	3.3	5.7	80.7	6.4	6.4	4.8	4.1
Anniston, AL	1.0	79.7	18.8	0.8	0.8	0.1	0.8	1.6	80.0	18.6	0.3	0.7	1.1
Appleton-Oshkosh-Neenah, WI	0.9	95.4	1.0	1.3	2.2	0.1	0.9	1.9	97.4	0.3	0.9	1.2	0.7
Asheville, NC	1.2	90.9	7.3	0.9	0.8	0.1	1.4	2.7	90.9	8.2	0.3	0.4	0.7
Athens, GA	1.2	74.2	20.9	0.5	2.7	0.1	2.9	5.1	79.4	18.6	0.2	1.5	1.3
Atlanta, GA	1.7	64.2	29.6	0.7	3.7	0.1	3.6	6.5	71.3	26.0	0.2	1.8	2.0
Auburn-Opalika, AL	0.9	74.9	22.9	0.6	1.9	0.1	0.7	1.4	74.5	23.4	0.2	1.8	0.6
Augusta-Aiken, GA-SC	1.5	62.6	35.0	0.8	1.9	0.2	1.2	2.4	66.7	31.1	0.2	1.4	1.4
Austin-San Marcos, TX	2.6	74.7	8.5	1.1	4.1	0.2	14.3	26.2	76.8	9.2	0.4	2.4	20.5
Bakersfield, CA	4.1	65.1	6.6	2.6	4.2	0.3	25.6	38.4	69.6	5.5	1.3	3.0	28.0
Bangor, ME	1.0	97.5	0.7	1.4	0.9	0.1	0.4	0.6	97.3	0.5	1.1	0.9	0.6
Barnstable-Yarmouth, MA	1.7	95.6	2.4	1.0	0.8	0.1	1.9	1.3	96.2	1.5	0.6	0.5	0.0
Baton Rouge, LA	0.9	65.6	32.2	0.5	1.7	0.1	0.8	1.8	68.8	29.6	0.2	1.1	1.4
Beaumont-Port Arthur, TX	1.4	69.3	25.1	0.8	2.3	0.1	3.8	8.0	73.2	23.4	0.2	1.6	4.2
Bellingham, WA	2.7	90.8	1.1	3.8	3.7	0.3	3.2	5.2	93.3	0.5	3.1	1.8	2.9
Benton Harbor, MI	1.6	81.0	16.7	1.0	1.4	0.1	1.6	3.0	82.6	15.4	0.4	0.9	1.7
Billings, MT	1.9	94.5	0.8	4.1	0.8	0.1	1.7	3.7	95.2	0.5	2.9	0.5	2.8
Biloxi-Gulfport-Pascagoula, MS	1.4	77.1	19.8	0.9	2.4	0.1	1.1	2.3	79.3	17.8	0.3	2.3	1.8
Binghamton, NY	1.5	93.9	3.3	0.6	2.6	0.1	1.1	1.8	96.2	1.8	0.2	1.5	1.1
Birmingham, AL	0.8	68.0	30.3	0.6	1.0	0.1	0.9	1.8	72.2	27.1	0.2	0.4	0.4
Bismarck, ND	0.9	96.1	0.4	3.6	0.5	0.0	0.3	0.7	97.0	0.1	2.4	0.3	0.5
Bloomington, IN	1.6	92.3	3.5	0.7	3.9	0.1	1.2	1.9	94.3	2.6	0.2	2.5	1.3
Bloomington-Normal, IL	1.4	90.4	6.8	0.5	2.3	0.1	1.3	2.5	93.7	4.3	0.2	1.3	1.3
Boise City, ID	2.4	92.1	0.8	1.5	2.1	0.3	5.8	8.8	96.7	0.5	0.7	1.4	2.7
Boston-Worcester-Lawrence-Lowell-Brockton, MA-NH	2.2	87.0	5.8	0.6	4.3	0.1	4.5	6.0	88.9	5.7	0.2	2.9	4.6
Brownsville-Harlingen-San Benito, TX	2.3	82.4	0.6	0.6	0.6	0.1	18.0	84.3	82.4	0.3	0.2	0.3	81.9
Bryan-College Station, TX	2.0	76.2	11.0	0.8	4.4	0.1	9.5	17.9	77.8	11.2	0.2	3.5	13.7
Buffalo-Niagara Falls, NY	1.3	84.8	12.3	1.0	1.5	0.1	1.7	2.9	87.2	10.3	0.6	0.9	2.0
Burlington, VT	1.4	96.7	1.0	1.3	1.8	0.1	0.6	0.9	97.8	0.6	0.2	1.1	0.9
Canton-Massillon, OH	1.4	92.1	7.4	0.7	0.7	0.0	0.5	0.9	92.8	6.4	0.3	0.4	0.7
Casper, WY	1.7	95.7	1.1	1.8	0.6	0.1	2.5	4.9	96.9	0.7	0.7	0.5	3.7
Cedar Rapids, IA	1.4	95.2	3.3	0.6	1.7	0.1	0.7	1.4	96.7	2.0	0.2	0.8	0.9
Champaign-Urbana, IL	2.0	80.4	12.0	0.7	7.1	0.1	1.8	2.9	84.7	9.6	0.2	4.6	2.0
Charleston, WV	1.1	93.0	6.2	0.6	1.0	0.0	0.4	0.6	93.6	5.6	0.1	0.6	0.4
Charleston-North Charleston, SC	1.3	66.1	31.3	0.8	1.7	0.1	1.3	2.4	67.8	30.2	0.3	1.2	1.5
Charlotte-Gastonia-Rock Hill, NC-SC	1.2	74.6	21.0	0.7	2.2	0.1	2.8	5.1	78.5	19.9	0.4	1.0	0.9
Charlottesville, VA	1.5	81.9	14.7	0.5	3.4	0.1	1.1	2.2	83.2	14.4	0.1	2.0	1.1
Chattanooga, TN-GA	1.0	83.7	14.6	0.7	1.2	0.1	0.9	1.5	85.5	13.4	0.2	0.7	0.6
Cheyenne, WY	2.6	91.2	3.2	1.7	1.5	0.2	4.9	10.9	90.6	3.0	0.7	1.1	10.0
Chicago-Gary-Kenosha, IL-IN-WI	2.2	68.7	19.2	0.6	4.7	0.1	9.0	16.4	71.6	19.2	0.2	3.2	11.1
Chicago, IL	2.3	67.7	19.4	0.6	5.1	0.1	9.5	17.1	67.5	22.0	0.2	3.8	12.1
Gary, IN	1.7	74.8	20.1	0.7	1.1	0.1	5.0	10.5	76.2	19.4	0.2	0.6	8.0
Kankakee, IL	1.4	81.1	16.0	0.6	0.9	0.1	2.9	4.8	83.3	15.0	0.2	0.7	2.0
Kenosha, WI	1.9	90.1	5.8	0.9	1.2	0.1	4.0	7.2	93.0	4.1	0.4	0.5	4.4
Chico-Paradise, CA	3.9	88.0	1.9	3.6	4.1	0.3	6.3	10.5	90.7	1.3	1.8	2.8	7.5
Cincinnati-Hamilton, OH-KY-IN	1.1	86.3	12.1	0.6	1.5	0.1	0.7	1.1	87.2	11.7	0.1	0.8	0.5
Cincinnati, OH-KY-IN	1.1	85.0	13.5	0.6	1.4	0.1	0.6	1.1	85.8	13.1	0.1	0.8	0.5
Hamilton-Middletown, OH	1.1	92.2	5.7	0.6	1.8	0.1	0.8	1.4	94.3	4.5	0.1	0.9	0.5
Clarksville-Hopkinsville, TN-KY	2.7	74.2	21.9	1.2	2.2	0.4	3.0	5.0	75.9	20.5	0.4	1.6	3.3
Cleveland-Akron, OH	1.5	80.3	17.4	0.6	1.6	0.1	1.6	2.7	81.9	16.0	0.2	1.0	1.9
Akron, OH	1.3	87.0	11.6	0.7	1.5	0.1	0.5	0.8	88.8	9.9	0.2	0.9	0.6
Cleveland-Lorain-Elyria, OH	1.6	78.2	19.2	0.6	1.6	0.1	2.0	3.3	78.4	19.4	0.2	1.1	1.9
Colorado Springs, CO	3.9	84.5	7.7	2.0	3.6	0.5	6.0	11.3	86.0	7.2	0.8	2.5	8.7
Columbia, MO	1.9	87.1	9.4	1.0	3.4	0.1	1.1	1.8	89.0	7.5	0.4	2.8	1.1

[1] Hispanic persons may be of any race.

Table C. Metropolitan Areas

Area Name	Under 5 years	5 to 17 years	18 to 24 years	25 to 34 years	35 to 44 years	45 to 54 years	55 to 64 years	65 to 74 years	75 years and over	Median age (years)	Percent Female
	28	29	30	31	32	33	34	35	36	37	38
Abilene, TX	7.2	19.4	13.8	13.1	14.7	11.5	7.8	6.5	5.9	32.2	51.5
Albany, GA	7.6	20.7	11.4	14.0	14.8	13.1	7.9	5.9	4.7	32.3	52.6
Albany-Schenectady-Troy, NY	6.0	17.9	9.5	13.0	16.1	14.4	8.8	7.1	7.2	37.3	51.5
Albuquerque, NM	7.0	19.3	9.8	14.0	16.3	14.0	8.4	6.0	5.3	34.9	51.0
Alexandria, LA	7.1	20.2	9.5	12.6	15.3	13.2	9.2	7.1	6.0	35.5	52.2
Allentown-Bethlehem-Easton, PA	5.7	17.8	8.4	12.4	16.4	14.1	9.1	8.0	8.1	38.6	51.5
Altoona, PA	5.6	17.1	8.9	12.0	15.0	14.3	9.7	8.6	8.8	39.5	52.1
Amarillo, TX	7.6	19.5	11.1	13.8	15.5	12.6	8.0	6.4	5.4	33.4	50.5
Anchorage, AK	7.7	21.5	9.6	15.4	18.5	14.9	7.0	3.4	2.1	32.4	49.4
Anniston, AL	6.2	17.4	10.4	12.9	15.0	14.2	9.8	8.0	6.2	37.2	52.2
Appleton-Oshkosh-Neenah, WI	6.5	19.6	10.0	14.0	17.2	13.2	7.9	5.9	5.7	35.0	50.1
Asheville, NC	5.7	16.2	8.8	13.5	15.6	14.8	10.1	8.0	7.5	38.9	51.9
Athens, GA	5.8	15.6	23.3	15.3	13.1	11.3	6.9	4.6	4.1	28.1	51.1
Atlanta, GA	7.5	19.1	9.5	17.6	17.8	13.5	7.4	4.2	3.3	32.9	50.6
Auburn-Opalika, AL	6.3	17.0	22.7	14.5	13.6	11.0	6.8	4.6	3.5	27.5	50.8
Augusta-Aiken, GA-SC	6.9	20.2	9.9	13.7	16.1	13.7	8.5	6.2	4.8	34.6	51.5
Austin-San Marcos, TX	7.4	17.9	13.4	18.3	17.0	12.5	6.3	4.0	3.3	30.9	49.2
Bakersfield, CA	8.4	23.5	10.2	14.1	15.7	11.6	7.1	5.2	4.2	30.6	48.7
Bangor, ME	5.4	17.5	11.3	12.5	16.5	14.6	9.2	7.2	5.8	37.2	51.2
Barnstable-Yarmouth, MA	4.8	15.7	5.2	9.7	15.3	14.8	11.5	11.9	11.2	44.6	52.7
Baton Rouge, LA	7.3	20.0	12.8	14.2	15.4	13.1	7.8	5.2	4.2	31.9	51.6
Beaumont-Port Arthur, TX	6.7	19.7	9.6	13.1	15.8	13.2	8.6	7.1	6.1	35.6	50.1
Bellingham, WA	6.1	18.0	14.2	12.8	14.6	14.4	8.2	5.9	5.7	34.0	50.7
Benton Harbor, MI	6.5	19.5	8.3	12.1	15.4	14.1	9.6	7.5	6.9	37.4	51.5
Billings, MT	6.6	18.9	9.3	12.6	16.2	14.4	8.8	6.8	6.5	36.9	51.2
Biloxi-Gulfport-Pascagoula, MS	7.0	19.5	10.0	13.8	16.1	13.2	9.1	6.6	4.6	34.7	50.3
Binghamton, NY	5.8	18.1	10.2	11.3	16.0	13.6	9.5	7.9	7.8	38.1	51.5
Birmingham, AL	6.7	18.4	9.2	14.3	16.0	14.0	8.7	6.8	5.9	35.9	52.2
Bismarck, ND	6.3	19.0	10.2	12.6	16.4	14.3	8.2	6.8	6.2	36.3	50.9
Bloomington, IN	5.1	12.9	27.7	14.7	12.6	11.1	6.7	4.9	4.3	27.6	50.9
Bloomington-Normal, IL	6.5	17.0	18.6	14.2	15.0	12.2	6.9	5.0	4.7	30.5	51.7
Boise City, ID	8.1	20.3	10.4	15.5	15.8	13.0	7.3	4.9	4.8	32.1	50.0
Boston-Worcester-Lawrence-Lowell-Brockton, MA-NH	6.4	17.6	8.9	15.0	17.2	13.8	8.5	6.4	6.3	36.2	51.6
Brownsville-Harlingen-San Benito, TX	9.5	24.3	10.5	13.8	12.9	10.7	7.1	6.3	4.8	29.0	52.1
Bryan-College Station, TX	6.2	15.3	32.0	14.5	11.4	8.6	5.2	3.5	3.2	23.6	49.5
Buffalo-Niagara Falls, NY	6.1	18.3	8.7	12.4	16.0	13.7	9.1	8.0	7.8	38.0	52.1
Burlington, VT	6.1	18.6	11.5	14.2	17.6	14.2	8.1	5.4	4.5	34.8	51.0
Canton-Massillon, OH	6.4	18.5	8.2	12.1	15.6	14.5	9.6	7.7	7.3	38.3	51.9
Casper, WY	6.5	19.5	10.1	12.1	15.8	14.7	8.6	7.1	5.6	36.4	50.6
Cedar Rapids, IA	7.0	18.3	10.1	14.3	15.9	13.6	8.5	6.2	6.1	35.2	51.0
Champaign-Urbana, IL	5.8	15.3	23.1	14.7	13.5	11.4	6.6	5.1	4.7	28.6	49.7
Charleston, WV	5.9	16.2	8.2	12.8	15.8	15.6	10.1	8.2	7.2	39.6	52.1
Charleston-North Charleston, SC	6.7	19.1	11.2	14.7	16.1	13.4	8.6	5.8	4.5	33.9	50.9
Charlotte-Gastonia-Rock Hill, NC-SC	7.1	18.3	9.1	16.7	17.1	13.4	8.2	5.6	4.6	34.3	50.9
Charlottesville, VA	5.9	16.3	14.6	14.3	15.5	13.3	8.4	6.5	5.3	34.3	52.4
Chattanooga, TN-GA	6.2	17.6	9.3	13.6	15.5	14.5	9.8	7.4	6.1	37.2	51.9
Cheyenne, WY	6.6	19.2	9.6	14.2	16.3	14.1	8.6	6.1	5.3	35.3	49.8
Chicago-Gary-Kenosha, IL-IN-WI	7.4	19.5	9.5	15.3	16.3	13.0	8.1	5.7	5.2	33.9	51.1
Chicago, IL	7.5	19.5	9.5	15.6	16.3	13.0	8.0	5.6	5.1	33.7	51.1
Gary, IN	7.0	19.6	9.4	12.6	15.8	14.1	9.0	6.8	5.8	36.0	51.6
Kankakee, IL	7.0	20.1	9.7	12.9	15.3	13.2	8.8	6.7	6.3	35.2	51.1
Kenosha, WI	6.9	20.1	9.4	13.9	17.4	12.9	7.9	5.9	5.6	34.8	50.4
Chico-Paradise, CA	5.7	18.3	13.6	11.4	13.4	13.2	8.6	7.5	8.3	35.8	51.0
Cincinnati-Hamilton, OH-KY-IN	7.0	19.4	9.5	14.1	16.6	13.5	8.2	6.3	5.4	35.0	51.4
Cincinnati, OH-KY-IN	7.1	19.5	9.0	14.2	16.6	13.4	8.3	6.3	5.6	35.1	51.5
Hamilton-Middletown, OH	6.9	19.0	11.9	13.4	16.4	13.6	8.1	6.1	4.6	34.2	51.2
Clarksville-Hopkinsville, TN-KY	9.0	19.4	13.5	17.9	15.0	10.2	6.6	4.8	3.7	29.3	49.3
Cleveland-Akron, OH	6.6	18.7	8.2	13.2	16.1	14.0	9.0	7.3	7.0	37.2	52.0
Akron, OH	6.5	18.2	9.5	13.2	16.2	14.2	8.7	7.1	6.4	36.6	51.7
Cleveland-Lorain-Elyria, OH	6.6	18.8	7.8	13.1	16.1	13.9	9.0	7.4	7.2	37.3	52.1
Colorado Springs, CO	7.6	20.0	10.5	14.9	17.6	13.4	7.3	4.9	3.8	33.0	49.8
Columbia, MO	6.2	16.6	19.9	15.2	14.7	12.1	6.6	4.4	4.2	29.5	51.7

Table C. Metropolitan Areas

Area Name	Under 5 years	5 to 17 years	18 to 24 years	25 to 34 years	35 to 44 years	45 to 54 years	55 to 64 years	65 to 74 years	75 years and over	Percent Female	2000	1990	1980	1990–2000	1980–1990
	Age (percent)										Total persons			Percent change	
	39	40	41	42	43	44	45	46	47	48	49	50	51	52	53
Abilene, TX	8.2	19.0	13.4	17.3	13.3	8.8	7.9	6.6	5.4	51.4	126 555	119 655	110 932	5.8	7.9
Albany, GA	8.3	22.4	11.6	15.9	14.9	9.5	7.8	5.9	3.7	52.5	120 822	112 571	112 394	7.3	0.2
Albany-Schenectady-Troy, NY	6.8	16.4	11.7	16.8	15.3	10.0	8.8	8.0	6.2	51.7	875 583	861 623	824 729	1.6	4.5
Albuquerque, NM	7.7	18.4	10.5	18.7	16.2	10.1	7.9	6.4	4.1	51.2	712 738	589 131	485 430	21.0	21.4
Alexandria, LA	7.7	21.4	10.3	16.5	13.8	9.9	8.4	7.0	5.0	52.1	126 337	131 556	135 282	-4.0	-2.8
Allentown-Bethlehem-Easton, PA	6.7	16.4	9.9	16.4	15.3	10.4	9.7	8.9	6.3	51.7	637 958	595 043	551 052	7.2	8.0
Altoona, PA	6.3	18.1	9.2	14.5	14.5	10.2	10.2	9.8	7.2	52.9	129 144	130 542	136 621	-1.1	-4.4
Amarillo, TX	8.2	19.9	10.4	17.2	14.5	9.5	8.7	6.7	4.9	51.9	217 858	187 514	173 699	16.2	8.0
Anchorage, AK	9.5	20.0	10.6	21.5	19.2	10.3	5.3	2.7	1.0	48.6	260 283	226 338	174 431	15.0	29.8
Anniston, AL	6.4	18.6	12.9	15.9	14.5	10.2	9.1	7.4	5.0	51.7	112 249	116 032	119 761	-3.3	-3.1
Appleton-Oshkosh-Neenah, WI	7.7	19.1	11.0	17.9	14.9	9.7	8.0	6.5	5.4	50.8	358 365	315 121	291 369	13.7	8.2
Asheville, NC	6.3	16.0	9.4	15.4	15.7	11.2	9.9	9.2	6.9	52.5	225 965	191 310	177 761	18.1	7.9
Athens, GA	6.6	16.5	20.5	16.9	13.9	9.2	6.7	5.5	4.2	51.7	153 444	126 262	104 672	21.5	20.6
Atlanta, GA	7.7	18.1	10.9	20.3	17.5	10.7	6.9	4.8	3.2	51.3	4 112 198	2 959 500	2 233 229	38.9	32.5
Auburn-Opalika, AL	6.2	15.7	26.0	15.6	12.5	8.6	6.7	5.0	3.6	50.4	115 092	87 146	76 283	32.1	14.2
Augusta-Aiken, GA-SC	7.9	20.0	11.1	17.7	15.4	9.9	8.1	6.2	3.7	51.3	477 441	415 220	363 451	15.0	14.2
Austin-San Marcos, TX	7.8	17.5	15.3	21.2	16.4	8.6	5.8	4.3	3.1	50.1	1 249 763	846 227	585 051	47.7	44.6
Bakersfield, CA	9.6	21.8	10.0	18.2	14.3	9.0	7.2	5.9	3.8	49.6	661 645	544 981	403 089	21.4	35.2
Bangor, ME	6.3	16.1	16.6	16.6	15.0	9.5	8.3	6.4	5.3	51.6	144 919	146 601	137 015	-1.1	7.0
Barnstable-Yarmouth, MA	6.4	14.6	7.5	14.6	14.9	9.4	10.6	12.5	9.5	53.0	222 230	186 605	147 925	19.1	26.1
Baton Rouge, LA	7.8	20.8	12.9	17.5	15.3	9.6	7.1	5.5	3.4	51.7	602 894	528 261	494 151	14.1	6.9
Beaumont-Port Arthur, TX	7.3	20.3	9.4	15.9	14.2	10.2	9.6	7.7	5.4	51.7	385 090	361 218	373 211	6.6	-3.2
Bellingham, WA	6.9	18.2	13.1	15.7	16.4	9.6	7.6	7.0	5.5	50.8	166 814	127 780	106 701	30.5	19.8
Benton Harbor, MI	7.4	19.6	9.7	15.5	14.4	10.4	9.3	8.0	5.7	52.1	162 453	161 378	171 276	0.7	-5.8
Billings, MT	7.4	19.8	8.9	16.7	16.0	10.3	8.6	7.2	5.2	51.5	129 352	113 419	108 035	14.0	5.0
Biloxi-Gulfport-Pascagoula, MS	7.9	19.6	11.6	17.4	13.8	9.6	8.8	7.1	4.2	50.2	363 988	312 368	300 176	16.5	4.1
Binghamton, NY	7.0	16.9	11.2	16.8	14.2	10.4	9.3	8.1	6.1	51.6	252 320	264 497	263 460	-4.6	0.4
Birmingham, AL	7.0	18.4	9.9	16.8	15.5	10.2	9.0	7.6	5.6	52.7	921 106	839 942	815 333	9.7	3.0
Bismarck, ND	7.4	21.1	9.2	17.2	15.7	9.6	8.3	6.3	5.1	51.2	94 719	83 831	79 988	13.0	4.8
Bloomington, IN	5.5	12.9	29.0	16.8	12.8	8.0	6.5	4.9	3.7	51.7	120 563	108 978	98 787	10.6	10.3
Bloomington-Normal, IL	6.6	16.5	20.7	16.3	14.0	8.6	6.9	5.7	4.8	52.3	150 433	129 180	119 149	16.5	8.4
Boise City, ID	7.7	20.6	9.8	17.7	16.9	10.0	6.8	6.0	4.4	50.8	432 345	295 851	256 881	46.1	15.2
Boston-Worcester-Lawrence-Lowell-Brockton, MA-NH	6.9	15.3	11.9	19.3	15.7	10.3	8.4	6.9	5.5	51.8	6 057 826	5 685 769	5 336 242	6.5	6.5
Brownsville-Harlingen-San Benito, TX	8.9	26.4	11.3	14.6	12.8	8.1	7.3	6.4	4.2	52.1	335 227	260 120	209 727	28.9	24.0
Bryan-College Station, TX	6.8	14.7	32.0	17.5	11.0	6.7	4.7	3.7	3.0	48.6	152 415	121 862	93 588	25.1	30.2
Buffalo-Niagara Falls, NY	6.9	16.7	10.5	16.4	14.3	10.0	9.9	9.0	6.2	52.3	1 170 111	1 189 340	1 242 826	-1.6	-4.3
Burlington, VT	7.2	16.2	16.5	19.1	16.2	9.8	6.8	4.7	3.5	51.5	198 889	177 059	154 935	12.3	14.3
Canton-Massillon, OH	6.9	18.4	9.3	15.5	15.2	10.7	9.6	8.5	5.8	52.1	406 934	394 106	404 421	3.3	-2.6
Casper, WY	7.6	21.5	8.3	16.6	16.5	10.0	8.9	6.7	3.9	50.9	66 533	61 226	71 856	8.7	-14.8
Cedar Rapids, IA	7.1	18.1	11.0	17.2	15.5	10.6	8.4	6.8	5.4	51.4	191 701	168 767	169 775	13.6	-0.6
Champaign-Urbana, IL	6.8	15.0	22.7	18.9	13.6	7.9	6.4	5.0	3.8	49.4	179 669	173 025	168 392	3.8	2.8
Charleston, WV	6.0	17.8	8.5	15.5	15.9	11.0	10.3	8.9	6.0	52.5	251 662	250 454	269 595	0.5	-7.1
Charleston-North Charleston, SC	8.6	19.0	13.0	19.7	15.0	9.2	6.9	5.5	3.1	50.1	549 033	506 877	430 346	8.3	17.8
Charlotte-Gastonia-Rock Hill, NC-SC	7.3	17.4	11.1	18.3	15.8	10.7	8.4	6.6	4.3	51.8	1 499 293	1 161 546	971 447	29.1	19.6
Charlottesville, VA	6.8	14.9	16.6	18.7	15.0	9.4	7.7	6.3	4.5	51.7	159 576	131 373	113 568	21.5	15.7
Chattanooga, TN-GA	6.6	18.1	10.1	15.9	15.5	11.2	9.5	7.5	5.5	52.3	465 161	424 176	417 838	9.7	1.6
Cheyenne, WY	8.0	19.8	9.9	17.8	15.8	10.2	8.1	6.1	4.2	50.2	81 607	73 142	68 649	11.6	6.5
Chicago-Gary-Kenosha, IL-IN-WI	7.7	18.4	10.4	18.3	15.2	10.3	8.3	6.7	4.6	51.4	9 157 540	8 239 820	8 114 844	11.1	1.5
Chicago, IL	7.6	17.8	10.5	18.6	15.0	10.2	8.5	7.0	4.9	51.7	8 272 768	7 410 858	7 246 048	11.6	2.3
Gary, IN	7.1	20.8	9.7	15.9	15.0	10.5	9.1	7.4	4.4	51.8	631 362	604 526	642 733	4.4	-5.9
Kankakee, IL	7.6	20.6	9.9	15.3	14.3	10.1	8.6	7.9	5.8	51.6	103 833	96 255	102 926	7.9	-6.5
Kenosha, WI	7.9	18.9	10.3	17.2	14.5	10.2	8.3	7.2	5.4	51.1	149 577	128 181	123 137	16.7	4.1
Chico-Paradise, CA	6.8	16.8	13.8	14.5	13.9	8.7	8.4	10.1	7.2	51.0	203 171	182 120	143 851	11.6	26.6
Cincinnati-Hamilton, OH-KY-IN	7.8	18.9	10.7	17.5	14.9	9.9	8.5	6.7	5.0	52.0	1 979 202	1 817 542	1 726 430	8.9	5.3
Cincinnati, OH-KY-IN	7.9	18.9	10.2	17.7	14.9	9.8	8.6	6.9	5.2	52.0	1 646 395	1 526 063	1 467 643	7.9	4.0
Hamilton-Middletown, OH	7.4	18.8	13.2	16.7	15.2	10.1	8.5	6.1	4.1	51.6	332 807	291 479	258 787	14.2	12.6
Clarksville-Hopkinsville, TN-KY	8.6	17.7	16.6	19.9	13.3	8.3	6.9	5.0	3.7	47.7	207 033	169 439	150 220	22.2	12.8
Cleveland-Akron, OH	7.1	17.7	9.9	16.6	15.0	10.3	9.4	8.3	5.6	52.3	2 945 831	2 859 662	2 938 277	3.0	-2.7
Akron, OH	6.9	17.5	11.8	16.5	15.2	10.1	9.2	7.8	5.1	51.9	694 960	657 575	660 328	5.7	-0.4
Cleveland-Lorain-Elyria, OH	7.1	17.5	9.2	16.7	14.9	10.4	9.6	8.7	5.9	52.6	2 250 871	2 202 087	2 277 949	2.2	-3.3
Colorado Springs, CO	8.5	19.1	12.2	19.6	16.1	9.6	7.0	5.0	3.0	49.8	516 929	397 014	309 424	30.2	28.3
Columbia, MO	7.1	15.5	22.1	18.9	14.2	8.1	5.8	4.6	3.8	51.6	135 454	112 379	100 376	20.5	12.0

Table C. Metropolitan Areas

Area Name	Total population	Total in households	House-holder	Spouse	Child: Total	Child: Own child under 18 years	Other relatives: Total	Other relatives: Under 18 years	Nonrelatives: Total	Nonrelatives: Unmarried partner	Total in group quarters	Correctional institutions	Nursing homes	Other institutions	College dormitories	Military quarters	Other
	54	55	56	57	58	59	60	61	62	63	64	65	66	67	68	69	70
Abilene, TX	126 555	95.0	37.4	20.1	28.8	23.8	4.3	2.1	4.5	1.5	5.0	0.3	0.6	0.0	2.2	0.7	1.1
Albany, GA	120 822	95.6	36.2	16.5	31.7	23.8	7.1	3.7	4.1	1.9	4.4	1.5	0.5	0.0	1.0	0.2	1.3
Albany-Schenectady-Troy, NY	875 583	96.3	40.0	19.4	28.2	22.1	3.2	1.1	5.4	2.6	3.7	0.3	0.9	0.2	1.8	0.0	0.5
Albuquerque, NM	712 738	98.2	38.6	18.6	29.6	23.1	5.7	2.5	5.7	2.6	1.8	0.4	0.3	0.1	0.3	0.1	0.6
Alexandria, LA	126 337	95.6	37.3	18.5	30.6	23.4	5.8	3.0	3.4	1.7	4.4	1.1	1.1	0.5	0.4	0.0	1.3
Allentown-Bethlehem-Easton, PA	637 958	96.6	38.7	21.1	28.3	21.6	3.9	1.3	4.4	2.3	3.4	0.3	1.1	0.2	1.4	0.0	0.4
Altoona, PA	129 144	96.8	39.9	21.0	28.4	20.8	3.5	1.4	4.1	2.0	3.2	0.2	1.7	0.1	0.7	0.0	0.6
Amarillo, TX	217 858	96.0	37.6	19.7	29.6	24.2	4.8	2.3	4.1	1.7	4.0	2.4	0.7	0.1	0.5	0.0	0.3
Anchorage, AK	260 283	97.3	36.4	18.6	31.5	26.7	3.8	1.5	6.9	2.7	2.7	0.4	0.1	0.2	0.2	0.8	1.0
Anniston, AL	112 249	97.8	40.4	21.1	27.5	20.4	5.4	2.6	3.5	1.4	2.2	0.3	0.4	0.1	1.0	0.0	0.4
Appleton-Oshkosh-Neenah, WI	358 365	96.7	38.1	21.7	30.2	24.9	1.9	0.6	4.7	2.1	3.3	0.9	0.6	0.1	1.2	0.0	0.4
Asheville, NC	225 965	96.6	41.5	21.2	25.0	19.6	4.0	1.5	4.8	2.0	3.4	0.5	0.8	0.3	1.0	0.0	0.7
Athens, GA	153 444	94.4	38.2	16.4	24.1	19.0	4.9	1.9	10.9	1.9	5.6	0.4	0.5	0.0	4.3	0.2	0.2
Atlanta, GA	4 112 198	98.2	36.6	18.8	29.9	23.6	6.6	2.4	6.2	1.9	1.8	0.5	0.3	0.1	0.5	0.0	0.4
Auburn-Opalika, AL	115 092	96.1	39.7	17.5	25.9	20.9	4.6	2.0	8.4	1.5	3.9	0.2	0.3	0.2	3.1	0.0	0.2
Augusta-Aiken, GA-SC	477 441	96.5	37.0	18.9	31.0	23.7	5.8	2.8	3.8	1.7	3.5	1.2	0.3	0.1	0.2	0.9	0.8
Austin-San Marcos, TX	1 249 763	97.0	37.8	18.2	27.6	22.7	5.7	2.1	7.7	2.1	3.0	0.7	0.4	0.1	1.2	0.0	0.5
Bakersfield, CA	661 645	95.5	31.5	17.2	34.6	28.0	7.2	3.1	4.9	2.0	4.5	3.6	0.3	0.1	0.0	0.1	0.4
Bangor, ME	144 919	95.5	40.1	20.6	25.8	21.0	2.5	0.8	6.5	3.0	4.5	0.2	0.6	0.1	2.6	0.0	0.8
Barnstable-Yarmouth, MA	222 230	97.4	42.7	22.3	24.6	18.9	3.1	1.0	4.8	2.1	2.6	0.1	1.0	0.1	0.3	0.0	1.0
Baton Rouge, LA	602 894	97.3	37.0	18.3	31.4	23.8	5.7	2.8	4.8	1.8	2.7	0.4	0.5	0.1	1.3	0.0	0.3
Beaumont-Port Arthur, TX	385 090	95.7	37.0	19.4	30.4	23.2	5.6	2.6	3.3	1.5	4.3	3.3	0.6	0.0	0.2	0.0	0.2
Bellingham, WA	166 814	97.0	38.6	19.8	27.2	22.4	3.1	1.1	8.4	2.3	3.0	0.2	0.4	0.1	1.9	0.0	0.4
Benton Harbor, MI	162 453	97.3	39.1	20.0	29.3	23.0	4.3	2.1	4.5	2.1	2.7	0.3	0.4	0.2	0.5	0.0	1.2
Billings, MT	129 352	97.7	40.3	20.9	28.7	23.6	2.8	1.2	5.1	2.1	2.3	0.4	0.8	0.1	0.6	0.0	0.4
Biloxi-Gulfport-Pascagoula, MS	363 988	97.3	37.4	19.3	30.2	23.1	5.6	2.8	4.9	2.1	2.7	0.4	0.4	0.2	0.0	1.3	0.3
Binghamton, NY	252 320	96.2	39.8	19.8	28.0	22.0	3.0	1.1	5.5	2.4	3.8	0.2	1.0	0.2	2.0	0.0	0.4
Birmingham, AL	921 106	97.8	39.2	20.0	29.6	22.2	5.7	2.5	3.3	1.2	2.2	0.6	0.6	0.1	0.6	0.0	0.4
Bismarck, ND	94 719	96.8	39.7	21.9	29.4	24.2	1.8	0.6	4.1	1.8	3.2	0.8	1.0	0.1	0.9	0.0	0.3
Bloomington, IN	120 563	88.1	38.9	16.2	20.0	16.6	2.2	0.8	10.7	2.3	11.9	0.2	0.4	0.3	10.7	0.0	0.3
Bloomington-Normal, IL	150 433	92.5	37.7	19.2	26.3	22.1	2.3	0.9	6.9	1.8	7.5	0.1	0.6	0.1	6.5	0.0	0.3
Boise City, ID	432 345	97.7	36.6	20.8	31.2	26.4	3.6	1.3	5.4	2.0	2.3	1.0	0.5	0.1	0.4	0.0	0.4
Boston-Worcester-Lawrence-Lowell-Brockton, MA-NH	6 057 826	96.9	38.2	19.1	29.4	22.2	4.4	1.3	5.7	2.1	3.1	0.4	0.8	0.1	1.4	0.0	0.0
Brownsville-Harlingen-San Benito, TX	335 227	98.8	29.0	17.6	38.5	28.0	10.9	5.2	2.7	1.0	1.2	0.4	0.4	0.2	0.1	0.0	0.2
Bryan-College Station, TX	152 415	91.2	36.2	15.0	23.3	19.2	4.7	1.6	12.0	1.3	8.8	1.2	0.4	0.0	7.0	0.0	0.2
Buffalo-Niagara Falls, NY	1 170 111	97.0	40.1	18.9	30.1	22.5	3.6	1.4	4.3	2.0	3.0	0.6	0.9	0.1	0.9	0.0	0.5
Burlington, VT	198 889	96.0	38.2	20.0	27.8	23.2	2.4	0.8	7.5	2.9	4.0	0.2	0.4	0.1	2.9	0.0	0.3
Canton-Massillon, OH	406 934	97.7	39.2	21.4	29.4	22.6	3.7	1.6	4.0	2.0	2.3	0.1	1.1	0.1	0.6	0.0	0.3
Casper, WY	66 533	97.7	40.3	20.7	28.5	23.7	2.8	1.3	5.3	2.6	2.3	0.5	0.7	0.1	0.5	0.0	0.5
Cedar Rapids, IA	191 701	97.4	40.0	21.3	28.5	23.6	2.4	0.9	5.2	2.2	2.6	0.2	0.7	0.0	1.1	0.0	0.6
Champaign-Urbana, IL	179 669	91.7	39.3	17.1	23.2	19.4	2.7	1.1	9.5	2.0	8.3	0.2	0.6	0.0	7.1	0.0	0.3
Charleston, WV	251 662	98.6	42.2	21.9	27.2	20.1	3.8	1.6	3.6	1.9	1.4	0.2	0.5	0.0	0.3	0.0	0.5
Charleston-North Charleston, SC	549 033	96.6	37.9	18.5	29.2	22.5	5.7	2.8	5.3	1.9	3.4	0.9	0.4	0.0	0.9	0.6	0.6
Charlotte-Gastonia-Rock Hill, NC-SC	1 499 293	97.9	38.4	20.3	28.5	22.7	5.4	2.2	5.2	1.9	2.1	0.3	0.6	0.1	0.7	0.0	0.4
Charlottesville, VA	159 576	94.1	38.7	19.0	25.0	20.3	3.7	1.5	7.8	2.0	5.9	0.8	0.8	0.1	3.9	0.0	0.3
Chattanooga, TN-GA	465 161	97.8	39.8	21.2	28.0	21.0	5.2	2.2	3.7	1.5	2.2	0.4	0.6	0.1	0.8	0.0	0.3
Cheyenne, WY	81 607	96.0	39.1	21.1	28.5	23.7	2.9	1.3	4.3	2.0	4.0	2.2	0.6	0.0	0.1	0.7	0.5
Chicago-Gary-Kenosha, IL-IN-WI	9 157 540	98.1	36.1	18.1	31.9	23.6	7.3	2.7	4.7	1.7	1.9	0.2	0.6	0.1	0.5	0.1	0.4
Chicago, IL	8 272 768	98.1	35.9	18.0	31.8	23.6	7.5	2.8	4.8	1.7	1.9	0.2	0.6	0.1	0.5	0.1	0.4
Gary, IN	631 362	98.5	37.4	19.2	32.3	23.4	5.5	2.5	4.0	1.9	1.5	0.2	0.6	0.0	0.4	0.0	0.3
Kankakee, IL	103 833	96.1	36.8	19.4	30.8	24.2	4.5	2.1	4.5	2.1	3.9	0.2	1.2	0.9	1.0	0.0	0.6
Kenosha, WI	149 577	97.3	37.5	19.8	31.1	24.7	3.9	1.6	5.0	2.4	2.7	0.4	0.6	0.0	1.2	0.0	0.4
Chico-Paradise, CA	203 171	97.1	39.2	18.3	26.5	21.4	4.3	1.8	8.9	2.5	2.9	0.3	0.5	0.0	1.3	0.0	0.8
Cincinnati-Hamilton, OH-KY-IN	1 979 202	97.8	38.8	20.0	30.8	24.3	3.9	1.7	4.4	2.0	2.2	0.5	0.8	0.1	0.7	0.0	0.3
Cincinnati, OH-KY-IN	1 646 395	98.0	39.2	19.7	30.9	24.3	3.9	1.7	4.3	2.0	2.0	0.1	0.3	0.0	0.1	0.0	0.1
Hamilton-Middletown, OH	332 807	96.6	37.0	21.1	30.0	23.9	3.7	1.6	4.9	1.9	3.4	0.2	0.7	0.0	2.3	0.0	0.2
Clarksville-Hopkinsville, TN-KY	207 033	95.0	35.4	20.5	31.1	26.0	3.8	1.8	4.2	1.5	5.0	0.4	0.6	0.1	0.4	3.3	0.3
Cleveland-Akron, OH	2 945 831	97.9	39.6	19.4	30.2	22.8	4.5	1.9	4.2	1.9	2.1	0.3	0.8	0.1	0.6	0.0	0.4
Akron, OH	694 960	97.6	39.5	20.2	29.4	22.7	3.8	1.5	4.7	2.0	2.4	0.2	0.7	0.1	1.1	0.0	0.3
Cleveland-Lorain-Elyria, OH	2 250 871	98.0	39.7	19.1	30.4	22.9	4.7	2.0	4.1	1.9	2.0	0.4	0.8	0.1	0.4	0.0	0.4
Colorado Springs, CO	516 929	97.0	37.2	20.7	30.3	25.4	3.6	1.5	5.2	1.8	3.0	0.4	0.4	0.1	0.3	1.6	0.3
Columbia, MO	135 454	93.4	39.2	17.8	25.1	21.3	2.6	0.9	8.7	2.3	6.6	0.2	0.5	0.0	5.5	0.0	0.4

Table C. Metropolitan Areas

Area Name	Total households	Family households Total	Family households With own children under 18 years	Married couple Total	Married couple With own children under 18 years	Female householder[1] Total	Female householder[1] With own children under 18 years	Nonfamily households Total	Householder living alone Total	Householder living alone 65 years and over	Average household size	Average family size	Total households (1990)	Female householder[1] (1990)	Householder living alone (1990)
	71	72	73	74	75	76	77	78	79	80	81	82	83	84	85
Abilene, TX	47 274	68.8	34.7	53.8	25.0	11.5	7.5	31.2	25.7	9.7	2.54	3.07	43 301	9.3	24.7
Albany, GA	43 781	71.0	35.8	45.6	20.6	21.3	13.1	29.0	24.4	8.0	2.64	3.15	39 362	20.8	22.2
Albany-Schenectady-Troy, NY	350 284	63.7	30.3	48.5	21.3	11.3	7.0	36.3	29.4	11.0	2.41	3.00	330 484	10.6	26.8
Albuquerque, NM	275 028	66.3	32.9	48.2	22.1	12.8	7.8	33.7	26.7	7.7	2.55	3.11	221 619	11.8	24.6
Alexandria, LA	47 120	70.3	34.6	49.7	22.4	16.8	10.1	29.7	26.0	10.3	2.56	3.09	45 941	15.3	23.0
Allentown-Bethlehem-Easton, PA	247 148	68.6	30.6	54.6	22.9	10.2	5.7	31.4	26.0	11.4	2.49	3.01	225 831	9.3	23.6
Altoona, PA	51 518	67.7	29.3	52.6	21.0	11.2	6.0	32.3	27.8	13.3	2.43	2.96	50 332	11.4	25.9
Amarillo, TX	82 000	68.6	34.3	52.5	24.4	12.1	7.7	31.4	26.5	9.3	2.55	3.10	71 897	10.6	26.2
Anchorage, AK	94 822	67.6	38.9	51.1	27.3	11.5	8.3	32.4	23.4	3.8	2.67	3.19	82 702	10.1	22.9
Anniston, AL	45 307	69.1	29.5	52.2	20.7	13.4	7.1	30.9	26.9	10.7	2.42	2.94	42 983	12.4	23.2
Appleton-Oshkosh-Neenah, WI	136 597	68.0	34.0	56.9	27.0	7.8	5.1	32.0	25.3	9.0	2.54	3.08	115 515	7.7	22.7
Asheville, NC	93 776	65.3	27.6	51.1	19.7	10.6	6.0	34.7	28.7	10.7	2.33	2.85	77 290	10.6	26.4
Athens, GA	58 557	58.6	27.9	42.9	19.2	12.3	7.3	41.4	26.1	6.1	2.47	3.02	47 066	12.1	25.5
Atlanta, GA	1 504 871	69.2	35.8	51.4	25.7	13.6	8.1	30.8	23.3	5.0	2.68	3.18	1 102 578	12.9	24.5
Auburn-Opalika, AL	45 702	59.7	29.7	44.1	20.9	11.8	7.1	40.3	27.8	5.7	2.42	3.03	33 097	11.1	26.1
Augusta-Aiken, GA-SC	176 867	71.4	35.6	50.9	23.4	16.5	10.0	28.6	24.3	8.2	2.61	3.10	149 093	14.9	22.8
Austin-San Marcos, TX	471 855	62.7	32.8	48.3	24.5	10.2	6.4	37.3	26.6	4.7	2.57	3.18	325 995	10.2	28.4
Bakersfield, CA	208 652	75.0	42.2	54.6	29.1	14.5	9.7	25.0	20.3	7.8	3.03	3.50	181 480	12.3	20.3
Bangor, ME	58 096	65.0	30.0	52.0	21.0	10.0	7.0	35.0	27.0	10.0	2.38	2.88	54 063	9.9	22.6
Barnstable-Yarmouth, MA	94 822	64.0	24.0	52.0	18.0	9.0	5.0	36.0	30.0	14.0	2.28	2.82	77 586	9.8	27.2
Baton Rouge, LA	223 349	69.2	35.4	49.4	23.9	15.6	9.3	30.8	24.4	6.9	2.63	3.16	188 377	14.4	22.8
Beaumont-Port Arthur, TX	142 327	71.1	34.0	52.5	23.2	14.5	8.7	28.9	25.2	10.4	2.59	3.11	134 238	12.9	23.9
Bellingham, WA	64 446	63.8	30.4	51.2	22.4	8.8	5.9	36.2	25.6	8.4	2.51	3.03	48 543	8.0	24.9
Benton Harbor, MI	63 569	68.2	31.2	51.2	20.9	13.2	8.3	31.8	27.1	10.8	2.49	3.01	61 025	13.3	24.4
Billings, MT	52 084	65.7	31.6	51.8	22.6	10.1	6.6	34.3	27.9	10.1	2.43	2.98	44 689	9.7	26.5
Biloxi-Gulfport-Pascagoula, MS	136 111	70.6	34.5	51.5	23.1	14.4	8.9	29.4	23.9	8.0	2.60	3.09	111 828	13.5	22.3
Binghamton, NY	100 474	64.3	29.5	49.8	20.8	10.6	6.5	35.7	29.3	11.8	2.42	2.99	100 681	9.8	25.5
Birmingham, AL	361 304	69.1	32.2	50.9	22.7	14.8	8.1	30.9	26.7	9.1	2.49	3.04	319 774	14.1	24.9
Bismarck, ND	37 559	66.9	33.2	55.1	25.5	8.7	6.0	33.1	27.5	9.9	2.44	3.00	31 361	8.5	24.9
Bloomington, IN	46 898	52.7	24.3	41.8	17.5	8.1	5.1	47.3	32.4	7.2	2.27	2.87	39 351	8.3	28.5
Bloomington-Normal, IL	56 746	62.5	31.5	50.9	24.0	8.8	5.9	37.5	27.6	8.1	2.45	3.03	46 796	8.3	26.1
Boise City, ID	158 426	70.3	37.2	56.7	28.4	9.6	6.4	29.7	22.6	7.2	2.67	3.16	108 759	9.2	22.9
Boston-Worcester-Lawrence-Lowell-Brockton, MA-NH	2 313 452	65.0	32.0	50.0	24.0	11.0	6.0	35.0	27.0	10.0	2.54	3.20	2 111 440	11.6	25.2
Brownsville-Harlingen-San Benito, TX	97 267	82.2	45.8	60.8	34.0	17.4	9.9	17.8	15.4	7.6	3.40	3.81	73 278	16.1	16.0
Bryan-College Station, TX	55 202	55.1	27.9	41.3	20.4	10.0	6.1	44.9	25.5	5.0	2.52	3.16	43 725	9.1	25.2
Buffalo-Niagara Falls, NY	468 719	64.4	29.9	47.2	20.3	13.5	7.9	35.6	30.2	12.4	2.42	3.04	461 803	12.9	27.5
Burlington, VT	75 978	65.0	33.0	52.0	25.0	9.0	6.0	35.0	25.0	8.0	2.51	3.03	64 783	9.1	22.2
Canton-Massillon, OH	159 442	69.6	31.0	54.7	22.5	11.2	6.6	30.4	25.9	10.9	2.49	3.00	149 240	10.7	23.7
Casper, WY	26 819	66.2	32.2	51.4	22.1	10.6	7.4	33.8	27.5	9.4	2.42	2.95	23 837	9.7	25.9
Cedar Rapids, IA	76 753	65.6	31.8	53.2	23.8	9.0	6.0	34.4	27.5	8.9	2.43	2.99	65 501	8.5	25.0
Champaign-Urbana, IL	70 597	55.7	27.2	43.6	19.5	9.2	6.1	44.3	31.4	7.8	2.33	2.96	63 900	8.4	28.7
Charleston, WV	106 254	67.0	28.2	51.9	20.2	11.6	6.3	33.0	28.9	11.6	2.34	2.87	100 408	11.3	25.9
Charleston-North Charleston, SC	207 957	68.0	33.1	48.8	22.0	15.3	9.1	32.0	24.8	7.2	2.55	3.07	177 668	13.5	21.3
Charlotte-Gastonia-Rock Hill, NC-SC	575 293	69.1	33.3	52.9	24.3	12.1	7.1	30.9	24.5	7.0	2.55	3.04	440 670	12.0	23.1
Charlottesville, VA	61 688	62.7	29.5	49.2	21.4	10.4	6.4	37.3	27.4	7.7	2.43	2.97	48 709	10.2	24.6
Chattanooga, TN-GA	185 144	69.6	30.3	53.1	21.6	12.8	7.0	30.4	26.1	9.8	2.46	2.96	163 117	12.5	24.0
Cheyenne, WY	31 927	67.7	33.2	53.9	24.1	9.9	6.8	32.3	27.2	8.9	2.45	2.98	28 092	9.7	25.3
Chicago-Gary-Kenosha, IL-IN-WI	3 302 211	68.0	34.0	50.3	25.0	13.4	7.2	32.0	26.2	8.5	2.72	3.34	2 969 099	13.3	25.3
Chicago, IL	2 971 690	67.8	34.0	50.2	25.2	13.3	7.1	32.2	26.4	8.4	2.73	3.36	2 671 540	13.3	25.6
Gary, IN	236 282	70.6	33.3	51.3	22.9	14.9	8.4	29.4	24.9	9.2	2.63	3.16	215 907	14.3	22.4
Kankakee, IL	38 182	70.1	34.4	52.8	23.8	13.1	8.2	29.9	24.9	10.4	2.61	3.12	34 623	12.5	24.3
Kenosha, WI	56 057	68.6	34.8	52.7	25.0	11.5	7.4	31.4	25.5	9.1	2.60	3.13	47 029	11.6	23.2
Chico-Paradise, CA	79 566	62.1	28.4	46.7	18.8	11.2	7.1	37.9	27.2	11.1	2.48	3.02	71 665	9.7	25.4
Cincinnati-Hamilton, OH-KY-IN	768 130	67.3	33.7	51.5	24.1	12.2	7.5	32.7	27.3	9.0	2.52	3.09	679 137	12.1	25.3
Cincinnati, OH-KY-IN	645 048	66.5	33.3	50.4	23.6	12.4	7.7	33.5	28.2	9.3	2.50	3.09	574 602	12.5	26.1
Hamilton-Middletown, OH	123 082	71.4	35.5	57.0	26.8	10.7	6.6	28.6	22.7	7.6	2.61	3.07	104 535	10.4	20.8
Clarksville-Hopkinsville, TN-KY	73 187	74.2	40.8	58.1	30.3	12.7	8.5	25.8	20.9	6.6	2.69	3.11	55 981	11.6	19.1
Cleveland-Akron, OH	1 166 799	66.2	30.6	49.0	21.0	13.4	7.7	33.8	28.7	10.6	2.47	3.06	1 094 413	12.9	26.3
Akron, OH	274 237	67.0	31.0	51.3	22.0	12.1	7.2	33.0	27.0	9.7	2.47	3.02	249 227	11.8	24.7
Cleveland-Lorain-Elyria, OH	892 562	65.9	30.4	48.3	20.8	13.8	7.9	34.1	29.2	10.9	2.47	3.08	845 186	13.2	26.8
Colorado Springs, CO	192 409	69.6	36.7	55.6	27.5	10.2	6.9	30.4	23.9	6.1	2.61	3.11	146 965	9.8	23.7
Columbia, MO	53 094	59.1	30.3	45.5	21.3	10.4	7.2	40.9	28.7	6.2	2.38	2.97	41 937	9.5	27.5

[1] No spouse present.

Table C. Metropolitan Areas

| Area Name | Percent change of households, 1990–2000 | Total housing units | Occupied housing units (percent) | Vacant housing units | | Homeowner vacancy rate (percent) | Rental vacancy rate (percent) | Occupied housing units | | | Average household size of owner-occupied units | Average household size of renter-occupied units |
| | | | | Total | For seasonal, recreational, or occasional use | | | Total | Percent owner-occupied housing units | Percent renter-occupied housing units | | |
	86	87	88	89	90	91	92	93	94	95	96	97
Abilene, TX	9.2	52 056	90.8	9.2	0.5	2.3	10.5	47 274	61.6	38.4	2.62	2.41
Albany, GA	11.2	48 469	90.3	9.7	0.4	2.5	10.7	43 781	58.2	41.8	2.66	2.61
Albany-Schenectady-Troy, NY	6.0	386 262	90.7	9.3	2.7	1.9	7.2	350 284	64.6	35.4	2.60	2.05
Albuquerque, NM	24.1	298 583	92.1	7.9	0.9	1.9	11.5	275 028	67.6	32.4	2.68	2.26
Alexandria, LA	2.6	52 038	90.5	9.5	0.8	1.6	9.7	47 120	68.0	32.0	2.60	2.48
Allentown-Bethlehem-Easton, PA	9.4	266 112	92.9	7.1	2.1	1.6	6.7	247 148	71.6	28.4	2.62	2.16
Altoona, PA	2.4	55 061	93.6	6.4	0.6	1.2	7.5	51 518	72.9	27.1	2.55	2.09
Amarillo, TX	14.1	87 859	93.3	6.7	0.4	1.7	8.1	82 000	65.2	34.8	2.67	2.33
Anchorage, AK	14.7	100 368	94.5	5.5	1.1	1.4	5.3	94 822	60.1	39.9	2.81	2.46
Anniston, AL	5.4	51 322	88.3	11.7	0.5	2.7	14.3	45 307	72.5	27.5	2.48	2.28
Appleton-Oshkosh-Neenah, WI	18.3	143 093	95.5	4.5	1.1	1.1	5.7	136 597	71.3	28.7	2.72	2.07
Asheville, NC	21.3	103 695	90.4	9.6	2.6	1.9	8.6	93 776	70.8	29.2	2.40	2.14
Athens, GA	24.4	62 174	94.2	5.8	0.4	1.6	5.2	58 557	54.3	45.7	2.61	2.32
Atlanta, GA	36.5	1 589 568	94.7	5.3	0.4	1.7	6.1	1 504 871	66.4	33.6	2.79	2.48
Auburn-Opalika, AL	38.1	50 329	90.8	9.2	1.2	2.3	10.6	45 702	62.1	37.9	2.62	2.09
Augusta-Aiken, GA-SC	18.6	195 759	90.3	9.7	0.7	2.5	10.8	176 867	69.4	30.6	2.67	2.46
Austin-San Marcos, TX	44.7	496 004	95.1	4.9	1.0	1.2	3.8	471 855	58.2	41.8	2.79	2.26
Bakersfield, CA	15.0	231 564	90.1	9.9	2.5	2.6	8.2	208 652	62.1	37.9	3.02	3.04
Bangor, ME	7.5	66 847	87.0	13.0	7.0	2.3	6.2	58 096	70.0	30.0	2.56	1.98
Barnstable-Yarmouth, MA	22.2	147 083	65.0	36.0	32.0	1.4	7.4	94 822	78.0	22.0	2.34	2.09
Baton Rouge, LA	18.6	242 827	92.0	8.0	0.7	1.5	9.9	223 349	67.9	32.1	2.75	2.37
Beaumont-Port Arthur, TX	6.0	156 697	90.8	9.2	0.7	1.6	11.0	142 327	70.6	29.4	2.65	2.45
Bellingham, WA	32.8	73 893	87.2	12.8	8.0	2.2	5.7	64 446	63.4	36.6	2.63	2.31
Benton Harbor, MI	4.2	73 445	86.6	13.4	7.2	1.9	8.1	63 569	72.3	27.7	2.54	2.35
Billings, MT	16.5	54 563	95.5	4.5	0.5	1.2	5.4	52 084	69.2	30.8	2.58	2.10
Biloxi-Gulfport-Pascagoula, MS	21.7	152 386	89.3	10.7	3.1	1.8	10.9	136 111	68.9	31.1	2.67	2.46
Binghamton, NY	-0.2	110 227	91.2	8.8	1.5	2.1	9.9	100 474	67.6	32.4	2.57	2.10
Birmingham, AL	13.0	395 925	91.3	8.7	1.0	1.9	10.3	361 304	70.7	29.3	2.60	2.23
Bismarck, ND	19.8	39 590	94.9	5.1	0.6	1.3	6.0	37 559	70.0	30.0	2.66	1.93
Bloomington, IN	19.2	50 846	92.2	7.8	1.9	2.3	6.8	46 898	54.0	46.0	2.48	2.02
Bloomington-Normal, IL	21.3	59 972	94.6	5.4	0.4	1.8	6.6	56 746	66.5	33.5	2.63	2.11
Boise City, ID	45.7	166 481	95.2	4.8	0.4	2.0	5.6	158 426	71.4	28.6	2.76	2.44
Boston-Worcester-Lawrence-Lowell-Brockton, MA-NH	9.6	2 416 623	95.7	4.3	1.4	0.6	3.1	2 313 452	61.6	38.4	2.76	2.17
Brownsville-Harlingen-San Benito, TX	32.7	119 654	81.3	18.7	9.8	1.6	14.1	97 267	67.7	32.3	3.45	3.31
Bryan-College Station, TX	26.2	59 023	93.5	6.5	0.7	1.6	6.2	55 202	45.6	54.4	2.80	2.28
Buffalo-Niagara Falls, NY	1.5	511 583	91.6	8.4	0.5	1.8	9.2	468 719	66.2	33.8	2.60	2.07
Burlington, VT	17.3	82 718	92.0	8.0	6.0	0.7	2.1	75 978	69.0	31.0	2.69	2.13
Canton-Massillon, OH	6.8	170 040	93.8	6.2	1.0	1.4	8.0	159 442	72.9	27.1	2.61	2.19
Casper, WY	12.5	29 882	89.7	10.3	3.1	1.5	8.4	26 819	69.9	30.1	2.52	2.19
Cedar Rapids, IA	17.2	80 551	95.3	4.7	0.6	1.6	5.6	76 753	72.7	27.3	2.58	2.03
Champaign-Urbana, IL	10.5	75 280	93.8	6.2	0.3	1.6	6.9	70 597	55.7	44.3	2.53	2.09
Charleston, WV	5.8	115 409	92.1	7.9	0.7	1.9	8.5	106 254	72.9	27.1	2.43	2.09
Charleston-North Charleston, SC	17.0	232 985	89.3	10.7	3.2	1.4	9.9	207 957	66.5	33.5	2.65	2.36
Charlotte-Gastonia-Rock Hill, NC-SC	30.5	615 923	93.4	6.6	0.6	2.1	8.1	575 293	68.4	31.6	2.62	2.39
Charlottesville, VA	26.6	65 315	94.4	5.6	1.4	1.2	3.3	61 688	62.7	37.3	2.56	2.22
Chattanooga, TN-GA	13.5	200 427	92.4	7.6	0.6	1.8	9.0	185 144	69.9	30.1	2.55	2.23
Cheyenne, WY	13.7	34 213	93.3	6.7	0.7	1.5	7.7	31 927	69.1	30.9	2.54	2.25
Chicago-Gary-Kenosha, IL-IN-WI	11.2	3 485 845	94.7	5.3	0.5	1.3	5.4	3 302 211	65.2	34.8	2.87	2.43
Chicago, IL	11.2	3 132 638	94.9	5.1	0.4	1.3	5.3	2 971 690	64.6	35.4	2.89	2.44
Gary, IN	9.4	252 608	93.5	6.5	0.5	1.6	7.0	236 282	70.7	29.3	2.74	2.38
Kankakee, IL	10.3	40 610	94.0	6.0	0.9	2.2	6.0	38 182	69.4	30.6	2.69	2.43
Kenosha, WI	19.2	59 989	93.4	6.6	2.8	1.2	5.1	56 057	69.1	30.9	2.74	2.29
Chico-Paradise, CA	11.0	85 523	93.0	7.0	1.6	2.1	5.2	79 566	60.7	39.3	2.48	2.48
Cincinnati-Hamilton, OH-KY-IN	13.1	820 756	93.6	6.4	0.5	1.5	8.3	768 130	67.1	32.9	2.71	2.13
Cincinnati, OH-KY-IN	12.3	690 963	93.4	6.6	0.6	1.5	8.4	645 048	66.2	33.8	2.71	2.10
Hamilton-Middletown, OH	17.7	129 793	94.8	5.2	0.3	1.6	7.3	123 082	71.6	28.4	2.72	2.34
Clarksville-Hopkinsville, TN-KY	30.7	79 349	92.2	7.8	0.3	2.6	7.2	73 187	60.7	39.3	2.71	2.65
Cleveland-Akron, OH	6.6	1 246 124	93.6	6.4	0.6	1.4	8.6	1 166 799	68.8	31.2	2.62	2.14
Akron, OH	10.0	290 976	94.2	5.8	0.6	1.4	7.8	274 237	70.5	29.5	2.61	2.15
Cleveland-Lorain-Elyria, OH	5.6	955 148	93.4	6.6	0.6	1.4	8.8	892 562	68.3	31.7	2.63	2.14
Colorado Springs, CO	30.9	202 428	95.1	4.9	0.7	1.3	6.0	192 409	64.7	35.3	2.72	2.40
Columbia, MO	26.6	56 678	93.7	6.3	0.4	2.2	7.3	53 094	57.5	42.5	2.58	2.12

Table C. Metropolitan Areas

CMSA/ MSA/ PMSA/ NECMA code[1]	Area Name	Population, 2000				Population, 1990				Population and population characteristics, 2000					
										Race (percent)					
										One race					
		Land area, 2000[2] (sq km)	Total persons	Rank	Per square kilometer	Land area, 1990[2] (sq km)	Total persons	Rank	Per square kilometer	White	Black or African American	American Indian or Alaska Native	Asian	Native Hawaiian and other Pacific Islander	Some other race
		1	2	3	4	5	6	7	8	9	10	11	12	13	14
1760	Columbia, SC	3 770	536 691	99	142.4	3 774	453 847	99	120.3	63.9	32.1	0.3	1.4	0.1	1.0
1800	Columbus, GA-AL	4 066	274 624	165	67.5	4 066	260 862	157	64.2	54.4	40.4	0.4	1.3	0.1	1.7
1840	Columbus, OH	8 136	1 540 157	41	189.3	8 139	1 345 460	38	165.3	81.3	13.4	0.3	2.4	0.0	0.8
1880	Corpus Christi, TX	3 956	380 783	132	96.3	3 957	349 894	127	88.4	72.9	4.0	0.6	1.1	0.1	18.2
1890	Corvallis, OR	1 752	78 153	315	44.6	1 752	70 811	314	40.4	89.2	0.8	0.8	4.5	0.2	1.9
1900	Cumberland, MD-WV	1 951	102 008	300	52.3	1 951	101 643	290	52.1	93.9	4.6	0.1	0.4	0.0	0.2
31	Dallas-Fort Worth, TX	23 579	5 221 801	X	221.5	23 582	4 037 282	X	171.2	69.5	13.8	0.6	3.7	0.1	9.9
1920	Dallas, TX	16 021	3 519 176	10	219.7	16 025	2 676 248	10	167.0	67.2	15.1	0.6	4.0	0.1	10.7
2800	Fort Worth-Arlington, TX	7 557	1 702 625	31	225.3	7 557	1 361 034	37	180.1	74.3	11.2	0.6	3.2	0.1	8.3
1950	Danville, VA	2 626	110 156	292	42.0	2 627	108 728	281	41.4	65.7	32.6	0.2	0.4	0.0	0.4
1960	Davenport-Moline-Rock Island, IA-IL	4 423	359 062	138	81.2	4 423	350 855	126	79.3	88.4	6.0	0.3	1.2	0.0	2.5
2000	Dayton-Springfield, OH	4 360	950 558	65	218.0	4 361	951 262	55	218.1	82.3	14.2	0.2	1.2	0.0	0.5
2020	Daytona Beach, FL	4 114	493 175	103	119.9	4 120	399 438	110	97.0	86.2	9.2	0.3	1.0	0.0	1.7
2030	Decatur, AL	3 304	145 867	247	44.2	3 304	131 556	244	39.8	83.3	11.7	1.8	0.4	0.1	1.0
2040	Decatur, IL	1 504	114 706	285	76.3	1 504	117 206	267	77.9	83.5	14.1	0.2	0.6	0.0	0.3
34	Denver-Boulder-Greeley, CO	22 003	2 581 506	X	117.3	22 004	1 980 140	X	90.0	80.6	4.6	0.9	2.8	0.1	8.1
1125	Boulder-Longmont, CO	1 923	291 288	161	151.5	1 923	225 339	174	117.2	88.5	0.9	0.6	3.1	0.1	4.7
2080	Denver, CO	9 740	2 109 282	25	216.6	9 740	1 622 980	27	166.6	79.4	5.5	0.9	3.0	0.1	8.1
3060	Greeley, CO	10 340	180 936	213	17.5	10 341	131 821	242	12.7	81.7	0.6	0.9	0.8	0.1	13.3
2120	Des Moines, IA	4 474	456 022	112	101.9	4 475	392 928	116	87.8	89.8	4.1	0.2	2.3	0.1	2.1
35	Detroit-Ann Arbor-Flint, MI	17 004	5 456 428	X	320.9	17 005	5 187 171	X	305.0	73.1	21.1	0.4	2.4	0.0	1.1
0440	Ann Arbor, MI	5 255	578 736	93	110.1	5 255	490 058	93	93.3	85.3	7.3	0.4	3.7	0.0	1.2
2160	Detroit, MI	10 093	4 441 551	7	440.1	10 093	4 266 654	6	422.7	71.2	22.9	0.3	2.3	0.0	1.1
2640	Flint, MI	1 657	436 141	118	263.3	1 657	430 459	103	259.8	75.3	20.4	0.6	0.8	0.0	0.8
2180	Dothan, AL	2 956	137 916	256	46.7	2 956	130 964	247	44.3	73.5	23.1	0.5	0.8	0.1	0.7
2190	Dover, DE	1 527	126 697	268	83.0	1 530	110 993	278	72.5	73.5	20.7	0.6	1.7	0.1	1.3
2200	Dubuque, IA	1 575	89 143	308	56.6	1 575	86 403	305	54.9	97.1	0.9	0.1	0.6	0.1	0.5
2240	Duluth-Superior, MN-WI	19 514	243 815	179	12.5	19 515	239 990	169	12.3	94.9	0.8	2.0	0.7	0.0	0.2
2290	Eau Claire, WI	4 268	148 337	242	34.8	4 269	137 543	237	32.2	96.0	0.4	0.5	1.9	0.0	0.3
2320	El Paso, TX	2 624	679 622	79	259.0	2 624	591 610	82	225.5	73.9	3.1	0.8	1.0	0.1	17.9
2330	Elkhart-Goshen, IN	1 201	182 791	211	152.2	1 201	156 198	212	130.1	86.4	5.2	0.3	0.9	0.0	5.4
2335	Elmira, NY	1 057	91 070	307	86.1	1 057	95 195	299	90.1	91.0	5.8	0.2	0.8	0.0	0.7
2340	Enid, OK	2 741	57 813	318	21.1	2 742	56 735	318	20.7	88.7	3.3	2.1	0.8	0.5	2.0
2360	Erie, PA	2 077	280 843	163	135.2	2 077	275 575	152	132.7	90.9	6.1	0.2	0.7	0.0	0.9
2400	Eugene-Springfield, OR	11 795	322 959	151	27.4	11 795	282 912	149	24.0	90.6	0.8	1.1	2.0	0.2	1.9
2440	Evansville-Henderson, IN-KY	3 800	296 195	159	77.9	3 801	278 990	150	73.4	91.8	6.1	0.2	0.6	0.0	0.3
2520	Fargo-Moorhead, ND-MN	7 279	174 367	218	24.0	7 280	153 296	214	21.1	94.8	0.7	1.2	1.1	0.0	0.8
2560	Fayetteville, NC	1 691	302 963	157	179.2	1 692	274 713	153	162.4	55.2	34.9	1.5	1.9	0.3	3.1
2580	Fayetteville-Springdale-Rogers, AR	4 651	311 121	156	66.9	4 645	210 939	180	45.4	89.4	1.3	1.4	1.3	0.3	4.2
2620	Flagstaff, AZ-UT	58 558	122 366	276	2.1	58 564	101 760	289	1.7	64.7	1.0	27.2	0.8	0.1	4.0
2650	Florence, AL	3 274	142 950	250	43.7	3 274	131 327	246	40.1	85.7	12.5	0.3	0.3	0.0	0.4
2655	Florence, SC	2 072	125 761	272	60.7	2 070	114 344	273	55.2	58.7	39.3	0.2	0.7	0.0	0.4
2670	Fort Collins-Loveland, CO	6 737	251 494	174	37.3	6 738	186 136	193	27.6	91.4	0.7	0.7	1.6	0.1	3.4
2700	Fort Myers-Cape Coral, FL	2 081	440 888	116	211.8	2 081	335 113	134	161.0	87.7	6.6	0.3	0.8	0.0	3.1
2710	Fort Pierce-Port St. Lucie, FL	2 922	319 426	153	109.3	2 922	251 071	164	85.9	83.4	11.4	0.3	0.8	0.1	2.5
2720	Fort Smith, AR-OK	4 676	207 290	198	44.3	4 676	175 911	199	37.6	82.2	4.0	5.1	2.3	0.0	2.6
2750	Fort Walton Beach, FL	2 423	170 498	220	70.4	2 424	143 777	228	59.3	83.4	9.1	0.6	2.5	0.1	1.3
2760	Fort Wayne, IN	6 339	502 141	102	79.2	6 339	456 281	98	72.0	88.1	7.5	0.3	1.0	0.0	1.6
2840	Fresno, CA	20 975	922 516	66	44.0	20 984	755 569	69	36.0	55.4	5.1	1.7	7.1	0.1	25.7
2880	Gadsden, AL	1 385	103 459	298	74.7	1 385	99 840	292	72.1	82.9	14.7	0.3	0.4	0.0	0.7
2900	Gainesville, FL	2 264	217 955	191	96.3	2 264	181 596	196	80.2	73.5	19.3	0.2	3.5	0.0	1.4
2975	Glens Falls, NY	4 415	124 345	273	28.2	4 417	118 539	266	26.8	96.2	1.8	0.2	0.4	0.0	0.5
2980	Goldsboro, NC	1 431	113 329	286	79.2	1 431	104 666	286	73.1	61.3	33.0	0.4	1.0	0.0	3.1
2985	Grand Forks, ND-MN	8 827	97 478	303	11.0	8 828	103 272	288	11.7	93.4	1.0	2.0	0.8	0.1	1.3
2995	Grand Junction, CO	8 619	116 255	282	13.5	8 619	93 145	301	10.8	92.3	0.5	0.9	0.5	0.1	3.7
3000	Grand Rapids-Muskegon-Holland, MI	7 144	1 088 514	59	152.4	7 145	937 891	57	131.3	85.7	7.3	0.5	1.6	0.0	3.0
3040	Great Falls, MT	6 988	80 357	314	11.5	6 988	77 691	311	11.1	90.7	1.1	4.2	0.8	0.1	0.7
3080	Green Bay, WI	1 369	226 778	187	165.6	1 369	194 594	182	142.1	91.1	1.2	2.3	2.2	0.0	1.9
3120	Greensboro—Winston-Salem—High Point, NC	10 052	1 251 509	47	124.5	10 056	1 050 304	49	104.4	74.4	20.2	0.4	1.4	0.0	2.4
3150	Greenville, NC	1 688	133 798	260	79.3	1 688	108 480	282	64.3	62.1	33.6	0.3	1.1	0.0	1.8
3160	Greenville-Spartanburg-Anderson, SC	8 310	962 441	64	115.8	8 316	830 499	68	99.9	79.0	17.5	0.2	1.2	0.0	1.1
3240	Harrisburg-Lebanon-Carlisle, PA	5 156	629 401	83	122.1	5 157	587 986	84	114.0	87.8	7.8	0.1	1.5	0.0	1.4

[1] MSA = Metropolitan Statistical Area. PMSA = Primary MSA. NECMA = New England County Metropolitan Area. See Appendix A for explanation of these concepts. See Appendix B for list of metropolitan areas identified by type, with component counties.
[2] Dry land or land partially or temporarily covered by water.

Table C. Metropolitan Areas

	Population and population characteristics, 2000 (cont'd)								Population and population characteristics, 1990				
	Race (percent) (cont'd)								Race (percent)				
	Race alone or in combination												
Area Name	Two or more races	White	Black	American Indian or Alaska Native	Asian	Native Hawaiian and other Pacific Islander	Some other race	Hispanic[1]	White	Black or African American	American Indian or Alaska Native	Asian and Pacific Islander	Hispanic[1]
	15	16	17	18	19	20	21	22	23	24	25	26	27
Columbia, SC	1.2	64.8	32.6	0.6	1.8	0.1	1.4	2.4	67.8	30.4	0.2	1.1	1.3
Columbus, GA-AL	1.7	55.7	41.2	0.8	1.7	0.3	2.3	4.0	59.4	37.6	0.3	1.3	3.0
Columbus, OH	1.9	82.7	14.4	0.8	2.7	0.1	1.3	1.8	86.0	12.0	0.2	1.5	0.8
Corpus Christi, TX	3.1	75.6	4.4	1.1	1.4	0.2	20.5	54.7	75.7	3.9	0.4	0.8	52.0
Corvallis, OR	2.6	91.5	1.2	1.7	5.4	0.5	2.6	4.7	92.0	0.9	0.8	5.5	2.5
Cumberland, MD-WV	0.8	94.5	5.0	0.4	0.6	0.1	0.3	0.7	97.2	2.2	0.1	0.4	0.4
Dallas-Fort Worth, TX	2.4	71.5	14.3	1.1	4.2	0.2	11.3	21.5	75.3	14.3	0.5	2.5	13.4
Dallas, TX	2.4	69.2	15.5	1.1	4.5	0.1	12.1	23.0	72.6	16.1	0.5	2.6	14.4
Fort Worth-Arlington, TX	2.4	76.3	11.6	1.2	3.6	0.2	9.5	18.2	80.3	10.8	0.5	2.3	11.3
Danville, VA	0.7	66.3	33.0	0.4	0.5	0.0	0.6	1.2	67.9	31.6	0.1	0.3	0.5
Davenport-Moline-Rock Island, IA-IL	1.7	89.9	6.7	0.7	1.4	0.1	3.0	5.8	92.0	5.4	0.3	0.7	3.7
Dayton-Springfield, OH	1.5	83.6	15.0	0.7	1.6	0.1	0.7	1.2	85.3	13.3	0.2	1.0	0.8
Daytona Beach, FL	1.4	87.4	9.7	0.8	1.3	0.1	2.3	6.4	88.6	9.0	0.2	0.7	4.0
Decatur, AL	1.7	84.9	12.0	3.0	0.5	0.1	1.3	2.8	86.4	11.3	1.9	0.3	0.5
Decatur, IL	1.4	84.7	14.9	0.5	0.7	0.1	0.5	1.0	87.2	12.1	0.1	0.4	0.5
Denver-Boulder-Greeley, CO	2.9	83.0	5.3	1.6	3.5	0.2	9.4	18.5	86.6	5.3	0.8	2.3	12.2
Boulder-Longmont, CO	2.2	90.5	1.2	1.2	3.7	0.2	5.5	10.5	93.3	0.9	0.6	2.4	6.7
Denver, CO	3.0	81.9	6.2	1.7	3.6	0.2	9.5	18.8	85.6	5.9	0.8	2.3	13.0
Greeley, CO	2.7	84.1	0.8	1.6	1.2	0.2	14.8	27.0	88.9	0.4	0.6	0.9	20.9
Des Moines, IA	1.5	91.1	4.6	0.6	2.6	0.1	2.6	4.2	93.8	3.8	0.3	1.6	1.7
Detroit-Ann Arbor-Flint, MI	2.1	74.8	21.7	1.0	2.7	0.1	1.9	2.9	76.5	20.9	0.4	1.5	1.9
Ann Arbor, MI	2.0	87.1	8.0	1.0	4.2	0.1	1.7	3.1	83.5	11.2	0.4	4.1	2.0
Detroit, MI	2.1	73.0	23.5	0.9	2.7	0.1	2.0	2.9	76.0	21.5	0.4	1.3	1.9
Flint, MI	2.2	77.1	21.3	1.6	1.1	0.1	1.2	2.3	78.2	19.6	0.7	0.7	2.1
Dothan, AL	1.4	74.7	23.5	1.0	1.1	0.1	1.0	2.0	77.0	21.2	0.4	0.9	1.3
Dover, DE	2.2	75.1	21.8	1.3	2.2	0.1	1.9	3.2	78.7	18.6	0.6	1.3	2.3
Dubuque, IA	0.8	97.8	1.1	0.4	0.7	0.1	0.7	1.2	98.8	0.4	0.1	0.5	0.5
Duluth-Superior, MN-WI	1.4	96.2	1.1	2.8	0.9	0.1	0.4	0.8	96.9	0.5	1.9	0.6	0.5
Eau Claire, WI	0.9	96.8	0.6	0.8	2.2	0.1	0.4	0.8	97.5	0.2	0.4	1.7	0.4
El Paso, TX	3.2	76.8	3.5	1.1	1.3	0.2	20.4	78.2	76.5	3.7	0.4	1.1	69.6
Elkhart-Goshen, IN	1.8	88.0	5.8	0.7	1.2	0.1	6.1	8.9	93.8	4.5	0.3	0.6	1.9
Elmira, NY	1.4	92.3	6.7	0.6	1.0	0.0	1.0	1.8	92.8	5.5	0.2	0.7	1.5
Enid, OK	2.6	91.0	3.8	3.6	1.2	0.6	2.5	4.1	92.4	3.6	2.2	1.0	1.9
Erie, PA	1.2	92.0	6.7	0.5	0.9	0.1	1.2	2.2	93.6	5.2	0.2	0.5	1.2
Eugene-Springfield, OR	3.3	93.7	1.3	2.6	2.8	0.4	2.8	4.6	95.4	0.7	1.1	2.0	2.4
Evansville-Henderson, IN-KY	0.9	92.7	6.5	0.5	0.8	0.1	0.5	0.9	93.5	5.8	0.2	0.4	0.5
Fargo-Moorhead, ND-MN	1.3	96.0	1.0	1.7	1.5	0.1	1.2	1.9	97.2	0.3	1.0	0.9	1.2
Fayetteville, NC	3.1	57.4	36.3	2.4	2.7	0.5	4.1	6.9	61.9	31.9	1.6	2.1	4.8
Fayetteville-Springdale-Rogers, AR	2.0	91.2	1.6	2.5	1.6	0.4	4.7	8.5	95.9	1.5	1.3	0.9	1.3
Flagstaff, AZ-UT	2.3	66.7	1.3	28.4	1.1	0.2	4.8	10.5	92.9	2.3	0.2	1.7	7.1
Florence, AL	0.8	86.5	12.7	0.7	0.4	0.0	0.5	1.1	87.1	12.4	0.2	0.2	0.4
Florence, SC	0.7	59.2	39.6	0.5	0.9	0.1	0.6	1.1	60.8	38.7	0.1	0.3	0.4
Fort Collins-Loveland, CO	2.2	93.5	1.0	1.4	2.1	0.2	4.2	8.3	94.5	0.6	0.6	1.5	6.6
Fort Myers-Cape Coral, FL	1.6	88.9	7.1	0.6	1.0	0.1	3.9	9.5	91.4	6.6	0.2	0.6	4.5
Fort Pierce-Port St. Lucie, FL	1.5	84.5	12.0	0.6	1.1	0.1	3.3	7.9	85.3	12.2	0.2	0.6	4.3
Fort Smith, AR-OK	3.8	85.8	4.4	8.0	2.6	0.1	3.1	4.9	88.4	3.9	5.1	2.1	1.2
Fort Walton Beach, FL	3.0	85.9	9.9	1.4	3.7	0.3	2.0	4.3	87.1	9.0	0.5	2.5	3.1
Fort Wayne, IN	1.4	89.4	8.1	0.7	1.2	0.1	2.0	3.3	89.8	8.4	0.3	0.8	1.7
Fresno, CA	4.8	59.2	5.7	2.8	8.2	0.3	28.8	44.0	63.3	5.0	1.1	8.6	35.5
Gadsden, AL	0.9	83.7	14.9	0.8	0.5	0.1	0.9	1.7	85.4	13.8	0.3	0.4	0.3
Gainesville, FL	2.0	75.1	20.0	0.8	4.1	0.1	2.1	5.7	77.6	19.1	0.2	2.3	3.5
Glens Falls, NY	0.8	97.0	2.0	0.6	0.6	0.1	0.7	1.5	97.1	2.0	0.2	0.3	1.5
Goldsboro, NC	1.3	62.2	33.6	0.7	1.3	0.1	3.4	4.9	66.1	32.3	0.3	0.8	1.3
Grand Forks, ND-MN	1.5	94.7	1.4	2.7	1.1	0.1	1.6	2.9	94.5	2.0	1.8	1.2	1.5
Grand Junction, CO	2.0	94.2	0.7	1.8	0.8	0.2	4.4	10.0	94.7	0.4	0.7	0.7	8.1
Grand Rapids-Muskegon-Holland, MI	1.9	87.3	8.0	1.1	1.8	0.1	3.7	6.3	90.6	6.0	0.5	1.1	3.3
Great Falls, MT	2.4	92.9	1.5	5.7	1.3	0.2	1.0	2.4	93.1	1.4	4.0	1.0	1.8
Green Bay, WI	1.3	92.2	1.5	2.9	2.4	0.1	2.2	3.8	95.9	0.5	2.0	1.3	0.8
Greensboro—Winston-Salem—High Point, NC	1.2	75.4	20.7	0.7	1.6	0.1	2.9	5.0	79.4	19.3	0.3	0.7	0.8
Greenville, NC	1.1	62.9	34.1	0.5	1.3	0.1	2.2	3.2	65.5	33.3	0.2	0.7	0.9
Greenville-Spartanburg-Anderson, SC	1.0	79.9	17.8	0.5	1.4	0.1	1.5	2.7	81.6	17.4	0.1	0.7	0.8
Harrisburg-Lebanon-Carlisle, PA	1.3	88.9	8.5	0.4	1.8	0.1	1.8	3.1	91.3	6.7	0.1	1.1	1.7

[1] Hispanic persons may be of any race.

Table C. Metropolitan Areas

Area Name	Population and population characteristics, 2000										
	Age (percent)										
	Under 5 years	5 to 17 years	18 to 24 years	25 to 34 years	35 to 44 years	45 to 54 years	55 to 64 years	65 to 74 years	75 years and over	Median age (years)	Percent Female
	28	29	30	31	32	33	34	35	36	37	38
Columbia, SC	6.5	18.4	11.6	15.1	16.5	13.8	8.1	5.4	4.5	33.9	51.6
Columbus, GA-AL	7.2	19.5	11.8	14.7	15.2	12.2	7.8	6.5	5.0	32.7	50.7
Columbus, OH	7.2	18.3	10.7	16.0	16.6	13.3	7.9	5.5	4.5	33.6	50.9
Corpus Christi, TX	7.8	21.1	10.4	13.3	15.4	13.0	8.0	6.2	4.9	33.0	50.9
Corvallis, OR	5.1	16.2	20.2	12.9	13.8	14.2	7.2	5.1	5.2	31.1	50.2
Cumberland, MD-WV	5.2	16.2	10.5	12.5	14.4	13.6	10.6	8.8	8.4	39.1	50.4
Dallas-Fort Worth, TX	8.0	20.0	10.0	16.8	17.2	12.6	7.3	4.5	3.6	32.1	50.2
Dallas, TX	8.1	19.9	10.1	17.4	17.2	12.5	7.1	4.3	3.4	31.8	50.1
Fort Worth-Arlington, TX	7.8	20.2	9.7	15.7	17.1	13.0	7.6	4.9	3.9	32.8	50.4
Danville, VA	5.8	17.3	7.6	11.8	15.5	14.7	10.6	8.8	7.9	40.0	52.6
Davenport-Moline-Rock Island, IA-IL	6.6	18.6	9.3	12.8	15.4	14.2	9.3	7.0	6.8	36.9	51.2
Dayton-Springfield, OH	6.5	18.3	10.0	13.0	15.4	14.0	9.4	7.2	6.3	36.6	51.8
Daytona Beach, FL	4.8	15.2	7.8	10.6	14.2	13.3	11.3	11.9	10.9	43.1	51.5
Decatur, AL	6.5	18.9	8.4	13.8	16.3	14.0	9.8	6.9	5.3	36.4	51.0
Decatur, IL	6.4	18.2	9.8	11.6	14.8	14.4	9.6	7.9	7.3	38.0	52.3
Denver-Boulder-Greeley, CO	7.1	18.6	9.8	16.4	17.4	14.2	7.6	4.8	4.1	33.8	49.9
Boulder-Longmont, CO	6.0	16.9	13.4	16.0	17.6	15.0	7.2	4.2	3.6	33.4	49.4
Denver, CO	7.2	18.6	9.0	16.7	17.5	14.3	7.7	4.9	4.1	34.1	50.0
Greeley, CO	7.8	20.4	13.2	14.3	15.4	12.6	7.4	4.8	4.1	30.9	49.9
Des Moines, IA	7.5	18.6	9.2	15.3	16.5	13.6	8.1	5.7	5.5	34.6	51.4
Detroit-Ann Arbor-Flint, MI	7.0	19.4	8.7	14.5	16.5	13.9	8.4	6.2	5.5	35.3	51.3
Ann Arbor, MI	6.5	18.0	12.9	14.8	16.6	14.3	8.0	4.8	4.1	33.5	50.0
Detroit, MI	7.0	19.5	8.1	14.6	16.5	13.8	8.4	6.3	5.8	35.5	51.4
Flint, MI	7.3	20.2	8.9	13.6	16.0	13.7	8.7	6.6	5.0	35.0	51.9
Dothan, AL	7.0	19.1	8.7	13.8	15.5	13.4	9.5	7.2	5.9	35.9	51.8
Dover, DE	7.2	20.0	10.1	13.5	16.2	12.5	8.7	6.6	5.0	34.4	51.8
Dubuque, IA	6.6	18.9	10.2	12.0	15.3	13.4	8.9	7.3	7.4	36.5	51.4
Duluth-Superior, MN-WI	5.3	17.2	11.2	11.0	15.3	15.0	9.2	7.5	8.4	38.8	50.8
Eau Claire, WI	6.1	18.5	13.6	12.3	15.0	13.5	8.0	6.5	6.6	34.7	51.1
El Paso, TX	8.7	23.3	10.6	14.5	14.8	11.3	7.1	5.7	4.0	30.0	51.8
Elkhart-Goshen, IN	8.1	20.8	9.5	14.5	15.3	12.8	8.1	5.6	5.2	33.0	50.3
Elmira, NY	6.0	18.4	8.8	12.3	16.0	13.9	9.0	7.8	7.8	37.9	50.6
Enid, OK	6.7	18.3	9.1	12.1	15.3	13.0	9.4	7.9	8.1	37.7	51.6
Erie, PA	6.2	18.8	10.8	12.5	15.1	13.6	8.6	7.1	7.2	36.2	51.2
Eugene-Springfield, OR	5.8	17.1	12.0	13.0	14.5	15.3	9.0	6.6	6.7	36.6	50.8
Evansville-Henderson, IN-KY	6.3	18.1	9.9	12.6	16.1	14.0	9.0	7.2	6.8	37.1	51.9
Fargo-Moorhead, ND-MN	6.5	17.4	16.3	14.5	15.2	12.7	6.9	5.3	5.3	31.5	50.4
Fayetteville, NC	8.2	19.7	13.7	17.3	15.6	10.9	6.8	4.8	2.9	29.6	49.4
Fayetteville-Springdale-Rogers, AR	7.5	18.3	12.0	15.0	14.9	12.0	8.3	6.6	5.5	33.0	50.3
Flagstaff, AZ-UT	7.2	21.5	14.1	13.7	15.0	13.5	7.4	4.6	2.9	29.9	50.1
Florence, AL	6.0	17.3	9.3	12.9	15.0	13.8	10.5	8.2	7.0	38.0	52.2
Florence, SC	6.5	19.4	9.7	13.6	15.3	14.4	9.2	6.3	5.5	35.5	53.0
Fort Collins-Loveland, CO	6.1	17.7	14.2	14.4	16.3	14.2	7.6	5.1	4.5	33.2	50.0
Fort Myers-Cape Coral, FL	5.2	14.4	7.6	10.5	13.4	12.4	12.4	13.7	11.7	45.2	51.1
Fort Pierce-Port St. Lucie, FL	5.1	15.9	6.1	9.9	14.3	12.6	11.2	13.0	11.9	44.0	51.1
Fort Smith, AR-OK	7.3	19.5	8.8	13.5	15.5	13.2	9.5	6.8	5.8	35.6	50.9
Fort Walton Beach, FL	6.4	18.4	9.6	13.9	17.2	13.1	9.3	7.4	4.7	36.1	49.5
Fort Wayne, IN	7.5	20.3	9.2	13.6	15.8	13.5	8.1	6.1	5.9	34.6	50.9
Fresno, CA	8.4	23.4	10.9	13.9	14.6	11.7	7.1	5.3	4.8	30.2	50.2
Gadsden, AL	6.4	17.4	8.7	13.0	14.3	14.1	10.0	8.5	7.5	38.3	52.1
Gainesville, FL	5.1	15.0	23.2	14.4	13.3	12.2	7.1	5.0	4.6	29.0	51.2
Glens Falls, NY	5.5	18.8	7.9	12.5	16.3	14.4	10.0	7.8	6.8	38.3	50.1
Goldsboro, NC	7.0	19.2	9.9	14.2	16.3	13.0	8.9	6.8	4.8	34.8	50.7
Grand Forks, ND-MN	6.3	17.9	17.7	12.9	14.6	12.2	7.2	5.7	6.5	31.9	49.5
Grand Junction, CO	6.3	18.8	9.4	11.4	15.4	14.4	9.3	7.9	7.3	38.1	51.0
Grand Rapids-Muskegon-Holland, MI	7.5	20.8	10.3	14.1	16.2	12.8	7.5	5.5	5.3	33.2	50.7
Great Falls, MT	6.6	19.4	9.1	12.3	15.8	13.3	9.4	7.2	6.7	36.7	50.5
Green Bay, WI	6.9	19.2	10.5	14.8	17.1	13.4	7.6	5.4	5.3	34.2	50.3
Greensboro—Winston-Salem—High Point, NC	6.6	17.4	9.5	14.9	16.1	13.8	9.2	6.8	5.7	36.0	51.7
Greenville, NC	6.5	17.1	17.5	15.4	14.5	12.3	7.1	5.2	4.3	30.4	52.6
Greenville-Spartanburg-Anderson, SC	6.6	17.8	10.2	14.3	15.7	13.7	9.4	6.6	5.7	35.7	51.3
Harrisburg-Lebanon-Carlisle, PA	5.9	17.6	8.7	13.0	16.1	14.7	9.3	7.6	7.1	38.1	51.5

Table C. Metropolitan Areas

Area Name	Population and population characteristics, 1990										Population—change, 1980–2000				
	Age (percent)									Percent Female	Total persons			Percent change	
	Under 5 years	5 to 17 years	18 to 24 years	25 to 34 years	35 to 44 years	45 to 54 years	55 to 64 years	65 to 74 years	75 years and over		2000	1990	1980	1990–2000	1980–1990
	39	40	41	42	43	44	45	46	47	48	49	50	51	52	53
Columbia, SC	7.1	17.9	13.2	19.0	16.2	9.9	7.5	5.8	3.4	51.3	536 691	453 847	409 953	18.3	10.7
Columbus, GA-AL	8.1	18.9	13.5	18.0	13.7	9.0	8.3	6.4	4.2	50.4	274 624	260 862	254 660	5.3	2.4
Columbus, OH	7.5	17.7	12.4	19.0	15.6	9.9	7.9	5.9	4.1	51.2	1 540 157	1 345 460	1 214 291	14.5	10.8
Corpus Christi, TX	8.3	22.6	10.0	16.9	14.7	9.4	8.1	6.1	4.0	51.0	380 783	349 894	326 228	8.8	7.3
Corvallis, OR	6.2	16.1	21.1	16.0	15.7	8.8	6.5	5.7	4.0	49.4	78 153	70 811	68 211	10.4	3.8
Cumberland, MD-WV	6.0	16.7	11.6	13.2	13.5	10.9	10.6	10.1	7.4	52.6	102 008	101 643	107 782	0.4	-5.7
Dallas-Fort Worth, TX	8.4	18.8	11.0	21.0	16.1	10.0	6.8	4.7	3.3	50.6	5 221 801	4 037 282	3 046 136	29.3	32.5
Dallas, TX	8.4	18.8	11.0	21.3	16.2	10.0	6.6	4.5	3.2	50.7	3 519 176	2 676 248	2 055 284	31.5	30.2
Fort Worth-Arlington, TX	8.4	18.9	10.9	20.4	15.7	10.0	7.1	5.1	3.5	50.5	1 702 625	1 361 034	990 852	25.1	37.4
Danville, VA	6.3	17.2	9.2	15.2	14.7	11.1	10.4	9.5	6.4	52.6	110 156	108 728	111 789	1.3	-2.7
Davenport-Moline-Rock Island, IA-IL	7.3	19.5	9.5	15.6	15.0	10.5	8.9	7.7	5.9	51.7	359 062	350 855	384 749	2.3	-8.8
Dayton-Springfield, OH	7.2	18.1	10.8	16.5	15.0	10.9	9.2	7.4	4.9	51.9	950 558	951 262	942 083	-0.1	1.0
Daytona Beach, FL	5.7	14.0	9.5	14.8	13.0	9.4	10.9	13.3	9.5	51.6	493 175	399 438	269 675	23.5	48.1
Decatur, AL	7.0	19.3	9.8	16.7	15.0	11.4	9.0	6.9	4.8	51.2	145 867	131 556	120 401	10.9	9.3
Decatur, IL	6.8	19.1	9.3	14.8	14.9	10.8	9.6	8.2	6.3	52.3	114 706	117 206	131 375	-2.1	-10.8
Denver-Boulder-Greeley, CO	7.8	17.8	9.7	19.6	18.0	10.5	7.4	5.5	3.7	50.8	2 581 506	1 980 140	1 741 899	30.4	13.7
Boulder-Longmont, CO	7.0	16.0	14.5	19.6	18.7	10.2	6.2	4.3	3.3	49.9	291 288	225 339	189 625	29.3	18.8
Denver, CO	7.9	18.1	9.1	19.6	17.9	10.6	7.6	5.6	3.7	50.9	2 109 282	1 622 980	1 428 836	30.0	13.6
Greeley, CO	7.9	20.2	13.2	16.4	15.3	9.6	7.2	5.7	4.5	50.6	180 936	131 821	123 438	37.3	6.8
Des Moines, IA	7.5	18.0	10.6	18.2	15.6	10.2	8.1	6.5	5.2	52.2	456 022	392 928	367 561	16.1	6.9
Detroit-Ann Arbor-Flint, MI	7.6	18.3	10.6	17.6	15.5	10.4	8.6	7.0	4.6	51.8	5 456 428	5 187 171	5 293 161	5.2	-2.0
Ann Arbor, MI	6.8	14.8	19.6	19.9	16.1	9.3	6.1	4.4	3.1	50.5	578 736	490 058	454 977	18.1	7.7
Detroit, MI	7.6	18.5	10.0	17.4	15.5	10.4	8.7	7.2	4.7	51.9	4 441 551	4 266 654	4 387 735	4.1	-2.8
Flint, MI	7.8	20.3	10.3	16.9	15.0	10.8	8.7	6.1	4.1	52.1	436 141	430 459	450 449	1.3	-4.4
Dothan, AL	7.8	19.9	10.9	17.4	14.3	10.1	8.3	6.6	4.7	51.4	137 916	130 964	122 453	5.3	7.0
Dover, DE	8.4	18.8	11.9	17.8	14.2	10.1	8.4	6.1	4.2	51.1	126 697	110 993	98 219	14.1	13.0
Dubuque, IA	7.0	20.1	10.8	15.2	14.1	10.0	8.7	7.6	6.5	51.7	89 143	86 403	93 745	3.2	-7.8
Duluth-Superior, MN-WI	6.3	18.3	10.1	14.4	15.2	9.8	9.1	9.0	7.7	51.4	243 815	239 990	266 650	1.6	-10.0
Eau Claire, WI	7.2	18.9	13.9	15.4	14.5	9.1	7.8	7.2	5.9	51.5	148 337	137 543	130 932	7.8	5.0
El Paso, TX	9.0	23.6	12.3	17.2	13.7	8.7	7.4	5.1	3.0	51.4	679 622	591 610	479 899	14.9	23.3
Elkhart-Goshen, IN	8.5	20.0	10.2	16.6	15.2	10.3	8.0	6.4	4.8	51.1	182 791	156 198	137 330	17.0	13.7
Elmira, NY	7.1	18.2	10.2	15.6	14.5	10.0	9.3	8.8	6.3	51.4	91 070	95 195	97 656	-4.3	-2.5
Enid, OK	6.9	19.3	8.7	16.3	13.9	10.1	9.3	8.1	7.3	52.0	57 813	56 735	62 820	1.9	-9.7
Erie, PA	7.2	18.7	12.0	15.5	14.4	9.6	8.9	8.4	5.4	51.7	280 843	275 575	279 780	1.9	-1.5
Eugene-Springfield, OR	6.7	17.8	11.8	15.6	16.9	10.3	7.9	7.6	5.5	51.3	322 959	282 912	275 226	14.2	2.8
Evansville-Henderson, IN-KY	7.0	18.4	9.6	16.7	15.0	10.3	9.0	7.9	6.1	52.2	296 195	278 990	276 252	6.2	1.0
Fargo-Moorhead, ND-MN	7.3	17.7	16.8	17.5	14.7	8.5	7.1	5.6	4.9	50.8	174 367	153 296	137 574	13.7	11.4
Fayetteville, NC	9.1	18.9	17.1	20.3	13.6	8.4	6.5	4.1	2.1	48.3	302 963	274 713	247 160	10.3	11.1
Fayetteville-Springdale-Rogers, AR	6.9	17.8	15.2	16.8	14.4	9.8	7.7	6.3	4.9	50.6	311 121	210 939	178 609	47.5	18.1
Flagstaff, AZ-UT	7.8	16.8	11.4	18.4	14.8	9.2	8.2	7.6	5.7	51.7	122 366	101 760	79 032	20.2	28.8
Florence, AL	6.5	17.6	10.7	15.1	14.2	11.4	10.1	8.6	5.8	52.2	142 950	131 327	135 065	8.9	-2.8
Florence, SC	7.3	21.1	10.6	15.6	15.5	10.5	8.3	7.0	4.2	52.9	125 761	114 344	110 163	10.0	3.8
Fort Collins-Loveland, CO	7.3	18.0	14.3	17.9	16.9	9.4	6.5	5.5	4.1	50.5	251 494	186 136	149 184	35.1	24.8
Fort Myers-Cape Coral, FL	5.9	13.6	7.3	14.1	12.5	9.5	12.1	15.3	9.4	51.7	440 888	335 113	205 266	31.6	63.3
Fort Pierce-Port St. Lucie, FL	6.2	14.6	7.3	14.6	12.8	9.3	11.6	14.9	8.7	51.0	319 426	251 071	151 196	27.2	66.1
Fort Smith, AR-OK	7.3	19.9	9.4	16.0	14.5	10.9	8.7	7.5	5.9	51.4	207 290	175 911	162 813	17.8	8.0
Fort Walton Beach, FL	7.8	18.1	11.0	19.8	14.6	10.4	9.1	6.3	3.0	49.4	170 498	143 777	109 920	18.6	30.8
Fort Wayne, IN	7.9	20.0	9.8	17.3	15.5	9.8	8.1	6.6	4.9	51.4	502 141	456 281	444 772	10.1	2.6
Fresno, CA	9.4	22.0	11.3	17.1	14.1	8.8	7.1	6.1	4.3	50.4	922 516	755 569	577 737	22.1	30.8
Gadsden, AL	6.0	18.6	9.7	14.2	14.6	10.8	10.3	9.4	6.5	52.7	103 459	99 840	103 057	3.6	-3.1
Gainesville, FL	6.5	15.5	20.6	18.2	14.5	8.5	6.6	5.7	3.9	50.2	217 955	181 596	151 369	20.0	20.0
Glens Falls, NY	7.0	18.3	10.1	16.7	14.9	10.3	8.9	7.8	5.9	50.2	124 345	118 539	109 649	4.9	8.1
Goldsboro, NC	7.6	18.6	10.8	18.9	15.0	10.3	8.7	6.4	3.8	50.2	113 329	104 666	97 054	8.3	7.8
Grand Forks, ND-MN	8.4	17.6	19.1	20.0	13.3	7.1	5.7	4.7	4.1	48.9	97 478	103 272	100 944	-5.6	2.3
Grand Junction, CO	7.1	19.8	8.8	14.9	15.7	10.2	9.1	8.6	5.9	51.5	116 255	93 145	81 530	24.8	14.2
Grand Rapids-Muskegon-Holland, MI	8.7	19.9	11.1	18.3	14.9	9.2	7.3	5.9	4.6	51.3	1 088 514	937 891	840 824	16.1	11.5
Great Falls, MT	8.2	19.5	9.1	17.0	14.6	10.3	8.6	7.2	5.4	50.7	80 357	77 691	80 696	3.4	-3.7
Green Bay, WI	7.8	19.3	11.1	18.5	15.6	9.6	7.4	5.9	4.9	51.2	226 778	194 594	175 280	16.5	11.0
Greensboro—Winston-Salem—High Point, NC	6.6	16.4	11.4	17.4	15.7	11.2	9.2	7.2	5.0	52.2	1 251 509	1 050 304	950 763	19.2	10.5
Greenville, NC	7.1	17.0	17.9	17.4	14.5	8.8	7.4	6.0	3.9	52.5	133 798	108 480	90 146	23.3	20.3
Greenville-Spartanburg-Anderson, SC	6.8	17.5	12.2	16.5	15.2	11.0	8.7	7.3	4.8	51.7	962 441	830 499	744 428	15.9	11.6
Harrisburg-Lebanon-Carlisle, PA	6.6	16.8	10.5	16.5	15.7	10.6	9.5	8.1	5.8	51.7	629 401	587 986	556 242	7.0	5.7

Table C. Metropolitan Areas

Area Name	Total population	In households (percent)			Child		Other relatives		Nonrelatives		In group quarters (percent)	Institutionalized population			Noninstitutionalized population		
		Total in house-holds	House-holder	Spouse	Total	Own child under 18 years	Total	Under 18 years	Total	Unmar-ried partner	Total in group quarters	Correc-tional institu-tions	Nurs-ing homes	Other institu-tions	Col-lege dormi-tories	Mili-tary quar-ters	Other
	54	55	56	57	58	59	60	61	62	63	64	65	66	67	68	69	70
Columbia, SC	536 691	94.2	37.9	18.6	28.1	22.0	4.8	2.2	4.8	1.8	5.8	1.2	0.5	0.4	1.6	1.3	0.6
Columbus, GA-AL	274 624	94.6	36.9	17.4	30.2	23.2	6.1	2.9	4.0	1.7	5.4	0.8	0.5	0.1	0.1	3.5	0.3
Columbus, OH	1 540 157	97.3	39.7	19.2	28.6	23.3	3.9	1.6	5.9	2.3	2.7	0.8	0.6	0.1	1.0	0.0	0.2
Corpus Christi, TX	380 783	98.1	34.8	18.5	33.0	24.4	7.5	3.8	4.3	1.9	1.9	0.3	0.4	0.1	0.2	0.3	0.6
Corvallis, OR	78 153	93.6	38.6	19.4	23.7	20.0	2.5	0.7	9.4	2.2	6.4	0.0	0.3	0.1	5.5	0.0	0.4
Cumberland, MD-WV	102 008	93.5	39.3	20.7	25.8	19.3	3.3	1.3	4.3	1.9	6.5	3.2	1.0	0.3	1.7	0.0	0.3
Dallas-Fort Worth, TX	5 221 801	98.4	36.5	19.3	30.8	24.9	6.8	2.6	5.1	1.7	1.6	0.5	0.4	0.1	0.3	0.0	0.2
Dallas, TX	3 519 176	98.5	36.4	18.9	30.7	24.8	7.2	2.7	5.3	1.7	1.5	0.4	0.4	0.1	0.3	0.0	0.2
Fort Worth-Arlington, TX	1 702 625	98.3	36.7	19.9	31.0	25.1	6.0	2.4	4.6	1.7	1.7	0.7	0.5	0.1	0.3	0.0	0.2
Danville, VA	110 156	98.1	41.1	20.4	27.6	19.9	6.0	2.8	3.0	1.5	1.9	0.5	0.6	0.1	0.3	0.0	0.4
Davenport-Moline-Rock Island, IA-IL	359 062	97.6	39.9	20.7	29.1	23.0	3.3	1.6	4.6	2.2	2.4	0.5	0.8	0.1	0.7	0.0	0.3
Dayton-Springfield, OH	950 558	97.0	39.9	20.1	28.6	22.5	3.9	1.7	4.5	2.0	3.0	0.3	0.9	0.1	1.4	0.0	0.3
Daytona Beach, FL	493 175	96.9	41.8	21.6	23.2	17.6	4.8	1.8	5.6	2.5	3.1	0.5	0.9	0.2	0.9	0.0	0.6
Decatur, AL	145 867	98.7	39.2	22.8	29.7	23.1	4.3	1.9	2.6	1.2	1.3	0.6	0.5	0.0	0.0	0.0	0.2
Decatur, IL	114 706	96.9	40.6	20.6	27.8	22.1	3.6	1.8	4.3	1.9	3.1	0.5	0.9	0.1	1.4	0.0	0.3
Denver-Boulder-Greeley, CO	2 581 506	98.3	38.9	19.4	28.5	23.3	5.0	1.8	6.6	2.2	1.7	0.3	0.4	0.1	0.5	0.0	0.4
Boulder-Longmont, CO	291 288	97.1	39.4	19.3	25.5	21.6	3.2	1.0	9.8	2.4	2.9	0.2	0.4	0.0	2.1	0.0	0.2
Denver, CO	2 109 282	98.6	39.1	19.4	28.7	23.4	5.2	1.9	6.2	2.2	1.4	0.4	0.4	0.1	0.1	0.0	0.4
Greeley, CO	180 936	97.2	35.0	20.1	30.7	25.3	5.4	2.2	6.1	1.8	2.8	0.4	0.4	0.1	1.6	0.0	0.3
Des Moines, IA	456 022	97.6	39.3	20.8	29.1	24.1	3.3	1.3	4.9	2.2	2.4	0.3	0.8	0.1	0.8	0.0	0.4
Detroit-Ann Arbor-Flint, MI	5 456 428	98.3	38.2	18.7	31.4	23.6	5.3	2.2	4.7	2.0	1.7	0.4	0.4	0.1	0.4	0.0	0.5
Ann Arbor, MI	578 736	95.1	37.4	20.3	28.2	22.8	2.9	1.1	6.3	1.9	4.9	1.0	0.3	0.2	2.8	0.0	0.5
Detroit, MI	4 441 551	98.6	38.2	18.6	31.8	23.6	5.7	2.4	4.5	2.0	1.4	0.3	0.4	0.1	0.1	0.0	0.5
Flint, MI	436 141	98.8	38.9	18.5	31.9	24.4	4.6	2.3	4.9	2.4	1.2	0.2	0.4	0.0	0.1	0.0	0.5
Dothan, AL	137 916	98.0	39.7	21.2	29.7	23.6	4.3	2.1	3.1	1.4	2.0	0.3	0.7	0.1	0.0	0.9	0.1
Dover, DE	126 697	97.1	37.3	19.7	30.4	24.3	4.7	2.2	5.1	2.5	2.9	0.1	0.9	0.1	1.4	0.3	0.2
Dubuque, IA	89 143	94.9	37.8	21.5	30.2	24.4	1.9	0.7	3.5	1.6	5.1	0.1	1.2	0.1	2.4	0.0	1.3
Duluth-Superior, MN-WI	243 815	95.8	41.2	20.3	26.4	21.0	2.2	0.8	5.7	2.3	4.2	0.5	1.1	0.1	1.7	0.0	0.8
Eau Claire, WI	148 337	95.8	38.5	20.6	28.2	23.2	2.0	0.7	6.5	2.3	4.2	0.2	0.9	0.3	2.4	0.0	0.4
El Paso, TX	679 622	98.1	30.9	17.5	37.2	27.1	9.5	4.4	2.9	1.1	1.9	0.9	0.2	0.0	0.0	0.4	0.3
Elkhart-Goshen, IN	182 791	98.5	36.2	20.6	31.7	26.1	4.7	1.9	5.4	2.2	1.5	0.3	0.6	0.0	0.4	0.0	0.2
Elmira, NY	91 070	93.9	38.5	19.2	28.0	22.1	3.3	1.5	5.0	2.7	6.1	3.3	1.1	0.2	1.2	0.0	0.4
Enid, OK	57 813	97.0	40.1	21.7	27.9	22.8	3.6	1.7	3.7	1.6	3.0	0.4	1.6	0.1	0.0	0.4	0.5
Erie, PA	280 843	95.0	37.9	19.2	29.7	22.8	3.5	1.5	4.8	2.1	5.0	0.9	1.1	0.3	2.1	0.0	0.6
Eugene-Springfield, OR	322 959	97.7	40.4	19.8	25.5	20.7	3.5	1.3	8.5	2.8	2.3	0.2	0.3	0.1	1.0	0.0	0.7
Evansville-Henderson, IN-KY	296 195	97.0	40.2	21.2	28.5	22.4	3.2	1.5	4.1	1.9	3.0	0.3	1.0	0.1	1.2	0.0	0.3
Fargo-Moorhead, ND-MN	174 367	95.3	40.1	19.7	27.1	22.9	1.8	0.5	6.7	2.1	4.7	0.1	0.7	0.1	3.3	0.0	0.5
Fayetteville, NC	302 963	93.9	35.4	18.7	30.5	24.8	4.8	2.4	4.5	1.6	6.1	0.1	0.4	0.0	0.6	4.6	0.3
Fayetteville-Springdale-Rogers, AR	311 121	97.4	38.0	21.9	28.2	23.6	4.2	1.6	5.0	1.7	2.6	0.2	0.6	0.2	1.5	0.0	0.1
Flagstaff, AZ-UT	122 366	97.4	34.9	17.6	31.0	24.9	6.3	3.3	7.5	2.5	2.6	0.1	0.1	0.1	2.0	0.0	0.3
Florence, AL	142 950	98.4	41.0	22.9	28.0	21.2	3.9	1.7	2.7	1.1	1.6	0.2	0.7	0.1	0.5	0.0	0.2
Florence, SC	125 761	96.9	37.5	18.6	30.5	22.1	6.9	3.3	3.4	1.5	3.1	0.4	0.9	0.3	0.8	0.0	0.6
Fort Collins-Loveland, CO	251 494	97.2	38.6	20.7	26.6	22.4	2.8	0.9	8.4	2.2	2.8	0.1	0.4	0.0	1.8	0.0	0.4
Fort Myers-Cape Coral, FL	440 888	98.7	42.8	23.7	21.9	17.4	4.5	1.6	5.8	2.5	1.3	0.3	0.6	0.1	0.1	0.0	0.3
Fort Pierce-Port St. Lucie, FL	319 426	98.1	41.4	22.8	23.7	18.6	4.9	1.8	5.3	2.3	1.9	0.8	0.5	0.0	0.1	0.0	0.5
Fort Smith, AR-OK	207 290	98.4	38.5	21.5	30.0	24.0	4.7	2.1	3.8	1.6	1.6	0.3	0.6	0.2	0.0	0.0	0.4
Fort Walton Beach, FL	170 498	96.8	38.9	21.8	27.7	22.6	3.4	1.5	4.9	1.8	3.2	1.4	0.5	0.2	0.0	0.9	0.2
Fort Wayne, IN	502 141	98.2	38.2	20.8	31.7	25.7	3.2	1.4	4.2	2.0	1.8	0.2	0.8	0.1	0.3	0.0	0.4
Fresno, CA	922 516	97.2	31.3	16.8	35.1	27.6	8.2	3.3	5.7	2.0	2.8	1.6	0.4	0.1	0.2	0.0	0.6
Gadsden, AL	103 459	98.0	40.2	21.8	28.0	20.7	5.2	2.4	2.8	1.2	2.0	0.4	0.8	0.2	0.1	0.0	0.5
Gainesville, FL	217 955	94.1	40.2	15.6	22.6	18.0	4.3	1.6	11.5	2.4	5.9	0.7	0.2	0.2	3.9	0.0	0.9
Glens Falls, NY	124 345	95.9	38.8	20.7	28.2	22.3	3.2	1.2	5.1	2.8	4.1	2.3	0.8	0.0	0.4	0.0	0.5
Goldsboro, NC	113 329	95.9	37.6	19.4	29.4	23.0	5.4	2.5	4.2	1.7	4.1	1.5	0.7	0.5	0.2	0.5	0.7
Grand Forks, ND-MN	97 478	93.9	38.5	19.7	28.3	23.5	1.7	0.6	5.8	1.8	6.1	0.2	1.2	0.0	3.6	0.5	0.5
Grand Junction, CO	116 255	97.2	39.4	21.8	27.5	22.8	3.5	1.4	5.0	1.9	2.8	0.4	0.3	0.2	0.6	0.0	1.3
Grand Rapids-Muskegon-Holland, MI	1 088 514	97.3	36.4	20.2	32.2	26.2	3.5	1.4	5.0	1.9	2.7	0.5	0.7	0.1	0.8	0.0	0.6
Great Falls, MT	80 357	97.6	40.5	21.2	28.9	24.3	2.6	1.1	4.4	1.9	2.4	0.6	0.6	0.5	0.0	0.5	0.3
Green Bay, WI	226 778	96.6	38.5	20.5	29.8	24.7	2.4	0.8	5.4	2.5	3.4	1.0	0.6	0.0	1.2	0.0	0.5
Greensboro—Winston-Salem—High Point, NC	1 251 509	97.4	39.9	20.8	27.4	21.6	4.8	1.9	4.6	1.8	2.6	0.2	0.7	0.1	1.2	0.0	0.4
Greenville, NC	133 798	95.3	39.3	17.0	26.2	20.6	5.5	2.4	7.3	2.0	4.7	0.2	0.4	0.1	3.5	0.0	0.5
Greenville-Spartanburg-Anderson, SC	962 441	97.0	38.9	20.7	28.2	21.8	5.1	2.2	4.1	1.7	3.0	0.5	0.5	0.0	1.5	0.0	0.4
Harrisburg-Lebanon-Carlisle, PA	629 401	95.9	39.6	21.1	27.7	21.6	3.3	1.3	4.2	2.1	4.1	0.9	1.3	0.2	1.3	0.0	0.4

Table C. Metropolitan Areas

Area Name	Households by type, 2000												Households, 1990		
		Family households						Nonfamily households							
				Married couple		Female householder[1]			Householder living alone						
	Total households	Total	With own children under 18 years	Total	With own children under 18 years	Total	With own children under 18 years	Total	Total	65 years and over	Average household size	Average family size	Total households	Female householder[1]	Householder living alone
	71	72	73	74	75	76	77	78	79	80	81	82	83	84	85
Columbia, SC	203 341	67.0	33.1	49.0	22.5	14.4	8.8	33.0	26.4	7.1	2.49	3.03	163 223	13.5	23.6
Columbus, GA-AL	101 314	69.8	35.0	47.3	21.9	18.4	11.0	30.2	25.7	9.3	2.56	3.09	92 695	17.0	23.6
Columbus, OH	610 757	64.2	32.1	48.4	22.5	11.9	7.5	35.8	28.1	7.6	2.45	3.03	513 498	11.6	25.8
Corpus Christi, TX	132 458	73.2	37.2	53.3	25.9	14.9	8.6	26.8	22.0	7.9	2.82	3.32	118 516	13.4	21.2
Corvallis, OR	30 145	60.5	28.4	50.4	22.2	7.2	4.7	39.5	26.1	6.7	2.32	2.95	26 126	7.1	25.2
Cumberland, MD-WV	40 106	66.3	27.6	52.6	20.0	10.1	5.7	33.7	28.7	14.2	2.38	2.91	39 209	10.6	26.4
Dallas-Fort Worth, TX	1 906 764	69.2	36.7	52.7	27.2	12.0	7.4	30.8	24.7	5.6	2.70	3.25	1 508 031	11.0	25.2
Dallas, TX	1 281 957	68.6	36.5	52.0	27.1	12.1	7.4	31.4	25.1	5.4	2.70	3.27	1 001 750	11.3	25.9
Fort Worth-Arlington, TX	624 807	70.4	36.9	54.3	27.4	11.7	7.3	29.6	24.0	6.1	2.68	3.20	506 281	10.4	23.8
Danville, VA	45 291	68.8	28.5	49.6	18.6	15.3	8.2	31.2	28.2	12.3	2.39	2.91	42 325	14.1	24.9
Davenport-Moline-Rock Island, IA-IL	143 102	66.6	31.2	52.0	21.9	11.0	7.2	33.4	28.0	11.1	2.45	3.00	136 269	10.8	26.4
Dayton-Springfield, OH	379 626	66.7	30.7	50.3	20.9	12.7	7.8	33.3	27.9	9.8	2.43	2.97	364 300	12.0	24.8
Daytona Beach, FL	206 017	65.9	23.7	51.7	16.1	10.6	5.9	34.1	27.3	13.4	2.32	2.80	165 296	9.3	25.9
Decatur, AL	57 140	72.9	33.8	58.1	25.5	11.2	6.5	27.1	24.3	9.4	2.52	2.99	49 209	10.3	21.5
Decatur, IL	46 561	66.5	29.6	50.7	19.7	12.2	7.9	33.5	28.8	11.6	2.39	2.93	45 996	11.4	26.4
Denver-Boulder-Greeley, CO	1 003 218	63.9	32.6	49.9	24.2	9.9	6.2	36.1	27.4	6.6	2.53	3.13	785 276	10.1	28.0
Boulder-Longmont, CO	114 680	60.0	30.7	48.9	23.7	7.7	5.1	40.0	26.3	5.5	2.47	3.03	88 402	7.9	26.3
Denver, CO	825 291	63.9	32.5	49.5	23.9	10.2	6.4	36.1	28.0	6.7	2.52	3.13	649 404	10.5	28.7
Greeley, CO	63 247	71.5	37.2	57.6	28.6	9.4	6.1	28.5	21.0	6.9	2.78	3.25	47 470	9.1	22.3
Des Moines, IA	179 404	66.3	33.1	52.9	24.8	10.0	6.4	33.7	27.0	8.6	2.48	3.04	153 100	9.9	25.9
Detroit-Ann Arbor-Flint, MI	2 081 797	67.5	32.7	49.1	22.7	14.2	8.1	32.5	27.0	9.1	2.58	3.15	1 916 409	14.8	24.3
Ann Arbor, MI	216 641	66.1	32.7	54.1	25.7	8.8	5.4	33.9	25.3	6.4	2.54	3.08	175 050	8.9	22.7
Detroit, MI	1 695 331	67.6	32.6	48.6	22.5	14.6	8.2	32.4	27.2	9.5	2.58	3.17	1 580 063	15.3	24.6
Flint, MI	169 825	68.3	33.7	47.4	20.7	16.3	10.5	31.7	26.6	9.0	2.54	3.07	161 296	16.7	23.9
Dothan, AL	54 712	70.8	34.0	53.4	23.3	13.9	8.9	29.2	25.7	9.7	2.47	2.97	48 418	12.7	23.0
Dover, DE	47 224	71.2	35.5	52.9	23.9	13.8	8.9	28.8	23.0	8.4	2.61	3.06	39 655	11.9	21.2
Dubuque, IA	33 690	68.6	33.1	56.8	25.9	8.7	5.5	31.4	26.7	10.8	2.51	3.07	30 799	8.5	24.4
Duluth-Superior, MN-WI	100 427	62.4	27.9	49.2	19.6	9.5	6.3	37.6	31.0	12.8	2.33	2.90	95 275	9.5	28.7
Eau Claire, WI	57 178	65.2	31.4	53.4	23.8	8.4	5.6	34.8	26.2	10.4	2.49	3.02	50 359	8.3	24.2
El Paso, TX	210 022	79.1	44.9	54.7	32.2	18.0	10.5	20.9	17.8	6.7	3.18	3.63	178 366	15.8	17.0
Elkhart-Goshen, IN	66 154	72.0	36.4	56.8	26.6	10.5	7.0	28.0	22.6	8.4	2.72	3.18	56 713	9.1	21.6
Elmira, NY	35 049	66.4	31.0	49.8	20.5	12.4	8.1	33.6	27.9	12.2	2.44	2.97	35 275	11.5	25.5
Enid, OK	23 175	68.2	31.4	54.2	22.6	10.5	6.7	31.8	27.7	12.1	2.42	2.95	22 460	9.1	26.9
Erie, PA	106 507	66.7	31.6	50.5	22.0	12.1	7.4	33.3	27.6	11.2	2.51	3.07	101 564	11.5	25.4
Eugene-Springfield, OR	130 453	63.0	28.5	48.9	19.6	10.0	6.5	37.0	26.6	9.1	2.42	2.92	110 799	9.4	25.1
Evansville-Henderson, IN-KY	118 361	67.4	31.4	53.1	22.8	10.9	6.7	32.6	27.5	11.0	2.43	2.96	108 663	10.5	25.8
Fargo-Moorhead, ND-MN	69 985	60.3	30.9	49.0	23.6	8.0	5.5	39.7	29.9	8.4	2.38	3.01	57 771	7.9	26.7
Fayetteville, NC	107 358	72.3	39.4	52.9	27.0	15.5	10.1	27.7	22.4	5.9	2.65	3.11	91 500	14.1	19.4
Fayetteville-Springdale-Rogers, AR	118 363	70.1	33.5	57.6	25.8	8.8	5.6	29.9	23.5	7.8	2.56	3.04	80 927	7.5	22.4
Flagstaff, AZ-UT	42 685	66.9	34.8	50.5	24.4	11.9	7.6	33.1	22.1	4.8	2.79	3.36	31 642	11.2	19.9
Florence, AL	58 549	70.4	30.4	55.9	22.6	11.3	6.4	29.6	26.3	11.2	2.40	2.90	51 001	10.6	23.2
Florence, SC	47 147	71.7	33.8	49.7	22.1	18.1	10.0	28.3	24.5	8.2	2.59	3.08	40 217	17.3	21.8
Fort Collins-Loveland, CO	97 164	65.0	31.7	53.6	24.5	7.9	5.3	35.0	23.4	6.3	2.52	2.99	70 472	7.6	23.0
Fort Myers-Cape Coral, FL	188 599	67.7	22.4	55.5	15.4	8.7	5.1	32.3	25.8	13.1	2.31	2.73	140 124	8.2	23.0
Fort Pierce-Port St. Lucie, FL	132 221	68.4	24.3	55.2	16.8	9.5	5.6	31.6	25.8	13.9	2.37	2.81	101 196	8.5	22.3
Fort Smith, AR-OK	79 763	71.3	34.2	55.9	24.9	11.3	7.1	28.7	24.7	9.6	2.56	3.05	66 884	10.1	23.6
Fort Walton Beach, FL	66 269	70.2	33.1	56.2	24.3	10.2	6.6	29.8	23.5	7.5	2.49	2.94	53 313	9.5	20.9
Fort Wayne, IN	192 052	68.9	34.6	54.5	25.3	10.7	7.0	31.1	26.1	9.2	2.57	3.12	168 806	9.8	23.7
Fresno, CA	289 095	74.5	41.1	53.6	28.4	14.9	9.4	25.5	20.1	7.8	3.10	3.58	249 303	13.6	20.5
Gadsden, AL	41 615	70.8	29.9	54.2	21.3	13.1	7.1	29.2	26.3	12.4	2.44	2.93	38 675	11.8	24.3
Gainesville, FL	87 509	54.6	25.2	38.8	16.3	12.3	7.4	45.4	29.1	6.4	2.34	2.94	71 258	12.0	28.1
Glens Falls, NY	48 184	68.2	31.9	53.5	22.8	10.4	6.4	31.8	25.8	11.1	2.48	2.97	42 815	10.0	22.9
Goldsboro, NC	42 612	71.0	34.7	51.6	23.2	15.4	9.3	29.0	24.5	9.0	2.55	3.03	36 889	14.4	22.4
Grand Forks, ND-MN	37 505	63.1	32.3	51.2	24.4	8.7	6.1	36.9	28.5	10.0	2.44	3.05	37 324	8.0	25.7
Grand Junction, CO	45 823	68.9	31.4	55.3	22.7	9.8	6.3	31.1	25.1	10.3	2.47	2.94	36 250	9.8	24.8
Grand Rapids-Muskegon-Holland, MI	396 047	70.2	36.5	55.6	27.2	10.9	7.2	29.8	23.8	8.2	2.67	3.19	333 911	10.8	21.5
Great Falls, MT	32 547	65.9	32.2	52.3	23.0	9.9	6.8	34.1	28.8	10.9	2.41	2.97	30 133	9.3	26.2
Green Bay, WI	87 295	65.9	33.9	53.2	25.5	8.9	6.2	34.1	26.5	8.4	2.51	3.08	72 280	9.0	24.1
Greensboro—Winston-Salem—High Point, NC	498 751	68.3	31.3	52.1	22.1	12.3	7.3	31.7	26.4	9.0	2.44	2.95	414 793	11.9	25.0
Greenville, NC	52 539	61.4	29.9	43.4	19.5	14.4	8.7	38.6	28.3	7.3	2.43	3.02	40 491	14.5	25.7
Greenville-Spartanburg-Anderson, SC	374 741	69.8	31.9	53.2	22.7	12.6	7.2	30.2	25.4	8.9	2.49	2.98	312 740	12.1	23.3
Harrisburg-Lebanon-Carlisle, PA	248 931	67.2	30.0	53.4	21.9	10.3	6.1	32.8	27.5	10.4	2.43	2.96	226 353	9.6	25.3

[1] No spouse present.

Table C. Metropolitan Areas

Area Name	Percent change of households, 1990–2000	Total housing units	Occupied housing units (percent)	Vacant housing units — Total	For seasonal, recreational, or occasional use	Homeowner vacancy rate (percent)	Rental vacancy rate (percent)	Occupied housing units — Total	Percent owner-occupied housing units	Percent renter-occupied housing units	Average household size of owner-occupied units	Average household size of renter-occupied units
	86	87	88	89	90	91	92	93	94	95	96	97
Columbia, SC	24.6	220 771	92.1	7.9	0.9	1.9	9.8	203 341	67.9	32.1	2.60	2.26
Columbus, GA-AL.................	9.3	112 617	90.0	10.0	1.2	1.8	11.2	101 314	59.3	40.7	2.58	2.54
Columbus, OH	18.9	653 067	93.5	6.5	0.5	1.7	8.0	610 757	62.3	37.7	2.62	2.18
Corpus Christi, TX	11.8	147 905	89.6	10.4	2.5	2.1	9.8	132 458	62.5	37.5	2.93	2.64
Corvallis, OR	15.4	31 980	94.3	5.7	0.4	1.9	7.2	30 145	57.3	42.7	2.02	2.16
Cumberland, MD-WV	1.2	45 078	89.0	11.0	2.0	2.7	9.8	40 106	72.3	27.7	2.46	2.17
Dallas-Fort Worth, TX..........	26.4	2 031 348	93.9	6.1	0.7	1.6	7.4	1 906 764	60.4	39.6	2.86	2.44
Dallas, TX..................	28.0	1 366 060	93.8	6.2	0.7	1.6	7.2	1 281 957	58.9	41.1	2.87	2.46
Fort Worth-Arlington, TX	23.4	665 288	93.9	6.1	0.7	1.5	7.7	624 807	63.6	36.4	2.83	2.41
Danville, VA........................	7.0	51 119	88.6	11.4	2.1	2.0	10.8	45 291	70.1	29.9	2.43	2.29
Davenport-Moline-Rock Island, IA-IL	5.0	151 408	94.5	5.5	0.4	1.4	7.2	143 102	71.3	28.7	2.57	2.16
Dayton-Springfield, OH.........	4.2	408 277	93.0	7.0	0.4	1.7	9.0	379 626	67.2	32.8	2.52	2.23
Daytona Beach, FL..............	24.6	236 390	87.2	12.8	7.4	2.0	8.2	206 017	76.2	23.8	2.35	2.23
Decatur, AL........................	16.1	62 397	91.6	8.4	0.6	1.7	11.8	57 140	75.5	24.5	2.58	2.32
Decatur, IL.........................	1.2	50 241	92.7	7.3	0.3	1.6	11.0	46 561	71.6	28.4	2.46	2.21
Denver-Boulder-Greeley, CO	27.8	1 042 779	96.2	3.8	0.6	1.1	4.2	1 003 218	66.4	33.6	2.67	2.26
Boulder-Longmont, CO......	29.7	119 900	95.6	4.4	1.7	0.8	3.4	114 680	64.7	35.3	2.59	2.23
Denver, CO.....................	27.1	856 685	96.3	3.7	0.5	1.1	4.4	825 291	66.5	33.5	2.66	2.24
Greeley, CO....................	33.2	66 194	95.5	4.5	0.3	1.7	4.0	63 247	68.6	31.4	2.85	2.63
Des Moines, IA....................	17.2	188 265	95.3	4.7	0.3	1.6	6.1	179 404	70.4	29.6	2.65	2.08
Detroit-Ann Arbor-Flint, MI	8.6	2 208 124	94.3	5.7	0.7	1.4	6.6	2 081 797	72.2	27.8	2.70	2.25
Ann Arbor, MI	23.8	229 757	94.3	5.7	2.0	1.3	4.6	216 641	70.0	30.0	2.73	2.10
Detroit, MI......................	7.3	1 794 737	94.5	5.5	0.6	1.3	6.4	1 695 331	72.4	27.6	2.71	2.26
Flint, MI..........................	5.3	183 630	92.5	7.5	0.5	2.1	10.6	169 825	73.2	26.8	2.62	2.31
Dothan, AL.........................	13.0	61 350	89.2	10.8	0.7	2.2	12.9	54 712	67.7	32.3	2.50	2.40
Dover, DE	19.1	50 481	93.5	6.5	0.7	1.6	6.7	47 224	70.0	30.0	2.66	2.49
Dubuque, IA	9.4	35 505	94.9	5.1	0.5	1.0	8.4	33 690	73.5	26.5	2.68	2.03
Duluth-Superior, MN-WI	5.4	116 156	86.5	13.5	9.2	1.1	6.0	100 427	74.1	25.9	2.48	1.89
Eau Claire, WI	13.5	60 295	94.8	5.2	1.8	0.9	3.9	57 178	69.0	31.0	2.65	2.11
El Paso, TX	17.7	224 447	93.6	6.4	0.4	1.5	7.8	210 022	63.6	36.4	3.32	2.92
Elkhart-Goshen, IN	16.6	69 791	94.8	5.2	0.5	1.7	6.7	66 154	72.2	27.8	2.81	2.49
Elmira, NY	-0.6	37 745	92.9	7.1	0.7	1.8	9.2	35 049	68.9	31.1	2.54	2.22
Enid, OK	3.2	26 047	89.0	11.0	0.5	3.1	11.0	23 175	70.3	29.7	2.43	2.40
Erie, PA	4.9	114 322	93.2	6.8	1.0	1.6	7.9	106 501	69.2	30.8	2.65	2.17
Eugene-Springfield, OR........	17.7	138 946	93.9	6.1	1.2	1.8	6.3	130 453	62.3	37.7	2.52	2.25
Evansville-Henderson, IN-KY	8.9	127 388	92.9	7.1	0.6	1.8	8.1	118 361	70.9	29.1	2.56	2.09
Fargo-Moorhead, ND-MN......	21.1	73 536	95.2	4.8	0.5	1.5	5.3	69 985	58.9	41.1	2.70	1.90
Fayetteville, NC	17.3	118 425	90.7	9.3	0.3	2.7	10.1	107 358	59.4	40.6	2.68	2.61
Fayetteville-Springdale-Rogers, AR	46.3	128 611	92.0	8.0	1.6	2.6	6.8	118 363	65.7	34.3	2.62	2.44
Flagstaff, AZ-UT	34.9	57 210	74.6	25.4	18.2	2.4	6.7	42 685	62.3	37.7	2.91	2.59
Florence, AL	14.8	65 404	89.5	10.5	2.0	2.0	11.7	58 549	74.2	25.8	2.49	2.16
Florence, SC	17.2	51 836	91.0	9.0	0.7	1.4	10.0	47 147	73.0	27.0	2.65	2.40
Fort Collins-Loveland, CO	37.9	105 392	92.2	7.8	4.6	1.2	4.1	97 164	67.7	32.3	2.62	2.29
Fort Myers-Cape Coral, FL ...	34.6	245 405	76.9	23.1	16.1	2.7	15.2	188 599	76.5	23.5	2.29	2.38
Fort Pierce-Port St. Lucie, FL	30.7	156 733	84.4	15.6	10.1	2.3	10.9	132 221	78.8	21.2	2.31	2.58
Fort Smith, AR-OK	19.3	87 566	91.1	8.9	1.4	2.4	8.2	79 763	68.7	31.3	2.62	2.43
Fort Walton Beach, FL	24.3	78 593	84.3	15.7	5.4	2.2	19.3	66 269	66.4	33.6	2.51	2.45
Fort Wayne, IN	13.8	206 237	93.1	6.9	0.5	1.7	10.2	192 052	73.9	26.1	2.71	2.17
Fresno, CA	16.0	311 154	92.9	7.1	1.7	1.6	5.4	289 095	57.7	42.3	3.02	3.22
Gadsden, AL........................	7.6	45 959	90.5	9.5	0.5	2.1	9.8	41 615	74.4	25.6	2.48	2.31
Gainesville, FL.....................	22.8	95 113	92.0	8.0	0.7	2.0	7.9	87 509	54.9	45.1	2.51	2.14
Glens Falls, NY	12.5	61 646	78.2	21.8	15.9	2.5	7.7	48 184	71.9	28.1	2.58	2.21
Goldsboro, NC	15.5	47 313	90.1	9.9	0.4	1.7	8.0	42 612	65.4	34.6	2.58	2.50
Grand Forks, ND-MN	0.5	41 381	90.6	9.4	2.5	2.5	7.1	37 505	60.4	39.6	2.67	2.09
Grand Junction, CO..............	26.4	48 427	94.6	5.4	1.0	1.7	5.8	45 823	72.7	27.3	2.52	2.32
Grand Rapids-Muskegon-Holland, MI	18.6	422 704	93.7	6.3	2.0	1.4	6.3	396 047	74.9	25.1	2.80	2.28
Great Falls, MT	8.0	35 225	92.4	7.6	1.3	1.7	6.6	32 547	64.9	35.1	2.53	2.19
Green Bay, WI.....................	20.8	90 199	96.8	3.2	0.5	0.9	3.8	87 295	65.4	34.6	2.72	2.11
Greensboro—Winston-Salem—High Point, NC......	20.2	535 837	93.1	6.9	0.6	1.8	8.1	498 751	68.7	31.3	2.50	2.32
Greenville, NC	29.8	58 408	90.0	10.0	0.4	2.1	6.0	52 539	58.1	41.9	2.60	2.18
Greenville-Spartanburg-Anderson, SC	19.8	411 402	91.1	8.9	1.0	2.2	10.8	374 741	71.5	28.5	2.57	2.30
Harrisburg-Lebanon-Carlisle, PA................	10.0	266 345	93.5	6.5	1.0	1.8	7.7	248 931	70.3	29.7	2.56	2.11

Table C. Metropolitan Areas

Table C. Metropolitan Areas

CMSA/ MSA/ PMSA/ NECMA code[1]	Area Name	Population, 2000				Population, 1990				Population and population characteristics, 2000					
										Race (percent)					
										One race					
		Land area, 2000[2] (sq km)	Total persons	Rank	Per square kilometer	Land area, 1990[2] (sq km)	Total persons	Rank	Per square kilometer	White	Black or African American	American Indian or Alaska Native	Asian	Native Hawaiian and other Pacific Islander	Some other race
		1	2	3	4	5	6	7	8	9	10	11	12	13	14
3283	Hartford, CT	3 923	1 148 618	53	292.8	3 923	1 123 678	46	286.4	80.7	9.6	0.2	2.3	0.0	5.1
3285	Hattiesburg, MS	2 496	111 674	289	44.7	2 497	98 738	293	39.5	71.7	26.3	0.2	0.7	0.0	0.4
3290	Hickory-Morganton-Lenoir, NC	4 244	341 851	145	80.6	4 244	292 405	146	68.9	87.5	6.9	0.2	2.3	0.1	2.0
3320	Honolulu, HI	1 553	876 156	68	564.0	1 554	836 231	67	538.1	21.3	2.4	0.2	46.0	8.9	1.3
3350	Houma, LA	6 060	194 477	204	32.1	6 061	182 842	194	30.2	78.1	15.4	3.9	0.7	0.0	0.6
42	Houston-Galveston-Brazoria, TX	19 956	4 669 571	X	234.0	19 960	3 731 014	X	186.9	62.6	16.9	0.4	4.9	0.1	12.4
1145	Brazoria, TX	3 591	241 767	181	67.3	3 592	191 707	185	53.4	77.1	8.5	0.5	2.0	0.0	9.6
2920	Galveston-Texas City, TX	1 032	250 158	177	242.4	1 033	217 396	177	210.5	72.7	15.4	0.5	2.1	0.0	7.2
3360	Houston, TX	15 333	4 177 646	8	272.5	15 335	3 321 911	8	216.6	61.1	17.5	0.4	5.2	0.1	12.9
3400	Huntington-Ashland, WV-KY-OH	5 592	315 538	154	56.4	5 595	312 529	140	55.9	96.2	2.2	0.2	0.4	0.0	0.1
3440	Huntsville, AL	3 556	342 376	144	96.3	3 556	293 047	144	82.4	74.3	21.0	0.7	1.6	0.1	0.7
3480	Indianapolis, IN	9 125	1 607 486	37	176.2	9 126	1 380 491	35	151.3	82.1	13.9	0.2	1.2	0.0	1.3
3500	Iowa City, IA	1 591	111 006	290	69.7	1 592	96 119	298	60.4	90.1	2.9	0.3	4.1	0.0	1.0
3520	Jackson, MI	1 830	158 422	230	86.6	1 830	149 756	220	81.8	88.5	7.9	0.4	0.5	0.0	0.8
3560	Jackson, MS	6 114	440 801	117	72.1	6 120	395 396	114	64.6	52.6	45.6	0.1	0.7	0.0	0.3
3580	Jackson, TN	2 190	107 377	293	49.0	2 190	90 801	302	41.5	68.5	29.2	0.2	0.6	0.0	0.6
3600	Jacksonville, FL	6 825	1 100 491	57	161.2	6 826	906 727	59	132.8	72.6	21.7	0.3	2.3	0.1	1.2
3605	Jacksonville, NC	1 986	150 355	239	75.7	1 986	149 838	219	75.4	72.1	18.5	0.7	1.7	0.2	3.6
3610	Jamestown, NY	2 751	139 750	254	50.8	2 751	141 895	231	51.6	94.0	2.2	0.4	0.4	0.0	1.7
3620	Janesville-Beloit, WI	1 866	152 307	236	81.6	1 866	139 510	233	74.8	91.0	4.6	0.3	0.8	0.0	1.8
3660	Johnson City-Kingsport-Bristol, TN-VA	7 422	480 091	105	64.7	7 422	436 068	101	58.8	96.2	2.1	0.2	0.4	0.0	0.3
3680	Johnstown, PA	4 565	232 621	185	51.0	4 566	241 280	168	52.8	96.3	2.4	0.1	0.3	0.0	0.3
3700	Jonesboro, AR	1 841	82 148	312	44.6	1 841	68 956	315	37.5	89.3	7.8	0.3	0.6	0.0	0.9
3710	Joplin, MO	3 279	157 322	231	48.0	3 280	134 910	239	41.1	92.8	1.2	1.6	0.6	0.1	1.4
3720	Kalamazoo-Battle Creek, MI	4 873	452 851	113	92.9	4 874	429 453	104	88.1	84.9	9.3	0.6	1.4	0.0	1.6
3760	Kansas City, MO-KS	14 002	1 776 062	28	126.8	14 004	1 582 874	29	113.0	80.8	12.8	0.5	1.6	0.1	2.3
3810	Killeen-Temple, TX	5 469	312 952	155	57.2	5 467	255 299	161	46.7	63.9	20.8	0.8	2.4	0.5	8.0
3840	Knoxville, TN	6 344	687 249	78	108.3	6 343	585 960	86	92.4	91.3	5.8	0.3	1.0	0.0	0.5
3850	Kokomo, IN	1 433	101 541	301	70.8	1 433	96 946	296	67.7	91.1	5.5	0.3	0.9	0.0	0.8
3870	La Crosse, WI-MN	2 619	126 838	267	48.4	2 619	116 401	269	44.4	94.8	0.8	0.4	2.7	0.0	0.2
3920	Lafayette, IN	2 344	182 821	210	78.0	2 344	161 572	207	68.9	89.9	2.1	0.3	3.7	0.0	2.8
3880	Lafayette, LA	6 717	385 647	129	57.4	6 717	345 053	128	51.4	69.7	28.2	0.2	0.7	0.0	0.4
3960	Lake Charles, LA	2 774	183 577	209	66.2	2 774	168 134	206	60.6	73.6	24.0	0.3	0.6	0.0	0.4
3980	Lakeland-Winter Haven, FL	4 855	483 924	104	99.7	4 856	405 382	109	83.5	79.6	13.5	0.4	0.9	0.0	3.8
4000	Lancaster, PA	2 458	470 658	109	191.5	2 458	422 822	106	172.0	91.5	2.8	0.1	1.4	0.0	2.9
4040	Lansing-East Lansing, MI	4 421	447 728	114	101.3	4 421	432 684	102	97.9	84.4	8.1	0.5	2.6	0.0	1.9
4080	Laredo, TX	8 694	193 117	205	22.2	8 695	133 239	241	15.3	82.2	0.4	0.5	0.4	0.0	14.0
4100	Las Cruces, NM	9 861	174 682	217	17.7	9 861	135 510	238	13.7	67.8	1.6	1.5	0.8	0.1	24.7
4120	Las Vegas, NV-AZ	101 964	1 563 282	40	15.3	101 969	852 646	64	8.4	73.8	8.1	1.0	4.7	0.4	8.0
4150	Lawrence, KS	1 183	99 962	302	84.5	1 184	81 798	308	69.1	86.1	4.2	2.6	3.1	0.1	1.2
4200	Lawton, OK	2 770	114 996	284	41.5	2 770	111 486	277	40.2	65.2	19.0	5.1	2.1	0.4	3.5
4243	Lewiston-Auburn, ME	1 218	103 793	297	85.2	1 218	105 259	285	86.4	97.0	0.7	0.3	0.6	0.0	0.3
4280	Lexington, KY	4 971	479 198	106	96.4	4 973	405 936	108	81.6	86.4	9.5	0.2	1.6	0.0	1.0
4320	Lima, OH	2 087	155 084	232	74.3	2 087	154 340	213	74.0	88.9	8.6	0.2	0.5	0.0	0.5
4360	Lincoln, NE	2 173	250 291	176	115.2	2 173	213 641	179	98.3	90.1	2.8	0.6	2.9	0.1	1.7
4400	Little Rock-North Little Rock, AR	7 531	583 845	92	77.5	7 534	513 026	91	68.1	74.5	21.9	0.4	1.0	0.0	0.9
4420	Longview-Marshall, TX	4 559	208 780	196	45.8	4 560	193 801	184	42.5	74.6	19.5	0.5	0.5	0.0	3.6
49	Los Angeles-Riverside-Orange County, CA	87 944	16 373 645	X	186.2	87 970	14 531 529	X	165.2	55.1	7.6	0.9	10.4	0.3	21.0
4480	Los Angeles-Long Beach, CA	10 518	9 519 338	1	905.1	10 515	8 863 052	1	842.9	48.7	9.8	0.8	11.9	0.3	23.5
5945	Orange County, CA	2 045	2 846 289	14	1 392.1	2 045	2 410 668	16	1 178.8	64.8	1.7	0.7	13.6	0.3	14.8
6780	Riverside-San Bernardino, CA	70 603	3 254 821	11	46.1	70 629	2 588 793	12	36.7	62.1	7.7	1.2	4.2	0.3	19.8
8735	Ventura, CA	4 779	753 197	72	157.6	4 781	669 016	72	139.9	69.9	1.9	0.9	5.3	0.2	17.7
4520	Louisville, KY-IN	5 366	1 025 598	61	191.1	5 367	949 012	56	176.8	82.8	13.9	0.2	1.1	0.0	0.6
4600	Lubbock, TX	2 330	242 628	180	104.1	2 330	222 636	176	95.6	74.3	7.7	0.6	1.3	0.0	14.1
4640	Lynchburg, VA	4 637	214 911	193	46.3	4 639	193 926	183	41.8	79.6	17.9	0.3	0.7	0.0	0.4
4680	Macon, GA	3 967	322 549	152	81.3	3 968	291 079	148	73.4	59.2	37.5	0.2	1.1	0.0	0.7
4720	Madison, WI	3 113	426 526	120	137.0	3 114	367 085	122	117.9	89.0	4.0	0.3	3.5	0.0	1.4
4800	Mansfield, OH	2 328	175 818	215	75.5	2 329	174 007	201	74.7	90.8	7.1	0.2	0.5	0.0	0.3
4880	McAllen-Edinburg-Mission, TX	4 066	569 463	94	140.1	4 064	383 545	118	94.4	77.7	0.5	0.4	0.6	0.0	18.6
4890	Medford-Ashland, OR	7 214	181 269	212	25.1	7 214	146 387	226	20.3	91.6	0.4	1.1	0.9	0.2	2.9
4900	Melbourne-Titusville-Palm Bay, FL	2 637	476 230	108	180.6	2 638	398 978	112	151.2	86.8	8.4	0.4	1.5	0.1	1.1
4920	Memphis, TN-AR-MS	7 787	1 135 614	54	145.8	7 790	1 007 306	51	129.3	52.9	43.4	0.2	1.4	0.0	1.1

[1] MSA = Metropolitan Statistical Area. PMSA = Primary MSA. NECMA = New England County Metropolitan Area. See Appendix A for explanation of these concepts. See Appendix B for list of metropolitan areas identified by type, with component counties.
[2] Dry land or land partially or temporarily covered by water.

Table C. Metropolitan Areas

Area Name	Population and population characteristics, 2000 (cont'd)								Population and population characteristics, 1990				
	Race (percent) (cont'd)								Race (percent)				
	Race alone or in combination												
	Two or more races	White	Black	American Indian or Alaska Native	Asian	Native Hawaiian and other Pacific Islander	Some other race	Hispanic[1]	White	Black or African American	American Indian or Alaska Native	Asian and Pacific Islander	Hispanic[1]
	15	16	17	18	19	20	21	22	23	24	25	26	27
Hartford, CT	2.1	82.2	10.5	0.6	2.7	0.1	6.1	9.4	86.0	8.7	0.2	1.5	7.0
Hattiesburg, MS	0.7	72.3	26.6	0.5	0.8	0.0	0.5	1.2	74.2	25.0	0.1	0.6	0.7
Hickory-Morganton-Lenoir, NC	1.0	88.3	7.2	0.5	2.6	0.1	2.3	4.0	90.9	7.9	0.2	0.8	0.7
Honolulu, HI	19.9	35.2	3.4	1.8	61.6	21.6	3.7	6.7	31.6	3.1	0.4	63.0	6.8
Houma, LA	1.2	79.2	15.7	4.7	0.9	0.1	0.8	1.5	80.6	14.6	3.7	0.7	1.4
Houston-Galveston-Brazoria, TX	2.7	64.8	17.4	0.8	5.4	0.1	14.3	28.9	67.6	17.9	0.3	3.6	20.8
Brazoria, TX	2.2	79.1	8.8	1.0	2.3	0.1	11.0	22.8	80.8	8.3	0.4	1.0	17.6
Galveston-Texas City, TX	2.1	74.5	15.8	0.9	2.5	0.1	8.4	18.0	75.5	17.6	0.3	1.6	14.2
Houston, TX	2.8	63.4	17.9	0.8	5.8	0.1	14.8	29.9	66.3	18.5	0.3	3.8	21.4
Huntington-Ashland, WV-KY-OH	0.8	97.0	2.5	0.6	0.5	0.0	0.3	0.7	97.3	2.2	0.1	0.3	0.4
Huntsville, AL	1.7	75.7	21.5	1.5	1.9	0.1	1.0	2.0	77.1	20.1	0.7	1.8	1.2
Indianapolis, IN	1.3	83.1	14.5	0.6	1.5	0.1	1.6	2.7	84.9	13.8	0.2	0.8	0.9
Iowa City, IA	1.5	91.5	3.4	0.6	4.6	0.1	1.4	2.5	93.3	2.1	0.2	4.0	1.5
Jackson, MI	1.7	90.1	8.7	1.1	0.7	0.1	1.2	2.2	90.5	8.0	0.4	0.4	1.5
Jackson, MS	0.6	53.1	45.9	0.3	0.9	0.1	0.4	1.0	56.9	42.5	0.1	0.4	0.5
Jackson, TN	0.9	69.2	29.6	0.5	0.8	0.0	0.8	1.6	68.5	31.0	0.1	0.3	0.5
Jacksonville, FL	1.8	74.1	22.2	0.8	2.9	0.2	1.8	3.8	77.4	20.0	0.3	1.7	2.5
Jacksonville, NC	3.2	74.6	19.7	1.6	2.6	0.4	1.8	7.2	74.7	19.9	0.6	2.0	5.4
Jamestown, NY	1.2	95.2	2.6	0.8	0.5	0.1	2.2	4.2	96.1	1.7	0.4	0.4	2.9
Janesville-Beloit, WI	1.5	92.4	5.2	0.7	1.0	0.1	2.2	3.9	93.8	4.8	0.3	0.7	1.3
Johnson City-Kingsport-Bristol, TN-VA	0.7	96.9	2.3	0.6	0.5	0.0	0.4	0.9	97.4	2.0	0.2	0.3	0.4
Johnstown, PA	0.6	96.9	2.7	0.2	0.4	0.0	0.4	0.8	98.0	1.6	0.1	0.2	0.5
Jonesboro, AR	1.1	90.2	8.0	0.8	0.8	0.1	1.2	2.1	93.5	5.5	0.3	0.6	0.6
Joplin, MO	2.2	94.9	1.6	3.1	0.7	0.2	1.8	3.0	96.4	1.0	1.8	0.6	0.9
Kalamazoo-Battle Creek, MI	2.1	86.8	10.3	1.4	1.6	0.1	2.1	3.6	88.4	8.9	0.5	1.4	1.8
Kansas City, MO-KS	2.0	82.5	13.4	1.2	2.0	0.2	2.9	5.2	84.3	12.8	0.5	1.1	2.9
Killeen-Temple, TX	3.8	66.7	22.2	1.5	3.4	0.8	9.5	15.7	71.0	19.5	0.6	2.8	12.2
Knoxville, TN	1.1	92.3	6.1	0.8	1.2	0.1	0.7	1.3	92.8	6.0	0.2	0.8	0.5
Kokomo, IN	1.4	92.4	6.1	0.7	1.1	0.1	1.0	1.9	94.3	4.5	0.3	0.5	1.2
La Crosse, WI-MN	0.9	95.6	1.1	0.7	3.1	0.1	0.4	0.9	96.3	0.4	0.3	2.7	0.7
Lafayette, IN	1.3	91.0	2.4	0.6	4.0	0.1	3.2	5.6	93.4	2.0	0.2	3.7	1.6
Lafayette, LA	0.8	70.3	28.5	0.5	0.9	0.1	0.6	1.3	73.8	24.6	0.2	0.9	1.5
Lake Charles, LA	1.0	74.5	24.4	0.7	0.8	0.1	0.7	1.3	76.2	22.9	0.2	0.4	1.1
Lakeland-Winter Haven, FL	1.7	80.9	14.1	0.8	1.2	0.1	4.7	9.5	84.4	13.4	0.3	0.6	4.1
Lancaster, PA	1.3	92.5	3.3	0.4	1.6	0.1	3.4	5.7	94.1	2.4	0.1	1.1	3.7
Lansing-East Lansing, MI	2.4	86.5	9.1	1.2	3.0	0.1	2.6	4.7	88.1	7.2	0.6	1.9	3.9
Laredo, TX	2.5	84.5	0.5	0.6	0.6	0.0	16.3	94.3	70.3	0.1	0.2	0.4	93.9
Las Cruces, NM	3.6	71.0	2.0	2.2	1.1	0.2	27.3	63.4	91.1	1.6	0.7	0.9	56.4
Las Vegas, NV-AZ	4.0	77.1	8.9	1.7	5.9	0.9	9.9	20.6	81.3	9.5	0.9	3.5	11.2
Lawrence, KS	2.7	88.5	5.2	3.6	3.7	0.2	1.8	3.3	89.1	4.1	2.6	3.2	2.6
Lawton, OK	4.7	69.0	20.6	7.0	3.2	0.7	4.6	8.4	71.5	17.9	4.6	2.7	6.2
Lewiston-Auburn, ME	1.2	98.1	1.0	0.8	0.8	0.1	0.5	1.0	98.5	0.5	0.2	0.6	0.6
Lexington, KY	1.3	87.6	10.0	0.6	1.8	0.1	1.3	2.5	87.7	10.7	0.2	1.2	0.9
Lima, OH	1.3	90.1	9.3	0.6	0.7	0.0	0.7	1.2	91.0	8.0	0.2	0.5	1.0
Lincoln, NE	1.9	91.7	3.5	1.1	3.3	0.1	2.3	3.4	94.9	2.2	0.6	1.6	1.8
Little Rock-North Little Rock, AR	1.3	75.6	22.3	1.0	1.3	0.1	1.2	2.1	78.9	19.9	0.4	0.7	0.8
Longview-Marshall, TX	1.3	75.8	19.8	1.0	0.6	0.1	4.1	7.1	75.3	22.1	0.4	0.4	3.1
Los Angeles-Riverside-Orange County, CA	4.7	59.1	8.3	1.6	11.5	0.5	24.0	40.3	64.6	8.5	0.6	9.2	32.9
Los Angeles-Long Beach, CA	4.9	52.8	10.5	1.5	13.1	0.5	26.9	44.6	56.8	11.2	0.5	10.8	37.8
Orange County, CA	4.1	68.3	2.1	1.3	14.9	0.6	17.1	30.8	78.6	1.8	0.5	10.3	23.4
Riverside-San Bernardino, CA	4.7	66.0	8.6	2.1	5.2	0.5	22.6	37.8	74.6	6.9	1.0	3.9	26.5
Ventura, CA	3.9	73.3	2.4	1.8	6.5	0.5	19.7	33.4	79.1	2.3	0.7	5.2	26.4
Louisville, KY-IN	1.3	83.9	14.5	0.6	1.3	0.1	1.6	1.6	86.0	13.1	0.2	0.6	0.6
Lubbock, TX	2.0	76.0	8.0	1.0	1.6	0.1	15.4	27.5	79.1	7.7	0.3	1.2	22.9
Lynchburg, VA	1.0	80.5	18.4	0.7	0.9	0.1	0.6	1.0	78.0	21.2	0.2	0.5	0.6
Macon, GA	1.1	60.0	38.0	0.6	1.5	0.1	1.0	2.1	64.2	34.6	0.2	0.7	1.0
Madison, WI	1.8	90.5	4.7	0.8	3.9	0.1	1.9	3.4	93.9	2.9	0.3	2.4	1.6
Mansfield, OH	1.1	91.8	7.6	0.7	0.6	0.1	0.5	0.9	91.2	7.9	0.2	0.5	0.7
McAllen-Edinburg-Mission, TX	2.1	79.7	0.6	0.6	0.7	0.0	20.6	88.3	74.8	0.2	0.2	0.3	85.2
Medford-Ashland, OR	2.9	94.4	0.7	2.4	1.4	0.4	3.8	6.7	95.8	0.2	1.3	1.0	4.1
Melbourne-Titusville-Palm Bay, FL	1.8	88.3	9.0	0.9	2.0	0.2	1.7	4.6	89.8	7.9	0.3	1.3	3.1
Memphis, TN-AR-MS	1.0	53.6	43.8	0.5	1.6	0.1	1.4	2.4	58.1	40.6	0.2	0.8	0.8

[1] Hispanic persons may be of any race.

Table C. Metropolitan Areas

Area Name	Population and population characteristics, 2000										
	Age (percent)										
	Under 5 years	5 to 17 years	18 to 24 years	25 to 34 years	35 to 44 years	45 to 54 years	55 to 64 years	65 to 74 years	75 years and over	Median age (years)	Percent Female
	28	29	30	31	32	33	34	35	36	37	38
Hartford, CT.........................	6.3	17.9	8.3	13.1	16.9	14.3	9.1	6.9	7.1	37.6	51.6
Hattiesburg, MS..................	7.1	18.7	15.6	14.4	14.2	11.7	7.6	5.8	5.0	30.8	52.4
Hickory-Morganton-Lenoir, NC..	6.5	17.6	8.5	14.7	15.8	14.1	10.0	7.2	5.6	36.7	50.4
Honolulu, HI........................	6.5	17.3	10.1	14.9	15.7	13.4	8.7	7.1	6.3	35.7	49.7
Houma, LA...........................	7.2	21.1	10.3	13.7	16.1	12.7	8.5	6.0	4.4	33.5	51.0
Houston-Galveston-											
Brazoria, TX.......................	8.1	21.0	9.8	15.9	16.9	13.3	7.3	4.5	3.2	31.9	50.2
Brazoria, TX.....................	7.7	20.8	8.6	14.4	18.0	13.6	7.9	5.3	3.6	34.0	48.4
Galveston-Texas City, TX ..	7.0	19.7	8.7	13.2	17.0	14.4	8.9	6.3	4.8	35.9	51.0
Houston, TX......................	8.1	21.1	10.0	16.2	16.8	13.2	7.1	4.3	3.1	31.6	50.2
Huntington-Ashland, WV-KY-OH	5.8	16.7	10.2	13.1	14.6	14.1	10.5	8.3	6.7	38.1	51.7
Huntsville, AL......................	6.8	18.7	9.3	14.0	17.6	13.5	9.3	6.4	4.5	35.7	50.8
Indianapolis, IN	7.4	19.2	8.8	15.3	17.0	13.3	8.1	5.8	5.1	34.6	51.2
Iowa City, IA	5.8	14.3	23.4	16.6	14.1	12.2	6.1	3.9	3.5	28.4	50.2
Jackson, MI	6.6	19.1	8.1	13.6	16.8	14.2	8.8	6.6	6.2	36.6	49.0
Jackson, MS	7.4	20.1	10.8	14.5	15.9	13.1	7.8	5.6	4.8	33.0	52.4
Jackson, TN	6.9	18.7	11.5	13.4	15.4	13.3	8.4	6.5	6.0	34.6	52.0
Jacksonville, FL	6.9	19.2	9.0	14.5	16.9	13.8	8.6	6.1	5.0	35.3	51.4
Jacksonville, NC	8.8	17.3	23.8	15.8	13.4	8.6	5.8	4.0	2.3	25.0	44.8
Jamestown, NY	5.8	18.7	10.3	11.3	15.0	13.6	9.3	8.0	8.0	37.9	51.2
Janesville-Beloit, WI	6.7	19.8	8.6	13.5	16.3	13.6	8.8	6.7	6.0	35.9	50.8
Johnson City-Kingsport-Bristol, TN-VA...................	5.6	15.9	8.6	13.6	15.2	14.5	11.2	8.3	7.0	39.2	51.6
Johnstown, PA.....................	5.1	16.4	8.5	11.8	15.0	14.4	9.7	9.4	9.8	40.9	51.0
Jonesboro, AR.....................	6.9	17.2	14.0	14.4	14.3	12.8	8.6	6.2	5.5	33.0	51.6
Joplin, MO	7.2	18.7	10.3	12.9	14.8	12.9	9.2	7.2	6.7	35.6	51.4
Kalamazoo-Battle Creek, MI .	6.5	18.8	12.1	13.1	15.2	13.6	8.5	6.4	5.8	34.7	51.3
Kansas City, MO-KS	7.2	19.4	9.4	14.6	16.9	13.7	8.3	6.0	5.4	35.2	51.2
Killeen-Temple, TX	8.6	19.6	14.5	17.7	15.3	10.1	6.1	4.4	3.7	28.8	49.5
Knoxville, TN	6.0	16.6	10.0	13.8	15.9	14.4	9.9	7.3	6.2	37.3	51.6
Kokomo, IN	6.9	18.6	8.1	13.0	15.2	14.4	10.3	7.3	6.3	37.3	51.6
La Crosse, WI-MN...............	5.9	18.2	14.2	12.4	15.0	13.3	7.8	6.4	6.7	34.4	51.4
Lafayette, IN	6.1	16.0	22.4	14.3	13.1	11.2	6.9	5.0	5.1	28.5	49.1
Lafayette, LA	7.5	21.0	10.6	13.5	15.9	12.6	8.1	6.1	4.8	33.2	51.6
Lake Charles, LA	7.2	20.2	10.3	13.0	15.7	13.2	8.6	6.8	5.1	34.5	51.3
Lakeland-Winter Haven, FL...	6.4	18.0	8.3	12.3	14.2	12.3	10.3	9.9	8.4	38.6	50.9
Lancaster, PA	6.9	19.7	9.2	12.6	15.7	13.2	8.6	6.9	7.1	36.1	51.2
Lansing-East Lansing, MI......	6.4	18.3	14.7	13.6	15.1	13.8	8.0	5.3	4.8	32.7	51.4
Laredo, TX	10.6	25.6	11.4	15.9	13.4	9.6	6.0	4.3	3.3	26.5	51.8
Las Cruces, NM..................	7.8	21.9	13.3	12.9	14.1	11.5	7.7	6.2	4.4	30.2	50.9
Las Vegas, NV-AZ...............	7.3	18.0	8.8	15.5	15.7	13.0	9.9	7.2	4.6	35.2	49.2
Lawrence, KS	5.6	14.8	26.4	15.2	13.1	11.2	5.8	4.1	3.9	26.6	50.3
Lawton, OK	7.9	19.8	13.9	15.5	15.2	10.7	7.2	5.6	4.1	30.1	48.2
Lewiston-Auburn, ME	5.9	18.0	9.1	13.2	16.5	13.9	9.0	7.1	7.3	37.2	51.5
Lexington, KY	6.4	16.3	13.8	16.0	15.9	13.3	8.0	5.5	4.7	33.3	51.1
Lima, OH	6.7	19.7	9.3	12.3	15.5	13.7	8.6	7.2	7.0	36.4	50.3
Lincoln, NE	6.7	16.8	15.4	15.3	15.1	13.1	7.2	5.3	5.1	32.0	50.0
Little Rock-North Little Rock, AR.......................................	7.0	18.6	10.0	14.8	16.0	13.7	8.7	6.0	5.2	34.7	51.6
Longview-Marshall, TX.........	6.8	20.0	9.8	12.2	15.4	13.2	9.2	7.2	6.2	35.8	51.5
Los Angeles-Riverside-Orange County, CA...........	7.8	20.7	10.0	15.9	16.1	12.2	7.4	5.3	4.6	32.3	50.4
Los Angeles-Long Beach, CA.......................................	7.7	20.3	10.3	16.6	15.9	12.1	7.3	5.2	4.6	32.0	50.6
Orange County, CA	7.6	19.4	9.4	16.4	16.8	12.7	7.9	5.2	4.6	33.3	50.2
Riverside-San Bernardino, CA.......................................	8.1	23.2	9.8	13.7	15.8	11.7	7.1	5.7	4.9	31.6	50.2
Ventura, CA	7.5	21.0	9.0	13.8	16.9	13.6	8.1	5.3	4.9	34.2	50.1
Louisville, KY-IN	6.7	18.0	8.8	14.0	16.7	14.3	8.9	6.8	5.8	36.5	51.6
Lubbock, TX	7.2	18.5	16.3	13.8	14.0	11.7	7.5	6.0	5.1	30.5	51.1
Lynchburg, VA	5.8	17.5	9.8	12.4	15.5	14.3	10.2	7.8	6.7	38.0	52.0
Macon, GA...........................	7.1	20.0	10.0	13.8	16.2	13.3	8.5	6.2	4.9	34.4	52.5
Madison, WI........................	6.1	16.5	14.3	16.0	16.4	14.1	7.2	4.7	4.6	33.2	50.5
Mansfield, OH	6.4	18.4	8.3	12.8	15.5	14.1	10.0	7.7	6.7	37.8	50.2
McAllen-Edinburg-Mission, TX.......................................	10.2	25.1	11.3	14.9	12.8	9.8	6.2	5.5	4.2	27.2	51.4
Medford-Ashland, OR..........	6.0	18.4	8.7	11.2	14.3	15.4	10.0	7.9	8.1	39.2	51.4
Melbourne-Titusville-Palm Bay,FL................................	5.2	16.8	6.8	10.6	16.5	13.3	11.0	10.9	9.0	41.4	51.0
Memphis, TN-AR-MS	7.6	20.7	9.5	14.9	16.1	13.4	7.8	5.4	4.5	33.2	52.0

Table C. Metropolitan Areas

Area Name	Under 5 years	5 to 17 years	18 to 24 years	25 to 34 years	35 to 44 years	45 to 54 years	55 to 64 years	65 to 74 years	75 years and over	Percent Female	2000	1990	1980	1990–2000	1980–1990
	39	40	41	42	43	44	45	46	47	48	49	50	51	52	53
Hartford, CT	6.9	15.9	10.4	18.2	15.8	10.7	8.9	7.7	5.6	51.5	1 148 618	1 123 678	1 051 606	2.2	6.9
Hattiesburg, MS	7.5	19.7	15.5	16.5	13.3	8.9	7.5	6.4	4.9	52.7	111 674	98 738	89 839	13.1	9.9
Hickory-Morganton-Lenoir, NC	6.4	17.5	10.4	16.5	15.6	11.8	9.5	7.4	4.8	51.2	341 851	292 405	270 457	16.9	8.1
Honolulu, HI	7.4	17.1	11.9	18.7	15.6	9.8	8.5	7.0	4.0	49.1	876 156	836 231	762 565	4.8	9.7
Houma, LA	8.5	22.8	11.2	17.3	14.0	9.8	7.6	5.4	3.3	51.1	194 477	182 842	176 876	6.4	3.4
Houston-Galveston-Brazoria, TX	8.5	20.4	10.5	19.7	16.7	9.9	6.9	4.5	2.8	50.2	4 669 571	3 731 014	3 118 480	25.2	19.6
Brazoria, TX	8.1	21.2	9.5	19.2	16.3	10.3	7.6	4.8	3.0	48.1	241 767	191 707	169 587	26.1	13.0
Galveston-Texas City, TX	7.6	19.9	9.2	17.7	15.7	10.5	8.8	6.5	4.0	50.8	250 158	217 396	195 738	15.1	11.1
Houston, TX	8.6	20.3	10.7	19.9	16.8	9.9	6.7	4.4	2.7	50.3	4 177 646	3 321 911	2 753 155	25.8	20.7
Huntington-Ashland, WV-KY-OH	5.9	18.6	10.5	14.6	14.6	11.4	10.1	8.4	6.0	52.2	315 538	312 529	336 410	1.0	-7.1
Huntsville, AL	7.3	17.3	11.6	19.9	14.8	11.3	8.8	5.6	3.3	50.7	342 376	293 047	242 971	16.8	20.6
Indianapolis, IN	7.7	18.6	9.9	18.8	15.4	10.2	8.2	6.5	4.6	51.9	1 607 486	1 380 491	1 305 911	16.4	5.7
Iowa City, IA	6.4	13.7	24.8	20.3	14.5	7.5	5.4	4.1	3.4	50.5	111 006	96 119	81 717	15.5	17.6
Jackson, MI	7.3	18.5	9.5	17.6	15.7	10.3	8.8	7.2	5.1	49.2	158 422	149 756	151 495	5.8	-1.1
Jackson, MS	7.6	20.4	11.4	17.6	15.1	9.5	7.8	6.0	4.5	52.7	440 801	395 396	362 038	11.5	9.2
Jackson, TN	7.1	19.0	11.1	16.2	14.8	9.6	8.4	7.5	6.3	52.9	107 377	90 801	87 273	18.3	4.0
Jacksonville, FL	7.8	18.1	10.8	18.6	15.5	10.0	8.1	6.7	4.2	51.1	1 100 491	906 727	722 252	21.4	25.5
Jacksonville, NC	9.1	15.2	27.4	22.3	11.3	5.8	4.5	2.9	1.5	40.2	150 355	149 838	112 784	0.3	32.9
Jamestown, NY	6.9	18.4	11.0	14.7	13.9	9.8	9.5	8.5	7.2	51.8	139 750	141 895	146 925	-1.5	-3.4
Janesville-Beloit, WI	7.7	19.4	9.8	16.4	14.6	10.6	8.9	7.0	5.6	51.3	152 307	139 510	139 420	9.2	0.1
Johnson City-Kingsport-Bristol, TN-VA	5.7	16.6	10.5	15.2	15.1	12.1	10.2	8.6	6.0	51.9	480 091	436 068	433 638	10.1	0.6
Johnstown, PA	5.9	17.9	9.0	14.1	14.4	9.8	10.7	10.8	7.3	52.0	232 621	241 280	264 506	-3.6	-8.8
Jonesboro, AR	7.0	17.7	14.4	16.2	13.9	10.3	8.4	6.8	5.4	51.9	82 148	68 956	63 239	19.1	9.0
Joplin, MO	6.9	18.9	9.9	15.4	14.1	10.3	9.2	8.3	6.9	52.0	157 322	134 910	127 513	16.6	5.8
Kalamazoo-Battle Creek, MI	7.3	17.1	15.5	16.9	15.1	9.8	7.6	6.0	4.6	51.9	452 851	429 453	420 771	5.4	2.1
Kansas City, MO-KS	7.7	18.7	9.2	18.3	15.8	10.4	8.3	6.7	5.0	51.7	1 776 062	1 582 874	1 449 380	12.2	9.2
Killeen-Temple, TX	9.3	18.9	16.9	20.3	13.0	7.7	6.0	4.6	3.4	47.7	312 952	255 299	214 587	22.6	19.0
Knoxville, TN	6.3	16.6	11.4	16.5	15.5	11.2	9.3	7.8	5.4	52.0	687 249	585 960	546 488	17.3	7.2
Kokomo, IN	7.0	19.6	9.0	15.5	15.1	12.1	9.5	7.1	5.1	52.1	101 541	96 946	103 715	4.7	-6.5
La Crosse, WI-MN	7.1	17.6	15.5	16.2	14.4	8.9	7.6	6.8	6.0	52.0	126 838	116 401	109 438	9.0	6.4
Lafayette, IN	6.3	14.7	26.0	16.3	12.7	8.1	6.4	5.4	4.1	49.3	182 821	161 572	153 247	13.2	5.4
Lafayette, LA	8.6	21.2	11.8	18.6	14.8	9.1	7.4	5.1	3.4	51.5	385 647	345 053	330 784	11.8	4.3
Lake Charles, LA	7.8	21.4	10.2	16.5	14.5	10.0	8.9	6.6	4.3	51.4	183 577	168 134	167 223	9.2	0.5
Lakeland-Winter Haven, FL	7.0	17.1	9.2	14.7	13.1	10.0	10.3	11.3	7.3	51.5	483 924	405 382	321 652	19.4	26.0
Lancaster, PA	7.9	18.6	10.6	16.6	14.7	9.9	8.6	7.4	5.7	51.4	470 658	422 822	362 346	11.3	16.7
Lansing-East Lansing, MI	7.3	18.2	16.2	17.3	15.4	9.6	6.9	5.2	3.8	51.6	447 728	432 684	419 750	3.5	3.1
Laredo, TX	10.1	26.5	12.5	16.0	12.4	8.1	6.5	4.6	3.3	52.0	193 117	133 239	99 258	44.9	34.2
Las Cruces, NM	8.6	21.8	14.5	16.9	13.3	8.6	7.5	5.5	3.3	50.3	174 682	135 510	96 340	28.9	40.7
Las Vegas, NV-AZ	7.7	16.8	10.2	18.8	15.6	11.3	9.1	7.2	3.3	49.3	1 563 282	852 646	528 000	83.3	61.5
Lawrence, KS	6.3	14.2	28.0	17.6	13.1	7.3	5.5	4.4	3.7	50.2	99 962	81 798	67 640	22.2	20.9
Lawton, OK	8.5	19.8	15.5	19.0	13.1	8.4	7.1	5.2	3.5	48.1	114 996	111 486	112 456	3.1	-0.9
Lewiston-Auburn, ME	7.3	17.9	11.4	16.9	14.1	9.6	8.7	7.7	6.4	51.9	103 793	105 259	99 509	-1.4	5.8
Lexington, KY	6.9	17.0	13.2	19.0	16.0	10.0	7.7	6.0	4.3	52.0	479 198	405 936	370 900	18.0	9.4
Lima, OH	7.7	20.2	9.6	16.0	14.5	9.7	8.8	7.7	5.7	50.7	155 084	154 340	154 795	0.5	-0.3
Lincoln, NE	7.1	16.8	15.6	18.3	15.3	8.8	7.2	5.9	4.9	51.1	250 291	213 641	192 884	17.2	10.8
Little Rock-North Little Rock, AR	7.3	19.2	10.6	17.8	15.5	10.3	7.9	6.6	4.8	52.0	583 845	513 026	474 463	13.8	8.1
Longview-Marshall, TX	7.4	20.4	9.8	15.9	14.3	10.0	8.7	7.3	6.0	52.0	208 780	193 801	180 355	7.7	7.5
Los Angeles-Riverside-Orange County, CA	8.4	18.3	11.9	19.6	15.1	9.6	7.3	5.8	4.0	50.0	16 373 645	14 531 529	11 497 549	12.7	26.4
Los Angeles-Long Beach, CA	8.3	17.9	12.3	19.8	15.1	9.5	7.3	5.7	4.0	50.1	9 519 338	8 863 052	7 477 239	7.4	18.5
Orange County, CA	7.7	16.8	12.5	20.1	15.6	10.6	7.5	5.4	3.8	49.6	2 846 289	2 410 668	1 932 921	18.1	24.7
Riverside-San Bernardino, CA	9.4	20.4	10.4	18.7	14.6	8.6	7.0	6.5	4.3	49.9	3 254 821	2 588 793	1 558 215	25.7	66.1
Ventura, CA	8.0	19.3	10.7	18.1	16.4	10.7	7.4	5.5	3.9	49.6	753 197	669 016	529 174	12.6	26.4
Louisville, KY-IN	6.8	18.4	9.6	17.2	15.8	10.5	9.1	7.4	5.3	52.3	1 025 598	949 012	953 520	8.1	-0.5
Lubbock, TX	7.7	18.8	16.4	17.7	13.3	8.7	7.5	5.7	4.1	50.7	242 628	222 636	211 651	9.0	5.2
Lynchburg, VA	6.7	16.6	13.1	15.5	14.3	10.7	9.2	7.9	6.1	52.9	214 911	193 926	182 207	10.8	6.4
Macon, GA	7.7	19.5	10.8	17.4	14.9	10.3	8.5	6.6	4.2	52.4	322 549	291 079	272 945	10.8	6.6
Madison, WI	7.0	15.7	15.7	19.9	16.6	9.2	6.6	5.2	4.1	50.9	426 526	367 085	323 545	16.2	13.5
Mansfield, OH	6.9	19.2	9.4	15.5	14.8	11.3	9.8	7.7	5.2	51.0	175 818	174 007	181 280	1.0	-4.0
McAllen-Edinburg-Mission, TX	9.3	27.3	11.7	14.6	12.7	7.8	6.6	6.0	4.0	51.7	569 463	383 545	283 323	48.5	35.4
Medford-Ashland, OR	6.7	18.4	8.5	13.7	16.3	10.9	9.4	9.5	6.7	51.2	181 269	146 387	132 456	23.8	10.5
Melbourne-Titusville-Palm Bay, FL	6.6	15.3	8.8	17.5	13.6	10.5	11.0	10.8	5.8	50.6	476 230	398 978	272 959	19.4	46.2
Memphis, TN-AR-MS	8.1	19.7	11.1	17.9	15.5	9.7	7.7	6.1	4.3	52.2	1 135 614	1 007 306	938 777	12.7	7.3

Table C. Metropolitan Areas

Area Name	Total population	Total in house-holds	House-holder	Spouse	Child Total	Own child under 18 years	Other relatives Total	Under 18 years	Nonrelatives Total	Unmar-ried partner	Total in group quarters	Correc-tional institu-tions	Nurs-ing homes	Other institu-tions	Col-lege dormi-tories	Mili-tary quar-ters	Other
	54	55	56	57	58	59	60	61	62	63	64	65	66	67	68	69	70
Hartford, CT	1 148 618	96.2	38.8	19.7	28.8	22.3	4.2	1.5	4.6	2.1	3.8	0.8	1.1	0.1	1.5	0.0	0.0
Hattiesburg, MS	111 674	94.7	37.2	18.0	29.0	22.5	5.4	2.6	5.1	1.5	5.3	0.5	0.7	0.5	3.1	0.2	0.3
Hickory-Morganton-Lenoir, NC	341 851	97.9	39.2	22.0	27.6	21.4	4.9	2.0	4.3	2.0	2.1	0.6	0.6	0.3	0.2	0.0	0.4
Honolulu, HI	876 156	96.5	32.7	17.8	29.0	19.1	11.0	4.0	6.0	1.6	3.5	0.3	0.2	0.1	0.4	1.6	0.9
Houma, LA	194 477	98.4	35.0	20.3	33.1	24.6	6.0	3.1	4.0	2.1	1.6	0.4	0.5	0.2	0.4	0.0	0.2
Houston-Galveston-Brazoria, TX	4 669 571	98.4	35.1	18.8	32.6	25.7	7.4	2.8	4.5	1.6	1.6	0.7	0.3	0.1	0.2	0.0	0.3
Brazoria, TX	241 767	95.5	33.9	21.1	31.8	25.7	5.3	2.3	3.3	1.5	4.5	3.9	0.4	0.0	0.0	0.0	0.2
Galveston-Texas City, TX	250 158	98.3	37.9	19.9	30.4	23.6	5.9	2.6	4.3	1.9	1.7	0.5	0.6	0.1	0.3	0.0	0.2
Houston, TX	4 177 646	98.6	35.0	18.6	32.8	25.8	7.6	2.9	4.5	1.6	1.4	0.6	0.3	0.1	0.2	0.0	0.3
Huntington-Ashland, WV-KY-OH	315 538	97.7	40.6	22.1	27.5	20.3	3.9	1.6	3.6	1.6	2.3	0.6	0.6	0.2	0.7	0.0	0.3
Huntsville, AL	342 376	97.1	39.3	21.5	29.2	23.2	4.1	1.8	3.1	1.3	2.9	0.9	0.4	0.0	1.2	0.2	0.2
Indianapolis, IN	1 607 486	97.8	39.2	19.9	29.7	24.1	4.1	1.8	5.0	2.3	2.2	0.7	0.7	0.1	0.3	0.0	0.4
Iowa City, IA	111 006	92.8	39.7	17.4	22.6	19.2	1.9	0.5	11.2	2.4	7.2	0.8	0.4	0.2	5.6	0.0	0.2
Jackson, MI	158 422	93.7	36.7	19.8	29.0	23.1	3.5	1.7	4.7	2.3	6.3	4.6	0.7	0.0	0.5	0.0	0.5
Jackson, MS	440 801	96.1	36.4	17.2	31.6	23.4	6.9	3.5	4.0	1.7	3.9	0.9	0.6	0.6	1.3	0.0	0.5
Jackson, TN	107 377	95.9	38.4	19.6	29.1	22.6	5.0	2.3	3.8	1.5	4.1	0.4	1.0	0.0	2.5	0.0	0.3
Jacksonville, FL	1 100 491	98.2	38.7	19.5	29.3	23.2	5.2	2.3	5.4	2.2	1.8	0.3	0.5	0.0	0.3	0.4	0.3
Jacksonville, NC	150 355	87.1	32.0	19.5	28.2	24.2	3.1	1.4	4.2	1.4	12.9	0.1	0.1	0.0	0.0	12.3	0.3
Jamestown, NY	139 750	95.4	39.0	19.9	28.5	22.4	2.8	1.2	5.2	2.5	4.6	1.0	0.9	0.2	1.6	0.0	0.9
Janesville-Beloit, WI	152 307	97.7	38.5	20.6	29.9	24.3	3.4	1.4	5.3	2.6	2.3	0.3	0.6	0.2	0.6	0.0	0.5
Johnson City-Kingsport-Bristol, TN-VA	480 091	97.6	41.5	23.2	26.0	19.5	3.9	1.5	3.1	1.4	2.4	0.3	0.5	0.1	0.8	0.0	0.3
Johnstown, PA	232 621	94.9	39.4	21.6	27.8	19.9	3.3	1.2	2.8	1.6	5.1	2.0	0.9	0.3	1.1	0.0	0.7
Jonesboro, AR	82 148	96.6	39.3	21.0	27.5	21.9	4.1	1.7	4.6	1.5	3.4	0.3	0.8	0.0	1.8	0.0	0.5
Joplin, MO	157 322	97.7	39.1	21.6	28.8	23.4	3.5	1.6	4.7	2.0	2.3	0.2	0.8	0.0	0.8	0.0	0.5
Kalamazoo-Battle Creek, MI	452 851	96.2	38.8	19.3	28.3	22.9	3.5	1.6	6.3	2.3	3.8	0.3	0.6	0.2	1.8	0.0	0.9
Kansas City, MO-KS	1 776 062	98.2	39.1	20.2	30.1	24.2	4.2	1.8	4.6	1.9	1.8	0.5	0.7	0.1	0.2	0.0	0.3
Killeen-Temple, TX	312 952	91.7	33.7	19.6	30.3	25.8	3.9	1.9	4.2	1.4	8.3	3.1	0.6	0.2	0.4	3.9	0.2
Knoxville, TN	687 249	97.5	41.0	21.9	26.5	20.5	4.0	1.6	4.1	1.6	2.5	0.2	0.6	0.1	1.2	0.0	0.3
Kokomo, IN	101 541	98.7	40.6	22.0	29.3	23.3	3.1	1.5	3.6	1.8	1.3	0.2	0.8	0.0	0.0	0.0	0.2
La Crosse, WI-MN	126 838	95.5	38.8	20.0	27.6	22.8	2.0	0.7	7.1	2.2	4.5	0.2	1.1	0.1	2.6	0.0	0.5
Lafayette, IN	182 821	91.3	37.1	18.2	24.8	20.6	3.0	1.0	8.2	2.0	8.7	0.3	1.0	0.1	7.3	0.0	0.1
Lafayette, LA	385 647	97.9	37.1	18.8	33.0	25.5	4.9	2.5	4.2	2.1	2.1	0.5	0.8	0.1	0.5	0.0	0.3
Lake Charles, LA	183 577	97.5	37.4	19.7	31.6	24.2	5.0	2.5	3.9	1.8	2.5	0.7	0.7	0.3	0.6	0.0	0.3
Lakeland-Winter Haven, FL	483 924	97.4	38.7	21.0	26.7	20.8	6.0	2.7	5.0	2.2	2.6	1.0	0.6	0.2	0.4	0.0	0.5
Lancaster, PA	470 658	96.9	36.7	22.0	31.2	24.9	3.2	1.2	3.9	1.9	3.1	0.2	1.2	0.0	1.1	0.0	0.4
Lansing-East Lansing, MI	447 728	95.7	38.5	18.9	28.4	22.8	3.2	1.3	6.8	2.2	4.3	0.2	0.4	0.1	3.2	0.0	0.4
Laredo, TX	193 117	98.4	26.3	16.5	41.6	30.3	11.6	5.3	2.5	0.8	1.6	0.6	0.2	0.2	0.2	0.0	0.4
Las Cruces, NM	174 682	97.1	34.1	17.9	33.4	25.9	6.7	3.3	5.1	2.2	2.9	0.9	0.2	0.0	1.3	0.0	0.3
Las Vegas, NV-AZ	1 563 282	98.7	37.6	18.7	27.6	22.1	7.2	2.4	7.6	2.7	1.3	0.6	0.2	0.1	0.1	0.1	0.4
Lawrence, KS	99 962	91.3	38.5	16.6	22.6	19.2	2.4	0.8	11.1	2.1	8.7	0.1	0.5	0.0	7.9	0.0	0.3
Lawton, OK	114 996	91.0	34.6	18.9	29.9	24.7	4.0	2.1	3.6	1.4	9.0	1.9	0.7	0.1	0.2	5.7	0.3
Lewiston-Auburn, ME	103 793	96.5	40.5	20.1	27.2	22.2	2.9	0.9	5.9	3.2	3.5	0.1	1.3	0.1	1.5	0.0	1.0
Lexington, KY	479 198	95.4	39.9	19.7	26.0	20.8	3.7	1.4	6.1	2.0	4.6	0.8	0.6	0.1	2.9	0.0	0.3
Lima, OH	155 084	95.3	37.4	20.9	30.6	24.3	3.1	1.5	3.4	1.7	4.7	2.2	1.2	0.0	0.7	0.0	0.5
Lincoln, NE	250 291	95.1	39.6	19.3	26.7	22.2	2.5	0.8	6.9	2.1	4.9	1.1	0.4	0.1	2.8	0.0	0.4
Little Rock-North Little Rock, AR	583 845	97.5	39.5	20.3	28.8	22.9	4.7	2.1	4.1	1.6	2.5	0.4	0.6	0.1	0.6	0.2	0.5
Longview-Marshall, TX	208 780	97.5	37.9	20.7	29.7	23.4	5.7	2.8	3.5	1.5	2.5	0.5	0.7	0.1	1.0	0.0	0.2
Los Angeles-Riverside-Orange County, CA	16 373 645	98.1	32.7	16.7	32.5	24.5	9.7	3.2	6.5	1.9	1.9	0.4	0.3	0.1	0.3	0.1	0.6
Los Angeles-Long Beach, CA	9 519 338	98.2	32.9	15.7	32.3	23.9	10.6	3.4	6.7	2.0	1.8	0.3	0.4	0.1	0.4	0.0	0.6
Orange County, CA	2 846 289	98.5	32.9	18.4	31.1	23.6	8.9	2.6	7.3	1.6	1.5	0.2	0.3	0.1	0.4	0.0	0.6
Riverside-San Bernardino, CA	3 254 821	97.6	31.8	17.8	34.4	27.2	8.1	3.3	5.4	1.9	2.4	1.0	0.3	0.2	0.2	0.2	0.6
Ventura, CA	753 197	98.2	32.3	19.2	32.7	24.9	7.8	2.7	6.2	1.6	1.8	0.3	0.3	0.0	0.2	0.2	0.8
Louisville, KY-IN	1 025 598	98.0	40.2	19.8	29.1	22.2	4.4	2.0	4.5	2.1	2.0	0.6	0.7	0.1	0.3	0.0	0.3
Lubbock, TX	242 628	96.0	38.1	18.4	28.1	22.3	5.6	2.7	5.9	1.7	4.0	0.8	0.5	0.2	2.0	0.0	0.4
Lynchburg, VA	214 911	95.3	39.3	21.2	26.9	20.9	4.2	1.8	3.8	1.7	4.7	0.5	0.8	0.4	2.4	0.0	0.5
Macon, GA	322 549	97.1	37.7	18.3	31.1	23.7	5.9	2.9	4.1	1.7	2.9	0.6	0.7	0.1	0.8	0.5	0.2
Madison, WI	426 526	96.3	40.7	19.1	25.3	21.4	2.2	0.7	8.9	2.7	3.7	0.4	0.5	0.2	2.1	0.0	0.5
Mansfield, OH	175 818	96.0	39.0	21.2	28.6	22.5	3.4	1.6	3.8	2.0	4.0	2.9	0.6	0.1	0.0	0.0	0.5
McAllen-Edinburg-Mission, TX	569 463	99.0	27.5	17.9	40.5	29.7	10.7	5.1	2.4	0.8	1.0	0.6	0.2	0.1	0.0	0.0	0.1
Medford-Ashland, OR	181 269	98.0	39.5	21.0	27.1	22.1	4.0	1.5	6.4	2.4	2.0	0.2	0.6	0.0	0.5	0.0	0.7
Melbourne-Titusville-Palm Bay, FL	476 230	98.0	41.6	22.0	25.1	19.7	4.1	1.6	5.1	2.3	2.0	0.5	0.5	0.3	0.2	0.0	0.4
Memphis, TN-AR-MS	1 135 614	98.1	37.4	17.1	31.9	24.2	7.3	3.5	4.5	1.8	1.9	0.7	0.5	0.1	0.3	0.0	0.3

Table C. Metropolitan Areas

Area Name	Households by type, 2000												Households, 1990		
	Family households						Nonfamily households								
			Married couple		Female householder[1]			Householder living alone							
	Total	With own children under 18 years	Total	With own children under 18 years	Total	With own children under 18 years	Total	Total	65 years and over	Average household size	Average family size	Total households	Female householder[1]	Householder living alone
	Total households														
	71	72	73	74	75	76	77	78	79	80	81	82	83	84	85
Hartford, CT	445 870	67.0	31.0	51.0	22.0	12.0	7.0	33.0	27.0	10.0	2.48	3.04	423 651	11.6	24.4
Hattiesburg, MS	41 579	67.4	33.6	48.5	22.6	15.3	9.1	32.6	25.7	8.2	2.54	3.09	36 033	15.3	25.1
Hickory-Morganton-Lenoir, NC	133 966	71.4	31.4	56.1	23.1	10.8	6.0	28.6	24.2	9.2	2.50	2.95	112 387	10.6	21.8
Honolulu, HI	286 450	71.8	31.8	54.5	24.6	12.3	5.3	28.2	21.6	7.0	2.95	3.46	265 304	10.5	19.2
Houma, LA	68 054	76.0	38.6	58.0	28.2	13.3	7.8	24.0	19.4	7.5	2.81	3.23	60 672	12.3	17.4
Houston-Galveston-Brazoria, TX	1 639 401	71.3	38.7	53.6	28.6	13.0	7.9	28.7	23.4	5.5	2.80	3.35	1 338 775	12.1	24.6
Brazoria, TX	81 954	77.0	40.8	62.2	31.7	10.4	6.5	23.0	19.1	6.4	2.82	3.23	64 019	8.6	18.5
Galveston-Texas City, TX	94 782	69.8	33.8	52.4	24.0	13.1	7.7	30.2	25.1	8.1	2.60	3.12	81 451	12.6	24.3
Houston, TX	1 462 665	71.1	38.9	53.2	28.7	13.2	7.9	28.9	23.6	5.3	2.82	3.37	1 193 305	12.3	24.9
Huntington-Ashland, WV-KY-OH	128 039	69.4	29.3	54.6	21.4	11.3	6.2	30.6	26.5	11.5	2.41	2.90	119 640	11.1	23.8
Huntsville, AL	134 643	69.5	33.3	54.6	24.7	11.6	7.0	30.5	26.5	7.7	2.47	3.00	110 893	10.4	23.4
Indianapolis, IN	629 655	66.9	33.4	50.7	23.5	12.1	7.6	33.1	27.0	8.3	2.50	3.05	529 814	11.7	25.4
Iowa City, IA	44 080	53.5	26.5	43.9	20.7	6.8	4.4	46.5	30.2	5.6	2.34	2.97	36 067	6.7	27.8
Jackson, MI	58 168	70.2	33.5	53.8	22.9	12.0	7.8	29.8	24.6	9.6	2.55	3.03	53 660	11.5	23.2
Jackson, MS	160 338	70.3	35.5	47.4	22.4	18.7	11.0	29.7	25.1	7.7	2.64	3.18	140 157	17.1	23.8
Jackson, TN	41 212	70.0	33.5	51.1	22.3	15.3	9.4	30.0	25.7	9.5	2.50	3.00	34 167	12.9	24.5
Jacksonville, FL	425 584	68.5	33.5	50.5	22.7	14.0	8.6	31.5	24.8	7.7	2.54	3.04	343 526	12.6	24.4
Jacksonville, NC	48 122	76.0	42.6	61.0	32.5	11.6	8.0	24.0	18.6	5.2	2.72	3.09	40 658	9.5	15.4
Jamestown, NY	54 515	66.0	30.5	50.9	21.0	10.8	7.0	34.0	28.1	12.6	2.45	2.99	53 696	10.3	26.1
Janesville-Beloit, WI	58 617	68.9	33.6	53.5	23.6	10.9	7.4	31.1	25.1	9.7	2.54	3.03	52 252	10.6	23.4
Johnson City-Kingsport-Bristol, TN-VA	199 218	69.5	28.4	56.0	21.5	10.2	5.3	30.5	26.8	11.0	2.35	2.84	170 569	10.1	23.4
Johnstown, PA	91 753	68.3	27.8	54.7	21.3	9.8	4.8	31.7	28.5	15.0	2.41	2.95	91 578	9.8	25.7
Jonesboro, AR	32 301	68.4	32.3	53.3	23.7	11.4	6.9	31.6	25.2	9.1	2.46	2.96	26 285	10.5	23.5
Joplin, MO	61 552	69.3	32.4	55.1	23.4	10.4	6.7	30.7	25.7	10.8	2.50	2.99	53 020	9.1	25.7
Kalamazoo-Battle Creek, MI	175 561	65.2	31.5	49.7	21.6	11.6	7.6	34.8	27.1	9.2	2.48	3.02	160 916	11.7	24.3
Kansas City, MO-KS	694 468	67.1	33.2	51.6	23.9	11.8	7.3	32.9	27.1	8.6	2.51	3.07	608 459	11.2	26.0
Killeen-Temple, TX	105 457	73.7	41.6	58.2	30.8	12.1	8.6	26.3	21.3	6.4	2.72	3.16	83 927	10.1	20.4
Knoxville, TN	281 472	67.4	29.3	53.4	21.6	10.6	6.0	32.6	27.2	9.4	2.38	2.90	231 254	11.0	25.2
Kokomo, IN	41 269	68.6	31.5	54.2	22.4	10.9	7.0	31.4	27.4	10.5	2.43	2.95	37 549	10.7	24.5
La Crosse, WI-MN	49 232	63.0	30.6	51.6	23.2	8.2	5.5	37.0	27.9	10.1	2.46	3.03	43 506	8.7	25.7
Lafayette, IN	67 771	61.2	29.7	49.1	22.4	8.4	5.5	38.8	27.2	8.1	2.46	3.03	57 068	8.0	24.8
Lafayette, LA	143 006	70.4	36.9	50.7	24.9	15.3	9.6	29.6	24.4	8.6	2.64	3.17	121 807	14.1	22.7
Lake Charles, LA	68 613	71.5	35.6	52.6	24.4	14.7	9.0	28.5	24.0	8.9	2.61	3.11	60 328	13.2	22.2
Lakeland-Winter Haven, FL	187 233	70.7	29.0	54.4	19.6	12.0	7.1	29.3	24.1	11.1	2.52	2.96	155 969	10.8	22.4
Lancaster, PA	172 560	71.9	33.7	59.9	26.6	8.6	5.2	28.1	23.1	9.3	2.64	3.14	150 956	7.9	20.9
Lansing-East Lansing, MI	172 413	63.8	31.8	49.0	22.4	11.1	7.3	36.2	27.4	7.8	2.48	3.05	156 887	11.1	24.0
Laredo, TX	50 740	85.6	53.2	62.6	41.0	18.3	10.2	14.4	12.4	5.1	3.75	4.10	34 438	17.6	12.7
Las Cruces, NM	59 556	72.1	38.4	52.4	25.9	14.7	9.7	27.9	21.3	6.9	2.85	3.36	45 043	12.0	19.6
Las Vegas, NV-AZ	588 371	66.6	30.9	49.6	21.1	11.4	6.8	33.4	24.5	7.3	2.62	3.13	330 490	10.6	25.1
Lawrence, KS	38 486	55.0	27.4	43.1	19.9	8.5	5.6	45.0	28.5	5.8	2.37	2.97	30 138	7.6	27.0
Lawton, OK	39 808	72.5	39.0	54.6	27.2	14.1	9.4	27.5	23.4	7.9	2.63	3.10	37 569	12.1	20.4
Lewiston-Auburn, ME	42 028	65.0	31.0	50.0	21.0	11.0	8.0	35.0	28.0	11.0	2.38	2.91	40 017	10.9	24.4
Lexington, KY	191 006	64.1	30.4	49.4	21.8	11.4	6.9	35.9	27.7	7.7	2.39	2.93	154 089	11.5	25.3
Lima, OH	58 022	70.6	33.6	55.8	24.3	11.0	7.1	29.4	25.4	11.0	2.55	3.06	55 384	10.5	22.8
Lincoln, NE	99 187	61.2	30.3	48.8	22.5	9.1	6.0	38.8	29.1	8.3	2.40	3.00	82 759	8.7	27.5
Little Rock-North Little Rock, AR	230 864	68.3	32.7	51.3	22.5	13.3	8.3	31.7	26.6	8.3	2.47	2.99	195 437	12.1	24.9
Longview-Marshall, TX	79 064	71.7	33.8	54.6	24.0	13.1	7.7	28.3	24.7	10.5	2.57	3.07	72 092	11.7	24.3
Los Angeles-Riverside-Orange County, CA	5 347 107	70.4	37.8	51.2	27.4	13.5	7.7	29.6	22.8	7.3	3.00	3.56	4 900 720	12.0	23.0
Los Angeles-Long Beach, CA	3 133 774	68.2	36.8	47.6	25.9	14.7	8.2	31.8	24.6	7.1	2.98	3.61	2 989 552	13.1	25.0
Orange County, CA	935 287	71.4	37.0	55.9	29.1	10.7	5.7	28.6	21.1	7.2	3.00	3.48	827 066	9.7	20.7
Riverside-San Bernardino, CA	1 034 812	75.1	41.4	56.1	29.8	13.4	8.4	24.9	19.5	7.9	3.07	3.53	866 804	11.0	19.7
Ventura, CA	243 234	75.2	39.7	59.5	31.0	10.9	6.2	24.8	18.9	7.4	3.04	3.46	217 298	9.8	17.5
Louisville, KY-IN	412 050	66.8	31.4	49.3	21.4	13.6	8.1	33.2	27.8	9.5	2.44	2.99	366 364	13.5	25.3
Lubbock, TX	92 516	65.0	31.7	48.2	22.0	12.6	7.6	35.0	26.9	7.9	2.52	3.10	81 534	10.4	25.5
Lynchburg, VA	84 414	69.5	30.4	53.9	21.5	12.0	7.0	30.5	26.0	10.0	2.43	2.92	72 689	11.4	23.5
Macon, GA	121 505	70.4	34.6	48.7	21.8	17.7	10.8	29.6	25.0	8.2	2.58	3.09	106 478	16.6	23.5
Madison, WI	173 484	58.1	29.0	47.1	21.9	7.9	5.3	41.9	29.4	7.0	2.37	2.97	142 786	8.0	26.4
Mansfield, OH	68 491	69.3	31.0	54.5	21.9	11.1	6.9	30.7	26.5	11.0	2.46	2.97	65 956	10.3	24.0
McAllen-Edinburg-Mission, TX	156 824	84.7	49.7	65.0	38.7	15.7	9.2	15.3	13.1	6.3	3.60	3.96	103 479	15.0	13.4
Medford-Ashland, OR	71 532	67.7	30.3	53.2	21.0	10.5	6.8	32.3	25.1	11.0	2.48	2.95	57 238	9.1	24.0
Melbourne-Titusville-Palm Bay, FL	198 195	66.8	26.5	53.0	18.5	10.2	6.0	33.2	26.9	11.6	2.35	2.84	161 365	9.1	23.7
Memphis, TN-AR-MS	424 202	69.4	35.0	45.8	21.5	18.9	11.3	30.6	25.5	7.5	2.63	3.17	365 450	17.9	24.4

[1] No spouse present.

Table C. Metropolitan Areas

Area Name	Housing occupancy, 2000							Housing tenure, 2000				
				Vacant housing units				Occupied housing units				
	Percent change of households, 1990–2000	Total housing units	Occupied housing units (percent)	Total	For seasonal, recreational, or occasional use	Homeowner vacancy rate (percent)	Rental vacancy rate (percent)	Total	Percent owner-occupied housing units	Percent renter-occupied housing units	Average household size of owner-occupied units	Average household size of renter-occupied units
	86	87	88	89	90	91	92	93	94	95	96	97
Hartford, CT....................	5.2	471 877	95.0	6.0	1.0	0.9	5.9	445 870	66.0	34.0	2.63	2.17
Hattiesburg, MS..................	15.4	45 346	91.7	8.3	0.6	1.7	9.6	41 579	65.6	34.4	2.68	2.29
Hickory-Morganton-Lenoir, NC..........................	19.2	144 874	92.5	7.5	1.8	1.5	7.3	133 966	74.3	25.7	2.53	2.41
Honolulu, HI..................	8.0	315 988	90.7	9.3	2.2	1.6	8.6	286 450	54.6	45.4	3.13	2.74
Houma, LA..................	12.2	74 973	90.8	9.2	3.1	1.0	8.3	68 054	76.7	23.3	2.89	2.56
Houston-Galveston-Brazoria, TX..........	22.5	1 777 902	92.2	7.8	1.1	1.6	9.1	1 639 401	60.7	39.3	2.96	2.56
Brazoria, TX..................	28.0	90 628	90.4	9.6	1.7	1.6	13.0	81 954	74.0	26.0	2.90	2.58
Galveston-Texas City, TX ..	16.4	111 733	84.8	15.2	6.8	2.3	13.3	94 782	66.2	33.8	2.71	2.37
Houston, TX..................	22.6	1 575 541	92.8	7.2	0.7	1.6	8.7	1 462 665	59.5	40.5	2.98	2.57
Huntington-Ashland, WV-KY-OH..........................	7.0	141 398	90.6	9.4	0.9	1.9	9.5	128 039	72.9	27.1	2.49	2.18
Huntsville, AL..................	21.4	147 185	91.5	8.5	0.7	2.3	12.2	134 643	71.2	28.8	2.58	2.19
Indianapolis, IN..................	18.8	681 144	92.4	7.6	0.4	1.8	10.6	629 655	67.8	32.2	2.64	2.20
Iowa City, IA..................	22.2	45 831	96.2	3.8	0.4	1.9	2.9	44 080	56.6	43.4	2.58	2.02
Jackson, MI..................	8.4	62 906	92.5	7.5	3.0	1.4	6.4	58 168	76.5	23.5	2.64	2.27
Jackson, MS..................	14.4	174 138	92.1	7.9	0.6	1.7	10.0	160 338	68.5	31.5	2.73	2.45
Jackson, TN..................	20.6	44 383	92.9	7.1	0.5	1.7	8.9	41 212	68.4	31.6	2.58	2.31
Jacksonville, FL..................	23.9	467 451	91.0	9.0	1.7	1.8	9.8	425 584	67.3	32.7	2.64	2.33
Jacksonville, NC..................	18.4	55 726	86.4	13.6	5.2	2.9	10.3	48 122	58.1	41.9	2.70	2.75
Jamestown, NY..................	1.5	64 900	84.0	16.0	9.0	1.9	9.6	54 515	69.2	30.8	2.56	2.18
Janesville-Beloit, WI..........	12.2	62 187	94.3	5.7	1.2	1.4	7.3	58 617	71.1	28.9	2.64	2.29
Johnson City-Kingsport-Bristol, TN-VA..........	16.8	218 190	91.3	8.7	1.1	1.9	10.0	199 218	74.2	25.8	2.42	2.16
Johnstown, PA..................	0.2	102 959	89.1	10.9	4.3	1.6	9.0	91 753	75.9	24.1	2.52	2.04
Jonesboro, AR..................	22.9	35 133	91.9	8.1	0.4	2.2	9.9	32 301	63.9	36.1	2.54	2.31
Joplin, MO..................	16.1	67 468	91.2	8.8	0.4	2.9	9.9	61 552	70.1	29.9	2.55	2.37
Kalamazoo-Battle Creek, MI .	9.1	191 916	91.5	8.5	2.7	1.8	8.2	175 561	70.2	29.8	2.62	2.16
Kansas City, MO-KS..........	14.1	740 884	93.7	6.3	0.4	1.5	7.8	694 468	67.9	32.1	2.67	2.18
Killeen-Temple, TX..........	25.7	114 558	92.1	7.9	0.6	2.2	8.1	105 457	55.5	44.5	2.77	2.66
Knoxville, TN..................	21.7	313 394	89.8	10.2	2.6	2.2	11.0	281 472	70.5	29.5	2.49	2.12
Kokomo, IN..................	9.9	44 452	92.8	7.2	0.7	1.7	9.7	41 269	73.0	27.0	2.51	2.20
La Crosse, WI-MN..............	13.2	51 647	95.3	4.7	1.0	1.0	4.9	49 232	67.5	32.5	2.64	2.09
Lafayette, IN..................	18.8	71 610	94.6	5.4	0.3	1.6	5.6	67 771	59.1	40.9	2.62	2.23
Lafayette, LA..................	17.4	157 792	90.6	9.4	2.0	1.3	9.9	143 006	69.9	30.1	2.74	2.40
Lake Charles, LA..................	13.7	75 995	90.3	9.7	0.9	1.7	14.1	68 613	71.6	28.4	2.68	2.44
Lakeland-Winter Haven, FL...	20.0	226 376	82.7	17.3	8.4	2.9	12.9	187 233	73.4	26.6	2.51	2.53
Lancaster, PA..................	14.3	179 990	95.9	4.1	0.4	1.4	4.9	172 560	70.8	29.2	2.78	2.31
Lansing-East Lansing, MI......	9.9	181 804	94.8	5.2	0.5	1.4	6.2	172 413	67.3	32.7	2.65	2.14
Laredo, TX..................	47.3	55 206	91.9	8.1	1.6	1.4	5.9	50 740	65.7	34.3	3.91	3.42
Las Cruces, NM..................	32.2	65 210	91.3	8.7	0.8	1.8	10.3	59 556	67.5	32.5	2.98	2.58
Las Vegas, NV-AZ..................	78.0	655 795	89.7	10.3	2.9	2.8	9.8	588 371	61.1	38.9	2.69	2.51
Lawrence, KS..................	27.7	40 250	95.6	4.4	0.4	1.7	3.8	38 486	51.9	48.1	2.63	2.10
Lawton, OK..................	6.0	45 416	87.7	12.3	0.6	4.3	13.2	39 808	60.3	39.7	2.62	2.65
Lewiston-Auburn, ME	5.0	45 960	91.0	9.0	3.0	1.4	8.2	42 028	63.0	37.0	2.59	2.02
Lexington, KY..................	24.0	204 857	93.2	6.8	0.6	1.5	8.1	191 006	59.8	40.2	2.54	2.18
Lima, OH..................	4.8	62 715	92.5	7.5	0.5	1.6	10.6	58 022	73.8	26.2	2.64	2.29
Lincoln, NE..................	19.9	104 217	95.2	4.8	0.3	1.2	6.2	99 187	60.5	39.5	2.62	2.06
Little Rock-North Little Rock, AR........................	18.1	250 255	92.3	7.7	0.6	1.9	9.1	230 864	65.9	34.1	2.56	2.27
Longview-Marshall, TX..........	9.7	87 550	90.3	9.7	1.5	1.9	10.3	79 064	70.9	29.1	2.62	2.45
Los Angeles-Riverside-Orange County, CA..........	9.1	5 678 148	94.2	5.8	1.7	1.7	3.8	5 347 107	54.8	45.2	3.08	2.91
Los Angeles-Long Beach, CA..........................	4.8	3 270 909	95.8	4.2	0.4	1.6	3.3	3 133 774	47.9	52.1	3.13	2.85
Orange County, CA..........	13.1	969 484	96.5	3.5	0.9	0.9	3.0	935 287	61.4	38.6	2.96	3.05
Riverside-San Bernardino, CA..........................	19.4	1 186 043	87.2	12.8	5.9	2.8	7.3	1 034 812	66.6	33.4	3.09	3.03
Ventura, CA..................	11.9	251 712	96.6	3.4	1.1	0.9	2.6	243 234	67.6	32.4	3.03	3.08
Louisville, KY-IN..................	12.5	438 235	94.0	6.0	0.5	1.5	7.5	412 050	68.6	31.4	2.56	2.18
Lubbock, TX..................	13.5	100 595	92.0	8.0	0.3	1.6	10.0	92 516	59.2	40.8	2.67	2.30
Lynchburg, VA..................	16.1	92 229	91.5	8.5	1.9	1.7	7.0	84 414	73.9	26.1	2.51	2.18
Macon, GA..................	14.1	134 359	90.4	9.6	0.4	2.1	12.6	121 505	65.4	34.6	2.64	2.46
Madison, WI..................	21.5	180 398	96.2	3.8	0.6	1.0	4.2	173 484	57.6	42.4	2.61	2.03
Mansfield, OH..................	3.8	73 240	93.5	6.5	0.6	1.4	8.6	68 491	71.8	28.2	2.55	2.25
McAllen-Edinburg-Mission, TX..........................	51.6	192 658	81.4	18.6	9.1	1.4	10.7	156 824	73.1	26.9	3.69	3.34
Medford-Ashland, OR..........	25.0	75 737	94.4	5.6	1.1	1.8	5.0	71 532	66.5	33.5	2.52	2.40
Melbourne-Titusville-Palm Bay,FL..........................	22.8	222 072	89.2	10.8	4.7	2.3	10.6	198 195	74.6	25.4	2.40	2.23
Memphis, TN-AR-MS	16.1	454 534	93.3	6.7	0.4	1.9	8.1	424 202	65.4	34.6	2.73	2.43

Table C. Metropolitan Areas

CMSA/ MSA/ PMSA/ NECMA code[1]	Area Name	Land area, 2000[2] (sq km)	Total persons	Rank	Per square kilometer	Land area, 1990[2] (sq km)	Total persons	Rank	Per square kilometer	White	Black or African American	American Indian or Alaska Native	Asian	Native Hawaiian and other Pacific Islander	Some other race
		1	2	3	4	5	6	7	8	9	10	11	12	13	14
4940	Merced, CA....................	4 995	210 554	195	42.2	4 996	178 403	197	35.7	56.2	3.8	1.2	6.8	0.2	26.1
56	Miami-Fort Lauderdale, FL....	8 162	3 876 380	X	474.9	8 167	3 192 725	X	390.9	70.1	20.4	0.2	1.8	0.0	3.9
2680	Fort Lauderdale, FL..........	3 122	1 623 018	36	519.9	3 131	1 255 531	42	401.0	70.6	20.5	0.2	2.3	0.1	3.0
5000	Miami, FL....................	5 040	2 253 362	23	447.1	5 036	1 937 194	24	384.7	69.7	20.3	0.2	1.4	0.0	4.6
63	Milwaukee-Racine, WI.........	4 644	1 689 572	X	363.8	4 645	1 607 183	X	346.0	77.8	15.1	0.5	1.9	0.0	3.0
5080	Milwaukee-Waukesha, WI ..	3 781	1 500 741	42	396.9	3 782	1 432 149	34	378.7	77.1	15.7	0.5	2.1	0.0	2.9
6600	Racine, WI...................	863	188 831	208	218.9	863	175 034	200	202.8	83.0	10.5	0.4	0.7	0.0	3.7
5120	Minneapolis-St. Paul, MN-WI	15 703	2 968 806	13	189.1	15 709	2 538 776	13	161.6	86.1	5.3	0.7	4.1	0.0	1.6
5140	Missoula, MT.................	6 729	95 802	304	14.2	6 729	78 687	310	11.7	94.0	0.3	2.3	1.0	0.1	0.4
5160	Mobile, AL...................	7 328	540 258	98	73.7	7 329	476 923	97	65.1	69.3	27.4	0.6	1.1	0.0	0.4
5170	Modesto, CA..................	3 869	446 997	115	115.5	3 871	370 522	120	95.7	69.3	2.6	1.3	4.2	0.3	16.8
5200	Monroe, LA...................	1 581	147 250	245	93.1	1 582	142 191	230	89.9	64.5	33.6	0.2	0.6	0.0	0.3
5240	Montgomery, AL...............	5 198	333 055	148	64.1	5 200	292 517	145	56.3	58.6	38.9	0.3	0.8	0.0	0.4
5280	Muncie, IN...................	1 019	118 769	281	116.6	1 019	119 659	263	117.4	90.7	6.7	0.2	0.7	0.1	0.5
5330	Myrtle Beach, SC.............	2 936	196 629	203	67.0	2 936	144 053	227	49.1	81.0	15.5	0.4	0.8	0.1	1.2
5345	Naples, FL...................	5 246	251 377	175	47.9	5 246	152 099	215	29.0	86.1	4.5	0.3	0.6	0.1	6.2
5360	Nashville, TN................	10 548	1 231 311	49	116.7	10 549	985 026	53	93.4	79.4	15.6	0.3	1.6	0.0	1.6
5523	New London-Norwich, CT	1 725	259 088	169	150.2	1 725	254 957	162	147.8	87.0	5.3	1.0	2.0	0.1	2.1
5560	New Orleans, LA	8 805	1 337 726	45	151.9	8 806	1 285 262	41	146.0	57.3	37.5	0.4	2.1	0.0	1.2
70	New York-Northern New Jersey-Long Island, NY-NJ-CT-PA	27 065	21 199 865	X	783.3	26 329	19 480 002	X	739.9	64.1	17.2	0.3	6.8	0.0	8.2
0875	Bergen-Passaic, NJ	1 086	1 373 167	44	1 264.0	1 086	1 296 252	40	1 193.6	72.7	8.1	0.3	8.2	0.0	7.9
2281	Dutchess County, NY	2 076	280 150	164	134.9	2 076	259 462	159	125.0	83.7	9.3	0.2	2.5	0.0	2.4
3640	Jersey City, NJ	121	608 975	86	5 036.2	121	553 099	87	4 571.1	55.6	13.5	0.4	9.4	0.1	15.5
5015	Middlesex-Somerset-Hunterdon, NJ	2 705	1 169 641	52	432.4	2 708	1 019 786	50	376.6	73.9	8.0	0.2	11.2	0.0	4.4
5190	Monmouth-Ocean, NJ	2 870	1 126 217	56	392.4	2 870	986 395	52	343.7	88.3	5.8	0.1	2.7	0.0	1.5
5380	Nassau-Suffolk, NY	3 105	2 753 913	16	886.9	3 103	2 609 212	11	840.9	82.0	8.5	0.2	3.6	0.0	3.6
5483	New Haven-Bridgeport-Stamford-Danbury-Water-bury, CT	3 189	1 706 575	30	535.1	3 190	1 631 864	26	511.6	79.4	10.6	0.2	2.8	0.0	4.6
5600	New York, NY	2 957	9 314 235	2	3 150.1	2 972	8 546 846	2	2 875.8	48.8	24.6	0.5	9.1	0.1	12.3
5640	Newark, NJ	4 086	2 032 989	26	497.5	4 087	1 915 724	25	468.7	65.9	22.3	0.2	4.0	0.0	4.9
5660	Newburgh, NY-PA	2 114	387 669	128	183.4	3 531	335 603	133	95.0	84.8	7.5	0.3	1.4	0.0	3.8
8480	Trenton, NJ	585	350 761	141	599.4	585	325 759	136	556.9	68.5	19.8	0.2	4.9	0.1	4.3
5720	Norfolk-Virginia Beach-Newport News, VA-NC.......	6 083	1 569 541	39	258.0	6 082	1 444 710	33	237.5	62.5	30.9	0.4	2.7	0.1	1.2
5790	Ocala, FL....................	4 089	258 916	170	63.3	4 090	194 835	181	47.6	84.2	11.5	0.4	0.7	0.0	1.7
5800	Odessa-Midland, TX..........	4 665	237 132	182	50.8	4 666	225 545	173	48.3	75.5	5.8	0.7	0.8	0.0	14.8
5880	Oklahoma City, OK............	10 999	1 083 346	60	98.5	11 002	958 839	54	87.2	75.7	10.6	4.2	2.5	0.1	3.2
5920	Omaha, NE-IA	6 411	716 998	74	111.8	6 412	639 580	75	99.7	85.2	8.3	0.5	1.5	0.1	2.7
5960	Orlando, FL..................	9 041	1 644 561	34	181.9	9 042	1 224 844	43	135.5	75.0	13.9	0.3	2.7	0.1	5.1
5990	Owensboro, KY	1 198	91 545	306	76.4	1 198	87 189	303	72.8	93.7	4.3	0.1	0.4	0.0	0.4
6015	Panama City, FL..............	1 978	148 217	243	74.9	1 978	126 994	253	64.2	84.2	10.6	0.8	1.7	0.1	0.7
6020	Parkersburg-Marietta, WV-OH	2 596	151 237	237	58.3	2 596	149 169	222	57.5	97.3	1.0	0.2	0.5	0.0	0.1
6080	Pensacola, FL................	4 349	412 153	122	94.8	4 350	344 406	129	79.2	77.6	16.5	0.9	2.0	0.1	0.8
6120	Peoria-Pekin, IL.............	4 652	347 387	142	74.7	4 654	339 172	131	72.9	88.0	8.9	0.2	1.1	0.0	0.6
77	Philadelphia-Wilmington-Atlantic City, PA-NJ-DE-MD...	15 372	6 188 463	X	402.6	15 373	5 893 019	X	383.3	72.5	19.6	0.2	3.2	0.0	2.7
0560	Atlantic-Cape May, NJ........	2 114	354 878	140	167.9	2 114	319 416	137	151.1	75.0	14.0	0.2	3.8	0.0	4.7
6160	Philadelphia, PA-NJ..........	9 985	5 100 931	5	510.9	9 986	4 922 257	5	492.9	72.1	20.1	0.2	3.4	0.0	2.5
8760	Vineland-Millville-Bridgeton, NJ	1 267	146 438	246	115.6	1 267	138 053	236	109.0	65.9	20.2	1.0	1.0	0.1	9.1
9160	Wilmington-Newark, DE-MD	2 006	586 216	91	292.3	2 006	513 293	90	255.9	76.1	17.8	0.2	2.3	0.0	2.0
6200	Phoenix-Mesa, AZ.............	37 743	3 251 876	12	86.2	37 746	2 238 498	19	59.3	77.0	3.7	2.2	2.1	0.1	12.1
6240	Pine Bluff, AR...............	2 292	84 278	310	36.8	2 292	85 487	306	37.3	48.5	49.6	0.2	0.7	0.0	0.3
6280	Pittsburgh, PA...............	11 980	2 358 695	22	196.9	11 974	2 394 811	17	200.0	89.5	8.1	0.1	1.1	0.0	0.3
6323	Pittsfield, MA...............	2 412	134 953	259	55.9	2 412	139 352	234	57.8	95.0	2.0	0.1	1.0	0.0	0.6
6340	Pocatello, ID................	2 883	75 565	316	26.2	2 883	66 026	316	22.9	91.3	0.6	2.9	1.0	0.2	2.1
6403	Portland, ME.................	2 164	265 612	166	122.7	2 164	243 135	167	112.4	95.7	1.1	0.3	1.4	0.0	0.3
79	Portland-Salem, OR-WA	18 007	2 265 223	X	125.8	18 009	1 793 476	X	99.6	84.3	2.4	1.0	4.1	0.3	4.6
6440	Portland-Vancouver, OR-WA	13 022	1 918 009	27	147.3	13 021	1 515 452	31	116.4	84.5	2.7	0.9	4.6	0.3	3.8
7080	Salem, OR....................	4 986	347 214	143	69.6	4 988	278 024	151	55.7	83.0	0.8	1.5	1.6	0.3	9.5
6483	Providence-Warwick-Pawtucket, RI	2 437	962 886	63	395.1	2 436	916 270	58	376.1	84.4	4.5	0.5	2.3	0.1	5.4
6520	Provo-Orem, UT	5 176	368 536	135	71.2	5 176	263 590	156	50.9	92.4	0.3	0.6	1.1	0.6	3.2
6560	Pueblo, CO...................	6 187	141 472	252	22.9	6 187	123 051	257	19.9	79.5	1.9	1.6	0.7	0.1	12.9
6580	Punta Gorda, FL..............	1 796	141 627	251	78.8	1 797	110 975	279	61.8	92.6	4.4	0.2	0.9	0.0	0.8
6640	Raleigh-Durham-Chapel Hill, NC.......................	9 036	1 187 941	50	131.5	9 041	858 516	63	95.0	69.4	22.7	0.4	2.9	0.0	3.1
6660	Rapid City, SD...............	7 190	88 565	309	12.3	7 191	81 343	309	11.3	86.7	0.9	8.1	0.9	0.1	0.7

[1]MSA = Metropolitan Statistical Area. PMSA = Primary MSA. NECMA = New England County Metropolitan Area. See Appendix A for explanation of these concepts. See Appendix B for list of metropolitan areas identified by type, with component counties.
[2]Dry land or land partially or temporarily covered by water.

Items 1—14

Table C. Metropolitan Areas

Area Name	Population and population characteristics, 2000 (cont'd)								Population and population characteristics, 1990				
	Race (percent) (cont'd)								Race (percent)				
	Race alone or in combination												
	Two or more races	White	Black	American Indian or Alaska Native	Asian	Native Hawaiian and other Pacific Islander	Some other race	Hispanic[1]	White	Black or African American	American Indian or Alaska Native	Asian and Pacific Islander	Hispanic[1]
	15	16	17	18	19	20	21	22	23	24	25	26	27
Merced, CA	5.7	60.9	4.5	2.3	8.0	0.5	29.8	45.3	67.4	4.8	0.8	8.5	32.6
Miami-Fort Lauderdale, FL	3.6	72.4	21.9	0.5	2.2	0.2	6.7	40.3	76.4	18.5	0.2	1.4	33.3
Fort Lauderdale, FL	3.4	72.4	22.2	0.5	2.8	0.2	5.4	16.7	81.7	15.4	0.2	1.4	8.6
Miami, FL	3.8	72.3	21.6	0.4	1.8	0.2	7.6	57.3	72.9	20.5	0.2	1.4	49.2
Milwaukee-Racine, WI	1.7	79.1	15.8	0.9	2.2	0.1	3.6	6.5	83.1	13.3	0.5	1.2	3.8
Milwaukee-Waukesha, WI	1.7	78.5	16.3	1.0	2.4	0.1	3.6	6.3	82.6	13.8	0.6	1.3	3.6
Racine, WI	1.7	84.5	11.2	0.8	0.9	0.1	4.3	7.9	86.9	9.7	0.3	0.6	5.2
Minneapolis-St. Paul, MN-WI	2.1	87.7	6.2	1.3	4.7	0.1	2.2	3.3	92.1	3.6	1.0	2.6	1.5
Missoula, MT	1.9	95.8	0.5	3.4	1.4	0.2	0.8	1.6	96.1	0.2	2.3	1.1	1.2
Mobile, AL	1.0	70.2	27.7	1.1	1.3	0.1	0.7	1.4	71.2	27.4	0.5	0.8	0.9
Modesto, CA	5.4	73.9	3.2	2.5	5.5	0.8	19.9	31.7	80.2	1.7	1.1	5.2	21.8
Monroe, LA	0.7	65.0	33.8	0.5	0.8	0.1	0.5	1.2	68.1	31.0	0.2	0.5	0.8
Montgomery, AL	1.0	59.3	39.3	0.7	1.1	0.1	0.6	1.2	63.0	36.0	0.2	0.6	0.7
Muncie, IN	1.1	91.8	7.2	0.6	0.9	0.1	0.6	1.1	93.0	6.0	0.2	0.5	0.7
Myrtle Beach, SC	1.1	82.0	15.9	0.8	1.0	0.1	1.4	2.6	81.3	17.5	0.2	0.8	0.9
Naples, FL	2.2	87.4	5.5	0.5	0.8	0.1	7.9	19.6	91.4	4.6	0.3	0.4	13.6
Nashville, TN	1.4	80.6	16.0	0.7	2.0	0.1	2.1	3.3	83.1	15.5	0.2	1.0	0.8
New London-Norwich, CT	2.7	89.1	6.5	1.9	2.5	0.2	2.8	5.1	92.2	4.5	0.5	1.3	3.2
New Orleans, LA	1.4	58.4	38.0	0.8	2.4	0.1	1.8	4.4	62.2	34.7	0.3	1.7	4.3
New York-Northern New Jersey-Long Island, NY-NJ-CT-PA	3.4	66.3	18.4	0.8	7.5	0.2	10.5	18.2	70.2	18.2	0.3	4.8	15.4
Bergen-Passaic, NJ	2.9	74.9	8.8	0.5	8.8	0.1	9.9	17.3	81.6	8.3	0.2	5.2	11.6
Dutchess County, NY	1.9	85.1	10.2	0.7	2.9	0.1	3.1	6.4	88.3	8.4	0.1	2.2	3.8
Jersey City, NJ	5.6	59.9	14.7	0.8	10.3	0.2	19.9	39.8	68.8	14.4	0.3	6.6	33.2
Middlesex-Somerset-Hunterdon, NJ	2.2	75.5	8.6	0.5	11.9	0.1	5.7	11.2	84.8	6.9	0.1	5.6	7.0
Monmouth-Ocean, NJ	1.5	89.5	6.3	0.4	3.1	0.1	2.2	5.7	90.8	6.0	0.1	1.9	3.7
Nassau-Suffolk, NY	2.1	83.5	9.2	0.5	4.0	0.1	4.9	10.3	88.4	7.4	0.2	2.4	6.3
New Haven-Bridgeport-Stamford-Danbury-Waterbury, CT	2.3	81.1	11.5	0.6	3.2	0.1	6.0	11.0	83.3	12.1	0.2	1.6	6.2
New York, NY	4.6	51.6	26.3	1.0	10.1	0.2	15.7	25.1	56.5	26.3	0.3	6.5	22.1
Newark, NJ	2.7	67.7	23.3	0.5	4.5	0.1	6.7	13.3	70.2	23.2	0.2	2.9	10.3
Newburgh, NY-PA	2.1	86.5	8.4	0.8	1.7	0.1	4.7	10.8	88.9	7.2	0.3	1.2	7.0
Trenton, NJ	2.2	70.0	20.7	0.5	5.5	0.2	5.4	9.7	75.1	18.9	0.2	3.1	6.0
Norfolk-Virginia Beach-Newport News, VA-NC	2.2	64.1	31.9	1.0	3.5	0.2	1.7	3.1	67.8	28.5	0.3	2.5	2.3
Ocala, FL	1.4	85.3	12.0	1.0	0.9	0.1	2.3	6.0	85.8	12.8	0.3	0.5	3.0
Odessa-Midland, TX	2.4	77.6	6.1	1.2	1.0	0.1	16.5	35.8	76.8	4.7	0.5	0.6	31.4
Oklahoma City, OK	3.9	79.0	11.4	6.6	3.0	0.2	3.9	6.7	81.1	10.5	4.8	1.9	3.6
Omaha, NE-IA	1.7	86.7	8.9	1.0	1.9	0.1	3.2	5.5	89.1	8.3	0.5	1.0	2.6
Orlando, FL	2.9	77.0	14.9	0.8	3.3	0.2	6.8	16.5	82.9	12.4	0.3	1.9	9.0
Owensboro, KY	0.9	94.6	4.8	0.4	0.6	0.1	0.6	0.9	95.4	4.2	0.1	0.3	0.4
Panama City, FL	1.9	85.8	11.2	1.5	2.3	0.2	1.0	2.4	86.3	10.8	0.7	1.8	1.8
Parkersburg-Marietta, WV-OH	0.8	98.1	1.3	0.6	0.6	0.1	0.2	0.6	98.3	1.1	0.2	0.3	0.3
Pensacola, FL	2.1	79.4	17.0	1.8	2.6	0.2	1.2	2.6	80.6	16.2	1.0	1.7	1.8
Peoria-Pekin, IL	1.2	89.1	9.4	0.6	1.3	0.1	0.9	1.6	91.2	7.4	0.2	0.8	1.1
Philadelphia-Wilmington-Atlantic City, PA-NJ-DE-MD	1.7	73.7	20.3	0.6	3.6	0.1	3.4	5.6	77.0	18.7	0.2	2.1	3.8
Atlantic-Cape May, NJ	2.2	76.6	14.9	0.7	4.2	0.1	9.6	9.6	81.5	13.9	0.2	1.7	5.6
Philadelphia, PA-NJ	1.6	73.3	20.9	0.5	3.8	0.1	3.2	5.1	76.5	19.1	0.2	2.2	3.6
Vineland-Millville-Bridgeton, NJ	2.9	67.9	21.5	1.7	1.2	0.2	10.6	19.0	73.5	16.9	0.9	0.8	13.3
Wilmington-Newark, DE-MD	1.6	77.3	18.5	0.6	2.6	0.1	2.5	4.7	78.9	20.0	0.4	0.5	0.8
Phoenix-Mesa, AZ	2.9	79.4	4.2	2.8	2.6	0.3	13.7	25.1	84.8	3.5	1.8	1.7	16.3
Pine Bluff, AR	0.8	49.0	49.9	0.5	0.8	0.1	0.4	1.0	56.0	43.1	0.3	0.4	0.5
Pittsburgh, PA	0.9	90.3	8.6	0.4	1.3	0.1	0.4	0.7	91.0	8.0	0.1	0.7	0.6
Pittsfield, MA	1.2	96.1	2.5	0.5	1.3	0.1	0.8	1.7	96.7	2.1	0.2	0.7	1.0
Pocatello, ID	2.0	93.1	0.9	3.6	1.5	0.3	2.7	4.7	93.5	0.7	2.5	1.1	4.1
Portland, ME	1.1	96.7	1.4	0.7	1.7	0.1	0.6	1.0	98.2	0.6	0.3	0.9	0.6
Portland-Salem, OR-WA	3.3	87.2	3.0	2.0	5.1	0.6	5.7	8.7	90.7	3.1	0.9	3.7	3.6
Portland-Vancouver, OR-WA	3.3	87.4	3.4	1.9	5.6	0.6	4.8	7.4	91.4	2.8	0.9	3.5	3.4
Salem, OR	3.2	85.9	1.2	2.7	2.2	0.5	10.8	15.6	91.8	0.8	1.5	1.7	7.6
Providence-Warwick-Pawtucket, RI	2.8	86.3	5.6	1.0	2.8	0.2	7.0	9.2	90.2	4.7	0.5	2.2	4.8
Provo-Orem, UT	1.9	94.0	0.5	1.0	1.6	1.0	3.9	7.0	96.2	0.1	0.7	1.5	3.2
Pueblo, CO	3.4	82.4	2.3	2.6	1.0	0.2	15.1	38.0	84.8	1.8	0.8	0.6	35.8
Punta Gorda, FL	1.1	93.5	4.8	0.5	1.1	0.1	1.2	3.3	95.0	3.8	0.2	0.7	2.5
Raleigh-Durham-Chapel Hill, NC	1.6	70.6	23.3	0.8	3.3	0.1	3.7	6.1	72.5	24.9	0.3	1.9	1.2
Rapid City, SD	2.7	89.2	1.4	9.9	1.3	0.1	1.0	2.6	89.5	1.6	7.2	1.1	2.2

[1] Hispanic persons may be of any race.

Table C. Metropolitan Areas

Area Name	Population and population characteristics, 2000										
	Age (percent)										
	Under 5 years	5 to 17 years	18 to 24 years	25 to 34 years	35 to 44 years	45 to 54 years	55 to 64 years	65 to 74 years	75 years and over	Median age (years)	Percent Female
	28	29	30	31	32	33	34	35	36	37	38
Merced, CA................	8.9	25.6	10.3	13.4	14.4	10.9	7.0	5.3	4.2	29.0	50.2
Miami-Fort Lauderdale, FL....	6.4	17.9	8.3	14.7	16.5	12.8	8.9	7.2	7.3	36.5	51.7
Fort Lauderdale, FL...........	6.3	17.2	7.2	14.2	17.2	13.3	8.4	7.2	8.9	37.8	51.7
Miami, FL........	6.5	18.3	9.1	15.0	16.1	12.5	9.2	7.2	6.1	35.6	51.7
Milwaukee-Racine, WI..........	6.9	19.6	9.0	13.7	16.4	13.7	8.2	6.4	6.2	35.5	51.4
Milwaukee-Waukesha, WI..	6.9	19.5	9.1	13.8	16.3	13.7	8.1	6.4	6.2	35.4	51.5
Racine, WI............	7.0	20.0	8.3	13.0	16.9	13.9	8.6	6.4	5.9	36.1	50.5
Minneapolis-St. Paul, MN-WI	7.2	19.6	9.2	15.4	17.8	13.7	7.6	4.9	4.7	34.2	50.6
Missoula, MT	5.7	17.2	15.4	14.0	15.1	14.6	7.9	5.0	5.0	33.2	50.0
Mobile, AL..............	7.0	19.7	9.3	13.0	15.4	13.3	9.3	7.1	5.8	35.7	51.9
Modesto, CA..............	8.0	23.2	9.8	13.6	15.4	12.1	7.4	5.5	5.0	31.7	50.8
Monroe, LA..............	7.2	20.7	12.0	13.5	14.4	12.2	8.1	6.5	5.4	32.3	52.8
Montgomery, AL	6.9	19.3	10.7	14.4	15.9	13.1	8.4	6.1	5.2	34.2	51.7
Muncie, IN	5.9	16.2	16.9	12.4	13.2	12.5	9.4	7.1	6.4	33.8	52.0
Myrtle Beach, SC	5.7	15.6	9.4	14.2	15.1	13.7	11.3	9.4	5.6	38.3	50.9
Naples, FL	5.3	14.5	6.6	11.2	13.3	11.7	12.7	14.0	10.5	44.1	49.9
Nashville, TN	6.9	17.9	10.2	15.8	17.1	13.8	8.3	5.5	4.5	34.5	51.1
New London-Norwich, CT	6.3	18.1	8.6	13.6	17.6	13.9	8.9	6.7	6.3	37.0	50.5
New Orleans, LA	6.9	19.9	9.7	13.8	16.0	13.9	8.5	6.2	5.2	34.8	52.2
New York-Northern New Jersey-Long Island, NY-NJ-CT-PA	6.8	18.0	8.7	15.0	16.6	13.5	8.9	6.6	6.1	35.9	51.9
Bergen-Passaic, NJ............	6.7	17.4	7.6	13.9	16.9	14.0	9.4	7.2	6.9	37.6	51.8
Dutchess County, NY	6.2	18.8	9.4	12.5	17.7	14.2	9.0	6.5	5.5	36.7	50.0
Jersey City, NJ	6.4	16.2	10.4	19.6	16.0	11.9	8.2	6.0	5.3	33.6	50.9
Middlesex-Somerset-Hunterdon, NJ	6.8	17.6	8.2	14.8	18.1	14.1	8.6	6.3	5.5	36.4	50.9
Monmouth-Ocean, NJ	6.6	18.2	6.8	11.8	16.7	13.8	9.3	8.4	8.5	39.1	51.9
Nassau-Suffolk, NY	6.8	18.6	7.5	12.9	17.2	14.3	9.4	7.2	6.2	37.5	51.4
New Haven-Bridgeport-Stamford-Danbury-Waterbury, CT	6.9	18.2	7.8	13.5	16.9	13.9	9.0	6.8	7.1	37.1	51.8
New York, NY	6.8	17.6	9.6	16.5	15.9	12.9	8.7	6.3	5.6	34.6	52.5
Newark, NJ	7.1	18.5	7.9	14.2	17.2	13.9	9.0	6.3	5.9	36.3	51.8
Newburgh, NY-PA	7.4	21.4	8.3	12.4	17.4	13.9	8.4	5.9	5.0	35.3	49.9
Trenton, NJ	6.3	17.7	10.2	14.0	16.5	14.0	8.6	6.4	6.1	36.0	51.3
Norfolk-Virginia Beach-Newport News, VA-NC	7.0	19.4	11.2	14.7	17.0	12.6	7.8	5.7	4.6	33.6	50.7
Ocala, FL	5.2	16.2	6.4	10.2	13.6	12.1	11.8	13.6	10.9	43.8	51.7
Odessa-Midland, TX	7.8	22.5	9.7	12.5	15.7	12.9	7.7	6.5	4.8	33.0	51.5
Oklahoma City, OK.............	7.0	18.6	11.4	14.2	15.7	13.3	8.5	6.2	5.2	34.1	51.0
Omaha, NE-IA	7.4	19.8	9.8	14.8	16.3	13.3	7.8	5.7	4.9	33.7	50.9
Orlando, FL	6.5	18.3	9.5	15.1	16.7	13.0	8.5	6.8	5.6	35.3	50.8
Owensboro, KY	6.7	19.1	9.0	12.6	15.8	13.7	9.2	7.3	6.5	36.8	51.9
Panama City, FL	6.1	18.0	8.7	13.3	16.9	13.7	10.0	7.9	5.4	37.4	50.5
Parkersburg-Marietta, WV-OH	5.8	17.4	8.3	12.2	15.6	14.7	10.7	8.1	7.2	39.2	51.7
Pensacola, FL	6.2	18.2	10.8	13.5	16.1	13.2	9.4	7.2	5.5	35.9	50.2
Peoria-Pekin, IL	6.6	18.4	9.4	12.8	15.0	14.1	9.2	7.4	7.1	37.0	51.4
Philadelphia-Wilmington-Atlantic City, PA-NJ-DE-MD..	6.5	18.9	8.8	13.7	16.5	13.6	8.7	6.9	6.5	36.4	51.9
Atlantic-Cape May, NJ........	6.1	18.3	7.6	12.4	16.7	13.6	9.7	8.1	7.4	38.4	51.7
Philadelphia, PA-NJ...........	6.5	18.9	8.8	13.6	16.4	13.6	8.7	6.9	6.6	36.4	52.1
Vineland-Millville-Bridgeton, NJ	6.3	19.1	8.5	15.1	16.1	13.2	8.7	6.6	6.4	35.6	49.0
Wilmington-Newark, DE-MD	6.7	18.6	9.9	14.6	16.8	13.5	8.4	6.1	5.3	35.1	51.3
Phoenix-Mesa, AZ	7.8	19.0	10.1	15.7	15.4	11.9	8.0	6.4	5.6	33.2	49.8
Pine Bluff, AR	6.9	19.4	10.8	12.8	15.1	13.4	8.7	6.6	6.3	35.1	51.1
Pittsburgh, PA....................	5.6	16.7	8.1	12.2	15.9	14.4	9.5	8.8	8.9	40.0	52.3
Pittsfield, MA....................	5.2	17.2	8.4	10.9	15.4	14.9	10.1	8.6	9.3	40.5	52.2
Pocatello, ID	8.1	20.0	14.6	13.7	13.5	12.7	7.4	5.2	4.9	29.8	50.6
Portland, ME	5.8	17.5	8.4	13.9	17.5	14.9	8.7	6.6	6.7	37.6	51.6
Portland-Salem, OR-WA	7.1	18.6	9.5	15.2	16.2	14.6	8.0	5.2	5.5	34.7	50.3
Portland-Vancouver, OR-WA	7.0	18.5	9.3	15.5	16.5	14.8	8.0	5.1	5.3	34.8	50.4
Salem, OR	7.4	19.6	10.5	13.6	14.4	13.4	8.2	6.2	6.6	34.2	50.0
Providence-Warwick-Pawtucket, RI	6.1	17.6	10.3	13.4	16.2	13.4	8.4	7.0	7.5	36.6	52.0
Provo-Orem, UT	11.0	23.1	21.0	15.2	10.6	7.9	4.8	3.4	3.0	23.3	50.4
Pueblo, CO	6.7	19.1	9.4	12.4	14.8	13.5	8.9	8.0	7.2	36.7	51.1
Punta Gorda, FL..................	3.7	12.0	4.5	7.6	11.2	11.8	14.5	18.4	16.3	54.3	52.2
Raleigh-Durham-Chapel Hill, NC..................	6.9	17.3	11.6	17.6	17.3	13.3	7.3	4.7	3.9	33.0	50.9
Rapid City, SD	7.1	19.5	10.5	12.9	16.3	13.7	8.2	6.4	5.4	35.0	50.4

Table C. Metropolitan Areas

Area Name	Age (percent) Under 5 years	5 to 17 years	18 to 24 years	25 to 34 years	35 to 44 years	45 to 54 years	55 to 64 years	65 to 74 years	75 years and over	Percent Female	Total persons 2000	1990	1980	Percent change 1990–2000	1980–1990
	39	40	41	42	43	44	45	46	47	48	49	50	51	52	53
Merced, CA....................	10.2	23.8	10.8	17.4	13.2	8.3	7.0	5.7	3.5	49.5	210 554	178 403	134 558	18.0	32.6
Miami-Fort Lauderdale, FL....	6.9	15.8	9.3	17.1	14.5	10.5	9.2	8.8	7.9	52.1	3 876 380	3 192 725	2 643 766	21.4	20.8
Fort Lauderdale, FL...........	6.3	14.1	8.2	17.1	14.8	9.9	8.8	10.6	10.1	52.1	1 623 018	1 255 531	1 018 257	29.3	23.3
Miami, FL.....................	7.2	10.9	10.0	17.1	14.4	10.9	9.4	7.5	6.4	52.1	2 253 362	1 937 194	1 625 509	16.3	19.2
Milwaukee-Racine, WI..........	7.7	18.8	10.0	17.6	15.1	9.9	8.6	7.0	5.4	51.8	1 689 572	1 607 183	1 570 152	5.1	2.4
Milwaukee-Waukesha, WI..	7.7	18.6	10.1	17.7	15.1	9.8	8.6	7.0	5.5	51.9	1 500 741	1 432 149	1 397 020	4.8	2.5
Racine, WI....................	7.8	20.0	9.0	17.1	15.1	10.4	8.6	6.9	5.1	51.5	188 831	175 034	173 132	7.9	1.1
Minneapolis-St. Paul, MN-WI ...	8.1	18.2	10.1	20.2	16.4	10.0	7.1	5.5	4.4	51.1	2 968 806	2 538 776	2 198 190	16.9	15.5
Missoula, MT	7.3	18.4	13.0	17.1	17.1	9.8	6.9	5.8	4.5	50.8	95 802	78 687	76 016	21.8	3.5
Mobile, AL	7.6	20.4	10.0	16.0	14.5	10.2	8.7	7.5	5.0	52.3	540 258	476 923	443 536	13.3	7.5
Modesto, CA	9.1	21.5	9.8	17.6	14.7	9.3	7.2	6.3	4.5	50.8	446 997	370 522	265 900	20.6	39.3
Monroe, LA	8.0	21.3	12.6	15.7	13.6	9.4	8.1	6.4	4.8	52.8	147 250	142 191	139 241	3.6	2.1
Montgomery, AL	7.6	19.9	11.0	16.9	15.0	10.0	8.2	6.6	4.8	52.1	333 055	292 517	272 687	13.9	7.3
Muncie, IN	6.1	16.0	19.0	13.9	13.0	10.6	8.8	7.3	5.4	52.5	118 769	119 659	128 587	-0.7	-6.9
Myrtle Beach, SC	6.6	17.2	10.4	17.8	14.7	10.3	10.3	8.8	3.9	51.0	196 629	144 053	101 419	36.5	42.0
Naples, FL	6.0	13.9	7.8	14.6	12.8	10.0	12.1	14.4	8.4	50.4	251 377	152 099	85 971	65.3	76.9
Nashville, TN	7.2	17.9	10.9	18.7	16.1	10.5	8.0	6.1	4.5	51.7	1 231 311	985 026	850 505	25.0	15.8
New London-Norwich, CT	7.3	16.2	12.0	19.0	14.7	9.9	8.5	7.3	5.1	49.6	259 088	254 957	238 409	1.6	6.9
New Orleans, LA	7.7	20.2	10.3	17.3	15.4	9.8	8.1	6.6	4.4	52.4	1 337 726	1 285 262	1 304 212	4.1	-1.5
New York-Northern New Jersey-Long Island, NY-NJ-CT-PA	6.8	16.2	10.3	17.8	15.5	11.1	9.3	7.5	5.6	52.2	21 199 865	19 480 002	18 829 146	8.8	3.4
Bergen-Passaic, NJ...........	6.4	15.3	9.7	16.9	15.3	11.5	10.3	8.5	6.0	51.9	1 373 167	1 296 252	1 292 970	5.9	-1.1
Dutchess County, NY	7.1	16.8	11.1	17.9	16.1	11.1	8.5	6.4	5.0	49.7	280 150	259 462	245 055	8.0	5.9
Jersey City, NJ	6.7	15.5	11.1	20.4	14.4	10.1	9.1	7.5	5.2	51.5	608 975	553 099	556 972	10.1	-0.7
Middlesex-Somerset-Hunterdon, NJ	6.8	15.1	10.8	19.4	16.2	11.2	9.2	7.1	4.1	50.7	1 169 641	1 019 786	886 383	14.7	15.1
Monmouth-Ocean, NJ	6.9	16.7	8.6	15.6	15.4	10.4	9.1	9.7	7.6	52.1	1 126 217	986 395	849 211	14.2	16.1
Nassau-Suffolk, NY	6.6	16.7	10.3	16.5	16.5	15.5	11.7	10.2	7.6	4.9	51.4	2 753 913	2 609 212	2 605 813	5.5	0.1
New Haven-Bridgeport-Stamford-Danbury-Waterbury, CT	6.9	15.7	11.3	17.7	15.4	10.2	8.7	8.0	6.1	52.0	1 706 575	1 631 864	1 568 468	4.6	4.0
New York, NY	6.9	16.1	10.5	18.4	15.3	10.8	9.0	7.3	5.8	52.9	9 314 235	8 546 846	8 274 961	9.0	3.3
Newark, NJ	6.9	16.7	10.1	17.4	15.7	11.4	9.3	7.3	5.2	52.0	2 032 989	1 915 724	1 963 576	6.1	-2.4
Newburgh, NY-PA	8.3	19.3	10.7	17.3	16.1	10.3	7.4	5.9	4.5	49.7	387 669	335 603	277 874	15.5	20.8
Trenton, NJ	6.7	15.8	11.9	17.3	15.7	10.7	9.0	7.8	5.2	51.6	350 761	325 759	307 863	7.7	5.8
Norfolk-Virginia Beach-Newport News, VA-NC.......	8.4	18.1	13.8	20.1	14.7	8.9	7.0	5.7	3.3	49.9	1 569 541	1 444 710	1 200 998	8.6	20.3
Ocala, FL	6.3	15.8	7.7	13.8	12.5	9.8	11.9	14.4	7.7	51.8	258 916	194 835	122 488	32.9	59.1
Odessa-Midland, TX	9.1	22.6	9.6	17.5	14.3	9.3	8.4	5.8	3.5	51.1	237 132	225 545	198 010	5.1	13.9
Oklahoma City, OK.............	7.4	19.2	11.0	17.8	15.2	10.1	8.2	6.3	4.7	51.3	1 083 346	958 839	860 969	13.0	11.4
Omaha, NE-IA	8.1	19.7	10.2	18.3	15.4	9.7	7.9	6.1	4.5	51.5	716 998	639 580	605 419	12.1	5.6
Orlando, FL	7.3	17.1	11.6	19.6	15.6	10.0	8.1	6.6	4.2	50.7	1 644 561	1 224 844	804 774	34.3	52.2
Owensboro, KY	7.3	19.9	9.7	16.1	14.5	10.4	9.3	7.5	5.4	52.2	91 545	87 189	85 949	5.0	1.4
Panama City, FL	7.3	18.1	9.9	17.8	14.5	10.8	9.6	7.7	4.3	50.7	148 217	126 994	97 740	16.7	29.9
Parkersburg-Marietta, WV-OH	6.4	18.6	9.2	15.1	15.1	11.6	9.6	8.1	6.2	52.2	151 237	149 169	157 893	1.4	-5.5
Pensacola, FL.................	7.5	18.2	11.4	17.4	14.4	10.7	9.0	7.1	4.2	51.1	412 153	344 406	289 782	19.7	18.9
Peoria-Pekin, IL..............	7.0	19.5	9.8	15.1	15.0	10.6	9.2	7.7	6.2	51.8	347 387	339 172	365 864	2.4	-7.3
Philadelphia-Wilmington-Atlantic City, PA-NJ-DE-MD...	7.2	17.1	10.6	17.5	15.0	10.2	9.1	7.9	5.4	52.0	6 188 463	5 893 019	5 649 031	5.0	4.3
Atlantic-Cape May, NJ........	7.0	15.7	9.9	17.6	14.2	9.7	9.6	9.3	6.9	51.9	354 878	319 416	276 385	11.1	15.6
Philadelphia, PA-NJ..........	7.3	17.1	10.4	17.4	14.9	10.2	9.1	8.0	5.5	52.1	5 100 931	4 922 257	4 781 235	3.6	2.9
Vineland-Millville-Bridgeton, NJ..................	7.3	18.7	10.2	16.6	14.5	10.3	8.9	7.9	5.6	51.2	146 438	138 053	132 866	6.1	3.9
Wilmington-Newark, DE-MD	6.2	16.6	12.5	16.5	16.0	10.7	9.0	7.8	4.7	52.6	586 216	513 293	458 545	14.2	11.9
Phoenix-Mesa, AZ	8.0	18.2	10.7	18.5	14.8	9.6	7.7	7.4	5.1	50.7	3 251 876	2 238 498	1 600 093	45.3	39.9
Pine Bluff, AR.................	7.3	21.0	11.5	15.0	13.7	9.8	8.3	7.5	6.0	51.9	84 278	85 487	90 718	-1.4	-5.8
Pittsburgh, PA................	6.2	15.7	9.3	15.7	14.7	10.3	10.7	10.4	7.0	52.8	2 358 695	2 394 811	2 571 223	-1.5	-6.9
Pittsfield, MA.................	6.6	16.6	8.9	16.0	15.0	10.3	9.9	9.3	7.3	52.1	134 953	139 352	145 110	-3.2	-4.0
Pocatello, ID	8.4	24.1	10.9	15.8	14.8	9.0	6.9	5.9	4.3	50.4	75 565	66 026	65 421	14.4	0.9
Portland, ME	6.9	16.4	10.5	18.6	16.6	9.9	8.2	7.1	5.8	52.1	265 612	243 135	215 789	9.2	12.7
Portland-Salem, OR-WA	7.3	17.8	9.3	17.5	17.8	10.4	7.5	6.8	5.4	51.1	2 265 223	1 793 476	1 583 518	26.3	13.3
Portland-Vancouver, OR-WA	7.4	18.3	9.3	17.4	17.7	10.5	7.5	6.7	5.2	51.0	1 918 009	1 515 452	1 333 623	26.6	13.6
Salem, OR	7.3	19.1	10.0	15.6	15.6	10.0	8.0	7.9	6.5	50.6	347 214	278 024	249 895	24.9	11.3
Providence-Warwick-Pawtucket, RI	6.5	15.5	12.5	17.1	14.8	9.6	8.9	8.6	6.5	52.1	962 886	916 270	865 771	5.1	5.8
Provo-Orem, UT	10.7	27.0	18.8	15.1	10.1	6.3	4.9	4.0	3.0	50.6	368 536	263 590	218 106	39.8	20.9
Pueblo, CO	6.9	19.5	9.2	14.9	14.6	9.8	10.0	8.8	6.4	51.6	141 472	123 051	125 972	15.0	-2.3
Punta Gorda, FL	4.4	11.2	5.8	10.8	10.3	8.7	15.0	20.9	12.9	51.8	141 627	110 975	58 460	27.6	89.8
Raleigh-Durham-Chapel Hill, NC............................	6.9	15.6	14.3	20.7	16.8	9.9	6.9	5.3	3.7	51.7	1 187 941	858 516	664 788	38.4	29.1
Rapid City, SD	9.2	20.0	11.0	18.6	14.7	8.9	7.5	5.7	4.3	50.5	88 565	81 343	70 361	8.9	15.6

Table C. Metropolitan Areas

Area Name	Total population	Total in households	House-holder	Spouse	Child Total	Own child under 18 years	Other relatives Total	Under 18 years	Nonrelatives Total	Unmarried partner	Total in group quarters	Correctional institutions	Nursing homes	Other institutions	College dormitories	Military quarters	Other
	54	55	56	57	58	59	60	61	62	63	64	65	66	67	68	69	70
Merced, CA	210 554	98.6	30.3	17.5	38.0	30.3	8.0	3.2	4.8	2.0	1.4	0.3	0.2	0.0	0.0	0.0	0.8
Miami-Fort Lauderdale, FL	3 876 380	98.3	36.9	17.4	28.9	21.0	9.0	2.8	6.1	2.2	1.7	0.6	0.4	0.1	0.2	0.0	0.4
Fort Lauderdale, FL	1 623 018	98.8	40.3	18.6	27.4	21.0	6.4	2.1	6.0	2.6	1.2	0.4	0.3	0.1	0.0	0.0	0.4
Miami, FL	2 253 362	98.0	34.5	16.5	30.0	21.0	10.8	3.3	6.2	2.0	2.0	0.7	0.4	0.2	0.3	0.0	0.4
Milwaukee-Racine, WI	1 689 572	97.7	39.0	19.0	30.5	24.0	4.2	1.8	5.0	2.1	2.3	0.4	0.7	0.1	0.5	0.0	0.5
Milwaukee-Waukesha, WI	1 500 741	97.8	39.2	18.9	30.4	23.9	4.2	1.8	5.1	2.1	2.2	0.3	0.7	0.1	0.6	0.0	0.4
Racine, WI	188 831	97.1	37.5	20.3	31.0	24.5	4.0	1.8	4.4	2.1	2.9	1.3	0.5	0.1	0.0	0.0	1.0
Minneapolis-St. Paul, MN-WI	2 968 806	97.9	38.3	20.0	30.6	25.1	3.2	1.1	5.8	2.2	2.1	0.3	0.6	0.1	0.6	0.0	0.5
Missoula, MT	95 802	96.2	40.1	19.0	25.9	21.3	2.5	0.9	8.7	2.7	3.8	0.4	0.4	0.0	2.1	0.0	0.8
Mobile, AL	540 258	98.1	38.0	19.8	30.8	23.3	6.0	2.9	3.5	1.5	1.9	0.4	0.5	0.2	0.6	0.0	0.3
Modesto, CA	446 997	98.3	32.5	18.2	34.9	27.2	7.6	3.0	5.2	2.0	1.7	0.2	0.5	0.1	0.1	0.0	0.8
Monroe, LA	147 250	96.6	37.5	17.9	31.4	24.0	6.0	3.2	3.9	1.8	3.4	0.5	0.8	0.4	1.3	0.0	0.4
Montgomery, AL	333 055	94.7	37.5	18.4	29.7	22.8	5.8	2.8	3.3	1.4	5.3	2.2	0.5	0.2	0.9	1.1	0.4
Muncie, IN	118 769	94.2	39.7	19.3	25.0	19.9	3.1	1.4	7.1	2.1	5.8	0.1	1.0	0.2	4.2	0.0	0.2
Myrtle Beach, SC	196 629	98.7	41.6	21.4	24.6	18.7	5.0	2.1	6.2	2.4	1.3	0.2	0.4	0.0	0.4	0.0	0.2
Naples, FL	251 377	98.1	41.0	23.8	21.7	17.4	5.4	1.7	6.3	2.1	1.9	0.3	0.6	0.1	0.0	0.0	1.0
Nashville, TN	1 231 311	97.2	38.9	19.9	28.3	22.3	4.9	2.0	5.2	1.8	2.8	0.6	0.4	0.2	1.2	0.0	0.3
New London-Norwich, CT	259 088	95.4	38.5	20.2	28.2	22.5	3.4	1.2	5.1	2.4	4.6	1.4	0.8	0.1	1.1	0.8	0.0
New Orleans, LA	1 337 726	98.0	37.8	16.9	31.5	22.6	7.4	3.6	4.4	2.1	2.0	0.6	0.5	0.1	0.4	0.0	0.4
New York-Northern New Jersey-Long Island, NY-NJ-CT-PA	21 199 865	97.7	36.5	17.7	30.8	21.9	7.6	2.3	5.2	1.7	2.3	0.3	0.6	0.1	0.6	0.0	0.6
Bergen-Passaic, NJ	1 373 167	98.4	36.0	20.1	31.1	21.9	7.1	1.9	4.1	1.5	1.6	0.2	0.5	0.1	0.3	0.0	0.5
Dutchess County, NY	280 150	93.5	35.5	19.7	29.5	22.9	4.2	1.4	4.5	2.0	6.5	2.3	0.6	0.3	2.3	0.0	0.9
Jersey City, NJ	608 975	98.4	37.9	15.1	29.0	19.6	9.5	2.6	7.0	2.3	1.6	0.4	0.4	0.1	0.3	0.0	0.3
Middlesex-Somerset-Hunterdon, NJ	1 169 641	97.5	35.8	21.1	30.3	22.5	5.8	1.5	4.6	1.6	2.5	0.6	0.5	0.2	0.8	0.0	0.4
Monmouth-Ocean, NJ	1 126 217	98.4	37.7	21.6	30.7	23.0	4.6	1.5	3.7	1.6	1.6	0.1	0.7	0.1	0.2	0.1	0.3
Nassau-Suffolk, NY	2 753 913	98.2	33.3	20.8	32.7	22.8	6.9	2.0	4.5	1.3	1.8	0.1	0.6	0.1	0.6	0.0	0.5
New Haven-Bridgeport-Stamford-Danbury-Water-bury, CT	1 706 575	97.3	37.7	19.6	30.1	23.0	5.2	1.7	4.7	1.8	2.7	0.4	0.9	0.1	1.0	0.0	0.4
New York, NY	9 314 235	97.7	37.4	14.9	30.3	20.9	9.1	2.8	6.0	1.9	2.3	0.3	0.6	0.2	0.5	0.0	0.8
Newark, NJ	2 032 989	97.9	35.9	18.7	31.5	22.8	7.2	2.4	4.7	1.8	2.1	0.4	0.7	0.2	0.5	0.0	0.4
Newburgh, NY-PA	387 669	96.4	34.1	20.0	33.5	26.5	4.7	1.7	4.1	1.9	3.6	0.9	0.5	0.2	0.3	1.0	0.7
Trenton, NJ	350 761	94.0	35.9	18.1	28.8	21.4	6.1	2.2	5.1	1.9	6.0	1.2	0.6	0.2	3.5	0.0	0.5
Norfolk-Virginia Beach-Newport News, VA-NC	1 569 541	95.8	36.8	18.8	29.7	23.4	5.1	2.4	5.3	1.8	4.2	1.0	0.5	0.1	0.7	1.7	0.3
Ocala, FL	258 916	97.3	41.2	22.9	23.8	18.6	4.8	2.0	4.6	2.2	2.7	1.5	0.6	0.1	0.1	0.0	0.4
Odessa-Midland, TX	237 132	98.6	36.5	20.4	33.1	26.9	5.5	2.9	3.1	1.6	1.4	0.5	0.6	0.0	0.1	0.0	0.2
Oklahoma City, OK	1 083 346	96.8	39.2	19.8	28.7	23.0	4.6	2.0	4.6	1.7	3.2	1.0	0.6	0.1	1.0	0.0	0.4
Omaha, NE-IA	716 998	97.8	38.4	19.9	31.0	25.0	3.6	1.4	5.0	1.9	2.2	0.3	0.6	0.3	0.5	0.1	0.3
Orlando, FL	1 644 561	98.3	38.0	19.5	28.1	21.9	5.9	2.2	6.7	2.5	1.7	0.6	0.4	0.1	0.2	0.0	0.4
Owensboro, KY	91 545	97.2	39.4	21.1	29.9	23.4	3.3	1.6	3.5	1.7	2.8	0.2	1.0	0.3	0.5	0.0	0.9
Panama City, FL	148 217	97.7	40.2	20.9	27.3	21.5	4.3	1.9	5.1	2.3	2.3	1.1	0.5	0.1	0.0	0.4	0.3
Parkersburg-Marietta, WV-OH	151 237	98.0	40.6	22.7	27.6	21.3	3.3	1.4	3.8	2.0	2.0	0.1	0.9	0.1	0.7	0.0	0.2
Pensacola, FL	412 153	94.1	37.6	19.5	27.7	21.6	4.7	2.2	4.7	1.9	5.9	2.2	0.7	0.2	1.1	1.5	0.2
Peoria-Pekin, IL	347 387	96.8	39.1	21.2	29.1	22.8	3.2	1.5	4.1	1.8	3.2	0.7	1.0	0.1	0.9	0.0	0.5
Philadelphia-Wilmington-Atlantic City, PA-NJ-DE-MD	6 188 463	96.9	37.5	18.4	30.5	22.4	5.8	2.4	4.7	2.0	3.1	0.7	0.7	0.2	0.9	0.0	0.6
Atlantic-Cape May, NJ	354 878	97.4	38.7	18.4	28.6	21.6	6.3	2.3	5.4	2.5	2.6	0.3	0.8	0.2	0.6	0.1	0.7
Philadelphia, PA-NJ	5 100 931	97.0	37.5	18.3	30.8	22.5	5.9	2.4	4.5	1.9	3.0	0.2	0.2	0.0	0.1	0.0	0.1
Vineland-Millville-Bridgeton, NJ	146 438	91.6	33.6	16.3	29.5	21.4	6.9	3.2	5.4	2.6	8.4	6.3	0.8	0.0	0.0	0.0	1.2
Wilmington-Newark, DE-MD	586 216	96.8	37.6	19.1	29.4	22.5	5.1	2.2	5.6	2.3	3.2	0.8	0.5	0.1	1.3	0.0	0.5
Phoenix-Mesa, AZ	3 251 876	98.2	36.7	19.1	29.3	23.7	6.4	2.5	6.6	2.3	1.8	0.8	0.2	0.1	0.2	0.0	0.5
Pine Bluff, AR	84 278	93.7	36.3	17.2	29.7	21.8	7.5	3.9	3.1	1.4	6.3	3.9	0.9	0.1	1.2	0.0	0.2
Pittsburgh, PA	2 358 695	97.1	41.0	20.7	28.1	20.5	3.7	1.3	3.6	1.7	2.9	0.3	0.9	0.2	0.9	0.0	0.6
Pittsfield, MA	134 953	95.5	41.5	19.9	26.4	20.5	2.8	0.9	4.8	2.4	4.5	0.2	1.3	0.2	2.1	0.0	1.0
Pocatello, ID	75 565	97.0	36.0	20.4	32.2	26.2	3.3	1.4	5.1	1.7	3.0	0.7	0.4	0.0	1.5	0.0	0.4
Portland, ME	265 612	96.8	40.7	20.4	26.7	21.9	2.7	0.8	6.4	2.8	3.2	0.3	0.6	0.1	1.3	0.1	1.0
Portland-Salem, OR-WA	2 265 223	98.0	38.3	19.7	28.7	23.5	4.5	1.5	6.9	2.5	2.0	0.5	0.4	0.1	0.4	0.0	0.5
Portland-Vancouver, OR-WA	1 918 009	98.3	38.7	19.7	28.5	23.3	4.4	1.5	7.0	2.5	1.7	0.4	0.4	0.0	0.4	0.0	0.5
Salem, OR	347 214	96.4	35.9	19.5	29.5	24.2	5.1	1.8	6.4	2.1	3.6	1.3	0.6	0.4	0.6	0.0	0.7
Providence-Warwick-Pawtucket, RI	962 886	96.2	38.8	18.6	29.1	21.8	4.7	1.4	5.0	2.2	3.8	0.4	0.9	0.1	2.0	0.0	0.0
Provo-Orem, UT	368 536	97.4	27.1	18.9	39.1	31.8	4.6	1.7	7.6	0.4	2.6	0.1	0.2	0.3	1.3	0.0	0.6
Pueblo, CO	141 472	97.1	38.6	19.3	29.5	22.6	5.1	2.4	4.6	2.0	2.9	0.7	0.8	0.6	0.3	0.0	0.5
Punta Gorda, FL	141 627	98.2	45.1	26.7	18.4	13.9	3.7	1.3	4.3	2.1	1.8	0.8	0.9	0.0	0.0	0.0	0.1
Raleigh-Durham-Chapel Hill, NC	1 187 941	96.4	38.8	19.6	26.8	22.1	4.6	1.6	6.6	1.9	3.6	0.5	0.5	0.1	2.2	0.0	0.3
Rapid City, SD	88 565	97.3	39.1	20.1	29.4	24.5	3.1	1.3	5.6	2.4	2.7	0.4	0.6	0.1	0.9	0.0	0.8

Table C. Metropolitan Areas

Area Name	Households by type, 2000												Households, 1990		
		Family households						Nonfamily households							
				Married couple		Female householder¹			Householder living alone						
	Total households	Total	With own children under 18 years	Total	With own children under 18 years	Total	With own children under 18 years	Total	Total	65 years and over	Average household size	Average family size	Total households	Female householder¹	Householder living alone
	71	72	73	74	75	76	77	78	79	80	81	82	83	84	85
Merced, CA	63 815	78.0	45.4	57.8	32.5	14.1	9.2	22.0	17.7	7.4	3.25	3.69	55 331	12.5	17.7
Miami-Fort Lauderdale, FL	1 431 219	67.1	31.8	47.0	21.5	15.1	8.2	32.9	26.2	10.3	2.66	3.23	1 220 797	12.8	26.9
Fort Lauderdale, FL	654 445	62.9	29.3	46.1	20.1	12.5	7.2	37.1	29.6	12.4	2.45	3.07	520 442	10.0	29.5
Miami, FL	776 774	70.6	33.8	47.7	22.6	17.2	9.1	29.4	23.3	8.6	2.84	3.35	692 355	14.9	24.9
Milwaukee-Racine, WI	658 476	65.5	32.0	48.9	22.0	12.8	8.1	34.5	28.2	9.7	2.51	3.11	601 458	12.9	25.1
Milwaukee-Waukesha, WI	587 657	64.9	31.7	48.2	21.8	12.9	8.1	35.1	28.7	9.7	2.50	3.11	537 722	13.0	25.5
Racine, WI	70 819	70.4	34.5	54.0	24.2	12.3	8.0	29.6	24.5	9.2	2.59	3.09	63 736	12.3	22.0
Minneapolis-St. Paul, MN-WI	1 136 615	65.5	34.1	52.2	25.9	9.7	6.3	34.5	26.7	7.5	2.56	3.15	960 170	9.7	24.8
Missoula, MT	38 439	60.2	29.2	47.4	21.0	9.2	6.1	39.8	28.0	7.5	2.40	2.96	30 782	9.5	27.3
Mobile, AL	205 515	71.5	33.6	52.1	22.7	15.7	9.2	28.5	24.4	9.0	2.58	3.08	173 943	15.3	22.9
Modesto, CA	145 146	75.5	41.2	56.0	29.6	13.7	8.4	24.5	19.4	7.9	3.03	3.47	125 375	11.5	19.9
Monroe, LA	55 216	69.4	34.2	47.7	21.2	17.9	11.0	30.6	25.8	9.3	2.58	3.12	50 518	17.0	24.1
Montgomery, AL	124 808	69.5	34.0	49.1	22.2	16.7	10.0	30.5	26.5	8.8	2.53	3.07	105 531	15.7	24.5
Muncie, IN	47 131	63.0	27.8	48.5	19.0	10.9	6.9	37.0	28.2	10.4	2.37	2.90	45 177	10.6	25.9
Myrtle Beach, SC	81 800	66.6	26.3	51.4	17.7	11.5	6.6	33.4	25.8	8.5	2.37	2.84	55 764	11.2	22.3
Naples, FL	102 973	69.2	22.7	58.1	16.5	7.2	4.4	30.8	24.5	11.9	2.39	2.79	61 703	7.1	22.6
Nashville, TN	479 569	67.1	32.5	51.0	23.3	12.3	7.3	32.9	26.3	7.1	2.49	3.03	375 831	12.2	24.6
New London-Norwich, CT	99 835	67.0	32.0	53.0	23.0	11.0	7.0	33.0	26.0	10.0	2.48	3.00	93 245	9.6	23.1
New Orleans, LA	505 579	67.5	32.9	44.7	20.5	18.2	10.3	32.5	27.1	8.5	2.59	3.19	469 823	17.5	26.1
New York-Northern New Jersey-Long Island, NY-NJ-CT-PA	7 735 264	67.6	32.4	48.5	23.2	14.7	7.7	32.4	26.7	9.7	2.68	3.27	7 126 646	14.0	26.3
Bergen-Passaic, NJ	494 673	71.7	33.3	55.8	26.5	11.8	5.4	28.3	23.8	10.0	2.73	3.26	464 149	11.2	22.7
Dutchess County, NY	99 536	69.5	34.5	55.5	26.6	10.3	6.0	30.5	24.6	9.0	2.63	3.16	89 567	9.3	22.2
Jersey City, NJ	230 546	62.3	29.6	39.8	18.7	16.6	8.8	37.7	29.5	9.6	2.60	3.27	208 739	16.5	28.7
Middlesex-Somerset-Hunterdon, NJ	418 477	72.2	35.0	58.9	29.0	9.7	4.6	27.8	22.3	8.0	2.72	3.21	365 085	9.2	20.8
Monmouth-Ocean, NJ	424 638	70.2	32.0	57.3	26.0	9.6	4.7	29.8	25.3	12.8	2.61	3.15	365 717	9.3	23.3
Nassau-Suffolk, NY	916 686	77.2	36.2	62.5	30.2	10.9	4.6	22.8	18.6	8.5	2.95	3.35	856 234	10.3	16.5
New Haven-Bridgeport-Stamford-Danbury-Waterbury, CT	643 272	68.0	33.0	52.0	24.0	13.0	7.0	32.0	26.0	10.0	2.58	3.13	609 741	11.9	24.4
New York, NY	3 484 108	62.7	30.4	39.8	19.0	18.1	9.8	37.3	30.8	9.9	2.61	3.31	3 252 399	17.1	31.6
Newark, NJ	729 062	71.1	34.7	52.1	25.5	14.4	7.4	28.9	24.0	9.0	2.73	3.25	686 032	13.8	23.3
Newburgh, NY-PA	132 221	73.7	38.9	58.6	30.3	10.9	6.4	26.3	21.4	8.5	2.83	3.31	112 042	9.9	19.7
Trenton, NJ	125 807	68.6	32.8	50.6	23.7	13.8	7.4	31.4	25.6	9.9	2.62	3.16	116 941	13.2	24.2
Norfolk-Virginia Beach-Newport News, VA-NC	577 659	70.0	35.6	51.1	24.1	14.9	9.3	30.0	23.4	7.5	2.60	3.08	511 136	13.0	21.1
Ocala, FL	106 755	69.9	24.7	55.6	16.5	10.7	6.3	30.1	25.0	13.0	2.36	2.79	78 177	10.3	22.9
Odessa-Midland, TX	86 591	72.4	38.9	55.8	28.3	12.6	8.2	27.6	24.1	8.7	2.70	3.23	81 242	10.6	23.1
Oklahoma City, OK	424 764	66.8	32.4	50.6	22.5	12.3	7.7	33.2	27.5	8.5	2.47	3.03	367 775	11.4	26.3
Omaha, NE-IA	275 565	66.7	34.0	51.7	24.8	11.4	7.3	33.3	26.9	8.3	2.55	3.12	240 149	11.2	25.2
Orlando, FL	625 248	68.0	31.9	51.2	22.3	12.4	7.4	32.0	23.5	7.6	2.58	3.07	465 275	10.6	22.8
Owensboro, KY	36 033	68.9	32.9	53.6	23.8	11.8	7.2	31.1	27.1	11.1	2.47	3.00	33 036	11.5	24.8
Panama City, FL	59 597	67.9	30.6	52.0	20.8	12.0	7.5	32.1	26.0	8.8	2.43	2.92	48 938	11.1	23.0
Parkersburg-Marietta, WV-OH	61 412	69.3	29.9	55.8	22.2	10.1	5.9	30.7	26.4	11.4	2.41	2.90	57 804	9.8	23.9
Pensacola, FL	154 842	69.4	31.8	51.9	21.4	13.8	8.3	30.6	24.7	8.8	2.50	2.99	128 508	13.1	22.4
Peoria-Pekin, IL	135 857	68.3	31.1	54.3	22.4	10.7	6.9	31.7	27.0	10.8	2.47	3.00	129 363	10.3	25.4
Philadelphia-Wilmington-Atlantic City, PA-NJ-DE-MD	2 320 719	67.5	32.0	49.0	22.4	14.2	7.6	32.5	26.9	10.0	2.58	3.16	2 160 142	13.5	25.1
Atlantic-Cape May, NJ	137 172	66.0	30.0	47.7	20.2	13.6	7.5	34.0	28.0	11.9	2.52	3.09	122 979	12.6	26.9
Philadelphia, PA-NJ	1 914 246	67.4	31.9	48.8	22.5	14.3	7.5	32.6	27.1	10.1	2.58	3.17	1 801 159	13.7	25.3
Vineland-Millville-Bridgeton, NJ	49 143	71.6	34.1	48.7	21.0	17.3	10.1	28.4	23.6	11.1	2.73	3.19	47 118	15.8	21.6
Wilmington-Newark, DE-MD	220 158	68.3	33.1	50.9	23.3	13.1	7.6	31.7	24.9	8.3	2.58	3.09	188 886	11.8	23.2
Phoenix-Mesa, AZ	1 194 250	67.7	32.8	51.9	23.5	10.8	6.6	32.3	24.4	8.0	2.67	3.20	846 714	10.2	24.8
Pine Bluff, AR	30 555	70.4	33.1	47.4	19.9	18.8	11.2	29.6	26.2	10.6	2.59	3.13	30 001	16.0	24.2
Pittsburgh, PA	966 500	65.3	27.6	50.5	20.3	11.4	5.9	34.7	30.0	13.1	2.37	2.96	947 248	11.5	27.3
Pittsfield, MA	56 006	63.0	28.0	48.0	19.0	11.0	7.0	37.0	32.0	14.0	2.30	2.89	54 315	10.8	27.5
Pocatello, ID	27 192	70.7	36.5	56.7	27.8	10.0	6.5	29.3	22.8	7.6	2.69	3.20	23 412	8.8	23.9
Portland, ME	107 989	63.0	30.0	50.0	22.0	10.0	6.0	37.0	28.0	10.0	2.38	2.95	94 512	9.8	25.2
Portland-Salem, OR-WA	866 475	65.7	32.6	51.5	23.9	10.0	6.3	34.3	25.9	8.0	2.56	3.10	691 102	9.8	25.7
Portland-Vancouver, OR-WA	741 776	65.0	32.3	51.0	23.8	9.9	6.2	35.0	26.3	7.7	2.54	3.09	589 441	9.7	26.0
Salem, OR	124 699	69.4	34.1	54.3	24.6	10.7	7.0	30.6	23.7	9.6	2.68	3.17	101 661	10.1	24.1
Providence-Warwick-Pawtucket, RI	373 196	65.0	31.0	48.0	21.0	13.0	8.0	35.0	28.0	11.0	2.48	3.08	345 290	11.9	26.3
Provo-Orem, UT	99 937	80.8	48.3	69.8	42.5	8.0	4.6	19.2	11.2	4.7	3.59	3.86	70 168	7.8	12.2
Pueblo, CO	54 579	68.4	31.5	50.1	20.7	13.3	8.1	31.6	26.6	11.1	2.52	3.04	47 057	13.7	25.8
Punta Gorda, FL	63 864	69.1	17.4	59.2	12.2	7.2	3.8	30.9	26.0	16.7	2.18	2.56	48 433	6.0	23.0
Raleigh-Durham-Chapel Hill, NC	461 097	64.9	32.4	50.5	24.1	11.0	6.7	35.1	26.4	6.2	2.48	3.03	334 506	11.2	26.2
Rapid City, SD	34 641	67.2	33.5	51.3	22.7	11.7	8.3	32.8	26.1	8.4	2.49	3.00	30 553	10.2	23.4

¹No spouse present.

Table C. Metropolitan Areas

Area Name	Percent change of households, 1990–2000	Total housing units	Occupied housing units (percent)	Vacant housing units				Occupied housing units				
				Total	For seasonal, recreational, or occasional use	Homeowner vacancy rate (percent)	Rental vacancy rate (percent)	Total	Percent owner-occupied housing units	Percent renter-occupied housing units	Average household size of owner-occupied units	Average household size of renter-occupied units
	86	87	88	89	90	91	92	93	94	95	96	97
Merced, CA	15.3	68 373	93.3	6.7	1.2	1.4	4.2	63 815	58.7	41.3	3.14	3.42
Miami-Fort Lauderdale, FL	17.2	1 593 321	89.8	10.2	4.8	2.4	6.0	1 431 219	63.2	36.8	2.74	2.52
Fort Lauderdale, FL	23.8	741 043	88.3	11.7	6.3	2.6	6.5	654 445	69.5	30.5	2.49	2.35
Miami, FL	12.2	852 278	91.1	8.9	3.5	2.1	5.7	776 774	57.8	42.2	3.00	2.63
Milwaukee-Racine, WI	9.5	692 962	95.0	5.0	0.6	1.0	5.5	658 476	62.1	37.9	2.69	2.21
Milwaukee-Waukesha, WI	9.3	618 244	95.1	4.9	0.5	1.0	5.5	587 657	61.1	38.9	2.69	2.20
Racine, WI	11.1	74 718	94.8	5.2	1.2	1.0	6.3	70 819	70.6	29.4	2.69	2.35
Minneapolis-St. Paul, MN-WI	18.4	1 169 775	97.2	2.8	0.8	0.6	2.8	1 136 615	72.4	27.6	2.75	2.04
Missoula, MT	24.9	41 319	93.0	7.0	3.2	1.1	4.0	38 439	61.9	38.1	2.60	2.08
Mobile, AL	18.2	239 386	85.9	14.1	5.7	2.1	12.8	205 515	71.7	28.3	2.64	2.41
Modesto, CA	15.8	150 807	96.2	3.8	0.3	1.3	3.2	145 146	61.9	38.1	3.03	3.03
Monroe, LA	9.3	60 154	91.8	8.2	0.7	1.4	9.0	55 216	64.1	35.9	2.62	2.50
Montgomery, AL	18.3	138 832	89.9	10.1	1.0	2.2	10.7	124 808	69.4	30.6	2.59	2.39
Muncie, IN	4.3	51 032	92.4	7.6	0.4	1.7	9.0	47 131	67.2	32.8	2.44	2.23
Myrtle Beach, SC	46.7	122 085	67.0	33.0	20.4	3.2	30.2	81 800	73.0	27.0	2.39	2.33
Naples, FL	66.9	144 536	71.2	28.8	23.8	2.6	9.8	102 973	75.6	24.4	2.31	2.65
Nashville, TN	27.6	509 293	94.2	5.8	0.4	1.9	6.8	479 569	66.0	34.0	2.63	2.22
New London-Norwich, CT	7.1	110 674	90.0	10.0	5.0	1.3	6.4	99 835	67.0	33.0	2.60	2.23
New Orleans, LA	7.6	556 234	90.9	9.1	1.2	1.6	7.9	505 579	61.8	38.2	2.73	2.37
New York-Northern New Jersey-Long Island, NY-NJ-CT-PA	8.5	8 213 523	94.2	5.8	1.9	1.1	3.5	7 735 264	53.0	47.0	2.86	2.48
Bergen-Passaic, NJ	6.6	509 868	97.0	3.0	0.4	0.8	2.7	494 673	63.4	36.6	2.87	2.49
Dutchess County, NY	11.1	106 103	93.8	6.2	2.3	1.3	4.5	99 536	69.0	31.0	2.81	2.23
Jersey City, NJ	10.4	240 618	95.8	4.2	0.3	1.2	2.7	230 546	30.7	69.3	2.81	2.51
Middlesex-Somerset-Hunterdon, NJ	14.6	430 692	97.2	2.8	0.4	0.8	2.8	418 477	71.2	28.8	2.83	2.45
Monmouth-Ocean, NJ	16.1	489 595	86.7	13.3	8.4	1.4	7.4	424 638	78.7	21.3	2.68	2.35
Nassau-Suffolk, NY	7.1	980 474	93.5	6.5	4.2	0.7	2.7	916 686	80.0	20.0	3.05	2.54
New Haven-Bridgeport-Stamford-Danbury-Waterbury, CT	5.5	680 198	95.0	5.0	1.0	1.1	5.3	643 272	66.0	34.0	2.72	2.32
New York, NY	7.1	3 680 360	94.7	5.3	0.9	1.5	3.2	3 484 108	34.7	65.3	2.83	2.50
Newark, NJ	6.3	766 020	95.2	4.8	0.8	1.0	4.2	729 062	60.8	39.2	2.92	2.44
Newburgh, NY-PA	18.0	157 435	84.0	16.0	11.2	1.9	4.4	132 221	69.4	30.6	2.91	2.63
Trenton, NJ	7.6	133 280	94.4	5.6	0.3	1.6	5.4	125 807	67.0	33.0	2.75	2.37
Norfolk-Virginia Beach-Newport News, VA-NC	13.0	619 335	93.3	6.7	1.4	1.8	5.6	577 659	63.0	37.0	2.68	2.47
Ocala, FL	36.6	122 663	87.0	13.0	4.3	2.7	9.8	106 755	79.8	20.2	2.35	2.42
Odessa-Midland, TX	6.6	97 560	88.8	11.2	0.4	2.1	18.5	86 591	69.1	30.9	2.85	2.36
Oklahoma City, OK	15.5	466 230	91.1	8.9	0.6	2.0	10.8	424 764	64.7	35.3	2.56	2.30
Omaha, NE-IA	14.7	291 001	94.7	5.3	0.6	1.1	7.3	275 565	66.0	34.0	2.73	2.19
Orlando, FL	34.4	683 551	91.5	8.5	2.9	1.8	7.7	625 248	66.3	33.7	2.67	2.42
Owensboro, KY	9.1	38 432	93.8	6.2	0.4	1.7	7.9	36 033	70.3	29.7	2.57	2.22
Panama City, FL	21.8	78 435	76.0	24.0	11.2	2.9	22.7	59 597	68.6	31.4	2.48	2.33
Parkersburg-Marietta, WV-OH	6.2	67 545	90.9	9.1	1.6	1.9	9.1	61 412	74.5	25.5	2.49	2.18
Pensacola, FL	20.5	173 766	89.1	10.9	2.3	2.3	12.8	154 842	71.0	29.0	2.53	2.43
Peoria-Pekin, IL	5.0	144 664	93.9	6.1	0.3	1.5	8.7	135 857	72.2	27.8	2.59	2.17
Philadelphia-Wilmington-Atlantic City, PA-NJ-DE-MD	7.4	2 539 825	91.4	8.6	2.5	1.4	6.7	2 320 719	69.9	30.1	2.74	2.21
Atlantic-Cape May, NJ	11.5	205 137	66.9	33.1	26.7	2.3	12.2	137 172	68.8	31.2	2.60	2.34
Philadelphia, PA-NJ	6.3	2 047 843	93.5	6.5	0.3	1.4	6.2	1 914 246	69.9	30.1	2.76	2.17
Vineland-Millville-Bridgeton, NJ	4.3	52 863	93.0	7.0	1.6	1.9	5.5	49 143	67.9	32.1	2.73	2.74
Wilmington-Newark, DE-MD	16.6	233 982	94.1	5.9	0.9	1.3	7.3	220 158	70.8	29.2	2.68	2.32
Phoenix-Mesa, AZ	41.0	1 331 385	89.7	10.3	4.6	2.0	9.0	1 194 250	68.0	32.0	2.73	2.55
Pine Bluff, AR	1.8	34 350	89.0	11.0	1.1	1.6	8.5	30 555	66.2	33.8	2.59	2.57
Pittsburgh, PA	2.0	1 046 094	92.4	7.6	0.6	1.7	8.7	966 500	71.3	28.7	2.53	1.97
Pittsfield, MA	3.1	66 301	85.0	16.0	9.0	1.7	8.2	56 006	67.0	33.0	2.47	1.95
Pocatello, ID	16.1	29 102	93.4	6.6	0.9	2.1	8.4	27 192	70.7	29.3	2.83	2.36
Portland, ME	14.3	122 600	88.0	12.0	9.0	0.7	3.7	107 989	67.0	33.0	2.58	1.97
Portland-Salem, OR-WA	25.4	918 935	94.3	5.7	0.6	2.3	6.7	866 475	63.0	37.0	2.68	2.36
Portland-Vancouver, OR-WA	25.8	786 300	94.3	5.7	0.6	2.2	6.7	741 776	62.9	37.1	2.68	2.32
Salem, OR	22.7	132 635	94.0	6.0	0.7	2.5	6.8	124 699	64.0	36.0	2.71	2.64
Providence-Warwick-Pawtucket, RI	8.1	400 276	93.0	7.0	3.0	1.0	5.0	373 196	60.0	40.0	2.68	2.19
Provo-Orem, UT	42.4	104 315	95.8	4.2	0.8	1.7	3.2	99 937	66.8	33.2	3.78	3.21
Pueblo, CO	16.0	58 926	92.6	7.4	1.0	1.8	8.5	54 579	70.4	29.6	2.57	2.38
Punta Gorda, FL	31.9	79 758	80.1	19.9	13.2	2.2	14.2	63 864	83.7	16.3	2.16	2.28
Raleigh-Durham-Chapel Hill, NC	37.8	495 612	93.0	7.0	0.6	2.3	8.0	461 097	64.5	35.5	2.60	2.27
Rapid City, SD	13.4	37 249	93.0	7.0	2.6	1.0	6.4	34 641	66.2	33.8	2.60	2.26

Table C. Metropolitan Areas

CMSA/ MSA/ PMSA/ NECMA code[1]	Area Name	Population, 2000				Population, 1990				Population and population characteristics, 2000					
										Race (percent)					
										One race					
		Land area, 2000[2] (sq km)	Total persons	Rank	Per square kilometer	Land area, 1990[2] (sq km)	Total persons	Rank	Per square kilometer	White	Black or African American	American Indian or Alaska Native	Asian	Native Hawaiian and other Pacific Islander	Some other race
		1	2	3	4	5	6	7	8	9	10	11	12	13	14
6680	Reading, PA	2 224	373 638	133	168.0	2 225	336 523	132	151.2	88.2	3.7	0.2	1.0	0.0	5.4
6690	Redding, CA	9 804	163 256	226	16.7	9 805	147 036	224	15.0	89.3	0.8	2.8	1.9	0.1	1.7
6720	Reno, NV	16 426	339 486	146	20.7	16 427	254 667	163	15.5	80.4	2.1	1.8	4.3	0.5	7.7
6740	Richland-Kennewick-Pasco, WA	7 629	191 822	206	25.1	7 628	150 033	218	19.7	80.0	1.3	0.8	2.1	0.1	12.7
6760	Richmond-Petersburg, VA	7 626	996 512	62	130.7	7 628	865 640	60	113.5	64.9	30.2	0.4	2.1	0.0	1.1
6800	Roanoke, VA	2 204	235 932	183	107.0	2 204	224 592	175	101.9	83.9	13.0	0.2	1.2	0.0	0.5
6820	Rochester, MN	1 691	124 277	274	73.5	1 691	106 470	284	63.0	90.3	2.7	0.3	4.3	0.0	0.9
6840	Rochester, NY	8 872	1 098 201	58	123.8	8 873	1 062 470	48	119.7	84.0	10.3	0.3	1.8	0.0	1.9
6880	Rockford, IL	4 024	371 236	134	92.2	4 026	329 676	135	81.9	85.1	8.1	0.3	1.4	0.0	3.4
6895	Rocky Mount, NC	2 707	143 026	249	52.8	2 707	133 369	240	49.3	53.4	43.1	0.4	0.4	0.0	1.9
82	Sacramento-Yolo, CA	13 194	1 796 857	X	136.2	13 193	1 506 792	X	114.2	70.0	7.1	1.1	9.0	0.5	7.2
6920	Sacramento, CA	10 569	1 628 197	35	154.0	10 571	1 365 580	36	129.2	70.2	7.7	1.1	8.9	0.5	6.5
9270	Yolo, CA	2 624	168 660	222	64.3	2 622	141 212	232	53.9	67.7	2.0	1.2	9.9	0.3	13.8
6960	Saginaw-Bay City-Midland, MI	4 596	403 070	124	87.7	4 596	399 320	111	86.9	84.8	10.3	0.4	0.9	0.0	1.9
7120	Salinas, CA	8 604	401 762	125	46.7	8 604	355 660	125	41.3	55.9	3.7	1.0	6.0	0.4	27.8
7160	Salt Lake City-Ogden, UT	4 189	1 333 914	46	318.4	4 190	1 072 227	47	255.9	87.6	1.1	0.8	2.2	0.9	5.0
7200	San Angelo, TX	3 942	104 010	295	26.4	3 942	98 458	294	25.0	79.1	4.1	0.7	0.9	0.1	12.8
7240	San Antonio, TX	8 615	1 592 383	38	184.8	8 617	1 324 749	39	153.7	70.6	6.6	0.8	1.5	0.1	16.9
7320	San Diego, CA	10 878	2 813 833	15	258.7	10 890	2 498 016	14	229.4	66.5	5.7	0.9	8.9	0.5	12.8
84	San Francisco-Oakland-San Jose, CA	19 083	7 039 362	X	368.9	19 085	6 277 523	X	328.9	58.7	7.3	0.7	18.4	0.5	9.5
5775	Oakland, CA	3 775	2 392 557	21	633.8	3 776	2 108 078	21	558.3	55.4	12.7	0.6	16.7	0.5	8.6
7360	San Francisco, CA	2 630	1 731 183	29	658.2	2 630	1 603 678	28	609.8	58.6	5.3	0.4	22.7	0.8	7.7
7400	San Jose, CA	3 343	1 682 585	32	503.3	3 344	1 497 577	32	447.8	53.8	2.8	0.7	25.6	0.3	12.1
7485	Santa Cruz-Watsonville, CA	1 153	255 602	171	221.7	1 155	229 734	171	198.9	75.1	1.0	1.0	3.4	0.1	15.0
7500	Santa Rosa, CA	4 082	458 614	111	112.4	4 082	388 222	117	95.1	81.6	1.4	1.2	3.1	0.2	8.4
8720	Vallejo-Fairfield-Napa, CA	4 100	518 821	100	126.5	4 098	450 234	100	109.9	62.0	11.7	0.8	10.4	0.6	8.7
7460	San Luis Obispo-Atascadero-Paso Robles, CA	8 558	246 681	178	28.8	8 559	217 162	178	25.4	84.6	2.0	0.9	2.7	0.1	6.2
7480	Santa Barbara-Santa Maria-Lompoc, CA	7 089	399 347	126	56.3	7 093	369 608	121	52.1	72.7	2.3	1.2	4.1	0.2	15.2
7490	Santa Fe, NM	5 228	147 635	244	28.2	5 228	117 043	268	22.4	75.6	0.6	2.8	1.2	0.1	15.9
7510	Sarasota-Bradenton, FL	3 400	589 959	90	173.5	3 401	489 483	94	143.9	89.8	6.0	0.2	0.8	0.0	1.9
7520	Savannah, GA	3 520	293 000	160	83.2	3 527	257 899	160	73.1	61.2	34.9	0.3	1.5	0.1	0.8
7560	Scranton—Wilkes-Barre—Hazleton, PA	5 781	624 776	84	108.1	5 783	638 524	76	110.4	96.8	1.4	0.1	0.6	0.0	0.4
91	Seattle-Tacoma-Bremerton, WA	18 714	3 554 760	X	190.0	18 710	2 970 300	X	158.8	79.3	4.7	1.2	7.9	0.6	2.2
1150	Bremerton, WA	1 026	231 969	186	226.2	1 026	189 731	187	184.9	84.3	2.9	1.6	4.4	0.8	1.4
5910	Olympia, WA	1 883	207 355	197	110.1	1 883	161 238	209	85.6	85.7	2.4	1.5	4.4	0.5	1.7
7600	Seattle-Bellevue-Everett, WA	11 457	2 414 616	19	210.8	11 461	2 033 128	23	177.4	78.6	4.4	1.0	9.4	0.5	2.4
8200	Tacoma, WA	4 348	700 820	76	161.2	4 340	586 203	85	135.1	78.4	7.0	1.4	5.1	0.8	2.2
7610	Sharon, PA	1 740	120 293	279	69.1	1 740	121 003	261	69.5	93.1	5.3	0.1	0.4	0.0	0.2
7620	Sheboygan, WI	1 330	112 646	287	84.7	1 330	103 877	287	78.1	92.7	1.1	0.4	3.3	0.0	1.5
7640	Sherman-Denison, TX	2 418	110 595	291	45.7	2 418	95 019	300	39.3	87.2	5.9	1.3	0.6	0.0	2.9
7680	Shreveport-Bossier City, LA	6 000	392 302	127	65.4	6 000	376 330	119	62.7	59.7	37.4	0.4	0.8	0.0	0.5
7720	Sioux City, IA-NE	2 943	124 130	275	42.2	2 944	115 018	272	39.1	86.1	1.8	1.7	2.5	0.0	5.8
7760	Sioux Falls, SD	3 594	172 412	219	48.0	3 593	139 236	235	38.8	93.7	1.4	1.7	0.9	0.0	0.9
7800	South Bend, IN	1 185	265 559	167	224.2	1 185	247 052	166	208.5	82.4	11.5	0.4	1.3	0.1	2.5
7840	Spokane, WA	4 568	417 939	121	91.5	4 568	361 333	123	79.1	91.4	1.6	1.4	1.9	0.2	0.8
7880	Springfield, IL	3 062	201 437	201	65.8	3 063	189 550	188	61.9	88.1	9.1	0.2	1.0	0.0	0.4
8003	Springfield, MA	2 972	608 479	87	204.7	2 972	602 878	79	202.9	82.1	6.6	0.2	1.8	0.1	7.0
7920	Springfield, MO	4 743	325 721	150	68.7	4 744	264 346	155	55.7	94.4	1.8	0.6	0.9	0.1	0.6
6980	St. Cloud, MN	4 540	167 392	223	36.9	4 539	149 509	221	32.9	96.0	0.8	0.3	1.5	0.0	0.4
7000	St. Joseph, MO	2 188	102 490	299	46.8	2 188	97 715	295	44.7	93.6	3.7	0.4	0.4	0.0	0.6
7040	St. Louis, MO-IL	16 555	2 603 607	17	157.3	16 556	2 492 348	15	150.5	78.3	18.3	0.2	1.4	0.0	0.5
8050	State College, PA	2 868	135 758	257	47.3	2 869	124 812	255	43.5	91.4	2.6	0.1	4.0	0.1	0.7
8080	Steubenville-Weirton, OH-WV	1 506	132 008	261	87.7	1 506	142 523	229	94.6	94.5	3.9	0.2	0.3	0.0	0.2
8120	Stockton-Lodi, CA	3 624	563 598	95	155.5	3 625	480 628	96	132.6	58.1	6.7	1.1	11.4	0.3	16.3
8140	Sumter, SC	1 723	104 646	294	60.7	1 724	101 276	291	58.7	50.1	46.7	0.3	0.9	0.1	0.8
8160	Syracuse, NY	7 984	732 117	73	91.7	7 985	742 237	70	93.0	88.9	6.5	0.7	1.5	0.0	0.8
8240	Tallahassee, FL	3 064	284 539	162	92.9	3 064	233 609	170	76.2	62.0	33.6	0.3	1.6	0.0	1.1
8280	Tampa-St. Petersburg-Clearwater, FL	6 615	2 395 997	20	362.2	6 617	2 067 959	22	312.5	82.9	10.2	0.3	1.9	0.1	2.7
8320	Terre Haute, IN	2 636	149 192	241	56.6	2 636	147 585	223	56.0	92.9	4.4	0.3	0.9	0.0	0.3
8360	Texarkana, TX-Texarkana, AR	3 916	129 749	263	33.1	3 916	120 132	262	30.7	73.5	23.3	0.6	0.4	0.0	0.9
8400	Toledo, OH	3 534	618 203	85	174.9	3 535	614 128	77	173.7	82.1	12.8	0.3	1.1	0.0	1.8
8440	Topeka, KS	1 424	169 871	221	119.3	1 424	160 976	210	113.0	82.9	9.0	1.2	1.0	0.0	3.2

[1]MSA = Metropolitan Statistical Area. PMSA = Primary MSA. NECMA = New England County Metropolitan Area. See Appendix A for explanation of these concepts. See Appendix B for list of metropolitan areas identified by type, with component counties.
[2]Dry land or land partially or temporarily covered by water.

Table C. Metropolitan Areas

Area Name	Population and population characteristics, 2000 (cont'd)								Population and population characteristics, 1990				
	Race (percent) (cont'd)								Race (percent)				
	Race alone or in combination												
	Two or more races	White	Black	American Indian or Alaska Native	Asian	Native Hawaiian and other Pacific Islander	Some other race	Hispanic[1]	White	Black or African American	American Indian or Alaska Native	Asian and Pacific Islander	Hispanic[1]
	15	16	17	18	19	20	21	22	23	24	25	26	27
Reading, PA	1.5	89.4	4.3	0.4	1.2	0.1	6.2	9.7	93.5	3.0	0.1	0.8	5.1
Redding, CA	3.5	92.5	1.1	4.8	2.4	0.3	2.5	5.5	93.8	0.7	2.7	1.8	3.8
Reno, NV	3.3	83.2	2.6	2.7	5.2	0.7	9.1	16.6	88.4	2.2	1.9	3.9	9.0
Richland-Kennewick-Pasco, WA	3.1	82.8	1.7	1.5	2.6	0.2	14.3	21.3	86.5	1.6	0.7	2.1	13.3
Richmond-Petersburg, VA	1.3	65.9	30.8	0.8	2.4	0.1	1.5	2.3	68.8	29.2	0.3	1.4	1.1
Roanoke, VA	1.2	84.9	13.6	0.5	1.4	0.1	0.8	1.1	86.7	12.3	0.1	0.7	0.6
Rochester, MN	1.5	91.4	3.2	0.6	4.8	0.1	1.5	2.4	95.7	0.7	0.3	3.0	0.9
Rochester, NY	1.7	85.3	11.0	0.7	2.1	0.1	2.5	4.3	87.4	9.4	0.3	1.4	3.1
Rockford, IL	1.7	86.6	8.6	0.7	1.7	0.1	4.1	7.4	88.7	8.2	0.2	1.1	3.5
Rocky Mount, NC	0.8	54.0	43.5	0.6	0.6	0.1	2.2	3.1	57.4	41.9	0.2	0.2	0.6
Sacramento-Yolo, CA	5.2	74.1	8.2	2.4	10.8	0.9	9.2	15.5	77.1	7.7	1.2	8.5	12.1
Sacramento, CA	5.2	74.3	8.8	2.4	10.7	0.9	8.5	14.4	79.0	6.9	1.1	7.7	11.6
Yolo, CA	5.2	72.0	2.6	2.2	11.7	0.6	16.4	25.9	73.9	1.0	4.5	1.0	23.9
Saginaw-Bay City-Midland, MI	1.7	86.3	10.9	1.0	1.0	0.1	2.5	4.9	86.8	9.7	0.5	0.6	4.4
Salinas, CA	5.0	60.0	4.5	1.9	7.7	0.8	30.4	46.8	63.8	6.4	0.8	7.8	33.6
Salt Lake City-Ogden, UT	2.4	89.7	1.5	1.3	2.8	1.2	6.1	10.8	93.3	1.0	0.8	2.4	5.8
San Angelo, TX	2.4	81.1	4.6	1.2	1.2	0.1	14.2	30.7	80.8	4.2	0.4	1.0	25.9
San Antonio, TX	3.5	73.6	7.2	1.3	2.0	0.2	19.4	51.2	75.1	6.8	0.4	1.2	47.6
San Diego, CA	4.7	70.3	6.6	1.6	10.5	0.9	15.1	26.7	74.9	6.4	0.8	7.9	20.4
San Francisco-Oakland-San Jose, CA	4.9	62.7	8.1	1.5	20.3	1.0	11.7	19.7	69.3	8.6	0.7	14.8	15.5
Oakland, CA	5.4	59.7	13.8	1.6	18.8	1.0	11.0	18.5	65.9	14.6	0.7	12.9	13.1
San Francisco, CA	4.5	62.1	6.0	1.1	24.5	1.2	9.8	16.8	66.0	7.6	0.5	20.6	14.5
San Jose, CA	4.7	57.6	3.4	1.3	27.5	0.7	14.5	24.0	68.9	3.8	0.6	17.5	21.0
Santa Cruz-Watsonville, CA	4.4	78.9	1.5	2.1	4.7	0.4	17.2	26.8	83.9	1.1	0.8	3.7	20.4
Santa Rosa, CA	4.1	85.2	2.0	2.4	4.1	0.5	10.2	17.3	90.6	1.4	1.1	2.8	10.6
Vallejo-Fairfield-Napa, CA	5.8	66.5	13.0	2.0	12.6	1.3	10.9	19.1	72.2	10.4	0.9	10.4	13.6
San Luis Obispo-Atascadero-Paso Robles, CA	3.4	87.7	2.4	2.1	3.6	0.3	7.6	16.3	89.2	2.6	1.0	2.9	13.3
Santa Barbara-Santa Maria-Lompoc, CA	4.3	76.4	2.8	2.2	5.2	0.4	17.5	34.2	77.2	2.8	0.9	4.4	26.6
Santa Fe, NM	3.9	79.0	0.9	3.8	1.6	0.2	18.5	44.4	82.4	0.6	2.5	0.8	43.5
Sarasota-Bradenton, FL	1.2	90.8	6.3	0.6	1.1	0.1	2.4	6.6	94.6	4.3	0.2	0.5	2.1
Savannah, GA	1.3	62.2	35.4	0.6	1.8	0.2	1.2	2.2	62.9	35.5	0.2	1.0	1.2
Scranton—Wilkes-Barre—Hazleton, PA	0.6	97.4	1.7	0.3	0.7	0.0	0.6	1.2	98.2	1.0	0.1	0.5	0.8
Seattle-Tacoma-Bremerton, WA	4.2	82.7	5.7	2.3	9.5	1.0	3.3	5.2	86.4	4.8	1.3	6.4	3.0
Bremerton, WA	4.6	88.3	3.8	3.2	6.3	1.3	2.3	4.1	90.2	2.7	1.7	4.4	3.3
Olympia, WA	3.9	89.0	3.1	2.8	5.8	0.9	2.5	4.5	91.9	1.8	1.5	3.8	3.0
Seattle-Bellevue-Everett, WA	3.9	81.7	5.3	2.0	10.9	0.8	3.4	5.2	86.8	4.1	1.2	6.9	2.8
Tacoma, WA	5.1	82.7	8.6	2.8	7.0	1.4	3.3	5.5	85.1	7.2	1.4	5.0	3.5
Sharon, PA	0.9	94.0	5.7	0.4	0.5	0.0	0.3	0.7	94.6	4.9	0.1	0.3	0.4
Sheboygan, WI	1.1	93.5	1.3	0.7	3.6	0.1	1.8	3.4	96.6	0.4	0.3	2.0	1.6
Sherman-Denison, TX	2.1	89.1	6.3	2.4	0.8	0.1	3.5	6.8	90.0	6.9	1.1	0.4	2.9
Shreveport-Bossier City, LA	1.1	60.6	37.8	0.9	1.0	0.1	0.8	1.8	63.9	35.0	0.3	0.6	1.3
Sioux City, IA-NE	2.1	87.9	2.4	2.4	2.9	0.1	6.6	11.3	93.5	1.7	1.7	1.4	3.2
Sioux Falls, SD	1.4	94.9	1.8	2.1	1.2	0.1	1.4	1.9	97.3	0.6	1.4	0.6	0.5
South Bend, IN	2.0	84.1	12.3	0.9	1.7	0.1	3.1	4.7	87.8	9.8	0.3	1.0	2.1
Spokane, WA	2.8	93.9	2.2	2.4	2.6	0.3	1.4	2.8	94.6	1.4	1.5	1.8	1.9
Springfield, IL	1.2	89.1	9.7	0.6	1.3	0.1	0.5	1.0	91.3	7.6	0.2	0.7	0.7
Springfield, MA	2.2	83.8	7.4	0.7	2.2	0.2	8.1	12.2	86.4	6.6	0.2	1.0	9.0
Springfield, MO	1.6	95.9	2.2	1.5	1.2	0.1	0.9	1.7	96.9	1.6	0.6	0.7	0.8
St. Cloud, MN	0.8	96.8	1.1	0.6	1.7	0.1	0.6	1.3	98.5	0.4	0.3	0.6	0.5
St. Joseph, MO	1.2	94.8	4.2	0.9	0.6	0.1	0.8	2.2	95.5	3.2	0.3	0.3	2.1
St. Louis, MO-IL	1.2	79.3	18.8	0.6	1.7	0.1	0.8	1.5	81.2	17.3	0.2	1.0	1.1
State College, PA	1.1	92.3	2.9	0.4	4.4	0.2	1.0	1.7	94.2	2.3	0.1	3.1	1.1
Steubenville-Weirton, OH-WV	0.9	95.3	4.3	0.5	0.5	0.0	0.3	0.6	95.5	3.9	0.2	0.3	0.5
Stockton-Lodi, CA	6.0	62.7	7.5	2.3	13.6	0.8	19.5	30.5	73.5	5.6	1.1	12.4	23.4
Sumter, SC	1.2	51.0	47.2	0.6	1.2	0.1	1.1	1.8	55.3	43.2	0.2	0.9	1.2
Syracuse, NY	1.6	90.3	7.2	1.2	1.7	0.1	1.1	2.1	91.8	5.9	0.6	1.2	1.4
Tallahassee, FL	1.4	63.1	34.1	0.7	2.0	0.1	1.6	3.9	67.8	30.1	0.2	1.2	2.4
Tampa-St. Petersburg-Clearwater, FL	2.0	84.5	10.8	0.8	2.3	0.1	3.6	10.4	88.4	9.0	0.3	1.1	6.7
Terre Haute, IN	1.2	94.0	4.8	0.7	1.1	0.1	0.5	1.0	94.0	4.6	0.3	0.9	0.8
Texarkana, TX-Texarkana, AR	1.2	74.6	23.7	1.2	0.6	0.1	1.2	3.6	76.9	22.0	0.5	0.3	1.4
Toledo, OH	1.9	83.8	13.5	0.7	1.4	0.1	2.5	4.4	85.7	11.4	0.2	1.0	3.3
Topeka, KS	2.7	85.2	10.2	2.2	1.3	0.1	4.0	7.3	87.7	8.3	1.1	0.7	4.8

[1] Hispanic persons may be of any race.

Table C. Metropolitan Areas

Area Name	Population and population characteristics, 2000										
	Age (percent)										
	Under 5 years	5 to 17 years	18 to 24 years	25 to 34 years	35 to 44 years	45 to 54 years	55 to 64 years	65 to 74 years	75 years and over	Median age (years)	Percent Female
	28	29	30	31	32	33	34	35	36	37	38
Reading, PA	6.2	18.4	8.8	12.7	16.2	13.7	8.9	7.7	7.3	37.4	51.0
Redding, CA	5.9	20.2	8.2	10.3	15.0	14.7	10.5	7.9	7.3	38.9	51.3
Reno, NV	7.0	17.9	9.8	14.5	16.5	14.7	9.1	6.0	4.6	35.6	49.3
Richland-Kennewick-Pasco, WA	8.2	22.8	9.2	13.0	15.4	13.6	8.0	5.3	4.5	32.7	49.7
Richmond-Petersburg, VA	6.5	18.7	8.9	14.5	17.1	14.6	8.5	6.0	5.2	35.8	51.9
Roanoke, VA	5.8	16.8	7.7	12.9	15.9	15.3	9.8	8.1	7.7	39.4	52.6
Rochester, MN	7.2	19.8	8.5	14.5	17.7	13.3	8.3	5.4	5.4	35.0	50.9
Rochester, NY	6.3	19.4	9.3	12.9	16.4	14.1	8.7	6.4	6.5	36.3	51.4
Rockford, IL	7.0	19.9	8.1	13.5	16.2	13.7	9.0	6.5	6.1	35.9	50.9
Rocky Mount, NC	6.7	19.4	8.5	13.3	16.1	14.5	9.0	6.9	5.6	36.4	52.5
Sacramento-Yolo, CA	6.9	20.1	9.7	13.8	16.3	13.7	8.1	6.0	5.4	34.6	51.0
Sacramento, CA	7.0	20.3	8.8	13.8	16.6	13.8	8.2	6.1	5.4	35.1	50.9
Yolo, CA	6.5	18.7	18.3	14.0	14.2	12.0	6.9	4.8	4.6	29.5	51.1
Saginaw-Bay City-Midland, MI	6.5	19.6	8.8	12.4	15.7	14.2	9.3	6.9	6.6	36.9	51.6
Salinas, CA	7.8	20.6	10.9	15.9	15.4	12.3	7.1	5.3	4.7	31.7	48.2
Salt Lake City-Ogden, UT	9.1	22.3	12.7	15.4	14.4	11.4	6.5	4.4	3.9	28.6	49.7
San Angelo, TX	6.9	19.2	12.8	12.6	14.5	12.3	8.3	6.9	6.5	33.8	51.6
San Antonio, TX	7.8	20.6	10.3	14.7	15.6	12.6	7.8	5.8	4.9	32.7	51.3
San Diego, CA	7.1	18.7	11.3	15.8	16.3	12.5	7.3	5.7	5.5	33.2	49.7
San Francisco-Oakland-San Jose, CA	6.4	17.2	8.9	16.4	17.3	14.3	8.4	5.7	5.4	35.6	50.2
Oakland, CA	6.9	18.5	8.8	15.4	17.2	14.3	8.2	5.5	5.2	35.3	51.0
San Francisco, CA	5.2	13.6	8.1	18.7	17.4	14.8	9.0	6.7	6.5	37.3	49.9
San Jose, CA	7.1	17.7	9.3	17.8	17.6	13.0	8.0	5.2	4.4	34.0	49.3
Santa Cruz-Watsonville, CA	6.1	17.7	11.9	14.4	16.5	15.9	7.6	4.8	5.1	35.0	50.1
Santa Rosa, CA	6.0	18.4	8.8	12.7	16.5	16.1	8.8	6.0	6.7	37.5	50.8
Vallejo-Fairfield-Napa, CA	7.0	20.3	9.0	13.8	16.7	14.2	8.1	5.6	5.3	34.9	49.7
San Luis Obispo-Atascadero-Paso Robles, CA	5.0	16.6	13.6	11.4	15.6	14.7	8.6	7.3	7.1	37.3	48.6
Santa Barbara-Santa Maria-Lompoc, CA	6.5	18.4	13.3	13.9	15.1	12.3	7.8	6.3	6.4	33.4	50.0
Santa Fe, NM	6.1	18.2	7.7	12.8	16.7	17.3	10.3	6.2	4.7	38.3	50.9
Sarasota-Bradenton, FL	4.7	13.5	5.7	9.9	13.1	12.6	12.0	14.0	14.5	47.3	52.2
Savannah, GA	6.9	19.2	10.6	14.4	15.7	13.0	8.5	6.3	5.5	34.2	51.5
Scranton—Wilkes-Barre—Hazleton, PA	5.1	16.4	9.0	12.0	14.9	13.9	9.8	9.1	9.8	40.2	52.2
Seattle-Tacoma-Bremerton, WA	6.5	18.2	9.2	15.5	17.5	14.6	8.1	5.2	5.1	35.3	50.2
Bremerton, WA	6.7	20.1	9.2	12.9	16.8	15.2	8.6	5.4	5.2	35.8	49.3
Olympia, WA	6.2	19.1	9.3	13.0	16.3	15.7	8.9	5.8	5.6	36.5	51.0
Seattle-Bellevue-Everett, WA	6.4	17.5	9.0	16.2	17.8	14.7	8.1	5.1	5.1	35.5	50.2
Tacoma, WA	7.1	20.1	9.8	14.4	16.9	13.5	8.0	5.4	4.8	34.1	50.3
Sharon, PA	5.7	17.7	8.9	11.2	14.8	13.7	9.7	9.1	9.0	39.6	51.3
Sheboygan, WI	6.4	19.1	8.4	13.0	16.8	13.7	8.5	6.7	7.2	36.8	49.8
Sherman-Denison, TX	6.5	18.8	9.3	12.1	15.4	13.2	9.5	7.7	7.4	37.2	51.6
Shreveport-Bossier City, LA	7.0	19.9	9.9	13.0	15.0	13.1	8.9	7.0	6.2	35.1	52.2
Sioux City, IA-NE	7.8	20.0	10.2	13.7	14.7	12.8	7.8	6.4	6.4	33.7	50.8
Sioux Falls, SD	7.4	19.3	10.4	15.2	16.8	12.9	7.2	5.5	5.4	33.6	50.4
South Bend, IN	7.0	18.7	11.8	13.2	14.8	13.1	7.8	6.7	6.9	34.4	51.7
Spokane, WA	6.6	19.1	10.6	13.1	15.8	14.2	8.2	6.0	6.4	35.4	50.9
Springfield, IL	6.4	18.7	8.0	13.1	16.5	14.8	9.0	6.8	6.7	37.4	52.2
Springfield, MA	6.0	18.4	11.7	12.4	15.5	13.7	8.2	6.7	7.2	35.9	52.4
Springfield, MO	6.5	17.3	12.3	13.9	15.3	13.1	8.6	6.6	6.3	34.9	51.3
St. Cloud, MN	6.6	19.4	15.3	13.4	15.3	12.0	7.0	5.7	5.3	31.6	49.8
St. Joseph, MO	6.3	18.4	10.5	12.8	15.6	12.9	8.7	7.2	7.7	36.4	50.9
St. Louis, MO-IL	6.7	19.6	8.8	13.3	16.6	13.5	8.6	6.7	6.1	36.0	52.0
State College, PA	4.6	13.4	26.8	13.4	13.1	11.1	7.2	5.6	4.8	28.7	48.9
Steubenville-Weirton, OH-WV	5.2	15.9	8.4	11.3	14.8	15.4	10.7	9.7	8.8	41.5	52.2
Stockton-Lodi, CA	8.0	23.0	10.0	13.4	15.4	12.2	7.4	5.4	5.2	31.9	50.0
Sumter, SC	7.5	20.6	10.5	13.7	15.7	12.4	8.3	6.1	5.1	33.4	51.6
Syracuse, NY	6.3	19.4	9.8	12.6	16.2	13.7	8.6	6.8	6.5	36.1	51.5
Tallahassee, FL	5.9	16.2	19.5	14.5	14.4	13.2	7.3	4.7	4.2	30.3	52.4
Tampa-St. Petersburg-Clearwater, FL	5.8	16.2	7.5	12.8	15.5	13.3	9.8	9.4	9.8	40.0	51.8
Terre Haute, IN	6.2	17.3	12.6	12.8	14.6	13.2	8.8	7.1	7.4	35.8	51.0
Texarkana, TX-Texarkana, AR	6.7	18.6	9.5	13.9	15.4	13.3	9.0	7.0	6.6	35.8	50.1
Toledo, OH	6.7	19.2	11.1	13.4	15.3	13.5	8.2	6.5	6.2	34.7	51.8
Topeka, KS	6.8	18.5	8.8	12.8	15.6	14.6	9.1	7.1	6.6	37.1	51.6

Table C. Metropolitan Areas

	Population and population characteristics, 1990										Population—change, 1980–2000				
	Age (percent)										Total persons			Percent change	
Area Name	Under 5 years	5 to 17 years	18 to 24 years	25 to 34 years	35 to 44 years	45 to 54 years	55 to 64 years	65 to 74 years	75 years and over	Percent Female	2000	1990	1980	1990–2000	1980–1990
	39	40	41	42	43	44	45	46	47	48	49	50	51	52	53
Reading, PA	6.7	16.6	10.0	16.1	14.8	10.3	9.9	8.8	6.8	51.7	373 638	336 523	312 509	11.0	7.7
Redding, CA	7.7	19.8	8.1	14.7	15.6	11.0	9.1	8.6	5.5	51.0	163 256	147 036	115 613	11.0	27.2
Reno, NV	7.4	15.8	10.5	19.0	17.3	11.2	8.5	6.7	3.6	49.3	339 486	254 667	193 623	33.3	31.5
Richland-Kennewick-Pasco, WA	8.5	22.6	8.9	16.3	15.6	10.1	7.9	6.2	3.9	50.1	191 822	150 033	144 469	27.9	3.9
Richmond-Petersburg, VA	7.2	17.1	10.6	18.5	16.7	10.5	8.2	6.7	4.6	52.4	996 512	865 640	761 311	15.1	13.7
Roanoke, VA	6.2	15.9	9.7	16.1	16.1	11.0	9.9	8.7	6.5	52.8	235 932	224 592	220 393	5.0	1.9
Rochester, MN	8.6	19.1	9.2	20.1	15.4	10.5	7.1	5.3	4.7	51.5	124 277	106 470	92 006	16.7	15.7
Rochester, NY	7.6	17.4	11.3	17.4	15.4	10.3	8.2	7.0	5.4	51.7	1 098 201	1 062 470	1 030 630	3.4	3.1
Rockford, IL	7.6	18.8	9.5	16.9	15.3	10.7	8.7	7.3	5.2	51.4	371 236	329 676	325 852	12.6	1.2
Rocky Mount, NC	7.1	19.6	9.7	16.4	15.7	10.2	8.8	7.5	4.8	53.3	143 026	133 369	123 141	7.2	8.3
Sacramento-Yolo, CA	7.9	18.2	10.8	18.9	16.0	9.7	7.8	6.5	4.1	50.9	1 796 857	1 506 792	1 099 814	19.3	34.7
Sacramento, CA	7.8	18.3	10.5	18.5	16.3	9.9	7.9	6.6	4.1	50.8	1 628 197	1 365 580	986 440	19.2	35.8
Yolo, CA	8.7	21.6	9.8	15.3	14.1	9.6	7.9	7.1	5.9	50.3	168 660	141 212	113 374	19.4	24.6
Saginaw-Bay City-Midland, MI	7.5	19.9	10.0	15.9	15.1	10.9	8.6	7.0	5.0	51.8	403 070	399 320	421 518	0.9	-5.3
Salinas, CA	8.8	18.7	13.1	19.5	14.7	8.4	7.0	5.8	4.0	48.1	401 762	355 660	290 444	13.0	22.5
Salt Lake City-Ogden, UT	9.7	25.8	10.4	16.4	14.0	8.4	6.3	5.0	3.4	50.3	1 333 914	1 072 227	910 222	24.4	17.8
San Angelo, TX	7.8	19.3	12.9	16.4	13.9	9.0	8.1	7.0	5.7	51.5	104 010	98 458	84 784	5.6	16.1
San Antonio, TX	8.3	20.7	11.4	17.7	14.6	9.4	7.7	6.2	4.1	51.4	1 592 383	1 324 749	1 088 881	20.2	21.7
San Diego, CA	7.8	16.6	13.5	20.0	15.2	8.8	7.1	6.5	4.4	49.0	2 813 833	2 498 016	1 861 846	12.6	34.2
San Francisco-Oakland-San Jose, CA	7.1	16.0	10.4	19.5	17.3	10.8	7.9	6.5	4.6	50.2	7 039 362	6 277 523	5 367 900	12.1	16.9
Oakland, CA	7.5	16.7	10.4	18.8	17.3	10.8	7.7	6.3	4.4	50.8	2 392 557	2 108 078	1 761 710	13.5	18.1
San Francisco, CA	5.9	13.1	9.6	20.0	17.9	11.3	8.9	7.6	5.7	50.3	1 731 183	1 603 678	1 488 895	8.0	7.7
San Jose, CA	7.5	16.5	11.4	21.2	16.3	10.9	7.5	5.3	3.4	49.3	1 682 585	1 497 577	1 295 071	12.4	15.6
Santa Cruz-Watsonville, CA	7.2	16.6	12.2	17.7	18.8	9.7	6.6	6.1	5.2	50.3	255 602	229 734	188 141	11.3	22.1
Santa Rosa, CA	7.3	17.4	8.9	16.8	18.4	10.4	7.4	7.5	5.9	51.0	458 614	388 222	299 681	18.1	29.5
Vallejo-Fairfield-Napa, CA	8.2	19.2	10.0	18.4	16.9	9.9	7.2	6.1	4.1	49.2	518 821	450 234	334 402	15.2	34.6
San Luis Obispo-Atascadero-Paso Robles, CA	6.4	15.5	14.5	16.9	15.8	8.8	7.9	8.4	5.7	48.4	246 681	217 162	155 435	13.6	39.7
Santa Barbara-Santa Maria-Lompoc, CA	7.3	15.9	14.6	18.2	14.5	9.3	7.8	6.9	5.4	49.8	399 347	369 608	298 694	8.0	23.7
Santa Fe, NM	7.1	18.9	8.1	16.1	19.0	12.3	8.5	6.2	3.8	50.7	147 635	117 043	93 118	26.1	25.7
Sarasota-Bradenton, FL	4.6	11.2	6.2	12.0	12.0	9.5	12.4	17.9	14.2	53.2	589 959	489 483	350 696	20.5	39.6
Savannah, GA	7.9	19.0	11.0	17.4	14.4	9.7	8.3	7.5	4.8	51.9	293 000	257 899	230 728	13.6	11.8
Scranton—Wilkes-Barre—Hazleton, PA	6.2	16.1	10.4	14.6	14.1	10.1	10.3	10.5	7.8	52.5	624 776	638 524	659 387	-2.2	-3.2
Seattle-Tacoma-Bremerton, WA	7.5	17.1	10.1	19.4	17.3	10.5	7.5	6.3	4.4	50.5	3 554 760	2 970 300	2 408 749	19.7	23.3
Bremerton, WA	8.2	19.7	10.6	17.0	16.6	10.1	7.1	6.3	4.4	48.9	231 969	189 731	147 152	22.3	28.9
Olympia, WA	7.1	19.8	9.3	16.0	17.6	10.8	7.7	6.8	4.9	51.3	207 355	161 238	124 264	28.6	29.8
Seattle-Bellevue-Everett, WA	7.3	16.5	9.8	19.8	17.8	10.7	7.5	6.3	4.4	50.6	2 414 616	2 033 128	1 651 666	18.8	23.1
Tacoma, WA	8.2	19.0	11.4	18.2	15.4	9.7	7.6	6.2	4.3	50.0	700 820	586 203	485 667	19.6	20.7
Sharon, PA	6.2	17.2	10.3	14.2	13.8	10.3	10.7	10.0	7.2	51.5	120 293	121 003	128 299	-0.6	-5.7
Sheboygan, WI	7.1	19.7	8.7	16.6	14.9	9.9	8.6	7.9	6.7	50.5	112 646	103 877	100 935	8.4	2.9
Sherman-Denison, TX	6.8	18.6	9.5	15.1	13.9	10.3	9.5	8.8	7.5	52.3	110 595	95 019	89 796	16.4	5.8
Shreveport-Bossier City, LA	8.0	20.7	9.8	16.3	14.4	9.9	8.7	7.0	5.2	52.8	392 302	376 330	376 789	4.2	-0.1
Sioux City, IA-NE	7.7	20.7	9.6	15.8	14.3	9.0	8.7	7.8	6.5	51.7	124 130	115 018	117 457	7.9	-2.1
Sioux Falls, SD	7.9	19.1	10.6	19.1	15.0	8.9	7.7	6.4	5.2	51.9	172 412	139 236	123 377	23.8	12.9
South Bend, IN	7.3	18.0	12.4	15.9	14.5	9.1	8.8	8.0	6.1	51.8	265 559	247 052	241 617	7.5	2.2
Spokane, WA	7.4	19.0	10.6	16.4	15.6	9.8	7.9	7.4	5.8	51.4	417 939	361 333	341 835	15.7	5.7
Springfield, IL	7.2	18.5	8.6	17.0	16.0	10.4	8.7	7.5	5.8	52.9	201 437	189 550	187 770	6.3	0.9
Springfield, MA	7.1	17.1	11.6	16.7	14.6	9.5	8.7	8.4	6.2	52.7	608 479	602 878	581 831	0.9	3.6
Springfield, MO	6.5	17.1	14.0	16.4	14.7	10.0	8.3	7.2	5.9	52.0	325 721	264 346	228 118	23.2	15.9
St. Cloud, MN	8.0	21.0	15.3	17.1	13.7	8.4	6.7	5.4	4.5	49.8	167 392	149 509	133 348	12.0	12.1
St. Joseph, MO	7.2	18.6	9.8	15.8	13.5	9.5	9.2	8.7	7.7	52.6	102 490	97 715	101 868	4.9	-4.1
St. Louis, MO-IL	7.6	18.7	9.5	17.5	14.9	10.2	8.8	7.2	5.6	52.2	2 603 607	2 492 348	2 414 061	4.5	3.2
State College, PA	5.6	12.7	28.2	16.8	12.5	8.4	6.9	5.3	3.7	48.2	135 758	124 812	112 760	8.8	10.7
Steubenville-Weirton, OH-WV	5.4	17.8	9.1	13.5	15.0	11.0	11.3	10.1	6.6	52.4	132 008	142 523	163 734	-7.4	-13.0
Stockton-Lodi, CA	8.8	20.8	10.4	17.3	14.9	9.3	7.4	6.5	4.6	49.4	563 598	480 628	347 342	17.3	38.4
Sumter, SC	8.4	20.3	11.9	19.6	14.5	8.8	7.1	5.8	3.6	50.0	104 646	101 276	88 243	3.3	14.8
Syracuse, NY	7.5	17.7	12.7	17.0	14.6	9.7	8.5	7.2	5.2	51.8	732 117	742 237	722 865	-1.4	2.7
Tallahassee, FL	6.7	17.0	18.7	17.6	15.4	9.1	6.6	5.4	3.6	52.0	284 539	233 609	190 329	21.8	22.7
Tampa-St. Petersburg-Clearwater, FL	6.0	14.4	8.6	15.8	13.8	9.8	10.0	12.2	9.4	52.3	2 395 997	2 067 959	1 613 600	15.9	28.2
Terre Haute, IN	6.3	17.2	13.6	15.4	13.8	9.5	8.7	8.6	6.8	51.2	149 192	147 585	155 476	1.1	-5.1
Texarkana, TX-Texarkana, AR	7.2	20.4	9.2	15.4	14.5	10.3	8.8	8.0	6.2	51.8	129 749	120 132	113 067	8.0	6.2
Toledo, OH	7.5	18.7	12.3	16.6	14.6	9.5	8.4	7.2	5.2	52.2	618 203	614 128	616 864	0.7	-0.4
Topeka, KS	7.2	18.7	9.2	17.0	15.5	10.2	9.1	7.2	5.9	51.8	169 871	160 976	154 916	5.5	3.9

Table C. Metropolitan Areas

Area Name	Total population	Total in house-holds	House-holder	Spouse	Child Total	Child Own child under 18 years	Other relatives Total	Other relatives Under 18 years	Nonrelatives Total	Nonrelatives Unmarried partner	Total in group quarters	Correctional institutions	Nursing homes	Other institutions	College dormitories	Military quarters	Other
	54	55	56	57	58	59	60	61	62	63	64	65	66	67	68	69	70
Reading, PA	373 638	96.7	37.9	21.0	28.9	22.4	4.0	1.5	4.9	2.5	3.3	0.3	0.9	0.2	1.2	0.0	0.7
Redding, CA	163 256	97.9	38.9	20.6	28.5	23.1	4.4	1.9	5.6	2.3	2.1	0.4	0.4	0.2	0.4	0.0	0.7
Reno, NV	339 486	98.4	38.9	18.0	27.0	22.3	5.7	1.9	7.9	2.9	1.6	0.3	0.3	0.1	0.4	0.0	0.5
Richland-Kennewick-Pasco, WA	191 822	99.1	35.3	20.6	34.0	28.4	4.7	1.9	4.6	1.8	0.9	0.5	0.2	0.1	0.0	0.0	0.2
Richmond-Petersburg, VA	996 512	96.7	38.9	19.1	28.6	22.4	5.1	2.2	5.0	1.9	3.3	1.0	0.6	0.3	0.9	0.3	0.4
Roanoke, VA	235 932	97.0	41.7	20.9	26.2	20.3	4.2	1.7	4.0	1.8	3.0	0.5	1.1	0.1	0.7	0.0	0.5
Rochester, MN	124 277	97.5	38.5	21.8	30.3	25.8	2.2	0.7	4.8	1.8	2.5	0.8	0.5	0.1	0.1	0.0	1.0
Rochester, NY	1 098 201	96.1	38.3	19.1	29.8	23.6	3.6	1.5	5.3	2.4	3.9	0.7	0.8	0.1	1.7	0.0	0.6
Rockford, IL	371 236	98.4	38.2	20.9	30.6	24.4	4.1	1.8	4.5	2.1	1.6	0.2	0.8	0.1	0.1	0.0	0.3
Rocky Mount, NC	143 026	97.7	37.8	19.0	29.7	22.0	7.5	3.6	3.7	1.7	2.3	1.0	0.6	0.0	0.3	0.0	0.4
Sacramento-Yolo, CA	1 796 857	97.9	37.0	18.3	30.3	24.2	5.7	2.1	6.5	2.4	2.1	0.4	0.4	0.1	0.3	0.0	0.7
Sacramento, CA	1 628 197	98.2	37.2	18.5	30.6	24.3	5.8	2.2	6.1	2.4	1.8	0.4	0.4	0.1	0.1	0.0	0.7
Yolo, CA	168 660	95.5	35.2	16.8	28.0	22.6	5.3	1.9	10.3	2.0	4.5	0.2	0.5	0.0	2.9	0.0	0.8
Saginaw-Bay City-Midland, MI	403 070	97.8	38.7	20.6	30.9	23.8	3.4	1.6	4.1	2.0	2.2	0.5	0.5	0.1	0.4	0.0	0.7
Salinas, CA	401 762	94.8	30.2	16.9	31.1	24.0	10.0	3.5	6.6	1.7	5.2	3.0	0.2	0.1	0.4	0.6	0.9
Salt Lake City-Ogden, UT	1 333 914	98.4	32.4	19.5	36.6	28.7	5.2	2.0	4.7	1.3	1.6	0.5	0.3	0.1	0.2	0.0	0.5
San Angelo, TX	104 010	95.9	38.0	19.8	28.8	23.0	5.2	2.5	4.1	1.7	4.1	0.3	0.8	0.0	1.2	1.4	0.5
San Antonio, TX	1 592 383	97.6	35.2	18.3	32.5	24.5	7.2	3.3	4.4	1.8	2.4	0.4	0.5	0.1	0.3	0.6	0.4
San Diego, CA	2 813 833	96.6	35.3	17.9	29.3	22.7	6.8	2.3	7.2	2.1	3.4	0.4	0.3	0.1	0.5	1.5	0.7
San Francisco-Oakland-San Jose, CA	7 039 362	97.8	36.3	17.9	27.7	20.7	7.9	2.3	8.0	2.2	2.2	0.5	0.4	0.1	0.4	0.0	0.7
Oakland, CA	2 392 557	98.4	36.3	18.1	29.5	22.3	7.7	2.4	6.9	2.2	1.6	0.3	0.3	0.1	0.3	0.0	0.5
San Francisco, CA	1 731 183	97.6	39.5	16.6	23.2	16.3	8.1	2.0	10.2	2.6	2.4	0.6	0.4	0.1	0.3	0.0	1.0
San Jose, CA	1 682 585	98.2	33.6	18.5	28.9	21.5	9.4	2.6	7.9	1.8	1.8	0.3	0.3	0.1	0.6	0.0	0.5
Santa Cruz-Watsonville, CA	255 602	96.5	35.7	17.1	27.0	21.0	6.2	2.0	10.6	2.8	3.5	0.3	0.5	0.1	1.8	0.0	0.9
Santa Rosa, CA	458 614	97.6	37.6	18.9	27.7	21.8	5.4	1.7	7.9	2.7	2.4	0.3	0.4	0.1	0.3	0.1	1.3
Vallejo-Fairfield-Napa, CA	518 821	95.9	33.9	18.6	31.0	23.9	6.9	2.6	5.5	2.0	4.1	1.9	0.4	0.5	0.2	0.4	0.6
San Luis Obispo-Atascadero-Paso Robles, CA	246 681	93.7	37.6	19.0	24.6	19.5	4.1	1.4	8.4	2.0	6.3	3.0	0.4	0.8	1.5	0.0	0.6
Santa Barbara-Santa Maria-Lompoc, CA	399 347	95.8	34.2	17.6	27.7	21.8	6.9	2.4	9.4	1.8	4.2	1.0	0.4	0.1	1.7	0.1	0.8
Santa Fe, NM	147 635	98.3	40.6	19.4	27.6	22.0	4.6	1.8	6.1	2.8	1.7	0.5	0.3	0.0	0.5	0.0	0.3
Sarasota-Bradenton, FL	589 959	97.9	44.5	23.4	20.6	16.1	4.1	1.4	5.3	2.3	2.1	0.3	1.0	0.1	0.1	0.0	0.5
Savannah, GA	293 000	97.1	37.9	18.5	29.5	22.6	6.3	3.0	4.9	1.9	2.9	0.9	0.4	0.1	0.5	0.6	0.4
Scranton—Wilkes-Barre—Hazleton, PA	624 776	96.0	40.4	20.1	27.8	19.8	3.8	1.1	3.8	1.8	4.0	0.7	1.2	0.2	1.3	0.0	0.7
Seattle-Tacoma-Bremerton, WA	3 554 760	97.7	39.2	19.8	28.0	22.8	4.0	1.3	6.8	2.5	2.3	0.4	0.4	0.1	0.4	0.4	0.6
Bremerton, WA	231 969	96.9	37.3	21.5	29.7	24.8	3.1	1.3	5.3	2.1	3.1	1.0	0.6	0.0	0.0	1.2	0.2
Olympia, WA	207 355	98.4	39.4	20.9	28.3	23.1	3.4	1.3	6.3	2.5	1.6	0.4	0.4	0.2	0.4	0.0	0.4
Seattle-Bellevue-Everett, WA	2 414 616	98.0	39.9	19.6	27.2	22.0	4.1	1.2	7.2	2.5	2.0	0.3	0.3	0.1	0.5	0.1	0.7
Tacoma, WA	700 820	96.9	37.2	19.6	30.3	24.8	4.0	1.7	5.8	2.3	3.1	0.7	0.4	0.1	0.4	0.9	0.6
Sharon, PA	120 293	94.7	38.8	21.3	28.0	21.1	3.4	1.4	3.2	1.7	5.3	0.9	1.1	0.6	2.2	0.0	0.5
Sheboygan, WI	112 646	96.8	38.7	22.4	29.9	24.3	2.2	0.8	3.7	1.9	3.2	1.3	1.1	0.0	0.4	0.0	0.4
Sherman-Denison, TX	110 595	97.3	38.7	21.4	28.3	22.4	4.8	2.2	4.0	1.6	2.7	0.3	1.2	0.2	0.8	0.0	0.1
Shreveport-Bossier City, LA	392 302	97.6	38.5	17.7	30.5	22.8	6.7	3.5	4.1	1.8	2.4	0.6	0.8	0.2	0.2	0.2	0.4
Sioux City, IA-NE	124 130	97.5	37.3	19.5	31.1	25.3	4.3	1.7	5.5	2.3	2.5	0.2	0.8	0.1	0.8	0.0	0.5
Sioux Falls, SD	172 412	96.8	38.7	20.8	29.6	25.1	2.3	0.8	5.3	2.1	3.2	0.9	0.9	0.2	0.8	0.0	0.6
South Bend, IN	265 559	94.9	37.9	19.0	29.2	23.2	4.0	1.8	4.8	2.1	5.1	0.2	0.8	0.1	3.3	0.0	0.6
Spokane, WA	417 939	96.5	39.1	19.5	28.7	23.7	3.1	1.2	6.0	2.3	3.5	0.8	0.6	0.2	0.9	0.2	0.8
Springfield, IL	201 437	98.3	41.5	20.3	28.8	23.0	3.1	1.4	4.5	2.3	1.7	0.2	0.7	0.1	0.2	0.0	0.6
Springfield, MA	608 479	94.6	38.0	17.6	29.2	22.2	4.2	1.6	5.7	2.5	5.4	0.4	0.9	0.2	3.6	0.0	0.0
Springfield, MO	325 721	95.9	39.7	21.2	27.0	22.0	2.9	1.2	5.1	2.0	4.1	0.7	0.8	0.1	2.1	0.0	0.5
St. Cloud, MN	167 392	95.2	36.2	20.1	30.2	24.8	1.9	0.6	6.7	2.0	4.8	0.1	0.7	0.1	3.1	0.0	0.7
St. Joseph, MO	102 490	95.2	38.9	20.0	28.2	22.3	3.5	1.6	4.7	2.3	4.8	2.1	1.0	0.3	0.9	0.0	0.5
St. Louis, MO-IL	2 603 607	98.0	38.9	19.5	31.0	23.7	4.4	2.0	4.2	2.0	2.0	0.3	0.8	0.1	0.5	0.0	0.3
State College, PA	135 758	89.1	36.3	17.8	21.3	17.0	1.9	0.6	11.8	1.6	10.9	1.5	0.6	0.1	8.4	0.0	0.3
Steubenville-Weirton, OH-WV	132 008	97.5	41.3	22.1	26.7	19.1	3.9	1.4	3.5	1.9	2.5	0.2	0.9	0.0	1.1	0.0	0.3
Stockton-Lodi, CA	563 598	96.7	32.2	17.5	34.1	26.8	7.6	3.1	5.2	2.0	3.3	1.3	0.5	0.2	0.3	0.0	1.0
Sumter, SC	104 646	96.7	36.1	18.1	31.8	23.9	7.2	3.7	3.5	1.5	3.3	1.0	0.4	0.0	0.6	0.8	0.5
Syracuse, NY	732 117	96.3	38.6	19.0	29.9	23.8	3.3	1.3	5.6	2.6	3.7	0.6	0.6	0.1	1.9	0.0	0.5
Tallahassee, FL	284 539	94.4	39.5	16.0	25.0	19.5	5.0	2.1	8.9	2.1	5.6	1.3	0.5	0.3	3.1	0.0	0.4
Tampa-St. Petersburg-Clearwater, FL	2 395 997	98.0	42.1	20.3	24.9	19.4	4.9	1.9	5.8	2.6	2.0	0.3	0.7	0.1	0.3	0.0	0.6
Terre Haute, IN	149 192	94.1	38.9	19.9	27.2	21.4	3.4	1.5	4.8	2.2	5.9	1.3	1.0	0.3	2.9	0.0	0.3
Texarkana, TX-Texarkana, AR	129 749	93.9	37.5	19.4	28.7	22.2	5.2	2.7	3.1	1.4	6.1	4.7	0.9	0.1	0.0	0.0	0.4
Toledo, OH	618 203	97.2	39.4	18.8	30.0	23.6	3.8	1.7	5.3	2.3	2.8	0.1	0.8	0.0	1.4	0.0	0.4
Topeka, KS	169 871	97.1	40.6	20.1	28.2	22.9	3.6	1.7	4.6	2.0	2.9	0.8	1.1	0.6	0.2	0.0	0.3

Table C. Metropolitan Areas

Area Name	Households by type, 2000												Households, 1990		
		Family households						Nonfamily households							
				Married couple		Female householder[1]			Householder living alone						
	Total households	Total	With own children under 18 years	Total	With own children under 18 years	Total	With own children under 18 years	Total	Total	65 years and over	Average household size	Average family size	Total households	Female householder[1]	Householder living alone
	71	72	73	74	75	76	77	78	79	80	81	82	83	84	85
Reading, PA	141 570	69.6	31.7	55.5	23.6	9.9	5.8	30.4	24.6	10.7	2.55	3.05	127 649	9.1	23.5
Redding, CA	63 426	69.4	31.7	53.0	21.1	11.9	7.7	30.6	24.7	10.2	2.52	2.98	55 966	11.0	22.3
Reno, NV	132 084	63.4	31.1	47.9	21.8	10.3	6.4	36.6	27.0	7.7	2.53	3.09	102 294	9.4	27.6
Richland-Kennewick-Pasco, WA	67 706	73.4	39.7	58.3	29.3	10.4	7.4	26.6	22.0	7.6	2.81	3.29	54 423	9.7	22.6
Richmond-Petersburg, VA	387 721	67.2	32.9	49.2	22.5	14.4	8.6	32.8	26.4	8.0	2.48	3.02	331 824	13.6	25.1
Roanoke, VA	98 343	65.7	28.4	50.2	19.9	12.0	6.8	34.3	29.4	11.2	2.33	2.87	89 694	11.9	26.5
Rochester, MN	47 807	67.6	35.2	56.7	28.0	8.0	5.4	32.4	25.8	7.6	2.53	3.09	40 058	7.5	24.6
Rochester, NY	420 073	66.2	32.6	50.0	22.5	12.4	7.9	33.8	27.1	9.9	2.51	3.08	396 089	11.5	24.7
Rockford, IL	141 855	69.9	34.0	54.7	24.5	11.0	7.1	30.1	25.0	9.4	2.57	3.09	124 809	10.1	23.7
Rocky Mount, NC	54 036	71.7	32.8	50.3	21.4	17.1	9.4	28.3	24.6	9.8	2.59	3.07	49 360	16.7	23.6
Sacramento-Yolo, CA	665 298	67.0	34.0	49.5	23.5	12.7	7.9	33.0	25.0	7.9	2.65	3.19	556 448	11.8	23.9
Sacramento, CA	605 923	67.4	34.0	49.7	23.4	12.8	8.0	32.6	25.2	7.9	2.64	3.19	505 476	12.0	23.9
Yolo, CA	59 375	63.1	33.6	47.6	24.4	11.1	6.9	36.9	23.3	7.3	2.71	3.25	50 972	10.2	23.1
Saginaw-Bay City-Midland, MI	156 129	69.5	32.6	53.2	22.5	12.7	8.0	30.5	25.8	10.4	2.53	3.04	148 235	12.7	22.9
Salinas, CA	121 236	72.5	39.1	56.0	29.6	11.6	6.9	27.5	21.2	8.2	3.14	3.65	112 965	10.4	20.4
Salt Lake City-Ogden, UT	432 040	74.7	41.6	60.3	33.3	10.2	6.2	25.3	19.5	6.2	3.04	3.54	347 531	10.0	20.6
San Angelo, TX	39 503	67.8	33.0	52.1	23.4	11.9	7.4	32.2	27.2	10.8	2.52	3.09	35 408	10.5	24.8
San Antonio, TX	559 946	71.5	36.6	52.1	25.6	14.8	8.7	28.5	23.4	7.5	2.78	3.31	458 502	13.9	22.8
San Diego, CA	994 677	66.7	33.9	50.7	24.8	11.6	6.8	33.3	24.2	7.9	2.73	3.29	887 403	10.8	22.9
San Francisco-Oakland-San Jose, CA	2 557 158	64.6	31.4	49.2	23.7	10.8	5.7	35.4	25.8	7.9	2.69	3.28	2 329 808	10.7	25.9
Oakland, CA	867 495	67.0	33.7	50.0	24.8	12.4	6.8	33.0	24.8	7.6	2.71	3.27	779 806	12.1	25.1
San Francisco, CA	684 453	55.1	23.6	42.0	18.1	9.3	4.1	44.9	32.1	9.2	2.47	3.20	642 504	9.7	32.3
San Jose, CA	565 863	69.9	34.9	54.9	27.8	10.0	5.1	30.1	21.4	5.9	2.92	3.41	520 180	10.3	21.7
Santa Cruz-Watsonville, CA	91 139	62.7	31.9	48.0	23.2	10.2	6.1	37.3	25.1	8.2	2.71	3.25	83 566	9.6	24.1
Santa Rosa, CA	172 403	65.2	31.9	50.3	23.3	10.4	6.1	34.8	25.7	10.0	2.60	3.12	149 011	9.8	24.6
Vallejo-Fairfield-Napa, CA	175 805	72.8	37.7	55.0	27.1	12.8	7.7	27.2	21.2	7.8	2.83	3.29	154 741	10.9	20.2
San Luis Obispo-Atascadero-Paso Robles, CA	92 739	63.2	28.2	50.4	20.7	9.1	5.5	36.8	26.0	10.3	2.49	3.01	80 281	8.5	23.8
Santa Barbara-Santa Maria-Lompoc, CA	136 622	65.5	32.4	51.4	24.5	10.0	5.7	34.5	24.3	9.4	2.80	3.33	129 802	9.3	23.0
Santa Fe, NM	59 979	63.6	30.8	47.7	20.8	11.0	7.0	36.4	28.8	7.3	2.42	3.00	45 053	10.5	26.3
Sarasota-Bradenton, FL	262 397	64.1	20.3	52.7	14.1	8.4	4.7	35.9	29.6	16.1	2.20	2.69	216 553	7.8	27.4
Savannah, GA	111 105	68.8	33.0	48.8	21.6	15.9	9.4	31.2	25.2	8.7	2.56	3.08	94 940	15.3	24.4
Scranton—Wilkes-Barre—Hazleton, PA	252 582	65.1	27.1	49.7	20.0	11.2	5.4	34.9	30.5	15.2	2.37	2.97	246 491	11.5	27.9
Seattle-Tacoma-Bremerton, WA	1 392 393	64.2	32.1	50.6	23.7	9.8	6.2	35.8	27.1	7.4	2.50	3.06	1 155 361	9.3	26.0
Bremerton, WA	86 416	71.0	36.0	57.7	27.0	9.5	6.6	29.0	22.6	7.6	2.60	3.05	69 267	8.5	22.1
Olympia, WA	81 625	67.3	33.0	53.1	23.5	10.3	7.0	32.7	25.1	8.0	2.50	2.99	62 150	9.7	24.0
Seattle-Bellevue-Everett, WA	963 552	62.1	30.6	49.1	22.9	9.2	5.7	37.9	28.4	7.3	2.46	3.05	809 292	8.9	27.1
Tacoma, WA	260 800	69.1	35.9	52.8	25.2	11.8	7.9	30.9	24.3	7.6	2.60	3.10	214 652	10.9	23.4
Sharon, PA	46 712	69.3	29.3	54.8	21.4	10.9	6.1	30.7	27.0	13.2	2.44	2.96	45 591	10.3	24.6
Sheboygan, WI	43 545	68.7	32.3	58.0	25.6	7.3	4.8	31.3	26.1	10.4	2.50	3.05	38 592	7.1	23.3
Sherman-Denison, TX	42 849	70.5	32.1	55.2	23.2	11.4	6.7	29.5	25.5	11.4	2.51	3.00	36 847	10.2	25.2
Shreveport-Bossier City, LA	151 103	68.3	32.3	46.0	19.5	18.0	10.6	31.7	27.2	10.1	2.53	3.09	139 815	16.7	25.6
Sioux City, IA-NE	46 246	68.2	34.9	52.3	24.7	11.4	7.6	31.8	26.1	10.9	2.62	3.16	42 934	10.5	25.5
Sioux Falls, SD	66 778	66.3	34.7	53.7	26.3	9.1	6.4	33.7	26.7	8.5	2.50	3.06	53 142	8.5	26.4
South Bend, IN	100 743	66.3	32.0	50.0	22.1	12.4	7.8	33.7	27.9	10.7	2.50	3.07	92 365	11.4	26.4
Spokane, WA	163 611	64.8	32.4	49.9	22.5	11.0	7.4	35.2	28.1	9.6	2.46	3.02	141 619	10.8	27.5
Springfield, IL	83 595	63.9	30.9	49.0	21.1	11.5	7.4	36.1	30.5	10.6	2.37	2.97	76 345	11.1	29.0
Springfield, MA	231 279	65.0	31.0	46.0	20.0	14.0	9.0	35.0	28.0	11.0	2.49	3.07	219 958	14.1	25.4
Springfield, MO	129 357	66.4	30.8	53.4	22.6	9.6	6.1	33.6	26.8	9.3	2.41	2.94	101 791	8.9	25.0
St. Cloud, MN	60 669	67.0	35.0	55.4	27.7	7.8	5.3	33.0	24.1	8.5	2.63	3.15	50 711	7.5	22.0
St. Joseph, MO	39 830	66.7	31.2	51.4	21.8	11.2	7.0	33.3	27.9	12.2	2.45	2.99	37 915	10.8	26.7
St. Louis, MO-IL	1 012 419	67.4	32.9	50.2	22.9	13.5	8.0	32.6	27.4	9.9	2.52	3.09	942 119	12.5	25.7
State College, PA	49 323	57.8	25.5	48.9	20.7	6.1	3.4	42.2	26.6	7.6	2.45	2.95	42 683	6.2	23.6
Steubenville-Weirton, OH-WV	54 491	68.4	26.6	53.5	19.2	11.1	5.7	31.6	27.9	13.9	2.36	2.87	55 223	10.9	24.7
Stockton-Lodi, CA	181 629	74.2	40.5	54.3	28.5	14.0	8.8	25.8	20.7	8.4	3.00	3.48	158 156	12.7	20.9
Sumter, SC	37 728	73.2	36.5	50.2	23.8	18.3	10.5	26.8	23.2	8.5	2.68	3.17	32 723	16.7	19.0
Syracuse, NY	282 601	65.4	32.6	49.2	22.4	12.1	7.8	34.6	27.8	10.7	2.50	3.06	272 974	11.2	25.0
Tallahassee, FL	112 388	58.5	28.4	40.4	18.0	14.3	8.6	41.5	28.8	6.3	2.39	2.99	88 233	13.9	26.2
Tampa-St. Petersburg-Clearwater, FL	1 009 316	63.2	25.9	48.2	17.4	11.2	6.5	36.8	29.7	12.7	2.33	2.88	869 481	9.9	28.0
Terre Haute, IN	57 976	65.9	30.4	51.1	21.4	11.0	6.8	34.1	28.5	12.1	2.42	2.97	55 824	10.1	27.5
Texarkana, TX-Texarkana, AR	48 695	70.9	33.3	51.7	22.0	15.3	9.4	29.1	25.9	11.0	2.50	3.00	44 868	13.8	24.2
Toledo, OH	243 499	64.8	31.7	47.6	21.1	13.1	8.3	35.2	28.7	10.2	2.47	3.06	230 681	12.5	26.1
Topeka, KS	68 920	64.8	30.7	49.6	21.0	11.6	7.6	35.2	29.8	10.0	2.39	2.98	63 768	10.5	27.6

[1] No spouse present.

Table C. Metropolitan Areas

Area Name	Percent change of households, 1990–2000	Total housing units	Occupied housing units (percent)	Vacant housing units		For seasonal, recreational, or occasional use	Homeowner vacancy rate (percent)	Rental vacancy rate (percent)	Occupied housing units			Average household size of owner-occupied units	Average household size of renter-occupied units
				Total					Total	Percent owner-occupied housing units	Percent renter-occupied housing units		
	86	87	88	89	90	91	92		93	94	95	96	97
Reading, PA	10.9	150 222	94.2	5.8	0.5	1.7	6.3		141 570	74.0	26.0	2.65	2.27
Redding, CA	13.3	68 810	92.2	7.8	2.3	2.2	5.9		63 426	66.1	33.9	2.53	2.51
Reno, NV	29.1	143 908	91.8	8.2	2.5	2.0	7.8		132 084	59.3	40.7	2.65	2.35
Richland-Kennewick-Pasco, WA	24.4	72 047	94.0	6.0	0.4	1.6	7.9		67 706	68.1	31.9	2.87	2.67
Richmond-Petersburg, VA	16.8	410 394	94.5	5.5	0.4	1.4	6.5		387 721	67.7	32.3	2.60	2.24
Roanoke, VA	9.6	104 352	94.2	5.8	0.6	1.5	6.1		98 343	68.6	31.4	2.44	2.07
Rochester, MN	19.3	49 422	96.7	3.3	0.5	0.7	3.9		47 807	75.9	24.1	2.71	1.98
Rochester, NY	6.1	451 362	93.1	6.9	1.5	1.4	7.7		420 073	68.2	31.8	2.68	2.14
Rockford, IL	13.7	150 238	94.4	5.6	0.5	1.5	7.4		141 855	71.5	28.5	2.69	2.28
Rocky Mount, NC	9.5	61 053	88.5	11.5	0.5	1.5	6.0		54 036	66.4	33.6	2.61	2.53
Sacramento-Yolo, CA	19.6	714 981	93.1	6.9	3.0	1.3	4.9		665 298	61.3	38.7	2.71	2.54
Sacramento, CA	19.9	653 394	92.7	7.3	3.2	1.4	5.0		605 923	62.1	37.9	2.71	2.53
Yolo, CA	16.5	61 587	96.4	3.6	0.4	0.9	3.4		59 375	53.1	46.9	2.76	2.67
Saginaw-Bay City-Midland, MI	5.3	165 724	94.2	5.8	0.7	1.4	6.9		156 129	76.3	23.7	2.63	2.18
Salinas, CA	7.3	131 708	92.0	8.0	3.0	1.4	2.9		121 236	54.6	45.4	3.10	3.18
Salt Lake City-Ogden, UT	24.3	455 556	94.8	5.2	0.8	1.8	6.6		432 040	71.3	28.7	3.23	2.57
San Angelo, TX	11.6	43 916	90.0	10.0	0.9	2.3	11.4		39 503	64.1	35.9	2.65	2.30
San Antonio, TX	22.1	599 772	93.4	6.6	0.9	1.5	6.9		559 946	63.4	36.6	2.92	2.53
San Diego, CA	12.1	1 040 149	95.6	4.4	1.4	1.0	3.1		994 677	55.4	44.6	2.78	2.68
San Francisco-Oakland-San Jose, CA	9.8	2 651 275	96.5	3.5	1.0	0.7	2.4		2 557 158	57.8	42.2	2.82	2.51
Oakland, CA	11.2	894 760	97.0	3.0	0.4	0.7	2.6		867 495	60.5	39.5	2.83	2.54
San Francisco, CA	6.5	712 093	96.1	3.9	1.0	0.6	2.3		684 453	49.0	51.0	2.72	2.23
San Jose, CA	8.8	579 329	97.7	2.3	0.4	0.5	1.8		565 863	59.8	40.2	3.00	2.80
Santa Cruz-Watsonville, CA	9.1	98 873	92.2	7.8	5.1	0.8	2.5		91 139	60.0	40.0	2.71	2.70
Santa Rosa, CA	15.7	183 153	94.1	5.9	3.3	0.8	2.4		172 403	64.1	35.9	2.61	2.57
Vallejo-Fairfield-Napa, CA	13.6	183 067	96.0	4.0	1.1	1.0	3.5		175 805	65.2	34.8	2.86	2.78
San Luis Obispo-Atascadero-Paso Robles, CA	15.5	102 275	90.7	9.3	6.0	1.1	3.2		92 739	61.5	38.5	2.53	2.44
Santa Barbara-Santa Maria-Lompoc, CA	5.3	142 901	95.6	4.4	1.4	0.8	2.8		136 622	56.1	43.9	2.76	2.85
Santa Fe, NM	33.1	65 638	91.4	8.6	3.7	1.4	6.1		59 979	69.8	30.2	2.55	2.13
Sarasota-Bradenton, FL	21.2	320 595	81.8	18.2	11.6	2.2	12.6		262 397	76.8	23.2	2.19	2.25
Savannah, GA	17.0	122 527	90.7	9.3	1.1	1.8	9.6		111 105	64.3	35.7	2.65	2.41
Scranton—Wilkes-Barre—Hazleton, PA	2.5	280 494	90.0	10.0	2.5	1.9	8.5		252 582	69.9	30.1	2.52	2.03
Seattle-Tacoma-Bremerton, WA	20.5	1 467 176	94.9	5.1	1.1	1.5	4.9		1 392 393	62.9	37.1	2.65	2.23
Bremerton, WA	24.8	92 644	93.3	6.7	1.6	2.0	6.4		86 416	67.4	32.6	2.68	2.44
Olympia, WA	31.3	86 652	94.2	5.8	1.1	2.1	6.0		81 625	66.6	33.4	2.61	2.28
Seattle-Bellevue-Everett, WA	19.1	1 010 820	95.3	4.7	1.1	1.3	4.4		963 552	62.0	38.0	2.64	2.15
Tacoma, WA	21.5	277 060	94.1	5.9	0.9	1.8	6.1		260 800	63.5	36.5	2.71	2.42
Sharon, PA	2.5	49 859	93.7	6.3	1.0	1.5	6.7		46 712	76.3	23.7	2.54	2.12
Sheboygan, WI	12.8	45 947	94.8	5.2	1.7	1.1	5.4		43 545	71.4	28.6	2.67	2.10
Sherman-Denison, TX	16.3	48 315	88.7	11.3	3.6	2.0	9.2		42 849	70.6	29.4	2.56	2.39
Shreveport-Bossier City, LA	8.1	167 573	90.2	9.8	1.0	1.8	10.8		151 103	66.4	33.6	2.57	2.46
Sioux City, IA-NE	7.7	48 922	94.5	5.5	0.3	1.5	7.9		46 246	68.4	31.6	2.75	2.34
Sioux Falls, SD	25.7	69 368	96.3	3.7	0.2	1.0	5.3		66 778	66.6	33.4	2.73	2.03
South Bend, IN	9.1	107 013	94.1	5.9	0.4	1.5	7.3		100 743	71.7	28.3	2.62	2.21
Spokane, WA	15.5	175 005	93.5	6.5	0.6	2.0	8.7		163 611	65.5	34.5	2.61	2.19
Springfield, IL	9.5	90 744	92.1	7.9	0.4	2.0	10.2		83 595	70.5	29.5	2.49	2.09
Springfield, MA	5.1	244 520	95.0	5.0	1.0	0.9	4.8		231 279	63.0	37.0	2.63	2.26
Springfield, MO	27.1	138 396	93.5	6.5	0.4	2.4	7.4		129 357	66.8	33.2	2.53	2.18
St. Cloud, MN	19.6	63 751	95.2	4.8	2.3	0.7	3.4		60 669	72.4	27.6	2.84	2.06
St. Joseph, MO	5.1	43 236	92.1	7.9	0.5	1.8	7.2		39 830	69.5	30.5	2.55	2.23
St. Louis, MO-IL	7.5	1 092 915	92.6	7.4	0.7	1.6	8.4		1 012 419	71.4	28.6	2.66	2.16
State College, PA	15.6	53 161	92.8	7.2	2.9	1.2	3.7		49 323	60.2	39.8	2.61	2.22
Steubenville-Weirton, OH-WV	-1.3	59 169	92.1	7.9	0.5	1.5	8.9		54 491	75.5	24.5	2.44	2.12
Stockton-Lodi, CA	14.8	189 160	96.0	4.0	0.3	1.2	3.8		181 629	60.4	39.6	2.96	3.06
Sumter, SC	15.3	41 751	90.4	9.6	0.6	1.9	10.3		37 728	69.5	30.5	2.72	2.60
Syracuse, NY	3.5	313 587	90.1	9.9	3.1	2.0	9.4		282 601	67.6	32.4	2.66	2.15
Tallahassee, FL	27.4	121 677	92.4	7.6	0.8	1.8	8.2		112 388	60.0	40.0	2.55	2.15
Tampa-St. Petersburg-Clearwater, FL	16.1	1 143 979	88.2	11.8	5.1	2.2	9.7		1 009 316	70.8	29.2	2.38	2.19
Terre Haute, IN	3.9	63 705	91.0	9.0	0.7	2.3	10.8		57 976	70.9	29.1	2.53	2.16
Texarkana, TX-Texarkana, AR	8.5	54 190	89.9	10.1	0.7	2.1	12.7		48 695	70.0	30.0	2.53	2.44
Toledo, OH	5.6	259 959	93.7	6.3	0.3	1.5	7.7		243 499	67.3	32.7	2.62	2.15
Topeka, KS	8.1	73 768	93.4	6.6	0.2	1.3	7.3		68 920	67.4	32.6	2.53	2.12

Table C. Metropolitan Areas

CMSA/ MSA/ PMSA/ NECMA code[1]	Area Name	Population, 2000					Population, 1990			Population and population characteristics, 2000					
										Race (percent)					
										One race					
		Land area, 2000[2] (sq km)	Total persons	Rank	Per square kilometer	Land area, 1990[2] (sq km)	Total persons	Rank	Per square kilometer	White	Black or African American	American Indian or Alaska Native	Asian	Native Hawaiian and other Pacific Islander	Some other race
		1	2	3	4	5	6	7	8	9	10	11	12	13	14
8520	Tucson, AZ	23 792	843 746	70	35.5	23 794	666 957	73	28.0	75.1	3.0	3.2	2.0	0.1	13.3
8560	Tulsa, OK	12 987	803 235	71	61.8	12 988	708 954	71	54.6	76.0	8.8	6.9	1.2	0.0	2.1
8600	Tuscaloosa, AL	3 430	164 875	225	48.1	3 432	150 500	217	43.9	68.1	29.3	0.2	0.9	0.0	0.6
8640	Tyler, TX	2 405	174 706	216	72.7	2 405	151 309	216	62.9	72.6	19.1	0.4	0.7	0.0	5.7
8680	Utica-Rome, NY	6 796	299 896	158	44.1	6 798	316 645	138	46.6	91.8	4.6	0.2	1.0	0.0	0.9
8750	Victoria, TX	2 286	84 088	311	36.8	2 286	74 361	312	32.5	74.2	6.3	0.5	0.8	0.0	15.9
8780	Visalia-Tulare-Porterville, CA	12 494	368 021	136	29.5	12 495	311 932	142	25.0	58.1	1.6	1.6	3.3	0.1	30.8
8800	Waco, TX	2 698	213 517	194	79.1	2 699	189 123	189	70.1	72.2	15.2	0.5	1.1	0.0	9.2
97	Washington-Baltimore, DC-MD-VA-WV	24 803	7 608 070	X	306.7	24 807	6 726 395	X	271.1	63.0	26.2	0.3	5.3	0.1	2.7
0720	Baltimore, MD	6 757	2 552 994	18	377.8	6 757	2 382 172	18	352.5	67.3	27.4	0.3	2.7	0.0	0.7
3180	Hagerstown, MD	1 187	131 923	262	111.2	1 187	121 393	260	102.3	89.7	7.8	0.2	0.8	0.0	0.5
8840	Washington, DC-MD-VA-WV	16 859	4 923 153	6	292.0	16 863	4 222 830	7	250.4	60.1	26.0	0.3	6.7	0.1	3.9
8920	Waterloo-Cedar Falls, IA	1 469	128 012	266	87.2	1 469	123 798	256	84.3	88.4	8.0	0.2	1.0	0.0	0.9
8940	Wausau, WI	4 001	125 834	271	31.4	4 002	115 400	271	28.8	93.8	0.3	0.3	4.5	0.0	0.3
8960	West Palm Beach-Boca Raton, FL	5 113	1 131 184	55	221.2	5 269	863 503	61	163.9	79.1	13.8	0.2	1.5	0.1	3.0
9000	Wheeling, WV-OH	2 462	153 172	234	62.2	2 462	159 301	211	64.7	95.6	2.9	0.1	0.4	0.0	0.1
9080	Wichita Falls, TX	3 982	140 518	253	35.3	3 982	130 351	249	32.7	79.8	9.6	0.9	1.7	0.1	5.3
9040	Wichita, KS	7 683	545 220	97	71.0	7 687	485 270	95	63.1	81.8	7.8	1.1	2.9	0.1	3.8
9140	Williamsport, PA	3 198	120 044	280	37.5	3 198	118 710	265	37.1	93.9	4.3	0.2	0.4	0.0	0.3
9200	Wilmington, NC	2 729	233 450	184	85.5	2 729	171 269	203	62.8	80.7	16.2	0.5	0.7	0.1	1.0
9260	Yakima, WA	11 127	222 581	189	20.0	11 127	188 823	190	17.0	65.6	1.0	4.5	1.0	0.1	24.4
9280	York, PA	2 343	381 751	131	163.0	2 343	339 574	130	144.9	92.8	3.7	0.2	0.9	0.0	1.4
9320	Youngstown-Warren, OH	4 051	594 746	89	146.8	4 050	600 877	80	148.4	87.4	10.3	0.2	0.4	0.0	0.6
9340	Yuba City, CA	3 194	139 149	255	43.6	3 194	122 643	258	38.4	68.9	2.5	2.0	9.6	0.2	11.7
9360	Yuma, AZ	14 281	160 026	228	11.2	14 282	106 895	283	7.5	68.3	2.2	1.6	0.9	0.1	23.6

[1]MSA = Metropolitan Statistical Area. PMSA = Primary MSA. NECMA = New England County Metropolitan Area. See Appendix A for explanation of these concepts. See Appendix B for list of metropolitan areas identified by type, with component counties.
[2]Dry land or land partially or temporarily covered by water.

Table C. Metropolitan Areas

Area Name	Population and population characteristics, 2000 (cont'd)								Population and population characteristics, 1990				
	Race (percent) (cont'd)								Race (percent)				
	Race alone or in combination												
	Two or more races	White	Black	American Indian or Alaska Native	Asian	Native Hawaiian and other Pacific Islander	Some other race	Hispanic[1]	White	Black or African American	American Indian or Alaska Native	Asian and Pacific Islander	Hispanic[1]
	15	16	17	18	19	20	21	22	23	24	25	26	27
Tucson, AZ	3.2	77.8	3.7	4.0	2.7	0.2	15.1	29.3	78.7	3.1	3.0	1.8	24.5
Tulsa, OK	4.8	80.4	9.5	10.7	1.6	0.1	2.7	4.8	83.3	8.2	6.8	0.9	2.1
Tuscaloosa, AL	0.8	68.8	29.6	0.0	1.1	0.1	0.8	1.3	72.7	26.2	0.2	0.8	0.6
Tyler, TX	1.4	73.9	19.4	0.9	0.9	0.1	6.4	11.2	75.1	20.9	0.3	0.4	5.9
Utica-Rome, NY	1.4	93.1	5.1	0.6	1.2	0.1	1.5	2.7	94.0	4.4	0.2	0.7	1.9
Victoria, TX	2.2	76.2	6.7	0.9	0.9	0.1	17.5	39.2	79.7	6.6	0.3	0.3	34.1
Visalia-Tulare-Porterville, CA	4.6	62.0	2.0	2.5	4.0	0.3	34.0	50.8	65.7	1.5	1.3	4.3	38.8
Waco, TX	1.8	73.7	15.6	0.9	1.3	0.1	10.2	17.9	77.3	15.6	0.3	0.7	12.5
Washington-Baltimore, DC-MD-VA-WV	2.4	64.8	27.1	0.8	6.0	0.1	3.8	6.4	65.7	26.6	0.3	5.2	5.7
Baltimore, MD	1.5	68.5	28.1	0.7	3.1	0.1	1.2	2.0	71.8	25.9	0.3	1.8	1.3
Hagerstown, MD	1.0	90.7	8.2	0.5	1.0	0.1	0.6	1.2	92.9	6.0	0.2	0.7	0.7
Washington, DC-MD-VA-WV	2.9	62.2	27.1	0.8	7.6	0.2	5.2	8.8	65.7	26.6	0.3	5.2	5.7
Waterloo-Cedar Falls, IA	1.5	89.8	8.6	0.5	1.2	0.1	1.5	1.8	92.9	5.9	0.2	0.8	0.7
Wausau, WI	0.7	94.4	0.4	0.6	4.8	0.1	0.4	0.8	97.2	0.1	0.4	2.2	0.4
West Palm Beach-Boca Raton, FL	2.4	80.4	14.9	0.5	1.9	0.2	4.6	12.4	84.8	12.5	0.1	1.0	7.7
Wheeling, WV-OH	0.8	96.4	3.2	0.4	0.6	0.0	0.2	0.5	97.5	2.0	0.1	0.3	0.4
Wichita Falls, TX	2.6	82.0	10.2	1.7	2.2	0.2	6.4	11.8	83.7	9.2	0.7	1.5	8.6
Wichita, KS	2.6	84.1	8.6	2.1	3.3	0.1	4.6	7.4	87.3	7.6	1.1	1.9	4.1
Williamsport, PA	0.9	94.7	4.8	0.5	0.5	0.0	0.4	0.7	96.9	2.4	0.2	0.4	0.5
Wilmington, NC	1.0	81.5	16.5	0.9	0.8	0.1	1.3	2.2	82.5	14.8	0.2	1.3	2.4
Yakima, WA	3.5	68.6	1.4	5.6	1.5	0.2	26.4	35.9	73.9	1.0	4.5	1.0	23.9
York, PA	1.1	93.7	4.2	0.4	1.0	0.1	1.7	3.0	95.7	2.9	0.1	0.6	1.5
Youngstown-Warren, OH	1.2	88.4	10.8	0.6	0.6	0.0	0.8	1.8	87.7	11.1	0.2	0.4	1.5
Yuba City, CA	5.2	73.0	3.1	3.9	11.2	0.5	13.8	20.1	77.5	2.8	2.1	9.0	14.1
Yuma, AZ	3.2	71.1	2.6	2.2	1.4	0.3	25.8	50.5	75.5	2.9	1.3	1.3	40.6

[1] Hispanic persons may be of any race.

Table C. Metropolitan Areas

Area Name	Population and population characteristics, 2000											
	Age (percent)										
	Under 5 years	5 to 17 years	18 to 24 years	25 to 34 years	35 to 44 years	45 to 54 years	55 to 64 years	65 to 74 years	75 years and over	Median age (years)	Percent Female
	28	29	30	31	32	33	34	35	36	37	38
Tucson, AZ	6.6	18.0	10.9	13.5	14.9	13.1	8.8	7.5	6.7	35.7	51.1
Tulsa, OK...........................	7.2	19.5	9.3	13.8	15.8	13.7	8.8	6.4	5.4	35.1	51.2
Tuscaloosa, AL....................	6.4	17.0	16.5	13.9	14.1	13.0	7.8	6.3	5.0	31.9	51.9
Tyler, TX	7.1	19.5	9.8	12.9	14.5	12.9	9.2	7.5	6.6	35.5	52.1
Utica-Rome, NY..................	5.6	18.3	8.5	12.3	15.5	13.7	9.4	7.8	8.7	38.4	50.6
Victoria, TX	7.6	21.5	9.2	12.8	15.4	13.2	8.3	6.6	5.4	34.2	51.3
Visalia-Tulare-Porterville, CA	8.9	24.8	10.6	13.6	14.0	11.2	7.0	5.2	4.6	29.2	50.0
Waco, TX	7.1	19.5	14.6	12.4	14.0	11.8	7.8	6.5	6.3	31.9	51.5
Washington-Baltimore, DC-MD-VA-WV	6.8	18.5	8.7	15.3	17.6	14.4	8.6	5.5	4.7	35.4	51.5
Baltimore, MD.................	6.5	18.8	8.6	13.9	17.2	14.2	8.9	6.4	5.7	36.3	51.9
Hagerstown, MD	6.1	17.3	8.1	14.4	16.9	13.8	9.2	7.4	6.7	37.4	48.9
Washington, DC-MD-VA-WV	7.0	18.3	8.7	16.1	17.8	14.5	8.5	5.0	4.1	34.9	51.3
Waterloo-Cedar Falls, IA	6.1	17.0	15.7	11.9	13.3	13.6	8.4	6.8	7.2	34.4	52.0
Wausau, WI........................	6.4	20.4	8.2	13.0	16.5	13.9	8.6	6.4	6.6	36.3	50.1
West Palm Beach-Boca Raton, FL	5.6	15.7	6.6	11.8	15.2	12.5	9.6	10.8	12.3	41.8	51.7
Wheeling, WV-OH	5.1	16.7	8.5	11.6	15.0	15.2	9.9	9.0	8.9	40.7	51.7
Wichita Falls, TX	6.9	18.4	13.2	13.4	15.5	11.8	8.0	7.0	5.8	33.6	49.1
Wichita, KS........................	7.7	20.4	9.4	13.8	16.2	13.2	7.6	6.1	5.7	34.1	50.5
Williamsport, PA	5.5	17.8	9.7	12.0	15.6	14.1	9.4	8.2	7.8	38.4	51.1
Wilmington, NC...................	5.6	15.4	10.4	14.0	14.9	14.3	11.2	8.4	5.7	38.0	51.5
Yakima, WA........................	8.7	23.1	9.8	13.3	14.2	12.0	7.7	5.6	5.6	31.2	50.1
York, PA............................	6.1	18.5	7.5	13.1	17.2	14.6	9.4	7.1	6.4	37.8	50.8
Youngstown-Warren, OH	6.0	18.1	8.0	12.0	15.2	14.6	9.7	8.4	8.1	39.2	51.6
Yuba City, CA	7.7	22.2	9.8	13.2	14.9	12.2	8.4	6.4	5.2	32.9	50.1
Yuma, AZ...........................	7.9	21.0	10.0	12.5	13.1	9.9	9.0	10.0	6.6	33.9	49.5

Table C. Metropolitan Areas

Area Name	Population and population characteristics, 1990										Population—change, 1980–2000				
	Age (percent)										Total persons			Percent change	
	Under 5 years	5 to 17 years	18 to 24 years	25 to 34 years	35 to 44 years	45 to 54 years	55 to 64 years	65 to 74 years	75 years and over	Percent Female	2000	1990	1980	1990–2000	1980–1990
	39	40	41	42	43	44	45	46	47	48	49	50	51	52	53
Tucson, AZ	7.5	17.4	11.8	17.1	14.7	9.3	8.4	8.2	5.5	51.1	843 746	666 957	531 443	26.5	25.5
Tulsa, OK	7.6	19.2	9.6	17.2	15.7	10.6	8.6	6.7	4.8	51.5	803 235	708 954	657 173	13.3	7.9
Tuscaloosa, AL	6.4	17.3	17.5	15.7	14.2	9.2	8.3	6.6	4.8	51.7	164 875	150 500	137 541	9.6	9.4
Tyler, TX	7.4	19.3	10.2	16.0	14.4	10.0	9.0	7.8	5.9	51.9	174 706	151 309	128 366	15.5	17.9
Utica-Rome, NY	6.9	17.6	11.0	16.0	13.9	9.9	9.0	9.0	6.7	50.8	299 896	316 645	320 180	-5.3	-1.1
Victoria, TX	8.3	22.0	9.2	16.4	15.0	9.8	8.3	6.4	4.5	51.3	84 088	74 361	68 807	13.1	8.1
Visalia-Tulare-Porterville, CA	9.3	23.7	10.2	16.1	13.6	9.0	7.2	6.2	4.6	50.1	368 021	311 932	245 738	18.0	26.9
Waco, TX	7.5	18.5	14.6	15.3	13.0	9.1	8.4	7.5	6.1	51.5	213 517	189 123	170 755	12.9	10.8
Washington-Baltimore, DC-MD-VA-WV	7.3	16.2	11.1	20.4	17.6	11.5	7.4	5.2	3.3	51.3	7 608 070	6 726 395	5 790 555	13.1	16.2
Baltimore, MD	7.5	16.6	10.4	18.6	16.0	10.7	8.6	7.1	4.6	51.7	2 552 994	2 382 172	2 199 497	7.2	8.3
Hagerstown, MD	6.7	16.0	10.6	17.8	15.0	10.6	9.5	8.1	5.7	49.5	131 923	121 393	113 086	8.7	7.3
Washington, DC-MD-VA-WV	7.3	16.2	11.1	20.4	17.6	11.5	7.4	5.2	3.3	51.3	4 923 153	4 222 830	3 477 972	16.6	21.4
Waterloo-Cedar Falls, IA	6.6	18.8	13.5	13.9	14.5	10.0	8.6	7.9	6.3	52.3	128 012	123 798	137 961	3.4	-10.3
Wausau, WI	7.4	20.7	9.3	16.6	15.1	10.1	8.2	7.1	5.6	50.6	125 834	115 400	111 270	9.0	3.7
West Palm Beach-Boca Raton, FL	6.2	13.5	7.5	15.8	13.6	9.3	9.8	13.5	10.9	52.0	1 131 184	863 503	576 758	31.0	49.7
Wheeling, WV-OH	5.9	17.4	9.0	13.8	14.9	10.4	10.6	10.4	7.6	52.8	153 172	159 301	185 566	-3.8	-14.2
Wichita Falls, TX	7.6	18.5	12.3	17.3	13.2	9.3	8.9	7.1	5.7	51.0	140 518	130 351	128 348	7.8	1.6
Wichita, KS	8.3	19.4	9.6	18.1	15.0	9.3	8.3	6.9	5.0	51.1	545 220	485 270	442 401	12.4	9.7
Williamsport, PA	6.9	18.0	9.9	15.5	14.7	10.1	9.7	8.7	6.4	51.8	120 044	118 710	118 416	1.1	0.2
Wilmington, NC	7.2	17.4	11.5	17.9	15.3	10.4	8.7	7.1	4.5	51.4	233 450	171 269	139 248	36.3	23.0
Yakima, WA	8.7	21.6	9.8	15.3	14.1	9.6	7.9	7.1	5.9	50.3	222 581	188 823	172 508	17.9	9.5
York, PA	7.0	17.4	9.9	16.9	15.8	10.8	9.1	7.7	5.5	51.1	381 751	339 574	312 963	12.4	8.5
Youngstown-Warren, OH	6.6	18.2	9.0	14.6	14.8	10.5	10.4	9.8	6.0	52.4	594 746	600 877	644 922	-1.0	-6.8
Yuba City, CA	9.3	20.7	10.0	16.7	13.7	9.8	8.5	6.8	4.5	50.3	139 149	122 643	101 979	13.5	20.3
Yuma, AZ	8.5	21.1	11.4	16.0	12.4	8.3	8.4	8.9	4.9	49.1	160 026	106 895	76 205	49.7	40.3

Table C. Metropolitan Areas

Area Name		Household relationship, 2000															
		In households (percent)										In group quarters (percent)					
					Child		Other relatives		Nonrelatives				Institutionalized population			Noninstitutionalized population	
	Total population	Total in house-holds	House-holder	Spouse	Total	Own child under 18 years	Total	Under 18 years	Total	Unmar-ried partner	Total in group quarters	Correc-tional institu-tions	Nurs-ing homes	Other institu-tions	Col-lege dormi-tories	Mili-tary quar-ters	Other
	54	55	56	57	58	59	60	61	62	63	64	65	66	67	68	69	70
Tucson, AZ	843 746	97.4	39.4	18.8	27.6	21.6	5.5	2.3	6.1	2.5	2.6	0.8	0.2	0.1	0.8	0.1	0.6
Tulsa, OK	803 235	98.1	39.3	20.8	29.7	24.1	4.3	2.0	4.0	1.6	1.9	0.3	0.6	0.2	0.5	0.0	0.3
Tuscaloosa, AL	164 875	94.7	39.1	18.5	27.1	20.7	5.0	2.3	5.0	1.4	5.3	0.3	0.7	0.5	3.6	0.0	0.2
Tyler, TX	174 706	97.3	37.6	20.9	29.5	23.3	5.9	2.7	3.4	1.3	2.7	0.5	0.8	0.1	0.7	0.0	0.7
Utica-Rome, NY	299 896	94.5	38.8	19.2	28.8	22.1	3.2	1.2	4.5	2.4	5.5	2.2	1.1	0.5	1.1	0.0	0.6
Victoria, TX	84 088	98.2	35.8	20.3	32.3	25.3	6.1	3.0	3.7	1.7	1.8	0.6	0.6	0.3	0.0	0.0	0.4
Visalia-Tulare-Porterville, CA	368 021	98.4	30.0	17.4	37.1	29.2	8.7	3.6	5.2	1.9	1.6	0.3	0.4	0.3	0.0	0.0	0.6
Waco, TX	213 517	95.7	36.9	18.4	29.1	23.1	5.8	2.7	5.6	1.4	4.3	0.4	1.0	0.6	2.0	0.0	0.4
Washington-Baltimore, DC-MD-VA-WV	7 608 070	97.7	37.7	18.5	29.1	22.4	6.3	2.3	6.0	2.0	2.3	0.5	0.4	0.1	0.7	0.2	0.4
Baltimore, MD	2 552 994	97.3	38.2	18.3	29.2	22.0	6.2	2.7	5.4	2.2	2.7	0.7	0.5	0.1	0.7	0.2	0.5
Hagerstown, MD	131 923	92.9	37.7	20.3	27.0	21.3	3.4	1.4	4.4	2.4	7.1	5.5	0.9	0.2	0.0	0.0	0.5
Washington, DC-MD-VA-WV	4 923 153	98.0	37.5	18.6	29.1	22.6	6.3	2.2	6.4	1.9	2.0	0.3	0.4	0.1	0.8	0.1	0.4
Waterloo-Cedar Falls, IA	128 012	94.9	38.8	19.5	26.7	21.2	2.9	1.3	7.0	2.1	5.1	0.2	0.9	0.1	3.1	0.0	0.7
Wausau, WI	125 834	98.6	37.9	22.7	31.6	25.5	2.4	0.8	4.0	2.0	1.4	0.2	0.7	0.0	0.1	0.0	0.4
West Palm Beach-Boca Raton, FL	1 131 184	98.3	41.9	21.3	24.3	19.0	5.2	1.7	5.7	2.3	1.7	0.4	0.6	0.1	0.3	0.0	0.4
Wheeling, WV-OH	153 172	95.6	40.6	21.2	27.0	19.9	3.4	1.4	3.4	1.9	4.4	1.7	0.9	0.1	1.1	0.0	0.5
Wichita Falls, TX	140 518	92.0	36.9	19.6	27.8	22.7	4.1	2.0	3.7	1.5	8.0	3.0	0.7	0.3	0.5	3.3	0.3
Wichita, KS	545 220	98.2	38.6	20.6	31.2	25.8	3.9	1.7	3.9	1.6	1.8	0.5	0.6	0.0	0.2	0.1	0.3
Williamsport, PA	120 044	95.4	39.2	20.8	27.6	21.4	3.0	1.2	4.9	2.2	4.6	1.7	0.9	0.0	1.5	0.0	0.4
Wilmington, NC	233 450	97.9	42.2	21.2	23.9	18.8	4.2	1.7	6.3	2.1	2.1	0.3	0.3	0.0	0.8	0.1	0.6
Yakima, WA	222 581	98.3	33.2	18.6	34.1	27.7	7.1	3.1	5.3	2.2	1.7	0.5	0.5	0.1	0.0	0.0	0.6
York, PA	381 751	97.9	38.8	22.6	28.7	22.7	3.3	1.3	4.5	2.4	2.1	0.4	0.8	0.0	0.4	0.0	0.6
Youngstown-Warren, OH	594 746	97.5	39.4	20.5	29.7	21.7	4.4	1.9	3.4	1.8	2.5	1.2	0.9	0.1	0.2	0.0	0.3
Yuba City, CA	139 149	98.0	34.2	18.9	33.0	26.3	6.6	2.7	5.3	2.0	2.0	0.6	0.4	0.1	0.0	0.4	0.5
Yuma, AZ	160 026	96.3	33.6	21.0	31.9	25.5	6.2	3.0	3.6	1.7	3.7	1.7	0.4	0.0	0.1	1.0	0.3

Table C. Metropolitan Areas

Area Name	Households by type, 2000												Households, 1990		
		Family households						Nonfamily households							
				Married couple		Female householder[1]			Householder living alone						
	Total households	Total	With own children under 18 years	Total	With own children under 18 years	Total	With own children under 18 years	Total	Total	65 years and over	Average house-hold size	Average family size	Total house-holds	Female house-holder[1]	House-holder living alone
	71	72	73	74	75	76	77	78	79	80	81	82	83	84	85
Tucson, AZ	332 350	63.8	29.2	47.7	19.7	11.8	7.1	36.2	28.5	9.4	2.47	3.06	261 792	10.9	27.8
Tulsa, OK	315 532	68.2	33.3	53.0	23.9	11.5	7.3	31.8	27.0	8.7	2.50	3.04	277 202	10.4	26.3
Tuscaloosa, AL	64 517	64.6	30.3	47.2	20.6	14.0	8.3	35.4	28.4	8.3	2.42	3.00	55 354	13.0	25.8
Tyler, TX	65 692	71.4	33.1	55.5	24.1	12.3	7.2	28.6	24.7	9.8	2.59	3.10	56 000	11.3	24.3
Utica-Rome, NY	116 230	65.6	30.5	49.6	20.9	11.6	7.1	34.4	29.1	13.2	2.44	3.01	117 498	10.9	26.6
Victoria, TX	30 071	73.8	37.2	56.7	26.8	12.7	8.0	26.2	22.4	9.1	2.75	3.23	26 228	11.1	21.2
Visalia-Tulare-Porterville, CA	110 385	78.9	44.9	58.1	31.8	14.5	9.4	21.1	17.1	7.7	3.28	3.67	97 861	12.8	18.1
Waco, TX	78 859	67.1	33.0	49.7	22.8	13.6	8.3	32.9	26.0	9.7	2.59	3.15	70 208	12.1	25.8
Washington-Baltimore, DC-MD-VA-WV	2 871 861	66.5	32.8	49.1	23.4	13.2	7.5	33.5	26.4	7.3	2.59	3.15	2 491 041	12.7	24.4
Baltimore, MD	974 071	67.1	32.0	48.0	21.6	14.9	8.3	32.9	26.4	8.8	2.55	3.10	880 145	14.6	23.5
Hagerstown, MD	49 726	68.6	31.3	54.0	22.2	10.7	6.7	31.4	26.0	11.1	2.46	2.96	44 762	9.7	23.6
Washington, DC-MD-VA-WV	1 848 064	66.1	33.3	49.6	24.4	12.4	7.0	33.9	26.4	6.4	2.61	3.18	1 566 134	11.8	24.9
Waterloo-Cedar Falls, IA	49 683	64.3	29.5	50.2	20.6	10.8	7.2	35.7	27.1	10.9	2.45	2.97	46 932	10.4	25.6
Wausau, WI	47 702	71.0	34.0	59.9	27.3	7.4	4.7	29.0	23.6	9.5	2.60	3.11	41 547	7.2	21.0
West Palm Beach-Boca Raton, FL	474 175	64.1	24.9	50.8	17.5	9.7	5.7	35.9	29.2	14.6	2.34	2.89	365 558	8.6	27.5
Wheeling, WV-OH	62 249	66.7	27.8	52.1	20.1	11.1	6.0	33.3	29.6	14.9	2.35	2.90	62 858	10.9	27.4
Wichita Falls, TX	51 786	68.4	33.8	53.1	24.3	11.6	7.4	31.6	26.8	10.5	2.50	3.04	48 228	10.5	25.0
Wichita, KS	210 552	67.8	34.6	53.3	25.5	10.5	6.8	32.2	27.4	9.0	2.54	3.13	186 640	9.7	26.0
Williamsport, PA	47 003	67.4	29.9	53.1	21.1	10.3	6.3	32.6	26.9	11.9	2.44	2.95	44 949	9.9	24.1
Wilmington, NC	98 621	64.5	26.0	50.1	17.8	11.1	6.6	35.5	27.0	8.5	2.32	2.81	68 208	12.3	24.4
Yakima, WA	73 993	73.8	39.7	55.8	27.9	12.5	8.6	26.2	21.5	9.6	2.96	3.44	65 985	11.3	22.7
York, PA	148 219	71.2	32.5	58.3	24.6	9.0	5.5	28.8	23.3	9.2	2.52	2.98	128 666	8.4	21.3
Youngstown-Warren, OH	234 580	68.7	29.6	52.0	20.7	12.8	7.0	31.3	27.5	12.2	2.47	3.01	227 967	12.4	24.3
Yuba City, CA	47 568	73.0	38.0	55.4	27.0	12.4	7.9	27.0	21.4	8.4	2.87	3.34	42 887	11.8	21.1
Yuma, AZ	53 848	77.4	36.9	62.3	27.0	11.2	7.6	22.6	18.5	8.9	2.86	3.27	35 791	9.4	19.0

[1]No spouse present.

Table C. Metropolitan Areas

Area Name	Percent change of households, 1990–2000	Total housing units	Occupied housing units (percent)	Vacant housing units Total	For seasonal, recreational, or occasional use	Homeowner vacancy rate (percent)	Rental vacancy rate (percent)	Occupied housing units Total	Percent owner-occupied housing units	Percent renter-occupied housing units	Average household size of owner-occupied units	Average household size of renter-occupied units
	86	87	88	89	90	91	92	93	94	95	96	97
Tucson, AZ	27.0	366 737	90.6	9.4	2.9	1.8	9.2	332 350	64.3	35.7	2.59	2.26
Tulsa, OK..........................	13.8	341 415	92.4	7.6	0.8	1.7	8.8	315 532	66.9	33.1	2.60	2.29
Tuscaloosa, AL....................	16.6	71 429	90.3	9.7	0.7	1.7	12.3	64 517	63.5	36.5	2.58	2.14
Tyler, TX..........................	15.7	71 701	91.6	8.4	1.3	1.8	9.8	65 692	69.7	30.3	2.67	2.40
Utica-Rome, NY...................	-1.1	134 829	86.2	13.8	5.1	2.2	10.9	116 230	68.1	31.9	2.58	2.13
Victoria, TX	14.7	32 945	91.3	8.7	0.8	1.6	11.2	30 071	67.4	32.6	2.81	2.62
Visalia-Tulare-Porterville, CA	12.8	119 639	92.3	7.7	2.3	1.8	5.8	110 385	61.5	38.5	3.18	3.43
Waco, TX	12.3	84 795	93.0	7.0	0.5	1.6	6.5	78 859	60.2	39.8	2.69	2.44
Washington-Baltimore, DC-MD-VA-WV	15.3	3 043 659	94.4	5.6	0.7	1.5	4.8	2 871 861	65.0	35.0	2.73	2.32
Baltimore, MD....................	10.7	1 048 046	92.9	7.1	0.6	1.6	6.1	974 071	66.9	33.1	2.70	2.25
Hagerstown, MD..............	11.1	52 972	93.9	6.1	0.9	1.6	5.1	49 726	65.6	34.4	2.57	2.27
Washington, DC-MD-VA-WV	18.0	1 942 641	95.1	4.9	0.8	1.4	4.1	1 848 064	64.0	36.0	2.75	2.35
Waterloo-Cedar Falls, IA	5.9	51 759	96.0	4.0	0.2	0.8	5.0	49 683	68.9	31.1	2.54	2.25
Wausau, WI........................	14.8	50 360	94.7	5.3	1.1	1.3	7.5	47 702	75.7	24.3	2.75	2.14
West Palm Beach-Boca Raton, FL	29.7	556 428	85.2	14.8	9.5	2.0	8.7	474 175	74.7	25.3	2.34	2.37
Wheeling, WV-OH	-1.0	69 216	89.9	10.1	1.4	1.7	10.0	62 249	73.6	26.4	2.45	2.08
Wichita Falls, TX	7.4	57 175	90.6	9.4	0.7	2.3	11.1	51 786	63.5	36.5	2.57	2.37
Wichita, KS........................	12.8	227 687	92.5	7.5	0.3	1.9	11.2	210 552	67.7	32.3	2.69	2.24
Williamsport, PA	4.6	52 464	89.6	10.4	4.8	1.6	7.6	47 003	69.4	30.6	2.57	2.14
Wilmington, NC....................	44.6	131 047	75.3	24.7	15.2	3.4	17.1	98 621	70.1	29.9	2.38	2.17
Yakima, WA........................	12.1	79 174	93.5	6.5	1.1	1.6	6.6	73 993	64.4	35.6	2.95	2.96
York, PA............................	15.2	156 720	94.6	5.4	0.6	1.5	7.4	148 219	76.1	23.9	2.61	2.23
Youngstown-Warren, OH	2.9	252 962	92.7	7.3	0.6	1.7	9.5	234 580	73.9	26.1	2.57	2.19
Yuba City, CA	10.9	50 955	93.4	6.6	1.0	1.6	5.7	47 568	58.3	41.7	2.83	2.92
Yuma, AZ............................	50.5	74 140	72.6	27.4	15.7	1.8	14.1	53 848	72.3	27.7	2.83	2.96

TABLE D:

Cities of 25,000 or More

(For explanation of symbols, see page xi.)

Page

Page	
488	**AL**(Auburn)—**CA**(Atascadero)
495	**CA**(Azusa)—**CA**(Hollister)
502	**CA**(Huntington Beach)—**CA**(Placentia)
509	**CA**(Pleasant Hill)—**CA**(Visalia)
516	**CA**(Vista)—**FL**(Bradenton)
523	**FL**(Cape Coral)—**GA**(Alpharetta)
530	**GA**(Athens-Clarke County)—**IL**(Elk Grove Village)
537	**IL**(Elmhurst)—**IN**(Kokomo)
544	**IN**(Lafayette)—**KY**(Richmond)
551	**LA**(Alexandria)—**MA**(Worcester)
558	**MI**(Allen Park)—**MN**(Oakdale)
565	**MN**(Plymouth)—**NE**(Omaha)
572	**NV**(Carson City)—**NY**(Hempstead)
579	**NY**(Ithaca)—**OH**(Dayton)
586	**OH**(Delaware)—**OR**(Keizer)
593	**OR**(Lake Oswego)—**TN**(Germantown)
600	**TN**(Hendersonville)—**TX**(McAllen)
607	**TX**(McKinney)—**VA**(Leesburg)
614	**VA**(Lynchburg)—**WI**(Oshkosh)
621	**WI**(Racine)—**WY**(Laramie)

Table C—Metropolitan Areas

Table D. Cities

STATE Place code	City	Population, 2000				Population, 1990				Population and population characteristics, 2000					
										Race (percent)					
										One race					
		Land area, 2000[1] (sq km)	Total persons	Rank	Per square kilometer	Land area, 1990[1] (sq km)	Total persons	Rank	Per square kilometer	White	Black or African American	American Indian or Alaska Native	Asian	Native Hawaiian and other Pacific Islander	Some other race
		1	2	3	4	5	6	7	8	9	10	11	12	13	14
00 00000	UNITED STATES	9 161 924	281 421 906	X	30.7	9 159 127	248 790 925	X	27.2	75.1	12.3	0.9	3.6	0.1	5.5
01 00000	ALABAMA...................	131 426.4	4 447 100	X	33.8	131 443.1	4 040 389	X	30.7	71.1	26.0	0.5	0.7	0.0	0.7
01 03076	Auburn	101.3	42 987	801	424.4	84.2	33 830	897	401.8	78.1	16.8	0.2	3.3	0.0	0.6
01 05980	Bessemer	105.4	29 672	1 242	281.5	100.2	33 581	912	335.1	28.9	69.6	0.3	0.2	0.0	0.3
01 07000	Birmingham	388.3	242 820	73	625.3	384.6	265 347	60	689.9	24.1	73.5	0.2	0.8	0.0	0.6
01 20104	Decatur	138.3	53 929	612	389.9	122.3	49 917	559	408.2	75.5	19.6	0.6	0.7	0.1	2.2
01 21184	Dothan	224.3	57 737	533	257.4	206.4	54 131	486	262.3	67.3	30.1	0.3	0.9	0.0	0.5
01 26896	Florence	64.6	36 264	976	561.4	60.9	36 426	824	598.1	78.4	19.2	0.2	0.6	0.0	0.5
01 28696	Gadsden	93.2	38 978	899	418.2	92.1	42 523	681	461.7	62.7	34.0	0.3	0.5	0.1	1.2
01 35800	Homewood	21.5	25 043	1 504	1 164.8	19.1	23 644	1 386	1 237.9	79.8	15.3	0.2	2.6	0.0	1.0
01 35896	Hoover	111.7	62 742	470	561.7	61.8	39 988	743	647.1	87.7	6.8	0.2	2.9	0.0	1.4
01 37000	Huntsville	450.8	158 216	131	351.0	425.8	159 880	111	375.5	64.5	30.2	0.5	2.2	0.1	0.7
01 45784	Madison	60.0	29 329	1 260	488.8	51.8	14 792	2 206	285.6	80.1	13.0	0.6	3.5	0.1	0.7
01 50000	Mobile	305.4	198 915	94	651.3	305.7	199 973	78	654.1	50.4	46.3	0.2	1.5	0.0	0.5
01 51000	Montgomery	402.4	201 568	89	500.9	349.6	190 350	84	544.5	47.7	49.6	0.2	1.1	0.0	0.4
01 59472	Phenix City	63.7	28 265	1 312	443.7	52.8	25 311	1 273	479.4	52.9	45.0	0.2	0.5	0.0	0.6
01 62496	Prichard	65.8	28 633	1 291	435.2	65.8	34 320	880	521.6	14.2	84.5	0.3	0.1	0.0	0.1
01 77256	Tuscaloosa	145.7	77 906	355	534.7	122.0	77 866	291	638.2	54.1	42.7	0.2	1.5	0.0	0.6
02 00000	ALASKA.....................	1 481 346.9	626 932	X	0.4	1 477 267.5	550 043	X	0.4	69.3	3.5	15.6	4.0	0.5	1.6
02 03000	Anchorage	4 395.8	260 283	67	59.2	4 396.9	226 338	69	51.5	72.2	5.8	7.3	5.5	0.9	2.2
02 24230	Fairbanks	82.5	30 224	1 213	366.4	80.1	30 843	1 019	380.3	66.7	11.2	9.9	2.7	0.5	2.4
02 36400	Juneau	7 036.1	30 711	1 195	4.4	6 717.3	26 751	1 193	4.0	74.8	0.8	11.4	4.7	0.4	1.1
04 00000	ARIZONA....................	294 312.2	5 130 632	X	17.4	294 333.5	3 665 339	X	12.5	75.5	3.1	5.0	1.8	0.1	11.6
04 02830	Apache Junction..........	88.7	31 814	1 143	358.7	42.6	18 092	1 817	424.7	92.7	0.6	1.0	0.5	0.1	3.1
04 04720	Avondale....................	106.9	35 883	991	335.7	57.3	17 595	1 874	307.1	63.3	5.2	1.3	1.9	0.1	24.3
04 08220	Bullhead City	117.1	33 769	1 071	288.4	111.6	21 951	1 498	196.7	85.6	1.0	1.3	1.0	0.1	8.3
04 10530	Casa Grande	124.8	25 224	1 493	202.1	56.4	19 076	1 717	338.2	64.9	4.3	4.9	1.2	0.1	21.1
04 12000	Chandler	149.9	176 581	118	1 178.0	123.2	89 862	233	729.4	77.2	3.5	1.2	4.2	0.1	10.8
04 23620	Flagstaff	164.7	52 894	628	321.2	163.8	45 857	625	280.0	77.9	1.8	10.0	1.2	0.1	6.1
04 27400	Gilbert	111.3	109 697	212	985.6	70.3	29 149	1 085	414.6	85.7	2.4	0.6	3.6	0.1	4.8
04 27820	Glendale	144.2	218 812	82	1 517.4	135.2	147 070	120	1 087.8	75.5	4.7	1.5	2.7	0.1	12.0
04 39370	Lake Havasu City	111.5	41 938	821	376.1	111.5	24 363	1 335	218.5	94.3	0.3	0.7	0.6	0.1	2.5
04 46000	Mesa	323.7	396 375	44	1 224.5	281.3	289 199	53	1 028.1	81.7	2.5	1.7	1.5	0.2	9.7
04 51600	Oro Valley town...........	82.4	29 700	1 238	360.4	NA	8 627	3 250	NA	93.1	1.1	0.4	1.9	0.1	1.8
04 54050	Peoria	358.0	108 364	218	302.7	159.2	51 080	537	320.9	84.9	2.8	0.7	1.9	0.1	7.1
04 55000	Phoenix	1 229.9	1 321 045	6	1 074.1	1 087.6	988 015	9	908.4	71.1	5.1	2.0	2.0	0.1	16.4
04 57380	Prescott	96.0	33 938	1 061	353.5	83.9	26 592	1 206	316.9	92.9	0.5	1.3	0.8	0.1	2.8
04 65000	Scottsdale	477.1	202 705	88	424.9	477.5	130 099	141	272.5	92.2	1.2	0.6	2.0	0.1	2.3
04 66820	Sierra Vista................	397.5	37 775	935	95.0	368.7	32 983	936	89.5	73.3	10.9	0.8	3.6	0.5	6.0
04 71510	Surprise city...............	180.0	30 848	1 190	171.4	NA	7 122	3 367	NA	86.0	2.6	0.4	1.1	0.1	7.9
04 73000	Tempe	103.8	158 625	130	1 528.2	102.4	141 993	125	1 386.7	77.5	3.7	2.0	4.7	0.3	8.5
04 77000	Tucson	504.2	486 699	32	965.3	404.8	415 444	34	1 026.3	70.2	4.3	2.3	2.5	0.2	16.8
04 85540	Yuma	276.2	77 515	358	280.6	56.6	56 966	449	1 006.5	68.3	3.2	1.5	1.5	0.2	21.4
05 00000	ARKANSAS	134 855.9	2 673 400	X	19.8	134 875.1	2 350 624	X	17.4	80.0	15.7	0.7	0.8	0.1	1.5
05 15190	Conway.......................	90.8	43 167	796	475.4	62.4	26 481	1 215	424.4	84.0	12.1	0.4	1.3	0.0	1.0
05 23290	Fayetteville	112.5	58 047	529	516.0	104.2	42 247	686	405.4	86.5	5.1	1.3	2.6	0.2	2.0
05 24550	Fort Smith	130.4	80 268	337	615.6	121.0	72 798	319	601.6	77.0	8.6	1.7	4.6	0.1	5.0
05 33400	Hot Springs	85.2	35 750	996	419.6	74.7	33 095	933	443.0	78.9	16.9	0.5	0.8	0.0	1.0
05 34750	Jacksonville	68.3	29 916	1 225	438.0	50.9	29 101	1 090	571.7	68.9	24.8	0.5	2.0	0.1	1.1
05 35710	Jonesboro	206.3	55 515	579	269.1	189.8	46 535	610	245.2	85.4	11.3	0.3	0.8	0.0	1.1
05 41000	Little Rock	301.0	183 133	114	608.4	266.4	175 727	98	659.6	55.1	40.4	0.3	1.7	0.0	1.3
05 50450	North Little Rock.........	116.1	60 433	493	520.5	102.9	61 829	405	600.9	62.6	34.0	0.4	0.6	0.0	1.2
05 55310	Pine Bluff	118.1	55 085	588	466.4	109.8	57 140	447	520.4	32.3	65.9	0.2	0.7	0.0	0.2
05 60410	Rogers	86.8	38 829	906	447.3	57.5	24 692	1 307	429.4	85.8	0.5	1.0	1.4	0.1	9.4
05 66080	Springdale	81.1	45 798	747	564.7	76.8	29 945	1 055	389.9	81.6	0.8	0.9	1.7	1.6	11.1
05 68810	Texarkana	82.5	26 448	1 413	320.6	43.0	22 631	1 453	526.3	65.9	31.0	0.5	0.5	0.0	0.6
05 74540	West Memphis.............	68.6	27 666	1 346	403.3	37.2	28 259	1 128	759.7	42.2	55.9	0.2	0.5	0.0	0.5
06 00000	CALIFORNIA	403 932.8	33 871 648	X	83.9	403 970.3	29 785 857	X	73.7	59.5	6.7	1.0	10.9	0.3	16.8
06 00562	Alameda	28.0	72 259	391	2 580.7	27.8	73 979	313	2 661.1	56.9	6.2	0.7	26.1	0.6	3.3
06 00884	Alhambra	19.7	85 804	306	4 355.5	19.7	82 087	273	4 166.9	30.0	1.7	0.7	47.2	0.1	16.3
06 02000	Anaheim	126.8	328 014	57	2 586.9	114.7	266 406	59	2 322.6	54.8	2.7	0.9	12.0	0.4	24.2
06 02252	Antioch.......................	69.8	90 532	282	1 297.0	50.7	62 195	399	1 226.7	65.3	9.7	0.9	7.4	0.4	9.2
06 02364	Apple Valley	189.9	54 239	604	285.6	174.1	46 079	620	264.7	76.4	7.9	1.0	2.2	0.2	7.9
06 02462	Arcadia	28.4	53 054	623	1 868.1	28.2	48 284	586	1 712.2	45.6	1.1	0.2	45.4	0.1	4.2
06 03064	Atascadero	69.2	26 411	1 416	381.7	65.4	23 138	1 413	353.8	88.8	2.4	0.9	1.3	0.1	3.2

[1]Dry land or land partially or temporarily covered by water.

Table D. Cities

City	Two or more races	White	Black	American Indian or Alaska Native	Asian	Native Hawaiian and other Pacific Islander	Some other race	Hispanic[1]	White	Black or African American	American Indian or Alaska Native	Asian and Pacific Islander	Hispanic[1]
	15	16	17	18	19	20	21	22	23	24	25	26	27
UNITED STATES	2.4	77.1	12.9	1.5	4.2	0.3	6.6	12.5	80.3	12.1	0.8	2.9	9.0
ALABAMA	1.0	72.0	26.3	1.0	0.9	0.1	0.9	1.7	73.6	25.3	0.4	0.5	0.6
Auburn	1.1	79.0	17.1	0.6	3.7	0.1	0.8	1.5	79.9	16.3	0.2	3.4	0.9
Bessemer	0.7	29.4	70.0	0.6	0.4	0.0	0.5	1.1	41.4	58.4	0.1	0.1	0.2
Birmingham	0.8	24.6	74.0	0.5	1.0	0.1	0.9	1.6	36.0	63.3	0.1	0.6	0.4
Decatur	1.3	76.6	20.0	1.1	0.9	0.2	2.6	5.6	82.4	16.5	0.3	0.6	0.8
Dothan	1.0	68.1	30.5	0.6	1.0	0.1	0.7	1.3	71.5	27.3	0.3	0.8	0.7
Florence	1.0	79.3	19.5	0.6	0.8	0.1	0.8	1.3	82.1	17.1	0.3	0.4	0.5
Gadsden	1.2	63.6	34.5	0.7	0.7	0.2	1.5	2.7	70.8	28.2	0.1	0.7	0.4
Homewood	1.2	80.7	15.6	0.5	2.9	0.1	1.4	2.8	90.0	8.2	0.2	1.3	0.8
Hoover	1.1	88.5	7.0	0.4	3.3	0.1	1.9	3.8	95.2	3.3	0.1	1.2	0.9
Huntsville	1.8	65.9	30.9	1.3	2.7	0.1	1.0	2.0	72.6	24.4	0.5	2.1	1.2
Madison	2.0	81.8	13.4	1.4	4.2	0.1	1.1	2.3	88.6	7.8	0.5	2.7	1.7
Mobile	1.0	51.1	46.7	0.6	1.7	0.1	0.8	1.4	59.6	38.9	0.2	1.0	1.0
Montgomery	1.0	48.4	50.1	0.5	1.4	0.1	0.6	1.2	56.5	42.3	0.2	0.7	0.8
Phenix City	0.8	53.5	45.3	0.5	0.8	0.1	0.8	1.5	59.4	40.0	0.2	0.3	0.6
Prichard	0.8	14.6	85.1	0.7	0.3	0.1	0.2	0.6	20.1	79.4	0.4	0.0	0.3
Tuscaloosa	0.9	54.8	43.1	0.4	1.8	0.1	0.9	1.4	62.8	35.5	0.1	1.3	0.8
ALASKA	5.4	74.0	4.3	19.0	5.2	0.9	2.4	4.1	75.5	4.1	15.6	3.6	3.2
Anchorage	6.0	77.2	7.2	10.4	7.1	1.4	3.3	5.7	80.7	6.4	6.4	4.8	4.1
Fairbanks	6.6	72.3	12.9	13.3	4.0	1.0	3.6	6.1	72.4	13.0	9.2	3.3	5.4
Juneau	6.9	80.5	1.4	16.6	6.7	0.7	1.8	3.4	80.6	1.1	12.9	4.3	2.8
ARIZONA	2.9	77.9	3.6	5.7	2.3	0.3	13.2	25.3	80.8	3.0	5.6	1.5	18.8
Apache Junction	2.0	94.5	0.8	1.8	0.9	0.2	3.9	8.8	96.4	0.4	0.8	0.4	5.6
Avondale	3.9	66.6	5.9	2.0	2.6	0.3	26.7	46.2	58.9	4.6	1.3	1.3	51.2
Bullhead City	2.8	88.1	1.2	2.1	1.4	0.2	9.8	20.2	95.3	0.5	0.8	0.7	6.5
Casa Grande	3.6	67.8	4.9	6.0	1.4	0.2	23.4	39.1	76.1	5.2	3.3	0.8	34.5
Chandler	3.0	79.7	4.1	1.8	5.1	0.3	12.3	21.0	85.2	2.6	1.2	2.4	17.3
Flagstaff	2.9	80.4	2.2	11.3	1.7	0.2	7.3	16.1	79.6	2.5	9.2	1.4	15.2
Gilbert	2.8	88.2	3.0	1.1	4.4	0.3	6.0	11.9	90.3	1.6	0.5	1.7	11.6
Glendale	3.5	78.5	5.5	2.1	3.5	0.3	13.8	24.8	85.0	3.0	0.9	2.1	15.5
Lake Havasu City	1.5	95.7	0.4	1.3	0.9	0.2	3.0	7.9	97.9	0.2	0.6	0.5	3.7
Mesa	2.8	84.1	3.1	2.3	2.0	0.4	11.1	19.7	90.1	1.9	1.0	1.5	10.9
Oro Valley town	1.6	94.5	1.4	0.7	2.4	0.2	2.4	7.5	96.7	0.6	0.4	1.0	6.5
Peoria	2.5	87.1	3.3	1.2	2.6	0.3	8.2	15.4	86.9	2.2	0.6	1.4	15.5
Phoenix	3.3	73.8	5.8	2.7	2.5	0.3	18.4	34.1	81.7	5.2	1.9	1.7	20.0
Prescott	1.6	94.4	0.7	2.0	1.2	0.2	3.3	8.2	95.2	0.5	1.2	0.6	7.1
Scottsdale	1.7	93.6	1.5	1.0	2.5	0.2	2.9	7.0	96.0	0.8	0.6	1.2	4.8
Sierra Vista	4.9	77.3	12.5	1.9	5.4	0.9	7.5	15.8	77.4	12.0	0.6	5.2	11.8
Surprise city	2.0	87.8	3.0	0.8	1.4	0.1	8.9	23.3	54.7	1.6	0.5	0.1	55.0
Tempe	3.3	80.2	4.4	2.7	5.6	0.5	10.2	17.9	86.8	3.2	1.3	4.1	10.9
Tucson	3.8	73.3	5.1	3.2	3.2	0.3	19.0	35.7	75.2	4.3	1.6	2.2	29.3
Yuma	3.9	71.7	3.8	2.2	2.1	0.3	23.9	45.7	73.0	3.8	1.1	1.7	35.6
ARKANSAS	1.3	81.2	16.0	1.4	1.0	0.1	1.8	3.2	82.7	15.9	0.5	0.5	0.8
Conway	1.2	85.1	12.5	0.7	1.5	0.1	1.3	2.3	88.8	10.0	0.3	0.7	0.5
Fayetteville	2.4	88.6	5.8	2.3	3.1	0.4	2.5	4.9	93.1	3.8	1.1	1.6	1.4
Fort Smith	3.0	79.6	9.4	3.2	5.1	0.1	5.8	8.8	86.3	7.7	1.4	4.1	1.4
Hot Springs	1.9	80.5	17.5	1.5	1.0	0.1	1.3	3.8	83.1	15.5	0.5	0.4	1.3
Jacksonville	2.6	71.0	25.9	1.1	2.8	0.2	1.7	3.4	79.4	17.0	0.5	2.3	2.3
Jonesboro	1.1	86.4	11.6	0.8	1.1	0.1	1.3	2.3	90.8	8.0	0.3	0.8	0.5
Little Rock	1.3	56.1	41.0	0.7	1.9	0.1	1.6	2.7	64.7	34.0	0.3	0.9	0.8
North Little Rock	1.3	63.5	34.6	1.0	0.8	0.1	1.4	2.4	75.3	23.6	0.3	0.4	0.8
Pine Bluff	0.7	32.8	66.3	0.5	0.9	0.1	0.3	0.8	45.8	53.5	0.2	0.5	0.4
Rogers	1.8	87.4	0.7	1.7	1.7	0.1	10.3	19.3	97.7	0.1	0.9	0.8	1.9
Springdale	2.3	83.4	1.1	1.8	2.0	2.0	12.2	19.7	97.2	0.1	1.1	1.0	1.5
Texarkana	1.5	67.2	31.5	1.2	0.6	0.0	1.0	1.8	67.2	31.7	0.3	0.5	0.8
West Memphis	0.6	42.6	56.3	0.5	0.6	0.1	0.6	1.0	56.9	42.1	0.2	0.5	0.5
CALIFORNIA	4.7	63.4	7.4	1.9	12.3	0.7	19.4	32.4	69.0	7.4	0.8	9.6	25.8
Alameda	6.1	61.9	7.5	1.6	28.9	1.2	5.5	9.3	69.9	6.7	0.7	19.2	9.1
Alhambra	4.0	33.0	2.1	1.2	48.8	0.3	18.8	35.5	40.9	2.0	0.4	38.1	36.1
Anaheim	5.0	59.0	3.2	1.5	13.2	0.7	27.6	46.8	71.4	2.5	0.5	9.4	31.4
Antioch	7.0	71.2	11.1	2.3	9.6	0.9	12.5	22.1	85.4	2.6	1.1	4.8	15.6
Apple Valley	4.4	80.3	8.8	2.3	3.0	0.4	9.9	18.6	86.8	3.9	1.0	2.5	12.6
Arcadia	3.4	47.9	1.5	0.7	47.2	0.5	5.9	10.6	71.5	0.8	0.4	23.4	10.7
Atascadero	3.3	91.9	2.8	2.2	2.0	0.3	4.4	10.5	94.0	1.1	1.2	1.1	8.5

[1] Hispanic persons may be of any race.

Table D. Cities

City	Population and population characteristics, 2000										
	Age (percent)										
	Under 5 years	5 to 17 years	18 to 24 years	25 to 34 years	35 to 44 years	45 to 54 years	55 to 64 years	65 to 74 years	75 years and over	Median age (years)	Percent Female
	28	29	30	31	32	33	34	35	36	37	38
UNITED STATES	6.8	18.9	9.7	14.2	16.0	13.4	8.6	6.5	5.9	35.3	50.9
ALABAMA	6.7	18.6	9.9	13.6	15.4	13.5	9.3	7.1	5.9	35.8	51.7
Auburn..........................	4.1	11.2	44.6	12.7	9.2	7.4	4.3	3.2	3.2	22.6	50.1
Bessemer......................	7.7	19.1	9.6	12.3	13.7	12.6	8.5	8.2	8.2	35.9	54.7
Birmingham...................	6.8	18.2	11.1	14.9	15.1	12.9	7.5	6.7	6.7	34.3	53.9
Decatur........................	6.8	18.6	8.8	13.7	15.9	13.8	9.3	7.0	6.1	36.3	52.0
Dothan.........................	6.9	18.6	8.4	12.9	15.3	14.0	9.4	7.6	6.9	37.2	53.1
Florence.......................	5.8	15.7	13.7	12.4	13.2	12.5	9.2	8.7	8.8	36.9	54.3
Gadsden.......................	6.6	16.5	9.5	12.7	12.6	12.8	9.2	9.7	10.4	39.0	54.0
Homewood....................	6.3	14.0	17.8	19.6	14.3	11.5	5.8	4.5	6.1	30.5	53.8
Hoover.........................	6.6	18.2	7.9	15.3	17.4	15.3	8.4	5.8	5.1	36.2	51.3
Huntsville.....................	6.2	17.0	10.7	13.5	15.9	13.3	10.1	7.7	5.7	36.7	51.9
Madison........................	7.8	22.5	6.8	13.9	21.9	14.5	7.1	3.4	2.1	34.5	50.6
Mobile.........................	7.3	19.2	10.8	13.6	14.4	12.7	8.3	6.9	6.8	34.3	53.2
Montgomery...................	7.1	18.9	12.1	14.7	15.0	12.6	7.7	6.1	5.7	32.9	53.1
Phenix City...................	7.1	19.2	9.6	14.0	14.7	12.4	8.8	8.0	6.3	35.1	53.7
Prichard.......................	7.8	23.6	11.4	10.3	14.3	12.7	8.3	6.0	5.5	31.8	54.3
Tuscaloosa	5.7	14.1	24.5	13.5	11.9	11.5	6.9	6.3	5.5	28.4	52.4
ALASKA	7.6	22.8	9.1	14.3	18.2	15.1	7.1	3.6	2.1	32.4	48.3
Anchorage.....................	7.7	21.5	9.6	15.4	18.5	14.9	7.0	3.4	2.1	32.4	49.4
Fairbanks......................	9.6	19.8	14.7	18.5	14.4	10.8	5.6	3.6	3.0	27.6	48.7
Juneau.........................	6.5	20.9	8.1	14.0	18.8	18.0	7.7	3.5	2.6	35.3	49.6
ARIZONA	7.5	19.2	10.0	14.5	15.0	12.2	8.6	7.1	5.9	34.2	50.1
Apache Junction	6.3	14.2	6.9	11.6	12.1	11.0	12.6	14.4	10.9	44.1	51.1
Avondale.......................	9.8	24.5	9.7	16.8	16.2	11.5	6.2	3.2	2.1	29.0	49.4
Bullhead City	6.4	16.1	7.3	11.3	13.2	13.0	13.6	11.5	7.7	41.8	50.3
Casa Grande	8.7	22.2	9.3	13.1	13.3	11.0	8.6	8.2	5.6	32.3	50.7
Chandler.......................	9.1	20.7	8.6	19.0	19.0	11.8	6.0	3.4	2.4	31.2	50.1
Flagstaff.......................	6.7	17.6	21.7	16.4	14.1	12.2	6.1	3.1	2.2	26.8	50.4
Gilbert.........................	10.3	23.9	7.4	18.4	19.4	11.7	5.2	2.4	1.4	30.1	50.3
Glendale.......................	8.5	21.6	10.8	15.5	16.4	12.7	7.1	4.0	3.4	30.8	50.1
Lake Havasu City	4.7	14.8	5.7	8.8	12.8	12.7	15.0	15.2	10.3	47.5	50.8
Mesa...........................	8.2	19.1	11.2	15.5	14.2	11.1	7.3	6.7	6.6	32.0	50.5
Oro Valley town	5.0	16.5	4.5	8.3	15.3	14.8	12.9	14.3	8.4	45.3	51.5
Peoria.........................	7.4	21.0	6.7	13.9	16.8	11.9	8.0	6.9	7.5	35.6	52.0
Phoenix........................	8.7	20.3	10.9	17.2	16.0	11.9	6.9	4.4	3.7	30.7	49.1
Prescott.......................	3.7	12.1	11.2	8.1	10.8	13.9	13.4	13.8	13.0	47.8	50.8
Scottsdale	5.2	14.2	6.6	14.3	16.1	15.1	11.9	9.2	7.5	41.0	51.8
Sierra Vista	7.7	18.1	13.0	15.4	13.8	11.0	8.9	7.1	5.0	32.0	49.8
Surprise city	7.3	12.6	7.0	13.6	8.8	8.9	16.4	17.1	8.4	46.1	50.9
Tempe.........................	5.7	14.1	21.3	19.4	13.8	11.8	6.7	3.9	3.3	28.8	48.3
Tucson.........................	7.2	17.3	13.8	15.7	14.9	11.8	7.3	6.0	5.9	32.1	51.0
Yuma...........................	8.7	20.9	11.9	13.5	13.6	10.1	7.4	7.4	6.5	31.2	50.2
ARKANSAS	6.8	18.7	9.8	13.2	14.9	13.1	9.6	7.4	6.6	36.0	51.2
Conway.........................	6.9	16.4	22.4	15.7	13.5	10.3	5.8	4.3	4.7	27.3	52.5
Fayetteville....................	6.5	13.4	25.7	17.3	12.6	10.5	5.3	4.1	4.6	26.9	49.3
Fort Smith	7.6	17.8	9.8	14.3	15.0	13.1	8.7	6.7	7.0	35.3	51.5
Hot Springs	5.9	14.3	8.2	11.4	13.9	12.9	10.1	10.7	12.6	42.4	53.1
Jacksonville...................	9.5	19.5	12.8	17.7	15.6	10.6	7.1	4.7	2.7	29.5	49.9
Jonesboro.....................	6.7	16.2	16.6	14.5	13.6	12.5	8.1	6.2	5.6	31.8	52.1
Little Rock.....................	7.1	17.6	10.0	16.1	15.6	14.1	7.9	5.7	5.9	34.5	52.9
North Little Rock.............	7.1	18.3	9.0	13.4	14.9	13.8	8.7	7.3	7.3	36.5	53.3
Pine Bluff	7.4	20.1	12.2	12.7	14.2	12.0	7.7	6.6	7.1	33.1	52.7
Rogers.........................	8.9	20.6	9.0	15.9	15.6	11.1	7.2	5.7	6.1	32.3	51.2
Springdale.....................	9.3	19.7	10.7	16.3	15.1	11.1	7.6	5.2	5.0	31.0	50.4
Texarkana......................	7.6	18.3	10.1	14.2	14.3	12.8	8.7	6.9	7.1	34.8	52.1
West Memphis................	8.5	23.0	9.8	13.7	14.5	11.9	8.1	5.4	5.0	31.3	53.6
CALIFORNIA	7.3	20.0	9.9	15.4	16.2	12.8	7.7	5.6	5.0	33.3	50.2
Alameda........................	5.6	15.9	7.0	15.3	18.2	15.8	8.8	6.5	6.8	38.3	52.0
Alhambra	6.2	16.1	9.7	18.0	16.0	12.9	7.9	6.4	6.8	35.0	52.9
Anaheim........................	9.2	21.0	10.5	17.8	15.7	11.0	6.7	4.4	3.8	30.3	50.0
Antioch.........................	8.6	23.6	8.2	14.0	18.4	13.0	6.7	4.1	3.3	32.3	51.0
Apple Valley	7.1	24.4	7.8	10.0	15.1	12.7	9.0	7.9	5.9	35.4	51.6
Arcadia.........................	4.6	18.7	7.5	10.8	16.4	16.3	10.3	7.5	8.0	40.5	53.0
Atascadero....................	5.4	20.3	8.3	10.9	17.8	17.1	8.7	6.1	5.4	38.2	48.5

Table D. Cities

City	Age (percent)										Population—change, 1980–2000				
											Total persons			Percent change	
	Under 5 years	5 to 17 years	18 to 24 years	25 to 34 years	35 to 44 years	45 to 54 years	55 to 64 years	65 to 74 years	75 years and over	Percent Female	2000	1990	1980	1990–2000	1980–1990
	39	40	41	42	43	44	45	46	47	48	49	50	51	52	53
UNITED STATES	7.4	18.2	10.8	17.4	15.1	10.1	8.5	7.3	5.3	51.3	281 421 906	248 790 925	226 542 204	13.1	9.8
ALABAMA	7.0	19.2	11.0	16.0	14.4	10.4	9.0	7.5	5.5	52.1	4 447 100	4 040 389	3 894 025	10.1	3.8
Auburn	4.1	10.9	47.3	13.8	8.0	6.4	4.0	3.1	2.4	49.3	42 987	33 830	28 471	27.1	18.8
Bessemer	7.5	19.2	9.8	14.6	12.7	8.9	9.5	9.6	8.1	54.7	29 672	33 581	31 729	-11.6	5.8
Birmingham	7.4	18.0	10.5	17.8	14.4	8.4	8.6	8.0	6.8	54.3	242 820	265 347	284 413	-8.5	-6.7
Decatur	7.0	18.6	9.1	17.5	14.9	11.7	9.0	7.3	4.9	52.4	53 929	49 917	42 002	8.0	18.8
Dothan	7.4	20.5	9.0	15.9	15.9	9.9	8.8	7.6	5.1	53.1	57 737	54 143	48 750	6.6	11.1
Florence	6.8	15.9	13.6	14.9	12.9	9.9	9.6	9.3	7.1	54.2	36 264	36 426	37 029	-0.4	-1.6
Gadsden	6.3	16.8	9.6	14.0	12.5	9.5	10.9	11.5	8.8	54.5	38 978	42 523	47 565	-8.3	-10.6
Homewood	6.0	12.1	15.8	22.2	15.8	7.3	7.0	7.7	6.1	55.0	25 043	23 644	21 412	5.9	10.4
Hoover	6.5	17.1	9.1	18.3	18.7	11.7	8.8	6.6	3.3	52.7	62 742	40 000	19 792	56.9	102.1
Huntsville	6.5	16.8	12.0	18.8	14.4	12.0	9.6	6.2	3.8	51.4	158 216	159 880	142 513	-1.0	12.2
Madison	9.9	15.8	8.8	29.2	16.7	10.5	5.6	2.2	1.3	49.4	29 329	14 792	NA	98.3	NA
Mobile	7.5	18.8	10.9	16.8	14.4	9.4	8.6	8.0	5.7	53.6	198 915	196 263	200 396	1.4	-2.1
Montgomery	7.8	20.1	10.9	17.2	14.9	9.4	8.0	6.7	5.0	53.5	201 568	190 350	177 857	5.9	7.0
Phenix City	7.5	18.8	9.5	15.9	13.9	10.0	9.8	8.6	5.9	53.7	28 265	25 311	26 941	11.7	-6.1
Prichard	8.9	26.3	10.0	14.5	13.7	8.2	7.3	6.7	4.5	54.5	28 633	34 320	39 518	-16.6	-13.2
Tuscaloosa	5.6	15.1	23.5	15.7	12.3	8.3	8.0	6.7	4.8	52.2	77 906	77 759	75 211	0.2	3.4
ALASKA	10.0	21.4	10.2	20.5	18.7	9.8	5.4	2.8	1.2	47.3	626 932	550 043	401 851	14.0	36.9
Anchorage	9.4	19.9	10.3	21.6	19.1	10.8	5.3	2.6	1.0	48.6	260 283	226 338	174 431	15.0	29.8
Fairbanks	10.9	18.1	16.4	22.8	14.4	7.5	5.1	3.1	1.9	46.4	30 224	30 843	22 645	-2.0	36.2
Juneau	9.0	20.5	7.8	19.1	21.5	11.6	5.3	3.2	2.0	49.3	30 711	26 751	19 528	14.8	37.0
ARIZONA	8.0	18.8	10.7	17.3	14.4	9.5	8.2	7.9	5.1	50.6	5 130 632	3 665 339	2 716 546	40.0	34.9
Apache Junction	6.1	16.2	5.8	13.2	11.1	10.3	11.9	15.5	9.8	51.3	31 814	18 092	NA	75.8	NA
Avondale	11.2	24.8	11.7	17.2	12.4	9.7	6.1	4.5	2.5	49.6	35 883	17 595	NA	103.9	NA
Bullhead City	5.8	12.1	7.4	14.4	14.1	11.3	14.0	14.7	6.2	49.9	33 769	21 951	10 364	53.8	111.3
Casa Grande	9.9	22.8	10.2	15.2	14.7	9.4	7.3	6.3	4.1	51.0	25 224	19 076	NA	32.2	NA
Chandler	10.5	21.3	9.0	24.5	17.1	8.1	4.6	3.3	1.7	50.4	176 581	89 862	29 720	96.5	202.4
Flagstaff	7.0	17.7	26.3	17.7	14.4	8.2	4.3	2.9	1.5	50.4	52 894	45 857	34 743	15.3	32.0
Gilbert	10.9	24.8	10.0	21.4	17.1	8.6	3.9	2.3	0.9	50.1	109 697	29 149	NA	276.3	NA
Glendale	8.2	20.9	11.1	18.2	16.9	10.4	6.5	4.6	3.3	51.0	218 812	147 864	97 172	48.0	52.2
Lake Havasu City	4.9	14.4	6.0	12.5	12.5	11.1	14.7	16.7	7.1	50.4	41 938	24 363	NA	72.1	NA
Mesa	8.7	19.9	10.8	19.0	14.1	8.6	6.6	7.3	5.1	50.9	396 375	289 199	152 453	37.1	89.7
Oro Valley town	NA	NA	NA	NA	NA	NA	NA	NA	NA	NA	29 700	8 627	NA	244.3	NA
Peoria	9.4	19.6	5.9	20.1	14.3	8.2	7.4	8.2	6.8	52.1	108 364	50 675	12 251	113.8	313.6
Phoenix	8.5	18.6	10.5	19.7	15.5	10.1	7.4	6.0	3.7	50.4	1 321 045	984 310	789 704	34.2	24.6
Prescott	4.7	12.9	10.0	11.1	11.7	10.6	12.9	15.4	10.7	51.3	33 938	26 592	20 055	27.6	32.6
Scottsdale	5.1	12.7	8.6	17.5	15.2	13.2	11.5	9.9	6.3	52.9	202 705	130 075	88 412	55.8	47.1
Sierra Vista	7.8	18.9	13.9	21.2	14.1	9.8	7.0	5.0	2.2	48.6	37 775	32 983	24 937	14.5	32.3
Surprise city	NA	NA	NA	NA	NA	NA	NA	NA	NA	NA	30 848	7 122	NA	333.1	NA
Tempe	6.5	14.9	20.4	21.4	15.2	9.3	5.8	4.0	2.6	48.6	158 625	141 993	106 743	11.7	33.0
Tucson	7.7	16.7	14.3	19.0	14.0	8.2	7.5	7.3	5.3	51.3	486 699	411 480	330 537	18.3	24.5
Yuma	9.9	20.7	10.5	18.0	13.0	8.5	7.0	7.5	4.9	50.6	77 515	56 966	42 433	36.1	34.2
ARKANSAS	7.0	19.4	10.1	15.3	13.9	10.4	9.1	8.3	6.6	51.8	2 673 400	2 350 624	2 286 357	13.7	2.8
Conway	6.3	14.7	25.8	15.4	12.5	7.5	5.9	6.3	5.5	53.7	43 167	26 481	20 375	63.0	30.0
Fayetteville	6.5	14.0	25.4	18.5	12.5	7.9	5.6	5.1	4.5	50.0	58 047	42 247	36 608	37.4	15.4
Fort Smith	7.5	17.9	9.6	17.0	14.6	10.2	8.4	8.3	6.5	52.2	80 268	72 798	71 626	10.3	1.6
Hot Springs	5.9	14.3	7.8	13.3	12.1	9.6	11.4	12.6	12.8	54.7	35 750	32 462	35 781	10.1	-9.3
Jacksonville	10.3	20.7	13.8	21.9	13.2	8.1	6.1	3.4	2.6	49.7	29 916	29 101	NA	2.8	NA
Jonesboro	7.1	16.4	17.1	16.8	13.7	9.7	8.2	6.3	4.8	52.1	55 515	46 535	31 530	19.3	47.6
Little Rock	7.3	17.6	10.3	18.9	16.0	9.7	7.7	7.0	5.5	53.6	183 133	175 727	158 461	4.2	10.9
North Little Rock	7.0	18.3	8.9	16.4	14.6	10.5	8.9	9.1	6.3	53.1	60 433	61 829	64 288	-2.3	-3.8
Pine Bluff	7.8	21.1	11.2	14.8	12.9	8.6	8.5	8.0	7.0	54.3	55 085	57 140	56 636	-3.6	0.9
Rogers	7.5	18.0	9.1	17.3	13.8	9.9	8.2	8.7	7.6	52.1	38 829	24 692	17 429	57.3	41.7
Springdale	7.8	18.8	10.2	17.0	14.3	11.1	8.2	7.1	5.5	52.1	45 798	29 945	23 440	52.9	27.8
Texarkana	7.5	20.5	9.6	15.9	12.7	9.7	8.4	8.0	7.6	53.6	26 448	22 631	21 459	16.9	5.5
West Memphis	9.0	22.0	10.5	16.3	14.5	9.7	7.7	6.3	4.1	53.6	27 666	28 259	28 138	-2.1	0.4
CALIFORNIA	8.1	18.0	11.5	19.1	15.6	9.8	7.5	6.2	4.3	49.9	33 871 648	29 758 213	23 667 765	13.8	25.7
Alameda	6.4	13.5	12.7	21.2	17.7	9.6	7.1	6.7	5.0	47.2	72 259	73 979	63 852	-2.3	15.9
Alhambra	7.2	15.8	11.7	21.3	15.4	8.8	7.1	6.5	6.3	52.4	85 804	82 087	64 615	4.5	27.0
Anaheim	8.6	17.3	13.1	21.2	14.5	9.7	7.5	5.0	3.1	49.4	328 014	266 406	219 311	23.1	21.5
Antioch	10.0	21.1	9.3	19.2	17.6	9.4	5.9	4.5	3.0	50.7	90 532	62 195	42 683	45.6	45.7
Apple Valley	9.6	22.1	8.4	17.1	14.8	10.0	8.1	7.0	3.0	50.6	54 239	46 079	14 305	17.7	222.1
Arcadia	4.5	17.1	8.8	13.6	15.6	14.3	10.2	9.0	6.9	52.9	53 054	48 284	45 994	9.9	5.0
Atascadero	8.2	20.6	8.8	16.6	18.7	9.6	6.5	6.5	4.6	50.7	26 411	23 138	16 232	14.1	42.5

Table D. Cities

City	Total population	Total in households	House-holder	Spouse	Child Total	Child Own child under 18 years	Other relatives Total	Other relatives Under 18 years	Nonrelatives Total	Nonrelatives Unmarried partner	Total in group quarters	Correctional institutions	Nursing homes	Other institutions	College dormitories	Military quarters	Other
	54	55	56	57	58	59	60	61	62	63	64	65	66	67	68	69	70
UNITED STATES	281 421 906	97.2	37.5	19.4	29.6	22.9	5.6	2.1	5.2	1.9	2.8	0.7	0.6	0.1	0.7	0.1	0.5
ALABAMA......................	4 447 100	97.4	39.1	20.4	29.3	22.3	5.4	2.5	3.3	1.3	2.6	0.8	0.6	0.1	0.7	0.1	0.3
Auburn......................	42 987	91.0	42.9	12.3	17.1	14.1	3.1	0.9	15.7	1.2	9.0	0.0	0.2	0.1	8.2	0.0	0.4
Bessemer...................	29 672	97.9	38.9	13.5	32.1	21.1	10.6	5.3	2.9	1.3	2.1	0.7	1.0	0.3	0.0	0.0	0.1
Birmingham................	242 820	96.4	40.7	12.6	29.5	20.1	8.9	4.3	4.7	1.8	3.6	0.7	0.8	0.2	0.9	0.0	1.2
Decatur.....................	53 929	98.3	40.5	20.5	29.3	23.1	4.7	1.9	3.3	1.3	1.7	0.6	0.6	0.0	0.0	0.0	0.6
Dothan......................	57 737	98.0	41.0	20.1	29.0	22.8	4.7	2.2	3.3	1.5	2.0	0.7	1.0	0.2	0.0	0.0	0.2
Florence....................	36 264	95.9	43.6	19.0	25.4	19.5	3.7	1.5	4.2	1.3	4.1	0.6	1.3	0.1	1.7	0.0	0.3
Gadsden....................	38 978	96.3	42.2	17.1	26.1	18.7	7.1	3.4	3.8	1.5	3.7	1.0	1.2	0.1	0.2	0.0	1.2
Homewood..................	25 043	92.3	42.7	17.5	23.2	19.3	3.1	0.8	5.8	1.3	7.7	0.1	0.0	0.5	7.2	0.0	0.0
Hoover......................	62 742	99.2	40.2	23.8	28.5	23.8	3.1	0.8	3.6	1.0	0.8	0.0	0.7	0.0	0.0	0.0	0.1
Huntsville..................	158 216	96.5	42.2	19.2	26.6	20.7	4.5	2.0	4.0	1.5	3.5	0.6	0.5	0.0	2.1	0.0	0.3
Madison....................	29 329	99.1	38.0	22.8	33.5	29.0	2.3	0.9	2.5	1.0	0.9	0.0	0.6	0.1	0.0	0.0	0.2
Mobile......................	198 915	96.9	39.5	16.2	30.3	22.6	6.8	3.4	4.1	1.6	3.1	0.5	0.8	0.1	1.3	0.0	0.4
Montgomery...............	201 568	94.9	38.9	16.5	29.5	22.4	6.2	3.0	3.8	1.6	5.1	0.7	0.8	0.1	1.5	1.7	0.4
Phenix City................	28 265	97.6	40.7	16.1	30.7	22.6	6.7	3.2	3.5	1.8	2.4	1.0	1.1	0.0	0.0	0.0	0.2
Prichard....................	28 633	97.4	34.4	11.3	36.9	24.6	11.5	6.3	3.4	1.7	2.6	0.8	0.6	0.0	0.9	0.0	0.2
Tuscaloosa.................	77 906	89.6	40.3	14.1	22.6	16.9	5.3	2.5	7.3	1.6	10.4	0.6	0.9	1.0	7.6	0.0	0.3
ALASKA......................	626 932	96.9	35.3	18.6	32.9	27.8	3.9	1.7	6.2	2.6	3.1	0.5	0.1	0.1	0.3	0.6	1.4
Anchorage	260 283	97.3	36.4	18.6	31.5	26.7	3.8	1.5	6.9	2.7	2.7	0.4	0.1	0.2	0.2	0.8	1.0
Fairbanks..................	30 224	93.7	36.6	17.3	31.0	27.3	2.8	1.3	6.0	2.7	6.3	0.7	0.3	0.1	0.0	4.1	1.1
Juneau	30 711	97.8	37.6	19.2	29.5	24.9	3.5	1.3	8.0	3.0	2.2	0.5	0.1	0.1	0.4	0.0	1.0
ARIZONA.....................	5 130 632	97.9	37.1	19.2	29.2	23.3	6.2	2.6	6.2	2.3	2.1	0.9	0.3	0.1	0.3	0.1	0.5
Apache Junction..........	31 814	99.3	43.3	22.9	22.1	18.0	4.6	1.8	6.4	2.8	0.7	0.0	0.0	0.0	0.0	0.0	0.7
Avondale...................	35 883	99.6	29.7	18.7	36.7	29.1	9.3	4.3	5.3	2.1	0.4	0.1	0.3	0.0	0.0	0.0	0.0
Bullhead City.............	33 769	99.7	41.2	20.2	23.8	19.2	6.1	2.4	8.3	3.8	0.3	0.0	0.2	0.0	0.0	0.0	0.1
Casa Grande..............	25 224	98.9	35.4	18.5	32.6	26.6	6.9	3.5	5.5	2.6	1.1	0.0	0.5	0.0	0.0	0.0	0.6
Chandler...................	176 581	99.6	35.3	20.3	32.7	27.5	5.2	1.7	6.1	2.2	0.4	0.0	0.2	0.0	0.0	0.0	0.2
Flagstaff...................	52 894	94.6	36.5	16.0	26.4	22.0	4.2	1.6	11.5	2.9	5.4	0.1	0.1	0.1	4.6	0.0	0.4
Gilbert......................	109 697	99.9	32.3	22.4	37.5	32.5	3.7	1.3	4.0	1.6	0.1	0.0	0.0	0.0	0.0	0.0	0.0
Glendale	218 812	98.7	34.6	18.5	33.2	26.8	6.3	2.5	6.1	2.4	1.3	0.0	0.5	0.0	0.2	0.3	0.4
Lake Havasu City	41 938	99.2	42.7	25.4	21.8	17.3	4.0	1.5	5.4	2.5	0.8	0.0	0.6	0.0	0.0	0.0	0.2
Mesa........................	396 375	99.0	37.0	19.5	30.4	24.7	5.6	2.0	6.6	2.3	1.0	0.0	0.4	0.1	0.0	0.0	0.4
Oro Valley town	29 700	99.5	41.2	28.8	24.7	20.6	2.1	0.6	2.6	1.3	0.5	0.0	0.1	0.0	0.0	0.0	0.4
Peoria......................	108 364	98.6	36.2	22.4	31.5	26.1	4.4	1.7	4.1	1.7	1.4	0.0	0.8	0.0	0.0	0.0	0.6
Phoenix.....................	1 321 045	98.3	35.3	16.5	30.9	24.9	8.0	3.1	7.6	2.6	1.7	0.7	0.1	0.1	0.0	0.0	0.7
Prescott....................	33 938	94.0	44.5	21.7	17.9	14.0	3.1	1.2	6.8	2.1	6.0	0.1	2.2	0.3	2.7	0.0	0.8
Scottsdale.................	202 705	99.2	44.7	22.2	22.6	18.1	3.3	0.9	6.3	2.3	0.8	0.0	0.2	0.0	0.0	0.0	0.6
Sierra Vista...............	37 775	93.2	37.6	21.2	27.6	23.8	3.0	1.4	3.7	1.6	6.8	0.0	0.7	0.0	0.0	5.9	0.2
Surprise city..............	30 848	99.6	40.5	28.1	21.2	17.2	5.7	2.2	4.0	1.7	0.4	0.0	0.2	0.0	0.0	0.0	0.2
Tempe......................	158 625	96.7	40.1	15.4	22.8	17.7	5.2	1.6	13.2	2.8	3.3	0.0	0.2	0.0	2.9	0.0	0.2
Tucson......................	486 699	96.1	39.6	15.7	27.4	21.4	6.0	2.5	7.4	2.8	3.9	1.3	0.2	0.1	1.4	0.1	0.8
Yuma	77 515	95.9	34.4	19.5	32.3	26.5	5.6	2.6	4.2	1.9	4.1	0.6	0.7	0.0	0.3	2.1	0.2
ARKANSAS	2 673 400	97.2	39.0	21.2	28.4	22.5	4.9	2.3	3.7	1.5	2.8	0.8	0.8	0.1	0.7	0.0	0.3
Conway.....................	43 167	90.6	37.2	18.2	25.9	21.8	2.8	0.9	6.6	1.4	9.4	0.3	0.9	0.0	6.4	0.0	1.7
Fayetteville................	58 047	90.8	41.0	15.5	21.4	18.3	3.0	0.9	10.0	2.4	9.2	0.5	1.4	0.5	6.4	0.0	0.3
Fort Smith.................	80 268	97.5	40.4	19.0	28.1	22.7	5.1	2.0	5.0	2.1	2.5	0.7	0.8	0.6	0.0	0.0	0.4
Hot Springs...............	35 750	95.6	45.0	18.1	22.4	17.3	5.2	2.2	4.8	2.0	4.4	0.9	2.0	0.2	0.9	0.0	0.5
Jacksonville...............	29 916	96.0	36.4	20.1	31.8	26.6	3.8	1.9	3.9	1.7	4.0	0.0	0.1	0.0	0.0	3.6	0.3
Jonesboro	55 515	95.4	40.0	19.6	26.1	20.8	4.1	1.6	5.5	1.6	4.6	0.4	0.9	0.0	2.7	0.0	0.6
Little Rock	183 133	97.3	42.2	17.1	27.5	21.5	5.6	2.5	4.9	1.8	2.7	0.7	0.6	0.3	0.4	0.0	0.8
North Little Rock.........	60 433	99.1	42.3	17.7	29.0	22.3	6.0	2.7	4.3	1.6	0.9	0.0	0.7	0.0	0.0	0.0	0.2
Pine Bluff..................	55 085	93.1	36.2	14.0	30.6	22.3	8.6	3.6	3.6	1.6	6.9	3.4	1.4	0.0	1.9	0.0	0.3
Rogers	38 829	98.8	36.1	21.1	31.7	27.0	5.4	1.8	4.5	1.7	1.2	0.0	1.1	0.0	0.0	0.0	0.1
Springdale.................	45 798	98.7	35.3	20.5	31.0	25.7	7.1	2.6	4.9	1.6	1.3	0.1	0.6	0.4	0.0	0.0	0.1
Texarkana.................	26 448	96.0	39.3	17.8	29.4	22.4	5.9	2.9	3.7	1.6	4.0	2.2	1.1	0.1	0.0	0.0	0.6
West Memphis............	27 666	98.1	36.3	14.7	33.5	25.8	9.4	5.2	4.3	2.3	1.9	0.9	0.8	0.0	0.0	0.0	0.2
CALIFORNIA	33 871 648	97.6	34.0	17.4	31.1	23.7	8.4	2.8	6.8	2.0	2.4	0.7	0.4	0.1	0.4	0.2	0.7
Alameda....................	72 259	98.5	41.8	18.3	26.2	19.7	5.9	1.5	6.2	2.6	1.5	0.0	0.5	0.2	0.0	0.3	0.5
Alhambra...................	85 804	97.8	33.9	16.4	29.0	19.5	12.6	2.5	5.8	1.5	2.2	0.0	1.1	0.0	0.9	0.0	0.2
Anaheim....................	328 014	98.8	29.6	16.6	33.7	25.9	11.3	3.4	7.7	1.8	1.2	0.0	0.4	0.0	0.0	0.0	0.8
Antioch.....................	90 532	99.5	32.4	19.5	35.9	26.6	6.6	2.6	5.1	2.0	0.5	0.0	0.3	0.0	0.0	0.0	0.2
Apple Valley	54 239	99.3	34.2	19.8	34.4	27.7	5.9	2.8	5.1	2.2	0.7	0.0	0.3	0.1	0.0	0.0	0.3
Arcadia.....................	53 054	98.9	36.1	20.9	30.5	21.6	8.0	1.4	3.5	1.0	1.1	0.0	0.8	0.0	0.0	0.0	0.3
Atascadero................	26 411	94.4	36.1	20.0	29.3	23.6	3.6	1.3	5.5	2.3	5.6	0.0	0.2	4.6	0.0	0.0	0.7

Table D. Cities

City	Households by type, 2000												Households, 1990		
		Family households						Nonfamily households							
				Married couple		Female householder[1]			Householder living alone						
	Total households	Total	With own children under 18 years	Total	With own children under 18 years	Total	With own children under 18 years	Total	Total	65 years and over	Average household size	Average family size	Total households	Female householder[1]	Householder living alone
	71	72	73	74	75	76	77	78	79	80	81	82	83	84	85
UNITED STATES	105 480 101	68.1	32.8	51.7	23.5	12.2	7.2	31.9	25.8	9.2	2.59	3.14	91 947 410	11.6	24.6
ALABAMA	1 737 080	70.0	32.3	52.2	22.5	14.2	8.1	30.0	26.1	9.8	2.49	3.01	1 506 790	13.4	23.8
Auburn	18 421	39.3	18.6	28.6	13.4	7.7	4.4	60.7	36.8	4.5	2.12	2.93	13 444	8.3	32.5
Bessemer	11 537	68.2	30.5	34.6	13.2	29.2	15.9	31.8	29.0	13.0	2.52	3.12	12 584	23.8	27.8
Birmingham	98 782	60.0	27.7	31.1	12.5	24.6	13.6	40.0	34.4	10.4	2.37	3.09	105 437	21.7	31.9
Decatur	21 824	67.6	31.8	50.7	21.7	13.4	8.3	32.4	28.9	10.7	2.43	2.99	19 134	12.2	26.1
Dothan	23 685	67.7	31.5	48.9	20.2	15.4	9.8	32.3	28.4	10.6	2.39	2.94	20 685	14.8	26.1
Florence	15 820	60.4	25.9	43.6	16.4	14.0	8.5	39.6	33.8	13.3	2.20	2.82	14 910	13.3	29.6
Gadsden	16 456	62.3	24.9	40.5	13.6	18.1	9.9	37.7	33.9	16.9	2.28	2.91	17 512	15.6	30.7
Homewood	10 688	55.0	27.2	41.0	19.6	11.4	6.4	45.0	36.2	9.4	2.16	2.87	10 193	10.6	38.5
Hoover	25 191	69.1	33.4	59.4	28.2	7.2	4.2	30.9	25.9	6.3	2.47	3.00	16 064	7.7	24.6
Huntsville	66 742	62.5	27.6	45.5	17.8	13.7	8.3	37.5	32.3	9.2	2.29	2.91	63 058	11.8	27.1
Madison	11 143	72.4	42.5	60.1	33.8	9.6	7.1	27.6	23.9	3.4	2.61	3.13	5 967	6.7	24.1
Mobile	78 480	64.7	30.9	41.1	17.5	19.9	11.9	35.3	30.2	10.5	2.46	3.09	75 442	18.3	28.4
Montgomery	78 384	65.2	32.1	42.4	18.8	19.1	11.7	34.8	30.1	9.4	2.44	3.06	69 968	17.7	27.4
Phenix City	11 517	65.7	31.7	39.4	16.3	22.1	13.5	34.3	30.4	11.5	2.40	2.99	9 745	20.5	27.1
Prichard	9 841	73.9	36.3	32.8	13.9	36.0	20.5	26.1	23.4	9.0	2.84	3.35	11 121	33.9	20.7
Tuscaloosa	31 381	54.0	23.9	35.0	13.6	15.7	9.2	46.0	35.2	9.3	2.22	2.93	29 467	14.5	31.9
ALASKA	221 600	68.7	39.9	52.5	28.5	10.8	7.8	31.3	23.5	4.1	2.74	3.28	188 915	9.6	22.1
Anchorage	94 822	67.6	38.9	51.1	27.3	11.5	8.3	32.4	23.4	3.8	2.67	3.19	82 702	10.1	22.9
Fairbanks	11 075	64.9	39.9	47.2	26.8	12.6	9.6	35.1	27.4	6.0	2.56	3.15	10 885	10.6	26.4
Juneau	11 543	66.2	36.7	51.2	26.3	10.5	7.3	33.8	24.4	4.3	2.60	3.10	9 902	10.2	23.6
ARIZONA	1 901 327	67.7	32.0	51.9	22.6	11.1	6.8	32.3	24.8	8.6	2.64	3.18	1 368 843	10.4	24.7
Apache Junction	13 775	65.4	22.0	52.9	14.6	8.5	5.0	34.6	27.2	13.0	2.29	2.75	7 705	8.0	25.9
Avondale	10 640	82.0	47.9	62.9	36.5	12.7	7.7	18.0	12.9	3.1	3.36	3.66	4 917	17.1	17.9
Bullhead City	13 909	65.5	24.7	49.1	14.6	11.1	7.0	34.5	25.3	11.2	2.42	2.86	8 824	7.8	23.6
Casa Grande	8 920	73.4	37.1	52.3	22.6	15.1	10.3	26.6	21.7	8.9	2.80	3.24	6 495	13.3	21.1
Chandler	62 377	72.8	41.1	57.5	31.4	10.5	7.0	27.2	19.3	3.6	2.82	3.26	31 490	10.4	17.9
Flagstaff	19 306	60.1	32.8	44.0	21.9	11.6	8.2	39.9	23.2	3.8	2.59	3.13	14 417	11.1	20.4
Gilbert	35 405	81.7	50.8	69.5	42.9	8.3	5.5	18.3	12.7	1.8	3.10	3.42	9 381	8.8	14.0
Glendale	75 700	71.8	39.9	53.5	28.2	12.8	8.4	28.2	21.3	5.8	2.85	3.33	53 669	11.8	22.0
Lake Havasu City	17 911	71.0	22.5	59.4	15.7	7.7	4.5	29.0	22.8	11.8	2.32	2.69	9 919	6.0	18.6
Mesa	146 643	68.1	33.4	52.7	24.0	10.6	6.7	31.9	24.2	9.1	2.68	3.20	107 863	9.3	24.0
Oro Valley town	12 249	76.6	27.0	69.8	22.9	4.9	3.1	23.4	19.4	8.2	2.41	2.76	2 846	NA	NA
Peoria	39 184	74.8	37.7	62.0	29.7	9.1	5.8	25.2	20.5	10.3	2.73	3.16	18 254	7.5	19.6
Phoenix	465 834	66.0	35.7	46.9	24.3	12.9	8.1	34.0	25.4	6.3	2.79	3.39	369 921	11.8	26.1
Prescott	15 098	59.4	18.1	48.7	11.8	7.9	4.6	40.6	32.1	15.2	2.11	2.62	11 479	7.6	30.4
Scottsdale	90 669	60.1	22.6	49.6	17.1	7.5	4.1	39.9	30.8	9.7	2.22	2.79	57 583	8.4	29.7
Sierra Vista	14 196	70.4	34.9	56.5	24.8	10.4	7.8	29.6	25.1	7.7	2.48	2.96	11 672	8.7	22.3
Surprise city	12 484	77.9	21.5	69.5	17.0	5.4	2.9	22.1	17.9	8.9	2.46	2.75	2 254	NA	NA
Tempe	63 602	52.9	24.4	38.4	16.8	9.7	5.6	47.1	28.5	4.6	2.41	3.05	55 540	9.3	26.2
Tucson	192 891	58.3	29.0	39.7	17.9	13.8	8.5	41.7	32.3	9.3	2.42	3.12	162 685	12.4	31.3
Yuma	26 649	73.6	38.8	56.6	27.3	13.1	9.1	26.4	21.7	9.8	2.79	3.27	19 282	10.9	21.2
ARKANSAS	1 042 696	70.2	32.1	54.3	22.7	12.1	7.4	29.8	25.6	10.4	2.49	2.99	891 179	11.1	24.0
Conway	16 039	63.4	33.0	49.0	23.8	11.2	7.5	36.6	26.1	7.2	2.44	2.99	9 437	10.7	26.1
Fayetteville	23 798	51.0	25.5	37.7	17.3	9.6	6.5	49.0	34.0	5.7	2.21	2.91	16 894	8.8	32.2
Fort Smith	32 398	63.7	30.8	47.1	20.7	12.3	7.8	36.3	30.7	10.9	2.42	3.03	29 646	10.5	29.7
Hot Springs	16 096	56.3	22.0	40.2	13.2	12.4	7.2	43.7	38.4	18.3	2.12	2.80	14 488	12.2	36.7
Jacksonville	10 890	73.5	40.2	55.1	27.7	14.6	10.1	26.5	22.0	5.9	2.64	3.08	9 854	11.2	17.8
Jonesboro	22 219	64.6	30.1	48.9	21.1	12.2	7.5	35.4	27.5	9.0	2.38	2.93	17 976	11.2	25.3
Little Rock	77 352	60.1	28.6	40.5	17.0	16.1	9.9	39.9	33.8	9.1	2.30	2.98	72 573	14.5	32.1
North Little Rock	25 542	63.1	28.9	41.9	16.0	17.6	11.3	36.9	32.0	12.2	2.35	2.97	24 987	15.2	29.0
Pine Bluff	19 956	66.9	32.9	38.7	16.3	23.8	14.6	33.1	29.2	11.8	2.57	3.20	20 871	19.4	27.2
Rogers	14 005	72.9	39.4	58.4	30.2	10.1	6.6	27.1	22.2	8.9	2.74	3.21	9 705	8.7	23.4
Springdale	16 149	73.4	38.8	58.2	29.7	10.5	6.6	26.6	22.0	8.6	2.80	3.26	11 432	9.3	21.8
Texarkana	10 384	67.8	32.5	45.3	18.5	18.7	12.0	32.2	28.3	11.6	2.45	2.99	8 700	18.9	27.3
West Memphis	10 051	71.0	36.7	40.4	17.9	25.1	16.0	29.0	24.8	8.6	2.70	3.23	9 879	20.8	21.4
CALIFORNIA	11 502 870	68.9	35.8	51.1	26.0	12.6	7.3	31.1	23.5	7.8	2.87	3.43	10 381 206	11.5	23.4
Alameda	30 226	59.1	27.7	43.7	19.8	11.4	6.2	40.9	32.2	9.4	2.35	3.04	29 078	11.0	31.5
Alhambra	29 111	71.0	33.1	48.3	23.5	16.4	7.5	29.0	22.5	7.7	2.88	3.41	28 239	14.1	24.5
Anaheim	96 969	75.8	43.0	56.3	32.4	13.1	7.5	24.2	18.1	6.1	3.34	3.75	87 588	11.6	19.9
Antioch	29 338	79.0	46.3	60.3	34.5	13.5	8.8	21.0	15.9	5.4	3.07	3.42	21 401	12.2	16.9
Apple Valley	18 557	77.4	38.8	57.8	26.1	14.2	9.3	22.6	18.0	8.4	2.90	3.27	15 588	9.9	14.6
Arcadia	19 149	73.9	35.2	57.8	28.2	11.9	5.5	26.1	22.3	9.6	2.74	3.23	18 352	9.7	23.9
Atascadero	9 531	71.5	35.9	55.5	25.1	11.4	7.8	28.5	22.0	8.1	2.62	3.05	8 484	9.6	20.7

[1] No spouse present.

Table D. Cities

City	Percent change of households, 1990–2000	Total housing units	Occupied housing units (percent)	Vacant housing units Total	For seasonal, recreational, or occasional use	Homeowner vacancy rate (percent)	Rental vacancy rate (percent)	Occupied housing units Total	Percent owner-occupied housing units	Percent renter-occupied housing units	Average household size of owner-occupied units	Average household size of renter-occupied units
	86	87	88	89	90	91	92	93	94	95	96	97
UNITED STATES	14.7	115 904 641	91.0	9.0	3.1	1.7	6.8	105 480 101	66.2	33.8	2.69	2.40
ALABAMA	15.3	1 963 711	88.5	11.5	2.4	2.0	11.8	1 737 080	72.5	27.5	2.57	2.30
Auburn	37.0	20 043	91.9	8.1	0.5	3.0	8.8	18 421	40.9	59.1	2.45	1.90
Bessemer	-8.3	12 790	90.2	9.8	0.1	1.9	7.0	11 537	59.2	40.8	2.53	2.49
Birmingham	-6.3	111 927	88.3	11.7	0.3	2.7	11.6	98 782	53.7	46.3	2.49	2.23
Decatur	14.1	23 950	91.1	8.9	0.3	2.3	12.9	21 824	63.8	36.2	2.52	2.26
Dothan	14.5	25 920	91.4	8.6	0.5	2.3	10.5	23 685	62.9	37.1	2.47	2.26
Florence	6.1	17 707	89.3	10.7	0.6	3.0	12.6	15 820	58.5	41.5	2.33	2.02
Gadsden	-6.0	18 797	87.5	12.5	0.3	3.5	10.8	16 456	63.6	36.4	2.29	2.27
Homewood	4.9	11 494	93.0	7.0	0.3	1.6	9.5	10 688	54.6	45.4	2.34	1.95
Hoover	56.8	27 150	92.8	7.2	0.2	1.9	12.1	25 191	66.0	34.0	2.68	2.07
Huntsville	5.8	73 670	90.6	9.4	0.7	2.7	12.8	66 742	61.6	38.4	2.42	2.07
Madison	86.7	12 121	91.9	8.1	0.7	3.2	13.4	11 143	70.3	29.7	2.81	2.13
Mobile	4.0	86 187	91.1	8.9	0.5	1.7	9.1	78 480	59.3	40.7	2.55	2.32
Montgomery	12.0	86 787	90.3	9.7	0.3	2.5	9.9	78 384	61.9	38.1	2.51	2.33
Phenix City	18.2	13 250	86.9	13.1	0.2	3.6	15.9	11 517	52.7	47.3	2.47	2.31
Prichard	-11.5	11 336	86.8	13.2	0.2	1.7	12.6	9 841	58.4	41.6	2.81	2.87
Tuscaloosa	6.5	34 857	90.0	10.0	0.4	2.1	11.3	31 381	47.7	52.3	2.43	2.04
ALASKA	17.3	260 978	84.9	15.1	8.2	1.9	7.8	221 600	62.5	37.5	2.89	2.49
Anchorage	14.7	100 368	94.5	5.5	1.1	1.4	5.3	94 822	60.1	39.9	2.81	2.46
Fairbanks	1.7	12 357	89.6	10.4	1.0	2.4	10.0	11 075	34.9	65.1	2.62	2.53
Juneau	16.6	12 282	94.0	6.0	1.5	0.9	5.7	11 543	63.7	36.3	2.78	2.29
ARIZONA	38.9	2 189 189	86.9	13.1	6.5	2.1	9.2	1 901 327	68.0	32.0	2.69	2.53
Apache Junction	78.8	22 771	60.5	39.5	29.8	5.3	26.7	13 775	82.1	17.9	2.27	2.38
Avondale	116.4	11 419	93.2	6.8	0.5	2.7	12.2	10 640	77.6	22.4	3.35	3.39
Bullhead City	57.6	18 430	75.5	24.5	13.3	4.4	9.2	13 909	60.3	39.7	2.31	2.58
Casa Grande	37.3	11 041	80.8	19.2	7.8	2.7	18.4	8 920	64.0	36.0	2.80	2.79
Chandler	98.1	66 592	93.7	6.3	1.6	1.5	10.2	62 377	73.6	26.4	2.86	2.70
Flagstaff	33.9	21 396	90.2	9.8	4.6	2.1	5.3	19 306	48.2	51.8	2.74	2.46
Gilbert	277.4	37 007	95.7	4.3	0.7	2.1	5.2	35 405	84.9	15.1	3.16	2.72
Glendale	41.0	79 667	95.0	5.0	0.4	1.4	6.7	75 700	64.8	35.2	2.97	2.63
Lake Havasu City	80.6	23 018	77.8	22.2	17.3	2.3	7.8	17 911	77.6	22.4	2.29	2.45
Mesa	36.0	175 701	83.5	16.5	10.3	2.4	10.7	146 643	66.4	33.6	2.74	2.54
Oro Valley town	330.4	13 946	87.8	12.2	6.3	2.2	14.5	12 249	84.2	15.8	2.47	2.12
Peoria	114.7	42 573	92.0	8.0	3.0	2.3	10.0	39 184	84.3	15.7	2.78	2.45
Phoenix	25.9	495 832	93.9	6.1	0.9	1.4	7.9	465 834	60.7	39.3	2.89	2.63
Prescott	31.5	17 144	88.1	11.9	6.0	2.7	6.1	15 098	65.2	34.8	2.14	2.07
Scottsdale	57.5	104 974	86.4	13.6	7.6	2.3	10.6	90 669	69.6	30.4	2.32	1.97
Sierra Vista	21.6	15 685	90.5	9.5	1.1	2.0	10.7	14 196	52.2	47.8	2.43	2.53
Surprise city	453.9	16 260	76.8	23.2	13.3	3.2	31.6	12 484	88.3	11.7	2.37	3.14
Tempe	14.5	67 068	94.8	5.2	0.8	1.0	6.1	63 602	51.0	49.0	2.59	2.22
Tucson	18.6	209 609	92.0	8.0	1.7	1.6	8.1	192 891	53.4	46.6	2.58	2.24
Yuma	38.2	34 475	77.3	22.7	11.7	1.6	12.3	26 649	63.5	36.5	2.80	2.78
ARKANSAS	17.0	1 173 043	88.9	11.1	2.5	2.5	9.6	1 042 696	69.4	30.6	2.54	2.40
Conway	70.0	17 289	92.8	7.2	0.3	3.2	8.3	16 039	55.1	44.9	2.66	2.17
Fayetteville	40.9	25 467	93.4	6.6	0.5	2.7	6.1	23 798	42.2	57.8	2.45	2.04
Fort Smith	9.3	35 341	91.7	8.3	0.4	2.5	8.1	32 398	56.3	43.7	2.52	2.29
Hot Springs	11.1	18 813	85.6	14.4	2.9	3.2	11.9	16 096	57.3	42.7	2.18	2.05
Jacksonville	10.5	11 890	91.6	8.4	0.5	2.3	8.9	10 890	47.3	52.7	2.58	2.69
Jonesboro	23.6	24 263	91.6	8.4	0.4	2.5	10.4	22 219	57.7	42.3	2.49	2.24
Little Rock	6.6	84 793	91.2	8.8	0.5	1.7	9.7	77 352	57.4	42.6	2.46	2.10
North Little Rock	2.2	27 567	92.7	7.3	0.3	2.2	8.4	25 542	57.5	42.5	2.39	2.29
Pine Bluff	-4.4	22 484	88.8	11.2	0.3	2.0	9.2	19 956	58.8	41.2	2.56	2.58
Rogers	44.3	14 836	94.4	5.6	0.4	2.6	5.9	14 005	63.2	36.8	2.77	2.69
Springdale	41.3	16 962	95.2	4.8	0.3	2.3	4.4	16 149	60.4	39.6	2.77	2.85
Texarkana	19.4	11 721	88.6	11.4	0.4	2.8	15.1	10 384	60.9	39.1	2.46	2.42
West Memphis	1.7	11 022	91.2	8.8	0.3	1.7	10.2	10 051	56.0	44.0	2.73	2.66
CALIFORNIA	10.8	12 214 549	94.2	5.8	1.9	1.4	3.7	11 502 870	56.9	43.1	2.93	2.79
Alameda	3.9	31 644	95.5	4.5	0.5	0.5	2.4	30 226	47.9	52.1	2.50	2.22
Alhambra	3.1	30 069	96.8	3.2	0.3	1.3	2.1	29 111	39.2	60.8	3.04	2.78
Anaheim	10.7	99 719	97.2	2.8	0.2	0.9	3.2	96 969	50.0	50.0	3.24	3.45
Antioch	37.1	30 116	97.4	2.6	0.1	0.9	3.4	29 338	71.0	29.0	3.14	2.90
Apple Valley	19.0	20 163	92.0	8.0	0.7	3.4	7.8	18 557	70.0	30.0	2.83	3.08
Arcadia	4.3	19 970	95.9	4.1	0.6	1.8	2.4	19 149	62.3	37.7	2.91	2.47
Atascadero	12.3	9 848	96.8	3.2	0.7	0.9	2.7	9 531	65.6	34.4	2.71	2.44

Table D. Cities

STATE Place code	City	Population, 2000				Population, 1990				Population and population characteristics, 2000					
										Race (percent)					
										One race					
		Land area, 2000[1] (sq km)	Total persons	Rank	Per square kilometer	Land area, 1990[1] (sq km)	Total persons	Rank	Per square kilometer	White	Black or African American	American Indian or Alaska Native	Asian	Native Hawaiian and other Pacific Islander	Some other race
		1	2	3	4	5	6	7	8	9	10	11	12	13	14
	CALIFORNIA—Cont'd														
06 03386	Azusa	23.1	44 712	771	1 935.6	23.3	41 203	708	1 768.4	52.3	3.8	1.3	6.1	0.2	30.5
06 03526	Bakersfield	292.9	247 057	71	843.5	237.9	176 264	97	740.9	61.9	9.2	1.4	4.3	0.1	18.7
06 03666	Baldwin Park	17.3	75 837	371	4 383.6	17.1	69 330	346	4 054.4	40.2	1.6	1.4	11.6	0.1	40.5
06 04870	Bell	6.4	36 664	959	5 728.8	6.6	34 365	879	5 206.8	48.5	1.3	1.3	1.1	0.1	43.1
06 04982	Bellflower	15.7	72 878	386	4 641.9	15.7	61 815	406	3 937.3	46.1	13.1	0.9	9.7	0.7	24.4
06 04996	Bell Gardens	6.4	44 054	781	6 883.4	6.5	42 315	684	6 510.0	48.1	1.0	1.7	0.6	0.1	43.9
06 05108	Belmont	11.7	25 123	1 501	2 147.3	11.7	24 165	1 343	2 065.4	75.2	1.7	0.3	15.4	0.5	2.6
06 05290	Benicia	33.4	26 865	1 389	804.3	33.1	24 437	1 326	738.3	78.9	4.8	0.6	7.6	0.3	2.7
06 06000	Berkeley	27.1	102 743	235	3 791.3	27.1	102 724	196	3 790.6	59.2	13.6	0.5	16.4	0.1	4.6
06 06308	Beverly Hills	14.7	33 784	1 070	2 298.2	14.7	31 971	973	2 174.9	85.1	1.8	0.1	7.1	0.0	1.5
06 08100	Brea	27.3	35 410	1 008	1 297.1	25.9	32 873	943	1 269.2	77.3	1.3	0.5	9.1	0.2	7.8
06 08786	Buena Park	27.4	78 282	352	2 857.0	27.5	68 784	348	2 501.2	53.0	3.8	1.0	21.1	0.5	15.2
06 08954	Burbank	44.9	100 316	247	2 234.2	44.9	93 649	222	2 085.7	72.2	2.1	0.5	9.2	0.1	9.9
06 09066	Burlingame	11.2	28 158	1 316	2 514.1	11.3	26 666	1 200	2 359.8	76.9	1.1	0.2	13.8	0.5	3.6
06 09710	Calexico	16.1	27 109	1 377	1 683.8	10.7	18 633	1 763	1 741.4	46.6	0.5	0.7	1.8	0.0	47.0
06 10046	Camarillo	49.0	57 077	545	1 164.8	47.8	52 297	518	1 094.1	80.7	1.5	0.5	7.2	0.2	6.3
06 10345	Campbell	14.5	38 138	925	2 630.2	14.5	36 088	832	2 488.8	72.8	2.5	0.7	14.2	0.2	4.9
06 11194	Carlsbad	97.0	78 247	353	806.7	97.6	63 292	392	648.5	86.6	1.0	0.4	4.2	0.2	4.6
06 11530	Carson	48.8	89 730	287	1 838.7	48.8	83 995	269	1 721.2	25.7	25.4	0.6	22.3	3.0	18.0
06 12048	Cathedral City	49.7	42 647	808	858.1	49.0	30 085	1 051	614.0	65.3	2.7	1.0	3.7	0.1	23.1
06 12524	Ceres	18.0	34 609	1 040	1 922.7	14.4	26 413	1 220	1 834.2	64.5	2.7	1.4	5.0	0.4	20.4
06 12552	Cerritos	22.3	51 488	648	2 308.9	22.3	53 244	503	2 387.6	26.9	6.7	0.3	58.4	0.2	3.7
06 13014	Chico	71.9	59 954	504	833.9	58.1	39 970	744	688.0	82.4	2.0	1.3	4.2	0.2	5.7
06 13210	Chino	54.5	67 168	432	1 232.4	44.2	59 682	425	1 350.3	55.7	7.8	0.9	4.9	0.2	25.6
06 13392	Chula Vista	126.6	173 556	124	1 370.9	75.1	135 160	133	1 799.7	55.1	4.6	0.8	11.0	0.6	22.1
06 13756	Claremont	34.0	33 998	1 060	999.9	28.5	32 610	949	1 144.2	73.5	5.0	0.6	11.5	0.1	5.2
06 14218	Clovis	44.3	68 468	420	1 545.6	37.1	50 323	553	1 356.4	75.8	1.9	1.5	6.5	0.2	9.5
06 14890	Colton	39.1	47 662	711	1 219.0	36.6	40 213	732	1 098.7	42.7	11.0	1.3	5.3	0.2	34.5
06 15044	Compton	26.2	93 493	269	3 568.4	26.3	90 454	232	3 439.3	16.7	40.3	0.7	0.3	1.1	37.3
06 16000	Concord	78.1	121 780	184	1 559.3	76.3	111 308	168	1 458.8	70.7	3.0	0.6	9.4	0.5	9.7
06 16350	Corona	91.0	124 966	176	1 373.8	73.8	75 943	298	1 029.0	62.0	6.4	0.9	7.5	0.3	17.5
06 16532	Costa Mesa	40.5	108 724	217	2 684.5	40.3	96 357	213	2 391.0	69.5	1.4	0.8	6.9	0.6	16.6
06 16742	Covina	18.0	46 837	725	2 602.1	17.9	43 332	664	2 420.8	62.1	5.0	0.9	9.8	0.2	17.2
06 17568	Culver City	13.2	38 816	908	2 940.6	13.2	38 793	768	2 938.9	59.2	12.0	0.7	12.0	0.2	10.2
06 17610	Cupertino	28.3	50 546	661	1 786.1	26.7	39 967	745	1 496.9	50.1	0.7	0.2	44.4	0.1	1.3
06 17750	Cypress	17.1	46 229	740	2 703.5	17.1	42 655	677	2 494.4	65.6	2.8	0.6	20.8	0.4	5.4
06 17918	Daly City	19.6	103 621	231	5 286.8	19.5	92 088	228	4 722.5	25.9	4.6	0.4	50.7	0.9	11.3
06 17946	Dana Point	17.2	35 110	1 020	2 041.3	17.2	31 896	977	1 854.4	87.2	0.8	0.6	2.5	0.1	5.9
06 17988	Danville	46.9	41 715	826	889.4	45.8	31 306	997	683.5	86.3	0.9	0.2	9.0	0.1	0.9
06 18100	Davis	27.1	60 308	496	2 225.4	21.9	46 322	614	2 115.2	70.1	2.3	0.7	17.5	0.2	4.3
06 18394	Delano	26.2	38 824	907	1 481.8	22.1	22 762	1 440	1 030.0	26.2	5.4	0.9	15.9	0.1	47.1
06 19192	Diamond Bar	38.2	56 287	561	1 473.5	39.1	53 672	494	1 372.7	41.0	4.8	0.3	42.8	0.1	6.8
06 19766	Downey	32.2	107 323	220	3 333.0	32.2	91 444	231	2 839.9	53.5	3.8	0.9	7.7	0.2	29.1
06 20018	Dublin	32.6	29 973	1 223	919.4	22.2	23 229	1 404	1 046.4	69.4	10.1	0.7	10.3	0.3	5.3
06 20956	East Palo Alto	6.6	29 506	1 248	4 470.6	6.6	23 451	1 391	3 553.2	27.0	23.0	0.8	2.2	7.6	34.7
06 21712	El Cajon	37.7	94 869	263	2 516.4	37.3	88 918	238	2 383.9	74.0	5.4	1.0	2.8	0.4	10.5
06 21782	El Centro	24.8	37 835	933	1 525.6	16.2	31 405	995	1 938.9	46.9	3.2	1.0	3.5	0.1	41.7
06 22230	El Monte	24.7	115 965	200	4 694.9	24.6	106 162	188	4 315.5	35.7	0.8	1.4	18.5	0.1	39.3
06 22678	Encinitas	49.5	58 014	530	1 172.0	46.5	55 406	466	1 191.5	86.6	0.6	0.5	3.1	0.1	6.3
06 22804	Escondido	94.0	133 559	166	1 420.8	92.3	108 648	181	1 177.1	67.8	2.3	1.2	4.5	0.2	19.2
06 23042	Eureka	24.5	26 128	1 439	1 066.4	24.5	27 025	1 183	1 103.1	82.5	1.6	4.2	3.6	0.3	2.7
06 23182	Fairfield	97.5	96 178	255	986.4	92.9	78 650	286	846.6	56.2	15.0	0.8	10.9	0.9	8.8
06 24638	Folsom	56.3	51 884	640	921.6	55.5	29 802	1 061	537.0	77.9	6.0	0.6	7.2	0.2	4.7
06 24680	Fontana	93.5	128 929	169	1 378.9	92.3	87 535	243	948.4	45.0	11.8	1.1	4.4	0.3	31.9
06 25338	Foster City	9.7	28 803	1 283	2 969.4	9.7	28 176	1 133	2 904.7	59.3	2.1	0.1	32.5	0.6	1.2
06 25380	Fountain Valley	23.1	54 978	591	2 380.0	23.1	53 691	493	2 324.3	64.0	1.1	0.5	25.8	0.4	4.0
06 26000	Fremont	198.6	203 413	87	1 024.2	199.5	173 339	99	868.9	47.7	3.1	0.5	37.0	0.4	5.5
06 27000	Fresno	270.3	427 652	39	1 582.1	256.8	354 091	47	1 378.9	50.2	8.4	1.6	11.2	0.1	23.4
06 28000	Fullerton	57.5	126 003	175	2 191.4	57.3	114 144	162	1 992.0	61.9	2.3	0.7	16.1	0.2	14.8
06 28168	Gardena	15.1	57 746	532	3 824.2	13.7	51 481	529	3 757.7	23.8	26.0	0.6	26.8	0.7	16.9
06 29000	Garden Grove	46.7	165 196	128	3 537.4	46.5	142 965	122	3 074.5	46.9	1.3	0.6	30.9	0.7	15.4
06 29504	Gilroy	41.1	41 464	831	1 008.9	26.6	31 487	992	1 183.7	58.9	1.8	1.6	4.4	0.3	27.7
06 30000	Glendale	79.4	194 973	100	2 455.6	79.3	180 038	93	2 270.3	63.6	1.3	0.3	16.1	0.1	8.6
06 30014	Glendora	49.6	49 415	679	996.3	50.4	47 832	591	949.0	80.3	1.5	0.6	6.2	0.1	7.2
06 31960	Hanford	33.9	41 686	827	1 229.7	29.9	30 463	1 041	1 018.8	64.1	5.0	1.4	2.9	0.2	20.8
06 32548	Hawthorne	15.7	84 112	317	5 357.5	15.4	71 349	330	4 633.1	29.3	33.0	0.7	6.7	0.9	24.2
06 33000	Hayward	114.8	140 030	156	1 219.8	112.5	114 705	160	1 019.6	43.0	11.0	0.8	19.0	1.9	16.8
06 33182	Hemet	66.4	58 812	519	885.7	45.5	43 366	663	953.1	80.5	2.6	1.2	1.5	0.1	10.6
06 33434	Hesperia	174.4	62 582	472	358.8	125.1	50 418	550	403.0	74.3	4.0	1.3	1.1	0.2	14.5
06 33588	Highland	35.3	44 605	772	1 263.6	35.1	34 439	876	981.2	56.2	12.1	1.3	6.1	0.3	18.6
06 34120	Hollister	17.0	34 413	1 047	2 024.3	14.6	19 318	1 700	1 323.2	59.1	1.4	1.1	2.8	0.1	30.0

[1] Dry land or land partially or temporarily covered by water.

Table D. Cities

City	Population and population characteristics, 2000 (cont'd)								Population and population characteristics, 1990				
	Race (percent) (cont'd)								Race (percent)				
	Race alone or in combination												
	Two or more races	White	Black	American Indian or Alaska Native	Asian	Native Hawaiian and other Pacific Islander	Some other race	Hispanic[1]	White	Black or African American	American Indian or Alaska Native	Asian and Pacific Islander	Hispanic[1]
	15	16	17	18	19	20	21	22	23	24	25	26	27
CALIFORNIA—Cont'd													
Azusa	5.7	57.2	4.4	2.1	7.2	0.5	34.7	63.8	66.0	3.8	0.7	6.6	53.4
Bakersfield	4.4	65.5	10.0	2.5	5.3	0.3	21.1	32.5	72.7	9.4	1.1	3.6	20.5
Baldwin Park	4.5	43.9	1.9	2.0	12.3	0.3	44.2	78.7	55.6	2.4	0.7	12.3	70.8
Bell	4.8	52.9	1.5	1.6	1.4	0.1	47.4	90.9	42.0	1.0	0.8	1.4	86.1
Bellflower	5.1	50.1	14.1	1.7	10.8	1.1	27.6	43.2	69.8	6.3	0.9	10.1	23.9
Bell Gardens	4.7	52.3	1.1	2.0	0.8	0.2	48.2	93.4	38.2	0.5	1.2	1.3	87.5
Belmont	4.2	78.8	2.0	0.8	17.6	1.1	4.3	8.3	86.8	1.6	0.4	10.0	7.3
Benicia	5.2	83.5	5.8	2.0	9.6	0.8	4.2	9.0	84.0	5.3	0.8	7.9	7.4
Berkeley	5.6	63.7	15.3	1.6	18.7	0.4	6.5	9.7	62.1	18.8	0.6	14.8	8.4
Beverly Hills	4.5	89.3	2.1	0.4	8.7	0.1	4.1	4.6	91.3	1.7	0.2	5.5	5.4
Brea	3.8	80.7	1.6	1.2	10.2	0.5	9.9	20.3	87.0	1.1	0.4	6.2	15.4
Buena Park	5.5	57.4	4.5	1.8	22.7	0.9	18.5	33.5	70.9	2.5	0.7	14.4	24.5
Burbank	6.0	77.7	2.6	1.2	10.5	0.3	14.0	24.9	82.6	1.7	0.5	6.8	22.6
Burlingame	4.0	80.3	1.4	0.7	15.4	0.8	5.5	10.6	87.4	1.0	0.4	8.9	10.2
Calexico	3.5	49.5	0.6	0.9	2.3	0.1	50.2	95.3	67.8	0.2	0.2	2.6	95.6
Camarillo	3.6	83.8	1.9	1.2	8.7	0.5	7.7	15.5	86.3	1.6	0.5	6.3	12.1
Campbell	4.8	77.0	3.0	1.4	16.0	0.6	6.9	13.3	83.6	2.0	0.6	9.5	10.6
Carlsbad	3.0	89.2	1.3	1.1	5.5	0.4	5.7	11.7	89.8	1.2	0.5	3.2	13.8
Carson	5.1	29.0	26.6	1.3	24.2	3.8	20.6	34.9	34.7	26.1	0.6	25.0	27.9
Cathedral City	4.1	68.9	3.3	1.6	4.5	0.2	25.9	50.0	74.3	2.2	1.0	3.6	37.2
Ceres	5.5	69.0	3.3	2.8	6.3	0.7	23.7	37.9	78.0	1.7	1.4	5.0	22.6
Cerritos	3.8	29.5	7.2	0.8	60.7	0.7	5.1	10.4	42.3	7.4	0.3	45.2	12.5
Chico	4.3	86.1	2.8	2.6	5.2	0.4	7.5	12.3	89.5	1.8	1.1	4.0	8.7
Chino	4.9	59.8	8.3	1.7	5.9	0.5	28.9	47.4	67.3	9.8	0.5	3.4	36.2
Chula Vista	5.8	59.9	5.4	1.4	13.1	1.0	25.4	49.6	67.7	4.6	0.6	8.9	37.3
Claremont	4.1	77.1	5.8	1.3	13.1	0.5	6.7	15.4	82.2	5.0	0.4	8.5	10.3
Clovis	4.6	79.8	2.4	2.8	7.7	0.3	11.8	20.3	83.2	1.7	1.4	5.5	16.3
Colton	5.1	46.7	12.0	2.0	6.3	0.5	37.9	60.7	58.2	8.7	0.9	4.3	49.7
Compton	3.6	19.4	41.2	1.2	0.5	1.2	40.3	56.8	10.6	54.8	0.3	1.9	43.7
Concord	5.9	75.8	3.8	1.8	11.6	1.0	12.5	21.8	84.0	2.4	0.7	8.7	11.5
Corona	5.3	66.5	7.2	1.6	9.0	0.6	20.7	35.7	75.9	2.8	0.8	7.1	30.4
Costa Mesa	4.3	73.2	1.8	1.4	8.0	0.9	19.1	31.8	84.3	1.3	0.5	6.6	20.0
Covina	4.8	66.2	5.6	1.7	11.2	0.5	20.0	40.3	80.3	4.1	0.5	7.6	25.6
Culver City	5.7	63.8	13.6	1.8	13.9	0.6	12.8	23.7	69.2	10.4	0.6	12.0	19.8
Cupertino	3.1	52.8	1.0	0.6	46.3	0.3	2.2	4.0	74.4	0.9	0.3	23.0	4.9
Cypress	4.4	69.3	3.4	1.4	22.8	0.7	7.1	15.7	79.2	2.0	0.5	13.7	13.5
Daly City	6.2	30.2	5.4	1.0	53.6	1.6	14.8	22.3	39.5	7.7	0.4	43.8	22.4
Dana Point	2.8	89.8	1.2	1.2	3.4	0.4	7.0	15.5	89.6	0.6	0.6	2.3	13.9
Danville	2.5	88.6	1.1	0.6	10.4	0.3	1.8	4.7	91.6	0.8	0.3	6.5	4.1
Davis	4.9	74.2	3.1	1.5	19.9	0.5	6.0	9.6	79.7	3.0	0.7	13.2	7.4
Delano	4.5	29.2	5.8	1.4	17.6	0.2	50.4	68.5	24.3	2.3	0.6	21.5	62.4
Diamond Bar	4.2	44.1	5.3	0.9	44.8	0.5	8.9	18.5	63.7	5.7	0.4	24.9	17.0
Downey	4.9	57.6	4.2	1.4	8.6	0.4	32.8	57.9	72.5	3.4	0.6	8.8	32.3
Dublin	3.9	72.7	10.5	1.4	12.1	0.7	6.7	13.5	77.7	11.5	0.8	6.0	10.5
East Palo Alto	4.6	30.0	24.2	1.6	3.2	8.6	37.5	58.8	31.7	42.9	0.7	9.6	36.4
El Cajon	6.0	79.3	6.5	2.0	4.2	0.7	13.7	22.5	87.4	2.9	1.0	2.8	14.0
El Centro	3.7	50.0	3.5	1.5	4.1	0.1	44.6	74.6	60.0	4.5	0.7	2.5	65.3
El Monte	4.3	39.2	1.0	1.9	19.2	0.2	42.8	72.4	62.2	1.0	0.6	11.8	72.5
Encinitas	2.9	89.3	0.9	1.0	4.2	0.3	7.4	14.8	89.4	0.6	0.4	2.9	15.2
Escondido	4.8	72.0	2.9	2.3	5.4	0.5	22.0	38.7	85.2	1.5	0.8	3.7	23.4
Eureka	5.1	86.9	2.5	7.3	4.3	0.7	3.8	7.8	88.2	1.4	4.6	4.4	4.8
Fairfield	7.4	61.9	17.1	2.1	14.0	1.8	11.4	18.8	68.2	13.8	1.0	10.7	13.2
Folsom	3.4	80.9	6.4	1.3	8.6	0.5	6.1	9.5	84.0	9.9	0.7	3.5	10.9
Fontana	5.4	49.3	12.9	2.0	5.2	0.6	35.6	57.7	67.7	8.7	0.9	4.5	36.1
Foster City	4.1	62.8	2.5	0.6	34.9	1.1	2.6	5.3	73.5	3.2	0.2	22.0	5.8
Fountain Valley	4.3	67.8	1.5	1.2	27.7	0.8	5.6	10.7	78.2	0.9	0.6	17.7	8.1
Fremont	5.8	52.4	3.8	1.3	39.8	1.0	8.0	13.5	70.6	3.8	0.7	19.4	13.3
Fresno	5.2	54.0	9.2	2.6	12.6	0.4	26.6	39.9	59.2	8.3	1.1	12.5	29.9
Fullerton	4.0	65.2	2.7	1.4	17.4	0.5	17.2	30.2	74.7	2.2	0.5	12.2	21.3
Gardena	5.1	27.5	27.2	1.3	28.8	1.3	19.5	31.8	32.2	23.5	0.5	33.2	23.1
Garden Grove	4.1	50.3	1.8	1.4	32.2	1.0	17.7	32.5	67.3	1.5	0.6	20.5	23.5
Gilroy	5.3	63.6	2.3	2.4	5.7	0.6	31.2	53.8	68.2	1.2	0.7	4.0	47.3
Glendale	10.1	73.1	1.6	0.7	17.6	0.3	17.0	19.7	74.0	1.3	0.3	14.1	21.0
Glendora	4.0	83.9	1.8	1.2	7.5	0.4	9.5	21.7	88.5	1.1	0.5	5.6	15.2
Hanford	5.7	69.2	5.6	2.3	3.9	0.4	24.6	38.7	74.1	5.3	0.8	3.1	29.6
Hawthorne	5.2	33.0	34.4	1.4	7.7	1.2	27.8	44.3	42.3	28.3	0.5	11.0	31.1
Hayward	7.5	48.2	12.3	1.9	21.8	3.4	20.6	34.2	61.8	9.8	1.0	15.5	23.9
Hemet	3.5	83.6	3.2	2.1	2.1	0.3	12.4	23.1	90.9	0.7	0.9	1.2	14.9
Hesperia	4.7	78.5	4.7	2.5	1.8	0.4	17.1	29.4	85.7	2.5	0.9	1.4	19.0
Highland	5.2	60.5	13.3	2.4	7.3	0.6	21.5	36.6	73.1	11.0	1.1	4.8	22.8
Hollister	5.4	63.8	1.8	2.2	4.2	0.5	33.4	55.1	63.5	0.6	0.8	2.5	56.1

[1] Hispanic persons may be of any race.

Table D. Cities

City	Population and population characteristics, 2000										
	Age (percent)										
	Under 5 years	5 to 17 years	18 to 24 years	25 to 34 years	35 to 44 years	45 to 54 years	55 to 64 years	65 to 74 years	75 years and over	Median age (years)	Percent Female
	28	29	30	31	32	33	34	35	36	37	38
CALIFORNIA—Cont'd											
Azusa	9.3	21.6	15.5	17.2	14.2	9.5	5.8	3.9	3.0	27.1	50.6
Bakersfield	8.8	23.9	10.1	14.4	15.5	12.0	6.6	4.5	4.2	30.1	51.4
Baldwin Park	9.7	25.3	11.9	16.4	14.2	10.6	5.9	3.6	2.5	26.9	50.0
Bell	10.8	24.5	12.9	19.0	13.3	9.3	4.8	3.0	2.4	25.9	49.5
Bellflower	9.5	22.3	10.3	16.8	15.2	11.0	6.4	4.3	4.1	29.7	51.3
Bell Gardens	11.4	28.0	12.9	18.2	13.3	8.1	4.1	2.4	1.6	23.8	49.4
Belmont	6.0	13.3	6.5	16.8	19.1	15.0	10.1	7.0	6.2	38.8	50.8
Benicia	5.6	21.5	6.5	10.2	18.1	19.2	9.6	5.2	4.1	38.9	51.4
Berkeley	4.0	10.1	21.6	17.9	13.9	13.9	8.4	4.9	5.3	32.5	50.9
Beverly Hills	3.7	16.2	6.3	14.1	15.2	15.8	10.9	8.1	9.5	41.3	54.5
Brea	6.1	19.6	8.5	13.7	16.7	14.9	9.3	6.4	4.9	36.4	51.2
Buena Park	8.1	21.4	9.7	15.8	16.6	11.9	7.3	5.5	3.8	32.0	50.4
Burbank	5.7	16.5	7.7	17.3	18.1	13.3	8.5	6.0	6.8	36.4	51.5
Burlingame	5.6	13.6	5.5	18.1	18.7	14.4	8.7	6.5	8.8	38.4	52.2
Calexico	7.8	27.1	9.9	12.5	14.7	11.0	6.6	6.4	4.0	29.2	53.4
Camarillo	6.6	18.7	6.5	11.9	16.6	13.7	9.0	7.2	9.8	38.9	51.6
Campbell	6.5	15.0	7.6	20.4	19.9	13.5	7.4	5.0	4.7	35.2	50.4
Carlsbad	6.4	16.9	6.2	13.4	18.5	16.0	8.6	7.1	6.9	38.9	51.1
Carson	6.9	21.5	9.9	13.5	15.0	12.7	9.8	6.6	4.1	33.7	51.7
Cathedral City	8.8	22.3	8.8	15.0	15.6	10.1	7.1	6.7	5.5	32.0	49.3
Ceres	8.6	25.7	10.1	13.7	16.3	11.2	6.3	4.7	3.4	29.4	50.8
Cerritos	4.7	19.8	8.8	10.9	14.9	17.9	13.4	6.1	3.6	39.3	51.3
Chico	6.0	15.1	27.0	15.1	11.7	10.2	5.0	3.9	6.0	25.9	50.9
Chino	7.2	21.3	12.3	16.3	17.9	13.1	6.1	3.3	2.5	30.9	44.6
Chula Vista	7.8	20.9	9.4	15.2	16.4	11.8	7.4	6.0	5.0	33.0	51.5
Claremont	4.3	16.3	18.6	9.8	13.0	14.2	9.1	7.1	7.5	35.8	53.0
Clovis	7.6	23.1	9.2	13.2	17.2	13.5	6.9	4.7	4.6	32.8	52.0
Colton	10.0	24.9	11.9	16.7	14.9	10.0	5.2	3.7	2.7	26.8	50.7
Compton	10.4	28.1	11.5	15.0	13.7	8.8	5.6	4.2	2.7	25.0	51.0
Concord	7.1	18.2	9.0	15.5	17.3	13.9	8.3	5.7	5.0	35.1	50.6
Corona	9.8	23.6	8.9	17.3	17.8	11.1	5.7	3.2	2.6	29.9	50.5
Costa Mesa	7.1	16.1	11.2	21.5	17.5	11.5	6.5	4.6	3.9	32.0	48.8
Covina	7.4	20.7	9.5	14.7	16.4	12.6	7.8	6.0	4.9	33.5	52.1
Culver City	5.5	15.4	6.6	15.1	18.2	15.8	9.5	7.0	6.9	39.1	53.3
Cupertino	6.1	20.6	5.2	12.1	21.0	15.4	8.7	5.8	5.2	38.0	50.1
Cypress	6.0	21.0	7.9	12.4	17.8	14.3	10.1	6.6	4.0	36.7	51.3
Daly City	6.0	16.4	10.5	16.4	15.8	13.7	9.0	6.9	5.2	35.4	50.8
Dana Point	5.6	15.0	7.1	14.2	17.1	17.2	10.8	7.4	5.7	39.8	50.0
Danville	7.1	21.5	4.2	8.2	19.4	18.6	10.7	5.3	5.0	39.9	51.5
Davis	4.6	14.0	30.9	14.9	12.2	11.3	5.4	3.3	3.4	25.2	52.3
Delano	9.1	23.4	12.4	17.2	15.5	9.3	5.6	4.1	3.4	27.9	43.5
Diamond Bar	5.7	21.3	8.8	11.9	17.7	17.6	9.5	4.7	2.8	36.5	51.0
Downey	8.0	21.2	9.8	16.5	14.7	11.5	7.3	5.3	5.7	31.6	51.4
Dublin	5.9	15.1	9.3	21.4	22.8	14.2	6.7	3.1	1.5	34.3	47.3
East Palo Alto	10.0	25.0	13.4	18.6	13.9	8.8	5.1	3.2	1.9	25.8	48.5
El Cajon	8.2	19.7	11.2	15.5	15.8	11.3	7.0	5.6	5.8	31.9	51.2
El Centro	8.4	25.3	9.7	13.8	15.1	11.7	6.7	5.5	3.9	30.0	50.9
El Monte	10.0	24.1	12.1	17.4	14.1	9.7	5.7	4.0	3.0	27.1	49.5
Encinitas	5.9	17.2	7.2	14.7	18.6	18.1	7.8	4.9	5.5	37.9	50.2
Escondido	8.8	20.9	10.4	15.9	15.5	11.0	6.5	4.9	6.1	31.2	50.4
Eureka	5.7	16.6	11.6	13.8	15.0	15.2	8.3	6.5	7.2	36.6	50.5
Fairfield	8.5	21.3	11.1	14.9	16.4	12.0	6.8	5.0	3.9	31.1	50.2
Folsom	6.9	17.3	6.6	17.2	21.8	14.6	6.8	4.4	4.4	35.9	44.8
Fontana	10.3	27.5	10.3	16.3	16.0	10.1	4.6	2.7	2.0	26.2	50.4
Foster City	5.9	15.3	5.9	16.8	18.5	16.2	11.4	6.1	4.0	38.1	50.8
Fountain Valley	6.0	17.5	7.9	13.4	16.7	14.8	12.4	6.6	4.7	38.1	51.1
Fremont	7.4	18.3	7.7	17.3	19.5	13.7	7.7	4.9	3.5	34.5	49.7
Fresno	9.1	23.8	11.8	14.8	14.1	11.0	6.2	4.7	4.6	28.5	50.9
Fullerton	7.0	18.2	11.5	16.6	15.7	12.0	7.7	5.9	5.5	32.9	50.6
Gardena	7.5	18.3	8.7	16.5	15.8	12.0	8.8	7.0	5.4	34.4	51.3
Garden Grove	7.9	20.5	9.2	16.9	16.6	11.6	7.7	5.5	4.0	32.3	49.9
Gilroy	9.4	23.1	10.0	16.4	16.3	11.9	6.1	3.7	3.1	29.9	50.2
Glendale	5.7	16.7	8.4	14.9	17.3	14.1	9.0	7.2	6.7	37.5	52.3
Glendora	6.3	21.3	7.6	12.0	17.1	14.1	9.1	6.7	5.9	36.9	51.7
Hanford	8.7	22.9	9.8	14.7	14.9	11.6	7.1	5.2	5.1	30.9	51.0
Hawthorne	10.1	21.6	11.3	19.5	15.3	10.3	5.8	3.5	2.7	28.7	51.9
Hayward	7.9	18.9	10.9	17.5	15.8	11.9	6.9	5.2	4.9	31.9	50.4
Hemet	6.5	16.0	7.2	10.2	10.4	8.6	8.0	12.8	20.2	44.6	54.2
Hesperia	7.9	24.9	9.3	11.6	15.7	12.2	7.4	6.1	4.9	32.0	50.7
Highland	9.5	26.1	9.0	14.1	15.9	12.2	6.7	4.0	2.5	29.3	51.2
Hollister	10.0	24.6	9.5	16.4	17.4	10.7	5.1	3.6	2.7	29.0	49.5

Table D. Cities

City	Population and population characteristics, 1990										Population—change, 1980–2000				
	Age (percent)										Total persons			Percent change	
	Under 5 years	5 to 17 years	18 to 24 years	25 to 34 years	35 to 44 years	45 to 54 years	55 to 64 years	65 to 74 years	75 years and over	Percent Female	2000	1990	1980	1990–2000	1980–1990
	39	40	41	42	43	44	45	46	47	48	49	50	51	52	53
CALIFORNIA—Cont'd															
Azusa	9.8	19.2	15.9	22.1	12.6	7.6	6.2	4.0	2.6	49.9	44 712	41 203	29 380	8.5	40.2
Bakersfield	9.8	21.0	10.2	19.2	15.4	8.8	6.4	5.4	3.7	51.4	247 057	176 264	105 611	40.2	66.9
Baldwin Park	10.6	24.8	13.4	18.6	13.4	8.1	5.4	3.5	2.1	49.5	75 837	69 330	50 554	9.4	37.1
Bell	11.8	22.6	14.6	20.4	11.9	7.1	5.3	3.2	3.2	49.0	36 664	34 365	25 450	6.7	35.0
Bellflower	9.3	16.8	11.4	21.1	14.1	9.2	7.4	6.3	4.4	50.9	72 878	61 815	53 441	17.9	15.7
Bell Gardens	12.8	27.6	15.0	18.8	12.3	5.9	3.8	2.4	1.6	48.9	44 054	42 315	34 117	4.1	24.0
Belmont	5.9	11.8	9.2	20.9	16.8	13.4	10.4	7.6	4.0	51.2	25 123	24 165	24 505	4.0	-1.4
Benicia	8.0	19.5	6.8	16.6	20.5	13.2	7.2	5.1	3.0	50.7	26 865	24 437	15 376	9.9	58.9
Berkeley	4.5	9.7	22.1	18.8	17.1	10.9	6.0	6.0	4.9	50.3	102 743	102 724	103 328	0.0	-0.6
Beverly Hills	3.2	12.6	8.1	14.4	15.8	14.3	11.5	10.2	9.9	55.5	33 784	31 971	32 367	5.7	-1.2
Brea	6.3	16.5	11.4	18.6	17.5	11.9	8.8	5.8	3.1	50.3	35 410	32 873	27 913	7.7	17.8
Buena Park	8.4	18.1	11.4	20.2	14.5	10.6	8.8	5.2	2.7	49.9	78 282	68 784	64 165	13.8	7.2
Burbank	6.2	13.8	9.8	20.5	15.5	11.4	8.1	8.1	6.5	51.4	100 316	93 649	84 625	7.1	10.7
Burlingame	5.2	10.7	8.1	20.1	16.2	11.5	9.0	9.4	9.9	53.3	28 158	26 666	26 173	5.6	1.9
Calexico	8.7	29.1	10.7	13.2	13.7	8.5	7.9	5.7	2.6	52.8	27 109	18 633	14 412	45.5	29.3
Camarillo	6.9	17.6	7.9	15.7	16.2	10.7	8.2	9.5	7.2	50.8	57 077	52 297	37 797	9.1	38.4
Campbell	7.3	12.7	10.1	26.4	16.3	10.7	7.2	5.3	4.0	50.5	38 138	36 088	27 067	5.7	33.3
Carlsbad	6.7	14.8	8.9	19.5	17.8	10.7	8.7	8.6	4.4	49.4	78 247	63 292	35 490	23.6	78.3
Carson	7.7	19.7	11.3	17.0	14.5	12.6	9.1	5.4	2.8	50.9	89 730	83 995	81 221	6.8	3.4
Cathedral City	8.9	18.3	9.9	19.6	13.7	8.2	7.8	8.0	5.6	49.5	42 647	30 085	NA	41.8	NA
Ceres	10.0	23.0	8.9	19.7	15.3	8.3	6.6	5.1	3.1	51.1	34 609	26 413	13 281	31.0	98.9
Cerritos	5.7	22.1	11.1	12.3	18.4	17.5	7.3	3.9	1.6	50.7	51 488	53 244	53 020	-3.3	0.4
Chico	5.8	12.6	33.4	17.9	12.7	5.0	3.7	4.6	4.4	49.8	59 954	39 970	26 603	50.0	50.2
Chino	7.9	20.1	20.7	17.0	15.8	8.7	4.9	3.3	1.7	43.2	67 168	59 682	40 165	12.5	48.6
Chula Vista	8.2	18.0	11.1	19.1	14.1	9.6	8.5	7.1	4.3	50.9	173 556	135 160	83 927	28.4	61.0
Claremont	4.6	16.9	18.1	11.8	15.6	11.5	8.9	6.9	5.6	51.5	33 998	32 610	30 950	4.3	5.4
Clovis	9.3	21.4	10.3	20.7	17.3	7.9	5.3	4.3	3.4	51.7	68 468	50 323	33 021	36.1	52.4
Colton	11.2	20.9	12.4	22.8	13.6	7.5	5.1	4.1	2.4	50.6	47 662	40 273	21 310	18.3	89.0
Compton	11.0	25.6	12.8	18.6	11.8	8.1	6.3	4.0	1.8	51.0	93 493	90 454	81 286	3.4	11.3
Concord	7.7	16.8	10.1	20.1	17.0	11.0	7.9	5.9	3.5	50.8	121 780	111 308	103 255	9.4	7.8
Corona	10.7	20.4	11.4	21.9	15.8	9.0	5.1	3.5	2.2	49.3	124 966	75 943	37 791	64.6	101.0
Costa Mesa	6.9	12.7	13.4	26.3	16.0	9.3	7.3	5.1	3.0	48.9	108 724	96 357	82 562	12.8	16.7
Covina	7.7	17.5	11.1	18.9	15.6	9.9	8.8	6.6	3.9	52.0	46 837	43 332	33 751	8.1	28.4
Culver City	5.7	12.9	8.5	20.1	18.0	12.1	9.4	8.0	5.3	52.2	38 816	38 793	38 139	0.1	1.7
Cupertino	6.0	15.7	7.8	18.3	20.3	13.7	9.8	5.1	3.3	50.1	50 546	39 967	34 015	26.5	17.5
Cypress	6.6	18.1	11.2	17.4	16.3	13.5	9.6	5.0	2.4	50.8	46 229	42 655	40 391	8.4	5.6
Daly City	7.0	16.7	11.0	19.2	15.5	10.8	9.1	6.5	4.2	51.3	103 621	92 088	78 594	12.5	17.2
Dana Point	6.3	14.2	9.7	19.9	18.9	12.2	8.8	6.7	3.3	49.1	35 110	31 896	10 602	10.1	200.8
Danville	6.1	19.3	6.8	12.2	20.2	17.8	9.1	6.0	2.4	50.8	41 715	31 306	26 446	33.2	18.4
Davis	4.7	11.8	32.3	18.8	13.6	7.6	5.0	3.7	2.5	51.3	60 308	46 322	36 640	30.2	26.4
Delano	10.3	24.1	11.2	16.5	11.8	8.7	7.0	6.4	4.0	49.9	38 824	22 762	16 491	70.6	38.0
Diamond Bar	8.0	20.4	9.5	17.7	20.8	13.0	6.3	2.9	1.2	50.3	56 287	53 672	28 045	4.9	91.4
Downey	7.4	17.2	10.4	18.1	14.0	10.8	9.0	8.2	5.1	50.8	107 323	91 444	82 602	17.4	10.7
Dublin	7.4	14.7	8.9	26.5	21.3	11.5	6.4	2.5	0.9	44.8	29 973	23 229	13 496	29.0	72.1
East Palo Alto	10.7	22.0	12.1	20.0	14.3	8.9	6.1	4.1	1.8	49.0	29 506	23 451	18 191	25.8	28.9
El Cajon	9.1	17.2	12.6	20.9	13.9	8.4	6.8	6.3	4.8	51.3	94 869	88 918	73 892	6.7	20.3
El Centro	10.1	26.0	9.5	16.8	14.9	8.1	6.2	5.2	3.2	51.0	37 835	31 405	23 996	20.5	30.9
El Monte	10.9	23.2	14.5	19.6	12.8	7.6	5.1	4.0	2.5	48.6	115 965	106 162	79 494	9.2	33.5
Encinitas	6.7	15.2	9.5	21.3	21.3	10.2	6.4	5.2	4.2	48.5	58 014	55 406	10 796	4.7	413.2
Escondido	9.1	17.5	10.9	20.8	14.0	8.3	6.5	6.7	6.2	50.9	133 559	108 648	64 355	22.9	68.8
Eureka	6.9	17.9	9.8	16.3	16.5	9.4	7.9	8.3	7.1	51.4	26 128	27 025	24 074	-3.3	12.3
Fairfield	9.5	20.8	11.3	20.5	15.5	9.1	6.9	4.5	2.0	49.7	96 178	78 650	58 099	22.3	35.4
Folsom	6.8	14.0	8.6	25.6	20.2	10.2	5.9	5.2	3.5	40.0	51 884	29 802	11 003	74.1	170.9
Fontana	12.4	23.8	10.3	22.0	14.4	7.3	4.3	3.4	2.3	50.6	128 929	87 535	37 111	47.3	135.9
Foster City	5.2	15.1	8.9	19.7	19.9	15.4	9.1	4.8	2.0	50.1	28 803	28 176	23 287	2.2	21.0
Fountain Valley	5.4	18.4	11.8	14.8	17.0	16.2	9.1	4.7	2.6	50.2	54 978	53 691	55 080	2.4	-2.5
Fremont	8.2	17.7	9.3	22.0	18.0	11.2	7.0	4.2	2.3	49.9	203 413	173 339	131 945	17.3	31.4
Fresno	9.9	21.8	11.5	18.2	14.1	8.1	6.4	5.7	4.3	51.4	427 652	354 091	218 202	20.8	62.3
Fullerton	6.7	15.9	13.8	19.9	14.1	10.8	8.6	6.4	3.9	49.9	126 003	114 144	102 034	10.4	11.9
Gardena	7.6	15.9	9.5	21.0	15.0	11.0	9.2	6.8	4.2	50.5	57 746	51 481	45 165	12.2	14.0
Garden Grove	8.7	17.6	11.5	21.1	14.5	9.9	8.1	5.7	3.1	49.3	165 196	142 965	123 307	15.5	15.9
Gilroy	9.4	22.6	11.1	18.5	15.8	9.0	6.0	4.2	3.4	50.0	41 464	31 487	21 641	31.7	45.5
Glendale	6.5	15.2	9.9	19.8	15.7	11.2	8.5	7.0	6.3	51.9	194 973	180 038	139 060	8.3	29.5
Glendora	7.6	18.5	9.2	17.0	15.6	12.1	9.5	6.5	4.0	51.3	49 415	47 832	38 654	3.3	23.7
Hanford	9.4	20.9	10.0	17.4	14.0	9.7	7.4	6.1	5.1	51.5	41 686	30 463	20 995	36.8	45.1
Hawthorne	9.0	16.4	12.7	24.4	15.0	8.7	6.6	4.7	2.6	50.5	84 112	71 349	56 447	17.9	26.4
Hayward	7.8	17.0	10.8	20.7	15.6	9.4	8.3	6.5	3.9	50.8	140 030	114 705	94 167	22.1	21.8
Hemet	6.1	11.3	6.4	12.0	7.6	5.4	9.2	20.5	21.6	54.8	58 812	43 366	22 454	35.6	93.1
Hesperia	9.3	23.3	8.6	16.9	14.6	8.8	7.1	7.2	4.1	50.2	62 582	50 418	13 540	24.1	272.4
Highland	10.2	22.5	10.7	18.9	15.4	8.8	6.9	4.1	2.4	50.8	44 605	34 439	NA	29.5	NA
Hollister	9.8	23.3	10.4	19.9	14.0	7.4	6.4	5.1	3.6	49.8	34 413	19 318	11 488	78.1	68.2

Table D. Cities

City	Total population	Total in house-holds	House-holder	Spouse	Child Total	Own child under 18 years	Other relatives Total	Under 18 years	Nonrelatives Total	Unmar-ried partner	Total in group quarters	Correctional institu-tions	Nurs-ing homes	Other institu-tions	Col-lege dormi-tories	Mili-tary quar-ters	Other
	54	55	56	57	58	59	60	61	62	63	64	65	66	67	68	69	70
CALIFORNIA—Cont'd																	
Azusa	44 712	95.6	28.1	13.9	34.0	25.5	12.3	4.4	7.4	1.9	4.4	0.0	0.1	0.0	3.7	0.0	0.5
Bakersfield	247 057	98.5	33.8	17.6	35.5	29.0	6.4	2.8	5.2	2.1	1.5	0.3	0.5	0.1	0.1	0.0	0.7
Baldwin Park	75 837	99.2	22.4	14.0	38.7	27.4	17.3	6.2	6.7	1.4	0.8	0.0	0.3	0.0	0.0	0.0	0.4
Bell	36 664	98.5	24.3	14.1	39.3	29.8	14.6	4.6	6.2	1.8	1.5	0.0	0.3	0.0	0.0	0.0	1.2
Bellflower	72 878	99.1	32.1	15.1	35.7	27.8	10.1	3.3	6.2	2.4	0.9	0.0	0.3	0.0	0.0	0.0	0.5
Bell Gardens	44 054	99.0	21.5	12.9	43.9	34.3	14.5	4.6	6.2	1.9	1.0	0.0	0.3	0.4	0.0	0.0	0.4
Belmont	25 123	97.5	41.5	21.8	23.6	18.1	3.9	0.9	6.7	2.4	2.5	0.0	0.4	0.0	1.2	0.0	0.9
Benicia	26 865	99.8	38.4	20.9	31.7	25.1	4.0	1.6	4.8	2.3	0.2	0.0	0.1	0.0	0.0	0.0	0.1
Berkeley	102 743	94.3	43.8	12.6	16.5	12.4	4.3	1.2	17.2	3.2	5.7	0.0	0.2	0.1	4.5	0.0	1.0
Beverly Hills	33 784	99.9	44.5	19.5	26.5	19.1	3.5	0.6	5.9	1.6	0.1	0.0	0.0	0.0	0.0	0.0	0.1
Brea	35 410	99.6	36.9	20.9	31.7	23.5	5.5	1.8	4.7	1.4	0.4	0.0	0.0	0.1	0.0	0.0	0.3
Buena Park	78 282	98.8	29.8	17.6	34.8	25.2	10.9	3.5	5.7	1.6	1.2	0.0	0.4	0.0	0.0	0.0	0.8
Burbank	100 316	99.2	41.5	17.7	27.7	20.4	6.5	1.5	5.8	2.2	0.8	0.0	0.5	0.0	0.0	0.0	0.3
Burlingame	28 158	98.3	44.4	20.0	23.7	18.2	4.0	0.8	6.1	2.6	1.7	0.0	1.5	0.0	0.0	0.0	0.2
Calexico	27 109	99.6	25.1	15.4	40.0	27.5	15.4	6.6	3.7	0.8	0.4	0.0	0.0	0.0	0.0	0.0	0.4
Camarillo	57 077	98.4	37.6	22.4	29.6	23.1	4.6	1.6	4.2	1.4	1.6	0.3	0.4	0.0	0.2	0.0	0.7
Campbell	38 138	99.2	41.7	17.8	25.4	19.8	5.2	1.3	9.1	3.0	0.8	0.0	0.3	0.0	0.0	0.0	0.5
Carlsbad	78 247	99.0	40.3	21.9	27.0	22.0	3.5	0.9	6.3	2.1	1.0	0.0	0.7	0.0	0.0	0.0	0.3
Carson	89 730	98.7	27.5	16.1	34.3	21.5	15.5	5.8	5.3	1.2	1.3	0.0	0.3	0.0	0.5	0.0	0.6
Cathedral City	42 647	99.7	32.9	16.7	33.1	27.1	9.6	3.2	7.3	2.7	0.3	0.0	0.0	0.0	0.0	0.0	0.3
Ceres	34 609	99.7	30.2	18.0	38.3	30.1	8.3	3.4	4.9	2.0	0.3	0.0	0.2	0.0	0.0	0.0	0.1
Cerritos	51 488	99.8	29.9	22.1	34.7	21.5	10.5	2.7	2.6	0.6	0.2	0.0	0.1	0.0	0.0	0.0	0.1
Chico	59 954	94.9	39.2	13.5	22.9	19.6	3.1	1.0	16.2	2.7	5.1	0.0	0.8	0.0	3.3	0.0	1.0
Chino	67 168	88.4	25.8	16.1	33.0	24.3	9.0	3.5	4.5	1.3	11.6	11.4	0.0	0.0	0.0	0.0	0.3
Chula Vista	173 556	99.4	33.2	18.5	33.9	25.0	8.8	3.1	4.9	1.7	0.6	0.2	0.1	0.1	0.0	0.0	0.2
Claremont	33 998	85.0	33.2	18.5	25.2	18.8	4.2	1.4	4.0	1.2	15.0	0.0	1.1	0.2	13.1	0.0	0.6
Clovis	68 468	99.3	35.6	19.4	35.1	28.2	4.6	1.9	4.6	1.9	0.7	0.0	0.3	0.0	0.0	0.0	0.3
Colton	47 662	99.4	30.5	14.7	37.8	29.8	10.6	4.5	5.9	2.4	0.6	0.0	0.3	0.0	0.0	0.0	0.3
Compton	93 493	99.3	23.9	11.3	40.0	29.1	17.4	7.7	6.8	1.5	0.7	0.0	0.1	0.0	0.0	0.0	0.6
Concord	121 780	98.9	36.1	18.6	29.8	22.7	7.0	2.0	7.4	2.3	1.1	0.0	0.6	0.0	0.0	0.0	0.5
Corona	124 966	99.5	30.3	19.3	37.0	30.0	7.8	2.7	5.1	1.8	0.5	0.0	0.3	0.1	0.0	0.0	0.2
Costa Mesa	108 724	97.0	36.1	15.4	26.0	20.2	7.6	2.0	11.9	2.5	3.0	0.1	0.2	0.9	0.6	0.0	1.2
Covina	46 837	98.7	34.1	17.6	33.5	24.4	8.2	2.8	5.4	2.0	1.3	0.0	0.5	0.1	0.0	0.0	0.7
Culver City	38 816	98.7	42.8	17.5	26.0	19.0	6.0	1.6	6.4	2.2	1.3	0.0	0.4	0.2	0.0	0.0	0.7
Cupertino	50 546	99.1	36.0	23.0	31.3	25.6	4.7	0.8	4.2	1.1	0.9	0.0	0.7	0.0	0.0	0.0	0.1
Cypress	46 229	99.3	33.9	20.3	33.8	24.1	7.1	2.4	4.2	1.4	0.7	0.0	0.0	0.0	0.0	0.0	0.7
Daly City	103 621	99.2	29.7	16.2	29.4	18.0	16.3	3.9	7.7	1.4	0.8	0.0	0.5	0.0	0.0	0.0	0.2
Dana Point	35 110	99.3	41.2	21.2	24.7	18.8	4.3	1.3	8.0	2.4	0.7	0.0	0.3	0.0	0.0	0.0	0.4
Danville	41 715	98.9	35.5	25.1	33.1	27.8	2.3	0.6	2.9	1.2	1.1	0.0	0.2	0.0	0.0	0.0	0.9
Davis	60 308	95.1	38.1	14.6	20.5	17.6	2.3	0.5	19.6	2.1	4.9	0.0	0.4	0.0	3.9	0.0	0.6
Delano	38 824	87.0	21.7	13.1	36.0	27.6	11.9	4.4	4.3	1.3	13.0	12.4	0.5	0.0	0.0	0.0	0.2
Diamond Bar	56 287	99.8	31.4	21.4	34.8	24.7	8.7	1.9	3.5	0.9	0.2	0.0	0.1	0.0	0.0	0.0	0.1
Downey	107 323	98.4	31.7	17.1	34.5	25.1	10.2	3.1	4.9	1.9	1.6	0.0	0.4	0.9	0.0	0.0	0.1
Dublin	29 973	82.3	31.1	17.7	24.9	19.6	3.6	1.0	5.0	2.1	17.7	17.5	0.0	0.0	0.0	0.1	0.1
East Palo Alto	29 506	99.4	23.6	11.4	34.7	26.0	18.9	7.1	10.7	1.5	0.6	0.0	0.1	0.0	0.0	0.0	0.5
El Cajon	94 869	97.4	36.0	16.6	31.5	25.1	5.8	2.0	7.5	2.7	2.6	0.0	1.5	0.0	0.2	0.0	0.9
El Centro	37 835	97.7	30.2	16.3	38.1	28.7	9.3	4.4	3.7	1.6	2.3	1.5	0.3	0.2	0.0	0.0	0.4
El Monte	115 965	98.9	23.3	13.3	37.4	27.6	17.3	5.3	7.7	1.6	1.1	0.0	0.5	0.0	0.0	0.0	0.6
Encinitas	58 014	99.0	39.4	19.7	26.7	21.3	4.3	1.2	9.0	2.4	1.0	0.0	0.7	0.0	0.0	0.0	0.2
Escondido	133 559	98.7	32.8	17.7	32.2	25.9	8.4	2.8	7.6	2.0	1.3	0.0	0.5	0.0	0.0	0.0	0.8
Eureka	26 128	94.8	41.9	14.6	24.7	19.5	4.1	1.6	9.4	4.0	5.2	1.3	0.4	0.2	0.0	0.0	3.3
Fairfield	96 178	95.6	32.1	18.7	32.9	26.1	6.6	2.8	5.3	1.8	4.4	0.8	1.0	0.1	0.0	2.1	0.3
Folsom	51 884	86.6	33.1	20.4	27.3	23.1	2.6	0.8	3.2	1.5	13.4	6.0	0.2	0.0	0.0	0.0	7.2
Fontana	128 929	99.6	26.4	16.5	40.7	32.8	10.8	4.2	5.2	1.9	0.4	0.0	0.1	0.0	0.0	0.0	0.2
Foster City	28 803	99.7	40.3	23.3	26.6	20.2	4.2	0.8	5.3	1.9	0.3	0.0	0.2	0.0	0.0	0.0	0.1
Fountain Valley	54 978	99.1	33.0	20.9	31.2	20.7	8.7	2.4	5.2	1.2	0.9	0.0	0.3	0.0	0.0	0.0	0.6
Fremont	203 413	99.1	33.5	21.0	30.8	23.4	8.2	1.9	5.6	1.6	0.9	0.0	0.2	0.1	0.0	0.0	0.5
Fresno	427 652	98.1	32.8	15.1	35.8	28.8	8.0	3.2	6.4	2.4	1.9	0.6	0.4	0.1	0.3	0.0	0.5
Fullerton	126 003	97.8	34.6	17.9	29.6	22.0	8.1	2.3	7.6	1.8	2.2	0.0	0.7	0.0	0.7	0.0	0.8
Gardena	57 746	98.6	35.2	15.7	31.4	21.8	10.7	3.4	5.7	1.9	1.4	0.0	0.9	0.1	0.0	0.0	0.4
Garden Grove	165 196	98.6	27.7	16.6	33.6	23.9	13.8	3.7	7.0	1.3	1.4	0.1	0.4	0.0	0.0	0.0	0.9
Gilroy	41 464	99.0	28.6	17.4	35.9	27.7	10.0	3.7	7.0	1.9	1.0	0.0	0.3	0.2	0.0	0.0	0.5
Glendale	194 973	98.5	36.8	19.3	29.7	20.6	8.8	1.5	3.9	1.4	1.5	0.0	0.9	0.0	0.0	0.0	0.6
Glendora	49 415	98.0	34.0	20.5	33.6	25.0	5.9	2.1	4.0	1.3	2.0	0.0	1.4	0.2	0.1	0.0	0.4
Hanford	41 686	98.0	33.4	18.0	35.1	28.2	6.3	2.7	5.1	2.3	2.0	0.9	0.9	0.0	0.0	0.0	0.3
Hawthorne	84 112	99.4	33.9	13.1	35.4	27.5	10.2	3.5	6.7	2.8	0.6	0.0	0.4	0.0	0.0	0.0	0.2
Hayward	140 030	98.5	32.0	16.1	30.9	22.6	11.9	3.5	7.6	2.0	1.5	0.0	0.5	0.0	0.5	0.0	0.5
Hemet	58 812	97.1	42.9	19.4	24.8	20.1	4.9	1.9	5.2	2.4	2.9	0.0	1.5	0.1	0.0	0.0	1.3
Hesperia	62 582	99.5	31.9	18.8	35.9	28.2	7.6	3.6	5.3	2.0	0.5	0.1	0.2	0.0	0.0	0.0	0.2
Highland	44 605	99.5	30.2	16.6	38.4	30.9	8.7	3.8	5.5	2.3	0.5	0.0	0.2	0.0	0.0	0.0	0.5
Hollister	34 413	99.5	28.2	18.4	38.6	30.4	8.8	3.4	5.5	1.8	0.5	0.0	0.3	0.0	0.0	0.0	0.0

City	Households by type, 2000												Households, 1990		
	Family households						Nonfamily households								
			Married couple		Female householder[1]			Householder living alone							
	Total households	Total	With own children under 18 years	Total	With own children under 18 years	Total	With own children under 18 years	Total	Total	65 years and over	Average house-hold size	Average family size	Total house-holds	Female house-holder[1]	House-holder living alone
	71	72	73	74	75	76	77	78	79	80	81	82	83	84	85
CALIFORNIA—Cont'd															
Azusa	12 549	74.1	43.5	49.7	30.1	17.1	9.8	25.9	18.7	6.2	3.41	3.90	12 651	14.8	20.6
Bakersfield	83 441	73.1	42.5	52.1	28.6	15.5	10.6	26.9	21.5	7.2	2.92	3.41	62 467	14.0	23.0
Baldwin Park	16 961	88.8	55.9	62.8	42.2	17.5	9.7	11.2	8.1	3.9	4.44	4.53	16 614	16.3	10.5
Bell	8 918	85.4	57.6	58.0	41.5	18.3	11.5	14.6	11.0	5.1	4.05	4.27	9 013	15.1	17.3
Bellflower	23 367	73.3	43.7	47.0	27.7	19.0	12.1	26.7	21.1	7.5	3.09	3.59	22 905	13.8	25.3
Bell Gardens	9 466	89.9	67.3	60.1	47.0	19.6	14.3	10.1	7.2	2.8	4.61	4.69	9 244	18.2	9.3
Belmont	10 418	62.8	26.4	52.6	21.7	7.1	3.3	37.2	27.2	7.3	2.35	2.89	10 105	7.0	27.0
Benicia	10 328	70.1	36.7	54.2	26.9	11.9	7.5	29.9	23.6	6.7	2.60	3.10	9 208	9.8	21.3
Berkeley	44 955	41.5	17.8	28.9	11.8	9.5	4.7	58.5	38.1	7.9	2.16	2.84	43 453	10.7	39.8
Beverly Hills	15 035	55.0	24.4	43.8	18.8	8.1	4.4	45.0	38.2	11.3	2.24	3.02	14 564	8.1	38.1
Brea	13 067	71.2	34.6	56.6	27.1	10.5	5.6	28.8	23.0	8.5	2.70	3.21	12 224	8.0	21.7
Buena Park	23 332	80.3	43.0	59.0	32.5	14.8	7.6	19.7	14.4	5.4	3.32	3.64	22 210	12.8	15.1
Burbank	41 608	58.6	28.5	42.8	20.6	11.5	6.1	41.4	33.6	9.8	2.39	3.14	39 275	10.7	32.0
Burlingame	12 511	55.6	24.1	45.1	19.5	7.7	3.5	44.4	35.6	10.0	2.21	2.93	12 329	7.6	37.3
Calexico	6 814	87.8	53.4	61.2	38.9	22.0	12.6	12.2	10.4	6.9	3.96	4.21	4 729	21.6	10.8
Camarillo	21 438	71.1	33.0	59.7	26.6	8.2	4.7	28.9	24.1	13.6	2.62	3.12	18 109	7.3	18.1
Campbell	15 920	57.3	28.0	42.6	20.5	10.1	5.3	42.7	30.4	7.0	2.38	3.02	15 306	10.6	29.0
Carlsbad	31 521	66.3	30.7	54.3	24.0	8.6	5.0	33.7	24.8	8.2	2.46	2.96	24 995	8.1	23.2
Carson	24 648	82.1	39.2	58.7	29.8	17.2	6.9	17.9	14.2	5.9	3.59	3.92	23 808	14.2	14.2
Cathedral City	14 027	68.6	39.3	50.7	28.2	11.9	7.8	31.4	23.2	11.0	3.03	3.63	10 918	8.8	25.4
Ceres	10 435	81.8	48.6	59.8	35.2	15.7	10.0	18.2	14.1	6.0	3.31	3.62	8 581	11.7	15.7
Cerritos	15 390	88.7	40.9	73.9	35.4	10.9	4.2	11.3	8.9	3.1	3.34	3.54	15 026	9.5	7.4
Chico	23 476	49.6	27.1	34.4	16.9	11.3	7.9	50.4	29.3	8.1	2.42	3.03	15 508	10.5	29.6
Chino	17 304	81.5	47.3	62.5	37.0	12.9	7.4	18.5	14.1	5.2	3.43	3.77	15 636	10.8	14.7
Chula Vista	57 705	75.5	40.7	55.7	29.8	14.9	8.5	24.5	19.5	7.9	2.99	3.44	47 824	12.4	21.8
Claremont	11 281	69.2	31.3	55.7	24.1	10.4	5.8	30.8	24.9	10.6	2.56	3.08	10 472	8.9	21.3
Clovis	24 347	72.6	41.7	54.4	30.0	13.2	8.5	27.4	22.3	8.1	2.79	3.29	18 259	12.7	21.5
Colton	14 520	75.1	46.5	48.3	29.8	19.5	12.8	24.9	19.4	4.6	3.26	3.76	13 466	15.3	21.9
Compton	22 327	83.4	50.7	47.3	31.1	27.7	15.5	16.6	13.2	5.5	4.16	4.45	22 323	27.5	13.6
Concord	44 020	68.9	34.4	51.4	25.0	12.3	6.8	31.1	23.2	7.2	2.74	3.22	41 940	11.1	22.4
Corona	37 839	80.3	49.6	63.8	39.7	11.2	7.0	19.7	14.4	3.8	3.29	3.64	23 920	9.3	14.4
Costa Mesa	39 206	58.1	29.2	42.8	21.5	10.3	5.5	41.9	28.1	6.3	2.69	3.34	37 467	9.9	27.2
Covina	15 971	73.6	38.4	51.6	26.2	16.3	9.2	26.4	20.8	7.7	2.89	3.36	15 531	13.0	22.5
Culver City	16 611	57.3	26.1	40.8	17.8	12.8	6.9	42.7	34.5	9.3	2.31	3.02	16 166	11.4	31.6
Cupertino	18 204	74.8	41.6	63.9	36.4	7.8	3.9	25.2	19.6	6.4	2.75	3.19	15 358	8.0	20.0
Cypress	15 654	78.2	38.8	60.0	29.6	13.3	6.9	21.8	17.6	6.6	2.93	3.31	14 279	11.5	15.0
Daly City	30 775	75.0	34.1	54.5	26.5	14.2	5.5	25.0	18.1	6.7	3.34	3.78	29 010	13.5	19.9
Dana Point	14 456	64.2	26.2	51.4	19.4	8.8	4.7	35.8	26.0	7.1	2.41	2.90	12 701	8.3	23.2
Danville	14 816	80.1	42.2	70.7	36.6	7.1	4.2	19.9	15.5	5.6	2.78	3.13	11 064	6.7	12.8
Davis	22 948	49.2	26.4	38.3	19.9	8.2	5.2	50.8	25.0	5.2	2.50	3.00	17 926	7.3	24.3
Delano	8 409	86.2	56.3	60.3	40.4	18.4	11.7	13.8	10.8	5.4	4.02	4.27	6 236	15.4	14.6
Diamond Bar	17 651	83.9	44.4	68.3	37.0	11.1	5.6	16.1	12.5	2.7	3.18	3.47	16 901	8.5	11.6
Downey	33 989	76.5	41.8	54.1	29.6	15.8	9.0	23.5	19.1	8.1	3.11	3.55	33 013	12.2	23.0
Dublin	9 325	69.8	35.4	56.9	28.1	9.1	5.4	30.2	21.3	2.8	2.65	3.13	6 802	8.3	14.5
East Palo Alto	6 976	75.6	47.3	48.2	32.7	19.8	11.0	24.4	18.2	4.5	4.20	4.64	6 953	20.8	25.2
El Cajon	34 199	67.7	37.0	46.0	23.3	16.0	10.4	32.3	24.1	8.5	2.70	3.21	32 893	14.7	22.9
El Centro	11 439	77.9	47.4	53.9	31.9	18.7	12.4	22.1	18.8	7.3	3.23	3.71	9 633	15.5	18.6
El Monte	27 034	85.1	53.3	57.0	38.0	18.5	11.0	14.9	10.9	4.9	4.24	4.43	26 131	16.3	13.7
Encinitas	22 830	62.6	31.0	50.1	23.9	8.8	5.2	37.4	25.7	6.9	2.52	3.06	20 782	8.9	23.3
Escondido	43 817	71.1	39.1	53.9	28.5	11.7	7.5	28.9	22.4	10.1	3.01	3.50	39 267	10.3	23.3
Eureka	10 957	53.7	25.8	34.8	13.7	14.0	9.2	46.3	35.3	11.8	2.26	2.93	11 137	12.2	32.5
Fairfield	30 870	77.8	43.1	58.4	31.2	14.2	9.0	22.2	17.0	5.5	2.98	3.33	25 425	12.5	16.9
Folsom	17 196	72.8	39.1	61.7	32.0	8.0	5.1	27.2	21.8	7.1	2.61	3.08	8 757	7.5	19.9
Fontana	34 014	85.3	57.6	62.5	43.1	15.5	10.2	14.7	10.9	3.6	3.78	4.02	26 385	13.7	14.6
Foster City	11 613	68.3	30.5	57.7	25.5	7.7	3.8	31.7	23.6	5.0	2.47	2.97	11 210	7.6	23.1
Fountain Valley	18 162	78.3	34.3	63.4	28.4	10.5	4.4	21.7	16.0	5.5	3.00	3.35	17 407	9.6	13.5
Fremont	68 237	76.5	40.2	62.7	33.6	9.2	4.6	23.5	16.5	4.1	2.96	3.34	60 198	9.2	16.8
Fresno	140 079	69.9	40.4	46.1	25.4	17.6	11.5	30.1	23.3	7.9	2.99	3.57	121 807	16.2	24.1
Fullerton	43 609	67.9	33.0	51.8	25.1	11.0	5.7	32.1	23.5	7.3	2.83	3.37	40 872	9.7	22.4
Gardena	20 324	69.0	33.5	44.5	21.2	18.1	9.8	31.0	25.5	8.2	2.80	3.38	18 126	14.4	25.9
Garden Grove	45 791	79.6	42.6	59.7	33.8	13.0	6.1	20.4	15.2	6.0	3.56	3.90	44 538	11.9	16.7
Gilroy	11 869	80.8	47.7	60.8	35.9	14.2	8.6	19.2	14.3	5.9	3.46	3.74	9 512	14.3	15.2
Glendale	71 805	69.1	32.9	52.3	26.3	11.8	5.2	30.9	25.7	8.7	2.68	3.27	68 604	10.5	27.8
Glendora	16 819	76.5	38.6	60.1	30.1	12.1	6.3	23.5	19.1	7.9	2.88	3.30	16 327	9.7	17.5
Hanford	13 931	74.5	42.3	53.9	28.5	15.4	10.5	25.5	20.6	8.7	2.93	3.39	10 855	14.9	21.8
Hawthorne	28 536	69.3	43.7	38.6	23.8	23.5	15.9	30.7	24.5	4.5	2.93	3.50	27 137	16.1	30.1
Hayward	44 804	71.3	37.0	50.3	26.5	14.5	7.7	28.7	20.9	7.3	3.08	3.58	40 117	13.1	22.3
Hemet	25 252	60.1	23.0	45.1	14.1	11.2	6.7	39.9	34.4	23.2	2.26	2.90	17 397	7.9	36.3
Hesperia	19 966	79.0	42.6	58.9	30.0	13.8	8.7	21.0	16.5	7.6	3.12	3.47	16 551	10.0	15.6
Highland	13 478	80.0	47.9	55.1	32.0	19.0	12.3	20.0	15.4	4.8	3.29	3.64	11 317	16.1	17.2
Hollister	9 716	82.8	52.2	65.3	41.2	12.2	7.6	17.2	12.7	4.7	3.52	3.82	5 896	12.2	17.0

[1] No spouse present.

Table D. Cities

City	Percent change of households, 1990–2000	Total housing units	Occupied housing units (percent)	Vacant housing units		Homeowner vacancy rate (percent)	Rental vacancy rate (percent)	Occupied housing units			Average household size of owner-occupied units	Average household size of renter-occupied units
				Total	For seasonal, recreational, or occasional use			Total	Percent owner-occupied housing units	Percent renter-occupied housing units		
	86	87	88	89	90	91	92	93	94	95	96	97
CALIFORNIA—Cont'd												
Azusa	-0.8	13 013	96.4	3.6	0.2	1.1	4.0	12 549	50.5	49.5	3.34	3.48
Bakersfield	33.6	88 262	94.5	5.5	0.3	2.0	6.2	83 441	60.5	39.5	3.01	2.77
Baldwin Park	2.1	17 430	97.3	2.7	0.1	1.2	1.9	16 961	61.0	39.0	4.43	4.45
Bell	-1.1	9 215	96.8	3.2	0.5	1.7	1.9	8 918	30.9	69.1	4.36	3.91
Bellflower	2.0	24 247	96.4	3.6	0.2	1.8	3.0	23 367	40.3	59.7	3.20	3.02
Bell Gardens	2.4	9 788	96.7	3.3	0.1	2.7	1.7	9 466	23.8	76.2	4.67	4.59
Belmont	3.1	10 577	98.5	1.5	0.2	0.3	1.0	10 418	60.2	39.8	2.59	1.99
Benicia	12.2	10 547	97.9	2.1	0.4	0.5	2.4	10 328	70.7	29.3	2.73	2.27
Berkeley	3.5	46 875	95.9	4.1	0.6	0.7	2.8	44 955	42.7	57.3	2.40	1.98
Beverly Hills	3.2	15 856	94.8	5.2	0.9	1.6	3.3	15 035	43.4	56.6	2.73	1.87
Brea	6.9	13 327	98.0	2.0	0.3	0.5	2.1	13 067	64.2	35.8	2.88	2.37
Buena Park	5.1	23 826	97.9	2.1	0.1	0.8	2.2	23 332	57.1	42.9	3.28	3.36
Burbank	5.9	42 847	97.1	2.9	0.4	0.9	2.1	41 608	43.5	56.5	2.61	2.22
Burlingame	1.5	12 869	97.2	2.8	0.6	0.4	2.2	12 511	47.9	52.1	2.58	1.87
Calexico	44.1	6 983	97.6	2.4	0.3	1.0	1.1	6 814	55.2	44.8	4.19	3.68
Camarillo	18.4	21 946	97.7	2.3	0.3	0.9	1.9	21 438	73.5	26.5	2.63	2.59
Campbell	4.0	16 286	97.8	2.2	0.6	0.4	1.5	15 920	48.2	51.8	2.55	2.22
Carlsbad	26.1	33 798	93.3	6.7	2.6	2.2	4.1	31 521	67.4	32.6	2.52	2.33
Carson	3.5	25 337	97.3	2.7	0.1	1.1	2.6	24 648	77.9	22.1	3.57	3.68
Cathedral City	28.5	17 893	78.4	21.6	10.5	4.1	5.2	14 027	65.2	34.8	2.95	3.18
Ceres	21.6	10 773	96.9	3.1	0.1	1.0	3.8	10 435	66.2	33.8	3.29	3.34
Cerritos	2.4	15 607	98.6	1.4	0.2	0.4	1.7	15 390	83.5	16.5	3.30	3.56
Chico	51.4	24 386	96.3	3.7	0.3	1.8	2.6	23 476	40.4	59.6	2.52	2.35
Chino	10.7	17 898	96.7	3.3	0.1	0.9	5.2	17 304	68.7	31.3	3.51	3.26
Chula Vista	20.7	59 495	97.0	3.0	0.4	1.0	3.1	57 705	57.4	42.6	3.09	2.85
Claremont	7.7	11 559	97.6	2.4	0.4	0.7	2.2	11 281	66.7	33.3	2.74	2.20
Clovis	33.3	25 250	96.4	3.6	0.2	1.5	4.0	24 347	60.4	39.6	2.95	2.56
Colton	7.8	15 680	92.6	7.4	0.3	3.4	7.0	14 520	52.0	48.0	3.53	2.97
Compton	0.0	23 795	93.8	6.2	0.1	3.7	5.1	22 327	56.3	43.7	4.16	4.15
Concord	5.0	45 083	97.6	2.4	0.3	0.5	2.3	44 020	62.6	37.4	2.69	2.81
Corona	58.2	39 271	96.4	3.6	0.2	1.9	3.8	37 839	67.5	32.5	3.39	3.06
Costa Mesa	4.6	40 406	97.0	3.0	0.3	0.8	2.8	39 206	40.5	59.5	2.66	2.71
Covina	2.8	16 364	97.6	2.4	0.1	0.8	2.5	15 971	58.4	41.6	3.02	2.72
Culver City	2.8	17 130	97.0	3.0	0.2	1.2	2.1	16 611	54.4	45.6	2.34	2.26
Cupertino	18.5	18 682	97.4	2.6	0.4	0.6	1.8	18 204	63.6	36.4	2.83	2.62
Cypress	9.6	16 028	97.7	2.3	0.6	0.6	2.9	15 654	69.4	30.6	2.96	2.87
Daly City	6.1	31 311	98.3	1.7	0.3	0.3	1.7	30 775	59.8	40.2	3.48	3.13
Dana Point	13.8	15 682	92.2	7.8	4.6	1.2	4.2	14 456	62.0	38.0	2.38	2.46
Danville	33.9	15 130	97.9	2.1	0.3	0.6	5.5	14 816	89.1	10.9	2.83	2.38
Davis	28.0	23 617	97.2	2.8	0.4	0.8	2.7	22 948	44.6	55.4	2.64	2.39
Delano	34.8	8 830	95.2	4.8	0.3	1.1	5.6	8 409	59.4	40.6	4.16	3.80
Diamond Bar	4.4	17 959	98.3	1.7	0.2	0.7	1.9	17 651	82.6	17.4	3.21	3.05
Downey	3.0	34 759	97.8	2.2	0.2	1.0	1.5	33 989	51.8	48.2	3.26	2.94
Dublin	37.1	9 872	94.5	5.5	0.4	0.7	8.1	9 325	64.9	35.1	2.80	2.37
East Palo Alto	0.3	7 091	98.4	1.6	0.2	0.3	1.0	6 976	43.5	56.5	4.69	3.83
El Cajon	4.0	35 190	97.2	2.8	0.3	0.6	2.7	34 199	40.5	59.5	2.67	2.72
El Centro	18.7	12 263	93.3	6.7	2.4	1.2	4.9	11 439	50.2	49.8	3.34	3.12
El Monte	3.5	27 758	97.4	2.6	0.2	1.2	1.4	27 034	41.0	59.0	4.03	4.39
Encinitas	9.9	23 843	95.8	4.2	1.9	0.9	2.6	22 830	64.2	35.8	2.61	2.35
Escondido	11.6	45 050	97.3	2.7	0.2	1.0	2.7	43 817	53.2	46.8	2.93	3.10
Eureka	-1.6	11 637	94.2	5.8	0.5	2.0	4.7	10 957	46.5	53.5	2.29	2.23
Fairfield	21.4	31 792	97.1	2.9	0.2	0.7	3.9	30 870	59.7	40.3	2.99	2.97
Folsom	96.4	17 968	95.7	4.3	0.4	1.6	7.1	17 196	76.3	23.7	2.75	2.18
Fontana	28.9	35 908	94.7	5.3	0.1	3.1	4.2	34 014	68.1	31.9	3.87	3.58
Foster City	3.6	12 009	96.7	3.3	1.1	0.3	2.6	11 613	61.5	38.5	2.64	2.21
Fountain Valley	4.3	18 473	98.3	1.7	0.3	0.5	2.3	18 162	74.7	25.3	3.07	2.79
Fremont	13.4	69 452	98.3	1.7	0.3	0.6	1.7	68 237	64.5	35.5	3.08	2.73
Fresno	15.0	149 025	94.0	6.0	0.2	1.9	6.4	140 079	50.6	49.4	2.94	3.05
Fullerton	6.7	44 771	97.4	2.6	0.2	0.8	2.8	43 609	53.9	46.1	2.87	2.77
Gardena	12.1	21 041	96.6	3.4	0.2	1.2	3.3	20 324	47.3	52.7	2.85	2.76
Garden Grove	2.8	46 703	98.0	2.0	0.2	0.7	2.0	45 791	59.6	40.4	3.49	3.67
Gilroy	24.8	12 152	97.7	2.3	0.1	0.6	1.6	11 869	61.2	38.8	3.27	3.75
Glendale	4.7	73 713	97.4	2.6	0.3	0.9	1.9	71 805	38.4	61.6	2.72	2.65
Glendora	3.0	17 145	98.1	1.9	0.2	0.6	2.1	16 819	73.6	26.4	2.97	2.62
Hanford	28.3	14 721	94.6	5.4	0.4	2.1	6.0	13 931	59.0	41.0	2.96	2.89
Hawthorne	5.2	29 629	96.3	3.7	0.2	1.4	3.3	28 536	25.9	74.1	3.36	2.78
Hayward	11.7	45 922	97.6	2.4	0.2	0.6	2.6	44 804	53.2	46.8	3.13	3.02
Hemet	45.2	29 401	85.9	14.1	2.6	3.1	19.2	25 252	64.6	35.4	2.15	2.46
Hesperia	20.6	21 348	93.5	6.5	0.4	2.7	7.3	19 966	72.3	27.7	3.08	3.23
Highland	19.1	14 858	90.7	9.3	0.2	3.7	12.6	13 478	66.6	33.4	3.22	3.44
Hollister	64.8	9 924	97.9	2.1	0.2	0.6	2.3	9 716	67.0	33.0	3.51	3.55

Table D. Cities

STATE Place code	City	Land area, 2000[1] (sq km)	Total persons	Rank	Per square kilometer	Land area, 1990[1] (sq km)	Total persons	Rank	Per square kilometer	White	Black or African American	American Indian or Alaska Native	Asian	Native Hawaiian and other Pacific Islander	Some other race
		1	2	3	4	5	6	7	8	9	10	11	12	13	14
	CALIFORNIA—Cont'd														
06 36000	Huntington Beach	68.4	189 594	103	2 771.8	68.4	181 519	91	2 653.8	79.2	0.8	0.6	9.3	0.2	5.8
06 36056	Huntington Park	7.8	61 348	484	7 865.1	7.9	56 129	459	7 104.0	41.4	0.8	1.0	0.8	0.1	51.1
06 36294	Imperial Beach	11.1	26 992	1 382	2 431.7	11.0	26 512	1 211	2 410.2	62.3	5.3	1.1	6.5	0.6	17.8
06 36448	Indio	69.1	49 116	689	710.8	44.1	36 850	818	835.6	48.7	2.8	1.0	1.5	0.1	42.0
06 36546	Inglewood	23.7	112 580	208	4 750.2	23.7	109 602	175	4 624.6	19.1	47.1	0.7	1.1	0.4	27.4
06 36770	Irvine	119.6	143 072	152	1 196.3	109.6	110 330	172	1 006.7	61.1	1.4	0.2	29.8	0.1	2.5
06 39248	Laguna Niguel	38.0	61 891	477	1 628.7	37.9	44 723	641	1 180.0	83.5	1.3	0.3	7.7	0.1	3.5
06 39290	La Habra	19.0	58 974	516	3 103.9	19.0	51 263	535	2 698.1	63.0	1.6	1.0	5.9	0.2	23.7
06 39486	Lake Elsinore	87.6	28 928	1 277	330.2	60.7	19 733	1 669	325.1	65.6	5.2	1.3	2.0	0.3	20.3
06 39496	Lake Forest	32.4	58 707	522	1 811.9	NA	56 065	460	NA	76.0	1.8	0.5	9.7	0.2	7.5
06 39892	Lakewood	24.4	79 345	346	3 251.8	24.3	73 553	314	3 026.9	62.7	7.3	0.6	13.5	0.6	10.1
06 40004	La Mesa	24.0	54 749	595	2 281.2	23.9	52 911	509	2 213.8	80.6	4.9	0.7	4.1	0.4	5.1
06 40032	La Mirada	20.3	46 783	729	2 304.6	20.3	40 452	728	1 992.7	64.5	1.9	0.7	14.9	0.3	13.6
06 40130	Lancaster	243.5	118 718	191	487.5	230.0	97 300	210	423.0	62.8	16.0	1.0	3.8	0.2	11.1
06 40340	La Puente	9.0	41 063	843	4 562.6	9.0	36 955	816	4 106.1	39.1	2.0	1.3	7.2	0.2	45.1
06 40830	La Verne	21.5	31 638	1 152	1 471.5	20.2	30 843	1 019	1 526.9	77.1	3.2	0.6	7.2	0.2	7.4
06 40886	Lawndale	5.1	31 711	1 148	6 217.8	5.1	27 331	1 167	5 359.0	42.2	12.6	1.0	9.6	0.9	27.1
06 41992	Livermore	62.0	73 345	382	1 183.0	50.9	56 741	453	1 114.8	81.9	1.6	0.6	5.8	0.3	5.3
06 42202	Lodi	31.7	56 999	547	1 798.1	27.5	51 874	526	1 886.3	74.4	0.6	0.9	5.1	0.1	14.0
06 42524	Lompoc	30.1	41 103	842	1 365.5	29.1	37 649	802	1 293.8	65.8	7.3	1.6	3.9	0.3	15.7
06 43000	Long Beach	130.6	461 522	36	3 533.9	129.5	429 321	32	3 315.2	45.2	14.9	0.8	12.0	1.2	20.6
06 43280	Los Altos	16.4	27 693	1 344	1 688.6	16.5	26 599	1 205	1 612.1	80.3	0.5	0.2	15.4	0.2	0.7
06 44000	Los Angeles	1 214.9	3 694 820	2	3 041.3	1 215.6	3 485 557	2	2 867.4	46.9	11.2	0.8	10.0	0.2	25.7
06 44028	Los Banos	20.8	25 869	1 457	1 243.7	18.1	14 519	2 244	802.2	58.6	4.3	1.4	2.3	0.3	26.9
06 44112	Los Gatos	27.7	28 592	1 294	1 032.2	26.9	27 357	1 164	1 017.0	86.7	0.8	0.3	7.6	0.1	1.3
06 44574	Lynwood	12.6	69 845	408	5 543.3	12.6	61 945	402	4 916.3	33.6	13.5	1.2	0.8	0.4	46.1
06 45022	Madera	31.8	43 207	795	1 358.7	26.7	29 283	1 079	1 096.7	48.1	3.9	2.8	1.4	0.1	38.0
06 45400	Manhattan Beach	10.2	33 852	1 066	3 318.8	10.2	32 063	969	3 143.4	89.0	0.6	0.2	6.0	0.1	1.2
06 45484	Manteca	41.2	49 258	686	1 195.6	22.8	40 773	721	1 788.3	74.2	2.9	1.3	3.5	0.4	11.6
06 45778	Marina	22.7	25 101	1 502	1 105.8	22.7	26 512	1 211	1 167.9	43.7	14.3	0.7	16.3	2.1	14.8
06 46114	Martinez	31.7	35 866	992	1 131.4	29.0	31 800	982	1 096.6	81.0	3.3	0.7	6.6	0.2	3.3
06 46492	Maywood	3.0	28 083	1 319	9 361.0	3.0	27 893	1 145	9 297.7	43.0	0.4	1.1	0.4	0.1	50.5
06 46870	Menlo Park	26.2	30 785	1 192	1 175.0	26.1	28 403	1 119	1 088.2	72.4	7.0	0.4	7.1	1.3	8.6
06 46898	Merced	51.4	63 893	457	1 243.1	41.8	56 155	458	1 343.4	52.4	6.3	1.3	11.4	0.2	23.2
06 47766	Milpitas	35.1	62 698	471	1 786.3	35.6	50 690	543	1 423.9	30.9	3.7	0.6	51.8	0.6	7.5
06 48256	Mission Viejo	48.3	93 102	270	1 927.6	45.2	79 464	283	1 758.1	83.2	1.1	0.4	7.7	0.2	3.8
06 48354	Modesto	92.7	188 856	105	2 037.3	78.2	164 746	105	2 106.7	69.6	4.0	1.2	6.0	0.5	12.7
06 48648	Monrovia	35.6	36 929	951	1 037.3	34.6	35 733	837	1 032.7	62.9	8.7	0.9	7.0	0.1	15.6
06 48788	Montclair	13.2	33 049	1 095	2 503.7	13.1	28 434	1 117	2 170.5	44.8	6.4	1.0	8.1	0.3	34.6
06 48816	Montebello	21.4	62 150	476	2 904.2	21.4	59 564	426	2 783.4	46.8	0.9	1.2	11.6	0.1	33.9
06 48872	Monterey	21.9	29 674	1 241	1 355.0	21.8	31 954	974	1 465.8	80.8	2.5	0.6	7.4	0.3	3.9
06 48914	Monterey Park	19.8	60 051	501	3 032.9	19.8	60 738	414	3 067.6	21.3	0.4	0.7	61.8	0.1	12.4
06 49138	Moorpark	49.3	31 415	1 164	637.2	31.8	25 494	1 265	801.7	74.4	1.5	0.5	5.6	0.1	13.9
06 49270	Moreno Valley	132.7	142 381	154	1 073.0	127.3	118 779	156	933.1	46.8	19.9	0.9	5.9	0.5	20.1
06 49278	Morgan Hill	30.2	33 556	1 080	1 111.1	27.1	23 928	1 360	883.0	72.4	1.7	1.1	6.0	0.2	13.4
06 49670	Mountain View	31.2	70 708	402	2 266.3	31.2	67 365	359	2 159.1	63.8	2.5	0.4	20.7	0.3	8.3
06 50076	Murrieta	73.5	44 282	776	602.5	NA	18 557	1 775	NA	81.6	3.4	0.7	4.0	0.2	5.8
06 50258	Napa	45.8	72 585	389	1 584.8	45.1	61 865	403	1 371.7	80.3	0.5	0.9	1.7	0.2	12.6
06 50398	National City	19.1	54 260	603	2 840.8	19.6	54 249	485	2 767.8	35.1	5.6	0.9	18.6	0.9	33.5
06 50916	Newark	36.2	42 471	811	1 173.2	36.2	37 861	792	1 045.9	52.2	4.0	0.6	21.3	1.0	13.7
06 51182	Newport Beach	38.3	70 032	407	1 828.5	36.3	66 643	364	1 835.9	92.2	0.5	0.3	4.0	0.1	1.1
06 52526	Norwalk	25.1	103 298	233	4 115.5	25.3	94 279	221	3 726.4	44.8	4.6	1.2	11.5	0.4	32.7
06 52582	Novato	71.8	47 630	712	663.4	71.4	47 585	594	666.5	82.8	2.0	0.5	5.2	0.2	5.4
06 53000	Oakland	145.2	399 484	43	2 751.3	145.2	372 242	40	2 563.7	31.3	35.7	0.7	15.2	0.5	11.7
06 53322	Oceanside	105.1	161 029	129	1 532.2	105.3	128 090	142	1 216.4	66.4	6.3	0.9	5.5	1.3	14.5
06 53896	Ontario	128.9	158 007	132	1 225.8	95.2	133 179	136	1 398.9	47.8	7.5	1.1	3.9	0.4	34.1
06 53980	Orange	60.6	128 821	170	2 125.8	60.4	110 658	171	1 832.1	70.5	1.6	0.8	9.3	0.2	13.8
06 54652	Oxnard	65.6	170 358	126	2 596.9	63.3	142 560	124	2 252.1	42.1	3.8	1.3	7.4	0.4	40.4
06 54806	Pacifica	32.7	38 390	916	1 174.0	32.7	37 670	801	1 152.0	69.5	3.3	0.5	15.3	0.7	4.2
06 55156	Palmdale	271.8	116 670	198	429.2	201.0	73 314	316	364.7	54.8	14.5	1.0	3.8	0.2	20.4
06 55184	Palm Desert	63.1	41 155	839	652.2	49.4	23 252	1 403	470.7	86.8	1.2	0.5	2.6	0.1	6.5
06 55254	Palm Springs	244.1	42 807	804	175.4	198.3	40 144	735	202.4	78.3	3.9	0.9	3.8	0.1	9.8
06 55282	Palo Alto	61.3	58 598	523	955.9	61.3	55 900	462	911.9	75.8	2.0	0.2	17.2	0.1	1.4
06 55520	Paradise	47.3	26 408	1 418	558.3	48.3	25 401	1 270	525.9	93.7	0.2	1.1	1.0	0.1	1.2
06 55618	Paramount	12.3	55 266	584	4 493.2	12.2	47 669	592	3 907.3	34.7	13.6	1.1	3.3	0.8	41.7
06 56000	Pasadena	59.8	133 936	165	2 239.7	59.5	131 586	139	2 211.5	53.4	14.4	0.7	10.0	0.1	16.0
06 56700	Perris	81.3	36 189	978	445.1	76.9	21 500	1 527	279.6	41.2	15.9	1.5	2.7	0.3	32.6
06 56784	Petaluma	35.7	54 548	599	1 528.0	31.9	43 166	665	1 353.2	84.2	1.2	0.5	3.9	0.2	6.1
06 56924	Pico Rivera	21.5	63 428	463	2 950.1	20.7	59 177	431	2 858.8	49.4	0.7	1.4	2.7	0.1	40.3
06 57456	Pittsburg	40.4	56 769	550	1 405.2	28.2	47 607	593	1 688.2	43.5	18.9	0.7	12.6	0.9	16.1
06 57526	Placentia	17.1	46 488	734	2 718.6	17.1	41 259	707	2 412.8	67.8	1.8	0.8	11.2	0.2	14.7

[1] Dry land or land partially or temporarily covered by water.

Table D. Cities

City	Population and population characteristics, 2000 (cont'd.)								Population and population characteristics, 1990				
	Race (percent) (cont'd.)								Race (percent)				
	Race alone or in combination												
	Two or more races	White	Black	American Indian or Alaskan Native	Asian	Native Hawaiian and other Pacific Islander	Some other race	Hispanic[1]	White	Black or African American	American Indian or Alaskan Native	Asian and Pacific Islander	Hispanic[1]
	15	16	17	18	19	20	21	22	23	24	25	26	27
CALIFORNIA—Cont'd													
Huntington Beach	3.9	82.7	1.1	1.5	10.9	0.6	7.4	14.7	86.1	0.9	0.6	8.3	11.2
Huntington Park	4.9	45.9	1.0	1.3	1.0	0.1	55.6	95.6	31.2	1.1	0.5	1.8	91.9
Imperial Beach	6.5	67.5	6.4	2.1	9.2	1.3	20.5	40.1	72.9	4.9	1.2	8.3	28.3
Indio	3.9	52.1	3.1	1.5	2.0	0.2	45.2	75.4	54.5	4.0	0.8	1.6	68.1
Inglewood	4.2	21.9	48.7	1.4	1.6	0.5	30.4	46.0	17.4	51.9	0.4	2.5	38.5
Irvine	4.8	65.2	1.8	0.6	32.3	0.4	4.7	7.4	77.9	1.8	0.2	18.1	6.3
Laguna Niguel	3.6	86.8	1.6	0.8	9.2	0.3	5.2	10.4	88.5	1.4	0.3	7.8	7.8
La Habra	4.7	67.1	2.0	1.6	6.9	0.5	26.9	49.0	76.6	0.9	0.7	4.1	33.9
Lake Elsinore	5.2	69.8	6.2	2.5	3.1	0.6	23.3	38.0	76.9	3.9	1.1	2.3	26.0
Lake Forest	4.2	79.8	2.3	1.2	11.3	0.5	9.4	18.6	85.6	1.8	0.4	9.2	10.3
Lakewood	5.2	66.8	8.1	1.6	15.5	1.2	12.4	22.8	81.1	3.7	0.7	9.4	14.6
La Mesa	4.3	84.4	5.8	1.5	5.4	0.7	6.8	13.5	90.2	3.0	0.5	3.1	9.8
La Mirada	4.1	67.9	2.3	1.4	16.0	0.5	16.0	33.5	81.2	1.4	0.6	8.2	25.9
Lancaster	5.0	67.0	17.5	2.3	4.9	0.5	13.4	24.1	79.4	7.4	0.9	3.7	15.2
La Puente	5.2	43.4	2.4	1.9	7.9	0.4	49.4	83.1	63.9	3.5	0.6	7.8	74.9
La Verne	4.3	80.9	3.7	1.3	8.4	0.4	9.8	23.1	83.0	3.0	0.6	7.2	18.4
Lawndale	6.6	47.5	13.6	1.8	11.1	1.2	31.7	52.1	60.6	8.3	0.9	12.1	34.2
Livermore	4.5	85.9	2.1	1.6	7.5	0.7	7.1	14.4	89.4	1.5	0.7	4.6	9.8
Lodi	4.9	78.4	0.9	1.8	6.7	0.4	17.0	27.1	89.3	0.3	0.9	4.7	16.9
Lompoc	5.4	70.3	8.4	3.0	5.3	0.7	18.1	37.3	70.5	7.8	1.3	5.4	26.8
Long Beach	5.3	48.9	16.0	1.7	13.7	1.7	23.6	35.8	58.4	13.7	0.6	13.6	23.6
Los Altos	2.8	82.9	0.6	0.5	17.2	0.3	1.5	3.0	89.0	0.4	0.2	10.0	3.0
Los Angeles	5.2	51.2	12.0	1.4	11.0	0.4	29.4	46.5	52.8	14.0	0.5	9.8	39.9
Los Banos	6.2	63.7	5.1	2.5	3.7	0.7	30.8	50.4	70.8	2.7	0.6	1.9	35.9
Los Gatos	3.3	89.7	1.1	0.8	9.2	0.3	2.5	5.2	92.8	0.7	0.4	5.0	5.0
Lynwood	4.4	37.3	14.0	1.7	1.0	0.5	50.0	82.3	24.0	23.7	0.4	2.2	70.3
Madera	5.7	52.9	4.4	3.9	2.1	0.2	42.3	67.8	57.6	4.6	0.9	1.6	53.8
Manhattan Beach	2.8	91.6	0.9	0.6	7.6	0.3	1.9	5.2	93.5	0.6	0.3	4.4	5.1
Manteca	6.2	79.6	3.5	2.8	5.1	0.9	14.8	25.1	89.5	1.5	1.2	3.5	17.8
Marina	8.0	49.4	16.3	2.2	20.4	3.4	17.1	23.2	53.6	19.0	0.7	20.8	10.7
Martinez	4.7	85.2	4.0	2.0	8.4	0.6	4.9	10.2	87.7	3.3	0.8	5.7	8.4
Maywood	4.5	47.2	0.5	1.4	0.5	0.2	54.8	96.3	31.4	0.4	0.6	0.8	93.1
Menlo Park	3.2	74.9	7.6	1.0	8.5	1.6	9.9	15.6	79.1	12.4	0.4	5.9	9.7
Merced	5.2	56.3	7.3	2.5	12.7	0.5	26.2	41.4	61.7	6.9	0.9	15.2	29.9
Milpitas	4.9	34.4	4.4	1.3	54.3	1.2	9.7	16.6	52.1	5.9	0.9	34.7	18.6
Mission Viejo	3.6	86.4	1.6	0.9	9.2	0.4	5.3	12.1	90.3	0.9	0.3	6.3	7.7
Modesto	5.9	74.2	4.8	2.6	7.7	1.2	15.8	25.6	80.6	2.7	1.0	7.9	16.3
Monrovia	4.8	66.9	9.5	1.8	8.2	0.4	18.2	35.2	69.7	10.1	0.5	4.5	28.5
Montclair	4.8	48.7	6.9	1.7	9.1	0.5	38.1	60.0	61.6	9.4	0.8	6.8	38.2
Montebello	5.5	51.5	1.1	1.8	12.5	0.2	38.5	74.6	47.0	1.0	0.5	15.1	67.6
Monterey	4.4	84.8	3.2	1.5	9.3	0.6	5.4	10.9	86.6	2.9	0.6	7.3	7.8
Monterey Park	3.4	23.7	0.7	1.0	63.6	0.3	14.3	28.9	26.7	0.6	0.3	57.5	31.3
Moorpark	3.9	77.8	1.9	1.2	6.8	0.4	15.9	27.8	78.9	1.6	0.5	6.6	22.0
Moreno Valley	5.8	51.4	21.6	1.9	7.4	0.9	23.1	38.4	67.4	13.8	0.7	6.6	22.9
Morgan Hill	5.1	76.7	2.2	2.1	7.9	0.7	16.1	27.5	83.0	1.6	0.7	5.3	23.4
Mountain View	4.1	67.2	3.1	0.9	22.5	0.6	10.1	18.3	72.7	5.0	0.6	14.7	16.0
Murrieta	4.3	85.4	4.1	1.6	5.5	0.6	7.5	17.5	91.0	0.8	1.7	0.6	17.2
Napa	3.7	83.8	0.8	2.0	2.5	0.4	14.6	26.8	90.3	0.4	0.8	2.1	15.2
National City	5.4	39.1	6.6	1.6	20.4	1.3	36.9	59.1	40.9	8.5	0.7	17.7	49.6
Newark	7.1	57.8	4.7	1.6	24.4	2.0	17.2	28.6	68.6	4.3	0.6	15.9	22.9
Newport Beach	1.7	93.8	0.7	0.6	4.8	0.3	1.7	4.7	95.8	0.3	0.3	2.9	4.0
Norwalk	4.7	48.6	5.1	1.8	12.5	0.6	36.2	62.9	55.8	3.2	0.9	12.4	47.9
Novato	3.9	86.2	2.7	1.3	6.7	0.4	6.9	13.1	89.6	2.8	0.5	5.0	7.3
Oakland	5.0	34.7	37.6	1.7	16.6	0.8	14.1	21.9	32.5	43.9	0.6	14.8	13.9
Oceanside	5.2	70.6	7.4	1.7	7.4	1.9	16.7	30.2	74.7	7.9	0.7	6.1	22.6
Ontario	5.3	52.2	8.3	1.8	4.8	0.6	37.9	59.9	64.6	7.3	0.7	3.9	41.7
Orange	3.8	73.7	2.0	1.4	10.4	0.5	15.9	32.2	83.0	1.4	0.5	7.9	22.8
Oxnard	4.7	45.9	4.4	2.0	8.6	0.7	43.4	66.2	58.7	5.2	0.8	8.6	54.4
Pacifica	6.6	75.0	4.2	1.6	18.6	1.5	6.3	14.6	76.3	5.2	0.7	13.6	13.5
Palmdale	5.2	59.1	15.8	1.9	4.9	0.4	23.5	37.7	75.7	6.4	0.9	4.4	22.0
Palm Desert	2.4	88.9	1.6	0.9	3.1	0.2	7.8	17.1	91.3	1.0	0.4	1.8	13.7
Palm Springs	3.1	81.0	4.4	1.6	4.4	0.3	11.5	23.7	83.2	4.5	0.7	3.3	18.7
Palo Alto	3.2	78.6	2.5	0.7	19.1	0.3	2.3	4.6	84.9	2.9	0.3	10.4	5.0
Paradise	2.6	96.2	0.4	2.3	1.6	0.3	2.0	4.3	97.1	0.1	0.9	1.0	3.4
Paramount	4.8	38.5	14.3	1.7	4.0	1.0	45.5	72.3	48.2	10.7	0.7	5.8	60.8
Pasadena	5.4	57.7	15.6	1.5	11.3	0.3	19.3	33.4	57.3	19.0	0.4	8.1	27.3
Perris	5.8	45.8	17.3	2.5	3.7	0.6	36.2	56.2	70.5	13.0	1.0	3.3	35.9
Petaluma	4.0	87.8	1.7	1.5	5.2	0.5	7.7	14.6	92.1	1.3	0.6	3.3	9.2
Pico Rivera	5.4	54.3	0.9	1.9	3.1	0.2	45.1	88.3	58.8	0.7	0.6	3.2	83.2
Pittsburg	7.2	48.9	20.7	1.9	15.0	1.5	19.8	32.2	58.6	17.6	0.8	12.2	23.7
Placentia	3.6	70.8	2.1	1.5	12.2	0.4	16.8	31.1	76.2	1.9	0.5	8.2	24.7

[1] Hispanic persons may be of any race.

Table D. Cities

City	Population and population characteristics, 2000										
	Age (percent)										
	Under 5 years	5 to 17 years	18 to 24 years	25 to 34 years	35 to 44 years	45 to 54 years	55 to 64 years	65 to 74 years	75 years and over	Median age (years)	Percent Female
	28	29	30	31	32	33	34	35	36	37	38
CALIFORNIA—Cont'd											
Huntington Beach	6.2	16.1	8.4	17.4	17.5	14.2	9.8	5.9	4.5	36.0	49.9
Huntington Park	10.4	25.4	13.0	18.7	13.6	9.0	4.8	3.1	2.0	25.6	49.9
Imperial Beach	8.4	21.1	13.9	17.0	15.3	11.0	5.8	4.4	3.1	28.6	50.1
Indio	10.4	24.9	11.1	15.7	13.7	8.9	6.3	5.2	3.9	27.3	49.7
Inglewood	9.1	23.3	10.2	16.4	15.5	11.5	6.9	4.1	3.0	29.6	52.5
Irvine	5.6	17.9	14.4	15.0	17.3	14.9	7.7	3.9	3.3	33.1	51.6
Laguna Niguel	7.0	19.6	6.0	12.7	20.2	16.8	8.8	5.1	3.8	37.5	51.3
La Habra	8.4	20.7	10.3	16.4	15.3	11.2	7.0	5.4	5.4	31.5	50.7
Lake Elsinore	9.8	26.2	9.3	14.7	17.4	10.5	5.4	3.9	2.8	28.7	50.1
Lake Forest	7.1	19.9	8.0	15.0	18.3	15.1	8.1	4.0	4.6	35.1	50.8
Lakewood	7.1	20.5	8.1	13.9	17.2	13.6	7.8	6.1	5.8	35.3	51.6
La Mesa	5.7	14.1	9.9	16.5	16.4	12.8	7.5	7.1	10.0	37.3	52.8
La Mirada	6.3	19.9	10.7	12.4	16.1	12.1	8.7	7.7	6.1	35.4	51.7
Lancaster	8.0	24.3	9.5	13.8	17.5	11.6	6.6	4.6	4.0	31.1	49.2
La Puente	9.0	24.8	11.6	16.7	14.3	9.7	6.2	4.7	2.9	27.7	50.0
La Verne	5.8	19.4	9.7	11.2	16.2	15.1	9.4	6.6	6.6	37.7	51.9
Lawndale	9.3	22.6	10.2	19.5	16.4	10.6	5.9	3.5	2.1	29.3	49.4
Livermore	7.7	20.4	7.1	14.8	20.3	14.0	8.1	4.3	3.2	35.0	50.0
Lodi	7.9	20.3	9.6	13.3	14.8	12.1	7.7	6.5	7.8	34.1	51.2
Lompoc	8.0	22.0	8.9	15.6	17.7	11.4	7.1	5.3	4.0	32.2	46.9
Long Beach	8.4	20.8	10.9	17.2	15.7	11.6	6.4	4.4	4.7	30.8	50.9
Los Altos	5.9	17.8	3.5	7.2	17.3	16.9	12.2	9.0	10.3	44.2	51.8
Los Angeles	7.7	18.8	11.1	18.2	15.8	11.6	7.0	5.1	4.6	31.6	50.2
Los Banos	9.4	25.8	8.9	13.7	16.1	10.6	6.2	5.0	4.3	29.7	50.2
Los Gatos	5.0	16.2	4.3	12.9	18.5	16.1	11.7	7.4	7.9	41.2	52.5
Lynwood	10.6	27.4	13.1	17.3	13.9	9.0	4.5	2.4	1.8	24.4	48.9
Madera	10.7	24.7	12.5	15.7	12.6	9.4	5.5	4.7	4.2	26.2	49.3
Manhattan Beach	6.5	15.8	4.1	17.7	19.8	16.1	9.6	5.9	4.5	37.7	49.6
Manteca	7.5	24.1	8.8	13.1	17.4	12.8	7.0	4.9	4.4	32.5	51.0
Marina	5.7	15.6	14.0	19.7	18.7	11.6	6.8	5.2	2.7	32.3	42.8
Martinez	5.6	17.1	7.3	13.4	19.2	17.5	9.8	5.4	4.8	38.6	50.4
Maywood	11.4	25.6	13.2	19.4	13.2	8.5	4.5	2.5	1.7	24.9	49.0
Menlo Park	6.6	15.3	6.2	17.4	17.4	13.3	8.0	6.7	9.2	37.4	51.5
Merced	9.2	25.5	11.4	13.8	13.6	10.8	6.3	4.9	4.6	27.8	51.1
Milpitas	7.2	17.5	9.5	19.0	19.0	13.3	7.5	4.6	2.4	33.4	47.4
Mission Viejo	6.9	20.2	6.6	11.7	18.8	15.5	9.4	5.5	5.4	37.5	51.1
Modesto	7.6	22.5	9.6	13.5	15.5	12.8	7.6	5.6	5.5	32.7	51.5
Monrovia	8.0	19.3	8.0	16.9	17.1	12.7	7.5	5.0	5.4	33.7	52.0
Montclair	8.9	24.3	10.7	15.7	14.7	11.0	6.5	4.4	3.9	29.0	50.1
Montebello	8.1	20.5	10.4	16.6	13.8	10.6	7.6	6.7	5.7	31.4	52.0
Monterey	5.0	11.6	13.1	18.1	15.6	13.6	8.1	6.7	8.2	36.1	50.8
Monterey Park	5.6	15.7	8.4	15.0	15.2	13.0	9.3	9.6	8.3	38.4	52.0
Moorpark	8.1	26.1	8.6	12.4	19.9	14.8	5.6	2.7	1.8	31.5	50.1
Moreno Valley	8.8	28.0	10.5	12.9	16.6	12.1	5.6	3.4	2.0	27.1	51.1
Morgan Hill	8.1	22.4	7.6	13.5	18.2	14.8	7.9	3.9	3.6	34.0	50.4
Mountain View	6.0	11.9	8.3	24.6	18.8	12.6	7.2	5.3	5.2	34.6	48.3
Murrieta	7.5	26.2	6.4	10.9	19.9	11.0	6.6	7.1	4.3	34.4	51.0
Napa	6.8	19.0	8.5	14.1	15.5	13.9	8.5	6.2	7.6	36.1	50.9
National City	8.1	22.0	14.0	15.0	14.0	10.0	5.9	6.0	5.1	28.7	49.4
Newark	7.2	20.0	9.5	16.5	17.8	12.8	8.3	4.9	3.0	33.1	49.6
Newport Beach	4.0	11.7	6.5	17.0	16.0	15.2	12.0	8.8	8.8	41.6	50.5
Norwalk	8.6	23.5	10.7	15.7	14.8	10.9	6.7	5.1	3.9	29.7	50.5
Novato	5.9	17.2	6.4	12.6	17.4	16.9	10.7	6.6	6.4	39.6	51.6
Oakland	7.1	17.9	9.7	18.1	15.8	13.5	7.4	5.2	5.3	33.3	51.7
Oceanside	7.6	20.0	10.2	14.8	16.2	11.1	6.5	6.7	6.9	33.3	50.5
Ontario	9.7	24.7	11.2	16.9	15.4	10.6	5.5	3.3	2.6	27.6	49.9
Orange	7.4	19.3	9.9	16.5	16.8	12.6	7.9	5.4	4.3	33.2	49.8
Oxnard	8.9	22.8	11.8	16.2	14.7	10.8	6.5	4.7	3.4	28.9	48.9
Pacifica	5.7	17.5	7.7	14.4	18.4	17.3	9.3	5.8	4.0	37.6	50.7
Palmdale	9.3	28.7	8.5	12.7	18.4	11.3	5.4	3.4	2.2	28.2	50.9
Palm Desert	4.5	12.8	6.2	10.1	12.5	12.8	13.4	14.6	12.9	48.0	51.9
Palm Springs	4.7	12.3	6.1	10.4	13.8	13.8	12.6	12.9	13.4	46.9	48.1
Palo Alto	5.1	16.1	4.9	14.5	17.9	16.0	9.9	7.1	8.5	40.2	51.1
Paradise	4.3	16.1	5.9	7.8	13.3	14.6	10.8	11.3	15.9	46.6	53.4
Paramount	11.0	25.9	12.0	18.1	13.8	8.9	5.1	2.9	2.2	25.6	50.9
Pasadena	6.9	16.2	9.3	18.5	16.4	12.5	8.0	5.8	6.3	34.5	51.1
Perris	10.8	28.8	9.9	15.7	15.1	8.7	4.8	3.4	2.8	25.4	51.0
Petaluma	6.6	19.6	7.2	12.9	18.6	15.7	8.4	5.2	5.9	37.1	51.1
Pico Rivera	8.2	22.7	10.5	15.5	14.2	10.6	7.2	6.3	4.7	30.6	50.9
Pittsburg	8.3	22.5	10.4	14.9	16.3	12.5	6.8	4.5	3.7	30.9	50.9
Placentia	7.4	19.6	9.5	16.2	15.8	13.2	9.2	5.4	3.7	33.3	50.4

Table D. Cities

City	Population and population characteristics, 1990										Population—change, 1980–2000				
	Age (percent)										Total persons			Percent change	
	Under 5 years	5 to 17 years	18 to 24 years	25 to 34 years	35 to 44 years	45 to 54 years	55 to 64 years	65 to 74 years	75 years and over	Percent Female	2000	1990	1980	1990–2000	1980–1990
	39	40	41	42	43	44	45	46	47	48	49	50	51	52	53
CALIFORNIA—Cont'd															
Huntington Beach	6.0	14.7	12.2	21.3	16.6	12.9	8.0	5.1	3.1	49.5	189 594	181 519	170 505	4.4	6.5
Huntington Park	11.3	23.1	15.9	20.4	12.2	7.4	4.2	3.3	2.3	49.1	61 348	56 129	46 223	9.3	21.4
Imperial Beach	10.4	18.5	16.0	23.8	13.7	5.9	5.6	4.2	1.8	48.8	26 992	26 512	22 689	1.8	16.8
Indio	10.6	23.0	13.5	19.1	12.3	7.7	6.1	4.8	2.9	49.3	49 116	36 850	21 611	33.3	70.5
Inglewood	9.8	20.2	12.1	20.9	14.6	10.0	5.6	4.0	2.9	51.5	112 580	109 602	94 245	2.7	16.3
Irvine	6.8	17.5	13.7	19.2	19.8	11.8	5.6	3.5	2.1	51.6	143 072	110 330	62 134	29.7	77.6
Laguna Niguel	8.4	15.3	8.1	21.7	20.9	12.2	6.5	4.7	2.2	50.7	61 891	44 723	12 237	38.4	265.5
La Habra	8.2	16.8	11.9	20.6	13.3	9.7	8.5	7.1	3.8	50.4	58 974	51 263	45 232	15.0	13.3
Lake Elsinore	11.9	21.7	9.4	21.5	14.7	6.7	5.9	5.1	3.2	49.1	28 928	19 733	NA	46.6	NA
Lake Forest	NA	NA	NA	NA	NA	NA	NA	NA	NA	NA	58 707	56 065	NA	4.7	NA
Lakewood	7.2	17.4	8.6	18.9	16.0	10.3	9.4	8.5	3.6	50.7	79 345	73 553	74 654	7.9	-1.5
La Mesa	5.8	11.4	11.8	20.9	14.8	8.6	8.6	9.6	8.6	52.9	54 749	52 911	50 308	3.5	5.2
La Mirada	6.9	17.3	12.1	16.7	13.8	11.2	10.9	8.0	3.2	50.9	46 783	40 452	40 986	15.7	-1.3
Lancaster	9.7	20.3	10.3	21.7	14.5	8.8	6.7	5.0	3.0	49.9	118 718	97 300	48 027	22.0	102.6
La Puente	9.4	22.9	13.8	18.8	12.7	9.6	7.1	3.6	2.1	49.4	41 063	36 955	30 882	11.1	19.7
La Verne	7.2	18.9	10.1	14.8	17.8	11.0	7.4	7.1	5.7	51.8	31 638	30 843	23 508	2.6	31.2
Lawndale	9.3	16.9	13.0	25.3	14.8	9.5	5.5	3.5	2.1	48.4	31 711	27 331	23 460	16.0	16.5
Livermore	8.3	18.9	9.1	20.3	17.5	11.8	7.0	4.4	2.7	50.2	73 345	56 741	48 349	29.3	17.4
Lodi	7.8	17.1	9.5	18.4	14.4	8.9	8.1	7.8	8.0	51.0	56 999	51 874	35 221	9.9	47.3
Lompoc	9.6	19.3	8.5	22.4	15.3	9.3	7.3	5.3	2.9	47.3	41 103	37 649	26 267	9.2	43.3
Long Beach	8.6	16.8	13.0	21.5	14.6	8.5	6.3	6.4	4.7	49.5	461 522	429 321	361 334	7.5	18.8
Los Altos	5.0	15.6	4.6	10.2	16.9	16.8	12.3	11.8	6.8	51.6	27 693	26 599	25 769	4.1	3.2
Los Angeles	8.0	16.7	12.7	21.0	15.0	9.4	7.2	5.8	4.1	49.8	3 694 820	3 485 557	2 966 850	6.0	17.5
Los Banos	9.4	22.4	8.6	16.8	12.5	8.3	9.1	8.1	4.8	51.1	25 869	14 519	10 341	78.2	40.4
Los Gatos	5.1	13.3	7.9	17.2	17.2	16.3	10.2	6.9	6.0	52.2	28 592	27 357	26 906	4.5	1.7
Lynwood	11.4	25.9	14.3	18.9	13.0	7.1	4.2	3.1	2.2	49.5	69 845	61 945	48 548	12.8	27.6
Madera	9.9	23.7	10.9	16.6	12.6	8.1	6.8	6.1	5.2	51.4	43 207	29 283	21 732	47.5	34.7
Manhattan Beach	5.6	10.7	8.2	23.3	21.1	13.7	8.9	6.1	2.5	48.9	33 852	32 063	31 542	5.6	1.7
Manteca	9.3	23.1	9.3	19.2	15.7	9.1	6.0	5.3	3.1	49.8	49 258	40 773	24 925	20.8	63.6
Marina	10.5	18.6	16.5	24.2	14.8	5.6	5.4	3.1	1.3	47.2	25 101	26 512	20 647	-5.3	28.4
Martinez	6.9	16.0	8.7	20.4	19.8	12.2	7.2	5.3	3.5	50.5	35 866	31 810	22 582	12.8	40.9
Maywood	11.9	24.6	16.5	19.7	12.4	6.9	3.8	2.3	1.9	48.2	28 083	27 893	21 810	0.7	27.9
Menlo Park	6.3	12.4	6.5	19.9	17.5	9.9	9.1	10.1	8.3	52.5	30 785	28 403	26 369	8.4	7.7
Merced	11.1	23.6	11.0	18.3	13.1	7.6	6.5	5.4	3.5	50.6	63 893	56 155	36 499	13.8	53.9
Milpitas	7.9	18.4	10.6	23.9	18.0	10.7	5.6	3.2	1.6	47.0	62 698	50 690	37 820	23.7	34.0
Mission Viejo	7.8	19.9	8.3	17.4	20.5	12.0	6.4	5.4	2.5	50.5	93 102	72 820	50 666	27.9	43.7
Modesto	9.1	21.1	9.3	18.0	15.6	9.6	6.8	6.2	4.3	51.5	188 856	164 746	106 602	14.6	54.5
Monrovia	8.7	16.8	11.3	21.3	15.2	8.9	6.9	6.1	4.8	51.4	36 929	35 733	30 531	3.3	17.0
Montclair	10.0	20.9	11.6	19.8	13.9	9.2	6.8	4.6	3.3	50.1	33 049	28 434	22 628	16.2	25.7
Montebello	8.3	18.5	12.5	18.5	12.6	9.3	8.4	7.1	4.7	51.6	62 150	59 564	52 929	4.3	12.5
Monterey	6.9	10.9	15.4	24.4	14.6	8.2	6.9	6.9	5.7	49.3	29 674	31 954	27 558	-7.1	16.0
Monterey Park	6.2	16.3	11.4	17.4	14.0	10.6	10.3	8.8	5.0	51.3	60 051	60 738	54 338	-1.1	11.8
Moorpark	11.4	22.0	8.3	22.6	19.6	8.3	3.9	2.9	1.1	49.1	31 415	25 494	NA	23.2	NA
Moreno Valley	11.4	25.5	8.5	21.5	17.0	7.7	4.5	2.8	1.1	50.2	142 381	118 779	NA	19.9	NA
Morgan Hill	8.1	22.4	8.6	17.4	18.6	11.8	5.6	4.5	3.1	49.9	33 556	23 928	17 060	40.2	40.3
Mountain View	6.7	10.6	10.2	28.5	17.3	9.4	7.5	5.9	3.9	49.0	70 708	67 365	58 655	5.0	14.8
Murrieta	NA	NA	NA	NA	NA	NA	NA	NA	NA	NA	44 282	18 557	NA	138.6	NA
Napa	7.6	17.4	8.8	16.8	16.0	10.5	8.1	8.0	6.8	51.5	72 585	61 865	50 879	17.3	21.6
National City	8.9	18.8	19.0	19.5	12.2	6.0	6.2	5.4	3.9	47.0	54 260	54 249	48 772	0.0	11.2
Newark	8.9	19.5	9.9	21.6	15.3	12.1	7.3	3.5	1.8	49.6	42 471	37 861	32 126	12.2	17.9
Newport Beach	3.9	9.5	9.8	19.6	16.5	14.0	11.3	9.4	6.1	50.6	70 032	66 643	62 556	5.1	6.5
Norwalk	8.7	21.1	11.6	19.2	14.0	9.3	7.7	5.7	2.7	49.8	103 298	94 279	85 286	9.6	10.5
Novato	7.7	17.4	8.4	17.8	18.4	12.5	8.1	6.5	3.3	51.4	47 630	47 585	43 916	0.1	8.4
Oakland	8.0	16.9	10.1	19.2	16.8	9.8	7.0	6.7	5.5	52.0	399 484	372 242	339 337	7.3	9.7
Oceanside	9.5	16.7	11.3	20.8	13.4	7.0	7.2	8.7	5.4	50.4	161 029	128 090	76 698	25.7	67.0
Ontario	10.6	22.1	12.2	21.2	14.7	7.7	5.2	3.7	2.5	49.6	158 007	133 179	88 820	18.6	49.9
Orange	7.8	16.5	12.6	19.9	15.3	11.0	8.1	5.3	3.4	49.6	128 821	110 658	91 788	16.4	20.6
Oxnard	9.3	21.4	12.5	19.0	13.9	9.2	7.2	4.8	2.7	48.9	170 358	142 560	108 195	19.5	31.8
Pacifica	7.6	17.1	9.0	19.4	19.8	11.7	8.0	4.9	2.5	50.5	38 390	37 670	36 866	1.9	2.2
Palmdale	13.0	22.5	8.8	24.0	15.1	7.4	4.6	3.2	1.6	49.6	116 670	70 262	12 277	66.0	472.3
Palm Desert	4.8	12.3	7.9	14.9	13.6	10.8	12.4	15.0	8.3	51.0	41 155	23 252	11 801	77.0	97.0
Palm Springs	5.3	11.1	7.9	14.3	13.3	10.8	11.6	13.8	11.9	51.0	42 807	40 144	32 271	6.6	24.4
Palo Alto	4.9	12.5	7.0	19.1	18.3	13.2	9.2	8.9	6.8	51.1	58 598	55 900	55 225	4.8	1.2
Paradise	5.7	15.2	4.1	11.5	13.6	8.9	10.2	16.2	14.5	53.4	26 408	25 401	22 571	4.0	12.5
Paramount	11.3	23.5	13.9	19.9	12.9	7.3	5.0	3.8	2.3	49.8	55 266	47 669	36 407	15.9	30.9
Pasadena	7.3	14.5	11.1	21.5	15.4	9.4	7.7	6.4	6.6	51.2	133 936	131 586	118 550	1.8	11.0
Perris	12.8	21.3	10.7	21.7	11.5	6.4	6.0	6.3	3.3	50.5	36 189	21 500	NA	68.3	NA
Petaluma	8.0	17.9	8.4	17.7	19.1	10.2	6.9	6.5	5.2	51.4	54 548	43 166	33 834	26.4	27.6
Pico Rivera	8.7	21.4	12.4	17.1	12.9	9.4	8.5	6.3	3.1	50.4	63 428	59 177	53 459	7.2	10.7
Pittsburg	9.8	21.2	10.4	20.8	15.5	8.5	6.2	4.6	3.1	50.3	56 769	47 607	33 034	19.2	44.1
Placentia	7.0	18.7	12.9	17.5	15.6	13.2	8.3	4.3	2.6	49.7	46 488	41 259	35 041	12.7	17.7

Table D. Cities

City	Household relationship, 2000																
	In households (percent)										In group quarters (percent)						
					Child		Other relatives		Nonrelatives			Institutionalized population			Noninstitutionalized population		
	Total population	Total in households	House-holder	Spouse	Total	Own child under 18 years	Total	Under 18 years	Total	Unmarried partner	Total in group quarters	Correctional institutions	Nursing homes	Other institutions	College dormitories	Military quarters	Other
	54	55	56	57	58	59	60	61	62	63	64	65	66	67	68	69	70
CALIFORNIA—Cont'd																	
Huntington Beach	180 594	99.6	38.8	19.7	27.2	20.1	5.5	1.6	8.3	2.2	0.4	0.0	0.2	0.0	0.0	0.0	0.2
Huntington Park	61 348	99.7	24.2	13.4	40.0	30.3	15.5	4.8	0.5	1.0	0.3	0.0	0.0	0.0	0.0	0.0	0.3
Imperial Beach	26 992	97.5	34.4	15.5	32.4	25.3	7.2	2.9	8.1	2.7	2.5	0.0	0.0	0.0	0.0	0.0	2.5
Indio	49 116	98.3	28.2	15.8	37.5	29.7	11.7	4.9	5.0	2.0	1.7	0.7	0.4	0.1	0.0	0.0	0.6
Inglewood	112 580	98.8	32.7	12.6	36.4	27.4	11.3	4.1	5.8	2.0	1.2	0.1	0.4	0.2	0.0	0.0	0.6
Irvine	143 072	95.0	35.8	19.3	28.4	22.4	4.4	0.8	7.2	1.3	5.0	0.0	0.1	0.0	4.8	0.0	0.1
Laguna Niguel	61 891	99.5	37.5	22.6	30.7	25.5	3.6	0.8	5.0	1.7	0.5	0.0	0.1	0.0	0.0	0.0	0.4
La Habra	58 974	99.0	32.1	17.5	34.1	25.4	9.3	3.1	6.0	1.7	1.0	0.0	0.4	0.0	0.0	0.0	0.6
Lake Elsinore	28 928	99.7	30.5	17.5	37.9	32.0	7.7	3.1	6.1	2.3	0.3	0.0	0.0	0.0	0.0	0.0	0.3
Lake Forest	58 707	98.6	34.1	20.1	31.7	24.6	6.1	1.7	6.5	1.7	1.4	0.0	1.0	0.0	0.0	0.0	0.5
Lakewood	79 345	99.8	33.8	19.6	33.6	24.2	8.2	2.9	4.6	1.6	0.2	0.0	0.1	0.0	0.0	0.0	0.1
La Mesa	54 749	98.1	44.2	17.6	23.6	18.0	4.4	1.3	8.3	2.9	1.9	0.0	1.4	0.1	0.0	0.0	0.4
La Mirada	46 783	96.5	31.2	20.0	32.6	22.6	8.8	3.1	4.0	1.0	3.5	0.0	0.5	0.0	3.0	0.0	0.0
Lancaster	118 718	94.1	32.2	15.9	34.3	28.1	6.0	2.6	5.6	2.1	5.9	4.2	0.6	0.6	0.1	0.0	0.4
La Puente	41 063	99.9	23.0	13.9	37.1	25.2	18.3	7.2	7.5	1.3	0.1	0.0	0.0	0.0	0.0	0.0	0.1
La Verne	31 638	97.8	35.0	21.0	32.0	22.7	5.7	1.9	4.1	1.4	2.2	0.0	0.5	0.0	1.4	0.0	0.4
Lawndale	31 711	99.7	30.1	13.8	35.6	27.3	12.7	3.9	7.5	2.3	0.3	0.0	0.0	0.0	0.0	0.0	0.3
Livermore	73 345	99.7	35.6	21.8	32.2	26.1	4.6	1.4	5.6	2.0	0.3	0.0	0.0	0.0	0.0	0.0	0.1
Lodi	56 999	98.2	36.3	18.8	31.6	25.4	6.2	2.1	5.3	2.3	1.8	0.0	1.1	0.1	0.0	0.0	0.6
Lompoc	41 103	91.6	31.8	16.2	32.2	26.6	6.3	2.6	5.1	2.1	8.4	7.6	0.3	0.0	0.0	0.0	0.5
Long Beach	461 522	97.8	35.3	13.9	32.3	25.4	8.9	3.0	7.4	2.7	2.2	0.1	0.5	0.2	0.5	0.0	1.0
Los Altos	27 693	98.5	37.8	26.2	28.4	22.9	2.7	0.6	3.3	1.0	1.5	0.0	1.1	0.0	0.0	0.0	0.4
Los Angeles	3 694 820	97.8	34.5	14.5	30.2	22.6	10.6	3.2	7.9	2.2	2.2	0.4	0.3	0.1	0.6	0.0	0.8
Los Banos	25 869	99.3	29.8	18.7	38.0	31.1	8.0	3.2	4.7	1.9	0.7	0.0	0.6	0.0	0.0	0.0	0.1
Los Gatos	28 592	97.5	41.9	21.3	25.1	20.2	2.8	0.8	6.3	2.0	2.5	0.0	1.9	0.0	0.0	0.0	0.5
Lynwood	69 845	96.9	20.6	12.5	40.2	30.4	16.9	6.3	6.6	1.4	3.1	1.7	0.6	0.0	0.0	0.0	0.8
Madera	43 207	99.0	27.7	14.9	37.4	30.1	11.1	4.1	7.9	2.1	1.0	0.0	0.5	0.0	0.0	0.0	0.5
Manhattan Beach	33 852	100.0	42.8	21.3	25.5	21.5	2.2	0.6	8.2	2.0	0.0	0.0	0.0	0.0	0.0	0.0	0.0
Manteca	49 258	99.0	33.2	19.0	35.4	27.9	6.2	2.8	5.2	2.2	1.0	0.0	0.6	0.0	0.0	0.0	0.4
Marina	25 101	74.9	26.9	13.7	22.9	17.3	6.6	2.4	4.8	1.8	25.1	16.3	0.0	0.0	5.6	0.0	3.3
Martinez	35 866	96.2	39.9	19.7	26.7	20.3	4.0	1.4	5.9	2.6	3.8	2.0	0.6	0.8	0.0	0.0	0.4
Maywood	28 083	99.7	23.0	14.0	40.9	31.5	15.5	4.8	6.2	1.9	0.3	0.0	0.3	0.0	0.0	0.0	0.0
Menlo Park	30 785	96.9	40.2	18.6	24.4	19.7	5.9	1.8	7.7	2.1	3.1	0.0	1.0	1.0	0.2	0.0	0.9
Merced	63 893	97.9	32.0	15.1	37.6	30.7	7.4	3.1	5.8	2.4	2.1	0.8	0.3	0.1	0.0	0.0	0.9
Milpitas	62 698	94.9	27.3	17.8	29.9	21.1	13.2	3.0	6.8	1.1	5.1	4.9	0.0	0.0	0.0	0.0	0.1
Mission Viejo	93 102	98.9	34.9	23.0	32.7	25.6	4.3	1.2	4.0	1.3	1.1	0.0	0.0	0.0	0.0	0.0	1.1
Modesto	188 856	98.3	34.4	17.7	33.7	26.4	7.0	2.8	5.5	2.2	1.7	0.2	0.7	0.1	0.0	0.0	0.7
Monrovia	36 929	99.2	36.6	17.0	31.4	24.0	8.0	2.6	6.3	2.2	0.8	0.0	0.2	0.0	0.0	0.0	0.5
Montclair	33 049	98.1	26.6	15.0	36.9	27.4	12.9	4.8	6.7	1.8	1.9	0.0	0.5	0.0	0.0	0.0	1.3
Montebello	62 150	99.5	30.3	15.6	35.5	23.9	12.8	4.1	5.2	1.8	0.5	0.0	0.4	0.0	0.0	0.0	0.1
Monterey	29 674	90.4	42.5	16.8	19.4	15.3	3.5	0.9	8.3	2.5	9.6	0.0	1.0	0.0	0.0	8.3	0.2
Monterey Park	60 051	99.5	32.6	18.0	29.9	18.1	13.8	2.8	5.3	1.0	0.5	0.0	0.1	0.0	0.0	0.0	0.3
Moorpark	31 415	100.0	28.6	20.6	38.7	31.1	7.2	2.5	4.8	1.2	0.0	0.0	0.0	0.0	0.0	0.0	0.0
Moreno Valley	142 381	99.5	27.5	17.0	40.2	31.5	9.7	4.2	5.0	1.7	0.5	0.0	0.0	0.0	0.0	0.0	0.5
Morgan Hill	33 556	98.5	32.3	20.4	34.5	27.3	6.2	2.3	5.0	1.8	1.5	0.0	0.5	0.4	0.0	0.0	0.6
Mountain View	70 708	99.3	44.2	17.7	20.7	16.3	6.0	1.3	10.7	2.7	0.7	0.0	0.4	0.0	0.0	0.0	0.3
Murrieta	44 282	99.6	32.3	22.7	36.9	31.5	4.2	1.7	3.4	1.3	0.4	0.0	0.1	0.0	0.0	0.0	0.3
Napa	72 585	98.0	37.2	18.9	28.9	22.9	6.6	2.0	6.4	2.1	2.0	0.3	0.6	0.0	0.0	0.0	1.1
National City	54 260	93.8	27.7	13.9	35.1	25.0	11.7	4.5	5.5	1.8	6.2	0.0	0.4	0.0	0.0	4.9	0.9
Newark	42 471	99.8	30.6	19.0	32.7	23.2	11.4	3.6	6.1	1.6	0.2	0.0	0.0	0.0	0.0	0.0	0.2
Newport Beach	70 032	98.7	47.2	20.1	19.1	15.0	2.3	0.5	9.9	2.1	1.3	0.0	0.6	0.0	0.4	0.0	0.3
Norwalk	103 298	98.7	26.0	15.7	36.5	25.5	14.9	5.6	5.5	1.4	1.3	0.0	0.6	0.4	0.0	0.0	0.4
Novato	47 630	97.9	38.9	20.5	27.5	21.5	4.4	1.1	6.7	2.1	2.1	0.0	1.1	0.2	0.0	0.0	0.8
Oakland	399 484	98.2	37.7	12.8	28.1	20.4	10.5	3.7	9.0	2.8	1.8	0.2	0.4	0.1	0.1	0.0	0.9
Oceanside	161 029	99.2	35.1	19.0	30.3	23.9	7.5	2.8	7.3	2.0	0.8	0.0	0.1	0.0	0.0	0.0	0.7
Ontario	158 007	99.3	27.5	15.7	37.6	28.8	11.8	4.5	6.7	1.9	0.7	0.0	0.3	0.0	0.0	0.0	0.5
Orange	128 821	95.9	31.8	18.1	30.2	22.8	8.5	2.5	7.3	1.6	4.1	1.9	0.2	0.5	0.7	0.0	0.9
Oxnard	170 358	98.5	25.6	15.2	35.1	24.6	14.6	5.2	8.0	1.5	1.5	0.0	0.3	0.0	0.0	0.0	1.2
Pacifica	38 390	99.5	36.5	19.5	29.1	20.4	7.0	2.3	7.5	2.5	0.5	0.0	0.3	0.0	0.0	0.0	0.1
Palmdale	116 670	99.9	29.4	17.6	40.5	33.9	7.5	3.0	5.0	1.9	0.1	0.0	0.0	0.0	0.0	0.0	0.1
Palm Desert	41 155	99.4	46.6	22.6	19.6	15.7	4.2	1.2	6.5	2.6	0.6	0.0	0.4	0.0	0.0	0.0	0.2
Palm Springs	42 807	98.4	47.9	16.3	19.3	14.7	5.9	1.9	9.0	4.1	1.6	0.0	0.7	0.0	0.0	0.0	1.0
Palo Alto	58 598	98.9	43.0	20.9	24.8	20.3	2.8	0.6	7.3	1.9	1.1	0.0	0.6	0.2	0.0	0.0	0.4
Paradise	26 408	97.7	43.9	21.4	23.5	18.1	3.6	1.4	5.3	2.4	2.3	0.0	1.1	0.1	0.0	0.0	1.1
Paramount	55 266	99.4	25.3	13.0	39.8	30.7	15.0	5.4	6.3	2.0	0.6	0.0	0.3	0.3	0.0	0.0	0.0
Pasadena	133 936	97.4	38.7	15.9	26.8	19.9	8.5	2.6	7.4	2.1	2.6	0.0	0.9	0.1	0.4	0.0	1.2
Perris	36 189	99.4	26.7	15.5	40.5	33.5	11.2	4.9	5.5	1.8	0.6	0.0	0.3	0.0	0.0	0.0	0.3
Petaluma	54 548	98.6	36.5	20.2	30.6	24.1	4.8	1.5	6.5	2.3	1.4	0.0	0.6	0.0	0.0	0.0	0.8
Pico Rivera	63 428	99.4	26.0	15.2	36.6	23.5	16.3	6.5	5.4	1.4	0.6	0.0	0.5	0.0	0.0	0.0	0.0
Pittsburg	56 769	99.1	31.3	16.4	34.6	25.9	10.5	4.0	6.3	2.2	0.9	0.0	0.3	0.0	0.0	0.0	0.6
Placentia	46 488	99.3	32.3	19.9	32.5	23.6	8.4	2.7	6.2	1.5	0.7	0.0	0.2	0.0	0.0	0.0	0.5

Table D. Cities

City	Households by type, 2000												Households, 1990		
		Family households						Nonfamily households							
				Married couple		Female householder[1]			Householder living alone						
	Total households	Total	With own children under 18 years	Total	With own children under 18 years	Total	With own children under 18 years	Total	Total	65 years and over	Average household size	Average family size	Total households	Female householder[1]	Householder living alone
	71	72	73	74	75	76	77	78	79	80	81	82	83	84	85
CALIFORNIA—Cont'd															
Huntington Beach	73 657	64.8	29.0	50.7	22.0	9.6	4.9	35.2	24.3	6.7	2.56	3.08	68 879	9.5	21.5
Huntington Park	14 860	85.2	58.3	55.4	40.3	20.3	13.2	14.8	10.9	4.8	4.12	4.34	13 903	17.2	13.8
Imperial Beach	9 272	69.6	40.2	45.2	24.0	18.1	12.3	30.4	21.4	5.5	2.84	3.30	9 080	14.6	17.8
Indio	13 871	79.8	48.2	55.9	33.2	16.7	11.0	20.2	16.0	7.0	3.48	3.88	10 747	14.2	18.6
Inglewood	36 805	70.2	42.7	38.5	23.8	24.9	15.3	29.8	25.3	6.4	3.02	3.63	36 102	21.2	26.9
Irvine	51 199	67.1	36.0	53.8	28.8	9.8	5.7	32.9	22.8	5.0	2.66	3.17	40 257	9.2	19.7
Laguna Niguel	23 217	72.3	38.1	60.2	30.9	8.8	5.4	27.7	20.6	4.7	2.65	3.10	17 172	7.3	18.5
La Habra	18 947	74.0	39.3	54.5	29.0	13.5	7.4	26.0	21.0	8.0	3.08	3.56	18 112	11.5	22.0
Lake Elsinore	8 817	78.0	49.2	57.5	35.7	13.8	9.8	22.0	16.2	5.5	3.27	3.66	6 066	11.0	20.7
Lake Forest	20 008	73.7	39.2	59.1	31.4	10.3	5.6	26.3	19.4	5.1	2.89	3.31	21 717	NA	NA
Lakewood	26 853	76.5	38.0	57.8	29.4	13.4	6.3	23.5	18.4	8.2	2.95	3.37	26 102	10.3	17.7
La Mesa	24 186	55.3	24.7	39.8	16.4	11.6	6.3	44.7	34.2	12.9	2.22	2.86	23 206	10.7	31.1
La Mirada	14 580	79.0	37.4	64.1	31.5	10.4	3.9	21.0	17.3	10.0	3.10	3.49	12 731	9.1	14.7
Lancaster	38 224	72.4	42.8	49.4	27.2	17.0	11.8	27.6	22.1	6.9	2.92	3.41	32 901	11.1	20.4
La Puente	9 461	86.5	50.0	60.4	37.6	17.9	9.0	13.5	10.1	4.4	4.34	4.48	9 019	16.4	11.5
La Verne	11 070	75.4	35.5	60.0	27.9	11.5	5.7	24.6	19.6	9.6	2.79	3.23	10 740	8.5	19.3
Lawndale	9 555	73.5	45.5	45.8	29.6	19.0	11.6	26.5	18.8	4.5	3.31	3.80	9 227	14.8	21.7
Livermore	26 123	74.7	40.2	61.1	32.1	9.3	5.6	25.3	18.8	5.4	2.80	3.20	20 643	9.5	18.8
Lodi	20 692	69.3	35.8	51.7	24.9	12.2	7.9	30.7	25.4	11.2	2.71	3.25	19 001	11.3	24.0
Lompoc	13 059	71.3	41.1	51.0	27.6	14.8	10.0	28.7	23.5	8.3	2.88	3.42	12 504	13.0	22.1
Long Beach	163 088	61.1	35.0	39.2	21.6	16.1	10.6	38.9	29.6	7.4	2.77	3.55	158 895	13.0	30.8
Los Altos	10 462	76.7	33.6	69.4	30.5	5.4	2.2	23.3	18.7	9.8	2.61	2.98	9 837	5.4	16.3
Los Angeles	1 275 412	62.6	33.5	41.9	22.6	14.5	8.8	37.4	28.5	7.4	2.83	3.56	1 217 405	13.6	28.5
Los Banos	7 721	80.6	48.9	62.5	37.5	12.4	7.8	19.4	15.8	7.0	3.33	3.69	4 772	13.3	20.9
Los Gatos	11 988	60.9	27.3	50.9	21.8	7.2	4.0	39.1	29.7	10.0	2.33	2.93	11 273	8.3	26.8
Lynwood	14 395	89.9	63.5	60.5	45.5	20.6	13.3	10.1	7.7	2.6	4.70	4.76	14 158	20.3	12.0
Madera	11 978	78.8	48.4	53.7	32.3	17.5	11.9	21.2	16.8	7.9	3.57	3.90	9 159	16.9	20.2
Manhattan Beach	14 474	58.0	28.1	49.8	23.9	5.8	3.1	42.0	29.3	6.5	2.34	2.98	13 992	6.4	27.2
Manteca	16 368	76.3	43.3	57.2	31.2	13.0	8.3	23.7	18.6	7.1	2.98	3.39	13 440	11.9	16.4
Marina	6 745	71.3	35.5	51.1	23.6	15.1	9.2	28.7	21.4	6.4	2.79	3.25	7 908	11.0	12.4
Martinez	14 300	64.4	30.0	49.4	21.9	11.0	6.1	35.6	27.4	6.9	2.41	2.96	12 515	10.4	26.1
Maywood	6 469	88.1	62.9	60.8	45.8	16.9	11.7	11.9	8.4	3.2	4.33	4.47	6 446	16.1	10.5
Menlo Park	12 387	57.5	26.6	46.3	20.9	8.5	4.5	42.5	32.1	11.4	2.41	3.12	11 816	9.1	33.1
Merced	20 435	71.6	42.9	47.2	26.6	18.2	12.7	28.4	22.6	8.5	3.06	3.62	18 282	15.7	21.7
Milpitas	17 132	81.7	43.0	65.1	36.0	10.9	5.0	18.3	11.5	2.9	3.47	3.72	14 099	10.9	12.0
Mission Viejo	32 449	77.7	39.7	66.1	33.6	8.1	4.5	22.3	17.3	6.0	2.84	3.22	25 174	7.3	14.3
Modesto	64 959	71.8	38.7	51.5	26.2	14.7	9.2	28.2	22.5	8.6	2.86	3.36	57 958	12.1	22.1
Monrovia	13 502	67.3	35.4	46.4	24.0	15.4	8.6	32.7	26.0	8.8	2.71	3.29	13 242	14.1	25.8
Montclair	8 800	80.1	47.5	56.3	34.3	16.3	9.1	19.9	15.0	6.3	3.69	4.04	8 538	14.6	16.5
Montebello	18 844	78.9	40.2	51.5	26.7	20.1	10.5	21.1	17.1	8.0	3.28	3.67	18 618	17.6	18.3
Monterey	12 600	51.4	21.8	39.5	15.6	8.4	4.4	48.6	37.0	11.0	2.13	2.82	12 693	7.6	31.8
Monterey Park	19 564	77.9	31.3	55.4	23.5	15.8	6.0	22.1	17.3	8.7	3.06	3.43	19 505	13.7	17.3
Moorpark	8 994	85.6	54.7	72.0	46.4	9.7	6.1	14.4	9.9	2.2	3.49	3.71	7 621	6.7	9.2
Moreno Valley	39 225	85.1	54.0	61.6	38.6	17.1	11.6	14.9	11.0	3.1	3.61	3.86	34 965	10.6	10.5
Morgan Hill	10 846	79.6	44.0	63.2	34.0	11.1	7.0	20.4	15.1	5.5	3.05	3.38	7 808	9.4	15.5
Mountain View	31 242	50.9	21.9	40.0	17.2	7.3	3.3	49.1	35.6	7.0	2.25	2.97	29 990	8.0	35.1
Murrieta	14 320	81.7	47.5	70.2	39.7	8.1	5.6	18.3	14.5	6.7	3.08	3.42	568	NA	NA
Napa	26 978	66.5	32.9	50.7	23.7	11.1	6.6	33.5	26.8	12.1	2.64	3.20	23 914	10.6	25.9
National City	15 018	78.6	44.6	50.4	28.6	21.1	12.8	21.4	16.7	8.0	3.39	3.79	14 773	19.7	17.9
Newark	12 992	79.6	40.2	62.2	32.1	11.6	5.7	20.4	14.1	4.2	3.26	3.59	12 015	10.4	13.8
Newport Beach	33 071	51.3	18.0	42.5	13.9	6.1	2.9	48.7	35.3	10.1	2.09	2.71	30 860	6.2	31.9
Norwalk	26 887	83.8	46.6	60.1	35.5	16.6	8.1	16.2	12.7	5.8	3.79	4.08	26 346	13.7	13.6
Novato	18 524	67.0	32.1	52.7	23.9	10.3	6.1	33.0	25.2	9.3	2.52	3.01	18 236	9.7	21.3
Oakland	150 790	57.3	28.6	34.0	16.5	17.7	9.9	42.7	32.5	8.6	2.60	3.38	144 521	18.5	33.3
Oceanside	56 488	69.5	35.0	54.1	25.8	11.0	6.7	30.5	22.7	10.2	2.83	3.33	46 741	9.7	20.8
Ontario	43 525	79.7	49.4	56.9	36.0	15.5	9.4	20.3	15.1	4.6	3.60	3.96	40 277	13.3	16.8
Orange	40 930	73.7	37.1	57.1	28.8	11.6	6.0	26.3	19.5	6.6	3.02	3.43	36 791	10.9	18.9
Oxnard	43 576	80.2	46.1	59.4	34.9	14.1	8.0	19.8	14.6	5.6	3.85	4.16	39 302	12.9	15.4
Pacifica	13 994	69.0	32.0	53.5	24.7	11.0	5.3	31.0	21.2	6.4	2.73	3.21	13 340	10.8	18.8
Palmdale	34 285	82.0	54.6	59.8	39.4	16.2	11.4	18.0	13.9	3.8	3.40	3.72	21 952	10.4	14.4
Palm Desert	19 184	59.5	18.9	48.5	12.6	7.7	4.6	40.5	32.4	15.2	2.13	2.67	10 595	6.8	31.5
Palm Springs	20 516	46.1	16.3	34.0	10.3	8.5	4.4	53.9	41.6	18.3	2.05	2.88	18 622	8.0	36.6
Palo Alto	25 216	57.9	27.2	48.5	22.4	7.0	3.6	42.1	32.6	10.8	2.30	2.95	24 206	7.5	32.5
Paradise	11 591	62.5	23.0	48.7	14.8	10.3	6.0	37.5	32.0	18.1	2.22	2.77	11 045	8.1	29.3
Paramount	13 972	81.1	55.1	51.3	36.2	21.7	14.3	18.9	14.6	4.6	3.93	4.31	12 993	17.2	17.6
Pasadena	51 844	57.6	27.1	41.2	19.2	12.1	6.1	42.4	33.7	9.3	2.52	3.30	50 199	12.2	32.0
Perris	9 652	84.1	56.8	58.2	39.4	18.8	13.0	15.9	12.2	4.5	3.73	4.00	6 726	12.4	16.7
Petaluma	19 932	70.3	36.6	55.3	28.1	10.6	6.0	29.7	22.6	9.1	2.70	3.16	16 062	9.7	22.5
Pico Rivera	16 468	84.2	43.5	58.7	32.0	17.8	8.3	15.8	12.8	6.6	3.83	4.12	16 002	15.2	13.8
Pittsburg	17 741	76.0	42.2	52.5	28.9	17.2	10.1	24.0	18.0	5.8	3.17	3.59	15 643	14.3	17.8
Placentia	15 037	77.7	37.9	61.5	30.4	11.2	5.3	22.3	16.0	4.9	3.07	3.42	13 369	10.9	14.7

[1] No spouse present.

Table D. Cities

City	Percent change of households, 1990-2000	Total housing units	Occupied housing units (percent)	Vacant housing units Total	For seasonal, recreational, or occasional use	Homeowner vacancy rate (percent)	Rental vacancy rate (percent)	Occupied housing units Total	Percent owner-occupied housing units	Percent renter-occupied housing units	Average household size of owner-occupied units	Average household size of renter-occupied units
	86	87	88	89	90	91	92	93	94	95	96	97
CALIFORNIA—Cont'd												
Huntington Beach	6.9	75 662	97.4	2.6	0.7	0.9	2.0	73 657	60.6	39.4	2.58	2.54
Huntington Park	6.9	15 335	96.9	3.1	0.1	2.3	1.9	14 860	27.4	72.6	4.65	3.92
Imperial Beach	2.1	9 739	95.2	4.8	1.8	0.8	3.0	9 272	30.0	70.0	2.79	2.80
Indio	29.1	16 909	82.0	18.0	12.8	2.4	4.9	13 871	56.2	43.8	3.45	3.51
Inglewood	1.9	38 648	95.2	4.8	0.1	1.5	3.5	36 805	36.3	63.7	3.24	2.90
Irvine	27.2	53 711	95.3	4.7	0.7	1.1	3.5	51 199	60.0	40.0	2.78	2.46
Laguna Niguel	35.2	23 885	97.2	2.8	0.8	0.8	3.3	23 217	75.0	25.0	2.68	2.56
La Habra	4.6	19 441	97.5	2.5	0.2	1.3	2.1	18 947	56.6	43.4	3.04	3.13
Lake Elsinore	45.4	9 505	92.8	7.2	0.9	3.3	7.0	8 817	64.6	35.4	3.29	3.25
Lake Forest	-7.9	20 486	97.7	2.3	0.1	0.8	4.1	20 008	72.0	28.0	2.93	2.79
Lakewood	2.9	27 310	98.3	1.7	0.1	0.6	1.9	26 853	72.0	28.0	2.94	2.97
La Mesa	4.2	24 943	97.0	3.0	0.3	0.7	2.8	24 186	47.2	52.8	2.35	2.10
La Mirada	14.5	14 811	98.4	1.6	0.2	0.7	1.7	14 580	82.0	18.0	3.15	2.85
Lancaster	16.2	41 745	91.6	8.4	0.3	3.4	8.8	38 224	61.4	38.6	3.01	2.78
La Puente	4.9	9 660	97.9	2.1	0.1	1.2	1.3	9 461	60.9	39.1	4.50	4.09
La Verne	3.1	11 286	98.1	1.9	0.2	0.6	2.6	11 070	77.5	22.5	2.84	2.63
Lawndale	3.6	9 869	96.8	3.2	0.3	1.3	2.5	9 555	33.2	66.8	3.41	3.26
Livermore	26.5	26 610	98.2	1.8	0.2	0.4	2.0	26 123	72.2	27.8	2.86	2.65
Lodi	8.9	21 378	96.8	3.2	0.2	1.2	2.9	20 692	54.6	45.4	2.65	2.77
Lompoc	4.4	13 621	95.9	4.1	0.2	0.8	4.0	13 059	51.6	48.4	2.83	2.94
Long Beach	2.6	171 632	95.0	5.0	0.4	2.2	4.2	163 088	41.0	59.0	2.81	2.74
Los Altos	6.4	10 727	97.5	2.5	0.3	0.3	6.2	10 462	85.6	14.4	2.67	2.21
Los Angeles	4.8	1 337 706	95.3	4.7	0.4	1.8	3.5	1 275 412	38.6	61.4	2.99	2.73
Los Banos	61.8	8 049	95.9	4.1	0.6	1.3	3.1	7 721	67.9	32.1	3.29	3.40
Los Gatos	6.3	12 367	96.9	3.1	0.9	0.5	2.3	11 988	65.3	34.7	2.54	1.92
Lynwood	1.7	14 987	96.0	4.0	0.2	2.4	2.7	14 395	47.1	52.9	5.09	4.35
Madera	30.8	12 521	95.7	4.3	0.2	1.5	3.8	11 978	52.7	47.3	3.38	3.78
Manhattan Beach	3.4	15 034	96.3	3.7	1.1	1.0	3.0	14 474	65.1	34.9	2.60	1.85
Manteca	21.8	16 937	96.6	3.4	0.2	1.1	3.1	16 368	63.0	37.0	3.06	2.85
Marina	-14.7	8 537	79.0	21.0	0.3	6.4	2.9	6 745	45.8	54.2	2.77	2.80
Martinez	14.3	14 597	98.0	2.0	0.1	0.5	2.0	14 300	68.8	31.2	2.53	2.16
Maywood	-0.4	6 701	96.5	3.5	0.1	1.8	1.6	6 469	29.4	70.6	4.74	4.15
Menlo Park	4.8	12 714	97.4	2.6	0.8	0.3	1.5	12 387	57.0	43.0	2.67	2.07
Merced	11.8	21 532	94.9	5.1	0.2	1.6	5.1	20 435	46.5	53.5	2.93	3.18
Milpitas	21.5	17 364	98.7	1.3	0.1	0.4	2.1	17 132	69.8	30.2	3.49	3.44
Mission Viejo	28.9	32 985	98.4	1.6	0.3	0.6	2.3	32 449	81.4	18.6	2.87	2.71
Modesto	12.1	67 179	96.7	3.3	0.2	1.2	3.3	64 959	58.7	41.3	2.89	2.81
Monrovia	2.0	13 957	96.7	3.3	0.2	1.0	2.5	13 502	47.9	52.1	2.75	2.68
Montclair	3.1	9 066	97.1	2.9	0.1	1.2	3.6	8 800	60.6	39.4	3.59	3.84
Montebello	1.2	19 416	97.1	2.9	0.2	1.0	2.7	18 844	47.5	52.5	3.28	3.28
Monterey	-0.7	13 382	94.2	5.8	2.7	1.0	2.3	12 600	38.5	61.5	2.29	2.03
Monterey Park	0.3	20 209	96.8	3.2	0.3	1.9	1.9	19 564	54.0	46.0	2.97	3.16
Moorpark	18.0	9 094	98.9	1.1	0.1	0.5	1.2	8 994	82.1	17.9	3.43	3.78
Moreno Valley	12.2	41 431	94.7	5.3	0.2	2.8	5.9	39 225	71.1	28.9	3.63	3.56
Morgan Hill	38.9	11 091	97.8	2.2	0.3	0.6	2.6	10 846	72.5	27.5	2.98	3.21
Mountain View	4.2	32 432	96.3	3.7	0.9	0.6	1.6	31 242	41.5	58.5	2.30	2.21
Murrieta	2 421.1	14 921	96.0	4.0	0.7	1.7	5.1	14 320	79.7	20.3	3.18	2.70
Napa	12.8	27 776	97.1	2.9	0.6	0.8	1.9	26 978	60.6	39.4	2.59	2.71
National City	1.7	15 422	97.4	2.6	0.1	0.5	2.3	15 018	35.0	65.0	3.63	3.26
Newark	8.1	13 150	98.8	1.2	0.2	0.4	1.2	12 992	70.6	29.4	3.22	3.37
Newport Beach	7.2	37 288	88.7	11.3	5.3	1.8	8.0	33 071	55.7	44.3	2.30	1.83
Norwalk	2.1	27 554	97.6	2.4	0.1	1.4	2.0	26 887	65.8	34.2	3.85	3.67
Novato	1.6	18 994	97.5	2.5	0.3	0.9	2.5	18 524	67.6	32.4	2.50	2.56
Oakland	4.3	157 508	95.7	4.3	0.3	1.0	2.7	150 790	41.4	58.6	2.76	2.49
Oceanside	20.9	59 581	94.8	5.2	2.4	1.0	3.2	56 488	62.1	37.9	2.82	2.85
Ontario	8.1	45 182	96.3	3.7	0.2	1.6	3.3	43 525	57.6	42.4	3.64	3.55
Orange	11.3	41 904	97.7	2.3	0.2	1.1	2.0	40 930	62.6	37.4	2.91	3.20
Oxnard	10.9	45 166	96.5	3.5	1.6	1.0	1.8	43 576	57.3	42.7	3.79	3.94
Pacifica	4.9	14 245	98.2	1.8	0.3	0.2	1.9	13 994	68.6	31.4	2.88	2.41
Palmdale	56.2	37 096	92.4	7.6	0.3	3.1	9.6	34 285	71.0	29.0	3.43	3.33
Palm Desert	81.1	28 021	68.5	31.5	23.0	2.3	8.3	19 184	66.9	33.1	2.12	2.16
Palm Springs	10.2	30 823	66.6	33.4	23.5	3.2	11.0	20 516	60.8	39.2	2.03	2.09
Palo Alto	4.2	26 048	96.8	3.2	0.8	0.6	2.0	25 216	57.2	42.8	2.55	1.96
Paradise	4.9	12 374	93.7	6.3	0.8	2.5	6.2	11 591	70.9	29.1	2.23	2.21
Paramount	7.5	14 591	95.8	4.2	0.2	3.4	3.1	13 972	42.9	57.1	3.91	3.95
Pasadena	3.3	54 132	95.8	4.2	0.6	1.4	2.9	51 844	45.8	54.2	2.64	2.41
Perris	43.5	10 553	91.5	8.5	1.0	4.0	7.2	9 652	68.1	31.9	3.79	3.58
Petaluma	24.1	20 304	98.2	1.8	0.3	0.5	1.7	19 932	70.1	29.9	2.75	2.59
Pico Rivera	2.9	16 807	98.0	2.0	0.0	0.9	2.3	16 468	70.4	29.6	3.90	3.67
Pittsburg	13.4	18 300	96.9	3.1	0.2	0.9	3.8	17 741	62.8	37.2	3.24	3.05
Placentia	12.5	15 326	98.1	1.9	0.2	0.6	2.3	15 037	69.0	31.0	2.92	3.40

Table D. Cities

STATE Place code	City	Population, 2000				Population, 1990				Population and population characteristics, 2000					
										Race (percent)					
										One race					
		Land area, 2000[1] (sq km)	Total persons	Rank	Per square kilometer	Land area, 1990[1] (sq km)	Total persons	Rank	Per square kilometer	White	Black or African American	American Indian or Alaska Native	Asian	Native Hawaiian and other Pacific Islander	Some other race
		1	2	3	4	5	6	7	8	9	10	11	12	13	14
	CALIFORNIA—Cont'd														
06 57764	Pleasant Hill	18.4	32 837	1 104	1 784.6	17.6	31 583	990	1 794.5	81.8	1.5	0.5	9.4	0.3	2.3
06 57792	Pleasanton	56.1	63 654	459	1 134.7	42.0	50 570	548	1 204.0	80.4	1.4	0.3	11.7	0.1	2.3
06 58072	Pomona	59.2	149 473	142	2 524.9	59.1	131 700	138	2 228.4	41.8	9.6	1.3	7.2	0.2	34.9
06 58240	Porterville	36.3	39 615	882	1 091.3	29.1	29 521	1 069	1 014.5	54.8	1.3	1.7	4.6	0.2	32.7
06 58520	Poway	101.6	48 044	705	472.9	101.7	43 396	662	426.7	82.9	1.7	0.5	7.5	0.3	3.3
06 59451	Rancho Cucamonga	97.0	127 743	173	1 316.9	97.9	101 409	199	1 035.8	66.5	7.9	0.7	6.0	0.3	13.3
06 59514	Rancho Palos Verdes	35.4	41 145	840	1 162.3	35.4	41 667	703	1 177.0	67.2	2.0	0.2	25.9	0.1	1.2
06 59920	Redding	151.4	80 865	334	534.1	132.7	66 176	367	498.7	88.7	1.1	2.2	3.0	0.1	1.6
06 59962	Redlands	91.9	63 591	460	692.0	63.0	62 667	396	994.7	73.7	4.3	0.9	5.1	0.2	11.3
06 60018	Redondo Beach	16.3	63 261	466	3 881.0	16.3	60 167	419	3 691.2	78.6	2.5	0.5	9.1	0.4	4.4
06 60102	Redwood City	50.4	75 402	373	1 496.1	49.3	66 072	368	1 340.2	69.0	2.5	0.5	8.9	0.9	14.0
06 60466	Rialto	56.6	91 873	276	1 623.2	55.0	72 395	322	1 316.3	39.4	22.3	1.1	2.5	0.4	29.2
06 60620	Richmond	77.6	99 216	248	1 278.6	77.0	86 019	253	1 117.1	31.4	36.1	0.6	12.3	0.5	13.9
06 62000	Riverside	202.3	255 166	69	1 261.3	201.2	226 546	68	1 126.0	59.3	7.4	1.1	5.7	0.4	21.0
06 62364	Rocklin	41.9	36 330	970	867.1	32.7	18 806	1 746	575.1	88.3	0.9	0.8	4.2	0.2	1.9
06 62546	Rohnert Park	16.7	42 236	815	2 529.1	16.6	36 326	827	2 188.3	80.3	2.0	0.8	5.6	0.4	5.7
06 62896	Rosemead	13.3	53 505	616	4 022.9	13.3	51 638	528	3 882.6	26.6	0.7	0.9	48.8	0.1	19.7
06 62938	Roseville	78.9	79 921	340	1 012.9	77.4	44 685	642	577.3	86.0	1.3	0.7	4.3	0.2	3.9
06 64000	Sacramento	251.6	407 018	42	1 617.7	249.4	369 365	42	1 481.0	48.3	15.5	1.3	16.6	0.9	11.0
06 64224	Salinas	49.2	151 060	139	3 070.3	48.2	108 777	178	2 256.8	45.2	3.3	1.3	6.2	0.3	38.7
06 65000	San Bernardino	152.3	185 401	112	1 217.3	142.7	170 036	102	1 191.6	45.2	16.4	1.4	4.2	0.4	27.1
06 65028	San Bruno	14.1	40 165	867	2 848.6	16.7	38 961	765	2 333.0	57.7	2.0	0.5	18.7	2.9	10.8
06 65042	San Buenaventura (Ventura)	54.6	100 916	244	1 848.3	53.1	92 557	227	1 743.1	78.8	1.4	1.2	3.0	0.2	11.1
06 65070	San Carlos	15.3	27 718	1 343	1 811.6	14.6	26 382	1 223	1 807.0	84.5	0.8	0.2	7.9	0.4	2.4
06 65084	San Clemente	45.6	49 936	670	1 095.1	45.2	41 100	712	909.3	87.9	0.8	0.6	2.6	0.1	5.1
06 66000	San Diego	840.0	1 223 400	7	1 456.4	839.2	1 110 623	6	1 323.4	60.2	7.9	0.6	13.6	0.5	12.4
06 66070	San Dimas	40.2	34 980	1 027	870.1	40.2	32 398	956	805.9	74.7	3.3	0.7	9.4	0.2	7.3
06 67000	San Francisco	120.9	776 733	14	6 424.6	121.0	723 959	14	5 983.1	49.7	7.8	0.4	30.8	0.5	6.5
06 67042	San Gabriel	10.7	39 804	876	3 720.0	10.7	37 120	810	3 469.2	33.4	1.1	0.8	48.9	0.1	12.4
06 68000	San Jose	452.9	894 943	11	1 976.0	443.6	782 224	11	1 763.4	47.5	3.5	0.8	26.9	0.4	15.9
06 68028	San Juan Capistrano	36.8	33 826	1 069	919.2	36.9	26 183	1 235	709.6	78.5	0.8	1.1	1.9	0.1	14.2
06 68084	San Leandro	34.0	79 452	344	2 336.8	34.0	68 223	352	2 006.6	51.3	9.9	0.8	23.0	0.9	8.5
06 68154	San Luis Obispo	27.6	44 174	779	1 600.5	24.0	41 958	696	1 748.3	84.1	1.5	0.6	5.3	0.1	4.8
06 68196	San Marcos	61.5	54 977	592	893.9	60.1	38 974	764	648.5	67.4	2.0	0.8	4.7	0.2	20.4
06 68252	San Mateo	31.6	92 482	273	2 926.6	31.6	85 619	256	2 709.5	66.2	2.6	0.5	15.1	1.6	8.9
06 68294	San Pablo	6.7	30 215	1 214	4 509.7	6.7	25 158	1 279	3 754.9	31.6	18.3	0.9	16.4	0.5	25.4
06 68364	San Rafael	43.0	56 063	565	1 303.8	43.0	48 410	584	1 125.8	75.8	2.2	0.6	5.6	0.2	11.2
06 68378	San Ramon	30.0	44 722	770	1 490.7	29.5	35 303	853	1 196.7	76.8	1.9	0.4	14.9	0.2	2.2
06 69000	Santa Ana	70.3	337 977	53	4 807.6	70.2	293 827	52	4 185.6	42.7	1.7	1.2	8.8	0.3	40.6
06 69070	Santa Barbara	49.1	92 325	274	1 880.3	48.9	85 571	257	1 749.9	74.0	1.8	1.1	2.8	0.1	16.4
06 69084	Santa Clara	47.6	102 361	236	2 150.4	47.4	93 613	223	1 975.0	55.6	2.3	0.5	29.3	0.4	6.9
06 69088	Santa Clarita	123.9	151 088	138	1 219.4	104.8	120 050	153	1 145.5	79.5	2.1	0.6	5.2	0.1	8.5
06 69112	Santa Cruz	32.5	54 593	598	1 679.8	34.5	49 711	561	1 440.9	78.7	1.7	0.9	4.9	0.1	9.1
06 69196	Santa Maria	50.1	77 423	360	1 545.4	44.5	61 552	408	1 383.2	58.1	1.9	1.8	4.7	0.2	28.0
06 70000	Santa Monica	21.4	84 084	318	3 929.2	21.4	86 905	248	4 061.0	78.3	3.8	0.5	7.3	0.1	6.0
06 70042	Santa Paula	11.9	28 598	1 293	2 403.2	11.9	25 062	1 283	2 106.1	55.2	0.4	1.4	0.7	0.2	37.4
06 70098	Santa Rosa	103.9	147 595	145	1 420.5	87.3	113 261	164	1 297.4	77.6	2.2	1.4	3.8	0.3	10.3
06 70224	Santee	41.6	52 975	626	1 273.4	41.1	52 902	510	1 287.2	86.7	1.5	0.8	2.5	0.4	4.0
06 70280	Saratoga	31.4	29 843	1 232	950.4	31.0	28 061	1 140	905.2	67.4	0.4	0.2	29.1	0.1	0.6
06 70742	Seaside	22.9	31 696	1 150	1 384.1	22.9	38 826	767	1 695.5	49.2	12.6	1.0	10.1	1.3	18.4
06 72016	Simi Valley	105.1	111 351	210	1 097.1	85.6	100 218	202	1 170.8	81.3	1.3	0.7	6.3	0.1	6.5
06 73080	South Gate	19.1	96 375	254	5 045.8	19.0	86 284	252	4 541.3	41.6	1.0	0.9	0.8	0.1	51.0
06 73262	South San Francisco	23.4	60 552	491	2 587.7	23.2	54 312	483	2 341.0	44.0	2.8	0.6	28.9	1.6	15.0
06 73962	Stanton	8.1	37 403	944	4 617.7	8.1	30 491	1 039	3 764.3	49.6	2.3	1.1	15.5	0.9	25.7
06 75000	Stockton	141.7	243 771	72	1 720.3	136.2	210 943	75	1 548.8	43.3	11.2	1.1	19.9	0.4	17.3
06 75630	Suisun City	10.4	26 118	1 440	2 511.3	9.2	22 704	1 448	2 467.8	44.4	19.3	0.7	17.7	1.0	8.5
06 77000	Sunnyvale	56.8	131 760	167	2 319.7	56.7	117 334	158	2 069.2	53.3	2.2	0.5	32.3	0.3	7.2
06 78120	Temecula	68.0	57 716	535	848.8	68.4	27 177	1 175	397.3	78.9	3.4	0.9	4.7	0.3	7.4
06 78148	Temple City	10.4	33 377	1 090	3 209.3	10.4	31 153	1 003	2 995.5	48.7	0.9	0.4	38.9	0.1	7.5
06 78582	Thousand Oaks	142.1	117 005	196	823.4	128.4	104 381	192	812.9	85.1	1.1	0.5	5.9	0.1	4.5
06 80000	Torrance	53.2	137 946	161	2 593.0	53.2	133 107	137	2 502.0	59.2	2.2	0.4	28.6	0.3	4.6
06 80238	Tracy	54.4	56 929	548	1 046.5	24.8	33 558	915	1 353.1	65.2	5.5	0.9	8.1	0.6	13.1
06 80644	Tulare	43.0	43 994	782	1 023.1	36.9	33 249	927	901.0	56.4	5.0	1.4	2.0	0.1	29.1
06 80812	Turlock	34.5	55 810	572	1 617.7	24.8	42 224	687	1 702.6	72.3	1.4	0.9	4.5	0.3	15.2
06 80854	Tustin	29.5	67 504	428	2 288.3	29.2	50 689	544	1 735.9	58.7	2.9	0.7	14.9	0.3	17.9
06 81204	Union City	49.9	66 869	435	1 340.1	48.6	53 762	491	1 106.2	30.2	6.7	0.5	43.4	0.9	11.5
06 81344	Upland	39.2	68 393	421	1 744.7	39.1	63 374	391	1 620.8	67.2	7.6	0.8	7.3	0.1	12.3
06 81554	Vacaville	70.1	88 625	290	1 264.3	58.6	71 476	328	1 219.7	72.1	10.0	1.0	4.2	0.5	6.7
06 81666	Vallejo	78.2	116 760	197	1 493.1	78.3	109 199	176	1 394.6	36.0	23.7	0.7	24.2	1.1	7.9
06 82590	Victorville	188.5	64 029	456	339.7	108.3	50 103	555	462.6	61.1	11.9	1.1	3.5	0.2	16.3
06 82954	Visalia	74.0	91 565	278	1 237.4	60.8	75 659	302	1 244.4	69.5	1.9	1.3	5.1	0.1	17.8

[1] Dry land or land partially or temporarily covered by water.

Table D. Cities

	Population and population characteristics, 2000 (cont'd)								Population and population characteristics, 1990				
	Race (percent) (cont'd)								Race (percent)				
	Race alone or in combination												
City	Two or more races	White	Black	American Indian or Alaska Native	Asian	Native Hawaiian and other Pacific Islander	Some other race	Hispanic[1]	White	Black or African American	American Indian or Alaska Native	Asian and Pacific Islander	Hispanic[1]
	15	16	17	18	19	20	21	22	23	24	25	26	27

City	15	16	17	18	19	20	21	22	23	24	25	26	27
CALIFORNIA—Cont'd													
Pleasant Hill	4.2	85.4	2.1	1.3	11.3	0.6	3.8	8.4	89.3	1.4	0.6	7.0	6.6
Pleasanton	3.7	83.6	1.7	0.9	13.6	0.4	3.7	7.9	90.7	1.4	0.4	5.8	6.7
Pomona	5.0	45.6	10.4	2.0	8.2	0.4	38.6	64.5	57.0	14.4	0.6	6.7	51.3
Porterville	4.7	58.6	1.7	2.9	5.6	0.3	35.9	49.4	65.0	1.0	1.3	6.5	34.8
Poway	4.0	86.5	2.1	1.2	9.1	0.6	4.8	10.4	89.9	1.4	0.5	6.2	6.9
Rancho Cucamonga	5.4	71.0	8.9	1.6	7.3	0.6	16.3	27.8	78.6	5.9	0.6	5.4	20.0
Rancho Palos Verdes	3.4	70.1	2.4	0.6	27.8	0.3	2.4	5.7	76.2	1.9	0.2	20.5	5.3
Redding	3.3	91.7	1.5	3.8	3.7	0.3	2.5	5.4	92.6	1.1	2.2	3.3	4.0
Redlands	4.4	77.4	5.1	1.8	6.3	0.5	13.5	24.1	79.6	3.8	0.7	4.4	19.0
Redondo Beach	4.6	82.7	3.1	1.2	11.1	0.7	6.2	13.5	87.0	1.6	0.6	6.8	11.5
Redwood City	4.2	72.6	3.0	1.2	10.3	1.3	16.1	31.2	82.8	3.6	0.5	6.3	24.1
Rialto	5.2	43.3	23.7	2.1	3.3	0.7	32.4	51.2	57.9	20.4	0.9	3.5	31.5
Richmond	5.3	35.0	37.8	1.6	13.8	0.8	16.7	26.5	36.2	43.8	0.6	11.8	14.5
Riverside	5.1	63.6	8.4	2.1	6.7	0.7	23.9	38.1	70.8	7.4	0.8	5.2	26.0
Rocklin	3.7	91.7	1.3	1.8	5.8	0.5	3.0	7.9	93.6	0.8	1.0	2.6	7.0
Rohnert Park	5.2	84.9	2.9	2.1	7.3	1.0	7.6	13.6	89.2	2.6	1.0	4.8	8.9
Rosemead	3.4	29.0	0.9	1.4	50.0	0.3	22.0	41.3	35.4	0.6	0.5	34.3	49.7
Roseville	3.5	89.2	1.7	1.6	5.5	0.5	5.2	11.5	91.5	0.9	1.0	3.3	10.8
Sacramento	6.4	52.6	17.3	2.8	18.9	1.7	13.7	21.6	60.1	15.3	1.2	15.0	16.2
Salinas	5.1	49.4	3.9	2.0	7.7	0.6	41.9	64.1	54.6	3.0	0.9	8.1	50.6
San Bernardino	5.3	49.4	17.8	2.5	5.1	0.6	30.4	47.5	60.6	16.0	1.0	4.0	34.6
San Bruno	7.5	63.1	2.6	1.2	21.8	4.4	14.8	24.1	71.6	4.1	0.8	17.9	18.6
San Buenaventura (Ventura)	4.3	82.7	2.0	2.5	4.1	0.4	13.0	24.3	86.1	1.7	1.1	2.7	17.6
San Carlos	3.8	88.1	1.0	0.7	9.6	0.7	4.0	7.7	91.3	0.9	0.3	6.1	6.5
San Clemente	2.8	90.4	1.1	1.3	3.6	0.4	6.2	15.9	91.6	0.7	0.4	2.7	12.9
San Diego	4.8	63.9	8.9	1.3	15.5	0.9	14.7	25.4	67.1	9.4	0.6	11.8	20.7
San Dimas	4.4	78.5	3.8	1.5	10.7	0.5	9.7	23.3	81.7	3.8	0.5	8.6	17.3
San Francisco	4.3	53.0	8.6	1.2	32.6	0.8	8.5	14.1	53.6	10.9	0.5	29.1	13.9
San Gabriel	3.3	35.9	1.3	1.3	50.5	0.3	14.2	30.7	48.0	1.1	0.5	32.4	36.3
San Jose	5.0	51.5	4.1	1.5	28.8	0.8	18.7	30.2	62.8	4.7	0.7	19.5	26.6
San Juan Capistrano	3.4	81.7	1.1	1.7	2.7	0.3	16.2	33.1	89.4	0.4	0.8	2.2	21.8
San Leandro	5.8	55.9	11.0	1.7	24.9	1.6	11.3	20.1	74.1	5.8	0.7	13.8	15.2
San Luis Obispo	3.6	87.2	1.9	1.5	6.5	0.4	6.3	11.7	88.7	1.9	0.8	5.1	9.4
San Marcos	4.5	71.3	2.8	1.5	5.9	0.5	22.8	36.9	84.7	1.5	0.8	2.9	27.5
San Mateo	5.0	70.2	3.1	1.1	17.2	2.4	11.4	20.5	78.6	3.6	0.4	13.3	15.5
San Pablo	6.8	36.3	19.9	2.0	18.4	1.1	29.6	44.6	49.4	21.3	1.3	17.2	26.8
San Rafael	4.5	79.6	3.0	1.3	6.8	0.5	13.7	23.3	83.5	2.9	0.3	5.5	14.4
San Ramon	3.6	79.9	2.3	0.9	17.0	0.6	3.2	7.2	87.1	2.0	0.3	9.0	5.8
Santa Ana	4.6	46.6	2.1	1.7	9.4	0.5	44.3	76.1	68.0	2.6	0.5	9.7	65.2
Santa Barbara	3.8	77.5	2.2	1.9	3.6	0.3	18.6	35.0	77.7	2.2	0.9	2.3	31.5
Santa Clara	5.0	59.6	2.8	1.1	31.4	0.9	9.4	16.0	73.7	2.6	0.5	18.6	15.2
Santa Clarita	3.9	83.0	2.6	1.3	6.6	0.4	10.3	20.5	87.3	1.5	0.6	4.2	13.4
Santa Cruz	4.5	82.7	2.5	2.1	6.6	0.4	10.8	17.4	85.9	2.3	0.9	4.6	13.6
Santa Maria	5.4	62.5	2.3	3.1	5.9	0.3	31.4	59.7	61.6	2.2	0.9	6.1	45.7
Santa Monica	4.1	81.9	4.5	1.1	8.7	0.3	7.9	13.4	82.8	4.5	0.4	6.4	14.0
Santa Paula	4.7	59.4	0.7	2.1	1.1	0.4	41.0	71.2	59.3	0.3	0.8	1.0	58.9
Santa Rosa	4.4	81.4	2.9	2.6	5.1	0.5	12.3	19.2	89.4	1.8	1.2	3.4	9.5
Santee	4.0	90.3	2.0	1.7	4.0	0.9	5.4	11.4	91.1	1.7	0.8	3.0	10.7
Saratoga	2.3	69.4	0.5	0.4	30.7	0.3	1.2	3.1	83.7	0.4	0.2	15.0	3.3
Seaside	7.3	54.5	14.8	2.2	13.3	2.4	21.0	34.5	52.7	23.5	1.0	13.5	17.4
Simi Valley	3.7	84.7	1.7	1.6	7.6	0.4	8.1	16.8	88.2	1.5	0.6	5.5	12.7
South Gate	4.5	45.8	1.2	1.3	1.1	0.2	55.2	92.0	41.6	1.7	0.4	1.6	83.1
South San Francisco	7.0	49.6	3.5	1.4	31.7	2.4	18.9	31.8	61.5	4.0	0.7	24.6	27.1
Stanton	5.0	53.6	2.7	1.7	16.8	1.4	29.2	48.9	73.1	2.3	0.5	12.1	33.5
Stockton	6.8	47.7	12.5	2.3	22.9	1.0	20.8	32.5	57.5	9.6	1.0	22.8	25.0
Suisun City	8.3	50.6	21.7	2.1	21.5	2.2	11.3	17.8	59.6	14.3	1.1	17.1	16.1
Sunnyvale	4.3	56.7	2.7	1.1	34.2	0.7	9.1	15.5	71.6	3.4	0.5	19.3	13.2
Temecula	4.4	82.6	4.3	1.7	6.3	0.7	9.1	19.0	90.7	1.5	0.6	2.8	14.5
Temple City	3.5	51.5	1.1	0.9	40.3	0.3	9.5	20.5	71.9	0.6	0.4	19.5	18.8
Thousand Oaks	2.8	87.7	1.4	1.0	7.0	0.3	5.6	13.1	90.4	1.2	0.4	4.8	9.6
Torrance	4.7	63.1	2.7	1.1	31.1	0.8	6.3	12.8	73.0	1.5	0.4	21.9	10.1
Tracy	6.6	70.9	6.4	2.0	10.3	1.1	16.4	27.7	86.3	2.5	1.0	4.6	24.3
Tulare	6.0	61.6	5.8	2.4	2.6	0.4	33.3	45.6	65.6	6.2	1.1	2.5	33.8
Turlock	5.4	77.0	1.8	1.8	5.7	0.6	18.6	29.4	82.5	1.2	0.9	4.4	21.0
Tustin	4.6	62.5	3.5	1.3	16.4	0.6	20.5	34.2	73.2	5.7	0.5	10.4	20.7
Union City	6.7	34.9	7.6	1.3	46.9	1.9	14.7	24.0	43.9	8.6	0.6	33.4	25.1
Upland	4.7	71.1	8.4	1.6	8.4	0.4	15.0	27.5	78.9	5.3	0.5	7.0	17.5
Vacaville	5.5	76.8	11.2	2.1	6.3	1.0	8.7	17.9	78.8	8.9	1.0	3.8	15.9
Vallejo	6.6	40.4	25.8	1.8	27.2	2.0	10.1	15.9	50.5	21.2	0.7	23.0	10.8
Victorville	6.0	66.0	13.4	2.4	4.7	0.5	19.3	33.5	73.1	9.6	1.1	3.7	23.0
Visalia	4.2	73.1	2.3	2.4	6.0	0.3	20.3	35.6	74.8	1.5	1.0	6.4	25.1

[1] Hispanic persons may be of any race.

Table D. Cities

City	Under 5 years	5 to 17 years	18 to 24 years	25 to 34 years	35 to 44 years	45 to 54 years	55 to 64 years	65 to 74 years	75 years and over	Median age (years)	Percent Female
	28	29	30	31	32	33	34	35	36	37	38
CALIFORNIA—Cont'd											
Pleasant Hill	6.1	15.3	7.2	14.4	18.0	16.8	9.0	6.2	7.0	39.0	51.5
Pleasanton	6.8	21.4	5.5	12.5	20.8	16.5	8.9	4.3	3.3	36.9	50.9
Pomona	9.4	25.2	13.0	15.9	14.6	10.2	5.3	3.5	2.9	26.5	49.4
Porterville	9.5	24.8	10.8	14.0	14.0	11.2	6.3	4.4	5.0	28.6	50.9
Poway	6.0	24.7	7.1	9.5	18.6	17.0	8.5	4.5	4.1	36.9	50.8
Rancho Cucamonga	7.0	22.9	9.9	14.6	18.6	14.4	6.6	3.5	2.6	32.2	50.0
Rancho Palos Verdes	4.9	18.1	4.7	7.0	16.0	16.5	14.2	11.1	7.6	44.7	51.6
Redding	6.6	19.5	9.7	11.8	14.6	13.4	8.9	7.5	8.0	36.7	52.1
Redlands	6.2	20.0	10.7	13.0	14.9	14.2	8.4	5.9	6.7	35.1	52.8
Redondo Beach	5.7	13.1	6.1	20.9	22.1	15.5	8.0	4.7	3.7	36.7	49.6
Redwood City	7.5	15.7	8.4	18.9	18.5	13.2	7.6	4.7	5.5	34.8	49.7
Rialto	9.5	28.2	10.4	13.8	15.3	10.8	5.6	3.9	2.6	26.4	51.1
Richmond	7.7	20.0	9.9	15.9	15.5	13.3	7.9	5.2	4.7	32.8	51.4
Riverside	8.0	22.1	12.9	14.6	15.3	11.6	6.4	4.6	4.4	29.8	50.7
Rocklin	7.9	22.1	7.0	13.9	19.8	13.8	7.0	4.9	3.7	34.5	51.1
Rohnert Park	6.3	19.0	14.8	15.1	16.9	13.4	6.4	3.9	4.2	31.5	51.5
Rosemead	7.5	20.0	10.5	16.3	15.3	12.0	7.7	6.1	4.6	32.3	50.9
Roseville	7.3	19.5	7.0	13.8	17.0	12.7	8.3	7.5	6.9	36.4	52.1
Sacramento	7.1	20.2	10.4	15.6	15.1	12.8	7.4	5.7	5.7	32.8	51.4
Salinas	9.3	22.8	11.8	17.9	15.7	10.2	5.3	3.8	3.3	28.5	46.8
San Bernardino	9.8	25.4	11.0	14.7	14.9	10.1	5.9	4.3	3.9	27.6	50.8
San Bruno	6.1	16.9	8.2	16.4	18.0	14.6	8.5	6.1	5.2	36.3	50.6
San Buenaventura (Ventura)	6.6	18.5	7.8	14.1	17.4	14.6	8.3	6.3	6.5	36.8	50.8
San Carlos	7.0	15.1	4.3	13.5	19.6	16.4	9.8	6.5	7.8	39.9	51.9
San Clemente	6.5	17.6	7.2	13.7	17.9	15.4	8.6	6.9	6.2	38.0	49.4
San Diego	6.7	17.3	12.4	17.7	16.2	12.1	7.0	5.4	5.1	32.5	49.6
San Dimas	5.9	19.7	8.9	12.0	16.1	15.8	9.8	5.8	6.1	37.3	52.0
San Francisco	4.1	10.5	9.1	23.2	17.2	13.9	8.4	6.9	6.7	36.5	49.2
San Gabriel	6.7	16.8	8.6	16.7	16.6	12.8	8.3	6.3	7.1	35.6	52.0
San Jose	7.6	18.8	9.9	18.0	17.4	12.4	7.6	4.7	3.6	32.6	49.2
San Juan Capistrano	7.2	20.9	7.8	12.0	15.4	14.6	9.1	6.2	6.9	36.4	50.8
San Leandro	6.3	15.9	7.8	15.2	16.8	13.7	8.3	7.4	8.6	37.7	51.8
San Luis Obispo	3.4	10.8	33.6	12.4	11.2	10.7	5.8	5.0	7.1	26.2	48.6
San Marcos	8.8	20.3	9.4	16.4	15.9	10.9	6.4	5.4	6.4	32.1	50.4
San Mateo	6.1	14.3	7.2	17.7	17.4	13.7	8.5	6.7	8.4	37.5	51.1
San Pablo	9.1	22.6	10.9	17.0	14.8	10.7	6.2	4.1	4.5	29.5	50.9
San Rafael	5.8	13.7	8.1	16.6	16.7	15.4	9.4	6.5	7.9	38.5	50.5
San Ramon	7.4	18.9	5.8	14.7	21.0	17.4	8.8	3.4	2.7	36.5	50.7
Santa Ana	10.3	23.9	12.8	19.5	14.5	8.7	4.8	3.1	2.4	26.5	48.2
Santa Barbara	5.6	14.1	13.8	17.1	15.2	13.1	7.3	5.8	7.9	34.6	50.8
Santa Clara	6.5	13.4	11.3	21.9	17.2	11.7	7.4	5.6	5.1	33.4	49.1
Santa Clarita	7.8	22.5	8.1	14.2	19.4	13.9	6.9	3.8	3.3	33.4	50.5
Santa Cruz	4.9	12.5	20.5	17.1	15.5	14.7	6.3	4.0	4.5	31.7	50.2
Santa Maria	9.0	22.6	11.6	15.7	13.9	9.7	6.2	5.6	5.7	29.2	49.2
Santa Monica	4.1	10.5	6.1	20.3	19.8	15.7	9.1	6.4	7.9	39.3	51.8
Santa Paula	8.8	22.6	10.9	15.6	14.1	10.4	6.8	5.3	5.3	29.6	49.1
Santa Rosa	6.5	17.8	9.5	14.3	15.7	14.4	7.9	5.9	8.0	36.2	51.2
Santee	6.7	21.5	8.4	13.7	19.1	14.3	7.3	4.7	4.2	34.8	51.8
Saratoga	5.4	20.7	4.0	5.8	18.0	17.5	12.4	9.1	7.1	43.2	50.9
Seaside	9.7	20.6	11.1	19.4	15.1	10.1	5.7	5.2	3.3	29.5	49.1
Simi Valley	7.3	21.1	7.9	14.1	18.7	14.7	8.4	4.5	3.1	34.7	50.5
South Gate	10.1	25.5	12.5	17.5	14.0	9.6	5.2	2.9	2.5	26.0	50.4
South San Francisco	6.5	17.8	9.2	15.4	16.6	13.3	8.6	7.0	5.6	35.7	50.4
Stanton	9.3	21.1	10.5	18.4	14.9	9.7	6.5	4.9	4.7	30.0	49.4
Stockton	8.6	23.8	11.0	13.6	13.6	11.8	7.1	5.2	5.0	29.8	51.3
Suisun City	7.7	24.9	8.9	13.5	19.1	13.9	6.4	3.4	2.3	31.7	50.5
Sunnyvale	7.0	13.4	7.7	23.2	18.1	11.9	8.0	5.7	4.9	34.3	48.6
Temecula	8.9	25.8	7.8	13.5	19.7	11.6	5.5	4.4	2.7	31.3	50.6
Temple City	5.7	18.3	8.1	12.5	16.4	15.5	9.6	6.6	7.3	38.6	52.4
Thousand Oaks	6.7	19.3	7.1	12.3	17.6	15.8	10.1	5.8	5.3	37.7	50.9
Torrance	5.7	17.3	6.8	13.4	18.9	14.6	9.2	7.5	6.5	38.7	51.4
Tracy	9.4	25.0	7.5	15.5	19.6	11.3	5.4	3.3	3.1	30.9	50.0
Tulare	9.6	25.0	10.5	14.2	14.5	10.4	6.4	4.9	4.4	28.5	51.4
Turlock	8.1	21.8	11.4	14.4	14.4	11.4	6.7	5.6	6.2	30.9	51.9
Tustin	8.6	18.2	9.3	20.4	17.7	11.5	7.1	4.1	3.1	31.8	51.0
Union City	7.3	20.5	9.8	16.0	16.8	13.8	7.8	4.6	3.5	32.8	50.3
Upland	7.0	20.3	9.6	13.8	15.4	14.3	8.8	5.9	4.9	34.5	51.9
Vacaville	6.6	20.3	9.0	16.3	19.2	13.4	6.9	4.5	3.7	33.9	45.8
Vallejo	7.2	20.4	9.0	13.6	16.0	14.6	8.0	5.6	5.6	34.9	51.6
Victorville	8.6	25.6	8.6	13.2	15.5	10.6	6.8	6.2	5.0	30.7	51.6
Visalia	8.1	23.2	9.6	13.7	14.8	12.4	7.3	5.3	5.5	31.7	51.8

Table D. Cities

City	Population and population characteristics, 1990										Population—change, 1980–2000				
	Age (percent)										Total persons			Percent change	
	Under 5 years	5 to 17 years	18 to 24 years	25 to 34 years	35 to 44 years	45 to 54 years	55 to 64 years	65 to 74 years	75 years and over	Percent Female	2000	1990	1980	1990–2000	1980–1990
	39	40	41	42	43	44	45	46	47	48	49	50	51	52	53
CALIFORNIA—Cont'd															
Pleasant Hill	6.6	13.8	7.7	21.0	18.8	11.7	8.3	7.6	4.4	51.3	32 837	31 583	25 124	4.0	25.7
Pleasanton	7.4	18.1	9.3	18.1	20.5	14.6	6.5	3.3	2.2	50.4	63 654	50 570	35 160	25.9	43.8
Pomona	11.1	21.8	13.1	20.7	14.1	7.5	5.0	3.7	3.0	48.7	149 473	131 700	92 742	13.5	42.0
Porterville	9.4	22.2	10.5	15.6	14.5	8.0	6.7	6.8	6.2	52.0	39 615	29 521	19 692	34.2	49.9
Poway	7.7	22.3	8.4	15.7	20.1	12.3	6.5	4.5	2.4	50.1	48 044	43 396	32 263	10.7	34.5
Rancho Cucamonga	9.3	22.4	9.7	20.4	18.0	10.2	5.0	3.4	1.6	50.6	127 743	101 409	55 250	26.0	83.5
Rancho Palos Verdes	4.6	16.6	8.0	10.4	15.9	17.9	14.6	8.7	3.3	50.8	41 145	41 667	36 577	-1.3	13.9
Redding	8.2	18.6	9.5	16.2	15.4	9.5	8.3	8.3	6.1	51.9	80 865	66 462	41 995	21.7	58.3
Redlands	7.7	19.3	10.4	16.9	15.9	10.7	7.3	6.5	5.3	52.1	63 591	62 667	43 619	1.5	43.7
Redondo Beach	5.7	10.2	9.9	30.0	19.4	10.8	6.8	4.7	2.5	48.8	63 261	60 167	57 102	5.1	5.4
Redwood City	7.9	13.9	9.9	22.5	17.1	9.8	7.4	6.7	4.7	49.6	75 402	66 072	54 951	14.1	20.2
Rialto	10.9	24.8	8.9	19.0	15.4	7.9	6.3	4.5	2.1	51.1	91 873	72 395	37 474	26.9	93.2
Richmond	8.4	17.7	9.6	18.9	15.9	10.3	7.8	7.3	4.2	52.3	99 216	86 019	74 676	15.3	15.2
Riverside	8.8	20.0	13.0	19.7	14.5	8.5	6.4	5.3	3.7	50.3	255 166	226 546	170 876	12.6	32.6
Rocklin	8.1	20.0	8.4	18.4	18.3	10.6	6.9	6.1	3.2	50.3	36 330	18 806	NA	93.2	NA
Rohnert Park	8.5	18.0	14.2	21.3	17.6	7.8	5.0	4.7	2.8	51.2	42 236	36 326	22 965	16.3	58.2
Rosemead	8.7	21.7	11.8	18.8	13.9	8.8	7.4	4.7	4.2	50.4	53 505	51 638	42 604	3.6	21.2
Roseville	7.9	19.5	7.5	18.6	18.0	10.2	7.2	6.2	5.0	51.7	79 921	44 685	24 347	78.9	83.5
Sacramento	8.2	18.1	10.1	19.6	15.7	9.0	7.3	6.9	5.1	51.6	407 018	369 365	275 741	10.2	34.0
Salinas	10.2	21.8	12.0	20.0	13.9	7.8	6.2	4.8	3.4	50.0	151 060	108 777	80 479	38.9	35.2
San Bernardino	10.7	21.1	11.4	19.9	13.0	7.8	6.3	5.8	4.1	50.5	185 401	170 036	117 490	9.0	44.7
San Bruno	6.6	15.1	9.9	22.1	17.3	10.2	8.5	6.8	3.6	49.2	40 165	38 961	35 417	3.1	10.0
San Buenaventura (Ventura).	7.1	16.2	9.7	19.6	16.7	10.3	8.0	7.1	5.4	50.6	100 916	92 557	74 393	9.0	24.4
San Carlos	6.1	12.5	6.3	17.1	19.6	13.5	9.4	9.0	6.5	52.0	27 718	26 382	24 710	5.1	6.8
San Clemente	7.5	13.3	9.5	20.6	16.3	11.0	9.0	8.1	4.8	49.3	49 936	41 100	27 325	21.5	50.4
San Diego	7.3	15.9	14.4	21.3	15.3	8.8	6.9	6.1	4.0	49.0	1 223 400	1 110 623	875 538	10.2	26.9
San Dimas	6.9	19.3	9.6	16.0	17.9	13.3	7.6	5.9	3.5	50.6	34 980	32 398	24 014	8.0	34.9
San Francisco	4.9	11.3	9.8	22.2	18.0	10.7	8.6	8.0	6.6	49.9	776 733	723 959	678 974	7.3	6.6
San Gabriel	7.8	16.5	11.3	19.2	14.9	9.9	7.0	7.0	6.4	52.0	39 804	37 120	30 072	7.2	23.4
San Jose	8.3	18.4	11.2	21.6	16.0	10.6	6.7	4.3	2.8	49.2	894 943	782 224	629 442	14.4	24.3
San Juan Capistrano	7.4	19.5	8.5	14.8	18.0	11.3	7.6	7.1	5.8	50.4	33 826	26 183	18 959	29.2	38.1
San Leandro	5.8	13.1	8.2	18.1	15.1	10.1	10.5	11.5	7.6	52.4	79 452	68 223	63 952	16.5	6.7
San Luis Obispo	3.8	9.8	33.1	16.8	12.1	6.5	5.5	6.4	5.9	48.9	44 174	41 958	34 252	5.3	22.5
San Marcos	8.7	18.4	11.7	18.9	13.8	7.8	6.1	8.0	6.6	49.9	54 977	38 974	17 479	41.1	123.0
San Mateo	5.7	12.8	8.7	20.0	16.3	11.3	9.0	8.8	7.4	51.5	92 482	85 619	77 561	8.0	10.4
San Pablo	10.0	20.5	9.9	20.1	14.6	8.1	6.3	5.9	4.7	52.0	30 215	25 158	19 750	20.1	27.4
San Rafael	5.9	11.6	9.1	19.0	18.1	12.9	9.2	8.0	6.2	50.9	56 063	48 410	44 800	15.8	8.1
San Ramon	7.2	19.6	8.9	18.6	23.2	13.0	5.2	3.0	1.3	50.3	44 722	35 303	22 356	26.7	57.9
Santa Ana	10.0	20.4	16.7	22.7	12.7	7.2	4.9	3.4	2.1	46.8	337 977	293 827	203 713	15.0	44.2
Santa Barbara	6.2	12.0	12.5	21.4	16.1	8.4	7.2	7.6	8.6	51.0	92 325	85 571	74 414	7.9	15.0
Santa Clara	6.2	12.6	13.0	24.5	15.7	10.0	8.2	6.3	3.6	49.2	102 361	93 613	87 746	9.3	6.7
Santa Clarita	8.9	19.0	10.2	20.5	18.8	10.6	5.6	4.1	2.2	50.0	151 088	120 050	NA	25.9	NA
Santa Cruz	5.4	12.6	21.2	18.7	18.3	8.3	5.3	5.4	4.9	50.5	54 593	49 711	41 483	9.8	19.8
Santa Maria	9.8	20.2	11.2	18.9	12.3	8.7	7.3	7.1	4.6	50.4	77 423	61 552	39 685	25.8	55.1
Santa Monica	4.4	9.2	7.3	22.7	20.5	11.1	8.5	8.1	8.2	52.8	84 084	86 905	88 314	-3.2	-1.6
Santa Paula	9.0	21.1	11.2	18.0	13.0	8.4	7.1	6.6	5.6	49.0	28 598	25 062	20 552	14.1	21.9
Santa Rosa	7.1	16.6	9.6	16.7	17.2	9.3	7.1	8.7	7.6	52.2	147 595	113 261	83 320	30.3	35.9
Santee	8.4	20.5	9.6	20.5	17.6	9.0	6.1	5.0	3.4	50.5	52 975	52 902	47 080	0.1	12.4
Saratoga	4.6	15.8	7.3	9.7	17.2	18.4	13.7	8.4	4.9	50.8	29 843	28 061	29 261	6.4	-4.1
Seaside	9.8	17.3	21.8	21.9	12.5	6.1	5.2	3.9	1.4	43.0	31 696	38 826	36 567	-18.4	6.2
Simi Valley	8.0	19.9	10.8	19.0	18.2	12.3	6.5	3.4	1.8	49.7	111 351	100 218	77 500	11.1	29.3
South Gate	10.7	23.8	14.1	18.7	12.6	8.0	4.9	4.1	3.1	50.1	96 375	86 284	66 784	11.7	29.2
South San Francisco	7.4	16.6	9.6	19.1	15.8	10.4	9.7	7.4	3.8	50.9	60 552	54 312	49 393	11.5	10.0
Stanton	9.3	16.4	12.6	22.5	15.0	8.0	6.5	4.6	5.1	49.8	37 403	30 491	23 723	22.7	28.5
Stockton	9.4	22.3	10.9	16.6	14.6	8.9	6.9	6.0	4.4	50.5	243 771	210 943	149 779	15.6	40.8
Suisun City	10.4	26.7	8.3	20.6	17.7	8.6	4.3	2.2	1.2	49.7	26 118	22 704	11 087	15.0	104.8
Sunnyvale	6.4	12.6	9.7	25.4	15.7	11.0	9.0	6.5	3.7	49.4	131 760	117 324	106 618	12.3	10.0
Temecula	11.2	21.5	9.1	20.9	17.4	7.4	6.3	4.6	1.7	49.1	57 716	27 099	NA	113.0	NA
Temple City	6.8	16.7	10.1	15.4	15.7	12.1	8.5	7.7	7.0	52.4	33 377	31 153	28 972	7.1	7.5
Thousand Oaks	6.6	18.3	9.9	15.9	18.4	14.0	8.0	5.1	3.9	50.4	117 005	104 381	77 072	12.1	35.4
Torrance	6.0	14.4	8.7	19.7	16.6	12.2	10.4	7.6	4.4	50.9	137 946	133 107	129 881	3.6	2.5
Tracy	10.3	20.7	8.9	22.1	15.8	8.5	5.5	5.2	2.9	49.8	56 929	33 558	18 428	69.6	82.1
Tulare	9.9	24.8	8.7	17.4	13.2	8.6	6.8	6.0	4.5	52.0	43 994	33 249	22 498	32.3	47.8
Turlock	8.9	20.3	11.4	18.0	14.1	8.0	6.7	6.5	6.1	52.0	55 810	42 224	26 278	32.2	60.7
Tustin	8.8	14.9	14.8	24.2	14.3	9.2	6.3	4.5	3.1	49.6	67 504	50 689	32 317	33.2	56.8
Union City	8.3	21.5	10.4	17.9	18.3	11.1	5.7	4.1	2.7	50.5	66 869	53 762	39 406	24.4	36.4
Upland	7.5	19.2	10.8	17.1	15.8	12.5	7.9	5.7	3.5	51.2	68 393	63 374	47 647	7.9	33.0
Vacaville	8.0	18.4	10.4	23.1	17.9	9.7	5.8	4.4	2.4	44.8	88 625	71 476	43 367	24.0	64.8
Vallejo	8.7	19.2	10.4	18.0	16.6	9.5	6.8	6.8	4.1	50.1	116 760	109 199	80 303	6.9	36.0
Victorville	10.0	20.8	9.8	19.8	12.9	7.5	7.5	7.9	3.9	50.4	64 029	50 103	14 229	27.8	252.1
Visalia	9.4	22.1	9.5	16.6	15.3	9.5	6.6	6.0	4.9	51.7	91 565	75 659	49 729	21.0	52.1

Table D. Cities

City	Total population	Total in households	House-holder	Spouse	Child Total	Child Own child under 18 years	Other relatives Total	Other relatives Under 18 years	Nonrelatives Total	Nonrelatives Unmarried partner	Total in group quarters	Correctional institutions	Nursing homes	Other institutions	College dormitories	Military quarters	Other
	54	55	56	57	58	59	60	61	62	63	64	65	66	67	68	69	70
CALIFORNIA—Cont'd																	
Pleasant Hill	32 837	98.6	41.9	20.3	25.9	19.9	3.6	1.0	7.0	2.4	1.4	0.0	0.9	0.0	0.0	0.0	0.5
Pleasanton	63 654	99.6	36.6	23.3	32.4	27.0	3.1	0.8	4.2	1.5	0.4	0.0	0.3	0.0	0.0	0.0	0.1
Pomona	149 473	96.6	25.3	13.8	37.2	28.6	13.2	4.9	7.1	1.8	3.4	0.0	0.5	0.7	1.5	0.0	0.6
Porterville	39 615	95.9	30.0	15.9	37.0	30.2	7.8	3.2	5.2	2.1	4.1	0.0	0.7	2.1	0.0	0.0	1.3
Poway	48 044	99.1	32.2	22.1	36.1	28.6	4.6	1.6	4.1	1.2	0.9	0.0	0.7	0.0	0.0	0.0	0.1
Rancho Cucamonga	127 743	97.2	32.0	19.3	35.2	26.9	6.2	2.4	4.5	1.7	2.8	1.4	0.0	0.1	0.0	0.0	1.4
Rancho Palos Verdes	41 145	98.8	37.1	26.2	29.3	21.8	3.8	1.0	2.3	0.8	1.2	0.0	0.4	0.0	0.2	0.0	0.6
Redding	80 865	97.1	39.7	19.1	28.3	23.6	3.8	1.6	6.2	2.5	2.9	0.5	0.6	0.4	0.6	0.0	0.8
Redlands	63 591	96.9	37.1	18.8	30.5	23.3	5.5	2.3	5.0	1.8	3.1	0.0	0.8	0.0	1.8	0.0	0.4
Redondo Beach	63 261	99.7	45.2	18.3	22.2	17.1	4.5	1.1	9.6	2.9	0.3	0.0	0.0	0.1	0.0	0.0	0.1
Redwood City	75 402	97.4	37.2	18.3	26.8	20.8	7.2	1.8	7.9	2.2	2.6	1.4	0.4	0.2	0.0	0.0	0.6
Rialto	91 873	99.1	26.8	15.5	40.1	31.2	11.5	5.2	5.2	1.8	0.9	0.0	0.3	0.0	0.0	0.0	0.6
Richmond	99 216	98.4	34.9	14.1	31.1	22.5	11.3	4.3	6.9	2.3	1.6	0.7	0.2	0.1	0.0	0.0	0.7
Riverside	255 166	96.9	32.1	16.2	33.5	25.8	8.3	3.2	6.9	2.1	3.1	0.4	0.5	0.2	1.1	0.0	0.8
Rocklin	36 330	99.9	36.5	22.7	33.5	28.4	3.0	1.2	4.2	1.8	0.1	0.0	0.0	0.0	0.0	0.0	0.0
Rohnert Park	42 236	97.4	36.7	17.1	29.0	23.0	4.9	1.6	9.6	2.7	2.6	0.0	0.0	0.0	2.2	0.0	0.4
Rosemead	53 505	98.9	26.0	15.1	34.5	22.4	18.0	4.4	5.3	1.1	1.1	0.0	0.5	0.2	0.0	0.0	0.4
Roseville	79 921	98.8	38.5	22.0	30.1	25.0	3.5	1.2	4.7	2.0	1.2	0.0	0.8	0.1	0.0	0.0	0.3
Sacramento	407 018	97.8	38.0	14.6	30.2	23.4	7.9	3.0	7.2	2.7	2.2	0.5	0.5	0.2	0.2	0.0	0.8
Salinas	151 060	92.8	25.4	14.6	34.0	26.6	12.3	4.2	6.6	1.6	7.2	5.4	0.2	0.2	0.1	0.0	1.3
San Bernardino	185 401	96.8	30.4	13.7	36.9	29.5	9.8	4.4	6.1	2.4	3.2	1.2	0.4	0.5	0.2	0.0	0.9
San Bruno	40 165	99.4	36.5	18.9	29.2	20.3	8.5	2.3	6.3	2.0	0.6	0.0	0.3	0.0	0.0	0.0	0.2
San Buenaventura (Ventura)	100 916	97.7	38.2	18.8	29.0	22.4	5.3	1.9	6.4	2.3	2.3	0.7	0.4	0.3	0.0	0.0	1.0
San Carlos	27 718	99.3	41.3	23.3	26.5	21.2	3.1	0.7	5.1	2.1	0.7	0.0	0.5	0.0	0.0	0.0	0.1
San Clemente	49 936	99.4	38.8	21.6	27.5	22.3	4.4	1.3	7.1	2.2	0.6	0.0	0.1	0.0	0.0	0.0	0.5
San Diego	1 223 400	96.3	36.8	16.4	27.5	21.0	7.1	2.4	8.3	2.3	3.7	0.2	0.3	0.1	1.1	1.4	0.8
San Dimas	34 980	96.5	34.8	20.1	31.3	22.4	6.0	2.1	4.4	1.5	3.5	0.0	0.6	0.4	0.7	0.0	1.7
San Francisco	776 733	97.5	42.4	13.4	19.0	12.0	9.0	2.0	13.6	3.2	2.5	0.2	0.2	0.1	0.5	0.0	1.5
San Gabriel	39 804	98.1	31.6	17.1	30.1	20.4	13.4	2.7	5.9	1.2	1.9	0.0	1.3	0.4	0.0	0.0	0.2
San Jose	894 943	98.8	30.9	17.3	30.6	22.3	11.7	3.3	8.2	1.7	1.2	0.1	0.2	0.1	0.3	0.0	0.5
San Juan Capistrano	33 826	98.7	32.3	20.3	31.4	24.5	7.7	2.4	7.0	1.4	1.3	0.4	0.5	0.0	0.0	0.0	0.4
San Leandro	79 452	99.0	38.6	18.2	27.5	19.4	8.9	2.3	5.8	2.2	1.0	0.0	0.6	0.1	0.0	0.0	0.4
San Luis Obispo	44 174	95.8	42.2	13.2	16.6	13.2	2.6	0.6	21.1	2.1	4.2	0.0	0.8	0.0	2.1	0.0	1.3
San Marcos	54 977	99.7	32.9	19.3	31.9	25.6	8.0	2.7	7.6	1.9	0.3	0.0	0.0	0.0	0.0	0.0	0.2
San Mateo	92 482	98.6	40.4	18.9	24.6	18.2	7.0	1.6	7.7	2.1	1.4	0.0	0.5	0.1	0.0	0.0	0.8
San Pablo	30 215	98.5	30.0	13.3	34.9	26.7	13.3	4.2	6.9	2.0	1.5	0.0	1.2	0.0	0.0	0.0	0.3
San Rafael	56 063	96.4	39.9	17.7	22.0	17.5	5.7	1.2	11.1	2.5	3.6	0.6	1.4	0.0	0.4	0.0	1.2
San Ramon	44 722	99.8	37.9	23.4	31.0	25.4	3.2	0.7	4.4	1.9	0.2	0.0	0.0	0.1	0.0	0.0	0.1
Santa Ana	337 977	98.3	21.6	13.1	35.0	26.6	17.8	5.8	10.9	1.3	1.7	0.7	0.2	0.1	0.0	0.0	0.6
Santa Barbara	92 325	95.1	38.6	15.3	22.4	17.0	6.8	2.1	12.0	2.5	4.9	0.0	0.5	0.0	3.0	0.0	1.4
Santa Clara	102 361	97.3	37.6	18.2	24.2	17.6	7.9	2.0	9.3	2.0	2.7	0.0	0.4	0.0	2.0	0.0	0.2
Santa Clarita	151 088	99.1	33.6	20.5	34.7	28.3	5.1	1.5	5.2	1.7	0.9	0.0	0.2	0.0	0.5	0.0	0.2
Santa Cruz	54 593	91.5	37.4	13.9	19.9	15.7	4.0	1.1	16.3	3.6	8.5	0.6	0.1	0.0	5.8	0.0	2.1
Santa Maria	77 423	97.2	28.6	16.1	33.7	26.4	11.6	4.1	7.2	1.7	2.8	1.2	0.5	0.2	0.0	0.0	0.9
Santa Monica	84 084	97.0	52.9	14.5	17.7	13.5	3.6	0.8	8.2	2.8	3.0	0.0	0.9	0.2	0.0	0.0	1.9
Santa Paula	28 598	99.2	28.4	16.8	35.5	26.3	12.0	4.4	6.4	1.7	0.8	0.0	0.5	0.0	0.1	0.0	0.3
Santa Rosa	147 595	97.4	38.0	17.8	26.9	21.4	6.1	1.9	8.6	2.8	2.6	0.4	0.4	0.2	0.0	0.0	1.5
Santee	52 975	98.0	34.9	20.1	33.1	25.7	4.6	1.9	5.3	1.9	2.0	1.3	0.4	0.0	0.0	0.0	0.3
Saratoga	29 843	99.2	35.0	26.3	31.1	25.0	4.1	0.8	2.7	0.8	0.8	0.0	0.7	0.0	0.0	0.0	0.1
Seaside	31 696	99.7	31.0	17.0	32.2	25.2	11.3	4.0	8.2	1.9	0.3	0.0	0.1	0.0	0.0	0.0	0.2
Simi Valley	111 351	99.3	32.7	20.9	33.8	25.8	6.0	2.0	5.9	1.7	0.7	0.0	0.1	0.0	0.0	0.0	0.6
South Gate	96 375	99.9	24.1	14.4	40.6	29.9	15.1	4.9	5.7	1.7	0.1	0.0	0.1	0.0	0.0	0.0	0.1
South San Francisco	60 552	99.3	32.5	18.1	30.9	20.6	11.6	3.1	6.2	1.5	0.7	0.0	0.2	0.0	0.0	0.0	0.5
Stanton	37 403	98.6	28.8	14.5	33.1	25.2	13.5	4.1	8.8	1.7	1.4	0.0	0.7	0.0	0.0	0.0	0.6
Stockton	243 771	97.8	32.2	15.5	35.5	28.0	8.8	3.6	5.8	2.2	2.2	0.0	0.7	0.0	0.8	0.0	0.7
Suisun City	26 118	99.6	30.6	19.1	36.6	28.2	8.3	3.4	5.0	1.6	0.4	0.0	0.2	0.0	0.0	0.0	0.1
Sunnyvale	131 760	99.3	39.9	20.0	24.3	18.5	6.9	1.6	8.3	1.9	0.7	0.0	0.4	0.0	0.0	0.0	0.3
Temecula	57 716	100.0	31.7	21.8	38.3	32.8	4.3	1.4	3.9	1.4	0.0	0.0	0.0	0.0	0.0	0.0	0.0
Temple City	33 377	98.5	34.0	19.3	31.5	21.6	9.6	2.0	4.1	1.3	1.5	0.0	1.2	0.0	0.0	0.0	0.3
Thousand Oaks	117 005	98.3	35.7	22.3	30.8	24.3	4.2	1.2	5.3	1.4	1.7	0.0	0.2	0.0	0.7	0.0	0.7
Torrance	137 946	99.1	39.5	20.6	29.1	21.3	5.4	1.4	4.4	1.5	0.9	0.0	0.4	0.1	0.0	0.0	0.4
Tracy	56 929	99.4	31.0	20.1	37.7	31.5	6.4	2.3	4.2	1.9	0.6	0.0	0.3	0.0	0.0	0.0	0.3
Tulare	43 994	99.0	30.8	17.2	37.5	29.8	8.1	3.7	5.3	2.3	1.0	0.0	0.4	0.1	0.0	0.0	0.5
Turlock	55 810	96.3	33.0	18.1	33.4	26.3	6.7	2.3	5.1	2.0	3.7	0.0	0.9	0.0	0.6	0.0	2.2
Tustin	67 504	99.4	35.3	17.7	29.9	24.0	8.6	2.1	7.8	2.1	0.6	0.0	0.0	0.0	0.0	0.0	0.6
Union City	66 869	99.5	27.9	18.6	34.4	23.4	13.6	3.8	5.1	1.1	0.5	0.0	0.3	0.0	0.0	0.0	0.2
Upland	68 393	99.1	35.9	19.1	32.3	24.3	6.5	2.4	5.4	2.1	0.9	0.0	0.5	0.0	0.0	0.0	0.4
Vacaville	88 625	89.6	31.7	18.1	30.3	24.3	4.5	2.0	5.0	1.9	10.4	10.0	0.3	0.0	0.0	0.0	0.1
Vallejo	116 760	98.5	33.9	16.7	32.0	23.0	10.1	3.8	5.9	2.2	1.5	0.0	0.6	0.1	0.0	0.0	0.8
Victorville	64 029	99.0	32.6	17.7	36.2	29.7	7.3	3.5	5.1	2.0	1.0	0.2	0.4	0.0	0.0	0.0	0.4
Visalia	91 565	98.2	33.7	18.5	34.5	28.0	6.1	2.4	5.3	2.1	1.8	0.0	0.7	0.2	0.0	0.0	0.8

Table D. Cities

City	Households by type, 2000												Households, 1990		
		Family households						Nonfamily households							
			Married couple		Female householder[1]				Householder living alone						
	Total households	Total	With own children under 18 years	Total	With own children under 18 years	Total	With own children under 18 years	Total	Total	65 years and over	Average household size	Average family size	Total households	Female householder[1]	Householder living alone
	71	72	73	74	75	76	77	78	79	80	81	82	83	84	85
CALIFORNIA—Cont'd															
Pleasant Hill	10 753	61.1	28.0	48.4	21.7	9.1	4.5	38.9	29.1	9.5	2.35	2.95	13 004	8.3	26.7
Pleasanton	23 311	74.6	40.8	63.7	34.6	7.8	4.6	25.4	19.3	5.2	2.72	3.15	18 484	8.0	16.8
Pomona	37 855	78.7	49.8	54.7	35.8	16.3	10.0	21.3	15.4	5.5	3.82	4.22	36 443	14.2	18.2
Porterville	11 884	77.2	47.5	53.1	30.9	17.7	12.6	22.8	19.1	8.3	3.20	3.62	9 586	16.0	22.5
Poway	15 467	83.2	47.0	68.8	38.1	10.5	6.6	16.8	12.6	4.7	3.08	3.35	13 888	8.4	10.8
Rancho Cucamonga	40 863	77.9	44.7	60.2	34.1	12.8	7.9	22.1	16.8	4.1	3.04	3.44	33 635	9.8	16.1
Rancho Palos Verdes	15 256	80.1	32.6	70.8	28.7	6.8	2.9	19.9	16.8	7.6	2.66	3.00	14 943	6.2	14.0
Redding	32 103	65.4	31.9	48.1	20.2	13.0	8.8	34.6	27.6	11.4	2.44	2.97	26 105	12.2	25.6
Redlands	23 593	67.9	33.5	50.6	23.3	13.0	7.7	32.1	26.0	9.2	2.61	3.18	21 985	11.0	24.4
Redondo Beach	28 566	53.4	23.3	40.6	17.0	9.0	4.7	46.6	33.1	5.9	2.21	2.87	26 717	9.0	29.4
Redwood City	28 060	63.8	31.3	49.2	23.9	9.9	5.4	36.2	27.1	8.0	2.62	3.20	25 493	10.0	27.5
Rialto	24 659	83.2	52.8	57.6	36.8	18.6	12.0	16.8	13.4	5.4	3.69	4.01	21 893	13.9	15.7
Richmond	34 625	66.5	33.7	40.5	20.2	20.1	10.9	33.5	26.2	7.4	2.82	3.44	32 749	20.3	27.2
Riverside	82 005	70.9	39.8	50.3	27.7	14.8	9.0	29.1	21.5	7.2	3.02	3.54	75 463	12.5	20.6
Rocklin	13 258	75.5	42.6	62.3	33.8	9.4	6.3	24.5	18.7	6.3	2.74	3.15	7 063	9.1	18.1
Rohnert Park	15 503	63.2	35.1	46.7	25.2	11.9	7.3	36.8	24.0	7.7	2.65	3.20	13 409	10.8	22.0
Rosemead	13 913	83.6	43.6	58.0	33.3	17.4	7.9	16.4	12.6	5.3	3.80	4.11	13 701	15.4	14.3
Roseville	30 783	71.0	35.4	57.1	26.7	10.1	6.4	29.0	23.1	9.2	2.57	3.03	16 606	10.7	20.8
Sacramento	154 581	59.0	30.2	38.4	18.2	15.4	9.4	41.0	32.0	9.2	2.57	3.35	144 444	14.3	30.9
Salinas	38 298	78.4	49.2	57.6	36.4	14.8	9.6	21.6	17.1	6.5	3.66	4.07	33 360	14.2	19.3
San Bernardino	56 330	73.0	44.1	44.9	26.2	21.1	13.9	27.0	21.1	7.5	3.19	3.72	54 482	17.5	23.4
San Bruno	14 677	67.6	31.4	51.8	24.3	11.2	5.1	32.4	25.5	6.8	2.72	3.29	14 640	10.0	27.0
San Buenaventura (Ventura)	38 524	65.5	32.1	49.2	22.7	11.7	6.8	34.5	26.5	9.7	2.56	3.12	35 408	10.7	24.6
San Carlos	11 455	66.4	29.7	56.5	24.9	7.2	3.5	33.6	25.7	9.6	2.40	2.93	11 044	7.5	24.5
San Clemente	19 395	67.1	30.9	55.6	24.6	7.8	4.4	32.9	23.4	7.8	2.56	3.05	16 701	7.0	23.5
San Diego	450 691	60.2	30.2	44.6	21.8	11.4	6.5	39.8	28.0	7.4	2.61	3.30	406 096	11.2	26.3
San Dimas	12 163	73.9	35.5	57.7	27.0	11.6	6.1	26.1	21.0	8.7	2.78	3.23	10 948	10.1	18.3
San Francisco	329 700	44.0	16.6	31.6	12.2	8.9	3.4	56.0	38.6	9.8	2.30	3.22	305 584	9.9	39.3
San Gabriel	12 587	76.0	35.7	54.1	27.0	15.2	6.7	24.0	18.2	6.4	3.10	3.52	12 216	13.8	20.5
San Jose	276 598	73.6	38.3	56.0	29.9	11.7	6.0	26.4	18.4	4.9	3.20	3.62	250 218	11.9	18.4
San Juan Capistrano	10 930	75.0	36.9	62.7	30.9	8.5	4.0	25.0	19.7	10.3	3.06	3.45	9 015	8.8	19.1
San Leandro	30 642	64.7	28.8	47.1	20.9	12.7	6.0	35.3	28.5	11.6	2.57	3.19	29 128	10.4	30.8
San Luis Obispo	18 639	41.3	17.7	31.3	12.6	7.2	4.0	58.7	32.7	9.5	2.27	2.86	16 952	7.4	27.9
San Marcos	18 111	73.0	39.1	58.6	30.9	9.6	5.5	27.0	20.3	10.6	3.03	3.46	13 617	9.9	20.2
San Mateo	37 338	59.8	25.9	46.9	20.3	9.1	4.1	40.2	31.6	11.7	2.44	3.09	35 480	9.0	31.1
San Pablo	9 051	71.7	44.0	44.5	28.5	19.7	12.0	28.3	22.5	8.1	3.29	3.87	8 703	19.5	26.6
San Rafael	22 371	57.1	25.8	44.3	19.0	9.0	5.2	42.9	32.1	10.9	2.42	2.99	20 295	8.9	30.8
San Ramon	16 944	71.7	37.9	61.8	32.0	7.0	4.2	28.3	21.1	3.6	2.63	3.12	12 845	7.2	18.0
Santa Ana	73 002	81.9	53.2	60.6	42.1	13.5	7.6	18.1	12.7	4.6	4.55	4.72	71 611	11.8	16.6
Santa Barbara	35 605	53.2	24.3	35.7	17.5	9.5	5.1	46.8	32.9	11.4	2.47	3.17	34 348	9.5	32.4
Santa Clara	38 526	62.6	27.4	48.4	21.6	9.5	4.2	37.4	25.9	6.8	2.58	3.14	36 545	10.2	27.0
Santa Clarita	50 787	75.3	44.4	61.0	35.8	9.8	6.1	24.7	18.7	6.1	2.95	3.38	38 474	8.2	18.1
Santa Cruz	20 442	50.9	25.1	37.0	16.9	9.6	5.9	49.1	29.3	7.6	2.44	2.98	18 121	10.1	27.2
Santa Maria	22 146	75.2	42.3	56.4	31.2	13.3	8.3	24.8	20.0	9.3	3.40	3.85	19 907	12.6	19.7
Santa Monica	44 497	37.7	15.8	27.5	10.9	7.5	3.9	62.3	51.2	10.6	1.83	2.80	44 860	7.9	49.6
Santa Paula	8 136	79.1	44.1	59.1	33.2	13.4	7.6	20.9	17.2	9.4	3.49	3.86	7 664	12.0	17.9
Santa Rosa	56 036	62.7	30.9	46.9	21.6	11.0	6.6	37.3	27.8	11.9	2.57	3.14	45 708	10.6	27.5
Santee	18 470	75.9	40.9	57.7	29.9	13.0	7.9	24.1	18.2	6.9	2.81	3.19	17 770	12.1	16.3
Saratoga	10 450	82.3	38.7	75.0	35.7	4.9	2.0	17.7	14.3	7.6	2.83	3.13	10 050	5.4	13.7
Seaside	9 833	75.2	42.2	54.8	31.4	13.9	7.3	24.8	18.1	6.7	3.21	3.59	10 641	12.3	16.5
Simi Valley	36 421	79.5	42.5	63.9	33.9	10.7	5.9	20.5	14.7	4.9	3.04	3.33	31 998	9.5	12.6
South Gate	23 213	86.4	58.2	64.9	42.4	18.4	11.3	13.6	10.4	4.8	4.15	4.37	22 428	15.4	15.1
South San Francisco	19 677	74.5	35.2	55.8	27.7	13.2	5.6	25.5	19.9	9.0	3.05	3.51	18 519	12.4	20.9
Stanton	10 767	72.5	41.8	50.2	30.6	14.8	8.0	27.5	21.5	9.3	3.43	3.93	10 306	13.0	23.8
Stockton	78 556	71.5	40.8	48.1	26.2	17.3	11.2	28.5	22.9	8.6	3.04	3.59	68 794	15.5	23.4
Suisun City	7 987	80.7	47.8	62.4	36.1	13.1	8.4	19.3	14.3	3.0	3.26	3.59	6 693	11.1	11.5
Sunnyvale	52 539	62.2	27.6	50.0	22.4	8.2	3.8	37.8	27.1	6.4	2.49	3.06	48 296	9.0	28.1
Temecula	18 293	82.9	52.4	68.8	42.6	10.0	7.0	17.1	12.6	3.5	3.15	3.45	9 130	7.4	13.8
Temple City	11 338	76.4	36.5	56.8	27.9	14.3	6.7	23.6	19.7	7.9	2.90	3.33	11 055	12.3	21.9
Thousand Oaks	41 793	74.6	37.3	62.4	30.7	8.7	4.7	25.4	19.6	7.1	2.75	3.15	36 457	8.2	17.2
Torrance	54 542	66.5	31.1	52.1	24.4	10.3	5.0	33.5	27.5	9.1	2.51	3.10	52 615	9.3	25.3
Tracy	17 620	81.2	51.7	65.0	41.1	10.7	7.1	18.8	14.4	4.9	3.21	3.56	11 208	10.5	18.0
Tulare	13 543	79.4	46.3	55.9	30.9	17.1	11.5	20.6	16.7	8.0	3.22	3.57	10 859	16.6	18.5
Turlock	18 408	73.0	40.3	54.8	29.4	13.1	8.2	27.0	21.2	9.1	2.92	3.42	14 689	12.0	21.6
Tustin	23 831	67.4	36.8	50.2	27.4	12.3	7.1	32.6	24.1	5.2	2.82	3.37	18 332	11.6	23.6
Union City	18 642	84.2	45.3	66.6	37.2	12.2	6.0	15.8	11.3	3.8	3.57	3.83	15 701	12.1	12.8
Upland	24 551	72.8	36.3	53.2	24.9	14.3	8.6	27.2	21.1	7.0	2.76	3.21	23 077	11.2	20.9
Vacaville	28 105	74.6	41.4	57.0	29.7	12.4	8.4	25.4	19.2	6.4	2.83	3.24	22 627	10.4	17.3
Vallejo	39 601	71.3	36.5	49.1	24.1	16.5	9.5	28.7	22.7	8.0	2.90	3.43	37 383	13.1	21.7
Victorville	20 893	76.0	43.8	54.3	29.6	16.1	11.0	24.0	19.4	8.5	3.03	3.47	14 241	11.4	20.2
Visalia	30 883	74.2	41.1	54.9	28.3	14.1	9.6	25.8	20.7	8.4	2.91	3.37	26 111	12.3	21.2

[1]No spouse present.

Table D. Cities

City	Percent change of households, 1990–2000	Total housing units	Occupied housing units (percent)	Vacant housing units — Total	For seasonal, recreational, or occasional use	Homeowner vacancy rate (percent)	Rental vacancy rate (percent)	Occupied housing units — Total	Percent owner-occupied housing units	Percent renter-occupied housing units	Average household size of owner-occupied units	Average household size of renter-occupied units
	86	87	88	89	90	91	92	93	94	95	96	97
CALIFORNIA—Cont'd												
Pleasant Hill	5.8	14 034	98.0	2.0	0.5	0.5	1.4	13 753	63.5	36.5	2.53	2.05
Pleasanton	26.1	23 968	97.3	2.7	0.7	0.5	3.2	23 311	73.4	26.6	2.87	2.30
Pomona	3.9	39 598	95.6	4.4	0.2	2.2	3.2	37 855	57.3	42.7	3.86	3.76
Porterville	24.0	12 691	93.6	6.4	0.4	2.0	7.2	11 884	56.4	43.6	3.19	3.20
Poway	11.4	15 714	98.4	1.6	0.2	0.3	2.1	15 467	77.7	22.3	3.12	2.95
Rancho Cucamonga	21.5	42 134	97.0	3.0	0.1	1.2	4.1	40 863	70.2	29.8	3.20	2.66
Rancho Palos Verdes	2.1	15 709	97.1	2.9	0.7	0.8	3.7	15 256	81.6	18.4	2.67	2.65
Redding	23.0	33 802	95.0	5.0	0.5	1.9	4.6	32 103	56.7	43.3	2.47	2.41
Redlands	7.3	24 790	95.2	4.8	0.4	2.2	5.0	23 593	60.4	39.6	2.71	2.46
Redondo Beach	6.9	29 543	96.7	3.3	0.6	1.2	2.6	28 566	49.5	50.5	2.37	2.05
Redwood City	10.1	28 921	97.0	3.0	0.8	0.4	2.3	28 060	53.0	47.0	2.61	2.63
Rialto	12.6	26 045	94.7	5.3	0.1	2.9	5.6	24 659	68.4	31.6	3.74	3.59
Richmond	5.7	36 044	96.1	3.9	0.3	1.2	3.1	34 625	53.3	46.7	2.87	2.76
Riverside	8.7	85 974	95.4	4.6	0.3	1.9	4.8	82 005	56.6	43.4	3.18	2.81
Rocklin	87.7	14 421	91.9	8.1	0.3	1.7	17.1	13 258	72.7	27.3	2.88	2.35
Rohnert Park	15.6	15 808	98.1	1.9	0.4	0.5	2.2	15 503	58.4	41.6	2.83	2.40
Rosemead	1.5	14 345	97.0	3.0	0.2	1.0	2.2	13 913	48.8	51.2	3.67	3.92
Roseville	85.4	31 925	96.4	3.6	0.4	1.3	4.5	30 783	69.5	30.5	2.67	2.34
Sacramento	7.0	163 957	94.3	5.7	0.4	2.0	5.4	154 581	50.1	49.9	2.65	2.50
Salinas	14.8	39 659	96.6	3.4	0.2	1.0	3.8	38 298	50.1	49.9	3.65	3.67
San Bernardino	3.4	63 535	88.7	11.3	0.2	6.1	9.7	56 330	52.4	47.6	3.25	3.12
San Bruno	0.3	14 980	98.0	2.0	0.5	0.4	1.7	14 677	63.0	37.0	2.76	2.66
San Buenaventura (Ventura).	8.8	39 803	96.8	3.2	0.9	0.8	2.8	38 524	58.7	41.3	2.62	2.46
San Carlos	3.7	11 691	98.0	2.0	0.3	0.3	2.0	11 455	72.7	27.3	2.55	2.02
San Clemente	16.1	20 653	93.9	6.1	3.7	0.9	2.5	19 395	62.4	37.6	2.59	2.51
San Diego	11.0	469 689	96.0	4.0	1.1	0.8	3.2	450 691	49.5	50.5	2.71	2.52
San Dimas	11.1	12 503	97.3	2.7	0.4	1.0	2.6	12 163	73.7	26.3	2.87	2.51
San Francisco	7.9	346 527	95.1	4.9	1.1	0.8	2.5	329 700	35.0	65.0	2.73	2.06
San Gabriel	3.0	12 909	97.5	2.5	0.3	0.9	1.8	12 587	47.6	52.4	3.15	3.06
San Jose	10.5	281 841	98.1	1.9	0.3	0.4	1.8	276 598	61.8	38.2	3.22	3.16
San Juan Capistrano	21.2	11 320	96.6	3.4	0.6	1.0	6.1	10 930	78.9	21.1	2.91	3.60
San Leandro	5.2	31 334	97.8	2.2	0.3	0.6	2.2	30 642	60.6	39.4	2.70	2.36
San Luis Obispo	10.0	19 306	96.5	3.5	0.6	1.1	2.3	18 639	41.9	58.1	2.35	2.22
San Marcos	33.0	18 862	96.0	4.0	0.3	1.4	3.3	18 111	66.0	34.0	2.83	3.40
San Mateo	5.2	38 249	97.6	2.4	0.6	0.5	1.6	37 338	53.9	46.1	2.53	2.34
San Pablo	4.0	9 340	96.9	3.1	0.4	0.9	2.1	9 051	49.1	50.9	3.40	3.18
San Rafael	10.2	22 948	97.5	2.5	0.5	0.9	1.7	22 371	53.8	46.2	2.31	2.53
San Ramon	31.9	17 552	96.5	3.5	0.7	0.4	3.5	16 944	71.3	28.7	2.84	2.12
Santa Ana	1.9	74 588	97.9	2.1	0.1	0.8	1.9	73 002	49.3	50.7	4.54	4.57
Santa Barbara	3.7	37 076	96.0	4.0	1.4	0.7	2.3	35 605	42.0	58.0	2.51	2.43
Santa Clara	5.4	39 630	97.2	2.8	0.6	0.4	1.8	38 526	46.1	53.9	2.69	2.49
Santa Clarita	32.0	52 442	96.8	3.2	0.2	1.2	4.8	50 787	74.7	25.3	3.00	2.78
Santa Cruz	12.8	21 504	95.1	4.9	2.4	0.7	1.4	20 442	46.6	53.4	2.51	2.39
Santa Maria	11.2	22 847	96.9	3.1	0.2	0.9	3.1	22 146	55.9	44.1	3.18	3.68
Santa Monica	-0.8	47 863	93.0	7.0	1.6	1.4	4.3	44 497	29.8	70.2	2.24	1.66
Santa Paula	6.2	8 341	97.5	2.5	0.2	0.5	2.2	8 136	57.7	42.3	3.29	3.75
Santa Rosa	22.6	57 578	97.3	2.7	0.5	0.7	2.1	56 036	58.5	41.5	2.56	2.57
Santee	3.9	18 833	98.1	1.9	0.2	0.5	2.2	18 470	71.0	29.0	2.80	2.84
Saratoga	4.0	10 649	98.1	1.9	0.3	0.3	3.4	10 450	90.0	10.0	2.88	2.37
Seaside	-7.6	11 005	89.4	10.6	0.2	2.9	1.5	9 833	44.0	56.0	2.99	3.39
Simi Valley	13.8	37 272	97.7	2.3	0.1	0.9	3.8	36 421	77.6	22.4	3.09	2.85
South Gate	3.5	24 269	95.6	4.4	1.5	2.1	1.7	23 213	46.9	53.1	4.42	3.90
South San Francisco	6.3	20 138	97.7	2.3	0.3	0.7	1.3	19 677	62.5	37.5	3.02	3.11
Stanton	4.5	11 011	97.8	2.2	0.2	0.9	2.0	10 767	48.9	51.1	3.18	3.66
Stockton	14.2	82 042	95.8	4.2	0.2	1.4	4.3	78 556	51.6	48.4	2.99	3.08
Suisun City	19.3	8 146	98.0	2.0	0.1	0.8	3.1	7 987	73.6	26.4	3.34	3.03
Sunnyvale	8.8	53 753	97.7	2.3	0.6	0.5	1.3	52 539	47.6	52.4	2.60	2.39
Temecula	100.4	19 099	95.8	4.2	0.4	1.4	7.2	18 293	73.4	26.6	3.27	2.84
Temple City	2.6	11 674	97.1	2.9	0.4	0.9	1.9	11 338	63.1	36.9	2.96	2.79
Thousand Oaks	14.6	42 958	97.3	2.7	0.5	0.9	2.9	41 793	75.3	24.7	2.80	2.61
Torrance	3.7	55 967	97.5	2.5	0.3	1.0	2.4	54 542	56.0	44.0	2.68	2.29
Tracy	57.2	18 087	97.4	2.6	0.2	1.1	2.8	17 620	72.2	27.8	3.28	3.02
Tulare	24.7	14 253	95.0	5.0	0.3	1.3	5.4	13 543	60.5	39.5	3.16	3.30
Turlock	25.3	19 095	96.4	3.6	0.3	1.7	2.8	18 408	55.8	44.2	2.98	2.85
Tustin	30.0	25 501	93.5	6.5	0.4	0.9	2.5	23 831	49.6	50.4	2.70	2.93
Union City	18.7	18 877	98.8	1.2	0.1	0.5	1.3	18 642	71.3	28.7	3.59	3.52
Upland	6.4	25 467	96.4	3.6	0.2	1.6	3.9	24 551	58.9	41.1	2.83	2.66
Vacaville	24.2	28 696	97.9	2.1	0.2	0.7	2.8	28 105	66.7	33.3	2.90	2.68
Vallejo	5.9	41 219	96.1	3.9	0.3	1.2	4.5	39 601	63.2	36.8	2.99	2.76
Victorville	46.7	22 498	92.9	7.1	0.5	2.8	7.9	20 893	65.1	34.9	3.05	3.00
Visalia	18.3	32 654	94.6	5.4	0.3	2.2	6.4	30 883	62.7	37.3	2.88	2.97

Table D. Cities

STATE Place code	City	Land area, 2000[1] (sq km)	Total persons	Rank	Per square kilometer	Land area, 1990[1] (sq km)	Total persons	Rank	Per square kilometer	White	Black or African American	American Indian or Alaska Native	Asian	Native Hawaiian and other Pacific Islander	Some other race
		1	2	3	4	5	6	7	8	9	10	11	12	13	14
	CALIFORNIA—Cont'd														
06 82996	Vista	48.4	89 857	285	1 856.5	46.5	71 861	325	1 545.4	64.3	4.2	1.0	3.7	0.7	21.3
06 83332	Walnut	23.3	30 004	1 221	1 287.7	23.0	29 105	1 089	1 265.4	28.4	4.2	0.2	55.8	0.1	7.7
06 83346	Walnut Creek	51.6	64 296	453	1 246.0	50.0	60 569	416	1 211.4	83.9	1.1	0.3	9.4	0.1	2.0
06 83668	Watsonville	16.4	44 265	777	2 699.1	15.3	31 099	1 005	2 032.6	43.0	0.8	1.7	3.3	0.1	45.9
06 84200	West Covina	41.7	105 080	228	2 519.9	42.0	96 226	215	2 291.1	43.9	6.4	0.8	22.7	0.2	21.2
06 84410	West Hollywood	4.9	35 716	998	7 289.0	4.9	36 118	831	7 371.0	86.4	3.1	0.4	3.8	0.1	2.9
06 84550	Westminster	26.2	88 207	294	3 366.7	26.0	78 293	289	3 011.3	45.8	1.0	0.6	38.1	0.5	10.2
06 84816	West Sacramento	54.2	31 615	1 157	583.3	54.3	28 898	1 094	532.2	65.0	2.6	1.8	7.2	0.6	16.0
06 85292	Whittier	37.9	83 680	320	2 207.9	32.5	77 671	292	2 389.9	63.2	1.2	1.3	3.3	0.2	25.8
06 86328	Woodland	26.7	49 151	688	1 840.9	23.8	40 230	731	1 690.3	66.8	1.3	1.5	3.8	0.3	21.5
06 86832	Yorba Linda	50.2	58 918	518	1 173.7	45.3	52 422	513	1 157.2	81.5	1.2	0.4	11.1	0.1	2.7
06 86972	Yuba City	24.3	36 758	956	1 512.7	17.9	27 385	1 163	1 529.9	67.0	2.8	1.7	8.9	0.3	14.4
06 87042	Yucaipa	71.9	41 207	837	573.1	68.7	32 819	945	477.7	85.2	0.9	1.1	1.2	0.1	8.0
08 00000	**COLORADO**	268 627.2	4 301 261	X	16.0	268 659.5	3 294 473	X	12.3	82.8	3.8	1.0	2.2	0.1	7.2
08 03455	Arvada	84.6	102 153	239	1 207.5	57.3	89 261	237	1 557.8	91.0	0.7	0.7	2.2	0.1	3.1
08 04000	Aurora	369.1	276 393	63	748.8	343.2	222 103	72	647.2	68.9	13.4	0.8	4.4	0.2	8.1
08 07850	Boulder	63.1	94 673	264	1 500.4	58.4	85 127	260	1 457.7	88.3	1.2	0.5	4.0	0.1	3.5
08 09280	Broomfield	70.2	38 272	921	545.2	57.8	24 638	1 312	426.3	88.6	0.9	0.6	4.1	0.0	3.2
08 16000	Colorado Springs	481.1	360 890	50	750.1	474.5	280 430	54	591.0	80.7	6.6	0.9	2.8	0.2	5.0
08 20000	Denver	397.2	554 636	26	1 396.4	397.0	467 610	28	1 177.9	65.3	11.1	1.3	2.8	0.1	15.6
08 24785	Englewood	17.0	31 727	1 146	1 866.3	16.9	29 396	1 075	1 739.4	87.8	1.5	1.3	1.9	0.1	5.0
08 27425	Fort Collins	120.5	118 652	192	984.7	106.7	87 491	245	820.0	89.6	1.0	0.6	2.5	0.1	3.6
08 31660	Grand Junction	79.8	41 986	820	526.1	38.5	32 893	941	854.4	91.8	0.6	0.9	0.8	0.1	3.8
08 32155	Greeley	77.5	76 930	364	992.6	73.6	60 454	418	821.4	80.4	0.9	0.8	1.2	0.1	13.8
08 43000	Lakewood	107.7	144 126	150	1 338.2	105.7	126 475	146	1 196.5	87.2	1.5	1.1	2.7	0.1	4.9
08 45255	Littleton	35.0	40 340	862	1 152.6	31.9	33 711	905	1 056.8	91.8	1.2	0.7	1.7	0.1	2.7
08 45970	Longmont	56.4	71 093	400	1 260.5	34.0	51 976	523	1 528.7	84.8	0.5	1.0	1.8	0.1	9.7
08 46465	Loveland	63.6	50 608	659	795.7	55.4	37 357	808	674.3	92.9	0.4	0.7	0.8	0.0	3.2
08 54330	Northglenn	19.2	31 575	1 159	1 644.5	18.1	27 195	1 174	1 502.5	83.0	1.5	1.1	3.1	0.1	8.1
08 62000	Pueblo	116.7	102 121	240	875.1	93.0	98 640	209	1 060.6	76.2	2.4	1.7	0.7	0.1	15.2
08 77290	Thornton	69.6	82 384	326	1 183.7	53.5	55 031	471	1 028.6	82.7	1.5	1.1	2.5	0.1	9.0
08 83835	Westminster	81.6	100 940	243	1 237.0	69.4	74 619	310	1 075.2	84.2	1.2	0.7	5.5	0.1	5.5
08 84440	Wheat Ridge	23.5	32 913	1 099	1 400.6	23.0	29 419	1 073	1 279.1	89.2	0.8	0.9	1.4	0.1	5.0
09 00000	**CONNECTICUT**	12 548.0	3 405 565	X	271.4	12 549.6	3 287 116	X	261.9	81.6	9.1	0.3	2.4	0.0	4.3
09 08000	Bridgeport	41.4	139 529	158	3 370.3	41.5	141 686	126	3 414.1	45.0	30.8	0.5	3.3	0.1	14.8
09 08420	Bristol	68.7	60 062	499	874.3	68.7	60 640	415	882.7	91.6	2.7	0.2	1.5	0.0	2.4
09 18430	Danbury	109.1	74 848	377	686.0	109.1	65 585	375	601.1	76.0	6.8	0.3	5.5	0.0	7.6
09 37000	Hartford	44.8	121 578	186	2 713.8	44.8	139 739	130	3 119.2	27.7	38.1	0.5	1.6	0.1	26.5
09 46450	Meriden	61.5	58 244	527	947.1	61.5	59 479	428	967.1	80.2	6.4	0.4	1.4	0.0	8.6
09 47290	Middletown	105.9	43 167	796	407.6	105.9	42 762	674	403.8	80.0	12.3	0.2	2.7	0.0	2.0
09 47500	Milford	58.4	52 305	638	895.6	58.0	48 139	587	830.0	93.6	1.9	0.1	2.3	0.0	0.9
09 49880	Naugatuck Borough	42.4	30 989	1 178	730.9	42.5	30 625	1 031	720.6	91.8	2.8	0.3	1.7	0.0	1.6
09 50370	New Britain	34.5	71 538	396	2 073.6	34.5	75 491	304	2 188.1	69.4	10.9	0.4	2.4	0.1	13.1
09 52000	New Haven	48.8	123 626	182	2 533.3	48.8	130 474	140	2 673.6	43.5	37.4	0.4	3.9	0.1	10.9
09 52280	New London	14.3	25 671	1 468	1 795.2	14.3	28 540	1 115	1 995.8	63.5	18.6	0.9	2.1	0.1	9.1
09 55990	Norwalk	59.1	82 951	324	1 403.6	59.1	78 331	288	1 325.4	73.9	15.3	0.2	3.3	0.0	4.3
09 56200	Norwich	73.4	36 117	981	492.1	73.4	37 391	807	509.4	83.1	6.8	1.2	2.1	0.0	2.8
09 68100	Shelton	79.2	38 101	926	481.1	79.2	35 418	847	447.2	94.4	1.1	0.1	2.1	0.0	0.9
09 73000	Stamford	97.8	117 083	195	1 197.2	97.7	108 056	182	1 106.0	69.8	15.4	0.2	5.0	0.0	6.5
09 76500	Torrington	103.1	35 202	1 017	341.4	103.1	33 687	907	326.7	93.0	2.2	0.2	1.8	0.0	1.3
09 80000	Waterbury	74.0	107 271	221	1 449.6	74.0	108 961	177	1 472.4	67.1	16.3	0.4	1.5	0.1	10.9
09 82800	West Haven	28.1	52 360	636	1 863.3	28.1	54 021	489	1 922.5	74.1	16.3	0.2	2.9	0.1	3.6
10 00000	**DELAWARE**	5 059.7	783 600	X	154.9	5 062.5	666 168	X	131.6	74.6	19.2	0.3	2.1	0.0	2.0
10 21200	Dover	58.0	32 135	1 130	554.1	55.2	27 630	1 150	500.5	54.9	37.2	0.5	3.2	0.0	1.6
10 50670	Newark	23.1	28 547	1 299	1 235.8	22.3	26 463	1 217	1 186.7	87.3	6.0	0.2	4.1	0.0	0.9
10 77580	Wilmington	28.1	72 664	388	2 585.9	27.9	71 529	327	2 563.8	35.5	56.4	0.3	0.7	0.0	5.2
11 00000	**DISTRICT OF COLUMBIA**	159.0	572 059	X	3 597.9	159.1	606 900	X	3 814.6	30.8	60.0	0.3	2.7	0.1	3.8
11 50000	Washington	159.0	572 059	22	3 597.9	159.1	606 900	19	3 814.6	30.8	60.0	0.3	2.7	0.1	3.8
12 00000	**FLORIDA**	139 669.8	15 982 378	X	114.4	139 852.4	12 938 071	X	92.5	78.0	14.6	0.3	1.7	0.1	3.0
12 00950	Altamonte Springs	23.0	41 200	838	1 791.3	22.1	35 167	857	1 591.3	79.2	9.7	0.3	2.9	0.0	4.8
12 01700	Apopka	62.3	26 642	1 399	427.6	23.6	13 611	2 385	576.7	73.8	15.6	0.4	1.9	0.1	5.4
12 07300	Boca Raton	70.4	74 764	378	1 062.0	70.4	61 486	409	873.4	90.8	3.8	0.2	2.0	0.0	1.4
12 07875	Boynton Beach	41.1	60 389	494	1 469.3	39.2	46 284	616	1 180.7	70.4	22.9	0.2	1.5	0.0	2.4
12 07950	Bradenton	31.4	49 504	677	1 576.6	29.7	43 769	655	1 473.7	78.1	15.1	0.3	0.8	0.0	3.9

[1] Dry land or land partially or temporarily covered by water.

Table D. Cities

City	Population and population characteristics, 2000 (cont'd)								Population and population characteristics, 1990				
	Race (percent) (cont'd)								Race (percent)				
	Race alone or in combination												
	Two or more races	White	Black	American Indian or Alaska Native	Asian	Native Hawaiian and other Pacific Islander	Some other race	Hispanic¹	White	Black or African American	American Indian or Alaska Native	Asian and Pacific Islander	Hispanic¹
	15	16	17	18	19	20	21	22	23	24	25	26	27
CALIFORNIA—Cont'd													
Vista	4.8	68.3	5.1	1.9	5.0	1.1	23.8	38.9	80.7	4.5	0.8	4.0	24.8
Walnut	3.7	30.8	4.6	0.6	57.7	0.5	9.7	19.3	48.0	6.6	0.4	37.5	23.5
Walnut Creek	3.2	86.8	1.5	0.9	10.7	0.3	3.2	6.0	90.6	1.0	0.3	6.7	4.7
Watsonville	5.2	47.3	1.1	2.6	4.3	0.3	49.9	75.1	55.1	0.7	1.0	5.6	60.9
West Covina	4.9	47.5	7.1	1.4	24.3	0.5	24.4	45.7	59.8	8.5	0.5	17.2	34.6
West Hollywood	3.4	89.4	3.7	0.9	4.7	0.3	4.6	8.8	90.2	3.4	0.4	3.1	8.7
Westminster	3.8	49.0	1.4	1.4	39.5	0.7	12.1	21.7	69.6	1.1	0.6	22.5	19.1
West Sacramento	6.9	70.2	3.3	3.3	9.6	1.3	19.7	30.0	71.3	2.4	2.0	9.1	24.4
Whittier	5.0	67.6	1.6	2.1	4.2	0.4	29.5	55.9	73.4	1.3	0.6	3.3	39.0
Woodland	4.9	71.0	1.7	2.6	5.0	0.5	24.4	38.8	77.5	1.3	1.3	3.1	26.2
Yorba Linda	3.1	84.2	1.5	1.0	12.5	0.3	3.9	10.3	85.7	1.1	0.4	10.1	9.4
Yuba City	4.9	70.7	3.4	3.2	10.6	0.6	16.6	24.6	76.1	2.6	1.7	7.7	17.9
Yucaipa	3.5	88.3	1.2	2.2	1.8	0.3	9.8	18.3	92.6	0.5	0.9	1.0	11.0
COLORADO	2.8	85.2	4.4	1.9	2.8	0.2	8.5	17.1	88.2	4.0	0.8	1.8	12.9
Arvada	2.3	93.1	1.0	1.4	2.8	0.2	4.1	9.8	94.3	0.6	0.5	2.0	7.4
Aurora	4.2	72.3	15.0	1.8	5.3	0.4	9.9	19.8	82.4	11.4	0.6	3.8	6.6
Boulder	2.4	90.5	1.6	1.0	4.9	0.2	4.4	8.2	92.5	1.3	0.5	3.9	4.8
Broomfield	2.5	90.8	1.2	1.3	4.9	0.2	4.2	9.1	94.3	0.7	0.6	2.1	5.6
Colorado Springs	3.9	83.9	7.8	1.9	3.9	0.4	6.3	12.0	85.9	7.0	0.8	2.4	9.1
Denver	3.7	68.3	12.1	2.2	3.4	0.2	17.7	31.7	72.1	12.8	1.2	2.4	23.0
Englewood	2.5	90.0	1.9	2.3	2.3	0.2	6.0	13.0	93.8	1.2	0.9	1.5	8.0
Fort Collins	2.5	92.0	1.4	1.3	3.2	0.3	4.6	8.8	93.3	1.0	0.5	2.4	7.1
Grand Junction	2.0	93.6	0.9	1.8	1.1	0.2	4.6	10.9	91.8	0.8	0.8	1.0	11.1
Greeley	2.8	82.9	1.2	1.5	1.7	0.3	15.4	29.5	89.1	0.7	0.6	1.0	20.4
Lakewood	2.6	89.5	1.9	2.0	3.3	0.2	5.9	14.5	93.2	1.0	0.7	1.9	9.1
Littleton	2.0	93.6	1.5	1.4	2.1	0.2	3.3	8.4	96.1	0.9	0.6	1.4	5.2
Longmont	2.2	86.7	0.8	1.6	2.2	0.1	10.9	19.1	92.7	0.4	0.7	1.2	11.1
Loveland	2.0	94.7	0.6	1.4	1.2	0.1	4.1	8.6	94.9	0.3	0.5	0.7	6.8
Northglenn	2.9	85.7	2.0	2.0	3.7	0.3	9.6	20.3	90.7	1.6	0.8	2.0	14.6
Pueblo	3.7	79.4	2.9	2.7	1.0	0.2	17.6	44.1	83.0	2.2	0.8	0.6	39.5
Thornton	3.1	85.5	1.9	2.0	3.1	0.3	10.5	21.3	89.7	1.3	0.9	1.7	16.9
Westminster	2.8	86.6	1.6	1.5	6.3	0.2	6.7	15.2	90.6	1.0	0.6	3.7	11.5
Wheat Ridge	2.5	91.5	1.2	1.9	1.8	0.2	6.1	13.5	94.7	0.6	0.6	1.5	7.3
CONNECTICUT	2.2	83.3	10.0	0.7	2.8	0.1	5.5	9.4	87.0	8.3	0.2	1.5	6.5
Bridgeport	5.6	48.5	33.2	1.0	3.8	0.3	19.0	31.9	58.5	26.6	0.3	2.3	26.5
Bristol	1.6	93.0	3.4	0.7	1.7	0.1	2.8	5.3	96.0	2.1	0.2	0.8	2.7
Danbury	4.0	79.2	7.6	0.7	6.1	0.1	10.3	15.8	86.8	6.6	0.2	3.9	7.7
Hartford	5.4	30.8	40.6	1.2	2.2	0.4	30.6	40.5	40.0	38.9	0.3	1.4	31.6
Meriden	2.9	82.7	7.7	0.8	1.6	0.1	10.2	21.1	89.7	4.3	0.2	0.7	13.7
Middletown	2.8	82.2	13.7	0.8	3.2	0.1	3.0	5.3	85.4	11.1	0.2	1.9	3.3
Milford	1.1	94.6	2.2	0.4	2.6	0.1	1.3	3.3	97.1	1.4	0.1	0.7	2.0
Naugatuck Borough	1.8	93.4	3.5	0.7	1.9	0.0	2.4	4.5	96.2	1.9	0.2	0.9	3.1
New Britain	3.8	72.5	12.3	0.8	2.6	0.1	15.7	26.8	81.6	7.6	0.2	1.8	16.3
New Haven	3.9	45.9	39.3	1.2	4.4	0.3	13.0	21.4	53.9	36.1	0.3	2.4	13.2
New London	5.7	67.6	21.8	2.3	2.9	0.3	11.5	19.7	73.0	16.8	0.7	2.2	12.1
Norwalk	2.9	76.1	16.3	0.6	3.7	0.1	6.3	15.6	79.3	15.5	0.1	1.6	9.4
Norwich	3.9	85.8	9.0	2.4	2.6	0.1	4.3	6.1	91.3	5.3	0.6	1.1	3.1
Shelton	1.3	95.6	1.3	0.5	2.2	0.0	1.7	3.5	97.1	1.0	0.2	1.3	2.5
Stamford	3.1	71.9	16.5	0.5	5.5	0.1	8.7	16.8	76.3	17.8	0.1	2.6	9.8
Torrington	1.5	94.3	2.7	0.6	2.1	0.1	1.8	3.3	96.7	1.7	0.2	1.2	1.1
Waterbury	3.7	69.7	18.0	1.0	1.9	0.2	13.2	21.8	79.6	13.0	0.3	0.7	13.4
West Haven	2.8	76.2	17.4	0.7	3.3	0.1	5.2	9.1	84.1	12.4	0.2	2.0	3.6
DELAWARE	1.7	75.9	20.1	0.8	2.4	0.1	2.6	4.8	80.3	16.9	0.3	1.4	2.4
Dover	2.6	56.7	38.8	1.2	3.8	0.2	2.4	4.1	65.5	30.9	0.5	2.0	2.8
Newark	1.6	88.7	6.5	0.5	4.7	0.1	1.3	2.5	90.4	5.7	0.1	3.5	1.5
Wilmington	2.0	36.6	57.8	0.8	0.8	0.1	6.0	9.8	42.1	52.4	0.2	0.4	7.1
DISTRICT OF COLUMBIA	2.4	32.2	61.3	0.8	3.1	0.1	5.0	7.9	29.6	65.8	0.2	1.8	5.4
Washington	2.4	32.2	61.3	0.8	3.1	0.1	5.0	7.9	29.6	65.8	0.2	1.8	5.4
FLORIDA	2.4	79.7	15.5	0.7	2.1	0.2	4.4	16.8	83.1	13.6	0.3	1.2	12.2
Altamonte Springs	2.9	81.6	10.7	0.8	3.6	0.2	6.3	15.9	89.9	5.9	0.3	1.8	8.5
Apopka	2.8	76.0	16.5	0.7	2.3	0.1	7.2	18.1	81.4	14.0	0.3	1.3	8.4
Boca Raton	1.9	92.1	4.3	0.4	2.5	0.1	2.6	8.5	94.4	2.9	0.1	1.9	5.6
Boynton Beach	2.6	71.4	24.6	0.4	1.9	0.2	4.2	9.2	77.7	20.1	0.1	0.6	6.8
Bradenton	1.7	79.4	15.8	0.6	1.0	0.1	4.8	11.3	82.9	14.4	0.2	0.6	5.4

¹Hispanic persons may be of any race.

Table D. Cities

City	Population and population characteristics, 2000										
	Age (percent)										
	Under 5 years	5 to 17 years	18 to 24 years	25 to 34 years	35 to 44 years	45 to 54 years	55 to 64 years	65 to 74 years	75 years and over	Median age (years)	Percent Female
	28	29	30	31	32	33	34	35	36	37	38
CALIFORNIA—Cont'd											
Vista	8.6	21.1	11.4	16.5	16.2	10.7	5.5	4.8	5.2	30.3	50.0
Walnut	4.9	22.9	9.8	9.8	17.4	19.5	8.9	4.3	2.6	37.2	50.8
Walnut Creek	4.4	13.2	5.2	12.2	14.8	14.5	10.3	9.8	15.5	45.1	53.8
Watsonville	9.3	24.7	11.8	16.4	14.1	9.7	5.4	4.2	4.4	27.4	49.8
West Covina	7.6	20.9	10.0	14.9	15.6	12.7	7.9	5.8	4.5	32.7	51.4
West Hollywood	1.6	4.0	6.3	26.4	22.2	13.8	8.5	8.0	9.0	39.4	44.8
Westminster	7.3	18.7	8.8	16.8	15.8	12.4	9.2	6.6	4.5	34.1	50.0
West Sacramento	7.7	22.1	9.1	12.5	15.2	12.2	8.5	7.0	5.6	34.0	50.6
Whittier	7.8	20.5	10.0	15.1	15.5	11.7	6.9	5.8	6.7	32.8	51.4
Woodland	8.1	21.7	9.6	14.6	15.7	12.7	7.2	4.9	5.6	32.4	51.0
Yorba Linda	6.0	23.3	7.3	9.6	18.9	18.1	9.2	4.5	3.2	37.4	50.9
Yuba City	8.1	20.9	10.7	14.9	14.5	11.4	7.3	6.0	6.2	31.8	51.1
Yucaipa	6.5	22.0	7.6	11.0	16.2	13.0	8.2	7.0	8.4	36.8	51.7
COLORADO	6.9	18.7	10.0	15.4	17.1	14.3	7.9	5.3	4.4	34.3	49.6
Arvada	6.4	19.8	7.8	12.4	18.0	15.5	9.4	6.2	4.5	37.2	51.0
Aurora	8.1	19.5	10.1	17.7	17.0	13.3	6.9	4.1	3.3	31.7	50.5
Boulder	4.1	10.7	25.9	19.5	13.6	12.4	6.0	3.7	4.1	29.0	48.4
Broomfield	7.8	21.5	7.7	16.2	20.1	13.9	6.2	4.1	2.5	33.2	49.8
Colorado Springs	7.5	19.0	10.3	15.4	17.4	13.5	7.4	5.1	4.5	33.6	50.5
Denver	6.8	15.1	10.7	20.5	15.6	12.8	7.2	5.5	5.7	33.1	49.5
Englewood	5.8	14.5	9.6	18.2	17.7	12.9	7.1	5.6	8.6	36.2	50.5
Fort Collins	5.9	15.6	22.1	16.9	14.6	11.7	5.4	3.8	4.0	28.2	49.8
Grand Junction	5.6	15.6	11.9	11.9	14.4	13.9	8.8	8.3	9.6	38.8	51.3
Greeley	7.5	18.2	19.0	14.3	13.0	11.4	6.5	4.9	5.2	28.5	51.0
Lakewood	6.1	16.2	9.6	15.7	16.8	14.2	9.4	6.5	5.6	36.5	50.6
Littleton	5.7	17.6	8.2	13.0	17.1	15.1	9.1	7.2	7.0	38.6	51.4
Longmont	7.8	20.1	8.5	15.1	18.0	13.8	7.4	4.6	4.6	34.0	50.5
Loveland	7.0	19.9	7.8	13.6	17.0	14.0	8.1	6.3	6.2	36.0	51.0
Northglenn	7.3	19.4	9.9	16.1	16.8	11.4	8.8	6.7	3.5	33.2	50.0
Pueblo	6.7	18.4	10.3	12.5	14.1	13.0	8.4	8.2	8.4	36.5	51.6
Thornton	8.8	21.2	9.6	18.0	18.0	13.0	5.8	3.2	2.4	30.8	50.3
Westminster	7.3	19.6	9.6	17.6	18.4	14.3	6.8	3.8	2.7	32.6	50.0
Wheat Ridge	6.1	15.1	7.6	13.3	16.0	14.0	9.0	7.8	11.2	40.0	52.7
CONNECTICUT	6.6	18.2	8.0	13.3	17.1	14.1	9.1	6.8	7.0	37.4	51.6
Bridgeport	8.2	20.3	11.2	15.9	14.7	11.1	7.3	5.5	5.9	31.4	52.3
Bristol	6.3	16.9	7.2	15.1	17.4	13.5	8.8	7.3	7.6	37.6	51.6
Danbury	6.5	15.1	10.2	17.8	17.6	13.4	8.3	5.6	5.4	35.2	51.0
Hartford	8.3	21.8	12.6	15.5	14.3	11.0	7.1	4.9	4.6	29.7	52.2
Meriden	7.1	18.6	8.1	14.1	16.1	13.5	8.3	6.6	7.5	36.2	51.6
Middletown	6.5	15.2	8.3	17.6	17.5	13.0	8.5	6.2	7.2	36.3	51.7
Milford	6.0	16.3	5.9	14.0	17.7	15.2	10.0	7.4	7.5	39.4	51.6
Naugatuck Borough	6.9	19.9	7.3	14.9	18.2	13.1	7.9	5.4	6.3	35.5	51.4
New Britain	6.6	17.5	12.5	14.9	14.0	11.5	7.1	6.9	8.8	33.9	52.1
New Haven	7.1	18.4	16.4	17.8	13.4	10.2	6.6	4.8	5.4	29.3	52.1
New London	6.7	16.2	17.6	15.0	14.6	11.2	6.7	5.6	6.5	31.2	51.1
Norwalk	6.9	15.2	7.0	17.7	17.9	13.3	9.3	6.9	5.9	36.6	51.2
Norwich	6.4	17.7	8.9	14.0	16.2	13.4	8.1	7.3	8.1	36.9	52.5
Shelton	6.2	17.4	5.8	12.2	17.8	15.2	10.5	7.3	7.5	39.8	51.6
Stamford	6.9	15.2	7.4	17.8	17.3	12.9	8.7	7.1	6.8	36.4	51.6
Torrington	6.0	17.1	6.4	13.4	17.6	13.5	8.6	7.5	10.1	39.1	51.6
Waterbury	7.6	18.9	8.9	14.8	15.1	11.7	8.0	6.7	8.2	34.9	52.7
West Haven	6.2	16.9	9.7	14.9	16.3	13.4	8.4	6.9	7.3	36.4	52.3
DELAWARE	6.6	18.3	9.6	13.9	16.3	13.3	9.1	7.2	5.8	36.0	51.4
Dover	6.7	16.9	15.7	13.7	14.2	11.5	8.0	6.7	6.7	32.9	52.9
Newark	3.0	9.5	43.6	11.2	8.7	9.0	5.9	4.6	4.5	22.6	54.0
Wilmington	6.8	19.0	9.8	16.4	15.6	12.2	7.6	6.1	6.5	33.7	52.3
DISTRICT OF COLUMBIA	5.7	14.4	12.7	17.8	15.3	13.2	8.7	6.3	5.9	34.6	52.9
Washington	5.7	14.4	12.7	17.8	15.3	13.2	8.7	6.3	5.9	34.6	52.9
FLORIDA	5.9	16.9	8.3	13.0	15.5	12.9	9.8	9.1	8.5	38.7	51.2
Altamonte Springs	5.9	14.5	10.8	20.8	16.3	12.8	8.2	5.3	5.4	33.8	51.9
Apopka	8.5	19.7	8.6	16.2	17.4	11.9	7.6	5.7	4.4	33.3	51.6
Boca Raton	4.7	14.2	8.1	10.6	15.8	15.2	11.5	9.8	10.0	42.9	51.3
Boynton Beach	5.7	14.1	6.4	13.3	14.8	11.0	8.7	11.0	14.8	41.8	53.2
Bradenton	6.1	15.4	7.7	12.2	13.1	11.5	8.4	10.4	15.0	41.5	52.6

Table D. Cities

City	Population and population characteristics, 1990										Population—change, 1980–2000				
	Age (percent)										Total persons			Percent change	
	Under 5 years	5 to 17 years	18 to 24 years	25 to 34 years	35 to 44 years	45 to 54 years	55 to 64 years	65 to 74 years	75 years and over	Percent Female	2000	1990	1980	1990–2000	1980–1990
	39	40	41	42	43	44	45	46	47	48	49	50	51	52	53
CALIFORNIA—Cont'd															
Vista	9.6	17.4	12.5	21.2	13.5	7.2	6.2	6.8	5.5	50.1	89 857	71 861	35 834	25.0	100.5
Walnut	8.7	24.0	9.4	14.8	22.6	11.5	5.3	2.5	1.3	50.4	30 004	29 105	12 478	3.1	133.3
Walnut Creek	4.5	12.1	7.0	15.4	16.2	12.0	10.1	10.9	11.8	53.7	64 296	60 569	53 643	6.2	12.9
Watsonville	10.2	20.6	11.2	18.5	12.6	7.5	6.8	6.6	6.0	50.8	44 265	31 099	23 543	42.3	32.1
West Covina	7.8	19.7	11.3	18.4	15.8	10.3	8.1	5.9	2.7	50.9	105 080	96 226	80 291	9.2	19.8
West Hollywood	2.5	4.5	6.6	29.2	20.5	9.5	8.8	8.7	9.8	46.8	35 716	36 118	35 703	-1.1	1.2
Westminster	7.4	17.8	12.0	20.0	13.7	11.1	8.9	5.7	3.4	49.3	88 207	78 293	71 133	12.7	10.1
West Sacramento	8.2	19.6	8.5	17.2	13.8	10.0	9.8	8.1	4.8	49.8	31 615	28 898	10 875	9.4	165.7
Whittier	8.4	17.5	10.4	18.9	14.5	8.3	8.0	8.2	5.7	51.1	83 680	77 671	69 717	7.7	11.4
Woodland	8.5	20.5	9.4	18.2	16.2	8.6	7.2	6.1	5.2	51.1	49 151	40 230	30 235	22.2	33.1
Yorba Linda	8.4	21.5	8.5	16.3	20.7	13.1	6.6	3.5	1.5	50.3	58 918	52 422	28 254	12.4	85.5
Yuba City	10.1	18.4	12.2	18.2	13.8	8.8	6.8	6.4	5.3	52.0	36 758	27 385	18 731	34.2	46.2
Yucaipa	6.8	17.8	6.3	14.1	13.5	9.2	8.3	10.8	13.1	53.0	41 207	32 819	23 345	25.6	40.6
COLORADO	7.7	18.5	10.2	18.6	17.2	10.2	7.6	5.9	4.1	50.5	4 301 261	3 294 473	2 889 735	30.6	14.0
Arvada	7.4	20.0	8.6	17.2	18.4	12.3	8.4	4.9	2.7	51.0	102 153	89 261	84 619	14.4	5.5
Aurora	8.6	18.8	9.5	22.0	18.5	9.8	6.1	4.3	2.3	51.4	276 393	222 103	158 588	24.4	40.1
Boulder	4.7	10.3	26.3	20.7	17.1	8.0	5.2	4.0	3.8	49.5	94 673	85 127	76 685	11.2	11.0
Broomfield	8.6	22.2	8.4	19.9	19.2	9.7	6.4	3.8	1.8	49.4	38 272	24 638	20 722	55.3	18.9
Colorado Springs	8.5	18.3	10.9	20.2	16.4	9.6	7.0	5.6	3.6	51.1	360 890	280 430	215 150	28.7	30.3
Denver	7.3	14.6	9.5	20.9	16.7	9.3	8.1	7.6	6.1	51.3	554 636	467 610	492 365	18.6	-5.0
Englewood	6.8	14.7	8.9	22.6	15.0	8.3	7.8	8.9	6.9	51.9	31 727	29 396	30 021	7.9	-2.1
Fort Collins	6.9	15.5	21.9	19.8	16.0	7.3	4.9	4.3	3.6	50.4	118 652	87 491	65 092	35.6	34.4
Grand Junction	6.5	15.7	11.3	15.3	13.1	9.4	9.5	10.2	9.1	52.7	41 986	32 893	28 144	27.6	16.9
Greeley	7.5	17.1	18.5	16.5	14.2	8.4	6.6	5.8	5.2	51.5	76 930	60 454	53 006	27.3	14.1
Lakewood	6.9	15.3	9.9	19.3	16.3	12.5	9.1	6.5	4.2	51.5	144 126	126 475	112 860	14.0	12.1
Littleton	7.4	16.7	9.1	17.4	16.2	11.7	9.5	7.4	4.5	51.8	40 340	33 711	28 655	19.7	17.6
Longmont	8.7	19.5	8.9	19.1	16.8	11.0	6.5	5.2	4.5	51.1	71 093	51 976	42 942	36.8	21.0
Loveland	8.0	20.5	7.7	17.1	16.6	10.0	7.1	6.9	6.0	51.7	50 608	37 357	30 244	35.5	23.5
Northglenn	7.4	18.9	10.6	17.7	15.6	12.6	10.0	4.9	2.4	50.4	31 575	27 195	29 847	16.1	-8.9
Pueblo	7.1	19.1	9.3	15.4	14.2	9.2	9.9	9.0	6.9	52.0	102 121	98 640	101 686	3.5	-3.0
Thornton	10.0	22.5	9.5	21.4	18.1	8.4	4.9	3.0	2.1	50.9	82 384	55 031	40 343	49.7	36.4
Westminster	8.9	20.5	9.5	22.5	19.5	8.9	5.4	3.1	1.7	50.8	100 940	74 619	50 176	35.3	48.7
Wheat Ridge	6.6	13.7	7.9	18.0	14.7	10.1	9.6	10.3	9.1	53.1	32 913	29 419	30 280	11.9	-2.8
CONNECTICUT	6.9	15.9	10.5	17.8	15.5	10.8	9.0	7.8	5.8	51.5	3 405 565	3 287 116	3 107 564	3.6	5.8
Bridgeport	8.1	18.0	11.1	19.7	13.1	8.9	7.5	7.6	6.0	52.5	139 529	141 686	142 546	-1.5	-0.6
Bristol	7.0	15.0	10.4	20.3	14.5	10.1	9.0	8.0	5.5	51.6	60 062	60 640	57 370	-1.0	5.7
Danbury	7.2	14.4	11.6	20.9	14.8	11.2	8.1	6.3	5.4	50.8	74 848	65 585	60 470	14.1	8.5
Hartford	8.3	18.9	15.2	20.3	12.9	8.2	6.5	5.4	4.4	52.3	121 578	139 739	136 392	-13.0	2.5
Meriden	7.8	16.4	9.2	19.3	15.1	9.2	8.2	8.4	6.3	52.1	58 244	59 479	57 118	-2.1	4.1
Middletown	6.7	12.6	15.9	22.2	14.1	9.3	7.2	6.9	5.1	51.5	43 167	42 762	39 040	0.9	9.5
Milford	6.5	15.3	9.1	18.0	16.1	11.4	9.7	9.0	4.8	51.4	52 305	49 938	NA	4.7	NA
Naugatuck Borough	8.2	18.1	9.1	20.8	15.8	8.3	7.4	7.2	5.1	51.2	30 989	30 625	26 456	1.2	15.8
New Britain	6.8	14.3	13.3	20.0	12.8	7.1	8.8	10.0	6.9	52.2	71 538	75 491	73 840	-5.2	2.2
New Haven	7.8	15.6	16.9	20.5	12.6	8.1	6.4	6.3	5.9	53.0	123 626	130 474	126 109	-5.2	3.5
New London	7.1	12.5	23.1	19.2	11.6	7.2	6.5	6.8	6.1	49.7	25 671	28 540	28 842	-10.1	-1.0
Norwalk	6.8	13.3	9.0	21.7	15.3	11.7	9.6	7.4	5.1	51.8	82 951	78 331	77 767	5.9	0.7
Norwich	7.7	16.2	10.7	18.9	13.7	8.5	8.7	8.9	6.8	52.3	36 117	37 391	38 074	-3.4	-1.8
Shelton	7.1	16.1	9.0	17.3	16.0	12.7	9.2	7.2	5.4	50.7	38 101	35 418	31 314	7.6	13.1
Stamford	6.8	13.5	9.0	20.7	15.5	11.3	10.1	7.8	5.4	52.2	117 083	108 056	102 453	8.4	5.5
Torrington	6.8	13.9	9.6	18.5	14.7	9.2	8.7	10.0	8.5	51.9	35 202	33 687	30 987	4.5	8.7
Waterbury	7.8	15.6	10.5	19.1	13.1	8.7	8.7	9.1	7.3	52.7	107 271	108 961	103 266	-1.6	5.5
West Haven	7.0	14.2	10.9	20.7	14.4	9.5	8.5	9.0	5.8	52.1	52 360	54 021	53 184	-3.1	1.6
DELAWARE	7.3	17.2	11.4	17.9	14.8	10.2	9.0	7.4	4.7	51.5	783 600	666 168	594 338	17.6	12.1
Dover	6.9	16.2	18.5	16.8	13.6	9.7	7.4	6.1	4.7	51.5	32 135	27 630	23 504	16.3	17.6
Newark	3.9	10.1	42.7	11.4	10.4	7.0	6.1	4.9	3.6	52.8	28 547	26 463	25 247	7.9	4.8
Wilmington	7.1	17.8	9.7	19.3	14.8	8.9	7.7	8.1	6.7	53.5	72 664	71 529	70 195	1.6	1.9
DISTRICT OF COLUMBIA	6.0	13.2	13.4	20.2	15.7	10.3	8.4	7.4	5.4	53.4	572 059	606 900	638 432	-5.7	-4.9
Washington	6.0	13.2	13.4	20.2	15.7	10.3	8.4	7.4	5.4	53.4	572 059	606 900	638 432	-5.7	-4.9
FLORIDA	6.6	15.6	9.4	16.4	14.0	10.0	9.8	10.6	7.7	51.6	15 982 378	12 938 071	9 746 961	23.5	32.7
Altamonte Springs	5.8	14.3	12.7	25.0	16.0	9.8	7.0	5.6	3.8	52.0	41 200	35 167	22 028	17.2	59.6
Apopka	8.6	17.3	8.9	22.6	14.3	9.5	8.0	7.8	3.1	51.0	26 642	13 611	NA	95.7	NA
Boca Raton	5.0	12.1	8.5	15.3	15.2	11.6	10.7	11.1	10.4	52.0	74 764	61 486	49 505	21.6	24.2
Boynton Beach	5.8	12.3	6.8	15.5	11.9	8.6	9.0	14.0	16.1	53.3	60 389	46 284	35 624	30.5	29.9
Bradenton	5.9	13.4	7.5	14.9	12.4	7.9	9.6	14.4	14.0	53.5	49 504	43 769	30 170	13.1	45.1

Table D. Cities

City	Total population	Total in households	Householder	Spouse	Child Total	Child Own child under 18 years	Other relatives Total	Other relatives Under 18 years	Nonrelatives Total	Nonrelatives Unmarried partner	Total in group quarters	Institutionalized population Correctional institutions	Institutionalized population Nursing homes	Institutionalized population Other institutions	Noninstitutionalized population College dormitories	Noninstitutionalized population Military quarters	Noninstitutionalized population Other
	54	55	56	57	58	59	60	61	62	63	64	65	66	67	68	69	70
CALIFORNIA—Cont'd																	
Vista	89 857	97.5	32.1	17.2	32.0	25.8	8.2	2.8	8.0	2.1	2.5	1.0	0.4	0.0	0.0	0.0	1.1
Walnut	30 004	99.9	27.5	21.2	37.2	25.0	11.0	2.4	3.0	0.6	0.1	0.0	0.1	0.0	0.0	0.0	0.1
Walnut Creek	64 296	98.5	47.1	21.5	21.4	16.7	3.0	0.6	5.4	1.9	1.5	0.0	0.8	0.0	0.0	0.0	0.7
Watsonville	44 265	98.8	25.7	14.5	37.0	28.3	13.8	4.6	7.7	1.5	1.2	0.0	0.5	0.0	0.0	0.0	0.7
West Covina	105 080	99.2	29.9	17.4	34.4	23.9	12.3	3.8	5.2	1.5	0.8	0.0	0.2	0.0	0.0	0.0	0.6
West Hollywood	35 716	99.4	64.7	10.6	8.2	5.2	3.1	0.4	12.7	4.8	0.6	0.0	0.0	0.0	0.0	0.0	0.6
Westminster	88 207	99.4	29.9	17.5	32.1	22.0	13.0	3.2	6.8	1.3	0.6	0.0	0.2	0.0	0.0	0.0	0.4
West Sacramento	31 615	99.3	36.1	16.3	33.6	26.1	7.5	3.1	5.8	2.4	0.7	0.0	0.4	0.0	0.0	0.0	0.3
Whittier	83 680	97.2	33.8	17.7	32.7	24.5	7.7	2.7	5.2	2.0	2.8	0.0	0.4	0.9	0.9	0.0	0.6
Woodland	49 151	98.4	34.1	18.7	33.2	26.4	7.3	2.6	5.1	2.1	1.6	0.0	0.8	0.1	0.0	0.0	0.7
Yorba Linda	58 918	99.8	32.7	23.6	36.3	27.8	4.2	1.2	3.0	1.0	0.2	0.0	0.0	0.0	0.0	0.0	0.2
Yuba City	36 758	97.5	36.2	17.2	31.8	25.8	6.4	2.4	5.9	2.2	2.5	0.7	1.2	0.0	0.0	0.0	0.6
Yucaipa	41 207	98.6	36.9	20.0	31.9	25.4	5.4	2.2	4.5	1.7	1.4	0.0	0.8	0.2	0.0	0.0	0.3
COLORADO	4 301 261	97.6	38.6	20.0	28.3	23.4	4.4	1.6	6.4	2.1	2.4	0.7	0.4	0.1	0.5	0.2	0.4
Arvada	102 153	99.3	38.2	22.0	30.5	24.1	3.9	1.5	4.7	1.8	0.7	0.0	0.1	0.0	0.0	0.0	0.6
Aurora	276 393	99.2	38.2	17.9	30.1	24.7	6.4	2.1	6.6	2.4	0.8	0.1	0.3	0.1	0.0	0.1	0.2
Boulder	94 673	92.1	41.8	13.9	16.4	14.0	2.4	0.5	17.5	2.8	7.9	0.6	0.7	0.0	6.5	0.0	0.0
Broomfield	38 272	100.0	36.2	22.3	32.9	27.6	3.6	1.2	5.0	1.8	0.0	0.0	0.0	0.0	0.0	0.0	0.0
Colorado Springs	360 890	98.0	39.2	20.2	29.1	24.4	3.7	1.5	5.8	2.0	2.0	0.4	0.5	0.1	0.5	0.1	0.4
Denver	554 636	97.7	43.1	15.0	23.8	18.6	7.3	2.7	8.6	2.8	2.3	0.5	0.5	0.1	0.4	0.0	0.8
Englewood	31 727	97.7	45.4	16.6	22.9	18.0	4.7	1.5	8.1	3.0	2.3	0.0	1.8	0.1	0.1	0.0	0.3
Fort Collins	118 652	94.9	38.7	17.4	23.8	20.4	2.5	0.7	12.6	2.4	5.1	0.3	0.5	0.0	3.8	0.0	0.5
Grand Junction	41 986	94.8	42.5	19.6	23.4	19.4	3.3	1.2	6.0	2.1	5.2	1.2	0.5	0.3	1.7	0.0	1.5
Greeley	76 930	94.5	35.9	17.5	27.7	23.0	5.2	1.9	8.2	2.0	5.5	0.7	0.0	0.0	3.7	0.0	0.0
Lakewood	144 126	97.4	42.0	18.9	25.4	20.2	4.2	1.4	6.8	2.6	2.6	0.8	0.9	0.2	0.2	0.0	0.5
Littleton	40 340	98.5	42.9	20.3	26.7	21.6	3.5	1.2	5.1	2.0	1.5	0.5	0.8	0.0	0.0	0.0	0.2
Longmont	71 093	99.1	37.5	20.5	30.5	25.5	4.9	1.7	5.7	2.1	0.9	0.0	0.6	0.0	0.1	0.0	0.2
Loveland	50 608	99.3	39.0	22.4	30.3	25.3	3.0	1.1	4.5	1.9	0.7	0.0	0.5	0.0	0.0	0.0	0.1
Northglenn	31 575	99.5	36.8	19.7	30.4	23.2	6.8	2.9	5.8	2.1	0.5	0.0	0.5	0.0	0.0	0.0	0.0
Pueblo	102 121	96.2	39.5	17.6	28.9	21.8	5.4	2.6	4.9	2.2	3.8	1.0	1.1	0.8	0.4	0.0	0.5
Thornton	82 384	99.3	35.1	20.3	33.2	27.3	5.2	2.1	5.6	2.4	0.7	0.0	0.5	0.1	0.0	0.0	0.1
Westminster	100 940	99.5	38.0	20.4	30.4	24.7	4.7	1.6	6.1	2.4	0.5	0.0	0.3	0.1	0.0	0.0	0.1
Wheat Ridge	32 913	97.4	44.2	18.3	24.4	19.3	4.0	1.4	6.5	2.5	2.6	0.0	1.4	0.1	0.0	0.0	1.0
CONNECTICUT	3 405 565	96.8	38.2	19.9	29.5	22.7	4.6	1.5	4.7	2.0	3.2	0.6	0.9	0.1	1.1	0.1	0.4
Bridgeport	139 529	97.4	36.1	12.6	32.8	24.0	9.4	3.8	6.5	2.7	2.6	0.6	0.7	0.1	0.9	0.0	0.3
Bristol	60 062	98.7	41.4	20.6	28.2	21.6	3.6	1.1	4.9	2.5	1.3	0.0	1.0	0.0	0.0	0.0	0.3
Danbury	74 848	95.8	36.3	18.6	26.4	19.3	7.0	1.9	7.5	2.0	4.2	1.8	0.8	0.0	1.2	0.0	0.2
Hartford	121 578	95.6	37.0	9.3	33.4	24.9	9.4	4.3	6.5	3.0	4.4	0.9	0.8	0.3	1.5	0.0	1.0
Meriden	58 244	98.0	39.4	17.9	30.4	23.2	5.1	1.8	5.3	2.8	2.0	0.0	1.4	0.1	0.0	0.0	0.5
Middletown	43 167	95.7	43.0	17.7	24.4	19.2	3.6	1.3	7.0	2.9	4.3	0.0	1.3	2.0	0.0	0.0	1.0
Milford	52 305	99.0	40.0	21.7	28.6	20.6	4.5	1.4	4.2	1.9	1.0	0.0	0.8	0.0	0.0	0.0	0.2
Naugatuck Borough	30 989	99.3	38.2	20.3	32.8	25.3	3.8	1.1	4.1	2.1	0.7	0.0	0.6	0.0	0.0	0.0	0.1
New Britain	71 538	95.7	39.9	14.6	28.6	21.3	6.0	2.2	6.5	3.0	4.3	0.0	1.3	0.0	2.3	0.0	0.8
New Haven	123 626	91.4	38.1	10.5	28.0	21.4	7.3	3.1	7.6	2.5	8.6	1.1	0.9	0.1	5.7	0.0	0.7
New London	25 671	89.5	39.7	12.1	24.9	19.8	5.0	2.0	7.9	3.4	10.5	0.0	1.0	0.0	8.7	0.1	0.8
Norwalk	82 951	99.0	39.4	18.9	27.3	19.6	7.0	2.1	6.4	2.1	1.0	0.0	0.6	0.0	0.0	0.0	0.4
Norwich	36 117	97.9	41.8	17.0	27.9	21.7	4.3	1.5	7.0	3.3	2.1	0.0	1.0	0.0	0.0	0.0	1.0
Shelton	38 101	98.5	37.2	23.4	30.5	22.1	4.5	1.2	2.8	1.4	1.5	0.0	0.9	0.5	0.0	0.0	0.1
Stamford	117 083	98.5	38.8	18.8	27.0	19.9	7.0	1.8	7.0	1.8	1.5	0.0	0.7	0.1	0.0	0.0	0.7
Torrington	35 202	97.6	41.9	20.0	27.6	21.4	3.2	1.0	5.0	2.5	2.4	0.0	1.9	0.0	0.0	0.0	0.5
Waterbury	107 271	97.9	39.7	15.4	31.2	23.4	6.2	2.3	5.4	3.0	2.1	0.2	1.3	0.0	0.2	0.0	0.4
West Haven	52 360	97.6	40.3	16.9	29.0	20.6	5.8	2.1	5.6	2.5	2.4	0.0	0.7	0.2	1.5	0.0	0.0
DELAWARE	783 600	96.9	38.1	19.5	28.6	22.0	5.1	2.2	5.5	2.3	3.1	0.8	0.6	0.1	1.2	0.0	0.4
Dover	32 135	90.3	38.4	15.5	25.9	20.5	4.7	2.3	5.8	2.4	9.7	0.4	2.2	0.1	5.4	1.2	0.5
Newark	28 547	76.4	31.5	12.8	15.1	11.6	2.2	0.7	14.9	1.3	23.6	0.0	0.5	0.0	23.0	0.0	0.1
Wilmington	72 664	94.2	39.4	10.5	28.0	20.0	9.4	4.9	7.0	2.8	5.8	3.0	0.8	0.1	0.0	0.0	2.0
DISTRICT OF COLUMBIA	572 059	93.8	43.4	9.9	22.6	15.5	8.8	3.9	9.1	2.6	6.2	0.5	0.7	0.2	3.4	0.2	1.3
Washington	572 059	93.8	43.4	9.9	22.6	15.5	8.8	3.9	9.1	2.6	6.2	0.5	0.7	0.2	3.4	0.2	1.3
FLORIDA	15 982 378	97.6	39.7	20.0	26.1	20.0	6.0	2.2	5.9	2.3	2.4	0.9	0.6	0.1	0.3	0.1	0.5
Altamonte Springs	41 200	99.0	45.7	16.9	23.9	18.6	4.5	1.3	7.9	3.5	1.0	0.0	1.0	0.0	0.0	0.0	0.0
Apopka	26 642	99.2	35.9	20.0	30.9	25.1	6.5	2.4	5.9	2.3	0.8	0.0	0.5	0.0	0.0	0.0	0.3
Boca Raton	74 764	96.2	42.6	22.6	22.6	18.0	3.1	0.7	5.3	1.9	3.8	0.0	0.7	0.0	2.6	0.0	0.4
Boynton Beach	60 389	98.2	43.4	19.7	22.6	17.2	6.3	2.2	6.1	2.5	1.8	0.0	1.5	0.0	0.0	0.0	0.3
Bradenton	49 504	96.8	43.2	18.8	23.3	18.4	5.6	2.3	6.0	2.6	3.2	0.7	2.0	0.1	0.0	0.0	0.3

Table D. Cities

City	Households by type, 2000												Households, 1990		
	Total households	Family households						Nonfamily households			Average house-hold size	Average family size	Total house-holds	Female house-holder[1]	House-holder living alone
		Total	With own children under 18 years	Married couple		Female householder[1]		Total	Householder living alone						
				Total	With own children under 18 years	Total	With own children under 18 years		Total	65 years and over					
	71	72	73	74	75	76	77	78	79	80	81	82	83	84	85
CALIFORNIA—Cont'd															
Vista	28 877	72.0	40.4	53.7	28.9	12.7	8.2	28.0	20.5	7.2	3.03	3.48	25 371	10.4	20.0
Walnut	8 260	91.8	50.6	77.1	44.8	9.9	4.2	8.2	5.8	1.3	3.63	3.74	7 846	7.0	5.5
Walnut Creek	30 301	54.6	20.9	45.7	16.6	6.7	3.3	45.4	38.0	19.7	2.09	2.78	28 347	6.3	35.8
Watsonville	11 381	77.9	49.2	56.3	36.1	16.4	10.3	22.1	17.6	9.0	3.84	4.26	9 437	13.7	21.3
West Covina	31 411	80.4	41.9	58.2	31.4	15.8	7.9	19.6	14.8	6.0	3.32	3.67	30 096	13.5	14.7
West Hollywood	23 120	22.5	5.8	16.4	3.7	4.4	1.7	77.5	60.5	12.0	1.53	2.50	22 568	4.6	59.3
Westminster	26 406	77.3	37.8	54.8	29.8	12.4	5.8	22.7	16.9	7.4	3.32	3.71	25 077	10.8	17.5
West Sacramento	11 404	66.6	34.6	45.2	22.1	15.4	9.4	33.4	27.1	10.6	2.75	3.39	11 052	14.2	28.4
Whittier	28 271	72.4	37.8	52.5	26.9	14.3	8.0	27.6	22.4	9.4	2.88	3.38	27 637	12.0	22.8
Woodland	16 751	73.3	40.1	54.8	29.0	12.9	8.0	26.7	21.0	8.4	2.89	3.37	14 198	12.1	20.9
Yorba Linda	19 252	83.6	44.8	72.3	38.8	8.3	4.5	16.4	12.4	4.7	3.05	3.35	16 774	7.2	10.8
Yuba City	13 290	67.3	36.7	47.6	23.8	14.3	9.7	32.7	26.5	9.7	2.70	3.28	10 583	15.0	28.1
Yucaipa	15 193	70.3	35.4	54.2	25.9	11.6	6.9	29.7	25.3	13.4	2.67	3.21	13 319	8.3	28.6
COLORADO	1 658 238	65.4	32.8	51.8	24.4	9.6	6.2	34.6	26.3	7.0	2.53	3.09	1 282 489	9.7	26.6
Arvada	39 019	71.1	34.2	57.5	26.1	9.7	5.9	28.9	23.1	7.7	2.60	3.07	32 744	9.9	19.5
Aurora	105 625	65.2	35.5	46.9	24.0	13.1	8.8	34.8	27.4	5.7	2.60	3.19	89 132	11.8	25.5
Boulder	39 596	42.4	20.0	33.3	14.6	6.5	4.2	57.6	33.7	6.2	2.20	2.84	34 681	7.1	33.4
Broomfield	13 842	74.2	41.2	61.8	33.3	8.2	5.5	25.8	19.3	4.2	2.76	3.19	8 719	8.1	18.3
Colorado Springs	141 516	65.8	34.0	51.5	24.7	10.6	7.1	34.2	27.0	6.9	2.50	3.06	110 862	10.1	26.7
Denver	239 235	49.9	23.2	34.7	15.0	10.8	6.4	50.1	39.3	9.4	2.27	3.14	210 952	11.5	40.4
Englewood	14 392	51.9	23.6	36.7	14.9	10.8	6.3	48.1	37.9	9.5	2.15	2.88	13 252	10.9	35.9
Fort Collins	45 882	56.2	29.0	44.9	22.1	7.9	5.3	43.8	26.0	5.9	2.45	3.01	33 689	7.6	26.2
Grand Junction	17 865	59.0	25.5	46.1	17.5	9.4	5.9	41.0	33.2	13.8	2.23	2.84	12 810	11.6	37.2
Greeley	27 647	64.0	33.1	48.7	23.5	10.8	7.1	36.0	25.6	8.3	2.63	3.19	22 647	10.1	27.0
Lakewood	60 531	60.3	27.4	45.1	18.3	10.8	6.8	39.7	30.7	7.8	2.32	2.92	51 657	10.7	27.5
Littleton	17 313	60.0	28.0	47.3	20.4	9.2	5.8	40.0	33.3	11.1	2.29	2.96	13 905	9.8	29.5
Longmont	26 667	69.2	36.9	54.6	27.4	10.1	6.7	30.8	23.7	7.3	2.64	3.15	19 570	10.0	23.7
Loveland	19 741	71.1	35.3	57.5	26.2	9.8	6.9	28.9	23.4	8.8	2.55	3.01	14 049	9.4	21.9
Northglenn	11 610	70.7	33.8	53.6	24.1	11.8	6.8	29.3	23.0	5.5	2.71	3.19	9 829	10.9	20.3
Pueblo	40 307	64.8	29.8	44.5	17.8	15.1	9.2	35.2	30.0	12.9	2.44	3.03	38 324	14.9	27.9
Thornton	28 882	74.5	42.3	57.8	31.5	11.5	7.7	25.5	18.7	3.8	2.83	3.25	19 055	12.2	18.4
Westminster	38 343	67.9	35.7	53.6	27.2	9.6	6.0	32.1	23.7	4.5	2.62	3.15	27 828	10.2	21.9
Wheat Ridge	14 559	57.1	25.0	41.4	15.8	11.4	7.0	42.9	35.4	13.7	2.20	2.85	13 138	10.4	33.2
CONNECTICUT	1 301 670	67.7	32.2	52.0	23.6	12.1	7.0	32.3	26.4	10.1	2.53	3.08	1 230 479	11.4	24.2
Bridgeport	50 307	65.1	34.3	35.0	16.8	24.0	14.9	34.9	29.0	11.3	2.70	3.34	52 328	20.6	29.4
Bristol	24 886	65.0	29.6	49.6	21.0	11.5	6.6	35.0	28.9	10.7	2.38	2.94	23 956	10.3	24.9
Danbury	27 183	65.8	30.3	51.1	23.6	10.5	5.3	34.2	26.2	8.5	2.64	3.18	24 094	10.5	25.8
Hartford	44 986	60.4	34.4	25.2	11.7	29.6	20.1	39.6	33.2	9.6	2.58	3.33	51 464	27.6	32.8
Meriden	22 951	65.2	31.3	45.4	19.5	15.2	9.6	34.8	28.9	10.7	2.49	3.08	23 240	12.8	26.8
Middletown	18 554	56.0	25.7	41.3	17.1	11.6	7.2	44.0	35.0	10.1	2.23	2.90	16 821	11.9	31.0
Milford	20 900	67.3	29.1	54.4	23.4	9.7	4.4	32.7	26.6	10.3	2.48	3.04	18 851	9.7	22.5
Naugatuck Borough	11 829	70.1	36.3	53.3	26.5	12.8	7.9	29.9	24.9	9.6	2.60	3.13	11 330	10.4	23.1
New Britain	28 558	59.3	28.3	36.6	14.8	17.7	11.3	40.7	33.1	12.7	2.40	3.08	30 170	14.6	29.9
New Haven	47 094	54.9	29.3	27.5	12.3	22.9	15.1	45.1	36.1	10.5	2.40	3.19	48 986	21.6	34.0
New London	10 181	52.9	27.6	30.4	12.9	17.8	12.2	47.1	37.8	10.7	2.26	3.00	10 712	15.5	34.7
Norwalk	32 711	64.1	28.5	47.9	20.9	12.2	6.4	35.9	28.2	8.7	2.51	3.10	30 560	11.7	25.8
Norwich	15 091	60.1	29.0	40.7	16.7	15.0	9.9	39.9	32.0	12.5	2.34	2.96	15 018	13.0	27.8
Shelton	14 190	74.3	32.8	62.9	27.8	8.5	4.1	25.7	21.8	9.2	2.65	3.11	12 454	8.0	18.1
Stamford	45 399	63.8	28.7	48.5	21.7	11.5	5.7	36.2	28.7	9.8	2.54	3.13	41 945	12.4	26.5
Torrington	14 743	61.9	28.5	47.7	20.3	10.3	6.1	38.1	32.1	13.7	2.33	2.96	13 883	9.8	29.0
Waterbury	42 622	63.1	31.2	38.8	16.5	19.1	12.2	36.9	31.4	12.1	2.46	3.11	43 164	15.4	29.7
West Haven	21 090	62.2	28.5	41.9	17.7	15.6	8.8	37.8	31.0	10.7	2.42	3.06	21 284	13.0	27.5
DELAWARE	298 736	68.5	31.9	51.3	21.9	13.1	7.7	31.5	25.0	9.1	2.54	3.04	247 497	11.8	23.2
Dover	12 340	60.8	30.0	40.4	16.7	16.7	11.2	39.2	31.4	10.6	2.35	2.98	9 903	14.0	27.2
Newark	8 989	50.0	20.7	40.5	16.1	7.2	3.7	50.0	27.2	9.3	2.43	2.91	7 469	7.5	23.4
Wilmington	28 617	55.5	27.1	26.6	10.9	23.8	14.0	44.5	37.1	13.0	2.39	3.19	28 556	21.8	36.4
DISTRICT OF COLUMBIA	248 338	46.0	19.8	22.8	8.4	18.9	9.9	54.0	43.8	10.0	2.16	3.07	249 634	19.5	41.5
Washington	248 338	46.0	19.8	22.8	8.4	18.9	9.9	54.0	43.8	10.0	2.16	3.07	249 634	19.5	41.5
FLORIDA	6 337 929	66.4	28.1	50.4	19.2	12.0	6.9	33.6	26.6	11.2	2.46	2.98	5 134 869	10.7	25.5
Altamonte Springs	18 821	53.2	24.8	37.1	15.4	12.0	7.3	46.8	36.1	6.7	2.17	2.86	15 432	10.0	32.6
Apopka	9 562	75.0	38.2	55.8	26.6	14.4	9.1	25.0	18.6	5.8	2.76	3.13	5 112	12.0	19.0
Boca Raton	31 848	62.8	24.1	53.1	19.1	7.1	4.0	37.2	29.5	11.6	2.26	2.81	26 297	6.7	28.3
Boynton Beach	26 210	59.8	22.2	45.4	14.6	10.9	6.0	40.2	33.0	17.8	2.26	2.87	20 292	9.5	30.0
Bradenton	21 379	59.5	23.0	43.5	13.5	12.1	7.5	40.5	34.1	17.8	2.24	2.85	18 871	10.1	30.9

[1] No spouse present.

Table D. Cities

City	Percent change of households, 1990–2000	Total housing units	Occupied housing units (percent)	Vacant housing units — Total	For seasonal, recreational, or occasional use	Homeowner vacancy rate (percent)	Rental vacancy rate (percent)	Occupied housing units — Total	Percent owner-occupied housing units	Percent renter-occupied housing units	Average household size of owner-occupied units	Average household size of renter-occupied units
	86	87	88	89	90	91	92	93	94	95	96	97
CALIFORNIA—Cont'd												
Vista	13.8	29 814	96.9	3.1	0.2	1.0	3.3	28 877	54.2	45.8	2.89	3.20
Walnut	5.3	8 395	98.4	1.6	0.3	0.7	2.2	8 260	88.9	11.1	3.62	3.73
Walnut Creek	6.9	31 425	96.4	3.6	0.6	1.1	2.8	30 301	68.3	31.7	2.16	1.94
Watsonville	20.6	11 695	97.3	2.7	0.3	0.6	2.9	11 381	48.1	51.9	3.55	4.11
West Covina	4.4	32 058	98.0	2.0	0.1	0.7	2.2	31 411	66.5	33.5	3.38	3.19
West Hollywood	2.4	24 110	95.9	4.1	0.8	1.7	2.4	23 120	21.6	78.4	1.55	1.53
Westminster	5.3	26 940	98.0	2.0	0.1	0.7	2.3	26 406	60.2	39.8	3.21	3.48
West Sacramento	3.2	12 133	94.0	6.0	0.3	1.3	6.6	11 404	54.5	45.5	2.60	2.94
Whittier	2.3	28 977	97.6	2.4	0.2	0.9	2.1	28 271	57.8	42.2	2.94	2.80
Woodland	18.0	17 120	97.8	2.2	0.2	0.7	2.1	16 751	58.5	41.5	2.93	2.82
Yorba Linda	14.8	19 567	98.4	1.6	0.2	0.6	1.9	19 252	84.7	15.3	3.11	2.71
Yuba City	25.6	13 912	95.5	4.5	0.3	1.4	4.7	13 290	47.4	52.6	2.76	2.64
Yucaipa	14.1	16 112	94.3	5.7	0.4	2.0	6.6	15 193	74.2	25.8	2.64	2.79
COLORADO	29.3	1 808 037	91.7	8.3	4.0	1.4	5.5	1 658 238	67.3	32.7	2.64	2.30
Arvada	19.2	39 733	98.2	1.8	0.1	0.6	2.5	39 019	75.7	24.3	2.70	2.30
Aurora	18.5	109 260	96.7	3.3	0.2	1.1	3.5	105 625	63.9	36.1	2.65	2.50
Boulder	14.2	40 726	97.2	2.8	0.6	0.6	2.2	39 596	49.5	50.5	2.30	2.11
Broomfield	58.8	14 322	96.6	3.4	0.4	1.0	6.3	13 842	76.8	23.2	2.90	2.32
Colorado Springs	27.7	148 690	95.2	4.8	0.5	1.2	6.2	141 516	60.8	39.2	2.65	2.27
Denver	13.4	251 435	95.1	4.9	0.6	1.7	4.5	239 235	52.5	47.5	2.41	2.10
Englewood	8.6	14 916	96.5	3.5	0.1	0.7	4.3	14 392	52.2	47.8	2.32	1.98
Fort Collins	36.2	47 755	96.1	3.9	0.4	1.4	4.1	45 882	57.0	43.0	2.61	2.24
Grand Junction	39.5	18 784	95.1	4.9	0.4	1.7	5.9	17 865	62.6	37.4	2.35	2.03
Greeley	22.1	28 972	95.4	4.6	0.2	1.9	4.8	27 647	58.4	41.6	2.76	2.45
Lakewood	17.2	62 422	97.0	3.0	0.3	0.7	3.6	60 531	60.9	39.1	2.41	2.17
Littleton	24.5	18 084	95.7	4.3	0.3	0.7	7.2	17 313	62.1	37.9	2.49	1.97
Longmont	36.3	27 394	97.3	2.7	0.3	1.1	2.6	26 667	65.6	34.4	2.72	2.50
Loveland	40.5	20 299	97.3	2.7	0.3	1.0	2.8	19 741	69.4	30.6	2.62	2.37
Northglenn	18.1	12 051	96.3	3.7	0.2	0.7	6.8	11 610	67.4	32.6	2.88	2.34
Pueblo	5.2	43 121	93.5	6.5	0.2	1.7	8.5	40 307	65.6	34.4	2.49	2.34
Thornton	51.6	29 573	97.7	2.3	0.1	0.9	4.7	28 882	77.7	22.3	2.91	2.57
Westminster	37.8	39 318	97.5	2.5	0.3	0.5	4.3	38 343	69.7	30.3	2.75	2.31
Wheat Ridge	10.8	14 931	97.5	2.5	0.3	0.6	2.4	14 559	54.6	45.4	2.29	2.10
CONNECTICUT	5.8	1 385 975	93.9	6.1	1.7	1.1	5.6	1 301 670	66.8	33.2	2.67	2.25
Bridgeport	-3.9	54 367	92.5	7.5	0.2	1.9	5.6	50 307	43.2	56.8	2.74	2.67
Bristol	3.9	26 125	95.3	4.7	0.3	1.1	5.2	24 886	61.9	38.1	2.60	2.03
Danbury	12.8	28 519	95.3	4.7	1.3	1.1	3.4	27 183	58.3	41.7	2.67	2.59
Hartford	-12.6	50 644	88.8	11.2	0.3	2.0	9.2	44 986	24.6	75.4	2.76	2.52
Meriden	-1.2	24 631	93.2	6.8	0.2	1.7	7.3	22 951	59.9	40.1	2.59	2.34
Middletown	10.3	19 697	94.2	5.8	0.5	1.5	5.8	18 554	51.3	48.7	2.49	1.95
Milford	10.9	21 962	95.2	4.8	1.6	0.7	6.1	20 900	77.3	22.7	2.61	2.02
Naugatuck Borough	4.4	12 341	95.9	4.1	0.2	0.9	5.0	11 829	66.5	33.5	2.79	2.22
New Britain	-5.3	31 164	91.6	8.4	0.2	1.7	6.1	28 558	42.7	57.3	2.50	2.32
New Haven	-3.9	52 941	89.0	11.0	0.3	3.7	7.1	47 094	29.6	70.4	2.60	2.32
New London	-5.0	11 560	88.1	11.9	1.1	2.5	9.8	10 181	37.9	62.1	2.39	2.17
Norwalk	7.0	33 753	96.9	3.1	0.6	0.6	2.9	32 711	62.0	38.0	2.61	2.35
Norwich	0.5	16 600	90.9	9.1	1.3	2.3	7.0	15 091	52.5	47.5	2.51	2.16
Shelton	13.9	14 707	96.5	3.5	0.7	0.9	5.8	14 190	81.8	18.2	2.76	2.15
Stamford	8.2	47 317	95.9	4.1	1.0	0.6	3.0	45 399	56.7	43.3	2.65	2.39
Torrington	6.2	16 147	91.3	8.7	2.7	1.9	7.0	14 743	64.6	35.4	2.50	2.02
Waterbury	-1.3	46 827	91.0	9.0	0.3	2.2	7.6	42 622	47.6	52.4	2.58	2.36
West Haven	-0.9	22 336	94.4	5.6	0.3	1.5	6.6	21 090	55.2	44.8	2.62	2.18
DELAWARE	20.7	343 072	87.1	12.9	7.6	1.5	8.2	298 736	72.3	27.7	2.61	2.37
Dover	24.6	13 195	93.5	6.5	0.4	2.0	6.7	12 340	52.3	47.7	2.50	2.19
Newark	20.4	9 294	96.7	3.3	0.2	1.1	4.0	8 989	54.5	45.5	2.53	2.31
Wilmington	0.2	32 138	89.0	11.0	0.2	2.6	8.4	28 617	50.1	49.9	2.45	2.33
DISTRICT OF COLUMBIA.	-0.5	274 845	90.4	9.6	0.8	2.9	5.9	248 338	40.8	59.2	2.31	2.06
Washington	-0.5	274 845	90.4	9.6	0.8	2.9	5.9	248 338	40.8	59.2	2.31	2.06
FLORIDA	23.4	7 302 947	86.8	13.2	6.6	2.2	9.3	6 337 929	70.1	29.9	2.49	2.39
Altamonte Springs	22.0	19 992	94.1	5.9	1.0	1.5	5.7	18 821	41.8	58.2	2.38	2.02
Apopka	87.1	10 091	94.8	5.2	1.3	1.8	4.5	9 562	75.8	24.2	2.75	2.81
Boca Raton	21.1	37 547	84.8	15.2	11.2	1.4	7.0	31 848	75.6	24.4	2.33	2.04
Boynton Beach	29.2	30 643	85.5	14.5	9.6	2.1	7.8	26 210	72.8	27.2	2.27	2.24
Bradenton	13.3	24 887	85.9	14.1	7.5	2.1	9.4	21 379	61.7	38.3	2.25	2.22

Table D. Cities

STATE Place code	City	Land area, 2000[1] (sq km)	Population, 2000			Land area, 1990[1] (sq km)	Population, 1990			Population and population characteristics, 2000					
										Race (percent)					
										One race					
			Total persons	Rank	Per square kilometer		Total persons	Rank	Per square kilometer	White	Black or African American	American Indian or Alaska Native	Asian	Native Hawaiian and other Pacific Islander	Some other race
		1	2	3	4	5	6	7	8	9	10	11	12	13	14
	FLORIDA—Cont'd														
12 10275	Cape Coral	272.4	102 286	238	375.5	272.3	74 991	308	275.4	93.0	2.0	0.3	0.9	0.1	2.2
12 12875	Clearwater	65.5	108 787	216	1 660.9	64.4	98 669	208	1 532.1	83.9	9.8	0.3	1.6	0.1	2.5
12 13275	Coconut Creek	29.9	43 566	788	1 457.1	28.9	27 269	1 170	943.6	86.3	6.2	0.1	2.4	0.1	2.9
12 14125	Cooper City	16.4	27 939	1 325	1 703.6	16.4	21 335	1 536	1 300.9	89.1	3.1	0.2	4.1	0.0	1.7
12 14250	Coral Gables	34.0	42 249	814	1 242.6	30.6	40 091	737	1 310.2	91.8	3.3	0.1	1.7	0.0	1.5
12 14400	Coral Springs	61.9	117 549	193	1 899.0	60.8	78 864	284	1 297.1	81.5	9.2	0.2	3.5	0.1	3.0
12 16475	Davie	86.6	75 720	372	874.4	83.7	47 143	603	563.2	87.1	4.6	0.2	2.8	0.0	2.9
12 16525	Daytona Beach	152.0	64 112	455	421.8	83.5	61 991	401	742.4	62.3	32.7	0.3	1.7	0.1	1.0
12 16725	Deerfield Beach	34.8	64 583	452	1 855.8	27.0	46 997	606	1 740.6	77.3	16.0	0.2	1.4	0.0	2.4
12 17100	Delray Beach	39.8	60 020	502	1 508.0	38.4	47 184	601	1 228.8	66.5	26.6	0.2	1.1	0.1	1.6
12 18575	Dunedin	26.9	35 691	1 000	1 326.8	26.8	34 427	877	1 284.6	94.9	2.0	0.2	1.1	0.0	0.6
12 24000	Fort Lauderdale	82.2	152 397	135	1 854.0	81.2	149 238	119	1 837.9	64.3	28.9	0.2	1.0	0.0	1.8
12 24125	Fort Myers	82.4	48 208	701	585.0	56.9	44 947	636	789.9	56.4	33.4	0.4	1.0	0.1	5.7
12 24300	Fort Pierce	38.2	37 516	941	982.1	31.8	36 830	819	1 158.2	49.5	40.9	0.3	0.8	0.1	5.4
12 25175	Gainesville	124.8	95 447	260	764.8	90.3	91 482	230	1 013.1	68.4	23.2	0.2	4.5	0.0	1.5
12 27322	Greenacres City	12.1	27 569	1 350	2 278.4	10.5	18 683	1 756	1 779.3	83.2	6.5	0.3	1.8	0.0	5.6
12 28450	Hallandale	10.9	34 282	1 049	3 145.1	10.9	30 997	1 009	2 843.8	77.3	16.0	0.2	1.0	0.0	2.8
12 30000	Hialeah	49.8	226 419	77	4 546.6	49.8	188 008	87	3 775.3	88.0	2.4	0.1	0.4	0.0	5.5
12 32000	Hollywood	70.8	139 357	159	1 968.3	70.6	121 720	152	1 724.1	78.4	12.1	0.3	2.0	0.1	4.0
12 32275	Homestead	37.0	31 909	1 138	862.4	30.1	26 694	1 197	886.8	61.0	22.5	0.5	0.8	0.1	9.8
12 35000	Jacksonville	1 962.4	735 617	15	374.9	2 004.0	635 042	15	316.9	64.5	29.0	0.3	2.8	0.1	1.3
12 35875	Jupiter town	51.8	39 328	887	759.2	34.0	26 753	1 192	786.9	94.9	1.2	0.2	1.1	0.1	1.4
12 36550	Key West	15.4	25 478	1 480	1 654.4	14.2	24 832	1 297	1 748.7	84.9	9.3	0.4	1.3	0.1	1.9
12 36950	Kissimmee	43.2	47 814	709	1 106.8	32.2	30 337	1 043	942.1	67.2	10.0	0.5	3.4	0.1	14.1
12 38250	Lakeland	118.7	78 452	350	660.9	99.4	70 576	338	710.0	73.5	21.3	0.3	1.3	0.1	1.8
12 39075	Lake Worth	14.6	35 133	1 019	2 406.4	14.5	28 564	1 114	1 969.9	65.1	18.9	0.8	0.7	0.1	9.6
12 39425	Largo	40.6	69 371	411	1 708.6	36.6	65 910	370	1 800.8	92.7	2.7	0.3	1.7	0.1	1.0
12 39525	Lauderdale Lakes	9.3	31 705	1 149	3 409.1	9.3	27 341	1 165	2 939.9	24.0	67.7	0.1	1.0	0.1	1.9
12 39550	Lauderhill	18.9	57 585	538	3 046.8	19.0	49 015	572	2 579.7	33.8	58.8	0.1	1.6	0.1	1.6
12 43125	Margate	22.8	53 909	614	2 364.4	22.9	42 985	669	1 877.1	78.8	11.6	0.3	2.8	0.1	2.9
12 43975	Melbourne	78.2	71 382	397	912.8	74.3	60 034	421	808.0	84.5	9.3	0.3	2.3	0.1	1.2
12 45000	Miami	92.4	362 470	49	3 922.8	92.1	358 648	46	3 894.1	66.6	22.3	0.2	0.7	0.0	5.4
12 45025	Miami Beach	18.2	87 933	296	4 831.5	18.2	92 639	226	5 090.1	86.7	4.0	0.2	1.4	0.0	4.0
12 45975	Miramar	76.4	72 739	387	952.1	76.9	40 663	723	528.8	43.6	43.3	0.2	3.0	0.1	4.7
12 49425	North Lauderdale	10.0	32 264	1 126	3 226.4	10.0	26 473	1 216	2 647.3	50.0	35.2	0.3	3.1	0.1	5.9
12 49450	North Miami	21.9	59 880	505	2 734.2	21.8	50 001	558	2 293.6	34.8	54.9	0.3	1.9	0.0	3.2
12 49475	North Miami Beach	12.8	40 786	849	3 186.4	12.9	35 361	849	2 741.2	46.7	39.0	0.3	4.0	0.1	4.6
12 50575	Oakland Park	16.3	30 966	1 180	1 899.8	16.5	26 326	1 226	1 595.5	66.0	22.6	0.2	1.9	0.1	4.5
12 50750	Ocala	100.1	45 943	744	459.0	74.7	42 045	693	562.9	72.9	22.1	0.4	1.2	0.0	1.8
12 53000	Orlando	242.2	185 951	109	767.8	174.2	164 674	106	945.3	61.1	26.9	0.3	2.7	0.1	5.4
12 53150	Ormond Beach	66.7	36 301	973	544.2	65.3	29 721	1 065	455.1	94.3	2.8	0.2	1.4	0.0	0.3
12 53575	Oviedo	39.2	26 316	1 423	671.3	34.7	11 114	2 857	320.3	83.5	8.8	0.3	2.4	0.0	2.6
12 54000	Palm Bay	164.8	79 413	345	481.9	164.8	62 543	397	379.5	81.5	11.3	0.4	1.7	0.0	2.4
12 54075	Palm Beach Gardens	144.2	35 058	1 025	243.1	68.1	24 139	1 349	354.5	93.8	2.3	0.1	2.2	0.0	0.7
12 54700	Panama City	53.1	36 417	964	685.8	40.1	34 396	878	857.8	73.6	21.5	0.6	1.5	0.1	0.8
12 55775	Pembroke Pines	85.6	137 427	163	1 605.5	82.7	65 566	376	792.8	75.6	13.3	0.2	3.8	0.0	3.7
12 55925	Pensacola	58.8	56 255	564	956.7	58.6	59 198	430	1 010.2	64.9	30.6	0.5	1.8	0.1	0.5
12 56975	Pinellas Park	38.2	45 658	751	1 195.2	35.9	43 571	659	1 213.7	89.0	2.1	0.4	4.3	0.0	2.0
12 57425	Plantation	56.3	82 934	325	1 473.1	56.3	66 814	362	1 186.7	78.3	13.8	0.2	2.9	0.0	2.0
12 57550	Plant City	58.6	29 915	1 226	510.5	54.8	22 754	1 443	415.2	71.7	16.2	0.4	0.9	0.0	9.1
12 58050	Pompano Beach	53.2	78 191	354	1 469.8	52.7	72 411	321	1 374.0	67.8	25.4	0.2	0.8	0.0	2.0
12 58575	Port Orange	64.0	45 823	746	716.0	52.1	35 399	848	679.4	95.6	1.6	0.3	1.1	0.0	0.5
12 58715	Port St. Lucie	195.6	88 769	289	453.8	196.6	55 761	463	283.6	87.9	7.1	0.2	1.2	0.0	1.8
12 60975	Riviera Beach	21.6	29 884	1 229	1 383.5	19.4	27 646	1 148	1 425.1	27.8	67.8	0.1	1.0	0.1	1.1
12 63000	St. Petersburg	154.4	248 232	70	1 607.7	153.3	240 318	65	1 567.6	71.4	22.4	0.3	2.7	0.1	1.1
12 63650	Sanford	49.5	38 291	919	773.6	44.8	32 387	957	722.9	59.7	32.1	0.5	1.1	0.1	4.3
12 64175	Sarasota	38.6	52 715	632	1 365.7	37.9	50 897	540	1 342.9	76.9	16.0	0.4	1.0	0.0	3.7
12 69700	Sunrise	47.1	85 779	308	1 821.2	47.2	65 683	373	1 391.6	69.5	20.5	0.2	3.1	0.1	3.5
12 70600	Tallahassee	247.9	150 624	140	607.6	163.9	124 773	149	761.3	60.4	34.2	0.2	2.4	0.1	1.0
12 70675	Tamarac	29.5	55 588	577	1 884.3	29.8	44 822	639	1 504.1	82.1	10.5	0.2	1.5	0.0	2.9
12 71000	Tampa	290.2	303 447	59	1 045.6	281.5	280 015	55	994.7	64.2	26.1	0.4	2.2	0.1	4.2
12 71900	Titusville	55.1	40 670	852	738.1	50.5	39 394	756	780.1	83.8	12.6	0.4	0.9	0.0	0.7
12 76582	Weston city	61.5	49 286	685	801.4	NA	NA	NA	NA	87.8	3.7	0.1	3.2	0.0	2.9
12 76600	West Palm Beach	142.8	82 103	328	575.0	127.8	67 764	355	530.2	58.1	32.2	0.3	1.5	0.2	4.3
12 78275	Winter Haven	45.8	26 487	1 410	578.3	31.6	24 725	1 305	782.4	71.5	23.2	0.2	1.0	0.0	1.9
12 78325	Winter Springs	37.2	31 666	1 151	851.2	35.1	22 151	1 481	631.1	88.7	4.6	0.2	1.9	0.0	2.5
13 00000	GEORGIA	149 976.2	8 186 453	X	54.6	150 009.5	6 478 149	X	43.2	65.1	28.7	0.3	2.1	0.1	2.4
13 01052	Albany	143.8	76 939	363	535.0	143.6	78 804	285	548.8	33.2	64.8	0.2	0.6	0.0	0.4
13 01696	Alpharetta	55.3	34 854	1 034	630.3	49.3	13 002	2 477	263.7	83.6	6.5	0.2	5.7	0.0	2.4

[1] Dry land or land partially or temporarily covered by water.

Table D. Cities

City	Two or more races	White	Black	American Indian or Alaska Native	Asian	Native Hawaiian and other Pacific Islander	Some other race	Hispanic[1]	White	Black or African American	American Indian or Alaska Native	Asian and Pacific Islander	Hispanic[1]
	15	16	17	18	19	20	21	22	23	24	25	26	27
FLORIDA—Cont'd													
Cape Coral	1.6	94.4	2.4	0.6	1.2	0.1	2.9	8.3	97.5	1.0	0.2	0.6	3.7
Clearwater	1.8	85.4	10.4	0.7	1.9	0.1	3.3	9.0	89.1	9.0	0.2	1.0	2.9
Coconut Creek	2.1	87.9	6.8	0.3	3.0	0.1	4.2	11.7	97.1	1.5	0.1	0.8	4.1
Cooper City	1.9	90.6	3.6	0.4	4.7	0.1	2.8	15.6	94.3	2.0	0.1	2.7	10.7
Coral Gables	1.5	93.2	3.6	0.3	2.0	0.1	2.4	46.6	93.0	3.4	0.1	1.7	41.8
Coral Springs	2.5	83.3	10.2	0.4	4.1	0.1	4.6	15.5	93.1	3.5	0.2	2.1	7.1
Davie	2.4	88.9	5.2	0.6	3.4	0.1	4.3	18.8	92.8	3.9	0.2	1.7	10.0
Daytona Beach	1.8	63.6	33.5	0.8	2.1	0.2	1.7	3.5	67.4	30.7	0.2	1.1	2.5
Deerfield Beach	2.8	78.9	17.2	0.4	1.7	0.1	4.6	8.7	81.6	16.7	0.1	0.8	3.9
Delray Beach	4.0	67.5	29.7	0.4	1.5	0.4	4.6	7.0	72.0	26.3	0.1	0.7	6.1
Dunedin	1.1	95.9	2.2	0.6	1.3	0.1	1.1	3.3	98.1	1.1	0.2	0.4	1.8
Fort Lauderdale	3.8	65.6	31.5	0.5	1.4	0.2	4.7	9.5	69.6	28.1	0.2	0.9	7.2
Fort Myers	3.1	57.8	35.2	0.7	1.3	0.2	7.9	14.5	64.2	32.2	0.2	0.8	7.7
Fort Pierce	3.0	50.9	42.8	0.7	1.0	0.2	7.6	15.0	53.7	42.4	0.3	0.5	6.4
Gainesville	2.2	70.1	24.0	0.7	5.2	0.1	2.2	6.4	73.4	21.4	0.2	3.9	4.4
Greenacres City	2.5	85.0	7.3	0.6	2.3	0.1	7.3	21.2	95.1	1.8	0.2	1.1	8.3
Hallandale	2.7	79.1	17.0	0.5	1.4	0.2	4.8	18.8	84.0	14.2	0.1	0.5	8.8
Hialeah	3.6	91.2	2.9	0.3	0.6	0.1	8.6	90.3	89.9	1.9	0.1	0.5	87.6
Hollywood	3.3	80.7	13.2	0.6	2.5	0.2	6.3	22.5	88.2	8.5	0.2	1.3	11.9
Homestead	5.3	64.1	25.0	0.8	1.1	0.3	14.2	51.8	66.4	23.0	0.3	0.9	35.3
Jacksonville	2.0	66.0	29.7	0.8	3.4	0.2	2.1	4.2	72.7	24.4	0.4	1.9	2.4
Jupiter town	1.1	95.8	1.4	0.4	1.5	0.2	1.9	7.3	97.8	1.0	0.1	0.9	2.9
Key West	2.2	86.7	10.0	0.8	1.7	0.1	3.0	16.5	86.1	10.4	0.3	1.4	16.5
Kissimmee	4.7	70.8	11.3	1.0	4.1	0.2	17.5	41.7	83.6	9.3	0.3	2.4	14.5
Lakeland	1.8	74.8	22.1	0.7	1.7	0.1	2.5	6.4	78.1	20.2	0.2	0.9	3.3
Lake Worth	4.8	67.4	21.3	1.4	1.1	0.3	13.4	29.7	80.5	14.9	0.3	0.9	15.7
Largo	1.5	94.0	3.1	0.7	2.0	0.1	1.6	4.2	97.6	1.0	0.2	0.8	1.9
Lauderdale Lakes	5.2	25.1	72.0	0.4	1.5	0.3	6.0	5.5	51.6	45.6	0.2	1.4	6.0
Lauderhill	4.0	35.0	61.9	0.4	2.1	0.3	4.5	6.9	58.6	38.5	0.1	1.5	6.8
Margate	3.6	81.0	13.1	0.6	3.5	0.2	5.4	15.3	93.1	3.7	0.2	1.5	7.7
Melbourne	2.2	86.4	10.1	0.9	3.0	0.2	1.9	5.5	87.4	9.5	0.3	2.1	3.5
Miami	4.7	69.5	24.2	0.5	0.9	0.2	9.5	65.8	65.6	27.4	0.2	0.6	62.5
Miami Beach	3.5	89.8	4.8	0.5	1.8	0.2	6.6	53.4	88.3	5.2	0.2	1.2	46.8
Miramar	5.1	46.2	46.2	0.4	3.9	0.3	8.3	29.4	79.3	15.7	0.2	2.3	17.3
North Lauderdale	5.5	52.7	38.3	0.6	3.9	0.3	9.9	21.1	80.1	14.5	0.2	2.9	12.1
North Miami	4.9	36.7	58.1	0.7	2.6	0.4	6.6	23.2	62.4	31.9	0.2	2.4	24.6
North Miami Beach	5.3	49.3	41.8	0.6	4.9	0.3	8.6	30.0	71.6	21.8	0.2	3.4	22.1
Oakland Park	4.6	68.4	25.1	0.6	2.5	0.3	7.9	17.9	83.2	12.9	0.2	1.7	11.9
Ocala	1.6	74.2	22.7	0.9	1.4	0.1	2.5	5.7	74.9	23.8	0.3	0.6	2.2
Orlando	3.5	63.4	28.3	0.7	3.3	0.3	7.7	17.5	68.8	26.9	0.3	1.6	8.7
Ormond Beach	1.0	95.2	2.9	0.5	1.7	0.0	0.7	2.2	95.1	3.5	0.1	1.0	1.7
Oviedo	2.3	85.3	9.5	0.7	3.1	0.2	3.6	12.2	84.2	12.2	0.2	1.6	6.9
Palm Bay	2.7	83.6	12.2	0.8	2.3	0.2	3.7	8.6	89.3	7.5	0.3	1.8	5.3
Palm Beach Gardens	1.0	94.6	2.6	0.3	2.4	0.1	1.1	5.6	97.2	0.8	0.1	1.5	3.5
Panama City	1.9	75.2	22.0	1.4	2.1	0.2	1.1	2.9	75.5	21.8	0.6	1.7	1.3
Pembroke Pines	3.5	78.0	14.6	0.4	4.7	0.2	5.9	28.2	91.3	5.3	0.2	2.0	11.5
Pensacola	1.6	66.1	31.2	1.1	2.2	0.1	0.9	2.1	65.7	31.9	0.5	1.6	1.6
Pinellas Park	2.2	91.1	2.5	1.1	4.7	0.1	2.9	6.3	96.1	1.0	0.3	1.9	3.3
Plantation	2.8	80.0	15.1	0.4	3.6	0.2	3.8	13.1	90.7	6.2	0.1	1.8	8.1
Plant City	1.8	73.0	16.6	0.7	1.2	0.1	10.2	17.4	75.6	21.3	0.2	0.6	8.3
Pompano Beach	3.7	69.3	27.7	0.5	1.2	0.2	4.9	9.9	70.0	28.5	0.1	0.6	5.4
Port Orange	0.9	96.4	1.7	0.6	1.4	0.1	0.8	2.5	97.7	1.0	0.3	0.8	2.0
Port St. Lucie	1.8	89.2	7.7	0.6	1.6	0.1	2.6	7.5	94.2	3.8	0.2	0.9	4.0
Riviera Beach	2.1	28.5	69.4	0.5	1.2	0.2	2.5	4.5	28.7	69.7	0.2	0.8	2.6
St. Petersburg	2.2	73.0	23.2	0.9	3.2	0.1	2.0	4.2	78.0	19.6	0.2	1.7	2.6
Sanford	2.3	61.5	33.1	1.0	1.4	0.1	5.2	10.4	68.8	28.5	0.4	0.9	4.9
Sarasota	1.9	78.4	16.8	0.9	1.3	0.1	4.5	11.9	82.0	16.2	0.2	0.7	4.7
Sunrise	3.3	71.5	21.9	0.4	3.8	0.3	5.6	17.1	89.3	7.4	0.1	1.9	8.6
Tallahassee	1.7	61.7	34.9	0.7	2.9	0.1	1.6	4.2	68.2	29.1	0.2	1.8	5.4
Tamarac	2.8	84.0	11.6	0.4	1.9	0.2	4.9	14.9	96.0	2.3	0.1	0.9	5.4
Tampa	2.9	66.3	27.2	0.9	2.7	0.2	5.8	19.3	70.9	25.0	0.3	1.4	15.0
Titusville	1.5	85.0	13.2	0.9	1.3	0.1	1.1	3.5	87.3	11.0	0.4	0.8	2.8
Weston city	2.2	89.7	4.2	0.2	3.7	0.1	4.5	30.2	0.0	0.0	0.0	0.0	0.0
West Palm Beach	3.4	59.7	34.0	0.8	1.8	0.3	6.9	18.2	63.4	32.6	0.1	0.9	14.2
Winter Haven	2.2	72.5	24.5	0.5	1.3	0.1	3.3	4.9	76.0	22.6	0.2	0.6	2.5
Winter Springs	2.0	90.5	5.2	0.6	2.3	0.1	3.5	10.5	94.2	3.0	0.2	1.5	5.8
GEORGIA	1.4	66.1	29.2	0.6	2.4	0.1	2.9	5.3	71.0	27.0	0.2	1.2	1.7
Albany	0.7	33.7	65.2	0.5	0.8	0.1	0.6	1.2	44.2	55.0	0.2	0.4	0.8
Alpharetta	1.5	84.9	6.8	0.5	6.2	0.1	3.1	5.5	95.2	2.6	0.2	1.4	1.8

[1] Hispanic persons may be of any race.

Table D. Cities

City	Under 5 years	5 to 17 years	18 to 24 years	25 to 34 years	35 to 44 years	45 to 54 years	55 to 64 years	65 to 74 years	75 years and over	Median age (years)	Percent Female
	28	29	30	31	32	33	34	35	36	37	38
FLORIDA—Cont'd											
Cape Coral	5.5	17.1	5.8	11.2	15.6	13.9	11.4	10.5	9.1	41.6	51.5
Clearwater	5.2	14.0	8.0	12.8	14.8	13.7	10.1	9.7	11.8	41.8	52.1
Coconut Creek	6.2	11.8	5.6	16.0	15.3	10.5	8.1	9.5	17.0	41.3	53.5
Cooper City	6.1	25.3	6.3	9.4	20.8	18.1	7.5	4.1	2.6	36.7	51.5
Coral Gables	4.9	12.5	13.9	13.7	15.3	13.9	10.0	7.5	8.3	38.1	53.3
Coral Springs	6.9	23.8	7.9	13.2	19.1	16.4	6.7	3.1	2.9	33.8	51.3
Davie	6.7	19.7	8.2	14.5	18.9	14.5	8.2	5.4	4.0	35.5	51.3
Daytona Beach	5.0	12.6	16.6	13.1	12.5	11.5	9.0	9.4	10.4	37.2	50.1
Deerfield Beach	4.8	10.8	6.5	14.2	14.2	11.0	9.2	10.8	18.5	44.6	53.4
Delray Beach	5.0	13.2	6.3	12.4	14.7	12.6	9.8	10.8	15.1	43.8	52.3
Dunedin	3.8	11.8	5.4	10.3	14.2	13.6	11.0	12.9	17.0	48.2	54.2
Fort Lauderdale	5.3	14.1	7.7	15.1	17.7	14.9	9.9	7.8	7.5	39.3	47.6
Fort Myers	8.1	18.2	11.4	15.8	14.5	10.8	6.8	6.2	8.1	32.4	50.6
Fort Pierce	7.6	19.6	9.8	12.5	13.5	11.0	8.5	8.7	8.8	35.4	50.7
Gainesville	4.6	13.2	29.4	15.0	11.6	10.5	5.9	4.8	5.0	26.4	51.1
Greenacres City	6.1	14.8	7.6	14.7	13.8	10.7	8.7	11.9	11.7	39.6	53.2
Hallandale	4.0	9.2	5.3	11.0	11.9	11.1	11.7	14.7	21.1	52.7	53.9
Hialeah	5.8	17.2	8.2	14.2	15.1	12.0	10.9	9.5	7.1	37.7	51.9
Hollywood	5.9	15.4	7.0	14.4	16.9	13.7	9.4	8.0	9.4	39.2	51.5
Homestead	10.6	22.5	12.8	17.3	13.8	9.3	5.7	4.2	3.7	27.2	48.3
Jacksonville	7.3	19.4	9.7	15.5	16.8	13.1	7.8	5.5	4.8	33.8	51.6
Jupiter town	5.2	15.5	5.1	11.4	17.5	14.8	11.6	11.1	7.8	42.4	50.7
Key West	4.7	11.3	8.4	18.0	19.2	16.9	9.9	6.3	5.5	38.9	45.0
Kissimmee	7.8	19.2	12.0	18.7	16.2	11.5	6.9	4.5	3.1	30.6	50.5
Lakeland	6.2	15.2	10.3	12.5	12.2	11.2	9.4	10.6	12.4	39.7	53.5
Lake Worth	7.1	15.8	10.6	16.2	16.5	12.0	7.6	6.3	7.9	35.2	47.9
Largo	4.2	11.4	6.1	11.4	13.7	11.9	11.1	13.4	16.7	47.5	53.5
Lauderdale Lakes	7.6	20.1	8.7	12.7	14.2	10.8	8.1	7.1	10.7	35.7	55.2
Lauderhill	7.5	19.1	8.7	14.8	15.5	11.5	6.8	6.2	9.9	34.9	54.2
Margate	6.0	14.9	6.5	13.6	15.6	12.2	9.5	7.9	13.8	40.4	52.8
Melbourne	5.4	15.3	9.3	12.6	15.8	12.4	9.6	9.7	10.0	39.8	51.5
Miami	5.9	15.9	8.8	15.0	15.4	12.2	9.9	8.9	8.1	37.7	50.3
Miami Beach	3.9	9.5	7.8	20.9	17.3	12.4	8.9	8.8	10.5	39.0	48.8
Miramar	8.7	22.3	8.6	16.4	19.0	12.1	6.6	3.8	2.5	31.8	52.4
North Lauderdale	8.0	21.8	10.7	17.5	17.7	11.7	5.6	3.2	3.7	30.5	51.6
North Miami	8.1	20.0	11.3	15.8	16.0	12.5	7.1	4.8	4.4	31.8	51.9
North Miami Beach	7.1	20.2	9.4	14.2	16.8	13.3	7.7	5.5	5.8	34.5	52.2
Oakland Park	6.7	14.1	9.0	18.6	20.2	13.7	7.6	5.4	4.7	35.8	47.8
Ocala	5.9	17.3	9.3	12.1	14.1	11.7	9.2	9.0	11.4	39.0	52.7
Orlando	6.6	15.4	10.7	21.1	16.2	11.6	7.0	5.7	5.7	32.9	51.6
Ormond Beach	4.2	15.0	4.5	8.5	13.9	14.8	11.7	13.3	14.2	47.5	53.3
Oviedo	8.4	23.6	7.1	15.1	21.5	12.8	5.8	3.6	2.2	32.8	50.5
Palm Bay	6.1	20.4	7.6	12.1	17.5	12.6	8.9	8.7	6.0	37.2	51.2
Palm Beach Gardens	4.5	14.2	5.1	10.6	15.6	15.4	13.4	11.4	9.7	45.0	52.6
Panama City	6.1	16.9	9.6	13.8	16.0	13.0	8.7	7.8	8.1	37.2	51.4
Pembroke Pines	7.1	18.5	6.4	14.9	18.6	12.2	7.1	7.0	8.2	36.5	53.4
Pensacola	5.7	17.2	8.9	12.1	14.8	14.5	9.6	8.9	8.3	39.4	53.0
Pinellas Park	5.5	15.8	6.7	13.3	15.9	12.3	9.8	9.5	11.0	40.2	52.3
Plantation	6.0	17.1	7.1	14.7	17.3	15.2	9.5	6.2	6.9	37.9	52.5
Plant City	8.3	21.1	8.9	14.2	14.9	12.0	8.2	6.6	5.7	33.3	51.8
Pompano Beach	5.3	12.5	7.4	13.5	15.6	12.5	10.0	9.9	13.5	42.2	50.7
Port Orange	4.5	15.3	5.9	10.3	14.6	14.2	11.5	12.4	11.2	44.6	52.4
Port St. Lucie	5.8	18.5	5.9	11.4	16.7	13.0	9.8	10.5	8.3	39.9	51.4
Riviera Beach	7.1	22.1	8.0	12.0	13.8	11.8	10.3	8.3	6.7	35.6	52.3
St. Petersburg	5.7	15.8	7.7	13.8	16.5	13.9	9.2	8.1	9.3	39.3	52.3
Sanford	7.5	19.3	10.7	16.6	15.9	12.2	7.2	5.5	5.0	32.5	50.3
Sarasota	5.3	13.1	9.2	13.4	14.6	12.8	9.6	9.6	12.4	41.1	51.4
Sunrise	6.4	18.5	7.3	14.7	16.9	11.9	6.5	6.5	11.2	36.6	53.2
Tallahassee	5.2	12.2	29.7	15.9	11.9	10.9	5.9	4.1	4.1	26.3	52.8
Tamarac	4.4	9.0	5.3	12.1	11.3	10.1	10.0	14.4	23.4	52.9	55.3
Tampa	6.8	17.9	10.0	15.8	16.5	12.7	7.9	6.4	6.1	34.7	51.2
Titusville	5.7	17.3	6.9	10.9	15.3	12.4	10.8	11.2	9.6	41.0	52.4
Weston city	9.0	23.4	5.0	14.5	21.7	13.3	6.4	4.2	2.5	34.1	51.5
West Palm Beach	6.1	15.3	9.8	16.0	15.5	12.6	8.8	7.6	8.4	36.7	50.7
Winter Haven	5.7	15.2	6.8	11.0	12.5	11.5	9.8	11.8	15.6	44.0	54.0
Winter Springs	6.0	21.0	7.3	11.5	17.9	16.4	9.0	6.3	4.5	37.4	51.5
GEORGIA	7.3	19.2	10.2	15.9	16.5	13.2	8.1	5.3	4.3	33.4	50.8
Albany	7.8	20.0	13.0	14.2	13.5	12.0	7.6	6.3	5.6	31.1	54.0
Alpharetta	8.5	18.6	7.2	19.2	21.3	13.1	6.3	3.4	2.4	33.3	50.4

Table D. Cities

City	Under 5 years	5 to 17 years	18 to 24 years	25 to 34 years	35 to 44 years	45 to 54 years	55 to 64 years	65 to 74 years	75 years and over	Percent Female	2000	1990	1980	1990–2000	1980–1990
	39	40	41	42	43	44	45	46	47	48	49	50	51	52	53
FLORIDA—Cont'd															
Cape Coral	6.2	15.3	6.8	14.7	13.6	9.7	11.7	14.1	8.0	51.8	102 286	74 991	32 103	36.4	133.6
Clearwater	4.8	12.9	7.9	14.6	13.1	10.5	10.7	12.9	12.6	53.9	108 787	98 669	85 528	10.3	15.4
Coconut Creek	4.9	7.2	6.1	16.7	11.0	7.3	10.4	21.9	14.4	54.4	43 566	27 269	NA	59.8	NA
Cooper City	8.0	21.4	7.3	15.8	22.0	11.8	6.7	4.4	2.6	51.1	27 939	21 335	10 140	31.0	110.4
Coral Gables	4.6	10.8	15.8	15.8	14.3	12.1	9.3	9.6	7.7	52.6	42 249	40 091	43 241	5.4	-7.3
Coral Springs	7.1	23.6	9.5	15.4	20.9	11.9	4.7	3.9	3.0	51.2	117 549	78 864	37 349	49.1	111.2
Davie	7.7	17.1	10.0	20.3	17.6	11.1	7.2	6.1	2.8	51.1	75 720	47 143	20 877	60.6	125.8
Daytona Beach	5.2	11.6	17.1	15.7	11.5	8.1	9.4	11.1	10.3	50.7	64 112	61 991	54 176	3.4	14.4
Deerfield Beach	4.8	8.7	6.5	15.8	11.3	7.7	8.9	15.6	20.7	54.6	64 583	46 997	39 193	37.4	19.9
Delray Beach	5.4	10.2	6.3	15.1	12.0	8.9	10.3	16.5	15.2	53.0	60 020	47 184	34 325	27.2	37.5
Dunedin	4.0	10.8	6.9	12.5	12.1	9.5	11.0	15.5	17.7	55.0	35 691	34 427	30 203	3.7	14.0
Fort Lauderdale	6.0	12.8	8.1	19.1	15.6	10.8	9.6	9.3	8.7	49.6	152 397	149 238	153 279	2.1	-2.6
Fort Myers	8.6	16.9	11.0	18.2	12.8	8.6	7.9	8.0	8.1	51.3	48 208	44 947	36 638	7.3	22.7
Fort Pierce	8.5	17.9	8.7	14.6	11.5	9.0	9.7	12.3	7.7	52.1	37 516	36 830	33 802	1.9	9.0
Gainesville	5.8	13.5	27.1	17.7	13.6	7.1	5.8	5.3	4.0	50.8	95 447	85 075	81 371	12.2	4.6
Greenacres City	6.0	12.5	8.4	18.6	13.0	8.0	10.3	16.1	7.1	52.6	27 569	18 683	NA	47.6	NA
Hallandale	3.5	6.4	4.7	10.6	7.6	7.2	11.9	19.7	28.5	56.0	34 282	30 997	36 511	10.6	-15.1
Hialeah	6.5	16.8	9.8	15.6	12.5	12.7	12.3	8.1	5.8	52.2	226 419	188 008	145 254	20.4	29.4
Hollywood	5.6	13.4	7.6	15.9	13.6	10.7	10.3	10.7	12.2	52.6	139 357	121 720	121 323	14.5	0.3
Homestead	10.8	20.1	11.9	19.4	12.5	8.7	6.0	4.5	4.4	49.2	31 909	26 694	20 668	19.5	29.2
Jacksonville	8.0	17.9	11.1	19.6	15.1	9.8	7.8	6.5	4.2	51.2	735 617	672 971	NA	9.3	NA
Jupiter town	6.0	13.6	6.7	18.4	17.6	9.3	11.1	11.2	6.0	51.2	39 328	24 907	NA	57.9	NA
Key West	7.3	12.2	10.3	22.8	18.2	9.9	7.7	6.7	4.9	46.6	25 478	24 832	24 382	2.6	1.8
Kissimmee	8.0	17.2	13.0	20.8	15.0	9.9	7.3	5.0	3.9	51.0	47 814	30 337	15 487	57.6	95.9
Lakeland	6.3	15.0	10.4	14.4	12.1	9.3	9.9	12.1	10.6	53.8	78 452	70 576	47 406	11.2	48.9
Lake Worth	6.8	12.8	8.7	17.8	13.2	8.3	8.1	10.2	14.0	50.7	35 133	28 564	27 048	23.0	5.6
Largo	4.4	9.5	7.5	15.4	11.2	8.8	10.8	16.4	16.1	54.1	69 371	65 910	58 977	5.3	11.8
Lauderdale Lakes	6.7	14.2	7.6	15.8	11.9	7.7	5.8	10.9	19.4	55.5	31 705	27 341	25 426	16.0	7.5
Lauderhill	7.3	15.0	8.5	18.8	13.8	8.2	7.1	10.7	10.6	53.7	57 585	49 015	37 271	17.5	31.5
Margate	5.2	11.9	7.6	14.9	12.7	9.1	8.4	14.8	15.4	52.8	53 909	42 985	36 044	25.4	19.3
Melbourne	6.1	14.3	11.6	18.7	13.1	9.5	9.8	10.0	6.9	51.1	71 382	60 034	46 497	18.9	29.1
Miami	7.1	15.9	9.1	16.3	13.3	10.8	10.8	9.3	7.5	51.7	362 470	358 648	346 865	1.1	3.4
Miami Beach	4.6	9.6	7.5	16.1	12.6	9.4	10.0	11.8	18.5	53.4	87 933	92 639	96 298	-5.1	-3.8
Miramar	8.0	18.3	8.8	20.6	16.2	10.6	8.1	5.7	3.7	51.8	72 739	40 663	32 813	78.9	23.9
North Lauderdale	8.7	19.5	10.8	24.0	17.8	8.0	4.7	4.0	2.4	50.3	32 264	26 473	NA	21.9	NA
North Miami	7.2	15.5	9.9	19.9	15.4	9.0	8.1	7.7	7.3	52.7	59 880	50 001	42 566	19.8	17.5
North Miami Beach	6.3	15.6	7.3	17.1	15.5	10.3	8.6	9.1	10.2	53.5	40 786	35 361	36 553	15.3	-3.3
Oakland Park	6.8	10.9	10.0	25.2	16.3	9.3	8.6	7.2	5.8	49.8	30 966	26 326	23 035	17.6	14.3
Ocala	6.9	16.6	9.0	14.2	12.0	10.6	9.9	11.5	9.3	53.7	45 943	42 045	37 161	9.3	13.1
Orlando	6.8	14.2	16.1	22.7	13.7	8.2	7.0	6.4	4.9	49.7	185 951	164 674	128 291	12.9	28.4
Ormond Beach	4.6	13.6	6.6	12.1	13.5	11.5	13.0	14.8	10.3	52.6	36 301	29 721	21 378	22.1	39.0
Oviedo	11.1	20.3	8.5	24.4	17.9	7.4	5.7	3.2	1.6	50.2	26 316	11 114	NA	136.8	NA
Palm Bay	8.6	18.4	8.7	21.8	14.7	8.2	8.3	7.9	3.5	50.2	79 413	62 543	18 560	27.0	237.0
Palm Beach Gardens	5.6	15.3	6.8	15.8	17.3	13.3	10.9	9.1	6.0	51.4	35 058	24 139	14 407	45.2	67.6
Panama City	6.8	17.6	9.3	16.5	13.3	10.2	9.4	9.5	7.4	53.2	36 417	34 396	33 346	5.9	3.1
Pembroke Pines	6.2	14.1	7.7	18.4	15.5	9.8	9.0	11.6	7.9	53.2	137 427	65 566	35 776	109.6	83.3
Pensacola	6.5	17.3	9.5	15.3	14.7	10.1	9.9	9.9	6.7	53.6	56 255	59 198	57 619	-5.0	2.7
Pinellas Park	6.5	13.9	8.6	17.0	12.7	9.6	8.5	12.3	10.8	53.0	45 658	43 571	32 811	4.8	32.8
Plantation	5.5	15.5	8.9	16.5	16.8	13.4	9.1	7.6	6.7	52.1	82 934	66 814	48 501	24.1	37.8
Plant City	8.9	20.6	8.2	16.6	13.0	10.0	9.0	7.7	6.1	53.0	29 915	22 754	19 270	31.5	18.1
Pompano Beach	5.9	11.2	7.4	17.3	13.0	9.3	10.6	12.9	12.4	51.9	78 191	72 411	52 618	8.0	37.6
Port Orange	5.2	14.2	7.0	15.3	15.1	9.3	11.4	14.7	7.8	51.8	45 823	35 399	18 756	29.4	88.7
Port St. Lucie	7.5	17.3	6.4	18.3	14.5	8.5	10.4	12.2	4.8	50.6	88 769	55 761	14 690	59.2	279.6
Riviera Beach	8.9	19.4	8.8	15.5	11.9	10.7	9.2	9.3	6.2	52.7	29 884	27 646	26 473	8.1	4.4
St. Petersburg	5.9	13.8	8.3	16.4	14.0	9.7	9.6	10.9	11.3	53.6	248 232	240 318	238 647	3.3	0.7
Sanford	8.6	18.0	10.9	19.7	14.7	7.5	7.6	7.6	5.5	51.2	38 291	32 387	23 176	18.2	39.7
Sarasota	5.9	12.3	9.1	15.9	12.6	9.6	9.5	12.1	13.1	53.0	52 715	50 897	48 876	3.6	4.1
Sunrise	6.9	14.8	7.4	17.9	15.1	8.2	6.6	11.9	11.1	53.0	85 779	65 683	39 681	30.6	65.5
Tallahassee	5.5	13.8	26.4	18.1	13.8	7.9	5.7	5.2	3.5	52.4	150 624	124 773	81 548	20.7	53.0
Tamarac	3.0	5.7	5.3	11.9	8.3	6.8	11.4	25.0	22.6	54.6	55 588	44 822	29 376	24.0	52.6
Tampa	7.4	15.5	10.8	19.0	14.0	9.9	8.8	8.3	6.3	52.0	303 447	280 015	271 523	8.4	3.1
Titusville	7.0	16.1	8.1	18.1	12.7	10.8	11.4	9.8	6.0	51.6	40 670	39 394	31 910	3.2	23.5
Weston city	NA	NA	NA	NA	NA	NA	NA	NA	NA	NA	49 286	9 829	NA	401.4	NA
West Palm Beach	6.8	13.5	9.5	19.6	14.1	9.5	8.8	9.4	8.9	52.2	82 103	67 764	63 305	21.2	7.0
Winter Haven	5.7	13.8	7.5	13.2	11.2	9.2	11.4	14.8	13.2	54.6	26 487	24 725	21 169	7.1	16.8
Winter Springs	6.9	19.9	9.1	16.6	20.1	10.7	7.8	6.4	2.6	50.6	31 666	22 151	10 475	43.0	111.5
GEORGIA	7.6	19.0	11.4	18.1	15.7	10.3	7.7	6.0	4.1	51.5	8 186 453	6 478 149	5 462 982	26.4	18.6
Albany	8.6	22.3	12.0	15.5	13.9	9.0	7.8	6.5	4.2	53.6	76 939	78 804	74 059	-2.4	6.4
Alpharetta	8.7	15.2	9.4	24.6	18.9	10.9	5.8	4.3	2.4	51.6	34 854	13 002	NA	168.1	NA

City	Total population	Total in house-holds	House-holder	Spouse	Child Total	Child Own child under 18 years	Other relatives Total	Other relatives Under 18 years	Nonrelatives Total	Nonrelatives Unmarried partner	Total in group quarters	Correctional institutions	Nursing homes	Other institutions	College dormitories	Military quarters	Other
	54	55	56	57	58	59	60	61	62	63	64	65	66	67	68	69	70
FLORIDA—Cont'd																	
Cape Coral	102 286	99.4	39.9	24.4	26.0	20.8	4.2	1.3	5.0	2.4	0.6	0.0	0.5	0.0	0.0	0.0	0.0
Clearwater	108 787	96.4	44.5	18.6	21.7	16.8	4.9	1.6	6.8	2.8	3.6	0.0	1.3	0.0	0.4	0.0	1.8
Coconut Creek	43 566	99.5	46.1	22.8	20.8	16.7	4.1	0.9	5.7	2.7	0.5	0.0	0.3	0.0	0.0	0.0	0.2
Cooper City	27 939	100.0	32.7	23.1	37.6	30.1	3.9	1.0	2.8	1.2	0.0	0.0	0.0	0.0	0.0	0.0	0.0
Coral Gables	42 249	91.7	39.7	19.6	22.7	16.6	4.4	0.6	5.2	1.6	8.3	0.0	0.1	0.1	8.0	0.0	0.1
Coral Springs	117 549	99.5	33.6	20.6	36.0	29.0	4.7	1.3	4.6	2.0	0.5	0.0	0.3	0.0	0.0	0.0	0.2
Davie	75 720	99.9	37.9	19.6	30.7	24.4	5.4	1.5	6.4	2.6	0.1	0.0	0.0	0.0	0.0	0.0	0.1
Daytona Beach	64 112	92.0	44.6	13.4	19.4	14.3	5.5	2.4	9.1	3.3	8.0	0.0	2.1	0.3	5.0	0.0	0.7
Deerfield Beach	64 583	98.2	48.6	18.6	18.5	13.4	5.7	1.9	6.8	2.7	1.8	0.5	0.5	0.0	0.0	0.0	0.8
Delray Beach	60 020	99.1	44.6	18.9	21.2	15.3	6.8	2.4	7.5	2.5	0.9	0.0	0.4	0.1	0.0	0.0	0.4
Dunedin	35 691	97.4	48.4	21.2	19.4	14.4	3.1	0.8	5.3	2.6	2.6	0.0	0.6	0.0	0.1	0.0	2.0
Fort Lauderdale	152 397	96.4	44.9	14.5	21.7	16.2	6.5	2.5	8.7	3.6	3.6	2.0	0.4	0.2	0.2	0.0	0.9
Fort Myers	48 208	95.2	39.6	12.8	27.2	22.2	6.8	3.1	8.8	3.3	4.8	2.5	1.6	0.5	0.0	0.0	0.2
Fort Pierce	37 516	98.1	43.8	13.8	28.8	22.6	8.9	3.7	8.2	2.7	1.9	0.0	0.0	0.0	0.3	0.0	1.5
Gainesville	95 447	87.9	39.1	12.7	19.8	15.6	4.1	1.5	12.4	2.2	12.1	1.5	0.4	0.2	8.9	0.0	1.1
Greenacres City	27 569	100.0	43.7	20.1	23.4	18.6	6.0	1.8	6.8	3.0	0.0	0.0	0.0	0.0	0.0	0.0	0.0
Hallandale	34 282	98.9	52.7	18.9	16.3	11.2	5.5	1.7	5.6	2.7	1.1	0.0	0.4	0.0	0.0	0.0	0.7
Hialeah	226 419	98.4	31.2	17.9	29.1	18.9	13.6	3.5	6.6	1.7	1.6	0.0	0.7	0.3	0.0	0.0	0.6
Hollywood	139 357	98.7	42.8	17.8	25.3	18.7	6.4	2.0	6.5	2.9	1.3	0.0	0.6	0.0	0.0	0.0	0.6
Homestead	31 909	98.2	31.6	12.7	34.3	28.4	10.0	3.6	9.6	2.9	1.8	0.0	1.3	0.1	0.0	0.0	0.4
Jacksonville	735 617	97.9	38.7	18.0	29.8	23.5	5.7	2.6	5.6	2.3	2.1	0.4	0.5	0.0	0.3	0.5	0.3
Jupiter town	39 328	99.8	43.1	24.0	23.7	19.5	3.1	0.8	5.9	2.3	0.2	0.0	0.2	0.0	0.0	0.0	0.1
Key West	25 478	96.5	43.2	16.3	18.5	14.3	4.7	1.3	13.7	4.3	3.5	1.7	0.4	0.0	0.0	0.4	1.0
Kissimmee	47 814	99.0	35.8	16.9	30.0	23.8	7.6	2.6	8.6	3.2	1.0	0.2	0.4	0.1	0.0	0.0	0.3
Lakeland	78 452	95.3	42.7	18.6	23.4	18.3	5.3	2.4	5.3	2.3	4.7	0.1	1.4	0.1	1.9	0.0	1.2
Lake Worth	35 133	97.8	39.4	14.5	25.1	19.5	8.3	2.3	10.6	3.4	2.2	0.0	1.8	0.0	0.0	0.0	0.3
Largo	69 371	97.4	49.1	20.5	18.1	14.0	3.5	1.0	6.2	3.1	2.6	0.0	1.0	0.3	0.0	0.0	1.2
Lauderdale Lakes	31 705	98.9	38.2	14.0	31.3	23.4	9.6	3.7	5.9	2.5	1.1	0.0	1.1	0.0	0.0	0.0	0.0
Lauderhill	57 585	98.5	39.6	14.8	29.5	22.8	8.2	3.0	6.3	2.7	1.5	0.0	0.2	0.2	0.0	0.0	1.1
Margate	53 909	99.4	42.1	20.7	25.5	18.9	5.7	1.5	5.3	2.3	0.6	0.0	0.5	0.0	0.0	0.0	0.2
Melbourne	71 382	95.7	43.1	19.0	23.4	18.0	4.1	1.6	6.1	2.6	4.3	0.0	1.0	1.1	1.5	0.0	0.7
Miami	362 470	96.8	37.0	13.6	26.3	17.5	11.9	3.6	8.0	2.4	3.2	1.6	0.4	0.3	0.0	0.0	0.9
Miami Beach	87 933	98.5	52.5	14.4	16.8	12.1	5.5	1.0	9.2	3.4	1.5	0.0	0.8	0.1	0.1	0.1	0.5
Miramar	72 739	100.0	31.7	17.8	35.8	27.4	9.9	3.2	4.7	2.0	0.0	0.0	0.0	0.0	0.0	0.0	0.0
North Lauderdale	32 264	100.0	33.5	15.7	34.4	26.4	8.8	2.8	7.7	2.6	0.0	0.0	0.0	0.0	0.0	0.0	0.0
North Miami	59 880	97.9	34.3	13.4	32.8	24.2	10.8	3.3	6.6	2.6	2.1	0.0	0.8	0.1	0.8	0.0	0.4
North Miami Beach	40 786	99.0	34.3	15.2	32.8	23.5	10.6	3.2	6.1	2.2	1.0	0.0	0.9	0.0	0.0	0.0	0.1
Oakland Park	30 966	98.6	43.6	14.1	23.7	18.3	6.9	1.9	10.3	4.1	1.4	0.0	0.0	0.0	0.0	0.0	1.4
Ocala	45 943	92.9	40.6	16.6	25.4	20.0	5.0	2.3	5.3	2.4	7.1	2.9	2.3	0.3	0.4	0.0	1.2
Orlando	185 951	97.8	43.5	14.1	24.1	18.8	6.7	2.7	9.4	3.6	2.2	0.1	0.6	0.7	0.1	0.0	0.8
Ormond Beach	36 301	97.9	43.1	24.0	23.1	17.9	3.5	1.0	4.2	1.9	2.1	0.0	1.3	0.3	0.0	0.0	0.5
Oviedo	26 316	99.7	32.5	23.0	35.7	30.0	4.3	1.5	4.1	1.5	0.3	0.0	0.2	0.0	0.0	0.0	0.1
Palm Bay	79 413	99.5	38.2	21.0	29.8	23.8	4.9	2.0	5.6	2.5	0.5	0.0	0.3	0.0	0.0	0.0	0.2
Palm Beach Gardens	35 058	99.1	44.5	23.9	22.6	17.6	3.2	0.8	4.9	2.2	0.9	0.0	0.4	0.0	0.0	0.0	0.5
Panama City	36 417	93.5	40.7	17.0	25.8	20.0	4.8	2.1	5.3	2.2	6.5	4.1	1.4	0.2	0.0	0.0	0.7
Pembroke Pines	137 427	99.1	37.8	21.3	30.1	23.8	5.8	1.4	4.0	1.8	0.9	0.5	0.1	0.3	0.0	0.0	0.0
Pensacola	56 255	99.1	43.6	17.3	26.6	19.5	6.0	2.9	5.5	2.1	0.9	0.1	0.5	0.0	0.0	0.0	0.3
Pinellas Park	45 658	98.2	42.6	19.8	24.4	18.9	4.9	1.7	6.6	3.1	1.8	0.0	0.7	0.4	0.0	0.0	0.7
Plantation	82 934	99.4	40.1	20.9	27.9	21.3	5.2	1.4	5.3	2.4	0.6	0.0	0.5	0.0	0.0	0.0	0.1
Plant City	29 915	98.9	36.3	19.1	31.9	25.5	6.6	3.1	5.0	2.1	1.1	0.0	0.9	0.0	0.1	0.0	0.2
Pompano Beach	78 191	95.9	45.0	16.8	19.7	14.2	7.0	3.0	7.3	3.1	4.1	2.8	0.6	0.0	0.0	0.0	0.8
Port Orange	45 823	98.9	42.7	23.4	23.8	18.0	3.8	1.3	5.3	2.4	1.1	0.0	0.9	0.0	0.0	0.0	0.2
Port St. Lucie	88 769	99.4	38.2	23.6	27.7	22.0	4.8	1.7	5.0	2.3	0.6	0.0	0.4	0.0	0.0	0.0	0.3
Riviera Beach	29 884	99.0	38.1	14.1	31.6	23.6	9.4	5.0	5.7	2.5	1.0	0.0	0.4	0.1	0.0	0.0	0.6
St. Petersburg	248 232	97.4	44.2	16.9	24.2	18.4	5.6	2.4	6.5	3.1	2.6	0.1	1.1	0.1	0.4	0.0	0.8
Sanford	38 291	95.6	37.2	14.7	28.9	22.2	7.6	3.5	7.3	3.0	4.4	3.2	0.1	0.1	0.0	0.0	1.0
Sarasota	52 715	94.1	44.4	15.7	20.1	15.7	5.6	2.1	8.2	3.1	5.9	1.4	2.1	0.0	1.3	0.0	1.0
Sunrise	85 779	98.8	38.8	18.9	29.5	22.7	6.5	1.8	5.1	2.3	1.2	0.0	0.8	0.1	0.0	0.0	0.3
Tallahassee	150 624	91.3	42.0	12.6	19.6	15.4	4.1	1.5	13.0	2.3	8.7	1.7	0.6	0.2	5.8	0.0	0.5
Tamarac	55 588	98.9	49.3	22.1	17.1	12.1	4.9	1.1	5.4	2.6	1.1	0.0	0.6	0.0	0.0	0.0	0.5
Tampa	303 447	97.1	41.1	14.9	27.0	21.0	6.7	2.9	7.3	3.0	2.9	0.7	0.3	0.1	1.2	0.1	0.6
Titusville	40 670	98.0	42.3	20.3	26.1	20.3	4.5	2.0	4.9	2.4	2.0	0.0	1.3	0.3	0.0	0.0	0.5
Weston city	49 286	100.0	33.6	23.9	36.1	31.5	3.5	0.7	2.8	1.3	0.0	0.0	0.0	0.0	0.0	0.0	0.0
West Palm Beach	82 103	95.6	42.3	14.5	23.2	17.6	7.2	2.7	8.3	2.9	4.4	0.1	0.9	0.2	0.9	0.0	2.4
Winter Haven	26 487	97.1	44.7	18.8	23.1	17.7	5.6	2.6	4.9	2.4	2.9	0.0	1.6	0.0	0.0	0.0	1.2
Winter Springs	31 666	99.9	37.2	22.7	31.8	25.2	3.8	1.3	4.4	1.9	0.1	0.0	0.0	0.0	0.0	0.0	0.1
GEORGIA	8 186 453	97.1	36.7	18.9	29.8	23.2	6.4	2.7	5.3	1.8	2.9	1.0	0.4	0.1	0.6	0.3	0.4
Albany	76 939	94.5	37.2	13.6	30.9	22.5	8.1	4.3	4.7	2.1	5.5	1.4	0.6	0.1	1.5	0.0	1.9
Alpharetta	34 854	99.8	39.9	21.6	29.5	26.2	3.3	0.6	5.4	1.7	0.2	0.0	0.0	0.0	0.0	0.0	0.2

Table D. Cities

City	Households by type, 2000												Households, 1990		
	Family households						Nonfamily households								
			Married couple		Female householder[1]			Householder living alone							
	Total households	Total	With own children under 18 years	Total	With own children under 18 years	Total	With own children under 18 years	Total	Total	65 years and over	Average household size	Average family size	Total households	Female householder[1]	Householder living alone
	71	72	73	74	75	76	77	78	79	80	81	82	83	84	85
FLORIDA—Cont'd															
Cape Coral	40 768	74.1	29.5	61.2	22.0	9.3	5.5	25.9	19.7	9.7	2.49	2.85	29 748	7.8	17.1
Clearwater	48 449	56.6	21.7	41.7	13.3	11.3	6.8	43.4	35.5	15.4	2.17	2.79	44 138	10.2	33.0
Coconut Creek	20 093	59.9	22.0	49.4	16.7	7.7	3.9	40.1	32.5	18.0	2.16	2.73	13 575	6.1	30.2
Cooper City	9 123	85.8	51.5	70.8	42.2	11.9	7.7	14.2	10.8	3.1	3.06	3.30	6 976	8.6	12.7
Coral Gables	16 793	61.0	24.2	49.2	19.7	9.1	3.7	39.0	31.5	9.8	2.31	2.92	15 460	9.5	31.2
Coral Springs	39 522	79.2	48.4	61.4	36.4	13.3	9.4	20.8	15.2	4.0	2.96	3.30	27 014	9.9	16.5
Davie	28 682	68.9	36.7	51.8	26.7	12.6	7.6	31.1	22.3	6.3	2.64	3.13	17 907	10.9	20.7
Daytona Beach	28 605	48.4	18.0	30.1	7.9	14.5	8.4	51.6	39.4	14.4	2.06	2.77	27 546	12.9	37.6
Deerfield Beach	31 392	51.1	16.3	38.2	10.4	9.6	4.6	48.9	40.3	22.5	2.02	2.72	23 118	7.4	38.1
Delray Beach	26 787	56.3	18.9	42.4	12.1	10.2	5.3	43.7	35.3	18.3	2.22	2.87	21 390	9.2	31.8
Dunedin	17 258	55.3	18.2	43.9	12.1	8.8	4.8	44.7	37.9	20.6	2.01	2.63	15 888	8.0	34.1
Fort Lauderdale	68 468	48.2	19.6	32.2	11.1	11.5	6.5	51.8	40.3	11.7	2.14	2.97	66 440	11.3	38.2
Fort Myers	19 107	56.2	28.9	32.3	13.4	18.4	12.7	43.8	33.8	12.5	2.40	3.10	18 144	16.5	32.3
Fort Pierce	14 407	61.2	28.1	36.1	13.3	19.3	12.1	38.8	31.1	13.9	2.56	3.19	14 171	18.6	27.8
Gainesville	37 279	49.2	22.3	32.5	12.9	13.3	8.1	50.8	32.6	7.9	2.25	2.90	31 924	12.8	30.0
Greenacres City	12 059	62.9	24.5	45.9	14.4	12.5	7.9	37.1	29.7	15.1	2.29	2.80	8 235	9.6	25.2
Hallandale	18 051	48.2	12.5	35.8	6.9	9.1	4.4	51.8	45.2	25.8	1.88	2.60	17 135	7.2	45.7
Hialeah	70 704	81.3	36.2	57.4	25.6	17.4	8.4	18.7	14.7	7.8	3.15	3.39	59 381	14.9	13.9
Hollywood	59 673	57.8	24.9	41.5	16.4	11.9	6.5	42.2	34.4	13.1	2.31	3.00	52 904	9.9	33.4
Homestead	10 095	70.9	42.7	40.0	22.4	22.4	16.4	29.1	20.9	6.9	3.10	3.54	9 317	18.8	22.6
Jacksonville	284 499	67.0	33.9	46.7	21.7	16.0	9.9	33.0	26.2	7.7	2.53	3.07	257 245	13.4	25.3
Jupiter town	16 945	67.3	26.6	55.8	19.8	8.4	5.1	32.7	25.8	10.4	2.32	2.75	10 674	7.8	23.7
Key West	11 016	49.6	19.9	37.7	14.2	8.2	4.3	50.4	31.4	8.1	2.23	2.84	10 424	8.0	30.4
Kissimmee	17 121	69.0	37.4	47.2	23.9	15.8	10.3	31.0	20.9	4.9	2.77	3.21	11 318	12.5	20.6
Lakeland	33 509	60.8	23.5	43.5	13.3	13.7	8.4	39.2	32.9	14.9	2.23	2.82	29 656	12.3	30.6
Lake Worth	13 828	55.6	26.0	36.9	16.2	11.5	6.8	44.4	33.6	11.4	2.49	3.19	12 565	9.5	36.7
Largo	34 041	54.0	17.0	41.8	10.6	9.0	4.8	46.0	38.5	19.3	1.99	2.59	31 921	8.0	34.7
Lauderdale Lakes	12 099	64.0	32.1	36.7	15.4	22.2	14.2	36.0	30.1	16.9	2.59	3.25	11 962	13.5	33.8
Lauderhill	22 810	62.6	31.8	37.4	16.1	20.1	13.2	37.4	31.0	13.6	2.49	3.12	21 131	13.0	30.4
Margate	22 714	63.1	25.8	49.1	19.0	10.2	5.2	36.9	30.8	18.0	2.36	2.95	18 930	7.4	28.1
Melbourne	30 788	59.3	24.0	44.0	15.5	11.5	6.5	40.7	32.9	13.3	2.22	2.82	25 065	10.8	29.1
Miami	134 198	62.1	26.3	36.6	14.7	18.7	9.2	37.9	30.4	12.5	2.61	3.25	130 252	18.6	28.9
Miami Beach	46 194	39.7	14.0	27.4	8.9	8.5	3.9	60.3	48.7	14.8	1.87	2.76	49 305	9.1	50.7
Miramar	23 058	80.9	48.2	56.0	33.5	19.1	11.7	19.1	14.3	3.3	3.15	3.48	14 395	13.3	17.7
North Lauderdale	10 799	72.4	42.4	46.8	26.2	19.3	12.9	27.6	19.6	5.5	2.99	3.43	9 071	12.0	15.1
North Miami	20 541	66.1	37.6	39.0	21.6	20.1	12.6	33.9	26.9	6.8	2.85	3.51	20 127	13.9	33.2
North Miami Beach	13 987	70.1	37.6	44.3	23.3	19.5	11.4	29.9	23.9	8.6	2.89	3.44	13 968	13.9	29.2
Oakland Park	13 502	51.4	24.5	32.3	14.1	13.3	8.1	48.6	35.1	7.4	2.26	3.00	12 097	10.7	34.9
Ocala	18 646	60.5	26.8	40.9	14.8	15.9	10.0	39.5	33.0	15.0	2.29	2.91	17 393	15.3	31.3
Orlando	80 883	52.4	24.5	32.4	13.0	15.4	9.4	47.6	35.0	8.5	2.25	2.97	65 703	14.2	33.0
Ormond Beach	15 629	67.4	23.5	55.7	17.8	8.8	4.3	32.6	27.1	15.3	2.27	2.75	12 703	8.7	24.9
Oviedo	8 556	83.9	50.4	70.8	42.3	9.9	6.2	16.1	10.5	2.4	3.07	3.31	3 795	9.5	12.8
Palm Bay	30 336	71.8	34.0	55.0	23.7	12.2	7.7	28.2	21.8	8.3	2.60	3.03	23 328	8.8	17.9
Palm Beach Gardens	15 599	65.5	23.4	53.8	17.0	8.9	4.8	34.5	27.7	10.5	2.23	2.70	9 557	8.9	24.1
Panama City	14 819	61.0	27.6	41.8	16.2	15.4	9.5	39.0	32.2	12.4	2.30	2.92	14 053	15.0	30.5
Pembroke Pines	51 989	70.9	36.2	56.4	28.3	11.1	6.3	29.1	24.1	12.5	2.62	3.13	26 722	8.5	24.6
Pensacola	24 524	59.8	24.6	39.7	14.2	16.7	9.0	40.2	32.9	11.7	2.27	2.92	23 983	16.6	29.8
Pinellas Park	19 444	62.5	25.7	46.6	16.4	11.6	6.6	37.5	30.2	14.1	2.31	2.84	18 185	10.3	26.4
Plantation	33 244	66.8	30.9	52.0	23.0	11.2	6.2	33.2	25.8	8.5	2.48	3.02	26 489	8.7	22.9
Plant City	10 849	72.3	36.9	52.7	24.9	14.8	9.1	27.7	22.9	9.3	2.73	3.20	8 395	15.0	23.1
Pompano Beach	35 197	52.4	17.4	37.4	10.1	10.9	5.6	47.6	38.6	17.1	2.13	2.85	32 157	10.5	34.7
Port Orange	19 574	67.6	24.8	54.7	17.9	9.6	5.2	32.4	25.7	13.4	2.32	2.76	14 964	8.0	23.1
Port St. Lucie	33 909	75.9	31.6	61.8	23.4	10.0	6.0	24.1	18.2	8.9	2.60	2.94	20 675	6.9	13.2
Riviera Beach	11 387	66.1	29.3	37.1	12.2	23.5	14.8	33.9	27.6	10.3	2.60	3.19	10 333	21.8	25.7
St. Petersburg	109 663	56.2	24.0	38.3	14.1	13.8	7.9	43.8	35.6	13.1	2.20	2.88	105 703	12.4	35.1
Sanford	14 237	64.4	31.8	39.5	17.3	19.2	11.7	35.6	27.0	9.6	2.57	3.13	12 119	16.0	26.9
Sarasota	23 427	51.5	19.7	35.3	10.8	12.3	7.2	48.5	38.3	16.3	2.12	2.81	22 822	12.6	34.2
Sunrise	33 308	66.8	33.4	48.6	23.2	13.8	8.2	33.2	27.2	14.4	2.54	3.12	26 314	8.9	25.1
Tallahassee	63 217	46.6	21.8	30.1	12.4	13.2	8.0	53.4	34.7	6.0	2.17	2.86	50 442	13.2	31.6
Tamarac	27 423	57.4	15.4	44.8	9.9	9.4	4.2	42.6	36.3	23.0	2.00	2.56	22 906	5.2	31.4
Tampa	124 758	57.1	27.6	36.4	15.8	16.1	9.5	42.9	33.7	10.2	2.36	3.07	114 800	15.5	32.3
Titusville	17 200	64.5	26.7	47.9	16.5	12.6	7.9	35.5	29.9	13.9	2.32	2.86	16 207	10.9	25.6
Weston city	16 576	82.4	51.3	71.0	43.8	9.0	6.1	17.6	13.8	3.3	2.97	3.29	NA	NA	NA
West Palm Beach	34 769	52.5	22.4	34.3	12.4	13.6	7.9	47.5	37.6	11.8	2.26	3.02	28 787	13.3	35.2
Winter Haven	11 833	58.6	21.6	42.1	12.4	12.8	7.4	41.4	36.0	18.9	2.17	2.81	10 941	12.1	33.2
Winter Springs	11 774	75.6	38.1	61.2	29.4	11.1	6.9	24.4	18.8	6.4	2.69	3.08	8 011	9.1	16.3
GEORGIA	3 006 369	70.2	35.0	51.5	24.4	14.5	8.6	29.8	23.6	7.0	2.65	3.14	2 366 615	13.9	22.7
Albany	28 620	66.0	32.3	36.6	15.1	25.2	15.3	34.0	28.8	9.6	2.54	3.14	27 926	24.1	25.0
Alpharetta	13 911	64.1	36.2	54.1	30.3	7.3	4.6	35.9	27.7	4.2	2.50	3.13	5 265	9.1	24.3

[1]No spouse present.

Table D. Cities

City	Percent change of households, 1990–2000	Total housing units	Occupied housing units (percent)	Vacant housing units Total	For seasonal, recreational, or occasional use	Homeowner vacancy rate (percent)	Rental vacancy rate (percent)	Occupied housing units Total	Percent owner-occupied housing units	Percent renter-occupied housing units	Average household size of owner-occupied units	Average household size of renter-occupied units
	86	87	88	89	90	91	92	93	94	95	96	97
FLORIDA—Cont'd												
Cape Coral	37.0	45 653	89.3	10.7	6.2	1.8	7.9	40 768	80.0	20.0	2.48	2.54
Clearwater	9.8	56 802	85.3	14.7	7.6	2.4	9.3	48 449	62.1	37.9	2.19	2.12
Coconut Creek	48.0	22 182	90.6	9.4	4.1	2.4	10.0	20 093	75.5	24.5	2.17	2.13
Cooper City	30.8	9 289	98.2	1.8	0.5	0.7	2.9	9 123	92.2	7.8	3.07	3.00
Coral Gables	8.6	17 849	94.1	5.9	1.7	1.5	4.2	16 793	65.8	34.2	2.56	1.83
Coral Springs	46.3	41 337	95.6	4.4	0.7	1.6	5.1	39 522	65.0	35.0	3.08	2.73
Davie	60.2	31 284	91.7	8.3	3.3	2.6	5.3	28 682	76.5	23.5	2.74	2.29
Daytona Beach	3.8	33 345	85.8	14.2	6.4	2.6	8.4	28 605	47.3	52.7	2.15	1.98
Deerfield Beach	35.8	37 343	84.1	15.9	10.2	1.8	5.5	31 392	70.2	29.8	1.98	2.12
Delray Beach	25.2	31 702	84.5	15.5	11.0	1.5	7.8	26 787	69.7	30.3	2.19	2.30
Dunedin	8.6	19 952	86.5	13.5	6.2	2.3	13.8	17 258	71.4	28.6	2.09	1.81
Fort Lauderdale	3.1	80 862	84.7	15.3	8.5	2.5	7.7	68 468	55.4	44.6	2.18	2.10
Fort Myers	5.3	21 836	87.5	12.5	3.7	3.7	10.0	19 107	39.7	60.3	2.50	2.34
Fort Pierce	1.7	17 170	83.9	16.1	6.1	3.1	13.0	14 407	53.2	46.8	2.40	2.73
Gainesville	16.8	40 105	93.0	7.0	0.4	2.0	6.8	37 279	47.7	52.3	2.39	2.12
Greenacres City	46.4	14 153	85.2	14.8	8.4	2.3	10.5	12 059	70.9	29.1	2.17	2.56
Hallandale	5.3	25 022	72.1	27.9	19.7	2.6	9.0	18 051	66.6	33.4	1.80	2.03
Hialeah	19.1	72 142	98.0	2.0	0.2	1.0	1.7	70 704	50.7	49.3	3.35	2.95
Hollywood	12.8	68 426	87.2	12.8	7.2	2.2	7.1	59 673	62.2	37.8	2.43	2.10
Homestead	8.4	11 162	90.4	9.6	1.3	3.7	8.0	10 095	36.0	64.0	2.74	3.31
Jacksonville	10.6	308 826	92.1	7.9	0.3	1.8	9.0	284 499	63.2	36.8	2.64	2.34
Jupiter town	58.8	20 943	80.9	19.1	14.4	1.4	11.1	16 945	81.3	18.7	2.31	2.33
Key West	5.7	13 306	82.8	17.2	8.3	2.3	9.3	11 016	45.6	54.4	2.24	2.23
Kissimmee	51.3	19 642	87.2	12.8	5.6	2.6	9.2	17 121	44.9	55.1	2.88	2.67
Lakeland	13.0	38 980	86.0	14.0	5.5	3.5	9.4	33 509	60.3	39.7	2.24	2.22
Lake Worth	10.1	15 861	87.2	12.8	5.5	2.6	7.9	13 828	52.4	47.6	2.41	2.57
Largo	6.6	40 261	84.6	15.4	8.6	3.0	10.2	34 041	67.4	32.6	2.01	1.93
Lauderdale Lakes	1.1	14 325	84.5	15.5	9.7	2.9	6.8	12 099	62.2	37.8	2.41	2.89
Lauderhill	7.9	25 751	88.6	11.4	5.3	3.1	5.8	22 810	59.4	40.6	2.40	2.62
Margate	20.0	24 740	91.8	8.2	3.9	2.3	6.2	22 714	80.1	19.9	2.37	2.33
Melbourne	22.8	33 678	91.4	8.6	2.5	2.3	8.5	30 788	62.1	37.9	2.34	2.02
Miami	3.0	148 388	90.4	9.6	2.0	2.9	6.6	134 198	34.9	65.1	2.79	2.52
Miami Beach	-6.3	59 723	77.3	22.7	12.8	7.6	8.8	46 194	36.6	63.4	2.00	1.80
Miramar	60.2	25 905	89.0	11.0	0.4	9.7	6.6	23 058	80.1	19.9	3.23	2.83
North Lauderdale	19.0	11 444	94.4	5.6	0.9	3.1	5.8	10 799	63.7	36.3	3.03	2.92
North Miami	2.1	22 281	92.2	7.8	1.6	2.2	5.8	20 541	50.5	49.5	3.10	2.61
North Miami Beach	0.1	15 350	91.1	8.9	3.9	2.6	4.7	13 987	61.8	38.2	2.98	2.74
Oakland Park	11.6	14 509	93.1	6.9	2.8	2.0	4.6	13 502	50.7	49.3	2.23	2.29
Ocala	7.2	20 501	91.0	9.0	1.6	2.3	8.0	18 646	57.2	42.8	2.34	2.22
Orlando	23.1	88 486	91.4	8.6	1.3	1.8	8.3	80 883	40.8	59.2	2.38	2.16
Ormond Beach	23.0	17 258	90.6	9.4	4.7	1.7	10.4	15 629	81.7	18.3	2.32	2.02
Oviedo	125.5	8 977	95.3	4.7	0.3	1.4	11.9	8 556	85.6	14.4	3.09	2.92
Palm Bay	30.0	32 902	92.2	7.8	2.0	2.6	9.0	30 336	75.3	24.7	2.63	2.54
Palm Beach Gardens	63.2	18 317	85.2	14.8	10.0	1.6	10.0	15 599	79.5	20.5	2.26	2.08
Panama City	5.5	16 548	89.6	10.4	0.9	2.5	11.2	14 819	57.8	42.2	2.35	2.23
Pembroke Pines	94.6	55 296	94.0	6.0	2.1	2.1	5.8	51 989	80.2	19.8	2.65	2.48
Pensacola	2.3	26 995	90.8	9.2	0.7	2.2	10.0	24 524	63.3	36.7	2.34	2.16
Pinellas Park	6.9	21 843	89.0	11.0	4.5	2.6	8.9	19 444	75.1	24.9	2.29	2.36
Plantation	25.5	34 999	95.0	5.0	1.7	1.3	5.2	33 244	71.7	28.3	2.58	2.23
Plant City	29.2	11 797	92.0	8.0	0.9	2.4	7.8	10 849	65.7	34.3	2.73	2.71
Pompano Beach	9.5	44 496	79.1	20.9	15.8	1.9	7.1	35 197	62.8	37.2	2.07	2.23
Port Orange	30.8	21 102	92.8	7.2	3.5	1.7	5.6	19 574	82.1	17.9	2.33	2.24
Port St. Lucie	64.0	36 785	92.2	7.8	3.6	2.0	8.1	33 909	83.3	16.7	2.55	2.83
Riviera Beach	10.2	14 220	80.1	19.9	13.8	1.9	8.6	11 387	59.2	40.8	2.47	2.78
St. Petersburg	3.7	124 618	88.0	12.0	3.9	2.4	9.1	109 663	63.5	36.5	2.32	2.00
Sanford	17.5	15 623	91.1	8.9	0.9	2.7	6.6	14 237	55.4	44.6	2.63	2.49
Sarasota	2.7	26 898	87.1	12.9	6.6	2.2	7.8	23 427	58.4	41.6	2.08	2.17
Sunrise	26.6	35 661	93.4	6.6	1.9	2.4	5.8	33 308	73.8	26.2	2.58	2.43
Tallahassee	25.3	68 417	92.4	7.6	0.6	2.1	7.7	63 217	43.8	56.2	2.35	2.04
Tamarac	19.7	29 750	92.2	7.8	3.3	2.7	4.8	27 423	79.9	20.1	1.94	2.27
Tampa	8.7	135 776	91.9	8.1	0.6	2.1	7.8	124 758	55.0	45.0	2.49	2.20
Titusville	6.1	19 178	89.7	10.3	3.4	2.3	10.6	17 200	68.0	32.0	2.33	2.28
Weston city	NA	18 943	87.5	12.5	4.7	2.8	5.3	16 576	81.8	18.2	3.02	2.78
West Palm Beach	20.8	40 461	85.9	14.1	5.0	2.9	10.3	34 769	52.0	48.0	2.31	2.20
Winter Haven	8.2	13 912	85.1	14.9	5.5	3.8	11.8	11 833	59.1	40.9	2.26	2.05
Winter Springs	47.0	12 306	95.7	4.3	0.7	1.2	9.0	11 774	80.3	19.7	2.72	2.55
GEORGIA	27.0	3 281 737	91.6	8.4	1.5	1.9	8.2	3 006 369	67.5	32.5	2.71	2.51
Albany	2.5	32 062	89.3	10.7	0.4	2.7	10.7	28 620	47.4	52.6	2.54	2.54
Alpharetta	164.2	14 670	94.8	5.2	0.7	1.7	5.6	13 911	60.3	39.7	2.81	2.02

Table D. Cities

STATE Place code	City	Land area, 2000[1] (sq km)	Total persons	Rank	Per square kilometer	Land area, 1990[1] (sq km)	Total persons	Rank	Per square kilometer	White	Black or African American	American Indian or Alaska Native	Asian	Native Hawaiian and other Pacific Islander	Some other race
		1	2	3	4	5	6	7	8	9	10	11	12	13	14
	GEORGIA—Cont'd														
13 03436	Athens Clarke County	312.8	101 489	241	324.5	NA	NA	NA	NA	64.9	27.3	0.2	3.1	0.0	3.1
13 04000	Atlanta	341.2	416 474	41	1 220.6	341.3	303 929	36	1 154.2	33.2	61.4	0.2	1.9	0.0	2.0
13 04200	Augusta-Richmond County	839.3	199 775	91	238.0	NA	NA	NA	NA	45.6	49.8	0.3	1.5	0.1	1.0
13 19000	Columbus	560.1	186 291	107	332.6	560.0	178 685	94	319.1	50.4	43.7	0.4	1.5	0.1	1.9
13 21380	Dalton city	51.3	27 912	1 326	544.1	46.6	22 218	1 477	476.8	66.2	7.7	0.4	1.7	0.1	21.2
13 25720	East Point	35.6	39 595	883	1 112.2	35.6	34 595	870	971.8	16.1	78.2	0.2	0.6	0.1	3.4
13 31908	Gainesville	70.1	25 578	1 474	364.9	58.8	17 885	1 835	304.2	65.2	15.7	0.3	2.7	0.1	14.3
13 38964	Hinesville	42.0	30 392	1 205	723.6	32.0	21 596	1 522	674.9	41.5	46.0	0.5	2.3	0.6	5.0
13 44340	La Grange	75.0	25 998	1 448	346.6	67.2	25 574	1 261	380.6	49.2	47.5	0.2	0.8	0.1	1.2
13 49000	Macon	144.5	97 255	252	673.0	124.0	107 365	185	865.8	35.5	62.5	0.2	0.6	0.0	0.5
13 49756	Marietta	56.7	58 748	520	1 036.1	52.8	44 129	650	835.8	56.5	29.5	0.3	3.0	0.1	8.0
13 59724	Peachtree City	60.3	31 580	1 158	523.7	60.4	19 027	1 721	315.0	87.7	6.1	0.2	3.7	0.0	0.9
13 66668	Rome	76.1	34 980	1 027	459.7	62.7	30 425	1 042	485.2	63.1	27.7	0.4	1.4	0.2	5.6
13 67284	Roswell	98.5	79 334	347	805.4	84.4	47 986	588	568.6	81.5	8.5	0.2	3.7	0.0	4.1
13 69000	Savannah	193.6	131 510	168	679.3	162.1	137 812	132	850.2	38.9	57.1	0.2	1.5	0.1	0.9
13 71492	Smyrna	36.0	40 999	845	1 138.9	29.5	32 453	954	1 100.1	59.4	27.2	0.4	3.9	0.0	6.6
13 78800	Valdosta	77.5	43 724	787	564.2	68.6	40 038	740	583.6	47.7	48.5	0.2	1.4	0.0	0.9
13 80508	Warner Robins	59.0	48 804	691	827.2	43.2	43 861	653	1 015.3	62.5	32.1	0.3	1.8	0.1	1.2
15 00000	HAWAII	16 634.5	1 211 537	X	72.8	16 636.5	1 108 229	X	66.6	24.3	1.8	0.3	41.6	9.4	1.3
15 14650	Hilo CDP	140.6	40 759	850	289.9	140.6	37 808	796	268.9	17.1	0.4	0.3	38.3	13.1	0.9
15 17000	Honolulu CDP	222.0	371 657	48	1 674.1	214.5	377 059	39	1 757.9	19.7	1.6	0.2	55.9	6.8	0.9
15 23150	Kailua CDP	17.2	36 513	961	2 122.8	17.2	36 818	820	2 140.6	43.8	0.8	0.3	21.1	8.1	0.9
15 28250	Kaneohe CDP	17.0	34 970	1 029	2 057.1	17.0	35 448	846	2 085.2	20.5	0.8	0.2	38.5	11.4	0.7
15 51050	Mililani CDP	10.1	28 608	1 292	2 832.5	10.1	29 359	1 076	2 906.8	20.4	3.1	0.2	46.9	4.6	1.3
15 62600	Pearl City CDP	12.9	30 976	1 179	2 401.2	12.9	30 993	1 010	2 402.6	17.2	2.7	0.3	53.4	6.1	1.4
15 77750	Waimalu CDP	15.3	29 371	1 255	1 919.7	15.3	29 967	1 054	1 958.6	17.1	2.3	0.3	55.3	5.6	1.1
15 79700	Waipahu CDP	6.7	33 108	1 092	4 941.5	6.7	31 435	994	4 691.8	4.7	0.9	0.1	65.8	12.3	0.9
16 00000	IDAHO	214 314.3	1 293 953	X	6.0	214 325.0	1 006 734	X	4.7	91.0	0.4	1.4	0.9	0.1	4.2
16 08830	Boise City	165.2	185 787	110	1 124.6	119.5	126 685	145	1 060.1	92.2	0.8	0.7	2.1	0.2	1.7
16 12250	Caldwell	29.4	25 967	1 450	883.2	23.0	18 586	1 771	808.1	75.1	0.5	0.9	0.8	0.1	19.7
16 16750	Coeur d'Alene	34.0	34 514	1 043	1 015.1	27.6	24 561	1 318	889.9	95.8	0.2	0.8	0.6	0.1	0.6
16 39700	Idaho Falls	44.2	50 730	656	1 147.7	37.6	43 973	651	1 169.5	92.1	0.6	0.8	1.1	0.1	3.8
16 46540	Lewiston	42.7	30 904	1 186	723.7	42.6	28 082	1 139	659.2	95.1	0.3	1.6	0.8	0.1	0.5
16 52120	Meridian city	30.5	34 919	1 033	1 144.9	NA	9 596	3 129	NA	94.3	0.5	0.5	1.3	0.1	1.3
16 56260	Nampa	51.4	51 867	642	1 009.1	28.0	28 365	1 122	1 013.0	83.4	0.4	0.9	0.9	0.2	11.2
16 64090	Pocatello	73.1	51 466	650	704.0	71.5	46 117	619	645.0	92.3	0.7	1.3	1.1	0.2	2.2
16 82810	Twin Falls	31.1	34 469	1 045	1 108.3	27.3	27 634	1 149	1 012.2	91.8	0.2	0.7	1.1	0.1	3.7
17 00000	ILLINOIS	143 960.8	12 419 293	X	86.3	143 986.6	11 430 602	X	79.4	73.5	15.1	0.2	3.4	0.0	5.8
17 00243	Addison	24.4	35 914	990	1 471.9	22.3	32 053	970	1 437.4	75.4	2.5	0.4	7.9	0.0	11.4
17 01114	Alton	40.5	30 496	1 201	753.0	38.9	33 060	934	849.9	72.3	24.7	0.2	0.4	0.0	0.7
17 02154	Arlington Heights	42.5	76 031	369	1 789.0	41.9	75 463	305	1 801.0	90.6	1.0	0.1	6.0	0.0	1.2
17 03012	Aurora	99.8	142 990	153	1 432.8	86.7	99 672	205	1 149.6	68.1	11.1	0.4	3.1	0.0	14.5
17 04013	Bartlett	38.4	36 706	957	955.9	36.3	19 395	1 690	534.3	87.2	2.0	0.1	7.8	0.0	1.4
17 04845	Belleville	48.8	41 410	832	848.6	36.2	42 806	672	1 182.5	81.5	15.5	0.3	0.8	0.1	0.4
17 05573	Berwyn	10.1	54 016	608	5 348.1	10.1	45 426	629	4 497.6	73.4	1.3	0.4	2.6	0.0	18.6
17 06613	Bloomington	58.3	64 808	451	1 111.6	43.3	51 889	524	1 198.4	84.9	8.6	0.2	3.0	0.0	1.4
17 07133	Bolingbrook	53.1	56 321	560	1 060.7	29.1	40 843	719	1 403.5	64.5	20.4	0.2	6.4	0.1	5.6
17 09447	Buffalo Grove	23.8	42 909	803	1 802.9	20.7	36 417	825	1 759.3	88.7	0.8	0.1	8.4	0.0	0.9
17 09642	Burbank	10.8	27 902	1 328	2 583.5	10.7	27 600	1 152	2 579.4	90.7	0.3	0.2	1.8	0.0	3.9
17 10487	Calumet City	18.8	39 071	892	2 078.2	18.8	37 840	793	2 012.8	38.7	52.9	0.2	0.5	0.1	5.4
17 11332	Carol Stream	23.0	40 438	858	1 758.2	20.2	31 759	983	1 572.2	78.5	4.2	0.2	11.2	0.0	3.8
17 11358	Carpentersville	19.3	30 586	1 198	1 584.8	14.0	23 049	1 419	1 646.4	68.8	4.2	0.6	2.0	0.1	20.8
17 12385	Champaign	44.0	67 518	427	1 534.5	33.5	63 502	388	1 895.6	73.2	15.6	0.2	6.8	0.0	1.9
17 14000	Chicago	588.3	2 896 016	3	4 922.7	588.5	2 783 726	3	4 730.2	42.0	36.8	0.4	4.3	0.1	13.6
17 14026	Chicago Heights	24.8	32 776	1 108	1 321.6	23.4	32 966	937	1 408.8	45.0	37.9	0.4	0.4	0.0	13.5
17 14351	Cicero	15.1	85 616	310	5 669.9	15.1	67 436	358	4 466.0	48.3	1.1	0.9	1.0	0.0	44.7
17 17887	Crystal Lake	42.1	38 000	930	902.6	36.6	24 692	1 307	674.6	94.1	0.6	0.2	2.0	0.0	2.2
17 18563	Danville	44.0	33 904	1 062	770.5	39.3	33 828	898	860.8	70.2	24.4	0.2	1.2	0.0	2.1
17 18823	Decatur	107.6	81 860	330	760.8	96.0	83 900	270	874.0	77.6	19.5	0.2	0.7	0.0	0.4
17 19161	De Kalb	32.7	39 018	897	1 193.2	20.8	35 076	859	1 686.3	79.5	9.1	0.2	4.6	0.1	4.3
17 19642	Des Plaines	37.4	58 720	521	1 570.1	36.8	53 414	498	1 451.5	84.4	1.0	0.3	7.6	0.0	4.6
17 20292	Dolton	11.8	25 614	1 472	2 170.7	11.7	23 956	1 358	2 047.5	14.3	82.4	0.2	0.6	0.0	1.4
17 20591	Downers Grove	36.9	48 724	692	1 320.4	35.3	47 464	597	1 344.6	90.1	1.9	0.1	5.7	0.0	1.0
17 22255	East St. Louis	36.4	31 542	1 160	866.5	36.4	40 944	717	1 124.8	1.2	97.7	0.2	0.1	0.0	0.2
17 23074	Elgin	64.8	94 487	266	1 458.1	56.8	77 014	294	1 355.9	70.5	6.8	0.4	3.9	0.1	15.4
17 23256	Elk Grove Village	28.6	34 727	1 038	1 214.2	27.8	33 429	921	1 202.5	86.0	1.4	0.1	8.8	0.0	2.3

[1] Dry land or land partially or temporarily covered by water.

Table D. Cities

City	Population and population characteristics, 2000 (cont'd)								Population and population characteristics, 1990				
	Race (percent) (cont'd)								Race (percent)				
	Race alone or in combination												
	Two or more races	White	Black	American Indian or Alaska Native	Asian	Native Hawaiian and other Pacific Islander	Some other race	Hispanic¹	White	Black or African American	American Indian or Alaska Native	Asian and Pacific Islander	Hispanic¹
	15	16	17	18	19	20	21	22	23	24	25	26	27
GEORGIA—Cont'd													
Athens-Clarke County	1.4	66.1	27.8	0.5	3.6	0.1	3.5	6.3	66.4	29.6	0.1	3.3	1.6
Atlanta	1.2	34.0	62.1	0.5	2.2	0.1	2.5	4.5	31.0	67.1	0.1	0.9	1.9
Augusta-Richmond County	1.8	46.8	50.7	0.7	2.0	0.2	1.5	2.8	43.0	56.0	0.2	0.6	0.8
Columbus	1.9	51.8	44.6	0.8	2.0	0.2	2.5	4.5	59.0	38.0	0.3	1.4	2.9
Dalton city	2.8	68.6	8.2	0.7	2.0	0.2	23.2	40.2	83.4	10.6	0.3	1.0	6.5
East Point	1.4	16.9	79.0	0.6	0.9	0.2	4.0	7.6	31.6	66.3	0.2	0.7	1.9
Gainesville	1.7	66.5	16.1	0.6	2.9	0.2	15.4	33.2	68.8	23.5	0.1	1.2	7.9
Hinesville	4.2	44.2	48.2	1.1	3.3	0.9	6.7	9.1	57.3	35.6	0.5	3.3	6.9
La Grange	0.9	50.0	47.9	0.5	1.0	0.2	1.5	2.4	56.7	42.3	0.1	0.8	0.6
Macon	0.8	35.9	62.9	0.4	0.8	0.1	0.7	1.2	47.1	52.2	0.1	0.4	0.6
Marietta	2.6	58.4	30.5	0.8	3.4	0.2	9.5	16.9	76.3	20.5	0.3	1.8	3.2
Peachtree City	1.4	88.9	6.5	0.6	4.2	0.1	1.3	3.7	92.4	4.0	0.1	3.2	2.4
Rome	1.6	64.5	28.2	0.7	1.7	0.2	6.4	10.3	68.8	29.7	0.2	0.7	1.7
Roswell	1.9	82.9	9.1	0.6	4.3	0.1	5.0	10.6	92.2	4.9	0.1	1.8	2.7
Savannah	1.3	39.8	57.8	0.6	1.9	0.2	1.3	2.2	46.8	51.3	0.2	1.1	1.4
Smyrna	2.4	61.3	28.1	0.9	4.4	0.2	7.8	13.8	80.2	15.9	0.3	2.3	3.5
Valdosta	1.2	48.6	49.0	0.6	1.7	0.1	1.3	2.2	55.2	43.5	0.2	0.9	1.1
Warner Robins	2.0	64.1	32.8	0.8	2.5	0.2	1.7	3.8	72.7	25.0	0.3	1.4	1.8
HAWAII	21.4	39.3	2.8	2.1	58.0	23.3	3.9	7.2	33.4	2.5	0.5	61.8	7.3
Hilo CDP	29.7	38.7	1.2	2.6	61.8	34.2	4.3	8.8	26.6	0.6	0.6	70.2	8.5
Honolulu CDP	14.9	30.1	2.4	1.4	67.7	15.6	2.4	4.4	26.7	1.3	0.3	70.5	4.6
Kailua CDP	25.0	64.3	1.6	2.4	39.1	24.7	3.0	6.1	57.7	1.4	0.5	39.1	5.5
Kaneohe CDP	27.9	41.3	1.5	2.1	60.7	31.0	2.9	7.2	31.2	1.2	0.4	65.6	6.9
Mililani CDP	23.5	38.3	4.3	1.9	66.7	17.8	3.9	7.8	34.2	2.9	0.3	61.2	5.4
Pearl City CDP	18.8	30.1	3.6	1.6	69.0	17.8	3.9	7.3	21.4	2.5	0.3	74.1	6.6
Waimalu CDP	18.3	29.7	3.5	1.6	70.5	15.9	3.6	6.0	28.1	2.3	0.4	67.8	5.6
Waipahu CDP	15.3	13.7	1.7	1.4	78.1	22.4	3.5	6.1	11.6	2.0	0.5	83.8	11.5
IDAHO	2.0	92.8	0.6	2.1	1.3	0.2	5.0	7.9	94.4	0.3	1.4	0.9	5.3
Boise City	2.4	94.4	1.1	1.4	2.7	0.3	2.6	4.5	96.4	0.6	0.6	1.6	2.7
Caldwell	2.9	77.6	0.8	1.8	1.4	0.3	21.1	28.1	85.5	0.3	0.7	1.2	20.6
Coeur d'Alene	1.9	97.6	0.4	1.8	1.0	0.2	1.0	2.7	98.1	0.2	0.8	0.6	1.8
Idaho Falls	1.6	93.6	0.9	1.3	1.4	0.1	4.4	7.2	95.3	0.6	0.6	1.2	4.2
Lewiston	1.6	96.7	0.4	2.6	1.1	0.2	0.8	1.9	97.4	0.1	1.4	0.7	1.2
Meridian city	2.1	96.3	0.7	1.0	2.0	0.3	1.9	3.7	97.7	0.3	0.4	0.7	2.4
Nampa	2.9	86.1	0.7	1.7	1.5	0.3	12.7	17.9	89.5	0.3	1.0	1.1	12.8
Pocatello	2.1	94.2	1.0	2.1	1.7	0.4	2.9	4.9	94.1	0.9	1.4	1.3	4.5
Twin Falls	2.3	94.0	0.4	1.4	1.4	0.2	5.0	8.9	94.8	0.2	0.7	1.6	6.8
ILLINOIS	1.9	75.1	15.6	0.6	3.8	0.1	6.8	12.3	78.3	14.8	0.2	2.5	7.9
Addison	2.4	77.5	2.7	0.6	8.5	0.1	13.1	28.4	87.9	1.7	0.1	5.9	13.4
Alton	1.7	73.8	25.7	0.7	0.6	0.1	1.0	1.5	75.6	23.1	0.5	0.3	1.1
Arlington Heights	1.2	91.6	1.1	0.2	6.5	0.1	1.7	4.5	94.8	0.6	0.1	3.7	2.7
Aurora	2.9	70.5	11.9	0.7	3.5	0.1	16.2	32.6	74.1	11.9	0.2	1.3	23.0
Bartlett	1.5	88.4	2.3	0.4	8.4	0.1	2.0	5.5	93.7	1.6	0.2	3.5	3.4
Belleville	1.4	82.8	16.1	0.6	1.1	0.1	0.7	1.6	92.1	6.8	0.2	0.6	1.3
Berwyn	3.6	76.8	1.6	0.9	3.1	0.1	21.3	38.0	95.6	0.1	0.1	1.7	7.9
Bloomington	1.8	86.5	9.5	0.5	3.4	0.1	1.9	3.3	90.9	6.7	0.2	1.5	1.6
Bolingbrook	2.8	66.7	21.6	0.7	7.2	0.1	6.7	13.1	76.8	15.6	0.3	5.0	5.9
Buffalo Grove	1.1	89.7	0.9	0.1	9.0	0.1	1.4	3.3	94.2	1.0	0.1	4.4	2.0
Burbank	3.2	93.8	0.4	0.5	2.1	0.1	6.4	11.1	97.5	0.0	0.2	1.1	4.7
Calumet City	2.1	40.3	53.9	0.7	0.7	0.1	6.7	10.9	73.3	23.7	0.1	0.6	6.4
Carol Stream	2.1	80.2	4.7	0.5	11.9	0.1	4.8	10.0	88.4	3.4	0.2	5.8	5.7
Carpentersville	3.5	72.0	4.7	1.0	2.4	0.2	23.4	40.6	85.1	4.4	0.3	1.3	16.7
Champaign	2.2	74.9	16.5	0.6	7.5	0.1	2.6	4.0	80.7	14.2	0.2	4.1	1.9
Chicago	2.9	44.3	37.4	0.7	4.9	0.2	15.6	26.0	45.4	39.1	0.3	3.7	19.6
Chicago Heights	2.7	47.2	38.9	0.8	0.6	0.1	15.1	23.8	55.0	35.1	0.2	0.3	15.0
Cicero	4.0	51.9	1.3	1.3	1.2	0.1	48.2	77.4	75.2	0.2	0.4	1.6	37.0
Crystal Lake	1.1	95.0	0.7	0.4	2.4	0.1	2.6	7.0	97.6	0.2	0.1	1.2	2.5
Danville	1.9	71.8	25.5	0.6	1.4	0.1	2.7	4.6	78.3	19.1	0.2	1.1	2.1
Decatur	1.7	79.1	20.6	0.5	0.8	0.1	0.7	1.2	82.5	16.7	0.1	0.5	0.5
De Kalb	2.1	81.2	9.7	0.6	5.1	0.2	5.3	9.0	88.9	4.7	0.1	4.5	4.1
Des Plaines	2.0	86.1	1.2	0.6	8.2	0.1	5.8	14.0	92.0	0.6	0.1	4.7	6.6
Dolton	1.1	15.0	83.1	0.5	0.8	0.0	1.8	3.1	58.5	38.1	0.1	1.2	4.5
Downers Grove	1.1	91.1	2.1	0.3	6.2	0.0	1.4	3.6	93.2	1.7	0.1	4.2	2.4
East St. Louis	0.6	1.5	98.2	0.5	0.2	0.0	0.3	0.7	1.6	98.1	0.1	0.1	0.4
Elgin	3.0	73.0	7.5	0.8	4.4	0.1	17.2	34.3	77.8	7.3	0.2	3.5	18.9
Elk Grove Village	1.3	87.1	1.6	0.3	9.4	0.1	2.8	6.2	91.5	0.8	0.1	6.8	3.6

¹Hispanic persons may be of any race.

Table D. Cities

City	Population and population characteristics, 2000 Age (percent)									Median age (years)	Percent Female
	Under 5 years	5 to 17 years	18 to 24 years	25 to 34 years	35 to 44 years	45 to 54 years	55 to 64 years	65 to 74 years	75 years and over		
	28	29	30	31	32	33	34	35	36	37	38
GEORGIA—Cont'd											
Athens-Clarke County	5.2	12.6	31.3	16.4	11.0	9.5	5.9	4.1	3.9	25.4	51.2
Atlanta	6.4	15.9	13.3	19.7	15.5	12.0	7.4	5.0	4.7	31.9	50.4
Augusta-Richmond County	7.1	19.7	12.0	14.8	15.0	12.6	7.9	6.0	4.8	32.3	51.8
Columbus	7.3	19.5	11.9	14.6	15.2	12.2	7.5	6.5	5.2	32.6	51.4
Dalton city	8.9	18.4	12.0	17.0	13.3	11.4	7.5	5.6	5.9	31.1	49.0
East Point	8.7	20.6	11.9	16.1	15.2	12.8	6.7	4.1	3.9	30.0	52.8
Gainesville	8.3	16.7	15.1	18.3	12.3	10.3	6.6	5.7	6.8	29.9	50.5
Hinesville	10.6	23.6	13.8	19.1	16.9	8.9	4.1	2.0	1.1	25.9	50.7
La Grange	7.7	20.7	11.0	13.8	13.1	11.7	7.5	6.8	7.7	32.8	53.9
Macon	7.8	19.2	11.3	13.6	13.8	12.3	7.8	7.1	7.2	33.6	55.6
Marietta	7.9	14.5	14.1	24.1	15.4	10.2	5.5	3.7	4.6	30.0	49.7
Peachtree City	6.1	25.5	5.8	8.8	19.7	18.0	8.2	4.2	3.8	37.5	51.2
Rome	6.7	17.5	12.1	14.2	13.5	11.8	8.3	7.6	8.3	34.6	52.6
Roswell	6.9	17.5	8.2	17.0	18.1	16.3	8.4	4.0	3.5	35.2	50.0
Savannah	7.0	18.6	13.2	14.8	13.7	11.6	7.9	6.5	6.8	32.3	52.8
Smyrna	6.9	12.6	10.8	26.7	17.1	11.3	6.2	4.4	3.9	32.0	51.2
Valdosta	7.7	18.4	18.4	14.6	12.6	11.0	6.8	5.4	5.0	28.2	53.7
Warner Robins	7.2	20.3	9.6	15.5	16.4	12.1	8.1	6.4	4.4	33.3	51.5
HAWAII	6.5	18.0	9.5	14.1	15.8	14.1	8.8	7.0	6.2	36.2	49.8
Hilo CDP	5.6	19.0	10.3	10.7	13.7	14.3	9.6	8.5	8.2	38.6	51.1
Honolulu CDP	5.1	14.1	8.9	14.5	15.4	14.4	9.7	8.7	9.1	39.7	50.9
Kailua CDP	5.7	18.4	7.2	12.0	16.6	16.5	9.7	7.6	6.1	39.1	50.5
Kaneohe CDP	5.8	18.8	8.2	12.6	16.5	14.1	9.3	8.3	6.5	38.0	51.0
Mililani CDP	5.8	21.4	9.2	11.9	16.5	18.6	9.5	4.6	2.5	36.2	50.1
Pearl City CDP	5.1	13.7	13.7	14.7	12.4	11.1	12.0	10.5	6.6	37.0	46.5
Waimalu CDP	5.4	16.0	9.5	14.8	16.6	17.2	10.2	6.3	3.8	37.8	49.4
Waipahu CDP	6.9	19.6	9.5	13.4	13.3	11.6	9.8	8.6	7.2	35.5	50.6
IDAHO	7.5	21.0	10.7	13.1	14.9	13.2	8.3	5.9	5.4	33.2	49.9
Boise City	7.1	18.3	11.7	16.3	16.1	13.6	7.0	4.8	5.3	32.8	50.5
Caldwell	9.6	21.3	13.1	14.6	12.7	10.6	7.0	5.1	5.9	28.8	51.1
Coeur d'Alene	6.9	18.1	11.7	13.7	14.3	13.0	7.6	6.6	8.2	34.8	51.6
Idaho Falls	8.2	22.1	10.1	12.9	14.6	13.0	7.9	5.8	5.4	32.3	50.5
Lewiston	5.9	17.3	10.7	12.3	14.5	13.4	8.9	8.0	9.1	37.9	51.2
Meridian city	11.4	22.3	6.9	19.8	17.3	10.4	5.4	3.6	2.9	30.1	50.9
Nampa	10.5	20.4	12.5	17.6	12.7	9.2	5.9	5.0	6.2	28.5	51.0
Pocatello	8.3	18.3	16.7	14.7	12.6	12.0	6.9	5.2	5.2	28.8	50.8
Twin Falls	7.8	18.6	12.1	12.8	13.4	12.1	8.1	6.7	8.3	33.8	52.0
ILLINOIS	7.1	19.1	9.8	14.6	16.0	13.1	8.4	6.2	5.9	34.7	51.0
Addison	7.6	18.6	11.3	16.6	15.4	12.8	9.3	5.3	3.1	32.2	49.2
Alton	7.2	18.5	9.1	14.5	14.5	12.0	8.0	7.3	8.7	35.4	53.1
Arlington Heights	6.0	17.1	6.0	13.2	16.6	14.7	10.3	7.9	8.2	39.7	51.9
Aurora	10.6	21.2	10.2	19.4	16.5	10.6	5.4	3.1	3.1	29.3	49.6
Bartlett	10.7	21.1	5.4	16.4	21.4	13.4	6.1	3.3	2.3	33.5	50.6
Belleville	6.2	17.3	9.0	14.1	16.2	12.5	7.6	7.8	9.4	37.2	52.9
Berwyn	7.9	18.3	9.6	16.1	15.6	11.7	7.3	6.0	7.4	33.8	51.3
Bloomington	7.4	17.6	12.5	16.8	16.5	12.8	6.5	5.0	5.0	32.4	51.5
Bolingbrook	9.5	22.7	8.4	16.8	18.4	13.5	6.4	2.4	1.9	31.0	50.1
Buffalo Grove	6.6	22.3	5.3	11.7	20.5	16.8	7.8	5.2	3.9	37.4	51.6
Burbank	5.9	19.3	9.9	12.2	15.9	13.2	9.6	7.7	6.3	36.9	51.2
Calumet City	7.7	21.0	8.6	14.7	16.0	11.6	7.6	6.3	6.4	33.7	53.5
Carol Stream	8.2	22.7	9.1	16.5	20.2	12.6	5.0	2.6	3.1	31.3	50.7
Carpentersville	10.5	22.6	10.9	19.7	15.7	10.0	5.3	3.6	1.7	28.1	48.4
Champaign	5.0	12.8	31.7	15.1	11.6	10.0	5.4	4.5	3.9	25.3	49.3
Chicago	7.5	18.7	11.2	18.4	15.0	11.4	7.5	5.5	4.8	31.5	51.5
Chicago Heights	9.2	22.5	10.2	14.2	13.7	11.0	7.4	6.4	5.5	30.6	51.3
Cicero	10.9	23.7	12.7	18.2	13.7	8.8	4.8	3.4	3.7	26.4	48.6
Crystal Lake	8.1	23.5	6.7	13.4	19.7	13.0	6.6	4.5	4.5	34.1	50.6
Danville	7.1	17.8	9.5	13.6	14.1	12.7	8.6	7.9	8.7	36.6	50.2
Decatur	6.7	17.3	11.1	12.1	13.9	13.5	9.0	8.2	8.2	37.2	53.2
De Kalb	5.4	11.6	39.2	14.0	9.7	7.6	4.4	3.8	4.3	23.1	50.5
Des Plaines	5.9	16.5	7.5	12.9	16.3	14.0	9.8	8.3	8.9	39.7	51.6
Dolton	7.5	24.5	8.3	12.3	17.5	13.5	7.1	4.8	4.4	33.3	53.6
Downers Grove	6.2	18.5	6.6	12.1	17.2	16.0	9.0	6.5	7.9	39.1	52.0
East St. Louis	8.6	24.2	9.7	11.9	12.7	11.8	8.5	7.1	5.4	31.2	55.1
Elgin	9.2	19.8	10.7	17.5	16.1	11.8	6.4	4.2	4.4	30.9	50.0
Elk Grove Village	6.0	18.9	7.4	13.1	18.7	15.1	9.1	7.0	4.8	37.7	51.3

Table D. Cities

City	Population and population characteristics, 1990 — Age (percent)									Percent Female	Population—change, 1980–2000 — Total persons			Percent change	
	Under 5 years	5 to 17 years	18 to 24 years	25 to 34 years	35 to 44 years	45 to 54 years	55 to 64 years	65 to 74 years	75 years and over		2000	1990	1980	1990–2000	1980–1990
	39	40	41	42	43	44	45	46	47	48	49	50	51	52	53
GEORGIA—Cont'd															
Athens-Clarke County	5.2	10.7	39.2	15.2	8.9	5.7	5.0	5.4	4.8	53.7	101 489	NA	NA	NA	NA
Atlanta....................................	7.6	16.5	13.0	19.4	15.4	9.7	7.2	6.0	5.3	52.3	416 474	393 929	425 022	5.7	-7.3
Augusta-Richmond County....	7.8	16.5	10.7	16.9	11.9	8.7	8.6	10.3	8.5	55.1	199 775	NA	NA	NA	NA
Columbus...............................	8.2	18.9	12.1	18.3	14.0	9.2	8.5	6.7	4.1	51.4	186 291	179 280	NA	3.9	NA
Dalton city.............................	6.3	17.1	12.6	17.0	14.0	10.9	8.8	7.2	6.1	51.6	27 912	22 218	20 939	25.6	6.1
East Point..............................	8.0	18.8	10.4	19.0	15.7	9.8	6.7	7.1	4.5	53.7	39 595	34 595	37 486	14.5	-7.7
Gainesville............................	7.6	16.5	12.4	17.6	14.4	8.7	8.9	7.9	6.1	53.9	25 578	17 885	15 280	43.0	17.0
Hinesville..............................	12.1	21.8	15.6	24.2	14.4	6.1	3.3	1.5	0.9	50.7	30 392	21 596	11 309	40.7	91.0
La Grange..............................	7.9	19.6	11.4	15.4	12.4	8.7	8.9	8.3	7.4	55.0	25 998	25 574	24 163	1.7	5.8
Macon....................................	7.7	18.8	11.4	16.5	13.6	8.7	8.8	8.5	6.1	54.7	97 255	107 365	116 903	-9.4	-8.2
Marietta.................................	7.4	12.4	15.9	25.7	13.8	7.8	6.3	5.9	4.7	51.7	58 748	44 129	30 829	33.1	43.1
Peachtree City.......................	8.3	25.4	5.9	14.4	23.5	11.3	4.8	4.4	2.0	50.9	31 580	19 027	NA	66.0	NA
Rome......................................	6.8	17.1	10.8	15.2	13.0	9.9	9.5	9.6	8.3	54.4	34 980	30 326	29 609	15.3	2.4
Roswell..................................	7.0	18.2	9.3	17.9	20.2	14.1	6.5	4.3	2.5	51.0	79 334	47 986	23 337	65.3	105.6
Savannah...............................	8.2	18.6	11.8	17.3	13.0	9.3	8.1	8.2	5.6	52.9	131 510	137 812	141 378	-4.6	-2.5
Smyrna..................................	5.7	11.4	12.3	29.4	15.4	10.3	7.1	5.0	3.4	52.5	40 999	32 453	20 312	26.3	59.8
Valdosta................................	8.5	19.5	16.7	16.1	12.9	8.6	6.8	6.2	4.6	53.6	43 724	40 038	37 533	9.2	6.7
Warner Robins.......................	8.4	19.7	9.6	20.0	14.7	10.8	8.6	5.9	2.3	51.7	48 804	43 861	39 879	11.3	10.0
HAWAII	7.5	17.8	10.9	18.1	16.1	9.8	8.5	7.1	4.2	49.1	1 211 537	1 108 229	964 691	9.3	14.9
Hilo CDP................................	6.8	20.7	8.4	13.9	15.8	10.2	9.7	8.9	5.6	51.2	40 759	37 808	35 269	7.8	7.2
Honolulu CDP.........................	5.4	14.7	9.8	17.8	16.2	10.8	10.3	9.8	6.1	50.6	371 657	377 059	365 048	-1.4	3.3
Kailua CDP............................	6.6	17.5	9.9	16.5	17.0	12.0	9.6	7.6	3.3	49.5	36 513	36 818	35 812	-0.8	2.8
Kaneohe CDP.........................	7.3	17.7	9.9	18.8	15.4	10.5	9.5	6.4	4.5	50.2	34 970	35 448	29 919	-1.3	18.5
Mililani CDP...........................	8.3	24.3	7.9	17.4	22.3	11.4	4.8	2.7	1.0	49.6	28 608	29 359	21 365	-2.6	37.4
Pearl City CDP.......................	6.8	17.5	12.1	17.2	13.0	13.1	11.6	6.5	2.2	49.5	30 976	30 993	42 575	-0.1	-27.2
Waimalu CDP.........................	6.9	16.8	10.8	20.9	19.9	11.1	7.5	4.9	1.2	49.5	29 371	29 967	NA	-2.0	NA
Waipahu CDP.........................	8.4	20.9	12.7	16.6	12.2	9.6	9.1	6.7	3.8	49.9	33 108	31 435	29 139	5.3	7.9
IDAHO	8.0	22.7	9.8	15.2	14.8	9.8	7.7	6.9	5.1	50.2	1 293 953	1 006 734	944 127	28.5	6.6
Boise City	7.4	18.1	11.2	18.4	16.9	9.1	7.0	6.7	5.2	51.7	185 787	126 685	102 451	46.7	23.7
Caldwell.................................	8.5	21.7	11.1	15.0	13.7	8.3	7.2	7.5	7.0	51.7	25 967	18 400	17 699	41.1	4.0
Coeur d'Alene.......................	7.3	17.4	10.7	15.6	14.9	9.2	7.7	8.9	8.2	52.3	34 514	24 561	20 054	40.5	22.5
Idaho Falls............................	9.2	22.7	10.0	16.7	14.8	8.8	7.6	6.1	4.1	50.0	50 730	43 973	39 590	15.4	11.1
Lewiston................................	6.4	17.9	10.0	15.4	15.1	9.9	9.2	9.0	7.0	51.2	30 904	28 082	27 986	10.0	0.3
Meridian city..........................	NA	NA	NA	NA	NA	NA	NA	NA	NA	NA	34 919	9 596	NA	263.9	NA
Nampa...................................	9.0	19.6	12.6	16.2	11.3	8.4	6.6	8.3	8.1	52.1	51 867	28 365	25 112	82.9	13.0
Pocatello...............................	8.5	21.6	12.4	16.8	14.7	8.2	6.9	6.5	4.5	50.9	51 466	46 117	46 340	11.6	-0.5
Twin Falls	8.0	20.6	9.5	15.4	13.8	9.2	8.0	8.2	7.3	52.0	34 469	27 634	26 209	24.7	5.4
ILLINOIS	7.4	18.4	10.6	17.4	14.9	10.2	8.5	7.2	5.4	51.4	12 419 293	11 430 602	11 427 409	8.6	0.0
Addison..................................	8.1	18.9	11.7	19.6	14.0	12.8	8.4	4.5	2.0	50.0	35 914	32 053	29 759	12.0	7.7
Alton......................................	8.1	18.0	9.2	17.3	13.3	8.2	8.6	8.4	8.8	53.3	30 496	33 064	34 171	-7.8	-3.2
Arlington Heights	6.8	15.9	8.2	18.0	16.3	12.5	10.0	6.9	5.3	51.9	76 031	75 463	66 116	0.8	14.1
Aurora....................................	10.5	20.6	11.3	21.1	13.9	8.5	5.6	4.7	3.8	50.6	142 990	99 672	81 293	43.5	22.6
Bartlett...................................	10.3	21.9	7.6	21.5	20.3	9.1	4.7	3.3	1.4	50.5	36 706	19 395	13 254	89.3	46.3
Belleville................................	6.7	16.2	8.6	17.8	14.3	8.1	9.3	9.5	9.6	53.3	41 410	42 806	41 580	-3.3	2.9
Berwyn...................................	6.3	12.9	8.3	18.4	13.7	9.3	9.7	11.3	10.1	53.5	54 016	45 426	46 849	18.9	-3.0
Bloomington...........................	7.5	16.6	13.2	20.0	15.0	8.6	7.1	6.1	5.9	53.1	64 808	51 889	44 189	24.9	17.4
Bolingbrook............................	9.3	25.2	9.7	18.7	20.4	9.7	3.7	2.1	1.2	50.2	56 321	40 843	37 245	37.9	9.7
Buffalo Grove........................	9.5	19.2	6.4	21.8	21.1	10.1	6.2	4.0	1.7	51.0	42 909	36 417	22 238	17.8	63.8
Burbank..................................	6.5	18.2	9.9	16.5	13.4	11.2	10.6	8.8	4.9	51.3	27 902	27 600	28 462	1.1	-3.0
Calumet City..........................	6.7	16.3	8.9	18.8	13.7	10.7	9.2	10.0	5.5	52.7	39 071	37 840	39 697	3.3	-4.7
Carol Stream.........................	11.3	19.5	9.6	27.4	18.0	5.8	3.2	2.6	2.5	50.6	40 438	31 759	15 514	27.3	104.7
Carpentersville......................	10.2	24.2	10.7	20.1	13.1	9.3	7.2	4.2	1.0	49.9	30 586	23 049	23 275	32.7	-1.0
Champaign	5.9	12.1	31.8	17.6	12.2	6.8	5.5	4.9	3.3	48.2	67 518	63 502	58 133	6.3	9.2
Chicago..................................	7.7	18.3	11.3	19.3	13.9	9.5	8.1	7.0	4.9	52.1	2 896 016	2 783 726	3 005 078	4.0	-7.4
Chicago Heights	9.1	21.2	10.8	15.9	12.4	9.5	8.5	7.6	5.0	52.5	32 776	32 966	37 026	-0.6	-11.0
Cicero....................................	8.9	19.5	10.7	18.5	13.0	8.3	7.5	7.9	5.7	50.2	85 616	67 436	61 232	27.0	10.1
Crystal Lake..........................	8.4	21.0	8.1	18.9	17.7	10.0	6.4	5.4	4.0	51.0	38 000	24 696	18 590	53.9	32.8
Danville..................................	7.4	19.1	8.3	14.2	13.6	9.8	10.1	9.9	7.6	53.6	33 904	33 828	39 019	0.2	-13.3
Decatur..................................	6.9	18.1	9.7	15.2	14.3	9.8	9.8	8.9	7.2	53.2	81 860	83 900	94 081	-2.4	-10.8
De Kalb..................................	4.7	10.0	43.9	14.7	9.1	6.0	4.8	3.8	3.1	51.1	39 018	35 076	33 099	11.2	6.0
Des Plaines	6.3	14.3	8.6	17.3	14.4	12.0	11.7	9.0	6.2	51.7	58 720	53 414	53 568	9.9	-0.3
Dolton	6.5	19.7	7.8	17.2	15.3	10.8	9.4	8.0	5.3	52.4	25 614	23 956	24 766	6.9	-3.3
Downers Grove......................	7.7	17.2	7.8	18.0	17.8	11.0	8.3	6.9	5.2	51.7	48 724	46 845	42 572	4.0	10.0
East St. Louis	9.4	25.2	11.7	13.8	12.2	8.7	8.1	6.3	4.6	55.0	31 542	40 944	55 200	-23.0	-25.8
Elgin.......................................	9.2	19.3	10.9	20.7	14.6	8.7	6.3	5.6	4.7	50.6	94 487	77 010	63 798	22.7	20.7
Elk Grove Village	8.0	18.2	8.7	20.3	17.1	11.4	8.9	4.7	2.6	50.9	34 727	33 429	28 907	3.9	15.6

Table D. Cities

City	Total population (54)	Total in house-holds (55)	House-holder (56)	Spouse (57)	Child — Total (58)	Child — Own child under 18 years (59)	Other relatives — Total (60)	Other relatives — Under 18 years (61)	Nonrelatives — Total (62)	Nonrelatives — Unmarried partner (63)	Total in group quarters (64)	Institutionalized — Correctional institutions (65)	Institutionalized — Nursing homes (66)	Institutionalized — Other institutions (67)	Noninstitutionalized — College dormitories (68)	Noninstitutionalized — Military quarters (69)	Other (70)
GEORGIA—Cont'd																	
Athens-Clarke County	101 489	91.9	39.1	12.8	19.9	15.4	5.2	1.9	15.0	2.1	8.1	0.6	0.6	0.0	6.5	0.2	0.2
Atlanta	416 474	93.0	40.4	9.9	24.4	17.5	8.0	1.0	9.5	2.7	7.0	1.8	0.3	0.1	3.2	0.0	1.6
Augusta-Richmond County	199 775	94.5	37.0	15.5	30.3	22.7	6.9	3.5	4.8	2.0	5.5	1.2	0.2	0.1	0.4	2.2	1.3
Columbus	186 291	95.1	37.5	16.7	30.2	23.1	6.2	3.1	4.4	1.8	4.9	1.0	0.6	0.1	0.2	2.6	0.4
Dalton city	27 912	97.5	34.7	17.3	29.0	23.2	10.4	3.1	6.1	1.5	2.5	0.4	1.3	0.1	0.0	0.0	0.6
East Point	39 595	98.9	36.8	10.6	32.1	23.7	11.4	5.0	8.0	2.9	1.1	0.0	0.3	0.0	0.4	0.0	0.4
Gainesville	25 578	93.1	33.4	14.4	25.8	20.3	10.6	3.4	8.9	1.4	6.9	2.5	0.7	1.4	1.2	0.0	1.0
Hinesville	30 392	100.0	34.6	19.4	36.1	31.4	4.1	2.2	5.7	1.5	0.0	0.0	0.0	0.0	0.0	0.0	0.0
La Grange	25 998	96.6	38.5	14.1	30.6	23.6	8.2	4.1	5.0	2.2	3.4	0.0	0.5	1.1	1.4	0.0	0.4
Macon	97 255	96.3	39.5	13.0	30.6	22.3	8.2	4.1	5.0	2.2	3.7	0.7	0.9	0.1	1.7	0.0	0.2
Marietta	58 748	97.3	40.7	14.4	23.7	19.7	7.3	2.0	11.3	2.6	2.7	0.0	0.8	0.0	0.6	0.0	1.2
Peachtree City	31 580	99.5	34.4	24.4	36.2	30.5	2.6	0.9	1.9	0.6	0.5	0.0	0.5	0.0	0.0	0.0	0.0
Rome	34 980	94.0	38.1	15.7	26.4	20.2	7.7	3.2	6.1	1.9	6.0	1.8	1.4	0.8	1.5	0.0	0.5
Roswell	79 334	99.2	38.1	21.7	28.0	23.0	4.8	1.0	6.6	1.6	0.8	0.1	0.0	0.0	0.0	0.0	0.7
Savannah	131 510	95.8	39.1	13.8	28.7	20.7	8.4	4.2	5.9	2.0	4.2	1.0	0.5	0.2	0.8	1.2	0.5
Smyrna	40 999	98.9	44.8	16.2	21.3	16.9	6.9	1.9	9.6	2.6	1.1	0.1	0.1	0.0	0.0	0.0	1.0
Valdosta	43 724	95.5	38.2	14.6	28.8	22.4	6.4	3.1	7.6	2.1	4.5	0.0	0.8	0.3	3.2	0.0	0.2
Warner Robins	48 804	99.2	40.1	18.5	31.2	24.7	4.6	2.3	4.7	2.1	0.8	0.0	0.6	0.0	0.0	0.0	0.2
HAWAII	1 211 537	97.0	33.3	17.8	29.0	19.8	10.5	4.0	6.4	1.9	3.0	0.3	0.2	0.1	0.4	1.2	0.8
Hilo CDP	40 759	96.6	35.8	17.4	28.6	20.3	8.2	3.5	6.6	2.4	3.4	0.0	1.1	0.0	1.2	0.0	1.0
Honolulu CDP	371 657	97.0	37.8	17.2	24.9	15.6	10.3	3.1	6.9	1.9	3.0	0.2	0.4	0.2	0.8	0.2	1.2
Kailua CDP	36 513	99.8	33.5	19.8	29.7	19.4	9.9	4.2	6.8	1.7	0.2	0.0	0.0	0.0	0.0	0.0	0.2
Kaneohe CDP	34 970	98.6	31.4	19.0	31.1	19.1	11.6	4.8	5.6	1.5	1.4	0.0	0.4	0.4	0.0	0.0	0.6
Mililani CDP	28 608	100.0	31.5	22.2	35.5	24.0	7.1	2.8	3.8	1.2	0.0	0.0	0.0	0.0	0.0	0.0	0.0
Pearl City CDP	30 976	91.2	28.8	18.4	27.2	13.3	12.7	5.1	4.1	1.0	8.8	0.0	0.4	0.0	0.0	8.1	0.4
Waimalu CDP	29 371	99.7	35.8	20.0	29.1	18.0	8.6	3.0	6.1	1.9	0.3	0.0	0.0	0.0	0.0	0.0	0.3
Waipahu CDP	33 108	96.6	22.9	13.7	30.3	17.1	21.4	7.8	8.3	1.3	3.4	0.0	0.1	0.0	0.0	0.0	3.3
IDAHO	1 293 953	97.6	36.3	21.4	31.5	26.5	3.4	1.4	5.0	1.7	2.4	0.6	0.4	0.4	0.6	0.1	0.4
Boise City	185 787	97.8	40.1	19.5	28.2	23.8	3.1	1.0	7.0	2.4	2.2	0.7	0.6	0.1	0.4	0.0	0.4
Caldwell	25 967	96.4	34.5	17.8	32.8	27.7	5.6	2.3	5.7	2.1	3.6	1.2	0.7	0.1	1.4	0.0	0.2
Coeur d'Alene	34 514	96.9	40.5	19.3	27.1	22.7	3.0	1.1	7.0	2.4	3.1	0.6	1.5	0.3	0.0	0.0	0.6
Idaho Falls	50 730	98.1	37.0	20.9	33.5	28.4	3.0	1.2	3.7	1.6	1.9	0.7	0.2	0.4	0.0	0.0	0.5
Lewiston	30 904	97.9	41.4	21.2	26.2	21.3	3.0	1.2	6.0	2.5	2.1	0.1	1.2	0.0	0.5	0.0	0.3
Meridian city	34 919	99.2	33.9	23.2	36.2	32.3	2.4	0.9	3.7	1.4	0.8	0.0	0.4	0.0	0.0	0.0	0.3
Nampa	51 867	96.4	34.9	19.4	32.7	28.5	4.3	1.6	5.1	2.0	3.6	0.1	1.0	0.2	1.3	0.0	1.0
Pocatello	51 466	96.8	37.6	19.8	30.2	24.9	3.0	1.1	6.2	1.9	3.2	0.0	0.5	0.0	2.2	0.0	0.5
Twin Falls	34 469	96.6	38.5	19.9	29.4	24.4	3.5	1.4	5.3	2.1	3.4	0.6	1.0	0.1	0.5	0.0	1.2
ILLINOIS	12 419 293	97.4	37.0	19.0	30.7	23.2	6.1	2.3	4.7	1.8	2.6	0.5	0.7	0.1	0.7	0.1	0.4
Addison	35 914	99.4	32.4	20.3	33.6	23.6	8.5	2.0	4.6	1.4	0.6	0.0	0.0	0.0	0.0	0.0	0.6
Alton	30 496	96.9	41.0	16.1	29.3	22.4	5.2	2.6	5.3	2.6	3.1	0.0	1.4	0.7	0.0	0.0	1.0
Arlington Heights	76 031	98.8	40.5	23.6	28.8	22.3	2.9	0.6	3.0	1.1	1.2	0.0	1.0	0.0	0.2	0.0	0.2
Aurora	142 990	98.7	32.5	18.4	34.6	28.4	8.0	2.8	5.2	1.9	1.3	0.1	0.6	0.0	0.2	0.0	0.4
Bartlett	36 706	99.7	33.2	24.1	36.4	30.5	3.7	1.0	2.3	1.2	0.3	0.0	0.0	0.1	0.0	0.0	0.2
Belleville	41 410	96.4	42.5	17.8	27.7	21.2	3.5	1.4	4.9	2.5	3.6	0.8	2.2	0.1	0.0	0.0	0.4
Berwyn	54 016	99.7	36.5	17.1	32.0	23.1	9.4	2.7	4.6	1.9	0.3	0.0	0.3	0.0	0.0	0.0	0.1
Bloomington	64 808	96.2	41.1	19.0	27.6	23.4	2.8	1.0	5.7	2.2	3.8	0.3	0.5	0.0	2.4	0.0	0.5
Bolingbrook	56 321	99.5	30.9	20.6	37.3	29.0	6.8	2.6	3.9	1.4	0.5	0.0	0.5	0.0	0.0	0.0	0.0
Buffalo Grove	42 909	99.4	36.6	24.2	34.0	28.2	2.5	0.6	2.2	1.1	0.6	0.0	0.5	0.0	0.0	0.0	0.2
Burbank	27 902	99.6	33.4	20.3	35.2	22.2	8.1	2.7	2.6	1.1	0.4	0.0	0.2	0.0	0.0	0.0	0.1
Calumet City	39 071	99.9	38.7	14.8	34.0	24.6	7.6	3.4	4.7	2.3	0.1	0.0	0.2	0.0	0.0	0.0	0.0
Carol Stream	40 438	99.8	34.3	20.5	35.9	29.5	4.9	1.1	4.1	1.5	0.2	0.0	0.2	0.0	0.0	0.0	0.0
Carpentersville	30 586	100.0	29.0	18.3	36.6	29.1	10.6	3.5	5.6	1.7	0.0	0.0	0.0	0.0	0.0	0.0	0.0
Champaign	67 518	89.3	40.1	13.8	19.2	16.0	3.0	1.2	13.2	2.1	10.7	0.0	0.4	0.0	9.9	0.0	0.4
Chicago	2 896 016	97.9	36.7	12.9	30.3	20.9	11.4	4.6	6.6	2.2	2.1	0.4	0.5	0.1	0.5	0.0	0.6
Chicago Heights	32 776	98.0	32.7	14.7	36.2	26.3	9.6	4.3	5.0	1.7	2.0	0.0	0.7	0.0	0.0	0.0	1.2
Cicero	85 616	99.8	27.0	15.2	38.6	29.9	13.6	4.1	5.5	1.7	0.2	0.0	0.2	0.0	0.0	0.0	0.0
Crystal Lake	38 000	99.3	34.4	22.0	36.3	30.5	3.0	0.8	3.6	1.2	0.7	0.0	0.0	0.0	0.0	0.0	0.1
Danville	33 904	92.6	39.3	16.5	27.2	21.7	4.6	2.3	4.9	2.4	7.4	5.8	1.1	0.1	0.0	0.0	0.5
Decatur	81 860	95.8	41.6	18.3	26.7	21.3	4.0	2.0	5.1	2.2	4.2	0.8	1.1	0.1	1.9	0.0	0.4
De Kalb	39 018	81.1	33.5	12.4	18.7	15.7	2.9	0.7	13.6	1.9	18.9	0.0	1.0	0.0	17.7	0.0	0.3
Des Plaines	58 720	98.3	38.1	20.9	29.6	20.6	6.3	1.5	3.5	1.2	1.7	0.0	1.5	0.0	0.0	0.0	0.2
Dolton	25 614	99.1	33.2	14.8	37.0	25.7	9.6	5.0	4.5	2.1	0.9	0.0	0.9	0.0	0.0	0.0	0.0
Downers Grove	48 724	98.4	39.0	23.0	30.7	23.7	3.1	0.8	2.7	1.1	1.6	0.0	0.8	0.0	0.6	0.0	0.1
East St. Louis	31 542	99.1	35.4	7.8	37.9	25.1	13.2	6.8	4.9	2.0	0.9	0.0	0.4	0.2	0.0	0.0	0.3
Elgin	94 487	98.0	33.4	18.2	32.5	26.0	8.2	2.5	5.6	1.8	2.0	0.3	0.6	0.3	0.5	0.0	0.3
Elk Grove Village	34 727	99.4	38.2	22.3	32.0	23.8	3.9	0.9	2.9	1.3	0.6	0.0	0.4	0.0	0.0	0.0	0.2

Table D. Cities

City	Households by type, 2000												Households, 1990		
	Total households	Family households						Nonfamily households			Average household size	Average family size	Total households	Female householder[1]	Householder living alone
		Total	With own children under 18 years	Married couple		Female householder[1]		Total	Householder living alone						
				Total	With own children under 18 years	Total	With own children under 18 years		Total	65 years and over					
	71	72	73	74	75	76	77	78	79	80	81	82	83	84	85
GEORGIA—Cont'd															
Athens-Clarke County	39 706	49.6	22.5	32.6	13.4	13.3	7.9	50.4	29.7	5.8	2.35	2.95	NA	14.7	34.7
Atlanta	168 147	49.5	22.4	24.5	9.2	20.7	11.8	50.5	38.5	8.3	2.30	3.16	155 752	23.4	35.0
Augusta-Richmond County	73 920	67.0	33.6	41.8	18.7	20.8	12.7	33.0	27.7	8.5	2.55	3.13	NA	23.1	39.2
Columbus	69 819	68.3	34.6	44.7	20.7	19.6	11.8	31.7	26.7	9.4	2.54	3.08	65 858	17.1	24.5
Dalton city	9 689	67.2	34.3	49.9	25.8	11.5	6.1	32.8	27.6	10.8	2.81	3.43	8 733	13.9	30.1
East Point	14 553	64.8	34.5	28.7	13.3	28.9	17.8	35.2	27.4	5.5	2.69	3.27	13 373	22.5	28.2
Gainesville	8 537	63.7	31.2	43.1	20.1	15.2	9.2	36.3	29.5	10.7	2.79	3.39	6 940	17.2	29.9
Hinesville	10 528	76.3	50.2	56.0	34.5	16.7	13.2	23.7	17.4	2.4	2.89	3.26	7 504	14.1	15.7
La Grange	10 022	64.9	32.4	36.6	15.9	23.5	14.3	35.1	30.1	12.2	2.50	3.12	9 772	20.2	28.9
Macon	38 444	63.0	30.1	33.0	12.7	25.7	15.5	37.0	31.7	12.1	2.44	3.08	41 175	22.7	29.6
Marietta	23 895	54.5	27.8	35.4	16.6	13.8	9.1	45.5	32.8	6.9	2.39	3.05	19 866	11.3	35.8
Peachtree City	10 876	81.6	47.1	70.8	39.8	8.4	5.8	18.4	16.0	5.7	2.89	3.25	6 210	7.3	11.8
Rome	13 320	63.3	29.1	41.2	17.6	17.0	9.4	36.7	30.9	14.1	2.47	3.07	12 008	17.1	32.0
Roswell	30 207	69.3	34.6	57.1	27.9	8.6	5.2	30.7	23.1	4.5	2.61	3.07	18 189	8.3	20.5
Savannah	51 375	61.1	28.5	35.2	14.4	21.7	12.4	38.9	31.4	11.5	2.45	3.13	51 938	19.8	29.5
Smyrna	18 372	51.7	22.5	36.2	14.4	11.4	6.6	48.3	37.5	5.5	2.21	2.92	14 835	9.5	38.8
Valdosta	16 692	61.3	30.9	38.1	16.9	19.5	12.3	38.7	28.4	8.7	2.50	3.13	14 143	19.6	24.8
Warner Robins	19 550	66.9	34.3	46.3	20.7	16.6	11.2	33.1	28.1	7.5	2.48	3.03	16 721	14.0	24.2
HAWAII	403 240	71.2	32.1	53.6	24.0	12.4	5.9	28.8	21.9	7.1	2.92	3.42	356 267	10.5	19.4
Hilo CDP	14 577	69.3	30.6	48.5	19.5	15.2	8.4	30.7	24.1	10.6	2.70	3.19	13 324	13.9	22.1
Honolulu CDP	140 337	62.3	23.7	45.5	17.5	12.1	4.7	37.7	29.7	10.0	2.57	3.23	134 563	11.0	27.4
Kailua CDP	12 229	76.2	32.1	59.2	25.0	12.2	5.0	23.8	16.6	6.0	2.98	3.33	11 843	10.3	11.4
Kaneohe CDP	10 976	79.1	32.7	60.4	25.2	13.7	5.6	20.9	15.4	6.5	3.14	3.48	10 610	10.8	11.7
Mililani CDP	9 010	85.4	43.1	70.4	35.4	10.2	5.5	14.6	10.6	2.0	3.17	3.41	8 776	6.9	8.1
Pearl City CDP	8 921	81.7	25.2	63.9	20.1	12.3	3.6	18.3	14.9	6.6	3.17	3.48	8 876	9.1	8.2
Waimalu CDP	10 524	71.4	29.2	55.9	22.5	11.1	5.0	28.6	21.0	3.4	2.78	3.26	10 372	8.3	17.3
Waipahu CDP	7 566	85.0	36.2	59.8	26.0	18.1	7.9	15.0	11.1	6.0	4.23	4.37	7 567	17.7	9.2
IDAHO	469 645	71.5	36.3	58.9	28.1	8.7	5.8	28.5	22.4	8.3	2.69	3.17	360 723	8.0	22.4
Boise City	74 438	62.5	32.5	48.7	23.6	10.0	6.6	37.5	28.0	7.9	2.44	3.03	50 852	9.7	27.8
Caldwell	8 963	70.9	39.5	51.7	26.9	13.9	9.4	29.1	23.3	10.2	2.79	3.30	6 703	11.5	25.9
Coeur d'Alene	13 985	63.3	31.7	47.7	21.1	11.5	8.0	36.7	28.2	11.3	2.39	2.93	10 304	10.5	30.9
Idaho Falls	18 793	70.1	37.5	56.5	28.3	10.2	7.0	29.9	25.3	9.1	2.65	3.21	16 017	8.4	24.6
Lewiston	12 795	64.7	28.7	51.3	20.2	9.3	5.9	35.3	27.9	12.0	2.36	2.88	11 515	8.2	27.8
Meridian city	11 829	80.4	49.0	68.4	40.2	8.8	6.5	19.6	14.5	4.3	2.93	3.26	3 612	NA	NA
Nampa	18 090	72.0	40.6	55.6	29.7	11.4	7.8	28.0	22.6	9.6	2.77	3.25	10 213	11.7	26.7
Pocatello	19 334	67.1	34.5	52.6	25.4	10.5	6.8	32.9	25.0	7.8	2.58	3.10	17 183	9.5	26.5
Twin Falls	13 274	66.8	32.9	51.7	23.1	11.0	7.2	33.2	26.8	10.7	2.51	3.05	10 472	9.7	26.3
ILLINOIS	4 591 779	67.6	33.0	51.3	24.3	12.3	6.9	32.4	26.8	9.6	2.63	3.23	4 202 240	12.0	25.7
Addison	11 649	78.1	38.3	62.7	30.9	10.2	5.5	21.9	16.9	4.8	3.07	3.46	10 722	10.3	17.5
Alton	12 518	61.1	29.3	39.3	15.9	17.4	11.0	38.9	33.3	13.8	2.36	3.02	12 969	15.4	30.5
Arlington Heights	30 763	66.7	29.2	58.4	25.7	6.3	2.8	33.3	29.0	11.5	2.44	3.05	28 810	6.2	23.7
Aurora	46 489	73.6	44.2	56.5	34.0	12.0	7.7	26.4	20.6	5.3	3.04	3.55	33 710	12.2	22.7
Bartlett	12 179	82.0	48.6	72.5	43.3	7.0	4.0	18.0	14.2	3.3	3.00	3.36	6 365	7.0	13.2
Belleville	17 603	59.2	28.4	42.0	18.1	13.5	8.3	40.8	35.1	14.0	2.27	2.95	17 739	11.6	33.5
Berwyn	19 702	65.6	33.0	47.0	24.8	12.8	5.9	34.4	29.4	12.4	2.73	3.45	19 298	10.7	34.0
Bloomington	26 642	59.0	30.7	46.3	22.6	9.7	6.5	41.0	32.8	9.1	2.34	3.04	21 480	9.6	33.7
Bolingbrook	17 416	81.8	48.0	66.5	39.3	10.9	6.6	18.2	14.2	2.8	3.22	3.56	12 387	9.9	13.2
Buffalo Grove	15 708	74.2	42.7	66.0	38.0	6.6	3.8	25.8	22.1	6.4	2.72	3.23	13 335	5.8	20.7
Burbank	9 317	78.0	34.4	60.8	28.6	12.1	4.2	22.0	18.9	10.3	2.98	3.44	9 171	10.9	17.0
Calumet City	15 139	66.1	34.6	38.3	18.3	22.4	13.5	33.9	29.8	11.5	2.58	3.21	15 434	14.6	29.5
Carol Stream	13 872	73.1	45.4	59.7	37.6	9.6	6.0	26.9	21.1	6.0	2.91	3.45	11 333	7.4	19.4
Carpentersville	8 872	81.6	48.6	63.1	38.0	11.5	6.9	18.4	13.9	3.9	3.45	3.77	6 904	14.2	11.8
Champaign	27 071	46.0	22.0	34.4	15.0	9.0	5.8	54.0	36.6	6.9	2.23	2.95	24 173	8.8	34.2
Chicago	1 061 928	59.6	28.9	35.1	16.9	18.9	10.0	40.4	32.6	8.7	2.67	3.50	1 025 174	19.6	32.1
Chicago Heights	10 703	73.1	38.1	45.0	22.0	22.3	13.4	26.9	22.9	9.7	3.00	3.53	10 932	22.0	21.1
Cicero	23 115	78.3	50.7	56.1	39.3	13.7	7.9	21.7	17.5	8.1	3.70	4.18	23 179	14.3	26.5
Crystal Lake	13 070	75.4	44.6	64.1	37.9	8.4	5.2	24.6	20.2	8.1	2.89	3.36	8 651	8.3	19.2
Danville	13 327	61.2	28.3	42.0	16.2	15.1	9.6	38.8	33.9	15.5	2.35	3.01	13 791	14.0	32.4
Decatur	34 086	61.9	27.6	44.1	16.2	14.1	9.4	38.1	32.7	13.0	2.30	2.90	34 013	13.4	29.9
De Kalb	13 081	50.2	25.9	37.0	17.6	9.4	6.5	49.8	29.6	7.3	2.42	3.02	10 557	8.1	29.5
Des Plaines	22 362	67.4	29.1	54.8	24.3	9.0	3.6	32.6	28.5	13.3	2.58	3.21	19 990	8.2	23.6
Dolton	8 512	76.3	41.6	44.6	23.3	26.1	15.4	23.7	20.8	7.9	2.98	3.42	8 337	16.2	18.8
Downers Grove	18 979	68.6	32.2	59.1	28.1	7.2	3.3	31.4	27.4	12.0	2.53	3.13	17 660	6.4	23.8
East St. Louis	11 178	68.6	33.2	21.9	7.6	40.6	23.3	31.4	27.8	10.4	2.80	3.42	13 057	39.7	25.4
Elgin	31 543	71.0	39.6	54.6	30.2	11.3	7.0	29.0	23.3	7.4	2.94	3.49	26 865	10.9	24.2
Elk Grove Village	13 278	70.0	33.5	58.4	28.1	8.6	4.1	30.0	25.6	8.6	2.60	3.17	12 002	7.2	20.0

[1] No spouse present.

Table D. Cities

City	Percent change of households, 1990–2000	Total housing units	Occupied housing units (percent)	Vacant housing units Total	Vacant housing units For seasonal, recreational, or occasional use	Homeowner vacancy rate (percent)	Rental vacancy rate (percent)	Occupied housing units Total	Percent owner-occupied housing units	Percent renter-occupied housing units	Average household size of owner-occupied units	Average household size of renter-occupied units
	86	87	88	89	90	91	92	93	94	95	96	97
GEORGIA—Cont'd												
Athens-Clarke County	NA	42 126	91.3	5.7	0.4	1.6	4.9	39 706	42.0	58.0	2.45	2.27
Atlanta..................................	8.0	186 925	90.0	10.0	0.6	4.1	7.2	168 147	43.7	56.3	2.37	2.25
Augusta-Richmond County....	NA	82 312	89.8	10.2	0.3	2.6	10.7	73 920	58.0	42.0	2.62	2.46
Columbus.............................	6.0	76 182	91.6	8.4	0.3	1.7	10.5	69 819	56.4	43.6	2.57	2.49
Dalton city	10.9	10 229	94.7	5.3	0.2	1.5	5.3	9 689	47.9	52.1	2.71	2.90
East Point	8.8	15 637	93.1	6.9	0.2	1.7	5.2	14 553	45.4	54.6	2.63	2.74
Gainesville...........................	23.0	9 076	94.1	5.9	0.3	2.0	5.7	8 537	43.7	56.3	2.67	2.88
Hinesville.............................	40.3	11 742	89.7	10.3	0.3	4.9	10.0	10 528	49.6	50.4	3.02	2.75
La Grange............................	2.6	11 000	91.1	8.9	0.4	2.1	8.4	10 022	46.8	53.2	2.49	2.52
Macon..................................	-6.6	44 341	86.7	13.3	0.2	2.9	14.2	38 444	50.1	49.9	2.46	2.41
Marietta...............................	20.3	25 227	94.7	5.3	0.2	1.5	5.2	23 895	37.6	62.4	2.36	2.41
Peachtree City	75.1	11 313	96.1	3.9	0.6	1.2	7.9	10 876	81.2	18.8	2.95	2.65
Rome...................................	10.9	14 508	91.8	8.2	0.3	2.2	9.1	13 320	53.0	47.0	2.50	2.43
Roswell................................	66.1	31 300	96.5	3.5	0.3	1.0	5.3	30 207	67.0	33.0	2.68	2.46
Savannah.............................	-1.1	57 437	89.4	10.6	0.3	1.7	9.1	51 375	50.3	49.7	2.52	2.38
Smyrna................................	23.8	19 633	93.6	6.4	0.4	3.3	4.5	18 372	50.1	49.9	2.18	2.23
Valdosta..............................	18.0	18 907	88.3	11.7	0.3	3.1	13.2	16 692	47.7	52.3	2.56	2.45
Warner Robins.....................	16.9	21 688	90.1	9.9	0.2	2.8	12.1	19 550	57.5	42.5	2.49	2.45
HAWAII	13.2	460 542	87.6	12.4	5.6	1.6	8.2	403 240	56.5	43.5	3.07	2.71
Hilo CDP..............................	9.4	16 026	91.0	9.0	1.3	1.2	10.9	14 577	60.9	39.1	2.78	2.58
Honolulu CDP.......................	4.3	158 663	88.4	11.6	3.3	1.7	10.2	140 337	46.9	53.1	2.75	2.40
Kailua CDP...........................	3.3	12 780	95.7	4.3	1.3	0.8	4.1	12 229	69.7	30.3	3.09	2.72
Kaneohe CDP.......................	3.4	11 472	95.7	4.3	0.4	0.8	5.5	10 976	68.1	31.9	3.19	3.03
Mililani CDP..........................	2.7	9 280	97.1	2.9	0.2	1.0	4.9	9 010	75.9	24.1	3.16	3.21
Pearl City CDP......................	0.5	9 181	97.2	2.8	0.2	0.6	3.2	8 921	68.7	31.3	3.24	3.00
Waimalu CDP........................	1.5	10 999	95.7	4.3	0.3	1.1	6.0	10 524	62.1	37.9	2.94	2.53
Waipahu CDP........................	0.0	8 033	94.2	5.8	0.0	1.0	8.0	7 566	53.4	46.6	4.63	3.76
IDAHO	30.2	527 824	89.0	11.0	5.2	2.2	7.6	469 645	72.4	27.6	2.75	2.52
Boise City	46.4	77 850	95.6	4.4	0.5	1.5	5.2	74 438	64.0	36.0	2.58	2.19
Caldwell	33.7	9 603	93.3	6.7	0.2	2.5	7.9	8 963	65.3	34.7	2.83	2.72
Coeur d'Alene......................	35.7	14 929	93.7	6.3	0.6	2.4	7.6	13 985	61.8	38.2	2.48	2.25
Idaho Falls	17.3	19 771	95.1	4.9	0.4	1.5	5.9	18 793	68.3	31.7	2.80	2.32
Lewiston...............................	11.1	13 394	95.5	4.5	0.4	1.2	5.4	12 795	66.8	33.2	2.48	2.12
Meridian city	227.5	12 293	96.2	3.8	0.2	2.7	2.9	11 829	84.3	15.7	2.98	2.67
Nampa.................................	77.1	19 379	93.3	6.7	0.3	3.4	7.5	18 090	69.5	30.5	2.80	2.69
Pocatello..............................	12.5	20 627	93.7	6.3	0.4	2.3	7.8	19 334	66.2	33.8	2.72	2.30
Twin Falls	26.8	14 162	93.7	6.3	0.4	2.0	8.1	13 274	62.5	37.5	2.57	2.41
ILLINOIS	9.3	4 885 615	94.0	6.0	0.6	1.5	6.2	4 591 779	67.3	32.7	2.76	2.37
Addison................................	8.6	11 805	98.7	1.3	0.2	0.4	1.4	11 649	68.4	31.6	3.09	3.01
Alton....................................	-3.5	13 894	90.1	9.9	0.2	2.3	10.1	12 518	65.4	34.6	2.42	2.24
Arlington Heights	6.8	31 725	97.0	3.0	0.3	1.2	4.6	30 763	76.7	23.3	2.60	1.91
Aurora.................................	37.9	48 797	95.3	4.7	0.2	1.6	6.1	46 489	70.1	29.9	3.17	2.71
Bartlett................................	91.3	12 356	98.6	1.4	0.1	0.6	4.7	12 179	93.1	6.9	3.03	2.72
Belleville..............................	-0.8	19 142	92.0	8.0	0.1	2.1	8.9	17 603	60.2	39.8	2.44	2.00
Berwyn.................................	2.1	20 691	95.2	4.8	0.2	1.3	4.4	19 702	61.5	38.5	3.05	2.23
Bloomington.........................	24.0	28 431	93.7	6.3	0.2	2.1	8.1	26 642	63.1	36.9	2.59	1.92
Bolingbrook..........................	40.6	17 884	97.4	2.6	0.1	1.2	4.4	17 416	85.2	14.8	3.30	2.75
Buffalo Grove.......................	17.8	16 166	97.2	2.8	1.7	0.4	2.9	15 708	87.1	12.9	2.80	2.13
Burbank...............................	1.6	9 518	97.9	2.1	0.1	0.8	2.2	9 317	83.0	17.0	3.09	2.46
Calumet City	-1.9	15 947	94.9	5.1	0.1	2.1	6.3	15 139	63.3	36.7	2.74	2.31
Carol Stream	22.4	14 200	97.7	2.3	0.1	0.9	3.5	13 872	70.5	29.5	3.15	2.34
Carpentersville.....................	28.5	9 113	97.4	2.6	0.1	0.9	3.1	8 872	79.9	20.1	3.46	3.40
Champaign...........................	12.0	28 556	94.8	5.2	0.2	1.4	5.1	27 071	47.4	52.6	2.43	2.05
Chicago...............................	3.6	1 152 868	92.1	7.9	0.4	1.7	5.7	1 061 928	43.8	56.2	2.90	2.49
Chicago Heights	-2.1	11 444	93.5	6.5	0.1	2.6	6.5	10 703	62.8	37.2	3.02	2.97
Cicero..................................	-0.3	24 640	93.8	6.2	0.3	2.0	3.4	23 115	55.2	44.8	3.94	3.40
Crystal Lake.........................	51.1	13 459	97.1	2.9	0.3	1.1	4.3	13 070	79.3	20.7	3.04	2.30
Danville................................	-3.4	14 886	89.5	10.5	0.3	3.1	11.8	13 327	62.5	37.5	2.42	2.25
Decatur................................	0.2	37 239	91.5	8.5	0.3	1.9	11.7	34 086	66.4	33.6	2.35	2.20
De Kalb................................	23.9	13 619	96.0	4.0	0.3	1.6	3.6	13 081	41.9	58.1	2.67	2.24
Des Plaines..........................	11.9	22 851	97.9	2.1	0.2	0.6	3.5	22 362	79.3	20.7	2.70	2.13
Dolton..................................	2.1	8 944	95.2	4.8	0.1	2.7	4.9	8 512	81.6	18.4	3.10	2.47
Downers Grove.....................	7.5	19 477	97.4	2.6	0.3	0.9	3.5	18 979	79.2	20.8	2.70	1.86
East St. Louis	-14.4	12 899	86.7	13.3	0.1	1.9	7.7	11 178	52.9	47.1	2.78	2.82
Elgin....................................	17.4	32 665	96.6	3.4	0.2	1.1	4.9	31 543	70.2	29.8	3.01	2.77
Elk Grove Village..................	10.6	13 513	98.3	1.7	0.2	0.3	4.3	13 278	76.7	23.3	2.74	2.12

Table D. Cities

STATE Place code	City	Population, 2000				Population, 1990				Population and population characteristics, 2000					
		Land area, 2000[1] (sq km)	Total persons	Rank	Per square kilometer	Land area, 1990[1] (sq km)	Total persons	Rank	Per square kilometer	Race (percent) — One race					
										White	Black or African American	American Indian or Alaska Native	Asian	Native Hawaiian and other Pacific Islander	Some other race
		1	2	3	4	5	6	7	8	9	10	11	12	13	14
	ILLINOIS—Cont'd														
17 23620	Elmhurst	26.6	42 762	805	1 607.6	26.3	42 029	694	1 598.1	93.4	0.9	0.1	3.7	0.0	1.0
17 23724	Elmwood Park	4.9	25 405	1 483	5 184.7	4.9	23 206	1 407	4 735.9	91.5	0.5	0.2	2.1	0.0	3.3
17 24582	Evanston	20.1	74 239	380	3 693.5	20.1	73 233	317	3 643.4	65.2	22.5	0.2	6.1	0.1	2.9
17 27884	Freeport	29.6	26 443	1 414	893.3	26.7	25 840	1 250	907.8	81.8	13.8	0.2	1.0	0.0	1.0
17 28326	Galesburg	43.8	33 706	1 075	769.5	43.7	33 530	916	767.3	84.2	10.2	0.2	1.0	0.0	2.5
17 29730	Glendale Heights	14.0	31 765	1 144	2 268.9	13.3	27 915	1 144	2 098.9	63.8	4.8	0.3	20.0	0.1	8.1
17 29756	Glen Ellyn	17.1	26 999	1 381	1 578.9	15.9	24 919	1 291	1 567.2	89.5	2.1	0.1	4.7	0.0	1.8
17 29938	Glenview	34.8	41 847	822	1 202.5	31.0	38 436	775	1 239.9	85.6	1.6	0.1	10.1	0.0	1.3
17 30926	Granite City	43.2	31 301	1 170	724.6	32.4	32 766	948	1 011.3	94.7	2.0	0.5	0.5	0.0	0.9
17 32018	Gurnee	34.7	28 834	1 280	831.0	28.7	13 715	2 363	477.9	82.1	5.1	0.2	8.2	0.1	2.2
17 32746	Hanover Park	17.6	38 278	920	2 174.9	15.7	32 918	939	2 096.7	68.1	6.1	0.3	11.9	0.0	10.4
17 33383	Harvey	16.0	30 000	1 222	1 875.0	16.0	29 771	1 062	1 860.7	10.0	79.6	0.3	0.4	0.1	7.9
17 34722	Highland Park	32.0	31 365	1 166	980.2	31.2	30 575	1 034	980.0	91.2	1.8	0.1	2.3	0.0	3.5
17 35411	Hoffman Estates	51.0	49 495	678	970.5	48.4	46 363	613	957.9	74.4	4.4	0.2	15.1	0.0	3.8
17 38570	Joliet	98.6	106 221	225	1 077.3	72.0	77 217	293	1 072.5	69.3	18.2	0.3	1.1	0.0	9.0
17 38934	Kankakee	31.8	27 491	1 355	864.5	26.5	27 541	1 157	1 039.3	50.9	41.1	0.3	0.3	0.0	5.5
17 42028	Lansing	17.5	28 332	1 307	1 619.0	17.0	28 131	1 136	1 654.8	85.8	10.7	0.1	0.7	0.0	1.5
17 44407	Lombard	25.1	42 322	813	1 686.1	24.1	39 408	755	1 635.2	87.0	2.7	0.1	7.0	0.0	1.4
17 47774	Maywood	7.0	26 987	1 383	3 855.3	7.0	27 139	1 176	3 877.0	9.7	82.7	0.1	0.3	0.0	5.6
17 49867	Moline	40.4	43 768	786	1 083.4	38.9	43 080	668	1 107.5	88.4	3.1	0.2	1.4	0.0	5.1
17 51089	Mount Prospect	26.4	56 265	563	2 131.3	26.7	53 168	504	1 991.3	80.6	1.8	0.2	11.2	0.0	4.1
17 51349	Mundelein	22.3	30 935	1 183	1 387.2	19.5	21 224	1 547	1 088.4	78.7	1.6	0.3	6.6	0.1	10.7
17 51622	Naperville	91.6	128 358	171	1 401.3	72.4	85 806	255	1 185.2	85.2	3.0	0.1	9.6	0.0	0.8
17 53000	Niles	15.2	30 068	1 219	1 978.2	15.1	28 375	1 120	1 879.1	83.2	0.5	0.1	12.7	0.0	1.7
17 53234	Normal	35.3	45 386	756	1 285.7	31.5	40 023	741	1 270.6	87.6	7.7	0.1	2.2	0.0	0.9
17 53481	Northbrook	33.5	33 435	1 086	998.1	32.7	32 565	951	995.9	89.2	0.6	0.0	8.8	0.0	0.4
17 53559	North Chicago	20.3	35 918	989	1 769.4	19.2	34 978	863	1 821.8	47.7	36.3	0.8	3.6	0.1	7.7
17 54638	Oak Forest	14.6	28 051	1 321	1 921.3	14.0	26 202	1 234	1 871.6	90.4	3.6	0.1	2.7	0.0	1.7
17 54820	Oak Lawn	22.3	55 245	585	2 477.4	21.7	56 182	457	2 589.0	93.3	1.2	0.2	1.7	0.0	1.6
17 54885	Oak Park	12.2	52 524	634	4 305.2	12.2	53 648	495	4 397.4	68.8	22.4	0.2	4.1	0.0	1.6
17 56640	Orland Park	49.6	51 077	653	1 029.8	34.6	35 720	838	1 032.4	93.5	0.7	0.1	3.5	0.0	1.0
17 57225	Palatine	33.6	65 479	445	1 948.8	25.5	41 554	704	1 629.6	83.1	2.1	0.2	7.6	0.0	5.1
17 57875	Park Ridge	18.2	37 775	935	2 075.5	17.8	37 075	812	2 082.9	95.4	0.2	0.1	2.7	0.0	0.9
17 58447	Pekin	34.1	33 857	1 065	992.9	28.3	32 254	963	1 139.7	95.8	2.5	0.4	0.4	0.0	0.2
17 59000	Peoria	115.0	112 936	207	982.1	105.9	113 508	163	1 071.8	69.3	24.8	0.2	2.3	0.0	1.2
17 62367	Quincy	37.9	40 366	861	1 065.1	32.9	39 682	750	1 206.1	93.0	4.7	0.2	0.5	0.0	0.4
17 65000	Rockford	145.1	150 115	141	1 034.6	116.5	142 815	123	1 225.9	72.8	17.4	0.3	2.2	0.0	4.8
17 65078	Rock Island	41.2	39 684	878	963.2	39.2	40 630	725	1 036.5	77.1	17.2	0.3	0.8	0.1	2.4
17 66040	Round Lake Beach	12.9	25 859	1 458	2 004.6	10.2	16 406	1 981	1 608.4	74.4	3.1	0.6	2.1	0.0	17.0
17 66703	St. Charles	36.2	27 896	1 331	770.6	26.7	22 636	1 452	847.8	93.8	1.7	0.1	1.8	0.0	1.7
17 68003	Schaumburg	49.2	75 386	374	1 532.2	48.7	68 586	350	1 408.3	78.8	3.4	0.1	14.2	0.1	1.7
17 70122	Skokie	26.0	63 348	464	2 436.5	26.0	59 432	429	2 285.8	68.9	4.5	0.2	21.3	0.0	1.9
17 72000	Springfield	139.9	111 454	209	796.7	110.2	105 412	190	956.6	81.0	15.3	0.2	1.5	0.0	0.5
17 73157	Streamwood	18.9	36 407	965	1 926.3	17.6	31 197	1 002	1 772.6	77.5	3.8	0.3	8.6	0.0	7.1
17 75484	Tinley Park	38.7	48 401	700	1 250.7	27.1	37 115	811	1 369.6	93.2	1.9	0.1	2.4	0.0	1.1
17 77005	Urbana	27.2	36 395	966	1 338.1	20.2	36 383	826	1 801.1	67.0	14.3	0.2	14.2	0.0	1.8
17 79293	Waukegan	59.6	87 901	297	1 474.8	57.4	69 481	344	1 210.5	50.1	19.2	0.5	3.6	0.1	23.0
17 81048	Wheaton	29.1	55 416	582	1 904.3	28.7	51 441	530	1 792.4	89.8	2.8	0.1	4.8	0.0	1.0
17 81087	Wheeling	21.8	34 496	1 044	1 582.4	21.0	29 911	1 058	1 424.3	76.7	2.4	0.2	9.3	0.1	9.2
17 82075	Wilmette	13.9	27 651	1 349	1 989.3	13.9	26 694	1 197	1 920.4	89.7	0.6	0.0	8.2	0.0	0.4
17 83245	Woodridge	21.6	30 934	1 184	1 432.1	19.5	26 359	1 224	1 351.7	75.3	8.0	0.2	11.3	0.0	3.1
18 00000	INDIANA	92 894.8	6 080 485	X	65.5	92 903.7	5 544 156	X	59.7	87.5	8.4	0.3	1.0	0.0	1.6
18 01468	Anderson	103.7	59 734	506	576.0	98.1	59 518	427	606.7	82.0	14.9	0.3	0.5	0.0	0.9
18 05860	Bloomington	51.1	69 291	413	1 356.0	39.1	62 735	395	1 604.5	87.0	4.2	0.3	5.3	0.1	1.1
18 10342	Carmel	46.1	37 733	937	818.5	32.6	25 380	1 271	778.5	92.6	1.5	0.1	4.4	0.0	0.5
18 14734	Columbus	67.2	39 059	895	581.2	52.4	33 948	891	647.9	91.3	2.7	0.1	3.2	0.0	1.4
18 19486	East Chicago	31.0	32 414	1 122	1 045.6	31.0	33 892	893	1 093.3	36.5	36.1	0.5	0.2	0.1	24.0
18 20728	Elkhart	55.3	51 874	641	938.0	44.4	44 661	644	1 005.9	71.5	14.7	0.4	1.2	0.1	9.2
18 22000	Evansville	105.4	121 582	185	1 153.5	105.4	126 272	148	1 198.0	86.2	10.9	0.2	0.7	0.0	0.5
18 23278	Fishers town	56.2	37 835	933	673.2	NA	7 189	3 357	NA	92.3	2.9	0.1	3.1	0.0	0.5
18 25000	Fort Wayne	204.5	205 727	86	1 006.0	162.3	195 680	80	1 205.7	75.5	17.4	0.4	1.6	0.0	2.9
18 27000	Gary	130.1	102 746	234	789.7	130.1	116 646	159	896.6	11.9	84.0	0.2	0.1	0.0	2.0
18 28386	Goshen	34.2	29 383	1 253	859.2	29.3	23 794	1 370	812.1	83.1	1.5	0.3	1.1	0.0	12.0
18 29898	Greenwood	37.0	36 037	986	974.0	28.0	26 507	1 213	946.7	96.5	0.4	0.2	1.4	0.0	0.7
18 31000	Hammond	59.3	83 048	323	1 400.5	59.4	84 236	266	1 418.1	72.4	14.6	0.4	0.5	0.1	9.3
18 34114	Hobart	67.9	25 363	1 486	373.5	40.0	24 440	1 325	611.0	93.7	1.4	0.2	0.5	0.0	2.6
18 36000	Indianapolis	949.2	791 926	12	834.3	950.0	731 726	13	770.2	69.3	25.3	0.3	1.4	0.0	2.0
18 38358	Jeffersonville	35.2	27 362	1 365	777.3	24.7	24 016	1 355	972.3	82.5	13.7	0.3	0.8	0.1	0.7
18 40392	Kokomo	41.9	46 113	742	1 100.5	37.3	44 996	635	1 206.3	85.1	10.3	0.4	1.1	0.0	1.2

[1] Dry land or land partially or temporarily covered by water.

Table D. Cities

City	Population and population characteristics, 2000 (cont'd)								Population and population characteristics, 1990				
	Race (percent) (cont'd)								Race (percent)				
	Race alone or in combination												
	Two or more races	White	Black	American Indian or Alaska Native	Asian	Native Hawaiian and other Pacific Islander	Some other race	Hispanic[1]	White	Black or African American	American Indian or Alaska Native	Asian and Pacific Islander	Hispanic[1]
	15	16	17	18	19	20	21	22	23	24	25	26	27
ILLINOIS—Cont'd													
Elmhurst	0.9	94.2	1.0	0.3	4.1	0.1	1.3	4.0	95.9	0.4	0.1	3.0	2.7
Elmwood Park	2.3	93.8	0.7	0.4	2.4	0.1	5.1	11.0	97.6	0.1	0.1	1.0	4.3
Evanston	3.0	67.4	24.1	0.6	7.0	0.2	4.0	6.1	70.6	22.9	0.2	4.8	3.7
Freeport	2.2	83.8	15.2	0.5	1.3	0.1	1.5	2.1	87.1	11.6	0.2	0.9	0.8
Galesburg	1.8	85.9	11.3	0.6	1.2	0.1	2.9	5.0	88.6	8.4	0.2	0.9	3.8
Glendale Heights	2.9	66.1	5.4	0.6	21.0	0.2	9.8	18.4	81.7	2.8	0.2	13.3	6.2
Glen Ellyn	1.7	90.9	2.4	0.3	5.4	0.1	2.7	4.7	94.0	2.0	0.1	3.1	2.6
Glenview	1.4	86.8	1.7	0.3	10.8	0.1	1.8	4.1	91.0	0.8	0.1	7.4	2.4
Granite City	1.4	96.1	2.2	1.0	0.7	0.1	1.3	2.9	98.4	0.2	0.4	0.5	1.8
Gurnee	2.2	83.9	5.6	0.6	9.0	0.1	3.0	6.0	91.7	3.2	0.2	3.9	3.1
Hanover Park	3.1	70.7	6.6	0.7	12.9	0.1	12.2	26.7	85.5	3.6	0.2	7.4	11.0
Harvey	1.8	11.1	80.8	0.7	0.6	0.1	8.7	12.8	15.1	80.0	0.2	0.3	6.5
Highland Park	1.2	92.2	2.1	0.3	2.7	0.1	3.9	8.9	93.7	2.6	0.1	2.4	4.7
Hoffman Estates	2.2	76.1	4.8	0.5	16.1	0.1	4.7	10.5	87.2	2.9	0.2	8.0	5.5
Joliet	2.1	71.1	18.8	0.7	1.5	0.1	10.1	18.4	69.2	21.6	0.2	1.0	12.7
Kankakee	1.9	52.5	42.1	0.8	0.5	0.1	6.1	9.3	62.0	36.1	0.2	0.5	2.4
Lansing	1.1	86.7	11.0	0.5	0.9	0.0	2.1	5.7	95.7	3.0	0.1	0.4	2.8
Lombard	1.6	88.3	3.0	0.5	7.7	0.1	2.1	4.8	93.4	1.3	0.1	4.4	2.8
Maywood	1.6	10.8	83.8	0.6	0.4	0.1	6.3	10.5	12.0	83.8	0.1	0.5	6.6
Moline	1.8	90.1	3.7	0.6	1.6	0.0	5.9	11.9	94.1	2.0	0.2	0.9	6.8
Mount Prospect	2.0	82.2	2.1	0.5	11.8	0.1	5.3	11.8	90.2	1.1	0.1	6.4	6.4
Mundelein	2.1	80.5	1.9	0.6	7.2	0.1	11.8	24.2	89.5	0.9	0.2	2.9	13.5
Naperville	1.2	86.2	3.3	0.3	10.3	0.1	1.1	3.2	92.6	2.1	0.1	4.8	1.8
Niles	1.9	84.7	0.6	0.4	13.5	0.1	2.6	5.0	91.6	0.4	0.1	7.0	3.6
Normal	1.4	88.8	8.4	0.4	2.5	0.1	1.3	2.6	92.4	5.0	0.1	1.9	1.5
Northbrook	1.0	90.1	0.7	0.1	9.4	0.1	0.7	1.8	93.0	0.2	0.0	6.4	1.6
North Chicago	3.8	50.7	37.7	1.7	4.6	0.5	9.1	18.2	56.7	34.4	0.5	3.6	9.2
Oak Forest	1.5	91.7	3.8	0.5	3.1	0.0	2.5	5.9	97.1	0.6	0.2	1.5	2.5
Oak Lawn	1.9	95.1	1.3	0.4	2.1	0.0	2.9	5.3	98.3	0.1	0.1	1.1	2.4
Oak Park	2.8	71.1	23.9	0.7	5.0	0.1	2.4	4.5	77.0	18.3	0.1	3.3	3.6
Orland Park	1.1	94.6	0.8	0.2	3.8	0.1	1.7	3.7	95.4	0.4	0.1	3.6	2.3
Palatine	1.9	84.7	2.5	0.4	8.2	0.1	6.0	14.1	94.2	0.9	0.1	3.2	3.6
Park Ridge	0.7	96.1	0.3	0.2	3.0	0.1	1.1	2.9	97.4	0.1	0.1	2.2	1.3
Pekin	0.7	96.5	2.7	0.7	0.5	0.0	0.3	1.3	99.2	0.1	0.2	0.4	0.6
Peoria	2.2	71.1	26.2	0.6	2.6	0.1	1.7	2.5	76.5	20.9	0.2	1.7	1.6
Quincy	1.2	94.1	5.4	0.5	0.7	0.0	0.6	0.9	94.9	4.1	0.2	0.5	0.4
Rockford	2.5	74.9	18.4	0.8	2.6	0.1	5.8	10.2	81.1	15.0	0.3	1.5	4.2
Rock Island	2.2	79.1	18.5	0.7	1.0	0.1	3.0	5.9	80.7	17.2	0.2	0.6	3.8
Round Lake Beach	2.9	77.0	3.6	1.2	2.6	0.1	18.5	31.3	91.6	1.0	0.3	1.3	14.3
St. Charles	0.9	94.6	1.9	0.4	2.1	0.0	2.0	5.5	97.7	0.4	0.1	1.2	2.6
Schaumburg	1.8	80.2	3.7	0.4	14.9	0.1	2.5	5.3	90.6	2.1	0.1	6.5	2.7
Skokie	3.2	71.6	5.0	0.4	22.6	0.1	3.6	5.7	81.2	2.2	0.1	15.6	4.1
Springfield	1.5	82.3	16.2	0.6	1.7	0.1	0.7	1.2	85.6	13.0	0.2	1.0	0.8
Streamwood	2.6	79.7	4.3	0.7	9.4	0.2	8.5	16.8	91.2	2.0	0.2	4.2	7.4
Tinley Park	1.3	94.3	2.1	0.3	2.7	0.0	1.8	4.1	96.2	1.6	0.1	1.4	2.5
Urbana	2.4	69.0	15.2	0.6	15.2	0.2	2.4	3.5	75.7	11.4	0.2	11.7	2.7
Waukegan	3.5	53.0	20.3	1.0	4.1	0.1	25.2	44.8	64.3	19.8	0.4	3.1	23.7
Wheaton	1.3	91.0	3.1	0.3	5.4	0.1	1.5	3.7	93.0	2.5	0.1	3.8	2.0
Wheeling	2.1	78.5	2.7	0.5	9.8	0.1	10.6	20.7	90.1	1.7	0.2	4.6	8.4
Wilmette	1.2	90.7	0.7	0.2	8.9	0.1	0.6	2.1	92.4	0.5	0.0	6.9	1.7
Woodridge	2.1	77.0	8.7	0.5	11.9	0.1	4.1	9.2	86.4	6.1	0.1	6.2	4.1
INDIANA	1.2	88.6	8.8	0.6	1.2	0.1	2.0	3.5	90.6	7.8	0.2	0.7	1.8
Anderson	1.4	83.3	15.7	0.8	0.7	0.1	1.1	2.1	84.9	14.2	0.3	0.4	0.6
Bloomington	2.0	88.8	4.9	0.8	6.0	0.2	1.6	2.5	91.2	4.0	0.2	4.0	1.6
Carmel	0.9	93.4	1.7	0.4	4.7	0.1	0.6	1.7	97.0	0.5	0.1	2.3	0.9
Columbus	1.2	92.4	3.2	0.4	3.5	0.1	1.7	2.8	95.4	2.5	0.2	1.6	0.9
East Chicago	2.6	38.5	36.8	0.8	0.3	0.1	26.1	51.6	38.0	33.6	0.2	0.2	47.8
Elkhart	2.9	74.1	16.0	1.1	1.5	0.1	10.3	14.8	84.0	14.0	0.4	0.8	2.0
Evansville	1.4	87.5	11.7	0.6	0.9	0.1	0.7	1.1	89.6	9.5	0.2	0.6	0.6
Fishers town	1.0	93.2	3.2	0.3	3.6	0.1	0.7	2.0	97.4	1.0	0.1	1.3	1.0
Fort Wayne	2.3	77.4	18.5	0.9	1.9	0.1	3.6	5.8	80.5	16.7	0.3	1.0	2.7
Gary	1.7	13.0	85.3	0.7	0.3	0.1	2.7	4.9	16.3	80.6	0.2	0.2	5.7
Goshen	1.9	84.9	2.1	0.6	1.4	0.0	13.1	19.3	95.7	1.1	0.3	0.8	4.9
Greenwood	0.7	97.2	0.6	0.4	1.6	0.1	0.8	1.9	98.5	0.1	0.2	1.1	0.8
Hammond	2.8	74.8	15.3	1.0	0.7	0.1	11.0	21.0	84.8	9.2	0.2	0.4	11.8
Hobart	1.5	95.1	1.4	0.6	0.8	0.0	3.4	8.1	98.4	0.2	0.1	0.2	4.8
Indianapolis	1.6	70.7	26.1	0.7	1.7	0.1	2.4	3.9	76.2	22.3	0.2	0.9	1.0
Jeffersonville	2.0	84.3	14.9	0.8	1.1	0.1	0.9	1.8	86.4	12.7	0.2	0.5	0.6
Kokomo	1.8	86.8	11.3	0.9	1.3	0.1	1.5	2.6	89.5	8.9	0.3	0.7	1.7

[1] Hispanic persons may be of any race.

Table D. Cities

City	Population and population characteristics, 2000										
	Age (percent)										
	Under 5 years	5 to 17 years	18 to 24 years	25 to 34 years	35 to 44 years	45 to 54 years	55 to 64 years	65 to 74 years	75 years and over	Median age (years)	Percent Female
	28	29	30	31	32	33	34	35	36	37	38
ILLINOIS—Cont'd											
Elmhurst	7.0	18.6	7.0	11.3	17.2	14.0	9.0	7.1	8.9	38.7	51.9
Elmwood Park	5.7	16.2	8.2	13.9	16.6	13.4	9.4	8.1	8.5	38.6	52.4
Evanston	5.8	14.4	16.4	17.3	14.7	12.8	7.9	5.1	5.7	32.5	52.9
Freeport	6.6	17.8	8.5	12.8	15.0	12.4	8.8	8.1	10.0	37.9	53.4
Galesburg	5.7	15.4	11.8	12.9	14.1	13.2	8.7	8.4	9.7	38.1	49.9
Glendale Heights	8.0	18.9	11.5	20.1	16.7	13.0	6.9	3.1	1.9	30.5	49.0
Glen Ellyn	7.8	20.5	6.2	12.1	17.9	15.3	8.7	6.2	5.1	37.0	51.2
Glenview	6.5	19.1	5.2	9.5	15.8	16.5	11.4	8.6	7.4	41.3	52.0
Granite City	6.0	18.7	8.3	12.9	16.2	12.7	8.8	8.5	7.8	37.6	52.0
Gurnee	9.6	20.7	5.5	15.8	21.3	13.4	6.5	4.1	3.1	34.2	51.5
Hanover Park	8.8	22.7	10.9	17.3	17.8	12.3	6.2	2.6	1.5	29.7	48.5
Harvey	9.6	25.5	10.8	13.5	13.1	10.9	7.9	5.0	3.6	27.9	52.0
Highland Park	7.4	19.6	4.6	9.6	15.9	16.4	11.4	8.5	6.5	40.6	51.0
Hoffman Estates	7.2	20.9	8.7	15.4	18.5	15.3	7.3	3.9	2.8	33.6	50.2
Joliet	9.3	20.2	10.1	17.6	15.5	10.1	6.2	5.1	6.0	31.0	50.5
Kankakee	8.3	21.1	9.7	14.3	14.4	11.6	7.1	5.9	7.4	32.3	52.1
Lansing	6.4	17.9	7.8	12.8	16.3	13.7	9.4	8.0	7.7	38.4	52.6
Lombard	6.1	16.8	7.9	16.1	17.3	13.0	8.2	6.4	8.1	36.7	51.5
Maywood	8.0	23.7	10.4	13.6	14.1	11.8	8.7	6.0	3.6	30.7	53.2
Moline	6.5	17.6	9.2	12.8	15.0	14.2	9.4	7.7	7.7	37.9	52.2
Mount Prospect	6.6	16.4	8.2	15.3	16.0	12.9	9.9	8.5	6.3	37.2	50.3
Mundelein	9.2	22.2	8.3	16.2	19.7	12.7	5.4	3.7	2.5	31.7	48.9
Naperville	8.4	23.4	6.4	13.1	20.6	15.4	6.5	3.1	3.1	34.2	51.1
Niles	3.8	12.9	6.9	10.5	13.5	13.4	11.3	12.4	15.4	46.8	53.3
Normal	4.9	12.6	38.1	12.3	10.8	8.7	5.0	3.9	3.7	23.0	53.0
Northbrook	5.7	19.8	4.4	6.7	15.1	17.0	12.6	9.9	8.7	44.1	51.7
North Chicago	8.0	16.1	34.7	17.0	10.5	5.7	3.5	2.5	2.0	22.0	39.0
Oak Forest	6.7	19.3	9.1	13.8	17.2	15.1	9.6	5.2	4.0	35.6	50.2
Oak Lawn	5.4	16.6	7.2	11.2	15.0	13.0	9.9	10.5	11.3	41.5	53.1
Oak Park	6.9	17.3	6.7	17.3	17.9	16.5	7.9	4.5	5.1	36.0	53.5
Orland Park	5.4	19.0	7.1	9.2	15.5	16.3	11.0	8.9	7.5	41.4	52.2
Palatine	7.3	17.5	8.5	18.0	17.8	13.7	8.3	5.0	3.8	34.3	50.2
Park Ridge	5.8	18.7	5.5	8.3	16.2	15.1	10.7	9.6	10.1	42.5	52.6
Pekin	6.5	16.7	9.3	14.4	15.9	12.9	8.5	8.1	7.6	37.1	50.9
Peoria	7.4	18.3	12.0	13.8	13.4	12.7	8.1	6.8	7.4	33.8	52.7
Quincy	5.9	17.4	10.0	12.1	13.8	12.3	8.7	8.5	11.4	38.4	53.1
Rockford	7.7	18.9	9.2	14.9	14.8	12.5	7.9	6.7	7.4	34.4	51.8
Rock Island	6.4	16.5	13.1	12.0	13.7	13.3	8.6	7.6	8.7	36.4	52.8
Round Lake Beach	11.3	23.7	9.4	18.9	17.5	9.9	4.7	2.5	2.1	28.5	49.6
St. Charles	6.3	21.5	7.4	12.3	17.4	16.7	8.3	5.0	5.2	36.6	50.2
Schaumburg	6.0	15.9	8.3	19.2	17.1	14.9	9.1	4.7	4.8	35.3	51.3
Skokie	5.2	17.8	7.0	10.2	14.7	15.5	10.0	9.2	10.3	41.9	52.6
Springfield	6.6	17.4	8.8	14.3	15.5	14.4	8.6	7.0	7.4	36.9	53.0
Streamwood	8.7	19.4	8.2	18.7	18.6	12.8	7.5	3.8	2.3	32.5	49.9
Tinley Park	6.6	20.0	8.1	12.9	18.2	15.5	8.0	5.7	5.0	36.5	51.6
Urbana	4.4	10.5	36.2	16.3	10.1	8.4	4.8	4.2	5.2	24.6	47.3
Waukegan	9.6	20.6	12.1	18.4	15.0	10.6	5.8	4.2	3.7	29.0	49.2
Wheaton	6.3	19.8	10.5	12.2	16.5	15.4	8.0	5.4	5.8	35.8	51.3
Wheeling	6.6	16.8	9.4	18.0	17.1	13.9	7.8	5.3	4.9	34.5	50.8
Wilmette	7.1	22.6	3.6	5.5	16.2	17.2	10.6	8.6	8.6	42.2	52.1
Woodridge	7.6	19.7	9.2	17.2	18.8	14.7	7.5	3.3	2.0	32.8	50.3
INDIANA	7.0	18.9	10.1	13.7	15.8	13.4	8.7	6.5	5.9	35.2	51.0
Anderson	6.9	16.3	11.2	14.0	13.6	12.2	9.1	8.0	8.6	36.1	52.6
Bloomington	4.1	8.6	42.3	15.4	9.2	7.9	4.7	3.8	4.0	23.3	51.4
Carmel	7.9	22.4	4.8	11.0	18.9	16.4	8.9	5.1	4.6	37.2	51.4
Columbus	7.4	18.3	8.0	14.2	15.3	13.8	9.3	6.9	6.8	36.4	51.9
East Chicago	9.1	21.4	11.1	13.4	13.4	10.8	7.5	7.4	5.9	30.8	52.2
Elkhart	9.4	19.0	11.1	17.1	14.6	11.0	6.9	5.2	5.5	30.8	50.8
Evansville	6.4	16.3	11.5	13.7	14.9	12.5	8.4	7.7	8.5	36.5	53.0
Fishers town	11.9	20.3	5.4	23.4	21.4	10.2	4.0	2.2	1.2	30.7	51.1
Fort Wayne	7.8	19.2	10.7	15.2	14.9	12.4	7.3	6.0	6.4	32.8	51.6
Gary	8.4	21.5	10.1	11.5	13.5	13.1	9.0	7.5	5.3	33.6	54.2
Goshen	7.9	18.0	12.9	16.3	13.7	10.5	7.0	5.6	8.0	31.5	49.8
Greenwood	7.7	17.6	9.6	16.5	15.6	12.6	8.1	5.8	6.5	34.1	52.1
Hammond	8.1	19.2	9.8	14.4	15.7	12.2	7.6	6.5	6.5	33.9	51.2
Hobart	6.1	17.5	8.6	13.6	16.1	13.8	9.2	7.6	7.5	37.7	51.5
Indianapolis	7.3	18.3	10.1	16.5	16.3	12.7	7.6	5.8	5.2	33.6	51.6
Jeffersonville	6.7	16.9	8.7	15.1	16.2	14.6	9.2	6.9	5.7	36.7	52.0
Kokomo	7.8	17.1	9.4	14.7	14.3	13.1	9.2	7.2	7.2	35.7	52.7

Table D. Cities

City	Under 5 years	5 to 17 years	18 to 24 years	25 to 34 years	35 to 44 years	45 to 54 years	55 to 64 years	65 to 74 years	75 years and over	Percent Female	2000	1990	1980	1990–2000	1980–1990
					Age (percent)						Total persons			Percent change	
	39	40	41	42	43	44	45	46	47	48	49	50	51	52	53
ILLINOIS—Cont'd															
Elmhurst	7.2	16.6	8.6	16.5	15.8	11.2	10.0	8.5	5.7	51.7	42 762	42 029	44 276	1.7	-5.1
Elmwood Park	5.3	12.6	9.0	16.9	13.1	11.1	11.1	11.3	9.6	54.3	25 405	23 206	24 016	9.5	-3.4
Evanston	5.6	12.3	18.0	19.5	15.4	9.6	7.2	5.8	6.6	53.1	74 239	73 233	73 706	1.4	-0.6
Freeport	7.2	17.0	9.7	16.2	12.0	10.5	8.9	9.8	8.7	53.6	26 443	25 840	26 266	2.3	-1.6
Galesburg	6.3	16.0	10.8	15.8	14.8	8.5	9.6	9.5	8.5	51.1	33 706	33 530	35 305	0.5	-5.0
Glendale Heights	8.6	20.3	11.3	24.0	17.0	10.3	4.5	2.4	1.5	49.4	31 765	27 915	23 163	13.8	20.5
Glen Ellyn	8.0	17.8	8.5	16.7	17.4	12.5	8.7	6.2	4.1	50.9	26 999	24 919	23 649	8.3	5.4
Glenview	7.1	17.2	8.0	13.6	16.5	13.8	11.1	8.6	4.3	51.3	41 847	38 436	32 060	8.9	19.9
Granite City	6.9	18.0	9.2	16.7	12.9	10.6	10.4	9.1	6.1	52.1	31 301	32 766	36 815	-4.5	-11.0
Gurnee	9.0	16.4	9.3	22.3	18.0	10.7	7.4	4.5	2.3	51.1	28 834	13 715	NA	110.2	NA
Hanover Park	10.3	22.3	10.7	23.3	16.7	9.7	4.1	2.2	0.7	48.6	38 278	32 918	28 850	16.3	14.1
Harvey	9.6	24.6	11.5	16.3	13.7	8.9	7.0	5.1	3.1	52.0	30 000	29 771	35 779	0.8	-16.8
Highland Park	7.3	17.2	7.3	13.2	17.7	14.0	11.0	7.5	4.9	51.1	31 365	30 575	30 611	2.6	-0.1
Hoffman Estates	8.6	20.2	10.0	21.9	18.4	11.1	5.6	2.8	1.6	49.8	49 495	46 363	37 272	6.8	24.4
Joliet	8.1	19.2	11.3	17.2	13.0	8.8	7.9	7.6	6.8	51.4	106 221	77 217	77 956	37.6	-0.9
Kankakee	8.8	20.4	9.6	16.0	13.0	8.9	7.7	8.2	7.4	53.0	27 491	27 541	30 141	-0.2	-8.6
Lansing	6.5	16.4	9.0	17.2	15.1	10.7	10.2	9.7	5.1	52.3	28 332	28 131	29 039	0.7	-3.1
Lombard	7.5	16.1	9.3	20.9	14.8	10.4	8.5	7.0	5.6	51.5	42 322	39 408	37 295	7.4	5.7
Maywood	7.8	22.8	11.1	16.0	13.5	11.6	8.6	5.1	3.5	53.0	26 987	27 139	27 998	-0.6	-3.1
Moline	7.1	17.9	8.4	15.9	14.9	10.2	9.6	9.2	6.8	52.8	43 768	43 080	45 709	1.6	-5.8
Mount Prospect	6.5	14.5	10.3	19.3	13.5	12.4	11.3	7.9	4.2	50.3	56 265	53 168	52 634	5.8	1.0
Mundelein	10.2	19.3	8.5	22.8	16.9	8.7	6.8	4.9	1.8	49.4	30 935	21 224	17 053	45.8	24.5
Naperville	9.0	21.5	8.1	18.0	21.4	11.2	5.4	3.2	2.2	50.8	128 358	85 806	42 346	49.6	102.6
Niles	4.6	10.9	8.6	14.0	11.3	12.2	13.9	13.3	11.2	53.1	30 068	28 375	30 363	6.0	-6.5
Normal	4.8	12.4	41.9	13.1	10.3	6.3	4.7	3.8	2.6	53.1	45 386	40 023	35 672	13.4	12.2
Northbrook	6.2	18.1	6.7	10.1	16.2	15.2	13.0	8.8	5.8	51.3	33 435	32 572	30 778	2.6	5.8
North Chicago	7.9	15.4	35.9	18.1	9.7	4.3	3.7	3.1	1.8	34.8	35 918	34 978	38 774	2.7	-9.8
Oak Forest	7.8	20.6	10.5	17.6	16.8	12.5	6.9	5.1	2.2	50.7	28 051	26 202	26 096	7.1	0.4
Oak Lawn	5.6	14.5	9.2	14.8	12.3	10.6	12.7	11.8	8.4	53.5	55 245	56 182	60 590	-1.7	-7.3
Oak Park	7.1	16.1	8.0	20.9	19.5	10.4	6.7	5.6	5.7	53.4	52 524	53 648	54 887	-2.1	-2.3
Orland Park	7.1	19.8	9.3	15.2	17.0	12.8	8.9	6.9	2.9	51.2	51 077	35 720	23 045	43.0	55.0
Palatine	6.9	16.9	9.6	20.2	16.6	12.5	8.5	5.3	3.5	51.2	65 479	41 554	32 166	57.6	29.2
Park Ridge	5.5	15.1	7.8	12.3	14.6	12.9	12.8	10.7	8.2	53.1	37 775	37 075	38 704	1.9	-4.2
Pekin	7.1	18.8	9.1	15.5	13.5	10.6	9.9	8.7	6.9	52.9	33 857	32 254	33 967	5.0	-5.0
Peoria	7.4	18.5	12.1	15.5	14.0	9.6	8.6	7.9	6.5	52.8	112 936	113 513	124 160	-0.5	-8.6
Quincy	6.7	17.3	9.9	14.6	12.4	9.6	9.3	10.2	9.9	53.7	40 366	39 682	42 554	1.7	-6.7
Rockford	8.1	17.8	9.7	17.6	14.4	9.2	8.4	8.2	6.5	52.5	150 115	141 787	139 712	5.9	1.5
Rock Island	6.9	17.8	12.3	13.7	13.6	8.8	9.3	9.5	8.0	53.2	39 684	40 630	47 036	-2.3	-13.6
Round Lake Beach	9.8	25.6	11.0	20.6	16.9	6.7	4.2	3.1	2.1	50.6	25 859	16 406	12 921	57.6	27.0
St. Charles	7.5	20.7	8.1	16.4	18.8	11.7	7.3	5.3	4.2	51.1	27 896	22 620	17 487	23.3	29.4
Schaumburg	6.5	17.0	10.4	22.6	18.8	11.8	5.6	4.0	3.2	51.2	75 386	68 586	53 303	9.9	28.7
Skokie	5.1	15.1	7.0	13.0	15.2	11.5	12.4	12.3	8.4	53.2	63 348	59 432	60 278	6.6	-1.4
Springfield	7.3	17.0	9.3	18.2	15.6	9.4	8.5	7.7	7.1	54.0	111 454	105 417	99 637	5.7	5.8
Streamwood	10.1	19.5	10.3	24.9	16.4	10.0	5.5	2.1	1.2	50.0	36 407	31 197	23 456	16.7	33.0
Tinley Park	8.5	20.3	8.1	20.0	18.5	9.5	6.3	5.8	3.0	51.3	48 401	37 115	26 169	30.4	41.8
Urbana	5.9	10.3	32.7	20.2	11.0	5.6	5.2	4.7	4.4	51.1	36 395	36 383	35 978	0.0	1.1
Waukegan	8.2	18.8	11.3	19.9	14.0	9.4	7.6	6.1	4.6	50.7	87 901	69 481	67 653	26.5	2.7
Wheaton	7.8	18.3	11.3	16.8	17.4	11.5	7.6	5.3	4.1	51.7	55 416	51 441	43 043	7.7	19.5
Wheeling	8.4	14.5	8.3	27.0	16.9	9.2	7.4	5.0	3.2	51.2	34 496	29 911	23 270	15.3	28.5
Wilmette	6.9	17.7	6.1	10.0	17.4	13.7	12.0	9.5	6.7	52.6	27 651	26 694	28 229	3.6	-5.4
Woodridge	9.4	18.6	10.8	23.9	18.4	10.0	5.1	2.9	1.0	50.2	30 934	26 359	22 322	17.4	18.1
INDIANA	7.2	19.1	10.9	16.5	14.8	10.3	8.7	7.3	5.3	51.5	6 080 485	5 544 156	5 490 214	9.7	1.0
Anderson	6.9	17.3	11.7	15.3	13.4	10.0	9.3	9.1	7.0	53.3	59 734	59 518	64 714	0.4	-8.0
Bloomington	4.0	8.4	45.2	16.5	9.6	5.1	4.5	3.7	3.1	52.5	69 291	62 015	52 044	11.7	19.2
Carmel	7.1	21.5	7.2	13.4	20.4	13.1	8.3	5.0	4.0	51.9	37 733	25 380	18 272	48.7	38.9
Columbus	7.2	17.6	9.7	16.2	15.2	11.1	9.0	7.8	6.1	52.8	39 059	33 948	30 614	15.1	10.9
East Chicago	7.5	23.7	9.7	15.6	12.3	8.5	9.8	8.3	4.5	52.5	32 414	33 892	39 786	-4.4	-14.8
Elkhart	9.2	17.9	10.5	18.7	13.9	9.0	7.7	7.3	5.9	52.5	51 874	44 661	41 305	16.2	8.1
Evansville	6.9	16.1	10.3	17.5	13.3	9.4	9.3	9.4	7.7	53.6	121 582	126 272	130 496	-3.7	-3.2
Fishers town	NA	NA	NA	NA	NA	NA	NA	NA	NA	NA	37 835	7 189	NA	426.3	NA
Fort Wayne	8.0	18.4	10.9	18.8	14.2	8.4	7.9	7.4	6.0	52.4	205 727	191 839	172 196	7.2	11.4
Gary	8.0	23.7	9.4	14.5	13.5	10.2	9.4	7.4	4.0	54.0	102 746	116 646	151 953	-11.9	-23.2
Goshen	8.3	17.1	13.3	18.2	13.4	8.9	6.8	6.8	7.1	51.3	29 383	23 794	19 665	23.5	21.0
Greenwood	7.0	17.7	10.5	18.8	16.0	10.4	7.6	6.1	5.9	53.0	36 037	26 507	19 327	36.0	37.2
Hammond	7.4	19.2	9.6	18.1	13.5	8.9	9.1	9.1	5.2	51.6	83 048	84 236	93 714	-1.4	-10.1
Hobart	6.0	19.3	8.6	16.1	15.7	10.5	9.6	8.9	5.2	51.4	25 363	24 440	22 987	3.8	6.3
Indianapolis	7.9	17.7	10.4	20.2	14.6	9.4	8.2	6.8	4.8	52.5	791 926	741 866	NA	6.7	NA
Jeffersonville	6.8	17.7	9.7	17.6	14.4	10.9	9.2	7.5	6.1	53.4	27 362	24 016	21 220	13.9	13.2
Kokomo	7.5	18.7	9.3	17.0	14.6	10.3	9.1	7.8	5.7	53.5	46 113	44 996	47 808	2.5	-5.9

Table D. Cities

City	Total population	Total in house-holds	House-holder	Spouse	Child Total	Own child under 18 years	Other relatives Total	Under 18 years	Nonrelatives Total	Unmar-ried partner	Total in group quarters	Correc-tional institu-tions	Nurs-ing homes	Other institu-tions	Col-lege dormi-tories	Mili-tary quar-ters	Other
	54	55	56	57	58	59	60	61	62	63	64	65	66	67	68	69	70
ILLINOIS—Cont'd																	
Elmhurst	42 762	96.3	36.5	22.7	31.8	24.6	2.9	0.8	2.3	0.9	3.7	0.0	1.9	0.1	1.7	0.0	0.0
Elmwood Park	25 405	99.0	38.8	19.3	30.6	20.2	6.8	1.5	3.6	1.6	1.0	0.0	0.9	0.0	0.0	0.0	0.0
Evanston	74 239	90.6	39.9	16.1	23.0	18.1	4.5	1.8	7.0	1.8	9.4	0.0	0.8	0.0	7.3	0.0	1.4
Freeport	26 443	97.2	42.4	19.1	27.5	22.2	3.3	1.5	4.8	2.5	2.8	0.3	1.7	0.0	0.0	0.0	0.7
Galesburg	33 706	87.9	39.3	17.1	23.5	18.8	3.1	1.4	4.9	2.4	12.1	5.5	1.9	0.2	3.1	0.0	1.4
Glendale Heights	31 765	99.9	34.0	18.9	33.2	24.3	8.7	2.2	5.1	1.8	0.1	0.0	0.0	0.0	0.0	0.0	0.0
Glen Ellyn	26 999	99.6	37.8	23.1	33.1	27.2	2.8	0.7	2.9	1.0	0.4	0.0	0.1	0.0	0.0	0.0	0.3
Glenview	41 847	98.7	37.0	25.1	31.9	24.9	3.1	0.6	1.8	0.7	1.3	0.0	0.7	0.0	0.0	0.0	0.5
Granite City	31 301	99.1	40.8	19.4	29.7	22.0	4.4	2.0	4.8	2.4	0.9	0.0	0.7	0.0	0.0	0.0	0.3
Gurnee	28 834	99.9	36.9	23.1	34.1	29.3	2.9	0.8	3.0	1.5	0.1	0.0	0.0	0.0	0.0	0.0	0.1
Hanover Park	38 278	99.8	29.0	18.7	36.9	28.0	9.9	2.8	5.4	1.5	0.2	0.0	0.0	0.1	0.0	0.0	0.1
Harvey	30 000	98.8	30.0	10.9	38.1	25.8	14.1	7.8	5.8	1.9	1.2	0.0	0.3	0.2	0.0	0.0	0.7
Highland Park	31 365	99.4	36.7	25.7	30.5	26.0	3.3	0.8	3.2	0.8	0.6	0.0	0.0	0.0	0.0	0.0	0.6
Hoffman Estates	49 495	99.5	34.4	21.3	34.4	26.5	5.6	1.3	3.7	1.3	0.5	0.0	0.5	0.0	0.0	0.0	0.0
Joliet	106 221	95.8	34.1	17.7	33.1	25.9	6.3	2.6	4.6	1.9	4.2	1.5	1.5	0.4	0.3	0.0	0.6
Kankakee	27 491	94.7	36.4	13.3	31.7	25.1	7.1	3.3	6.2	2.6	5.3	0.5	1.1	2.9	0.0	0.0	0.7
Lansing	28 332	100.0	40.3	21.5	31.3	22.5	3.7	1.4	3.2	1.6	0.0	0.0	0.0	0.0	0.0	0.0	0.0
Lombard	42 322	96.8	39.0	21.0	29.0	21.8	3.8	1.0	4.0	1.3	3.2	0.0	1.6	0.0	0.9	0.0	0.7
Maywood	26 987	99.3	29.4	12.0	35.5	21.2	17.3	9.4	5.1	1.6	0.7	0.0	0.0	0.0	0.0	0.0	0.7
Moline	43 768	99.2	42.3	20.6	28.3	22.1	3.4	1.4	4.7	2.3	0.8	0.0	0.5	0.2	0.0	0.0	0.1
Mount Prospect	56 265	99.9	38.4	22.9	29.2	21.6	5.6	1.2	3.9	1.2	0.1	0.0	0.0	0.0	0.0	0.0	0.1
Mundelein	30 935	99.4	31.9	20.7	35.1	29.2	7.0	1.8	4.8	1.2	0.6	0.0	0.0	0.0	0.5	0.0	0.1
Naperville	128 358	98.5	34.1	23.6	36.3	31.2	2.2	0.4	2.3	1.0	1.5	0.0	0.6	0.1	0.6	0.0	0.2
Niles	30 068	95.5	39.9	21.6	25.5	15.5	6.2	1.0	2.4	0.9	4.5	0.0	3.9	0.0	0.0	0.0	0.6
Normal	45 386	81.1	33.4	14.2	19.7	16.5	1.6	0.5	12.2	1.4	18.9	0.0	0.8	0.1	17.9	0.0	0.1
Northbrook	33 435	97.8	36.5	26.4	31.3	24.8	2.2	0.5	1.3	0.5	2.2	0.0	1.5	0.0	0.1	0.0	0.6
North Chicago	35 918	65.8	21.3	10.3	24.6	20.4	6.1	2.6	3.5	1.1	34.2	0.5	0.0	4.2	0.0	29.0	0.4
Oak Forest	28 051	98.1	34.9	21.3	34.3	24.3	4.4	1.4	3.2	1.4	1.9	0.0	0.0	1.7	0.0	0.0	0.2
Oak Lawn	55 245	99.1	40.2	20.9	30.3	20.3	5.2	1.5	2.5	1.1	0.9	0.0	0.9	0.0	0.0	0.0	0.0
Oak Park	52 524	99.3	43.9	18.5	28.6	22.6	3.7	1.3	4.5	2.1	0.7	0.0	0.4	0.0	0.0	0.0	0.3
Orland Park	51 077	99.1	36.6	24.3	32.6	23.2	3.9	1.0	1.9	0.8	0.9	0.0	0.8	0.0	0.0	0.0	0.1
Palatine	65 479	99.7	39.0	20.8	29.5	23.3	5.1	1.1	5.4	1.8	0.3	0.0	0.2	0.0	0.0	0.0	0.1
Park Ridge	37 775	98.2	37.6	23.9	32.0	23.7	3.1	0.7	1.6	0.7	1.8	0.0	1.3	0.0	0.0	0.0	0.5
Pekin	33 857	93.5	39.5	20.0	27.0	21.3	2.8	1.3	4.1	2.2	6.5	5.0	0.9	0.0	0.0	0.0	0.6
Peoria	112 936	95.2	40.0	16.6	28.3	22.5	4.4	2.2	5.9	2.2	4.8	0.2	1.1	0.3	2.3	0.0	0.9
Quincy	40 366	94.1	41.0	19.0	26.7	21.3	2.9	1.3	4.6	2.2	5.9	0.3	3.5	0.2	1.3	0.0	0.5
Rockford	150 115	97.1	39.4	17.3	29.5	23.4	5.3	2.3	5.6	2.5	2.9	0.5	1.2	0.2	0.2	0.0	0.7
Rock Island	39 684	93.9	40.7	16.8	26.4	20.1	4.3	2.2	5.7	2.4	6.1	0.3	1.1	0.1	3.9	0.0	0.6
Round Lake Beach	25 859	99.5	28.4	18.8	38.1	31.1	9.0	3.1	5.1	1.5	0.5	0.0	0.5	0.0	0.0	0.0	0.0
St. Charles	27 896	97.1	37.1	22.7	31.4	25.3	2.6	0.8	3.3	1.2	2.9	0.0	0.6	1.8	0.0	0.0	0.5
Schaumburg	75 386	99.4	42.2	21.0	28.0	20.8	3.9	0.9	4.3	1.8	0.6	0.0	0.6	0.0	0.0	0.0	0.0
Skokie	63 348	98.2	36.7	22.2	30.7	21.2	6.4	1.2	2.2	0.8	1.8	0.0	1.0	0.1	0.1	0.0	0.6
Springfield	111 454	97.7	43.6	18.0	27.2	21.7	3.6	1.6	5.3	2.6	2.3	0.3	0.9	0.1	0.2	0.0	0.7
Streamwood	36 407	99.4	33.2	21.3	33.8	25.6	7.3	2.2	3.8	1.5	0.6	0.0	0.5	0.1	0.0	0.0	0.0
Tinley Park	48 401	98.5	36.1	22.2	34.2	25.3	3.5	1.0	2.4	1.2	1.5	0.0	0.2	1.1	0.0	0.0	0.2
Urbana	36 395	84.2	39.4	12.7	16.1	13.7	2.4	0.9	13.6	1.7	15.8	0.6	1.1	0.0	13.9	0.0	0.1
Waukegan	87 901	97.6	31.6	15.7	32.8	25.8	10.8	3.5	6.8	1.9	2.4	0.7	0.4	0.0	0.0	0.0	1.2
Wheaton	55 416	92.4	35.0	21.5	30.8	25.3	2.3	0.6	2.9	0.9	7.6	1.3	1.7	0.1	3.8	0.0	0.7
Wheeling	34 496	98.9	38.5	19.7	28.4	21.4	7.2	1.6	5.2	1.6	1.1	0.0	1.1	0.0	0.0	0.0	0.0
Wilmette	27 651	99.2	36.3	25.0	34.6	29.3	1.8	0.4	1.6	0.5	0.8	0.0	0.5	0.0	0.0	0.0	0.3
Woodridge	30 934	99.7	36.8	21.0	32.9	25.6	5.1	1.4	4.0	1.7	0.3	0.0	0.0	0.0	0.0	0.0	0.3
INDIANA	6 080 485	97.1	38.4	20.6	29.6	23.6	3.8	1.6	4.7	2.1	2.9	0.6	0.8	0.1	1.1	0.0	0.3
Anderson	59 734	96.4	42.3	17.5	26.1	20.3	4.7	2.2	5.7	2.9	3.6	0.4	1.0	0.0	1.8	0.0	0.4
Bloomington	69 291	79.8	38.2	11.2	13.8	11.7	1.6	0.4	15.0	2.2	20.2	0.3	0.5	0.5	18.6	0.0	0.4
Carmel	37 733	98.6	36.0	25.0	34.0	29.7	1.6	0.4	2.0	0.9	1.4	0.0	1.2	0.0	0.0	0.0	0.2
Columbus	39 059	97.9	40.9	21.2	28.5	23.8	2.9	1.2	4.4	2.0	2.1	0.4	1.4	0.2	0.0	0.0	0.1
East Chicago	32 414	99.4	36.1	12.6	37.1	25.7	9.4	4.2	4.2	1.9	0.6	0.0	0.3	0.0	0.0	0.0	0.3
Elkhart	51 874	98.7	38.7	15.8	29.8	24.7	6.5	2.6	7.9	3.3	1.3	0.0	0.6	0.0	0.2	0.0	0.5
Evansville	121 582	96.1	43.0	17.5	26.1	20.2	4.0	1.8	5.5	2.5	3.9	0.4	1.3	0.3	1.3	0.0	0.6
Fishers town	37 835	100.0	37.1	24.0	34.1	31.6	1.5	0.4	3.3	1.6	0.0	0.0	0.0	0.0	0.0	0.0	0.0
Fort Wayne	205 727	97.6	40.5	17.0	30.0	24.2	4.3	1.9	5.8	2.5	2.4	0.3	1.0	0.1	0.4	0.0	0.7
Gary	102 746	99.2	37.2	11.3	34.7	22.9	10.9	5.9	5.2	2.3	0.8	0.0	0.5	0.0	0.0	0.0	0.3
Goshen	29 383	94.8	36.3	18.5	27.1	22.9	6.1	2.0	6.8	2.2	5.2	1.6	1.3	0.1	1.9	0.0	0.4
Greenwood	36 037	98.4	41.4	21.1	28.5	23.9	2.9	1.0	4.5	2.1	1.6	0.0	1.0	0.2	0.1	0.0	0.3
Hammond	83 048	99.5	38.6	16.6	32.9	23.8	6.6	2.8	4.9	2.5	0.5	0.0	0.1	0.0	0.0	0.0	0.3
Hobart	25 363	99.0	38.9	21.9	29.9	21.5	4.3	1.5	4.2	2.0	1.0	0.0	0.8	0.0	0.0	0.0	0.1
Indianapolis	791 926	97.7	41.0	16.7	28.3	22.5	5.3	2.3	6.6	2.8	2.3	0.6	0.7	0.2	0.5	0.0	0.4
Jeffersonville	27 362	97.7	42.6	18.4	27.4	20.9	4.5	2.0	4.8	2.6	2.3	0.9	0.7	0.1	0.0	0.0	0.6
Kokomo	46 113	98.5	44.0	18.6	27.9	22.4	3.6	1.7	4.4	2.3	1.5	0.0	0.9	0.3	0.0	0.0	0.3

Table D. Cities

City	Households by type, 2000												Households, 1990		
		Family households						Nonfamily households							
				Married couple		Female householder[1]			Householder living alone						House-holder living alone
	Total households	Total	With own children under 18 years	Total	With own children under 18 years	Total	With own children under 18 years	Total	Total	65 years and over	Average house-hold size	Average family size	Total house-holds	Female house-holder[1]	
	71	72	73	74	75	76	77	78	79	80	81	82	83	84	85
ILLINOIS—Cont'd															
Elmhurst	15 627	71.9	33.9	62.0	30.0	7.4	3.1	28.1	24.6	11.4	2.63	3.19	15 135	7.6	20.3
Elmwood Park	9 858	66.2	29.5	49.6	22.9	12.4	5.2	33.8	29.2	13.1	2.55	3.20	9 474	11.3	30.1
Evanston	29 651	53.8	25.4	40.4	18.0	10.9	6.2	46.2	36.3	9.0	2.27	3.03	27 954	10.7	34.2
Freeport	11 222	61.0	28.4	45.1	17.8	12.6	8.6	39.0	33.7	15.1	2.29	2.93	10 843	10.9	32.1
Galesburg	13 237	59.7	26.3	43.6	16.0	12.4	8.3	40.3	34.6	16.1	2.24	2.87	13 272	11.2	33.3
Glendale Heights	10 791	70.4	38.2	55.5	30.9	9.9	5.3	29.6	22.8	3.1	2.94	3.54	9 613	8.5	19.7
Glen Ellyn	10 207	70.5	36.7	61.0	32.2	6.8	3.6	29.5	25.2	9.3	2.63	3.21	9 413	7.2	23.2
Glenview	15 464	76.8	35.6	67.9	31.5	6.9	3.4	23.2	20.7	9.6	2.67	3.11	13 348	7.0	18.7
Granite City	12 773	66.2	30.0	47.6	19.3	13.7	7.8	33.8	29.4	13.3	2.43	2.98	13 008	12.9	26.6
Gurnee	10 629	72.6	42.3	62.6	36.1	7.8	5.1	27.4	22.7	6.4	2.71	3.25	5 360	7.7	22.7
Hanover Park	11 105	82.0	49.1	64.4	39.7	11.8	6.9	18.0	13.5	2.1	3.44	3.75	10 053	9.5	12.0
Harvey	8 990	75.2	39.1	36.4	17.9	31.8	18.3	24.8	20.7	7.1	3.30	3.80	9 052	28.9	21.6
Highland Park	11 521	77.4	36.9	69.9	33.0	5.8	3.1	22.6	19.5	9.3	2.71	3.09	11 023	6.1	17.0
Hoffman Estates	17 034	74.7	41.3	61.9	34.5	9.6	5.6	25.3	19.9	4.0	2.89	3.39	15 924	8.0	17.4
Joliet	36 182	70.2	38.8	51.9	28.6	13.3	7.9	29.8	24.7	10.0	2.81	3.39	26 779	14.7	27.0
Kankakee	10 020	62.6	34.4	36.4	17.1	21.2	14.5	37.4	31.5	13.9	2.60	3.28	10 397	19.3	32.5
Lansing	11 416	68.1	30.3	53.3	22.9	11.4	5.9	31.9	27.9	12.6	2.48	3.06	10 881	8.8	23.8
Lombard	16 487	65.0	29.8	53.9	25.0	7.9	3.5	35.0	28.7	10.3	2.49	3.13	15 046	7.7	24.4
Maywood	7 937	77.5	36.2	40.7	18.8	30.2	15.0	22.5	19.1	6.8	3.38	3.84	8 036	26.6	18.4
Moline	18 492	62.7	28.8	48.8	20.2	10.4	6.7	37.3	31.9	12.6	2.35	2.97	18 265	10.7	31.0
Mount Prospect	21 585	70.2	30.5	59.7	26.4	7.2	3.1	29.8	25.1	10.0	2.60	3.14	20 281	6.8	22.3
Mundelein	9 858	78.3	47.2	65.0	40.0	9.0	5.3	21.7	17.0	4.5	3.12	3.52	7 120	8.3	16.1
Naperville	43 751	76.9	47.3	69.2	42.6	5.9	3.8	23.1	18.8	4.5	2.89	3.37	29 101	5.5	17.6
Niles	12 002	66.2	21.9	54.0	18.6	8.5	2.4	33.8	30.6	18.2	2.39	3.01	10 776	8.1	25.5
Normal	15 157	54.0	27.3	42.4	19.6	9.3	6.4	46.0	26.6	6.2	2.43	2.96	11 856	8.2	21.0
Northbrook	12 203	79.3	35.4	72.3	32.2	5.3	2.5	20.7	18.9	11.3	2.68	3.07	11 391	5.6	15.8
North Chicago	7 661	72.8	46.3	48.5	31.4	18.9	12.3	27.2	21.8	6.0	3.09	3.64	7 142	18.3	19.0
Oak Forest	9 785	75.0	36.9	61.0	30.8	9.7	4.4	25.0	20.7	5.9	2.81	3.30	8 865	8.8	17.8
Oak Lawn	22 220	65.5	25.8	52.0	21.4	10.1	3.4	34.5	30.9	17.0	2.46	3.14	21 459	9.6	26.2
Oak Park	23 079	56.2	29.5	42.1	21.7	11.6	6.6	43.8	37.0	8.6	2.26	3.06	22 607	12.0	34.3
Orland Park	18 675	76.9	32.2	66.3	28.3	7.9	3.1	23.1	20.6	10.0	2.71	3.16	12 096	6.9	15.6
Palatine	25 518	65.0	32.2	53.3	26.4	8.3	4.5	35.0	27.5	6.2	2.56	3.18	15 158	7.6	24.8
Park Ridge	14 219	73.6	32.3	63.4	28.5	8.0	3.1	26.4	24.1	12.8	2.61	3.13	13 466	8.2	21.0
Pekin	13 380	65.8	31.1	50.7	21.1	11.4	7.7	34.2	29.5	13.2	2.37	2.92	13 078	10.4	28.4
Peoria	45 199	60.5	29.0	41.6	16.7	15.5	10.5	39.5	33.2	11.7	2.38	3.04	44 976	14.7	31.6
Quincy	16 546	61.1	28.6	46.3	19.1	11.6	7.6	38.9	33.7	15.3	2.30	2.94	16 086	11.1	33.4
Rockford	59 158	63.1	31.5	43.8	19.2	14.8	9.8	36.9	30.7	11.3	2.46	3.09	54 839	13.4	28.6
Rock Island	16 148	59.1	26.4	41.2	15.3	14.2	9.1	40.9	34.5	14.3	2.31	2.97	16 239	13.8	32.6
Round Lake Beach	7 349	82.0	53.4	66.2	43.6	10.5	7.0	18.0	14.0	4.5	3.50	3.83	4 902	11.6	14.5
St. Charles	10 351	71.7	36.4	61.1	30.6	8.0	4.6	28.3	23.5	8.0	2.62	3.13	8 133	7.9	20.8
Schaumburg	31 799	60.7	28.4	49.9	23.1	8.1	4.2	39.3	32.3	7.8	2.36	3.07	27 589	7.8	28.4
Skokie	23 223	73.4	32.2	60.5	27.0	9.9	4.2	26.6	23.6	13.6	2.68	3.20	22 708	8.5	22.2
Springfield	48 621	57.5	27.5	41.1	17.3	12.9	8.2	42.5	36.1	11.7	2.24	2.94	45 006	12.7	35.0
Streamwood	12 095	77.8	40.7	64.2	34.1	9.2	4.8	22.2	17.3	3.0	2.99	3.41	9 931	7.7	10.9
Tinley Park	17 478	73.2	36.4	61.5	31.1	8.6	4.1	26.8	23.1	8.7	2.73	3.27	12 678	7.9	20.2
Urbana	14 327	43.4	20.1	32.2	13.2	8.7	5.9	56.6	36.6	8.1	2.14	2.83	13 210	8.3	35.4
Waukegan	27 787	70.0	40.4	49.5	28.4	14.6	9.2	30.0	24.2	7.5	3.09	3.68	24 545	13.3	25.7
Wheaton	19 377	70.8	36.7	61.4	31.9	7.3	3.9	29.2	24.5	7.5	2.64	3.20	17 770	7.2	20.6
Wheeling	13 280	63.7	31.5	51.1	25.6	9.0	4.6	36.3	30.1	8.2	2.57	3.26	12 468	8.4	29.9
Wilmette	10 039	77.0	40.6	68.9	36.5	6.4	3.3	23.0	21.1	12.1	2.73	3.19	9 720	7.4	18.6
Woodridge	11 382	71.1	38.3	57.1	30.5	10.5	6.3	28.9	23.5	3.2	2.71	3.26	9 622	9.7	21.4
INDIANA	2 336 306	68.6	32.9	53.6	23.8	11.1	6.9	31.4	25.9	9.5	2.53	3.05	2 065 355	10.5	24.1
Anderson	25 274	61.0	27.0	41.4	15.0	15.1	9.4	39.0	33.1	14.0	2.28	2.87	24 311	14.2	30.8
Bloomington	26 468	39.5	17.9	29.2	11.6	7.8	5.2	60.5	39.1	7.1	2.09	2.76	20 983	8.5	35.5
Carmel	13 597	77.7	43.2	69.3	37.7	6.6	4.3	22.3	18.9	6.3	2.74	3.16	9 111	6.7	18.7
Columbus	15 985	66.1	31.8	51.9	23.0	11.0	7.0	33.9	29.1	10.7	2.39	2.94	12 850	11.1	27.7
East Chicago	11 707	67.8	35.6	34.8	16.8	26.7	16.3	32.2	28.6	11.2	2.75	3.41	12 122	25.8	27.4
Elkhart	20 072	62.3	33.4	40.9	19.1	15.3	10.7	37.7	30.3	10.3	2.55	3.16	17 519	14.0	29.7
Evansville	52 273	58.4	26.6	40.8	16.1	13.7	8.5	41.6	35.1	13.5	2.24	2.90	52 948	12.8	32.9
Fishers town	14 044	73.3	46.3	64.7	40.0	6.6	4.8	26.7	20.7	2.3	2.69	3.19	2 682	NA	NA
Fort Wayne	83 333	60.8	31.5	41.9	19.3	14.6	9.8	39.2	32.6	10.3	2.41	3.08	69 627	13.8	31.0
Gary	38 244	67.0	31.2	30.2	11.0	30.9	17.9	33.0	28.9	9.4	2.66	3.28	40 968	29.1	25.6
Goshen	10 675	66.4	32.6	50.8	22.9	10.1	6.8	33.6	27.5	12.5	2.61	3.14	9 029	7.9	27.0
Greenwood	14 931	64.3	32.4	51.0	23.8	9.9	6.7	35.7	29.9	9.9	2.37	2.97	10 594	9.4	27.4
Hammond	32 026	65.2	31.8	42.9	19.6	16.9	9.7	34.8	29.7	10.9	2.58	3.23	32 146	14.4	27.7
Hobart	9 855	70.8	30.6	56.3	23.5	10.4	5.0	29.2	24.1	10.4	2.55	3.04	8 073	9.2	21.7
Indianapolis	324 342	60.3	29.8	40.7	18.0	15.0	9.4	39.7	32.0	8.6	2.39	3.03	296 297	13.6	29.1
Jeffersonville	11 643	62.2	28.8	43.3	17.9	14.8	8.9	37.8	32.1	10.1	2.30	2.90	8 745	16.0	29.0
Kokomo	20 273	60.2	28.5	42.2	17.0	14.1	9.3	39.8	35.2	12.5	2.24	2.90	18 664	13.9	31.0

[1]No spouse present.

Table D. Cities

City	Percent change of households, 1990–2000	Total housing units	Occupied housing units (percent)	Vacant housing units		Homeowner vacancy rate (percent)	Rental vacancy rate (percent)	Occupied housing units			Average household size of owner-occupied units	Average household size of renter-occupied units
				Total	For seasonal, recreational, or occasional use			Total	Percent owner-occupied housing units	Percent renter-occupied housing units		
	86	87	88	89	90	91	92	93	94	95	96	97
ILLINOIS—Cont'd												
Elmhurst	3.3	16 147	96.8	3.2	0.8	1.0	4.8	15 627	83.3	16.7	2.78	1.92
Elmwood Park	4.1	10 150	97.1	2.9	0.2	0.9	2.8	9 858	65.6	34.4	2.79	2.09
Evanston	6.1	30 817	96.2	3.8	0.4	1.2	3.2	29 651	52.7	47.3	2.50	2.01
Freeport	3.5	12 471	90.0	10.0	0.3	2.0	14.6	11 222	68.2	31.8	2.42	2.02
Galesburg	-0.3	14 133	93.7	6.3	0.2	1.8	7.5	13 237	64.3	35.7	2.35	2.03
Glendale Heights	12.3	11 105	97.2	2.8	0.1	0.5	5.0	10 791	70.1	29.9	3.22	2.28
Glen Ellyn	8.4	10 515	97.1	2.9	0.4	0.8	3.2	10 207	77.4	22.6	2.78	2.14
Glenview	15.9	15 853	97.5	2.5	0.5	0.7	3.2	15 464	88.0	12.0	2.70	2.45
Granite City	-1.8	14 022	91.1	8.9	0.1	1.7	13.6	12 773	70.5	29.5	2.51	2.23
Gurnee	98.3	10 929	97.3	2.7	0.4	0.5	5.9	10 629	78.4	21.6	2.92	1.96
Hanover Park	10.5	11 343	97.9	2.1	0.0	0.5	5.1	11 105	82.3	17.7	3.38	3.72
Harvey	-0.7	10 158	88.5	11.5	0.1	3.3	8.9	8 990	56.4	43.6	3.38	3.19
Highland Park	4.5	11 934	96.5	3.5	0.8	1.1	3.2	11 521	82.1	17.9	2.72	2.66
Hoffman Estates	7.0	17 387	98.0	2.0	0.1	0.6	4.3	17 034	76.5	23.5	3.06	2.33
Joliet	35.1	38 176	94.8	5.2	0.1	1.6	6.7	36 182	70.4	29.6	2.93	2.52
Kankakee	-3.6	10 965	91.4	8.6	0.2	3.6	8.4	10 020	53.4	46.6	2.68	2.50
Lansing	4.9	11 748	97.2	2.8	0.1	1.3	4.9	11 416	75.3	24.7	2.61	2.09
Lombard	9.6	17 019	96.9	3.1	0.4	0.7	6.0	16 487	74.9	25.1	2.64	2.02
Maywood	-1.2	8 475	93.7	6.3	0.1	2.3	6.9	7 937	62.8	37.2	3.65	2.91
Moline	1.2	19 487	94.9	5.1	0.4	1.1	6.4	18 492	67.3	32.7	2.47	2.09
Mount Prospect	6.4	21 952	98.3	1.7	0.1	0.5	2.5	21 585	71.5	28.5	2.67	2.43
Mundelein	38.5	10 167	97.0	3.0	0.2	1.2	6.3	9 858	79.7	20.3	3.10	3.18
Naperville	50.3	45 651	95.8	4.2	0.5	1.3	8.7	43 751	79.7	20.3	3.11	2.02
Niles	11.4	12 256	97.9	2.1	0.3	0.4	1.1	12 002	76.5	23.5	2.50	2.03
Normal	27.8	15 683	96.6	3.4	0.2	1.0	4.0	15 157	55.2	44.8	2.57	2.25
Northbrook	7.1	12 492	97.7	2.3	0.5	0.7	2.5	12 203	91.7	8.3	2.74	1.97
North Chicago	7.3	8 377	91.5	8.5	0.3	2.0	5.2	7 661	36.3	63.7	3.14	3.06
Oak Forest	10.4	10 022	97.6	2.4	0.1	1.3	3.1	9 785	81.7	18.3	3.00	2.00
Oak Lawn	3.5	22 846	97.3	2.7	0.2	1.4	4.0	22 220	82.9	17.1	2.56	1.99
Oak Park	2.1	23 723	97.3	2.7	0.2	0.8	2.7	23 079	56.3	43.7	2.67	1.73
Orland Park	54.4	19 045	98.1	1.9	0.3	0.9	3.4	18 675	91.1	8.9	2.76	2.20
Palatine	68.3	26 223	97.3	2.7	0.3	0.6	4.5	25 518	69.3	30.7	2.65	2.34
Park Ridge	5.6	14 646	97.1	2.9	0.3	1.2	4.3	14 219	87.6	12.4	2.71	1.88
Pekin	2.3	14 038	95.3	4.7	0.2	1.3	5.4	13 380	67.2	32.8	2.50	2.08
Peoria	0.5	49 125	92.0	8.0	0.2	1.9	10.3	45 199	59.7	40.3	2.49	2.21
Quincy	2.9	18 043	91.7	8.3	0.3	1.8	9.9	16 546	66.4	33.6	2.43	2.03
Rockford	7.9	63 570	93.1	6.9	0.2	1.7	8.4	59 158	61.1	38.9	2.59	2.26
Rock Island	-0.6	17 542	92.1	7.9	0.2	1.8	9.8	16 148	65.1	34.9	2.41	2.12
Round Lake Beach	49.9	7 608	96.6	3.4	0.3	1.6	3.2	7 349	84.6	15.4	3.54	3.27
St. Charles	27.3	11 072	93.5	6.5	1.0	2.3	10.5	10 351	74.0	26.0	2.81	2.06
Schaumburg	15.3	33 093	96.1	3.9	0.4	0.5	6.8	31 799	69.4	30.6	2.52	1.99
Skokie	2.3	23 702	98.0	2.0	0.3	0.8	1.9	23 223	75.2	24.8	2.77	2.41
Springfield	8.0	53 733	90.5	9.5	0.3	2.4	11.0	48 621	62.8	37.2	2.38	2.01
Streamwood	21.8	12 371	97.8	2.2	0.1	1.3	3.2	12 095	89.6	10.4	3.00	2.96
Tinley Park	37.9	18 037	96.9	3.1	0.1	1.6	3.4	17 478	84.9	15.1	2.86	1.99
Urbana	8.5	15 311	93.6	6.4	0.3	1.5	7.3	14 327	37.0	63.0	2.35	2.02
Waukegan	13.2	29 243	95.0	5.0	0.2	1.5	6.0	27 787	56.5	43.5	3.35	2.74
Wheaton	9.0	19 881	97.5	2.5	0.2	0.7	3.8	19 377	74.1	25.9	2.84	2.08
Wheeling	6.5	13 697	97.0	3.0	0.4	0.5	4.9	13 280	66.6	33.4	2.78	2.15
Wilmette	3.3	10 319	97.3	2.7	0.7	0.7	2.7	10 039	86.8	13.2	2.83	2.11
Woodridge	18.3	11 708	97.2	2.8	0.2	0.8	4.6	11 382	67.2	32.8	2.94	2.24
INDIANA	13.1	2 532 319	92.3	7.7	1.3	1.8	8.8	2 336 306	71.4	28.6	2.64	2.24
Anderson	4.0	27 643	91.4	8.6	0.4	2.3	9.2	25 274	63.8	36.2	2.31	2.21
Bloomington	26.1	28 400	93.2	6.8	0.6	2.7	6.3	26 468	35.3	64.7	2.30	1.97
Carmel	49.2	14 107	96.4	3.6	0.3	1.5	7.0	13 597	79.1	20.9	2.92	2.03
Columbus	24.4	17 162	93.1	6.9	0.4	2.2	8.6	15 985	64.9	35.1	2.50	2.20
East Chicago	-3.4	13 261	88.3	11.7	0.2	2.2	8.8	11 707	44.6	55.4	2.95	2.59
Elkhart	14.6	21 688	92.5	7.5	0.4	2.4	8.2	20 072	53.5	46.5	2.64	2.45
Evansville	-1.3	57 065	91.6	8.4	0.4	2.2	8.1	52 273	60.0	40.0	2.38	2.02
Fishers town	423.6	15 241	92.1	7.9	0.4	2.3	18.8	14 044	77.5	22.5	2.90	1.98
Fort Wayne	19.7	90 915	91.7	8.3	0.3	1.9	10.7	83 333	61.6	38.4	2.57	2.14
Gary	-6.6	43 630	87.7	12.3	0.2	2.5	8.3	38 244	55.8	44.2	2.66	2.68
Goshen	18.2	11 264	94.8	5.2	0.5	2.0	5.4	10 675	63.6	36.4	2.65	2.55
Greenwood	40.9	16 042	93.1	6.9	0.5	2.3	10.7	14 931	62.5	37.5	2.64	1.93
Hammond	-0.4	34 139	93.8	6.2	0.2	1.6	6.4	32 026	63.2	36.8	2.70	2.37
Hobart	22.1	10 299	95.7	4.3	0.3	1.8	5.8	9 855	80.2	19.8	2.63	2.21
Indianapolis	9.5	356 980	90.9	9.1	0.3	2.0	11.0	324 342	58.7	41.3	2.53	2.18
Jeffersonville	33.1	12 402	93.9	6.1	0.4	1.6	7.7	11 643	62.2	37.8	2.41	2.11
Kokomo	8.6	22 292	90.9	9.1	0.7	2.3	10.3	20 273	61.1	38.9	2.31	2.12

Table D. Cities

STATE Place code	City	Land area, 2000[1] (sq km)	Population, 2000 Total persons	Rank	Per square kilometer	Land area, 1990[1] (sq km)	Population, 1990 Total persons	Rank	Per square kilometer	White	Black or African American	American Indian or Alaska Native	Asian	Native Hawaiian and other Pacific Islander	Some other race
		1	2	3	4	5	6	7	8	9	10	11	12	13	14
	INDIANA—Cont'd														
18 40788	Lafayette	52.0	56 397	556	1 084.6	34.7	45 933	623	1 323.7	88.9	3.2	0.4	1.2	0.0	4.6
18 42426	Lawrence	52.0	38 915	904	748.4	52.0	26 849	1 189	516.3	78.6	15.5	0.3	1.8	0.1	1.9
18 46908	Marion	34.4	31 320	1 169	910.5	32.3	32 607	950	1 009.5	79.6	15.6	0.5	0.7	0.0	1.4
18 48528	Merrillville	86.2	30 560	1 200	354.5	80.3	27 257	1 171	339.4	69.7	22.9	0.3	1.5	0.0	3.4
18 48798	Michigan City	50.8	32 900	1 100	647.6	50.8	33 822	900	665.8	69.4	26.3	0.3	0.5	0.0	1.1
18 49932	Mishawaka	40.7	46 557	732	1 143.9	36.0	42 635	679	1 184.3	91.6	3.6	0.4	1.4	0.0	1.1
18 51876	Muncie	62.6	67 430	429	1 077.2	59.0	71 170	332	1 206.3	85.7	11.0	0.3	0.8	0.1	0.7
18 52326	New Albany	37.9	37 603	940	992.2	34.6	36 322	828	1 049.8	90.0	6.9	0.3	0.4	0.0	0.7
18 54180	Noblesville city, IN	46.4	28 590	1 295	616.2	22.4	17 655	1 863	788.2	96.3	1.1	0.2	0.8	0.1	0.6
18 61092	Portage	65.9	33 496	1 085	508.3	53.9	29 062	1 091	539.2	92.5	1.4	0.3	0.6	0.1	3.2
18 64260	Richmond	60.1	39 124	889	651.0	47.6	38 705	771	813.1	86.8	8.9	0.3	0.8	0.1	1.1
18 71000	South Bend	100.2	107 789	219	1 075.7	94.3	105 511	189	1 118.9	66.1	24.6	0.4	1.2	0.1	4.9
18 75428	Terre Haute	80.9	59 614	508	736.9	71.6	57 475	443	802.7	86.3	9.8	0.3	1.2	0.0	0.5
18 78326	Valparaiso	28.2	27 428	1 358	972.6	26.3	24 414	1 328	928.3	94.4	1.6	0.2	1.5	0.0	0.8
18 82862	West Lafayette	14.3	28 778	1 284	2 012.4	12.7	26 144	1 236	2 058.6	83.3	2.4	0.2	11.3	0.0	1.2
19 00000	**IOWA**	144 701.0	2 926 324	X	20.2	144 716.0	2 776 831	X	19.2	93.9	2.1	0.3	1.3	0.0	1.3
19 01855	Ames	55.9	50 731	655	907.5	50.9	47 198	600	927.3	87.3	2.6	0.1	7.7	0.0	0.8
19 02305	Ankeny	43.4	27 117	1 376	624.8	34.1	18 482	1 781	542.0	96.9	0.8	0.1	0.9	0.0	0.4
19 06355	Bettendorf	55.0	31 275	1 173	568.6	55.0	28 139	1 135	511.6	95.0	1.6	0.2	1.4	0.0	0.7
19 09550	Burlington	36.4	26 839	1 391	737.3	34.3	27 208	1 173	793.2	91.6	5.0	0.2	0.7	0.0	0.9
19 11755	Cedar Falls	73.3	36 145	980	493.1	73.7	34 298	881	465.4	95.1	1.6	0.2	1.6	0.0	0.4
19 12000	Cedar Rapids	163.5	120 758	188	738.6	138.5	108 772	179	785.4	91.9	3.7	0.3	1.8	0.1	0.6
19 14430	Clinton	92.1	27 772	1 338	301.5	91.9	29 201	1 083	317.7	93.8	3.2	0.3	0.8	0.0	0.5
19 16860	Council Bluffs	96.8	58 268	525	601.9	95.3	54 315	482	569.9	94.8	1.1	0.5	0.6	0.0	1.8
19 19000	Davenport	162.6	98 359	249	604.9	158.9	95 333	219	600.0	83.7	9.2	0.4	2.0	0.0	2.3
19 21000	Des Moines	196.3	198 682	95	1 012.1	194.9	193 189	81	991.2	82.3	8.1	0.4	3.5	0.0	3.5
19 22395	Dubuque	68.6	57 686	537	840.9	59.7	57 538	442	963.8	96.2	1.2	0.2	0.7	0.1	0.7
19 28515	Fort Dodge	37.7	25 136	1 499	666.7	37.3	26 057	1 239	698.6	92.5	3.8	0.2	0.9	0.0	1.3
19 38595	Iowa City	62.6	62 220	474	993.9	57.0	59 735	423	1 048.0	87.3	3.7	0.3	5.6	0.0	1.3
19 49485	Marion	31.1	26 294	1 426	845.5	24.7	20 422	1 598	826.8	97.0	0.6	0.2	0.9	0.0	0.4
19 49755	Marshalltown	46.7	26 009	1 446	556.9	39.1	25 178	1 278	643.9	86.8	1.3	0.4	1.0	0.1	8.6
19 50160	Mason City	66.8	29 172	1 268	436.7	66.3	29 040	1 092	438.0	95.4	1.2	0.2	0.8	0.0	1.1
19 73335	Sioux City	141.9	85 013	314	599.1	140.6	80 505	278	572.6	85.2	2.4	2.0	2.8	0.0	5.3
19 79950	Urbandale	53.6	29 072	1 272	542.4	27.8	23 775	1 374	855.2	95.2	1.5	0.1	1.7	0.1	0.5
19 82425	Waterloo	157.3	68 747	418	437.0	156.9	66 467	365	423.6	81.6	13.9	0.2	0.9	0.0	1.4
19 83910	West Des Moines	69.4	46 403	737	668.6	46.4	31 702	986	683.2	92.7	1.9	0.1	2.8	0.0	1.3
20 00000	**KANSAS**	211 899.6	2 688 418	X	12.7	211 921.6	2 477 588	X	11.7	86.1	5.7	0.9	1.7	0.0	3.4
20 18250	Dodge City	32.7	25 176	1 496	769.9	31.3	21 129	1 555	675.0	71.4	1.9	0.7	2.4	0.2	20.8
20 21275	Emporia	25.6	26 760	1 393	1 045.3	23.8	25 512	1 264	1 071.9	78.6	3.0	0.5	2.7	0.0	12.7
20 25325	Garden City	22.1	28 451	1 304	1 287.4	19.1	24 097	1 351	1 261.6	68.8	1.5	1.1	3.5	0.1	22.3
20 33625	Hutchinson	54.7	40 787	848	745.6	53.6	39 308	758	733.4	88.6	4.3	0.7	0.6	0.0	3.7
20 36000	Kansas City	321.8	146 866	147	456.4	279.2	151 521	117	542.7	55.8	30.1	0.8	1.7	0.0	8.6
20 38900	Lawrence	72.8	80 098	338	1 100.2	59.4	65 608	374	1 104.5	83.8	5.1	2.9	3.8	0.1	1.4
20 39000	Leavenworth	60.9	35 420	1 007	581.6	58.8	38 495	774	654.7	76.8	16.3	0.8	1.5	0.2	1.7
20 39075	Leawood	39.1	27 656	1 347	707.3	38.8	19 693	1 671	507.6	95.2	1.5	0.1	2.2	0.0	0.3
20 39350	Lenexa	88.8	40 238	864	453.1	75.2	34 110	888	453.6	89.5	3.3	0.4	3.6	0.0	1.6
20 44250	Manhattan	38.9	44 831	767	1 152.5	28.6	43 081	667	1 506.3	87.3	4.9	0.5	3.9	0.1	1.3
20 52575	Olathe	140.3	92 962	271	662.6	109.5	63 402	389	579.0	88.6	3.7	0.4	2.7	0.0	2.6
20 53775	Overland Park	147.0	149 080	144	1 014.1	144.2	111 790	167	775.2	90.6	2.5	0.3	3.8	0.0	1.2
20 62700	Salina	58.9	45 679	750	775.5	54.4	42 299	685	777.6	87.8	3.6	0.6	2.0	0.0	3.8
20 64500	Shawnee	108.1	47 996	706	444.0	108.2	37 962	789	350.9	90.3	3.0	0.3	2.7	0.0	1.9
20 71000	Topeka	145.1	122 377	183	843.4	142.9	119 883	154	838.9	78.5	11.7	1.3	1.1	0.0	4.1
20 79000	Wichita	351.6	344 284	52	979.2	298.2	304 017	51	1 019.5	75.2	11.4	1.2	4.0	0.1	5.1
21 00000	**KENTUCKY**	102 895.5	4 041 769	X	39.3	102 906.8	3 686 892	X	35.8	90.1	7.3	0.2	0.7	0.0	0.6
21 08902	Bowling Green	91.7	49 296	684	537.6	75.0	41 688	701	555.8	80.8	12.7	0.2	1.9	0.1	2.2
21 17848	Covington	34.0	43 370	792	1 275.6	34.3	43 646	658	1 272.5	87.0	10.1	0.2	0.3	0.0	0.6
21 28900	Frankfort	38.2	27 741	1 341	726.2	37.7	26 535	1 210	703.8	81.8	14.7	0.1	0.9	0.0	0.8
21 35866	Henderson	38.8	27 373	1 363	705.5	33.7	25 945	1 244	769.9	87.3	10.5	0.2	0.4	0.0	0.6
21 37918	Hopkinsville	62.2	30 089	1 218	483.7	52.7	29 809	1 060	565.6	66.1	30.9	0.2	0.8	0.1	0.6
21 40222	Jeffersontown	25.8	26 633	1 400	1 032.3	25.1	23 223	1 405	925.2	86.7	8.7	0.2	1.8	0.0	1.1
21 46027	Lexington-Fayette	736.9	260 512	66	353.5	736.9	225 366	70	305.8	81.0	13.5	0.2	2.5	0.0	1.2
21 48000	Louisville	160.9	256 231	68	1 592.5	160.9	269 555	58	1 675.3	62.9	33.0	0.2	1.4	0.0	0.7
21 58620	Owensboro	45.1	54 067	607	1 198.8	38.8	53 577	496	1 380.9	90.6	6.9	0.1	0.5	0.0	0.5
21 58836	Paducah	50.5	26 307	1 425	520.9	45.5	27 256	1 172	599.0	72.8	24.1	0.3	0.6	0.1	0.5
21 65226	Richmond	49.5	27 152	1 373	548.5	22.0	21 183	1 551	962.9	88.3	8.3	0.3	1.1	0.0	0.4

[1] Dry land or land partially or temporarily covered by water.

Table D. Cities

City	Population and population characteristics, 2000 (cont'd)								Population and population characteristics, 1990				
	Race (percent) (cont'd)								Race (percent)				
	Race alone or in combination												
	Two or more races	White	Black	American Indian or Alaska Native	Asian	Native Hawaiian and other Pacific Islander	Some other race	Hispanic[1]	White	Black or African American	American Indian or Alaska Native	Asian and Pacific Islander	Hispanic[1]
	15	16	17	18	19	20	21	22	23	24	25	26	27
INDIANA—Cont'd													
Lafayette	1.6	90.4	3.6	0.9	1.4	0.1	5.2	9.1	95.8	2.1	0.3	1.1	1.7
Lawrence	1.9	80.2	16.4	0.7	2.2	0.1	2.3	4.7	86.7	10.7	0.3	1.7	1.7
Marion	2.2	81.6	16.8	1.1	0.9	0.1	2.0	3.6	82.6	14.8	0.4	0.7	3.2
Merrillville	2.2	71.6	23.6	0.8	1.8	0.1	4.6	9.7	91.7	5.0	0.1	0.9	6.9
Michigan City	2.4	71.4	27.7	0.9	0.7	0.1	1.7	3.1	75.8	22.5	0.3	0.7	1.8
Mishawaka	1.9	93.3	4.3	1.0	1.7	0.1	1.6	2.8	97.1	1.6	0.4	0.7	1.1
Muncie	1.5	87.1	11.7	0.7	1.1	0.2	0.9	1.4	89.1	9.5	0.3	0.7	0.9
New Albany	1.6	91.5	7.9	0.8	0.7	0.1	0.9	1.4	93.2	6.2	0.2	0.3	0.5
Noblesville city, IN	0.8	97.2	1.4	0.5	1.1	0.1	0.8	1.4	98.1	1.0	0.2	0.6	0.5
Portage	1.9	94.2	1.8	0.8	0.9	0.1	4.1	9.9	97.1	0.4	0.2	0.5	6.4
Richmond	2.1	88.8	10.2	0.8	1.0	0.1	1.4	2.0	89.6	9.2	0.3	0.6	0.7
South Bend	2.8	68.4	26.1	1.0	1.6	0.2	5.8	8.5	76.0	20.9	0.4	0.9	3.4
Terre Haute	1.9	88.0	10.7	0.9	1.5	0.1	0.9	1.6	88.6	9.4	0.4	1.1	1.3
Valparaiso	1.5	95.7	1.9	0.7	1.9	0.1	1.4	3.3	97.8	0.6	0.2	1.1	1.4
West Lafayette	1.6	84.6	2.7	0.4	12.2	0.2	1.7	3.2	88.7	2.2	0.2	8.3	2.0
IOWA	1.1	94.9	2.5	0.6	1.5	0.1	1.6	2.8	96.6	1.7	0.3	0.9	1.2
Ames	1.4	88.4	3.0	0.4	8.3	0.1	1.1	2.0	89.9	2.4	0.1	6.9	1.6
Ankeny	0.8	97.7	1.0	0.3	1.2	0.1	0.6	1.1	98.8	0.4	0.1	0.5	0.6
Bettendorf	1.1	96.0	1.9	0.6	1.7	0.1	0.9	2.5	96.8	1.4	0.2	1.0	2.2
Burlington	1.4	92.9	5.9	0.7	0.9	0.1	1.2	2.1	94.1	4.5	0.2	0.7	1.3
Cedar Falls	1.1	96.1	2.0	0.4	1.9	0.1	0.7	1.1	96.9	1.1	0.2	1.4	0.8
Cedar Rapids	1.8	93.5	4.6	0.7	2.1	0.1	0.9	1.7	95.5	2.9	0.2	1.0	1.1
Clinton	1.3	95.1	3.8	0.8	0.9	0.0	0.8	1.7	96.5	2.4	0.3	0.5	0.7
Council Bluffs	1.3	95.9	1.4	0.9	0.8	0.1	2.2	4.5	97.8	0.8	0.3	0.4	2.4
Davenport	2.4	85.8	10.4	1.0	2.3	0.1	3.0	5.4	89.1	7.9	0.4	1.0	3.5
Des Moines	2.2	84.1	8.9	0.8	4.0	0.1	4.4	6.6	89.2	7.1	0.4	2.4	2.4
Dubuque	1.0	97.0	1.5	0.5	0.9	0.2	0.9	1.6	98.4	0.6	0.1	0.6	0.6
Fort Dodge	1.4	93.7	4.4	0.6	1.0	0.1	1.6	2.9	95.4	3.3	0.3	0.5	1.5
Iowa City	1.7	88.8	4.4	0.6	6.2	0.1	1.7	2.9	91.1	2.5	0.2	5.6	1.7
Marion	0.8	97.8	0.9	0.4	1.1	0.1	0.6	1.1	98.6	0.4	0.1	0.7	0.7
Marshalltown	1.8	88.4	1.8	0.7	1.3	0.1	9.6	12.6	97.1	1.0	0.3	1.1	1.0
Mason City	1.4	96.7	1.7	0.5	1.0	0.1	1.6	3.4	97.3	0.9	0.1	0.5	2.9
Sioux City	2.3	87.2	3.1	2.8	3.2	0.1	6.0	10.9	92.6	2.3	2.0	1.5	3.3
Urbandale	0.9	96.0	1.9	0.3	1.9	0.2	0.8	1.6	97.2	1.0	0.1	1.5	0.8
Waterloo	2.0	83.4	14.7	0.6	1.1	0.1	2.2	2.6	86.6	12.1	0.2	0.7	0.8
West Des Moines	1.3	93.8	2.2	0.4	3.1	0.1	1.7	3.0	96.3	1.3	0.1	1.6	1.9
KANSAS	2.1	87.9	6.3	1.8	2.1	0.1	4.0	7.0	90.1	5.8	0.9	1.3	3.8
Dodge City	2.6	73.7	2.4	1.2	2.6	0.2	22.6	42.9	79.3	2.2	0.6	3.0	18.2
Emporia	2.5	80.9	3.6	1.2	3.0	0.0	13.9	21.5	89.3	2.8	0.6	2.6	7.8
Garden City	2.7	71.1	1.9	1.6	3.9	0.2	24.1	43.9	78.3	1.7	0.7	4.0	25.3
Hutchinson	2.2	90.6	5.0	1.4	0.8	0.1	4.4	7.7	91.5	4.1	0.6	0.4	5.4
Kansas City	3.0	58.1	31.3	1.7	2.1	0.1	9.9	16.8	65.0	29.3	0.7	1.2	7.1
Lawrence	3.0	86.4	6.2	4.0	4.5	0.2	2.0	3.6	87.1	4.9	3.0	3.9	3.0
Leavenworth	2.8	79.1	17.6	1.6	2.1	0.4	2.4	5.1	79.8	15.8	0.7	2.0	4.7
Leawood	0.8	95.9	1.6	0.3	2.5	0.0	0.4	1.3	96.6	1.0	0.2	2.2	0.9
Lenexa	1.6	90.9	3.7	0.9	4.1	0.1	2.1	4.0	94.6	2.4	0.4	2.0	1.7
Manhattan	2.1	89.0	5.6	1.0	4.6	0.2	1.8	3.5	90.1	5.0	0.5	3.3	2.8
Olathe	1.8	90.2	4.3	0.9	3.2	0.1	3.2	5.4	94.3	3.0	0.4	1.7	1.8
Overland Park	1.4	91.9	2.9	0.7	4.3	0.1	1.7	3.8	95.4	1.8	0.3	1.9	2.0
Salina	2.3	89.8	4.5	1.3	2.3	0.1	4.4	6.7	93.1	3.5	0.5	1.2	2.7
Shawnee	1.8	92.0	3.5	0.8	3.1	0.1	2.5	4.4	94.9	2.1	0.4	1.7	2.6
Topeka	3.3	81.2	13.2	2.5	1.5	0.1	5.1	8.9	84.7	10.6	1.3	0.8	5.8
Wichita	3.1	77.8	12.4	2.3	4.5	0.2	6.1	9.6	82.3	11.3	1.2	2.6	5.0
KENTUCKY	1.1	91.0	7.7	0.6	0.9	0.1	0.8	1.5	92.0	7.1	0.2	0.5	0.6
Bowling Green	2.0	82.6	13.3	0.6	2.3	0.3	3.0	4.1	86.4	12.2	0.2	1.1	0.7
Covington	1.6	88.5	11.0	0.7	0.5	0.1	0.9	1.4	91.5	7.7	0.2	0.4	0.7
Frankfort	1.6	83.2	15.7	0.5	1.3	0.1	1.0	1.5	87.4	11.7	0.2	0.6	0.6
Henderson	1.0	88.2	11.0	0.5	0.5	0.0	0.8	1.3	88.9	10.5	0.2	0.3	0.4
Hopkinsville	1.4	67.2	31.6	0.6	1.0	0.2	0.9	1.7	69.9	29.0	0.2	0.6	0.9
Jeffersontown	1.5	88.0	9.2	0.6	2.0	0.1	1.7	2.5	92.4	6.6	0.1	0.8	1.0
Lexington-Fayette	1.6	82.4	14.1	0.6	2.8	0.1	1.7	3.3	84.5	13.4	0.2	1.6	1.1
Louisville	1.7	64.2	33.9	0.7	1.7	0.1	1.2	1.9	69.2	29.7	0.2	0.7	0.7
Owensboro	1.3	91.8	7.6	0.5	0.7	0.1	0.7	1.0	93.0	6.4	0.1	0.3	0.4
Paducah	1.6	74.2	25.0	0.8	0.9	0.1	0.7	1.4	78.4	20.9	0.2	0.3	0.6
Richmond	1.6	89.7	9.1	0.8	1.3	0.1	0.7	1.2	88.7	10.2	0.2	0.7	0.4

[1] Hispanic persons may be of any race.

Table D. Cities

City	Under 5 years	5 to 17 years	18 to 24 years	25 to 34 years	35 to 44 years	45 to 54 years	55 to 64 years	65 to 74 years	75 years and over	Median age (years)	Percent Female
	Population and population characteristics, 2000										
	Age (percent)										
	28	29	30	31	32	33	34	35	36	37	38
INDIANA—Cont'd											
Lafayette	7.0	16.2	14.2	17.4	13.9	11.8	7.4	5.9	6.1	31.7	50.6
Lawrence	9.1	20.9	7.7	17.3	18.9	11.8	6.2	4.5	3.7	32.4	51.2
Marion	6.5	16.7	12.5	12.5	13.5	12.1	9.2	8.3	8.7	36.3	53.0
Merrillville	6.6	18.0	8.7	13.7	15.7	13.7	8.5	6.9	8.2	37.0	52.3
Michigan City	7.6	17.4	9.6	15.1	15.6	12.6	8.0	6.9	7.2	35.2	49.6
Mishawaka	7.1	16.9	11.8	16.3	14.4	12.0	7.4	6.5	7.5	33.5	52.7
Muncie	5.8	13.9	24.6	12.9	11.2	10.3	8.0	6.6	6.6	28.9	52.7
New Albany	6.9	17.2	9.6	14.0	15.2	13.2	8.6	7.6	7.8	36.6	53.1
Noblesville city, IN	9.3	20.2	7.3	17.0	17.5	13.0	7.2	4.4	4.1	33.0	50.9
Portage	7.2	18.9	9.4	13.8	16.1	14.2	8.6	6.0	5.8	35.4	51.5
Richmond	6.8	16.6	11.0	13.7	13.7	12.5	9.1	8.1	8.3	36.3	53.0
South Bend	8.3	19.0	10.4	15.5	13.8	11.5	6.7	6.8	8.0	32.7	52.3
Terre Haute	6.2	15.2	18.7	13.4	13.2	11.2	7.2	6.5	8.3	32.1	50.7
Valparaiso	5.9	15.3	17.4	14.5	13.6	13.0	7.2	5.8	7.3	32.7	52.1
West Lafayette	2.5	7.9	54.6	10.2	6.7	6.5	3.9	3.1	4.6	22.3	42.8
IOWA	6.4	18.6	10.2	12.4	15.2	13.4	8.8	7.2	7.7	36.6	50.9
Ames	4.4	10.2	40.0	14.2	9.6	8.7	5.2	3.9	3.8	23.6	47.8
Ankeny	8.4	18.8	11.4	16.9	16.5	13.0	7.1	4.2	3.7	31.9	51.5
Bettendorf	6.2	20.1	6.7	11.4	16.6	16.9	9.7	6.5	5.9	38.7	51.5
Burlington	6.6	17.9	8.9	12.4	14.3	13.7	9.0	7.9	9.3	37.9	52.4
Cedar Falls	4.4	13.6	30.6	9.5	11.0	12.0	7.0	5.4	6.5	26.0	53.1
Cedar Rapids	7.1	17.3	10.8	15.2	15.5	13.0	8.0	6.4	6.7	34.7	51.3
Clinton	6.6	18.0	9.1	11.6	15.1	13.1	9.4	8.0	9.1	38.3	52.3
Council Bluffs	7.2	18.8	10.3	14.2	15.4	12.5	8.2	7.2	6.1	34.6	51.6
Davenport	7.4	18.8	10.7	15.1	14.9	13.0	7.9	6.0	6.2	33.6	51.4
Des Moines	7.5	17.3	10.6	16.3	15.5	12.6	7.8	6.0	6.4	33.8	51.6
Dubuque	6.2	17.4	11.8	11.9	14.6	13.1	8.5	7.7	8.9	36.9	52.6
Fort Dodge	6.8	17.5	10.7	11.3	13.9	12.8	8.5	8.2	10.4	38.0	52.5
Iowa City	4.6	11.6	32.8	16.4	11.7	10.6	5.2	3.5	3.5	25.4	51.0
Marion	7.4	19.0	8.2	15.3	16.6	13.5	8.6	5.9	5.5	35.1	51.4
Marshalltown	6.7	17.8	8.9	12.3	13.7	13.7	9.2	8.1	9.5	38.4	50.5
Mason City	6.2	17.3	10.2	11.9	14.8	13.2	8.5	8.4	9.4	38.2	52.6
Sioux City	7.9	19.2	11.0	14.2	14.3	12.6	7.6	6.6	6.7	33.4	51.2
Urbandale	6.7	19.6	7.0	13.4	17.9	15.6	9.0	6.1	4.6	37.0	51.7
Waterloo	7.0	17.6	10.6	13.6	13.8	13.6	8.4	7.3	8.0	35.9	52.0
West Des Moines	7.7	16.9	9.7	19.2	16.3	13.0	7.3	5.3	4.5	33.0	52.1
KANSAS	7.0	19.5	10.3	13.0	15.6	13.2	8.2	6.5	6.7	35.2	50.6
Dodge City	9.9	21.3	12.3	16.3	13.7	10.3	6.2	4.6	5.3	28.9	48.4
Emporia	7.3	18.0	19.4	13.9	13.3	10.8	6.2	4.8	6.2	28.4	51.1
Garden City	10.2	22.5	11.6	16.2	14.9	10.5	6.1	4.1	4.1	28.6	49.4
Hutchinson	6.6	16.6	11.0	12.8	15.1	12.7	8.5	7.8	9.1	37.1	49.6
Kansas City	8.1	20.4	10.6	14.5	14.9	12.1	7.7	6.1	5.5	32.3	51.1
Lawrence	5.4	13.1	30.7	16.2	12.2	10.2	4.9	3.6	3.6	25.3	50.3
Leavenworth	8.2	19.5	8.8	15.6	19.2	12.1	6.9	4.9	4.8	34.1	47.1
Leawood	6.3	23.8	4.2	5.9	17.4	19.6	10.1	7.0	5.6	41.3	51.0
Lenexa	6.4	19.3	9.5	14.7	17.3	16.5	7.7	3.5	5.1	35.1	51.1
Manhattan	4.6	11.2	39.2	14.0	10.0	8.6	4.6	3.6	4.2	23.5	48.5
Olathe	9.4	21.5	9.2	18.0	18.7	12.8	5.4	2.8	2.4	30.8	50.1
Overland Park	7.1	19.0	7.0	14.6	17.9	14.9	8.0	5.8	5.6	36.3	51.6
Salina	7.1	18.8	10.0	13.6	15.1	12.8	8.3	7.1	7.1	35.3	51.1
Shawnee	7.7	19.1	7.8	15.8	18.4	14.6	8.1	5.0	3.5	34.8	50.8
Topeka	7.0	17.2	9.9	14.0	14.8	13.5	8.4	7.4	7.7	36.3	52.0
Wichita	8.0	19.1	10.1	15.0	15.7	12.8	7.4	6.0	5.9	33.4	50.7
KENTUCKY	6.6	18.0	9.9	14.1	15.9	13.8	9.2	6.8	5.7	35.9	51.1
Bowling Green	6.0	14.2	23.5	14.5	12.4	10.4	7.1	5.9	6.0	28.6	51.6
Covington	7.8	18.0	10.0	17.3	16.0	11.9	7.1	5.9	6.0	33.1	51.1
Frankfort	6.2	15.4	11.7	15.3	15.0	13.6	8.8	7.0	6.9	35.9	52.3
Henderson	6.7	16.9	9.2	14.1	15.3	13.7	8.8	7.8	7.4	37.0	52.8
Hopkinsville	7.4	19.0	9.7	13.7	14.6	12.1	8.7	7.6	7.3	35.1	53.2
Jeffersontown	7.2	17.5	7.7	16.2	17.2	14.6	8.7	6.0	4.8	35.7	51.9
Lexington-Fayette	6.2	15.1	14.6	17.1	16.1	13.2	7.6	5.3	4.7	33.0	50.9
Louisville	6.6	17.0	10.4	14.7	15.7	13.2	7.8	7.3	7.4	35.8	52.7
Owensboro	6.8	17.4	9.8	12.7	14.7	13.1	9.2	8.2	8.1	37.4	53.3
Paducah	6.5	16.0	8.5	12.3	13.9	13.2	9.2	8.8	11.4	39.9	54.5
Richmond	6.0	11.6	31.7	16.6	10.9	8.3	5.5	4.6	4.9	25.3	52.5

Table D. Cities

City	Population and population characteristics, 1990										Population—change, 1980-2000				
	Age (percent)										Total persons			Percent change	
	Under 5 years	5 to 17 years	18 to 24 years	25 to 34 years	35 to 44 years	45 to 54 years	55 to 64 years	65 to 74 years	75 years and over	Percent Female	2000	1990	1980	1990–2000	1980–1990
	39	40	41	42	43	44	45	46	47	48	49	50	51	52	53
INDIANA—Cont'd															
Lafayette	7.4	16.9	11.2	18.9	14.5	9.7	8.2	7.5	5.7	51.6	56 397	44 622	43 011	26.4	3.7
Lawrence	8.6	18.0	9.6	23.2	15.0	8.8	7.8	5.6	3.4	51.2	38 915	26 849	25 591	44.9	4.9
Marion	6.5	17.8	10.5	14.7	12.8	11.0	10.1	9.1	7.4	52.4	31 320	32 607	35 874	-3.9	-9.1
Merrillville	6.0	17.1	8.9	15.5	15.1	11.3	10.3	9.3	6.5	52.1	30 560	27 257	27 677	12.1	-1.5
Michigan City	7.2	18.2	9.5	18.4	14.6	9.3	8.9	8.3	5.5	50.2	32 900	33 822	36 833	-2.7	-8.2
Mishawaka	7.4	18.0	10.8	18.4	14.4	8.5	7.9	8.1	6.7	53.2	46 557	42 635	40 201	9.2	6.1
Muncie	6.1	13.4	26.0	13.6	11.1	8.4	8.1	7.7	5.5	53.4	67 430	71 170	77 216	-5.3	-7.8
New Albany	7.2	17.5	9.6	16.8	13.4	9.7	9.4	9.3	7.1	53.8	37 603	36 322	37 103	3.5	-2.1
Noblesville city, IN	8.3	19.9	8.7	18.8	16.4	11.2	6.9	5.7	4.1	51.8	28 590	17 655	12 056	61.9	46.4
Portage	7.0	21.1	9.2	16.9	16.2	11.0	8.4	6.7	3.5	51.3	33 496	29 062	27 409	15.3	6.0
Richmond	7.1	17.4	12.1	15.3	12.8	9.5	9.3	9.2	7.3	53.4	39 124	38 705	41 327	1.1	-6.3
South Bend	8.1	17.8	9.8	17.4	13.9	7.7	8.7	9.3	7.4	52.8	107 789	105 511	109 727	2.2	-3.8
Terre Haute	6.3	14.8	18.2	15.9	12.0	8.0	7.9	9.0	7.8	51.1	59 614	57 475	61 125	3.7	-6.0
Valparaiso	5.7	16.1	19.3	15.4	15.1	8.4	7.6	6.3	6.1	53.0	27 428	24 414	22 247	12.3	9.7
West Lafayette	3.5	7.4	49.7	14.0	7.9	5.1	4.0	4.4	3.9	46.2	28 778	26 144	21 247	10.1	23.0
IOWA	7.0	18.9	10.2	15.4	14.2	9.9	9.0	8.2	7.2	51.6	2 926 324	2 776 831	2 913 808	5.4	-4.7
Ames	5.1	10.1	40.8	16.3	10.7	5.4	4.9	3.6	3.1	46.8	50 731	47 198	45 775	7.5	3.1
Ankeny	8.2	19.7	14.7	19.3	17.8	9.5	5.7	3.0	2.1	51.5	27 117	18 482	15 429	46.7	19.8
Bettendorf	6.8	21.1	7.5	14.9	18.4	12.6	8.6	6.4	3.7	51.5	31 275	28 139	27 376	11.1	2.8
Burlington	7.0	18.8	8.4	14.9	14.6	10.0	9.1	9.3	7.8	53.1	26 839	27 208	29 529	-1.4	-7.9
Cedar Falls	5.1	15.6	27.5	11.9	13.5	8.4	6.9	6.0	5.1	53.0	36 145	34 298	36 310	5.4	-5.5
Cedar Rapids	7.0	17.2	11.3	17.8	15.0	10.0	8.5	7.4	5.8	52.0	120 758	108 772	110 217	11.0	-1.3
Clinton	7.0	18.4	8.5	15.4	13.6	10.0	9.5	9.6	8.0	52.9	27 772	29 201	32 828	-4.9	-11.0
Council Bluffs	8.0	18.9	9.5	17.7	13.7	8.9	9.6	7.8	5.9	52.8	58 268	54 315	56 449	7.3	-3.8
Davenport	8.1	19.3	10.6	17.6	14.8	8.8	8.1	7.1	5.6	52.1	98 359	95 333	103 264	3.2	-7.7
Des Moines	7.8	16.4	11.9	18.9	14.4	9.1	8.1	7.3	6.0	52.9	198 682	193 189	191 003	2.8	1.1
Dubuque	6.6	18.4	11.5	15.1	14.1	9.3	9.0	8.4	7.6	52.9	57 686	57 538	62 321	0.3	-7.7
Fort Dodge	7.6	17.8	9.1	14.7	14.3	8.1	9.5	9.4	9.4	53.5	25 136	25 894	29 423	-2.9	-12.0
Iowa City	5.6	11.2	33.7	19.7	13.1	5.8	4.3	3.4	3.1	50.5	62 220	59 735	50 508	4.2	18.3
Marion	8.0	18.8	9.1	18.5	16.1	11.6	7.8	5.5	4.7	51.1	26 294	20 422	19 474	28.8	4.9
Marshalltown	6.4	17.7	8.5	14.7	14.3	10.8	9.2	9.6	8.7	51.5	26 009	25 178	26 938	3.3	-6.5
Mason City	7.0	17.3	10.3	16.0	13.5	8.9	9.7	8.8	8.4	53.5	29 172	29 040	30 144	0.5	-3.7
Sioux City	7.7	19.8	10.5	15.9	14.0	8.7	8.7	8.1	6.7	52.1	85 013	80 505	82 003	5.6	-1.8
Urbandale	7.4	19.0	8.4	19.1	17.7	12.1	8.8	4.9	2.6	51.6	29 072	23 775	17 869	22.3	33.1
Waterloo	7.1	19.0	9.2	15.0	14.8	9.9	9.3	9.0	6.7	52.8	68 747	66 467	75 985	3.4	-12.5
West Des Moines	6.6	16.8	10.2	19.7	16.3	11.9	7.9	6.2	4.4	52.7	46 403	31 702	21 894	46.4	44.8
KANSAS	7.6	19.1	10.3	16.7	14.6	9.5	8.4	7.5	6.4	51.0	2 688 418	2 477 588	2 364 236	8.5	4.8
Dodge City	9.4	19.5	13.8	17.1	13.4	7.9	7.1	6.5	5.2	49.8	25 176	21 129	18 001	19.2	17.4
Emporia	7.8	18.1	19.5	16.9	12.8	7.3	5.7	5.6	6.3	51.8	26 760	25 512	25 287	4.9	0.9
Garden City	9.7	23.4	11.4	18.8	13.9	8.1	5.8	5.5	3.3	49.9	28 451	24 097	18 256	18.1	32.0
Hutchinson	7.0	16.9	10.5	16.8	14.1	9.3	8.8	8.7	7.8	50.9	40 787	39 308	40 284	3.8	-2.4
Kansas City	8.4	20.2	9.4	17.7	13.6	9.0	8.7	7.4	5.5	52.4	146 866	151 521	161 093	-3.1	-5.9
Lawrence	6.0	12.9	31.8	18.5	12.1	6.6	4.9	3.9	3.3	50.2	80 098	65 608	52 738	22.1	24.4
Leavenworth	7.3	18.6	8.3	20.5	21.3	8.8	6.0	5.3	3.9	43.6	35 420	38 495	33 656	-8.0	14.4
Leawood	7.1	21.5	4.5	8.8	22.7	12.5	10.2	8.6	4.0	50.8	27 656	19 693	13 360	40.4	47.4
Lenexa	8.5	19.8	10.0	19.9	21.2	10.6	4.6	2.7	2.9	51.3	40 238	34 110	18 639	18.0	83.0
Manhattan	6.3	13.8	30.5	17.9	12.4	6.3	4.7	4.4	3.7	48.4	44 831	43 081	32 645	4.1	32.0
Olathe	10.1	22.2	9.8	22.5	18.7	7.4	4.2	2.7	2.4	50.9	92 962	63 402	37 258	46.6	70.2
Overland Park	7.2	17.5	8.3	19.1	18.2	11.2	8.6	6.5	3.4	52.3	149 080	111 790	81 784	33.4	36.7
Salina	7.6	18.7	9.7	17.4	14.1	9.7	8.4	7.8	6.6	52.1	45 679	42 299	41 843	8.0	1.1
Shawnee	7.5	18.8	9.3	19.6	18.1	11.5	7.9	4.8	2.4	50.8	47 996	37 962	29 625	26.4	28.1
Topeka	7.4	17.2	9.8	18.1	14.4	9.3	9.1	8.0	6.7	52.4	122 377	119 883	115 266	2.1	4.0
Wichita	8.6	18.0	10.2	19.5	14.6	8.7	8.0	7.3	5.1	51.4	344 284	304 017	279 272	13.2	8.9
KENTUCKY	6.8	19.1	10.9	16.6	14.9	10.4	8.8	7.3	5.4	51.6	4 041 769	3 686 891	3 660 324	9.6	0.7
Bowling Green	5.9	15.1	21.5	15.5	12.3	8.7	7.8	7.3	5.8	53.9	49 296	41 688	40 450	18.2	3.1
Covington	8.4	18.6	10.3	19.0	13.5	7.9	7.9	7.7	6.7	52.5	43 370	43 646	49 569	-0.6	-11.9
Frankfort	6.6	15.9	10.9	17.1	15.4	10.6	9.3	8.1	6.2	53.0	27 741	26 535	25 973	4.5	2.2
Henderson	6.9	18.5	9.5	16.7	14.5	9.8	8.8	8.3	7.0	53.8	27 373	25 945	24 834	5.5	4.5
Hopkinsville	7.3	18.8	9.9	15.5	14.3	10.0	9.0	8.0	7.2	54.1	30 089	29 818	27 318	0.9	9.2
Jeffersontown	7.6	18.1	8.9	19.9	17.8	11.6	7.8	5.0	3.3	52.1	26 633	23 223	15 736	14.7	47.6
Lexington-Fayette	6.7	15.6	14.5	20.3	16.1	9.5	7.3	5.8	4.1	52.2	260 512	225 366	204 165	15.6	10.4
Louisville	6.8	16.7	9.9	17.9	14.1	8.8	9.4	9.1	7.5	53.7	256 231	269 555	298 455	-4.9	-9.7
Owensboro	7.2	18.1	10.2	15.9	13.9	10.2	9.6	8.5	6.5	53.7	54 067	53 577	54 450	0.9	-1.6
Paducah	6.1	16.7	7.4	15.0	12.7	9.6	10.3	11.3	10.9	55.3	26 307	27 256	29 315	-3.5	-7.0
Richmond	4.9	11.1	36.5	15.1	8.7	6.6	6.0	5.8	5.5	54.4	27 152	21 183	21 705	28.2	-2.4

Table D. Cities

City	Total population	Total in house-holds	House-holder	Spouse	Child Total	Child Own child under 18 years	Other relatives Total	Other relatives Under 18 years	Nonrelatives Total	Nonrelatives Unmar-ried partner	Total in group quarters	Correc-tional institu-tions	Nurs-ing homes	Other institu-tions	Col-lege dormi-tories	Mili-tary quar-ters	Other
	54	55	56	57	58	59	60	61	62	63	64	65	66	67	68	69	70
INDIANA—Cont'd																	
Lafayette	56 397	98.7	42.7	18.1	25.7	21.1	4.1	1.4	8.2	2.9	1.3	0.0	0.9	0.0	0.0	0.0	0.3
Lawrence	38 915	99.3	38.2	19.9	32.6	27.7	4.0	1.6	4.6	2.3	0.7	0.0	0.7	0.0	0.0	0.0	0.1
Marion	31 320	91.6	39.8	16.7	25.5	20.2	4.4	2.3	5.2	2.4	8.4	0.7	2.0	0.9	4.3	0.0	0.6
Merrillville	30 560	98.2	38.2	20.2	30.9	22.1	5.2	2.0	3.7	1.6	1.8	0.0	1.3	0.1	0.0	0.0	0.4
Michigan City	32 900	91.9	38.1	15.3	27.9	21.6	5.3	2.7	5.3	2.7	8.1	6.7	1.2	0.0	0.0	0.0	0.2
Mishawaka	46 557	97.2	43.5	17.5	27.1	21.8	3.4	1.4	5.8	2.9	2.8	0.0	0.5	0.3	1.4	0.0	0.6
Muncie	67 430	90.8	40.5	14.8	21.8	17.2	3.6	1.7	10.1	2.5	9.2	0.3	0.9	0.4	7.5	0.0	0.2
New Albany	37 603	98.2	42.4	18.0	28.2	21.7	4.1	1.6	5.5	2.7	1.8	0.3	1.4	0.0	0.0	0.0	0.2
Noblesville city, IN	28 590	97.7	37.0	22.9	32.4	28.2	2.1	0.8	3.3	1.8	2.3	1.2	0.8	0.2	0.0	0.0	0.1
Portage	33 496	98.8	38.1	20.4	31.6	23.6	4.1	1.7	4.6	2.5	1.2	0.0	1.1	0.0	0.0	0.0	0.1
Richmond	39 124	95.3	41.6	17.9	25.9	20.7	4.0	1.8	5.8	2.9	4.7	0.4	1.1	0.7	2.0	0.0	0.4
South Bend	107 789	97.4	39.8	15.5	29.7	23.7	5.8	2.7	6.5	2.6	2.6	0.4	1.0	0.2	0.1	0.0	1.0
Terre Haute	59 614	87.6	38.4	15.0	24.1	19.0	3.6	1.6	6.6	2.5	12.4	3.2	1.1	0.4	7.0	0.0	0.6
Valparaiso	27 428	90.1	39.6	18.2	24.6	20.1	2.0	0.6	5.7	2.1	9.9	0.7	1.8	0.2	6.2	0.0	0.9
West Lafayette	28 778	82.1	36.4	10.0	11.8	10.0	1.7	0.2	22.2	0.9	17.9	0.0	0.7	0.0	17.1	0.0	0.0
IOWA	2 926 324	96.4	39.3	21.6	28.4	23.4	2.5	1.0	4.6	1.9	3.6	0.4	1.1	0.2	1.4	0.0	0.4
Ames	50 731	82.0	35.6	15.0	16.1	14.0	1.6	0.3	13.7	1.7	18.0	0.1	0.3	0.0	17.0	0.0	0.6
Ankeny	27 117	97.9	38.1	23.1	30.4	26.1	1.6	0.6	4.7	1.9	2.1	0.0	0.9	0.0	1.0	0.0	0.2
Bettendorf	31 275	99.1	39.9	23.7	30.4	25.1	2.0	0.8	3.1	1.6	0.9	0.0	0.6	0.0	0.0	0.0	0.4
Burlington	26 839	97.6	41.4	19.9	28.6	22.5	2.9	1.4	4.8	2.4	2.4	0.4	1.3	0.1	0.0	0.0	0.6
Cedar Falls	36 145	87.0	35.5	17.4	21.1	17.2	1.5	0.5	11.6	1.5	13.0	0.0	1.4	0.0	11.1	0.0	0.5
Cedar Rapids	120 758	97.2	41.3	20.0	27.4	22.7	2.6	1.1	6.0	2.5	2.8	0.3	0.8	0.0	1.0	0.0	0.6
Clinton	27 772	97.2	41.1	20.1	28.0	22.6	3.1	1.3	4.8	2.6	2.8	0.2	0.4	0.6	0.7	0.0	1.0
Council Bluffs	58 268	97.7	39.3	18.3	29.2	22.8	4.9	2.2	6.0	2.8	2.3	0.5	0.7	0.3	0.6	0.0	0.3
Davenport	98 359	97.1	39.8	18.3	29.1	23.4	3.9	1.9	6.0	2.8	2.9	0.3	0.9	0.3	1.0	0.0	0.5
Des Moines	198 682	96.7	40.5	17.7	27.5	22.1	4.7	1.9	6.2	2.7	3.3	0.3	0.8	0.3	1.2	0.0	0.7
Dubuque	57 686	92.8	39.1	19.7	27.6	22.3	2.2	0.8	4.2	1.8	7.2	0.2	1.5	0.2	3.6	0.0	1.8
Fort Dodge	25 136	95.4	41.7	19.1	27.4	22.6	2.5	1.2	4.6	2.1	4.6	0.3	2.4	0.5	1.2	0.0	0.2
Iowa City	62 220	90.2	40.5	14.3	18.1	15.4	1.8	0.4	15.5	2.3	9.8	0.2	0.2	0.4	8.8	0.0	0.3
Marion	26 294	98.4	39.8	22.7	29.9	25.1	2.0	0.7	4.0	2.0	1.6	0.0	0.9	0.0	0.0	0.0	0.8
Marshalltown	26 009	95.3	39.1	19.8	27.1	22.2	4.2	1.6	5.0	2.1	4.7	0.3	3.9	0.1	0.1	0.0	0.2
Mason City	29 172	96.1	42.4	20.1	27.0	22.1	1.9	0.8	4.8	2.3	3.9	0.3	1.6	0.2	1.2	0.0	0.5
Sioux City	85 013	96.9	37.7	18.5	30.2	24.5	4.5	1.7	5.9	2.4	3.1	0.3	0.9	0.2	1.2	0.0	0.6
Urbandale	29 072	99.0	39.5	24.0	30.0	25.3	1.9	0.7	3.6	1.5	1.0	0.0	0.5	0.0	0.0	0.0	0.2
Waterloo	68 747	97.7	41.0	18.9	28.0	22.1	4.0	1.8	5.9	2.5	2.3	0.4	0.6	0.2	0.0	0.0	1.1
West Des Moines	46 403	99.4	42.7	21.3	27.3	23.7	2.1	0.7	5.9	2.2	0.6	0.0	0.5	0.0	0.0	0.0	0.2
KANSAS	2 688 418	97.0	38.6	21.1	29.5	24.5	3.3	1.4	4.4	1.6	3.0	0.6	0.9	0.1	0.9	0.2	0.3
Dodge City	25 176	98.0	33.3	18.4	32.4	27.7	7.5	2.5	6.4	1.6	2.0	0.3	0.8	0.0	0.4	0.0	0.4
Emporia	26 760	94.5	38.3	17.4	27.1	23.1	4.0	1.4	7.7	2.4	5.5	0.5	0.7	0.0	4.0	0.0	0.3
Garden City	28 451	98.0	32.8	18.5	34.7	29.3	6.4	2.3	5.6	1.7	2.0	0.2	0.5	0.1	0.8	0.0	0.4
Hutchinson	40 787	92.7	40.0	19.8	25.7	21.3	2.9	1.3	4.3	1.9	7.3	5.2	1.4	0.1	0.5	0.0	0.1
Kansas City	146 866	99.1	37.8	15.6	31.8	24.1	8.1	3.7	5.8	2.2	0.9	0.2	0.4	0.0	0.0	0.0	0.3
Lawrence	80 098	90.1	39.2	14.9	20.5	17.4	2.4	0.7	13.0	2.3	9.9	0.1	0.4	0.0	9.1	0.0	0.3
Leavenworth	35 420	88.4	34.0	18.0	29.7	25.6	3.2	1.7	3.5	1.7	11.6	8.9	0.4	0.5	0.6	0.6	0.6
Leawood	27 656	99.8	35.6	27.0	34.5	29.7	1.4	0.4	1.3	0.6	0.2	0.0	0.1	0.0	0.0	0.0	0.0
Lenexa	40 238	98.3	38.7	22.2	29.9	24.8	2.5	0.7	5.0	1.6	1.7	0.0	1.7	0.0	0.0	0.0	0.0
Manhattan	44 831	87.1	37.8	15.0	17.7	15.1	2.1	0.6	14.5	1.5	12.9	0.1	0.7	0.1	11.4	0.5	0.3
Olathe	92 962	98.3	34.8	22.2	34.2	29.2	3.0	0.9	4.2	1.4	1.7	0.0	0.7	0.1	0.6	0.0	0.3
Overland Park	149 080	98.9	40.0	22.7	29.8	25.3	2.4	0.7	4.0	1.4	1.1	0.0	0.8	0.2	0.0	0.0	0.1
Salina	45 679	97.0	40.6	20.2	28.1	23.7	3.1	1.3	5.1	2.2	3.0	0.4	0.9	0.1	0.9	0.0	0.6
Shawnee	47 996	99.5	38.6	23.3	30.8	25.5	2.9	1.0	4.0	1.6	0.5	0.0	0.4	0.0	0.0	0.0	0.1
Topeka	122 377	96.7	42.6	17.8	26.7	21.6	4.1	1.9	5.4	2.4	3.3	0.7	1.3	0.7	0.2	0.0	0.4
Wichita	344 284	98.6	40.4	19.1	30.0	24.6	4.5	1.9	4.6	1.8	1.4	0.5	0.4	0.0	0.1	0.0	0.4
KENTUCKY	4 041 769	97.2	39.4	21.2	28.8	22.3	3.9	1.7	3.9	1.8	2.8	0.7	0.7	0.1	0.8	0.2	0.3
Bowling Green	49 296	88.9	39.1	15.1	22.3	17.8	4.1	1.5	8.3	2.2	11.1	0.8	1.2	0.3	8.2	0.0	0.7
Covington	43 370	97.4	42.1	14.4	28.9	22.5	5.3	2.6	6.7	3.1	2.6	0.8	1.0	0.1	0.0	0.0	0.6
Frankfort	27 741	95.2	44.4	17.3	24.8	19.4	3.8	1.6	5.0	2.4	4.8	1.8	0.4	0.0	2.4	0.0	0.2
Henderson	27 373	97.0	42.7	19.4	27.2	21.3	3.6	1.6	4.2	2.3	3.0	1.2	1.3	0.0	0.0	0.0	0.5
Hopkinsville	30 089	96.7	40.5	18.2	29.7	23.4	4.7	2.4	3.6	1.8	3.3	1.3	1.5	0.2	0.0	0.0	0.3
Jeffersontown	26 633	98.5	40.0	21.7	29.2	23.1	3.5	1.3	4.0	1.7	1.5	0.0	1.5	0.0	0.0	0.0	0.0
Lexington-Fayette	260 512	95.1	41.6	18.1	24.2	19.4	3.8	1.4	7.5	2.2	4.9	1.1	0.5	0.1	2.6	0.0	0.5
Louisville	256 231	96.7	43.5	13.7	27.4	20.1	6.0	2.8	6.1	2.5	3.3	0.5	0.8	0.2	1.0	0.0	0.9
Owensboro	54 067	95.9	41.9	18.7	27.4	21.4	3.7	1.7	4.1	1.9	4.1	0.2	1.4	0.4	0.8	0.0	1.2
Paducah	26 307	95.4	45.0	16.6	25.6	20.0	4.3	2.0	4.0	1.9	4.6	1.7	2.4	0.2	0.0	0.0	0.3
Richmond	27 152	85.0	39.8	14.0	19.3	16.0	3.0	0.9	8.9	2.5	15.0	0.7	0.7	0.0	13.5	0.0	0.1

Table D. Cities

City	Households by type, 2000												Households, 1990		
	Total households	Family households		Married couple		Female householder[1]		Nonfamily households	Householder living alone		Average household size	Average family size	Total households	Female householder[1]	Householder living alone
		Total	With own children under 18 years	Total	With own children under 18 years	Total	With own children under 18 years	Total	Total	65 years and over					
	71	72	73	74	75	76	77	78	79	80	81	82	83	84	85
INDIANA—Cont'd															
Lafayette	24 060	56.8	27.0	42.5	18.2	10.2	6.6	43.2	33.2	9.4	2.31	2.98	18 074	9.6	31.1
Lawrence	14 853	69.6	39.8	52.1	28.2	13.0	9.1	30.4	24.8	5.9	2.60	3.13	10 612	12.0	25.6
Marion	12 462	61.2	27.3	42.1	15.2	14.7	9.4	38.8	33.8	14.2	2.30	2.91	12 693	15.0	30.1
Merrillville	11 678	69.6	32.2	52.9	23.9	12.6	6.7	30.4	26.1	11.8	2.57	3.12	10 006	9.1	21.2
Michigan City	12 550	63.0	30.6	40.0	16.4	18.1	11.5	37.0	30.9	11.6	2.41	3.02	12 562	15.9	29.3
Mishawaka	20 248	57.5	28.2	40.2	17.1	13.0	8.5	42.5	35.8	12.1	2.23	2.92	18 001	11.7	33.3
Muncie	27 322	53.4	23.7	36.4	13.5	13.0	8.0	46.6	34.1	11.8	2.24	2.86	27 188	12.7	31.0
New Albany	15 959	63.0	29.6	42.5	17.2	16.1	10.0	37.0	30.8	11.7	2.31	2.88	14 691	16.0	28.3
Noblesville city, IN	10 576	74.5	40.8	62.0	32.4	9.2	6.4	25.5	21.3	6.5	2.64	3.08	6 650	9.3	22.1
Portage	12 746	70.7	34.7	53.7	24.9	12.2	7.1	29.3	23.9	9.1	2.60	3.09	10 520	10.8	19.9
Richmond	16 287	60.9	27.8	43.1	16.6	13.9	8.8	39.1	33.0	13.7	2.29	2.89	15 579	14.3	30.2
South Bend	42 908	60.5	30.5	39.0	17.2	17.0	11.0	39.5	32.5	12.7	2.45	3.12	42 260	14.9	30.7
Terre Haute	22 870	57.0	27.2	39.0	16.1	14.0	8.8	43.0	34.9	14.1	2.28	2.95	21 488	13.4	33.5
Valparaiso	10 867	58.6	28.8	45.9	20.8	9.7	6.4	41.4	33.4	10.9	2.27	2.93	8 978	9.2	30.8
West Lafayette	10 462	34.3	14.9	27.6	12.2	4.4	2.1	65.7	32.7	7.3	2.26	2.89	9 153	4.4	29.5
IOWA	1 149 276	67.0	31.4	55.1	23.9	8.6	5.6	33.0	27.2	11.4	2.46	3.00	1 064 325	8.0	25.9
Ames	18 085	49.6	22.3	42.0	18.2	5.3	3.3	50.4	28.5	5.9	2.30	2.85	15 613	5.3	26.9
Ankeny	10 339	70.4	38.1	60.7	31.4	7.3	5.2	29.6	21.8	5.8	2.57	3.05	6 756	7.6	19.0
Bettendorf	12 474	69.9	34.0	59.5	27.3	8.1	5.5	30.1	26.0	9.7	2.48	3.01	10 663	8.2	22.1
Burlington	11 102	64.0	29.2	48.2	19.0	12.0	7.9	36.0	31.0	14.0	2.36	2.94	10 986	11.7	29.4
Cedar Falls	12 833	58.9	26.9	48.9	20.6	7.5	5.2	41.1	25.5	9.4	2.45	2.91	11 689	8.1	23.8
Cedar Rapids	49 820	61.9	29.9	48.4	21.2	10.0	6.7	38.1	30.2	9.7	2.36	2.96	43 674	9.9	27.5
Clinton	11 427	64.4	30.1	48.9	20.2	11.7	7.7	35.6	30.2	13.0	2.36	2.93	11 667	11.2	28.0
Council Bluffs	22 889	65.9	31.6	46.7	19.8	14.3	8.9	34.1	27.9	10.6	2.49	3.03	21 131	13.4	26.1
Davenport	39 124	63.4	31.8	46.0	20.4	13.4	9.1	36.6	29.5	9.4	2.44	3.03	37 205	12.9	28.0
Des Moines	80 504	60.5	29.5	43.7	19.3	12.6	7.9	39.5	31.9	10.2	2.39	3.04	78 453	11.9	30.7
Dubuque	22 560	63.4	30.0	50.3	21.9	10.0	6.4	36.6	31.0	12.6	2.37	2.99	21 437	9.6	27.7
Fort Dodge	10 470	60.9	29.0	45.9	19.1	11.4	7.7	39.1	33.8	14.1	2.29	2.94	10 502	11.2	31.2
Iowa City	25 202	44.4	21.2	35.2	15.9	6.7	4.2	55.6	33.8	6.1	2.23	2.90	21 951	6.8	29.7
Marion	10 458	68.6	34.5	57.1	27.0	8.4	5.5	31.4	26.0	7.9	2.47	3.00	7 772	8.1	23.1
Marshalltown	10 175	64.8	30.0	50.5	20.5	10.8	7.3	35.2	29.7	13.5	2.44	3.02	9 974	9.8	29.1
Mason City	12 368	60.7	28.4	47.4	19.6	10.3	6.8	39.3	33.5	14.6	2.27	2.90	12 027	9.5	31.5
Sioux City	32 054	65.8	33.4	49.1	22.7	12.2	8.1	34.2	27.7	11.3	2.57	3.14	30 488	11.4	27.1
Urbandale	11 484	70.0	35.0	60.7	29.3	7.1	4.3	30.0	24.2	7.2	2.51	3.02	9 013	7.5	20.3
Waterloo	28 169	63.0	29.0	46.0	18.3	13.3	8.7	37.0	30.0	12.1	2.39	2.97	27 037	12.4	28.9
West Des Moines	19 826	60.1	30.3	50.0	24.0	7.7	5.1	39.9	30.5	7.1	2.33	2.98	12 974	7.0	27.1
KANSAS	1 037 891	67.6	33.2	54.7	25.1	9.3	6.0	32.4	27.0	10.2	2.51	3.07	944 726	8.6	25.9
Dodge City	8 395	71.1	41.1	55.1	31.0	10.3	7.3	28.9	23.5	9.6	2.94	3.46	7 609	9.2	25.5
Emporia	10 253	58.9	31.5	45.4	22.2	9.4	6.7	41.1	31.1	10.2	2.47	3.15	9 753	8.8	31.5
Garden City	9 338	72.4	43.1	56.4	32.3	10.8	7.8	27.6	22.1	7.7	2.99	3.51	8 072	9.8	21.3
Hutchinson	16 335	63.3	28.9	49.3	19.8	10.3	6.8	36.7	31.7	13.5	2.31	2.91	15 656	9.8	30.3
Kansas City	55 500	65.3	32.5	41.2	18.5	18.2	11.1	34.7	29.2	9.9	2.62	3.25	57 146	16.9	28.0
Lawrence	31 388	50.1	25.1	38.0	17.5	8.7	5.8	49.9	30.6	5.6	2.30	2.93	24 513	8.0	28.8
Leavenworth	12 035	68.3	39.1	53.0	28.7	11.6	8.2	31.7	27.1	9.5	2.60	3.19	11 475	10.7	24.5
Leawood	9 841	82.5	41.4	76.0	37.4	5.1	3.3	17.5	15.2	6.5	2.81	3.14	6 888	4.4	12.1
Lenexa	15 574	67.8	35.1	57.4	28.7	7.6	4.8	32.2	24.3	5.8	2.54	3.08	12 713	7.9	21.8
Manhattan	16 949	48.7	22.7	39.6	17.6	6.6	4.1	51.3	30.5	6.3	2.30	2.89	14 689	6.7	28.2
Olathe	32 314	76.2	45.1	63.8	36.9	9.0	6.2	23.8	18.4	3.7	2.83	3.24	21 445	8.7	17.4
Overland Park	59 703	66.5	33.9	56.8	28.2	7.4	4.5	33.5	27.4	7.7	2.47	3.06	44 936	7.9	25.6
Salina	18 523	64.1	31.5	49.8	21.9	10.5	7.1	35.9	30.1	11.3	2.39	2.98	17 287	10.1	28.9
Shawnee	18 522	71.5	36.3	60.3	29.8	8.2	4.9	28.5	22.7	5.2	2.58	3.07	14 567	8.1	22.8
Topeka	52 190	58.8	28.0	41.8	17.1	13.1	8.6	41.2	35.0	11.7	2.27	2.94	49 936	11.9	32.0
Wichita	139 087	63.1	32.1	47.3	22.2	11.6	7.5	36.9	31.2	9.3	2.44	3.10	123 249	11.1	30.0
KENTUCKY	1 590 647	69.4	32.5	53.9	23.6	11.8	7.0	30.6	26.0	9.8	2.47	2.97	1 379 782	11.6	23.3
Bowling Green	19 277	55.5	26.2	38.5	16.1	13.1	8.3	44.5	33.5	10.6	2.27	2.91	15 973	13.3	31.8
Covington	18 257	55.5	28.8	34.3	16.1	16.5	10.4	44.5	36.5	12.0	2.31	3.08	17 319	16.7	34.0
Frankfort	12 314	56.4	26.4	38.9	15.9	14.1	8.7	43.6	37.6	13.1	2.14	2.83	11 037	13.9	32.9
Henderson	11 693	63.2	29.8	45.5	18.8	14.1	8.9	36.8	32.1	12.9	2.27	2.86	10 548	14.1	28.3
Hopkinsville	12 174	66.7	32.4	45.1	18.8	18.2	11.7	33.3	29.7	12.5	2.39	2.95	11 402	17.4	26.7
Jeffersontown	10 653	68.3	32.9	54.3	25.0	10.7	6.3	31.7	26.4	6.4	2.46	2.99	8 900	10.0	22.1
Lexington-Fayette	108 288	58.1	27.3	43.5	18.9	11.5	6.9	41.9	31.7	7.5	2.29	2.90	89 529	12.2	29.1
Louisville	111 414	55.1	25.7	31.6	12.3	19.2	11.5	44.9	37.9	12.4	2.22	2.97	113 065	18.3	35.0
Owensboro	22 659	62.2	28.8	44.7	18.5	13.9	8.5	37.8	33.3	14.0	2.29	2.91	21 672	13.8	30.1
Paducah	11 825	56.2	25.0	36.8	13.5	16.2	9.9	43.8	39.3	17.3	2.12	2.84	11 955	15.4	35.7
Richmond	10 795	51.4	24.4	35.2	14.3	12.8	8.4	48.6	34.7	8.8	2.14	2.78	7 209	13.7	30.7

[1] No spouse present.

Table D. Cities

City	Percent change of households, 1990–2000	Total housing units	Occupied housing units (percent)	Housing occupancy — Vacant housing units — Total	For seasonal, recreational, or occasional use	Homeowner vacancy rate (percent)	Rental vacancy rate (percent)	Housing tenure — Occupied housing units — Total	Percent owner-occupied housing units	Percent renter-occupied housing units	Average household size of owner-occupied units	Average household size of renter-occupied units
	86	87	88	89	90	91	92	93	94	95	96	97
INDIANA—Cont'd												
Lafayette	33.1	25 602	94.0	6.0	0.3	1.6	6.8	24 060	52.9	47.1	2.45	2.16
Lawrence	40.0	16 292	91.2	8.8	0.3	3.4	15.3	14 853	75.8	24.2	2.68	2.37
Marion	-1.8	13 820	90.2	9.8	0.2	2.4	10.6	12 462	62.1	37.9	2.42	2.11
Merrillville	16.7	12 303	94.9	5.1	0.3	1.9	8.3	11 678	70.6	29.4	2.79	2.03
Michigan City	-0.1	14 221	88.2	11.8	3.4	2.7	8.2	12 550	61.1	38.9	2.49	2.28
Mishawaka	12.5	21 572	93.9	6.1	0.4	1.6	6.7	20 248	56.8	43.2	2.47	1.92
Muncie	0.5	30 205	90.5	9.5	0.3	2.2	9.3	27 322	55.8	44.2	2.27	2.20
New Albany	8.6	17 098	93.3	6.7	0.3	1.7	7.4	15 959	59.3	40.7	2.40	2.18
Noblesville city, IN	59.0	11 294	93.6	6.4	0.6	1.7	11.1	10 576	74.1	25.9	2.79	2.21
Portage	21.2	13 375	95.3	4.7	0.4	1.3	8.0	12 746	72.5	27.5	2.70	2.33
Richmond	4.5	17 647	92.3	7.7	0.4	2.0	9.4	16 287	58.7	41.3	2.33	2.23
South Bend	1.5	46 349	92.6	7.4	0.5	2.0	7.6	42 908	63.1	36.9	2.50	2.35
Terre Haute	6.4	25 636	89.2	10.8	0.3	3.2	11.9	22 870	59.5	40.5	2.38	2.14
Valparaiso	21.0	11 559	94.0	6.0	0.5	1.5	7.4	10 867	55.1	44.9	2.56	1.92
West Lafayette	14.3	10 819	96.7	3.3	0.2	1.4	2.5	10 462	32.2	67.8	2.57	2.11
IOWA	8.0	1 232 511	93.2	6.8	1.3	1.7	6.8	1 149 276	72.3	27.7	2.57	2.15
Ames	15.8	18 757	96.4	3.6	0.3	1.2	3.3	18 085	46.1	53.9	2.52	2.11
Ankeny	53.0	10 882	95.0	5.0	0.2	3.4	5.5	10 339	71.8	28.2	2.79	2.00
Bettendorf	17.0	13 044	95.6	4.4	0.5	1.5	7.3	12 474	77.3	22.7	2.64	1.95
Burlington	1.1	11 985	92.6	7.4	0.4	2.0	9.1	11 102	70.2	29.8	2.49	2.06
Cedar Falls	9.8	13 271	96.7	3.3	0.2	0.8	3.4	12 833	64.3	35.7	2.55	2.27
Cedar Rapids	14.1	52 240	95.4	4.6	0.3	1.5	5.8	49 820	69.0	31.0	2.50	2.03
Clinton	-2.1	12 412	92.1	7.9	0.4	1.8	11.2	11 427	69.3	30.7	2.48	2.10
Council Bluffs	8.3	24 340	94.0	6.0	0.3	1.4	9.3	22 889	65.0	35.0	2.60	2.28
Davenport	5.2	41 350	94.6	5.4	0.3	1.6	7.3	39 124	65.2	34.8	2.58	2.18
Des Moines	2.6	85 067	94.6	5.4	0.2	1.4	6.8	80 504	64.7	35.3	2.53	2.12
Dubuque	5.2	23 819	94.7	5.3	0.3	0.8	8.0	22 560	67.5	32.5	2.58	1.95
Fort Dodge	-0.3	11 168	93.8	6.3	0.4	1.5	8.2	10 470	66.4	33.6	2.44	1.99
Iowa City	14.8	26 083	96.6	3.4	0.2	2.4	2.2	25 202	46.5	53.5	2.46	2.02
Marion	34.6	10 968	95.4	4.6	0.3	2.6	5.7	10 458	78.3	21.7	2.65	1.82
Marshalltown	2.0	10 857	93.7	6.3	0.6	1.7	7.8	10 175	70.1	29.9	2.53	2.20
Mason City	2.8	13 029	94.9	5.1	0.3	1.5	5.4	12 368	67.4	32.6	2.44	1.92
Sioux City	5.1	33 816	94.8	5.2	0.2	1.4	7.8	32 054	66.2	33.8	2.71	2.29
Urbandale	27.4	11 869	96.8	3.2	0.3	1.2	5.1	11 484	77.6	22.4	2.67	1.94
Waterloo	4.2	29 499	95.5	4.5	0.2	0.9	5.9	28 169	67.1	32.9	2.47	2.20
West Des Moines	52.8	20 815	95.2	4.8	0.7	1.6	5.9	19 826	62.1	37.9	2.58	1.90
KANSAS	9.9	1 131 200	91.8	8.2	0.9	2.0	8.8	1 037 891	69.2	30.8	2.63	2.25
Dodge City	10.3	8 976	93.5	6.5	0.3	1.5	8.3	8 395	60.7	39.3	3.01	2.84
Emporia	5.1	11 019	93.0	7.0	0.3	1.5	7.5	10 253	53.6	46.4	2.71	2.18
Garden City	15.7	9 907	94.3	5.7	0.2	1.5	7.3	9 338	61.6	38.4	3.16	2.71
Hutchinson	4.3	17 693	92.3	7.7	0.3	1.7	10.1	16 335	64.7	35.3	2.43	2.11
Kansas City	-2.9	61 446	90.3	9.7	0.3	1.9	8.4	55 500	62.0	38.0	2.69	2.52
Lawrence	28.0	32 761	95.8	4.2	0.1	1.9	3.6	31 388	45.9	54.1	2.57	2.07
Leavenworth	4.9	12 936	93.0	7.0	0.2	2.0	6.3	12 035	50.8	49.2	2.47	2.74
Leawood	42.9	10 129	97.2	2.8	0.7	0.7	7.4	9 841	92.8	7.2	2.87	2.01
Lenexa	22.5	16 378	95.1	4.9	0.4	0.7	8.4	15 574	62.7	37.3	2.85	2.01
Manhattan	15.4	17 690	95.8	4.2	0.3	1.3	3.4	16 949	42.9	57.1	2.54	2.12
Olathe	50.7	33 343	96.9	3.1	0.1	1.6	3.3	32 314	71.5	28.5	3.02	2.36
Overland Park	32.9	62 586	95.4	4.6	0.6	1.0	8.1	59 703	68.3	31.7	2.72	1.94
Salina	7.1	19 599	94.5	5.5	0.2	1.6	7.3	18 523	66.1	33.9	2.51	2.16
Shawnee	27.2	19 086	97.0	3.0	0.2	1.0	4.9	18 522	74.4	25.6	2.78	1.98
Topeka	4.5	56 435	92.5	7.5	0.2	1.6	7.2	52 190	60.7	39.3	2.40	2.07
Wichita	12.9	152 119	91.4	8.6	0.3	2.0	12.0	139 087	61.6	38.4	2.61	2.17
KENTUCKY	15.3	1 750 927	90.8	9.2	1.7	1.8	8.7	1 590 647	70.8	29.2	2.55	2.27
Bowling Green	20.7	21 290	90.5	9.5	0.4	2.6	10.1	19 277	47.0	53.0	2.34	2.21
Covington	5.4	20 448	89.3	10.7	0.3	3.1	9.7	18 257	49.3	50.7	2.53	2.11
Frankfort	11.6	13 422	91.7	8.3	0.5	1.5	9.9	12 314	52.0	48.0	2.27	2.01
Henderson	10.9	12 652	92.4	7.6	0.5	1.9	7.2	11 693	57.3	42.7	2.39	2.11
Hopkinsville	6.8	13 260	91.8	8.2	0.2	2.7	7.9	12 174	57.9	42.1	2.39	2.39
Jeffersontown	19.7	11 220	94.9	5.1	1.0	0.9	8.6	10 653	69.8	30.2	2.60	2.15
Lexington-Fayette	21.0	116 167	93.2	6.8	0.8	1.1	8.4	108 288	55.3	44.7	2.47	2.07
Louisville	-1.5	121 275	91.9	8.1	0.3	1.8	7.5	111 414	52.5	47.5	2.33	2.10
Owensboro	4.6	24 302	93.2	6.8	0.4	1.9	7.7	22 659	60.2	39.8	2.38	2.14
Paducah	-1.1	13 221	89.4	10.6	0.5	3.3	10.4	11 825	52.9	47.1	2.22	2.01
Richmond	49.7	11 857	91.0	9.0	0.3	3.5	8.8	10 795	35.2	64.8	2.31	2.05

Table D. Cities

STATE Place code	City	Land area, 2000¹ (sq km)	Total persons	Rank	Per square kilometer	Land area, 1990¹ (sq km)	Total persons	Rank	Per square kilometer	White	Black or African American	American Indian or Alaska Native	Asian	Native Hawaiian and other Pacific Islander	Some other race
		1	2	3	4	5	6	7	8	9	10	11	12	13	14
22 00000	LOUISIANA	112 824.7	4 468 976	X	39.6	112 836.0	4 221 826	X	37.4	63.9	32.5	0.6	1.2	0.0	0.7
22 00975	Alexandria...............	68.4	46 342	738	677.5	64.1	49 049	571	765.2	42.6	54.7	0.3	1.2	0.0	0.2
22 05000	Baton Rouge	199.0	227 818	76	1 144.8	191.5	219 531	73	1 146.4	45.7	50.0	0.2	2.6	0.0	0.5
22 08920	Bossier City	105.8	56 461	554	533.7	98.5	52 721	511	535.2	71.4	22.7	0.6	1.7	0.1	1.4
22 36255	Houma	36.3	32 393	1 124	892.4	35.1	30 495	1 038	868.8	67.5	26.1	3.4	0.7	0.0	0.7
22 39475	Kenner	39.2	70 517	404	1 798.9	39.2	72 033	323	1 837.6	68.1	22.5	0.4	2.8	0.1	3.8
22 40735	Lafayette	123.3	110 257	211	894.2	106.0	101 865	197	961.0	68.2	28.5	0.2	1.4	0.0	0.6
22 41155	Lake Charles	104.0	71 757	395	690.0	83.1	70 580	337	849.3	50.2	46.8	0.2	1.1	0.0	0.5
22 51410	Monroe	74.3	53 107	620	714.8	67.8	54 909	474	809.9	36.8	61.1	0.1	1.1	0.0	0.2
22 54035	New Iberia	27.4	32 623	1 117	1 190.6	26.3	31 828	980	1 210.2	57.0	38.4	0.2	2.6	0.0	0.5
22 55000	New Orleans	467.6	484 674	33	1 036.5	467.9	496 938	24	1 062.1	28.1	67.3	0.2	2.3	0.0	0.4
22 70000	Shreveport	267.1	200 145	90	749.3	255.4	198 518	79	777.3	46.7	50.8	0.3	0.8	0.0	0.4
22 70805	Slidell	30.5	25 695	1 467	842.5	24.2	24 124	1 350	996.9	83.1	13.6	0.5	0.7	0.1	0.6
23 00000	MAINE	79 931.1	1 274 923	X	16.0	79 939.2	1 227 928	X	15.4	96.9	0.5	0.6	0.7	0.0	0.2
23 02795	Bangor	89.2	31 473	1 161	352.8	89.2	33 181	929	372.0	95.0	1.0	1.0	1.2	0.1	0.4
23 38740	Lewiston	88.3	35 690	1 001	404.2	88.3	39 757	748	450.2	95.7	1.1	0.3	0.8	0.0	0.4
23 60545	Portland	54.9	64 249	454	1 170.3	58.6	64 157	382	1 094.8	91.3	2.6	0.5	3.1	0.1	0.7
24 00000	MARYLAND...............	25 314.1	5 296 486	X	209.2	25 316.3	4 780 753	X	188.8	64.0	27.9	0.3	4.0	0.0	1.8
24 01600	Annapolis...............	17.4	35 838	993	2 059.7	16.4	33 195	928	2 024.1	62.7	31.4	0.2	1.8	0.0	2.2
24 04000	Baltimore	209.3	651 154	18	3 111.1	209.3	736 014	12	3 516.6	31.6	64.3	0.3	1.5	0.0	0.7
24 08775	Bowie	41.7	50 269	665	1 205.5	33.3	37 642	803	1 130.4	62.6	30.8	0.3	2.9	0.0	0.9
24 30325	Frederick	52.9	52 767	630	997.5	47.1	40 186	733	853.2	77.0	14.7	0.3	3.2	0.1	2.3
24 31175	Gaithersburg	26.1	52 613	633	2 015.8	23.6	39 676	751	1 681.2	58.2	14.6	0.4	13.8	0.1	8.6
24 36075	Hagerstown	27.6	36 687	958	1 329.2	25.7	35 306	852	1 373.8	85.9	10.1	0.2	1.0	0.0	0.8
24 67675	Rockville	34.8	47 388	715	1 361.7	31.4	44 830	638	1 427.7	67.8	9.1	0.3	14.8	0.0	4.8
25 00000	MASSACHUSETTS.......	20 305.6	6 349 097	X	312.7	20 300.3	6 016 425	X	296.4	84.5	5.4	0.2	3.8	0.0	3.7
25 00765	Agawam	60.2	28 144	1 318	467.5	NA	27 323	1 168	NA	96.7	0.9	0.1	1.0	0.0	0.4
25 02690	Attleboro	71.3	42 068	818	590.0	71.3	38 383	777	538.3	91.3	1.6	0.2	3.2	0.0	1.8
25 03600	Barnstable Town	155.5	47 821	708	307.5	NA	40 949	716	NA	91.9	2.7	0.6	0.8	0.0	1.7
25 05595	Beverly	43.0	39 862	873	927.0	40.0	38 195	779	954.9	96.0	1.0	0.2	1.3	0.0	0.5
25 07000	Boston	125.4	589 141	21	4 698.1	125.4	574 283	20	4 579.6	54.5	25.3	0.4	7.5	0.1	7.8
25 09000	Brockton	55.6	94 304	267	1 696.1	55.6	92 788	224	1 668.8	61.5	17.8	0.4	2.2	0.0	10.3
25 11000	Cambridge	16.7	101 355	242	6 069.2	16.7	95 802	216	5 736.6	68.1	11.9	0.3	11.9	0.1	3.2
25 13205	Chelsea	5.7	35 080	1 022	6 154.4	5.7	28 710	1 105	5 036.8	57.9	7.3	0.5	4.7	0.1	22.9
25 13660	Chicopee	59.2	54 653	597	923.2	59.3	56 632	454	955.0	89.8	2.3	0.2	0.9	0.1	4.9
25 21990	Everett	8.8	38 037	928	4 322.4	8.8	35 701	841	4 056.9	79.7	6.3	0.3	3.2	0.1	5.0
25 23000	Fall River	80.3	91 938	275	1 144.9	80.3	92 703	225	1 154.5	91.2	2.5	0.2	2.2	0.0	1.4
25 23875	Fitchburg	71.9	39 102	890	543.8	71.9	41 194	709	572.9	81.9	3.6	0.4	4.3	0.0	6.8
25 25100	Franklin	69.3	29 560	1 247	426.6	NA	22 095	1 492	NA	96.0	1.1	0.1	1.7	0.0	0.3
25 26010	Gloucester	67.2	30 273	1 210	450.5	67.3	28 716	1 104	426.7	97.0	0.6	0.1	0.7	0.0	0.5
25 29405	Haverhill	86.3	58 969	517	683.3	86.3	51 418	532	595.8	89.7	2.4	0.2	1.4	0.0	4.3
25 30840	Holyoke	55.1	39 838	874	723.0	55.1	43 704	657	793.2	65.8	3.7	0.4	0.8	0.1	26.4
25 34550	Lawrence	18.0	72 043	393	4 002.4	18.0	70 207	342	3 900.4	48.6	4.9	0.8	2.7	0.1	36.7
25 35075	Leominster	74.8	41 303	833	552.2	74.8	38 145	782	510.0	87.1	3.7	0.2	2.4	0.1	4.3
25 37000	Lowell	35.7	105 167	226	2 945.9	35.7	103 439	195	2 897.5	68.6	4.2	0.2	16.5	0.0	6.5
25 37490	Lynn	28.0	89 050	288	3 180.4	28.0	81 245	275	2 901.6	67.9	10.5	0.4	6.4	0.1	9.8
25 37875	Malden	13.1	56 340	559	4 300.8	13.2	53 884	490	4 082.1	72.1	8.2	0.1	14.0	0.1	2.1
25 38715	Marlborough	54.6	36 255	977	664.0	54.6	31 813	981	582.7	87.7	2.2	0.2	3.8	0.0	3.3
25 39835	Medford	21.1	55 765	573	2 642.9	21.1	57 407	444	2 720.7	86.5	6.1	0.1	3.9	0.0	1.1
25 40115	Melrose	12.2	27 134	1 375	2 224.1	12.2	28 150	1 134	2 307.4	95.2	0.9	0.1	2.0	0.0	0.4
25 40710	Methuen	58.0	43 789	784	755.0	NA	39 990	742	NA	89.4	1.3	0.2	2.4	0.0	4.9
25 45000	New Bedford.............	52.1	93 768	268	1 799.8	52.2	99 922	204	1 914.2	78.9	4.4	0.6	0.7	0.0	9.5
25 45560	Newton	46.8	83 829	319	1 791.2	46.8	82 585	271	1 764.6	88.1	2.0	0.1	7.7	0.0	0.7
25 46330	Northampton	89.2	28 978	1 275	324.9	89.3	29 289	1 078	328.0	90.0	2.1	0.3	3.1	0.1	2.4
25 52490	Peabody	42.5	48 129	702	1 132.4	42.5	47 264	599	1 112.1	93.9	1.0	0.1	1.4	0.0	1.8
25 53960	Pittsfield	105.5	45 793	748	434.1	105.5	48 622	580	460.9	92.6	3.7	0.1	1.2	0.0	0.8
25 55745	Quincy	43.5	88 025	295	2 023.6	43.5	84 985	261	1 953.7	79.6	2.2	0.2	15.4	0.0	0.9
25 56585	Revere	15.3	47 283	720	3 090.4	15.3	42 786	673	2 796.5	84.4	2.9	0.3	4.5	0.1	4.1
25 59105	Salem	21.0	40 407	859	1 924.1	21.0	38 091	786	1 813.9	85.4	3.2	0.2	2.0	0.0	6.7
25 62535	Somerville	10.6	77 478	359	7 309.2	10.6	76 210	295	7 189.6	77.0	6.5	0.2	6.4	0.0	5.0
25 67000	Springfield	83.1	152 082	136	1 830.1	83.2	156 983	113	1 886.8	56.1	21.0	0.4	1.9	0.1	16.4
25 69170	Taunton	120.7	55 976	568	463.8	120.7	49 832	560	412.9	91.7	2.7	0.2	0.6	0.0	2.6
25 72600	Waltham	32.9	59 226	514	1 800.2	32.9	57 878	440	1 759.2	83.0	4.4	0.2	7.3	0.1	3.2
25 76030	Westfield	120.6	40 072	870	332.3	120.7	38 372	778	317.9	94.5	0.9	0.2	0.8	0.0	2.1
25 81035	Woburn	32.8	37 258	947	1 135.9	32.8	35 943	834	1 095.8	90.6	1.9	0.1	4.8	0.1	1.4
25 82000	Worcester	97.3	172 648	125	1 774.4	97.3	169 759	104	1 744.7	77.1	6.9	0.4	4.9	0.1	7.2

¹ Dry land or land partially or temporarily covered by water.

Table D. Cities

City	Population and population characteristics, 2000 (cont'd)								Population and population characteristics, 1990				
	Race (percent) (cont'd)								Race (percent)				
	Race alone or in combination												
	Two or more races	White	Black	American Indian or Alaska Native	Asian	Native Hawaiian and other Pacific Islander	Some other race	Hispanic[1]	White	Black or African American	American Indian or Alaska Native	Asian and Pacific Islander	Hispanic[1]
	15	16	17	18	19	20	21	22	23	24	25	26	27
LOUISIANA	1.1	64.8	32.9	1.0	1.4	0.1	1.1	2.4	67.3	30.8	0.4	1.0	2.2
Alexandria	0.9	43.2	55.3	0.6	1.4	0.1	0.5	1.0	49.6	49.3	0.2	0.7	1.0
Baton Rouge	1.0	40.4	50.4	0.5	2.9	0.1	0.8	1.7	53.9	43.9	0.1	1.7	1.6
Bossier City	2.0	73.1	23.4	1.1	2.4	0.2	1.9	4.0	79.3	18.1	0.4	1.5	2.6
Houma	1.6	68.7	26.7	4.4	0.9	0.1	1.0	1.8	71.0	25.0	3.0	0.8	1.4
Kenner	2.2	70.1	22.9	0.8	3.2	0.1	5.3	13.6	77.4	18.1	0.3	1.7	10.1
Lafayette	1.0	69.0	28.9	0.5	1.6	0.1	1.0	1.9	70.8	27.2	0.2	1.3	1.7
Lake Charles	1.1	51.1	47.5	0.7	1.2	0.1	0.8	1.4	57.3	41.6	0.2	0.5	1.1
Monroe	0.6	37.2	61.4	0.3	1.2	0.1	0.4	1.0	43.3	55.6	0.1	0.8	0.8
New Iberia	1.2	57.8	38.9	0.6	3.0	0.1	0.9	1.5	64.2	33.3	0.2	2.0	2.3
New Orleans	1.3	28.9	67.9	0.5	2.5	0.1	1.5	3.1	34.9	61.9	0.2	1.9	3.5
Shreveport	1.0	47.4	51.2	0.7	1.0	0.1	0.7	1.6	54.3	44.8	0.2	0.5	1.1
Slidell	1.4	84.4	14.0	1.0	1.0	0.1	1.0	2.7	87.9	10.8	0.4	0.6	2.5
MAINE	1.0	97.9	0.7	1.0	0.9	0.1	0.4	0.7	98.4	0.4	0.5	0.5	0.6
Bangor	1.4	96.3	1.4	1.6	1.5	0.1	0.6	1.0	97.1	0.9	0.7	1.0	0.6
Lewiston	1.7	97.3	1.6	1.0	1.1	0.1	0.7	1.3	98.2	0.7	0.2	0.7	0.7
Portland	1.9	92.8	3.2	1.0	3.6	0.1	1.2	1.5	96.6	1.1	0.4	1.7	0.8
MARYLAND	2.0	65.4	28.8	0.7	4.5	0.1	2.5	4.3	71.0	24.9	0.3	2.9	2.6
Annapolis	1.7	63.8	32.1	0.6	2.3	0.1	2.8	6.4	64.9	33.0	0.2	1.3	1.5
Baltimore	1.5	32.6	65.2	0.8	1.8	0.1	1.2	1.7	39.1	59.2	0.3	1.1	1.0
Bowie	2.3	64.4	32.0	1.0	3.7	0.1	1.5	2.9	91.4	5.7	0.3	2.3	2.2
Frederick	2.5	79.1	16.0	0.8	3.8	0.1	2.9	4.8	84.3	12.8	0.3	1.9	2.1
Gaithersburg	4.4	61.6	15.7	0.8	14.9	0.3	11.2	19.8	72.2	12.9	0.4	10.2	9.3
Hagerstown	1.8	87.6	11.2	0.7	1.2	0.1	1.1	1.8	92.5	6.3	0.1	0.7	0.8
Rockville	3.1	70.2	9.9	0.9	16.1	0.2	6.2	11.7	79.2	8.3	0.3	9.8	8.6
MASSACHUSETTS	2.3	86.2	6.3	0.6	4.2	0.1	5.1	6.8	89.8	5.0	0.2	2.4	4.8
Agawam	0.8	97.4	1.1	0.4	1.1	0.1	0.7	1.8	0.0	0.0	0.0	0.0	0.0
Attleboro	1.8	92.7	2.0	0.6	3.8	0.2	2.6	4.3	95.5	1.0	0.2	2.4	2.9
Barnstable Town	2.3	93.8	3.5	1.1	1.1	0.1	3.0	1.7	0.0	0.0	0.0	0.0	0.0
Beverly	1.0	96.9	1.4	0.4	1.5	0.1	0.7	1.8	97.6	0.9	0.1	1.0	1.1
Boston	4.4	56.8	27.7	0.9	8.1	0.3	10.9	14.4	62.8	25.6	0.3	5.3	10.8
Brockton	7.8	64.4	23.3	0.9	2.7	0.2	16.5	8.0	80.2	13.0	0.3	1.7	6.3
Cambridge	4.6	71.2	13.8	0.8	13.1	0.2	5.7	7.4	75.3	13.5	0.3	8.4	6.8
Chelsea	6.6	63.3	8.7	0.9	5.1	0.3	28.5	48.4	69.7	5.2	0.3	5.0	31.4
Chicopee	1.8	91.4	2.8	0.5	1.1	0.2	5.9	8.8	95.4	1.8	0.1	0.6	3.6
Everett	5.4	84.1	7.5	0.7	3.7	0.2	9.4	9.5	93.5	3.2	0.3	1.8	3.8
Fall River	2.6	93.3	3.2	0.6	2.5	0.3	2.8	3.3	97.2	1.0	0.1	1.3	1.7
Fitchburg	3.1	84.2	4.7	0.9	4.9	0.1	8.4	15.0	89.4	3.4	0.2	2.6	9.6
Franklin	0.8	96.7	1.3	0.3	2.0	0.1	0.5	1.1	98.3	0.7	0.1	0.8	0.7
Gloucester	1.0	97.9	0.9	0.4	0.9	0.1	0.9	1.5	99.3	0.2	0.1	0.3	0.9
Haverhill	2.0	91.4	3.0	0.6	1.7	0.1	5.3	8.8	94.9	2.0	0.2	0.8	5.3
Holyoke	2.8	68.0	4.6	0.8	1.0	0.2	28.4	41.4	73.1	3.6	0.2	0.8	31.1
Lawrence	6.2	53.5	7.6	1.3	3.0	0.3	41.0	59.7	65.0	6.4	0.5	1.9	41.6
Leominster	2.2	88.9	4.4	0.5	2.9	0.1	5.6	11.0	93.1	2.3	0.2	1.6	8.3
Lowell	3.9	71.4	5.0	0.6	17.9	0.3	9.0	14.0	81.1	2.4	0.2	11.1	10.1
Lynn	4.9	71.0	12.6	0.9	7.5	0.2	12.8	18.4	83.1	8.1	0.3	3.7	9.1
Malden	3.5	74.2	9.7	0.5	14.6	0.2	4.5	4.8	89.4	4.2	0.2	5.2	2.6
Marlborough	2.9	90.3	2.6	0.6	4.2	0.1	5.0	6.1	94.8	1.8	0.2	1.9	4.2
Medford	2.3	88.2	7.1	0.4	4.3	0.1	2.4	2.6	93.4	4.1	0.1	2.0	1.7
Melrose	1.4	96.4	1.3	0.4	2.4	0.1	1.0	1.0	98.1	0.6	0.1	1.1	0.8
Methuen	1.8	90.9	1.8	0.4	2.7	0.1	6.0	9.6	0.0	0.0	0.0	0.0	0.0
New Bedford	5.9	82.9	6.8	1.4	0.9	0.3	14.0	10.2	87.6	4.1	0.4	0.4	6.7
Newton	1.5	89.3	2.4	0.3	8.3	0.1	1.2	2.5	92.8	2.1	0.1	4.6	2.0
Northampton	2.0	91.7	2.8	0.9	3.7	0.1	3.0	5.2	93.0	1.8	0.2	2.9	4.1
Peabody	1.8	95.5	1.3	0.3	1.6	0.1	3.0	3.4	96.8	1.2	0.0	1.1	2.9
Pittsfield	1.6	94.0	4.6	0.6	1.4	0.1	1.1	2.0	95.5	3.1	0.2	0.8	1.1
Quincy	1.8	81.0	2.6	0.4	15.9	0.1	1.8	2.1	91.7	1.1	0.2	6.6	1.4
Revere	3.8	86.9	3.6	0.6	5.7	0.3	6.9	9.4	93.2	1.4	0.2	3.7	3.8
Salem	2.5	87.4	3.9	0.6	2.4	0.2	8.2	11.2	93.0	2.7	0.3	1.4	6.7
Somerville	4.8	80.6	7.9	0.6	7.2	0.2	8.6	8.8	88.7	5.6	0.1	3.7	6.3
Springfield	4.0	58.7	22.9	1.0	2.3	0.5	18.9	27.2	68.6	19.2	0.2	1.0	16.9
Taunton	2.2	93.4	3.5	0.5	0.9	0.2	3.8	3.9	95.3	2.0	0.2	0.5	4.7
Waltham	1.9	84.4	5.0	0.4	7.8	0.1	4.4	8.5	91.4	3.1	0.1	3.6	5.6
Westfield	1.3	95.8	1.2	0.6	1.1	0.1	2.6	5.0	96.5	0.9	0.1	0.8	4.1
Woburn	1.1	91.5	2.2	0.3	5.2	0.1	1.9	3.1	96.6	1.0	0.2	1.5	2.3
Worcester	3.4	79.8	8.0	1.0	5.3	0.2	9.3	15.1	87.1	4.5	0.3	2.8	9.6

[1] Hispanic persons may be of any race.

Table D. Cities

City	Population and population characteristics, 2000										
	Age (percent)										
	Under 5 years	5 to 17 years	18 to 24 years	25 to 34 years	35 to 44 years	45 to 54 years	55 to 64 years	65 to 74 years	75 years and over	Median age (years)	Percent Female
	28	29	30	31	32	33	34	35	36	37	38
LOUISIANA	7.1	20.2	10.6	13.5	15.5	13.1	8.5	6.3	5.2	34.0	51.6
Alexandria	7.3	20.8	9.2	11.8	14.4	12.7	8.7	7.5	7.6	35.6	54.5
Baton Rouge	6.8	17.6	17.5	13.9	13.3	11.9	7.5	5.8	5.6	30.4	52.5
Bossier City	8.0	20.2	11.0	14.7	15.6	11.5	7.9	6.1	4.8	32.1	51.4
Houma	7.4	20.5	9.8	13.3	16.0	12.6	8.3	6.6	5.7	34.3	51.3
Kenner	7.0	20.3	9.4	14.1	16.4	15.1	8.7	5.2	3.7	34.5	52.0
Lafayette	6.4	18.6	13.3	14.0	15.5	13.3	7.7	6.3	4.9	33.1	51.8
Lake Charles	6.9	18.6	11.5	12.5	14.4	12.9	8.5	7.7	6.9	35.3	52.4
Monroe	7.6	22.0	15.0	12.4	12.7	11.0	6.5	6.2	6.6	29.1	54.3
New Iberia	8.2	21.6	9.7	12.4	14.4	12.2	8.1	6.8	6.6	33.6	53.2
New Orleans	6.9	19.8	11.4	14.5	14.8	13.1	7.8	6.0	5.7	33.1	53.1
Shreveport	7.1	19.8	10.7	13.2	14.1	13.0	8.2	6.9	7.0	34.3	53.4
Slidell	6.7	20.3	7.6	12.5	16.0	13.8	9.5	7.2	6.5	37.0	52.1
MAINE	5.5	18.1	8.1	12.4	16.7	15.1	9.7	7.5	6.8	38.6	51.3
Bangor	5.7	15.5	12.4	14.7	15.6	13.9	8.1	6.7	7.4	36.1	52.8
Lewiston	5.6	15.2	12.6	12.9	14.0	12.7	9.3	8.3	9.4	37.6	52.4
Portland	5.1	13.6	10.7	19.3	16.8	13.3	7.3	6.3	7.6	35.7	52.1
MARYLAND	6.7	18.9	8.5	14.1	17.3	14.3	8.9	6.1	5.2	36.0	51.7
Annapolis	6.7	15.0	9.3	17.7	15.7	14.3	9.3	6.3	5.7	35.7	52.6
Baltimore	6.4	18.4	10.9	14.3	15.6	12.8	8.4	6.9	6.3	35.0	53.4
Bowie	7.5	19.4	5.7	14.5	20.5	13.8	9.2	5.7	3.7	36.3	52.2
Frederick	7.5	17.7	9.3	17.7	17.6	12.4	6.7	5.3	6.0	33.8	52.4
Gaithersburg	8.2	16.8	9.0	18.9	18.8	13.4	6.6	3.5	4.8	33.6	51.3
Hagerstown	7.9	17.6	9.0	15.8	15.3	12.3	7.8	6.8	7.6	34.8	53.2
Rockville	6.3	17.1	7.0	14.2	17.9	14.8	9.7	6.8	6.3	37.8	51.2
MASSACHUSETTS	6.3	17.4	9.1	14.6	16.7	13.8	8.6	6.7	6.8	36.5	51.8
Agawam	5.5	16.5	6.5	12.6	17.0	15.4	9.7	7.4	9.3	40.3	52.5
Attleboro	7.0	18.4	6.8	15.7	18.2	12.7	8.3	6.4	6.5	36.1	51.4
Barnstable Town	5.2	16.7	5.6	10.4	16.4	14.9	10.6	10.5	9.6	42.3	52.2
Beverly	6.3	15.4	9.0	13.6	17.2	14.5	8.3	7.2	8.4	38.3	52.7
Boston	5.4	14.3	16.2	21.2	14.7	10.8	7.0	5.3	5.1	31.1	51.9
Brockton	7.3	20.6	9.1	14.6	15.9	12.4	8.4	5.8	5.9	34.0	52.1
Cambridge	4.1	9.2	21.2	24.9	13.8	11.0	6.8	4.6	4.5	30.4	51.0
Chelsea	8.1	19.2	10.6	19.0	15.6	9.8	6.5	5.4	5.8	31.3	49.8
Chicopee	5.5	17.2	8.5	13.2	15.6	13.3	9.2	8.5	9.1	38.7	52.4
Everett	5.9	15.7	8.9	18.4	16.4	11.8	8.1	7.5	7.2	35.6	52.4
Fall River	6.4	17.8	9.2	15.6	14.2	11.7	8.3	7.6	9.4	35.7	53.3
Fitchburg	6.7	19.1	11.6	13.9	14.9	11.7	7.5	6.7	7.9	34.1	52.3
Franklin	9.4	20.9	6.5	13.6	21.5	13.3	6.6	4.6	3.6	34.8	51.0
Gloucester	5.8	16.2	6.5	12.5	17.4	16.1	9.9	8.3	7.3	40.2	52.1
Haverhill	7.4	18.3	7.7	15.7	17.8	12.8	7.6	5.9	6.9	35.5	52.5
Holyoke	7.9	21.5	9.0	13.0	13.8	11.5	7.7	6.7	8.9	34.0	53.2
Lawrence	9.0	23.0	11.1	15.8	14.6	10.5	6.2	4.4	5.4	29.5	52.2
Leominster	7.1	18.4	7.2	14.9	17.5	13.1	8.2	6.8	6.9	36.3	51.9
Lowell	7.3	19.6	11.9	17.1	15.3	11.0	6.8	5.4	5.4	31.4	50.7
Lynn	7.3	19.7	9.1	15.1	15.9	12.4	7.7	6.3	6.5	34.2	51.6
Malden	5.8	14.1	8.5	20.2	16.7	12.5	8.3	7.0	6.8	35.7	51.9
Marlborough	7.0	16.2	7.0	17.5	19.2	13.2	8.4	5.8	5.7	36.1	50.7
Medford	4.9	13.1	11.0	17.0	15.6	12.4	8.7	8.1	9.2	37.5	53.1
Melrose	6.7	15.3	5.4	14.5	17.5	15.2	9.1	7.6	8.7	39.4	53.0
Methuen	6.3	18.5	7.3	13.6	17.4	13.5	8.1	7.1	8.3	37.5	52.1
New Bedford	6.7	18.2	9.5	14.3	14.4	11.9	8.2	7.7	9.0	35.9	52.9
Newton	5.2	16.0	10.3	12.9	15.3	16.0	9.2	7.1	8.0	38.7	53.5
Northampton	4.1	12.9	15.4	14.1	15.8	16.3	7.6	5.9	7.9	37.3	56.9
Peabody	5.8	16.4	6.2	12.4	17.1	14.5	10.2	9.1	8.4	40.3	52.1
Pittsfield	5.9	17.2	6.9	12.6	15.7	13.7	9.4	8.8	9.8	39.6	52.5
Quincy	5.1	12.4	8.1	19.7	16.3	13.1	9.0	8.0	8.3	37.6	52.3
Revere	5.8	15.2	7.9	16.5	16.1	12.4	9.4	8.3	8.3	37.6	51.6
Salem	5.6	14.6	10.4	17.0	16.3	13.7	8.2	6.9	7.2	36.4	53.6
Somerville	4.5	10.3	15.9	27.6	15.0	10.1	6.2	5.2	5.2	31.1	51.3
Springfield	7.6	21.3	11.4	14.0	14.4	11.6	7.2	6.1	6.4	31.9	52.8
Taunton	7.1	17.8	8.0	15.9	17.3	12.7	8.4	6.3	6.6	35.7	51.9
Waltham	4.7	10.8	16.8	19.1	15.3	12.0	8.2	6.6	6.5	34.2	50.7
Westfield	5.9	17.9	12.6	12.3	15.7	13.7	8.2	6.6	7.1	35.8	51.6
Woburn	5.8	15.3	6.9	17.3	17.6	12.9	8.8	8.6	6.8	37.7	51.1
Worcester	6.5	17.1	13.3	15.5	14.8	11.4	7.2	6.3	7.8	33.4	52.0

Table D. Cities

City	Population and population characteristics, 1990										Population—change, 1980–2000				
	Age (percent)										Total persons			Percent change	
	Under 5 years	5 to 17 years	18 to 24 years	25 to 34 years	35 to 44 years	45 to 54 years	55 to 64 years	65 to 74 years	75 years and over	Percent Female	2000	1990	1980	1990–2000	1980–1990
	39	40	41	42	43	44	45	46	47	48	49	50	51	52	53
LOUISIANA	7.9	21.2	11.0	16.7	14.4	9.6	8.1	6.5	4.6	51.9	4 468 976	4 220 164	4 206 116	5.9	0.3
Alexandria	7.8	21.5	10.0	15.6	13.1	9.3	8.5	7.8	6.4	54.3	46 342	49 049	51 565	-5.5	-4.9
Baton Rouge	7.1	17.0	10.4	16.5	13.8	9.2	7.8	7.0	4.5	52.7	227 818	219 531	219 419	3.8	0.1
Bossier City	8.8	20.3	11.2	19.1	14.1	9.8	7.9	5.6	3.3	51.7	56 461	52 721	50 861	7.1	3.7
Houma	8.5	22.7	9.1	16.8	14.3	9.0	8.0	7.4	4.3	52.4	32 393	30 495	32 608	6.2	-6.5
Kenner	8.1	21.7	10.6	18.3	17.5	10.6	6.9	3.8	2.7	51.8	70 517	72 033	66 382	-2.1	8.5
Lafayette	7.5	19.1	13.6	18.1	14.8	9.2	8.2	5.9	3.6	51.9	110 257	101 852	81 961	8.3	24.3
Lake Charles	7.5	20.2	10.8	16.1	13.5	9.4	9.4	8.0	5.2	52.7	71 757	70 580	75 226	1.7	-6.2
Monroe	8.8	21.9	14.9	14.2	12.1	7.1	7.6	7.0	6.4	54.8	53 107	54 909	57 597	-3.3	-4.7
New Iberia	8.7	22.9	10.2	15.9	12.8	8.9	8.2	7.5	4.8	52.6	32 623	31 828	32 766	2.5	-2.9
New Orleans	7.7	19.8	11.1	17.1	14.4	9.1	7.9	7.4	5.6	53.5	484 674	496 938	557 515	-2.5	-10.9
Shreveport	7.9	20.6	9.6	15.9	14.2	9.4	8.6	7.7	6.0	53.9	200 145	198 525	205 776	0.8	-3.5
Slidell	7.1	21.9	8.3	14.2	16.6	12.8	8.6	6.6	3.9	51.4	25 695	24 124	26 718	6.5	-9.7
MAINE	7.0	18.2	10.1	16.7	15.7	10.2	8.8	7.5	5.8	51.3	1 274 923	1 227 928	1 125 043	3.8	9.1
Bangor	7.2	14.8	14.0	19.1	14.1	9.3	7.9	7.0	6.7	53.1	31 473	33 181	31 643	-5.1	4.9
Lewiston	7.0	15.5	14.1	15.7	12.4	9.5	9.4	9.0	7.4	52.9	35 690	39 757	40 481	-10.2	-1.8
Portland	6.7	13.1	12.8	21.7	14.8	8.2	7.7	7.6	7.4	53.5	64 249	64 157	61 572	0.1	4.2
MARYLAND	7.5	16.8	10.6	18.8	16.3	10.9	8.3	6.6	4.2	51.5	5 296 486	4 780 753	4 216 933	10.8	13.4
Annapolis	6.8	14.6	10.7	20.0	15.4	11.6	8.7	7.2	5.0	53.5	35 838	33 195	31 740	8.0	4.6
Baltimore	7.7	16.7	11.1	18.8	14.1	9.5	8.4	7.9	5.7	53.3	651 154	736 014	786 775	-11.5	-6.5
Bowie	7.6	16.4	9.8	20.5	15.7	13.8	9.9	4.9	1.4	49.9	50 269	37 642	33 695	33.5	11.7
Frederick	8.5	15.4	12.5	21.8	15.1	8.4	6.4	6.3	5.7	53.2	52 767	40 186	28 086	31.3	43.1
Gaithersburg	9.1	15.4	10.7	26.4	16.9	10.3	4.7	3.0	3.5	51.6	52 613	39 676	26 424	32.6	50.2
Hagerstown	8.2	15.2	10.8	18.6	13.6	8.8	8.7	9.1	6.9	53.9	36 687	35 306	34 132	3.9	3.4
Rockville	6.7	16.3	9.2	18.4	17.5	12.3	9.2	6.3	4.1	50.8	47 388	44 830	43 811	5.7	2.3
MASSACHUSETTS	6.9	15.6	11.8	18.3	15.3	10.0	8.6	7.6	6.0	52.0	6 349 097	6 016 425	5 737 093	5.5	4.9
Agawam	NA	NA	NA	NA	NA	NA	NA	NA	NA	NA	28 144	27 323	NA	3.0	NA
Attleboro	8.8	16.3	10.0	20.7	13.9	10.2	8.2	7.0	5.0	51.2	42 068	38 383	34 196	9.6	12.2
Barnstable Town	NA	NA	NA	NA	NA	NA	NA	NA	NA	NA	47 821	40 949	NA	16.8	NA
Beverly	6.9	14.4	10.7	18.5	15.7	9.8	9.0	8.3	6.7	53.2	39 862	38 195	37 655	4.4	1.4
Boston	6.2	12.8	17.3	23.2	13.6	8.2	7.1	6.3	5.2	51.9	589 141	574 283	562 994	2.6	2.0
Brockton	8.4	17.9	11.1	18.5	14.1	9.7	7.9	6.7	5.7	51.9	94 304	92 788	95 172	1.6	-2.5
Cambridge	4.8	9.3	19.6	25.1	16.0	8.8	6.0	5.8	4.6	51.4	101 355	95 802	95 322	5.8	0.5
Chelsea	9.1	16.7	11.8	21.3	11.9	7.6	8.2	7.5	5.9	51.1	35 080	28 710	25 431	22.2	12.9
Chicopee	6.3	15.5	10.9	17.0	13.4	9.7	10.0	10.7	6.5	52.6	54 653	56 632	55 112	-3.5	2.8
Everett	6.7	12.8	10.8	20.5	13.3	9.1	10.2	9.1	7.5	53.5	38 037	35 701	37 195	6.5	-4.0
Fall River	7.4	16.8	11.3	16.9	11.7	9.0	8.8	10.2	8.0	53.8	91 938	92 703	92 574	-0.8	0.1
Fitchburg	8.0	16.0	14.3	18.1	12.3	7.8	8.0	8.3	7.2	52.6	39 102	41 194	39 580	-5.1	4.1
Franklin	NA	NA	NA	NA	NA	NA	NA	NA	NA	NA	29 560	22 095	NA	33.8	NA
Gloucester	6.6	14.8	9.1	17.0	17.0	10.0	10.2	8.5	6.9	51.8	30 273	28 716	27 717	5.4	3.6
Haverhill	8.4	15.6	10.4	21.5	13.7	9.2	7.1	7.5	6.7	52.3	58 969	51 418	46 865	14.7	9.7
Holyoke	9.3	19.3	10.5	16.0	11.4	8.7	7.8	8.6	8.4	53.8	39 838	43 704	44 678	-8.8	-2.2
Lawrence	9.9	21.8	11.0	18.4	12.6	7.5	6.3	6.8	5.6	52.2	72 043	70 207	63 175	2.6	11.1
Leominster	7.6	15.5	10.2	20.7	14.6	9.9	8.5	7.5	5.5	51.7	41 303	38 145	34 508	8.3	10.5
Lowell	8.6	17.6	14.1	20.5	12.1	7.6	7.2	7.1	5.1	51.3	105 167	103 439	92 418	1.7	11.9
Lynn	8.2	16.4	10.4	19.0	13.9	9.0	8.2	8.2	6.8	52.2	89 050	81 245	78 471	9.6	3.5
Malden	6.7	12.8	11.1	22.1	14.2	8.9	8.9	8.3	7.1	52.7	56 340	53 884	53 386	4.6	0.9
Marlborough	7.7	14.4	10.4	22.4	16.7	9.6	7.3	6.5	4.9	50.8	36 255	31 813	30 617	14.0	3.9
Medford	5.5	11.9	13.6	19.6	13.6	9.2	9.7	9.2	7.6	53.4	55 765	57 407	58 076	-2.9	-1.2
Melrose	6.1	14.7	9.1	16.9	16.6	10.8	9.1	8.4	8.4	53.7	27 134	28 150	30 055	-3.6	-6.3
Methuen	NA	NA	NA	NA	NA	NA	NA	NA	NA	NA	43 789	39 990	NA	9.5	NA
New Bedford	7.5	17.5	10.4	16.8	12.4	8.9	9.2	9.6	7.8	53.1	93 768	99 922	98 478	-6.2	1.5
Newton	5.5	13.1	13.5	16.5	16.6	10.9	8.9	7.9	7.1	53.9	83 829	82 585	83 622	1.5	-1.2
Northampton	4.7	12.8	17.3	17.7	17.4	8.0	7.3	7.5	7.2	56.3	28 978	29 289	29 286	-1.1	0.0
Peabody	6.3	15.1	9.2	17.7	15.2	11.1	11.1	8.8	5.4	52.0	48 129	47 264	45 976	1.8	2.8
Pittsfield	6.8	15.9	9.5	16.8	14.3	9.5	9.9	9.7	7.6	52.5	45 793	48 622	51 974	-5.8	-6.4
Quincy	5.8	10.9	12.2	21.8	13.3	10.0	9.3	9.1	7.6	53.5	88 025	84 985	84 743	3.6	0.3
Revere	6.0	12.6	10.8	18.7	13.6	10.3	10.8	9.7	7.4	51.7	47 283	42 786	42 423	10.5	0.9
Salem	6.5	12.1	13.1	21.7	14.3	8.9	8.3	8.5	6.7	53.7	40 407	38 091	38 220	6.1	-0.3
Somerville	5.0	10.2	16.8	26.6	13.8	7.7	7.7	6.8	5.4	52.2	77 478	76 210	77 372	1.7	-1.5
Springfield	8.5	18.5	12.2	18.2	13.0	8.3	7.6	7.9	5.8	52.9	152 082	156 983	152 319	-3.1	3.1
Taunton	7.5	16.9	10.2	19.4	14.6	9.2	8.2	8.2	6.0	52.2	55 976	49 832	45 001	12.3	10.7
Waltham	4.9	10.6	19.4	20.9	13.8	8.5	8.6	7.3	6.0	51.5	59 226	57 878	58 200	2.3	-0.6
Westfield	6.8	16.2	14.7	16.2	14.6	9.9	8.0	8.2	5.6	52.4	40 072	38 372	36 465	4.4	5.2
Woburn	6.5	14.4	10.8	21.7	13.6	9.9	10.5	8.1	4.5	51.3	37 258	35 943	36 626	3.7	-1.9
Worcester	7.2	15.1	14.8	18.6	12.2	8.0	8.0	8.6	7.4	52.4	172 648	169 759	161 799	1.7	4.9

Table D. Cities

City	Total population	Total in households	House-holder	Spouse	Child Total	Child Own child under 18 years	Other relatives Total	Other relatives Under 18 years	Nonrelatives Total	Nonrelatives Unmarried partner	Total in group quarters	Correctional institutions	Nursing homes	Other institutions	College dormitories	Military quarters	Other
	54	55	56	57	58	59	60	61	62	63	64	65	66	67	68	69	70
LOUISIANA	4 468 976	97.0	37.1	18.1	31.4	23.5	6.3	3.2	4.1	1.9	3.0	1.1	0.7	0.2	0.6	0.1	0.3
Alexandria	46 342	96.2	38.4	14.8	31.2	22.9	8.0	4.4	3.8	1.8	3.8	0.9	1.6	0.2	0.0	0.0	1.1
Baton Rouge	227 818	94.5	39.1	14.0	27.9	20.4	7.1	3.5	6.4	2.0	5.5	0.8	0.6	0.1	3.4	0.0	0.6
Bossier City	56 461	97.0	37.5	18.9	31.5	25.3	4.7	2.4	4.4	1.8	3.0	0.0	1.0	0.5	0.0	1.4	0.1
Houma	32 393	97.5	35.9	17.8	32.3	23.5	7.3	3.7	4.3	2.2	2.5	1.7	0.4	0.1	0.0	0.0	0.4
Kenner	70 517	99.0	36.4	18.5	33.0	23.7	6.9	3.2	4.2	2.1	1.0	0.0	0.6	0.0	0.0	0.0	0.4
Lafayette	110 257	96.0	39.5	17.3	29.3	22.6	4.4	2.0	5.5	2.1	4.0	0.8	0.8	0.1	1.6	0.0	0.6
Lake Charles	71 757	95.0	39.0	16.2	29.4	21.8	6.0	3.1	4.4	1.9	5.0	1.4	1.1	0.6	1.4	0.0	0.5
Monroe	53 107	93.0	36.6	12.2	31.9	24.2	7.8	4.3	4.6	2.0	7.0	0.4	1.3	0.8	3.7	0.0	0.7
New Iberia	32 623	97.1	36.0	16.2	33.6	25.2	7.3	3.9	4.0	2.1	2.9	0.0	1.1	0.3	0.0	0.0	1.4
New Orleans	484 674	96.4	38.8	12.0	30.7	21.2	9.4	4.9	5.5	2.3	3.6	1.3	0.6	0.1	1.0	0.1	0.6
Shreveport	200 145	97.3	39.3	15.0	30.5	22.1	7.9	4.1	4.6	2.0	2.7	0.6	1.0	0.1	0.4	0.0	0.6
Slidell	25 695	98.6	36.9	21.2	31.6	24.0	5.3	2.6	3.7	1.6	1.4	0.1	1.2	0.0	0.0	0.0	0.1
MAINE	1 274 923	97.3	40.6	21.3	26.9	21.9	2.6	0.9	5.8	3.0	2.7	0.2	0.7	0.1	1.1	0.1	0.6
Bangor	31 473	92.5	43.6	15.7	23.2	19.0	2.4	0.7	7.6	3.4	7.5	0.6	1.5	0.4	1.7	0.0	3.3
Lewiston	35 690	92.9	42.8	17.5	23.6	19.0	2.8	0.8	6.0	3.3	7.1	0.0	1.9	0.2	4.2	0.0	0.8
Portland	64 249	96.2	46.2	14.9	21.8	17.3	3.1	0.9	10.2	3.9	3.8	0.6	0.8	0.0	0.5	0.0	1.8
MARYLAND	5 296 486	97.5	37.4	18.8	29.6	22.6	6.2	2.4	5.5	2.1	2.5	0.7	0.5	0.1	0.7	0.1	0.4
Annapolis	35 838	98.0	42.7	15.6	24.6	18.5	6.5	2.7	8.6	2.7	2.0	0.0	0.6	0.0	0.8	0.0	0.6
Baltimore	651 154	96.0	39.6	10.6	27.3	18.4	11.0	5.5	7.6	2.8	4.0	1.2	0.6	0.1	1.4	0.0	0.6
Bowie	50 269	99.1	36.2	21.7	31.5	24.7	5.1	1.7	4.6	1.6	0.9	0.0	0.7	0.0	0.0	0.0	0.3
Frederick	52 767	96.0	39.6	17.6	27.8	22.9	4.3	1.6	6.7	2.9	4.0	0.0	1.8	0.0	0.8	0.5	0.9
Gaithersburg	52 613	98.8	37.3	18.1	28.6	22.8	7.2	1.7	7.6	2.0	1.2	0.0	0.5	0.0	0.0	0.0	0.7
Hagerstown	36 687	97.7	43.2	15.9	27.9	22.9	4.0	1.9	6.7	3.7	2.3	0.0	1.1	0.1	0.0	0.0	1.1
Rockville	47 388	96.5	36.4	20.6	28.1	21.5	5.4	1.4	6.1	1.2	3.5	1.1	1.4	0.2	0.0	0.0	0.8
MASSACHUSETTS	6 349 097	96.5	38.5	18.9	29.0	21.8	4.5	1.4	5.6	2.1	3.5	0.4	0.9	0.1	1.6	0.0	0.5
Agawam	28 144	97.4	40.0	21.4	28.5	20.6	3.5	1.1	4.0	2.0	2.6	0.0	2.6	0.0	0.0	0.0	0.0
Attleboro	42 068	98.0	38.1	20.4	30.5	23.6	4.2	1.3	4.8	2.3	2.0	0.0	1.4	0.0	0.0	0.0	0.5
Barnstable Town	47 821	97.5	41.0	21.5	25.9	20.2	3.6	1.1	5.4	1.9	2.5	0.6	1.9	0.0	0.0	0.0	1.3
Beverly	39 862	94.6	39.5	19.8	26.9	20.4	3.5	0.9	4.8	1.8	5.4	0.0	1.9	0.0	2.9	0.0	0.6
Boston	589 141	94.0	40.7	11.2	24.2	17.0	7.0	2.2	11.1	2.5	6.0	0.4	0.7	0.4	3.4	0.0	1.0
Brockton	94 304	98.0	35.7	15.0	33.9	24.3	7.7	2.8	5.7	2.6	2.0	0.0	1.0	0.5	0.0	0.0	0.5
Cambridge	101 355	85.5	42.0	12.2	16.1	12.1	3.3	0.8	11.8	2.6	14.5	0.2	0.3	0.0	13.0	0.0	0.9
Chelsea	35 080	97.3	33.9	12.5	31.4	23.7	10.3	2.8	9.2	2.4	2.7	0.0	2.5	0.0	0.0	0.0	0.2
Chicopee	54 653	98.2	42.3	18.0	28.3	20.5	4.2	1.3	5.3	2.8	1.8	0.0	0.6	0.0	0.3	0.0	0.9
Everett	38 037	99.4	40.6	17.0	29.3	19.8	6.6	1.6	6.0	1.9	0.6	0.0	0.6	0.0	0.0	0.0	0.0
Fall River	91 938	97.9	42.2	17.0	30.0	22.1	4.1	1.3	4.7	2.7	2.1	0.0	1.5	0.1	0.0	0.0	0.5
Fitchburg	39 102	95.5	38.2	16.5	29.7	23.4	4.8	1.7	6.4	2.8	4.5	0.0	1.3	0.1	2.5	0.0	0.5
Franklin	29 560	97.9	34.3	22.8	35.6	29.3	2.6	0.8	2.5	1.2	2.1	0.0	0.2	0.0	1.9	0.0	0.0
Gloucester	30 273	98.8	41.6	20.3	28.1	20.5	3.8	1.1	5.0	2.4	1.2	0.0	0.9	0.0	0.0	0.0	0.3
Haverhill	58 969	97.6	39.0	18.3	30.6	23.7	4.3	1.4	5.5	2.7	2.4	0.0	1.3	0.1	0.5	0.0	0.4
Holyoke	39 838	96.5	37.6	13.7	33.4	25.7	5.9	2.6	6.0	2.9	3.5	0.0	3.0	0.0	0.0	0.0	0.5
Lawrence	72 043	98.6	34.0	12.4	35.4	27.9	8.8	3.2	6.8	3.1	1.4	0.3	0.8	0.0	0.0	0.0	0.3
Leominster	41 303	99.0	39.9	19.8	30.5	23.9	4.0	1.2	4.9	2.5	1.0	0.0	0.7	0.0	0.0	0.0	0.2
Lowell	105 167	96.3	36.0	14.5	31.9	23.9	7.2	2.4	6.8	2.7	3.7	0.0	1.1	0.0	1.8	0.0	0.8
Lynn	89 050	98.5	37.6	15.0	32.2	23.7	7.5	2.6	6.2	2.5	1.5	0.0	0.7	0.0	0.0	0.0	0.7
Malden	56 340	98.9	40.8	17.5	27.1	18.2	6.9	1.5	6.7	2.2	1.1	0.0	0.7	0.0	0.0	0.0	0.4
Marlborough	36 255	98.7	40.0	20.6	28.1	21.8	4.3	1.2	5.6	2.3	1.3	0.0	1.0	0.0	0.0	0.0	0.4
Medford	55 765	96.0	39.6	18.0	25.9	16.5	5.3	1.2	7.2	1.7	4.0	0.0	1.0	0.0	2.8	0.0	0.2
Melrose	27 134	98.8	40.5	21.6	29.4	20.7	3.6	1.1	3.7	1.6	1.2	0.0	1.1	0.0	0.0	0.0	0.1
Methuen	43 789	98.9	37.8	20.1	31.7	22.9	5.4	1.5	3.9	2.0	1.1	0.0	0.7	0.0	0.0	0.0	0.4
New Bedford	93 768	97.9	40.7	16.1	30.7	22.5	4.9	1.7	5.5	2.8	2.1	0.2	1.4	0.0	0.0	0.1	0.5
Newton	83 829	93.3	37.2	20.5	26.2	20.4	3.0	0.6	6.4	1.4	6.7	0.0	0.7	0.0	5.7	0.0	0.3
Northampton	28 978	87.6	41.0	15.0	20.7	15.8	2.1	0.7	8.7	3.6	12.4	0.8	2.3	0.6	7.8	0.0	0.8
Peabody	48 129	98.5	38.6	21.6	29.7	20.5	5.1	1.4	3.6	1.6	1.5	0.0	1.1	0.0	0.0	0.0	0.4
Pittsfield	45 793	97.2	43.0	18.5	27.3	21.3	3.1	1.1	5.3	2.6	2.8	0.6	1.4	0.0	0.0	0.0	0.8
Quincy	88 025	98.2	44.2	17.1	24.4	16.0	5.9	1.2	6.6	2.2	1.8	0.0	0.7	0.1	0.6	0.0	0.4
Revere	47 283	99.3	41.2	17.2	28.0	18.7	7.2	1.9	5.8	2.2	0.7	0.0	0.5	0.0	0.0	0.0	0.1
Salem	40 407	97.1	43.3	16.8	25.6	18.5	4.4	1.3	7.0	2.8	2.9	0.0	0.4	0.0	2.2	0.0	0.2
Somerville	77 478	96.8	40.7	13.1	19.8	13.1	6.1	1.4	17.0	2.7	3.2	0.0	0.4	0.0	2.4	0.0	0.5
Springfield	152 082	96.4	37.6	13.0	32.8	25.0	6.6	2.9	6.3	2.9	3.6	0.1	0.5	0.4	2.1	0.0	0.4
Taunton	55 976	98.5	39.4	18.9	30.6	22.7	4.6	1.7	5.0	2.6	1.5	0.0	0.7	0.4	0.0	0.0	0.4
Waltham	59 226	89.9	39.2	16.2	21.2	14.1	4.9	1.0	8.4	2.1	10.1	0.0	0.8	0.5	8.0	0.0	0.9
Westfield	40 072	93.8	36.9	19.6	28.9	22.1	3.4	1.0	5.1	2.2	6.2	0.0	0.9	0.4	4.7	0.0	0.2
Woburn	37 258	99.3	40.3	19.9	29.1	19.5	5.2	1.4	4.9	1.8	0.7	0.0	0.3	0.0	0.0	0.0	0.4
Worcester	172 648	93.6	38.8	14.9	27.7	21.2	5.3	1.7	6.9	2.5	6.4	0.0	1.5	0.2	4.0	0.0	0.7

Table D. Cities

City	Households by type, 2000												Households, 1990		
		Family households						Nonfamily households							
				Married couple		Female householder[1]			Householder living alone						
	Total households	Total	With own children under 18 years	Total	With own children under 18 years	Total	With own children under 18 years	Total	Total	65 years and over	Average household size	Average family size	Total households	Female householder[1]	Householder living alone
	71	72	73	74	75	76	77	78	79	80	81	82	83	84	85
LOUISIANA	1 656 053	69.8	34.5	48.9	22.6	16.6	9.8	30.2	25.3	9.0	2.62	3.16	1 499 269	15.6	23.7
Alexandria	17 816	65.8	31.9	38.5	16.2	23.2	13.9	34.2	30.4	12.1	2.50	3.13	18 134	21.1	28.0
Baton Rouge	88 973	59.2	28.1	35.8	15.3	19.0	11.1	40.8	31.7	8.6	2.42	3.12	83 340	17.7	29.7
Bossier City	21 197	70.3	36.8	50.4	23.9	15.8	10.6	29.7	24.7	8.4	2.58	3.09	19 032	13.8	22.4
Houma	11 634	71.2	35.4	49.5	23.3	16.7	9.4	28.8	24.1	10.3	2.72	3.24	10 658	16.7	22.2
Kenner	25 652	72.0	36.3	50.9	24.7	16.3	9.3	28.0	23.2	6.1	2.72	3.23	25 056	14.0	21.8
Lafayette	43 506	62.3	31.3	43.9	20.2	14.6	9.1	37.7	29.4	8.0	2.43	3.07	36 326	13.8	28.9
Lake Charles	27 974	64.4	30.5	41.6	17.1	18.7	11.4	35.6	30.0	11.1	2.44	3.06	26 815	17.2	27.7
Monroe	19 421	62.6	32.3	33.4	14.5	25.3	16.0	37.4	31.3	11.7	2.54	3.26	19 131	24.2	29.7
New Iberia	11 756	70.9	36.6	45.1	21.1	20.5	12.9	29.1	25.2	10.8	2.70	3.24	11 143	18.0	23.1
New Orleans	188 251	60.0	29.2	30.8	13.3	24.5	14.0	40.0	33.2	9.7	2.48	3.23	188 235	24.1	32.2
Shreveport	78 662	64.1	30.1	38.3	15.5	21.5	12.6	35.9	30.8	10.9	2.48	3.12	75 645	19.9	28.7
Slidell	9 480	75.5	36.0	57.4	25.9	14.0	8.1	24.5	20.4	8.7	2.67	3.09	8 322	11.8	17.1
MAINE	518 200	65.7	30.4	52.5	21.8	9.5	6.2	34.3	27.0	10.7	2.39	2.90	465 312	9.5	23.3
Bangor	13 713	52.4	26.1	36.0	15.2	12.8	8.7	47.6	37.6	11.5	2.12	2.81	13 392	12.7	31.1
Lewiston	15 290	56.6	25.4	40.9	14.7	11.8	8.4	43.4	35.9	13.7	2.17	2.81	15 823	12.6	29.7
Portland	29 714	45.6	21.4	32.1	13.3	10.5	6.6	54.4	40.1	11.5	2.08	2.89	28 235	12.2	35.3
MARYLAND	1 980 859	68.6	33.4	50.2	23.3	14.1	8.0	31.4	25.0	8.1	2.61	3.13	1 748 991	13.3	22.6
Annapolis	15 303	56.7	24.5	36.6	13.2	16.3	9.8	43.3	32.9	9.2	2.30	2.93	14 061	16.7	31.8
Baltimore	257 996	57.0	25.5	26.7	10.0	25.0	13.3	43.0	34.9	11.3	2.42	3.16	276 484	24.6	30.5
Bowie	18 188	74.6	37.7	60.0	30.0	11.0	6.0	25.4	19.7	5.2	2.74	3.16	12 891	8.0	12.7
Frederick	20 891	61.2	32.3	44.4	21.9	12.8	8.2	38.8	30.0	8.8	2.42	3.05	15 671	12.4	27.3
Gaithersburg	19 621	64.1	34.8	48.6	26.2	11.2	6.6	35.9	27.8	7.2	2.65	3.25	15 202	11.6	25.7
Hagerstown	15 849	57.3	29.5	36.8	15.3	15.9	11.2	42.7	35.4	12.9	2.26	2.93	15 063	14.4	32.3
Rockville	17 247	69.6	33.0	56.6	26.7	9.5	5.0	30.4	23.8	8.9	2.65	3.13	15 660	9.9	20.0
MASSACHUSETTS	2 443 580	64.5	30.6	49.0	22.4	11.9	6.7	35.5	28.0	10.5	2.51	3.11	2 247 110	12.1	25.8
Agawam	11 260	66.3	28.9	53.4	22.6	9.8	5.0	33.7	28.0	11.3	2.43	3.01	NA	NA	NA
Attleboro	16 019	68.2	33.4	53.6	25.0	10.6	6.4	31.8	25.7	9.4	2.57	3.12	14 180	10.6	23.1
Barnstable Town	19 626	66.3	26.9	52.4	19.2	10.7	6.3	33.7	27.7	12.5	2.38	2.88	NA	NA	NA
Beverly	15 750	62.9	28.8	50.1	22.6	9.7	5.1	37.1	29.9	11.4	2.39	3.02	14 796	11.2	26.7
Boston	239 528	48.1	22.7	27.4	11.8	16.4	9.5	51.9	37.1	9.1	2.31	3.17	228 464	16.8	35.5
Brockton	33 675	67.6	35.0	42.0	19.9	19.9	12.5	32.4	26.6	9.5	2.74	3.35	32 850	17.4	24.6
Cambridge	42 615	41.3	17.6	29.1	11.3	9.7	5.5	58.7	41.4	9.2	2.03	2.83	39 405	10.7	42.3
Chelsea	11 888	64.0	36.4	36.9	20.2	20.1	13.0	36.0	28.8	10.8	2.87	3.50	10 553	20.7	30.4
Chicopee	23 117	61.2	26.5	42.6	16.2	14.2	8.3	38.8	32.7	14.1	2.32	2.96	22 625	13.4	28.3
Everett	15 435	61.9	27.6	41.8	18.3	15.2	7.7	38.1	31.3	11.8	2.45	3.11	14 528	14.8	29.7
Fall River	38 759	60.8	29.9	40.3	17.0	16.5	11.0	39.2	34.2	14.2	2.32	3.00	37 303	14.8	30.1
Fitchburg	14 943	62.7	31.0	43.1	18.8	14.6	9.6	37.3	30.3	12.0	2.50	3.13	15 363	14.0	27.6
Franklin	10 152	77.6	44.6	66.4	38.9	8.5	4.5	22.4	18.3	6.7	2.85	3.29	3 448	NA	NA
Gloucester	12 592	62.7	27.6	48.8	20.2	10.6	5.9	37.3	30.7	11.4	2.38	3.00	11 579	11.2	28.2
Haverhill	22 976	64.7	33.0	47.0	22.6	13.4	8.3	35.3	28.6	10.3	2.51	3.11	19 575	12.8	25.8
Holyoke	14 967	63.3	33.3	36.5	15.8	22.1	15.2	36.7	30.9	13.5	2.57	3.23	15 850	23.0	28.2
Lawrence	24 463	69.1	41.4	36.6	19.5	25.7	18.3	30.9	25.5	10.0	2.90	3.46	24 270	24.2	26.2
Leominster	16 491	66.1	32.9	49.5	22.7	12.5	8.0	33.9	27.9	10.7	2.48	3.05	14 834	10.4	24.5
Lowell	37 887	63.3	34.0	40.1	20.1	17.4	11.1	36.7	29.0	9.3	2.67	3.35	37 019	17.0	27.5
Lynn	33 511	62.8	32.5	39.7	18.8	17.6	11.2	37.2	31.0	11.8	2.62	3.31	31 554	16.9	31.1
Malden	23 009	59.0	25.4	42.8	18.5	12.3	5.8	41.0	32.2	11.5	2.42	3.13	21 921	12.4	31.1
Marlborough	14 501	64.0	30.4	51.5	24.0	9.0	4.9	36.0	28.4	8.3	2.47	3.07	12 152	10.0	25.1
Medford	22 067	61.2	23.6	45.6	18.0	11.8	4.7	38.8	28.7	12.4	2.43	3.04	21 829	12.2	26.0
Melrose	10 982	64.7	28.8	53.4	24.7	8.7	3.4	35.3	29.7	13.2	2.44	3.08	10 941	10.0	27.7
Methuen	16 532	69.8	33.1	53.3	25.1	12.2	6.4	30.2	25.3	11.6	2.62	3.17	NA	NA	NA
New Bedford	38 788	63.1	31.2	39.5	16.5	18.9	12.3	36.9	31.6	13.6	2.40	3.01	38 788	17.1	28.1
Newton	31 201	65.7	31.1	55.2	26.6	8.0	3.7	34.3	25.5	11.1	2.51	3.04	29 455	9.0	22.4
Northampton	11 880	49.5	22.9	36.7	15.4	10.1	6.2	50.5	37.3	10.7	2.14	2.87	11 164	10.5	33.5
Peabody	18 581	69.9	29.7	55.9	23.8	10.4	4.7	30.1	25.4	12.2	2.55	3.09	17 556	10.8	22.4
Pittsfield	19 704	60.0	27.3	42.9	17.0	13.1	8.3	40.0	34.0	14.3	2.26	2.89	19 916	12.7	29.1
Quincy	38 883	52.8	20.7	38.7	15.3	10.5	4.4	47.2	37.6	13.4	2.22	3.03	35 678	12.1	33.6
Revere	19 463	61.0	25.5	41.8	16.7	13.9	7.0	39.0	32.7	12.4	2.41	3.09	17 438	13.6	29.9
Salem	17 492	55.5	24.2	38.8	15.0	13.3	7.7	44.5	34.9	11.5	2.24	2.95	15 806	12.7	31.6
Somerville	31 555	46.5	18.8	32.2	13.1	10.3	4.6	53.5	31.0	8.8	2.38	3.06	30 319	12.3	30.1
Springfield	57 130	63.7	33.7	34.7	15.2	23.8	16.1	36.3	30.2	11.4	2.57	3.19	57 769	21.2	27.8
Taunton	22 045	65.7	32.3	48.0	22.1	13.4	7.9	34.3	28.2	9.9	2.50	3.09	18 849	13.5	24.9
Waltham	23 207	53.7	20.3	41.3	16.0	8.9	3.4	46.3	34.2	10.0	2.29	3.01	20 728	10.6	30.4
Westfield	14 797	67.7	31.5	53.0	23.4	10.6	6.2	32.3	25.9	10.9	2.54	3.07	13 823	11.4	23.7
Woburn	14 997	64.4	26.8	49.5	20.5	10.9	4.9	35.6	28.7	10.1	2.47	3.09	13 485	11.5	24.4
Worcester	67 028	58.5	29.0	38.3	17.2	15.6	9.9	41.5	33.0	12.2	2.41	3.11	63 884	15.7	30.1

[1] No spouse present.

City	Percent change of households, 1990–2000	Total housing units	Occupied housing units (percent)	Housing occupancy — Vacant housing units — Total	For seasonal, recreational, or occasional use	Homeowner vacancy rate (percent)	Rental vacancy rate (percent)	Housing tenure — Occupied housing units — Total	Percent owner-occupied housing units	Percent renter-occupied housing units	Average household size of owner-occupied units	Average household size of renter-occupied units
	86	87	88	89	90	91	92	93	94	95	96	97
LOUISIANA	10.5	1 847 181	89.7	10.3	2.1	1.6	9.3	1 656 053	67.9	32.1	2.70	2.44
Alexandria	-1.8	19 806	90.0	10.0	0.3	2.0	10.7	17 816	57.4	42.6	2.53	2.47
Baton Rouge	6.8	97 388	91.4	8.6	0.3	1.6	8.8	88 973	52.2	47.8	2.58	2.25
Bossier City	11.4	23 026	92.1	7.9	0.5	2.1	9.8	21 197	60.0	40.0	2.60	2.56
Houma	9.2	12 514	93.0	7.0	0.1	1.3	8.0	11 634	67.7	32.3	2.80	2.54
Kenner	2.4	27 378	93.7	6.3	0.3	0.9	10.1	25 652	60.8	39.2	2.87	2.49
Lafayette	19.8	46 865	92.8	7.2	0.5	1.4	9.1	43 506	58.3	41.7	2.63	2.15
Lake Charles	4.3	31 429	89.0	11.0	0.4	2.1	13.6	27 974	57.6	42.4	2.51	2.34
Monroe	1.5	21 278	91.3	8.7	0.3	1.8	7.6	19 421	49.6	50.4	2.56	2.52
New Iberia	5.5	12 880	91.3	8.7	0.4	1.5	7.2	11 756	62.6	37.4	2.70	2.69
New Orleans	0.0	215 091	87.5	12.5	1.1	2.2	7.9	188 251	46.5	53.5	2.60	2.37
Shreveport	4.0	86 802	90.6	9.4	0.4	1.8	10.9	78 662	59.0	41.0	2.52	2.41
Slidell	13.9	10 133	93.6	6.4	0.4	1.5	11.2	9 480	76.1	23.9	2.71	2.57
MAINE	11.4	651 901	79.5	20.5	15.6	1.7	7.0	518 200	71.6	28.4	2.54	2.03
Bangor	2.4	14 587	94.0	6.0	1.0	2.0	4.2	13 713	47.5	52.5	2.43	1.85
Lewiston	-3.4	16 470	92.8	7.2	0.4	1.3	8.8	15 290	47.2	52.8	2.44	1.92
Portland	5.2	31 862	93.3	6.7	3.0	0.5	3.6	29 714	42.5	57.5	2.41	1.84
MARYLAND	13.3	2 145 283	92.3	7.7	1.8	1.6	6.1	1 980 859	67.7	32.3	2.73	2.35
Annapolis	8.8	16 165	94.7	5.3	1.2	1.4	3.8	15 303	51.7	48.3	2.36	2.23
Baltimore	-6.7	300 477	85.9	14.1	0.5	3.6	7.6	257 996	50.3	49.7	2.57	2.27
Bowie	41.1	18 718	97.2	2.8	0.2	1.2	4.5	18 188	85.0	15.0	2.79	2.45
Frederick	33.3	22 106	94.5	5.5	0.3	2.7	5.3	20 891	55.6	44.4	2.59	2.22
Gaithersburg	29.1	20 674	94.9	5.1	0.5	1.5	6.1	19 621	52.6	47.4	2.86	2.42
Hagerstown	5.2	17 089	92.7	7.3	0.2	3.4	5.7	15 849	41.9	58.1	2.36	2.19
Rockville	10.1	17 786	97.0	3.0	0.2	0.8	4.5	17 247	67.7	32.3	2.71	2.54
MASSACHUSETTS	8.7	2 621 989	93.2	6.8	3.6	0.7	3.5	2 443 580	61.7	38.3	2.72	2.17
Agawam	NA	11 659	96.6	3.4	0.6	0.8	4.2	11 260	73.6	26.4	2.63	1.90
Attleboro	13.0	16 554	96.8	3.2	0.2	0.7	3.8	16 019	63.8	36.2	2.81	2.16
Barnstable Town	NA	25 018	78.4	21.6	19.0	1.1	3.7	19 626	76.2	23.8	2.43	2.19
Beverly	6.4	16 275	96.8	3.2	0.8	0.4	3.1	15 750	60.0	40.0	2.70	1.93
Boston	4.8	251 935	95.1	4.9	0.6	1.0	3.0	239 528	32.2	67.8	2.51	2.22
Brockton	2.5	34 837	96.7	3.3	0.1	0.5	3.3	33 675	54.6	45.4	2.98	2.46
Cambridge	8.1	44 725	95.3	4.7	1.3	0.9	2.6	42 615	32.3	67.7	2.16	1.97
Chelsea	12.7	12 337	96.4	3.6	0.2	1.1	1.6	11 888	28.9	71.1	2.87	2.87
Chicopee	2.2	24 424	94.6	5.4	0.4	0.9	4.8	23 117	59.3	40.7	2.46	2.11
Everett	6.2	15 908	97.0	3.0	0.1	0.5	2.2	15 435	41.4	58.6	2.67	2.29
Fall River	3.9	41 857	92.6	7.4	0.2	1.4	6.7	38 759	34.9	65.1	2.66	2.14
Fitchburg	-2.7	16 002	93.4	6.6	0.2	1.4	6.5	14 943	51.6	48.4	2.64	2.35
Franklin	194.4	10 327	98.3	1.7	0.3	0.3	2.9	10 152	81.2	18.8	3.06	1.92
Gloucester	8.7	13 958	90.2	9.8	6.9	0.8	2.7	12 592	59.7	40.3	2.60	2.04
Haverhill	17.4	23 737	96.8	3.2	0.3	0.5	3.1	22 976	60.2	39.8	2.69	2.23
Holyoke	-5.6	16 210	92.3	7.7	0.2	0.9	6.9	14 967	41.5	58.5	2.66	2.50
Lawrence	0.8	25 601	95.6	4.4	0.2	1.0	3.0	24 463	32.2	67.8	3.02	2.85
Leominster	11.2	16 976	97.1	2.9	0.2	0.5	2.6	16 491	57.9	42.1	2.71	2.16
Lowell	2.3	39 468	96.0	4.0	0.2	1.2	3.1	37 887	43.0	57.0	2.87	2.53
Lynn	6.2	34 637	96.7	3.3	0.2	0.7	2.3	33 511	45.6	54.4	2.81	2.46
Malden	5.0	23 634	97.4	2.6	0.3	0.4	2.1	23 009	43.3	56.7	2.86	2.08
Marlborough	19.3	14 903	97.3	2.7	0.4	0.5	2.4	14 501	61.0	39.0	2.68	2.13
Medford	1.1	22 687	97.3	2.7	0.2	0.5	2.5	22 067	58.6	41.4	2.62	2.15
Melrose	0.4	11 248	97.6	2.4	0.4	0.4	1.6	10 982	67.0	33.0	2.78	1.75
Methuen	NA	16 885	97.9	2.1	0.2	0.3	2.8	16 532	71.9	28.1	2.79	2.19
New Bedford	-1.6	41 511	92.0	8.0	0.3	1.9	6.9	38 178	43.8	56.2	2.60	2.25
Newton	5.9	32 112	97.2	2.8	0.8	0.5	2.1	31 201	69.5	30.5	2.70	2.08
Northampton	6.4	12 405	95.8	4.2	1.0	0.4	3.4	11 880	53.5	46.5	2.44	1.79
Peabody	5.8	18 898	98.3	1.7	0.3	0.3	1.7	18 581	71.2	28.8	2.75	2.06
Pittsfield	-1.1	21 366	92.2	7.8	1.2	1.5	9.0	19 704	60.8	39.2	2.45	1.97
Quincy	9.0	40 093	97.0	3.0	0.5	0.4	2.7	38 883	49.0	51.0	2.59	1.87
Revere	11.6	20 181	96.4	3.6	0.4	0.5	2.3	19 463	50.0	50.0	2.64	2.19
Salem	10.7	18 175	96.2	3.8	0.4	0.9	2.5	17 492	49.1	50.9	2.40	2.09
Somerville	4.1	32 477	97.2	2.8	0.3	0.8	1.6	31 555	30.6	69.4	2.59	2.28
Springfield	-1.1	61 172	93.4	6.6	0.3	1.3	6.1	57 130	49.9	50.1	2.61	2.52
Taunton	17.0	22 908	96.2	3.8	0.1	0.6	4.7	22 045	61.2	38.8	2.73	2.14
Waltham	12.0	23 880	97.2	2.8	0.5	0.3	2.2	23 207	46.0	54.0	2.60	2.03
Westfield	7.0	15 441	95.8	4.2	0.5	1.0	2.8	14 797	67.8	32.2	2.68	2.25
Woburn	11.2	15 391	97.4	2.6	0.5	0.4	2.2	14 997	61.2	38.8	2.74	2.04
Worcester	4.9	70 723	94.8	5.2	0.4	0.9	4.1	67 028	43.3	56.7	2.57	2.28

STATE Place code	City	Population, 2000				Population, 1990				Population and population characteristics, 2000					
										Race (percent)					
										One race					
		Land area, 2000[1] (sq km)	Total persons	Rank	Per square kilometer	Land area, 1990[1] (sq km)	Total persons	Rank	Per square kilometer	White	Black or African American	American Indian or Alaska Native	Asian	Native Hawaiian and other Pacific Islander	Some other race
		1	2	3	4	5	6	7	8	9	10	11	12	13	14
26 00000	MICHIGAN	147 121.2	9 938 444	X	67.6	147 135.8	9 295 287	X	63.2	80.2	14.2	0.6	1.8	0.0	1.3
26 01380	Allen Park	18.2	29 376	1 254	1 614.1	18.2	31 092	1 006	1 708.4	95.6	0.7	0.4	0.8	0.0	1.2
26 03000	Ann Arbor	70.0	114 024	203	1 628.9	67.1	109 608	174	1 633.5	74.7	8.8	0.3	11.9	0.0	1.2
26 05920	Battle Creek	110.9	53 364	618	481.2	110.9	53 516	497	482.6	74.7	17.8	0.8	1.9	0.0	2.1
26 06020	Bay City	27.0	36 817	954	1 363.6	26.9	38 936	766	1 447.4	91.2	2.7	0.7	0.5	0.0	2.5
26 12060	Burton	60.8	30 308	1 209	498.5	60.8	27 437	1 161	451.3	92.1	3.5	0.8	0.7	0.0	0.8
26 21000	Dearborn	63.1	97 775	250	1 549.5	63.1	89 286	236	1 415.0	86.9	1.3	0.3	1.5	0.0	0.7
26 21020	Dearborn Heights	30.3	58 264	526	1 922.9	30.3	60 838	413	2 007.9	91.6	2.1	0.4	2.2	0.0	0.8
26 22000	Detroit	359.4	951 270	10	2 646.8	359.3	1 027 974	7	2 861.0	12.3	81.6	0.3	1.0	0.0	2.5
26 24120	East Lansing	29.1	46 525	733	1 598.8	24.6	50 677	545	2 060.0	80.9	7.4	0.3	8.2	0.1	1.0
26 24290	Eastpointe	13.2	34 077	1 056	2 581.6	13.2	35 283	854	2 673.0	92.1	4.7	0.4	0.9	0.0	0.3
26 27440	Farmington Hills	86.2	82 111	327	952.6	86.2	74 614	311	865.6	82.9	6.9	0.2	7.5	0.0	0.5
26 29000	Flint	87.1	124 943	177	1 434.5	87.6	140 925	127	1 608.7	41.4	53.3	0.6	0.4	0.0	1.1
26 31420	Garden City	15.2	30 047	1 220	1 976.8	15.2	31 846	979	2 095.1	96.2	1.1	0.4	0.7	0.0	0.3
26 34000	Grand Rapids	115.6	197 800	96	1 711.1	114.6	189 126	85	1 650.3	67.3	20.4	0.7	1.6	0.1	6.6
26 38640	Holland	42.9	35 048	1 026	817.0	36.7	30 745	1 024	837.7	78.2	2.5	0.6	3.6	0.0	12.4
26 40680	Inkster	16.2	30 115	1 217	1 859.0	16.2	30 772	1 021	1 899.5	25.1	67.5	0.4	3.4	0.0	0.7
26 41420	Jackson	28.7	36 316	971	1 265.4	28.6	37 425	806	1 308.6	73.9	19.7	0.6	0.5	0.0	1.7
26 42160	Kalamazoo	63.9	77 145	362	1 207.3	63.6	80 277	280	1 262.2	70.8	20.6	0.6	2.4	0.1	2.4
26 42820	Kentwood	54.5	45 255	759	830.4	54.5	37 826	794	694.1	80.9	9.1	0.5	5.6	0.0	1.4
26 46000	Lansing	90.8	119 128	190	1 312.0	87.8	127 321	144	1 450.1	65.3	21.9	0.8	2.8	0.1	4.5
26 47800	Lincoln Park	15.2	40 008	871	2 632.1	15.1	41 832	698	2 770.3	93.3	2.1	0.5	0.5	0.0	1.8
26 49000	Livonia	92.5	100 545	246	1 087.0	92.5	100 850	200	1 090.3	95.5	0.9	0.2	1.9	0.0	0.3
26 50560	Madison Heights	18.6	31 101	1 177	1 672.1	18.6	32 196	966	1 731.0	89.6	1.8	0.4	5.0	0.0	0.5
26 53780	Midland	86.0	41 685	828	484.7	71.5	38 053	787	532.2	93.4	1.8	0.3	2.7	0.1	0.6
26 56020	Mount Pleasant	20.2	25 946	1 451	1 284.5	18.7	23 299	1 400	1 245.9	89.1	3.7	1.5	2.8	0.1	0.9
26 56320	Muskegon	37.2	40 105	868	1 078.1	37.2	39 809	747	1 070.1	60.6	31.7	1.0	0.5	0.0	2.7
26 59440	Novi	78.9	47 386	716	600.6	78.9	32 998	935	418.2	87.3	1.9	0.2	8.7	0.0	0.5
26 59920	Oak Park	13.0	29 793	1 233	2 291.8	13.0	30 468	1 040	2 343.7	47.0	46.0	0.2	2.2	0.0	0.6
26 65440	Pontiac	51.8	66 337	440	1 280.6	51.8	71 136	333	1 373.3	39.1	47.9	0.6	2.4	0.0	6.5
26 65560	Portage	83.4	44 897	766	538.3	83.4	41 042	713	492.1	90.8	3.7	0.3	2.6	0.0	0.7
26 65820	Port Huron	20.9	32 338	1 125	1 547.3	20.7	33 694	906	1 627.7	86.7	7.7	0.9	0.6	0.0	1.3
26 69035	Rochester Hills	85.1	68 825	416	808.8	85.1	61 766	407	725.8	88.8	2.4	0.2	6.8	0.0	0.5
26 69800	Roseville	25.4	48 129	702	1 894.8	25.4	51 412	533	2 024.1	93.4	2.6	0.4	1.6	0.0	0.3
26 70040	Royal Oak	30.6	60 062	499	1 962.8	30.6	65 410	378	2 137.6	94.8	1.5	0.3	1.6	0.1	0.4
26 70520	Saginaw	45.2	61 799	480	1 367.2	45.2	69 512	343	1 537.9	47.0	43.3	0.5	0.3	0.0	5.9
26 70760	St. Clair Shores	29.9	63 096	468	2 110.2	29.9	68 107	353	2 277.8	96.9	0.7	0.3	0.8	0.0	0.2
26 74900	Southfield	67.9	78 296	351	1 153.1	67.9	75 727	301	1 115.3	38.8	54.2	0.2	3.1	0.0	0.6
26 74960	Southgate	17.8	30 136	1 216	1 693.0	17.8	30 771	1 022	1 728.7	93.7	2.1	0.5	1.7	0.0	0.8
26 76460	Sterling Heights	94.9	124 471	179	1 311.6	94.9	117 810	157	1 241.4	90.7	1.3	0.2	4.9	0.0	0.3
26 79000	Taylor	61.2	65 868	443	1 076.3	61.2	70 811	335	1 157.0	86.1	8.7	0.7	1.6	0.0	0.7
26 80700	Troy	86.9	80 959	333	931.6	86.9	72 884	318	838.7	82.3	2.1	0.2	13.3	0.0	0.4
26 84000	Warren	88.8	138 247	160	1 556.8	88.8	144 864	121	1 631.4	91.3	2.7	0.4	3.1	0.0	0.3
26 86000	Westland	53.0	86 602	301	1 634.0	53.0	84 724	262	1 598.6	87.2	6.8	0.5	2.8	0.0	0.7
26 88900	Wyandotte	13.7	28 006	1 324	2 044.2	13.7	30 938	1 015	2 258.2	96.3	0.5	0.5	0.3	0.0	0.7
26 88980	Wyoming	63.3	69 368	412	1 095.9	62.9	63 891	385	1 015.8	84.3	4.8	0.6	2.9	0.0	4.7
27 00000	MINNESOTA	206 189.1	4 919 479	X	23.9	206 207.1	4 375 665	X	21.2	89.4	3.5	1.1	2.9	0.0	1.3
27 01486	Andover	88.3	26 588	1 403	301.1	88.4	15 216	2 141	172.1	96.5	0.5	0.4	1.1	0.0	0.3
27 01900	Apple Valley	44.9	45 527	752	1 014.0	44.9	34 598	869	770.6	91.8	1.9	0.3	3.4	0.0	0.9
27 06382	Blaine	87.7	44 942	763	512.5	87.9	38 975	763	443.4	93.5	0.9	0.6	2.5	0.0	0.7
27 06616	Bloomington	91.9	85 172	312	926.8	92.0	86 335	251	938.4	88.1	3.4	0.3	5.1	0.0	1.3
27 07948	Brooklyn Center	20.6	29 172	1 268	1 416.1	20.6	28 887	1 095	1 402.3	71.4	14.1	0.9	8.8	0.0	1.5
27 07966	Brooklyn Park	67.5	67 388	430	998.3	67.5	56 381	456	835.3	71.4	14.3	0.6	9.2	0.1	1.5
27 08794	Burnsville	64.4	60 220	497	935.1	64.4	51 288	534	796.4	87.5	4.1	0.5	4.1	0.1	1.4
27 13114	Coon Rapids	58.7	61 607	483	1 049.5	59.1	52 978	508	896.4	93.2	2.2	0.7	1.6	0.0	0.6
27 13456	Cottage Grove	88.0	30 582	1 199	347.5	88.0	22 935	1 427	260.6	93.5	2.4	0.4	1.4	0.1	0.9
27 17000	Duluth	176.1	86 918	298	493.6	175.1	85 493	258	488.3	92.7	1.6	2.4	1.1	0.0	0.3
27 17288	Eagan	83.7	63 557	462	759.3	83.5	47 409	598	567.8	88.0	3.4	0.3	5.3	0.1	1.0
27 18116	Eden Prairie	83.9	54 901	593	654.4	83.9	39 311	757	468.5	90.7	2.3	0.2	4.8	0.0	0.5
27 18188	Edina	40.8	47 425	714	1 162.4	40.8	46 075	621	1 129.3	94.3	1.2	0.1	3.0	0.0	0.3
27 22814	Fridley	26.3	27 449	1 356	1 043.7	26.2	28 335	1 123	1 081.5	88.7	3.4	0.8	2.9	0.1	1.2
27 31076	Inver Grove Heights	74.2	29 751	1 236	401.0	74.2	22 477	1 464	302.9	91.8	2.1	0.5	2.0	0.0	1.7
27 35180	Lakeville	93.7	43 128	798	460.3	93.8	24 854	1 292	265.0	94.3	1.3	0.4	2.0	0.0	0.8
27 39878	Mankato	39.4	32 427	1 121	823.0	30.0	31 459	993	1 048.6	92.5	1.9	0.3	2.8	0.1	0.9
27 40166	Maple Grove	85.1	50 365	663	591.8	85.1	38 736	769	455.2	94.7	1.0	0.2	2.5	0.0	0.3
27 40382	Maplewood	44.9	34 947	1 031	778.3	44.9	30 954	1 013	689.4	88.7	3.5	0.6	4.5	0.1	0.7
27 43000	Minneapolis	142.2	382 618	47	2 690.7	142.3	368 383	43	2 588.8	65.1	18.0	2.2	6.1	0.1	4.1
27 43252	Minnetonka	70.3	51 301	652	729.7	70.2	48 370	585	689.0	94.4	1.5	0.2	2.3	0.0	0.6
27 43864	Moorhead	34.8	32 177	1 128	924.6	26.1	32 295	961	1 237.4	92.1	0.8	1.9	1.3	0.0	2.1
27 47680	Oakdale	28.7	26 653	1 398	928.7	25.6	18 377	1 794	717.9	92.2	2.3	0.4	2.5	0.0	0.8

[1] Dry land or land partially or temporarily covered by water.

Table D. Cities

City	Population and population characteristics, 2000 (cont'd)								Population and population characteristics, 1990				
	Race (percent) (cont'd)								Race (percent)				
		Race alone or in combination											
	Two or more races	White	Black	American Indian or Alaska Native	Asian	Native Hawaiian and other Pacific Islander	Some other race	Hispanic[1]	White	Black or African American	American Indian or Alaska Native	Asian and Pacific Islander	Hispanic[1]
	15	16	17	18	19	20	21	22	23	24	25	26	27
MICHIGAN	1.9	81.8	14.8	1.3	2.1	0.1	2.0	3.3	83.4	13.9	0.6	1.1	2.2
Allen Park	1.3	96.8	0.8	0.9	1.0	0.1	1.7	4.7	98.0	0.5	0.2	0.7	3.2
Ann Arbor	3.1	77.3	9.9	0.9	13.0	0.1	2.1	3.3	82.0	9.0	0.4	7.7	2.6
Battle Creek	2.7	76.9	19.4	1.7	2.2	0.1	2.7	4.6	80.7	16.5	0.6	1.3	1.8
Bay City	2.3	93.4	3.5	1.7	0.7	0.0	3.2	6.7	93.6	2.4	0.8	0.4	5.6
Burton	2.0	94.0	4.1	1.8	1.0	0.1	1.3	2.3	95.2	2.6	1.0	0.5	2.1
Dearborn	9.4	96.1	1.5	0.6	2.6	0.1	8.7	3.0	97.6	0.6	0.3	0.9	2.8
Dearborn Heights	2.8	94.3	2.4	0.9	2.8	0.1	2.4	3.4	97.3	0.5	0.4	1.3	2.3
Detroit	2.3	13.8	82.8	0.9	1.3	0.1	3.6	5.0	21.6	75.7	0.4	0.8	2.8
East Lansing	2.1	82.7	8.1	0.7	8.9	0.2	1.6	2.7	84.6	6.9	0.3	7.0	2.5
Eastpointe	1.6	93.7	5.1	1.2	1.1	0.1	0.5	1.3	98.7	0.2	0.4	0.6	0.8
Farmington Hills	1.9	84.7	7.4	0.6	8.2	0.1	1.2	1.5	93.9	1.9	0.2	3.8	1.2
Flint	3.1	43.7	55.3	2.2	0.7	0.1	1.6	3.0	49.6	47.9	0.7	0.5	2.9
Garden City	1.3	97.4	1.3	0.9	1.0	0.0	0.7	2.0	98.6	0.2	0.4	0.5	1.5
Grand Rapids	3.2	69.9	22.0	1.5	1.9	0.2	7.9	13.1	76.4	18.5	0.8	1.1	5.0
Holland	2.7	80.4	3.2	1.1	4.1	0.0	14.0	22.2	87.7	1.1	0.3	3.2	14.1
Inkster	2.8	27.1	69.5	1.4	3.7	0.1	1.3	1.6	36.1	62.4	0.4	0.7	1.1
Jackson	3.7	77.0	22.0	1.7	0.8	0.1	2.4	4.0	80.2	17.7	0.6	0.4	2.5
Kalamazoo	3.2	73.5	22.4	1.6	2.9	0.2	3.2	4.3	77.3	18.8	0.6	1.9	2.7
Kentwood	2.5	83.0	10.2	1.0	6.2	0.1	2.2	3.9	91.3	5.6	0.4	2.0	2.0
Lansing	4.6	69.0	24.4	2.0	3.3	0.1	6.1	10.0	73.9	18.6	1.0	1.8	7.9
Lincoln Park	1.8	94.9	2.4	1.3	0.7	0.0	2.5	6.4	97.3	0.9	0.5	0.4	3.8
Livonia	1.1	96.5	1.1	0.6	2.3	0.0	0.7	1.7	98.0	0.3	0.2	1.3	1.3
Madison Heights	2.7	92.1	2.1	1.1	5.6	0.1	1.8	1.6	95.9	0.9	0.5	2.4	1.2
Midland	1.2	94.5	2.1	0.7	3.0	0.1	0.8	1.9	95.6	1.7	0.4	1.9	1.7
Mount Pleasant	1.8	90.7	4.3	2.2	3.2	0.1	1.4	2.5	94.6	2.3	1.0	1.5	1.6
Muskegon	3.5	63.5	33.4	2.3	0.8	0.1	3.6	6.4	69.9	27.1	1.0	0.3	3.5
Novi	1.5	88.6	2.2	0.5	9.3	0.1	0.9	1.8	96.0	0.8	0.3	2.6	1.1
Oak Park	4.1	50.5	47.3	0.8	2.7	0.1	3.0	1.3	62.8	34.3	0.1	2.4	1.5
Pontiac	3.5	41.8	49.9	1.5	2.8	0.1	7.6	12.8	51.3	42.2	0.8	1.4	8.0
Portage	1.8	92.4	4.5	0.9	3.0	0.1	1.1	1.9	94.3	2.8	0.4	2.1	1.4
Port Huron	2.8	89.2	9.2	1.8	0.8	0.1	2.0	4.3	90.1	6.8	0.8	0.6	3.5
Rochester Hills	1.4	90.0	2.7	0.6	7.2	0.1	0.8	2.3	95.0	1.4	0.2	3.2	1.4
Roseville	1.6	94.9	3.0	1.1	1.9	0.1	0.7	1.5	97.3	1.0	0.5	1.1	1.2
Royal Oak	1.4	96.1	1.8	0.7	2.0	0.1	0.8	1.3	97.9	0.5	0.2	1.1	1.1
Saginaw	3.0	49.4	44.9	1.2	0.6	0.1	7.1	11.7	52.3	40.3	0.5	0.4	10.5
St. Clair Shores	1.1	97.9	0.8	0.9	1.1	0.0	0.4	1.2	98.7	0.2	0.3	0.6	0.9
Southfield	3.0	41.0	55.8	0.9	3.6	0.1	1.9	1.2	67.9	29.1	0.3	2.4	1.7
Southgate	1.2	94.8	2.3	0.9	1.9	0.1	1.2	4.0	96.5	1.2	0.5	1.1	2.8
Sterling Heights	2.5	93.0	1.5	0.6	5.4	0.1	1.9	1.3	96.3	0.4	0.2	2.9	1.1
Taylor	2.0	87.9	9.5	1.5	1.9	0.1	1.3	3.2	93.2	4.2	0.6	1.3	2.8
Troy	1.8	83.9	2.3	0.5	14.0	0.1	1.2	1.5	91.5	1.3	0.2	6.8	1.3
Warren	2.2	93.3	3.1	1.1	3.6	0.1	1.1	1.4	97.3	0.7	0.5	1.3	1.1
Westland	2.0	89.0	7.4	1.1	3.2	0.1	1.4	2.5	94.7	3.3	0.6	1.0	1.9
Wyandotte	1.6	97.8	0.8	1.3	0.5	0.1	1.1	2.9	98.2	0.2	0.6	0.4	2.1
Wyoming	2.6	86.6	5.8	1.3	3.3	0.1	5.7	9.7	93.5	2.7	0.5	1.5	3.5
MINNESOTA	1.7	90.8	4.1	1.6	3.3	0.1	1.8	2.9	94.4	2.2	1.1	1.8	1.2
Andover	1.2	97.6	0.9	0.8	1.4	0.0	0.5	1.0	97.8	0.3	0.6	0.9	1.0
Apple Valley	1.7	93.3	2.5	0.6	4.0	0.1	1.3	2.0	96.7	0.9	0.2	1.9	1.0
Blaine	1.7	95.1	1.4	1.3	3.0	0.1	1.0	1.7	97.2	0.3	0.8	1.4	1.0
Bloomington	1.7	89.5	4.1	0.7	5.7	0.1	1.7	2.7	94.7	1.6	0.3	3.1	0.9
Brooklyn Center	3.4	73.8	15.9	1.5	9.6	0.2	2.5	2.8	90.9	5.2	0.9	2.3	1.3
Brooklyn Park	2.9	73.6	15.9	1.1	10.0	0.2	2.4	2.9	90.6	4.9	0.6	3.4	1.2
Burnsville	2.4	89.5	5.2	0.9	4.8	0.2	2.0	2.9	94.8	2.3	0.3	2.3	1.0
Coon Rapids	1.7	94.8	2.7	1.1	2.1	0.1	1.0	1.5	97.3	0.5	0.8	1.1	0.9
Cottage Grove	1.3	94.7	2.8	0.8	1.8	0.1	1.2	2.5	96.6	1.2	0.3	1.1	1.8
Duluth	1.8	94.3	2.2	3.4	1.4	0.1	0.5	1.1	95.9	0.9	2.1	0.9	0.6
Eagan	1.9	89.7	4.1	0.7	5.9	0.2	1.5	2.2	93.7	2.4	0.3	3.1	1.3
Eden Prairie	1.5	91.9	2.8	0.4	5.4	0.1	0.9	1.6	96.4	1.1	0.2	2.1	0.7
Edina	1.1	95.2	1.5	0.3	3.5	0.1	0.6	1.1	97.2	0.7	0.1	1.7	0.7
Fridley	2.9	91.2	4.4	1.5	3.5	0.2	2.3	2.6	95.7	1.0	0.7	2.2	1.0
Inver Grove Heights	1.9	93.5	2.8	0.9	2.5	0.1	2.3	4.2	97.1	0.7	0.5	0.6	2.5
Lakeville	1.3	95.4	1.7	0.7	2.5	0.1	1.0	1.9	97.4	0.7	0.4	1.3	0.8
Mankato	1.4	93.6	2.4	0.7	3.2	0.1	1.4	2.2	96.3	0.7	0.3	2.3	1.1
Maple Grove	1.1	95.8	1.4	0.5	2.9	0.1	0.5	1.1	97.1	0.9	0.3	1.6	0.8
Maplewood	1.9	90.3	4.4	1.0	5.0	0.1	1.2	2.2	94.4	2.5	0.6	2.0	1.5
Minneapolis	4.4	68.0	20.5	3.3	7.0	0.2	5.8	7.6	78.4	13.0	3.3	4.3	2.1
Minnetonka	1.0	95.3	1.8	0.4	2.7	0.1	0.8	1.3	97.1	0.9	0.2	1.6	0.8
Moorhead	1.8	93.8	1.1	2.6	1.8	0.1	2.6	4.5	95.3	0.5	1.4	1.1	2.8
Oakdale	1.9	93.9	3.0	0.8	2.9	0.1	1.3	2.7	97.0	1.0	0.4	1.0	1.6

[1] Hispanic persons may be of any race.

Table D. Cities

City	Population and population characteristics, 2000										
	Age (percent)										
	Under 5 years	5 to 17 years	18 to 24 years	25 to 34 years	35 to 44 years	45 to 54 years	55 to 64 years	65 to 74 years	75 years and over	Median age (years)	Percent Female
	28	29	30	31	32	33	34	35	36	37	38
MICHIGAN	6.8	19.4	9.4	13.7	16.1	13.8	8.7	6.5	5.8	35.5	51.0
Allen Park	5.3	16.8	6.5	12.0	16.3	13.7	8.5	9.2	11.7	41.0	52.4
Ann Arbor	5.0	11.7	26.8	18.3	13.0	11.3	6.0	4.1	3.8	28.1	50.6
Battle Creek	7.3	19.9	8.7	14.5	15.0	13.1	8.0	6.7	6.9	34.7	52.1
Bay City	7.0	18.5	9.4	14.8	15.6	12.7	7.8	6.5	7.6	35.2	51.8
Burton	7.3	20.1	8.4	14.9	17.1	12.8	8.2	6.5	4.6	34.6	51.1
Dearborn	8.3	19.6	8.3	14.5	14.6	11.9	7.2	6.5	9.0	34.5	50.3
Dearborn Heights	6.4	16.1	7.5	14.0	15.5	12.4	9.3	9.8	9.0	38.9	51.8
Detroit	8.0	23.1	9.7	15.2	14.4	12.2	7.1	5.6	4.9	30.9	52.9
East Lansing	2.5	6.5	58.6	10.6	5.8	6.2	3.7	2.5	3.6	21.7	51.9
Eastpointe	6.4	18.1	7.6	15.2	17.1	12.6	6.6	7.7	8.8	36.6	51.5
Farmington Hills	6.0	17.1	6.7	14.5	16.8	15.3	9.3	7.0	7.4	38.6	51.6
Flint	9.0	21.6	10.3	15.1	14.3	11.9	7.3	5.8	4.7	30.8	53.0
Garden City	6.2	18.9	7.6	14.7	17.9	12.9	8.2	8.5	5.0	36.5	50.6
Grand Rapids	8.3	18.8	13.1	17.2	14.3	10.8	6.0	5.2	6.4	30.4	51.1
Holland	8.0	18.2	17.5	14.4	13.0	9.9	5.6	5.4	8.2	29.2	52.6
Inkster	8.0	21.8	9.2	15.8	14.5	11.9	7.9	6.1	4.7	31.8	52.3
Jackson	9.1	20.6	9.8	15.8	14.6	11.4	6.8	5.6	6.4	31.3	52.3
Kalamazoo	6.2	14.1	27.6	15.0	11.8	9.6	5.6	4.5	5.6	26.1	51.8
Kentwood	7.7	18.9	10.4	17.1	16.6	12.6	6.9	5.0	4.9	32.4	51.8
Lansing	8.2	18.6	11.4	17.6	15.2	12.4	6.9	5.2	4.5	31.4	52.0
Lincoln Park	6.9	17.4	8.5	16.4	16.3	12.9	7.4	7.1	7.0	35.5	51.1
Livonia	5.6	18.2	6.3	11.3	17.4	14.9	9.4	8.9	8.0	40.2	51.5
Madison Heights	6.2	15.9	8.1	17.9	17.5	12.3	7.9	8.0	6.2	36.1	51.1
Midland	6.5	19.4	10.2	12.2	15.7	14.0	8.2	6.8	7.1	36.2	52.1
Mount Pleasant	3.4	8.1	54.1	9.8	7.0	6.5	3.7	3.1	4.3	21.8	54.8
Muskegon	7.6	18.1	11.6	16.6	15.5	11.6	6.4	5.5	6.9	32.3	47.7
Novi	7.4	20.2	6.7	15.2	20.4	14.7	7.2	4.3	3.8	35.2	50.8
Oak Park	6.8	21.4	8.0	14.4	15.4	14.0	7.8	5.9	6.3	34.6	53.2
Pontiac	8.9	21.7	10.3	17.4	14.9	11.5	6.8	4.7	3.8	30.0	51.3
Portage	6.9	19.5	8.5	13.8	16.0	14.7	8.7	6.5	5.3	35.8	52.1
Port Huron	7.8	19.2	9.7	14.8	14.9	12.1	7.5	6.5	7.6	34.0	52.4
Rochester Hills	6.5	19.4	6.7	12.1	18.0	17.1	9.5	5.5	5.2	38.1	51.3
Roseville	6.5	16.6	8.2	16.5	16.5	12.4	7.8	7.9	7.5	36.2	51.6
Royal Oak	5.2	12.6	7.5	21.2	17.6	13.6	7.4	6.7	8.3	36.9	51.2
Saginaw	8.6	23.0	9.9	14.1	14.2	12.1	6.6	5.8	5.6	30.7	53.4
St. Clair Shores	5.1	15.1	6.2	12.6	16.2	13.7	9.4	11.1	10.7	42.0	52.4
Southfield	5.6	16.0	7.9	15.8	14.8	15.4	9.3	6.8	8.4	38.3	54.1
Southgate	5.4	16.1	8.3	14.8	15.9	14.2	9.1	8.4	7.8	38.5	51.8
Sterling Heights	6.2	17.9	8.5	14.3	16.1	15.0	10.3	5.8	5.9	37.0	51.0
Taylor	7.5	19.7	9.3	15.3	15.7	12.6	8.9	6.7	4.2	33.9	51.8
Troy	6.2	20.0	6.7	12.1	17.6	17.0	10.1	5.8	4.5	38.1	50.5
Warren	6.4	16.6	7.6	14.9	15.9	11.8	9.7	9.1	8.2	37.9	51.1
Westland	6.9	16.3	9.0	17.3	16.5	12.4	8.2	7.0	6.3	35.2	51.9
Wyandotte	5.6	17.1	8.3	14.2	17.4	14.1	7.6	7.6	8.2	38.0	51.0
Wyoming	8.0	20.0	10.9	17.3	16.4	11.8	6.2	5.1	4.3	31.2	50.6
MINNESOTA	6.7	19.5	9.6	13.7	16.8	13.5	8.2	6.0	6.1	35.4	50.5
Andover	9.2	26.3	6.0	14.5	21.9	13.1	6.1	1.7	1.1	31.9	49.2
Apple Valley	7.2	22.5	7.2	13.9	19.2	16.3	8.2	3.3	2.2	34.5	51.1
Blaine	7.8	21.3	8.7	15.8	19.1	14.2	7.8	3.7	1.6	32.7	49.9
Bloomington	5.3	15.3	8.0	13.6	15.8	15.1	11.3	8.7	7.0	40.1	51.7
Brooklyn Center	6.7	18.3	9.6	14.8	15.3	11.6	8.1	8.3	7.1	35.3	51.3
Brooklyn Park	8.1	20.7	9.7	16.8	18.2	14.0	6.9	3.7	1.9	31.9	50.3
Burnsville	7.1	19.1	10.1	16.9	17.1	13.7	8.7	4.4	2.8	33.0	50.7
Coon Rapids	7.5	21.2	8.9	15.2	18.1	13.6	8.2	4.6	2.7	33.3	51.3
Cottage Grove	8.5	24.2	7.4	15.6	18.8	13.6	7.2	3.6	1.3	31.9	50.2
Duluth	5.4	15.9	16.2	12.1	14.1	13.4	7.9	6.5	8.6	35.4	51.7
Eagan	8.1	21.9	7.4	16.7	21.6	14.2	6.0	2.7	1.5	32.8	50.8
Eden Prairie	7.8	22.6	6.2	14.6	21.0	16.1	6.8	3.0	1.9	34.2	50.9
Edina	5.4	17.5	4.4	8.8	14.8	15.9	10.6	10.1	12.6	44.5	54.2
Fridley	6.7	15.9	10.2	15.4	15.6	13.4	11.0	7.7	4.2	36.3	50.6
Inver Grove Heights	7.2	20.1	9.2	15.4	18.5	13.9	7.8	4.7	3.1	33.8	50.5
Lakeville	10.1	26.0	5.9	15.2	22.6	12.1	5.3	1.9	0.9	31.5	49.4
Mankato	4.9	12.0	32.5	13.1	10.8	9.8	5.6	4.9	6.4	25.3	50.8
Maple Grove	7.4	23.3	6.6	13.7	21.2	17.0	6.7	2.6	1.5	34.4	50.5
Maplewood	6.5	18.2	7.7	13.0	16.9	13.8	8.7	7.4	7.7	37.8	52.2
Minneapolis	6.6	15.4	14.4	20.6	15.9	12.0	5.9	4.0	5.1	31.2	49.8
Minnetonka	5.3	17.8	6.0	11.7	16.8	18.1	10.3	7.2	6.8	40.8	52.1
Moorhead	5.8	16.8	23.1	10.9	13.3	10.9	6.3	5.8	6.9	28.7	53.1
Oakdale	7.7	21.3	7.2	15.0	19.6	13.2	7.5	4.7	3.7	34.3	51.8

Table D. Cities

City	Under 5 years	5 to 17 years	18 to 24 years	25 to 34 years	35 to 44 years	45 to 54 years	55 to 64 years	65 to 74 years	75 years and over	Percent Female	2000	1990	1980	1990–2000	1980–1990
			Population and population characteristics, 1990 — Age (percent)								Population—change, 1980–2000 — Total persons			Percent change	
	39	40	41	42	43	44	45	46	47	48	49	50	51	52	53
MICHIGAN	7.6	18.9	10.8	16.9	15.1	10.2	8.5	7.1	4.9	51.5	9 938 444	9 295 287	9 262 044	6.9	0.4
Allen Park	6.0	14.8	7.3	16.2	14.4	9.9	11.4	13.1	6.9	51.9	29 376	31 092	34 196	-5.5	-9.1
Ann Arbor	5.7	11.4	27.1	20.9	14.8	7.4	5.4	4.1	3.2	50.5	114 024	109 608	107 960	4.0	1.5
Battle Creek	8.4	19.3	8.9	16.7	14.9	9.2	8.3	7.9	6.5	53.0	53 364	53 516	35 724	-0.3	49.8
Bay City	7.7	18.4	10.1	17.3	14.4	8.5	8.4	8.9	6.4	52.5	36 817	38 936	41 593	-5.4	-6.4
Burton	7.4	19.5	9.8	17.5	14.3	11.1	9.4	7.1	3.0	51.8	30 308	27 437	29 976	10.5	-8.5
Dearborn	7.1	16.0	8.9	17.4	13.9	9.5	9.4	10.8	7.2	51.6	97 775	89 286	90 660	9.5	-1.5
Dearborn Heights	6.0	14.6	9.0	17.2	13.0	10.8	12.6	11.1	5.7	52.0	58 264	60 838	67 706	-4.2	-10.1
Detroit	9.0	20.4	11.0	16.6	14.1	8.8	7.9	7.3	4.9	53.6	951 270	1 027 974	1 203 339	-7.5	-14.6
East Lansing	3.3	7.3	57.0	12.8	8.0	4.6	2.7	2.5	1.9	51.5	46 525	50 677	51 392	-8.2	-1.4
Eastpointe	7.0	15.7	8.2	18.4	13.1	8.2	10.6	11.9	6.9	52.7	34 077	35 283	38 280	-3.4	-7.8
Farmington Hills	6.6	16.1	8.3	18.8	17.1	11.9	9.4	7.4	4.4	51.3	82 111	74 614	58 056	10.0	28.5
Flint	9.4	21.1	11.2	17.6	13.4	8.8	7.8	6.2	4.5	53.2	124 943	140 925	159 611	-11.3	-11.7
Garden City	6.9	18.4	9.4	19.1	13.9	10.7	11.7	7.3	2.6	50.6	30 047	31 846	35 640	-5.6	-10.6
Grand Rapids	9.4	18.2	12.5	19.6	13.3	7.1	6.9	6.8	6.2	52.5	197 800	189 126	181 843	4.6	4.0
Holland	8.6	18.2	15.6	17.4	12.4	7.4	6.7	6.9	6.7	52.9	35 048	30 745	26 281	14.0	17.0
Inkster	8.1	20.6	11.1	17.0	14.5	9.3	8.0	7.5	3.8	52.9	30 115	30 772	35 190	-2.1	-12.6
Jackson	9.7	18.7	10.7	18.4	12.7	7.8	7.8	7.5	6.5	53.1	36 316	37 425	39 739	-3.0	-5.8
Kalamazoo	7.4	14.7	24.4	17.9	12.0	7.0	6.0	5.5	5.2	52.9	77 145	80 277	79 722	-3.9	0.7
Kentwood	7.9	18.5	11.1	21.6	15.2	9.3	6.8	5.6	4.0	52.2	45 255	37 826	30 438	19.6	24.3
Lansing	9.2	18.4	11.7	21.4	15.0	7.9	6.7	5.8	3.9	52.6	119 128	127 321	130 414	-6.4	-2.4
Lincoln Park	7.0	17.2	9.4	18.8	14.6	8.9	9.7	9.5	4.9	51.7	40 008	41 832	45 105	-4.4	-7.3
Livonia	6.6	16.3	8.6	16.2	15.8	11.5	11.8	8.3	4.8	51.4	100 545	100 850	104 814	-0.3	-3.8
Madison Heights	7.2	15.7	10.4	21.5	13.7	10.1	10.0	6.9	4.5	51.7	31 101	32 196	35 375	-3.4	-9.0
Midland	7.1	17.9	11.2	16.7	15.6	11.0	8.5	6.7	5.2	51.7	41 685	38 053	37 257	9.5	2.1
Mount Pleasant	3.9	9.1	52.7	10.4	7.9	4.8	3.8	3.8	3.5	54.4	25 946	23 299	23 746	11.4	-1.9
Muskegon	8.7	17.9	11.8	19.4	13.2	7.4	7.1	7.7	6.9	50.5	40 105	39 809	40 823	0.7	-2.5
Novi	7.7	18.1	8.1	21.7	18.2	11.1	7.1	5.1	2.8	51.7	47 386	32 998	22 525	43.6	46.5
Oak Park	8.2	20.0	8.3	17.4	15.6	10.1	7.9	8.0	4.4	52.1	29 793	30 468	31 537	-2.2	-3.4
Pontiac	9.8	20.6	12.5	19.3	13.3	9.1	6.6	5.2	3.5	51.6	66 337	71 136	76 715	-6.7	-7.3
Portage	7.4	19.4	9.3	17.2	18.3	11.1	8.6	5.7	2.9	51.5	44 897	41 042	38 157	9.4	7.6
Port Huron	8.7	19.8	10.7	17.7	13.1	8.3	7.8	7.4	6.5	53.4	32 338	33 694	33 981	-4.0	-0.8
Rochester Hills	7.2	19.1	8.4	17.1	19.8	11.8	7.8	4.8	3.9	51.4	68 825	61 766	NA	11.4	NA
Roseville	7.2	16.8	9.8	20.1	13.8	8.8	9.9	8.9	4.8	52.1	48 129	51 412	54 311	-6.4	-5.3
Royal Oak	6.8	13.9	7.6	22.5	16.1	8.5	8.8	9.3	6.4	52.8	60 062	65 410	70 893	-8.2	-7.7
Saginaw	9.7	22.3	10.3	16.9	13.5	8.0	7.4	6.9	5.0	53.9	61 799	69 512	77 508	-11.1	-10.3
St. Clair Shores	5.7	14.1	8.1	16.5	13.3	10.4	13.3	11.4	7.2	52.6	63 096	68 107	76 210	-7.4	-10.6
Southfield	5.7	14.4	8.7	17.9	15.9	11.0	9.5	8.8	8.0	53.2	78 296	75 727	75 568	3.4	0.2
Southgate	6.0	16.0	10.0	17.9	16.2	10.0	10.6	9.2	4.1	51.5	30 136	30 771	32 058	-2.1	-4.0
Sterling Heights	6.5	19.5	11.1	16.3	17.3	12.7	7.3	5.9	3.3	51.2	124 471	117 810	108 999	5.7	8.1
Taylor	8.2	19.5	11.6	18.5	14.2	11.1	8.9	5.2	2.7	51.4	65 868	70 811	77 568	-7.0	-8.7
Troy	6.7	19.8	8.5	15.4	19.7	13.4	8.1	5.2	3.1	51.0	80 959	72 884	67 102	11.1	8.6
Warren	6.2	14.8	10.4	17.7	12.2	11.7	12.0	9.5	5.4	51.4	138 247	144 864	161 134	-4.6	-10.1
Westland	7.3	16.4	11.3	21.0	13.6	10.7	8.9	6.3	4.5	52.0	86 602	84 724	84 603	2.2	0.1
Wyandotte	7.1	17.0	9.0	18.4	14.9	8.2	9.1	10.3	5.9	51.7	28 006	30 938	34 006	-9.5	-9.0
Wyoming	8.8	18.9	11.1	21.4	14.1	8.1	7.8	6.1	3.6	51.5	69 368	63 891	59 616	8.6	7.2
MINNESOTA	7.7	19.0	10.1	17.8	15.2	9.8	7.9	6.7	5.8	51.0	4 919 479	4 375 665	4 075 970	12.4	7.4
Andover	9.6	26.1	8.9	19.8	18.3	12.2	3.4	1.4	0.3	49.0	26 588	15 216	NA	74.7	NA
Apple Valley	9.3	25.5	7.6	18.4	21.0	12.1	3.5	1.5	1.1	50.1	45 527	34 598	21 818	31.6	58.6
Blaine	9.7	22.6	9.9	22.0	17.4	10.3	5.0	2.3	0.8	49.8	44 942	38 975	28 558	15.3	36.5
Bloomington	6.2	15.2	9.9	18.9	15.7	13.1	10.9	6.6	3.7	51.6	85 172	86 335	81 831	-1.3	5.5
Brooklyn Center	7.2	16.2	10.3	18.5	13.8	9.6	12.1	8.0	4.4	51.9	29 172	28 887	31 230	1.0	-7.5
Brooklyn Park	9.2	20.6	11.2	22.9	18.2	9.5	5.0	2.5	0.8	50.8	67 388	56 381	43 332	19.5	30.1
Burnsville	9.1	19.2	10.9	22.3	16.7	12.0	6.1	2.7	1.1	50.5	60 220	51 288	35 674	17.4	43.8
Coon Rapids	9.2	22.2	10.0	20.5	16.7	10.9	5.7	2.8	1.9	50.6	61 607	52 978	35 826	16.3	47.9
Cottage Grove	9.5	26.3	7.9	18.7	18.5	11.0	5.5	1.7	0.8	49.7	30 582	22 935	18 994	33.3	20.7
Duluth	6.4	16.5	13.7	15.0	14.3	8.9	8.0	8.8	8.4	52.9	86 918	85 493	92 811	1.7	-7.9
Eagan	11.2	18.6	9.1	28.7	18.5	8.5	3.4	1.3	0.6	50.4	63 557	47 409	20 700	34.1	129.0
Eden Prairie	10.5	18.8	7.6	25.1	21.9	8.9	4.1	2.2	0.9	51.0	54 901	39 311	16 263	39.7	141.7
Edina	5.3	14.7	6.2	12.1	16.3	12.4	12.5	11.3	9.1	54.6	47 425	46 075	46 073	2.9	0.0
Fridley	6.6	16.8	11.9	18.6	14.6	13.1	10.7	5.2	2.5	50.7	27 449	28 335	30 228	-3.1	-6.3
Inver Grove Heights	9.4	20.3	10.3	21.1	16.2	10.3	6.7	3.4	2.3	50.8	29 751	22 477	17 147	32.4	31.1
Lakeville	11.9	23.6	7.7	24.5	18.6	7.9	3.4	1.7	0.7	49.4	43 128	24 854	14 790	73.5	68.0
Mankato	5.4	12.6	33.7	14.8	10.4	6.4	5.8	5.8	5.1	50.8	32 427	31 459	28 650	3.1	9.8
Maple Grove	10.1	24.4	6.5	21.9	21.3	10.0	3.7	1.5	0.6	50.1	50 365	38 736	20 525	30.0	88.7
Maplewood	8.0	17.2	9.2	18.9	15.0	10.7	9.4	6.7	5.1	51.5	34 947	30 954	26 990	12.9	14.7
Minneapolis	7.3	13.3	13.3	23.5	15.7	7.9	6.2	6.3	6.6	51.5	382 618	368 383	370 951	3.9	-0.7
Minnetonka	6.7	17.5	7.6	17.5	19.3	12.3	9.3	6.5	3.3	51.5	51 301	48 370	38 683	6.1	25.0
Moorhead	6.8	15.6	26.6	14.1	11.8	7.2	6.7	5.9	5.2	53.5	32 177	32 295	29 998	-0.4	7.7
Oakdale	9.7	20.6	8.6	23.7	16.3	10.2	5.9	3.6	1.5	51.4	26 653	18 377	12 126	45.0	51.6

Table D. Cities

City	Total population	In households (percent)									In group quarters (percent)						
		Total in house-holds	House-holder	Spouse	Child Total	Own child under 18 years	Other relatives Total	Under 18 years	Nonrelatives Total	Unmarried partner	Total in group quarters	Correctional institutions	Nursing homes	Other institutions	College dormitories	Military quarters	Other
	54	55	56	57	58	59	60	61	62	63	64	65	66	67	68	69	70
MICHIGAN	9 938 444	97.5	38.1	19.6	30.6	23.6	4.4	1.8	4.9	2.0	2.5	0.7	0.5	0.1	0.7	0.0	0.5
Allen Park	29 376	99.0	40.8	22.4	29.4	20.5	3.6	1.4	2.7	1.3	1.0	0.0	1.0	0.0	0.0	0.0	0.0
Ann Arbor	114 024	80.1	40.1	15.2	18.9	15.9	2.1	0.5	12.9	1.9	10.9	0.0	0.3	0.2	10.0	0.0	0.4
Battle Creek	53 364	97.1	40.0	16.8	29.7	24.1	4.6	2.1	6.0	2.7	2.9	0.0	0.7	0.0	0.0	0.0	0.8
Bay City	36 817	98.4	41.3	17.5	30.3	22.9	3.9	1.7	5.4	2.7	1.6	0.5	0.0	0.0	0.0	0.0	1.1
Burton	30 308	99.6	38.6	20.0	32.0	24.9	4.1	1.9	5.0	2.6	0.4	0.0	0.0	0.0	0.0	0.0	0.4
Dearborn	97 775	99.6	37.6	19.2	34.2	26.0	5.7	1.6	2.9	1.1	0.4	0.0	0.2	0.0	0.0	0.0	0.2
Dearborn Heights	58 264	98.8	39.9	21.1	29.3	20.4	4.9	1.5	3.5	1.6	1.2	0.0	0.6	0.3	0.0	0.0	0.3
Detroit	951 270	97.9	35.4	9.4	34.6	24.2	12.1	5.9	6.4	2.5	2.1	0.4	0.5	0.2	0.1	0.0	0.9
East Lansing	46 525	68.7	30.9	8.5	10.2	8.6	1.2	0.2	17.9	1.1	31.3	0.0	0.5	0.0	29.8	0.0	1.0
Eastpointe	34 077	99.8	39.9	19.4	31.1	22.2	4.9	1.7	4.5	2.2	0.2	0.0	0.0	0.0	0.0	0.0	0.2
Farmington Hills	82 111	98.4	40.9	22.9	28.3	22.0	3.1	0.7	3.3	1.4	1.6	0.0	0.5	0.1	0.1	0.0	0.9
Flint	124 943	98.0	39.0	11.3	33.7	25.6	7.5	4.0	6.5	3.0	2.0	0.6	0.1	0.1	0.3	0.0	1.0
Garden City	30 047	99.9	38.2	21.4	32.1	22.7	4.3	1.8	3.9	1.8	0.1	0.0	0.0	0.0	0.0	0.0	0.1
Grand Rapids	197 800	95.1	37.0	14.9	29.6	23.8	5.8	2.3	7.8	2.3	4.9	0.7	1.3	0.2	1.8	0.0	0.9
Holland	35 048	91.2	34.2	17.6	28.6	23.5	4.5	1.6	6.4	1.6	8.8	0.0	1.5	0.0	6.0	0.0	1.4
Inkster	30 115	99.2	37.1	12.6	34.5	24.3	9.0	4.6	6.0	2.4	0.8	0.0	0.2	0.0	0.0	0.0	0.6
Jackson	36 316	97.0	39.1	14.0	31.7	25.8	5.0	2.5	7.1	3.2	3.0	0.6	0.9	0.2	0.4	0.0	1.0
Kalamazoo	77 145	87.6	38.1	11.7	21.7	17.9	3.6	1.5	12.5	2.6	12.4	0.7	0.6	0.3	9.2	0.0	1.5
Kentwood	45 255	99.2	40.8	19.7	30.5	25.0	3.1	1.0	5.0	2.0	0.8	0.0	0.3	0.1	0.0	0.0	0.4
Lansing	119 128	99.3	41.6	14.9	29.7	23.5	5.1	2.3	8.1	3.4	0.7	0.0	0.3	0.1	0.0	0.0	0.3
Lincoln Park	40 008	99.7	40.5	18.7	30.0	21.6	5.2	2.1	5.2	2.6	0.3	0.0	0.0	0.0	0.0	0.0	0.0
Livonia	100 545	98.1	37.9	23.8	31.1	22.8	3.0	0.9	2.3	1.0	1.9	0.0	1.0	0.1	0.1	0.0	0.6
Madison Heights	31 101	99.5	42.8	19.3	28.0	20.2	4.7	1.4	4.7	2.0	0.5	0.0	0.4	0.0	0.0	0.0	0.1
Midland	41 685	97.1	40.2	21.9	29.3	24.9	1.5	0.6	4.2	1.6	2.9	0.2	0.9	0.0	1.6	0.0	0.2
Mount Pleasant	25 946	77.4	32.6	8.4	12.8	10.8	1.4	0.3	22.2	1.7	22.6	0.6	1.0	0.8	19.4	0.0	0.8
Muskegon	40 105	88.0	36.3	12.1	27.7	22.0	5.5	2.8	6.4	2.9	12.0	9.8	0.8	0.5	0.4	0.0	0.5
Novi	47 386	99.4	39.5	22.2	31.8	26.8	2.3	0.5	3.6	1.7	0.6	0.0	0.4	0.0	0.0	0.0	0.1
Oak Park	29 793	99.9	37.3	16.4	34.8	24.8	7.3	2.9	4.2	1.7	0.1	0.0	0.0	0.0	0.0	0.0	0.1
Pontiac	66 337	97.8	36.5	11.5	32.9	24.7	9.0	4.6	7.9	3.2	2.2	0.2	0.4	0.4	0.1	0.0	1.1
Portage	44 897	99.1	40.4	22.0	30.3	25.2	2.1	0.8	4.3	2.1	0.9	0.0	0.3	0.0	0.0	0.0	0.7
Port Huron	32 338	97.4	40.1	16.0	30.5	24.1	4.3	1.9	6.6	3.1	2.6	0.8	0.6	0.0	0.0	0.1	1.2
Rochester Hills	68 825	98.9	38.8	24.0	31.7	25.2	2.3	0.6	2.6	1.1	1.1	0.0	0.4	0.0	0.4	0.0	0.4
Roseville	48 129	99.6	41.5	19.3	29.7	21.1	4.4	1.6	4.7	2.4	0.4	0.0	0.3	0.0	0.0	0.0	0.1
Royal Oak	60 062	99.2	48.1	19.2	23.0	16.8	2.7	0.6	6.3	2.2	0.8	0.0	0.3	0.0	0.0	0.0	0.5
Saginaw	61 799	97.7	37.5	12.3	35.1	27.0	7.1	3.9	5.7	2.9	2.3	0.6	0.5	0.1	0.0	0.0	1.1
St. Clair Shores	63 096	99.2	43.5	21.5	27.4	18.7	3.5	1.1	3.3	1.7	0.8	0.0	0.6	0.0	0.0	0.0	0.2
Southfield	78 296	98.4	43.4	17.5	27.2	18.8	6.1	2.3	4.3	1.7	1.6	0.1	0.8	0.0	0.4	0.0	0.3
Southgate	30 136	99.3	42.6	21.0	28.1	19.8	3.8	1.4	3.9	1.9	0.7	0.0	0.3	0.0	0.0	0.0	0.1
Sterling Heights	124 471	99.0	37.2	22.5	32.4	22.8	4.4	1.0	2.5	1.2	1.0	0.0	0.5	0.0	0.0	0.0	0.4
Taylor	65 868	98.9	37.6	18.3	32.7	24.2	5.3	2.4	5.0	2.6	1.1	0.0	0.7	0.2	0.0	0.0	0.2
Troy	80 959	99.7	37.1	23.9	33.0	25.4	3.3	0.6	2.5	0.9	0.3	0.0	0.0	0.0	0.0	0.0	0.3
Warren	138 247	99.1	40.2	20.0	29.4	20.8	5.1	1.6	4.4	2.1	0.9	0.0	0.7	0.0	0.0	0.0	0.2
Westland	86 602	98.9	42.2	18.7	28.5	21.3	4.1	1.5	5.4	2.6	1.1	0.0	0.7	0.3	0.0	0.0	0.1
Wyandotte	28 006	99.7	42.2	19.5	28.8	20.4	4.5	1.8	4.7	2.4	0.3	0.0	0.1	0.0	0.0	0.0	0.2
Wyoming	69 368	99.5	38.3	19.0	32.1	25.8	4.2	1.6	5.9	2.5	0.5	0.0	0.1	0.0	0.1	0.0	0.2
MINNESOTA	4 919 479	97.2	38.5	20.7	29.9	24.6	2.8	1.0	5.3	2.0	2.8	0.3	0.8	0.1	0.9	0.0	0.6
Andover	26 588	100.0	30.5	24.4	40.2	34.2	2.1	0.9	2.8	1.2	0.0	0.0	0.0	0.0	0.0	0.0	0.0
Apple Valley	45 527	99.5	35.9	22.9	34.9	28.6	2.3	0.8	3.5	1.5	0.5	0.0	0.4	0.0	0.0	0.0	0.1
Blaine	44 942	99.8	35.4	21.6	34.2	27.1	3.5	1.4	5.1	2.3	0.2	0.0	0.0	0.0	0.0	0.0	0.2
Bloomington	85 172	98.4	42.7	21.9	25.1	19.3	3.0	0.9	5.7	2.0	1.6	0.0	0.8	0.1	0.0	0.0	0.6
Brooklyn Center	29 172	98.7	39.2	18.2	29.7	22.6	5.5	1.9	6.1	2.4	1.3	0.0	0.6	0.0	0.0	0.0	0.7
Brooklyn Park	67 388	99.7	36.3	19.8	33.1	26.7	5.2	1.7	5.3	2.2	0.3	0.0	0.0	0.0	0.0	0.0	0.3
Burnsville	60 220	99.4	39.3	20.8	30.1	24.9	2.9	0.9	6.4	2.5	0.6	0.0	0.0	0.2	0.0	0.0	0.4
Coon Rapids	61 607	99.4	36.6	21.0	33.7	27.0	3.1	1.2	5.0	2.2	0.6	0.0	0.3	0.0	0.0	0.0	0.3
Cottage Grove	30 582	99.8	32.5	23.7	38.4	31.3	2.2	0.9	3.1	1.4	0.2	0.0	0.0	0.0	0.0	0.0	0.2
Duluth	86 918	92.5	40.8	16.9	24.5	19.7	2.2	0.8	8.0	2.4	7.5	0.9	1.3	0.3	3.8	0.0	1.2
Eagan	63 557	99.7	37.4	21.6	33.6	29.0	2.3	0.7	4.8	1.8	0.3	0.0	0.0	0.0	0.0	0.0	0.3
Eden Prairie	54 901	99.7	37.3	22.8	33.8	29.9	1.7	0.3	4.1	1.5	0.3	0.0	0.1	0.0	0.0	0.0	0.2
Edina	47 425	99.4	44.3	23.8	26.5	22.3	1.6	0.4	3.2	1.1	0.6	0.0	0.6	0.0	0.0	0.0	0.1
Fridley	27 449	99.2	41.3	20.1	27.3	20.8	3.7	1.3	6.9	2.9	0.8	0.0	0.2	0.0	0.0	0.0	0.6
Inver Grove Heights	29 751	99.1	37.8	21.4	31.9	26.1	2.6	0.8	5.5	2.3	0.9	0.0	0.5	0.2	0.0	0.0	0.2
Lakeville	43 128	99.9	31.6	23.2	39.8	34.9	1.9	0.7	3.4	1.4	0.1	0.0	0.0	0.0	0.0	0.0	0.1
Mankato	32 427	88.2	38.1	14.0	19.5	16.1	1.9	0.4	14.6	2.4	11.8	0.2	0.8	0.0	9.4	0.0	1.4
Maple Grove	50 365	99.9	34.8	24.2	36.1	30.1	1.8	0.5	2.9	1.3	0.1	0.0	0.0	0.0	0.0	0.0	0.1
Maplewood	34 947	97.7	39.4	20.8	29.6	23.2	3.2	1.1	4.7	2.0	2.3	0.0	1.0	0.0	0.0	0.0	1.4
Minneapolis	382 618	95.3	42.4	12.3	23.4	19.0	5.8	2.1	11.3	3.3	4.7	0.2	1.1	0.2	2.0	0.0	1.3
Minnetonka	51 301	98.8	41.7	23.6	27.3	22.2	1.8	0.5	4.4	1.6	1.2	0.0	0.4	0.3	0.0	0.0	0.6
Moorhead	32 177	88.1	36.2	17.1	25.7	21.5	1.8	0.6	7.3	1.7	11.9	0.4	1.2	0.1	9.4	0.0	0.9
Oakdale	26 653	99.6	38.4	21.2	33.4	27.7	2.5	0.9	4.0	1.9	0.4	0.0	0.0	0.0	0.2	0.0	0.1

Table D. Cities

City	Total households	Family households Total	Family households With own children under 18 years	Married couple Total	Married couple With own children under 18 years	Female householder[1] Total	Female householder[1] With own children under 18 years	Nonfamily households Total	Householder living alone Total	Householder living alone 65 years and over	Average household size	Average family size	Households 1990 Total households	Households 1990 Female householder[1]	Households 1990 Householder living alone
	71	72	73	74	75	76	77	78	79	80	81	82	83	84	85
MICHIGAN	3 785 661	68.0	32.7	51.4	23.1	12.5	7.5	32.0	26.2	9.4	2.56	3.10	3 419 331	12.9	23.7
Allen Park	11 974	68.5	27.5	55.0	22.5	9.9	3.7	31.5	28.2	14.9	2.43	2.99	12 030	9.2	23.5
Ann Arbor	45 693	47.5	23.0	37.8	17.6	7.5	4.4	52.5	35.5	6.6	2.22	2.90	41 657	8.1	31.4
Battle Creek	21 348	62.6	32.3	41.9	18.6	16.1	11.0	37.4	31.6	12.1	2.43	3.04	21 457	16.4	29.3
Bay City	15 208	61.3	30.2	42.4	18.7	14.7	9.1	38.7	32.9	12.8	2.38	3.04	15 570	14.4	29.9
Burton	11 699	69.8	35.0	51.8	23.8	12.8	8.2	30.2	25.3	9.0	2.58	3.08	10 447	14.2	22.4
Dearborn	36 770	64.9	31.3	51.0	25.7	9.4	4.3	35.1	30.9	14.7	2.65	3.42	35 442	10.4	29.0
Dearborn Heights	23 276	67.8	27.5	52.7	21.8	10.8	4.2	32.2	28.0	13.0	2.47	3.04	23 432	10.6	23.4
Detroit	336 428	64.9	33.9	26.7	12.5	31.6	18.6	35.1	29.7	9.2	2.77	3.45	374 057	30.3	29.8
East Lansing	14 390	35.4	16.1	27.6	11.8	5.7	3.5	64.6	36.2	7.2	2.22	2.82	13 500	6.5	28.7
Eastpointe	13 595	65.9	30.2	48.6	22.9	12.3	5.3	34.1	28.8	13.8	2.50	3.11	13 443	11.5	23.0
Farmington Hills	33 559	65.0	29.5	56.0	25.3	6.6	3.3	35.0	29.6	10.2	2.41	3.04	29 234	6.0	25.5
Flint	48 744	62.1	33.5	29.0	12.6	27.5	18.1	37.9	31.9	9.9	2.51	3.16	53 894	26.3	29.3
Garden City	11 479	71.7	32.5	56.0	25.3	11.2	5.1	28.3	24.0	9.7	2.62	3.11	11 213	11.1	17.6
Grand Rapids	73 217	60.6	32.0	40.3	19.4	15.8	10.3	39.4	30.8	10.0	2.57	3.24	69 029	16.1	27.2
Holland	11 971	66.2	34.5	51.4	25.0	10.8	7.2	33.8	26.8	11.7	2.67	3.24	10 572	9.6	23.4
Inkster	11 169	66.8	33.1	34.0	14.8	26.8	15.7	33.2	27.9	9.2	2.67	3.26	11 201	24.2	26.8
Jackson	14 210	61.0	33.7	35.8	16.5	19.9	13.9	39.0	32.0	10.8	2.48	3.12	14 723	18.7	31.4
Kalamazoo	29 413	48.8	24.9	30.6	12.8	14.7	10.3	51.2	34.8	9.6	2.30	2.99	29 409	15.2	31.1
Kentwood	18 477	62.4	33.3	48.3	24.4	10.8	7.1	37.6	30.9	8.2	2.43	3.10	15 247	9.7	28.3
Lansing	49 505	57.3	30.0	35.8	16.1	17.0	11.3	42.7	33.2	8.1	2.39	3.08	50 635	16.6	29.1
Lincoln Park	16 204	65.3	30.2	46.3	21.0	13.3	6.4	34.7	29.3	11.3	2.46	3.04	16 257	12.6	25.2
Livonia	38 089	73.7	32.5	62.8	28.0	8.0	3.4	26.3	22.9	11.1	2.59	3.07	35 916	7.7	17.7
Madison Heights	13 299	60.2	26.9	45.2	20.0	10.5	5.2	39.8	33.8	12.3	2.33	3.02	12 850	11.1	28.7
Midland	16 743	65.7	33.2	54.4	25.7	8.7	5.9	34.3	28.6	11.4	2.42	3.00	14 812	7.7	25.4
Mount Pleasant	8 449	37.0	18.8	25.9	11.6	8.5	5.8	63.0	29.6	8.8	2.38	2.88	6 661	10.2	26.5
Muskegon	14 569	58.6	31.1	33.2	14.4	20.2	13.7	41.4	34.4	12.9	2.42	3.13	14 770	20.2	31.6
Novi	18 726	65.8	36.3	56.2	31.0	7.1	4.1	34.2	28.1	5.9	2.52	3.17	12 699	8.2	23.2
Oak Park	11 104	68.4	34.4	44.0	21.9	19.5	10.4	31.6	26.6	10.4	2.68	3.29	10 885	15.9	22.0
Pontiac	24 234	63.0	33.9	31.5	14.9	25.2	15.9	37.0	29.4	8.0	2.68	3.32	24 777	25.5	26.3
Portage	18 138	66.9	34.2	54.4	25.8	9.7	6.6	33.1	27.2	8.4	2.45	3.01	15 467	8.6	21.6
Port Huron	12 961	62.1	32.4	39.8	17.6	17.5	12.1	37.9	31.9	13.2	2.43	3.04	13 158	18.2	28.5
Rochester Hills	26 315	72.1	35.7	62.8	30.8	6.8	3.7	27.9	24.0	8.4	2.59	3.11	22 353	6.8	19.5
Roseville	19 976	63.7	28.6	46.4	20.5	12.7	6.1	36.3	30.8	12.6	2.40	3.02	19 537	12.6	24.7
Royal Oak	28 880	50.0	20.4	39.9	16.3	7.5	3.3	50.0	40.8	11.6	2.06	2.86	28 344	9.2	32.3
Saginaw	23 182	65.2	35.4	32.9	14.1	27.3	18.8	34.8	29.5	9.9	2.60	3.23	26 179	26.0	28.1
St. Clair Shores	27 434	63.0	24.1	49.5	19.1	10.0	3.8	37.0	32.7	16.3	2.28	2.92	27 218	9.8	26.3
Southfield	33 987	58.2	25.3	40.2	16.4	14.3	7.5	41.8	36.2	11.9	2.27	3.01	32 112	9.7	32.3
Southgate	12 836	62.7	26.7	49.2	20.6	9.7	4.5	37.3	32.3	14.1	2.33	2.98	12 128	9.5	26.9
Sterling Heights	46 319	72.1	32.9	60.4	27.8	8.5	4.0	27.9	24.1	8.5	2.66	3.21	40 835	8.4	19.1
Taylor	24 776	71.6	34.9	48.7	21.4	17.4	10.7	28.4	23.1	7.6	2.63	3.09	24 861	16.4	18.2
Troy	30 018	72.9	36.9	64.5	33.2	6.0	2.9	27.1	22.8	7.8	2.69	3.23	26 167	6.3	20.5
Warren	55 551	66.1	27.8	49.7	20.3	11.7	5.5	33.9	28.8	12.0	2.47	3.05	54 602	11.4	22.7
Westland	36 533	60.9	28.6	44.4	19.9	12.1	6.6	39.1	32.6	11.3	2.34	3.00	33 110	11.7	27.1
Wyandotte	11 816	62.8	27.7	46.3	20.0	11.9	5.6	37.2	31.9	13.3	2.36	2.99	12 319	12.4	28.3
Wyoming	26 536	66.1	35.7	49.6	25.4	12.0	7.8	33.9	26.6	7.4	2.60	3.19	24 168	10.4	23.6
MINNESOTA	1 895 127	66.2	33.0	53.7	25.2	8.9	5.9	33.8	26.9	9.3	2.52	3.09	1 647 853	8.6	25.1
Andover	8 107	88.2	55.1	80.0	49.7	5.5	3.7	11.8	8.4	2.3	3.28	3.48	4 430	5.1	5.7
Apple Valley	16 344	75.9	42.5	63.7	34.6	9.0	6.0	24.1	19.3	4.0	2.77	3.21	11 145	8.1	12.7
Blaine	15 898	76.6	41.1	61.1	31.7	11.1	7.1	23.4	17.0	3.3	2.82	3.19	12 825	10.0	12.8
Bloomington	36 400	62.5	25.1	51.2	19.0	8.2	4.7	37.5	29.6	9.9	2.30	2.87	34 488	8.2	23.4
Brooklyn Center	11 430	64.6	29.7	46.3	18.8	13.4	8.4	35.4	28.2	11.0	2.52	3.11	11 226	12.8	21.8
Brooklyn Park	24 432	71.0	39.2	54.6	28.9	12.1	8.1	29.0	22.0	3.7	2.75	3.26	20 386	11.7	19.2
Burnsville	23 687	66.0	34.1	52.8	25.5	10.0	6.8	34.0	24.8	4.8	2.53	3.07	19 127	9.2	19.5
Coon Rapids	22 578	73.4	39.1	57.3	28.7	12.2	8.4	26.6	20.1	5.1	2.71	3.15	17 449	10.6	13.3
Cottage Grove	9 932	85.2	49.8	72.9	41.7	8.8	6.2	14.8	11.0	2.7	3.07	3.32	6 856	7.7	7.2
Duluth	35 500	56.1	26.6	41.4	17.2	11.4	7.6	43.9	34.5	13.3	2.26	2.90	34 563	11.1	31.7
Eagan	23 773	69.1	41.2	57.9	33.8	8.4	5.8	30.9	23.0	2.6	2.67	3.23	17 427	7.9	19.0
Eden Prairie	20 457	71.3	42.6	61.3	35.6	7.7	5.6	28.7	22.0	3.4	2.68	3.20	14 447	7.3	18.0
Edina	20 996	61.3	26.5	53.8	22.6	5.8	3.1	38.7	34.0	18.5	2.24	2.91	19 860	6.2	29.7
Fridley	11 328	64.6	28.2	48.6	18.4	11.6	7.4	35.4	26.8	6.3	2.40	2.91	10 909	11.7	20.6
Inver Grove Heights	11 257	70.4	37.3	56.4	28.1	10.3	7.1	29.6	21.5	4.7	2.62	3.09	7 803	11.9	16.3
Lakeville	13 609	84.7	56.0	73.6	48.0	7.5	5.7	15.3	10.7	1.9	3.17	3.43	7 851	7.0	11.0
Mankato	12 367	49.0	23.6	36.7	16.0	8.8	6.0	51.0	32.2	9.9	2.31	2.90	11 220	8.7	27.2
Maple Grove	17 532	79.6	46.3	69.5	39.8	7.5	5.0	20.4	15.8	2.6	2.87	3.24	12 531	6.8	11.3
Maplewood	13 758	66.8	31.6	52.8	23.5	10.5	6.5	33.2	27.0	11.1	2.48	3.04	11 496	11.0	21.5
Minneapolis	162 352	45.5	22.6	29.0	12.8	12.3	7.9	54.5	40.3	8.0	2.25	3.15	160 682	12.7	38.5
Minnetonka	21 393	65.9	29.1	56.6	24.0	6.8	3.9	34.1	27.3	9.3	2.37	2.92	18 687	6.7	21.3
Moorhead	11 660	60.3	31.4	47.3	22.4	9.8	7.2	39.7	29.2	11.1	2.43	3.04	11 063	10.3	24.8
Oakdale	10 243	69.6	38.5	55.2	28.7	11.1	7.9	30.4	25.2	7.2	2.59	3.14	6 699	11.6	19.6

[1] No spouse present.

Table D. Cities

City	Percent change of households, 1990–2000	Total housing units	Occupied housing units (percent)	Housing occupancy — Vacant housing units				Housing tenure — Occupied housing units				
				Total	For seasonal, recreational, or occasional use	Homeowner vacancy rate (percent)	Rental vacancy rate (percent)	Total	Percent owner-occupied housing units	Percent renter-occupied housing units	Average household size of owner-occupied units	Average household size of renter-occupied units
	86	87	88	89	90	91	92	93	94	95	96	97
MICHIGAN	10.7	4 234 279	89.4	10.6	5.5	1.6	6.8	3 785 661	73.8	26.2	2.67	2.24
Allen Park	-0.5	12 254	97.7	2.3	0.2	0.6	4.4	11 974	87.9	12.1	2.51	1.82
Ann Arbor	9.7	47 218	96.8	3.2	0.5	1.0	2.6	45 693	45.3	54.7	2.43	2.06
Battle Creek	-0.5	23 525	90.7	9.3	0.4	2.5	12.1	21 348	65.8	34.2	2.52	2.25
Bay City	-2.3	16 259	93.5	6.5	0.4	1.7	7.4	15 208	69.5	30.5	2.51	2.09
Burton	12.0	12 348	94.7	5.3	0.2	2.7	5.3	11 699	80.8	19.2	2.67	2.23
Dearborn	3.7	38 981	94.3	5.7	1.2	1.5	6.1	36 770	73.4	26.6	2.75	2.38
Dearborn Heights	-0.7	23 913	97.3	2.7	0.3	0.9	3.8	23 276	85.4	14.6	2.53	2.14
Detroit	-10.1	375 096	89.7	10.3	0.2	1.6	8.3	336 428	54.9	45.1	2.84	2.68
East Lansing	6.6	15 321	93.9	6.1	0.3	1.2	6.3	14 390	32.0	68.0	2.41	2.13
Eastpointe	1.1	13 965	97.4	2.6	0.2	0.9	4.5	13 595	88.0	12.0	2.56	2.09
Farmington Hills	14.8	34 858	96.3	3.7	0.8	0.5	5.1	33 559	66.9	33.1	2.72	1.77
Flint	-9.6	55 464	87.9	12.1	0.3	2.7	13.1	48 744	58.8	41.2	2.45	2.59
Garden City	2.4	11 719	98.0	2.0	0.2	0.5	3.6	11 479	86.2	13.8	2.71	2.03
Grand Rapids	6.1	77 960	93.9	6.1	0.3	1.3	6.6	73 217	59.7	40.3	2.69	2.39
Holland	13.2	12 533	95.5	4.5	0.9	1.4	3.3	11 971	67.1	32.9	2.73	2.55
Inkster	-0.3	12 013	93.0	7.0	0.2	1.7	7.7	11 169	58.0	42.0	2.76	2.55
Jackson	-3.5	15 241	93.2	6.8	0.3	1.5	7.9	14 210	57.6	42.4	2.55	2.38
Kalamazoo	0.0	31 798	92.5	7.5	0.4	2.1	6.9	29 413	47.7	52.3	2.43	2.18
Kentwood	21.2	19 507	94.7	5.3	0.5	1.3	7.0	18 477	61.0	39.0	2.71	1.99
Lansing	-2.2	53 159	93.1	6.9	0.4	2.0	7.2	49 505	57.5	42.5	2.49	2.26
Lincoln Park	-0.3	16 821	96.3	3.7	0.3	1.0	5.8	16 204	79.1	20.9	2.57	2.06
Livonia	6.1	38 658	98.5	1.5	0.2	0.4	2.7	38 089	88.8	11.2	2.68	1.86
Madison Heights	3.5	13 623	97.6	2.4	0.3	0.8	3.0	13 299	70.1	29.9	2.50	1.93
Midland	13.0	17 773	94.2	5.8	0.8	1.7	6.7	16 743	69.7	30.3	2.63	1.92
Mount Pleasant	26.8	8 878	95.2	4.8	0.4	1.7	4.5	8 449	34.3	65.7	2.43	2.35
Muskegon	-1.4	15 999	91.1	8.9	0.5	2.9	7.8	14 569	56.9	43.1	2.58	2.21
Novi	47.5	19 649	95.3	4.7	0.5	1.2	7.0	18 726	71.1	28.9	2.78	1.88
Oak Park	2.0	11 370	97.7	2.3	0.2	1.1	2.7	11 104	74.8	25.2	2.74	2.52
Pontiac	-2.2	26 336	92.0	8.0	0.2	2.0	8.6	24 234	52.8	47.2	2.76	2.59
Portage	17.3	18 880	96.1	3.9	0.4	1.4	5.2	18 138	68.9	31.1	2.71	1.88
Port Huron	-1.5	14 003	92.6	7.4	0.7	2.0	7.9	12 961	57.2	42.8	2.54	2.29
Rochester Hills	17.7	27 263	96.5	3.5	0.5	1.0	6.1	26 315	79.1	20.9	2.76	1.92
Roseville	2.2	20 519	97.4	2.6	0.3	0.9	3.3	19 976	75.2	24.8	2.53	2.01
Royal Oak	1.9	29 942	96.5	3.5	0.7	0.8	4.5	28 880	70.1	29.9	2.24	1.65
Saginaw	-11.4	25 639	90.4	9.6	0.2	2.2	7.6	23 182	63.6	36.4	2.61	2.59
St. Clair Shores	0.8	28 208	97.3	2.7	0.5	0.8	4.0	27 434	85.8	14.2	2.36	1.81
Southfield	5.8	35 698	95.2	4.8	0.3	1.1	5.8	33 987	54.1	45.9	2.64	1.83
Southgate	5.8	13 361	96.1	3.9	0.5	1.2	4.8	12 836	70.6	29.4	2.58	1.73
Sterling Heights	13.4	47 547	97.4	2.6	0.3	0.9	3.7	46 319	79.0	21.0	2.87	1.88
Taylor	-0.3	25 905	95.6	4.4	0.2	1.5	5.8	24 776	70.8	29.2	2.67	2.53
Troy	14.7	30 872	97.2	2.8	0.7	0.5	3.7	30 018	77.3	22.7	2.92	1.91
Warren	1.7	57 249	97.0	3.0	0.3	0.8	4.4	55 551	80.4	19.6	2.55	2.12
Westland	10.3	38 077	95.9	4.1	0.3	1.5	5.2	36 533	62.7	37.3	2.57	1.97
Wyandotte	-4.1	12 303	96.0	4.0	0.3	1.1	4.4	11 816	73.0	27.0	2.53	1.91
Wyoming	9.8	27 506	96.5	3.5	0.2	1.0	5.6	26 536	67.6	32.4	2.80	2.18
MINNESOTA	15.0	2 065 946	91.7	8.3	5.1	0.9	4.1	1 895 127	74.6	25.4	2.69	2.03
Andover	83.0	8 205	98.8	1.2	0.1	0.6	1.1	8 107	95.7	4.3	3.32	2.34
Apple Valley	46.6	16 536	98.8	1.2	0.2	0.3	2.2	16 344	88.0	12.0	2.86	2.14
Blaine	24.0	16 169	98.3	1.7	0.1	0.8	0.9	15 898	90.5	9.5	2.87	2.32
Bloomington	5.5	37 104	98.1	1.9	0.4	0.3	3.0	36 400	70.6	29.4	2.48	1.88
Brooklyn Center	1.8	11 598	98.6	1.4	0.2	0.4	2.3	11 430	68.7	31.3	2.70	2.13
Brooklyn Park	19.8	24 846	98.3	1.7	0.2	0.4	2.9	24 432	73.4	26.6	2.94	2.22
Burnsville	23.8	24 261	97.6	2.4	0.4	0.4	3.4	23 687	68.1	31.9	2.71	2.14
Coon Rapids	29.4	22 828	98.9	1.1	0.2	0.5	1.1	22 578	80.4	19.6	2.81	2.30
Cottage Grove	44.9	10 024	99.1	0.9	0.1	0.2	4.3	9 932	91.4	8.6	3.09	2.92
Duluth	2.7	36 994	96.0	4.0	0.5	1.0	3.4	35 500	64.1	35.9	2.46	1.91
Eagan	36.4	24 390	97.5	2.5	0.3	0.2	5.6	23 773	75.0	25.0	2.85	2.11
Eden Prairie	41.6	21 026	97.3	2.7	0.7	0.4	3.9	20 457	78.3	21.7	2.83	2.11
Edina	5.7	21 669	96.9	3.1	1.4	0.5	2.5	20 996	76.5	23.5	2.42	1.66
Fridley	3.8	11 504	98.5	1.5	0.2	0.4	2.0	11 328	67.7	32.3	2.51	2.19
Inver Grove Heights	44.3	11 457	98.3	1.7	0.2	0.6	2.2	11 257	77.5	22.5	2.72	2.27
Lakeville	73.3	13 799	98.6	1.4	0.2	0.5	2.3	13 609	91.8	8.2	3.22	2.55
Mankato	10.2	12 759	96.9	3.1	0.2	0.9	2.6	12 367	52.9	47.1	2.51	2.09
Maple Grove	39.9	17 745	98.8	1.2	0.2	0.3	2.3	17 532	92.7	7.3	2.92	2.24
Maplewood	19.7	14 004	98.2	1.8	0.4	0.4	1.9	13 758	75.7	24.3	2.67	1.90
Minneapolis	1.0	168 606	96.3	3.7	0.5	0.7	2.8	162 352	51.4	48.6	2.43	2.05
Minnetonka	14.5	22 228	96.2	3.8	1.1	0.4	5.0	21 393	75.7	24.3	2.55	1.79
Moorhead	5.4	12 180	95.7	4.3	0.2	0.8	6.3	11 660	63.7	36.3	2.65	2.05
Oakdale	52.9	10 394	98.5	1.5	0.2	0.5	1.8	10 243	80.5	19.5	2.75	1.94

Table D. Cities

STATE Place code	City	Land area, 2000[1] (sq km)	Total persons	Rank	Per square kilometer	Land area, 1990[1] (sq km)	Total persons	Rank	Per square kilometer	White	Black or African American	American Indian or Alaska Native	Asian	Native Hawaiian and other Pacific Islander	Some other race
		Population, 2000				Population, 1990				Population and population characteristics, 2000 — Race (percent) — One race					
		1	2	3	4	5	6	7	8	9	10	11	12	13	14
	MINNESOTA—Cont'd														
27 51730	Plymouth	85.2	65 894	442	773.4	85.3	50 889	541	596.6	91.4	2.7	0.3	3.8	0.0	0.5
27 54214	Richfield	17.9	34 439	1 046	1 924.0	17.8	35 710	839	2 006.2	81.2	6.6	0.7	5.3	0.0	3.4
27 54880	Rochester	102.6	85 806	305	836.3	76.3	70 729	336	927.0	87.5	3.6	0.3	5.6	0.0	1.2
27 55852	Roseville	34.3	33 690	1 077	982.2	34.3	33 485	919	976.2	89.5	2.8	0.3	4.9	0.1	0.8
27 56896	St. Cloud	78.1	59 107	515	756.8	37.6	48 812	574	1 298.2	91.7	2.4	0.7	3.1	0.1	0.6
27 57220	St. Louis Park	27.7	44 126	780	1 593.0	27.7	43 787	654	1 580.8	88.9	4.4	0.4	3.2	0.1	1.3
27 58000	St. Paul	136.7	287 151	61	2 100.6	136.7	272 235	57	1 991.5	67.0	11.7	1.1	12.4	0.1	3.8
27 59998	Shoreview	29.0	25 924	1 453	893.9	29.0	24 587	1 317	847.8	93.3	1.0	0.2	3.6	0.1	0.4
27 71032	Winona	47.2	27 069	1 379	573.5	30.7	25 435	1 268	828.5	94.5	1.1	0.2	2.7	0.0	0.5
27 71428	Woodbury	90.6	46 463	735	512.8	90.7	20 075	1 635	221.3	90.0	2.5	0.2	5.0	0.0	0.6
28 00000	**MISSISSIPPI**	121 488.5	2 844 658	X	23.4	121 506.4	2 575 475	X	21.2	61.4	36.3	0.4	0.7	0.0	0.5
28 06220	Biloxi	98.5	50 644	658	514.2	50.9	46 319	615	910.0	71.4	19.0	0.5	5.1	0.1	1.4
28 15380	Columbus	55.5	25 944	1 452	467.5	29.7	23 799	1 368	801.3	43.6	54.4	0.1	0.6	0.0	0.5
28 29180	Greenville	69.6	41 633	829	598.2	67.6	45 226	632	669.0	28.9	69.6	0.1	0.7	0.0	0.2
28 29700	Gulfport	147.4	71 127	399	482.5	58.6	64 045	383	1 092.9	62.2	33.5	0.4	1.3	0.1	0.9
28 31020	Hattiesburg	127.6	44 779	769	350.9	65.8	45 325	630	688.8	49.9	47.3	0.2	1.2	0.0	0.5
28 36000	Jackson	271.7	184 256	113	678.2	282.3	202 062	77	715.8	27.8	70.6	0.1	0.6	0.0	0.2
28 46640	Meridian	116.9	39 968	872	341.9	92.3	41 036	714	444.6	44.0	54.4	0.2	0.6	0.0	0.3
28 55360	Pascagoula	39.3	26 200	1 436	666.7	39.3	25 899	1 246	659.0	67.2	29.0	0.2	1.0	0.0	1.7
28 69280	Southaven	87.5	28 977	1 276	331.2	33.0	18 705	1 752	566.8	90.3	6.7	0.3	0.7	0.0	1.1
28 74840	Tupelo	132.4	34 211	1 052	258.4	132.5	30 685	1 029	231.6	69.4	28.3	0.1	0.9	0.0	0.5
28 76720	Vicksburg	85.2	26 407	1 419	309.9	34.8	26 886	1 185	772.6	37.8	60.4	0.2	0.6	0.0	0.4
29 00000	**MISSOURI**	178 413.7	5 595 211	X	31.4	178 446.0	5 116 901	X	28.7	84.9	11.2	0.4	1.1	0.1	0.8
29 03160	Ballwin	23.2	31 283	1 171	1 348.4	16.3	27 054	1 180	1 659.8	93.4	1.5	0.2	3.3	0.0	0.5
29 06652	Blue Springs	47.1	48 080	704	1 020.8	41.7	40 103	736	961.7	93.2	2.9	0.4	1.0	0.1	0.8
29 11242	Cape Girardeau	62.9	35 349	1 010	562.0	59.6	34 475	874	578.4	87.3	9.3	0.4	1.1	0.0	0.4
29 13600	Chesterfield	81.6	46 802	728	573.6	77.6	42 325	683	545.4	91.3	1.9	0.1	5.6	0.0	0.4
29 15670	Columbia	137.4	84 531	315	615.2	114.8	69 133	347	602.2	81.5	10.9	0.4	4.3	0.0	0.8
29 24778	Florissant	29.4	50 497	662	1 717.6	26.4	51 038	538	1 933.3	85.7	11.5	0.2	0.6	0.0	0.5
29 27190	Gladstone	20.7	26 365	1 421	1 273.7	20.8	26 243	1 232	1 261.7	93.2	2.0	0.5	1.3	0.1	1.1
29 31276	Hazelwood	41.1	26 206	1 434	637.6	12.7	15 512	2 097	1 221.4	80.2	16.0	0.2	1.2	0.1	0.5
29 35000	Independence	202.9	113 288	206	558.3	202.5	112 301	166	554.6	91.9	2.6	0.6	0.7	0.5	1.4
29 37000	Jefferson City	70.6	39 636	881	561.4	68.9	35 517	845	515.5	81.5	14.7	0.4	1.2	0.1	0.6
29 37592	Joplin	81.4	45 504	753	559.0	76.9	41 175	710	535.4	91.4	2.7	1.5	0.7	0.0	1.0
29 38000	Kansas City	812.1	441 545	38	543.7	806.9	434 829	31	538.9	60.7	31.2	0.5	1.9	0.1	3.2
29 39044	Kirkwood	23.9	27 324	1 368	1 143.3	23.4	28 318	1 125	1 210.2	90.8	7.1	0.1	0.8	0.0	0.3
29 41348	Lee's Summit	154.1	70 700	403	458.8	153.1	46 418	612	303.2	93.2	3.5	0.4	1.0	0.1	0.5
29 42032	Liberty	69.8	26 232	1 430	375.8	69.7	20 459	1 596	293.5	93.7	2.6	0.4	0.6	0.1	1.0
29 46586	Maryland Heights	55.4	25 756	1 462	464.9	54.3	25 440	1 267	468.5	85.4	5.6	0.2	7.1	0.0	0.7
29 54074	O'Fallon	58.2	46 169	741	793.3	41.2	17 427	1 888	423.0	95.3	2.2	0.2	0.7	0.0	0.4
29 60788	Raytown	25.7	30 388	1 206	1 182.4	25.7	30 601	1 032	1 190.7	84.2	11.7	0.4	0.8	0.2	0.9
29 64082	St. Charles	52.7	60 321	495	1 144.6	42.9	50 634	546	1 180.3	93.3	3.5	0.3	1.0	0.0	0.7
29 64550	St. Joseph	113.5	73 990	381	651.9	112.3	71 852	326	639.8	91.9	5.0	0.5	0.5	0.0	0.7
29 65000	St. Louis	160.4	348 189	51	2 170.8	160.4	396 685	35	2 473.1	43.8	51.2	0.3	2.0	0.0	0.8
29 65126	St. Peters	54.9	51 381	651	935.9	40.9	40 660	724	994.1	94.3	2.8	0.2	1.2	0.0	0.4
29 70000	Springfield	189.5	151 580	137	799.9	176.0	140 494	129	798.3	91.7	3.3	0.8	1.4	0.1	0.9
29 75220	University City	15.2	37 428	943	2 462.4	15.2	40 087	738	2 637.3	49.3	45.4	0.2	2.8	0.0	0.6
29 79820	Wildwood	171.0	32 884	1 102	192.3	NA	NA	NA	NA	94.7	1.6	0.1	2.4	0.0	0.3
30 00000	**MONTANA**	376 979.1	902 195	X	2.4	376 990.9	799 065	X	2.1	90.6	0.3	6.2	0.5	0.1	0.6
30 06550	Billings	87.3	89 847	286	1 029.2	84.4	81 125	276	961.2	91.9	0.6	3.4	0.6	0.0	1.4
30 08950	Bozeman	32.6	27 509	1 353	843.8	25.3	22 660	1 450	895.7	94.7	0.3	1.2	1.6	0.1	0.5
30 11390	Butte-Silver Bow	1 860.4	34 606	1 041	18.6	1 860.0	33 252	926	17.9	95.4	0.2	2.0	0.4	0.1	0.6
30 32800	Great Falls	50.5	56 690	551	1 122.6	40.0	55 125	469	1 378.1	90.0	1.0	5.1	0.9	0.1	0.6
30 35600	Helena	36.3	25 780	1 460	710.2	35.0	24 609	1 316	703.1	94.8	0.2	2.1	0.8	0.1	0.4
30 50200	Missoula	61.6	57 053	546	926.2	43.1	42 918	670	995.8	93.6	0.4	2.4	1.2	0.1	0.5
31 00000	**NEBRASKA**	199 098.6	1 711 263	X	8.6	199 113.2	1 578 417	X	7.9	89.6	4.0	0.9	1.3	0.0	2.8
31 03950	Bellevue	34.4	44 382	775	1 290.2	20.8	39 240	759	1 886.5	85.8	6.1	0.5	2.1	0.1	2.8
31 17670	Fremont	19.2	25 174	1 497	1 311.1	17.2	23 680	1 383	1 376.7	95.3	0.6	0.3	0.6	0.1	2.3
31 19595	Grand Island	55.6	42 940	802	772.3	53.2	39 487	753	742.2	86.7	0.4	0.3	1.3	0.2	9.6
31 25055	Kearney	28.4	27 431	1 357	965.9	22.2	24 396	1 330	1 098.9	95.2	0.6	0.4	0.9	0.0	1.7
31 28000	Lincoln	193.3	225 581	78	1 167.0	163.9	191 972	82	1 171.3	89.2	3.1	0.7	3.1	0.1	1.8
31 37000	Omaha	299.7	390 007	46	1 301.3	260.7	344 463	48	1 321.3	78.4	13.3	0.7	1.7	0.1	3.9

[1] Dry land or land partially or temporarily covered by water.

Table D. Cities

	Population and population characteristics, 2000 (cont'd)								Population and population characteristics, 1990				
	Race (percent) (cont'd)								Race (percent)				
	Race alone or in combination												
City	Two or more races	White	Black	American Indian or Alaska Native	Asian	Native Hawaiian and other Pacific Islander	Some other race	Hispanic[1]	White	Black or African American	American Indian or Alaska Native	Asian and Pacific Islander	Hispanic[1]
	15	16	17	18	19	20	21	22	23	24	25	26	27
MINNESOTA—Cont'd													
Plymouth	1.3	92.5	3.2	0.6	4.2	0.1	0.8	1.6	95.7	1.6	0.4	2.0	1.0
Richfield	2.6	83.2	7.9	1.3	6.0	0.1	4.3	6.3	93.5	2.6	0.6	2.8	1.1
Rochester	1.8	88.7	4.3	0.6	6.3	0.1	1.9	3.0	94.2	1.0	0.3	4.1	1.2
Roseville	1.7	90.9	3.5	0.7	5.4	0.2	1.1	2.0	95.1	1.6	0.3	2.6	1.1
St. Cloud	1.4	92.9	2.9	1.2	3.5	0.1	0.8	1.3	96.8	1.0	0.6	1.3	0.6
St. Louis Park	1.7	90.3	5.2	0.9	3.7	0.1	1.7	2.9	95.3	1.9	0.4	2.1	1.0
St. Paul	3.9	69.6	13.4	2.1	13.5	0.4	5.2	7.9	82.3	7.4	1.4	7.1	4.2
Shoreview	1.4	94.5	1.2	0.6	4.2	0.1	0.8	1.3	96.4	0.7	0.3	2.3	0.9
Winona	1.0	95.3	1.3	0.6	3.1	0.1	0.8	1.3	97.6	0.7	0.2	1.2	0.9
Woodbury	1.6	91.4	3.1	0.6	5.6	0.1	0.9	2.1	94.6	1.6	0.3	3.1	1.7
MISSISSIPPI	0.7	61.9	36.6	0.7	0.8	0.1	0.7	1.4	63.5	35.6	0.3	0.5	0.6
Biloxi	2.4	73.4	19.8	1.1	6.0	0.3	2.0	3.6	74.6	18.6	0.3	5.7	2.8
Columbus	0.8	44.1	54.9	0.3	0.8	0.1	0.7	1.1	48.3	51.2	0.1	0.3	0.8
Greenville	0.5	29.2	69.9	0.2	0.9	0.1	0.3	0.7	39.8	59.6	0.1	0.4	0.6
Gulfport	1.6	63.5	34.1	1.0	1.7	0.2	1.3	2.6	69.9	28.6	0.3	0.9	1.5
Hattiesburg	0.8	50.6	47.7	0.4	1.4	0.1	0.7	0.8	58.2	40.4	0.1	1.1	1.0
Jackson	0.7	28.2	71.1	0.4	0.7	0.1	0.3	1.1	43.6	55.7	0.1	0.5	0.4
Meridian	0.6	44.4	54.7	0.4	0.7	0.1	0.4	1.1	54.0	45.4	0.1	0.4	0.6
Pascagoula	1.0	68.0	29.3	0.5	1.2	0.1	2.0	3.9	77.2	21.5	0.2	0.9	1.0
Southaven	0.8	91.0	6.8	0.6	0.9	0.1	1.4	2.3	96.7	2.5	0.2	0.3	0.6
Tupelo	0.8	70.1	28.7	0.3	1.0	0.0	0.7	1.4	75.2	24.4	0.1	0.3	0.5
Vicksburg	0.6	38.1	60.8	0.4	0.7	0.0	0.6	1.0	40.5	59.0	0.1	0.3	0.5
MISSOURI	1.5	86.1	11.7	1.1	1.4	0.1	1.2	2.1	87.7	10.7	0.4	0.8	1.2
Ballwin	1.1	94.4	1.7	0.5	3.7	0.1	0.8	1.9	96.5	1.6	0.1	1.7	1.0
Blue Springs	1.6	94.6	3.4	1.0	1.2	0.2	1.2	2.8	95.6	2.4	0.4	1.1	1.6
Cape Girardeau	1.4	88.5	9.9	0.9	1.4	0.1	0.6	1.1	90.2	8.0	0.2	1.3	0.6
Chesterfield	0.7	92.0	2.0	0.3	5.9	0.0	0.5	1.6	93.7	2.4	0.1	3.6	1.2
Columbia	2.1	83.3	11.7	0.9	4.8	0.1	1.3	2.1	85.1	9.9	0.3	4.1	1.3
Florissant	1.5	86.9	12.2	0.6	0.9	0.1	0.9	1.5	95.0	4.1	0.2	0.5	1.0
Gladstone	1.6	94.7	2.4	1.1	1.5	0.3	1.7	3.6	97.1	1.0	0.5	0.8	2.5
Hazelwood	1.8	81.7	16.8	0.7	1.6	0.1	0.9	1.6	87.8	10.6	0.2	1.0	1.4
Independence	2.3	94.0	3.2	1.6	1.0	0.6	2.0	3.7	96.2	1.4	0.6	1.0	2.0
Jefferson City	1.5	82.7	15.4	1.0	1.6	0.1	0.9	1.6	88.8	10.1	0.3	0.5	0.8
Joplin	2.6	93.9	3.3	3.0	1.0	0.1	1.4	2.5	95.0	2.1	1.9	0.6	1.2
Kansas City	2.4	62.5	32.3	1.2	2.3	0.2	4.1	6.9	66.8	29.6	0.5	1.2	3.9
Kirkwood	0.9	91.6	7.5	0.4	1.0	0.1	0.4	1.1	93.1	5.9	0.1	0.7	0.7
Lee's Summit	1.4	94.5	3.9	0.8	1.3	0.1	0.9	2.0	96.9	1.7	0.3	0.6	1.0
Liberty	1.6	95.3	3.0	1.1	0.9	0.1	1.4	2.7	95.8	3.0	0.4	0.4	1.4
Maryland Heights	1.0	86.2	5.9	0.5	7.5	0.1	0.9	2.3	93.5	3.6	0.2	2.4	1.1
O'Fallon	1.0	96.3	2.6	0.6	1.0	0.1	0.6	1.5	97.9	1.1	0.4	0.3	1.6
Raytown	1.8	85.8	12.4	1.1	1.1	0.2	1.3	2.3	95.3	3.2	0.4	0.5	1.4
St. Charles	1.2	94.4	3.9	0.7	1.3	0.1	1.0	2.0	95.9	2.8	0.3	0.7	1.0
St. Joseph	1.4	93.2	5.7	0.9	0.7	0.1	1.0	2.6	95.0	3.6	0.3	0.4	2.2
St. Louis	1.9	45.2	52.1	0.8	2.3	0.1	1.5	2.0	50.9	47.5	0.2	0.9	1.3
St. Peters	1.1	95.2	3.1	0.5	1.5	0.1	0.7	1.5	96.4	2.2	0.2	1.0	1.1
Springfield	2.0	93.5	3.9	1.7	1.7	0.2	1.2	2.3	95.7	2.5	0.7	0.9	1.0
University City	1.8	50.6	46.4	0.6	3.3	0.1	0.9	1.6	49.1	48.2	0.1	2.2	1.1
Wildwood	0.8	95.5	1.8	0.4	2.7	0.0	0.5	1.4	0.0	0.0	0.0	0.0	0.0
MONTANA	1.7	92.2	0.5	7.4	0.8	0.1	0.9	2.0	92.7	0.3	6.0	0.5	1.5
Billings	2.1	93.7	0.9	4.5	0.9	0.1	1.9	4.2	94.6	0.5	3.2	0.6	3.1
Bozeman	1.5	96.1	0.5	1.9	2.1	0.2	0.9	1.6	95.9	0.3	1.8	1.5	1.4
Butte-Silver Bow	1.4	96.7	0.3	3.0	0.7	0.1	0.8	2.7	97.4	0.0	1.1	0.6	2.2
Great Falls	2.5	92.2	1.4	6.6	1.4	0.2	0.9	2.4	93.1	1.0	4.6	0.8	1.7
Helena	1.7	96.4	0.4	3.0	1.1	0.1	0.7	1.7	96.6	0.2	2.3	0.6	1.3
Missoula	1.9	95.3	0.6	3.4	1.6	0.2	0.8	1.8	95.5	0.3	2.4	1.4	1.3
NEBRASKA	1.4	90.8	4.4	1.3	1.6	0.1	3.3	5.5	93.8	3.6	0.8	0.8	2.3
Bellevue	2.5	88.0	7.0	1.1	3.0	0.2	3.4	5.9	89.4	6.5	0.4	2.4	3.9
Fremont	0.8	96.0	0.7	0.7	0.8	0.2	2.6	4.3	98.7	0.3	0.4	0.4	0.7
Grand Island	1.4	88.0	0.6	0.6	1.5	0.2	10.5	15.9	96.0	0.3	0.3	1.3	4.8
Kearney	1.2	96.2	1.0	0.7	1.2	0.1	2.1	4.1	97.3	0.5	0.3	0.5	2.7
Lincoln	2.0	91.0	3.8	1.2	3.5	0.1	2.4	3.6	94.5	2.4	0.6	1.7	2.0
Omaha	1.9	80.0	14.2	1.2	2.1	0.1	4.5	7.5	83.9	13.1	0.7	1.0	3.1

[1] Hispanic persons may be of any race.

Table D. Cities

| City | Population and population characteristics, 2000 — Age (percent) | | | | | | | | | | |
| | Under 5 years | 5 to 17 years | 18 to 24 years | 25 to 34 years | 35 to 44 years | 45 to 54 years | 55 to 64 years | 65 to 74 years | 75 years and over | Median age (years) | Percent Female |
	28	29	30	31	32	33	34	35	36	37	38
MINNESOTA—Cont'd											
Plymouth	7.0	20.1	7.4	13.8	19.2	16.1	8.9	4.8	2.8	36.1	50.7
Richfield	6.0	14.2	9.3	16.9	16.5	12.7	8.0	7.1	9.3	37.1	51.0
Rochester	7.5	18.3	9.1	16.2	17.2	12.5	7.7	5.5	6.0	34.3	51.4
Roseville	4.6	13.7	11.1	12.4	14.4	13.3	10.4	9.2	11.0	41.0	53.5
St. Cloud	5.5	15.2	24.1	14.2	13.4	11.1	6.2	5.2	5.1	28.2	49.6
St. Louis Park	6.0	12.7	8.7	21.2	16.5	12.8	7.4	6.1	8.6	35.7	52.5
St. Paul	7.6	19.5	12.5	16.8	15.3	11.9	6.2	4.6	5.7	31.0	51.6
Shoreview	5.5	20.6	6.9	10.3	18.2	18.8	9.9	5.9	3.8	39.2	51.5
Winona	4.5	13.5	27.5	10.5	11.7	11.0	7.0	5.8	8.4	28.8	53.0
Woodbury	9.6	21.0	5.9	16.8	20.2	13.8	6.6	3.6	2.5	33.4	51.5
MISSISSIPPI	7.2	20.1	10.9	13.4	15.0	12.7	8.6	6.5	5.5	33.8	51.7
Biloxi	7.3	16.9	14.3	15.1	15.2	11.5	7.7	6.7	5.3	32.5	49.5
Columbus	7.1	18.9	12.0	13.5	13.1	11.7	8.1	7.3	8.2	33.8	54.8
Greenville	8.6	22.8	10.1	12.6	13.6	12.6	7.8	6.0	5.8	31.5	53.9
Gulfport	7.1	18.9	11.1	14.8	15.6	12.7	8.3	6.5	4.9	33.6	50.4
Hattiesburg	6.7	14.8	24.4	15.0	11.3	9.6	6.3	5.5	6.3	27.1	54.0
Jackson	7.8	20.7	12.4	14.5	14.6	12.1	7.0	5.5	5.4	31.0	53.5
Meridian	7.6	19.6	9.9	13.3	13.3	11.8	8.0	7.8	8.7	34.6	54.3
Pascagoula	7.8	19.0	12.0	14.2	14.7	12.0	8.3	6.5	5.4	32.6	49.6
Southaven	7.6	19.6	9.0	16.7	15.8	12.9	9.7	5.5	3.4	33.1	51.2
Tupelo	7.5	20.0	8.1	14.5	16.0	12.8	8.7	6.1	6.3	34.9	53.0
Vicksburg	7.9	20.4	9.3	13.3	14.6	12.0	7.6	6.9	7.9	34.3	54.7
MISSOURI	6.6	18.9	9.6	13.2	15.9	13.3	9.1	7.0	6.5	36.1	51.4
Ballwin	7.3	19.8	6.4	12.1	17.8	14.8	9.7	7.6	4.6	37.6	51.5
Blue Springs	7.4	22.1	8.7	14.8	17.2	15.1	7.7	3.9	3.2	33.1	51.1
Cape Girardeau	5.4	15.2	18.4	12.7	12.9	12.2	7.7	6.9	8.6	33.6	52.8
Chesterfield	5.6	19.1	5.9	8.9	16.2	18.0	11.7	7.3	7.4	41.8	52.2
Columbia	5.8	14.0	26.7	15.9	12.8	10.5	5.8	4.1	4.5	26.8	52.1
Florissant	6.5	18.1	8.2	13.5	16.5	11.7	8.4	9.0	8.1	37.1	52.8
Gladstone	5.4	15.6	8.6	13.1	15.1	15.3	11.1	8.8	7.0	40.0	51.9
Hazelwood	6.1	18.5	9.7	14.8	16.9	13.6	8.8	6.6	5.0	35.6	52.0
Independence	6.6	17.3	8.7	13.2	15.7	13.4	9.6	8.1	7.4	37.8	52.2
Jefferson City	5.8	15.0	11.0	15.6	16.4	14.2	7.8	6.7	7.3	36.5	48.7
Joplin	7.1	16.1	13.5	13.6	13.7	12.1	8.2	7.4	8.3	34.7	52.5
Kansas City	7.2	18.2	9.7	16.4	16.1	12.8	7.9	6.2	5.6	34.0	51.7
Kirkwood	6.0	17.4	5.9	11.9	15.7	15.7	9.2	8.1	10.1	41.1	54.3
Lee's Summit	8.0	21.1	6.6	14.1	19.0	13.6	7.3	4.7	5.6	35.1	52.1
Liberty	6.7	20.9	10.4	13.4	16.8	13.7	7.7	5.2	5.2	34.0	52.1
Maryland Heights	5.9	15.6	9.8	20.2	17.1	12.9	9.1	5.6	3.9	34.2	50.6
O'Fallon	10.5	22.9	6.4	18.6	20.2	9.7	5.6	3.8	2.3	31.1	50.7
Raytown	5.8	16.7	7.8	12.4	15.6	13.3	9.2	9.5	9.8	39.8	53.0
St. Charles	6.2	17.1	12.0	14.1	16.4	13.3	8.7	6.4	5.8	35.4	50.9
St. Joseph	6.4	17.7	11.6	13.4	15.1	12.2	8.1	7.2	8.2	35.6	51.1
St. Louis	6.7	19.0	10.6	15.6	15.3	11.8	7.2	6.6	7.1	33.7	53.0
St. Peters	7.4	22.5	7.4	13.9	19.7	14.5	6.7	4.4	3.4	34.2	51.3
Springfield	5.9	14.0	17.4	14.5	13.5	11.8	7.9	7.0	7.9	33.5	51.8
University City	6.1	15.7	11.3	16.4	14.8	13.1	9.4	6.8	6.5	35.4	54.3
Wildwood	8.2	25.0	4.8	10.0	21.5	17.6	7.6	3.4	2.1	36.1	50.8
MONTANA	6.1	19.4	9.5	11.4	15.7	15.0	9.4	6.9	6.5	37.5	50.2
Billings	6.5	17.5	10.1	13.2	15.5	13.7	8.6	7.2	7.7	36.8	51.9
Bozeman	5.0	11.1	33.0	17.1	11.5	10.1	4.3	3.2	4.8	25.4	47.4
Butte-Silver Bow	5.8	17.9	9.6	11.2	15.4	14.2	9.8	7.7	8.3	38.9	50.6
Great Falls	6.4	18.5	9.0	12.0	15.8	13.2	9.5	7.7	8.0	37.8	51.5
Helena	5.8	16.6	11.1	11.4	15.2	16.7	9.3	6.4	7.5	38.8	52.4
Missoula	5.3	14.4	20.7	15.7	13.7	13.1	6.6	4.7	5.6	30.3	50.3
NEBRASKA	6.8	19.5	10.2	13.0	15.4	13.2	8.3	6.8	6.8	35.3	50.7
Bellevue	7.1	20.3	10.2	14.7	16.3	12.7	9.0	6.0	3.5	33.5	50.4
Fremont	6.3	17.9	11.0	11.9	14.8	12.3	8.4	8.4	9.1	37.0	52.4
Grand Island	7.8	19.1	9.5	13.8	14.9	12.9	7.8	6.9	7.3	34.8	50.5
Kearney	6.7	15.5	23.9	13.9	12.3	11.1	6.0	4.7	6.0	27.3	51.9
Lincoln	6.7	16.3	16.4	15.9	14.8	12.6	6.9	5.2	5.2	31.3	50.2
Omaha	7.2	18.4	11.0	15.5	15.4	12.9	7.8	6.1	5.7	33.5	51.3

Table D. Cities

	Population and population characteristics, 1990										Population—change, 1980–2000				
	Age (percent)										Total persons			Percent change	
City	Under 5 years	5 to 17 years	18 to 24 years	25 to 34 years	35 to 44 years	45 to 54 years	55 to 64 years	65 to 74 years	75 years and over	Percent Female	2000	1990	1980	1990–2000	1980–1990
	39	40	41	42	43	44	45	46	47	48	49	50	51	52	53
MINNESOTA—Cont'd															
Plymouth	8.0	19.5	9.2	19.7	19.1	13.0	6.6	3.6	1.3	50.3	65 894	50 889	31 614	29.5	61.0
Richfield	6.2	13.1	10.0	20.6	14.2	9.3	9.7	10.8	6.1	52.3	34 439	35 710	37 851	-3.6	-5.7
Rochester	8.7	17.1	10.0	21.7	14.9	9.7	7.0	5.4	5.6	52.3	85 806	70 729	57 890	21.3	22.2
Roseville	5.5	13.8	11.3	16.3	13.2	11.8	11.3	9.8	7.0	53.2	33 690	33 485	35 820	0.6	-6.5
St. Cloud	6.2	14.3	28.0	17.5	11.3	6.3	6.2	5.5	4.7	50.9	59 107	48 812	42 566	21.1	14.7
St. Louis Park	6.4	11.4	9.5	24.3	14.8	9.2	8.3	8.6	7.5	53.6	44 126	43 787	42 931	0.8	2.0
St. Paul	8.4	16.1	12.2	20.4	14.6	7.6	6.9	7.0	6.8	52.8	287 151	272 235	270 230	5.5	0.7
Shoreview	8.4	19.7	7.4	19.1	19.9	12.7	7.2	4.3	1.3	50.9	25 924	24 587	17 300	5.4	42.1
Winona	5.3	13.7	26.1	13.0	11.8	7.1	7.0	7.4	8.8	53.1	27 069	25 435	25 075	6.4	1.4
Woodbury	9.0	22.0	6.8	19.2	20.5	11.6	6.1	2.6	2.1	51.7	46 463	20 075	10 297	131.4	95.0
MISSISSIPPI	7.6	21.4	11.4	15.5	13.6	9.6	8.3	7.0	5.5	52.2	2 844 658	2 575 475	2 520 770	10.5	2.2
Biloxi	8.6	16.9	16.9	19.6	11.5	7.0	8.0	6.9	4.6	48.4	50 644	46 319	49 311	9.3	-6.1
Columbus	7.9	19.9	13.0	14.2	13.1	8.2	9.1	8.2	6.3	55.0	25 944	23 799	27 383	9.0	-13.1
Greenville	8.5	25.2	9.6	14.5	13.5	8.6	7.9	6.9	5.4	53.8	41 633	45 226	40 613	-7.9	11.4
Gulfport	7.4	17.9	10.8	17.4	12.9	9.6	9.5	8.9	5.6	51.0	71 127	64 045	39 676	11.1	61.4
Hattiesburg	7.1	16.5	22.6	16.5	11.2	7.1	6.4	6.6	6.1	54.2	44 779	45 325	40 829	-1.2	11.0
Jackson	7.7	19.8	12.1	17.9	14.4	8.8	7.7	6.6	5.0	53.7	184 256	202 062	202 893	-8.8	-0.4
Meridian	7.5	19.7	9.8	15.3	14.1	8.2	8.9	9.2	7.2	54.5	39 968	41 036	46 577	-2.6	-11.9
Pascagoula	8.1	20.0	10.8	16.7	13.4	10.9	8.6	6.8	4.7	51.2	26 200	25 899	29 318	1.2	-11.7
Southaven	7.1	21.2	10.4	17.0	15.9	14.3	7.8	4.2	2.3	51.4	28 977	17 949	16 071	61.4	11.7
Tupelo	7.9	20.0	8.7	17.4	14.7	11.1	8.0	6.6	5.6	53.4	34 211	30 685	23 905	11.5	28.4
Vicksburg	7.5	21.0	8.6	15.7	12.3	8.3	8.1	9.8	8.8	55.1	26 407	26 886	25 434	-1.8	5.7
MISSOURI	7.2	18.5	10.1	16.7	14.4	10.2	8.9	7.7	6.3	51.8	5 595 211	5 116 901	4 916 766	9.3	4.1
Ballwin	7.4	19.7	8.2	17.1	18.1	11.9	8.9	5.8	2.9	51.3	31 283	21 406	12 656	46.1	69.1
Blue Springs	8.6	24.5	8.7	17.9	19.5	9.8	4.8	3.5	2.6	51.2	48 080	40 103	25 927	19.9	54.7
Cape Girardeau	6.2	15.2	19.5	15.2	12.2	9.3	8.0	7.5	7.0	53.1	35 349	34 475	34 361	2.5	0.3
Chesterfield	5.8	21.3	8.2	11.4	19.7	15.8	8.6	4.9	4.3	51.1	46 802	42 325	NA	10.6	NA
Columbia	6.0	12.6	30.0	18.5	12.2	6.9	5.1	4.5	4.1	52.0	84 531	69 133	62 061	22.3	11.4
Florissant	6.8	16.8	8.8	18.5	12.7	10.6	12.1	8.9	4.8	52.2	50 497	51 038	55 372	-1.1	-7.8
Gladstone	6.4	16.3	9.8	16.6	15.4	13.3	10.8	7.6	3.8	52.3	26 365	26 243	24 990	0.5	5.0
Hazelwood	6.7	15.5	10.6	20.7	14.7	11.3	10.8	6.6	3.3	52.0	26 206	15 512	12 935	68.9	19.9
Independence	7.1	16.9	9.4	17.6	13.4	11.3	9.9	8.6	5.7	52.5	113 288	112 301	111 806	0.9	0.4
Jefferson City	6.0	15.5	10.8	17.5	15.9	9.7	8.9	8.0	7.7	51.0	39 636	35 517	33 618	11.6	5.6
Joplin	7.1	15.8	11.5	16.8	13.1	9.6	8.9	9.2	8.0	53.7	45 504	40 866	38 869	11.3	5.1
Kansas City	7.7	17.1	9.8	19.7	14.5	9.8	8.6	7.4	5.6	52.4	441 545	434 829	448 154	1.5	-3.0
Kirkwood	6.6	16.4	6.0	15.5	17.2	10.3	9.8	9.6	8.6	54.2	27 324	28 318	27 987	-3.5	1.2
Lee's Summit	8.6	19.8	8.1	19.1	17.2	10.1	6.4	4.3	6.4	52.7	70 700	46 418	28 742	52.3	61.5
Liberty	7.9	18.7	13.5	17.0	15.4	10.5	7.2	5.9	3.9	51.8	26 232	20 459	16 217	28.2	26.2
Maryland Heights	6.5	13.5	12.0	26.1	15.2	12.2	7.5	4.2	2.8	50.5	25 756	25 440	NA	1.2	NA
O'Fallon	10.6	20.5	10.4	23.5	14.4	8.0	6.2	4.0	2.5	51.1	46 169	17 427	NA	164.9	NA
Raytown	6.2	15.2	7.9	16.3	14.6	9.9	12.0	11.0	6.9	53.4	30 388	30 601	31 759	-0.7	-3.6
St. Charles	7.7	17.1	11.2	21.3	15.1	9.9	7.9	5.6	4.3	51.2	60 321	50 634	37 379	19.1	35.5
St. Joseph	7.3	18.8	9.6	16.0	13.1	9.1	9.1	8.9	8.1	53.1	73 990	71 852	76 691	3.0	-6.3
St. Louis	8.0	17.3	10.3	18.4	12.8	8.1	8.5	8.5	8.2	54.5	348 189	396 685	453 085	-12.2	-12.4
St. Peters	10.6	23.0	7.1	21.8	20.6	8.3	4.1	3.1	1.4	50.6	51 381	40 660	15 700	26.4	159.0
Springfield	6.2	14.4	17.8	16.4	12.9	8.9	8.1	8.1	7.2	52.7	151 580	140 494	133 116	7.9	5.5
University City	7.1	16.4	10.4	18.1	15.7	10.5	8.0	7.1	6.8	54.1	37 428	40 087	42 738	-6.6	-6.2
Wildwood	NA	NA	NA	NA	NA	NA	NA	NA	NA	NA	32 884	16 527	NA	99.0	NA
MONTANA	7.4	20.4	8.8	15.4	15.9	10.3	8.6	7.6	5.7	50.5	902 195	799 065	786 690	12.9	1.6
Billings	7.4	18.4	9.4	17.4	15.3	10.0	8.6	7.8	5.7	52.3	89 847	81 125	66 798	10.8	21.4
Bozeman	5.5	12.7	30.3	18.1	13.2	6.5	4.6	4.8	4.2	48.8	27 509	22 660	21 645	21.4	4.7
Butte-Silver Bow	6.8	18.2	9.0	14.5	14.7	10.3	9.5	9.4	7.6	50.9	34 606	33 941	NA	2.0	NA
Great Falls	7.4	18.7	8.5	16.5	14.7	10.6	9.1	8.2	6.3	52.1	56 690	55 125	56 725	2.8	-2.8
Helena	6.8	18.1	9.7	15.5	17.2	11.0	7.6	7.4	6.5	52.6	25 780	24 609	23 938	4.8	2.8
Missoula	6.6	16.0	16.8	17.8	16.0	8.2	6.3	6.3	6.0	51.6	57 053	42 918	33 387	32.9	28.5
NEBRASKA	7.6	19.6	9.9	16.3	14.5	9.5	8.6	7.5	6.7	51.3	1 711 263	1 578 417	1 569 825	8.4	0.5
Bellevue	7.8	19.6	12.7	19.2	15.2	10.8	7.9	4.6	2.3	50.0	44 382	39 240	21 813	13.1	79.9
Fremont	6.8	18.3	10.2	15.0	13.8	9.3	9.5	8.8	8.3	52.8	25 174	23 680	23 979	6.3	-1.2
Grand Island	7.9	20.3	8.5	16.6	14.5	9.1	8.4	7.9	6.8	51.9	42 940	39 487	33 180	8.7	19.0
Kearney	6.8	16.2	25.7	15.7	12.0	6.9	5.7	5.4	5.5	52.1	27 431	24 396	21 158	12.4	15.3
Lincoln	7.2	16.2	16.6	18.8	14.9	8.4	7.0	5.9	5.1	51.4	225 581	191 972	171 932	17.5	11.7
Omaha	7.6	17.9	10.9	18.5	14.2	9.5	8.6	7.2	5.6	52.2	390 007	342 862	314 267	13.8	9.1

Table D. Cities

City	Total population	Total in households	House-holder	Spouse	Child Total	Own child under 18 years	Other relatives Total	Under 18 years	Nonrelatives Total	Unmar-ried partner	Total in group quarters	Correctional institutions	Nursing homes	Other institutions	College dormitories	Military quarters	Other
	54	55	56	57	58	59	60	61	62	63	64	65	66	67	68	69	70
MINNESOTA—Cont'd																	
Plymouth	65 894	97.8	37.7	23.0	31.1	26.4	1.9	0.4	4.1	1.6	2.2	1.2	0.1	0.1	0.2	0.0	0.6
Richfield	34 439	98.6	43.8	19.0	24.5	18.6	4.5	1.2	6.9	2.4	1.4	0.0	0.7	0.0	0.0	0.0	0.7
Rochester	85 806	96.6	39.8	20.6	28.5	24.5	2.4	0.7	5.3	1.9	3.4	1.1	0.6	0.1	0.1	0.0	1.4
Roseville	33 690	95.1	43.3	21.3	22.8	17.4	2.4	0.6	5.3	1.9	4.9	0.2	1.9	0.0	2.5	0.0	0.3
St. Cloud	59 107	92.0	38.3	15.9	23.6	19.5	2.0	0.5	12.2	2.6	8.0	1.5	0.9	0.4	4.2	0.0	1.0
St. Louis Park	44 126	97.9	47.1	18.5	22.0	17.7	2.8	0.7	7.5	2.5	2.1	0.0	1.2	0.0	0.0	0.0	0.8
St. Paul	287 151	96.1	39.0	14.1	29.9	24.3	5.3	2.0	7.7	2.7	3.9	0.2	0.8	0.1	1.8	0.0	0.9
Shoreview	25 924	99.3	39.1	23.6	31.4	25.4	1.9	0.6	3.4	1.5	0.7	0.0	0.0	0.0	0.0	0.0	0.7
Winona	27 069	86.5	38.1	15.4	21.1	17.0	1.6	0.5	10.3	2.1	13.5	0.1	2.0	0.0	10.3	0.0	1.1
Woodbury	46 463	99.1	35.9	24.0	34.1	29.8	2.0	0.5	3.1	1.5	0.9	0.0	0.8	0.0	0.0	0.0	0.2
MISSISSIPPI	2 844 658	96.6	36.8	18.3	31.1	23.1	6.8	3.6	3.7	1.6	3.4	0.9	0.6	0.2	1.0	0.2	0.3
Biloxi	50 644	93.5	38.7	17.2	27.5	21.7	4.7	2.0	5.4	2.1	6.5	0.1	0.4	0.5	0.1	5.1	0.2
Columbus	25 944	93.9	38.8	14.8	29.3	21.3	7.3	3.9	3.8	1.7	6.1	0.8	1.9	0.8	2.4	0.0	0.2
Greenville	41 633	98.3	35.5	13.4	34.3	24.5	10.9	6.5	4.1	2.3	1.7	0.4	0.9	0.1	0.0	0.0	0.3
Gulfport	71 127	95.2	37.9	16.1	28.9	21.8	6.5	3.3	5.9	2.5	4.8	1.5	0.3	0.3	0.1	1.6	0.9
Hattiesburg	44 779	88.5	38.6	12.0	23.6	17.6	6.6	3.3	7.7	1.9	11.5	1.0	1.3	0.8	7.7	0.0	0.6
Jackson	184 256	96.1	36.8	13.0	32.5	23.3	8.6	4.5	5.2	2.2	3.9	0.5	0.6	0.3	1.8	0.0	0.8
Meridian	39 968	95.4	39.9	14.5	31.0	23.4	6.3	3.1	3.7	1.7	4.6	0.5	1.0	1.9	0.7	0.0	0.5
Pascagoula	26 200	94.9	37.7	16.8	30.6	23.1	5.2	2.6	4.6	1.9	5.1	1.2	0.5	0.0	0.0	3.2	0.2
Southaven	28 977	99.6	38.0	21.7	30.8	24.6	4.7	2.0	4.4	1.8	0.4	0.0	0.4	0.0	0.0	0.0	0.0
Tupelo	34 211	96.7	39.2	18.9	30.5	24.4	4.9	2.4	3.3	1.5	3.3	0.5	1.6	0.5	0.0	0.0	0.6
Vicksburg	26 407	97.7	39.2	13.7	32.0	23.4	8.1	4.3	4.7	2.4	2.3	0.5	1.4	0.0	0.0	0.0	0.4
MISSOURI	5 595 211	97.1	39.2	20.4	29.2	23.1	3.8	1.7	4.5	2.0	2.9	0.6	0.9	0.1	0.8	0.1	0.4
Ballwin	31 283	100.0	37.7	24.7	32.7	26.1	2.4	0.7	2.5	1.0	0.0	0.0	0.0	0.0	0.0	0.0	0.0
Blue Springs	48 080	99.5	36.0	22.7	34.2	27.8	3.1	1.3	3.6	1.7	0.5	0.0	0.4	0.0	0.0	0.0	0.1
Cape Girardeau	35 349	91.3	40.7	17.8	23.6	18.7	3.2	1.2	6.1	1.9	8.7	0.1	2.7	0.1	5.4	0.0	0.5
Chesterfield	46 802	97.7	38.6	25.3	29.7	23.9	1.9	0.5	2.2	0.9	2.3	0.0	2.1	0.1	0.0	0.0	0.0
Columbia	84 531	90.0	39.9	15.2	21.6	18.4	2.6	0.9	10.8	2.2	10.0	0.0	0.6	0.1	8.8	0.0	0.5
Florissant	50 497	98.5	40.4	20.1	30.5	22.3	3.9	1.7	3.5	1.8	1.5	0.0	1.1	0.0	0.1	0.0	0.3
Gladstone	26 365	98.9	43.6	22.2	25.4	19.3	3.5	1.4	4.3	2.1	1.1	0.0	0.9	0.0	0.0	0.0	0.2
Hazelwood	26 206	99.5	41.8	18.6	29.6	22.3	4.3	1.8	5.2	2.6	0.5	0.0	0.0	0.0	0.0	0.0	0.5
Independence	113 288	99.0	41.8	20.0	27.5	21.0	4.5	2.1	5.1	2.4	1.0	0.0	0.3	0.2	0.0	0.0	0.5
Jefferson City	39 636	88.1	39.8	17.7	23.7	19.4	2.6	0.9	4.2	1.7	11.9	8.9	1.2	0.0	1.3	0.0	0.6
Joplin	45 504	95.8	42.0	18.6	25.7	20.8	3.4	1.4	6.1	2.6	4.2	0.1	1.4	0.1	2.2	0.0	0.5
Kansas City	441 545	97.9	41.7	15.9	28.2	21.9	6.0	2.7	6.2	2.5	2.1	0.4	0.5	0.2	0.3	0.0	0.6
Kirkwood	27 324	98.8	43.1	21.8	28.1	22.1	2.7	1.1	3.1	1.3	1.2	0.0	0.8	0.1	0.0	0.0	0.3
Lee's Summit	70 700	98.9	37.4	23.2	33.0	27.9	2.3	0.9	3.1	1.4	1.1	0.0	1.1	0.0	0.0	0.0	0.0
Liberty	26 232	95.1	36.3	21.5	31.0	25.9	2.7	1.1	3.7	1.6	4.9	0.7	0.9	0.1	2.4	0.0	0.8
Maryland Heights	25 756	98.7	43.9	19.4	25.5	19.8	3.5	1.2	6.3	2.2	1.3	0.0	1.0	0.2	0.0	0.0	0.1
O'Fallon	46 169	99.2	33.3	23.3	37.0	31.9	2.6	1.0	3.0	1.7	0.8	0.0	0.2	0.0	0.0	0.0	0.6
Raytown	30 388	98.2	42.3	20.6	26.7	19.9	4.2	1.8	4.4	2.0	1.8	0.0	1.5	0.2	0.0	0.0	0.1
St. Charles	60 321	95.6	40.1	19.8	27.8	21.9	2.7	1.0	5.2	2.4	4.4	0.4	0.7	0.1	2.8	0.0	0.3
St. Joseph	73 990	93.8	39.2	18.3	27.3	21.6	3.7	1.7	5.2	2.4	6.2	2.9	1.0	0.4	1.3	0.0	0.7
St. Louis	348 189	96.9	42.2	11.0	29.1	21.0	8.2	3.9	6.4	2.8	3.1	0.3	0.8	0.2	0.8	0.0	0.9
St. Peters	51 381	99.7	35.9	22.5	35.3	28.3	2.9	1.2	3.1	1.5	0.3	0.0	0.2	0.0	0.0	0.0	0.0
Springfield	151 580	92.7	42.7	17.3	22.4	18.0	3.2	1.2	7.2	2.5	7.3	1.0	0.9	0.1	4.5	0.0	0.7
University City	37 428	98.9	44.0	16.0	25.9	18.6	5.9	2.8	7.2	2.0	1.1	0.0	0.6	0.1	0.0	0.0	0.5
Wildwood	32 884	99.5	33.0	26.0	37.8	32.6	1.4	0.4	1.3	0.7	0.5	0.0	0.2	0.1	0.0	0.0	0.2
MONTANA	902 195	97.3	39.8	21.3	28.2	23.5	2.9	1.3	5.1	2.0	2.7	0.5	0.7	0.2	0.8	0.0	0.6
Billings	89 847	97.0	41.8	19.7	27.1	22.2	2.9	1.2	5.6	2.3	3.0	0.6	1.1	0.1	0.8	0.0	0.4
Bozeman	27 509	89.5	39.5	14.2	17.6	15.3	1.8	0.3	16.2	2.6	10.5	0.2	1.0	0.0	9.3	0.0	0.1
Butte-Silver Bow	34 606	96.8	41.7	19.9	28.0	21.8	2.8	1.2	4.4	1.9	3.2	0.8	1.1	0.2	0.6	0.0	0.5
Great Falls	56 690	97.3	42.0	19.9	27.8	23.1	2.6	1.1	5.0	2.1	2.7	0.8	0.8	0.6	0.0	0.0	0.5
Helena	25 780	95.7	44.8	19.0	24.8	21.1	2.1	0.7	5.0	2.1	4.3	0.2	1.0	0.0	1.9	0.0	1.2
Missoula	57 053	94.2	42.3	16.0	22.2	18.3	2.3	0.7	11.4	3.1	5.8	0.6	0.2	0.0	3.6	0.0	1.3
NEBRASKA	1 711 263	97.0	38.9	21.1	29.6	24.6	2.8	1.1	4.7	1.7	3.0	0.4	0.9	0.2	1.1	0.0	0.3
Bellevue	44 382	99.5	38.2	21.1	31.8	25.2	3.4	1.5	5.0	1.9	0.5	0.0	0.2	0.0	0.1	0.0	0.2
Fremont	25 174	96.3	40.4	21.4	27.4	22.7	2.3	0.9	4.8	1.9	3.7	0.1	1.4	0.0	2.0	0.0	0.3
Grand Island	42 940	97.5	38.3	20.3	29.4	24.7	4.1	1.5	5.4	2.0	2.5	0.3	1.5	0.1	0.0	0.0	0.7
Kearney	27 431	91.2	38.5	17.6	24.4	21.0	2.0	0.5	8.8	2.1	8.8	0.2	1.0	0.2	7.1	0.0	0.3
Lincoln	225 581	94.8	40.1	18.6	26.1	21.7	2.6	0.8	7.4	2.2	5.2	1.2	0.4	0.0	3.1	0.0	0.4
Omaha	390 007	97.3	40.2	17.6	29.2	23.2	4.3	1.7	6.0	2.2	2.7	0.4	0.7	0.3	0.7	0.0	0.5

Table D. Cities

City	Households by type, 2000												Households, 1990		
	Total households	Family households						Nonfamily households			Average house-hold size	Average family size	Total house-holds	Female house-holder[1]	House-holder living alone
		Total	With own children under 18 years	Married couple		Female householder[1]		Total	Householder living alone						
				Total	With own children under 18 years	Total	With own children under 18 years		Total	65 years and over					
	71	72	73	74	75	76	77	78	79	80	81	82	83	84	85
MINNESOTA—Cont'd															
Plymouth	24 820	71.1	37.8	61.2	31.6	7.6	5.0	28.9	21.8	4.7	2.60	3.09	18 361	7.5	17.7
Richfield	15 073	57.9	24.4	43.4	16.7	10.5	6.0	42.1	33.7	12.0	2.25	2.89	15 551	9.8	29.8
Rochester	34 116	63.0	32.6	51.8	25.3	8.5	5.7	37.0	29.7	8.5	2.43	3.06	27 913	8.3	29.1
Roseville	14 598	58.9	22.2	49.2	17.3	7.2	3.9	41.1	33.6	13.9	2.20	2.82	13 562	7.8	27.0
St. Cloud	22 652	54.1	27.3	41.4	19.1	9.4	6.4	45.9	30.2	8.0	2.40	3.00	17 926	10.4	27.9
St. Louis Park	20 782	50.8	22.0	39.3	15.8	8.6	5.0	49.2	37.9	10.4	2.08	2.81	19 925	8.4	33.4
St. Paul	112 109	54.4	29.1	36.1	17.8	13.9	9.2	45.6	35.9	9.4	2.46	3.32	110 249	13.0	34.7
Shoreview	10 125	70.8	35.1	60.3	29.1	7.9	4.9	29.2	24.1	6.5	2.54	3.06	8 991	7.7	19.3
Winona	10 301	51.7	23.9	40.4	17.1	8.4	5.4	48.3	35.2	12.8	2.27	2.94	9 334	8.3	32.3
Woodbury	16 676	75.9	43.8	66.8	37.9	6.9	4.6	24.1	18.8	3.3	2.76	3.20	6 927	7.9	16.1
MISSISSIPPI	1 046 434	71.4	34.7	49.8	22.4	17.3	10.1	28.6	24.6	9.6	2.63	3.14	911 374	15.9	23.4
Biloxi	19 588	63.2	31.4	44.6	20.1	14.0	9.0	36.8	30.1	10.6	2.42	3.02	16 644	13.0	28.9
Columbus	10 062	63.8	29.8	38.0	14.9	21.7	13.1	36.2	31.3	12.2	2.42	3.07	9 138	21.7	30.7
Greenville	14 784	70.5	35.8	37.8	16.5	27.7	16.7	29.5	25.8	10.4	2.77	3.34	15 322	24.8	24.3
Gulfport	26 943	65.5	32.1	42.6	18.6	18.2	11.0	34.5	27.7	8.5	2.51	3.07	15 797	16.5	29.6
Hattiesburg	17 295	54.3	25.3	31.1	12.0	19.4	11.7	45.7	34.4	9.3	2.29	3.01	15 911	19.0	33.4
Jackson	67 841	65.6	33.7	35.4	16.1	25.3	15.3	34.4	28.9	9.0	2.61	3.24	71 865	20.4	27.5
Meridian	15 966	62.8	31.1	36.2	15.0	23.3	14.6	37.2	33.2	14.0	2.39	3.06	16 170	20.7	31.0
Pascagoula	9 878	68.1	34.5	44.6	19.6	18.8	12.5	31.9	27.0	9.7	2.52	3.05	9 774	16.3	25.7
Southaven	11 007	73.9	36.8	57.1	26.6	12.4	7.7	26.1	21.3	5.7	2.62	3.04	6 115	11.7	13.0
Tupelo	13 395	68.0	34.9	48.3	22.6	16.2	10.4	32.0	28.0	8.8	2.47	3.04	11 705	14.5	26.1
Vicksburg	10 364	63.8	32.2	34.9	15.0	24.2	14.7	36.2	32.0	13.6	2.49	3.15	8 268	21.7	33.3
MISSOURI	2 194 594	67.3	31.9	52.0	22.7	11.6	7.1	32.7	27.3	10.3	2.48	3.02	1 961 206	10.6	26.0
Ballwin	11 797	75.8	37.2	65.6	31.4	8.0	4.6	24.2	20.6	7.3	2.65	3.09	7 849	7.9	17.6
Blue Springs	17 286	77.3	42.5	63.1	33.0	10.5	7.0	22.7	18.1	4.8	2.77	3.16	13 529	9.5	14.9
Cape Girardeau	14 380	57.7	25.7	43.8	17.6	10.9	6.7	42.3	33.6	11.5	2.24	2.90	13 442	10.1	30.5
Chesterfield	18 060	72.6	33.2	65.5	29.3	5.4	3.0	27.4	23.6	8.8	2.53	3.03	13 115	5.1	17.4
Columbia	33 689	51.3	26.1	38.2	17.5	10.3	7.1	48.7	33.1	6.5	2.26	2.92	25 841	9.7	32.2
Florissant	20 399	67.1	30.7	49.8	21.3	13.2	7.4	32.9	28.8	12.3	2.44	3.01	19 177	9.8	21.6
Gladstone	11 484	64.3	25.7	51.0	18.3	10.3	5.9	35.7	29.9	9.1	2.27	2.82	10 535	8.8	24.0
Hazelwood	10 954	61.3	29.6	44.4	19.8	12.7	7.5	38.7	32.1	9.7	2.38	3.05	6 355	11.3	28.4
Independence	47 390	64.5	28.1	47.9	18.5	12.3	7.3	35.5	30.1	11.3	2.37	2.93	45 322	10.3	26.1
Jefferson City	15 794	58.3	27.9	44.4	19.1	10.8	7.1	41.7	36.1	11.9	2.21	2.90	14 162	9.5	34.4
Joplin	19 101	60.3	27.5	44.4	17.6	12.3	7.7	39.7	32.4	12.5	2.28	2.89	17 474	10.9	32.7
Kansas City	183 981	58.4	28.1	38.0	16.2	16.0	9.8	41.6	34.1	9.4	2.35	3.06	177 607	15.1	32.5
Kirkwood	11 763	61.7	28.0	50.5	22.3	9.0	4.6	38.3	33.5	14.9	2.29	2.98	11 212	8.8	28.6
Lee's Summit	26 417	73.8	40.8	62.1	32.9	8.9	6.1	26.2	22.0	9.2	2.65	3.12	17 632	8.6	23.4
Liberty	9 511	73.0	38.9	59.2	29.8	10.9	7.4	27.0	22.4	7.9	2.62	3.08	7 175	8.9	22.2
Maryland Heights	11 302	56.8	25.8	44.2	19.0	9.5	5.4	43.2	33.8	5.5	2.25	2.94	10 667	7.8	30.0
O'Fallon	15 389	81.9	50.6	69.8	42.3	8.6	6.0	18.1	14.1	3.4	2.98	3.30	6 382	8.9	16.2
Raytown	12 855	64.6	27.1	48.6	17.8	12.6	7.5	35.4	30.3	13.3	2.32	2.88	12 697	9.3	26.0
St. Charles	24 210	63.3	30.1	49.4	21.5	10.2	6.5	36.7	29.6	9.1	2.38	2.98	21 670	9.2	27.6
St. Joseph	29 026	63.6	30.1	46.7	19.6	12.8	8.0	36.4	30.4	13.2	2.39	2.98	28 411	12.2	29.1
St. Louis	147 076	52.3	25.4	26.2	10.8	21.3	12.4	47.7	40.3	12.9	2.30	3.19	164 931	20.5	39.2
St. Peters	18 435	75.6	42.3	62.8	34.3	9.7	6.2	24.4	20.3	6.4	2.78	3.24	15 223	7.1	14.4
Springfield	64 691	55.2	24.0	40.7	15.2	10.9	6.7	44.8	35.3	11.6	2.17	2.82	57 353	10.1	31.5
University City	16 453	55.4	23.7	36.3	14.5	16.3	8.2	44.6	34.2	10.2	2.25	2.96	16 556	16.2	30.1
Wildwood	10 837	85.3	51.0	79.0	46.7	4.6	3.2	14.7	12.4	4.0	3.02	3.32	NA	NA	NA
MONTANA	358 667	66.2	31.2	53.6	23.0	8.9	5.9	33.8	27.4	10.0	2.45	2.99	306 163	8.6	26.3
Billings	37 525	61.7	29.2	47.2	20.0	10.8	7.0	38.3	31.3	11.4	2.32	2.93	33 181	10.5	29.4
Bozeman	10 877	46.1	22.3	36.0	16.1	7.3	5.0	53.9	30.4	6.7	2.26	2.85	8 751	8.3	30.2
Butte-Silver Bow	14 432	61.9	28.0	47.8	19.7	10.5	6.2	38.1	32.8	13.7	2.32	2.97	13 899	8.8	31.5
Great Falls	23 834	62.3	30.1	47.4	19.9	11.1	7.8	37.7	31.9	12.4	2.31	2.92	22 639	10.4	29.5
Helena	11 541	56.1	27.1	42.5	17.7	10.4	7.4	43.9	37.5	11.3	2.14	2.83	10 428	11.2	35.1
Missoula	24 141	51.1	24.6	37.9	16.2	10.0	6.6	48.9	33.6	8.9	2.23	2.88	17 677	10.2	33.3
NEBRASKA	666 184	66.6	32.7	54.2	24.9	9.1	6.0	33.4	27.6	10.7	2.49	3.06	602 363	8.3	26.5
Bellevue	16 937	70.5	35.5	55.4	25.7	11.3	7.6	29.5	23.2	6.6	2.61	3.09	11 429	9.9	20.7
Fremont	10 171	65.6	30.7	53.0	22.2	9.4	6.4	34.4	29.1	14.0	2.38	2.93	9 427	7.6	28.7
Grand Island	16 426	67.2	34.3	53.0	24.7	10.4	7.3	32.8	27.1	11.1	2.55	3.09	15 244	9.3	27.8
Kearney	10 549	58.4	30.3	45.7	21.7	9.7	6.9	41.6	28.7	9.5	2.37	2.96	8 973	8.3	27.9
Lincoln	90 485	59.2	29.5	46.3	21.4	9.5	6.3	40.8	30.4	8.5	2.36	2.99	75 402	9.1	28.8
Omaha	156 738	60.6	30.0	43.8	20.0	13.0	8.2	39.4	31.9	9.4	2.42	3.10	133 842	13.3	30.6

[1] No spouse present.

Table D. Cities

City	Percent change of households, 1990–2000	Total housing units	Occupied housing units (percent)	Housing occupancy — Vacant housing units — Total	For seasonal, recreational, or occasional use	Homeowner vacancy rate (percent)	Rental vacancy rate (percent)	Occupied housing units — Total	Percent owner-occupied housing units	Percent renter-occupied housing units	Average household size of owner-occupied units	Average household size of renter-occupied units
	86	87	88	89	90	91	92	93	94	95	96	97
MINNESOTA—Cont'd												
Plymouth	35.2	25 258	98.3	1.7	0.5	0.3	2.1	24 820	76.5	23.5	2.76	2.08
Richfield	-3.1	15 357	98.2	1.8	0.2	0.4	2.4	15 073	67.6	32.4	2.42	1.91
Rochester	22.2	35 346	96.5	3.5	0.5	0.7	4.0	34 116	71.0	29.0	2.64	1.93
Roseville	7.6	14 917	97.9	2.1	0.5	0.5	2.3	14 598	67.5	32.5	2.44	1.69
St. Cloud	26.4	23 249	97.4	2.6	0.3	0.6	2.8	22 652	55.9	44.1	2.66	2.07
St. Louis Park	4.3	21 140	98.3	1.7	0.3	0.4	1.7	20 782	63.6	36.4	2.26	1.77
St. Paul	1.7	115 713	96.9	3.1	0.4	0.7	2.8	112 109	54.8	45.2	2.72	2.15
Shoreview	12.6	10 289	98.4	1.6	0.4	0.5	2.3	10 125	87.2	12.8	2.64	1.91
Winona	10.4	10 666	96.6	3.4	0.2	0.8	4.1	10 301	60.9	39.1	2.46	1.99
Woodbury	140.7	17 541	95.1	4.9	0.6	1.4	13.3	16 676	85.2	14.8	2.87	2.13
MISSISSIPPI	14.8	1 161 953	90.1	9.9	1.9	1.6	9.2	1 046 434	72.3	27.7	2.67	2.52
Biloxi	17.7	22 115	88.6	11.4	1.3	2.4	9.9	19 588	48.9	51.1	2.47	2.37
Columbus	10.1	11 112	90.6	9.4	0.5	2.2	9.2	10 062	54.3	45.7	2.48	2.35
Greenville	-3.5	16 251	91.0	9.0	0.1	1.9	8.6	14 784	55.8	44.2	2.72	2.83
Gulfport	70.6	29 559	91.1	8.9	1.1	2.0	10.3	26 943	58.7	41.3	2.57	2.43
Hattiesburg	8.7	19 258	89.8	10.2	0.5	2.4	9.9	17 295	44.6	55.4	2.47	2.15
Jackson	-5.6	75 678	89.6	10.4	0.4	2.2	11.7	67 841	58.0	42.0	2.68	2.51
Meridian	-1.3	17 890	89.2	10.8	0.3	3.3	8.8	15 966	56.3	43.7	2.43	2.33
Pascagoula	1.1	10 931	90.4	9.6	0.5	1.7	11.7	9 878	56.8	43.2	2.55	2.48
Southaven	80.0	11 462	96.0	4.0	0.2	1.6	5.4	11 007	72.3	27.7	2.65	2.54
Tupelo	14.4	14 551	92.1	7.9	0.4	1.4	10.9	13 395	62.2	37.8	2.59	2.28
Vicksburg	25.4	11 654	88.9	11.1	0.4	2.0	12.3	10 364	56.4	43.6	2.50	2.48
MISSOURI	11.9	2 442 017	89.9	10.1	2.7	2.1	9.0	2 194 594	70.3	29.7	2.59	2.20
Ballwin	50.3	12 062	97.8	2.2	0.2	0.5	5.6	11 797	82.9	17.1	2.76	2.11
Blue Springs	27.8	17 733	97.5	2.5	0.2	1.0	3.7	17 286	74.2	25.8	2.92	2.34
Cape Girardeau	7.0	15 827	90.9	9.1	0.5	2.9	11.3	14 380	57.3	42.7	2.42	2.01
Chesterfield	37.7	18 738	96.4	3.6	0.7	0.9	6.3	18 060	77.9	22.1	2.75	1.77
Columbia	30.4	35 916	93.8	6.2	0.3	2.5	6.2	33 689	47.3	52.7	2.50	2.04
Florissant	6.4	21 027	97.0	3.0	0.2	1.0	5.8	20 399	76.8	23.2	2.56	2.05
Gladstone	9.0	11 919	96.4	3.6	0.2	1.2	5.8	11 484	68.6	31.4	2.43	1.92
Hazelwood	72.4	11 433	95.8	4.2	0.4	1.5	5.5	10 954	64.6	35.4	2.62	1.95
Independence	4.6	50 213	94.4	5.6	0.2	1.6	7.2	47 390	67.8	32.2	2.47	2.15
Jefferson City	11.5	16 987	93.0	7.0	0.8	2.2	7.4	15 794	58.6	41.4	2.43	1.90
Joplin	9.3	21 328	89.6	10.4	0.3	3.5	10.8	19 101	57.6	42.4	2.36	2.18
Kansas City	3.6	202 334	90.9	9.1	0.3	1.9	9.6	183 981	57.7	42.3	2.52	2.11
Kirkwood	4.9	12 306	95.6	4.4	0.4	1.3	6.2	11 763	77.1	22.9	2.44	1.81
Lee's Summit	49.8	27 311	96.7	3.3	0.2	1.2	5.4	26 417	75.6	24.4	2.86	1.99
Liberty	32.6	9 973	95.4	4.6	0.3	1.8	6.4	9 511	73.5	26.5	2.76	2.24
Maryland Heights	6.0	11 846	95.4	4.6	0.5	0.7	7.4	11 302	62.6	37.4	2.46	1.89
O'Fallon	141.1	15 920	96.7	3.3	0.2	1.9	6.4	15 389	89.5	10.5	3.04	2.42
Raytown	1.2	13 309	96.6	3.4	0.1	1.1	5.5	12 855	73.9	26.1	2.42	2.05
St. Charles	11.7	25 283	95.8	4.2	0.4	0.9	6.2	24 210	64.6	35.4	2.63	1.93
St. Joseph	2.2	31 752	91.4	8.6	0.3	2.0	7.6	29 026	64.8	35.2	2.49	2.20
St. Louis	-10.8	176 354	83.4	16.6	0.3	3.5	11.8	147 076	46.9	53.1	2.49	2.12
St. Peters	21.1	18 776	98.2	1.8	0.2	0.8	3.8	18 435	85.4	14.6	2.89	2.13
Springfield	12.8	69 650	92.9	7.1	0.4	2.5	7.1	64 691	53.7	46.3	2.27	2.06
University City	-0.6	17 485	94.1	5.9	0.2	1.5	6.8	16 453	57.8	42.2	2.47	1.94
Wildwood	NA	11 229	96.5	3.5	0.3	0.8	11.4	10 837	90.4	9.6	3.13	1.98
MONTANA	17.1	412 633	86.9	13.1	5.9	2.2	7.6	358 667	69.1	30.9	2.55	2.22
Billings	13.1	39 293	95.5	4.5	0.4	1.2	5.3	37 525	64.0	36.0	2.48	2.04
Bozeman	24.3	11 577	94.0	6.0	0.9	2.1	4.9	10 877	42.9	57.1	2.43	2.13
Butte-Silver Bow	3.8	16 176	89.2	10.8	1.1	3.1	12.6	14 432	70.4	29.6	2.46	1.99
Great Falls	5.3	25 250	94.4	5.6	0.3	1.4	7.0	23 834	63.0	37.0	2.48	2.03
Helena	10.7	12 133	95.1	4.9	0.5	1.4	5.3	11 541	57.3	42.7	2.35	1.86
Missoula	36.6	25 225	95.7	4.3	0.5	1.0	3.6	24 141	50.2	49.8	2.47	1.98
NEBRASKA	10.6	722 668	92.2	7.8	1.6	1.8	7.6	666 184	67.4	32.6	2.63	2.20
Bellevue	48.2	17 439	97.1	2.9	0.1	0.8	4.1	16 937	66.1	33.9	2.76	2.32
Fremont	7.9	10 576	96.2	3.8	0.2	0.9	4.4	10 171	63.4	36.6	2.51	2.16
Grand Island	7.8	17 421	94.3	5.7	0.1	2.0	7.4	16 426	62.7	37.3	2.71	2.28
Kearney	17.6	11 099	95.0	5.0	0.3	1.9	5.3	10 549	56.5	43.5	2.59	2.08
Lincoln	20.0	95 199	95.0	5.0	0.3	1.3	6.2	90 485	58.0	42.0	2.59	2.05
Omaha	17.1	165 731	94.6	5.4	0.3	1.0	7.2	156 738	59.6	40.4	2.64	2.10

Table D. Cities

STATE Place code	City	Population, 2000				Population, 1990				Population and population characteristics, 2000					
										Race (percent)					
										One race					
		Land area, 2000[1] (sq km)	Total persons	Rank	Per square kilometer	Land area, 1990[1] (sq km)	Total persons	Rank	Per square kilometer	White	Black or African American	American Indian or Alaska Native	Asian	Native Hawaiian and other Pacific Islander	Some other race
		1	2	3	4	5	6	7	8	9	10	11	12	13	14
32 00000	NEVADA......................	284 448.0	1 998 257	X	7.0	284 397.2	1 201 675	X	4.2	75.2	6.8	1.3	4.5	0.4	8.0
32 09700	Carson City......................	371.3	52 457	635	141.3	371.8	40 443	729	108.8	85.3	1.8	2.4	1.8	0.1	6.5
32 31900	Henderson......................	206.4	175 381	120	849.7	185.3	64 948	381	350.5	84.5	3.8	0.7	4.0	0.4	3.2
32 40000	Las Vegas......................	293.5	478 434	34	1 630.1	215.7	258 877	63	1 200.2	69.9	10.4	0.7	4.8	0.4	9.7
32 51800	North Las Vegas	203.3	115 488	202	568.1	157.9	47 849	590	303.0	55.9	19.0	0.8	3.2	0.5	15.8
32 60600	Reno......................	179.0	180 480	116	1 008.3	148.9	134 230	134	901.5	77.5	2.6	1.3	5.3	0.6	9.3
32 68400	Sparks......................	62.0	66 346	439	1 070.1	36.9	53 367	499	1 446.3	78.4	2.4	1.2	5.0	0.5	9.1
33 00000	NEW HAMPSHIRE........	23 227.3	1 235 786	X	53.2	23 230.7	1 109 252	X	47.7	96.0	0.7	0.2	1.3	0.0	0.6
33 14200	Concord......................	166.5	40 687	851	244.4	166.5	36 006	833	216.3	95.5	1.0	0.3	1.5	0.0	0.3
33 18820	Dover......................	69.2	26 884	1 388	388.5	69.2	25 042	1 284	361.9	94.5	1.1	0.2	2.4	0.1	0.3
33 45140	Manchester......................	85.5	107 006	222	1 251.5	85.5	99 332	207	1 161.8	91.7	2.1	0.3	2.3	0.0	1.8
33 50260	Nashua......................	80.0	86 605	300	1 082.6	80.1	79 662	282	994.5	89.2	2.0	0.3	3.9	0.0	3.1
33 65140	Rochester......................	116.9	28 461	1 302	243.5	117.0	26 630	1 202	227.6	97.1	0.5	0.2	0.9	0.0	0.3
34 00000	NEW JERSEY............	19 210.8	8 414 350	X	438.0	19 214.8	7 747 750	X	403.2	72.6	13.6	0.2	5.7	0.0	5.4
34 02080	Atlantic City......................	29.4	40 517	855	1 378.1	29.4	37 986	788	1 292.0	26.7	44.2	0.5	10.4	0.1	13.8
34 03580	Bayonne......................	14.6	61 842	478	4 235.8	14.6	61 464	410	4 209.9	78.6	5.5	0.2	4.1	0.0	7.5
34 05170	Bergenfield Borough..........	7.5	26 247	1 429	3 499.6	7.5	24 458	1 324	3 261.1	62.9	6.9	0.2	20.4	0.0	6.5
34 10000	Camden......................	22.8	79 904	341	3 504.6	22.8	87 492	244	3 837.4	16.8	53.3	0.5	2.5	0.1	22.8
34 13690	Clifton......................	29.3	78 672	349	2 685.1	29.3	71 984	324	2 456.8	76.2	2.9	0.2	6.4	0.0	9.6
34 19390	East Orange......................	10.2	69 824	409	6 845.5	10.2	73 552	315	7 211.0	3.8	89.5	0.3	0.4	0.1	2.1
34 21000	Elizabeth......................	31.7	120 568	189	3 803.4	31.9	110 002	173	3 448.3	55.8	20.0	0.5	2.3	0.0	15.5
34 21480	Englewood......................	12.8	26 203	1 435	2 047.1	12.8	24 850	1 293	1 941.4	42.5	39.0	0.3	5.2	0.0	8.5
34 22470	Fair Lawn Borough	13.4	31 637	1 153	2 361.0	13.4	30 548	1 035	2 279.7	91.5	0.7	0.0	4.9	0.0	1.4
34 24420	Fort Lee Borough	6.6	35 461	1 006	5 372.9	6.6	31 997	972	4 848.0	62.8	1.7	0.1	31.4	0.1	1.7
34 25770	Garfield......................	5.5	29 786	1 234	5 415.6	5.5	26 727	1 194	4 859.5	82.1	3.0	0.3	2.7	0.0	8.1
34 28680	Hackensack......................	10.7	42 677	806	3 988.5	10.7	37 049	814	3 462.5	52.6	24.6	0.4	7.5	0.1	9.7
34 32250	Hoboken......................	3.3	38 577	913	11 690.0	3.3	33 397	923	10 120.3	80.8	4.3	0.2	4.3	0.1	7.6
34 36000	Jersey City......................	38.6	240 055	74	6 219.0	38.5	228 517	67	5 935.5	34.0	28.3	0.4	16.2	0.1	15.1
34 36510	Kearny......................	23.7	40 513	856	1 709.4	23.7	34 874	865	1 471.5	75.7	4.0	0.4	5.5	0.1	10.0
34 40350	Linden......................	28.0	39 394	886	1 406.9	28.0	36 701	821	1 310.8	66.1	22.8	0.1	2.3	0.0	4.9
34 41310	Long Branch......................	13.5	31 340	1 167	2 321.5	13.5	28 658	1 108	2 122.8	68.0	18.7	0.4	1.6	0.0	7.1
34 46680	Millville......................	109.7	26 847	1 390	244.7	109.7	25 992	1 243	236.9	76.1	15.0	0.5	0.8	0.0	5.2
34 51000	Newark......................	61.6	273 546	65	4 440.7	61.7	275 221	56	4 460.6	26.5	53.5	0.4	1.2	0.0	14.0
34 51210	New Brunswick..............	13.5	48 573	696	3 598.0	13.5	41 711	700	3 089.7	48.8	23.0	0.5	5.3	0.1	18.1
34 55950	Paramus Borough	27.1	25 737	1 466	949.7	27.1	25 004	1 285	922.7	79.2	1.1	0.0	17.2	0.0	0.9
34 56550	Passaic......................	8.1	67 861	426	8 377.9	8.0	58 041	437	7 255.1	35.4	13.8	0.8	5.5	0.0	39.4
34 57000	Paterson......................	21.9	149 222	143	6 813.8	21.9	140 891	128	6 433.4	30.8	32.9	0.6	1.9	0.1	27.6
34 58200	Perth Amboy..................	12.4	47 303	719	3 814.8	12.4	41 967	695	3 384.4	46.4	10.0	0.7	1.5	0.1	35.6
34 59190	Plainfield......................	15.6	47 829	707	3 066.0	15.6	46 577	609	2 985.7	21.4	61.8	0.4	0.9	0.1	10.8
34 61530	Rahway......................	10.3	26 500	1 408	2 572.8	10.3	25 325	1 272	2 458.7	60.2	27.1	0.2	3.6	0.1	5.6
34 65790	Sayreville Borough	41.2	40 377	860	980.0	41.8	34 998	861	837.3	76.5	8.6	0.1	10.6	0.0	2.1
34 74000	Trenton......................	19.8	85 403	311	4 313.3	19.8	88 675	240	4 478.5	32.6	52.1	0.4	0.8	0.2	10.8
34 74630	Union City......................	3.3	67 088	433	20 329.7	3.3	58 012	438	17 579.4	58.4	3.6	0.7	2.1	0.1	28.2
34 76070	Vineland......................	177.9	56 271	562	316.3	177.9	54 780	477	307.9	67.5	13.6	0.5	1.2	0.1	14.0
34 79040	Westfield......................	17.4	29 644	1 243	1 703.7	17.4	28 870	1 096	1 659.2	90.0	3.9	0.1	4.1	0.0	0.6
34 79610	West New York	2.6	45 768	749	17 603.1	2.6	38 125	785	14 663.5	60.1	3.6	0.7	2.9	0.0	25.2
35 00000	NEW MEXICO..............	314 309.4	1 819 046	X	5.8	314 334.1	1 515 069	X	4.8	66.8	1.9	9.5	1.1	0.1	17.0
35 01780	Alamogordo..................	50.1	35 582	1 003	710.2	44.3	27 596	1 153	622.9	75.4	5.6	1.1	1.5	0.2	12.1
35 02000	Albuquerque..................	467.9	448 607	37	958.8	342.4	384 915	38	1 124.2	71.6	3.1	3.9	2.2	0.1	14.8
35 12150	Carlsbad......................	73.5	25 625	1 470	348.6	70.6	24 952	1 289	353.4	77.4	2.2	1.3	0.7	0.1	15.8
35 16420	Clovis......................	58.0	32 667	1 113	563.2	35.8	30 954	1 013	864.6	71.3	7.3	1.0	1.6	0.1	15.0
35 25800	Farmington..................	68.8	37 844	932	550.1	60.9	33 997	890	558.2	70.7	0.8	17.0	0.5	0.1	7.8
35 32520	Hobbs......................	49.0	28 657	1 289	584.8	48.9	29 121	1 088	595.5	63.5	6.8	1.1	0.4	0.0	24.4
35 39380	Las Cruces..................	134.9	74 267	379	550.5	97.1	62 360	398	642.2	69.0	2.3	1.7	1.2	0.1	21.6
35 63460	Rio Rancho..................	190.2	51 765	645	272.2	118.3	32 512	953	274.8	78.4	2.7	2.4	1.5	0.2	10.9
35 64930	Roswell......................	74.9	45 293	757	604.7	75.5	44 260	649	586.2	71.0	2.5	1.3	0.6	0.1	21.3
35 70500	Santa Fe......................	96.7	62 203	475	643.3	94.8	56 537	455	596.4	76.3	0.7	2.2	1.3	0.1	15.3
36 00000	NEW YORK..................	122 283.1	18 976 457	X	155.2	122 309.7	17 990 778	X	147.1	67.9	15.9	0.4	5.5	0.0	7.1
36 01000	Albany......................	55.4	95 658	258	1 726.7	55.4	100 031	203	1 805.6	63.1	28.1	0.3	3.3	0.0	2.2
36 03078	Auburn......................	21.7	28 574	1 298	1 316.8	21.7	31 258	1 001	1 440.5	88.6	7.6	0.3	0.6	0.0	1.4
36 06607	Binghamton..................	27.0	47 380	717	1 754.8	26.9	53 008	507	1 970.6	83.2	8.4	0.3	3.3	0.0	1.7
36 11000	Buffalo......................	105.2	292 648	60	2 781.8	105.2	328 175	50	3 119.5	54.4	37.2	0.8	1.4	0.0	3.7
36 24229	Elmira......................	18.9	30 940	1 182	1 637.0	19.0	33 724	903	1 774.9	82.0	13.1	0.4	0.5	0.0	1.4
36 27485	Freeport......................	11.9	43 783	785	3 679.2	11.9	39 894	746	3 352.4	42.9	32.6	0.5	1.4	0.1	17.2
36 29113	Glen Cove..................	17.2	26 622	1 401	1 547.8	17.2	24 149	1 348	1 404.0	80.3	6.4	0.3	4.1	0.1	5.7
36 33139	Hempstead..................	9.5	56 554	553	5 953.1	9.5	45 982	622	4 840.2	25.7	52.5	0.5	1.3	0.1	15.2

[1]Dry land or land partially or temporarily covered by water.

Table D. Cities

City	Population and population characteristics, 2000 (cont'd)								Population and population characteristics, 1990				
	Race (percent) (cont'd)								Race (percent)				
	Race alone or in combination												
	Two or more races	White	Black	American Indian or Alaska Native	Asian	Native Hawaiian and other Pacific Islander	Some other race	Hispanic[1]	White	Black or African American	American Indian or Alaska Native	Asian and Pacific Islander	Hispanic[1]
	15	16	17	18	19	20	21	22	23	24	25	26	27
NEVADA	3.8	78.4	7.5	2.1	5.6	0.8	9.7	19.7	84.3	6.6	1.6	3.2	10.4
Carson City	2.1	87.2	2.1	3.3	2.2	0.3	7.2	14.2	90.7	1.7	2.7	1.4	7.7
Henderson	3.5	87.5	4.4	1.4	5.3	0.9	4.4	10.7	91.4	2.7	1.0	2.0	8.1
Las Vegas	4.1	73.2	11.3	1.5	6.0	0.9	11.6	23.6	78.4	11.4	0.9	3.6	12.5
North Las Vegas	4.7	59.8	20.2	1.5	4.4	1.0	18.2	37.6	45.2	37.4	1.0	2.4	22.2
Reno	3.6	80.5	3.2	2.1	6.3	0.9	10.8	19.2	86.1	2.9	1.4	4.9	11.1
Sparks	3.5	81.4	2.9	1.9	6.0	0.8	10.7	19.7	88.4	2.4	1.4	4.5	8.6
NEW HAMPSHIRE	1.1	97.0	1.0	0.6	1.6	0.1	0.9	1.7	98.0	0.6	0.2	0.8	1.0
Concord	1.3	96.7	1.4	0.8	1.8	0.1	0.7	1.5	98.2	0.6	0.3	0.7	1.0
Dover	1.5	95.8	1.5	0.7	2.7	0.1	0.7	1.1	97.4	1.1	0.2	1.1	1.0
Manchester	1.7	93.3	2.6	0.7	2.7	0.1	2.5	4.6	97.0	1.0	0.2	1.1	2.1
Nashua	1.5	90.5	2.5	0.6	4.3	0.1	3.7	6.2	95.2	1.6	0.2	1.9	3.0
Rochester	1.0	98.0	0.8	0.6	1.1	0.1	0.5	0.9	98.7	0.3	0.2	0.6	0.7
NEW JERSEY	2.5	74.4	14.4	0.6	6.2	0.1	6.9	13.3	79.3	13.4	0.2	3.5	9.6
Atlantic City	4.5	29.2	45.9	1.2	11.5	0.2	16.7	24.9	35.4	51.3	0.5	4.0	15.3
Bayonne	4.0	82.0	6.3	0.5	4.8	0.2	10.4	17.8	90.4	4.7	0.1	1.8	9.5
Bergenfield Borough	3.1	64.9	7.8	0.7	21.4	0.1	8.3	17.0	83.9	4.2	0.1	9.1	9.2
Camden	3.9	19.0	55.3	1.2	3.0	0.3	25.4	38.8	19.0	56.4	0.4	1.3	31.2
Clifton	4.6	80.3	3.3	0.5	7.2	0.1	13.4	19.8	92.8	1.4	0.1	3.5	6.8
East Orange	3.8	4.5	92.8	0.9	0.7	0.3	4.9	4.7	7.2	89.9	0.4	0.6	4.1
Elizabeth	5.9	60.2	21.6	0.8	2.8	0.2	20.5	49.5	65.5	19.8	0.3	2.7	39.1
Englewood	4.5	44.8	41.5	1.0	5.9	0.2	11.5	21.8	49.2	39.5	0.3	4.9	15.7
Fair Lawn Borough	1.4	92.7	1.0	0.2	5.4	0.1	2.1	5.5	96.0	0.6	0.1	2.9	3.5
Fort Lee Borough	2.3	64.6	2.1	0.2	32.3	0.1	2.9	7.9	77.2	1.3	0.1	20.3	5.6
Garfield	3.8	85.4	4.0	0.6	3.1	0.1	10.7	20.1	93.8	2.2	0.1	1.7	9.0
Hackensack	5.1	56.3	26.5	1.1	8.1	0.1	13.3	25.9	66.4	24.8	0.2	3.7	15.1
Hoboken	2.8	83.1	5.1	0.5	4.9	0.1	9.3	20.2	79.0	5.5	0.2	4.4	30.1
Jersey City	5.8	37.7	30.0	1.0	17.6	0.3	19.6	28.3	48.2	29.7	0.3	11.4	24.2
Kearny	4.3	79.5	4.6	0.6	6.0	0.2	13.5	27.3	90.5	1.2	0.2	4.7	17.1
Linden	3.7	68.5	24.4	0.5	2.7	0.1	7.7	14.4	76.8	20.0	0.1	1.5	7.4
Long Branch	4.2	71.5	20.0	0.8	2.1	0.2	9.9	20.7	73.5	19.5	0.2	1.5	13.6
Millville	2.4	77.9	16.2	1.2	1.0	0.1	6.1	11.2	86.6	8.4	0.4	0.6	7.6
Newark	4.4	29.4	55.0	0.8	1.6	0.2	17.6	29.5	28.6	58.5	0.2	1.2	26.1
New Brunswick	4.2	51.7	24.5	1.2	5.9	0.2	21.0	39.0	57.4	29.6	0.3	4.0	19.3
Paramus Borough	1.5	80.4	1.3	0.2	18.0	0.0	1.6	4.9	88.2	0.8	0.0	10.5	3.6
Passaic	5.0	39.0	15.2	1.2	6.1	0.2	43.5	62.5	45.3	20.6	0.5	7.1	50.0
Paterson	6.2	35.0	34.6	1.0	2.5	0.3	32.9	50.1	41.2	36.0	0.3	1.4	41.0
Perth Amboy	5.6	50.9	11.4	1.1	1.8	0.2	40.3	69.8	59.8	11.8	0.4	1.6	55.5
Plainfield	4.6	24.4	63.9	1.1	1.2	0.3	14.0	25.2	26.5	65.7	0.5	1.1	15.0
Rahway	3.3	62.3	28.7	0.8	4.0	0.1	7.6	13.9	75.4	20.2	0.2	2.4	7.5
Sayreville Borough	2.1	78.0	9.1	0.4	11.3	0.1	3.3	7.3	93.1	3.2	0.1	3.0	4.0
Trenton	3.2	34.5	53.6	0.8	1.2	0.4	12.9	21.5	42.2	49.3	0.3	0.7	14.1
Union City	6.9	64.2	5.3	1.2	2.6	0.2	33.7	82.3	74.7	5.1	0.2	2.1	75.6
Vineland	3.1	69.8	14.8	1.1	1.4	0.2	16.1	30.0	73.0	11.5	0.3	0.9	23.6
Westfield	1.3	91.1	4.3	0.3	4.7	0.1	1.0	2.8	91.5	4.6	0.1	3.5	2.0
West New York	7.6	66.7	4.8	1.1	3.4	0.1	31.8	78.7	76.7	4.0	0.4	1.9	73.3
NEW MEXICO	3.6	69.9	2.3	10.5	1.5	0.2	19.4	42.1	75.6	2.0	8.9	0.9	38.2
Alamogordo	4.2	79.1	6.4	1.8	2.4	0.3	14.5	32.0	82.7	6.0	0.8	1.9	25.0
Albuquerque	4.3	75.3	3.8	4.9	2.9	0.2	17.5	39.9	78.2	3.0	3.0	1.7	34.5
Carlsbad	2.5	79.7	2.6	1.9	0.9	0.1	17.4	36.7	81.2	2.6	0.5	0.7	33.4
Clovis	3.6	74.3	8.3	1.8	2.2	0.2	17.0	33.4	72.8	7.0	0.7	1.7	26.8
Farmington	3.1	73.4	1.3	18.4	0.8	0.1	9.2	17.7	77.1	0.8	13.8	0.4	16.0
Hobbs	3.7	66.9	7.4	1.8	0.5	0.1	27.2	42.2	78.7	7.4	0.6	0.5	30.1
Las Cruces	4.1	72.6	2.9	2.7	1.7	0.2	24.2	51.7	88.2	1.9	0.9	1.1	46.9
Rio Rancho	4.1	82.0	3.4	3.4	2.1	0.3	13.1	27.7	84.1	2.6	2.1	1.2	21.8
Roswell	3.3	73.9	2.9	2.1	1.0	0.1	23.6	44.3	81.7	2.6	0.7	0.6	36.5
Santa Fe	4.2	80.1	1.0	3.3	1.7	0.2	18.3	47.8	81.2	0.6	2.2	0.6	47.4
NEW YORK	3.1	70.0	17.0	0.9	6.2	0.2	9.1	15.1	74.4	15.9	0.3	3.9	12.3
Albany	3.0	65.1	29.9	1.0	3.9	0.1	3.2	5.6	75.5	20.6	0.3	2.3	3.1
Auburn	1.5	89.9	8.6	0.8	0.7	0.1	1.7	2.8	91.9	6.8	0.3	0.5	2.2
Binghamton	3.1	85.7	10.0	0.8	3.9	0.1	2.8	3.9	91.9	4.9	0.3	2.1	1.8
Buffalo	2.5	56.2	38.6	1.4	1.7	0.1	4.7	7.5	64.7	30.7	0.8	1.0	4.9
Elmira	2.6	84.4	14.9	0.9	0.7	0.1	1.9	3.1	85.4	12.3	0.3	0.6	2.7
Freeport	5.4	46.8	34.7	1.2	1.8	0.2	21.1	33.5	56.5	32.3	0.4	1.3	21.2
Glen Cove	3.1	82.9	7.0	0.6	4.8	0.2	7.8	20.0	85.8	7.8	0.1	3.4	11.5
Hempstead	4.7	28.5	54.7	1.4	1.8	0.2	18.4	31.8	32.4	58.8	0.5	1.7	19.1

[1] Hispanic persons may be of any race.

City	Population and population characteristics, 2000										
	Age (percent)										
	Under 5 years	5 to 17 years	18 to 24 years	25 to 34 years	35 to 44 years	45 to 54 years	55 to 64 years	65 to 74 years	75 years and over	Median age (years)	Percent Female
	28	29	30	31	32	33	34	35	36	37	38
NEVADA	7.3	18.3	9.0	15.3	16.1	13.5	9.5	6.6	4.4	35.0	49.1
Carson City	6.3	17.1	7.9	12.9	16.0	14.7	10.2	7.8	7.1	38.7	48.3
Henderson	6.8	18.3	7.9	15.4	17.1	14.4	10.0	6.4	3.7	35.9	50.4
Las Vegas	7.7	18.2	8.8	16.1	15.9	12.5	9.2	7.1	4.5	34.5	49.2
North Las Vegas	10.4	23.6	9.6	18.5	15.8	10.0	6.4	3.7	2.0	28.8	49.0
Reno	7.0	16.2	11.8	15.9	15.6	13.6	8.5	6.1	5.3	34.5	48.9
Sparks	7.4	19.5	9.2	14.7	16.9	13.8	8.3	5.6	4.6	34.5	50.6
NEW HAMPSHIRE	6.1	18.9	8.4	13.0	17.9	14.9	8.9	6.3	5.6	37.1	50.8
Concord	5.8	17.3	8.3	15.2	17.8	14.3	7.7	5.8	7.9	37.0	50.5
Dover	5.7	15.2	11.2	17.2	16.7	12.6	7.7	6.5	7.3	35.5	52.0
Manchester	6.7	17.0	9.5	16.9	16.5	12.9	7.6	6.1	6.8	34.9	51.0
Nashua	6.5	18.1	8.1	15.9	17.6	13.6	8.5	6.1	5.5	35.8	50.6
Rochester	6.8	18.5	7.7	14.2	17.4	13.4	8.6	7.3	6.2	36.7	51.4
NEW JERSEY	6.7	18.1	8.0	14.1	17.1	13.8	9.0	6.8	6.4	36.7	51.5
Atlantic City	7.5	18.2	8.9	15.8	15.2	11.5	8.7	7.3	6.8	34.7	51.0
Bayonne	5.8	16.3	8.2	14.6	16.1	13.8	8.7	8.0	8.6	38.1	52.7
Bergenfield Borough	6.8	18.1	7.3	13.4	17.6	14.3	9.0	6.9	6.9	37.6	52.2
Camden	9.1	25.5	12.0	15.3	14.1	9.9	6.4	4.5	3.1	27.2	51.5
Clifton	6.0	15.6	7.7	14.4	16.3	13.8	8.7	7.9	9.7	38.8	52.3
East Orange	7.9	20.2	9.8	15.2	14.9	12.1	8.7	6.3	5.0	33.0	55.0
Elizabeth	7.7	18.6	10.8	17.2	16.5	11.6	7.7	5.2	4.8	32.6	50.5
Englewood	6.9	17.0	7.4	14.6	15.9	14.3	10.5	7.3	6.0	37.4	53.0
Fair Lawn Borough	5.3	17.5	6.0	10.3	16.5	16.3	9.3	8.9	9.8	41.8	52.5
Fort Lee Borough	5.3	12.2	5.1	15.3	17.2	13.9	10.9	10.2	10.0	41.6	53.3
Garfield	6.1	16.3	9.6	17.0	16.2	13.0	7.8	6.7	7.4	35.6	51.3
Hackensack	5.8	12.4	8.6	20.7	17.7	13.4	8.9	6.3	6.2	36.2	50.3
Hoboken	3.2	7.3	15.3	37.9	13.9	8.1	5.4	4.6	4.5	30.4	49.1
Jersey City	6.9	17.8	10.7	19.4	15.7	11.8	7.9	5.2	4.5	32.4	51.2
Kearny	5.7	15.7	10.7	18.5	17.2	13.1	8.2	5.6	5.2	34.7	48.4
Linden	6.0	16.5	8.2	14.6	15.8	13.5	9.1	7.5	8.8	38.0	52.5
Long Branch	7.0	16.8	10.2	16.5	15.9	12.6	8.2	6.6	6.3	34.7	51.5
Millville	7.0	21.0	8.6	13.4	15.4	13.2	8.5	6.5	6.4	35.0	52.8
Newark	7.8	20.2	12.1	16.9	15.1	10.9	7.8	5.3	4.0	30.8	51.5
New Brunswick	7.0	13.1	34.0	17.6	10.6	7.1	4.2	3.2	3.3	23.6	50.4
Paramus Borough	5.2	18.1	5.5	9.0	15.7	14.4	10.7	10.5	11.0	42.9	51.4
Passaic	9.6	21.2	12.5	17.5	14.2	10.5	6.4	4.2	3.9	28.6	50.1
Paterson	8.4	21.4	11.2	16.5	15.5	11.3	7.5	4.6	3.7	30.5	51.4
Perth Amboy	8.0	20.4	11.4	16.5	15.1	11.3	7.0	5.1	5.1	31.2	50.4
Plainfield	7.9	19.6	10.2	15.9	16.7	12.2	8.3	5.0	4.2	32.8	51.1
Rahway	6.3	17.6	7.8	14.7	17.3	13.5	8.3	7.2	7.3	37.1	52.3
Sayreville Borough	6.7	16.8	7.3	16.3	18.0	13.8	8.7	6.5	5.9	36.5	51.0
Trenton	7.6	20.1	10.1	16.7	15.2	11.5	7.4	5.8	5.6	32.2	50.6
Union City	7.4	17.9	11.0	18.0	16.3	11.4	8.0	5.9	4.1	32.5	49.9
Vineland	6.2	19.5	8.3	13.6	15.4	13.8	9.1	6.9	7.2	36.5	52.1
Westfield	8.0	20.4	4.0	11.2	18.4	15.7	8.8	6.6	6.9	38.6	52.1
West New York	6.7	15.6	10.9	18.6	15.5	11.1	8.8	7.3	5.4	34.0	50.9
NEW MEXICO	7.2	20.8	9.8	12.9	15.5	13.5	8.7	6.5	5.2	34.6	50.8
Alamogordo	7.6	21.0	9.2	14.2	15.5	11.5	8.3	7.4	5.3	33.5	50.6
Albuquerque	6.9	17.7	10.6	15.0	16.0	13.8	8.2	6.1	5.8	34.9	51.4
Carlsbad	7.3	19.8	8.4	11.1	13.6	13.5	9.1	8.1	9.1	37.7	51.8
Clovis	8.3	21.7	9.4	13.1	14.9	11.5	8.0	6.7	6.3	33.1	52.0
Farmington	7.6	21.7	9.9	12.5	16.0	13.7	7.9	5.8	4.9	33.6	51.0
Hobbs	8.1	22.3	10.3	13.1	14.9	11.5	7.8	6.7	5.2	32.1	50.0
Las Cruces	7.0	18.1	16.0	13.4	13.4	11.1	7.8	7.1	6.0	31.2	51.5
Rio Rancho	7.5	21.7	7.0	13.7	18.4	13.1	7.0	5.7	6.0	35.1	51.5
Roswell	7.4	21.1	9.9	11.3	13.6	12.3	8.3	7.8	8.2	35.2	51.8
Santa Fe	5.4	14.9	8.9	13.7	15.3	17.3	10.7	7.3	6.6	39.8	52.2
NEW YORK	6.5	18.2	9.3	14.5	16.2	13.5	8.9	6.7	6.2	35.9	51.8
Albany	5.6	14.3	19.3	15.9	13.4	11.3	6.9	5.9	7.4	31.4	52.5
Auburn	6.3	16.5	9.3	14.8	15.5	12.6	7.2	7.2	10.6	36.9	50.3
Binghamton	6.1	15.5	13.2	13.0	13.7	12.5	8.5	7.7	9.9	36.7	52.7
Buffalo	7.1	19.2	11.3	14.4	14.9	12.0	7.6	6.8	6.7	33.6	53.0
Elmira	7.0	18.1	13.0	14.2	15.7	11.5	6.7	6.5	7.3	33.4	49.7
Freeport	6.9	19.5	9.1	15.1	16.9	13.5	8.5	5.7	4.8	34.6	51.9
Glen Cove	6.2	15.0	8.1	14.7	15.9	13.0	9.5	8.1	9.4	38.6	51.9
Hempstead	7.9	18.4	16.3	17.1	14.4	10.5	7.1	4.3	4.1	29.4	52.2

Table D. Cities

City	Under 5 years	5 to 17 years	18 to 24 years	25 to 34 years	35 to 44 years	45 to 54 years	55 to 64 years	65 to 74 years	75 years and over	Percent Female	2000	1990	1980	1990–2000	1980–1990
	39	40	41	42	43	44	45	46	47	48	49	50	51	52	53
NEVADA	7.7	17.0	9.9	18.5	16.0	11.3	9.0	7.1	3.5	49.1	1 998 257	1 201 675	800 508	66.3	50.1
Carson City	6.9	15.4	8.3	16.6	16.1	12.3	9.7	9.4	5.4	48.9	52 457	40 443	32 022	29.7	26.3
Henderson	8.1	20.1	9.0	19.2	16.9	10.7	7.6	5.8	2.6	50.3	175 381	64 948	NA	170.0	NA
Las Vegas	8.2	16.6	9.9	19.8	15.5	10.9	8.8	7.0	3.3	49.3	478 434	258 204	164 674	85.3	56.8
North Las Vegas	10.6	23.5	11.7	18.1	13.2	9.7	6.5	4.6	2.2	50.5	115 488	47 849	42 739	141.4	12.0
Reno	7.1	13.4	12.6	20.2	16.0	10.7	8.3	7.3	4.4	49.2	180 480	133 850	100 756	34.8	32.8
Sparks	7.8	17.3	10.1	19.5	17.1	10.9	8.0	5.6	3.7	50.7	66 346	53 367	40 780	24.3	30.9
NEW HAMPSHIRE	7.6	17.5	10.6	18.5	16.5	10.1	8.0	6.4	4.8	51.0	1 235 786	1 109 252	920 610	11.4	20.5
Concord	7.1	16.1	9.8	20.8	16.4	8.3	7.5	6.8	7.2	51.5	40 687	36 006	30 400	13.0	18.4
Dover	6.4	13.6	15.3	20.8	13.2	9.5	8.3	7.2	5.8	52.2	26 884	25 042	22 387	7.4	11.9
Manchester	7.8	15.2	11.9	20.9	14.0	8.5	8.0	7.8	5.8	52.1	107 006	99 332	90 936	7.7	9.2
Nashua	8.0	16.1	10.2	21.8	15.7	10.1	7.9	5.9	4.2	50.9	86 605	79 662	67 865	8.7	17.4
Rochester	8.5	17.8	9.3	19.3	15.1	8.9	8.5	7.4	5.4	51.4	28 461	26 630	21 560	6.9	23.5
NEW JERSEY	6.9	16.4	10.1	17.6	15.5	10.9	9.3	7.9	5.5	51.7	8 414 350	7 730 188	7 365 011	8.9	5.0
Atlantic City	7.4	15.2	10.1	17.0	12.9	8.6	9.8	9.7	9.3	52.8	40 517	37 986	40 199	6.7	-5.5
Bayonne	5.5	14.3	8.9	17.4	13.6	10.7	10.6	11.9	7.0	52.8	61 842	61 464	65 047	0.6	-5.5
Bergenfield Borough	6.6	14.1	9.1	16.7	16.2	11.7	10.2	9.5	6.0	52.0	26 247	24 458	25 568	7.3	-4.3
Camden	10.7	24.9	12.1	17.5	11.8	8.3	6.4	5.3	3.1	52.4	79 904	87 492	84 910	-8.7	3.0
Clifton	5.4	12.4	8.6	17.6	14.3	10.0	11.0	12.1	8.6	52.7	78 672	71 984	74 388	9.3	-3.2
East Orange	7.9	17.9	10.8	18.6	14.0	11.0	8.1	6.6	5.1	54.7	69 824	73 552	77 690	-5.1	-5.3
Elizabeth	7.5	17.2	10.7	20.0	14.0	10.2	8.5	6.8	5.2	51.3	120 568	110 002	106 201	9.6	3.6
Englewood	6.9	15.0	8.5	17.5	16.4	11.6	10.2	8.1	5.8	53.2	26 203	24 850	23 701	5.4	4.8
Fair Lawn Borough	5.6	14.8	7.0	13.5	15.3	11.4	12.2	12.2	7.9	52.3	31 637	30 548	32 229	3.6	-5.2
Fort Lee Borough	5.8	9.8	5.1	20.2	16.1	10.6	12.1	11.6	8.9	52.9	35 461	31 997	32 449	10.8	-1.4
Garfield	6.5	13.1	10.0	20.6	14.0	8.9	9.2	10.4	7.0	52.2	29 786	26 727	26 803	11.4	-0.3
Hackensack	5.1	10.6	9.8	23.7	16.1	11.2	8.9	8.0	6.6	50.7	42 677	37 049	36 039	15.2	2.8
Hoboken	4.8	11.9	13.3	29.8	14.7	7.9	6.5	6.6	4.5	50.9	38 577	33 397	42 460	15.5	-21.3
Jersey City	7.3	17.1	11.4	21.0	14.9	9.7	7.7	6.4	4.5	51.4	240 055	228 517	223 532	5.0	2.2
Kearny	6.2	15.2	10.5	19.8	14.3	11.7	9.5	7.9	5.0	50.6	40 513	34 874	35 735	16.2	-2.4
Linden	5.7	14.1	8.9	17.1	14.5	10.3	10.2	11.4	7.7	52.4	39 394	36 701	37 836	7.3	-3.0
Long Branch	7.1	15.6	9.5	20.3	13.8	9.4	8.9	8.5	6.9	53.0	31 340	28 658	29 819	9.4	-3.9
Millville	7.6	19.0	10.7	16.2	14.5	9.8	8.7	8.4	5.1	52.6	26 847	25 992	24 815	3.3	4.7
Newark	7.9	20.7	12.5	18.5	13.5	9.9	7.7	5.7	3.6	52.2	273 546	275 221	329 248	-0.6	-16.4
New Brunswick	5.8	11.0	33.9	18.3	10.5	5.8	5.3	5.4	3.9	52.5	48 573	41 711	41 442	16.5	0.6
Paramus Borough	4.7	15.3	9.1	12.7	14.4	13.2	13.8	11.2	5.7	51.6	25 737	25 004	26 474	2.9	-5.6
Passaic	8.8	18.7	12.2	19.0	14.1	9.7	7.1	5.7	4.6	51.0	67 861	58 041	52 463	16.9	10.6
Paterson	8.8	20.3	12.1	18.5	13.8	9.8	7.1	5.5	4.0	51.9	149 222	140 891	137 970	5.9	2.1
Perth Amboy	7.5	18.4	11.3	17.9	14.1	9.5	7.6	7.8	5.8	51.6	47 303	41 967	38 951	12.7	7.7
Plainfield	8.0	17.9	11.7	19.3	15.3	10.3	7.6	5.6	4.2	52.1	47 829	46 577	45 555	2.7	2.2
Rahway	6.6	14.2	9.6	18.9	16.2	9.9	9.5	9.7	5.5	51.9	26 500	25 325	26 723	4.6	-5.2
Sayreville Borough	7.0	14.5	9.7	20.4	14.8	11.0	10.0	8.8	3.8	51.3	40 377	34 998	29 969	15.4	16.8
Trenton	8.5	18.0	10.9	19.1	14.5	8.3	7.8	7.7	5.2	51.5	85 403	88 675	92 124	-3.7	-3.7
Union City	7.3	16.8	10.8	19.7	14.4	11.2	9.7	6.3	4.0	51.0	67 088	58 012	55 593	15.6	4.4
Vineland	7.0	18.5	10.1	16.0	14.4	10.5	9.0	8.4	6.1	52.9	56 271	54 780	53 753	2.7	1.9
Westfield	6.9	17.0	7.1	14.6	18.0	12.2	10.9	8.0	5.4	52.0	29 644	28 870	30 447	2.7	-5.2
West New York	6.6	14.9	10.3	18.4	12.7	12.1	11.4	8.1	5.5	52.0	45 768	38 125	39 194	20.0	-2.7
NEW MEXICO	8.3	21.2	10.0	16.9	15.0	9.7	8.0	6.4	4.3	50.8	1 819 046	1 515 069	1 303 302	20.1	16.2
Alamogordo	8.6	20.2	9.7	18.3	14.7	9.3	8.8	6.6	3.9	50.5	35 582	27 596	24 024	28.9	14.9
Albuquerque	7.3	17.7	10.4	19.0	16.3	10.3	7.9	6.7	4.4	51.5	448 607	384 915	331 767	16.5	16.0
Carlsbad	7.3	21.2	7.3	14.3	12.8	10.0	9.0	10.2	7.9	52.0	25 625	24 952	25 457	2.7	-2.0
Clovis	8.3	21.2	10.1	17.6	12.5	9.8	8.2	6.5	5.7	52.0	32 667	30 954	31 194	5.5	-0.8
Farmington	9.1	24.1	7.4	18.1	16.4	8.7	7.7	5.7	2.8	51.0	37 844	33 997	31 222	11.3	8.9
Hobbs	9.0	24.4	9.1	16.2	13.9	7.9	8.3	6.6	4.5	51.6	28 657	29 121	29 153	-1.6	-0.1
Las Cruces	7.6	19.1	13.9	17.6	13.2	9.4	7.9	6.7	4.6	51.0	74 267	62 360	45 060	19.1	38.4
Rio Rancho	10.1	20.0	6.1	22.0	16.1	7.3	6.5	6.4	4.0	51.3	51 765	32 512	NA	59.2	NA
Roswell	8.1	22.0	9.5	14.7	12.6	9.0	8.4	8.6	7.1	51.6	45 293	44 260	39 676	2.3	11.6
Santa Fe	6.4	16.7	8.9	15.8	18.5	12.5	8.6	7.4	5.1	52.5	62 203	56 537	48 953	10.0	15.5
NEW YORK	7.0	16.7	10.9	17.4	15.1	10.6	9.1	7.5	5.6	52.1	18 976 457	17 990 778	17 558 165	5.5	2.5
Albany	6.0	12.1	19.8	18.8	13.2	7.4	7.2	7.4	8.0	53.5	95 658	100 031	101 727	-4.4	-1.7
Auburn	7.2	16.1	10.0	18.3	14.2	7.7	8.1	9.7	8.7	51.1	28 574	31 258	32 501	-8.6	-3.8
Binghamton	6.6	13.2	13.9	17.2	12.9	8.5	8.6	9.9	9.1	53.4	47 380	53 008	55 860	-10.6	-5.1
Buffalo	7.8	16.5	12.5	18.5	13.0	8.3	8.5	8.5	6.4	53.4	292 648	328 175	357 870	-10.8	-8.3
Elmira	8.5	17.8	14.0	16.9	12.5	7.5	7.8	8.3	6.6	51.5	30 940	33 724	35 327	-8.3	-4.5
Freeport	7.4	16.5	11.3	18.4	15.2	11.9	9.1	6.2	3.9	51.6	43 783	39 894	38 272	9.7	4.2
Glen Cove	5.9	14.1	10.1	17.1	13.4	11.8	11.2	9.1	7.3	52.2	26 622	24 149	24 618	10.2	-1.9
Hempstead	7.1	16.6	18.0	18.6	13.8	10.5	7.2	4.8	3.5	53.2	56 554	45 982	40 404	23.0	13.8

Table D. Cities

City	Total population	Total in house-holds	House-holder	Spouse	Child Total	Child Own child under 18 years	Other relatives Total	Other relatives Under 18 years	Nonrelatives Total	Nonrelatives Unmar-ried partner	Total in group quarters	Correc-tional institu-tions	Nurs-ing homes	Other institu-tions	Col-lege dormi-tories	Mili-tary quar-ters	Other
	54	55	56	57	58	59	60	61	62	63	64	65	66	67	68	69	70
NEVADA	1 998 257	98.3	37.6	18.7	28.0	22.6	6.7	2.2	7.4	2.7	1.7	0.8	0.2	0.1	0.1	0.1	0.4
Carson City	52 457	93.9	38.5	19.2	25.5	20.9	5 1	1 8	5.6	2.4	6.1	5.4	0.5	0.0	0.0	0.0	0.2
Henderson	175 381	99.4	37.8	21.3	28.5	22.8	5.3	1.7	6.5	2.7	0.6	0.1	0.3	0.0	0.0	0.0	0.2
Las Vegas	478 434	98.3	36.9	17.8	28.1	22.5	7.8	2.6	7.6	2.6	1.7	0.8	0.3	0.1	0.0	0.0	0.6
North Las Vegas	115 488	98.8	29.5	16.9	35.4	29.3	10.3	3.9	6.8	2.2	1.2	0.6	0.5	0.0	0.0	0.0	0.1
Reno	180 480	97.5	40.9	16.6	25.1	20.6	5.8	1.8	9.1	3.1	2.5	0.5	0.4	0.1	0.7	0.0	0.8
Sparks	66 346	99.1	37.1	18.6	29.9	24.0	6.5	2.2	7.0	2.7	0.9	0.0	0.6	0.2	0.0	0.0	0.1
NEW HAMPSHIRE	1 235 786	97.1	38.4	21.2	28.8	23.4	3.0	1.0	5.6	2.6	2.9	0.3	0.8	0.1	1.4	0.0	0.3
Concord	40 687	92.0	40.0	17.7	25.7	21.5	2.6	0.8	5.9	3.0	8.0	4.1	1.7	1.1	0.6	0.0	0.5
Dover	26 884	97.2	43.0	18.3	24.0	19.6	2.9	0.8	9.0	3.6	2.8	0.5	1.8	0.0	0.0	0.0	0.4
Manchester	107 006	97.5	41.4	17.6	27.4	21.8	3.8	1.1	7.3	3.5	2.5	0.4	0.8	0.1	0.5	0.0	0.7
Nashua	86 605	98.4	40.0	19.7	28.8	23.0	3.7	1.1	6.2	2.8	1.6	0.0	0.7	0.1	0.7	0.0	0.2
Rochester	28 461	99.0	40.2	20.4	29.0	23.5	3.0	1.1	6.3	3.3	1.0	0.0	0.7	0.0	0.0	0.0	0.3
NEW JERSEY	8 414 350	97.7	36.4	19.5	30.8	22.3	6.5	2.0	4.6	1.8	2.3	0.6	0.6	0.1	0.5	0.0	0.4
Atlantic City	40 517	96.4	39.1	9.7	27.7	20.9	11.1	4.1	8.8	2.9	3.6	0.0	0.8	0.0	0.0	0.0	2.8
Bayonne	61 842	99.8	41.3	17.7	30.5	20.4	6.2	1.5	4.1	1.9	0.2	0.0	0.0	0.0	0.0	0.0	0.2
Bergenfield Borough	26 247	99.8	34.2	20.5	33.2	22.8	8.2	1.8	3.7	1.2	0.2	0.0	0.0	0.0	0.0	0.0	0.2
Camden	79 904	94.5	30.3	7.9	36.4	26.8	12.9	6.7	7.1	3.0	5.5	3.8	0.5	0.0	0.6	0.0	0.6
Clifton	78 672	99.5	38.4	19.7	29.7	19.8	7.6	1.5	4.1	1.6	0.5	0.0	0.3	0.0	0.0	0.0	0.2
East Orange	69 824	98.1	37.3	9.7	31.8	21.4	13.1	5.9	6.3	2.7	1.9	0.0	0.8	0.5	0.0	0.0	0.5
Elizabeth	120 568	97.6	33.6	14.4	31.8	22.4	11.0	3.3	6.8	2.5	2.4	1.4	0.4	0.1	0.0	0.0	0.5
Englewood	26 203	98.9	35.4	16.9	29.7	20.2	10.1	3.1	6.7	1.8	1.1	0.0	0.6	0.0	0.0	0.0	0.5
Fair Lawn Borough	31 637	99.5	37.3	23.7	31.2	21.8	4.8	0.9	2.5	1.0	0.5	0.0	0.4	0.0	0.0	0.0	0.1
Fort Lee Borough	35 461	99.9	46.7	21.8	23.2	16.6	5.0	0.7	3.3	1.4	0.1	0.0	0.0	0.0	0.0	0.0	0.1
Garfield	29 786	99.8	37.8	17.6	30.4	20.4	8.4	1.6	5.7	2.1	0.2	0.0	0.0	0.0	0.0	0.0	0.2
Hackensack	42 677	96.1	42.4	14.8	22.9	15.4	9.0	2.2	7.0	2.5	3.9	1.5	0.7	0.1	0.0	0.0	1.6
Hoboken	38 577	96.7	50.3	12.0	14.6	9.0	4.1	1.3	15.7	3.4	3.3	0.4	0.0	0.0	2.3	0.0	0.7
Jersey City	240 055	98.6	36.9	13.4	30.5	20.7	10.9	3.6	6.8	2.4	1.4	0.0	0.6	0.1	0.4	0.0	0.4
Kearny	40 513	93.8	33.4	18.0	29.9	19.5	7.3	1.6	5.1	1.7	6.2	5.4	0.4	0.2	0.0	0.0	0.2
Linden	39 394	99.4	38.2	17.8	30.2	19.4	8.6	2.7	4.5	1.7	0.6	0.0	0.6	0.0	0.0	0.0	0.0
Long Branch	31 340	99.3	40.2	14.8	28.2	20.5	7.8	2.7	8.4	2.8	0.7	0.0	0.2	0.0	0.0	0.0	0.4
Millville	26 847	99.0	37.4	17.4	32.5	24.3	6.2	2.9	5.6	3.2	1.0	0.0	0.5	0.0	0.0	0.0	0.5
Newark	273 546	95.3	33.4	10.4	32.1	21.8	12.7	5.2	6.8	2.5	4.7	1.6	0.9	0.3	1.2	0.0	0.7
New Brunswick	48 573	86.7	26.9	8.0	20.5	15.1	11.4	3.6	20.0	2.0	13.3	0.0	0.2	0.0	11.8	0.0	1.2
Paramus Borough	25 737	94.1	31.4	23.0	32.3	21.7	5.8	1.2	1.7	0.4	5.9	0.0	2.5	2.3	0.0	0.0	1.0
Passaic	67 861	99.1	28.7	12.5	35.3	25.3	14.6	4.8	8.1	2.3	0.9	0.0	0.3	0.0	0.1	0.0	0.4
Paterson	149 222	97.4	30.0	11.8	34.6	23.7	14.2	5.4	6.9	2.6	2.6	1.3	0.1	0.0	0.0	0.0	1.1
Perth Amboy	47 303	98.5	30.8	13.7	34.1	24.0	12.2	3.7	7.8	2.8	1.5	0.0	0.8	0.0	0.0	0.0	0.7
Plainfield	47 829	98.1	31.6	12.4	30.8	20.8	13.6	5.6	9.7	2.6	1.9	0.0	0.8	0.3	0.1	0.0	0.7
Rahway	26 500	99.4	37.8	17.7	30.6	20.3	8.5	3.1	4.8	2.0	0.6	0.0	0.4	0.0	0.0	0.0	0.2
Sayreville Borough	40 377	99.4	37.0	21.3	31.6	21.9	5.9	1.5	3.6	1.7	0.6	0.0	0.5	0.0	0.0	0.0	0.1
Trenton	85 403	94.8	34.5	10.0	30.6	21.6	11.5	5.0	8.3	2.9	5.2	2.6	0.6	0.7	0.0	0.0	1.3
Union City	67 088	99.5	34.1	14.5	31.4	21.9	11.7	2.9	7.9	2.6	0.5	0.0	0.3	0.0	0.0	0.0	0.3
Vineland	56 271	95.7	35.4	17.3	30.6	22.0	6.8	2.9	5.6	2.8	4.3	0.8	1.1	0.0	0.0	0.0	2.4
Westfield	29 644	99.1	35.8	24.4	33.8	27.6	2.6	0.7	2.5	0.9	0.9	0.0	0.6	0.0	0.0	0.0	0.3
West New York	45 768	99.9	36.5	15.3	28.6	19.2	11.6	2.7	8.0	2.3	0.1	0.0	0.0	0.0	0.0	0.0	0.1
NEW MEXICO	1 819 046	98.0	37.3	18.8	31.2	24.5	5.8	2.8	4.9	2.4	2.0	0.6	0.4	0.1	0.4	0.1	0.4
Alamogordo	35 582	98.8	38.5	21.4	31.2	26.0	4.1	2.1	3.6	1.5	1.2	0.5	0.5	0.1	0.0	0.0	0.2
Albuquerque	448 607	97.9	40.8	17.8	27.8	21.9	5.1	2.1	6.4	2.8	2.1	0.4	0.4	0.1	0.5	0.0	0.7
Carlsbad	25 625	97.4	38.9	20.2	29.7	23.8	5.0	2.7	3.6	2.0	2.6	0.5	1.5	0.0	0.0	0.0	0.5
Clovis	32 667	98.2	38.1	19.0	32.0	26.7	4.9	2.7	4.2	1.9	1.8	0.6	0.9	0.0	0.0	0.0	0.3
Farmington	37 844	98.7	36.9	20.1	32.1	26.3	4.7	2.2	4.8	2.3	1.3	0.2	0.6	0.1	0.0	0.0	0.4
Hobbs	28 657	95.3	35.0	19.0	33.0	27.1	5.0	2.6	3.3	1.8	4.7	3.7	0.6	0.0	0.2	0.0	0.2
Las Cruces	74 267	96.8	39.3	16.6	28.2	22.2	5.2	2.3	7.5	2.8	3.2	1.2	0.3	0.0	1.1	0.0	0.6
Rio Rancho	51 765	99.2	36.7	21.8	32.8	27.2	3.9	1.5	4.1	2.0	0.8	0.0	0.5	0.0	0.0	0.0	0.3
Roswell	45 293	97.4	37.7	18.5	31.1	24.7	5.6	2.9	4.5	2.2	2.6	0.5	0.7	0.1	0.8	0.0	0.6
Santa Fe	62 203	97.6	44.3	16.7	23.8	17.8	5.2	1.9	7.6	3.2	2.4	0.0	0.7	0.0	1.2	0.0	0.5
NEW YORK	18 976 457	96.9	37.2	17.3	30.2	21.9	6.7	2.2	5.5	2.0	3.1	0.6	0.7	0.2	0.9	0.0	0.7
Albany	95 658	89.6	42.6	10.8	22.3	17.3	4.4	1.7	9.6	3.1	10.4	0.0	1.5	0.7	7.1	0.0	1.1
Auburn	28 574	90.8	39.9	14.9	27.1	20.9	3.3	1.2	5.6	3.0	9.2	6.0	1.6	0.2	0.2	0.0	1.3
Binghamton	47 380	97.4	44.5	14.1	25.0	19.5	4.0	1.4	9.8	3.0	2.6	0.2	1.3	0.4	0.0	0.0	0.7
Buffalo	292 648	96.2	41.9	11.6	30.3	23.0	5.6	2.5	6.8	2.7	3.8	0.5	0.9	0.4	1.4	0.0	0.7
Elmira	30 940	87.9	37.1	13.1	27.6	22.3	3.7	1.7	6.5	3.4	12.1	6.6	1.1	0.4	3.3	0.0	0.6
Freeport	43 783	98.5	30.8	15.3	31.9	21.0	12.8	4.6	7.6	1.8	1.5	0.0	0.9	0.0	0.0	0.0	0.6
Glen Cove	26 622	96.7	35.5	19.0	28.4	18.9	8.0	1.9	5.7	1.5	3.3	0.0	2.1	0.0	0.3	0.0	0.9
Hempstead	56 554	91.6	26.9	10.5	29.3	19.8	14.7	5.2	10.3	1.9	8.4	0.0	1.8	0.0	6.1	0.0	0.6

Table D. Cities

City	Households by type, 2000												Households, 1990		
		Family households						Nonfamily households							
				Married couple		Female householder[1]			Householder living alone						House-holder living alone
	Total households	Total	With own children under 18 years	Total	With own children under 18 years	Total	With own children under 18 years	Total	Total	65 years and over	Average house-hold size	Average family size	Total house-holds	Female house-holder[1]	
	71	72	73	74	75	76	77	78	79	80	81	82	83	84	85
NEVADA	751 165	66.3	31.8	49.7	22.1	11.1	6.7	33.7	24.9	7.1	2.62	3.14	466 297	10.2	25.7
Carson City	20 171	65.7	29.8	50.0	20.3	11.0	6.7	34.3	27.8	11.0	2.44	2.97	15 895	9.6	27.2
Henderson	66 331	71.0	33.0	56.4	24.3	10.0	6.0	29.0	20.3	5.0	2.63	3.05	23 237	9.7	18.0
Las Vegas	176 750	66.5	31.9	48.3	21.6	12.2	7.3	33.5	25.0	7.5	2.66	3.19	99 735	12.0	26.2
North Las Vegas	34 018	79.7	47.8	57.3	34.0	15.2	9.7	20.3	13.6	3.2	3.36	3.67	14 525	23.2	17.1
Reno	73 904	56.4	27.6	40.5	18.2	10.6	6.7	43.6	32.6	9.2	2.38	3.06	57 286	9.6	33.7
Sparks	24 601	67.6	35.2	50.0	24.8	12.0	7.3	32.4	24.3	7.7	2.67	3.19	20 561	11.2	23.7
NEW HAMPSHIRE	474 606	68.2	33.4	55.3	25.4	9.1	5.7	31.8	24.4	8.5	2.53	3.03	411 186	8.5	22.0
Concord	16 281	59.1	30.6	44.3	20.5	11.4	8.0	40.9	32.7	11.2	2.30	2.95	14 222	9.9	30.4
Dover	11 573	56.1	26.3	42.5	18.0	10.3	6.5	43.9	31.0	9.2	2.26	2.87	10 345	9.5	27.7
Manchester	44 247	59.0	29.4	42.6	19.2	11.7	7.5	41.0	31.7	10.3	2.36	3.00	40 338	11.1	29.2
Nashua	34 614	63.8	31.6	49.3	22.8	10.4	6.5	36.2	28.3	8.7	2.46	3.05	31 051	9.3	24.8
Rochester	11 434	66.9	32.8	50.9	22.0	11.4	7.8	33.1	25.7	9.6	2.46	2.95	10 221	10.0	22.5
NEW JERSEY	3 064 645	70.3	33.5	53.5	25.3	12.6	6.4	29.7	24.5	9.8	2.68	3.21	2 794 711	12.1	23.1
Atlantic City	15 848	54.9	27.7	24.8	10.8	23.2	14.0	45.1	37.2	15.4	2.46	3.26	15 731	22.8	40.6
Bayonne	25 545	62.7	28.3	42.8	19.4	15.1	7.3	37.3	32.8	15.0	2.42	3.10	25 309	13.7	31.4
Bergenfield Borough	8 981	75.2	36.4	59.8	30.7	11.8	4.6	24.8	20.8	9.9	2.92	3.41	8 799	10.6	19.8
Camden	24 177	72.1	42.2	26.1	13.6	37.7	24.5	27.9	22.5	7.8	3.12	3.62	26 626	36.9	23.6
Clifton	30 244	67.3	28.9	51.3	22.9	11.5	4.6	32.7	27.9	13.7	2.59	3.20	29 041	10.3	28.1
East Orange	26 024	61.8	31.9	26.0	12.0	28.8	16.7	38.2	33.0	11.0	2.63	3.37	27 210	26.4	35.1
Elizabeth	40 482	69.6	36.6	42.9	22.8	19.1	10.7	30.4	24.6	8.4	2.91	3.45	39 101	17.2	26.7
Englewood	9 273	69.9	31.0	47.9	21.8	17.4	7.4	30.1	24.8	9.0	2.79	3.29	8 971	15.8	24.5
Fair Lawn Borough	11 806	75.4	33.4	63.5	29.0	9.0	3.5	24.6	21.3	12.3	2.67	3.12	11 493	8.7	20.4
Fort Lee Borough	16 544	56.8	22.6	46.7	19.0	7.4	2.9	43.2	39.0	15.2	2.14	2.88	15 236	6.6	38.6
Garfield	11 250	66.0	30.5	46.5	22.6	13.8	6.1	34.0	27.4	12.2	2.64	3.26	10 946	11.8	28.9
Hackensack	18 113	52.7	21.9	34.8	13.9	13.0	6.4	47.3	39.8	9.4	2.26	3.08	16 464	11.9	39.7
Hoboken	19 418	35.2	11.4	23.8	6.6	9.0	4.1	64.8	41.8	8.0	1.92	2.73	15 036	12.8	37.8
Jersey City	88 632	62.8	31.1	36.4	17.6	20.2	11.2	37.2	29.2	8.2	2.67	3.37	82 381	20.4	28.7
Kearny	13 539	72.4	34.6	53.8	26.5	13.2	6.1	27.6	21.8	8.8	2.81	3.28	12 470	12.2	22.1
Linden	15 052	67.0	29.0	46.7	20.8	15.3	6.5	33.0	27.9	13.6	2.60	3.21	14 369	13.1	26.9
Long Branch	12 594	57.6	27.0	36.9	15.9	15.9	9.2	42.4	34.1	10.5	2.47	3.19	11 544	15.5	32.1
Millville	10 043	69.8	35.0	46.5	20.8	17.9	11.1	30.2	25.1	11.6	2.65	3.15	9 640	15.0	23.8
Newark	91 382	67.8	35.2	31.0	15.1	29.3	17.1	32.2	26.6	8.8	2.85	3.43	91 552	28.6	27.5
New Brunswick	13 057	55.2	29.1	29.6	15.8	18.0	10.0	44.8	24.3	8.4	3.23	3.69	12 711	17.5	28.3
Paramus Borough	8 082	83.9	37.0	73.3	33.7	8.0	2.6	16.1	14.4	9.4	3.00	3.32	7 776	8.3	11.3
Passaic	19 458	74.3	42.0	43.7	25.6	21.7	12.5	25.7	20.3	8.4	3.46	3.93	18 735	20.2	23.3
Paterson	44 710	74.6	40.9	39.4	21.3	26.8	15.7	25.4	20.4	7.9	3.25	3.71	43 946	23.7	21.3
Perth Amboy	14 562	73.9	40.3	44.6	23.8	21.0	12.2	26.1	20.6	8.8	3.20	3.63	14 207	17.6	24.2
Plainfield	15 137	72.0	35.5	39.3	18.8	24.5	13.0	28.0	21.1	7.4	3.10	3.49	15 146	21.5	21.8
Rahway	10 028	67.1	30.0	46.7	20.8	15.6	7.4	32.9	28.0	11.7	2.63	3.24	9 623	12.8	24.9
Sayreville Borough	14 955	73.0	34.3	57.5	27.7	11.1	5.0	27.0	22.3	8.7	2.68	3.17	12 749	9.9	19.7
Trenton	29 437	63.5	32.4	29.0	13.3	27.1	15.7	36.5	29.7	12.0	2.75	3.38	30 744	24.6	28.8
Union City	22 872	70.2	36.6	42.4	22.1	19.3	11.1	29.8	23.0	7.5	2.92	3.40	20 612	18.5	23.7
Vineland	19 930	71.3	33.9	48.8	21.4	16.8	9.6	28.7	23.7	11.2	2.70	3.17	18 732	15.2	21.1
Westfield	10 622	77.0	40.8	68.0	36.8	7.1	3.2	23.0	19.3	9.4	2.77	3.20	10 289	7.3	17.2
West New York	16 719	66.0	31.1	41.9	19.9	16.9	8.5	34.0	27.5	11.3	2.74	3.30	14 419	16.2	26.6
NEW MEXICO	677 971	68.8	34.7	50.4	23.3	13.2	8.3	31.2	25.4	8.2	2.63	3.18	542 709	11.9	23.0
Alamogordo	13 704	71.0	36.3	55.6	25.7	11.7	8.2	29.0	25.2	8.8	2.57	3.07	10 482	10.1	23.1
Albuquerque	183 236	61.5	30.2	43.6	19.4	12.9	8.0	38.5	30.5	8.4	2.40	3.02	153 818	12.1	28.2
Carlsbad	9 957	69.8	32.9	52.1	21.5	13.1	8.5	30.2	26.6	12.0	2.51	3.03	9 273	11.0	23.9
Clovis	12 458	69.0	36.3	49.8	23.1	14.9	10.4	31.0	26.8	10.3	2.57	3.12	11 676	12.5	23.9
Farmington	13 982	72.2	37.9	54.3	25.9	12.4	8.1	27.8	22.6	7.2	2.67	3.13	11 979	10.1	20.6
Hobbs	10 040	73.4	39.8	54.1	26.9	14.6	10.0	26.6	23.4	10.1	2.72	3.22	10 242	12.6	22.2
Las Cruces	29 184	62.1	30.4	42.3	18.0	15.1	9.9	37.9	27.9	8.9	2.46	3.05	23 797	12.7	25.1
Rio Rancho	18 995	74.3	40.3	59.4	30.9	10.3	6.5	25.7	20.8	7.9	2.70	3.14	11 658	8.7	17.1
Roswell	17 068	68.8	34.5	49.1	21.7	14.9	9.7	31.2	27.1	13.4	2.58	3.13	16 195	12.8	24.9
Santa Fe	27 569	54.3	24.1	37.6	14.6	12.1	7.0	45.7	36.4	10.2	2.20	2.90	22 789	12.3	31.0
NEW YORK	7 056 860	65.7	31.6	46.6	21.6	14.7	8.1	34.3	28.1	10.1	2.61	3.22	6 639 322	13.8	27.2
Albany	40 709	45.2	22.0	25.3	9.7	16.1	10.5	54.8	41.9	11.5	2.11	2.95	42 121	14.7	38.6
Auburn	11 411	57.3	28.1	37.3	15.7	14.7	9.6	42.7	36.3	16.6	2.27	2.98	11 936	14.5	32.2
Binghamton	21 089	49.4	23.3	31.6	12.6	13.8	8.7	50.6	40.3	15.5	2.19	2.96	22 617	13.2	36.2
Buffalo	122 720	54.6	28.6	27.6	12.0	22.3	14.4	45.4	37.7	12.1	2.29	3.07	136 436	20.2	35.6
Elmira	11 475	58.4	31.1	35.3	15.5	18.4	12.8	41.6	34.5	13.6	2.37	3.05	12 428	17.2	32.1
Freeport	13 504	73.4	36.4	49.7	25.0	17.8	9.0	26.6	21.2	8.1	3.20	3.65	13 240	15.4	22.4
Glen Cove	9 461	70.3	29.9	53.5	23.3	12.7	5.4	29.7	24.1	11.3	2.72	3.22	8 466	12.4	20.4
Hempstead	15 188	73.6	38.7	39.0	20.6	27.0	14.9	26.4	20.8	6.7	3.41	3.76	14 586	22.6	23.5

[1] No spouse present.

City	Percent change of households, 1990–2000	Total housing units	Occupied housing units (percent)	Housing occupancy — Vacant housing units: Total	For seasonal, recreational, or occasional use	Homeowner vacancy rate (percent)	Rental vacancy rate (percent)	Housing tenure — Occupied housing units: Total	Percent owner-occupied housing units	Percent renter-occupied housing units	Average household size of owner-occupied units	Average household size of renter-occupied units
	86	87	88	89	90	91	92	93	94	95	96	97
NEVADA	61.1	827 457	90.8	9.2	2.0	2.6	9.7	751 165	60.9	39.1	2.71	2.47
Carson City	26.9	21 283	94.8	5.2	0.5	1.5	6.0	20 171	63.1	36.9	2.48	2.41
Henderson	185.5	71 149	93.2	6.8	1.2	2.2	9.4	66 331	70.5	29.5	2.71	2.43
Las Vegas	77.2	190 724	92.7	7.3	0.9	2.5	8.4	176 750	59.1	40.9	2.76	2.52
North Las Vegas	134.2	36 600	92.9	7.1	0.2	2.1	12.0	34 018	70.1	29.9	3.27	3.56
Reno	29.0	79 453	93.0	7.0	0.5	2.2	7.9	73 904	47.5	52.5	2.53	2.25
Sparks	19.6	26 025	94.5	5.5	0.2	2.4	7.0	24 601	59.7	40.3	2.76	2.54
NEW HAMPSHIRE	15.4	547 024	86.8	13.2	10.3	1.0	3.5	474 606	69.7	30.3	2.70	2.14
Concord	14.5	16 881	96.4	3.6	0.7	0.8	2.9	16 281	51.4	48.6	2.62	1.96
Dover	11.9	11 924	97.1	2.9	0.6	0.7	1.8	11 573	51.2	48.8	2.54	1.96
Manchester	9.7	45 892	96.4	3.6	0.5	0.5	3.1	44 247	46.0	54.0	2.61	2.14
Nashua	11.5	35 387	97.8	2.2	0.5	0.4	1.6	34 614	56.9	43.1	2.66	2.20
Rochester	11.9	11 836	96.6	3.4	0.7	0.9	2.8	11 434	66.8	33.2	2.56	2.26
NEW JERSEY	9.7	3 310 275	92.6	7.4	3.3	1.2	4.5	3 064 645	65.6	34.4	2.81	2.43
Atlantic City	0.7	20 219	78.4	21.6	9.6	6.2	7.3	15 848	28.9	71.1	2.66	2.38
Bayonne	0.9	26 826	95.2	4.8	0.2	0.9	3.6	25 545	40.0	60.0	2.61	2.28
Bergenfield Borough	2.1	9 147	98.2	1.8	0.2	0.4	1.8	8 981	71.1	28.9	3.09	2.49
Camden	-9.2	29 769	81.2	18.8	0.1	5.1	6.1	24 177	46.1	53.9	3.16	3.09
Clifton	4.1	31 060	97.4	2.6	0.2	0.7	2.4	30 244	60.9	39.1	2.75	2.33
East Orange	-4.4	28 485	91.4	8.6	0.1	2.3	6.8	26 024	26.6	73.4	3.27	2.40
Elizabeth	3.5	42 838	94.5	5.5	0.3	1.5	3.4	40 482	29.7	70.3	3.25	2.76
Englewood	3.4	9 614	96.5	3.5	0.4	1.0	2.5	9 273	59.4	40.6	2.91	2.63
Fair Lawn Borough	2.7	12 006	98.3	1.7	0.2	0.4	1.9	11 806	80.0	20.0	2.80	2.11
Fort Lee Borough	8.6	17 446	94.8	5.2	1.5	1.3	3.9	16 544	56.2	43.8	2.13	2.15
Garfield	2.8	11 698	96.2	3.8	0.3	0.8	2.9	11 250	40.2	59.8	2.80	2.54
Hackensack	10.0	18 945	95.6	4.4	0.6	1.3	3.8	18 113	32.4	67.6	2.49	2.15
Hoboken	29.1	19 915	97.5	2.5	0.3	0.6	1.7	19 418	22.6	77.4	1.96	1.91
Jersey City	7.6	93 648	94.6	5.4	0.3	1.9	3.3	88 632	28.2	71.8	2.98	2.55
Kearny	8.6	13 872	97.6	2.4	0.2	0.6	2.1	13 539	48.0	52.0	3.00	2.63
Linden	4.8	15 567	96.7	3.3	0.2	1.1	3.0	15 052	58.7	41.3	2.75	2.39
Long Branch	9.1	13 983	90.1	9.9	5.0	1.3	3.6	12 594	42.4	57.6	2.61	2.37
Millville	4.2	10 652	94.3	5.7	0.5	2.0	5.8	10 043	63.9	36.1	2.71	2.54
Newark	-0.2	100 141	91.3	8.7	0.1	2.0	5.6	91 382	23.8	76.2	3.22	2.74
New Brunswick	2.7	13 893	94.0	6.0	0.3	2.0	3.4	13 057	26.3	73.7	3.01	3.30
Paramus Borough	3.9	8 209	98.5	1.5	0.2	0.5	2.2	8 082	90.7	9.3	3.00	2.94
Passaic	3.9	20 194	96.4	3.6	0.2	2.0	1.9	19 458	27.0	73.0	3.63	3.40
Paterson	1.7	47 169	94.8	5.2	0.1	1.7	3.8	44 710	31.5	68.5	3.59	3.10
Perth Amboy	2.5	15 236	95.6	4.4	0.2	1.5	2.8	14 562	40.5	59.5	3.24	3.17
Plainfield	-0.1	16 180	93.6	6.4	0.1	2.3	5.0	15 137	50.1	49.9	3.16	3.04
Rahway	4.2	10 381	96.6	3.4	0.1	1.2	3.3	10 028	62.7	37.3	2.84	2.26
Sayreville Borough	17.3	15 235	98.2	1.8	0.1	0.6	1.6	14 955	67.7	32.3	2.84	2.35
Trenton	-4.3	33 843	87.0	13.0	0.1	4.0	8.4	29 437	45.5	54.5	2.83	2.69
Union City	11.0	23 741	96.3	3.7	0.2	1.0	2.3	22 872	18.2	81.8	2.98	2.90
Vineland	6.4	20 958	95.1	4.9	0.5	1.7	4.4	19 930	66.2	33.8	2.74	2.63
Westfield	3.2	10 819	98.2	1.8	0.4	0.3	2.7	10 622	81.7	18.3	2.94	1.99
West New York	16.0	17 360	96.3	3.7	0.3	1.4	2.5	16 719	19.9	80.1	2.70	2.74
NEW MEXICO	24.9	780 579	86.9	13.1	4.1	2.2	11.6	677 971	70.0	30.0	2.72	2.41
Alamogordo	30.7	15 920	86.1	13.9	1.1	3.5	18.0	13 704	60.7	39.3	2.61	2.49
Albuquerque	19.1	198 465	92.3	7.7	0.4	1.9	11.8	183 236	60.4	39.6	2.55	2.16
Carlsbad	7.4	11 421	87.2	12.8	0.6	3.3	20.1	9 957	71.5	28.5	2.56	2.38
Clovis	6.7	14 269	87.3	12.7	0.5	5.1	12.2	12 458	62.3	37.7	2.58	2.57
Farmington	16.7	15 077	92.7	7.3	0.7	1.5	9.5	13 982	68.4	31.6	2.74	2.51
Hobbs	-2.0	11 968	83.9	16.1	0.3	4.0	21.1	10 040	67.9	32.1	2.76	2.64
Las Cruces	22.6	31 682	92.1	7.9	0.7	2.3	9.3	29 184	58.1	41.9	2.60	2.28
Rio Rancho	62.9	20 209	94.0	6.0	0.5	2.3	12.2	18 995	81.5	18.5	2.75	2.51
Roswell	5.4	19 327	88.3	11.7	0.6	3.3	14.2	17 068	68.4	31.6	2.64	2.47
Santa Fe	21.0	30 533	90.3	9.7	5.2	1.7	5.5	27 569	58.2	41.8	2.31	2.05
NEW YORK	6.3	7 679 307	91.9	8.1	3.1	1.6	4.6	7 056 860	53.0	47.0	2.78	2.41
Albany	-3.4	45 288	89.9	10.1	0.2	3.3	7.0	40 709	37.6	62.4	2.31	1.98
Auburn	-4.4	12 637	90.3	9.7	0.2	2.7	11.4	11 411	51.9	48.1	2.48	2.05
Binghamton	-6.8	23 971	88.0	12.0	0.3	3.9	11.2	21 089	43.0	57.0	2.33	2.08
Buffalo	-10.1	145 574	84.3	15.7	0.2	4.2	11.1	122 720	43.5	56.5	2.47	2.16
Elmira	-7.7	12 895	89.0	11.0	0.3	3.2	10.9	11 475	48.3	51.7	2.49	2.26
Freeport	2.0	13 819	97.7	2.3	0.3	1.1	1.1	13 504	65.2	34.8	3.23	3.14
Glen Cove	11.8	9 734	97.2	2.8	0.7	0.9	1.3	9 461	58.5	41.5	2.75	2.67
Hempstead	4.1	15 579	97.5	2.5	0.1	1.1	1.7	15 188	43.2	56.8	3.70	3.19

Table D. Cities

STATE Place code	City	Population, 2000				Population, 1990				Population and population characteristics, 2000					
										Race (percent)					
										One race					
		Land area, 2000[1] (sq km)	Total persons	Rank	Per square kilometer	Land area, 1990[1] (sq km)	Total persons	Rank	Per square kilometer	White	Black or African American	American Indian or Alaska Native	Asian	Native Hawaiian and other Pacific Islander	Some other race
		1	2	3	4	5	6	7	8	9	10	11	12	13	14
	NEW YORK—Cont'd														
36 38077	Ithaca	14.1	29 287	1 263	2 077.1	14.1	29 541	1 068	2 095.1	74.0	6.7	0.4	13.7	0.1	1.9
36 38264	Jamestown	23.3	31 730	1 145	1 361.8	22.9	34 681	868	1 514.5	91.5	3.4	0.6	0.4	0.1	1.8
36 42554	Lindenhurst	9.7	27 819	1 336	2 867.9	9.7	26 879	1 186	2 771.0	94.2	0.8	0.1	1.4	0.0	1.7
36 43335	Long Beach	5.5	35 462	1 005	6 447.6	5.5	33 510	918	6 092.7	84.2	6.2	0.2	2.3	0.1	4.7
36 47042	Middletown	13.3	25 388	1 485	1 908.9	12.8	24 160	1 345	1 887.5	68.7	15.1	0.7	1.7	0.0	9.3
36 49121	Mount Vernon	11.3	68 381	422	6 051.4	11.4	67 153	361	5 890.6	28.6	59.6	0.3	2.1	0.1	4.8
36 50034	Newburgh	9.9	28 259	1 314	2 854.4	9.9	26 454	1 218	2 672.1	42.3	33.0	0.7	0.8	0.1	18.1
36 50617	New Rochelle	26.8	72 182	392	2 693.4	26.8	67 265	360	2 509.9	67.9	19.2	0.2	3.2	0.0	6.3
36 51000	New York	785.6	8 008 278	1	10 193.8	800.2	7 322 564	1	9 150.9	44.7	26.6	0.5	9.8	0.1	13.4
36 51055	Niagara Falls	36.4	55 593	576	1 527.3	36.4	61 840	404	1 698.9	76.2	18.7	1.6	0.7	0.0	0.7
36 53682	North Tonawanda	26.2	33 262	1 091	1 269.5	26.2	34 989	862	1 335.5	97.9	0.3	0.3	0.5	0.0	0.3
36 59223	Port Chester	6.1	27 867	1 333	4 568.4	6.1	24 728	1 303	4 053.8	60.7	7.0	0.4	2.1	0.0	23.0
36 59641	Poughkeepsie	13.3	29 871	1 230	2 245.9	13.3	28 844	1 097	2 168.7	52.8	35.7	0.4	1.6	0.0	5.3
36 63000	Rochester	92.8	219 773	81	2 368.2	92.7	230 356	66	2 485.0	48.3	38.5	0.5	2.2	0.0	6.6
36 63418	Rome	194.1	34 950	1 030	180.1	194.1	44 350	648	228.5	87.9	7.6	0.3	0.9	0.0	1.4
36 65255	Saratoga Springs	73.6	26 186	1 437	355.8	73.6	25 001	1 286	339.7	93.5	3.1	0.2	1.0	0.0	0.6
36 65508	Schenectady	28.1	61 821	479	2 200.0	28.1	65 566	376	2 333.3	76.8	14.8	0.4	2.0	0.0	2.5
36 70420	Spring Valley	5.4	25 464	1 481	4 715.6	5.4	21 802	1 510	4 037.4	38.2	44.0	0.4	5.6	0.2	5.3
36 73000	Syracuse	65.0	147 306	146	2 266.2	65.0	163 860	107	2 520.9	64.3	25.3	1.1	3.4	0.0	2.2
36 75484	Troy	27.0	49 170	687	1 821.1	27.0	54 269	484	2 010.0	80.2	11.4	0.3	3.5	0.0	2.2
36 76540	Utica	42.3	60 651	489	1 433.8	42.3	68 637	349	1 622.6	79.4	12.9	0.3	2.2	0.0	2.2
36 76705	Valley Stream	8.9	36 368	968	4 086.3	8.9	33 946	892	3 814.2	78.8	7.5	0.1	6.9	0.0	4.1
36 78608	Watertown	23.2	26 705	1 394	1 151.1	22.5	29 429	1 072	1 308.0	89.1	4.9	0.5	1.2	0.1	1.7
36 81677	White Plains	25.4	53 077	621	2 089.6	25.4	48 718	577	1 918.0	64.9	15.9	0.3	4.5	0.1	10.4
36 84000	Yonkers	46.8	196 086	98	4 189.9	46.8	188 082	86	4 018.8	60.2	16.6	0.4	4.9	0.0	13.4
37 00000	NORTH CAROLINA	126 160.6	8 049 313	X	63.8	126 179.9	6 632 448	X	52.6	72.1	21.6	1.2	1.4	0.0	2.3
37 02140	Asheville	106.0	68 889	415	649.9	90.5	63 379	390	700.3	78.0	17.6	0.3	0.9	0.1	1.5
37 09060	Burlington	55.1	44 917	764	815.2	52.7	39 498	752	749.5	66.3	25.1	0.3	1.7	0.0	5.2
37 10740	Cary	109.0	94 536	265	867.3	80.7	44 394	647	550.1	82.2	6.1	0.3	8.1	0.0	1.5
37 11800	Chapel Hill	51.2	48 715	693	951.5	42.8	38 711	770	904.5	77.9	11.4	0.4	7.2	0.0	1.2
37 12000	Charlotte	627.5	540 828	28	861.9	451.3	419 558	33	929.7	58.3	32.7	0.3	3.4	0.1	3.6
37 14100	Concord	133.6	55 977	567	419.0	56.5	29 591	1 067	523.7	78.8	15.1	0.3	1.2	0.0	3.3
37 19000	Durham	245.1	187 035	106	763.1	179.4	138 894	131	774.2	45.5	43.8	0.3	3.6	0.0	4.7
37 22920	Fayetteville	152.2	121 015	187	795.1	105.1	75 850	300	721.7	48.8	42.4	1.1	2.2	0.2	2.5
37 25580	Gastonia	119.3	66 277	441	555.5	78.7	54 725	478	695.4	70.2	25.6	0.2	1.2	0.0	1.8
37 26880	Goldsboro	64.2	39 043	896	608.1	54.5	40 736	722	747.4	43.0	52.2	0.4	1.4	0.1	1.1
37 28000	Greensboro	271.2	223 891	79	825.6	206.7	185 125	89	895.6	55.5	37.4	0.4	2.8	0.0	2.1
37 28080	Greenville	66.2	60 476	492	913.5	46.7	46 274	617	990.9	61.4	34.1	0.3	1.8	0.0	1.0
37 31060	Hickory	72.7	37 222	948	512.0	52.6	28 474	1 116	541.3	77.2	14.1	0.2	3.9	0.1	3.1
37 31400	High Point	127.0	85 839	303	675.9	111.4	69 428	345	623.2	60.6	31.8	0.5	3.3	0.0	2.3
37 34200	Jacksonville	115.2	66 715	437	579.1	33.7	78 031	290	2 315.5	63.9	24.0	0.8	2.1	0.2	5.4
37 35200	Kannapolis	77.3	36 910	952	477.5	40.7	31 592	988	776.2	77.7	16.5	0.3	0.9	0.0	3.4
37 43920	Monroe	63.6	26 228	1 433	412.4	35.9	18 623	1 766	518.7	60.1	27.8	0.4	0.6	0.0	9.4
37 55000	Raleigh	296.8	276 093	64	930.2	228.3	218 859	74	958.6	63.3	27.8	0.4	3.4	0.0	3.2
37 57500	Rocky Mount	92.1	55 893	571	606.9	64.7	53 078	505	820.4	40.9	56.0	0.3	0.7	0.0	0.9
37 58860	Salisbury	46.0	26 462	1 412	575.3	42.4	23 626	1 388	557.2	57.3	37.6	0.3	1.4	0.1	1.9
37 74440	Wilmington	106.2	75 838	370	714.1	76.9	55 530	465	722.1	70.6	25.8	0.4	0.9	0.1	1.1
37 74540	Wilson	60.3	44 405	774	736.4	47.9	38 400	776	801.7	46.7	47.5	0.3	0.6	0.0	3.9
37 75000	Winston-Salem	281.9	185 776	111	659.0	184.2	162 292	108	881.1	55.6	37.1	0.3	1.1	0.0	4.3
38 00000	NORTH DAKOTA	178 646.8	642 200	X	3.6	178 695.2	638 800	X	3.6	92.4	0.6	4.9	0.6	0.0	0.4
38 07200	Bismarck	69.6	55 532	578	797.9	63.0	49 272	569	782.1	94.8	0.3	3.4	0.5	0.0	0.2
38 25700	Fargo	98.3	90 599	281	921.7	77.2	74 084	312	959.6	94.2	1.0	1.2	1.6	0.0	0.4
38 32060	Grand Forks	49.8	49 321	683	990.4	37.4	49 417	566	1 321.3	93.3	0.9	2.8	1.0	0.1	0.6
38 53380	Minot	37.7	36 567	960	969.9	34.3	34 544	872	1 007.1	93.2	1.3	2.8	0.6	0.1	0.5
39 00000	OHIO	106 055.8	11 353 140	X	107.0	106 067.2	10 847 115	X	102.3	85.0	11.5	0.2	1.2	0.0	0.8
39 01000	Akron	160.8	217 074	83	1 350.0	161.1	223 019	71	1 384.4	67.2	28.5	0.3	1.5	0.0	0.4
39 03828	Barberton	23.3	27 899	1 329	1 197.4	19.7	27 623	1 151	1 402.2	92.4	5.3	0.3	0.4	0.0	0.2
39 04720	Beavercreek	68.4	37 984	931	555.3	66.7	33 626	910	504.1	93.4	1.4	0.2	3.5	0.0	0.3
39 07972	Bowling Green	26.3	29 636	1 244	1 126.8	20.5	28 303	1 126	1 380.6	91.8	2.8	0.2	1.8	0.0	1.8
39 09680	Brunswick	32.5	33 388	1 088	1 027.3	29.8	28 218	1 131	946.9	97.1	0.7	0.1	0.9	0.0	0.4
39 12000	Canton	53.2	80 806	335	1 518.9	52.4	84 161	267	1 606.1	74.5	21.0	0.5	0.3	0.0	0.6
39 15000	Cincinnati	201.9	331 285	56	1 640.8	200.0	364 114	45	1 820.6	53.0	42.9	0.2	1.5	0.0	0.6
39 16000	Cleveland	200.9	478 403	35	2 381.3	199.5	505 616	23	2 534.4	41.5	51.0	0.3	1.3	0.0	3.6
39 16014	Cleveland Heights	21.0	49 958	669	2 379.0	21.0	54 052	488	2 573.9	52.5	41.8	0.2	2.6	0.0	0.7
39 18000	Columbus	544.6	711 470	16	1 306.4	494.5	632 945	16	1 280.0	67.9	24.5	0.3	3.4	0.1	1.2
39 19778	Cuyahoga Falls	66.2	49 374	680	745.8	66.1	48 950	573	740.5	95.8	1.9	0.2	1.1	0.0	0.2
39 21000	Dayton	144.5	166 179	127	1 150.0	142.5	182 011	90	1 277.3	53.4	43.1	0.3	0.6	0.0	0.7

[1] Dry land or land partially or temporarily covered by water.

Table D. Cities

City	Population and population characteristics, 2000 (cont'd)								Population and population characteristics, 1990				
	Race (percent) (cont'd)								Race (percent)				
		Race alone or in combination											
	Two or more races	White	Black	American Indian or Alaska Native	Asian	Native Hawaiian and other Pacific Islander	Some other race	Hispanic[1]	White	Black or African American	American Indian or Alaska Native	Asian and Pacific Islander	Hispanic[1]
	15	16	17	18	19	20	21	22	23	24	25	26	27
NEW YORK—Cont'd													
Ithaca	3.4	76.4	7.8	1.0	15.1	0.5	2.8	5.3	81.8	6.5	0.3	10.0	3.6
Jamestown	2.2	93.5	4.5	1.2	0.6	0.1	2.4	4.9	94.9	2.6	0.5	0.5	3.0
Lindenhurst	1.8	95.8	1.1	0.4	1.7	0.1	2.8	6.5	97.9	0.5	0.1	1.0	4.1
Long Beach	2.3	85.9	6.8	0.5	2.8	0.2	6.2	12.8	87.0	7.8	0.3	1.7	10.8
Middletown	4.4	72.1	17.4	1.5	2.1	0.2	11.4	25.1	82.2	11.1	0.5	1.4	13.3
Mount Vernon	4.4	30.9	62.2	0.9	2.7	0.3	7.8	10.4	39.8	55.3	0.4	1.8	7.8
Newburgh	5.1	45.9	35.5	1.5	1.1	0.2	21.1	36.3	51.2	34.8	0.3	0.5	23.2
New Rochelle	3.2	70.2	20.3	0.6	3.8	0.1	8.4	20.1	76.0	18.1	0.1	2.9	10.8
New York	4.9	47.5	28.4	1.1	10.9	0.2	17.0	27.0	52.3	28.7	0.4	7.0	24.4
Niagara Falls	2.0	77.9	19.8	2.4	0.9	0.1	1.1	2.0	82.2	15.6	1.6	0.3	1.2
North Tonawanda	0.7	98.5	0.5	0.6	0.7	0.0	0.4	1.1	98.9	0.2	0.3	0.4	0.8
Port Chester	6.8	67.0	7.6	0.7	2.3	0.2	29.3	46.2	79.4	10.2	0.1	1.7	30.1
Poughkeepsie	4.1	55.3	38.5	1.2	1.9	0.1	7.2	10.6	65.4	31.5	0.4	1.5	3.8
Rochester	3.8	50.9	40.7	1.3	2.7	0.2	8.4	12.8	61.1	31.5	0.5	1.8	8.7
Rome	2.0	89.7	8.5	0.6	1.2	0.1	2.1	4.7	89.4	8.0	0.2	1.3	3.9
Saratoga Springs	1.4	94.8	3.8	0.7	1.3	0.0	0.9	1.9	95.5	3.3	0.2	0.7	1.4
Schenectady	3.5	79.6	16.8	1.0	2.6	0.2	3.6	5.9	88.6	8.7	0.3	1.1	2.7
Spring Valley	6.3	40.3	48.3	0.8	6.2	0.7	10.2	15.4	49.4	43.1	0.4	5.2	7.5
Syracuse	3.6	67.1	27.5	2.2	3.8	0.1	3.2	5.3	75.0	20.3	1.3	2.2	2.9
Troy	2.3	82.2	12.6	0.7	3.9	0.1	3.1	4.3	88.3	7.6	0.2	3.0	2.1
Utica	3.0	82.0	14.0	0.7	2.6	0.1	3.7	5.8	86.7	10.5	0.3	1.1	3.4
Valley Stream	2.5	80.4	8.3	0.4	7.7	0.2	5.8	12.3	94.9	0.4	0.0	3.6	4.5
Watertown	2.4	91.2	6.1	1.2	1.6	0.3	2.3	3.6	93.8	3.8	0.5	0.8	2.0
White Plains	3.9	67.5	17.1	0.8	5.0	0.5	13.2	23.5	73.7	19.0	0.2	3.1	14.2
Yonkers	4.4	63.2	18.1	0.9	5.5	0.2	16.8	25.9	76.2	14.1	0.2	3.0	16.7
NORTH CAROLINA	1.3	73.1	22.1	1.6	1.7	0.1	2.8	4.7	75.6	22.0	1.2	0.8	1.2
Asheville	1.6	79.3	18.2	0.8	1.2	0.1	2.1	3.8	79.1	19.8	0.3	0.6	0.9
Burlington	1.4	67.3	25.6	0.7	2.0	0.1	5.8	10.1	76.3	22.6	0.2	0.8	0.6
Cary	1.8	83.7	6.6	0.6	8.8	0.1	2.2	4.3	89.8	5.5	0.3	3.8	1.6
Chapel Hill	1.9	79.4	12.1	0.9	7.9	0.1	1.6	3.2	82.3	12.5	0.3	4.3	1.6
Charlotte	1.7	59.4	33.4	0.7	3.8	0.1	4.4	7.4	65.6	31.8	0.4	1.8	1.4
Concord	1.2	79.8	15.5	0.6	1.4	0.1	3.9	7.8	78.6	20.6	0.2	0.5	0.5
Durham	1.9	46.8	44.6	0.8	4.1	0.1	5.6	8.6	51.7	45.7	0.2	2.0	1.2
Fayetteville	2.8	50.7	43.8	1.8	3.0	0.4	3.4	5.7	57.6	38.3	1.3	1.5	3.1
Gastonia	1.0	71.0	26.1	0.5	1.4	0.1	2.1	5.5	74.0	24.9	0.2	0.7	0.5
Goldsboro	1.6	44.2	53.2	0.8	1.9	0.1	1.6	2.7	50.3	47.4	0.3	1.3	1.5
Greensboro	1.7	56.6	38.2	0.9	3.2	0.1	2.8	4.4	63.9	33.9	0.5	1.4	1.0
Greenville	1.3	62.4	34.7	0.6	2.2	0.1	1.5	2.1	64.2	34.1	0.2	1.2	0.8
Hickory	1.5	78.3	14.6	0.5	4.4	0.1	3.8	7.7	81.4	17.1	0.3	1.0	0.8
High Point	1.6	61.6	32.3	0.8	3.9	0.1	3.0	4.9	68.1	30.2	0.5	0.9	0.8
Jacksonville	3.7	66.6	25.5	1.6	3.2	0.5	6.6	10.0	67.6	26.7	0.5	3.0	5.2
Kannapolis	1.2	78.7	16.9	0.6	1.1	0.1	3.8	6.3	81.3	18.0	0.1	0.2	0.6
Monroe	1.6	61.4	28.2	0.7	0.8	0.1	10.4	21.4	58.3	40.2	0.3	0.6	1.3
Raleigh	1.9	64.7	28.6	0.8	3.8	0.1	4.0	7.0	69.2	27.6	0.3	2.5	1.4
Rocky Mount	1.1	41.7	56.5	0.6	0.9	0.1	1.3	1.8	49.6	49.6	0.2	0.4	0.5
Salisbury	1.5	58.4	38.2	0.7	1.7	0.1	2.4	4.3	63.8	35.2	0.2	0.7	0.6
Wilmington	1.1	71.5	26.3	0.7	1.1	0.1	1.5	2.6	64.9	33.9	0.3	0.6	0.9
Wilson	1.0	47.4	47.9	0.5	0.8	0.1	4.4	7.3	52.4	46.9	0.1	0.3	0.7
Winston-Salem	1.6	56.7	37.9	0.6	1.4	0.1	4.9	8.6	59.5	39.3	0.2	0.8	0.9
NORTH DAKOTA	1.2	93.4	0.8	5.5	0.8	0.1	0.6	1.2	94.6	0.6	4.1	0.5	0.7
Bismarck	0.9	95.6	0.4	3.9	0.6	0.1	0.3	0.7	96.7	0.1	2.6	0.4	0.7
Fargo	1.5	95.4	1.4	1.7	2.0	0.1	0.9	1.3	97.1	0.4	1.1	1.3	0.7
Grand Forks	1.4	94.6	1.2	3.5	1.3	0.1	0.8	1.9	95.5	0.8	2.3	1.1	1.2
Minot	1.5	94.6	1.8	3.5	0.9	0.1	0.7	1.5	95.8	1.1	2.1	0.8	0.8
OHIO	1.4	86.1	12.1	0.7	1.4	0.1	1.1	1.9	87.8	10.6	0.2	0.8	1.3
Akron	2.1	68.9	29.7	0.9	1.8	0.1	0.8	1.2	73.8	24.5	0.3	1.2	0.7
Barberton	1.4	93.7	5.9	0.8	0.5	0.0	0.4	0.6	94.1	5.3	0.3	0.3	0.3
Beavercreek	1.1	94.5	1.6	0.5	4.0	0.1	0.5	1.1	96.3	0.9	0.2	2.3	1.0
Bowling Green	1.5	93.1	3.2	0.6	2.2	0.1	2.3	3.5	93.9	2.6	0.2	2.1	2.2
Brunswick	0.8	97.8	0.9	0.4	1.1	0.0	0.6	1.4	98.6	0.4	0.1	0.8	0.8
Canton	3.1	77.1	22.9	1.5	0.5	0.1	1.2	1.2	80.7	18.2	0.5	0.3	1.1
Cincinnati	1.7	54.2	44.0	0.8	1.8	0.1	1.0	1.3	60.5	37.9	0.2	1.1	0.7
Cleveland	2.2	43.2	52.1	0.9	1.6	0.1	4.6	7.3	49.5	46.6	0.3	1.0	4.6
Cleveland Heights	2.3	54.2	43.3	0.8	3.0	0.1	1.2	1.6	60.2	37.1	0.2	2.1	1.1
Columbus	2.6	69.8	26.0	1.0	3.9	0.1	2.0	2.5	74.4	22.6	0.2	2.4	1.1
Cuyahoga Falls	0.9	96.6	2.1	0.5	1.2	0.0	0.4	0.6	98.1	1.1	0.1	0.6	0.4
Dayton	1.8	54.8	44.3	1.0	0.9	0.1	1.0	1.6	58.4	40.4	0.2	0.6	0.7

[1] Hispanic persons may be of any race.

Table D. Cities

City	Population and population characteristics, 2000										
	Age (percent)										
	Under 5 years	5 to 17 years	18 to 24 years	25 to 34 years	35 to 44 years	45 to 54 years	55 to 64 years	65 to 74 years	75 years and over	Median age (years)	Percent Female
	28	29	30	31	32	33	34	35	36	37	38
NEW YORK—Cont'd											
Ithaca	2.5	6.8	53.8	12.6	7.4	7.1	3.5	2.8	3.5	22.0	49.4
Jamestown	7.6	18.3	9.1	13.5	14.7	12.9	8.0	7.5	8.5	36.2	52.3
Lindenhurst	6.9	19.8	7.1	14.5	19.5	13.5	7.6	6.3	4.7	35.8	51.4
Long Beach	4.9	13.7	6.6	16.5	17.9	14.9	8.9	7.6	9.1	39.6	51.9
Middletown	7.9	19.9	9.4	15.3	15.6	12.4	7.5	5.4	6.6	33.4	51.7
Mount Vernon	7.1	18.3	8.3	14.9	16.2	13.1	9.3	6.5	6.4	35.8	54.9
Newburgh	9.8	23.4	12.7	15.1	13.7	9.4	6.7	4.5	4.6	27.8	52.6
New Rochelle	6.8	17.3	8.7	14.0	15.5	13.1	9.2	7.6	7.9	37.0	52.5
New York	6.8	17.5	10.0	17.1	15.8	12.6	8.5	6.2	5.5	34.2	52.6
Niagara Falls	6.4	18.3	8.6	12.4	15.3	12.5	7.9	8.7	9.9	38.0	53.2
North Tonawanda	5.7	18.1	8.6	12.3	16.7	14.8	8.3	8.2	7.5	38.4	51.4
Port Chester	7.0	15.5	10.8	18.5	16.7	11.5	7.1	6.3	6.6	34.0	49.4
Poughkeepsie	7.6	18.3	12.2	15.0	14.2	11.4	7.7	6.6	7.0	32.7	52.2
Rochester	7.8	20.3	11.6	17.1	15.0	11.4	6.7	4.5	5.5	30.8	52.2
Rome	5.9	16.3	8.5	14.3	15.6	13.2	9.2	7.8	9.4	38.2	48.8
Saratoga Springs	5.3	14.0	15.5	13.2	14.3	14.6	8.8	6.1	8.2	36.3	52.5
Schenectady	7.0	17.3	11.6	14.4	15.3	11.7	7.4	6.6	8.6	34.8	52.2
Spring Valley	9.6	22.5	10.7	16.4	15.3	11.5	7.3	3.8	2.9	29.4	50.3
Syracuse	6.9	18.0	16.8	14.5	13.4	11.0	6.5	5.8	7.1	30.5	52.9
Troy	6.4	15.7	17.6	14.9	13.6	10.9	7.2	6.5	7.2	31.7	50.5
Utica	6.7	17.4	10.0	13.2	13.7	11.8	8.4	8.1	10.7	37.0	53.0
Valley Stream	5.8	17.7	7.7	12.6	16.6	14.7	8.7	8.2	8.1	39.0	52.3
Watertown	7.8	18.2	10.4	15.1	14.5	11.4	7.1	6.8	8.7	34.0	52.5
White Plains	6.2	15.0	7.5	16.0	16.5	13.9	9.7	7.6	7.5	38.1	52.7
Yonkers	7.0	17.3	8.8	15.4	15.2	12.3	8.9	7.7	7.3	35.8	53.0
NORTH CAROLINA	6.7	17.7	10.0	15.1	16.0	13.5	9.0	6.6	5.4	35.3	51.0
Asheville	5.4	14.2	10.3	14.3	14.4	14.0	9.1	8.6	9.7	39.2	53.2
Burlington	6.5	17.2	8.9	14.6	14.4	12.6	8.8	8.5	8.5	36.9	53.0
Cary	8.1	21.0	6.6	16.9	21.6	14.1	6.3	3.1	2.3	33.7	50.2
Chapel Hill	3.6	11.5	37.1	14.2	10.2	9.9	5.5	3.9	4.2	24.0	54.9
Charlotte	7.1	17.6	10.4	19.1	17.1	12.9	7.1	4.7	4.1	32.7	51.0
Concord	7.9	18.3	8.9	17.1	16.4	12.3	7.9	5.6	5.5	33.6	51.1
Durham	7.2	15.8	14.1	20.1	15.5	11.8	6.3	4.6	4.7	31.0	51.9
Fayetteville	7.5	17.9	12.7	16.4	14.8	11.7	8.0	6.5	4.5	31.9	52.1
Gastonia	7.0	17.9	8.8	15.4	15.1	13.4	8.6	7.3	6.5	35.6	52.7
Goldsboro	7.1	17.9	11.4	14.6	15.2	12.0	8.0	7.3	6.4	34.3	50.8
Greensboro	6.3	15.9	14.1	16.7	14.9	12.5	7.6	6.1	5.8	33.0	52.8
Greenville	5.6	13.3	28.7	16.6	11.6	9.9	5.6	4.6	4.2	26.0	53.7
Hickory	6.9	16.3	11.2	16.1	14.6	12.8	8.5	7.0	6.6	34.6	51.9
High Point	7.5	18.5	9.3	15.6	16.2	13.0	8.0	6.1	5.7	34.4	52.2
Jacksonville	9.6	14.6	36.3	15.8	10.1	5.6	3.1	2.8	2.0	22.4	39.0
Kannapolis	7.0	17.1	9.0	15.1	15.4	12.0	8.8	7.6	8.0	36.0	51.6
Monroe	8.8	18.1	11.6	18.2	14.4	10.6	7.4	5.7	5.2	30.9	49.4
Raleigh	6.3	14.5	15.9	20.7	15.9	11.9	6.4	4.4	4.0	30.9	50.5
Rocky Mount	7.0	20.7	8.9	13.1	15.4	13.8	8.1	6.7	6.3	35.2	54.0
Salisbury	6.4	15.4	13.1	12.4	12.7	11.9	8.2	8.3	11.6	37.1	52.6
Wilmington	5.3	13.1	17.2	15.5	13.0	12.1	8.5	7.7	7.6	34.1	53.3
Wilson	7.4	18.6	9.8	14.0	14.9	13.4	8.4	7.1	6.3	35.1	53.2
Winston-Salem	6.7	16.6	11.7	15.6	14.8	12.7	8.2	7.0	6.7	34.6	53.0
NORTH DAKOTA	6.1	18.9	11.4	12.0	15.3	13.3	8.3	7.1	7.6	36.2	50.1
Bismarck	6.0	17.5	11.1	13.2	15.9	14.1	8.3	7.0	6.8	36.5	51.6
Fargo	6.4	14.8	19.2	16.7	14.4	12.2	6.3	5.0	5.1	30.1	50.0
Grand Forks	5.9	15.5	22.9	14.2	13.5	11.9	6.4	4.7	5.1	28.3	49.5
Minot	6.6	16.6	13.3	13.4	14.0	12.7	7.9	7.2	8.1	35.0	51.8
OHIO	6.6	18.8	9.3	13.4	15.9	13.8	8.9	7.0	6.3	36.2	51.4
Akron	7.2	18.1	10.5	15.3	15.0	12.7	7.6	6.7	6.8	34.2	52.2
Barberton	7.7	17.1	8.4	13.7	14.6	12.8	8.4	8.5	8.8	37.2	53.3
Beavercreek	5.2	20.1	6.3	9.5	17.5	17.8	11.5	7.0	5.2	40.5	50.6
Bowling Green	3.7	9.4	46.6	11.0	8.5	8.4	4.8	3.7	4.0	22.4	53.2
Brunswick	7.3	20.5	8.1	14.9	17.8	14.4	8.8	4.9	3.4	34.6	50.9
Canton	7.8	18.8	9.8	14.4	14.8	12.5	7.6	6.8	7.5	34.4	53.3
Cincinnati	7.2	17.3	12.9	16.9	14.7	11.7	7.0	6.0	6.3	32.1	52.8
Cleveland	8.1	20.4	9.5	15.0	15.4	11.5	7.5	6.6	5.9	33.0	52.6
Cleveland Heights	6.2	17.7	9.2	16.7	15.0	15.0	8.6	6.2	5.5	35.2	53.3
Columbus	7.5	16.7	14.0	19.6	15.5	11.4	6.5	4.7	4.1	30.6	51.4
Cuyahoga Falls	6.5	15.9	7.9	15.9	16.1	13.2	8.4	8.1	8.0	37.2	52.5
Dayton	7.1	18.0	14.2	14.1	14.9	12.1	7.6	6.4	5.6	32.4	51.8

Table D. Cities

City	| Population and population characteristics, 1990 — Age (percent) — Under 5 years	5 to 17 years	18 to 24 years	25 to 34 years	35 to 44 years	45 to 54 years	55 to 64 years	65 to 74 years	75 years and over	Percent Female	Population—change, 1980–2000 — Total persons — 2000	1990	1980	Percent change 1990–2000	1980–1990
	39	40	41	42	43	44	45	46	47	48	49	50	51	52	53
NEW YORK—Cont'd															
Ithaca	2.9	7.0	51.4	14.6	8.7	4.0	3.7	3.7	3.9	48.3	29 287	29 541	28 732	-0.9	2.8
Jamestown	8.1	17.3	10.4	16.7	13.0	8.4	8.8	8.5	8.7	53.2	31 730	34 681	35 775	-8.5	-3.1
Lindenhurst	7.8	16.2	10.4	19.8	15.1	10.2	9.6	7.2	3.8	51.2	27 819	26 879	26 919	3.5	-0.1
Long Beach	6.2	11.4	8.3	20.9	14.7	10.4	9.5	8.2	10.5	52.4	35 462	33 510	34 073	5.8	-1.7
Middletown	8.6	17.5	10.7	19.2	14.0	8.7	7.0	7.2	7.1	52.5	25 388	24 160	21 454	5.1	12.6
Mount Vernon	6.9	16.0	9.8	17.9	14.4	11.2	8.8	8.1	6.9	54.8	68 381	67 153	66 713	1.8	0.7
Newburgh	10.0	20.3	13.3	17.3	12.7	8.5	7.1	6.2	4.5	53.3	28 259	26 454	23 438	6.8	12.9
New Rochelle	6.1	14.0	9.8	16.3	14.6	11.5	10.6	8.9	8.2	53.2	72 182	67 265	70 794	7.3	-5.0
New York	6.9	16.1	10.3	18.7	15.2	10.9	8.9	7.3	5.7	53.1	8 008 278	7 322 564	7 071 639	9.4	3.5
Niagara Falls	7.3	16.5	9.3	16.6	12.7	8.2	10.3	11.3	7.8	53.8	55 593	61 840	71 384	-10.1	-13.4
North Tonawanda	7.1	17.8	9.3	17.0	16.1	8.6	9.7	9.1	5.4	52.1	33 262	34 989	35 760	-4.9	-2.2
Port Chester	6.3	13.7	10.9	21.8	13.7	9.5	9.3	8.2	6.7	51.3	27 867	24 728	23 565	12.7	4.9
Poughkeepsie	8.4	14.9	10.3	20.0	13.9	8.3	8.3	8.0	7.8	52.9	29 871	28 844	29 757	3.6	-3.1
Rochester	9.5	16.6	13.0	21.7	13.4	7.8	6.1	6.1	5.9	52.8	219 773	230 356	241 741	-4.6	-4.7
Rome	7.8	16.6	12.7	20.0	13.0	8.6	7.5	8.0	5.8	48.2	34 950	44 350	43 826	-21.2	1.2
Saratoga Springs	5.7	14.7	18.3	15.4	15.0	10.2	7.1	6.7	7.0	52.4	26 186	25 001	23 906	4.7	4.6
Schenectady	7.9	14.1	13.0	19.2	12.6	8.1	8.0	9.0	8.0	52.9	61 821	65 566	67 972	-5.7	-3.5
Spring Valley	9.7	19.4	9.6	20.4	13.7	10.9	7.5	4.9	4.0	52.2	25 464	21 802	20 537	16.8	6.2
Syracuse	7.6	15.0	17.8	18.4	12.0	7.6	7.0	7.6	7.1	53.4	147 306	163 860	170 105	-10.1	-3.7
Troy	7.0	14.5	19.8	17.8	11.6	7.1	8.0	7.4	6.8	50.7	49 170	54 269	56 638	-9.4	-4.2
Utica	7.2	15.5	11.6	16.6	11.7	8.8	9.3	10.5	8.8	53.2	60 651	68 637	75 632	-11.6	-9.2
Valley Stream	5.9	15.3	9.2	15.2	15.9	9.8	11.7	11.0	6.0	52.3	36 368	33 946	35 769	7.1	-5.1
Watertown	8.8	17.7	11.6	18.8	12.1	8.3	7.8	7.3	7.6	53.4	26 705	29 429	27 861	-9.3	5.6
White Plains	5.3	12.5	8.9	20.0	15.6	11.7	10.1	8.1	7.7	53.4	53 077	48 718	46 999	8.9	3.7
Yonkers	6.7	14.7	9.6	17.9	13.8	10.2	10.6	9.3	7.2	53.4	196 086	188 082	195 351	4.3	-3.7
NORTH CAROLINA	6.9	17.3	11.8	17.3	15.2	10.5	8.9	7.3	4.8	51.5	8 049 313	6 632 448	5 880 095	21.4	12.8
Asheville	6.1	14.6	9.1	15.5	15.1	9.5	9.8	11.2	9.1	54.6	68 889	63 379	53 583	8.7	18.3
Burlington	6.4	15.2	9.5	15.9	13.7	11.1	11.0	10.2	6.9	53.9	44 917	39 498	37 324	13.7	5.8
Cary	8.1	17.8	8.8	24.0	19.7	11.4	5.8	2.9	1.5	50.6	94 536	44 397	21 708	112.9	104.5
Chapel Hill	3.9	10.2	36.3	17.1	11.4	7.5	4.9	4.9	3.8	54.3	48 715	38 711	32 461	25.8	19.3
Charlotte	7.5	16.8	10.6	21.1	16.3	10.3	7.7	5.9	3.8	52.5	540 828	419 539	314 447	28.9	33.4
Concord	6.6	15.5	11.4	16.3	14.3	9.9	9.3	9.3	7.3	53.5	55 977	29 591	16 942	89.2	74.7
Durham	7.3	14.8	14.9	21.9	15.1	8.2	6.6	6.1	5.2	53.5	187 035	138 894	100 847	34.7	37.7
Fayetteville	7.7	17.4	13.4	18.3	13.9	9.7	9.1	6.9	3.7	52.7	121 015	75 850	59 507	59.5	27.5
Gastonia	7.1	18.5	10.0	16.1	14.8	9.8	9.4	8.3	6.1	53.4	66 277	54 725	47 285	21.1	15.7
Goldsboro	8.5	17.2	11.7	22.7	13.9	7.9	7.7	6.5	3.9	48.8	39 043	40 709	31 895	-4.1	27.6
Greensboro	6.4	15.2	14.8	18.5	15.3	9.8	8.2	7.0	4.8	53.6	223 891	183 894	155 684	21.8	18.1
Greenville	5.8	14.0	29.8	15.9	12.4	7.4	6.5	5.0	3.2	52.7	60 476	46 305	35 740	30.6	29.6
Hickory	6.1	14.6	13.6	17.4	14.3	10.3	9.2	8.3	6.3	53.5	37 222	28 474	20 753	30.7	37.2
High Point	7.3	17.1	10.5	17.4	14.9	9.9	8.8	7.5	6.6	53.7	85 839	69 428	63 355	23.6	9.6
Jacksonville	10.3	19.2	13.9	21.9	13.0	7.4	6.7	5.0	2.6	52.2	66 715	78 031	17 056	-14.5	357.5
Kannapolis	6.9	15.9	10.0	16.5	12.8	9.4	10.1	10.8	7.8	53.7	36 910	31 592	34 564	16.8	-8.6
Monroe	8.6	19.4	11.3	17.5	13.6	9.6	8.0	7.7	4.2	53.1	26 228	18 623	12 639	40.8	47.3
Raleigh	6.2	13.4	17.5	22.7	16.0	9.0	6.6	5.3	3.5	51.5	276 093	212 092	150 255	30.2	41.2
Rocky Mount	7.7	20.0	9.4	16.5	15.9	9.3	8.3	7.6	5.2	54.7	55 893	49 438	41 283	13.1	19.8
Salisbury	6.5	14.5	12.6	13.6	11.9	9.5	10.7	11.1	9.5	53.4	26 462	23 626	22 677	12.0	4.2
Wilmington	6.3	15.5	15.1	16.3	13.3	8.8	8.7	9.4	6.5	54.7	75 838	55 530	44 000	36.6	26.2
Wilson	6.9	19.6	11.0	15.3	14.1	9.9	9.4	8.5	5.4	54.4	44 405	38 400	34 424	15.6	11.6
Winston-Salem	6.7	15.1	12.8	18.4	14.3	9.9	8.9	7.9	6.2	54.1	185 776	150 958	131 885	23.1	14.5
NORTH DAKOTA	7.5	20.0	10.6	16.3	14.1	8.9	8.4	7.4	6.8	50.2	642 200	638 800	652 717	0.5	-2.1
Bismarck	7.3	19.7	9.7	18.0	16.1	9.5	8.2	6.2	5.2	52.2	55 532	49 272	44 485	12.7	10.8
Fargo	7.1	15.2	18.2	20.1	14.8	7.7	6.8	5.4	4.7	50.4	90 599	74 084	61 383	22.3	20.7
Grand Forks	7.5	15.8	21.6	19.2	12.8	7.8	6.0	4.9	4.3	50.0	49 321	49 417	43 765	-0.2	12.9
Minot	7.2	18.0	12.5	17.3	14.5	8.4	8.1	7.1	6.8	52.3	36 567	34 544	32 843	5.9	5.2
OHIO	7.2	18.6	10.5	16.5	14.9	10.3	9.0	7.6	5.3	51.8	11 353 140	10 847 115	10 797 603	4.7	0.5
Akron	7.5	17.0	12.1	17.5	14.1	8.4	8.5	8.6	6.2	52.8	217 074	223 019	237 177	-2.7	-6.0
Barberton	7.1	18.2	9.2	16.9	13.3	8.6	9.9	9.9	6.9	53.2	27 899	27 623	29 751	1.0	-7.2
Beavercreek	5.8	20.1	8.2	13.2	19.6	14.2	9.8	5.9	3.3	50.3	37 984	33 626	31 589	13.0	6.4
Bowling Green	3.8	9.1	50.6	12.0	8.4	5.2	4.3	3.7	3.1	54.7	29 636	28 303	25 728	4.7	10.0
Brunswick	7.2	22.7	10.4	16.8	18.3	12.0	6.5	4.1	2.1	50.6	33 388	28 218	28 104	18.3	0.4
Canton	7.9	18.2	9.9	16.5	13.8	8.5	8.8	9.2	7.2	53.8	80 806	84 161	94 730	-4.0	-11.2
Cincinnati	8.4	16.7	12.8	19.6	13.0	7.9	7.8	7.2	6.7	53.5	331 285	364 114	385 457	-9.0	-5.5
Cleveland	8.7	18.2	10.4	18.1	12.6	8.9	9.1	8.2	5.8	53.1	478 403	505 616	573 822	-5.4	-11.9
Cleveland Heights	6.6	18.4	9.1	18.0	18.0	9.6	7.3	6.8	6.0	53.1	49 958	54 052	56 438	-7.6	-4.2
Columbus	7.9	15.8	15.5	22.3	14.4	8.0	7.0	5.4	3.7	51.7	711 470	632 945	564 866	12.4	12.1
Cuyahoga Falls	6.8	16.0	8.8	19.4	14.9	9.2	9.6	9.4	5.9	52.6	49 374	48 950	43 890	0.9	11.5
Dayton	8.5	17.4	13.1	18.0	12.9	8.3	8.6	8.0	5.2	52.9	166 179	182 005	203 371	-8.7	-10.5

Table D. Cities

City	Total population	Total in house-holds	House-holder	Spouse	Child Total	Child Own child under 18 years	Other relatives Total	Other relatives Under 18 years	Nonrelatives Total	Nonrelatives Unmarried partner	Total in group quarters	Correctional institutions	Nursing homes	Other institutions	College dormitories	Military quarters	Other
	54	55	56	57	58	59	60	61	62	63	64	65	66	67	68	69	70
NEW YORK—Cont'd																	
Ithaca	29 287	74.7	35.1	6.7	10.2	8.3	1.4	0.5	21.3	2.0	25.3	0.0	0.6	0.0	24.2	0.0	0.5
Jamestown	31 730	97.7	42.7	16.7	28.5	23.2	3.1	1.3	6.6	3.6	2.3	0.0	0.9	0.1	0.0	0.0	1.2
Lindenhurst	27 819	99.6	32.6	20.2	34.7	24.3	1.9	1.9	5.1	1.6	0.4	0.0	0.0	0.0	0.0	0.0	0.4
Long Beach	35 462	95.2	42.1	16.8	23.4	16.2	5.9	1.7	6.9	2.4	4.8	0.0	2.3	0.2	0.2	0.0	2.1
Middletown	25 388	97.7	37.3	14.9	31.2	24.3	7.1	2.6	7.2	3.0	2.3	0.0	0.8	0.0	0.0	0.0	1.5
Mount Vernon	68 381	98.9	37.6	13.9	31.1	20.7	10.4	3.8	5.9	2.0	1.1	0.0	0.8	0.0	0.0	0.0	0.3
Newburgh	28 259	96.1	32.4	11.0	34.5	27.4	10.8	4.6	7.4	3.0	3.9	0.0	0.1	0.6	2.0	0.0	1.2
New Rochelle	72 182	97.1	36.3	18.3	30.1	21.8	7.2	1.9	5.2	1.4	2.9	0.0	1.5	0.0	0.9	0.0	0.5
New York	8 008 278	97.7	37.7	14.0	30.1	20.5	9.6	3.0	6.3	1.9	2.3	0.3	0.5	0.1	0.5	0.0	0.9
Niagara Falls	55 593	98.6	43.3	15.7	29.9	22.1	4.7	2.0	4.9	2.5	1.4	0.0	0.9	0.0	0.0	0.0	0.5
North Tonawanda	33 262	99.7	41.1	20.9	31.2	22.5	2.6	0.9	3.9	2.1	0.3	0.0	0.2	0.0	0.0	0.0	0.1
Port Chester	27 867	99.0	34.2	16.1	28.1	19.5	11.5	2.5	9.1	1.8	1.0	0.0	0.7	0.0	0.0	0.0	0.2
Poughkeepsie	29 871	96.7	40.2	12.0	28.0	21.7	7.2	2.9	9.3	3.1	3.3	1.0	0.6	0.3	0.0	0.0	1.4
Rochester	219 773	95.7	40.5	10.1	30.5	24.1	6.3	3.1	8.3	3.5	4.3	0.4	1.2	0.2	1.6	0.0	0.9
Rome	34 950	90.0	39.1	16.7	26.3	20.2	2.9	1.1	5.0	2.9	10.0	7.0	1.4	0.6	0.0	0.0	1.0
Saratoga Springs	26 186	91.2	41.2	17.8	22.7	18.0	2.5	0.9	7.1	2.4	8.8	0.0	1.4	0.2	6.4	0.0	0.7
Schenectady	61 821	94.7	42.5	13.6	27.3	21.8	4.1	1.5	7.3	3.6	5.3	0.5	1.1	0.2	2.4	0.0	1.0
Spring Valley	25 464	98.8	29.7	13.2	36.1	28.0	11.2	3.2	8.6	1.7	1.2	0.0	0.3	0.0	0.0	0.0	0.8
Syracuse	147 306	92.5	40.4	11.1	27.6	22.0	4.8	2.2	8.7	3.0	7.5	0.3	1.1	0.1	4.8	0.0	1.2
Troy	49 170	91.9	40.7	13.3	25.9	20.1	3.8	1.4	8.2	3.0	8.1	0.5	1.2	0.0	5.7	0.0	0.7
Utica	60 651	94.4	41.4	14.7	28.6	21.7	4.5	1.7	5.1	2.4	5.6	0.0	1.9	0.9	1.6	0.0	1.1
Valley Stream	36 368	99.8	34.3	21.1	33.4	21.3	8.0	2.0	3.0	1.0	0.2	0.0	0.0	0.0	0.0	0.0	0.2
Watertown	26 705	95.9	41.3	16.8	28.8	23.8	3.0	1.1	6.0	2.9	4.1	0.5	2.3	0.0	0.0	0.0	1.3
White Plains	53 077	97.3	39.4	18.0	25.9	18.5	7.2	1.8	6.7	1.6	2.7	0.0	1.2	0.0	0.2	0.0	1.3
Yonkers	196 086	98.8	37.9	16.8	31.5	21.7	7.8	2.2	4.7	1.9	1.2	0.0	0.4	0.0	0.4	0.0	0.4
NORTH CAROLINA	8 049 313	96.8	38.9	20.4	27.6	21.7	5.1	2.2	4.8	1.8	3.2	0.6	0.6	0.1	0.9	0.5	0.4
Asheville	68 889	95.3	44.5	17.0	22.2	17.1	4.7	1.8	6.9	2.4	4.7	0.8	1.1	0.1	1.3	0.0	1.3
Burlington	44 917	97.5	40.7	18.4	26.8	20.9	6.1	2.2	5.6	1.9	2.5	0.0	1.6	0.0	0.0	0.0	0.8
Cary	94 536	99.4	36.9	23.4	32.0	28.2	2.7	0.6	4.4	1.4	0.6	0.0	0.5	0.0	0.0	0.0	0.1
Chapel Hill	48 715	81.0	36.6	13.2	16.3	14.2	1.9	0.5	13.0	1.4	19.0	0.0	0.6	0.1	17.7	0.0	0.5
Charlotte	540 828	97.7	39.8	17.4	27.2	21.8	6.1	2.3	7.2	2.2	2.3	0.4	0.4	0.1	0.9	0.0	0.4
Concord	55 977	97.6	37.4	20.9	29.1	23.6	5.6	2.0	4.6	1.7	2.4	0.2	1.1	0.0	0.6	0.0	0.4
Durham	187 035	95.0	40.1	15.3	24.9	20.0	6.5	2.4	8.2	2.2	5.0	0.4	0.9	0.0	3.3	0.0	0.4
Fayetteville	121 015	96.7	40.0	17.9	28.0	21.9	5.5	2.9	5.3	1.8	3.3	0.3	0.9	0.0	1.6	0.0	0.5
Gastonia	66 277	97.8	39.1	18.5	28.2	21.4	6.7	2.9	5.2	2.0	2.2	0.4	1.4	0.0	0.0	0.0	0.5
Goldsboro	39 043	90.0	37.5	15.4	27.5	21.6	5.6	2.8	4.0	1.4	10.0	4.3	1.2	1.3	0.0	1.4	1.6
Greensboro	223 891	94.9	41.3	16.4	25.2	19.8	5.2	1.9	6.9	2.1	5.1	0.0	0.8	0.0	3.5	0.0	0.7
Greenville	60 476	90.8	41.7	12.8	20.6	16.6	4.5	1.8	11.1	2.4	9.2	0.0	0.6	0.1	7.7	0.0	0.7
Hickory	37 222	96.9	41.3	18.4	25.9	20.8	5.4	1.9	5.8	2.2	3.1	0.0	1.1	0.0	1.7	0.0	0.4
High Point	85 839	97.3	39.0	18.4	29.2	23.1	5.9	2.5	4.9	1.8	2.7	0.4	0.7	0.0	1.0	0.0	0.6
Jacksonville	66 715	72.9	25.7	16.4	25.6	22.9	2.2	1.0	3.0	0.9	27.1	0.2	0.3	0.1	0.0	25.9	0.5
Kannapolis	36 910	98.6	40.1	20.2	27.4	21.0	6.2	2.5	4.8	1.9	1.4	0.0	1.1	0.3	0.0	0.0	0.0
Monroe	26 228	97.4	34.4	16.9	28.4	21.9	10.1	3.8	7.6	1.9	2.6	0.3	1.4	0.1	0.0	0.0	0.6
Raleigh	276 093	93.7	40.8	16.1	22.7	18.8	4.9	1.5	9.2	2.2	6.3	1.2	0.4	0.2	3.9	0.0	0.6
Rocky Mount	55 893	97.9	38.4	16.6	30.9	23.3	7.9	3.8	4.2	1.8	2.1	0.0	0.8	0.0	0.8	0.0	0.5
Salisbury	26 462	88.7	38.8	15.1	23.9	18.5	5.8	2.6	5.0	1.9	11.3	0.7	4.1	0.0	4.4	0.0	2.0
Wilmington	75 838	95.3	45.3	15.2	20.8	15.9	4.6	1.9	9.4	2.4	4.7	0.4	0.5	0.0	2.5	0.0	1.2
Wilson	44 405	96.3	39.0	16.4	28.5	22.0	7.5	3.5	4.9	1.9	3.7	0.5	1.8	0.0	0.9	0.0	0.6
Winston-Salem	185 776	95.1	41.0	16.5	25.8	20.3	6.2	2.5	5.5	1.9	4.9	0.6	1.1	0.0	2.7	0.0	0.5
NORTH DAKOTA	642 200	96.3	40.0	21.4	28.4	23.8	2.0	0.8	4.5	1.8	3.7	0.2	1.1	0.1	1.6	0.2	0.4
Bismarck	55 532	96.9	41.8	20.9	27.5	22.6	1.9	0.5	4.8	1.9	3.1	1.3	1.1	0.0	0.4	0.0	0.3
Fargo	90 599	95.6	43.3	18.1	23.8	20.3	1.9	0.4	8.4	2.6	4.4	0.1	0.7	0.1	2.9	0.0	0.6
Grand Forks	49 321	92.3	39.9	17.2	25.1	20.6	1.7	0.4	8.3	2.3	7.7	0.2	0.9	0.0	6.3	0.0	0.3
Minot	36 567	96.4	42.4	19.8	26.4	21.8	2.0	0.7	5.7	2.2	3.6	0.1	1.1	0.2	1.2	0.0	0.9
OHIO	11 353 140	97.4	39.2	20.1	29.7	23.2	3.9	1.7	4.4	2.0	2.6	0.6	0.8	0.1	0.8	0.0	0.3
Akron	217 074	97.7	41.5	15.6	28.9	22.2	5.3	2.4	6.5	2.6	2.3	0.5	0.5	0.0	0.8	0.0	0.5
Barberton	27 899	98.6	41.3	18.6	29.3	22.1	4.4	1.8	5.0	2.6	1.4	0.0	0.9	0.3	0.0	0.0	0.3
Beavercreek	37 984	98.5	37.0	26.2	30.5	24.2	2.3	0.8	2.5	0.9	1.5	0.0	1.2	0.0	0.0	0.0	0.3
Bowling Green	29 636	76.5	34.6	11.5	14.7	12.1	1.4	0.4	14.3	1.8	23.5	0.1	0.9	0.2	21.5	0.0	0.7
Brunswick	33 388	99.2	35.6	23.2	34.1	26.0	3.4	1.4	3.0	1.6	0.8	0.0	0.6	0.0	0.0	0.0	0.2
Canton	80 806	96.2	40.2	14.9	29.5	22.9	5.6	2.7	6.0	2.8	3.8	0.5	1.4	0.0	1.0	0.0	0.8
Cincinnati	331 285	95.9	44.7	11.9	26.9	21.2	5.4	2.6	7.1	2.8	4.1	0.7	1.0	0.2	1.4	0.0	0.7
Cleveland	478 403	97.2	39.8	11.3	31.8	23.7	8.2	4.0	6.0	2.8	2.8	0.6	0.8	0.1	0.6	0.0	0.8
Cleveland Heights	49 958	99.5	41.9	14.3	28.3	20.9	5.3	2.5	6.7	1.9	0.5	0.0	0.3	0.0	0.0	0.0	0.2
Columbus	711 470	97.5	42.4	15.3	26.5	21.5	4.9	2.0	8.5	3.0	2.5	0.1	0.5	0.1	1.4	0.0	0.3
Cuyahoga Falls	49 374	99.2	43.9	21.2	27.3	21.2	2.6	0.9	4.2	2.1	0.8	0.0	0.6	0.0	0.0	0.0	0.2
Dayton	166 179	93.5	40.6	12.2	27.7	21.1	6.3	3.1	6.8	2.7	6.5	1.2	0.6	0.2	3.8	0.0	0.7

Table D. Cities

City	Households by type, 2000										Average household size	Average family size	Households, 1990		
	Family households						Nonfamily households								
			Married couple		Female householder[1]			Householder living alone							
	Total households	Total	With own children under 18 years	Total	With own children under 18 years	Total	With own children under 18 years	Total	Total	65 years and over	Average household size	Average family size	Total households	Female householder[1]	Householder living alone
	71	72	73	74	75	76	77	78	79	80	81	82	83	84	85
NEW YORK—Cont'd															
Ithaca	10 287	28.8	14.2	19.0	8.0	7.8	5.1	71.2	43.3	7.4	2.13	2.81	9 617	8.3	36.5
Jamestown	13 558	58.3	29.4	39.1	16.1	14.5	10.4	41.7	35.0	13.9	2.29	2.94	14 269	13.3	31.9
Lindenhurst	9 061	78.1	39.5	62.0	33.1	11.8	4.9	21.9	17.0	7.4	3.06	3.43	8 600	10.9	14.6
Long Beach	14 923	54.3	21.6	40.0	15.5	10.8	4.9	45.7	36.7	10.7	2.26	3.02	13 592	10.2	34.3
Middletown	9 466	63.0	34.0	40.0	20.0	16.7	10.8	37.0	30.0	12.3	2.62	3.27	8 790	15.1	26.5
Mount Vernon	25 729	64.8	31.1	36.9	16.8	23.0	12.3	35.2	30.0	10.7	2.63	3.27	25 175	20.5	29.0
Newburgh	9 144	66.5	40.0	34.1	19.0	25.4	17.2	33.5	27.1	11.0	2.97	3.62	9 008	23.2	27.0
New Rochelle	26 189	67.0	32.7	50.5	25.3	12.5	6.0	33.0	28.0	11.8	2.68	3.29	25 317	11.8	28.8
New York	3 021 588	61.3	29.7	37.2	17.6	19.1	10.3	38.7	31.9	9.9	2.59	3.32	2 819 401	18.0	32.9
Niagara Falls	24 099	59.2	27.8	36.2	14.3	18.3	11.4	40.8	35.9	15.2	2.27	2.96	25 970	16.5	33.1
North Tonawanda	13 671	65.7	30.2	50.8	22.0	11.1	6.3	34.3	29.5	12.8	2.43	3.03	13 635	10.6	26.0
Port Chester	9 531	66.9	31.7	47.0	23.4	13.6	6.2	33.1	26.7	11.2	2.89	3.44	9 104	13.7	27.7
Poughkeepsie	12 014	54.6	28.3	29.8	12.6	19.7	13.3	45.4	35.4	13.2	2.40	3.15	11 874	17.1	33.8
Rochester	88 999	53.0	30.0	25.1	11.3	23.3	16.4	47.0	37.1	9.2	2.36	3.19	93 607	20.6	35.3
Rome	13 653	61.0	28.1	42.6	16.2	13.9	9.2	39.0	33.2	14.6	2.30	2.93	15 754	11.8	27.2
Saratoga Springs	10 784	55.5	25.3	43.1	18.1	9.6	5.7	44.5	35.0	12.3	2.21	2.88	9 688	9.7	32.1
Schenectady	26 265	53.5	27.2	32.0	13.4	16.7	11.1	46.5	38.6	13.8	2.23	2.98	27 748	14.6	36.0
Spring Valley	7 566	73.0	42.2	44.4	26.2	21.4	13.2	27.0	20.6	5.9	3.33	3.79	7 513	17.1	26.1
Syracuse	59 482	51.0	27.5	27.5	11.9	19.3	13.3	49.0	38.2	11.9	2.29	3.11	64 945	16.9	35.8
Troy	19 996	53.7	27.0	32.6	13.6	16.3	10.9	46.3	36.6	12.6	2.26	2.97	20 761	14.8	33.7
Utica	25 100	56.7	27.0	35.5	14.4	16.9	10.7	43.3	37.4	15.5	2.28	3.04	28 358	15.4	35.6
Valley Stream	12 484	76.9	33.9	61.5	28.6	11.5	4.2	23.1	20.2	11.3	2.91	3.37	11 851	9.9	18.4
Watertown	11 036	58.9	31.9	40.7	19.3	14.2	10.1	41.1	34.5	13.8	2.32	2.99	11 430	13.6	29.3
White Plains	20 921	60.7	26.9	45.7	20.6	11.3	5.1	39.3	33.4	11.8	2.47	3.14	19 432	11.7	33.9
Yonkers	74 351	66.3	30.9	44.2	19.5	17.2	9.7	33.7	29.2	11.9	2.61	3.23	72 101	15.3	28.3
NORTH CAROLINA	3 132 013	68.9	31.8	52.5	22.6	12.5	7.3	31.1	25.4	8.6	2.49	2.98	2 517 026	12.3	23.7
Asheville	30 690	54.5	22.2	38.1	13.2	13.0	7.4	45.5	36.8	13.8	2.14	2.81	27 027	13.9	35.2
Burlington	18 280	64.3	29.0	45.1	18.3	14.9	8.8	35.7	30.3	12.2	2.40	2.96	16 627	13.7	28.9
Cary	34 906	72.0	41.7	63.3	36.2	6.3	4.3	28.0	21.0	3.0	2.69	3.18	16 908	6.8	21.1
Chapel Hill	17 808	45.7	22.4	36.2	16.7	7.5	5.0	54.3	31.2	6.6	2.22	2.88	13 780	8.1	32.8
Charlotte	215 449	61.4	30.6	43.6	20.5	13.7	8.3	38.6	29.5	6.3	2.45	3.07	158 991	14.0	28.0
Concord	20 962	71.5	35.2	55.7	26.3	11.5	6.7	28.5	23.6	8.0	2.61	3.08	10 807	13.8	27.4
Durham	74 981	58.1	28.7	38.2	17.1	15.9	9.9	41.9	31.9	7.2	2.37	3.01	56 001	16.1	32.6
Fayetteville	48 414	65.4	31.8	44.7	19.2	17.1	10.6	34.6	28.2	7.8	2.42	2.96	29 639	16.8	26.3
Gastonia	25 945	68.3	30.6	47.3	19.4	16.3	9.1	31.7	26.5	9.8	2.50	3.00	20 983	17.0	24.5
Goldsboro	14 630	64.7	32.1	41.1	17.7	20.4	12.7	35.3	30.5	11.9	2.40	3.00	13 423	20.0	26.8
Greensboro	92 394	58.4	27.5	39.8	17.0	14.6	8.9	41.6	32.6	8.7	2.30	2.94	74 905	13.8	30.5
Greenville	25 204	47.6	23.0	30.8	13.1	13.8	8.7	52.4	35.4	6.4	2.18	2.91	17 017	14.4	30.6
Hickory	15 372	60.9	27.9	44.6	18.9	12.3	7.1	39.1	32.2	10.9	2.35	2.98	11 800	13.2	31.5
High Point	33 519	67.2	32.9	46.9	21.1	16.3	10.1	32.8	27.2	9.5	2.49	3.03	27 529	16.6	27.0
Jacksonville	17 175	78.8	49.5	63.8	38.7	12.3	8.9	21.2	16.6	5.1	2.83	3.18	10 916	13.1	18.4
Kannapolis	14 804	68.5	30.0	50.4	20.4	13.5	7.5	31.5	26.5	11.4	2.46	2.96	12 018	14.1	26.2
Monroe	9 029	70.8	33.7	49.0	21.9	15.9	9.2	29.2	23.3	8.3	2.83	3.27	5 935	19.6	25.4
Raleigh	112 608	54.5	26.5	39.5	17.9	11.4	7.2	45.5	33.1	6.2	2.30	2.97	85 822	11.3	32.2
Rocky Mount	21 435	68.5	32.9	43.3	18.7	20.9	12.2	31.5	27.4	10.3	2.55	3.11	18 871	19.9	26.4
Salisbury	10 276	60.2	26.5	39.0	13.8	17.4	10.9	39.8	34.3	14.5	2.29	2.92	9 162	15.4	32.9
Wilmington	34 359	50.5	20.4	33.5	10.8	14.0	8.4	49.5	36.6	11.3	2.10	2.77	23 557	18.0	32.8
Wilson	17 296	65.5	31.6	42.0	18.3	19.3	11.6	34.5	29.4	10.9	2.47	3.06	14 461	20.5	29.4
Winston-Salem	76 247	60.6	28.0	40.2	16.1	16.6	10.1	39.4	33.4	10.7	2.32	2.95	59 919	16.7	33.8
NORTH DAKOTA	257 152	64.6	31.3	53.4	24.1	7.8	5.3	35.4	29.3	11.5	2.41	3.00	240 878	7.3	26.5
Bismarck	23 185	62.3	30.2	50.1	22.4	9.3	6.2	37.7	31.0	10.5	2.32	2.94	19 315	9.5	27.5
Fargo	39 268	52.8	26.5	41.8	19.6	7.8	5.3	47.2	34.6	8.0	2.20	2.91	30 149	7.7	31.4
Grand Forks	19 677	56.2	28.7	43.2	20.0	10.0	7.1	43.8	31.4	8.5	2.31	2.96	18 531	9.5	29.1
Minot	15 520	59.7	28.6	46.6	20.0	10.0	6.8	40.3	32.5	12.0	2.27	2.90	13 965	9.9	30.8
OHIO	4 445 773	67.3	31.7	51.4	22.4	12.1	7.3	32.7	27.3	10.0	2.49	3.04	4 087 546	11.7	25.0
Akron	90 116	59.6	28.5	37.5	15.4	17.7	10.9	40.4	33.1	11.2	2.35	3.01	89 923	16.6	30.8
Barberton	11 523	64.6	29.5	44.9	18.1	15.4	9.3	35.4	30.1	14.0	2.39	2.96	11 082	14.3	28.2
Beavercreek	14 071	78.8	35.2	70.7	30.8	5.8	3.4	21.2	17.5	5.7	2.66	3.02	11 693	5.5	13.6
Bowling Green	10 266	43.2	20.2	33.2	13.8	7.5	5.1	56.8	34.3	7.0	2.21	2.84	8 502	6.8	29.0
Brunswick	11 883	78.1	39.3	65.3	32.1	9.3	5.4	21.9	17.7	5.2	2.79	3.18	9 032	8.1	12.7
Canton	32 489	60.9	30.0	37.1	15.4	19.1	12.1	39.1	33.0	12.4	2.39	3.04	33 452	17.0	31.2
Cincinnati	148 095	49.0	25.1	26.6	10.9	18.6	12.4	51.0	42.8	11.1	2.15	3.02	154 342	18.2	39.5
Cleveland	190 638	58.7	29.9	28.5	12.2	24.8	15.3	41.3	35.2	11.1	2.44	3.19	199 787	22.7	33.5
Cleveland Heights	20 913	58.2	26.8	41.2	16.0	14.1	7.7	41.8	32.6	8.5	2.38	3.09	21 012	13.0	29.5
Columbus	301 534	54.8	28.0	36.1	16.5	14.5	9.3	45.2	34.1	7.0	2.30	3.01	256 996	14.2	31.3
Cuyahoga Falls	21 655	61.5	27.0	48.3	19.7	10.1	5.7	38.5	32.6	12.3	2.26	2.90	20 383	9.7	29.1
Dayton	67 409	55.8	27.3	30.2	12.3	20.6	12.4	44.2	36.8	11.3	2.30	3.04	72 670	20.6	33.4

[1]No spouse present.

Table D. Cities

City	Percent change of households, 1990–2000	Total housing units	Occupied housing units (percent)	Vacant housing units				Occupied housing units				
				Total	For seasonal, recreational, or occasional use	Homeowner vacancy rate (percent)	Rental vacancy rate (percent)	Total	Percent owner-occupied housing units	Percent renter-occupied housing units	Average household size of owner-occupied units	Average household size of renter-occupied units
	86	87	88	89	90	91	92	93	94	95	96	97
NEW YORK—Cont'd												
Ithaca	7.0	10 736	95.8	4.2	0.4	2.1	2.7	10 287	26.0	74.0	2.30	2.07
Jamestown	-5.0	15 027	90.2	9.8	0.2	2.6	9.8	13 558	51.3	48.7	2.46	2.10
Lindenhurst	5.4	9 277	97.7	2.3	0.3	0.7	2.6	9 061	80.6	19.4	3.21	2.43
Long Beach	9.8	16 128	92.5	7.5	4.2	1.0	3.2	14 923	53.4	46.6	2.45	2.05
Middletown	7.7	10 124	93.5	6.5	0.2	2.0	4.2	9 466	45.7	54.3	2.68	2.57
Mount Vernon	2.2	27 048	95.1	4.9	0.2	2.0	4.0	25 729	36.5	63.5	2.93	2.45
Newburgh	1.5	10 476	87.3	12.7	0.3	6.8	7.6	9 144	30.7	69.3	2.88	3.01
New Rochelle	3.4	26 995	97.0	3.0	0.6	0.6	2.3	26 189	50.3	49.7	2.87	2.48
New York	7.2	3 200 912	94.4	5.6	0.9	1.7	3.2	3 021 588	30.2	69.8	2.81	2.50
Niagara Falls	-7.2	27 837	86.6	13.4	0.2	2.7	16.0	24 099	57.6	42.4	2.40	2.10
North Tonawanda	0.3	14 425	94.8	5.2	0.2	1.3	7.8	13 671	68.7	31.3	2.65	1.93
Port Chester	4.7	9 772	97.5	2.5	0.2	1.4	1.4	9 531	43.2	56.8	2.76	3.00
Poughkeepsie	1.2	13 153	91.3	8.7	0.5	3.3	5.8	12 014	36.8	63.2	2.46	2.37
Rochester	-4.9	99 789	89.2	10.8	0.2	3.8	9.0	88 999	40.2	59.8	2.54	2.24
Rome	-13.3	16 272	83.9	16.1	0.2	3.3	14.6	13 653	57.1	42.9	2.45	2.11
Saratoga Springs	11.3	11 584	93.1	6.9	2.9	1.2	3.6	10 784	55.8	44.2	2.49	1.87
Schenectady	-5.3	30 272	86.8	13.2	0.3	4.6	9.3	26 265	44.7	55.3	2.37	2.12
Spring Valley	0.7	7 812	96.9	3.1	0.2	2.2	2.3	7 566	31.4	68.6	3.41	3.29
Syracuse	-8.4	68 192	87.2	12.8	0.3	4.8	11.8	59 482	40.3	59.7	2.48	2.16
Troy	-3.7	23 093	86.6	13.4	0.5	4.2	9.2	19 996	40.1	59.9	2.45	2.13
Utica	-11.5	29 186	86.0	14.0	0.3	3.6	12.9	25 100	48.8	51.2	2.41	2.15
Valley Stream	5.3	12 688	98.4	1.6	0.2	0.6	1.8	12 484	80.3	19.7	3.06	2.27
Watertown	-3.4	12 450	88.6	11.4	0.3	4.5	11.5	11 036	43.0	57.0	2.51	2.18
White Plains	7.7	21 576	97.0	3.0	0.8	0.8	2.1	20 921	52.2	47.8	2.53	2.41
Yonkers	3.1	77 589	95.8	4.2	0.4	1.3	3.5	74 351	43.2	56.8	2.68	2.55
NORTH CAROLINA	24.4	3 523 944	88.9	11.1	3.8	2.0	8.8	3 132 013	69.4	30.6	2.54	2.37
Asheville	13.6	33 567	91.4	8.6	1.3	2.6	8.1	30 690	56.8	43.2	2.24	2.01
Burlington	9.9	19 567	93.4	6.6	0.3	2.1	7.7	18 280	59.4	40.6	2.39	2.40
Cary	106.4	36 863	94.7	5.3	0.6	1.9	8.2	34 906	72.8	27.2	2.86	2.23
Chapel Hill	29.2	18 976	93.8	6.2	0.7	1.4	6.5	17 808	42.9	57.1	2.49	2.01
Charlotte	35.5	230 434	93.5	6.5	0.3	2.2	8.4	215 449	57.5	42.5	2.56	2.30
Concord	94.0	22 485	93.2	6.8	0.3	2.4	7.3	20 962	67.6	32.4	2.65	2.52
Durham	33.9	80 797	92.8	7.2	0.6	2.6	6.7	74 981	48.9	51.1	2.44	2.30
Fayetteville	63.3	53 565	90.4	9.6	0.3	2.8	10.4	48 414	53.3	46.7	2.50	2.32
Gastonia	23.6	27 857	93.1	6.9	0.2	2.1	7.4	25 945	56.7	43.3	2.54	2.44
Goldsboro	9.0	16 372	89.4	10.6	0.2	2.5	6.8	14 630	42.5	57.5	2.37	2.42
Greensboro	23.3	99 305	93.0	7.0	0.4	2.0	7.2	92 394	53.0	47.0	2.42	2.17
Greenville	48.1	28 145	89.6	10.4	0.4	3.0	5.6	25 204	39.3	60.7	2.39	2.04
Hickory	30.3	16 571	92.8	7.2	0.4	2.1	8.0	15 372	55.0	45.0	2.39	2.30
High Point	21.8	35 952	93.2	6.8	0.5	2.2	7.0	33 519	59.0	41.0	2.53	2.44
Jacksonville	57.3	18 312	93.8	6.2	0.2	2.9	5.2	17 175	39.2	60.8	2.67	2.94
Kannapolis	23.2	15 941	92.9	7.1	0.2	1.8	7.9	14 804	66.7	33.3	2.43	2.52
Monroe	52.1	9 621	93.8	6.2	0.3	3.3	4.3	9 029	56.1	43.9	2.66	3.04
Raleigh	31.2	120 699	93.3	6.7	0.4	2.1	8.3	112 608	51.6	48.4	2.43	2.15
Rocky Mount	13.6	24 167	88.7	11.3	0.3	2.2	6.3	21 435	55.0	45.0	2.56	2.54
Salisbury	12.2	11 288	91.0	9.0	0.5	3.1	7.0	10 276	53.5	46.5	2.29	2.28
Wilmington	45.9	38 678	88.8	11.2	1.3	3.6	11.0	34 359	48.6	51.4	2.20	2.01
Wilson	19.6	18 660	92.7	7.3	0.3	2.4	4.8	17 296	51.0	49.0	2.50	2.44
Winston-Salem	27.3	82 593	92.3	7.7	0.3	2.2	9.7	76 247	55.8	44.2	2.34	2.28
NORTH DAKOTA	6.8	289 677	88.8	11.2	2.9	2.7	8.2	257 152	66.6	33.4	2.60	2.02
Bismarck	20.0	24 217	95.7	4.3	0.4	1.1	5.5	23 185	63.4	36.6	2.59	1.86
Fargo	30.2	41 200	95.3	4.7	0.5	1.6	5.1	39 268	47.1	52.9	2.61	1.84
Grand Forks	6.2	20 838	94.4	5.6	0.4	2.4	6.7	19 677	50.7	49.3	2.68	1.94
Minot	11.1	16 475	94.2	5.8	0.6	1.7	6.2	15 520	62.4	37.6	2.51	1.87
OHIO	8.8	4 783 051	92.9	7.1	1.0	1.6	8.3	4 445 773	69.1	30.9	2.62	2.19
Akron	0.2	97 315	92.6	7.4	0.3	1.8	8.8	90 116	59.4	40.6	2.45	2.21
Barberton	4.0	12 163	94.7	5.3	0.2	1.5	5.4	11 523	65.1	34.9	2.44	2.29
Beavercreek	20.3	14 769	95.3	4.7	0.5	1.3	13.6	14 071	84.5	15.5	2.74	2.22
Bowling Green	20.7	10 667	96.2	3.8	0.3	1.1	3.8	10 266	42.2	57.8	2.45	2.03
Brunswick	31.6	12 251	97.0	3.0	0.1	0.9	7.0	11 883	80.6	19.4	2.92	2.23
Canton	-2.9	35 502	91.5	8.5	0.1	2.2	10.2	32 489	59.7	40.3	2.51	2.22
Cincinnati	-4.0	166 012	89.2	10.8	0.4	2.2	9.9	148 095	39.0	61.0	2.43	1.97
Cleveland	-4.6	215 856	88.3	11.7	0.4	2.1	10.8	190 638	48.5	51.5	2.56	2.32
Cleveland Heights	-0.5	21 798	95.9	4.1	0.2	1.2	5.0	20 913	62.1	37.9	2.63	1.95
Columbus	17.3	327 175	92.2	7.8	0.3	2.0	8.3	301 534	49.1	50.9	2.48	2.13
Cuyahoga Falls	6.2	22 727	95.3	4.7	0.3	1.2	6.7	21 655	65.7	34.3	2.46	1.89
Dayton	-7.2	77 321	87.2	12.8	0.2	3.0	12.7	67 409	52.8	47.2	2.36	2.24

Table D. Cities

STATE Place code	City	Land area, 2000[1] (sq km)	Population, 2000 Total persons	Rank	Per square kilometer	Land area, 1990[1] (sq km)	Population, 1990 Total persons	Rank	Per square kilometer	White	Black or African American	American Indian or Alaska Native	Asian	Native Hawaiian and other Pacific Islander	Some other race
		1	2	3	4	5	6	7	8	9	10	11	12	13	14
	OHIO—Cont'd														
39 21434	Delaware	38.8	25 243	1 491	650.6	27.0	19 900	1 647	739.5	92.8	3.8	0.2	0.8	0.1	0.5
39 22694	Dublin	54.7	31 392	1 165	573.9	45.9	16 366	1 989	356.6	89.7	1.7	0.1	7.4	0.0	0.2
39 23380	East Cleveland	8.0	27 217	1 370	3 402.1	8.0	33 096	932	4 137.0	4.6	93.4	0.2	0.2	0.0	0.2
39 25256	Elyria	51.5	55 953	570	1 086.5	50.3	56 746	452	1 128.2	81.3	14.2	0.3	0.6	0.0	1.0
39 25704	Euclid	27.7	52 717	631	1 903.1	27.7	54 875	475	1 981.0	66.4	30.6	0.1	0.9	0.0	0.3
39 25914	Fairborn	33.8	32 052	1 135	948.3	29.0	31 300	998	1 079.3	87.3	6.3	0.4	3.3	0.1	0.5
39 25970	Fairfield	54.4	42 097	817	773.8	54.0	39 709	749	735.4	89.9	6.1	0.1	2.3	0.0	0.5
39 27048	Findlay	44.5	38 967	901	875.7	35.1	35 703	840	1 017.2	93.7	1.4	0.2	1.8	0.0	1.7
39 29106	Gahanna	32.1	32 636	1 116	1 016.7	34.1	23 898	1 363	700.8	86.5	8.1	0.2	3.3	0.0	0.5
39 29428	Garfield Heights	18.7	30 734	1 194	1 643.5	18.7	31 739	985	1 697.3	80.7	16.8	0.2	0.9	0.0	0.4
39 32592	Grove City	36.1	27 075	1 378	750.0	26.2	19 661	1 673	750.4	96.2	1.5	0.2	0.6	0.0	0.3
39 33012	Hamilton	56.0	60 690	488	1 083.8	51.7	61 438	411	1 188.4	88.9	7.5	0.3	0.5	0.0	1.5
39 36610	Huber Heights	54.5	38 212	924	701.1	53.9	38 696	772	717.9	84.9	9.8	0.3	2.2	0.1	0.6
39 39872	Kent	22.5	27 906	1 327	1 240.3	22.6	28 835	1 099	1 275.9	86.1	9.1	0.2	2.1	0.0	0.4
39 40040	Kettering	48.4	57 502	540	1 188.1	48.3	60 569	416	1 254.0	95.2	1.7	0.2	1.4	0.0	0.3
39 41664	Lakewood	14.4	56 646	552	3 933.8	14.4	59 718	424	4 147.1	93.1	2.0	0.2	1.4	0.0	0.6
39 41720	Lancaster	46.8	35 335	1 011	755.0	40.5	34 507	873	852.0	97.4	0.6	0.3	0.5	0.0	0.2
39 43554	Lima	33.1	40 081	869	1 210.9	32.8	45 553	627	1 388.8	69.3	26.5	0.3	0.5	0.0	1.0
39 44856	Lorain	62.2	68 652	419	1 103.7	62.3	71 245	331	1 143.6	69.7	15.9	0.4	0.3	0.0	9.6
39 47138	Mansfield	77.5	49 346	681	636.7	72.3	50 627	547	700.2	76.8	19.6	0.3	0.6	0.0	0.6
39 47306	Maple Heights	13.4	26 156	1 438	1 951.9	13.4	27 089	1 179	2 021.6	51.6	44.3	0.1	1.7	0.0	0.5
39 47754	Marion	29.4	35 318	1 012	1 201.3	20.8	34 075	889	1 638.2	90.4	7.0	0.2	0.5	0.0	0.6
39 48244	Massillon	43.4	31 325	1 168	721.8	34.2	30 969	1 011	905.5	88.2	9.4	0.2	0.3	0.0	0.3
39 48790	Medina	28.8	25 139	1 498	872.9	26.4	19 231	1 707	728.4	94.6	2.8	0.2	0.7	0.0	0.3
39 49056	Mentor	69.3	50 278	664	725.5	69.3	47 491	596	685.3	97.3	0.6	0.0	1.2	0.0	0.2
39 49840	Middletown	66.5	51 605	647	776.0	52.3	46 758	608	894.0	87.0	10.6	0.2	0.4	0.0	0.4
39 54040	Newark	50.6	46 279	739	914.6	46.7	44 396	646	950.7	94.1	3.1	0.3	0.6	0.0	0.3
39 56882	North Olmsted	30.1	34 113	1 054	1 133.3	29.8	34 204	885	1 147.8	94.0	1.0	0.1	2.7	0.0	0.5
39 57008	North Royalton	55.1	28 648	1 290	519.9	55.1	23 197	1 408	421.0	96.2	0.7	0.1	2.0	0.0	0.2
39 61000	Parma	51.7	85 655	309	1 656.8	51.8	87 876	242	1 696.4	95.7	1.1	0.1	1.6	0.0	0.4
39 66390	Reynoldsburg	27.4	32 069	1 132	1 170.4	24.3	25 748	1 253	1 059.6	85.0	10.4	0.3	1.7	0.0	0.7
39 70380	Sandusky	26.0	27 844	1 335	1 070.9	26.0	29 764	1 063	1 144.8	74.5	21.1	0.3	0.3	0.0	1.0
39 71682	Shaker Heights	16.3	29 405	1 251	1 804.0	16.3	30 955	1 012	1 899.1	59.9	34.1	0.1	3.2	0.0	0.5
39 74118	Springfield	58.2	65 358	446	1 123.0	50.6	70 487	339	1 393.0	78.0	18.2	0.3	0.7	0.0	0.5
39 74944	Stow	44.3	32 139	1 129	725.5	44.4	27 998	1 141	630.6	95.2	1.5	0.1	1.9	0.0	0.3
39 75098	Strongsville	63.8	43 858	783	687.4	63.8	35 308	851	553.4	94.2	1.3	0.0	3.2	0.0	0.3
39 77000	Toledo	208.8	313 619	58	1 502.0	208.7	332 943	49	1 595.3	70.2	23.5	0.3	1.0	0.0	2.3
39 77504	Trotwood city	79.1	27 420	1 360	346.6	NA	8 816	3 233	NA	38.7	58.3	0.3	0.2	0.0	0.4
39 79002	Upper Arlington	25.3	33 686	1 078	1 331.5	24.9	34 128	887	1 370.6	94.7	0.6	0.1	3.5	0.0	0.3
39 80892	Warren	41.7	46 832	726	1 123.1	41.4	50 793	542	1 226.9	71.9	25.2	0.1	0.4	0.0	0.3
39 83342	Westerville	32.1	35 318	1 012	1 100.2	27.3	30 269	1 044	1 108.8	93.5	3.2	0.1	1.6	0.0	0.4
39 83622	Westlake	41.2	31 719	1 147	769.9	41.2	27 018	1 184	655.8	92.9	0.9	0.1	4.2	0.0	0.3
39 88000	Youngstown	87.8	82 026	329	934.2	87.5	95 732	217	1 094.1	50.9	43.8	0.3	0.3	0.0	2.2
39 88084	Zanesville	29.1	25 586	1 473	879.2	27.0	26 778	1 191	991.8	85.5	10.8	0.4	0.2	0.0	0.4
40 00000	OKLAHOMA	177 846.9	3 450 654	X	19.4	177 877.5	3 145 576	X	17.7	76.2	7.6	7.9	1.4	0.1	2.4
40 04450	Bartlesville	54.7	34 748	1 036	635.2	54.7	34 256	883	626.3	82.1	3.2	7.2	1.0	0.0	1.0
40 09050	Broken Arrow	116.5	74 859	376	642.6	104.5	58 082	436	555.8	85.3	3.7	4.0	1.9	0.1	1.2
40 23200	Edmond	220.5	68 315	424	309.8	220.9	52 310	517	236.8	86.6	4.0	2.3	3.3	0.1	0.9
40 23950	Enid	191.6	47 045	724	245.5	187.0	45 309	631	242.3	87.2	3.9	2.1	1.0	0.6	2.4
40 41850	Lawton	194.6	92 757	272	476.7	132.5	80 561	277	608.0	61.3	23.1	3.8	2.5	0.4	4.0
40 48350	Midwest City	63.7	54 088	605	849.1	63.5	52 267	519	823.1	69.5	19.5	3.5	1.6	0.1	1.5
40 49200	Moore	56.3	41 138	841	730.7	55.7	40 318	730	723.8	84.6	2.9	4.1	1.6	0.0	1.8
40 50050	Muskogee	96.7	38 310	917	396.2	89.3	37 708	800	422.3	61.1	17.9	12.3	0.9	0.0	1.6
40 52500	Norman	458.4	95 694	257	208.8	458.5	80 071	281	174.6	82.4	4.3	4.5	3.5	0.1	1.4
40 55000	Oklahoma City	1 572.1	506 132	31	321.9	1 575.1	444 724	30	282.3	68.4	15.4	3.5	3.5	0.1	5.3
40 59850	Ponca City	46.9	25 919	1 454	552.6	45.0	26 359	1 224	585.8	84.2	3.0	6.3	0.7	0.0	2.1
40 66800	Shawnee	109.5	28 692	1 287	262.0	108.2	26 017	1 241	240.5	77.0	4.1	12.8	1.0	0.0	0.7
40 70300	Stillwater	72.1	39 065	893	541.8	70.6	36 676	822	519.5	82.5	4.3	3.9	5.1	0.0	0.9
40 75000	Tulsa	473.1	393 049	45	830.8	475.3	367 302	44	772.8	70.1	15.5	4.7	1.8	0.1	3.5
41 00000	OREGON	248 630.5	3 421 399	X	13.8	248 646.7	2 842 337	X	11.4	86.6	1.6	1.3	3.0	0.2	4.2
41 01000	Albany	41.1	40 852	847	994.0	29.7	33 523	917	1 128.7	91.7	0.5	1.2	1.1	0.2	2.7
41 05350	Beaverton	42.3	76 129	368	1 799.7	35.8	53 307	501	1 489.0	78.3	1.7	0.7	9.7	0.4	5.5
41 05800	Bend	82.9	52 029	639	627.6	34.8	23 740	1 376	682.2	94.0	0.3	0.8	1.0	0.1	1.7
41 15800	Corvallis	35.2	49 322	682	1 401.2	33.5	44 757	640	1 336.0	86.0	1.2	0.8	6.4	0.3	2.5
41 23850	Eugene	104.9	137 893	162	1 314.5	98.5	112 733	165	1 144.5	88.1	1.3	0.9	3.6	0.2	2.2
41 31250	Gresham	57.4	90 205	284	1 571.5	57.1	68 285	351	1 195.9	82.7	1.9	0.9	3.3	0.3	7.0
41 34100	Hillsboro	55.9	70 186	405	1 255.6	49.9	37 598	804	753.5	77.5	1.2	0.8	6.5	0.3	10.4
41 38500	Keizer	18.7	32 203	1 127	1 722.1	18.8	21 884	1 504	1 164.0	85.5	0.8	1.4	1.5	0.2	7.2

[1] Dry land or land partially or temporarily covered by water.

Table D. Cities

City	Two or more races	White	Black	American Indian or Alaska Native	Asian	Native Hawaiian and other Pacific Islander	Some other race	Hispanic[1]	White	Black or African American	American Indian or Alaska Native	Asian and Pacific Islander	Hispanic[1]
	15	16	17	18	19	20	21	22	23	24	25	26	27
OHIO—Cont'd													
Delaware	1.7	94.3	4.6	0.9	1.1	0.1	0.8	1.2	94.1	4.6	0.2	0.8	0.8
Dublin	0.9	90.5	2.0	0.3	7.9	0.1	0.3	1.0	94.3	0.9	0.1	4.5	0.7
East Cleveland	1.4	5.2	94.6	0.9	0.4	0.1	0.5	0.8	5.3	93.7	0.1	0.7	0.6
Elyria	2.6	83.7	15.6	1.1	0.9	0.1	1.4	2.8	85.0	13.7	0.2	0.5	1.5
Euclid	1.6	67.6	31.6	0.6	1.2	0.1	0.7	1.1	82.9	16.0	0.1	0.9	0.8
Fairborn	2.1	89.2	7.1	1.0	4.0	0.1	0.9	1.7	92.4	4.1	0.4	2.6	1.3
Fairfield	1.1	90.9	6.6	0.4	2.5	0.1	0.8	1.5	95.0	3.3	0.1	1.4	0.7
Findlay	1.3	94.8	1.8	0.5	2.0	0.1	2.1	3.9	95.9	1.3	0.2	0.8	3.4
Gahanna	1.4	87.7	8.8	0.6	3.7	0.1	0.7	1.3	90.3	7.9	0.1	1.3	0.8
Garfield Heights	1.0	81.5	17.2	0.5	1.1	0.0	0.6	1.3	84.4	14.8	0.1	0.5	0.8
Grove City	1.1	97.2	1.9	0.6	0.9	0.0	0.5	1.2	98.8	0.5	0.2	0.4	0.5
Hamilton	1.3	90.1	8.0	0.8	0.6	0.1	1.7	2.6	91.9	7.3	0.2	0.4	0.5
Huber Heights	2.2	86.8	10.9	0.8	2.8	0.1	1.0	1.7	90.7	6.9	0.2	1.7	1.5
Kent	2.0	87.9	10.2	0.7	2.5	0.1	0.9	1.3	89.9	7.1	0.2	2.5	0.9
Kettering	1.2	96.3	2.0	0.5	1.8	0.1	0.6	1.1	97.8	0.7	0.1	1.2	0.8
Lakewood	2.7	95.6	2.5	0.7	1.8	0.1	2.1	2.2	97.5	0.8	0.2	1.0	1.5
Lancaster	1.0	98.3	1.0	0.8	0.6	0.1	0.3	0.8	98.8	0.5	0.2	0.4	0.5
Lima	2.4	71.5	28.2	0.9	0.7	0.0	1.3	2.0	74.5	24.0	0.2	0.5	1.5
Lorain	4.0	73.2	17.8	1.2	0.5	0.1	11.5	21.0	78.2	13.8	0.4	0.3	16.9
Mansfield	2.1	78.5	20.9	1.0	0.8	0.1	0.8	1.2	80.7	18.1	0.2	0.6	0.9
Maple Heights	1.7	52.8	45.4	0.6	2.1	0.0	0.9	1.2	83.8	14.7	0.1	1.1	0.7
Marion	1.2	91.4	7.6	0.6	0.7	0.0	0.9	1.3	94.7	4.2	0.3	0.5	0.8
Massillon	1.6	89.6	10.4	0.8	0.4	0.0	0.5	1.0	89.4	9.8	0.2	0.2	0.9
Medina	1.4	96.0	3.5	0.6	0.9	0.1	0.4	1.0	96.6	2.6	0.2	0.6	0.7
Mentor	0.6	97.9	0.8	0.2	1.4	0.0	0.3	0.7	98.6	0.3	0.1	0.9	0.6
Middletown	1.4	88.2	11.4	0.7	0.5	0.1	0.6	0.9	88.3	11.0	0.1	0.4	0.4
Newark	1.5	95.6	3.9	0.8	0.8	0.1	0.5	0.8	96.0	3.2	0.2	0.4	0.7
North Olmsted	1.7	95.6	1.2	0.4	3.2	0.0	1.4	1.7	97.1	0.7	0.1	1.7	1.2
North Royalton	0.8	96.9	0.8	0.2	2.3	0.1	0.5	1.0	97.7	0.4	0.1	1.7	0.6
Parma	1.1	96.7	1.3	0.3	1.9	0.1	0.9	1.5	97.9	0.7	0.1	1.1	0.9
Reynoldsburg	1.8	86.6	11.2	0.7	2.2	0.1	1.1	1.8	93.9	4.1	0.3	1.5	0.9
Sandusky	2.9	77.0	23.1	0.8	0.5	0.1	1.6	3.1	79.7	18.9	0.2	0.3	2.3
Shaker Heights	2.2	61.7	35.4	0.7	3.8	0.1	1.0	1.2	66.9	30.7	0.2	1.9	1.1
Springfield	2.1	79.9	19.6	1.1	0.9	0.1	0.8	1.2	81.6	17.4	0.2	0.5	0.6
Stow	0.9	96.1	1.8	0.4	2.3	0.0	0.5	0.9	97.1	1.1	0.1	1.6	0.5
Strongsville	1.0	95.1	1.5	0.2	3.6	0.0	0.6	1.3	96.6	0.8	0.1	2.4	1.0
Toledo	2.6	72.4	24.8	0.9	1.3	0.1	3.2	5.5	77.0	19.7	0.3	1.0	4.0
Trotwood city	2.0	40.1	59.8	1.0	0.4	0.1	0.8	0.8	54.5	43.9	0.3	0.5	1.2
Upper Arlington	0.8	95.4	0.8	0.3	3.9	0.0	0.4	1.0	97.3	0.3	0.1	2.3	0.7
Warren	2.0	73.6	26.5	0.7	0.6	0.1	0.6	1.0	77.9	21.3	0.2	0.3	0.7
Westerville	1.2	94.6	3.7	0.4	1.8	0.1	0.6	1.1	96.8	1.7	0.1	1.2	0.7
Westlake	1.5	94.4	1.1	0.2	4.7	0.0	1.1	1.3	96.3	0.6	0.1	2.9	0.9
Youngstown	2.5	52.6	45.5	1.1	0.5	0.1	3.0	5.2	59.3	38.1	0.2	0.3	4.0
Zanesville	2.7	88.0	12.7	1.3	0.4	0.0	0.6	0.8	88.3	10.8	0.5	0.2	0.4
OKLAHOMA	4.5	80.3	8.3	11.4	1.7	0.1	3.0	5.2	82.1	7.4	8.0	1.1	2.7
Bartlesville	5.5	87.4	3.8	11.8	1.3	0.1	1.5	3.0	88.6	3.3	6.4	1.1	1.8
Broken Arrow	3.7	88.8	4.2	6.6	2.3	0.1	1.8	3.6	91.7	3.1	3.6	1.0	2.1
Edmond	2.9	89.2	4.5	4.0	3.8	0.2	1.4	2.8	91.8	3.1	2.5	2.0	1.8
Enid	2.8	89.7	4.5	3.7	1.4	0.7	2.9	4.7	91.0	4.4	2.3	1.3	2.1
Lawton	4.9	65.2	25.0	5.5	3.7	0.8	5.2	9.4	70.8	19.3	3.3	3.3	6.3
Midwest City	4.2	73.0	20.9	5.9	2.4	0.3	2.1	4.1	77.1	16.3	3.9	1.7	2.7
Moore	4.9	89.2	3.6	7.5	2.2	0.2	2.4	5.1	90.2	1.8	5.3	1.3	3.4
Muskogee	6.2	66.3	19.3	17.8	1.1	0.1	1.9	3.3	69.0	18.9	11.0	0.5	1.5
Norman	4.0	86.0	5.0	7.0	4.1	0.1	1.9	3.9	87.5	3.6	4.8	3.2	2.4
Oklahoma City	3.9	71.7	16.4	5.7	4.0	0.2	6.2	10.1	74.8	16.0	4.2	2.4	5.0
Ponca City	3.8	87.7	3.3	9.2	1.0	0.1	2.5	4.4	90.2	2.9	5.5	0.7	1.9
Shawnee	4.4	80.9	4.8	16.3	1.3	0.1	1.2	2.7	82.6	3.4	12.5	0.8	2.0
Stillwater	3.4	85.5	4.8	5.8	5.7	0.1	1.5	2.5	87.6	3.7	3.4	4.6	1.8
Tulsa	4.4	73.9	16.5	7.7	2.2	0.1	4.2	7.2	79.3	13.6	4.7	1.4	2.6
OREGON	3.1	89.3	2.1	2.5	3.7	0.5	5.2	8.0	92.8	1.6	1.4	2.4	4.0
Albany	2.6	94.0	0.8	2.4	1.8	0.4	3.4	6.1	96.1	0.3	1.1	1.3	3.0
Beaverton	3.7	81.5	2.4	1.4	11.2	0.8	6.7	11.1	89.4	1.0	0.5	7.7	3.3
Bend	2.1	96.0	0.5	1.7	1.5	0.3	2.2	4.6	97.5	0.2	0.9	0.7	2.4
Corvallis	2.8	88.6	1.6	1.6	7.5	0.6	3.3	5.7	89.1	1.2	0.7	8.0	2.8
Eugene	3.7	91.5	2.0	2.3	4.6	0.5	3.1	5.0	93.4	1.3	0.9	3.5	2.7
Gresham	3.8	86.1	2.6	2.0	4.4	0.6	8.5	11.9	93.8	1.1	1.0	2.7	3.3
Hillsboro	3.3	80.4	1.7	1.6	7.6	0.6	11.7	18.9	88.6	0.5	0.6	2.2	11.2
Keizer	3.4	88.6	1.2	2.5	2.2	0.4	8.7	12.3	93.0	0.5	2.0	1.4	5.6

[1] Hispanic persons may be of any race.

Table D. Cities

City	Under 5 years	5 to 17 years	18 to 24 years	25 to 34 years	35 to 44 years	45 to 54 years	55 to 64 years	65 to 74 years	75 years and over	Median age (years)	Percent Female
	28	29	30	31	32	33	34	35	36	37	38
OHIO—Cont'd											
Delaware	7.9	16.7	14.5	16.2	14.8	11.7	7.2	5.6	5.3	31.6	52.2
Dublin	8.2	23.0	4.0	12.2	21.2	17.6	6.7	3.1	2.3	35.4	50.5
East Cleveland	7.4	22.3	9.0	12.5	14.1	12.2	9.2	7.8	5.5	33.9	55.7
Elyria	7.9	18.7	8.9	14.8	15.5	12.9	8.4	6.6	6.4	34.8	52.0
Euclid	6.3	16.0	6.8	14.5	16.2	12.7	8.3	8.3	10.8	38.9	54.3
Fairborn	6.0	15.1	18.4	15.3	13.9	11.7	8.0	6.9	4.7	31.3	51.4
Fairfield	6.3	18.0	9.5	15.9	16.4	14.6	8.6	6.1	4.6	35.2	51.3
Findlay	7.0	16.8	11.9	14.1	14.6	12.8	8.6	6.7	7.4	35.1	52.3
Gahanna	6.8	22.1	6.5	12.0	19.7	16.1	8.2	4.9	3.8	36.5	51.5
Garfield Heights	6.3	17.7	7.3	13.5	15.8	12.7	8.0	8.3	10.3	38.3	53.3
Grove City	7.7	20.5	7.4	14.4	17.2	13.5	8.2	6.3	4.8	35.0	51.4
Hamilton	7.5	18.3	9.8	14.6	15.3	12.5	7.7	7.5	6.8	34.9	51.9
Huber Heights	7.3	20.1	8.6	15.1	16.0	14.3	9.3	6.0	3.3	34.4	51.3
Kent	5.0	11.4	40.0	13.0	10.0	8.8	4.2	3.7	3.9	22.9	54.2
Kettering	5.8	16.7	7.5	14.2	15.2	13.1	9.2	9.3	9.0	38.9	52.5
Lakewood	5.9	15.1	9.5	20.7	16.5	13.0	7.0	5.7	6.5	34.2	51.9
Lancaster	7.7	16.9	9.3	14.7	14.3	12.2	9.0	8.0	8.0	35.9	52.7
Lima	8.1	19.0	11.5	14.1	14.6	11.8	7.6	6.6	6.7	32.9	49.8
Lorain	8.0	20.4	9.0	13.5	14.7	12.5	8.0	7.2	6.7	34.4	52.6
Mansfield	7.2	16.7	9.3	14.8	14.9	12.9	8.7	7.7	7.7	36.4	50.4
Maple Heights	6.3	19.4	6.7	13.5	17.4	12.6	7.5	7.9	8.6	37.4	53.3
Marion	7.0	18.2	9.3	15.1	15.7	13.2	8.2	6.9	6.4	35.2	53.3
Massillon	6.6	18.7	7.9	13.1	15.0	13.1	9.4	8.2	7.9	37.6	51.9
Medina	9.2	20.7	7.2	16.1	17.7	12.6	6.3	4.7	5.6	33.2	52.1
Mentor	6.0	19.9	6.5	11.1	17.8	16.5	9.9	6.6	5.6	38.9	51.5
Middletown	7.2	17.8	9.3	14.0	15.3	13.0	8.6	7.8	7.1	36.2	52.2
Newark	7.5	17.8	9.4	13.8	15.3	12.7	8.4	7.2	7.7	35.9	52.7
North Olmsted	5.5	18.2	7.3	11.5	16.1	15.6	10.9	8.2	6.8	39.9	51.7
North Royalton	5.4	18.9	7.7	12.2	18.5	16.7	8.7	6.4	5.6	38.6	51.2
Parma	5.8	16.5	7.0	13.8	15.9	12.6	8.9	9.0	10.6	39.4	52.3
Reynoldsburg	7.1	19.5	8.0	14.8	17.1	14.9	8.5	6.0	4.2	35.4	52.4
Sandusky	7.2	18.6	9.2	13.1	15.4	12.9	8.4	7.5	7.6	36.2	52.8
Shaker Heights	6.2	20.0	5.3	11.7	15.7	15.7	9.8	7.9	7.7	39.6	54.5
Springfield	7.5	18.0	11.5	13.5	13.5	12.5	8.2	7.1	8.1	34.5	52.8
Stow	6.6	19.4	7.4	13.5	17.7	15.3	8.2	6.1	5.9	36.9	51.6
Strongsville	6.2	20.0	6.2	10.5	18.0	17.3	10.3	6.4	4.9	39.1	51.2
Toledo	7.3	18.9	11.0	15.2	14.6	12.2	7.6	6.6	6.5	33.2	52.1
Trotwood city	6.2	20.1	7.5	11.8	14.8	14.0	9.8	7.7	8.2	38.4	54.4
Upper Arlington	5.5	19.4	4.4	9.6	15.5	16.9	10.2	9.0	9.6	42.6	52.8
Warren	7.9	18.4	8.6	13.3	13.9	12.2	8.9	8.3	8.5	36.3	53.5
Westerville	6.1	20.8	9.1	10.1	17.0	17.8	8.8	5.4	5.0	37.8	52.6
Westlake	5.1	17.7	5.6	11.1	15.7	16.7	9.9	7.6	10.7	42.0	52.8
Youngstown	7.1	18.7	10.1	12.5	13.9	12.4	8.0	8.6	8.8	36.4	52.1
Zanesville	8.1	18.6	9.5	14.0	13.7	12.1	8.4	7.4	8.1	34.8	54.0
OKLAHOMA	6.8	19.0	10.3	13.1	15.2	13.1	9.2	7.0	6.2	35.5	50.9
Bartlesville	6.2	18.8	8.1	10.8	13.9	13.9	9.8	9.1	9.4	40.0	52.6
Broken Arrow	8.0	22.9	7.7	14.1	18.2	14.6	7.0	4.3	3.2	33.3	51.2
Edmond	7.0	20.5	11.3	12.8	16.8	14.8	8.0	4.7	4.1	33.6	51.6
Enid	6.9	17.8	9.6	12.6	15.0	12.6	8.9	7.9	8.5	37.2	51.8
Lawton	8.4	19.5	15.3	16.6	14.8	9.9	6.4	5.2	4.1	28.9	47.9
Midwest City	7.3	19.1	10.7	13.8	14.9	12.9	7.9	7.1	6.1	34.2	52.2
Moore	7.7	21.8	9.3	15.5	17.0	13.1	8.4	4.6	2.6	32.0	51.6
Muskogee	7.5	18.2	9.7	12.1	13.7	12.7	8.7	7.9	9.5	36.9	53.0
Norman	5.9	15.3	21.4	15.0	14.1	12.3	7.0	4.8	4.2	29.3	49.8
Oklahoma City	7.3	18.2	10.7	15.1	15.7	13.2	8.3	6.1	5.4	34.0	51.1
Ponca City	7.2	19.1	8.5	11.2	14.4	13.4	8.7	8.4	9.2	38.2	52.4
Shawnee	7.4	16.9	15.2	12.5	13.0	11.3	8.3	7.5	7.8	33.3	51.9
Stillwater	4.7	10.5	38.2	14.4	10.0	8.2	5.3	3.7	4.9	23.9	49.3
Tulsa	7.2	17.6	10.9	14.9	15.0	13.3	8.2	6.6	6.2	34.5	51.7
OREGON	6.5	18.2	9.6	13.8	15.4	14.8	8.9	6.4	6.4	36.3	50.4
Albany	7.6	18.8	9.6	14.5	14.9	13.7	8.2	5.6	7.1	34.6	51.4
Beaverton	7.2	17.7	10.6	18.4	16.7	13.6	6.8	4.0	5.0	32.6	50.6
Bend	6.9	17.6	10.2	15.5	15.6	14.3	7.5	6.0	6.4	34.8	50.7
Corvallis	4.9	12.8	28.4	14.8	12.1	11.3	5.5	4.4	5.6	27.0	50.2
Eugene	5.3	15.0	17.3	14.9	13.5	14.6	7.2	5.3	6.8	33.0	51.0
Gresham	8.0	19.6	11.1	14.7	15.6	13.7	7.5	4.7	5.1	32.5	50.6
Hillsboro	9.3	19.0	11.4	21.2	15.8	11.3	5.7	3.1	3.1	29.7	48.6
Keizer	8.1	19.7	8.2	15.0	15.1	13.5	8.4	6.0	6.2	34.4	51.5

Population and population characteristics, 2000

Age (percent)

Table D. Cities

City	Under 5 years	5 to 17 years	18 to 24 years	25 to 34 years	35 to 44 years	45 to 54 years	55 to 64 years	65 to 74 years	75 years and over	Percent Female	2000	1990	1980	1990–2000	1980–1990
	39	40	41	42	43	44	45	46	47	48	49	50	51	52	53
OHIO—Cont'd															
Delaware	7.1	17.5	17.2	16.2	14.1	9.4	7.4	5.6	5.4	52.1	25 243	19 966	18 780	26.4	6.3
Dublin	8.8	23.5	4.8	14.3	26.1	12.5	5.7	3.1	1.3	49.8	31 392	16 366	NA	91.8	NA
East Cleveland	8.4	20.5	10.2	16.6	14.8	10.0	9.1	6.3	4.1	56.4	27 217	33 096	36 957	-17.8	-10.4
Elyria	8.3	19.3	10.2	18.3	14.7	9.2	8.2	7.3	4.5	52.0	55 953	56 746	57 538	-1.4	-1.4
Euclid	6.2	13.6	7.5	18.2	13.3	9.2	9.9	12.3	9.8	54.4	52 717	54 875	59 999	-3.9	-8.5
Fairborn	7.0	15.8	17.2	18.8	12.9	9.8	8.8	6.8	2.9	50.8	32 052	31 300	29 702	2.4	5.4
Fairfield	7.3	18.1	10.3	20.4	16.8	10.7	7.9	5.2	3.2	51.5	42 097	39 709	30 777	6.0	29.0
Findlay	7.6	17.5	11.1	17.6	14.3	9.9	8.5	7.6	6.0	52.3	38 967	35 703	35 594	9.1	0.3
Gahanna	9.0	20.6	8.7	18.4	18.3	10.6	6.7	4.9	2.8	51.8	32 636	23 898	18 001	36.6	32.8
Garfield Heights	6.4	15.9	8.5	16.9	13.6	8.9	10.3	12.5	7.0	53.6	30 734	31 739	34 938	-3.2	-9.2
Grove City	7.2	18.8	10.0	17.3	16.8	10.2	9.3	6.3	4.1	52.2	27 075	19 661	16 849	37.7	16.7
Hamilton	8.2	19.2	9.3	17.8	13.1	8.9	9.4	8.2	6.0	53.0	60 690	61 436	63 189	-1.2	-2.8
Huber Heights	8.0	20.8	9.4	19.3	17.0	11.7	7.9	4.4	1.6	50.7	38 212	38 696	35 480	-1.3	9.1
Kent	5.1	11.7	41.9	14.6	10.3	5.1	4.5	4.1	2.9	53.9	27 906	28 835	26 164	-3.2	10.2
Kettering	6.2	15.1	8.5	17.7	14.3	10.2	11.1	10.3	6.6	52.7	57 502	60 569	61 186	-5.1	-1.0
Lakewood	6.6	16.6	9.4	22.2	15.5	8.7	7.4	7.2	6.4	53.6	56 646	59 718	61 963	-5.1	-3.6
Lancaster	7.3	17.6	9.8	16.5	13.8	10.0	9.3	8.6	7.1	53.2	35 335	34 507	34 953	2.4	-1.3
Lima	8.2	19.4	11.1	18.5	13.2	8.4	7.9	7.5	5.8	49.5	40 081	45 553	47 381	-12.0	-3.9
Lorain	8.1	20.9	9.2	16.6	13.4	9.4	9.1	8.3	5.0	52.6	68 652	71 245	75 416	-3.6	-5.5
Mansfield	7.3	16.9	11.3	17.1	13.2	10.4	8.9	8.5	6.4	51.1	49 346	50 627	53 927	-2.5	-6.1
Maple Heights	6.7	16.0	8.0	17.6	14.0	8.5	10.4	11.9	6.9	52.8	26 156	27 089	29 735	-3.4	-8.9
Marion	8.4	19.9	9.8	16.6	14.4	9.4	8.5	7.7	5.4	52.5	35 318	34 075	37 040	3.6	-8.0
Massillon	7.1	17.8	9.3	16.8	13.3	9.9	9.7	8.9	7.2	52.6	31 325	30 969	30 557	1.1	1.3
Medina	8.8	21.5	7.4	18.7	17.4	8.2	7.0	5.7	5.3	52.8	25 139	19 231	15 268	30.7	26.0
Mentor	7.5	19.9	8.2	16.5	18.5	11.8	8.3	6.4	3.0	51.2	50 278	47 491	42 065	5.9	12.9
Middletown	7.9	17.9	10.0	16.9	14.1	9.0	9.6	8.7	5.9	52.7	51 605	46 022	43 719	12.1	5.3
Newark	7.9	18.0	9.7	17.8	13.4	9.4	8.6	8.1	7.2	53.1	46 279	44 396	41 200	4.2	7.8
North Olmsted	6.2	18.3	8.9	15.0	16.0	12.6	10.1	8.1	4.8	52.1	34 113	34 204	36 486	-0.3	-6.3
North Royalton	6.9	17.4	8.6	19.0	17.9	10.3	8.6	6.9	4.4	51.0	28 648	23 197	17 671	23.5	31.3
Parma	6.3	15.0	8.0	17.7	13.2	9.9	10.9	12.2	6.9	52.6	85 655	87 876	92 548	-2.5	-5.0
Reynoldsburg	7.1	19.1	10.5	18.2	18.4	10.7	8.3	5.3	2.4	52.0	32 069	25 748	20 661	24.5	24.6
Sandusky	8.0	18.9	9.6	17.5	14.1	8.1	9.1	9.1	5.6	53.0	27 844	29 764	31 360	-6.5	-5.1
Shaker Heights	5.8	18.0	6.4	14.2	17.9	12.3	10.7	8.4	6.3	53.9	29 405	30 955	32 487	-5.0	-4.7
Springfield	7.8	18.1	12.6	15.5	13.6	8.8	8.2	8.3	7.0	53.4	65 358	70 487	72 563	-7.3	-2.9
Stow	7.6	19.2	8.5	18.1	18.6	10.2	8.2	5.9	3.6	51.5	32 139	27 998	25 303	14.8	10.7
Strongsville	7.1	20.2	8.1	14.9	20.1	13.4	8.2	5.7	2.2	50.8	43 858	35 308	28 577	24.2	23.6
Toledo	8.1	18.0	11.7	17.7	13.5	8.9	8.5	7.9	5.7	52.6	313 619	332 943	354 635	-5.8	-6.1
Trotwood city	NA	NA	NA	NA	NA	NA	NA	NA	NA	NA	27 420	8 816	NA	211.0	NA
Upper Arlington	5.8	16.6	5.7	11.6	17.5	12.4	11.8	10.5	8.2	53.5	33 686	34 128	35 648	-1.3	-4.3
Warren	8.0	18.0	8.4	15.8	13.4	9.3	10.1	10.1	6.9	53.9	46 832	50 793	56 629	-7.8	-10.3
Westerville	6.8	22.3	9.9	13.5	21.0	11.8	6.5	4.1	3.9	52.7	35 318	30 269	23 416	16.7	29.3
Westlake	6.0	17.7	7.0	15.2	17.2	12.3	9.1	8.1	7.4	52.5	31 719	27 018	19 483	17.4	38.7
Youngstown	7.4	18.9	9.3	15.0	12.3	8.7	10.1	11.0	7.2	53.7	82 026	95 732	115 435	-14.3	-17.1
Zanesville	8.4	18.8	10.1	15.7	12.3	9.0	8.9	8.9	7.8	54.7	25 586	26 778	28 655	-4.5	-6.6
OKLAHOMA	7.2	19.4	10.2	16.2	14.4	10.3	8.9	7.5	6.0	51.3	3 450 654	3 145 576	3 025 487	9.7	4.0
Bartlesville	6.8	19.0	7.5	14.1	14.1	11.6	10.0	9.6	7.2	52.7	34 748	34 256	34 568	1.4	-0.9
Broken Arrow	9.4	24.3	6.8	20.0	19.8	9.0	5.1	3.3	2.2	50.7	74 859	58 043	35 761	29.0	62.3
Edmond	8.1	20.9	11.1	18.3	17.4	11.1	6.3	3.8	3.2	51.4	68 315	52 310	34 637	30.6	51.0
Enid	6.9	18.1	9.1	17.1	13.9	9.0	9.9	8.1	7.9	52.1	47 045	45 309	50 363	3.8	-10.0
Lawton	8.9	20.5	12.2	19.4	13.2	9.1	7.6	5.5	3.6	51.3	92 757	80 561	80 054	15.1	0.6
Midwest City	8.1	19.6	10.1	18.6	14.5	9.2	8.8	7.8	3.4	52.2	54 088	52 267	49 559	3.5	5.5
Moore	8.2	24.1	9.1	19.4	17.0	11.1	6.1	3.2	1.8	51.1	41 138	40 318	35 063	2.0	15.0
Muskogee	7.0	19.6	8.5	14.9	12.9	9.2	9.1	9.9	8.8	53.9	38 310	37 708	40 011	1.6	-5.8
Norman	6.5	15.7	21.0	18.8	15.0	8.5	6.3	4.8	3.4	50.1	95 694	80 071	67 996	19.5	17.8
Oklahoma City	7.7	18.2	9.9	19.0	14.9	10.2	8.3	6.8	5.0	51.8	506 132	444 724	403 243	13.8	10.3
Ponca City	7.7	18.9	7.7	15.4	14.6	9.6	9.2	8.9	8.1	52.7	25 919	26 359	26 238	-1.7	0.5
Shawnee	7.1	17.6	12.7	14.8	12.2	8.9	8.6	8.8	9.3	54.0	28 692	26 017	26 506	10.3	-1.8
Stillwater	5.3	11.9	36.3	17.8	10.0	6.0	4.4	4.0	4.2	49.3	39 065	36 676	38 268	6.5	-4.2
Tulsa	7.3	17.0	10.7	18.4	15.1	10.2	8.7	7.4	5.3	52.2	393 049	367 302	360 919	7.0	1.8
OREGON	7.1	18.4	9.4	15.9	16.7	10.4	8.3	7.9	5.9	50.8	3 421 399	2 842 337	2 633 156	20.4	7.9
Albany	8.0	18.1	11.0	17.0	14.7	10.1	7.1	7.7	6.4	51.9	40 852	33 523	26 544	21.9	26.3
Beaverton	7.9	17.1	9.8	22.3	18.0	9.8	6.1	5.0	4.0	52.1	76 129	53 307	30 582	42.8	74.3
Bend	7.4	17.5	10.4	18.5	17.8	8.8	6.1	7.0	6.5	51.2	52 029	23 740	17 263	119.2	37.5
Corvallis	5.8	12.6	29.5	17.2	13.3	7.1	4.9	5.3	4.3	49.1	49 322	44 757	40 960	10.2	9.3
Eugene	5.9	15.2	16.7	16.6	17.5	8.9	6.5	6.9	5.8	51.9	137 893	112 733	105 624	22.3	6.7
Gresham	7.9	19.6	9.9	17.7	17.3	10.6	7.0	5.7	4.3	51.5	90 205	68 249	33 005	32.2	106.8
Hillsboro	8.8	22.1	9.4	18.0	18.0	9.1	6.0	4.7	3.9	50.5	70 186	37 598	27 664	86.7	35.9
Keizer	7.4	18.7	8.2	16.0	16.1	11.0	8.6	7.8	6.3	52.1	32 203	21 884	18 592	47.2	17.7

Table D. Cities

City	Total population	Total in house-holds	House-holder	Spouse	Child Total	Child Own child under 18 years	Other relatives Total	Other relatives Under 18 years	Nonrelatives Total	Nonrelatives Unmarried partner	Total in group quarters	Correctional institutions	Nursing homes	Other institutions	College dormitories	Military quarters	Other
	54	55	56	57	58	59	60	61	62	63	64	65	66	67	68	69	70
OHIO—Cont'd																	
Delaware	25 243	92.4	37.7	19.7	27.8	23.2	2.5	1.0	4.7	2.2	7.6	0.0	1.4	0.0	6.1	0.0	0.1
Dublin	31 392	99.8	35.7	25.3	35.5	31.8	1.2	0.2	2.1	1.0	0.2	0.0	0.2	0.0	0.0	0.0	0.0
East Cleveland	27 217	98.4	41.2	8.7	32.7	23.2	10.4	5.6	5.4	2.8	1.6	0.1	1.1	0.1	0.0	0.0	0.4
Elyria	55 953	98.3	40.0	18.6	30.3	23.5	4.4	2.2	5.0	2.7	1.7	0.7	0.7	0.1	0.0	0.0	0.1
Euclid	52 717	98.8	46.2	16.8	27.3	20.4	4.4	1.6	4.2	2.2	1.2	0.1	0.8	0.0	0.0	0.0	0.2
Fairborn	32 052	96.8	42.5	18.2	25.0	19.4	3.2	1.2	7.9	2.3	3.2	0.0	0.3	0.0	2.9	0.0	0.0
Fairfield	42 097	98.4	40.3	21.6	28.9	22.7	3.2	1.3	4.5	2.5	1.6	0.0	1.0	0.0	0.0	0.0	0.6
Findlay	38 967	96.1	40.8	20.1	26.6	21.9	2.8	1.2	5.8	2.3	3.9	0.2	1.4	0.0	1.8	0.0	0.5
Gahanna	32 636	99.3	36.7	22.9	33.4	27.5	3.0	1.0	3.2	1.4	0.7	0.0	0.6	0.0	0.0	0.0	0.0
Garfield Heights	30 734	98.6	40.5	18.9	30.4	21.4	5.2	2.1	3.6	1.9	1.4	0.0	0.8	0.1	0.0	0.0	0.5
Grove City	27 075	99.0	37.9	22.6	31.8	26.2	3.2	1.4	3.4	1.8	1.0	0.0	0.7	0.0	0.0	0.0	0.4
Hamilton	60 690	97.8	39.9	18.1	29.3	22.5	5.4	2.5	5.1	2.5	2.2	0.7	0.8	0.2	0.0	0.0	0.5
Huber Heights	38 212	99.5	37.7	22.1	32.0	25.1	3.8	1.7	3.9	1.9	0.5	0.0	0.2	0.0	0.0	0.0	0.3
Kent	27 906	79.5	35.0	11.5	19.1	15.4	1.9	0.6	12.0	2.2	20.5	0.0	0.3	0.0	19.9	0.0	0.3
Kettering	57 502	99.2	44.6	21.7	26.4	21.3	2.4	0.9	4.0	1.9	0.8	0.0	0.6	0.0	0.1	0.0	0.1
Lakewood	56 646	98.6	47.1	16.0	25.7	19.8	3.3	1.0	6.6	2.8	1.4	0.0	0.7	0.0	0.4	0.0	0.3
Lancaster	35 335	98.7	42.0	20.1	28.2	22.5	3.5	1.4	5.0	2.8	1.3	0.3	0.9	0.0	0.0	0.0	0.1
Lima	40 081	93.2	38.4	14.3	29.9	23.7	5.1	2.7	5.4	2.6	6.8	4.5	0.8	0.1	0.8	0.0	0.6
Lorain	68 652	98.9	38.5	16.8	32.8	24.8	5.7	2.8	5.1	2.7	1.1	0.0	0.7	0.0	0.0	0.0	0.3
Mansfield	49 346	93.2	40.9	16.6	26.1	20.8	4.4	2.2	5.2	2.6	6.8	5.0	0.7	0.1	0.0	0.0	0.9
Maple Heights	26 156	99.1	40.1	18.1	31.3	22.5	6.1	2.7	3.5	1.8	0.9	0.0	0.7	0.0	0.0	0.0	0.1
Marion	35 318	93.8	38.4	17.8	27.9	22.4	4.3	2.0	5.5	2.8	6.2	5.4	0.6	0.0	0.0	0.0	0.3
Massillon	31 325	97.3	40.5	19.3	28.8	22.0	4.0	1.8	4.6	2.4	2.7	0.0	0.9	1.3	0.0	0.0	0.5
Medina	25 139	97.9	37.7	21.6	33.4	28.9	2.1	0.6	3.1	1.7	2.1	0.9	1.1	0.0	0.0	0.0	0.1
Mentor	50 278	99.1	37.4	23.8	32.4	24.8	2.8	0.8	2.7	1.3	0.9	0.0	0.6	0.0	0.0	0.0	0.3
Middletown	51 605	98.9	41.6	19.1	28.5	22.3	4.7	2.2	5.0	2.7	1.1	0.1	0.8	0.0	0.0	0.0	0.2
Newark	46 279	98.0	41.7	19.0	28.5	23.1	3.2	1.4	5.6	2.9	2.0	0.4	1.3	0.0	0.0	0.0	0.3
North Olmsted	34 113	99.1	39.6	22.8	30.5	22.3	3.4	1.1	2.8	1.3	0.9	0.0	0.8	0.0	0.0	0.0	0.1
North Royalton	28 648	98.7	39.3	22.9	31.0	23.5	2.7	0.6	2.8	1.6	1.3	0.0	0.8	0.0	0.0	0.0	0.4
Parma	85 655	98.6	41.0	21.6	29.1	20.8	3.6	1.0	3.3	1.7	1.4	0.0	1.1	0.2	0.0	0.0	0.1
Reynoldsburg	32 069	99.7	40.1	21.1	30.5	24.7	3.5	1.4	4.4	2.1	0.3	0.0	0.3	0.0	0.0	0.0	0.0
Sandusky	27 844	98.3	42.6	16.5	29.1	22.5	4.7	2.6	5.5	3.1	1.7	0.0	1.2	0.0	0.0	0.0	0.5
Shaker Heights	29 405	99.3	41.6	20.8	30.2	24.2	3.6	1.5	3.2	1.2	0.7	0.0	0.3	0.1	0.0	0.0	0.2
Springfield	65 358	95.7	40.2	16.3	28.2	22.3	5.0	2.3	6.1	2.9	4.3	0.3	1.5	0.2	1.9	0.0	0.4
Stow	32 139	98.3	38.3	22.9	31.4	25.1	2.3	0.7	3.4	1.6	1.7	0.0	1.4	0.0	0.0	0.0	0.2
Strongsville	43 858	99.2	37.0	25.0	32.3	25.4	2.8	0.7	2.2	1.1	0.8	0.0	0.6	0.0	0.0	0.0	0.2
Toledo	313 619	97.8	41.1	15.7	29.8	23.1	4.9	2.4	6.3	2.8	2.2	0.2	0.6	0.0	0.8	0.0	0.6
Trotwood city	27 420	97.4	40.5	16.3	30.1	22.1	6.1	3.3	4.4	2.3	2.6	0.0	2.1	0.1	0.0	0.0	0.4
Upper Arlington	33 686	99.1	41.5	24.5	29.1	24.5	1.5	0.3	2.4	0.9	0.9	0.0	0.7	0.3	0.0	0.0	0.0
Warren	46 832	97.5	41.2	15.8	30.4	23.2	5.3	2.6	4.7	2.5	2.5	0.7	1.5	0.0	0.0	0.0	0.3
Westerville	35 318	95.6	35.9	23.2	31.7	25.9	2.2	0.7	2.5	1.0	4.4	0.0	1.6	0.0	2.7	0.0	0.1
Westlake	31 719	96.0	40.4	22.6	28.4	22.2	2.2	0.5	2.4	1.2	4.0	0.0	3.0	0.4	0.0	0.0	0.6
Youngstown	82 026	93.9	39.2	13.0	29.4	21.0	7.4	3.8	4.8	2.1	6.1	3.0	0.9	0.3	1.0	0.0	0.8
Zanesville	25 586	97.4	41.3	15.9	29.8	23.8	4.4	2.1	6.0	3.3	2.6	0.5	1.3	0.2	0.0	0.0	0.6
OKLAHOMA	3 450 654	96.7	38.9	20.8	28.7	23.1	4.4	2.1	3.9	1.5	3.3	1.0	0.8	0.1	0.8	0.2	0.3
Bartlesville	34 748	98.4	41.9	23.0	27.7	23.2	2.9	1.2	2.9	1.3	1.6	0.1	0.7	0.0	0.6	0.0	0.2
Broken Arrow	74 859	99.3	34.9	23.8	35.1	29.3	2.8	1.2	2.7	0.9	0.7	0.0	0.6	0.1	0.0	0.0	0.1
Edmond	68 315	97.3	37.0	22.9	31.3	26.3	2.3	0.8	3.8	1.0	2.7	0.0	0.6	0.1	1.7	0.0	0.4
Enid	47 045	96.3	40.3	20.8	27.3	22.4	3.7	1.7	4.2	1.8	3.7	0.4	2.0	0.2	0.0	0.5	0.6
Lawton	92 757	89.5	34.3	17.7	29.7	24.9	3.9	2.0	3.8	1.5	10.5	2.3	0.8	0.2	0.2	6.8	0.2
Midwest City	54 088	99.1	41.0	18.9	29.9	23.3	4.9	2.5	4.4	1.8	0.9	0.1	0.6	0.0	0.0	0.0	0.1
Moore	41 138	99.4	36.1	21.8	33.7	26.9	4.3	2.0	3.5	1.4	0.6	0.0	0.5	0.0	0.2	0.0	0.0
Muskogee	38 310	96.7	40.5	18.3	27.9	22.0	5.8	2.7	4.2	1.7	3.3	0.7	1.6	0.1	0.2	0.0	0.7
Norman	95 694	93.7	40.6	18.3	24.1	19.6	3.2	1.1	7.5	1.8	6.3	0.1	0.8	0.2	5.0	0.0	0.2
Oklahoma City	506 132	97.4	40.4	18.5	28.2	22.6	5.3	2.3	5.0	1.9	2.6	1.0	0.6	0.1	0.4	0.1	0.5
Ponca City	25 919	97.7	41.0	21.1	28.5	23.8	3.3	1.5	3.9	1.9	2.3	0.0	1.2	0.3	0.0	0.0	0.8
Shawnee	28 692	93.9	39.4	18.2	26.9	21.3	4.8	2.3	4.5	1.6	6.1	0.3	1.1	0.0	4.5	0.0	0.2
Stillwater	39 065	84.9	39.9	14.4	17.2	14.3	2.3	0.6	11.1	1.6	15.1	0.2	0.5	0.0	13.5	0.0	0.8
Tulsa	393 049	97.3	42.2	18.2	27.2	22.1	4.7	2.0	5.2	2.0	2.7	0.3	0.6	0.3	0.9	0.0	0.5
OREGON	3 421 399	97.7	39.0	20.2	27.4	22.4	4.2	1.5	6.9	2.5	2.3	0.6	0.4	0.1	0.6	0.0	0.6
Albany	40 852	98.3	39.4	20.2	28.8	24.0	3.7	1.5	6.3	2.5	1.7	0.5	0.4	0.3	0.0	0.0	0.5
Beaverton	76 129	98.8	40.5	19.0	27.6	23.4	4.1	0.9	7.7	2.6	1.2	0.0	0.3	0.1	0.0	0.0	0.8
Bend	52 029	98.1	40.5	20.3	26.5	22.8	2.7	0.9	8.1	2.9	1.9	0.5	0.5	0.0	0.2	0.0	0.8
Corvallis	49 322	90.1	39.8	16.2	19.5	16.8	2.2	0.4	12.3	2.4	9.9	0.1	0.5	0.1	8.8	0.0	0.5
Eugene	137 893	95.6	42.1	17.1	22.6	18.8	2.7	0.8	11.1	3.1	4.4	0.6	0.5	0.1	2.3	0.0	0.9
Gresham	90 205	98.7	36.9	18.8	30.7	25.0	5.1	1.6	7.2	2.4	1.3	0.0	0.7	0.1	0.0	0.0	0.5
Hillsboro	70 186	98.6	35.7	19.6	30.2	25.7	5.8	1.8	7.4	2.2	1.4	0.9	0.3	0.0	0.0	0.0	0.2
Keizer	32 203	99.1	37.6	21.0	30.2	25.3	4.4	1.6	6.0	2.2	0.9	0.0	0.7	0.0	0.0	0.0	0.1

Table D. Cities

City	Total households	Total	With own children under 18 years	Total	With own children under 18 years	Total	With own children under 18 years	Total	Total	65 years and over	Average household size	Average family size	Total households	Female householder[1]	Householder living alone
													(1990)		
	71	72	73	74	75	76	77	78	79	80	81	82	83	84	85
OHIO—Cont'd															
Delaware	9 520	66.8	34.7	52.1	25.0	11.1	7.5	33.2	26.9	9.1	2.45	2.98	7 137	11.2	26.5
Dublin	11 209	77.4	46.6	70.7	42.0	5.0	3.5	22.6	18.5	3.8	2.80	3.24	5 522	4.9	12.7
East Cleveland	11 210	57.3	28.5	21.2	7.4	30.3	18.6	42.7	38.0	11.4	2.39	3.20	13 362	31.4	34.3
Elyria	22 409	66.2	31.9	46.4	19.7	15.1	9.7	33.8	28.5	10.6	2.46	3.01	21 423	13.9	24.8
Euclid	24 353	55.4	24.9	36.3	14.7	15.2	8.6	44.6	39.7	16.1	2.14	2.89	24 894	11.9	37.1
Fairborn	13 615	58.9	26.7	42.8	16.8	12.4	7.9	41.1	31.0	8.3	2.28	2.86	12 673	11.4	26.1
Fairfield	16 960	67.0	32.5	53.7	24.1	9.7	6.3	33.0	26.6	6.5	2.44	2.99	15 289	8.3	22.9
Findlay	15 905	62.9	29.2	49.3	20.4	9.9	6.6	37.1	30.2	10.2	2.36	2.93	14 117	9.2	28.0
Gahanna	11 990	74.5	40.4	62.4	33.2	9.2	5.6	25.5	20.9	6.6	2.70	3.17	9 453	10.3	16.5
Garfield Heights	12 452	65.9	28.9	46.5	19.7	15.3	7.5	34.1	30.0	14.4	2.43	3.04	12 483	13.7	26.0
Grove City	10 265	73.5	37.8	59.5	29.1	10.3	6.4	26.5	22.4	8.3	2.61	3.07	7 382	10.8	21.3
Hamilton	24 188	65.6	31.5	45.5	19.4	15.3	9.4	34.4	29.3	11.7	2.45	3.02	23 992	14.9	26.7
Huber Heights	14 392	74.9	36.9	58.7	26.9	12.0	7.5	25.1	20.5	5.9	2.64	3.05	13 509	9.9	15.5
Kent	9 772	49.1	25.8	32.8	14.4	13.3	9.6	50.9	32.4	8.1	2.27	2.89	8 808	12.9	28.0
Kettering	25 657	61.3	26.9	48.7	19.4	9.5	5.9	38.7	33.4	12.7	2.22	2.85	26 098	8.5	30.0
Lakewood	26 693	47.0	23.0	34.0	15.8	9.7	5.8	53.0	43.6	11.3	2.09	3.03	26 999	10.7	41.0
Lancaster	14 852	64.4	30.5	47.9	20.2	12.9	8.1	35.6	30.3	13.5	2.35	2.91	13 981	12.4	27.4
Lima	15 410	62.1	31.9	37.3	15.5	19.7	13.5	37.9	32.1	12.6	2.42	3.06	16 311	17.9	28.3
Lorain	26 434	68.0	33.3	43.6	17.9	19.2	12.6	32.0	27.4	10.7	2.57	3.11	26 198	16.7	24.5
Mansfield	20 182	59.6	27.3	40.5	15.4	15.2	9.7	40.4	34.8	13.8	2.28	2.93	20 197	13.8	32.1
Maple Heights	10 489	66.4	30.9	45.2	20.0	17.0	8.9	33.6	29.9	12.5	2.47	3.08	10 551	12.0	25.2
Marion	13 551	65.1	31.6	46.3	19.8	14.1	8.8	34.9	29.3	12.0	2.44	3.00	13 179	13.3	26.5
Massillon	12 677	65.7	29.8	47.8	19.4	13.8	8.1	34.3	29.6	13.6	2.40	2.96	12 110	13.2	27.5
Medina	9 467	70.6	40.3	57.5	31.4	10.6	7.3	29.4	25.1	9.5	2.60	3.15	7 102	11.0	23.5
Mentor	18 797	75.7	35.8	63.6	29.7	8.9	4.6	24.3	20.5	8.1	2.65	3.08	16 730	8.4	17.2
Middletown	21 469	64.9	29.9	45.9	18.6	14.6	8.9	35.1	29.6	11.4	2.38	2.94	18 362	14.4	26.4
Newark	19 312	62.7	30.8	45.5	19.6	13.4	8.9	37.3	31.5	12.7	2.35	2.94	17 802	12.3	29.1
North Olmsted	13 517	69.3	29.6	57.4	24.3	8.6	4.0	30.7	26.5	9.9	2.50	3.07	12 657	8.9	22.4
North Royalton	11 250	68.4	31.5	58.4	26.7	7.4	3.7	31.6	26.7	7.0	2.51	3.11	8 771	7.5	23.6
Parma	35 126	66.4	27.6	52.7	21.6	10.2	4.6	33.6	29.2	13.6	2.40	2.99	34 685	10.0	24.7
Reynoldsburg	12 849	68.5	34.8	52.8	24.7	12.3	7.9	31.5	25.8	7.2	2.49	3.01	9 981	9.7	23.1
Sandusky	11 851	59.4	28.9	38.7	15.7	16.4	10.7	40.6	34.9	13.1	2.31	2.99	12 059	14.7	31.8
Shaker Heights	12 220	65.8	32.1	50.1	23.5	12.9	7.3	34.2	30.2	11.6	2.39	3.00	12 648	11.2	27.7
Springfield	26 254	61.8	29.9	40.5	16.7	16.6	10.5	38.2	32.2	13.5	2.38	2.99	27 247	15.7	29.5
Stow	12 317	71.0	35.3	59.8	28.9	8.4	4.9	29.0	23.7	8.0	2.57	3.08	10 086	8.2	19.6
Strongsville	16 209	76.4	35.9	67.5	31.5	6.4	3.3	23.6	19.9	7.0	2.69	3.13	12 284	6.0	16.7
Toledo	128 925	60.0	29.8	38.2	16.3	17.2	11.0	40.0	32.8	11.0	2.38	3.04	130 883	15.7	29.7
Trotwood city	11 110	66.1	30.3	40.3	14.6	21.5	13.2	33.9	29.8	10.9	2.40	2.96	3 604	NA	NA
Upper Arlington	13 985	68.0	31.9	59.1	26.9	6.9	4.0	32.0	28.2	12.9	2.39	2.95	13 956	6.8	25.6
Warren	19 288	62.4	29.5	38.4	14.8	19.4	12.4	37.6	32.9	13.7	2.37	3.01	20 314	17.2	29.6
Westerville	12 663	75.4	39.3	64.8	32.5	8.3	5.5	24.6	20.9	8.0	2.67	3.11	10 178	8.8	17.6
Westlake	12 826	63.9	28.5	55.9	24.6	5.8	2.9	36.1	32.0	12.7	2.37	3.06	10 262	6.1	26.9
Youngstown	32 177	61.3	27.2	33.2	11.9	22.9	13.2	38.7	34.0	14.7	2.36	3.07	37 037	21.5	29.5
Zanesville	10 572	60.9	30.7	38.5	16.0	18.0	12.1	39.1	33.4	14.5	2.36	2.99	10 819	17.4	32.3
OKLAHOMA	1 342 293	68.7	32.4	53.5	23.2	11.4	7.0	31.3	26.7	10.1	2.49	3.02	1 206 135	10.4	25.6
Bartlesville	14 565	67.5	30.1	54.9	22.1	9.7	6.3	32.5	29.5	14.0	2.35	2.89	14 013	8.3	26.8
Broken Arrow	26 159	80.9	45.5	68.0	36.9	9.7	6.7	19.1	15.7	4.7	2.84	3.18	19 256	8.4	13.3
Edmond	25 256	73.6	39.3	61.9	31.7	9.1	6.3	26.4	20.6	6.1	2.63	3.08	18 756	9.3	19.1
Enid	18 955	66.3	30.9	51.6	21.5	11.2	7.2	33.7	29.1	12.5	2.39	2.94	18 215	9.7	28.6
Lawton	31 778	70.9	39.6	51.7	26.8	15.3	10.5	29.1	24.6	7.8	2.61	3.12	29 566	13.2	21.9
Midwest City	22 161	66.6	31.8	46.2	18.9	16.5	10.6	33.4	28.6	9.5	2.42	2.97	20 390	13.7	25.7
Moore	14 848	77.9	41.8	60.4	30.5	13.3	8.7	22.1	18.2	5.1	2.75	3.13	13 567	11.5	14.3
Muskogee	15 523	64.1	29.3	45.2	18.4	15.4	9.0	35.9	31.8	14.8	2.39	3.00	15 088	14.5	30.7
Norman	38 834	58.1	27.7	44.1	20.3	9.5	5.8	41.9	30.3	6.5	2.31	2.93	31 907	9.2	30.0
Oklahoma City	204 434	63.3	30.8	45.8	20.2	13.2	8.4	36.7	30.7	8.8	2.41	3.04	178 662	12.6	30.0
Ponca City	10 636	66.0	31.4	51.3	21.5	11.1	7.5	34.0	30.0	13.7	2.38	2.95	10 733	8.4	28.9
Shawnee	11 311	64.6	29.7	46.2	18.7	14.4	8.8	35.4	30.4	13.3	2.38	2.96	10 337	12.1	30.9
Stillwater	15 604	46.9	20.8	36.1	14.9	7.7	4.7	53.1	34.6	6.9	2.13	2.81	14 172	7.2	32.9
Tulsa	165 743	59.8	28.5	43.1	18.3	12.9	8.2	40.2	33.9	9.8	2.31	2.98	155 447	11.8	32.7
OREGON	1 333 723	65.8	30.8	51.9	22.2	9.8	6.2	34.2	26.1	9.1	2.51	3.02	1 103 313	9.2	25.3
Albany	16 108	67.1	33.3	51.1	22.5	11.7	7.9	32.9	26.1	10.4	2.49	2.99	11 786	11.5	26.8
Beaverton	30 821	60.5	32.3	46.8	23.9	9.7	6.3	39.5	29.7	7.1	2.44	3.07	22 100	9.4	28.7
Bend	21 062	63.6	31.9	50.2	22.5	9.7	7.1	36.4	26.1	8.6	2.42	2.92	8 526	9.9	29.5
Corvallis	19 630	50.8	24.0	40.8	18.0	7.2	4.7	49.2	31.5	7.5	2.26	2.88	16 743	7.3	30.4
Eugene	58 110	53.9	25.8	40.6	17.2	9.7	6.5	46.1	31.7	9.4	2.27	2.87	46 274	9.2	31.0
Gresham	33 327	68.1	36.2	50.9	25.3	12.0	7.9	31.9	24.3	7.8	2.67	3.17	25 705	10.3	25.3
Hillsboro	25 079	68.1	37.9	54.7	29.3	9.0	6.2	31.9	23.4	5.3	2.76	3.28	12 849	10.8	19.4
Keizer	12 110	71.4	35.6	55.8	25.6	11.2	7.3	28.6	22.4	8.4	2.64	3.07	8 332	10.5	22.5

[1] No spouse present.

Table D. Cities

City	Percent change of households, 1990-2000	Total housing units	Occupied housing units (percent)	Vacant housing units		Homeowner vacancy rate (percent)	Rental vacancy rate (percent)	Occupied housing units			Average household size of owner-occupied units	Average household size of renter-occupied units
				Total	For seasonal, recreational, or occasional use			Total	Percent owner-occupied housing units	Percent renter-occupied housing units		
	86	87	88	89	90	91	92	93	94	95	96	97
OHIO—Cont'd												
Delaware	33.4	10 208	93.3	6.7	0.3	1.7	9.2	9 520	60.3	39.7	2.63	2.17
Dublin	103.0	12 038	93.1	6.9	1.7	1.3	12.8	11 209	76.8	23.2	3.04	1.99
East Cleveland	-16.1	13 491	83.1	16.9	0.1	3.6	15.4	11 210	35.5	64.5	2.75	2.19
Elyria	4.6	23 841	94.0	6.0	0.3	1.5	8.8	22 409	64.6	35.4	2.57	2.25
Euclid	-2.2	26 123	93.2	6.8	0.1	1.4	9.8	24 353	59.5	40.5	2.34	1.84
Fairborn	7.4	14 419	94.4	5.6	0.4	1.7	6.6	13 615	51.7	48.3	2.39	2.15
Fairfield	10.9	17 789	95.3	4.7	0.4	0.9	7.6	16 960	65.4	34.6	2.63	2.09
Findlay	12.7	17 152	92.7	7.3	0.5	2.0	8.5	15 905	64.8	35.2	2.47	2.14
Gahanna	26.8	12 390	96.8	3.2	0.5	0.6	5.9	11 990	77.7	22.3	2.86	2.16
Garfield Heights	-0.2	12 998	95.8	4.2	0.1	1.3	7.6	12 452	79.9	20.1	2.51	2.15
Grove City	39.1	10 712	95.8	4.2	0.3	1.9	5.5	10 265	72.5	27.5	2.73	2.29
Hamilton	0.8	25 913	93.3	6.7	0.3	1.5	7.1	24 188	60.7	39.3	2.52	2.35
Huber Heights	6.5	14 938	96.3	3.7	0.2	1.3	5.8	14 392	72.0	28.0	2.64	2.64
Kent	10.9	10 435	93.6	6.4	0.2	1.8	6.4	9 772	37.8	62.2	2.58	2.08
Kettering	-1.7	26 936	95.3	4.7	0.5	1.3	6.9	25 657	66.6	33.4	2.39	1.90
Lakewood	-1.1	28 416	93.9	6.1	0.5	0.9	6.4	26 693	45.2	54.8	2.53	1.74
Lancaster	6.2	15 891	93.5	6.5	0.8	1.6	7.1	14 852	59.4	40.6	2.41	2.26
Lima	-5.5	17 631	87.4	12.6	0.4	2.5	12.9	15 410	56.8	43.2	2.44	2.40
Lorain	0.9	28 231	93.6	6.4	0.2	1.6	7.2	26 434	61.2	38.8	2.61	2.51
Mansfield	-0.1	22 267	90.6	9.4	0.4	2.1	10.6	20 182	57.6	42.4	2.36	2.17
Maple Heights	-0.6	10 935	95.9	4.1	0.1	1.8	5.7	10 489	83.8	16.2	2.55	2.09
Marion	2.8	14 713	92.1	7.9	0.2	2.3	8.0	13 551	63.5	36.5	2.52	2.32
Massillon	4.7	13 567	93.4	6.6	0.2	1.8	7.2	12 677	69.0	31.0	2.50	2.20
Medina	33.3	9 924	95.4	4.6	0.2	1.4	6.4	9 467	66.3	33.7	2.86	2.09
Mentor	12.4	19 301	97.4	2.6	0.4	0.9	5.6	18 797	87.5	12.5	2.69	2.33
Middletown	16.9	23 144	92.8	7.2	0.2	2.2	8.5	21 469	60.1	39.9	2.47	2.24
Newark	8.5	20 625	93.6	6.4	0.3	2.1	6.8	19 312	58.2	41.8	2.47	2.18
North Olmsted	6.8	14 059	96.1	3.9	0.4	1.1	7.9	13 517	79.7	20.3	2.62	2.01
North Royalton	28.3	11 754	95.7	4.3	0.4	1.5	7.0	11 250	74.9	25.1	2.75	1.80
Parma	1.3	36 414	96.5	3.5	0.2	0.8	7.2	35 126	77.5	22.5	2.52	2.00
Reynoldsburg	28.7	13 434	95.6	4.4	0.3	1.2	7.1	12 849	65.1	34.9	2.63	2.23
Sandusky	-1.7	13 323	89.0	11.0	3.5	2.0	9.6	11 851	56.5	43.5	2.42	2.17
Shaker Heights	-3.4	12 982	94.1	5.9	0.4	1.1	8.2	12 220	64.9	35.1	2.66	1.89
Springfield	-3.6	29 309	89.6	10.4	0.4	2.6	10.7	26 254	57.2	42.8	2.42	2.33
Stow	22.1	12 852	95.8	4.2	0.4	1.4	6.4	12 317	72.1	27.9	2.79	1.99
Strongsville	32.0	16 863	96.1	3.9	0.5	0.9	10.1	16 209	82.7	17.3	2.85	1.92
Toledo	-1.5	139 871	92.2	7.8	0.3	1.5	8.8	128 925	59.8	40.2	2.50	2.19
Trotwood city	208.3	12 020	92.4	7.6	0.2	2.1	9.6	11 110	62.6	37.4	2.46	2.30
Upper Arlington	0.2	14 432	96.9	3.1	0.7	0.9	4.1	13 985	81.3	18.7	2.51	1.85
Warren	-5.1	21 279	90.6	9.4	0.2	2.5	11.5	19 288	58.4	41.6	2.39	2.33
Westerville	24.4	13 143	96.3	3.7	0.3	1.0	8.4	12 663	79.2	20.8	2.82	2.09
Westlake	25.0	13 648	94.0	6.0	0.7	1.9	8.9	12 826	74.8	25.2	2.61	1.67
Youngstown	-13.1	37 159	86.6	13.4	0.2	2.3	11.5	32 177	64.0	36.0	2.40	2.38
Zanesville	-2.3	11 662	90.7	9.3	0.2	3.4	7.6	10 572	54.6	45.4	2.42	2.28
OKLAHOMA	11.3	1 514 400	88.6	11.4	2.1	2.5	10.6	1 342 293	68.4	31.6	2.55	2.36
Bartlesville	3.9	16 091	90.5	9.5	0.6	1.9	7.9	14 565	70.4	29.6	2.39	2.24
Broken Arrow	35.8	27 085	96.6	3.4	0.1	1.3	6.9	26 159	78.7	21.3	2.90	2.62
Edmond	34.7	26 380	95.7	4.3	0.2	1.4	6.3	25 256	72.8	27.2	2.78	2.23
Enid	4.1	21 255	89.2	10.8	0.4	2.9	11.2	18 955	67.2	32.8	2.40	2.37
Lawton	7.5	36 433	87.2	12.8	0.2	4.9	13.5	31 778	54.7	45.3	2.58	2.65
Midwest City	8.7	23 853	92.9	7.1	0.3	2.1	9.1	22 161	61.2	38.8	2.43	2.40
Moore	9.4	15 801	94.0	6.0	0.8	1.7	9.3	14 848	75.8	24.2	2.75	2.76
Muskogee	2.9	17 517	88.6	11.4	0.4	2.6	10.2	15 523	61.9	38.1	2.45	2.27
Norman	21.7	41 547	93.5	6.5	0.4	1.7	8.0	38 834	55.2	44.8	2.53	2.04
Oklahoma City	14.4	228 149	89.6	10.4	0.5	2.2	12.3	204 434	59.4	40.6	2.51	2.27
Ponca City	-0.9	11 871	89.6	10.4	0.8	2.3	11.0	10 636	68.1	31.9	2.41	2.33
Shawnee	9.4	12 651	89.4	10.6	1.1	2.4	9.1	11 311	59.9	40.1	2.40	2.36
Stillwater	10.1	16 827	92.7	7.3	0.4	2.2	5.8	15 604	41.8	58.2	2.38	1.94
Tulsa	6.6	179 405	92.4	7.6	0.5	1.6	8.7	165 743	55.6	44.4	2.41	2.18
OREGON	20.9	1 452 709	91.8	8.2	2.5	2.3	7.3	1 333 723	64.3	35.7	2.59	2.36
Albany	36.7	17 374	92.7	7.3	0.3	2.6	9.8	16 108	59.5	40.5	2.57	2.38
Beaverton	39.5	32 500	94.8	5.2	0.3	2.0	6.0	30 821	47.7	52.3	2.67	2.23
Bend	147.0	22 507	93.6	6.4	1.5	2.6	5.5	21 062	62.9	37.1	2.48	2.32
Corvallis	17.2	20 909	93.9	6.1	0.3	2.2	7.1	19 630	44.9	55.1	2.50	2.07
Eugene	25.6	61 444	94.6	5.4	0.4	1.7	6.6	58 110	51.8	48.2	2.47	2.05
Gresham	29.7	35 309	94.4	5.6	0.3	2.4	6.9	33 327	54.9	45.1	2.78	2.54
Hillsboro	95.2	27 211	92.2	7.8	0.6	4.0	8.2	25 079	52.3	47.7	2.92	2.58
Keizer	45.3	12 774	94.8	5.2	0.2	2.8	6.7	12 110	64.7	35.3	2.67	2.57

Table D. Cities

STATE Place code	City	Population, 2000				Population, 1990				Population and population characteristics, 2000					
										Race (percent)					
										One race					
		Land area, 2000[1] (sq km)	Total persons	Rank	Per square kilometer	Land area, 1990[1] (sq km)	Total persons	Rank	Per square kilometer	White	Black or African American	American Indian or Alaska Native	Asian	Native Hawaiian and other Pacific Islander	Some other race
		1	2	3	4	5	6	7	8	9	10	11	12	13	14
	OREGON—Cont'd														
41 40550	Lake Oswego	26.8	35 278	1 016	1 316.3	24.7	30 576	1 033	1 237.9	91.1	0.6	0.3	4.6	0.2	0.7
41 45000	McMinnville	25.6	26 499	1 409	1 035.1	22.1	17 894	1 834	809.7	86.4	0.7	1.4	1.2	0.2	7.3
41 47000	Medford	56.2	63 154	467	1 123.7	47.3	47 021	605	994.1	90.0	0.5	1.1	1.1	0.3	3.9
41 55200	Oregon City	21.1	25 754	1 463	1 220.6	12.2	14 698	2 225	1 204.8	92.4	0.6	1.1	1.1	0.1	2.1
41 59000	Portland	347.9	529 121	30	1 520.9	322.9	485 975	26	1 505.0	77.9	6.6	1.1	6.3	0.4	3.5
41 64900	Salem	118.4	136 924	146	1 156.5	107.6	107 793	183	1 001.8	83.1	1.3	1.5	2.4	0.5	7.9
41 69600	Springfield	37.3	52 864	629	1 417.3	34.8	44 664	643	1 283.4	89.6	0.7	1.4	1.1	0.3	3.1
41 73650	Tigard	28.1	41 223	836	1 467.0	26.4	29 435	1 071	1 115.0	85.4	1.1	0.6	5.6	0.5	3.8
42 00000	PENNSYLVANIA	116 074.5	12 281 054	X	105.8	116 082.8	11 882 842	X	102.4	85.4	10.0	0.1	1.8	0.0	1.5
42 02000	Allentown	45.9	106 632	223	2 323.1	45.9	105 301	191	2 294.1	72.5	7.8	0.3	2.3	0.1	13.4
42 02184	Altoona	25.3	49 523	676	1 957.4	25.3	51 881	525	2 050.6	96.0	2.5	0.1	0.3	0.0	0.2
42 06064	Bethel Park Borough	30.3	33 556	1 080	1 107.5	30.3	33 823	899	1 116.3	97.1	1.0	0.0	1.1	0.0	0.1
42 06088	Bethlehem	49.9	71 329	398	1 429.4	49.9	71 427	329	1 431.4	81.8	3.6	0.3	2.2	0.0	9.4
42 13208	Chester	12.6	36 854	953	2 924.9	12.5	41 856	697	3 348.5	18.9	75.7	0.2	0.6	0.0	3.0
42 21648	Easton	11.0	26 263	1 428	2 387.5	11.0	26 276	1 230	2 388.7	78.5	12.7	0.2	1.7	0.1	3.7
42 24000	Erie	56.9	103 717	230	1 822.8	56.9	108 718	180	1 910.7	80.6	14.2	0.2	0.7	0.0	1.9
42 32800	Harrisburg	21.0	48 950	690	2 331.0	21.0	52 376	514	2 494.1	31.7	54.8	0.4	2.8	0.1	6.5
42 41216	Lancaster	19.2	56 348	558	2 934.8	19.1	55 551	464	2 908.4	61.6	14.1	0.4	2.5	0.1	17.4
42 52330	Monroeville Borough	51.3	29 349	1 257	572.1	51.2	29 169	1 084	569.7	85.6	8.3	0.1	4.4	0.0	0.3
42 53368	New Castle	22.1	26 309	1 424	1 190.5	22.1	28 334	1 124	1 282.1	86.8	10.8	0.1	0.2	0.0	0.3
42 54656	Norristown	9.1	31 282	1 172	3 437.6	9.1	30 749	1 023	3 379.6	54.3	34.8	0.2	3.0	0.0	4.6
42 60000	Philadelphia	349.9	1 517 550	5	4 337.1	350.0	1 585 577	5	4 530.2	45.0	43.2	0.3	4.5	0.0	4.8
42 61000	Pittsburgh	144.0	334 563	54	2 323.4	144.1	369 879	41	2 566.8	67.6	27.1	0.2	2.7	0.0	0.7
42 61536	Plum Borough	74.1	26 940	1 385	363.6	74.2	25 609	1 259	345.1	95.6	2.8	0.1	0.9	0.0	0.3
42 63624	Reading	25.4	81 207	332	3 197.1	25.3	78 380	287	3 098.0	59.2	12.2	0.4	1.6	0.0	22.3
42 69000	Scranton	65.3	76 415	366	1 170.2	65.3	81 805	274	1 252.8	93.5	3.0	0.1	1.1	0.0	1.2
42 73808	State College Borough	11.8	38 420	915	3 255.9	11.6	38 981	762	3 360.4	84.3	3.7	0.2	8.8	0.1	1.4
42 85152	Wilkes-Barre	17.7	43 123	799	2 436.3	17.7	47 523	595	2 684.9	92.3	5.1	0.1	0.8	0.0	0.5
42 85312	Williamsport	23.0	30 706	1 196	1 335.0	23.0	31 933	975	1 388.4	84.1	12.7	0.4	0.6	0.0	0.5
42 87048	York	13.5	40 862	846	3 026.8	13.5	42 192	688	3 125.3	59.8	25.1	0.4	1.4	0.1	9.4
44 00000	RHODE ISLAND	2 706.3	1 048 319	X	387.4	2 706.5	1 003 464	X	370.8	85.0	4.5	0.5	2.3	0.1	5.0
44 19180	Cranston	74.0	79 269	348	1 071.2	74.0	76 060	296	1 027.8	89.2	3.7	0.3	3.3	0.0	1.9
44 22960	East Providence	34.7	48 688	694	1 403.1	34.7	50 380	551	1 451.9	86.5	5.0	0.5	1.1	0.0	2.8
44 49960	Newport	20.6	26 475	1 411	1 285.2	20.6	28 227	1 130	1 370.2	84.1	7.8	0.8	1.3	0.1	2.4
44 54640	Pawtucket	22.6	72 958	385	3 228.2	22.6	72 644	320	3 214.3	75.4	7.3	0.3	0.9	0.1	10.7
44 59000	Providence	47.8	173 618	123	3 632.2	47.8	160 728	109	3 362.5	54.5	14.5	1.1	6.0	0.2	17.6
44 74300	Warwick	91.9	85 808	304	933.7	92.0	85 427	259	928.6	95.2	1.2	0.2	1.5	0.0	0.6
44 80780	Woonsocket	20.0	43 224	794	2 161.2	20.0	43 877	652	2 193.9	83.1	4.4	0.3	4.1	0.0	4.9
45 00000	SOUTH CAROLINA	77 983.2	4 012 012	X	51.4	77 987.8	3 486 310	X	44.7	67.2	29.5	0.3	0.9	0.0	1.0
45 00550	Aiken	41.9	25 337	1 487	604.7	35.2	20 386	1 608	579.1	66.6	30.3	0.3	1.3	0.0	0.4
45 01360	Anderson	35.8	25 514	1 478	712.7	32.1	26 385	1 222	822.0	63.1	34.0	0.2	0.8	0.0	0.7
45 13330	Charleston	251.2	96 650	253	384.8	111.9	88 256	241	788.7	63.1	34.0	0.2	1.2	0.1	0.5
45 16000	Columbia	324.3	116 278	199	358.6	303.4	110 734	170	365.0	49.2	46.0	0.3	1.7	0.1	1.4
45 25810	Florence	45.8	30 248	1 212	660.4	38.2	29 913	1 057	783.1	53.0	44.8	0.2	1.2	0.0	0.2
45 29815	Goose Creek	82.1	29 208	1 265	355.8	81.1	24 692	1 307	304.5	78.5	14.2	0.6	2.7	0.1	1.6
45 30850	Greenville	67.5	56 002	566	829.7	65.0	58 256	435	896.2	62.1	33.9	0.1	1.3	0.1	1.4
45 34045	Hilton Head Island	108.9	33 862	1 064	310.9	108.9	23 694	1 381	217.6	85.3	8.3	0.1	0.6	0.0	4.5
45 48535	Mount Pleasant	108.5	47 609	713	438.8	56.4	30 108	1 048	533.8	90.2	7.3	0.2	1.2	0.0	0.4
45 50875	North Charleston	151.6	79 641	342	525.3	129.6	70 304	341	542.5	44.8	49.4	0.4	1.6	0.1	1.8
45 61405	Rock Hill	80.4	49 765	671	619.0	60.0	42 112	691	701.9	58.7	37.3	0.5	1.4	0.0	1.0
45 68290	Spartanburg	49.6	39 673	879	799.9	46.9	43 479	661	927.1	47.2	49.6	0.2	1.3	0.1	0.8
45 70270	Summerville	39.8	27 752	1 339	697.3	36.1	22 519	1 462	623.8	77.2	19.4	0.5	0.9	0.1	0.7
45 70405	Sumter	68.9	39 643	880	575.4	58.9	40 977	715	695.7	49.6	46.3	0.2	1.3	0.1	1.1
46 00000	SOUTH DAKOTA	196 540.3	754 844	X	3.8	196 575.2	696 004	X	3.5	88.7	0.6	8.3	0.6	0.0	0.5
46 52980	Rapid City	115.5	59 607	509	516.1	91.5	54 523	480	595.9	84.3	1.0	10.1	1.0	0.1	0.7
46 59020	Sioux Falls	145.9	123 975	181	849.7	116.7	100 836	201	864.1	91.9	1.8	2.1	1.0	0.1	1.2
47 00000	TENNESSEE	106 751.8	5 689 283	X	53.3	106 758.5	4 877 203	X	45.7	80.2	16.4	0.3	1.0	0.0	1.0
47 03440	Bartlett	49.4	40 543	854	820.7	37.3	27 038	1 181	724.9	92.4	4.9	0.3	1.2	0.0	0.4
47 14000	Chattanooga	350.2	155 554	134	444.2	306.7	152 393	115	496.9	59.7	36.1	0.3	1.5	0.1	1.0
47 15160	Clarksville	245.7	103 455	232	421.1	189.3	75 542	303	399.1	67.9	23.2	0.5	2.2	0.3	2.6
47 15400	Cleveland	64.6	37 192	950	575.7	51.4	32 236	964	627.2	89.0	7.0	0.2	1.0	0.0	1.3
47 16420	Collierville	63.6	31 872	1 142	501.1	32.2	14 501	2 248	450.3	89.9	7.3	0.2	1.5	0.0	0.3
47 16540	Columbia	76.7	33 055	1 094	431.0	76.2	28 583	1 112	375.1	74.6	21.1	0.3	0.4	0.0	2.1
47 27740	Franklin	77.8	41 842	823	537.8	66.1	20 098	1 633	304.1	84.5	10.3	0.2	1.6	0.0	2.2
47 28960	Germantown	45.5	37 348	945	820.8	39.8	33 159	930	833.1	92.9	2.3	0.2	3.5	0.0	0.2

[1] Dry land or land partially or temporarily covered by water.

Table D. Cities

City	Population and population characteristics, 2000 (cont'd)								Population and population characteristics, 1990				
	Race (percent) (cont'd)								Race (percent)				
	Race alone or in combination							Hispanic¹	White	Black or African American	American Indian or Alaska Native	Asian and Pacific Islander	Hispanic¹
	Two or more races	White	Black	American Indian or Alaska Native	Asian	Native Hawaiian and other Pacific Islander	Some other race						
	15	16	17	18	19	20	21	22	23	24	25	26	27
OREGON—Cont'd													
Lake Oswego	2.5	93.4	0.9	0.8	5.8	0.4	1.3	2.3	96.2	0.5	0.3	2.7	1.6
McMinnville	2.9	89.0	1.0	2.4	2.0	0.4	8.3	14.6	94.5	0.2	1.0	1.7	7.8
Medford	3.2	93.0	0.8	2.2	1.7	0.4	5.1	9.2	94.8	0.3	1.2	1.2	5.1
Oregon City	2.5	94.8	1.1	2.1	1.8	0.3	2.7	5.0	96.9	0.3	0.9	1.2	2.2
Portland	4.1	81.3	7.9	2.3	7.5	0.7	4.9	6.8	84.6	7.7	1.2	5.3	3.2
Salem	3.4	86.1	1.8	2.7	3.1	0.7	9.1	14.6	91.2	1.5	1.6	2.4	6.1
Springfield	3.8	93.1	1.3	3.2	1.9	0.6	3.9	6.9	95.4	0.7	1.5	1.5	2.9
Tigard	3.0	88.0	1.7	1.3	6.7	0.9	4.6	8.9	94.3	0.7	0.6	3.4	2.4
PENNSYLVANIA	1.2	86.3	10.5	0.4	2.0	0.1	1.9	3.2	88.5	9.2	0.1	1.2	2.0
Allentown	3.6	75.5	9.3	0.7	2.6	0.2	15.5	24.4	86.2	5.0	0.2	1.3	11.7
Altoona	0.8	96.8	3.0	0.3	0.4	0.1	0.4	0.7	98.0	1.5	0.1	0.3	0.4
Bethel Park Borough	0.6	97.6	1.2	0.2	1.4	0.1	0.2	0.5	98.1	1.0	0.1	0.8	0.5
Bethlehem	2.6	83.9	4.5	0.6	2.5	0.1	11.0	18.2	87.6	2.9	0.1	1.7	13.0
Chester	1.5	19.7	76.9	0.6	0.8	0.1	3.6	5.4	32.0	65.2	0.2	0.4	3.8
Easton	3.1	81.0	14.4	0.9	2.0	0.2	4.8	9.8	86.8	9.4	0.2	1.7	4.4
Erie	2.3	82.6	15.5	0.7	1.0	0.1	2.6	4.4	86.1	12.0	0.2	0.5	2.4
Harrisburg	3.6	34.3	57.5	1.1	3.2	0.2	7.8	11.7	42.6	50.6	0.3	1.8	7.7
Lancaster	3.9	64.5	16.3	1.0	2.8	0.2	19.4	30.8	70.9	12.2	0.2	2.0	20.6
Monroeville Borough	1.2	86.5	9.0	0.4	4.8	0.1	0.5	0.8	90.2	6.6	0.1	2.9	0.7
New Castle	1.9	88.5	12.0	0.5	0.3	0.0	0.6	0.8	91.5	8.0	0.1	0.2	0.5
Norristown	3.1	56.7	36.7	0.9	3.3	0.1	5.7	10.5	70.8	26.4	0.2	1.7	2.7
Philadelphia	2.2	46.4	44.3	0.7	4.9	0.2	6.0	8.5	53.5	39.9	0.2	2.7	5.6
Pittsburgh	1.6	68.8	28.1	0.7	3.1	0.1	1.1	1.3	72.1	25.8	0.2	1.6	0.9
Plum Borough	0.5	96.0	3.0	0.2	1.0	0.0	0.2	0.6	97.1	2.0	0.0	0.8	0.6
Reading	4.2	62.4	14.1	1.0	1.9	0.2	24.8	37.3	78.6	9.7	0.1	1.4	18.5
Scranton	1.1	94.5	3.6	0.3	1.3	0.0	1.5	2.6	97.2	1.6	0.1	0.9	0.7
State College Borough	1.6	85.4	4.1	0.4	9.5	0.4	1.9	3.0	88.5	3.4	0.1	7.3	2.0
Wilkes-Barre	1.2	93.3	5.8	0.4	1.0	0.1	0.8	1.6	96.1	2.9	0.1	0.6	0.7
Williamsport	1.7	85.7	13.9	0.7	0.7	0.0	0.7	1.1	92.3	6.7	0.2	0.5	0.8
York	3.8	62.8	27.6	1.0	1.8	0.2	10.7	17.2	72.5	21.3	0.2	1.1	7.7
RHODE ISLAND	2.7	86.9	5.5	1.0	2.7	0.2	6.6	8.7	91.4	3.9	0.4	1.8	4.6
Cranston	1.6	90.4	4.2	0.6	3.7	0.1	2.7	4.6	95.1	2.4	0.2	1.8	2.0
East Providence	4.0	89.2	6.9	1.3	1.4	0.2	5.3	1.9	92.1	4.4	0.5	0.6	1.7
Newport	3.4	86.6	9.7	1.8	1.9	0.3	3.5	5.5	88.6	8.1	0.7	1.4	2.8
Pawtucket	5.3	78.6	9.7	0.8	1.1	0.4	15.0	13.9	89.3	3.6	0.3	0.6	7.2
Providence	6.1	58.1	17.1	2.2	7.0	0.4	21.7	30.0	69.9	14.8	0.9	5.9	15.5
Warwick	1.3	96.3	1.6	0.7	1.8	0.0	1.0	1.6	98.0	0.8	0.2	0.8	1.0
Woonsocket	3.1	85.5	5.7	0.8	4.9	0.1	6.4	9.3	93.3	2.6	0.2	3.0	2.6
SOUTH CAROLINA	1.0	68.0	29.9	0.7	1.1	0.1	1.3	2.4	69.0	29.8	0.2	0.6	0.9
Aiken	1.1	67.5	30.8	0.7	1.6	0.1	0.7	1.5	68.0	30.9	0.1	0.6	0.9
Anderson	1.2	64.0	34.6	0.6	1.0	0.1	1.0	1.5	65.1	34.3	0.2	0.3	0.5
Charleston	0.9	63.8	34.4	0.4	1.5	0.1	0.8	1.5	57.2	41.6	0.1	0.9	0.8
Columbia	1.4	50.1	46.7	0.6	2.1	0.2	1.8	3.0	53.7	43.7	0.3	1.4	2.0
Florence	0.7	53.5	45.0	0.4	1.3	0.0	0.4	0.8	52.3	47.0	0.1	0.5	0.6
Goose Creek	2.4	80.5	15.0	1.2	3.6	0.3	2.0	4.0	83.0	12.7	0.5	2.6	4.1
Greenville	1.1	63.0	34.4	0.4	1.5	0.1	1.8	3.4	63.6	35.2	0.1	0.8	1.0
Hilton Head Island	1.2	86.4	8.5	0.3	0.7	0.0	5.3	11.5	89.5	9.5	0.1	0.5	1.4
Mount Pleasant	0.8	90.9	7.4	0.4	1.4	0.1	0.7	1.3	89.9	9.2	0.1	0.6	0.9
North Charleston	1.9	46.2	50.3	1.0	2.1	0.2	2.3	4.0	62.7	34.3	0.5	1.6	2.5
Rock Hill	1.0	59.5	37.7	0.8	1.6	0.1	1.3	2.5	60.4	38.1	0.4	0.8	0.6
Spartanburg	1.0	47.8	50.1	0.4	1.6	0.1	1.1	1.8	53.1	45.6	0.1	0.9	0.8
Summerville	1.3	78.2	19.9	0.9	1.3	0.1	1.0	2.0	80.6	17.8	0.4	0.7	1.5
Sumter	1.4	50.5	46.9	0.6	1.8	0.2	1.6	2.4	59.8	38.2	0.3	1.2	1.6
SOUTH DAKOTA	1.3	89.9	0.9	9.0	0.8	0.1	0.7	1.4	91.6	0.5	7.3	0.4	0.8
Rapid City	2.8	86.8	1.5	12.0	1.4	0.1	1.1	2.8	88.2	1.3	8.9	1.0	2.2
Sioux Falls	1.7	93.4	2.4	2.6	1.5	0.1	1.8	2.5	96.8	0.7	1.6	0.7	0.6
TENNESSEE	1.1	81.2	16.8	0.7	1.2	0.1	1.3	2.2	83.0	16.0	0.2	0.7	0.7
Bartlett	0.8	93.1	5.0	0.5	1.5	0.1	0.5	1.1	96.4	2.4	0.1	1.0	0.7
Chattanooga	1.3	60.7	36.7	0.7	1.8	0.2	1.4	2.1	65.0	33.7	0.2	1.0	0.6
Clarksville	3.3	70.5	24.7	1.3	3.2	0.5	3.5	6.0	75.0	20.9	0.4	2.2	3.9
Cleveland	1.5	90.3	7.5	0.8	1.2	0.1	1.7	2.9	91.6	7.2	0.3	0.5	1.4
Collierville	0.8	90.6	7.5	0.4	1.7	0.1	0.6	1.5	88.2	11.1	0.2	0.4	0.8
Columbia	1.5	75.9	21.9	0.6	0.5	0.1	2.6	4.7	78.5	20.6	0.2	0.4	0.7
Franklin	1.1	85.5	10.6	0.5	1.9	0.1	2.6	4.8	81.0	18.0	0.2	0.5	0.8
Germantown	0.9	93.7	2.5	0.4	3.8	0.0	0.5	1.1	95.2	1.9	0.2	2.7	0.8

¹Hispanic persons may be of any race.

Table D. Cities

| City | Population and population characteristics, 2000 Age (percent) | | | | | | | | | | |
| | Under 5 years | 5 to 17 years | 18 to 24 years | 25 to 34 years | 35 to 44 years | 45 to 54 years | 55 to 64 years | 65 to 74 years | 75 years and over | Median age (years) | Percent Female |
	28	29	30	31	32	33	34	35	36	37	38
OREGON—Cont'd											
Lake Oswego	4.9	19.8	6.1	9.9	16.9	20.6	10.4	5.7	5.7	41.2	51.9
McMinnville	7.6	18.7	14.7	13.6	13.3	11.2	6.7	6.2	8.0	31.5	51.6
Medford	7.0	18.8	8.6	12.8	14.5	13.5	8.3	7.2	9.4	37.0	52.1
Oregon City	8.4	18.6	10.3	16.5	16.1	13.3	7.1	4.5	5.3	32.7	50.8
Portland	6.1	15.0	10.3	18.3	16.4	14.8	7.6	5.3	6.2	35.2	50.6
Salem	7.4	18.0	11.4	15.1	15.0	13.3	7.3	5.5	6.9	33.6	49.8
Springfield	8.2	19.0	11.1	15.9	15.5	12.7	7.2	4.9	5.4	32.1	51.1
Tigard	7.7	17.8	9.0	16.3	17.7	14.2	7.2	4.5	5.6	34.5	51.0
PENNSYLVANIA	5.9	17.9	8.9	12.7	15.9	13.9	9.2	7.9	7.7	38.0	51.7
Allentown	7.1	17.6	11.2	14.8	15.0	11.6	7.5	7.1	8.0	34.5	52.1
Altoona	6.3	16.6	10.9	12.7	14.6	13.1	8.9	8.2	8.6	37.4	53.1
Bethel Park Borough	5.3	18.4	5.0	9.9	16.8	15.6	10.9	9.6	8.5	42.1	52.1
Bethlehem	5.4	15.5	14.4	12.9	13.7	12.0	8.1	8.1	9.8	36.2	52.2
Chester	8.4	21.4	13.0	12.9	14.0	11.3	7.3	6.0	5.8	30.6	52.9
Easton	6.2	17.1	16.3	15.0	14.9	11.6	7.0	5.8	6.2	32.0	50.7
Erie	7.2	18.2	11.6	14.3	14.2	11.7	7.5	7.1	8.2	34.1	52.4
Harrisburg	8.1	20.1	9.2	15.5	15.4	13.2	7.6	5.7	5.1	33.0	53.0
Lancaster	7.9	19.6	13.9	15.6	14.8	11.0	6.7	5.3	5.2	30.4	51.2
Monroeville Borough	4.9	15.4	6.2	12.1	15.3	15.4	10.5	10.0	10.3	42.6	53.0
New Castle	6.7	17.1	8.1	12.5	13.6	12.4	8.9	9.2	11.5	39.4	54.0
Norristown	6.9	18.2	10.5	16.5	16.1	12.0	8.1	6.2	5.6	33.7	51.3
Philadelphia	6.5	18.8	11.1	14.8	14.5	12.0	8.3	7.1	7.0	34.2	53.5
Pittsburgh	5.3	14.6	14.8	14.6	14.0	12.3	8.0	7.9	8.5	35.5	52.4
Plum Borough	6.3	18.5	6.1	13.4	17.6	14.4	10.4	7.1	6.0	38.4	51.2
Reading	8.7	21.3	11.7	15.1	13.9	10.3	6.8	6.1	6.3	30.6	51.7
Scranton	5.3	15.5	12.3	11.8	13.8	12.5	8.7	9.0	11.1	38.8	53.5
State College Borough	1.8	3.9	65.5	11.3	4.9	4.1	2.6	2.5	3.3	21.8	47.9
Wilkes-Barre	4.9	15.0	12.6	12.3	13.8	12.1	8.7	9.5	11.1	38.8	51.8
Williamsport	6.0	16.5	18.0	12.7	13.9	11.9	7.4	6.4	7.0	32.4	50.6
York	8.0	20.4	11.4	15.5	14.6	11.6	7.5	5.5	5.4	31.3	51.8
RHODE ISLAND	6.1	17.5	10.2	13.4	16.2	13.5	8.5	7.0	7.5	36.7	52.0
Cranston	5.3	16.3	7.7	14.0	17.4	13.7	8.3	8.0	9.3	39.0	51.1
East Providence	5.4	16.3	7.4	13.4	16.0	13.2	9.4	8.8	10.1	39.6	53.5
Newport	5.8	13.9	14.6	16.0	15.6	13.1	8.2	6.2	6.7	34.9	51.8
Pawtucket	6.7	18.1	9.1	15.3	16.0	12.0	7.9	7.2	7.7	35.4	52.6
Providence	7.3	18.8	18.9	15.6	13.0	10.0	6.0	4.9	5.6	28.1	52.2
Warwick	5.4	16.5	6.7	12.8	17.3	14.8	9.5	8.3	8.7	40.0	52.4
Woonsocket	7.6	18.2	9.2	15.3	14.7	12.0	7.7	7.0	8.2	34.8	52.3
SOUTH CAROLINA	6.6	18.6	10.2	14.0	15.6	13.7	9.3	6.7	5.4	35.4	51.4
Aiken	5.8	17.4	9.4	11.3	14.2	14.2	9.8	8.7	9.2	39.5	53.4
Anderson	6.7	15.5	10.7	13.2	13.1	12.1	8.3	8.8	11.7	38.0	54.8
Charleston	5.4	14.6	17.2	15.2	13.6	12.4	8.1	6.7	6.8	33.2	52.7
Columbia	5.6	14.5	22.9	16.8	13.3	10.6	6.0	5.0	5.3	28.6	51.0
Florence	6.4	18.6	8.7	13.6	14.6	14.2	8.9	7.4	7.7	36.8	54.7
Goose Creek	8.6	21.0	18.2	16.2	16.2	9.8	5.6	2.8	1.4	26.3	46.4
Greenville	5.6	14.3	13.8	16.8	14.5	12.5	7.9	6.4	8.0	34.6	52.7
Hilton Head Island	4.4	12.9	6.9	11.8	12.8	13.4	13.9	14.0	10.1	46.0	50.0
Mount Pleasant	7.5	17.6	6.5	16.7	18.6	14.8	8.0	5.3	5.0	35.9	52.1
North Charleston	8.0	19.8	13.4	16.8	15.2	10.9	6.8	5.0	4.0	29.9	50.5
Rock Hill	7.0	18.0	14.8	16.2	14.2	11.5	6.9	5.1	6.2	31.0	54.2
Spartanburg	6.5	18.7	12.2	13.0	13.6	12.5	8.0	7.1	8.4	34.7	55.7
Summerville	7.0	21.8	7.8	14.6	16.6	14.2	7.5	5.4	5.2	34.4	52.6
Sumter	8.1	19.7	12.5	13.9	14.3	10.8	7.1	6.4	7.2	31.9	52.8
SOUTH DAKOTA	6.8	20.1	10.3	12.1	15.3	12.9	8.3	7.0	7.3	35.6	50.4
Rapid City	7.0	18.3	11.8	13.2	15.5	13.0	7.9	6.7	6.5	34.8	51.0
Sioux Falls	7.3	17.9	11.8	16.0	16.3	12.5	7.1	5.6	5.5	33.0	50.7
TENNESSEE	6.6	18.0	9.6	14.3	15.9	13.8	9.4	6.7	5.6	35.9	51.3
Bartlett	6.6	22.4	6.8	11.1	18.9	16.9	8.6	5.2	3.4	36.6	51.2
Chattanooga	6.1	16.3	10.8	14.3	14.5	13.6	9.1	7.8	7.4	36.8	52.8
Clarksville	9.0	19.8	13.6	19.0	15.7	9.8	5.8	4.2	3.1	28.8	49.8
Cleveland	6.5	15.5	15.4	13.9	13.6	11.9	9.3	7.2	6.7	34.0	52.8
Collierville	7.6	25.8	5.8	10.4	22.0	15.7	6.6	3.7	2.3	35.2	50.6
Columbia	7.5	18.3	9.8	13.3	15.3	12.8	8.2	7.4	7.4	35.7	52.6
Franklin	8.5	19.4	7.5	18.7	19.4	13.1	6.1	3.7	3.7	33.0	51.7
Germantown	5.2	22.8	5.8	6.6	16.9	21.7	11.7	5.7	3.5	41.3	51.3

Table D. Cities

City	Under 5 years	5 to 17 years	18 to 24 years	25 to 34 years	35 to 44 years	45 to 54 years	55 to 64 years	65 to 74 years	75 years and over	Percent Female	2000	1990	1980	1990–2000	1980–1990
					Age (percent)						Total persons			Percent change	
	39	40	41	42	43	44	45	46	47	48	49	50	51	52	53
OREGON—Cont'd															
Lake Oswego	5.7	18.0	6.1	14.5	21.2	14.9	8.4	6.8	4.5	52.0	35 278	30 576	22 909	15.4	33.5
McMinnville	7.8	18.4	13.9	14.7	14.2	7.9	7.1	8.6	7.4	52.1	26 499	17 894	14 080	48.1	27.1
Medford	7.7	17.4	8.7	15.7	15.7	9.4	8.2	9.2	8.0	52.5	63 154	47 021	39 603	34.3	18.7
Oregon City	8.2	20.1	10.1	17.2	16.0	10.3	5.9	6.0	6.1	51.8	25 754	14 698	14 673	75.2	0.2
Portland	7.0	15.0	10.0	18.9	18.1	9.2	7.3	7.8	6.7	51.5	529 121	463 634	366 423	14.1	26.5
Salem	7.3	17.0	10.5	18.0	16.3	9.1	7.1	7.8	7.0	50.3	136 924	107 793	89 233	27.0	20.8
Springfield	8.8	18.8	12.2	19.1	15.3	8.6	6.3	6.1	4.7	51.7	52 864	44 664	41 621	18.4	7.3
Tigard	8.0	16.3	8.5	21.5	18.4	9.3	6.6	6.2	5.1	52.0	41 223	29 435	14 286	40.0	106.0
PENNSYLVANIA	6.7	16.8	10.3	16.1	14.7	10.2	9.8	9.0	6.4	52.1	12 281 054	11 882 842	11 864 720	3.4	0.2
Allentown	7.2	14.7	11.3	18.7	13.2	8.8	9.2	9.3	7.6	52.7	106 632	105 301	103 758	1.3	1.5
Altoona	6.6	17.9	9.2	15.0	13.3	9.6	9.8	10.7	8.0	54.2	49 523	51 881	57 078	-4.5	-9.1
Bethel Park Borough	7.0	16.6	7.1	15.8	15.8	12.9	11.1	8.8	4.8	52.0	33 556	33 823	34 755	-0.8	-2.7
Bethlehem	6.1	14.9	14.8	15.6	13.0	8.9	9.5	10.5	6.7	52.0	71 329	71 427	70 419	-0.1	1.4
Chester	9.3	18.7	13.0	16.4	12.6	8.6	7.8	8.2	5.4	54.0	36 854	41 856	45 794	-12.0	-8.6
Easton	7.5	15.9	16.8	18.0	12.3	8.1	7.5	7.2	6.6	51.0	26 263	26 276	26 027	0.0	1.0
Erie	7.9	17.4	12.1	16.6	13.2	8.2	8.6	9.5	6.6	52.8	103 717	108 718	119 123	-4.6	-8.7
Harrisburg	8.9	17.8	10.4	18.7	15.5	8.4	7.2	6.8	6.2	53.5	48 950	52 376	53 264	-6.5	-1.7
Lancaster	8.4	18.0	14.0	18.7	13.6	7.6	7.4	7.2	5.1	51.9	56 348	55 551	54 725	1.4	1.5
Monroeville Borough	5.9	15.1	8.2	16.9	15.9	12.0	11.7	9.1	5.2	52.2	29 349	29 169	NA	0.6	NA
New Castle	6.8	15.3	8.8	14.3	12.6	9.0	10.5	12.5	10.2	54.8	26 309	28 334	33 621	-7.1	-15.7
Norristown	8.0	15.3	9.1	21.0	14.6	8.2	9.2	8.7	5.8	52.9	31 282	30 754	34 684	1.7	-11.3
Philadelphia	7.3	16.6	11.4	17.4	13.4	9.5	9.1	8.7	6.5	53.5	1 517 550	1 585 577	1 688 210	-4.3	-6.1
Pittsburgh	6.1	13.8	13.7	17.1	13.2	8.5	9.6	10.2	7.8	53.6	334 563	369 879	423 938	-9.5	-12.8
Plum Borough	7.4	18.4	9.0	18.9	16.9	12.4	8.9	5.5	2.4	50.6	26 940	25 609	25 390	5.2	0.9
Reading	8.2	17.2	11.7	17.1	11.6	8.6	8.8	8.9	7.8	53.1	81 207	78 380	78 686	3.6	-0.4
Scranton	6.0	15.0	11.8	14.4	11.9	9.0	10.0	12.0	10.0	54.2	76 415	81 805	88 117	-6.6	-7.2
State College Borough	2.2	4.1	65.8	12.2	5.5	3.1	2.7	2.8	1.9	46.0	38 420	38 981	36 130	-1.4	7.9
Wilkes-Barre	5.6	14.4	13.1	14.3	12.4	8.6	10.7	11.5	9.5	54.0	43 123	47 523	51 551	-9.3	-7.8
Williamsport	7.7	17.4	13.7	16.9	12.6	8.4	8.2	8.6	6.4	52.8	30 706	31 933	33 401	-3.8	-4.4
York	8.8	17.6	11.9	18.8	13.0	8.8	7.6	7.5	6.0	52.9	40 862	42 192	44 619	-3.2	-5.4
RHODE ISLAND	6.7	15.8	12.0	17.3	14.7	9.6	8.9	8.5	6.5	52.0	1 048 319	1 003 464	947 154	4.5	5.9
Cranston	5.7	13.6	9.6	17.8	15.2	9.4	10.1	10.7	7.9	51.9	79 269	76 060	71 992	4.2	5.7
East Providence	6.0	14.9	9.1	17.1	13.9	9.9	10.0	10.7	8.4	53.5	48 688	50 380	50 980	-3.4	-1.2
Newport	6.4	13.9	16.6	19.4	14.1	9.2	7.0	7.4	6.0	51.7	26 475	28 227	29 258	-6.2	-3.5
Pawtucket	7.4	15.3	10.4	19.6	12.8	8.9	9.2	9.4	7.0	53.0	72 958	72 644	71 204	0.4	2.0
Providence	7.8	16.1	17.6	18.1	12.0	7.7	7.0	7.1	6.5	52.4	173 618	160 728	156 804	8.0	2.5
Warwick	6.0	15.5	8.7	16.9	15.1	10.9	10.1	10.0	6.8	52.5	85 808	85 427	87 123	0.4	-1.9
Woonsocket	7.7	16.7	10.9	17.6	12.9	9.1	8.9	8.9	7.4	52.9	43 224	43 877	45 914	-1.5	-4.4
SOUTH CAROLINA	7.4	19.0	11.7	17.0	15.0	10.2	8.4	7.1	4.3	51.6	4 012 012	3 486 310	3 120 729	15.1	11.7
Aiken	7.4	18.2	7.8	16.4	15.7	9.4	8.8	9.3	7.1	53.3	25 337	20 386	14 978	24.3	36.1
Anderson	6.7	16.4	11.1	14.8	12.5	8.3	9.6	10.8	9.7	55.8	25 514	26 385	27 313	-3.3	-3.4
Charleston	7.1	15.1	17.3	18.1	13.8	8.2	7.6	8.0	4.9	52.8	96 650	79 925	69 510	20.9	15.0
Columbia	6.1	13.8	22.7	20.0	12.8	7.0	5.8	6.5	5.2	50.8	116 278	110 734	101 208	5.0	9.4
Florence	7.4	19.0	10.0	16.4	14.7	9.7	8.5	8.7	5.6	54.6	30 248	29 913	30 104	1.1	-0.6
Goose Creek	12.8	27.0	8.3	25.5	15.2	6.0	3.2	1.5	0.4	48.7	29 208	24 692	17 811	18.3	38.6
Greenville	6.8	15.4	13.5	18.3	14.0	8.5	7.7	9.0	6.8	54.5	56 002	58 256	58 242	-3.9	0.0
Hilton Head Island	6.1	11.8	7.8	17.0	13.9	10.2	12.9	14.5	5.7	52.2	33 862	23 694	11 344	42.9	108.9
Mount Pleasant	7.7	16.7	9.0	22.2	19.5	8.9	6.8	5.8	3.4	51.1	47 609	30 108	13 838	58.1	117.6
North Charleston	10.0	16.4	20.9	24.2	11.4	6.6	4.7	3.4	2.3	45.6	79 641	70 304	62 534	13.3	12.4
Rock Hill	7.6	17.1	17.0	17.2	12.7	8.9	6.9	6.8	5.7	54.5	49 765	41 610	35 386	19.6	17.6
Spartanburg	7.8	17.3	12.7	16.0	13.4	9.5	8.0	8.7	6.6	55.2	39 673	43 479	43 838	-8.8	-0.8
Summerville	9.6	20.1	10.5	20.7	15.5	8.9	5.7	5.0	3.9	51.6	27 752	22 519	NA	23.2	NA
Sumter	8.2	18.5	13.0	22.2	13.9	7.4	6.4	6.4	4.0	48.6	39 643	40 977	24 896	-3.3	64.6
SOUTH DAKOTA	7.8	20.7	9.8	15.7	13.7	9.0	8.6	7.8	6.9	50.8	754 844	696 004	690 768	8.5	0.8
Rapid City	8.5	19.1	11.4	18.1	14.8	8.7	7.8	6.4	5.2	51.1	59 607	54 523	46 492	9.3	17.3
Sioux Falls	7.9	17.9	11.4	19.9	14.9	8.6	7.7	6.5	5.2	52.4	123 975	100 836	81 341	22.9	24.0
TENNESSEE	6.8	18.1	10.8	16.7	15.2	10.8	8.9	7.3	5.4	51.8	5 689 283	4 877 203	4 591 023	16.7	6.2
Bartlett	6.8	25.3	7.9	14.4	23.3	11.0	6.0	3.6	1.6	51.0	40 543	26 989	17 170	50.2	57.2
Chattanooga	6.8	16.5	10.8	16.5	14.1	10.2	9.9	8.5	6.8	53.8	155 554	152 393	169 550	2.1	-10.1
Clarksville	8.9	17.1	18.1	20.9	13.8	7.8	6.2	4.2	3.0	48.3	103 455	75 542	54 777	37.0	37.9
Cleveland	6.1	16.0	13.3	15.5	13.6	11.0	9.7	8.2	6.6	53.5	37 192	32 236	26 432	15.4	22.0
Collierville	8.0	26.2	7.5	15.5	20.7	11.0	5.3	3.4	2.4	50.9	31 872	14 501	NA	119.8	NA
Columbia	7.3	17.5	9.4	16.9	13.8	10.1	9.9	8.5	6.5	53.5	33 055	28 583	26 372	15.6	8.4
Franklin	8.1	18.1	9.2	20.9	17.8	8.5	6.7	5.3	5.4	53.4	41 842	20 098	12 407	108.2	62.0
Germantown	6.0	25.1	6.8	8.7	23.4	17.0	7.6	4.0	1.4	50.7	37 348	33 016	20 459	13.1	61.4

Table D. Cities

City	Total population	Total in house-holds	House-holder	Spouse	Child Total	Own child under 18 years	Other relatives Total	Under 18 years	Nonrelatives Total	Unmar-ried partner	Total in group quarters	Correc-tional institu-tions	Nurs-ing homes	Other institu-tions	Col-lege dormi-tories	Mili-tary quar-ters	Other
	54	55	56	57	58	59	60	61	62	63	64	65	66	67	68	69	70
OREGON—Cont'd																	
Lake Oswego	35 278	99.5	41.9	23.5	28.0	23.9	1.8	0.4	4.3	1.7	0.5	0.0	0.0	0.2	0.0	0.0	0.2
McMinnville	26 499	94.0	35.3	18.9	28.4	24.0	4.6	1.6	6.7	1.9	6.0	0.9	1.2	0.0	3.6	0.0	0.3
Medford	63 154	98.0	39.7	20.0	28.2	23.6	3.8	1.4	6.3	2.5	2.0	0.3	0.7	0.1	0.0	0.0	1.0
Oregon City	25 754	96.5	36.8	19.5	30.4	24.9	3.6	1.3	6.3	2.4	3.5	1.9	1.3	0.0	0.0	0.0	0.3
Portland	529 121	97.2	42.3	16.1	23.7	18.6	4.9	1.6	10.1	3.4	2.8	0.5	0.5	0.1	0.9	0.0	0.9
Salem	136 924	93.5	37.0	17.7	27.3	22.8	4.6	1.6	6.9	2.5	6.5	3.2	0.8	0.6	1.0	0.0	0.9
Springfield	52 864	98.8	38.8	17.7	29.7	24.7	4.3	1.6	8.3	3.3	1.2	0.0	0.2	0.0	0.0	0.0	1.0
Tigard	41 223	99.5	40.0	20.8	28.2	24.0	3.8	1.0	6.5	2.4	0.5	0.0	0.3	0.0	0.0	0.0	0.3
PENNSYLVANIA	12 281 054	96.5	38.9	20.1	28.9	21.6	4.3	1.6	4.3	1.9	3.5	0.6	0.9	0.2	1.2	0.0	0.6
Allentown	106 632	95.3	39.4	15.5	28.0	21.8	5.8	2.2	6.6	3.2	4.7	1.0	0.8	0.3	2.0	0.0	0.6
Altoona	49 523	96.1	40.5	18.0	28.3	20.7	3.9	1.6	5.4	2.2	3.9	0.0	0.8	0.1	1.8	0.0	1.2
Bethel Park Borough	33 556	98.9	39.8	24.7	30.2	22.8	2.4	0.7	1.8	1.0	1.1	0.0	0.8	0.0	0.0	0.0	0.3
Bethlehem	71 329	92.1	39.4	17.4	25.3	19.0	4.1	1.5	5.8	2.4	7.9	0.4	1.4	0.0	5.4	0.0	0.7
Chester	36 854	91.9	34.8	8.6	33.0	23.5	10.1	5.4	5.5	2.6	8.1	2.6	1.1	0.0	3.3	0.0	1.1
Easton	26 263	89.5	36.3	13.7	26.6	20.2	5.7	2.2	7.2	3.1	10.5	2.4	1.2	0.0	6.5	0.0	0.5
Erie	103 717	94.4	39.5	15.1	29.2	22.4	4.7	2.1	5.9	2.6	5.6	0.6	1.1	0.5	2.3	0.0	1.1
Harrisburg	48 950	97.4	42.0	9.8	30.1	23.3	8.1	4.0	7.4	3.4	2.6	0.3	0.7	0.2	0.0	0.0	1.4
Lancaster	56 348	93.5	37.1	12.4	29.5	23.4	6.4	3.0	8.1	3.6	6.5	1.8	1.1	0.1	2.6	0.0	0.9
Monroeville Borough	29 349	96.8	42.2	22.2	26.5	19.1	3.2	1.1	2.7	1.5	3.2	0.0	1.3	0.3	0.1	0.0	1.5
New Castle	26 309	96.2	40.8	16.8	29.3	21.0	5.3	2.1	4.0	2.2	3.8	0.9	1.8	0.1	0.0	0.0	1.0
Norristown	31 282	96.8	38.5	13.0	29.2	20.9	8.5	3.4	7.7	2.7	3.2	0.0	0.7	2.0	0.0	0.0	0.5
Philadelphia	1 517 550	96.4	38.9	12.5	29.9	20.4	9.2	4.2	6.0	2.3	3.6	0.5	0.7	0.2	1.4	0.0	0.8
Pittsburgh	334 563	93.2	43.0	13.4	24.4	17.3	5.3	2.1	7.1	2.4	6.8	1.4	0.8	0.3	3.7	0.0	0.7
Plum Borough	26 940	99.1	38.1	24.2	31.6	23.7	2.8	0.9	2.3	1.4	0.9	0.0	0.2	0.0	0.0	0.0	0.7
Reading	81 207	97.4	37.1	12.7	32.3	25.7	7.8	3.3	7.5	3.7	2.6	0.0	0.3	0.0	1.4	0.0	0.9
Scranton	76 415	93.6	41.0	16.3	27.0	18.9	4.3	1.3	5.0	1.9	6.4	0.8	1.2	0.1	3.0	0.0	1.3
State College Borough	38 420	72.1	31.3	7.0	6.5	5.4	1.1	0.1	26.2	1.1	27.9	0.0	0.5	0.0	27.2	0.0	0.2
Wilkes-Barre	43 123	91.5	41.7	15.2	25.0	17.3	4.6	1.4	5.0	2.1	8.5	2.5	1.7	0.9	2.6	0.0	0.8
Williamsport	30 706	91.5	39.8	13.9	25.7	20.1	3.7	1.6	8.5	3.0	8.5	1.1	0.5	0.1	5.6	0.0	1.1
York	40 862	97.8	39.5	12.2	30.1	24.0	6.9	3.4	9.1	3.9	2.2	0.1	0.3	0.0	0.1	0.0	1.7
RHODE ISLAND	1 048 319	96.3	39.0	18.8	29.0	21.8	4.5	1.4	5.1	2.2	3.7	0.3	0.9	0.1	2.0	0.1	0.3
Cranston	79 269	94.1	39.0	19.2	27.6	19.7	4.6	1.3	3.7	1.9	5.9	4.1	0.3	0.7	0.4	0.0	0.4
East Providence	48 688	98.4	42.2	19.5	28.4	19.9	4.5	1.5	3.8	2.0	1.6	0.0	1.3	0.0	0.0	0.0	0.2
Newport	26 475	92.1	43.7	14.1	22.6	18.3	3.0	0.9	8.8	2.7	7.9	0.0	0.9	0.0	3.4	3.2	0.4
Pawtucket	72 958	99.1	41.2	16.3	30.5	22.7	5.6	1.7	5.4	2.7	0.9	0.0	0.6	0.0	0.0	0.0	0.3
Providence	173 618	92.1	35.9	11.5	29.7	23.2	6.9	2.3	8.1	2.6	7.9	0.0	0.8	0.1	6.5	0.0	0.5
Warwick	85 808	98.8	41.4	21.0	28.2	20.1	4.0	1.3	4.3	2.2	1.2	0.0	0.7	0.0	0.2	0.0	0.2
Woonsocket	43 224	97.5	41.1	16.2	30.0	23.8	4.2	1.3	6.1	3.5	2.5	0.0	1.7	0.0	0.0	0.0	0.8
SOUTH CAROLINA	4 012 012	96.6	38.2	19.5	28.8	21.8	5.9	2.8	4.3	1.8	3.4	0.9	0.5	0.1	1.0	0.4	0.4
Aiken	25 337	95.0	40.6	19.9	26.3	20.7	4.5	2.0	3.8	1.4	5.0	0.8	2.1	0.1	1.3	0.0	0.7
Anderson	25 514	92.6	41.7	15.4	25.2	18.8	6.2	2.9	4.1	2.0	7.4	1.1	2.8	0.0	2.4	0.0	1.1
Charleston	96 650	94.3	42.2	15.2	23.1	17.1	5.7	2.6	8.1	2.0	5.7	0.0	0.5	0.0	3.9	0.1	1.2
Columbia	116 278	80.2	36.3	11.4	21.2	16.5	4.9	2.2	6.4	1.8	19.8	3.5	0.5	1.2	7.5	6.1	0.9
Florence	30 248	96.2	39.4	16.5	29.2	21.0	7.2	3.4	3.8	1.6	3.8	0.0	1.2	1.4	0.0	0.0	1.2
Goose Creek	29 208	90.1	30.6	21.1	32.3	27.8	3.2	1.4	2.9	1.0	9.9	0.0	0.1	0.0	0.0	9.6	0.2
Greenville	56 002	92.0	43.5	14.3	22.7	17.1	5.8	2.3	5.7	2.0	8.0	1.5	0.4	0.0	4.7	0.0	1.3
Hilton Head Island	33 862	98.7	42.5	25.4	19.4	15.8	4.3	1.2	7.1	1.5	1.3	0.0	0.6	0.1	0.0	0.6	0.0
Mount Pleasant	47 609	98.6	40.0	22.7	28.3	24.0	2.6	0.9	5.0	1.6	1.4	0.0	1.0	0.2	0.0	0.0	0.2
North Charleston	79 641	93.8	37.4	13.5	30.1	23.9	6.6	3.3	6.2	2.6	6.2	2.1	0.6	0.2	1.6	0.7	1.1
Rock Hill	49 765	93.7	37.7	15.7	27.6	21.4	6.4	2.9	6.3	2.4	6.3	0.0	1.3	0.1	3.9	0.0	0.9
Spartanburg	39 673	93.9	40.3	13.7	28.4	21.3	7.0	3.4	4.5	1.9	6.1	0.3	0.7	0.0	3.5	0.0	1.6
Summerville	27 752	97.8	37.4	20.6	31.8	26.0	4.1	2.0	3.9	1.8	2.2	0.0	1.0	0.0	0.0	0.0	1.2
Sumter	39 643	94.4	36.7	16.9	30.8	24.1	6.6	3.3	3.4	1.4	5.6	0.0	0.8	0.0	1.6	2.1	1.1
SOUTH DAKOTA	754 844	96.2	38.5	20.9	29.5	24.6	3.0	1.4	4.5	1.8	3.8	0.6	1.0	0.3	1.2	0.1	0.6
Rapid City	59 607	96.3	40.2	18.8	28.0	23.1	3.3	1.4	6.0	2.4	3.7	0.5	0.9	0.0	1.3	0.0	1.1
Sioux Falls	123 975	96.1	40.1	19.4	27.8	23.5	2.6	0.8	6.2	2.4	3.9	1.2	0.8	0.2	1.1	0.0	0.6
TENNESSEE	5 689 283	97.4	39.2	20.6	28.3	21.8	5.0	2.2	4.1	1.7	2.6	0.7	0.7	0.1	0.8	0.0	0.3
Bartlett	40 543	99.2	34.0	25.3	34.7	27.0	3.6	1.5	1.6	0.6	0.8	0.0	0.4	0.4	0.0	0.0	0.0
Chattanooga	155 554	96.3	42.1	16.5	25.9	18.8	6.6	2.9	5.2	1.9	3.7	0.7	0.8	0.3	1.2	0.0	0.8
Clarksville	103 455	96.1	35.7	20.1	31.3	26.3	3.9	1.8	5.0	1.7	3.9	0.4	0.5	0.0	0.7	2.0	0.3
Cleveland	37 192	94.2	40.4	18.8	25.3	19.7	4.4	1.7	5.2	1.5	5.8	0.3	1.3	0.1	3.7	0.0	0.3
Collierville	31 872	99.7	32.5	24.7	38.2	32.0	2.8	1.3	1.5	0.6	0.3	0.0	0.3	0.0	0.0	0.0	0.0
Columbia	33 055	97.2	39.5	18.5	28.9	22.1	5.5	2.5	4.8	1.9	2.8	0.0	2.0	0.6	0.0	0.0	0.2
Franklin	41 842	98.3	38.5	21.7	31.1	26.4	3.4	1.2	3.6	1.2	1.7	0.8	0.5	0.0	0.0	0.0	0.4
Germantown	37 348	99.9	35.4	26.8	34.1	27.2	2.5	0.8	1.2	0.4	0.1	0.0	0.1	0.0	0.0	0.0	0.0

Table D. Cities

City	Total households	Family households						Nonfamily households			Average household size	Average family size	Households, 1990		
			Married couple		Female householder[1]			Householder living alone					Total house-holds	Female house-holder[1]	House-holder living alone
		Total	With own children under 18 years	Total	With own children under 18 years	Total	With own children under 18 years	Total	Total	65 years and over					
	71	72	73	74	75	76	77	78	79	80	81	82	83	84	85
OREGON—Cont'd															
Lake Oswego	14 769	65.4	32.0	50.2	26.5	6.9	4.3	34.6	27.9	7.9	2.38	2.95	12 487	7.1	25.3
McMinnville	9 367	69.0	35.4	53.5	25.1	10.8	7.5	31.0	23.9	11.5	2.66	3.13	6 007	10.5	25.5
Medford	25 093	65.8	31.7	50.3	21.1	11.7	8.0	34.2	27.7	12.6	2.47	2.99	18 867	10.7	26.8
Oregon City	9 471	70.4	36.6	53.0	25.4	12.3	8.1	29.6	22.4	7.8	2.62	3.06	5 479	11.8	24.1
Portland	223 737	52.9	24.5	38.1	16.2	10.8	6.3	47.1	34.6	9.0	2.30	3.00	187 268	11.0	34.9
Salem	50 676	63.8	32.4	47.7	22.0	11.6	7.8	36.2	28.3	10.5	2.53	3.10	40 936	11.2	29.9
Springfield	20 514	65.7	35.3	45.7	21.7	14.3	10.0	34.3	25.4	7.8	2.55	3.03	17 447	13.5	24.9
Tigard	16 507	65.1	33.5	52.0	25.2	9.2	6.3	34.9	26.7	7.8	2.48	3.03	12 055	8.5	26.0
PENNSYLVANIA	4 777 003	67.2	30.0	51.7	21.8	11.6	6.2	32.8	27.7	11.6	2.48	3.04	4 495 966	11.3	25.6
Allentown	42 032	59.8	28.8	39.4	16.3	15.1	9.6	40.2	33.1	12.8	2.42	3.09	42 775	12.7	31.7
Altoona	20 059	62.7	28.4	44.6	18.3	13.8	7.6	37.3	31.6	14.7	2.37	2.98	20 684	14.0	28.9
Bethel Park Borough	13 362	71.4	30.3	62.0	26.4	7.2	3.1	28.6	26.1	12.0	2.48	3.01	12 692	7.5	20.5
Bethlehem	28 116	60.8	26.3	44.1	16.8	12.8	7.6	39.2	32.3	14.4	2.34	2.95	27 268	12.0	27.9
Chester	12 814	63.4	32.7	24.8	10.5	32.1	19.1	36.6	31.2	11.2	2.64	3.34	14 537	29.4	27.8
Easton	9 544	60.1	30.5	37.7	17.5	16.6	10.0	39.9	31.6	11.0	2.46	3.10	9 397	14.3	29.8
Erie	40 938	59.8	29.2	38.2	16.2	16.8	10.5	40.2	33.4	13.3	2.39	3.08	42 131	15.6	30.8
Harrisburg	20 561	53.1	28.5	23.4	9.7	24.4	16.0	46.9	39.3	10.4	2.32	3.15	21 520	23.1	37.9
Lancaster	20 933	58.1	31.6	33.4	15.4	19.0	12.9	41.9	33.1	9.9	2.52	3.23	21 189	16.4	32.5
Monroeville Borough	12 376	65.0	25.8	52.7	20.0	9.7	4.8	35.0	30.8	12.1	2.30	2.89	11 828	8.5	26.4
New Castle	10 727	62.7	27.0	41.2	15.5	16.9	9.4	37.3	33.5	17.2	2.36	3.01	11 374	15.6	30.9
Norristown	12 028	59.4	28.7	33.7	14.8	19.8	11.6	40.6	32.7	9.2	2.52	3.22	12 187	15.0	35.2
Philadelphia	590 071	59.7	27.6	32.1	13.5	22.3	11.8	40.3	33.8	11.9	2.48	3.22	603 075	20.3	31.6
Pittsburgh	143 739	51.6	21.9	31.2	11.4	16.5	9.0	48.4	39.4	13.7	2.17	2.95	153 483	17.2	36.2
Plum Borough	10 270	74.9	34.1	63.6	28.6	8.5	4.3	25.1	21.5	8.6	2.60	3.06	9 067	8.4	16.2
Reading	30 113	61.2	33.7	34.4	16.3	20.2	13.5	38.8	31.7	12.4	2.63	3.33	31 403	16.4	32.6
Scranton	31 303	57.9	24.4	39.8	15.8	13.8	6.9	42.1	36.7	18.1	2.29	3.01	32 637	13.8	34.0
State College Borough	12 024	27.5	10.5	22.4	8.3	3.4	1.8	72.5	33.5	5.9	2.30	2.69	10 938	3.4	27.4
Wilkes-Barre	17 961	55.0	23.0	36.5	14.1	14.0	7.2	45.0	39.0	18.6	2.20	2.96	19 435	14.5	36.1
Williamsport	12 219	55.1	27.4	34.9	14.1	15.5	10.3	44.9	35.1	12.9	2.30	2.97	12 588	15.1	31.3
York	16 137	57.3	30.9	31.0	13.3	20.6	14.1	42.7	33.1	10.7	2.48	3.17	16 887	17.9	31.9
RHODE ISLAND	408 424	65.0	30.6	48.2	21.0	12.9	7.8	35.0	28.6	11.4	2.47	3.07	377 977	11.7	26.2
Cranston	30 954	65.4	28.7	49.2	20.9	12.5	6.3	34.6	29.4	13.1	2.41	3.01	29 349	11.2	27.1
East Providence	20 530	62.6	27.1	46.3	18.7	12.7	6.9	37.4	32.4	14.6	2.33	2.99	19 950	11.0	28.5
Newport	11 566	48.8	22.9	32.3	12.4	13.6	9.1	51.2	39.4	10.9	2.11	2.86	11 196	14.0	33.8
Pawtucket	30 047	61.6	30.5	39.7	17.2	16.8	10.8	38.4	32.3	12.5	2.41	3.07	29 711	13.7	30.6
Providence	62 389	57.5	32.3	31.9	15.7	20.5	14.2	42.5	32.3	10.1	2.56	3.33	58 905	18.4	31.8
Warwick	35 517	64.7	27.4	50.7	20.8	10.2	4.9	35.3	29.8	13.2	2.39	2.99	33 437	9.6	26.5
Woonsocket	17 750	60.7	31.2	39.4	16.5	16.2	11.8	39.3	32.7	12.5	2.37	3.02	17 572	14.1	29.3
SOUTH CAROLINA	1 533 854	69.9	32.3	51.1	21.8	14.8	8.5	30.1	25.0	8.6	2.53	3.02	1 258 044	14.0	22.4
Aiken	10 287	65.7	28.1	48.9	18.5	13.7	8.2	34.3	29.6	11.6	2.34	2.90	7 749	13.2	27.5
Anderson	10 641	59.2	25.4	36.9	13.1	18.7	10.8	40.8	36.0	16.3	2.22	2.89	10 509	18.0	33.3
Charleston	40 791	54.3	23.2	36.0	13.7	15.2	8.4	45.7	33.7	10.1	2.23	2.92	30 753	17.0	30.8
Columbia	42 245	52.4	25.4	31.5	13.3	17.6	10.8	47.6	37.0	9.8	2.21	2.97	33 919	16.5	34.0
Florence	11 925	66.1	30.2	41.9	17.7	20.7	11.1	33.9	29.5	10.4	2.44	3.03	11 074	20.7	27.7
Goose Creek	8 947	83.2	49.7	68.9	39.7	10.6	7.6	16.8	12.9	2.9	2.94	3.22	7 396	7.0	12.9
Greenville	24 382	51.6	22.3	32.7	12.3	15.5	8.8	48.4	40.8	12.8	2.11	2.90	24 101	16.7	36.6
Hilton Head Island	14 408	68.7	20.9	59.6	16.1	6.2	3.6	31.3	23.8	11.3	2.32	2.68	10 344	7.6	21.8
Mount Pleasant	19 025	67.6	33.9	56.9	27.8	8.3	5.0	32.4	24.1	6.0	2.47	2.99	11 788	9.2	23.0
North Charleston	29 783	63.7	34.4	36.0	16.6	22.8	15.3	36.3	28.6	6.6	2.51	3.10	23 499	16.6	24.9
Rock Hill	18 750	64.5	32.1	41.6	18.9	18.3	11.1	35.5	27.5	8.5	2.49	3.05	14 669	18.4	24.6
Spartanburg	15 989	60.8	28.9	34.0	12.9	23.0	14.3	39.2	34.0	13.2	2.33	3.00	16 712	21.0	31.2
Summerville	10 391	72.4	39.1	55.0	27.7	14.0	9.4	27.6	23.0	8.4	2.61	3.08	8 103	11.8	20.0
Sumter	14 564	69.0	35.6	46.0	22.6	19.3	11.2	31.0	27.3	11.7	2.57	3.14	12 737	18.2	22.0
SOUTH DAKOTA	290 245	67.0	32.8	54.2	24.5	9.0	6.1	33.0	27.6	11.1	2.50	3.07	259 034	8.0	26.4
Rapid City	23 969	63.5	31.2	46.7	19.9	12.6	8.8	36.5	29.4	10.0	2.39	2.96	21 152	11.3	26.4
Sioux Falls	49 731	61.9	32.1	48.4	23.1	10.0	7.0	38.1	29.8	8.9	2.40	3.00	39 790	9.4	28.7
TENNESSEE	2 232 905	69.3	31.7	52.6	22.4	12.9	7.4	30.7	25.8	9.0	2.48	2.99	1 853 725	12.6	23.9
Bartlett	13 773	85.8	44.0	74.6	38.0	8.7	4.7	14.2	12.1	4.3	2.92	3.18	8 456	7.9	8.4
Chattanooga	65 499	60.5	25.3	39.2	14.0	17.3	9.6	39.5	33.5	11.6	2.29	2.92	62 177	17.1	31.1
Clarksville	36 969	72.9	41.3	56.4	30.1	13.1	9.0	27.1	21.1	5.3	2.69	3.12	25 442	11.4	19.4
Cleveland	15 037	63.3	28.4	46.6	18.9	13.0	7.7	36.7	30.4	10.8	2.33	2.90	11 996	12.1	27.4
Collierville	10 368	86.2	52.4	76.1	46.2	8.0	4.9	13.8	11.8	3.4	3.06	3.34	4 429	9.2	11.0
Columbia	13 059	67.4	32.4	46.8	20.4	16.3	9.9	32.6	27.8	10.8	2.46	2.98	11 267	15.2	26.3
Franklin	16 128	69.6	38.6	56.2	30.6	10.8	6.7	30.4	25.0	5.4	2.55	3.09	7 828	13.0	25.4
Germantown	13 220	83.7	41.2	75.7	36.7	6.1	3.5	16.3	14.6	4.7	2.82	3.14	10 713	5.9	10.9

[1]No spouse present.

Table D. Cities

City	Percent change of households, 1990–2000	Housing occupancy		Vacant housing units		Homeowner vacancy rate (percent)	Rental vacancy rate (percent)	Housing tenure			Average household size of owner-occupied units	Average household size of renter-occupied units
		Total housing units	Occupied housing units (percent)	Total	For seasonal, recreational, or occasional use			Occupied housing units				
								Total	Percent owner-occupied housing units	Percent renter-occupied housing units		
	86	87	88	89	90	91	92	93	94	95	96	97
OREGON—Cont'd												
Lake Oswego	18.3	15 741	93.8	6.2	0.8	3.0	7.8	14 769	70.6	29.4	2.58	1.89
McMinnville	41.8	9 834	95.3	4.7	0.2	1.8	6.0	9 367	60.4	39.6	2.71	2.58
Medford	33.0	26 297	95.4	4.6	0.3	1.8	4.9	25 093	57.3	42.7	2.52	2.39
Oregon City	72.9	10 110	93.7	6.3	0.2	3.4	7.7	9 471	59.8	40.2	2.74	2.45
Portland	19.5	237 307	94.3	5.7	0.4	2.3	6.2	223 737	55.8	44.2	2.47	2.08
Salem	23.8	53 817	94.2	5.8	0.3	2.5	7.0	50 676	57.1	42.9	2.59	2.44
Springfield	17.6	21 500	95.4	4.6	0.3	2.1	4.3	20 514	53.6	46.4	2.57	2.52
Tigard	36.9	17 369	95.0	5.0	0.3	1.9	6.9	16 507	58.3	41.7	2.66	2.24
PENNSYLVANIA	6.3	5 249 750	91.0	9.0	2.8	1.6	7.2	4 777 003	71.3	28.7	2.62	2.12
Allentown	-1.7	45 960	91.5	8.5	0.3	2.6	8.4	42 032	53.0	47.0	2.55	2.26
Altoona	-3.0	21 681	92.5	7.5	0.1	1.4	9.7	20 059	65.9	34.1	2.51	2.11
Bethel Park Borough	5.3	13 871	96.3	3.7	0.4	1.4	6.0	13 362	79.9	20.1	2.69	1.66
Bethlehem	3.1	29 631	94.9	5.1	0.3	1.7	5.2	28 116	58.1	41.9	2.44	2.19
Chester	-11.9	14 976	85.6	14.4	0.2	3.2	7.4	12 814	47.7	52.3	2.69	2.60
Easton	1.6	10 545	90.5	9.5	0.2	4.6	9.4	9 544	48.5	51.5	2.67	2.27
Erie	-2.8	44 971	91.0	9.0	0.3	2.1	9.6	40 938	56.2	43.8	2.51	2.24
Harrisburg	-4.5	24 314	84.6	15.4	0.8	5.4	12.0	20 561	42.3	57.7	2.44	2.23
Lancaster	-1.2	23 024	90.9	9.1	0.2	4.3	8.5	20 933	46.6	53.4	2.58	2.46
Monroeville Borough	4.6	13 159	94.0	6.0	0.5	0.9	11.2	12 376	69.7	30.3	2.52	1.78
New Castle	-5.7	11 709	91.6	8.4	0.2	2.5	9.3	10 727	64.6	35.4	2.47	2.15
Norristown	-1.3	13 531	88.9	11.1	0.2	4.6	10.1	12 028	48.1	51.9	2.70	2.35
Philadelphia	-2.2	661 958	89.1	10.9	0.3	1.9	7.0	590 071	59.3	40.7	2.65	2.23
Pittsburgh	-6.3	163 366	88.0	12.0	0.5	2.8	8.8	143 739	52.1	47.9	2.37	1.95
Plum Borough	13.3	10 624	96.7	3.3	0.2	0.8	5.9	10 270	79.8	20.2	2.74	2.03
Reading	-4.1	34 314	87.8	12.2	0.2	4.9	9.1	30 113	51.0	49.0	2.74	2.51
Scranton	-4.1	35 336	88.6	11.4	0.3	2.8	10.1	31 303	54.5	45.5	2.49	2.04
State College Borough	9.9	12 488	96.3	3.7	0.7	0.8	2.9	12 024	22.8	77.2	2.32	2.30
Wilkes-Barre	-7.6	20 294	88.5	11.5	0.3	2.8	11.9	17 961	53.5	46.5	2.41	1.95
Williamsport	-2.9	13 524	90.4	9.6	0.2	2.9	8.7	12 219	44.8	55.2	2.47	2.16
York	-4.4	18 534	87.1	12.9	0.1	4.1	12.8	16 137	46.8	53.2	2.51	2.45
RHODE ISLAND	8.1	439 837	92.9	7.1	3.0	1.0	5.0	408 424	60.0	40.0	2.66	2.19
Cranston	5.5	32 068	96.5	3.5	0.3	0.9	4.1	30 954	66.9	33.1	2.64	1.96
East Providence	2.9	21 309	96.3	3.7	0.3	0.7	3.5	20 530	58.9	41.1	2.63	1.92
Newport	3.3	13 226	87.4	12.6	6.5	1.5	6.7	11 566	41.9	58.1	2.22	2.03
Pawtucket	1.1	31 819	94.4	5.6	0.2	1.1	5.5	30 047	44.4	55.6	2.59	2.26
Providence	5.9	67 915	91.9	8.1	0.5	2.3	6.1	62 389	34.6	65.4	2.71	2.49
Warwick	6.2	37 085	95.8	4.2	1.3	1.1	3.9	35 517	72.7	27.3	2.58	1.87
Woonsocket	1.0	18 757	94.6	5.4	0.2	0.9	5.1	17 750	35.0	65.0	2.66	2.22
SOUTH CAROLINA	21.9	1 753 670	87.5	12.5	4.0	1.9	12.0	1 533 854	72.2	27.8	2.59	2.37
Aiken	32.8	11 373	90.5	9.5	1.0	3.1	10.6	10 287	66.1	33.9	2.42	2.19
Anderson	1.3	12 068	88.2	11.8	0.3	3.4	13.5	10 641	53.4	46.6	2.27	2.16
Charleston	32.6	44 563	91.5	8.5	1.1	1.8	6.5	40 791	51.1	48.9	2.43	2.03
Columbia	24.5	46 142	91.6	8.4	0.5	2.2	7.7	42 245	45.6	54.4	2.29	2.14
Florence	7.7	13 090	91.1	8.9	0.4	2.1	9.4	11 925	61.4	38.6	2.52	2.32
Goose Creek	21.0	9 482	94.4	5.6	0.1	1.5	3.2	8 947	63.5	36.5	2.89	3.03
Greenville	1.2	27 295	89.3	10.7	0.7	2.4	10.9	24 382	47.0	53.0	2.21	2.03
Hilton Head Island	39.3	24 647	58.5	41.5	29.9	1.5	40.6	14 408	77.7	22.3	2.21	2.70
Mount Pleasant	61.4	20 197	94.2	5.8	0.8	1.5	8.7	19 025	74.0	26.0	2.61	2.05
North Charleston	26.7	33 631	88.6	11.4	0.3	2.1	10.6	29 783	46.4	53.6	2.52	2.50
Rock Hill	27.8	20 287	92.4	7.6	0.3	3.1	7.8	18 750	53.4	46.6	2.57	2.39
Spartanburg	-4.3	17 696	90.4	9.6	0.3	3.0	9.6	15 989	49.8	50.2	2.40	2.26
Summerville	28.2	11 087	93.7	6.3	0.4	1.7	6.8	10 391	65.7	34.3	2.81	2.23
Sumter	14.3	16 032	90.8	9.2	0.4	2.2	8.2	14 564	53.1	46.9	2.58	2.55
SOUTH DAKOTA	12.0	323 208	89.8	10.2	3.0	1.8	8.0	290 245	68.2	31.8	2.64	2.22
Rapid City	13.3	25 096	95.5	4.5	0.4	0.9	5.7	23 969	59.3	40.7	2.53	2.20
Sioux Falls	25.0	51 680	96.2	3.8	0.2	1.0	5.2	49 731	61.1	38.9	2.65	2.00
TENNESSEE	20.5	2 439 443	91.5	8.5	1.5	2.0	8.8	2 232 905	69.9	30.1	2.57	2.29
Bartlett	62.9	14 021	98.2	1.8	0.1	1.0	4.2	13 773	92.2	7.8	2.93	2.81
Chattanooga	5.3	72 108	90.8	9.2	0.4	2.5	8.9	65 499	54.9	45.1	2.40	2.15
Clarksville	45.3	40 041	92.3	7.7	0.2	3.0	7.3	36 969	57.5	42.5	2.79	2.55
Cleveland	25.4	16 431	91.5	8.5	0.3	2.2	9.8	15 037	51.8	48.2	2.48	2.17
Collierville	134.1	10 770	96.3	3.7	0.6	2.1	4.7	10 368	86.4	13.6	3.15	2.51
Columbia	15.9	14 322	91.2	8.8	0.2	2.6	11.5	13 059	63.5	36.5	2.50	2.38
Franklin	106.0	17 296	93.2	6.8	0.3	3.7	6.2	16 128	63.5	36.5	2.78	2.15
Germantown	23.4	13 676	96.7	3.3	0.4	1.2	10.3	13 220	89.0	11.0	2.89	2.25

Table D. Cities

STATE Place code	City	Population, 2000				Population, 1990				Population and population characteristics, 2000 Race (percent) One race					
		Land area, 2000[1] (sq km)	Total persons	Rank	Per square kilometer	Land area, 1990[1] (sq km)	Total persons	Rank	Per square kilometer	White	Black or African American	American Indian or Alaska Native	Asian	Native Hawaiian and other Pacific Islander	Some other race
		1	2	3	4	5	6	7	8	9	10	11	12	13	14
	TENNESSEE—Cont'd														
47 33280	Hendersonville	70.8	40 620	853	573.7	57.2	32 188	967	562.7	92.9	4.1	0.3	1.1	0.0	0.7
47 37640	Jackson	128.2	59 643	507	465.2	104.5	49 145	570	470.3	55.1	42.1	0.2	0.8	0.0	0.9
47 38320	Johnson City	101.7	55 469	580	545.4	79.2	50 354	552	635.8	90.1	6.4	0.3	1.2	0.0	0.7
47 39560	Kingsport	114.1	44 905	765	393.6	83.8	40 457	727	482.8	93.3	4.2	0.2	0.8	0.0	0.3
47 40000	Knoxville	240.0	173 890	121	724.5	200.1	169 761	103	848.4	79.7	16.2	0.3	1.5	0.0	0.7
47 48000	Memphis	723.4	650 100	19	898.7	663.2	618 652	18	932.8	34.4	61.4	0.2	1.5	0.0	1.5
47 51560	Murfreesboro	101.0	68 816	417	681.3	78.6	44 922	637	571.5	79.8	13.9	0.3	2.7	0.0	1.9
47 52004	Nashville-Davidson	1 300.9	569 891	23	438.1	1 301.0	488 188	25	375.2	67.0	25.9	0.3	2.3	0.1	2.4
47 55120	Oak Ridge	221.6	27 387	1 362	123.6	221.6	27 310	1 169	123.2	87.0	8.2	0.3	2.1	0.0	0.8
47 69420	Smyrna	59.1	25 569	1 476	432.6	47.6	14 720	2 217	309.2	87.2	7.8	0.3	1.2	0.1	1.8
48 00000	TEXAS	678 051.4	20 851 820	X	30.8	678 357.8	16 986 335	X	25.0	71.0	11.5	0.6	2.7	0.1	11.7
48 01000	Abilene	272.3	115 930	201	425.7	267.0	106 707	187	399.7	78.1	8.8	0.6	1.3	0.1	8.7
48 01924	Allen	68.2	43 554	789	638.6	49.2	19 315	1 701	392.6	87.1	4.4	0.5	3.7	0.0	2.4
48 03000	Amarillo	232.7	173 627	122	746.1	227.8	157 571	112	691.7	77.5	6.0	0.8	2.1	0.0	11.3
48 04000	Arlington	248.2	332 969	55	1 341.5	240.9	261 717	61	1 086.4	67.7	13.7	0.5	6.0	0.1	8.9
48 05000	Austin	651.4	656 562	17	1 007.9	564.0	472 020	27	836.9	65.4	10.0	0.6	4.7	0.1	16.2
48 06128	Baytown	84.6	66 430	438	785.2	81.1	63 843	386	787.2	67.9	13.4	0.5	1.0	0.1	14.4
48 07000	Beaumont	220.2	113 866	204	517.1	207.3	114 323	161	551.5	46.4	45.8	0.2	2.5	0.0	3.5
48 07132	Bedford	25.9	47 152	723	1 820.5	25.9	43 762	656	1 689.7	87.6	3.7	0.5	3.6	0.3	2.4
48 08236	Big Spring	49.5	25 233	1 492	509.8	49.3	23 093	1 416	468.4	76.7	5.3	0.6	0.6	0.0	14.4
48 10768	Brownsville	208.2	139 722	157	671.1	72.3	107 027	186	1 480.3	81.6	0.4	0.4	0.5	0.0	14.7
48 10912	Bryan	112.2	65 660	444	585.2	84.6	55 002	473	650.1	64.7	17.7	0.4	1.7	0.1	13.3
48 13024	Carrollton	94.5	109 576	213	1 159.5	90.0	82 169	272	913.0	71.9	6.3	0.5	10.9	0.1	7.7
48 13492	Cedar Hill	91.0	32 093	1 131	352.7	87.1	19 988	1 643	229.5	56.7	33.6	0.5	2.0	0.0	4.9
48 13552	Cedar Park	44.0	26 049	1 444	592.0	NA	5 161	3 432	NA	86.4	3.3	0.3	2.6	0.1	5.1
48 15364	Cleburne	72.0	26 005	1 447	361.2	50.4	22 205	1 479	440.6	86.3	4.4	0.5	0.4	0.2	6.4
48 15976	College Station	104.3	67 890	425	650.9	76.3	52 443	512	687.3	80.5	5.4	0.3	7.3	0.1	4.5
48 16432	Conroe	97.9	36 811	955	376.0	54.2	27 675	1 147	510.6	71.2	11.1	0.4	0.9	0.0	13.4
48 16612	Coppell	38.5	35 958	987	934.0	38.1	16 881	1 933	443.1	83.2	3.3	0.3	9.3	0.0	1.9
48 16624	Copperas Cove	36.1	29 592	1 245	819.7	24.3	24 079	1 352	990.9	65.4	20.4	0.6	2.7	0.6	5.0
48 17000	Corpus Christi	400.5	277 454	62	692.8	349.6	257 428	64	736.4	71.6	4.7	0.6	1.3	0.1	18.6
48 19000	Dallas	887.2	1 188 580	8	1 339.7	886.8	1 007 618	8	1 136.2	50.8	25.9	0.5	2.7	0.0	17.2
48 19624	Deer Park	26.8	28 520	1 300	1 064.2	26.9	27 424	1 162	1 019.5	90.0	1.3	0.4	1.1	0.1	5.2
48 19792	Del Rio	40.0	33 867	1 063	846.7	38.2	30 705	1 028	803.8	77.1	1.2	0.7	0.5	0.1	17.8
48 19972	Denton	159.3	80 537	336	505.6	136.3	66 270	366	486.2	75.6	9.1	0.6	3.4	0.1	8.8
48 20092	DeSoto	55.9	37 646	938	673.5	55.9	30 544	1 036	546.4	48.8	45.5	0.3	1.3	0.0	2.6
48 21628	Duncanville	29.2	36 081	983	1 235.7	29.2	35 008	860	1 198.9	63.9	24.8	0.3	2.0	0.1	6.8
48 22660	Edinburg	96.8	48 465	698	500.7	36.6	31 091	1 007	849.5	73.3	0.6	0.5	0.6	0.0	22.7
48 24000	El Paso	645.1	563 662	24	873.8	635.5	515 342	22	810.9	73.3	3.1	0.8	1.1	0.1	18.2
48 24768	Euless	42.1	46 005	743	1 092.8	41.5	38 149	781	919.3	75.5	6.5	0.6	7.1	1.9	5.4
48 25452	Farmers Branch	31.1	27 508	1 354	884.5	31.1	24 250	1 340	779.7	78.4	2.4	0.5	2.9	0.0	13.0
48 26232	Flower Mound	105.9	50 702	657	478.8	83.0	15 527	2 093	187.1	90.2	2.9	0.4	3.1	0.1	1.8
48 27000	Fort Worth	757.7	534 694	29	705.7	728.0	447 619	29	614.9	59.7	20.3	0.6	2.6	0.1	14.0
48 27648	Friendswood	54.4	29 037	1 273	533.8	53.7	22 814	1 438	424.8	90.1	2.7	0.4	2.4	0.0	2.8
48 27684	Frisco	181.0	33 714	1 073	186.3	NA	6 138	3 405	NA	87.3	3.8	0.4	2.3	0.0	4.3
48 28068	Galveston	119.5	57 247	543	479.1	119.6	59 067	432	493.9	58.7	25.5	0.4	3.2	0.1	9.7
48 29000	Garland	147.9	215 768	84	1 458.9	148.5	180 635	92	1 216.4	65.3	11.9	0.6	7.3	0.1	12.0
48 29336	Georgetown	59.1	28 339	1 306	479.5	34.8	14 840	2 197	426.4	85.4	3.4	0.4	0.7	0.1	8.3
48 30464	Grand Prairie	184.9	127 427	174	689.2	177.4	99 606	206	561.5	62.0	13.5	0.8	4.4	0.1	15.9
48 30644	Grapevine	83.6	42 059	819	503.1	81.0	29 407	1 074	363.0	88.2	2.4	0.6	2.6	0.1	4.6
48 31928	Haltom City	32.1	39 018	897	1 215.5	32.0	32 856	944	1 026.8	76.8	2.8	0.7	7.7	0.1	9.2
48 32372	Harlingen	88.2	57 564	539	652.7	69.7	48 746	575	699.4	78.7	0.9	0.5	0.9	0.0	16.4
48 35000	Houston	1 500.7	1 953 631	4	1 301.8	1 398.3	1 654 348	4	1 183.1	49.3	25.3	0.4	5.3	0.1	16.5
48 35528	Huntsville	80.0	35 078	1 023	438.5	54.3	30 628	1 030	564.1	65.8	26.1	0.3	1.1	0.1	4.9
48 35576	Hurst	25.6	36 273	975	1 416.9	25.6	33 574	914	1 311.5	86.0	4.1	0.6	1.8	0.3	5.2
48 37000	Irving	174.1	191 615	102	1 100.6	175.1	155 037	114	885.4	64.2	10.2	0.6	8.2	0.1	13.4
48 38632	Keller	47.8	27 345	1 367	572.1	47.4	13 683	2 370	288.7	93.7	1.4	0.4	1.8	0.0	1.2
48 39148	Killeen	91.5	86 911	299	949.8	71.7	63 535	387	886.1	45.8	33.5	0.8	4.3	0.9	9.0
48 39352	Kingsville	35.8	25 575	1 475	714.4	32.9	25 276	1 275	768.3	71.1	4.3	0.6	1.7	0.1	18.8
48 40588	Lake Jackson	49.3	26 386	1 420	535.2	35.7	22 771	1 439	637.8	86.2	3.9	0.4	2.5	0.0	5.2
48 41212	Lancaster	75.9	25 894	1 456	341.2	75.5	22 117	1 486	292.9	37.6	53.0	0.5	0.4	0.1	6.6
48 41440	La Porte	49.1	31 880	1 141	649.3	49.9	27 923	1 143	559.6	81.4	6.3	0.5	1.1	0.1	8.5
48 41464	Laredo	203.2	176 576	119	869.0	85.1	122 893	151	1 444.1	82.3	0.4	0.4	0.5	0.0	13.9
48 41980	League City	132.7	45 444	754	342.5	133.1	30 159	1 046	226.6	84.0	5.1	0.4	3.2	0.1	5.3
48 42508	Lewisville	95.3	77 737	357	815.7	93.3	46 521	611	498.6	77.2	7.4	0.7	3.9	0.0	8.3
48 43888	Longview	141.6	73 344	383	518.0	135.5	70 311	340	518.9	70.1	22.1	0.5	0.8	0.0	4.9
48 45000	Lubbock	297.4	199 564	92	671.0	269.7	186 206	88	690.4	72.9	8.7	0.6	1.5	0.0	14.3
48 45072	Lufkin	69.2	32 709	1 112	472.7	61.1	30 210	1 045	494.4	59.9	26.6	0.3	1.4	0.0	10.3
48 45384	McAllen	119.1	106 414	224	893.5	84.0	84 021	268	1 000.3	78.5	0.6	0.4	1.9	0.0	15.8

[1] Dry land or land partially or temporarily covered by water.

Table D. Cities

City	Population and population characteristics, 2000 (cont'd)								Population and population characteristics, 1990				
	Race (percent) (cont'd)								Race (percent)				
	Race alone or in combination												
	Two or more races	White	Black	American Indian or Alaska Native	Asian	Native Hawaiian and other Pacific Islander	Some other race	Hispanic¹	White	Black or African American	American Indian or Alaska Native	Asian and Pacific Islander	Hispanic¹
	15	16	17	18	19	20	21	22	23	24	25	26	27
TENNESSEE—Cont'd													
Hendersonville	0.9	93.8	4.3	0.6	1.3	0.1	0.9	1.7	96.7	2.3	0.2	0.6	0.8
Jackson	1.0	55.9	42.5	0.5	1.0	0.1	1.1	2.2	59.1	40.3	0.1	0.4	0.5
Johnson City	1.3	91.3	7.0	0.7	1.4	0.0	1.0	1.9	93.1	5.9	0.2	0.7	0.6
Kingsport	1.1	94.3	4.6	0.7	1.0		0.6	1.0	94.8	4.4	0.1	0.6	0.3
Knoxville	1.6	81.1	16.8	0.9	1.7	0.1	1.1	1.6	82.7	15.8	0.2	1.0	0.7
Memphis	1.0	35.2	61.9	0.5	1.7	0.1	1.8	3.0	44.0	54.8	0.2	0.8	0.7
Murfreesboro	1.4	80.9	14.4	0.7	3.1	0.1	2.3	3.5	82.3	14.5	0.2	2.8	0.8
Nashville-Davidson	2.0	68.5	26.6	0.7	2.8	0.1	3.3	4.6	74.8	23.4	0.3	1.3	0.8
Oak Ridge	1.7	88.5	8.9	0.9	2.4	0.1	0.9	1.9	89.4	8.0	0.4	2.1	1.0
Smyrna	1.6	88.7	8.4	0.7	1.5	0.1	2.4	4.3	92.5	6.7	0.3	0.3	1.1
TEXAS	2.5	73.1	12.0	1.0	3.1	0.1	13.3	32.0	75.2	11.9	0.4	1.9	25.5
Abilene	2.4	80.1	9.5	1.1	1.9	0.1	9.8	19.4	82.4	7.0	0.4	1.3	15.5
Allen	1.7	88.7	4.8	1.0	4.2	0.1	3.1	7.0	93.2	3.2	0.6	1.2	4.4
Amarillo	2.3	79.5	6.4	1.4	2.3	0.1	12.6	21.9	82.7	6.0	0.8	1.9	14.7
Arlington	2.9	70.1	14.5	1.2	6.6	0.2	10.4	18.3	82.6	8.4	0.5	3.9	8.9
Austin	3.0	67.8	10.7	1.1	5.4	0.2	18.0	30.5	70.6	12.4	0.4	3.0	23.0
Baytown	2.8	70.2	14.0	0.9	1.2	0.2	16.3	34.2	73.0	12.0	0.3	0.8	23.2
Beaumont	1.5	47.5	46.4	0.6	2.8	0.1	4.2	7.9	55.0	41.3	0.2	1.7	4.3
Bedford	1.9	89.3	4.0	1.1	4.1	0.4	3.1	7.2	92.8	2.6	0.4	2.5	4.6
Big Spring	2.4	78.8	5.7	1.2	0.9	0.1	16.0	44.6	74.0	5.1	0.6	0.6	30.2
Brownsville	2.3	83.8	0.5	0.6	0.7	0.1	16.7	91.3	84.8	0.2	0.1	0.3	90.1
Bryan	2.2	66.5	18.2	0.8	1.9	0.1	14.7	27.8	69.9	17.2	0.2	1.5	19.8
Carrollton	2.7	74.1	6.7	0.9	11.8	0.1	9.2	19.5	83.1	4.9	0.4	6.8	10.2
Cedar Hill	2.3	58.4	34.4	1.0	2.4	0.1	6.0	11.9	80.5	14.2	0.4	1.8	8.1
Cedar Park	2.2	88.4	3.6	0.9	3.2	0.1	6.0	13.5	93.5	0.8	0.4	0.6	10.7
Cleburne	1.7	87.9	4.8	1.0	0.5	0.3	7.3	19.9	88.5	5.6	0.3	0.4	10.5
College Station	1.9	82.2	5.7	0.7	7.9	0.2	5.4	10.0	83.0	6.3	0.2	6.5	8.9
Conroe	2.9	73.8	11.5	0.8	1.3	0.1	15.6	32.6	74.5	13.4	0.3	0.9	17.4
Coppell	2.0	84.7	3.6	0.7	10.3	0.1	2.7	6.9	89.5	2.3	0.3	5.4	6.0
Copperas Cove	5.1	69.4	22.3	1.8	4.3	1.0	6.8	11.7	75.1	16.5	0.7	3.7	9.0
Corpus Christi	3.1	74.4	5.1	1.1	1.7	0.2	20.9	54.3	76.1	4.8	0.4	0.9	50.4
Dallas	2.7	53.0	26.5	1.0	3.1	0.1	19.2	35.6	55.3	29.5	0.5	2.2	20.9
Deer Park	1.8	91.6	1.4	0.9	1.5	0.2	6.1	15.2	92.2	1.1	0.4	1.2	10.8
Del Rio	2.7	79.5	1.4	1.1	0.7	0.1	20.0	81.0	65.5	1.4	0.4	0.4	77.2
Denton	2.4	77.7	9.6	1.2	3.9	0.1	10.0	16.4	82.0	9.5	0.5	2.8	9.0
DeSoto	1.4	49.9	46.1	0.7	1.5	0.1	3.2	7.3	76.0	20.8	0.3	1.1	5.0
Duncanville	2.1	65.6	25.4	0.8	2.4	0.1	7.9	15.3	82.5	12.1	0.3	2.1	6.7
Edinburg	2.3	75.4	0.7	0.7	0.8	0.1	24.7	88.7	74.3	0.5	0.2	0.4	85.9
El Paso	3.4	76.3	3.5	1.2	1.5	0.2	20.8	76.6	76.9	3.4	0.4	1.2	69.0
Euless	3.0	77.7	7.1	1.2	8.1	2.1	6.9	13.3	86.5	4.6	0.6	5.1	7.9
Farmers Branch	2.7	80.8	2.7	1.0	3.4	0.0	14.8	37.2	84.9	2.8	0.7	2.3	20.2
Flower Mound	1.6	91.7	3.2	0.9	3.6	0.1	2.3	5.6	94.8	2.1	0.4	1.0	4.2
Fort Worth	2.7	62.0	20.8	1.1	3.1	0.1	15.7	29.8	63.8	22.0	0.4	2.0	19.5
Friendswood	1.6	91.5	3.0	0.8	2.9	0.0	3.4	8.8	93.8	2.7	0.3	1.7	6.1
Frisco	1.9	89.0	4.1	0.8	2.9	0.1	5.1	11.0	83.4	2.1	0.6	0.5	21.7
Galveston	2.4	60.7	26.0	0.9	3.6	0.2	11.3	25.8	61.5	29.1	0.2	2.3	21.4
Garland	2.9	67.7	12.4	1.1	7.9	0.1	13.7	25.6	79.7	8.9	0.5	4.5	11.6
Georgetown	1.8	87.0	3.7	0.7	1.0	0.1	9.4	18.1	86.8	5.2	0.4	0.6	20.9
Grand Prairie	3.3	64.8	14.1	1.3	5.0	0.1	18.1	33.0	75.8	9.7	0.8	3.0	20.5
Grapevine	1.7	89.6	2.6	1.1	3.0	0.2	5.3	11.6	94.7	1.8	0.5	1.1	5.7
Haltom City	2.6	78.9	3.1	1.3	8.4	0.2	10.7	19.9	89.8	1.3	0.7	4.8	8.5
Harlingen	2.6	81.1	1.1	0.8	1.0	0.1	18.6	72.8	80.1	0.8	0.2	0.4	71.0
Houston	3.1	51.8	25.9	0.8	5.8	0.1	18.8	37.4	52.7	28.1	0.3	4.1	27.6
Huntsville	1.6	67.1	26.6	0.7	1.3	0.2	5.8	16.2	64.7	26.7	0.4	0.9	13.0
Hurst	1.9	87.7	4.5	1.3	2.2	0.4	6.0	11.0	93.4	2.6	0.5	1.2	5.2
Irving	3.2	66.8	10.8	1.2	8.9	0.2	15.4	31.2	78.7	7.5	0.6	4.6	16.3
Keller	1.4	95.0	1.7	0.9	2.2	0.1	1.7	4.5	97.5	0.6	0.5	0.7	2.9
Killeen	5.7	49.7	36.1	1.7	6.1	1.4	11.2	17.8	58.1	30.1	0.5	5.8	14.0
Kingsville	3.3	74.1	4.7	1.1	2.1	0.1	21.4	67.1	66.8	3.8	0.3	1.6	62.4
Lake Jackson	1.8	87.9	4.2	0.8	2.8	0.0	6.1	14.7	89.5	3.2	0.3	2.2	10.8
Lancaster	1.9	39.1	53.8	1.0	0.6	0.1	7.5	11.6	65.0	29.8	0.5	0.5	8.0
La Porte	2.2	83.2	6.6	1.0	1.4	0.1	9.9	20.5	85.3	7.1	0.5	1.0	14.3
Laredo	2.5	84.6	0.5	0.6	0.6	0.0	16.2	94.1	70.8	0.1	0.2	0.4	93.9
League City	2.0	85.7	5.5	0.8	3.7	0.1	6.3	13.5	88.1	5.1	0.3	2.3	11.7
Lewisville	2.5	79.3	7.9	1.3	4.4	0.1	9.6	17.8	88.6	4.6	0.6	1.9	8.7
Longview	1.5	71.4	22.5	1.0	1.0	0.1	5.6	10.3	76.6	19.9	0.4	0.6	4.1
Lubbock	2.0	74.6	9.1	1.0	1.8	0.1	15.6	27.5	77.6	8.6	0.3	1.4	22.5
Lufkin	1.5	61.2	27.1	0.6	1.6	0.0	11.2	17.6	65.2	27.2	0.2	0.8	9.6
McAllen	2.7	81.0	0.7	0.6	2.2	0.1	18.2	80.3	70.9	0.3	0.2	0.7	77.0

¹Hispanic persons may be of any race.

Table D. Cities

City	Population and population characteristics, 2000										
	Age (percent)										
	Under 5 years	5 to 17 years	18 to 24 years	25 to 34 years	35 to 44 years	45 to 54 years	55 to 64 years	65 to 74 years	75 years and over	Median age (years)	Percent Female
	28	29	30	31	32	33	34	35	36	37	38
TENNESSEE—Cont'd											
Hendersonville	6.6	19.2	7.8	14.2	17.2	14.8	10.0	5.7	4.4	36.2	51.3
Jackson	7.2	18.6	12.8	14.3	14.4	12.0	7.5	6.4	6.8	32.8	53.4
Johnson City	5.5	14.3	13.7	13.9	14.2	14.1	9.3	7.9	8.0	36.9	52.3
Kingsport	5.7	16.0	6.5	12.1	14.1	14.1	11.2	9.5	10.8	41.9	54.3
Knoxville	5.9	13.7	16.8	15.7	13.8	11.9	7.7	6.9	7.5	33.4	52.6
Memphis	7.8	20.1	10.8	15.8	14.9	12.4	7.2	5.6	5.3	31.9	52.7
Murfreesboro	6.5	16.2	20.5	16.4	14.4	11.0	6.3	4.6	4.2	28.7	50.3
Nashville-Davidson	6.6	15.6	11.6	17.6	16.4	13.2	7.9	5.9	5.3	34.1	51.6
Oak Ridge	4.8	17.7	6.6	9.5	14.1	15.7	10.6	9.7	11.4	43.4	53.2
Smyrna	8.6	19.0	10.5	17.3	17.8	12.4	7.5	3.9	2.9	31.7	51.1
TEXAS	7.8	20.4	10.5	15.2	15.9	12.5	7.7	5.5	4.5	32.3	50.4
Abilene	7.1	18.5	15.3	14.1	14.7	10.9	7.3	6.3	5.7	31.1	49.5
Allen	10.7	24.3	5.4	17.4	23.2	11.7	4.5	1.7	1.1	31.4	50.1
Amarillo	8.0	19.9	10.2	13.9	14.9	12.5	8.0	6.7	5.9	33.5	52.0
Arlington	8.3	20.0	11.0	18.5	17.2	12.3	6.5	3.6	2.5	30.7	50.0
Austin	7.1	15.4	16.6	21.1	16.0	11.6	5.6	3.5	3.2	29.6	48.6
Baytown	8.7	21.3	11.2	15.2	14.2	12.4	7.0	4.9	5.0	30.6	51.5
Beaumont	7.1	20.0	10.4	13.2	14.8	13.0	8.2	6.8	6.6	34.5	52.5
Bedford	5.9	16.6	9.7	15.9	17.1	16.7	9.5	4.8	3.9	36.2	51.8
Big Spring	6.1	17.5	9.9	16.3	16.4	12.2	7.6	7.2	6.9	35.1	44.4
Brownsville	9.9	24.8	11.2	14.6	12.9	10.6	6.6	5.4	4.1	27.7	52.9
Bryan	8.0	19.0	18.1	16.6	13.2	9.7	6.1	4.5	4.8	27.6	50.2
Carrollton	7.9	20.3	8.0	17.3	19.8	14.3	7.1	3.2	2.1	33.0	50.5
Cedar Hill	8.5	24.1	7.7	15.9	19.9	13.7	5.6	2.6	2.1	31.5	52.3
Cedar Park	11.0	22.6	6.0	19.2	21.1	11.0	4.8	2.4	1.9	31.1	50.6
Cleburne	8.2	19.7	9.7	14.7	13.9	12.3	7.8	6.5	7.3	33.2	51.5
College Station	4.5	10.0	51.2	13.0	8.3	6.0	3.4	1.9	1.7	21.9	48.9
Conroe	8.7	19.4	13.4	17.5	14.1	10.6	6.7	4.9	4.8	29.4	49.7
Coppell	9.5	25.2	4.5	13.7	25.3	14.5	4.7	1.6	1.0	33.5	50.7
Copperas Cove	10.2	21.8	14.2	17.8	15.5	9.2	6.1	3.3	1.7	26.9	50.5
Corpus Christi	7.8	20.4	10.6	13.6	15.6	13.2	7.8	6.1	5.0	33.2	51.1
Dallas	8.3	18.2	11.8	19.8	15.5	11.1	6.5	4.5	4.1	30.5	49.6
Deer Park	6.3	22.7	9.4	12.1	18.2	15.9	8.0	4.6	2.8	34.7	50.3
Del Rio	8.6	23.1	8.8	14.2	13.4	11.4	8.8	6.5	5.2	31.7	51.5
Denton	6.2	14.5	25.0	17.9	12.9	9.9	5.8	3.8	4.1	26.8	50.8
DeSoto	7.0	21.1	7.6	12.5	17.7	16.0	8.8	4.9	4.4	36.1	53.0
Duncanville	6.5	21.6	8.5	12.3	15.4	16.1	10.0	5.7	3.9	35.8	52.6
Edinburg	9.8	23.2	13.1	16.3	13.5	9.9	6.0	4.8	3.5	27.2	51.2
El Paso	8.5	22.6	10.0	14.3	14.8	11.7	7.5	6.2	4.4	31.1	52.5
Euless	7.4	17.5	9.8	20.5	19.2	12.5	7.3	3.8	2.0	32.2	50.4
Farmers Branch	7.3	18.4	9.5	15.4	16.0	12.0	9.3	7.5	4.6	34.7	49.7
Flower Mound	10.7	24.1	4.2	14.8	24.7	13.9	4.9	1.6	1.1	33.3	50.2
Fort Worth	8.5	19.8	11.3	17.0	15.7	11.5	6.7	5.0	4.6	30.9	50.7
Friendswood	6.6	23.5	6.2	10.4	19.0	16.5	9.2	4.8	3.8	37.2	51.6
Frisco	12.8	18.0	5.3	25.6	20.3	9.5	5.0	2.2	1.4	30.9	50.5
Galveston	6.6	16.7	11.3	14.5	15.3	13.1	8.7	7.5	6.2	35.5	51.7
Garland	8.2	21.6	9.6	16.0	17.0	13.1	7.4	4.2	2.9	31.7	50.4
Georgetown	6.4	17.0	11.4	12.6	13.7	11.4	9.8	9.6	8.0	36.9	51.3
Grand Prairie	8.9	21.7	10.1	17.2	16.9	12.1	6.7	3.7	2.6	30.5	50.5
Grapevine	7.4	21.9	7.5	14.5	22.1	15.7	6.2	2.5	2.2	34.3	49.9
Haltom City	8.2	18.9	10.2	17.1	15.8	11.9	7.5	5.8	4.6	32.3	49.8
Harlingen	9.1	21.7	9.6	13.9	12.7	11.0	7.0	7.5	7.6	31.8	52.4
Houston	8.2	19.2	11.2	18.1	15.6	12.0	7.1	4.8	3.6	28.3	50.1
Huntsville	4.6	10.5	29.3	15.0	15.7	10.5	5.9	4.4	4.1	36.6	39.5
Hurst	7.2	18.2	8.3	13.6	16.7	13.3	10.3	7.4	5.0	36.6	51.4
Irving	8.1	17.0	11.9	22.8	16.7	10.8	6.5	3.7	2.4	30.3	49.0
Keller	8.6	25.1	4.7	11.6	23.1	15.6	7.0	2.8	1.6	35.0	50.3
Killeen	10.1	19.8	16.0	20.7	15.0	8.9	4.6	3.2	1.7	26.7	49.8
Kingsville	8.0	18.9	17.3	15.3	11.8	10.6	7.7	5.6	4.9	28.4	50.1
Lake Jackson	7.4	23.2	7.6	12.5	17.8	14.3	7.4	5.5	4.4	34.5	51.2
Lancaster	8.2	22.2	8.6	15.2	17.1	12.8	6.8	4.5	4.5	32.3	53.9
La Porte	7.9	21.8	8.9	15.1	17.6	14.7	7.1	3.9	3.0	32.6	50.4
Laredo	10.5	25.0	11.4	16.1	13.4	9.7	6.1	4.4	3.4	26.9	52.0
League City	8.1	21.3	6.6	15.1	20.7	14.8	7.4	3.4	2.5	34.4	50.2
Lewisville	9.1	17.5	11.8	23.4	17.8	10.6	5.5	2.5	1.8	29.8	50.0
Longview	7.4	19.4	10.8	13.7	15.0	12.4	8.1	6.9	6.4	34.0	51.8
Lubbock	7.2	17.8	17.9	14.2	13.5	11.3	7.1	5.9	5.2	29.7	51.4
Lufkin	8.0	19.0	10.6	13.6	13.7	11.8	8.3	7.1	8.1	34.0	52.9
McAllen	8.7	22.1	10.5	15.3	14.0	11.8	7.1	5.6	4.9	30.5	52.6

Table D. Cities

City	Under 5 years	5 to 17 years	18 to 24 years	25 to 34 years	35 to 44 years	45 to 54 years	55 to 64 years	65 to 74 years	75 years and over	Percent Female	2000	1990	1980	1990–2000	1980–1990
	39	40	41	42	43	44	45	46	47	48	49	50	51	52	53
TENNESSEE—Cont'd															
Hendersonville	6.6	20.1	9.5	16.3	17.8	13.5	7.7	5.1	3.3	51.7	40 620	32 188	26 561	26.2	21.2
Jackson	7.2	17.9	12.8	15.8	13.6	8.8	8.6	7.9	7.5	54.4	59 643	49 115	49 131	21.4	0.0
Johnson City	5.2	14.5	15.1	15.6	13.3	10.6	9.8	8.9	6.9	52.4	55 469	50 354	39 738	10.2	26.7
Kingsport	6.1	15.6	8.3	13.3	13.0	12.5	11.4	11.5	8.4	54.9	44 905	40 457	32 027	11.0	26.3
Knoxville	5.9	13.9	16.5	18.0	13.1	8.7	8.5	8.6	6.8	53.3	173 890	169 761	175 030	2.4	-3.0
Memphis	8.1	18.8	11.2	18.1	14.2	9.2	8.4	7.1	5.1	53.3	650 100	618 652	646 356	5.1	-4.3
Murfreesboro	6.4	16.1	21.8	17.5	13.4	8.1	6.8	5.6	4.2	52.3	68 816	44 922	32 845	53.2	36.8
Nashville-Davidson	7.0	15.8	11.4	20.6	15.4	10.0	8.2	6.6	5.0	52.5	569 891	510 786	NA	11.6	NA
Oak Ridge	5.3	16.9	6.9	13.5	16.1	11.3	11.6	12.1	6.3	52.9	27 387	27 310	27 662	0.3	-1.3
Smyrna	8.9	21.0	10.7	20.2	15.5	9.5	6.4	4.9	3.0	51.4	25 569	14 717	NA	73.7	NA
TEXAS	8.2	20.3	11.1	18.2	14.9	9.6	7.6	5.9	4.2	50.7	20 851 820	16 986 335	14 225 513	22.8	19.4
Abilene	8.3	18.7	14.0	17.8	13.3	8.5	7.7	6.5	5.1	51.3	115 930	106 707	98 312	8.6	8.5
Allen	10.5	24.5	7.3	25.3	18.8	7.9	3.0	1.7	1.0	50.0	43 554	19 315	NA	125.5	NA
Amarillo	8.3	19.7	9.7	17.7	14.9	9.0	8.7	6.9	5.1	52.1	173 627	157 571	149 230	10.2	5.6
Arlington	8.8	18.1	12.4	23.9	16.8	9.5	5.4	3.2	1.7	49.9	332 969	261 717	160 113	27.2	63.5
Austin	7.5	15.6	17.2	23.0	15.7	8.0	5.6	4.2	3.1	50.1	656 562	472 020	345 544	39.1	36.6
Baytown	8.9	22.0	10.9	17.7	15.1	9.0	6.8	5.5	4.1	50.7	66 430	63 843	56 923	4.1	12.2
Beaumont	7.4	19.5	10.1	16.8	14.3	9.5	8.7	7.7	6.0	52.4	113 866	114 323	118 102	-0.4	-3.2
Bedford	7.1	18.7	10.1	20.7	20.2	12.5	6.1	3.0	1.7	51.0	47 152	43 762	20 821	7.7	110.2
Big Spring	8.0	18.7	9.2	16.4	12.7	9.5	9.6	9.0	6.9	50.2	25 233	23 093	24 804	9.3	-6.9
Brownsville	9.0	27.5	11.7	15.0	13.0	8.2	6.9	5.3	3.4	52.8	139 722	107 027	84 997	30.5	25.9
Bryan	8.5	18.4	16.4	20.3	12.8	8.0	5.9	5.3	4.5	50.4	65 660	55 002	44 337	19.4	24.1
Carrollton	9.5	18.8	8.0	25.0	20.3	10.3	4.8	2.2	1.1	50.8	109 576	82 169	40 587	33.4	102.5
Cedar Hill	10.6	22.9	7.4	24.6	18.3	7.9	3.9	2.9	1.6	51.3	32 093	19 988	NA	60.6	NA
Cedar Park	NA	NA	NA	NA	NA	NA	NA	NA	NA	NA	26 049	5 161	NA	404.7	NA
Cleburne	7.8	20.9	8.9	15.1	14.7	8.8	7.3	8.2	8.4	53.0	26 005	22 205	19 218	17.1	15.5
College Station	4.5	9.2	54.3	14.8	8.0	4.3	2.1	1.4	1.3	46.4	67 890	52 443	37 272	29.5	40.7
Conroe	8.5	20.5	12.0	18.7	13.9	9.3	6.9	5.4	4.9	50.5	36 811	27 675	18 034	33.0	53.5
Coppell	11.6	19.3	5.1	29.1	21.0	9.5	2.7	1.1	0.7	50.4	35 958	16 881	NA	113.0	NA
Copperas Cove	11.2	22.5	14.0	21.4	13.7	8.7	5.2	2.5	0.9	49.9	29 592	24 079	19 469	22.9	23.7
Corpus Christi	8.2	21.9	9.7	18.0	14.8	9.5	7.9	6.1	3.9	51.2	277 454	257 453	231 999	7.8	11.0
Dallas	8.0	17.0	11.4	22.8	14.8	9.3	7.2	5.6	4.0	50.8	1 188 580	1 007 618	904 074	18.0	11.5
Deer Park	7.6	24.8	8.8	17.0	18.9	11.8	6.3	3.1	1.6	49.8	28 520	27 424	22 648	4.0	21.1
Del Rio	8.6	24.8	10.6	14.7	13.7	9.3	8.0	6.3	4.0	51.4	33 867	30 705	30 034	10.3	2.2
Denton	6.4	13.7	27.1	19.0	12.9	7.6	5.1	4.3	3.9	52.0	80 537	66 270	48 063	21.5	37.9
DeSoto	7.6	21.5	8.6	17.5	19.1	12.6	6.5	3.8	2.8	51.6	37 646	30 544	15 538	23.3	96.6
Duncanville	7.1	22.3	9.1	15.9	18.5	13.0	7.5	4.3	2.3	51.4	36 081	35 008	27 781	3.1	26.0
Edinburg	8.9	24.5	13.9	16.5	12.7	8.0	6.4	5.6	3.5	52.1	48 465	31 091	24 075	55.9	29.1
El Paso	8.7	23.1	11.6	17.1	13.8	9.4	7.7	5.5	3.2	52.0	563 662	515 342	425 259	9.4	21.2
Euless	8.6	16.8	10.8	26.8	15.6	11.2	6.1	2.8	1.3	50.3	46 005	38 149	24 002	20.6	58.9
Farmers Branch	7.8	16.5	9.2	17.9	14.4	12.7	11.6	7.4	2.5	50.3	27 508	24 250	24 863	13.4	-2.5
Flower Mound	10.4	23.5	6.0	21.3	22.3	10.0	3.8	2.1	0.8	49.6	50 702	15 527	NA	226.5	NA
Fort Worth	8.6	17.9	11.7	20.8	13.9	8.5	7.4	6.5	4.7	50.8	534 694	447 619	385 166	19.5	16.2
Friendswood	7.4	22.6	7.6	16.3	19.8	13.5	7.1	3.4	2.3	50.6	29 037	22 814	10 719	27.3	112.8
Frisco	NA	NA	NA	NA	NA	NA	NA	NA	NA	NA	33 714	6 138	NA	449.3	NA
Galveston	7.1	17.8	9.8	19.6	14.0	9.4	8.7	7.9	5.7	51.7	57 247	59 067	61 902	-3.1	-4.6
Garland	9.3	20.5	9.9	20.9	17.5	10.5	6.0	3.5	2.0	50.6	215 768	180 635	138 857	19.4	30.1
Georgetown	7.8	20.1	14.7	14.6	14.5	7.9	6.5	6.4	7.4	52.2	28 339	14 842	NA	90.9	NA
Grand Prairie	9.3	20.8	10.6	20.8	17.0	8.9	6.2	4.2	2.2	50.3	127 427	99 606	71 457	27.9	39.4
Grapevine	9.2	19.1	8.0	23.3	21.6	10.1	4.5	2.3	2.1	50.0	42 059	29 198	11 801	44.0	147.4
Haltom City	8.1	17.1	11.3	19.5	14.1	9.6	8.2	7.4	4.6	50.8	39 018	32 856	29 014	18.8	13.2
Harlingen	9.1	23.4	9.9	15.6	13.0	8.0	8.0	7.1	6.0	52.5	57 564	48 746	43 543	18.1	11.9
Houston	8.3	18.4	11.6	21.1	15.3	9.8	7.3	5.1	3.1	50.4	1 953 631	1 637 859	1 595 167	19.3	2.7
Huntsville	5.1	10.8	28.5	22.0	14.8	6.8	4.6	3.5	4.0	39.7	35 078	27 925	23 936	25.6	16.7
Hurst	7.2	17.8	10.1	17.4	14.8	13.4	10.4	6.2	2.8	51.1	36 273	33 574	31 420	8.0	6.9
Irving	8.3	15.8	13.3	26.6	14.3	10.0	6.3	3.4	1.9	49.8	191 615	155 037	109 943	23.6	41.0
Keller	8.8	21.7	6.8	18.8	20.2	12.7	6.0	2.6	2.4	50.1	27 345	13 683	NA	99.8	NA
Killeen	11.5	18.8	18.3	22.9	12.2	7.3	5.0	2.6	1.4	49.6	86 911	63 535	46 296	36.8	37.2
Kingsville	8.3	20.1	17.2	15.7	12.3	9.4	6.8	6.1	4.0	50.6	25 575	25 276	28 808	1.2	-12.3
Lake Jackson	8.3	21.3	7.9	19.5	17.5	11.3	7.3	4.4	2.4	50.1	26 386	22 771	19 102	15.9	19.2
Lancaster	8.5	21.8	8.6	20.2	15.1	9.3	6.8	5.3	4.4	52.8	25 894	22 117	14 807	17.1	49.4
La Porte	9.2	23.2	8.9	19.4	18.0	9.8	6.3	3.3	2.0	50.2	31 880	27 923	14 062	14.2	98.6
Laredo	9.9	26.1	12.2	16.2	12.5	8.4	6.6	4.8	3.2	52.2	176 576	122 899	91 449	43.7	34.4
League City	8.9	21.3	8.0	22.5	17.7	11.5	5.4	3.0	1.6	49.9	45 444	30 159	16 575	50.7	82.0
Lewisville	9.3	17.7	12.5	25.9	16.2	9.4	4.5	2.5	1.9	50.0	77 737	46 521	24 273	67.1	91.7
Longview	7.9	19.1	10.2	17.3	14.4	9.6	8.4	7.2	5.8	52.1	73 344	70 311	62 762	4.3	12.0
Lubbock	7.6	18.0	17.4	18.2	13.2	8.6	7.3	5.6	4.1	50.9	199 564	186 206	173 979	7.2	7.0
Lufkin	7.7	20.3	9.8	18.2	13.0	9.3	8.8	7.9	7.3	52.9	32 709	30 206	28 562	8.3	5.8
McAllen	8.2	25.2	10.5	15.6	14.3	9.1	6.8	6.0	4.3	52.4	106 414	84 021	66 281	26.7	26.8

Table D. Cities

City	Total population	Total in house-holds	House-holder	Spouse	Child Total	Child Own child under 18 years	Other relatives Total	Other relatives Under 18 years	Nonrelatives Total	Nonrelatives Unmar-ried partner	Total in group quarters	Institutionalized Correctional institutions	Institutionalized Nursing homes	Institutionalized Other institutions	Noninstitutionalized College dormitories	Noninstitutionalized Military quarters	Other
	54	55	56	57	58	59	60	61	62	63	64	65	66	67	68	69	70
TENNESSEE—Cont'd																	
Hendersonville	40 020	99.4	39.0	23.1	30.3	24.1	3.7	1.5	3.4	1.3	0.6	0.0	0.5	0.0	0.0	0.0	0.0
Jackson	59 643	94.7	39.4	16.3	28.7	22.6	5.6	2.6	4.7	1.8	5.3	0.5	1.5	0.0	2.9	0.0	0.4
Johnson City	55 469	93.9	42.8	18.9	23.4	18.0	3.8	1.3	5.1	1.9	6.1	0.1	1.3	0.8	3.5	0.0	0.5
Kingsport	44 905	97.4	43.8	21.2	25.5	19.7	4.0	1.6	2.9	1.3	2.6	0.1	2.0	0.0	0.0	0.0	0.5
Knoxville	173 890	93.7	44.1	15.5	22.4	17.1	4.7	1.8	7.0	2.1	6.3	0.1	1.1	0.4	4.0	0.0	0.8
Memphis	650 100	97.4	38.6	13.1	31.1	22.8	8.9	4.3	5.7	2.1	2.6	1.0	0.6	0.2	0.6	0.0	0.4
Murfreesboro	68 816	93.2	38.5	16.9	25.5	20.8	3.8	1.4	8.5	1.9	6.8	0.9	0.9	0.0	4.5	0.0	0.4
Nashville-Davidson	569 891	95.8	41.7	16.6	25.1	19.3	5.7	2.3	6.6	2.2	4.2	1.0	0.4	0.4	2.0	0.0	0.4
Oak Ridge	27 387	98.5	44.0	21.9	26.3	20.7	3.3	1.4	2.9	1.4	1.5	0.0	1.0	0.0	0.0	0.0	0.5
Smyrna	25 569	98.6	37.6	20.7	31.0	25.2	4.6	1.9	4.8	2.1	1.4	0.0	0.7	0.6	0.0	0.0	0.1
TEXAS	20 851 820	97.3	35.5	19.1	31.5	24.8	6.8	2.9	4.4	1.6	2.7	1.2	0.5	0.1	0.4	0.2	0.3
Abilene	115 930	90.6	35.9	18.7	27.3	22.6	4.1	2.1	4.6	1.5	9.4	4.3	0.7	0.0	2.4	0.8	1.2
Allen	43 554	100.0	32.6	24.3	38.1	33.8	2.7	0.9	2.3	0.9	0.0	0.0	0.0	0.0	0.0	0.0	0.0
Amarillo	173 627	98.7	39.0	19.7	30.5	24.8	5.2	2.5	4.2	1.8	1.3	0.0	0.8	0.1	0.1	0.0	0.3
Arlington	332 969	99.3	37.4	19.3	31.3	25.9	5.7	1.9	5.5	1.9	0.7	0.0	0.2	0.0	0.3	0.0	0.2
Austin	656 562	96.9	40.5	15.4	24.3	19.7	6.5	2.2	10.3	2.6	3.1	0.5	0.3	0.2	1.4	0.0	0.6
Baytown	66 430	99.1	35.3	18.7	33.8	26.3	7.0	3.1	4.2	1.9	0.9	0.0	0.6	0.0	0.0	0.0	0.3
Beaumont	113 866	97.3	39.0	16.9	30.5	23.1	6.8	3.2	4.1	1.7	2.7	1.0	0.7	0.1	0.5	0.0	0.4
Bedford	47 152	98.9	42.9	21.4	26.4	21.0	3.5	1.2	4.6	2.0	1.1	0.1	1.0	0.0	0.0	0.0	0.0
Big Spring	25 233	81.0	32.3	15.6	25.2	20.4	4.8	2.6	3.2	1.6	19.0	15.7	0.6	1.1	1.0	0.0	0.6
Brownsville	139 722	98.8	27.3	16.2	39.9	28.2	12.8	5.9	2.6	0.8	1.2	0.5	0.5	0.0	0.3	0.0	0.3
Bryan	65 660	96.0	36.2	16.0	28.9	23.1	6.6	2.6	8.3	1.7	4.0	2.8	0.3	0.0	0.0	0.0	0.2
Carrollton	109 576	99.5	35.7	21.5	31.7	26.3	6.1	1.6	4.4	1.5	0.5	0.0	0.0	0.0	0.0	0.0	0.2
Cedar Hill	32 093	99.2	33.5	21.4	36.4	30.1	4.8	2.1	3.1	1.3	0.8	0.0	0.4	0.0	0.4	0.0	0.0
Cedar Park	26 049	99.4	33.1	23.3	36.1	31.9	3.7	1.2	3.2	1.4	0.6	0.0	0.5	0.0	0.0	0.0	0.1
Cleburne	26 005	97.3	35.9	20.2	30.7	24.4	6.3	2.8	4.2	1.3	2.7	1.2	1.3	0.0	0.0	0.0	0.2
College Station	67 890	84.2	36.4	11.7	15.7	13.6	2.8	0.6	17.6	1.0	15.8	0.0	0.3	0.0	15.3	0.0	0.1
Conroe	36 811	97.7	35.7	17.0	29.9	24.2	8.3	3.0	6.7	2.0	2.3	1.5	0.5	0.1	0.0	0.0	0.2
Coppell	35 958	100.0	34.0	23.7	37.5	34.0	2.6	0.5	2.2	1.0	0.0	0.0	0.0	0.0	0.0	0.0	0.0
Copperas Cove	29 592	99.0	34.7	21.6	34.1	29.4	3.7	1.9	5.0	1.4	1.0	0.0	0.6	0.0	0.3	0.0	0.0
Corpus Christi	277 454	98.1	35.6	18.1	32.2	23.8	7.4	3.6	4.7	2.0	1.9	0.4	0.5	0.1	0.3	0.1	0.6
Dallas	1 188 580	98.2	38.0	14.7	28.4	22.1	10.1	3.8	7.0	2.1	1.8	0.7	0.5	0.2	0.1	0.0	0.3
Deer Park	28 520	98.9	33.7	22.5	34.7	26.5	4.8	2.1	3.1	1.3	1.1	0.0	0.3	0.0	0.0	0.0	0.8
Del Rio	33 867	98.4	31.8	18.9	36.3	26.8	9.2	4.6	2.3	1.0	1.6	0.7	0.5	0.0	0.0	0.0	0.3
Denton	80 537	90.3	38.4	15.3	22.1	18.1	4.7	1.5	9.9	2.1	9.7	1.0	0.8	1.2	6.3	0.0	0.3
DeSoto	37 646	98.8	36.4	21.4	32.5	25.3	5.6	2.5	2.9	1.2	1.2	0.0	1.1	0.0	0.0	0.0	0.0
Duncanville	36 081	99.8	35.7	21.2	33.1	24.8	6.6	2.9	3.0	1.2	0.2	0.0	0.2	0.0	0.0	0.0	0.1
Edinburg	48 465	96.3	29.3	16.7	37.8	27.9	9.3	4.2	3.3	1.0	3.7	2.2	0.2	0.8	0.4	0.0	0.1
El Paso	563 662	99.1	32.3	17.6	36.5	26.3	9.4	4.3	3.2	1.2	0.9	0.3	0.2	0.1	0.0	0.0	0.3
Euless	46 005	99.5	41.8	18.9	27.8	22.8	5.1	1.7	6.0	2.5	0.5	0.0	0.4	0.0	0.0	0.0	0.1
Farmers Branch	27 508	99.4	35.5	20.1	29.0	22.1	9.3	3.0	5.6	1.5	0.6	0.0	0.2	0.0	0.3	0.0	0.2
Flower Mound	50 702	99.6	31.9	25.7	38.0	33.9	2.3	0.7	1.7	0.8	0.4	0.0	0.2	0.1	0.0	0.0	0.1
Fort Worth	534 694	97.2	36.5	16.7	30.7	24.3	8.0	3.3	5.3	1.8	2.8	1.1	0.6	0.1	0.6	0.1	0.4
Friendswood	29 037	99.2	34.8	23.8	35.0	28.6	3.2	1.2	2.3	1.0	0.8	0.0	0.8	0.0	0.0	0.0	0.1
Frisco	33 714	99.7	35.8	25.5	32.3	29.5	3.1	0.9	2.9	1.3	0.3	0.0	0.2	0.0	0.0	0.0	0.1
Galveston	57 247	95.9	41.6	15.2	26.7	19.9	6.8	2.9	5.4	2.3	4.1	1.6	0.6	0.0	1.4	0.0	0.5
Garland	215 768	99.5	33.9	19.3	33.4	26.5	8.2	2.8	4.8	1.5	0.5	0.0	0.2	0.0	0.0	0.0	0.2
Georgetown	28 339	92.5	36.7	22.6	25.8	21.5	4.0	1.5	3.5	1.2	7.5	2.0	1.7	0.1	3.4	0.0	0.3
Grand Prairie	127 427	99.7	34.4	18.9	33.8	26.8	7.7	3.2	4.9	1.8	0.3	0.0	0.3	0.0	0.0	0.0	0.0
Grapevine	42 059	99.5	37.4	22.0	32.3	28.0	3.2	0.9	4.6	1.4	0.5	0.0	0.5	0.0	0.0	0.0	0.0
Haltom City	39 018	99.7	38.2	18.9	30.3	23.8	7.0	2.7	5.2	2.1	0.3	0.0	0.3	0.0	0.0	0.0	0.0
Harlingen	57 564	97.2	33.0	18.4	34.4	26.0	8.0	3.7	3.4	1.3	2.8	0.0	1.3	0.8	0.4	0.0	0.4
Houston	1 953 631	98.3	36.7	15.9	30.6	23.3	9.4	3.5	5.7	1.9	1.7	0.6	0.3	0.1	0.2	0.0	0.5
Huntsville	35 078	67.6	29.3	10.8	16.5	13.5	3.5	1.2	7.5	1.4	32.4	24.7	0.7	0.0	6.5	0.0	0.5
Hurst	36 273	99.4	38.8	22.2	29.2	23.1	5.0	1.9	4.2	1.6	0.6	0.0	0.6	0.0	0.0	0.0	0.1
Irving	191 615	99.4	39.8	17.5	27.5	22.4	7.6	2.2	7.0	2.2	0.6	0.0	0.1	0.0	0.2	0.0	0.1
Keller	27 345	99.9	32.3	26.2	37.4	32.6	2.4	0.9	1.6	0.7	0.1	0.0	0.0	0.0	0.0	0.0	0.0
Killeen	86 911	99.6	37.3	20.1	31.7	27.1	4.2	2.0	6.2	1.7	0.4	0.0	0.3	0.0	0.0	0.0	0.0
Kingsville	25 575	95.4	35.0	17.2	30.6	23.2	6.9	3.0	5.8	1.8	4.6	0.5	0.6	0.0	3.5	0.0	0.0
Lake Jackson	26 386	99.6	36.3	23.5	33.9	28.9	3.2	1.3	2.6	1.2	0.4	0.0	0.4	0.0	0.0	0.0	0.0
Lancaster	25 894	98.1	35.5	17.5	33.8	26.1	7.7	3.9	3.6	1.7	1.9	0.0	1.0	1.0	0.0	0.0	0.0
La Porte	31 880	99.3	34.3	21.5	34.1	26.6	5.7	2.5	3.7	1.7	0.7	0.0	0.1	0.0	0.0	0.0	0.6
Laredo	176 576	98.3	26.5	16.5	41.1	29.7	11.7	5.3	2.6	0.8	1.7	0.7	0.2	0.2	0.2	0.0	0.5
League City	45 444	99.1	35.6	23.3	32.9	27.6	3.8	1.3	3.5	1.5	0.9	0.0	0.6	0.0	0.0	0.0	0.1
Lewisville	77 737	99.5	38.6	20.2	28.8	24.6	5.3	1.5	6.5	2.2	0.5	0.0	0.1	0.0	0.9	0.0	0.3
Longview	73 344	96.6	38.7	18.9	29.2	23.4	5.5	2.6	4.2	1.7	3.4	0.9	1.1	0.2	0.0	0.0	0.3
Lubbock	199 564	95.8	38.8	17.7	27.1	21.6	5.6	2.7	6.5	1.8	4.2	0.5	0.5	0.3	2.4	0.0	0.6
Lufkin	32 709	96.6	37.4	18.5	29.8	23.0	7.1	3.5	3.7	1.6	3.4	0.3	1.9	0.3	0.3	0.0	0.5
McAllen	106 414	99.1	31.2	18.4	36.7	26.2	9.6	4.0	3.2	0.9	0.9	0.0	0.7	0.0	0.0	0.0	0.2

Table D. Cities

City	Total households	Family households — Total	With own children under 18 years	Married couple — Total	With own children under 18 years	Female householder¹ — Total	With own children under 18 years	Nonfamily households — Total	Householder living alone — Total	65 years and over	Average household size	Average family size	Households, 1990 — Total households	Female householder¹	Householder living alone
	71	72	73	74	75	76	77	78	79	80	81	82	83	84	85
TENNESSEE—Cont'd															
Hendersonville	15 823	73.1	35.7	59.3	27.4	10.7	6.5	26.9	22.3	6.5	2.55	3.00	11 441	9.3	16.7
Jackson	23 503	64.4	32.1	41.5	17.8	19.4	12.6	35.6	30.3	10.4	2.40	2.99	19 206	18.8	29.2
Johnson City	23 720	59.1	25.0	44.1	16.8	11.6	6.6	40.9	33.9	11.5	2.20	2.82	19 675	12.0	30.7
Kingsport	19 662	64.3	26.5	48.5	18.0	12.7	7.1	35.7	32.5	14.7	2.22	2.80	15 629	12.6	30.1
Knoxville	76 650	52.4	22.8	35.3	13.3	13.7	8.0	47.6	38.3	11.4	2.12	2.84	69 973	14.3	35.5
Memphis	250 721	63.2	31.3	34.1	14.8	23.8	14.2	36.8	30.5	8.9	2.52	3.18	229 829	21.9	28.3
Murfreesboro	26 511	59.4	30.7	43.8	21.1	11.9	7.8	40.6	28.3	7.0	2.42	3.02	17 110	12.0	29.9
Nashville-Davidson	237 405	58.2	26.7	39.9	16.5	14.3	8.4	41.8	33.4	8.2	2.30	2.96	207 530	14.0	30.1
Oak Ridge	12 062	63.8	26.8	49.7	18.4	11.1	6.8	36.2	32.7	15.0	2.24	2.83	11 763	10.4	29.8
Smyrna	9 608	73.5	39.8	55.0	27.5	14.2	9.8	26.5	21.1	4.3	2.62	3.04	4 836	14.2	17.8
TEXAS	7 393 354	71.0	36.8	54.0	27.1	12.7	7.6	29.0	23.7	7.3	2.74	3.28	6 070 937	11.6	23.9
Abilene	41 570	67.6	34.2	52.0	24.2	11.9	7.7	32.4	26.6	9.8	2.53	3.07	38 395	9.6	25.0
Allen	14 205	84.8	55.5	74.6	48.5	7.4	5.1	15.2	11.9	1.6	3.07	3.35	5 896	7.3	11.4
Amarillo	67 699	67.6	33.9	50.6	23.5	12.8	8.1	32.4	27.7	9.9	2.53	3.10	61 137	11.0	27.2
Arlington	124 686	68.2	38.0	51.6	27.6	11.8	8.0	31.8	24.7	3.8	2.65	3.20	100 651	9.4	24.8
Austin	265 649	53.3	26.8	38.1	18.5	10.8	6.5	46.7	32.8	4.6	2.40	3.14	192 148	11.0	34.1
Baytown	23 483	72.5	39.2	52.9	27.2	14.2	9.0	27.5	23.0	8.0	2.80	3.32	22 422	12.5	22.0
Beaumont	44 361	65.6	31.8	43.5	19.0	18.1	10.9	34.4	29.5	10.7	2.50	3.12	43 357	15.9	28.1
Bedford	20 251	61.8	29.0	49.8	21.7	8.8	5.6	38.2	31.6	5.5	2.30	2.93	17 586	7.8	27.3
Big Spring	8 155	67.0	32.8	48.3	21.3	14.1	8.7	33.0	29.2	14.6	2.51	3.10	8 256	12.8	25.8
Brownsville	38 174	84.3	50.1	59.3	36.4	20.9	11.8	15.7	13.7	6.7	3.62	3.99	26 322	20.3	15.2
Bryan	23 759	62.6	32.3	44.2	21.6	14.0	8.8	37.4	26.1	7.7	2.65	3.27	20 705	12.2	25.5
Carrollton	39 136	73.9	41.3	60.1	33.2	9.9	6.3	26.1	20.1	2.9	2.78	3.25	30 452	9.0	19.2
Cedar Hill	10 748	81.3	49.5	63.8	37.7	14.4	9.9	18.7	15.0	2.8	2.96	3.30	6 571	9.6	12.9
Cedar Park	8 621	83.0	52.8	70.3	44.2	9.6	6.7	17.0	12.5	2.1	3.00	3.29	1 666	NA	NA
Cleburne	9 335	72.5	35.8	56.2	27.0	11.9	6.6	27.5	24.0	11.6	2.71	3.20	8 150	11.1	23.8
College Station	24 691	42.0	21.0	32.2	16.4	6.8	3.9	58.0	27.1	2.4	2.32	2.98	17 878	6.3	26.7
Conroe	13 145	66.4	35.3	47.5	24.1	13.5	8.7	33.6	27.2	9.5	2.73	3.33	10 016	13.7	25.5
Coppell	12 211	80.1	54.6	69.7	46.8	8.1	6.2	19.9	16.1	1.5	2.94	3.34	5 997	6.7	14.8
Copperas Cove	10 273	78.1	47.3	62.2	35.1	12.7	9.9	21.9	16.7	3.2	2.85	3.19	8 074	9.8	14.6
Corpus Christi	98 791	71.3	36.1	50.9	24.5	15.4	8.9	28.7	23.2	7.9	2.75	3.27	89 468	13.8	22.5
Dallas	451 833	59.0	30.3	38.8	19.4	14.9	8.8	41.0	32.9	6.5	2.58	3.37	402 060	13.9	34.2
Deer Park	9 615	82.6	43.6	66.8	34.0	11.5	7.1	17.4	14.0	4.2	2.93	3.23	8 822	9.0	10.9
Del Rio	10 778	79.0	42.0	59.3	31.0	15.8	9.0	21.0	18.7	8.4	3.09	3.56	9 465	14.2	17.8
Denton	30 895	53.1	26.1	39.8	18.7	9.5	5.9	46.9	31.5	6.0	2.35	3.06	25 719	8.6	32.5
DeSoto	13 709	76.3	39.5	58.8	28.7	14.1	9.1	23.7	20.6	6.1	2.71	3.14	10 754	10.3	16.8
Duncanville	12 896	79.4	38.4	59.3	26.6	16.1	9.6	20.6	17.6	5.7	2.79	3.15	12 509	11.7	16.9
Edinburg	14 183	80.5	46.9	56.9	33.7	19.0	11.3	19.5	15.4	5.5	3.29	3.71	8 474	19.9	15.7
El Paso	182 063	77.5	42.4	54.6	29.7	18.5	10.6	22.5	19.2	7.2	3.07	3.54	160 545	16.4	17.9
Euless	19 218	60.5	31.6	45.3	22.1	10.9	7.3	39.5	31.0	3.0	2.38	3.05	15 456	9.6	28.0
Farmers Branch	9 766	71.0	32.1	56.5	25.1	9.8	5.1	29.0	22.9	7.6	2.80	3.31	8 771	9.9	18.2
Flower Mound	16 179	88.2	56.8	80.6	51.7	5.4	3.7	11.8	9.1	1.1	3.12	3.34	5 019	5.2	10.8
Fort Worth	195 078	65.4	34.7	45.8	23.7	14.7	8.7	34.6	28.6	7.7	2.67	3.33	168 274	13.3	29.0
Friendswood	10 107	80.0	43.7	68.5	36.8	8.7	5.4	20.0	17.0	6.3	2.85	3.23	7 756	8.2	14.8
Frisco	12 065	80.0	46.7	71.3	41.1	6.3	4.3	20.0	15.6	1.7	2.78	3.13	2 070	NA	NA
Galveston	23 842	57.6	26.3	36.6	14.8	16.9	9.6	42.4	35.6	11.2	2.30	3.03	24 157	16.6	34.3
Garland	73 241	75.7	41.6	56.7	30.6	13.7	8.5	24.3	19.8	5.0	2.93	3.37	63 193	11.3	18.4
Georgetown	10 393	74.2	31.8	61.6	24.2	9.5	6.1	25.8	21.5	9.3	2.52	2.92	5 179	10.5	24.9
Grand Prairie	43 791	73.8	41.3	54.9	29.8	13.7	8.8	26.2	20.7	4.5	2.90	3.38	34 958	11.4	20.6
Grapevine	15 712	72.0	42.1	58.9	33.5	9.4	6.8	28.0	22.2	3.7	2.66	3.14	10 969	7.6	20.8
Haltom City	14 922	67.0	33.7	49.4	24.0	12.0	6.8	33.0	27.1	8.0	2.61	3.19	12 756	11.2	25.7
Harlingen	19 021	75.5	38.6	55.6	27.3	16.2	9.5	24.5	20.9	10.3	2.94	3.44	15 398	14.6	20.1
Houston	717 945	63.7	33.1	43.2	22.2	15.3	8.8	36.3	29.6	6.2	2.67	3.39	616 691	14.6	31.0
Huntsville	10 266	53.3	25.3	37.0	15.6	12.5	8.0	46.7	30.8	7.5	2.31	2.97	7 853	11.9	32.8
Hurst	14 076	72.9	33.5	57.2	24.5	11.6	6.8	27.1	22.4	7.2	2.56	2.99	12 779	10.5	20.1
Irving	76 241	60.6	31.3	44.1	21.8	11.2	7.1	39.4	31.3	3.8	2.50	3.19	63 236	9.9	30.1
Keller	8 827	89.0	53.2	81.3	48.0	5.6	3.8	11.0	8.9	2.0	3.09	3.30	4 487	5.4	9.0
Killeen	32 447	70.8	42.0	53.9	29.5	13.4	10.3	29.2	22.3	3.3	2.67	3.12	23 248	11.3	20.3
Kingsville	8 943	68.6	34.5	49.1	23.4	14.9	9.0	31.4	23.5	7.7	2.73	3.28	8 529	13.5	22.8
Lake Jackson	9 588	76.6	42.6	64.7	34.5	8.5	5.8	23.4	20.0	7.3	2.74	3.18	8 141	6.5	18.0
Lancaster	9 182	75.1	40.6	49.4	24.7	20.8	13.4	24.9	21.3	6.3	2.77	3.22	7 703	15.3	19.2
La Porte	10 928	78.5	43.2	62.8	33.6	11.4	7.0	21.5	17.4	4.6	2.90	3.28	9 144	9.4	15.3
Laredo	46 852	85.3	52.3	62.0	40.2	18.7	10.2	14.7	12.7	5.2	3.70	4.05	32 029	18.2	12.9
League City	16 189	77.0	42.6	65.4	35.0	8.2	5.5	23.0	18.4	3.2	2.78	3.19	10 586	7.9	17.1
Lewisville	30 043	66.0	36.2	52.3	27.8	9.6	6.4	34.0	25.2	2.9	2.58	3.13	17 683	8.8	23.3
Longview	28 363	67.4	33.2	48.9	22.0	14.5	9.1	32.6	27.9	10.7	2.50	3.06	27 206	12.3	26.7
Lubbock	77 527	62.6	30.3	45.6	20.4	12.9	7.8	37.4	28.3	8.0	2.47	3.07	69 143	10.7	26.8
Lufkin	12 247	68.3	32.9	49.4	22.3	14.7	8.6	31.7	27.9	11.9	2.58	3.17	11 222	13.6	27.1
McAllen	33 151	78.7	43.2	59.0	32.7	16.0	9.0	21.3	17.9	6.4	3.18	3.64	24 905	15.0	17.4

¹No spouse present.

Table D. Cities

City	Percent change of households, 1990–2000	Total housing units	Occupied housing units (percent)	Total	For seasonal, recreational, or occasional use	Homeowner vacancy rate (percent)	Rental vacancy rate (percent)	Total	Percent owner-occupied housing units	Percent renter-occupied housing units	Average household size of owner-occupied units	Average household size of renter-occupied units
	86	87	88	89	90	91	92	93	94	95	96	97
TENNESSEE—Cont'd												
Hendersonville	38.3	16 507	95.9	4.1	0.3	1.9	6.2	15 823	71.4	28.6	2.72	2.13
Jackson	22.4	25 501	92.2	7.8	0.4	2.2	9.1	23 503	56.7	43.3	2.50	2.28
Johnson City	20.6	25 730	92.2	7.8	0.4	2.9	8.5	23 720	57.2	42.8	2.36	1.98
Kingsport	25.8	21 796	90.2	9.8	0.4	3.5	12.8	19 662	64.8	35.2	2.31	2.08
Knoxville	9.5	84 981	90.2	9.8	0.3	2.9	10.5	76 650	51.2	48.8	2.29	1.95
Memphis	9.1	271 552	92.3	7.7	0.3	2.0	8.4	250 721	55.8	44.2	2.62	2.40
Murfreesboro	54.9	28 815	92.0	8.0	0.4	3.1	9.8	26 511	52.1	47.9	2.63	2.19
Nashville-Davidson	14.4	252 977	93.8	6.2	0.4	2.0	6.5	237 405	55.3	44.7	2.43	2.13
Oak Ridge	2.5	13 417	89.9	10.1	0.4	2.3	18.3	12 062	68.4	31.6	2.33	2.03
Smyrna	98.7	10 016	95.9	4.1	0.1	1.8	5.3	9 608	64.5	35.5	2.76	2.38
TEXAS	21.8	8 157 575	90.6	9.4	2.1	1.8	8.5	7 393 354	63.8	36.2	2.87	2.53
Abilene	8.3	45 618	91.1	8.9	0.4	2.3	10.4	41 570	58.6	41.4	2.61	2.40
Allen	140.9	15 227	93.3	6.7	0.4	1.6	26.3	14 205	85.7	14.3	3.13	2.69
Amarillo	10.7	72 408	93.5	6.5	0.3	1.7	8.1	67 699	63.3	36.7	2.64	2.34
Arlington	23.9	130 628	95.5	4.5	0.3	1.4	6.1	124 686	54.7	45.3	2.87	2.38
Austin	38.3	276 842	96.0	4.0	0.5	1.0	3.5	265 649	44.8	55.2	2.65	2.19
Baytown	4.7	26 203	89.6	10.4	0.6	1.4	14.3	23 483	59.6	40.4	2.91	2.64
Beaumont	2.3	48 815	90.9	9.1	0.4	1.7	9.9	44 361	59.9	40.1	2.58	2.37
Bedford	15.2	21 113	95.9	4.1	0.2	0.7	6.7	20 251	55.0	45.0	2.64	1.89
Big Spring	-1.2	9 865	82.7	17.3	0.4	4.9	23.7	8 155	63.6	36.4	2.53	2.47
Brownsville	45.0	42 323	90.2	9.8	3.0	1.1	8.0	38 174	61.2	38.8	3.74	3.42
Bryan	14.8	25 703	92.4	7.6	0.6	2.0	7.7	23 759	50.8	49.2	2.80	2.51
Carrollton	28.5	40 458	96.7	3.3	0.4	1.0	5.0	39 136	65.7	34.3	2.90	2.56
Cedar Hill	63.6	11 075	97.0	3.0	0.1	1.3	2.8	10 748	81.0	19.0	3.03	2.67
Cedar Park	417.5	8 914	96.7	3.3	0.1	1.5	4.6	8 621	84.4	15.6	3.04	2.80
Cleburne	14.5	9 910	94.2	5.8	0.3	1.9	4.6	9 335	66.8	33.2	2.71	2.70
College Station	38.1	26 054	94.8	5.2	0.4	1.4	5.0	24 691	30.6	69.4	2.78	2.11
Conroe	31.2	14 378	91.4	8.6	0.3	1.5	10.0	13 145	47.3	52.7	3.00	2.50
Coppell	103.6	12 587	97.0	3.0	0.3	1.2	5.5	12 211	77.2	22.8	3.15	2.23
Copperas Cove	27.2	11 120	92.4	7.6	0.2	2.6	9.9	10 273	54.2	45.8	2.94	2.76
Corpus Christi	10.4	107 831	91.6	8.4	1.0	2.0	9.5	98 791	59.6	40.4	2.89	2.56
Dallas	12.4	484 117	93.3	6.7	0.3	1.4	7.0	451 833	43.2	56.8	2.78	2.44
Deer Park	9.0	9 921	96.9	3.1	0.2	0.4	8.3	9 615	79.3	20.7	2.97	2.79
Del Rio	13.9	11 895	90.6	9.4	0.7	1.9	8.4	10 778	64.6	35.4	3.17	2.96
Denton	20.1	32 716	94.4	5.6	0.2	2.0	5.5	30 895	41.9	58.1	2.67	2.12
DeSoto	27.5	14 069	97.4	2.6	0.2	1.2	2.6	13 709	72.2	27.8	2.88	2.30
Duncanville	3.1	13 290	97.0	3.0	0.1	1.0	4.6	12 896	71.7	28.3	2.84	2.66
Edinburg	67.4	16 031	88.5	11.5	2.5	1.7	8.2	14 183	61.7	38.3	3.45	3.03
El Paso	13.4	193 663	94.0	6.0	0.4	1.6	7.9	182 063	61.4	38.6	3.20	2.86
Euless	24.3	20 136	95.4	4.6	0.3	1.0	5.9	19 218	43.8	56.2	2.66	2.17
Farmers Branch	11.3	10 115	96.5	3.5	0.3	1.1	4.8	9 766	68.0	32.0	2.70	3.02
Flower Mound	222.4	16 833	96.1	3.9	0.1	1.6	17.2	16 179	92.9	7.1	3.15	2.74
Fort Worth	15.9	211 035	92.4	7.6	0.3	1.9	9.1	195 078	55.9	44.1	2.84	2.44
Friendswood	30.3	10 405	97.1	2.9	0.2	1.1	6.1	10 107	80.1	19.9	3.00	2.25
Frisco	482.9	13 683	88.2	11.8	0.2	2.0	34.9	12 065	81.3	18.7	2.86	2.44
Galveston	-1.3	30 017	79.4	20.6	7.5	3.2	15.9	23 842	43.6	56.4	2.43	2.20
Garland	15.9	75 300	97.3	2.7	0.1	1.1	3.5	73 241	65.6	34.4	2.98	2.84
Georgetown	100.7	10 902	95.3	4.7	0.6	2.2	3.6	10 393	68.7	31.3	2.54	2.48
Grand Prairie	25.3	46 425	94.3	5.7	0.6	1.2	7.8	43 791	61.2	38.8	3.06	2.65
Grapevine	43.2	16 486	95.3	4.7	0.3	0.6	9.2	15 712	65.0	35.0	2.88	2.26
Haltom City	17.0	15 716	94.9	5.1	0.4	1.1	5.4	14 922	59.5	40.5	2.77	2.37
Harlingen	23.5	23 008	82.7	17.3	8.9	2.3	13.1	19 021	61.1	38.9	2.94	2.94
Houston	16.4	782 009	91.8	8.2	0.4	1.6	8.7	717 945	45.8	54.2	2.84	2.54
Huntsville	30.7	11 508	89.2	10.8	0.5	2.3	11.5	10 266	43.5	56.5	2.54	2.13
Hurst	10.1	14 729	95.6	4.4	0.2	0.7	9.1	14 076	66.1	33.9	2.60	2.48
Irving	20.6	80 293	95.0	5.0	0.6	1.1	5.2	76 241	37.2	62.8	2.76	2.35
Keller	96.7	9 216	95.8	4.2	0.1	2.9	6.9	8 827	92.7	7.3	3.12	2.74
Killeen	39.6	35 343	91.8	8.2	0.2	3.0	9.1	32 447	46.4	53.6	2.92	2.45
Kingsville	4.9	10 427	85.8	14.2	0.4	2.3	17.1	8 943	55.0	45.0	2.85	2.58
Lake Jackson	17.8	10 475	91.5	8.5	0.8	1.6	16.7	9 588	71.1	28.9	2.87	2.41
Lancaster	19.2	9 590	95.7	4.3	0.2	1.6	5.2	9 182	65.6	34.4	2.88	2.55
La Porte	19.5	11 720	93.2	6.8	0.4	1.9	11.4	10 928	77.2	22.8	2.98	2.61
Laredo	46.3	50 319	93.1	6.9	0.4	1.3	5.8	46 852	64.4	35.6	3.87	3.40
League City	52.9	17 280	93.7	6.3	0.6	2.3	11.5	16 189	77.0	23.0	2.92	2.32
Lewisville	69.9	31 764	94.6	5.4	0.2	1.5	7.7	30 043	53.9	46.1	2.92	2.18
Longview	4.3	30 726	92.3	7.7	0.4	2.0	10.1	28 363	58.3	41.7	2.61	2.34
Lubbock	12.1	84 066	92.2	7.8	0.3	1.7	10.1	77 527	55.8	44.2	2.64	2.25
Lufkin	9.1	13 402	91.4	8.6	0.5	2.2	8.3	12 247	60.0	40.0	2.64	2.49
McAllen	33.1	37 922	87.4	12.6	4.5	2.2	10.7	33 151	63.3	36.7	3.33	2.92

Table D. Cities

STATE Place code	City	Land area, 2000[1] (sq km)	Total persons	Rank	Per square kilometer	Land area, 1990[1] (sq km)	Total persons	Rank	Per square kilometer	White	Black or African American	American Indian or Alaska Native	Asian	Native Hawaiian and other Pacific Islander	Some other race
		1	2	3	4	5	6	7	8	9	10	11	12	13	14
	TEXAS—Cont'd														
48 45744	McKinney	150.3	54 369	602	361.7	115.0	21 283	1 539	185.1	78.4	7.2	0.5	1.5	0.1	10.2
48 46452	Mansfield	94.5	28 031	1 322	296.6	100.3	15 615	2 077	155.7	86.4	4.4	0.6	1.2	0.0	5.7
48 47892	Mesquite	112.4	124 523	178	1 107.9	110.9	101 484	198	915.1	73.5	13.3	0.6	3.7	0.1	6.4
48 48072	Midland	172.5	94 996	261	550.7	170.5	89 343	235	524.0	75.5	8.4	0.6	1.0	0.0	12.5
48 48768	Mission	62.5	45 408	755	726.5	36.0	28 653	1 109	795.9	77.6	0.4	0.4	0.6	0.0	18.6
48 48804	Missouri City	76.9	52 913	627	688.1	60.1	36 143	829	601.4	44.3	38.3	0.2	10.6	0.0	4.5
48 50256	Nacogdoches	65.3	29 914	1 227	458.1	64.6	30 872	1 018	477.9	66.0	25.1	0.3	1.1	0.1	5.8
48 50820	New Braunfels	75.8	36 494	962	481.5	65.9	27 334	1 166	414.8	84.3	1.4	0.6	0.6	0.0	10.9
48 52356	North Richland Hills	47.2	55 635	575	1 178.7	47.2	45 895	624	972.4	88.5	2.7	0.5	2.7	0.2	3.4
48 53388	Odessa	95.3	90 943	280	954.3	91.6	89 699	234	979.2	73.4	5.9	0.8	0.9	0.0	16.1
48 55080	Paris	110.7	25 898	1 455	233.9	70.4	24 799	1 301	352.3	72.9	22.3	0.9	0.7	0.0	1.6
48 56000	Pasadena	114.4	141 674	155	1 238.4	113.4	119 604	155	1 054.7	71.4	1.6	0.7	1.8	0.0	21.3
48 56348	Pearland	101.9	37 640	939	369.4	51.0	18 927	1 730	371.1	82.6	5.3	0.4	3.6	0.0	6.1
48 57200	Pharr	53.9	46 660	731	865.7	40.9	32 921	938	804.9	79.5	0.2	0.7	0.2	0.0	17.3
48 58016	Plano	185.4	222 030	80	1 197.6	171.6	127 885	143	745.3	78.3	5.0	0.4	10.2	0.0	3.9
48 58820	Port Arthur	214.8	57 755	531	268.9	200.0	58 551	433	292.8	39.0	43.7	0.5	5.9	0.0	8.9
48 61796	Richardson	74.0	91 802	277	1 240.6	73.2	74 840	309	1 022.4	75.4	6.2	0.4	11.7	0.1	3.7
48 63500	Round Rock	67.7	61 136	486	903.0	49.5	30 923	1 017	624.7	76.8	7.7	0.5	2.9	0.1	9.5
48 63572	Rowlett	52.4	44 503	773	849.3	48.4	23 260	1 401	480.6	81.8	9.0	0.5	3.3	0.1	3.5
48 64472	San Angelo	144.8	88 439	291	610.8	124.0	84 462	263	681.1	77.1	4.7	0.7	1.0	0.1	14.0
48 65000	San Antonio	1 055.6	1 144 646	9	1 084.4	862.6	976 514	10	1 132.1	67.7	6.8	0.8	1.6	0.1	19.3
48 65516	San Juan	28.5	26 229	1 432	920.3	9.5	12 561	2 545	1 322.2	81.2	0.3	0.5	0.1	0.0	15.9
48 65600	San Marcos	47.2	34 733	1 037	735.9	45.1	28 738	1 102	637.2	72.6	5.5	0.7	1.2	0.1	17.0
48 67496	Sherman	99.8	35 082	1 021	351.5	96.8	31 584	989	326.3	78.5	11.2	1.3	1.1	0.0	5.3
48 68636	Socorro	45.3	27 152	1 373	599.4	45.3	22 995	1 425	507.6	73.4	0.4	1.3	0.1	0.0	22.0
48 70808	Sugar Land	62.4	63 328	465	1 014.9	31.8	33 712	904	1 060.1	66.0	5.2	0.2	23.8	0.0	2.3
48 72176	Temple	169.3	54 514	600	322.0	111.3	46 150	618	414.6	69.8	16.5	0.5	1.5	0.1	9.2
48 72368	Texarkana	66.4	34 782	1 035	523.8	54.5	32 294	962	592.6	59.2	37.0	0.3	0.7	0.0	1.4
48 72392	Texas City	161.5	41 521	830	257.1	160.9	40 822	720	253.7	60.7	27.5	0.5	0.9	0.0	8.2
48 72530	The Colony	35.4	26 531	1 406	749.5	30.3	22 113	1 487	729.8	84.5	5.2	0.7	1.7	0.0	5.3
48 74144	Tyler	127.7	83 650	321	655.1	102.7	75 450	306	734.7	61.9	26.6	0.3	1.0	0.0	8.5
48 75428	Victoria	85.4	60 603	490	709.6	78.0	55 076	470	706.1	71.2	7.6	0.5	1.0	0.0	17.3
48 76000	Waco	218.1	113 726	205	521.4	196.3	103 590	194	527.7	60.8	22.6	0.5	1.4	0.1	12.4
48 77272	Weslaco	32.9	26 935	1 386	818.7	21.7	22 739	1 444	1 047.9	74.9	0.3	0.5	1.1	0.1	20.9
48 79000	Wichita Falls	183.1	104 197	229	569.1	140.2	96 259	214	686.6	75.1	12.4	0.9	2.2	0.1	6.4
49 00000	UTAH	212 751.1	2 233 169	X	10.5	212 815.5	1 722 850	X	8.1	89.2	0.8	1.3	1.7	0.7	4.2
49 07690	Bountiful	34.9	41 301	834	1 183.4	27.6	37 544	805	1 360.3	95.6	0.2	0.3	1.1	0.3	1.1
49 13850	Clearfield	20.1	25 974	1 449	1 292.2	19.3	21 435	1 532	1 110.6	83.2	3.6	1.6	2.8	0.3	4.8
49 20120	Draper	78.6	25 220	1 494	320.9	NA	7 143	3 364	NA	91.2	1.5	0.7	1.3	0.4	2.7
49 43660	Layton	53.6	58 474	524	1 090.9	47.3	41 784	699	883.4	89.9	1.6	0.5	2.1	0.3	3.1
49 45860	Logan	42.8	42 670	807	997.0	36.6	32 771	947	895.4	88.9	0.6	0.8	3.6	0.3	4.1
49 49710	Midvale	15.1	27 029	1 380	1 790.0	8.9	11 886	2 684	1 335.5	82.4	1.2	1.3	1.8	0.6	10.0
49 53230	Murray	24.9	34 024	1 059	1 366.4	24.7	31 274	1 000	1 266.2	91.6	1.0	0.6	1.8	0.3	2.8
49 55980	Ogden	69.0	77 226	361	1 119.2	67.6	63 943	384	945.9	79.0	2.3	1.2	1.4	0.2	12.9
49 57300	Orem	47.8	84 324	316	1 764.1	46.5	67 561	356	1 452.9	90.8	0.3	0.7	1.5	0.9	3.6
49 62470	Provo	102.7	105 166	227	1 024.0	100.0	86 835	249	868.4	88.5	0.5	0.8	1.8	0.8	5.1
49 64340	Riverton	32.6	25 011	1 505	767.2	21.1	11 261	2 816	533.7	96.4	0.2	0.2	0.7	0.2	1.0
49 65110	Roy	19.7	32 885	1 101	1 669.3	17.5	24 560	1 319	1 403.4	90.7	1.2	0.6	1.8	0.1	3.6
49 65330	St. George	166.8	49 663	673	297.7	148.9	28 572	1 113	191.9	92.3	0.2	1.6	0.6	0.6	2.9
49 67000	Salt Lake City	282.5	181 743	115	643.3	282.4	159 928	110	566.3	79.2	1.9	1.3	3.6	1.9	8.5
49 67440	Sandy	57.8	88 418	292	1 529.7	51.8	75 240	307	1 452.5	93.5	0.5	0.4	2.2	0.3	1.5
49 70850	South Jordan	54.0	29 437	1 250	545.1	52.2	12 215	2 613	234.0	95.5	0.3	0.1	1.0	0.5	1.3
49 75360	Taylorsville	27.7	57 439	541	2 073.6	NA	NA	NA	NA	85.5	0.9	1.0	3.0	1.6	5.4
49 82950	West Jordan	80.0	68 336	423	854.2	69.5	42 915	671	617.5	88.8	0.6	0.6	2.0	0.9	4.8
49 83470	West Valley City	91.7	108 896	215	1 187.5	88.1	86 969	247	987.2	78.2	1.1	1.2	4.3	2.9	8.7
50 00000	VERMONT	23 956.2	608 827	X	25.4	23 955.7	562 758	X	23.5	96.8	0.5	0.4	0.9	0.0	0.2
50 10675	Burlington	27.4	38 889	905	1 419.3	27.3	39 127	760	1 433.2	92.3	1.8	0.5	2.7	0.0	0.5
51 00000	VIRGINIA	102 548.2	7 078 515	X	69.0	102 558.3	6 189 197	X	60.3	72.3	19.6	0.3	3.7	0.1	2.0
51 01000	Alexandria	39.3	128 283	172	3 264.2	39.6	111 182	169	2 807.6	59.8	22.5	0.3	5.7	0.1	7.4
51 07784	Blacksburg	50.1	39 573	884	789.9	48.6	34 590	871	711.7	84.4	4.4	0.1	7.8	0.1	0.9
51 14968	Charlottesville	26.6	45 049	761	1 693.6	26.6	40 475	726	1 521.6	69.6	22.2	0.1	4.9	0.0	1.0
51 16000	Chesapeake	882.5	199 184	93	225.7	882.4	151 982	116	172.2	66.9	28.5	0.4	1.8	0.1	0.7
51 21344	Danville	111.5	48 411	699	434.2	111.5	53 056	506	475.8	53.9	44.1	0.2	0.6	0.0	0.5
51 35000	Hampton	134.1	146 437	148	1 092.0	134.2	133 811	135	997.1	49.5	44.7	0.4	1.8	0.1	1.0
51 35624	Harrisonburg	45.5	40 468	857	889.4	45.5	30 707	1 027	674.9	84.8	5.9	0.2	3.1	0.0	3.3
51 44984	Leesburg	30.0	28 311	1 309	943.7	29.9	16 202	2 007	541.9	83.3	9.2	0.2	2.6	0.0	2.5

[1] Dry land or land partially or temporarily covered by water.

Table D. Cities

City	Population and population characteristics, 2000 (cont'd)								Population and population characteristics, 1990				
	Race (percent) (cont'd)								Race (percent)				
	Race alone or in combination												
	Two or more races	White	Black	American Indian or Alaska Native	Asian	Native Hawaiian and other Pacific Islander	Some other race	Hispanic[1]	White	Black or African American	American Indian or Alaska Native	Asian and Pacific Islander	Hispanic[1]
	15	16	17	18	19	20	21	22	23	24	25	26	27
TEXAS—Cont'd													
McKinney	2.1	80.3	7.7	1.1	1.8	0.1	11.3	18.2	75.9	12.9	0.5	0.5	16.9
Mansfield	1.7	87.9	4.8	1.0	1.5	0.1	6.6	12.8	92.9	2.7	0.5	0.4	8.6
Mesquite	2.3	75.6	13.8	1.2	4.1	0.1	7.6	15.7	87.2	5.8	0.5	2.6	8.8
Midland	2.0	77.2	8.7	1.0	1.2	0.1	13.7	29.0	79.8	9.1	0.4	1.0	21.3
Mission	2.3	79.8	0.5	0.6	0.8	0.0	20.7	81.0	75.4	0.2	0.2	0.1	80.1
Missouri City	2.1	45.7	39.1	0.5	11.2	0.1	5.5	10.9	60.6	29.4	0.3	6.3	9.2
Nacogdoches	1.6	67.3	25.4	0.7	1.4	0.2	6.6	10.8	73.5	22.5	0.2	0.9	5.1
New Braunfels	2.2	86.3	1.6	1.0	0.8	0.1	12.5	34.5	85.5	1.3	0.2	0.3	34.8
North Richland Hills	2.1	90.3	2.9	1.2	3.1	0.2	4.3	9.5	93.6	1.8	0.5	1.6	5.8
Odessa	2.9	76.1	6.2	1.3	1.1	0.1	18.2	41.4	75.4	6.0	0.5	0.7	31.1
Paris	1.6	74.3	22.9	1.7	0.8	0.1	1.9	4.1	75.9	22.1	1.0	0.6	1.2
Pasadena	3.1	74.2	1.9	1.1	2.1	0.1	23.8	48.2	83.7	1.0	0.5	1.6	28.8
Pearland	1.8	84.3	5.6	0.8	4.1	0.1	7.0	16.2	90.9	1.7	0.3	1.4	12.4
Pharr	2.0	81.4	0.3	0.8	0.3	0.0	19.2	90.6	70.2	0.1	0.2	0.1	88.4
Plano	2.3	80.2	5.4	0.8	11.0	0.1	4.9	10.1	88.5	4.1	0.3	4.0	6.2
Port Arthur	2.1	40.6	44.3	0.8	6.2	0.1	10.2	17.5	49.3	42.2	0.3	4.8	8.2
Richardson	2.6	77.5	6.6	1.0	12.6	0.2	4.8	10.3	86.8	4.7	0.3	6.6	4.3
Round Rock	2.6	78.9	8.4	0.9	3.6	0.2	10.7	22.1	84.6	5.5	0.4	1.1	18.7
Rowlett	1.8	83.4	9.4	0.8	3.8	0.1	4.4	8.8	90.5	5.4	0.4	1.4	6.0
San Angelo	2.5	79.2	5.2	1.2	1.3	0.2	15.5	33.2	78.8	4.8	0.4	1.1	28.0
San Antonio	3.7	70.8	7.4	1.3	2.1	0.2	22.0	58.7	72.2	7.0	0.4	1.1	55.6
San Juan	1.9	82.9	0.5	0.8	0.1	0.1	17.6	95.1	78.4	0.1	0.2	0.1	90.8
San Marcos	2.9	75.0	6.0	1.2	1.7	0.2	18.8	36.5	78.4	5.3	0.2	0.9	37.4
Sherman	2.6	80.8	11.9	2.4	1.4	0.2	6.1	12.1	83.2	12.6	0.9	0.8	4.4
Socorro	2.8	76.1	0.5	1.5	0.1	0.0	24.6	96.4	78.6	0.1	0.3	0.0	95.5
Sugar Land	2.4	67.8	5.5	0.5	25.1	0.1	3.5	8.0	79.2	5.0	0.2	12.9	8.5
Temple	2.4	71.8	17.3	1.0	2.0	0.2	10.4	17.8	72.8	17.1	0.4	0.9	13.7
Texarkana	1.2	60.1	37.6	0.8	1.0	0.1	1.7	2.9	63.0	35.9	0.4	0.5	1.1
Texas City	2.1	62.5	28.0	0.8	1.1	0.1	9.6	20.5	67.1	25.1	0.4	1.1	15.9
The Colony	2.6	86.9	5.7	1.3	2.2	0.1	6.5	13.3	88.6	4.8	0.6	1.8	8.6
Tyler	1.6	63.3	27.0	0.7	1.2	0.1	9.4	15.8	66.1	28.2	0.3	0.5	8.9
Victoria	2.4	73.2	8.0	0.8	1.2	0.1	19.1	42.9	76.9	7.9	0.3	0.4	37.9
Waco	2.3	62.6	23.3	1.0	1.7	0.1	13.7	23.6	67.6	23.1	0.3	0.9	16.3
Weslaco	2.2	76.9	0.4	0.7	1.2	0.1	22.9	83.8	79.4	0.2	0.2	0.5	79.7
Wichita Falls	3.0	77.6	13.2	1.7	2.8	0.2	7.7	14.0	80.4	11.2	0.7	1.8	10.0
UTAH	2.1	91.1	1.1	1.8	2.2	1.0	5.1	9.0	93.8	0.7	1.4	1.9	4.9
Bountiful	1.3	96.8	0.4	0.5	1.7	0.6	1.5	2.9	98.2	0.1	0.3	0.9	1.6
Clearfield	3.7	86.2	4.5	2.4	4.1	0.7	6.1	10.6	85.7	4.6	1.7	4.0	8.3
Draper	2.1	93.0	1.8	1.3	1.9	0.7	3.5	5.8	90.6	3.1	1.4	1.4	7.7
Layton	2.5	92.1	2.1	1.1	3.1	0.5	3.9	7.0	92.7	2.1	0.7	2.3	5.6
Logan	1.6	90.3	0.9	1.1	4.1	0.4	4.8	8.2	91.4	0.6	1.3	5.1	3.1
Midvale	2.7	84.8	1.6	1.7	2.4	0.8	11.5	20.8	87.0	0.4	1.2	3.9	15.3
Murray	1.9	93.3	1.4	0.9	2.3	0.6	3.5	7.5	95.8	0.7	0.5	1.5	4.2
Ogden	2.9	81.5	2.9	1.9	2.0	0.3	14.4	23.6	87.4	2.7	1.1	1.8	12.0
Orem	2.2	92.7	0.6	1.2	2.0	1.3	4.5	8.6	96.4	0.1	0.8	1.5	3.0
Provo	2.4	90.7	0.7	1.3	2.6	1.4	6.0	10.5	94.1	0.3	1.1	2.7	4.2
Riverton	1.2	97.5	0.4	0.5	1.0	0.4	1.5	3.2	98.1	0.1	0.1	0.6	2.8
Roy	2.0	92.6	1.5	0.9	2.4	0.2	4.4	7.7	94.5	1.0	0.5	1.7	5.2
St. George	1.8	93.9	0.5	2.2	0.9	1.0	3.5	6.7	96.8	0.2	1.6	0.7	2.0
Salt Lake City	3.5	82.2	2.5	1.9	4.3	2.3	10.6	18.8	87.0	1.7	1.6	4.7	9.7
Sandy	1.7	95.0	0.7	0.6	2.8	0.6	2.1	4.4	97.1	0.2	0.3	1.7	2.5
South Jordan	1.3	96.7	0.4	0.4	1.5	0.8	1.7	3.3	98.0	0.1	0.2	0.9	2.1
Taylorsville	2.6	87.7	1.3	1.4	3.6	2.0	6.6	12.2	0.0	0.0	0.0	0.0	0.0
West Jordan	2.3	90.8	0.9	1.0	2.6	1.3	5.8	10.1	94.0	0.3	0.6	1.9	6.5
West Valley City	3.5	81.1	1.6	1.7	5.0	3.5	10.7	18.5	90.8	0.8	1.1	4.0	7.1
VERMONT	1.2	97.9	0.7	1.1	1.1	0.1	0.4	0.9	98.6	0.3	0.3	0.6	0.7
Burlington	2.3	94.2	2.4	1.3	3.2	0.1	1.2	1.4	96.8	1.0	0.3	1.5	1.2
VIRGINIA	2.0	73.9	20.4	0.7	4.3	0.1	2.7	4.7	77.4	18.8	0.2	2.6	2.6
Alexandria	4.3	62.7	24.0	0.7	6.7	0.2	10.1	14.7	69.1	21.9	0.3	4.2	9.7
Blacksburg	2.4	86.2	4.9	0.5	8.8	0.2	1.9	2.3	87.4	4.3	0.1	7.7	1.8
Charlottesville	2.1	71.2	23.2	0.5	5.7	0.2	1.5	2.4	76.1	21.2	0.1	2.3	1.2
Chesapeake	1.6	68.1	29.2	0.9	2.4	0.1	1.0	2.0	70.7	27.4	0.3	1.2	1.3
Danville	0.8	54.5	44.5	0.4	0.7	0.1	0.7	1.3	62.7	36.6	0.1	0.5	0.5
Hampton	2.4	51.1	46.1	1.1	2.5	0.2	1.6	2.8	58.4	38.9	0.3	1.7	2.0
Harrisonburg	2.6	87.1	6.7	0.5	4.1	0.1	4.3	8.8	91.1	6.6	0.1	1.5	1.6
Leesburg	2.2	85.2	10.0	0.5	3.2	0.1	3.3	5.9	85.3	12.3	0.2	1.4	2.4

[1] Hispanic persons may be of any race.

Table D. Cities

City	Population and population characteristics, 2000										
	Age (percent)										
	Under 5 years	5 to 17 years	18 to 24 years	25 to 34 years	35 to 44 years	45 to 54 years	55 to 64 years	65 to 74 years	75 years and over	Median age (years)	Percent Female
	28	29	30	31	32	33	34	35	36	37	38
TEXAS—Cont'd											
McKinney	10.1	20.9	9.3	18.1	18.3	10.7	5.8	3.5	3.3	30.6	49.4
Mansfield	8.4	23.4	7.8	14.9	19.7	13.2	6.9	3.4	2.3	32.3	49.3
Mesquite	7.7	22.8	9.2	15.2	18.7	12.4	6.9	4.3	2.8	31.9	51.8
Midland	7.5	22.4	9.0	12.2	16.0	13.1	7.4	6.9	5.4	34.1	52.0
Mission	9.2	22.9	9.8	13.8	13.0	10.1	6.9	7.4	6.8	30.5	52.3
Missouri City	7.3	23.5	7.0	11.3	19.7	17.8	7.9	3.5	1.9	35.5	51.6
Nacogdoches	5.8	14.4	30.9	12.1	10.2	9.5	6.0	5.2	5.9	24.4	53.3
New Braunfels	7.1	18.6	8.5	14.2	14.2	12.6	8.0	7.6	9.3	36.2	52.1
North Richland Hills	7.1	20.2	9.0	14.3	18.3	14.4	7.9	5.0	3.9	34.7	50.8
Odessa	8.0	21.8	10.6	12.9	14.9	12.3	7.7	6.5	5.2	32.3	51.8
Paris	7.4	17.9	10.0	12.7	13.1	11.6	9.2	7.7	10.3	36.5	53.7
Pasadena	9.3	22.3	11.4	15.8	15.4	11.4	6.5	4.5	3.4	29.2	50.0
Pearland	8.0	20.9	7.3	15.1	19.1	13.7	7.5	5.0	3.4	34.3	50.9
Pharr	10.6	24.2	11.3	14.6	11.7	9.2	6.7	6.8	5.1	27.4	52.4
Plano	8.3	20.4	7.0	16.0	20.5	15.4	7.5	2.9	2.1	34.1	50.2
Port Arthur	7.8	20.8	9.7	12.1	14.1	12.0	7.9	7.7	7.8	34.6	52.3
Richardson	6.7	18.1	8.7	15.2	17.5	14.5	9.4	5.9	4.1	35.8	50.6
Round Rock	9.7	22.2	8.5	19.6	19.2	11.6	4.7	2.3	2.2	30.1	50.2
Rowlett	8.7	24.8	5.6	15.1	21.9	13.2	5.6	3.1	2.1	32.8	50.6
San Angelo	7.1	18.8	13.8	13.0	13.9	11.7	7.9	6.9	6.9	32.8	52.1
San Antonio	8.1	20.5	10.8	15.5	15.3	12.1	7.3	5.6	4.8	31.7	51.7
San Juan	10.5	26.9	11.9	15.1	12.3	10.0	5.5	4.4	3.3	25.5	51.7
San Marcos	4.9	10.4	41.9	16.0	8.8	6.5	4.2	3.3	3.9	23.3	50.8
Sherman	7.2	17.3	13.1	13.6	14.2	11.6	7.7	6.9	8.3	34.0	52.1
Socorro	9.2	26.9	11.5	13.6	14.3	11.5	6.7	4.2	2.1	26.6	51.6
Sugar Land	6.1	25.0	6.2	9.0	19.7	19.7	7.5	3.8	3.0	37.4	51.1
Temple	7.8	18.5	9.2	14.2	14.4	12.3	7.8	7.1	8.7	35.2	52.2
Texarkana	7.1	18.9	10.0	13.1	14.5	12.6	8.1	7.3	8.5	35.7	52.9
Texas City	6.8	19.9	9.6	12.9	14.9	14.1	8.3	7.3	6.1	35.5	52.8
The Colony	8.4	25.6	7.4	16.4	21.5	12.9	4.9	1.9	1.0	30.8	50.3
Tyler	7.4	18.7	11.7	13.3	13.6	12.0	8.0	7.3	7.9	34.1	53.2
Victoria	7.9	20.9	9.7	13.1	14.9	13.0	8.0	6.6	6.0	33.9	51.9
Waco	7.6	17.8	20.3	12.9	12.0	9.7	6.3	6.2	7.2	27.9	52.3
Weslaco	9.5	22.3	9.9	14.2	11.7	10.1	7.1	7.5	7.6	30.8	53.2
Wichita Falls	7.1	17.5	15.2	14.3	15.0	11.3	7.3	6.5	5.8	31.9	48.5
UTAH	9.4	22.8	14.2	14.6	13.4	10.6	6.4	4.5	4.0	27.1	49.9
Bountiful	8.0	21.7	11.6	11.3	12.6	11.2	9.4	7.8	6.5	32.5	51.4
Clearfield	12.2	24.0	16.0	18.0	12.6	7.6	3.8	2.8	2.9	24.0	49.3
Draper	10.5	21.5	11.2	20.5	17.8	10.0	4.8	2.2	1.5	28.6	43.5
Layton	10.3	24.7	12.1	15.3	14.9	11.2	5.6	3.5	2.2	26.8	49.6
Logan	9.5	13.9	34.3	17.6	7.9	6.1	3.6	3.1	4.0	23.5	52.1
Midvale	9.5	16.3	16.7	19.2	12.7	9.4	7.2	4.8	4.2	28.1	49.3
Murray	7.5	19.8	13.3	14.2	14.4	12.3	7.3	6.0	5.4	31.0	51.1
Ogden	9.8	18.9	14.6	15.9	13.2	10.1	6.2	5.3	6.0	28.6	49.4
Orem	10.6	24.8	17.4	14.8	11.0	9.2	5.3	3.6	3.3	23.9	50.3
Provo	8.7	13.6	40.2	16.5	6.7	5.1	3.5	2.8	2.9	22.9	51.9
Riverton	12.4	30.2	8.9	15.8	16.3	9.2	3.9	2.0	1.3	23.7	49.7
Roy	10.1	23.4	11.6	16.2	14.4	10.1	5.9	4.8	3.6	28.0	50.5
St. George	8.6	19.7	13.7	11.5	10.4	8.9	7.8	9.8	9.5	31.4	51.4
Salt Lake City	7.9	15.7	15.2	19.7	13.8	10.8	5.9	4.9	6.1	30.0	49.4
Sandy	7.9	26.5	11.1	11.4	16.0	14.9	6.9	2.8	2.4	29.1	49.8
South Jordan	8.4	30.8	10.5	10.6	16.5	12.5	6.0	2.7	2.0	25.3	49.8
Taylorsville	8.4	22.3	14.7	15.0	13.9	12.7	6.8	3.8	2.5	27.8	50.0
West Jordan	11.3	26.5	12.2	17.0	15.1	10.4	4.4	1.9	1.3	25.0	49.8
West Valley City	10.6	23.1	12.9	16.9	13.8	10.8	6.6	3.4	2.0	26.8	49.4
VERMONT	5.6	18.6	9.3	12.2	16.7	15.4	9.3	6.7	6.0	37.7	51.0
Burlington	4.6	11.7	25.4	17.5	13.5	10.5	6.3	5.0	5.5	29.2	51.7
VIRGINIA	6.5	18.0	9.6	14.6	17.0	14.1	8.9	6.1	5.1	35.7	51.0
Alexandria	6.2	10.6	9.2	25.4	18.1	13.8	7.8	4.4	4.6	34.4	51.7
Blacksburg	2.9	6.7	57.4	12.3	6.6	5.7	3.5	2.6	2.4	21.9	44.1
Charlottesville	4.4	10.8	33.8	14.6	11.2	9.3	5.9	5.1	5.0	25.6	53.3
Chesapeake	7.2	21.6	8.2	13.5	18.9	13.8	7.9	5.1	3.8	34.7	51.4
Danville	6.0	17.3	8.0	11.5	14.0	13.8	9.8	9.7	9.9	40.5	54.5
Hampton	6.3	17.9	12.6	14.8	17.7	12.4	8.0	5.8	4.5	34.0	50.4
Harrisonburg	4.7	10.7	40.9	11.3	9.9	8.0	5.2	4.3	5.0	22.6	52.6
Leesburg	9.8	19.6	6.4	18.3	20.6	12.6	6.7	3.1	3.0	33.1	50.9

Table D. Cities

City	Population and population characteristics, 1990										Population—change, 1980–2000				
	Age (percent)										Total persons			Percent change	
	Under 5 years	5 to 17 years	18 to 24 years	25 to 34 years	35 to 44 years	45 to 54 years	55 to 64 years	65 to 74 years	75 years and over	Percent Female	2000	1990	1980	1990– 2000	1980– 1990
	39	40	41	42	43	44	45	46	47	48	49	50	51	52	53
TEXAS—Cont'd															
McKinney	8.6	19.2	13.7	18.3	13.5	8.0	7.3	5.5	5.8	50.9	54 369	21 283	16 256	155.5	30.9
Mansfield	9.5	22.0	9.8	18.8	17.2	10.2	6.1	3.9	2.6	50.5	28 031	15 615	NA	79.5	NA
Mesquite	9.3	21.1	9.7	22.1	16.3	9.8	6.4	3.2	2.0	51.6	124 523	101 484	67 053	22.7	51.3
Midland	9.8	21.2	8.6	18.5	15.0	9.0	8.5	5.9	3.6	51.8	94 996	89 443	70 525	6.2	26.8
Mission	8.6	25.1	11.1	13.5	12.4	7.7	7.4	9.0	5.3	52.2	45 408	28 653	22 551	58.5	27.1
Missouri City	8.5	23.2	7.3	16.8	23.2	11.1	5.7	3.0	1.1	50.9	52 913	36 176	24 533	46.3	47.5
Nacogdoches	5.4	14.4	33.2	13.3	11.2	6.4	5.3	5.4	5.5	52.6	29 914	30 872	27 149	-3.1	13.7
New Braunfels	7.4	19.8	8.0	15.0	14.0	8.8	9.0	9.2	8.8	52.8	36 494	27 334	22 404	33.5	22.0
North Richland Hills	8.7	19.2	10.1	20.3	17.5	10.4	6.9	4.6	2.2	51.0	55 635	45 895	30 592	21.2	50.0
Odessa	9.0	21.9	9.6	17.6	13.9	9.7	8.3	6.2	3.8	51.6	90 943	89 699	90 027	1.4	-0.4
Paris	7.5	17.8	10.8	14.1	11.4	10.1	8.4	9.5	10.4	54.1	25 898	24 799	25 498	4.4	-2.7
Pasadena	8.9	21.0	11.3	19.5	14.6	9.6	7.6	4.9	2.7	50.1	141 674	119 604	112 560	18.5	6.3
Pearland	7.5	21.5	7.8	18.2	18.0	11.6	7.3	4.9	3.1	51.0	37 640	18 927	13 219	98.9	43.2
Pharr	8.9	27.4	12.1	13.6	11.4	8.3	7.1	7.0	4.3	51.9	46 660	32 921	21 381	41.7	54.0
Plano	8.6	21.6	8.2	19.9	21.4	12.3	4.4	2.2	1.4	50.1	222 030	127 885	72 329	73.6	76.8
Port Arthur	8.0	20.2	8.4	15.5	12.2	8.9	9.8	9.7	7.2	52.8	57 755	58 551	61 251	-1.4	-4.4
Richardson	7.1	19.6	7.3	16.3	18.9	14.3	9.2	4.9	2.6	51.3	91 802	74 840	72 480	22.7	3.3
Round Rock	9.9	23.3	9.3	23.2	17.8	7.6	3.9	2.7	2.2	50.8	61 136	30 923	11 762	97.7	162.9
Rowlett	11.5	22.0	6.4	25.2	20.1	7.5	4.3	1.8	1.3	50.2	44 503	23 260	NA	91.3	NA
San Angelo	7.8	19.1	13.1	16.9	13.4	8.6	8.0	7.1	5.9	51.9	88 439	84 462	73 240	4.7	15.3
San Antonio	8.4	20.7	11.5	18.2	14.2	9.1	7.6	6.3	4.1	51.8	1 144 646	959 295	785 809	19.3	22.1
San Juan	7.7	27.1	12.2	12.5	13.9	8.1	7.2	6.3	5.0	52.7	26 229	12 561	NA	108.8	NA
San Marcos	4.9	12.8	42.3	15.1	8.3	5.5	4.1	3.5	3.5	51.1	34 733	28 738	23 420	20.9	22.7
Sherman	6.9	17.8	12.3	15.9	12.9	8.8	8.5	8.8	7.9	53.2	35 082	31 584	30 413	11.1	3.9
Socorro	10.1	30.0	13.3	15.6	13.3	8.2	5.4	2.4	1.6	50.7	27 152	22 995	NA	18.1	NA
Sugar Land	9.2	21.9	5.5	16.9	22.1	11.7	6.1	3.8	2.8	50.7	63 328	33 712	NA	87.9	NA
Temple	7.9	18.1	9.3	17.1	13.8	8.9	8.5	8.7	7.7	51.9	54 514	46 150	42 483	18.1	8.6
Texarkana	7.4	20.1	8.9	15.1	14.5	8.6	8.3	9.5	7.6	54.4	34 782	32 294	31 271	7.7	3.3
Texas City	7.3	21.2	9.1	15.6	15.7	10.5	9.5	6.9	4.1	51.4	41 521	40 822	41 403	1.7	-1.4
The Colony	11.9	25.5	7.4	25.7	18.9	6.1	2.7	1.1	0.6	49.8	26 531	22 113	11 596	20.0	90.7
Tyler	7.2	18.4	12.0	16.1	13.6	9.4	8.5	7.6	7.1	53.0	83 650	75 450	70 501	10.9	7.0
Victoria	8.1	22.2	9.2	16.9	14.7	10.0	7.9	6.6	4.5	51.9	60 603	55 076	50 695	10.0	8.6
Waco	7.6	16.8	18.8	15.7	11.0	7.4	7.9	7.9	6.9	52.2	113 726	103 590	101 262	9.8	2.3
Weslaco	8.2	23.8	11.1	13.1	11.7	8.0	7.6	8.6	8.0	53.1	26 935	22 739	19 331	18.5	17.6
Wichita Falls	8.0	18.1	13.3	18.0	13.3	8.4	8.3	6.9	5.7	50.9	104 197	96 259	94 201	8.2	2.2
UTAH	9.8	26.6	11.6	16.0	13.0	8.0	6.2	5.1	3.6	50.3	2 233 169	1 722 850	1 461 037	29.6	17.9
Bountiful	8.4	26.8	9.6	12.5	11.0	11.2	9.6	6.9	3.9	51.1	41 301	37 544	32 877	10.0	14.2
Clearfield	11.6	26.9	15.3	18.8	12.1	5.4	4.2	3.6	2.0	47.6	25 974	21 435	17 982	21.2	19.2
Draper	NA	NA	NA	NA	NA	NA	NA	NA	NA	NA	25 220	7 143	NA	253.1	NA
Layton	11.4	28.3	9.5	18.2	14.3	8.3	5.5	3.3	1.2	49.9	58 474	41 784	22 862	39.9	82.8
Logan	10.7	17.4	25.8	19.3	9.3	4.4	4.2	4.0	4.8	50.1	42 670	32 771	26 844	30.2	22.1
Midvale	10.5	19.0	16.1	18.9	10.1	8.8	6.3	6.4	4.0	51.0	27 029	11 886	10 146	127.4	17.1
Murray	8.9	21.7	10.0	18.4	13.3	9.6	7.7	6.8	3.5	51.6	34 024	31 274	25 750	8.8	21.5
Ogden	9.2	19.7	11.9	16.9	11.7	7.8	8.1	8.0	6.6	51.2	77 226	63 943	64 407	20.8	-0.7
Orem	12.6	31.7	11.3	15.2	11.2	7.0	4.9	3.8	2.3	50.6	84 324	67 561	52 399	24.8	28.9
Provo	9.4	16.3	36.4	17.1	5.9	4.5	3.8	3.5	3.0	51.5	105 166	86 835	74 108	21.1	17.2
Riverton	11.6	35.6	7.4	16.7	14.5	7.6	3.0	2.2	1.4	49.6	25 011	11 261	NA	122.1	NA
Roy	9.9	26.8	9.4	17.4	13.4	8.4	6.8	5.4	2.6	51.2	32 885	24 595	19 694	33.7	24.9
St. George	9.1	23.5	12.3	12.1	10.1	6.7	8.2	10.8	7.3	51.4	49 663	28 572	11 350	73.8	151.7
Salt Lake City	8.3	16.7	12.3	19.8	13.9	7.5	6.9	7.5	7.0	50.7	181 743	159 928	163 033	13.6	-1.9
Sandy	10.7	33.5	7.5	14.6	18.9	8.2	3.2	2.1	1.4	49.8	88 418	75 240	50 546	17.5	48.9
South Jordan	9.6	37.3	7.8	12.2	15.8	9.1	4.2	2.8	1.2	49.6	29 437	12 215	NA	141.0	NA
Taylorsville	NA	NA	NA	NA	NA	NA	NA	NA	NA	NA	57 439	51 426	NA	11.7	NA
West Jordan	12.2	34.4	8.5	18.1	15.2	6.3	2.8	1.8	0.8	49.8	68 336	42 915	27 192	59.2	57.8
West Valley City	10.7	28.9	10.8	17.6	14.4	8.5	4.9	2.7	1.4	50.1	108 896	86 969	72 378	25.2	20.2
VERMONT	7.3	18.1	11.2	16.9	16.4	10.2	8.0	6.6	5.2	51.0	608 827	562 758	511 456	8.2	10.0
Burlington	5.3	10.7	30.5	17.9	12.1	6.7	6.2	5.5	5.1	53.4	38 889	39 127	37 712	-0.6	3.8
VIRGINIA	7.2	17.2	11.6	18.4	16.0	10.7	8.1	6.5	4.3	51.0	7 078 515	6 189 197	5 346 797	14.4	15.8
Alexandria	5.5	9.8	10.9	27.6	18.0	10.8	7.1	5.9	4.3	52.6	128 283	111 182	103 217	15.4	7.7
Blacksburg	3.5	7.3	53.8	15.0	8.5	4.5	3.3	2.6	1.5	44.8	39 573	34 590	30 638	14.4	12.9
Charlottesville	6.0	11.9	23.5	19.7	12.9	7.2	6.7	6.4	5.8	53.1	45 049	40 475	39 916	11.3	1.4
Chesapeake	8.2	20.7	9.3	19.1	16.8	10.3	7.2	5.6	2.8	51.0	199 184	151 982	114 486	31.1	32.8
Danville	6.5	16.0	9.3	14.4	13.6	10.7	10.8	10.9	7.7	54.4	48 411	53 056	45 642	-8.8	16.2
Hampton	7.9	17.1	13.3	19.8	14.0	10.5	7.9	6.4	3.1	51.2	146 437	133 811	122 617	9.4	9.1
Harrisonburg	4.7	10.9	37.0	14.1	10.1	7.1	5.7	5.4	5.0	53.8	40 468	30 707	19 671	31.8	56.1
Leesburg	9.3	16.2	11.2	23.6	16.9	9.7	5.4	4.4	3.4	52.0	28 311	16 202	NA	74.7	NA

Table D. Cities

City	Total population	Total in house-holds	House-holder	Spouse	Child Total	Own child under 18 years	Other relatives Total	Under 18 years	Nonrelatives Total	Unmar-ried partner	Total in group quarters	Correc-tional institu-tions	Nurs-ing homes	Other institu-tions	Col-lege dormi-tories	Mili-tary quar-ters	Other
	54	55	56	57	58	59	60	61	62	63	64	65	66	67	68	69	70
TEXAS—Cont'd																	
McKinney	54 369	96.6	33.4	21.3	32.5	28.4	5.1	1.7	4.3	1.3	3.4	1.3	0.7	0.0	0.0	0.0	1.4
Mansfield	28 031	97.7	31.7	23.6	35.0	29.5	4.5	1.8	2.8	0.9	2.3	1.7	0.2	0.1	0.0	0.0	0.3
Mesquite	124 523	99.4	35.3	19.9	34.1	27.6	6.1	2.4	4.1	1.6	0.6	0.0	0.5	0.0	0.0	0.0	0.0
Midland	94 996	98.5	37.6	20.8	32.4	26.8	4.8	2.5	2.9	1.4	1.5	0.3	0.8	0.1	0.1	0.0	0.3
Mission	45 408	99.8	30.3	19.6	37.8	27.4	9.6	4.4	2.4	0.8	0.2	0.0	0.2	0.0	0.0	0.0	0.0
Missouri City	52 913	99.7	32.3	22.7	36.5	28.3	6.1	2.3	2.2	0.9	0.3	0.0	0.0	0.0	0.0	0.0	0.2
Nacogdoches	29 914	86.2	37.5	13.4	22.0	17.7	4.9	2.2	8.3	1.4	13.8	0.6	1.0	0.0	11.7	0.0	0.5
New Braunfels	36 494	96.8	37.2	20.6	29.2	22.6	5.8	2.5	4.0	1.7	3.2	0.7	1.5	0.0	0.0	0.0	1.0
North Richland Hills	55 635	99.5	37.4	22.4	31.3	25.3	4.3	1.5	4.2	1.7	0.5	0.0	0.3	0.0	0.0	0.0	0.1
Odessa	90 943	98.0	37.0	19.1	32.6	26.1	5.8	3.1	3.4	1.8	2.0	1.0	0.7	0.0	0.2	0.0	0.1
Paris	25 898	95.9	40.8	17.4	27.6	21.7	6.0	3.0	4.1	1.7	4.1	0.7	1.9	0.2	0.9	0.0	0.3
Pasadena	141 674	99.3	33.2	18.5	35.2	28.0	7.7	3.0	4.6	1.8	0.7	0.0	0.5	0.1	0.0	0.0	0.1
Pearland	37 640	99.5	35.0	23.7	33.4	26.8	4.4	1.6	2.9	1.3	0.5	0.0	0.4	0.0	0.0	0.0	0.0
Pharr	46 660	100.0	27.4	17.6	39.8	28.0	13.0	6.4	2.2	0.7	0.0	0.0	0.0	0.0	0.0	0.0	0.0
Plano	222 030	99.5	36.4	23.4	32.1	27.4	4.0	1.0	3.6	1.2	0.5	0.0	0.2	0.0	0.1	0.0	0.2
Port Arthur	57 755	98.7	37.8	16.1	33.0	24.3	8.0	3.8	3.8	1.6	1.3	0.0	0.8	0.0	0.0	0.0	0.4
Richardson	91 802	99.1	38.3	22.3	28.6	23.1	5.0	1.3	4.9	1.3	0.9	0.0	0.6	0.0	0.0	0.0	0.3
Round Rock	61 136	99.1	34.5	20.9	34.3	29.7	4.6	1.6	4.9	1.8	0.9	0.0	0.7	0.0	0.0	0.0	0.2
Rowlett	44 503	99.2	32.1	24.1	36.9	31.7	3.7	1.4	2.4	1.0	0.8	0.0	0.6	0.0	0.0	0.0	0.1
San Angelo	88 439	95.5	38.5	19.0	28.4	22.7	5.3	2.6	4.4	1.8	4.5	0.3	0.9	0.1	1.4	1.6	0.2
San Antonio	1 144 646	98.0	35.4	17.0	32.8	24.3	8.0	3.6	4.7	1.9	2.0	0.4	0.5	0.2	0.4	0.2	0.4
San Juan	26 229	99.5	25.2	17.4	43.3	31.3	11.7	5.7	2.0	0.6	0.5	0.0	0.5	0.0	0.0	0.0	0.0
San Marcos	34 733	84.1	36.4	10.2	16.5	12.3	5.6	2.2	15.3	2.2	15.9	0.8	1.0	0.5	12.7	0.0	1.0
Sherman	35 082	95.0	39.2	18.3	26.9	21.6	5.3	2.2	5.2	1.8	5.0	0.8	1.6	0.3	2.2	0.0	0.2
Socorro	27 152	100.0	24.9	17.3	42.0	28.5	13.7	7.2	2.2	0.9	0.0	0.0	0.0	0.0	0.0	0.0	0.0
Sugar Land	63 328	99.2	32.4	24.1	36.7	29.9	4.5	1.1	1.5	0.6	0.8	0.0	0.4	0.0	0.0	0.0	0.3
Temple	54 514	96.3	39.5	19.1	28.6	23.3	5.1	2.4	4.0	1.6	3.7	0.0	2.0	0.9	0.2	0.0	0.6
Texarkana	34 782	94.5	39.0	16.6	29.0	22.3	6.0	3.1	3.9	1.7	5.5	2.5	1.9	0.2	0.1	0.0	0.8
Texas City	41 521	97.8	37.3	18.1	30.7	22.2	7.6	3.9	4.1	1.8	2.2	0.9	1.1	0.1	0.0	0.0	0.1
The Colony	26 531	100.0	31.9	22.2	38.1	31.9	4.4	1.7	3.4	1.4	0.0	0.0	0.0	0.0	0.0	0.0	0.0
Tyler	83 650	96.4	38.9	18.2	28.8	22.7	6.5	2.8	4.1	1.5	3.6	0.9	1.2	0.1	0.7	0.0	0.7
Victoria	60 603	98.0	36.5	19.1	31.8	25.0	6.4	3.2	4.1	1.8	2.0	0.8	0.8	0.0	0.0	0.0	0.4
Waco	113 726	92.6	37.2	14.3	26.8	21.4	6.6	3.1	7.8	1.6	7.4	0.7	1.4	0.9	3.8	0.0	0.6
Weslaco	26 935	98.7	30.8	18.2	36.9	26.3	10.7	5.2	2.1	0.9	1.3	0.1	1.2	0.0	0.0	0.0	0.0
Wichita Falls	104 197	89.5	36.4	18.1	26.8	22.0	4.0	2.0	4.1	1.6	10.5	4.0	0.7	0.3	0.6	4.5	0.3
UTAH	2 233 169	98.2	31.4	19.8	37.1	29.7	4.7	1.9	5.1	1.1	1.8	0.4	0.3	0.1	0.4	0.1	0.4
Bountiful	41 301	98.6	32.3	22.4	37.5	27.6	4.2	1.8	2.1	0.5	1.4	0.0	1.0	0.0	0.0	0.0	0.3
Clearfield	25 974	95.1	30.5	18.4	38.4	33.0	3.6	1.5	4.1	1.4	4.9	0.1	0.4	0.0	0.0	0.0	4.5
Draper	25 220	84.9	25.0	19.4	35.7	30.4	2.7	1.0	2.1	0.5	15.1	14.4	0.3	0.3	0.0	0.0	0.1
Layton	58 474	99.8	31.3	21.1	40.6	33.1	3.7	1.5	3.2	1.0	0.2	0.0	0.0	0.0	0.0	0.0	0.2
Logan	42 670	95.0	32.6	18.0	26.1	22.1	3.3	0.9	15.0	0.9	5.0	0.2	0.7	0.0	3.8	0.0	0.3
Midvale	27 029	99.3	37.3	17.8	29.2	22.5	6.8	2.2	8.1	2.3	0.7	0.0	0.0	0.0	0.0	0.0	0.7
Murray	34 024	99.7	37.2	19.8	32.9	25.1	4.6	1.7	5.1	1.6	0.3	0.0	0.2	0.0	0.0	0.0	0.0
Ogden	77 226	96.9	35.5	17.2	31.5	25.2	6.5	2.6	6.3	2.1	3.1	0.6	0.4	0.3	0.6	0.0	1.2
Orem	84 324	99.1	27.7	19.1	41.7	32.8	5.4	1.8	5.1	0.4	0.9	0.0	0.4	0.4	0.0	0.0	0.2
Provo	105 166	92.8	27.8	15.8	25.1	20.2	4.7	1.3	19.4	0.4	7.2	0.0	0.2	0.6	4.4	0.0	1.9
Riverton	25 011	99.8	25.4	21.4	47.6	40.5	3.6	1.6	1.8	0.5	0.2	0.0	0.0	0.0	0.0	0.0	0.2
Roy	32 885	99.5	32.5	21.4	38.1	30.9	4.1	1.9	3.4	1.2	0.5	0.0	0.4	0.1	0.0	0.0	0.0
St. George	49 663	98.3	35.0	22.2	31.7	26.3	4.0	1.5	5.3	0.9	1.7	0.0	0.7	0.1	0.3	0.0	0.7
Salt Lake City	181 743	97.5	39.3	16.2	26.5	20.9	6.6	2.1	9.0	2.1	2.5	0.1	0.4	0.1	0.9	0.0	1.0
Sandy	88 418	99.4	29.1	21.2	42.1	32.4	4.0	1.7	3.0	0.8	0.6	0.0	0.3	0.0	0.0	0.0	0.2
South Jordan	29 437	100.0	25.5	21.2	47.3	37.1	4.2	1.8	1.7	0.4	0.0	0.0	0.0	0.0	0.0	0.0	0.0
Taylorsville	57 439	99.7	32.3	19.2	36.5	27.5	6.4	2.6	5.3	1.5	0.3	0.0	0.1	0.0	0.0	0.0	0.2
West Jordan	68 336	99.4	27.7	19.9	43.1	34.8	5.2	2.2	3.5	1.0	0.6	0.0	0.2	0.2	0.0	0.0	0.2
West Valley City	108 896	99.5	29.6	18.2	38.0	29.6	8.5	3.3	5.3	1.6	0.5	0.1	0.1	0.1	0.0	0.0	0.3
VERMONT	608 827	96.6	39.5	20.8	27.5	22.7	2.4	0.8	6.4	3.0	3.4	0.2	0.7	0.1	2.1	0.0	0.4
Burlington	38 889	89.7	40.8	12.8	18.6	15.0	2.3	0.7	15.1	3.5	10.3	0.0	1.2	0.0	8.1	0.1	1.0
VIRGINIA	7 078 515	96.7	38.1	20.1	28.1	22.1	5.0	2.0	5.3	1.8	3.3	0.9	0.5	0.1	0.9	0.5	0.3
Alexandria	128 283	98.5	48.2	15.5	18.8	14.8	6.1	1.5	9.9	2.8	1.5	0.3	0.7	0.1	0.0	0.0	0.3
Blacksburg	39 573	78.7	33.3	9.5	10.6	9.2	1.5	0.2	23.8	1.4	21.3	0.0	0.5	0.0	20.8	0.0	0.1
Charlottesville	45 049	84.8	37.4	10.9	16.7	13.2	3.6	1.4	16.1	2.0	15.2	0.0	0.8	0.0	13.8	0.0	0.6
Chesapeake	199 184	97.9	35.1	20.9	32.7	25.6	5.4	2.5	3.8	1.4	2.1	1.1	0.4	0.2	0.0	0.2	0.3
Danville	48 411	96.5	42.6	16.7	27.0	19.5	6.8	3.3	3.5	1.6	3.5	0.7	1.3	0.2	0.6	0.0	0.7
Hampton	146 437	91.5	36.8	17.0	27.4	21.0	5.1	2.6	5.2	1.7	8.5	5.7	0.5	0.0	1.8	0.1	0.2
Harrisonburg	40 468	82.2	32.5	11.8	17.1	14.0	3.0	1.0	17.9	1.5	17.8	0.8	1.5	0.0	15.2	0.0	0.3
Leesburg	28 311	98.2	36.5	20.9	31.8	27.6	3.8	1.2	5.2	1.9	1.8	0.5	1.1	0.1	0.0	0.0	0.1

Table D. Cities

City	Total households	Family households Total	With own children under 18 years	Married couple Total	With own children under 18 years	Female householder¹ Total	With own children under 18 years	Nonfamily households Total	Householder living alone Total	65 years and over	Average household size	Average family size	Households, 1990 Total households	Female householder¹	Householder living alone
	71	72	73	74	75	76	77	78	79	80	81	82	83	84	85
TEXAS—Cont'd															
McKinney	18 186	76.8	45.1	63.6	36.8	9.5	6.5	23.2	19.0	5.3	2.89	3.29	7 596	12.3	26.0
Mansfield	8 881	86.1	50.4	74.5	43.1	8.3	6.6	13.9	10.9	3.2	3.08	3.32	5 130	8.1	12.8
Mesquite	43 926	74.9	43.1	56.4	31.5	14.0	9.0	25.1	20.6	4.9	2.82	3.27	35 856	11.7	19.1
Midland	35 674	70.7	37.9	55.4	28.1	11.9	7.8	29.3	25.8	9.2	2.62	3.19	33 169	10.3	25.0
Mission	13 766	82.7	43.4	64.8	33.7	14.5	8.2	17.3	15.3	9.1	3.29	3.68	8 315	15.4	14.4
Missouri City	17 069	85.8	48.6	70.2	39.7	12.5	7.3	14.2	11.9	2.4	3.09	3.36	11 544	10.1	10.4
Nacogdoches	11 220	52.9	25.3	35.7	15.4	13.7	8.6	47.1	33.5	9.6	2.30	3.04	11 306	12.6	30.8
New Braunfels	13 558	70.8	33.4	55.4	24.5	11.5	6.8	29.2	24.8	12.0	2.60	3.11	9 997	10.5	24.1
North Richland Hills	20 793	74.1	38.0	59.9	29.5	10.3	6.3	25.9	20.4	5.6	2.66	3.09	16 901	9.5	18.6
Odessa	33 661	70.4	37.9	51.6	25.7	14.5	9.6	29.6	25.7	9.6	2.65	3.21	32 826	12.2	24.2
Paris	10 570	63.5	29.4	42.7	17.0	17.0	10.5	36.5	32.5	15.2	2.35	2.97	9 806	15.1	30.3
Pasadena	47 031	74.8	43.1	55.8	31.8	13.1	8.3	25.2	20.4	6.2	2.99	3.48	42 044	11.5	21.6
Pearland	13 192	80.8	43.2	67.6	35.5	9.7	5.9	19.2	15.8	4.8	2.84	3.17	6 591	9.3	16.2
Pharr	12 798	85.0	47.1	64.2	36.0	16.9	9.4	15.0	13.3	7.6	3.64	4.02	8 659	16.1	12.0
Plano	80 875	74.9	42.0	64.3	35.6	7.5	4.8	25.1	20.2	2.9	2.73	3.18	44 352	7.6	15.7
Port Arthur	21 839	67.2	33.2	42.6	19.2	19.7	11.9	32.8	29.4	13.6	2.61	3.25	22 326	17.2	28.6
Richardson	35 191	70.4	33.7	58.1	27.0	8.9	5.2	29.6	22.9	5.5	2.59	3.07	27 220	9.9	17.1
Round Rock	21 076	75.6	47.5	60.5	37.0	11.0	8.1	24.4	18.1	3.0	2.87	3.29	10 568	11.1	18.1
Rowlett	14 266	86.6	53.8	75.3	46.4	8.0	5.4	13.4	10.6	2.3	3.09	3.33	7 561	6.1	9.4
San Angelo	34 006	65.9	32.3	49.5	22.3	12.5	7.8	34.1	28.8	11.5	2.48	3.08	30 661	11.3	26.1
San Antonio	405 474	69.3	35.9	48.1	24.1	16.4	9.5	30.7	25.1	7.6	2.77	3.36	326 761	15.7	25.0
San Juan	6 606	90.1	56.7	69.0	44.4	17.1	10.5	9.9	8.6	4.2	3.95	4.19	2 784	17.9	10.3
San Marcos	12 660	42.5	19.2	27.9	12.3	10.1	5.3	57.5	31.0	5.7	2.31	3.08	9 849	10.0	30.3
Sherman	13 739	64.2	30.9	46.7	20.5	13.4	8.2	35.8	30.4	12.5	2.42	3.01	12 454	12.6	29.4
Socorro	6 756	91.6	56.9	69.4	44.4	17.0	9.9	8.4	7.1	2.9	4.02	4.20	5 239	14.1	6.1
Sugar Land	20 515	85.4	51.2	74.5	44.5	8.4	5.4	14.6	12.6	2.9	3.06	3.36	8 100	6.0	12.9
Temple	21 543	65.5	32.1	48.4	21.4	13.6	8.9	34.5	29.9	11.8	2.44	3.04	18 153	12.8	29.2
Texarkana	13 569	65.9	31.5	42.5	17.5	19.3	12.0	34.1	29.9	12.1	2.42	3.01	12 475	17.6	29.1
Texas City	15 479	70.9	33.1	48.6	20.8	17.3	9.8	29.1	24.8	9.3	2.62	3.13	15 110	14.7	23.7
The Colony	8 462	84.4	53.7	69.7	43.8	10.4	7.1	15.6	11.4	1.8	3.14	3.41	6 771	6.9	9.6
Tyler	32 555	64.8	30.8	46.7	20.5	14.5	8.8	35.2	30.2	11.5	2.48	3.12	29 381	13.5	30.1
Victoria	22 129	71.2	36.1	52.4	24.5	14.3	9.2	28.8	24.5	10.0	2.68	3.21	19 777	12.7	23.3
Waco	42 279	58.6	29.5	38.4	17.4	16.2	10.2	41.4	31.1	10.9	2.49	3.19	39 482	14.9	30.8
Weslaco	8 295	79.6	41.1	59.2	30.4	17.0	9.1	20.4	18.4	10.8	3.21	3.68	6 591	14.9	19.5
Wichita Falls	37 970	65.8	33.1	49.7	23.0	12.3	8.0	34.2	28.7	10.7	2.46	3.04	35 470	11.6	26.6
UTAH	701 281	76.3	42.7	63.2	35.0	9.4	5.8	23.7	17.8	6.3	3.13	3.57	537 273	9.1	18.9
Bountiful	13 341	80.7	38.1	69.3	32.2	8.9	4.7	19.3	16.7	7.6	3.05	3.46	11 152	8.3	14.8
Clearfield	7 921	79.1	52.2	60.4	38.4	13.9	10.7	20.9	16.3	4.3	3.12	3.51	6 168	11.8	16.2
Draper	6 305	86.1	54.7	77.8	49.2	5.6	3.8	13.9	10.6	2.0	3.40	3.69	1 373	NA	NA
Layton	18 282	80.8	48.9	67.4	40.2	9.7	6.6	19.2	15.2	3.5	3.19	3.59	12 730	9.7	14.9
Logan	13 902	66.0	33.4	55.1	27.2	7.7	4.7	34.0	17.9	5.7	2.92	3.20	11 034	6.5	21.7
Midvale	10 089	65.8	31.7	47.8	21.6	12.7	7.5	34.2	25.3	6.5	2.66	3.19	4 630	15.2	27.6
Murray	12 673	68.8	34.1	53.3	25.6	11.3	6.4	31.2	24.6	8.0	2.68	3.24	11 712	10.8	25.6
Ogden	27 384	67.2	35.2	48.4	24.2	13.1	8.1	32.8	26.2	9.6	2.73	3.32	24 239	12.5	28.8
Orem	23 382	81.6	48.8	69.0	42.1	9.5	5.4	18.4	12.4	5.1	3.57	3.93	17 584	8.7	10.8
Provo	29 192	68.3	33.8	57.0	28.8	7.8	3.9	31.7	11.8	4.6	3.34	3.40	23 805	7.6	12.8
Riverton	6 348	92.7	65.3	84.4	59.7	5.7	4.0	7.3	5.8	1.9	3.93	4.09	2 745	5.2	7.1
Roy	10 689	80.5	46.5	65.8	37.3	10.3	6.5	19.5	15.8	4.8	3.06	3.43	7 655	9.8	14.5
St. George	17 367	75.1	34.2	63.6	26.9	8.6	5.7	24.9	19.4	10.2	2.81	3.21	9 450	8.4	18.0
Salt Lake City	71 461	55.7	27.0	41.1	19.4	10.2	5.8	44.3	33.2	9.7	2.48	3.24	66 657	10.2	35.8
Sandy	25 737	84.6	51.3	72.9	44.0	8.6	5.5	15.4	11.6	3.4	3.42	3.73	19 423	7.1	8.1
South Jordan	7 507	90.2	58.7	83.3	54.5	5.0	3.2	9.8	7.9	3.4	3.92	4.16	2 829	4.6	5.6
Taylorsville	18 530	76.4	42.2	59.5	32.1	11.9	7.4	23.6	17.6	4.3	3.09	3.52	NA	NA	NA
West Jordan	18 897	85.9	57.3	72.0	48.1	10.0	6.8	14.1	10.2	2.0	3.60	3.87	11 143	10.3	10.0
West Valley City	32 253	80.4	47.1	61.3	35.8	13.2	8.2	19.6	14.7	3.9	3.36	3.71	25 933	12.7	14.3
VERMONT	240 634	65.6	31.8	52.5	23.2	9.3	6.1	34.4	26.2	9.5	2.44	2.96	210 650	9.2	23.4
Burlington	15 885	44.4	21.3	31.4	13.0	10.0	6.8	55.6	35.6	8.2	2.19	2.86	14 680	10.2	32.1
VIRGINIA	2 699 173	68.5	32.7	52.8	23.9	11.9	6.9	31.5	25.1	8.0	2.54	3.04	2 291 830	11.1	22.9
Alexandria	61 889	44.8	18.6	32.2	12.4	9.2	5.0	55.2	43.4	6.8	2.04	2.87	53 280	9.1	42.0
Blacksburg	13 162	36.3	16.3	28.7	12.3	5.3	3.2	63.7	26.6	3.7	2.37	2.79	11 175	5.4	24.5
Charlottesville	16 851	45.3	20.5	29.2	10.9	13.1	8.3	54.7	34.9	8.2	2.27	2.85	16 009	12.9	30.6
Chesapeake	69 900	77.5	41.0	60.3	30.3	14.0	8.7	22.5	18.0	5.9	2.79	3.17	51 965	12.7	16.1
Danville	20 607	62.8	26.1	39.2	13.4	19.6	11.1	37.2	33.9	15.3	2.27	2.89	21 712	17.3	30.2
Hampton	53 887	66.6	32.5	48.0	20.2	16.4	10.3	33.4	26.6	7.9	2.49	3.02	49 673	13.5	23.7
Harrisonburg	13 133	49.1	23.3	36.4	15.8	9.3	5.7	50.9	28.3	8.6	2.53	3.00	10 310	10.2	28.2
Leesburg	10 325	70.3	41.2	57.3	33.1	9.7	6.4	29.7	22.9	4.5	2.69	3.20	6 342	10.6	25.2

¹No spouse present.

Table D. Cities

City	Percent change of households, 1990–2000	Total housing units	Occupied housing units (percent)	Vacant housing units Total	For seasonal, recreational, or occasional use	Homeowner vacancy rate (percent)	Rental vacancy rate (percent)	Occupied housing units Total	Percent owner-occupied housing units	Percent renter-occupied housing units	Average household size of owner-occupied units	Average household size of renter-occupied units
	86	87	88	89	90	91	92	93	94	95	96	97
TEXAS—Cont'd												
McKinney	139.4	19 462	93.4	6.6	0.2	2.7	10.4	18 186	70.2	29.8	3.00	2.62
Mansfield	73.1	9 172	96.8	3.2	0.2	1.4	5.0	8 881	86.6	13.4	3.08	3.08
Mesquite	22.5	46 245	95.0	5.0	0.2	1.4	8.5	43 926	65.5	34.5	2.99	2.50
Midland	7.6	39 855	89.5	10.5	0.3	2.3	17.7	35 674	66.1	33.9	2.81	2.25
Mission	65.6	17 723	77.7	22.3	15.0	1.7	7.9	13 766	74.9	25.1	3.27	3.36
Missouri City	47.9	17 481	97.6	2.4	0.1	1.3	3.5	17 069	90.8	9.2	3.08	3.18
Nacogdoches	-0.8	12 329	91.0	9.0	0.6	1.7	8.9	11 220	43.5	56.5	2.49	2.15
New Braunfels	35.6	14 896	91.0	9.0	1.7	1.4	11.2	13 558	64.4	35.6	2.69	2.45
North Richland Hills	23.0	21 600	96.3	3.7	0.2	0.8	7.0	20 793	67.1	32.9	2.81	2.36
Odessa	2.5	37 966	88.7	11.3	0.4	2.0	17.3	33 661	64.1	35.9	2.80	2.38
Paris	7.8	11 777	89.8	10.2	0.6	2.3	9.2	10 570	54.3	45.7	2.34	2.36
Pasadena	11.9	50 367	93.4	6.6	0.2	1.3	9.5	47 031	56.1	43.9	3.10	2.85
Pearland	100.2	13 922	94.8	5.2	0.1	1.9	10.8	13 192	79.4	20.6	2.95	2.41
Pharr	47.8	16 537	77.4	22.6	11.9	1.5	16.6	12 798	73.2	26.8	3.68	3.55
Plano	82.3	86 078	94.0	6.0	0.3	1.4	12.6	80 875	68.8	31.2	2.97	2.21
Port Arthur	-2.2	24 713	88.4	11.6	0.6	1.8	8.4	21 839	62.2	37.8	2.69	2.48
Richardson	29.3	36 530	96.3	3.7	0.2	1.0	5.5	35 191	64.4	35.6	2.70	2.37
Round Rock	99.4	21 766	96.8	3.2	0.3	1.0	3.5	21 076	65.3	34.7	3.03	2.58
Rowlett	88.7	14 580	97.8	2.2	0.1	1.1	4.9	14 266	92.2	7.8	3.09	3.16
San Angelo	10.9	37 699	90.2	9.8	0.7	2.2	11.2	34 006	60.8	39.2	2.62	2.27
San Antonio	24.1	433 122	93.6	6.4	0.5	1.4	6.9	405 474	58.1	41.9	2.95	2.51
San Juan	137.3	7 719	85.6	14.4	7.0	1.2	6.9	6 606	76.7	23.3	4.03	3.69
San Marcos	28.5	13 340	94.9	5.1	0.3	1.3	4.5	12 660	30.2	69.8	2.75	2.12
Sherman	10.3	14 926	92.0	8.0	0.3	2.0	8.9	13 739	56.4	43.6	2.53	2.29
Socorro	29.0	7 140	94.6	5.4	0.4	0.6	6.3	6 756	81.1	18.9	4.11	3.64
Sugar Land	153.3	21 090	97.3	2.7	0.3	1.1	5.1	20 515	84.1	15.9	3.15	2.61
Temple	18.7	23 511	91.6	8.4	0.3	2.5	8.4	21 543	55.9	44.1	2.59	2.25
Texarkana	8.8	15 105	89.8	10.2	0.4	2.2	11.5	13 569	58.7	41.3	2.44	2.40
Texas City	2.4	16 715	92.6	7.4	0.3	1.6	9.5	15 479	63.3	36.7	2.72	2.45
The Colony	25.0	8 812	96.0	4.0	0.0	2.3	7.2	8 462	82.5	17.5	3.14	3.12
Tyler	10.7	35 337	92.0	8.0	0.4	1.9	9.4	32 525	56.2	43.8	2.63	2.28
Victoria	11.9	24 192	91.5	8.5	0.5	1.4	11.3	22 129	60.8	39.2	2.76	2.57
Waco	7.1	45 819	92.3	7.7	0.3	1.9	6.6	42 279	46.4	53.6	2.60	2.40
Weslaco	25.9	10 230	81.1	18.9	10.2	1.5	9.2	8 295	65.4	34.6	3.29	3.06
Wichita Falls	7.0	41 916	90.6	9.4	0.4	2.6	11.2	37 970	57.8	42.2	2.54	2.34
UTAH	30.5	768 594	91.2	8.8	3.9	2.1	6.5	701 281	71.5	28.5	3.28	2.75
Bountiful	19.6	13 819	96.5	3.5	0.3	1.5	4.8	13 341	77.7	22.3	3.19	2.59
Clearfield	28.4	8 374	94.6	5.4	0.2	3.3	5.8	7 921	55.1	44.9	3.19	3.04
Draper	359.2	6 588	95.7	4.3	0.4	2.2	4.9	6 305	83.8	16.2	3.54	2.63
Layton	43.6	19 145	95.5	4.5	0.3	2.4	6.5	18 282	74.5	25.5	3.42	2.52
Logan	26.0	14 692	94.6	5.4	0.6	2.3	4.6	13 902	44.0	56.0	3.05	2.81
Midvale	117.9	10 730	94.0	6.0	0.6	1.4	6.9	10 089	48.1	51.9	2.66	2.66
Murray	8.2	13 327	95.1	4.9	0.2	2.1	6.9	12 673	66.7	33.3	2.81	2.40
Ogden	13.0	29 763	92.0	8.0	0.3	3.2	9.9	27 384	61.2	38.8	2.84	2.57
Orem	33.0	24 166	96.8	3.2	0.3	1.2	3.4	23 382	67.1	32.9	3.82	3.06
Provo	22.6	30 374	96.1	3.9	0.4	2.2	2.4	29 192	42.6	57.4	3.45	3.27
Riverton	131.3	6 555	96.8	3.2	0.2	1.3	5.0	6 348	94.0	6.0	3.96	3.50
Roy	39.6	11 053	96.7	3.3	0.2	2.0	5.6	10 689	84.3	15.7	3.11	2.81
St. George	83.8	21 083	82.4	17.6	11.9	3.7	6.6	17 367	67.9	32.1	2.78	2.88
Salt Lake City	7.2	77 054	92.7	7.3	0.8	2.1	6.8	71 461	51.2	48.8	2.69	2.26
Sandy	32.5	26 579	96.8	3.2	0.3	1.3	6.7	25 737	84.3	15.7	3.53	2.82
South Jordan	165.4	7 721	97.2	2.8	0.1	1.0	8.8	7 507	89.7	10.3	4.09	2.44
Taylorsville	NA	19 159	96.7	3.3	0.3	1.3	4.8	18 530	71.2	28.8	3.25	2.70
West Jordan	69.6	19 597	96.4	3.6	0.1	1.7	6.4	18 897	81.9	18.1	3.72	3.05
West Valley City	24.4	33 488	96.3	3.7	0.1	1.7	5.1	32 253	72.6	27.4	3.48	3.05
VERMONT	14.2	294 382	81.7	18.3	14.6	1.4	4.2	240 634	70.6	29.4	2.58	2.11
Burlington	8.2	16 395	96.9	3.1	1.1	0.6	1.6	15 885	41.5	58.5	2.39	2.06
VIRGINIA	17.8	2 904 192	92.9	7.1	1.9	1.5	5.2	2 699 173	68.1	31.9	2.62	2.36
Alexandria	16.2	64 251	96.3	3.7	0.8	1.0	2.4	61 889	40.0	60.0	2.03	2.05
Blacksburg	17.8	13 732	95.8	4.2	0.4	1.6	3.2	13 162	30.4	69.6	2.45	2.33
Charlottesville	5.3	17 591	95.8	4.2	0.4	1.1	2.4	16 851	40.8	59.2	2.27	2.26
Chesapeake	34.5	72 672	96.2	3.8	0.3	1.4	3.6	69 900	74.9	25.1	2.87	2.56
Danville	-5.1	23 108	89.2	10.8	0.4	2.8	11.6	20 607	58.1	41.9	2.28	2.25
Hampton	8.5	57 311	94.0	6.0	0.5	2.0	5.6	53 887	58.6	41.4	2.55	2.40
Harrisonburg	27.4	13 689	95.9	4.1	0.3	1.7	3.3	13 133	39.0	61.0	2.52	2.54
Leesburg	62.8	10 671	96.8	3.2	0.4	0.6	3.4	10 325	67.9	32.1	2.88	2.30

Table D. Cities

STATE Place code	City	Land area, 2000¹ (sq km)	Total persons	Rank	Per square kilometer	Land area, 1990¹ (sq km)	Total persons	Rank	Per square kilometer	White	Black or African American	American Indian or Alaska Native	Asian	Native Hawaiian and other Pacific Islander	Some other race
		Population, 2000				Population, 1990				Population and population characteristics, 2000 — Race (percent) — One race					
		1	2	3	4	5	6	7	8	9	10	11	12	13	14
	VIRGINIA—Cont'd														
51 47672	Lynchburg	127.9	65 269	447	510.3	127.9	66 049	369	516.4	66.6	29.7	0.3	1.3	0.0	0.6
51 48952	Manassas	25.7	35 135	1 018	1 367.1	25.9	27 957	1 142	1 079.4	72.1	12.9	0.4	3.4	0.1	7.9
51 56000	Newport News	176.9	180 150	117	1 018.4	177.0	171 439	100	968.6	53.5	39.1	0.4	2.3	0.1	1.8
51 57000	Norfolk	139.2	234 403	75	1 683.9	139.2	261 250	62	1 876.8	48.4	44.1	0.5	2.8	0.1	1.7
51 61832	Petersburg	59.3	33 740	1 072	569.0	59.3	37 027	815	624.4	18.5	79.0	0.2	0.7	0.0	0.6
51 64000	Portsmouth	85.9	100 565	245	1 170.7	85.8	103 910	193	1 211.1	45.8	50.6	0.5	0.8	0.1	0.6
51 67000	Richmond	155.6	197 790	97	1 271.1	155.7	202 798	76	1 302.5	38.3	57.2	0.2	1.2	0.1	1.5
51 68000	Roanoke	111.1	94 911	262	854.3	111.1	96 509	211	868.7	69.4	26.7	0.2	1.2	0.0	0.7
51 76432	Suffolk	1 036.0	63 677	458	61.5	1 036.2	52 143	522	50.3	53.8	43.5	0.3	0.8	0.0	0.4
51 82000	Virginia Beach	643.1	425 257	40	661.3	643.2	393 089	37	611.1	71.4	19.0	0.4	4.9	0.1	1.5
53 00000	**WASHINGTON**	172 348.3	5 894 121	X	34.2	172 447.2	4 866 669	X	28.2	81.8	3.2	1.6	5.5	0.4	3.9
53 03180	Auburn	55.1	40 314	863	731.7	51.0	33 650	909	659.8	82.8	2.4	2.5	3.5	0.5	3.7
53 05210	Bellevue	79.6	109 569	214	1 376.5	68.4	95 213	220	1 392.0	74.3	2.0	0.3	17.4	0.2	2.5
53 05280	Bellingham	66.4	67 171	431	1 011.6	57.0	52 179	521	915.4	87.9	1.0	1.5	4.2	0.2	2.2
53 07380	Bothell	31.2	30 150	1 215	966.3	13.8	12 575	2 543	911.2	87.3	1.2	0.6	6.0	0.2	1.8
53 07695	Bremerton	58.7	37 259	946	634.7	51.5	38 142	783	740.6	75.0	7.5	1.9	5.5	0.9	2.6
53 17635	Des Moines	16.4	29 267	1 264	1 784.6	8.8	20 830	1 569	2 367.0	74.2	7.2	1.0	8.3	1.3	3.3
53 20750	Edmonds	23.1	39 515	885	1 710.6	18.9	30 743	1 025	1 626.6	87.7	1.3	0.8	5.6	0.3	1.3
53 22640	Everett	84.2	91 488	279	1 086.6	77.4	70 937	334	916.5	81.1	3.3	1.6	6.3	0.4	3.1
53 35275	Kennewick	59.4	54 693	596	920.8	52.1	42 148	689	809.0	82.9	1.1	0.9	2.1	0.1	9.4
53 35415	Kent	72.6	79 524	343	1 095.4	49.0	37 960	790	774.7	70.8	8.2	1.0	9.4	0.8	4.4
53 35940	Kirkland	27.6	45 054	760	1 632.4	27.7	40 059	739	1 446.2	85.3	1.6	0.5	7.8	0.2	1.7
53 36745	Lacey	41.3	31 226	1 174	756.1	26.2	19 279	1 704	735.8	78.2	4.8	1.3	7.8	1.1	2.2
53 40245	Longview	35.5	34 660	1 039	976.3	31.1	31 499	991	1 012.8	89.3	0.7	1.8	2.2	0.1	3.0
53 40840	Lynnwood	19.8	33 847	1 067	1 709.4	18.0	28 637	1 110	1 590.9	74.3	3.3	1.0	13.9	0.4	2.8
53 43955	Marysville	24.8	25 315	1 488	1 020.8	12.0	12 248	2 604	1 020.7	88.2	1.0	1.6	3.8	0.4	1.9
53 47560	Mount Vernon	28.8	26 232	1 430	910.8	21.8	17 647	1 866	809.5	75.4	0.7	1.0	2.6	0.2	17.1
53 51300	Olympia	43.3	42 514	810	981.8	41.8	33 729	902	806.9	85.3	1.9	1.3	5.8	0.3	1.7
53 53545	Pasco	72.7	32 066	1 134	441.1	59.1	20 337	1 609	344.1	52.8	3.2	0.8	1.8	0.1	37.4
53 56695	Puyallup	31.4	33 011	1 097	1 051.3	26.6	23 878	1 364	897.7	87.9	1.5	1.0	3.3	0.3	1.9
53 57535	Redmond	41.1	45 256	758	1 101.1	37.4	35 800	835	957.2	79.3	1.5	0.4	13.0	0.2	2.5
53 57745	Renton	44.1	50 052	667	1 135.0	42.1	41 688	701	990.2	68.1	8.5	0.7	13.4	0.5	4.2
53 58235	Richland	90.2	38 708	909	429.1	83.0	32 315	959	389.3	89.5	1.4	0.8	4.1	0.1	1.9
53 61115	Sammamish	46.8	34 104	1 055	728.7	NA	NA	NA	NA	87.8	0.8	0.3	7.9	0.1	0.6
53 63000	Seattle	217.2	563 374	25	2 593.8	217.3	516 259	21	2 375.8	70.1	8.4	1.0	13.1	0.5	2.4
53 63960	Shoreline	30.2	53 025	624	1 755.8	NA	NA	NA	NA	77.0	2.8	0.9	13.2	0.3	1.5
53 67000	Spokane	149.6	195 629	99	1 307.7	144.8	177 165	95	1 223.5	89.5	2.1	1.8	2.2	0.2	0.9
53 70000	Tacoma	129.7	193 556	101	1 492.3	124.4	176 664	96	1 420.1	69.1	11.2	2.0	7.6	0.9	2.9
53 74060	Vancouver	110.8	143 560	151	1 295.7	36.6	62 065	400	1 695.8	84.8	2.5	1.0	4.5	0.5	2.9
53 75775	Walla Walla	28.0	29 686	1 239	1 060.2	26.7	26 482	1 214	991.8	83.8	2.6	1.1	1.2	0.2	8.3
53 77105	Wenatchee	17.8	27 856	1 334	1 564.9	15.8	21 746	1 513	1 376.3	80.9	0.4	1.1	0.9	0.1	14.0
53 80010	Yakima	52.1	71 845	394	1 379.0	38.7	58 427	434	1 509.7	68.8	2.0	2.0	1.2	0.1	22.0
54 00000	**WEST VIRGINIA**	62 361.0	1 808 344	X	29.0	62 384.2	1 793 477	X	28.7	95.0	3.2	0.2	0.5	0.0	0.2
54 14600	Charleston	81.9	53 421	617	652.3	76.3	57 287	445	750.8	80.6	15.1	0.2	1.8	0.0	0.3
54 39460	Huntington	41.2	51 475	649	1 249.4	38.6	54 844	476	1 420.8	89.6	7.5	0.2	0.8	0.0	0.3
54 55756	Morgantown	25.4	26 809	1 392	1 055.5	20.0	25 879	1 247	1 294.0	89.5	4.2	0.2	4.2	0.0	0.5
54 62140	Parkersburg	30.6	33 099	1 093	1 081.7	28.9	33 862	894	1 171.7	96.4	1.7	0.2	0.4	0.1	0.2
54 86452	Wheeling	36.0	31 419	1 163	872.8	35.7	34 882	864	977.1	92.7	5.0	0.1	0.9	0.0	0.2
55 00000	**WISCONSIN**	140 662.5	5 363 675	X	38.1	140 672.5	4 891 769	X	34.8	88.9	5.7	0.9	1.7	0.0	1.6
55 02375	Appleton	54.1	70 087	406	1 295.5	44.4	65 695	372	1 479.6	91.5	1.0	0.6	4.6	0.0	1.3
55 06500	Beloit	42.6	35 775	994	839.8	41.9	35 571	844	848.9	75.6	15.4	0.4	1.2	0.1	4.6
55 10025	Brookfield	70.4	38 649	910	549.0	69.5	35 184	856	506.2	94.2	0.8	0.1	3.8	0.0	0.2
55 22300	Eau Claire	78.4	61 704	482	787.0	71.7	56 806	451	792.3	93.4	0.7	0.5	3.7	0.0	0.3
55 26275	Fond du Lac	43.7	42 203	816	965.7	33.1	37 755	798	1 140.6	93.6	1.9	0.5	1.5	0.0	1.3
55 27300	Franklin	89.7	29 494	1 249	328.8	89.7	21 855	1 506	243.6	90.8	5.2	0.4	2.1	0.0	0.7
55 31000	Green Bay	113.6	102 313	237	900.6	113.5	96 466	212	849.9	85.9	1.4	3.3	3.8	0.0	3.7
55 31175	Greenfield	29.9	35 476	1 004	1 186.5	29.9	33 403	922	1 117.2	93.7	1.0	0.4	2.3	0.0	1.3
55 37825	Janesville	71.3	59 498	511	834.5	60.9	52 210	520	857.3	95.3	1.3	0.2	1.0	0.0	1.0
55 39225	Kenosha	61.7	90 352	283	1 464.4	55.8	80 426	279	1 441.3	83.6	7.7	0.4	1.0	0.0	4.8
55 40775	La Crosse	52.2	51 818	643	992.7	47.5	51 140	536	1 076.6	91.6	1.6	0.5	4.7	0.0	0.4
55 48000	Madison	177.9	208 054	85	1 169.5	149.6	190 766	83	1 275.2	84.0	5.8	0.4	5.8	0.0	1.7
55 48500	Manitowoc	43.7	34 053	1 057	779.2	37.3	32 521	952	871.9	93.1	0.6	0.6	3.8	0.1	0.9
55 51000	Menomonee Falls	86.2	32 647	1 115	378.7	86.2	26 840	1 190	311.4	96.5	1.5	0.2	0.9	0.0	0.2
55 53000	Milwaukee	248.8	596 974	20	2 399.4	248.8	628 088	17	2 524.5	50.0	37.3	0.9	2.9	0.1	6.1
55 56375	New Berlin	95.4	38 220	922	400.6	95.4	33 592	911	352.1	95.8	0.4	0.2	2.3	0.0	0.5
55 58800	Oak Creek	74.1	28 456	1 303	384.0	74.1	19 513	1 682	263.3	92.0	1.8	0.6	2.4	0.0	1.7
55 60500	Oshkosh	61.2	62 916	469	1 028.0	46.5	55 006	472	1 182.9	92.7	2.2	0.5	3.0	0.0	0.5

¹Dry land or land partially or temporarily covered by water.

Table D. Cities

City	Population and population characteristics, 2000 (cont'd)								Population and population characteristics, 1990				
	Race (percent) (cont'd)								Race (percent)				
	Race alone or in combination												
	Two or more races	White	Black	American Indian or Alaska Native	Asian	Native Hawaiian and other Pacific Islander	Some other race	Hispanic¹	White	Black or African American	American Indian or Alaska Native	Asian and Pacific Islander	Hispanic¹
	15	16	17	18	19	20	21	22	23	24	25	26	27
VIRGINIA—Cont'd													
Lynchburg	1.5	67.8	30.6	0.7	1.5	0.1	0.9	1.3	72.5	26.4	0.2	0.8	0.7
Manassas	3.3	74.8	13.9	0.8	4.0	0.2	9.7	15.1	83.5	10.3	0.3	3.1	5.7
Newport News	2.8	55.4	40.6	1.1	3.1	0.3	2.6	4.2	62.6	33.6	0.3	2.3	2.8
Norfolk	2.5	50.1	45.3	1.1	3.6	0.3	2.4	3.8	56.7	39.1	0.4	2.6	2.9
Petersburg	1.0	19.1	79.6	0.5	0.9	0.1	0.8	1.4	26.6	72.1	0.2	0.8	1.2
Portsmouth	1.6	47.0	51.5	1.1	1.1	0.2	0.9	1.7	51.2	47.3	0.3	0.8	1.3
Richmond	1.5	39.2	58.1	0.7	1.5	0.2	2.0	2.6	43.4	55.2	0.2	0.9	0.9
Roanoke	1.8	70.8	27.7	0.7	1.4	0.1	1.3	1.5	74.6	24.3	0.2	0.7	0.7
Suffolk	1.2	54.7	44.1	0.8	1.1	0.1	0.6	1.3	54.7	44.6	0.2	0.4	0.6
Virginia Beach	2.7	73.6	20.0	1.0	6.0	0.3	2.2	4.2	80.5	13.9	0.4	4.3	3.1
WASHINGTON	3.6	84.9	4.0	2.7	6.7	0.7	4.9	7.5	88.5	3.1	1.7	4.3	4.4
Auburn	4.6	86.8	3.5	4.0	4.9	1.0	4.9	7.5	92.4	1.4	2.1	3.0	3.1
Bellevue	3.2	77.0	2.6	0.8	19.0	0.5	3.5	5.3	86.5	2.2	0.4	9.9	2.5
Bellingham	3.1	90.6	1.6	2.5	5.4	0.4	2.9	4.6	93.8	0.8	1.8	2.8	2.4
Bothell	3.0	89.9	1.7	1.2	7.4	0.6	2.4	4.4	94.7	0.8	0.8	3.4	1.9
Bremerton	6.6	80.4	9.4	4.1	7.8	1.7	3.8	6.6	83.9	7.1	1.7	5.3	4.8
Des Moines	4.8	78.0	8.7	2.1	10.1	1.8	4.6	6.6	88.9	3.7	1.0	5.2	3.1
Edmonds	3.0	90.4	1.9	1.7	6.9	0.5	1.9	3.3	93.5	0.9	0.9	4.0	2.0
Everett	4.2	84.7	4.3	2.8	7.6	0.7	4.4	7.1	91.7	1.7	1.7	3.9	2.8
Kennewick	3.4	86.1	1.7	1.7	2.8	0.2	11.0	15.5	89.9	1.1	0.8	2.0	8.7
Kent	5.4	75.0	9.9	2.2	11.4	1.3	6.3	8.1	89.2	3.8	1.4	4.4	3.9
Kirkland	2.9	87.8	2.1	1.1	9.2	0.4	2.4	4.1	92.8	1.5	0.6	4.3	2.4
Lacey	4.7	82.2	6.0	2.5	9.7	1.5	3.2	5.9	88.9	3.0	1.1	6.0	3.5
Longview	2.9	92.0	1.2	3.1	2.8	0.4	3.6	5.8	94.7	0.5	1.5	2.1	2.0
Lynnwood	4.4	78.0	4.2	2.0	15.4	0.8	4.3	7.0	88.5	2.0	1.1	7.6	3.0
Marysville	3.1	90.9	1.5	2.3	5.1	0.7	2.7	4.8	95.0	0.3	2.4	1.9	2.4
Mount Vernon	2.9	78.1	1.1	1.7	3.3	0.3	18.7	25.1	89.6	0.4	1.1	1.4	10.9
Olympia	3.8	88.6	2.7	2.5	7.1	0.7	2.5	4.4	92.0	1.2	1.2	4.8	2.6
Pasco	3.9	56.2	3.7	1.4	2.3	0.3	40.3	56.3	59.9	5.6	0.9	2.5	40.8
Puyallup	4.1	91.5	2.3	2.1	4.9	0.8	2.9	4.7	94.7	0.8	1.2	2.7	2.1
Redmond	3.1	81.8	2.1	1.1	14.6	0.5	3.4	5.6	91.1	1.3	0.5	6.3	2.5
Renton	4.6	71.7	10.0	1.8	15.0	0.9	5.6	7.6	83.5	6.6	1.2	7.7	3.0
Richland	2.3	91.6	1.8	1.5	4.7	0.3	2.6	4.7	93.0	1.4	0.7	3.3	3.0
Sammamish	2.5	90.1	1.2	0.7	9.3	0.2	1.0	2.5	0.0	0.0	0.0	0.0	0.0
Seattle	4.5	73.4	9.9	2.1	15.0	0.9	3.7	5.3	75.3	10.1	1.4	11.8	3.6
Shoreline	4.3	80.5	3.6	2.0	15.2	0.7	2.6	3.9	0.0	0.0	0.0	0.0	0.0
Spokane	3.4	92.6	3.0	3.0	3.0	0.4	1.7	3.0	93.3	1.9	2.0	2.1	2.1
Tacoma	6.3	74.1	13.7	3.6	9.7	1.5	4.4	6.9	78.1	11.4	2.0	6.9	3.8
Vancouver	3.8	88.2	3.3	2.1	5.6	0.9	4.0	6.3	92.3	2.3	1.3	3.2	3.0
Walla Walla	2.8	86.3	3.0	2.0	1.9	0.4	9.5	17.4	88.1	2.2	1.0	1.3	10.2
Wenatchee	2.5	83.2	0.6	1.9	1.5	0.2	15.2	21.5	91.6	0.2	1.1	1.0	8.6
Yakima	3.9	72.2	2.7	3.1	1.7	0.3	24.2	33.7	82.5	2.4	2.0	1.3	16.3
WEST VIRGINIA	0.9	95.9	3.5	0.6	0.7	0.0	0.3	0.7	96.2	3.1	0.1	0.4	0.5
Charleston	1.9	82.3	16.2	0.9	2.1	0.1	0.6	0.8	84.1	14.2	0.2	1.3	0.6
Huntington	1.5	91.0	8.2	0.8	1.1	0.1	0.5	0.8	92.5	6.7	0.1	0.5	0.5
Morgantown	1.5	90.8	4.7	0.5	4.7	0.2	0.8	1.5	92.0	3.5	0.1	4.1	1.1
Parkersburg	1.0	97.3	2.2	0.6	0.5	0.1	0.3	0.8	97.7	1.7	0.2	0.3	0.3
Wheeling	1.1	93.7	5.6	0.3	1.1	0.1	0.3	0.6	94.7	4.5	0.1	0.7	0.3
WISCONSIN	1.2	90.0	6.1	1.3	1.9	0.1	2.0	3.6	92.2	5.0	0.8	1.1	1.9
Appleton	1.3	92.5	1.3	1.0	5.1	0.2	1.4	2.5	96.6	0.2	0.4	2.4	0.9
Beloit	2.8	78.1	16.8	0.9	1.5	0.1	5.5	9.1	81.8	15.7	0.3	1.2	1.9
Brookfield	0.8	94.9	1.0	0.2	4.3	0.1	0.4	1.2	96.9	0.4	0.2	2.4	0.7
Eau Claire	1.3	94.5	1.0	1.0	4.1	0.2	0.6	1.0	95.1	0.4	0.6	3.8	0.6
Fond du Lac	1.2	94.7	2.2	1.0	1.8	0.0	1.6	2.9	97.8	0.3	0.5	0.8	1.5
Franklin	0.9	91.6	5.4	0.6	2.3	0.1	1.0	2.6	94.6	3.7	0.4	0.8	1.6
Green Bay	2.0	87.5	1.9	4.1	4.1	0.1	4.3	7.1	94.2	0.5	2.5	2.3	1.1
Greenfield	1.3	94.9	1.3	0.7	2.5	0.1	1.9	3.9	97.6	0.4	0.4	1.0	2.0
Janesville	1.2	96.4	1.7	0.6	1.2	0.1	1.3	2.6	98.1	0.6	0.2	0.8	1.1
Kenosha	2.4	85.7	8.6	1.0	1.3	0.1	5.7	10.0	89.8	6.4	0.4	0.6	5.9
La Crosse	1.3	92.6	2.0	0.9	5.1	0.2	0.6	1.1	93.8	0.7	0.4	4.9	0.9
Madison	2.3	86.0	6.8	0.9	6.5	0.1	2.2	4.1	90.7	4.2	0.4	3.9	2.0
Manitowoc	1.0	94.0	0.8	0.9	4.1	0.1	1.2	2.5	96.4	0.2	0.5	2.5	1.1
Menomonee Falls	0.7	97.2	1.7	0.4	1.0	0.0	0.3	1.2	98.8	0.3	0.2	0.5	0.6
Milwaukee	2.7	52.1	38.6	1.5	3.4	0.1	7.2	12.0	63.4	30.5	0.9	1.9	6.3
New Berlin	0.7	96.5	0.6	0.4	2.5	0.0	0.6	1.6	98.4	0.2	0.2	1.0	0.8
Oak Creek	1.5	93.3	2.2	1.0	2.8	0.0	2.4	4.5	96.9	0.7	0.5	0.9	3.2
Oshkosh	1.0	93.6	2.4	0.8	3.4	0.1	0.7	1.7	96.3	0.8	0.5	2.2	0.8

¹Hispanic persons may be of any race.

Table D. Cities

City	Population and population characteristics, 2000 Age (percent) Under 5 years	5 to 17 years	18 to 24 years	25 to 34 years	35 to 44 years	45 to 54 years	55 to 64 years	65 to 74 years	75 years and over	Median age (years)	Percent Female
	28	29	30	31	32	33	34	35	36	37	38
VIRGINIA—Cont'd											
Lynchburg	5.8	16.3	15.5	12.2	13.1	12.4	8.4	7.5	8.8	35.1	54.3
Manassas	8.6	21.0	9.8	17.4	18.4	13.1	6.3	3.1	2.3	31.3	49.1
Newport News	7.9	19.6	11.5	15.8	16.4	11.5	7.3	5.4	4.7	32.0	51.6
Norfolk	7.1	17.0	18.2	15.6	14.3	10.7	6.2	5.5	5.4	29.6	48.9
Petersburg	6.4	18.7	8.9	13.0	14.5	13.2	9.7	8.0	7.6	36.9	54.3
Portsmouth	7.1	18.6	11.1	14.0	15.1	12.3	8.0	6.8	6.9	34.5	54.3
Richmond	6.3	15.6	13.1	16.6	15.1	12.6	7.5	6.5	6.7	33.9	53.5
Roanoke	6.5	16.1	8.2	15.2	15.3	13.8	8.5	7.8	8.6	37.6	53.1
Suffolk	7.3	20.6	7.1	13.4	17.8	13.4	9.2	6.3	5.2	36.0	52.2
Virginia Beach	7.2	20.3	10.0	16.4	17.8	12.7	7.1	4.9	3.6	32.7	50.5
WASHINGTON	6.7	19.0	9.5	14.3	16.5	14.4	8.4	5.7	5.5	35.3	50.2
Auburn	7.7	18.9	9.5	15.1	16.5	12.5	8.2	5.7	5.9	34.1	50.4
Bellevue	5.6	15.5	7.8	16.0	16.6	14.8	10.2	7.1	6.4	38.2	50.4
Bellingham	5.2	12.5	23.8	14.3	12.2	12.9	6.6	5.3	7.2	30.4	51.9
Bothell	6.0	19.2	8.1	14.8	18.4	15.8	8.1	4.6	5.0	36.0	51.0
Bremerton	8.1	16.4	15.5	16.1	14.3	10.8	6.4	5.1	7.4	30.9	49.1
Des Moines	6.6	17.2	8.3	14.5	16.6	13.5	8.5	6.0	8.9	37.0	51.8
Edmonds	5.0	15.6	7.0	11.5	15.9	16.8	11.5	8.8	7.8	42.0	52.7
Everett	7.8	17.3	12.3	17.0	16.3	12.3	6.7	4.7	5.6	32.2	49.1
Kennewick	8.4	21.2	10.3	13.8	15.5	13.3	7.3	5.2	5.0	32.3	50.4
Kent	8.4	19.3	10.3	17.4	17.5	12.7	7.0	4.0	3.3	31.8	50.4
Kirkland	5.5	13.0	9.3	19.9	18.2	15.3	8.6	5.0	5.2	36.1	51.3
Lacey	7.7	18.6	9.7	15.0	15.6	13.0	7.0	5.3	8.0	34.2	52.2
Longview	7.1	18.8	8.9	13.1	14.0	13.8	8.8	6.8	8.6	36.6	51.8
Lynnwood	7.1	17.3	10.4	15.4	16.7	13.1	8.1	6.0	5.8	34.9	51.3
Marysville	8.2	21.9	7.9	15.5	17.4	11.3	6.4	4.9	6.4	33.0	51.2
Mount Vernon	8.4	20.6	11.9	14.9	14.1	11.4	6.2	5.3	7.2	31.1	51.0
Olympia	5.4	16.0	11.9	15.2	15.1	15.1	7.8	5.8	7.6	36.0	52.2
Pasco	11.1	24.4	11.8	15.6	12.9	9.8	5.8	4.6	4.1	26.6	48.4
Puyallup	6.9	20.3	10.2	13.9	17.0	13.6	7.2	4.8	6.1	34.1	51.7
Redmond	6.4	15.1	9.5	20.8	17.1	14.1	7.8	3.9	5.4	34.0	49.9
Renton	7.0	14.8	10.2	19.8	17.1	12.9	7.9	4.9	5.4	34.0	50.3
Richland	6.6	20.6	7.5	11.5	15.6	15.4	10.0	6.7	6.1	37.7	51.0
Sammamish	8.4	25.0	4.8	11.2	22.0	18.0	6.7	2.4	1.6	35.3	49.6
Seattle	4.7	10.9	11.9	21.7	16.9	14.5	7.5	5.2	6.8	35.4	50.1
Shoreline	5.2	17.3	7.7	12.8	17.6	16.3	8.5	6.8	7.8	39.3	51.8
Spokane	7.0	17.8	11.1	14.5	15.1	13.1	7.4	6.2	7.8	34.7	51.8
Tacoma	7.0	18.8	10.4	15.4	16.2	12.9	7.4	5.4	6.5	33.9	51.2
Vancouver	8.0	18.7	9.8	16.3	15.8	13.1	7.5	5.2	5.5	33.1	50.8
Walla Walla	6.0	16.8	15.2	13.5	14.0	12.3	7.2	6.2	8.9	33.8	48.0
Wenatchee	8.0	19.4	10.0	14.0	14.3	12.2	7.1	6.8	8.2	34.0	51.1
Yakima	8.9	20.5	10.8	14.5	13.1	11.0	7.2	5.9	8.2	31.4	51.1
WEST VIRGINIA	5.6	16.6	9.5	12.7	15.1	15.0	10.2	8.2	7.1	38.9	51.4
Charleston	5.5	15.1	8.4	12.6	15.4	15.6	9.7	8.5	9.1	40.8	53.4
Huntington	4.9	12.9	17.5	12.7	12.2	12.8	9.0	8.7	9.3	36.7	53.0
Morgantown	3.0	8.1	44.7	11.9	8.5	8.4	5.0	4.8	5.6	23.1	48.9
Parkersburg	5.6	15.6	9.1	12.9	14.2	13.7	10.0	9.1	9.7	39.9	53.3
Wheeling	4.9	15.7	9.1	10.5	13.8	14.6	9.8	10.1	11.5	42.4	54.3
WISCONSIN	6.4	19.1	9.7	13.2	16.3	13.7	8.5	6.6	6.5	36.0	50.6
Appleton	6.9	20.5	9.7	14.7	17.1	12.9	6.9	5.5	5.8	33.8	50.8
Beloit	7.7	20.0	11.5	14.1	14.5	11.9	7.5	6.3	6.6	32.7	52.1
Brookfield	5.4	21.4	4.6	6.8	16.4	16.9	10.9	9.6	8.0	42.5	51.6
Eau Claire	5.8	15.9	22.1	13.2	12.8	12.0	6.2	5.5	6.4	29.4	52.4
Fond du Lac	6.5	17.6	10.7	14.1	15.3	13.1	7.4	6.5	8.8	35.7	53.0
Franklin	5.6	17.8	8.4	13.1	19.7	16.9	8.7	6.0	3.9	37.9	47.8
Green Bay	7.2	18.3	11.6	15.7	16.0	12.5	7.0	5.7	6.1	33.2	50.7
Greenfield	4.5	14.4	8.1	13.1	15.2	14.4	9.9	9.3	11.1	41.7	53.1
Janesville	7.0	19.2	8.3	15.1	16.2	12.7	8.7	6.8	6.1	35.3	51.1
Kenosha	7.5	19.7	10.1	15.0	16.5	11.8	7.2	5.9	6.3	33.6	50.8
La Crosse	4.8	14.0	24.4	12.6	12.4	10.3	6.7	6.6	8.3	30.1	52.9
Madison	5.2	12.7	21.4	17.8	14.4	12.8	6.5	4.6	4.7	30.6	50.9
Manitowoc	6.2	18.0	8.2	12.2	15.7	12.9	8.5	8.2	10.2	38.6	51.6
Menomonee Falls	6.6	18.4	5.4	11.9	18.6	15.9	9.8	8.9	6.8	39.2	51.6
Milwaukee	8.0	20.7	12.2	15.8	14.4	11.4	6.6	5.5	5.4	30.6	52.2
New Berlin	6.0	18.8	6.4	10.8	18.2	16.7	10.4	7.6	5.1	39.8	50.8
Oak Creek	6.7	18.3	9.3	16.7	18.7	13.7	7.8	5.3	3.5	34.5	50.2
Oshkosh	5.4	15.3	18.1	14.8	14.9	11.5	6.8	6.0	7.1	32.4	50.0

Table D. Cities

City	Under 5 years	5 to 17 years	18 to 24 years	25 to 34 years	35 to 44 years	45 to 54 years	55 to 64 years	65 to 74 years	75 years and over	Percent Female	2000	1990	1980	1990–2000	1980–1990
	Population and population characteristics, 1990 — Age (percent)										**Population—change, 1980–2000 — Total persons**			**Percent change**	
	39	40	41	42	43	44	45	46	47	48	49	50	51	52	53
VIRGINIA—Cont'd															
Lynchburg	6.9	15.8	15.5	14.7	13.0	9.0	8.6	8.8	7.7	55.0	65 269	66 049	66 743	-1.2	-1.0
Manassas	9.7	18.6	12.0	23.5	17.6	9.4	4.4	2.9	2.0	49.0	35 135	27 957	15 438	25.7	81.1
Newport News	9.2	18.2	12.1	21.7	13.9	8.6	7.0	5.9	3.4	51.0	180 150	171 439	144 903	5.1	18.3
Norfolk	8.3	14.7	21.6	20.1	11.7	6.6	6.5	6.3	4.1	46.7	234 403	261 250	266 979	-10.3	-2.1
Petersburg	7.4	15.9	11.8	17.0	13.8	9.7	9.5	9.0	6.0	53.8	33 740	37 027	41 055	-8.9	-9.8
Portsmouth	8.4	18.2	11.1	18.0	12.9	9.1	8.5	8.7	5.0	52.4	100 565	103 910	104 577	-3.2	-0.6
Richmond	6.9	14.0	12.9	19.5	14.4	8.6	8.4	8.5	6.8	54.3	197 790	202 798	219 214	-2.5	-7.5
Roanoke	7.1	15.2	9.4	18.0	14.6	9.2	9.4	9.4	7.6	53.7	94 911	96 509	100 220	-1.7	-3.7
Suffolk	7.7	19.4	8.5	16.8	14.2	11.3	9.1	8.0	5.0	52.6	63 677	52 143	47 621	22.1	9.5
Virginia Beach	8.9	19.0	12.8	22.6	15.8	9.1	6.0	3.9	2.0	49.2	425 257	393 089	262 199	8.2	49.9
WASHINGTON	7.5	18.4	10.0	17.6	16.5	10.3	7.8	6.9	4.9	50.4	5 894 121	4 866 669	4 132 353	21.1	17.8
Auburn	8.4	17.2	10.7	20.3	14.6	9.5	7.8	6.6	4.9	51.2	40 314	33 650	26 417	19.8	27.4
Bellevue	5.7	15.3	9.9	18.2	16.6	13.9	10.0	6.8	3.6	51.1	109 569	86 872	73 883	26.1	17.6
Bellingham	5.4	13.8	21.1	15.8	15.5	7.7	6.6	6.8	7.3	52.4	67 171	52 179	45 805	28.7	13.9
Bothell	7.5	17.6	8.5	18.0	17.0	11.5	7.3	7.3	5.3	52.1	30 150	12 345	NA	144.2	NA
Bremerton	9.4	14.1	19.2	19.6	11.3	6.9	6.1	7.1	6.4	46.9	37 259	38 142	36 209	-2.3	5.3
Des Moines	6.8	13.6	10.1	20.9	14.4	9.6	7.2	7.8	9.6	52.8	29 267	17 283	NA	69.3	NA
Edmonds	5.9	15.0	8.5	15.2	16.5	13.3	10.9	9.0	5.6	52.7	39 515	30 743	27 679	28.5	11.1
Everett	8.6	16.4	11.1	20.9	14.3	9.0	6.7	6.9	6.3	50.4	91 488	70 937	54 413	29.0	30.4
Kennewick	9.1	21.5	10.2	18.6	15.7	9.4	6.4	5.5	3.7	51.0	54 693	42 148	34 397	29.8	22.5
Kent	8.7	15.7	13.5	24.4	14.8	9.9	6.4	4.0	2.6	49.8	79 524	37 960	23 152	109.5	64.0
Kirkland	6.7	14.0	10.9	23.3	18.3	10.4	6.7	5.6	4.0	52.1	45 054	40 059	18 779	12.5	113.3
Lacey	7.2	18.3	10.7	15.7	15.6	9.5	7.2	7.0	8.8	52.8	31 226	19 279	13 940	62.0	38.3
Longview	7.5	18.6	9.1	15.5	15.6	10.2	8.6	8.0	6.9	51.7	34 660	31 499	31 041	10.0	1.5
Lynnwood	8.0	16.8	11.1	21.3	15.4	10.3	7.4	5.8	3.9	51.3	33 847	28 637	22 641	18.2	26.5
Marysville	9.9	16.3	10.2	20.5	13.0	6.7	6.6	7.8	9.0	52.9	25 315	12 248	NA	106.7	NA
Mount Vernon	8.4	18.4	9.9	18.4	15.6	8.1	7.0	7.0	7.1	52.1	26 232	17 647	13 009	48.6	35.7
Olympia	6.3	16.2	10.3	16.9	18.4	9.7	7.6	8.0	6.5	52.6	42 514	33 729	27 447	26.0	22.9
Pasco	10.2	23.6	12.7	16.8	12.2	6.6	6.7	6.3	4.8	48.8	32 066	20 337	17 944	57.7	13.3
Puyallup	8.0	20.1	8.8	17.6	15.7	10.3	6.7	6.0	6.8	52.0	33 011	23 878	18 239	38.2	30.9
Redmond	6.9	18.3	9.8	21.1	19.9	11.4	5.8	3.7	3.1	50.8	45 256	35 800	23 318	26.4	53.5
Renton	7.2	14.8	10.9	23.3	15.9	10.0	7.3	6.3	4.2	50.3	50 052	41 688	30 612	20.1	36.2
Richland	7.2	19.1	8.1	16.2	15.6	11.8	9.5	7.9	4.7	51.2	38 708	32 315	33 578	19.8	-3.8
Sammamish	NA	NA	NA	NA	NA	NA	NA	NA	NA	NA	34 104	NA	NA	NA	NA
Seattle	5.6	10.7	11.9	21.9	18.0	9.2	7.4	8.2	7.0	51.2	563 374	516 259	493 846	9.1	4.5
Shoreline	NA	NA	NA	NA	NA	NA	NA	NA	NA	NA	53 025	49 229	NA	7.7	NA
Spokane	7.5	16.9	10.8	17.7	14.4	8.7	7.8	8.6	7.7	52.3	195 629	177 165	171 300	10.4	3.4
Tacoma	8.2	17.7	10.9	18.9	14.6	8.7	7.3	7.2	6.4	51.6	193 556	176 664	158 501	9.6	11.5
Vancouver	7.9	15.4	11.4	18.4	14.1	8.7	8.7	8.7	7.7	52.2	143 560	54 651	42 834	162.7	27.6
Walla Walla	6.7	17.2	12.8	16.1	14.2	8.7	7.3	8.4	8.6	48.9	29 686	26 482	25 631	12.1	3.3
Wenatchee	7.7	17.7	9.2	16.0	14.6	8.7	8.6	8.8	8.8	52.4	27 856	21 746	17 257	28.1	26.0
Yakima	8.8	17.8	10.4	16.7	13.7	8.4	7.8	8.2	8.2	51.8	71 845	58 427	49 826	23.0	17.3
WEST VIRGINIA	5.9	18.8	10.0	14.6	15.1	10.7	9.9	8.7	6.3	52.0	1 808 344	1 793 477	1 950 186	0.8	-8.0
Charleston	6.0	15.7	8.0	16.0	15.2	10.2	10.6	10.2	8.1	54.5	53 421	57 287	63 968	-6.7	-10.4
Huntington	4.9	14.5	15.0	13.3	12.3	9.6	10.4	10.9	9.0	54.6	51 475	54 844	63 684	-6.1	-13.9
Morgantown	3.8	8.1	43.0	12.5	9.6	5.7	5.9	6.5	4.9	50.3	26 809	25 879	27 605	3.6	-6.3
Parkersburg	6.0	16.1	8.7	14.5	14.0	10.3	10.7	10.4	9.3	54.3	33 099	33 862	39 967	-2.3	-15.3
Wheeling	5.6	15.3	8.6	13.3	13.3	10.6	11.4	12.3	9.7	54.6	31 419	34 882	43 067	-9.9	-19.0
WISCONSIN	7.4	19.0	10.5	16.8	14.8	9.8	8.5	7.3	6.0	51.1	5 363 675	4 891 769	4 705 642	9.6	4.0
Appleton	8.1	19.3	9.9	19.0	15.2	9.3	7.3	6.3	5.7	51.8	70 087	65 695	59 040	6.7	11.3
Beloit	8.8	19.8	11.6	16.4	12.9	9.0	8.0	7.4	6.1	53.2	35 775	35 571	35 207	0.6	1.0
Brookfield	6.3	19.5	6.8	11.2	17.0	13.7	12.9	8.3	4.3	50.7	38 649	35 184	34 035	9.8	3.4
Eau Claire	7.0	16.1	21.6	15.2	13.6	7.3	6.6	6.9	5.8	53.1	61 704	56 806	51 516	8.6	10.3
Fond du Lac	7.2	18.9	9.7	16.5	14.5	8.6	8.2	8.3	8.0	53.0	42 203	37 755	35 863	11.8	5.3
Franklin	7.1	18.6	9.1	19.1	19.7	10.8	8.3	5.2	2.1	48.1	29 494	21 855	16 871	35.0	29.5
Green Bay	8.1	17.8	11.2	19.5	14.8	8.6	7.4	6.9	5.8	52.2	102 313	96 466	87 899	6.1	9.7
Greenfield	5.3	13.7	9.6	17.3	15.9	10.3	10.7	9.7	7.4	53.0	35 476	33 403	31 467	6.2	6.2
Janesville	8.1	18.3	9.6	17.9	14.6	10.7	8.8	6.7	5.3	51.5	59 498	52 210	51 071	14.0	2.2
Kenosha	8.3	18.8	10.5	17.9	14.2	8.9	7.9	7.4	6.1	51.9	90 352	80 426	77 685	12.3	3.5
La Crosse	6.6	13.7	22.4	15.7	11.7	6.8	7.6	7.8	7.9	53.7	51 818	51 140	48 347	1.3	5.8
Madison	6.2	12.3	22.2	20.3	15.2	8.3	6.3	5.0	4.2	51.3	208 054	190 766	170 616	9.1	11.8
Manitowoc	6.6	17.3	8.1	15.9	14.0	8.9	9.3	9.7	10.1	52.7	34 053	32 521	32 547	4.7	-0.1
Menomonee Falls	6.7	17.1	8.1	16.5	13.7	13.5	12.8	7.4	4.3	50.7	32 647	26 840	27 845	21.6	-3.6
Milwaukee	8.6	18.8	12.0	19.1	13.5	8.0	7.6	6.9	5.5	52.7	596 974	628 088	636 212	-5.0	-1.3
New Berlin	6.7	19.0	7.9	15.8	17.7	13.6	10.7	5.8	2.7	50.1	38 220	33 592	30 529	13.8	10.0
Oak Creek	6.9	19.4	9.9	19.3	15.9	11.7	8.8	5.4	2.8	50.4	28 456	19 513	16 932	45.8	15.2
Oshkosh	6.6	14.6	19.0	17.2	13.1	7.8	7.6	7.1	6.9	52.3	62 916	55 006	49 620	14.4	10.9

Table D. Cities

City	Total population	Total in house-holds	House-holder	Spouse	Child Total	Child Own child under 18 years	Other relatives Total	Other relatives Under 18 years	Nonrelatives Total	Nonrelatives Unmar-ried partner	Total in group quarters	Correc-tional institu-tions	Nurs-ing homes	Other institu-tions	Col-lege dormi-tories	Mili-tary quar-ters	Other
	54	55	56	57	58	59	60	61	62	63	64	65	66	67	68	69	70
VIRGINIA—Cont'd																	
Lynchburg	65 269	90.0	39.0	16.2	25.0	19.4	4.7	2.0	5.0	1.7	10.0	0.7	1.7	0.3	6.8	0.0	0.6
Manassas	35 135	97.5	33.5	18.7	32.6	26.9	6.1	1.9	6.8	2.0	2.5	1.5	0.6	0.0	0.0	0.0	0.3
Newport News	180 150	96.8	38.7	17.3	30.4	24.4	4.9	2.4	5.6	2.0	3.2	0.4	0.6	0.1	0.4	1.4	0.3
Norfolk	234 403	90.1	36.8	13.6	26.2	20.4	6.1	3.0	7.4	2.3	9.9	0.6	0.5	0.2	1.4	7.0	0.3
Petersburg	33 740	97.3	40.9	12.3	28.3	19.6	9.2	4.6	6.6	2.8	2.7	0.5	1.0	0.3	0.0	0.0	0.9
Portsmouth	100 565	95.2	38.0	15.6	28.6	20.8	7.6	3.9	5.4	2.1	4.8	1.2	0.4	0.2	0.0	2.5	0.5
Richmond	197 790	94.3	42.7	11.6	23.8	17.5	7.6	3.6	8.6	2.6	5.7	0.8	0.7	0.1	2.9	0.0	1.2
Roanoke	94 911	97.3	44.3	16.4	25.5	19.5	5.6	2.5	5.6	2.5	2.7	0.7	1.1	0.0	0.1	0.0	0.8
Suffolk	63 677	98.5	36.6	20.2	31.7	24.2	6.4	3.0	3.6	1.5	1.5	0.7	0.7	0.0	0.0	0.0	0.2
Virginia Beach	425 257	98.2	36.3	20.2	31.2	25.1	4.5	1.8	6.0	1.9	1.8	0.2	0.4	0.0	0.0	1.0	0.1
WASHINGTON	5 894 121	97.7	38.5	20.1	28.7	23.5	4.0	1.5	6.4	2.4	2.3	0.5	0.4	0.1	0.5	0.2	0.6
Auburn	40 314	98.5	40.0	17.5	29.4	24.2	4.2	1.7	7.4	3.2	1.5	0.1	0.4	0.0	0.0	0.0	0.9
Bellevue	109 569	99.3	41.8	22.2	25.2	19.9	3.9	0.9	6.2	1.7	0.7	0.0	0.2	0.0	0.0	0.0	0.5
Bellingham	67 171	93.2	41.7	15.6	20.1	16.5	2.5	0.7	13.3	2.9	6.8	0.4	1.0	0.1	4.7	0.0	0.5
Bothell	30 150	99.3	39.5	21.3	29.5	23.9	3.3	0.9	5.7	2.1	0.7	0.0	0.6	0.0	0.0	0.0	0.1
Bremerton	37 259	93.1	40.5	15.6	26.2	22.2	3.3	1.4	7.5	2.8	6.9	0.0	0.9	0.1	0.0	5.4	0.5
Des Moines	29 267	95.7	38.7	18.3	27.1	21.4	5.0	1.7	6.7	2.6	4.3	0.0	4.2	0.1	0.0	0.0	0.1
Edmonds	39 515	99.1	42.8	22.3	24.9	19.3	3.5	1.0	5.7	2.0	0.9	0.0	0.4	0.0	0.2	0.0	0.3
Everett	91 488	95.4	39.7	16.7	27.5	22.9	4.0	1.3	7.5	3.0	4.6	0.6	0.2	0.1	0.0	2.3	1.3
Kennewick	54 693	98.9	38.0	19.6	32.3	27.2	3.9	1.6	5.2	2.3	1.1	0.5	0.3	0.1	0.0	0.0	0.2
Kent	79 524	99.1	39.1	17.7	30.4	25.4	4.9	1.5	7.0	2.9	0.9	0.1	0.1	0.0	0.0	0.0	0.7
Kirkland	45 054	98.1	46.0	19.3	21.7	17.4	3.1	0.7	7.9	2.6	1.9	0.0	0.6	0.0	0.8	0.0	0.4
Lacey	31 226	98.5	39.9	20.0	29.2	24.3	3.5	1.4	5.8	2.4	1.5	0.0	1.0	0.0	0.3	0.0	0.2
Longview	34 660	97.5	40.6	18.9	28.0	23.4	3.6	1.5	6.4	2.8	2.5	0.2	1.2	0.2	0.0	0.0	0.9
Lynnwood	33 847	98.5	39.4	18.2	28.8	22.4	5.3	1.4	6.7	2.2	1.5	0.1	0.0	0.0	0.0	0.0	1.4
Marysville	25 315	98.9	37.1	20.1	32.6	28.3	3.4	1.1	5.6	2.6	1.1	0.1	0.4	0.0	0.0	0.0	0.6
Mount Vernon	26 232	97.1	35.4	18.1	30.9	25.9	5.9	2.0	6.8	2.2	2.9	0.5	1.3	0.1	0.5	0.0	0.5
Olympia	42 514	96.9	43.9	17.4	23.9	19.9	2.7	0.9	9.0	3.2	3.1	1.0	1.1	0.0	0.0	0.0	1.0
Pasco	32 066	98.9	30.0	16.4	37.2	31.0	9.4	3.6	5.9	2.0	1.1	0.4	0.4	0.0	0.0	0.0	0.3
Puyallup	33 011	98.5	39.0	19.4	30.8	25.3	3.4	1.3	5.9	2.5	1.5	0.0	0.8	0.0	0.0	0.0	0.7
Redmond	45 256	98.2	42.2	20.6	24.9	20.4	3.3	0.7	7.1	2.2	1.8	0.0	0.6	0.2	0.0	0.0	1.1
Renton	50 052	99.2	43.4	17.7	24.7	19.7	5.5	1.4	7.9	3.0	0.8	0.1	0.5	0.0	0.0	0.0	0.2
Richland	38 708	99.7	40.2	22.5	30.8	25.7	2.5	1.0	3.6	1.6	0.3	0.0	0.2	0.0	0.0	0.0	0.1
Sammamish	34 104	100.0	32.6	25.9	37.1	32.7	1.8	0.5	2.5	1.1	0.0	0.0	0.0	0.0	0.0	0.0	0.0
Seattle	563 374	95.3	45.9	15.0	18.1	13.8	4.5	1.2	11.8	3.6	4.7	0.6	0.5	0.1	1.9	0.0	1.6
Shoreline	53 025	97.5	39.1	20.0	27.6	21.0	4.1	1.0	6.8	2.1	2.5	0.0	0.7	0.4	0.0	0.0	1.4
Spokane	195 629	96.9	41.7	17.2	27.3	22.6	3.3	1.3	7.3	2.8	3.1	0.4	0.8	0.2	0.8	0.0	1.0
Tacoma	193 556	96.5	39.3	16.4	28.3	22.6	5.3	2.2	7.3	2.7	3.5	0.7	0.6	0.3	0.7	0.0	1.2
Vancouver	143 560	98.5	39.4	18.7	29.4	24.5	4.0	1.4	7.0	2.8	1.5	0.4	0.4	0.1	0.0	0.0	0.5
Walla Walla	29 686	87.1	35.7	16.6	25.2	20.6	4.0	1.6	5.6	1.8	12.9	8.2	1.3	0.0	2.9	0.0	0.4
Wenatchee	27 856	97.6	38.6	19.1	29.8	24.9	4.6	1.7	5.5	2.2	2.4	0.9	0.7	0.1	0.1	0.0	0.6
Yakima	71 845	97.0	36.9	16.3	31.2	25.9	6.2	2.5	6.5	2.7	3.0	1.2	1.0	0.1	0.1	0.0	0.6
WEST VIRGINIA	1 808 344	97.6	40.7	22.0	27.2	20.1	3.8	1.6	3.9	1.9	2.4	0.6	0.6	0.1	0.8	0.0	0.3
Charleston	53 421	96.9	45.9	17.8	24.7	18.7	4.0	1.6	4.5	2.2	3.1	0.7	0.8	0.0	0.6	0.0	1.0
Huntington	51 475	94.4	44.6	16.5	22.1	15.6	4.3	1.5	7.0	2.0	5.6	0.5	0.9	0.5	3.2	0.0	0.4
Morgantown	26 809	83.9	40.2	11.7	13.5	10.3	2.2	0.4	16.2	1.8	16.1	0.2	0.3	0.1	15.1	0.0	0.4
Parkersburg	33 099	97.4	43.7	18.9	25.4	18.8	4.3	1.7	5.1	2.6	2.6	0.3	1.1	0.1	0.5	0.0	0.6
Wheeling	31 419	94.8	43.7	18.2	25.2	18.6	3.6	1.4	4.1	2.1	5.2	0.2	1.5	0.1	2.3	0.0	1.0
WISCONSIN	5 363 675	97.1	38.9	20.7	29.4	23.7	3.0	1.1	5.2	2.2	2.9	0.6	0.8	0.1	1.0	0.0	0.5
Appleton	70 087	96.6	38.3	20.7	31.0	26.2	2.1	0.6	4.6	2.1	3.4	0.8	0.7	0.0	1.4	0.0	0.6
Beloit	35 775	96.1	37.4	16.6	30.3	24.4	5.3	2.3	6.4	3.0	3.9	0.0	1.0	0.0	2.7	0.0	0.3
Brookfield	38 649	98.3	35.9	26.3	32.3	26.1	2.2	0.6	1.6	0.8	1.7	0.0	1.2	0.0	0.0	0.0	0.4
Eau Claire	61 704	92.5	38.9	17.3	24.5	20.4	1.9	0.6	9.9	2.4	7.5	0.5	0.6	0.3	5.5	0.0	0.6
Fond du Lac	42 203	93.6	39.4	19.1	27.5	22.7	2.2	0.8	5.5	2.4	6.4	2.7	2.0	0.0	0.9	0.0	0.8
Franklin	29 494	92.9	35.9	22.7	28.9	22.3	2.3	0.6	3.0	1.4	7.1	6.4	0.0	0.0	0.0	0.0	0.8
Green Bay	102 313	97.4	40.7	17.9	28.5	23.7	3.2	1.1	7.0	3.1	2.6	0.2	0.8	0.1	1.0	0.0	0.5
Greenfield	35 476	97.4	44.2	20.9	24.3	17.6	3.1	0.9	4.8	2.4	2.6	0.0	1.7	0.0	0.0	0.0	0.9
Janesville	59 498	98.5	40.2	20.5	29.5	24.3	2.7	1.1	5.6	2.7	1.5	0.0	0.6	0.2	0.0	0.0	0.6
Kenosha	90 352	96.7	38.1	17.9	30.9	24.6	4.4	1.9	4.5	2.6	3.3	0.7	0.9	0.0	1.2	0.0	0.5
La Crosse	51 818	90.7	40.7	14.7	21.3	17.4	2.1	0.6	11.9	2.6	9.3	0.5	1.2	0.2	6.4	0.0	0.9
Madison	208 054	93.8	42.8	15.8	20.0	16.7	2.4	0.7	12.8	3.0	6.2	0.4	0.5	0.4	4.4	0.0	0.6
Manitowoc	34 053	97.2	41.8	20.5	27.9	22.9	2.3	0.7	4.7	2.3	2.8	0.6	1.0	0.0	0.0	0.0	1.1
Menomonee Falls	32 647	99.3	39.3	25.0	30.3	24.2	2.1	0.6	2.5	1.2	0.7	0.0	0.6	0.0	0.0	0.0	0.1
Milwaukee	596 974	97.3	38.9	12.5	31.1	24.1	7.3	3.5	7.5	2.8	2.7	0.4	0.6	0.1	1.1	0.0	0.5
New Berlin	38 220	99.4	37.9	25.8	30.8	23.9	2.2	0.6	2.8	1.3	0.6	0.0	0.3	0.0	0.0	0.0	0.2
Oak Creek	28 456	99.7	39.5	22.3	30.5	23.8	2.7	0.8	4.7	2.5	0.3	0.0	0.1	0.0	0.0	0.0	0.3
Oshkosh	62 916	88.3	38.3	16.9	23.4	19.4	2.0	0.7	7.7	2.5	11.7	4.0	1.0	0.6	5.4	0.0	0.7

Table D. Cities

City	Households by type, 2000												Households, 1990		
		Family households						Nonfamily households							
				Married couple		Female householder[1]			Householder living alone						
	Total households	Total	With own children under 18 years	Total	With own children under 18 years	Total	With own children under 18 years	Total	Total	65 years and over	Average household size	Average family size	Total households	Female householder[1]	Householder living alone
	71	72	73	74	75	76	77	78	79	80	81	82	83	84	85
VIRGINIA—Cont'd															
Lynchburg	25 477	61.2	27.8	41.6	16.3	16.0	9.7	38.8	32.7	12.9	2.30	2.92	25 143	15.6	30.5
Manassas	11 757	71.8	42.3	55.8	32.4	11.3	7.3	28.2	21.1	3.7	2.92	3.39	9 481	9.2	17.0
Newport News	69 686	66.5	35.7	44.6	21.4	17.9	12.1	33.5	27.0	8.1	2.50	3.04	63 952	15.1	23.7
Norfolk	86 210	60.2	30.3	36.9	16.4	18.8	11.7	39.8	30.2	9.6	2.45	3.07	89 478	16.1	26.8
Petersburg	13 799	61.7	27.6	30.1	10.2	26.1	15.0	38.3	32.2	11.7	2.38	2.98	14 730	23.0	30.3
Portsmouth	38 170	66.8	30.6	41.1	16.4	20.9	12.0	33.2	27.5	10.8	2.51	3.05	38 741	19.3	24.5
Richmond	84 549	51.6	23.1	27.1	9.6	20.4	11.9	48.4	37.6	10.9	2.21	2.95	85 337	19.8	35.9
Roanoke	42 003	57.7	25.5	37.1	13.8	16.5	9.7	42.3	35.9	12.8	2.20	2.86	41 030	15.7	32.3
Suffolk	23 283	76.1	36.6	55.1	25.0	16.8	9.6	23.9	20.2	8.1	2.69	3.09	18 516	17.1	20.4
Virginia Beach	154 455	71.8	38.8	55.7	28.6	12.4	8.0	28.2	20.4	5.5	2.70	3.14	135 566	9.5	17.1
WASHINGTON	2 271 398	66.0	32.7	52.0	23.8	9.9	6.5	34.0	26.2	8.1	2.53	3.07	1 872 431	9.4	25.4
Auburn	16 108	62.4	32.8	43.7	20.4	13.4	9.1	37.6	29.1	9.1	2.47	3.05	13 357	12.8	27.6
Bellevue	45 836	63.4	27.5	53.0	22.2	7.5	4.1	36.6	28.4	7.9	2.37	2.93	35 756	7.9	26.0
Bellingham	27 999	50.0	23.1	37.5	15.2	9.2	6.2	50.0	33.0	10.3	2.24	2.83	21 189	9.1	31.6
Bothell	11 923	66.5	33.9	53.9	26.4	8.9	5.4	33.5	25.7	7.1	2.51	3.05	4 919	8.7	24.8
Bremerton	15 096	56.1	30.2	38.4	17.8	13.3	9.4	43.9	35.4	11.9	2.30	2.98	14 718	10.9	32.6
Des Moines	11 337	64.3	30.4	47.1	19.6	12.2	8.2	35.7	27.8	6.9	2.47	3.02	7 054	11.3	30.2
Edmonds	16 904	64.0	26.1	52.0	19.7	8.7	4.7	36.0	29.0	10.1	2.32	2.85	12 628	8.7	25.1
Everett	36 325	59.5	31.9	42.1	20.2	12.5	8.6	40.5	31.7	8.5	2.40	3.04	28 679	12.2	30.1
Kennewick	20 786	68.2	37.6	51.5	25.6	12.2	8.9	31.8	26.1	8.6	2.60	3.15	16 074	11.5	25.7
Kent	31 113	63.0	35.5	45.1	23.4	12.8	9.2	37.0	28.5	5.8	2.53	3.15	16 246	11.2	30.8
Kirkland	20 736	53.2	23.3	42.0	16.8	8.1	4.8	46.8	35.6	6.7	2.13	2.80	17 211	9.0	30.1
Lacey	12 459	65.4	34.1	50.1	23.6	11.4	8.1	34.6	28.2	11.0	2.47	3.02	7 722	10.0	27.9
Longview	14 066	63.5	30.9	46.5	19.0	12.3	8.8	36.5	30.1	12.4	2.40	2.96	12 875	10.7	29.2
Lynnwood	13 328	62.5	32.1	46.3	22.7	11.5	7.0	37.5	29.3	9.4	2.50	3.13	11 331	11.9	26.6
Marysville	9 400	70.3	40.5	54.1	29.3	11.3	8.1	29.7	23.5	10.4	2.66	3.15	4 288	10.1	30.5
Mount Vernon	9 276	66.9	36.5	51.3	25.9	11.4	8.2	33.1	26.1	10.9	2.75	3.32	6 885	11.3	28.8
Olympia	18 670	53.4	26.8	39.6	17.6	10.4	7.2	46.6	35.2	10.7	2.21	2.88	14 951	10.0	34.5
Pasco	9 619	75.5	45.6	54.7	32.0	14.3	9.9	24.5	20.1	8.5	3.30	3.79	6 842	15.3	25.1
Puyallup	12 870	66.2	36.0	49.7	24.8	11.7	8.2	33.8	26.9	9.5	2.53	3.08	8 944	9.7	25.1
Redmond	19 102	59.4	28.5	48.9	22.4	7.6	4.7	40.6	30.4	6.1	2.33	2.95	14 153	8.8	25.1
Renton	21 708	56.4	26.8	40.9	17.5	10.8	6.9	43.6	34.0	8.1	2.29	2.96	18 219	9.9	32.5
Richland	15 549	68.7	34.1	56.0	25.1	9.3	6.7	31.3	27.2	9.4	2.48	3.02	13 162	8.4	28.0
Sammamish	11 131	86.7	53.3	79.5	48.5	5.3	3.7	13.3	9.4	1.5	3.06	3.29	NA	NA	NA
Seattle	258 499	43.9	17.9	32.7	12.5	8.1	4.2	56.1	40.8	9.3	2.08	2.87	236 702	9.0	39.8
Shoreline	20 716	65.1	30.6	51.2	23.2	10.0	5.5	34.9	26.4	9.1	2.50	3.03	NA	NA	NA
Spokane	81 512	58.0	29.4	41.3	18.4	12.4	8.3	42.0	33.9	11.7	2.32	2.98	75 147	12.4	33.8
Tacoma	76 152	60.3	30.9	41.6	19.0	13.9	9.0	39.7	31.7	10.4	2.45	3.10	69 939	13.3	31.3
Vancouver	56 628	64.1	33.4	47.3	22.3	12.1	8.3	35.9	27.6	8.3	2.50	3.06	20 138	13.2	35.7
Walla Walla	10 596	61.6	30.6	46.4	20.5	11.0	7.5	38.4	31.9	15.1	2.44	3.08	9 912	10.5	32.1
Wenatchee	10 741	64.1	33.4	49.4	24.0	10.2	6.7	35.9	30.1	13.4	2.53	3.17	8 986	10.5	31.7
Yakima	26 498	63.5	34.4	44.2	21.2	14.2	10.1	36.5	30.3	14.0	2.63	3.29	21 596	12.1	30.7
WEST VIRGINIA	736 481	68.4	28.9	54.0	21.3	10.7	5.7	31.6	27.1	11.9	2.40	2.90	688 557	10.7	24.5
Charleston	24 505	55.6	23.7	38.9	14.3	13.5	7.9	44.4	38.9	14.5	2.11	2.82	25 306	13.9	35.7
Huntington	22 955	63.4	20.6	36.9	12.7	13.1	6.6	46.7	37.6	15.1	2.12	2.80	23 419	13.2	35.6
Morgantown	10 782	38.8	15.0	29.1	10.9	7.0	3.3	61.2	37.3	9.5	2.08	2.76	9 588	6.9	34.8
Parkersburg	14 467	60.6	25.0	43.2	15.4	13.5	7.7	39.4	34.0	15.1	2.23	2.83	14 463	13.0	31.5
Wheeling	13 719	56.9	23.4	41.8	15.5	12.2	6.4	43.1	38.3	18.6	2.17	2.89	15 038	12.5	36.3
WISCONSIN	2 084 544	66.5	31.9	53.2	23.7	9.6	5.8	33.5	26.8	9.9	2.50	3.05	1 822 118	9.6	24.3
Appleton	26 864	65.8	35.0	53.9	27.2	8.7	5.8	34.2	27.6	9.1	2.52	3.13	24 818	8.6	24.8
Beloit	13 370	66.6	34.0	44.5	19.5	16.6	11.5	33.4	27.5	11.3	2.57	3.10	13 307	16.1	26.3
Brookfield	13 891	80.8	36.1	73.1	32.6	5.5	2.6	19.2	16.7	9.0	2.74	3.09	11 939	5.1	11.3
Eau Claire	24 016	66.5	27.7	44.4	19.8	9.3	6.3	43.5	30.0	10.5	2.38	2.99	21 118	9.4	27.8
Fond du Lac	16 638	61.8	30.6	48.4	21.8	9.8	6.7	38.2	30.9	12.5	2.38	3.00	14 637	9.9	28.4
Franklin	10 602	72.6	33.8	63.2	28.8	6.6	3.7	27.4	22.5	6.9	2.58	3.06	7 434	5.9	18.0
Green Bay	41 591	59.3	30.6	44.1	20.5	10.8	7.6	40.7	31.6	9.9	2.40	3.06	38 383	10.8	29.1
Greenfield	15 697	58.4	22.6	47.3	17.3	8.0	3.8	41.6	34.6	14.4	2.20	2.87	13 785	8.0	28.6
Janesville	23 894	65.9	32.7	51.1	22.8	10.5	7.2	34.1	27.4	9.7	2.45	2.99	20 388	10.0	25.2
Kenosha	34 411	65.5	34.1	47.1	22.5	13.9	9.1	34.5	28.4	10.3	2.54	3.13	29 919	14.0	25.7
La Crosse	21 110	48.4	22.0	36.1	14.4	9.3	6.0	51.6	37.0	13.0	2.23	2.93	19 970	10.1	33.2
Madison	89 019	47.7	22.1	37.0	15.7	7.8	5.0	52.3	35.3	7.1	2.19	2.87	77 361	8.3	31.2
Manitowoc	14 235	61.9	28.6	49.0	20.3	9.1	6.1	38.1	32.5	14.6	2.32	2.96	13 144	8.4	31.1
Menomonee Falls	12 844	72.4	32.4	63.6	28.0	6.5	3.2	27.6	23.7	11.2	2.52	3.01	9 817	5.9	17.9
Milwaukee	232 188	58.2	30.5	32.2	14.3	21.1	13.9	41.8	33.5	9.5	2.50	3.25	240 540	19.8	30.5
New Berlin	14 495	76.2	34.0	68.0	30.1	5.7	2.9	23.8	19.0	7.0	2.62	3.03	11 695	5.4	13.7
Oak Creek	11 239	67.0	33.3	56.4	27.2	7.1	4.3	33.0	25.3	7.0	2.52	3.10	7 081	7.0	20.3
Oshkosh	24 082	56.7	27.3	44.3	19.3	9.1	6.1	43.3	32.4	11.7	2.31	2.95	20 957	9.2	29.7

[1] No spouse present.

Table D. Cities

City	Percent change of households, 1990–2000	Total housing units	Occupied housing units (percent)	Vacant housing units — Total	For seasonal, recreational, or occasional use	Homeowner vacancy rate (percent)	Rental vacancy rate (percent)	Occupied housing units — Total	Percent owner-occupied housing units	Percent renter-occupied housing units	Average household size of owner-occupied units	Average household size of renter-occupied units
	86	87	88	89	90	91	92	93	94	95	96	97
VIRGINIA—Cont'd												
Lynchburg	1.3	27 640	92.2	7.8	0.5	2.2	7.1	25 477	58.5	41.5	2.44	2.12
Manassas	24.0	12 114	97.1	2.9	0.2	1.0	3.6	11 757	69.8	30.2	2.98	2.78
Newport News	9.0	74 117	94.0	6.0	0.3	1.9	6.2	69 686	52.4	47.6	2.61	2.39
Norfolk	-3.7	94 416	91.3	8.7	0.3	3.2	6.9	86 210	45.5	54.5	2.51	2.40
Petersburg	-6.3	15 955	86.5	13.5	0.1	3.4	12.4	13 799	51.5	48.5	2.40	2.36
Portsmouth	-1.5	41 605	91.7	8.3	0.3	2.6	6.9	38 170	58.6	41.4	2.52	2.49
Richmond	-0.9	92 282	91.6	8.4	0.3	2.4	6.4	84 549	46.1	53.9	2.30	2.12
Roanoke	2.4	45 257	92.8	7.2	0.4	2.0	6.4	42 003	56.3	43.7	2.30	2.07
Suffolk	25.7	24 704	94.2	5.8	0.3	1.7	6.2	23 283	72.2	27.8	2.71	2.64
Virginia Beach	13.9	162 277	95.2	4.8	1.4	1.5	4.0	154 455	65.6	34.4	2.79	2.54
WASHINGTON	21.3	2 451 075	92.7	7.3	2.5	1.8	5.9	2 271 398	64.6	35.4	2.65	2.32
Auburn	20.6	16 767	96.1	3.9	0.1	1.7	4.0	16 108	54.2	45.8	2.55	2.37
Bellevue	28.2	48 396	94.7	5.3	1.1	1.6	5.3	45 836	61.5	38.5	2.54	2.10
Bellingham	32.1	29 474	95.0	5.0	0.5	2.3	4.6	27 999	48.2	51.8	2.36	2.12
Bothell	142.4	12 303	96.9	3.1	0.2	1.0	4.6	11 923	68.0	32.0	2.69	2.14
Bremerton	2.6	16 631	90.8	9.2	0.4	4.3	7.8	15 096	41.4	58.6	2.34	2.27
Des Moines	60.7	11 777	96.3	3.7	0.5	1.2	4.4	11 337	61.0	39.0	2.56	2.33
Edmonds	33.9	17 508	96.6	3.4	0.5	1.3	3.3	16 904	68.1	31.9	2.46	2.01
Everett	26.7	38 512	94.3	5.7	0.2	1.9	6.2	36 325	46.0	54.0	2.51	2.32
Kennewick	29.3	22 043	94.3	5.7	0.3	1.3	8.1	20 786	59.7	40.3	2.75	2.38
Kent	91.5	32 488	95.8	4.2	0.3	1.1	4.9	31 113	48.8	51.2	2.70	2.38
Kirkland	20.5	21 831	95.0	5.0	0.7	1.7	5.2	20 736	57.0	43.0	2.30	1.91
Lacey	61.3	13 160	94.7	5.3	0.3	2.5	6.0	12 459	55.5	44.5	2.59	2.31
Longview	9.3	15 225	92.4	7.6	0.3	2.5	10.6	14 066	57.8	42.2	2.45	2.34
Lynnwood	17.6	13 808	96.5	3.5	0.2	1.3	3.8	13 328	53.0	47.0	2.63	2.35
Marysville	119.2	9 730	96.6	3.4	0.4	1.2	3.8	9 400	63.4	36.6	2.83	2.37
Mount Vernon	34.7	9 686	95.8	4.2	0.3	2.1	4.3	9 276	57.3	42.7	2.74	2.75
Olympia	24.9	19 738	94.6	5.4	0.4	1.6	6.4	18 670	50.3	49.7	2.43	1.98
Pasco	40.6	10 341	93.0	7.0	0.3	2.5	7.4	9 619	60.0	40.0	3.26	3.35
Puyallup	43.9	13 467	95.6	4.4	0.2	0.9	6.1	12 870	54.9	45.1	2.83	2.15
Redmond	35.0	20 248	94.3	5.7	1.1	1.5	5.7	19 102	55.1	44.9	2.53	2.07
Renton	19.2	22 676	95.7	4.3	0.4	1.2	4.7	21 708	50.0	50.0	2.47	2.11
Richland	18.1	16 458	94.5	5.5	0.3	1.5	7.1	15 549	66.3	33.7	2.61	2.23
Sammamish	NA	11 599	96.0	4.0	0.6	2.1	6.5	11 131	90.1	9.9	3.12	2.52
Seattle	9.2	270 524	95.6	4.4	0.7	1.2	3.5	258 499	48.4	51.6	2.32	1.84
Shoreline	NA	21 338	97.1	2.9	0.3	1.1	3.2	20 716	68.0	32.0	2.60	2.27
Spokane	8.5	87 941	92.7	7.3	0.3	2.4	9.4	81 512	58.8	41.2	2.47	2.11
Tacoma	8.9	81 102	93.9	6.1	0.3	1.9	6.4	76 152	54.7	45.3	2.60	2.27
Vancouver	181.2	60 039	94.3	5.7	0.4	2.3	6.4	56 628	52.9	47.1	2.57	2.42
Walla Walla	6.9	11 400	92.9	7.1	0.4	2.2	7.6	10 596	59.1	40.9	2.56	2.27
Wenatchee	19.5	11 486	93.5	6.5	0.2	3.4	6.9	10 741	57.7	42.3	2.64	2.37
Yakima	22.7	28 643	92.5	7.5	0.4	2.0	8.7	26 498	53.2	46.8	2.67	2.58
WEST VIRGINIA	7.0	844 623	87.2	12.8	3.9	2.2	9.1	736 481	75.2	24.8	2.47	2.17
Charleston	-3.2	27 131	90.3	9.7	0.6	2.7	9.3	24 505	58.1	41.9	2.27	1.90
Huntington	-2.0	25 888	88.7	11.3	0.3	3.0	8.7	22 955	54.6	45.4	2.27	1.94
Morgantown	12.5	11 721	92.0	8.0	0.4	3.1	6.6	10 782	41.7	58.3	2.26	1.96
Parkersburg	0.0	16 100	89.9	10.1	0.8	2.4	10.0	14 467	62.0	38.0	2.28	2.13
Wheeling	-8.8	15 706	87.3	12.7	0.3	2.5	14.7	13 719	62.7	37.3	2.36	1.85
WISCONSIN	14.4	2 321 144	89.8	10.2	6.1	1.2	5.6	2 084 544	68.4	31.6	2.66	2.15
Appleton	8.2	27 736	96.9	3.1	0.3	1.1	4.4	26 864	68.7	31.3	2.72	2.08
Beloit	0.5	14 262	93.7	6.3	0.1	1.9	8.2	13 370	61.9	38.1	2.60	2.53
Brookfield	16.3	14 208	97.8	2.2	0.6	0.6	3.8	13 891	89.9	10.1	2.81	2.06
Eau Claire	13.7	24 895	96.5	3.5	0.3	1.0	3.5	24 016	57.3	42.7	2.57	2.12
Fond du Lac	13.7	17 519	95.0	5.0	0.2	1.4	7.5	16 638	61.7	38.3	2.59	2.03
Franklin	42.6	10 936	96.9	3.1	0.2	0.8	6.0	10 602	78.4	21.6	2.75	1.97
Green Bay	8.4	43 123	96.4	3.6	0.3	0.9	4.1	41 591	56.0	44.0	2.56	2.19
Greenfield	13.9	16 203	96.9	3.1	0.3	0.9	3.4	15 697	59.5	40.5	2.49	1.78
Janesville	17.2	25 083	95.3	4.7	0.3	1.3	7.4	23 894	68.2	31.8	2.60	2.14
Kenosha	15.0	36 004	95.6	4.4	0.3	1.3	4.9	34 411	62.2	37.8	2.69	2.29
La Crosse	5.7	22 233	94.9	5.1	0.5	1.0	5.1	21 110	50.9	49.1	2.39	2.06
Madison	15.1	92 394	96.3	3.7	0.3	0.8	3.9	89 019	47.7	52.3	2.40	2.00
Manitowoc	8.3	15 007	94.9	5.1	0.4	1.1	7.7	14 235	67.6	32.4	2.51	1.93
Menomonee Falls	30.8	13 140	97.7	2.3	0.3	0.8	2.8	12 844	77.4	22.6	2.75	1.75
Milwaukee	-3.5	249 225	93.2	6.8	0.2	1.3	6.0	232 188	45.3	54.7	2.60	2.42
New Berlin	23.9	14 921	97.1	2.9	0.2	1.1	4.8	14 495	81.3	18.7	2.79	1.91
Oak Creek	58.7	11 897	94.5	5.5	0.1	1.2	8.7	11 239	60.9	39.1	2.89	1.95
Oshkosh	14.9	25 420	94.7	5.3	0.4	1.3	6.5	24 082	57.5	42.5	2.49	2.06

Table D. Cities

STATE Place code	City	Land area, 2000[1] (sq km)	Total persons	Rank	Per square kilometer	Land area, 1990[1] (sq km)	Total persons	Rank	Per square kilometer	White	Black or African American	American Indian or Alaska Native	Asian	Native Hawaiian and other Pacific Islander	Some other race
			Population, 2000				Population, 1990			Population and population characteristics, 2000					
										Race (percent)					
										One race					
		1	2	3	4	5	6	7	8	9	10	11	12	13	14
	WISCONSIN—Cont'd														
55 66000	Racine	40.2	81 855	331	2 036.2	40.0	84 298	265	2 107.5	68.9	20.3	0.4	0.6	0.1	7.1
55 72975	Sheboygan	36.0	50 792	654	1 410.9	34.3	49 587	562	1 445.7	87.6	0.9	0.5	6.5	0.0	2.8
55 78650	Superior	95.7	27 368	1 364	286.0	95.7	27 134	1 177	283.5	94.3	0.7	2.2	0.8	0.0	0.3
55 84250	Waukesha	56.0	64 825	450	1 157.6	44.8	56 894	450	1 270.0	91.2	1.3	0.3	2.2	0.0	3.3
55 84475	Wausau	42.7	38 426	914	899.9	36.5	37 060	813	1 015.3	85.9	0.5	0.6	11.4	0.0	0.3
55 84675	Wauwatosa	34.3	47 271	721	1 378.2	34.3	49 366	568	1 439.2	94.0	2.0	0.3	1.9	0.1	0.5
55 85300	West Allis	29.4	61 254	485	2 083.5	29.3	63 221	393	2 157.7	94.0	1.3	0.7	1.3	0.0	1.2
55 85350	West Bend	32.9	28 152	1 317	855.7	26.0	24 470	1 322	941.2	97.3	0.3	0.4	0.5	0.0	0.6
56 00000	WYOMING	251 488.9	493 782	X	2.0	251 500.8	453 589	X	1.8	92.1	0.8	2.3	0.6	0.1	2.5
56 13150	Casper	62.0	49 644	674	800.7	53.4	46 765	607	875.7	94.0	0.9	1.0	0.5	0.0	2.0
56 13900	Cheyenne	54.7	53 011	625	969.1	48.7	50 008	557	1 026.9	88.1	2.8	0.8	1.1	0.1	4.4
56 45050	Laramie	28.8	27 204	1 371	944.6	28.8	26 687	1 199	926.6	90.8	1.2	0.9	1.9	0.1	2.9

[1]Dry land or land partially or temporarily covered by water.

Table D. Cities

City	Population and population characteristics, 2000 (cont'd)								Population and population characteristics, 1990				
	Race (percent) (cont'd)								Race (percent)				
		Race alone or in combination											
	Two or more races	White	Black	American Indian or Alaska Native	Asian	Native Hawaiian and other Pacific Islander	Some other race	Hispanic[1]	White	Black or African American	American Indian or Alaska Native	Asian and Pacific Islander	Hispanic[1]
	15	16	17	18	19	20	21	22	23	24	25	26	27
WISCONSIN—Cont'd													
Racine................	2.6	71.1	21.6	0.9	0.8	0.1	8.2	14.0	76.4	18.4	0.3	0.5	8.1
Sheboygan............	1.7	88.8	1.1	0.9	7.1	0.2	3.5	6.0	94.4	0.2	0.4	3.9	2.5
Superior..............	1.7	95.8	1.1	3.2	1.1	0.1	0.5	0.8	96.1	0.5	2.4	0.8	0.5
Waukesha............	1.7	92.7	1.7	0.8	2.5	0.1	4.0	8.6	95.4	0.6	0.3	1.3	5.9
Wausau...............	1.2	86.8	0.8	1.1	12.0	0.2	0.5	1.0	93.1	0.1	0.7	6.0	0.7
Wauwatosa...........	1.2	95.0	2.5	0.5	2.3	0.1	0.8	1.7	97.3	1.2	0.2	1.0	1.0
West Allis............	1.4	95.3	1.8	1.2	1.6	0.1	1.6	3.5	98.2	0.3	0.5	0.6	1.5
West Bend...........	0.8	98.0	0.5	0.8	0.7	0.0	0.8	1.8	98.7	0.1	0.4	0.5	0.9
WYOMING............	1.8	93.7	1.0	3.0	0.8	0.1	3.2	6.4	94.2	0.8	2.1	0.6	5.7
Casper................	1.6	95.5	1.2	1.6	0.7	0.1	2.6	5.4	96.5	0.9	0.5	0.5	3.9
Cheyenne............	2.7	90.4	3.4	1.6	1.7	0.2	5.5	12.5	89.6	3.1	0.7	1.2	11.8
Laramie...............	2.2	92.9	1.5	1.7	2.3	0.2	3.7	7.9	93.1	0.9	0.8	2.3	6.7

[1] Hispanic persons may be of any race.

Table D. Cities

City	Population and population characteristics, 2000										
	Age (percent)										
	Under 5 years	5 to 17 years	18 to 24 years	25 to 34 years	35 to 44 years	45 to 54 years	55 to 64 years	65 to 74 years	75 years and over	Median age (years)	Percent Female
	28	29	30	31	32	33	34	35	36	37	38
WISCONSIN—Cont'd											
Racine...................	8.0	20.7	9.9	14.3	15.7	12.0	7.2	6.0	6.3	33.1	51.3
Sheboygan.............	7.0	18.6	9.2	14.6	15.4	11.8	7.7	6.9	8.9	35.4	51.0
Superior................	6.0	16.7	12.9	13.1	14.8	13.7	7.9	6.4	8.6	35.9	52.0
Waukesha..............	7.4	17.3	10.8	17.2	16.4	13.0	7.2	5.0	5.6	33.4	51.1
Wausau..................	6.2	19.2	9.6	13.0	14.5	12.5	7.9	7.3	9.8	36.5	52.0
Wauwatosa............	6.5	16.8	5.5	14.5	16.7	14.2	7.6	7.4	10.8	39.1	53.7
West Allis..............	5.8	15.7	8.4	15.3	16.9	12.9	7.7	7.5	9.8	37.8	51.8
West Bend.............	7.2	18.3	8.6	15.4	15.7	12.6	7.7	6.4	8.0	35.3	51.8
WYOMING.............	6.3	19.8	10.1	12.1	16.0	15.0	9.0	6.3	5.3	36.2	49.7
Casper..................	6.6	19.3	10.5	12.3	15.4	14.1	8.2	7.3	6.3	36.1	51.3
Cheyenne..............	6.5	18.5	8.8	13.9	15.8	14.0	8.8	7.0	6.8	36.6	51.2
Laramie.................	5.1	12.4	31.8	15.0	10.9	11.1	5.7	4.0	4.1	25.3	48.3

Table D. Cities

City	Population and population characteristics, 1990										Population—change, 1980–2000				
	Age (percent)										Total persons			Percent change	
	Under 5 years	5 to 17 years	18 to 24 years	25 to 34 years	35 to 44 years	45 to 54 years	55 to 64 years	65 to 74 years	75 years and over	Percent Female	2000	1990	1980	1990–2000	1980–1990
	39	40	41	42	43	44	45	46	47	48	49	50	51	52	53
WISCONSIN—Cont'd															
Racine	8.8	20.4	9.4	18.1	14.1	8.2	8.1	7.2	5.8	52.6	81 855	84 298	85 730	-2.9	-1.7
Sheboygan	7.5	18.1	9.0	17.5	13.9	8.6	8.4	8.8	8.2	52.0	50 792	49 587	48 085	2.4	3.1
Superior	7.0	18.0	11.0	15.4	14.3	8.8	8.0	8.9	8.6	52.8	27 368	27 134	29 571	0.9	-8.2
Waukesha	8.0	18.6	11.4	20.2	15.9	9.2	6.7	5.2	4.7	51.7	64 825	56 894	50 319	13.9	13.1
Wausau	7.6	17.1	10.0	16.7	14.3	8.1	8.8	9.0	8.4	53.2	38 426	37 060	32 426	3.7	14.3
Wauwatosa	6.7	15.4	6.0	17.3	15.5	9.5	9.8	9.5	10.3	53.8	47 271	49 366	51 308	-4.2	-3.8
West Allis	6.6	15.0	9.0	20.0	13.5	8.8	9.2	9.7	8.2	52.7	61 254	63 221	63 982	-3.1	-1.2
West Bend	8.2	20.4	10.0	17.6	14.9	9.7	7.2	6.4	5.6	51.2	28 152	24 470	21 484	15.0	13.9
WYOMING	7.7	22.2	9.1	16.4	16.4	10.0	7.8	6.1	4.3	50.0	493 782	453 589	469 557	8.9	-3.4
Casper	7.7	21.3	8.3	16.8	16.4	9.6	8.7	7.1	4.2	51.6	49 644	46 765	51 016	6.2	-8.3
Cheyenne	7.6	18.8	9.2	17.6	16.5	9.9	8.6	7.0	4.8	51.1	53 011	50 008	47 283	6.0	5.8
Laramie	6.2	14.4	28.1	18.2	12.8	7.4	5.3	4.3	3.3	48.4	27 204	26 687	24 410	1.9	9.3

Table D. Cities

City	Total population	Total in house-holds	House-holder	Spouse	Child Total	Child Own child under 18 years	Other relatives Total	Other relatives Under 18 years	Nonrelatives Total	Nonrelatives Unmar-ried partner	Total in group quarters	Institutionalized population Correc-tional institu-tions	Institutionalized population Nurs-ing homes	Institutionalized population Other institu-tions	Noninstitutionalized population Col-lege dormi-tories	Noninstitutionalized population Mili-tary quar-ters	Other
	54	55	56	57	58	59	60	61	62	63	64	65	66	67	68	69	70
WISCONSIN—Cont'd																	
Racine	81 855	97.7	38.4	16.2	31.7	25.0	5.8	2.7	5.6	2.6	2.3	1.2	0.6	0.1	0.0	0.0	0.4
Sheboygan	50 792	97.6	40.9	19.7	29.2	24.0	2.8	1.0	4.9	2.5	2.4	0.4	1.4	0.0	0.0	0.0	0.5
Superior	27 368	95.9	42.4	17.5	26.8	21.1	2.5	0.9	6.7	3.2	4.1	0.3	1.1	0.1	1.8	0.0	0.8
Waukesha	64 825	96.2	39.6	19.9	28.8	23.4	2.6	0.8	5.3	2.2	3.8	1.1	0.8	0.0	1.5	0.0	0.4
Wausau	38 426	96.6	40.8	19.0	28.9	23.9	2.7	0.8	5.3	2.4	3.4	0.6	1.6	0.0	0.4	0.0	0.7
Wauwatosa	47 271	97.9	43.1	21.6	27.6	22.4	2.0	0.5	3.7	1.5	2.1	0.0	1.0	0.7	0.0	0.0	0.3
West Allis	61 254	98.5	45.1	18.5	26.5	20.1	3.1	0.9	5.4	2.6	1.5	0.1	0.9	0.0	0.0	0.0	0.5
West Bend	28 152	98.6	40.4	21.6	29.9	24.3	2.0	0.7	4.7	2.3	1.4	0.4	0.8	0.0	0.0	0.0	0.3
WYOMING	493 782	97.1	39.2	21.5	28.6	24.0	2.8	1.3	5.0	2.1	2.9	0.8	0.6	0.2	0.8	0.1	0.4
Casper	49 644	97.5	41.0	20.3	28.4	23.8	2.6	1.1	5.2	2.6	2.5	0.0	0.9	0.2	0.7	0.0	0.7
Cheyenne	53 011	98.1	42.1	20.7	27.8	22.9	2.9	1.3	4.5	2.1	1.9	0.3	0.9	0.0	0.0	0.0	0.6
Laramie	27 204	91.3	41.7	15.9	19.4	16.5	2.4	0.6	11.8	2.2	8.7	0.1	0.4	0.0	7.9	0.0	0.3

Table D. Cities

City	Total households	Family households							Nonfamily households			Average household size	Average family size	Households, 1990		
		Total	With own children under 18 years	Married couple	With own children under 18 years	Female householder[1]	With own children under 18 years	Total	Householder living alone				Total house-holds	Female house-holder[1]	House-holder living alone
				Total		Total			Total	65 years and over					
	71	72	73	74	75	76	77	78	79	80	81	82	83	84	85
WISCONSIN—Cont'd															
Racine	31 449	64.9	33.9	42.2	19.2	17.9	12.1	35.1	29.4	10.5	2.54	3.15	31 767	17.0	26.1
Sheboygan	20 779	61.8	29.7	48.2	21.0	9.4	6.4	38.4	32.2	12.6	2.39	3.05	19 703	8.7	28.3
Superior	11 609	57.7	27.9	41.3	17.1	12.3	8.5	42.3	34.2	13.9	2.26	2.91	11 001	13.5	31.6
Waukesha	25 663	63.5	32.5	50.2	24.1	9.8	6.5	36.5	29.0	9.2	2.43	3.04	21 235	10.0	25.4
Wausau	15 678	59.5	27.8	46.7	19.8	9.5	6.0	40.5	33.6	14.1	2.37	3.08	14 718	9.4	29.0
Wauwatosa	20 388	60.4	28.3	50.0	22.9	7.9	4.2	39.6	33.9	15.4	2.27	2.96	19 848	7.7	29.0
West Allis	27 604	55.7	25.5	41.2	17.2	10.6	6.3	44.3	37.3	14.0	2.19	2.92	26 797	10.0	31.7
West Bend	11 375	66.1	32.7	53.3	24.6	9.4	6.1	33.9	27.5	12.0	2.44	3.00	8 686	8.7	21.5
WYOMING	193 608	67.4	32.7	54.8	24.3	8.7	6.0	32.6	26.3	8.8	2.48	3.00	168 839	8.3	24.5
Casper	20 343	64.6	31.8	49.6	21.4	11.1	7.9	35.4	29.1	10.2	2.38	2.94	18 504	10.2	27.6
Cheyenne	22 324	63.5	30.4	49.2	21.0	10.6	7.2	36.5	31.3	10.6	2.33	2.93	20 243	10.3	28.4
Laramie	11 336	49.5	23.0	38.3	16.3	8.0	5.2	50.5	33.2	6.4	2.19	2.83	10 400	8.3	30.6

[1] No spouse present.

Table D. Cities

City	Percent change of households, 1990–2000	Total housing units	Occupied housing units (percent)	Housing occupancy				Housing tenure				
				Vacant housing units		Homeowner vacancy rate (percent)	Rental vacancy rate (percent)	Occupied housing units				
				Total	For seasonal, recreational, or occasional use			Total	Percent owner-occupied housing units	Percent renter-occupied housing units	Average household size of owner-occupied units	Average household size of renter-occupied units
	86	87	88	89	90	91	92	93	94	95	96	97
WISCONSIN—Cont'd												
Racine	-1.0	33 414	94.1	5.9	0.2	1.0	7.2	31 449	60.3	39.7	2.61	2.44
Sheboygan	5.5	21 762	95.5	4.5	0.4	1.2	5.1	20 779	61.1	38.9	2.55	2.13
Superior	5.5	12 196	95.2	4.8	0.3	0.6	6.2	11 609	61.7	38.3	2.47	1.93
Waukesha	20.9	26 856	95.6	4.4	0.2	0.7	6.3	25 663	56.5	43.5	2.71	2.06
Wausau	6.5	16 668	94.1	5.9	0.4	1.6	7.7	15 678	61.7	38.3	2.54	2.10
Wauwatosa	2.7	20 917	97.5	2.5	0.2	0.5	3.5	20 388	67.8	32.2	2.55	1.68
West Allis	3.0	28 708	96.2	3.8	0.1	1.1	4.5	27 604	58.1	41.9	2.47	1.80
West Bend	31.0	11 926	95.4	4.6	0.3	2.0	6.1	11 375	62.2	37.8	2.65	2.08
WYOMING	14.7	223 854	86.5	13.5	5.5	2.1	9.7	193 608	70.0	30.0	2.58	2.25
Casper	9.9	21 872	93.0	7.0	0.5	1.5	8.1	20 343	66.9	33.1	2.50	2.13
Cheyenne	10.3	23 782	93.9	6.1	0.4	1.3	7.9	22 324	66.0	34.0	2.47	2.06
Laramie	9.0	11 994	94.5	5.5	0.5	1.9	4.9	11 336	47.5	52.5	2.41	1.99

Towns of 25,000 or More in Selected States

(For explanation of symbols, see page xi.)

Page

630   **CT**(Branford town)—**MA**(Dartmouth town)
637   **MA**(Dracut town)—**MI**(East pointe city)
644   **MI**(Farmington Hills city)—**MN**(Maple Grove city)
651   **MN**(Maplewood city)—**NJ**(Long Branch city)
658   **NJ**(Manalapan township)—**NY**(East Fishkill town)
665   **NY**(Elmira city)—**NY**(Yorktown town))
672   **PA**(Abington township)—**WI**(Brookfield city)
679   **WI**(Fond du Lac city)—**WI**(West Bend city)

Table E. Towns

STATE MCD code	Town	Population, 2000				Population, 1990				Population and population characteristics, 2000					
										Race (percent)					
										One race					
		Land area, 2000[1] (sq km)	Total persons	Rank within state	Per square kilometer	Land area, 1990[1] (sq km)	Total persons	Rank within state	Per square kilometer	White	Black or African American	American Indian or Alaska Native	Asian	Native Hawaiian and other Pacific Islander	Some other race
		1	2	3	4	5	6	7	8	9	10	11	12	13	14
00 00000	UNITED STATES	9 161 924	281 421 906	X	30.7	9 159 127	248 790 925	X	27.2	75.1	12.3	0.9	3.6	0.1	5.5
09 00000	CONNECTICUT............	12 548	3 405 565	X	271.4	12 550	3 287 116	X	261.9	81.6	9.1	0.3	2.4	0.0	4.3
09 07310	Branford town	56.9	28 683	35	504.1	57.0	27 603	35	484.3	94.0	1.3	0.1	2.7	0.1	0.5
09 08070	Bridgeport town	41.4	139 529	1	3 370.3	41.5	141 686	1	3 414.1	45.0	30.8	0.5	3.3	0.1	14.8
09 08490	Bristol town	68.7	60 062	9	874.3	68.7	60 640	9	882.7	91.6	2.7	0.2	1.5	0.0	2.4
09 14160	Cheshire town	85.2	28 543	37	335.0	85.2	25 684	37	301.5	89.4	4.7	0.1	2.6	0.0	1.9
09 18500	Danbury town	109.1	74 848	8	686.0	109.1	65 585	8	601.1	76.0	6.8	0.3	5.5	0.0	7.6
09 22630	East Hartford town	46.7	49 575	17	1 061.6	46.7	50 452	17	1 080.3	64.7	18.8	0.3	4.0	0.0	8.7
09 22910	East Haven town	31.8	28 189	36	886.4	31.8	26 144	36	822.1	93.9	1.4	0.1	1.9	0.0	1.5
09 25990	Enfield town	86.5	45 212	20	522.7	86.6	45 532	20	525.8	89.7	5.6	0.2	1.3	0.0	1.6
09 26620	Fairfield town	77.8	57 340	14	737.0	77.8	53 418	14	686.6	95.3	1.1	0.1	2.0	0.0	0.5
09 31240	Glastonbury town	133.0	31 876	33	239.7	133.1	27 901	33	209.6	93.1	1.5	0.1	3.4	0.0	0.9
09 33620	Greenwich town	123.9	61 101	12	493.1	124.0	58 441	12	471.3	90.0	1.7	0.1	5.2	0.0	1.5
09 34250	Groton town	81.1	39 907	21	492.1	81.1	45 144	21	556.6	83.6	7.0	0.8	3.3	0.2	1.7
09 35650	Hamden town	84.9	56 913	15	670.4	84.9	52 434	15	617.6	77.3	15.5	0.1	3.5	0.0	1.6
09 37070	Hartford town	44.8	121 578	2	2 713.8	44.8	139 739	2	3 119.2	27.7	38.1	0.5	1.6	0.1	26.5
09 44700	Manchester town	70.6	54 740	16	775.4	70.6	51 618	16	731.1	82.8	8.4	0.2	3.2	0.0	3.1
09 46520	Meriden town	61.5	58 244	11	947.1	61.5	59 479	11	967.1	80.2	6.4	0.4	1.4	0.0	8.6
09 47360	Middletown town	105.9	43 167	22	407.6	105.9	42 762	22	403.8	80.0	12.3	0.2	2.7	0.0	2.0
09 47535	Milford town	58.4	52 305	18	895.6	58.5	49 938	18	853.6	93.6	1.9	0.1	2.3	0.0	0.9
09 49950	Naugatuck town	42.4	30 989	29	730.9	42.5	30 625	29	720.6	91.8	2.8	0.3	1.7	0.0	1.6
09 50440	New Britain town	34.5	71 538	7	2 073.6	34.6	75 491	7	2 181.8	69.4	10.9	0.4	2.4	0.1	13.1
09 52070	New Haven town	48.8	123 626	3	2 533.3	48.8	130 474	3	2 673.6	43.5	37.4	0.4	3.9	0.1	10.9
09 52140	Newington town	34.1	29 306	31	859.4	34.1	29 208	31	856.5	92.5	2.1	0.1	2.8	0.0	1.2
09 52350	New London town	14.3	25 671	32	1 795.2	14.4	28 540	32	1 981.9	63.5	18.6	0.9	2.1	0.1	9.1
09 52630	New Milford town	159.5	27 121	40	170.0	159.5	23 629	40	148.1	94.3	1.4	0.1	1.9	0.0	0.7
09 52980	Newtown town	149.6	25 031	41	167.3	149.6	20 779	41	138.9	95.1	1.7	0.1	1.4	0.0	0.6
09 56060	Norwalk town	59.1	82 951	6	1 403.6	59.1	78 331	6	1 325.4	73.9	15.3	0.2	3.3	0.0	4.3
09 56270	Norwich town	73.4	36 117	25	492.1	73.4	37 391	25	509.4	83.1	6.8	1.2	2.1	0.0	2.8
09 68170	Shelton town	79.2	38 101	26	481.1	79.2	35 418	26	447.2	94.4	1.1	0.1	2.1	0.0	0.9
09 70550	Southington town	93.2	39 728	24	426.3	93.2	38 518	24	413.3	96.4	0.9	0.1	1.0	0.0	0.6
09 73070	Stamford town	97.8	117 083	5	1 197.2	97.7	108 056	5	1 106.0	69.8	15.4	0.2	5.0	0.0	6.5
09 74190	Stratford town	45.5	49 976	19	1 098.4	45.5	49 389	19	1 085.5	84.8	9.8	0.2	1.4	0.0	2.1
09 76570	Torrington town	103.1	35 202	27	341.4	103.1	33 687	27	326.7	93.0	2.2	0.2	1.8	0.0	1.3
09 77200	Trumbull town	60.3	34 243	28	567.9	60.4	32 016	28	530.1	94.0	1.9	0.1	2.4	0.0	0.7
09 78250	Vernon town	45.9	28 063	30	611.4	45.9	29 841	30	650.1	90.0	4.0	0.2	2.7	0.0	1.2
09 78740	Wallingford town	101.1	43 026	23	425.6	101.1	40 822	23	403.8	94.8	1.0	0.2	1.8	0.0	1.2
09 80070	Waterbury town	74.0	107 271	4	1 449.6	74.0	108 961	4	1 472.4	67.1	16.3	0.4	1.5	0.1	10.9
09 82590	West Hartford town	56.9	63 589	10	1 117.6	56.9	60 110	10	1 056.4	86.0	4.8	0.1	4.8	0.1	2.6
09 82870	West Haven town	28.1	52 360	13	1 863.3	28.1	54 021	13	1 922.5	74.1	16.3	0.2	2.9	0.1	3.6
09 83500	Westport town	51.8	25 749	39	497.1	51.8	24 410	39	471.2	95.2	1.1	0.0	2.4	0.0	0.4
09 84900	Wethersfield town	32.1	26 271	38	818.4	32.1	25 651	38	799.1	93.2	2.1	0.1	1.6	0.0	1.8
09 87000	Windsor town	76.7	28 237	34	368.1	76.8	27 817	34	362.2	65.1	27.1	0.2	3.1	0.0	2.1
23 00000	MAINE	79 931	1 274 923	X	16.0	79 939	1 227 928	X	15.4	96.9	0.5	0.6	0.7	0.0	0.2
23 02795	Bangor city	89.2	31 473	3	352.8	89.2	33 181	3	372.0	95.0	1.0	1.0	1.2	0.1	0.4
23 38740	Lewiston city	88.3	35 690	2	404.2	88.3	39 757	2	450.2	95.7	1.1	0.3	0.8	0.0	0.4
23 60545	Portland city	54.9	64 249	1	1 170.3	58.6	64 157	1	1 094.8	91.3	2.6	0.5	3.1	0.1	0.7
25 00000	MASSACHUSETTS........	20 306	6 349 097	X	312.7	20 300	6 016 425	X	296.4	84.5	5.4	0.2	3.8	0.0	3.7
25 00765	Agawam city	60.2	28 144	57	467.5	60.2	27 323	57	453.9	96.7	0.9	0.2	1.0	0.0	0.4
25 01325	Amherst town	71.8	34 874	40	485.7	71.7	35 228	40	491.3	79.3	5.1	0.2	9.0	0.1	2.9
25 01465	Andover town	80.3	31 247	48	389.1	80.3	29 151	48	363.0	91.6	0.7	0.1	5.7	0.0	0.8
25 01605	Arlington town	13.4	42 389	26	3 163.4	13.4	44 630	26	3 330.6	91.0	1.7	0.1	5.0	0.0	0.7
25 02690	Attleboro city	71.3	42 068	32	590.0	71.3	38 383	32	538.3	91.3	1.6	0.2	3.2	0.0	1.8
25 03600	Barnstable Town city	155.5	47 821	30	307.5	155.5	40 949	30	263.3	91.9	2.7	0.6	0.8	0.0	1.7
25 05595	Beverly city	43.0	39 862	34	927.0	40.0	38 195	34	954.9	96.0	1.0	0.2	1.3	0.0	0.5
25 05805	Billerica town	67.0	38 981	37	581.8	67.1	37 609	37	560.5	94.7	1.1	0.1	2.8	0.0	0.3
25 07000	Boston city	125.4	589 141	1	4 698.1	125.4	574 283	1	4 579.6	54.5	25.3	0.4	7.5	0.1	7.8
25 07665	Braintree town	36.0	33 828	41	939.7	36.0	33 836	41	939.9	94.0	1.2	0.1	3.1	0.0	0.6
25 08085	Bridgewater town	71.2	25 185	71	353.7	71.2	21 249	71	298.4	87.3	4.0	0.2	1.1	0.0	6.2
25 09000	Brockton city	55.6	94 304	7	1 696.1	55.6	92 788	7	1 668.8	61.5	17.8	0.4	2.2	0.0	10.3
25 09175	Brookline town	17.6	57 107	18	3 244.7	17.6	54 718	18	3 109.0	81.1	2.7	0.1	12.8	0.0	1.0
25 11000	Cambridge city	16.7	101 355	6	6 069.2	16.7	95 802	6	5 736.6	68.1	11.9	0.3	11.9	0.1	3.2
25 13135	Chelmsford town	58.7	33 858	43	576.8	58.7	32 383	43	551.7	93.1	0.8	0.1	4.6	0.0	0.5
25 13205	Chelsea city	5.7	35 080	51	6 154.4	5.7	28 710	51	5 036.8	57.9	7.3	0.5	4.7	0.1	22.9
25 13660	Chicopee city	59.2	54 653	17	923.2	59.3	56 632	17	955.0	89.8	2.3	0.2	0.9	0.1	4.9
25 16250	Danvers town	34.4	25 212	67	732.9	34.4	24 174	67	702.7	97.7	0.3	0.1	1.1	0.0	0.2
25 16425	Dartmouth town	159.5	30 666	59	192.3	159.4	27 244	59	170.9	90.8	1.1	0.2	1.2	0.0	5.1

[1] Dry land or land partially or temporarily covered by water.

Table E. Towns

Town	Population and population characteristics, 2000 (cont'd)								Population and population characteristics, 1990				
	Race (percent) (cont'd)								Race (percent)				
	Race alone or in combination												
	Two or more races	White	Black	American Indian or Alaska Native	Asian	Native Hawaiian and other Pacific Islander	Some other race	Hispanic[1]	White	Black or African American	American Indian or Alaska Native	Asian and Pacific Islander	Hispanic[1]
	15	16	17	18	19	20	21	22	23	24	25	26	27
UNITED STATES	2.4	77.1	12.9	1.5	4.2	0.3	6.6	12.5	80.3	12.1	0.8	2.9	9.0
CONNECTICUT	2.2	83.3	10.0	0.7	2.8	0.1	5.5	9.4	87.0	8.3	0.2	1.5	6.5
Branford town	1.2	95.1	1.7	0.5	3.1	0.1	0.9	2.6	97.0	1.2	0.1	1.3	1.6
Bridgeport town	5.6	48.5	33.2	1.0	3.8	0.3	19.0	31.9	58.5	26.6	0.3	2.3	26.5
Bristol town	1.6	93.0	3.4	0.7	1.7	0.1	2.8	5.3	96.0	2.1	0.2	0.8	2.7
Cheshire town	1.2	90.2	5.1	0.7	2.9	0.1	2.3	3.8	93.1	3.9	0.1	1.9	2.8
Danbury town	4.0	79.2	7.6	0.7	6.1	0.1	10.3	15.8	86.8	6.6	0.2	3.9	7.7
East Hartford town	3.4	66.8	20.5	0.9	4.5	0.2	10.6	15.2	86.8	8.4	0.2	2.2	6.0
East Haven town	1.1	94.9	1.6	0.4	2.1	0.0	2.1	4.4	98.1	0.9	0.1	0.4	1.9
Enfield town	1.5	90.9	6.2	0.6	1.6	0.1	2.1	3.7	95.7	2.7	0.1	1.0	2.3
Fairfield town	1.0	96.1	1.3	0.2	2.5	0.1	0.9	2.3	97.6	0.8	0.1	1.3	1.9
Glastonbury town	0.9	93.9	1.8	0.3	3.8	0.0	1.2	2.5	96.0	0.9	0.1	2.4	2.0
Greenwich town	1.6	91.4	2.0	0.3	5.7	0.1	2.3	6.3	93.3	2.1	0.1	3.5	4.4
Groton town	3.5	86.4	8.4	2.0	4.2	0.4	2.4	5.0	89.2	6.6	0.7	2.2	3.7
Hamden town	1.9	78.7	16.4	0.6	3.8	0.1	2.4	4.3	88.9	8.7	0.1	1.8	2.0
Hartford town	5.4	30.8	40.6	1.2	2.2	0.4	30.6	40.5	40.0	38.9	0.3	1.4	31.6
Manchester town	2.3	84.6	9.4	0.7	3.7	0.1	4.0	6.5	93.5	3.9	0.2	1.7	2.4
Meriden town	2.9	82.7	7.7	0.8	1.6	0.1	10.2	21.1	89.7	4.3	0.2	0.7	13.7
Middletown town	2.8	82.2	13.7	0.8	3.2	0.1	3.0	5.3	85.4	11.1	0.2	1.9	3.3
Milford town	1.1	94.6	2.2	0.4	2.6	0.1	1.3	3.3	96.8	1.5	0.1	1.0	2.3
Naugatuck town	1.8	93.4	3.5	0.7	1.9	0.0	2.4	4.5	96.2	1.9	0.2	0.9	3.1
New Britain town	3.8	72.5	12.3	0.8	2.6	0.1	15.7	26.8	81.6	7.6	0.2	1.8	16.3
New Haven town	3.9	45.9	39.3	1.2	4.4	0.3	13.0	21.4	53.9	36.1	0.3	2.4	13.2
Newington town	1.3	93.5	2.4	0.4	3.2	0.1	1.7	3.7	96.5	1.4	0.1	2.4	2.1
New London town	5.7	67.6	21.8	2.3	2.9	0.3	11.5	19.7	73.0	16.8	0.7	2.2	12.1
New Milford town	1.5	95.7	1.8	0.5	2.2	0.0	1.3	2.8	96.6	1.5	0.2	1.3	1.9
Newtown town	0.9	95.9	2.0	0.3	1.7	0.1	0.9	2.4	97.3	1.0	0.2	1.3	1.7
Norwalk town	2.9	76.1	16.3	0.6	3.7	0.1	6.3	15.6	79.3	15.5	0.1	1.6	9.4
Norwich town	3.9	85.8	9.0	2.4	2.6	0.1	4.3	6.1	91.3	5.3	0.6	1.1	3.1
Shelton town	1.3	95.6	1.3	0.5	2.2	0.0	1.7	3.5	97.1	1.0	0.1	1.3	2.5
Southington town	1.0	97.4	1.2	0.4	1.2	0.0	0.8	2.0	98.0	0.9	0.1	0.7	1.3
Stamford town	3.1	71.9	16.5	0.5	5.5	0.1	8.7	16.8	76.3	17.8	0.1	2.6	9.8
Stratford town	1.7	86.0	10.6	0.5	1.7	0.1	2.9	6.8	90.1	7.9	0.1	0.8	3.6
Torrington town	1.5	94.3	2.7	0.6	2.1	0.1	1.8	3.3	96.7	1.7	0.2	1.2	1.1
Trumbull town	0.9	94.8	2.1	0.3	2.6	0.0	1.1	2.7	96.8	1.3	0.1	1.7	1.8
Vernon town	1.9	91.5	4.8	0.7	3.1	0.1	1.9	3.6	94.8	2.3	0.2	2.0	2.0
Wallingford town	1.1	95.7	1.3	0.6	2.0	0.0	1.5	4.5	97.1	1.0	0.1	0.9	3.2
Waterbury town	3.7	69.7	18.0	1.0	1.9	0.2	13.2	21.8	79.6	13.0	0.3	0.7	13.4
West Hartford town	1.7	87.1	5.3	0.4	5.3	0.2	3.4	6.3	94.0	2.2	0.1	2.8	3.1
West Haven town	2.8	76.2	17.4	0.7	3.3	0.1	5.2	9.1	84.1	12.4	0.2	2.0	3.6
Westport town	0.8	95.9	1.3	0.2	2.9	0.0	0.6	2.3	97.0	1.1	0.1	1.6	2.2
Wethersfield town	1.2	94.1	2.5	0.2	1.9	0.1	2.5	4.2	97.5	1.1	0.1	0.8	1.6
Windsor town	2.4	66.5	28.6	0.7	3.6	0.1	3.1	5.0	79.0	17.2	0.1	2.4	3.4
MAINE	1.0	97.9	0.7	1.0	0.9	0.1	0.4	0.7	98.4	0.4	0.5	0.5	0.6
Bangor city	1.4	96.3	1.4	1.6	1.5	0.1	0.6	1.0	97.1	0.9	0.7	1.0	0.6
Lewiston city	1.7	97.3	1.6	1.0	1.1	0.1	0.7	1.3	98.2	0.7	0.2	0.7	0.7
Portland city	1.9	92.8	3.2	1.0	3.6	0.1	1.2	1.5	96.6	1.1	0.4	1.7	0.8
MASSACHUSETTS	2.3	86.2	6.3	0.6	4.2	0.1	5.1	6.8	89.8	5.0	0.2	2.4	4.8
Agawam city	0.8	97.4	1.1	0.4	1.1	0.1	0.7	1.8	98.0	1.0	0.1	0.5	1.1
Amherst town	3.4	82.0	6.4	0.9	10.2	0.2	4.0	6.2	85.0	4.6	0.3	7.9	4.7
Andover town	1.0	92.4	0.9	0.2	6.3	0.1	1.1	1.8	95.0	0.8	0.1	3.8	1.5
Arlington town	1.6	92.3	2.2	0.3	5.6	0.1	1.2	1.9	95.2	1.3	0.1	3.0	1.7
Attleboro city	1.8	92.7	2.0	0.6	3.8	0.2	2.6	4.3	95.5	1.0	0.2	2.4	2.9
Barnstable Town city	2.3	93.8	3.5	1.1	1.1	0.1	3.0	1.7	94.5	2.7	0.7	0.7	1.7
Beverly city	1.0	96.9	1.4	0.4	1.5	0.1	0.7	1.8	97.6	0.9	0.1	1.0	1.1
Billerica town	1.0	95.6	1.4	0.4	3.0	0.1	0.7	1.5	96.8	1.1	0.1	1.5	1.3
Boston city	4.4	56.8	27.7	0.9	8.1	0.3	10.9	14.4	62.8	25.6	0.3	5.3	10.8
Braintree town	0.9	94.8	1.5	0.3	3.4	0.1	1.0	1.2	97.4	0.6	0.1	1.6	0.9
Bridgewater town	1.1	88.2	4.5	0.6	1.3	0.0	6.6	2.8	92.8	4.7	0.3	0.8	3.2
Brockton city	7.8	64.4	23.3	0.9	2.7	0.2	16.5	8.0	80.2	13.0	0.3	1.7	6.3
Brookline town	2.2	82.9	3.3	0.5	13.8	0.1	1.8	3.5	87.4	3.1	0.1	8.4	2.9
Cambridge city	4.6	71.2	13.8	0.8	13.1	0.2	5.7	7.4	75.3	13.5	0.3	8.4	6.8
Chelmsford town	0.9	93.9	1.0	0.3	5.0	0.0	0.8	1.2	96.1	0.5	0.1	3.1	1.0
Chelsea city	6.6	63.3	8.7	0.9	5.1	0.3	28.5	48.4	69.7	5.2	0.3	5.0	31.4
Chicopee city	1.8	91.4	2.8	0.5	1.1	0.2	5.9	8.8	95.4	1.8	0.1	0.6	3.6
Danvers town	0.5	98.1	0.5	0.2	1.2	0.0	0.4	0.8	98.2	0.5	0.0	1.0	1.1
Dartmouth town	1.6	92.1	1.5	0.4	1.4	0.2	6.1	1.5	97.0	0.7	0.1	0.8	1.0

[1] Hispanic persons may be of any race.

Table E. Towns

Town	Population and population characteristics, 2000										
	Age (percent)										
	Under 5 years	5 to 17 years	18 to 24 years	25 to 34 years	35 to 44 years	45 to 54 years	55 to 64 years	65 to 74 years	75 years and over	Median age (years)	Percent Female
	28	29	30	31	32	33	34	35	36	37	38
UNITED STATES	6.8	18.9	9.7	14.2	16.0	13.4	8.6	6.5	5.9	35.3	50.9
CONNECTICUT................	6.6	18.2	8.0	13.3	17.1	14.1	9.1	6.8	7.0	37.4	51.6
Branford town	5.4	15.2	5.4	12.7	17.8	16.1	10.5	8.0	8.8	41.4	52.9
Bridgeport town	8.2	20.3	11.2	15.9	14.7	11.1	7.3	5.5	5.9	31.4	52.3
Bristol town	6.3	16.9	7.2	15.1	17.4	13.5	8.8	7.3	7.6	37.6	51.6
Cheshire town	5.8	19.5	7.7	11.2	18.2	16.1	8.8	5.9	6.7	38.4	46.8
Danbury town	6.5	15.1	10.2	17.8	17.6	13.4	8.3	5.6	5.4	35.2	51.0
East Hartford town............	6.5	17.6	7.8	14.2	16.0	12.9	9.5	8.0	7.6	37.4	52.3
East Haven town	5.8	16.4	6.9	14.3	17.3	13.7	9.0	8.3	8.3	38.8	52.2
Enfield town	5.6	17.0	7.6	15.2	19.1	12.5	9.4	7.9	5.9	37.3	47.6
Fairfield town	7.2	16.6	9.8	10.7	16.8	13.7	9.0	7.5	8.8	38.5	52.5
Glastonbury town	7.1	19.7	4.1	10.2	18.8	17.2	10.2	6.3	6.4	39.8	52.6
Greenwich town	7.0	18.4	4.1	11.1	17.8	14.9	10.8	8.1	7.8	40.2	52.6
Groton town	8.1	16.8	11.8	17.6	15.4	11.0	7.3	5.9	6.2	32.5	48.8
Hamden town	5.3	15.5	12.1	13.1	14.9	13.2	8.4	7.6	10.0	37.7	54.2
Hartford town	8.3	21.8	12.6	15.5	14.3	11.0	7.1	4.9	4.6	29.7	52.2
Manchester town	6.3	16.4	8.0	16.6	16.4	13.5	8.6	6.2	8.0	36.5	52.3
Meriden town	7.1	18.6	8.1	14.1	16.1	13.5	8.3	6.6	7.5	36.2	51.6
Middletown town	6.5	15.2	8.3	17.6	17.5	13.0	8.5	6.2	7.2	36.3	51.7
Milford town	6.0	16.3	5.9	14.0	17.7	15.2	10.0	7.4	7.5	39.4	51.6
Naugatuck town.................	6.9	19.9	7.3	14.9	18.2	13.1	7.9	5.4	6.3	35.5	51.4
New Britain town	6.6	17.5	12.5	14.9	14.0	11.5	7.1	6.9	8.8	33.9	52.1
New Haven town	7.1	18.4	16.4	17.8	13.4	10.2	6.6	4.8	5.4	29.3	52.1
Newington town	5.2	15.4	5.6	12.3	16.4	15.0	11.2	9.2	9.6	41.9	53.0
New London town	6.7	16.2	17.6	15.0	14.6	11.2	6.7	5.6	6.5	31.2	51.1
New Milford town................	7.1	20.3	5.8	13.1	20.0	15.4	8.8	5.0	4.5	36.8	50.8
Newtown town	8.1	21.2	4.4	11.1	21.4	16.0	9.1	4.8	3.9	37.5	48.8
Norwalk town	6.9	15.2	7.0	17.7	17.9	13.3	9.3	6.9	5.9	36.6	51.2
Norwich town	6.4	17.7	8.9	14.0	16.2	13.4	8.1	7.3	8.1	36.9	52.5
Shelton town	6.2	17.4	5.8	12.2	17.8	15.2	10.5	7.3	7.5	39.8	51.6
Southington town...............	6.0	17.8	5.9	12.3	17.0	15.4	10.8	7.5	7.2	39.7	51.5
Stamford town	6.9	15.2	7.4	17.8	17.3	12.9	8.7	7.1	6.8	36.4	51.6
Stratford town	6.0	17.1	5.8	12.3	16.1	13.8	9.7	9.1	10.1	40.3	52.9
Torrington town	6.0	17.1	6.4	13.4	17.6	13.5	8.6	7.5	10.1	39.1	51.6
Trumbull town	6.9	19.1	5.0	9.6	17.9	14.1	10.0	8.5	8.8	40.3	51.9
Vernon town	6.1	16.0	7.7	15.7	16.7	14.1	9.8	7.0	7.0	37.7	52.2
Wallingford town................	6.1	17.9	6.0	12.9	17.8	15.2	8.9	6.8	8.4	39.1	51.8
Waterbury town	7.6	18.9	8.9	14.8	15.1	11.7	8.0	6.7	8.2	34.9	52.7
West Hartford town	5.7	16.4	9.8	11.0	14.7	14.4	8.5	7.9	11.5	40.0	54.0
West Haven town	6.2	16.9	9.7	14.9	16.3	13.4	8.4	6.9	7.3	36.4	52.3
Westport town	7.5	20.5	2.7	7.2	19.0	16.7	11.4	8.4	6.7	41.4	52.4
Wethersfield town	5.3	14.8	4.8	10.8	15.8	14.4	10.7	11.1	12.4	44.1	53.6
Windsor town	6.0	18.6	5.9	11.4	17.3	16.2	10.1	6.6	7.9	39.8	52.7
MAINE	5.5	18.1	8.1	12.4	16.7	15.1	9.7	7.5	6.8	38.6	51.3
Bangor city	5.7	15.5	12.4	14.7	15.6	13.9	8.1	6.7	7.4	36.1	52.8
Lewiston city	5.6	15.2	12.6	12.9	14.0	12.7	9.3	8.3	9.4	37.6	52.4
Portland city	5.1	13.6	10.7	19.3	16.8	13.3	7.3	6.3	7.6	35.7	52.1
MASSACHUSETTS...........	6.3	17.4	9.1	14.6	16.7	13.8	8.6	6.7	6.8	36.5	51.8
Agawam city	5.5	16.5	6.5	12.6	17.0	15.4	9.7	7.4	9.3	40.3	52.5
Amherst town.....................	2.8	10.0	50.0	9.3	7.9	8.7	4.6	3.3	3.4	21.8	51.9
Andover town	6.6	22.2	4.7	9.0	18.5	17.1	9.6	6.2	6.0	39.5	51.8
Arlington town....................	6.0	12.3	5.1	17.5	18.5	14.6	9.1	8.2	8.6	39.5	53.6
Attleboro city	7.0	18.4	6.8	15.7	18.2	12.7	8.3	6.4	6.5	36.1	51.4
Barnstable Town city............	5.2	16.7	5.6	10.4	16.4	14.9	10.6	10.5	9.6	42.3	52.2
Beverly city	6.3	15.4	9.0	13.6	17.2	14.5	8.3	7.2	8.4	38.3	52.7
Billerica town	6.9	18.8	7.3	15.2	19.4	14.0	10.0	5.0	3.4	35.9	49.1
Boston city	5.4	14.3	16.2	21.2	14.7	10.8	7.0	5.3	5.1	31.1	51.9
Braintree town	6.2	16.3	6.5	12.8	16.1	13.7	10.2	9.0	9.1	40.0	52.9
Bridgewater town	6.2	16.7	14.7	14.9	18.0	13.5	7.3	4.7	3.9	33.6	47.5
Brockton city	7.3	20.6	9.1	14.6	15.9	12.4	8.4	5.8	5.9	34.0	52.1
Brookline town	4.6	12.0	11.7	22.5	14.8	13.6	8.3	5.8	6.7	34.5	54.8
Cambridge city...................	4.1	9.2	21.2	24.9	13.8	11.0	6.8	4.6	4.5	30.4	51.0
Chelmsford town................	6.7	18.3	5.2	12.3	18.6	15.2	10.7	7.0	6.0	38.9	51.7
Chelsea city	8.1	19.2	10.6	19.0	15.6	9.8	6.5	5.4	5.8	31.3	49.8
Chicopee city.....................	5.5	17.2	8.5	13.2	15.6	13.3	9.2	8.5	9.1	38.7	52.4
Danvers town.....................	5.5	17.7	6.4	11.0	17.7	14.7	9.8	8.6	8.6	40.4	53.5
Dartmouth town	4.5	16.0	14.1	10.7	15.0	14.8	9.4	7.5	8.0	38.2	50.6

Table E. Towns

| | Population and population characteristics, 1990 | | | | | | | | | | Population—change, 1980–2000 | | | | |
| | Age (percent) | | | | | | | | | Percent Female | Total persons | | | Percent change | |
Town	Under 5 years	5 to 17 years	18 to 24 years	25 to 34 years	35 to 44 years	45 to 54 years	55 to 64 years	65 to 74 years	75 years and over		2000	1990	1980	1990–2000	1980–1990
	39	40	41	42	43	44	45	46	47	48	49	50	51	52	53
UNITED STATES	7.4	18.2	10.8	17.4	15.1	10.1	8.5	7.3	5.3	51.3	281 421 906	248 790 925	226 542 204	13.1	9.8
CONNECTICUT	6.9	15.9	10.5	17.8	15.5	10.8	9.0	7.8	5.8	51.5	3 405 565	3 287 116	3 107 564	3.6	5.8
Branford town	6.2	12.9	8.1	19.8	17.1	11.1	9.5	9.0	6.1	52.5	28 683	27 603	23 363	3.9	18.1
Bridgeport town	8.1	18.0	11.1	19.7	13.1	8.9	7.5	7.6	6.0	52.6	139 529	141 686	142 546	-1.5	-0.6
Bristol town	7.0	15.0	10.4	20.3	14.5	10.1	9.0	8.0	5.5	51.6	60 062	60 640	57 370	-1.0	5.7
Cheshire town	6.2	18.3	10.3	14.3	18.0	12.7	8.1	6.2	5.8	48.4	28 543	25 684	21 788	11.1	17.9
Danbury town	7.2	14.4	11.6	20.9	14.8	11.2	8.1	6.3	5.4	51.4	74 848	65 585	60 470	14.1	8.5
East Hartford town	6.3	13.3	10.4	19.6	13.0	11.5	10.4	9.6	6.0	51.2	49 575	50 452	52 563	-1.7	-4.0
East Haven town	6.7	13.5	9.7	19.8	14.3	10.4	10.3	9.7	5.6	52.0	28 189	26 144	25 028	7.8	4.5
Enfield town	7.1	16.0	9.6	21.2	14.0	11.2	10.1	6.6	4.2	49.5	45 212	45 532	42 695	-0.7	6.6
Fairfield town	5.8	13.8	11.3	14.2	15.5	11.5	10.8	9.7	7.4	52.2	57 340	53 418	54 849	7.3	-2.6
Glastonbury town	5.7	17.4	7.8	14.0	19.4	14.1	9.8	7.2	4.7	51.7	31 876	27 901	24 327	14.2	14.7
Greenwich town	5.5	14.8	7.4	14.7	15.4	14.1	11.9	9.1	6.9	52.8	61 101	58 441	59 578	4.6	-1.9
Groton town	9.4	14.8	16.9	24.8	11.9	7.0	6.2	5.5	3.6	44.4	39 907	45 144	41 062	-11.6	9.9
Hamden town	6.2	12.9	10.8	16.3	14.5	10.0	9.5	10.6	9.1	53.9	56 913	52 434	51 071	8.5	2.7
Hartford town	8.3	18.9	15.2	20.3	12.9	8.2	6.5	5.4	4.4	52.5	121 578	139 739	136 392	-13.0	2.5
Manchester town	6.9	14.6	9.6	19.8	15.3	10.0	8.1	8.8	6.9	52.5	54 740	51 618	49 761	6.0	3.7
Meriden town	7.8	16.4	9.2	19.3	15.1	9.2	8.2	8.4	6.3	52.5	58 244	59 479	57 118	-2.1	4.1
Middletown town	6.7	12.6	15.9	22.2	14.1	9.3	7.2	6.9	5.1	51.6	43 167	42 762	39 040	0.9	9.5
Milford town	6.5	15.3	9.1	18.0	16.1	11.4	9.7	9.0	4.8	51.4	52 305	49 938	50 898	4.7	-1.9
Naugatuck town	8.2	18.1	9.1	20.8	15.8	8.3	7.4	7.2	5.1	51.4	30 989	30 625	26 456	1.2	15.8
New Britain town	6.8	14.3	13.3	20.0	12.8	7.1	8.8	10.0	6.9	52.5	71 538	75 491	73 840	-5.2	2.2
New Haven town	7.8	15.6	16.9	20.5	12.6	8.1	6.4	6.3	5.9	52.9	123 626	130 474	126 109	-5.2	3.5
Newington town	5.2	14.4	8.1	16.3	15.6	12.3	10.8	10.3	7.0	52.3	29 306	29 208	28 841	0.3	1.3
New London town	7.1	12.5	23.1	19.2	11.6	7.2	6.5	6.8	6.1	49.0	25 671	28 540	28 842	-10.1	-1.0
New Milford town	8.1	18.4	8.7	19.6	18.1	11.3	6.7	4.5	4.5	50.5	27 121	23 629	19 420	14.8	21.7
Newtown town	7.1	18.5	7.5	15.3	20.1	14.0	8.5	5.2	3.9	49.9	25 031	20 779	19 107	20.5	8.8
Norwalk town	6.8	13.3	9.0	21.7	15.3	11.7	9.6	7.4	5.1	52.0	82 951	78 331	77 767	5.9	0.7
Norwich town	7.7	16.2	10.7	18.9	13.7	8.5	8.7	8.9	6.8	52.1	36 117	37 391	38 074	-3.4	-1.8
Shelton town	7.1	16.1	9.0	17.3	16.0	12.7	9.2	7.2	5.4	50.7	38 101	35 418	31 314	7.6	13.1
Southington town	6.4	17.4	9.5	15.4	17.4	12.7	9.2	7.7	4.2	51.0	39 728	38 518	36 879	3.1	4.4
Stamford town	6.8	13.5	9.0	20.7	15.5	11.3	10.1	7.8	5.4	52.3	117 083	108 056	102 453	8.4	5.5
Stratford town	5.9	14.5	7.9	15.7	14.8	10.7	10.9	11.8	7.8	52.9	49 976	49 389	50 541	1.2	-2.3
Torrington town	6.8	13.9	9.6	18.5	14.7	9.2	8.7	10.0	8.5	52.0	35 202	33 687	30 987	4.5	8.7
Trumbull town	6.0	16.3	8.3	12.5	15.3	13.9	12.0	9.6	6.0	51.6	34 243	32 016	32 989	7.0	-2.9
Vernon town	7.3	15.4	10.5	20.3	14.3	11.9	8.5	7.1	4.8	51.5	28 063	29 841	27 974	-6.0	6.7
Wallingford town	6.9	16.2	8.4	17.8	16.4	11.2	9.0	7.8	6.3	51.4	43 026	40 822	37 274	5.4	9.5
Waterbury town	7.8	15.6	10.5	19.1	13.1	8.7	8.7	9.1	7.3	53.0	107 271	108 961	103 266	-1.6	5.5
West Hartford town	5.4	14.3	8.0	13.6	15.5	10.2	10.8	11.0	11.2	54.7	63 589	60 110	61 301	5.8	-1.9
West Haven town	7.0	14.2	10.9	20.7	14.4	9.5	8.5	9.0	5.8	52.1	52 360	54 021	53 184	-3.1	1.6
Westport town	5.6	14.4	7.2	12.7	17.1	16.6	12.9	8.7	4.9	52.0	25 749	24 410	25 290	5.5	-3.5
Wethersfield town	5.2	13.0	7.1	13.8	13.8	11.6	12.8	12.4	10.3	53.3	26 271	25 651	26 013	2.4	-1.4
Windsor town	6.6	16.5	8.3	17.1	17.5	11.4	8.7	8.0	5.9	51.7	28 237	27 817	25 204	1.5	10.4
MAINE	7.0	18.2	10.1	16.7	15.7	10.2	8.8	7.5	5.8	51.3	1 274 923	1 227 928	1 125 043	3.8	9.1
Bangor city	7.2	14.8	14.0	19.1	14.1	9.3	7.9	7.0	6.7	53.1	31 473	33 181	31 643	-5.1	4.9
Lewiston city	7.0	14.5	14.1	15.7	12.4	9.5	9.4	9.0	7.4	53.0	35 690	39 757	40 481	-10.2	-1.8
Portland city	6.7	13.1	12.8	21.7	14.8	8.2	7.7	7.6	7.4	53.6	64 249	64 157	61 572	0.1	4.2
MASSACHUSETTS	6.9	15.6	11.8	18.3	15.3	10.0	8.6	7.6	6.0	52.0	6 349 097	6 016 425	5 737 093	5.5	4.9
Agawam city	6.2	15.8	9.6	17.3	16.7	10.6	8.7	8.5	6.6	52.3	28 144	27 323	26 271	3.0	4.0
Amherst town	3.4	8.5	53.3	11.6	9.4	5.3	3.5	2.7	2.4	51.3	34 874	35 228	33 229	-1.0	6.0
Andover town	6.7	19.4	8.2	13.2	18.4	14.4	9.1	6.3	4.3	51.7	31 247	29 151	26 370	7.2	10.5
Arlington town	5.6	11.0	8.8	21.1	16.2	9.6	10.0	9.3	8.5	54.1	42 389	44 630	48 219	-5.0	-7.4
Attleboro city	8.8	16.3	10.0	20.7	13.9	10.2	8.2	7.0	5.0	51.1	42 068	38 383	34 196	9.6	12.2
Barnstable Town city	6.6	14.8	7.9	15.6	14.8	9.9	10.0	11.9	8.5	52.3	47 821	40 949	30 898	16.8	32.5
Beverly city	6.9	14.4	10.7	18.5	15.7	9.8	9.0	8.3	6.7	53.3	39 862	38 195	37 655	4.4	1.4
Billerica town	7.4	18.3	12.1	19.9	16.2	12.3	6.9	4.2	2.6	49.1	38 981	37 609	36 727	3.6	2.4
Boston city	6.2	12.8	17.3	23.2	13.6	8.2	7.1	6.3	5.2	52.2	589 141	574 283	562 994	2.6	2.0
Braintree town	5.7	14.2	10.4	16.4	13.2	12.0	11.1	9.6	7.4	52.8	33 828	33 836	36 337	0.0	-6.9
Bridgewater town	6.0	15.5	18.9	19.6	16.4	10.3	5.5	5.0	2.8	46.8	25 185	21 249	17 202	18.5	23.5
Brockton city	8.4	17.9	11.1	18.5	14.1	9.7	7.9	6.7	5.7	51.7	94 304	92 788	95 172	1.6	-2.5
Brookline town	4.8	10.8	11.9	22.6	16.7	10.3	7.2	6.7	8.9	55.4	57 107	54 718	55 062	4.4	-0.6
Cambridge city	4.8	9.3	19.6	25.1	16.0	8.8	6.0	5.8	4.6	51.7	101 355	95 802	95 322	5.8	0.5
Chelmsford town	6.6	16.8	9.7	17.0	16.8	13.6	9.7	5.9	3.8	50.9	33 858	32 383	31 174	4.6	3.9
Chelsea city	9.1	16.7	11.8	21.3	11.9	7.6	8.2	7.5	5.9	51.1	35 080	28 710	25 431	22.2	12.9
Chicopee city	6.3	15.5	10.9	17.0	13.4	9.7	10.0	10.7	6.5	52.4	54 653	56 632	55 112	-3.5	2.8
Danvers town	6.1	15.1	9.1	17.2	14.8	12.1	10.7	8.5	6.4	52.7	25 212	24 174	24 100	4.3	0.3
Dartmouth town	4.9	16.7	15.3	11.6	16.2	10.3	9.3	9.6	6.2	52.1	30 666	27 244	23 966	12.6	13.7

Table E. Towns

Town	Total population	In households (percent)			Child		Other relatives		Nonrelatives		In group quarters (percent)	Institutionalized population			Noninstitutionalized population		
		Total in households	House-holder	Spouse	Total	Own child under 18 years	Total	Under 18 years	Total	Unmar-ried partner	Total in group quarters	Correc-tional institu-tions	Nurs-ing homes	Other institu-tions	Col-lege dormi-tories	Mili-tary quar-ters	Other
	54	55	56	57	58	59	60	61	62	63	64	65	66	67	68	69	70
UNITED STATES	281 421 906	97.2	37.5	19.4	29.6	22.9	5.6	2.1	5.2	1.9	2.8	0.7	0.6	0.1	0.7	0.1	0.5
CONNECTICUT	3 405 565	96.8	38.2	19.9	29.5	22.7	4.6	1.5	4.7	2.0	3.2	0.6	0.9	0.1	1.1	0.1	0.4
Branford town	28 683	99.0	43.7	21.0	25.9	19.3	3.9	1.0	4.6	2.3	1.0	0.0	0.7	0.2	0.0	0.0	0.1
Bridgeport town	139 529	97.4	36.1	12.6	32.8	24.0	9.4	3.8	6.5	2.7	2.6	0.6	0.7	0.1	0.9	0.0	0.3
Bristol town	60 062	98.7	41.4	20.6	28.2	21.6	3.6	1.1	4.9	2.5	1.3	0.0	1.0	0.0	0.0	0.0	0.3
Cheshire town	28 543	88.9	32.8	22.4	29.5	23.0	2.3	0.5	1.8	0.9	11.1	9.2	1.4	0.0	0.0	0.0	0.6
Danbury town	74 848	95.8	36.3	18.6	26.4	19.3	7.0	1.9	7.5	2.0	4.2	1.8	0.9	0.0	1.2	0.0	0.2
East Hartford town	49 575	98.6	40.8	16.9	29.0	21.4	6.1	2.1	5.8	2.9	1.4	0.0	1.2	0.0	0.0	0.0	0.2
East Haven town	28 189	99.2	39.8	20.1	29.0	20.0	6.2	1.9	4.1	2.0	0.8	0.0	0.5	0.0	0.0	0.0	0.3
Enfield town	45 212	91.7	36.3	20.2	27.6	21.0	3.6	1.3	4.0	1.9	8.3	7.4	0.7	0.0	0.0	0.0	0.1
Fairfield town	57 340	92.8	35.6	22.0	28.6	22.8	3.0	0.8	3.7	1.1	7.2	0.0	1.7	0.0	5.4	0.0	0.1
Glastonbury town	31 876	99.0	38.5	24.5	31.2	26.1	2.3	0.5	2.5	1.1	1.0	0.0	0.8	0.0	0.0	0.0	0.2
Greenwich town	61 101	98.9	38.0	22.6	30.5	24.5	3.2	0.8	4.6	1.2	1.1	0.0	0.8	0.0	0.0	0.0	0.3
Groton town	39 907	93.4	38.8	19.6	27.6	23.4	2.6	0.9	4.8	2.1	6.6	0.0	1.2	0.0	0.0	5.2	0.2
Hamden town	56 913	92.6	39.4	19.0	25.6	18.9	4.2	1.3	4.4	1.6	7.4	0.0	1.2	0.2	5.4	0.0	0.7
Hartford town	121 578	95.6	37.0	9.3	33.4	24.9	9.4	4.3	6.5	3.0	4.4	0.9	0.8	0.3	1.5	0.0	1.0
Manchester town	54 740	98.1	42.4	18.5	27.1	21.1	3.8	1.2	6.3	2.9	1.9	0.0	1.4	0.0	0.0	0.0	0.5
Meriden town	58 244	98.0	39.4	17.9	30.4	23.2	5.1	1.8	5.3	2.8	2.0	0.0	1.4	0.1	0.0	0.0	0.5
Middletown town	43 167	95.7	43.0	17.7	24.4	19.2	3.6	1.3	7.0	2.9	4.3	0.0	1.3	2.0	0.0	0.0	1.0
Milford town	52 305	99.0	40.0	21.7	28.6	20.6	4.5	1.4	4.2	1.9	1.0	0.0	0.8	0.0	0.0	0.0	0.2
Naugatuck town	30 989	99.3	38.2	20.3	32.8	25.3	3.8	1.1	4.1	2.1	0.7	0.0	0.6	0.0	0.0	0.0	0.1
New Britain town	71 538	95.7	39.9	14.6	28.6	21.3	6.0	2.2	6.5	3.0	4.3	0.0	1.3	0.0	2.3	0.0	0.8
New Haven town	123 626	91.4	38.1	10.5	28.0	21.4	7.3	3.1	7.6	2.5	8.6	1.1	0.9	0.1	5.7	0.0	0.7
Newington town	29 306	98.1	41.0	22.5	27.6	19.6	3.9	0.8	3.1	1.5	1.9	0.0	1.4	0.2	0.0	0.0	0.4
New London town	25 671	89.5	39.7	12.1	24.9	19.8	5.0	2.0	7.9	3.4	10.5	0.0	1.0	0.0	8.7	0.1	0.8
New Milford town	27 121	99.0	36.9	22.1	32.2	26.0	3.4	1.1	4.4	2.2	1.0	0.0	0.8	0.0	0.0	0.0	0.1
Newtown town	25 031	96.4	33.3	24.4	33.8	28.5	2.4	0.6	2.6	1.1	3.6	2.8	0.7	0.0	0.0	0.0	0.1
Norwalk town	82 951	99.0	39.4	18.9	27.3	19.6	7.0	2.1	6.4	2.1	1.0	0.0	0.6	0.0	0.0	0.0	0.4
Norwich town	36 117	97.9	41.8	17.0	27.9	21.7	4.3	1.5	7.0	3.3	2.1	0.0	0.9	0.5	0.0	0.0	1.0
Shelton town	38 101	98.5	37.2	23.4	30.5	22.1	4.5	1.2	2.8	1.4	1.5	0.0	1.2	0.0	0.2	0.0	0.1
Southington town	39 728	98.5	38.0	23.9	30.0	22.5	3.5	1.0	3.2	1.7	1.5	0.0	1.2	0.0	0.0	0.0	0.7
Stamford town	117 083	98.5	38.8	18.8	27.0	19.9	7.0	1.8	7.0	1.8	1.5	0.0	0.7	0.1	0.0	0.0	0.1
Stratford town	49 976	99.3	39.8	20.9	29.4	20.8	5.4	1.8	3.7	1.6	0.7	0.0	0.6	0.0	0.0	0.0	0.1
Torrington town	35 202	97.6	41.9	20.0	27.6	21.4	3.2	1.0	5.0	2.5	2.4	0.0	1.9	0.0	0.0	0.0	0.5
Trumbull town	34 243	98.1	34.8	25.0	32.5	24.8	4.1	1.0	1.8	0.7	1.9	0.0	1.3	0.0	0.5	0.0	0.1
Vernon town	28 063	98.8	43.7	19.8	26.4	20.7	3.0	0.9	5.9	3.3	1.2	0.0	0.9	0.0	0.0	0.0	0.3
Wallingford town	43 026	98.0	38.8	22.2	29.7	22.6	3.7	1.1	3.5	1.9	2.0	0.0	2.0	0.0	0.0	0.0	0.1
Waterbury town	107 271	97.9	39.7	15.4	31.2	23.4	6.2	2.3	5.4	3.0	2.1	0.2	1.3	0.0	0.2	0.0	0.4
West Hartford town	63 589	92.4	38.6	20.4	26.5	21.1	3.2	0.8	3.6	1.4	7.6	0.0	2.1	0.0	5.1	0.0	0.4
West Haven town	52 360	97.6	40.3	16.9	24.2	20.6	5.8	2.1	5.6	2.5	2.4	0.0	0.7	0.2	1.5	0.0	0.0
Westport town	25 749	99.1	37.2	24.6	31.6	27.2	2.2	0.5	3.5	1.0	0.9	0.0	0.4	0.2	0.0	0.0	0.3
Wethersfield town	26 271	98.8	42.7	23.0	26.6	19.1	3.9	0.8	2.7	1.3	1.2	0.0	1.2	0.0	0.0	0.0	0.1
Windsor town	28 237	97.9	37.5	20.9	30.3	22.1	5.3	1.9	4.0	1.7	2.1	0.0	2.0	0.0	0.0	0.0	0.1
MAINE	1 274 923	97.3	40.6	21.3	26.9	21.9	2.6	0.9	5.8	3.0	2.7	0.2	0.7	0.1	1.1	0.1	0.6
Bangor city	31 473	92.5	43.6	15.7	23.2	19.0	2.4	0.7	7.6	3.4	7.5	0.6	1.5	0.4	1.7	0.0	3.3
Lewiston city	35 690	92.9	42.8	17.5	23.6	19.0	2.8	0.8	6.0	3.3	7.1	0.0	1.9	0.2	4.2	0.0	0.8
Portland city	64 249	96.2	46.2	14.9	21.8	17.3	3.1	0.9	10.2	3.9	3.8	0.6	0.8	0.0	0.5	0.0	1.8
MASSACHUSETTS	6 349 097	96.5	38.5	18.9	29.0	21.8	4.5	1.4	5.6	2.1	3.5	0.4	0.9	0.1	1.6	0.0	0.5
Agawam city	28 144	97.4	40.0	21.4	28.5	20.6	3.5	1.1	4.0	2.0	2.6	0.0	2.6	0.0	0.0	0.0	0.0
Amherst town	34 874	64.4	26.3	9.6	14.7	12.1	1.4	0.4	12.3	1.5	35.6	0.0	0.4	0.0	35.1	0.0	0.1
Andover town	31 247	99.0	36.2	23.7	34.6	28.0	2.5	0.7	2.1	0.9	1.0	0.0	0.9	0.0	0.0	0.0	0.1
Arlington town	42 389	99.6	44.8	20.4	24.8	17.6	3.4	0.6	6.2	2.2	0.4	0.0	0.2	0.0	0.0	0.0	0.2
Attleboro city	42 068	98.0	38.1	20.4	30.5	23.6	4.2	1.3	4.8	2.3	2.0	0.0	1.4	0.0	0.0	0.0	0.5
Barnstable Town city	47 821	97.5	41.0	21.5	25.9	20.2	3.6	1.1	5.4	1.9	2.5	0.6	0.7	0.0	0.0	0.0	1.3
Beverly city	39 862	94.6	39.5	19.8	26.9	20.4	3.5	0.9	4.8	1.8	5.4	0.0	1.9	0.0	2.9	0.0	0.6
Billerica town	38 981	96.9	33.1	21.9	33.5	23.5	5.1	1.8	3.2	1.3	3.1	2.5	0.3	0.0	0.0	0.0	0.3
Boston city	589 141	94.0	40.7	11.2	24.2	17.0	7.0	2.2	11.1	2.5	6.0	0.4	0.7	0.4	3.4	0.0	1.0
Braintree town	33 828	97.6	37.4	20.7	31.3	20.8	4.8	1.4	3.4	1.5	2.4	0.1	1.9	0.3	0.0	0.0	0.1
Bridgewater town	25 185	84.0	29.9	18.4	28.6	21.6	3.4	1.1	3.7	1.4	16.0	8.9	0.1	0.0	6.9	0.0	0.5
Brockton city	94 304	98.0	35.7	15.0	33.9	24.3	7.7	2.8	5.7	2.6	2.0	0.0	1.0	0.5	0.0	0.0	0.5
Brookline town	57 107	97.6	44.8	17.2	20.0	16.0	2.7	0.4	12.9	1.9	2.4	0.0	0.8	0.1	1.2	0.0	0.3
Cambridge town	101 355	85.5	42.0	12.2	16.1	12.1	3.3	0.8	11.8	2.6	14.5	0.2	0.3	0.0	13.0	0.0	0.9
Chelmsford town	33 858	98.6	37.8	23.1	31.3	23.7	3.5	1.0	2.8	1.4	1.4	0.7	0.6	0.0	0.0	0.0	0.0
Chelsea city	35 080	97.3	33.9	12.5	31.4	23.7	10.3	2.8	9.2	2.4	2.7	0.0	2.5	0.0	0.0	0.0	0.2
Chicopee city	54 653	98.2	42.3	18.0	28.3	20.5	4.2	1.3	5.3	2.8	1.8	0.0	0.6	0.0	0.3	0.0	0.9
Danvers town	25 212	96.0	37.9	21.3	29.5	21.6	4.0	1.3	3.3	1.5	4.0	0.0	2.2	0.7	0.9	0.0	0.3
Dartmouth town	30 666	89.5	34.4	21.1	27.6	18.8	3.7	1.3	2.7	1.3	10.5	2.7	0.5	0.0	7.0	0.0	0.2

Table E. Towns

	Households by type, 2000												Households, 1990		
	Family households						Nonfamily households								
			Married couple		Female householder[1]			Householder living alone							
Town	Total households	Total	With own children under 18 years	Total	With own children under 18 years	Total	With own children under 18 years	Total	Total	65 years and over	Average household size	Average family size	Total households	Female householder[1]	Householder living alone
	71	72	73	74	75	76	77	78	79	80	81	82	83	84	85
UNITED STATES	105 480 101	68.1	32.8	51.7	23.5	12.2	7.2	31.9	25.8	9.2	2.59	3.14	91 947 410	11.6	24.6
CONNECTICUT	1 301 670	67.7	32.2	52.0	23.6	12.1	7.0	32.3	26.4	10.1	2.53	3.08	1 230 479	11.4	24.2
Branford town	12 543	61.1	25.7	47.9	19.3	9.8	4.9	38.9	32.4	11.6	2.26	2.90	11 663	8.0	29.6
Bridgeport town	50 307	65.1	34.3	35.0	16.8	24.0	14.9	34.9	29.0	11.3	2.70	3.34	52 328	20.0	28.8
Bristol town	24 886	65.0	29.6	49.6	21.0	11.5	6.6	35.0	28.9	10.7	2.38	2.94	23 956	9.4	24.7
Cheshire town	9 349	77.6	39.1	68.5	34.5	6.9	3.6	22.4	19.4	9.6	2.71	3.14	8 340	7.4	17.2
Danbury town	27 183	65.8	30.3	51.1	23.6	10.5	5.3	34.2	26.2	8.5	2.64	3.18	24 094	9.8	24.4
East Hartford town	20 206	63.5	29.2	41.5	16.2	17.4	11.0	36.5	30.2	11.3	2.42	3.01	20 343	12.2	26.9
East Haven town	11 219	66.8	28.2	50.6	21.2	12.0	5.3	33.2	27.8	11.1	2.49	3.08	10 059	9.7	23.7
Enfield town	16 418	69.4	31.1	55.7	23.8	10.2	5.7	30.6	25.0	9.5	2.53	3.04	15 985	9.5	18.8
Fairfield town	20 397	72.6	33.9	61.8	29.7	8.5	3.5	27.4	22.0	10.3	2.61	3.07	19 371	8.9	20.9
Glastonbury town	12 257	73.3	37.1	63.7	31.7	7.5	4.5	26.7	22.6	8.8	2.57	3.06	10 553	6.3	20.4
Greenwich town	23 230	69.9	33.5	59.4	28.8	8.0	3.8	30.1	24.8	9.9	2.60	3.12	22 192	9.1	22.9
Groton town	15 473	64.5	33.4	50.5	24.5	10.5	7.1	35.5	29.2	9.5	2.41	2.99	14 853	8.5	21.8
Hamden town	22 408	62.6	26.7	48.2	20.1	11.3	5.5	37.4	31.1	13.6	2.35	2.98	20 641	8.1	27.6
Hartford town	44 986	60.4	34.4	25.2	11.7	29.6	20.1	39.6	33.2	9.6	2.58	3.33	51 464	28.2	32.6
Manchester town	23 197	60.4	28.2	43.8	18.2	13.0	8.3	39.6	31.1	10.1	2.32	2.93	20 745	10.7	25.5
Meriden town	22 951	65.2	31.3	45.4	19.5	15.2	9.6	34.8	28.9	10.7	2.49	3.08	23 240	12.7	25.9
Middletown town	18 554	56.0	25.7	41.3	17.1	11.6	7.2	44.0	35.0	10.1	2.23	2.90	16 821	11.8	30.7
Milford town	20 900	67.3	29.1	54.4	23.4	9.7	4.4	32.7	26.6	10.3	2.48	3.04	18 851	9.7	22.5
Naugatuck town	11 829	70.1	36.3	53.3	26.5	12.8	7.9	29.9	24.9	9.6	2.60	3.13	11 330	9.5	22.9
New Britain town	28 558	59.3	28.3	36.6	14.8	17.7	11.3	40.7	33.1	12.7	2.40	3.08	30 170	14.9	29.4
New Haven town	47 094	54.9	29.3	27.5	12.3	22.9	15.1	45.1	36.1	10.5	2.40	3.19	48 986	21.5	33.5
Newington town	12 014	68.7	27.7	54.9	21.6	10.7	5.1	31.3	26.8	11.6	2.39	2.92	11 223	10.1	22.3
New London town	10 181	52.9	27.6	30.4	12.9	17.8	12.2	47.1	37.8	10.7	2.26	3.00	10 712	15.3	34.4
New Milford town	10 018	72.6	38.0	60.0	30.9	9.0	5.1	27.4	21.3	6.4	2.68	3.15	8 419	7.3	19.8
Newtown town	8 325	81.4	44.7	73.3	40.9	5.8	2.8	18.6	14.8	5.8	2.90	3.24	6 798	6.5	14.0
Norwalk town	32 711	64.1	28.5	47.9	20.9	12.2	6.4	35.9	28.2	8.7	2.51	3.10	30 560	10.9	25.6
Norwich town	15 091	60.1	29.0	40.7	16.7	15.0	9.9	39.9	32.0	12.5	2.34	2.96	15 018	12.5	27.6
Shelton town	14 190	74.3	32.8	62.9	27.8	8.5	4.1	25.7	21.8	9.2	2.65	3.11	12 454	7.0	18.1
Southington town	15 083	74.8	33.0	62.9	27.2	8.9	4.4	25.2	20.8	9.7	2.59	3.02	13 766	8.0	17.5
Stamford town	45 399	63.8	28.7	48.5	21.7	11.5	5.7	36.2	28.7	9.8	2.54	3.13	41 945	12.4	26.2
Stratford town	19 898	68.5	28.5	52.5	21.7	12.5	5.6	31.5	27.1	14.1	2.49	3.04	19 310	9.9	24.4
Torrington town	14 743	61.9	28.5	47.7	20.3	10.3	6.1	38.1	32.1	13.7	2.33	2.96	13 883	8.9	28.6
Trumbull town	11 911	81.5	37.5	71.7	34.0	7.4	2.9	18.5	16.2	9.6	2.82	3.17	10 843	6.9	13.6
Vernon town	12 269	59.3	26.5	45.3	17.8	10.5	6.7	40.7	33.0	10.6	2.26	2.90	12 137	9.5	26.2
Wallingford town	16 697	69.4	32.3	57.3	26.3	9.0	4.6	30.6	25.6	10.3	2.52	3.07	15 167	8.3	22.5
Waterbury town	42 622	63.1	31.2	38.8	16.5	19.1	12.2	36.9	31.4	12.1	2.46	3.11	43 164	14.8	29.4
West Hartford town	24 576	64.8	29.8	52.9	23.7	9.3	5.0	35.2	29.6	14.4	2.39	3.00	23 916	8.8	27.1
West Haven town	21 090	62.2	28.5	41.9	17.7	15.6	8.8	37.8	31.0	10.7	2.42	3.06	21 284	12.5	27.1
Westport town	9 586	74.8	38.4	66.1	34.1	6.8	3.6	25.2	20.8	8.8	2.66	3.10	9 276	7.2	19.2
Wethersfield town	11 214	66.1	25.2	53.9	20.3	9.6	4.1	33.9	30.2	15.9	2.31	2.89	10 470	8.7	26.3
Windsor town	10 577	71.9	32.8	55.7	24.3	13.0	7.0	28.1	23.2	8.8	2.61	3.10	9 838	8.9	19.3
MAINE	518 200	65.7	30.4	52.5	21.8	9.5	6.2	34.3	27.0	10.7	2.39	2.90	465 312	9.5	23.3
Bangor city	13 713	52.4	26.1	36.0	15.2	12.8	8.7	47.6	37.6	11.5	2.12	2.81	13 392	11.8	30.7
Lewiston city	15 290	56.6	25.4	40.9	14.7	11.8	8.4	43.4	35.9	13.7	2.17	2.81	15 823	12.6	29.8
Portland city	29 714	45.6	21.4	32.1	13.3	10.5	6.6	54.4	40.1	11.5	2.08	2.89	28 235	11.5	35.2
MASSACHUSETTS	2 443 580	64.5	30.6	49.0	22.4	11.9	6.7	35.5	28.0	10.5	2.51	3.11	2 247 110	12.1	25.8
Agawam city	11 260	66.3	28.9	53.4	22.6	9.8	5.0	33.7	28.0	11.3	2.43	3.01	10 432	8.5	23.8
Amherst town	9 174	49.6	27.0	36.4	18.0	10.8	7.7	50.4	28.6	8.6	2.45	2.97	8 477	11.6	22.8
Andover town	11 305	75.1	40.3	65.6	35.3	7.5	4.2	24.9	21.6	9.2	2.74	3.24	10 415	7.5	20.4
Arlington town	19 011	56.7	23.1	45.4	19.1	8.8	3.4	43.3	34.2	12.5	2.22	2.91	18 819	9.7	30.6
Attleboro city	16 019	68.2	33.4	53.6	25.0	10.6	6.4	31.8	25.7	9.4	2.57	3.12	14 180	9.4	23.1
Barnstable Town city	19 626	66.3	26.9	52.4	19.2	10.7	6.3	33.7	27.7	12.5	2.38	2.88	16 601	10.5	26.2
Beverly city	15 750	62.9	28.8	50.1	22.6	9.7	5.1	37.1	29.9	11.4	2.39	3.02	14 796	10.7	26.7
Billerica town	12 919	79.3	37.4	66.1	32.0	9.4	4.1	20.7	16.4	5.3	2.92	3.30	11 695	9.1	14.0
Boston city	239 528	48.1	22.7	27.4	11.8	16.4	9.5	51.9	37.1	9.1	2.31	3.17	228 464	16.5	35.2
Braintree town	12 652	70.4	29.6	55.4	24.1	11.7	4.7	29.6	24.4	11.9	2.61	3.16	11 896	11.5	21.0
Bridgewater town	7 526	74.2	38.6	61.5	32.4	9.5	4.9	25.8	19.6	7.7	2.81	3.27	5 947	8.3	19.6
Brockton city	33 675	67.6	35.0	42.0	19.9	19.9	12.5	32.4	26.6	9.5	2.74	3.35	32 850	17.3	23.8
Brookline town	25 594	47.8	21.9	38.4	17.5	7.1	3.8	52.2	36.7	10.1	2.18	2.86	24 357	7.8	38.7
Cambridge city	42 615	41.3	17.6	29.1	11.3	9.7	5.5	58.7	41.4	9.2	2.03	2.83	39 405	9.8	42.1
Chelmsford town	12 812	72.6	34.4	61.0	29.0	9.0	4.4	27.4	23.1	9.6	2.61	3.11	11 453	8.9	17.2
Chelsea city	11 888	64.0	36.4	36.9	20.2	20.1	13.0	36.0	28.8	10.8	2.87	3.50	10 553	21.3	30.4
Chicopee city	23 117	61.2	26.5	42.6	16.2	14.2	8.3	38.8	32.7	14.1	2.32	2.96	22 625	13.3	28.1
Danvers town	9 555	68.7	30.9	56.2	25.4	9.4	4.4	31.3	26.6	10.8	2.53	3.11	8 813	9.4	22.2
Dartmouth town	10 555	74.1	31.9	61.3	25.8	9.6	4.7	25.9	22.3	12.5	2.60	3.06	9 190	8.9	19.5

[1]No spouse present.

Table E. Towns

Town	Housing occupancy							Housing tenure				
				Vacant housing units				Occupied housing units				
	Percent change of households, 1990–2000	Total housing units	Occupied housing units (percent)	Total	For seasonal, recreational, or occasional use	Homeowner vacancy rate (percent)	Rental vacancy rate (percent)	Total	Percent owner-occupied housing units	Percent renter-occupied housing units	Average household size of owner-occupied units	Average household size of renter-occupied units
	86	87	88	89	90	91	92	93	94	95	96	97
UNITED STATES	14.7	115 904 641	91.0	9.0	3.1	1.7	6.8	105 480 101	66.2	33.8	2.69	2.40
CONNECTICUT	5.8	1 385 075	93.9	6.1	1.7	1.1	5.6	1 301 670	66.8	33.2	2.67	2.25
Branford town	7.5	13 342	94.0	6.0	2.8	0.9	5.0	12 543	68.6	31.4	2.41	1.95
Bridgeport town	-3.9	54 367	92.5	7.5	0.2	1.9	5.6	50 307	43.2	56.8	2.74	2.67
Bristol town	3.9	26 125	95.3	4.7	0.3	1.1	5.2	24 886	61.9	38.1	2.60	2.03
Cheshire town	12.1	9 588	97.5	2.5	0.5	0.9	3.5	9 349	86.6	13.4	2.84	1.88
Danbury town	12.8	28 519	95.3	4.7	1.3	1.1	3.4	27 183	58.3	41.7	2.67	2.59
East Hartford town	-0.7	21 273	95.0	5.0	0.4	1.2	6.2	20 206	57.5	42.5	2.53	2.26
East Haven town	11.5	11 698	95.9	4.1	1.2	1.2	4.0	11 219	72.8	27.2	2.66	2.05
Enfield town	2.7	17 043	96.3	3.7	0.4	1.0	5.6	16 418	75.6	24.4	2.66	2.10
Fairfield town	5.3	21 029	97.0	3.0	0.9	0.5	3.0	20 397	83.2	16.8	2.70	2.15
Glastonbury town	16.1	12 614	97.2	2.8	0.4	0.7	4.4	12 257	81.7	18.3	2.71	1.96
Greenwich town	4.7	24 511	94.8	5.2	1.8	1.1	2.8	23 230	68.8	31.2	2.74	2.29
Groton town	4.2	16 817	92.0	8.0	3.1	1.0	4.6	15 473	50.5	49.5	2.40	2.41
Hamden town	8.6	23 464	95.5	4.5	0.5	0.9	6.0	22 408	67.2	32.8	2.53	1.98
Hartford town	-12.6	50 644	88.8	11.2	0.3	2.0	9.2	44 986	24.6	75.4	2.76	2.52
Manchester town	11.8	24 256	95.6	4.4	0.6	1.1	4.7	23 197	56.3	43.7	2.49	2.09
Meriden town	-1.2	24 631	93.2	6.8	0.2	1.7	7.3	22 951	59.9	40.1	2.59	2.34
Middletown town	10.3	19 697	94.2	5.8	0.5	1.5	5.8	18 554	51.3	48.7	2.49	1.95
Milford town	10.9	21 962	95.2	4.8	1.6	0.7	6.1	20 900	77.3	22.7	2.61	2.02
Naugatuck town	4.4	12 341	95.9	4.1	0.2	0.9	5.0	11 829	66.5	33.5	2.79	2.22
New Britain town	-5.3	31 164	91.6	8.4	0.2	1.7	6.1	28 558	42.7	57.3	2.50	2.32
New Haven town	-3.9	52 941	89.0	11.0	0.3	3.7	7.1	47 094	29.6	70.4	2.60	2.32
Newington town	7.0	12 264	98.0	2.0	0.3	0.6	2.8	12 014	80.6	19.4	2.48	2.04
New London town	-5.0	11 560	88.1	11.9	1.1	2.5	9.8	10 181	37.9	62.1	2.39	2.17
New Milford town	19.0	10 710	93.5	6.5	3.5	0.8	4.9	10 018	77.6	22.4	2.82	2.21
Newtown town	22.5	8 601	96.8	3.2	1.2	0.7	2.9	8 325	91.9	8.1	2.97	2.11
Norwalk town	7.0	33 753	96.9	3.1	0.6	0.6	2.9	32 711	62.0	38.0	2.61	2.35
Norwich town	0.5	16 600	90.9	9.1	1.3	2.3	7.0	15 091	52.5	47.5	2.51	2.16
Shelton town	13.9	14 707	96.5	3.5	0.7	0.9	5.8	14 190	81.8	18.2	2.76	2.15
Southington town	9.6	15 557	97.0	3.0	0.5	0.6	5.9	15 083	81.4	18.6	2.69	2.17
Stamford town	8.2	47 317	95.9	4.1	1.0	0.6	3.0	45 399	56.7	43.3	2.65	2.39
Stratford town	3.0	20 596	96.6	3.4	0.8	0.8	4.1	19 898	80.4	19.6	2.56	2.23
Torrington town	6.2	16 147	91.3	8.7	2.7	1.9	7.0	14 743	64.6	35.4	2.50	2.02
Trumbull town	9.8	12 160	98.0	2.0	0.6	0.4	1.6	11 911	90.9	9.1	2.88	2.21
Vernon town	1.1	12 867	95.4	4.6	0.4	0.7	4.9	12 269	56.5	43.5	2.51	1.93
Wallingford town	10.1	17 306	96.5	3.5	0.3	0.7	5.3	16 697	72.7	27.3	2.72	1.99
Waterbury town	-1.3	46 827	91.0	9.0	0.3	2.2	7.6	42 622	47.6	52.4	2.58	2.36
West Hartford town	2.8	25 332	97.0	3.0	0.7	0.6	4.2	24 576	71.9	28.1	2.57	1.93
West Haven town	-0.9	22 336	94.4	5.6	0.3	1.5	6.6	21 090	55.2	44.8	2.62	2.18
Westport town	3.3	10 065	95.2	4.8	2.2	1.0	4.1	9 586	85.6	14.4	2.76	2.10
Wethersfield town	7.1	11 454	97.9	2.1	0.5	0.5	1.9	11 214	77.9	22.1	2.46	1.81
Windsor town	7.5	10 900	97.0	3.0	0.4	1.0	3.8	10 577	80.3	19.7	2.73	2.15
MAINE	11.4	651 901	79.5	20.5	15.6	1.7	7.0	518 200	71.6	28.4	2.54	2.03
Bangor city	2.4	14 587	94.0	6.0	1.0	2.0	4.2	13 713	47.5	52.5	2.43	1.85
Lewiston city	-3.4	16 470	92.8	7.2	0.4	1.3	8.8	15 290	47.2	52.8	2.44	1.92
Portland city	5.2	31 862	93.3	6.7	3.0	0.5	3.6	29 714	42.5	57.5	2.41	1.84
MASSACHUSETTS	8.7	2 621 989	93.2	6.8	3.6	0.7	3.5	2 443 580	61.7	38.3	2.72	2.17
Agawam city	7.9	11 659	96.6	3.4	0.6	0.8	4.2	11 260	73.6	26.4	2.63	1.90
Amherst town	8.2	9 427	97.3	2.7	0.7	0.4	1.7	9 174	45.0	55.0	2.62	2.31
Andover town	8.5	11 590	97.5	2.5	0.7	0.4	2.8	11 305	78.6	21.4	2.97	1.89
Arlington town	1.0	19 411	97.9	2.1	0.3	0.4	1.5	19 011	58.8	41.2	2.47	1.87
Attleboro city	13.0	16 554	96.8	3.2	0.2	0.7	3.8	16 019	63.8	36.2	2.81	2.16
Barnstable Town city	18.2	25 018	78.4	21.6	19.0	1.1	3.7	19 626	76.2	23.8	2.43	2.19
Beverly city	6.4	16 275	96.8	3.2	0.8	0.4	3.1	15 750	60.0	40.0	2.70	1.93
Billerica town	10.5	13 071	98.8	1.2	0.1	0.2	2.0	12 919	84.4	15.6	3.06	2.20
Boston city	4.8	251 935	95.1	4.9	0.6	1.0	3.0	239 528	32.2	67.8	2.51	2.22
Braintree town	6.4	12 973	97.5	2.5	0.4	0.3	3.3	12 652	77.5	22.5	2.79	2.00
Bridgewater town	26.6	7 652	98.4	1.6	0.2	0.4	1.7	7 526	74.6	25.4	3.05	2.10
Brockton city	2.5	34 837	96.7	3.3	0.1	0.5	3.3	33 675	54.6	45.4	2.98	2.46
Brookline town	5.1	26 413	96.9	3.1	0.7	0.5	2.1	25 594	45.3	54.7	2.39	2.00
Cambridge city	8.1	44 725	95.3	4.7	1.3	0.9	2.6	42 615	32.3	67.7	2.16	1.97
Chelmsford town	11.9	13 025	98.4	1.6	0.3	0.2	1.9	12 812	83.9	16.1	2.74	1.93
Chelsea city	12.7	12 337	96.4	3.6	0.2	1.1	1.6	11 888	28.9	71.1	2.87	2.87
Chicopee city	2.2	24 424	94.6	5.4	0.4	0.9	4.8	23 117	59.3	40.7	2.46	2.11
Danvers town	8.4	9 762	97.9	2.1	0.5	0.4	2.3	9 555	77.1	22.9	2.72	1.91
Dartmouth town	14.9	11 283	93.5	6.5	3.9	0.5	3.0	10 555	80.7	19.3	2.75	1.96

Table E. Towns

STATE MCD code	Town	Population, 2000				Population, 1990				Population and population characteristics, 2000					
										Race (percent)					
										One race					
		Land area, 2000[1] (sq km)	Total persons	Rank within state	Per square kilometer	Land area, 1990[1] (sq km)	Total persons	Rank within state	Per square kilometer	White	Black or African American	American Indian or Alaska Native	Asian	Native Hawaiian and other Pacific Islander	Some other race
		1	2	3	4	5	6	7	8	9	10	11	12	13	14
	MASSACHUSETTS—Cont'd														
25 17475	Dracut town	54.1	28 562	63	527.9	54.1	25 594	63	473.1	95.1	0.8	0.1	2.6	0.0	0.4
25 21990	Everett city	8.8	38 037	39	4 322.4	8.8	35 701	39	4 056.9	79.7	6.3	0.3	3.2	0.1	5.0
25 23000	Fall River city	80.3	91 938	8	1 144.9	80.3	92 703	8	1 154.5	91.2	2.5	0.2	2.2	0.0	1.4
25 23105	Falmouth town	114.6	32 660	54	285.0	114.6	27 960	54	244.0	93.4	1.8	0.5	0.9	0.0	1.4
25 23875	Fitchburg city	71.9	39 102	29	543.8	71.9	41 194	29	572.9	81.9	3.6	0.4	4.3	0.0	6.8
25 24925	Framingham town	65.1	66 910	14	1 027.8	65.1	64 989	14	998.3	79.8	5.1	0.2	5.3	0.0	6.3
25 25100	Franklin city	69.3	29 560	70	426.6	69.3	22 095	70	318.8	96.0	1.1	0.1	1.7	0.0	0.3
25 26150	Gloucester city	67.2	30 273	50	450.5	67.3	28 716	50	426.7	97.0	0.6	0.1	0.7	0.0	0.5
25 29405	Haverhill city	86.3	58 969	21	683.3	86.3	51 418	21	595.8	89.7	2.4	0.2	1.4	0.0	4.3
25 30840	Holyoke city	55.1	39 838	27	723.0	55.1	43 704	27	793.2	65.8	3.7	0.4	0.8	0.1	26.4
25 34550	Lawrence city	18.0	72 043	13	4 002.4	18.0	70 207	13	3 900.4	48.6	4.9	0.8	2.7	0.1	36.7
25 35075	Leominster city	74.8	41 303	35	552.2	74.8	38 145	35	510.0	87.1	3.7	0.2	2.4	0.1	4.3
25 35215	Lexington town	42.5	30 355	49	714.2	42.5	28 974	49	681.7	86.1	1.1	0.1	10.9	0.0	0.3
25 37000	Lowell city	35.7	105 167	4	2 945.9	35.7	103 439	4	2 897.5	68.6	4.2	0.2	16.5	0.1	6.5
25 37490	Lynn city	28.0	89 050	11	3 180.4	28.0	81 245	11	2 901.6	67.9	10.5	0.4	6.4	0.1	9.8
25 37875	Malden city	13.1	56 340	20	4 300.8	13.2	53 884	20	4 082.1	72.1	8.2	0.1	14.0	0.1	2.1
25 38715	Marlborough city	54.6	36 255	44	664.0	54.6	31 813	44	582.7	87.7	2.2	0.2	3.8	0.0	3.3
25 39835	Medford city	21.1	55 765	16	2 642.9	21.1	57 407	16	2 720.7	86.5	6.1	0.1	3.9	0.0	1.1
25 40115	Melrose city	12.2	27 134	53	2 224.1	12.2	28 150	53	2 307.4	95.2	0.9	0.1	2.0	0.0	0.4
25 40710	Methuen city	58.0	43 789	31	755.0	58.0	39 990	31	689.5	89.4	1.3	0.2	2.4	0.0	4.9
25 41165	Milford town	37.8	26 799	65	709.0	37.8	25 355	65	670.8	92.9	1.4	0.1	1.8	0.1	2.0
25 41690	Milton town	33.8	26 062	62	771.1	33.8	25 725	62	761.1	85.4	10.2	0.1	2.0	0.0	0.6
25 43895	Natick town	39.1	32 170	45	822.8	39.1	30 510	45	780.3	92.0	1.6	0.1	3.9	0.1	0.8
25 44105	Needham town	32.7	28 911	55	884.1	32.7	27 557	55	842.7	94.8	0.7	0.0	3.5	0.0	0.3
25 45000	New Bedford city	52.1	93 768	5	1 799.8	52.2	99 922	5	1 914.2	78.9	4.4	0.6	0.7	0.0	9.5
25 45560	Newton city	46.8	83 829	10	1 791.2	46.8	82 585	10	1 764.6	88.1	2.0	0.1	7.7	0.0	0.7
25 46330	Northampton city	89.2	28 978	47	324.9	89.3	29 289	47	328.0	90.0	2.1	0.3	3.1	0.1	2.4
25 46365	North Andover town	69.0	27 202	69	394.2	69.1	22 792	69	329.8	93.7	0.7	0.1	4.0	0.0	0.7
25 46575	North Attleborough town	48.3	27 143	66	562.0	48.3	25 038	66	518.4	96.0	0.9	0.1	1.7	0.0	0.4
25 50250	Norwood town	27.2	28 587	52	1 051.0	27.1	28 700	52	1 059.0	90.5	2.3	0.1	5.1	0.0	0.8
25 52490	Peabody city	42.5	48 129	24	1 132.4	42.5	47 264	24	1 112.1	93.9	1.0	0.1	1.4	0.0	1.8
25 53960	Pittsfield city	105.5	45 793	23	434.1	105.5	48 622	23	460.9	92.6	3.7	0.1	1.2	0.0	0.8
25 54310	Plymouth town	249.8	51 701	25	207.0	249.9	45 608	25	182.5	94.8	1.9	0.3	0.6	0.0	0.9
25 55745	Quincy city	43.5	88 025	9	2 023.6	43.5	84 985	9	1 953.7	79.6	2.2	0.2	15.4	0.0	0.9
25 55955	Randolph town	26.1	30 963	46	1 186.3	26.1	30 093	46	1 153.0	62.8	20.9	0.2	10.2	0.0	2.5
25 56585	Revere city	15.3	47 283	28	3 090.4	15.3	42 786	28	2 796.5	84.4	2.9	0.3	4.5	0.1	4.1
25 59105	Salem city	21.0	40 407	36	1 924.1	21.0	38 091	36	1 813.9	85.4	3.2	0.2	2.0	0.0	6.7
25 60015	Saugus town	28.5	26 078	64	915.0	28.5	25 549	64	896.5	97.3	0.4	0.1	1.2	0.0	0.3
25 61800	Shrewsbury town	53.7	31 640	68	589.2	53.7	24 146	68	449.6	89.1	1.5	0.1	7.6	0.0	0.7
25 62535	Somerville city	10.6	77 478	12	7 309.2	10.7	76 210	12	7 122.4	77.0	6.5	0.2	6.4	0.1	5.0
25 67000	Springfield city	83.1	152 082	3	1 830.1	83.2	156 983	3	1 886.8	56.1	21.0	0.4	1.9	0.1	16.4
25 67945	Stoughton town	41.5	27 149	60	654.2	41.5	26 777	60	645.2	88.5	5.7	0.1	2.1	0.0	1.3
25 69170	Taunton city	120.7	55 976	22	463.8	120.7	49 832	22	412.9	91.7	2.7	0.2	0.6	0.0	2.6
25 69415	Tewksbury town	53.7	28 851	58	537.3	53.7	27 266	58	507.7	96.4	0.7	0.1	1.6	0.0	0.4
25 72600	Waltham city	32.9	59 226	15	1 800.2	32.9	57 878	15	1 759.2	83.0	4.4	0.2	7.3	0.1	3.2
25 73440	Watertown city	10.6	32 986	42	3 111.9	10.7	33 284	42	3 110.7	91.4	1.7	0.0	3.9	0.0	0.9
25 74175	Wellesley town	26.4	26 613	61	1 008.1	26.4	26 615	61	1 008.1	90.0	1.6	0.1	6.4	0.0	0.5
25 76030	Westfield city	120.6	40 072	33	332.3	120.7	38 372	33	317.9	94.5	0.9	0.2	0.8	0.0	2.1
25 77850	West Springfield town	43.4	27 899	56	642.8	43.4	27 537	56	634.5	90.7	2.1	0.2	2.0	0.0	2.9
25 78865	Weymouth town	44.1	53 988	19	1 224.2	44.1	54 063	19	1 225.9	94.9	1.4	0.2	1.6	0.1	0.6
25 81035	Woburn city	32.8	37 258	38	1 135.9	32.9	35 943	38	1 092.5	90.6	1.9	0.1	4.8	0.1	1.4
25 82000	Worcester city	97.3	172 648	2	1 774.4	97.3	169 759	2	1 744.7	77.1	6.9	0.4	4.9	0.1	7.2
26 00000	MICHIGAN	147 121	9 938 444	X	67.6	147 136	9 295 287	X	63.2	80.2	14.2	0.6	1.8	0.0	1.3
26 01380	Allen Park city	18.2	29 376	47	1 614.1	18.2	31 092	47	1 708.4	95.6	0.7	0.4	0.8	0.0	1.2
26 03000	Ann Arbor city	70.0	114 024	6	1 628.9	67.1	109 608	6	1 633.5	74.7	8.8	0.3	11.9	0.0	1.2
26 05920	Battle Creek city	110.9	53 364	27	481.2	110.9	53 516	27	482.6	74.7	17.8	0.8	1.9	0.0	2.1
26 06020	Bay City city	27.0	36 817	35	1 363.6	26.9	38 936	35	1 447.4	91.2	2.7	0.7	0.5	0.0	2.5
26 06740	Bedford township	101.3	28 606	60	282.4	101.2	23 748	60	234.7	97.6	0.4	0.2	0.5	0.0	0.4
26 09110	Bloomfield township	64.6	43 023	31	666.0	64.6	42 473	31	657.5	87.7	4.3	0.1	6.5	0.1	0.3
26 12060	Burton city	60.8	30 308	52	498.5	60.8	27 437	52	451.3	92.1	3.5	0.8	0.7	0.0	0.8
26 13120	Canton township	93.2	76 366	24	819.4	93.2	57 040	24	612.0	83.9	4.5	0.3	8.7	0.0	0.6
26 15340	Chesterfield township	72.2	37 405	55	518.1	72.3	25 905	55	358.3	93.4	3.0	0.4	0.9	0.0	0.9
26 16520	Clinton township	73.0	95 648	9	1 310.2	73.0	85 866	9	1 176.2	91.1	4.7	0.3	1.7	0.0	0.4
26 17640	Commerce township	71.4	34 764	53	486.9	71.5	26 883	53	376.0	96.7	0.5	0.2	1.3	0.0	0.3
26 21000	Dearborn city	63.1	97 775	8	1 549.5	63.1	89 286	8	1 415.0	86.9	1.3	0.3	1.5	0.0	0.7
26 21020	Dearborn Heights city	30.3	58 264	23	1 922.9	30.3	60 838	23	2 007.9	91.6	2.1	0.4	2.2	0.0	0.8
26 21520	Delta charter township	89.4	29 682	54	332.0	89.4	26 129	54	292.3	85.6	8.0	0.4	2.6	0.0	1.3
26 22000	Detroit city	359.4	951 270	1	2 646.8	359.3	1 027 974	1	2 861.0	12.3	81.6	0.3	1.0	0.0	2.5
26 24290	Eastpointe city	13.2	34 077	40	2 581.6	13.2	35 283	40	2 673.0	92.1	4.7	0.4	0.9	0.0	0.3

[1]Dry land or land partially or temporarily covered by water.

Table E. Towns

Town	Population and population characteristics, 2000 (cont'd)								Population and population characteristics, 1990				
	Race (percent) (cont'd)								Race (percent)				
	Race alone or in combination												
	Two or more races	White	Black	American Indian or Alaska Native	Asian	Native Hawaiian and other Pacific Islander	Some other race	Hispanic[1]	White	Black or African American	American Indian or Alaska Native	Asian and Pacific Islander	Hispanic[1]
	15	16	17	18	19	20	21	22	23	24	25	26	27
MASSACHUSETTS— Cont'd													
Dracut town	1.0	96.0	1.0	0.4	2.8	0.1	0.7	1.6	97.8	0.5	0.1	1.2	0.9
Everett city	5.4	84.1	7.5	0.7	3.7	0.2	9.4	9.5	93.5	3.2	0.3	1.8	3.8
Fall River city	2.6	93.3	3.2	0.6	2.5	0.3	2.8	3.3	97.2	1.0	0.1	1.3	1.7
Falmouth town	1.9	94.9	2.6	1.0	1.2	0.1	2.3	1.3	94.6	1.8	0.6	0.7	1.5
Fitchburg city	3.1	84.2	4.7	0.9	4.9	0.1	8.4	15.0	89.4	3.4	0.2	2.6	9.6
Framingham town	3.4	82.6	5.9	0.5	5.8	0.1	8.7	10.9	90.1	3.7	0.2	2.9	8.1
Franklin city	0.8	96.7	1.3	0.3	2.0	0.1	0.5	1.1	98.0	0.7	0.1	1.0	0.6
Gloucester city	1.0	97.9	0.9	0.4	0.9	0.1	0.9	1.5	99.3	0.2	0.1	0.3	0.9
Haverhill city	2.0	91.4	3.0	0.6	1.7	0.1	5.3	8.8	94.9	2.0	0.2	0.8	5.3
Holyoke city	2.8	68.0	4.6	0.8	1.0	0.2	28.4	41.4	73.1	3.6	0.2	0.8	31.1
Lawrence city	6.2	53.5	7.6	1.3	3.0	0.3	41.0	59.7	65.0	6.4	0.5	1.9	41.6
Leominster city	2.2	88.9	4.4	0.5	2.9	0.1	5.6	11.0	93.1	2.3	0.2	1.6	8.3
Lexington town	1.4	87.4	1.5	0.2	11.8	0.0	0.6	1.4	92.2	1.1	0.1	6.5	1.2
Lowell city	3.9	71.4	5.0	0.6	17.9	0.3	9.0	14.0	81.1	2.4	0.2	11.1	10.1
Lynn city	4.9	71.0	12.6	0.9	7.5	0.2	12.8	18.4	83.1	8.1	0.3	3.7	9.1
Malden city	3.5	74.2	9.7	0.5	14.6	0.2	4.5	4.8	89.4	4.2	0.2	5.2	2.6
Marlborough city	2.9	90.3	2.6	0.6	4.2	0.1	5.0	6.1	94.8	1.8	0.2	1.9	4.2
Medford city	2.3	88.2	7.1	0.4	4.3	0.1	2.4	2.6	93.4	4.1	0.1	2.0	1.7
Melrose city	1.4	96.4	1.3	0.4	2.4	0.1	1.0	1.0	98.1	0.6	0.1	1.1	0.8
Methuen city	1.8	90.9	1.8	0.4	2.7	0.1	6.0	9.6	94.7	1.0	0.1	1.3	5.2
Milford town	1.8	94.6	1.7	0.3	2.0	0.1	3.1	4.4	96.2	1.3	0.1	1.0	4.0
Milton town	1.6	86.5	11.2	0.4	2.4	0.1	1.2	1.7	93.8	4.7	0.1	1.2	1.0
Natick town	1.6	93.4	2.1	0.4	4.4	0.1	1.4	2.0	95.1	2.0	0.1	2.4	1.8
Needham town	0.7	95.4	0.9	0.1	3.9	0.0	0.4	1.2	97.0	0.7	0.1	2.2	1.0
New Bedford city	5.9	82.9	6.8	1.4	0.9	0.3	14.0	10.2	87.6	4.1	0.4	0.4	6.7
Newton city	1.5	89.3	2.4	0.3	8.3	0.1	1.2	2.5	92.8	2.1	0.1	4.6	2.0
Northampton city	2.0	91.7	2.8	0.9	3.7	0.1	3.0	5.2	93.0	1.8	0.2	2.9	4.1
North Andover town	0.8	94.4	0.8	0.2	4.3	0.0	1.1	2.0	96.9	0.8	0.1	2.0	1.3
North Attleborough town	0.8	96.7	1.1	0.4	2.0	0.0	0.7	1.3	98.0	0.5	0.1	1.2	0.8
Norwood town	1.2	91.5	2.7	0.2	5.4	0.0	1.4	1.7	96.6	1.6	0.1	1.5	1.1
Peabody city	1.8	95.5	1.3	0.3	1.6	0.1	3.0	3.4	96.8	1.2	0.0	1.1	2.9
Pittsfield city	1.6	94.0	4.6	0.6	1.4	0.1	1.1	2.0	95.5	3.1	0.2	0.8	1.1
Plymouth town	1.5	96.0	2.5	0.7	0.8	0.1	1.6	1.7	96.6	1.9	0.2	0.6	1.2
Quincy city	1.8	81.0	2.6	0.4	15.9	0.1	1.8	2.1	91.7	1.1	0.2	6.6	1.4
Randolph town	3.4	64.3	23.2	0.8	10.7	0.2	4.6	3.2	85.4	8.2	0.2	5.6	1.8
Revere city	3.8	86.9	3.6	0.6	5.7	0.3	6.9	9.4	93.2	1.4	0.2	3.7	3.8
Salem city	2.5	87.4	3.9	0.6	2.4	0.2	8.2	11.2	93.0	2.7	0.3	1.4	6.7
Saugus town	0.7	97.9	0.6	0.3	1.4	0.0	0.6	1.0	98.4	0.5	0.1	0.8	0.9
Shrewsbury town	1.0	89.9	1.6	0.3	8.1	0.0	1.1	1.6	94.8	1.1	0.1	3.7	1.4
Somerville city	4.8	80.6	7.9	0.6	7.2	0.2	8.6	8.8	88.7	5.6	0.1	3.7	6.3
Springfield city	4.0	58.7	22.9	1.0	2.3	0.5	18.9	27.2	68.6	19.2	0.2	1.0	16.9
Stoughton town	2.3	90.3	6.5	0.4	2.5	0.1	2.6	1.5	94.2	4.0	0.1	1.1	1.8
Taunton city	2.2	93.4	3.5	0.5	0.9	0.2	3.8	3.9	95.3	2.0	0.2	0.5	4.7
Tewksbury town	0.8	97.1	0.9	0.3	1.8	0.1	0.6	1.2	97.5	0.8	0.2	1.3	0.9
Waltham city	1.9	84.4	5.0	0.4	7.8	0.1	4.4	8.5	91.4	3.1	0.1	3.6	5.6
Watertown city	1.9	93.2	2.1	0.4	4.5	0.1	1.9	2.7	96.1	1.3	0.1	2.2	2.0
Wellesley town	1.4	91.3	1.9	0.3	7.2	0.1	0.8	2.3	94.0	1.6	0.1	3.9	2.2
Westfield city	1.3	95.8	1.2	0.6	1.1	0.1	2.6	5.0	96.5	0.9	0.1	0.8	4.1
West Springfield town	2.1	92.6	2.5	0.6	2.3	0.1	4.1	5.8	96.0	1.4	0.2	1.1	3.0
Weymouth town	1.2	95.9	1.7	0.5	1.9	0.1	1.2	1.3	97.6	1.0	0.1	0.9	1.0
Woburn city	1.1	91.5	2.2	0.3	5.2	0.1	1.9	3.1	96.6	1.0	0.2	1.5	2.3
Worcester city	3.4	79.8	8.0	1.0	5.3	0.2	9.3	15.1	87.1	4.5	0.3	2.8	9.6
MICHIGAN	1.9	81.8	14.8	1.3	2.1	0.1	2.0	3.3	83.4	13.9	0.6	1.1	2.2
Allen Park city	1.3	96.8	0.8	0.9	1.0	0.1	1.7	4.7	98.0	0.5	0.2	0.7	3.2
Ann Arbor city	3.1	77.3	9.9	0.9	13.0	0.1	2.1	3.3	82.0	9.0	0.4	7.7	2.6
Battle Creek city	2.7	76.9	19.4	1.7	2.2	0.1	2.7	4.6	80.7	16.5	0.6	1.3	1.8
Bay City city	2.3	93.4	3.5	1.7	0.7	0.0	3.2	6.7	93.6	2.4	0.8	0.4	5.6
Bedford township	0.9	98.5	0.5	0.6	0.7	0.0	0.7	1.9	98.8	0.2	0.2	0.4	1.2
Bloomfield township	1.1	88.6	4.5	0.3	7.0	0.1	0.6	1.4	91.7	2.4	0.1	5.6	1.2
Burton city	2.0	94.0	4.1	1.8	1.0	0.1	1.3	2.3	95.2	2.6	1.0	0.5	2.1
Canton township	1.9	85.5	5.0	0.8	9.6	0.1	1.2	2.3	92.9	2.0	0.3	4.5	1.4
Chesterfield township	1.6	94.9	3.5	1.0	1.0	0.1	1.2	2.5	97.1	1.5	0.3	0.8	1.1
Clinton township	1.8	92.8	5.2	0.9	2.1	0.1	1.0	1.7	95.4	3.0	0.3	1.1	1.2
Commerce township	0.9	97.6	0.6	0.6	1.6	0.0	0.5	1.2	98.8	0.1	0.4	0.4	0.9
Dearborn city	9.4	96.1	1.5	0.6	2.6	0.1	8.7	3.0	97.6	0.6	0.3	0.9	2.8
Dearborn Heights city	2.8	94.3	2.4	0.9	2.8	0.1	2.4	3.4	97.3	0.5	0.4	1.3	2.3
Delta charter township	2.1	87.5	8.9	1.0	2.9	0.1	2.0	3.7	92.5	5.0	0.4	0.9	2.5
Detroit city	2.3	13.8	82.8	0.9	1.3	0.1	3.6	5.0	21.6	75.7	0.4	0.8	2.8
Eastpointe city	1.6	93.7	5.1	1.2	1.1	0.1	0.5	1.3	98.7	0.2	0.4	0.6	0.8

[1] Hispanic persons may be of any race.

Table E. Towns

Town	Population and population characteristics, 2000										
	Age (percent)										
	Under 5 years	5 to 17 years	18 to 24 years	25 to 34 years	35 to 44 years	45 to 54 years	55 to 64 years	65 to 74 years	75 years and over	Median age (years)	Percent Female
	28	29	30	31	32	33	34	35	36	37	38
MASSACHUSETTS— Cont'd											
Dracut town	6.8	18.8	7.3	15.2	18.3	14.1	8.1	6.5	5.1	36.1	51.0
Everett city	5.9	15.7	8.9	18.4	16.4	11.8	8.1	7.5	7.2	35.6	52.4
Fall River city	6.4	17.8	9.2	15.6	14.2	11.7	8.3	7.6	9.4	35.7	53.3
Falmouth town	4.5	16.2	4.8	9.2	15.3	14.9	12.6	12.0	10.4	45.0	53.3
Fitchburg city	6.7	19.1	11.6	13.9	14.9	11.7	7.5	6.7	7.9	34.1	52.3
Framingham town	6.5	15.0	9.0	17.4	17.1	13.5	8.6	6.5	6.5	36.2	52.3
Franklin city	9.4	20.9	6.5	13.6	21.5	13.3	6.6	4.6	3.6	34.8	51.0
Gloucester city	5.8	16.2	6.5	12.5	17.4	16.1	9.9	8.3	7.3	40.2	52.1
Haverhill city	7.4	18.3	7.7	15.7	17.8	12.8	7.6	5.9	6.9	35.5	52.5
Holyoke city	7.9	21.5	9.0	13.0	13.8	11.5	7.7	6.7	8.9	34.0	53.2
Lawrence city	9.0	23.0	11.1	15.8	14.6	10.5	6.2	4.4	5.4	29.5	52.2
Leominster city	7.1	18.4	7.2	14.9	17.5	13.1	8.2	6.8	6.9	36.3	51.9
Lexington town	5.7	20.7	3.5	6.5	16.1	17.6	10.9	8.9	10.1	43.7	53.0
Lowell city	7.3	19.6	11.9	17.1	15.3	11.0	6.8	5.4	5.4	31.4	50.7
Lynn city	7.3	19.7	9.1	15.1	15.9	12.4	7.7	6.3	6.5	34.2	51.6
Malden city	5.8	14.1	8.5	20.2	16.7	12.5	8.3	7.0	6.8	35.7	51.9
Marlborough city	7.0	16.2	7.0	17.5	19.2	13.2	8.4	5.8	5.7	36.1	50.7
Medford city	4.9	13.1	11.0	17.0	15.6	12.4	8.7	8.1	9.2	37.5	53.1
Melrose city	6.7	15.3	5.4	14.5	17.5	15.2	9.1	7.6	8.7	39.4	53.0
Methuen city	6.3	18.5	7.3	13.6	17.4	13.5	8.1	7.1	8.3	37.5	52.1
Milford town	7.2	17.6	6.5	15.6	17.6	14.1	8.5	5.9	7.0	36.6	51.5
Milton town	6.3	19.5	8.0	9.7	16.2	15.9	8.2	7.5	8.8	39.3	52.7
Natick town	7.4	15.6	5.1	15.5	18.8	14.1	9.2	7.3	7.0	38.2	52.7
Needham town	7.4	18.8	5.3	8.7	17.1	15.5	9.2	7.8	10.1	40.8	52.6
New Bedford city	6.7	18.2	9.5	14.3	14.4	11.9	8.2	7.7	9.0	35.9	52.9
Newton city	5.2	16.0	10.3	12.9	15.3	16.0	9.2	7.1	8.0	38.7	53.5
Northampton city	4.1	12.9	15.4	14.1	15.8	16.3	7.6	5.9	7.9	37.3	56.9
North Andover town	7.0	18.4	9.5	11.0	18.1	14.6	8.0	5.7	7.7	37.2	51.8
North Attleborough town	7.2	19.7	6.6	15.4	19.0	14.6	7.9	5.1	4.6	35.6	51.4
Norwood town	5.9	14.8	6.4	16.6	16.6	13.1	9.0	8.5	9.1	38.6	52.7
Peabody city	5.8	16.4	6.2	12.4	17.1	14.5	10.2	9.1	8.4	40.3	52.1
Pittsfield city	5.9	17.2	6.9	12.6	15.7	13.7	9.4	8.8	9.8	39.6	52.5
Plymouth town	6.7	19.1	7.1	14.5	17.5	15.3	8.5	5.2	6.1	36.5	50.3
Quincy city	5.1	12.4	8.1	19.7	16.3	13.1	9.0	8.0	8.3	37.6	52.3
Randolph town	6.0	17.3	7.2	13.8	17.1	14.8	9.5	7.3	7.0	38.3	52.2
Revere city	5.8	15.2	7.9	16.5	16.1	12.4	9.4	8.3	8.3	37.6	51.6
Salem city	5.6	14.6	10.4	17.0	16.3	13.7	8.2	6.9	7.2	36.4	53.6
Saugus town	5.0	15.5	6.5	12.7	16.6	15.0	11.1	9.2	8.4	41.3	52.2
Shrewsbury town	7.8	17.8	5.0	14.1	19.3	13.9	8.5	6.8	6.7	37.6	51.4
Somerville city	4.5	10.3	15.9	27.6	15.0	10.1	6.2	5.2	5.2	31.1	51.3
Springfield city	7.6	21.3	11.4	14.0	14.4	11.6	7.2	6.1	6.4	31.9	52.8
Stoughton town	5.6	16.8	6.8	13.3	17.1	14.8	10.4	7.8	7.4	39.2	52.0
Taunton city	7.1	17.8	8.0	15.9	17.3	12.7	8.4	6.3	6.6	35.7	51.9
Tewksbury town	7.0	18.0	6.2	13.6	19.2	14.9	9.7	6.7	4.8	37.6	51.0
Waltham city	4.7	10.8	16.8	19.1	15.3	12.0	8.2	6.6	6.5	34.2	50.7
Watertown city	4.7	9.5	9.4	23.0	16.8	12.2	7.7	7.9	8.8	36.7	53.7
Wellesley town	7.3	17.7	13.9	7.1	15.8	14.8	9.4	6.8	7.2	37.6	56.2
Westfield city	5.9	17.9	12.6	12.3	15.7	13.7	8.2	6.6	7.1	35.8	51.6
West Springfield town	5.8	17.6	7.8	13.6	15.9	14.1	9.1	8.0	7.9	38.2	51.2
Weymouth town	6.4	15.6	6.6	15.3	17.4	13.9	9.5	8.0	7.4	38.4	52.5
Woburn city	5.8	15.3	6.9	17.3	17.6	12.9	8.8	8.6	6.8	37.7	51.1
Worcester city	6.5	17.1	13.3	15.5	14.8	11.4	7.2	6.3	7.8	33.4	52.0
MICHIGAN	6.8	19.4	9.4	13.7	16.1	13.8	8.7	6.5	5.8	35.5	51.0
Allen Park city	5.3	16.8	6.5	12.0	16.3	13.7	8.5	9.2	11.7	41.0	52.4
Ann Arbor city	5.0	11.7	26.8	18.3	13.0	11.3	6.0	4.1	3.8	28.1	50.6
Battle Creek city	7.3	19.9	8.7	14.5	15.0	13.1	8.0	6.7	6.9	34.7	52.1
Bay City city	7.0	18.5	9.4	14.8	15.6	12.7	7.8	6.5	7.6	35.2	51.8
Bedford township	6.1	21.9	6.6	11.0	18.1	15.8	9.5	6.3	4.6	37.5	50.9
Bloomfield township	4.9	18.9	4.2	6.9	14.8	18.7	13.8	10.2	7.6	45.1	51.5
Burton city	7.3	20.1	8.4	14.9	17.1	12.8	8.2	6.5	4.6	34.6	51.1
Canton township	8.8	20.2	8.0	16.1	18.9	15.0	7.1	3.4	2.6	33.4	50.5
Chesterfield township	8.6	21.2	7.9	17.0	19.4	12.8	6.5	3.5	3.1	32.7	50.4
Clinton township	6.1	16.3	9.1	15.1	15.8	14.3	9.2	7.4	6.9	37.3	52.0
Commerce township	8.1	21.4	5.6	12.8	21.3	15.4	8.3	4.5	2.6	36.0	49.7
Dearborn city	8.3	19.6	8.3	14.5	14.6	11.9	7.2	6.5	9.0	34.5	50.3
Dearborn Heights city	6.4	16.1	7.5	14.0	15.5	12.4	9.3	9.8	9.0	38.9	51.8
Delta charter township	5.6	17.2	9.5	13.0	15.0	16.2	10.3	6.8	6.3	38.4	52.8
Detroit city	8.0	23.1	9.7	15.2	14.4	12.2	7.1	5.6	4.9	30.9	52.9
Eastpointe city	6.4	18.1	7.6	15.2	17.1	12.6	6.6	7.7	8.8	36.6	51.5

Table E. Towns

	Population and population characteristics, 1990										Population—change, 1980–2000				
	Age (percent)										Total persons			Percent change	
Town	Under 5 years	5 to 17 years	18 to 24 years	25 to 34 years	35 to 44 years	45 to 54 years	55 to 64 years	65 to 74 years	75 years and over	Percent Female	2000	1990	1980	1990–2000	1980–1990
	39	40	41	42	43	44	45	46	47	48	49	50	51	52	53
MASSACHUSETTS—Cont'd															
Dracut town	7.6	17.6	10.2	20.4	15.6	10.2	8.4	6.9	3.2	50.6	28 562	25 594	21 249	11.6	20.4
Everett city	6.7	12.8	10.8	20.5	13.3	9.1	10.2	9.1	7.5	54.1	38 037	35 701	37 195	6.5	-4.0
Fall River city	7.4	16.8	11.3	16.9	11.7	9.0	8.8	10.2	8.0	53.9	91 938	92 703	92 574	-0.8	0.1
Falmouth town	6.4	15.9	6.6	15.3	15.7	10.0	11.1	11.1	7.8	53.0	32 660	27 960	23 640	16.8	18.3
Fitchburg city	8.0	16.0	14.3	18.1	12.3	7.8	8.0	8.3	7.2	52.2	39 102	41 194	39 580	-5.1	4.1
Framingham town	6.3	13.1	12.6	20.3	15.1	11.1	9.0	6.9	5.6	52.8	66 910	64 989	65 113	3.0	-0.2
Franklin city	8.6	16.9	12.6	20.1	15.8	10.4	7.4	5.0	3.2	51.0	29 560	22 095	18 217	33.8	21.3
Gloucester city	6.6	14.8	9.1	17.0	17.0	10.0	10.2	8.5	6.9	51.8	30 273	28 716	27 768	5.4	3.4
Haverhill city	8.4	15.6	10.4	21.5	13.7	9.2	7.1	7.5	6.7	52.5	58 969	51 418	46 865	14.7	9.7
Holyoke city	9.3	19.3	10.5	16.0	11.4	8.7	7.8	8.6	8.4	54.3	39 838	43 704	44 678	-8.8	-2.2
Lawrence city	9.9	21.8	11.0	18.4	12.6	7.5	6.3	6.8	5.6	52.3	72 043	70 207	63 175	2.6	11.1
Leominster city	7.6	15.5	10.2	20.7	14.6	9.9	8.5	7.5	5.5	51.3	41 303	38 145	34 508	8.3	10.5
Lexington town	5.5	16.1	6.9	11.3	16.9	14.4	12.1	9.5	7.3	52.4	30 355	28 974	29 479	4.8	-1.7
Lowell city	8.6	17.6	14.1	20.5	12.1	7.6	7.2	7.1	5.1	51.4	105 167	103 439	92 418	1.7	11.9
Lynn city	8.2	16.4	10.4	19.0	13.9	9.0	8.2	8.2	6.8	52.2	89 050	81 245	78 471	9.6	3.5
Malden city	6.7	12.8	11.1	22.1	14.2	8.9	8.9	8.3	7.1	52.7	56 340	53 884	53 386	4.6	0.9
Marlborough city	7.7	14.4	10.4	22.4	16.7	9.6	7.3	6.5	4.9	51.3	36 255	31 813	30 617	14.0	3.9
Medford city	5.5	11.9	13.6	19.6	13.6	9.2	9.7	9.2	7.6	53.3	55 765	57 407	58 076	-2.9	-1.2
Melrose city	6.1	14.7	9.1	16.9	16.6	10.8	9.1	8.4	8.4	53.7	27 134	28 150	30 055	-3.6	-6.3
Methuen city	6.9	16.9	8.6	17.3	15.2	9.6	9.0	9.8	6.8	52.1	43 789	39 990	36 701	9.5	9.0
Milford town	7.3	16.7	10.2	18.3	15.6	11.1	7.8	7.9	5.2	52.0	26 799	25 355	23 390	5.7	8.4
Milton town	6.6	15.5	10.8	13.5	15.9	10.0	10.0	9.3	8.4	52.7	26 062	25 725	25 860	1.3	-0.5
Natick town	6.5	13.9	8.5	21.1	16.4	11.1	9.7	7.7	5.3	51.9	32 170	30 510	29 461	5.4	3.6
Needham town	6.6	16.0	7.5	13.8	16.3	12.1	10.8	8.7	8.2	53.1	28 911	27 557	27 901	4.9	-1.2
New Bedford city	7.5	17.5	10.4	16.8	12.4	8.9	9.2	9.6	7.8	53.3	93 768	99 922	98 478	-6.2	1.5
Newton city	5.5	13.1	13.5	16.5	16.6	10.9	8.9	7.9	7.1	54.1	83 829	82 585	83 622	1.5	-1.2
Northampton city	4.7	12.8	17.3	17.7	17.4	8.0	7.3	7.5	7.2	56.1	28 978	29 289	29 286	-1.1	0.0
North Andover town	6.6	17.0	13.4	14.1	16.7	12.0	7.9	6.8	5.5	51.8	27 202	22 792	20 129	19.3	13.2
North Attleborough town	8.1	17.1	10.8	19.9	17.1	10.1	7.2	5.6	4.1	51.1	27 143	25 038	21 095	8.4	18.7
Norwood town	5.7	13.4	10.5	19.7	13.3	10.4	10.4	9.1	7.4	53.3	28 587	28 700	29 711	-0.4	-3.4
Peabody city	6.3	15.1	9.2	17.7	15.2	11.1	11.1	8.8	5.4	52.0	48 129	47 264	45 976	1.8	2.8
Pittsfield city	6.8	15.9	9.5	16.8	14.3	9.5	9.9	9.7	7.6	52.3	45 793	48 622	51 974	-5.8	-6.4
Plymouth town	7.9	19.5	9.2	17.7	17.5	9.8	6.4	6.9	5.2	50.9	51 701	45 608	35 913	13.4	27.0
Quincy city	5.8	10.9	12.2	21.8	13.3	10.0	9.3	9.1	7.6	53.5	88 025	84 985	84 743	3.6	0.3
Randolph town	6.8	14.8	9.2	18.8	14.6	11.5	9.8	8.2	6.3	51.9	30 963	30 093	28 218	2.9	6.6
Revere city	6.0	12.6	10.8	18.7	13.6	10.3	10.8	9.7	7.4	51.4	47 283	42 786	42 423	10.5	0.9
Salem city	6.5	12.1	13.1	21.7	14.3	8.9	8.3	8.5	6.7	53.5	40 407	38 091	38 220	6.1	-0.3
Saugus town	5.6	14.4	10.4	16.6	14.3	12.4	11.0	9.0	6.3	52.0	26 078	25 549	24 746	2.1	3.2
Shrewsbury town	6.3	15.8	8.6	17.5	16.5	11.3	9.9	8.5	5.6	51.0	31 640	24 146	22 674	31.0	6.5
Somerville city	5.0	10.2	16.8	26.6	13.8	7.7	7.7	6.8	5.4	52.4	77 478	76 210	77 372	1.7	-1.5
Springfield city	8.5	18.5	12.2	18.2	13.0	8.3	7.6	7.9	5.8	53.1	152 082	156 983	152 319	-3.1	3.1
Stoughton town	6.4	15.8	10.3	17.9	15.3	11.6	9.6	7.7	5.3	51.8	27 149	26 777	26 710	1.4	0.3
Taunton city	7.5	16.9	10.2	19.4	14.6	9.2	8.2	8.2	6.0	52.5	55 976	49 832	45 001	12.3	10.7
Tewksbury town	7.8	17.0	9.8	19.6	16.0	11.7	8.7	5.7	3.7	49.8	28 851	27 266	24 635	5.8	10.7
Waltham city	4.9	10.6	19.4	20.9	13.8	8.5	8.6	7.3	5.9	51.6	59 226	57 878	58 200	2.3	-0.6
Watertown city	4.8	9.3	10.4	26.0	14.2	8.6	9.6	9.3	7.8	55.0	32 986	33 284	34 384	-0.9	-3.2
Wellesley town	5.9	14.6	18.3	10.5	15.3	12.2	9.1	7.4	6.6	55.8	26 613	26 615	27 209	0.0	-2.2
Westfield city	6.8	16.2	14.7	16.2	14.6	9.9	8.0	8.2	5.6	52.6	40 072	38 372	36 465	4.4	5.2
West Springfield town	6.5	14.7	9.8	17.5	14.6	10.7	10.4	8.9	6.8	51.9	27 899	27 537	27 042	1.3	1.8
Weymouth town	6.4	13.9	10.5	20.2	15.0	10.3	9.9	8.4	5.4	52.3	53 988	54 063	55 601	-0.1	-2.8
Woburn city	6.5	14.4	10.8	21.7	13.6	9.9	10.5	8.1	4.5	51.3	37 258	35 943	36 626	3.7	-1.9
Worcester city	7.2	15.1	14.8	18.6	12.2	8.0	8.0	8.6	7.4	52.3	172 648	169 759	161 799	1.7	4.9
MICHIGAN	7.6	18.9	10.8	16.9	15.1	10.2	8.5	7.1	4.9	51.5	9 938 444	9 295 287	9 262 044	6.9	0.4
Allen Park city	6.0	14.8	7.3	16.2	14.4	9.9	11.4	13.1	6.9	52.2	29 376	31 092	34 196	-5.5	-9.1
Ann Arbor city	5.7	11.4	27.1	20.9	14.8	7.4	5.4	4.1	3.2	50.7	114 024	109 608	107 966	4.0	1.5
Battle Creek city	8.4	19.3	8.9	16.7	14.9	9.2	8.3	7.9	6.5	52.7	53 364	53 516	56 339	-0.3	-5.0
Bay City city	7.7	18.4	10.1	17.3	14.4	8.5	8.4	8.9	6.4	52.3	36 817	38 936	41 593	-5.4	-6.4
Bedford township	7.7	20.8	9.2	16.0	17.1	11.7	8.8	5.5	3.2	50.3	28 606	23 748	22 902	20.5	3.7
Bloomfield township	4.9	16.9	7.3	10.1	16.9	16.4	14.1	9.4	3.9	51.0	43 023	42 473	42 876	1.3	-0.9
Burton city	7.4	19.5	9.8	17.5	14.3	11.1	9.4	7.1	3.9	52.0	30 308	27 437	29 976	10.5	-8.5
Canton township	8.4	22.7	9.7	19.4	20.0	10.5	4.7	3.1	1.5	50.9	76 366	57 040	48 616	33.9	17.3
Chesterfield township	8.7	21.2	9.5	20.4	18.4	10.2	5.3	4.1	2.2	49.9	37 405	25 905	NA	44.4	NA
Clinton township	7.4	17.1	10.5	19.0	16.0	10.3	8.7	6.9	3.9	52.1	95 648	85 866	NA	11.4	NA
Commerce township	8.4	18.7	8.8	20.1	18.6	11.7	7.5	4.4	1.8	49.7	34 764	26 883	23 757	29.3	13.2
Dearborn city	7.1	16.0	8.9	17.4	13.9	9.5	9.4	10.8	7.2	51.4	97 775	89 286	90 660	9.5	-1.5
Dearborn Heights city	6.0	14.6	9.0	17.2	13.0	10.8	12.6	11.1	5.7	51.9	58 264	60 838	67 706	-4.2	-10.1
Delta charter township	6.2	18.2	9.4	16.5	17.8	13.0	8.9	6.3	3.6	52.1	29 682	26 129	NA	13.6	NA
Detroit city	9.0	20.4	11.0	16.6	14.1	8.8	7.9	7.3	4.9	53.7	951 270	1 027 974	1 203 339	-7.5	-14.6
Eastpointe city	7.0	15.7	8.2	18.4	13.1	8.2	10.6	11.9	6.9	52.7	34 077	35 283	38 280	-3.4	-7.8

Table E. Towns

Town	Total population	Total in house-holds	House-holder	Spouse	Child Total	Child Own child under 18 years	Other relatives Total	Other relatives Under 18 years	Nonrelatives Total	Nonrelatives Unmar-ried partner	Total in group quarters	Correc-tional institu-tions	Nurs-ing homes	Other institu-tions	Col-lege dormi-tories	Mili-tary quar-ters	Other
	54	55	56	57	58	59	60	61	62	63	64	65	66	67	68	69	70
MASSACHUSETTS— Cont'd																	
Dracut town	28 562	99.9	36.6	21.3	32.9	23.6	5.2	1.5	3.9	2.0	0.1	0.0	0.0	0.0	0.0	0.0	0.1
Everett city	38 037	99.4	40.6	17.0	29.3	19.8	6.6	1.6	6.0	1.9	0.6	0.0	0.6	0.0	0.0	0.0	0.0
Fall River city	91 938	97.9	42.2	17.0	30.0	22.1	4.1	1.3	4.7	2.7	2.1	0.0	1.5	0.1	0.0	0.0	0.5
Falmouth town	32 660	97.4	42.4	22.0	25.1	18.8	3.4	1.3	4.4	1.9	2.6	0.0	1.2	0.0	0.1	0.0	1.3
Fitchburg city	39 102	95.5	38.2	16.5	29.7	23.4	4.8	1.7	6.4	2.8	4.5	0.0	1.3	0.1	2.5	0.0	0.5
Framingham town	66 910	95.0	39.1	19.5	26.1	20.0	4.5	1.0	5.9	1.9	5.0	1.2	1.4	0.0	1.8	0.0	0.5
Franklin city	29 560	97.9	34.3	22.8	35.6	29.3	2.6	0.8	2.5	1.2	2.1	0.0	0.2	0.0	1.9	0.0	0.0
Gloucester city	30 273	98.8	41.6	20.3	28.1	20.5	3.8	1.1	5.0	2.4	1.2	0.0	0.9	0.0	0.0	0.0	0.3
Haverhill city	58 969	97.6	39.0	18.3	30.6	23.7	4.3	1.4	5.5	2.7	2.4	0.0	1.3	0.1	0.5	0.0	0.4
Holyoke city	39 838	96.5	37.6	13.7	33.4	25.7	5.9	2.6	6.0	2.9	3.5	0.0	3.0	0.0	0.0	0.0	0.5
Lawrence city	72 043	98.6	34.0	12.4	36.5	27.9	8.8	3.2	6.8	3.1	1.4	0.3	0.8	0.0	0.0	0.0	0.3
Leominster city	41 303	99.0	39.9	19.8	30.5	23.9	4.0	1.2	4.9	2.5	1.0	0.0	0.7	0.0	0.0	0.0	0.2
Lexington town	30 355	97.4	36.6	24.2	31.5	25.4	2.7	0.7	2.4	0.7	2.6	0.0	2.0	0.0	0.0	0.0	0.6
Lowell city	105 167	96.3	36.0	14.5	31.9	23.9	7.2	2.4	6.8	2.7	3.7	0.0	1.1	0.0	1.8	0.0	0.8
Lynn city	89 050	98.5	37.6	15.0	32.2	23.7	7.5	2.6	6.2	2.5	1.5	0.0	0.8	0.0	0.0	0.0	0.7
Malden city	56 340	98.9	40.8	17.5	27.1	18.2	6.9	1.5	6.7	2.2	1.1	0.0	0.7	0.0	0.0	0.0	0.4
Marlborough city	36 255	98.7	40.0	20.6	28.1	21.8	4.3	1.2	5.6	2.3	1.3	0.0	1.0	0.0	0.0	0.0	0.4
Medford city	55 765	96.0	39.6	18.0	25.9	16.5	5.3	1.2	7.2	1.7	4.0	0.0	1.0	0.0	2.8	0.0	0.2
Melrose city	27 134	98.8	40.5	21.6	29.4	20.7	3.6	1.1	3.7	1.6	1.2	0.0	1.1	0.0	0.0	0.0	0.1
Methuen city	43 789	98.9	37.8	20.1	31.7	22.9	5.4	1.5	3.9	2.0	1.1	0.0	0.7	0.0	0.0	0.0	0.4
Milford town	26 799	98.8	38.9	21.0	30.9	23.4	4.0	1.0	4.0	1.9	1.2	0.0	1.0	0.0	0.0	0.0	0.2
Milton town	26 062	96.0	34.5	20.7	34.1	24.6	4.1	1.0	2.7	0.9	4.0	0.0	1.0	0.0	2.9	0.0	0.1
Natick town	32 170	98.3	40.7	22.2	28.3	22.0	3.0	0.8	4.2	1.7	1.7	0.0	1.3	0.0	0.0	0.1	0.3
Needham town	28 911	96.7	36.7	23.8	31.9	25.6	2.0	0.5	2.2	0.8	3.3	0.0	1.4	0.0	1.5	0.0	0.4
New Bedford city	93 768	97.9	40.7	16.1	30.7	22.5	4.9	1.7	5.5	2.8	2.1	0.2	1.4	0.0	0.0	0.1	0.5
Newton city	83 829	93.3	37.2	20.5	26.2	20.4	3.0	0.6	6.4	1.4	6.7	0.0	0.7	0.0	5.7	0.0	0.3
Northampton city	28 978	87.6	41.0	15.0	20.7	15.8	2.1	0.7	8.7	3.6	12.4	0.8	2.3	0.6	7.8	0.0	0.8
North Andover town	27 202	93.2	35.7	21.5	30.8	24.5	2.6	0.7	2.5	1.2	6.8	0.0	1.9	0.0	4.8	0.0	0.1
North Attleborough town	27 143	99.4	38.3	21.8	32.4	25.5	3.1	1.1	3.9	2.1	0.6	0.0	0.5	0.0	0.0	0.0	0.1
Norwood town	28 587	98.0	40.7	20.7	28.5	19.9	3.7	0.7	4.5	1.5	2.0	0.0	1.5	0.1	0.0	0.0	0.4
Peabody city	48 129	98.5	38.6	21.6	29.7	20.5	5.1	1.4	3.6	1.6	1.5	0.0	1.1	0.0	0.0	0.0	0.4
Pittsfield city	45 793	97.2	43.0	18.5	27.3	21.3	3.1	1.1	5.3	2.6	2.8	0.6	1.4	0.0	0.0	0.0	0.8
Plymouth town	51 701	95.3	35.6	20.8	31.1	23.8	3.4	1.2	4.3	2.0	4.7	2.9	1.3	0.2	0.0	0.0	0.3
Quincy city	88 025	98.2	44.2	17.1	24.4	16.0	5.9	1.2	6.6	2.2	1.8	0.0	0.7	0.1	0.6	0.0	0.4
Randolph town	30 963	99.1	36.5	19.4	31.2	20.8	7.4	2.1	4.5	1.6	0.9	0.0	0.8	0.0	0.0	0.0	0.1
Revere city	47 283	99.3	41.2	17.2	28.0	18.7	7.2	1.9	5.8	2.2	0.7	0.0	0.5	0.0	0.0	0.0	0.1
Salem city	40 407	97.1	43.3	16.8	25.6	18.5	4.4	1.3	7.0	2.8	2.9	0.0	0.4	0.0	2.2	0.0	0.2
Saugus town	26 078	99.1	38.3	21.8	30.2	18.8	5.7	1.5	3.1	1.2	0.9	0.0	0.6	0.0	0.0	0.0	0.2
Shrewsbury town	31 640	99.4	39.1	23.5	30.8	24.7	3.2	0.7	2.9	1.5	0.6	0.0	0.3	0.0	0.0	0.0	0.2
Somerville city	77 478	96.8	40.7	13.1	19.8	13.1	6.1	1.4	17.0	2.7	3.2	0.0	0.4	0.0	2.4	0.0	0.5
Springfield city	152 082	96.4	37.6	13.0	32.8	25.0	6.6	2.9	6.3	2.9	3.6	0.1	0.5	0.4	2.1	0.0	0.4
Stoughton town	27 149	98.3	37.8	21.1	30.5	20.4	5.4	1.8	3.6	1.7	1.7	0.0	1.1	0.5	0.0	0.0	0.0
Taunton city	55 976	98.5	39.4	18.9	30.6	22.7	4.6	1.7	5.0	2.6	1.5	0.0	0.7	0.4	0.0	0.0	0.4
Tewksbury town	28 851	97.2	34.5	22.5	32.2	22.9	5.0	1.8	2.9	1.3	2.8	0.0	0.6	1.7	0.0	0.0	0.6
Waltham city	59 226	89.9	39.2	16.2	21.2	14.1	4.9	1.0	8.4	2.1	10.1	0.0	0.8	0.5	8.0	0.0	0.9
Watertown city	32 986	96.2	44.3	16.8	20.0	13.2	4.5	0.7	10.6	2.5	3.8	0.0	1.1	0.4	2.0	0.0	0.4
Wellesley town	26 613	87.1	32.3	21.7	29.4	24.6	1.6	0.3	2.1	0.7	12.9	0.0	1.3	0.2	11.4	0.0	0.0
Westfield city	40 072	93.8	36.9	19.6	28.9	22.1	3.4	1.0	5.1	2.2	6.2	0.0	0.9	0.4	4.7	0.0	0.2
West Springfield town	27 899	98.6	40.4	18.9	28.6	21.4	4.0	1.2	4.7	2.4	1.4	0.0	0.9	0.3	0.0	0.0	0.1
Weymouth town	53 988	98.7	40.8	19.8	29.4	20.4	4.4	1.3	4.3	1.9	1.3	0.0	1.0	0.0	0.0	0.0	0.3
Woburn city	37 258	99.3	40.3	19.9	29.1	19.5	5.2	1.4	4.9	1.8	0.7	0.0	0.3	0.0	0.0	0.0	0.4
Worcester city	172 648	93.6	38.8	14.9	27.7	21.2	5.3	1.7	6.9	2.5	6.4	0.0	1.5	0.2	4.0	0.0	0.7
MICHIGAN	9 938 444	97.5	38.1	19.6	30.6	23.6	4.4	1.8	4.9	2.0	2.5	0.7	0.5	0.1	0.7	0.0	0.5
Allen Park city	29 376	99.0	40.8	22.4	29.4	20.5	3.6	1.4	2.7	1.3	1.0	0.0	1.0	0.0	0.0	0.0	0.0
Ann Arbor city	114 024	89.1	40.1	15.2	18.9	15.9	2.1	0.5	12.9	1.9	10.9	0.0	0.3	0.2	10.0	0.0	0.4
Battle Creek city	53 364	97.1	40.0	16.8	29.7	24.1	4.6	2.1	6.0	2.7	2.9	1.3	0.7	0.0	0.0	0.0	0.8
Bay City city	36 817	98.4	41.3	17.5	30.3	22.9	3.9	1.7	5.4	2.7	1.6	0.5	0.0	0.0	0.0	0.0	1.1
Bedford township	28 606	99.6	36.1	24.0	34.0	26.4	2.9	1.3	2.7	1.5	0.4	0.0	0.0	0.0	0.0	0.0	0.4
Bloomfield township	43 023	99.0	39.1	26.6	29.5	23.2	2.0	0.5	1.8	0.8	1.0	0.0	0.5	0.0	0.0	0.0	0.5
Burton city	30 308	99.6	38.6	20.0	32.0	24.9	4.1	1.9	5.0	2.6	0.4	0.0	0.0	0.0	0.0	0.0	0.4
Canton township	76 366	99.9	36.0	22.8	35.0	27.9	3.0	0.9	3.1	1.5	0.1	0.0	0.0	0.0	0.0	0.0	0.1
Chesterfield township	37 405	99.4	35.7	22.2	35.0	28.3	2.7	0.9	3.9	2.0	0.6	0.0	0.4	0.0	0.0	0.0	0.2
Clinton township	95 648	99.2	42.1	20.5	28.8	20.9	3.5	1.1	4.3	2.1	0.8	0.0	0.5	0.1	0.0	0.0	0.2
Commerce township	34 764	99.9	35.6	24.3	34.4	28.3	2.6	0.9	3.0	1.5	0.1	0.0	0.0	0.0	0.0	0.0	0.1
Dearborn city	97 775	99.6	37.6	19.2	34.2	26.0	5.7	1.6	2.9	1.1	0.4	0.0	0.2	0.0	0.0	0.0	0.2
Dearborn Heights city	58 264	98.8	39.9	21.1	29.3	20.4	4.9	1.5	3.5	1.6	1.2	0.0	0.6	0.3	0.0	0.0	0.3
Delta charter township	29 682	98.8	42.3	22.1	27.5	21.5	2.6	1.1	4.3	1.9	1.2	0.0	0.4	0.0	0.4	0.0	0.4
Detroit city	951 270	97.9	35.4	9.4	34.6	24.2	12.1	5.9	6.4	2.5	2.1	0.4	0.5	0.2	0.1	0.0	0.9
Eastpointe city	34 077	99.8	39.9	19.4	31.1	22.2	4.9	1.7	4.5	2.2	0.2	0.0	0.0	0.0	0.0	0.0	0.2

Table E. Towns

Town	Households by type, 2000												Households, 1990		
		Family households						Nonfamily households							
				Married couple		Female householder[1]			Householder living alone						
	Total households	Total	With own children under 18 years	Total	With own children under 18 years	Total	With own children under 18 years	Total	Total	65 years and over	Average household size	Average family size	Total households	Female householder[1]	Householder living alone
	71	72	73	74	75	76	77	78	79	80	81	82	83	84	85
MASSACHUSETTS—Cont'd															
Dracut town	10 451	74.0	35.9	58.3	28.2	11.6	5.9	26.0	20.9	8.0	2.73	3.19	8 992	9.6	17.6
Everett city	15 435	61.9	27.6	41.8	18.3	15.2	7.7	38.1	31.3	11.8	2.45	3.11	14 528	14.0	29.0
Fall River city	38 759	60.8	29.9	40.3	17.0	16.5	11.0	39.2	34.2	14.2	2.32	3.00	37 303	14.1	29.8
Falmouth town	13 859	64.8	24.2	52.0	17.5	10.1	5.5	35.2	29.8	14.0	2.30	2.84	11 274	11.4	26.3
Fitchburg city	14 943	62.7	31.0	43.1	18.8	14.6	9.6	37.3	30.3	12.0	2.50	3.13	15 363	14.3	27.3
Framingham town	26 153	63.4	29.1	50.0	22.3	10.2	5.8	36.6	28.7	9.1	2.43	3.02	25 113	9.9	28.3
Franklin city	10 152	77.6	44.6	66.4	38.9	8.5	4.5	22.4	18.3	6.7	2.85	3.29	7 406	7.6	16.9
Gloucester city	12 592	62.7	27.6	48.8	20.2	10.6	5.9	37.3	30.7	11.4	2.38	3.00	11 579	11.3	28.0
Haverhill city	22 976	64.7	33.0	47.0	22.6	13.4	8.3	35.3	28.6	10.3	2.51	3.11	19 575	13.0	25.4
Holyoke city	14 967	63.3	33.3	36.5	15.8	22.1	15.2	36.7	30.9	13.5	2.57	3.23	15 850	21.8	27.5
Lawrence city	24 463	69.1	41.4	36.6	19.5	25.7	18.3	30.9	25.5	10.0	2.90	3.46	24 270	22.9	25.7
Leominster city	16 491	66.1	32.9	49.5	22.7	12.5	8.0	33.9	27.9	10.7	2.48	3.05	14 834	9.7	24.1
Lexington town	11 110	75.9	37.8	66.0	33.4	7.7	3.6	24.1	20.8	12.3	2.66	3.10	10 515	7.1	18.1
Lowell city	37 887	63.3	34.0	40.1	20.1	17.4	11.1	36.7	29.0	9.3	2.67	3.35	37 019	16.9	27.0
Lynn city	33 511	62.8	32.5	39.7	18.8	17.6	11.2	37.2	31.0	11.8	2.62	3.31	31 554	16.0	30.8
Malden city	23 009	59.0	25.4	42.8	18.5	12.3	5.8	41.0	32.2	11.5	2.42	3.13	21 921	11.8	31.0
Marlborough city	14 501	64.0	30.4	51.5	24.0	9.0	4.9	36.0	28.4	8.3	2.47	3.07	12 152	9.7	25.3
Medford city	22 067	61.2	23.6	48.6	18.0	11.8	4.7	38.8	28.7	12.4	2.43	3.04	21 829	12.4	25.9
Melrose city	10 982	64.7	28.8	53.4	24.7	8.7	3.4	35.3	29.7	13.2	2.44	3.08	10 941	10.9	27.4
Methuen city	16 532	69.8	33.1	53.3	25.1	12.2	6.4	30.2	25.3	11.6	2.62	3.17	14 647	11.8	22.6
Milford town	10 420	69.1	33.4	54.0	25.5	11.2	6.4	30.9	25.6	9.5	2.54	3.08	9 362	12.0	21.5
Milton town	8 982	75.2	37.5	60.1	31.7	11.9	4.9	24.8	21.2	12.7	2.79	3.27	8 749	12.1	20.3
Natick town	13 080	65.2	30.3	54.5	25.5	8.2	3.9	34.8	28.3	9.8	2.42	3.02	12 009	7.4	24.8
Needham town	10 612	73.3	37.0	64.9	33.2	6.9	3.2	26.7	23.4	13.9	2.63	3.15	10 160	8.1	21.4
New Bedford city	38 178	63.1	31.2	39.5	16.5	18.9	12.3	36.9	31.6	13.6	2.40	3.01	38 788	16.4	27.6
Newton city	31 201	65.7	31.1	55.2	26.6	8.0	3.7	34.3	25.5	11.1	2.51	3.04	29 455	8.6	22.4
Northampton city	11 880	49.5	22.9	36.7	15.4	10.1	6.2	50.5	37.3	10.7	2.14	2.87	11 164	11.7	33.6
North Andover town	9 724	71.0	36.8	60.2	31.0	8.5	4.8	29.0	25.1	11.8	2.61	3.16	7 891	8.8	21.6
North Attleborough town	10 391	69.6	36.0	57.0	28.9	9.4	5.6	30.4	24.7	7.3	2.60	3.15	9 235	10.1	21.2
Norwood town	11 623	63.5	27.2	50.9	22.4	9.9	4.2	36.5	29.4	12.0	2.41	3.05	11 018	10.4	25.8
Peabody city	18 581	69.9	29.7	55.9	23.8	10.4	4.7	30.1	25.4	12.2	2.55	3.09	17 556	10.5	22.1
Pittsfield city	19 704	60.0	27.3	42.9	17.0	13.1	8.3	40.0	34.0	14.3	2.26	2.89	19 916	12.7	29.3
Plymouth town	18 423	72.0	36.0	58.4	28.3	10.4	6.1	28.0	21.7	8.5	2.67	3.16	15 875	10.3	20.0
Quincy city	38 883	52.8	20.7	38.7	15.3	10.5	4.4	47.2	37.6	13.4	2.22	3.03	35 678	11.3	33.4
Randolph town	11 313	70.6	31.7	53.0	24.1	13.4	6.3	29.4	23.6	10.5	2.71	3.25	10 886	10.1	20.4
Revere city	19 463	61.0	25.5	41.8	16.7	13.9	7.0	39.0	32.7	12.4	2.41	3.09	17 438	13.6	29.3
Salem city	17 492	55.5	24.2	38.8	15.0	13.3	7.7	44.5	34.9	11.5	2.24	2.95	15 806	12.6	31.4
Saugus town	9 975	71.6	27.5	57.0	22.4	10.7	4.0	28.4	24.3	12.1	2.59	3.11	9 286	9.0	20.7
Shrewsbury town	12 366	70.3	34.5	60.1	29.7	7.5	3.8	29.7	25.3	10.5	2.54	3.09	9 302	7.5	24.5
Somerville city	31 555	46.5	18.8	32.2	13.1	10.3	4.6	53.5	31.0	8.8	2.38	3.06	30 319	12.2	30.1
Springfield city	57 130	63.7	33.7	34.7	15.2	23.8	16.1	36.3	30.2	11.4	2.57	3.19	57 769	20.7	27.5
Stoughton town	10 254	70.9	30.3	55.8	23.6	11.6	5.5	29.1	24.4	9.9	2.60	3.13	9 394	11.1	20.3
Taunton city	22 045	65.7	32.3	48.0	22.1	13.4	7.9	34.3	28.2	9.9	2.50	3.20	18 849	11.0	24.7
Tewksbury town	9 964	77.2	35.9	65.1	30.9	9.1	4.0	22.8	18.9	7.2	2.81	3.24	8 744	7.4	14.4
Waltham city	23 207	53.7	20.3	41.3	16.0	8.9	3.4	46.3	34.2	10.0	2.29	3.01	20 728	10.0	30.2
Watertown city	14 629	50.1	17.8	37.9	13.9	8.7	3.1	49.9	34.1	12.4	2.17	2.86	14 190	9.7	30.3
Wellesley town	8 594	76.1	39.9	67.2	35.8	7.1	3.4	23.9	20.7	10.5	2.70	3.14	8 472	8.3	19.4
Westfield city	14 797	67.7	31.5	53.0	23.4	10.6	6.2	32.3	25.9	10.9	2.54	3.07	13 823	11.5	23.5
West Springfield town	11 823	60.2	27.0	44.7	18.7	11.4	6.5	39.8	34.0	11.2	2.33	3.02	11 485	11.2	30.6
Weymouth town	22 028	63.2	27.3	48.6	21.2	11.1	4.9	36.8	30.6	11.1	2.42	3.08	20 829	11.7	26.5
Woburn city	14 997	64.4	26.8	49.5	20.5	10.9	4.9	35.6	28.7	10.1	2.47	3.09	13 485	10.7	24.5
Worcester city	67 028	58.5	29.0	38.3	17.2	15.6	9.9	41.5	33.0	12.2	2.41	3.11	63 884	15.3	29.7
MICHIGAN	3 785 661	68.0	32.7	51.4	23.1	12.5	7.5	32.0	26.2	9.4	2.56	3.10	3 419 331	12.9	23.7
Allen Park city	11 974	68.5	27.5	55.0	22.5	9.9	3.7	31.5	28.2	14.9	2.43	2.99	12 030	9.4	23.3
Ann Arbor city	45 693	47.5	23.0	37.8	17.6	7.5	4.4	52.5	35.5	6.6	2.22	2.90	41 657	7.9	31.7
Battle Creek city	21 348	62.6	32.3	41.9	18.6	16.1	11.0	37.4	31.6	12.1	2.43	3.04	21 457	16.5	29.0
Bay City city	15 208	61.3	30.2	42.4	18.7	14.7	9.1	38.7	32.9	12.8	2.38	3.04	15 570	13.8	29.9
Bedford township	10 327	78.3	38.0	66.5	31.5	8.4	4.6	21.7	18.3	8.0	2.76	3.15	8 058	7.6	15.0
Bloomfield township	16 804	75.6	31.1	68.1	27.7	5.7	2.7	24.4	21.6	9.3	2.53	2.97	15 734	5.1	16.5
Burton city	11 699	69.8	35.0	51.8	23.8	12.8	8.2	30.2	25.3	9.0	2.58	3.08	10 447	13.2	22.4
Canton township	27 490	74.8	42.0	63.4	35.2	8.6	5.3	25.2	20.5	4.8	2.77	3.26	19 542	10.1	17.5
Chesterfield township	13 347	75.5	43.1	62.1	34.3	9.5	6.4	24.5	19.2	4.7	2.78	3.22	8 916	8.5	16.9
Clinton township	40 299	63.4	28.1	48.7	20.5	10.9	5.9	36.6	30.8	10.8	2.35	2.98	32 459	10.5	22.7
Commerce township	12 379	78.8	42.4	68.4	36.5	7.3	4.1	21.2	17.0	4.3	2.81	3.19	9 358	9.0	13.9
Dearborn city	36 770	64.9	31.3	51.0	25.7	9.4	4.3	35.1	30.9	14.7	2.65	3.42	35 442	9.7	28.8
Dearborn Heights city	23 276	67.8	27.5	52.7	21.8	10.8	4.2	32.2	28.0	13.0	2.47	3.04	23 432	9.8	23.4
Delta charter township	12 559	64.3	28.4	52.1	21.3	9.4	5.7	35.7	29.4	9.0	2.33	2.92	10 250	8.0	24.3
Detroit city	336 428	64.9	33.9	26.7	12.5	31.6	18.6	35.1	29.7	9.2	2.77	3.45	374 057	30.4	29.5
Eastpointe city	13 595	65.9	30.2	48.6	22.9	12.3	5.3	34.1	28.8	13.8	2.50	3.11	13 443	11.0	22.8

[1] No spouse present.

Table E. Towns

Town	Percent change of households, 1990–2000	Total housing units	Occupied housing units (percent)	Vacant housing units Total	For seasonal, recreational, or occasional use	Homeowner vacancy rate (percent)	Rental vacancy rate (percent)	Occupied housing units Total	Percent owner-occupied housing units	Percent renter-occupied housing units	Average household size of owner-occupied units	Average household size of renter-occupied units
	86	87	88	89	90	91	92	93	94	95	96	97
MASSACHUSETTS— Cont'd												
Dracut town	16.2	10 643	98.2	1.8	0.4	0.4	2.7	10 451	78.5	21.5	2.89	2.15
Everett city	6.2	15 908	97.0	3.0	0.1	0.5	2.2	15 435	41.4	58.6	2.67	2.29
Fall River city	3.9	41 857	92.6	7.4	0.2	1.4	6.7	38 759	34.9	65.1	2.66	2.14
Falmouth town	22.9	20 055	69.1	30.9	28.0	1.0	5.7	13 859	77.6	22.4	2.37	2.03
Fitchburg city	-2.7	16 002	93.4	6.6	0.2	1.4	6.5	14 943	51.6	48.4	2.64	2.35
Framingham town	4.1	26 734	97.8	2.2	0.5	0.2	1.7	26 153	55.5	44.5	2.63	2.19
Franklin city	37.1	10 327	98.3	1.7	0.3	0.3	2.9	10 152	81.2	18.8	3.06	1.92
Gloucester city	8.7	13 958	90.2	9.8	6.9	0.8	2.7	12 592	59.7	40.3	2.60	2.04
Haverhill city	17.4	23 737	96.8	3.2	0.3	0.5	3.1	22 976	60.2	39.8	2.69	2.23
Holyoke city	-5.6	16 210	92.3	7.7	0.2	0.9	6.9	14 967	41.5	58.5	2.66	2.50
Lawrence city	0.8	25 601	95.6	4.4	0.2	1.0	3.0	24 463	32.2	67.8	3.02	2.85
Leominster city	11.2	16 976	97.1	2.9	0.2	0.5	2.6	16 491	57.9	42.1	2.71	2.16
Lexington town	5.7	11 333	98.0	2.0	0.5	0.4	1.7	11 110	82.6	17.4	2.77	2.16
Lowell city	2.3	39 468	96.0	4.0	0.2	1.2	3.1	37 887	43.0	57.0	2.87	2.53
Lynn city	6.2	34 637	96.7	3.3	0.2	0.7	2.3	33 511	45.6	54.4	2.81	2.46
Malden city	5.0	23 634	97.4	2.6	0.3	0.4	2.1	23 009	43.3	56.7	2.86	2.08
Marlborough city	19.3	14 903	97.3	2.7	0.4	0.5	2.4	14 501	61.0	39.0	2.68	2.13
Medford city	1.1	22 687	97.3	2.7	0.2	0.5	2.5	22 067	58.6	41.4	2.62	2.15
Melrose city	0.4	11 248	97.6	2.4	0.4	0.4	1.6	10 982	67.0	33.0	2.78	1.75
Methuen city	12.9	16 885	97.9	2.1	0.2	0.3	2.8	16 532	71.9	28.1	2.79	2.19
Milford town	11.3	10 713	97.3	2.7	0.3	0.4	2.9	10 420	64.7	35.3	2.76	2.14
Milton town	2.7	9 161	98.0	2.0	0.2	0.4	2.9	8 982	84.1	15.9	2.92	2.09
Natick town	8.9	13 368	97.8	2.2	0.2	0.4	2.6	13 080	71.1	28.9	2.65	1.84
Needham town	4.4	10 846	97.8	2.2	0.5	0.3	2.2	10 612	80.9	19.1	2.82	1.84
New Bedford city	-1.6	41 511	92.0	8.0	0.3	1.9	6.9	38 178	43.8	56.2	2.60	2.25
Newton city	5.9	32 112	97.2	2.8	0.8	0.5	2.1	31 201	69.5	30.5	2.70	2.08
Northampton city	6.4	12 405	95.8	4.2	1.0	0.4	3.4	11 880	53.5	46.5	2.44	1.79
North Andover town	23.2	9 943	97.8	2.2	0.5	0.4	2.3	9 724	72.5	27.5	2.84	2.00
North Attleborough town	12.5	10 635	97.7	2.3	0.3	0.5	2.9	10 391	68.5	31.5	2.87	2.00
Norwood town	5.5	11 945	97.3	2.7	0.3	0.5	2.8	11 623	57.2	42.8	2.68	2.05
Peabody city	5.8	18 898	98.3	1.7	0.3	0.3	1.7	18 581	71.2	28.8	2.75	2.06
Pittsfield city	-1.1	21 366	92.2	7.8	1.2	1.5	9.0	19 704	60.8	39.2	2.45	1.97
Plymouth town	16.1	21 250	86.7	13.3	10.6	0.8	3.3	18 423	77.6	22.4	2.81	2.20
Quincy city	9.0	40 093	97.0	3.0	0.5	0.4	2.7	38 883	49.0	51.0	2.59	1.87
Randolph town	3.9	11 533	98.1	1.9	0.3	0.3	2.3	11 313	72.3	27.7	2.92	2.18
Revere city	11.6	20 181	96.4	3.6	0.4	0.5	2.3	19 463	50.0	50.0	2.64	2.19
Salem city	10.7	18 175	96.2	3.8	0.4	0.9	2.5	17 492	49.1	50.9	2.40	2.09
Saugus town	7.4	10 122	98.5	1.5	0.1	0.3	1.6	9 975	80.0	20.0	2.78	1.86
Shrewsbury town	32.9	12 696	97.4	2.6	0.7	0.6	3.1	12 366	73.1	26.9	2.81	1.84
Somerville city	4.1	32 477	97.2	2.8	0.3	0.8	1.6	31 555	30.6	69.4	2.59	2.28
Springfield city	-1.1	61 172	93.4	6.6	0.3	1.3	6.1	57 130	49.9	50.1	2.61	2.52
Stoughton town	9.2	10 488	97.8	2.2	0.6	0.5	2.2	10 254	74.5	25.5	2.78	2.07
Taunton city	17.0	22 908	96.2	3.8	0.1	0.6	4.7	22 045	61.2	38.8	2.73	2.14
Tewksbury town	14.0	10 158	98.1	1.9	0.3	0.4	5.6	9 964	89.1	10.9	2.90	2.08
Waltham city	12.0	23 880	97.2	2.8	0.5	0.3	2.2	23 207	46.0	54.0	2.60	2.03
Watertown city	3.1	15 008	97.5	2.5	0.3	0.4	1.6	14 629	47.0	53.0	2.31	2.05
Wellesley town	1.4	8 861	97.0	3.0	0.8	0.8	2.4	8 594	83.1	16.9	2.84	1.98
Westfield city	7.0	15 441	95.8	4.2	0.5	1.0	2.8	14 797	67.8	32.2	2.68	2.25
West Springfield town	2.9	12 259	96.4	3.6	0.5	0.6	3.7	11 823	58.2	41.8	2.56	2.00
Weymouth town	5.8	22 573	97.6	2.4	0.5	0.4	2.1	22 028	67.3	32.7	2.67	1.91
Woburn city	11.2	15 391	97.4	2.6	0.5	0.4	2.2	14 997	61.2	38.8	2.74	2.04
Worcester city	4.9	70 723	94.8	5.2	0.4	0.9	4.1	67 028	43.3	56.7	2.57	2.28
MICHIGAN	10.7	4 234 279	89.4	10.6	5.5	1.6	6.8	3 785 661	73.8	26.2	2.67	2.24
Allen Park city	-0.5	12 254	97.7	2.3	0.2	0.6	4.4	11 974	87.9	12.1	2.51	1.82
Ann Arbor city	9.7	47 218	96.8	3.2	0.5	1.0	2.6	45 693	45.3	54.7	2.43	2.06
Battle Creek city	-0.5	23 525	90.7	9.3	0.4	2.5	12.1	21 348	65.8	34.2	2.52	2.25
Bay City city	-2.3	16 259	93.5	6.5	0.4	1.7	7.4	15 208	69.5	30.5	2.51	2.09
Bedford township	28.2	10 659	96.9	3.1	0.5	0.8	5.6	10 327	88.9	11.1	2.83	2.17
Bloomfield township	6.8	17 455	96.3	3.7	1.2	0.8	5.3	16 804	90.3	9.7	2.59	2.02
Burton city	12.0	12 348	94.7	5.3	0.2	2.7	5.3	11 699	80.8	19.2	2.67	2.23
Canton township	40.7	28 430	96.7	3.3	0.3	1.2	5.3	27 490	79.1	20.9	2.94	2.14
Chesterfield township	49.7	13 967	95.6	4.4	0.4	1.7	6.3	13 347	81.4	18.6	2.83	2.58
Clinton township	24.2	41 803	96.4	3.6	0.3	1.0	5.3	40 299	69.5	30.5	2.55	1.90
Commerce township	32.3	12 924	95.8	4.2	1.2	1.4	4.3	12 379	92.5	7.5	2.85	2.30
Dearborn city	3.7	38 981	94.3	5.7	1.2	1.5	6.1	36 770	73.4	26.6	2.75	2.38
Dearborn Heights city	-0.7	23 913	97.3	2.7	0.3	0.9	3.8	23 276	85.4	14.6	2.53	2.14
Delta charter township	22.5	13 112	95.8	4.2	0.6	1.2	5.2	12 559	64.3	35.7	2.60	1.85
Detroit city	-10.1	375 096	89.7	10.3	0.2	1.6	8.3	336 428	54.9	45.1	2.84	2.68
Eastpointe city	1.1	13 965	97.4	2.6	0.2	0.9	4.5	13 595	88.0	12.0	2.56	2.09

Table E. Towns

STATE MCD code	Town	Population, 2000				Population, 1990				Population and population characteristics, 2000					
										Race (percent)					
										One race					
		Land area, 2000[1] (sq km)	Total persons	Rank within state	Per square kilometer	Land area, 1990[1] (sq km)	Total persons	Rank within state	Per square kilometer	White	Black or African American	American Indian or Alaska Native	Asian	Native Hawaiian and other Pacific Islander	Some other race
		1	2	3	4	5	6	7	8	9	10	11	12	13	14
	MICHIGAN—Cont'd														
26 27440	Farmington Hills city	86.2	82 111	13	952.6	86.2	74 614	13	865.6	82.9	6.9	0.2	7.5	0.0	0.5
26 29000	Flint city	87.1	124 943	4	1 434.5	87.6	140 925	4	1 608.7	41.4	53.3	0.6	0.4	0.0	1.1
26 29020	Flint township	61.2	33 691	41	550.5	61.4	34 072	41	554.9	77.8	16.1	0.6	2.2	0.0	0.7
26 31420	Garden City city	15.2	30 047	46	1 976.8	15.2	31 846	46	2 095.1	96.2	1.1	0.4	0.7	0.0	0.3
26 31880	Georgetown township	86.7	41 658	44	480.5	86.7	32 672	44	376.8	97.0	0.6	0.2	0.9	0.0	0.5
26 33300	Grand Blanc township	84.5	29 827	56	353.0	84.7	25 392	56	299.8	88.1	6.7	0.4	2.5	0.0	0.6
26 34000	Grand Rapids city	115.6	197 800	2	1 711.1	114.6	189 126	2	1 650.3	67.3	20.4	0.7	1.6	0.1	6.6
26 38660	Holland township	70.4	28 911	66	410.7	70.6	17 523	66	248.2	79.2	2.2	0.4	7.9	0.0	7.6
26 40400	Independence township	91.2	32 581	58	357.2	92.4	24 722	58	267.6	95.8	0.8	0.2	1.2	0.0	0.6
26 40680	Inkster city	16.2	30 115	49	1 859.0	16.2	30 772	49	1 899.5	25.1	67.5	0.4	3.4	0.0	0.7
26 41420	Jackson city	28.7	36 316	38	1 265.4	28.6	37 425	38	1 308.6	73.9	19.7	0.6	0.5	0.0	1.7
26 42160	Kalamazoo city	63.9	77 145	11	1 207.3	63.6	80 277	11	1 262.2	70.8	20.6	0.6	2.4	0.1	2.4
26 42820	Kentwood city	54.5	45 255	36	830.4	54.5	37 826	36	694.1	80.9	9.1	0.5	5.6	0.0	1.4
26 47800	Lincoln Park city	15.2	40 008	32	2 632.1	15.2	41 832	32	2 752.1	93.3	2.1	0.5	0.5	0.0	1.8
26 49000	Livonia city	92.5	100 545	7	1 087.0	92.5	100 850	7	1 090.3	95.5	0.9	0.2	1.9	0.0	0.3
26 50480	Macomb township	93.9	50 478	63	537.6	94.0	22 714	63	241.6	96.1	0.8	0.2	1.4	0.0	0.3
26 50560	Madison Heights city	18.6	31 101	45	1 672.1	18.6	32 196	45	1 731.0	89.6	1.8	0.4	5.0	0.0	0.5
26 53140	Meridian charter township	80.3	39 116	39	487.1	82.4	35 644	39	432.6	86.4	4.0	0.3	6.5	0.1	0.7
26 56020	Mount Pleasant city	20.2	25 946	62	1 284.5	18.7	23 299	62	1 245.9	89.1	3.7	1.5	2.8	0.1	0.9
26 56320	Muskegon city	37.2	40 105	34	1 078.1	37.2	39 809	34	1 070.1	60.6	31.7	1.0	0.5	0.0	2.7
26 59440	Novi city	78.9	47 386	43	600.6	78.9	32 998	43	418.2	87.3	1.9	0.2	8.7	0.0	0.5
26 59920	Oak Park city	13.0	29 793	51	2 291.8	13.0	30 468	51	2 343.7	47.0	46.0	0.3	2.2	0.0	0.6
26 61100	Orion township	86.4	33 463	59	387.3	86.4	24 076	59	278.7	95.4	1.3	0.3	1.2	0.0	0.6
26 64560	Pittsfield charter township	71.3	30 167	65	423.1	72.8	17 650	65	242.4	70.4	14.3	0.4	10.0	0.0	1.7
26 64660	Plainfield township	91.0	30 195	57	331.8	91.0	24 946	57	274.1	95.7	1.2	0.3	0.9	0.0	0.6
26 65080	Plymouth township	41.2	27 798	61	674.7	41.2	23 648	61	574.0	92.4	3.0	0.3	2.7	0.0	0.4
26 65440	Pontiac city	51.8	66 337	15	1 280.6	51.8	71 136	15	1 373.3	39.1	47.9	0.6	2.4	0.0	6.5
26 65560	Portage city	83.4	44 897	33	538.3	83.4	41 042	33	492.1	90.8	3.7	0.3	2.6	0.0	0.7
26 65820	Port Huron city	20.9	32 338	42	1 547.3	20.7	33 694	42	1 627.7	86.7	7.7	0.9	0.6	0.0	1.3
26 67625	Redford township	29.1	51 622	26	1 774.0	29.1	54 387	26	1 869.0	88.0	8.5	0.4	0.8	0.0	0.6
26 69035	Rochester Hills city	85.1	68 825	22	808.8	85.1	61 766	22	725.8	88.8	2.4	0.2	6.8	0.0	0.5
26 69800	Roseville city	25.4	48 129	28	1 894.8	25.4	51 412	28	2 024.1	93.4	2.6	0.4	1.6	0.0	0.3
26 70040	Royal Oak city	30.6	60 062	20	1 962.8	30.6	65 410	20	2 137.6	94.8	1.5	0.3	1.6	0.1	0.4
26 70520	Saginaw city	45.2	61 799	17	1 367.2	45.2	69 512	17	1 537.9	47.0	43.3	0.5	0.3	0.0	5.9
26 70540	Saginaw charter township	63.8	39 657	37	621.6	63.8	37 684	37	590.7	88.8	5.3	0.3	2.7	0.0	1.5
26 70760	St. Clair Shores city	29.9	63 096	18	2 110.2	29.9	68 107	18	2 277.8	96.9	0.7	0.3	0.8	0.0	0.2
26 72820	Shelby charter township	89.8	65 159	29	725.6	90.0	48 655	29	540.6	95.0	0.8	0.2	2.1	0.0	0.4
26 74900	Southfield city	67.9	78 296	12	1 153.1	67.9	75 727	12	1 115.3	38.8	54.2	0.2	3.1	0.0	0.6
26 74960	Southgate city	17.8	30 136	50	1 693.0	17.8	30 771	50	1 728.7	93.7	2.1	0.5	1.7	0.0	0.8
26 76460	Sterling Heights city	94.9	124 471	5	1 311.6	94.9	117 810	5	1 241.4	90.7	1.3	0.2	4.9	0.0	0.3
26 79000	Taylor city	61.2	65 868	16	1 076.3	61.2	70 811	16	1 157.0	86.1	8.7	0.7	1.6	0.0	0.7
26 80700	Troy city	86.9	80 959	14	931.6	86.9	72 884	14	838.7	82.3	2.1	0.2	13.3	0.0	0.4
26 84000	Warren city	88.8	138 247	3	1 556.8	88.8	144 864	3	1 631.4	91.3	2.7	0.4	3.1	0.0	0.3
26 84240	Waterford township	81.2	73 150	19	900.9	81.2	66 692	19	821.3	92.7	2.9	0.4	1.3	0.0	1.1
26 85480	West Bloomfield township	70.8	64 860	25	916.1	70.8	54 516	25	770.0	84.2	5.2	0.1	7.8	0.0	0.4
26 86000	Westland city	53.0	86 602	10	1 634.0	53.0	84 724	10	1 598.6	87.2	6.8	0.5	2.8	0.0	0.7
26 86860	White Lake township	87.2	28 219	64	323.6	87.1	22 677	64	260.4	96.6	0.8	0.5	0.6	0.0	0.3
26 88900	Wyandotte city	13.7	28 006	48	2 044.2	13.8	30 938	48	2 241.9	96.3	0.5	0.5	0.3	0.0	0.7
26 88940	Wyoming city	63.3	69 368	21	1 095.9	62.9	63 891	21	1 015.8	84.3	4.8	0.6	2.9	0.0	4.7
26 89160	Ypsilanti township	78.1	49 182	30	629.7	78.2	45 307	30	579.4	67.5	25.5	0.5	2.0	0.0	1.2
27 00000	MINNESOTA	206 189	4 919 479	X	23.9	206 207	4 375 665	X	21.2	89.4	3.5	1.1	2.9	0.0	1.3
27 01486	Andover city	88.3	26 588	32	301.1	88.4	15 216	32	172.1	96.5	0.5	0.4	1.1	0.0	0.3
27 01900	Apple Valley city	44.9	45 527	18	1 014.0	44.9	34 598	18	770.6	91.8	1.9	0.3	3.4	0.0	0.9
27 06382	Blaine city	87.2	44 942	15	515.4	87.5	38 975	15	445.4	93.5	0.9	0.6	2.5	0.0	0.7
27 06616	Bloomington city	91.9	85 172	3	926.8	92.0	86 335	3	938.4	88.1	3.4	0.3	5.1	0.0	1.3
27 07948	Brooklyn Center city	20.6	29 172	23	1 416.1	20.6	28 887	23	1 402.3	71.4	14.1	0.9	8.8	0.0	1.5
27 07966	Brooklyn Park city	67.5	67 388	6	998.3	67.5	56 381	6	835.3	71.4	14.3	0.6	9.2	0.1	1.5
27 08794	Burnsville city	64.4	60 220	8	935.1	64.4	51 288	8	796.4	87.5	4.1	0.5	4.1	0.1	1.4
27 13114	Coon Rapids city	58.7	61 607	7	1 049.5	59.1	52 978	7	896.4	93.2	2.2	0.7	1.6	0.0	0.6
27 13456	Cottage Grove city	88.0	30 582	28	347.5	88.0	22 935	28	260.6	93.5	2.4	0.4	1.4	0.1	0.9
27 17000	Duluth city	176.1	86 918	4	493.6	175.1	85 493	4	488.3	92.7	1.6	2.4	1.1	0.0	0.3
27 17288	Eagan city	83.7	63 557	11	759.3	83.5	47 409	11	567.8	88.0	3.4	0.3	5.3	0.1	1.0
27 18116	Eden Prairie city	83.9	54 901	14	654.4	83.9	39 311	14	468.5	90.7	2.3	0.2	4.8	0.0	0.5
27 18188	Edina city	40.8	47 425	12	1 162.4	40.8	46 075	12	1 129.3	94.3	1.2	0.1	3.0	0.0	0.3
27 22814	Fridley city	26.3	27 449	24	1 043.7	26.2	28 335	24	1 081.5	88.7	3.4	0.8	2.9	0.1	1.2
27 31076	Inver Grove Heights city	74.2	29 751	29	401.0	74.2	22 477	29	302.9	91.8	2.1	0.5	2.0	0.0	1.7
27 35180	Lakeville city	93.7	43 128	26	460.3	93.8	24 854	26	265.0	94.3	1.3	0.4	2.0	0.0	0.8
27 39878	Mankato city	38.7	32 427	21	837.9	29.3	31 444	21	1 073.2	92.5	1.9	0.3	2.8	0.0	0.9
27 40166	Maple Grove city	85.1	50 365	16	591.8	85.1	38 736	16	455.2	94.7	1.0	0.2	2.5	0.0	0.3

[1]Dry land or land partially or temporarily covered by water.

Table E. Towns

Town	Population and population characteristics, 2000 (cont'd)								Population and population characteristics, 1990				
	Race (percent) (cont'd)								Race (percent)				
		Race alone or in combination											
	Two or more races	White	Black	American Indian or Alaska Native	Asian	Native Hawaiian and other Pacific Islander	Some other race	Hispanic¹	White	Black or African American	American Indian or Alaska Native	Asian and Pacific Islander	Hispanic¹
	15	16	17	18	19	20	21	22	23	24	25	26	27
MICHIGAN—Cont'd													
Farmington Hills city	1.9	84.7	7.4	0.6	8.2	0.1	1.2	1.5	93.9	1.9	0.2	3.8	1.2
Flint city	3.1	43.7	55.3	2.2	0.7	0.1	1.6	3.0	49.6	47.9	0.7	0.5	2.9
Flint township	2.5	80.0	16.9	1.7	2.6	0.1	1.4	2.3	88.7	7.6	1.0	2.0	1.6
Garden City city	1.3	97.4	1.3	0.9	1.0	0.0	0.7	2.0	98.6	0.2	0.4	0.5	1.5
Georgetown township	0.8	97.8	0.8	0.4	1.1	0.1	0.7	1.7	98.7	0.3	0.1	0.6	0.9
Grand Blanc township	1.6	89.6	7.1	0.9	2.9	0.1	1.1	2.1	92.3	4.9	0.5	1.8	1.7
Grand Rapids city	3.2	69.9	22.0	1.5	1.9	0.2	7.9	13.1	76.4	18.5	0.8	1.1	5.0
Holland township	2.6	81.4	2.8	0.9	8.6	0.2	8.9	15.8	91.2	0.5	0.3	3.3	9.3
Independence township	1.2	97.0	1.1	0.7	1.5	0.0	0.9	2.5	98.3	0.2	0.4	0.6	1.6
Inkster city	2.8	27.1	69.5	1.4	3.7	0.1	1.3	1.6	36.1	62.4	0.4	0.7	1.1
Jackson city	3.7	77.0	22.0	1.7	0.8	0.1	2.4	4.0	80.2	17.7	0.6	0.4	2.5
Kalamazoo city	3.2	73.5	22.4	1.6	2.9	0.2	3.2	4.3	77.3	18.8	0.6	1.9	2.7
Kentwood city	2.5	83.0	10.2	1.0	6.2	0.1	2.2	3.9	91.3	5.6	0.4	2.0	2.0
Lincoln Park city	1.8	94.9	2.4	1.3	0.7	0.0	2.5	6.4	97.3	0.9	0.5	0.4	3.8
Livonia city	1.1	96.5	1.1	0.6	2.3	0.0	0.7	1.7	98.0	0.3	0.2	1.3	1.3
Macomb township	1.1	97.2	1.0	0.5	1.7	0.0	0.7	1.5	98.3	0.5	0.3	0.8	1.1
Madison Heights city	2.7	92.1	2.1	1.1	5.6	0.1	1.8	1.6	95.9	0.9	0.5	2.4	1.2
Meridian charter township	2.0	88.1	4.7	0.8	7.3	0.1	1.3	2.5	91.3	3.7	0.5	3.9	2.1
Mount Pleasant city	1.8	90.7	4.3	2.2	3.2	0.1	1.4	2.5	94.6	2.3	1.0	1.5	1.6
Muskegon city	3.5	63.5	33.4	2.3	0.8	0.1	3.6	6.4	69.9	27.1	1.0	0.3	3.5
Novi city	1.5	88.6	2.2	0.5	9.3	0.1	0.9	1.8	96.0	0.8	0.3	2.6	1.1
Oak Park city	4.1	50.5	47.3	0.8	2.7	0.1	3.0	1.3	62.8	34.3	0.1	2.4	1.5
Orion township	1.2	96.6	1.5	0.8	1.5	0.0	0.9	2.6	98.0	0.6	0.4	0.3	1.8
Pittsfield charter township	3.2	73.1	15.5	1.1	10.9	0.2	2.8	4.0	78.2	16.6	0.4	4.0	2.1
Plainfield township	1.2	96.8	1.6	0.8	1.2	0.1	0.9	1.8	97.5	0.9	0.2	1.0	1.2
Plymouth township	1.2	93.5	3.2	0.7	3.1	0.0	0.7	1.6	96.7	1.2	0.2	1.6	1.1
Pontiac city	3.5	41.8	49.9	1.5	2.8	0.1	7.6	12.8	51.3	42.2	0.8	1.4	8.0
Portage city	1.8	92.4	4.5	0.9	3.0	0.1	1.1	1.9	94.3	2.8	0.4	2.1	1.4
Port Huron city	2.8	89.2	9.2	1.8	0.8	0.1	2.0	4.3	90.1	6.8	0.8	0.6	3.5
Redford township	1.7	89.6	9.1	1.0	1.1	0.1	1.0	2.0	98.1	0.7	0.4	0.6	1.5
Rochester Hills city	1.4	90.0	2.7	0.6	7.2	0.1	0.8	2.3	95.0	1.4	0.2	3.2	1.4
Roseville city	1.6	94.9	3.0	1.1	1.9	0.1	0.7	1.5	97.3	1.0	0.5	1.1	1.2
Royal Oak city	1.4	96.1	1.8	0.7	2.0	0.1	0.8	1.3	97.9	0.5	0.2	1.1	1.1
Saginaw city	3.0	49.4	44.9	1.2	0.6	0.1	7.1	11.7	52.3	40.3	0.5	0.4	10.5
Saginaw charter township	1.5	90.1	5.7	0.6	3.1	0.0	2.0	4.2	93.5	2.8	0.2	1.9	3.4
St. Clair Shores city	1.1	97.9	0.8	0.9	1.1	0.0	0.4	1.2	98.7	0.2	0.3	0.6	0.9
Shelby charter township	1.4	96.2	1.0	0.6	2.4	0.0	1.1	1.7	98.0	0.3	0.3	1.2	1.0
Southfield city	3.0	41.0	55.8	0.9	3.6	0.1	1.9	1.2	67.9	29.1	0.3	2.4	1.7
Southgate city	1.2	94.8	2.3	0.9	1.9	0.1	1.2	4.0	96.5	1.2	0.5	1.1	2.8
Sterling Heights city	2.5	93.0	1.5	0.6	5.4	0.1	1.9	1.3	96.3	0.4	0.2	2.9	1.1
Taylor city	2.0	87.9	9.5	1.5	1.9	0.1	1.3	3.2	93.2	4.2	0.6	1.3	2.8
Troy city	1.8	83.9	2.3	0.5	14.0	0.1	1.2	1.5	91.5	1.3	0.2	6.8	1.3
Warren city	2.2	93.3	3.1	1.1	3.6	0.1	1.1	1.4	97.3	0.7	0.5	1.3	1.1
Waterford township	1.7	94.2	3.2	0.9	1.6	0.0	1.8	3.9	96.9	1.1	0.6	0.7	2.3
West Bloomfield township	2.2	86.3	5.5	0.4	8.4	0.1	1.7	1.4	92.5	2.0	0.1	5.2	1.2
Westland city	2.0	89.0	7.4	1.1	3.2	0.1	1.4	2.5	94.7	3.3	0.6	1.0	1.9
White Lake township	1.3	97.8	1.0	1.2	0.8	0.1	0.5	1.8	98.0	0.7	0.6	0.4	1.3
Wyandotte city	1.6	97.8	0.8	1.3	0.5	0.1	1.1	2.9	98.2	0.2	0.6	0.4	2.1
Wyoming city	2.6	86.6	5.8	1.3	3.3	0.1	5.7	9.7	93.5	2.7	0.5	1.5	3.5
Ypsilanti township	3.3	70.3	27.1	1.4	2.5	0.1	2.2	2.8	79.4	18.2	0.4	1.4	1.6
MINNESOTA	1.7	90.8	4.1	1.6	3.3	0.1	1.8	2.9	94.4	2.2	1.1	1.8	1.2
Andover city	1.2	97.6	0.9	0.8	1.4	0.0	0.5	1.0	97.8	0.3	0.6	0.9	1.0
Apple Valley city	1.7	93.3	2.5	0.6	4.0	0.1	1.3	2.0	96.7	0.9	0.2	1.9	1.0
Blaine city	1.7	95.1	1.4	1.3	3.0	0.1	1.0	1.7	97.2	0.3	0.8	1.4	1.0
Bloomington city	1.7	89.5	4.1	0.7	5.7	0.1	1.7	2.7	94.7	1.6	0.3	3.1	0.9
Brooklyn Center city	3.4	73.8	15.9	1.5	9.6	0.2	2.5	2.8	90.9	5.2	0.9	2.3	1.3
Brooklyn Park city	2.9	73.6	15.9	1.1	10.0	0.2	2.4	2.9	90.6	4.9	0.6	3.4	1.2
Burnsville city	2.4	89.5	5.2	0.9	4.8	0.2	2.0	2.9	94.8	2.3	0.3	2.3	1.0
Coon Rapids city	1.7	94.8	2.7	1.1	2.1	0.1	1.0	1.5	97.3	0.5	0.8	1.1	0.9
Cottage Grove city	1.3	94.7	2.8	0.8	1.8	0.1	1.2	2.5	96.6	1.2	0.3	1.1	1.8
Duluth city	1.8	94.3	2.2	3.4	1.4	0.1	0.5	1.1	95.9	0.9	2.1	0.9	0.6
Eagan city	1.9	89.7	4.1	0.7	5.9	0.2	1.5	2.2	93.7	2.4	0.3	3.1	1.3
Eden Prairie city	1.5	91.9	2.8	0.4	5.4	0.1	0.9	1.6	96.4	1.1	0.2	2.1	0.7
Edina city	1.1	95.2	1.5	0.3	3.5	0.1	0.6	1.1	97.2	0.7	0.1	1.7	0.7
Fridley city	2.9	91.2	4.4	1.5	3.5	0.2	2.3	2.6	95.7	1.0	0.7	2.2	1.0
Inver Grove Heights city	1.9	93.3	2.8	0.9	2.5	0.1	2.3	4.2	97.1	0.7	0.5	0.6	2.5
Lakeville city	1.3	95.4	1.7	0.7	2.5	0.1	1.0	1.9	97.4	0.7	0.4	1.3	0.8
Mankato city	1.4	93.6	2.4	0.7	3.2	0.1	1.4	2.2	96.3	0.7	0.3	2.3	1.1
Maple Grove city	1.1	95.8	1.4	0.5	2.9	0.1	0.5	1.1	97.1	0.9	0.3	1.6	0.8

¹Hispanic persons may be of any race.

Table E. Towns

Town	Population and population characteristics, 2000										
	Age (percent)										
	Under 5 years	5 to 17 years	18 to 24 years	25 to 34 years	35 to 44 years	45 to 54 years	55 to 64 years	65 to 74 years	75 years and over	Median age (years)	Percent Female
	28	29	30	31	32	33	34	35	36	37	38
MICHIGAN—Cont'd											
Farmington Hills city	6.0	17.1	6.7	14.5	16.8	15.3	9.3	7.0	7.4	38.6	51.6
Flint city	9.0	21.6	10.3	15.1	14.3	11.9	7.3	5.8	4.7	30.8	53.0
Flint township	5.9	18.5	8.6	12.5	15.5	13.6	9.3	8.3	7.9	38.1	53.3
Garden City city	6.2	18.9	7.6	14.7	17.9	12.9	8.2	8.5	5.0	36.5	50.6
Georgetown township	7.0	22.4	10.9	11.4	16.1	13.4	8.2	5.5	5.1	33.8	51.3
Grand Blanc township	6.7	18.8	7.8	15.0	17.1	14.7	9.1	6.1	4.7	36.0	51.1
Grand Rapids city	8.3	18.8	13.1	17.2	14.3	10.8	6.0	5.2	6.4	30.4	51.1
Holland township	10.1	21.2	10.4	18.8	15.7	10.5	6.3	4.0	3.1	29.3	49.5
Independence township	7.3	20.4	6.9	13.0	18.7	16.3	9.4	4.9	3.2	36.4	50.2
Inkster city	8.0	21.8	9.2	15.8	14.5	11.9	7.9	6.1	4.7	31.8	52.3
Jackson city	9.1	20.6	9.8	15.8	14.6	11.4	6.8	5.6	6.4	31.3	52.3
Kalamazoo city	6.2	14.1	27.6	15.0	11.8	9.6	5.6	4.5	5.6	26.1	51.8
Kentwood city	7.7	18.9	10.4	17.1	16.6	12.6	6.9	5.0	4.9	32.4	51.8
Lincoln Park city	6.9	17.4	8.5	16.4	16.3	12.9	7.4	7.1	7.0	35.5	51.1
Livonia city	5.6	18.2	6.3	11.3	17.4	14.9	9.4	8.9	8.0	40.2	51.5
Macomb township	9.0	21.2	6.9	15.7	19.5	13.4	6.9	4.6	2.8	33.6	50.1
Madison Heights city	6.2	15.9	8.1	17.9	17.5	12.3	7.9	8.0	6.2	36.1	51.1
Meridian charter township	5.3	18.4	13.4	12.5	15.1	16.9	8.5	5.1	4.9	35.4	52.2
Mount Pleasant city	3.4	8.1	54.1	9.8	7.0	6.5	3.7	3.1	4.3	21.8	54.8
Muskegon city	7.6	18.1	11.6	16.6	15.5	11.6	6.4	5.5	6.9	32.3	47.7
Novi city	7.4	20.2	6.7	15.2	20.4	14.7	7.2	4.3	3.8	35.2	50.8
Oak Park city	6.8	21.4	8.0	14.4	15.4	14.0	7.8	5.9	6.3	34.6	53.2
Orion township	8.6	19.9	7.3	15.9	20.5	14.1	7.6	3.4	2.8	34.1	49.3
Pittsfield charter township	7.4	16.5	11.8	20.9	18.6	13.2	5.8	3.1	2.6	31.6	48.1
Plainfield township	7.2	22.8	8.0	11.8	18.2	14.7	8.0	5.6	3.7	35.1	50.3
Plymouth township	6.0	16.6	6.5	12.6	17.8	17.2	11.0	7.1	5.2	39.6	49.8
Pontiac city	8.9	21.7	10.3	17.4	14.9	11.5	6.8	4.7	3.8	30.0	51.3
Portage city	6.9	19.5	8.5	13.8	16.0	14.7	8.7	6.5	5.3	35.8	52.1
Port Huron city	7.8	19.2	9.7	14.8	14.9	12.1	7.5	6.5	7.6	34.0	52.4
Redford township	6.9	18.5	7.0	16.1	18.0	12.2	6.5	6.8	8.1	35.9	51.0
Rochester Hills city	6.5	19.4	6.7	12.1	18.0	17.1	9.5	5.5	5.2	38.1	51.3
Roseville city	6.5	16.6	8.2	16.5	16.5	12.4	7.8	7.8	7.5	36.2	51.6
Royal Oak city	5.2	12.6	7.5	21.2	17.6	13.6	7.4	6.7	8.3	36.9	51.2
Saginaw city	8.6	23.0	9.9	14.1	14.2	12.1	6.6	5.8	5.6	30.7	53.4
Saginaw charter township	5.1	16.0	9.2	11.1	13.7	15.4	10.3	8.7	10.6	41.7	53.1
St. Clair Shores city	5.1	15.1	6.2	12.6	16.2	13.7	9.4	11.1	10.7	42.0	52.4
Shelby charter township	6.2	18.7	8.5	13.9	17.0	15.1	10.0	6.2	4.3	36.6	50.1
Southfield city	5.6	16.0	7.9	15.8	14.8	15.4	9.3	6.8	8.4	38.3	54.1
Southgate city	5.4	16.1	8.3	14.8	15.9	14.2	9.1	8.4	7.8	38.5	51.8
Sterling Heights city	6.2	17.9	8.5	14.3	16.1	15.0	10.3	5.8	5.9	37.0	51.0
Taylor city	7.5	19.7	9.3	15.3	15.7	12.6	8.9	6.7	4.2	33.9	51.8
Troy city	6.2	20.0	6.7	12.1	17.6	17.0	10.1	5.8	4.5	38.1	50.5
Warren city	6.4	16.6	7.6	14.9	15.9	11.8	9.7	9.1	8.2	37.9	51.1
Waterford township	7.2	16.0	8.2	17.7	18.3	13.8	8.1	5.7	5.1	35.5	50.1
West Bloomfield township	6.5	19.9	5.2	9.8	17.3	17.1	10.8	7.3	6.1	40.2	50.8
Westland city	6.9	16.3	9.0	17.3	16.5	12.4	8.2	7.0	6.3	35.2	51.9
White Lake township	7.2	20.5	6.8	13.0	19.9	16.3	8.6	4.8	3.1	36.4	50.0
Wyandotte city	5.6	17.1	8.3	14.2	17.4	14.1	7.6	7.6	8.2	38.0	51.0
Wyoming city	8.0	20.0	10.9	17.3	16.4	11.8	6.2	5.1	4.3	31.2	50.6
Ypsilanti township	8.2	18.1	11.1	19.5	15.7	13.0	7.1	4.3	2.9	31.2	50.9
MINNESOTA	6.7	19.5	9.6	13.7	16.8	13.5	8.2	6.0	6.1	35.4	50.5
Andover city	9.2	26.3	6.0	14.5	21.9	13.1	6.1	1.7	1.1	31.9	49.2
Apple Valley city	7.2	22.5	7.2	13.9	19.2	16.3	8.2	3.3	2.2	34.5	51.1
Blaine city	7.8	21.3	8.7	15.8	19.1	14.2	7.8	3.7	1.6	32.7	49.9
Bloomington city	5.3	15.3	8.0	13.6	15.8	15.1	11.3	8.7	7.0	40.1	51.7
Brooklyn Center city	6.7	18.3	9.6	14.8	15.3	11.6	8.1	8.3	7.1	35.3	51.3
Brooklyn Park city	8.1	20.7	9.7	16.8	18.2	14.0	6.9	3.7	1.9	31.9	50.3
Burnsville city	7.1	19.1	10.1	16.9	17.1	13.7	8.7	4.4	2.8	33.0	50.7
Coon Rapids city	7.5	21.2	8.9	15.2	18.1	13.6	8.2	4.6	2.7	33.3	51.3
Cottage Grove city	8.5	24.2	7.4	15.6	18.6	13.6	7.2	3.6	1.3	31.9	50.2
Duluth city	5.4	15.9	16.2	12.1	14.1	13.4	7.9	6.5	8.6	35.4	51.7
Eagan city	8.1	21.9	7.4	16.7	21.6	14.2	6.0	2.7	1.5	32.8	50.8
Eden Prairie city	7.8	22.6	6.2	14.6	21.0	16.1	6.8	3.0	1.9	34.2	50.9
Edina city	5.4	17.5	4.4	8.8	14.8	15.9	10.6	10.1	12.6	44.5	54.2
Fridley city	6.7	15.9	10.2	15.4	15.6	13.1	11.0	7.7	4.2	36.3	50.6
Inver Grove Heights city	7.2	20.1	9.2	15.4	18.5	13.9	7.8	4.7	3.1	33.8	50.5
Lakeville city	10.1	26.0	5.9	15.2	22.6	12.1	5.3	1.9	0.9	31.5	49.4
Mankato city	4.9	12.0	32.5	13.1	10.8	9.8	5.6	4.9	6.4	25.3	50.8
Maple Grove city	7.4	23.3	6.6	13.7	21.2	17.0	6.7	2.6	1.5	34.4	50.5

Table E. Towns

Town	Under 5 years	5 to 17 years	18 to 24 years	25 to 34 years	35 to 44 years	45 to 54 years	55 to 64 years	65 to 74 years	75 years and over	Percent Female	2000	1990	1980	1990–2000	1980–1990
	39	40	41	42	43	44	45	46	47	48	49	50	51	52	53
MICHIGAN—Cont'd															
Farmington Hills city	6.6	16.1	8.3	18.8	17.1	11.9	9.4	7.4	4.4	51.4	82 111	74 614	58 056	10.0	28.5
Flint city	9.4	21.1	11.2	17.6	13.4	8.8	7.8	6.2	4.5	53.2	124 943	140 925	159 611	-11.3	-11.7
Flint township	6.2	17.4	9.5	16.9	14.4	11.7	10.6	7.8	5.4	53.0	33 691	34 072	NA	-1.1	NA
Garden City city	6.9	18.4	9.4	19.1	13.9	10.7	11.7	7.3	2.6	50.5	30 047	31 846	35 640	-5.6	-10.6
Georgetown township	8.3	23.0	11.0	15.6	15.6	11.5	6.8	4.6	3.6	50.7	41 658	32 672	26 104	27.5	25.2
Grand Blanc township	6.5	18.4	9.8	17.8	17.1	13.2	9.1	5.9	2.3	50.7	29 827	25 392	NA	17.5	NA
Grand Rapids city	9.4	18.2	12.5	19.6	13.3	7.1	6.9	6.8	6.2	52.6	197 800	189 126	181 843	4.6	4.0
Holland township	9.2	20.0	11.2	20.6	14.3	9.8	7.0	5.1	3.0	49.9	28 911	17 523	13 739	65.0	27.5
Independence township	6.7	19.8	9.1	15.4	19.2	14.3	8.4	4.2	2.8	50.5	32 581	24 722	21 537	31.8	14.8
Inkster city	8.1	20.6	11.1	17.0	14.5	9.3	8.0	7.5	3.8	52.8	30 115	30 772	35 190	-2.1	-12.6
Jackson city	9.7	18.7	10.7	18.4	12.7	7.8	7.8	7.5	6.5	53.1	36 316	37 425	39 739	-3.0	-5.8
Kalamazoo city	7.4	14.7	24.4	17.9	12.0	7.0	6.0	5.5	5.2	53.2	77 145	80 277	79 722	-3.9	0.7
Kentwood city	7.9	18.5	11.1	21.6	15.2	9.3	6.8	5.6	4.0	51.8	45 255	37 826	30 438	19.6	24.3
Lincoln Park city	7.0	17.2	9.4	18.8	14.6	8.9	9.7	9.5	4.9	51.6	40 008	41 832	45 105	-4.4	-7.3
Livonia city	6.6	16.3	8.6	16.2	15.8	11.5	11.8	8.3	4.8	51.4	100 545	100 850	104 814	-0.3	-3.8
Macomb township	9.4	21.9	8.5	19.6	18.7	8.9	6.5	4.7	1.8	50.4	50 478	22 714	NA	122.2	NA
Madison Heights city	7.2	15.7	10.4	21.5	13.7	10.1	10.0	6.9	4.5	51.7	31 101	32 196	35 375	-3.4	-9.0
Meridian charter township	6.5	18.7	12.4	16.9	19.6	10.4	6.6	4.8	4.2	52.6	39 116	35 644	NA	9.7	NA
Mount Pleasant city	3.9	9.1	52.7	10.4	7.9	4.8	3.8	3.8	3.5	54.6	25 946	23 299	NA	11.4	NA
Muskegon city	8.7	17.9	11.8	19.4	13.2	7.4	7.1	7.7	6.9	50.3	40 105	39 809	40 823	0.7	-2.5
Novi city	7.7	18.1	8.1	21.7	18.2	11.1	7.1	5.1	2.8	51.8	47 386	32 998	22 525	43.6	46.5
Oak Park city	8.2	20.0	8.3	17.4	15.6	10.1	7.9	8.0	4.4	52.1	29 793	30 468	31 537	-2.2	-3.4
Orion township	7.6	18.4	10.2	19.3	17.9	12.3	6.7	4.5	2.9	49.8	33 463	24 076	22 473	39.0	7.1
Pittsfield charter township	6.7	13.9	15.8	28.7	18.1	7.6	3.8	2.9	2.4	50.5	30 167	17 650	12 997	70.9	35.8
Plainfield township	7.9	21.4	9.8	16.4	17.1	11.4	7.9	5.5	2.5	50.6	30 195	24 946	20 611	21.0	21.0
Plymouth township	6.1	16.5	8.9	15.4	18.1	15.1	10.2	6.0	3.9	49.9	27 798	23 648	23 028	17.5	2.7
Pontiac city	9.8	20.6	12.5	19.3	13.3	9.1	6.6	5.2	3.5	51.6	66 337	71 136	76 715	-6.7	-7.3
Portage city	7.4	19.4	9.3	17.2	18.3	11.1	8.6	5.7	2.9	51.6	44 897	41 042	38 157	9.4	7.6
Port Huron city	8.7	19.8	10.7	17.7	13.1	8.3	7.8	7.4	6.5	53.3	32 338	33 694	33 981	-4.0	-0.8
Redford township	7.7	16.8	7.4	20.0	13.9	8.0	9.8	10.5	6.0	51.6	51 622	54 387	58 441	-5.1	-6.9
Rochester Hills city	7.2	19.1	8.4	17.1	19.8	11.8	7.8	4.8	3.9	51.5	68 825	61 766	40 779	11.4	51.5
Roseville city	7.2	16.8	9.8	20.1	13.8	8.8	9.9	8.9	4.8	52.0	48 129	51 412	54 311	-6.4	-5.3
Royal Oak city	6.8	13.9	7.6	22.5	16.1	8.5	8.8	9.3	6.4	52.9	60 062	65 410	70 893	-8.2	-7.7
Saginaw city	9.7	22.3	10.3	16.9	13.5	8.0	7.4	6.9	5.0	53.7	61 799	69 512	77 508	-11.1	-10.3
Saginaw charter township	5.7	17.1	8.9	14.1	15.9	12.1	10.1	9.0	7.0	52.9	39 657	37 684	38 668	5.2	-2.5
St. Clair Shores city	5.7	14.1	8.1	16.5	13.3	10.4	13.3	11.4	7.2	52.7	63 096	68 107	76 210	-7.4	-10.6
Shelby charter township	6.3	18.7	12.0	16.8	16.2	13.9	8.7	5.2	2.2	49.9	65 159	48 655	NA	33.9	NA
Southfield city	5.7	14.4	8.7	17.9	15.9	11.0	9.5	8.8	8.0	53.3	78 296	75 727	75 568	3.4	0.2
Southgate city	6.0	16.0	10.0	17.9	16.2	10.0	10.6	9.2	4.1	51.2	30 136	30 771	32 058	-2.1	-4.0
Sterling Heights city	6.5	19.5	11.1	16.3	17.3	12.7	7.3	5.9	3.3	51.3	124 471	117 810	108 999	5.7	8.1
Taylor city	8.2	19.5	11.6	18.5	14.2	11.1	8.9	5.2	2.7	51.3	65 868	70 811	77 568	-7.0	-8.7
Troy city	6.7	19.8	8.5	15.4	19.7	13.4	8.1	5.2	3.1	51.0	80 959	72 884	67 102	11.1	8.6
Warren city	6.2	14.8	10.4	17.7	12.2	11.7	12.0	9.5	5.4	51.3	138 247	144 864	161 134	-4.6	-10.1
Waterford township	7.2	16.8	10.3	20.8	16.4	10.3	8.4	6.0	3.8	51.0	73 150	66 692	64 437	9.7	3.5
West Bloomfield township	6.8	18.5	7.1	14.5	19.0	13.7	10.6	6.6	3.3	50.4	64 860	54 516	41 962	19.0	29.9
Westland city	7.3	16.4	11.3	21.0	13.6	10.7	8.9	6.3	4.5	52.1	86 602	84 724	84 603	2.2	0.1
White Lake township	7.5	19.6	9.3	19.0	18.4	11.8	7.5	4.3	2.6	50.1	28 219	22 677	21 870	24.4	3.7
Wyandotte city	7.1	17.0	9.0	18.4	14.9	8.2	9.1	10.3	5.9	51.6	28 006	30 938	34 006	-9.5	-9.0
Wyoming city	8.8	18.9	11.1	21.4	14.1	8.1	7.8	6.1	3.6	51.4	69 368	63 891	59 616	8.6	7.2
Ypsilanti township	8.5	18.3	12.2	22.3	15.6	9.8	7.0	4.6	1.8	51.4	49 182	45 307	44 511	8.6	1.8
MINNESOTA	7.7	19.0	10.1	17.8	15.2	9.8	7.9	6.7	5.8	51.0	4 919 479	4 375 665	4 075 970	12.4	7.4
Andover city	9.6	26.1	8.9	19.8	18.3	12.2	3.4	1.4	0.3	49.0	26 588	15 216	NA	74.7	NA
Apple Valley city	9.3	25.5	7.6	18.4	21.0	12.1	3.5	1.5	1.1	50.0	45 527	34 598	21 818	31.6	58.6
Blaine city	9.7	22.6	9.9	22.0	17.4	10.3	5.0	2.3	0.8	49.9	44 942	38 975	28 558	15.3	36.5
Bloomington city	6.2	15.2	9.9	18.9	15.7	13.1	10.9	6.6	3.7	51.6	85 172	86 335	81 831	-1.3	5.5
Brooklyn Center city	7.2	16.2	10.3	18.5	13.8	9.6	12.1	8.0	4.4	51.3	29 172	28 887	31 230	1.0	-7.5
Brooklyn Park city	9.2	20.6	11.2	22.9	18.2	9.5	5.0	2.5	0.8	50.6	67 388	56 381	43 332	19.5	30.1
Burnsville city	9.1	19.2	10.9	22.3	16.7	12.0	6.1	2.7	1.1	50.5	60 220	51 288	35 674	17.4	43.8
Coon Rapids city	9.2	22.2	10.0	20.5	16.7	10.9	5.7	2.8	1.9	50.6	61 607	52 978	35 826	16.3	47.9
Cottage Grove city	9.5	26.3	7.9	18.7	18.5	11.0	5.5	1.7	0.8	49.9	30 582	22 935	NA	33.3	NA
Duluth city	6.4	16.5	13.7	15.0	14.3	8.9	8.0	8.8	8.4	52.7	86 918	85 493	92 811	1.7	-7.9
Eagan city	11.2	18.6	9.1	28.7	18.5	8.5	3.4	1.3	0.6	50.3	63 557	47 409	20 700	34.1	129.0
Eden Prairie city	10.5	18.8	7.6	25.1	21.9	8.9	4.1	2.2	0.9	51.0	54 901	39 311	16 263	39.7	141.7
Edina city	5.3	14.7	6.2	12.1	16.3	12.4	12.5	11.3	9.1	54.7	47 425	46 075	46 073	2.9	0.0
Fridley city	6.6	14.8	11.9	18.6	14.6	13.1	10.7	5.2	2.5	50.5	27 449	28 335	30 228	-3.1	-6.3
Inver Grove Heights city	9.4	20.3	10.3	21.1	16.2	10.3	6.7	3.4	2.3	50.8	29 751	22 477	NA	32.4	NA
Lakeville city	11.9	23.6	7.7	24.5	18.6	7.9	3.4	1.7	0.7	49.6	43 128	24 854	NA	73.5	NA
Mankato city	5.4	12.6	33.7	14.7	10.4	6.4	5.8	5.8	5.1	50.9	32 427	31 444	28 650	3.1	9.8
Maple Grove city	10.1	24.4	6.5	21.9	21.3	10.0	3.7	1.5	0.6	50.4	50 365	38 736	20 525	30.0	88.7

Table E. Towns

Town	Total population	Total in house-holds	House-holder	Spouse	Child Total	Child Own child under 18 years	Other relatives Total	Other relatives Under 18 years	Nonrelatives Total	Nonrelatives Unmarried partner	Total in group quarters	Institutionalized population Correctional institutions	Institutionalized population Nursing homes	Institutionalized population Other institutions	Noninstitutionalized population College dormitories	Noninstitutionalized population Military quarters	Other
	54	55	56	57	58	59	60	61	62	63	64	65	66	67	68	69	70
MICHIGAN—Cont'd																	
Farmington Hills city	82 111	98.4	40.9	22.9	28.3	22.0	3.1	0.7	3.3	1.4	1.6	0.0	0.5	0.1	0.1	0.0	0.9
Flint city	124 943	98.0	39.0	11.3	33.7	25.6	7.5	4.0	6.5	3.0	2.0	0.6	0.1	0.1	0.3	0.0	1.0
Flint township	33 691	98.0	41.5	18.9	29.2	22.1	3.8	1.7	4.6	2.5	2.0	0.0	1.2	0.2	0.5	0.0	0.2
Garden City city	30 047	99.9	38.2	21.4	32.1	22.7	4.3	1.8	3.9	1.8	0.1	0.0	0.0	0.0	0.0	0.0	0.1
Georgetown township	41 658	98.8	33.8	24.3	35.5	28.7	1.5	0.6	3.7	0.7	1.2	0.0	0.8	0.0	0.0	0.0	0.4
Grand Blanc township	29 827	98.9	39.5	22.8	30.0	23.9	2.7	1.1	3.9	2.0	1.1	0.0	0.8	0.0	0.0	0.0	0.3
Grand Rapids city	197 800	95.1	37.0	14.9	29.6	23.8	5.8	2.3	7.8	2.3	4.9	0.7	1.3	0.2	1.8	0.0	0.9
Holland township	28 911	97.6	34.0	20.6	34.0	28.9	4.3	1.5	4.7	1.9	2.4	0.0	0.0	0.0	0.0	0.0	2.4
Independence township	32 581	99.1	36.1	24.0	33.2	26.4	2.5	0.9	3.3	1.5	0.9	0.0	0.4	0.0	0.0	0.0	0.5
Inkster city	30 115	99.2	37.1	12.6	34.5	24.3	9.0	4.6	6.0	2.4	0.8	0.0	0.2	0.0	0.0	0.0	0.6
Jackson city	36 316	97.0	39.1	14.0	31.7	25.8	5.0	2.5	7.1	3.2	3.0	0.6	0.9	0.2	0.4	0.0	1.0
Kalamazoo city	77 145	87.6	38.1	11.7	21.7	17.9	3.6	1.5	12.5	2.6	12.4	0.7	0.6	0.3	9.2	0.0	1.5
Kentwood city	45 255	99.2	40.8	19.7	30.5	25.0	3.1	1.0	5.0	2.0	0.8	0.0	0.3	0.1	0.0	0.0	0.4
Lincoln Park city	40 008	99.7	40.5	18.7	30.0	21.6	5.2	2.1	5.2	2.6	0.3	0.0	0.3	0.0	0.0	0.0	0.0
Livonia city	100 545	98.1	37.9	23.8	31.1	22.8	3.0	0.9	2.3	1.0	1.9	0.0	1.0	0.1	0.1	0.0	0.6
Macomb township	50 478	99.9	33.6	24.8	36.4	29.2	2.8	0.8	2.3	1.2	0.1	0.0	0.0	0.0	0.0	0.0	0.1
Madison Heights city	31 101	99.5	42.8	19.3	28.0	20.2	4.7	1.4	4.7	2.0	0.5	0.0	0.4	0.0	0.0	0.0	0.1
Meridian charter township	39 116	98.9	42.0	20.5	27.3	22.9	2.0	0.5	7.1	1.8	1.1	0.0	1.0	0.0	0.0	0.0	0.2
Mount Pleasant city	25 946	77.4	32.6	8.4	12.8	10.8	1.4	0.3	22.2	1.7	22.6	0.6	1.0	0.8	19.4	0.0	0.8
Muskegon city	40 105	88.0	36.3	12.1	27.7	22.0	5.5	2.8	6.4	2.9	12.0	9.8	0.8	0.5	0.4	0.0	0.5
Novi city	47 386	99.4	39.5	22.2	31.8	26.8	2.3	0.5	3.6	1.7	0.6	0.0	0.4	0.0	0.0	0.0	0.1
Oak Park city	29 793	99.9	37.3	16.4	34.8	24.8	7.3	2.9	4.2	1.7	0.1	0.0	0.0	0.0	0.0	0.0	0.1
Orion township	33 463	99.2	36.6	23.0	33.3	27.3	2.4	0.9	3.8	1.8	0.8	0.0	0.6	0.0	0.0	0.0	0.2
Pittsfield charter township	30 167	94.6	39.2	19.0	26.4	22.7	3.3	0.9	6.8	2.4	5.4	4.6	0.3	0.1	0.0	0.0	0.4
Plainfield township	30 195	99.8	36.6	22.8	35.1	28.7	2.1	0.8	3.3	1.5	0.2	0.0	0.0	0.0	0.0	0.0	0.1
Plymouth township	27 798	96.5	38.7	24.4	28.7	21.8	2.3	0.7	2.4	1.1	3.5	3.4	0.0	0.0	0.0	0.0	0.1
Pontiac city	66 337	97.8	36.5	11.5	32.9	24.7	9.0	4.6	7.9	3.2	2.2	0.2	0.4	0.4	0.1	0.0	1.1
Portage city	44 897	99.1	40.4	22.0	30.3	25.2	2.1	0.8	4.3	2.1	0.9	0.0	0.3	0.0	0.0	0.0	0.7
Port Huron city	32 338	97.4	40.1	16.0	30.5	24.1	4.3	1.9	6.6	3.1	2.6	0.8	0.6	0.0	0.0	0.1	1.2
Redford township	51 622	99.3	39.1	19.7	31.4	23.1	4.6	1.7	4.5	2.1	0.7	0.0	0.5	0.0	0.0	0.0	0.2
Rochester Hills city	68 825	98.9	38.2	24.0	31.7	25.2	2.3	0.6	2.6	1.1	1.1	0.0	0.4	0.0	0.4	0.0	0.4
Roseville city	48 129	99.6	41.5	19.3	29.7	21.1	4.4	1.6	4.7	2.4	0.4	0.0	0.3	0.0	0.0	0.0	0.1
Royal Oak city	60 062	99.2	48.1	19.2	23.0	16.8	2.7	0.6	6.3	2.2	0.8	0.0	0.3	0.0	0.0	0.0	0.5
Saginaw city	61 799	97.7	37.5	12.3	35.1	27.0	7.1	3.9	5.7	2.9	2.3	0.6	0.5	0.1	0.0	0.0	1.1
Saginaw charter township	39 657	97.8	43.1	22.1	26.3	19.9	2.2	0.8	4.1	1.6	2.2	0.0	0.9	0.1	0.0	0.0	1.1
St. Clair Shores city	63 096	99.2	43.5	21.5	27.4	18.7	3.5	1.1	3.3	1.7	0.8	0.0	0.6	0.0	0.0	0.0	0.2
Shelby charter township	65 159	99.6	37.6	23.5	31.9	23.7	3.2	0.9	3.4	1.6	0.4	0.0	0.3	0.0	0.0	0.0	0.1
Southfield city	78 296	98.4	43.4	17.5	27.2	18.8	6.1	2.3	4.3	1.7	1.6	0.1	0.8	0.0	0.4	0.0	0.3
Southgate city	30 136	99.3	42.6	21.0	28.1	19.8	3.8	1.4	3.9	1.9	0.7	0.0	0.3	0.2	0.0	0.0	0.1
Sterling Heights city	124 471	99.0	37.2	22.5	32.4	22.8	4.4	1.0	2.5	1.2	1.0	0.0	0.5	0.0	0.0	0.0	0.4
Taylor city	65 868	98.9	37.6	18.3	32.7	24.2	5.3	2.4	5.0	2.6	1.1	0.0	0.7	0.2	0.0	0.0	0.2
Troy city	80 959	99.7	37.1	23.9	33.0	25.4	3.3	0.6	2.5	0.9	0.3	0.0	0.0	0.0	0.0	0.0	0.3
Warren city	138 247	99.1	40.2	20.0	29.4	20.8	5.1	1.6	4.4	2.1	0.9	0.0	0.7	0.0	0.0	0.0	0.2
Waterford township	73 150	97.4	40.2	20.7	27.8	21.4	3.4	1.2	5.2	2.4	2.6	1.8	0.4	0.0	0.0	0.0	0.4
West Bloomfield township	64 860	98.8	36.1	25.1	32.4	25.5	3.2	0.7	1.9	0.8	1.2	0.0	0.9	0.0	0.0	0.0	0.3
Westland city	86 602	98.9	42.2	18.7	28.5	21.3	4.1	1.5	5.4	2.6	1.1	0.0	0.7	0.3	0.0	0.0	0.1
White Lake township	28 219	99.0	35.8	23.3	33.3	26.1	3.1	1.2	3.6	1.9	1.0	0.5	0.2	0.0	0.0	0.0	0.3
Wyandotte city	28 006	99.7	42.2	19.5	28.8	20.4	4.5	1.8	4.7	2.4	0.3	0.0	0.0	0.1	0.0	0.0	0.2
Wyoming city	69 368	99.5	38.3	19.0	32.1	25.8	4.2	1.6	5.9	2.5	0.5	0.0	0.1	0.0	0.1	0.0	0.2
Ypsilanti township	49 182	99.9	41.1	17.0	29.5	23.3	5.2	2.4	7.0	3.1	0.1	0.0	0.0	0.1	0.0	0.0	0.1
MINNESOTA	4 919 479	97.2	38.5	20.7	29.9	24.6	2.8	1.0	5.3	2.0	2.8	0.3	0.8	0.1	0.9	0.0	0.6
Andover city	26 588	100.0	30.5	24.4	40.2	34.2	2.1	0.9	2.8	1.2	0.0	0.0	0.0	0.0	0.0	0.0	0.0
Apple Valley city	45 527	99.5	35.9	22.9	34.9	28.6	2.3	0.8	3.5	1.5	0.5	0.0	0.4	0.0	0.0	0.0	0.1
Blaine city	44 942	99.8	35.4	21.6	34.2	27.1	3.5	1.4	5.1	2.3	0.2	0.0	0.0	0.0	0.0	0.0	0.2
Bloomington city	85 172	98.4	42.7	21.9	25.1	19.3	3.0	0.9	5.7	2.0	1.6	0.0	0.8	0.1	0.1	0.0	0.6
Brooklyn Center city	29 172	98.7	39.2	18.2	29.7	22.6	5.5	1.9	6.1	2.4	1.3	0.0	0.6	0.0	0.0	0.0	0.7
Brooklyn Park city	67 388	99.7	36.3	19.8	33.1	26.7	5.2	1.7	5.3	2.2	0.3	0.0	0.0	0.0	0.0	0.0	0.3
Burnsville city	60 220	99.4	39.3	20.8	30.1	24.9	2.9	0.9	6.4	2.5	0.6	0.0	0.0	0.2	0.0	0.0	0.4
Coon Rapids city	61 607	99.4	36.6	21.0	33.7	27.0	3.1	1.2	5.0	2.2	0.6	0.0	0.3	0.0	0.0	0.0	0.3
Cottage Grove city	30 582	99.8	32.5	23.7	38.4	31.3	2.2	0.9	3.1	1.4	0.2	0.0	0.0	0.0	0.0	0.0	0.2
Duluth city	86 918	92.5	40.8	16.9	24.5	19.7	2.2	0.8	8.0	2.4	7.5	0.9	1.3	0.3	3.8	0.0	1.2
Eagan city	63 557	99.7	37.4	21.6	33.6	29.0	2.3	0.7	4.8	1.8	0.3	0.0	0.0	0.0	0.0	0.0	0.3
Eden Prairie city	54 901	99.7	37.3	22.8	33.8	29.9	1.7	0.3	4.1	1.5	0.3	0.0	0.1	0.0	0.0	0.0	0.2
Edina city	47 425	99.4	44.3	23.8	26.5	22.3	1.6	0.4	3.2	1.1	0.6	0.0	0.6	0.0	0.0	0.0	0.1
Fridley city	27 449	99.2	41.3	20.1	27.3	20.8	3.7	1.3	6.9	2.9	0.8	0.0	0.0	0.0	0.0	0.0	0.6
Inver Grove Heights city	29 751	99.1	37.8	21.4	31.9	26.1	2.6	0.8	5.5	2.3	0.9	0.0	0.5	0.2	0.0	0.0	0.2
Lakeville city	43 128	99.9	31.6	23.2	39.8	34.9	1.9	0.7	3.4	1.4	0.1	0.0	0.0	0.0	0.0	0.0	0.1
Mankato city	32 427	88.2	38.1	14.0	19.5	16.1	1.9	0.4	14.6	2.4	11.8	0.2	0.8	0.0	9.4	0.0	1.4
Maple Grove city	50 365	99.9	34.8	24.2	36.1	30.1	1.8	0.5	2.9	1.3	0.1	0.0	0.0	0.0	0.0	0.0	0.1

Table E. Towns

	Households by type, 2000												Households, 1990		
		Family households						Nonfamily households							
				Married couple		Female householder[1]			Householder living alone						House-holder living alone
Town	Total households	Total	With own children under 18 years	Total	With own children under 18 years	Total	With own children under 18 years	Total	Total	65 years and over	Average house-hold size	Average family size	Total house-holds	Female house-holder[1]	
	71	72	73	74	75	76	77	78	79	80	81	82	83	84	85
MICHIGAN—Cont'd															
Farmington Hills city	33 559	65.0	29.5	56.0	25.3	6.6	3.3	35.0	29.6	10.2	2.41	3.04	29 234	5.6	25.5
Flint city	48 744	62.1	33.5	29.0	12.6	27.5	18.1	37.9	31.9	9.9	2.51	3.16	53 894	26.0	29.1
Flint township	13 972	64.6	30.4	45.5	18.4	14.9	9.4	35.4	30.5	12.6	2.36	2.94	13 907	11.7	28.1
Garden City city	11 479	71.7	32.5	56.0	25.3	11.2	5.1	28.3	24.0	9.7	2.62	3.11	11 213	10.2	17.7
Georgetown township	14 099	79.0	41.0	71.9	36.7	5.1	3.2	21.0	15.7	7.6	2.92	3.29	10 230	4.2	10.8
Grand Blanc township	11 793	69.4	33.5	57.6	26.6	8.6	5.1	30.6	25.2	5.9	2.50	3.02	9 678	9.0	22.0
Grand Rapids city	73 217	60.6	32.0	40.3	19.4	15.8	10.3	39.4	30.8	10.0	2.57	3.24	69 029	15.6	27.0
Holland township	9 821	75.0	43.2	60.8	33.7	9.9	7.0	25.0	19.6	5.0	2.87	3.32	6 053	7.5	19.1
Independence township	11 765	77.3	39.1	66.5	33.0	7.9	4.5	22.7	17.9	4.7	2.75	3.14	8 408	7.5	13.3
Inkster city	11 169	66.8	33.1	34.0	14.8	26.8	15.7	33.2	27.9	9.2	2.67	3.26	11 201	24.5	26.8
Jackson city	14 210	61.0	33.7	35.8	16.5	19.9	13.9	39.0	32.0	10.8	2.48	3.12	14 723	18.9	31.4
Kalamazoo city	29 413	48.8	24.9	30.6	12.8	14.7	10.3	51.2	34.8	9.6	2.30	2.99	29 409	15.8	31.5
Kentwood city	18 477	62.4	33.3	48.3	24.4	10.8	7.1	37.6	30.9	8.2	2.43	3.10	15 247	9.5	28.2
Lincoln Park city	16 204	65.3	30.2	46.3	21.0	13.3	6.4	34.7	29.3	11.3	2.46	3.04	16 257	11.6	25.2
Livonia city	38 089	73.7	32.5	62.8	28.0	8.0	3.4	26.3	22.9	11.1	2.59	3.07	35 916	7.4	17.7
Macomb township	16 946	83.0	45.3	73.7	40.3	6.5	3.7	17.0	13.7	3.9	2.97	3.30	7 355	7.3	12.1
Madison Heights city	13 299	60.2	26.9	45.2	20.0	10.5	5.2	39.8	33.8	12.3	2.33	3.02	12 850	10.1	28.5
Meridian charter township	16 414	59.6	30.2	48.9	23.5	8.2	5.4	40.4	29.1	6.8	2.36	2.99	14 022	8.5	26.2
Mount Pleasant city	8 449	37.0	18.8	25.9	11.6	8.5	5.8	63.0	29.6	8.8	2.38	2.88	6 661	9.4	26.4
Muskegon city	14 569	58.6	31.1	33.2	14.4	20.2	13.7	41.4	34.4	12.9	2.42	3.13	14 770	19.2	31.3
Novi city	18 726	65.8	36.3	56.2	31.0	7.1	4.1	34.2	28.1	5.9	2.52	3.17	12 699	7.3	23.2
Oak Park city	11 104	68.4	34.4	44.0	21.9	19.5	10.4	31.6	26.6	10.4	2.68	3.29	10 885	16.2	21.7
Orion township	12 246	73.3	39.7	63.0	33.6	6.9	4.3	26.7	20.8	4.0	2.71	3.19	8 571	6.5	19.4
Pittsfield charter township	11 817	58.9	31.5	48.5	25.6	7.3	4.6	41.1	29.8	4.1	2.42	3.11	7 020	8.7	29.3
Plainfield township	11 038	74.0	39.9	62.3	32.2	8.7	6.0	26.0	21.7	6.7	2.73	3.22	8 884	7.7	19.3
Plymouth township	10 757	71.4	30.7	63.1	26.8	6.1	2.9	28.6	24.7	9.2	2.49	3.01	8 815	6.5	20.7
Pontiac city	24 234	63.0	33.9	31.5	14.9	25.2	15.9	37.0	29.4	8.0	2.68	3.32	24 777	24.9	26.0
Portage city	18 138	66.9	34.2	54.4	25.8	9.7	6.6	33.1	27.2	8.4	2.45	3.01	15 467	8.3	21.6
Port Huron city	12 961	62.1	32.4	39.8	17.6	17.5	12.1	37.9	31.9	13.2	2.43	3.04	13 158	18.4	28.1
Redford township	20 182	67.3	31.8	50.4	23.9	12.1	5.8	32.7	27.3	11.6	2.54	3.12	20 123	10.8	20.9
Rochester Hills city	26 315	72.1	35.7	62.8	30.8	6.8	3.7	27.9	24.0	8.4	2.59	3.11	22 353	6.6	19.3
Roseville city	19 976	63.7	28.6	46.4	20.5	12.7	6.1	36.3	30.8	12.6	2.40	3.02	19 537	12.4	24.7
Royal Oak city	28 880	50.0	20.4	39.9	16.3	7.5	3.3	50.0	40.8	11.6	2.06	2.86	28 344	8.5	32.2
Saginaw city	23 182	65.2	35.4	32.9	14.1	27.3	18.8	34.8	29.5	9.9	2.60	3.23	26 179	24.8	27.9
Saginaw charter township	17 096	62.5	25.8	51.3	19.6	8.8	5.0	37.5	31.9	15.0	2.27	2.88	15 293	8.7	27.4
St. Clair Shores city	27 434	63.0	24.1	49.5	19.1	10.0	3.8	37.0	32.7	16.3	2.28	2.92	27 218	9.2	26.0
Shelby charter township	24 486	73.2	33.7	62.6	28.4	7.3	3.8	26.8	21.6	6.6	2.65	3.13	16 836	7.2	15.3
Southfield city	33 987	58.2	25.3	40.2	16.4	14.3	7.5	41.8	36.2	11.9	2.27	3.01	32 112	9.6	32.2
Southgate city	12 836	62.7	26.7	49.2	20.6	9.7	4.5	37.3	32.3	14.1	2.33	2.98	12 128	8.9	26.9
Sterling Heights city	46 319	72.1	32.9	60.4	27.8	8.5	4.0	27.9	24.1	8.5	2.66	3.21	40 835	8.1	19.1
Taylor city	24 776	71.6	34.9	48.7	21.4	17.4	10.7	28.4	23.1	7.6	2.63	3.09	24 861	16.3	18.1
Troy city	30 018	72.9	36.9	64.5	33.2	6.0	2.9	27.1	22.8	7.8	2.69	3.23	26 167	6.3	20.3
Warren city	55 551	66.1	27.8	49.7	20.3	11.7	5.5	33.9	28.8	12.0	2.47	3.05	54 602	10.9	22.6
Waterford township	29 387	65.1	30.4	51.6	23.1	9.6	5.4	34.9	27.9	8.1	2.42	2.99	25 476	10.6	22.3
West Bloomfield township	23 414	77.7	37.0	69.5	33.1	5.8	2.9	22.3	19.4	7.5	2.74	3.17	19 226	5.5	15.6
Westland city	36 533	60.9	28.6	44.4	19.9	12.1	6.6	39.1	32.6	11.3	2.34	3.00	33 110	11.7	26.8
White Lake township	10 092	77.5	39.0	65.0	32.1	8.7	4.9	22.5	17.6	4.5	2.77	3.15	7 776	10.3	15.3
Wyandotte city	11 816	62.8	27.7	46.3	20.0	11.9	5.6	37.2	31.9	13.3	2.36	2.99	12 319	12.7	27.8
Wyoming city	26 536	66.1	35.7	49.6	25.4	12.0	7.8	33.9	26.6	7.4	2.60	3.19	24 168	10.2	23.4
Ypsilanti township	20 194	61.1	31.1	41.5	19.3	14.9	9.5	38.9	29.7	5.3	2.43	3.06	17 637	13.5	25.3
MINNESOTA	1 895 127	66.2	33.0	53.7	25.2	8.9	5.9	33.8	26.9	9.3	2.52	3.09	1 647 853	8.6	25.1
Andover city	8 107	88.2	55.1	80.0	49.7	5.5	3.7	11.8	8.4	2.3	3.28	3.48	4 430	4.3	5.6
Apple Valley city	16 344	75.9	42.5	63.7	34.6	9.0	6.0	24.1	19.3	4.0	2.77	3.21	11 145	8.3	12.7
Blaine city	15 898	76.6	41.1	61.1	31.7	11.1	7.1	23.4	17.0	3.3	2.82	3.19	12 825	9.9	12.5
Bloomington city	36 400	62.5	25.1	51.2	19.0	8.2	4.7	37.5	29.6	9.9	2.30	2.87	34 488	7.7	23.4
Brooklyn Center city	11 430	64.6	29.7	46.3	18.8	13.4	8.4	35.4	28.2	11.0	2.52	3.11	11 226	12.1	21.5
Brooklyn Park city	24 432	71.0	39.2	54.6	28.9	12.1	8.1	29.0	22.0	3.7	2.75	3.26	20 386	12.7	19.1
Burnsville city	23 687	66.0	34.1	52.8	25.5	10.0	6.8	34.0	24.8	4.8	2.53	3.07	19 127	9.2	19.5
Coon Rapids city	22 578	73.4	39.1	57.3	28.7	12.2	8.4	26.6	20.1	5.1	2.71	3.15	17 449	9.4	13.4
Cottage Grove city	9 932	85.2	49.8	72.9	41.7	8.8	6.2	14.8	11.0	2.7	3.07	3.32	6 856	6.3	7.1
Duluth city	35 500	56.1	26.6	41.4	17.2	11.4	7.6	43.9	34.5	13.3	2.26	2.90	34 563	10.9	31.3
Eagan city	23 773	69.1	41.2	57.9	33.8	8.4	5.8	30.9	23.0	2.6	2.67	3.23	17 427	7.0	18.9
Eden Prairie city	20 457	71.3	42.6	61.3	35.6	7.7	5.6	28.7	22.0	3.4	2.68	3.20	14 447	7.2	17.8
Edina city	20 996	64.6	26.5	53.8	22.6	5.8	3.1	38.7	34.0	18.5	2.24	2.91	19 860	5.4	29.7
Fridley city	11 328	64.6	28.2	48.6	18.4	11.6	7.4	35.4	26.8	6.3	2.40	2.91	10 909	11.6	20.4
Inver Grove Heights city	11 257	70.4	37.3	56.4	28.1	10.3	7.1	29.6	21.5	4.7	2.62	3.09	7 803	12.3	16.4
Lakeville city	13 609	84.7	56.0	73.6	48.0	7.5	5.7	15.3	10.7	1.9	3.17	3.43	7 851	6.7	10.8
Mankato city	12 367	49.0	23.6	36.7	16.0	8.8	6.0	51.0	32.2	9.9	2.31	2.90	11 217	7.7	27.2
Maple Grove city	17 532	79.6	46.3	69.5	39.8	7.5	5.0	20.4	15.8	2.6	2.87	3.24	12 531	6.6	11.2

[1] No spouse present.

Table E. Towns

Town	Percent change of households, 1990-2000	Total housing units	Occupied housing units (percent)	Vacant housing units Total	For seasonal, recreational, or occasional use	Homeowner vacancy rate (percent)	Rental vacancy rate (percent)	Occupied housing units Total	Percent owner-occupied housing units	Percent renter-occupied housing units	Average household size of owner-occupied units	Average household size of renter-occupied units
	86	87	88	89	90	91	92	93	94	95	96	97
MICHIGAN—Cont'd												
Farmington Hills city	14.8	34 858	96.3	3.7	0.8	0.5	5.1	33 559	66.9	33.1	2.72	1.77
Flint city	-9.6	55 464	87.9	12.1	0.3	2.7	13.1	48 744	58.8	41.2	2.45	2.59
Flint township	0.5	14 864	94.0	6.0	0.4	1.9	9.3	13 972	68.6	31.4	2.53	2.00
Garden City city	2.4	11 719	98.0	2.0	0.2	0.5	3.6	11 479	86.2	13.8	2.71	2.03
Georgetown township	37.8	14 442	97.6	2.4	0.3	0.9	2.6	14 099	83.7	16.3	3.06	2.20
Grand Blanc township	21.9	12 450	94.7	5.3	0.7	1.9	6.2	11 793	74.0	26.0	2.72	1.87
Grand Rapids city	6.1	77 960	93.9	6.1	0.3	1.3	6.6	73 217	59.7	40.3	2.69	2.39
Holland township	62.3	10 385	94.6	5.4	0.6	1.4	8.2	9 821	71.2	28.8	3.00	2.56
Independence township........	39.9	12 375	95.1	4.9	0.8	1.7	10.8	11 765	83.2	16.8	2.89	2.04
Inkster city	-0.3	12 013	93.0	7.0	0.2	1.7	7.7	11 169	58.0	42.0	2.76	2.55
Jackson city	-3.5	15 241	93.2	6.8	0.3	1.5	7.9	14 210	57.6	42.4	2.55	2.38
Kalamazoo city	0.0	31 798	92.5	7.5	0.4	2.1	6.9	29 413	47.7	52.3	2.43	2.18
Kentwood city	21.2	19 507	94.7	5.3	0.5	1.3	7.0	18 477	61.0	39.0	2.71	1.99
Lincoln Park city	-0.3	16 821	96.3	3.7	0.3	1.0	5.8	16 204	79.1	20.9	2.57	2.06
Livonia city	6.1	38 658	98.5	1.5	0.2	0.4	2.7	38 089	88.8	11.2	2.68	1.86
Macomb township	130.4	17 922	94.6	5.4	0.1	2.8	11.6	16 946	96.5	3.5	3.00	2.28
Madison Heights city	3.5	13 623	97.6	2.4	0.3	0.8	3.0	13 299	70.1	29.9	2.50	1.93
Meridian charter township	17.1	17 120	95.9	4.1	0.6	0.7	5.2	16 414	62.1	37.9	2.63	1.90
Mount Pleasant city	26.8	8 878	95.2	4.8	0.4	1.7	4.5	8 449	34.3	65.7	2.43	2.35
Muskegon city	-1.4	15 999	91.1	8.9	0.5	2.9	7.8	14 569	56.9	43.1	2.58	2.21
Novi city	47.5	19 649	95.3	4.7	0.5	1.2	7.0	18 726	71.1	28.9	2.78	1.88
Oak Park city	2.0	11 370	97.7	2.3	0.2	1.1	2.7	11 104	74.8	25.2	2.74	2.52
Orion township.....................	42.9	12 837	95.4	4.6	1.1	1.6	5.0	12 246	81.7	18.3	2.86	2.01
Pittsfield charter township	68.3	12 337	95.8	4.2	0.4	1.3	4.1	11 817	56.0	44.0	2.83	1.89
Plainfield township	24.2	11 456	96.4	3.6	0.5	1.5	4.9	11 038	82.1	17.9	2.88	2.06
Plymouth township	22.0	11 043	97.4	2.6	0.5	0.8	3.3	10 757	83.4	16.6	2.65	1.69
Pontiac city	-2.2	26 336	92.0	8.0	0.2	2.0	8.6	24 234	52.8	47.2	2.76	2.59
Portage city	17.3	18 880	96.1	3.9	0.4	1.4	5.2	18 138	68.9	31.1	2.71	1.88
Port Huron city	-1.5	14 003	92.6	7.4	0.7	2.0	7.9	12 961	57.2	42.8	2.54	2.29
Redford township	0.3	20 605	97.9	2.1	0.2	0.6	4.2	20 182	90.1	9.9	2.57	2.29
Rochester Hills city	17.7	27 263	96.5	3.5	0.5	1.0	6.1	26 315	79.1	20.9	2.76	1.92
Roseville city	2.2	20 519	97.4	2.6	0.3	0.9	3.3	19 976	75.2	24.8	2.53	2.01
Royal Oak city	1.9	29 942	96.5	3.5	0.7	0.8	4.5	28 880	70.1	29.9	2.24	1.65
Saginaw city	-11.4	25 639	90.4	9.6	0.2	2.2	7.6	23 182	63.6	36.4	2.61	2.59
Saginaw charter township	11.8	17 859	95.7	4.3	0.5	1.1	5.9	17 096	65.3	34.7	2.52	1.79
St. Clair Shores city	0.8	28 208	97.3	2.7	0.5	0.8	4.0	27 434	85.8	14.2	2.36	1.81
Shelby charter township	45.4	25 265	96.9	3.1	0.2	1.2	4.4	24 486	78.4	21.6	2.80	2.10
Southfield city	5.8	35 698	95.2	4.8	0.3	1.1	5.8	33 987	54.1	45.9	2.64	1.83
Southgate city	5.8	13 361	96.1	3.9	0.5	1.2	4.8	12 836	70.6	29.4	2.58	1.73
Sterling Heights city	13.4	47 547	97.4	2.6	0.3	0.9	3.7	46 319	79.0	21.0	2.87	1.88
Taylor city	-0.3	25 905	95.6	4.4	0.2	1.5	5.8	24 776	70.8	29.2	2.67	2.53
Troy city	14.7	30 872	97.2	2.8	0.7	0.5	3.7	30 018	77.3	22.7	2.92	1.91
Warren city	1.7	57 249	97.0	3.0	0.3	0.8	4.4	55 551	80.4	19.6	2.55	2.12
Waterford township	15.4	30 404	96.7	3.3	0.6	0.9	4.6	29 387	76.3	23.7	2.56	2.00
West Bloomfield township	21.8	24 410	95.9	4.1	1.3	1.0	6.6	23 414	86.7	13.3	2.82	2.20
Westland city	10.3	38 077	95.9	4.1	0.3	1.5	5.2	36 533	62.7	37.3	2.57	1.97
White Lake township	29.8	10 616	95.1	4.9	2.0	1.3	5.3	10 092	91.9	8.1	2.80	2.35
Wyandotte city	-4.1	12 303	96.0	4.0	0.3	1.1	4.4	11 816	73.0	27.0	2.53	1.91
Wyoming city	9.8	27 506	96.5	3.5	0.2	1.0	5.6	26 536	67.6	32.4	2.80	2.18
Ypsilanti township................	14.5	21 196	95.3	4.7	0.4	1.3	6.0	20 194	59.8	40.2	2.64	2.12
MINNESOTA	15.0	2 065 946	91.7	8.3	5.1	0.9	4.1	1 895 127	74.6	25.4	2.69	2.03
Andover city	83.0	8 205	98.8	1.2	0.1	0.6	1.1	8 107	95.7	4.3	3.32	2.34
Apple Valley city	46.6	16 536	98.8	1.2	0.2	0.3	2.2	16 344	88.0	12.0	2.86	2.14
Blaine city	24.0	16 169	98.3	1.7	0.1	0.8	0.9	15 898	90.5	9.5	2.87	2.32
Bloomington city	5.5	37 104	98.1	1.9	0.4	0.3	3.0	36 400	70.6	29.4	2.48	1.88
Brooklyn Center city	1.8	11 598	98.6	1.4	0.2	0.4	2.3	11 430	68.7	31.3	2.70	2.13
Brooklyn Park city	19.8	24 846	98.3	1.7	0.2	0.4	2.9	24 432	73.4	26.6	2.94	2.22
Burnsville city	23.8	24 261	97.6	2.4	0.4	0.4	3.4	23 687	68.1	31.9	2.71	2.14
Coon Rapids city	29.4	22 828	98.9	1.1	0.2	0.5	1.1	22 578	80.4	19.6	2.81	2.30
Cottage Grove city................	44.9	10 024	99.1	0.9	0.1	0.2	4.3	9 932	91.4	8.6	3.09	2.92
Duluth city	2.7	36 994	96.0	4.0	0.5	1.0	3.4	35 500	64.1	35.9	2.46	1.91
Eagan city	36.4	24 390	97.5	2.5	0.3	0.2	5.6	23 773	75.0	25.0	2.85	2.11
Eden Prairie city	41.6	21 026	97.3	2.7	0.7	0.4	3.9	20 457	78.3	21.7	2.83	2.11
Edina city	5.7	21 669	96.9	3.1	1.4	0.5	2.5	20 996	76.5	23.5	2.42	1.66
Fridley city	3.8	11 504	98.5	1.5	0.2	0.4	2.0	11 328	67.7	32.3	2.51	2.19
Inver Grove Heights city........	44.3	11 457	98.3	1.7	0.2	0.6	2.2	11 257	77.5	22.5	2.72	2.27
Lakeville city	73.3	13 799	98.6	1.4	0.2	0.5	2.3	13 609	91.8	8.2	3.22	2.55
Mankato city	10.3	12 759	96.9	3.1	0.2	0.9	2.6	12 367	52.9	47.1	2.51	2.09
Maple Grove city	39.9	17 745	98.8	1.2	0.2	0.3	2.3	17 532	92.7	7.3	2.92	2.24

Table E. Towns

STATE MCD code	Town	Land area, 2000[1] (sq km)	Population, 2000			Land area, 1990[1] (sq km)	Population, 1990			Population and population characteristics, 2000					
										White	Black or African American	American Indian or Alaska Native	Asian	Native Hawaiian and other Pacific Islander	Some other race
			Total persons	Rank within state	Per square kilometer		Total persons	Rank within state	Per square kilometer			Race (percent)			
												One race			
		1	2	3	4	5	6	7	8	9	10	11	12	13	14
	MINNESOTA—Cont'd														
27 40382	Maplewood city	44.9	34 947	22	778.3	44.9	30 954	22	689.4	88.7	3.5	0.6	4.5	0.1	0.7
27 43000	Minneapolis city	142.2	382 618	1	2 690.7	142.3	368 383	1	2 588.8	65.1	18.0	2.2	6.1	0.1	4.1
27 43252	Minnetonka city	70.3	51 301	10	729.7	70.2	48 370	10	689.0	94.4	1.5	0.2	2.3	0.0	0.6
27 43864	Moorhead city	34.8	32 177	20	924.6	26.1	32 295	20	1 237.4	92.1	0.8	1.9	1.3	0.0	2.1
27 47680	Oakdale city	28.7	26 653	31	928.7	25.7	18 377	31	715.1	92.2	2.3	0.4	2.5	0.0	0.8
27 51730	Plymouth city	85.2	65 894	9	773.4	85.3	50 889	9	596.6	91.4	2.7	0.3	3.8	0.0	0.5
27 54214	Richfield city	17.9	34 439	17	1 924.0	17.8	35 710	17	2 006.2	81.2	6.6	0.7	5.3	0.0	3.4
27 54880	Rochester city	102.6	85 806	5	836.3	76.3	70 729	5	927.0	87.5	3.6	0.3	5.6	0.0	1.2
27 55852	Roseville city	34.3	33 690	19	982.2	34.3	33 485	19	976.2	89.5	2.8	0.3	4.9	0.1	0.8
27 57220	St. Louis Park city	27.7	44 126	13	1 593.0	27.8	43 787	13	1 575.1	88.9	4.4	0.4	3.2	0.1	1.3
27 58000	St. Paul city	136.7	287 151	2	2 100.6	136.7	272 235	2	1 991.5	67.0	11.7	1.1	12.4	0.1	3.8
27 59998	Shoreview city	29.0	25 924	27	893.9	29.0	24 587	27	847.8	93.3	1.0	0.2	3.6	0.1	0.4
27 71032	Winona city	47.2	27 069	25	573.5	30.7	25 435	25	828.5	94.5	1.1	0.2	2.7	0.0	0.5
27 71428	Woodbury city	90.6	46 463	30	512.8	90.7	20 075	30	221.3	90.0	2.5	0.2	5.0	0.0	0.6
33 00000	**NEW HAMPSHIRE**	23 227	1 235 786	X	53.2	23 231	1 109 252	X	47.7	96.0	0.7	0.2	1.3	0.0	0.6
33 14200	Concord city	166.5	40 687	3	244.4	166.5	36 006	3	216.3	95.5	1.0	0.3	1.5	0.0	0.3
33 17940	Derry town	92.7	34 021	4	367.0	92.7	29 603	4	319.3	96.0	0.9	0.2	1.1	0.0	0.6
33 18820	Dover city	69.2	26 884	7	388.5	69.2	25 042	7	361.9	94.5	1.1	0.2	2.4	0.1	0.3
33 45140	Manchester city	85.5	107 006	1	1 251.5	85.5	99 332	1	1 161.8	91.7	2.1	0.3	2.3	0.0	1.8
33 47540	Merrimack town	84.4	25 119	8	297.6	84.5	22 156	8	262.2	96.6	0.7	0.2	1.5	0.0	0.2
33 50260	Nashua city	80.0	86 605	2	1 082.6	80.1	79 662	2	994.5	89.2	2.0	0.3	3.9	0.0	3.1
33 65140	Rochester city	116.9	28 461	5	243.5	117.0	26 630	5	227.6	97.1	0.5	0.2	0.9	0.0	0.3
33 66660	Salem town	64.0	28 112	6	439.3	64.0	25 746	6	402.3	95.0	0.6	0.2	2.3	0.1	0.8
34 00000	**NEW JERSEY**	19 211	8 414 350	X	438.0	19 215	7 747 750	X	403.2	72.6	13.6	0.2	5.7	0.0	5.4
34 02080	Atlantic City city	29.4	40 517	39	1 378.1	29.4	37 986	39	1 292.0	26.7	44.2	0.5	10.4	0.1	13.8
34 03580	Bayonne city	14.6	61 842	16	4 235.8	14.6	61 464	16	4 209.9	78.6	5.5	0.2	4.1	0.0	7.5
34 04695	Belleville township	8.7	35 928	51	4 129.7	8.7	34 213	51	3 932.5	69.4	5.4	0.2	11.3	0.1	9.8
34 05170	Bergenfield borough	7.5	26 247	84	3 499.6	7.5	24 458	84	3 261.1	62.9	6.9	0.2	20.4	0.0	6.5
34 05305	Berkeley township	111.1	39 991	42	360.0	111.1	37 319	42	335.9	97.1	1.3	0.05	0.5	0.0	0.4
34 06260	Bloomfield township	13.8	47 683	29	3 455.3	13.8	45 061	29	3 265.3	70.1	11.7	0.2	8.4	0.1	6.4
34 07420	Brick township	67.9	76 119	15	1 121.0	68.1	66 415	15	975.3	95.8	1.0	0.1	1.4	0.0	0.9
34 07720	Bridgewater township	84.0	42 940	55	511.2	84.0	32 509	55	387.0	85.1	2.2	0.1	10.5	0.0	0.9
34 10000	Camden city	22.8	79 904	8	3 504.6	22.8	87 492	8	3 837.4	16.8	53.3	0.5	2.5	0.1	22.8
34 12280	Cherry Hill township	62.8	69 965	13	1 114.1	62.8	69 348	13	1 104.3	84.7	4.5	0.1	8.9	0.0	0.7
34 13045	City of Orange township	5.7	32 868	62	5 766.3	5.7	29 925	62	5 250.0	13.2	75.1	0.3	1.3	0.1	5.2
34 13690	Clifton city	29.3	78 672	12	2 685.1	29.3	71 984	12	2 456.8	76.2	2.9	0.2	6.4	0.0	9.6
34 17710	Deptford township	45.3	26 763	85	590.8	45.3	24 137	85	532.8	83.4	12.4	0.2	1.5	0.0	1.0
34 18130	Dover township	106.1	89 706	10	845.5	106.5	76 388	10	717.3	93.6	1.7	0.1	2.5	0.0	0.9
34 19000	East Brunswick township	56.9	46 756	31	821.7	57.0	43 548	31	764.0	77.6	2.8	0.1	16.3	0.0	1.1
34 19390	East Orange city	10.2	69 824	11	6 845.5	10.2	73 552	11	7 211.0	3.8	89.5	0.3	0.4	0.1	2.1
34 20230	Edison township	78.0	97 687	6	1 252.4	78.2	88 680	6	1 134.0	59.5	6.9	0.1	29.3	0.0	2.0
34 20290	Egg Harbor township	174.4	30 726	83	176.2	174.3	24 544	83	140.8	79.4	10.4	0.2	5.1	0.0	2.8
34 21000	Elizabeth city	31.7	120 568	4	3 803.4	31.9	110 002	4	3 448.3	55.8	20.0	0.5	2.3	0.0	15.5
34 21480	Englewood city	12.8	26 203	80	2 047.1	12.8	24 850	80	1 941.4	42.5	39.0	0.3	5.2	0.0	8.5
34 22110	Evesham township	76.5	42 275	47	552.6	76.5	35 309	47	461.6	91.3	3.1	0.1	4.1	0.0	0.5
34 22185	Ewing township	39.7	35 707	52	899.4	39.7	34 185	52	861.1	69.0	24.8	0.2	2.3	0.1	1.8
34 22470	Fair Lawn borough	13.4	31 637	59	2 361.0	13.4	30 548	59	2 279.7	91.5	0.7	0.0	4.9	0.0	1.4
34 24420	Fort Lee borough	6.6	35 461	56	5 372.9	6.6	31 997	56	4 848.0	62.8	1.7	0.1	31.4	0.1	1.7
34 24900	Franklin township	121.1	50 903	32	420.3	121.2	42 780	32	353.0	55.1	26.0	0.2	12.7	0.0	3.6
34 25230	Freehold township	99.6	31 537	81	316.6	99.8	24 710	81	247.6	87.1	5.1	0.1	5.1	0.0	1.2
34 25560	Galloway township	234.4	31 209	86	133.1	234.1	23 330	86	99.7	77.2	9.8	0.2	8.0	0.0	2.6
34 25770	Garfield city	5.5	29 786	69	5 415.6	5.5	26 727	69	4 859.5	82.1	3.0	0.3	2.7	0.0	8.1
34 26760	Gloucester township	60.1	64 350	22	1 070.7	60.2	53 797	22	893.6	83.1	11.5	0.2	2.6	0.0	1.1
34 28680	Hackensack city	10.7	42 677	43	3 988.5	10.7	37 049	43	3 462.5	52.6	24.6	0.4	7.5	0.1	9.7
34 29310	Hamilton township	102.2	87 109	9	852.3	102.2	86 553	9	846.9	85.1	8.2	0.1	2.6	0.0	2.2
34 31890	Hillsborough township	141.6	36 634	64	258.7	141.6	28 808	64	203.4	86.0	3.8	0.1	7.3	0.1	1.3
34 32250	Hoboken city	3.3	38 577	53	11 690.0	3.3	33 397	53	10 120.3	80.8	4.3	0.2	4.3	0.1	7.6
34 33300	Howell township	157.8	48 903	37	309.9	157.8	38 987	37	247.1	90.0	3.6	0.1	3.6	0.0	1.3
34 34450	Irvington township	7.7	60 695	17	7 882.5	7.6	61 018	17	8 028.7	9.0	81.7	0.2	1.1	0.1	3.7
34 34680	Jackson township	259.1	42 816	54	165.2	259.2	33 233	54	128.2	91.3	3.9	0.1	2.1	0.0	1.0
34 36000	Jersey City city	38.6	240 055	2	6 219.0	38.5	228 517	2	5 935.5	34.0	28.3	0.4	16.2	0.1	15.1
34 36510	Kearny town	23.7	40 513	49	1 709.4	23.7	34 874	49	1 471.5	75.7	4.0	0.4	5.5	0.0	10.0
34 37380	Lacey township	217.6	25 346	88	116.5	217.6	22 141	88	101.8	97.8	0.4	0.1	0.5	0.0	0.4
34 38550	Lakewood township	64.3	60 352	30	938.6	64.3	45 048	30	700.6	78.8	12.0	0.2	1.4	0.0	4.6
34 39510	Lawrence township	57.3	29 159	75	508.9	57.4	25 787	75	449.3	79.2	9.3	0.1	7.9	0.1	1.8
34 40350	Linden city	28.0	39 394	44	1 406.9	28.0	36 701	44	1 310.8	66.1	22.8	0.1	2.3	0.0	4.9
34 40890	Livingston township	36.0	27 391	72	760.9	36.0	26 609	72	739.1	82.6	1.2	0.1	14.5	0.0	0.7
34 41310	Long Branch city	13.5	31 340	65	2 321.5	13.5	28 658	65	2 122.8	68.0	18.7	0.4	1.6	0.0	7.1

[1] Dry land or land partially or temporarily covered by water.

Table E. Towns

Town	Population and population characteristics, 2000 (cont'd)								Population and population characteristics, 1990				
	Race (percent) (cont'd)								Race (percent)				
	Race alone or in combination												
	Two or more races	White	Black	American Indian or Alaska Native	Asian	Native Hawaiian and other Pacific Islander	Some other race	Hispanic[1]	White	Black or African American	American Indian or Alaska Native	Asian and Pacific Islander	Hispanic[1]
	15	16	17	18	19	20	21	22	23	24	25	26	27
MINNESOTA—Cont'd													
Maplewood city	1.9	90.3	4.4	1.0	5.0	0.1	1.2	2.2	94.4	2.5	0.6	2.0	1.5
Minneapolis city	4.4	68.0	20.5	3.3	7.0	0.2	5.8	7.6	78.4	13.0	3.3	4.3	2.1
Minnetonka city	1.0	95.3	1.8	0.4	2.7	0.1	0.8	1.3	97.1	0.9	0.2	1.6	0.8
Moorhead city	1.8	93.8	1.1	2.6	1.8	0.1	2.6	4.5	95.3	0.5	1.4	1.1	2.8
Oakdale city	1.9	93.9	3.0	0.8	2.9	0.1	1.3	2.7	97.0	1.0	0.4	1.0	1.6
Plymouth city	1.3	92.5	3.2	0.6	4.2	0.1	0.8	1.6	95.7	1.6	0.4	2.0	1.0
Richfield city	2.6	83.2	7.9	1.3	6.0	0.1	4.3	6.3	93.5	2.6	0.6	2.8	1.1
Rochester city	1.8	88.7	4.3	0.6	6.3	0.1	1.9	3.0	94.2	1.0	0.3	4.1	1.2
Roseville city	1.7	90.9	3.5	0.7	5.4	0.2	1.1	2.0	95.1	1.6	0.3	2.6	1.1
St. Louis Park city	1.7	90.3	5.2	0.9	3.7	0.1	1.7	2.9	95.3	1.9	0.4	2.1	1.0
St. Paul city	3.9	69.6	13.4	2.1	13.5	0.4	5.2	7.9	82.3	7.4	1.4	7.1	4.2
Shoreview city	1.4	94.5	1.2	0.6	4.2	0.1	0.8	1.3	96.4	0.7	0.3	2.3	0.9
Winona city	1.0	95.3	1.3	0.6	3.1	0.1	0.8	1.3	97.6	0.7	0.2	1.2	0.9
Woodbury city	1.6	91.4	3.1	0.6	5.6	0.1	0.9	2.1	94.6	1.6	0.3	3.1	1.7
NEW HAMPSHIRE	1.1	97.0	1.0	0.6	1.6	0.1	0.9	1.7	98.0	0.6	0.2	0.8	1.0
Concord city	1.3	96.7	1.4	0.8	1.8	0.1	0.7	1.5	98.2	0.6	0.3	0.7	1.0
Derry town	1.1	97.1	1.2	0.6	1.4	0.1	1.9	1.9	97.6	0.9	0.2	0.8	1.4
Dover city	1.5	95.8	1.5	0.7	2.7	0.1	0.7	1.1	97.4	1.1	0.2	1.1	1.0
Manchester city	1.7	93.3	2.6	0.7	2.7	0.1	2.5	4.6	97.0	1.0	0.2	1.1	2.1
Merrimack town	0.7	97.3	0.9	0.3	1.8	0.1	0.4	1.1	97.6	1.0	0.1	1.0	1.0
Nashua city	1.5	90.5	2.5	0.6	4.3	0.1	3.7	6.2	95.2	1.6	0.2	1.9	3.0
Rochester city	1.0	98.0	0.8	0.6	1.1	0.1	0.5	0.9	98.7	0.3	0.2	0.6	0.7
Salem town	1.1	96.0	0.7	0.4	2.5	0.1	1.3	2.0	96.8	0.9	0.1	1.8	1.4
NEW JERSEY	2.5	74.4	14.4	0.6	6.2	0.1	6.9	13.3	79.3	13.4	0.2	3.5	9.6
Atlantic City city	4.5	29.2	45.9	1.2	11.5	0.2	16.7	24.9	35.4	51.3	0.5	4.0	15.3
Bayonne city	4.0	82.0	6.3	0.5	4.8	0.2	10.4	17.8	90.4	4.7	0.1	1.8	9.5
Belleville township	3.8	72.6	5.9	0.5	12.0	0.2	12.8	23.7	86.1	3.7	0.2	6.0	10.1
Bergenfield borough	3.1	64.9	7.8	0.7	21.4	0.1	8.3	17.0	83.9	4.2	0.1	9.1	9.2
Berkeley township	0.7	97.7	1.5	0.3	0.6	0.0	0.7	2.3	98.5	1.0	0.1	0.2	1.5
Bloomfield township	3.2	72.3	12.7	0.6	9.1	0.2	8.5	14.5	89.1	4.3	0.1	5.0	5.1
Brick township	1.0	96.7	1.2	0.4	1.4	0.0	1.3	3.8	97.8	0.6	0.1	0.8	2.6
Bridgewater township	1.3	86.1	2.4	0.3	11.1	0.0	1.4	4.8	92.6	1.6	0.1	5.1	2.5
Camden city	3.9	19.0	55.3	1.2	3.0	0.3	25.4	38.8	19.0	56.4	0.4	1.3	31.2
Cherry Hill township	1.2	85.6	4.8	0.3	9.4	0.1	1.1	2.5	89.8	3.2	0.1	6.1	2.0
City of Orange township	4.8	14.6	78.7	0.9	1.6	0.3	8.9	12.5	24.0	70.3	0.4	1.3	10.8
Clifton city	4.6	80.3	3.3	0.5	7.2	0.1	13.4	19.8	92.8	1.4	0.1	3.5	6.8
Deptford township	1.4	84.6	13.1	0.5	1.9	0.1	1.4	2.9	87.9	10.2	0.2	1.1	1.9
Dover township	1.1	94.6	2.1	0.4	2.8	0.1	1.4	4.5	97.1	0.8	0.1	1.5	2.5
East Brunswick township	2.1	79.4	3.2	0.3	16.9	0.1	2.4	4.2	88.1	2.2	0.1	9.1	2.9
East Orange city	3.8	4.5	92.8	0.9	0.7	0.3	4.9	4.7	7.2	89.9	0.4	0.6	4.1
Edison township	2.2	60.9	7.4	0.5	30.2	0.1	3.2	6.4	79.5	5.6	0.1	13.7	4.3
Egg Harbor township	2.1	81.0	11.1	0.6	5.6	0.1	3.7	6.8	86.9	9.3	0.2	2.5	3.0
Elizabeth city	5.9	60.2	21.6	0.8	2.8	0.2	20.5	49.5	65.5	19.8	0.3	2.7	39.1
Englewood city	4.5	44.8	41.5	1.0	5.9	0.2	11.5	21.8	49.2	39.5	0.3	4.9	15.7
Evesham township	1.0	92.1	3.4	0.3	4.5	0.0	0.7	2.0	93.6	2.8	0.1	3.2	1.3
Ewing township	1.8	70.2	25.8	0.7	2.6	0.1	2.6	4.4	78.7	18.3	0.1	1.8	2.7
Fair Lawn borough	1.4	92.7	1.0	0.2	5.4	0.1	2.1	5.5	96.0	0.6	0.1	2.9	3.5
Fort Lee borough	2.3	64.6	2.1	0.2	32.3	0.1	2.9	7.9	77.2	1.3	0.1	20.3	5.6
Franklin township	2.4	56.6	27.1	0.6	13.4	0.1	4.8	8.1	69.9	21.4	0.2	7.1	4.5
Freehold township	1.3	88.2	5.5	0.4	5.6	0.0	1.8	5.2	90.5	4.7	0.1	4.2	3.5
Galloway township	2.2	78.8	10.5	0.6	8.7	0.1	3.4	6.2	88.6	7.4	0.1	2.7	3.7
Garfield city	3.8	85.4	4.0	0.6	3.1	0.1	10.7	20.1	93.8	2.2	0.1	1.7	9.0
Gloucester township	1.4	84.2	12.2	0.5	3.0	0.1	1.6	3.0	91.2	6.1	0.2	2.0	1.5
Hackensack city	5.1	56.3	26.5	1.1	8.1	0.1	13.3	25.9	66.4	24.8	0.2	3.7	15.1
Hamilton township	1.8	86.3	8.9	0.4	2.9	0.1	3.2	5.1	92.0	5.1	0.1	2.1	2.3
Hillsborough township	1.5	87.1	4.1	0.3	8.0	0.1	2.0	4.7	91.4	3.3	0.1	4.6	2.7
Hoboken city	2.8	83.1	5.1	0.5	4.9	0.1	9.3	20.2	79.0	5.5	0.2	4.4	30.1
Howell township	1.5	91.2	4.0	0.4	4.1	0.1	1.8	5.3	92.4	3.1	0.1	3.5	4.3
Irvington township	4.2	9.8	85.2	0.6	1.4	0.3	7.1	8.4	22.4	70.1	0.2	2.2	10.6
Jackson township	1.7	92.7	4.3	0.5	2.4	0.1	1.7	5.8	94.5	3.1	0.2	1.5	4.4
Jersey City city	5.8	37.7	30.0	1.0	17.6	0.3	19.6	28.3	48.2	29.7	0.3	11.4	24.2
Kearny town	4.3	79.5	4.6	0.6	6.0	0.2	13.5	27.3	90.5	1.2	0.2	4.7	17.1
Lacey township	0.7	98.5	0.5	0.4	0.8	0.0	0.6	2.2	98.9	0.3	0.2	0.4	1.6
Lakewood township	3.0	81.2	12.9	0.5	1.7	0.1	6.7	14.8	79.8	14.1	0.2	1.4	10.3
Lawrence township	1.6	80.5	9.8	0.4	8.4	0.1	2.5	4.6	86.6	8.0	0.2	4.5	2.6
Linden city	3.7	68.5	24.4	0.5	2.7	0.1	7.7	14.4	76.8	20.0	0.1	1.5	7.4
Livingston township	0.9	83.3	1.4	0.2	15.0	0.1	1.0	2.5	89.3	1.1	0.1	9.3	1.9
Long Branch city	4.2	71.5	20.0	0.8	2.1	0.2	9.9	20.7	73.5	19.5	0.2	1.5	13.6

[1] Hispanic persons may be of any race.

Table E. Towns

Town	Population and population characteristics, 2000										
	Age (percent)										
	Under 5 years	5 to 17 years	18 to 24 years	25 to 34 years	35 to 44 years	45 to 54 years	55 to 64 years	65 to 74 years	75 years and over	Median age (years)	Percent Female
	28	29	30	31	32	33	34	35	36	37	38
MINNESOTA—Cont'd											
Maplewood city	6.5	18.2	7.7	13.0	16.9	13.8	8.7	7.4	7.7	37.8	52.2
Minneapolis city	6.6	15.4	14.4	20.6	15.9	12.0	5.9	4.0	5.1	31.2	49.8
Minnetonka city	5.3	17.8	6.0	11.7	16.8	18.1	10.3	7.2	6.8	40.8	52.1
Moorhead city	5.8	16.8	23.1	10.9	13.3	10.9	6.3	5.8	6.9	28.7	53.1
Oakdale city	7.7	21.3	7.2	15.0	19.6	13.2	7.5	4.7	3.7	34.3	51.8
Plymouth city	7.0	20.1	7.4	13.8	19.2	16.1	8.9	4.8	2.8	36.1	50.7
Richfield city	6.0	14.2	9.3	16.9	16.5	12.7	8.0	7.1	9.3	37.1	51.0
Rochester city	7.5	18.3	9.1	16.2	17.2	12.5	7.7	5.5	6.0	34.3	51.4
Roseville city	4.6	13.7	11.1	12.4	14.4	13.3	10.4	9.2	11.0	41.0	53.5
St. Louis Park city	6.0	12.7	8.7	21.2	16.5	12.8	7.4	6.1	8.6	35.7	52.5
St. Paul city	7.6	19.5	12.5	16.8	15.3	11.9	6.2	4.6	5.7	31.0	51.6
Shoreview city	5.5	20.6	6.9	10.3	18.2	18.8	9.9	5.9	3.8	39.2	51.5
Winona city	4.5	13.5	27.5	10.5	10.5	11.7	11.0	7.0	8.4	28.8	53.0
Woodbury city	9.6	21.0	5.9	16.8	20.2	13.8	6.6	3.6	2.5	33.4	51.5
NEW HAMPSHIRE	6.1	18.9	8.4	13.0	17.9	14.9	8.9	6.3	5.6	37.1	50.8
Concord city	5.8	17.3	8.3	15.2	17.8	14.3	7.7	5.8	7.9	37.0	50.5
Derry town	7.2	23.0	7.4	15.1	20.5	14.3	6.5	3.6	2.6	33.6	50.3
Dover city	5.7	15.2	11.2	17.2	16.7	12.6	7.7	6.5	7.3	35.5	52.0
Manchester city	6.7	17.0	9.5	16.9	16.5	12.9	7.6	6.1	6.8	34.9	51.0
Merrimack town	6.9	22.1	5.8	13.2	21.0	15.6	9.1	3.9	2.5	36.0	50.2
Nashua city	6.5	18.1	8.1	15.9	17.6	13.6	8.5	6.1	5.5	35.8	50.6
Rochester city	6.8	18.5	7.7	14.2	17.4	13.4	8.6	7.3	6.2	36.7	51.4
Salem town	6.3	19.0	6.2	12.7	19.0	15.1	10.2	6.6	5.0	38.1	50.2
NEW JERSEY	6.7	18.1	8.0	14.1	17.1	13.8	9.0	6.8	6.4	36.7	51.5
Atlantic City city	7.5	18.2	8.9	15.8	15.2	11.5	8.7	7.3	6.8	34.7	51.0
Bayonne city	5.8	16.3	8.2	14.6	16.1	13.8	8.7	8.0	8.6	38.1	52.7
Belleville township	5.9	15.9	8.7	17.4	16.5	13.5	8.7	6.6	6.7	36.2	51.8
Bergenfield borough	6.8	18.1	7.3	13.4	17.6	14.3	9.0	6.9	6.6	37.6	52.2
Berkeley township	2.7	8.7	3.6	6.0	8.6	8.0	10.3	22.6	29.4	66.3	55.6
Bloomfield township	5.9	15.1	8.4	16.9	17.1	13.7	8.6	6.8	7.5	37.1	52.4
Brick township	6.2	17.6	6.4	12.3	17.2	14.0	9.3	8.2	8.8	39.4	52.5
Bridgewater township	7.7	18.0	4.9	13.0	19.6	14.8	9.4	6.5	6.2	38.2	51.9
Camden city	9.1	25.5	12.0	15.3	14.1	9.9	6.4	4.5	3.1	27.2	51.5
Cherry Hill township	5.6	17.9	5.4	10.4	16.0	15.6	11.1	9.1	8.8	41.8	52.2
City of Orange township	8.5	19.2	10.0	16.5	15.7	11.5	7.8	5.8	5.0	32.5	53.8
Clifton city	6.0	15.6	7.7	14.4	16.3	13.8	8.7	7.9	9.7	38.8	52.3
Deptford township	6.2	17.6	7.4	14.6	17.6	12.5	9.1	8.1	6.9	37.3	51.8
Dover township	5.5	17.8	7.2	11.5	15.7	14.8	10.3	9.3	7.9	40.2	51.9
East Brunswick township	5.9	20.1	6.2	10.9	18.3	16.7	10.3	6.6	5.0	39.1	51.5
East Orange city	7.9	20.2	9.8	15.2	14.9	12.1	8.7	6.3	5.0	33.0	55.0
Edison township	6.4	16.4	7.8	17.0	17.0	14.4	9.0	6.5	5.5	36.3	50.9
Egg Harbor township	7.4	20.5	6.6	13.6	19.1	15.0	8.7	5.3	3.9	36.0	51.4
Elizabeth city	7.7	18.6	10.8	17.2	16.5	11.6	7.7	5.2	4.8	32.6	50.5
Englewood city	6.9	17.0	7.4	14.6	15.9	14.3	10.5	7.3	6.0	37.4	53.0
Evesham township	7.3	19.9	6.0	14.9	19.9	14.6	8.5	5.0	3.9	36.0	51.5
Ewing township	4.5	13.5	17.3	11.6	15.2	13.2	8.9	7.7	8.1	37.0	51.8
Fair Lawn borough	5.3	17.5	6.0	10.3	16.5	16.3	9.3	8.9	9.8	41.8	52.5
Fort Lee borough	5.3	12.2	5.1	15.3	17.2	13.9	10.9	10.2	10.0	41.6	53.3
Franklin township	7.3	15.3	6.8	18.1	18.8	13.8	8.4	5.9	5.6	36.1	52.2
Freehold township	6.8	18.5	6.1	12.3	18.8	15.4	10.1	6.2	5.8	38.3	50.6
Galloway township	6.5	19.3	13.6	12.1	18.7	13.2	7.5	5.4	3.7	34.0	52.0
Garfield city	6.1	16.3	9.6	17.0	16.2	13.0	7.8	6.7	7.4	35.6	51.3
Gloucester township	6.8	20.0	8.7	15.1	17.9	14.2	7.8	5.3	4.1	34.6	51.3
Hackensack city	5.8	12.4	8.6	20.7	17.7	13.4	8.9	6.3	6.2	36.2	50.3
Hamilton township	5.7	17.4	7.0	12.9	17.0	15.0	9.2	7.9	7.7	39.1	52.3
Hillsborough township	7.9	21.2	6.0	13.4	21.3	16.1	7.2	4.0	2.9	35.7	50.6
Hoboken city	3.2	7.3	15.3	37.9	13.9	8.1	5.4	4.6	4.5	30.4	49.1
Howell township	8.0	22.9	6.0	11.8	21.0	14.5	7.1	4.7	4.0	35.7	51.2
Irvington township	8.1	20.0	10.7	16.9	15.5	13.0	8.4	4.3	3.2	31.5	53.3
Jackson township	8.2	21.5	6.5	13.4	20.7	12.8	7.5	5.2	4.2	35.2	51.2
Jersey City city	6.9	17.8	10.7	19.4	15.7	11.8	7.9	5.2	4.5	32.4	51.2
Kearny town	5.7	15.7	10.7	18.5	17.2	13.1	8.2	5.6	5.2	34.7	48.4
Lacey township	6.2	19.4	6.5	11.5	16.7	14.7	9.8	8.0	7.2	38.9	51.3
Lakewood township	11.9	19.9	10.1	13.2	10.3	8.5	7.2	8.7	10.3	30.6	52.2
Lawrence township	5.8	15.9	12.4	13.3	16.1	14.5	8.4	6.6	7.0	36.7	53.2
Linden city	6.0	16.5	8.2	14.6	15.8	13.5	9.1	7.5	8.8	38.0	52.5
Livingston township	7.0	19.6	4.6	9.2	17.3	16.2	10.6	8.4	7.0	40.6	51.4
Long Branch city	7.0	16.8	10.2	16.5	15.9	12.6	8.2	6.6	6.3	34.7	51.5

Table E. Towns

Town	Population and population characteristics, 1990										Population—change, 1980–2000				
	Age (percent)										Total persons			Percent change	
	Under 5 years	5 to 17 years	18 to 24 years	25 to 34 years	35 to 44 years	45 to 54 years	55 to 64 years	65 to 74 years	75 years and over	Percent Female	2000	1990	1980	1990–2000	1980–1990
	39	40	41	42	43	44	45	46	47	48	49	50	51	52	53
MINNESOTA—Cont'd															
Maplewood city	8.0	17.2	9.2	18.9	15.0	10.7	9.4	6.7	5.1	51.5	34 947	30 954	26 990	12.9	14.7
Minneapolis city	7.3	13.3	13.3	23.5	15 7	7.9	6.2	6.3	6.6	51.5	382 618	368 383	370 951	3.9	-0.7
Minnetonka city	6.7	17.5	7.6	17.5	19.3	12.3	9.3	6.5	3.3	51.0	51 301	48 370	38 683	6.1	25.0
Moorhead city	6.8	15.6	26.6	14.1	11.8	7.2	6.7	5.9	5.2	53.4	32 177	32 295	29 998	-0.4	7.7
Oakdale city	9.7	20.6	8.6	23.7	16.3	10.2	5.9	3.6	1.5	51.5	26 653	18 377	NA	45.0	NA
Plymouth city	8.0	19.5	9.2	19.7	19.1	13.0	6.6	3.6	1.3	50.7	65 894	50 889	31 614	29.5	61.0
Richfield city	6.2	13.1	10.0	20.6	14.2	9.3	9.7	10.8	6.1	51.8	34 439	35 710	37 851	-3.6	-5.7
Rochester city	8.7	17.1	10.0	21.7	14.9	9.7	7.0	5.4	5.6	52.2	85 806	70 729	57 890	21.3	22.2
Roseville city	5.5	13.8	11.3	16.3	13.2	11.8	11.3	9.8	7.0	53.3	33 690	33 485	35 820	0.6	-6.5
St. Louis Park city	6.4	11.4	9.5	24.3	14.8	9.2	8.3	8.6	7.5	53.6	44 126	43 787	42 931	0.8	2.0
St. Paul city	8.4	16.1	12.2	20.4	14.6	7.6	6.9	7.0	6.8	53.0	287 151	272 235	270 230	5.5	0.7
Shoreview city	8.4	19.7	7.4	19.1	19.9	12.7	7.2	4.3	1.3	50.9	25 924	24 587	NA	5.4	NA
Winona city	5.3	13.7	26.1	13.0	11.8	7.1	7.0	7.4	8.8	53.1	27 069	25 435	25 075	6.4	1.4
Woodbury city	9.0	22.0	6.8	19.2	20.5	11.6	6.1	2.6	2.1	51.7	46 463	20 075	NA	131.4	NA
NEW HAMPSHIRE	7.6	17.5	10.6	18.5	16.5	10.1	8.0	6.4	4.8	51.0	1 235 786	1 109 252	920 610	11.4	20.5
Concord city	7.1	16.1	9.8	20.8	16.4	8.3	7.5	6.8	7.2	51.5	40 687	36 006	30 400	13.0	18.4
Derry town	10.1	18.7	9.0	25.1	17.8	8.9	4.6	3.2	2.6	50.4	34 021	29 603	18 875	14.9	56.8
Dover city	6.4	13.6	15.3	20.8	13.2	9.5	8.3	7.2	5.8	52.2	26 884	25 042	22 377	7.4	11.9
Manchester city	7.8	15.2	11.9	20.9	14.0	8.5	8.0	7.8	5.8	52.1	107 006	99 332	90 936	7.7	9.2
Merrimack town	8.6	20.4	8.9	20.6	18.0	13.3	5.5	2.9	1.8	49.8	25 119	22 156	15 406	13.4	43.8
Nashua city	8.0	16.1	10.2	21.8	15.7	10.1	7.9	5.9	4.2	50.9	86 605	79 662	67 865	8.7	17.4
Rochester city	8.5	17.8	9.3	19.3	15.1	8.9	8.5	7.4	5.4	51.4	28 461	26 630	21 560	6.9	23.5
Salem town	7.2	16.7	9.9	17.8	17.4	12.1	9.0	6.2	3.7	50.5	28 112	25 746	24 124	9.2	6.7
NEW JERSEY	6.9	16.4	10.1	17.6	15.5	10.9	9.3	7.9	5.5	51.7	8 414 350	7 747 750	7 365 011	8.6	5.0
Atlantic City city	7.4	15.2	10.1	17.0	12.9	8.6	9.8	9.7	9.3	53.4	40 517	37 986	40 199	6.7	-5.5
Bayonne city	5.5	14.3	8.9	17.4	13.6	10.7	10.6	11.9	7.0	53.0	61 842	61 464	65 047	0.6	-5.5
Belleville township	6.0	13.3	10.0	20.6	14.7	10.8	10.3	9.2	5.2	52.5	35 928	34 213	35 367	5.0	-3.3
Bergenfield borough	6.6	14.1	9.1	16.7	16.2	11.7	10.2	9.5	6.0	51.9	26 247	24 458	25 568	7.3	-4.3
Berkeley township	3.1	8.6	3.9	7.6	7.5	5.0	13.3	31.9	19.1	55.1	39 991	37 319	23 151	7.2	61.2
Bloomfield township	5.6	12.1	9.9	19.6	14.8	9.9	10.2	10.3	7.6	53.5	47 683	45 061	47 792	5.8	-5.7
Brick township	7.1	16.3	8.4	17.1	15.2	10.1	8.5	10.0	7.2	52.3	76 119	66 415	53 629	14.6	23.8
Bridgewater township	6.3	15.9	8.8	17.4	16.5	14.0	10.7	6.5	3.8	51.0	42 940	32 509	29 175	32.1	11.4
Camden city	10.7	24.9	12.1	17.5	11.8	8.3	6.4	5.3	3.1	52.4	79 904	87 492	84 910	-8.7	3.0
Cherry Hill township	5.9	16.7	7.9	13.9	15.7	13.6	12.1	8.8	5.4	51.7	69 965	69 348	68 785	0.9	0.8
City of Orange township	7.4	16.5	11.2	18.5	16.0	9.2	8.8	6.7	5.7	53.3	32 868	29 925	31 136	9.8	-3.9
Clifton city	5.4	12.4	8.6	17.6	14.3	10.0	11.0	12.1	8.6	52.6	78 672	71 984	74 388	9.3	-3.2
Deptford township	7.1	16.1	10.3	18.9	13.3	11.5	10.5	8.1	4.2	51.2	26 763	24 137	23 473	10.9	2.8
Dover township	6.3	18.3	9.1	14.4	15.6	11.4	9.2	9.0	6.8	52.0	89 706	76 388	64 455	17.4	18.5
East Brunswick township	6.6	17.3	9.6	16.4	18.0	13.8	9.7	6.0	2.6	50.6	46 756	43 548	37 711	7.4	15.5
East Orange city	7.9	17.9	10.8	18.6	14.0	11.0	8.1	6.6	5.1	54.8	69 824	73 552	77 878	-5.1	-5.6
Edison township	6.9	14.9	9.5	20.8	16.7	11.5	9.3	6.9	3.7	51.0	97 687	88 680	70 193	10.2	26.3
Egg Harbor township	7.5	18.7	9.4	18.9	17.2	11.4	7.8	6.3	2.9	51.2	30 726	24 544	19 381	25.2	26.6
Elizabeth city	7.5	17.2	10.7	20.0	14.0	10.2	8.5	6.8	5.2	51.0	120 568	110 002	106 201	9.6	3.6
Englewood city	6.9	15.0	8.5	17.5	16.4	11.6	10.2	8.1	5.8	53.1	26 203	24 850	23 701	5.4	4.8
Evesham township	8.3	18.3	9.0	21.3	18.5	11.5	6.8	3.9	2.4	51.4	42 275	35 309	21 508	19.7	64.2
Ewing township	4.8	12.3	16.0	14.3	14.6	10.5	10.6	10.0	6.9	52.9	35 707	34 185	34 842	4.5	-1.9
Fair Lawn borough	5.6	14.8	7.0	13.5	15.3	11.4	12.2	12.2	7.9	52.3	31 637	30 548	32 229	3.6	-5.2
Fort Lee borough	5.8	9.8	5.1	20.2	16.1	10.6	12.1	11.6	8.9	52.5	35 461	31 997	32 449	10.8	-1.4
Franklin township	7.3	13.3	8.5	24.8	16.5	10.8	8.7	5.7	4.3	51.6	50 903	42 780	31 358	19.0	36.4
Freehold township	5.8	17.7	9.9	17.1	16.6	14.5	8.8	5.4	4.2	49.7	31 537	24 710	19 202	27.6	28.7
Galloway township	8.2	14.9	17.2	21.7	15.0	8.9	6.8	4.9	2.5	50.8	31 209	23 330	12 176	33.8	91.6
Garfield city	6.5	13.1	10.0	20.6	14.0	8.9	9.2	10.4	7.0	52.0	29 786	26 727	26 803	11.4	-0.3
Gloucester township	8.0	20.0	9.5	19.6	17.5	9.9	7.3	5.6	2.7	51.1	64 350	53 797	45 156	19.6	19.1
Hackensack city	5.1	10.6	9.8	23.7	16.1	11.2	8.9	8.0	6.6	50.6	42 677	37 049	36 039	15.2	2.8
Hamilton township	6.1	15.7	8.7	17.0	16.4	11.1	10.1	9.4	5.5	52.5	87 109	86 553	82 801	0.6	4.5
Hillsborough township	9.0	17.9	7.3	21.2	21.0	11.1	6.7	3.6	2.1	50.9	36 634	28 808	19 061	27.2	51.1
Hoboken city	4.8	11.9	13.3	29.8	14.7	7.9	6.5	6.6	4.5	50.5	38 577	33 397	42 460	15.5	-21.3
Howell township	9.6	19.6	7.7	19.3	18.6	9.3	6.8	5.5	3.7	50.6	48 903	38 987	25 065	25.4	55.5
Irvington township	7.6	18.7	10.1	20.4	16.0	10.5	7.1	5.3	4.3	53.0	60 695	61 018	61 493	-0.5	-0.8
Jackson township	8.5	18.6	9.2	20.2	16.7	10.1	7.3	5.6	3.9	51.2	42 816	33 233	25 644	28.8	29.6
Jersey City city	7.3	17.1	11.4	21.0	14.9	9.7	7.7	6.4	4.5	51.4	240 055	228 517	223 532	5.0	2.2
Kearny town	6.2	15.2	10.5	19.8	14.3	11.7	9.5	7.9	5.0	50.7	40 513	34 874	35 735	16.2	-2.4
Lacey township	6.9	18.2	7.9	14.2	16.2	10.1	9.2	10.8	6.6	51.3	25 346	22 141	14 161	14.5	56.4
Lakewood township	9.8	18.1	8.9	15.3	12.0	7.3	6.5	8.7	13.4	54.0	60 352	45 048	38 464	34.0	17.1
Lawrence township	5.8	13.8	16.4	16.5	16.5	9.4	8.7	7.8	5.2	52.9	29 159	25 787	19 724	13.1	30.7
Linden city	5.7	14.1	8.9	17.1	14.5	10.3	10.2	11.4	7.7	52.7	39 394	36 701	37 836	7.3	-3.0
Livingston township	5.5	17.6	8.0	12.0	16.4	14.2	12.6	9.2	4.4	51.6	27 391	26 609	28 040	2.9	-5.1
Long Branch city	7.1	15.6	9.5	20.3	13.8	9.4	8.9	8.5	6.9	53.0	31 340	28 658	29 819	9.4	-3.9

Table E. Towns

Town	Total population	In households (percent)									In group quarters (percent)						
		Total in house-holds	House-holder	Spouse	Child Total	Child Own child under 18 years	Other relatives Total	Other relatives Under 18 years	Nonrelatives Total	Nonrelatives Unmar-ried partner	Total in group quarters	Institutionalized population Correc-tional institu-tions	Institutionalized population Nurs-ing homes	Institutionalized population Other institu-tions	Noninstitutionalized population Col-lege dormi-tories	Noninstitutionalized population Mili-tary quar-ters	Other
	54	55	56	57	58	59	60	61	62	63	64	65	66	67	68	69	70
MINNESOTA—Cont'd																	
Maplewood city	34 947	97.7	39.4	20.8	29.6	23.2	3.2	1.1	4.7	2.0	2.3	0.0	1.0	0.0	0.0	0.0	1.4
Minneapolis city	382 618	95.3	42.4	12.3	23.4	19.0	5.8	2.1	11.3	3.3	4.7	0.2	1.1	0.2	2.0	0.0	1.3
Minnetonka city	51 301	98.8	41.7	23.6	27.3	22.2	1.8	0.5	4.4	1.6	1.2	0.0	0.4	0.3	0.0	0.0	0.6
Moorhead city	32 177	88.1	36.2	17.1	25.7	21.5	1.8	0.6	7.3	1.7	11.9	0.4	1.2	0.1	9.4	0.0	0.9
Oakdale city	26 653	99.6	38.4	21.2	33.4	27.7	2.5	0.9	4.0	1.9	0.4	0.0	0.0	0.0	0.2	0.0	0.2
Plymouth city	65 894	97.8	37.7	23.0	31.1	26.4	1.9	0.4	4.1	1.6	2.2	1.2	0.1	0.1	0.2	0.0	0.6
Richfield city	34 439	98.6	43.8	19.0	24.5	18.6	4.5	1.2	6.9	2.4	1.4	0.0	0.7	0.0	0.1	0.0	0.7
Rochester city	85 806	96.6	39.8	20.6	28.5	24.5	2.4	0.7	5.3	1.9	3.4	1.1	0.6	0.1	0.1	0.0	1.4
Roseville city	33 690	95.1	43.3	21.3	22.8	17.4	2.4	0.6	5.3	1.9	4.9	0.2	1.9	0.0	2.5	0.0	0.3
St. Louis Park city	44 126	97.9	47.1	18.5	22.0	17.7	2.8	0.7	7.5	2.5	2.1	0.0	1.2	0.0	0.0	0.0	0.8
St. Paul city	287 151	96.1	39.0	14.1	29.9	24.3	5.3	2.0	7.7	2.7	3.9	0.2	0.8	0.1	1.8	0.0	0.9
Shoreview city	25 924	99.3	39.1	23.6	31.4	25.4	1.9	0.6	3.4	1.5	0.7	0.0	0.0	0.0	0.0	0.0	0.7
Winona city	27 069	86.5	38.1	15.4	21.1	17.0	1.6	0.5	10.3	2.1	13.5	0.1	2.0	0.0	10.3	0.0	1.1
Woodbury city	46 463	99.1	35.9	24.0	34.1	29.8	2.0	0.5	3.1	1.5	0.9	0.0	0.8	0.0	0.0	0.0	0.2
NEW HAMPSHIRE	1 235 786	97.1	38.4	21.2	28.8	23.4	3.0	1.0	5.6	2.6	2.9	0.3	0.8	0.1	1.4	0.0	0.3
Concord city	40 687	92.0	40.0	17.7	25.7	21.5	2.6	0.8	5.9	3.0	8.0	4.1	1.7	1.1	0.6	0.0	0.5
Derry town	34 021	99.3	36.2	20.4	34.4	28.4	3.1	1.1	5.2	2.7	0.7	0.0	0.5	0.0	0.0	0.0	0.2
Dover city	26 884	97.2	43.0	18.3	24.0	19.6	2.9	0.8	9.0	3.6	2.8	0.5	1.8	0.0	0.0	0.0	0.4
Manchester city	107 006	97.5	41.4	17.6	27.4	21.8	3.8	1.1	7.3	3.5	2.5	0.4	0.8	0.1	0.5	0.0	0.7
Merrimack town	25 119	99.7	35.2	24.0	34.1	27.5	2.9	1.1	3.6	1.7	0.3	0.0	0.0	0.0	0.2	0.0	0.1
Nashua city	86 605	98.4	40.0	19.7	28.8	23.0	3.7	1.1	6.2	2.8	1.6	0.0	0.7	0.1	0.7	0.0	0.2
Rochester city	28 461	99.0	40.2	20.4	29.0	23.5	3.0	1.1	6.3	3.3	1.0	0.0	0.7	0.1	0.0	0.0	0.3
Salem town	28 112	99.5	37.0	22.4	31.6	23.5	4.5	1.5	4.0	1.9	0.5	0.0	0.4	0.0	0.0	0.0	0.1
NEW JERSEY	8 414 350	97.7	36.4	19.5	30.8	22.3	6.5	2.0	4.6	1.8	2.3	0.6	0.6	0.1	0.5	0.0	0.4
Atlantic City city	40 517	96.4	39.1	9.7	27.7	20.9	11.1	4.1	8.8	2.9	3.6	0.0	0.8	0.0	0.0	0.0	2.8
Bayonne city	61 842	99.8	41.3	17.7	30.5	20.4	6.2	1.5	4.1	1.9	0.2	0.0	0.0	0.0	0.0	0.0	0.2
Belleville township	35 928	99.4	38.2	18.0	30.1	19.7	8.3	1.9	4.8	2.1	0.6	0.0	0.5	0.0	0.0	0.0	0.1
Bergenfield borough	26 247	99.8	34.2	20.5	33.2	22.8	8.2	1.8	3.7	1.2	0.2	0.0	0.0	0.0	0.0	0.0	0.2
Berkeley township	39 991	98.5	49.6	26.3	16.3	10.3	3.7	0.9	2.6	1.3	1.5	0.0	0.5	0.0	0.0	0.0	0.9
Bloomfield township	47 683	99.1	39.9	18.6	29.0	19.3	6.9	1.6	4.6	2.0	0.9	0.0	0.2	0.0	0.4	0.0	0.2
Brick township	76 119	99.1	38.8	22.0	30.3	22.2	4.4	1.3	3.7	1.9	0.9	0.0	0.7	0.0	0.0	0.0	0.2
Bridgewater township	42 940	98.2	36.2	24.1	31.4	24.7	3.7	0.8	2.8	1.1	1.8	0.0	1.5	0.0	0.0	0.0	0.3
Camden city	79 904	94.5	30.3	7.9	36.4	26.8	12.9	6.7	7.1	3.0	5.5	3.8	0.5	0.0	0.6	0.0	0.6
Cherry Hill township	69 965	97.8	37.5	23.5	30.3	22.1	3.9	1.1	2.6	1.1	2.2	0.0	1.6	0.0	0.0	0.0	0.6
City of Orange township	32 868	98.6	36.2	11.1	31.6	21.8	12.7	5.1	7.0	2.4	1.4	0.0	1.0	0.0	0.0	0.0	0.4
Clifton city	78 672	99.5	38.4	19.7	29.7	19.8	7.6	1.5	4.1	1.6	0.5	0.0	0.3	0.0	0.0	0.0	0.2
Deptford township	26 763	97.9	37.4	20.2	30.4	21.2	5.6	2.2	4.3	2.3	2.1	0.0	1.7	0.0	0.0	0.0	0.4
Dover township	89 706	97.8	37.4	22.1	30.4	21.5	4.4	1.4	3.6	1.7	2.2	0.4	0.6	0.7	0.0	0.0	0.2
East Brunswick township	46 756	99.5	35.0	24.0	33.7	24.9	4.7	1.0	2.1	0.9	0.5	0.0	0.1	0.0	0.0	0.0	0.4
East Orange city	69 824	98.1	37.3	9.7	31.8	21.4	13.1	5.9	6.3	2.7	1.9	0.0	0.8	0.5	0.0	0.0	0.5
Edison township	97 687	97.9	36.0	22.0	29.6	21.0	6.5	1.3	3.8	1.3	2.1	0.0	1.1	0.0	0.1	0.0	0.9
Egg Harbor township	30 726	99.8	36.4	20.2	32.7	25.1	5.9	2.4	4.6	2.5	0.2	0.0	0.0	0.0	0.0	0.0	0.2
Elizabeth city	120 568	97.6	33.6	14.4	31.8	22.4	11.0	3.3	6.8	2.5	2.4	1.4	0.4	0.1	0.0	0.0	0.5
Englewood city	26 203	98.9	35.4	16.9	29.7	20.2	10.1	3.1	6.7	1.8	1.1	0.0	0.6	0.0	0.0	0.0	0.5
Evesham township	42 275	99.6	37.2	22.8	33.4	26.0	3.2	1.0	3.0	1.5	0.4	0.0	0.2	0.0	0.0	0.0	0.2
Ewing township	35 707	86.0	35.1	17.5	23.0	15.4	5.5	2.1	4.9	1.7	14.0	3.2	0.6	0.3	9.8	0.0	0.2
Fair Lawn borough	31 637	99.5	37.3	23.7	31.2	21.8	4.8	0.9	2.5	1.0	0.5	0.0	0.4	0.0	0.0	0.0	0.1
Fort Lee borough	35 461	99.9	46.7	21.8	23.2	16.6	5.0	0.7	3.3	1.4	0.1	0.0	0.0	0.0	0.0	0.0	0.1
Franklin township	50 903	98.0	38.0	20.2	27.6	20.3	6.8	2.1	5.3	1.8	2.0	0.0	1.4	0.0	0.0	0.0	0.6
Freehold township	31 537	94.6	34.3	22.6	31.6	24.0	3.8	0.9	2.4	1.1	5.4	3.3	1.6	0.2	0.0	0.0	0.3
Galloway township	31 209	93.3	34.5	18.8	29.7	23.8	5.1	1.7	5.1	2.3	6.7	0.0	0.1	0.0	6.5	0.0	0.2
Garfield city	29 786	99.8	37.8	17.6	30.4	20.4	8.4	1.6	5.7	2.1	0.2	0.0	0.0	0.0	0.0	0.0	0.2
Gloucester township	64 350	98.9	36.0	20.1	33.7	24.6	5.0	1.8	4.2	2.4	1.1	0.0	0.4	0.2	0.0	0.0	0.5
Hackensack city	42 677	96.1	42.4	14.8	22.9	15.4	9.0	2.2	7.0	2.5	3.9	1.5	0.7	0.1	0.0	0.0	1.6
Hamilton township	87 109	99.2	38.5	21.3	30.5	21.3	5.2	1.6	3.7	1.8	0.8	0.0	0.7	0.0	0.0	0.0	0.1
Hillsborough township	36 634	99.3	34.5	23.4	34.9	28.2	3.5	0.7	3.0	1.4	0.7	0.0	0.4	0.0	0.0	0.0	0.3
Hoboken city	38 577	96.7	50.3	12.0	14.6	9.0	4.1	1.3	15.7	3.4	3.3	0.4	0.0	0.0	2.3	0.0	0.7
Howell township	48 903	99.8	32.8	22.8	37.2	29.3	4.2	1.2	2.7	1.2	0.2	0.0	0.0	0.0	0.0	0.0	0.1
Irvington township	60 695	99.6	36.3	11.0	32.8	22.1	13.0	5.2	6.5	2.9	0.4	0.1	0.3	0.0	0.0	0.0	0.1
Jackson township	42 816	99.1	33.1	22.1	35.6	27.7	4.8	1.6	3.5	1.8	0.9	0.0	0.6	0.1	0.4	0.0	0.4
Jersey City city	240 055	98.6	36.9	13.4	30.5	20.7	10.9	3.6	6.8	2.4	1.4	0.0	0.4	0.2	0.0	0.0	0.4
Kearny town	40 513	93.8	33.4	18.0	29.9	19.5	7.3	1.6	5.1	1.7	6.2	5.4	0.4	0.0	0.0	0.0	0.2
Lacey township	25 346	99.9	36.8	23.8	31.8	23.9	4.0	1.1	3.4	1.8	0.1	0.0	0.0	0.1	0.0	0.0	0.1
Lakewood township	60 352	96.3	32.9	17.6	35.3	29.2	5.5	2.0	4.9	1.4	3.7	0.0	2.0	0.4	1.3	0.0	0.1
Lawrence township	29 159	92.1	37.0	20.0	26.8	20.2	4.2	1.2	4.1	1.5	7.9	0.0	0.9	0.0	6.4	0.0	0.5
Linden city	39 394	99.4	38.2	17.8	30.2	19.4	8.6	2.7	4.5	1.7	0.6	0.0	0.6	0.0	0.0	0.0	0.0
Livingston township	27 391	99.5	34.0	25.8	34.1	25.8	4.0	0.7	1.6	0.4	0.5	0.0	0.2	0.0	0.0	0.0	0.1
Long Branch city	31 340	99.3	40.2	14.8	28.2	20.5	7.8	2.7	8.4	2.8	0.7	0.0	0.0	0.0	0.0	0.0	0.4

Table E. Towns

Town	Households by type, 2000												Households, 1990		
	Family households						Nonfamily households								
			Married couple		Female householder[1]			Householder living alone							
	Total households	Total	With own children under 18 years	Total	With own children under 18 years	Total	With own children under 18 years	Total	Total	65 years and over	Average household size	Average family size	Total households	Female householder[1]	Householder living alone
	71	72	73	74	75	76	77	78	79	80	81	82	83	84	85
MINNESOTA—Cont'd															
Maplewood city	13 758	66.8	31.6	52.8	23.5	10.5	6.5	33.2	27.0	11.1	2.48	3.04	11 496	11.8	21.5
Minneapolis city	162 352	45.5	22.6	29.0	12.8	12.3	7.9	54.5	40.3	8.0	2.25	3.15	160 682	12.3	38.3
Minnetonka city	21 393	65.9	29.1	56.6	24.0	6.8	3.9	34.I	27.3	9.3	2.37	2.92	18 687	6.8	20.0
Moorhead city	11 660	60.3	31.4	47.3	22.4	9.8	7.2	39.7	29.2	11.1	2.43	3.04	11 063	8.9	24.9
Oakdale city	10 243	69.6	38.5	55.2	28.7	11.1	7.9	30.4	25.2	7.2	2.59	3.14	6 699	10.0	19.3
Plymouth city	24 820	71.1	37.8	61.2	31.6	7.6	5.0	28.9	21.8	4.7	2.60	3.09	18 361	6.3	17.9
Richfield city	15 073	57.9	24.4	43.4	16.7	10.5	6.0	42.1	33.7	12.0	2.60	2.89	15 551	9.1	29.7
Rochester city	34 116	63.0	32.6	51.8	25.3	8.5	5.7	37.0	29.7	8.5	2.43	3.06	27 913	8.0	29.1
Roseville city	14 598	58.9	22.2	49.2	17.3	7.2	3.9	41.1	33.6	13.9	2.20	2.82	13 562	7.3	26.6
St. Louis Park city	20 782	50.8	22.0	39.3	15.8	8.6	5.0	49.2	37.9	10.4	2.08	2.81	19 925	7.8	33.5
St. Paul city	112 109	54.4	29.1	36.1	17.8	13.9	9.2	45.6	35.9	9.4	2.46	3.32	110 249	12.9	34.8
Shoreview city	10 125	70.8	35.1	60.3	29.1	7.9	4.9	29.2	24.1	6.5	2.54	3.06	8 991	6.7	19.3
Winona city	10 301	51.7	23.9	40.4	17.1	8.4	5.4	48.3	35.2	12.8	2.27	2.94	9 334	7.0	32.5
Woodbury city	16 676	75.9	43.8	66.8	37.9	6.9	4.6	24.1	18.8	3.3	2.76	3.20	6 927	7.1	16.3
NEW HAMPSHIRE	474 606	68.2	33.4	55.3	25.4	9.1	5.7	31.8	24.4	8.5	2.53	3.03	411 186	8.5	22.0
Concord city	16 281	59.1	30.6	44.3	20.5	11.4	8.0	40.9	32.7	11.2	2.30	2.95	14 222	9.3	30.1
Derry town	12 327	71.3	42.6	56.4	32.4	10.6	7.5	28.7	21.6	4.9	2.74	3.24	10 767	7.8	19.7
Dover city	11 573	56.1	26.3	42.5	18.0	10.3	6.5	43.9	31.0	9.2	2.26	2.87	10 345	9.4	27.7
Manchester city	44 247	59.0	29.4	42.6	19.2	11.7	7.5	41.0	31.7	10.3	2.36	3.00	40 338	10.3	29.2
Merrimack town	8 832	79.1	41.9	68.1	35.3	7.8	4.9	20.9	15.8	3.8	2.84	3.19	7 439	6.0	13.2
Nashua city	34 614	68.4	31.6	49.3	22.8	10.4	6.5	36.2	28.3	8.7	2.46	3.05	31 051	8.7	24.7
Rochester city	11 434	66.9	32.8	50.9	22.0	11.4	7.8	33.1	25.7	9.6	2.46	2.95	10 221	9.4	22.3
Salem town	10 402	73.1	34.3	60.6	28.4	8.7	4.3	26.9	21.2	7.5	2.69	3.16	9 185	7.9	19.3
NEW JERSEY	3 064 645	70.3	33.5	53.5	25.3	12.6	6.4	29.7	24.5	9.8	2.68	3.21	2 794 711	12.1	23.1
Atlantic City city	15 848	54.9	27.7	24.8	10.8	23.2	14.0	45.1	37.2	15.4	2.46	3.26	15 731	22.8	41.0
Bayonne city	25 545	62.7	28.3	42.8	19.4	15.1	7.3	37.3	32.8	15.0	2.42	3.10	25 309	12.7	31.2
Belleville township	13 771	66.2	29.5	47.0	21.5	13.9	6.1	33.8	27.9	9.1	2.60	3.23	13 374	11.4	26.6
Bergenfield borough	8 981	75.2	36.4	59.8	30.7	11.8	4.6	24.8	20.8	9.9	2.92	3.41	8 799	10.8	19.6
Berkeley township	19 828	61.4	11.1	53.1	8.8	6.2	1.6	38.6	35.9	29.8	1.99	2.52	17 614	5.3	28.1
Bloomfield township	19 017	63.5	28.2	46.7	21.3	12.4	5.4	36.5	30.4	10.6	2.49	3.16	18 455	10.5	30.5
Brick township	29 511	70.4	31.6	56.8	25.1	10.2	5.0	29.6	25.0	12.7	2.56	3.07	24 965	8.9	21.2
Bridgewater township	15 561	76.4	38.0	66.6	33.5	7.3	3.6	23.6	19.8	7.6	2.71	3.14	11 292	7.7	14.4
Camden city	24 177	72.1	42.2	26.1	13.6	37.7	24.5	27.9	22.5	7.8	3.12	3.62	26 626	37.4	23.3
Cherry Hill township	26 227	74.0	32.1	62.8	27.5	8.3	3.5	26.0	22.5	11.0	2.61	3.08	24 529	7.9	18.0
City of Orange township	11 885	64.3	33.4	30.7	15.3	26.3	15.1	35.7	30.2	10.5	2.73	3.38	11 580	22.0	34.3
Clifton city	30 244	67.3	28.9	51.3	22.9	11.5	4.6	32.7	27.9	13.7	2.59	3.20	29 041	9.6	27.9
Deptford township	10 013	70.7	31.6	53.9	23.6	11.9	5.5	29.3	24.3	9.3	2.62	3.12	8 554	9.8	20.5
Dover township	33 510	70.1	31.2	59.1	24.9	10.5	5.0	27.1	22.7	11.0	2.62	3.09	27 357	9.1	20.5
East Brunswick township	16 372	79.9	40.5	68.6	35.4	8.5	4.2	20.1	17.2	7.0	2.84	3.23	14 921	7.2	14.8
East Orange city	26 024	61.8	31.9	26.0	12.0	28.8	16.7	38.2	33.0	11.0	2.63	3.37	27 210	26.4	34.4
Edison township	35 136	73.7	34.3	61.1	29.7	9.1	3.7	26.3	21.1	7.2	2.72	3.19	31 771	8.3	19.4
Egg Harbor township	11 199	72.4	37.5	55.3	28.1	12.6	6.9	27.6	22.0	7.1	2.74	3.23	9 068	9.7	21.9
Elizabeth city	40 482	69.6	36.6	42.9	22.8	19.1	10.7	30.4	24.6	8.4	2.91	3.45	39 101	17.2	26.2
Englewood city	9 273	69.3	31.0	47.9	21.8	17.4	7.4	30.1	24.8	9.0	2.79	3.29	8 971	16.1	23.8
Evesham township	15 712	72.2	38.2	61.2	32.4	8.5	4.6	27.8	22.8	6.0	2.68	3.21	12 562	7.0	19.1
Ewing township	12 551	65.4	25.3	49.7	18.8	12.2	5.3	34.6	27.7	12.1	2.45	3.00	12 102	10.7	24.1
Fair Lawn borough	11 806	75.4	33.4	63.5	29.0	9.0	3.5	24.6	21.3	12.3	2.67	3.12	11 493	8.7	20.1
Fort Lee borough	16 544	56.8	22.6	46.7	19.0	7.4	2.9	43.2	39.0	15.2	2.14	2.88	15 236	5.9	38.5
Franklin township	19 355	67.1	30.8	53.1	24.6	10.3	4.9	32.9	25.7	5.8	2.58	3.14	16 158	8.8	21.9
Freehold township	10 814	76.6	37.8	65.9	33.4	8.0	3.5	23.4	20.0	7.7	2.76	3.21	8 207	7.3	16.7
Galloway township	10 772	71.3	38.4	54.5	28.2	12.4	7.7	28.7	21.5	6.6	2.70	3.18	7 937	9.1	18.5
Garfield city	11 250	66.0	30.5	46.5	22.6	13.8	6.1	34.0	27.4	12.2	2.64	3.26	10 946	11.7	28.9
Gloucester township	23 150	72.9	37.8	55.9	28.5	12.5	6.8	27.1	21.4	6.2	2.75	3.24	18 527	9.8	19.2
Hackensack city	18 113	52.7	21.9	34.8	13.9	13.0	6.4	47.3	39.8	9.4	2.26	3.08	16 464	13.1	39.6
Hamilton township	33 523	70.6	31.2	55.3	24.3	11.5	5.3	29.4	24.5	10.8	2.58	3.10	32 576	9.5	22.3
Hillsborough township	12 649	77.5	44.9	67.6	39.7	7.5	4.1	22.5	17.8	4.0	2.88	3.31	10 088	7.9	16.4
Hoboken city	19 418	35.2	11.4	23.8	6.6	9.0	4.1	64.8	41.8	8.0	1.92	2.73	15 036	11.8	37.6
Howell township	16 063	81.0	47.1	69.4	41.4	8.6	4.5	19.0	15.4	7.1	3.04	3.42	12 777	7.4	13.6
Irvington township	22 032	65.4	33.9	30.2	14.9	27.6	15.6	34.6	29.3	6.4	2.74	3.39	22 188	22.6	28.2
Jackson township	14 176	79.5	44.0	66.7	37.4	8.9	4.8	20.5	16.0	6.1	2.99	3.38	11 116	8.2	15.3
Jersey City city	88 632	62.8	31.1	36.4	17.6	20.2	11.2	37.2	29.2	8.2	2.67	3.37	82 381	19.7	28.4
Kearny town	13 539	72.4	34.6	53.8	26.5	13.2	6.1	27.6	21.8	8.8	2.81	3.28	12 470	12.9	21.3
Lacey township	9 336	77.6	35.1	64.5	28.4	9.4	5.0	22.4	18.4	9.3	2.71	3.08	7 957	7.7	16.8
Lakewood township	19 876	67.2	32.2	53.3	25.5	10.6	5.3	32.8	28.5	19.5	2.92	3.64	16 352	9.7	31.9
Lawrence township	10 797	67.0	31.4	53.9	25.3	10.5	5.1	33.0	26.8	9.7	2.49	3.05	9 107	9.8	22.9
Linden city	15 052	67.0	29.0	46.7	20.8	15.3	6.5	33.0	27.9	13.6	2.60	3.21	14 369	12.3	26.6
Livingston township	9 300	85.3	41.8	76.0	38.5	7.0	2.6	14.7	13.0	8.4	2.93	3.21	8 789	7.0	10.6
Long Branch city	12 594	57.6	27.0	36.9	15.9	15.9	9.2	42.4	34.1	10.5	2.47	3.19	11 544	15.8	31.7

[1] No spouse present.

Table E. Towns

Town	Percent change of households, 1990–2000	Total housing units	Occupied housing units (percent)	Vacant housing units Total	For seasonal, recreational, or occasional use	Homeowner vacancy rate (percent)	Rental vacancy rate (percent)	Occupied housing units Total	Percent owner-occupied housing units	Percent renter-occupied housing units	Average household size of owner-occupied units	Average household size of renter-occupied units
	86	87	88	89	90	91	92	93	94	95	96	97
MINNESOTA—Cont'd												
Maplewood city	19.7	14 004	98.2	1.8	0.4	0.4	1.9	13 758	75.7	24.3	2.67	1.90
Minneapolis city	1.0	168 606	96.3	3.7	0.5	0.7	2.8	162 352	51.4	48.6	2.43	2.05
Minnetonka city	14.5	22 228	96.2	3.8	1.1	0.4	5.0	21 393	75.7	24.3	2.55	1.79
Moorhead city	5.4	12 180	95.7	4.3	0.2	0.8	6.3	11 660	63.7	36.3	2.65	2.05
Oakdale city	52.9	10 394	98.5	1.5	0.2	0.5	1.8	10 243	80.5	19.5	2.75	1.94
Plymouth city	35.2	25 258	98.3	1.7	0.5	0.3	2.1	24 820	76.5	23.5	2.76	2.08
Richfield city	-3.1	15 357	98.2	1.8	0.2	0.4	2.4	15 073	67.6	32.4	2.42	1.91
Rochester city	22.2	35 346	96.5	3.5	0.5	0.7	4.0	34 116	71.0	29.0	2.64	1.93
Roseville city	7.6	14 917	97.9	2.1	0.5	0.5	2.3	14 598	67.5	32.5	2.44	1.69
St. Louis Park city	4.3	21 140	98.3	1.7	0.3	0.4	1.7	20 782	63.6	36.4	2.26	1.77
St. Paul city	1.7	115 713	96.9	3.1	0.4	0.7	2.8	112 109	54.8	45.2	2.72	2.15
Shoreview city	12.6	10 289	98.4	1.6	0.4	0.5	2.3	10 125	87.2	12.8	2.64	1.91
Winona city	10.4	10 666	96.6	3.4	0.2	0.8	4.1	10 301	60.9	39.1	2.46	1.99
Woodbury city	140.7	17 541	95.1	4.9	0.6	1.4	13.3	16 676	85.2	14.8	2.87	2.13
NEW HAMPSHIRE	15.4	547 024	86.8	13.2	10.3	1.0	3.5	474 606	69.7	30.3	2.70	2.14
Concord city	14.5	16 881	96.4	3.6	0.7	0.8	2.9	16 281	51.4	48.6	2.62	1.96
Derry town	14.5	12 735	96.8	3.2	1.2	0.5	2.3	12 327	64.7	35.3	3.03	2.22
Dover city	11.9	11 924	97.1	2.9	0.6	0.7	1.8	11 573	51.2	48.8	2.54	1.96
Manchester city	9.7	45 892	96.4	3.6	0.5	0.5	3.1	44 247	46.0	54.0	2.61	2.14
Merrimack town	18.7	8 959	98.6	1.4	0.5	0.2	1.8	8 832	86.1	13.9	2.92	2.34
Nashua city	11.5	35 387	97.8	2.2	0.5	0.4	1.6	34 614	56.9	43.1	2.66	2.20
Rochester city	11.9	11 836	96.6	3.4	0.7	0.9	2.8	11 434	66.8	33.2	2.56	2.26
Salem town	13.2	10 866	95.7	4.3	2.5	0.5	2.6	10 402	78.2	21.8	2.86	2.06
NEW JERSEY	9.7	3 310 275	92.6	7.4	3.3	1.2	4.5	3 064 645	65.6	34.4	2.81	2.43
Atlantic City city	0.7	20 219	78.4	21.6	9.6	6.2	7.3	15 848	28.9	71.1	2.66	2.38
Bayonne city	0.9	26 826	95.2	4.8	0.2	0.9	3.6	25 545	40.0	60.0	2.61	2.28
Belleville township	2.7	14 144	97.1	2.9	0.2	1.0	2.5	13 731	51.0	49.0	2.91	2.28
Bergenfield borough	2.1	9 147	98.2	1.8	0.2	0.4	1.8	8 981	71.1	28.9	3.09	2.49
Berkeley township	12.6	22 288	89.0	11.0	6.8	1.8	6.3	19 828	92.9	7.1	1.97	2.16
Bloomfield township	3.0	19 508	97.5	2.5	0.2	0.7	2.5	19 017	53.4	46.6	2.86	2.05
Brick township	18.2	32 689	90.3	9.7	6.5	0.9	4.4	29 511	83.4	16.6	2.60	2.32
Bridgewater township	37.8	15 879	98.0	2.0	0.3	0.5	3.1	15 561	86.0	14.0	2.79	2.19
Camden city	-9.2	29 769	81.2	18.8	0.1	5.1	6.1	24 177	46.1	53.9	3.16	3.09
Cherry Hill township	6.9	27 074	96.9	3.1	0.7	0.6	6.5	26 227	83.0	17.0	2.74	1.95
City of Orange township	2.6	12 665	93.8	6.2	0.2	2.5	4.2	11 885	25.5	74.5	3.25	2.55
Clifton city	4.1	31 060	97.4	2.6	0.2	0.7	2.4	30 244	60.9	39.1	2.75	2.33
Deptford township	17.1	10 647	94.0	6.0	0.2	1.1	11.6	10 013	77.4	22.6	2.76	2.13
Dover township	22.5	41 116	81.5	18.5	10.6	1.5	9.7	33 510	83.7	16.3	2.66	2.42
East Brunswick township	9.7	16 640	98.4	1.6	0.1	0.4	3.6	16 372	84.0	16.0	2.94	2.30
East Orange city	-4.4	28 485	91.4	8.6	0.1	2.3	6.8	26 024	26.6	73.4	3.27	2.40
Edison township	10.6	36 018	97.6	2.4	0.2	0.6	2.8	35 136	63.8	36.2	2.90	2.41
Egg Harbor township	23.5	12 067	92.8	7.2	2.6	2.4	6.9	11 199	84.9	15.1	2.81	2.36
Elizabeth city	3.5	42 838	94.5	5.5	0.3	1.5	3.4	40 482	29.7	70.3	3.25	2.76
Englewood city	3.4	9 614	96.5	3.5	0.4	1.0	2.5	9 273	59.4	40.6	2.91	2.63
Evesham township	25.1	16 324	96.3	3.7	0.2	1.3	6.9	15 712	77.7	22.3	2.91	1.89
Ewing township	3.7	12 924	97.1	2.9	0.3	0.9	2.9	12 551	74.0	26.0	2.58	2.07
Fair Lawn borough	2.7	12 006	98.3	1.7	0.2	0.4	1.9	11 806	80.0	20.0	2.80	2.11
Fort Lee borough	8.6	17 446	94.8	5.2	1.5	1.3	3.9	16 544	56.2	43.8	2.13	2.15
Franklin township	19.8	19 789	97.8	2.2	0.3	0.6	2.2	19 355	72.0	28.0	2.65	2.38
Freehold township	31.8	11 032	98.0	2.0	0.2	0.5	3.6	10 814	86.8	13.2	2.85	2.15
Galloway township	35.7	11 406	94.4	5.6	1.9	1.3	5.2	10 772	74.5	25.5	2.81	2.39
Garfield city	2.8	11 698	96.2	3.8	0.3	0.8	2.9	11 250	40.2	59.8	2.80	2.54
Gloucester township	25.0	24 257	95.4	4.6	0.3	1.4	5.2	23 150	74.1	25.9	2.95	2.18
Hackensack city	10.0	18 945	95.6	4.4	0.6	1.3	3.8	18 113	32.4	67.6	2.49	2.15
Hamilton township	2.9	34 535	97.1	2.9	0.1	1.2	3.9	33 523	75.1	24.9	2.75	2.05
Hillsborough township	25.4	12 854	98.4	1.6	0.2	0.4	1.1	12 649	83.1	16.9	2.98	2.38
Hoboken city	29.1	19 915	97.5	2.5	0.3	0.6	1.7	19 418	22.6	77.4	1.96	1.91
Howell township	25.7	16 572	96.9	3.1	0.3	1.1	4.0	16 063	89.2	10.8	3.10	2.56
Irvington township	-0.7	24 116	91.4	8.6	0.1	3.6	5.2	22 032	29.7	70.3	3.30	2.51
Jackson township	27.5	14 640	96.8	3.2	0.5	0.9	2.9	14 176	87.1	12.9	3.06	2.54
Jersey City city	7.6	93 648	94.6	5.4	0.3	1.9	3.3	88 632	28.2	71.8	2.98	2.55
Kearny town	8.6	13 872	97.6	2.4	0.2	0.6	2.1	13 539	48.0	52.0	3.00	2.63
Lacey township	17.3	10 580	88.2	11.8	9.2	0.9	3.7	9 336	90.7	9.3	2.69	2.88
Lakewood township	21.6	21 214	93.7	6.3	1.3	2.0	4.0	19 876	63.1	36.9	2.65	3.38
Lawrence township	18.6	11 180	96.6	3.4	0.7	1.0	4.0	10 797	70.8	29.2	2.64	2.12
Linden city	4.8	15 567	96.7	3.3	0.2	1.1	3.0	15 052	58.7	41.3	2.75	2.39
Livingston township	5.8	9 457	98.3	1.7	0.3	0.5	1.6	9 300	93.5	6.5	2.97	2.41
Long Branch city	9.1	13 983	90.1	9.9	5.0	1.3	3.6	12 594	42.4	57.6	2.61	2.37

Table E. Towns

STATE MCD code	Town	Land area, 2000[1] (sq km)	Total persons	Rank within state	Per square kilometer	Land area, 1990[1] (sq km)	Total persons	Rank within state	Per square kilometer	White	Black or African American	American Indian or Alaska Native	Asian	Native Hawaiian and other Pacific Islander	Some other race
		1	2	3	4	5	6	7	8	9	10	11	12	13	14
	NEW JERSEY—Cont'd														
34 42990	Manalapan township..........	79.8	33 423	70	418.8	79.3	26 716	70	336.9	91.8	2.0	0.0	4.5	0.0	0.5
34 43140	Manchester township.....	213.9	38 928	46	182.0	214.0	35 976	46	168.1	94.3	3.1	0.1	0.9	0.0	0.7
34 44070	Marlboro township	79.2	36 398	67	459.6	79.2	27 074	67	353.2	83.8	2.1	0.0	12.7	0.0	0.5
34 45990	Middletown township	106.5	66 327	14	622.8	106.5	68 183	14	640.2	94.7	1.2	0.1	2.6	0.0	0.5
34 46680	Millville city	109.7	26 847	73	244.7	109.7	25 992	73	236.9	76.1	15.0	0.5	0.8	0.0	5.2
34 47250	Monroe township (Gloucester)	120.6	28 967	71	240.2	120.6	26 703	71	221.4	84.8	11.2	0.2	1.2	0.0	1.0
34 47280	Monroe township (Middlesex)	108.6	27 999	87	257.8	109.4	22 256	87	203.4	93.3	2.9	0.1	2.3	0.1	0.7
34 47500	Montclair township	16.3	38 977	41	2 391.2	16.3	37 487	41	2 299.8	59.8	32.1	0.2	3.2	0.0	1.8
34 49020	Mount Laurel township	56.5	40 221	60	711.9	56.5	30 270	60	535.8	87.1	6.9	0.1	3.8	0.0	0.6
34 49890	Neptune township	21.3	27 690	66	1 300.0	21.2	28 148	66	1 327.7	55.9	38.2	0.2	1.2	0.0	0.8
34 51000	Newark city	61.6	273 546	1	4 440.7	61.7	275 221	1	4 460.6	26.5	53.5	0.4	1.2	0.0	14.0
34 51210	New Brunswick city	13.5	48 573	35	3 598.0	13.5	41 711	35	3 089.7	48.8	23.0	0.5	5.3	0.1	18.1
34 52470	North Bergen township.......	13.5	58 092	25	4 303.1	13.5	48 414	25	3 586.2	67.4	2.7	0.4	6.5	0.0	15.5
34 52560	North Brunswick township..	31.1	36 287	58	1 166.8	31.2	31 287	58	1 002.8	62.7	15.3	0.2	14.2	0.0	4.7
34 53680	Nutley township	8.7	27 362	68	3 145.1	8.7	27 099	68	3 114.8	87.9	1.9	0.1	7.1	0.0	1.8
34 54270	Ocean township	28.6	26 959	78	942.6	28.6	25 058	78	876.2	84.3	5.7	0.1	6.3	0.1	1.6
34 54705	Old Bridge township	98.6	60 456	20	613.1	98.5	56 493	20	573.5	79.5	5.3	0.2	10.8	0.0	1.9
34 55950	Paramus borough	27.1	25 737	79	949.7	27.2	25 004	79	919.3	79.2	1.1	0.0	17.2	0.0	0.9
34 56460	Parsippany-Troy Hills township..............	62.0	50 649	24	816.9	61.9	48 478	24	783.2	74.3	3.1	0.1	18.1	0.1	1.9
34 56550	Passaic city	8.1	67 861	18	8 377.9	8.0	58 041	18	7 255.1	35.4	13.8	0.8	5.5	0.0	39.4
34 57000	Paterson city......................	21.9	149 222	3	6 813.8	21.9	140 891	3	6 433.4	30.8	32.9	0.6	1.9	0.1	27.6
34 57510	Pemberton township	159.7	28 691	57	179.7	160.0	31 342	57	195.9	66.0	23.1	0.5	3.2	0.1	2.9
34 57660	Pennsauken township	27.3	35 737	50	1 309.0	27.3	34 738	50	1 272.5	60.1	24.2	0.3	4.6	0.0	8.3
34 58200	Perth Amboy city	12.4	47 303	33	3 814.8	12.4	41 967	33	3 384.4	46.4	10.0	0.7	1.5	0.1	35.6
34 59010	Piscataway township	48.6	50 482	26	1 038.7	48.7	47 089	26	966.9	48.8	20.3	0.2	24.8	0.0	3.1
34 59190	Plainfield city	15.6	47 829	28	3 066.0	15.6	46 577	28	2 985.7	21.4	61.8	0.4	0.9	0.1	10.8
34 61530	Rahway city	10.3	26 500	77	2 572.8	10.3	25 325	77	2 458.7	60.2	27.1	0.2	3.6	0.1	5.6
34 65790	Sayreville borough	41.2	40 377	48	980.0	41.8	34 998	48	837.3	76.5	8.6	0.1	10.6	0.0	2.1
34 68790	South Brunswick township .	105.8	37 734	74	356.7	106.1	25 798	74	243.1	70.5	7.9	0.1	18.0	0.0	1.4
34 72360	Teaneck township	15.7	39 260	40	2 500.6	15.7	37 825	40	2 409.2	56.2	28.8	0.2	7.1	0.0	4.2
34 74000	Trenton city........................	19.8	85 403	7	4 313.3	19.8	88 675	7	4 478.5	32.6	52.1	0.4	0.8	0.2	10.8
34 74480	Union township	23.6	54 405	23	2 305.3	23.6	50 024	23	2 119.7	67.7	19.8	0.1	7.7	0.0	2.4
34 74630	Union City city	3.3	67 088	19	20 329.7	3.3	58 012	19	17 579.4	58.4	3.6	0.7	2.1	0.1	28.2
34 76070	Vineland city	177.9	56 271	21	316.3	177.9	54 780	21	307.9	67.5	13.6	0.5	1.2	0.1	14.0
34 76220	Voorhees township	30.1	28 126	82	934.4	30.1	24 559	82	815.9	78.3	8.0	0.1	11.4	0.0	0.6
34 76460	Wall township	79.3	25 261	89	318.5	79.3	20 244	89	255.3	97.1	0.6	0.1	1.3	0.0	0.3
34 77180	Washington township	55.3	47 114	34	852.0	55.4	41 960	34	757.4	90.2	4.9	0.1	3.3	0.0	0.5
34 77840	Wayne township	61.7	54 069	27	876.3	61.7	47 025	27	762.2	90.0	1.7	0.1	5.7	0.0	1.2
34 79040	Westfield town	17.4	29 644	63	1 703.7	17.4	28 870	63	1 659.2	90.0	3.9	0.1	4.1	0.0	0.6
34 79460	West Milford township	195.4	26 410	76	135.2	195.4	25 430	76	130.1	95.1	1.2	0.6	1.0	0.0	0.6
34 79610	West New York town..........	2.6	45 768	38	17 603.1	2.6	38 125	38	14 663.5	60.1	3.6	0.7	2.9	0.0	25.2
34 79800	West Orange township	31.4	44 943	36	1 431.3	31.4	39 103	36	1 245.3	67.6	17.5	0.1	8.1	0.0	3.5
34 81440	Willingboro township	19.9	33 008	45	1 658.7	20.0	36 291	45	1 814.6	24.7	66.7	0.3	1.7	0.0	2.6
34 81740	Winslow township	149.4	34 611	61	231.7	149.4	30 087	61	201.4	65.5	29.3	0.3	1.3	0.0	1.6
34 82000	Woodbridge township	59.6	97 203	5	1 630.9	59.7	93 092	5	1 559.3	70.8	8.8	0.2	14.5	0.0	3.3
36 00000	NEW YORK	122 283	18 976 457	X	155.2	122 310	17 990 778	X	147.1	67.9	15.9	0.4	5.5	0.0	7.1
36 01000	Albany city	55.4	95 658	19	1 726.7	55.4	100 031	19	1 802.4	63.1	28.1	0.3	3.3	0.0	2.2
36 02000	Amherst town	137.9	116 510	18	844.9	138.0	111 711	18	809.5	89.3	3.9	0.1	5.2	0.0	0.4
36 03078	Auburn city.........................	21.7	28 574	60	1 316.8	21.7	31 258	60	1 440.5	88.6	7.6	0.3	0.6	0.0	1.4
36 04000	Babylon town	135.4	211 792	13	1 564.2	135.6	202 793	13	1 495.5	76.3	15.6	0.3	1.9	0.0	3.4
36 06354	Bethlehem town	126.4	31 304	74	247.7	126.4	27 552	74	218.0	94.7	2.3	0.2	1.7	0.0	0.3
36 06607	Binghamton city	27.0	47 380	37	1 754.8	26.9	53 008	37	1 970.6	83.2	8.4	0.3	3.3	0.0	1.7
36 08246	Brighton town	40.0	35 588	52	889.7	40.1	34 455	52	859.2	86.1	3.7	0.1	8.1	0.0	0.6
36 08510	Bronx borough	108.8	1 332 650	4	12 248.6	108.9	1 203 789	4	11 054.1	29.9	35.6	0.9	3.0	0.1	24.7
36 10000	Brookhaven town	671.6	448 248	6	667.4	671.6	407 779	6	607.2	88.4	4.3	0.2	2.9	0.0	2.2
36 10022	Brooklyn borough	182.9	2 465 326	1	13 479.1	182.7	2 300 664	1	12 592.6	41.2	36.4	0.4	7.5	0.1	10.1
36 11000	Buffalo city.........................	105.2	292 648	8	2 781.8	105.2	328 175	8	3 119.5	54.4	37.2	0.8	1.4	0.0	3.7
36 12529	Carmel town	93.5	33 006	69	353.0	93.6	28 816	69	307.9	94.6	1.1	0.1	1.2	0.0	1.5
36 15011	Cheektowaga town	76.5	94 019	20	1 229.0	76.5	99 314	20	1 298.2	94.9	2.9	0.2	0.9	0.0	0.3
36 15462	Chili town	102.9	27 638	80	268.6	102.9	25 178	80	244.7	91.1	5.7	0.2	1.1	0.0	0.5
36 15704	Cicero town	125.5	27 982	79	223.0	125.5	25 560	79	203.7	96.3	1.2	0.4	0.7	0.0	0.2
36 15825	Clarence town	138.3	26 123	91	188.9	138.4	20 041	91	144.8	97.0	0.6	0.2	1.4	0.0	0.2
36 15968	Clarkstown town	99.8	82 082	25	822.5	99.8	79 346	25	795.1	80.0	7.9	0.1	7.9	0.1	2.0
36 16067	Clay town	124.3	58 805	33	473.1	124.3	59 749	33	480.7	92.1	3.5	0.5	2.0	0.0	0.4
36 16353	Clifton Park town	125.8	32 995	64	262.3	125.8	30 117	64	239.4	94.9	1.2	0.1	2.5	0.0	0.4
36 17343	Colonie town	145.2	79 258	26	545.9	145.3	76 497	26	526.5	90.6	4.0	0.2	3.6	0.0	0.6
36 18410	Cortlandt town	102.7	38 467	47	374.6	102.7	37 357	47	363.7	88.6	4.6	0.2	2.6	0.0	2.3
36 21820	Eastchester town	12.7	31 318	61	2 466.0	12.7	30 867	61	2 430.5	87.3	2.8	0.1	6.8	0.0	1.4
36 21996	East Fishkill town...............	147.4	25 589	90	173.6	147.4	22 101	90	149.9	92.5	2.3	0.0	2.8	0.0	0.9

[1] Dry land or land partially or temporarily covered by water.

Table E. Towns

Town	Two or more races	White	Black	American Indian or Alaska Native	Asian	Native Hawaiian and other Pacific Islander	Some other race	Hispanic[1]	White	Black or African American	American Indian or Alaska Native	Asian and Pacific Islander	Hispanic[1]
	15	16	17	18	19	20	21	22	23	24	25	26	27
NEW JERSEY—Cont'd													
Manalapan township............	1.1	92.8	2.3	0.2	4.9	0.1	1.0	3.5	92.8	3.1	0.1	3.6	2.7
Manchester township...........	0.9	95.2	3.4	0.4	1.0	0.1	1.0	2.6	95.8	3.3	0.1	0.5	2.0
Marlboro township	1.0	84.6	2.2	0.2	13.2	0.1	0.8	2.9	90.1	3.6	0.1	5.8	2.1
Middletown township	0.9	95.5	1.4	0.2	2.9	0.1	0.9	3.4	95.0	1.9	0.1	2.7	2.7
Millville city......................	2.4	77.9	16.2	1.2	1.0	0.1	6.1	11.2	86.6	8.4	0.4	0.6	7.6
Monroe township (Gloucester)	1.5	86.1	11.8	0.6	1.6	0.1	1.5	2.7	85.7	12.5	0.2	1.0	2.1
Monroe township (Middlesex)	0.6	93.8	3.1	0.2	2.5	0.1	0.9	2.4	94.9	3.1	0.1	1.7	1.8
Montclair township	3.0	61.8	34.1	0.9	3.8	0.1	2.7	5.1	65.5	31.0	0.2	2.3	3.3
Mount Laurel township	1.4	88.2	7.6	0.5	4.3	0.1	0.9	2.2	90.8	6.0	0.1	2.6	1.6
Neptune township................	2.6	57.3	39.9	0.9	1.5	0.2	2.9	5.6	62.9	33.8	0.3	1.2	4.2
Newark city	4.4	29.4	55.0	0.8	1.6	0.2	17.6	29.5	28.6	58.5	0.2	1.2	26.1
New Brunswick city	4.2	51.7	24.5	1.2	5.9	0.2	21.0	39.0	57.4	29.6	0.3	4.0	19.3
North Bergen township	7.5	74.0	3.6	0.8	7.3	0.1	21.8	57.3	84.2	2.1	0.2	4.8	41.2
North Brunswick township	2.9	64.7	16.3	0.7	15.1	0.1	6.3	10.4	80.0	11.1	0.2	6.8	5.8
Nutley township	1.2	89.0	2.0	0.2	7.5	0.1	2.4	6.7	92.7	1.8	0.0	4.7	3.3
Ocean township	1.9	85.6	6.4	0.4	6.8	0.2	2.6	4.5	90.4	5.2	0.1	3.7	2.7
Old Bridge township	2.3	81.1	5.8	0.5	11.7	0.1	3.2	7.6	89.4	3.4	0.1	6.1	5.0
Paramus borough	1.5	80.4	1.3	0.2	18.0	0.0	1.6	4.9	88.2	0.8	0.0	10.5	3.6
Parsippany-Troy Hills township	2.5	76.1	3.6	0.4	19.2	0.1	3.1	7.0	85.1	3.6	0.1	10.1	4.2
Passaic city.......................	5.0	39.0	15.2	1.2	6.1	0.2	43.5	62.5	45.3	20.6	0.5	7.1	50.0
Paterson city	6.2	35.0	34.6	1.0	2.5	0.3	32.9	50.1	41.2	36.0	0.3	1.4	41.0
Pemberton township............	4.2	69.2	25.3	1.3	4.6	0.2	4.0	8.6	68.8	22.8	0.5	4.4	8.1
Pennsauken township	2.5	61.8	25.3	0.7	5.2	0.1	9.6	14.3	80.5	14.7	0.4	1.8	4.9
Perth Amboy city	5.6	50.9	11.4	1.1	1.8	0.2	40.3	69.8	59.8	11.8	0.4	1.6	55.5
Piscataway township	2.8	50.7	21.3	0.7	25.9	0.1	4.2	7.9	65.9	17.6	0.2	13.9	5.9
Plainfield city	4.6	24.4	63.9	1.1	1.2	0.3	14.0	25.2	26.5	65.7	0.5	1.1	15.0
Rahway city	3.3	62.3	28.7	0.8	4.0	0.1	7.6	13.9	75.4	20.2	0.2	2.4	7.5
Sayreville borough...............	2.1	78.0	9.1	0.4	11.3	0.1	3.3	7.3	93.1	3.2	0.1	3.0	4.0
South Brunswick township	2.0	72.0	8.6	0.5	18.8	0.1	2.1	5.1	84.1	6.2	0.1	8.8	3.7
Teaneck township................	3.5	58.5	30.5	0.8	8.0	0.1	6.0	10.5	66.6	26.2	0.2	5.6	6.3
Trenton city	3.2	34.5	53.6	0.8	1.2	0.4	12.9	21.5	42.2	49.3	0.3	0.7	14.1
Union township	2.2	69.2	20.6	0.4	8.2	0.1	3.9	8.9	86.5	9.4	0.1	3.3	4.5
Union City city	6.9	64.2	5.3	1.2	2.6	0.2	33.7	82.3	74.7	5.1	0.2	2.1	75.6
Vineland city	3.1	69.8	14.8	1.1	1.4	0.2	16.1	30.0	73.0	11.5	0.3	0.9	23.6
Voorhees township	1.6	79.5	8.5	0.4	12.1	0.1	1.1	2.5	85.1	6.5	0.1	7.8	1.9
Wall township	0.6	97.6	0.8	0.3	1.4	0.0	0.4	1.5	98.4	0.6	0.0	0.8	1.0
Washington township	1.0	91.0	5.2	0.3	3.7	0.1	0.9	2.0	92.5	3.7	0.1	3.3	1.4
Wayne township	1.3	91.2	1.9	0.3	6.1	0.0	1.9	5.1	95.0	1.1	0.1	3.1	3.1
Westfield town	1.3	91.1	4.3	0.3	4.7	0.1	1.0	2.8	91.5	4.6	0.1	3.5	2.0
West Milford township	1.4	96.2	1.7	1.2	1.3	0.0	1.0	3.4	97.2	1.0	0.4	0.9	2.1
West New York town...........	7.6	66.7	4.8	1.1	3.4	0.1	31.8	78.7	76.7	4.0	0.4	1.9	73.3
West Orange township	3.2	69.5	18.9	0.5	8.8	0.1	5.6	10.0	87.6	5.7	0.1	5.6	4.4
Willingboro township............	4.0	26.9	69.9	1.3	2.4	0.2	3.8	6.1	39.7	56.1	0.3	1.9	5.3
Winslow township	2.0	67.0	30.4	0.8	1.6	0.1	2.3	4.3	74.6	23.0	0.3	1.1	3.1
Woodbridge township	2.5	72.5	9.3	0.5	15.3	0.1	4.7	9.2	86.6	6.5	0.1	5.5	5.6
NEW YORK	3.1	70.0	17.0	0.9	6.2	0.2	9.1	15.1	74.4	15.9	0.3	3.9	12.3
Albany city	3.0	65.1	29.9	1.0	3.9	0.1	3.2	5.6	75.5	20.6	0.3	2.3	3.1
Amherst town......................	1.1	90.2	4.3	0.3	5.6	0.1	0.7	1.4	92.9	2.8	0.2	3.9	1.1
Auburn city	1.5	89.9	8.6	0.8	0.7	0.1	1.7	2.8	91.9	6.8	0.3	0.5	2.2
Babylon town......................	2.5	78.0	16.6	0.7	2.3	0.1	4.9	10.0	82.1	14.9	0.3	1.2	6.2
Bethlehem town...................	0.8	95.5	2.5	0.3	2.0	0.1	0.5	1.7	96.5	1.9	0.1	1.3	1.1
Binghamton city	3.1	85.7	10.0	0.8	3.9	0.1	2.8	3.9	91.9	4.9	0.3	2.1	1.8
Brighton town......................	1.3	87.2	4.1	0.3	8.8	0.1	1.0	2.3	92.1	3.0	0.1	4.3	1.6
Bronx borough	5.8	33.1	38.3	1.5	3.6	0.3	29.2	48.4	35.7	37.3	0.5	3.0	43.5
Brookhaven town.................	1.9	89.9	5.0	0.6	3.3	0.1	3.1	8.0	93.1	3.6	0.2	2.0	5.5
Brooklyn borough	4.3	43.7	38.1	0.8	8.4	0.2	13.2	19.8	46.9	37.9	0.3	4.8	20.1
Buffalo city	2.5	56.2	38.6	1.4	1.7	0.1	4.7	7.5	64.7	30.7	0.8	1.0	4.9
Carmel town	1.5	96.0	1.4	0.4	1.4	0.1	2.4	5.9	97.8	0.7	0.1	0.9	2.5
Cheektowaga town...............	0.7	95.6	3.3	0.4	1.1	0.0	0.4	1.0	98.4	1.0	0.1	0.4	0.5
Chili town	1.2	92.2	6.2	0.5	1.4	0.1	0.9	1.6	93.8	4.6	0.2	1.0	1.1
Cicero town........................	1.2	97.4	1.6	0.8	1.0	0.0	0.4	0.9	97.2	1.5	0.4	0.6	0.9
Clarence town.....................	0.6	97.5	0.8	0.3	1.6	0.1	0.3	0.8	98.6	0.4	0.2	0.8	0.4
Clarkstown town	2.0	81.3	8.8	0.4	8.4	0.2	3.1	6.9	86.5	7.5	0.1	5.1	4.2
Clay town...........................	1.5	93.5	4.2	0.9	2.3	0.1	0.6	1.4	95.1	2.8	0.4	1.5	1.0
Clifton Park town	0.9	95.6	1.4	0.3	2.9	0.0	0.7	1.4	96.6	1.1	0.2	1.9	1.0
Colonie town	1.1	91.4	4.3	0.4	3.9	0.0	1.0	1.9	94.6	2.8	0.1	2.2	1.2
Cortland town	1.7	90.0	5.2	0.5	3.0	0.0	3.0	7.2	93.5	3.8	0.1	1.9	3.6
Eastchester town	1.5	88.7	3.1	0.2	7.3	0.1	2.2	4.5	88.2	3.5	0.1	7.7	2.8
East Fishkill town................	1.3	93.7	2.7	0.5	3.2	0.1	1.3	4.0	93.8	2.2	0.2	3.5	2.5

[1] Hispanic persons may be of any race.

Table E. Towns

| Town | Population and population characteristics, 2000 | | | | | | | | | | |
| | Age (percent) | | | | | | | | | | |
	Under 5 years	5 to 17 years	18 to 24 years	25 to 34 years	35 to 44 years	45 to 54 years	55 to 64 years	65 to 74 years	75 years and over	Median age (years)	Percent Female
	28	29	30	31	32	33	34	35	36	37	38
NEW JERSEY—Cont'd											
Manalapan township	6.6	23.7	5.8	8.5	19.1	16.5	8.1	4.9	6.7	38.2	52.0
Manchester township	2.6	8.1	3.5	5.7	7.7	7.5	10.3	21.2	33.3	67.7	57.7
Marlboro township	7.5	22.7	5.6	9.5	19.3	17.5	9.1	5.3	3.5	37.6	50.4
Middletown township	6.8	19.5	6.4	10.7	17.9	16.2	9.7	6.5	6.3	38.8	51.4
Millville city	7.0	21.0	8.6	13.4	15.4	13.2	8.5	6.5	6.4	35.0	52.8
Monroe township (Gloucester)	6.6	19.1	7.4	13.4	16.6	14.2	9.8	7.2	5.7	37.1	51.7
Monroe township (Middlesex)	4.0	12.0	4.2	6.3	10.0	9.6	10.4	19.7	23.9	58.9	54.1
Montclair township	7.0	18.6	6.6	13.3	18.5	16.0	8.1	5.8	6.1	37.5	53.7
Mount Laurel township	6.1	17.0	5.4	14.4	18.3	14.3	9.8	8.6	6.1	38.9	52.8
Neptune township	6.0	17.1	6.7	12.6	17.1	14.0	9.8	8.1	8.6	39.4	53.4
Newark city	7.8	20.2	12.1	16.9	15.1	10.9	7.8	5.3	4.0	30.8	51.5
New Brunswick city	7.0	13.1	34.0	17.6	10.6	7.1	4.2	3.2	3.3	23.6	50.4
North Bergen township	6.4	16.3	9.0	16.7	16.5	12.2	9.1	7.0	6.8	35.9	52.2
North Brunswick township	6.7	16.3	8.0	18.2	18.3	14.2	8.4	5.6	4.4	35.4	52.2
Nutley township	5.5	16.3	6.4	14.4	17.2	14.8	9.3	8.0	8.1	39.3	50.3
Ocean township	6.3	19.2	6.7	12.2	17.6	16.2	9.6	6.8	5.3	38.4	51.8
Old Bridge township	7.0	18.8	7.0	14.4	19.3	14.4	8.5	6.2	4.4	36.5	51.1
Paramus borough	5.2	18.1	5.5	9.0	15.7	14.4	10.7	10.5	11.0	42.9	51.4
Parsippany-Troy Hills township	6.1	14.9	6.7	17.1	18.1	15.2	10.7	6.6	4.6	37.6	50.6
Passaic city	9.6	21.2	12.5	17.5	14.2	10.5	6.4	4.2	3.9	28.6	50.1
Paterson city	8.4	21.4	11.2	16.5	15.5	11.3	7.5	4.6	3.7	30.5	51.4
Pemberton township	6.7	20.9	9.5	13.8	17.7	13.2	8.5	6.3	3.4	34.4	50.7
Pennsauken township	6.2	21.3	7.6	13.0	16.6	13.1	8.0	7.0	7.2	36.1	52.1
Perth Amboy city	8.0	20.4	11.4	16.5	15.1	11.3	7.0	5.1	5.1	31.2	50.4
Piscataway township	6.2	15.7	14.1	16.7	16.5	13.4	8.7	5.2	3.4	33.3	50.5
Plainfield city	7.9	19.6	10.2	15.9	16.7	12.2	8.3	5.0	4.2	32.8	51.1
Rahway city	6.3	17.6	7.8	14.7	17.3	13.5	8.3	7.2	7.3	37.1	52.3
Sayreville borough	6.7	16.8	7.3	16.3	18.0	13.8	8.7	6.5	5.9	36.5	51.0
South Brunswick township	8.1	20.4	5.7	15.7	21.0	14.2	7.6	4.5	2.8	35.0	51.6
Teaneck township	6.4	19.4	8.5	10.8	15.4	15.2	10.2	7.2	7.0	38.4	52.7
Trenton city	7.6	20.1	10.1	16.7	15.2	11.5	7.4	5.8	5.6	32.2	50.6
Union township	5.5	16.8	8.9	12.8	16.5	13.5	8.8	7.7	9.6	38.7	53.2
Union City city	7.4	17.9	11.0	18.0	16.3	11.4	8.0	5.9	4.1	32.5	49.9
Vineland city	6.2	19.5	8.3	13.6	15.4	13.8	9.1	6.9	7.2	36.5	52.1
Voorhees township	6.3	20.1	6.3	13.6	18.1	16.1	8.5	4.8	6.1	37.2	52.0
Wall township	6.6	18.6	5.1	10.1	18.3	15.9	10.9	8.0	6.4	40.3	51.9
Washington township	6.2	22.6	8.0	11.7	18.0	16.4	8.3	5.0	4.0	36.0	51.5
Wayne township	6.1	17.0	8.1	10.4	17.2	14.5	10.4	8.4	7.8	40.0	52.5
Westfield town	8.0	20.4	4.0	11.2	18.4	15.7	8.8	6.6	6.9	38.6	52.1
West Milford township	7.1	20.2	6.0	12.7	20.9	15.7	9.1	4.8	3.6	37.0	49.9
West New York town	6.7	15.6	10.9	18.6	15.5	11.1	8.8	7.3	5.4	34.0	50.9
West Orange township	6.6	16.6	6.2	13.1	16.6	14.1	9.3	7.6	9.8	39.4	53.0
Willingboro township	6.1	21.3	7.5	10.7	15.4	14.5	11.5	8.8	4.1	37.9	52.6
Winslow township	8.2	20.6	7.0	15.3	19.1	13.7	7.6	4.3	4.2	34.4	50.8
Woodbridge township	6.3	16.0	7.1	16.7	18.2	13.6	8.7	7.2	6.2	37.1	50.0
NEW YORK	6.5	18.2	9.3	14.5	16.2	13.5	8.9	6.7	6.2	35.9	51.8
Albany city	5.6	14.3	19.3	15.9	13.4	11.3	6.9	5.9	7.4	31.4	52.5
Amherst town	5.4	16.8	10.8	10.7	14.6	14.7	9.3	8.3	9.4	39.6	52.8
Auburn city	6.3	16.5	9.3	14.8	15.5	12.6	7.2	7.2	10.6	36.9	50.3
Babylon town	7.0	19.0	7.5	14.5	18.0	12.9	8.7	7.0	5.4	36.1	51.8
Bethlehem town	6.5	21.0	5.2	10.0	17.1	17.1	8.7	6.8	7.6	39.6	52.4
Binghamton city	6.1	15.5	13.2	13.0	13.7	12.5	8.5	7.7	9.9	36.7	52.7
Brighton town	5.3	14.7	7.5	15.5	14.4	14.7	8.7	7.3	11.8	40.0	53.0
Bronx borough	8.2	21.6	10.6	15.6	15.0	11.2	7.7	5.3	4.7	31.2	53.5
Brookhaven town	7.1	19.6	8.9	14.0	17.5	14.2	8.5	5.3	4.8	35.2	50.8
Brooklyn borough	7.4	19.5	10.3	15.8	15.0	12.5	8.2	6.1	5.4	33.1	53.1
Buffalo city	7.1	19.2	11.3	14.4	14.9	12.0	7.6	6.8	6.7	33.6	53.0
Carmel town	7.2	20.1	6.7	11.8	19.3	15.5	9.9	5.5	4.0	37.1	50.4
Cheektowaga town	5.4	15.2	7.1	13.4	15.2	13.0	10.2	10.2	10.3	40.9	53.1
Chili town	5.8	19.8	8.6	12.4	17.0	14.8	9.4	6.9	5.2	37.1	51.3
Cicero town	7.4	20.7	5.9	14.0	19.2	13.3	8.8	6.5	4.1	36.0	50.9
Clarence town	6.3	21.7	5.7	8.2	18.1	15.8	9.6	7.6	6.9	39.8	51.5
Clarkstown town	6.4	18.3	6.6	11.8	16.5	16.5	11.6	7.3	5.0	39.1	51.5
Clay town	7.2	20.6	7.3	14.9	17.7	14.9	8.2	5.4	3.9	35.0	51.8
Clifton Park town	6.5	20.0	5.4	12.0	18.0	17.0	10.7	6.1	4.0	38.7	50.5
Colonie town	5.0	16.8	8.9	11.8	16.0	15.5	9.5	8.4	8.0	39.7	51.9
Cortlandt town	7.4	19.1	5.3	10.9	19.2	15.7	9.6	6.5	6.3	38.9	51.1
Eastchester town	6.8	17.1	5.4	12.3	17.5	14.2	10.0	8.4	8.3	39.9	53.3
East Fishkill town	7.9	21.8	6.4	11.1	19.3	16.4	9.0	5.1	3.0	36.6	50.3

Table E. Towns

Town	Population and population characteristics, 1990										Population—change, 1980–2000				
	Age (percent)									Percent Female	Total persons			Percent change	
	Under 5 years	5 to 17 years	18 to 24 years	25 to 34 years	35 to 44 years	45 to 54 years	55 to 64 years	65 to 74 years	75 years and over		2000	1990	1980	1990–2000	1980–1990
	39	40	41	42	43	44	45	46	47	48	49	50	51	52	53
NEW JERSEY—Cont'd															
Manalapan township	7.3	21.4	8.3	12.5	19.8	11.6	6.3	7.0	5.7	51.7	33 423	26 716	18 914	25.1	41.2
Manchester township	3.0	8.8	3.8	6.7	7.5	3.9	8.4	28.0	30.0	57.7	38 928	35 976	27 987	8.2	28.5
Marlboro township	6.8	21.9	8.4	11.6	22.6	14.1	7.2	5.3	2.0	49.7	36 398	27 974	17 560	30.1	59.3
Middletown township	6.8	18.6	9.4	14.7	17.5	12.6	8.8	7.0	4.6	50.7	66 327	68 183	62 574	-2.7	9.0
Millville city	7.6	19.0	10.7	16.2	14.5	9.8	8.7	8.4	5.1	51.8	26 847	25 992	24 815	3.3	4.7
Monroe township (Gloucester)	7.4	20.1	9.3	16.1	16.5	11.0	7.8	7.7	4.1	51.4	28 967	26 703	21 639	8.5	23.4
Monroe township (Middlesex)	4.0	12.8	7.1	8.3	11.4	8.1	12.4	22.7	13.4	52.9	27 999	22 256	15 858	25.8	40.3
Montclair township	6.1	14.3	9.1	17.9	17.2	11.6	8.9	7.6	7.4	53.9	38 977	37 487	38 321	4.0	-2.2
Mount Laurel township	6.4	15.4	8.5	20.6	17.6	11.3	10.2	6.9	3.0	52.0	40 221	30 270	17 614	32.9	71.9
Neptune township	6.8	15.1	7.7	17.3	13.8	11.5	10.7	9.0	8.0	54.0	27 690	28 148	28 366	-1.6	-0.8
Newark city	7.9	20.7	12.5	18.5	13.5	9.9	7.7	5.7	3.6	52.1	273 546	275 221	329 248	-0.6	-16.4
New Brunswick city	5.8	11.0	33.9	18.3	10.5	5.8	5.3	5.4	3.9	52.5	48 573	41 711	41 442	16.5	0.6
North Bergen township	6.2	14.2	8.6	19.5	14.1	11.6	10.6	8.7	6.4	52.0	58 092	48 414	47 019	20.0	3.0
North Brunswick township	6.5	13.4	12.4	22.6	16.6	11.2	8.0	6.0	3.3	50.1	36 287	31 287	22 220	16.0	40.8
Nutley township	5.7	13.3	8.8	17.1	16.7	10.5	11.0	10.2	6.8	53.1	27 362	27 099	28 998	1.0	-6.5
Ocean township	6.7	18.2	8.8	16.2	18.0	11.9	9.2	6.9	4.2	51.3	26 959	25 058	23 570	7.6	6.3
Old Bridge township	7.8	16.2	9.5	20.9	16.9	10.9	8.8	6.3	3.3	50.9	60 456	56 493	51 515	7.0	9.7
Paramus borough	4.7	15.3	9.1	12.7	14.4	13.2	13.9	11.2	5.7	52.3	25 737	25 004	26 474	2.9	-5.6
Parsippany-Troy Hills township	5.7	14.3	10.1	21.1	16.9	13.0	10.0	5.4	3.7	50.7	50 649	48 478	49 868	4.5	-2.8
Passaic city	8.8	18.7	12.2	19.0	14.1	9.7	7.1	5.7	4.6	50.2	67 861	58 041	52 463	16.9	10.6
Paterson city	8.8	20.3	12.1	18.5	13.8	9.8	7.1	5.5	4.0	52.1	149 222	140 891	137 970	5.9	2.1
Pemberton township	8.2	22.4	10.0	19.7	15.4	10.1	8.0	4.1	2.1	50.5	28 691	31 342	29 720	-8.5	5.5
Pennsauken township	7.6	17.1	8.2	18.3	14.6	9.1	9.4	9.3	6.3	52.4	35 737	34 738	33 775	2.9	2.9
Perth Amboy city	7.5	18.4	11.3	17.9	14.1	9.5	7.6	7.8	5.8	51.7	47 303	41 967	38 951	12.7	7.7
Piscataway township	6.2	13.6	22.2	18.7	14.3	10.6	7.7	4.5	2.3	49.4	50 482	47 089	42 223	7.2	11.5
Plainfield city	8.0	17.9	11.7	19.3	15.3	10.3	7.6	5.6	4.2	52.2	47 829	46 577	45 555	2.7	2.2
Rahway city	6.6	14.2	9.6	18.9	16.2	9.9	9.5	9.7	5.5	51.7	26 500	25 325	26 723	4.6	-5.2
Sayreville borough	7.0	14.5	9.7	20.4	14.8	11.0	10.0	8.8	3.8	51.2	40 377	34 998	29 969	15.4	16.8
South Brunswick township	8.5	17.0	7.7	22.2	18.6	11.9	7.7	4.2	2.2	50.7	37 734	25 798	17 127	46.3	50.6
Teaneck township	6.7	16.1	10.2	13.0	16.4	12.7	10.7	8.4	5.9	53.2	39 260	37 825	39 007	3.8	-3.0
Trenton city	8.5	18.0	10.9	19.1	14.5	8.3	7.8	7.7	5.2	51.6	85 403	88 675	92 124	-3.7	-3.7
Union township	4.8	12.7	10.1	14.8	14.2	10.8	11.2	11.9	9.5	53.1	54 405	50 024	50 184	8.8	-0.3
Union City city	7.3	16.8	10.8	19.7	14.4	11.2	9.7	6.3	4.0	51.1	67 088	58 012	55 593	15.6	4.4
Vineland city	7.0	18.5	10.1	16.0	14.4	10.5	9.0	8.4	6.1	52.6	56 271	54 780	53 753	2.7	1.9
Voorhees township	7.9	17.1	8.4	19.4	19.8	11.3	6.7	4.2	5.3	52.3	28 126	24 559	12 919	14.5	90.1
Wall township	6.3	18.1	8.2	13.3	17.0	13.2	9.7	8.1	6.4	51.8	25 261	20 244	18 952	24.8	6.8
Washington township	8.5	22.1	9.1	17.2	20.0	10.5	6.3	4.1	2.1	50.6	47 114	41 960	27 878	12.3	50.5
Wayne township	5.7	14.8	11.2	14.1	15.6	13.2	12.1	7.7	5.5	51.8	54 069	47 025	46 474	15.0	1.2
Westfield town	6.9	17.0	7.1	14.6	18.0	12.2	10.9	8.0	5.4	51.7	29 644	28 870	30 447	2.7	-5.2
West Milford township	8.4	18.6	8.7	19.0	19.9	11.7	7.0	3.9	2.7	49.3	26 410	25 430	22 750	3.9	11.8
West New York town	6.6	14.9	10.3	18.4	12.7	12.1	11.4	8.1	5.5	52.2	45 768	38 125	39 194	20.0	2.7
West Orange township	6.1	13.3	7.9	16.8	16.0	10.1	10.0	10.0	8.9	52.9	44 943	39 103	39 510	14.9	-1.0
Willingboro township	6.7	20.7	10.1	15.4	15.3	13.4	11.7	5.1	1.6	51.6	33 008	36 291	39 912	-9.0	-9.1
Winslow township	9.4	19.9	8.8	21.6	17.1	9.1	6.2	5.2	2.6	50.4	34 611	30 087	20 034	15.0	50.2
Woodbridge township	5.8	13.6	9.0	20.7	15.8	10.6	11.3	9.3	3.8	49.5	97 203	93 092	90 074	4.4	3.4
NEW YORK	7.0	16.7	10.9	17.4	15.1	10.6	9.1	7.5	5.6	52.1	18 976 457	17 990 778	17 558 165	5.5	2.5
Albany city	6.0	12.1	19.8	18.8	13.2	7.4	7.2	7.4	8.0	53.5	95 658	100 031	101 727	-4.4	-1.7
Amherst town	6.3	15.7	11.9	14.1	15.3	11.4	10.1	8.5	6.6	52.5	116 510	111 711	NA	4.3	NA
Auburn city	7.2	16.1	10.0	18.3	14.2	7.7	8.1	9.7	8.7	51.0	28 574	31 258	32 501	-8.6	-3.8
Babylon town	7.4	16.1	10.8	19.2	14.2	11.2	10.0	7.0	3.9	51.6	211 792	202 793	NA	4.4	NA
Bethlehem town	7.0	18.7	7.0	14.0	18.9	10.9	9.4	8.3	5.8	51.8	31 304	27 552	NA	13.6	NA
Binghamton city	6.6	13.2	13.9	17.2	12.9	8.5	8.6	9.9	9.1	53.3	47 380	53 008	55 860	-10.6	-5.1
Brighton town	5.6	12.6	7.9	16.6	16.6	11.3	9.6	9.6	10.2	54.3	35 588	34 455	NA	3.3	NA
Bronx borough	8.4	19.1	11.4	17.8	13.5	10.1	8.0	6.2	5.4	54.0	1 332 650	1 203 789	1 168 972	10.7	3.0
Brookhaven town	7.5	19.6	11.1	17.6	16.8	10.9	6.8	5.5	4.1	50.9	448 248	407 779	NA	9.9	NA
Brooklyn borough	7.7	18.6	10.4	17.6	14.6	10.3	8.4	7.2	5.3	53.5	2 465 326	2 300 664	2 231 028	7.2	3.1
Buffalo city	7.8	16.5	12.5	18.5	13.0	8.3	8.5	8.5	6.4	53.5	292 648	328 175	357 870	-10.8	-8.3
Carmel town	7.2	18.5	9.9	16.7	17.0	14.4	8.5	4.5	3.2	49.9	33 006	28 816	NA	14.5	NA
Cheektowaga town	5.6	13.9	10.0	16.4	13.0	11.0	11.8	11.9	6.4	52.7	94 019	99 314	NA	-5.3	NA
Chili town	7.3	18.6	11.8	16.3	17.1	11.4	8.8	5.8	3.0	51.5	27 638	25 178	NA	9.8	NA
Cicero town	8.5	19.2	8.7	19.8	15.7	11.0	8.7	5.8	2.7	50.4	27 982	25 560	NA	9.5	NA
Clarence town	6.5	19.0	7.1	13.2	17.0	11.7	11.1	8.1	6.3	51.6	26 123	20 041	NA	30.3	NA
Clarkstown town	5.7	19.0	9.7	13.8	16.9	14.7	10.5	5.3	4.2	51.6	82 082	79 346	NA	3.4	NA
Clay town	8.6	20.6	9.3	19.7	17.9	10.2	6.7	4.6	2.3	51.2	58 805	59 749	NA	-1.6	NA
Clifton Park town	7.5	21.1	7.6	15.3	20.4	14.2	8.0	4.1	1.9	50.1	32 995	30 117	NA	9.6	NA
Colonie town	5.7	15.5	11.2	15.8	15.7	11.1	10.3	8.7	6.0	52.0	79 258	76 497	NA	3.6	NA
Cortlandt town	7.3	15.8	7.8	16.2	17.6	13.0	9.4	7.4	5.7	50.7	38 467	37 357	NA	3.0	NA
Eastchester town	6.2	13.5	8.9	15.3	16.1	11.7	11.1	9.2	8.0	53.9	31 318	30 867	NA	1.5	NA
East Fishkill town	7.9	22.4	8.6	14.6	20.1	13.0	7.0	4.0	2.3	49.9	25 589	22 101	NA	15.8	NA

Table E. Towns

Town	Total population	Total in house-holds	House-holder	Spouse	Child Total	Child Own child under 18 years	Other relatives Total	Other relatives Under 18 years	Nonrelatives Total	Nonrelatives Unmar-ried partner	Total in group quarters	Correc-tional institu-tions	Nurs-ing homes	Other institu-tions	Col-lege dormi-tories	Mili-tary quar-ters	Other
	54	55	56	57	58	59	60	61	62	63	64	65	66	67	68	69	70
NEW JERSEY—Cont'd																	
Manalapan township..........	33 423	99.5	32.3	24.5	37.8	29.3	3.6	0.9	1.4	0.6	0.5	0.0	0.4	0.0	0.0	0.0	0.1
Manchester township........	30 928	98.1	63.1	24.3	15.0	9.7	3.1	0.9	2.5	1.3	1.9	0.0	1.3	0.0	0.0	0.5	0.1
Marlboro township.............	36 398	99.2	31.5	25.6	36.9	29.4	3.8	0.6	1.3	0.6	0.8	0.4	0.0	0.0	0.0	0.0	0.4
Middletown township..........	66 327	99.4	35.0	23.6	34.3	24.9	4.2	1.2	2.3	1.1	0.6	0.0	0.4	0.0	0.0	0.0	0.2
Millville city...................	26 847	99.0	37.4	17.4	32.5	24.3	6.2	2.9	5.6	3.2	1.0	0.0	0.5	0.0	0.0	0.0	0.5
Monroe township (Gloucester).............	28 967	99.3	36.3	21.3	32.3	23.1	5.6	2.2	3.8	2.0	0.7	0.0	0.5	0.0	0.0	0.0	0.2
Monroe township (Middlesex).....	27 999	96.5	44.8	27.1	19.4	13.7	3.3	0.9	1.8	0.9	3.5	0.0	1.2	1.9	0.0	0.0	0.4
Montclair township............	38 977	97.5	38.5	18.2	30.1	23.4	5.4	1.8	5.3	1.8	2.5	0.0	0.8	0.0	1.0	0.0	0.8
Mount Laurel township	40 221	99.1	41.2	23.0	28.4	22.1	3.2	0.9	3.4	1.7	0.9	0.0	0.8	0.0	0.0	0.0	0.1
Neptune township.............	27 690	97.0	39.4	16.8	28.2	19.2	7.6	3.4	5.0	2.3	3.0	0.0	2.0	0.0	0.0	0.0	0.9
Newark city..................	273 546	95.3	33.4	10.4	32.1	21.8	5.2	2.5	6.8	2.5	4.7	1.6	0.9	0.3	1.2	0.0	0.7
New Brunswick city	48 573	86.7	26.9	8.0	20.5	15.1	11.4	3.6	20.0	2.0	13.3	0.0	0.2	0.0	11.8	0.0	1.2
North Bergen township.......	58 092	98.9	36.6	17.3	30.1	20.4	9.6	2.0	5.3	2.0	1.1	0.0	1.1	0.0	0.0	0.0	0.0
North Brunswick township.....	36 287	96.9	37.6	20.1	28.7	21.2	5.8	1.3	4.7	2.1	3.1	2.6	0.0	0.3	0.1	0.0	0.1
Nutley township	27 362	99.9	39.8	21.5	30.1	20.5	5.4	1.1	3.2	1.4	0.1	0.0	0.0	0.0	0.0	0.0	0.1
Ocean township	26 959	99.9	38.0	22.2	32.4	24.2	3.8	1.0	3.5	1.7	0.1	0.0	0.0	0.0	0.0	0.0	0.1
Old Bridge township	60 456	99.1	35.5	21.7	33.3	24.2	5.7	1.4	3.0	1.6	0.9	0.0	0.6	0.0	0.0	0.0	0.2
Paramus borough..............	25 737	94.1	31.4	23.0	32.3	21.7	5.8	1.2	1.7	0.4	5.9	0.0	2.5	2.3	0.0	0.0	1.0
Parsippany-Troy Hills township................	50 649	98.1	38.7	21.8	27.7	19.5	5.9	1.2	3.9	1.6	1.9	0.0	0.4	1.3	0.0	0.0	0.2
Passaic city..................	67 861	99.1	28.7	12.5	35.3	25.3	14.6	4.8	8.1	2.3	0.9	0.0	0.3	0.0	0.1	0.0	0.4
Paterson city................	149 222	97.4	30.0	11.8	34.6	23.7	14.2	5.4	6.9	2.6	2.6	1.3	0.1	0.0	0.0	0.0	1.1
Pemberton township	28 691	98.2	35.0	18.7	32.7	23.6	6.4	3.1	5.4	2.5	1.8	0.8	0.6	0.1	0.0	0.0	0.3
Pennsauken township	35 737	98.1	34.7	17.9	33.8	23.7	7.7	3.2	4.0	1.9	1.9	0.0	1.3	0.0	0.0	0.0	0.6
Perth Amboy city	47 303	98.5	30.8	13.7	34.1	24.0	12.2	3.7	7.8	2.8	1.5	0.0	0.8	0.0	0.0	0.0	0.7
Piscataway township	50 482	92.8	32.7	19.8	28.5	19.6	7.7	2.0	4.1	1.2	7.2	0.0	0.1	0.0	7.0	0.0	0.1
Plainfield city................	47 829	98.1	31.6	12.4	30.8	20.8	13.6	5.6	9.7	2.6	1.9	0.0	0.8	0.3	0.1	0.0	0.7
Rahway city.................	26 500	99.4	37.8	17.7	30.6	20.3	8.5	3.1	4.8	2.0	0.6	0.0	0.4	0.0	0.0	0.0	0.2
Sayreville borough............	40 377	99.4	37.0	21.3	31.6	21.9	5.9	1.5	3.6	1.7	0.6	0.0	0.5	0.0	0.0	0.0	0.1
South Brunswick township	37 734	99.7	35.6	22.7	33.6	27.2	4.4	1.0	3.4	1.6	0.3	0.0	0.2	0.0	0.0	0.0	0.1
Teaneck township	39 260	97.7	34.2	20.3	32.7	23.1	7.1	2.3	3.4	1.0	2.3	0.0	0.3	0.0	1.8	0.0	0.2
Trenton city..................	85 403	94.8	34.5	10.0	30.6	21.6	11.5	5.0	8.3	2.9	5.2	2.6	0.6	0.7	0.0	0.0	1.3
Union township	54 405	97.4	35.9	19.9	31.1	20.3	7.5	1.8	3.0	1.2	2.6	0.0	0.6	0.0	2.0	0.0	0.1
Union City city	67 088	99.5	34.1	14.5	31.4	21.9	11.7	2.9	7.9	2.6	0.5	0.0	0.3	0.0	0.0	0.0	0.3
Vineland city.................	56 271	95.7	35.4	17.3	30.6	22.0	6.8	2.9	5.6	2.8	4.3	0.8	1.1	0.0	0.0	0.0	2.4
Voorhees township	28 126	96.8	37.3	21.2	31.2	24.9	3.6	0.9	3.4	1.7	3.2	0.0	2.2	0.4	0.0	0.0	0.7
Wall township	25 261	98.7	37.4	23.5	31.6	24.0	3.5	1.0	2.7	1.3	1.3	0.0	1.0	0.0	0.0	0.0	0.3
Washington township	47 114	99.5	33.1	22.6	37.5	27.3	3.9	1.2	2.4	1.4	0.5	0.0	0.3	0.0	0.0	0.0	0.3
Wayne township	54 069	94.9	34.7	23.0	30.7	22.0	4.4	1.0	2.2	0.9	5.1	0.0	1.5	0.0	2.8	0.0	0.8
Westfield town	29 644	99.1	35.8	24.4	33.8	27.6	2.6	0.7	2.5	0.9	0.9	0.0	0.6	0.0	0.0	0.0	0.3
West Milford township	26 410	98.9	34.8	23.4	33.6	25.7	3.6	1.0	3.4	1.8	1.1	0.0	0.4	0.0	0.0	0.0	0.7
West New York town............	45 768	99.9	36.5	15.3	28.6	19.2	11.6	2.7	8.0	2.3	0.1	0.0	0.0	0.0	0.0	0.0	0.1
West Orange township	44 943	97.4	36.7	20.5	30.0	21.6	6.5	1.5	3.7	1.4	2.6	0.0	2.1	0.2	0.0	0.0	0.3
Willingboro township...........	33 008	99.5	32.5	18.8	33.5	20.8	10.6	5.8	4.1	1.4	0.5	0.0	0.1	0.1	0.0	0.0	0.3
Winslow township..............	34 611	96.7	33.7	20.0	33.9	25.6	5.4	2.5	3.8	1.9	3.3	1.0	0.0	2.0	0.0	0.0	0.3
Woodbridge township...........	97 203	96.5	35.6	20.6	29.9	20.4	6.7	1.7	3.7	1.4	3.5	2.7	0.2	0.0	0.0	0.0	0.6
NEW YORK	18 976 457	96.9	37.2	17.3	30.2	21.9	6.7	2.2	5.5	2.0	3.1	0.6	0.7	0.2	0.9	0.0	0.7
Albany city	95 658	89.6	42.6	10.8	22.3	17.3	4.4	1.7	9.6	3.1	10.4	0.0	1.5	0.7	7.1	0.0	1.1
Amherst town.................	116 510	93.7	38.7	21.5	27.8	21.4	2.3	0.5	3.4	1.2	6.3	0.0	1.5	0.0	4.1	0.0	0.7
Auburn city...................	28 574	90.8	39.9	14.9	27.1	20.9	3.3	1.2	5.6	3.0	9.2	6.0	1.6	0.2	0.2	0.0	1.3
Babylon town..................	211 792	98.8	32.6	18.8	32.8	22.3	9.0	3.0	5.7	1.6	1.2	0.0	0.5	0.1	0.2	0.0	0.5
Bethlehem town...............	31 304	97.8	38.7	23.2	31.0	26.0	1.9	0.6	2.9	1.7	2.2	0.0	0.6	0.1	1.1	0.0	0.4
Binghamton city...............	47 380	97.4	44.5	14.1	25.0	19.5	4.0	1.4	9.8	3.0	2.6	0.2	1.3	0.4	0.0	0.0	0.7
Brighton town..................	35 588	95.3	44.5	20.4	23.1	19.3	1.9	0.4	5.4	2.2	4.7	1.2	2.6	0.3	0.0	0.0	0.6
Bronx borough..................	1 332 650	96.5	34.8	10.9	34.8	24.8	10.2	3.9	5.7	2.3	3.5	1.0	0.9	0.2	0.4	0.0	1.0
Brookhaven town...............	448 248	97.1	32.8	20.4	33.7	24.4	5.6	1.7	4.7	1.7	2.9	0.1	0.5	0.1	1.4	0.0	0.8
Brooklyn borough..............	2 465 326	98.4	35.7	13.8	33.2	22.8	10.1	3.4	5.6	1.8	1.6	0.1	0.4	0.2	0.1	0.0	0.8
Buffalo city....................	292 648	96.2	41.9	11.6	30.3	23.0	5.6	2.5	6.8	2.7	3.8	0.5	0.5	0.4	1.4	0.0	0.7
Carmel town....................	33 006	99.1	32.9	22.9	34.8	25.6	5.2	1.4	3.4	1.1	0.9	0.3	0.0	0.4	0.0	0.0	0.3
Cheektowaga town.............	94 019	99.0	42.6	21.1	28.1	19.3	3.4	1.0	3.8	2.0	1.0	0.0	0.6	0.0	0.0	0.0	0.4
Chili town......................	27 638	98.0	36.8	22.7	31.2	23.9	3.3	1.2	4.0	1.8	2.0	0.0	0.0	0.1	1.5	0.0	0.4
Cicero town....................	27 982	100.0	37.7	22.2	33.0	26.5	2.5	0.9	4.6	2.4	0.0	0.0	0.0	0.0	0.0	0.0	0.0
Clarence town..................	26 123	98.1	35.0	24.6	34.4	27.3	2.1	0.6	1.9	1.0	1.9	0.0	1.6	0.0	0.0	0.0	0.3
Clarkstown town	82 082	97.8	33.7	22.8	32.4	22.9	5.8	1.4	3.1	1.1	2.2	0.2	0.7	0.2	0.1	0.0	1.0
Clay town......................	58 805	99.6	37.9	21.6	32.8	26.2	2.8	1.0	4.6	2.5	0.4	0.0	0.2	0.0	0.0	0.0	0.2
Clifton Park town	32 995	99.7	38.1	25.1	31.4	25.6	2.1	0.5	3.0	1.6	0.3	0.0	0.0	0.0	0.0	0.0	0.3
Colonie town...................	79 258	94.8	39.1	20.8	27.7	20.5	3.3	1.0	3.9	2.0	5.2	0.9	1.2	0.1	2.4	0.0	0.6
Cortlandt town	38 467	96.7	35.1	22.6	32.1	23.2	3.9	1.0	3.0	1.2	3.3	0.0	1.6	0.5	0.2	0.0	1.0
Eastchester town..............	31 318	99.1	40.3	22.5	30.1	23.0	3.5	0.8	2.6	1.1	0.9	0.0	0.0	0.0	0.8	0.0	0.1
East Fishkill town...............	25 589	99.8	32.2	24.4	36.6	28.1	4.3	1.3	2.4	1.1	0.2	0.0	0.0	0.0	0.0	0.0	0.2

Table E. Towns

Town	Households by type, 2000												Households, 1990		
	Family households						Nonfamily households								
			Married couple		Female householder[1]			Householder living alone						
	Total households	Total	With own children under 18 years	Total	With own children under 18 years	Total	With own children under 18 years	Total	Total	65 years and over	Average household size	Average family size	Total households	Female householder[1]	Householder living alone
	71	72	73	74	75	76	77	78	79	80	81	82	83	84	85
NEW JERSEY—Cont'd															
Manalapan township	10 781	83.5	47.0	75.9	43.8	5.7	2.5	16.5	14.9	10.4	3.09	3.45	8 490	4.5	14.1
Manchester township	20 688	52.3	9.9	45.8	8.3	5.0	1.2	47.7	45.0	39.0	1.85	2.53	18 512	4.3	40.6
Marlboro township	11 478	88.6	50.4	81.3	46.8	5.6	2.9	11.4	9.7	4.7	3.15	3.38	8 149	5.7	7.6
Middletown township	23 236	77.9	37.9	67.3	33.6	7.8	3.3	22.1	18.9	10.1	2.84	3.27	22 637	7.4	16.3
Millville city	10 043	69.8	35.0	46.5	20.8	17.9	11.1	30.2	25.1	11.6	2.65	3.15	9 640	13.7	23.3
Monroe township (Gloucester)	10 521	74.6	34.1	58.5	26.2	11.7	5.5	25.4	21.0	9.6	2.73	3.18	9 170	11.4	18.3
Monroe township (Middlesex)	12 536	65.7	15.9	60.6	14.6	3.9	1.0	34.3	32.0	28.0	2.15	2.70	9 291	3.9	26.7
Montclair township	15 020	64.5	34.3	47.2	25.5	14.1	7.5	35.5	29.3	8.6	2.53	3.16	14 518	13.1	28.7
Mount Laurel township	16 570	66.8	30.4	55.7	24.8	8.5	4.4	33.2	27.9	8.9	2.41	2.98	11 844	6.2	23.8
Neptune township	10 907	62.4	26.3	42.6	16.7	15.8	8.2	37.6	31.5	11.8	2.46	3.14	10 395	13.4	26.3
Newark city	91 382	67.8	35.2	31.0	15.1	29.3	17.1	32.2	26.6	8.8	2.85	3.43	91 552	28.3	26.5
New Brunswick city	13 057	55.2	29.1	29.6	15.8	18.0	10.0	44.8	24.3	8.4	3.23	3.69	12 711	17.9	27.8
North Bergen township	21 236	67.1	32.0	47.4	22.7	14.2	7.1	32.9	27.7	11.2	2.70	3.33	18 970	11.6	29.6
North Brunswick township	13 635	68.7	33.3	53.4	25.5	11.6	6.3	31.3	24.5	7.5	2.58	3.12	11 555	6.5	23.0
Nutley township	10 884	67.7	29.3	54.0	24.3	10.5	4.1	32.3	27.9	11.4	2.51	3.11	10 594	9.1	26.6
Ocean township	10 254	71.6	35.4	58.3	28.5	10.3	5.5	28.4	24.0	8.4	2.63	3.14	9 261	9.9	20.8
Old Bridge township	21 438	74.4	37.8	61.2	32.0	9.5	4.4	25.6	21.1	6.8	2.80	3.30	19 984	10.1	18.3
Paramus borough	8 082	83.9	37.0	73.3	33.7	8.0	2.6	16.1	14.4	9.4	3.00	3.32	7 776	8.7	11.9
Parsippany-Troy Hills township	19 624	74.1	29.5	56.2	25.4	7.6	3.1	32.9	27.1	6.7	2.53	3.13	18 369	6.8	24.0
Passaic city	19 458	74.3	42.0	43.7	25.6	21.7	12.5	25.7	20.3	8.4	3.46	3.93	18 735	20.3	23.6
Paterson city	44 710	74.6	40.9	39.4	21.3	26.8	15.7	25.4	20.4	7.9	3.25	3.71	43 946	22.9	21.1
Pemberton township	10 050	74.5	37.5	53.3	24.8	15.7	9.4	25.5	20.4	6.3	2.80	3.22	10 051	12.8	15.0
Pennsauken township	12 389	73.4	36.5	51.6	25.0	16.2	8.6	26.6	23.1	10.4	2.83	3.34	12 406	12.6	21.2
Perth Amboy city	14 562	73.9	40.3	44.6	23.8	21.0	12.2	26.1	20.6	8.8	3.20	3.63	14 207	18.5	23.6
Piscataway township	16 500	74.7	34.6	60.6	28.9	10.4	4.5	25.3	19.5	5.4	2.84	3.29	14 033	8.1	17.6
Plainfield city	15 137	72.0	35.5	39.3	18.8	24.5	13.0	28.0	21.1	7.4	3.10	3.49	15 146	21.0	21.5
Rahway city	10 028	67.1	30.0	46.7	20.8	15.6	7.4	32.9	28.0	11.7	2.63	3.24	9 623	13.7	24.6
Sayreville borough	14 955	73.0	34.3	57.5	27.7	11.1	5.0	27.0	22.3	8.7	2.68	3.17	12 749	9.2	19.7
South Brunswick township	13 428	75.1	43.0	63.8	36.8	8.6	4.9	24.9	19.6	4.3	2.80	3.27	9 408	7.2	18.9
Teaneck township	13 418	75.1	34.9	59.3	28.7	12.3	5.1	24.9	21.2	10.5	2.86	3.34	13 000	9.6	19.9
Trenton city	29 437	63.5	32.4	29.0	13.3	27.1	15.7	36.5	29.7	12.0	2.75	3.38	30 744	23.6	28.5
Union township	19 534	72.5	32.0	55.5	25.8	13.1	5.0	27.5	23.8	13.3	2.71	3.25	18 882	10.5	23.8
Union City city	22 872	70.2	36.6	42.4	22.1	19.3	11.1	29.8	23.0	7.5	2.92	3.40	20 612	19.1	23.5
Vineland city	19 930	71.3	33.9	48.8	21.4	16.8	9.6	28.7	23.7	11.2	2.70	3.17	18 732	14.9	20.7
Voorhees township	10 489	67.4	37.0	57.0	31.2	7.9	4.5	32.6	26.9	8.5	2.60	3.23	9 107	6.5	26.9
Wall township	9 437	73.4	33.8	63.0	29.4	8.0	3.5	26.6	22.7	9.7	2.64	3.14	7 364	8.0	21.9
Washington township	15 609	81.1	43.8	68.3	37.1	9.8	5.4	18.9	15.4	5.8	3.00	3.38	13 150	7.2	12.0
Wayne township	18 755	76.6	34.4	66.4	30.9	7.6	2.7	23.4	20.2	10.1	2.74	3.19	15 757	7.3	15.7
Westfield town	10 622	77.0	40.8	68.0	36.8	7.1	3.2	23.0	19.3	9.4	2.77	3.20	10 289	6.7	17.0
West Milford township	9 190	78.2	39.9	67.3	34.7	7.8	3.9	21.8	16.7	5.5	2.84	3.23	8 383	6.8	13.4
West New York town	16 719	66.0	31.1	41.9	19.9	16.9	8.5	34.0	27.5	11.3	2.74	3.30	14 419	16.2	26.3
West Orange township	16 480	70.9	32.2	56.0	25.9	11.2	4.9	29.1	24.6	11.6	2.66	3.19	14 821	9.3	24.8
Willingboro township	10 713	82.0	33.7	58.1	23.6	18.6	8.1	18.0	15.0	6.2	3.07	3.36	11 044	13.2	10.2
Winslow township	11 661	77.2	41.7	59.2	31.1	13.5	8.1	22.8	18.8	6.9	2.87	3.28	9 736	10.8	17.3
Woodbridge township	34 562	73.6	33.0	58.1	27.0	11.4	4.6	26.4	21.7	9.0	2.71	3.19	33 473	10.0	20.7
NEW YORK	7 056 860	65.7	31.6	46.6	21.6	14.7	8.1	34.3	28.1	10.1	2.61	3.22	6 639 322	13.8	27.2
Albany city	40 709	45.2	22.0	25.3	9.7	16.1	10.5	54.8	41.9	11.5	2.11	2.95	42 121	14.0	38.3
Amherst town	45 076	66.3	29.7	55.6	24.3	8.3	4.5	33.7	28.3	13.4	2.42	3.01	41 320	7.3	23.9
Auburn city	11 411	57.3	28.1	37.3	15.7	14.7	9.6	42.7	36.3	16.6	2.27	2.98	11 936	14.8	31.7
Babylon town	69 048	75.9	35.7	57.6	28.2	13.7	5.9	24.1	19.1	8.5	3.03	3.45	64 506	12.3	15.4
Bethlehem town	12 112	70.6	36.6	60.0	30.6	8.0	4.6	29.4	25.0	11.7	2.53	3.06	10 341	7.0	22.6
Binghamton city	21 089	49.4	23.3	31.6	12.6	13.8	8.7	50.6	40.3	15.5	2.19	2.96	22 617	12.4	35.8
Brighton town	15 854	54.8	24.7	45.9	19.6	6.8	4.0	45.2	36.3	13.8	2.14	2.86	15 142	6.7	32.8
Bronx borough	463 212	68.0	38.1	31.4	16.2	30.4	19.2	32.0	27.4	9.4	2.78	3.37	424 112	28.6	27.6
Brookhaven town	146 828	76.9	38.9	62.3	31.9	10.6	5.3	23.1	17.9	7.2	2.97	3.37	129 092	9.5	15.3
Brooklyn borough	880 727	66.3	33.3	38.6	19.1	22.3	12.2	33.7	27.8	9.8	2.75	3.41	828 199	21.6	28.1
Buffalo city	122 720	54.6	28.6	27.6	12.0	22.3	14.4	45.4	37.7	12.1	2.29	3.07	136 436	19.9	35.0
Carmel town	10 847	80.7	41.3	69.6	36.6	7.9	3.7	19.3	15.2	5.4	3.02	3.37	9 334	6.8	13.2
Cheektowaga town	40 045	64.6	25.5	49.5	18.8	11.4	5.3	35.4	30.4	15.5	2.32	2.91	39 695	10.0	25.0
Chili town	10 159	74.4	34.7	61.7	27.5	9.1	5.3	25.6	20.2	7.5	2.67	3.09	8 571	7.8	15.4
Cicero town	10 538	73.0	38.7	58.9	29.4	10.1	6.9	27.0	21.3	8.3	2.65	3.10	9 014	8.8	16.8
Clarence town	9 154	78.7	38.6	70.3	34.5	6.1	3.1	21.3	18.4	9.0	2.80	3.22	6 967	6.2	17.3
Clarkstown town	27 697	79.4	36.9	67.4	31.9	9.1	4.0	20.6	16.9	6.5	2.90	3.27	25 357	8.0	14.0
Clay town	22 294	71.5	38.0	56.9	28.7	11.0	7.1	28.5	22.3	6.4	2.63	3.11	21 095	7.9	18.4
Clifton Park town	12 581	74.4	36.4	65.9	31.7	6.1	3.7	25.6	20.6	6.0	2.62	3.07	10 418	5.9	15.6
Colonie town	30 980	66.3	29.2	53.3	22.7	9.6	5.0	33.7	28.1	11.1	2.43	3.00	28 578	8.6	23.9
Cortlandt town	13 517	75.0	39.3	64.3	34.2	7.9	4.2	25.0	21.3	8.8	2.75	3.22	13 178	6.3	20.7
Eastchester town	12 626	66.6	31.4	55.7	26.8	8.7	3.9	33.4	29.8	13.1	2.46	3.09	12 381	7.9	28.2
East Fishkill town	8 233	85.1	45.8	75.7	41.4	6.5	3.1	14.9	11.9	3.9	3.10	3.38	6 796	6.8	10.5

[1] No spouse present.

Table E. Towns

Town	Percent change of households, 1990–2000	Total housing units	Occupied housing units (percent)	Vacant housing units Total	For seasonal, recreational, or occasional use	Homeowner vacancy rate (percent)	Rental vacancy rate (percent)	Occupied housing units Total	Percent owner-occupied housing units	Percent renter-occupied housing units	Average household size of owner-occupied units	Average household size of renter-occupied units
	86	87	88	89	90	91	92	93	94	95	96	97
NEW JERSEY—Cont'd												
Manalapan township	27.0	11 066	97.4	2.6	0.7	0.9	2.9	10 781	94.3	5.7	3.13	2.32
Manchester township	11.8	22 681	91.2	8.8	2.2	3.3	8.0	20 688	91.9	8.1	1.84	1.88
Marlboro township	40.9	11 896	96.5	3.5	0.7	1.6	2.3	11 478	96.6	3.4	3.16	2.80
Middletown township	2.6	23 841	97.5	2.5	0.4	0.6	2.3	23 236	86.4	13.6	2.96	2.09
Millville city	4.2	10 652	94.3	5.7	0.5	2.0	5.8	10 043	63.9	36.1	2.71	2.54
Monroe township (Gloucester)	14.7	11 069	95.0	5.0	0.4	1.1	4.5	10 521	84.0	16.0	2.83	2.25
Monroe township (Middlesex)	34.9	13 259	94.5	5.5	2.8	1.2	3.4	12 536	94.8	5.2	2.17	1.87
Montclair township	3.5	15 531	96.7	3.3	0.3	1.0	3.1	15 020	56.4	43.6	2.91	2.03
Mount Laurel township	39.9	17 163	96.5	3.5	0.4	1.2	6.7	16 570	83.7	16.3	2.48	2.04
Neptune township	4.9	12 217	89.3	10.7	5.6	1.7	5.6	10 907	65.5	34.5	2.66	2.10
Newark city	-0.2	100 141	91.3	8.7	0.1	2.0	5.6	91 382	23.8	76.2	3.22	2.74
New Brunswick city	2.7	13 893	94.0	6.0	0.3	2.0	3.4	13 057	26.3	73.7	3.01	3.30
North Bergen township	11.9	22 009	96.5	3.5	0.3	0.9	2.4	21 236	37.5	62.5	3.03	2.51
North Brunswick township	18.0	13 932	97.9	2.1	0.1	0.7	2.1	13 635	62.8	37.2	2.76	2.27
Nutley township	2.7	11 118	97.9	2.1	0.2	0.5	2.0	10 884	66.9	33.1	2.80	1.94
Ocean township	10.7	10 756	95.3	4.7	2.3	0.7	2.9	10 254	67.2	32.8	2.86	2.14
Old Bridge township	7.3	21 896	97.9	2.1	0.2	0.8	2.0	21 438	69.4	30.6	3.04	2.24
Paramus borough	3.9	8 209	98.5	1.5	0.2	0.5	2.2	8 082	90.7	9.3	3.00	2.94
Parsippany-Troy Hills township	6.8	20 066	97.8	2.2	0.3	0.4	2.6	19 624	60.5	39.5	2.87	2.01
Passaic city	3.9	20 194	96.4	3.6	0.2	2.0	1.9	19 458	27.0	73.0	3.63	3.40
Paterson city	1.7	47 169	94.8	5.2	0.1	1.7	3.8	44 710	31.5	68.5	3.59	3.10
Pemberton township	0.0	10 778	93.2	6.8	0.3	2.5	5.5	10 050	73.4	26.6	2.87	2.63
Pennsauken township	-0.1	12 945	95.7	4.3	0.1	1.9	5.0	12 389	80.4	19.6	2.97	2.27
Perth Amboy city	2.5	15 236	95.6	4.4	0.2	1.5	2.8	14 562	40.5	59.5	3.24	3.17
Piscataway township	17.6	16 946	97.4	2.6	0.2	1.3	3.1	16 500	69.2	30.8	3.06	2.35
Plainfield city	-0.1	16 180	93.6	6.4	0.1	2.3	5.0	15 137	50.1	49.9	3.16	3.04
Rahway city	4.2	10 381	96.6	3.4	0.1	1.2	3.3	10 028	62.7	37.3	2.84	2.26
Sayreville borough	17.3	15 235	98.2	1.8	0.1	0.6	1.6	14 955	67.7	32.3	2.84	2.35
South Brunswick township	42.7	13 862	96.9	3.1	0.2	0.7	3.5	13 428	76.2	23.8	2.97	2.26
Teaneck township	3.2	13 719	97.8	2.2	0.3	0.7	2.4	13 418	77.6	22.4	3.05	2.19
Trenton city	-4.3	33 843	87.0	13.0	0.1	4.0	8.4	29 437	45.5	54.5	2.83	2.69
Union township	3.5	20 001	97.7	2.3	0.2	0.7	2.7	19 534	76.5	23.5	2.86	2.22
Union City city	11.0	23 741	96.3	3.7	0.2	1.0	2.3	22 872	18.2	81.8	2.98	2.90
Vineland city	6.4	20 958	95.1	4.9	0.5	1.7	4.4	19 930	66.2	33.8	2.74	2.63
Voorhees township	15.2	11 084	94.6	5.4	0.3	1.0	9.8	10 489	67.3	32.7	2.95	1.87
Wall township	28.2	9 957	94.8	5.2	3.0	0.9	3.3	9 437	85.9	14.1	2.74	2.03
Washington township	18.7	16 020	97.4	2.6	0.2	0.8	5.0	15 609	87.2	12.8	3.12	2.22
Wayne township	19.0	19 218	97.6	2.4	0.4	0.7	3.0	18 755	82.0	18.0	2.91	1.97
Westfield town	3.2	10 819	98.2	1.8	0.4	0.3	2.7	10 622	81.7	18.3	2.94	1.99
West Milford township	9.6	9 909	92.7	7.3	4.2	1.5	2.8	9 190	89.6	10.4	2.88	2.48
West New York town	16.0	17 360	96.3	3.7	0.3	1.4	2.5	16 719	19.9	80.1	2.70	2.74
West Orange township	11.2	16 901	97.5	2.5	0.5	0.8	2.2	16 480	70.4	29.6	2.83	2.26
Willingboro township	-3.0	11 124	96.3	3.7	0.2	2.0	2.9	10 713	92.5	7.5	3.00	3.82
Winslow township	19.8	12 413	93.9	6.1	0.1	2.0	9.1	11 661	83.1	16.9	2.94	2.53
Woodbridge township	3.3	35 298	97.9	2.1	0.2	0.6	2.4	34 562	70.6	29.4	2.84	2.41
NEW YORK	6.3	7 679 307	91.9	8.1	3.1	1.6	4.6	7 056 860	53.0	47.0	2.78	2.41
Albany city	-3.4	45 288	89.9	10.1	0.2	3.3	7.0	40 709	37.6	62.4	2.31	1.98
Amherst town	9.1	46 803	96.3	3.7	0.6	1.0	4.8	45 076	74.0	26.0	2.59	1.94
Auburn city	-4.4	12 637	90.3	9.7	0.4	2.7	11.4	11 411	51.9	48.1	2.48	2.05
Babylon town	7.0	71 186	97.0	3.0	0.6	0.8	2.2	69 048	75.5	24.5	3.18	2.56
Bethlehem town	17.1	12 459	97.2	2.8	0.3	0.7	3.4	12 112	75.3	24.7	2.73	1.90
Binghamton city	-6.8	23 971	88.0	12.0	0.3	3.9	11.2	21 089	43.0	57.0	2.33	2.08
Brighton town	4.7	16 705	94.9	5.1	0.7	0.7	6.9	15 854	57.2	42.8	2.45	1.72
Bronx borough	9.2	490 659	94.4	5.6	0.2	2.0	4.2	463 212	19.6	80.4	2.83	2.76
Brookhaven town	13.7	155 406	94.5	5.5	2.7	1.0	2.9	146 828	78.9	21.1	3.08	2.53
Brooklyn borough	6.3	930 866	94.6	5.4	0.3	1.6	3.1	880 727	27.1	72.9	3.04	2.65
Buffalo city	-10.1	145 574	84.3	15.7	0.2	4.2	11.1	122 720	43.5	56.5	2.47	2.16
Carmel town	16.2	11 283	96.1	3.9	2.2	0.7	2.4	10 847	84.5	15.5	3.13	2.40
Cheektowaga town	0.9	41 901	95.6	4.4	0.2	1.3	5.3	40 045	71.8	28.2	2.46	1.98
Chili town	18.5	10 466	97.1	2.9	0.2	0.7	5.7	10 159	79.8	20.2	2.79	2.15
Cicero town	16.9	11 033	95.5	4.5	1.6	0.9	4.9	10 538	80.4	19.6	2.79	2.11
Clarence town	31.4	9 497	96.4	3.6	0.4	1.0	9.8	9 154	87.8	12.2	2.91	1.98
Clarkstown town	9.2	28 220	98.1	1.9	0.3	0.4	3.5	27 697	82.0	18.0	3.01	2.40
Clay town	5.7	23 398	95.3	4.7	0.4	1.9	7.3	22 294	72.8	27.2	2.81	2.15
Clifton Park town	20.8	13 069	96.3	3.7	0.5	1.1	5.9	12 581	78.3	21.7	2.81	1.90
Colonie town	8.4	32 280	96.0	4.0	0.5	0.9	5.7	30 980	71.8	28.2	2.62	1.93
Cortlandt town	2.6	14 065	96.1	3.9	1.9	0.7	3.2	13 517	77.7	22.3	2.95	2.08
Eastchester town	2.0	13 035	96.9	3.1	0.6	1.1	3.1	12 626	71.4	28.6	2.59	2.12
East Fishkill town	21.1	8 495	96.9	3.1	0.9	0.6	2.9	8 233	89.9	10.1	3.18	2.38

Table E. Towns

STATE MCD code	Town	Population, 2000				Population, 1990				Population and population characteristics, 2000 Race (percent) One race					
		Land area, 2000[1] (sq km)	Total persons	Rank within state	Per square kilometer	Land area, 1990[1] (sq km)	Total persons	Rank within state	Per square kilometer	White	Black or African American	American Indian or Alaska Native	Asian	Native Hawaiian and other Pacific Islander	Some other race
		1	2	3	4	5	6	7	8	9	10	11	12	13	14
	NEW YORK—Cont'd														
36 24229	Elmira city	18.9	30 940	54	1 637.0	19.0	33 724	54	1 774.9	82.0	13.1	0.4	0.5	0.0	1.4
36 28442	Gates town	39.5	29 275	71	741.1	39.5	28 583	71	723.6	88.6	6.4	0.2	2.4	0.0	1.1
36 29113	Glen Cove city	17.2	26 622	85	1 547.8	17.2	24 149	85	1 404.0	80.3	6.4	0.3	4.1	0.1	5.7
36 29366	Glenville town	129.2	28 183	70	218.1	129.2	28 771	70	222.7	97.4	0.7	0.1	0.9	0.0	0.1
36 30290	Greece town	122.8	94 141	22	766.6	122.8	90 106	22	733.8	93.4	2.9	0.2	1.5	0.0	0.9
36 30367	Greenburgh town	79.1	86 764	23	1 096.9	79.0	83 816	23	1 061.0	72.4	13.1	0.2	8.8	0.0	2.9
36 31104	Guilderland town	150.0	32 688	65	217.9	150.9	30 011	65	198.9	92.1	2.5	0.1	3.8	0.0	0.4
36 31654	Hamburg town	106.9	56 259	35	526.3	106.9	53 735	35	502.7	97.9	0.5	0.2	0.4	0.0	0.4
36 32765	Haverstraw town	58.1	33 811	57	581.9	58.1	32 712	57	563.0	66.2	10.3	0.4	3.2	0.1	15.7
36 34000	Hempstead town	310.7	755 924	5	2 433.0	311.2	725 605	5	2 331.6	74.6	14.8	0.2	3.5	0.0	4.5
36 34099	Henrietta town	91.7	39 028	48	425.6	91.6	36 376	48	397.1	84.3	6.9	0.3	5.5	0.0	1.0
36 37000	Huntington town	243.4	195 289	14	802.3	243.4	191 474	14	786.7	88.3	4.2	0.1	3.5	0.0	2.3
36 37726	Irondequoit town	39.3	52 354	36	1 332.2	39.5	53 657	36	1 358.4	93.0	3.5	0.2	1.0	0.0	1.0
36 38000	Islip town	272.7	322 612	9	1 183.0	272.6	299 587	9	1 099.0	77.2	9.0	0.3	2.2	0.0	8.3
36 38077	Ithaca city	14.1	29 287	66	2 077.1	14.1	29 541	66	2 095.1	74.0	6.7	0.4	13.7	0.1	1.9
36 38264	Jamestown city	23.3	31 730	51	1 361.8	22.9	34 681	51	1 514.5	91.5	3.4	0.6	0.4	0.1	1.8
36 41146	Lancaster town	98.0	39 019	58	398.2	98.1	32 181	58	328.0	98.0	0.8	0.2	0.4	0.0	0.1
36 43335	Long Beach city	5.5	35 462	55	6 447.6	5.5	33 510	55	6 092.7	84.2	6.2	0.2	2.3	0.1	4.7
36 44842	Mamaroneck town	17.1	28 967	73	1 694.0	17.2	27 706	73	1 610.8	88.9	2.8	0.1	3.1	0.0	2.9
36 44919	Manhattan borough	59.5	1 537 195	3	25 835.2	73.5	1 487 536	3	20 238.6	54.4	17.4	0.5	9.4	0.1	14.1
36 45029	Manlius town	128.5	31 872	62	248.0	128.5	30 656	62	238.6	94.7	0.9	0.2	2.9	0.0	0.2
36 47042	Middletown city	13.3	25 388	84	1 908.9	12.8	24 160	84	1 887.5	68.7	15.1	0.7	1.7	0.0	9.3
36 47999	Monroe town	52.0	31 407	87	604.0	52.0	23 035	87	443.0	94.9	1.2	0.3	1.4	0.0	1.2
36 49011	Mount Pleasant town	71.7	43 221	44	602.8	71.7	40 590	44	566.1	84.3	5.1	0.2	3.3	0.0	5.0
36 49121	Mount Vernon city	11.3	68 381	29	6 051.4	11.4	67 153	29	5 890.6	28.6	59.6	0.3	2.1	0.1	4.8
36 50034	Newburgh city	9.9	28 259	77	2 854.0	9.9	26 454	77	2 672.1	42.3	33.0	0.7	0.8	0.1	18.1
36 50045	Newburgh town	113.2	27 568	86	243.5	113.2	24 058	86	212.5	85.1	7.6	0.1	2.1	0.0	3.1
36 50617	New Rochelle city	26.8	72 182	28	2 693.4	26.8	67 265	28	2 509.9	67.9	19.2	0.2	3.2	0.0	6.3
36 51055	Niagara Falls city	36.4	55 593	31	1 527.3	36.4	61 840	31	1 698.9	76.2	18.7	1.6	0.7	0.0	0.7
36 53000	North Hempstead town	138.8	222 611	12	1 603.8	138.7	211 393	12	1 524.1	79.0	6.4	0.1	9.1	0.0	2.9
36 53682	North Tonawanda city	26.2	33 262	50	1 269.5	26.2	34 989	50	1 335.5	97.9	0.3	0.3	0.5	0.0	0.3
36 55211	Orangetown town	62.6	47 711	40	762.2	62.6	46 742	40	746.7	84.0	5.9	0.1	6.4	0.0	1.7
36 55277	Orchard Park town	99.7	27 637	82	277.2	99.7	24 632	82	247.1	97.6	0.5	0.1	1.1	0.0	0.2
36 55541	Ossining town	30.3	36 534	53	1 205.7	30.3	34 124	53	1 126.2	70.3	14.3	0.3	4.5	0.0	7.3
36 56000	Oyster Bay town	270.3	293 925	10	1 087.4	270.1	292 787	10	1 084.0	90.8	1.6	0.1	4.9	0.0	1.4
36 57144	Penfield town	97.1	34 645	63	356.8	97.1	30 219	63	311.2	93.5	2.1	0.1	3.1	0.0	0.3
36 57221	Perinton town	88.4	46 090	43	521.4	88.4	43 015	43	486.6	93.9	1.7	0.1	2.8	0.0	0.5
36 58365	Pittsford town	60.1	27 219	83	452.9	60.1	24 497	83	407.6	92.6	1.6	0.1	4.6	0.0	0.3
36 59641	Poughkeepsie city	13.3	29 871	68	2 245.9	13.3	28 844	68	2 168.7	52.8	35.7	0.4	1.6	0.0	5.3
36 59652	Poughkeepsie town	74.5	42 777	45	574.2	74.5	40 143	45	538.8	83.0	8.1	0.1	5.1	0.0	1.6
36 60323	Queens borough	282.9	2 229 379	2	7 880.4	283.4	1 951 598	2	6 886.4	44.1	20.0	0.5	17.6	0.1	11.7
36 60356	Queensbury town	163.2	25 441	89	155.9	163.2	22 630	89	138.7	97.5	0.6	0.2	0.7	0.0	0.2
36 60510	Ramapo town	158.6	108 905	21	686.7	158.6	93 861	21	591.8	72.5	17.0	0.3	4.6	0.1	2.6
36 61984	Riverhead town	174.5	27 680	88	158.6	174.5	23 011	88	131.9	85.2	10.5	0.3	0.9	0.1	1.4
36 63000	Rochester city	92.8	219 773	11	2 368.2	92.7	230 356	11	2 485.0	48.3	38.5	0.5	2.2	0.0	6.6
36 63418	Rome city	194.1	34 950	42	180.1	194.1	44 350	42	228.5	87.9	7.6	0.3	0.9	0.0	1.4
36 63935	Rotterdam town	93.2	28 316	72	303.8	93.2	28 395	72	304.7	97.3	0.9	0.2	0.6	0.0	0.2
36 64320	Rye town	18.0	43 880	46	2 437.8	18.1	39 524	46	2 183.6	71.3	5.1	0.3	2.9	0.0	15.4
36 64815	Salina town	35.7	33 290	49	932.5	35.7	35 145	49	984.5	93.9	2.2	0.5	1.6	0.0	0.4
36 65255	Saratoga Springs city	73.6	26 186	81	355.8	73.6	25 001	81	339.7	93.5	3.1	0.2	1.4	0.0	0.6
36 65508	Schenectady city	28.1	61 821	30	2 200.0	28.1	65 566	30	2 333.3	76.8	14.8	0.4	2.0	0.0	2.5
36 68000	Smithtown town	138.8	115 715	17	833.7	138.8	113 406	17	817.0	95.5	0.6	0.1	2.4	0.0	0.6
36 68473	Southampton town	359.7	54 712	41	152.1	359.7	44 976	41	125.0	88.0	6.6	0.4	0.9	0.1	2.3
36 70915	Staten Island borough	151.5	443 728	7	2 928.9	151.8	378 977	7	2 496.6	77.6	9.7	0.2	5.7	0.0	4.1
36 73000	Syracuse city	65.0	147 306	16	2 266.2	65.0	163 860	16	2 520.9	64.3	25.3	1.1	3.4	0.0	2.2
36 75000	Tonawanda town	48.7	78 155	24	1 604.8	48.7	82 464	24	1 693.3	96.0	1.4	0.3	1.1	0.0	0.4
36 75484	Troy city	27.0	49 170	34	1 821.1	27.0	54 269	34	2 010.0	80.2	11.4	0.3	3.5	0.0	2.2
36 76056	Union town	91.1	56 298	32	618.0	91.1	59 786	32	656.3	92.7	2.4	0.2	2.7	0.0	0.6
36 76540	Utica city	42.3	60 651	27	1 433.8	42.3	68 637	27	1 622.6	79.4	12.9	0.3	2.2	0.0	2.2
36 77255	Vestal town	135.1	26 535	76	196.4	135.1	26 733	76	197.9	87.1	2.2	0.2	8.3	0.0	1.0
36 78157	Wappinger town	70.6	26 274	78	372.2	70.7	26 008	78	367.9	86.2	5.0	0.2	4.3	0.0	2.4
36 78366	Warwick town	263.3	30 764	75	116.8	263.3	27 193	75	103.3	91.1	4.5	0.3	0.9	0.0	1.6
36 78608	Watertown city	23.2	26 705	67	1 151.1	22.5	29 429	67	1 308.0	89.1	4.9	0.5	1.2	0.1	1.7
36 78971	Webster town	88.2	37 926	59	430.0	88.2	31 639	59	358.7	95.0	1.6	0.1	2.0	0.0	0.5
36 80918	West Seneca town	55.3	45 920	39	830.4	55.4	47 830	39	863.4	98.1	0.5	0.2	0.5	0.0	0.2
36 81677	White Plains city	25.4	53 077	38	2 089.6	25.4	48 718	38	1 918.0	64.9	15.9	0.3	4.5	0.1	10.4
36 84000	Yonkers city	46.8	196 086	15	4 189.9	46.8	188 082	15	4 018.8	60.2	16.6	0.4	4.9	0.0	13.4
36 84077	Yorktown town	95.0	36 318	56	382.3	95.2	33 467	56	351.5	90.6	3.0	0.1	3.4	0.0	1.3

[1]Dry land or land partially or temporarily covered by water.

Table E. Towns

Town	Two or more races	White	Black	American Indian or Alaska Native	Asian	Native Hawaiian and other Pacific Islander	Some other race	Hispanic[1]	White	Black or African American	American Indian or Alaska Native	Asian and Pacific Islander	Hispanic[1]
	15	16	17	18	19	20	21	22	23	24	25	26	27
NEW YORK—Cont'd													
Elmira city	2.6	84.4	14.9	0.9	0.7	0.1	1.9	3.1	85.4	12.3	0.3	0.6	2.7
Gates town	1.3	89.8	6.8	0.4	2.7	0.1	1.6	2.9	93.2	4.5	0.1	1.5	1.8
Glen Cove city	3.1	82.9	7.0	0.6	4.8	0.2	7.8	20.0	85.8	7.8	0.1	3.4	11.5
Glenville town	0.7	98.0	1.0	0.4	1.1	0.1	0.3	1.2	98.4	0.5	0.1	0.9	0.8
Greece town	1.1	94.3	3.3	0.5	1.7	0.1	1.3	2.6	95.9	2.2	0.2	1.2	1.6
Greenburgh town	2.6	74.3	14.0	0.6	9.5	0.1	4.2	9.0	77.7	13.2	0.1	7.6	5.9
Guilderland town	1.0	92.9	2.8	0.4	4.2	0.0	0.7	1.8	96.1	2.1	0.1	1.4	1.2
Hamburg town	0.6	98.5	0.7	0.4	0.5	0.0	0.5	1.6	98.9	0.4	0.2	0.3	1.3
Haverstraw town	4.1	69.1	11.7	1.0	3.8	0.2	18.6	31.7	78.4	10.8	0.3	2.3	22.7
Hempstead town	2.3	76.1	15.7	0.5	4.0	0.1	6.0	11.5	83.4	12.1	0.2	2.4	6.6
Henrietta town	2.0	85.9	7.7	0.9	6.1	0.1	1.5	3.0	89.0	6.2	0.4	3.7	2.0
Huntington town	1.5	89.5	4.7	0.4	4.0	0.1	3.1	6.6	92.3	4.2	0.1	2.5	4.1
Irondequoit town	1.2	94.1	3.9	0.4	1.3	0.0	1.5	3.1	97.4	1.3	0.2	0.6	1.4
Islip town	2.9	79.3	10.1	0.7	2.7	0.1	10.3	20.2	87.2	6.8	0.2	1.6	13.1
Ithaca city	3.4	76.4	7.8	1.0	15.1	0.5	2.8	5.3	81.8	6.5	0.3	10.0	3.6
Jamestown city	2.2	93.5	4.5	1.2	0.6	0.1	2.4	4.9	94.9	2.6	0.5	0.5	3.0
Lancaster town	0.5	98.5	0.9	0.3	0.5	0.0	0.2	0.7	98.9	0.5	0.2	0.3	0.5
Long Beach city	2.3	85.9	6.8	0.5	2.8	0.2	6.2	12.8	87.0	7.8	0.3	1.7	10.8
Mamaroneck town	2.1	90.8	3.3	0.3	3.5	0.1	4.2	10.9	91.3	3.6	0.1	3.4	7.2
Manhattan borough	4.1	57.1	19.0	1.0	10.2	0.2	16.9	27.2	58.3	22.0	0.4	7.4	26.0
Manlius town	1.1	95.7	1.1	0.6	3.3	0.1	0.5	1.0	97.2	0.6	0.2	1.9	0.7
Middletown city	4.4	72.1	17.4	1.5	2.1	0.2	11.4	25.1	82.2	11.1	0.5	1.4	13.3
Monroe town	1.1	95.8	1.5	0.4	1.7	0.0	1.7	4.9	97.8	0.6	0.1	1.1	2.9
Mount Pleasant town	2.1	86.0	5.5	0.5	3.8	0.1	6.4	14.0	88.2	6.2	0.3	2.7	10.2
Mount Vernon city	4.4	30.9	62.2	0.9	2.7	0.3	7.8	10.4	39.8	55.3	0.4	1.8	7.8
Newburgh city	5.1	45.9	35.5	1.5	1.1	0.2	21.1	36.3	51.2	34.8	0.3	0.5	23.2
Newburgh town	2.1	86.7	8.4	0.7	2.4	0.1	3.8	9.6	92.7	4.3	0.1	1.5	5.5
New Rochelle city	3.2	70.2	20.3	0.6	3.8	0.1	8.4	20.1	76.0	18.1	0.1	2.9	10.8
Niagara Falls city	2.0	77.9	19.8	2.4	0.9	0.1	1.1	2.0	82.2	15.6	1.6	0.3	1.2
North Hempstead town	2.5	80.9	6.9	0.4	9.8	0.1	4.4	9.8	86.4	6.6	0.1	5.6	6.1
North Tonawanda city	0.7	98.5	0.5	0.6	0.7	0.0	0.4	1.1	98.9	0.2	0.3	0.4	0.8
Orangetown town	1.9	85.1	6.8	0.4	7.0	0.1	2.7	6.0	85.7	8.2	0.1	5.2	4.4
Orchard Park town	0.6	98.1	0.6	0.3	1.2	0.0	0.3	1.0	98.4	0.5	0.1	0.9	0.9
Ossining town	3.2	72.8	15.1	0.7	5.1	0.1	9.5	19.9	77.9	15.9	0.2	2.6	12.0
Oyster Bay town	1.2	91.8	1.9	0.2	5.3	0.1	2.1	5.1	94.7	1.7	0.1	2.9	3.4
Penfield town	0.9	94.3	2.3	0.3	3.4	0.1	0.5	1.4	95.3	1.8	0.1	2.6	0.8
Perinton town	1.0	94.8	2.0	0.3	3.2	0.0	0.7	1.4	95.8	1.6	0.1	2.3	0.9
Pittsford town	0.8	93.3	1.8	0.2	4.9	0.0	0.5	1.3	94.5	1.8	0.1	3.5	0.9
Poughkeepsie city	4.1	55.3	38.5	1.2	1.9	0.1	7.2	10.6	65.4	31.5	0.4	1.5	3.8
Poughkeepsie town	2.0	84.6	8.8	0.5	5.7	0.1	2.4	5.3	89.7	5.6	0.1	4.0	2.4
Queens borough	6.1	47.4	21.8	1.2	19.4	0.2	16.3	25.0	57.9	21.7	0.4	12.2	19.5
Queensbury town	0.8	98.3	0.7	0.6	0.9	0.0	0.4	1.1	98.6	0.4	0.1	0.8	0.8
Ramapo town	2.8	73.9	18.6	0.7	5.1	0.2	4.4	8.2	81.0	13.8	0.5	3.7	4.6
Riverhead town	1.6	86.5	11.1	0.8	1.1	0.2	2.0	6.1	86.0	12.7	0.2	0.6	2.6
Rochester city	3.8	50.9	40.7	1.3	2.7	0.2	8.4	12.8	61.1	31.5	0.5	1.8	8.7
Rome city	2.0	89.7	8.5	0.6	1.2	0.1	2.1	4.7	89.4	8.0	0.2	1.3	3.9
Rotterdam town	0.8	98.0	1.3	0.4	0.8	0.0	0.4	1.0	98.6	0.7	0.1	0.4	0.9
Rye town	4.9	75.8	5.7	0.6	3.3	0.1	19.7	32.5	84.2	7.2	0.1	2.6	21.2
Salina town	1.4	95.2	2.6	1.0	1.9	0.1	0.7	1.4	97.3	1.3	0.4	0.9	0.8
Saratoga Springs city	1.4	94.8	3.8	0.7	1.3	0.0	0.9	1.9	95.5	3.3	0.2	0.7	1.4
Schenectady city	3.5	79.6	16.8	1.0	2.6	0.2	3.6	5.9	88.6	8.7	0.3	1.1	2.7
Smithtown town	0.8	96.2	0.8	0.2	2.7	0.1	0.9	3.3	96.8	0.9	0.1	1.8	2.6
Southampton town	1.7	89.3	7.2	0.8	1.2	0.2	3.2	8.6	89.6	8.9	0.3	0.7	2.6
Staten Island borough	2.7	79.5	10.5	0.6	6.3	0.1	5.8	12.1	85.0	8.1	0.2	4.5	8.0
Syracuse city	3.6	67.1	27.5	2.2	3.8	0.1	3.2	5.3	75.0	20.3	1.3	2.2	2.9
Tonawanda town	0.8	96.7	1.7	0.5	1.4	0.1	0.6	1.3	98.1	0.7	0.2	0.9	0.8
Troy city	2.3	82.2	12.6	0.7	3.9	0.1	3.1	4.3	88.3	7.6	0.2	3.0	2.1
Union town	1.4	93.9	3.1	0.6	3.0	0.1	1.5	1.5	96.4	1.4	0.1	1.8	1.0
Utica city	3.0	82.0	14.0	0.7	2.6	0.1	3.7	5.8	86.7	10.5	0.3	1.1	3.4
Vestal town	1.2	88.1	2.5	0.4	8.8	0.0	1.4	2.4	93.0	1.8	0.1	4.5	1.8
Wappinger town	1.9	87.7	5.7	0.6	4.7	0.0	3.2	7.9	91.4	4.0	0.1	3.8	3.4
Warwick town	1.6	92.4	5.1	0.9	1.2	0.1	2.1	6.5	94.1	4.1	0.4	0.6	4.7
Watertown city	2.4	91.2	6.1	1.2	1.6	0.3	2.3	3.6	93.8	3.8	0.5	0.8	2.0
Webster town	0.9	95.8	1.9	0.4	2.3	0.0	0.7	1.6	96.8	1.3	0.1	1.5	0.9
West Seneca town	0.6	98.6	0.6	0.4	0.6	0.0	0.4	0.9	98.9	0.4	0.2	0.4	0.6
White Plains city	3.9	67.5	17.1	0.8	5.0	0.5	13.2	23.5	73.7	19.0	0.2	3.1	14.2
Yonkers city	4.4	63.2	18.1	0.9	5.5	0.2	16.8	25.9	76.2	14.1	0.2	3.0	16.7
Yorktown town	1.4	91.8	3.4	0.5	3.9	0.0	1.9	5.8	93.8	2.9	0.1	2.5	3.6

[1] Hispanic persons may be of any race.

Table E. Towns

Town	Population and population characteristics, 2000										
	Age (percent)										
	Under 5 years	5 to 17 years	18 to 24 years	25 to 34 years	35 to 44 years	45 to 54 years	55 to 64 years	65 to 74 years	75 years and over	Median age (years)	Percent Female
	28	29	30	31	32	33	34	35	36	37	38
NEW YORK—Cont'd											
Elmira city	7.0	18.1	13.0	14.2	15.7	11.5	6.7	6.5	7.3	33.4	49.7
Gates town	5.5	17.1	6.9	12.9	16.0	13.5	10.7	8.8	8.6	39.6	52.0
Glen Cove city	6.2	15.0	8.1	14.7	15.9	13.0	9.5	8.1	9.4	38.6	51.9
Glenville town	5.2	18.5	5.0	10.1	16.2	15.7	10.4	8.4	10.4	41.9	52.1
Greece town	5.7	19.3	7.0	11.8	16.5	15.2	9.1	7.7	7.6	39.0	52.0
Greenburgh town	6.3	17.4	5.9	12.4	17.3	15.9	10.3	7.9	6.6	39.7	52.5
Guilderland town	5.5	18.6	6.0	13.1	17.8	16.8	9.1	6.9	6.2	38.9	52.0
Hamburg town	6.0	18.8	6.9	12.2	16.4	15.2	9.5	7.5	7.5	38.9	52.4
Haverstraw town	6.9	19.4	8.6	14.6	16.6	13.6	9.9	5.9	4.5	35.3	51.6
Hempstead town	6.7	18.8	7.8	12.4	16.8	14.4	9.1	7.5	6.6	37.6	52.0
Henrietta town	5.0	15.4	23.9	12.4	14.4	11.7	7.9	5.7	3.6	29.8	47.2
Huntington town	7.3	18.2	5.8	12.0	18.2	15.1	10.4	7.4	7.7	38.7	51.0
Irondequoit town	5.3	16.6	5.2	11.4	15.3	14.8	8.9	9.1	13.4	42.6	54.0
Islip town	7.3	20.0	8.1	14.5	17.9	13.1	9.1	5.8	4.1	35.0	50.8
Ithaca city	2.5	6.8	53.8	12.6	7.4	7.1	3.5	2.8	3.5	22.0	49.4
Jamestown city	7.6	18.3	9.1	13.5	14.7	12.9	8.0	7.5	8.5	36.2	52.3
Lancaster town	6.5	18.6	6.5	13.1	18.2	14.2	8.6	7.1	7.1	38.0	51.6
Long Beach city	4.9	13.7	6.6	16.5	17.9	14.9	8.9	7.6	9.1	39.6	51.9
Mamaroneck town	7.2	18.8	5.1	12.5	17.2	14.8	9.6	7.4	7.4	38.8	52.3
Manhattan borough	4.9	11.8	10.2	21.5	16.7	13.4	9.2	6.4	5.7	35.7	52.5
Manlius town	5.9	20.5	4.7	9.5	17.3	16.5	10.1	8.1	7.4	40.7	52.3
Middletown city	7.9	19.9	9.4	15.3	15.6	12.4	7.5	5.4	6.6	33.4	51.7
Monroe town	12.8	28.7	11.6	11.6	13.2	11.2	5.0	3.3	2.6	22.5	48.1
Mount Pleasant town	6.9	19.1	8.3	13.1	17.6	14.2	8.5	6.7	5.7	36.5	49.3
Mount Vernon city	7.1	18.3	8.3	14.9	16.2	13.1	9.3	6.5	6.4	35.8	54.9
Newburgh city	9.8	23.4	12.7	15.1	13.7	9.4	6.7	4.5	4.6	27.8	52.6
Newburgh town	6.7	19.5	6.6	12.2	17.9	14.7	9.9	6.9	5.7	37.8	51.0
New Rochelle city	6.8	17.3	8.7	14.0	15.5	13.1	9.2	7.6	7.9	37.0	52.5
Niagara Falls city	6.4	18.3	8.6	12.4	15.3	12.5	7.9	8.7	9.9	38.0	53.2
North Hempstead town	6.2	17.4	7.5	11.6	15.6	15.0	10.2	8.4	8.2	39.9	51.9
North Tonawanda city	5.7	18.1	8.6	12.3	16.7	14.8	8.3	8.2	7.5	38.4	51.4
Orangetown town	6.1	16.4	8.1	12.0	16.9	13.9	11.0	8.9	6.7	39.3	51.9
Orchard Park town	5.5	19.8	5.7	9.4	16.1	16.1	10.7	8.4	8.3	41.4	51.9
Ossining town	6.3	15.5	7.8	15.7	18.8	14.0	8.8	6.5	6.5	37.4	48.5
Oyster Bay town	6.5	18.0	6.0	11.3	17.4	15.1	9.8	8.8	7.1	39.8	51.5
Penfield town	5.9	19.9	4.8	9.9	17.5	16.7	10.4	7.4	7.5	40.5	52.0
Perinton town	6.8	19.9	5.0	10.8	17.7	17.2	10.9	6.3	5.4	39.3	51.8
Pittsford town	5.8	19.5	9.4	6.6	15.5	16.3	10.9	8.2	7.7	40.9	53.3
Poughkeepsie city	7.6	18.3	12.2	15.0	14.2	11.4	7.7	6.6	7.0	32.7	52.2
Poughkeepsie town	5.4	17.2	16.9	10.8	15.6	12.5	8.7	7.2	5.7	34.8	52.1
Queens borough	6.4	16.4	9.6	16.8	16.3	12.9	8.8	6.6	6.1	35.4	51.8
Queensbury town	5.8	19.5	6.1	11.3	17.0	15.3	9.8	7.9	7.3	39.3	52.0
Ramapo town	9.5	24.2	8.8	11.9	14.1	12.9	8.5	5.6	4.6	31.6	50.7
Riverhead town	6.2	16.9	6.1	11.9	16.4	14.0	10.2	9.2	9.3	40.6	51.2
Rochester city	7.8	20.3	11.6	17.1	15.0	11.4	6.7	4.5	5.5	30.8	52.2
Rome city	5.9	16.3	8.5	14.3	15.6	13.2	9.2	7.8	9.4	38.2	48.8
Rotterdam town	5.4	17.7	5.8	11.6	16.4	14.2	9.9	9.8	9.3	40.9	51.8
Rye town	7.1	16.4	8.5	16.1	17.2	12.6	8.0	7.1	6.9	36.1	50.4
Salina town	5.4	16.4	7.0	14.0	16.0	13.7	9.5	9.3	8.8	39.4	52.6
Saratoga Springs city	5.3	14.0	15.5	13.2	14.3	14.6	8.8	6.1	8.2	36.3	52.5
Schenectady city	7.0	17.3	11.6	14.4	15.3	11.7	7.4	6.6	8.6	34.8	52.2
Smithtown town	7.5	18.5	5.4	12.1	18.2	13.7	11.0	7.5	5.9	38.4	51.4
Southampton town	5.7	15.5	7.7	11.7	16.9	15.3	10.7	8.6	8.0	40.4	50.2
Staten Island borough	6.7	18.8	8.5	14.3	16.6	14.3	9.2	6.3	5.3	35.9	51.7
Syracuse city	6.9	18.0	16.8	14.5	13.4	11.0	6.5	5.8	7.1	30.5	52.9
Tonawanda town	5.4	16.5	7.2	11.8	15.6	13.8	8.8	10.2	10.7	41.1	53.2
Troy city	6.4	15.7	17.6	14.9	13.6	10.9	7.2	6.5	7.2	31.7	50.5
Union town	5.8	16.1	8.4	12.8	15.7	13.2	9.2	8.6	10.2	39.5	52.6
Utica city	6.7	17.4	10.0	13.2	13.7	11.8	8.4	8.1	10.7	37.0	53.0
Vestal town	4.3	14.6	24.0	7.8	12.7	11.7	9.1	7.9	7.9	34.2	52.5
Wappinger town	6.5	18.8	7.6	14.5	18.0	14.5	9.6	6.3	4.1	36.3	50.3
Warwick town	6.5	20.7	5.6	11.1	20.2	15.8	8.8	6.0	5.3	38.3	49.8
Watertown city	7.8	18.2	10.4	15.1	14.5	11.4	7.1	6.8	8.7	34.0	52.5
Webster town	6.2	19.8	5.6	11.9	18.1	15.5	9.9	7.0	6.0	38.8	51.3
West Seneca town	5.2	17.1	6.9	11.3	15.9	14.5	10.9	9.4	8.8	41.1	52.4
White Plains city	6.2	15.0	7.5	16.0	16.5	13.9	9.7	7.6	7.5	38.1	52.7
Yonkers city	7.0	17.3	8.8	15.4	15.2	12.3	8.9	7.7	7.3	35.8	53.0
Yorktown town	6.9	20.6	5.4	9.8	18.7	15.7	9.6	6.7	6.6	39.0	51.8

Table E. Towns

Town	Under 5 years	5 to 17 years	18 to 24 years	25 to 34 years	35 to 44 years	45 to 54 years	55 to 64 years	65 to 74 years	75 years and over	Percent Female	2000	1990	1980	1990–2000	1980–1990
					Age (percent)						Total persons			Percent change	
	39	40	41	42	43	44	45	46	47	48	49	50	51	52	53
NEW YORK—Cont'd															
Elmira city	8.5	17.8	14.0	16.9	12.5	7.5	7.8	8.3	6.6	51.6	30 940	33 724	35 327	-8.3	-4.5
Gates town	6.0	15.2	9.0	10.2	13.7	13.0	10.7	9.2	6.5	52.3	29 275	28 583	NA	2.4	NA
Glen Cove city	5.9	14.1	10.1	17.1	13.4	11.8	11.2	9.1	7.3	52.3	26 622	24 149	NA	10.2	NA
Glenville town	6.1	17.5	7.1	13.6	16.2	11.7	10.1	10.8	6.9	52.0	28 183	28 771	NA	-2.0	NA
Greece town	7.4	17.9	8.7	17.1	16.9	10.2	9.3	8.1	4.6	51.8	94 141	90 106	NA	4.5	NA
Greenburgh town	6.5	14.7	7.7	16.2	16.6	12.8	11.4	8.4	5.7	52.6	86 764	83 816	NA	3.5	NA
Guilderland town	6.3	16.8	8.1	17.5	18.6	11.2	9.5	7.5	4.5	52.1	32 688	30 011	NA	8.9	NA
Hamburg town	6.7	18.4	8.9	15.8	16.0	11.1	9.3	8.3	5.5	52.7	56 259	53 735	NA	4.7	NA
Haverstraw town	7.9	18.1	9.9	18.7	16.4	11.5	8.3	5.3	3.9	51.2	33 811	32 712	NA	3.4	NA
Hempstead town	6.4	16.0	10.1	16.1	15.3	11.4	11.0	8.7	5.0	51.9	755 924	725 605	NA	4.2	NA
Henrietta town	6.1	15.2	22.8	18.0	14.4	9.1	7.5	5.0	2.0	48.1	39 028	36 376	NA	7.3	NA
Huntington town	6.1	17.0	9.5	15.8	16.3	13.5	11.2	6.6	4.1	51.1	195 289	191 474	NA	2.0	NA
Irondequoit town	5.7	13.6	6.9	14.3	15.3	9.6	11.2	13.5	9.8	53.5	52 354	53 657	NA	-2.4	NA
Islip town	7.4	18.1	11.5	18.2	15.3	12.0	8.9	5.3	3.2	51.0	322 612	299 587	NA	7.7	NA
Ithaca city	2.9	7.0	51.4	14.6	8.7	4.0	3.7	3.7	3.9	48.4	29 287	29 541	28 732	-0.9	2.8
Jamestown city	8.1	17.3	10.4	16.7	13.0	8.4	8.8	8.5	8.7	53.3	31 730	34 681	35 775	-8.5	-3.1
Lancaster town	7.4	16.8	9.1	18.2	15.2	10.0	9.5	8.5	5.3	51.8	39 019	32 181	NA	21.2	NA
Long Beach city	6.2	11.4	8.3	20.9	14.7	10.4	9.5	8.2	10.5	52.2	35 462	33 510	34 073	5.8	-1.7
Mamaroneck town	5.8	15.9	8.2	14.7	16.2	13.3	10.7	8.1	7.0	52.2	28 967	27 706	NA	4.6	NA
Manhattan borough	5.3	11.3	9.8	21.7	17.5	12.0	9.1	7.2	6.1	53.1	1 537 195	1 487 536	1 428 285	3.3	4.1
Manlius town	6.8	19.3	6.7	14.6	18.1	11.9	10.0	7.4	5.3	52.2	31 872	30 656	NA	4.0	NA
Middletown city	8.6	17.5	10.7	19.2	14.0	8.7	7.0	7.2	7.1	52.0	25 388	24 160	NA	5.1	NA
Monroe town	11.6	27.7	10.0	14.3	15.1	8.3	5.6	4.4	2.8	49.1	31 407	23 035	NA	36.3	NA
Mount Pleasant town	6.2	16.1	11.4	16.6	15.6	12.1	10.2	6.7	5.0	49.7	43 221	40 590	NA	6.5	NA
Mount Vernon city	6.9	16.0	9.8	17.9	14.4	11.2	8.8	8.1	6.9	55.2	68 381	67 153	66 713	1.8	0.7
Newburgh city	10.0	20.3	13.3	17.3	12.7	8.5	7.1	6.2	4.5	53.5	28 259	26 454	23 438	6.8	12.9
Newburgh town	6.9	17.4	8.9	16.9	15.8	12.4	9.9	7.2	4.7	50.9	27 568	24 058	NA	14.6	NA
New Rochelle city	6.1	14.0	9.8	16.3	14.6	11.5	10.6	8.9	8.2	53.0	72 182	67 265	70 794	7.3	-5.0
Niagara Falls city	7.3	16.5	9.3	16.6	12.7	8.2	10.3	11.3	7.8	54.1	55 593	61 840	71 384	-10.1	-13.4
North Hempstead town	5.5	15.3	8.8	14.3	15.3	12.6	11.9	10.1	6.1	51.8	222 611	211 393	NA	5.3	NA
North Tonawanda city	7.1	17.8	9.3	17.0	16.1	8.6	9.7	9.1	5.4	52.1	33 262	34 989	35 760	-4.9	-2.2
Orangetown town	5.7	14.4	10.6	16.2	14.2	13.0	11.9	8.3	5.4	51.4	47 711	46 742	NA	2.1	NA
Orchard Park town	6.0	18.0	8.4	13.0	16.8	13.1	10.6	8.3	5.6	51.5	27 637	24 632	NA	12.2	NA
Ossining town	6.6	12.7	10.8	21.8	16.9	10.8	8.7	6.1	5.6	49.5	36 534	34 124	NA	7.1	NA
Oyster Bay town	5.9	15.5	9.9	15.5	15.3	12.2	12.6	9.0	4.2	51.3	293 925	292 787	NA	0.4	NA
Penfield town	6.8	17.5	7.2	14.3	18.1	13.1	9.9	7.6	5.5	52.5	34 645	30 219	NA	14.6	NA
Perinton town	6.9	19.9	8.1	14.8	20.0	13.4	8.0	5.3	3.6	51.5	46 090	43 015	NA	7.1	NA
Pittsford town	5.9	17.4	12.8	9.9	17.5	14.4	10.9	6.9	4.2	52.1	27 219	24 497	NA	11.1	NA
Poughkeepsie city	8.4	14.9	10.3	20.0	13.9	8.3	8.3	8.0	7.8	53.3	29 871	28 844	29 757	3.6	-3.1
Poughkeepsie town	6.2	15.2	17.7	15.6	13.7	11.0	9.1	7.6	3.9	51.9	42 777	40 143	NA	6.6	NA
Queens borough	6.1	14.8	9.9	18.6	14.9	11.3	9.8	8.3	6.3	52.5	2 229 379	1 951 598	1 891 325	14.2	3.2
Queensbury town	6.5	19.4	9.3	15.0	17.5	10.9	8.8	7.6	5.6	52.2	25 441	22 630	NA	12.4	NA
Ramapo town	9.0	21.5	9.7	15.0	14.7	12.1	9.0	5.0	4.2	51.6	108 905	93 861	NA	16.0	NA
Riverhead town	6.4	16.5	7.6	13.9	14.3	10.5	9.8	11.6	9.0	51.7	27 680	23 011	NA	20.3	NA
Rochester city	9.5	16.6	13.0	21.7	13.4	7.8	6.1	6.1	5.9	52.9	219 773	230 356	241 741	-4.6	-4.7
Rome city	7.8	16.6	12.7	20.0	13.0	8.6	7.5	8.0	5.8	48.0	34 950	44 350	43 826	-21.2	1.2
Rotterdam town	5.8	15.9	8.4	15.0	14.0	11.8	11.9	10.6	6.6	52.3	28 316	28 395	NA	-0.3	NA
Rye town	6.5	13.9	10.0	19.2	14.5	10.5	10.3	8.5	6.6	52.2	43 880	39 524	NA	11.0	NA
Salina town	6.4	15.3	9.5	18.5	13.8	10.6	11.1	9.7	5.2	52.3	33 290	35 145	NA	-5.3	NA
Saratoga Springs city	5.7	14.7	18.3	15.4	15.0	10.2	7.1	6.7	7.0	52.6	26 186	25 001	23 906	4.7	4.6
Schenectady city	7.9	14.1	13.0	19.2	12.6	8.1	8.0	9.0	8.0	53.1	61 821	65 566	67 972	-5.7	-3.5
Smithtown town	6.1	16.4	10.7	15.4	15.0	14.8	11.0	5.9	4.6	51.0	115 715	113 406	NA	2.0	NA
Southampton town	5.8	13.9	8.9	15.3	16.1	10.7	10.3	10.4	8.7	52.4	54 712	44 976	NA	21.6	NA
Staten Island borough	7.4	17.6	10.2	17.7	16.1	11.5	8.5	6.6	4.5	51.7	443 728	378 977	352 029	17.1	7.7
Syracuse city	7.6	15.0	17.8	18.4	12.0	7.6	7.0	7.6	7.1	53.4	147 306	163 860	170 105	-10.1	-3.7
Tonawanda town	6.2	14.7	8.1	16.2	14.3	9.3	11.9	12.0	7.3	53.1	78 155	82 464	NA	-5.2	NA
Troy city	7.0	14.5	19.8	17.8	11.6	7.1	8.0	7.4	6.8	50.7	49 170	54 269	56 638	-9.4	-4.2
Union town	6.6	15.1	10.0	18.1	14.0	9.7	9.6	9.5	7.3	52.5	56 298	59 786	NA	-5.8	NA
Utica city	7.2	15.5	11.6	16.6	11.7	8.8	9.3	10.5	8.8	53.1	60 651	68 637	75 632	-11.6	-9.2
Vestal town	5.5	13.7	22.0	13.4	13.7	10.0	9.6	7.0	5.1	51.8	26 535	26 733	NA	-0.7	NA
Wappinger town	7.7	17.7	10.7	19.0	16.6	12.3	7.9	4.4	3.6	49.3	26 274	26 008	NA	1.0	NA
Warwick town	8.5	17.7	8.1	18.6	18.2	10.7	8.2	5.8	4.3	49.0	30 764	27 193	NA	13.1	NA
Watertown city	8.8	17.7	11.6	18.8	12.1	8.3	7.8	7.3	7.6	53.3	26 705	29 429	27 861	-9.3	5.6
Webster town	7.0	18.8	8.1	15.7	17.7	12.5	9.4	7.3	3.5	51.0	37 926	31 639	NA	19.9	NA
West Seneca town	5.6	16.3	10.3	15.2	14.9	11.5	11.2	9.6	5.4	51.7	45 920	47 830	NA	-4.0	NA
White Plains city	5.3	12.5	8.9	20.0	15.6	11.7	10.1	8.1	7.7	53.6	53 077	48 718	46 999	8.9	3.7
Yonkers city	6.7	14.7	9.6	17.9	13.8	10.2	10.6	9.3	7.2	53.4	196 086	188 082	195 351	4.3	-3.7
Yorktown town	7.0	17.6	8.6	14.7	17.3	13.0	9.8	6.1	5.8	51.2	36 318	33 467	NA	8.5	NA

Table E. Towns

Town	Total population	Total in house-holds	House-holder	Spouse	Child Total	Child Own child under 18 years	Other relatives Total	Other relatives Under 18 years	Nonrelatives Total	Nonrelatives Unmarried partner	Total in group quarters	Correctional institutions	Nursing homes	Other institutions	College dormitories	Military quarters	Other
	54	55	56	57	58	59	60	61	62	63	64	65	66	67	68	69	70
NEW YORK—Cont'd																	
Elmira city	30 940	87.9	37.1	13.1	27.6	22.3	3.7	1.7	6.5	3.4	12.1	6.6	1.1	0.4	3.3	0.0	0.6
Gates town	29 275	99.3	40.1	21.6	28.9	20.6	4.7	1.6	4.1	2.0	0.7	0.0	0.4	0.0	0.0	0.0	0.3
Glen Cove city	26 622	96.7	35.5	19.0	28.4	18.9	8.0	1.9	5.7	1.5	3.3	0.0	2.1	0.0	0.0	0.0	0.9
Glenville town	28 183	96.7	39.6	23.3	28.6	22.5	2.2	0.7	3.0	1.6	3.3	0.0	2.5	0.0	0.0	0.0	0.8
Greece town	94 141	98.9	39.3	21.9	30.8	23.4	3.3	1.1	3.7	2.0	1.1	0.0	0.6	0.1	0.0	0.0	0.4
Greenburgh town	86 764	97.8	38.1	21.8	28.9	21.6	5.1	1.3	4.0	1.3	2.2	0.0	0.2	0.2	0.7	0.0	1.1
Guilderland town	32 688	98.6	41.1	22.2	28.9	23.1	2.5	0.7	3.9	2.1	1.4	0.0	0.9	0.0	0.0	0.0	0.5
Hamburg town	56 259	98.3	39.1	21.8	31.3	23.4	2.7	1.0	3.4	1.8	1.7	0.0	1.0	0.0	0.1	0.0	0.6
Haverstraw town	33 811	97.9	33.3	18.1	33.2	23.1	8.4	2.7	4.8	1.7	2.1	0.0	0.8	0.1	0.0	0.0	1.3
Hempstead town	755 924	98.5	32.7	20.3	33.4	22.6	8.0	2.4	4.2	1.1	1.5	0.0	0.5	0.0	0.5	0.0	0.3
Henrietta town	39 028	85.6	32.9	17.7	24.7	18.7	3.2	1.2	7.2	1.8	14.4	0.0	0.0	0.0	14.0	0.0	0.4
Huntington town	195 289	98.4	33.8	22.8	32.4	23.6	5.3	1.5	4.2	1.2	1.6	0.0	0.7	0.2	0.0	0.0	0.7
Irondequoit town	52 354	98.5	42.5	21.6	27.3	20.6	3.4	1.0	3.7	2.0	1.5	0.0	1.0	0.0	0.0	0.0	0.5
Islip town	322 612	98.7	30.7	19.1	33.9	23.6	9.0	2.9	6.0	1.5	1.3	0.0	0.4	0.1	0.3	0.0	0.5
Ithaca city	29 287	74.7	35.1	6.7	10.2	8.3	1.4	0.5	21.3	2.0	25.3	0.0	0.6	0.0	24.2	0.0	0.5
Jamestown city	31 730	97.7	42.7	16.7	28.5	23.2	3.1	1.3	6.6	3.6	2.3	0.0	0.9	0.1	0.0	0.0	1.2
Lancaster town	39 019	98.4	38.6	22.5	31.7	24.1	2.6	0.7	3.1	1.7	1.6	0.0	1.0	0.0	0.0	0.0	0.6
Long Beach city	35 462	95.2	42.1	16.8	23.4	16.2	5.9	1.7	6.9	2.4	4.8	0.0	2.3	0.2	0.2	0.0	2.1
Mamaroneck town	28 967	98.8	37.7	22.6	31.2	25.0	3.6	0.9	3.6	1.1	1.2	0.0	1.0	0.0	0.0	0.0	0.2
Manhattan borough	1 537 195	96.1	48.1	12.1	20.3	13.9	6.7	2.3	8.9	2.3	3.9	0.2	0.4	0.2	1.8	0.0	1.3
Manlius town	31 872	98.9	39.4	23.7	30.9	25.3	2.2	0.7	2.8	1.4	1.1	0.0	0.5	0.0	0.0	0.0	0.6
Middletown city	25 388	99.7	37.3	14.9	31.2	24.3	7.1	2.6	7.2	3.0	2.3	0.0	0.8	0.0	0.0	0.0	1.5
Monroe town	31 407	97.3	26.2	19.5	46.1	39.6	3.2	1.2	2.3	0.7	2.7	0.0	0.0	0.0	2.2	0.0	0.5
Mount Pleasant town	43 221	92.0	31.8	20.7	30.4	22.8	5.0	1.1	4.2	0.9	8.0	2.9	1.2	1.8	1.3	0.0	0.7
Mount Vernon city	68 381	98.9	37.6	13.9	31.1	20.7	10.4	3.8	5.9	2.0	1.1	0.0	0.8	0.0	0.0	0.0	0.3
Newburgh city	28 259	96.1	32.4	11.0	34.5	27.4	10.8	4.6	7.4	3.0	3.9	0.0	0.1	0.6	2.0	0.0	1.2
Newburgh town	27 568	99.1	35.4	22.2	32.1	23.8	5.3	1.8	4.1	2.0	0.9	0.0	0.7	0.0	0.0	0.0	0.2
New Rochelle city	72 182	97.1	36.3	18.3	30.1	21.8	7.2	1.9	5.2	1.4	2.9	0.0	1.5	0.0	0.9	0.0	0.5
Niagara Falls city	55 593	98.6	43.3	15.7	29.9	22.1	4.7	2.0	4.9	2.5	1.4	0.0	0.9	0.0	0.0	0.0	0.5
North Hempstead town	222 611	98.0	34.5	22.1	31.1	21.7	6.5	1.5	3.9	0.9	2.0	0.0	0.6	0.0	1.2	0.0	0.2
North Tonawanda city	33 262	99.7	41.1	20.9	31.2	22.5	2.6	0.9	3.9	2.1	0.3	0.0	0.2	0.0	0.0	0.0	0.1
Orangetown town	47 711	95.1	36.3	20.7	28.9	20.7	5.0	1.4	4.1	1.2	4.9	0.0	0.0	1.4	2.4	0.0	1.1
Orchard Park town	27 637	97.5	37.2	23.9	31.6	24.2	2.5	0.8	2.3	1.3	2.5	0.0	1.8	0.0	0.0	0.0	0.7
Ossining town	36 534	89.1	33.8	18.4	25.9	20.0	5.7	1.4	5.3	1.6	10.9	6.2	2.5	0.1	1.3	0.0	0.7
Oyster Bay town	293 925	98.9	33.8	23.3	33.1	22.8	5.7	1.5	3.0	0.8	1.1	0.0	0.5	0.1	0.0	0.0	0.5
Penfield town	34 645	97.8	37.9	24.0	30.6	24.8	2.4	0.7	2.8	1.4	2.2	0.0	1.3	0.0	0.0	0.0	0.9
Perinton town	46 090	98.9	38.2	24.6	31.4	25.8	1.9	0.6	2.9	1.6	1.1	0.0	0.9	0.0	0.0	0.0	0.2
Pittsford town	27 219	91.9	34.7	24.4	29.2	24.8	1.6	0.4	2.0	0.8	8.1	0.0	1.1	0.0	5.9	0.0	1.1
Poughkeepsie city	29 871	96.7	40.2	12.0	28.0	21.7	7.2	2.9	9.3	3.1	3.3	1.0	0.6	0.3	0.0	0.0	1.4
Poughkeepsie town	42 777	87.8	34.1	19.0	27.0	20.8	3.6	1.2	4.0	1.7	12.2	0.0	0.0	0.7	10.6	0.0	0.9
Queens borough	2 229 379	98.8	35.1	16.5	29.8	19.4	11.3	2.8	6.1	1.5	1.2	0.0	0.5	0.1	0.0	0.0	0.5
Queensbury town	25 441	98.6	39.1	23.1	29.6	23.9	2.7	0.9	4.1	2.3	1.4	0.3	1.0	0.0	0.0	0.0	0.1
Ramapo town	108 905	97.6	29.0	18.6	39.5	31.3	6.3	1.7	4.2	1.0	2.4	0.0	1.1	0.2	0.2	0.0	0.9
Riverhead town	27 680	96.9	38.8	21.0	27.6	20.6	4.5	1.4	5.1	2.0	3.1	0.4	0.6	0.6	0.0	0.0	1.8
Rochester city	219 773	95.7	40.5	10.1	30.5	24.1	6.3	3.1	8.3	3.5	4.3	0.4	1.2	0.2	1.6	0.0	0.9
Rome city	34 950	90.0	39.1	16.7	26.3	20.2	7.2	1.1	5.0	2.9	10.0	7.0	1.4	0.6	0.0	0.0	1.0
Rotterdam town	28 316	99.7	40.8	22.7	29.0	21.4	3.6	1.3	3.6	2.1	0.3	0.0	0.3	0.0	0.0	0.0	0.1
Rye town	43 880	99.0	35.1	19.0	29.2	21.2	8.8	1.9	7.0	1.5	1.0	0.0	0.7	0.0	0.0	0.0	0.3
Salina town	33 290	99.5	43.3	20.1	27.0	19.9	3.6	1.3	5.5	2.7	0.5	0.0	0.1	0.0	0.0	0.0	0.3
Saratoga Springs city	26 186	91.2	41.2	17.8	22.7	18.0	2.5	0.9	7.1	2.4	8.8	0.5	1.4	0.2	6.4	0.0	0.7
Schenectady city	61 821	94.7	42.5	13.6	27.3	21.8	4.1	1.5	7.3	3.6	5.3	0.5	1.1	0.2	2.4	0.0	1.0
Smithtown town	115 715	98.0	33.3	23.8	33.8	24.5	4.5	1.2	2.6	0.9	2.0	0.0	1.4	0.0	0.0	0.0	0.3
Southampton town	54 712	96.2	39.3	20.0	25.2	19.0	5.0	1.5	6.7	2.2	3.8	1.8	0.4	0.1	0.9	0.0	0.5
Staten Island borough	443 728	97.9	35.2	19.4	33.8	23.4	6.2	1.7	3.3	1.4	2.1	0.2	0.7	0.2	0.2	0.0	1.2
Syracuse city	147 306	92.5	40.4	11.1	27.6	22.0	4.8	2.2	8.7	3.0	7.5	0.3	1.1	0.1	4.8	0.0	1.2
Tonawanda town	78 155	98.8	42.6	21.3	29.0	20.8	2.6	0.8	3.4	1.7	1.2	0.0	0.7	0.0	0.0	0.0	0.5
Troy city	49 170	91.9	40.7	13.3	25.9	20.1	3.8	1.4	8.2	3.0	8.1	0.5	1.2	0.0	5.7	0.0	0.7
Union town	56 298	97.8	43.6	19.6	26.7	20.4	2.9	1.0	5.1	2.5	2.2	0.0	1.5	0.0	0.3	0.0	0.4
Utica city	60 651	94.4	41.4	14.7	28.6	21.7	4.5	1.7	5.1	2.4	5.6	0.0	1.9	0.9	1.6	0.0	1.1
Vestal town	26 535	78.7	32.1	19.2	22.5	18.1	1.8	0.5	3.0	1.2	21.3	0.0	2.3	0.0	18.6	0.0	0.4
Wappinger town	26 274	99.3	37.3	21.7	31.5	23.4	4.6	1.5	4.3	2.0	0.7	0.0	0.2	0.0	0.0	0.0	0.4
Warwick town	30 764	96.7	35.3	21.8	32.9	25.9	3.5	1.0	3.2	1.7	3.3	2.4	0.6	0.0	0.0	0.0	0.3
Watertown city	26 705	95.9	41.3	16.8	28.8	23.8	3.0	1.1	6.0	2.9	4.1	0.5	2.3	0.0	0.0	0.0	1.3
Webster town	37 926	99.5	38.9	23.9	31.4	25.2	2.2	0.6	3.0	1.8	0.5	0.0	0.2	0.0	0.0	0.0	0.3
West Seneca town	45 920	98.7	39.9	22.4	30.5	20.9	3.1	1.0	2.8	1.6	1.3	0.0	0.3	0.1	0.0	0.0	0.8
White Plains city	53 077	97.3	39.4	18.0	25.9	18.5	7.2	1.8	6.7	1.6	2.7	0.0	1.2	0.0	0.4	0.0	1.3
Yonkers city	196 086	98.8	37.9	16.8	31.5	21.7	7.8	2.2	4.7	1.9	1.2	0.0	0.4	0.0	0.4	0.0	0.4
Yorktown town	36 318	97.9	34.6	23.9	33.6	26.2	3.7	0.9	2.1	0.9	2.1	0.0	1.1	0.7	0.0	0.0	0.3

Table E. Towns

Town	Households by type, 2000												Households, 1990		
	Total households	Family households		Married couple		Female householder[1]		Nonfamily households	Householder living alone		Average household size	Average family size	Total households	Female householder[1]	Householder living alone
		Total	With own children under 18 years	Total	With own children under 18 years	Total	With own children under 18 years	Total	Total	65 years and over					
	71	72	73	74	75	76	77	78	79	80	81	82	83	84	85
NEW YORK—Cont'd															
Elmira city	11 475	58.4	31.1	35.3	15.5	18.4	12.8	41.6	34.5	13.6	2.37	3.05	12 428	17.1	32.0
Gates town	11 730	68.6	28.6	53.8	21.3	10.7	6.4	31.4	26.5	12.1	2.48	3.01	10 914	10.0	21.7
Glen Cove city	9 461	70.3	29.9	53.5	23.3	12.7	5.4	29.7	24.1	11.3	2.72	3.22	8 466	12.0	20.5
Glenville town	11 150	70.2	30.9	59.0	24.6	8.4	4.7	29.8	26.0	12.5	2.44	2.95	10 740	5.9	23.3
Greece town	36 995	69.6	32.5	55.6	24.5	10.4	6.1	30.4	25.6	11.1	2.52	3.05	33 572	8.2	21.2
Greenburgh town	33 043	69.9	32.4	57.3	26.9	9.8	4.5	30.1	25.5	9.1	2.57	3.10	31 033	8.4	22.7
Guilderland town	13 422	65.3	31.6	54.2	25.3	8.5	4.9	34.7	28.5	8.6	2.40	3.00	11 450	7.9	25.9
Hamburg town	21 999	68.9	32.3	55.7	25.4	10.1	5.4	31.1	26.4	11.8	2.51	3.07	19 847	10.0	22.9
Haverstraw town	11 255	74.0	37.3	54.4	27.0	15.0	8.3	26.0	21.3	7.8	2.94	3.43	10 509	12.5	18.9
Hempstead town	246 828	78.4	36.5	62.2	30.3	12.3	5.0	21.6	18.1	9.2	3.02	3.41	239 304	10.8	16.7
Henrietta town	12 823	66.3	30.6	53.8	24.1	9.2	5.0	33.7	22.7	6.9	2.60	3.09	12 099	7.6	18.2
Huntington town	65 917	79.4	37.1	67.4	32.4	8.9	3.7	20.6	16.2	6.7	2.91	3.26	62 861	8.8	14.3
Irondequoit town	22 247	64.4	26.7	50.7	19.8	10.4	5.4	35.6	30.8	16.7	2.32	2.91	21 604	8.4	26.0
Islip town	98 936	79.4	39.4	62.4	31.9	12.3	5.7	20.6	16.2	6.4	3.22	3.55	89 726	11.3	13.3
Ithaca city	10 287	28.8	14.2	19.0	8.0	7.8	5.1	71.2	43.3	7.4	2.13	2.81	9 617	7.9	36.2
Jamestown city	13 558	58.3	29.4	39.1	16.1	14.5	10.4	41.7	35.0	13.9	2.29	2.94	14 269	13.0	31.6
Lancaster town	15 053	69.8	33.1	58.3	27.4	8.5	4.3	30.2	26.0	11.0	2.55	3.11	12 117	8.8	23.8
Long Beach city	14 923	54.3	21.6	40.0	15.5	10.8	4.9	45.7	36.7	10.7	2.26	3.02	13 592	8.9	34.2
Mamaroneck town	10 929	70.9	35.6	60.0	30.6	8.0	3.9	29.1	25.4	10.5	2.62	3.15	10 406	7.6	23.5
Manhattan borough	738 644	40.9	17.1	25.2	9.6	12.6	6.5	59.1	48.0	10.9	2.00	2.99	716 422	13.0	48.3
Manlius town	12 553	70.8	34.5	60.2	28.2	8.0	4.8	29.2	25.3	10.9	2.51	3.04	11 481	6.1	22.2
Middletown city	9 466	63.0	34.0	40.0	20.0	16.7	10.8	37.0	30.0	12.3	2.62	3.27	8 790	15.9	26.2
Monroe town	8 228	83.6	53.6	74.3	48.6	6.3	3.7	16.4	13.2	5.2	3.72	4.14	6 270	6.2	13.2
Mount Pleasant town	13 737	76.6	38.3	65.0	33.5	8.4	3.8	23.4	18.4	7.5	2.89	3.30	12 774	8.4	17.7
Mount Vernon city	25 729	64.8	31.1	36.9	16.8	23.0	12.3	35.2	30.0	10.7	2.63	3.27	25 175	20.6	28.6
Newburgh city	9 144	66.5	40.0	34.1	19.0	25.4	17.2	33.5	27.1	11.0	2.97	3.62	9 008	23.4	26.6
Newburgh town	9 765	77.0	36.4	62.6	29.3	10.2	5.1	23.0	17.9	7.1	2.80	3.19	8 302	7.6	16.0
New Rochelle city	26 189	67.0	32.7	50.5	25.3	12.5	6.0	33.0	28.0	11.8	2.68	3.29	25 317	11.5	28.3
Niagara Falls city	24 099	59.2	27.8	36.2	14.3	18.3	11.4	40.8	35.9	15.2	2.27	2.96	25 970	15.6	32.6
North Hempstead town	76 820	76.1	33.6	64.0	29.5	8.9	3.2	23.9	20.6	10.3	2.84	3.27	74 587	8.8	19.1
North Tonawanda city	13 671	65.7	30.2	50.8	22.0	11.1	6.3	34.3	29.5	12.8	2.43	3.03	13 635	9.8	25.7
Orangetown town	17 330	68.9	30.3	57.1	25.8	8.8	3.7	31.1	25.8	11.0	2.62	3.18	16 121	8.2	22.8
Orchard Park town	10 277	74.5	33.7	64.3	29.0	7.6	3.7	25.5	22.1	10.3	2.62	3.09	8 858	7.0	18.8
Ossining town	12 355	69.1	33.1	54.4	26.1	10.7	5.5	30.9	25.5	9.0	2.64	3.14	11 543	9.2	24.0
Oyster Bay town	99 355	80.8	36.0	68.9	32.3	8.9	3.0	19.2	16.1	8.5	2.93	3.27	95 566	8.5	13.3
Penfield town	13 144	73.3	34.9	63.4	29.5	7.4	4.2	26.7	22.3	8.5	2.58	3.05	11 358	7.7	21.2
Perinton town	17 591	73.7	36.4	64.4	31.1	7.1	4.2	26.3	21.7	7.5	2.59	3.06	15 603	7.5	19.4
Pittsford town	9 448	77.7	37.1	70.4	33.3	5.5	3.0	22.3	19.1	9.5	2.65	3.05	8 199	4.5	15.2
Poughkeepsie city	12 014	54.6	28.3	29.8	12.6	19.7	13.3	45.4	35.4	13.2	2.40	3.15	11 874	16.1	33.6
Poughkeepsie town	14 605	69.3	32.9	55.8	25.7	9.6	5.3	30.7	25.0	9.6	2.57	3.10	13 769	7.1	23.1
Queens borough	782 664	68.7	31.5	46.9	22.4	16.0	7.3	31.3	25.6	9.7	2.81	3.39	720 149	13.9	26.8
Queensbury town	9 948	72.0	34.0	59.1	26.4	9.4	5.6	28.0	22.6	11.0	2.52	2.97	8 310	7.4	20.1
Ramapo town	31 561	78.8	42.3	64.3	35.4	10.6	5.5	21.2	17.2	7.1	3.37	3.82	28 554	9.4	17.1
Riverhead town	10 749	67.8	28.1	54.0	21.3	10.3	5.4	32.2	26.4	14.1	2.50	3.01	8 736	11.3	23.6
Rochester city	88 999	53.0	30.0	25.1	11.3	23.3	16.4	47.0	37.1	9.2	2.36	3.19	93 607	20.7	34.9
Rome city	13 653	61.0	28.1	42.6	16.2	13.9	9.2	39.0	33.2	14.6	2.30	2.93	15 754	10.5	26.9
Rotterdam town	11 544	70.1	29.4	55.7	21.8	10.6	5.7	29.9	25.8	12.6	2.44	2.94	11 044	8.2	21.6
Rye town	15 389	70.3	33.6	54.1	27.0	11.4	5.0	29.7	24.3	10.3	2.82	3.31	14 511	11.2	24.3
Salina town	14 401	61.6	26.0	46.4	18.0	11.1	5.9	38.4	31.6	12.8	2.30	2.91	14 166	9.1	25.3
Saratoga Springs city	10 784	55.5	25.3	43.1	18.1	9.6	5.7	44.5	35.0	12.3	2.21	2.88	9 688	8.9	32.1
Schenectady city	26 265	53.5	27.2	32.0	13.4	16.7	11.1	46.5	38.6	13.8	2.23	2.98	27 748	14.1	35.8
Smithtown town	38 487	81.8	38.5	71.6	34.8	7.5	2.9	18.2	15.2	7.2	2.95	3.28	35 565	7.1	12.8
Southampton town	21 504	64.2	27.1	50.8	20.9	9.3	4.6	35.8	28.6	12.2	2.45	2.99	18 029	8.5	28.4
Staten Island borough	156 341	73.0	35.8	55.0	27.3	13.9	7.1	27.0	23.2	8.4	2.78	3.31	130 519	11.5	20.8
Syracuse city	59 482	51.0	27.5	27.5	11.9	19.3	13.3	49.0	38.2	11.9	2.29	3.11	64 945	16.7	35.8
Tonawanda town	33 278	63.6	26.8	49.9	20.1	10.6	5.3	36.4	31.8	15.4	2.32	2.95	33 765	8.7	27.1
Troy city	19 996	53.7	27.0	32.6	13.6	16.3	10.9	46.3	36.6	12.6	2.26	2.97	20 761	14.6	33.7
Union town	24 538	59.3	26.1	45.0	17.8	10.9	6.5	40.7	34.5	13.6	2.24	2.90	24 766	9.7	29.8
Utica city	25 100	56.7	27.0	35.5	14.4	16.9	10.7	43.3	37.4	15.5	2.28	3.04	28 358	15.7	35.5
Vestal town	8 525	69.5	29.6	59.9	24.5	7.0	3.7	30.5	25.1	10.7	2.45	2.95	8 575	5.4	19.6
Wappinger town	9 793	71.4	34.3	58.1	27.3	9.4	5.3	28.6	23.1	6.2	2.67	3.17	9 246	7.2	18.6
Warwick town	10 868	73.2	38.5	61.7	32.5	8.6	4.7	26.8	22.0	9.1	2.74	3.25	9 218	8.0	19.2
Watertown city	11 036	58.9	31.9	40.7	19.3	14.2	10.1	41.1	34.5	13.8	2.32	2.99	11 430	12.0	29.4
Webster town	14 750	72.4	34.6	61.5	28.1	8.1	5.0	27.6	23.1	9.0	2.56	3.04	11 687	7.9	19.0
West Seneca town	18 328	69.5	28.2	56.2	22.5	10.3	4.5	30.5	26.6	13.1	2.47	3.02	17 386	8.2	21.3
White Plains city	20 921	60.7	26.9	45.7	20.6	11.3	5.1	39.3	33.4	11.8	2.47	3.14	19 432	11.7	34.0
Yonkers city	74 351	66.3	30.9	44.2	19.5	17.2	9.7	33.7	29.2	11.9	2.61	3.23	72 101	15.7	28.1
Yorktown town	12 556	78.3	40.9	69.1	36.6	7.1	3.3	21.7	19.0	10.0	2.83	3.26	11 159	6.4	15.5

[1] No spouse present.

Table E. Towns

		Housing occupancy						Housing tenure				
				Vacant housing units				Occupied housing units				
Town	Percent change of households, 1990–2000	Total housing units	Occupied housing units (percent)	Total	For seasonal, recreational, or occasional use	Homeowner vacancy rate (percent)	Rental vacancy rate (percent)	Total	Percent owner-occupied housing units	Percent renter-occupied housing units	Average household size of owner-occupied units	Average household size of renter-occupied units
	86	87	88	89	90	91	92	93	94	95	96	97

Town	86	87	88	89	90	91	92	93	94	95	96	97
NEW YORK—Cont'd												
Elmira city	-7.7	12 895	89.0	11.0	0.3	3.2	10.9	11 475	48.3	51.7	2.49	2.26
Gates town	7.5	12 049	97.4	2.6	0.2	0.6	4.5	11 730	77.6	22.4	2.64	1.92
Glen Cove city	11.8	9 734	97.2	2.8	0.7	0.9	1.3	9 461	58.5	41.5	2.75	2.67
Glenville town	3.8	11 582	96.3	3.7	0.4	1.4	4.0	11 150	80.2	19.8	2.60	1.81
Greece town	10.2	38 315	96.6	3.4	0.4	0.9	5.9	36 995	74.5	25.5	2.72	1.92
Greenburgh town	6.5	34 084	96.9	3.1	0.8	0.7	2.6	33 043	69.8	30.2	2.70	2.28
Guilderland town	17.2	13 928	96.4	3.6	0.5	1.0	4.3	13 422	66.6	33.4	2.68	1.84
Hamburg town	10.8	22 833	96.3	3.7	0.5	0.8	4.3	21 999	74.2	25.8	2.72	1.93
Haverstraw town	7.1	11 553	97.4	2.6	0.2	0.6	2.9	11 255	63.4	36.6	3.02	2.81
Hempstead town	3.1	252 286	97.8	2.2	0.5	0.6	2.0	246 828	80.7	19.3	3.11	2.64
Henrietta town	6.0	13 243	96.8	3.2	0.4	0.5	5.0	12 823	72.0	28.0	2.74	2.26
Huntington town	4.9	67 708	97.4	2.6	0.6	0.5	3.3	65 917	85.3	14.7	2.99	2.50
Irondequoit town	3.0	23 037	96.6	3.4	0.6	1.0	5.2	22 247	79.3	20.7	2.45	1.83
Islip town	10.3	104 278	94.9	5.1	2.6	0.7	3.7	98 936	78.6	21.4	3.36	2.69
Ithaca city	7.0	10 736	95.8	4.2	0.4	2.1	2.7	10 287	26.0	74.0	2.30	2.07
Jamestown city	-5.0	15 027	90.2	9.8	0.2	2.6	9.8	13 558	51.3	48.7	2.46	2.10
Lancaster town	24.2	15 627	96.3	3.7	0.2	1.0	5.3	15 053	77.2	22.8	2.74	1.90
Long Beach city	9.8	16 128	92.5	7.5	4.2	1.0	3.2	14 923	53.4	46.6	2.45	2.05
Mamaroneck town	5.0	11 255	97.1	2.9	0.5	0.7	4.1	10 929	66.7	33.3	2.76	2.32
Manhattan borough	3.1	798 144	92.5	7.5	2.4	2.7	3.4	738 644	20.1	79.9	1.88	2.03
Manlius town	9.3	13 071	96.0	4.0	1.1	0.8	5.2	12 553	79.5	20.5	2.68	1.87
Middletown city	7.7	10 124	93.5	6.5	0.2	2.0	4.2	9 466	45.7	54.3	2.68	2.57
Monroe town	31.2	8 517	96.6	3.4	1.5	0.7	1.0	8 228	66.6	33.4	3.47	4.21
Mount Pleasant town	7.5	13 985	98.2	1.8	0.4	0.4	2.2	13 737	72.0	28.0	3.00	2.62
Mount Vernon city	2.2	27 048	95.1	4.9	0.2	2.0	4.0	25 729	36.5	63.5	2.93	2.45
Newburgh city	1.5	10 476	87.3	12.7	0.3	6.8	7.6	9 144	30.7	69.3	2.88	3.01
Newburgh town	17.6	10 122	96.5	3.5	0.8	0.9	3.4	9 765	82.4	17.6	2.86	2.52
New Rochelle city	3.4	26 995	97.0	3.0	0.6	0.6	2.3	26 189	50.3	49.7	2.87	2.48
Niagara Falls city	-7.2	27 837	86.6	13.4	0.2	2.7	16.0	24 099	57.6	42.4	2.40	2.10
North Hempstead town	3.0	78 927	97.3	2.7	0.6	0.6	2.2	76 820	78.5	21.5	2.92	2.54
North Tonawanda city	0.3	14 425	94.8	5.2	0.3	1.3	7.8	13 671	68.7	31.3	2.65	1.93
Orangetown town	7.5	17 827	97.2	2.8	0.6	0.8	2.3	17 330	71.2	28.8	2.88	1.96
Orchard Park town	16.0	10 644	96.6	3.4	0.4	0.9	6.2	10 277	78.7	21.3	2.81	1.93
Ossining town	7.0	12 733	97.0	3.0	0.5	1.1	3.1	12 355	63.8	36.2	2.69	2.54
Oyster Bay town	4.0	101 076	98.3	1.7	0.5	0.3	2.0	99 355	86.9	13.1	3.02	2.32
Penfield town	15.7	13 673	96.1	3.9	0.2	1.1	10.6	13 144	82.9	17.1	2.70	1.97
Perinton town	12.7	18 041	97.5	2.5	0.3	0.6	4.2	17 591	80.5	19.5	2.74	1.99
Pittsford town	15.2	9 709	97.3	2.7	0.6	0.6	4.4	9 448	86.9	13.1	2.77	1.84
Poughkeepsie city	1.2	13 153	91.3	8.7	0.5	3.3	5.8	12 014	36.8	63.2	2.46	2.37
Poughkeepsie town	6.1	15 132	96.5	3.5	0.5	1.2	4.2	14 605	69.8	30.2	2.77	2.13
Queens borough	8.7	817 250	95.8	4.2	0.6	1.3	2.3	782 664	42.8	57.2	2.99	2.68
Queensbury town	19.7	11 223	88.6	11.4	7.5	1.5	6.5	9 948	75.9	24.1	2.66	2.10
Ramapo town	10.5	32 422	97.3	2.7	0.4	0.8	2.7	31 561	63.9	36.1	3.35	3.39
Riverhead town	23.0	12 479	86.1	13.9	9.3	1.3	4.0	10 749	77.1	22.9	2.50	2.48
Rochester city	-4.9	99 789	89.2	10.8	0.2	3.8	9.0	88 999	40.2	59.8	2.54	2.24
Rome city	-13.3	16 272	83.9	16.1	0.3	3.3	14.6	13 653	57.1	42.9	2.45	2.11
Rotterdam town	4.5	11 990	96.3	3.7	0.4	1.1	5.7	11 544	81.4	18.6	2.54	2.00
Rye town	6.1	15 813	97.3	2.7	0.4	0.9	1.6	15 389	56.1	43.9	2.77	2.89
Salina town	1.7	14 979	96.1	3.9	0.4	1.3	3.5	14 401	68.5	31.5	2.45	1.98
Saratoga Springs city	11.3	11 584	93.1	6.9	2.9	1.2	3.6	10 784	55.8	44.2	2.49	1.87
Schenectady city	-5.3	30 272	86.8	13.2	0.3	4.6	9.3	26 265	44.7	55.3	2.37	2.12
Smithtown town	8.2	39 357	97.8	2.2	0.5	0.4	2.4	38 487	87.4	12.6	3.07	2.07
Southampton town	19.3	35 836	60.0	40.0	35.2	2.0	5.2	21 504	76.0	24.0	2.40	2.60
Staten Island borough	19.8	163 993	95.3	4.7	0.3	1.4	4.1	156 341	63.8	36.2	3.00	2.40
Syracuse city	-8.4	68 192	87.2	12.8	0.3	4.8	11.8	59 482	40.3	59.7	2.48	2.16
Tonawanda town	-1.4	34 634	96.1	3.9	0.2	0.9	5.9	33 278	72.9	27.1	2.50	1.84
Troy city	-3.7	23 093	86.6	13.4	0.5	4.2	9.2	19 996	40.1	59.9	2.45	2.13
Union town	-0.9	26 507	92.6	7.4	0.3	2.3	9.0	24 538	60.1	39.9	2.44	1.94
Utica city	-11.5	29 186	86.0	14.0	0.3	3.6	12.9	25 100	48.8	51.2	2.41	2.15
Vestal town	-0.6	8 898	95.8	4.2	0.5	1.3	5.0	8 525	78.7	21.3	2.58	1.97
Wappinger town	5.9	10 144	96.5	3.5	0.4	1.4	3.4	9 793	66.0	34.0	2.93	2.15
Warwick town	17.9	11 818	92.0	8.0	4.1	1.7	3.6	10 868	78.2	21.8	2.91	2.11
Watertown city	-3.4	12 450	88.6	11.4	0.3	4.5	11.5	11 036	43.0	57.0	2.51	2.18
Webster town	26.2	15 218	96.9	3.1	0.4	0.8	4.5	14 750	77.3	22.7	2.74	1.95
West Seneca town	5.4	18 982	96.6	3.4	0.2	0.8	6.7	18 328	78.4	21.6	2.62	1.95
White Plains city	7.7	21 576	97.0	3.0	0.8	0.8	2.1	20 921	52.2	47.8	2.53	2.41
Yonkers city	3.1	77 589	95.8	4.2	0.4	1.3	3.5	74 351	43.2	56.8	2.68	2.55
Yorktown town	12.5	12 852	97.7	2.3	0.7	0.7	2.3	12 556	85.9	14.1	2.97	2.01

Table E. Towns

STATE MCD code	Town	Population, 2000				Population, 1990				Population and population characteristics, 2000					
										Race (percent)					
										One race					
		Land area, 2000[1] (sq km)	Total persons	Rank within state	Per square kilometer	Land area, 1990[1] (sq km)	Total persons	Rank within state	Per square kilometer	White	Black or African American	American Indian or Alaska Native	Asian	Native Hawaiian and other Pacific Islander	Some other race
		1	2	3	4	5	6	7	8	9	10	11	12	13	14
42 00000	PENNSYLVANIA	116 074	12 281 054	X	105.8	116 083	11 882 842	X	102.4	85.4	10.0	0.1	1.8	0.0	1.5
42 00156	Abington township	40.0	56 103	11	1 402.6	40.0	56 358	11	1 409.0	84.1	10.8	0.1	3.3	0.0	0.5
42 02000	Allentown city....................	45.9	106 632	4	2 323.1	45.9	105 301	4	2 294.1	72.5	7.8	0.3	2.3	0.1	13.4
42 02184	Altoona city	25.3	49 523	14	1 957.4	25.3	51 881	14	2 050.6	96.0	2.5	0.1	0.3	0.0	0.2
42 05616	Bensalem township	51.7	58 434	10	1 130.3	51.7	56 788	10	1 098.4	82.9	6.9	0.2	6.6	0.1	1.6
42 06064	Bethel Park borough	30.3	33 556	28	1 107.5	30.3	33 823	28	1 116.3	97.1	1.0	0.0	1.1	0.0	0.1
42 08768	Bristol township	41.8	55 521	9	1 328.3	41.5	57 129	9	1 376.6	86.1	8.4	0.2	2.1	0.0	1.6
42 12968	Cheltenham township	23.4	36 875	27	1 575.9	23.4	34 900	27	1 491.5	66.4	24.6	0.1	6.4	0.1	0.8
42 13208	Chester city......................	12.6	36 854	22	2 924.9	12.5	41 856	22	3 348.5	18.9	75.7	0.2	0.6	0.0	3.0
42 21648	Easton city.......................	11.0	26 263	43	2 387.5	11.0	26 276	43	2 388.7	78.5	12.7	0.2	1.7	0.1	3.7
42 24000	Erie city...........................	56.9	103 717	3	1 822.8	57.0	108 718	3	1 907.3	80.6	14.2	0.2	0.7	0.0	1.9
42 25112	Falls township	57.7	34 865	26	604.2	57.7	35 047	26	607.4	90.2	4.9	0.2	2.6	0.0	0.8
42 32800	Harrisburg city..................	21.0	48 950	13	2 331.0	21.0	52 376	13	2 494.1	31.7	54.8	0.4	2.8	0.1	6.5
42 33144	Haverford township	25.9	48 498	16	1 872.5	25.9	49 848	16	1 924.6	94.0	2.1	0.1	2.8	0.0	0.2
42 33792	Hempfield township	198.4	40 721	20	205.2	198.4	42 609	20	214.8	97.4	1.1	0.1	0.8	0.0	0.1
42 41216	Lancaster city...................	19.2	56 348	12	2 934.8	19.1	55 551	12	2 908.4	61.6	14.1	0.4	2.5	0.1	17.4
42 44968	Lower Makefield township ..	46.5	32 681	46	702.8	46.5	25 083	46	539.4	93.3	1.8	0.1	3.7	0.0	0.3
42 44976	Lower Merion township	61.4	59 850	8	974.8	61.4	58 003	8	944.7	90.3	4.5	0.1	3.4	0.1	0.5
42 45056	Lower Paxton township	72.8	44 424	23	610.2	72.8	39 162	23	537.9	86.5	8.3	0.1	2.7	0.0	1.0
42 45900	McCandless township........	42.8	29 022	38	678.1	42.8	28 781	38	672.5	94.6	1.3	0.1	3.2	0.0	0.1
42 46896	Manheim township	62.7	33 697	37	537.4	62.1	28 880	37	465.1	93.2	1.5	0.1	3.1	0.0	1.0
42 49120	Middletown township	49.5	44 141	19	891.7	50.2	43 063	19	857.8	93.9	2.1	0.1	2.4	0.0	0.6
42 49548	Millcreek township	76.3	52 129	18	683.2	76.4	46 820	18	612.8	96.6	1.1	0.1	1.3	0.0	0.3
42 51696	Mount Lebanon township ...	15.7	33 017	30	2 103.0	15.7	33 362	30	2 125.0	96.2	0.6	0.1	2.3	0.0	0.2
42 52330	Municipality of Monroeville borough....................	51.3	29 349	36	572.1	51.2	29 169	36	569.7	85.6	8.3	0.1	4.4	0.0	0.3
42 53368	New Castle city.................	22.1	26 309	40	1 190.5	22.1	28 334	40	1 282.1	86.8	10.8	0.1	0.2	0.0	0.3
42 54656	Norristown borough	9.1	31 282	34	3 437.6	9.1	30 754	34	3 379.6	54.3	34.8	0.2	3.0	0.0	4.6
42 54688	Northampton township	66.9	39 384	25	588.7	66.9	35 406	25	529.2	97.0	0.4	0.0	1.8	0.0	0.2
42 55128	North Huntingdon township .	70.8	29 123	41	411.3	71.0	28 158	41	396.6	98.8	0.3	0.0	0.4	0.0	0.0
42 59032	Penn Hills township	49.3	46 809	15	949.5	49.3	51 479	15	1 044.2	73.6	24.2	0.1	0.5	0.0	0.3
42 60000	Philadelphia city................	349.9	1 517 550	1	4 337.1	350.0	1 585 577	1	4 530.2	45.0	43.2	0.3	4.5	0.0	4.8
42 61000	Pittsburgh city...................	144.0	334 563	2	2 323.4	144.1	369 879	2	2 566.8	67.6	27.1	0.2	2.7	0.0	0.7
42 61536	Plum borough	74.1	26 940	45	363.6	74.2	25 609	45	345.1	95.6	2.8	0.1	0.9	0.0	0.2
42 63264	Radnor township	35.6	30 878	39	867.4	35.6	28 703	39	806.3	89.6	3.1	0.1	5.7	0.0	0.6
42 63624	Reading city......................	25.4	81 207	7	3 197.1	25.3	78 380	7	3 098.0	59.2	12.2	0.4	1.6	0.0	22.3
42 64800	Ridley township	13.1	30 791	33	2 350.5	13.1	31 169	33	2 379.3	93.0	4.3	0.1	1.6	0.0	0.2
42 66264	Ross township	37.4	32 551	29	870.3	37.2	33 482	29	900.1	95.9	1.4	0.1	1.8	0.1	0.2
42 69000	Scranton city....................	65.3	76 415	5	1 170.2	65.3	81 805	5	1 252.8	93.5	3.0	0.1	1.1	0.0	1.2
42 69584	Shaler township	28.5	29 757	35	1 044.1	28.8	30 533	35	1 060.2	97.9	0.4	0.1	0.9	0.0	0.1
42 73808	State College borough........	11.8	38 420	24	3 255.9	11.6	38 981	24	3 360.4	84.3	3.7	0.2	8.8	0.1	1.4
42 77344	Tredyffrin township	51.4	29 062	42	565.4	51.4	28 028	42	545.3	90.9	2.8	0.1	5.1	0.0	0.3
42 79000	Upper Darby township........	20.4	81 821	6	4 010.8	20.4	81 177	6	3 979.3	77.3	11.3	0.1	8.9	0.0	0.5
42 79008	Upper Dublin township	34.2	25 878	47	756.7	34.2	24 028	47	702.6	87.5	5.4	0.1	6.2	0.0	0.2
42 79136	Upper Merion township	43.7	26 863	44	614.7	43.6	25 722	44	590.0	84.8	4.6	0.1	8.5	0.1	0.7
42 80952	Warminster township	26.6	31 383	31	1 179.8	26.4	32 832	31	1 243.6	91.0	3.3	0.1	2.0	0.1	2.2
42 85152	Wilkes-Barre city...............	17.7	43 123	17	2 436.3	17.7	47 523	17	2 684.9	92.3	5.1	0.1	0.8	0.0	0.5
42 85312	Williamsport city................	23.0	30 706	32	1 335.0	23.0	31 933	32	1 388.4	84.1	12.7	0.4	0.6	0.0	0.5
42 87048	York city...........................	13.5	40 862	21	3 026.8	13.5	42 192	21	3 125.3	59.8	25.1	0.4	1.4	0.1	9.4
44 00000	RHODE ISLAND..............	2 706	1 048 319	X	387.4	2 707	1 003 464	X	370.7	85.0	4.5	0.5	2.3	0.1	5.0
44 18640	Coventry town...................	154.2	33 668	8	218.3	154.2	31 083	8	201.6	97.6	0.4	0.1	0.6	0.0	0.3
44 19180	Cranston city.....................	74.0	79 269	3	1 071.2	74.0	76 060	3	1 027.8	89.2	3.7	0.3	3.3	0.0	1.9
44 20080	Cumberland town	69.4	31 840	10	458.8	69.4	29 038	10	418.4	96.7	0.6	0.1	0.8	0.0	0.8
44 22960	East Providence city..........	34.7	48 688	5	1 403.1	34.7	50 380	5	1 451.9	86.5	5.0	0.5	1.1	0.0	2.8
44 37720	Johnston town	61.3	28 195	12	460.0	61.3	26 542	12	433.0	96.7	0.7	0.1	1.1	0.0	0.5
44 49960	Newport city......................	20.6	26 475	11	1 285.2	20.6	28 227	11	1 370.2	84.1	7.8	0.8	1.3	0.1	2.4
44 51580	North Kingstown town	112.9	26 326	14	233.2	113.2	23 786	14	210.1	95.7	1.0	0.6	1.0	0.0	0.5
44 51760	North Providence town	14.7	32 411	7	2 204.8	14.7	32 090	7	2 183.0	92.0	2.7	0.2	1.8	0.0	1.6
44 54640	Pawtucket city...................	22.6	72 958	4	3 228.2	22.6	72 644	4	3 214.3	75.4	7.3	0.3	0.9	0.1	10.7
44 59000	Providence city.................	47.8	173 618	1	3 632.2	47.8	160 728	1	3 362.5	54.5	14.5	1.1	6.0	0.2	17.6
44 67460	South Kingstown town	147.9	27 921	13	188.8	147.9	24 612	13	166.4	91.1	1.6	1.6	3.1	0.1	0.7
44 74300	Warwick city......................	91.9	85 808	2	933.7	92.0	85 427	2	928.6	95.2	1.2	0.2	1.5	0.0	0.6
44 78440	West Warwick town	20.5	29 581	9	1 443.0	20.5	29 268	9	1 427.7	93.8	1.1	0.4	1.4	0.0	1.4
44 80780	Woonsocket city................	20.0	43 224	6	2 161.2	20.0	43 877	6	2 193.9	83.1	4.4	0.3	4.1	0.0	4.9
50 00000	VERMONT.....................	23 956	608 827	X	25.4	23 956	562 758	X	23.5	96.8	0.5	0.4	0.9	0.0	0.2
50 10675	Burlington city...................	27.4	38 889	1	1 419.3	27.3	39 127	1	1 433.2	92.3	1.8	0.5	2.7	0.0	0.5
55 00000	WISCONSIN...................	140 663	5 363 675	X	38.1	140 672	4 891 954	X	34.8	88.9	5.7	0.9	1.7	0.0	1.6
55 06500	Beloit city.........................	42.6	35 775	15	839.8	41.9	35 571	15	848.9	75.6	15.4	0.4	1.2	0.1	4.6
55 10025	Brookfield city...................	70.4	38 649	16	549.0	69.5	35 184	16	506.2	94.2	0.8	0.1	3.8	0.0	0.2

[1] Dry land or land partially or temporarily covered by water.

Table E. Towns

Town	Population and population characteristics, 2000 (cont'd)								Population and population characteristics, 1990				
	Race (percent) (cont'd)								Race (percent)				
	Race alone or in combination												
	Two or more races	White	Black	American Indian or Alaska Native	Asian	Native Hawaiian and other Pacific Islander	Some other race	Hispanic[1]	White	Black or African American	American Indian or Alaska Native	Asian and Pacific Islander	Hispanic[1]
	15	16	17	18	19	20	21	22	23	24	25	26	27
PENNSYLVANIA	1.2	86.3	10.5	0.4	2.0	0.1	1.9	3.2	88.5	9.2	0.1	1.2	2.0
Abington township	1.1	85.0	11.5	0.4	3.6	0.1	0.7	1.6	89.4	8.2	0.1	2.1	0.9
Allentown city	3.6	75.5	9.3	0.7	2.6	0.2	15.5	24.4	86.2	5.0	0.2	1.3	11.7
Altoona city	0.8	96.8	3.0	0.3	0.4	0.1	0.4	0.7	98.0	1.5	0.1	0.3	0.4
Bensalem township	1.7	84.2	7.4	0.6	7.2	0.1	2.3	4.3	88.7	6.9	0.2	3.7	2.2
Bethel Park borough	0.6	97.6	1.2	0.2	1.4	0.1	0.2	0.5	98.1	1.0	0.1	0.8	0.5
Bristol township	1.5	87.3	9.1	0.6	2.6	0.1	2.0	3.9	91.1	6.4	0.2	1.7	2.3
Cheltenham township	1.5	67.5	25.5	0.5	6.8	0.1	1.2	2.0	79.4	15.1	0.2	5.0	1.1
Chester city	1.5	19.7	76.9	0.6	0.8	0.1	3.6	5.4	32.0	65.2	0.2	0.4	3.8
Easton city	3.1	81.0	14.4	0.9	2.0	0.2	4.8	9.8	86.8	9.4	0.2	1.7	4.4
Erie city	2.3	82.6	15.5	0.7	1.0	0.1	2.6	4.4	86.1	12.0	0.2	0.5	2.4
Falls township	1.4	91.4	5.4	0.4	3.0	0.1	1.3	2.3	94.3	3.5	0.1	1.6	1.7
Harrisburg city	3.6	34.3	57.5	1.1	3.2	0.2	7.8	11.7	42.6	50.6	0.3	1.8	7.7
Haverford township	0.8	94.7	2.4	0.3	3.0	0.1	0.4	0.9	96.1	2.0	0.0	1.7	0.7
Hempfield township	0.4	97.8	1.2	0.2	0.9	0.1	0.4	0.2	97.5	1.8	0.1	0.6	0.4
Lancaster city	3.9	64.5	16.3	1.0	2.8	0.2	19.4	30.8	70.9	12.2	0.2	2.0	20.6
Lower Makefield township	0.8	94.0	2.1	0.2	4.1	0.0	0.4	1.4	95.3	1.4	0.1	3.0	1.1
Lower Merion township	1.1	91.2	5.0	0.3	3.8	0.1	0.8	1.6	93.1	4.5	0.1	2.2	1.2
Lower Paxton township	1.3	87.6	9.1	0.4	3.0	0.0	1.4	2.4	92.6	5.5	0.1	1.3	1.1
McCandless township	0.7	95.2	1.5	0.2	3.6	0.1	0.3	0.7	97.3	0.9	0.1	1.7	0.5
Manheim township	1.1	94.2	1.9	0.3	3.4	0.0	1.4	2.8	96.6	1.1	0.1	1.8	1.0
Middletown township	0.9	94.7	2.4	0.4	2.7	0.0	0.8	1.7	96.5	1.6	0.1	1.5	1.2
Millcreek township	0.6	97.1	1.3	0.2	1.6	0.1	0.4	1.0	98.0	0.8	0.1	1.0	0.4
Mount Lebanon township	0.6	96.8	0.8	0.1	2.6	0.0	0.4	0.8	97.7	0.5	0.0	1.7	0.8
Municipality of Monroeville borough	1.2	86.5	9.0	0.4	4.8	0.1	0.5	0.8	90.2	6.6	0.1	2.9	0.7
New Castle city	1.9	88.5	12.0	0.5	0.3	0.0	0.6	0.8	91.5	8.0	0.1	0.2	0.5
Norristown borough	3.1	56.7	36.7	0.9	3.3	0.1	5.7	10.5	70.8	26.4	0.2	1.7	2.7
Northampton township	0.6	97.5	0.5	0.1	2.1	0.0	0.3	0.8	97.9	0.4	0.0	1.5	0.7
North Huntingdon township	0.4	99.2	0.4	0.2	0.6	0.0	0.1	0.4	99.5	0.2	0.0	0.2	0.3
Penn Hills township	1.2	74.4	25.1	0.5	0.7	0.0	0.5	0.6	83.9	15.4	0.1	0.4	0.5
Philadelphia city	2.2	46.4	44.3	0.7	4.9	0.2	6.0	8.5	53.5	39.9	0.2	2.7	5.6
Pittsburgh city	1.6	68.8	28.1	0.7	3.1	0.1	1.1	1.3	72.1	25.8	0.2	1.6	0.9
Plum borough	0.5	96.0	3.0	0.2	1.0	0.0	0.2	0.6	97.1	2.0	0.0	0.8	0.6
Radnor township	1.0	90.4	3.5	0.3	6.2	0.0	0.8	2.0	93.0	3.2	0.1	3.6	1.7
Reading city	4.2	62.4	14.1	1.0	1.9	0.2	24.8	37.3	78.6	9.7	0.1	1.4	18.5
Ridley township	0.8	93.7	4.6	0.3	1.8	0.1	0.4	0.9	95.7	3.3	0.1	0.9	0.6
Ross township	0.5	96.4	1.6	0.2	1.9	0.1	0.3	0.7	97.9	1.1	0.0	0.9	0.4
Scranton city	1.1	94.5	3.6	0.3	1.3	0.0	1.5	2.6	97.2	1.6	0.1	0.9	0.7
Shaler township	0.6	98.4	0.5	0.2	1.1	0.0	0.3	0.5	98.9	0.2	0.0	0.7	0.4
State College borough	1.6	85.4	4.1	0.4	9.5	0.4	1.9	3.0	88.5	3.4	0.1	7.3	2.0
Tredyffrin township	0.7	91.5	3.0	0.2	5.5	0.0	0.5	1.2	93.7	3.9	0.1	2.1	0.9
Upper Darby township	1.9	78.6	12.1	0.4	9.4	0.1	1.4	1.6	92.5	3.0	0.1	4.2	1.0
Upper Dublin township	0.6	88.0	5.7	0.2	6.5	0.0	0.3	0.9	90.8	4.6	0.1	4.4	0.7
Upper Merion township	1.3	85.7	5.1	0.3	9.0	0.1	1.1	1.8	92.1	3.7	0.2	3.6	1.5
Warminster township	1.3	92.1	3.9	0.3	2.4	0.1	2.7	4.6	94.4	2.3	0.1	1.7	3.6
Wilkes-Barre city	1.2	93.3	5.8	0.4	1.0	0.1	0.8	1.6	96.1	2.9	0.1	0.6	0.7
Williamsport city	1.7	85.7	13.9	0.7	0.7	0.0	0.7	1.1	92.3	6.7	0.2	0.5	0.8
York city	3.8	62.8	27.6	1.0	1.8	0.2	10.7	17.2	72.5	21.3	0.2	1.1	7.7
RHODE ISLAND	2.7	86.9	5.5	1.0	2.7	0.2	6.6	8.7	91.4	3.9	0.4	1.8	4.6
Coventry town	1.0	98.5	0.7	0.5	0.8	0.1	0.6	1.1	99.0	0.3	0.1	0.4	0.8
Cranston city	1.6	90.4	4.2	0.6	3.7	0.1	2.7	4.6	95.1	2.4	0.2	1.8	2.0
Cumberland town	0.9	97.6	0.8	0.3	1.0	0.1	1.3	2.1	98.9	0.2	0.0	0.4	1.5
East Providence city	4.0	89.2	6.9	1.3	1.4	0.2	5.3	1.9	92.1	4.4	0.5	0.6	1.7
Johnston town	0.9	97.4	0.9	0.3	1.3	0.1	0.9	1.9	98.7	0.6	0.1	0.6	0.7
Newport city	3.4	86.6	9.7	1.8	1.9	0.3	3.5	5.5	88.6	8.1	0.7	1.4	2.8
North Kingstown town	1.3	96.8	1.5	1.0	1.2	0.1	0.8	1.8	96.9	1.3	0.4	1.0	1.1
North Providence town	1.8	93.4	3.1	0.4	2.2	0.1	2.6	3.8	97.1	1.0	0.1	1.2	1.8
Pawtucket city	5.3	78.6	9.7	0.8	1.1	0.4	15.0	13.9	89.3	3.6	0.3	0.6	7.2
Providence city	6.1	58.1	17.1	2.2	7.0	0.4	21.7	30.0	69.9	14.8	0.9	5.9	15.5
South Kingstown town	1.9	92.3	2.5	2.5	3.4	0.2	1.2	1.8	93.4	1.5	1.8	3.0	1.2
Warwick city	1.3	96.3	1.6	0.7	1.8	0.0	1.0	1.6	98.0	0.8	0.2	0.8	1.0
West Warwick town	1.9	95.4	1.6	0.9	1.8	0.1	2.2	3.1	97.6	0.8	0.2	1.0	1.9
Woonsocket city	3.1	85.5	5.7	0.8	4.9	0.1	6.4	9.3	93.3	2.6	0.2	3.0	2.6
VERMONT	1.2	97.9	0.7	1.1	1.1	0.1	0.4	0.9	98.6	0.3	0.3	0.6	0.7
Burlington city	2.3	94.2	2.4	1.3	3.2	0.1	1.2	1.4	96.8	1.0	0.3	1.5	1.2
WISCONSIN	1.2	90.0	6.1	1.3	1.9	0.1	2.0	3.6	92.2	5.0	0.8	1.1	1.9
Beloit city	2.8	78.1	16.8	0.9	1.5	0.1	5.5	9.1	81.8	15.7	0.3	1.2	1.9
Brookfield city	0.8	94.9	1.0	0.2	4.3	0.1	0.4	1.2	96.9	0.4	0.2	2.4	0.7

[1] Hispanic persons may be of any race.

Table E. Towns

	Population and population characteristics, 2000										
Town	Age (percent)										
	Under 5 years	5 to 17 years	18 to 24 years	25 to 34 years	35 to 44 years	45 to 54 years	55 to 64 years	65 to 74 years	75 years and over	Median age (years)	Percent Female
	28	29	30	31	32	33	34	35	36	37	38
PENNSYLVANIA	5.9	17.9	8.9	12.7	15.9	13.9	9.2	7.9	7.7	38.0	51.7
Abington township	5.8	17.8	6.1	11.5	16.2	14.1	9.4	9.0	10.0	40.6	52.8
Allentown city	7.1	17.6	11.2	14.8	15.0	11.6	7.5	7.1	8.0	34.5	52.1
Altoona city	6.3	16.6	10.9	12.7	14.8	13.1	8.9	8.2	8.6	37.4	53.1
Bensalem township	5.7	17.5	8.9	15.7	16.8	15.1	9.3	5.8	5.1	36.4	50.3
Bethel Park borough	5.3	18.4	5.0	9.9	16.8	15.6	10.9	9.6	8.5	42.1	52.1
Bristol township	6.6	19.3	8.8	13.9	17.4	13.4	8.0	7.3	5.4	35.9	50.6
Cheltenham township	5.1	17.7	8.5	11.6	14.4	14.9	9.2	8.2	10.4	40.3	53.7
Chester city	8.4	21.4	13.0	12.9	14.0	11.3	7.3	6.0	5.8	30.6	52.9
Easton city	6.2	17.1	16.3	15.0	14.9	11.6	7.0	5.8	6.2	32.0	50.7
Erie city	7.2	18.2	11.6	14.3	14.2	11.7	7.5	7.1	8.2	34.1	52.4
Falls township	6.2	19.6	7.9	13.9	18.0	13.9	7.9	7.3	5.4	36.4	51.3
Harrisburg city	8.1	20.1	9.2	15.5	15.4	13.2	7.6	5.7	5.1	33.0	53.0
Haverford township	6.6	18.3	6.3	12.0	16.5	14.2	8.4	8.1	9.3	39.2	52.5
Hempfield township	4.7	15.7	7.5	10.7	15.8	16.7	11.1	8.8	8.9	42.4	51.7
Lancaster city	7.9	19.6	13.9	15.6	14.8	11.0	6.7	5.3	5.2	30.4	51.2
Lower Makefield township	7.5	20.1	4.2	10.9	19.2	17.7	10.1	6.2	4.2	39.1	51.2
Lower Merion township	5.0	16.7	10.7	9.8	13.2	15.6	10.6	8.4	10.0	41.2	54.5
Lower Paxton township	5.6	16.9	7.3	13.8	17.1	16.0	9.2	7.5	6.6	38.9	52.2
McCandless township	5.9	17.7	6.8	11.7	16.1	16.6	9.2	7.9	8.1	40.3	52.4
Manheim township	5.5	17.6	5.8	9.9	15.0	15.3	9.9	9.0	12.0	42.6	53.1
Middletown township	5.8	20.4	7.7	11.5	18.1	15.6	7.8	6.7	6.3	37.8	51.3
Millcreek township	5.7	18.4	7.2	11.6	15.8	15.9	9.3	8.1	8.1	39.9	51.8
Mount Lebanon township	6.1	18.8	4.0	10.5	16.4	15.5	9.8	8.7	10.2	41.8	53.4
Municipality of Monroeville borough	4.9	15.4	6.2	12.1	15.3	15.4	10.5	10.0	10.3	42.6	53.0
New Castle city	6.7	17.1	8.1	12.5	13.6	12.4	8.9	9.2	11.5	39.4	54.0
Norristown borough	6.9	18.2	10.5	16.5	16.1	12.0	8.1	6.2	5.6	33.7	51.3
Northampton township	5.7	22.5	6.5	8.9	18.3	17.7	10.4	5.5	4.5	38.9	51.4
North Huntingdon township	5.3	16.5	6.0	11.0	16.7	15.7	11.1	9.7	8.0	41.9	51.6
Penn Hills township	5.5	16.1	6.3	11.3	15.7	15.1	10.2	10.3	9.4	41.9	53.0
Philadelphia city	6.5	18.8	11.1	14.8	14.5	12.0	8.3	7.1	7.0	34.2	53.5
Pittsburgh city	5.3	14.6	14.8	14.6	14.0	12.3	8.0	7.9	8.5	35.5	52.4
Plum borough	6.3	18.5	6.1	13.4	17.6	14.4	10.4	7.1	6.0	38.4	51.2
Radnor township	4.9	14.5	24.0	9.7	12.8	12.4	8.2	6.2	7.2	31.7	53.4
Reading city	8.7	21.3	11.7	15.1	13.9	10.3	6.8	6.1	6.3	30.6	51.7
Ridley township	6.1	18.3	7.1	13.3	17.0	12.6	8.4	9.1	8.1	38.1	52.0
Ross township	4.9	14.5	5.9	12.6	16.0	14.6	10.4	10.2	11.0	42.7	53.4
Scranton city	5.3	15.5	12.3	11.8	13.8	12.5	8.7	9.0	11.1	38.8	53.5
Shaler township	5.3	16.7	5.6	11.5	16.6	14.6	11.3	10.4	8.2	41.7	52.3
State College borough	1.8	3.9	65.5	11.3	4.9	4.1	2.6	2.5	3.3	21.8	47.9
Tredyffrin township	6.2	17.1	4.7	12.7	17.4	16.2	10.9	8.4	6.3	40.4	52.7
Upper Darby township	6.7	18.6	8.4	15.9	16.9	12.6	7.3	6.6	7.1	35.3	52.2
Upper Dublin township	6.0	21.4	4.9	8.9	16.5	17.8	10.8	7.9	5.8	40.9	51.2
Upper Merion township	5.5	13.2	7.5	18.2	15.6	13.9	10.4	9.1	6.6	38.2	50.8
Warminster township	6.3	18.2	7.6	13.2	15.9	12.7	10.9	9.1	6.1	37.9	51.1
Wilkes-Barre city	4.9	15.0	12.6	12.3	13.8	12.1	8.7	9.5	11.1	38.8	51.8
Williamsport city	6.0	16.5	18.0	12.7	13.9	11.9	7.4	6.4	7.0	32.4	50.6
York city	8.0	20.4	11.4	15.5	14.6	11.6	7.5	5.5	5.4	31.3	51.8
RHODE ISLAND	6.1	17.5	10.2	13.4	16.2	13.5	8.5	7.0	7.5	36.7	52.0
Coventry town	6.4	18.6	6.5	13.1	18.3	15.0	9.1	6.7	6.3	38.0	51.6
Cranston city	5.3	16.3	7.7	14.0	17.4	13.7	8.3	8.0	9.3	39.0	51.1
Cumberland town	6.2	18.0	5.8	12.3	18.0	14.4	9.3	8.2	7.8	39.3	52.3
East Providence city	5.4	16.3	7.4	13.4	16.0	13.2	9.4	8.8	10.1	39.6	53.5
Johnston town	5.4	15.5	6.3	13.2	16.8	14.0	9.9	8.6	10.2	40.7	53.1
Newport city	5.8	13.9	14.6	16.0	15.6	13.1	8.2	6.2	6.7	34.9	51.8
North Kingstown town	6.9	19.2	6.0	11.7	18.0	17.0	9.6	6.1	5.7	38.7	51.6
North Providence town	4.5	13.8	7.5	14.3	16.0	14.1	10.0	9.3	10.5	41.2	53.4
Pawtucket city	6.7	18.1	9.1	15.3	16.0	12.0	7.9	7.2	7.7	35.4	52.6
Providence city	7.3	18.8	18.9	15.6	13.0	10.0	6.0	4.9	5.6	28.1	52.2
South Kingstown town	5.3	17.2	19.8	9.3	15.1	14.1	7.5	5.8	5.8	33.6	52.5
Warwick city	5.4	16.5	6.7	12.8	17.3	14.8	9.5	8.3	8.7	40.0	52.4
West Warwick town	6.5	15.9	9.5	15.8	16.2	13.8	8.2	7.2	6.9	36.4	51.9
Woonsocket city	7.6	18.2	9.2	15.3	14.7	12.0	7.7	7.0	8.2	34.8	52.3
VERMONT	5.6	18.6	9.3	12.2	16.7	15.4	9.3	6.7	6.0	37.7	51.0
Burlington city	4.6	11.7	25.4	17.5	13.5	10.5	6.3	5.0	5.5	29.2	51.7
WISCONSIN	6.4	19.1	9.7	13.2	16.3	13.7	8.5	6.6	6.5	36.0	50.6
Beloit city	7.7	20.0	11.5	14.1	14.5	11.9	7.5	6.3	6.6	32.7	52.1
Brookfield city	5.4	21.4	4.6	6.8	16.4	16.9	10.9	9.6	8.0	42.5	51.6

Table E. Towns

Town	Under 5 years	5 to 17 years	18 to 24 years	25 to 34 years	35 to 44 years	45 to 54 years	55 to 64 years	65 to 74 years	75 years and over	Percent Female	2000	1990	1980	1990–2000	1980–1990
	39	40	41	42	43	44	45	46	47	48	49	50	51	52	53
PENNSYLVANIA	6.7	16.8	10.3	16.1	14.7	10.2	9.8	9.0	6.4	52.1	12 281 054	11 882 842	11 864 720	3.4	0.2
Abington township	6.5	15.3	7.5	15.3	14.2	10.6	11.3	10.7	8.6	53.1	56 103	56 358	NA	-0.5	NA
Allentown city	7.2	14.7	11.3	18.7	13.2	8.8	9.2	9.3	7.6	53.0	106 632	105 301	103 758	1.3	1.5
Altoona city	6.6	17.9	9.2	15.0	13.3	9.6	9.8	10.7	8.0	54.2	49 523	51 881	57 078	-4.5	-9.1
Bensalem township	8.0	18.4	10.3	20.7	17.0	9.9	6.8	5.5	3.5	50.1	58 434	56 788	NA	2.9	NA
Bethel Park borough	7.0	16.6	7.1	15.8	15.8	12.9	11.1	8.8	4.8	51.9	33 556	33 823	34 755	-0.8	-2.7
Bristol township	8.0	18.5	10.0	19.2	14.7	9.0	9.9	7.7	2.8	50.6	55 521	57 129	NA	-2.8	NA
Cheltenham township	6.1	14.4	8.2	13.7	15.3	11.0	11.1	11.0	9.1	53.8	36 875	34 900	NA	5.7	NA
Chester city	9.3	18.7	13.0	16.4	12.6	8.6	7.8	8.2	5.4	54.2	36 854	41 856	45 794	-12.0	-8.6
Easton city	7.5	15.9	16.8	18.0	12.3	8.1	7.5	7.2	6.6	51.5	26 263	26 276	26 027	0.0	1.0
Erie city	7.9	17.4	12.1	16.6	13.2	8.2	8.6	9.5	6.6	52.8	103 717	108 718	119 123	-4.6	-8.7
Falls township	7.4	18.5	8.9	19.2	16.0	9.5	9.8	8.0	2.6	50.4	34 865	35 047	NA	-0.5	NA
Harrisburg city	8.9	17.8	10.4	18.7	15.5	8.4	7.2	6.8	6.2	53.3	48 950	52 376	53 264	-6.5	-1.7
Haverford township	6.9	15.2	10.1	15.2	15.7	9.4	10.2	9.9	7.6	52.2	48 498	49 848	NA	-2.7	NA
Hempfield township	5.7	17.0	8.6	15.0	16.3	12.2	10.3	9.0	6.0	51.3	40 721	42 609	NA	-4.4	NA
Lancaster city	8.4	18.0	14.0	18.7	13.6	7.6	7.4	7.2	5.1	51.6	56 348	55 551	54 725	1.4	1.5
Lower Makefield township	7.3	19.2	7.4	13.3	18.7	15.7	10.2	5.6	2.7	50.7	32 681	25 083	NA	30.3	NA
Lower Merion township	5.5	14.5	10.3	11.3	15.5	13.1	10.7	10.1	9.0	55.1	59 850	58 003	NA	3.2	NA
Lower Paxton township	6.4	15.1	8.9	18.6	17.3	10.8	9.9	7.9	4.9	52.7	44 424	39 162	NA	13.4	NA
McCandless township	6.8	17.1	7.7	14.5	18.6	11.4	9.9	8.4	5.8	52.8	29 022	28 781	NA	0.8	NA
Manheim township	5.8	16.2	6.8	12.1	16.3	11.5	10.6	9.6	11.1	53.8	33 697	28 880	NA	16.7	NA
Middletown township	8.0	19.0	8.6	18.0	17.7	9.1	9.2	6.5	3.9	51.3	44 141	43 063	NA	2.5	NA
Millcreek township	6.5	18.0	8.4	15.6	16.3	10.9	10.2	9.7	4.4	51.8	52 129	46 820	NA	11.3	NA
Mount Lebanon township	6.6	15.9	5.7	14.8	15.7	12.4	10.4	9.6	8.8	54.0	33 017	33 362	NA	-1.0	NA
Municipality of Monroeville borough	5.9	15.1	8.2	16.9	15.9	12.0	11.7	9.1	5.2	52.6	29 349	29 169	NA	0.6	NA
New Castle city	6.8	15.3	8.8	14.3	12.6	9.0	10.5	12.5	10.2	54.8	26 309	28 334	33 621	-7.1	-15.7
Norristown borough	8.0	15.3	9.1	21.0	14.6	8.2	9.2	8.7	5.8	52.9	31 282	30 754	34 684	1.7	-11.3
Northampton township	6.4	22.2	9.5	13.5	19.6	13.6	7.8	4.1	3.3	51.0	39 384	35 406	NA	11.2	NA
North Huntingdon township	5.5	17.6	8.2	13.7	16.1	12.7	11.7	9.5	5.0	51.3	29 123	28 158	NA	3.4	NA
Penn Hills township	5.9	15.6	8.2	15.9	15.3	10.8	12.0	10.6	5.7	52.2	46 809	51 479	NA	-9.1	NA
Philadelphia city	7.3	16.6	11.4	17.4	13.4	9.5	9.1	8.7	6.5	53.5	1 517 550	1 585 577	1 688 210	-4.3	-6.1
Pittsburgh city	6.1	13.8	13.7	17.1	13.2	8.5	9.6	10.2	7.8	53.5	334 563	369 879	423 938	-9.5	-12.8
Plum borough	7.4	18.4	9.0	18.9	16.9	12.4	8.9	5.5	2.4	50.6	26 940	25 609	25 390	5.2	0.9
Radnor township	4.6	12.1	23.0	12.3	13.3	10.7	9.9	7.9	6.1	51.9	30 878	28 703	NA	7.6	NA
Reading city	8.2	17.2	11.7	17.1	11.6	8.6	8.8	8.9	7.8	53.2	81 207	78 380	78 686	3.6	-0.4
Ridley township	7.0	15.3	9.3	18.5	12.7	9.7	11.3	11.0	5.2	51.6	30 791	31 169	NA	-1.2	NA
Ross township	5.8	13.5	7.5	17.0	14.6	11.4	11.7	10.7	7.8	53.9	32 551	33 482	NA	-2.8	NA
Scranton city	6.0	15.0	11.8	14.4	11.9	9.0	10.0	12.0	10.0	54.2	76 415	81 805	88 117	-6.6	-7.2
Shaler township	6.4	14.6	8.0	16.0	14.6	12.5	12.2	10.2	5.6	52.2	29 757	30 533	NA	-2.5	NA
State College borough	2.2	4.1	65.8	12.2	5.5	3.1	2.7	2.8	1.9	45.9	38 420	38 981	36 130	-1.4	7.9
Tredyffrin township	6.0	14.7	7.8	17.0	17.5	13.6	11.8	7.6	4.1	51.8	29 062	28 028	NA	3.7	NA
Upper Darby township	7.4	15.0	9.8	20.1	13.9	8.5	8.9	9.7	6.8	52.8	81 821	81 177	NA	0.8	NA
Upper Dublin township	6.4	17.7	9.5	13.8	17.0	14.1	10.9	7.2	3.6	51.3	25 878	24 028	NA	7.7	NA
Upper Merion township	5.6	12.7	10.3	19.0	14.5	12.9	12.7	8.9	3.5	51.3	26 863	25 722	NA	4.4	NA
Warminster township	6.9	18.5	10.7	17.5	13.9	12.3	10.5	6.2	3.4	50.6	31 383	32 832	NA	-4.4	NA
Wilkes-Barre city	5.6	14.4	13.1	14.3	12.4	8.6	10.7	11.5	9.5	53.8	43 123	47 523	51 551	-9.3	-7.8
Williamsport city	7.7	17.4	13.7	16.9	12.6	8.4	8.2	8.6	6.4	52.5	30 706	31 933	33 401	-3.8	-4.4
York city	8.8	17.6	11.9	18.8	13.0	8.8	7.6	7.5	6.0	52.7	40 862	42 192	44 619	-3.2	-5.4
RHODE ISLAND	6.7	15.8	12.0	17.3	14.7	9.6	8.9	8.5	6.5	52.0	1 048 319	1 003 464	947 154	4.5	5.9
Coventry town	6.5	18.0	8.6	16.9	16.5	11.4	9.2	8.0	5.0	51.5	33 668	31 083	NA	8.3	NA
Cranston city	5.7	13.6	9.6	17.8	15.2	9.4	10.1	10.7	7.9	51.8	79 269	76 060	71 992	4.2	5.7
Cumberland town	6.2	15.9	9.0	16.5	14.8	11.9	11.2	9.3	5.2	52.2	31 840	29 038	NA	9.6	NA
East Providence city	6.0	14.9	9.1	17.1	13.9	9.9	10.0	10.7	8.4	53.4	48 688	50 380	50 980	-3.4	-1.2
Johnston town	5.7	14.9	8.8	17.6	15.6	10.0	10.2	10.3	6.9	52.3	28 195	26 542	NA	6.2	NA
Newport city	6.4	13.9	16.6	19.4	14.1	9.2	7.0	7.4	6.0	51.4	26 475	28 227	29 258	-6.2	-3.5
North Kingstown town	6.9	18.5	8.1	16.5	18.9	10.9	8.2	7.1	4.8	51.1	26 326	23 786	NA	10.7	NA
North Providence town	5.2	12.4	10.4	18.2	14.4	10.2	10.4	10.7	8.0	53.5	32 411	32 090	NA	1.0	NA
Pawtucket city	7.4	15.3	10.4	19.6	12.8	8.9	9.2	9.4	7.0	52.8	72 958	72 644	71 204	0.4	2.0
Providence city	7.8	16.1	17.6	18.1	12.0	7.7	7.0	7.1	6.5	52.9	173 618	160 728	156 804	8.0	2.5
South Kingstown town	5.0	14.0	27.7	13.3	13.7	8.2	6.6	6.4	5.0	52.0	27 921	24 612	NA	13.4	NA
Warwick city	6.0	15.5	8.7	16.9	15.1	10.9	10.1	10.0	6.8	52.5	85 808	85 427	87 123	0.4	-1.9
West Warwick town	6.9	15.4	11.1	19.9	15.0	9.0	8.8	9.0	4.9	51.9	29 581	29 268	NA	1.1	NA
Woonsocket city	7.7	16.7	10.9	17.6	12.9	9.1	8.9	8.9	7.4	52.7	43 224	43 877	45 914	-1.5	-4.4
VERMONT	7.3	18.1	11.2	16.9	16.4	10.2	8.0	6.6	5.2	51.0	608 827	562 758	511 456	8.2	10.0
Burlington city	5.3	10.7	30.5	17.9	12.1	6.7	6.2	5.5	5.1	53.6	38 889	39 127	37 712	-0.6	3.8
WISCONSIN	7.4	19.0	10.5	16.8	14.8	9.8	8.5	7.3	6.0	51.1	5 363 675	4 891 954	4 705 642	9.6	4.0
Beloit city	8.8	19.8	11.6	16.4	12.9	9.0	8.0	7.4	6.1	53.4	35 775	35 571	35 207	0.6	1.0
Brookfield city	6.3	19.5	6.8	11.2	17.0	13.7	12.9	8.3	4.3	50.5	38 649	35 184	34 035	9.8	3.4

Table E. Towns

Town	Total population	Total in house-holds	House-holder	Spouse	Child Total	Child Own child under 18 years	Other relatives Total	Other relatives Under 18 years	Nonrelatives Total	Nonrelatives Unmarried partner	Total in group quarters	Correctional institutions	Nursing homes	Other institutions	College dormitories	Military quarters	Other
	54	55	56	57	58	59	60	61	62	63	64	65	66	67	68	69	70
PENNSYLVANIA	12 281 054	96.5	38.9	20.1	28.9	21.6	4.3	1.6	4.3	1.9	3.5	0.6	0.9	0.2	1.2	0.0	0.6
Abington township	56 103	98.2	38.7	22.2	30.1	21.9	4.3	1.5	3.0	1.3	1.8	0.0	1.1	0.0	0.2	0.0	0.5
Allentown city	106 632	95.3	39.4	15.5	28.0	21.8	5.8	2.2	6.6	3.2	4.7	1.0	0.8	0.3	2.0	0.0	0.6
Altoona city	49 523	96.1	40.5	18.0	28.3	20.7	3.9	1.6	5.4	2.2	3.9	0.0	0.8	0.1	1.8	0.0	1.2
Bensalem township	58 434	99.3	38.7	20.0	30.0	20.9	5.3	1.6	5.3	2.4	0.7	0.0	0.3	0.0	0.0	0.0	0.4
Bethel Park borough	33 556	98.9	39.8	24.7	30.2	22.8	2.4	0.7	1.8	1.0	1.1	0.0	0.8	0.0	0.0	0.0	0.3
Bristol township	55 521	99.3	35.5	19.3	32.8	22.5	7.0	2.8	4.7	2.2	0.7	0.0	0.4	0.0	0.0	0.0	0.3
Cheltenham township	36 875	96.2	38.9	20.8	28.4	21.0	4.3	1.4	3.8	1.6	3.8	0.0	1.5	0.0	2.0	0.0	0.4
Chester city	36 854	91.9	34.8	8.6	33.0	23.5	10.1	5.4	5.5	2.6	8.1	2.6	1.1	0.0	3.3	0.0	1.1
Easton city	26 263	89.5	36.3	13.7	26.6	20.2	5.7	2.2	7.2	3.1	10.5	2.4	1.2	0.0	6.5	0.0	0.5
Erie city	103 717	94.4	39.5	15.1	29.2	22.4	4.7	2.1	5.9	2.6	5.6	0.6	1.1	0.5	2.3	0.0	1.1
Falls township	34 865	99.8	37.8	20.6	32.5	23.6	4.8	1.8	4.1	2.3	0.2	0.0	0.0	0.0	0.0	0.0	0.2
Harrisburg city	48 950	97.4	42.0	9.8	30.1	23.3	8.1	4.0	7.4	3.4	2.6	0.3	0.7	0.2	0.0	0.0	1.4
Haverford township	48 498	98.8	37.2	22.7	32.2	23.8	3.4	0.9	3.2	0.9	1.2	0.0	0.9	0.0	0.0	0.0	0.3
Hempfield township	40 721	95.4	39.3	24.3	27.0	19.3	2.6	0.8	2.2	1.2	4.6	1.0	1.8	0.0	1.1	0.0	0.7
Lancaster city	56 348	93.5	37.1	12.4	29.5	23.4	6.4	3.0	8.1	3.6	6.5	1.8	1.1	0.1	2.6	0.0	0.9
Lower Makefield township	32 681	99.2	35.8	26.0	32.9	26.9	2.3	0.5	2.1	1.1	0.8	0.0	0.3	0.0	0.0	0.0	0.5
Lower Merion township	59 850	92.4	38.2	21.7	26.0	21.0	2.4	0.6	4.2	1.0	7.6	0.0	0.8	0.0	5.6	0.0	1.2
Lower Paxton township	44 424	98.2	41.8	22.2	27.2	21.1	3.1	1.0	3.8	2.0	1.8	0.0	1.4	0.1	0.0	0.0	0.2
McCandless township	29 022	95.7	38.5	24.1	28.9	22.8	2.0	0.6	2.2	1.0	4.3	0.0	1.9	0.1	1.4	0.0	0.9
Manheim township	33 697	94.9	38.5	24.3	27.3	22.3	2.4	0.7	2.5	1.2	5.1	0.0	3.2	0.0	0.8	0.0	1.0
Middletown township	44 141	97.6	34.7	22.0	33.4	24.5	4.2	1.3	3.3	1.5	2.4	0.0	1.7	0.0	0.4	0.0	0.3
Millcreek township	52 129	98.3	40.7	22.4	29.3	22.6	2.6	1.0	3.4	1.8	1.7	0.0	1.0	0.2	0.0	0.0	0.5
Mount Lebanon township	33 017	97.6	41.2	23.6	29.1	24.3	1.8	0.4	1.8	0.9	2.4	0.0	2.0	0.0	0.0	0.0	0.4
Municipality of Monroeville borough	29 349	96.8	42.2	22.2	26.5	19.1	3.2	1.1	2.7	1.5	3.2	0.0	1.3	0.3	0.1	0.0	1.5
New Castle city	26 309	96.2	40.8	16.8	29.3	21.0	5.3	2.1	4.0	2.2	3.8	0.9	1.8	0.1	0.0	0.0	1.0
Norristown borough	31 282	96.8	38.5	13.0	29.2	20.9	8.5	3.4	7.7	2.7	3.2	0.0	0.7	0.0	0.0	0.0	0.5
Northampton township	39 384	99.3	33.0	25.1	36.7	27.2	3.1	0.8	1.4	0.7	0.7	0.0	0.6	0.0	0.0	0.0	0.1
North Huntingdon township	29 123	98.4	38.5	25.6	29.7	20.6	2.9	1.0	1.8	1.0	1.6	0.0	1.1	0.0	0.0	0.0	0.5
Penn Hills township	46 809	99.1	41.6	21.3	28.5	19.4	4.5	1.9	3.2	1.6	0.9	0.0	0.6	0.0	0.0	0.0	0.2
Philadelphia city	1 517 550	96.4	38.9	12.5	29.9	20.4	9.2	4.2	6.0	2.3	3.6	0.5	0.7	0.2	1.4	0.0	0.8
Pittsburgh city	334 563	93.2	43.0	13.4	24.4	17.3	5.3	2.1	7.1	2.4	6.8	1.4	0.8	0.3	3.7	0.0	0.7
Plum borough	26 940	99.1	38.1	24.2	31.6	23.7	2.8	0.9	2.3	1.4	0.9	0.0	0.2	0.0	0.0	0.0	0.7
Radnor township	30 878	80.2	33.5	17.7	23.2	18.8	2.0	0.4	3.8	0.9	19.8	0.0	1.1	0.2	18.0	0.0	0.6
Reading city	81 207	97.4	37.1	12.7	32.3	25.7	7.8	3.3	7.5	3.7	2.6	0.0	0.3	0.0	1.4	0.0	0.9
Ridley township	30 791	99.8	39.4	20.6	31.9	22.4	4.6	1.7	3.3	1.7	0.2	0.0	0.0	0.0	0.0	0.0	0.2
Ross township	32 551	96.7	42.7	22.8	25.6	18.4	2.7	0.7	2.9	1.5	3.3	0.0	2.0	0.0	0.0	0.0	1.3
Scranton city	76 415	93.6	41.0	16.3	27.0	18.9	4.3	1.3	5.0	1.9	6.4	0.8	1.2	0.1	3.0	0.0	1.3
Shaler township	29 757	99.4	40.1	24.9	29.5	20.9	3.1	1.0	1.9	1.1	0.6	0.0	0.0	0.0	0.0	0.0	0.6
State College borough	38 420	72.1	31.3	7.0	6.5	5.4	1.1	0.1	26.2	1.1	27.9	0.0	0.5	0.0	27.2	0.0	0.2
Tredyffrin township	29 062	99.4	42.1	23.5	27.7	22.6	2.3	0.5	3.8	1.3	0.6	0.0	0.4	0.1	0.0	0.0	0.2
Upper Darby township	81 821	99.6	39.8	17.9	32.4	23.3	5.4	1.6	4.2	1.9	0.4	0.0	0.0	0.0	0.0	0.0	0.3
Upper Dublin township	25 878	98.6	35.5	24.6	33.2	25.9	3.5	1.0	1.9	1.0	1.4	0.0	0.7	0.3	0.0	0.0	0.4
Upper Merion township	26 863	99.3	43.1	22.5	24.6	17.5	3.6	1.0	5.4	1.9	0.7	0.0	0.7	0.0	0.0	0.0	0.1
Warminster township	31 383	99.0	36.2	22.4	32.4	22.7	4.6	1.5	3.3	1.4	1.0	0.0	0.0	0.0	0.0	0.0	0.2
Wilkes-Barre city	43 123	91.5	41.7	15.2	25.0	17.3	4.6	1.4	5.0	2.1	8.5	2.5	1.7	0.9	2.6	0.0	0.8
Williamsport city	30 706	91.5	39.8	13.9	25.7	20.1	3.7	1.6	8.5	3.0	8.5	1.1	0.5	0.1	5.6	0.0	1.1
York city	40 862	97.8	39.5	12.2	30.1	24.0	6.9	3.4	9.1	3.9	2.2	0.1	0.3	0.0	0.1	0.0	1.7
RHODE ISLAND	1 048 319	96.3	39.0	18.8	29.0	21.8	4.5	1.4	5.1	2.2	3.7	0.3	0.9	0.1	2.0	0.1	0.3
Coventry town	33 668	98.4	37.4	22.6	30.9	23.2	3.7	1.3	3.7	2.0	1.6	0.0	1.4	0.0	0.0	0.0	0.2
Cranston city	79 269	94.1	39.0	19.2	27.6	19.7	4.6	1.3	3.7	1.9	5.9	4.1	0.3	0.7	0.4	0.0	0.4
Cumberland town	31 840	99.2	38.3	23.7	30.6	22.8	3.8	1.0	2.8	1.6	0.8	0.0	0.6	0.0	0.0	0.0	0.1
East Providence city	48 688	98.4	42.2	19.5	28.4	19.9	4.5	1.5	3.8	2.0	1.6	0.0	1.3	0.0	0.0	0.0	0.2
Johnston town	28 195	98.3	39.7	21.4	28.7	19.3	5.2	1.4	3.3	1.6	1.7	0.0	1.6	0.0	0.0	0.0	0.2
Newport city	26 475	92.1	41.6	14.1	22.6	18.3	3.0	0.9	8.8	2.7	7.9	0.0	0.9	0.0	3.4	3.2	0.4
North Kingstown town	26 326	98.9	38.6	22.6	31.2	24.9	2.6	0.8	3.9	2.0	1.1	0.0	0.8	0.0	0.0	0.0	0.2
North Providence town	32 411	98.7	44.3	19.7	25.4	16.7	5.1	1.2	4.1	2.1	1.3	0.0	0.8	0.2	0.0	0.0	0.4
Pawtucket city	72 958	99.1	41.2	16.3	30.5	22.7	5.6	1.7	5.4	2.7	0.9	0.0	0.6	0.0	0.0	0.0	0.3
Providence city	173 618	92.1	35.9	11.5	29.7	23.2	6.9	2.3	8.1	2.6	7.9	0.0	0.8	0.1	6.5	0.0	0.5
South Kingstown town	27 921	85.0	33.2	18.7	26.0	21.1	2.7	1.1	4.4	1.6	15.0	0.0	0.6	0.0	14.0	0.0	0.3
Warwick city	85 808	98.8	41.4	21.0	28.2	20.1	4.0	1.3	4.3	2.2	1.2	0.0	0.7	0.0	0.2	0.0	0.3
West Warwick town	29 581	99.4	42.3	18.8	28.2	20.6	4.2	1.2	5.9	3.2	0.6	0.0	0.4	0.1	0.0	0.0	0.1
Woonsocket city	43 224	97.5	41.1	16.2	30.0	23.8	4.2	1.3	6.1	3.5	2.5	0.0	1.7	0.0	0.0	0.0	0.8
VERMONT	608 827	96.6	39.5	20.8	27.5	22.7	2.4	0.8	6.4	3.0	3.4	0.2	0.7	0.0	2.1	0.0	0.4
Burlington city	38 889	89.7	40.8	12.8	18.6	15.0	2.3	0.7	15.1	3.5	10.3	0.0	1.2	0.0	8.1	0.1	1.0
WISCONSIN	5 363 675	97.1	38.9	20.7	29.4	23.7	3.0	1.1	5.2	2.2	2.9	0.6	0.8	0.1	1.0	0.0	0.5
Beloit city	35 775	96.1	37.4	16.6	30.3	24.4	5.3	2.3	6.4	3.0	3.9	0.0	1.0	0.0	2.7	0.0	0.3
Brookfield city	38 649	98.3	35.9	26.3	32.3	26.1	2.2	0.6	1.6	0.8	1.7	0.0	1.2	0.0	0.0	0.0	0.4

Table E. Towns

Town	Total households	Family households Total	With own children under 18 years	Married couple Total	With own children under 18 years	Female householder[1] Total	With own children under 18 years	Nonfamily households Total	Householder living alone Total	65 years and over	Average household size	Average family size	Total households	Female householder[1]	Householder living alone
													1990	1990	1990
	71	72	73	74	75	76	77	78	79	80	81	82	83	84	85
PENNSYLVANIA	4 777 003	67.2	30.0	51.7	21.8	11.6	6.2	32.8	27.7	11.6	2.48	3.04	4 495 966	11.3	25.6
Abington township	21 690	69.8	30.0	57.4	25.2	9.6	3.8	30.2	25.9	12.9	2.54	3.10	21 543	8.9	24.0
Allentown city	42 032	59.8	28.8	39.4	16.3	15.1	9.6	40.2	33.1	12.8	2.42	3.09	42 775	12.6	31.4
Altoona city	20 059	62.7	28.4	44.6	18.3	13.8	7.6	37.3	31.6	14.7	2.37	2.98	20 684	13.2	28.5
Bensalem township	22 627	66.8	30.6	51.6	23.3	10.5	5.3	33.2	26.3	7.9	2.56	3.14	20 964	9.3	23.2
Bethel Park borough	13 362	71.4	30.3	62.0	26.4	7.2	3.1	28.6	26.1	12.0	2.48	3.01	12 692	7.2	20.6
Bristol township	19 733	73.5	33.6	54.3	24.6	13.4	6.3	26.5	21.2	8.3	2.79	3.26	19 314	10.9	17.7
Cheltenham township	14 346	67.2	30.4	53.4	23.4	10.6	5.7	32.8	27.6	12.5	2.47	3.05	13 747	7.8	27.0
Chester city	12 814	63.4	32.7	24.8	10.5	32.1	19.1	36.6	31.2	11.2	2.64	3.34	14 537	29.0	27.5
Easton city	9 544	60.1	30.5	37.7	17.5	16.6	10.0	39.9	31.6	11.0	2.46	3.10	9 397	12.8	29.5
Erie city	40 938	59.8	29.2	38.2	16.2	16.8	10.5	40.2	33.4	13.3	2.39	3.08	42 131	15.5	30.7
Falls township	13 170	71.4	35.1	54.5	25.9	12.1	6.7	28.6	23.4	9.0	2.64	3.15	12 546	9.1	18.4
Harrisburg city	20 561	53.1	28.5	23.4	9.7	24.4	16.0	46.9	39.3	10.4	2.32	3.15	21 520	22.6	37.2
Haverford township	18 061	72.1	33.3	60.9	29.3	8.6	3.2	27.9	23.3	12.4	2.65	3.17	17 720	7.8	20.6
Hempfield township	15 997	72.5	28.4	61.8	23.7	7.8	3.6	27.5	24.3	11.7	2.43	2.89	15 499	7.9	20.2
Lancaster city	20 933	58.1	31.6	33.4	15.4	19.0	12.9	41.9	33.1	9.9	2.52	3.23	21 189	16.0	32.3
Lower Makefield township	11 706	80.2	40.6	72.5	36.9	5.7	2.9	19.8	16.2	4.9	2.77	3.13	8 552	5.5	12.9
Lower Merion township	22 868	65.7	29.4	56.7	25.3	7.0	3.4	34.3	28.3	12.4	2.42	2.99	22 559	7.1	27.0
Lower Paxton township	18 584	65.4	29.0	53.2	22.3	9.2	5.1	34.6	28.8	8.4	2.35	2.92	16 060	7.5	26.1
McCandless township	11 159	71.0	32.2	62.8	28.2	6.1	3.0	29.0	25.0	8.9	2.49	3.02	10 524	6.1	21.5
Manheim township	12 961	71.6	31.0	63.1	26.1	6.4	3.8	28.4	24.8	12.8	2.47	2.96	10 656	7.0	20.9
Middletown township	15 321	76.1	38.2	63.3	31.7	9.3	4.7	23.9	19.4	7.3	2.81	3.25	14 481	8.5	17.5
Millcreek township	21 217	66.4	30.2	55.0	23.8	8.4	4.8	33.6	29.0	11.7	2.42	3.01	18 397	7.8	26.0
Mount Lebanon township	13 610	66.3	31.3	57.3	26.8	7.2	3.8	33.7	30.6	13.5	2.37	3.00	13 652	7.3	29.1
Municipality of Monroeville borough	12 376	65.0	25.8	52.7	20.0	9.7	4.8	35.0	30.8	12.1	2.30	2.89	11 828	8.9	26.5
New Castle city	10 727	62.7	27.0	41.2	15.5	16.9	9.4	37.3	33.5	17.2	2.36	3.01	11 374	15.0	30.5
Norristown borough	12 028	59.4	28.7	33.7	14.8	19.8	11.6	40.6	32.7	9.2	2.52	3.22	12 187	15.3	34.7
Northampton township	13 014	84.2	43.3	76.0	39.2	6.2	3.2	15.8	13.7	5.8	3.01	3.33	11 105	5.3	12.0
North Huntingdon township	11 216	76.9	29.7	66.3	25.7	8.0	3.1	23.1	20.8	10.1	2.56	2.96	10 214	6.6	17.3
Penn Hills township	19 490	68.1	26.3	51.1	18.4	13.5	6.6	31.9	28.2	13.2	2.38	2.91	19 798	9.9	21.6
Philadelphia city	590 071	59.7	27.6	32.1	13.5	22.3	11.8	40.3	33.8	11.9	2.48	3.22	603 075	20.1	31.2
Pittsburgh city	143 739	51.6	21.9	32.1	11.4	16.5	9.0	48.4	39.4	13.7	2.17	2.95	153 483	17.0	36.2
Plum borough	10 270	74.9	34.1	63.6	28.6	8.5	4.3	25.1	21.5	8.6	2.60	3.06	9 067	7.9	16.0
Radnor township	10 347	61.6	29.4	52.9	25.5	6.8	3.2	38.4	31.1	12.1	2.39	3.08	9 831	7.1	28.8
Reading city	30 113	61.2	33.7	34.4	16.3	20.2	13.5	38.8	31.7	12.4	2.63	3.33	31 403	15.9	32.1
Ridley township	12 121	67.8	30.2	52.3	23.3	11.7	5.3	32.2	28.0	12.9	2.54	3.14	11 926	9.7	24.6
Ross township	13 892	63.4	24.3	53.4	20.4	7.4	3.1	36.6	31.8	13.5	2.26	2.89	13 645	8.1	27.5
Scranton city	31 303	57.9	24.4	39.8	15.8	13.8	6.9	42.1	36.7	18.1	2.29	3.01	32 637	13.0	33.9
Shaler township	11 932	72.8	28.6	62.1	24.6	8.2	3.0	27.2	24.4	12.1	2.48	2.97	11 609	7.1	19.5
State College borough	12 024	27.5	10.5	22.4	8.3	3.4	1.8	72.5	33.5	5.9	2.30	2.69	10 938	2.7	27.4
Tredyffrin township	12 223	64.1	29.0	55.9	25.4	6.2	2.9	35.9	30.1	9.1	2.36	2.99	11 427	6.9	25.4
Upper Darby township	32 551	62.9	31.0	45.0	22.3	13.4	6.9	37.1	31.6	11.5	2.50	3.23	32 746	10.5	31.3
Upper Dublin township	9 174	79.3	38.2	69.4	33.8	7.5	3.6	20.7	17.8	6.5	2.78	3.18	8 206	8.2	15.7
Upper Merion township	11 575	61.7	23.1	52.3	19.6	6.8	2.6	38.3	29.7	7.7	2.30	2.91	10 541	6.5	25.5
Warminster township	11 350	76.0	32.5	62.1	26.1	10.3	4.8	24.0	20.0	8.5	2.74	3.16	10 846	9.0	15.8
Wilkes-Barre city	17 961	55.0	23.0	36.5	14.1	14.0	7.2	45.0	38.0	18.6	2.20	2.96	19 435	13.2	35.7
Williamsport city	12 219	55.1	27.4	34.9	14.1	15.5	10.3	44.9	35.1	12.9	2.30	2.97	12 588	14.7	30.9
York city	16 137	57.3	30.9	31.0	13.3	20.6	14.1	42.7	33.1	10.7	2.48	3.17	16 887	17.3	31.9
RHODE ISLAND	408 424	65.0	30.6	48.2	21.0	12.9	7.8	35.0	28.6	11.4	2.47	3.07	377 977	11.7	26.2
Coventry town	12 596	73.8	34.7	60.4	27.1	10.0	5.8	26.2	21.2	9.1	2.63	3.07	11 189	8.3	20.6
Cranston city	30 954	65.4	28.7	49.2	20.9	12.5	6.3	34.6	29.4	13.1	2.41	3.01	29 349	11.2	27.0
Cumberland town	12 198	74.1	33.2	61.9	27.0	9.2	5.0	25.9	22.2	11.2	2.59	3.05	10 764	8.1	19.9
East Providence city	20 530	62.6	27.1	46.3	18.7	12.7	6.9	37.4	32.4	14.6	2.33	2.99	19 950	10.1	28.2
Johnston town	11 197	69.0	27.8	53.9	21.4	11.4	5.2	31.0	26.6	13.2	2.47	3.02	9 995	10.3	22.8
Newport city	11 566	48.8	22.9	32.3	12.4	13.6	9.1	51.2	39.4	10.9	2.11	2.86	11 196	13.5	33.5
North Kingstown town	10 154	72.0	35.7	58.6	27.8	10.1	6.4	28.0	22.5	8.2	2.57	3.03	8 695	10.1	20.0
North Providence town	14 351	59.5	22.4	44.5	15.9	11.5	5.2	40.5	34.8	13.8	2.23	2.91	13 257	8.1	29.1
Pawtucket city	30 047	61.6	30.5	39.7	17.2	16.8	10.8	38.4	32.3	12.5	2.41	3.07	29 711	12.7	30.3
Providence city	62 389	57.5	32.3	31.9	15.7	20.5	14.2	42.5	32.3	10.1	2.56	3.33	58 905	17.7	31.2
South Kingstown town	9 268	69.0	34.0	56.4	27.1	9.4	5.5	31.0	24.2	9.6	2.56	3.07	7 428	9.0	23.1
Warwick city	35 517	64.7	27.4	50.7	20.8	10.2	4.9	35.3	29.8	13.2	2.39	2.99	33 437	9.4	26.2
West Warwick town	12 498	61.6	28.0	44.4	17.9	13.1	7.8	38.4	31.2	10.7	2.35	2.97	11 722	10.9	28.4
Woonsocket city	17 750	60.7	31.2	39.4	16.5	16.2	11.8	39.3	32.7	12.5	2.37	3.02	17 572	13.0	28.8
VERMONT	240 634	65.6	31.8	52.5	23.2	9.3	6.1	34.4	26.2	9.5	2.44	2.96	210 650	9.2	23.4
Burlington city	15 885	44.4	21.3	31.4	13.0	10.0	6.8	55.6	35.6	8.2	2.19	2.86	14 680	10.0	32.0
WISCONSIN	2 084 544	66.5	31.9	53.2	23.7	9.6	6.2	33.5	26.8	9.9	2.50	3.05	1 822 118	9.6	24.3
Beloit city	13 370	66.6	34.0	44.5	19.5	16.6	11.5	33.4	27.5	11.3	2.57	3.10	13 307	16.1	25.7
Brookfield city	13 891	80.8	36.1	73.1	32.6	5.5	2.6	19.2	16.7	9.0	2.74	3.09	11 939	5.0	11.3

[1]No spouse present.

Table E. Towns

| Town | Percent change of households, 1990–2000 | Total housing units | Occupied housing units (percent) | Vacant housing units | | Homeowner vacancy rate (percent) | Rental vacancy rate (percent) | Occupied housing units | | | Average household size of owner-occupied units | Average household size of renter-occupied units |
| | | | | Total | For seasonal, recreational, or occasional use | | | Total | Percent owner-occupied housing units | Percent renter-occupied housing units | | |
	86	87	88	89	90	91	92	93	94	95	96	97
PENNSYLVANIA	6.3	5 249 750	91.0	9.0	2.8	1.6	7.2	4 777 003	71.3	28.7	2.62	2.12
Abington township	0.7	22 367	97.0	3.0	0.3	0.8	5.7	21 690	79.3	20.7	2.72	1.85
Allentown city	-1.7	45 960	91.5	8.5	0.3	2.6	8.4	42 032	53.0	47.0	2.55	2.26
Altoona city	-3.0	21 681	92.5	7.5	0.1	1.4	9.7	20 059	65.9	34.1	2.51	2.11
Bensalem township	7.9	23 535	96.1	3.9	0.3	0.8	4.9	22 627	58.1	41.9	2.90	2.10
Bethel Park borough	5.3	13 871	96.3	3.7	0.4	1.4	6.0	13 362	79.9	20.1	2.69	1.66
Bristol township	2.2	20 486	96.3	3.7	0.4	0.8	5.0	19 733	76.3	23.7	2.94	2.33
Cheltenham township	4.4	14 897	96.3	3.7	0.7	0.6	5.0	14 346	64.5	35.5	2.77	1.93
Chester city	-11.9	14 976	85.6	14.4	0.2	3.2	7.4	12 814	47.7	52.3	2.69	2.60
Easton city	1.6	10 545	90.5	9.5	0.2	4.6	9.4	9 544	48.5	51.5	2.67	2.27
Erie city	-2.8	44 971	91.0	9.0	0.3	2.1	9.6	40 938	56.2	43.8	2.51	2.24
Falls township	5.0	13 528	97.4	2.6	0.1	0.7	3.8	13 170	73.5	26.5	2.84	2.11
Harrisburg city	-4.5	24 314	84.6	15.4	0.8	5.4	12.0	20 561	42.3	57.7	2.44	2.23
Haverford township	1.9	18 378	98.3	1.7	0.2	0.6	2.6	18 061	85.3	14.7	2.78	1.93
Hempfield township	3.2	16 799	95.2	4.8	0.3	1.3	9.4	15 997	84.4	15.6	2.52	1.93
Lancaster city	-1.2	23 024	90.9	9.1	0.2	4.3	8.5	20 933	46.6	53.4	2.58	2.46
Lower Makefield township	36.9	11 931	98.1	1.9	0.6	0.6	2.8	11 706	88.9	11.1	2.86	2.05
Lower Merion township	1.4	23 699	96.5	3.5	0.6	0.8	4.0	22 868	75.5	24.5	2.61	1.83
Lower Paxton township	15.7	19 606	94.8	5.2	0.4	1.4	8.6	18 584	65.9	34.1	2.58	1.89
McCandless township	6.0	11 697	95.4	4.6	0.4	0.9	10.7	11 159	78.2	21.8	2.68	1.79
Manheim township	21.6	13 434	96.5	3.5	0.8	1.3	4.3	12 961	76.0	24.0	2.61	2.03
Middletown township	5.8	15 713	97.5	2.5	0.2	0.7	3.9	15 321	77.4	22.6	3.06	1.97
Millcreek township	15.3	22 369	94.9	5.1	1.0	1.8	5.4	21 217	72.0	28.0	2.65	1.80
Mount Lebanon township	-0.3	14 089	96.6	3.4	0.4	1.0	5.4	13 610	75.3	24.7	2.61	1.64
Municipality of Monroeville borough	4.6	13 159	94.0	6.0	0.5	0.9	11.2	12 376	69.7	30.3	2.52	1.78
New Castle city	-5.7	11 709	91.6	8.4	0.2	2.5	9.3	10 727	64.6	35.4	2.47	2.15
Norristown borough	-1.3	13 531	88.9	11.1	0.2	4.6	10.1	12 028	48.1	51.9	2.70	2.35
Northampton township	17.2	13 138	99.1	0.9	0.2	0.1	3.0	13 014	93.1	6.9	3.09	1.93
North Huntingdon township	9.8	11 578	96.9	3.1	0.2	0.7	7.2	11 216	88.8	11.2	2.62	2.03
Penn Hills township	-1.6	20 355	95.8	4.2	0.1	1.4	4.7	19 490	79.7	20.3	2.47	2.01
Philadelphia city	-2.2	661 958	89.1	10.9	0.3	1.9	7.0	590 071	59.3	40.7	2.65	2.23
Pittsburgh city	-6.3	163 366	88.0	12.0	0.5	2.8	8.8	143 739	52.1	47.9	2.37	1.95
Plum borough	13.3	10 624	96.7	3.3	0.2	0.8	5.9	10 270	79.8	20.2	2.74	2.03
Radnor township	5.2	10 731	96.4	3.6	0.6	0.5	3.9	10 347	63.3	36.7	2.76	1.76
Reading city	-4.1	34 314	87.8	12.2	0.2	4.9	9.1	30 113	51.0	49.0	2.74	2.51
Ridley township	1.6	12 544	96.6	3.4	0.1	1.0	6.7	12 121	75.9	24.1	2.71	2.00
Ross township	1.8	14 422	96.3	3.7	0.4	0.9	5.5	13 892	74.9	25.1	2.46	1.67
Scranton city	-4.1	35 336	88.6	11.4	0.3	2.8	10.1	31 303	54.5	45.5	2.49	2.04
Shaler township	2.8	12 334	96.7	3.3	0.2	1.1	6.8	11 932	85.9	14.1	2.56	1.97
State College borough	9.9	12 488	96.3	3.7	0.7	0.8	2.9	12 024	22.8	77.2	2.32	2.30
Tredyffrin township	7.0	12 551	97.4	2.6	0.6	0.7	3.2	12 223	78.6	21.4	2.50	1.88
Upper Darby township	-0.6	34 322	94.8	5.2	0.1	2.0	6.0	32 551	62.3	37.7	2.80	2.01
Upper Dublin township	11.8	9 344	98.2	1.8	0.2	0.4	6.3	9 174	88.8	11.2	2.88	2.03
Upper Merion township	9.8	12 151	95.3	4.7	1.1	0.7	6.8	11 575	67.4	32.6	2.54	1.81
Warminster township	4.6	11 644	97.5	2.5	0.1	0.4	5.0	11 350	74.3	25.7	2.81	2.53
Wilkes-Barre city	-7.6	20 294	88.5	11.5	0.3	2.8	11.9	17 961	53.5	46.5	2.41	1.95
Williamsport city	-2.9	13 524	90.4	9.6	0.2	2.9	8.7	12 219	44.8	55.2	2.47	2.16
York city	-4.4	18 534	87.1	12.9	0.1	4.1	12.8	16 137	46.8	53.2	2.51	2.45
RHODE ISLAND	8.1	439 837	92.9	7.1	3.0	1.0	5.0	408 424	60.0	40.0	2.66	2.19
Coventry town	12.6	13 059	96.5	3.5	1.5	0.6	3.2	12 596	81.3	18.7	2.75	2.12
Cranston city	5.5	32 068	96.5	3.5	0.3	0.9	4.1	30 954	66.9	33.1	2.64	1.96
Cumberland town	13.3	12 572	97.0	3.0	0.3	0.4	4.0	12 198	76.7	23.3	2.76	2.03
East Providence city	2.9	21 309	96.3	3.7	0.3	0.7	3.5	20 530	58.9	41.1	2.63	1.92
Johnston town	12.0	11 574	96.7	3.3	0.4	0.7	4.1	11 197	71.4	28.6	2.70	1.90
Newport city	3.3	13 226	87.4	12.6	6.5	1.5	6.7	11 566	41.9	58.1	2.22	2.03
North Kingstown town	16.8	10 743	94.5	5.5	2.5	1.1	3.3	10 154	74.4	25.6	2.73	2.10
North Providence town	8.3	14 867	96.5	3.5	0.5	0.7	3.9	14 351	60.3	39.7	2.55	1.75
Pawtucket city	1.1	31 819	94.4	5.6	0.2	1.1	5.5	30 047	44.4	55.6	2.59	2.26
Providence city	5.9	67 915	91.9	8.1	0.5	2.3	6.1	62 389	34.6	65.4	2.71	2.49
South Kingstown town	24.8	11 291	82.1	17.9	15.3	0.7	3.9	9 268	74.9	25.1	2.72	2.10
Warwick city	6.2	37 085	95.8	4.2	1.3	1.1	3.9	35 517	72.7	27.3	2.58	1.87
West Warwick town	6.6	13 186	94.8	5.2	0.5	1.1	6.0	12 498	54.4	45.6	2.59	2.07
Woonsocket city	1.0	18 757	94.6	5.4	0.2	0.9	5.1	17 750	35.0	65.0	2.66	2.22
VERMONT	14.2	294 382	81.7	18.3	14.6	1.4	4.2	240 634	70.6	29.4	2.58	2.11
Burlington city	8.2	16 395	96.9	3.1	1.1	0.6	1.6	15 885	41.5	58.5	2.39	2.06
WISCONSIN	14.4	2 321 144	89.8	10.2	6.1	1.2	5.6	2 084 544	68.4	31.6	2.66	2.15
Beloit city	0.5	14 262	93.7	6.3	0.1	1.9	8.2	13 370	61.9	38.1	2.60	2.53
Brookfield city	16.3	14 208	97.8	2.2	0.6	0.6	3.8	13 891	89.9	10.1	2.81	2.06

Table E. Towns

STATE MCD code	Town	Population, 2000				Population, 1990				Population and population characteristics, 2000					
										Race (percent)					
										One race					
		Land area, 2000[1] (sq km)	Total persons	Rank within state	Per square kilometer	Land area, 1990[1] (sq km)	Total persons	Rank within state	Per square kilometer	White	Black or African American	American Indian or Alaska Native	Asian	Native Hawaiian and other Pacific Islander	Some other race
		1	2	3	4	5	6	7	8	9	10	11	12	13	14
	WISCONSIN—Cont'd														
55 26275	Fond du Lac city	43.7	42 203	13	965.7	33.1	37 755	13	1 140.6	93.6	1.9	0.5	1.5	0.0	1.3
55 27300	Franklin city	89.7	29 494	23	328.8	89.7	21 855	23	243.6	90.8	5.2	0.4	2.1	0.0	0.7
55 31000	Green Bay city	113.6	102 313	3	900.6	113.5	96 466	3	849.9	85.9	1.4	3.3	3.8	0.0	3.7
55 31175	Greenfield city	29.9	35 476	18	1 186.5	29.9	33 403	18	1 117.2	93.7	1.0	0.4	2.3	0.0	1.3
55 37825	Janesville city	71.3	59 498	9	834.5	60.9	52 210	9	857.3	95.3	1.3	0.2	1.0	0.0	1.0
55 39225	Kenosha city	61.7	90 352	5	1 464.4	55.8	80 426	5	1 441.3	83.6	7.7	0.4	1.0	0.0	4.8
55 40775	La Crosse city	52.2	51 818	10	992.7	47.6	51 140	10	1 074.4	91.6	1.6	0.5	4.7	0.0	0.4
55 48000	Madison city	177.9	208 054	2	1 169.5	149.6	190 766	2	1 275.2	84.0	5.8	0.4	5.8	0.0	1.7
55 48500	Manitowoc city	43.7	34 053	19	779.2	37.3	32 521	19	871.9	93.1	0.6	0.6	3.8	0.1	0.9
55 51000	Menomonee Falls village	86.2	32 647	21	378.7	86.2	26 840	21	311.4	96.5	1.5	0.2	0.9	0.0	0.2
55 53000	Milwaukee city	248.5	596 974	1	2 402.3	248.6	628 088	1	2 526.5	50.0	37.3	0.9	2.9	0.1	6.1
55 56375	New Berlin city	95.4	38 220	17	400.6	95.4	33 592	17	352.1	95.8	0.4	0.2	2.3	0.0	0.5
55 58800	Oak Creek city	74.1	28 456	24	384.0	74.1	19 513	24	263.3	92.0	1.8	0.6	2.4	0.0	1.7
55 60500	Oshkosh city	61.2	62 916	8	1 028.0	46.5	55 006	8	1 182.9	92.7	2.2	0.5	3.0	0.0	0.5
55 66000	Racine city	40.2	81 855	4	2 036.2	40.0	84 298	4	2 107.5	68.9	20.3	0.4	0.6	0.1	7.1
55 72975	Sheboygan city	36.0	50 792	11	1 410.9	34.3	49 587	11	1 445.7	87.6	0.9	0.5	6.5	0.0	2.8
55 78650	Superior city	95.7	27 368	20	286.0	95.7	27 134	20	283.5	94.3	0.7	2.2	0.8	0.0	0.3
55 84250	Waukesha city	56.0	64 825	7	1 157.6	44.9	56 894	7	1 267.1	91.2	1.3	0.3	2.2	0.0	3.3
55 84475	Wausau city	42.7	38 426	14	899.9	36.5	37 060	14	1 015.3	85.9	0.5	0.6	11.4	0.0	0.3
55 84675	Wauwatosa city	34.3	47 271	12	1 378.2	34.3	49 366	12	1 439.2	94.0	2.0	0.3	1.9	0.1	0.5
55 85300	West Allis city	29.4	61 254	6	2 083.5	29.4	63 221	6	2 150.4	94.0	1.3	0.7	1.3	0.0	1.2
55 85350	West Bend city	32.9	28 152	22	855.7	26.0	24 470	22	941.2	97.3	0.3	0.4	0.5	0.0	0.6

[1] Dry land or land partially or temporarily covered by water.

Table E. Towns

	Population and population characteristics, 2000 (cont'd)								Population and population characteristics, 1990				
	Race (percent) (cont'd)								Race (percent)				
	Race alone or in combination												
Town	Two or more races	White	Black	American Indian or Alaska Native	Asian	Native Hawaiian and other Pacific Islander	Some other race	Hispanic[1]	White	Black or African American	American Indian or Alaska Native	Asian and Pacific Islander	Hispanic[1]
	15	16	17	18	19	20	21	22	23	24	25	26	27
WISCONSIN—Cont'd												
Fond du Lac city	1.2	94.7	2.2	1.0	1.8	0.0	1.6	2.9	97.8	0.3	0.5	0.8	1.5
Franklin city	0.9	91.6	5.4	0.6	2.3	0.1	1.0	2.6	94.6	3.7	0.4	0.8	1.6
Green Bay city	2.0	87.5	1.9	4.1	4.1	0.1	4.3	7.1	94.2	0.5	2.5	2.3	1.1
Greenfield city	1.3	94.9	1.3	0.7	2.5	0.1	1.9	3.9	97.6	0.4	0.4	1.0	2.0
Janesville city	1.2	96.4	1.7	0.6	1.2	0.1	1.3	2.6	98.1	0.6	0.2	0.8	1.1
Kenosha city	2.4	85.7	8.6	1.0	1.3	0.1	5.7	10.0	89.8	6.4	0.4	0.6	5.9
La Crosse city	1.3	92.6	2.0	0.9	5.1	0.2	0.6	1.1	93.8	0.7	0.4	4.9	0.9
Madison city	2.3	86.0	6.8	0.9	6.5	0.1	2.2	4.1	90.7	4.2	0.4	3.9	2.0
Manitowoc city	1.0	94.0	0.8	0.9	4.1	0.1	1.2	2.5	96.4	0.2	0.5	2.5	1.1
Menomonee Falls village	0.7	97.2	1.7	0.4	1.0	0.0	0.3	1.2	98.8	0.3	0.2	0.5	0.6
Milwaukee city	2.7	52.1	38.6	1.5	3.4	0.1	7.2	12.0	63.4	30.5	0.9	1.9	6.3
New Berlin city	0.7	96.5	0.6	0.4	2.5	0.0	0.6	1.6	98.4	0.2	0.2	1.0	0.8
Oak Creek city	1.5	93.3	2.2	1.0	2.8	0.0	2.4	4.5	96.9	0.7	0.5	0.9	3.2
Oshkosh city	1.0	93.6	2.4	0.8	3.4	0.1	0.7	1.7	96.3	0.8	0.5	2.2	0.8
Racine city	2.6	71.1	21.6	0.9	0.8	0.1	8.2	14.0	76.4	18.4	0.3	0.5	8.1
Sheboygan city	1.7	88.8	1.1	0.9	7.1	0.2	3.5	6.0	94.4	0.2	0.4	3.9	2.5
Superior city	1.7	95.8	1.1	3.2	1.1	0.1	0.5	0.8	96.1	0.5	2.4	0.8	0.5
Waukesha city	1.7	92.7	1.7	0.8	2.5	0.1	4.0	8.6	95.4	0.6	0.3	1.3	5.9
Wausau city	1.2	86.8	0.8	1.1	12.0	0.2	0.5	1.0	93.1	0.1	0.7	6.0	0.7
Wauwatosa city	1.2	95.0	2.5	0.5	2.3	0.1	0.8	1.7	97.3	1.2	0.2	1.0	1.0
West Allis city	1.4	95.3	1.8	1.2	1.6	0.1	1.6	3.5	98.2	0.3	0.5	0.6	1.5
West Bend city	0.8	98.0	0.5	0.8	0.7	0.0	0.8	1.8	98.7	0.1	0.4	0.5	0.9

[1] Hispanic persons may be of any race.

Table E. Towns

Town	Population and population characteristics, 2000										
	Age (percent)										
	Under 5 years	5 to 17 years	18 to 24 years	25 to 34 years	35 to 44 years	45 to 54 years	55 to 64 years	65 to 74 years	75 years and over	Median age (years)	Percent Female
	28	29	30	31	32	33	34	35	36	37	38
WISCONSIN—Cont'd											
Fond du Lac city	6.5	17.6	10.7	14.1	15.3	13.1	7.4	6.5	8.8	35.7	53.0
Franklin city	5.6	17.8	8.4	13.1	19.7	16.9	8.7	6.0	3.9	37.9	47.8
Green Bay city	7.2	18.3	11.6	15.7	16.0	12.5	7.0	5.7	6.1	33.2	50.7
Greenfield city	4.5	14.4	8.1	13.1	15.2	14.4	9.9	9.3	11.1	41.7	53.1
Janesville city	7.0	19.2	8.3	15.1	16.2	12.7	8.7	6.8	6.1	35.3	51.1
Kenosha city	7.5	19.7	10.1	15.0	16.5	11.8	7.2	5.9	6.3	33.6	50.8
La Crosse city	4.8	14.0	24.4	12.6	12.4	10.3	6.7	6.6	8.3	30.1	52.9
Madison city	5.2	12.7	21.4	17.8	14.4	12.8	6.5	4.6	4.7	30.6	50.9
Manitowoc city	6.2	18.0	8.2	12.2	15.7	12.9	8.5	8.2	10.2	38.6	51.6
Menomonee Falls village	6.6	18.4	5.4	11.9	18.6	13.6	9.8	8.9	6.8	39.2	51.6
Milwaukee city	8.0	20.7	12.2	15.8	14.4	11.4	6.6	5.5	5.4	30.6	52.2
New Berlin city	6.0	18.8	6.4	10.8	18.2	16.7	10.4	7.6	5.1	39.8	50.8
Oak Creek city	6.7	18.3	9.3	16.7	18.7	13.7	7.8	5.3	3.5	34.5	50.2
Oshkosh city	5.4	15.3	18.1	14.8	14.9	11.5	6.8	6.0	7.1	32.4	50.0
Racine city	8.0	20.7	9.9	14.3	15.7	12.0	7.2	6.0	6.3	33.1	51.3
Sheboygan city	7.0	18.6	9.2	14.6	15.4	11.8	7.7	6.9	8.9	35.4	51.0
Superior city	6.0	16.7	12.9	13.1	14.8	13.7	7.9	6.4	8.6	35.9	52.0
Waukesha city	7.4	17.3	10.8	17.2	16.4	13.0	7.2	5.0	5.6	33.4	51.1
Wausau city	6.2	19.2	9.6	13.0	14.5	12.5	7.9	7.3	9.8	36.5	52.0
Wauwatosa city	6.5	16.8	5.5	14.5	16.7	14.2	7.6	7.4	10.8	39.1	53.7
West Allis city	5.8	15.7	8.4	15.3	16.9	12.9	7.7	7.5	9.8	37.8	51.8
West Bend city	7.2	18.3	8.6	15.4	15.7	12.6	7.7	6.4	8.0	35.3	51.8

Table E. Towns

Town	Population and population characteristics, 1990										Population—change, 1980–2000				
	Age (percent)										Total persons			Percent change	
	Under 5 years	5 to 17 years	18 to 24 years	25 to 34 years	35 to 44 years	45 to 54 years	55 to 64 years	65 to 74 years	75 years and over	Percent Female	2000	1990	1980	1990–2000	1980–1990
	39	40	41	42	43	44	45	46	47	48	49	50	51	52	53
WISCONSIN—Cont'd															
Fond du Lac city	7.2	18.9	9.7	16.5	14.5	8.6	8.2	8.3	8.0	53.1	42 203	37 755	35 863	11.8	5.3
Franklin city	7.1	10.6	0.1	19.1	19.7	10.8	8.3	5.2	2.1	48.1	29 494	21 855	NA	35.0	NA
Green Bay city	8.1	17.8	11.2	19.5	14.8	8.6	7.4	6.9	5.8	52.1	102 313	96 466	87 899	6.1	9.7
Greenfield city	5.3	13.7	9.6	17.3	15.9	10.3	10.7	9.7	7.4	53.0	35 476	33 403	31 467	6.2	6.2
Janesville city	8.1	18.3	9.6	17.9	14.6	10.7	8.8	6.7	5.3	51.6	59 498	52 210	51 071	14.0	2.2
Kenosha city	8.3	18.8	10.5	17.9	14.2	8.9	7.9	7.4	6.2	52.0	90 352	80 426	77 685	12.3	3.5
La Crosse city	6.6	13.7	22.4	15.7	11.7	6.8	7.6	7.8	7.9	53.8	51 818	51 140	48 347	1.3	5.8
Madison city	6.2	12.3	22.2	20.3	15.2	8.3	6.3	5.0	4.2	50.9	208 054	190 766	170 616	9.1	11.8
Manitowoc city	6.6	17.3	8.1	15.9	14.0	8.9	9.3	9.7	10.1	52.7	34 053	32 547	32 521	4.7	-0.1
Menomonee Falls village	6.7	17.1	8.1	16.5	13.7	13.5	12.8	7.4	4.3	50.7	32 647	26 840	27 845	21.6	-3.6
Milwaukee city	8.6	18.8	12.0	19.1	13.5	8.0	7.6	6.9	5.5	52.7	596 974	628 088	636 212	-5.0	-1.3
New Berlin city	6.7	19.0	7.9	15.8	17.7	13.6	10.7	5.8	2.7	50.1	38 220	33 592	30 529	13.8	10.0
Oak Creek city	6.9	19.4	9.9	19.3	15.9	11.7	8.8	5.4	2.8	50.4	28 456	19 513	NA	45.8	NA
Oshkosh city	6.6	14.6	19.0	17.2	13.1	7.8	7.6	7.1	6.9	52.3	62 916	55 006	49 620	14.4	10.9
Racine city	8.8	20.4	9.4	18.1	14.1	8.2	8.1	7.2	5.8	52.8	81 855	84 298	85 730	-2.9	-1.7
Sheboygan city	7.5	18.1	9.0	17.5	13.9	8.6	8.4	8.8	8.2	51.8	50 792	49 587	48 085	2.4	3.1
Superior city	7.0	18.0	11.0	15.4	14.3	8.8	8.0	8.9	8.6	52.8	27 368	27 134	29 571	0.9	-8.2
Waukesha city	8.0	18.6	11.4	20.2	15.9	9.2	6.7	5.2	4.7	51.5	64 825	56 894	50 319	13.9	13.1
Wausau city	7.6	17.1	10.0	16.7	14.3	8.1	8.8	9.0	8.4	53.3	38 426	37 060	32 426	3.7	14.3
Wauwatosa city	6.7	15.4	6.0	17.3	15.5	9.5	9.8	9.5	10.3	54.0	47 271	49 366	51 308	-4.2	-3.8
West Allis city	6.6	15.0	9.0	20.0	13.5	8.8	9.2	9.7	8.2	52.7	61 254	63 221	63 982	-3.1	-1.2
West Bend city	8.2	20.4	10.0	17.6	14.9	9.7	7.2	6.4	5.6	51.2	28 152	24 470	NA	15.0	NA

Table E. Towns

Town	Total population	Total in house-holds	House-holder	Spouse	Child		Other relatives		Nonrelatives		Total in group quarters	Institutionalized population			Noninstitutionalized population		
					Total	Own child under 18 years	Total	Under 18 years	Total	Unmar-ried partner		Correc-tional institu-tions	Nurs-ing homes	Other institu-tions	Col-lege dormi-tories	Mili-tary quar-ters	Other
	54	55	56	57	58	59	60	61	62	63	64	65	66	67	68	69	70
WISCONSIN—Cont'd																	
Fond du Lac city	42 203	93.6	39.4	19.1	27.5	22.7	2.2	0.8	5.5	2.4	6.4	2.7	2.0	0.0	0.9	0.0	0.8
Franklin city	29 494	92.9	35.9	22.7	28.9	22.3	2.3	0.6	3.0	1.4	7.1	6.4	0.0	0.0	0.0	0.0	0.8
Green Bay city	102 313	97.4	40.7	17.9	28.5	23.7	3.2	1.1	7.0	3.1	2.6	0.2	0.8	0.1	1.0	0.0	0.5
Greenfield city	35 476	97.4	44.2	20.9	24.3	17.6	3.1	0.9	4.8	2.4	2.6	0.0	1.7	0.0	0.0	0.0	0.9
Janesville city	59 498	98.5	40.2	20.5	29.5	24.3	2.7	1.1	5.6	2.7	1.5	0.0	0.6	0.2	0.0	0.0	0.7
Kenosha city	90 352	96.7	38.1	17.9	30.9	24.6	4.4	1.9	5.4	2.6	3.3	0.7	0.9	0.0	1.2	0.0	0.5
La Crosse city	51 818	90.7	40.7	14.7	21.3	17.4	2.1	0.6	11.9	2.6	9.3	0.5	1.2	0.2	6.4	0.0	0.9
Madison city	208 054	93.8	42.8	15.8	20.0	16.7	2.4	0.7	12.8	3.0	6.2	0.4	0.5	0.4	4.4	0.0	0.6
Manitowoc city	34 053	97.2	41.8	20.5	27.9	22.9	2.3	0.7	4.7	2.3	2.8	0.6	1.7	0.0	0.0	0.0	0.5
Menomonee Falls village	32 647	99.3	39.3	25.0	30.3	24.2	2.1	0.6	2.5	1.2	0.7	0.0	0.6	0.0	0.0	0.0	0.1
Milwaukee city	596 974	97.3	38.9	12.5	31.1	24.1	7.3	3.5	7.5	2.8	2.7	0.4	0.6	0.1	1.1	0.0	0.5
New Berlin city	38 220	99.4	37.9	25.8	30.8	23.9	2.2	0.6	2.8	1.3	0.6	0.0	0.3	0.0	0.0	0.0	0.2
Oak Creek city	28 456	99.7	39.5	22.3	30.5	23.8	2.7	0.8	4.7	2.5	0.3	0.0	0.1	0.0	0.0	0.0	0.3
Oshkosh city	62 916	88.3	38.3	16.9	23.4	19.4	2.0	0.7	7.7	2.5	11.7	4.0	1.0	0.6	5.4	0.0	0.7
Racine city	81 855	97.7	38.4	16.2	31.7	25.0	5.8	2.7	5.6	2.6	2.3	1.2	0.6	0.1	0.0	0.0	0.4
Sheboygan city	50 792	97.6	40.9	19.7	29.2	24.0	2.8	1.0	4.9	2.5	2.4	0.4	1.4	0.0	0.0	0.0	0.5
Superior city	27 368	95.9	42.4	17.5	26.8	21.1	2.5	0.9	6.7	3.2	4.1	0.3	1.1	0.1	1.8	0.0	0.8
Waukesha city	64 825	96.2	39.6	19.9	28.8	23.4	2.6	0.8	5.3	2.2	3.8	1.1	0.8	0.0	1.5	0.0	0.4
Wausau city	38 426	96.6	40.8	19.0	28.9	23.9	2.7	0.8	5.3	2.4	3.4	0.6	1.6	0.0	0.4	0.0	0.7
Wauwatosa city	47 271	97.9	43.1	21.6	27.6	22.4	2.0	0.5	3.7	1.5	2.1	0.0	1.0	0.7	0.0	0.0	0.3
West Allis city	61 254	98.5	45.1	18.5	26.5	20.1	3.1	0.9	5.4	2.6	1.5	0.1	0.9	0.0	0.0	0.0	0.5
West Bend city	28 152	98.6	40.4	21.6	29.9	24.3	2.0	0.7	4.7	2.3	1.4	0.4	0.8	0.0	0.0	0.0	0.3

Table E. Towns

	Households by type, 2000												Households, 1990		
Town		Family households						Nonfamily households							
				Married couple		Female householder[1]			Householder living alone						
	Total households	Total	With own children under 18 years	Total	With own children under 18 years	Total	With own children under 18 years	Total	Total	65 years and over	Average household size	Average family size	Total households	Female householder[1]	Householder living alone
	71	72	73	74	75	76	77	78	79	80	81	82	83	84	85

WISCONSIN—Cont'd

Fond du Lac city	16 638	61.8	30.6	48.4	21.8	9.8	6.7	38.2	30.9	12.5	2.38	3.00	14 637	9.4	28.0
Franklin city	10 602	72.6	33.8	63.2	28.8	6.0	3.7	27.4	22.5	6.9	2.58	3.06	7 434	5.8	18.1
Green Bay city	41 591	59.3	30.6	44.1	20.5	10.8	7.6	40.7	31.6	9.9	2.40	3.06	38 383	10.3	29.0
Greenfield city	15 697	58.4	22.6	47.3	17.3	8.0	3.8	41.6	34.6	14.4	2.20	2.87	13 785	8.3	28.7
Janesville city	23 894	65.9	32.7	51.1	22.8	10.5	7.2	34.1	27.4	9.7	2.45	2.99	20 388	9.6	25.1
Kenosha city	34 411	65.5	34.1	47.1	22.5	13.9	9.1	34.5	28.4	10.3	2.54	3.13	29 919	12.9	25.6
La Crosse city	21 110	48.4	22.0	36.1	14.4	9.3	6.0	51.6	37.0	13.0	2.23	2.93	19 970	9.4	33.2
Madison city	89 019	47.7	22.1	37.0	15.7	7.8	5.0	52.3	35.3	7.1	2.19	2.87	77 361	7.9	30.9
Manitowoc city	14 235	61.9	28.6	49.0	20.3	9.1	6.1	38.1	32.5	14.6	2.32	2.96	13 144	8.5	31.1
Menomonee Falls village	12 844	72.4	32.4	63.6	28.0	6.5	3.2	27.6	23.7	11.2	2.52	3.01	9 817	7.4	17.7
Milwaukee city	232 188	58.2	30.5	32.2	14.3	21.1	13.9	41.8	33.5	9.5	2.62	3.25	240 540	19.8	30.3
New Berlin city	14 495	76.2	34.0	68.0	30.1	5.7	2.9	23.8	19.0	7.0	2.52	3.03	11 695	5.3	13.6
Oak Creek city	11 239	67.0	33.3	56.4	27.2	7.1	4.3	33.0	25.3	7.0	2.52	3.10	7 081	5.7	20.3
Oshkosh city	24 082	56.7	27.3	44.3	19.3	9.1	6.1	43.3	32.4	11.7	2.31	2.95	20 957	9.6	29.7
Racine city	31 449	64.9	33.9	42.2	19.2	17.9	12.1	35.1	29.4	10.5	2.54	3.15	31 767	16.7	26.0
Sheboygan city	20 779	61.6	29.7	48.2	21.0	9.4	6.4	38.4	32.2	12.6	2.39	3.05	19 703	8.1	28.4
Superior city	11 609	57.7	27.9	41.3	17.1	12.3	8.5	42.3	34.2	13.9	2.26	2.91	11 001	13.8	31.3
Waukesha city	25 663	63.5	32.5	50.2	24.1	9.8	6.5	36.5	29.0	9.2	2.43	3.04	21 235	9.0	25.1
Wausau city	15 678	59.5	27.8	46.7	19.8	9.5	6.0	40.5	33.6	14.1	2.37	3.08	14 718	9.7	29.0
Wauwatosa city	20 388	60.4	28.3	50.0	22.9	7.9	4.2	39.6	33.9	15.4	2.27	2.96	19 848	7.2	28.8
West Allis city	27 604	55.7	25.5	41.2	17.2	10.6	6.3	44.3	37.3	14.0	2.19	2.92	26 797	9.8	31.5
West Bend city	11 375	66.1	32.7	53.3	24.6	9.4	6.1	33.9	27.5	12.0	2.44	3.00	8 686	8.9	21.3

[1] No spouse present.

Table E. Towns

Town	Percent change of households, 1990–2000	Total housing units	Occupied housing units (percent)	Housing occupancy					Housing tenure				
				Vacant housing units					Occupied housing units				
				Total	For seasonal, recreational, or occasional use	Homeowner vacancy rate (percent)	Rental vacancy rate (percent)		Total	Percent owner-occupied housing units	Percent renter-occupied housing units	Average household size of owner-occupied units	Average household size of renter-occupied units
	86	87	88	89	90	91	92		93	94	95	96	97
WISCONSIN—Cont'd													
Fond du Lac city	13.7	17 519	95.0	5.0	0.2	1.4	7.5		16 638	61.7	38.3	2.59	2.03
Franklin city	42.6	10 936	96.9	3.1	0.2	0.8	6.0		10 602	78.4	21.6	2.75	1.97
Green Bay city	8.4	43 123	96.4	3.6	0.3	0.9	4.1		41 591	56.0	44.0	2.56	2.19
Greenfield city	13.9	16 203	96.9	3.1	0.3	0.9	3.4		15 697	59.5	40.5	2.49	1.78
Janesville city	17.2	25 083	95.3	4.7	0.3	1.3	7.4		23 894	68.2	31.8	2.60	2.14
Kenosha city	15.0	36 004	95.6	4.4	0.3	1.3	4.9		34 411	62.2	37.8	2.69	2.29
La Crosse city	5.7	22 233	94.9	5.1	0.5	1.0	5.1		21 110	50.9	49.1	2.39	2.06
Madison city	15.1	92 394	96.3	3.7	0.3	0.8	3.9		89 019	47.7	52.3	2.40	2.00
Manitowoc city	8.3	15 007	94.9	5.1	0.4	1.1	7.7		14 235	67.6	32.4	2.51	1.93
Menomonee Falls village	30.8	13 140	97.7	2.3	0.3	0.8	2.8		12 844	77.4	22.6	2.75	1.75
Milwaukee city	-3.5	249 225	93.2	6.8	0.2	1.3	6.0		232 188	45.3	54.7	2.79	2.42
New Berlin city	23.9	14 921	97.1	2.9	0.2	1.1	4.8		14 495	81.3	18.7	2.89	1.91
Oak Creek city	58.7	11 897	94.5	5.5	0.1	1.2	8.7		11 239	60.9	39.1	2.49	1.95
Oshkosh city	14.9	25 420	94.7	5.3	0.4	1.3	6.5		24 082	57.5	42.5	2.61	2.06
Racine city	-1.0	33 414	94.1	5.9	0.2	1.0	7.2		31 449	60.3	39.7	2.55	2.44
Sheboygan city	5.5	21 762	95.5	4.5	0.4	1.2	5.1		20 779	61.1	38.9	2.47	2.13
Superior city	5.5	12 196	95.2	4.8	0.3	0.6	6.2		11 609	61.7	38.3	2.71	1.93
Waukesha city	20.9	26 856	95.6	4.4	0.2	0.7	6.3		25 663	56.5	43.5	2.54	2.06
Wausau city	6.5	16 668	94.1	5.9	0.4	1.6	7.7		15 678	61.7	38.3	2.55	2.10
Wauwatosa city	2.7	20 917	97.5	2.5	0.2	0.5	3.5		20 388	67.8	32.2	2.47	1.68
West Allis city	3.0	28 708	96.2	3.8	0.1	1.1	4.5		27 604	58.1	41.9	2.65	1.80
West Bend city	31.0	11 926	95.4	4.6	0.3	2.0	6.1		11 375	62.2	37.8		2.08

Congressional Districts of the 107th Congress

(For explanation of symbols, see page xi.)

Page

688	**AL**(District 1)—**CA**(District 44)
695	**CA**(District 45)—**GA**(District 11)
702	**HI**(District 1)—**LA**(District 6)
709	**LA**(District 7)—**MO**(District 3)
716	**MO**(District 4)—**NY**(District 24)
723	**NY**(District 25)—**PA**(District 7)
730	**PA**(District 8)—**TX**(District 27)
737	**TX**(District 28)—**WY**(At Large)

Table F—Congressional Districts

Table F. Congressional Districts 107th Congress

STATE District	Population, 2000 Land area, 2000[1] (sq km)	Total persons	Rank	Per square kilometer	Population, 1990 Land area, 1990[1] (sq km)	Total persons	Rank	Per square kilometer	Population and population characteristics, 2000 — Race (percent) — One race White	Black or African American	American Indian or Alaska Native	Asian	Native Hawaiian and other Pacific Islander	Some other race
	1	2	3	4	5	6	7	8	9	10	11	12	13	14
ALABAMA	131 426.0	4 447 100	X	33.8	131 443.0	4 040 389	X	30.7	71.1	26.0	0.5	0.7	0.0	0.7
District 1	17 572.1	646 181	X	36.8	17 574.0	577 226	X	33.0	68.0	28.6	1.0	1.0	0.0	0.4
District 2	26 235.3	650 321	X	24.8	26 241.0	577 227	X	22.0	69.3	28.0	0.4	0.7	0.0	0.5
District 3	22 582.4	643 525	X	28.5	22 583.0	577 227	X	20.0	72.6	25.3	0.3	0.5	0.0	0.5
District 4	23 668.5	643 275	X	27.2	23 671.0	577 227	X	24.0	90.3	6.3	0.7	0.2	0.0	1.4
District 5	11 418.3	654 886	X	57.4	11 419.0	577 227	X	51.0	79.9	16.2	0.7	1.0	0.0	0.7
District 6	7 370.6	664 795	X	90.2	7 372.0	577 226	X	78.0	82.1	14.9	0.3	1.2	0.0	0.7
District 7	22 579.0	544 117	X	24.1	22 583.0	577 227	X	26.0	28.7	70.0	0.2	0.2	0.0	0.3
ALASKA	1 481 347.0	626 932	X	0.4	1 477 268.0	550 043	X	0.4	69.3	3.5	15.6	4.0	0.5	1.6
At Large	1 481 346.9	626 932	X	0.4	1 477 268.0	550 043	X	0.0	69.3	3.5	15.6	4.0	0.5	1.6
ARIZONA	294 312.0	5 130 632	X	17.4	294 333.0	3 665 339	X	12.5	75.5	3.1	5.0	1.8	0.1	11.6
District 1	545.6	829 492	X	1 520.3	546.0	610 872	X	1 120.0	76.7	3.9	2.0	3.1	0.2	11.0
District 2	45 865.9	773 824	X	16.9	45 869.0	610 871	X	13.0	55.8	5.1	4.4	1.0	0.1	29.9
District 3	107 779.2	997 565	X	9.3	107 783.0	610 871	X	6.0	82.6	2.5	2.6	1.3	0.1	8.3
District 4	500.6	735 344	X	1 468.9	501.0	610 871	X	1 220.0	81.6	3.1	1.8	2.4	0.1	8.2
District 5	32 866.3	793 256	X	24.1	32 870.0	610 871	X	19.0	82.1	3.1	1.2	2.1	0.1	8.4
District 6	106 754.6	1 001 151	X	9.4	106 765.0	610 872	X	6.0	73.0	1.5	15.6	1.2	0.1	6.5
ARKANSAS	134 856.0	2 673 400	X	19.8	134 875.0	2 350 624	X	17.4	80.0	15.7	0.7	0.8	0.1	1.5
District 1	42 986.3	629 974	X	14.7	42 989.0	588 588	X	14.0	80.0	17.7	0.4	0.3	0.0	0.5
District 2	15 338.4	666 058	X	43.4	15 343.0	587 412	X	38.0	76.6	19.5	0.5	0.9	0.0	1.1
District 3	29 804.0	764 853	X	25.7	29 810.0	589 523	X	20.0	90.8	1.8	1.3	1.3	0.1	2.8
District 4	46 727.2	612 515	X	13.1	46 733.0	585 202	X	13.0	70.1	26.6	0.5	0.4	0.0	1.3
CALIFORNIA	403 933.0	33 871 648	X	83.9	403 970.0	29 811 427	X	73.8	59.5	6.7	1.0	10.9	0.3	16.8
District 1	27 977.8	644 525	X	23.0	27 981.0	573 082	X	21.0	76.6	4.6	2.8	3.6	0.3	7.4
District 2	73 589.3	633 808	X	8.6	73 595.0	573 322	X	8.0	86.3	1.6	2.4	2.5	0.1	3.4
District 3	19 828.2	675 618	X	34.1	19 827.0	571 374	X	29.0	73.2	3.8	1.3	6.4	0.3	9.9
District 4	27 988.1	725 180	X	25.9	27 990.0	571 033	X	20.0	87.7	1.6	1.1	2.7	0.2	3.5
District 5	391.4	669 412	X	1 710.3	391.0	573 684	X	1 468.0	52.6	13.6	1.2	15.5	0.8	9.8
District 6	4 120.1	644 600	X	156.5	4 121.0	571 227	X	139.0	82.6	2.1	0.9	3.8	0.2	6.6
District 7	906.2	636 367	X	702.2	903.0	572 773	X	634.0	50.5	16.5	0.7	15.1	0.6	10.5
District 8	89.1	617 094	X	6 925.9	89.0	573 247	X	6 432.0	49.5	9.1	0.5	28.4	0.6	7.6
District 9	188.8	597 285	X	3 163.6	189.0	573 458	X	3 037.0	41.3	26.2	0.6	17.4	0.4	8.9
District 10	2 650.2	713 341	X	269.2	2 651.0	572 008	X	216.0	77.2	3.7	0.5	9.3	0.3	4.6
District 11	4 730.2	684 178	X	144.6	4 731.0	571 772	X	121.0	60.4	6.6	1.1	11.0	0.4	14.5
District 12	277.3	615 370	X	2 219.1	277.0	571 535	X	2 060.0	52.9	2.7	0.4	30.9	1.0	6.8
District 13	619.0	678 177	X	1 095.6	619.0	572 441	X	925.0	44.5	7.4	0.6	30.1	0.9	10.3
District 14	1 236.0	615 917	X	498.3	1 236.0	571 131	X	462.0	64.9	3.2	0.4	18.9	0.8	8.1
District 15	1 172.3	612 416	X	522.4	1 172.0	572 485	X	489.0	69.5	2.1	0.5	17.6	0.3	5.4
District 16	2 450.3	689 817	X	281.5	2 452.0	571 551	X	233.0	41.3	3.6	1.0	26.9	0.4	21.7
District 17	12 655.2	653 209	X	51.6	12 657.0	570 981	X	45.0	61.2	2.7	1.1	5.0	0.3	24.8
District 18	10 715.6	683 642	X	63.8	10 719.0	571 393	X	53.0	65.0	3.1	1.2	4.9	0.3	20.1
District 19	19 786.1	709 622	X	35.9	19 793.0	573 043	X	29.0	63.7	4.5	1.8	7.2	0.1	18.0
District 20	17 763.1	711 574	X	40.1	17 760.0	573 282	X	32.0	43.0	5.9	1.6	4.7	0.1	40.3
District 21	23 091.1	666 684	X	28.9	23 093.0	571 300	X	25.0	68.1	4.5	1.6	3.0	0.2	18.3
District 22	15 633.9	631 659	X	40.4	15 638.0	572 891	X	37.0	77.3	2.2	1.1	3.6	0.2	11.6
District 23	4 613.9	642 427	X	139.2	4 616.0	571 483	X	124.0	66.9	2.1	1.0	5.3	0.2	20.3
District 24	786.2	629 832	X	801.1	786.0	572 563	X	728.0	75.5	2.9	0.5	7.8	0.1	8.9
District 25	5 328.1	699 526	X	131.3	5 330.0	573 105	X	108.0	67.4	7.9	0.8	7.6	0.2	11.6
District 26	181.0	660 224	X	3 647.6	181.0	571 523	X	3 159.0	46.4	5.1	1.0	6.6	0.1	35.1
District 27	789.5	600 986	X	761.2	789.0	572 594	X	726.0	62.5	6.6	0.5	13.2	0.1	10.2
District 28	1 202.4	609 233	X	506.7	1 203.0	572 927	X	476.0	56.9	4.8	0.7	19.4	0.2	13.7
District 29	305.3	584 823	X	1 915.6	305.0	571 566	X	1 871.0	76.5	3.3	0.3	9.8	0.1	5.4
District 30	96.5	582 745	X	6 038.8	96.0	572 538	X	5 935.0	34.7	3.0	1.0	19.6	0.1	36.0
District 31	195.6	600 376	X	3 069.4	195.0	572 643	X	2 932.0	34.9	1.3	1.1	28.2	0.1	30.2
District 32	121.9	586 031	X	4 807.5	122.0	572 595	X	4 695.0	31.8	32.9	0.7	7.8	0.2	21.6
District 33	123.8	600 695	X	4 852.1	124.0	570 943	X	4 610.0	37.6	3.9	1.2	4.5	0.1	47.8
District 34	234.1	617 343	X	2 637.1	234.0	573 047	X	2 449.0	46.9	1.9	1.2	8.9	0.2	36.0
District 35	112.8	607 944	X	5 389.6	113.0	570 882	X	5 062.0	22.9	34.6	0.8	4.3	0.4	32.6
District 36	599.7	591 448	X	986.2	600.0	573 663	X	957.0	67.5	3.9	0.5	15.3	0.4	7.7
District 37	187.0	616 103	X	3 294.7	187.0	572 049	X	3 060.0	24.6	25.9	0.9	8.3	1.3	34.6
District 38	196.3	634 392	X	3 231.7	192.0	572 657	X	2 978.0	52.1	10.7	0.9	8.9	0.7	21.5
District 39	271.1	622 921	X	2 297.8	271.0	573 574	X	2 113.0	59.3	3.1	0.7	18.4	0.3	13.8
District 40	77 476.1	674 431	X	8.7	77 473.0	573 625	X	7.0	71.9	6.6	1.6	3.5	0.3	11.4
District 41	595.4	666 225	X	1 119.0	595.0	572 663	X	963.0	52.8	5.9	0.8	14.7	0.2	21.0
District 42	543.5	700 491	X	1 288.9	543.0	571 844	X	1 052.0	48.8	12.4	1.2	3.7	0.3	28.3
District 43	1 939.6	736 634	X	379.8	1 936.0	571 231	X	295.0	64.7	6.2	1.0	4.6	0.3	18.4
District 44	16 464.0	742 718	X	45.1	16 470.0	571 583	X	35.0	65.3	6.5	1.3	2.7	0.2	20.1

[1]Dry land or land partially or temporarily covered by water.

Table F. Congressional Districts 107th Congress

STATE District	Population and population characteristics, 2000 (cont'd)								Population and population characteristics, 1990				
	Race (percent) (cont'd)								Race (percent)				
	Race alone or in combination												
	Two or more races	White	Black	American Indian or Alaska Native	Asian	Native Hawaiian and other Pacific Islander	Some other race	Hispanic[1]	White	Black or African American	American Indian or Alaska Native	Asian and Pacific Islander	Hispanic[1]
	15	16	17	18	19	20	21	22	23	24	25	26	27
ALABAMA	1.0	72.0	26.3	1.0	0.9	0.1	0.9	1.7	73.6	25.3	0.4	0.5	0.6
District 1	1.0	68.8	28.9	1.5	1.2	0.1	0.6	1.3	69.9	28.5	0.9	0.7	0.8
District 2	1.1	70.2	28.3	0.9	0.9	0.1	0.7	1.5	74.8	24.1	0.3	0.6	0.8
District 3	0.8	73.3	25.6	0.7	0.7	0.1	0.6	1.3	73.1	26.0	0.2	0.5	0.6
District 4	1.1	91.3	6.5	1.3	0.3	0.1	1.7	3.0	92.5	6.6	0.6	0.2	0.4
District 5	1.5	81.2	16.6	1.5	1.2	0.1	0.9	2.0	83.4	14.9	0.6	0.9	0.8
District 6	0.8	82.8	15.1	0.6	1.4	0.1	0.9	1.8	89.7	9.2	0.2	0.8	0.6
District 7	0.6	29.1	70.3	0.4	0.4	0.1	0.5	1.0	32.1	67.5	0.1	0.2	0.3
ALASKA	5.4	74.0	4.3	19.0	5.2	0.9	2.4	4.1	75.5	4.1	15.6	3.6	3.2
At Large	5.4	74.0	4.3	19.0	5.2	0.9	2.4	4.1	75.5	4.1	15.6	3.6	3.2
ARIZONA	2.9	77.9	3.6	5.7	2.3	0.3	13.2	25.3	80.8	3.0	5.6	1.5	18.8
District 1	3.1	79.3	4.5	2.7	3.8	0.4	12.7	22.7	86.9	3.2	1.7	2.3	13.2
District 2	3.7	58.9	5.6	5.2	1.3	0.2	32.6	62.5	60.1	6.8	4.5	1.3	50.5
District 3	2.5	84.8	3.0	3.3	1.8	0.2	9.5	18.1	87.6	1.9	3.3	1.1	11.8
District 4	2.9	84.0	3.7	2.4	3.0	0.3	9.7	18.8	92.1	1.9	1.2	1.8	7.8
District 5	3.0	84.7	3.7	2.0	2.8	0.3	9.8	20.5	88.0	3.0	0.9	1.9	16.5
District 6	2.2	74.8	1.8	16.4	1.5	0.2	7.6	14.2	70.3	1.3	21.7	0.7	13.0
ARKANSAS	1.3	81.2	16.0	1.4	1.0	0.1	1.8	3.2	82.7	15.9	0.5	0.5	0.8
District 1	1.0	80.9	18.0	1.0	0.5	0.1	0.7	1.6	81.3	17.9	0.3	0.3	0.6
District 2	1.3	77.8	19.9	1.0	1.2	0.1	1.4	2.4	81.2	17.6	0.4	0.6	0.8
District 3	1.8	92.5	2.1	2.4	1.5	0.2	3.2	5.8	95.9	1.6	1.1	1.0	1.1
District 4	1.1	71.0	27.0	1.0	0.5	0.1	1.6	2.7	72.4	26.6	0.4	0.2	0.8
CALIFORNIA	4.7	63.4	7.4	1.9	12.3	0.7	19.4	32.4	69.0	7.4	0.8	9.6	25.8
District 1	4.6	80.6	5.3	4.5	4.8	0.7	9.1	16.5	85.0	3.9	2.7	3.6	11.2
District 2	3.7	89.6	2.0	4.2	3.1	0.3	4.5	8.5	91.6	1.5	2.4	2.4	6.0
District 3	5.1	77.5	4.7	2.7	8.0	0.7	12.1	19.5	82.2	3.2	1.4	5.5	14.2
District 4	3.3	90.7	1.9	2.3	3.6	0.4	4.5	9.2	92.7	1.8	1.3	2.1	7.4
District 5	6.5	57.2	15.3	2.6	17.8	1.5	12.6	19.9	65.6	12.8	1.2	13.2	14.7
District 6	3.9	86.0	2.7	1.9	4.9	0.5	8.2	14.4	90.0	2.4	0.8	3.4	8.9
District 7	6.1	55.1	18.0	1.9	17.3	1.2	13.2	21.6	62.7	16.6	0.8	14.4	13.3
District 8	4.4	52.8	10.0	1.3	30.1	0.9	9.7	16.1	52.0	12.8	0.5	27.8	15.7
District 9	5.2	45.1	27.9	1.7	19.2	0.8	11.2	17.3	45.4	31.8	0.6	15.7	12.0
District 10	4.4	81.0	4.3	1.4	11.1	0.6	6.4	12.1	87.9	2.3	0.6	6.4	8.7
District 11	6.0	65.0	7.5	2.3	13.1	0.8	17.7	27.8	74.9	5.8	1.1	11.5	21.1
District 12	5.2	57.1	3.4	1.0	33.4	1.6	9.3	15.9	65.2	4.1	0.4	25.7	14.3
District 13	6.2	49.2	8.3	1.5	32.8	1.7	13.1	22.1	64.2	7.4	0.8	19.4	18.4
District 14	3.8	68.1	3.7	0.9	20.6	1.1	9.8	17.2	78.1	4.9	0.4	12.2	13.5
District 15	4.6	73.4	2.7	1.3	19.5	0.6	7.4	13.3	82.2	2.3	0.6	11.3	10.8
District 16	5.1	45.2	4.2	1.7	28.7	0.8	24.8	39.8	55.1	5.2	0.8	21.1	36.8
District 17	4.9	65.3	3.3	2.0	6.5	0.7	27.4	42.6	69.5	4.4	0.9	6.3	31.6
District 18	5.4	69.5	3.7	2.4	6.1	0.7	23.3	36.4	75.7	2.8	1.0	6.0	26.0
District 19	4.8	67.5	5.1	2.9	8.3	0.4	20.8	32.9	73.5	3.3	1.3	7.4	23.6
District 20	4.5	46.7	6.3	2.4	5.4	0.2	43.7	63.7	48.7	6.4	1.0	5.5	55.4
District 21	4.3	71.8	5.1	2.8	3.8	0.3	20.7	31.4	77.7	4.0	1.5	3.2	20.3
District 22	4.0	80.8	2.7	2.2	4.6	0.4	13.6	27.0	81.7	2.8	1.0	3.9	21.3
District 23	4.2	70.5	2.6	1.9	6.4	0.5	22.5	37.7	76.9	2.5	0.8	5.2	30.0
District 24	4.4	79.3	3.5	1.1	9.1	0.3	11.3	19.8	84.6	2.1	0.4	6.4	13.5
District 25	4.6	71.3	8.8	1.7	8.9	0.4	13.9	25.0	80.0	4.5	0.7	6.5	16.4
District 26	5.7	51.3	5.7	1.6	7.3	0.3	39.8	65.4	53.5	6.2	0.6	7.3	52.7
District 27	6.9	68.7	7.3	1.1	14.6	0.3	15.1	23.1	70.9	8.3	0.4	10.5	20.6
District 28	4.4	60.4	5.4	1.4	20.8	0.4	16.3	31.6	70.9	5.7	0.5	13.0	24.1
District 29	4.6	80.5	4.0	0.9	11.2	0.3	8.0	12.1	83.8	3.5	0.3	7.7	13.2
District 30	5.5	39.2	3.6	1.7	20.7	0.3	40.3	64.3	43.6	3.5	0.5	21.3	61.5
District 31	4.2	38.2	1.6	1.7	29.3	0.3	33.3	59.4	48.3	1.7	0.5	22.8	58.5
District 32	5.0	35.5	34.6	1.5	8.8	0.4	24.8	37.1	32.2	40.3	0.4	7.9	30.2
District 33	4.9	41.8	4.2	1.7	4.9	0.2	52.2	86.0	35.7	4.5	0.6	4.3	83.7
District 34	4.9	51.0	2.3	1.9	9.7	0.4	39.8	72.4	56.7	1.9	0.6	9.3	62.3
District 35	4.5	26.2	35.7	1.4	4.9	0.6	36.0	54.2	21.3	42.7	0.4	6.0	43.1
District 36	4.7	71.4	4.6	1.2	17.2	0.7	9.8	18.8	77.7	3.2	0.5	12.5	14.9
District 37	4.6	27.9	26.8	1.5	9.2	1.7	37.8	57.2	26.2	33.6	0.5	10.8	45.1
District 38	5.1	56.1	11.7	1.7	10.3	1.1	24.6	40.1	69.2	7.7	0.7	9.1	25.7
District 39	4.3	62.9	3.5	1.4	19.9	0.6	16.2	30.4	72.8	2.6	0.5	13.8	22.8
District 40	4.8	76.0	7.5	2.8	4.5	0.6	13.8	23.8	82.1	5.4	1.5	3.5	16.1
District 41	4.5	56.5	6.5	1.5	16.0	0.4	23.9	40.9	68.0	6.8	0.5	10.1	31.5
District 42	5.3	53.1	13.5	2.1	4.6	0.6	31.7	50.8	66.0	11.1	0.9	4.0	34.3
District 43	4.8	68.7	7.0	2.0	5.7	0.6	21.1	35.5	75.7	5.9	0.8	4.3	25.0
District 44	4.0	68.6	7.3	2.1	3.4	0.4	22.4	38.5	76.5	5.1	1.1	2.9	28.1

[1]Hispanic persons may be of any race.

Table F. Congressional Districts 107th Congress

STATE District	Population and population characteristics, 2000										
	Age (percent)										
	Under 5 years	5 to 17 years	18 to 24 years	25 to 34 years	35 to 44 years	45 to 54 years	55 to 64 years	65 to 74 years	75 years and over	Median age (years)	Percent Female
	28	29	30	31	32	33	34	35	36	37	38
ALABAMA	6.7	18.6	9.9	13.6	15.4	13.5	9.3	7.1	5.9	35.8	51.7
District 1	7.0	19.7	9.3	13.0	15.3	13.3	9.4	7.1	5.8	35.7	51.8
District 2	6.6	18.8	9.6	13.8	15.5	10.4	9.2	6.9	6.1	35.7	51.4
District 3	6.4	18.1	11.7	13.5	14.7	13.2	9.4	7.1	5.8	35.2	51.3
District 4	6.4	17.8	8.6	13.4	14.9	13.6	10.5	8.1	6.6	37.5	51.3
District 5	6.5	18.3	9.1	13.7	16.6	13.7	9.8	7.0	5.3	36.5	51.2
District 6	6.5	17.3	10.1	15.1	16.2	14.1	8.5	6.6	5.7	35.6	51.7
District 7	7.2	20.5	11.1	12.1	14.4	13.0	8.4	7.0	6.2	34.3	53.8
ALASKA	7.6	22.8	9.1	14.3	18.2	15.1	7.1	3.6	2.1	32.4	48.3
At Large	7.6	22.8	9.1	14.3	18.2	15.1	7.1	3.6	2.1	32.4	48.3
ARIZONA	7.5	19.2	10.0	14.5	15.0	12.2	8.6	7.1	5.9	34.2	50.1
District 1	7.7	18.1	12.9	18.3	16.3	11.9	6.6	4.3	3.9	30.8	49.4
District 2	9.3	22.9	12.0	15.3	13.7	10.2	6.9	5.6	3.9	28.6	49.0
District 3	6.9	18.4	7.7	12.4	14.2	12.2	10.1	9.7	8.5	38.3	50.7
District 4	7.2	18.1	10.0	15.5	16.0	13.6	8.7	5.8	5.1	34.5	50.3
District 5	6.1	17.1	10.0	12.7	14.9	13.5	9.8	8.5	7.4	37.9	50.8
District 6	7.7	20.5	8.5	13.4	15.0	12.2	9.1	7.7	5.9	35.0	50.1
ARKANSAS	6.8	18.7	9.8	13.2	14.9	13.1	9.6	7.4	6.6	36.0	51.2
District 1	6.8	19.2	9.4	12.6	14.6	12.9	10.0	7.7	6.7	36.3	51.4
District 2	6.8	18.3	10.2	14.4	15.6	13.5	8.9	6.5	5.7	35.2	51.5
District 3	7.0	18.5	10.0	13.4	14.8	12.8	9.6	7.5	6.5	35.8	50.7
District 4	6.5	18.7	9.5	12.3	14.5	13.1	9.9	8.1	7.5	37.2	51.3
CALIFORNIA	7.3	20.0	9.9	15.4	16.2	12.8	7.7	5.6	5.0	33.3	50.2
District 1	6.2	19.1	9.4	12.7	15.7	14.9	9.0	6.6	6.3	36.8	49.4
District 2	5.7	19.2	9.7	10.8	14.7	14.8	9.9	7.9	7.4	38.4	50.0
District 3	7.1	20.8	11.3	13.4	15.6	12.6	7.9	6.0	5.4	33.2	51.1
District 4	5.9	19.2	7.3	11.6	17.2	15.8	9.8	7.3	6.0	38.8	49.6
District 5	7.4	20.6	10.1	15.3	15.6	12.7	7.3	5.5	5.4	32.7	51.5
District 6	5.7	16.9	7.7	12.9	17.0	17.0	9.7	6.2	6.7	39.1	50.7
District 7	7.2	19.7	9.0	14.5	16.7	14.3	8.1	5.4	5.0	34.7	51.1
District 8	4.1	10.2	9.1	24.5	17.4	13.5	8.2	6.7	6.3	35.9	48.6
District 9	6.3	16.2	11.3	17.6	15.8	14.1	7.8	5.3	5.5	34.1	51.7
District 10	6.8	19.7	6.5	12.7	18.5	15.6	9.2	5.6	5.4	37.4	50.9
District 11	7.9	22.7	9.6	13.4	15.6	12.4	7.7	5.6	5.0	32.4	50.3
District 12	5.5	14.9	8.2	16.5	17.0	14.8	9.2	7.0	6.8	37.7	51.1
District 13	7.3	18.6	8.9	16.7	17.7	13.2	7.7	5.3	4.6	34.2	50.2
District 14	6.6	15.8	8.2	17.6	17.8	13.8	8.5	5.9	5.9	35.9	49.4
District 15	6.5	16.9	8.0	16.0	18.6	14.4	9.0	5.7	5.0	36.4	50.1
District 16	8.0	19.7	10.9	18.3	16.6	12.0	7.0	4.3	3.2	31.2	48.7
District 17	7.4	19.9	11.3	15.6	15.7	13.0	7.1	5.2	4.8	32.2	49.0
District 18	8.2	23.9	10.0	13.6	15.2	11.7	7.3	5.4	4.7	30.9	50.3
District 19	7.9	22.2	10.2	13.4	15.0	12.7	7.7	5.8	5.1	32.2	51.4
District 20	9.3	25.0	12.0	15.7	14.8	9.8	5.8	4.1	3.5	27.3	46.0
District 21	8.1	23.0	9.7	13.3	15.2	12.2	7.8	5.7	4.9	32.0	50.3
District 22	5.9	17.7	13.5	12.9	15.2	13.1	8.1	6.7	6.7	34.9	49.5
District 23	7.6	21.2	9.4	14.2	16.6	13.2	7.7	5.3	4.8	33.5	49.9
District 24	6.5	17.6	7.8	14.6	17.5	14.8	9.2	6.3	5.7	37.0	51.0
District 25	7.5	22.5	9.1	13.7	18.1	13.2	7.4	4.8	3.7	33.2	49.8
District 26	9.2	22.3	11.4	18.1	15.4	10.5	5.8	3.9	3.4	28.9	49.5
District 27	6.1	17.5	8.0	15.3	17.4	14.2	8.8	6.4	6.3	36.8	51.7
District 28	6.5	20.1	9.5	13.2	16.1	14.1	8.6	6.1	5.8	35.4	51.8
District 29	4.1	9.8	9.9	21.5	17.7	13.9	8.7	6.8	7.6	37.3	50.3
District 30	8.4	19.8	11.4	19.4	15.6	11.0	6.5	4.5	3.5	30.2	49.5
District 31	8.3	21.1	11.2	16.9	14.7	11.0	6.9	5.4	4.5	30.5	50.8
District 32	7.3	18.5	10.8	17.6	15.8	11.9	7.4	5.4	5.2	32.5	52.2
District 33	9.9	23.1	13.8	18.8	13.9	9.2	5.0	3.4	2.9	26.6	48.1
District 34	8.3	22.6	10.8	15.8	14.5	11.0	7.1	5.6	4.2	30.2	50.6
District 35	10.0	24.6	11.2	16.9	14.6	9.9	6.0	4.0	3.0	27.6	51.4
District 36	6.0	15.7	7.3	16.6	18.4	14.5	9.3	6.6	5.5	37.2	50.5
District 37	9.8	26.4	11.5	15.6	14.0	9.7	6.0	4.1	2.9	26.5	50.8
District 38	8.2	20.2	10.3	17.2	15.9	11.9	6.8	4.7	5.1	31.6	51.0
District 39	6.9	20.1	9.7	14.3	15.9	13.0	8.7	6.3	5.0	34.3	50.9
District 40	7.3	22.3	9.9	12.4	15.5	12.7	8.2	6.4	5.4	33.6	50.0
District 41	8.0	22.9	10.3	14.7	16.8	13.4	7.1	4.0	2.9	31.1	49.9
District 42	9.3	26.0	10.6	15.2	15.8	10.9	5.7	3.7	2.8	27.9	50.4
District 43	8.2	23.5	10.1	14.2	16.9	11.9	6.8	4.7	3.8	31.0	50.1
District 44	7.5	21.2	8.5	12.2	14.1	10.9	8.4	8.8	8.5	35.5	50.3

Table F. Congressional Districts 107th Congress

STATE District	Under 5 years	5 to 17 years	18 to 24 years	25 to 34 years	35 to 44 years	45 to 54 years	55 to 64 years	65 to 74 years	75 years and over	Percent Female	2000	1990	1980	1990–2000	1980–1990
	39	40	41	42	43	44	45	46	47	48	49	50	51	52	53
ALABAMA	7.0	19.2	11.0	16.0	14.4	10.4	9.0	7.5	5.5	52.1	4 447 100	4 040 389	3 894 025	10.1	3.8
District 1	7.5	20.7	10.0	15.8	14.3	10.3	8.8	7.4	5.2	52.2	646 181	577 226	NA	11.9	NA
District 2	7.2	19.5	10.5	16.2	14.6	10.3	8.7	7.4	5.7	51.7	650 321	577 227	NA	12.7	NA
District 3	6.7	18.9	13.4	15.2	13.8	10.1	9.0	7.5	5.4	51.6	643 525	577 227	NA	11.5	NA
District 4	6.4	18.8	9.8	14.8	14.2	11.3	10.0	8.4	6.3	51.9	643 275	577 227	NA	11.4	NA
District 5	6.9	18.0	10.7	17.7	14.8	11.4	9.2	6.8	4.4	51.2	654 886	577 227	NA	13.5	NA
District 6	6.6	16.9	11.4	17.7	16.1	10.5	8.8	7.0	5.1	52.0	664 795	577 226	NA	15.2	NA
District 7	7.8	21.7	10.9	15.0	13.3	8.8	8.6	7.7	6.3	54.1	544 117	577 227	NA	-5.7	NA
ALASKA	10.0	21.4	10.2	20.5	18.7	9.8	5.4	2.8	1.2	47.3	626 932	550 043	401 851	14.0	36.9
At Large	10.0	21.4	10.2	20.5	18.7	9.8	5.4	2.8	1.2	47.3	626 932	550 043	NA	14.0	NA
ARIZONA	8.0	18.8	10.7	17.3	14.4	9.5	8.2	7.9	5.1	50.6	5 130 632	3 665 339	2 716 546	40.0	34.9
District 1	8.0	17.0	13.2	21.5	15.5	9.1	6.5	5.3	3.9	50.3	829 492	610 872	NA	35.8	NA
District 2	9.8	22.4	12.2	17.3	13.1	8.4	7.2	6.0	3.7	49.7	773 824	610 871	NA	26.7	NA
District 3	7.3	17.9	7.8	15.1	13.5	9.2	9.4	11.8	8.0	50.9	997 565	610 871	NA	63.3	NA
District 4	7.0	17.0	10.2	17.9	16.3	11.7	8.7	6.9	4.3	51.3	735 344	610 871	NA	20.4	NA
District 5	6.9	16.9	11.0	16.5	14.9	9.9	9.0	9.0	5.9	50.9	793 256	610 871	NA	29.9	NA
District 6	8.9	21.5	9.9	15.7	13.2	9.0	8.3	8.5	5.1	50.5	1 001 151	610 872	NA	63.9	NA
ARKANSAS	7.0	19.4	10.1	15.3	13.9	10.4	9.1	8.3	6.6	51.8	2 673 400	2 350 624	2 286 357	13.7	2.8
District 1	7.2	20.5	9.6	14.5	13.3	10.4	9.3	8.4	6.8	52.1	629 974	588 588	NA	7.0	NA
District 2	7.2	18.9	10.8	17.1	15.0	10.3	8.4	7.1	5.2	51.9	666 058	587 412	NA	13.4	NA
District 3	6.8	18.5	10.3	15.1	13.9	10.4	9.3	8.9	6.8	51.2	764 853	589 523	NA	29.7	NA
District 4	6.8	19.8	9.7	14.3	13.4	10.2	9.4	8.9	7.4	52.0	612 515	585 202	NA	4.7	NA
CALIFORNIA	8.1	18.0	11.5	19.1	15.6	9.8	7.5	6.2	4.3	49.9	33 871 648	29 811 427	23 667 765	13.6	25.7
District 1	7.4	18.7	9.4	16.6	16.7	10.2	8.2	7.6	5.2	49.4	644 525	573 082	NA	12.5	NA
District 2	7.2	18.6	9.7	14.5	15.4	10.0	9.1	9.4	6.0	50.3	633 808	573 322	NA	10.6	NA
District 3	8.0	18.9	11.6	17.8	14.9	9.7	8.1	6.7	4.3	50.8	675 618	571 374	NA	18.2	NA
District 4	7.0	18.3	8.0	16.7	18.0	11.2	8.8	7.6	4.4	49.1	725 180	571 033	NA	27.0	NA
District 5	8.3	18.2	10.6	19.4	15.6	9.0	7.4	6.7	4.7	51.6	669 412	573 684	NA	16.7	NA
District 6	6.7	15.6	8.5	17.0	19.3	11.9	8.1	7.4	5.6	50.9	644 600	571 227	NA	12.8	NA
District 7	8.3	18.1	9.9	18.9	17.0	10.1	7.4	6.3	4.0	50.9	636 367	572 773	NA	11.1	NA
District 8	4.9	11.1	10.5	22.8	18.2	10.3	8.5	7.5	6.1	49.3	617 094	573 247	NA	7.6	NA
District 9	7.1	14.9	13.0	19.2	17.4	9.6	6.9	6.5	5.4	51.1	597 285	573 458	NA	4.2	NA
District 10	7.1	17.5	8.5	17.0	18.3	13.0	8.2	6.3	4.2	50.6	713 341	572 008	NA	24.7	NA
District 11	8.7	20.5	10.4	17.5	15.0	9.5	7.6	6.4	4.4	49.8	684 178	571 772	NA	19.7	NA
District 12	6.1	14.2	9.6	18.8	16.9	11.2	9.3	7.9	6.0	51.5	615 370	571 535	NA	7.7	NA
District 13	8.0	17.5	9.9	20.4	16.6	10.3	7.8	5.9	3.5	50.4	678 177	572 441	NA	18.5	NA
District 14	6.5	13.6	10.8	20.8	16.8	11.5	8.5	6.9	4.5	49.5	615 917	571 131	NA	7.8	NA
District 15	6.8	15.5	10.0	20.2	17.2	12.4	8.4	5.8	3.7	50.2	612 416	572 485	NA	7.0	NA
District 16	8.9	19.5	12.3	21.2	15.8	9.1	6.1	4.2	2.9	48.4	689 817	571 551	NA	20.7	NA
District 17	8.3	18.2	13.1	18.8	15.6	8.6	6.9	6.0	4.5	49.0	653 209	570 981	NA	14.4	NA
District 18	9.4	22.1	10.2	17.6	14.2	9.0	7.2	6.1	4.2	50.0	683 642	571 393	NA	19.6	NA
District 19	8.6	20.8	10.4	16.7	15.1	9.5	7.7	6.7	4.5	51.2	709 622	573 043	NA	23.8	NA
District 20	10.4	24.4	11.9	17.7	12.5	7.8	6.3	5.1	3.7	48.0	711 574	573 282	NA	24.1	NA
District 21	9.0	21.3	9.6	17.6	14.8	9.5	7.5	6.5	4.3	50.3	666 684	571 300	NA	16.7	NA
District 22	7.0	15.7	14.6	17.7	15.0	9.1	7.8	7.5	5.5	49.3	631 659	572 891	NA	10.3	NA
District 23	8.3	19.5	10.9	18.5	16.1	10.0	7.2	5.6	3.9	49.4	642 427	571 483	NA	12.4	NA
District 24	6.5	14.8	10.3	18.7	17.3	12.3	9.1	6.7	4.3	50.6	629 832	572 563	NA	10.0	NA
District 25	8.8	18.8	10.6	20.3	16.5	10.3	7.2	4.9	2.6	49.1	699 526	573 105	NA	22.1	NA
District 26	9.4	18.9	13.4	21.6	14.5	8.2	6.0	4.8	3.2	48.9	660 224	571 523	NA	15.5	NA
District 27	6.8	15.4	10.0	19.4	16.2	11.0	8.2	7.0	6.0	51.4	600 986	572 594	NA	5.0	NA
District 28	7.5	18.6	10.8	16.9	16.1	10.9	8.3	6.5	4.6	51.3	609 233	572 927	NA	6.3	NA
District 29	4.3	8.8	11.4	21.9	17.8	11.0	8.9	8.3	7.7	50.6	584 823	571 566	NA	2.3	NA
District 30	9.0	18.4	14.1	21.1	14.6	8.4	6.2	4.6	3.5	49.1	582 745	572 538	NA	1.8	NA
District 31	9.1	20.4	13.6	19.5	13.4	8.2	6.8	5.2	3.7	50.3	600 376	572 643	NA	4.8	NA
District 32	7.9	16.2	12.2	20.4	15.1	9.4	7.5	6.5	4.9	52.1	586 031	572 595	NA	2.3	NA
District 33	10.6	22.2	16.3	20.1	12.7	6.9	4.8	3.6	2.9	47.5	600 695	570 943	NA	5.2	NA
District 34	8.9	20.9	12.6	18.1	13.5	9.2	7.9	5.8	3.2	50.3	617 343	573 047	NA	7.7	NA
District 35	10.4	21.4	13.1	20.0	13.3	8.3	6.1	4.5	2.9	50.9	607 944	570 882	NA	6.5	NA
District 36	6.2	13.3	10.0	21.4	17.3	12.1	9.3	6.7	3.7	49.8	591 448	573 663	NA	3.1	NA
District 37	10.8	23.6	13.1	18.4	12.9	8.2	6.2	4.3	2.6	50.4	616 103	572 049	NA	7.7	NA
District 38	8.1	15.9	12.5	20.8	14.8	8.9	7.2	6.9	4.9	49.8	634 392	572 657	NA	10.8	NA
District 39	7.2	17.8	12.1	17.8	15.0	11.6	9.1	6.1	3.3	50.3	622 921	573 574	NA	8.6	NA
District 40	8.9	20.1	10.3	17.5	14.6	9.0	7.7	7.1	4.7	49.7	674 431	573 625	NA	17.6	NA
District 41	9.3	20.9	11.8	19.4	16.9	9.8	5.9	3.8	2.2	49.2	666 225	572 663	NA	16.3	NA
District 42	10.8	22.6	10.8	20.0	14.7	8.1	5.7	4.4	2.8	50.5	700 491	571 844	NA	22.5	NA
District 43	9.4	20.4	11.1	19.6	15.3	9.1	6.7	5.4	3.1	49.4	736 634	571 231	NA	29.0	NA
District 44	8.5	18.5	8.7	16.5	12.7	8.2	8.7	10.6	7.6	50.6	742 718	571 583	NA	29.9	NA

Table F. Congressional Districts 107th Congress

STATE District		Household relationship, 2000															
		In households (percent)										In group quarters (percent)					
					Child		Other relatives		Nonrelatives				Institutionalized population			Noninstitutionalized population		
	Total population	Total in households	House-holder	Spouse	Total	Own child under 18 years	Total	Under 18 years	Total	Unmarried partner	Total in group quarters	Correctional institutions	Nursing homes	Other institutions	College dormitories	Military quarters	Other
	54	55	56	57	58	59	60	61	62	63	64	65	66	67	68	69	70
ALABAMA	4 447 100	97.4	39.1	20.4	29.3	22.3	5.4	2.5	3.3	1.3	2.6	0.8	0.6	0.1	0.7	0.1	0.3
District 1	646 181	97.8	38.0	19.9	30.8	23.3	5.9	2.9	3.3	1.4	2.2	0.6	0.5	0.2	0.5	0.0	0.4
District 2	650 321	96.3	38.9	20.3	29.1	22.7	4.9	2.3	3.1	1.3	3.7	1.8	0.6	0.1	0.3	0.7	0.2
District 3	643 525	96.9	39.1	20.1	28.1	21.3	5.6	2.7	4.0	1.4	3.1	1.0	0.7	0.1	1.1	0.0	0.2
District 4	643 275	98.5	39.6	23.2	28.3	21.7	4.7	2.1	2.7	1.2	1.5	0.3	0.8	0.0	0.1	0.0	0.2
District 5	654 886	97.8	39.7	22.1	28.9	22.6	4.1	1.8	2.9	1.2	2.2	0.6	0.5	0.1	0.7	0.1	0.2
District 6	664 795	97.9	40.2	21.9	28.0	21.9	4.0	1.5	3.8	1.2	2.1	0.3	0.6	0.2	0.9	0.0	0.2
District 7	544 117	96.6	37.7	14.2	32.3	22.3	9.2	4.8	3.2	1.5	3.4	0.7	0.6	0.1	1.5	0.0	0.5
ALASKA	626 932	96.9	35.3	18.6	32.9	27.8	3.9	1.7	6.2	2.6	3.1	0.5	0.1	0.1	0.3	0.6	1.4
At Large	626 932	96.9	35.3	18.6	32.9	27.8	3.9	1.7	6.2	2.6	3.1	0.5	0.1	0.1	0.3	0.6	1.4
ARIZONA	5 130 632	97.9	37.1	19.2	29.2	23.3	6.2	2.6	6.2	2.3	2.1	0.9	0.3	0.1	0.3	0.1	0.5
District 1	829 492	98.7	38.2	17.3	28.5	23.2	5.9	2.0	8.8	2.7	1.3	0.0	0.3	0.1	0.6	0.0	0.4
District 2	773 824	96.8	30.6	15.2	34.1	26.4	10.7	5.0	6.2	2.2	3.2	1.7	0.2	0.1	0.0	0.2	0.9
District 3	997 565	98.3	38.2	22.0	27.5	22.3	5.3	2.2	5.3	2.2	1.7	0.6	0.4	0.2	0.2	0.1	0.3
District 4	735 344	99.3	39.5	18.3	28.2	22.5	5.9	2.0	7.4	2.7	0.7	0.0	0.1	0.0	0.1	0.0	0.5
District 5	793 256	96.5	40.4	20.6	26.1	20.9	4.1	1.6	5.4	2.2	3.5	1.4	0.3	0.1	0.9	0.4	0.5
District 6	1 001 151	97.5	35.5	20.8	30.7	24.7	5.9	2.9	4.6	1.9	2.5	1.6	0.2	0.1	0.3	0.0	0.3
ARKANSAS	2 673 400	97.2	39.0	21.2	28.4	22.5	4.9	2.3	3.7	1.5	2.8	0.8	0.8	0.1	0.7	0.0	0.3
District 1	629 974	97.3	38.7	21.0	29.0	22.8	5.3	2.8	3.2	1.5	2.7	1.2	0.9	0.0	0.3	0.0	0.2
District 2	666 058	97.2	39.6	20.6	28.3	22.4	4.7	2.1	4.0	1.5	2.8	0.4	0.7	0.1	0.9	0.2	0.5
District 3	764 853	97.9	38.9	22.5	28.2	23.1	4.2	1.7	4.2	1.6	2.1	0.2	0.7	0.2	0.8	0.0	0.3
District 4	612 515	96.5	38.9	20.4	28.2	21.7	5.7	2.9	3.3	1.4	3.5	1.4	1.0	0.1	0.7	0.0	0.4
CALIFORNIA	33 871 648	97.6	34.0	17.4	31.1	23.7	8.4	2.8	6.8	2.0	2.4	0.7	0.4	0.1	0.4	0.2	0.7
District 1	644 525	95.2	36.5	18.7	28.0	22.2	5.4	2.1	6.6	2.5	4.8	2.3	0.5	0.4	0.4	0.3	0.9
District 2	633 808	96.6	38.7	20.0	27.2	22.2	4.1	1.8	6.6	2.3	3.4	1.7	0.4	0.1	0.5	0.1	0.6
District 3	675 618	97.9	35.8	18.5	31.1	24.8	5.7	2.2	6.8	2.2	2.1	0.2	0.5	0.1	0.7	0.0	0.5
District 4	725 180	96.9	37.6	21.8	28.4	22.9	3.9	1.5	5.3	2.1	3.1	1.6	0.4	0.2	0.0	0.0	0.9
District 5	669 412	98.2	37.3	15.6	31.0	24.4	7.4	2.8	6.9	2.6	1.8	0.3	0.4	0.2	0.1	0.1	0.7
District 6	644 600	96.7	39.0	19.0	25.9	20.5	4.7	1.4	8.1	2.7	3.3	1.2	0.5	0.1	0.3	0.1	1.2
District 7	636 367	98.7	35.1	17.1	31.1	23.0	8.9	3.1	6.5	2.3	1.3	0.2	0.4	0.1	0.0	0.0	0.6
District 8	617 094	97.4	43.4	12.4	18.2	11.5	9.2	2.2	14.2	3.4	2.6	0.2	0.3	0.2	0.4	0.0	1.6
District 9	597 285	97.6	39.7	13.8	25.7	19.0	8.4	2.8	10.0	2.9	2.4	0.2	0.3	0.1	0.9	0.0	0.9
District 10	713 341	98.3	36.7	22.0	30.6	24.7	4.2	1.3	4.8	1.8	1.7	0.8	0.3	0.1	0.2	0.0	0.3
District 11	684 178	97.5	33.0	18.0	33.8	26.7	7.4	2.9	5.3	2.1	2.5	0.7	0.4	0.2	0.3	0.0	0.9
District 12	615 370	98.7	36.8	18.6	26.3	17.9	9.1	2.1	7.9	2.0	1.3	0.0	0.4	0.1	0.2	0.0	0.6
District 13	678 177	99.1	34.3	18.7	31.0	22.5	10.5	2.9	6.3	1.7	0.9	0.0	0.4	0.0	0.1	0.0	0.4
District 14	615 917	97.5	38.1	19.9	25.8	20.4	5.9	1.5	7.7	1.9	2.5	0.3	0.5	0.1	1.1	0.0	0.5
District 15	612 416	98.6	37.0	20.3	28.0	21.4	5.9	1.6	7.3	2.0	1.4	0.0	0.4	0.0	0.6	0.0	0.4
District 16	689 817	98.0	28.2	15.9	31.4	22.6	13.8	4.1	8.7	1.7	2.0	0.6	0.2	0.1	0.3	0.0	0.7
District 17	653 209	95.7	31.7	16.8	30.3	23.4	9.0	3.1	7.9	2.0	4.3	2.0	0.3	0.1	0.7	0.4	0.9
District 18	683 642	97.9	31.6	17.9	35.7	28.1	7.7	3.1	5.0	2.0	2.1	0.8	0.4	0.1	0.1	0.0	0.8
District 19	709 622	97.9	33.9	18.1	33.6	26.7	6.8	2.7	5.5	2.1	2.1	1.0	0.3	0.1	0.2	0.0	0.5
District 20	711 574	92.7	25.3	14.7	37.3	29.2	10.0	4.1	5.4	1.7	7.3	6.0	0.3	0.1	0.0	0.2	0.7
District 21	666 684	97.6	33.9	18.3	34.0	27.5	6.5	2.9	5.0	2.1	2.4	1.2	0.3	0.2	0.0	0.1	0.5
District 22	631 659	94.9	35.5	18.1	26.5	20.9	5.8	2.0	9.0	1.9	5.1	1.8	0.4	0.4	1.6	0.1	0.8
District 23	642 427	98.2	31.7	18.6	32.9	24.9	8.5	3.0	6.4	1.7	1.8	0.4	0.3	0.1	0.1	0.2	0.8
District 24	629 832	98.6	37.5	19.6	28.8	22.1	6.2	1.5	6.5	2.0	1.4	0.0	0.4	0.1	0.4	0.0	0.6
District 25	699 526	96.9	32.4	18.7	33.8	27.0	6.5	2.1	5.4	1.8	3.1	1.8	0.2	0.2	0.4	0.0	0.4
District 26	660 224	98.9	28.7	14.3	34.9	26.4	13.3	4.0	7.8	2.1	1.1	0.0	0.3	0.2	0.0	0.0	0.5
District 27	600 986	98.4	38.0	18.6	29.1	21.2	7.7	1.8	5.3	1.8	1.6	0.0	0.7	0.1	0.1	0.0	0.7
District 28	609 233	97.7	32.7	18.6	32.4	23.1	9.1	2.8	4.9	1.4	2.3	0.0	0.7	0.2	0.8	0.0	0.5
District 29	584 823	96.6	49.7	15.4	17.3	12.9	4.7	0.7	10.1	3.0	3.4	0.0	0.5	0.1	1.9	0.0	0.9
District 30	582 745	98.6	32.1	13.8	32.6	24.0	12.5	3.4	7.7	2.3	1.4	0.0	0.4	0.2	0.2	0.0	0.7
District 31	600 376	98.7	27.1	14.8	34.6	24.0	15.6	4.6	6.5	1.4	1.3	0.0	0.5	0.1	0.4	0.0	0.4
District 32	586 031	98.6	37.1	13.2	29.6	21.6	10.7	3.5	8.1	2.2	1.4	0.0	0.3	0.0	0.4	0.0	0.6
District 33	600 695	95.3	25.3	12.4	36.3	27.5	14.3	4.5	7.1	1.8	4.7	2.0	0.3	0.1	0.5	0.0	1.7
District 34	617 343	99.0	27.0	15.6	35.9	24.5	14.6	5.4	5.8	1.5	1.0	0.0	0.3	0.3	0.1	0.0	0.3
District 35	607 944	99.4	29.4	12.2	37.5	28.5	13.5	5.1	6.7	2.0	0.6	0.0	0.2	0.1	0.0	0.0	0.3
District 36	591 448	98.7	40.9	19.1	26.3	19.8	5.6	1.6	6.8	2.2	1.3	0.0	0.4	0.0	0.5	0.0	0.5
District 37	616 103	98.7	25.4	12.6	39.1	29.0	15.3	6.0	6.3	1.7	1.3	0.2	0.2	0.0	0.1	0.0	0.8
District 38	634 392	98.1	35.2	15.2	32.1	24.8	8.8	2.9	6.7	2.5	1.9	0.2	0.5	0.3	0.4	0.0	0.5
District 39	622 921	98.7	32.4	19.1	32.9	23.6	8.9	2.8	5.4	1.4	1.3	0.0	0.4	0.0	0.4	0.0	0.5
District 40	674 431	96.7	34.6	18.7	32.3	26.0	6.1	2.7	5.1	2.0	3.3	0.6	0.4	0.6	0.2	1.1	0.4
District 41	666 225	97.5	29.0	18.0	35.7	26.9	9.6	3.3	5.2	1.5	2.5	1.5	0.1	0.1	0.3	0.0	0.4
District 42	700 491	98.5	28.6	15.8	38.2	29.9	10.3	4.3	5.6	2.0	1.5	0.4	0.2	0.1	0.0	0.0	0.7
District 43	736 634	97.9	30.8	18.2	35.0	27.6	8.1	3.2	5.8	1.8	2.1	0.8	0.3	0.1	0.4	0.0	0.5
District 44	742 718	97.5	34.8	18.5	31.1	24.7	7.7	3.1	5.4	2.1	2.5	1.4	0.3	0.1	0.0	0.0	0.7

Table F. Congressional Districts 107th Congress

STATE District	Households by type, 2000												Households, 1990		
		Family households						Nonfamily households							House-holder living alone
				Married couple		Female householder[1]			Householder living alone						
	Total households	Total	With own children under 18 years	Total	With own children under 18 years	Total	With own children under 18 years	Total	Total	65 years and over	Average house-hold size	Average family size	Total house-holds	Female house-holder[1]	Householder living alone
	71	72	73	74	75	76	77	78	79	80	81	82	83	84	85
ALABAMA	1 737 080	70.0	32.3	52.2	22.5	14.2	8.1	30.0	26.1	9.8	2.49	3.01	1 506 790	13.4	23.8
District 1	245 355	71.7	33.8	52.4	23.0	15.6	9.1	28.3	24.5	9.3	2.58	3.08	209 370	15.1	22.8
District 2	252 944	70.0	33.2	52.2	22.8	14.3	8.7	30.0	26.4	10.2	2.47	2.99	215 137	12.6	24.2
District 3	251 525	69.0	31.1	51.4	21.6	13.7	7.7	31.0	26.1	9.7	2.48	3.00	212 651	13.0	23.2
District 4	255 047	72.8	31.8	58.5	24.2	10.7	5.8	27.2	24.6	11.2	2.49	2.95	220 788	9.9	22.2
District 5	260 271	70.4	32.6	55.7	24.2	11.4	6.7	29.6	26.0	9.0	2.46	2.97	219 452	10.4	22.9
District 6	267 020	67.6	31.4	54.5	24.5	10.2	5.6	32.4	27.2	8.2	2.44	2.99	223 443	9.0	24.9
District 7	204 918	68.3	32.4	37.7	16.0	26.1	14.7	31.7	28.4	11.0	2.56	3.16	205 949	24.4	26.1
ALASKA	221 600	68.7	39.9	52.5	28.5	10.8	7.8	31.3	23.5	4.1	2.74	3.28	188 915	9.6	22.1
At Large	221 600	68.7	39.9	52.5	28.5	10.8	7.8	31.3	23.5	4.1	2.74	3.28	188 915	9.6	22.1
ARIZONA	1 901 327	67.7	32.0	51.9	22.6	11.1	6.8	32.3	24.8	8.6	2.64	3.18	1 368 843	10.4	24.7
District 1	317 145	61.1	31.8	45.1	22.5	10.8	6.7	38.9	27.2	6.1	2.58	3.21	241 398	10.0	27.6
District 2	236 436	73.0	40.2	49.7	26.3	16.6	10.3	27.0	20.7	7.1	3.17	3.69	196 480	15.5	22.4
District 3	381 331	71.0	29.9	57.6	21.8	9.1	5.6	29.0	23.1	11.1	2.57	3.02	234 162	7.9	22.7
District 4	290 096	63.1	30.5	46.4	20.7	11.5	7.0	36.9	28.1	7.7	2.52	3.11	246 345	10.1	26.5
District 5	320 429	64.7	28.0	51.0	19.8	10.0	6.1	35.3	28.4	10.1	2.39	2.94	242 990	9.2	27.3
District 6	355 890	73.0	33.7	58.4	25.0	10.4	6.3	27.0	21.3	8.3	2.74	3.21	207 468	10.5	20.3
ARKANSAS	1 042 696	70.2	32.1	54.3	22.7	12.1	7.4	29.8	25.6	10.4	2.49	2.99	891 179	11.1	24.0
District 1	243 643	71.5	32.6	54.4	22.6	13.2	7.9	28.5	25.0	11.3	2.52	3.00	220 333	12.1	23.3
District 2	263 453	68.4	32.0	52.0	22.2	12.8	7.8	31.6	26.7	9.0	2.46	2.98	224 233	11.6	24.8
District 3	297 580	70.7	32.5	57.7	24.6	9.3	5.8	29.3	24.4	9.6	2.52	2.99	227 700	8.2	23.1
District 4	238 020	70.3	31.3	52.5	21.2	13.9	8.1	29.7	26.4	12.1	2.48	2.99	218 913	12.6	24.8
CALIFORNIA	11 502 870	68.9	35.8	51.1	26.0	12.6	7.3	31.1	23.5	7.8	2.87	3.43	10 381 206	11.5	23.4
District 1	234 984	67.7	32.8	51.2	22.6	11.6	7.3	32.3	24.8	9.5	2.61	3.11	208 711	10.3	22.9
District 2	245 147	66.8	30.1	51.7	20.4	10.9	7.0	33.2	25.6	10.5	2.50	2.99	219 020	9.9	23.4
District 3	242 105	69.2	35.9	51.6	25.2	12.5	7.8	30.8	23.0	8.4	2.73	3.23	209 586	11.2	22.0
District 4	272 937	71.4	33.0	57.8	24.7	9.4	5.9	28.6	22.1	8.1	2.57	3.01	210 045	8.6	19.9
District 5	249 892	62.1	32.6	41.8	20.5	15.1	9.4	37.9	29.5	8.4	2.63	3.33	223 134	13.8	28.9
District 6	251 423	62.6	29.8	48.7	21.8	9.8	5.8	37.4	27.8	9.9	2.48	3.03	226 960	9.4	26.5
District 7	223 309	69.4	35.3	48.8	24.1	15.2	8.5	30.6	23.5	7.4	2.81	3.34	208 202	13.6	22.9
District 8	268 026	40.8	15.4	28.6	10.8	8.7	3.6	59.2	41.3	9.7	2.24	3.24	245 820	10.0	41.7
District 9	237 212	54.2	26.5	34.8	16.3	14.8	8.2	45.8	33.7	8.6	2.46	3.23	227 756	15.4	34.4
District 10	261 663	72.3	36.8	60.1	29.8	8.7	5.1	27.7	21.4	7.6	2.68	3.14	213 366	8.1	20.5
District 11	225 687	73.9	39.8	54.6	28.1	13.7	8.5	26.1	20.7	7.9	2.96	3.43	192 038	12.5	20.5
District 12	226 199	65.2	28.1	50.7	22.5	10.2	4.1	34.8	25.3	8.9	2.69	3.26	215 787	10.0	26.1
District 13	220 965	74.6	38.0	57.3	29.9	12.0	5.9	25.4	18.5	6.2	3.04	3.48	198 910	11.2	19.4
District 14	234 612	63.8	30.2	52.3	24.7	7.9	4.0	36.2	26.5	7.6	2.56	3.12	223 976	8.3	27.2
District 15	226 831	68.5	32.6	54.9	26.0	9.2	4.7	31.5	22.3	6.4	2.66	3.14	214 252	9.6	21.5
District 16	194 697	75.8	40.7	56.4	31.3	12.7	6.7	24.2	16.9	4.7	3.47	3.86	168 563	12.8	17.6
District 17	206 835	69.3	37.2	53.2	27.8	11.3	6.7	30.7	22.3	8.3	3.02	3.55	189 099	10.4	21.8
District 18	215 784	76.3	42.5	56.8	30.6	13.7	8.6	23.7	18.8	7.7	3.10	3.54	186 489	11.7	19.1
District 19	240 272	72.7	38.3	53.4	26.4	13.8	8.7	27.3	21.6	8.0	2.89	3.38	202 858	12.3	21.6
District 20	180 223	81.8	50.3	57.9	35.6	16.5	10.7	18.2	14.3	6.5	3.66	3.99	158 379	15.4	16.0
District 21	225 835	73.5	39.8	54.1	27.2	14.0	9.2	26.5	21.7	8.6	2.88	3.36	199 642	11.7	21.3
District 22	224 371	64.6	30.6	51.0	22.9	9.6	5.6	35.4	25.0	9.7	2.67	3.20	205 198	9.0	23.3
District 23	203 699	75.2	40.0	58.8	30.8	11.3	6.5	24.8	18.9	7.6	3.10	3.52	183 312	10.1	17.8
District 24	236 137	67.1	32.9	52.4	25.4	10.1	5.4	32.9	25.0	7.2	2.63	3.17	219 354	8.9	24.8
District 25	226 900	75.3	42.5	57.7	31.9	12.4	7.7	24.7	18.7	5.7	2.99	3.42	190 996	9.2	17.6
District 26	189 181	73.3	44.8	50.1	31.8	15.5	9.2	26.7	19.9	5.6	3.45	3.98	177 447	12.9	23.1
District 27	228 095	64.7	31.4	48.4	23.8	11.7	5.8	35.3	28.6	8.6	2.59	3.25	219 623	11.0	28.3
District 28	199 315	75.4	37.9	56.9	28.9	13.3	6.7	24.6	19.7	7.9	2.99	3.44	192 695	11.3	19.7
District 29	290 778	40.4	15.8	30.9	11.8	6.6	3.0	59.6	45.8	9.5	1.94	2.83	278 690	6.6	44.1
District 30	187 303	67.1	38.2	42.8	25.5	16.5	9.5	32.9	24.8	6.2	3.07	3.73	177 284	15.1	24.7
District 31	162 708	80.1	43.2	54.8	31.4	17.4	8.8	19.9	15.2	6.2	3.64	4.00	158 775	15.4	16.7
District 32	217 323	60.1	31.1	35.5	18.5	18.7	10.2	39.9	31.3	8.6	2.66	3.40	212 744	18.1	31.0
District 33	151 990	75.7	49.9	48.9	34.2	17.7	11.4	24.3	19.2	6.8	3.77	4.29	145 328	16.5	19.9
District 34	166 460	82.0	44.0	58.0	32.5	16.9	8.4	18.0	14.2	6.4	3.67	3.99	162 272	14.6	14.8
District 35	178 561	74.0	45.8	41.6	26.5	24.7	15.3	26.0	21.3	6.3	3.38	3.91	174 747	22.5	23.8
District 36	241 826	60.3	27.4	46.6	20.7	9.6	5.0	39.7	30.3	7.5	2.41	3.07	233 720	8.7	28.0
District 37	156 506	81.4	50.2	49.7	32.1	23.6	14.2	18.6	14.6	5.5	3.89	4.24	153 884	21.6	16.8
District 38	223 510	64.4	35.7	43.2	23.2	15.5	9.6	35.6	27.4	7.8	2.79	3.48	215 601	12.1	29.0
District 39	201 697	76.3	37.8	58.9	29.4	12.2	6.1	23.7	18.3	7.1	3.05	3.47	190 832	10.5	17.3
District 40	233 208	72.4	37.5	54.0	25.9	13.2	8.5	27.6	22.3	8.7	2.80	3.28	201 282	10.5	20.9
District 41	192 901	81.0	46.3	62.2	36.0	13.0	7.4	19.0	14.2	4.5	3.37	3.70	172 941	11.0	15.2
District 42	200 503	79.1	48.9	55.1	34.1	17.2	11.0	20.9	16.1	5.2	3.44	3.84	181 408	14.2	18.3
District 43	226 619	76.9	43.7	59.0	33.1	12.4	7.5	23.1	17.1	6.0	3.18	3.59	182 767	10.2	17.0
District 44	258 703	69.8	33.7	53.1	23.6	11.9	7.4	30.2	24.4	12.7	2.80	3.36	209 956	9.2	24.1

[1] No spouse present.

Items 71—85

Table F. Congressional Districts 107th Congress

STATE District	Housing occupancy							Housing tenure				
	Percent change of households, 1990–2000	Total housing units	Occupied housing units (percent)	Vacant housing units		Homeowner vacancy rate (percent)	Rental vacancy rate (percent)	Occupied housing units			Average household size of owner-occupied units	Average household size of renter-occupied units
				Total	For seasonal, recreational, or occasional use			Total	Percent owner-occupied housing units	Percent renter-occupied housing units		
	86	87	88	89	90	91	92	93	94	95	96	97
ALABAMA	15.3	1 963 711	88.5	11.5	2.4	2.0	11.8	1 737 080	72.5	27.5	2.57	2.30
District 1	17.2	286 477	85.6	14.4	5.3	2.0	13.1	245 355	73.1	26.9	2.64	2.41
District 2	17.6	286 832	88.2	11.8	1.8	2.3	12.4	252 944	72.2	27.8	2.53	2.34
District 3	18.3	287 110	87.6	12.4	2.7	2.0	12.7	251 525	73.1	26.9	2.55	2.28
District 4	15.5	290 717	87.7	12.3	3.0	1.9	11.8	255 047	77.9	22.1	2.52	2.35
District 5	18.6	286 322	90.9	9.1	1.1	2.1	12.0	260 271	72.8	27.2	2.55	2.21
District 6	19.5	288 537	92.5	7.5	0.9	1.9	10.0	267 020	71.7	28.3	2.59	2.05
District 7	-0.5	237 716	86.2	13.8	1.9	1.9	10.9	204 918	64.9	35.1	2.61	2.47
ALASKA	17.3	260 978	84.9	15.1	8.2	1.9	7.8	221 600	62.5	37.5	2.89	2.49
At Large	17.3	260 978	84.9	15.1	8.2	1.9	7.8	221 600	62.5	37.5	2.89	2.49
ARIZONA	38.9	2 189 189	86.9	13.1	6.5	2.1	9.2	1 901 327	68.0	32.0	2.69	2.53
District 1	31.4	341 736	92.8	7.2	1.8	1.5	8.4	317 145	58.2	41.8	2.72	2.38
District 2	20.3	273 114	86.6	13.4	5.1	1.7	8.9	236 436	60.7	39.3	3.24	3.05
District 3	62.8	446 547	85.4	14.6	7.9	2.5	9.0	381 331	77.0	23.0	2.57	2.59
District 4	17.8	311 075	93.3	6.7	1.9	1.4	8.1	290 096	63.2	36.8	2.60	2.37
District 5	31.9	357 723	89.6	10.4	3.5	2.1	10.2	320 429	67.1	32.9	2.49	2.19
District 6	71.5	458 994	77.5	22.5	14.8	2.8	11.3	355 890	76.9	23.1	2.75	2.71
ARKANSAS	17.0	1 173 043	88.9	11.1	2.5	2.5	9.6	1 042 696	69.4	30.6	2.54	2.40
District 1	10.6	277 721	87.7	12.3	3.1	2.5	10.6	243 643	68.9	31.1	2.53	2.48
District 2	17.5	289 170	91.1	8.9	1.2	2.1	9.3	263 453	67.1	32.9	2.54	2.28
District 3	30.7	330 022	90.2	9.8	2.2	2.7	8.0	297 580	69.9	30.1	2.56	2.41
District 4	8.7	276 130	86.2	13.8	3.5	2.4	10.8	238 020	71.8	28.2	2.50	2.43
CALIFORNIA	10.8	12 214 549	94.2	5.8	1.9	1.4	3.7	11 502 870	56.9	43.1	2.93	2.79
District 1	12.6	259 066	90.7	9.3	4.6	1.6	4.4	234 984	63.3	36.7	2.60	2.63
District 2	11.9	280 010	87.5	12.5	6.2	2.2	6.3	245 147	65.4	34.6	2.48	2.52
District 3	15.5	253 858	95.4	4.6	0.8	1.3	4.5	242 105	60.4	39.6	2.76	2.69
District 4	29.9	325 350	83.9	16.1	12.1	1.4	6.2	272 937	72.1	27.9	2.63	2.43
District 5	12.0	262 801	95.1	4.9	0.3	1.6	5.1	249 892	53.5	46.5	2.72	2.53
District 6	10.8	265 191	94.8	5.2	2.7	0.7	2.3	251 423	63.2	36.8	2.52	2.41
District 7	7.3	230 279	97.0	3.0	0.3	0.9	3.0	223 309	62.8	37.2	2.85	2.75
District 8	9.0	282 902	94.7	5.3	1.2	0.9	2.6	268 026	29.9	70.1	2.74	2.03
District 9	4.2	247 728	95.8	4.2	0.4	0.9	2.7	237 212	43.0	57.0	2.63	2.33
District 10	22.6	269 431	97.1	2.9	0.7	0.7	2.9	261 663	73.9	26.1	2.78	2.40
District 11	17.5	235 469	95.8	4.2	0.4	1.3	3.9	225 687	61.7	38.3	2.93	3.00
District 12	4.8	232 219	97.4	2.6	0.5	0.5	2.0	226 199	60.2	39.8	2.83	2.47
District 13	11.1	225 237	98.1	1.9	0.2	0.5	2.0	220 965	63.4	36.6	3.12	2.91
District 14	4.7	241 415	97.2	2.8	0.7	0.5	1.7	234 612	56.0	44.0	2.67	2.41
District 15	5.9	232 968	97.4	2.6	0.8	0.4	1.9	226 831	63.4	36.6	2.74	2.52
District 16	15.5	199 218	97.7	2.3	0.3	0.6	2.0	194 697	61.6	38.4	3.47	3.47
District 17	9.4	223 825	92.4	7.6	3.6	1.1	2.7	206 835	56.0	44.0	2.99	3.06
District 18	15.7	226 584	95.2	4.8	0.6	1.3	3.5	215 784	61.0	39.0	3.06	3.17
District 19	18.4	261 230	92.0	8.0	2.7	1.7	5.7	240 272	61.0	39.0	2.86	2.93
District 20	13.8	192 793	93.5	6.5	0.4	1.8	5.5	180 223	54.6	45.4	3.55	3.79
District 21	13.1	250 569	90.1	9.9	3.0	2.5	7.9	225 835	62.7	37.3	2.88	2.89
District 22	9.3	239 652	93.6	6.4	3.3	0.9	2.8	224 371	58.3	41.7	2.66	2.69
District 23	11.1	211 625	96.3	3.7	1.3	0.9	2.8	203 699	65.5	34.5	3.07	3.14
District 24	7.7	244 732	96.5	3.5	0.6	1.1	3.3	236 137	62.2	37.8	2.75	2.42
District 25	18.8	240 072	94.5	5.5	0.4	2.0	6.1	226 900	69.8	30.2	3.06	2.83
District 26	6.6	195 283	96.9	3.1	0.2	1.4	2.6	189 181	43.2	56.8	3.67	3.29
District 27	3.9	235 618	96.8	3.2	0.4	1.0	2.2	228 095	48.5	51.5	2.72	2.47
District 28	3.4	204 939	97.3	2.7	0.3	1.0	2.5	199 315	67.2	32.8	3.09	2.77
District 29	4.3	306 023	95.0	5.0	1.0	1.4	3.3	290 778	35.0	65.0	2.25	1.78
District 30	5.7	196 223	95.5	4.5	0.2	2.1	3.1	187 303	23.7	76.3	3.24	3.02
District 31	2.5	167 871	96.9	3.1	0.2	1.3	2.1	162 708	48.0	52.0	3.63	3.65
District 32	2.2	228 581	95.1	4.9	0.2	1.9	3.8	217 323	35.5	64.5	2.86	2.55
District 33	4.6	160 886	94.5	5.5	0.5	2.8	3.8	151 990	24.1	75.9	4.43	3.56
District 34	2.6	170 607	97.6	2.4	0.1	1.0	2.1	166 460	62.5	37.5	3.74	3.56
District 35	2.2	190 301	93.8	6.2	0.1	3.1	4.3	178 561	36.2	63.8	3.57	3.28
District 36	3.5	252 358	95.8	4.2	0.9	1.1	3.0	241 826	53.4	46.6	2.56	2.24
District 37	1.7	165 423	94.6	5.4	0.2	3.0	4.2	156 506	50.1	49.9	3.94	3.83
District 38	3.7	232 783	96.0	4.0	0.4	1.6	3.4	223 510	45.6	54.4	2.86	2.72
District 39	5.7	206 250	97.8	2.2	0.2	0.7	2.6	201 697	64.4	35.6	3.05	3.05
District 40	15.9	289 847	80.5	19.5	10.9	3.7	9.3	233 208	65.3	34.7	2.78	2.83
District 41	11.5	198 764	97.1	2.9	0.2	1.2	3.2	192 901	68.4	31.6	3.38	3.33
District 42	10.5	214 607	93.4	6.6	0.2	3.2	6.6	200 503	63.0	37.0	3.54	3.26
District 43	24.0	238 580	95.0	5.0	0.7	1.9	4.7	226 619	68.0	32.0	3.27	2.98
District 44	23.2	324 238	79.8	20.2	11.2	3.2	9.5	258 703	69.1	30.9	2.73	2.95

Table F. Congressional Districts 107th Congress

STATE District	Land area, 2000[1] (sq km)	Total persons	Rank	Per square kilometer	Land area, 1990[1] (sq km)	Total persons	Rank	Per square kilometer	White	Black or African American	American Indian or Alaska Native	Asian	Native Hawaiian and other Pacific Islander	Some other race
	1	2	3	4	5	6	7	8	9	10	11	12	13	14
CALIFORNIA—Cont'd														
District 45	235.8	619 092	X	2 625.5	237.0	570 874	X	2 412.0	68.2	1.4	0.6	15.4	0.5	9.9
District 46	162.7	663 548	X	4 078.4	163.0	571 380	X	3 510.0	43.9	1.8	1.1	15.2	0.4	32.9
District 47	787.5	715 625	X	908.7	788.0	571 518	X	725.0	71.6	1.6	0.5	13.6	0.2	8.5
District 48	3 929.8	773 292	X	196.8	3 931.0	572 928	X	146.0	76.0	3.3	1.1	4.8	0.5	10.3
District 49	306.7	586 882	X	1 913.5	306.0	573 362	X	1 874.0	74.1	5.2	0.7	8.1	0.4	7.1
District 50	347.9	641 790	X	1 844.8	350.0	573 463	X	1 639.0	41.2	11.4	0.8	14.3	0.7	26.0
District 51	1 282.7	713 746	X	556.4	1 285.0	572 982	X	446.0	73.9	2.1	0.6	11.1	0.3	8.0
District 52	16 656.5	640 630	X	38.5	16 665.0	573 203	X	34.0	71.8	4.7	1.2	3.0	0.3	14.4
COLORADO	268 627.0	4 301 261	X	16.0	268 660.0	3 294 473	X	12.3	82.8	3.8	1.0	2.2	0.1	7.2
District 1	565.2	662 711	X	1 172.5	565.0	549 068	X	971.0	64.6	11.3	1.3	2.8	0.1	16.0
District 2	3 962.5	702 336	X	177.2	3 963.0	549 072	X	139.0	87.1	1.0	0.8	3.3	0.1	5.4
District 3	147 721.9	723 533	X	4.9	147 743.0	549 062	X	4.0	87.4	0.7	1.7	0.5	0.1	7.2
District 4	104 330.3	748 228	X	7.2	104 338.0	549 070	X	5.0	85.9	1.1	0.9	1.4	0.1	8.2
District 5	10 959.5	810 423	X	73.9	10 961.0	549 066	X	50.0	85.2	4.8	0.8	2.5	0.2	3.5
District 6	1 087.8	654 030	X	601.2	1 087.0	549 056	X	505.0	85.0	4.8	0.8	3.0	0.1	3.7
CONNECTICUT	12 548.0	3 405 565	X	271.4	12 550.0	3 287 116	X	261.9	81.6	9.1	0.3	2.4	0.0	4.3
District 1	1 223.2	552 127	X	451.4	1 223.0	548 016	X	448.0	71.1	15.6	0.2	2.7	0.1	7.7
District 2	4 413.5	568 007	X	128.7	4 414.0	548 041	X	124.0	89.1	4.2	0.6	1.9	0.0	2.0
District 3	1 100.9	561 576	X	510.1	1 101.0	547 765	X	497.0	78.8	12.8	0.2	2.7	0.0	3.5
District 4	656.7	574 101	X	874.2	657.0	547 765	X	834.0	74.2	13.4	0.2	3.5	0.0	5.9
District 5	1 518.7	581 903	X	383.2	1 519.0	547 764	X	361.0	85.3	5.7	0.2	2.2	0.0	4.4
District 6	3 635.0	567 851	X	156.2	3 635.0	547 765	X	151.0	91.0	3.2	0.2	1.5	0.0	2.5
DELAWARE	5 060.0	783 600	X	154.9	5 062.0	666 168	X	131.6	74.6	19.2	0.3	2.1	0.0	2.0
At Large	5 059.7	783 600	X	154.9	5 062.0	666 168	X	132.0	74.6	19.2	0.3	2.1	0.0	2.0
DISTRICT OF COLUMBIA	159.0	572 059	X	3 597.9	159.0	606 900	X	3 817.0	30.8	60.0	0.3	2.7	0.1	3.8
Delegate	159.0	572 059	X	3 597.9	159.0	606 900	X	3 816.0	30.8	60.0	0.3	2.7	0.1	3.8
FLORIDA	139 670.0	15 982 378	X	114.4	139 852.0	12 938 071	X	92.5	78.0	14.6	0.3	1.7	0.1	3.0
District 1	11 595.0	683 987	X	59.0	11 597.0	562 518	X	49.0	81.0	12.9	0.9	1.9	0.1	0.9
District 2	30 607.2	678 025	X	22.2	30 610.0	562 518	X	18.0	70.7	25.2	0.5	1.1	0.0	0.9
District 3	4 716.2	586 694	X	124.4	4 717.0	562 519	X	119.0	44.4	49.7	0.3	1.3	0.0	2.1
District 4	4 732.5	734 246	X	155.1	4 740.0	562 519	X	119.0	85.5	9.0	0.3	2.4	0.1	1.0
District 5	9 379.6	689 672	X	73.5	9 380.0	562 518	X	60.0	86.9	8.6	0.3	1.6	0.0	1.0
District 6	12 368.4	755 939	X	61.1	12 369.0	562 518	X	46.0	84.1	11.1	0.4	1.1	0.0	1.6
District 7	2 509.5	722 139	X	287.8	2 510.0	562 518	X	224.0	85.0	7.9	0.3	1.9	0.0	2.8
District 8	2 184.3	782 397	X	358.2	2 185.0	562 518	X	258.0	76.4	8.8	0.4	3.6	0.1	7.3
District 9	2 319.8	722 068	X	311.3	2 321.0	562 518	X	242.0	90.3	4.2	0.3	1.9	0.0	1.6
District 10	390.5	583 809	X	1 495.0	391.0	562 518	X	1 440.0	83.3	11.3	0.3	2.3	0.1	1.0
District 11	654.6	628 167	X	959.6	655.0	562 519	X	859.0	69.3	20.4	0.4	2.2	0.1	4.6
District 12	9 070.5	671 347	X	74.0	9 072.0	562 519	X	62.0	79.1	12.6	0.4	1.0	0.0	5.2
District 13	3 987.6	677 666	X	169.9	3 989.0	562 518	X	141.0	89.5	5.7	0.3	0.8	0.0	2.4
District 14	9 048.3	790 852	X	87.4	9 049.0	562 518	X	62.0	88.0	5.5	0.3	0.7	0.0	3.7
District 15	8 112.3	718 294	X	88.5	8 114.0	562 519	X	69.0	86.5	7.9	0.4	1.3	0.1	1.9
District 16	13 655.5	758 365	X	55.5	13 657.0	562 519	X	41.0	86.2	7.2	0.3	1.2	0.1	3.2
District 17	271.8	577 167	X	2 123.5	272.0	562 519	X	2 070.0	29.3	60.3	0.3	1.1	0.0	4.1
District 18	297.9	597 947	X	2 007.2	298.0	562 519	X	1 888.0	85.4	5.1	0.2	1.3	0.0	4.7
District 19	679.4	800 902	X	1 178.8	681.0	562 519	X	826.0	84.9	7.7	0.2	2.3	0.0	2.7
District 20	8 957.2	783 412	X	87.5	8 961.0	562 518	X	63.0	80.2	10.8	0.3	2.7	0.1	3.1
District 21	615.1	789 742	X	1 283.9	615.0	562 519	X	914.0	84.5	4.8	0.1	1.6	0.0	5.3
District 22	330.8	630 775	X	1 906.8	331.0	562 519	X	1 701.0	86.3	6.7	0.2	1.4	0.1	2.7
District 23	3 185.8	618 766	X	194.2	3 187.0	562 519	X	177.0	34.7	55.3	0.3	0.9	0.1	4.0
GEORGIA	149 976.0	8 186 453	X	54.6	150 010.0	6 478 149	X	43.2	65.1	28.7	0.3	2.1	0.1	2.4
District 1	21 133.6	692 199	X	32.8	21 143.0	588 541	X	28.0	64.4	31.1	0.3	1.1	0.1	1.7
District 2	29 678.7	650 392	X	21.9	29 683.0	587 583	X	20.0	55.9	40.5	0.3	0.6	0.0	1.8
District 3	7 944.2	781 694	X	98.4	7 947.0	589 630	X	74.0	63.8	30.6	0.3	2.0	0.1	1.7
District 4	771.9	744 717	X	964.8	772.0	589 322	X	763.0	37.7	49.5	0.3	5.3	0.1	4.8
District 5	1 033.0	646 184	X	625.5	1 033.0	589 359	X	570.0	31.1	62.9	0.2	2.3	0.0	2.3
District 6	1 526.9	943 373	X	617.8	1 528.0	589 600	X	386.0	79.6	10.9	0.2	4.7	0.0	2.8
District 7	9 585.7	752 161	X	78.5	9 589.0	589 405	X	62.0	76.8	18.2	0.3	0.9	0.0	2.5
District 8	29 785.3	662 811	X	22.3	29 791.0	587 912	X	20.0	64.4	32.3	0.2	0.7	0.0	1.3
District 9	15 088.0	814 305	X	54.0	15 088.0	589 420	X	39.0	90.5	3.2	0.3	0.7	0.1	4.1
District 10	25 107.0	662 201	X	26.4	25 111.0	588 046	X	23.0	58.2	38.5	0.2	1.1	0.1	0.8
District 11	8 322.0	836 416	X	100.5	8 324.0	589 398	X	71.0	78.9	14.6	0.2	2.9	0.0	2.0

[1] Dry land or land partially or temporarily covered by water.

Table F. Congressional Districts 107th Congress

	Population and population characteristics, 2000 (cont'd)								Population and population characteristics, 1990				
	Race (percent) (cont'd)								Race (percent)				
STATE District	Two or more races	Race alone or in combination						Hispanic[1]	White	Black or African American	American Indian or Alaska Native	Asian and Pacific Islander	Hispanic[1]
		White	Black	American Indian or Alaska Native	Asian	Native Hawaiian and other Pacific Islander	Some other race						
	15	16	17	18	19	20	21	22	23	24	25	26	27
CALIFORNIA—Cont'd													
District 45	4.0	71.7	1.7	1.4	16.8	0.8	11.9	21.2	82.1	1.2	0.6	11.0	14.8
District 46	4.7	47.0	2.3	1.6	16.0	0.7	36.4	62.3	66.5	2.5	0.6	12.3	50.0
District 47	4.0	75.0	2.0	1.0	15.2	0.5	10.5	19.7	83.6	1.8	0.4	9.6	13.1
District 48	4.1	79.5	3.9	1.8	6.2	0.8	12.1	22.5	83.3	4.0	1.1	4.5	17.2
District 49	4.4	77.7	6.1	1.5	9.7	0.8	9.0	16.7	82.1	5.3	0.7	6.6	12.8
District 50	5.7	45.3	12.7	1.4	16.2	1.1	29.3	50.8	46.5	14.4	0.6	14.8	40.6
District 51	4.0	77.4	2.7	1.2	12.8	0.6	9.7	17.6	84.6	1.8	0.6	8.2	13.6
District 52	4.5	75.7	5.4	2.1	4.3	0.7	16.7	29.7	83.6	3.1	1.1	3.0	22.6
COLORADO	2.8	85.2	4.4	1.9	2.8	0.2	8.5	17.1	88.2	4.0	0.8	1.8	12.9
District 1	3.9	67.7	12.4	2.2	3.4	0.3	18.2	33.4	73.0	12.9	1.1	2.4	21.9
District 2	2.5	89.3	1.3	1.5	3.9	0.2	6.5	13.7	92.7	0.8	0.6	2.4	9.5
District 3	2.3	89.5	1.0	2.6	0.8	0.1	8.4	18.9	91.7	0.7	1.4	0.5	17.4
District 4	2.5	88.1	1.4	1.6	1.8	0.2	9.4	18.4	91.3	0.7	0.6	1.1	14.7
District 5	3.1	87.8	5.7	1.7	3.4	0.4	4.5	9.3	88.8	5.6	0.7	2.2	7.4
District 6	2.7	87.3	5.5	1.5	3.7	0.2	4.7	10.5	91.7	3.5	0.5	2.3	6.4
CONNECTICUT	2.2	83.3	10.0	0.7	2.8	0.1	5.5	9.4	87.0	8.3	0.2	1.5	6.5
District 1	2.6	72.8	16.7	0.7	3.2	0.2	9.2	13.1	78.3	14.2	0.2	1.7	10.1
District 2	2.1	90.8	5.1	1.3	2.3	0.1	2.7	4.7	93.3	3.7	0.4	1.4	3.0
District 3	2.0	80.3	13.7	0.7	3.0	0.1	4.4	8.0	84.1	11.9	0.2	1.5	4.9
District 4	2.8	76.2	14.4	0.5	4.0	0.1	7.8	14.8	80.0	13.1	0.1	2.2	11.1
District 5	2.1	87.0	6.4	0.6	2.6	0.1	5.6	10.0	91.2	4.8	0.2	1.4	6.2
District 6	1.5	92.3	3.7	0.5	1.8	0.1	3.2	5.8	95.0	2.3	0.1	1.1	3.5
DELAWARE	1.7	75.9	20.1	0.8	2.4	0.1	2.6	4.8	80.3	16.9	0.3	1.4	2.4
At Large	1.7	75.9	20.1	0.8	2.4	0.1	2.6	4.8	80.3	16.9	0.3	1.4	2.4
DISTRICT OF COLUMBIA	2.4	32.2	61.3	0.8	3.1	0.1	5.0	7.9	29.6	65.8	0.2	1.8	5.4
Delegate	2.4	32.2	61.3	0.8	3.1	0.1	5.0	7.9	29.6	65.8	0.2	1.8	5.4
FLORIDA	2.4	79.7	15.5	0.7	2.1	0.2	4.4	16.8	83.1	13.6	0.3	1.2	12.2
District 1	2.3	83.0	13.5	1.7	2.6	0.2	1.3	3.0	84.0	12.8	0.9	1.8	2.1
District 2	1.5	71.9	25.7	1.1	1.5	0.1	1.3	3.4	74.0	24.1	0.5	0.9	1.9
District 3	2.1	45.7	50.8	0.7	1.7	0.2	3.2	5.8	50.4	47.0	0.3	1.0	3.4
District 4	1.7	86.9	9.4	0.8	3.0	0.1	1.6	4.0	91.0	6.4	0.3	1.7	2.7
District 5	1.5	88.2	9.0	0.8	1.9	0.1	1.5	4.5	89.6	8.5	0.2	1.1	2.7
District 6	1.5	85.4	11.6	0.9	1.5	0.1	2.1	5.3	87.1	11.0	0.3	0.9	2.8
District 7	2.0	86.6	8.6	0.8	2.3	0.1	3.8	10.0	93.2	4.0	0.3	1.3	5.5
District 8	3.4	78.9	9.9	0.8	4.3	0.2	9.4	23.0	88.8	5.2	0.3	2.3	11.4
District 9	1.6	91.7	4.6	0.7	2.3	0.1	2.3	7.4	94.6	3.4	0.3	1.0	4.1
District 10	1.7	84.7	11.8	0.8	2.7	0.1	1.7	4.1	88.6	9.4	0.2	1.3	2.3
District 11	2.9	71.5	21.5	1.0	2.8	0.2	6.3	20.0	78.7	17.2	0.3	1.4	13.9
District 12	1.7	80.4	13.1	0.9	1.2	0.1	6.1	12.3	84.1	12.6	0.3	0.6	6.1
District 13	1.2	90.6	6.1	0.6	1.1	0.1	2.9	7.5	92.8	5.4	0.2	0.5	4.3
District 14	1.7	89.2	6.1	0.6	1.0	0.1	4.8	11.9	91.9	5.7	0.2	0.5	6.6
District 15	1.8	88.0	8.5	0.8	1.8	0.1	2.7	7.2	90.2	7.6	0.3	1.1	3.4
District 16	1.8	87.5	7.8	0.7	1.5	0.1	4.3	11.8	93.0	4.0	0.4	0.8	6.3
District 17	4.8	31.3	63.4	0.6	1.5	0.3	7.9	27.4	36.6	58.4	0.2	1.3	23.0
District 18	3.3	88.2	5.7	0.4	1.6	0.1	7.4	70.5	88.7	4.2	0.1	1.2	66.7
District 19	2.3	86.4	8.5	0.4	2.7	0.1	4.2	12.2	94.8	2.7	0.1	1.4	6.2
District 20	2.8	82.2	11.8	0.6	3.3	0.2	4.9	23.1	92.1	4.4	0.3	1.6	12.3
District 21	3.6	87.7	5.4	0.3	2.0	0.1	8.3	77.5	87.6	4.1	0.1	1.5	69.6
District 22	2.7	88.2	7.5	0.5	1.8	0.1	4.6	20.6	94.2	3.0	0.1	1.1	12.8
District 23	4.7	36.1	58.7	0.6	1.3	0.3	7.7	13.1	44.8	51.6	0.2	0.9	9.4
GEORGIA	1.4	66.1	29.2	0.6	2.4	0.1	2.9	5.3	71.0	27.0	0.2	1.2	1.7
District 1	1.3	65.4	31.7	0.7	1.4	0.2	2.1	3.6	67.6	30.6	0.2	0.8	1.7
District 2	0.9	56.6	40.8	0.6	0.8	0.1	2.0	3.3	59.5	39.2	0.2	0.4	1.7
District 3	1.5	64.9	31.3	0.7	2.4	0.1	2.2	4.1	73.2	24.7	0.2	1.2	1.8
District 4	2.3	39.1	50.6	0.7	5.8	0.1	6.1	11.0	58.4	36.6	0.2	3.6	3.2
District 5	1.4	31.9	63.7	0.6	2.4	0.1	2.9	5.2	35.7	62.0	0.2	1.3	1.9
District 6	1.8	81.0	11.4	0.6	5.2	0.1	3.6	6.6	91.0	6.4	0.2	1.9	2.1
District 7	1.3	77.9	18.7	0.7	1.1	0.1	2.9	5.0	85.6	13.2	0.2	0.6	1.1
District 8	0.9	65.1	32.7	0.6	1.0	0.1	1.6	2.8	67.9	31.1	0.2	0.5	1.0
District 9	1.1	91.5	3.4	0.8	0.9	0.1	4.5	8.4	94.7	3.7	0.3	0.4	1.7
District 10	1.1	59.0	39.0	0.6	1.5	0.1	1.0	2.0	60.9	37.5	0.2	1.0	1.1
District 11	1.4	80.0	15.0	0.6	3.2	0.1	2.6	5.0	86.5	11.8	0.2	1.2	1.3

[1] Hispanic persons may be of any race.

Table F. Congressional Districts 107th Congress

Population and population characteristics, 2000 — Age (percent)

STATE / District	Under 5 years	5 to 17 years	18 to 24 years	25 to 34 years	35 to 44 years	45 to 54 years	55 to 64 years	65 to 74 years	75 years and over	Median age (years)	Percent Female
	28	29	30	31	32	33	34	35	36	37	38
CALIFORNIA—Cont'd											
District 45	6.6	16.8	9.0	17.5	16.6	12.8	9.0	6.1	5.5	35.0	50.1
District 46	9.7	22.8	11.8	18.9	15.1	9.5	5.5	3.8	3.0	28.0	48.6
District 47	6.9	17.8	9.0	15.7	17.5	13.7	8.4	5.4	5.6	35.3	51.3
District 48	7.8	20.1	10.2	14.0	17.2	13.0	7.3	5.5	4.9	33.6	49.4
District 49	5.1	11.8	14.8	20.3	15.9	11.9	7.5	6.3	6.5	33.8	48.1
District 50	8.4	23.0	11.2	15.8	15.3	10.9	6.5	5.0	3.9	29.7	50.3
District 51	7.1	19.2	8.1	14.1	17.8	14.5	7.7	5.6	5.9	35.8	50.5
District 52	7.1	20.6	9.9	13.9	16.6	13.1	7.7	6.0	5.3	34.0	50.3
COLORADO	6.9	18.7	10.0	15.4	17.1	14.3	7.9	5.3	4.4	34.3	49.6
District 1	7.2	16.0	11.0	20.1	15.5	12.4	7.0	5.4	5.4	32.5	49.2
District 2	6.7	18.4	10.7	15.6	17.8	14.6	7.7	4.8	3.8	34.1	49.9
District 3	6.2	18.3	9.5	13.5	16.2	15.0	9.1	6.6	5.5	36.7	49.2
District 4	7.1	19.9	11.5	14.0	16.5	13.6	7.6	5.2	4.6	33.2	49.6
District 5	7.7	20.4	8.8	14.8	18.7	14.5	7.5	4.4	3.2	33.9	49.4
District 6	6.5	18.6	8.6	15.0	17.9	15.6	8.5	5.2	4.2	35.8	50.5
CONNECTICUT	6.6	18.2	8.0	13.3	17.1	14.1	9.1	6.8	7.0	37.4	51.6
District 1	6.5	18.3	8.3	13.0	16.3	14.1	9.0	6.9	7.6	37.4	52.4
District 2	6.2	17.7	9.5	13.5	17.5	14.1	8.9	6.4	6.2	36.8	50.8
District 3	6.2	17.6	9.0	13.5	16.2	13.9	9.0	7.1	7.6	37.3	52.2
District 4	7.4	18.1	7.4	14.0	17.0	13.3	9.0	6.9	6.7	36.7	51.9
District 5	7.0	19.1	7.0	13.0	17.7	14.4	9.0	6.3	6.5	37.2	51.2
District 6	6.0	18.2	6.7	12.5	17.6	14.8	9.5	7.2	7.5	38.9	50.9
DELAWARE	6.6	18.3	9.6	13.9	16.3	13.3	9.1	7.2	5.8	36.0	51.4
At Large	6.6	18.3	9.6	13.9	16.3	13.3	9.1	7.2	5.8	36.0	51.4
DISTRICT OF COLUMBIA	5.7	14.4	12.7	17.8	15.3	13.2	8.7	6.3	5.9	34.6	52.9
Delegate	5.7	14.4	12.7	17.8	15.3	13.2	8.7	6.3	5.9	34.6	52.9
FLORIDA	5.9	16.9	8.3	13.0	15.5	12.9	9.8	9.1	8.5	38.7	51.2
District 1	6.1	18.0	10.0	13.5	16.4	13.4	9.7	7.5	5.4	36.5	49.8
District 2	5.9	17.2	13.5	13.8	15.3	13.4	9.0	6.5	5.3	34.7	50.0
District 3	7.4	20.8	9.8	13.5	15.3	12.5	8.5	6.7	5.5	33.9	51.7
District 4	6.1	16.9	8.2	14.0	16.7	14.4	9.5	7.6	6.6	37.8	51.2
District 5	4.8	14.6	11.1	10.8	12.7	12.1	10.8	11.7	11.2	41.8	52.0
District 6	5.7	17.1	6.9	11.6	14.9	12.5	11.2	11.4	8.8	40.8	50.5
District 7	5.8	17.6	8.3	13.0	16.4	14.0	9.5	8.2	7.2	38.3	51.3
District 8	6.5	17.5	11.2	16.9	17.3	12.7	7.6	5.6	4.7	33.7	50.2
District 9	5.6	16.2	6.4	12.2	16.3	14.0	10.0	9.6	9.8	40.9	51.9
District 10	5.0	14.2	6.5	11.8	15.6	14.0	10.5	10.4	11.9	43.0	52.2
District 11	6.9	18.0	10.4	16.2	16.3	12.7	8.2	6.1	5.3	34.1	51.2
District 12	6.6	18.9	8.6	12.3	14.5	12.4	9.7	9.2	7.8	37.5	50.4
District 13	4.7	13.5	5.7	9.7	12.8	12.3	11.9	14.3	15.1	47.7	52.3
District 14	5.0	14.0	6.0	10.3	13.0	12.1	12.9	14.6	12.0	46.3	50.8
District 15	5.3	16.8	6.7	10.8	15.8	13.1	10.9	11.1	9.4	41.5	51.0
District 16	5.4	16.3	6.4	10.9	14.8	12.6	10.4	11.8	11.4	42.4	51.1
District 17	7.8	23.0	10.7	13.8	15.1	12.1	8.0	5.5	4.1	31.2	51.7
District 18	5.5	15.2	8.8	15.1	15.6	12.5	10.2	8.9	8.2	38.2	51.3
District 19	5.4	14.9	6.1	12.0	15.0	12.2	8.9	10.8	14.5	42.6	52.8
District 20	6.5	18.3	6.8	13.8	18.2	14.3	8.6	6.6	6.8	37.4	51.5
District 21	6.6	18.5	8.9	15.9	17.0	12.4	9.1	6.7	4.9	35.1	51.9
District 22	4.5	10.9	5.9	13.9	16.2	14.1	11.1	10.8	12.7	44.1	50.9
District 23	7.6	21.5	9.9	14.5	16.0	11.8	7.6	5.6	5.4	32.6	50.4
GEORGIA	7.3	19.2	10.2	15.9	16.5	13.2	8.1	5.3	4.3	33.4	50.8
District 1	7.3	19.6	12.1	14.5	15.3	12.3	8.1	5.9	4.9	32.5	50.5
District 2	7.3	20.2	11.1	13.9	14.7	12.5	8.5	6.3	5.6	33.2	51.4
District 3	7.5	20.9	9.2	14.8	16.8	13.5	8.1	5.3	3.9	33.5	51.1
District 4	7.4	17.5	11.3	20.2	17.3	12.4	6.6	4.0	3.3	31.7	50.9
District 5	6.9	17.2	12.4	19.4	15.6	12.4	7.1	4.6	4.4	31.6	51.1
District 6	7.6	19.2	7.9	17.8	19.6	14.9	7.1	3.5	2.4	33.6	50.3
District 7	7.5	19.4	9.7	15.9	16.6	12.7	8.2	5.5	4.5	33.5	50.8
District 8	7.0	19.7	9.9	13.8	15.6	13.2	8.9	6.5	5.4	34.7	51.3
District 9	7.4	18.2	9.2	14.9	16.1	13.3	9.6	6.6	4.7	35.2	50.1
District 10	6.8	20.0	9.9	13.5	15.8	13.5	9.0	6.4	5.1	34.9	51.2
District 11	7.1	19.6	11.0	15.2	17.0	13.6	7.9	4.8	3.7	33.2	50.6

Table F. Congressional Districts 107th Congress

STATE District	Under 5 years	5 to 17 years	18 to 24 years	25 to 34 years	35 to 44 years	45 to 54 years	55 to 64 years	65 to 74 years	75 years and over	Percent Female	2000	1990	1980	1990–2000	1980–1990
	39	40	41	42	43	44	45	46	47	48	49	50	51	52	53
CALIFORNIA—Cont'd															
District 45	6.5	14.7	12.4	21.1	15.4	11.5	8.4	5.8	4.4	49.7	619 092	570 874	NA	8.4	NA
District 46	9.7	19.3	15.4	22.1	13.1	7.6	5.9	4.3	2.7	47.6	663 548	571 380	NA	16.1	NA
District 47	6.9	15.8	11.3	18.7	17.0	11.8	7.6	5.8	5.1	51.0	715 625	571 518	NA	25.2	NA
District 48	8.7	16.9	12.8	19.6	15.8	9.0	6.9	6.5	3.9	48.4	773 292	572 928	NA	35.0	NA
District 49	5.3	10.9	17.7	22.7	14.7	8.6	7.6	7.3	5.2	47.1	586 882	573 362	NA	2.4	NA
District 50	9.6	20.9	13.3	19.4	13.7	8.0	6.6	5.3	3.2	49.9	641 790	573 463	NA	11.9	NA
District 51	7.6	17.0	10.1	19.1	17.7	10.1	6.9	6.7	4.6	49.8	713 746	572 982	NA	24.6	NA
District 52	8.3	19.2	10.9	18.3	15.3	9.4	7.7	6.5	4.3	50.7	640 630	573 203	NA	11.8	NA
COLORADO	7.7	18.5	10.2	18.6	17.2	10.2	7.6	5.9	4.1	50.5	4 301 261	3 294 473	2 889 735	30.6	14.0
District 1	7.6	15.1	10.0	20.4	16.2	9.1	8.2	7.5	5.8	51.2	662 711	549 068	NA	20.7	NA
District 2	7.6	18.2	11.3	19.4	18.1	10.6	7.1	4.7	3.1	50.4	702 336	549 072	NA	27.9	NA
District 3	7.1	19.3	9.2	16.3	16.7	10.1	8.7	7.4	5.2	50.1	723 533	549 062	NA	31.8	NA
District 4	7.7	20.0	11.3	16.8	16.0	9.7	7.5	6.2	4.8	50.5	748 228	549 070	NA	36.3	NA
District 5	8.4	19.8	10.5	18.9	17.7	10.4	6.9	4.6	2.7	49.7	810 423	549 066	NA	47.6	NA
District 6	7.5	18.4	8.9	19.6	18.8	11.4	7.5	5.1	2.9	51.0	654 030	549 056	NA	19.1	NA
CONNECTICUT	6.9	15.9	10.5	17.8	15.5	10.8	9.0	7.8	5.8	51.5	3 405 565	3 287 116	3 107 564	3.6	5.8
District 1	6.8	15.9	10.4	17.6	15.4	10.5	8.9	8.0	6.3	52.2	552 127	548 016	NA	0.8	NA
District 2	7.1	16.1	12.8	18.6	15.3	10.2	8.1	6.8	5.0	50.3	568 007	548 041	NA	3.6	NA
District 3	6.7	15.4	11.0	17.5	15.4	10.4	9.0	8.4	6.1	52.2	561 576	547 765	NA	2.5	NA
District 4	6.9	15.3	9.8	17.6	15.0	11.5	10.0	8.0	5.9	52.3	574 101	547 765	NA	4.8	NA
District 5	7.3	16.7	9.5	17.6	16.1	11.3	8.7	7.4	5.5	51.2	581 903	547 764	NA	6.2	NA
District 6	6.8	15.8	9.5	17.6	16.2	11.1	9.2	8.1	5.8	51.1	567 851	547 765	NA	3.7	NA
DELAWARE	7.3	17.2	11.4	17.9	14.8	10.2	9.0	7.4	4.7	51.5	783 600	666 168	594 338	17.6	12.1
At Large	7.3	17.2	11.4	17.9	14.8	10.2	9.0	7.4	4.7	51.5	783 600	666 168	NA	17.6	NA
DISTRICT OF COLUMBIA	6.2	13.1	13.6	20.0	15.7	10.2	8.4	7.3	5.5	53.4	572 059	606 900	638 432	-5.7	-4.9
Delegate	6.2	13.1	13.6	20.0	15.7	10.2	8.4	7.3	5.5	53.4	572 059	606 900	NA	-5.7	NA
FLORIDA	6.6	15.6	9.4	16.4	14.0	10.0	9.8	10.6	7.7	51.6	15 982 378	12 938 071	9 746 961	23.5	32.7
District 1	7.4	18.0	10.9	17.8	14.4	10.7	9.4	7.3	4.1	50.6	683 987	562 518	NA	21.6	NA
District 2	6.8	18.4	13.6	16.5	14.5	10.0	8.4	6.9	4.8	50.9	678 025	562 518	NA	20.5	NA
District 3	8.3	19.6	10.9	17.0	13.5	9.4	8.7	7.6	5.0	51.9	586 694	562 519	NA	4.3	NA
District 4	6.9	15.9	10.3	18.2	15.8	10.2	9.0	8.3	5.4	50.8	734 246	562 519	NA	30.5	NA
District 5	5.4	13.6	11.2	13.3	11.8	8.8	11.1	15.2	9.6	52.1	689 672	562 518	NA	22.6	NA
District 6	6.7	17.1	8.5	15.2	13.5	10.1	10.4	11.5	6.9	50.6	755 939	562 518	NA	34.4	NA
District 7	6.4	16.1	9.2	17.4	15.5	10.3	9.4	9.6	6.2	51.3	722 139	562 518	NA	28.4	NA
District 8	6.9	15.6	13.1	20.5	15.1	9.5	8.1	6.8	4.3	50.3	782 397	562 518	NA	39.1	NA
District 9	5.8	14.5	7.5	15.4	14.9	10.0	10.0	12.6	9.2	52.2	722 068	562 518	NA	28.4	NA
District 10	5.3	12.5	7.6	14.9	13.4	9.7	10.5	13.2	12.9	53.3	583 809	562 518	NA	3.8	NA
District 11	7.3	16.1	11.6	19.6	14.7	10.2	8.5	7.1	4.9	51.6	628 167	562 519	NA	11.7	NA
District 12	7.2	18.2	9.3	14.8	13.6	10.1	9.8	10.4	6.8	51.3	671 347	562 519	NA	19.3	NA
District 13	5.1	12.2	6.7	12.5	11.7	9.0	11.9	17.4	13.5	52.8	677 666	562 518	NA	20.5	NA
District 14	5.7	13.2	7.2	13.8	12.2	9.6	12.7	16.0	9.6	51.3	790 852	562 518	NA	40.6	NA
District 15	6.5	15.2	8.4	16.5	13.4	10.3	11.2	11.9	6.7	50.7	718 294	562 519	NA	27.7	NA
District 16	6.1	14.3	7.1	15.1	13.4	9.4	10.8	14.3	9.5	51.6	758 365	562 519	NA	34.8	NA
District 17	9.2	21.3	10.8	17.1	14.4	9.7	7.6	5.7	4.2	51.9	577 167	562 519	NA	2.6	NA
District 18	5.8	14.2	10.0	16.0	13.6	11.8	11.3	9.4	7.9	51.9	597 947	562 519	NA	6.3	NA
District 19	5.4	12.5	6.9	15.0	13.8	8.8	9.3	15.7	12.5	52.6	800 902	562 519	NA	42.4	NA
District 20	6.4	15.3	8.1	17.0	16.4	11.2	9.3	9.4	6.8	51.1	783 412	562 518	NA	39.3	NA
District 21	7.5	17.1	10.4	19.4	15.1	11.5	9.0	6.1	3.9	51.7	789 742	562 519	NA	40.4	NA
District 22	4.1	8.6	6.6	14.8	13.0	10.2	11.6	14.3	16.6	53.2	630 775	562 519	NA	12.1	NA
District 23	8.6	18.9	10.2	18.4	14.1	9.2	7.4	6.7	6.4	51.1	618 766	562 519	NA	10.0	NA
GEORGIA	7.6	19.0	11.4	18.1	15.7	10.3	7.7	6.0	4.1	51.5	8 186 453	6 478 149	5 462 982	26.4	18.6
District 1	8.1	19.4	12.8	17.4	14.0	9.4	7.7	6.7	4.4	50.8	692 199	588 541	NA	17.6	NA
District 2	7.9	21.4	11.8	15.6	13.7	9.5	8.0	7.0	5.2	52.0	650 392	587 583	NA	10.7	NA
District 3	8.0	20.0	10.7	17.5	15.7	10.7	8.0	5.8	3.7	51.3	781 694	589 630	NA	32.6	NA
District 4	7.2	16.3	11.9	22.4	17.2	10.2	7.1	4.8	2.9	51.8	744 717	589 322	NA	26.4	NA
District 5	7.7	17.2	12.7	19.6	16.0	9.6	6.9	5.7	4.7	52.4	646 184	589 359	NA	9.6	NA
District 6	7.6	17.7	9.8	21.9	20.1	11.6	6.1	3.5	1.8	50.7	943 373	589 600	NA	60.0	NA
District 7	7.7	18.9	11.1	17.7	15.1	10.5	8.2	6.4	4.5	51.5	752 161	589 405	NA	27.6	NA
District 8	7.5	20.2	10.5	16.2	14.3	10.3	8.7	7.2	5.1	52.3	662 811	587 912	NA	12.7	NA
District 9	7.0	18.5	10.7	16.6	15.0	11.3	9.1	7.1	4.7	50.8	814 305	589 420	NA	38.2	NA
District 10	7.7	20.3	10.8	16.9	14.8	10.0	8.2	6.7	4.6	51.5	662 201	588 046	NA	12.6	NA
District 11	7.7	19.4	12.6	17.8	16.4	10.5	6.9	5.2	3.6	51.1	836 416	589 398	NA	41.9	NA

Population and population characteristics, 1990 — Age (percent); Population—change, 1980–2000 — Total persons; Percent change

Table F. Congressional Districts 107th Congress

STATE District	Household relationship, 2000															
	In households (percent)										In group quarters (percent)					
					Child		Other relatives		Nonrelatives			Institutionalized population			Noninstitutionalized population			
	Total population	Total in households	House-holder	Spouse	Total	Own child under 18 years	Total	Under 18 years	Total	Unmarried partner	Total in group quarters	Correctional institutions	Nursing homes	Other institutions	College dormitories	Military quarters	Other
	54	55	56	57	58	59	60	61	62	63	64	65	66	67	68	69	70
CALIFORNIA—Cont'd																	
District 45	619 092	98.6	36.1	18.0	28.1	20.5	8.0	2.2	8.4	1.9	1.4	0.0	0.5	0.2	0.1	0.0	0.6
District 46	663 548	98.2	24.0	14.1	34.7	26.1	16.0	4.9	9.5	1.4	1.8	0.7	0.3	0.1	0.0	0.0	0.7
District 47	715 625	98.0	36.4	20.0	29.0	22.6	6.0	1.6	6.6	1.7	2.0	0.1	0.2	0.1	1.1	0.0	0.5
District 48	773 292	97.1	34.1	20.6	31.2	25.5	5.4	1.8	5.8	1.7	2.9	0.2	0.1	0.0	0.0	0.0	0.5
District 49	586 882	92.6	42.7	15.3	19.5	15.0	4.3	1.3	10.8	2.9	7.4	0.4	0.4	0.1	1.8	3.2	1.4
District 50	641 790	97.9	29.5	15.5	35.9	26.4	11.2	4.3	5.9	1.7	2.1	1.1	0.1	0.0	0.0	0.4	0.4
District 51	713 746	98.6	35.8	20.9	30.2	24.2	5.6	1.6	6.1	1.8	1.4	0.0	0.4	0.0	0.0	0.6	0.4
District 52	640 630	96.7	34.1	18.4	31.8	24.3	6.5	2.6	6.0	2.0	3.3	1.7	0.6	0.1	0.3	0.0	0.6
COLORADO	4 301 261	97.6	38.6	20.0	28.3	23.4	4.4	1.6	6.4	2.1	2.4	0.7	0.5	0.1	0.5	0.2	0.4
District 1	662 711	97.9	41.7	15.0	25.0	19.7	7.8	2.8	8.5	2.7	2.1	0.5	0.5	0.1	0.3	0.0	0.7
District 2	702 336	98.4	38.5	20.1	28.2	23.1	4.2	1.5	7.4	2.3	1.6	0.1	0.4	0.0	0.9	0.0	0.3
District 3	723 533	97.2	39.1	20.9	26.9	22.3	3.6	1.5	6.6	2.1	2.8	0.7	0.5	0.2	0.6	0.0	0.8
District 4	748 228	97.0	36.3	20.8	29.8	24.8	4.1	1.6	6.0	1.9	3.0	1.0	0.6	0.0	1.1	0.0	0.3
District 5	810 423	96.8	36.3	21.9	30.9	26.3	3.1	1.2	4.5	1.7	3.2	1.4	0.3	0.1	0.2	1.0	0.2
District 6	654 030	98.7	40.2	20.5	28.4	23.2	3.8	1.3	5.8	2.2	1.3	0.3	0.5	0.1	0.1	0.0	0.2
CONNECTICUT	3 405 565	96.8	38.2	19.9	29.5	22.7	4.6	1.5	4.7	2.0	3.2	0.6	0.9	0.1	1.1	0.1	0.4
District 1	552 127	96.5	38.9	18.4	29.5	22.4	5.2	1.9	4.6	2.1	3.5	0.2	1.4	0.1	1.4	0.0	0.4
District 2	568 007	95.2	38.5	20.3	27.7	22.1	3.3	1.1	5.4	2.5	4.8	0.8	0.8	0.2	2.1	0.4	0.4
District 3	561 576	96.5	38.9	19.0	28.8	21.5	5.0	1.7	4.7	1.9	3.5	0.2	0.9	0.1	1.9	0.0	0.3
District 4	574 101	97.9	37.1	19.2	30.4	23.2	5.9	1.9	5.3	1.7	2.1	0.2	0.8	0.0	0.8	0.0	0.4
District 5	581 903	97.7	37.0	20.7	31.2	24.2	4.6	1.4	4.2	1.9	2.3	0.2	0.9	0.0	0.2	0.0	0.3
District 6	567 851	97.0	38.9	21.5	29.0	22.7	3.5	1.1	4.1	2.0	3.0	1.3	1.0	0.0	0.3	0.0	0.4
DELAWARE	783 600	96.9	38.1	19.5	28.6	22.0	5.1	2.2	5.5	2.3	3.1	0.8	0.6	0.1	1.2	0.0	0.4
At Large	783 600	96.9	38.1	19.5	28.6	22.0	5.1	2.2	5.5	2.3	3.1	0.8	0.6	0.1	1.2	0.0	0.4
DISTRICT OF COLUMBIA	572 059	93.8	43.4	9.9	22.6	15.5	8.8	3.9	9.1	2.6	6.2	0.5	0.7	0.2	3.4	0.2	1.3
Delegate	572 059	93.8	43.4	9.9	22.6	15.5	8.8	3.9	9.1	2.6	6.2	0.5	0.7	0.2	3.4	0.2	1.3
FLORIDA	15 982 378	97.6	39.7	20.0	26.1	20.0	6.0	2.2	5.9	2.3	2.4	0.9	0.6	0.1	0.3	0.1	0.5
District 1	683 987	95.1	38.4	20.4	27.2	21.5	4.3	1.9	4.8	1.9	4.9	2.1	0.6	0.2	0.6	1.1	0.2
District 2	678 025	93.0	37.9	18.0	25.9	20.1	5.1	2.3	6.1	2.0	7.0	4.3	0.6	0.3	1.3	0.1	0.4
District 3	586 694	96.8	37.0	14.5	30.5	22.9	8.6	4.3	6.1	2.5	3.2	1.0	0.5	0.2	0.4	0.2	1.0
District 4	734 246	98.2	40.7	21.8	26.4	21.1	3.9	1.4	5.4	2.2	1.8	0.2	0.7	0.0	0.3	0.4	0.2
District 5	689 672	97.0	42.5	21.4	22.0	17.2	4.3	1.6	6.8	2.4	3.0	0.4	0.7	0.1	1.2	0.0	0.5
District 6	755 939	96.2	39.1	22.8	25.4	20.1	4.6	2.0	4.4	2.0	3.8	2.7	0.6	0.1	0.0	0.0	0.3
District 7	722 139	98.6	39.5	21.3	27.2	21.1	4.8	1.7	5.7	2.4	1.4	0.2	0.5	0.0	0.4	0.0	0.3
District 8	782 397	97.7	37.9	18.5	27.5	21.5	5.9	1.9	7.9	2.7	2.3	0.9	0.4	0.2	0.5	0.0	0.2
District 9	722 068	98.5	41.8	22.7	25.2	20.0	3.9	1.2	4.9	2.3	1.5	0.1	0.6	0.0	0.1	0.0	0.6
District 10	583 809	97.4	45.3	19.3	22.1	16.8	4.5	1.7	6.1	2.9	2.6	0.6	1.0	0.2	0.2	0.0	0.7
District 11	628 167	97.8	40.3	16.3	27.5	21.5	6.4	2.6	7.3	3.0	2.2	0.5	0.3	0.1	0.7	0.1	0.6
District 12	671 347	97.3	37.3	20.9	27.8	21.8	6.1	2.8	5.2	2.0	2.7	0.9	0.6	0.2	0.4	0.0	0.6
District 13	677 666	97.9	44.3	23.5	20.6	16.1	4.3	1.5	5.2	2.3	2.1	0.3	1.1	0.1	0.1	0.0	0.6
District 14	790 852	98.4	42.6	24.3	21.1	16.8	4.6	1.5	5.7	2.3	1.6	0.4	0.7	0.1	0.0	0.0	0.5
District 15	718 294	97.9	41.0	22.4	25.1	19.6	4.5	1.8	5.0	2.2	2.1	0.6	0.5	0.3	0.2	0.0	0.5
District 16	758 365	98.6	41.4	22.8	24.4	19.4	4.6	1.6	5.4	2.3	1.4	0.5	0.4	0.1	0.0	0.0	0.4
District 17	577 167	97.5	31.4	11.7	34.7	24.1	13.1	5.8	6.5	2.3	2.5	0.7	0.6	0.2	0.3	0.0	0.6
District 18	597 947	97.9	36.9	17.2	26.3	17.7	10.3	2.5	7.1	1.9	2.1	0.5	0.4	0.2	0.7	0.0	0.3
District 19	800 902	98.7	42.6	22.8	24.0	18.9	4.3	1.1	5.0	2.2	1.3	0.0	0.7	0.0	0.3	0.0	0.2
District 20	783 412	99.0	38.1	20.6	29.2	22.8	5.7	1.6	5.4	2.3	1.0	0.4	0.2	0.1	0.0	0.0	0.2
District 21	789 742	98.3	32.0	18.6	31.2	22.0	11.1	2.6	5.4	1.7	1.7	0.8	0.4	0.2	0.0	0.0	0.3
District 22	630 775	98.7	36.1	19.0	18.6	13.9	4.7	1.1	7.2	3.1	1.3	0.0	0.4	0.0	0.2	0.0	0.6
District 23	618 766	96.5	34.2	13.0	31.6	23.5	10.4	4.6	7.3	2.6	3.5	2.0	0.4	0.1	0.0	0.0	0.9
GEORGIA	8 186 453	97.1	36.7	18.9	29.8	23.2	6.4	2.7	5.3	1.8	2.9	1.0	0.4	0.1	0.6	0.3	0.4
District 1	692 199	95.9	36.8	18.8	29.6	23.5	5.6	2.8	5.1	1.8	4.1	1.4	0.4	0.1	0.6	1.1	0.4
District 2	650 392	95.2	36.1	17.5	30.6	23.3	6.9	3.5	4.0	1.7	4.8	1.8	0.7	0.2	0.6	0.9	0.6
District 3	781 694	98.0	35.6	19.8	32.1	24.9	6.4	2.8	4.2	1.6	2.0	0.6	0.4	0.1	0.1	0.7	0.2
District 4	744 717	98.1	36.9	15.3	27.7	21.0	9.2	3.1	9.0	2.2	1.9	0.4	0.3	0.2	0.5	0.0	0.5
District 5	646 184	95.2	39.7	11.2	26.4	19.3	9.0	3.9	8.8	2.6	4.8	1.2	0.3	0.0	2.1	0.0	1.1
District 6	943 373	99.4	37.3	21.9	30.3	25.3	4.3	1.1	5.5	1.6	0.6	0.2	0.1	0.0	0.0	0.0	0.3
District 7	752 161	97.5	36.1	20.3	30.2	23.7	6.1	2.6	4.8	1.7	2.5	0.9	0.5	0.0	0.6	0.0	0.2
District 8	662 811	95.8	37.1	18.8	30.1	22.9	6.0	3.0	3.9	1.7	4.2	2.2	0.8	0.2	0.6	0.2	0.2
District 9	814 305	98.3	36.7	22.7	29.0	22.9	5.7	2.1	4.1	1.5	1.7	0.5	0.4	0.1	0.5	0.0	0.2
District 10	662 201	95.5	36.5	18.2	30.6	23.0	6.4	3.2	3.8	1.7	4.5	2.0	0.5	0.4	0.3	0.7	0.7
District 11	836 416	98.0	35.5	21.0	30.6	24.1	5.6	2.1	5.3	1.6	2.0	0.4	0.4	0.0	0.9	0.0	0.3

Table F. Congressional Districts 107th Congress

		Households by type, 2000											Households, 1990		
		Family households						Nonfamily households							
				Married couple		Female householder[1]			Householder living alone						
STATE District	Total households	Total	With own children under 18 years	Total	With own children under 18 years	Total	With own children under 18 years	Total	Total	65 years and over	Average house-hold size	Average family size	Total house-holds	Female house-holder[1]	House-holder living alone
	71	72	73	74	75	76	77	78	79	80	81	82	83	84	85
CALIFORNIA—Cont'd															
District 45	223 672	65.2	30.4	49.9	23.1	10.4	5.2	34.8	25.0	8.5	2.73	3.30	213 006	9.6	23.7
District 46	158 971	80.1	49.1	50.9	38.3	13.6	7.4	19.9	14.4	5.4	4.10	4.37	155 659	12.0	17.7
District 47	260 153	68.4	34.0	55.0	27.1	9.5	5.2	31.6	23.8	8.1	2.70	3.21	212 084	8.6	22.4
District 48	263 378	73.8	39.1	60.6	31.2	9.3	5.7	26.2	19.5	6.7	2.85	3.28	200 215	8.2	18.8
District 49	250 694	47.9	20.0	35.8	13.9	8.6	4.5	52.1	36.5	9.2	2.17	2.91	233 952	8.8	33.1
District 50	189 064	77.2	44.4	52.6	30.2	18.5	11.3	22.8	16.9	6.1	3.32	3.75	175 606	17.0	18.1
District 51	255 803	71.3	36.5	58.4	29.1	9.1	5.4	28.7	21.4	7.7	2.75	3.22	207 876	8.3	20.0
District 52	218 203	72.3	37.6	53.9	26.8	13.4	8.1	27.7	20.9	8.0	2.84	3.30	199 359	12.0	19.7
COLORADO	1 658 238	65.4	32.8	51.8	24.4	9.6	6.2	34.6	26.3	7.0	2.53	3.09	1 282 489	9.7	26.6
District 1	276 278	52.1	25.1	36.0	16.2	11.4	6.8	47.9	37.5	9.1	2.35	3.20	242 791	12.0	38.9
District 2	270 561	65.3	33.0	52.1	24.9	9.1	5.8	34.7	24.7	6.0	2.55	3.08	210 000	9.1	23.9
District 3	282 826	66.5	31.0	53.4	22.7	9.1	5.9	33.5	25.2	8.4	2.49	2.98	210 794	9.4	24.5
District 4	271 325	70.4	36.0	57.5	27.9	8.9	5.8	29.6	21.9	7.3	2.67	3.14	202 437	8.6	22.7
District 5	294 551	72.5	38.9	60.2	30.7	9.0	6.2	27.5	21.4	5.2	2.66	3.12	199 048	9.1	21.5
District 6	262 697	65.0	32.3	51.0	23.6	10.1	6.5	35.0	27.2	6.2	2.46	3.02	217 419	9.7	25.7
CONNECTICUT	1 301 670	67.7	32.2	52.0	23.6	12.1	7.0	32.3	26.4	10.1	2.53	3.08	1 230 479	11.4	24.2
District 1	214 887	65.8	31.4	47.3	20.8	14.8	9.0	34.2	28.4	10.7	2.48	3.07	208 723	13.9	25.8
District 2	218 951	66.7	31.7	52.6	23.3	10.4	6.5	33.3	26.4	9.5	2.47	2.99	200 769	9.5	23.3
District 3	218 716	65.5	30.2	48.9	21.4	13.1	7.3	34.5	28.4	11.0	2.48	3.07	207 515	12.4	25.7
District 4	212 711	68.6	33.3	51.9	24.9	13.0	7.0	31.4	25.5	9.8	2.64	3.18	204 373	12.7	24.2
District 5	215 500	71.1	35.1	55.8	26.8	11.6	6.7	28.9	23.9	9.3	2.64	3.15	201 115	10.5	22.6
District 6	220 905	68.5	31.7	55.2	24.5	9.8	5.6	31.5	26.0	10.6	2.49	3.03	207 984	9.3	23.2
DELAWARE	298 736	68.5	31.9	51.3	21.9	13.1	7.7	31.5	25.0	9.1	2.54	3.04	247 497	11.8	23.2
At Large	298 736	68.5	31.9	51.3	21.9	13.1	7.7	31.5	25.0	9.1	2.54	3.04	247 497	11.8	23.2
DISTRICT OF COLUMBIA	248 338	46.0	19.8	22.8	8.4	18.9	9.9	54.0	43.8	10.0	2.16	3.07	249 634	19.5	41.5
Delegate	248 338	46.0	19.8	22.8	8.4	18.9	9.9	54.0	43.8	10.0	2.16	3.07	249 634	19.5	41.5
FLORIDA	6 337 929	66.4	28.1	50.4	19.2	12.0	6.9	33.6	26.6	11.2	2.46	2.98	5 134 869	10.7	25.5
District 1	262 806	69.2	31.3	53.1	21.8	12.2	7.5	30.8	24.8	8.6	2.47	2.95	211 725	11.7	22.3
District 2	257 083	65.3	30.1	47.5	19.8	13.7	8.2	34.7	26.6	8.6	2.45	2.98	207 532	13.2	24.2
District 3	217 220	66.8	32.4	39.2	16.4	22.1	13.3	33.2	26.8	9.5	2.61	3.17	204 394	19.8	25.7
District 4	298 583	66.9	29.8	53.6	22.1	9.8	5.9	33.1	25.8	8.9	2.42	2.92	224 605	8.8	25.5
District 5	293 149	63.8	22.6	50.3	15.1	10.0	5.7	36.2	27.7	13.1	2.28	2.76	237 502	8.8	25.7
District 6	295 256	72.3	28.4	58.3	20.0	10.4	6.3	27.7	22.8	11.2	2.46	2.87	214 281	9.6	21.3
District 7	285 542	68.7	30.2	53.9	21.8	11.0	6.4	31.3	24.1	9.2	2.49	2.96	222 116	8.7	22.5
District 8	296 753	65.2	31.8	48.9	22.7	11.7	6.9	34.8	24.2	6.4	2.58	3.10	216 066	9.4	23.9
District 9	301 814	66.6	27.3	54.4	20.4	9.0	5.2	33.4	27.0	11.8	2.36	2.86	233 442	7.8	25.0
District 10	264 641	57.3	21.5	42.6	13.5	11.1	6.2	42.7	35.1	15.8	2.15	2.77	253 213	10.0	33.2
District 11	253 362	60.4	29.5	40.3	17.6	15.4	9.4	39.6	30.5	8.4	2.42	3.06	225 942	13.7	28.4
District 12	250 701	72.1	31.0	55.8	21.6	11.9	7.0	27.9	22.8	10.6	2.61	3.04	209 945	10.8	21.5
District 13	300 006	64.5	20.2	53.2	14.0	8.4	4.6	35.5	29.4	16.6	2.21	2.70	247 267	7.6	27.0
District 14	336 848	68.4	21.5	57.1	15.2	7.9	4.6	31.6	25.3	13.2	2.31	2.72	234 797	7.5	22.8
District 15	294 302	68.2	26.6	54.6	18.9	9.9	5.8	31.8	25.8	11.9	2.39	2.86	226 294	8.7	23.2
District 16	313 747	67.6	25.8	55.1	18.6	8.9	5.3	32.4	26.3	13.8	2.38	2.85	233 951	7.1	23.7
District 17	181 274	71.7	38.3	37.4	19.3	27.0	15.8	28.3	22.4	7.4	3.10	3.64	182 462	23.4	23.5
District 18	220 843	65.7	27.5	46.6	19.7	13.8	6.1	34.3	27.3	10.6	2.65	3.22	209 846	12.5	27.0
District 19	341 063	65.3	25.4	53.5	19.0	8.6	4.9	34.7	28.5	16.0	2.32	2.84	244 747	6.5	26.2
District 20	298 441	69.0	33.8	54.1	25.7	11.0	6.2	31.0	24.0	9.8	2.60	3.11	222 030	8.6	23.6
District 21	252 930	79.8	40.4	58.2	29.9	16.1	8.4	20.2	15.3	5.1	3.07	3.38	188 480	13.2	17.1
District 22	309 937	50.3	16.9	38.8	11.4	8.1	4.0	49.7	40.5	16.1	2.01	2.71	284 067	6.9	40.1
District 23	211 628	66.7	34.8	38.0	18.1	22.0	13.5	33.3	25.7	9.2	2.82	3.41	200 175	18.5	26.2
GEORGIA	3 006 369	70.2	35.0	51.5	24.4	14.5	8.6	29.8	23.6	7.0	2.65	3.14	2 366 615	13.9	22.7
District 1	254 736	69.9	35.1	51.1	23.9	14.8	9.1	30.1	24.0	8.3	2.61	3.10	209 008	14.2	22.8
District 2	234 942	71.4	34.8	48.3	21.4	18.8	11.2	28.6	24.4	9.6	2.64	3.13	203 783	18.1	22.6
District 3	278 057	75.3	38.7	55.5	27.1	15.5	9.4	24.7	20.4	6.5	2.75	3.17	208 344	14.1	19.3
District 4	274 954	63.5	32.2	41.4	20.1	16.8	10.0	36.5	26.4	4.7	2.66	3.22	228 142	13.6	25.3
District 5	256 317	54.0	26.0	28.4	11.8	20.9	12.3	46.0	35.2	7.4	2.40	3.18	231 179	21.5	32.2
District 6	352 341	70.3	38.0	58.7	31.3	8.5	5.2	29.7	22.0	3.3	2.66	3.15	226 407	7.8	21.7
District 7	271 642	73.8	36.6	56.1	26.6	13.1	7.7	26.2	21.3	7.5	2.70	3.12	214 189	11.8	20.6
District 8	245 698	71.2	34.2	50.7	22.4	16.4	9.7	28.8	24.8	9.5	2.58	3.08	214 046	15.7	23.5
District 9	298 794	75.8	34.9	62.0	27.6	9.7	5.3	24.2	20.3	7.8	2.68	3.07	217 009	9.7	19.7
District 10	241 693	71.7	34.8	49.8	22.2	17.7	10.5	28.3	24.2	8.8	2.62	3.11	206 840	16.6	22.8
District 11	297 195	74.2	37.7	59.0	29.2	11.3	6.6	25.8	19.3	5.6	2.76	3.17	207 668	10.3	18.4

[1]No spouse present.

Table F. Congressional Districts 107th Congress

| STATE District | Percent change of households, 1990–2000 | Total housing units | Occupied housing units (percent) | Vacant housing units | | Homeowner vacancy rate (percent) | Rental vacancy rate (percent) | Occupied housing units | | | Average household size of owner-occupied units | Average household size of renter-occupied units |
				Total	For seasonal, recreational, or occasional use			Total	Percent owner-occupied housing units	Percent renter-occupied housing units		
	86	87	88	89	90	91	92	93	94	95	96	97
CALIFORNIA—Cont'd												
District 45	5.0	232 605	96.2	3.8	1.2	1.0	3.0	223 672	56.6	43.4	2.72	2.74
District 46	2.1	163 716	97.1	2.9	0.2	0.8	2.2	158 971	48.8	51.2	4.07	4.13
District 47	22.7	271 810	95.7	4.3	1.0	1.0	3.6	260 153	66.0	34.0	2.72	2.64
District 48	31.5	276 579	95.2	4.8	1.8	1.1	3.5	263 378	67.8	32.2	2.84	2.87
District 49	7.2	265 213	94.5	5.5	2.1	0.9	3.3	250 694	41.7	58.3	2.24	2.11
District 50	7.7	194 913	97.0	3.0	0.3	0.9	2.9	189 064	49.6	50.4	3.35	3.30
District 51	23.1	266 342	96.0	4.0	1.2	1.0	3.4	255 803	67.8	32.2	2.76	2.73
District 52	9.5	229 965	94.9	5.1	2.0	0.9	3.2	218 203	59.9	40.1	2.88	2.78
COLORADO	29.3	1 808 037	91.7	8.3	4.0	1.4	5.5	1 658 238	67.3	32.7	2.64	2.30
District 1	13.8	290 212	95.2	4.8	0.5	1.6	4.4	276 278	52.6	47.4	2.48	2.20
District 2	28.8	281 469	96.1	3.9	1.4	0.7	3.6	270 561	68.9	31.1	2.67	2.29
District 3	34.2	361 493	78.2	21.8	15.2	2.4	9.5	282 826	70.5	29.5	2.54	2.36
District 4	34.0	292 604	92.7	7.3	2.3	1.7	5.5	271 325	71.5	28.5	2.75	2.48
District 5	48.0	311 042	94.7	5.3	1.3	1.3	6.5	294 551	71.5	28.5	2.77	2.38
District 6	20.8	271 217	96.9	3.1	0.4	0.8	4.2	262 697	68.6	31.4	2.58	2.19
CONNECTICUT	5.8	1 385 975	93.9	6.1	1.7	1.1	5.6	1 301 670	66.8	33.2	2.67	2.25
District 1	3.0	226 758	94.8	5.2	0.6	0.9	6.6	214 887	62.7	37.3	2.62	2.25
District 2	9.1	238 922	91.6	8.4	3.8	1.2	5.6	218 951	67.4	32.6	2.62	2.16
District 3	5.4	233 335	93.7	6.3	1.4	1.1	6.1	218 716	65.1	34.9	2.64	2.18
District 4	4.1	222 992	95.4	4.6	0.9	0.9	4.0	212 711	64.2	35.8	2.74	2.46
District 5	7.2	227 677	94.7	5.3	0.9	1.1	5.8	215 500	69.5	30.5	2.78	2.32
District 6	6.2	236 291	93.5	6.5	2.5	1.1	5.3	220 905	71.9	28.1	2.64	2.11
DELAWARE	20.7	343 072	87.1	12.9	7.6	1.5	8.2	298 736	72.3	27.7	2.61	2.37
At Large	20.7	343 072	87.1	12.9	7.6	1.5	8.2	298 736	72.3	27.7	2.61	2.37
DISTRICT OF COLUMBIA	-0.5	274 845	90.4	9.6	0.8	2.9	5.9	248 338	40.8	59.2	2.31	2.06
Delegate	-0.5	274 845	90.4	9.6	0.8	2.9	5.9	248 338	40.8	59.2	2.31	2.06
FLORIDA	23.4	7 302 947	86.8	13.2	6.6	2.2	9.3	6 337 929	70.1	29.9	2.49	2.39
District 1	24.1	321 368	81.8	18.2	7.5	2.5	19.2	262 806	70.5	29.5	2.50	2.42
District 2	23.9	296 410	86.7	13.3	3.8	2.2	11.6	257 083	69.5	30.5	2.53	2.28
District 3	6.3	243 578	89.2	10.8	1.5	2.5	9.2	217 220	59.7	40.3	2.66	2.55
District 4	32.9	330 467	90.4	9.6	3.7	1.6	9.6	298 583	70.4	29.6	2.52	2.16
District 5	23.4	334 792	87.6	12.4	5.2	2.5	9.6	293 149	74.7	25.3	2.31	2.22
District 6	37.8	336 735	87.7	12.3	4.6	2.3	10.5	295 256	79.9	20.1	2.46	2.48
District 7	28.6	312 624	91.3	8.7	4.1	1.7	6.8	285 542	73.8	26.2	2.56	2.32
District 8	37.3	321 059	92.4	7.6	2.2	1.7	7.4	296 753	61.3	38.7	2.71	2.36
District 9	29.3	341 054	88.5	11.5	5.6	2.0	11.2	301 814	76.7	23.3	2.42	2.15
District 10	4.5	310 847	85.1	14.9	7.7	2.4	10.4	264 641	70.1	29.9	2.20	2.02
District 11	12.1	274 304	92.4	7.6	0.7	1.9	8.1	253 362	56.3	43.7	2.57	2.23
District 12	19.4	294 689	85.1	14.9	7.0	2.7	10.7	250 701	74.1	25.9	2.59	2.65
District 13	21.3	364 368	82.3	17.7	11.3	2.2	12.3	300 006	77.5	22.5	2.19	2.27
District 14	43.5	448 629	75.1	24.9	18.5	2.6	13.7	336 848	77.3	22.7	2.27	2.46
District 15	30.1	341 080	86.3	13.7	7.2	2.3	11.9	294 302	76.0	24.0	2.42	2.31
District 16	34.1	375 769	83.5	16.5	10.2	2.5	10.6	313 747	78.8	21.2	2.35	2.49
District 17	-0.7	198 825	91.2	8.8	0.9	2.5	8.0	181 274	51.2	48.8	3.33	2.87
District 18	5.2	238 341	92.7	7.3	2.7	1.8	4.4	220 843	51.9	48.1	2.85	2.43
District 19	39.4	382 820	89.1	10.9	6.7	1.9	6.5	341 063	77.8	22.2	2.32	2.31
District 20	34.4	337 152	88.5	11.5	6.0	2.8	7.0	298 441	76.5	23.5	2.66	2.39
District 21	34.2	263 678	95.9	4.1	1.0	1.4	3.6	252 930	64.5	35.5	3.18	2.87
District 22	9.1	396 781	78.1	21.9	15.5	2.8	8.2	309 937	64.6	35.4	2.06	1.92
District 23	5.7	237 577	89.1	10.9	3.6	2.8	7.8	211 628	55.2	44.8	2.84	2.80
GEORGIA	27.0	3 281 737	91.6	8.4	1.5	1.9	8.2	3 006 369	67.5	32.5	2.71	2.51
District 1	21.9	289 826	87.9	12.1	2.6	2.1	11.1	254 736	65.4	34.6	2.66	2.51
District 2	15.3	266 501	88.2	11.8	1.9	2.1	10.9	234 942	66.5	33.5	2.65	2.61
District 3	33.5	296 472	93.8	6.2	0.6	1.6	8.1	278 057	71.5	28.5	2.80	2.64
District 4	20.5	287 284	95.7	4.3	0.3	1.4	4.7	274 954	56.9	43.1	2.71	2.59
District 5	10.9	281 538	91.0	9.0	0.5	3.4	7.1	256 317	45.4	54.6	2.50	2.32
District 6	55.6	367 828	95.8	4.2	0.3	1.4	6.3	352 341	70.1	29.9	2.83	2.28
District 7	26.8	289 303	93.9	6.1	0.5	1.6	7.0	271 642	72.1	27.9	2.73	2.61
District 8	14.8	277 419	88.6	11.4	1.0	2.1	13.0	245 698	69.7	30.3	2.63	2.49
District 9	37.7	335 762	89.0	11.0	5.0	1.9	7.8	298 794	76.9	23.1	2.67	2.72
District 10	16.9	275 102	87.9	12.1	3.0	2.1	10.3	241 693	70.8	29.2	2.67	2.50
District 11	43.1	314 702	94.4	5.6	0.9	1.6	6.0	297 195	73.9	26.1	2.83	2.55

STATE District	Population, 2000				Population, 1990				Population and population characteristics, 2000					
									Race (percent)					
									One race					
	Land area, 2000[1] (sq km)	Total persons	Rank	Per square kilometer	Land area, 1990[1] (sq km)	Total persons	Rank	Per square kilometer	White	Black or African American	American Indian or Alaska Native	Asian	Native Hawaiian and other Pacific Islander	Some other race
	1	2	3	4	5	6	7	8	9	10	11	12	13	14
HAWAII	16 635.0	1 211 537	X	72.8	16 636.0	1 108 229	X	66.6	24.3	1.8	0.3	41.6	9.4	1.3
District 1	470.1	568 524	X	1 209.4	470.0	554 119	X	1 179.0	19.5	2.1	0.2	53.5	6.8	1.0
District 2	16 164.4	643 013	X	39.8	16 166.0	554 110	X	34.0	28.5	1.6	0.4	31.1	11.7	1.5
IDAHO	214 314.0	1 293 953	X	6.0	214 325.0	1 006 734	X	4.7	91.0	0.4	1.4	0.9	0.1	4.2
District 1	102 436.0	702 521	X	6.9	102 441.0	503 357	X	5.0	91.6	0.3	1.3	1.0	0.1	3.6
District 2	111 878.2	591 432	X	5.3	111 884.0	503 392	X	5.0	90.3	0.5	1.4	0.8	0.1	4.9
ILLINOIS	143 961.0	12 419 293	X	86.3	143 987.0	11 430 602	X	79.4	73.5	15.1	0.2	3.4	0.0	5.8
District 1	143.7	560 239	X	3 898.7	144.0	571 530	X	3 976.0	23.0	70.3	0.2	1.4	0.0	3.6
District 2	322.3	556 482	X	1 726.6	322.0	571 530	X	1 773.0	18.1	75.8	0.2	0.5	0.0	4.0
District 3	327.5	629 597	X	1 922.4	328.0	571 531	X	1 744.0	78.5	4.5	0.3	1.7	0.0	12.1
District 4	102.3	625 941	X	6 118.7	102.0	571 530	X	5 587.0	44.7	8.1	0.7	2.6	0.1	39.6
District 5	136.6	635 824	X	4 654.6	137.0	571 530	X	4 181.0	76.8	2.0	0.3	6.1	0.1	11.1
District 6	476.5	615 419	X	1 291.5	477.0	571 530	X	1 199.0	83.8	2.4	0.2	7.7	0.0	4.0
District 7	131.5	569 470	X	4 330.6	132.0	571 530	X	4 345.0	28.0	63.3	0.2	4.8	0.1	2.2
District 8	1 117.2	699 513	X	626.1	1 118.0	571 530	X	511.0	83.4	2.7	0.2	7.4	0.0	4.4
District 9	139.1	593 205	X	4 264.6	139.0	571 530	X	4 106.0	66.8	12.2	0.3	12.1	0.1	4.9
District 10	632.8	627 793	X	992.1	633.0	571 530	X	903.0	79.1	6.7	0.2	5.7	0.0	6.3
District 11	6 725.6	635 653	X	94.5	6 729.0	571 528	X	85.0	79.4	13.2	0.2	0.7	0.0	4.8
District 12	9 081.0	560 912	X	61.8	9 082.0	571 530	X	63.0	78.3	18.5	0.3	0.9	0.0	0.8
District 13	1 044.3	759 124	X	726.9	1 046.0	571 531	X	547.0	85.8	4.5	0.1	6.2	0.0	1.8
District 14	6 350.5	720 663	X	113.5	6 352.0	571 530	X	90.0	83.4	4.5	0.3	2.5	0.0	7.5
District 15	19 402.3	595 833	X	30.7	19 404.0	571 532	X	30.0	85.5	8.8	0.2	2.6	0.0	1.4
District 16	8 009.9	691 356	X	86.3	8 013.0	571 530	X	71.0	88.9	5.1	0.2	1.3	0.0	2.9
District 17	21 569.1	567 712	X	26.3	21 571.0	571 530	X	27.0	92.2	3.7	0.2	0.7	0.0	1.9
District 18	15 987.3	597 447	X	37.4	15 989.0	571 580	X	36.0	90.9	6.4	0.2	0.9	0.0	0.6
District 19	27 790.5	575 769	X	20.7	27 798.0	571 530	X	21.0	93.6	4.6	0.2	0.4	0.0	0.3
District 20	24 470.7	601 341	X	24.6	24 473.0	571 480	X	23.0	92.4	5.6	0.2	0.5	0.0	0.4
INDIANA	92 895.0	6 080 485	X	65.5	92 904.0	5 544 156	X	59.7	87.5	8.4	0.3	1.0	0.0	1.6
District 1	1 682.9	571 747	X	339.7	1 683.0	554 416	X	329.0	71.0	21.6	0.3	0.9	0.0	4.4
District 2	10 070.2	567 204	X	56.3	10 071.0	554 416	X	55.0	93.3	4.3	0.2	0.6	0.0	0.6
District 3	4 702.5	610 182	X	129.8	4 703.0	554 416	X	118.0	85.3	8.4	0.3	1.0	0.0	3.2
District 4	9 341.2	619 891	X	66.4	9 342.0	554 416	X	59.0	89.6	6.2	0.3	0.9	0.0	1.7
District 5	18 031.3	585 988	X	32.5	18 033.0	554 415	X	31.0	94.4	2.4	0.4	0.4	0.0	1.3
District 6	5 277.6	724 143	X	137.2	5 278.0	554 416	X	105.0	94.2	2.3	0.2	1.5	0.0	0.8
District 7	12 306.7	633 484	X	51.5	12 308.0	554 416	X	45.0	94.1	2.2	0.3	1.5	0.0	0.9
District 8	13 535.7	590 205	X	43.6	13 538.0	554 416	X	41.0	93.7	3.5	0.2	1.1	0.0	0.4
District 9	17 437.7	608 430	X	34.9	17 439.0	554 416	X	32.0	96.1	2.0	0.2	0.4	0.0	0.6
District 10	509.1	569 211	X	1 118.1	509.0	554 416	X	1 089.0	59.7	34.3	0.3	1.3	0.0	2.5
IOWA	144 701.0	2 926 324	X	20.2	144 716.0	2 776 831	X	19.2	93.9	2.1	0.3	1.3	0.0	1.3
District 1	11 603.8	603 837	X	52.0	11 605.0	555 229	X	48.0	92.0	3.2	0.3	1.7	0.0	1.3
District 2	31 753.7	568 857	X	17.9	31 757.0	555 494	X	18.0	95.5	2.1	0.3	0.5	0.0	0.9
District 3	35 822.4	573 674	X	16.0	35 828.0	555 299	X	16.0	95.5	1.1	0.3	1.3	0.0	0.6
District 4	19 418.7	621 351	X	32.0	19 421.0	555 276	X	29.0	91.8	3.1	0.3	1.7	0.0	1.8
District 5	46 102.3	558 605	X	12.1	46 106.0	555 457	X	12.0	95.2	0.8	0.5	0.9	0.0	1.7
KANSAS	211 900.0	2 688 418	X	12.7	211 922.0	2 477 588	X	11.7	86.1	5.7	0.9	1.7	0.0	3.4
District 1	145 669.0	637 670	X	4.4	145 674.0	619 370	X	4.0	89.8	1.4	0.5	0.9	0.0	5.8
District 2	36 185.2	641 387	X	17.7	36 195.0	619 391	X	17.0	87.9	5.9	1.3	1.0	0.1	1.7
District 3	4 016.6	733 606	X	182.6	4 017.0	619 439	X	154.0	83.5	8.3	0.7	2.5	0.0	2.9
District 4	26 028.7	675 755	X	26.0	26 036.0	619 374	X	24.0	83.6	6.8	1.2	2.4	0.0	3.3
KENTUCKY	102 896.0	4 041 769	X	39.3	102 907.0	3 686 892	X	35.8	90.1	7.3	0.2	0.7	0.0	0.6
District 1	29 086.5	652 338	X	22.4	29 089.0	614 265	X	21.0	90.2	7.5	0.2	0.4	0.1	0.6
District 2	20 095.4	706 978	X	35.2	20 098.0	614 794	X	31.0	92.0	5.2	0.2	0.7	0.1	0.6
District 3	618.4	626 676	X	1 013.4	618.0	613 603	X	993.0	75.7	20.5	0.2	1.4	0.0	0.7
District 4	14 255.8	691 720	X	48.5	14 258.0	602 896	X	42.0	95.3	2.6	0.2	0.5	0.0	0.5
District 5	26 744.1	648 751	X	24.3	26 746.0	624 837	X	23.0	97.7	1.1	0.2	0.2	0.0	0.1
District 6	12 095.3	715 306	X	59.1	12 098.0	614 901	X	51.0	88.8	7.9	0.2	1.1	0.0	0.6
LOUISIANA	112 825.0	4 468 976	X	39.6	112 836.0	4 221 826	X	37.4	63.9	32.5	0.6	1.2	0.0	0.7
District 1	6 175.5	666 747	X	108.0	6 177.0	602 842	X	98.0	81.6	13.7	0.3	1.6	0.0	1.3
District 2	697.5	590 824	X	847.1	696.0	602 877	X	866.0	27.8	66.9	0.3	2.5	0.0	1.1
District 3	17 891.2	637 359	X	35.6	17 893.0	602 839	X	34.0	70.2	25.3	1.6	1.2	0.0	0.6
District 4	26 404.7	616 120	X	23.3	26 407.0	602 876	X	23.0	62.4	34.0	0.8	0.7	0.1	0.7
District 5	33 942.9	610 398	X	18.0	33 948.0	602 933	X	18.0	65.3	32.6	0.4	0.5	0.0	0.4
District 6	10 119.2	683 536	X	67.5	10 121.0	602 774	X	60.0	63.6	33.6	0.2	1.3	0.0	0.4

[1] Dry land or land partially or temporarily covered by water.

Table F. Congressional Districts 107th Congress

STATE District	Population and population characteristics, 2000 (cont'd)								Population and population characteristics, 1990				
	Race (percent) (cont'd)								Race (percent)				
	Race alone or in combination												
	Two or more races	White	Black	American Indian or Alaska Native	Asian	Native Hawaiian and other Pacific Islander	Some other race	Hispanic¹	White	Black or African American	American Indian or Alaska Native	Asian and Pacific Islander	Hispanic¹
	15	16	17	18	19	20	21	22	23	24	25	26	27
HAWAII	21.4	39.3	2.8	2.1	58.0	23.3	3.9	7.2	33.4	2.5	0.5	61.8	7.3
District 1	16.9	31.3	3.0	1.5	67.1	16.8	2.9	5.4	29.1	2.5	0.3	66.6	5.5
District 2	25.4	46.3	2.5	2.5	50.0	29.1	4.8	8.9	37.6	2.4	0.6	57.1	9.2
IDAHO	2.0	92.8	0.6	2.1	1.3	0.2	5.0	7.9	94.4	0.3	1.4	0.9	5.3
District 1	2.0	93.5	0.5	2.2	1.4	0.2	4.3	6.8	94.9	0.2	1.3	1.0	4.6
District 2	1.9	92.1	0.7	2.0	1.2	0.2	5.8	9.1	93.9	0.4	1.4	0.9	5.9
ILLINOIS	1.9	75.1	15.6	0.6	3.8	0.1	6.8	12.3	78.3	14.8	0.2	2.5	7.9
District 1	1.5	24.0	71.1	0.6	1.6	0.1	4.3	7.5	27.3	69.7	0.1	1.0	3.6
District 2	1.4	19.0	76.6	0.6	0.6	0.1	4.6	7.8	27.1	68.5	0.1	0.6	6.6
District 3	2.9	81.2	4.7	0.6	2.0	0.1	14.3	24.3	93.3	1.9	0.1	1.4	7.4
District 4	4.2	48.3	8.7	1.1	2.9	0.3	43.1	70.1	48.6	6.3	0.4	2.6	65.0
District 5	3.6	80.0	2.3	0.6	6.9	0.1	13.7	25.0	86.8	1.5	0.3	5.9	13.3
District 6	1.9	85.3	2.7	0.5	8.4	0.1	5.0	10.9	91.8	1.5	0.1	4.9	5.3
District 7	1.5	29.0	64.0	0.5	5.1	0.1	2.9	5.2	29.0	65.6	0.1	3.2	4.3
District 8	1.9	85.0	3.0	0.5	8.0	0.1	5.3	11.3	92.2	1.7	0.2	4.0	5.5
District 9	3.6	69.4	13.2	0.7	13.2	0.2	7.0	12.3	73.1	12.1	0.3	10.0	9.7
District 10	1.9	80.7	7.1	0.5	6.3	0.1	7.3	13.9	86.5	6.2	0.2	4.1	7.1
District 11	1.6	80.8	13.7	0.6	0.9	0.1	5.6	10.5	87.4	8.6	0.2	0.7	6.5
District 12	1.2	79.4	18.9	0.7	1.2	0.1	1.0	2.0	81.5	17.0	0.2	0.9	1.3
District 13	1.6	87.1	4.9	0.4	6.7	0.1	2.4	5.4	91.6	3.2	0.1	4.2	3.0
District 14	1.9	85.1	4.9	0.6	2.8	0.1	8.5	17.5	88.8	4.2	0.2	1.7	9.8
District 15	1.4	86.8	9.4	0.5	3.0	0.1	1.8	3.0	89.7	7.4	0.2	1.9	1.6
District 16	1.4	90.2	5.5	0.6	1.6	0.1	3.5	6.9	92.9	4.7	0.2	0.9	3.1
District 17	1.2	93.4	4.2	0.5	0.8	0.1	2.4	4.6	94.7	3.3	0.2	0.6	3.0
District 18	1.0	91.8	6.8	0.5	1.1	0.0	0.8	1.5	93.7	5.1	0.2	0.7	0.9
District 19	0.8	94.4	4.9	0.5	0.5	0.0	0.4	1.0	95.5	3.9	0.2	0.3	0.5
District 20	0.9	93.2	5.9	0.6	0.7	0.1	0.5	1.1	95.0	4.2	0.2	0.4	0.7
INDIANA	1.2	88.6	8.8	0.6	1.2	0.1	2.0	3.5	90.6	7.8	0.2	0.7	1.8
District 1	1.8	72.5	22.1	0.7	1.1	0.1	5.4	11.2	74.2	21.1	0.2	0.6	8.5
District 2	1.0	94.2	4.7	0.6	0.8	0.1	0.7	1.3	95.0	4.1	0.2	0.4	0.6
District 3	1.8	86.8	9.1	0.8	1.3	0.1	3.8	5.8	90.7	7.4	0.3	0.8	1.9
District 4	1.3	90.8	6.7	0.7	1.1	0.1	2.1	3.5	92.9	5.5	0.3	0.6	1.6
District 5	1.1	95.4	2.7	0.8	0.6	0.1	1.6	3.0	96.7	2.2	0.4	0.3	1.3
District 6	0.9	95.1	2.6	0.4	1.7	0.1	1.0	1.9	97.7	1.1	0.2	0.9	0.8
District 7	1.0	95.1	2.4	0.7	1.7	0.1	1.1	2.0	96.3	2.0	0.2	1.2	0.8
District 8	1.0	94.6	3.9	0.6	1.3	0.1	0.6	1.1	95.8	3.1	0.2	0.8	0.6
District 9	0.8	96.8	2.3	0.5	0.5	0.1	0.7	1.3	97.7	1.7	0.2	0.3	0.4
District 10	1.9	61.2	35.3	0.8	1.7	0.1	3.0	4.8	68.6	29.8	0.2	0.9	1.2
IOWA	1.1	94.9	2.5	0.6	1.5	0.1	1.6	2.8	96.6	1.7	0.3	0.9	1.2
District 1	1.5	93.3	3.8	0.6	2.0	0.1	1.7	3.2	95.0	2.6	0.2	1.3	2.0
District 2	0.8	96.3	2.4	0.6	0.7	0.1	0.8	1.4	97.3	1.7	0.2	0.5	0.7
District 3	0.9	96.3	1.4	0.5	1.5	0.1	1.2	2.0	97.5	0.9	0.2	1.1	0.8
District 4	1.3	92.9	3.5	0.6	2.0	0.1	2.2	3.7	95.3	2.8	0.2	1.2	1.5
District 5	0.9	95.9	1.1	0.8	1.1	0.1	2.0	3.7	98.0	0.6	0.4	0.6	0.9
KANSAS	2.1	87.9	6.3	1.8	2.1	0.1	4.0	7.0	90.1	5.8	0.9	1.3	3.8
District 1	1.6	91.2	1.8	1.1	1.1	0.1	6.4	11.1	94.2	1.3	0.4	0.8	5.2
District 2	2.2	89.8	6.6	2.2	1.3	0.2	2.2	4.1	90.1	6.3	1.2	1.1	3.0
District 3	2.0	85.2	9.0	1.4	2.9	0.1	3.5	6.4	87.2	8.9	0.7	1.7	3.3
District 4	2.6	85.9	7.5	2.4	2.8	0.1	4.0	6.5	88.8	6.6	1.2	1.6	3.7
KENTUCKY	1.1	91.0	7.7	0.6	0.9	0.1	0.8	1.5	92.0	7.1	0.2	0.5	0.6
District 1	1.0	91.1	7.9	0.6	0.5	0.1	0.8	1.5	91.4	7.8	0.2	0.3	0.7
District 2	1.1	93.0	5.6	0.6	0.9	0.1	0.9	1.5	93.4	5.5	0.2	0.6	0.8
District 3	1.5	76.9	21.2	0.6	1.7	0.1	1.1	1.8	80.6	18.3	0.2	0.7	0.7
District 4	0.9	96.1	2.9	0.5	0.7	0.1	0.7	1.3	97.3	2.2	0.1	0.3	0.4
District 5	0.6	98.3	1.2	0.6	0.3	0.0	0.2	0.7	98.7	0.9	0.1	0.2	0.3
District 6	1.2	89.8	8.4	0.6	1.4	0.1	1.1	2.0	90.8	8.1	0.1	0.8	0.6
LOUISIANA	1.1	64.8	32.9	1.0	1.4	0.1	1.1	2.4	67.3	30.8	0.4	1.0	2.2
District 1	1.4	82.8	14.0	0.7	2.0	0.1	1.9	4.8	85.5	12.1	0.3	1.1	4.3
District 2	1.3	28.7	67.5	0.7	2.8	0.1	1.7	3.6	35.8	60.7	0.3	2.2	3.6
District 3	1.2	71.2	25.6	2.1	1.4	0.1	1.0	2.1	73.6	23.6	1.5	0.9	2.2
District 4	1.3	63.5	34.4	1.4	1.0	0.1	1.0	2.1	66.0	32.5	0.4	0.7	1.8
District 5	0.7	65.9	32.9	0.7	0.6	0.1	0.6	1.2	68.1	31.1	0.2	0.4	0.9
District 6	0.8	64.2	33.8	0.5	1.5	0.1	0.7	1.6	66.9	31.8	0.2	0.9	1.4

¹Hispanic persons may be of any race.

Table F. Congressional Districts 107th Congress

	Population and population characteristics, 2000										
	Age (percent)										
STATE District	Under 5 years	5 to 17 years	18 to 24 years	25 to 34 years	35 to 44 years	45 to 54 years	55 to 64 years	65 to 74 years	75 years and over	Median age (years)	Percent Female
	28	29	30	31	32	33	34	35	36	37	38
HAWAII	6.5	18.0	9.5	14.1	15.8	14.1	8.8	7.0	6.2	36.2	49.8
District 1	5.8	15.7	9.3	14.9	15.9	14.0	9.2	7.8	7.4	37.6	50.1
District 2	7.1	10.0	9.7	13.4	15.6	14.2	8.5	6.3	5.2	34.9	49.5
IDAHO	7.5	21.0	10.7	13.1	14.9	13.2	8.3	5.9	5.4	33.2	49.9
District 1	7.4	20.4	9.6	13.2	15.3	13.7	8.7	6.1	5.5	34.6	49.9
District 2	7.8	21.6	12.1	13.0	14.4	12.5	7.8	5.6	5.2	31.4	49.8
ILLINOIS	7.1	19.1	9.8	14.6	16.0	13.1	8.4	6.2	5.9	34.7	51.0
District 1	7.7	20.8	10.1	14.0	14.5	11.9	8.1	6.8	6.1	33.1	54.2
District 2	8.0	23.1	9.3	12.9	14.7	12.3	9.0	6.3	4.4	32.5	53.7
District 3	7.3	18.9	9.1	14.3	15.6	12.7	8.3	6.8	7.0	35.3	51.2
District 4	9.4	21.8	13.6	20.6	14.3	9.3	5.2	3.3	2.5	27.3	47.7
District 5	6.2	13.9	10.4	21.4	15.8	12.4	8.1	5.9	5.9	33.9	50.9
District 6	6.6	17.8	8.5	14.3	16.7	13.9	8.9	6.6	6.6	36.7	51.0
District 7	7.4	20.3	10.6	16.4	15.2	12.3	7.8	5.5	4.4	31.9	53.3
District 8	7.8	19.5	7.6	15.8	18.4	14.1	8.2	4.8	3.7	34.6	50.2
District 9	5.6	13.6	10.6	18.4	15.8	12.9	8.4	6.8	7.7	36.0	51.1
District 10	7.3	20.3	8.7	12.1	16.3	14.5	8.8	6.4	5.6	36.1	50.4
District 11	7.1	20.1	8.7	13.2	16.4	13.3	8.6	6.4	6.2	35.6	51.0
District 12	6.4	19.1	10.7	13.2	15.6	12.8	8.4	7.2	6.7	35.4	51.1
District 13	7.6	20.5	7.5	14.3	18.3	14.7	8.1	4.8	4.3	35.1	50.7
District 14	8.2	21.0	10.2	14.5	17.1	13.1	7.3	4.5	4.0	32.5	49.8
District 15	6.3	17.3	15.3	13.4	14.6	12.4	8.0	6.4	6.3	33.2	50.8
District 16	7.4	20.6	7.7	13.6	17.3	13.7	8.5	5.9	5.3	35.5	50.5
District 17	5.9	17.6	10.0	11.7	14.7	13.7	9.8	8.1	8.5	38.5	51.1
District 18	6.3	18.5	8.9	12.4	15.5	14.4	9.4	7.3	7.3	37.7	51.4
District 19	5.9	17.7	9.9	11.7	14.8	13.3	9.9	8.3	8.6	38.4	51.3
District 20	6.1	18.4	9.0	12.7	15.9	13.5	9.2	7.5	7.6	37.4	50.5
INDIANA	7.0	18.9	10.1	13.7	15.8	13.4	8.7	6.5	5.9	35.2	51.0
District 1	7.1	19.5	9.5	12.7	15.6	14.1	8.9	6.8	5.9	35.9	51.8
District 2	6.5	17.9	10.2	13.0	14.9	13.5	9.7	7.5	6.7	36.6	51.3
District 3	7.3	19.3	10.3	13.7	15.2	13.3	8.2	6.4	6.2	34.5	50.6
District 4	7.6	20.5	9.3	13.6	15.6	13.3	8.2	6.1	5.7	34.3	50.6
District 5	6.6	19.3	8.8	12.5	15.5	13.8	9.8	7.3	6.4	36.9	50.6
District 6	7.5	19.7	7.3	14.6	17.7	14.2	8.3	5.7	5.1	35.5	51.1
District 7	6.5	18.1	13.3	13.5	15.5	12.9	8.5	6.1	5.6	34.0	50.0
District 8	6.1	17.1	13.4	12.8	15.0	13.2	8.9	7.0	6.6	35.5	51.1
District 9	6.7	19.2	8.5	13.3	16.4	14.1	9.4	6.8	5.7	36.5	50.6
District 10	7.7	18.5	11.0	16.9	16.1	11.9	7.3	5.6	5.0	32.4	51.7
IOWA	6.4	18.6	10.2	12.4	15.2	13.4	8.8	7.2	7.7	36.6	50.9
District 1	6.6	18.2	11.9	14.1	15.6	13.6	8.3	6.0	5.9	34.5	50.7
District 2	6.1	18.9	10.2	11.1	14.8	13.3	9.2	7.8	8.5	37.7	51.2
District 3	6.0	18.0	11.4	11.5	14.6	13.5	9.1	7.6	8.4	37.3	50.6
District 4	7.1	18.8	8.7	14.3	16.2	13.6	8.5	6.5	6.4	35.8	51.3
District 5	6.2	19.4	8.8	10.8	14.8	13.2	8.9	8.4	9.4	38.5	50.9
KANSAS	7.0	19.5	10.3	13.0	15.6	13.2	8.2	6.5	6.7	35.2	50.6
District 1	6.7	19.7	9.5	11.3	14.9	12.8	8.7	7.8	8.6	37.0	50.3
District 2	6.6	18.8	11.7	12.3	15.1	13.0	8.6	6.8	7.0	35.4	50.3
District 3	7.3	19.2	10.7	14.8	16.6	13.7	7.5	5.2	4.9	33.6	51.0
District 4	7.4	20.3	9.1	13.1	15.8	13.2	8.0	6.5	6.5	35.1	50.7
KENTUCKY	6.6	18.0	9.9	14.1	15.9	13.8	9.2	6.8	5.7	35.9	51.1
District 1	6.5	17.6	9.9	13.2	14.8	13.4	10.1	7.6	7.0	36.9	51.0
District 2	6.8	18.9	9.8	13.6	16.3	13.7	9.2	6.5	5.1	35.5	50.7
District 3	6.7	17.3	9.1	14.2	16.1	13.9	8.7	7.4	6.6	36.8	52.4
District 4	6.9	18.9	9.3	14.2	16.6	13.8	8.9	6.3	5.1	35.5	50.7
District 5	6.2	18.5	9.3	13.8	15.6	14.3	9.9	7.0	5.5	36.4	50.9
District 6	6.4	16.8	12.2	15.3	15.9	13.6	8.6	6.0	5.1	34.5	51.2
LOUISIANA	7.1	20.2	10.6	13.5	15.5	13.1	8.5	6.3	5.2	34.0	51.6
District 1	6.5	18.4	8.8	13.4	16.3	14.6	9.1	6.9	5.9	36.8	51.7
District 2	7.3	21.0	11.4	14.3	14.9	13.0	7.8	5.6	4.7	32.2	52.9
District 3	7.3	21.6	9.6	13.2	16.3	13.0	8.4	6.0	4.5	33.9	51.3
District 4	7.2	20.0	10.5	13.1	14.7	12.7	8.9	7.0	6.0	34.4	51.6
District 5	7.0	20.0	11.2	12.7	14.5	12.5	8.9	7.1	6.2	34.4	51.6
District 6	7.1	19.8	12.4	14.2	15.7	13.2	7.9	5.3	4.3	32.5	51.0

Table F. Congressional Districts 107th Congress

| | Population and population characteristics, 1990 | | | | | | | | | | Population—change, 1980–2000 | | | | |
| | Age (percent) | | | | | | | | | | Total persons | | | Percent change | |
STATE District	Under 5 years	5 to 17 years	18 to 24 years	25 to 34 years	35 to 44 years	45 to 54 years	55 to 64 years	65 to 74 years	75 years and over	Percent Female	2000	1990	1980	1990–2000	1980–1990
	39	40	41	42	43	44	45	46	47	48	49	50	51	52	53
HAWAII	7.5	17.8	10.9	18.1	16.1	9.8	8.5	7.1	4.2	49.1	1 211 537	1 108 229	964 691	9.3	14.9
District 1	6.6	15.6	10.9	18.7	16.2	10.3	9.2	7.9	4.6	49.7	568 524	554 119	NA	2.6	NA
District 2	8.5	20.0	10.9	17.5	15.9	9.3	7.8	6.3	3.7	48.5	643 013	554 110	NA	16.0	NA
IDAHO	8.0	22.7	9.8	15.2	14.8	9.8	7.7	6.9	5.1	50.2	1 293 953	1 006 734	944 127	28.5	6.6
District 1	7.4	21.3	9.1	15.0	15.5	10.5	8.2	7.4	5.5	50.4	702 521	503 357	NA	39.6	NA
District 2	8.5	24.0	10.4	15.4	14.1	9.2	7.3	6.5	4.7	50.1	591 432	503 392	NA	17.5	NA
ILLINOIS	7.4	18.4	10.6	17.4	14.9	10 2	8.5	7.2	5.4	51.4	12 419 293	11 430 602	11 427 409	8.6	0.0
District 1	7.8	18.9	10.7	16.8	13.2	9.5	9.2	8.2	5.7	54.2	560 239	571 530	NA	-2.0	NA
District 2	8.0	21.6	11.1	16.2	14.0	10.8	8.7	6.1	3.6	53.0	556 482	571 530	NA	-2.6	NA
District 3	6.7	15.9	9.4	17.2	14.1	10.4	10.1	9.8	6.4	52.0	629 597	571 531	NA	10.2	NA
District 4	10.1	22.8	13.4	19.3	13.1	7.7	5.9	4.7	3.0	48.7	625 941	571 530	NA	9.5	NA
District 5	5.8	12.4	10.3	21.8	15.2	10.1	9.2	8.6	6.6	51.9	635 824	571 530	NA	11.2	NA
District 6	7.2	16.3	9.9	18.6	15.5	11.1	9.4	7.1	4.9	51.1	615 419	571 530	NA	7.7	NA
District 7	8.5	20.3	11.6	18.6	14.2	9.2	7.6	6.0	4.0	53.0	569 470	571 530	NA	-0.4	NA
District 8	8.1	18.3	9.7	20.4	17.4	11.4	7.3	4.6	2.8	50.3	699 513	571 530	NA	22.4	NA
District 9	5.8	12.5	11.2	20.2	15.0	9.8	9.1	8.5	7.9	51.9	593 205	571 530	NA	3.8	NA
District 10	7.7	17.9	10.4	16.6	16.3	11.5	9.1	6.3	4.1	50.1	627 793	571 530	NA	9.8	NA
District 11	7.3	19.6	9.6	16.5	14.7	10.4	8.8	7.7	5.4	51.1	635 653	571 528	NA	11.2	NA
District 12	7.3	18.9	11.6	16.5	13.8	9.4	8.8	7.6	6.0	51.5	560 912	571 530	NA	-1.9	NA
District 13	8.1	19.7	9.2	18.6	18.3	11.4	6.9	4.8	2.9	50.5	759 124	571 531	NA	32.8	NA
District 14	8.5	20.2	11.5	18.0	16.0	9.8	6.9	5.2	4.0	50.3	720 663	571 530	NA	26.1	NA
District 15	6.8	17.4	15.4	16.6	13.8	9.2	8.0	7.1	5.8	51.0	595 833	571 532	NA	4.3	NA
District 16	7.8	19.5	9.0	17.0	15.7	10.8	8.2	6.9	5.1	50.9	691 356	571 530	NA	21.0	NA
District 17	6.5	18.6	10.1	14.4	14.0	10.4	9.5	9.0	7.6	51.6	567 712	571 530	NA	-0.7	NA
District 18	6.8	19.4	9.3	15.2	15.2	10.8	9.2	7.8	6.4	51.7	597 447	571 580	NA	4.5	NA
District 19	6.5	18.3	9.8	14.5	13.6	10.4	9.5	9.3	8.1	52.0	575 769	571 530	NA	0.7	NA
District 20	6.9	18.8	9.1	15.9	14.2	10.1	9.3	8.5	7.3	51.6	601 341	571 480	NA	5.2	NA
INDIANA	7.2	19.1	10.9	16.5	14.8	10.3	8.7	7.3	5.3	51.5	6 080 485	5 544 156	5 490 214	9.7	1.0
District 1	7.0	20.8	9.8	15.8	15.0	10.5	9.1	7.4	4.5	52.0	571 747	554 416	NA	3.1	NA
District 2	6.6	18.3	11.7	15.0	14.3	11.0	9.3	7.8	5.8	51.7	567 204	554 416	NA	2.3	NA
District 3	7.6	18.9	11.0	16.3	14.9	9.8	8.6	7.5	5.5	51.0	610 182	554 416	NA	10.1	NA
District 4	8.0	20.5	9.8	16.8	15.0	9.8	8.1	6.8	5.1	51.2	619 891	554 416	NA	11.8	NA
District 5	7.1	20.0	9.3	15.4	14.6	10.9	9.3	7.8	5.6	51.3	585 988	554 415	NA	5.7	NA
District 6	7.3	19.1	8.5	17.6	16.8	11.2	8.4	6.5	4.7	51.2	724 143	554 416	NA	30.6	NA
District 7	6.7	17.9	14.5	15.9	14.3	10.1	8.3	7.0	5.3	50.4	633 484	554 416	NA	14.3	NA
District 8	6.5	17.4	13.5	15.8	14.1	9.9	8.8	7.8	6.2	51.9	590 205	554 416	NA	6.5	NA
District 9	6.9	20.1	9.3	16.0	15.1	10.8	8.9	7.3	5.5	51.2	608 430	554 416	NA	9.7	NA
District 10	8.2	17.7	11.4	20.5	13.8	8.8	8.1	6.6	4.8	52.6	569 211	554 416	NA	2.7	NA
IOWA	7.0	18.9	10.2	15.4	14.2	9.9	9.0	8.2	7.2	51.6	2 926 324	2 776 831	2 913 808	5.4	-4.7
District 1	7.1	18.4	12.4	17.2	15.1	9.9	8.0	6.6	5.3	51.2	603 837	555 229	NA	8.8	NA
District 2	6.8	19.6	9.8	14.3	13.7	10.0	9.3	8.7	7.6	51.7	568 857	555 494	NA	2.4	NA
District 3	6.5	18.3	11.3	14.5	14.0	9.9	9.1	8.6	7.9	51.1	573 674	555 299	NA	3.3	NA
District 4	7.3	18.5	9.6	17.1	14.9	10.1	8.8	7.5	6.3	52.1	621 351	555 276	NA	11.9	NA
District 5	7.0	19.9	8.0	14.1	13.4	9.4	9.9	9.5	8.7	51.8	558 605	555 457	NA	0.6	NA
KANSAS	7.6	19.1	10.3	16.7	14.6	9.5	8.4	7.5	6.4	51.0	2 688 418	2 477 588	2 364 236	8.5	4.8
District 1	7.3	19.6	8.8	15.0	13.4	9.4	9.3	8.7	8.5	51.0	637 670	619 370	NA	3.0	NA
District 2	7.3	18.7	11.8	16.2	14.2	9.2	8.2	7.5	6.8	50.1	641 387	619 391	NA	3.6	NA
District 3	7.8	18.6	11.3	18.3	16.1	9.9	7.6	6.1	4.3	51.6	733 606	619 439	NA	18.4	NA
District 4	8.0	19.4	9.2	17.1	14.6	9.5	8.6	7.5	6.0	51.2	675 755	619 374	NA	9.1	NA
KENTUCKY	6.8	19.1	10.9	16.6	14.9	10.4	8.8	7.3	5.4	51.6	4 041 769	3 686 892	3 660 324	9.6	0.7
District 1	6.5	18.5	10.6	15.4	14.0	10.6	9.2	8.5	6.8	51.2	652 338	614 265	NA	6.2	NA
District 2	7.1	20.0	11.2	16.7	14.7	10.5	8.4	6.6	4.8	50.8	706 978	614 794	NA	15.0	NA
District 3	6.8	17.4	9.7	17.4	15.3	10.1	9.5	8.1	5.8	53.0	626 676	613 603	NA	2.1	NA
District 4	7.1	19.6	10.3	16.6	15.2	10.5	8.7	7.0	5.0	51.4	691 720	602 896	NA	14.7	NA
District 5	6.7	21.4	10.4	15.8	14.9	10.4	8.5	7.0	5.0	51.2	648 751	624 837	NA	3.8	NA
District 6	6.6	17.7	12.8	17.5	15.5	10.3	8.2	6.6	4.9	51.9	715 306	614 901	NA	16.3	NA
LOUISIANA	7.9	21.2	11.0	16.7	14.4	9.6	8.1	6.5	4.6	51.9	4 468 976	4 221 826	4 206 116	5.9	0.3
District 1	7.0	19.2	9.6	16.9	15.9	10.6	8.8	7.3	4.8	52.0	666 747	602 842	NA	10.6	NA
District 2	8.2	21.3	11.5	17.0	14.5	9.0	7.5	6.3	4.5	53.0	590 824	602 877	NA	-2.0	NA
District 3	8.6	22.8	10.4	17.4	14.2	9.6	7.8	5.7	3.6	51.3	637 359	602 839	NA	5.7	NA
District 4	8.1	20.7	11.2	16.1	13.6	9.5	8.5	7.0	5.4	51.6	616 120	602 876	NA	2.2	NA
District 5	7.6	21.6	11.5	15.0	13.1	9.5	8.6	7.4	5.7	52.3	610 398	602 933	NA	1.2	NA
District 6	7.8	20.7	12.5	17.7	15.3	9.6	7.2	5.6	3.6	51.1	683 536	602 774	NA	13.4	NA

Table F. Congressional Districts 107th Congress

STATE District	Total population	Total in house-holds	House-holder	Spouse	Child Total	Own child under 18 years	Other relatives Total	Under 18 years	Nonrelatives Total	Unmar-ried partner	Total in group quarters	Correc-tional institu-tions	Nurs-ing homes	Other institu-tions	Col-lege dormi-tories	Mili-tary quar-ters	Other
	54	55	56	57	58	59	60	61	62	63	64	65	66	67	68	69	70
HAWAII	1 211 537	97.0	33.3	17.8	29.0	19.8	10.5	4.0	6.4	1.9	3.0	0.3	0.2	0.1	0.4	1.2	0.8
District 1	568 524	96.8	35.2	18.0	27.2	17.6	10.3	3.4	6.1	1.7	3.2	0.4	0.3	0.1	0.5	0.9	0.9
District 2	643 013	97.2	31.0	17.7	30.6	21.7	10.7	4.5	6.6	2.1	2.8	0.1	0.2	0.1	0.3	1.4	0.7
IDAHO	1 293 953	97.6	36.3	21.4	31.5	26.5	3.4	1.4	5.0	1.7	2.4	0.6	0.4	0.4	0.6	0.1	0.4
District 1	702 521	97.5	36.9	21.8	30.5	25.7	3.5	1.4	4.9	1.9	2.5	0.8	0.5	0.1	0.7	0.0	0.4
District 2	591 432	97.6	35.6	20.9	32.7	27.4	3.3	1.3	5.2	1.6	2.4	0.3	0.3	0.7	0.6	0.1	0.4
ILLINOIS	12 419 293	97.4	37.0	19.0	30.7	23.2	6.1	2.3	4.7	1.8	2.6	0.5	0.7	0.1	0.7	0.1	0.4
District 1	560 239	98.0	36.8	11.3	32.6	21.9	11.9	5.7	5.3	2.0	2.0	0.0	0.5	0.1	1.0	0.0	0.4
District 2	556 482	99.1	32.9	12.7	35.4	23.0	13.3	7.0	4.9	1.9	0.9	0.0	0.4	0.0	0.0	0.0	0.4
District 3	629 597	99.1	35.6	18.9	33.1	23.4	7.8	2.4	3.7	1.5	0.9	0.0	0.6	0.1	0.1	0.0	0.1
District 4	625 941	97.8	29.5	13.2	35.2	26.4	12.5	4.0	7.3	2.1	2.2	1.7	0.2	0.0	0.0	0.0	0.3
District 5	635 824	98.7	40.4	16.8	25.8	17.8	8.2	1.9	7.4	2.1	1.3	0.0	0.5	0.1	0.4	0.0	0.3
District 6	615 419	98.1	37.0	21.3	30.8	22.8	5.3	1.3	3.8	1.3	1.9	0.1	1.0	0.0	0.6	0.0	0.3
District 7	569 470	97.1	37.6	11.3	30.4	20.5	12.1	6.3	5.7	2.2	2.9	0.2	0.5	0.1	1.0	0.0	1.0
District 8	699 513	99.4	36.2	22.0	32.3	25.7	4.8	1.3	4.1	1.5	0.6	0.0	0.4	0.1	0.0	0.0	0.1
District 9	593 205	96.3	43.0	16.5	24.1	17.4	6.4	1.5	6.4	2.1	3.7	0.0	1.3	0.1	1.3	0.0	1.0
District 10	627 793	96.4	34.7	21.6	31.9	25.8	4.8	1.4	3.4	1.1	3.6	0.1	0.7	0.2	0.3	1.7	0.5
District 11	635 653	98.0	36.4	20.4	32.7	24.6	4.8	2.0	3.8	1.7	2.0	0.6	0.8	0.1	0.2	0.0	0.3
District 12	560 912	96.3	38.7	18.8	29.9	22.8	4.4	2.1	4.6	2.0	3.7	1.3	0.9	0.2	0.9	0.1	0.4
District 13	759 124	98.5	35.4	22.8	33.8	26.8	3.6	1.0	2.9	1.3	1.5	0.4	0.6	0.1	0.3	0.0	0.2
District 14	720 663	97.5	33.5	20.7	33.3	26.8	5.4	1.8	4.5	1.5	2.5	0.4	0.5	0.2	1.1	0.0	0.3
District 15	595 833	93.7	38.6	19.2	26.5	21.7	3.0	1.3	6.4	1.9	6.3	1.0	1.0	0.2	3.8	0.0	0.3
District 16	691 356	98.8	37.0	21.8	32.1	25.9	3.8	1.5	4.1	1.9	1.2	0.2	0.6	0.1	0.0	0.0	0.3
District 17	567 712	95.8	39.7	21.4	27.5	21.5	3.0	1.4	4.2	2.0	4.2	1.0	1.3	0.1	1.5	0.0	0.3
District 18	597 447	96.4	39.1	21.8	28.8	22.8	2.9	1.3	3.9	1.8	3.6	1.1	1.0	0.2	0.8	0.0	0.5
District 19	575 769	96.2	40.2	21.8	27.5	21.6	2.9	1.3	3.8	1.7	3.8	1.2	1.3	0.2	0.9	0.0	0.3
District 20	601 341	95.8	39.0	21.4	28.7	22.6	2.9	1.3	3.7	1.9	4.2	2.0	1.0	0.2	0.7	0.0	0.3
INDIANA	6 080 485	97.1	38.4	20.6	29.6	23.6	3.8	1.6	4.7	2.1	2.9	0.6	0.8	0.1	1.1	0.0	0.3
District 1	571 747	98.6	37.5	18.8	32.3	23.3	5.8	2.6	4.1	2.0	1.4	0.0	0.6	0.0	0.5	0.0	0.3
District 2	567 204	96.8	39.5	21.4	27.9	22.2	3.3	1.5	4.7	2.1	3.2	0.7	0.9	0.1	1.2	0.0	0.2
District 3	610 182	96.1	37.2	19.9	30.0	24.1	4.2	1.8	4.9	2.1	3.9	1.1	0.8	0.1	1.5	0.0	0.4
District 4	619 891	98.3	37.7	21.0	32.1	26.0	3.3	1.4	4.2	2.0	1.7	0.2	0.8	0.1	0.3	0.0	0.3
District 5	585 988	97.4	38.2	22.4	29.7	23.6	3.3	1.5	3.8	1.8	2.6	0.6	0.8	0.2	0.8	0.0	0.3
District 6	724 143	98.6	38.4	23.1	30.7	25.7	2.6	1.0	3.7	1.7	1.4	0.1	0.7	0.1	0.1	0.0	0.3
District 7	633 484	94.4	37.4	21.0	27.8	22.7	3.0	1.2	5.1	1.9	5.6	1.3	0.9	0.1	3.2	0.0	0.2
District 8	590 205	94.9	39.4	20.6	26.8	21.3	2.9	1.2	5.2	1.9	5.1	0.6	1.0	0.2	3.1	0.0	0.3
District 9	608 430	98.2	38.3	22.4	30.2	23.7	3.5	1.5	3.9	2.0	1.8	0.4	0.9	0.1	0.2	0.0	0.3
District 10	569 211	97.2	40.8	14.3	28.4	22.3	6.3	2.9	7.3	3.2	2.8	0.8	0.7	0.2	0.6	0.0	0.5
IOWA	2 926 324	96.4	39.3	21.6	28.4	23.4	2.5	1.0	4.6	1.9	3.6	0.4	1.1	0.2	1.4	0.0	0.4
District 1	603 837	96.7	39.5	20.6	28.0	23.1	2.6	1.1	5.9	2.3	3.3	0.5	0.7	0.1	1.6	0.0	0.4
District 2	568 857	96.2	39.0	22.1	28.9	23.6	2.0	0.8	4.2	1.8	3.8	0.1	1.3	0.1	1.7	0.0	0.6
District 3	573 674	95.0	39.1	21.9	27.2	22.5	2.2	0.9	4.6	1.8	5.0	0.8	1.3	0.1	2.4	0.0	0.4
District 4	621 351	97.7	39.5	21.2	29.0	23.9	3.2	1.3	4.7	2.1	2.3	0.2	1.0	0.2	0.5	0.0	0.4
District 5	558 605	96.6	39.3	22.5	29.0	24.1	2.2	0.9	3.6	1.7	3.4	0.4	1.5	0.3	0.9	0.0	0.4
KANSAS	2 688 418	97.0	38.6	21.1	29.5	24.5	3.3	1.4	4.4	1.6	3.0	0.6	0.9	0.1	0.9	0.2	0.3
District 1	637 670	96.5	38.7	22.2	29.0	24.6	2.9	1.2	3.7	1.4	3.5	0.8	1.3	0.1	0.9	0.0	0.3
District 2	641 387	95.3	38.4	20.9	28.3	23.4	3.0	1.4	4.6	1.7	4.7	1.2	1.0	0.2	1.2	0.6	0.4
District 3	733 606	97.8	38.4	20.5	29.9	24.6	3.7	1.4	5.3	1.7	2.2	0.1	0.6	0.1	1.2	0.0	0.2
District 4	675 755	98.0	38.9	20.9	30.7	25.4	3.7	1.7	3.8	1.5	2.0	0.5	0.8	0.0	0.3	0.1	0.3
KENTUCKY	4 041 769	97.2	39.4	21.2	28.8	22.3	3.9	1.7	3.9	1.8	2.8	0.7	0.7	0.1	0.8	0.2	0.3
District 1	652 338	96.6	39.6	22.4	27.9	21.9	3.6	1.6	3.1	1.5	3.4	0.8	1.0	0.1	0.5	0.7	0.4
District 2	706 978	97.4	38.1	22.2	29.9	23.5	3.6	1.6	3.6	1.7	2.6	0.5	0.7	0.1	0.7	0.4	0.3
District 3	626 676	98.1	41.9	18.1	28.2	21.2	4.8	2.2	5.0	2.2	1.9	0.2	0.8	0.1	0.4	0.0	0.4
District 4	691 720	97.4	38.0	21.5	30.4	23.6	3.7	1.6	3.8	1.8	2.6	1.0	0.6	0.1	0.6	0.0	0.3
District 5	648 751	97.6	39.0	22.4	29.5	22.3	4.2	1.9	2.4	1.3	2.4	1.0	0.7	0.2	0.3	0.0	0.3
District 6	715 306	96.0	39.8	20.5	26.7	21.2	3.8	1.5	5.2	2.0	4.0	0.8	0.6	0.1	2.2	0.0	0.3
LOUISIANA	4 468 976	97.0	37.1	18.1	31.4	23.5	6.3	3.2	4.1	1.9	3.0	1.1	0.7	0.2	0.6	0.1	0.3
District 1	666 747	98.4	39.3	20.2	29.7	22.3	5.1	2.2	4.0	1.9	1.6	0.4	0.6	0.2	0.2	0.0	0.3
District 2	590 824	96.9	36.9	12.4	32.4	22.4	10.0	5.3	5.2	2.3	3.1	1.2	0.5	0.1	0.8	0.0	0.5
District 3	637 359	98.4	35.0	19.5	33.8	24.9	6.5	3.4	3.6	2.0	1.6	0.5	0.6	0.1	0.1	0.0	0.2
District 4	616 120	96.9	37.9	18.5	30.6	23.3	6.2	3.3	3.8	1.7	3.1	0.8	0.8	0.2	0.4	0.6	0.4
District 5	610 398	94.8	36.8	18.4	30.2	22.9	6.0	3.3	3.4	1.6	5.2	2.0	1.2	0.4	1.1	0.0	0.5
District 6	683 536	96.0	36.4	18.1	31.1	23.4	5.9	2.9	4.5	1.7	4.0	1.8	0.6	0.2	1.1	0.0	0.4

Table F. Congressional Districts 107th Congress

STATE District		Households by type, 2000											Households, 1990		
		Family households						Nonfamily households							
				Married couple		Female householder[1]			Householder living alone						
	Total households	Total	With own children under 18 years	Total	With own children under 18 years	Total	With own children under 18 years	Total	Total	65 years and over	Average household size	Average family size	Total households	Female householder[1]	Householder living alone
	71	72	73	74	75	76	77	78	79	80	81	82	83	84	85
HAWAII	403 240	71.2	32.1	53.6	24.0	12.4	5.9	28.8	21.9	7.1	2.92	3.42	356 267	10.5	19.4
District 1	199 979	67.6	28.1	51.0	21.7	11.8	4.8	32.4	25.3	8.1	2.75	3.34	188 969	10.3	22.5
District 2	203 261	74.8	36.0	56.1	26.3	13.0	6.9	25.2	18.5	6.1	3.08	3.50	167 298	10.8	15.8
IDAHO	469 645	71.5	36.3	58.9	28.1	8.7	5.8	28.5	22.4	8.3	2.69	3.17	360 723	8.0	22.4
District 1	258 947	72.0	35.7	59.1	27.3	8.8	5.9	28.0	21.9	8.2	2.65	3.10	185 172	8.2	22.3
District 2	210 698	70.8	37.1	58.6	29.2	8.5	5.7	29.2	22.9	8.3	2.74	3.25	175 551	7.8	22.5
ILLINOIS	4 591 779	67.6	33.0	51.3	24.3	12.3	6.9	32.4	26.8	9.6	2.63	3.23	4 202 240	12.0	25.7
District 1	206 431	63.3	30.3	30.7	13.8	27.0	14.3	36.7	31.8	11.4	2.66	3.39	210 872	25.6	31.1
District 2	183 180	73.7	35.3	38.5	17.2	29.0	15.5	26.3	22.6	7.7	3.01	3.53	183 227	25.6	20.6
District 3	224 008	70.1	33.7	53.1	26.5	12.1	5.4	29.9	25.6	11.4	2.79	3.40	214 647	10.8	25.1
District 4	184 540	69.7	42.2	44.9	28.8	16.6	10.0	30.3	21.7	5.5	3.32	3.97	170 646	18.7	22.2
District 5	257 076	55.7	24.4	41.6	19.1	9.6	3.9	44.3	34.4	8.9	2.44	3.26	243 577	9.9	35.6
District 6	227 495	69.8	32.7	57.5	27.4	8.7	4.1	30.2	25.2	9.6	2.65	3.22	210 552	8.1	22.5
District 7	213 996	58.7	27.7	30.2	12.4	23.9	13.5	41.3	34.9	8.4	2.58	3.44	204 386	25.8	32.3
District 8	253 199	72.3	37.6	60.8	31.6	8.1	4.6	27.7	22.3	6.0	2.75	3.26	205 605	7.7	20.0
District 9	254 817	51.2	22.1	38.4	16.7	9.2	4.4	48.8	39.6	10.8	2.24	3.14	245 104	9.4	38.2
District 10	217 949	74.0	38.4	62.3	32.0	8.7	5.1	26.0	22.1	8.5	2.78	3.27	199 839	8.3	20.4
District 11	231 272	72.0	35.3	56.0	26.5	11.8	6.7	28.0	23.8	9.9	2.69	3.21	204 630	10.6	22.4
District 12	216 943	66.8	32.0	48.5	21.2	14.2	8.7	33.2	27.9	11.3	2.49	3.05	213 212	13.5	25.8
District 13	268 835	74.8	39.6	64.4	34.2	7.7	4.2	25.2	20.8	6.2	2.78	3.27	197 921	7.0	18.9
District 14	241 604	75.0	40.8	61.8	33.2	9.1	5.6	25.0	19.7	6.6	2.91	3.36	192 838	8.6	19.6
District 15	230 288	62.9	30.1	49.7	21.7	9.9	6.4	37.1	28.9	10.4	2.43	3.00	213 068	9.1	27.0
District 16	255 764	72.3	36.7	58.9	28.5	9.6	6.1	27.7	22.9	8.6	2.67	3.16	210 646	9.0	21.8
District 17	225 434	67.0	29.4	53.9	21.4	9.6	6.1	33.0	28.2	13.1	2.41	2.95	221 563	9.2	27.1
District 18	233 363	68.9	31.5	55.8	23.4	9.9	6.3	31.1	26.6	11.1	2.47	2.99	217 008	9.3	25.0
District 19	231 235	67.2	29.8	54.2	21.9	9.6	5.9	32.8	28.5	13.6	2.39	2.93	223 161	9.0	26.7
District 20	234 350	68.4	31.8	54.9	23.6	9.9	6.1	31.6	27.1	12.2	2.46	2.99	219 738	9.3	25.9
INDIANA	2 336 306	68.6	32.9	53.6	23.8	11.1	6.9	31.4	25.9	9.5	2.53	3.05	2 065 355	10.5	24.1
District 1	214 620	70.1	33.1	50.0	22.2	15.6	8.8	29.9	25.3	9.4	2.63	3.16	198 750	14.8	22.8
District 2	224 019	68.5	30.8	54.2	22.1	10.6	6.5	31.5	26.2	10.9	2.45	2.94	209 961	10.2	24.0
District 3	226 778	69.1	33.6	53.5	24.0	11.4	7.3	30.9	25.4	9.8	2.58	3.10	203 314	10.4	24.1
District 4	233 944	69.8	34.9	55.7	26.0	10.3	6.7	30.2	25.3	9.1	2.60	3.14	202 849	9.4	23.0
District 5	223 852	71.7	32.8	58.6	24.8	9.3	5.7	28.3	24.3	10.4	2.55	3.02	205 013	8.8	22.3
District 6	278 176	71.3	36.1	60.2	29.2	8.0	5.1	28.7	23.6	7.7	2.57	3.06	209 027	7.7	21.9
District 7	237 174	68.7	32.9	56.1	25.0	9.0	5.7	31.3	24.7	9.1	2.52	3.01	200 596	8.5	23.2
District 8	232 639	65.2	29.9	52.3	22.2	9.5	5.9	34.8	28.3	11.0	2.41	2.96	211 519	9.2	26.2
District 9	232 808	72.6	34.2	58.5	25.9	10.0	6.0	27.4	23.1	9.4	2.57	3.02	202 651	9.6	21.5
District 10	232 296	58.5	29.7	35.1	15.4	18.1	11.4	41.5	33.4	8.6	2.38	3.06	221 675	16.4	30.8
IOWA	1 149 276	67.0	31.4	55.1	23.9	8.6	5.6	33.0	27.2	11.4	2.46	3.00	1 064 325	8.0	25.9
District 1	238 345	64.8	31.5	52.2	23.4	9.2	6.1	35.2	27.3	8.9	2.45	3.00	211 466	8.9	25.2
District 2	221 713	68.1	31.4	56.7	24.2	8.1	5.3	31.9	26.8	12.5	2.47	3.00	209 760	7.6	25.5
District 3	224 379	67.1	30.4	55.9	23.2	8.0	5.3	32.9	27.2	12.3	2.43	2.95	212 356	7.4	25.9
District 4	245 495	66.9	32.4	53.6	24.1	9.8	6.3	33.1	27.0	9.8	2.47	3.02	216 874	9.4	26.0
District 5	219 344	68.1	31.4	57.4	24.5	7.5	5.0	31.9	27.9	13.8	2.46	3.01	213 869	6.7	26.7
KANSAS	1 037 891	67.6	33.2	54.7	25.1	9.3	6.0	32.4	27.0	10.2	2.51	3.07	944 726	8.6	25.9
District 1	247 024	68.2	32.5	57.4	25.4	7.5	5.0	31.8	27.6	12.8	2.49	3.05	239 568	6.7	27.0
District 2	246 530	67.3	32.3	54.3	24.0	9.5	6.2	32.7	27.0	10.9	2.48	3.02	230 344	8.4	25.8
District 3	281 782	67.0	34.2	53.5	26.1	10.0	6.3	33.0	25.9	7.4	2.55	3.10	235 450	10.0	24.7
District 4	262 555	67.9	33.9	53.9	25.0	10.1	6.6	32.1	27.6	10.0	2.52	3.10	239 364	9.3	26.4
KENTUCKY	1 590 647	69.4	32.5	53.9	23.6	11.8	7.0	30.6	26.0	9.8	2.47	2.97	1 379 782	11.6	23.3
District 1	258 480	70.7	31.8	56.6	23.6	10.7	6.4	29.3	26.0	11.6	2.44	2.92	232 764	10.2	23.6
District 2	269 060	72.7	34.8	58.3	26.1	10.7	6.6	27.3	23.2	9.0	2.56	3.01	222 235	10.1	20.6
District 3	262 582	62.4	28.8	43.2	17.9	15.2	9.0	37.6	31.7	10.7	2.34	2.96	246 351	14.8	28.4
District 4	262 841	71.4	34.6	56.7	26.1	10.9	6.4	28.6	24.2	9.1	2.56	3.05	220 240	10.7	22.2
District 5	253 054	73.4	33.8	57.5	25.3	12.1	6.6	26.6	24.1	9.9	2.50	2.96	225 010	12.0	19.8
District 6	284 630	66.4	31.1	51.6	22.5	11.3	6.8	33.6	26.9	8.6	2.41	2.93	233 182	11.3	24.4
LOUISIANA	1 656 053	69.8	34.5	48.9	22.6	16.6	9.8	30.2	25.3	9.0	2.62	3.16	1 499 269	15.6	23.7
District 1	262 349	67.8	31.9	51.4	23.2	12.5	6.8	32.2	27.0	9.2	2.50	3.06	228 470	11.9	25.5
District 2	218 125	64.5	32.3	33.6	15.1	25.7	14.9	35.5	29.4	8.5	2.62	3.30	217 170	24.3	28.9
District 3	222 949	76.0	38.8	55.7	27.2	15.4	9.0	24.0	20.1	7.8	2.81	3.25	200 349	13.8	18.1
District 4	233 417	69.5	33.3	48.7	21.4	16.7	9.9	30.5	26.4	10.3	2.56	3.10	217 133	15.4	24.4
District 5	224 698	70.6	33.9	50.0	21.9	16.7	9.9	29.4	25.5	10.8	2.58	3.10	211 252	15.6	23.4
District 6	248 925	69.7	35.3	49.8	23.9	15.7	9.3	30.3	24.3	7.2	2.64	3.17	210 773	14.7	22.7

[1] No spouse present.

Table F. Congressional Districts 107th Congress

STATE District	Percent change of households, 1990–2000	Total housing units	Occupied housing units (percent)	Total	For seasonal, recreational, or occasional use	Homeowner vacancy rate (percent)	Rental vacancy rate (percent)	Total	Percent owner-occupied housing units	Percent renter-occupied housing units	Average household size of owner-occupied units	Average household size of renter-occupied units
	86	87	88	89	90	91	92	93	94	95	96	97
HAWAII	13.2	460 542	87.6	12.4	5.6	1.6	8.2	403 240	56.5	43.5	3.07	2.71
District 1	5.8	221 630	90.2	9.8	2.4	1.6	9.1	199 979	52.4	47.6	2.94	2.54
District 2	21.5	238 912	85.1	14.9	8.5	1.6	7.1	203 261	60.5	39.5	3.18	2.92
IDAHO	30.2	527 824	89.0	11.0	5.2	2.2	7.6	469 645	72.4	27.6	2.75	2.52
District 1	39.8	290 868	89.0	11.0	5.6	2.3	7.2	258 947	74.2	25.8	2.70	2.49
District 2	20.0	236 956	88.9	11.1	4.8	2.1	8.1	210 698	70.1	29.9	2.82	2.55
ILLINOIS	9.3	4 885 615	94.0	6.0	0.6	1.5	6.2	4 591 779	67.3	32.7	2.76	2.37
District 1	-2.1	227 978	90.5	9.5	0.1	1.9	8.2	206 431	46.7	53.3	2.91	2.44
District 2	0.0	198 576	92.2	7.8	0.1	2.2	8.3	183 180	63.0	37.0	3.10	2.86
District 3	4.4	232 199	96.5	3.5	0.2	1.2	4.0	224 008	74.6	25.4	2.92	2.39
District 4	8.1	201 297	91.7	8.3	0.4	1.9	4.6	184 540	36.6	63.4	3.62	3.14
District 5	5.5	268 267	95.8	4.2	0.5	1.1	3.0	257 076	50.9	49.1	2.70	2.17
District 6	8.0	233 285	97.5	2.5	0.3	0.7	3.6	227 495	74.9	25.1	2.78	2.26
District 7	4.7	239 224	89.5	10.5	0.7	2.3	6.6	213 996	42.5	57.5	2.77	2.45
District 8	23.1	262 127	96.6	3.4	0.8	0.9	5.0	253 199	78.4	21.6	2.85	2.36
District 9	4.0	265 542	96.0	4.0	0.3	1.0	3.9	254 817	48.2	51.8	2.47	2.03
District 10	9.1	225 759	96.5	3.5	0.5	1.0	4.7	217 949	77.0	23.0	2.85	2.52
District 11	13.0	243 450	95.0	5.0	0.4	1.6	6.0	231 272	76.2	23.8	2.79	2.38
District 12	1.7	236 325	91.8	8.2	0.5	1.7	8.8	216 943	68.3	31.7	2.58	2.30
District 13	35.8	278 574	96.5	3.5	0.3	1.3	6.1	268 835	81.3	18.7	2.93	2.12
District 14	25.3	251 038	96.2	3.8	0.4	1.3	5.1	241 604	76.4	23.6	3.02	2.56
District 15	8.1	246 424	93.5	6.5	0.5	1.9	7.3	230 288	65.7	34.3	2.55	2.18
District 16	21.4	272 048	94.0	6.0	1.4	1.4	7.2	255 764	76.0	24.0	2.78	2.32
District 17	1.7	243 018	92.8	7.2	1.2	1.7	7.4	225 434	73.0	27.0	2.50	2.18
District 18	7.5	249 498	93.5	6.5	0.7	1.7	8.5	233 363	74.1	25.9	2.57	2.17
District 19	3.6	255 346	90.6	9.4	1.4	2.2	10.0	231 235	75.3	24.7	2.46	2.19
District 20	6.6	255 640	91.7	8.3	1.2	1.8	8.2	234 350	75.2	24.8	2.55	2.19
INDIANA	13.1	2 532 319	92.3	7.7	1.3	1.8	8.8	2 336 306	71.4	28.6	2.64	2.24
District 1	8.0	229 889	93.4	6.6	0.4	1.6	7.1	214 620	69.7	30.3	2.73	2.38
District 2	6.7	240 126	93.3	6.7	0.5	1.7	8.2	224 019	72.0	28.0	2.52	2.28
District 3	11.5	244 198	92.9	7.1	1.9	1.6	7.2	226 778	72.9	27.1	2.68	2.32
District 4	15.3	256 096	91.4	8.6	2.5	1.7	9.8	233 944	74.9	25.1	2.74	2.20
District 5	9.2	245 592	91.1	8.9	3.0	1.6	7.8	223 852	76.6	23.4	2.61	2.35
District 6	33.1	294 257	94.5	5.5	0.5	1.5	10.0	278 176	75.9	24.1	2.73	2.07
District 7	18.2	255 761	92.7	7.3	1.1	1.8	7.9	237 174	71.5	28.5	2.64	2.23
District 8	10.0	254 109	91.6	8.4	1.3	2.1	8.6	232 639	70.4	29.6	2.54	2.08
District 9	14.9	252 309	92.3	7.7	2.0	1.6	7.7	232 808	76.5	23.5	2.65	2.29
District 10	4.8	259 982	89.4	10.6	0.3	2.4	11.3	232 296	53.3	46.7	2.49	2.26
IOWA	8.0	1 232 511	93.2	6.8	1.3	1.7	6.8	1 149 276	72.3	27.7	2.57	2.15
District 1	12.7	251 231	94.9	5.1	0.7	1.6	5.7	238 345	69.7	30.3	2.60	2.11
District 2	5.7	238 643	92.9	7.1	2.0	1.3	6.7	221 713	74.5	25.5	2.57	2.18
District 3	5.7	242 750	92.4	7.6	1.3	1.7	7.4	224 379	72.7	27.3	2.54	2.13
District 4	13.2	259 785	94.5	5.5	0.5	1.7	6.6	245 495	71.1	28.9	2.61	2.14
District 5	2.6	240 102	91.4	8.6	2.3	2.0	8.0	219 344	74.1	25.9	2.55	2.21
KANSAS	9.9	1 131 200	91.8	8.2	0.9	2.0	8.8	1 037 891	69.2	30.8	2.63	2.25
District 1	3.1	276 996	89.2	10.8	1.3	2.7	10.0	247 024	71.9	28.1	2.56	2.31
District 2	7.0	269 361	91.5	8.5	1.1	2.0	7.8	246 530	68.8	31.2	2.56	2.31
District 3	19.7	297 315	94.8	5.2	0.4	1.3	6.4	281 782	67.7	32.3	2.73	2.17
District 4	9.7	287 528	91.3	8.7	0.6	2.1	11.4	262 555	68.9	31.1	2.65	2.24
KENTUCKY	15.3	1 750 927	90.8	9.2	1.7	1.8	8.7	1 590 647	70.8	29.2	2.55	2.27
District 1	11.0	292 414	88.4	11.6	2.9	2.1	9.5	258 480	73.9	26.1	2.47	2.34
District 2	21.1	297 489	90.4	9.6	2.4	1.8	9.0	269 060	74.5	25.5	2.62	2.38
District 3	6.6	280 361	93.7	6.3	0.5	1.4	7.7	262 582	63.3	36.7	2.46	2.13
District 4	19.3	286 619	91.7	8.3	1.4	2.0	8.4	262 841	73.2	26.8	2.67	2.26
District 5	12.5	287 010	88.2	11.8	2.4	1.8	10.1	253 054	76.5	23.5	2.54	2.36
District 6	22.1	307 034	92.7	7.3	0.8	1.6	8.3	284 630	63.9	36.1	2.53	2.21
LOUISIANA	10.5	1 847 181	89.7	10.3	2.1	1.6	9.3	1 656 053	67.9	32.1	2.70	2.44
District 1	14.8	283 639	92.5	7.5	1.0	1.5	8.1	262 349	69.7	30.3	2.65	2.16
District 2	0.4	246 763	88.4	11.6	0.9	2.0	8.0	218 125	49.3	50.7	2.76	2.49
District 3	11.3	247 564	90.1	9.9	3.2	1.1	8.7	222 949	77.3	22.7	2.87	2.62
District 4	7.5	267 893	87.1	12.9	3.2	2.1	10.5	233 417	68.1	31.9	2.58	2.52
District 5	6.4	255 308	88.0	12.0	3.3	1.6	9.4	224 698	70.2	29.8	2.59	2.54
District 6	18.1	273 861	90.9	9.1	1.6	1.5	9.8	248 925	69.3	30.7	2.75	2.38

Table F. Congressional Districts 107th Congress

STATE District	Population, 2000				Population, 1990				Population and population characteristics, 2000					
									Race (percent)					
									One race					
	Land area, 2000[1] (sq km)	Total persons	Rank	Per square kilometer	Land area, 1990[1] (sq km)	Total persons	Rank	Per square kilometer	White	Black or African American	American Indian or Alaska Native	Asian	Native Hawaiian and other Pacific Islander	Some other race
	1	2	3	4	5	6	7	8	9	10	11	12	13	14
LOUISIANA—Cont'd														
District 7	17 593.6	663 992	X	37.7	17 595.0	602 832	X	34.0	72.7	25.0	0.3	0.7	0.0	0.4
MAINE	79 931.0	1 274 923	X	16.0	79 939.0	1 227 928	X	15.4	96.9	0.5	0.6	0.7	0.0	0.2
District 1	9 368.3	666 936	X	71.2	9 368.0	613 961	X	66.0	96.8	0.7	0.3	0.9	0.0	0.2
District 2	70 562.8	607 987	X	8.6	70 572.0	613 967	X	9.0	97.1	0.4	0.9	0.5	0.0	0.2
MARYLAND	25 314.0	5 296 486	X	209.2	25 316.0	4 780 753	X	188.8	64.0	27.9	0.3	4.0	0.0	1.8
District 1	9 003.0	682 770	X	75.8	9 004.0	597 684	X	66.0	81.0	15.1	0.3	1.5	0.0	0.8
District 2	2 341.0	652 938	X	278.9	2 341.0	597 683	X	255.0	87.2	8.2	0.3	2.4	0.0	0.5
District 3	552.3	643 935	X	1 165.9	553.0	597 680	X	1 082.0	66.5	26.8	0.3	3.2	0.0	1.1
District 4	499.7	648 764	X	1 298.3	500.0	597 690	X	1 196.0	22.1	64.7	0.3	4.9	0.1	4.9
District 5	4 058.9	714 886	X	176.1	4 059.0	597 681	X	147.0	62.9	29.1	0.4	3.7	0.1	1.7
District 6	7 387.9	723 196	X	97.9	7 389.0	597 688	X	81.0	89.4	6.1	0.2	2.5	0.0	0.6
District 7	282.0	539 439	X	1 912.9	282.0	597 680	X	2 120.0	21.3	74.6	0.2	2.0	0.0	0.4
District 8	1 189.3	690 558	X	580.6	1 189.0	597 682	X	503.0	70.3	10.6	0.3	11.3	0.0	4.3
MASSACHUSETTS	20 306.0	6 349 097	X	312.7	20 300.0	6 016 425	X	296.4	84.5	5.4	0.2	3.8	0.0	3.7
District 1	7 853.4	610 522	X	77.7	7 854.0	601 643	X	77.0	91.1	1.9	0.2	1.7	0.0	3.3
District 2	2 293.8	615 557	X	268.4	2 294.0	601 642	X	262.0	85.3	6.0	0.2	1.3	0.1	5.2
District 3	1 868.6	655 701	X	350.9	1 869.0	601 642	X	322.0	89.7	2.7	0.2	2.8	0.0	2.7
District 4	1 974.9	639 072	X	323.6	1 974.0	601 642	X	305.0	89.5	2.2	0.2	3.2	0.0	2.7
District 5	1 518.0	644 869	X	424.8	1 518.0	601 643	X	396.0	83.7	2.1	0.2	5.4	0.0	6.1
District 6	1 295.4	652 455	X	503.7	1 289.0	601 643	X	467.0	90.9	2.3	0.2	2.5	0.0	2.5
District 7	447.3	616 542	X	1 378.4	447.0	601 642	X	1 345.0	86.3	3.5	0.1	5.5	0.0	2.2
District 8	115.1	620 372	X	5 389.9	115.0	601 643	X	5 224.0	59.5	20.7	0.4	7.6	0.1	7.3
District 9	658.3	630 499	X	957.8	658.0	601 643	X	914.0	77.4	10.5	0.2	4.7	0.0	4.1
District 10	2 280.9	663 508	X	290.9	2 282.0	601 642	X	264.0	91.0	2.7	0.3	2.8	0.0	1.4
MICHIGAN	147 121.0	9 938 444	X	67.6	147 136.0	9 295 287	X	63.2	80.2	14.2	0.6	1.8	0.0	1.3
District 1	58 958.0	639 161	X	10.8	58 963.0	580 956	X	10.0	94.0	1.1	2.7	0.4	0.0	0.3
District 2	14 162.9	686 086	X	48.4	14 165.0	580 956	X	41.0	90.1	4.4	0.6	1.0	0.0	2.3
District 3	4 312.2	662 041	X	153.5	4 312.0	580 956	X	135.0	84.5	8.2	0.5	1.7	0.1	3.0
District 4	22 466.5	651 347	X	29.0	22 469.0	580 956	X	26.0	94.9	1.7	0.7	0.6	0.0	0.7
District 5	14 125.8	587 031	X	41.6	14 127.0	580 956	X	41.0	87.3	8.6	0.5	0.5	0.0	1.5
District 6	7 529.5	610 640	X	81.1	7 530.0	580 956	X	77.0	85.2	9.6	0.5	1.2	0.0	1.6
District 7	10 714.3	620 053	X	57.9	10 716.0	580 957	X	54.0	89.7	6.1	0.5	0.7	0.0	1.3
District 8	5 028.7	658 695	X	131.0	5 029.0	580 956	X	116.0	87.7	6.2	0.5	2.3	0.0	1.3
District 9	2 111.7	633 553	X	300.0	2 112.0	580 956	X	275.0	76.9	17.3	0.4	1.9	0.0	1.4
District 10	2 925.5	671 306	X	229.5	2 926.0	580 956	X	199.0	93.9	2.8	0.4	1.0	0.0	0.5
District 11	984.1	640 548	X	650.9	984.0	580 956	X	590.0	84.7	8.9	0.2	4.1	0.0	0.4
District 12	385.9	574 950	X	1 489.9	386.0	580 956	X	1 506.0	86.5	6.0	0.3	4.5	0.0	0.4
District 13	1 179.0	628 363	X	533.0	1 179.0	580 956	X	493.0	78.4	13.1	0.4	5.0	0.0	0.8
District 14	206.8	550 599	X	2 662.5	207.0	580 956	X	2 809.0	16.8	78.9	0.3	1.3	0.0	0.5
District 15	218.8	531 634	X	2 429.8	219.0	580 956	X	2 657.0	21.6	69.9	0.4	1.1	0.0	4.2
District 16	1 811.3	592 437	X	327.1	1 811.0	580 956	X	321.0	92.2	2.5	0.4	1.2	0.0	0.8
MINNESOTA	206 189.0	4 919 479	X	23.9	206 207.0	4 375 665	X	21.2	89.4	3.5	1.1	2.9	0.0	1.3
District 1	24 059.2	594 864	X	24.7	24 061.0	546 887	X	23.0	94.7	1.2	0.3	1.7	0.0	1.1
District 2	42 182.8	616 816	X	14.6	42 187.0	546 888	X	13.0	95.6	0.5	0.5	0.9	0.1	1.7
District 3	1 284.3	642 053	X	499.9	1 284.0	546 888	X	426.0	88.7	4.0	0.4	4.3	0.0	0.9
District 4	475.8	577 077	X	1 212.9	476.0	546 887	X	1 149.0	79.0	7.0	0.8	8.0	0.1	2.5
District 5	277.1	557 819	X	2 013.1	277.0	546 887	X	1 973.0	72.3	13.8	1.7	5.3	0.1	3.3
District 6	2 879.2	720 995	X	250.4	2 880.0	546 887	X	190.0	93.2	1.8	0.5	2.2	0.0	0.7
District 7	68 162.6	588 825	X	8.6	68 167.0	546 901	X	8.0	94.2	0.5	2.7	0.8	0.0	0.7
District 8	66 868.1	624 030	X	9.3	66 874.0	546 874	X	8.0	95.3	0.5	2.3	0.4	0.0	0.2
MISSISSIPPI	121 488.0	2 844 658	X	23.4	121 506.0	2 575 475	X	21.2	61.4	36.3	0.4	0.7	0.0	0.5
District 1	26 931.2	607 229	X	22.5	26 926.0	514 548	X	19.0	75.8	22.4	0.2	0.4	0.0	0.6
District 2	31 723.3	517 345	X	16.3	31 730.0	514 845	X	16.0	33.4	65.2	0.1	0.4	0.0	0.3
District 3	25 893.1	588 915	X	22.7	25 910.0	515 314	X	20.0	65.0	32.1	1.2	0.6	0.0	0.5
District 4	20 298.3	530 679	X	26.1	20 293.0	513 853	X	25.0	51.6	46.9	0.1	0.4	0.0	0.3
District 5	16 642.6	600 490	X	36.1	16 647.0	514 656	X	31.0	76.0	20.4	0.4	1.4	0.0	0.6
MISSOURI	178 414.0	5 595 211	X	31.4	178 446.0	5 116 901	X	28.7	84.9	11.2	0.4	1.1	0.1	0.8
District 1	377.3	514 264	X	1 363.0	377.0	568 285	X	1 506.0	36.6	59.9	0.2	1.3	0.0	0.5
District 2	1 391.3	610 984	X	439.1	1 391.0	568 306	X	409.0	90.4	5.1	0.2	2.7	0.0	0.5
District 3	3 263.7	596 066	X	182.6	3 264.0	568 326	X	174.0	90.0	6.4	0.3	1.4	0.0	0.6

[1] Dry land or land partially or temporarily covered by water.

Table F. Congressional Districts 107th Congress

STATE District	Population and population characteristics, 2000 (cont'd)								Population and population characteristics, 1990				
	Race (percent) (cont'd)								Race (percent)				
	Race alone or in combination												
	Two or more races	White	Black	American Indian or Alaska Native	Asian	Native Hawaiian and other Pacific Islander	Some other race	Hispanic[1]	White	Black or African American	American Indian or Alaska Native	Asian and Pacific Islander	Hispanic[1]
	15	16	17	18	19	20	21	22	23	24	25	26	27
LOUISIANA—Cont'd													
District 7	0.8	73.4	25.4	0.6	0.9	0.1	0.6	1.5	75.1	23.8	0.2	0.5	1.2
MAINE	1.0	97.9	0.7	1.0	0.9	0.1	0.4	0.7	98.4	0.4	0.5	0.5	0.6
District 1	1.0	97.7	0.9	0.7	1.2	0.1	0.4	0.8	98.5	0.5	0.3	0.7	0.6
District 2	1.0	98.0	0.6	1.4	0.7	0.1	0.4	0.7	98.3	0.4	0.7	0.4	0.5
MARYLAND	2.0	65.4	28.8	0.7	4.5	0.1	2.5	4.3	71.0	24.9	0.3	2.9	2.6
District 1	1.3	82.1	15.7	0.7	1.8	0.1	1.1	2.2	83.4	15.0	0.2	1.0	1.1
District 2	1.3	88.3	8.7	0.6	2.7	0.1	0.9	1.7	91.7	5.9	0.3	1.8	1.2
District 3	2.0	68.0	27.8	0.8	3.7	0.1	1.8	2.8	79.5	17.5	0.3	2.2	1.7
District 4	3.1	23.7	66.5	1.0	5.5	0.2	6.5	10.0	33.5	58.5	0.3	4.6	6.4
District 5	2.2	64.5	30.2	1.0	4.3	0.1	2.3	3.9	77.2	18.6	0.4	3.0	2.4
District 6	1.2	90.5	6.6	0.5	2.8	0.1	0.8	1.6	93.8	4.5	0.2	1.3	0.9
District 7	1.4	22.1	75.5	0.7	2.3	0.1	0.9	1.3	27.2	71.0	0.3	1.3	0.9
District 8	3.2	72.8	11.5	0.7	12.4	0.2	5.8	10.5	81.5	8.2	0.2	8.0	6.3
MASSACHUSETTS	2.3	86.2	6.3	0.6	4.2	0.1	5.1	6.8	89.8	5.0	0.2	2.4	4.8
District 1	1.7	92.6	2.5	0.7	2.1	0.1	3.9	6.5	94.2	1.7	0.2	1.3	4.8
District 2	1.9	86.7	6.7	0.6	1.6	0.2	6.1	9.5	89.6	5.6	0.2	1.0	6.0
District 3	1.8	91.2	3.2	0.6	3.2	0.1	3.6	5.5	94.4	1.8	0.2	1.8	3.7
District 4	2.1	91.1	3.0	0.6	3.6	0.1	3.9	3.1	93.5	2.2	0.2	2.1	2.5
District 5	2.3	85.6	2.8	0.5	6.0	0.1	7.4	11.1	89.4	2.3	0.2	3.6	8.1
District 6	1.6	92.2	2.9	0.4	2.8	0.1	3.3	5.0	95.3	1.9	0.1	1.5	2.9
District 7	2.3	88.1	4.2	0.4	6.0	0.1	3.6	4.8	93.8	2.3	0.1	2.8	3.0
District 8	4.5	62.3	22.6	0.8	8.3	0.2	10.4	14.5	65.5	23.3	0.3	5.6	10.6
District 9	3.0	79.1	12.1	0.6	5.1	0.2	6.1	6.2	87.6	6.7	0.2	2.8	4.6
District 10	1.8	92.3	3.4	0.7	3.0	0.1	2.4	1.7	95.1	2.1	0.4	1.5	1.4
MICHIGAN	1.9	81.8	14.8	1.3	2.1	0.1	2.0	3.3	83.4	13.9	0.6	1.1	2.2
District 1	1.5	95.4	1.3	3.8	0.6	0.1	0.5	1.0	96.2	0.8	2.4	0.4	0.6
District 2	1.6	91.5	4.8	1.3	1.2	0.1	2.8	5.0	92.9	4.4	0.6	0.6	3.0
District 3	2.1	86.3	9.0	1.1	1.9	0.1	3.7	6.4	89.6	7.5	0.5	1.0	2.8
District 4	1.3	96.1	2.0	1.4	0.8	0.1	1.0	2.2	97.1	1.1	0.7	0.4	1.8
District 5	1.6	88.8	9.1	1.2	0.7	0.1	1.9	3.8	88.9	8.4	0.6	0.5	3.4
District 6	1.9	86.9	10.4	1.3	1.4	0.1	2.1	3.6	88.1	9.5	0.5	0.9	1.8
District 7	1.7	91.2	6.7	1.1	0.9	0.1	1.8	3.3	92.3	5.6	0.4	0.5	2.4
District 8	2.0	89.5	7.0	1.2	2.6	0.1	1.8	3.4	90.4	5.8	0.6	1.7	2.9
District 9	2.0	78.6	18.1	1.2	2.2	0.1	1.9	3.8	79.4	17.8	0.6	1.0	2.8
District 10	1.4	95.2	3.2	0.9	1.3	0.1	0.9	1.8	96.5	2.0	0.4	0.7	1.3
District 11	1.7	86.1	9.3	0.7	4.5	0.1	1.1	1.6	93.0	4.1	0.3	2.4	1.3
District 12	2.2	88.5	6.5	0.9	5.0	0.1	1.4	1.4	93.3	3.7	0.4	2.4	1.2
District 13	2.3	80.3	14.0	1.0	5.6	0.1	1.4	2.4	85.2	11.0	0.4	2.9	1.7
District 14	2.2	18.3	80.2	0.9	1.7	0.1	1.4	1.2	29.2	69.1	0.3	1.0	1.1
District 15	2.7	23.6	71.0	1.0	1.5	0.1	5.7	8.2	26.4	70.0	0.4	0.7	4.3
District 16	2.9	94.9	2.8	1.0	1.6	0.1	2.6	3.3	96.6	1.4	0.4	1.0	2.4
MINNESOTA	1.7	90.8	4.1	1.6	3.3	0.1	1.8	2.9	94.4	2.2	1.1	1.8	1.2
District 1	1.0	95.5	1.5	0.6	2.0	0.1	1.5	2.7	97.8	0.3	0.3	1.2	1.0
District 2	0.8	96.3	0.7	0.8	1.1	0.1	1.9	3.3	98.5	0.1	0.4	0.5	1.0
District 3	1.7	90.1	4.7	0.7	4.8	0.1	1.3	2.0	95.4	1.8	0.4	2.1	0.9
District 4	2.8	81.0	8.1	1.5	8.8	0.3	3.4	5.4	89.0	4.2	0.9	4.6	2.9
District 5	3.6	74.8	15.8	2.6	6.0	0.2	4.6	6.2	83.9	9.4	2.4	3.5	1.8
District 6	1.6	94.6	2.3	1.0	2.7	0.1	1.1	1.9	96.8	0.9	0.6	1.4	1.1
District 7	1.1	95.2	0.7	3.4	1.0	0.1	0.9	1.6	96.7	0.2	2.2	0.5	0.8
District 8	1.1	96.4	0.8	3.0	0.6	0.1	0.4	0.9	97.0	0.4	2.1	0.4	0.5
MISSISSIPPI	0.7	61.9	36.6	0.7	0.8	0.1	0.7	1.4	63.5	35.6	0.3	0.5	0.6
District 1	0.6	76.3	22.6	0.4	0.5	0.1	0.8	1.5	76.8	22.8	0.1	0.3	0.5
District 2	0.5	33.7	65.5	0.3	0.5	0.1	0.5	1.2	36.6	63.0	0.1	0.3	0.5
District 3	0.6	65.4	32.3	1.4	0.8	0.1	0.6	1.4	67.0	31.3	1.1	0.5	0.6
District 4	0.6	52.0	47.2	0.4	0.5	0.1	0.5	0.9	58.8	40.7	0.1	0.3	0.4
District 5	1.2	77.0	20.8	0.8	1.7	0.1	0.9	1.9	78.3	20.0	0.2	1.2	1.1
MISSOURI	1.5	86.1	11.7	1.1	1.4	0.1	1.2	2.1	87.7	10.7	0.4	0.8	1.2
District 1	1.6	37.6	60.8	0.6	1.7	0.1	0.8	1.2	46.3	52.3	0.2	1.0	0.9
District 2	1.1	91.4	5.4	0.5	3.0	0.1	0.8	1.6	94.2	3.7	0.2	1.6	1.0
District 3	1.4	91.2	6.8	0.7	1.7	0.1	1.0	1.7	96.3	2.3	0.2	0.8	1.1

[1] Hispanic persons may be of any race.

Table F. Congressional Districts 107th Congress

STATE District	Population and population characteristics, 2000										
	Age (percent)										
	Under 5 years	5 to 17 years	18 to 24 years	25 to 34 years	35 to 44 years	45 to 54 years	55 to 64 years	65 to 74 years	75 years and over	Median age (years)	Percent Female
	28	29	30	31	32	33	34	35	36	37	38
LOUISIANA—Cont'd											
District 7	7.4	20.7	10.3	13.2	15.8	12.6	8.3	6.5	5.1	33.8	51.2
MAINE	5.5	18.1	8.1	12.4	16.7	15.1	9.7	7.5	6.8	38.6	51.3
District 1	5.7	18.1	7.7	12.8	17.1	15.2	9.4	7.2	6.8	38.5	51.5
District 2	5.4	18.1	8.7	11.9	16.2	15.0	9.9	7.9	6.9	38.8	51.2
MARYLAND	6.7	18.9	8.5	14.1	17.3	14.3	8.9	6.1	5.2	36.0	51.7
District 1	6.3	18.1	8.6	13.2	16.7	14.2	9.9	7.2	5.8	37.3	51.0
District 2	6.2	18.7	7.9	12.5	17.2	14.7	9.4	7.2	6.3	37.9	51.7
District 3	6.7	17.9	8.5	16.0	16.7	13.7	8.3	6.1	6.1	35.5	52.3
District 4	7.4	19.8	9.3	16.5	17.1	13.9	8.2	4.5	3.3	33.3	52.8
District 5	6.8	19.3	9.5	14.8	18.4	14.1	8.6	4.9	3.6	34.8	50.8
District 6	6.6	19.7	7.5	13.0	18.1	14.7	8.9	6.1	5.4	36.7	50.3
District 7	6.4	19.0	11.1	13.6	15.8	13.0	8.4	6.7	6.0	34.9	53.5
District 8	6.9	18.8	6.3	13.7	17.9	15.4	9.2	6.0	5.8	37.4	51.9
MASSACHUSETTS	6.3	17.4	9.1	14.6	16.7	13.8	8.6	6.7	6.8	36.5	51.8
District 1	5.8	18.3	10.6	12.1	16.2	14.4	8.5	6.8	7.3	37.1	51.6
District 2	6.4	19.0	8.7	13.1	16.6	13.9	8.5	6.7	7.2	36.7	52.2
District 3	6.7	18.6	8.6	13.7	17.4	13.7	8.3	6.4	6.7	36.4	51.4
District 4	6.4	18.0	8.9	13.6	16.7	14.4	8.8	6.5	6.7	36.8	52.2
District 5	7.4	20.0	7.3	13.7	18.3	14.1	8.4	5.7	5.1	35.9	50.8
District 6	6.5	17.8	7.0	12.8	17.7	14.8	9.1	7.2	7.0	38.3	51.9
District 7	6.0	15.0	8.1	16.0	16.9	13.7	9.0	7.6	7.8	37.8	52.3
District 8	5.1	13.0	18.4	22.5	14.1	10.3	6.7	5.0	4.8	30.3	51.6
District 9	6.3	16.8	7.8	15.9	16.9	13.5	8.6	6.9	7.3	36.7	52.0
District 10	5.9	16.9	6.2	12.8	16.7	14.7	10.1	8.6	8.2	39.9	52.0
MICHIGAN	6.8	19.4	9.4	13.7	16.1	13.8	8.7	6.5	5.8	35.5	51.0
District 1	5.5	17.9	8.7	11.2	15.6	14.5	10.4	8.5	7.7	39.5	49.7
District 2	7.0	20.8	9.3	12.6	16.1	13.3	8.7	6.4	5.8	35.1	50.4
District 3	7.6	20.5	10.5	14.8	16.3	12.7	7.2	5.3	5.1	32.7	50.4
District 4	6.1	18.9	10.9	11.8	15.4	13.5	10.1	7.4	5.9	36.6	50.3
District 5	6.3	19.8	8.1	11.9	15.5	14.0	9.9	7.7	6.8	37.7	51.2
District 6	6.6	19.1	10.9	12.7	15.3	13.8	8.9	6.6	6.0	35.5	51.1
District 7	6.4	19.4	8.7	13.0	16.2	14.4	9.2	6.7	6.0	36.6	50.1
District 8	6.6	18.9	11.9	13.4	16.6	14.5	8.3	5.3	4.5	34.4	50.9
District 9	7.7	19.9	8.6	15.0	17.2	14.0	8.2	5.2	4.2	34.3	51.0
District 10	6.6	18.4	7.9	14.3	17.2	14.0	8.8	6.8	6.0	36.6	50.9
District 11	6.4	18.5	6.4	13.2	17.6	15.4	9.2	6.9	6.4	38.3	51.3
District 12	6.2	17.2	7.8	15.7	16.6	13.9	9.0	6.9	6.8	36.9	51.3
District 13	6.8	16.8	13.0	16.6	16.0	13.3	7.8	5.3	4.4	33.0	51.1
District 14	7.9	23.5	9.1	14.9	14.6	12.6	7.3	5.4	4.7	31.3	53.4
District 15	7.9	21.8	9.8	14.8	14.4	12.2	7.2	6.1	5.7	31.9	52.0
District 16	6.8	18.9	8.2	13.8	16.1	13.8	8.6	7.1	6.7	36.5	51.0
MINNESOTA	6.7	19.5	9.6	13.7	16.8	13.5	8.2	6.0	6.1	35.4	50.5
District 1	6.3	19.4	10.9	12.1	15.9	13.2	8.5	6.6	7.1	35.9	50.4
District 2	6.9	20.8	8.1	12.2	16.5	12.9	8.4	6.7	7.5	36.3	50.1
District 3	6.9	19.8	7.5	14.2	18.4	15.2	8.5	5.3	4.3	36.0	50.9
District 4	6.8	18.6	11.0	14.8	15.7	13.2	7.7	5.9	6.3	34.2	51.9
District 5	6.4	15.2	12.2	19.3	16.1	12.4	6.7	5.1	6.5	33.2	50.5
District 6	7.8	22.0	7.5	14.7	19.6	14.1	7.6	4.0	2.7	33.8	50.1
District 7	6.1	19.7	11.5	11.0	15.0	12.8	8.9	7.4	7.6	36.2	50.1
District 8	6.0	19.4	8.7	11.3	16.0	14.1	9.6	7.6	7.3	38.0	50.1
MISSISSIPPI	7.2	20.1	10.9	13.4	15.0	12.7	8.6	6.5	5.5	33.8	51.7
District 1	6.9	19.3	10.4	13.7	15.0	12.8	9.3	6.7	5.8	34.7	51.5
District 2	7.7	22.2	11.2	12.6	14.2	12.3	8.0	6.1	5.7	32.0	52.4
District 3	7.1	19.4	11.1	13.8	15.1	12.9	8.5	6.5	5.6	34.0	51.8
District 4	7.2	20.3	10.9	13.0	14.8	12.7	8.3	6.8	6.0	33.9	52.4
District 5	7.1	19.5	11.1	13.8	15.5	12.9	9.0	6.5	4.7	34.0	50.7
MISSOURI	6.6	18.9	9.6	13.2	15.9	13.3	9.1	7.0	6.5	36.1	51.4
District 1	6.6	20.1	10.9	14.0	15.0	12.5	7.9	6.7	6.3	33.8	53.8
District 2	6.5	19.3	7.6	12.5	17.3	15.1	9.3	6.6	5.8	37.5	51.6
District 3	6.4	18.4	8.5	13.9	16.8	13.5	8.6	7.0	7.0	36.7	51.7

Table F. Congressional Districts 107th Congress

STATE District	Population and population characteristics, 1990										Population—change, 1980-2000				
	Age (percent)									Percent Female	Total persons			Percent change	
	Under 5 years	5 to 17 years	18 to 24 years	25 to 34 years	35 to 44 years	45 to 54 years	55 to 64 years	65 to 74 years	75 years and over		2000	1990	1980	1990–2000	1980–1990
	39	40	41	42	43	44	45	46	47	48	49	50	51	52	53
LOUISIANA—Cont'd															
District 7	8.2	21.9	10.3	16.7	13.9	9.6	8.5	6.4	4.5	51.7	663 992	602 832	NA	10.1	NA
MAINE	7.0	18.2	10.1	16.7	15.7	10.2	8.8	7.5	5.8	51.3	1 274 923	1 227 928	1 125 043	3.8	9.1
District 1	7.1	17.6	9.7	17.2	16.3	10.1	8.6	7.5	5.9	51.6	666 936	613 961	NA	8.6	NA
District 2	6.9	18.7	10.4	16.2	15.2	10.2	9.1	7.4	5.8	51.0	607 987	613 967	NA	-1.0	NA
MARYLAND	7.5	16.8	10.6	18.8	16.3	10.9	8.3	6.6	4.2	51.5	5 296 486	4 780 753	4 216 933	10.8	13.4
District 1	7.1	16.8	10.6	17.1	15.5	11.1	9.3	7.6	4.8	50.8	682 770	597 684	NA	14.2	NA
District 2	7.2	16.4	9.9	17.7	16.1	11.3	9.5	7.6	4.4	51.2	652 938	597 683	NA	9.2	NA
District 3	7.5	15.7	9.8	19.6	15.8	10.0	8.2	7.8	5.5	52.4	643 935	597 680	NA	7.7	NA
District 4	7.9	17.3	11.4	21.1	17.4	10.8	6.8	4.6	2.8	52.4	648 764	597 690	NA	8.5	NA
District 5	7.6	17.1	12.6	20.0	16.4	11.4	7.4	4.9	2.7	49.9	714 886	597 681	NA	19.6	NA
District 6	7.3	17.7	10.0	17.3	16.5	11.2	8.4	6.7	4.7	50.7	723 196	597 688	NA	21.0	NA
District 7	7.8	17.2	11.5	18.9	14.7	9.4	8.4	7.1	5.0	53.1	539 439	597 680	NA	-9.7	NA
District 8	7.5	16.4	8.6	18.8	17.6	12.1	8.5	6.3	4.1	51.6	690 558	597 682	NA	15.5	NA
MASSACHUSETTS	6.9	15.6	11.8	18.3	15.3	10.0	8.6	7.6	6.0	52.0	6 349 097	6 016 425	5 737 093	5.5	4.9
District 1	7.1	16.8	12.8	16.5	15.2	9.4	8.2	7.9	6.2	51.7	610 522	601 643	NA	1.5	NA
District 2	7.2	17.2	11.1	17.2	15.0	9.7	8.5	8.2	5.9	52.4	615 557	601 642	NA	2.3	NA
District 3	7.2	16.7	11.4	17.4	15.3	10.0	8.5	7.7	5.9	51.6	655 701	601 642	NA	9.0	NA
District 4	6.7	16.6	11.4	16.8	16.1	10.5	8.2	7.5	6.2	52.4	639 072	601 642	NA	6.2	NA
District 5	7.9	17.8	10.9	18.4	15.9	10.7	7.9	6.1	4.4	50.7	644 869	601 643	NA	7.2	NA
District 6	6.9	15.6	9.9	17.5	16.1	10.9	9.3	7.8	6.0	52.0	652 455	601 643	NA	8.4	NA
District 7	6.1	13.2	11.4	19.3	15.0	10.2	9.7	8.3	6.8	52.7	616 542	601 642	NA	2.5	NA
District 8	5.9	11.9	19.3	23.7	13.7	8.0	6.7	5.9	4.9	51.9	620 372	601 643	NA	3.1	NA
District 9	6.8	14.6	10.5	19.3	14.9	10.1	9.2	8.0	6.6	52.3	630 499	601 643	NA	4.8	NA
District 10	6.7	15.8	9.3	17.0	15.6	10.4	9.3	9.0	6.9	52.2	663 508	601 642	NA	10.3	NA
MICHIGAN	7.6	18.9	10.8	16.9	15.1	10.2	8.5	7.1	4.9	51.5	9 938 444	9 295 287	9 262 044	6.9	0.4
District 1	6.8	18.9	9.6	15.1	14.7	9.9	9.4	8.9	6.8	50.1	639 161	580 956	NA	10.0	NA
District 2	8.1	20.5	9.6	16.3	14.8	10.0	8.4	7.2	5.2	50.8	686 086	580 956	NA	18.1	NA
District 3	8.6	19.7	11.0	18.5	14.8	9.1	7.4	6.1	4.7	51.1	662 041	580 956	NA	14.0	NA
District 4	7.1	19.6	12.3	15.1	14.1	10.5	9.0	7.4	4.9	50.6	651 347	580 956	NA	12.1	NA
District 5	7.5	20.4	9.4	15.6	14.6	10.5	9.1	7.6	5.4	51.6	587 031	580 956	NA	1.0	NA
District 6	7.4	19.1	11.6	16.1	14.9	10.2	8.5	7.0	5.2	51.6	610 640	580 956	NA	5.1	NA
District 7	7.3	19.7	9.8	16.1	15.6	10.7	8.7	7.1	5.1	50.5	620 053	580 957	NA	6.7	NA
District 8	7.2	18.5	14.1	17.2	16.2	10.5	7.3	5.3	3.7	51.2	658 695	580 956	NA	13.4	NA
District 9	8.1	19.4	10.8	18.3	15.8	10.7	7.7	5.4	3.7	51.5	633 553	580 956	NA	9.1	NA
District 10	7.2	18.1	9.9	17.8	15.3	10.5	9.1	7.4	4.6	51.4	671 306	580 956	NA	15.6	NA
District 11	6.8	16.7	8.3	17.5	16.7	11.7	9.9	7.6	4.8	51.3	640 548	580 956	NA	10.3	NA
District 12	6.8	17.0	9.7	18.1	15.4	11.1	9.1	7.7	5.1	51.8	574 950	580 956	NA	-1.0	NA
District 13	7.1	16.7	15.1	19.5	15.7	9.9	7.4	5.2	3.4	51.2	628 363	580 956	NA	8.2	NA
District 14	8.9	20.7	11.1	16.4	14.6	9.0	7.7	6.9	4.6	53.9	550 599	580 956	NA	-5.2	NA
District 15	8.8	19.2	10.9	16.2	13.8	8.6	8.6	8.2	5.8	53.2	531 634	580 956	NA	-8.5	NA
District 16	7.1	18.1	9.7	17.0	15.1	10.4	9.5	8.1	4.9	51.4	592 437	580 956	NA	2.0	NA
MINNESOTA	7.7	19.0	10.1	17.8	15.2	9.8	7.9	6.7	5.8	51.0	4 919 479	4 375 665	4 075 970	12.4	7.4
District 1	7.4	19.6	11.2	15.9	14.1	9.6	8.1	7.3	6.8	51.0	594 864	546 887	NA	8.8	NA
District 2	7.7	21.0	8.2	15.4	13.9	9.7	8.5	8.0	7.6	50.6	613 816	546 888	NA	12.2	NA
District 3	8.2	18.4	9.1	20.3	17.7	11.3	7.5	4.7	2.8	51.0	642 053	546 888	NA	17.4	NA
District 4	7.9	16.7	11.3	19.1	15.0	9.3	8.0	6.9	5.8	52.3	577 077	546 887	NA	5.5	NA
District 5	7.1	13.4	12.0	22.1	15.4	8.5	7.4	7.3	6.9	52.0	557 819	546 887	NA	2.0	NA
District 6	9.1	22.0	9.0	20.4	17.7	10.7	5.9	3.3	2.0	49.9	720 995	546 887	NA	31.8	NA
District 7	7.3	20.4	11.8	14.6	13.2	9.1	8.5	7.8	7.2	50.4	588 825	546 901	NA	7.7	NA
District 8	6.9	20.4	8.4	14.6	14.8	10.1	9.1	8.6	7.1	50.6	624 030	546 874	NA	14.1	NA
MISSISSIPPI	7.6	21.4	11.4	15.5	13.6	9.6	8.3	7.0	5.5	52.2	2 844 658	2 575 475	2 520 770	10.5	2.2
District 1	7.2	20.1	11.5	15.2	13.7	10.4	8.6	7.3	5.9	51.9	607 229	514 548	NA	18.0	NA
District 2	8.3	24.5	11.2	14.3	12.5	8.6	7.6	7.0	6.0	53.2	517 345	514 845	NA	0.5	NA
District 3	7.4	20.7	11.7	15.9	14.1	9.6	8.3	6.7	5.5	52.0	588 915	515 314	NA	14.3	NA
District 4	7.4	21.0	10.9	15.8	13.7	9.4	8.6	7.4	5.8	52.8	530 679	513 853	NA	3.3	NA
District 5	7.7	20.7	11.7	16.5	13.9	10.1	8.5	6.6	4.3	51.0	600 490	514 656	NA	16.7	NA
MISSOURI	7.2	18.5	10.1	16.7	14.4	10.2	8.9	7.7	6.3	51.8	5 595 211	5 116 901	4 916 766	9.3	4.1
District 1	7.7	18.6	10.8	17.6	13.7	9.0	8.7	7.6	6.3	53.9	514 264	568 285	NA	-9.5	NA
District 2	7.3	18.6	8.6	17.6	16.9	11.8	8.7	6.1	4.2	51.4	610 984	568 306	NA	7.5	NA
District 3	7.3	17.3	8.8	18.1	14.7	9.9	9.1	8.0	6.8	52.2	596 066	568 326	NA	4.9	NA

Table F. Congressional Districts 107th Congress

STATE District	Total population	Total in house-holds	House-holder	Spouse	Child Total	Child Own child under 18 years	Other relatives Total	Other relatives Under 18 years	Nonrelatives Total	Nonrelatives Unmarried partner	Total in group quarters	Institutionalized population Correctional institutions	Institutionalized population Nursing homes	Institutionalized population Other institutions	Noninstitutionalized population College dormitories	Noninstitutionalized population Military quarters	Noninstitutionalized population Other
	54	55	56	57	58	59	60	61	62	63	64	65	66	67	68	69	70
LOUISIANA—Cont'd																	
District 7	663 992	97.2	37.0	19.2	32.3	25.0	4.8	2.5	3.9	1.9	2.8	1.1	0.8	0.2	0.4	0.0	0.3
MAINE	1 274 923	97.3	40.6	21.3	26.9	21.9	2.6	0.9	5.8	3.0	2.7	0.2	0.7	0.1	1.1	0.1	0.6
District 1	666 936	97.5	40.6	21.2	27.2	22.3	2.7	0.9	5.8	2.9	2.5	0.3	0.6	0.1	0.8	0.1	0.6
District 2	607 987	97.0	40.7	21.5	26.5	21.6	2.6	0.9	5.8	3.1	3.0	0.1	0.8	0.1	1.3	0.0	0.6
MARYLAND	5 296 486	97.5	37.4	18.8	29.6	22.6	6.2	2.4	5.5	2.1	2.5	0.7	0.5	0.1	0.7	0.1	0.4
District 1	682 770	97.0	38.3	20.4	28.0	21.7	4.9	2.1	5.4	2.4	3.0	0.8	0.6	0.1	0.6	0.5	0.4
District 2	652 938	98.3	38.4	21.3	29.6	22.7	4.5	1.6	4.6	2.0	1.7	0.2	0.4	0.1	0.6	0.0	0.3
District 3	643 935	97.6	39.8	17.8	28.3	21.7	5.6	2.3	6.0	2.4	2.4	0.6	0.5	0.1	0.5	0.2	0.6
District 4	648 764	99.0	36.5	15.0	31.3	22.8	9.6	3.8	6.5	2.2	1.0	0.2	0.3	0.1	0.1	0.1	0.3
District 5	714 886	96.9	35.3	19.5	30.4	23.3	5.9	2.3	5.8	2.0	3.1	0.6	0.4	0.1	1.5	0.1	0.4
District 6	723 196	96.4	36.2	22.0	30.6	24.5	3.7	1.3	4.0	1.9	3.6	1.6	0.6	0.2	0.6	0.0	0.4
District 7	539 439	95.4	38.3	10.7	27.9	18.6	11.5	5.8	7.0	2.6	4.6	1.4	0.8	0.2	1.6	0.0	0.7
District 8	690 558	98.9	36.9	21.4	30.2	24.0	5.2	1.3	5.2	1.4	1.1	0.1	0.5	0.1	0.0	0.1	0.4
MASSACHUSETTS	6 349 097	96.5	38.5	18.9	29.0	21.8	4.5	1.4	5.6	2.1	3.5	0.4	0.9	0.1	1.6	0.0	0.5
District 1	610 522	95.2	38.7	19.1	28.4	22.1	3.4	1.2	5.7	2.5	4.8	0.2	1.0	0.2	3.0	0.0	0.4
District 2	615 557	97.0	38.4	19.0	30.5	23.2	4.2	1.6	4.9	2.4	3.0	0.3	0.9	0.2	1.3	0.0	0.3
District 3	655 701	96.6	37.6	20.2	30.6	23.6	3.9	1.2	4.3	1.9	3.4	0.3	0.9	0.2	1.6	0.0	0.4
District 4	639 072	96.0	37.4	20.0	29.9	22.8	3.7	1.2	5.0	1.9	4.0	0.7	0.9	0.1	2.1	0.0	0.3
District 5	644 869	97.7	35.8	20.1	32.8	25.4	4.8	1.5	4.3	1.9	2.3	0.9	0.7	0.1	0.3	0.0	0.4
District 6	652 455	97.5	38.3	20.4	30.3	22.7	4.3	1.3	4.3	1.9	2.5	0.2	1.0	0.1	0.8	0.0	0.3
District 7	616 542	97.2	39.9	19.6	27.5	19.6	4.7	1.1	5.5	1.8	2.8	0.1	0.9	0.1	1.3	0.0	0.3
District 8	620 372	92.9	40.4	11.6	22.0	15.8	6.3	1.9	12.5	2.5	7.1	0.1	0.6	0.1	5.7	0.0	0.7
District 9	630 499	96.9	38.6	17.6	29.6	21.1	5.5	1.6	5.6	1.9	3.1	0.6	1.0	0.5	0.3	0.0	0.7
District 10	663 508	97.9	40.0	20.7	28.5	21.1	4.0	1.2	4.7	2.0	2.1	0.3	0.9	0.1	0.2	0.0	0.6
MICHIGAN	9 938 444	97.5	38.1	19.6	30.6	23.6	4.4	1.8	4.9	2.0	2.5	0.7	0.5	0.1	0.7	0.0	0.5
District 1	639 161	96.0	39.9	22.1	27.2	21.9	2.3	0.9	4.5	2.1	4.0	1.7	0.8	0.1	0.8	0.0	0.6
District 2	686 086	97.0	36.3	21.5	31.7	25.7	3.1	1.4	4.3	1.8	3.0	0.8	0.6	0.1	0.8	0.0	0.7
District 3	662 041	97.1	36.7	19.5	31.9	26.0	3.6	1.4	5.4	2.0	2.9	1.0	0.7	0.1	0.6	0.0	0.5
District 4	651 347	96.1	37.6	21.8	28.9	23.1	2.7	1.2	5.2	2.1	3.9	1.2	0.5	0.1	1.7	0.0	0.4
District 5	587 031	98.3	38.7	21.0	30.8	23.6	3.6	1.7	4.1	2.1	1.7	0.3	0.5	0.1	0.0	0.0	0.7
District 6	610 640	96.8	38.5	19.9	28.8	23.1	3.7	1.7	5.9	2.3	3.2	0.2	0.5	0.2	1.3	0.0	1.0
District 7	620 053	95.6	37.4	20.7	29.5	23.4	3.5	1.6	4.5	2.1	4.4	2.3	0.6	0.2	0.7	0.0	0.7
District 8	658 695	96.5	37.7	20.5	29.6	23.7	3.0	1.2	5.6	2.0	3.5	0.4	0.5	0.1	2.1	0.0	0.4
District 9	633 553	98.2	38.0	19.0	31.8	24.9	4.5	2.0	4.9	2.2	1.8	0.6	0.3	0.1	0.3	0.0	0.6
District 10	671 306	98.9	39.0	21.6	31.1	23.4	3.4	1.2	3.9	2.0	1.1	0.4	0.4	0.0	0.0	0.0	0.3
District 11	640 548	99.0	39.4	22.7	30.5	23.6	3.2	1.0	3.2	1.5	1.0	0.0	0.5	0.0	0.1	0.0	0.4
District 12	574 950	99.3	40.4	20.3	29.9	21.7	4.4	1.3	4.2	1.8	0.7	0.0	0.4	0.0	0.0	0.0	0.3
District 13	628 363	96.3	39.3	18.7	28.0	21.7	3.8	1.5	6.6	2.1	3.7	0.3	0.4	0.2	2.4	0.0	0.3
District 14	550 599	98.6	35.1	11.4	35.7	25.0	10.9	5.5	5.5	2.3	1.4	0.4	0.4	0.1	0.2	0.0	0.3
District 15	531 634	97.3	36.4	9.4	32.8	23.2	11.9	5.5	6.8	2.4	2.7	0.5	0.5	0.3	0.0	0.0	1.3
District 16	592 437	99.2	38.7	20.7	31.7	23.5	4.3	1.7	3.8	1.9	0.8	0.1	0.4	0.1	0.0	0.0	0.2
MINNESOTA	4 919 479	97.2	38.5	20.7	29.9	24.6	2.8	1.0	5.3	2.0	2.8	0.3	0.8	0.1	0.9	0.0	0.6
District 1	594 864	95.9	37.9	21.6	29.4	24.4	2.0	0.7	5.0	1.9	4.1	0.6	1.0	0.1	1.7	0.0	0.7
District 2	613 816	97.4	37.5	22.8	31.6	26.5	1.9	0.6	3.6	1.6	2.6	0.4	1.1	0.2	0.6	0.0	0.4
District 3	642 053	99.1	38.7	22.2	30.9	25.6	2.7	0.8	4.7	1.8	0.9	0.1	0.3	0.1	0.0	0.0	0.4
District 4	577 077	96.8	39.6	17.6	29.2	23.3	4.0	1.4	6.3	2.3	3.2	0.1	0.8	0.1	1.4	0.0	0.7
District 5	557 819	96.0	42.8	14.7	23.9	19.2	5.0	1.7	9.6	2.9	4.0	0.1	1.3	0.1	1.3	0.0	1.1
District 6	720 995	99.0	35.5	22.3	34.5	28.4	2.5	0.9	4.2	1.9	1.0	0.5	0.2	0.1	0.0	0.0	0.3
District 7	588 825	96.0	38.0	21.4	29.6	24.4	2.1	0.8	4.9	1.8	4.0	0.3	1.2	0.1	1.8	0.0	0.6
District 8	624 030	97.2	39.1	21.9	29.1	23.7	2.3	0.9	4.8	2.2	2.8	0.6	0.9	0.2	0.6	0.0	0.5
MISSISSIPPI	2 844 658	96.6	36.8	18.3	31.1	23.1	6.8	3.6	3.7	1.6	3.4	0.9	0.6	0.2	1.0	0.2	0.3
District 1	607 229	97.5	37.8	20.7	30.1	23.0	5.5	2.7	3.3	1.5	2.5	0.4	0.7	0.1	1.1	0.0	0.3
District 2	517 345	95.8	34.3	14.1	33.3	23.2	10.4	6.1	3.6	1.9	4.2	2.1	0.7	0.1	1.0	0.0	0.2
District 3	588 915	96.5	37.4	19.3	30.7	23.2	5.7	2.9	3.5	1.4	3.5	0.8	0.7	0.5	1.1	0.1	0.2
District 4	530 679	96.7	37.1	17.4	31.4	23.0	7.2	3.8	3.6	1.6	3.3	0.6	0.6	0.3	1.2	0.0	0.6
District 5	600 490	96.7	37.1	19.4	30.2	23.2	5.6	2.8	4.5	1.9	3.3	0.7	0.5	0.2	0.7	0.8	0.3
MISSOURI	5 595 211	97.1	39.2	20.4	29.2	23.1	3.8	1.7	4.5	2.0	2.9	0.6	0.9	0.1	0.8	0.1	0.4
District 1	514 264	96.8	40.0	12.8	30.7	22.0	7.9	4.0	5.3	2.3	3.2	0.4	0.7	0.2	1.3	0.0	0.6
District 2	610 984	98.3	38.7	22.5	30.9	24.4	2.8	1.0	3.4	1.5	1.7	0.2	0.8	0.1	0.4	0.0	0.2
District 3	596 066	98.6	40.3	20.0	29.8	22.6	3.9	1.6	4.6	2.3	1.4	0.0	0.9	0.1	0.1	0.0	0.4

Table F. Congressional Districts 107th Congress

	Households by type, 2000												Households, 1990		
	Family households						Nonfamily households								
			Married couple		Female householder[1]			Householder living alone							
STATE District	Total households	Total	With own children under 18 years	Total	With own children under 18 years	Total	With own children under 18 years	Total	Total	65 years and over	Average household size	Average family size	Total households	Female householder[1]	Householder living alone
	71	72	73	74	75	76	77	78	79	80	81	82	83	84	85
LOUISIANA—Cont'd															
District 7	245 590	70.9	36.4	51.8	24.9	14.8	0.3	29.1	24.4	9.2	2.63	3.15	214 122	13.5	22.6
MAINE	518 200	65.7	30.4	52.5	21.8	9.5	6.2	34.3	27.0	10.7	2.39	2.90	465 312	9.5	23.3
District 1	270 935	65.2	30.7	52.2	22.4	9.5	6.2	34.8	27.2	10.4	2.40	2.93	235 671	9.5	23.9
District 2	247 265	66.4	30.0	52.8	21.1	9.5	6.3	33.6	26.8	11.0	2.39	2.87	229 641	9.6	22.7
MARYLAND	1 980 859	68.6	33.4	50.2	23.3	14.1	8.0	31.4	25.0	8.1	2.61	3.13	1 748 991	13.3	22.6
District 1	261 214	69.6	31.7	53.4	22.4	12.1	7.1	30.4	24.0	9.0	2.53	3.00	221 366	11.3	21.8
District 2	250 863	70.3	32.9	55.5	24.8	10.8	6.1	29.7	24.1	9.4	2.56	3.05	222 476	9.8	20.9
District 3	256 468	63.3	30.5	44.6	20.1	14.5	8.4	36.7	29.2	9.3	2.45	3.05	232 681	13.3	25.9
District 4	236 537	68.1	35.4	41.3	20.5	21.1	12.3	31.9	25.3	5.1	2.71	3.26	216 758	18.1	23.5
District 5	252 640	72.1	36.4	55.1	26.9	12.4	7.2	27.9	21.1	5.3	2.74	3.19	204 414	10.1	18.2
District 6	261 822	73.4	36.7	60.8	29.2	9.1	5.5	26.6	21.4	8.3	2.66	3.11	214 745	8.7	20.0
District 7	206 339	59.9	27.1	27.9	10.8	26.6	14.1	40.1	32.9	10.3	2.49	3.19	216 574	26.1	28.5
District 8	254 976	70.5	35.7	58.0	29.1	9.4	5.2	29.5	23.6	8.1	2.68	3.18	219 977	8.5	21.2
MASSACHUSETTS	2 443 580	64.5	30.6	49.0	22.4	11.9	6.7	35.5	28.0	10.5	2.51	3.11	2 247 110	12.1	25.8
District 1	236 215	64.9	30.9	49.5	21.6	11.5	7.3	35.1	28.1	11.3	2.46	3.03	222 811	11.5	25.1
District 2	236 234	67.1	32.4	49.4	22.0	13.8	8.5	32.9	27.0	11.1	2.53	3.08	222 230	13.2	24.2
District 3	246 370	68.5	33.9	53.8	25.7	11.1	6.5	31.5	25.9	10.3	2.57	3.13	220 174	11.3	23.7
District 4	238 717	68.0	33.5	53.6	25.7	11.1	6.4	32.0	25.6	10.3	2.57	3.11	218 092	11.1	23.9
District 5	230 732	72.0	37.6	56.1	28.7	12.0	7.1	28.0	22.7	8.2	2.73	3.24	209 525	12.1	20.9
District 6	249 622	67.7	32.1	53.4	24.7	10.9	6.0	32.3	26.6	10.6	2.55	3.12	225 496	11.0	24.4
District 7	246 169	62.9	27.4	49.1	21.6	10.4	4.7	37.1	29.6	11.2	2.44	3.06	232 429	10.9	27.1
District 8	250 834	47.0	21.6	28.6	12.0	14.5	8.3	53.0	36.4	8.8	2.30	3.10	238 103	15.3	35.3
District 9	243 334	62.6	29.5	45.7	21.3	13.2	6.9	37.4	29.4	10.8	2.51	3.18	226 665	13.2	27.2
District 10	265 353	65.4	28.5	51.7	21.7	10.4	5.4	34.6	28.2	11.9	2.45	3.03	231 585	10.9	25.5
MICHIGAN	3 785 661	68.0	32.7	51.4	23.1	12.5	7.5	32.0	26.2	9.4	2.56	3.10	3 419 331	12.9	23.7
District 1	255 335	67.4	29.3	55.2	21.7	8.5	5.5	32.6	27.3	11.9	2.40	2.92	219 934	8.6	24.8
District 2	249 359	72.7	35.8	59.2	27.1	9.7	6.4	27.3	22.4	9.1	2.67	3.13	206 301	9.6	20.4
District 3	243 202	68.5	36.0	53.2	26.3	11.4	7.5	31.5	25.1	8.1	2.64	3.19	208 512	11.2	22.6
District 4	244 789	70.9	32.2	58.1	24.0	9.1	5.9	29.1	23.0	9.4	2.56	3.00	207 299	9.0	20.2
District 5	227 407	70.4	32.1	54.2	22.2	12.2	7.6	29.6	25.3	10.8	2.54	3.03	214 348	12.5	22.4
District 6	235 284	67.1	31.8	51.7	22.1	11.5	7.4	32.9	26.0	9.4	2.51	3.03	216 367	11.5	23.4
District 7	232 134	70.3	33.3	55.2	23.7	11.0	7.0	29.7	24.7	9.5	2.55	3.04	210 201	10.8	22.5
District 8	248 451	67.8	33.7	54.4	25.5	9.9	6.2	32.2	24.7	7.3	2.56	3.08	208 151	10.3	22.1
District 9	240 949	68.2	34.8	50.0	23.8	14.0	8.8	31.8	26.0	7.7	2.58	3.13	213 603	15.3	23.6
District 10	261 520	69.2	32.4	55.3	25.2	10.0	5.4	30.8	25.9	9.9	2.54	3.08	214 512	10.3	22.1
District 11	252 118	69.0	32.6	57.6	26.9	8.3	4.4	31.0	26.4	9.2	2.51	3.08	220 558	7.8	22.3
District 12	232 339	64.4	29.2	50.3	22.7	10.4	5.1	35.6	29.8	10.6	2.46	3.10	220 490	10.4	24.6
District 13	246 781	62.3	30.4	47.5	22.1	11.2	6.5	37.7	29.0	7.5	2.45	3.06	215 487	11.2	25.0
District 14	193 235	69.1	35.9	32.4	15.2	30.5	17.9	30.9	26.4	8.2	2.81	3.39	206 555	28.0	25.3
District 15	193 624	60.9	31.3	25.7	12.1	28.7	16.6	39.1	33.1	11.1	2.67	3.44	220 864	29.1	34.1
District 16	229 134	69.2	32.2	53.5	24.2	11.3	6.0	30.8	26.3	10.9	2.57	3.12	216 149	11.4	22.9
MINNESOTA	1 895 127	66.2	33.0	53.7	25.2	8.9	5.9	33.8	26.9	9.3	2.52	3.09	1 647 853	8.6	25.1
District 1	225 585	68.0	33.3	57.0	26.2	7.6	5.1	32.0	25.8	10.4	2.53	3.05	201 475	6.9	24.5
District 2	230 060	71.1	35.6	60.7	28.9	6.9	4.7	28.9	24.4	11.2	2.60	3.11	200 523	6.0	23.7
District 3	248 428	68.8	35.3	57.4	28.3	8.4	5.4	31.2	24.4	6.8	2.56	3.09	205 269	8.2	20.6
District 4	228 672	60.0	29.7	44.5	20.3	11.7	7.5	40.0	31.8	9.8	2.44	3.14	215 257	11.2	29.0
District 5	238 619	49.7	23.5	34.4	14.7	11.4	7.1	50.3	38.1	9.4	2.24	3.05	235 878	11.5	35.3
District 6	255 730	75.5	41.9	62.8	33.8	9.1	6.1	24.5	18.9	4.8	2.79	3.22	184 815	9.0	15.6
District 7	223 955	67.7	32.5	56.3	25.2	7.7	5.2	32.3	26.2	11.6	2.53	3.06	198 065	7.2	24.2
District 8	244 078	68.4	31.6	56.0	23.5	8.5	5.7	31.6	26.3	11.3	2.48	2.99	206 571	8.1	25.1
MISSISSIPPI	1 046 434	71.4	34.7	49.8	22.4	17.3	10.1	28.6	24.6	9.6	2.63	3.14	911 374	15.9	23.4
District 1	229 413	72.6	34.5	54.7	24.5	13.7	7.9	27.4	23.8	9.8	2.58	3.06	186 772	12.5	22.2
District 2	177 271	72.0	35.6	41.2	18.3	25.6	14.8	28.0	24.9	10.5	2.79	3.35	170 188	23.3	24.2
District 3	220 494	70.9	34.7	51.4	23.5	15.7	9.3	29.1	25.0	9.4	2.58	3.09	184 721	14.3	23.1
District 4	196 773	70.4	34.2	46.9	20.8	19.1	11.2	29.6	26.0	10.4	2.61	3.14	185 716	16.6	24.9
District 5	222 483	71.1	34.8	52.4	23.8	14.3	8.6	28.9	23.7	8.2	2.61	3.09	183 977	13.7	22.5
MISSOURI	2 194 594	67.3	31.9	52.0	22.7	11.6	7.1	32.7	27.3	10.8	2.48	3.02	1 961 206	10.6	26.0
District 1	205 933	59.7	29.0	32.0	13.3	23.1	13.7	40.3	34.3	11.0	2.42	3.15	220 470	20.3	32.0
District 2	236 472	70.1	34.2	58.2	27.3	9.1	5.3	29.9	25.0	8.4	2.54	3.07	210 097	8.1	21.4
District 3	239 965	65.0	30.8	49.8	22.2	11.2	6.5	35.0	29.3	10.8	2.45	3.05	225 237	9.8	28.0

[1] No spouse present.

Table F. Congressional Districts 107th Congress

STATE District	Percent change of households, 1990–2000	Total housing units	Occupied housing units (percent)	Vacant housing units Total	Vacant housing units For seasonal, recreational, or occasional use	Homeowner vacancy rate (percent)	Rental vacancy rate (percent)	Occupied housing units Total	Percent owner-occupied housing units	Percent renter-occupied housing units	Average household size of owner-occupied units	Average household size of renter-occupied units
	86	87	88	89	90	91	92	93	94	95	96	97
LOUISIANA—Cont'd												
District 7	14.7	272 153	90.2	9.8	1.8	1.5	10.9	245 590	70.5	29.5	2.71	2.44
MAINE	11.4	651 901	79.5	20.5	15.6	1.7	7.0	518 200	71.6	28.4	2.54	2.03
District 1	15.0	326 739	82.9	17.1	13.4	1.0	5.5	270 935	70.4	29.6	2.55	2.04
District 2	7.7	325 162	76.0	24.0	17.8	2.3	8.8	247 265	72.8	27.2	2.52	2.03
MARYLAND	13.3	2 145 283	92.3	7.7	1.8	1.6	6.1	1 980 859	67.7	32.3	2.73	2.35
District 1	18.0	309 920	84.3	15.7	7.9	1.6	10.7	261 214	72.3	27.7	2.60	2.36
District 2	12.8	262 384	95.6	4.4	0.5	1.1	5.8	250 863	72.9	27.1	2.70	2.19
District 3	10.2	274 846	93.3	6.7	0.5	2.1	5.5	256 468	64.2	35.8	2.58	2.22
District 4	9.1	249 039	95.0	5.0	0.2	2.4	4.2	236 537	54.9	45.1	2.85	2.55
District 5	23.6	267 475	94.5	5.5	1.3	1.5	5.3	252 640	74.3	25.7	2.83	2.48
District 6	21.9	280 025	93.5	6.5	2.0	1.5	6.0	261 822	75.0	25.0	2.80	2.27
District 7	-4.7	238 564	86.5	13.5	0.3	3.0	7.7	206 339	50.1	49.9	2.68	2.30
District 8	15.9	263 030	96.9	3.1	0.6	0.9	3.6	254 976	73.8	26.2	2.78	2.39
MASSACHUSETTS	8.7	2 621 989	93.2	6.8	3.6	0.7	3.5	2 443 580	61.7	38.3	2.72	2.17
District 1	6.0	257 925	91.6	8.4	3.8	1.2	5.3	236 215	65.1	34.9	2.63	2.14
District 2	6.3	248 879	94.9	5.1	1.0	0.9	4.9	236 234	65.7	34.3	2.69	2.22
District 3	11.9	256 925	95.9	4.1	0.8	0.6	4.2	246 370	64.4	35.6	2.80	2.16
District 4	9.5	252 307	94.6	5.4	1.9	0.7	4.3	238 717	66.4	33.6	2.79	2.13
District 5	10.1	237 692	97.1	2.9	0.4	0.5	3.0	230 732	68.3	31.7	2.89	2.39
District 6	10.7	260 034	96.0	4.0	1.6	0.5	3.0	249 622	67.7	32.3	2.76	2.12
District 7	5.9	252 621	97.4	2.6	0.4	0.4	2.1	246 169	58.6	41.4	2.69	2.07
District 8	5.3	262 078	95.7	4.3	0.7	0.9	2.4	250 834	30.1	69.9	2.45	2.23
District 9	7.4	252 532	96.4	3.6	0.4	0.6	3.4	243 334	59.4	40.6	2.76	2.15
District 10	14.6	340 996	77.8	22.2	19.3	0.9	4.2	265 353	72.0	28.0	2.61	2.04
MICHIGAN	10.7	4 234 279	89.4	10.6	5.5	1.6	6.8	3 785 661	73.8	26.2	2.67	2.24
District 1	16.1	359 404	71.0	29.0	23.1	2.0	9.3	255 335	78.8	21.2	2.49	2.09
District 2	20.9	296 544	84.1	15.9	11.1	1.7	6.9	249 359	80.8	19.2	2.74	2.35
District 3	16.6	256 584	94.8	5.2	1.0	1.2	6.0	243 202	71.6	28.4	2.80	2.24
District 4	18.1	310 666	78.8	21.2	16.7	1.8	6.7	244 789	80.0	20.0	2.62	2.30
District 5	6.1	266 492	85.3	14.7	8.9	2.4	7.8	227 407	79.5	20.5	2.61	2.26
District 6	8.7	266 067	88.4	11.6	6.0	1.8	7.2	235 284	72.1	27.9	2.62	2.24
District 7	10.4	254 090	91.4	8.6	3.5	1.6	7.7	232 134	76.3	23.7	2.65	2.23
District 8	19.4	264 149	94.1	5.9	1.6	1.5	6.5	248 451	73.9	26.1	2.71	2.12
District 9	12.8	258 212	93.3	6.7	0.7	1.8	8.9	240 949	71.6	28.4	2.71	2.27
District 10	21.9	274 462	95.3	4.7	1.0	1.4	5.5	261 520	79.2	20.8	2.66	2.06
District 11	14.3	262 114	96.2	3.8	0.8	0.9	5.4	252 118	78.7	21.3	2.68	1.89
District 12	5.4	239 301	97.1	2.9	0.4	0.8	3.8	232 339	75.2	24.8	2.63	1.94
District 13	14.5	257 264	95.9	4.1	0.4	1.3	4.8	246 781	64.5	35.5	2.67	2.05
District 14	-6.4	207 788	93.0	7.0	0.1	1.4	6.3	193 235	66.3	33.7	2.81	2.81
District 15	-12.3	221 628	87.4	12.6	0.2	1.8	9.4	193 624	47.4	52.6	2.80	2.55
District 16	6.0	239 514	95.7	4.3	0.5	1.5	5.4	229 134	77.4	22.6	2.68	2.19
MINNESOTA	15.0	2 065 946	91.7	8.3	5.1	0.9	4.1	1 895 127	74.6	25.4	2.69	2.03
District 1	12.0	237 552	95.0	5.0	1.6	1.0	4.7	225 585	77.2	22.8	2.67	2.05
District 2	14.7	248 682	92.5	7.5	2.8	1.5	7.5	230 060	80.1	19.9	2.73	2.07
District 3	21.0	254 283	97.7	2.3	0.6	0.5	2.9	248 428	75.7	24.3	2.74	1.99
District 4	6.2	234 507	97.5	2.5	0.4	0.5	2.5	228 672	64.1	35.9	2.66	2.05
District 5	1.2	246 203	96.9	3.1	0.4	0.6	2.6	238 619	57.2	42.8	2.43	2.00
District 6	38.4	260 966	98.0	2.0	0.4	0.5	3.3	255 730	84.3	15.7	2.91	2.15
District 7	13.1	270 558	82.8	17.2	12.5	1.6	6.2	223 955	76.4	23.6	2.67	2.04
District 8	18.2	313 195	77.9	22.1	18.1	1.2	5.4	244 078	80.5	19.5	2.61	1.98
MISSISSIPPI	14.8	1 161 953	90.1	9.9	1.9	1.6	9.2	1 046 434	72.3	27.7	2.67	2.52
District 1	22.8	252 982	90.7	9.3	1.9	1.7	9.5	229 413	76.4	23.6	2.62	2.44
District 2	4.2	195 483	90.7	9.3	1.7	1.3	7.0	177 271	66.1	33.9	2.79	2.81
District 3	19.4	243 081	90.7	9.3	1.2	1.6	8.6	220 494	74.2	25.8	2.64	2.40
District 4	6.0	221 527	88.8	11.2	1.9	1.7	10.4	196 773	72.6	27.4	2.64	2.51
District 5	20.9	248 880	89.4	10.6	2.7	1.7	10.7	222 483	71.1	28.9	2.68	2.44
MISSOURI	11.9	2 442 017	89.9	10.1	2.7	2.1	9.0	2 194 594	70.3	29.7	2.59	2.20
District 1	-6.6	234 077	88.0	12.0	0.3	2.8	10.5	205 933	57.2	42.8	2.60	2.18
District 2	12.6	245 696	96.2	3.8	0.5	0.9	6.4	236 472	77.3	22.7	2.70	1.99
District 3	6.5	258 790	92.7	7.3	0.8	1.4	8.1	239 965	72.1	27.9	2.60	2.06

Table F. Congressional Districts 107th Congress

STATE District	Population, 2000 Land area, 2000[1] (sq km)	Total persons	Rank	Per square kilometer	Population, 1990 Land area, 1990[1] (sq km)	Total persons	Rank	Per square kilometer	Population and population characteristics, 2000 — Race (percent) — One race White	Black or African American	American Indian or Alaska Native	Asian	Native Hawaiian and other Pacific Islander	Some other race
	1	2	3	4	5	6	7	8	9	10	11	12	13	14
MISSOURI—Cont'd														
District 4	36 518.7	659 533	X	18.1	36 523.0	569 146	X	16.0	93.4	3.1	0.5	0.6	0.1	0.8
District 5	968.2	577 050	X	596.0	968.0	569 130	X	588.0	66.8	26.1	0.5	1.4	0.2	2.7
District 6	35 145.8	635 835	X	18.1	35 149.0	569 131	X	16.0	93.9	2.8	0.4	0.8	0.1	0.7
District 7	24 050.4	695 069	X	28.9	24 065.0	568 017	X	24.0	94.4	1.2	1.0	0.6	0.1	1.0
District 8	45 243.3	611 537	X	13.5	45 248.0	568 385	X	13.0	93.0	4.4	0.6	0.4	0.0	0.3
District 9	31 455.0	694 873	X	22.1	31 461.0	568 347	X	18.0	93.2	4.0	0.3	0.9	0.0	0.4
MONTANA	376 979.0	902 195	X	2.4	376 991.0	799 065	X	2.1	90.6	0.3	6.2	0.5	0.1	0.6
At Large	376 979.1	902 195	X	2.4	376 991.0	799 065	X	2.0	90.6	0.3	6.2	0.5	0.1	0.6
NEBRASKA	199 099.0	1 711 263	X	8.6	199 113.0	1 578 417	X	7.9	89.6	4.0	0.9	1.3	0.0	2.8
District 1	34 701.1	581 488	X	16.8	34 705.0	526 297	X	15.0	92.1	1.4	1.2	1.6	0.1	2.2
District 2	1 550.6	594 207	X	383.2	1 551.0	526 567	X	340.0	82.9	9.9	0.6	1.7	0.1	3.0
District 3	162 846.9	535 568	X	3.3	162 857.0	525 521	X	3.0	94.3	0.3	0.8	0.5	0.0	3.1
NEVADA	284 448.0	1 998 257	X	7.0	284 397.0	1 201 675	X	4.2	75.2	6.8	1.3	4.5	0.4	8.0
District 1	597.2	936 104	X	1 567.5	598.0	600 957	X	1 005.0	68.9	9.6	0.8	5.3	0.5	10.5
District 2	283 850.8	1 062 153	X	3.7	283 798.0	600 876	X	2.0	80.7	4.3	1.8	3.8	0.4	5.7
NEW HAMPSHIRE	23 227.0	1 235 786	X	53.2	23 231.0	1 109 252	X	47.7	96.0	0.7	0.2	1.3	0.0	0.6
District 1	6 491.8	625 527	X	96.4	6 493.0	554 360	X	85.0	96.1	0.8	0.2	1.2	0.0	0.5
District 2	16 735.5	610 259	X	36.5	16 738.0	554 892	X	33.0	95.9	0.7	0.3	1.4	0.0	0.7
NEW JERSEY	19 211.0	8 414 350	X	438.0	19 215.0	7 747 750	X	403.2	72.6	13.6	0.2	5.7	0.0	5.4
District 1	831.8	609 847	X	733.2	832.0	594 630	X	715.0	73.3	17.4	0.3	2.7	0.0	4.4
District 2	4 951.9	652 730	X	131.8	4 952.0	594 630	X	120.0	75.3	14.8	0.4	2.5	0.0	4.9
District 3	2 502.5	647 095	X	258.6	2 503.0	594 630	X	238.0	86.3	8.3	0.2	2.7	0.0	1.0
District 4	1 810.4	674 193	X	372.4	1 811.0	594 630	X	328.0	80.4	12.5	0.2	2.1	0.1	3.0
District 5	2 787.3	638 669	X	229.1	2 787.0	594 630	X	213.0	89.8	1.5	0.2	6.2	0.0	1.1
District 6	521.7	632 202	X	1 211.8	523.0	594 630	X	1 138.0	71.9	12.2	0.2	9.4	0.0	3.9
District 7	708.0	642 715	X	907.8	708.0	594 629	X	840.0	74.2	11.7	0.1	8.7	0.0	3.1
District 8	270.6	640 015	X	2 365.2	271.0	594 629	X	2 197.0	63.2	13.9	0.3	5.1	0.0	13.6
District 9	239.6	647 240	X	2 701.3	240.0	594 630	X	2 481.0	70.9	7.2	0.2	11.3	0.0	6.9
District 10	142.2	597 384	X	4 201.0	142.0	594 630	X	4 180.0	25.5	60.9	0.3	3.0	0.1	6.4
District 11	1 651.2	665 932	X	403.3	1 651.0	594 630	X	360.0	87.6	2.7	0.1	6.4	0.0	1.7
District 12	2 645.5	709 867	X	268.3	2 647.0	594 630	X	225.0	84.1	5.3	0.1	7.8	0.0	1.1
District 13	148.0	656 461	X	4 435.5	148.0	594 630	X	4 019.0	55.7	12.9	0.5	6.0	0.1	19.0
NEW MEXICO	314 309.0	1 819 046	X	5.8	314 334.0	1 515 069	X	4.8	66.8	1.9	9.5	1.1	0.1	17.0
District 1	12 201.9	592 911	X	48.6	12 203.0	505 491	X	41.0	71.0	2.6	3.5	1.8	0.1	16.8
District 2	174 408.6	596 790	X	3.4	174 423.0	504 659	X	3.0	69.8	1.9	4.2	0.6	0.1	20.2
District 3	127 698.8	629 345	X	4.9	127 709.0	504 919	X	4.0	59.9	1.2	20.3	0.8	0.1	14.3
NEW YORK	122 283.0	18 976 457	X	155.2	122 310.0	17 990 778	X	147.1	67.9	15.9	0.4	5.5	0.0	7.1
District 1	1 653.1	642 032	X	388.4	1 651.0	580 338	X	352.0	89.1	4.3	0.3	2.4	0.0	2.1
District 2	491.0	612 961	X	1 248.4	491.0	580 337	X	1 182.0	77.5	11.1	0.3	2.4	0.0	6.0
District 3	400.9	588 611	X	1 468.2	401.0	580 337	X	1 448.0	89.8	2.6	0.1	3.9	0.0	2.2
District 4	217.7	611 953	X	2 811.0	218.0	580 338	X	2 660.0	68.1	18.8	0.2	5.0	0.0	5.2
District 5	393.3	615 731	X	1 565.6	393.0	580 337	X	1 476.0	72.2	3.5	0.1	18.7	0.0	3.0
District 6	97.0	664 941	X	6 855.1	97.0	580 337	X	5 971.0	18.0	52.5	0.7	9.9	0.1	10.6
District 7	57.7	684 573	X	11 864.4	67.0	580 337	X	8 680.0	51.0	9.0	0.6	16.8	0.1	16.6
District 8	36.9	618 987	X	16 774.7	40.0	580 337	X	14 350.0	75.2	6.5	0.2	10.4	0.1	4.5
District 9	94.8	652 370	X	6 881.5	97.0	580 338	X	5 970.0	70.5	4.5	0.3	13.4	0.1	7.6
District 10	43.0	621 305	X	14 449.0	44.0	580 335	X	13 266.0	20.7	63.9	0.4	2.4	0.1	8.6
District 11	27.8	586 819	X	21 108.6	26.0	580 337	X	22 392.0	19.3	68.6	0.3	3.4	0.0	4.6
District 12	41.4	620 677	X	14 992.2	36.0	580 340	X	16 277.0	36.8	12.6	0.8	16.4	0.1	27.3
District 13	168.6	670 006	X	3 973.9	169.0	580 337	X	3 440.0	76.3	6.7	0.2	9.6	0.0	3.9
District 14	32.1	608 017	X	18 941.3	35.0	580 337	X	16 756.0	77.4	4.6	0.2	9.3	0.1	4.7
District 15	24.9	607 324	X	24 390.5	28.0	580 337	X	20 568.0	24.4	36.7	0.9	2.7	0.1	29.0
District 16	40.0	647 437	X	16 185.9	40.0	580 338	X	14 505.0	21.2	36.0	1.1	1.9	0.1	33.1
District 17	55.7	627 566	X	11 266.9	56.0	580 337	X	10 393.0	28.6	43.6	0.7	3.5	0.1	18.1
District 18	243.3	620 213	X	2 549.2	243.0	580 337	X	2 384.0	70.6	8.5	0.2	11.1	0.0	6.0
District 19	2 796.0	626 776	X	224.2	2 797.0	580 338	X	208.0	84.3	7.5	0.2	2.8	0.0	3.2
District 20	3 336.0	635 820	X	190.6	3 336.0	580 338	X	174.0	81.0	8.9	0.3	4.3	0.1	3.2
District 21	2 814.8	573 294	X	203.7	2 816.0	580 337	X	206.0	85.7	8.7	0.2	2.4	0.0	1.2
District 22	16 858.9	619 548	X	36.7	16 861.0	580 337	X	34.0	94.7	2.5	0.2	0.8	0.0	0.7
District 23	15 503.0	563 385	X	36.3	15 504.0	580 337	X	37.0	94.1	3.1	0.3	0.8	0.0	0.7
District 24	32 092.7	582 371	X	18.1	32 098.0	580 338	X	18.0	93.3	3.0	1.0	0.6	0.0	1.0

[1] Dry land or land partially or temporarily covered by water.

Table F. Congressional Districts 107th Congress

	Population and population characteristics, 2000 (cont'd)								Population and population characteristics, 1990				
	Race (percent) (cont'd)								Race (percent)				
	Race alone or in combination												
STATE District	Two or more races	White	Black	American Indian or Alaska Native	Asian	Native Hawaiian and other Pacific Islander	Some other race	Hispanic[1]	White	Black or African American	American Indian or Alaska Native	Asian and Pacific Islander	Hispanic[1]
	15	16	17	18	19	20	21	22	23	24	25	26	27
MISSOURI—Cont'd													
District 4	1.4	94.8	3.5	1.2	0.8	0.1	1.1	2.0	95.4	3.2	0.5	0.6	1.1
District 5	2.4	68.6	27.1	1.3	1.7	0.3	3.4	5.8	73.2	23.7	0.5	1.0	3.2
District 6	1.3	95.1	3.2	1.0	1.0	0.1	1.1	2.3	96.5	2.1	0.4	0.5	1.5
District 7	1.7	96.1	1.4	2.0	0.8	0.1	1.3	2.4	97.3	0.9	1.0	0.5	0.8
District 8	1.2	94.2	4.6	1.3	0.6	0.1	0.5	1.0	94.8	4.4	0.3	0.4	0.5
District 9	1.2	94.2	4.4	0.8	1.1	0.1	0.6	1.2	95.0	3.7	0.3	0.8	0.7
MONTANA	1.7	92.2	0.5	7.4	0.8	0.1	0.9	2.0	92.7	0.3	6.0	0.5	1.5
At Large	1.7	92.2	0.5	7.4	0.8	0.1	0.9	2.0	92.7	0.3	6.0	0.5	1.5
NEBRASKA	1.4	90.8	4.4	1.3	1.6	0.1	3.3	5.5	93.8	3.6	0.8	0.8	2.3
District 1	1.3	93.3	1.8	1.7	1.8	0.1	2.7	4.2	96.4	1.1	1.1	0.9	1.4
District 2	1.8	84.4	10.6	1.1	2.2	0.1	3.6	6.1	87.5	9.7	0.6	1.2	2.8
District 3	1.0	95.2	0.4	1.2	0.6	0.1	3.5	6.2	97.6	0.2	0.7	0.3	2.9
NEVADA	3.8	78.4	7.5	2.1	5.6	0.8	9.7	19.7	84.3	6.6	1.6	3.2	10.4
District 1	4.4	72.5	10.5	1.5	6.6	0.9	12.7	26.6	79.5	10.5	0.8	3.8	12.2
District 2	3.3	83.5	4.9	2.6	4.8	0.7	7.0	13.6	89.0	2.7	2.4	2.6	8.5
NEW HAMPSHIRE	1.1	97.0	1.0	0.6	1.6	0.1	0.9	1.7	98.0	0.6	0.2	0.8	1.0
District 1	1.1	97.1	1.1	0.6	1.5	0.1	0.8	1.6	98.0	0.7	0.2	0.8	1.0
District 2	1.1	96.9	0.9	0.7	1.6	0.1	1.0	1.7	98.1	0.6	0.2	0.9	1.0
NEW JERSEY	2.5	74.4	14.4	0.6	6.2	0.1	6.9	13.3	79.3	13.4	0.2	3.5	9.6
District 1	1.9	74.7	18.2	0.6	3.1	0.1	5.2	8.5	78.4	15.8	0.2	1.7	6.3
District 2	2.1	76.8	15.7	0.9	2.8	0.1	5.9	10.3	80.7	14.1	0.4	1.2	6.6
District 3	1.5	87.5	9.0	0.5	3.1	0.1	1.5	3.6	88.9	8.0	0.2	2.1	2.6
District 4	1.8	81.7	13.2	0.5	2.5	0.1	3.9	7.8	83.7	12.5	0.2	1.5	5.2
District 5	1.3	90.8	1.8	0.4	6.6	0.1	1.6	4.4	93.5	1.3	0.2	4.5	2.8
District 6	2.4	73.6	13.0	0.6	10.0	0.1	5.2	10.6	81.8	11.2	0.2	4.8	6.1
District 7	2.1	75.7	12.3	0.4	9.3	0.1	4.3	9.3	83.6	10.2	0.1	4.6	5.0
District 8	3.8	66.0	14.9	0.6	5.7	0.2	16.5	25.8	74.7	13.0	0.2	3.6	17.8
District 9	3.5	73.7	7.9	0.6	12.0	0.1	9.4	18.9	83.7	6.5	0.1	6.6	11.4
District 10	4.0	27.3	63.2	0.8	3.4	0.2	9.3	15.8	32.6	60.2	0.3	2.4	12.3
District 11	1.5	88.8	3.0	0.3	6.9	0.1	2.4	6.8	92.3	2.7	0.1	3.9	4.1
District 12	1.5	85.3	5.8	0.4	8.3	0.1	1.7	4.1	89.6	5.2	0.1	4.4	2.7
District 13	5.8	60.3	14.2	0.9	6.7	0.2	23.8	47.2	67.4	13.7	0.3	4.6	41.5
NEW MEXICO	3.6	69.9	2.3	10.5	1.5	0.2	19.4	42.1	75.6	2.0	8.9	0.9	38.2
District 1	4.2	74.6	3.2	4.5	2.4	0.2	19.5	42.8	77.6	2.7	2.7	1.5	38.1
District 2	3.4	72.8	2.2	5.0	0.9	0.1	22.5	48.0	83.9	2.1	3.7	0.7	42.1
District 3	3.4	62.8	1.6	21.4	1.1	0.2	16.4	35.7	65.4	1.2	20.1	0.6	34.6
NEW YORK	3.1	70.0	17.0	0.9	6.2	0.2	9.1	15.1	74.4	15.9	0.3	3.9	12.3
District 1	1.7	90.5	4.9	0.7	2.8	0.1	2.9	7.6	93.0	4.1	0.3	1.7	4.7
District 2	2.7	79.3	12.1	0.7	2.9	0.1	7.7	15.4	85.5	9.8	0.2	1.7	9.7
District 3	1.5	90.9	2.9	0.3	4.3	0.1	3.0	6.9	94.4	2.0	0.1	2.6	4.4
District 4	2.7	69.8	19.8	0.6	5.6	0.1	7.0	13.3	78.3	16.2	0.2	3.2	7.5
District 5	2.5	74.1	3.9	0.4	19.7	0.1	4.5	9.2	84.0	3.5	0.1	10.6	7.3
District 6	8.1	20.2	56.5	2.1	12.8	0.4	16.6	18.1	29.3	56.2	0.6	6.3	16.9
District 7	6.0	55.4	10.1	1.1	18.2	0.2	21.3	39.1	70.0	10.1	0.3	11.5	21.3
District 8	3.2	77.7	7.2	0.6	11.3	0.1	6.4	11.5	80.4	8.6	0.2	6.3	12.7
District 9	3.6	73.0	5.2	0.6	14.6	0.1	10.2	17.0	87.6	3.3	0.1	6.2	8.5
District 10	4.0	22.6	66.2	0.9	2.9	0.3	11.4	17.1	26.8	60.7	0.4	2.3	19.7
District 11	3.9	20.6	71.1	0.8	4.2	0.3	7.2	10.8	18.7	74.0	0.4	2.8	11.5
District 12	6.0	40.9	14.2	1.4	17.4	0.3	32.0	48.6	33.8	13.7	0.5	19.7	57.9
District 13	3.2	78.8	7.4	0.5	10.4	0.1	6.1	11.1	86.7	5.6	0.2	5.5	7.5
District 14	3.7	80.3	5.3	0.5	10.4	0.1	7.3	12.2	85.9	4.6	0.2	5.6	10.9
District 15	6.1	28.1	39.4	1.7	3.3	0.3	33.7	50.5	27.6	46.9	0.7	2.4	46.4
District 16	6.6	24.8	39.1	1.9	2.5	0.3	38.3	62.9	20.0	42.2	0.6	2.1	60.2
District 17	5.5	31.6	46.2	1.3	4.2	0.3	22.1	35.9	40.3	41.9	0.4	3.7	29.1
District 18	3.6	73.3	9.3	0.5	12.0	0.2	8.5	15.3	81.1	7.5	0.1	8.2	10.4
District 19	2.0	85.9	8.2	0.6	3.2	0.1	4.1	9.0	89.0	7.3	0.2	2.3	5.2
District 20	2.3	82.5	9.9	0.7	4.8	0.1	4.4	9.6	86.6	8.2	0.2	3.4	6.1
District 21	1.8	87.1	9.6	0.6	2.7	0.1	1.8	3.4	91.3	6.3	0.2	1.5	2.1
District 22	1.1	95.7	2.8	0.6	1.0	0.1	1.0	2.1	96.6	2.2	0.2	0.7	1.5
District 23	1.2	95.1	3.4	0.6	0.9	0.1	1.1	2.1	95.8	2.9	0.2	0.6	1.5
District 24	1.0	94.2	3.3	1.4	0.8	0.1	1.3	2.3	95.4	2.6	0.8	0.6	1.6

[1] Hispanic persons may be of any race.

Table F. Congressional Districts 107th Congress

STATE District	Population and population characteristics, 2000										
	Age (percent)										
	Under 5 years	5 to 17 years	18 to 24 years	25 to 34 years	35 to 44 years	45 to 54 years	55 to 64 years	65 to 74 years	75 years and over	Median age (years)	Percent Female
	28	29	30	31	32	33	34	35	36	37	38
MISSOURI—Cont'd											
District 4	6.6	19.1	9.5	12.6	15.5	12.9	9.8	7.6	6.5	36.5	50.1
District 5	7.0	18.4	9.3	14.9	16.1	12.9	8.3	6.8	6.3	35.3	52.0
District 6	6.5	18.9	9.3	13.2	16.2	13.6	9.1	6.7	6.6	36.4	50.8
District 7	6.6	17.9	10.7	12.8	14.8	13.1	9.7	7.6	6.8	36.4	51.2
District 8	6.3	18.9	9.3	12.0	14.7	13.0	10.2	8.2	7.4	37.5	51.2
District 9	6.9	19.5	11.1	13.3	16.4	12.8	8.4	6.1	5.6	34.5	50.8
MONTANA	6.1	19.4	9.5	11.4	15.7	15.0	9.4	6.9	6.5	37.5	50.2
At Large	6.1	19.4	9.5	11.4	15.7	15.0	9.4	6.9	6.5	37.5	50.2
NEBRASKA	6.8	19.5	10.2	13.0	15.4	13.2	8.3	6.8	6.8	35.3	50.7
District 1	6.5	18.7	11.9	12.8	15.2	13.0	8.1	6.7	7.0	35.0	50.4
District 2	7.6	19.8	10.1	15.3	16.3	13.2	7.6	5.4	4.7	33.1	50.9
District 3	6.4	19.9	8.4	10.8	14.7	13.4	9.2	8.3	8.9	38.4	50.8
NEVADA	7.3	18.3	9.0	15.3	16.1	13.5	9.5	6.6	4.4	35.0	49.1
District 1	7.6	18.2	9.8	16.2	15.7	12.8	9.1	6.3	4.2	33.9	48.8
District 2	7.0	18.4	8.3	14.6	16.4	14.0	9.9	6.9	4.5	36.0	49.2
NEW HAMPSHIRE	6.1	18.9	8.4	13.0	17.9	14.9	8.9	6.3	5.6	37.1	50.8
District 1	6.2	18.8	8.4	13.4	18.2	14.6	8.6	6.2	5.5	36.8	51.0
District 2	6.0	19.1	8.3	12.4	17.6	15.1	9.1	6.5	5.8	37.5	50.7
NEW JERSEY	6.7	18.1	8.0	14.1	17.1	13.8	9.0	6.8	6.4	36.7	51.5
District 1	6.7	19.9	8.4	14.3	17.0	13.5	8.2	6.3	5.7	35.4	51.7
District 2	6.3	18.8	8.3	13.0	16.7	13.6	9.2	7.4	6.8	37.2	51.1
District 3	5.9	18.2	6.5	11.8	16.6	14.3	10.0	8.7	8.0	39.7	51.4
District 4	7.1	18.3	7.3	13.0	16.6	13.0	8.6	7.9	8.3	37.5	51.8
District 5	6.8	19.3	5.8	11.2	18.2	15.4	9.8	7.0	6.4	38.9	51.4
District 6	6.6	16.7	10.2	15.8	17.0	13.4	8.5	6.3	5.6	35.4	51.2
District 7	6.9	17.6	6.6	14.0	18.0	14.3	8.9	6.9	6.7	37.7	51.4
District 8	7.1	17.9	8.8	14.8	16.2	13.2	8.5	6.6	6.8	35.8	52.0
District 9	5.9	15.3	7.9	16.1	16.8	13.8	9.4	7.5	7.4	37.7	51.8
District 10	7.5	19.8	10.4	15.7	15.6	12.1	8.3	5.7	5.0	32.9	53.1
District 11	7.1	18.0	6.1	13.2	18.5	15.3	9.9	6.3	5.5	38.0	51.1
District 12	6.5	18.9	7.5	11.8	18.3	15.5	9.1	6.4	5.8	38.0	51.2
District 13	6.7	16.8	11.1	19.4	15.9	11.5	7.8	5.7	5.0	32.8	50.3
NEW MEXICO	7.2	20.8	9.8	12.9	15.5	13.5	8.7	6.5	5.2	34.6	50.8
District 1	6.9	18.8	10.0	13.9	16.2	14.2	8.5	6.1	5.4	35.2	51.0
District 2	7.3	21.5	10.2	11.9	14.5	12.5	9.0	7.4	5.6	34.3	50.6
District 3	7.3	21.9	9.1	12.9	15.8	13.8	8.7	5.9	4.7	34.1	50.9
NEW YORK	6.5	18.2	9.3	14.5	16.2	13.5	8.9	6.7	6.2	35.9	51.8
District 1	6.8	18.8	8.1	13.3	17.4	14.3	9.2	6.3	5.8	36.7	50.9
District 2	7.2	19.5	7.7	14.3	17.9	13.2	9.1	6.3	4.7	35.7	51.2
District 3	6.5	17.8	6.4	11.8	17.5	15.0	9.7	8.4	6.9	39.4	51.6
District 4	6.6	18.7	8.4	12.8	16.2	14.0	9.0	7.4	7.0	37.2	52.1
District 5	6.1	16.1	6.8	13.1	16.7	14.9	10.2	8.2	7.8	39.7	52.0
District 6	7.2	20.1	10.0	15.0	16.2	12.6	8.7	5.7	4.5	33.6	53.1
District 7	6.4	15.5	10.2	18.6	16.3	12.2	8.4	6.4	6.0	34.6	50.8
District 8	5.3	11.9	9.5	20.5	16.5	13.8	8.8	6.9	6.7	36.3	50.7
District 9	6.2	15.8	8.6	15.3	15.4	13.7	9.1	7.9	8.0	37.6	51.9
District 10	7.9	21.6	10.5	15.5	15.0	11.8	8.0	5.4	4.2	31.4	54.5
District 11	7.7	20.6	10.6	15.7	15.5	12.7	8.2	5.2	3.8	32.0	54.9
District 12	7.3	18.9	11.6	18.4	15.4	11.7	7.5	5.3	3.9	31.4	51.1
District 13	6.4	17.2	8.5	15.2	16.3	13.9	9.2	6.9	6.4	36.6	51.8
District 14	4.3	8.1	9.0	24.3	16.8	13.8	10.2	7.0	6.6	37.1	53.2
District 15	6.5	18.3	12.1	17.3	15.6	11.7	7.9	5.6	4.9	32.5	52.2
District 16	9.4	24.9	11.2	15.4	14.7	10.4	7.1	4.2	2.8	28.0	53.5
District 17	7.8	20.2	10.2	15.4	15.1	11.6	8.1	5.8	5.8	32.7	54.4
District 18	6.3	15.9	7.8	14.3	16.3	13.9	9.7	7.9	8.0	38.5	52.5
District 19	6.8	18.8	7.9	12.5	18.3	14.8	9.1	6.3	5.4	37.1	50.4
District 20	7.3	20.4	7.4	12.3	16.7	14.6	9.5	6.4	5.3	36.5	50.8
District 21	5.9	17.3	10.4	13.1	15.5	14.0	8.5	7.3	8.0	37.2	52.0
District 22	5.8	18.7	7.7	12.5	17.0	15.0	9.8	7.2	6.3	38.1	50.0
District 23	5.6	18.6	9.6	11.6	15.4	13.8	9.7	7.7	8.1	38.2	50.8
District 24	5.9	19.0	11.0	13.2	16.3	13.2	8.7	6.7	5.9	35.5	49.1

Table F. Congressional Districts 107th Congress

STATE District	Under 5 years	5 to 17 years	18 to 24 years	25 to 34 years	35 to 44 years	45 to 54 years	55 to 64 years	65 to 74 years	75 years and over	Percent Female	2000	1990	1980	1990–2000	1980–1990
	39	40	41	42	43	44	45	46	47	48	49	50	51	52	53
MISSOURI—Cont'd															
District 4	7.1	19.0	10.4	15.8	13.7	10.2	9.2	8.0	6.6	50.3	659 533	569 146	NA	15.9	NA
District 5	7.6	17.2	9.8	18.5	14.4	9.9	9.0	7.6	6.1	52.6	577 050	569 130	NA	1.4	NA
District 6	7.0	19.0	9.6	16.0	14.7	10.6	8.7	7.7	6.6	51.5	635 835	569 131	NA	11.7	NA
District 7	6.6	17.9	11.2	15.1	13.8	10.4	9.4	8.6	7.0	51.8	695 069	568 017	NA	22.4	NA
District 8	6.8	19.6	9.7	14.4	13.2	10.4	9.7	8.9	7.3	51.7	611 537	568 385	NA	7.6	NA
District 9	7.5	19.1	12.1	16.7	14.2	9.8	7.9	6.8	5.9	51.2	694 873	568 347	NA	22.3	NA
MONTANA	7.4	20.4	8.8	15.4	15.9	10.3	8.6	7.6	5.7	50.5	902 195	799 065	786 690	12.9	1.6
At Large	7.4	20.4	8.8	15.4	15.9	10.3	8.6	7.6	5.7	50.5	902 195	799 065	NA	12.9	NA
NEBRASKA	7.6	19.6	9.9	16.3	14.5	9.5	8.6	7.5	6.7	51.3	1 711 263	1 578 417	1 569 825	8.4	0.5
District 1	7.2	18.7	11.4	16.0	14.2	9.3	8.5	7.6	7.2	51.1	581 488	526 297	NA	10.5	NA
District 2	8.3	19.7	10.4	18.8	15.6	9.5	7.6	5.8	4.3	51.4	594 207	526 567	NA	12.8	NA
District 3	7.2	20.4	7.8	14.1	13.7	9.6	9.6	9.0	8.6	51.3	535 568	525 521	NA	1.9	NA
NEVADA	7.7	17.0	9.9	18.5	16.0	11.3	9.0	7.1	3.5	49.1	1 998 257	1 201 675	800 508	66.3	50.1
District 1	7.5	16.6	10.3	18.3	15.4	11.5	9.4	7.5	3.5	49.4	936 104	600 957	NA	55.8	NA
District 2	7.8	17.5	9.5	18.6	16.6	11.1	8.6	6.8	3.4	48.7	1 062 153	600 876	NA	76.8	NA
NEW HAMPSHIRE	7.6	17.5	10.6	18.5	16.5	10.1	8.0	6.4	4.8	51.0	1 235 786	1 109 252	920 610	11.4	20.5
District 1	7.7	17.2	10.8	19.3	16.3	9.8	7.7	6.4	4.7	51.1	625 527	554 360	NA	12.8	NA
District 2	7.5	17.8	10.4	17.6	16.6	10.4	8.2	6.5	5.0	50.9	610 259	554 892	NA	10.0	NA
NEW JERSEY	6.9	16.4	10.1	17.6	15.5	10.9	9.3	7.9	5.5	51.7	8 414 350	7 747 750	7 365 011	8.6	5.0
District 1	8.0	18.7	10.0	18.6	15.2	9.7	8.2	7.2	4.5	51.8	609 847	594 630	NA	2.6	NA
District 2	7.1	17.2	10.1	17.1	14.5	10.0	9.3	8.6	6.2	51.7	652 730	594 630	NA	9.8	NA
District 3	6.6	17.4	9.3	15.5	15.4	11.0	9.7	9.3	5.8	51.4	647 095	594 630	NA	8.8	NA
District 4	7.4	16.6	9.0	17.2	15.0	9.6	8.5	9.2	7.5	52.0	674 193	594 630	NA	13.4	NA
District 5	6.8	17.1	8.8	15.4	16.6	12.7	10.1	7.3	5.2	51.4	638 669	594 630	NA	7.4	NA
District 6	6.8	14.9	12.4	19.3	15.1	10.3	9.0	7.2	4.9	51.5	632 202	594 630	NA	6.3	NA
District 7	6.6	14.8	8.9	17.9	16.0	11.5	10.5	8.5	5.3	51.5	642 715	594 629	NA	8.1	NA
District 8	6.8	15.6	10.6	17.3	14.9	10.5	9.6	8.4	6.3	52.4	640 015	594 629	NA	7.6	NA
District 9	5.9	13.2	9.4	18.7	15.2	10.9	10.6	9.5	6.6	52.1	647 240	594 630	NA	8.8	NA
District 10	7.4	17.9	11.6	18.6	14.5	10.1	8.3	6.8	4.8	53.0	597 384	594 630	NA	0.5	NA
District 11	6.6	16.3	9.5	16.9	17.1	13.3	9.6	6.4	4.4	51.0	665 932	594 630	NA	12.0	NA
District 12	6.6	16.7	10.0	16.2	17.6	12.4	8.9	7.0	4.5	50.9	709 867	594 630	NA	19.4	NA
District 13	7.0	16.6	11.4	20.0	14.1	9.9	8.8	7.2	4.9	51.2	656 461	594 630	NA	10.4	NA
NEW MEXICO	8.3	21.2	10.0	16.9	15.0	9.7	8.0	6.4	4.3	50.8	1 819 046	1 515 069	1 303 302	20.1	16.2
District 1	7.8	18.7	10.3	18.6	16.2	10.1	7.9	6.4	4.1	51.1	592 911	505 491	NA	17.3	NA
District 2	8.3	22.2	10.5	15.8	13.5	9.2	8.6	7.0	4.8	50.4	596 790	504 659	NA	18.3	NA
District 3	8.8	22.7	9.3	16.4	15.4	9.9	7.6	5.9	4.0	50.9	629 345	504 919	NA	24.6	NA
NEW YORK	7.0	16.7	10.9	17.4	15.1	10.6	9.1	7.5	5.6	52.1	18 976 457	17 990 778	17 558 165	5.5	2.5
District 1	7.1	18.3	10.7	16.7	16.3	11.3	7.9	6.6	5.2	51.1	642 032	580 338	NA	10.6	NA
District 2	7.2	17.4	11.1	18.3	14.9	11.9	9.5	5.9	3.8	51.2	612 961	580 337	NA	5.6	NA
District 3	6.1	15.4	9.7	16.1	15.6	11.7	12.0	8.8	4.7	51.3	588 611	580 337	NA	1.4	NA
District 4	6.3	16.0	10.5	15.9	14.9	11.1	10.7	9.1	5.5	52.1	611 953	580 338	NA	5.4	NA
District 5	5.7	14.6	9.0	16.1	15.7	12.1	11.4	9.2	6.2	52.0	615 731	580 337	NA	6.1	NA
District 6	7.3	18.3	11.4	17.6	14.3	11.1	8.9	6.8	4.4	53.2	664 941	580 337	NA	14.6	NA
District 7	5.7	12.9	9.8	19.0	14.7	10.7	10.1	9.1	8.0	52.7	684 573	580 337	NA	18.0	NA
District 8	5.2	11.0	9.6	21.0	18.3	10.8	8.9	8.0	7.2	51.2	618 987	580 337	NA	6.7	NA
District 9	5.8	13.2	8.7	16.9	14.7	10.1	10.8	10.6	9.1	52.8	652 370	580 338	NA	12.4	NA
District 10	8.3	20.2	11.6	17.9	14.4	10.1	7.7	5.8	3.9	54.0	621 305	580 335	NA	7.1	NA
District 11	8.3	20.2	11.1	18.6	16.1	10.2	7.1	5.0	3.5	54.7	586 819	580 337	NA	1.1	NA
District 12	8.2	19.7	12.4	19.1	14.7	9.8	7.5	5.1	3.3	51.2	620 677	580 340	NA	7.0	NA
District 13	6.8	15.8	10.2	17.7	15.4	10.9	9.3	7.9	6.1	52.2	670 006	580 337	NA	15.5	NA
District 14	3.8	7.3	9.2	23.1	18.3	13.0	10.4	8.4	7.2	53.5	608 017	580 337	NA	4.8	NA
District 15	7.5	17.1	12.1	19.1	14.5	10.0	8.0	6.5	5.2	52.9	607 324	580 337	NA	4.7	NA
District 16	10.5	23.1	12.4	17.6	13.2	9.5	6.6	4.3	2.7	54.3	647 437	580 338	NA	11.6	NA
District 17	7.5	16.9	11.0	17.6	14.0	10.1	8.6	7.3	7.0	54.6	627 566	580 337	NA	8.1	NA
District 18	5.8	13.6	9.4	16.8	15.1	11.4	10.8	9.3	7.7	52.8	620 213	580 337	NA	6.9	NA
District 19	7.1	16.4	10.6	17.5	16.8	11.8	8.8	6.2	4.9	50.1	626 776	580 337	NA	8.0	NA
District 20	7.5	18.5	9.5	16.1	16.1	12.0	9.2	6.3	4.8	51.0	635 820	580 338	NA	9.6	NA
District 21	6.7	15.5	12.6	16.7	14.7	9.5	9.0	8.5	6.9	52.3	573 294	580 337	NA	-1.2	NA
District 22	7.1	18.0	9.8	16.6	16.0	10.9	8.8	7.3	5.5	50.3	619 548	580 337	NA	6.8	NA
District 23	6.9	17.9	12.0	15.3	14.0	10.1	8.9	8.5	6.4	51.0	563 385	580 337	NA	-2.9	NA
District 24	7.5	19.0	13.3	16.9	14.0	9.4	8.1	6.8	5.1	49.7	582 371	580 338	NA	0.4	NA

Table F. Congressional Districts 107th Congress

STATE District	Total population	Total in house- holds	House- holder	Spouse	Child Total	Own child under 18 years	Other relatives Total	Under 18 years	Nonrelatives Total	Unmar- ried partner	Total in group quarters	Correc- tional institu- tions	Nurs- ing homes	Other institu- tions	Col- lege dormi- tories	Mili- tary quar- ters	Other
	54	55	56	57	58	59	60	61	62	63	64	65	66	67	68	69	70
MISSOURI—Cont'd																	
District 4	659 533	96.1	38.2	22.3	28.6	23.6	3.0	1.3	4.0	1.9	3.9	1.1	0.9	0.2	0.6	0.8	0.3
District 5	677 050	08.0	41.3	16.9	28.5	22.0	5.7	2.0	5.7	2.4	2.0	0.3	0.7	0.2	0.2	0.0	0.6
District 6	635 835	96.7	38.8	21.9	29.0	23.5	3.0	1.3	4.0	1.9	3.3	1.3	0.9	0.1	0.7	0.0	0.3
District 7	695 069	96.9	39.7	22.0	27.4	22.3	3.2	1.4	4.7	1.9	3.1	0.3	0.8	0.1	1.5	0.0	0.4
District 8	611 537	96.9	39.4	21.8	28.4	22.7	3.5	1.7	3.8	1.9	3.1	0.7	1.2	0.1	0.6	0.0	0.4
District 9	694 873	95.9	37.2	21.3	29.8	24.5	2.8	1.2	4.8	1.9	4.1	1.2	0.8	0.1	1.7	0.0	0.3
MONTANA	902 195	97.3	39.8	21.3	28.2	23.5	2.9	1.3	5.1	2.0	2.7	0.5	0.7	0.2	0.8	0.0	0.6
At Large	902 195	97.3	39.8	21.3	28.2	23.5	2.9	1.3	5.1	2.0	2.7	0.5	0.7	0.2	0.8	0.0	0.6
NEBRASKA	1 711 263	97.0	38.9	21.1	29.6	24.6	2.8	1.1	4.7	1.7	3.0	0.4	0.9	0.2	1.1	0.0	0.3
District 1	581 488	96.0	38.8	21.1	28.5	23.8	2.5	0.9	5.1	1.8	4.0	0.6	0.9	0.2	2.0	0.0	0.3
District 2	594 207	97.8	38.5	19.5	31.1	25.2	3.6	1.4	5.1	1.9	2.2	0.3	0.6	0.3	0.5	0.1	0.4
District 3	535 568	97.3	39.6	22.9	29.0	24.7	2.2	0.9	3.6	1.5	2.7	0.2	1.3	0.1	0.7	0.0	0.3
NEVADA	1 998 257	98.3	37.6	18.7	28.0	22.6	6.7	2.2	7.4	2.7	1.7	0.8	0.2	0.1	0.1	0.1	0.4
District 1	936 104	98.6	37.0	16.8	28.2	22.2	8.3	2.8	8.3	2.8	1.4	0.5	0.2	0.1	0.1	0.0	0.5
District 2	1 062 153	98.1	38.1	20.3	27.7	22.9	5.3	1.8	6.6	2.6	1.9	1.0	0.3	0.1	0.1	0.1	0.3
NEW HAMPSHIRE	1 235 786	97.1	38.4	21.2	28.8	23.4	3.0	1.0	5.6	2.6	2.9	0.3	0.8	0.1	1.4	0.0	0.3
District 1	625 527	97.5	38.6	21.1	28.9	23.4	3.1	1.0	5.9	2.7	2.5	0.2	0.7	0.0	1.2	0.0	0.3
District 2	610 259	96.7	38.2	21.4	28.8	23.4	2.9	1.0	5.4	2.6	3.3	0.3	0.8	0.1	1.6	0.0	0.3
NEW JERSEY	8 414 350	97.7	36.4	19.5	30.8	22.3	6.5	2.0	4.6	1.8	2.3	0.6	0.6	0.1	0.5	0.0	0.4
District 1	609 847	98.2	36.6	18.2	32.6	23.6	6.2	2.5	4.6	2.3	1.8	0.6	0.6	0.2	0.1	0.0	0.4
District 2	652 730	96.0	36.9	18.4	29.5	22.0	6.1	2.5	5.1	2.4	4.0	1.6	0.7	0.1	0.7	0.1	0.8
District 3	647 095	97.8	37.6	22.2	30.1	22.0	4.4	1.6	3.5	1.7	2.2	0.9	0.7	0.1	0.0	0.2	0.3
District 4	674 193	97.7	37.2	20.1	30.7	23.1	5.4	1.9	4.3	1.8	2.3	0.8	0.9	0.1	0.1	0.0	0.3
District 5	638 669	98.3	35.4	23.3	32.8	24.8	4.0	1.0	2.8	1.2	1.7	0.0	0.9	0.1	0.3	0.0	0.3
District 6	632 202	97.3	36.7	18.9	29.3	20.8	6.5	2.0	5.8	1.9	2.7	0.1	0.6	0.0	1.5	0.0	0.5
District 7	642 715	98.4	35.8	21.4	31.0	22.6	6.0	1.6	4.0	1.4	1.6	0.4	0.6	0.1	0.2	0.0	0.4
District 8	640 015	98.0	34.9	17.8	31.7	22.0	8.8	2.7	4.9	1.8	2.0	0.3	0.6	0.1	0.4	0.0	0.6
District 9	647 240	99.0	38.8	19.4	28.8	19.4	7.4	1.6	4.7	1.7	1.0	0.2	0.3	0.1	0.1	0.0	0.4
District 10	597 384	97.3	35.3	12.1	32.1	21.6	12.0	4.9	5.9	2.4	2.7	0.8	0.5	0.2	0.7	0.0	0.5
District 11	665 932	98.0	36.0	22.9	31.2	23.8	4.2	1.0	3.6	1.3	2.0	0.3	0.7	0.2	0.5	0.0	0.3
District 12	709 867	96.0	35.7	22.9	30.8	24.3	3.6	0.9	3.0	1.2	4.0	0.8	0.5	0.3	1.9	0.2	0.3
District 13	656 461	98.0	36.4	14.5	29.6	20.2	9.9	2.8	7.5	2.4	2.0	0.6	0.6	0.0	0.4	0.0	0.4
NEW MEXICO	1 819 046	98.0	37.3	18.8	31.2	24.5	5.8	2.8	4.9	2.4	2.0	0.6	0.4	0.1	0.4	0.1	0.4
District 1	592 911	98.1	39.3	18.4	28.9	22.7	5.5	2.3	6.0	2.7	1.9	0.4	0.3	0.1	0.4	0.1	0.6
District 2	596 790	97.5	36.2	19.5	31.8	25.2	5.7	3.0	4.2	2.0	2.5	1.1	0.5	0.0	0.6	0.1	0.2
District 3	629 345	98.4	36.3	18.5	32.6	25.5	6.3	3.2	4.7	2.5	1.6	0.3	0.4	0.1	0.3	0.1	0.4
NEW YORK	18 976 457	96.9	37.2	17.3	30.2	21.9	6.7	2.2	5.5	2.0	3.1	0.6	0.7	0.2	0.9	0.0	0.7
District 1	642 032	97.2	34.2	20.8	32.1	23.4	5.3	1.6	4.8	1.7	2.8	0.2	0.6	0.1	1.1	0.0	0.7
District 2	612 961	98.6	31.5	19.4	33.4	23.1	8.6	2.8	5.7	1.5	1.4	0.0	0.5	0.1	0.2	0.0	0.6
District 3	588 611	98.9	34.5	22.6	32.6	22.5	5.9	1.5	3.4	1.0	1.1	0.0	0.4	0.0	0.1	0.0	0.5
District 4	611 953	98.3	32.2	19.4	33.1	22.0	8.9	2.7	4.7	1.0	1.7	0.2	0.4	0.0	0.7	0.0	0.4
District 5	615 731	98.4	36.5	21.8	30.0	20.7	6.4	1.3	3.7	1.1	1.6	0.0	0.8	0.1	0.3	0.0	0.4
District 6	664 941	98.4	30.6	14.1	34.2	21.5	14.2	4.8	5.3	1.5	1.6	0.0	0.6	0.2	0.0	0.0	0.8
District 7	684 573	99.0	35.8	15.5	28.2	18.8	11.5	2.5	7.9	1.7	1.0	0.0	0.5	0.2	0.1	0.0	0.2
District 8	618 987	96.0	47.3	15.0	21.6	15.8	4.7	1.2	7.3	2.7	4.0	0.6	0.4	0.1	1.7	0.0	1.2
District 9	652 370	98.8	38.2	18.7	29.4	20.0	8.0	1.7	4.5	1.4	1.2	0.1	0.5	0.0	0.0	0.0	0.6
District 10	621 305	97.5	35.4	10.9	34.6	23.9	10.9	4.6	5.7	2.1	2.5	0.1	0.4	0.4	0.3	0.0	1.3
District 11	586 819	98.6	35.4	11.2	34.2	23.1	11.7	4.4	6.1	2.1	1.4	0.0	0.4	0.1	0.1	0.0	0.8
District 12	620 677	98.6	34.1	12.7	32.4	21.8	11.5	3.8	7.9	2.1	1.4	0.0	0.2	0.1	0.1	0.0	1.0
District 13	670 006	98.4	36.8	19.2	31.9	21.7	6.9	1.6	3.5	1.4	1.6	0.1	0.6	0.1	0.2	0.0	0.5
District 14	608 017	97.5	53.9	15.5	15.6	11.3	3.9	0.7	8.8	2.6	2.5	0.1	0.4	0.2	1.0	0.0	0.8
District 15	607 324	93.8	36.5	8.8	29.2	19.4	11.4	4.3	8.0	2.1	6.2	2.2	0.5	0.2	1.7	0.0	1.5
District 16	647 437	98.1	32.6	8.9	38.6	28.0	11.7	4.9	6.3	2.4	1.9	0.1	0.3	0.1	0.0	0.0	1.4
District 17	627 566	97.1	36.4	11.9	33.2	23.6	9.9	3.6	5.7	2.2	2.9	0.0	1.3	0.1	0.7	0.0	0.7
District 18	620 213	98.0	37.8	19.8	29.2	20.4	6.8	1.4	4.4	1.3	2.0	0.0	0.9	0.0	0.7	0.0	0.3
District 19	626 776	95.1	35.0	20.9	30.6	23.8	4.4	1.3	4.2	1.5	4.9	1.4	0.7	0.4	1.2	0.6	0.7
District 20	635 820	97.1	33.8	20.5	33.6	25.6	5.3	1.6	3.9	1.5	2.9	0.5	0.6	0.3	0.4	0.0	1.0
District 21	573 294	95.4	40.8	18.1	27.5	21.4	3.4	1.2	5.7	2.6	4.6	0.2	1.1	0.2	2.3	0.0	0.6
District 22	619 548	95.9	38.2	21.2	28.6	22.7	3.0	1.1	4.9	2.6	4.1	1.9	0.7	0.2	0.7	0.0	0.6
District 23	563 385	94.4	38.4	19.7	28.3	22.2	3.0	1.1	5.1	2.6	5.6	1.3	1.0	0.4	2.2	0.0	0.6
District 24	582 371	93.2	36.9	19.5	28.4	22.9	2.7	1.1	5.7	2.9	6.8	2.7	0.7	0.1	2.1	0.8	0.5

Table F. Congressional Districts 107th Congress

STATE District	Households by type, 2000												Households, 1990		
		Family households						Nonfamily households							
				Married couple		Female householder[1]			Householder living alone						
	Total households	Total	With own children under 18 years	Total	With own children under 18 years	Total	With own children under 18 years	Total	Total	65 years and over	Average household size	Average family size	Total households	Female householder[1]	Householder living alone
	71	72	73	74	75	76	77	78	79	80	81	82	83	84	85
MISSOURI—Cont'd															
District 4	252 056	70.9	33.1	58.3	25.0	8.9	5.8	29.1	24.5	10.5	2.52	2.99	211 458	7.9	23.5
District 5	238 137	60.6	28.7	40.9	17.1	15.3	9.4	39.4	32.8	10.4	2.38	3.04	230 604	14.1	30.9
District 6	246 761	69.3	32.9	56.4	24.9	9.3	5.9	30.7	25.7	10.2	2.49	3.00	216 556	8.3	24.6
District 7	275 745	68.4	30.7	55.5	22.7	9.3	5.9	31.6	26.0	10.3	2.44	2.94	222 201	8.3	25.1
District 8	240 840	69.8	31.9	55.3	22.9	10.8	6.8	30.2	26.2	12.1	2.46	2.96	216 430	10.0	24.5
District 9	258 685	70.1	35.1	57.2	26.7	9.3	6.2	29.9	23.8	8.9	2.58	3.06	208 153	8.2	23.5
MONTANA	358 667	66.2	31.2	53.6	23.0	8.9	5.9	33.8	27.4	10.0	2.45	2.99	306 163	8.6	26.3
At Large	358 667	66.2	31.2	53.6	23.0	8.9	5.9	33.8	27.4	10.0	2.45	2.99	306 163	8.6	26.3
NEBRASKA	666 184	66.6	32.7	54.2	24.9	9.1	6.0	33.4	27.6	10.7	2.49	3.06	602 363	8.3	26.5
District 1	225 518	65.8	31.9	54.3	24.6	8.2	5.4	34.2	27.5	11.0	2.48	3.04	200 847	7.2	26.6
District 2	228 650	65.8	34.2	50.7	24.9	11.6	7.4	34.2	27.6	7.9	2.54	3.14	197 804	11.5	25.8
District 3	212 016	68.2	31.9	57.8	25.1	7.3	4.9	31.8	27.6	13.2	2.46	3.01	203 712	6.3	27.1
NEVADA	751 165	66.3	31.8	49.7	22.1	11.1	6.7	33.7	24.9	7.1	2.62	3.14	466 297	10.2	25.7
District 1	346 095	64.3	31.2	45.4	20.7	12.6	7.5	35.7	26.2	7.4	2.67	3.24	236 070	11.8	26.9
District 2	405 070	68.1	32.3	53.3	23.3	9.8	6.1	31.9	23.7	6.9	2.57	3.05	230 227	8.5	24.4
NEW HAMPSHIRE	474 606	68.2	33.4	55.3	25.4	9.1	5.7	31.8	24.4	8.5	2.53	3.03	411 186	8.5	22.0
District 1	241 411	67.7	33.3	54.6	25.2	9.2	5.8	32.3	24.6	8.3	2.53	3.03	206 495	8.6	22.1
District 2	233 195	68.7	33.4	56.0	25.5	8.9	5.6	31.3	24.3	8.8	2.53	3.02	204 691	8.3	21.8
NEW JERSEY	3 064 645	70.3	33.5	53.5	25.3	12.6	6.4	29.7	24.5	9.8	2.68	3.21	2 794 711	12.1	23.1
District 1	223 274	69.7	34.7	49.7	23.9	15.2	8.5	30.3	25.1	9.4	2.68	3.23	211 962	14.4	23.2
District 2	240 615	68.8	32.1	50.0	21.8	14.0	7.9	31.2	25.7	11.1	2.60	3.13	218 043	13.1	24.3
District 3	243 308	72.4	31.7	59.1	25.3	9.9	4.8	27.6	23.4	11.2	2.60	3.08	212 334	9.3	19.8
District 4	251 121	69.4	32.4	54.0	24.8	11.6	5.9	30.6	25.9	13.1	2.62	3.17	220 574	11.3	24.5
District 5	226 297	76.9	37.6	65.8	32.7	8.2	3.7	23.1	19.4	8.4	2.77	3.20	206 078	8.2	17.0
District 6	232 127	67.4	31.6	51.5	24.3	11.7	5.7	32.6	25.8	9.2	2.65	3.21	215 093	11.1	24.0
District 7	230 184	73.9	34.9	59.9	29.2	10.4	4.5	26.1	21.5	9.0	2.75	3.21	215 596	9.7	20.2
District 8	223 271	70.9	33.9	51.0	24.6	14.8	7.4	29.1	24.2	10.3	2.81	3.36	212 344	13.6	23.8
District 9	250 958	66.0	28.9	50.0	22.5	11.7	5.0	34.0	28.6	10.9	2.55	3.17	234 586	10.9	28.0
District 10	211 052	66.5	33.5	34.1	16.5	25.8	14.3	33.5	28.3	9.6	2.76	3.39	212 001	23.3	29.2
District 11	240 063	74.1	35.9	63.5	31.3	7.8	3.6	25.9	21.2	7.5	2.72	3.18	209 150	7.9	18.5
District 12	253 157	74.1	37.0	64.3	32.3	7.5	3.8	25.9	21.6	8.5	2.69	3.17	209 601	7.2	19.6
District 13	239 218	63.7	31.2	39.7	19.2	17.6	9.6	36.3	28.1	9.2	2.69	3.33	217 349	17.3	27.4
NEW MEXICO	677 971	68.8	34.7	50.4	23.3	13.2	8.3	31.2	25.4	8.2	2.63	3.18	542 709	11.9	23.0
District 1	233 136	64.8	31.8	46.8	21.0	12.8	7.8	35.2	27.9	7.9	2.50	3.08	194 425	11.8	25.7
District 2	216 085	71.8	35.9	53.8	24.4	13.2	8.6	28.2	23.6	9.3	2.69	3.19	175 354	11.3	21.2
District 3	228 750	70.1	36.4	50.8	24.5	13.7	8.4	29.9	24.5	7.5	2.71	3.25	172 930	12.7	21.8
NEW YORK	7 056 860	65.7	31.6	46.6	21.6	14.7	8.1	34.3	28.1	10.1	2.61	3.22	6 639 322	13.8	27.2
District 1	219 884	74.6	36.1	60.7	29.5	10.0	5.0	25.4	20.1	8.6	2.84	3.28	192 807	9.6	18.1
District 2	193 187	78.4	38.0	61.4	30.8	12.5	5.6	21.6	16.9	7.0	3.13	3.48	178 664	11.8	14.2
District 3	202 955	78.1	35.0	65.5	30.8	9.3	3.3	21.9	18.2	8.9	2.87	3.27	195 063	9.0	15.5
District 4	197 315	77.6	35.7	60.3	29.1	13.2	5.3	22.4	19.0	9.8	3.05	3.46	191 210	11.8	18.1
District 5	224 804	72.9	31.8	59.7	27.1	9.7	3.8	27.1	23.0	10.1	2.69	3.19	212 262	9.2	21.8
District 6	203 282	77.1	38.4	46.0	24.1	24.3	11.8	22.9	19.0	6.8	3.22	3.65	180 632	21.5	19.7
District 7	244 921	65.9	30.5	43.4	21.1	15.9	7.5	34.1	27.1	10.4	2.77	3.35	235 147	13.5	31.9
District 8	293 017	42.0	17.2	31.7	13.1	7.7	3.5	58.0	47.1	11.7	2.03	3.08	282 170	8.0	48.4
District 9	249 227	65.0	28.5	48.9	22.2	11.5	4.9	35.0	30.1	12.9	2.59	3.26	238 905	9.9	32.4
District 10	220 120	65.6	34.8	30.9	15.6	29.2	17.0	34.4	28.5	8.4	2.75	3.43	202 579	27.4	29.9
District 11	207 586	66.8	35.3	31.6	16.4	29.1	16.5	33.2	26.8	7.1	2.79	3.42	199 404	27.8	26.7
District 12	211 800	65.7	34.0	37.1	19.2	22.3	12.6	34.3	26.2	8.3	2.89	3.52	184 010	25.0	22.1
District 13	246 735	69.5	32.4	52.2	25.0	12.9	6.1	30.5	26.4	10.2	2.67	3.27	215 118	11.8	25.9
District 14	327 513	36.9	13.2	28.7	10.1	6.0	2.5	63.1	51.3	11.0	1.81	2.75	316 747	6.4	52.3
District 15	221 894	57.5	29.4	24.0	11.7	27.8	15.6	42.5	34.7	11.2	2.57	3.35	214 632	27.5	35.6
District 16	210 892	71.9	43.9	27.5	15.9	37.5	24.9	28.1	23.7	7.4	3.01	3.53	188 194	38.0	23.8
District 17	228 250	65.7	35.6	32.7	16.4	27.0	16.6	34.3	29.5	10.2	2.67	3.30	217 580	22.8	30.6
District 18	234 476	67.6	30.2	52.4	24.3	11.2	4.7	32.4	27.7	11.3	2.59	3.18	222 962	10.3	27.5
District 19	219 247	72.3	36.6	59.6	30.1	9.3	5.0	27.7	22.7	8.4	2.72	3.21	199 080	8.7	21.0
District 20	215 170	74.3	37.4	60.5	30.5	10.1	5.2	25.7	21.2	8.3	2.87	3.36	192 825	9.4	19.2
District 21	233 665	60.6	28.7	44.3	19.0	12.5	7.7	39.4	32.1	11.9	2.34	2.98	228 409	11.6	29.4
District 22	236 726	68.9	32.5	55.5	24.5	9.4	5.7	31.1	25.0	9.9	2.51	3.01	210 874	8.9	22.1
District 23	216 196	66.5	30.8	51.3	21.6	10.7	6.6	33.5	27.7	12.5	2.46	3.00	211 591	10.0	25.0
District 24	214 911	67.8	33.4	52.8	23.6	10.4	6.8	32.2	25.6	10.7	2.52	3.02	202 380	9.6	22.7

[1] No spouse present.

STATE District	Percent change of households, 1990–2000	Total housing units	Occupied housing units (percent)	Vacant housing units Total	For seasonal, recreational, or occasional use	Homeowner vacancy rate (percent)	Rental vacancy rate (percent)	Occupied housing units Total	Percent owner-occupied housing units	Percent renter-occupied housing units	Average household size of owner-occupied units	Average household size of renter-occupied units
	86	87	88	89	90	91	92	93	94	95	96	97
MISSOURI—Cont'd												
District 4	19.2	305 686	82.5	17.5	10.3	2.7	9.1	252 056	73.8	26.2	2.57	2.35
District 5	3.3	259 025	91.9	8.1	0.3	1.8	9.1	238 137	61.2	38.8	2.54	2.12
District 6	13.9	269 508	91.6	8.4	1.5	2.0	8.1	246 761	72.2	27.8	2.61	2.18
District 7	24.1	307 977	89.5	10.5	2.8	2.9	9.0	275 745	69.9	30.1	2.51	2.28
District 8	11.3	274 411	87.8	12.2	3.4	2.6	9.8	240 840	71.7	28.3	2.51	2.33
District 9	24.3	286 847	90.2	9.8	2.7	2.1	9.4	258 685	74.7	25.3	2.69	2.24
MONTANA	17.1	412 633	86.9	13.1	5.9	2.2	7.6	358 667	69.1	30.9	2.55	2.22
At Large	17.1	412 633	86.9	13.1	5.9	2.2	7.6	358 667	69.1	30.9	2.55	2.22
NEBRASKA	10.6	722 668	92.2	7.8	1.6	1.8	7.6	666 184	67.4	32.6	2.63	2.20
District 1	12.3	242 231	93.1	6.9	1.4	1.7	6.9	225 518	67.1	32.9	2.62	2.18
District 2	15.6	240 879	94.9	5.1	0.5	1.0	7.1	228 650	64.5	35.5	2.75	2.16
District 3	4.1	239 558	88.5	11.5	3.1	2.7	9.1	212 016	71.0	29.0	2.53	2.29
NEVADA	61.1	827 457	90.8	9.2	2.0	2.6	9.7	751 165	60.9	39.1	2.71	2.47
District 1	46.6	376 036	92.0	8.0	1.1	2.4	9.4	346 095	54.1	45.9	2.80	2.50
District 2	75.9	451 421	89.7	10.3	2.8	2.7	10.1	405 070	66.6	33.4	2.64	2.44
NEW HAMPSHIRE	15.4	547 024	86.8	13.2	10.3	1.0	3.5	474 606	69.7	30.3	2.70	2.14
District 1	16.9	279 758	86.3	13.7	10.9	0.9	3.5	241 411	68.6	31.4	2.70	2.14
District 2	13.9	267 266	87.3	12.7	9.6	1.1	3.5	233 195	70.8	29.2	2.69	2.14
NEW JERSEY	9.7	3 310 275	92.6	7.4	3.3	1.2	4.5	3 064 645	65.6	34.4	2.81	2.43
District 1	5.3	239 678	93.2	6.8	0.2	1.8	6.8	223 274	69.8	30.2	2.86	2.27
District 2	10.4	315 665	76.2	23.8	17.7	2.1	9.7	240 615	70.5	29.5	2.68	2.43
District 3	14.6	287 208	84.7	15.3	9.9	1.5	10.8	243 308	82.8	17.2	2.67	2.29
District 4	13.8	271 576	92.5	7.5	2.5	1.6	5.9	251 121	75.2	24.8	2.67	2.49
District 5	9.8	236 879	95.5	4.5	1.8	1.0	3.7	226 297	81.8	18.2	2.89	2.27
District 6	7.9	246 516	94.2	5.8	2.3	1.1	3.5	232 127	62.0	38.0	2.83	2.35
District 7	6.8	235 952	97.6	2.4	0.3	0.6	2.9	230 184	74.4	25.6	2.87	2.40
District 8	5.1	230 368	96.9	3.1	0.3	0.8	2.8	223 271	56.8	43.2	2.95	2.63
District 9	7.0	259 194	96.8	3.2	0.4	0.9	2.7	250 958	52.7	47.3	2.75	2.33
District 10	-0.4	227 122	92.9	7.1	0.1	1.8	5.1	211 052	35.5	64.5	3.11	2.56
District 11	14.8	247 084	97.2	2.8	0.9	0.6	2.7	240 063	78.2	21.8	2.87	2.19
District 12	20.8	262 114	96.6	3.4	0.8	0.8	3.5	253 157	80.7	19.3	2.81	2.18
District 13	10.1	250 919	95.3	4.7	0.3	1.3	3.0	239 218	29.0	71.0	2.90	2.60
NEW MEXICO	24.9	780 579	86.9	13.1	4.1	2.2	11.6	677 971	70.0	30.0	2.72	2.41
District 1	19.9	252 959	92.2	7.8	0.5	1.9	11.5	233 136	65.4	34.6	2.63	2.24
District 2	23.2	257 882	83.8	16.2	5.5	2.8	14.0	216 085	71.9	28.1	2.75	2.56
District 3	32.3	269 738	84.8	15.2	6.1	1.9	9.3	228 750	72.8	27.2	2.79	2.48
NEW YORK	6.3	7 679 307	91.9	8.1	3.1	1.6	4.6	7 056 860	53.0	47.0	2.78	2.41
District 1	14.0	263 454	83.5	16.5	13.2	1.1	3.7	219 884	79.2	20.8	2.93	2.50
District 2	8.1	201 234	96.0	4.0	1.6	0.7	3.1	193 187	78.3	21.7	3.26	2.65
District 3	4.0	207 596	97.8	2.2	0.8	0.4	2.1	202 955	83.8	16.2	2.98	2.31
District 4	3.2	201 802	97.8	2.2	0.5	0.6	2.0	197 315	77.8	22.2	3.15	2.71
District 5	5.9	231 867	97.0	3.0	0.8	0.7	1.9	224 804	67.1	32.9	2.82	2.45
District 6	12.5	215 094	94.5	5.5	0.2	1.6	3.4	203 282	54.3	45.7	3.49	2.89
District 7	4.2	255 038	96.0	4.0	0.3	1.3	2.5	244 921	30.7	69.3	2.83	2.74
District 8	3.8	311 980	93.9	6.1	1.9	1.6	2.8	293 017	26.1	73.9	2.24	1.95
District 9	4.3	261 776	95.2	4.8	1.0	1.2	2.6	249 227	42.6	57.4	2.82	2.42
District 10	8.7	238 316	92.4	7.6	0.2	2.5	4.4	220 120	27.1	72.9	3.10	2.62
District 11	4.1	218 092	95.2	4.8	0.2	1.5	3.1	207 586	20.7	79.3	3.20	2.68
District 12	15.1	224 074	94.5	5.5	0.3	1.9	3.0	211 800	17.7	82.3	2.97	2.87
District 13	14.7	257 828	95.7	4.3	0.3	1.3	3.0	246 735	53.3	46.7	2.95	2.36
District 14	3.4	354 899	92.3	7.7	3.8	2.2	2.6	327 513	27.5	72.5	1.95	1.76
District 15	3.4	238 423	93.1	6.9	0.3	5.8	4.2	221 894	8.0	92.0	2.21	2.60
District 16	12.1	224 859	93.8	6.2	0.1	2.6	4.5	210 892	9.8	90.2	3.28	2.98
District 17	4.9	239 914	95.1	4.9	0.2	2.3	3.7	228 250	24.3	75.7	2.74	2.65
District 18	5.2	242 329	96.8	3.2	0.5	1.0	2.4	234 476	53.7	46.3	2.75	2.41
District 19	10.1	230 023	95.3	4.7	1.8	1.0	3.3	219 247	71.9	28.1	2.87	2.33
District 20	11.6	230 191	93.5	6.5	3.4	1.0	3.4	215 170	71.0	29.0	2.97	2.62
District 21	2.3	254 528	91.8	8.2	0.7	2.2	7.3	233 665	59.5	40.5	2.55	2.03
District 22	12.3	284 769	83.1	16.9	11.3	2.0	7.3	236 726	73.7	26.3	2.64	2.15
District 23	2.2	253 879	85.2	14.8	6.8	2.4	10.3	216 196	71.2	28.8	2.59	2.15
District 24	6.2	278 159	77.3	22.7	15.7	2.6	9.0	214 911	69.6	30.4	2.64	2.27

Table F. Congressional Districts 107th Congress

STATE District	Land area, 2000[1] (sq km)	Total persons	Rank	Per square kilometer	Land area, 1990[1] (sq km)	Total persons	Rank	Per square kilometer	White	Black or African American	American Indian or Alaska Native	Asian	Native Hawaiian and other Pacific Islander	Some other race
	1	2	3	4	5	6	7	8	9	10	11	12	13	14
NEW YORK—Cont'd														
District 25	4 760.8	569 864	X	119.7	4 761.0	580 337	X	122.0	87.2	7.7	0.7	1.8	0.0	0.8
District 26	7 984.2	589 237	X	73.8	7 985.0	580 338	X	73.0	85.8	6.6	0.3	2.6	0.0	2.6
District 27	9 306.6	610 516	X	65.6	9 308.0	580 337	X	62.0	93.4	3.0	0.3	1.5	0.0	0.7
District 28	714.4	592 533	X	829.4	714.0	580 337	X	813.0	75.7	16.2	0.3	2.7	0.0	2.9
District 29	3 059.7	572 581	X	187.1	3 060.0	580 337	X	190.0	88.9	6.0	0.8	1.0	0.0	1.8
District 30	1 876.9	563 256	X	300.1	1 877.0	580 337	X	309.0	78.3	18.4	0.6	0.8	0.0	0.8
District 31	17 060.0	575 753	X	33.7	17 061.0	580 337	X	34.0	94.0	2.6	0.6	0.7	0.0	0.8
NORTH CAROLINA	126 161.0	8 049 313	X	63.8	126 180.0	6 632 448	X	52.6	72.1	21.6	1.2	1.4	0.0	2.3
District 1	18 881.3	587 830	X	31.1	21 110.0	552 394	X	26.0	45.9	50.5	0.7	0.4	0.0	1.6
District 2	9 790.0	730 266	X	74.6	10 709.0	552 378	X	52.0	66.4	26.9	0.5	1.1	0.0	3.7
District 3	15 952.7	615 614	X	38.6	19 510.0	552 387	X	28.0	75.1	19.5	0.5	1.0	0.1	2.2
District 4	4 975.4	765 876	X	153.9	4 755.0	552 387	X	116.0	71.9	19.9	0.3	3.7	0.0	2.5
District 5	8 995.6	637 158	X	70.8	10 990.0	552 386	X	50.0	81.2	14.3	0.3	0.8	0.0	2.4
District 6	7 955.5	689 529	X	86.7	6 368.0	552 385	X	87.0	84.1	10.9	0.4	1.3	0.0	2.2
District 7	16 574.5	690 054	X	41.6	9 361.0	552 386	X	59.0	65.6	23.0	6.8	0.6	0.1	2.4
District 8	10 214.4	661 112	X	64.7	11 496.0	552 387	X	48.0	65.1	26.4	2.7	1.2	0.1	2.7
District 9	2 960.4	693 042	X	234.1	2 700.0	552 387	X	205.0	79.9	14.8	0.3	2.2	0.0	1.6
District 10	10 922.2	655 413	X	60.0	11 309.0	552 386	X	49.0	89.5	6.0	0.2	1.4	0.0	1.8
District 11	16 743.8	656 619	X	39.2	15 724.0	552 387	X	35.0	91.1	4.8	1.5	0.5	0.0	1.0
District 12	2 194.7	666 800	X	303.8	2 148.0	552 387	X	257.0	47.6	44.6	0.4	2.3	0.0	3.4
NORTH DAKOTA	178 647.0	642 200	X	3.6	178 695.0	638 800	X	3.6	92.4	0.6	4.9	0.6	0.0	0.4
At Large	178 646.8	642 200	X	3.6	178 695.0	638 800	X	4.0	92.4	0.6	4.9	0.6	0.0	0.4
OHIO	106 056.0	11 353 140	X	107.0	106 067.0	10 847 115	X	102.3	85.0	11.5	0.2	1.2	0.0	0.8
District 1	457.9	542 618	X	1 185.0	458.0	570 900	X	1 247.0	62.5	34.0	0.2	1.3	0.0	0.5
District 2	5 043.8	634 061	X	125.7	5 045.0	570 902	X	113.0	94.5	2.6	0.2	1.4	0.0	0.3
District 3	1 116.9	556 039	X	497.8	1 117.0	570 901	X	511.0	76.4	20.0	0.2	1.3	0.0	0.5
District 4	11 737.9	591 795	X	50.4	11 738.0	570 901	X	49.0	92.5	5.2	0.2	0.5	0.0	0.5
District 5	13 468.6	589 716	X	43.8	13 470.0	570 901	X	42.0	94.3	2.3	0.2	0.4	0.0	1.6
District 6	16 499.9	620 901	X	37.6	16 502.0	570 901	X	35.0	95.6	2.2	0.3	0.6	0.0	0.2
District 7	8 993.5	620 156	X	69.0	8 996.0	570 902	X	64.0	92.0	5.2	0.3	0.9	0.0	0.4
District 8	7 065.0	625 445	X	88.5	7 066.0	570 901	X	81.0	94.0	3.3	0.2	1.1	0.0	0.5
District 9	2 845.2	569 053	X	200.0	2 845.0	570 901	X	201.0	81.0	13.8	0.3	1.1	0.0	1.8
District 10	403.2	573 874	X	1 423.0	403.0	570 903	X	1 416.0	87.8	5.1	0.2	1.8	0.0	2.9
District 11	270.2	532 337	X	1 970.2	270.0	570 901	X	2 118.0	31.7	64.5	0.2	1.4	0.0	0.6
District 12	2 647.3	661 049	X	249.7	2 648.0	570 902	X	216.0	71.8	22.8	0.3	2.2	0.0	1.4
District 13	4 369.7	645 068	X	147.6	4 370.0	570 894	X	131.0	91.6	4.7	0.2	0.7	0.0	0.3
District 14	1 292.6	586 402	X	453.7	1 293.0	570 900	X	442.0	84.5	12.3	0.2	1.3	0.0	0.3
District 15	2 262.1	649 980	X	287.3	2 262.0	570 902	X	252.0	85.9	7.7	0.3	3.2	0.0	1.0
District 16	5 527.5	605 661	X	109.6	5 528.0	570 902	X	103.0	92.9	4.9	0.2	0.5	0.0	0.3
District 17	3 483.5	563 164	X	161.7	3 484.0	570 900	X	164.0	86.8	10.8	0.2	0.4	0.0	0.6
District 18	15 723.6	586 247	X	37.3	15 725.0	570 900	X	36.0	95.7	2.6	0.2	0.3	0.0	0.2
District 19	2 847.4	599 574	X	210.6	2 848.0	570 901	X	200.0	93.8	2.9	0.1	1.6	0.0	0.5
OKLAHOMA	177 847.0	3 450 654	X	19.4	177 878.0	3 145 576	X	17.7	76.2	7.6	7.9	1.4	0.1	2.4
District 1	1 745.2	586 853	X	336.3	1 745.0	524 264	X	300.0	75.3	10.6	5.3	1.6	0.0	2.7
District 2	30 291.4	599 445	X	19.8	30 294.0	524 264	X	17.0	70.7	4.4	17.0	0.3	0.0	0.8
District 3	46 520.1	565 932	X	12.2	46 526.0	524 264	X	11.0	78.5	3.8	11.3	0.7	0.0	1.0
District 4	20 930.0	572 589	X	27.4	20 945.0	524 265	X	25.0	79.5	7.5	4.6	1.8	0.1	2.4
District 5	12 074.8	593 898	X	49.2	12 076.0	524 264	X	43.0	79.9	6.5	4.1	2.5	0.1	3.2
District 6	66 285.3	531 937	X	8.0	66 291.0	524 264	X	8.0	73.0	13.0	4.8	1.3	0.1	4.4
OREGON	248 631.0	3 421 399	X	13.8	248 647.0	2 842 337	X	11.4	86.6	1.6	1.3	3.0	0.2	4.2
District 1	7 662.7	743 195	X	97.0	7 663.0	568 461	X	74.0	85.4	1.2	0.8	5.0	0.2	4.5
District 2	182 830.5	701 847	X	3.8	182 842.0	568 464	X	3.0	89.3	0.4	2.1	0.8	0.2	4.8
District 3	2 108.8	650 092	X	308.3	2 109.0	568 465	X	270.0	79.3	5.5	1.0	5.6	0.4	4.2
District 4	41 649.3	633 335	X	15.2	41 649.0	568 465	X	14.0	91.9	0.5	1.4	1.4	0.2	1.6
District 5	14 379.2	692 930	X	48.2	14 383.0	568 466	X	40.0	87.0	0.7	1.3	2.0	0.3	5.9
PENNSYLVANIA	116 074.0	12 281 054	X	105.8	116 083.0	11 882 842	X	102.4	85.4	10.0	0.1	1.8	0.0	1.5
District 1	135.7	515 560	X	3 799.3	136.0	565 842	X	4 175.0	31.0	55.4	0.3	4.2	0.0	6.8
District 2	117.6	532 455	X	4 527.7	118.0	565 650	X	4 808.0	29.4	64.4	0.2	3.3	0.0	0.8
District 3	146.9	572 488	X	3 897.1	147.0	565 866	X	3 847.0	72.4	13.7	0.2	5.2	0.0	6.0
District 4	3 426.1	582 777	X	170.1	3 427.0	565 792	X	165.0	95.0	3.4	0.1	0.5	0.0	0.2
District 5	27 140.2	582 083	X	21.4	27 142.0	565 813	X	21.0	96.0	1.6	0.2	1.2	0.0	0.3
District 6	4 924.2	600 437	X	121.9	4 925.0	565 760	X	115.0	90.8	3.5	0.1	0.8	0.0	3.6
District 7	786.0	587 281	X	747.2	786.0	565 746	X	720.0	88.8	5.8	0.1	3.9	0.0	0.4

[1] Dry land or land partially or temporarily covered by water.

Table F. Congressional Districts 107th Congress

STATE District	Population and population characteristics, 2000 (cont'd)								Population and population characteristics, 1990				
	Race (percent) (cont'd)								Race (percent)				
	Two or more races	Race alone or in combination							White	Black or African American	American Indian or Alaska Native	Asian and Pacific Islander	Hispanic[1]
		White	Black	American Indian or Alaska Native	Asian	Native Hawaiian and other Pacific Islander	Some other race	Hispanic[1]					
	15	16	17	18	19	20	21	22	23	24	25	26	27
NEW YORK—Cont'd													
District 25	1.8	88.7	8.6	1.4	2.0	0.1	1.2	2.1	91.0	6.6	0.6	1.3	1.4
District 26	2.1	87.5	7.5	0.8	3.0	0.1	3.3	6.6	90.6	5.7	0.2	2.0	4.3
District 27	1.1	94.4	3.4	0.6	1.7	0.0	0.9	1.9	95.5	2.5	0.3	1.1	1.3
District 28	2.1	77.3	17.2	0.7	3.2	0.1	3.8	6.1	81.5	14.0	0.3	2.0	4.3
District 29	1.5	90.2	6.6	1.2	1.2	0.1	2.3	4.0	92.6	4.5	0.8	0.7	2.8
District 30	1.2	79.2	18.9	1.0	0.9	0.1	1.2	2.2	81.5	16.7	0.6	0.6	1.5
District 31	1.1	95.1	3.1	1.1	0.9	0.0	1.1	2.1	95.9	2.3	0.6	0.6	1.5
NORTH CAROLINA	1.3	73.1	22.1	1.6	1.7	0.1	2.8	4.7	75.6	22.0	1.2	0.8	1.2
District 1	0.8	46.5	50.9	1.0	0.5	0.1	1.9	3.0	41.6	57.3	0.6	0.2	0.7
District 2	1.3	67.4	27.5	0.9	1.3	0.1	4.2	6.5	76.2	21.9	0.6	0.7	1.2
District 3	1.6	76.4	20.1	0.9	1.5	0.2	2.6	4.2	76.6	21.5	0.4	0.7	1.6
District 4	1.6	73.2	20.5	0.7	4.1	0.1	3.1	5.3	77.2	20.1	0.3	1.9	1.3
District 5	1.0	82.0	14.7	0.6	0.9	0.1	2.8	4.7	83.9	15.2	0.2	0.4	0.8
District 6	1.1	85.0	11.3	0.8	1.5	0.1	2.5	4.4	91.3	7.5	0.4	0.6	0.7
District 7	1.3	66.6	23.5	7.4	0.9	0.1	2.9	4.4	71.5	18.7	7.3	1.1	2.9
District 8	1.7	66.4	27.1	3.2	1.6	0.2	3.3	5.9	72.8	23.2	2.5	0.8	1.4
District 9	1.2	80.8	15.2	0.6	2.5	0.1	2.1	4.1	89.1	8.9	0.3	1.3	1.1
District 10	0.9	90.3	6.3	0.5	1.6	0.1	2.1	4.0	93.7	5.5	0.2	0.4	0.7
District 11	1.0	92.0	5.1	2.0	0.6	0.1	1.3	2.6	90.9	7.2	1.4	0.3	0.7
District 12	1.6	48.7	45.3	0.8	2.7	0.1	4.2	6.8	41.8	56.6	0.4	0.9	0.9
NORTH DAKOTA	1.2	93.4	0.8	5.5	0.8	0.1	0.6	1.2	94.6	0.6	4.1	0.5	0.7
At Large	1.2	93.4	0.8	5.5	0.8	0.1	0.6	1.2	94.6	0.6	4.1	0.5	0.7
OHIO	1.4	86.1	12.1	0.7	1.4	0.1	1.1	1.9	87.8	10.6	0.2	0.8	1.3
District 1	1.5	63.6	34.9	0.7	1.5	0.1	0.8	1.1	68.6	30.1	0.2	0.9	0.6
District 2	0.9	95.3	2.9	0.6	1.6	0.0	0.5	1.0	96.7	2.3	0.1	0.8	0.5
District 3	1.5	77.7	20.7	0.7	1.7	0.1	0.8	1.3	80.7	17.8	0.2	1.0	0.8
District 4	1.1	93.4	5.7	0.6	0.7	0.0	0.7	1.2	94.4	4.6	0.2	0.4	0.9
District 5	1.2	95.3	2.7	0.6	0.5	0.0	2.0	3.7	95.9	2.1	0.2	0.3	3.1
District 6	1.1	96.6	2.6	0.9	0.7	0.0	0.3	0.7	97.1	2.1	0.2	0.5	0.4
District 7	1.3	93.2	5.8	0.8	1.1	0.1	0.5	1.0	93.6	5.3	0.2	0.7	0.7
District 8	1.0	94.9	3.7	0.6	1.3	0.1	0.6	1.1	96.2	2.8	0.1	0.7	0.5
District 9	2.0	82.7	14.6	0.8	1.4	0.1	2.6	4.5	84.9	12.2	0.2	1.0	3.4
District 10	2.1	89.7	5.7	0.7	2.2	0.1	3.9	6.3	94.1	2.1	0.2	1.4	4.0
District 11	1.6	32.7	65.7	0.7	1.7	0.1	1.0	1.5	39.8	58.6	0.2	1.0	1.1
District 12	2.2	73.3	24.2	0.8	2.5	0.1	1.5	1.8	74.8	23.2	0.2	1.4	0.8
District 13	1.4	92.8	5.3	0.6	0.9	0.0	1.8	3.4	93.6	4.5	0.2	0.5	2.9
District 14	1.4	85.7	13.0	0.7	1.6	0.1	0.6	0.9	87.7	10.9	0.2	1.0	0.6
District 15	1.8	87.4	8.5	0.8	3.7	0.1	1.5	2.3	92.4	4.9	0.2	2.2	1.0
District 16	1.2	94.0	5.5	0.6	0.7	0.0	0.4	0.9	94.4	4.8	0.2	0.4	0.6
District 17	1.2	87.8	11.3	0.6	0.6	0.0	0.9	1.9	89.2	9.8	0.2	0.4	1.3
District 18	1.0	96.6	3.1	0.7	0.4	0.0	0.3	0.6	97.1	2.4	0.2	0.2	0.3
District 19	1.0	94.7	3.3	0.4	1.8	0.0	0.8	1.5	96.8	1.8	0.1	1.0	0.9
OKLAHOMA	4.5	80.3	8.3	11.4	1.7	0.1	3.0	5.2	82.1	7.4	8.0	1.1	2.7
District 1	4.4	79.3	11.4	8.5	2.0	0.1	3.4	5.8	83.2	9.6	5.1	1.2	2.3
District 2	6.8	77.1	4.9	23.2	0.5	0.1	1.2	2.2	77.1	5.1	17.2	0.2	1.1
District 3	4.7	82.9	4.3	15.3	0.9	0.1	1.4	2.6	83.4	4.0	11.4	0.6	1.4
District 4	4.0	83.1	8.3	7.1	2.4	0.3	3.1	5.7	84.2	7.2	4.8	1.7	4.0
District 5	3.7	83.3	7.2	6.6	2.9	0.1	3.8	6.7	86.6	5.6	4.6	1.7	3.2
District 6	3.4	75.9	13.8	6.9	1.6	0.2	5.2	8.4	78.3	13.2	4.9	1.0	4.4
OREGON	3.1	89.3	2.1	2.5	3.7	0.5	5.2	8.0	92.8	1.6	1.4	2.4	4.0
District 1	2.9	88.0	1.6	1.6	6.1	0.5	5.4	8.9	93.2	0.8	0.8	3.4	4.0
District 2	2.5	91.6	0.7	3.3	1.2	0.3	5.5	8.6	93.7	0.3	2.3	0.9	5.4
District 3	4.1	82.7	6.6	2.3	6.6	0.7	5.5	7.7	87.3	5.9	1.2	4.5	3.2
District 4	3.0	94.8	0.9	3.0	2.0	0.3	2.3	4.2	96.0	0.5	1.4	1.4	2.4
District 5	2.9	89.7	1.1	2.4	2.6	0.5	6.9	10.4	93.6	0.6	1.2	2.0	5.0
PENNSYLVANIA	1.2	86.3	10.5	0.4	2.0	0.1	1.9	3.2	88.5	9.2	0.1	1.2	2.0
District 1	2.2	32.2	56.6	0.8	4.6	0.2	8.0	11.5	37.7	52.4	0.2	2.4	9.9
District 2	1.9	30.3	65.7	0.8	3.7	0.2	1.5	2.0	34.7	62.2	0.3	2.2	1.6
District 3	2.4	74.2	14.4	0.6	5.7	0.1	7.5	10.8	89.3	4.9	0.2	3.2	4.7
District 4	0.8	95.7	3.8	0.3	0.6	0.0	0.3	0.6	96.3	3.2	0.1	0.4	0.5
District 5	0.7	96.6	1.8	0.4	1.4	0.1	0.5	1.0	97.8	1.0	0.2	0.9	0.6
District 6	1.2	91.8	4.0	0.4	1.0	0.1	4.1	6.6	95.2	2.5	0.1	0.6	3.3
District 7	1.1	89.6	6.2	0.3	4.2	0.1	0.7	1.3	93.8	3.8	0.1	2.1	0.9

[1] Hispanic persons may be of any race.

Table F. Congressional Districts 107th Congress

STATE District	Population and population characteristics, 2000										
	Age (percent)										
	Under 5 years	5 to 17 years	18 to 24 years	25 to 34 years	35 to 44 years	45 to 54 years	55 to 64 years	65 to 74 years	75 years and over	Median age (years)	Percent Female
	28	29	30	31	32	33	34	35	36	37	38
NEW YORK—Cont'd											
District 25	6.4	19.3	9.8	12.6	16.1	13.6	8.5	7.0	6.7	36.2	52.0
District 26	5.7	17.6	12.3	12.2	15.7	13.6	9.0	7.0	6.7	36.4	50.9
District 27	5.8	19.1	8.8	11.8	16.8	14.6	9.2	7.0	6.8	37.8	50.7
District 28	6.5	19.0	9.5	13.6	15.8	13.8	8.4	6.4	7.0	35.9	52.0
District 29	6.0	18.4	9.1	12.8	16.3	13.8	8.8	7.5	7.3	37.4	51.8
District 30	6.3	18.7	8.3	12.6	16.0	13.4	9.2	8.0	7.6	37.8	52.2
District 31	5.9	19.2	9.5	11.6	15.4	14.0	9.4	7.7	7.3	37.6	50.6
NORTH CAROLINA	6.7	17.7	10.0	15.1	16.0	13.5	9.0	6.6	5.4	35.3	51.0
District 1	6.6	19.3	8.7	12.8	15.2	13.8	9.5	7.7	6.4	36.8	52.7
District 2	7.2	18.0	10.5	16.5	16.8	13.0	8.0	5.5	4.4	33.7	50.4
District 3	6.8	17.2	14.3	13.8	15.1	12.4	8.8	6.8	4.8	33.4	49.1
District 4	6.7	17.1	11.6	17.5	17.4	13.8	7.3	4.7	4.0	33.3	51.2
District 5	6.3	16.9	8.5	14.2	16.0	14.2	9.8	7.5	6.5	37.6	51.6
District 6	6.4	17.2	8.7	14.6	16.2	14.0	9.5	7.2	6.1	36.8	51.1
District 7	6.7	18.1	9.7	14.2	15.4	13.7	9.8	7.3	5.2	35.8	51.3
District 8	7.8	19.5	10.9	15.8	15.8	12.2	8.0	5.6	4.4	32.4	49.9
District 9	6.9	17.7	7.9	16.7	17.2	14.2	8.6	5.9	4.9	35.5	51.4
District 10	6.2	17.1	9.4	14.2	15.8	14.1	10.2	7.3	5.7	36.9	50.4
District 11	5.6	15.9	8.1	12.5	14.6	14.4	11.2	9.3	8.3	40.5	51.7
District 12	7.3	18.5	11.7	16.9	15.9	12.1	7.5	5.5	4.6	32.2	51.4
NORTH DAKOTA	6.1	18.9	11.4	12.0	15.3	13.3	8.3	7.1	7.6	36.2	50.1
At Large	6.1	18.9	11.4	12.0	15.3	13.3	8.3	7.1	7.6	36.2	50.1
OHIO	6.6	18.8	9.3	13.4	15.9	13.8	8.9	7.0	6.3	36.2	51.4
District 1	6.9	19.2	10.9	14.2	15.4	12.3	7.9	6.8	6.4	34.1	52.5
District 2	7.0	19.7	7.6	13.6	17.1	14.4	8.7	6.4	5.6	36.3	51.4
District 3	6.6	18.0	9.7	13.6	15.4	13.7	9.2	7.3	6.4	36.3	52.0
District 4	6.5	19.0	9.2	12.7	15.6	13.9	9.4	7.3	6.5	36.8	50.3
District 5	6.5	19.7	8.6	12.1	15.9	14.3	9.3	7.2	6.6	37.2	50.7
District 6	6.4	18.2	11.0	13.2	15.5	13.4	9.4	7.1	5.9	35.8	50.9
District 7	6.6	19.0	9.6	12.9	16.0	14.3	9.4	6.7	5.7	36.3	50.8
District 8	6.9	19.6	10.0	12.9	16.1	13.7	8.8	6.5	5.5	35.4	50.9
District 9	6.7	19.2	11.1	13.5	15.2	13.4	8.2	6.5	6.2	34.7	51.8
District 10	6.5	17.5	7.9	14.8	16.4	13.5	8.6	7.2	7.6	37.0	51.5
District 11	7.2	20.1	9.0	13.4	14.9	12.6	8.3	7.4	7.0	35.1	54.3
District 12	7.6	19.7	9.3	15.0	16.9	13.9	8.0	5.4	4.3	34.0	51.8
District 13	6.9	19.9	7.7	12.3	17.1	14.8	9.4	6.5	5.5	37.0	51.0
District 14	6.5	18.0	10.0	13.3	15.7	14.1	8.6	7.2	6.7	36.4	51.9
District 15	6.8	16.4	13.1	18.1	16.2	12.4	7.2	5.3	4.6	32.4	50.1
District 16	6.8	19.3	9.2	12.2	15.3	13.9	9.3	7.3	6.9	36.9	51.5
District 17	6.0	17.9	8.0	12.0	15.2	14.6	9.6	8.5	8.2	39.3	51.7
District 18	6.2	18.5	8.3	12.2	15.6	14.1	9.9	8.0	7.1	38.3	51.1
District 19	5.8	17.9	6.9	12.0	16.2	14.7	9.8	8.4	8.3	39.9	51.9
OKLAHOMA	6.8	19.0	10.3	13.1	15.2	13.1	9.2	7.0	6.2	35.5	50.9
District 1	7.3	19.0	9.9	14.6	15.8	13.5	8.2	6.2	5.5	34.4	51.5
District 2	6.8	19.9	8.7	11.8	14.8	13.4	10.5	7.8	6.4	37.1	50.9
District 3	6.4	18.5	11.2	12.0	14.2	12.8	9.9	7.9	7.1	36.4	50.7
District 4	6.9	19.0	12.0	13.7	15.6	12.7	8.6	6.3	5.2	33.8	50.1
District 5	6.9	18.5	10.1	13.6	15.7	13.7	8.7	6.6	6.2	35.6	51.6
District 6	6.8	19.1	10.2	12.9	15.0	12.6	9.1	7.4	6.8	35.7	50.3
OREGON	6.5	18.2	9.6	13.8	15.4	14.8	8.9	6.4	6.4	36.3	50.4
District 1	6.9	18.2	9.4	16.1	16.6	14.8	7.9	5.0	5.1	34.6	50.0
District 2	6.3	19.1	8.3	11.5	14.6	14.9	10.1	7.8	7.3	38.5	50.3
District 3	6.8	17.0	10.0	16.5	16.3	14.6	7.7	5.3	6.0	34.8	50.8
District 4	5.7	17.7	9.8	11.8	14.4	15.3	10.0	7.8	7.4	38.8	50.8
District 5	6.7	19.0	10.6	12.7	15.0	14.6	8.9	6.3	6.2	35.7	50.3
PENNSYLVANIA	5.9	17.9	8.9	12.7	15.9	13.9	9.2	7.9	7.7	38.0	51.7
District 1	7.0	20.8	11.0	14.2	14.6	11.9	8.1	6.6	5.7	32.8	53.7
District 2	5.9	17.3	13.1	15.2	14.1	12.1	8.3	7.0	7.0	33.9	54.7
District 3	6.6	18.6	8.9	14.7	15.0	12.2	8.2	7.4	8.2	35.7	52.2
District 4	5.8	17.9	6.8	11.2	16.7	14.6	9.6	8.8	8.5	40.2	52.0
District 5	5.3	16.9	13.6	12.2	14.7	13.1	9.4	7.8	7.1	36.5	50.0
District 6	5.8	17.7	8.2	12.8	15.9	13.8	9.2	8.3	8.2	38.4	50.9
District 7	6.0	17.8	8.2	12.7	16.6	14.0	9.0	7.9	7.7	38.2	52.0

Table F. Congressional Districts 107th Congress

| | Population and population characteristics, 1990 | | | | | | | | | | Population—change, 1980–2000 | | | | |
| | Age (percent) | | | | | | | | | | Total persons | | | Percent change | |
STATE District	Under 5 years	5 to 17 years	18 to 24 years	25 to 34 years	35 to 44 years	45 to 54 years	55 to 64 years	65 to 74 years	75 years and over	Percent Female	2000	1990	1980	1990–2000	1980–1990
	39	40	41	42	43	44	45	46	47	48	49	50	51	52	53
NEW YORK—Cont'd															
District 25	7.5	17.4	12.1	17.1	14.7	9.7	8.7	7.4	5.5	52.0	569 864	580 337	NA	-1.8	NA
District 26	6.9	16.2	13.5	17.0	14.6	10.0	8.7	7.4	5.7	50.9	589 237	580 338	NA	1.5	NA
District 27	7.1	18.1	10.6	16.1	15.6	10.7	9.0	7.3	5.5	50.9	610 516	580 337	NA	5.2	NA
District 28	7.7	16.6	11.2	17.9	15.2	10.0	8.2	7.3	5.8	52.2	592 533	580 337	NA	2.1	NA
District 29	7.0	16.9	10.6	17.0	14.6	9.8	9.4	8.6	6.0	52.1	572 581	580 337	NA	-1.3	NA
District 30	7.1	16.9	10.7	16.5	13.9	10.1	9.9	9.0	5.9	52.3	563 256	580 337	NA	-2.9	NA
District 31	7.2	19.0	10.7	15.1	14.3	10.0	9.2	8.2	6.4	51.1	575 753	580 337	NA	-0.8	NA
NORTH CAROLINA	6.9	17.3	11.8	17.3	15.2	10.5	8.9	7.3	4.8	51.5	8 049 313	6 632 448	5 880 095	21.4	12.8
District 1	7.4	20.2	10.2	15.6	13.9	9.6	9.2	8.3	5.7	53.5	587 830	552 394	NA	6.4	NA
District 2	6.8	17.2	10.8	17.2	15.5	10.5	9.0	7.9	5.1	51.9	730 266	552 378	NA	32.2	NA
District 3	7.3	17.9	12.0	17.2	14.6	10.2	9.2	7.3	4.3	50.9	615 614	552 387	NA	11.4	NA
District 4	6.9	15.5	14.4	20.8	17.0	10.1	6.9	5.1	3.4	51.4	765 876	552 387	NA	38.6	NA
District 5	6.2	16.2	11.6	16.5	15.0	11.1	9.5	7.9	5.9	52.1	637 158	552 386	NA	15.3	NA
District 6	6.3	16.2	11.0	16.8	15.9	11.7	9.6	7.5	4.9	51.6	689 529	552 385	NA	24.8	NA
District 7	7.7	17.3	17.6	18.5	13.7	8.9	7.5	5.7	3.1	47.1	690 054	552 386	NA	24.9	NA
District 8	7.6	19.4	10.7	16.6	14.9	10.5	8.6	7.1	4.7	51.6	661 112	552 387	NA	19.7	NA
District 9	7.0	16.6	10.7	19.3	16.7	10.9	8.4	6.2	4.0	51.5	693 042	552 387	NA	25.5	NA
District 10	6.3	17.4	9.8	16.3	16.1	12.2	9.7	7.4	4.8	51.1	655 413	552 386	NA	18.7	NA
District 11	5.9	16.2	9.8	14.2	14.4	11.3	10.6	10.2	7.5	52.2	656 619	552 387	NA	18.9	NA
District 12	7.7	17.7	12.7	18.1	14.6	9.4	8.0	6.7	4.9	53.2	666 800	552 387	NA	20.7	NA
NORTH DAKOTA	7.5	20.0	10.6	16.3	14.1	8.9	8.4	7.4	6.8	50.2	642 200	638 800	652 717	0.5	-2.1
At Large	7.5	20.0	10.6	16.3	14.1	8.9	8.4	7.4	6.8	50.2	642 200	638 800	NA	0.5	-2.1
OHIO	7.2	18.6	10.5	16.5	14.9	10.3	9.0	7.6	5.3	51.8	11 353 140	10 847 115	10 797 603	4.7	0.5
District 1	8.1	18.2	11.7	17.7	13.3	8.9	8.7	7.4	6.0	52.9	542 618	570 900	NA	-5.0	NA
District 2	7.5	19.3	8.9	17.3	16.0	10.7	8.7	6.7	4.8	51.4	634 061	570 902	NA	11.1	NA
District 3	7.4	17.5	10.6	17.5	14.8	10.5	9.3	7.6	5.0	52.1	556 039	570 901	NA	-2.6	NA
District 4	7.2	19.7	9.7	15.7	14.6	10.6	9.2	7.7	5.6	51.0	591 795	570 901	NA	3.7	NA
District 5	7.3	20.7	9.3	15.6	14.9	10.3	8.9	7.5	5.4	50.9	589 716	570 901	NA	3.3	NA
District 6	6.8	19.5	11.5	15.3	14.2	10.5	9.1	7.5	5.6	51.5	620 901	570 901	NA	8.8	NA
District 7	6.9	19.3	10.7	15.6	15.5	11.3	8.8	7.0	4.9	50.9	620 156	570 902	NA	8.6	NA
District 8	7.4	19.8	11.1	16.1	15.0	10.4	8.7	6.8	4.7	51.3	625 445	570 901	NA	9.6	NA
District 9	7.6	18.6	12.3	16.6	14.4	9.4	8.4	7.2	5.3	52.2	569 053	570 901	NA	-0.3	NA
District 10	7.1	16.6	9.3	17.9	14.6	10.0	9.3	9.0	6.2	52.1	573 874	570 903	NA	0.5	NA
District 11	7.7	17.9	10.0	16.8	13.9	9.4	9.4	8.6	6.3	54.2	532 337	570 901	NA	-6.8	NA
District 12	8.0	19.1	11.2	18.4	16.1	10.1	7.8	5.6	3.8	52.1	661 049	570 902	NA	15.8	NA
District 13	7.4	20.2	9.5	15.9	16.2	11.3	8.7	6.7	4.1	51.1	645 068	570 894	NA	13.0	NA
District 14	6.9	17.2	12.1	16.4	15.0	9.8	9.2	8.0	5.4	52.1	586 402	570 900	NA	2.7	NA
District 15	7.0	15.4	14.8	20.8	15.1	9.2	7.7	5.9	4.1	50.4	649 980	570 902	NA	13.9	NA
District 16	7.3	19.2	9.9	15.4	14.9	10.4	9.2	8.0	5.7	51.8	605 661	570 902	NA	6.1	NA
District 17	6.7	18.3	8.9	14.7	14.7	10.4	10.4	9.8	6.1	52.4	563 164	570 900	NA	-1.4	NA
District 18	6.8	19.3	8.8	15.0	14.5	10.6	9.9	8.7	6.4	52.1	586 247	570 900	NA	2.7	NA
District 19	6.4	17.1	8.6	15.7	15.2	11.1	10.5	9.4	5.9	52.0	599 574	570 901	NA	5.0	NA
OKLAHOMA	7.2	19.4	10.2	16.2	14.4	10.3	8.9	7.5	6.0	51.3	3 450 654	3 145 576	3 025 487	9.7	4.0
District 1	7.7	18.6	10.0	18.0	15.8	10.2	8.3	6.6	4.7	51.8	586 853	524 264	NA	11.9	NA
District 2	6.9	20.1	8.9	14.1	13.9	11.2	9.8	8.5	6.5	51.3	599 445	524 264	NA	14.3	NA
District 3	6.5	19.4	11.1	14.2	13.1	10.2	9.4	8.5	7.5	51.4	565 932	524 264	NA	7.9	NA
District 4	7.4	19.8	12.3	17.5	14.4	9.8	7.9	6.2	4.7	50.2	572 589	524 265	NA	9.2	NA
District 5	7.4	18.6	9.5	17.4	15.5	10.2	8.5	7.1	5.8	52.0	593 898	524 264	NA	13.3	NA
District 6	7.3	19.9	9.5	15.8	13.5	10.0	9.2	7.9	6.8	51.4	531 937	524 264	NA	1.5	NA
OREGON	7.1	18.4	9.4	15.9	16.7	10.4	8.3	7.9	5.9	50.8	3 421 399	2 842 337	2 633 156	20.4	7.9
District 1	7.2	17.9	9.2	17.8	18.1	10.7	7.4	6.5	5.1	50.7	743 195	568 461	NA	30.7	NA
District 2	7.1	19.4	8.1	14.0	15.7	10.6	9.4	9.2	6.5	50.5	701 847	568 464	NA	23.5	NA
District 3	7.4	17.2	9.7	17.7	17.3	9.7	7.6	7.4	6.1	51.6	650 092	568 465	NA	14.4	NA
District 4	6.8	18.5	9.7	14.7	16.1	10.6	8.9	8.6	5.9	50.9	633 335	568 465	NA	11.4	NA
District 5	7.0	18.9	10.4	15.2	16.3	10.5	8.2	7.7	5.7	50.6	692 930	568 466	NA	21.9	NA
PENNSYLVANIA	6.7	16.8	10.3	16.1	14.7	10.2	9.8	9.0	6.4	52.1	12 281 054	11 882 842	11 864 720	3.4	0.2
District 1	8.3	18.8	12.0	17.3	13.3	9.2	8.5	7.6	5.0	53.5	515 560	565 842	NA	-8.9	NA
District 2	6.9	15.5	12.9	18.0	13.7	9.3	8.8	8.3	6.6	54.5	532 455	565 650	NA	-5.9	NA
District 3	6.9	15.8	9.8	17.3	13.3	9.4	9.7	10.2	7.6	52.4	572 488	565 866	NA	1.2	NA
District 4	6.4	17.2	8.4	15.2	15.0	10.6	10.8	10.0	6.4	52.2	582 777	565 792	NA	3.0	NA
District 5	6.4	17.3	14.5	15.0	13.7	10.0	9.3	8.0	5.9	50.5	582 083	565 813	NA	2.9	NA
District 6	6.5	16.6	9.5	15.6	14.4	10.2	10.3	9.7	7.2	51.8	600 437	565 760	NA	6.1	NA
District 7	6.6	15.5	10.3	16.9	14.8	10.5	10.3	9.1	6.0	52.0	587 281	565 746	NA	3.8	NA

Table F. Congressional Districts 107th Congress

STATE District	Household relationship, 2000																
	In households (percent)										In group quarters (percent)						
					Child		Other relatives		Nonrelatives			Institutionalized population			Noninstitutionalized population		
	Total population	Total in house-holds	House-holder	Spouse	Total	Own child under 18 years	Total	Under 18 years	Total	Unmar-ried partner	Total in group quarters	Correc-tional institu-tions	Nurs-ing homes	Other institu-tions	Col-lege dormi-tories	Mili-tary quar-ters	Other
	54	55	56	57	58	59	60	61	62	63	64	65	66	67	68	69	70
NEW YORK—Cont'd																	
District 25	569 864	96.9	39.2	18.8	29.9	23.7	3.4	1.4	5.7	2.5	3.1	0.2	0.6	0.1	1.7	0.0	0.5
District 26	589 237	93.5	38.2	18.0	26.9	21.1	3.7	1.4	6.7	2.6	6.5	1.1	0.8	0.2	3.2	0.0	1.2
District 27	610 516	95.3	37.1	21.2	29.7	23.4	2.8	1.0	4.5	2.2	4.7	1.5	0.9	0.1	1.7	0.0	0.5
District 28	592 533	96.2	39.5	17.7	29.5	23.3	4.0	1.7	5.5	2.4	3.8	0.2	1.0	0.1	1.8	0.0	0.7
District 29	572 581	97.3	40.1	19.1	29.9	22.6	3.4	1.3	4.8	2.3	2.7	0.6	0.7	0.0	0.9	0.0	0.5
District 30	563 256	97.1	39.7	18.1	30.8	22.7	4.1	1.7	4.4	2.0	2.9	0.9	0.8	0.2	0.4	0.0	0.6
District 31	575 753	95.1	38.3	19.8	28.8	22.9	2.9	1.2	5.3	2.7	4.9	1.5	0.9	0.3	1.6	0.0	0.6
NORTH CAROLINA	8 049 313	96.8	38.9	20.4	27.6	21.7	5.1	2.2	4.8	1.8	3.2	0.6	0.6	0.1	0.9	0.5	0.4
District 1	587 830	97.4	38.7	17.6	29.3	21.5	7.7	3.8	4.1	1.8	2.6	0.9	0.8	0.1	0.2	0.0	0.5
District 2	730 266	95.6	37.4	19.5	28.0	22.3	5.5	2.3	5.2	1.8	4.4	1.4	0.5	0.3	1.7	0.0	0.4
District 3	615 614	93.6	37.3	20.9	26.8	21.6	4.0	1.8	4.5	1.7	6.4	0.8	0.4	0.3	0.9	3.7	0.3
District 4	765 876	97.1	39.6	20.0	26.5	22.0	4.2	1.4	6.8	1.8	2.9	0.1	0.6	0.0	1.9	0.0	0.3
District 5	637 158	97.6	40.5	22.0	26.9	21.0	4.5	1.7	3.8	1.6	2.4	0.2	0.9	0.0	0.8	0.0	0.4
District 6	689 529	98.1	39.9	22.6	27.1	21.5	4.2	1.6	4.3	1.7	1.9	0.3	0.6	0.1	0.6	0.0	0.4
District 7	690 054	97.8	39.3	20.1	27.8	21.4	5.6	2.6	5.0	1.9	2.2	0.7	0.4	0.0	0.5	0.0	0.6
District 8	661 112	95.7	35.7	19.9	30.3	24.0	5.8	2.7	4.0	1.6	4.3	0.8	0.6	0.1	0.4	2.2	0.2
District 9	693 042	98.7	39.8	21.5	27.9	22.4	4.7	1.8	4.8	1.9	1.3	0.1	0.6	0.1	0.3	0.0	0.3
District 10	655 413	97.3	39.2	22.4	27.2	20.9	4.5	1.8	4.2	1.8	2.7	0.6	0.6	0.0	0.9	0.0	0.4
District 11	656 619	97.1	41.5	22.9	24.8	19.3	4.0	1.6	3.9	1.7	2.9	0.4	0.9	0.1	0.8	0.0	0.6
District 12	666 800	96.0	37.9	15.7	28.5	21.9	7.4	3.2	6.5	2.1	4.0	0.6	0.7	0.1	1.9	0.0	0.7
NORTH DAKOTA	642 200	96.3	40.0	21.4	28.4	23.8	2.0	0.8	4.5	1.8	3.7	0.2	1.1	0.1	1.6	0.2	0.4
At Large	642 200	96.3	40.0	21.4	28.4	23.8	2.0	0.8	4.5	1.8	3.7	0.2	1.1	0.1	1.6	0.2	0.4
OHIO	11 353 140	97.4	39.2	20.1	29.7	23.2	3.9	1.7	4.4	2.0	2.6	0.6	0.8	0.1	0.8	0.0	0.3
District 1	542 618	97.1	41.1	15.6	30.2	23.2	5.0	2.4	5.2	2.2	2.9	0.4	0.9	0.1	0.9	0.0	0.5
District 2	634 061	99.0	38.8	22.3	31.0	24.9	3.2	1.3	3.6	1.8	1.0	0.1	0.8	0.0	0.0	0.0	0.2
District 3	556 039	97.2	41.0	19.0	28.3	22.2	4.2	1.9	4.7	2.2	2.8	0.4	0.9	0.1	1.1	0.0	0.3
District 4	591 795	95.9	38.1	21.4	29.3	23.3	3.2	1.5	3.9	1.9	4.1	2.2	0.8	0.0	0.7	0.0	0.4
District 5	589 716	98.0	38.2	22.3	30.7	24.2	3.0	1.4	3.9	1.9	2.0	0.5	0.9	0.0	0.2	0.0	0.3
District 6	620 901	96.0	38.2	21.3	28.6	22.4	3.5	1.6	4.5	2.0	4.0	1.2	0.9	0.2	1.5	0.0	0.2
District 7	620 156	96.2	37.5	21.8	29.4	23.4	3.3	1.5	4.1	1.9	3.8	1.4	0.9	0.1	1.2	0.1	0.3
District 8	625 445	97.6	37.4	22.1	30.7	24.5	3.3	1.4	4.1	1.8	2.4	0.2	0.8	0.0	1.2	0.0	0.3
District 9	569 053	97.1	39.3	18.5	30.1	23.5	3.9	1.8	5.2	2.3	2.9	0.1	0.8	0.0	1.6	0.0	0.4
District 10	573 874	97.9	41.2	18.8	29.2	22.1	4.2	1.5	4.5	2.2	2.1	0.4	0.9	0.1	0.3	0.0	0.4
District 11	532 337	97.3	40.7	12.9	31.0	22.7	7.8	3.9	5.0	2.1	2.7	0.2	0.9	0.2	0.9	0.0	0.6
District 12	661 049	97.9	39.4	18.9	30.5	24.9	4.3	1.9	4.9	2.2	2.1	0.1	0.6	0.2	0.9	0.0	0.2
District 13	645 068	98.2	36.7	22.4	32.1	24.8	3.7	1.5	3.3	1.7	1.8	0.4	0.6	0.1	0.4	0.0	0.2
District 14	586 402	97.5	39.9	19.6	29.0	22.4	3.8	1.6	5.0	2.1	2.5	0.2	0.7	0.1	1.2	0.0	0.3
District 15	649 980	96.3	40.6	18.3	26.1	21.3	3.7	1.4	7.5	2.5	3.7	1.5	0.5	0.1	1.4	0.0	0.2
District 16	605 661	97.1	37.8	21.4	30.8	24.0	3.4	1.4	3.8	1.8	2.9	0.1	1.2	0.2	1.1	0.0	0.3
District 17	563 164	97.3	39.6	20.4	29.5	21.5	4.4	1.9	3.4	1.8	2.7	1.2	0.9	0.1	0.2	0.0	0.3
District 18	586 247	97.7	39.2	21.9	29.3	22.6	3.4	1.5	3.9	2.1	2.3	0.9	0.9	0.1	0.3	0.0	0.2
District 19	599 574	98.6	40.1	22.2	29.5	22.1	3.5	1.2	3.3	1.7	1.4	0.1	0.9	0.1	0.1	0.0	0.3
OKLAHOMA	3 450 654	96.7	38.9	20.8	28.7	23.1	4.4	2.1	3.9	1.5	3.3	1.0	0.8	0.1	0.8	0.2	0.3
District 1	586 853	97.9	40.1	20.0	29.2	23.9	4.3	1.9	4.3	1.7	2.1	0.2	0.6	0.2	0.6	0.0	0.4
District 2	599 445	97.5	38.0	22.1	29.5	23.4	4.8	2.5	3.2	1.5	2.5	0.8	0.8	0.2	0.4	0.0	0.3
District 3	565 932	95.7	38.6	21.1	27.5	21.8	4.7	2.4	3.8	1.4	4.3	1.4	1.1	0.1	1.5	0.0	0.2
District 4	572 589	95.7	37.7	21.1	29.0	23.4	3.9	1.8	4.0	1.4	4.3	1.0	0.8	0.1	1.0	1.3	0.2
District 5	593 898	97.8	40.3	21.0	28.4	23.3	3.9	1.6	4.3	1.7	2.2	0.1	0.7	0.1	0.8	0.0	0.5
District 6	531 937	95.6	38.7	19.4	28.5	22.7	5.1	2.5	3.9	1.6	4.4	2.5	0.9	0.2	0.3	0.0	0.4
OREGON	3 421 399	97.7	39.0	20.2	27.4	22.4	4.2	1.5	6.9	2.5	2.3	0.6	0.9	0.1	0.6	0.0	0.6
District 1	743 195	98.0	39.5	20.4	27.8	23.3	3.9	1.2	6.5	2.3	2.0	0.5	0.3	0.0	0.4	0.0	0.7
District 2	701 847	97.6	38.7	21.5	27.7	22.9	3.9	1.6	5.7	2.3	2.4	0.9	0.5	0.1	0.2	0.0	0.6
District 3	650 092	97.9	39.4	17.4	26.7	21.1	5.3	1.8	9.1	3.1	2.1	0.3	0.5	0.1	0.6	0.0	0.6
District 4	633 335	98.2	40.1	21.1	26.1	21.1	3.8	1.5	7.0	2.6	1.8	0.3	0.4	0.1	0.5	0.0	0.6
District 5	692 930	97.0	37.2	20.6	28.5	23.4	4.4	1.6	6.4	2.2	3.0	0.8	0.5	0.2	0.9	0.0	0.6
PENNSYLVANIA	12 281 054	96.5	38.9	20.1	28.9	22.4	4.3	1.6	4.3	1.9	3.5	0.6	0.9	0.2	1.2	0.0	0.6
District 1	515 560	96.7	37.3	10.4	31.8	21.6	11.2	5.5	6.1	2.5	3.3	0.3	0.3	0.2	1.4	0.1	0.9
District 2	532 455	94.9	40.9	10.5	26.6	17.7	9.7	4.8	7.2	2.3	5.1	0.0	0.9	0.2	2.8	0.0	1.0
District 3	572 488	97.4	38.1	16.4	31.7	22.4	6.7	2.5	4.5	2.2	2.6	1.1	0.8	0.1	0.0	0.0	0.5
District 4	582 777	98.0	39.4	22.7	29.9	22.2	3.4	1.2	2.7	1.5	2.0	0.1	0.9	0.1	0.4	0.0	0.5
District 5	582 083	93.5	38.0	20.8	26.3	20.6	2.6	1.0	5.9	1.9	6.5	1.6	0.9	0.2	3.4	0.0	0.5
District 6	600 437	96.5	38.8	21.0	28.3	21.5	3.9	1.4	4.5	2.3	3.5	1.0	1.0	0.1	0.8	0.0	0.6
District 7	587 281	96.4	38.2	20.8	30.0	22.2	3.9	1.3	3.5	1.5	3.6	0.2	0.9	0.2	1.5	0.0	0.6

Table F. Congressional Districts 107th Congress

STATE District	Households by type, 2000												Households, 1990		
	Total households	Family households						Nonfamily households			Average household size	Average family size	Total households	Female householder¹	Householder living alone
		Total	With own children under 18 years	Married couple		Female householder¹		Total	Householder living alone						
				Total	With own children under 18 years	Total	With own children under 18 years		Total	65 years and over					
	71	72	73	74	75	76	77	78	79	80	81	82	83	84	85
NEW YORK—Cont'd															
District 25	223 335	64.4	32.0	48.0	21.8	12.4	8.0	35.6	28.6	10.8	2.47	3.06	217 749	11.4	25.7
District 26	224 952	62.6	29.8	47.1	20.5	11.4	7.0	37.4	29.4	10.9	2.45	3.04	213 391	10.5	25.8
District 27	226 542	70.2	33.3	57.2	25.6	9.3	5.6	29.8	24.0	10.5	2.57	3.06	206 855	8.7	21.3
District 28	234 324	62.5	31.1	44.6	20.0	14.3	9.3	37.5	30.2	10.3	2.43	3.07	225 411	13.3	27.8
District 29	229 815	63.9	30.1	47.7	20.7	12.3	7.4	36.1	30.2	11.7	2.42	3.04	225 954	11.5	27.7
District 30	223 660	65.1	30.3	45.5	19.5	15.5	9.0	34.9	29.8	12.5	2.45	3.05	223 708	15.0	27.1
District 31	220 459	67.0	31.4	51.8	21.8	10.7	6.9	33.0	27.1	11.8	2.48	3.01	213 009	10.2	24.7
NORTH CAROLINA	3 132 013	68.9	31.8	52.5	22.6	12.5	7.3	31.1	25.4	8.6	2.49	2.98	2 517 026	12.3	23.7
District 1	227 415	69.2	31.2	45.5	18.3	19.3	11.0	30.8	26.8	11.1	2.52	3.04	202 736	20.8	25.2
District 2	273 133	69.2	33.9	52.1	24.2	13.0	7.7	30.8	24.9	7.8	2.56	3.05	212 833	11.6	24.3
District 3	229 460	71.0	33.4	56.2	24.6	11.2	6.9	29.0	23.3	8.2	2.51	2.96	205 941	11.4	22.1
District 4	303 568	63.7	31.6	50.5	24.1	10.0	6.1	36.3	26.7	5.8	2.45	3.01	215 806	10.0	25.9
District 5	257 913	69.0	30.3	54.4	22.3	10.9	6.1	31.0	26.8	10.1	2.41	2.91	217 545	11.2	25.4
District 6	275 257	70.1	31.2	56.6	23.7	9.7	5.6	29.9	24.8	8.7	2.46	2.93	216 882	8.9	23.2
District 7	271 249	69.2	31.3	51.1	21.0	13.9	8.1	30.8	25.2	8.8	2.49	2.97	184 729	12.0	20.7
District 8	235 881	74.3	37.1	55.9	26.4	14.1	8.4	25.7	21.5	7.5	2.68	3.11	200 750	13.0	20.9
District 9	275 985	68.1	32.0	54.0	24.2	10.5	6.1	31.9	25.6	7.3	2.48	2.99	215 438	9.1	23.4
District 10	257 182	71.2	30.9	57.1	23.3	9.9	5.4	28.8	24.1	9.2	2.48	2.93	212 320	9.1	20.6
District 11	272 478	68.5	27.1	55.1	19.9	9.8	5.4	31.5	26.9	11.6	2.34	2.82	221 168	10.3	24.8
District 12	252 492	65.3	32.2	41.5	18.7	18.8	11.3	34.7	27.4	7.8	2.54	3.09	210 878	21.2	27.5
NORTH DAKOTA	257 152	64.6	31.3	53.4	24.1	7.8	5.3	35.4	29.3	11.5	2.41	3.00	240 878	7.3	26.5
At Large	257 152	64.6	31.3	53.4	24.1	7.8	5.3	35.4	29.3	11.5	2.41	3.00	240 878	7.3	26.5
OHIO	4 445 773	67.3	31.7	51.4	22.4	12.1	7.3	32.7	27.3	10.0	2.49	3.04	4 087 546	11.7	25.0
District 1	223 204	59.1	29.7	38.0	16.6	17.3	11.1	40.9	34.7	10.8	2.36	3.09	223 619	16.4	31.9
District 2	245 751	70.2	34.7	57.6	27.3	9.2	5.5	29.8	25.1	8.9	2.55	3.08	211 251	9.4	22.4
District 3	228 130	64.0	29.6	46.2	19.0	13.9	8.5	36.0	30.4	10.1	2.37	2.96	225 198	13.2	27.1
District 4	225 205	70.3	32.4	56.2	23.6	10.3	6.5	29.7	25.2	10.6	2.52	3.01	210 326	9.7	22.9
District 5	225 250	71.5	33.5	58.3	25.4	9.3	5.8	28.5	24.1	10.2	2.57	3.05	206 472	8.5	21.6
District 6	237 265	70.2	32.7	55.6	24.0	10.6	6.3	29.8	24.8	10.3	2.51	2.99	209 760	10.7	22.8
District 7	232 728	72.2	34.0	58.1	25.4	10.4	6.4	27.8	23.1	9.1	2.56	3.01	205 376	9.9	20.8
District 8	233 779	72.5	35.1	59.1	26.9	9.7	6.0	27.5	22.6	8.6	2.61	3.07	204 772	9.2	20.6
District 9	223 894	64.7	31.6	47.0	20.7	13.6	8.6	35.3	28.9	10.2	2.47	3.06	214 332	12.8	26.2
District 10	236 328	61.3	28.2	45.7	19.9	11.7	6.5	38.7	32.9	11.6	2.38	3.07	228 377	11.3	29.7
District 11	216 521	60.1	29.3	31.7	13.0	24.0	14.4	39.9	34.7	11.8	2.39	3.11	227 289	21.7	32.6
District 12	260 480	65.9	34.1	47.9	22.8	14.1	9.2	34.1	27.8	7.3	2.49	3.07	215 958	14.5	25.4
District 13	236 922	74.5	35.1	61.0	27.5	10.0	5.8	25.5	21.4	8.0	2.67	3.12	198 819	9.7	18.7
District 14	234 093	65.6	30.3	49.2	20.8	12.7	7.6	34.4	28.1	10.2	2.44	3.01	219 388	12.2	25.7
District 15	263 748	59.4	29.1	45.2	20.7	10.3	6.3	40.6	30.4	7.5	2.37	3.00	223 084	9.5	27.9
District 16	228 760	70.6	32.4	56.6	24.3	10.4	6.2	29.4	24.9	10.4	2.57	3.08	209 545	10.0	23.1
District 17	223 232	68.3	29.4	51.4	20.4	13.0	7.2	31.7	27.9	12.4	2.46	3.00	217 693	12.6	24.6
District 18	229 853	70.3	31.4	55.8	23.0	10.5	6.2	29.7	25.7	12.0	2.49	2.98	216 909	10.2	23.9
District 19	240 630	68.5	29.7	55.4	23.1	9.7	4.9	31.5	27.3	11.8	2.46	3.01	219 378	9.2	24.0
OKLAHOMA	1 342 293	68.7	32.4	53.5	23.2	11.4	7.0	31.3	26.7	10.1	2.49	3.02	1 206 135	10.4	25.6
District 1	235 245	65.6	32.5	49.8	22.7	12.0	7.7	34.4	29.1	8.8	2.44	3.04	209 563	11.0	28.3
District 2	227 511	72.9	33.1	58.1	24.4	10.9	6.5	27.1	23.8	10.7	2.57	3.04	196 048	10.0	23.0
District 3	218 611	69.5	30.9	54.6	22.4	11.0	6.4	30.5	26.2	11.6	2.48	2.99	199 724	10.1	25.4
District 4	216 057	70.7	34.5	56.0	25.4	11.0	6.9	29.3	24.3	8.6	2.54	3.02	192 106	9.9	22.8
District 5	239 228	66.3	31.9	52.1	23.1	10.6	6.8	33.7	28.4	9.5	2.43	3.00	209 157	9.8	27.6
District 6	205 641	67.4	31.4	50.2	21.2	12.8	7.9	32.6	28.3	11.4	2.47	3.04	199 537	11.6	26.5
OREGON	1 333 723	65.8	30.8	51.9	22.2	9.8	6.2	34.2	26.1	9.1	2.51	3.02	1 103 313	9.2	25.3
District 1	293 498	63.7	32.0	51.7	24.6	8.4	5.4	36.3	28.2	7.6	2.48	3.07	225 335	8.0	27.3
District 2	271 846	69.4	31.2	55.6	22.3	9.7	6.4	30.6	24.3	10.3	2.52	2.98	219 958	8.5	23.7
District 3	256 369	60.6	29.1	44.2	19.7	11.8	7.0	39.4	28.6	8.7	2.48	3.07	226 909	11.6	28.5
District 4	254 232	66.4	28.8	52.6	20.1	9.8	6.3	33.6	25.5	10.0	2.45	2.91	221 212	9.0	23.7
District 5	257 778	69.0	32.7	55.3	24.1	9.7	6.2	31.0	23.6	9.0	2.61	3.08	209 899	8.9	22.8
PENNSYLVANIA	4 777 003	67.2	30.0	51.7	21.8	11.6	6.2	32.8	27.7	11.6	2.48	3.04	4 495 966	11.3	25.6
District 1	192 395	61.6	29.4	27.8	11.7	27.8	15.1	38.4	32.2	10.9	2.59	3.32	202 744	26.3	29.2
District 2	217 640	53.6	23.6	25.8	9.9	23.0	11.7	46.4	38.4	11.6	2.32	3.14	222 487	21.9	35.3
District 3	218 382	65.1	30.8	43.0	19.2	16.8	9.2	34.9	30.1	12.9	2.55	3.21	218 642	13.1	29.1
District 4	229 541	71.1	30.6	57.7	24.0	10.1	5.2	28.9	25.5	12.5	2.49	3.00	215 984	10.0	23.3
District 5	221 140	66.6	29.2	54.7	22.2	8.2	4.9	33.4	26.3	11.4	2.46	2.96	205 789	8.2	23.8
District 6	233 266	68.3	30.1	53.9	22.3	10.1	5.6	31.7	26.5	12.4	2.48	3.00	218 537	9.4	25.1
District 7	224 353	67.5	30.8	54.4	24.8	9.8	4.6	32.5	27.4	10.9	2.52	3.12	211 077	9.4	24.6

¹No spouse present.

Table F. Congressional Districts 107th Congress

STATE District	Percent change of households, 1990–2000	Total housing units	Occupied housing units (percent)	Vacant housing units		Homeowner vacancy rate (percent)	Rental vacancy rate (percent)	Occupied housing units			Average household size of owner-occupied units	Average household size of renter-occupied units
				Total	For seasonal, recreational, or occasional use			Total	Percent owner-occupied housing units	Percent renter-occupied housing units		
	86	87	88	89	90	91	92	93	94	95	96	97
NEW YORK—Cont'd												
District 25	2.6	243 627	91.7	8.3	1.6	2.0	9.4	223 335	65.8	34.2	2.66	2.12
District 26	5.4	259 741	86.6	13.4	6.3	2.3	7.8	224 952	63.0	37.0	2.58	2.22
District 27	9.5	244 279	92.7	7.3	2.9	1.3	7.3	226 542	76.1	23.9	2.70	2.14
District 28	4.0	250 343	93.6	6.4	0.3	1.6	7.8	234 324	62.1	37.9	2.63	2.11
District 29	1.7	250 477	91.8	8.2	0.8	1.8	10.1	229 815	65.8	34.2	2.62	2.05
District 30	0.0	246 605	90.7	9.3	0.5	1.9	8.7	223 660	65.6	34.4	2.61	2.14
District 31	3.5	264 111	83.5	16.5	9.8	2.2	9.5	220 459	71.6	28.4	2.59	2.21
NORTH CAROLINA	24.4	3 523 944	88.9	11.1	3.8	2.0	8.8	3 132 013	69.4	30.6	2.54	2.37
District 1	12.2	259 633	87.6	12.4	2.6	1.7	7.0	227 415	65.7	34.3	2.55	2.46
District 2	28.3	298 266	91.6	8.4	0.7	2.3	9.0	273 133	68.7	31.3	2.61	2.45
District 3	11.4	289 023	79.4	20.6	13.0	2.1	9.0	229 460	68.7	31.3	2.52	2.48
District 4	40.7	325 100	93.4	6.6	0.5	2.2	8.0	303 568	63.3	36.7	2.60	2.19
District 5	18.6	282 340	91.3	8.7	1.8	1.8	9.3	257 913	72.8	27.2	2.47	2.25
District 6	26.9	297 098	92.6	7.4	1.2	1.8	7.9	275 257	73.8	26.2	2.52	2.29
District 7	46.8	326 076	83.2	16.8	7.7	2.4	13.2	271 249	72.1	27.9	2.54	2.36
District 8	17.5	260 116	90.7	9.3	1.9	1.9	8.8	235 881	70.2	29.8	2.68	2.68
District 9	28.1	294 889	93.6	6.4	0.5	2.0	8.8	275 985	69.4	30.6	2.58	2.25
District 10	21.1	290 060	88.7	11.3	5.2	1.5	7.8	257 182	75.3	24.7	2.51	2.38
District 11	23.2	328 867	82.9	17.1	9.4	1.9	9.8	272 478	75.5	24.5	2.38	2.21
District 12	19.7	272 476	92.7	7.3	0.3	2.2	7.8	252 492	56.2	43.8	2.56	2.50
NORTH DAKOTA	6.8	289 677	88.8	11.2	2.9	2.7	8.2	257 152	66.6	33.4	2.60	2.02
At Large	6.8	289 677	88.8	11.2	2.9	2.7	8.2	257 152	66.6	33.4	2.60	2.02
OHIO	8.8	4 783 051	92.9	7.1	1.0	1.6	8.3	4 445 773	69.1	30.9	2.62	2.19
District 1	-0.2	243 765	91.6	8.4	0.3	1.6	9.5	223 204	53.7	46.3	2.62	2.07
District 2	16.3	259 119	94.8	5.2	0.7	1.2	7.1	245 751	73.8	26.2	2.72	2.08
District 3	1.3	247 302	92.2	7.8	0.4	1.8	9.7	228 130	64.6	35.4	2.48	2.18
District 4	7.1	243 691	92.4	7.6	1.5	1.6	8.7	225 205	74.0	26.0	2.60	2.29
District 5	9.1	249 176	90.4	9.6	4.6	1.5	7.6	225 250	76.9	23.1	2.65	2.29
District 6	13.1	261 691	90.7	9.3	1.8	1.9	8.5	237 265	72.6	27.4	2.58	2.33
District 7	13.3	247 485	94.0	6.0	0.5	1.6	7.5	232 728	72.7	27.3	2.64	2.35
District 8	14.2	247 346	94.5	5.5	0.7	1.5	7.0	233 779	73.5	26.5	2.70	2.35
District 9	4.5	239 291	93.6	6.4	0.3	1.4	7.8	223 894	67.0	33.0	2.62	2.16
District 10	3.5	251 502	94.0	6.0	0.4	1.3	8.1	236 328	66.3	33.7	2.55	2.05
District 11	-4.7	241 395	89.7	10.3	0.3	1.9	10.7	216 521	52.7	47.3	2.57	2.19
District 12	20.6	281 548	92.5	7.5	0.4	2.0	9.1	260 480	60.8	39.2	2.67	2.20
District 13	19.2	248 531	95.3	4.7	0.6	1.3	7.3	236 922	79.1	20.9	2.78	2.29
District 14	6.7	248 507	94.2	5.8	0.4	1.5	7.8	234 093	68.2	31.8	2.58	2.14
District 15	18.2	279 735	94.3	5.7	0.4	1.5	7.2	263 748	60.0	40.0	2.54	2.12
District 16	9.2	242 655	94.3	5.7	0.7	1.4	7.6	228 760	72.8	27.2	2.69	2.24
District 17	2.5	241 009	92.6	7.4	0.6	1.7	9.5	223 232	73.5	26.5	2.56	2.18
District 18	6.0	255 443	90.0	10.0	2.9	1.7	8.0	229 853	75.0	25.0	2.56	2.28
District 19	9.7	253 860	94.8	5.2	1.2	1.2	7.4	240 630	76.2	23.8	2.59	2.03
OKLAHOMA	11.3	1 514 400	88.6	11.4	2.1	2.5	10.6	1 342 293	68.4	31.6	2.55	2.36
District 1	12.3	252 804	93.1	6.9	0.4	1.6	8.7	235 245	62.5	37.5	2.56	2.25
District 2	16.0	266 599	85.3	14.7	5.8	2.4	9.6	227 511	75.9	24.1	2.60	2.48
District 3	9.5	254 458	85.9	14.1	3.7	2.7	10.8	218 611	71.6	28.4	2.52	2.38
District 4	12.5	239 841	90.1	9.9	0.7	2.8	11.3	216 057	68.2	31.8	2.59	2.42
District 5	14.4	262 122	91.3	8.7	0.7	2.1	10.3	239 228	66.4	33.6	2.53	2.23
District 6	3.1	238 576	86.2	13.8	1.2	3.6	13.0	205 641	66.2	33.8	2.48	2.45
OREGON	20.9	1 452 709	91.8	8.2	2.5	2.3	7.3	1 333 723	64.3	35.7	2.59	2.36
District 1	30.2	315 425	93.0	7.0	1.5	2.4	7.0	293 498	60.4	39.6	2.67	2.19
District 2	23.6	305 018	89.1	10.9	4.7	2.2	7.7	271 846	68.4	31.6	2.54	2.47
District 3	13.0	272 768	94.0	6.0	0.8	2.3	6.5	256 369	60.3	39.7	2.58	2.34
District 4	14.9	274 811	92.5	7.5	1.6	2.1	7.8	254 232	66.1	33.9	2.50	2.33
District 5	22.8	284 687	90.5	9.5	3.9	2.6	7.8	257 778	66.3	33.7	2.66	2.50
PENNSYLVANIA	6.3	5 249 750	91.0	9.0	2.8	1.6	7.2	4 777 003	71.3	28.7	2.62	2.12
District 1	-5.1	224 129	85.8	14.2	0.2	2.2	7.0	192 395	56.6	43.4	2.70	2.45
District 2	-2.2	246 148	88.4	11.6	0.3	1.9	7.8	217 640	53.3	46.7	2.55	2.06
District 3	-0.1	234 029	93.3	6.7	0.2	1.8	5.8	218 382	67.9	32.1	2.71	2.23
District 4	6.3	244 744	93.8	6.2	0.4	1.6	8.2	229 541	78.0	22.0	2.61	2.06
District 5	7.5	274 681	80.5	19.5	14.6	1.6	6.1	221 140	72.4	27.6	2.57	2.17
District 6	6.7	251 561	92.7	7.3	0.7	2.0	7.4	233 266	74.0	26.0	2.59	2.18
District 7	6.3	233 364	96.1	3.9	0.3	1.1	5.7	224 353	74.1	25.9	2.73	1.95

Table F. Congressional Districts 107th Congress

	Population, 2000				Population, 1990			Population and population characteristics, 2000					
								Race (percent)					
								One race					
STATE District	Land area, 2000[1] (sq km)	Total persons	Rank	Per square kilometer	Land area, 1990[1] (sq km)	Total persons	Rank	Per square kilometer	White	Black or African American	American Indian or Alaska Native	Asian	Native Hawaiian and other Pacific Islander	Some other race
	1	2	3	4	5	6	7	8	9	10	11	12	13	14
PENNSYLVANIA—Cont'd														
District 8	1 620.9	624 248	X	385.1	1 622.0	565 787	X	349.0	92.4	3.3	0.1	2.4	0.0	0.8
District 9	17 261.0	588 138	X	34.1	17 262.0	565 803	X	33.0	97.0	1.6	0.1	0.3	0.0	0.3
District 10	14 403.5	613 459	X	42.6	14 406.0	565 681	X	39.0	94.9	2.6	0.2	0.6	0.0	0.8
District 11	6 147.5	579 470	X	94.3	6 149.0	565 913	X	92.0	96.2	1.9	0.1	0.6	0.0	0.5
District 12	10 915.4	556 856	X	51.0	10 911.0	565 794	X	52.0	97.2	1.7	0.1	0.3	0.0	0.2
District 13	946.7	628 203	X	663.6	947.0	565 793	X	597.0	85.9	7.9	0.1	4.2	0.0	0.7
District 14	501.3	529 299	X	1 055.9	501.0	565 787	X	1 129.0	77.3	18.4	0.2	2.3	0.0	0.5
District 15	2 045.9	612 265	X	299.3	2 046.0	565 810	X	277.0	89.4	3.1	0.2	1.7	0.0	4.0
District 16	3 313.9	647 575	X	195.4	3 314.0	565 835	X	171.0	88.7	5.4	0.2	1.6	0.0	2.7
District 17	3 847.6	608 390	X	158.1	3 848.0	565 742	X	147.0	87.9	7.6	0.1	1.5	0.0	1.5
District 18	685.1	535 432	X	781.5	685.0	565 781	X	826.0	86.9	10.5	0.1	1.2	0.0	0.3
District 19	4 964.1	632 862	X	127.5	4 965.0	565 831	X	114.0	93.5	3.1	0.2	0.9	0.0	1.2
District 20	5 534.0	570 336	X	103.1	5 534.0	565 815	X	102.0	94.9	3.4	0.1	0.7	0.0	0.2
District 21	7 210.9	581 440	X	80.6	7 212.0	565 802	X	79.0	93.4	4.4	0.1	0.5	0.0	0.5
RHODE ISLAND	2 706.0	1 048 319	X	387.4	2 707.0	1 003 464	X	370.7	85.0	4.5	0.5	2.3	0.1	5.0
District 1	838.0	510 287	X	608.9	838.0	501 677	X	599.0	86.4	4.2	0.3	1.8	0.0	4.4
District 2	1 868.3	538 032	X	288.0	1 868.0	501 787	X	269.0	83.7	4.7	0.6	2.7	0.1	5.6
SOUTH CAROLINA	77 983.0	4 012 012	X	51.4	77 988.0	3 486 310	X	44.7	67.2	29.5	0.3	0.9	0.0	1.0
District 1	8 168.8	684 765	X	83.8	8 169.0	581 133	X	71.0	74.9	21.0	0.4	1.2	0.1	1.1
District 2	12 973.1	731 022	X	56.3	12 974.0	581 099	X	45.0	68.2	27.7	0.3	1.2	0.1	1.4
District 3	14 512.1	670 139	X	46.2	14 508.0	581 116	X	40.0	76.7	20.9	0.2	0.6	0.0	0.8
District 4	5 660.0	670 335	X	118.4	5 662.0	581 113	X	103.0	76.2	19.8	0.2	1.3	0.0	1.3
District 5	17 687.2	655 525	X	37.1	17 689.0	581 131	X	33.0	66.5	30.6	0.6	0.5	0.0	0.8
District 6	18 982.0	600 226	X	31.6	18 986.0	581 111	X	31.0	37.2	60.9	0.2	0.4	0.0	0.5
SOUTH DAKOTA	196 540.0	754 844	X	3.8	196 575.0	696 004	X	3.5	88.7	0.6	8.3	0.6	0.0	0.5
At Large	196 540.3	754 844	X	3.8	196 571.0	696 004	X	4.0	88.7	0.6	8.3	0.6	0.0	0.5
TENNESSEE	106 752.0	5 689 283	X	53.3	106 759.0	4 877 203	X	45.7	80.2	16.4	0.3	1.0	0.0	1.0
District 1	10 923.4	628 443	X	57.5	10 924.0	541 875	X	50.0	96.2	2.0	0.2	0.4	0.0	0.4
District 2	6 443.0	636 383	X	98.8	6 443.0	541 864	X	84.0	90.7	6.3	0.3	1.0	0.0	0.6
District 3	11 171.7	595 855	X	53.3	11 176.0	541 866	X	49.0	85.2	11.9	0.3	0.9	0.0	0.6
District 4	24 192.7	635 355	X	26.3	24 191.0	541 868	X	22.0	94.1	3.4	0.3	0.3	0.0	1.0
District 5	2 278.0	607 853	X	266.8	2 278.0	541 910	X	238.0	68.3	24.9	0.3	2.2	0.1	2.3
District 6	13 898.4	738 663	X	53.1	13 899.0	541 977	X	39.0	91.0	5.7	0.3	1.0	0.0	1.0
District 7	17 115.7	728 956	X	42.6	17 117.0	541 937	X	32.0	80.3	15.5	0.3	1.4	0.1	1.1
District 8	20 096.8	604 894	X	30.1	20 072.0	541 907	X	27.0	74.1	23.5	0.3	0.5	0.0	0.7
District 9	632.2	512 881	X	811.3	657.0	541 981	X	825.0	30.1	66.2	0.2	1.2	0.0	1.3
TEXAS	678 051.0	20 851 820	X	30.8	678 358.0	16 986 335	X	25.0	71.0	11.5	0.6	2.7	0.1	11.7
District 1	29 949.4	622 475	X	20.8	29 959.0	566 217	X	19.0	77.1	17.0	0.6	0.4	0.0	3.6
District 2	36 763.4	669 591	X	18.2	36 767.0	566 217	X	15.0	77.6	15.5	0.5	0.5	0.0	4.6
District 3	945.0	835 040	X	883.6	945.0	567 648	X	601.0	72.9	9.6	0.5	8.0	0.1	6.4
District 4	17 670.7	707 329	X	40.0	17 674.0	566 217	X	32.0	85.1	7.7	0.7	0.6	0.0	4.2
District 5	17 026.4	657 495	X	38.6	17 048.0	567 457	X	33.0	67.0	17.4	0.6	1.5	0.0	11.3
District 6	2 157.5	759 418	X	352.0	2 158.0	565 469	X	262.0	81.8	8.0	0.5	3.7	0.1	3.7
District 7	1 206.9	772 147	X	639.8	1 207.0	564 900	X	468.0	72.3	7.5	0.4	7.2	0.1	9.5
District 8	7 990.4	776 623	X	97.2	7 991.0	565 090	X	71.0	85.7	5.3	0.4	2.5	0.1	4.3
District 9	5 316.5	636 960	X	119.8	5 317.0	564 322	X	106.0	67.3	21.7	0.4	2.7	0.0	5.9
District 10	2 068.5	791 117	X	382.5	2 069.0	566 217	X	274.0	67.5	9.5	0.6	4.6	0.1	14.9
District 11	29 261.8	663 275	X	22.7	29 262.0	566 217	X	19.0	70.3	16.4	0.6	1.5	0.2	8.2
District 12	4 462.9	661 753	X	148.3	4 463.0	566 217	X	127.0	74.4	8.6	0.7	2.1	0.2	11.6
District 13	82 231.1	597 401	X	7.3	82 250.0	566 217	X	7.0	74.3	8.5	0.8	1.4	0.0	12.6
District 14	39 824.0	688 604	X	17.3	39 829.0	566 217	X	14.0	75.7	9.1	0.5	0.7	0.0	11.8
District 15	21 887.9	780 310	X	35.7	21 886.0	566 217	X	26.0	76.8	1.8	0.5	0.6	0.0	18.1
District 16	1 256.4	620 847	X	494.1	1 256.0	566 217	X	451.0	74.3	3.0	0.8	1.0	0.1	17.5
District 17	72 843.1	618 958	X	8.5	72 894.0	566 217	X	8.0	84.1	4.0	0.6	0.5	0.0	8.8
District 18	406.4	606 441	X	1 492.2	406.0	567 364	X	1 396.0	38.8	40.4	0.4	3.1	0.0	14.7
District 19	52 282.1	607 535	X	11.6	52 286.0	566 217	X	11.0	81.0	3.0	0.7	1.0	0.0	12.3
District 20	753.3	624 384	X	828.9	753.0	566 217	X	752.0	66.3	5.9	1.0	1.4	0.1	21.2
District 21	44 845.1	801 078	X	17.9	44 851.0	566 217	X	13.0	86.4	3.2	0.5	1.6	0.1	6.1
District 22	4 334.0	784 759	X	181.1	4 335.0	568 160	X	131.0	62.8	14.7	0.4	10.0	0.0	9.3
District 23	151 274.6	762 627	X	5.0	151 286.0	566 217	X	4.0	77.0	2.7	0.6	1.0	0.1	15.9
District 24	5 319.2	680 808	X	128.0	5 484.0	567 454	X	104.0	55.1	21.2	0.7	2.6	0.1	17.4
District 25	748.7	662 264	X	884.6	749.0	564 724	X	754.0	53.5	23.8	0.4	5.4	0.1	13.9
District 26	1 771.2	845 541	X	477.4	1 771.0	564 843	X	319.0	79.7	6.0	0.5	4.7	0.0	6.9
District 27	10 554.9	664 428	X	62.9	10 557.0	566 217	X	54.0	76.3	2.3	0.5	0.8	0.1	17.3

[1] Dry land or land partially or temporarily covered by water.

Table F. Congressional Districts 107th Congress

STATE District	Population and population characteristics, 2000 (cont'd) Race (percent) (cont'd) Race alone or in combination								Population and population characteristics, 1990 Race (percent)				
	Two or more races	White	Black	American Indian or Alaska Native	Asian	Native Hawaiian and other Pacific Islander	Some other race	Hispanic[1]	White	Black or African American	American Indian or Alaska Native	Asian and Pacific Islander	Hispanic[1]
	15	16	17	18	19	20	21	22	23	24	25	26	27
PENNSYLVANIA—Cont'd													
District 8	1.0	93.2	3.6	0.4	2.7	0.1	1.1	2.3	95.0	2.8	0.1	1.6	1.6
District 9	0.6	97.6	1.8	0.3	0.5	0.0	0.5	0.9	98.3	1.2	0.1	0.3	0.4
District 10	0.9	95.7	3.0	0.5	0.8	0.0	1.1	2.1	98.1	1.1	0.1	0.5	0.8
District 11	0.7	96.8	2.1	0.3	0.8	0.0	0.7	1.7	98.4	0.9	0.1	0.4	0.7
District 12	0.5	97.7	1.9	0.3	0.4	0.0	0.3	0.6	98.3	1.3	0.1	0.3	0.4
District 13	1.1	86.8	8.5	0.4	4.5	0.1	1.1	2.0	91.0	6.1	0.1	2.5	1.2
District 14	1.3	78.3	19.2	0.5	2.6	0.1	0.8	1.1	80.5	17.8	0.1	1.3	0.8
District 15	1.6	90.8	3.6	0.4	1.9	0.1	4.8	8.2	94.0	2.2	0.1	1.1	4.7
District 16	1.3	89.8	6.0	0.4	1.8	0.1	3.2	5.9	91.4	5.2	0.1	1.1	3.8
District 17	1.3	89.0	8.3	0.4	1.7	0.1	1.9	3.4	91.3	6.7	0.1	1.0	1.9
District 18	1.0	87.7	11.1	0.4	1.4	0.0	0.5	0.7	91.2	7.8	0.1	0.7	0.6
District 19	1.0	94.4	3.6	0.4	1.1	0.1	1.5	2.7	95.9	2.6	0.1	0.7	1.3
District 20	0.8	95.6	3.8	0.3	0.8	0.0	0.3	0.6	96.2	3.2	0.1	0.5	0.5
District 21	1.0	94.3	4.9	0.4	0.7	0.1	0.7	1.4	95.2	3.9	0.1	0.4	0.8
RHODE ISLAND	2.7	86.9	5.5	1.0	2.7	0.2	6.6	8.7	91.4	3.9	0.4	1.8	4.6
District 1	2.9	88.4	5.4	0.8	2.2	0.2	6.1	7.0	92.8	3.3	0.3	1.3	3.8
District 2	2.5	85.4	5.7	1.2	3.2	0.2	7.0	10.2	90.0	4.5	0.5	2.4	5.3
SOUTH CAROLINA	1.0	68.0	29.9	0.7	1.1	0.1	1.3	2.4	69.0	29.8	0.2	0.6	0.9
District 1	1.3	76.0	21.4	0.8	1.6	0.1	1.4	2.5	78.0	20.1	0.3	1.2	1.4
District 2	1.2	69.1	28.2	0.7	1.5	0.1	1.7	3.2	73.2	25.1	0.2	1.0	1.4
District 3	0.8	77.4	21.2	0.6	0.7	0.1	1.0	1.9	78.3	21.1	0.1	0.4	0.5
District 4	1.1	77.1	20.2	0.5	1.6	0.1	1.7	3.2	79.3	19.7	0.1	0.7	0.8
District 5	0.8	67.2	31.0	1.0	0.7	0.1	1.0	1.8	68.2	30.8	0.4	0.4	0.6
District 6	0.7	37.7	61.3	0.5	0.6	0.1	0.7	1.4	37.2	62.2	0.2	0.3	0.6
SOUTH DAKOTA	1.3	89.9	0.9	9.0	0.8	0.1	0.7	1.4	91.6	0.5	7.3	0.4	0.8
At Large	1.3	89.9	0.9	9.0	0.8	0.1	0.7	1.4	91.6	0.5	7.3	0.4	0.8
TENNESSEE	1.1	81.2	16.8	0.7	1.2	0.1	1.3	2.2	83.0	16.0	0.2	0.7	0.7
District 1	0.8	97.0	2.2	0.6	0.5	0.0	0.5	1.0	97.5	1.9	0.2	0.3	0.4
District 2	1.1	91.7	6.6	0.8	1.2	0.1	0.8	1.4	92.3	6.6	0.2	0.7	0.6
District 3	1.1	86.2	12.3	0.8	1.1	0.1	0.8	1.5	87.4	11.6	0.2	0.6	0.6
District 4	0.9	95.0	3.6	0.7	0.4	0.1	1.1	2.1	95.8	3.6	0.2	0.2	0.4
District 5	1.9	69.8	25.6	0.7	2.6	0.1	3.1	4.5	75.4	22.8	0.2	1.3	0.9
District 6	0.9	91.9	6.0	0.6	1.2	0.1	1.2	2.2	93.3	5.7	0.2	0.6	0.6
District 7	1.4	81.4	16.0	0.7	1.8	0.1	1.4	2.5	86.2	12.4	0.2	0.9	1.1
District 8	0.9	74.9	23.8	0.6	0.7	0.1	0.9	1.6	79.5	19.7	0.2	0.4	0.7
District 9	0.9	30.8	66.6	0.5	1.4	0.1	1.7	2.8	39.7	59.2	0.2	0.7	0.7
TEXAS	2.5	73.1	12.0	1.0	3.1	0.1	13.3	32.0	75.2	11.9	0.4	1.9	25.5
District 1	1.3	78.2	17.3	1.1	0.5	0.1	4.1	7.3	79.5	18.1	0.4	0.3	3.2
District 2	1.3	78.8	15.8	1.0	0.6	0.1	5.2	10.1	79.4	16.7	0.4	0.3	5.6
District 3	2.5	75.0	10.1	1.0	8.7	0.1	7.7	15.4	83.4	7.4	0.4	4.5	8.3
District 4	1.7	86.6	8.0	1.4	0.8	0.1	4.8	8.8	88.3	8.4	0.6	0.4	4.3
District 5	2.2	68.9	17.8	1.1	1.7	0.1	12.7	23.0	74.6	15.8	0.5	1.2	14.4
District 6	2.1	83.6	8.5	1.1	4.3	0.2	4.6	9.6	90.0	5.1	0.4	2.3	5.7
District 7	3.0	74.8	8.0	0.8	8.1	0.1	11.4	23.6	80.4	6.1	0.3	5.5	16.4
District 8	1.8	87.2	5.6	0.8	2.9	0.1	5.2	11.3	89.6	5.1	0.3	1.9	7.1
District 9	1.9	68.9	22.1	0.8	3.1	0.1	7.0	14.4	72.4	21.7	0.3	2.1	9.4
District 10	2.9	69.9	10.1	1.1	5.2	0.2	16.6	28.8	72.9	11.2	0.4	2.9	21.4
District 11	2.7	72.4	17.3	1.2	2.1	0.4	9.4	16.4	76.0	15.9	0.4	1.6	12.3
District 12	2.5	76.6	9.0	1.3	2.5	0.2	13.0	25.0	80.1	8.0	0.5	1.9	16.3
District 13	2.3	76.3	9.0	1.5	1.7	0.1	13.9	24.6	78.9	8.0	0.6	1.2	19.4
District 14	2.1	77.5	9.5	1.0	1.0	0.1	13.1	27.9	77.7	10.6	0.3	0.6	23.6
District 15	2.2	78.9	1.9	0.7	0.7	0.1	20.0	78.9	75.5	1.1	0.2	0.3	74.5
District 16	3.2	77.2	3.4	1.1	1.4	0.2	20.0	78.0	76.5	3.6	0.4	1.1	70.4
District 17	1.9	85.8	4.3	1.2	0.8	0.1	9.8	20.7	85.7	3.5	0.4	0.5	17.2
District 18	2.6	40.9	40.9	0.8	3.4	0.1	16.6	33.4	40.2	44.7	0.2	2.7	23.4
District 19	2.0	82.8	3.3	1.1	1.2	0.1	13.6	26.1	86.1	2.5	0.4	0.9	19.6
District 20	4.2	69.9	6.5	1.5	2.0	0.2	24.3	67.0	71.8	5.8	0.4	1.3	60.7
District 21	2.1	88.3	3.6	1.0	2.1	0.1	7.1	18.3	91.3	2.5	0.4	1.0	14.1
District 22	2.8	65.0	15.2	0.8	10.8	0.1	11.0	22.3	71.5	12.7	0.3	6.9	17.0
District 23	2.7	79.4	3.0	1.0	1.3	0.1	18.0	66.3	73.9	2.9	0.4	0.7	62.5
District 24	2.9	57.6	21.7	1.2	2.9	0.2	19.4	34.5	64.0	20.4	0.6	2.1	21.0
District 25	2.9	55.8	24.4	0.8	5.9	0.2	16.0	31.1	63.3	23.0	0.3	3.8	18.6
District 26	2.2	81.6	6.4	0.9	5.2	0.1	8.1	17.1	86.7	5.4	0.4	2.9	9.5
District 27	2.7	78.7	2.5	0.9	1.0	0.1	19.5	70.5	78.7	2.4	0.3	0.6	66.2

[1] Hispanic persons may be of any race.

Table F. Congressional Districts 107th Congress

STATE District	Population and population characteristics, 2000										
	Age (percent)										
	Under 5 years	5 to 17 years	18 to 24 years	25 to 34 years	35 to 44 years	45 to 54 years	55 to 64 years	65 to 74 years	75 years and over	Median age (years)	Percent Female
	28	29	30	31	32	33	34	35	36	37	38
PENNSYLVANIA—Cont'd											
District 8	6.4	19.3	7.0	12.7	18.1	15.0	9.2	6.7	5.6	37.7	50.9
District 9	5.9	17.6	8.3	12.7	15.3	13.9	10.1	8.4	7.8	38.6	50.9
District 10	5.5	18.3	8.3	11.4	15.7	14.1	10.0	8.6	8.1	39.2	51.4
District 11	5.1	16.8	8.4	12.0	15.4	14.0	9.9	9.1	9.3	40.1	51.6
District 12	5.2	16.6	9.3	11.6	15.1	14.4	9.8	9.0	8.9	40.1	51.3
District 13	6.3	17.8	7.1	13.2	16.9	14.4	9.2	7.4	7.8	38.4	51.8
District 14	5.4	15.5	11.7	13.7	15.0	13.4	8.6	8.2	8.6	37.6	52.5
District 15	5.9	18.0	8.5	12.4	16.5	14.1	9.0	7.7	7.9	38.3	51.5
District 16	7.0	20.0	9.1	12.5	16.4	13.8	8.6	6.3	6.2	35.9	51.0
District 17	6.2	18.3	7.8	13.1	16.5	14.6	9.1	7.5	6.9	37.9	51.6
District 18	5.5	16.5	6.4	11.9	15.7	14.5	9.7	9.7	10.0	41.4	53.1
District 19	5.9	18.0	8.9	12.9	16.7	14.4	9.3	7.3	6.8	37.7	50.9
District 20	5.5	16.7	7.5	11.9	15.9	15.0	9.9	8.7	8.9	40.6	51.8
District 21	6.0	18.2	10.2	12.1	15.2	13.8	9.1	7.7	7.8	37.5	51.3
RHODE ISLAND	6.1	17.5	10.2	13.4	16.2	13.5	8.5	7.0	7.5	36.7	52.0
District 1	5.9	16.8	10.7	13.5	15.9	13.3	8.5	7.3	8.1	37.0	52.3
District 2	6.3	18.3	9.7	13.3	16.6	13.8	8.4	6.7	6.9	36.5	51.6
SOUTH CAROLINA	6.6	18.6	10.2	14.0	15.6	13.7	9.3	6.7	5.4	35.4	51.4
District 1	6.4	17.9	10.3	14.7	15.8	13.6	9.5	7.0	4.8	35.4	51.0
District 2	6.7	18.4	10.7	14.8	16.0	13.5	8.7	6.3	4.9	34.7	50.9
District 3	6.4	17.9	10.3	13.2	15.1	13.6	9.9	7.4	6.0	36.4	51.3
District 4	6.7	18.0	9.4	14.7	16.0	13.9	9.3	6.5	5.6	35.8	51.4
District 5	6.9	19.5	9.1	13.8	15.7	13.9	9.3	6.5	5.3	35.5	51.7
District 6	6.5	19.9	11.2	12.5	14.7	13.8	9.1	6.7	5.5	34.9	52.4
SOUTH DAKOTA	6.8	20.1	10.3	12.1	15.3	12.9	8.3	7.0	7.3	35.6	50.4
At Large	6.8	20.1	10.3	12.1	15.3	12.9	8.3	7.0	7.3	35.6	50.4
TENNESSEE	6.6	18.0	9.6	14.3	15.9	13.8	9.4	6.7	5.6	35.9	51.3
District 1	5.8	16.3	8.6	13.8	15.4	14.5	11.2	8.0	6.4	38.6	51.2
District 2	6.1	16.7	10.3	14.0	15.8	14.2	9.8	7.1	6.0	36.8	51.5
District 3	6.0	17.1	9.3	13.4	15.3	14.6	10.2	7.6	6.5	37.8	51.6
District 4	6.2	17.6	8.7	13.3	15.0	13.7	10.9	8.1	6.3	37.7	50.9
District 5	6.7	15.9	11.5	17.3	16.4	13.1	7.9	5.9	5.3	34.2	51.5
District 6	6.9	19.2	9.6	14.1	17.0	14.2	8.9	5.6	4.5	35.1	50.7
District 7	7.2	19.6	9.1	14.9	16.9	13.9	8.4	5.6	4.4	34.5	50.6
District 8	6.8	19.1	9.4	13.2	15.5	13.4	9.4	7.0	6.3	36.0	51.6
District 9	7.6	20.3	10.8	15.2	14.9	12.5	7.3	5.9	5.4	32.2	52.7
TEXAS	7.8	20.4	10.5	15.2	15.9	12.5	7.7	5.5	4.5	32.3	50.4
District 1	6.5	18.8	10.0	12.1	14.5	13.1	9.9	7.9	7.3	36.9	51.0
District 2	6.7	19.0	10.1	13.1	15.1	12.8	9.5	7.6	6.0	35.8	49.2
District 3	8.2	20.3	8.6	17.6	19.0	13.4	7.0	3.5	2.4	32.4	50.4
District 4	6.9	19.9	8.9	12.9	15.9	13.3	9.3	6.9	6.0	35.9	50.8
District 5	7.5	18.5	9.9	17.0	16.1	11.9	7.8	6.1	5.3	33.3	48.9
District 6	7.4	20.2	8.4	15.7	18.6	14.5	7.8	4.3	3.1	34.0	50.8
District 7	7.8	19.7	8.6	17.6	18.3	14.0	7.0	3.9	2.9	32.8	50.4
District 8	7.0	20.5	12.4	13.2	16.5	14.2	8.2	4.7	3.4	32.7	50.5
District 9	7.0	19.5	9.5	14.1	16.6	13.7	8.3	6.2	5.1	35.0	50.2
District 10	7.3	16.5	15.0	20.1	16.6	12.1	5.8	3.5	3.0	30.1	48.8
District 11	7.7	19.7	13.1	14.6	14.5	11.2	7.6	6.0	5.7	31.3	50.5
District 12	7.8	20.0	10.3	15.5	16.1	12.1	7.7	5.6	5.0	32.6	50.1
District 13	7.2	19.5	12.3	13.2	14.4	11.6	8.3	7.1	6.4	33.3	49.9
District 14	7.0	20.2	10.8	12.2	15.2	13.2	8.7	6.8	6.0	34.9	50.3
District 15	9.4	23.8	11.3	14.7	13.3	10.4	6.8	5.8	4.6	28.7	50.3
District 16	8.5	22.9	10.7	14.2	14.6	11.5	7.3	6.0	4.2	30.4	51.9
District 17	6.4	19.3	10.1	12.2	14.8	12.5	9.4	7.9	7.2	36.3	49.9
District 18	7.6	19.3	11.2	17.0	15.7	12.2	7.5	5.4	4.1	31.8	49.7
District 19	7.2	20.3	12.1	13.0	15.1	12.5	8.0	6.5	5.3	32.9	51.0
District 20	8.4	20.2	12.6	16.6	14.7	10.8	6.7	5.4	4.6	30.0	50.9
District 21	6.8	19.2	7.8	13.2	16.7	14.0	9.0	7.0	6.2	36.8	51.3
District 22	7.6	21.7	8.4	14.7	18.6	14.5	7.4	4.2	2.8	33.5	49.8
District 23	8.7	23.8	9.8	14.1	14.9	12.0	7.4	5.3	3.9	30.5	51.0
District 24	8.9	22.0	11.3	16.1	15.4	11.5	6.8	4.4	3.5	29.8	50.0
District 25	8.9	20.5	10.9	17.3	15.9	12.4	6.5	4.2	3.4	30.4	51.1
District 26	8.1	18.5	9.1	18.5	18.8	13.2	7.0	3.8	3.1	32.7	50.1
District 27	8.6	22.5	10.5	13.6	14.1	11.9	7.6	6.3	4.9	31.0	51.6

Table F. Congressional Districts 107th Congress

STATE District	Under 5 years	5 to 17 years	18 to 24 years	25 to 34 years	35 to 44 years	45 to 54 years	55 to 64 years	65 to 74 years	75 years and over	Percent Female	2000	1990	1980	1990–2000	1980–1990
	Population and population characteristics, 1990										Population—change, 1980–2000				
	Age (percent)										Total persons			Percent change	
	39	40	41	42	43	44	45	46	47	48	49	50	51	52	53
PENNSYLVANIA—Cont'd															
District 8	7.4	18.2	9.1	17.8	16.6	11.1	9.0	6.7	4.2	50.7	624 248	565 787	NA	10.3	NA
District 9	6.6	18.2	9.8	15.1	14.4	10.7	9.9	8.9	6.4	51.5	588 138	565 803	NA	3.9	NA
District 10	6.7	17.5	9.5	15.0	14.3	10.2	9.9	9.7	7.1	52.0	613 459	565 681	NA	8.4	NA
District 11	6.0	16.0	10.0	14.5	14.0	10.1	10.6	10.7	8.0	52.5	579 470	565 913	NA	2.4	NA
District 12	6.0	17.7	10.3	14.3	14.4	10.1	10.3	10.1	6.9	51.9	550 856	565 794	NA	-1.6	NA
District 13	6.7	15.7	8.9	16.8	15.6	11.0	9.9	8.7	6.7	52.1	628 203	565 793	NA	11.0	NA
District 14	6.3	14.3	11.9	16.8	14.2	9.2	9.9	10.0	7.5	53.4	529 299	565 787	NA	-6.4	NA
District 15	6.7	16.4	10.1	16.4	15.3	10.3	9.7	8.8	6.2	51.6	612 265	565 810	NA	8.2	NA
District 16	7.8	18.5	10.7	16.6	15.6	10.4	8.3	6.9	5.1	51.1	647 575	565 835	NA	14.4	NA
District 17	7.1	17.4	9.5	17.1	15.8	10.4	9.3	7.9	5.6	51.7	608 390	565 742	NA	7.5	NA
District 18	6.2	14.7	8.1	16.1	14.7	10.3	11.4	11.2	7.4	53.2	535 432	565 781	NA	-5.4	NA
District 19	6.7	17.0	10.9	16.6	15.6	10.7	9.1	7.7	5.6	51.2	632 862	565 831	NA	11.8	NA
District 20	6.0	16.8	9.0	14.8	15.3	10.8	10.6	10.1	6.7	52.3	570 336	565 815	NA	0.8	NA
District 21	6.8	18.1	11.6	15.0	14.4	10.0	9.4	8.8	6.0	51.6	581 440	565 802	NA	2.8	NA
RHODE ISLAND	6.7	15.8	12.0	17.3	14.7	9.6	8.9	8.5	6.5	52.0	1 048 319	1 003 464	947 154	4.5	5.9
District 1	6.5	15.2	12.5	17.4	14.2	9.5	9.1	8.7	6.9	52.2	510 287	501 677	NA	1.7	NA
District 2	6.8	16.4	11.5	17.2	15.2	9.7	8.7	8.3	6.1	51.9	538 032	501 787	NA	7.2	NA
SOUTH CAROLINA	7.4	19.0	11.7	17.0	15.0	10.2	8.4	7.1	4.3	51.6	4 012 012	3 486 310	3 120 729	15.1	11.7
District 1	8.0	18.4	12.2	19.6	15.2	9.5	7.7	6.2	3.1	50.2	684 765	581 133	NA	17.8	NA
District 2	7.4	18.4	12.4	18.3	15.6	9.8	7.8	6.5	3.7	51.0	731 022	581 099	NA	25.8	NA
District 3	6.7	18.4	11.8	15.5	14.6	10.8	9.3	7.8	5.1	51.7	670 139	581 116	NA	15.3	NA
District 4	6.9	17.8	10.9	16.6	15.4	11.1	8.9	7.4	4.9	52.0	670 335	581 113	NA	15.4	NA
District 5	7.3	19.9	10.7	16.2	15.0	10.5	8.5	7.2	4.6	51.9	655 525	581 131	NA	12.8	NA
District 6	7.8	21.3	11.9	15.5	14.2	9.4	8.1	7.2	4.6	52.8	600 226	581 111	NA	3.3	NA
SOUTH DAKOTA	7.8	20.7	9.8	15.7	13.7	9.0	8.6	7.8	6.9	50.8	754 844	696 004	690 768	8.5	0.8
At Large	7.8	20.7	9.8	15.7	13.7	9.0	8.6	7.8	6.9	50.8	754 844	696 004	NA	8.5	NA
TENNESSEE	6.8	18.1	10.8	16.7	15.2	10.8	8.9	7.3	5.4	51.8	5 689 283	4 877 203	4 591 023	16.7	6.2
District 1	5.8	16.9	10.5	15.3	15.1	12.2	10.2	8.3	5.7	51.6	628 443	541 875	NA	16.0	NA
District 2	6.4	16.7	11.7	16.6	15.5	11.1	9.1	7.7	5.4	52.1	636 383	541 864	NA	17.4	NA
District 3	6.4	17.9	10.1	15.6	15.3	11.3	9.7	8.0	5.7	52.1	595 855	541 866	NA	10.0	NA
District 4	6.4	18.7	9.9	14.9	14.3	11.6	9.9	8.3	6.0	51.6	635 355	541 868	NA	17.3	NA
District 5	7.1	16.1	11.5	20.2	15.4	9.8	8.3	6.6	5.0	52.4	607 853	541 910	NA	12.2	NA
District 6	6.9	19.4	10.7	16.3	16.2	11.3	8.1	6.3	4.6	51.0	738 663	541 977	NA	36.3	NA
District 7	7.4	19.3	10.6	17.6	16.3	10.6	7.9	5.8	4.3	50.7	728 956	541 937	NA	34.5	NA
District 8	6.9	18.9	11.1	15.4	14.2	10.5	9.0	7.9	6.2	51.7	604 894	541 907	NA	11.6	NA
District 9	8.2	19.0	11.2	18.0	14.3	8.7	8.2	7.1	5.3	53.4	512 881	541 981	NA	-5.4	NA
TEXAS	8.2	20.3	11.1	18.2	14.9	9.6	7.6	5.9	4.2	50.7	20 851 820	16 986 335	14 225 513	22.8	19.4
District 1	6.9	19.5	10.3	14.3	13.5	10.2	9.3	8.6	7.4	51.9	622 475	566 217	NA	9.9	NA
District 2	7.0	19.9	10.0	15.3	13.7	10.3	9.6	8.2	6.1	49.9	669 591	566 217	NA	18.3	NA
District 3	8.7	19.8	9.6	22.1	18.5	10.8	5.6	3.0	1.8	50.6	835 040	567 648	NA	47.1	NA
District 4	7.3	19.7	9.3	15.8	14.6	10.6	8.9	7.6	6.1	51.5	707 329	566 217	NA	24.9	NA
District 5	7.8	17.5	10.3	20.2	14.3	9.2	8.2	7.0	5.5	50.0	657 495	567 457	NA	15.9	NA
District 6	8.3	18.9	9.9	21.5	18.0	11.0	6.5	3.8	2.0	50.3	759 418	565 469	NA	34.3	NA
District 7	8.5	18.5	9.3	22.4	18.7	10.3	6.4	3.8	2.1	50.4	772 147	564 900	NA	36.7	NA
District 8	7.5	20.5	13.6	16.9	16.9	10.9	6.6	4.2	2.8	50.1	776 623	565 090	NA	37.4	NA
District 9	7.6	19.8	9.4	17.6	15.4	10.1	8.8	6.7	4.5	51.1	636 960	564 322	NA	12.9	NA
District 10	7.7	16.3	16.0	22.4	16.3	8.4	5.7	4.1	2.9	50.0	791 117	566 217	NA	39.7	NA
District 11	8.2	18.8	14.2	17.0	12.9	8.6	7.7	6.8	5.8	49.8	663 275	566 217	NA	17.1	NA
District 12	8.3	18.8	10.9	18.9	14.2	9.4	7.9	6.6	5.0	50.6	661 753	566 217	NA	16.9	NA
District 13	7.7	20.0	11.5	15.7	12.6	9.2	9.0	7.7	6.6	51.4	597 401	566 217	NA	5.5	NA
District 14	7.5	20.5	11.0	15.2	14.0	9.5	8.7	7.6	5.9	50.6	688 604	566 217	NA	21.6	NA
District 15	8.9	25.8	11.2	14.6	12.8	8.3	7.4	6.5	4.5	51.5	780 310	566 217	NA	37.8	NA
District 16	8.9	23.5	12.4	17.0	13.6	8.8	7.5	5.2	3.1	51.2	620 847	566 217	NA	9.6	NA
District 17	7.4	19.7	9.8	15.0	13.2	9.7	9.3	8.5	7.5	51.4	618 958	566 217	NA	9.3	NA
District 18	8.2	19.1	11.7	19.2	15.0	9.4	7.8	5.7	3.9	50.2	606 441	567 364	NA	6.9	NA
District 19	8.1	20.7	11.8	17.3	14.2	9.5	8.2	6.0	4.2	51.0	607 535	566 217	NA	7.3	NA
District 20	8.9	20.6	13.2	19.0	13.4	8.2	7.0	5.6	4.0	51.1	624 384	566 217	NA	10.3	NA
District 21	7.1	18.7	8.9	16.5	16.0	10.5	8.8	8.0	5.5	51.5	801 078	566 217	NA	41.5	NA
District 22	8.4	21.0	9.2	20.1	18.6	10.5	6.4	3.7	2.2	49.5	784 759	568 160	NA	38.1	NA
District 23	9.1	24.7	10.6	15.7	14.1	9.3	7.4	5.5	3.6	51.1	762 627	566 217	NA	34.7	NA
District 24	9.1	21.0	11.4	19.0	14.6	9.1	6.7	5.1	4.0	50.7	680 808	567 454	NA	20.0	NA
District 25	8.7	18.8	11.7	21.2	16.3	9.2	6.6	4.6	3.0	51.1	662 264	564 724	NA	17.3	NA
District 26	7.7	15.6	10.8	23.8	17.3	10.6	6.6	4.4	3.1	50.7	845 541	564 843	NA	49.7	NA
District 27	8.6	24.2	10.6	16.0	13.9	8.8	7.7	6.2	4.1	51.5	664 428	566 217	NA	17.3	NA

Table F. Congressional Districts 107th Congress

STATE District	Total population	Total in house-holds	House-holder	Spouse	Child Total	Child Own child under 18 years	Other relatives Total	Other relatives Under 18 years	Nonrelatives Total	Nonrelatives Unmar-ried partner	Total in group quarters	Correc-tional institu-tions	Nurs-ing homes	Other institu-tions	Col-lege dormi-tories	Mili-tary quar-ters	Other
	54	55	56	57	58	59	60	61	62	63	64	65	66	67	68	69	70
PENNSYLVANIA—Cont'd																	
District 8	624 248	98.5	36.6	22.4	32.0	24.1	3.9	1.3	3.5	1.7	1.5	0.1	0.7	0.1	0.2	0.0	0.3
District 9	588 138	96.7	38.9	22.6	28.4	21.7	3.1	1.2	3.6	2.0	3.3	1.1	1.1	0.2	0.7	0.0	0.3
District 10	613 459	96.6	39.0	21.1	28.9	22.0	3.6	1.2	4.1	2.0	3.4	0.7	0.8	0.1	1.1	0.0	0.6
District 11	579 470	96.2	40.0	20.6	27.7	20.1	3.8	1.1	4.0	2.0	3.8	1.0	1.1	0.3	0.8	0.0	0.6
District 12	556 856	95.9	39.5	21.9	27.9	20.1	3.2	1.2	3.5	1.6	4.1	0.9	0.8	0.2	1.3	0.0	0.9
District 13	628 203	97.9	37.9	21.9	29.5	22.6	3.6	1.1	3.6	1.5	3.5	0.8	1.1	0.2	0.9	0.0	0.5
District 14	529 299	94.9	42.4	16.4	25.9	18.8	4.5	1.6	5.7	2.1	5.1	0.9	0.8	0.3	2.4	0.0	0.7
District 15	612 265	96.5	38.4	21.2	28.6	21.9	3.9	1.3	4.4	2.2	3.5	0.3	1.1	0.2	1.4	0.0	0.4
District 16	647 575	96.5	35.8	21.6	31.5	25.1	3.5	1.3	4.1	1.7	3.5	0.3	1.1	0.2	1.4	0.0	0.6
District 17	608 390	97.4	39.5	21.5	28.9	22.6	3.4	1.4	4.1	2.1	2.6	0.3	1.0	0.2	0.5	0.0	0.5
District 18	535 432	98.4	42.6	20.5	28.3	20.3	3.7	1.3	3.3	1.8	1.6	0.0	0.9	0.1	0.0	0.0	0.6
District 19	632 862	96.1	38.4	22.3	28.7	22.1	3.0	1.2	4.5	2.2	3.9	0.8	1.1	0.1	1.5	0.0	0.4
District 20	570 336	96.9	40.0	22.1	28.3	20.6	3.5	1.2	3.0	1.6	3.1	0.7	0.9	0.2	0.8	0.0	0.6
District 21	581 440	95.1	38.3	20.3	28.8	22.1	3.3	1.3	4.3	2.0	4.9	0.8	1.1	0.4	2.1	0.0	0.6
RHODE ISLAND	1 048 319	96.3	39.0	18.8	29.0	21.8	4.5	1.4	5.1	2.2	3.7	0.3	0.9	0.1	2.0	0.1	0.3
District 1	510 287	95.7	39.8	18.7	28.0	21.0	4.2	1.2	5.0	2.2	4.3	0.1	1.1	0.0	2.6	0.2	0.3
District 2	538 032	96.9	38.1	18.9	29.9	22.5	4.8	1.5	5.1	2.2	3.1	0.6	0.7	0.1	1.3	0.0	0.4
SOUTH CAROLINA	4 012 012	96.6	38.2	19.5	28.8	21.8	5.9	2.8	4.3	1.8	3.4	0.9	0.5	0.1	1.0	0.4	0.4
District 1	684 765	97.7	39.3	20.3	27.6	21.5	5.0	2.3	5.5	2.0	2.3	0.4	0.4	0.0	0.6	0.5	0.3
District 2	731 022	95.2	37.9	20.0	28.1	22.4	4.7	2.1	4.5	1.7	4.8	1.3	0.5	0.2	0.7	1.8	0.3
District 3	670 139	96.6	38.7	20.8	28.0	21.3	5.3	2.5	3.8	1.6	3.4	0.8	0.6	0.1	1.4	0.0	0.5
District 4	670 335	97.2	39.1	20.5	28.4	21.9	5.3	2.2	4.0	1.7	2.8	0.6	0.4	0.0	1.1	0.0	0.5
District 5	655 525	97.7	37.7	19.6	30.2	22.6	6.5	3.2	3.7	1.8	2.3	0.7	0.6	0.1	0.5	0.1	0.3
District 6	600 226	95.3	36.6	15.4	30.4	21.1	9.0	4.7	3.9	1.7	4.7	1.5	0.5	0.3	1.7	0.0	0.7
SOUTH DAKOTA	754 844	96.2	38.5	20.9	29.5	24.6	3.0	1.4	4.5	1.8	3.8	0.6	1.0	0.3	1.2	0.1	0.6
At Large	754 844	96.2	38.5	20.9	29.5	24.6	3.0	1.4	4.5	1.8	3.8	0.6	1.0	0.3	1.2	0.1	0.6
TENNESSEE	5 689 283	97.4	39.2	20.6	28.3	21.8	5.0	2.2	4.1	1.7	2.6	0.7	0.7	0.1	0.8	0.0	0.3
District 1	628 443	97.6	40.9	23.0	26.2	19.8	4.1	1.7	3.4	1.6	2.4	0.5	0.8	0.2	0.7	0.0	0.2
District 2	636 383	97.5	40.8	21.9	26.6	20.7	4.0	1.6	4.1	1.5	2.5	0.1	0.6	0.1	1.4	0.0	0.3
District 3	595 855	97.4	40.2	21.3	27.3	20.5	5.0	2.1	3.7	1.6	2.6	0.7	0.7	0.1	0.7	0.0	0.3
District 4	635 355	98.0	39.4	23.0	27.9	21.3	4.5	1.9	3.2	1.5	2.0	0.6	0.8	0.0	0.3	0.0	0.3
District 5	607 853	95.9	41.2	16.9	25.5	19.7	5.7	2.3	6.5	2.1	4.1	1.0	0.4	0.3	1.9	0.0	0.4
District 6	738 663	98.2	37.5	22.6	30.0	23.9	4.1	1.7	4.0	1.5	1.8	0.2	0.5	0.1	0.7	0.0	0.3
District 7	728 956	97.7	37.3	22.0	30.5	24.3	4.3	1.9	3.6	1.5	2.3	0.8	0.6	0.1	0.2	0.3	0.2
District 8	604 894	97.0	38.2	20.4	29.5	22.8	5.4	2.6	3.5	1.6	3.0	1.1	0.9	0.0	0.6	0.0	0.3
District 9	512 881	96.9	38.2	12.3	31.2	22.4	9.6	4.8	5.6	2.1	3.1	1.2	0.5	0.2	0.7	0.0	0.5
TEXAS	20 851 820	97.3	35.5	19.1	31.5	24.8	6.8	2.9	4.4	1.6	2.7	1.2	0.5	0.1	0.4	0.2	0.3
District 1	622 475	96.1	38.0	20.9	28.2	22.1	5.5	2.7	3.4	1.4	3.9	1.6	1.0	0.1	1.0	0.0	0.2
District 2	669 591	93.5	35.6	20.2	28.5	22.4	5.7	2.7	3.5	1.4	6.5	5.0	0.7	0.2	0.4	0.0	0.2
District 3	835 040	99.6	36.8	21.1	31.7	26.4	5.5	1.7	4.5	1.5	0.4	0.0	0.2	0.0	0.0	0.0	0.2
District 4	707 329	97.5	37.1	21.9	29.7	23.9	5.1	2.3	3.7	1.4	2.5	0.6	0.9	0.2	0.4	0.0	0.4
District 5	657 495	95.3	37.2	17.5	28.1	22.3	7.3	2.9	5.3	1.9	4.7	3.5	0.7	0.1	0.1	0.0	0.3
District 6	759 418	99.4	38.1	22.5	31.0	25.6	4.0	1.5	3.9	1.6	0.6	0.0	0.3	0.0	0.1	0.0	0.1
District 7	772 147	99.5	38.2	20.5	30.8	25.6	5.4	1.5	4.6	1.6	0.5	0.0	0.3	0.1	0.0	0.0	0.1
District 8	776 623	98.0	35.9	21.7	31.0	25.4	4.3	1.6	5.0	1.4	2.0	0.0	0.4	0.1	1.4	0.0	0.1
District 9	636 960	96.5	37.3	19.3	30.2	23.4	5.7	2.5	4.0	1.7	3.5	2.5	0.5	0.0	0.2	0.0	0.2
District 10	791 117	97.4	39.5	16.5	25.8	21.1	6.3	2.1	9.4	2.4	2.6	0.4	0.3	0.2	1.2	0.0	0.6
District 11	663 275	93.9	35.6	19.6	29.5	24.3	4.8	2.3	4.4	1.4	6.1	1.8	1.0	0.4	0.8	1.8	0.3
District 12	661 753	97.1	35.8	18.6	30.6	24.2	7.1	3.0	4.9	1.7	2.9	1.4	0.8	0.0	0.4	0.0	0.3
District 13	597 401	93.8	36.7	19.1	28.6	23.2	5.3	2.7	4.1	1.6	6.2	2.9	0.9	0.3	1.1	0.8	0.2
District 14	688 604	96.3	35.9	20.3	30.1	23.7	5.7	2.7	4.2	1.6	3.7	1.1	0.8	0.1	1.3	0.0	0.4
District 15	780 310	96.9	28.8	18.0	37.9	28.1	9.5	4.6	2.6	1.0	3.1	2.3	0.4	0.1	0.2	0.1	0.1
District 16	620 847	98.1	31.2	17.4	36.8	26.4	9.7	4.5	3.0	1.2	1.9	0.9	0.2	0.1	0.0	0.4	0.3
District 17	618 958	94.1	37.0	20.9	28.0	22.7	4.6	2.3	3.5	1.4	5.9	3.3	1.0	0.2	0.9	0.1	0.4
District 18	606 441	96.4	35.8	13.5	30.0	21.3	11.1	4.8	5.9	2.0	3.6	1.6	0.3	0.2	0.5	0.0	0.9
District 19	607 535	97.5	37.7	21.1	30.3	24.9	4.4	2.1	4.0	1.4	2.5	0.6	0.5	0.1	1.1	0.0	0.3
District 20	624 384	96.0	34.4	15.5	32.7	24.1	8.5	3.9	5.0	2.0	4.0	1.0	0.5	0.1	0.3	1.5	0.5
District 21	801 078	98.1	38.3	23.0	29.2	24.0	3.9	1.5	3.7	1.5	1.9	0.2	0.7	0.1	0.5	0.2	0.3
District 22	784 759	97.7	33.7	20.8	33.5	26.7	6.3	2.2	3.4	1.3	2.3	1.6	0.3	0.0	0.0	0.0	0.3
District 23	762 627	98.0	31.3	19.5	36.7	28.3	7.8	3.7	2.8	1.1	2.0	1.1	0.3	0.1	0.2	0.0	0.3
District 24	680 808	98.4	33.0	17.1	33.6	26.4	9.4	3.8	5.4	1.7	1.6	0.4	0.4	0.1	0.4	0.0	0.2
District 25	662 264	99.2	36.4	17.3	32.7	25.8	7.9	2.9	5.0	1.9	0.8	0.0	0.3	0.0	0.2	0.0	0.3
District 26	845 541	99.1	39.0	20.9	29.2	24.9	4.8	1.3	5.2	1.7	0.9	0.0	0.3	0.1	0.3	0.0	0.1
District 27	664 428	98.5	32.0	18.0	35.6	26.0	9.3	4.5	3.6	1.5	1.5	0.4	0.4	0.1	0.1	0.1	0.4

Table F. Congressional Districts 107th Congress

STATE District	Total households	Family households Total	Married couple — With own children under 18 years	Married couple — Total	With own children under 18 years	Female householder[1] — Total	With own children under 18 years	Nonfamily households — Total	Householder living alone — Total	65 years and over	Average household size	Average family size	Total households (1990)	Female householder[1] (1990)	Householder living alone
	71	72	73	74	75	76	77	78	79	80	81	82	83	84	85
PENNSYLVANIA—Cont'd															
District 8	228 657	73.5	35.4	61.2	29.3	8.8	4.5	26.5	21.5	8.0	2.69	3.17	199 677	8.4	19.3
District 9	229 022	70.9	30.5	58.0	23.3	8.9	4.9	29.1	25.1	12.0	2.48	2.96	212 351	8.9	23.3
District 10	239 044	68.4	30.3	54.1	22.6	10.1	5.6	31.6	26.9	12.5	2.48	3.01	212 813	10.0	24.8
District 11	231 911	66.3	27.9	51.6	20.7	10.5	5.3	33.7	29.0	14.5	2.40	2.96	218 969	10.6	27.0
District 12	219 874	68.8	28.3	55.4	21.7	9.6	4.8	31.2	27.3	13.8	2.43	2.95	213 386	9.5	24.7
District 13	238 092	69.3	32.1	57.7	26.5	8.8	4.3	30.7	25.5	10.1	2.55	3.09	211 735	8.3	24.6
District 14	224 277	56.4	24.1	38.8	15.3	13.9	7.4	43.6	36.2	13.1	2.24	2.96	231 642	14.7	33.3
District 15	235 233	69.0	31.2	55.1	23.5	10.1	5.7	31.0	25.6	11.0	2.51	3.03	213 418	9.2	23.3
District 16	231 969	72.4	35.2	60.3	28.3	8.7	5.1	27.6	22.3	8.3	2.69	3.18	197 885	8.4	20.4
District 17	240 154	68.5	31.1	54.5	22.9	10.3	6.2	31.5	26.4	10.0	2.47	2.99	216 856	9.6	24.4
District 18	228 136	63.9	26.3	48.1	18.7	12.4	6.3	36.1	32.0	14.2	2.31	2.93	232 220	11.6	28.4
District 19	243 143	70.3	31.7	57.9	24.2	8.7	5.3	29.7	24.1	9.6	2.50	2.97	212 004	8.1	22.0
District 20	228 234	68.7	28.8	55.1	22.2	10.2	5.0	31.3	27.5	13.1	2.42	2.96	217 875	10.2	24.6
District 21	222 540	67.9	30.7	53.1	22.2	10.9	6.4	32.1	27.0	11.6	2.48	3.02	209 875	10.5	24.8
RHODE ISLAND	408 424	65.0	30.6	48.2	21.0	12.9	7.8	35.0	28.6	11.4	2.47	3.07	377 977	11.7	26.2
District 1	203 247	63.2	29.2	46.9	19.9	12.5	7.6	36.8	30.3	12.1	2.40	3.02	191 853	11.3	27.1
District 2	205 177	66.8	31.9	49.5	22.1	13.2	7.9	33.2	26.8	10.7	2.54	3.11	186 124	12.2	25.3
SOUTH CAROLINA	1 533 854	69.9	32.3	51.1	21.8	14.8	8.5	30.1	25.0	8.6	2.53	3.02	1 258 044	14.0	22.4
District 1	268 997	68.2	31.2	51.7	21.6	12.6	7.6	31.8	24.6	7.4	2.49	2.98	210 982	11.0	21.0
District 2	277 387	69.3	33.3	52.7	23.5	13.0	8.0	30.7	24.9	7.7	2.51	3.01	210 778	12.0	22.5
District 3	259 294	71.0	31.5	53.7	21.9	13.1	7.5	29.0	24.6	9.6	2.50	2.97	215 512	12.1	22.7
District 4	261 904	69.4	32.0	52.4	22.6	13.1	7.5	30.6	26.0	8.9	2.49	3.00	220 099	12.7	23.7
District 5	246 866	72.5	34.0	52.1	22.7	16.0	9.1	27.5	23.7	8.9	2.59	3.06	205 042	15.0	21.1
District 6	219 406	69.4	31.7	42.2	17.6	22.5	12.2	30.6	26.3	9.5	2.61	3.16	195 631	21.9	23.1
SOUTH DAKOTA	290 245	67.0	32.8	54.2	24.5	9.0	6.1	33.0	27.6	11.1	2.50	3.07	259 034	8.0	26.4
At Large	290 245	67.0	32.8	54.2	24.5	9.0	6.1	33.0	27.6	11.1	2.50	3.07	259 034	8.0	26.4
TENNESSEE	2 232 905	69.3	31.7	52.6	22.4	12.9	7.4	30.7	25.8	9.0	2.48	2.99	1 853 725	12.6	23.9
District 1	257 054	70.4	29.1	56.3	21.7	10.4	5.6	29.6	25.7	10.2	2.39	2.85	210 363	10.3	22.7
District 2	259 475	67.5	29.5	53.8	22.0	10.5	5.9	32.5	27.1	9.2	2.39	2.91	212 752	11.0	25.1
District 3	239 446	69.1	29.5	53.0	21.0	12.3	6.7	30.9	26.7	10.3	2.42	2.93	209 558	12.1	24.4
District 4	250 400	73.0	31.3	58.3	23.4	10.8	5.9	27.0	23.8	10.4	2.49	2.92	204 747	10.5	21.1
District 5	250 719	59.3	27.4	41.1	17.2	14.3	8.4	40.7	32.5	8.2	2.33	2.97	218 369	14.1	29.6
District 6	276 700	74.0	36.2	60.3	28.3	10.1	6.0	26.0	21.1	7.0	2.62	3.05	197 185	9.4	19.3
District 7	272 103	73.6	36.9	58.9	28.2	11.2	6.8	26.4	22.1	7.0	2.62	3.07	197 446	9.9	20.6
District 8	230 970	72.0	33.5	53.5	22.7	14.5	8.8	28.0	24.4	10.2	2.54	3.01	200 919	12.6	22.6
District 9	196 038	63.0	30.6	32.2	13.7	25.3	14.6	37.0	30.9	9.5	2.54	3.21	202 386	22.8	28.6
TEXAS	7 393 354	71.0	36.8	54.0	27.1	12.7	7.6	29.0	23.7	7.3	2.74	3.28	6 070 937	11.6	23.9
District 1	236 648	70.9	31.7	55.1	22.8	12.1	7.0	29.1	25.4	11.7	2.53	3.02	212 663	10.9	24.6
District 2	238 699	72.8	33.5	56.7	24.4	12.1	7.0	27.2	23.4	10.6	2.62	3.09	202 546	11.0	22.7
District 3	307 084	71.3	39.6	57.5	31.4	9.9	6.3	28.7	23.1	3.7	2.71	3.22	210 090	9.2	22.5
District 4	262 101	73.6	35.0	59.2	26.5	10.6	6.3	26.4	22.5	9.2	2.63	3.08	211 624	9.3	22.9
District 5	244 380	64.9	31.8	47.0	21.6	13.3	8.0	35.1	28.8	8.7	2.56	3.19	217 824	11.5	29.2
District 6	289 202	71.5	37.7	59.1	30.0	9.0	5.9	28.5	23.2	4.4	2.61	3.11	215 161	7.5	22.5
District 7	294 650	66.8	36.8	53.8	29.1	9.2	6.0	33.2	27.3	4.7	2.61	3.23	221 903	8.3	28.7
District 8	279 054	73.0	38.2	60.5	30.7	9.0	5.6	27.0	19.9	5.4	2.73	3.17	198 519	8.1	19.2
District 9	237 696	69.6	34.2	51.6	23.9	13.7	8.2	30.4	25.7	8.6	2.59	3.13	212 067	12.7	24.9
District 10	312 251	56.8	29.3	41.9	21.0	10.5	6.5	43.2	30.4	4.3	2.47	3.17	228 606	10.6	31.7
District 11	236 004	70.9	36.4	55.1	26.4	12.2	7.9	29.1	23.9	9.1	2.64	3.13	200 738	10.6	23.8
District 12	237 205	69.6	35.6	52.0	25.7	12.7	7.5	30.4	25.1	8.2	2.71	3.26	207 789	11.2	24.8
District 13	219 041	68.1	33.1	52.1	23.5	11.9	7.3	31.9	27.0	11.2	2.56	3.13	209 996	10.0	26.2
District 14	246 955	72.0	34.7	56.7	25.9	11.0	6.5	28.0	23.0	9.7	2.68	3.17	201 932	9.9	24.3
District 15	225 044	81.7	46.0	62.5	35.3	14.9	8.7	18.3	15.7	7.4	3.36	3.78	164 944	13.7	16.3
District 16	193 995	78.4	43.4	55.7	30.8	18.3	10.5	21.6	18.5	7.0	3.14	3.61	170 915	16.0	17.2
District 17	228 972	70.9	32.8	56.6	24.2	10.4	6.3	29.1	25.3	11.8	2.54	3.05	210 111	8.7	24.6
District 18	216 972	62.5	30.2	37.9	18.4	19.0	9.8	37.5	30.4	7.5	2.69	3.44	202 510	18.7	29.6
District 19	229 090	69.8	35.3	55.8	26.6	10.3	6.6	30.2	25.0	8.8	2.58	3.12	208 449	8.5	23.5
District 20	214 548	68.0	36.2	45.1	23.2	17.6	10.4	32.0	26.0	7.5	2.79	3.43	192 134	16.0	25.1
District 21	306 967	72.0	34.4	60.0	27.2	8.8	5.5	28.0	23.3	8.3	2.56	3.03	217 836	8.0	23.9
District 22	264 138	76.9	42.7	61.9	34.0	10.9	6.6	23.1	18.9	4.2	2.90	3.35	195 058	9.4	20.1
District 23	238 925	79.4	44.8	62.1	34.9	13.4	8.0	20.6	17.4	6.5	3.13	3.57	174 390	12.2	17.5
District 24	224 408	73.8	40.8	51.8	28.1	16.1	9.9	26.2	20.8	6.3	2.99	3.47	194 480	14.2	21.7
District 25	240 902	68.6	38.1	47.5	25.7	15.9	10.1	31.4	25.8	5.6	2.73	3.32	216 809	13.5	28.3
District 26	329 781	65.4	35.1	53.7	28.2	8.2	5.2	34.6	27.5	4.6	2.54	3.15	235 193	7.3	30.9
District 27	212 615	77.0	40.7	56.1	29.1	16.2	9.3	23.0	19.2	7.7	3.08	3.55	177 612	14.6	19.3

[1]No spouse present.

Table F. Congressional Districts 107th Congress

STATE District	Percent change of households, 1990–2000	Total housing units	Occupied housing units (percent)	Housing occupancy — Vacant housing units — Total	For seasonal, recreational, or occasional use	Homeowner vacancy rate (percent)	Rental vacancy rate (percent)	Housing tenure — Occupied housing units — Total	Percent owner-occupied housing units	Percent renter-occupied housing units	Average household size of owner-occupied units	Average household size of renter-occupied units
	86	87	88	89	90	91	92	93	94	95	96	97
PENNSYLVANIA—Cont'd												
District 8	14.5	235 622	97.0	3.0	0.4	0.8	4.1	228 657	77.3	22.7	2.87	2.09
District 9	7.9	257 307	89.0	11.0	5.4	1.5	7.1	229 022	76.1	23.9	2.57	2.19
District 10	12.3	306 272	78.0	22.0	15.8	2.2	7.8	239 044	73.1	26.9	2.60	2.15
District 11	5.9	266 860	86.9	13.1	5.7	2.1	8.4	231 911	73.0	27.0	2.52	2.08
District 12	3.0	244 110	90.1	9.9	3.5	1.5	8.3	219 874	75.7	24.3	2.53	2.11
District 13	12.4	247 186	96.3	3.7	0.3	1.0	5.4	238 092	74.2	25.8	2.74	1.99
District 14	-3.2	249 323	90.0	10.0	0.5	2.2	9.0	224 277	59.5	40.5	2.46	1.92
District 15	10.2	247 807	94.9	5.1	0.4	1.5	6.4	235 233	71.4	28.6	2.65	2.16
District 16	17.2	241 636	96.0	4.0	0.4	1.2	5.0	231 969	72.6	27.4	2.84	2.31
District 17	10.7	255 188	94.1	5.9	0.6	1.7	7.3	240 154	70.6	29.4	2.61	2.13
District 18	-1.8	244 847	93.2	6.8	0.2	1.7	8.7	228 136	70.2	29.8	2.48	1.92
District 19	14.7	257 015	94.6	5.4	0.8	1.5	6.8	243 143	75.1	24.9	2.60	2.21
District 20	4.8	245 527	93.0	7.0	0.7	1.7	8.8	228 234	75.9	24.1	2.54	2.04
District 21	6.0	242 394	91.8	8.2	2.6	1.6	7.6	222 540	72.7	27.3	2.61	2.14
RHODE ISLAND	8.1	439 837	92.9	7.1	3.0	1.0	5.0	408 424	60.0	40.0	2.66	2.19
District 1	5.9	215 819	94.2	5.8	1.6	0.8	4.7	203 247	56.1	43.9	2.62	2.12
District 2	10.2	224 018	91.6	8.4	4.2	1.1	5.4	205 177	63.9	36.1	2.69	2.27
SOUTH CAROLINA	21.9	1 753 670	87.5	12.5	4.0	1.9	12.0	1 533 854	72.2	27.8	2.59	2.37
District 1	27.5	334 321	80.5	19.5	10.3	2.1	17.7	268 997	70.1	29.9	2.55	2.34
District 2	31.6	313 960	88.4	11.6	4.1	1.8	11.6	277 387	72.3	27.7	2.58	2.33
District 3	20.3	293 232	88.4	11.6	2.8	2.0	11.6	259 294	75.6	24.4	2.55	2.35
District 4	19.0	285 823	91.6	8.4	0.7	2.3	10.2	261 904	70.2	29.8	2.57	2.30
District 5	20.4	273 892	90.1	9.9	1.7	1.8	9.6	246 866	74.9	25.1	2.63	2.48
District 6	12.2	252 442	86.9	13.1	3.2	1.6	9.5	219 406	70.0	30.0	2.67	2.47
SOUTH DAKOTA	12.0	323 208	89.8	10.2	3.0	1.8	8.0	290 245	68.2	31.8	2.64	2.22
At Large	12.0	323 208	89.8	10.2	3.0	1.8	8.0	290 245	68.2	31.8	2.64	2.22
TENNESSEE	20.5	2 439 443	91.5	8.5	1.5	2.0	8.8	2 232 905	69.9	30.1	2.57	2.29
District 1	22.2	288 818	89.0	11.0	3.2	1.9	10.9	257 054	74.8	25.2	2.45	2.21
District 2	22.0	282 919	91.7	8.3	1.0	2.3	10.0	259 475	70.8	29.2	2.50	2.12
District 3	14.3	261 973	91.4	8.6	1.2	1.9	9.6	239 446	70.1	29.9	2.52	2.21
District 4	22.3	280 570	89.2	10.8	3.1	2.0	9.4	250 400	76.7	23.3	2.51	2.40
District 5	14.8	267 000	93.9	6.1	0.4	1.9	6.5	250 719	56.3	43.7	2.46	2.15
District 6	40.3	297 376	93.0	7.0	0.9	2.1	8.0	276 700	75.4	24.6	2.71	2.34
District 7	37.8	293 777	92.6	7.4	1.3	1.9	8.4	272 103	73.1	26.9	2.72	2.33
District 8	15.0	254 310	90.8	9.2	2.0	2.0	9.2	230 970	71.6	28.4	2.58	2.45
District 9	-3.1	212 700	92.2	7.8	0.2	1.9	8.2	196 038	56.8	43.2	2.60	2.45
TEXAS	21.8	8 157 575	90.6	9.4	2.1	1.8	8.5	7 393 354	63.8	36.2	2.87	2.53
District 1	11.3	271 863	87.0	13.0	3.4	2.1	10.9	236 648	73.4	26.6	2.55	2.47
District 2	17.8	287 797	82.9	17.1	7.0	2.4	11.6	238 699	76.1	23.9	2.64	2.58
District 3	46.2	323 424	94.9	5.1	0.2	1.3	8.7	307 084	63.1	36.9	2.93	2.32
District 4	23.9	287 589	91.1	8.9	2.0	1.9	8.3	262 101	73.2	26.8	2.69	2.47
District 5	12.2	274 128	89.1	10.9	3.3	1.9	7.7	244 380	59.6	40.4	2.61	2.50
District 6	34.4	303 684	95.2	4.8	0.4	1.4	7.8	289 202	67.4	32.6	2.86	2.10
District 7	32.8	316 001	93.2	6.8	0.7	1.6	9.5	294 650	57.2	42.8	2.87	2.26
District 8	40.6	300 349	92.9	7.1	1.6	1.6	8.3	279 054	71.2	28.8	2.89	2.31
District 9	12.1	268 169	88.6	11.4	3.2	1.8	11.6	237 696	65.9	34.1	2.70	2.37
District 10	36.6	325 797	95.8	4.2	0.6	1.1	3.5	312 251	50.6	49.4	2.73	2.20
District 11	17.6	262 541	89.9	10.1	2.0	2.3	7.7	236 004	61.3	38.7	2.68	2.58
District 12	14.2	253 754	93.5	6.5	0.5	1.6	7.2	237 205	63.2	36.8	2.80	2.55
District 13	4.3	250 548	87.4	12.6	1.9	3.0	10.6	219 041	64.3	35.7	2.60	2.47
District 14	22.3	289 188	85.4	14.6	5.3	1.8	9.4	246 955	71.6	28.4	2.73	2.58
District 15	36.4	273 645	82.2	17.8	7.6	1.7	11.2	225 044	72.1	27.9	3.44	3.15
District 16	13.5	207 351	93.6	6.4	0.4	1.5	7.8	193 995	62.0	38.0	3.28	2.91
District 17	9.0	272 735	84.0	16.0	4.7	3.0	12.2	228 972	71.2	28.8	2.57	2.47
District 18	7.1	238 649	90.9	9.1	0.5	1.8	8.0	216 972	49.8	50.2	2.78	2.61
District 19	9.9	251 911	90.9	9.1	0.4	1.9	12.0	229 090	67.0	33.0	2.71	2.33
District 20	11.7	229 426	93.5	6.5	0.5	1.3	6.5	214 548	52.0	48.0	3.03	2.54
District 21	40.9	341 015	90.0	10.0	3.7	1.8	7.7	306 967	72.9	27.1	2.67	2.27
District 22	35.4	279 939	94.4	5.6	0.5	1.7	8.5	264 138	70.8	29.2	3.06	2.53
District 23	37.0	270 312	88.4	11.6	2.3	1.9	10.1	238 925	72.4	27.6	3.23	2.85
District 24	15.4	239 057	93.9	6.1	0.5	1.5	6.8	224 408	60.2	39.8	3.02	2.93
District 25	11.1	259 041	93.0	7.0	0.4	1.4	8.5	240 902	49.5	50.5	2.90	2.56
District 26	40.2	348 826	94.5	5.5	0.3	1.7	7.5	329 781	58.5	41.5	2.81	2.16
District 27	19.7	249 106	85.4	14.6	6.2	1.8	11.8	212 615	64.5	35.5	3.17	2.90

Table F. Congressional Districts 107th Congress

STATE District	Land area, 2000[1] (sq km)	Total persons	Rank	Per square kilometer	Land area, 1990[1] (sq km)	Total persons	Rank	Per square kilometer	White	Black or African American	American Indian or Alaska Native	Asian	Native Hawaiian and other Pacific Islander	Some other race
	Population, 2000				Population, 1990				Population and population characteristics, 2000 Race (percent) One race					
	1	2	3	4	5	6	7	8	9	10	11	12	13	14
TEXAS—Cont'd														
District 28	31 537.2	646 161	X	20.5	31 540.0	566 217	X	18.0	66.6	8.2	0.8	0.7	0.1	20.4
District 29	678.0	672 591	X	992.0	678.0	568 959	X	839.0	50.7	15.7	0.6	2.2	0.1	27.1
District 30	685.0	633 860	X	925.3	685.0	564 431	X	824.0	37.8	39.3	0.5	2.5	0.1	17.3
UTAH	212 751.0	2 233 169	X	10.5	212 816.0	1 722 850	X	8.1	89.2	0.8	1.3	1.7	0.7	4.2
District 1	88 233.2	765 156	X	8.7	88 280.0	574 286	X	7.0	91.2	0.9	0.9	1.2	0.3	3.7
District 2	1 187.0	702 102	X	591.5	1 187.0	574 241	X	484.0	89.4	0.9	0.7	2.2	0.7	3.8
District 3	123 330.9	765 911	X	6.2	123 348.0	574 323	X	5.0	87.2	0.6	2.3	1.6	1.1	5.0
VERMONT	23 956.0	608 827	X	25.4	23 956.0	562 758	X	23.5	96.8	0.5	0.4	0.9	0.0	0.2
At Large	23 956.2	608 827	X	25.4	23 956.0	562 758	X	24.0	96.8	0.5	0.4	0.9	0.0	0.2
VIRGINIA	102 548.0	7 078 515	X	69.0	102 558.0	6 189 197	X	60.3	72.3	19.6	0.3	3.7	0.1	2.0
District 1	11 430.3	709 060	X	62.0	9 053.0	562 757	X	62.0	75.4	19.7	0.4	1.5	0.1	1.1
District 2	746.6	574 058	X	768.9	735.0	562 276	X	765.0	67.5	23.1	0.4	4.5	0.1	1.6
District 3	2 995.3	567 683	X	189.5	4 557.0	562 351	X	123.0	38.3	56.6	0.5	1.4	0.1	1.3
District 4	11 619.8	645 733	X	55.6	14 648.0	562 466	X	38.0	57.4	39.1	0.3	1.2	0.0	0.7
District 5	22 857.7	620 104	X	27.1	22 860.0	562 268	X	25.0	73.4	24.0	0.2	0.9	0.0	0.6
District 6	13 458.8	609 802	X	45.3	13 460.0	562 572	X	42.0	85.2	11.7	0.2	1.0	0.0	0.7
District 7	8 788.3	699 196	X	79.6	6 588.0	562 643	X	85.0	81.6	13.5	0.3	2.4	0.0	1.0
District 8	419.2	627 849	X	1 497.7	420.0	562 484	X	1 340.0	66.8	14.0	0.3	8.7	0.1	6.2
District 9	20 434.4	582 943	X	28.5	20 435.0	562 380	X	28.0	95.1	2.8	0.2	0.8	0.0	0.4
District 10	9 154.2	792 534	X	86.6	9 156.0	562 664	X	62.0	83.2	6.7	0.2	5.3	0.1	2.3
District 11	643.6	649 553	X	1 009.2	644.0	562 497	X	873.0	66.6	11.3	0.3	12.2	0.1	5.5
WASHINGTON	172 348.0	5 894 121	X	34.2	172 447.0	4 866 669	X	28.2	81.8	3.2	1.6	5.5	0.4	3.9
District 1	971.1	632 484	X	651.3	971.0	540 745	X	557.0	83.6	1.7	0.9	8.4	0.3	1.6
District 2	16 112.3	719 487	X	44.7	16 117.0	540 739	X	34.0	87.5	1.3	1.9	3.2	0.2	2.8
District 3	21 719.3	698 038	X	32.1	21 827.0	540 745	X	25.0	89.5	1.3	1.2	2.7	0.3	2.0
District 4	61 408.0	672 059	X	10.9	61 396.0	540 744	X	9.0	75.8	0.9	2.8	1.2	0.1	16.1
District 5	45 778.2	625 971	X	13.7	45 781.0	540 744	X	12.0	90.0	1.4	1.8	1.8	0.2	2.3
District 6	16 184.9	611 292	X	37.8	16 188.0	540 742	X	33.0	80.9	5.5	2.3	4.1	0.7	1.9
District 7	327.1	590 062	X	1 803.9	327.0	540 747	X	1 653.0	69.5	8.6	1.0	13.2	0.5	2.6
District 8	7 614.0	695 277	X	91.3	7 605.0	540 742	X	71.0	83.6	2.4	0.9	7.7	0.3	1.8
District 9	2 233.5	649 451	X	290.8	2 233.0	540 744	X	242.0	73.9	7.0	1.4	7.9	1.1	3.4
WEST VIRGINIA	62 361.0	1 808 344	X	29.0	62 384.0	1 793 477	X	28.7	95.0	3.2	0.2	0.5	0.0	0.2
District 1	15 400.6	595 385	X	38.7	15 402.0	598 056	X	39.0	96.3	1.8	0.2	0.7	0.0	0.2
District 2	24 470.1	635 965	X	26.0	24 490.0	597 921	X	24.0	94.6	3.4	0.2	0.5	0.0	0.2
District 3	22 490.3	576 994	X	25.7	22 492.0	597 500	X	27.0	94.2	4.3	0.2	0.4	0.0	0.1
WISCONSIN	140 663.0	5 363 675	X	38.1	140 672.0	4 891 954	X	34.8	88.9	5.7	0.9	1.7	0.0	1.6
District 1	5 717.5	612 814	X	107.2	5 718.0	543 530	X	95.0	88.7	5.8	0.3	0.8	0.0	2.8
District 2	13 849.9	624 959	X	45.1	13 852.0	543 532	X	39.0	91.7	3.0	0.4	2.4	0.0	1.1
District 3	27 552.0	600 914	X	21.8	27 554.0	543 533	X	20.0	96.5	0.5	0.6	1.3	0.0	0.3
District 4	759.7	578 409	X	761.4	760.0	543 527	X	716.0	86.7	2.2	0.9	2.1	0.0	6.2
District 5	261.2	507 636	X	1 943.5	261.0	543 530	X	2 081.0	50.0	43.3	0.4	2.9	0.1	1.3
District 6	17 396.5	606 416	X	34.9	17 398.0	543 652	X	31.0	96.1	0.8	0.5	1.1	0.0	0.7
District 7	43 309.9	582 884	X	13.5	43 313.0	543 529	X	13.0	95.2	0.3	1.7	1.7	0.0	0.3
District 8	25 498.1	617 575	X	24.2	25 498.0	543 404	X	21.0	92.8	0.7	2.9	1.5	0.0	1.0
District 9	6 317.7	632 068	X	100.0	6 318.0	543 532	X	86.0	96.0	0.8	0.3	1.4	0.0	0.7
WYOMING	251 489.0	493 782	X	2.0	251 501.0	453 589	X	1.8	92.1	0.8	2.3	0.6	0.1	2.5
At Large	251 488.9	493 782	X	2.0	251 501.0	453 588	X	2.0	92.1	0.8	2.3	0.6	0.1	2.5

[1] Dry land or land partially or temporarily covered by water.

Table F. Congressional Districts 107th Congress

STATE District	Population and population characteristics, 2000 (cont'd) Race (percent) (cont'd) Race alone or in combination								Population and population characteristics, 1990 Race (percent)				
	Two or more races	White	Black	American Indian or Alaska Native	Asian	Native Hawaiian and other Pacific Islander	Some other race	Hispanic[1]	White	Black or African American	American Indian or Alaska Native	Asian and Pacific Islander	Hispanic[1]
	15	16	17	18	19	20	21	22	23	24	25	26	27
TEXAS—Cont'd													
District 28	3.2	69.5	8.6	1.2	1.1	0.1	22.9	65.0	68.5	8.5	0.3	0.7	60.4
District 29	3.5	53.8	16.1	1.0	2.6	0.1	30.0	60.9	57.4	15.4	0.3	2.1	45.1
District 30	2.6	39.9	39.8	0.9	2.8	0.1	19.0	34.7	41.8	44.5	0.5	2.1	18.4
UTAH	2.1	91.1	1.1	1.8	2.2	1.0	5.1	9.0	93.8	0.7	1.4	1.9	4.9
District 1	1.9	92.8	1.2	1.4	1.7	0.4	4.4	7.7	94.4	0.9	0.9	1.5	4.7
District 2	2.2	91.4	1.2	1.2	2.8	1.0	4.8	8.7	94.4	0.6	0.7	2.3	4.9
District 3	2.2	89.1	0.9	2.8	2.0	1.5	6.1	10.7	92.6	0.5	2.6	1.9	5.1
VERMONT	1.2	97.9	0.7	1.1	1.1	0.1	0.4	0.9	98.6	0.3	0.3	0.6	0.7
At Large	1.2	97.9	0.7	1.1	1.1	0.1	0.4	0.9	98.6	0.3	0.3	0.6	0.7
VIRGINIA	2.0	73.9	20.4	0.7	4.3	0.1	2.7	4.7	77.4	18.8	0.2	2.6	2.6
District 1	1.8	76.8	20.5	1.0	2.0	0.2	1.5	2.8	80.4	17.6	0.3	1.3	1.5
District 2	2.7	69.6	24.2	1.1	5.5	0.3	2.3	4.3	78.1	16.6	0.4	3.8	3.3
District 3	1.9	39.6	57.7	1.1	1.8	0.2	1.8	2.7	33.5	64.4	0.4	1.1	1.4
District 4	1.3	58.4	39.7	0.8	1.5	0.1	1.0	1.8	66.2	32.1	0.2	1.1	1.1
District 5	0.9	74.1	24.5	0.5	1.0	0.1	0.8	1.6	74.4	24.8	0.1	0.6	0.6
District 6	1.2	86.2	12.2	0.6	1.2	0.1	1.0	1.9	87.6	11.5	0.1	0.6	0.7
District 7	1.3	82.6	14.0	0.6	2.8	0.1	1.3	2.3	87.8	10.0	0.2	1.7	1.0
District 8	4.0	69.9	15.0	0.8	10.0	0.2	8.3	13.8	76.0	13.4	0.3	6.7	8.7
District 9	0.8	95.8	3.0	0.5	1.0	0.0	0.6	1.0	96.6	2.5	0.1	0.7	0.5
District 10	2.2	85.1	7.3	0.6	6.0	0.1	3.2	5.6	90.7	5.8	0.2	2.7	2.2
District 11	4.1	69.8	12.2	0.8	13.7	0.2	7.5	12.9	80.7	8.2	0.3	8.1	7.4
WASHINGTON	3.6	84.9	4.0	2.7	6.7	0.7	4.9	7.5	88.5	3.1	1.7	4.3	4.4
District 1	3.5	86.6	2.4	1.8	9.9	0.6	2.5	4.2	91.6	1.3	1.0	5.4	2.3
District 2	3.0	90.2	1.8	3.0	4.2	0.5	3.6	5.8	93.7	0.9	2.0	2.1	3.0
District 3	3.0	92.2	1.8	2.4	3.5	0.6	2.7	4.7	94.8	0.9	1.3	2.1	2.5
District 4	3.0	78.5	1.3	3.8	1.7	0.2	17.7	25.4	83.2	1.0	2.8	1.3	15.9
District 5	2.7	92.4	1.9	2.8	2.5	0.3	2.9	4.9	93.2	1.2	1.8	1.8	3.4
District 6	4.6	84.8	6.8	3.9	5.6	1.2	2.9	5.0	87.3	5.4	2.3	3.9	3.1
District 7	4.5	72.8	10.1	2.1	15.1	0.9	4.0	5.6	75.5	10.0	1.4	11.6	3.5
District 8	3.4	86.5	3.1	1.8	9.2	0.6	2.5	4.1	92.0	1.6	1.0	4.6	2.3
District 9	5.2	78.1	8.6	2.8	9.9	1.7	4.7	7.2	85.5	5.4	1.5	6.1	3.7
WEST VIRGINIA	0.9	95.9	3.5	0.6	0.7	0.0	0.3	0.7	96.2	3.1	0.1	0.4	0.5
District 1	0.8	97.1	2.1	0.5	0.8	0.1	0.3	0.7	97.6	1.6	0.2	0.5	0.5
District 2	1.0	95.5	3.8	0.6	0.6	0.0	0.4	0.8	96.0	3.3	0.1	0.4	0.5
District 3	0.8	94.9	4.6	0.6	0.5	0.0	0.2	0.6	95.0	4.5	0.1	0.3	0.4
WISCONSIN	1.2	90.0	6.1	1.3	1.9	0.1	2.0	3.6	92.2	5.0	0.8	1.1	1.9
District 1	1.6	90.2	6.3	0.7	1.0	0.1	3.4	6.3	92.0	5.4	0.3	0.6	3.4
District 2	1.4	92.9	3.5	0.8	2.8	0.1	1.5	2.7	95.5	2.1	0.3	1.7	1.2
District 3	0.8	97.2	0.7	0.9	1.5	0.1	0.4	0.9	98.0	0.2	0.4	1.2	0.5
District 4	2.0	88.5	2.6	1.3	2.4	0.1	7.2	12.5	93.9	0.9	0.8	1.3	6.3
District 5	2.1	51.4	44.6	1.0	3.3	0.1	1.9	3.3	61.3	35.2	0.5	1.7	2.6
District 6	0.8	96.9	0.9	0.8	1.3	0.1	0.8	1.8	98.1	0.4	0.4	0.7	0.9
District 7	0.9	96.0	0.4	2.1	1.9	0.1	0.4	0.9	97.2	0.2	1.5	0.9	0.5
District 8	1.1	93.8	0.9	3.5	1.7	0.1	1.2	2.2	96.0	0.3	2.6	0.9	0.6
District 9	0.8	96.7	1.0	0.5	1.6	0.1	0.9	2.1	98.1	0.4	0.2	0.9	1.0
WYOMING	1.8	93.7	1.0	3.0	0.8	0.1	3.2	6.4	94.2	0.8	2.1	0.6	5.7
At Large	1.8	93.7	1.0	3.0	0.8	0.1	3.2	6.4	94.2	0.8	2.1	0.6	5.7

[1] Hispanic persons may be of any race.

Table F. Congressional Districts 107th Congress

STATE District	Population and population characteristics, 2000										
	Age (percent)										
	Under 5 years	5 to 17 years	18 to 24 years	25 to 34 years	35 to 44 years	45 to 54 years	55 to 64 years	65 to 74 years	75 years and over	Median age (years)	Percent Female
	28	29	30	31	32	33	34	35	36	37	38
TEXAS—Cont'd											
District 28	8.3	23.0	9.8	13.7	14.6	11.9	7.9	6.1	4.8	31.5	51.1
District 29	9.8	23.3	12.4	17.0	14.7	10.6	5.9	3.8	2.5	27.5	49.3
District 30	8.5	20.8	12.0	18.0	15.1	11.0	6.9	4.5	3.3	29.6	50.0
UTAH	9.4	22.8	14.2	14.6	13.4	10.6	6.4	4.5	4.0	27.1	49.9
District 1	9.5	23.6	13.6	13.5	13.2	10.4	6.6	5.2	4.4	27.2	50.0
District 2	8.4	21.2	12.9	15.8	14.7	11.9	6.6	4.4	4.2	29.4	49.7
District 3	10.1	23.6	16.1	14.7	12.4	9.7	5.9	4.1	3.3	25.1	49.9
VERMONT	5.6	18.6	9.3	12.2	16.7	15.4	9.3	6.7	6.0	37.7	51.0
At Large	5.6	18.6	9.3	12.2	16.7	15.4	9.3	6.7	6.0	37.7	51.0
VIRGINIA	6.5	18.0	9.6	14.6	17.0	14.1	8.9	6.1	5.1	35.7	51.0
District 1	6.4	19.2	8.9	12.9	17.3	13.8	9.4	6.7	5.4	36.5	50.8
District 2	7.1	19.0	12.9	16.4	16.8	12.0	6.8	5.0	4.0	31.7	49.6
District 3	7.0	18.8	11.7	14.9	15.9	12.7	7.8	5.9	5.3	33.3	52.7
District 4	6.6	19.6	9.0	13.5	17.2	13.6	8.8	6.3	5.4	35.8	50.9
District 5	5.6	16.7	9.7	12.6	15.5	14.2	10.6	8.3	6.8	38.5	51.5
District 6	5.7	16.4	11.3	12.5	15.1	14.1	9.8	7.8	7.2	37.7	52.0
District 7	6.5	19.1	7.4	13.9	17.8	15.3	8.8	6.1	5.1	36.7	51.4
District 8	6.3	14.4	8.4	20.1	18.1	14.9	8.4	4.8	4.5	35.4	50.6
District 9	5.2	15.4	12.4	13.1	14.7	14.3	10.5	7.8	6.5	37.8	50.7
District 10	7.8	20.1	7.0	15.2	19.1	14.7	8.4	4.5	3.2	35.0	50.3
District 11	7.2	18.6	8.6	16.1	18.0	15.3	8.7	4.3	3.1	34.7	50.3
WASHINGTON	6.7	19.0	9.5	14.3	16.5	14.4	8.4	5.7	5.5	35.3	50.2
District 1	6.3	18.4	8.1	14.6	17.9	15.9	8.6	5.2	5.1	36.6	50.6
District 2	6.9	19.7	9.9	13.6	16.6	14.1	8.2	5.7	5.5	35.0	50.0
District 3	6.9	20.0	8.6	13.0	16.0	14.8	9.0	6.1	5.8	36.0	50.5
District 4	8.0	22.2	9.8	12.7	14.6	13.0	8.2	5.9	5.5	32.8	49.9
District 5	6.4	19.1	11.6	12.5	15.2	14.0	8.5	6.3	6.5	35.3	50.5
District 6	6.2	18.3	9.1	12.6	15.6	14.5	9.4	7.3	6.9	37.6	50.5
District 7	4.8	11.6	11.7	21.2	16.9	14.6	7.5	5.2	6.5	35.4	50.0
District 8	7.1	20.9	7.2	13.8	19.0	15.1	8.3	4.7	4.0	35.6	50.1
District 9	7.3	19.6	9.9	15.2	17.0	13.4	8.1	5.1	4.3	33.7	49.9
WEST VIRGINIA	5.6	16.6	9.5	12.7	15.1	15.0	10.2	8.2	7.1	38.9	51.4
District 1	5.4	16.4	10.5	12.4	14.7	14.6	10.2	8.2	7.6	38.7	51.5
District 2	5.9	17.2	8.5	12.8	15.7	15.0	10.3	8.0	6.6	38.7	51.2
District 3	5.6	16.2	9.6	12.8	14.7	15.3	10.2	8.5	7.2	39.3	51.5
WISCONSIN	6.4	19.1	9.7	13.2	16.3	13.7	8.5	6.6	6.5	36.0	50.6
District 1	6.7	19.8	9.4	13.2	16.7	13.5	8.5	6.3	5.9	35.5	50.5
District 2	6.1	17.5	12.1	14.9	16.6	14.1	7.8	5.6	5.5	34.7	50.3
District 3	6.0	19.0	12.5	12.1	15.3	13.3	8.4	6.6	6.8	35.2	50.4
District 4	6.7	17.7	9.1	14.7	16.6	13.5	8.2	6.8	6.7	36.1	50.7
District 5	7.6	20.9	11.3	14.9	14.5	12.3	6.9	5.7	5.9	31.7	53.3
District 6	6.0	19.1	8.7	12.4	16.6	13.7	9.1	7.4	7.1	37.4	50.0
District 7	6.0	19.4	8.7	11.7	16.0	13.9	9.4	7.5	7.5	37.8	50.3
District 8	6.2	19.4	8.6	12.9	16.6	13.6	9.1	7.0	6.6	36.8	50.2
District 9	6.4	19.8	7.1	12.0	17.7	14.7	9.2	6.7	6.3	37.8	50.3
WYOMING	6.3	19.8	10.1	12.1	16.0	15.0	9.0	6.3	5.3	36.2	49.7
At Large	6.3	19.8	10.1	12.1	16.0	15.0	9.0	6.3	5.3	36.2	49.7

STATE District	Under 5 years	5 to 17 years	18 to 24 years	25 to 34 years	35 to 44 years	45 to 54 years	55 to 64 years	65 to 74 years	75 years and over	Percent Female	2000	1990	1980	1990–2000	1980–1990
	39	40	41	42	43	44	45	46	47	48	49	50	51	52	53
TEXAS—Cont'd															
District 28	8.9	23.5	10.6	15.8	13.5	9.2	7.9	6.3	4.3	51.3	646 161	566 217	NA	14.1	NA
District 29	9.7	22.8	12.4	19.2	14.2	8.6	6.3	4.3	2.5	49.6	672 591	568 959	NA	18.2	NA
District 30	8.8	20.1	12.2	20.1	14.3	9.4	7.1	4.9	3.1	50.9	633 860	564 431	NA	12.3	NA
UTAH	9.8	26.6	11.6	16.0	13.0	8.0	6.2	5.1	3.6	50.3	2 233 169	1 722 850	1 461 037	29.6	17.9
District 1	9.9	27.4	10.8	15.1	12.5	8.2	6.7	5.6	3.8	50.1	765 156	574 286	NA	33.2	NA
District 2	9.3	24.6	10.4	17.4	14.6	8.5	6.2	5.2	3.8	50.5	702 102	574 241	NA	22.3	NA
District 3	10.3	27.7	13.6	15.3	12.0	7.4	5.8	4.6	3.1	50.4	765 911	574 323	NA	33.4	NA
VERMONT	7.3	18.1	11.2	16.9	16.4	10.2	8.0	6.6	5.2	51.0	608 827	562 758	511 456	8.2	10.0
At Large	7.3	18.1	11.2	16.9	16.4	10.2	8.0	6.6	5.2	51.0	608 827	562 758	NA	8.2	NA
VIRGINIA	7.2	17.2	11.6	18.4	16.0	10.7	8.1	6.5	4.3	51.0	7 078 515	6 189 197	5 346 797	14.4	15.8
District 1	7.3	18.1	10.7	17.4	15.6	10.8	8.6	7.1	4.6	50.9	709 060	562 757	NA	26.0	NA
District 2	8.5	16.9	17.1	22.0	14.5	7.8	6.0	4.6	2.6	47.4	574 058	562 276	NA	2.1	NA
District 3	8.4	18.2	12.8	18.6	13.6	8.9	8.1	7.0	4.4	53.2	567 683	562 351	NA	0.9	NA
District 4	7.5	18.7	10.0	17.7	15.6	10.6	8.5	7.1	4.4	51.0	645 733	562 466	NA	14.8	NA
District 5	6.3	16.6	11.6	15.8	14.4	11.0	9.8	8.5	5.9	51.7	620 104	562 268	NA	10.3	NA
District 6	6.2	16.0	12.3	15.6	15.0	10.8	9.6	8.3	6.3	52.2	609 802	562 572	NA	8.4	NA
District 7	7.2	17.3	9.3	18.7	17.8	10.7	8.0	6.5	4.5	51.9	699 196	562 643	NA	24.3	NA
District 8	6.3	13.1	10.6	22.8	18.6	11.7	7.6	5.8	3.6	50.6	627 849	562 484	NA	11.6	NA
District 9	5.7	17.2	13.5	15.0	14.7	11.1	9.4	7.8	5.6	51.3	582 943	562 380	NA	3.7	NA
District 10	8.0	18.8	9.4	19.0	17.9	12.2	7.1	4.6	2.9	50.0	792 534	562 664	NA	40.9	NA
District 11	7.4	17.9	10.7	20.3	18.7	12.3	6.8	3.9	2.1	50.4	649 553	562 497	NA	15.5	NA
WASHINGTON	7.5	18.4	10.0	17.6	16.5	10.3	7.8	6.9	4.9	50.4	5 894 121	4 866 669	4 132 353	21.1	17.8
District 1	7.6	18.2	8.9	18.6	18.6	11.2	7.4	5.8	3.7	50.7	632 484	540 745	NA	17.0	NA
District 2	7.8	19.0	9.8	17.2	16.4	9.8	7.7	7.2	5.1	50.0	719 487	540 739	NA	33.1	NA
District 3	7.4	20.1	8.8	15.6	16.5	10.8	8.2	7.4	5.4	50.8	698 038	540 745	NA	29.1	NA
District 4	8.3	21.4	9.6	15.3	14.9	9.9	8.2	7.2	5.3	50.1	672 059	540 744	NA	24.3	NA
District 5	7.2	19.1	11.8	15.6	15.1	9.8	8.0	7.5	5.9	50.8	625 971	540 744	NA	15.8	NA
District 6	7.4	18.0	9.9	16.4	15.4	9.9	8.7	8.4	5.8	50.4	611 292	540 742	NA	13.0	NA
District 7	5.8	11.4	11.8	21.5	18.1	9.3	7.4	8.0	6.7	51.0	590 062	540 747	NA	9.1	NA
District 8	8.1	20.0	8.3	18.4	18.1	11.9	7.4	5.0	2.9	50.1	695 277	540 742	NA	28.6	NA
District 9	8.2	18.3	11.4	19.5	15.6	10.2	7.5	5.7	3.5	49.7	649 451	540 744	NA	20.1	NA
WEST VIRGINIA	5.9	18.8	10.0	14.6	15.1	10.7	9.9	8.7	6.3	52.0	1 808 344	1 793 477	1 950 186	0.8	-8.0
District 1	5.8	17.8	11.1	14.3	14.8	10.7	9.8	8.9	6.7	52.0	595 385	598 056	NA	-0.4	NA
District 2	6.3	18.6	9.2	15.3	15.4	10.9	9.9	8.4	6.0	51.6	635 965	597 921	NA	6.4	NA
District 3	5.7	19.9	9.8	14.2	15.2	10.4	9.9	8.7	6.2	52.3	576 994	597 500	NA	-3.4	NA
WISCONSIN	7.4	19.0	10.5	16.8	14.8	9.8	8.5	7.3	6.0	51.1	5 363 675	4 891 954	4 705 642	9.6	4.0
District 1	7.6	19.3	10.4	16.6	14.8	10.3	8.5	7.0	5.5	51.2	612 814	543 530	NA	12.7	NA
District 2	7.1	17.0	13.3	18.5	15.9	9.4	7.4	6.3	5.1	50.7	624 959	543 532	NA	15.0	NA
District 3	7.2	19.5	12.6	15.3	14.2	9.3	8.0	7.4	6.5	50.8	600 914	543 533	NA	10.6	NA
District 4	7.2	17.4	9.6	18.4	15.1	9.9	9.1	7.8	5.6	51.5	578 409	543 527	NA	6.4	NA
District 5	8.4	18.7	11.8	18.3	14.0	8.3	7.7	6.7	6.1	53.2	507 636	543 530	NA	-6.6	NA
District 6	7.1	19.3	9.5	16.0	14.4	9.9	9.1	8.1	6.7	50.7	606 416	543 652	NA	11.5	NA
District 7	7.1	20.1	9.3	15.5	14.3	9.8	8.8	8.2	6.9	50.6	582 884	543 529	NA	7.2	NA
District 8	7.5	19.6	9.3	16.7	14.7	9.9	8.6	7.6	6.2	50.8	617 575	543 404	NA	13.6	NA
District 9	7.2	19.9	8.5	15.9	16.0	11.3	8.9	6.9	5.3	50.4	632 068	543 532	NA	16.3	NA
WYOMING	7.7	22.2	9.1	16.4	16.4	10.0	7.8	6.1	4.3	50.0	493 782	453 589	469 557	8.9	-3.4
At Large	7.7	22.2	9.1	16.4	16.4	10.0	7.8	6.1	4.3	50.0	493 782	453 588	NA	8.9	NA

Table F. Congressional Districts 107th Congress

STATE District	Total population	Total in house-holds	House-holder	Spouse	Child Total	Child Own child under 18 years	Other relatives Total	Other relatives Under 18 years	Nonrelatives Total	Nonrelatives Unmarried partner	Total in group quarters	Correctional institutions	Nursing homes	Other institutions	College dormitories	Military quarters	Other
	54	55	56	57	58	59	60	61	62	63	64	65	66	67	68	69	70
TEXAS—Cont'd																	
District 28	646 161	98.3	32.2	17.6	35.9	26.2	8.9	4.5	3.6	1.6	1.7	0.7	0.4	0.2	0.1	0.1	0.2
District 29	672 591	99.3	30.2	16.1	37.0	28.1	11.1	4.4	4.9	1.6	0.7	0.2	0.1	0.0	0.0	0.0	0.3
District 30	633 860	97.2	33.8	13.9	31.5	23.6	11.8	4.9	6.1	1.8	2.8	1.7	0.4	0.3	0.2	0.0	0.4
UTAH	2 233 169	98.2	31.4	19.8	37.1	29.7	4.7	1.9	5.1	1.1	1.8	0.4	0.3	0.1	0.4	0.1	0.4
District 1	765 156	98.3	31.4	20.9	38.1	30.8	3.9	1.7	4.0	1.0	1.7	0.3	0.4	0.1	0.3	0.2	0.4
District 2	702 102	98.1	33.7	19.4	34.9	27.2	4.8	1.8	5.3	1.4	1.9	0.8	0.3	0.1	0.2	0.0	0.4
District 3	765 911	98.1	29.2	19.2	38.1	30.9	5.5	2.2	6.1	0.9	1.9	0.3	0.2	0.2	0.7	0.0	0.4
VERMONT	608 827	96.6	39.5	20.8	27.5	22.7	2.4	0.8	6.4	3.0	3.4	0.2	0.7	0.1	2.1	0.0	0.4
At Large	608 827	96.6	39.5	20.8	27.5	22.7	2.4	0.8	6.4	3.0	3.4	0.2	0.7	0.1	2.1	0.0	0.4
VIRGINIA	7 078 515	96.7	38.1	20.1	28.1	22.1	5.0	2.0	5.3	1.8	3.3	0.9	0.5	0.1	0.9	0.5	0.3
District 1	709 060	96.3	37.0	21.5	29.0	23.0	4.5	2.0	4.3	1.8	3.7	1.6	0.6	0.1	1.0	0.2	0.3
District 2	574 058	95.2	36.2	18.8	29.4	23.6	4.6	1.9	6.3	2.0	4.8	0.2	0.4	0.1	0.3	3.6	0.2
District 3	567 683	96.2	39.6	14.1	28.5	21.5	7.2	3.6	6.8	2.3	3.8	0.7	0.6	0.1	1.2	0.5	0.6
District 4	645 733	95.1	36.2	18.9	29.8	22.6	6.1	2.9	4.1	1.7	4.9	2.6	0.5	0.3	0.3	0.9	0.3
District 5	620 104	96.0	39.8	20.8	26.1	19.5	5.1	2.3	4.3	1.7	4.0	1.3	0.6	0.1	1.7	0.0	0.3
District 6	609 802	94.7	39.6	20.4	25.7	19.9	4.1	1.7	5.0	1.8	5.3	0.7	1.0	0.3	2.8	0.0	0.5
District 7	699 196	97.5	38.3	22.2	29.1	23.6	3.9	1.5	4.0	1.7	2.5	0.9	0.6	0.2	0.5	0.0	0.1
District 8	627 849	98.4	42.0	18.5	24.0	19.0	5.8	1.5	8.2	2.0	1.6	0.6	0.4	0.0	0.1	0.3	0.2
District 9	582 943	95.7	40.2	22.2	25.0	18.6	3.8	1.5	4.5	1.4	4.3	1.0	0.7	0.1	2.2	0.0	0.4
District 10	792 534	99.2	35.9	22.4	31.5	25.9	4.5	1.4	4.9	1.8	0.8	0.2	0.3	0.0	0.1	0.0	0.2
District 11	649 553	98.7	35.5	20.5	30.0	23.7	6.2	1.6	6.4	1.5	1.3	0.2	0.4	0.0	0.4	0.0	0.2
WASHINGTON	5 894 121	97.7	38.5	20.1	28.7	23.5	4.0	1.5	6.4	2.4	2.3	0.5	0.4	0.1	0.5	0.2	0.6
District 1	632 484	98.7	39.1	21.6	28.6	23.2	3.5	1.0	5.9	2.1	1.3	0.3	0.3	0.1	0.1	0.1	0.4
District 2	719 487	97.8	37.7	20.7	29.4	24.5	3.6	1.3	6.4	2.3	2.2	0.4	0.3	0.1	0.5	0.5	0.6
District 3	698 038	98.7	38.3	20.9	29.9	24.6	3.7	1.5	5.8	2.4	1.3	0.3	0.4	0.1	0.1	0.0	0.3
District 4	672 059	98.3	35.1	19.9	32.7	27.1	5.4	2.2	5.2	2.1	1.7	0.4	0.4	0.1	0.3	0.0	0.5
District 5	625 971	95.7	38.5	19.8	28.2	23.4	3.2	1.3	6.0	2.2	4.3	1.0	0.6	0.2	1.7	0.1	0.8
District 6	611 292	97.0	39.8	20.0	27.3	22.1	3.9	1.6	6.1	2.5	3.0	1.4	0.5	0.1	0.2	0.3	0.4
District 7	590 062	95.5	45.1	15.2	19.0	14.5	4.7	1.3	11.5	3.5	4.5	0.6	0.5	0.1	1.8	0.0	1.5
District 8	695 277	99.4	36.7	22.4	31.8	26.3	3.5	1.1	5.0	1.9	0.6	0.0	0.2	0.0	0.0	0.0	0.4
District 9	649 451	97.7	37.5	19.2	30.0	24.4	4.8	1.8	6.3	2.5	2.3	0.2	0.4	0.0	0.2	1.0	0.4
WEST VIRGINIA	1 808 344	97.6	40.7	22.0	27.2	20.1	3.8	1.6	3.9	1.9	2.4	0.6	0.6	0.1	0.8	0.0	0.3
District 1	595 385	97.1	40.7	21.7	26.8	19.9	3.5	1.4	4.4	2.0	2.9	0.4	0.8	0.1	1.3	0.0	0.3
District 2	635 965	98.1	40.6	22.2	27.6	20.9	3.7	1.5	3.9	2.1	1.9	0.3	0.6	0.1	0.5	0.0	0.3
District 3	576 994	97.5	40.9	22.0	27.1	19.5	4.2	1.8	3.4	1.6	2.5	1.0	0.6	0.1	0.5	0.0	0.2
WISCONSIN	5 363 675	97.1	38.9	20.7	29.4	23.7	3.0	1.1	5.2	2.2	2.9	0.6	0.8	0.1	1.0	0.0	0.5
District 1	612 814	97.0	37.6	20.4	30.3	24.3	3.6	1.5	5.0	2.3	3.0	0.6	0.6	0.1	1.0	0.0	0.6
District 2	624 959	96.6	40.1	20.2	26.7	22.3	2.2	0.7	7.5	2.5	3.4	0.7	0.6	0.2	1.5	0.0	0.5
District 3	600 914	95.8	38.0	21.0	28.9	23.6	2.0	0.7	6.0	2.2	4.2	0.4	1.0	0.1	2.2	0.0	0.4
District 4	578 409	98.2	40.0	19.7	29.1	22.5	4.1	1.4	5.3	2.3	1.8	0.3	0.6	0.1	0.3	0.0	0.5
District 5	507 636	96.9	39.7	13.4	30.8	24.2	6.3	3.3	6.7	2.5	3.1	0.4	0.9	0.2	1.2	0.0	0.5
District 6	606 416	96.5	38.6	22.2	29.2	23.7	2.1	0.8	4.3	2.1	3.5	1.2	0.9	0.1	0.7	0.0	0.6
District 7	582 884	97.6	39.3	22.2	29.4	23.8	2.3	0.9	4.4	2.1	2.4	0.2	0.9	0.2	0.7	0.0	0.4
District 8	617 575	97.5	39.1	22.1	29.5	24.1	2.4	0.8	4.5	2.3	2.5	0.6	0.7	0.0	0.7	0.0	0.4
District 9	632 068	97.7	37.7	23.7	31.0	25.1	2.1	0.7	3.3	1.6	2.3	0.7	0.8	0.2	0.3	0.0	0.4
WYOMING	493 782	97.1	39.2	21.5	28.6	24.0	2.8	1.3	5.0	2.1	2.9	0.8	0.6	0.2	0.8	0.1	0.4
At Large	493 782	97.1	39.2	21.5	28.6	24.0	2.8	1.3	5.0	2.1	2.9	0.8	0.6	0.2	0.8	0.1	0.4

Table F. Congressional Districts 107th Congress

STATE District	Households by type, 2000												Households, 1990		
	Total households	Family households						Nonfamily households			Average house-hold size	Average family size	Total house-holds	Female house-holder[1]	House-holder living alone
		Total		Married couple		Female householder[1]		Total	Householder living alone						
			With own children under 18 years	Total	With own children under 18 years	Total	With own children under 18 years		Total	65 years and over					
	71	72	73	74	75	76	77	78	79	80	81	82	83	84	85
TEXAS—Cont'd															
District 28	208 259	77.4	40.7	54.5	28.1	17.6	9.9	22.6	19.2	8.3	3.05	3.50	178 888	15.7	18.0
District 29	203 259	76.5	45.3	53.3	32.4	16.5	10.0	23.5	18.8	4.9	3.29	3.78	184 101	14.5	21.6
District 30	214 509	68.1	35.7	41.2	21.4	20.6	11.8	31.9	25.9	6.0	2.87	3.48	196 049	19.5	25.0
UTAH	701 281	76.3	42.7	63.2	35.0	9.4	5.8	23.7	17.8	6.3	3.13	3.57	537 273	9.1	18.9
District 1	240 475	78.9	43.9	66.3	36.2	9.0	5.8	21.1	16.6	6.5	3.13	3.54	176 881	8.7	17.3
District 2	236 899	71.0	38.6	57.4	30.9	9.7	5.7	29.0	21.9	6.5	2.91	3.46	193 316	9.4	23.3
District 3	223 907	79.2	45.9	65.8	38.2	9.5	5.8	20.8	14.7	5.7	3.36	3.72	167 076	9.3	15.5
VERMONT	240 634	65.6	31.8	52.5	23.2	9.3	6.1	34.4	26.2	9.5	2.44	2.96	210 650	9.2	23.4
At Large	240 634	65.6	31.8	52.5	23.2	9.3	6.1	34.4	26.2	9.5	2.44	2.96	210 650	9.2	23.4
VIRGINIA	2 699 173	68.5	32.7	52.8	23.9	11.9	6.9	31.5	25.1	8.0	2.54	3.04	2 291 830	11.1	22.9
District 1	262 613	72.5	34.6	57.9	26.1	11.0	6.5	27.5	22.2	8.4	2.60	3.05	205 434	9.5	20.8
District 2	207 877	68.8	36.5	51.8	25.9	13.1	8.4	31.2	22.9	6.5	2.63	3.12	192 765	9.9	20.2
District 3	224 993	61.8	30.4	35.6	15.0	21.7	13.4	38.2	30.2	8.9	2.43	3.03	209 435	23.0	26.9
District 4	233 963	72.8	35.2	52.0	23.4	16.4	9.6	27.2	22.7	8.8	2.62	3.08	199 069	13.3	19.9
District 5	246 757	68.5	28.6	52.2	20.0	12.4	6.8	31.5	26.6	10.7	2.41	2.91	212 145	11.8	23.5
District 6	241 584	66.6	28.8	51.4	20.4	11.4	6.5	33.4	27.7	10.9	2.39	2.90	215 001	11.2	25.3
District 7	267 736	71.0	35.0	57.9	27.5	9.8	5.8	29.0	23.6	7.4	2.55	3.03	217 794	8.7	23.8
District 8	263 688	56.1	25.9	44.1	19.9	8.7	4.7	43.9	33.8	6.5	2.34	3.05	232 754	8.5	31.4
District 9	234 526	68.6	28.1	55.1	21.4	9.9	5.0	31.4	26.0	10.9	2.38	2.85	210 961	10.0	21.9
District 10	284 781	74.5	39.2	64.2	32.2	8.5	5.1	25.5	19.4	5.0	2.76	3.18	197 675	7.7	16.9
District 11	230 655	71.3	36.7	57.8	29.5	9.6	5.6	28.7	21.3	4.8	2.78	3.24	198 797	9.0	18.8
WASHINGTON	2 271 398	66.0	32.7	52.0	23.8	9.9	6.5	34.0	26.2	8.1	2.53	3.07	1 872 431	9.4	25.4
District 1	247 257	67.2	33.3	55.3	26.2	8.5	5.2	32.8	24.8	7.0	2.52	3.04	205 181	8.4	21.9
District 2	270 983	68.7	34.6	55.1	25.6	9.5	6.5	31.3	23.6	7.9	2.60	3.07	202 215	8.6	22.6
District 3	267 260	69.2	33.9	54.7	24.4	10.2	6.8	30.8	24.0	8.5	2.58	3.06	206 863	9.6	23.9
District 4	236 177	72.2	37.8	56.8	27.5	10.6	7.4	27.8	22.5	9.0	2.80	3.29	196 812	9.7	23.4
District 5	241 248	65.5	32.0	51.3	22.6	10.3	6.9	34.5	27.4	9.8	2.48	3.03	207 264	9.9	26.7
District 6	243 494	65.5	30.2	50.1	20.2	11.2	7.5	34.5	27.8	10.2	2.43	2.96	211 878	10.2	26.7
District 7	266 272	45.3	18.9	33.7	13.2	8.4	4.5	54.7	39.8	8.9	2.12	2.90	244 606	9.2	38.9
District 8	255 125	73.5	38.9	61.0	31.0	8.6	5.7	26.5	20.2	5.7	2.71	3.14	195 943	8.1	18.6
District 9	243 582	68.1	35.3	51.2	24.4	12.0	8.0	31.9	24.7	6.6	2.61	3.11	201 669	10.5	23.2
WEST VIRGINIA	736 481	68.4	28.9	54.0	21.3	10.7	5.7	31.6	27.1	11.9	2.40	2.90	688 557	10.7	24.5
District 1	242 584	66.9	28.1	53.2	20.9	10.2	5.4	33.1	27.8	12.3	2.38	2.91	230 990	10.0	25.4
District 2	258 077	69.3	30.0	54.8	22.0	10.5	5.9	30.7	26.4	11.0	2.42	2.91	230 330	10.3	24.0
District 3	235 820	69.1	28.6	53.9	21.0	11.6	5.9	30.9	27.2	12.4	2.39	2.89	227 237	11.7	24.1
WISCONSIN	2 084 544	66.5	31.9	53.2	23.7	9.6	6.2	33.5	26.8	9.9	2.50	3.05	1 822 118	9.6	24.3
District 1	230 453	69.4	34.1	54.3	24.6	10.9	7.1	30.6	24.7	9.2	2.58	3.08	198 940	10.8	22.7
District 2	250 519	61.5	30.1	50.3	23.0	7.8	5.2	38.5	28.2	8.3	2.41	2.99	208 577	7.7	25.6
District 3	228 360	66.6	32.0	55.2	24.7	7.8	5.1	33.4	25.7	10.5	2.52	3.05	197 728	7.6	24.1
District 4	231 445	63.7	29.9	49.1	21.8	10.4	6.2	36.3	29.7	10.7	2.45	3.08	210 102	10.5	26.3
District 5	201 567	58.3	30.5	33.7	14.8	20.6	13.7	41.7	33.7	9.8	2.44	3.18	207 859	19.3	30.1
District 6	234 087	68.8	32.0	57.6	25.1	7.6	4.9	31.2	25.5	10.7	2.50	3.02	201 139	7.3	23.5
District 7	228 895	68.3	31.4	56.5	24.1	8.0	5.1	31.7	26.1	11.3	2.49	3.01	202 076	7.8	23.9
District 8	241 200	68.2	32.3	56.5	24.8	8.0	5.3	31.8	25.8	10.0	2.50	3.02	202 772	7.9	23.5
District 9	238 018	73.0	34.8	62.9	28.8	7.0	4.3	27.0	22.3	9.2	2.59	3.06	192 925	6.7	19.0
WYOMING	193 608	67.4	32.7	54.8	24.3	8.7	6.0	32.6	26.3	8.8	2.48	3.00	168 839	8.3	24.5
At Large	193 608	67.4	32.7	54.8	24.3	8.7	6.0	32.6	26.3	8.8	2.48	3.00	168 839	8.3	24.5

[1] No spouse present.

Table F. Congressional Districts 107th Congress

STATE District	Percent change of households, 1990–2000	Total housing units	Occupied housing units (percent)	Housing occupancy — Vacant housing units — Total	For seasonal, recreational, or occasional use	Homeowner vacancy rate (percent)	Rental vacancy rate (percent)	Housing tenure — Occupied housing units — Total	Percent owner-occupied housing units	Percent renter-occupied housing units	Average household size of owner-occupied units	Average household size of renter-occupied units
	86	87	88	89	90	91	92	93	94	95	96	97
TEXAS—Cont'd												
District 28	16.4	232 177	89.7	10.3	2.0	1.5	8.2	208 259	70.7	29.3	3.08	2.97
District 29	10.4	219 601	92.6	7.4	0.3	1.3	8.4	203 259	53.6	46.4	3.45	3.10
District 30	9.4	229 952	93.3	6.7	0.3	1.2	6.4	214 509	46.1	53.9	3.03	2.73
UTAH	30.5	768 594	91.2	8.8	3.9	2.1	6.5	701 281	71.5	28.5	3.28	2.75
District 1	36.0	264 922	90.8	9.2	4.0	2.5	7.2	240 475	74.5	25.5	3.24	2.81
District 2	22.5	250 375	94.6	5.4	0.8	1.6	6.8	236 899	68.4	31.6	3.15	2.39
District 3	34.0	253 297	88.4	11.6	6.7	2.0	5.4	223 907	71.6	28.4	3.45	3.11
VERMONT	14.2	294 382	81.7	18.3	14.6	1.4	4.2	240 634	70.6	29.4	2.58	2.11
At Large	14.2	294 382	81.7	18.3	14.6	1.4	4.2	240 634	70.6	29.4	2.58	2.11
VIRGINIA	17.8	2 904 192	92.9	7.1	1.9	1.5	5.2	2 699 173	68.1	31.9	2.62	2.36
District 1	27.8	292 453	89.8	10.2	4.6	1.7	5.6	262 613	74.0	26.0	2.65	2.44
District 2	7.8	220 429	94.3	5.7	1.1	1.7	5.0	207 877	60.8	39.2	2.73	2.48
District 3	7.4	244 439	92.0	8.0	0.5	2.6	6.5	224 993	51.6	48.4	2.51	2.34
District 4	17.5	251 462	93.0	7.0	0.6	1.8	6.2	233 963	70.0	30.0	2.67	2.53
District 5	16.3	280 409	88.0	12.0	4.3	1.8	7.6	246 757	73.0	27.0	2.46	2.28
District 6	12.4	261 258	92.5	7.5	1.8	1.6	6.0	241 584	69.0	31.0	2.48	2.20
District 7	22.9	281 789	95.0	5.0	1.2	1.1	5.7	267 736	74.9	25.1	2.66	2.20
District 8	13.3	273 128	96.5	3.5	0.9	0.7	2.4	263 688	54.4	45.6	2.47	2.20
District 9	11.2	262 067	89.5	10.5	2.6	1.6	8.0	234 526	73.6	26.4	2.43	2.24
District 10	44.1	299 719	95.0	5.0	1.7	1.1	3.5	284 781	76.1	23.9	2.86	2.44
District 11	16.0	237 039	97.3	2.7	0.5	0.8	2.5	230 655	68.1	31.9	2.82	2.69
WASHINGTON	21.3	2 451 075	92.7	7.3	2.5	1.8	5.9	2 271 398	64.6	35.4	2.65	2.32
District 1	20.5	258 102	95.8	4.2	0.8	1.2	4.8	247 257	67.9	32.1	2.67	2.21
District 2	34.0	300 239	90.3	9.7	5.3	1.9	5.6	270 983	66.7	33.3	2.68	2.43
District 3	29.2	291 236	91.8	8.2	2.8	2.3	7.1	267 260	67.1	32.9	2.65	2.42
District 4	20.0	263 982	89.5	10.5	3.9	2.1	7.6	236 177	66.1	33.9	2.82	2.76
District 5	16.4	264 102	91.3	8.7	2.2	2.3	8.4	241 248	65.9	34.1	2.60	2.26
District 6	14.9	272 061	89.5	10.5	4.5	2.3	7.2	243 494	64.1	35.9	2.51	2.30
District 7	8.9	279 155	95.4	4.6	0.8	1.2	3.5	266 272	49.4	50.6	2.36	1.88
District 8	30.2	266 393	95.8	4.2	0.9	1.4	4.7	255 125	74.4	25.6	2.82	2.38
District 9	20.8	255 805	95.2	4.8	0.4	1.6	5.4	243 582	60.2	39.8	2.69	2.48
WEST VIRGINIA	7.0	844 623	87.2	12.8	3.9	2.2	9.1	736 481	75.2	24.8	2.47	2.17
District 1	5.0	274 341	88.4	11.6	2.9	2.1	9.5	242 584	74.0	26.0	2.48	2.12
District 2	12.0	296 608	87.0	13.0	5.2	2.0	7.9	258 077	75.8	24.2	2.49	2.20
District 3	3.8	273 674	86.2	13.8	3.4	2.4	9.9	235 820	75.7	24.3	2.45	2.20
WISCONSIN	14.4	2 321 144	89.8	10.2	6.1	1.2	5.6	2 084 544	68.4	31.6	2.66	2.15
District 1	15.8	251 704	91.6	8.4	4.3	1.3	6.1	230 453	70.5	29.5	2.69	2.32
District 2	20.1	265 855	94.2	5.8	2.1	1.2	4.7	250 519	62.8	37.2	2.62	2.06
District 3	15.5	247 250	92.4	7.6	3.7	1.2	4.8	228 360	71.7	28.3	2.68	2.12
District 4	10.2	241 938	95.7	4.3	0.2	0.9	5.1	231 445	60.6	39.4	2.65	2.15
District 5	-3.0	215 388	93.6	6.4	0.2	1.1	6.1	201 567	48.7	51.3	2.59	2.30
District 6	16.4	265 309	88.2	11.8	7.5	1.4	6.9	234 087	74.8	25.2	2.64	2.09
District 7	13.3	279 931	81.8	18.2	14.0	1.3	6.4	228 895	75.9	24.1	2.62	2.08
District 8	19.0	304 770	79.1	20.9	17.4	1.2	5.3	241 200	73.2	26.8	2.64	2.11
District 9	23.4	248 999	95.6	4.4	1.4	1.0	5.1	238 018	75.3	24.7	2.76	2.09
WYOMING	14.7	223 854	86.5	13.5	5.5	2.1	9.7	193 608	70.0	30.0	2.58	2.25
At Large	14.7	223 854	86.5	13.5	5.5	2.1	9.7	193 608	70.0	30.0	2.58	2.25

Appendices

Page

A-1   A. Geographic Concepts and Codes

B-1   B. Metropolitan Statistical Areas and Components

C-1   C. Metropolitan Statistical Areas and Components by State

D-1   D. Maps of States and Congressional Districts

E-1   E. Cities by County

F-1   F. Definitions

Appendices

APPENDIX A
GEOGRAPHIC CONCEPTS AND CODES

AREAS FOR WHICH DATA ARE PRESENTED

County and City Extra—Special Decennial Census Edition presents data for States (Table A), States and Counties (Table B), Metropolitan Areas (Table C), Cities (Table D), Towns in selected states (Table E), and Congressional Districts (Table F).

STATES AND COUNTIES

Data are presented for each of the 50 states, the District of Columbia, and the United States as a whole. The states are arranged alphabetically, and in Table B counties are arranged alphabetically within each state.

Data are presented for 3,141 counties and county equivalents. Maps of each state, showing their counties and county equivalents and their metropolitan areas are contained in Appendix D.

County equivalents

In Louisiana, the primary divisions of the state are known as parishes rather than counties. In Alaska, the county equivalents are the organized boroughs, together with the census areas that were developed for general statistical purposes by the State of Alaska and the U.S. Bureau of the Census. Four states—Maryland, Missouri, Nevada, and Virginia—have one or more incorporated places that are legally independent of any county and thus constitute primary divisions of their states. Within each state, independent cities are listed alphabetically following the list of counties. A list of independent cities is given at the end of this appendix. The District of Columbia is not divided into counties or county equivalents—data for the entire District are presented as a county equivalent. New York City contains five counties—Bronx, Kings, New York, Queens, and Richmond.

County changes since the 1990 Census

- Dade County in Florida officially became Miami-Dade County.
- Denali Borough in Alaska was formed primarily from the Yukon-Koyukuk census area and a small part of the Southeast Fairbanks census area.
- The Skagway-Yakutat-Angoon census area in Alaska was dissolved and replaced by Yakutat Borough and the Skagway-Hoonah-Angoon census area.
- South Boston City in Virginia, formerly an independent city, became a town within Halifax County.
- Yellowstone Park in Montana, which had not been part of any county, was dissolved as a county equivalent and became part of Park and Gallatin Counties.
- The city of Takoma Park, Maryland, formerly split between Montgomery and Prince George's Counties, moved its boundary, and now lies completely within Montgomery County.

METROPOLITAN AREAS

Table C presents data for 335 metropolitan areas comprising 248 metropolitan statistical areas (MSAs), 17 consolidated metropolitan statistical areas (CMSAs), 58 primary metropolitan statistical areas (PMSAs), and 12 New England county metropolitan areas (NECMAs). The left-hand column of each page provides an alphabetical listing of MSAs, CMSAs, and NECMAs—PMSAs are listed alphabetically under the CMSAs of which they are components.

The metropolitan areas used in this edition of *County and City Extra* are those defined by the U.S. government based on 1990 census data. The U.S. Office of Management and Budget first issued these definitions in December 1992. Additional revisions occurred throughout the decade, with the final revisions dated June 30, 1999.

In general, a metropolitan area is a geographic area consisting of a large population nucleus together with adjacent communities that have a high degree of economic and social integration with that nucleus. The major purpose of defining these areas is to enable all U.S. government agencies to use the same geographic definitions in tabulating and publishing data.

Metropolitan complexes with populations of one million or more may be divided into primary metropolitan statistical areas (PMSAs) with the support of local opinion. When PMSAs are defined, the larger metropolitan area of which they are components is designated a consolidated metropolitan statistical area (CMSA).

For most of the United States, metropolitan areas are defined in terms of counties because counties are the smallest geographical units for which a wide variety of statistical data can be obtained. In New England, however, the metropolitan area definitions are in terms of cities and towns because these subcounty units are of great local significance. An alternative concept for the New England states is the New England county metropolitan area (NECMA). NECMAs, rather than MSAs, CMSAs, and PMSAs, are presented for New England in this volume for consistency with other editions of *County and City Extra*.

In recent years, the Office of Management and Budget has issued new standards that will eventually replace the current metropolitan statistical areas. These will be based on the 2000 census and will be defined in 2003. The criteria will be new, and there will be smaller areas called micropolitan areas in addition to metropolitan areas.

CITIES

Table D presents data for 1,237 cities with 2000 census populations of 25,000 or more. Corresponding data for states are also provided. The states are arranged alphabetically, and the cities are arranged alphabetically within each state.

As used in this volume, the term *city* refers to places that have been incorporated as cities, boroughs, towns, or villages under the laws of their respective states. Towns in the New England states and six other states, however, are treated as minor civil divisions (MCDs) and are included separately in Table E. MCDs that are both incorporated places and towns in their respective states are included in both tables. For Hawaii, data for census designated places (CDPs) are included in the Cities table, since the U.S. Bureau of the Census does not recognize any incorporated places in Hawaii. CDPs are delineated by the U.S. Bureau of the Census, in cooperation with states and localities, as statistical counterparts of incorporated places for purposes of the decennial census. CDPs comprise densely settled concentrations of population that are identifiable by name but are not legally incorporated places.

A consolidated city is an incorporated place that has combined its governmental functions with a county or subcounty entity but contains one or more other semi-independent incorporated places that continue to function as local governments within the consolidated government. Consolidated cities included in this volume are Milford, CT; Athens-Clarke County, GA; Augusta-Richmond County, GA; Columbus, GA; Indianapolis, IN; Butte-Silver Bow, MT; and Nashville-Davidson, TN.

TOWNS

Table E presents data for 487 towns with 2000 census populations of 25,000 or more in Connecticut, Maine, Massachusetts, Michigan, Minnesota, New Hampshire, New Jersey, New York, Pennsylvania, Rhode Island, Vermont, and Wisconsin. In these 12 states, the towns serve as general-purpose local governments that generally can perform the same functions as incorporated places. These towns are referred to as minor civil divisions (MCDs) by the Census Bureau.

CONGRESSIONAL DISTRICTS

The congressional districts shown in this volume are the districts used for the election of the 107th Congress, which convened in January 2001. These are the districts that were established following the 1990 Census and are based on population data from that census. As a result of litigation, some boundaries have changed during the decade. The new data from the 2000 census will be used to draw boundaries for the 108th Congress. Data are shown for the 435 regular districts plus the District of Columbia, which has no representative. Corresponding data for each state also are included. States are listed alphabetically and districts numerically within each state. A map showing congressional districts of the 105th Congress is included in Appendix D. There have been no boundary changes since then.

GEOGRAPHIC CODES

Tables A, B, C, D, and E provide, in one or more columns at the beginning of the table, a geographic code or codes for each area.

In Table B (States and Counties), a five-digit state and county code is given for each state and county. The first two digits indicate the state; the remaining three represent the county. Within each state the counties are numbered in alphabetical order, beginning with 001, with even numbers usually omitted. Independent cities follow the counties and begin with the number 510. In the second column of Table B, a four-digit metropolitan area (MSA, PMSA, or NECMA) code is given for those counties that are within metropolitan areas. In Table A, a two-digit state code is provided. The state code is a sequential numbering, with some gaps, of the states and the District of Columbia in alphabetical order from Alabama (01) to Wyoming (56).

These codes have been established by the U.S. government as Federal Information Processing Standards and are often referred to as *FIPS codes*. They are used by U.S. government agencies and many other organizations for data presentation. The codes are provided in this volume for use in matching the data given here with other data sources in which counties may be identified by FIPS code. The metro area codes will also enable the user to identify the metro area of which a county is a component. Table C (Metropolitan Areas) provides the same metro area codes for each metropolitan area.

Table D (Cities) provides, in the first column, a seven-digit state and place code. The first two digits identify the state and are the same as the state FIPS codes described above. The remaining five digits are the place FIPS codes established by the U.S. government.

Table E (Towns) also includes a seven-digit code. The first two digits identify the state and the remaining five digits identify the minor civil division or town.

INDEPENDENT CITIES

Independent cities are not included in any county; data are presented separately in this volume.

MARYLAND:
  Baltimore: (Separate from Baltimore County)

MISSOURI:
  St. Louis: (Separate from St. Louis County)

NEVADA:
  Carson City

VIRGINIA:

Alexandria	Lynchburg
Bedford	Manassas
Bristol	Manassas Park
Buena Vista	Martinsville
Charlottesville	Newport News
Chesapeake	Norfolk
Clifton Forge	Norton
Colonial Heights	Petersburg
Covington	Poquoson
Danville	Portsmouth
Emporia	Radford
Fairfax	Richmond
Falls Church	Roanoke
Franklin	Salem
Fredericksburg	Staunton
Galax	Suffolk
Hampton	Virginia Beach
Harrisonburg	Waynesboro
Hopewell	Williamsburg
Lexington	Winchester

COUNTY TYPE

Table B (States and Counties) provides, in the third column, a *county type* code that identifies each county by its metropolitan/nonmetropolitan status and its size. These codes were developed by the Economic Research Service (ERS) of the U.S. Department of Agriculture and are commonly referred to as *Beale* codes after their originator, Calvin Beale. The ERS county typology scheme goes beyond the Beale codes to a detailed typology of economic and land-use classifications. In this volume, only the basic Beale codes, based on the 1990 Census, are used:

Metropolitan Counties

0. Central county of a metropolitan area of 1 million population or more.
1. Fringe county of a metropolitan area of 1 million population or more.
2. County in a metropolitan area of 250,000 to 1,000,000 population.
3. County in a metropolitan area of less than 250,000 population.

(Nonmetropolitan Counties

4. Urban population of 20,000 or more, adjacent to a metropolitan area.
5. Urban population of 20,000 or more, not adjacent to a metropolitan area.
6. Urban population of 2,500–19,999, adjacent to a metropolitan area.
7. Urban population of 2,500–19,999, not adjacent to a metropolitan area.
8. Completely rural (no places with a population of 2,500 or more), adjacent to a metropolitan area.
9. Completely rural (no places with a population of 2,500 or more), not adjacent to a metropolitan area.

MSA/ CMSA/ PMSA/ NECMA	State and County	Title and Geographic Components	2000 Population	MSA/ CMSA/ PMSA/ NECMA	State and County	Title and Geographic Components	2000 Population
0040		Abilene, TX MSA..................................	126 555		13 063	Clayton County, GA..........................	236 517
	48 441	Taylor County, TX........................	126 555		13 067	Cobb County, GA..............................	607 751
0080		Akron, OH PMSA................................	694 960		13 077	Coweta County, GA...........................	89 215
		(See Cleveland-Akron, OH CMSA)			13 089	De Kalb County, GA..........................	665 865
					13 097	Douglas County, GA..........................	92 174
					13 113	Fayette County, GA...........................	91 263
0120		Albany, GA MSA................................	120 822		13 117	Forsyth County, GA...........................	98 407
	13 095	Dougherty County, GA...................	96 065		13 121	Fulton County, GA............................	816 006
	13 177	Lee County, GA...........................	24 757		13 135	Gwinnett County, GA.........................	588 448
					13 151	Henry County, GA............................	119 341
0160		Albany-Schenectady-Troy, NY MSA..............	875 583		13 217	Newton County, GA...........................	62 001
	36 001	Albany County, NY.......................	294 565		13 223	Paulding County, GA.........................	81 678
	36 057	Montgomery County, NY...................	49 708		13 227	Pickens County, GA..........................	22 983
	36 083	Rensselaer County, NY...................	152 538		13 247	Rockdale County, GA.........................	70 111
	36 091	Saratoga County, NY.....................	200 635		13 255	Spalding County, GA.........................	58 417
	36 093	Schenectady County, NY..................	146 555		13 297	Walton County, GA...........................	60 687
	36 095	Schoharie County, NY....................	31 582	0560		Atlantic-Cape May, NJ PMSA...................	354 878
0200		Albuquerque, NM MSA..........................	712 738			(See Philadelphia-Wilmington-Atlantic City,	
	35 001	Bernalillo County, NM...................	556 678			PA-NJ-DE-MD CMSA)	
	35 043	Sandoval County, NM.....................	89 908				
	35 061	Valencia County, NM.....................	66 152	0580		Auburn-Opelika, AL MSA.......................	115 092
					01 081	Lee County, AL..............................	115 092
0220		Alexandria, LA MSA...........................	126 337				
	22 079	Rapides Parish, LA......................	126 337	0600		Augusta-Aiken, GA-SC MSA.....................	477 441
					13 073	Columbia County, GA..........................	89 288
0240		Allentown-Bethlehem-Easton, PA MSA............	637 958		13 189	McDuffie County, GA..........................	21 231
	42 025	Carbon County, PA.......................	58 802		13 245	Richmond County, GA..........................	199 775
	42 077	Lehigh County, PA.......................	312 090		45 003	Aiken County, SC.............................	142 552
	42 095	Northampton County, PA..................	267 066		45 037	Edgefield County, SC.........................	24 595
0280		Altoona, PA MSA..............................	129 144	0640		Austin-San Marcos, TX MSA....................	1 249 763
	42 013	Blair County, PA........................	129 144		48 021	Bastrop County, TX..........................	57 733
					48 055	Caldwell County, TX..........................	32 194
0320		Amarillo, TX MSA.............................	217 858		48 209	Hays County, TX.............................	97 589
	48 375	Potter County, TX.......................	113 546		48 453	Travis County, TX...........................	812 280
	48 381	Randall County, TX......................	104 312		48 491	Williamson County, TX........................	249 967
0380		Anchorage, AK MSA............................	260 283	0680		Bakersfield, CA MSA..........................	661 645
	02 020	Anchorage Borough, AK...................	260 283		06 029	Kern County, CA..............................	661 645
0440		Ann Arbor, MI PMSA...........................	578 736	0720	08 872	Baltimore, MD PMSA...........................	2 552 994
		(See Detroit-Ann Arbor-Flint, MI CMSA)				(See Washington-Baltimore, DC-MD-VA-WV	
						CMSA)	
0450		Anniston, AL MSA.............................	112 249				
	01 015	Calhoun County, AL......................	112 249	0733		Bangor, ME NECMA.............................	144 919
0460		Appleton-Oshkosh-Neenah, WI MSA................	358 365		23 019	Penobscot County, ME.........................	144 919
	55 015	Calumet County, WI......................	40 631	0743		Barnstable-Yarmouth, MA NECMA................	222 230
	55 087	Outagamie County, WI....................	160 971		25 001	Barnstable County, MA........................	222 230
	55 139	Winnebago County, WI....................	156 763	0760		Baton Rouge, LA MSA..........................	602 894
0480		Asheville, NC MSA............................	225 965		22 005	Ascension Parish, LA.........................	76 627
	37 021	Buncombe County, NC.....................	206 330		22 033	East Baton Rouge Parish, LA..................	412 852
	37 115	Madison County, NC......................	19 635		22 063	Livingston Parish, LA........................	91 814
0500		Athens, GA MSA...............................	153 444		22 121	West Baton Rouge Parish, LA..................	21 601
	13 059	Clarke County, GA.......................	101 489	0840		Beaumont-Port Arthur, TX MSA.................	385 090
	13 195	Madison County, GA......................	25 730		48 199	Hardin County, TX...........................	48 073
	13 219	Oconee County, GA.......................	26 225		48 245	Jefferson County, TX.........................	252 051
0520		Atlanta, GA MSA..............................	4 112 198		48 361	Orange County, TX...........................	84 966
	13 013	Barrow County, GA.......................	46 144	0860		Bellingham, WA MSA...........................	166 814
	13 015	Bartow County, GA.......................	76 019		53 073	Whatcom County, WA...........................	166 814
	13 045	Carroll County, GA......................	87 268				
	13 057	Cherokee County, GA.....................	141 903				

(MSA = metropolitan statistical area; CMSA = consolidated MSA; PMSA = primary MSA; and NECMA = New England county metropolitan area. For further information, see Appendix A.)

MSA/ CMSA/ PMSA/ NECMA	State and County	Tital and Geographic Components	2000 Population	MSA/ CMSA/ PMSA/ NECMA	State and County	Tital and Geographic Components	2000 Population
0870		Benton Harbor, MI MSA..........................	162 453	1260		Bryan-College Station, TX MSA..................	152 415
	26 021	Berrien County, MI........................	162 453		48 041	Brazos County, TX	152 415
0075		Bergen-Passaic, NJ PMSA	1 373 167	1280		Buffalo-Niagara Falls, NY MSA	1 170 111
		(See New York-Northern New Jersey-Long Island, NY-NJ-CT-PA CMSA)			36 029	Erie County, NY..........................	950 265
					36 063	Niagara County, NY......................	219 846
0880		Billings, MT MSA..................................	129 352	1303		Burlington, VT NECMA	198 889
	30 111	Yellowstone County, MT.....................	129 352		50 077	Chittenden County, VT	146 571
0920		Biloxi-Gulfport-Pascagoula, MS MSA	363 988		50 011	Franklin County, VT	45 417
	28 045	Hancock County, MS......................	42 967		50 013	Grand Isle County, VT	6 901
	28 047	Harrison County, MS	189 601	1320		Canton-Massillon, OH MSA.....................	406 934
	28 059	Jackson County, MS	131 420		39 019	Carroll County, OH	28 836
0960		Binghamton, NY MSA	252 320		39 151	Stark County, OH	378 098
	36 007	Broome County, NY	200 536	1350		Casper, WY MSA	66 533
	36 107	Tioga County, NY.........................	51 784		56 025	Natrona County, WY	66 533
1000		Birmingham, AL MSA	921 106	1360		Cedar Rapids, IA MSA	191 701
	01 009	Blount County, AL.........................	51 024		19 113	Linn County, IA	191 701
	01 073	Jefferson County, AL......................	662 047	1400		Champaign-Urbana, IL MSA	179 669
	01 115	St. Clair County, AL.......................	64 742		17 019	Champaign County, IL......................	179 669
	01 117	Shelby County, AL	143 293				
1010		Bismarck, ND MSA	94 719	1480		Charleston, WV MSA	251 662
1010	38 015	Burleigh County, ND.......................	69 416		54 039	Kanawha County, WV	200 073
1010	38 059	Morton County, ND........................	25 303		54 079	Putnam County, WV	51 589
1020		Bloomington, IN MSA	120 563	1440		Charleston-North Charleston, SC MSA	549 033
1020	18 105	Monroe County, IN	120 563		45 015	Berkeley County, SC	142 651
1040		Bloomington-Normal, IL MSA	150 433		45 019	Charleston County, SC	309 969
1040	17 113	McLean County, IL	150 433		45 035	Dorchester County, SC....................	96 413
1080		Boise City, ID MSA..............................	432 345	1520		Charlotte-Gastonia-Rock Hill, NC-SC MSA	1 499 293
1080	16 001	Ada County, ID	300 904		37 025	Cabarrus County, NC	131 063
1080	16 027	Canyon County, ID	131 441		37 071	Gaston County, NC	190 365
1123		Boston-Worcester-Lawrence-Lowell-Brockton, MA-NH NECMA	6 057 826		37 109	Lincoln County, NC	63 780
	25 005	Bristol County, MA........................	534 678		37 119	Mecklenburg County, NC	695 454
	25 009	Essex County, MA	723 419		37 159	Rowan County, NC	130 340
	25 017	Middlesex County, MA......................	1 465 396		37 179	Union County, NC........................	123 677
	25 021	Norfolk County, MA	650 308		45 091	York County, SC	164 614
	25 023	Plymouth County, MA	472 822	1540		Charlottesville, VA MSA	159 576
	25 025	Suffolk County, MA	689 807		51 003	Albemarle County, VA	79 236
	25 027	Worcester County, MA.....................	750 963		51 065	Fluvanna County, VA	20 047
	33 011	Hillsborough County, NH	380 841		51 079	Greene County, VA	15 244
	33 015	Rockingham County, NH	277 359		51 540	Charlottesville City, VA	45 049
	33 017	Strafford County, NH	112 233	1560		Chattanooga, TN-GA MSA......................	465 161
1125		Boulder-Longmont, CO PMSA	291 288		13 047	Catoosa County, GA......................	53 282
		(See Denver-Boulder-Greeley, CO CMSA)			13 083	Dade County, GA	15 154
1145		Brazoria, TX PMSA	241 767		13 295	Walker County, GA	61 053
		(See Houston-Galveston-Brazoria, TX CMSA)			47 065	Hamilton County, TN	307 896
					47 115	Marion County, TN	27 776
1150		Bremerton, WA PMSA	231 969	1580		Cheyenne, WY MSA	81 607
		(See Seattle-Tacoma-Bremerton, WA CMSA)			56 021	Laramie County, WY	81 607
1240		Brownsville-Harlingen-San Benito, TX MSA	335 227	14		Chicago-Gary-Kenosha, IL-IN-WI CMSA............	9 157 540
	48 061	Cameron County, TX.......................	335 227	1600		Chicago, IL PMSA.............................	8 272 768
					17 031	Cook County, IL	5 376 741
					17 037	De Kalb County, IL	88 969
					17 043	Du Page County, IL	904 161
					17 063	Grundy County, IL	37 535

Metropolitan Statistical Areas and Components – Continued

(MSA = metropolitan statistical area; CMSA = consolidated MSA; PMSA = primary MSA; and
NECMA = New England county metropolitan area. For further information, see Appendix A.)

Geographic Codes MSA/ CMSA/ PMSA/ NECMA	Geographic Codes State and County	Tital and Geographic Components	2000 Population	Geographic Codes MSA/ CMSA/ PMSA/ NECMA	Geographic Codes State and County	Tital and Geographic Components	2000 Population
	17 089	Kane County, IL	404 119	1800		Columbus, GA-AL MSA	274 624
	17 093	Kendall County, IL	54 544		01 113	Russell County, AL	49 756
	17 097	Lake County, IL	644 356		13 053	Chattahoochee County, GA	14 882
	17 111	McHenry County, IL	260 077		13 145	Harris County, GA	23 695
	17 197	Will County, IL	502 266		13 215	Muscogee County, GA	186 291
2960		Gary, IN PMSA	631 362	1840		Columbus, OH MSA	1 540 157
	18 089	Lake County, IN	484 564		39 041	Delaware County, OH	109 989
	18 127	Porter County, IN	146 798		39 045	Fairfield County, OH	122 759
					39 049	Franklin County, OH	1 068 978
3740		Kankakee, IL PMSA	103 833		39 089	Licking County, OH	145 491
	17 091	Kankakee County, IL	103 833		39 097	Madison County, OH	40 213
					39 129	Pickaway County, OH	52 727
3800		Kenosha, WI PMSA	149 577	1880		Corpus Christi, TX MSA	380 783
	55 059	Kenosha County, WI	149 577		48 355	Nueces County, TX	313 645
1620		Chico-Paradise, CA MSA	203 171		48 409	San Patricio County, TX	67 138
	06 007	Butte County, CA	203 171	1890		Corvallis, OR MSA	78 153
21		Cincinnati-Hamilton, OH-KY-IN CMSA	1 979 202		41 003	Benton County, OR	78 153
1640		Cincinnati, OH-KY-IN PMSA	1 646 395	1900		Cumberland, MD-WV MSA	102 008
	18 029	Dearborn County, IN	46 109		24 001	Allegany County, MD	74 930
	18 115	Ohio County, IN	5 623		54 057	Mineral County, WV	27 078
	21 015	Boone County, KY	85 991				
	21 037	Campbell County, KY	88 616	31		Dallas-Fort Worth, TX CMSA	5 221 801
	21 077	Gallatin County, KY	7 870				
	21 081	Grant County, KY	22 384	1920		Dallas, TX PMSA	3 519 176
	21 117	Kenton County, KY	151 464		48 085	Collin County, TX	491 675
	21 191	Pendleton County, KY	14 390		48 113	Dallas County, TX	2 218 899
	39 015	Brown County, OH	42 285		48 121	Denton County, TX	432 976
	39 025	Clermont County, OH	177 977		48 139	Ellis County, TX	111 360
	39 061	Hamilton County, OH	845 303		48 213	Henderson County, TX	73 277
	39 165	Warren County, OH	158 383		48 231	Hunt County, TX	76 596
					48 257	Kaufman County, TX	71 313
3200		Hamilton-Middletown, OH PMSA	332 807		48 397	Rockwall County, TX	43 080
	39 017	Butler County, OH	332 807	2800		Fort Worth-Arlington, TX PMSA	1 702 625
1660		Clarksville-Hopkinsville, TN-KY MSA	207 033		48 221	Hood County, TX	41 100
	21 047	Christian County, KY	72 265		48 251	Johnson County, TX	126 811
	47 125	Montgomery County, TN	134 768		48 367	Parker County, TX	88 495
					48 439	Tarrant County, TX	1 446 219
28		Cleveland-Akron, OH CMSA	2 945 831	1950		Danville, VA MSA	110 156
80		Akron, OH PMSA	694 960		51 143	Pittsylvania County, VA	61 745
	39 133	Portage County, OH	152 061		51 590	Danville City, VA	48 411
	39 153	Summit County, OH	542 899	1960		Davenport-Moline-Rock Island, IA-IL MSA	359 062
1680		Cleveland-Lorain-Elyria, OH PMSA	2 250 871		17 073	Henry County, IL	51 020
	39 007	Ashtabula County, OH	102 728		17 161	Rock Island County, IL	149 374
	39 035	Cuyahoga County, OH	1 393 978		19 163	Scott County, IA	158 668
	39 055	Geauga County, OH	90 895	2000		Dayton-Springfield, OH MSA	950 558
	39 085	Lake County, OH	227 511		39 023	Clark County, OH	144 742
	39 093	Lorain County, OH	284 664		39 057	Greene County, OH	147 886
	39 103	Medina County, OH	151 095		39 109	Miami County, OH	98 868
1720		Colorado Springs, CO MSA	516 929		39 113	Montgomery County, OH	559 062
	08 041	El Paso County, CO	516 929	2020		Daytona Beach, FL MSA	493 175
1740		Columbia, MO MSA	135 454		12 035	Flagler County, FL	49 832
	29 019	Boone County, MO	135 454		12 127	Volusia County, FL	443 343
1760		Columbia, SC MSA	536 691	2030		Decatur, AL MSA	145 867
	45 063	Lexington County, SC	216 014		01 079	Lawrence County, AL	34 803
	45 079	Richland County, SC	320 677		01 103	Morgan County, AL	111 064

Metropolitan Statistical Areas and Components – Continued

(MSA = metropolitan statistical area; CMSA = consolidated MSA; PMSA = primary MSA; and NECMA = New England county metropolitan area. For further information, see Appendix A.)

MSA/ CMSA/ PMSA/ NECMA	State and County	Tital and Geographic Components	2000 Population	MSA/ CMSA/ PMSA/ NECMA	State and County	Tital and Geographic Components	2000 Population
2040		Decatur, IL MSA	114 706	2330		Elkhart-Goshen, IN MSA	182 791
	17 115	Macon County, IL	114 706		18 039	Elkhart County, IN	182 791
34		Denver-Boulder-Greeley, CO CMSA	2 581 506	2335		Elmira, NY MSA	91 070
1125		Boulder-Longmont, CO PMSA	291 288		36 015	Chemung County, NY	91 070
	08 013	Boulder County, CO	291 288	2340		Enid, OK MSA	57 813
2080		Denver, CO PMSA	2 109 282		40 047	Garfield County, OK	57 813
	08 001	Adams County, CO	363 857	2360		Erie, PA MSA	280 843
	08 005	Arapahoe County, CO	487 967		42 049	Erie County, PA	280 843
	08 031	Denver County, CO	554 636	2400		Eugene-Springfield, OR MSA	322 959
	08 035	Douglas County, CO	175 766		41 039	Lane County, OR	322 959
	08 059	Jefferson County, CO	527 056	2440		Evansville-Henderson, IN-KY MSA	296 195
3060		Greeley, CO PMSA	180 936		18 129	Posey County, IN	27 061
	08 123	Weld County, CO	180 936		18 163	Vanderburgh County, IN	171 922
2120		Des Moines, IA MSA	456 022		18 173	Warrick County, IN	52 383
	19 049	Dallas County, IA	40 750		21 101	Henderson County, KY	44 829
	19 153	Polk County, IA	374 601	2520		Fargo-Moorhead, ND-MN MSA	174 367
	19 181	Warren County, IA	40 671		27 027	Clay County, MN	51 229
2162		Detroit-Ann Arbor-Flint, MI CMSA	5 456 428		38 017	Cass County, ND	123 138
0440		Ann Arbor, MI PMSA	578 736	2560		Fayetteville, NC MSA	302 963
	26 091	Lenawee County, MI	98 890		37 051	Cumberland County, NC	302 963
	26 093	Livingston County, MI	156 951	2580		Fayetteville-Springdale-Rogers, AR MSA	311 121
	26 161	Washtenaw County, MI	322 895		05 007	Benton County, AR	153 406
2160		Detroit, MI PMSA	4 441 551		05 143	Washington County, AR	157 715
	26 087	Lapeer County, MI	87 904	2620		Flagstaff, AZ-UT MSA	122 366
	26 099	Macomb County, MI	788 149		04 005	Coconino County, AZ	116 320
	26 115	Monroe County, MI	145 945		49 025	Kane County, UT	6 046
	26 125	Oakland County, MI	1 194 156	2640		Flint, MI PMSA	436 141
	26 147	St. Clair County, MI	164 235			(See Detroit-Ann Arbor-Flint, MI CMSA)	
	26 163	Wayne County, MI	2 061 162	2650		Florence, AL MSA	142 950
2640		Flint, MI PMSA	436 141		01 033	Colbert County, AL	54 984
	26 049	Genesee County, MI	436 141		01 077	Lauderdale County, AL	87 966
2180		Dothan, AL MSA	137 916	2655		Florence, SC MSA	125 761
	01 045	Dale County, AL	49 129		45 041	Florence County, SC	125 761
	01 069	Houston County, AL	88 787	2670		Fort Collins-Loveland, CO MSA	251 494
2190		Dover, DE MSA	126 697		08 069	Larimer County, CO	251 494
	10 001	Kent County, DE	126 697	2680		Fort Lauderdale, FL PMSA	1 623 018
2200		Dubuque, IA MSA	89 143			(See Miami-Fort Lauderdale, FL CMSA)	
	19 061	Dubuque County, IA	89 143	2700		Fort Myers-Cape Coral, FL MSA	440 888
2240		Duluth-Superior, MN-WI MSA	243 815		12 071	Lee County, FL	440 888
	27 137	St. Louis County, MN	200 528	2710		Fort Pierce-Port St. Lucie, FL MSA	319 426
	55 031	Douglas County, WI	43 287		12 085	Martin County, FL	126 731
2281		Dutchess County, NY PMSA	280 150		12 111	St. Lucie County, FL	192 695
		(See New York-Northern New Jersey-Long Island, NY-NJ-CT-PA CMSA)		2720		Fort Smith, AR-OK MSA	207 290
2290		Eau Claire, WI MSA	148 337		05 033	Crawford County, AR	53 247
	55 017	Chippewa County, WI	55 195		05 131	Sebastian County, AR	115 071
	55 035	Eau Claire County, WI	93 142		40 135	Sequoyah County, OK	38 972
2320		El Paso, TX MSA	679 622	2750		Fort Walton Beach, FL MSA	170 498
	48 141	El Paso County, TX	679 622		12 091	Okaloosa County, FL	170 498

Metropolitan Statistical Areas and Components – Continued

(MSA = metropolitan statistical area; CMSA = consolidated MSA; PMSA = primary MSA; and NECMA = New England county metropolitan area. For further information, see Appendix A.)

MSA/CMSA/PMSA/NECMA	State and County	Title and Geographic Components	2000 Population
2760		Fort Wayne, IN MSA	502 141
	18 001	Adams County, IN	33 625
	18 003	Allen County, IN	331 849
	18 033	De Kalb County, IN	40 285
	18 069	Huntington County, IN	38 075
	18 179	Wells County, IN	27 600
	18 183	Whitley County, IN	30 707
2800		Fort Worth-Arlington, TX PMSA	1 702 625
		(See Dallas-Fort Worth, TX CMSA)	
2840		Fresno, CA MSA	922 516
	06 019	Fresno County, CA	799 407
	06 039	Madera County, CA	123 109
2880		Gadsden, AL MSA	103 459
	01 055	Etowah County, AL	103 459
2900		Gainesville, FL MSA	217 955
	12 001	Alachua County, FL	217 955
2920		Galveston-Texas City, TX PMSA	250 158
		(See Houston-Galveston-Brazoria, TX CMSA)	
2975		Glens Falls, NY MSA	124 345
	36 113	Warren County, NY	63 303
	36 115	Washington County, NY	61 042
2980		Goldsboro, NC MSA	113 329
	37 191	Wayne County, NC	113 329
2985		Grand Forks, ND-MN MSA	97 478
	27 119	Polk County, MN	31 369
	38 035	Grand Forks County, ND	66 109
2995		Grand Junction, CO MSA	116 255
	08 077	Mesa County, CO	116 255
3000		Grand Rapids-Muskegon-Holland, MI MSA	1 088 514
	26 005	Allegan County, MI	105 665
	26 081	Kent County, MI	574 335
	26 121	Muskegon County, MI	170 200
	26 139	Ottawa County, MI	238 314
3040		Great Falls, MT MSA	80 357
	30 013	Cascade County, MT	80 357
3060		Greeley, CO PMSA	180 936
		(See Denver-Boulder-Greeley, CO CMSA)	
3080		Green Bay, WI MSA	226 778
	55 009	Brown County, WI	226 778
3120		Greensboro-Winston-Salem-High Point, NC MSA	1 251 509
	37 001	Alamance County, NC	130 800
	37 057	Davidson County, NC	147 246
	37 059	Davie County, NC	34 835
	37 067	Forsyth County, NC	306 067
	37 081	Guilford County, NC	421 048
	37 151	Randolph County, NC	130 454
	37 169	Stokes County, NC	44 711
	37 197	Yadkin County, NC	36 348
3150		Greenville, NC MSA	133 798
	37 147	Pitt County, NC	133 798
3160		Greenville-Spartanburg-Anderson, SC MSA	962 441
	45 007	Anderson County, SC	165 740
	45 021	Cherokee County, SC	52 537
	45 045	Greenville County, SC	379 616
	45 077	Pickens County, SC	110 757
	45 083	Spartanburg County, SC	253 791
3180		Hagerstown, MD PMSA	131 923
		(See Washington-Baltimore, DC-MD-VA-WV CMSA)	
3240		Harrisburg-Lebanon-Carlisle, PA MSA	629 401
	42 041	Cumberland County, PA	213 674
	42 043	Dauphin County, PA	251 798
	42 075	Lebanon County, PA	120 327
	42 099	Perry County, PA	43 602
3280		Hartford, CT NECMA	1 148 618
	09 003	Hartford County, CT	857 183
	09 007	Middlesex County, CT	155 071
	09 013	Tolland County, CT	136 364
3285		Hattiesburg, MS MSA	111 674
	28 035	Forrest County, MS	72 604
	28 073	Lamar County, MS	39 070
3290		Hickory-Morganton-Lenoir, NC MSA	341 851
	37 003	Alexander County, NC	33 603
	37 023	Burke County, NC	89 148
	37 027	Caldwell County, NC	77 415
	37 035	Catawba County, NC	141 685
3320		Honolulu, HI MSA	876 156
	15 003	Honolulu County, HI	876 156
3350		Houma, LA MSA	194 477
	22 057	Lafourche Parish, LA	89 974
	22 109	Terrebonne Parish, LA	104 503
3362		Houston-Galveston-Brazoria, TX CMSA	4 669 571
1145		Brazoria, TX PMSA	241 767
	48 039	Brazoria County, TX	241 767
2920		Galveston-Texas City, TX PMSA	250 158
		Galveston County, TX	250 158
3360		Houston, TX PMSA	4 177 646
	48 071	Chambers County, TX	26 031
	48 157	Fort Bend County, TX	354 452
	48 201	Harris County, TX	3 400 578
	48 291	Liberty County, TX	70 154
	48 339	Montgomery County, TX	293 768
	48 473	Waller County, TX	32 663
3400		Huntington-Ashland, WV-KY-OH MSA	315 538
	21 019	Boyd County, KY	49 752
	21 043	Carter County, KY	26 889
	21 089	Greenup County, KY	36 891
	39 087	Lawrence County, OH	62 319
	54 011	Cabell County, WV	96 784
	54 099	Wayne County, WV	42 903

Metropolitan Statistical Areas and Components – Continued

(MSA = metropolitan statistical area; CMSA = consolidated MSA; PMSA = primary MSA; and NECMA = New England county metropolitan area. For further information, see Appendix A.)

MSA/CMSA/PMSA/NECMA	State and County	Title and Geographic Components	2000 Population
3440		Huntsville, AL MSA	342 376
	01 083	Limestone County, AL	65 676
	01 089	Madison County, AL	276 700
3480		Indianapolis, IN MSA	1 607 486
	18 011	Boone County, IN	46 107
	18 057	Hamilton County, IN	182 740
	18 059	Hancock County, IN	55 391
	18 063	Hendricks County, IN	104 093
	18 081	Johnson County, IN	115 209
	18 095	Madison County, IN	133 358
	18 097	Marion County, IN	860 454
	18 109	Morgan County, IN	66 689
	18 145	Shelby County, IN	43 445
3500		Iowa City, IA MSA	111 006
	19 103	Johnson County, IA	111 006
3520		Jackson, MI MSA	158 422
	26 075	Jackson County, MI	158 422
3560		Jackson, MS MSA	440 801
	28 049	Hinds County, MS	250 800
	28 089	Madison County, MS	74 674
	28 121	Rankin County, MS	115 327
3580		Jackson, TN MSA	107 377
	47 023	Chester County, TN	15 540
	47 113	Madison County, TN	91 837
3600		Jacksonville, FL MSA	1 100 491
	12 019	Clay County, FL	140 814
	12 031	Duval County, FL	778 879
	12 089	Nassau County, FL	57 663
	12 109	St. Johns County, FL	123 135
3605		Jacksonville, NC MSA	150 355
	37 133	Onslow County, NC	150 355
3610		Jamestown, NY MSA	139 750
	36 013	Chautauqua County, NY	139 750
3620		Janesville-Beloit, WI MSA	152 307
	55 105	Rock County, WI	152 307
3640		Jersey City, NJ PMSA	608 975
		(See New York-Northern New Jersey-Long Island, NY-NJ-CT-PA CMSA)	
3660		Johnson City-Kingsport-Bristol, TN-VA MSA	480 091
	47 019	Carter County, TN	56 742
	47 073	Hawkins County, TN	53 563
	47 163	Sullivan County, TN	153 048
	47 171	Unicoi County, TN	17 667
	47 179	Washington County, TN	107 198
	51 169	Scott County, VA	23 403
	51 191	Washington County, VA	51 103
	51 520	Bristol City, VA	17 367
3680		Johnstown, PA MSA	232 621
	42 021	Cambria County, PA	152 598
	42 111	Somerset County, PA	80 023
3700		Jonesboro, AR MSA	82 148
	5 031	Craighead County, AR	82 148
3710		Joplin, MO MSA	157 322
	29 097	Jasper County, MO	104 686
	29 145	Newton County, MO	52 636
3720		Kalamazoo-Battle Creek, MI MSA	452 851
	26 025	Calhoun County, MI	137 985
	26 077	Kalamazoo County, MI	238 603
	26 159	Van Buren County, MI	76 263
3740		Kankakee, IL PMSA	103 833
		(See Chicago-Gary-Kenosha, IL-IN-WI CMSA)	
3760		Kansas City, MO-KS MSA	1 776 062
	20 091	Johnson County, KS	451 086
	20 103	Leavenworth County, KS	68 691
	20 121	Miami County, KS	28 351
	20 209	Wyandotte County, KS	157 882
	29 037	Cass County, MO	82 092
	29 047	Clay County, MO	184 006
	29 049	Clinton County, MO	18 979
	29 095	Jackson County, MO	654 880
	29 107	Lafayette County, MO	32 960
	29 165	Platte County, MO	73 781
	29 177	Ray County, MO	23 354
3800		Kenosha, WI PMSA	149 577
		(See Chicago-Gary-Kenosha, IL-IN-WI CMSA)	
3810		Killeen-Temple, TX MSA	312 952
	48 027	Bell County, TX	237 974
	48 099	Coryell County, TX	74 978
3840		Knoxville, TN MSA	687 249
	47 001	Anderson County, TN	71 330
	47 009	Blount County, TN	105 823
	47 093	Knox County, TN	382 032
	47 105	Loudon County, TN	39 086
	47 155	Sevier County, TN	71 170
	47 173	Union County, TN	17 808
3850		Kokomo, IN MSA	101 541
	18 067	Howard County, IN	84 964
	18 159	Tipton County, IN	16 577
3870		La Crosse, WI-MN MSA	126 838
	27 055	Houston County, MN	19 718
	55 063	La Crosse County, WI	107 120
3920		Lafayette, IN MSA	182 821
	18 023	Clinton County, IN	33 866
	18 157	Tippecanoe County, IN	148 955
3880		Lafayette, LA MSA	385 647
	22 001	Acadia Parish, LA	58 861
	22 055	Lafayette Parish, LA	190 503
	22 097	St. Landry Parish, LA	87 700
	22 099	St. Martin Parish, LA	48 583
3960		Lake Charles, LA MSA	183 577
	22 019	Calcasieu Parish, LA	183 577
3980		Lakeland-Winter Haven, FL MSA	483 924
	12 105	Polk County, FL	483 924

Metropolitan Statistical Areas and Components – Continued

(MSA = metropolitan statistical area; CMSA = consolidated MSA; PMSA = primary MSA; and NECMA = New England county metropolitan area. For further information, see Appendix A.)

MSA/CMSA/PMSA/NECMA	State and County	Title and Geographic Components	2000 Population
4000		Lancaster, PA MSA	470 658
	42 071	Lancaster County, PA	470 658
4040		Lansing-East Lansing, MI MSA	447 728
	26 037	Clinton County, MI	64 753
	26 045	Eaton County, MI	103 655
	26 065	Ingham County, MI	279 320
4080		Laredo, TX MSA	193 117
	48 479	Webb County, TX	193 117
4100		Las Cruces, NM MSA	174 682
	35 013	Dona Ana County, NM	174 682
4120		Las Vegas, NV-AZ MSA	1 563 282
	04 015	Mohave County, AZ	155 032
	32 003	Clark County, NV	1 375 765
	32 023	Nye County, NV	32 485
4150		Lawrence, KS MSA	99 962
	20 045	Douglas County, KS	99 962
4200		Lawton, OK MSA	114 996
	40 031	Comanche County, OK	114 996
4240		Lewiston-Auburn, ME NECMA	103 793
	23 001	Androscoggin County, ME	103 793
4280		Lexington, KY MSA	479 198
	21 017	Bourbon County, KY	19 360
	21 049	Clark County, KY	33 144
	21 067	Fayette County, KY	260 512
	21 113	Jessamine County, KY	39 041
	21 151	Madison County, KY	70 872
	21 209	Scott County, KY	33 061
	21 239	Woodford County, KY	23 208
4320		Lima, OH MSA	155 084
	39 003	Allen County, OH	108 473
	39 011	Auglaize County, OH	46 611
4360		Lincoln, NE MSA	250 291
	31 109	Lancaster County, NE	250 291
4400		Little Rock-North Little Rock, AR MSA	583 845
	05 045	Faulkner County, AR	86 014
	05 085	Lonoke County, AR	52 828
	05 119	Pulaski County, AR	361 474
	05 125	Saline County, AR	83 529
4420		Longview-Marshall, TX MSA	208 780
	48 183	Gregg County, TX	111 379
	48 203	Harrison County, TX	62 110
	48 459	Upshur County, TX	35 291
4472		Los Angeles-Riverside-Orange County, CA CMSA	16 373 645
4480		Los Angeles-Long Beach, CA PMSA	9 519 338
	06 037	Los Angeles County, CA	9 519 338
5945		Orange County, CA PMSA	2 846 289
	06 059	Orange County, CA	2 846 289
4520		Louisville, KY-IN MSA	1 025 598
	18 019	Clark County, IN	96 472
	18 043	Floyd County, IN	70 823
	18 061	Harrison County, IN	34 325
	18 143	Scott County, IN	22 960
	21 029	Bullitt County, KY	61 236
	21 111	Jefferson County, KY	693 604
	21 185	Oldham County, KY	46 178
4600		Lubbock, TX MSA	242 628
	48 303	Lubbock County, TX	242 628
4640		Lynchburg, VA MSA	214 911
	51 009	Amherst County, VA	31 894
	51 019	Bedford County, VA	60 371
	51 031	Campbell County, VA	51 078
	51 515	Bedford City, VA	6 299
	51 680	Lynchburg City, VA	65 269
4680		Macon, GA MSA	322 549
	13 021	Bibb County, GA	153 887
	13 153	Houston County, GA	110 765
	13 169	Jones County, GA	23 639
	13 225	Peach County, GA	23 668
	13 289	Twiggs County, GA	10 590
4720		Madison, WI MSA	426 526
	55 025	Dane County, WI	426 526
4800		Mansfield, OH MSA	175 818
	39 033	Crawford County, OH	46 966
	39 139	Richland County, OH	128 852
4880		McAllen-Edinburg-Mission, TX MSA	569 463
	48 215	Hidalgo County, TX	569 463
4890		Medford-Ashland, OR MSA	181 269
	41 029	Jackson County, OR	181 269
4900		Melbourne-Titusville-Palm Bay, FL MSA	476 230
	12 009	Brevard County, FL	476 230
4920		Memphis, TN-AR-MS MSA	1 135 614
	05 035	Crittenden County, AR	50 866
	28 033	De Soto County, MS	107 199
	47 047	Fayette County, TN	28 806
	47 157	Shelby County, TN	897 472
	47 167	Tipton County, TN	51 271
4940		Merced, CA MSA	210 554
	06 047	Merced County, CA	210 554
4992		Miami-Fort Lauderdale, FL CMSA	3 876 380
2680		Fort Lauderdale, FL PMSA	1 623 018
	12 011	Broward County, FL	1 623 018
5000		Miami, FL PMSA	2 253 362
	12 086	Miami-Dade County, FL	2 253 362
5082		Milwaukee-Racine, WI CMSA	1 689 572
5080		Milwaukee-Waukesha, WI PMSA	1 500 741
	55 079	Milwaukee County, WI	940 164
	55 089	Ozaukee County, WI	82 317
	55 131	Washington County, WI	117 493
	55 133	Waukesha County, WI	360 767

(MSA = metropolitan statistical area; CMSA = consolidated MSA; PMSA = primary MSA; and
NECMA = New England county metropolitan area. For further information, see Appendix A.)

Geographic Codes MSA/CMSA/PMSA/NECMA	State and County	Tital and Geographic Components	2000 Population	Geographic Codes MSA/CMSA/PMSA/NECMA	State and County	Tital and Geographic Components	2000 Population
6600		Racine, WI PMSA	188 831	5560		New Orleans, LA MSA	1 337 726
	55 101	Racine County, WI.........................	188 831		22 051	Jefferson Parish, LA	455 466
5120		Minneapolis-St. Paul, MN-WI MSA	2 968 806		22 071	Orleans Parish, LA	484 674
	27 003	Anoka County, MN	298 084		22 075	Plaquemines Parish, LA	26 757
	27 019	Carver County, MN	70 205		22 087	St. Bernard Parish, LA	67 229
	27 025	Chisago County, MN	41 101		22 089	St. Charles Parish, LA	48 072
	27 037	Dakota County, MN	355 904		22 093	St. James Parish, LA	21 216
	27 053	Hennepin County, MN	1 116 200		22 095	St. John the Baptist Parish, LA	43 044
	27 059	Isanti County, MN	31 287		22 103	St. Tammany Parish, LA	191 268
	27 123	Ramsey County, MN	511 035	5600		New York, NY PMSA	9 314 235
	27 139	Scott County, MN	89 498			(See New York-Northern New Jersey-Long	
	27 141	Sherburne County, MN	64 417			Island, NY-NJ-CT-PA CMSA)	
	27 163	Washington County, MN	201 130				
	27 171	Wright County, MN	89 986	70		New York-Northern New Jersey-Long Island,	21 199 865
	55 093	Pierce County, WI	36 804			NY-NJ-CT-PA CMSA	
	55 109	St. Croix County, WI	63 155				
				875		Bergen-Passaic, NJ PMSA	1 373 167
5140		Missoula, MT MSA	95 802		34 003	Bergen County, NJ	884 118
	30 063	Missoula County, MT	95 802		34 031	Passaic County, NJ	489 049
5160		Mobile, AL MSA	540 258	2281		Dutchess County, NY PMSA	280 150
	01 003	Baldwin County, AL	140 415		36 027	Dutchess County, NY	280 150
	01 097	Mobile County, AL	399 843				
5170		Modesto, CA MSA..........................	446 997	3640		Jersey City, NJ PMSA	608 975
	06 099	Stanislaus County, CA	446 997		34 017	Hudson County, NJ	608 975
				5015		Middlesex-Somerset-Hunterdon, NJ PMSA.......	1 169 641
5190		Monmouth-Ocean, NJ PMSA.................	1 126 217		34 019	Hunterdon County, NJ	121 989
		(See New York-Northern New Jersey-Long			34 023	Middlesex County, NJ.......................	750 162
		Island, NY-NJ-CT-PA CMSA)			34 035	Somerset County, NJ	297 490
5200		Monroe, LA MSA	147 250	5190		Monmouth-Ocean, NJ PMSA	1 126 217
	22 073	Ouachita Parish, LA	147 250		34 025	Monmouth County, NJ	615 301
					34 029	Ocean County, NJ	510 916
5240		Montgomery, AL MSA	333 055				
	01 001	Autauga County, AL	43 671	5380		Nassau-Suffolk, NY PMSA....................	2 753 913
	01 051	Elmore County, AL	65 874		36 059	Nassau County, NY	1 334 544
	01 101	Montgomery County, AL	223 510		36 103	Suffolk County, NY	1 419 369
5280		Muncie, IN MSA	118 769	5483		New Haven-Bridgeport-Stamford-Danbury-	1 706 575
	18 035	Delaware County, IN	118 769			Waterbury, CT NECMA........................	
					09 001	Fairfield County, CT........................	882 567
5330		Myrtle Beach, SC MSA	196 629		09 009	New Haven County, CT......................	824 008
	45 051	Horry County, SC	196 629				
				5600		New York, NY PMSA	9 314 235
5345		Naples, FL MSA	251 377		36 005	Bronx County, NY	1 332 650
	12 021	Collier County, FL.........................	251 377		36 047	Kings County, NY	2 465 326
					36 061	New York County, NY	1 537 195
5360		Nashville, TN MSA	1 231 311		36 079	Putnam County, NY	95 745
	47 021	Cheatham County, TN......................	35 912		36 081	Queens County, NY	2 229 379
	47 037	Davidson County, TN	569 891		36 085	Richmond County, NY	443 728
	47 043	Dickson County, TN........................	43 156		36 087	Rockland County, NY	286 753
	47 147	Robertson County, TN	54 433		36 119	Westchester County, NY	923 459
	47 149	Rutherford County, TN	182 023				
	47 165	Sumner County, TN........................	130 449	5640		Newark, NJ PMSA	2 032 989
	47 187	Williamson County, TN	126 638		34 013	Essex County, NJ	793 633
	47 189	Wilson County, TN.........................	88 809		34 027	Morris County, NJ	470 212
					34 037	Sussex County, NJ.........................	144 166
5380		Nassau-Suffolk, NY PMSA...................	2 753 913		34 039	Union County, NJ	522 541
		(See New York-Northern New Jersey-Long			34 041	Warren County, NJ	102 437
		Island, NY-NJ-CT-PA CMSA)					
				5660		Newburgh, NY-PA PMSA.....................	387 669
5520		New London-Norwich, CT NECMA..............	259 088		36 071	Orange County, NY	341 367
	09 011	New London County, CT....................	259 088		42 103	Pike County, PA	46 302

Metropolitan Statistical Areas and Components – Continued

(MSA = metropolitan statistical area; CMSA = consolidated MSA; PMSA = primary MSA; and
NECMA = New England county metropolitan area. For further information, see Appendix A.)

MSA/CMSA/PMSA/NECMA	State and County	Tital and Geographic Components	2000 Population	MSA/CMSA/PMSA/NECMA	State and County	Tital and Geographic Components	2000 Population
8480		Trenton, NJ PMSA	350 761	6020		Parkersburg-Marietta, WV-OH MSA	151 237
	34 021	Mercer County, NJ..........................	350 761		39 167	Washington County, OH.......................	63 251
5720		Norfolk-Virginia Beach-Newport News, VA-NC MSA............................	1 569 541		54 107	Wood County, WV...........................	87 986
	37 053	Currituck County, NC........................	18 190	6080		Pensacola, FL MSA	412 153
	51 073	Gloucester County, VA	34 780		12 033	Escambia County, FL	294 410
	51 093	Isle of Wight County, VA	29 728		12 113	Santa Rosa County, FL	117 743
	51 095	James City, VA.............................	48 102	6120		Peoria-Pekin, IL MSA........................	347 387
	51 115	Mathews County, VA	9 207		17 143	Peoria County, IL	183 433
	51 199	York County, VA............................	56 297		17 179	Tazewell County, IL	128 485
	51 550	Chesapeake City, VA	199 184		17 203	Woodford County, IL	35 469
	51 650	Hampton City, VA...........................	146 437	6162		Philadelphia-Wilmington-Atlantic City, PA-NJ-DE-MD CMSA	6 188 463
	51 700	Newport News City, VA......................	180 150				
	51 710	Norfolk City, VA............................	234 403	560		Atlantic-Cape May, NJ PMSA	354 878
	51 735	Poquoson City, VA..........................	11 566		34 001	Atlantic County, NJ	252 552
	51 740	Portsmouth City, VA.........................	100 565		34 009	Cape May County, NJ	102 326
	51 800	Suffolk City, VA............................	63 677	6160		Philadelphia, PA-NJ PMSA	5 100 931
	51 810	Virginia Beach City, VA......................	425 257		34 005	Burlington County, NJ	423 394
	51 830	Williamsburg City, VA	11 998		34 007	Camden County, NJ	508 932
5775		Oakland, CA PMSA..........................	2 392 557		34 015	Gloucester County, NJ	254 673
		(See San Francisco-Oakland-San Jose, CA CMSA)			34 033	Salem County, NJ...........................	64 285
					42 017	Bucks County, PA...........................	597 635
5790		Ocala, FL MSA.............................	258 916		42 029	Chester County, PA	433 501
	12 083	Marion County, FL	258 916		42 045	Delaware County, PA	550 864
5800		Odessa-Midland, TX MSA....................	237 132		42 091	Montgomery County, PA	750 097
	48 135	Ector County, TX	121 123		42 101	Philadelphia County, PA	1 517 550
	48 329	Midland County, TX	116 009	8760		Vineland-Millville-Bridgeton, NJ PMSA	146 438
5880		Oklahoma City, OK MSA	1 083 346		34 011	Cumberland County, NJ	146 438
	40 017	Canadian County, OK........................	87 697				
	40 027	Cleveland County, OK........................	208 016	9160		Wilmington-Newark, DE-MD PMSA	586 216
	40 083	Logan County, OK	33 924		10 003	New Castle County, DE.......................	500 265
	40 087	McClain County, OK.........................	27 740		24 015	Cecil County, MD	85 951
	40 109	Oklahoma County, OK	660 448	6200		Phoenix-Mesa, AZ MSA......................	3 251 876
	40 125	Pottawatomie County, OK	65 521		04 013	Maricopa County, AZ	3 072 149
5910		Olympia, WA PMSA	207 355		04 021	Pinal County, AZ............................	179 727
		(See Seattle-Tacoma-Bremerton, WA CMSA)		6240		Pine Bluff, AR MSA	84 278
5920		Omaha, NE-IA MSA	716 998		05 069	Jefferson County, AR	84 278
	19 155	Pottawattamie County, IA	87 704	6280		Pittsburgh, PA MSA	2 358 695
	31 025	Cass County, NE	24 334		42 003	Allegheny County, PA	1 281 666
	31 055	Douglas County, NE.........................	463 585		42 007	Beaver County, PA..........................	181 412
	31 153	Sarpy County, NE	122 595		42 019	Butler County, PA...........................	174 083
	31 177	Washington County, NE	18 780		42 051	Fayette County, PA	148 644
5945		Orange County, CA PMSA	2 846 289		42 125	Washington County, PA	202 897
		(See Los Angeles-Long Beach, CA PMSA)			42 129	Westmoreland County, PA	369 993
5960		Orlando, FL MSA	1 644 561	6323		Pittsfield, MA NECMA	134 953
	12 069	Lake County, FL	210 528		25 003	Berkshire County, MA........................	134 953
	12 095	Orange County, FL	896 344	6340		Pocatello, ID MSA	75 565
	12 097	Osceola County, FL	172 493		16 005	Bannock County, ID..........................	75 565
	12 117	Seminole County, FL	365 196	6403		Portland, ME NECMA	265 612
5990		Owensboro, KY MSA	91 545		23 005	Cumberland County, ME	265 612
	21 059	Daviess County, KY	91 545	6442		Portland-Salem, OR-WA CMSA................	2 265 223
6015		Panama City, FL MSA	148 217	6440		Portland-Vancouver, OR-WA PMSA.................	1 918 009
	12 005	Bay County, FL.............................	148 217		41 005	Clackamas County, OR.......................	338 391

Metropolitan Statistical Areas and Components – Continued

(MSA = metropolitan statistical area; CMSA = consolidated MSA; PMSA = primary MSA; and NECMA = New England county metropolitan area. For further information, see Appendix A.)

MSA/ CMSA/ PMSA/ NECMA	State and County	Tital and Geographic Components	2000 Population	MSA/ CMSA/ PMSA/ NECMA	State and County	Tital and Geographic Components	2000 Population
	41 009	Columbia County, OR	43 560				
	41 051	Multnomah County, OR	660 486	6780		Riverside-San Bernardino, CA PMSA	3 254 821
	41 067	Washington County, OR	445 342			(See Los Angeles-Riverside-Orange County, CA CMSA)	
	41 071	Yamhill County, OR	84 992				
	53 011	Clark County, WA	345 238				
				6800		Roanoke, VA MSA	235 932
7080		Salem, OR PMSA	347 214		51 023	Botetourt County, VA	30 496
	41 047	Marion County, OR	284 834		51 161	Roanoke County, VA	85 778
	41 053	Polk County, OR	62 380		51 770	Roanoke City, VA	94 911
					51 775	Salem City, VA	24 747
6483		Providence-Warwick-Pawtucket, RI NECMA	962 886				
	44 001	Bristol County, RI	50 648	6820		Rochester, MN MSA	124 277
	44 003	Kent County, RI	167 090		27 109	Olmsted County, MN	124 277
	44 007	Providence County, RI	621 602				
	44 009	Washington County, RI	123 546	6840		Rochester, NY MSA	1 098 201
					36 037	Genesee County, NY	60 370
6520		Provo-Orem, UT MSA	368 536		36 051	Livingston County, NY	64 328
	49 049	Utah County, UT	368 536		36 055	Monroe County, NY	735 343
					36 069	Ontario County, NY	100 224
6560		Pueblo, CO MSA	141 472		36 073	Orleans County, NY	44 171
	08 101	Pueblo County, CO	141 472		36 117	Wayne County, NY	93 765
6580		Punta Gorda, FL MSA	141 627	6880		Rockford, IL MSA	371 236
	12 015	Charlotte County, FL	141 627		17 007	Boone County, IL	41 786
					17 141	Ogle County, IL	51 032
6600		Racine, WI PMSA	188 831		17 201	Winnebago County, IL	278 418
		(See Milwaukee-Waukesha, WI PMSA)					
				6895		Rocky Mount, NC MSA	143 026
6640		Raleigh-Durham-Chapel Hill, NC MSA	1 187 941		37 065	Edgecombe County, NC	55 606
	37 037	Chatham County, NC	49 329		37 127	Nash County, NC	87 420
	37 063	Durham County, NC	223 314				
	37 069	Franklin County, NC	47 260	6922		Sacramento-Yolo, CA CMSA	1 796 857
	37 101	Johnston County, NC	121 965				
	37 135	Orange County, NC	118 227	6920		Sacramento, CA PMSA	1 628 197
	37 183	Wake County, NC	627 846		06 017	El Dorado County, CA	156 299
					06 061	Placer County, CA	248 399
6660		Rapid City, SD MSA	88 565		06 067	Sacramento County, CA	1 223 499
	46 103	Pennington County, SD	88 565				
				9270		Yolo, CA PMSA	168 660
6680		Reading, PA MSA	373 638		06 113	Yolo County, CA	168 660
	42 011	Berks County, PA	373 638				
				6960		Saginaw-Bay City-Midland, MI MSA	403 070
6690		Redding, CA MSA	163 256		26 017	Bay County, MI	110 157
	06 089	Shasta County, CA	163 256		26 111	Midland County, MI	82 874
					26 145	Saginaw County, MI	210 039
6720		Reno, NV MSA	339 486				
	32 031	Washoe County, NV	339 486	6980		St. Cloud, MN MSA	167 392
					27 009	Benton County, MN	34 226
6740		Richland-Kennewick-Pasco, WA MSA	191 822		27 145	Stearns County, MN	133 166
	53 005	Benton County, WA	142 475				
	53 021	Franklin County, WA	49 347	7000		St. Joseph, MO MSA	102 490
					29 003	Andrew County, MO	16 492
6760		Richmond-Petersburg, VA MSA	996 512		29 021	Buchanan County, MO	85 998
	51 036	Charles City, VA	6 926				
	51 041	Chesterfield County, VA	259 903	7040		St. Louis, MO-IL MSA	2 603 607
	51 053	Dinwiddie County, VA	24 533		17 027	Clinton County, IL	35 535
	51 075	Goochland County, VA	16 863		17 083	Jersey County, IL	21 668
	51 085	Hanover County, VA	86 320		17 119	Madison County, IL	258 941
	51 087	Henrico County, VA	262 300		17 133	Monroe County, IL	27 619
	51 127	New Kent County, VA	13 462		17 163	St. Clair County, IL	256 082
	51 145	Powhatan County, VA	22 377		29 071	Franklin County, MO	93 807
	51 149	Prince George County, VA	33 047		29 099	Jefferson County, MO	198 099
	51 570	Colonial Heights City, VA	16 897		29 113	Lincoln County, MO	38 944
	51 670	Hopewell City, VA	22 354		29 183	St. Charles County, MO	283 883
	51 730	Petersburg City, VA	33 740		29 189	St. Louis County, MO	1 016 315
	51 760	Richmond City, VA	197 790		29 219	Warren County, MO	24 525

Metropolitan Statistical Areas and Components – Continued

(MSA = metropolitan statistical area; CMSA = consolidated MSA; PMSA = primary MSA; and NECMA = New England county metropolitan area. For further information, see Appendix A.)

MSA/CMSA/PMSA/NECMA	State and County	Title and Geographic Components	2000 Population
	29 510	St. Louis City, MO	348 189
7080		Salem, OR PMSA	347 214
		(See Portland-Vancouver, OR-WA PMSA)	
7120		Salinas, CA MSA	401 762
	06 053	Monterey County, CA	401 762
7160		Salt Lake City-Ogden, UT MSA	1 333 914
	49 011	Davis County, UT	238 994
	49 035	Salt Lake County, UT	898 387
	49 057	Weber County, UT	196 533
7200		San Angelo, TX MSA	104 010
	48 451	Tom Green County, TX	104 010
7240		San Antonio, TX MSA	1 592 383
	48 029	Bexar County, TX	1 392 931
	48 091	Comal County, TX	78 021
	48 187	Guadalupe County, TX	89 023
	48 493	Wilson County, TX	32 408
7320		San Diego, CA MSA	2 813 833
	06 073	San Diego County, CA	2 813 833
7362		San Francisco-Oakland-San Jose, CA CMSA	7 039 362
5775		Oakland, CA PMSA	2 392 557
	06 001	Alameda County, CA	1 443 741
	06 013	Contra Costa County, CA	948 816
7360		San Francisco, CA PMSA	1 731 183
	06 041	Marin County, CA	247 289
	06 075	San Francisco County, CA	776 733
	06 081	San Mateo County, CA	707 161
7400		San Jose, CA PMSA	1 682 585
	06 085	Santa Clara County, CA	1 682 585
7485		Santa Cruz-Watsonville, CA PMSA	255 602
	06 087	Santa Cruz County, CA	255 602
7500		Santa Rosa, CA PMSA	458 614
	06 097	Sonoma County, CA	458 614
8720		Vallejo-Fairfield-Napa, CA PMSA	518 821
	06 055	Napa County, CA	124 279
	06 095	Solano County, CA	394 542
7460		San Luis Obispo-Atascadero-Paso Robles, CA MSA	246 681
	06 079	San Luis Obispo County, CA	246 681
7480		Santa Barbara-Santa Maria-Lompoc, CA MSA	399 347
	06 083	Santa Barbara County, CA	399 347
7490		Santa Fe, NM MSA	147 635
	35 028	Los Alamos County, NM	18 343
	35 049	Santa Fe County, NM	129 292
7510		Sarasota-Bradenton, FL MSA	589 959
	12 081	Manatee County, FL	264 002
	12 115	Sarasota County, FL	325 957
7520		Savannah, GA MSA	293 000
	13 029	Bryan County, GA	23 417

MSA/CMSA/PMSA/NECMA	State and County	Title and Geographic Components	2000 Population
	13 051	Chatham County, GA	232 048
	13 103	Effingham County, GA	37 535
7560		Scranton-Wilkes-Barre-Hazleton, PA MSA	624 776
	42 037	Columbia County, PA	64 151
	42 069	Lackawanna County, PA	213 295
	42 079	Luzerne County, PA	319 250
	42 131	Wyoming County, PA	28 080
7602		Seattle-Tacoma-Bremerton, WA CMSA	3 554 760
1150		Bremerton, WA PMSA	231 969
	53 035	Kitsap County, WA	231 969
5910		Olympia, WA PMSA	207 355
	53 067	Thurston County, WA	207 355
7600		Seattle-Bellevue-Everett, WA PMSA	2 414 616
	53 029	Island County, WA	71 558
	53 033	King County, WA	1 737 034
	53 061	Snohomish County, WA	606 024
8200		Tacoma, WA PMSA	700 820
	53 053	Pierce County, WA	700 820
7610		Sharon, PA MSA	120 293
	42 085	Mercer County, PA	120 293
7620		Sheboygan, WI MSA	112 646
	55 117	Sheboygan County, WI	112 646
7640		Sherman-Denison, TX MSA	110 595
	48 181	Grayson County, TX	110 595
7680		Shreveport-Bossier City, LA MSA	392 302
	22 015	Bossier Parish, LA	98 310
	22 017	Caddo Parish, LA	252 161
	22 119	Webster Parish, LA	41 831
7720		Sioux City, IA-NE MSA	124 130
	19 193	Woodbury County, IA	103 877
	31 043	Dakota County, NE	20 253
7760		Sioux Falls, SD MSA	172 412
	46 083	Lincoln County, SD	24 131
	46 099	Minnehaha County, SD	148 281
7800		South Bend, IN MSA	265 559
	18 141	St. Joseph County, IN	265 559
7840		Spokane, WA MSA	417 939
	53 063	Spokane County, WA	417 939
7880		Springfield, IL MSA	201 437
	17 129	Menard County, IL	12 486
	17 167	Sangamon County, IL	188 951
8003		Springfield, MA NECMA	608 479
	25 013	Hampden County, MA	456 228
	25 015	Hampshire County, MA	152 251
7920		Springfield, MO MSA	325 721
	29 043	Christian County, MO	54 285
	29 077	Greene County, MO	240 391
	29 225	Webster County, MO	31 045

(MSA = metropolitan statistical area; CMSA = consolidated MSA; PMSA = primary MSA; and
NECMA = New England county metropolitan area. For further information, see Appendix A.)

MSA/ CMSA/ PMSA/ NECMA	State and County	Tital and Geographic Components	2000 Population	MSA/ CMSA/ PMSA/ NECMA	State and County	Tital and Geographic Components	2000 Population
8050		State College, PA MSA	135 758				
	42 027	Centre County, PA	135 758	8640		Tyler, TX MSA	174 706
8080		Steubenville-Weirton, OH-WV MSA	132 008		48 423	Smith County, TX	174 706
	39 081	Jefferson County, OH	73 894	8680		Utica-Rome, NY MSA	299 896
	54 009	Brooke County, WV	25 447		36 043	Herkimer County, NY	64 427
	54 029	Hancock County, WV	32 667		36 065	Oneida County, NY	235 469
8120		Stockton-Lodi, CA MSA	563 598	8720		Vallejo-Fairfield-Napa, CA PMSA	518 821
	06 077	San Joaquin County, CA	563 598			(See San Francisco-Oakland-San Jose, CA CMSA)	
8140		Sumter, SC MSA	104 646				
	45 085	Sumter County, SC	104 646	8735		Ventura, CA PMSA	753 197
8160		Syracuse, NY MSA	732 117			(See Los Angeles-Riverside-Orange County, CA CMSA)	753 197
	36 011	Cayuga County, NY	81 963				
	36 053	Madison County, NY	69 441	8750		Victoria, TX MSA	84 088
	36 067	Onondaga County, NY	458 336		48 469	Victoria County, TX	84 088
	36 075	Oswego County, NY	122 377				
8200		Tacoma, WA PMSA	700 820	8760		Vineland-Millville-Bridgeton, NJ PMSA	146 438
		(See Seattle-Tacoma-Bremerton, WA CMSA)				(See Philadelphia-Wilmington-Atlantic City, PA-NJ-DE-MD CMSA)	
8240		Tallahassee, FL MSA	284 539	8780		Visalia-Tulare-Porterville, CA MSA	368 021
	12 039	Gadsden County, FL	45 087		06 107	Tulare County, CA	368 021
	12 073	Leon County, FL	239 452				
8280		Tampa-St. Petersburg-Clearwater, FL MSA	2 395 997	8800		Waco, TX MSA	213 517
	12 053	Hernando County, FL	130 802		48 309	McLennan County, TX	213 517
	12 057	Hillsborough County, FL	998 948				
	12 101	Pasco County, FL	344 765	8872		Washington-Baltimore, DC-MD-VA-WV CMSA	7 608 070
	12 103	Pinellas County, FL	921 482	720		Baltimore, MD PMSA	2 552 994
8320		Terre Haute, IN MSA	149 192		24 003	Anne Arundel County, MD	489 656
	18 021	Clay County, IN	26 556		24 005	Baltimore County, MD	754 292
	18 165	Vermillion County, IN	16 788		24 013	Carroll County, MD	150 897
	18 167	Vigo County, IN	105 848		24 025	Harford County, MD	218 590
8360		Texarkana, TX-Texarkana, AR MSA	129 749		24 027	Howard County, MD	247 842
	05 091	Miller County, AR	40 443		24 035	Queen Anne's County, MD	40 563
	48 037	Bowie County, TX	89 306		24 510	Baltimore City, MD	651 154
8400		Toledo, OH MSA	618 203	3180		Hagerstown, MD PMSA	131 923
	39 051	Fulton County, OH	42 084		24 043	Washington County, MD	131 923
	39 095	Lucas County, OH	455 054				
	39 173	Wood County, OH	121 065	8840		Washington, DC-MD-VA-WV PMSA	4 923 153
8440		Topeka, KS MSA	169 871		11 001	District of Columbia	572 059
	20 177	Shawnee County, KS	169 871		24 009	Calvert County, MD	74 563
					24 017	Charles County, MD	120 546
8480		Trenton, NJ PMSA	350 761		24 021	Frederick County, MD	195 277
		(See New York-Northern New Jersey-Long Island, NY-NJ-CT-PA CMSA)			24 031	Montgomery County, MD	873 341
					24 033	Prince George's County, MD	801 515
8520		Tucson, AZ MSA	843 746		51 013	Arlington County, VA	189 453
	04 019	Pima County, AZ	843 746		51 043	Clarke County, VA	12 652
					51 047	Culpeper County, VA	34 262
8560		Tulsa, OK MSA	803 235		51 059	Fairfax County, VA	969 749
	40 037	Creek County, OK	67 367		51 061	Fauquier County, VA	55 139
	40 113	Osage County, OK	44 437		51 099	King George County, VA	16 803
	40 131	Rogers County, OK	70 641		51 107	Loudoun County, VA	169 599
	40 143	Tulsa County, OK	563 299		51 153	Prince William County, VA	280 813
	40 145	Wagoner County, OK	57 491		51 177	Spotsylvania County, VA	90 395
					51 179	Stafford County, VA	92 446
8600		Tuscaloosa, AL MSA	164 875		51 187	Warren County, VA	31 584
	01 125	Tuscaloosa County, AL	164 875		51 510	Alexandria City, VA	128 283
					51 600	Fairfax City, VA	21 498
					51 610	Falls Church City, VA	10 377
					51 630	Fredericksburg City, VA	19 279
					51 683	Manassas City, VA	35 135

Metropolitan Statistical Areas and Components – Continued

(MSA = metropolitan statistical area; CMSA = consolidated MSA; PMSA = primary MSA; and NECMA = New England county metropolitan area. For further information, see Appendix A.)

Geographic Codes		Title and Geographic Components	2000 Population
MSA/ CMSA/ PMSA/ NECMA	State and County		
	51 685	Manassas Park City, VA	10 290
	54 003	Berkeley County, WV	75 905
	54 037	Jefferson County, WV	42 190
8920		Waterloo-Cedar Falls, IA MSA	128 012
	19 013	Black Hawk County, IA	128 012
8940		Wausau, WI MSA	125 834
	55 073	Marathon County, WI	125 834
8960		West Palm Beach-Boca Raton, FL MSA	1 131 184
	12 099	Palm Beach County, FL	1 131 184
9000		Wheeling, WV-OH MSA	153 172
	39 013	Belmont County, OH	70 226
	54 051	Marshall County, WV	35 519
	54 069	Ohio County, WV	47 427
9080		Wichita Falls, TX MSA	140 518
	48 009	Archer County, TX	8 854
	48 485	Wichita County, TX	131 664
9040		Wichita, KS MSA	545 220
	20 015	Butler County, KS	59 482
	20 079	Harvey County, KS	32 869
	20 173	Sedgwick County, KS	452 869
9140		Williamsport, PA MSA	120 044
	42 081	Lycoming County, PA	120 044
9200		Wilmington, NC MSA	233 450
	37 019	Brunswick County, NC	73 143
	37 129	New Hanover County, NC	160 307
9160		Wilmington-Newark, DE-MD PMSA (See Philadelphia-Wilmington-Atlantic City, PA-NJ-DE-MD CMSA)	586 216
9260		Yakima, WA MSA	222 581
	53 077	Yakima County, WA	222 581
9270		Yolo, CA PMSA (See Sacramento-Yolo, CA CMSA)	168 660
9280		York, PA MSA	381 751
9280	42 133	York County, PA	381 751
9320		Youngstown-Warren, OH MSA	594 746
9320	39 029	Columbiana County, OH	112 075
9320	39 099	Mahoning County, OH	257 555
9320	39 155	Trumbull County, OH	225 116
9340		Yuba City, CA MSA	139 149
9340	06 101	Sutter County, CA	78 930
9340	06 115	Yuba County, CA	60 219
9360		Yuma, AZ MSA	160 026
9360	04 027	Yuma County, AZ	160 026

APPENDIX C
METROPOLITAN STATISTICAL AREAS AND COMPONENTS BY STATE

The following table is arranged alphabetically by state. Under each state heading, all of the metropolitan areas that lie wholly or partly within that state are listed alphabetically along with their component counties, which are also listed alphabetically. For metropolitan areas that cross state lines, only the counties within a particular state are included under that state. However, the metropolitan area names include the two letter abbreviation for each state involved, and the remaining counties can be located under their respective state headings.

For states containing Consolidated Metropolitan Statistical Areas (CMSAs), or parts of such areas, the CMSAs appear first, followed by the Primary Metropolitan Statistical Areas (PMSAs) that make up the CMSA, and their component counties.

(MSA = metropolitan statistical area; CMSA = consolidated MSA; PMSA = primary MSA; and
NECMA = New England county metropolitan area. For further information, see Appendix A.)

Geographic Codes MSA/CMSA/ PMSA/ NECMA	State and County	Title and Geographic Components	Geographic Codes MSA/CMSA/ PMSA/ NECMA	State and County	Title and Geographic Components
		ALABAMA	9360		YUMA, AZ MSA
0450		ANNISTON, AL MSA	9360	04 027	Yuma
	01 015	Calhoun			
0580		AUBURN-OPELIKA, AL MSA			**ARKANSAS**
	01 081	Lee	2580		FAYETTEVILLE-SPRINGDALE-ROGERS, AR MSA
1000		BIRMINGHAM, AL MSA		05 007	Benton
	01 009	Blount		05 143	Washington
	01 073	Jefferson	2720		FORT SMITH, AR-OK MSA
	01 115	St. Clair		05 033	Crawford
	01 117	Shelby		05 131	Sebastian
1800		COLUMBUS, GA-AL MSA	3700		JONESBORO, AR MSA
	01 113	Russell		5 031	Craighead
2030		DECATUR, AL MSA	4400		LITTLE ROCK-NORTH LITTLE ROCK, AR MSA
	01 079	Lawrence		05 045	Faulkner
	01 103	Morgan		05 085	Lonoke
2180		DOTHAN, AL MSA		05 119	Pulaski
	01 045	Dale		05 125	Saline
	01 069	Houston	4920		MEMPHIS, TN-AR-MS MSA
2650		FLORENCE, AL MSA		05 035	Crittenden
	01 033	Colbert	6240		PINE BLUFF, AR MSA
	01 077	Lauderdale		05 069	Jefferson
2880		GADSDEN, AL MSA	8360		TEXARKANA, TX-TEXARKANA, AR MSA
	01 055	Etowah		05 091	Miller
3440		HUNTSVILLE, AL MSA			
	01 083	Limestone			**CALIFORNIA**
	01 089	Madison	4472		LOS ANGELES-RIVERSIDE-ORANGE COUNTY, CA
5160		MOBILE, AL MSA			CMSA
	01 003	Baldwin	4480		LOS ANGELES-LONG BEACH, CA PMSA
	01 097	Mobile		06 037	Los Angeles
5240		MONTGOMERY, AL MSA	5945		ORANGE COUNTY, CA PMSA
	01 001	Autauga		06 059	Orange
	01 051	Elmore	6780		RIVERSIDE-SAN BERNARDINO, CA PMSA
	01 101	Montgomery			SAN BERNARDINO, CA
8600		TUSCALOOSA, AL MSA			RIVERSIDE, CA
	01 125	Tuscaloosa	6922		SACRAMENTO-YOLO, CA CMSA
			6920		SACRAMENTO, CA PMSA
		ALASKA		06 017	El Dorado
0380		ANCHORAGE, AK MSA		06 061	Placer
	02 020	Anchorage		06 067	Sacramento
			9270		YOLO, CA PMSA
		ARIZONA		06 113	Yolo
2620		FLAGSTAFF, AZ-UT MSA	7362		SAN FRANCISCO-OAKLAND-SAN JOSE, CA CMSA
	04 005	Coconino	5775		OAKLAND, CA PMSA
4120		LAS VEGAS, NV-AZ MSA		06 001	Alameda
	04 015	Mohave		06 013	Contra Costa
6200		PHOENIX-MESA, AZ MSA	7360		SAN FRANCISCO, CA PMSA
	04 013	Maricopa		06 041	Marin
	04 021	Pinal		06 075	San Francisco
8520		TUCSON, AZ MSA		06 081	San Mateo
	04 019	Pima	7400		SAN JOSE, CA PMSA
				06 085	Santa Clara

(MSA = metropolitan statistical area; CMSA = consolidated MSA; PMSA = primary MSA; and
NECMA = New England county metropolitan area. For further information, see Appendix A.)

Geographic Codes MSA/CMSA/ PMSA/ NECMA	State and County	Title and Geographic Components	Geographic Codes MSA/CMSA/ PMSA/ NECMA	State and County	Title and Geographic Components
7485		SANTA CRUZ-WATSONVILLE, CA PMSA		09 007	Middlesex
	06 087	Santa Cruz		09 013	Tolland
7500		SANTA ROSA, CA PMSA	5520		NEW LONDON-NORWICH, CT NECMA
	06 097	Sonoma		09 011	New London
8720		VALLEJO-FAIRFIELD-NAPA, CA PMSA			
	06 055	Napa			**DELAWARE**
	06 095	Solano	6162		PHILADELPHIA-WILMINGTON-ATLANTIC CITY, PA-NJ-DE-MD CMSA
0680		BAKERSFIELD, CA MSA	9160		WILMINGTON-NEWARK, DE-MD PMSA
	06 029	Kern		10 003	New Castle
1620		CHICO-PARADISE, CA MSA	2190		DOVER, DE MSA
	06 007	Butte		10 001	Kent
2840		FRESNO, CA MSA			
	06 019	Fresno			**FLORIDA**
	06 039	Madera	4992		MIAMI-FORT LAUDERDALE, FL CMSA
4940		MERCED, CA MSA	2680		FORT LAUDERDALE, FL PMSA
	06 047	Merced		12 011	Broward
5170		MODESTO, CA MSA	5000		MIAMI, FL PMSA
	06 099	Stanislaus		12 086	Miami-Dade
6690		REDDING, CA MSA	2020		DAYTONA BEACH, FL MSA
	06 089	Shasta		12 035	Flagler
7120		SALINAS, CA MSA		12 127	Volusia
	06 053	Monterey	2700		FORT MYERS-CAPE CORAL, FL MSA
7320		SAN DIEGO, CA MSA		12 071	Lee
	06 073	San Diego	2710		FORT PIERCE-PORT ST. LUCIE, FL MSA
7460		SAN LUIS OBISPO-ATASCADERO-PASO ROBLES, CA MSA		12 085	Martin
	06 079	San Luis Obispo		12 111	St. Lucie
7480		SANTA BARBARA-SANTA MARIA-LOMPOC, CA MSA	2750		FORT WALTON BEACH, FL MSA
	06 083	Santa Barbara		12 091	Okaloosa
8120		STOCKTON-LODI, CA MSA	2900		GAINESVILLE, FL MSA
	06 077	San Joaquin		12 001	Alachua
8780		VISALIA-TULARE-PORTERVILLE, CA MSA	3600		JACKSONVILLE, FL MSA
	06 107	Tulare		12 019	Clay
9340		YUBA CITY, CA MSA		12 031	Duval
	06 101	Sutter		12 089	Nassau
	06 115	Yuba		12 109	St. Johns
			3980		LAKELAND-WINTER HAVEN, FL MSA
		COLORADO		12 105	Polk
34		DENVER-BOULDER-GREELEY, CO CMSA	4900		MELBOURNE-TITUSVILLE-PALM BAY, FL MSA
1125		BOULDER-LONGMONT, CO PMSA		12 009	Brevard
	08 013	Boulder	5345		NAPLES, FL MSA
2080		DENVER, CO PMSA		12 021	Collier
	08 001	Adams	5790		OCALA, FL MSA
	08 005	Arapahoe		12 083	Marion
	08 031	Denver	5960		ORLANDO, FL MSA
	08 035	Douglas		12 069	Lake
	08 059	Jefferson		12 095	Orange
3060		GREELEY, CO PMSA		12 097	Osceola
	08 123	Weld		12 117	Seminole
1720		COLORADO SPRINGS, CO MSA	6015		PANAMA CITY, FL MSA
	08 041	El Paso		12 005	Bay
2670		FORT COLLINS-LOVELAND, CO MSA	6080		PENSACOLA, FL MSA
	08 069	Larimer		12 033	Escambia
2995		GRAND JUNCTION, CO MSA		12 113	Santa Rosa
	08 077	Mesa	6580		PUNTA GORDA, FL MSA
6560		PUEBLO, CO MSA		12 015	Charlotte
	08 101	Pueblo	7510		SARASOTA-BRADENTON, FL MSA
				12 081	Manatee
		CONNECTICUT		12 115	Sarasota
70		NEW YORK-NORTHERN NEW JERSEY-LONG ISLAND, NY-NJ-CT-PA CMSA	8240		TALLAHASSEE, FL MSA
5483		NEW HAVEN-BRIDGEPORT-STAMFORD-DANBURY-WATERBURY, CT NECMA		12 039	Gadsden
		FAIRFIELD COUNTY, CT		12 073	Leon
		NEW HAVEN COUNTY, CT	8280		TAMPA-ST. PETERSBURG-CLEARWATER, FL MSA
3280		HARTFORD, CT NECMA		12 053	Hernando
	09 003	Hartford		12 057	Hillsborough
				12 101	Pasco
				12 103	Pinellas

Metropolitan Statistical Areas and Components by State – Continued

(MSA = metropolitan statistical area; CMSA = consolidated MSA; PMSA = primary MSA; and
NECMA = New England county metropolitan area. For further information, see Appendix A.)

Geographic Codes MSA/CMSA/ PMSA/ NECMA	State and County	Title and Geographic Components	Geographic Codes MSA/CMSA/ PMSA/ NECMA	State and County	Title and Geographic Components
8960		WEST PALM BEACH-BOCA RATON, FL MSA			**ILLINOIS**
	12 099	Palm Beach	1040		BLOOMINGTON-NORMAL, IL MSA
			1040	17 113	McLean
		GEORGIA	1400		CHAMPAIGN-URBANA, IL MSA
0120		ALBANY, GA MSA		17 019	Champaign
	13 095	DOUGHERTY COUNTY, GA	14		CHICAGO-GARY-KENOSHA, IL-IN-WI CMSA
	13 177	LEE COUNTY, GA	1600		CHICAGO, IL PMSA
0500		ATHENS, GA MSA		17 031	Cook
	13 059	Clarke		17 037	De Kalb
	13 195	Madison		17 043	Du Page
	13 219	Oconee		17 063	Grundy
0520		ATLANTA, GA MSA		17 089	Kane
	13 013	Barrow		17 093	Kendall
	13 015	Bartow		17 097	Lake
	13 045	Carroll		17 111	McHenry
	13 057	Cherokee		17 197	Will
	13 063	Clayton	3740		KANKAKEE, IL PMSA
	13 067	Cobb		17 091	Kankakee
	13 077	Coweta	1960		DAVENPORT-MOLINE-ROCK ISLAND, IA-IL MSA
	13 089	De Kalb		17 073	Henry
	13 097	Douglas		17 161	Rock Island
	13 113	Fayette	2040		DECATUR, IL MSA
	13 117	Forsyth		17 115	Macon
	13 121	Fulton	6120		PEORIA-PEKIN, IL MSA
	13 135	Gwinnett		17 143	Peoria
	13 151	Henry		17 179	Tazewell
	13 217	Newton		17 203	Woodford
	13 223	Paulding	6880		ROCKFORD, IL MSA
	13 227	Pickens		17 007	Boone
	13 247	Rockdale		17 141	Ogle
	13 255	Spalding		17 201	Winnebago
	13 297	Walton	7040		ST. LOUIS, MO-IL MSA
0600		AUGUSTA-AIKEN, GA-SC MSA		17 027	Clinton
	13 073	Columbia		17 083	Jersey
	13 189	McDuffie		17 119	Madison
	13 245	Richmond		17 133	Monroe
1560		CHATTANOOGA, TN-GA MSA		17 163	St. Clair
	13 047	Catoosa	7880		SPRINGFIELD, IL MSA
	13 083	Dade		17 129	Menard
	13 295	Walker		17 167	Sangamon
1800		COLUMBUS, GA-AL MSA			
	13 053	Chattahoochee			**INDIANA**
	13 145	Harris	1020		BLOOMINGTON, IN MSA
	13 215	Muscogee	1020	18 105	Monroe
4680		MACON, GA MSA	14		CHICAGO-GARY-KENOSHA, IL-IN-WI CMSA
	13 021	Bibb	2960		GARY, IN PMSA
	13 153	Houston		18 089	Lake
	13 169	Jones		18 127	Porter
	13 225	Peach	21		CINCINNATI-HAMILTON, OH-KY-IN CMSA
	13 289	Twiggs	1640		CINCINNATI, OH-KY-IN PMSA
7520		SAVANNAH, GA MSA		18 029	Dearborn
	13 029	Bryan		18 115	Ohio
	13 051	Chatham	2330		ELKHART-GOSHEN, IN MSA
	13 103	Effingham		18 039	Elkhart
			2440		EVANSVILLE-HENDERSON, IN-KY MSA
		HAWAII		18 129	Posey
3320		HONOLULU, HI MSA		18 163	Vanderburgh
	15 003	Honolulu		18 173	Warrick
			2760		FORT WAYNE, IN MSA
		IDAHO		18 001	Adams
1080		BOISE CITY, ID MSA		18 003	Allen
1080	16 001	Ada		18 033	De Kalb
1080	16 027	Canyon		18 069	Huntington
6340		POCATELLO, ID MSA		18 179	Wells
	16 005	Bannock		18 183	Whitley
			3480		INDIANAPOLIS, IN MSA
				18 011	Boone

Metropolitan Statistical Areas and Components by State – Continued

(MSA = metropolitan statistical area; CMSA = consolidated MSA; PMSA = primary MSA; and
NECMA = New England county metropolitan area. For further information, see Appendix A.)

Geographic Codes MSA/CMSA/ PMSA/ NECMA	State and County	Title and Geographic Components	Geographic Codes MSA/CMSA/ PMSA/ NECMA	State and County	Title and Geographic Components
	18 057	Hamilton		21 037	Campbell
	18 059	Hancock		21 077	Gallatin
	18 063	Hendricks		21 081	Grant
	18 081	Johnson		21 117	Kenton
	18 095	Madison		21 191	Pendleton
	18 097	Marion	1660		CLARKSVILLE-HOPKINSVILLE, TN-KY MSA
	18 109	Morgan		21 047	Christian
	18 145	Shelby	2440		EVANSVILLE-HENDERSON, IN-KY MSA
3850		KOKOMO, IN MSA		21 101	Henderson
	18 067	Howard	3400		HUNTINGTON-ASHLAND, WV-KY-OH MSA
	18 159	Tipton		21 019	Boyd
3920		LAFAYETTE, IN MSA		21 043	Carter
	18 023	Clinton		21 089	Greenup
	18 157	Tippecanoe	4280		LEXINGTON, KY MSA
4520		LOUISVILLE, KY-IN MSA		21 017	Bourbon
	18 019	Clark		21 049	Clark
	18 043	Floyd		21 067	Fayette
	18 061	Harrison		21 113	Jessamine
	18 143	Scott		21 151	Madison
7800		SOUTH BEND, IN MSA		21 209	Scott
	18 141	St. Joseph		21 239	Woodford
5280		MUNCIE, IN MSA	4520		LOUISVILLE, KY-IN MSA
	18 035	Delaware		21 029	Bullitt
8320		TERRE HAUTE, IN MSA		21 111	Jefferson
	18 021	Clay		21 185	Oldham
	18 165	Vermillion	5990		OWENSBORO, KY MSA
	18 167	Vigo		21 059	Daviess
		IOWA			**LOUISIANA**
1360		CEDAR RAPIDS, IA MSA	0220		ALEXANDRIA, LA MSA
	19 113	Linn		22 079	Rapides
1960		DAVENPORT-MOLINE-ROCK ISLAND, IA-IL MSA	0760		BATON ROUGE, LA MSA
	19 163	Scott		22 005	Ascension
2120		DES MOINES, IA MSA		22 033	East Baton Rouge
	19 049	Dallas		22 063	Livingston
	19 153	Polk		22 121	West Baton Rouge
	19 181	Warren	3350		HOUMA, LA MSA
2200		DUBUQUE, IA MSA		22 057	Lafourche
	19 061	Dubuque		22 109	Terrebonne
3500		IOWA CITY, IA MSA	3880		LAFAYETTE, LA MSA
	19 103	Johnson		22 001	Acadia
5920		OMAHA, NE-IA MSA		22 055	Lafayette
	19 155	Pottawattamie		22 097	St. Landry
7720		SIOUX CITY, IA-NE MSA		22 099	St. Martin
	19 193	Woodbury	3960		LAKE CHARLES, LA MSA
8920		WATERLOO-CEDAR FALLS, IA MSA		22 019	Calcasieu
	19 013	Black Hawk	5200		MONROE, LA MSA
				22 073	Ouachita
		KANSAS	5560		NEW ORLEANS, LA MSA
3760		KANSAS CITY, MO-KS MSA		22 051	Jefferson
	20 091	Johnson		22 071	Orleans
	20 103	Leavenworth		22 075	Plaquemines
	20 121	Miami		22 087	St. Bernard
	20 209	Wyandotte		22 089	St. Charles
4150		LAWRENCE, KS MSA		22 093	St. James
	20 045	Douglas		22 095	St. John the Baptist
8440		TOPEKA, KS MSA		22 103	St. Tammany
	20 177	Shawnee	7680		SHREVEPORT-BOSSIER CITY, LA MSA
9040		WICHITA, KS MSA		22 015	Bossier
	20 015	Butler		22 017	Caddo
	20 079	Harvey		22 119	Webster
	20 173	Sedgwick			
					MAINE
		KENTUCKY	0733		BANGOR, ME NECMA
21		CINCINNATI-HAMILTON, OH-KY-IN CMSA		23 019	Penobscot
1640		CINCINNATI, OH-KY-IN PMSA	4240		LEWISTON-AUBURN, ME NECMA
	21 015	Boone		23 001	Androscoggin

Metropolitan Statistical Areas and Components by State – Continued

(MSA = metropolitan statistical area; CMSA = consolidated MSA; PMSA = primary MSA; and
NECMA = New England county metropolitan area. For further information, see Appendix A.)

Geographic Codes MSA/CMSA/ PMSA/ NECMA	State and County	Title and Geographic Components	Geographic Codes MSA/CMSA/ PMSA/ NECMA	State and County	Title and Geographic Components
6403		PORTLAND, ME NECMA		26 139	Ottawa
	23 005	Cumberland	3520		JACKSON, MI MSA
				26 075	Jackson
		MARYLAND	3720		KALAMAZOO-BATTLE CREEK, MI MSA
6162		PHILADELPHIA-WILMINGTON-ATLANTIC CITY, PA-NJ-DE-MD CMSA		26 025	Calhoun
				26 077	Kalamazoo
9160		WILMINGTON-NEWARK, DE-MD PMSA		26 159	Van Buren
	24 015	Cecil	4040		LANSING-EAST LANSING, MI MSA
8872		WASHINGTON-BALTIMORE, DC-MD-VA-WV CMSA		26 037	Clinton
0720		BALTIMORE, MD PMSA		26 045	Eaton
	24 003	Anne Arundel		26 065	Ingham
	24 005	Baltimore	6960		SAGINAW-BAY CITY-MIDLAND, MI MSA
	24 013	Carroll		26 017	Bay
	24 025	Harford		26 111	Midland
	24 027	Howard		26 145	Saginaw
	24 035	Queen Anne's			
	24 510	BALTIMORE CITY, MD			**MINNESOTA**
3180		HAGERSTOWN, MD PMSA	2240		DULUTH-SUPERIOR, MN-WI MSA
	24 043	Washington		27 137	St. Louis
8840		WASHINGTON, DC-MD-VA-WV PMSA	2520		FARGO-MOORHEAD, ND-MN MSA
	24 009	Calvert		27 027	Clay
	24 017	Charles	2985		GRAND FORKS, ND-MN MSA
	24 021	Frederick		27 119	Polk
	24 031	Montgomery	3870		LA CROSSE, WI-MN MSA
	24 033	Prince George's		27 055	Houston
1900		CUMBERLAND, MD-WV MSA	5120		MINNEAPOLIS-ST. PAUL, MN-WI MSA
	24 001	Allegany		27 003	Anoka
				27 019	Carver
		MASSACHUSETTS		27 025	Chisago
0743		BARNSTABLE-YARMOUTH, MA NECMA		27 037	Dakota
	25 001	Barnstable		27 053	Hennepin
1123		BOSTON-WORCESTER-LAWRENCE-LOWELL-BROCKTON, MA-NH NECMA		27 059	Isanti
				27 123	Ramsey
	25 005	Bristol		27 139	Scott
	25 009	Essex		27 141	Sherburne
	25 017	Middlesex		27 163	Washington
	25 021	Norfolk		27 171	Wright
	25 023	Plymouth	6820		ROCHESTER, MN MSA
	25 025	Suffolk		27 109	Olmsted
	25 027	Worcester	6980		ST. CLOUD, MN MSA
6323		PITTSFIELD, MA NECMA		27 009	Benton
	25 003	Berkshire		27 145	Stearns
8003		SPRINGFIELD, MA NECMA			
	25 013	Hampden			**MISSISSIPPI**
	25 015	Hampshire	0920		BILOXI-GULFPORT-PASCAGOULA, MS MSA
				28 045	Hancock
		MICHIGAN		28 047	Harrison
2162		DETROIT-ANN ARBOR-FLINT, MI CMSA		28 059	Jackson
0440		ANN ARBOR, MI PMSA	3285		HATTIESBURG, MS MSA
	26 091	Lenawee		28 035	Forrest
	26 093	Livingston		28 073	Lamar
	26 161	Washtenaw	3560		JACKSON, MS MSA
2160		DETROIT, MI PMSA		28 049	Hinds
	26 087	Lapeer		28 089	Madison
	26 099	Macomb		28 121	Rankin
	26 115	Monroe	4920		MEMPHIS, TN-AR-MS MSA
	26 125	Oakland		28 033	De Soto
	26 147	St. Clair			
	26 163	Wayne			**MISSOURI**
2640		FLINT, MI PMSA	1740		COLUMBIA, MO MSA
	26 049	Genesee		29 019	Boone
0870		BENTON HARBOR, MI MSA	3710		JOPLIN, MO MSA
	26 021	Berrien		29 097	Jasper
3000		GRAND RAPIDS-MUSKEGON-HOLLAND, MI MSA		29 145	Newton
	26 005	Allegan	3760		KANSAS CITY, MO-KS MSA
	26 081	Kent		29 037	Cass
	26 121	Muskegon		29 047	Clay

(MSA = metropolitan statistical area; CMSA = consolidated MSA; PMSA = primary MSA; and NECMA = New England county metropolitan area. For further information, see Appendix A.)

Geographic Codes MSA/CMSA/ PMSA/ NECMA	State and County	Title and Geographic Components
	29 049	Clinton
	29 095	Jackson
	29 107	Lafayette
	29 165	Platte
	29 177	Ray
7000		ST. JOSEPH, MO MSA
	29 003	Andrew
	29 021	Buchanan
7040		ST. LOUIS, MO-IL MSA
	29 071	Franklin
	29 099	Jefferson
	29 113	Lincoln
	29 183	St. Charles
	29 189	St. Louis
	29 219	Warren
	29 510	St. Louis City
7920		SPRINGFIELD, MO MSA
	29 043	Christian
	29 077	Greene
	29 225	Webster
		MONTANA
0880		BILLINGS, MT MSA
	30 111	Yellowstone
3040		GREAT FALLS, MT MSA
	30 013	Cascade
5140		MISSOULA, MT MSA
	30 063	Missoula
		NEBRASKA
4360		LINCOLN, NE MSA
	31 109	Lancaster
5920		OMAHA, NE-IA MSA
	31 025	Cass
	31 055	Douglas
	31 153	Sarpy
	31 177	Washington
7720		SIOUX CITY, IA-NE MSA
	31 043	Dakota
		NEVADA
4120		LAS VEGAS, NV-AZ MSA
	32 003	Clark
	32 023	Nye
6720		RENO, NV MSA
	32 031	Washoe
		NEW HAMPSHIRE
1123		BOSTON-WORCESTER-LAWRENCE-LOWELL-BROCKTON, MA-NH NECMA
	33 011	Hillsborough
	33 015	Rockingham
	33 017	Strafford
		NEW JERSEY
70		NEW YORK-NORTHERN NEW JERSEY-LONG ISLAND, NY-NJ-CT-PA CMSA
0875		BERGEN-PASSAIC, NJ PMSA
	34 003	Bergen
	34 031	Passaic
3640		JERSEY CITY, NJ PMSA
	34 017	HUDSON COUNTY, NJ
5015		MIDDLESEX-SOMERSET-HUNTERDON, NJ PMSA
	34 019	Hunterdon
	34 023	Middlesex
	34 035	Somerset

Geographic Codes MSA/CMSA/ PMSA/ NECMA	State and County	Title and Geographic Components
5190		MONMOUTH-OCEAN, NJ PMSA
	34 025	Monmouth
	34 029	Ocean
5640		NEWARK, NJ PMSA
	34 013	Essex
	34 027	Morris
	34 037	Sussex
	34 039	Union
	34 041	Warren
8480		TRENTON, NJ PMSA
	34 021	Mercer
560		ATLANTIC-CAPE MAY, NJ PMSA
	34 001	Atlantic
	34 009	Cape May
6160		PHILADELPHIA, PA-NJ PMSA
	34 005	Burlington
	34 007	Camden
	34 015	Gloucester
	34 033	Salem
8760		VINELAND-MILLVILLE-BRIDGETON, NJ PMSA
	34 011	Cumberland
		NEW MEXICO
0200		ALBUQUERQUE, NM MSA
	35 001	Bernalillo
	35 043	Sandoval
	35 061	Valencia
4100		LAS CRUCES, NM MSA
	35 013	Dona Ana
7490		SANTA FE, NM MSA
	35 028	Los Alamos
	35 049	Santa Fe
		NEW YORK
70		NEW YORK-NORTHERN NEW JERSEY-LONG ISLAND, NY-NJ-CT-PA CMSA
2281		DUTCHESS COUNTY, NY PMSA
	36 027	Dutchess
5380		NASSAU-SUFFOLK, NY PMSA
	36 059	Nassau
	36 103	Suffolk
5600		NEW YORK, NY PMSA
	36 005	Bronx
	36 047	Kings
	36 061	New York
	36 079	Putnam
	36 081	Queens
	36 085	Richmond
	36 087	Rockland
	36 119	Westchester
5660		NEWBURGH, NY-PA PMSA
	36 071	Orange
0160		ALBANY-SCHENECTADY-TROY, NY MSA
	36 001	ALBANY COUNTY, NY
	36 057	MONTGOMERY COUNTY, NY
	36 083	RENSSELAER COUNTY, NY
	36 091	SARATOGA COUNTY, NY
	36 093	SCHENECTADY COUNTY, NY
	36 095	SCHOHARIE COUNTY, NY
0960		BINGHAMTON, NY MSA
	36 007	Broome
	36 107	Tioga
1280		BUFFALO-NIAGARA FALLS, NY MSA
	36 029	Erie
	36 063	Niagara
2335		ELMIRA, NY MSA
	36 015	Chemung

Metropolitan Statistical Areas and Components by State – Continued

(MSA = metropolitan statistical area; CMSA = consolidated MSA; PMSA = primary MSA; and NECMA = New England county metropolitan area. For further information, see Appendix A.)

Geographic Codes MSA/CMSA/ PMSA/ NECMA	State and County	Title and Geographic Components	Geographic Codes MSA/CMSA/ PMSA/ NECMA	State and County	Title and Geographic Components
2281		DUTCHESS COUNTY, NY PMSA	6895		ROCKY MOUNT, NC MSA
2975		GLENS FALLS, NY MSA		37 065	Edgecombe
	36 113	Warren		37 127	Nash
	36 115	Washington	9200		WILMINGTON, NC MSA
3610		JAMESTOWN, NY MSA		37 019	Brunswick
	36 013	Chautauqua		37 129	New Hanover
6840		ROCHESTER, NY MSA			
	36 037	Genesee			**NORTH DAKOTA**
	36 051	Livingston	1010		BISMARCK, ND MSA
	36 055	Monroe	1010	38 015	Burleigh
	36 069	Ontario	1010	38 059	Morton
	36 073	Orleans	2520		FARGO-MOORHEAD, ND-MN MSA
	36 117	Wayne		38 017	Cass
8160		SYRACUSE, NY MSA	2985		GRAND FORKS, ND-MN MSA
	36 011	Cayuga		38 035	Grand Forks
	36 053	Madison			
	36 067	Onondaga			**OHIO**
	36 075	Oswego	21		CINCINNATI-HAMILTON, OH-KY-IN CMSA
8680		UTICA-ROME, NY MSA	1640		CINCINNATI, OH-KY-IN PMSA
	36 043	Herkimer		39 015	Brown
	36 065	Oneida		39 025	Clermont
				39 061	Hamilton
		NORTH CAROLINA		39 165	Warren
0480		ASHEVILLE, NC MSA	3200		HAMILTON-MIDDLETOWN, OH PMSA
	37 021	Buncombe		39 017	Butler
	37 115	Madison	28		CLEVELAND-AKRON, OH CMSA
1520		CHARLOTTE-GASTONIA-ROCK HILL, NC-SC MSA	0080		AKRON, OH PMSA
	37 025	Cabarrus		39 133	PORTAGE COUNTY, OH
	37 071	Gaston		39 153	SUMMIT COUNTY, OH
	37 109	Lincoln	1680		CLEVELAND-LORAIN-ELYRIA, OH PMSA
	37 119	Mecklenburg		39 007	Ashtabula
	37 159	Rowan		39 035	Cuyahoga
	37 179	Union		39 055	Geauga
2560		FAYETTEVILLE, NC MSA		39 085	Lake
	37 051	Cumberland		39 093	Lorain
2980		GOLDSBORO, NC MSA		39 103	Medina
	37 191	Wayne	1320		CANTON-MASSILLON, OH MSA
3120		GREENSBORO-WINSTON-SALEM-HIGH POINT, NC MSA		39 019	Carroll
				39 151	Stark
	37 001	Alamance	1840		COLUMBUS, OH MSA
	37 057	Davidson		39 041	Delaware
	37 059	Davie		39 045	Fairfield
	37 067	Forsyth		39 049	Franklin
	37 081	Guilford		39 089	Licking
	37 151	Randolph		39 097	Madison
	37 169	Stokes		39 129	Pickaway
	37 197	Yadkin	2000		DAYTON-SPRINGFIELD, OH MSA
3150		GREENVILLE, NC MSA		39 023	Clark
	37 147	Pitt		39 057	Greene
3290		HICKORY-MORGANTON-LENOIR, NC MSA		39 109	Miami
	37 003	Alexander		39 113	Montgomery
	37 023	Burke	3400		HUNTINGTON-ASHLAND, WV-KY-OH MSA
	37 027	Caldwell		39 087	Lawrence
	37 035	Catawba	4320		LIMA, OH MSA
3605		JACKSONVILLE, NC MSA		39 003	Allen
	37 133	Onslow		39 011	Auglaize
5720		NORFOLK-VIRGINIA BEACH-NEWPORT NEWS, VA-NC MSA	4800		MANSFIELD, OH MSA
				39 033	Crawford
	37 053	Currituck		39 139	Richland
6640		RALEIGH-DURHAM-CHAPEL HILL, NC MSA	6020		PARKERSBURG-MARIETTA, WV-OH MSA
	37 037	Chatham		39 167	Washington
	37 063	Durham	8080		STEUBENVILLE-WEIRTON, OH-WV MSA
	37 069	Franklin		39 081	Jefferson
	37 101	Johnston	8400		TOLEDO, OH MSA
	37 135	Orange		39 051	Fulton
	37 183	Wake		39 095	Lucas
				39 173	Wood

(MSA = metropolitan statistical area; CMSA = consolidated MSA; PMSA = primary MSA; and
NECMA = New England county metropolitan area. For further information, see Appendix A.)

Geographic Codes MSA/CMSA/ PMSA/ NECMA	State and County	Title and Geographic Components	Geographic Codes MSA/CMSA/ PMSA/ NECMA	State and County	Title and Geographic Components
9000		WHEELING, WV-OH MSA	3240		HARRISBURG-LEBANON-CARLISLE, PA MSA
	39 013	Belmont		42 041	Cumberland
9320		YOUNGSTOWN-WARREN, OH MSA		42 043	Dauphin
9320	39 029	Columbiana		42 075	Lebanon
9320	39 099	Mahoning		42 099	Perry
9320	39 155	Trumbull	3680		JOHNSTOWN, PA MSA
				42 021	Cambria
		OKLAHOMA		42 111	Somerset
2340		ENID, OK MSA	4000		LANCASTER, PA MSA
	40 047	Garfield		42 071	Lancaster
2720		FORT SMITH, AR-OK MSA	6280		PITTSBURGH, PA MSA
	40 135	Sequoyah		42 003	Allegheny
4200		LAWTON, OK MSA		42 007	Beaver
	40 031	Comanche		42 019	Butler
5880		OKLAHOMA CITY, OK MSA		42 051	Fayette
	40 017	Canadian		42 125	Washington
	40 027	Cleveland		42 129	Westmoreland
	40 083	Logan	6680		READING, PA MSA
	40 087	McClain		42 011	Berks
	40 109	Oklahoma	7560		SCRANTON-WILKES-BARRE-HAZLETON, PA MSA
	40 125	Pottawatomie		42 037	Columbia
8560		TULSA, OK MSA		42 069	Lackawanna
	40 037	Creek		42 079	Luzerne
	40 113	Osage		42 131	Wyoming
	40 131	Rogers	7610		SHARON, PA MSA
	40 143	Tulsa		42 085	Mercer
	40 145	Wagoner	8050		STATE COLLEGE, PA MSA
				42 027	Centre
		OREGON	9140		WILLIAMSPORT, PA MSA
1890		CORVALLIS, OR MSA		42 081	Lycoming
	41 003	Benton	9280		YORK, PA MSA
6442		PORTLAND-SALEM, OR-WA CMSA	9280	42 133	York
6440		PORTLAND-VANCOUVER, OR-WA PMSA			
	41 005	Clackamas			**RHODE ISLAND**
	41 009	Columbia	6483		PROVIDENCE-WARWICK-PAWTUCKET, RI NECMA
	41 051	Multnomah		44 001	Bristol
	41 067	Washington		44 003	Kent
	41 071	Yamhill		44 007	Providence
7080		SALEM, OR PMSA		44 009	Washington
	41 047	Marion			
	41 053	Polk			**SOUTH CAROLINA**
2400		EUGENE-SPRINGFIELD, OR MSA	0600		AUGUSTA-AIKEN, GA-SC MSA
	41 039	Lane		45 003	Aiken
4890		MEDFORD-ASHLAND, OR MSA		45 037	Edgefield
	41 029	Jackson	1440		CHARLESTON-NORTH CHARLESTON, SC MSA
				45 015	Berkeley
		PENNSYLVANIA		45 019	Charleston
70		NEW YORK-NORTHERN NEW JERSEY-LONG ISLAND, NY-NJ-CT-PA CMSA		45 035	Dorchester
5660		NEWBURGH, NY-PA PMSA	1520		CHARLOTTE-GASTONIA-ROCK HILL, NC-SC MSA
	42 103	Pike		45 091	York
6162		PHILADELPHIA-WILMINGTON-ATLANTIC CITY, PA-NJ-DE-MD CMSA	1760		COLUMBIA, SC MSA
				45 063	Lexington
6160		PHILADELPHIA, PA-NJ PMSA		45 079	Richland
	42 017	Bucks	2655		FLORENCE, SC MSA
	42 029	Chester		45 041	Florence
	42 045	Delaware	3160		GREENVILLE-SPARTANBURG-ANDERSON, SC MSA
	42 091	Montgomery		45 007	Anderson
	42 101	Philadelphia		45 021	Cherokee
0240		ALLENTOWN-BETHLEHEM-EASTON, PA MSA		45 045	Greenville
	42 025	CARBON COUNTY, PA		45 077	Pickens
	42 077	Lehigh		45 083	Spartanburg
	42 095	Northampton	5330		MYRTLE BEACH, SC MSA
0280		ALTOONA, PA MSA		45 051	Horry
	42 013	Blair	8140		SUMTER, SC MSA
2360		ERIE, PA MSA		45 085	Sumter
	42 049	Erie			

Metropolitan Statistical Areas and Components by State – Continued

(MSA = metropolitan statistical area; CMSA = consolidated MSA; PMSA = primary MSA; and
NECMA = New England county metropolitan area. For further information, see Appendix A.)

Geographic Codes MSA/CMSA/ PMSA/ NECMA	State and County	Title and Geographic Components	Geographic Codes MSA/CMSA/ PMSA/ NECMA	State and County	Title and Geographic Components
		SOUTH DAKOTA		48 201	Harris
6660		RAPID CITY, SD MSA		48 291	Liberty
	46 103	PENNINGTON COUNTY, SD		48 339	Montgomery
7760		SIOUX FALLS, SD MSA		48 473	Waller
	46 083	LINCOLN COUNTY, SD	0040		ABILENE, TX MSA
	46 099	MINNEHAHA COUNTY, SD		48 441	TAYLOR COUNTY, TX
			0320		AMARILLO, TX MSA
		TENNESSEE		48 375	Potter
1560		CHATTANOOGA, TN-GA MSA		48 381	Randall
	47 065	Hamilton	0640		AUSTIN-SAN MARCOS, TX MSA
	47 115	Marion		48 021	Bastrop
1660		CLARKSVILLE-HOPKINSVILLE, TN-KY MSA		48 055	Caldwell
	47 125	Montgomery		48 209	Hays
3580		JACKSON, TN MSA		48 453	Travis
	47 023	Chester		48 491	Williamson
	47 113	Madison	0840		BEAUMONT-PORT ARTHUR, TX MSA
3660		JOHNSON CITY-KINGSPORT-BRISTOL, TN-VA MSA		48 199	Hardin
	47 019	Carter		48 245	Jefferson
	47 073	Hawkins		48 361	Orange
	47 163	Sullivan	1240		BROWNSVILLE-HARLINGEN-SAN BENITO, TX MSA
	47 171	Unicoi		48 061	Cameron
	47 179	Washington	1260		BRYAN-COLLEGE STATION, TX MSA
3840		KNOXVILLE, TN MSA		48 041	Brazos
	47 001	Anderson	1880		CORPUS CHRISTI, TX MSA
	47 009	Blount		48 355	Nueces
	47 093	Knox		48 409	San Patricio
	47 105	Loudon	2320		EL PASO, TX MSA
	47 155	Sevier		48 141	El Paso
	47 173	Union	3810		KILLEEN-TEMPLE, TX MSA
4920		MEMPHIS, TN-AR-MS MSA		48 027	Bell
	47 047	Fayette		48 099	Coryell
	47 157	Shelby	4080		LAREDO, TX MSA
	47 167	Tipton		48 479	Webb
5360		NASHVILLE, TN MSA	4420		LONGVIEW-MARSHALL, TX MSA
	47 021	Cheatham		48 183	Gregg
	47 037	Davidson		48 203	Harrison
	47 043	Dickson		48 459	Upshur
	47 147	Robertson	4600		LUBBOCK, TX MSA
	47 149	Rutherford		48 303	Lubbock
	47 165	Sumner	4880		MCALLEN-EDINBURG-MISSION, TX MSA
	47 187	Williamson		48 215	Hidalgo
	47 189	Wilson	5800		ODESSA-MIDLAND, TX MSA
				48 135	Ector
		TEXAS		48 329	Midland
31		DALLAS-FORT WORTH, TX CMSA	7200		SAN ANGELO, TX MSA
1920		DALLAS, TX PMSA		48 451	Tom Green
	48 085	Collin	7240		SAN ANTONIO, TX MSA
	48 113	Dallas		48 029	Bexar
	48 121	Denton		48 091	Comal
	48 139	Ellis		48 187	Guadalupe
	48 213	Henderson		48 493	Wilson
	48 231	Hunt	7640		SHERMAN-DENISON, TX MSA
	48 257	Kaufman		48 181	Grayson
	48 397	Rockwall	8360		TEXARKANA, TX-TEXARKANA, AR MSA
2800		FORT WORTH-ARLINGTON, TX PMSA		48 037	Bowie
	48 221	Hood	8640		TYLER, TX MSA
	48 251	Johnson		48 423	Smith
	48 367	Parker	8750		VICTORIA, TX MSA
	48 439	Tarrant		48 469	Victoria
3362		HOUSTON-GALVESTON-BRAZORIA, TX CMSA	8800		WACO, TX MSA
1145		BRAZORIA, TX PMSA		48 309	McLennan
	48 039	Brazoria	9080		WICHITA FALLS, TX MSA
2920		GALVESTON-TEXAS CITY, TX PMSA		48 009	Archer
		GALVESTON COUNTY, TX		48 485	Wichita
3360		HOUSTON, TX PMSA			
	48 071	Chambers			
	48 157	Fort Bend			

(MSA = metropolitan statistical area; CMSA = consolidated MSA; PMSA = primary MSA; and
NECMA = New England county metropolitan area. For further information, see Appendix A.)

Geographic Codes MSA/CMSA/ PMSA/ NECMA	State and County	Title and Geographic Components	Geographic Codes MSA/CMSA/ PMSA/ NECMA	State and County	Title and Geographic Components
		UTAH		51 800	Suffolk City
2620		FLAGSTAFF, AZ-UT MSA		51 810	Virginia Beach City
	49 025	Kane		51 830	Williamsburg City
6520		PROVO-OREM, UT MSA	6760		RICHMOND-PETERSBURG, VA MSA
	49 049	Utah		51 036	Charles City
7160		SALT LAKE CITY-OGDEN, UT MSA		51 041	Chesterfield
	49 011	Davis		51 053	Dinwiddie
	49 035	Salt Lake		51 075	Goochland
	49 057	Weber		51 085	Hanover
				51 087	Henrico
				51 127	New Kent
		VERMONT		51 145	Powhatan
1303		BURLINGTON, VT NECMA		51 149	Prince George
	50 077	Chittenden		51 570	Colonial Heights City
	50 011	Franklin		51 670	Hopewell City
	50 013	Grand Isle		51 730	Petersburg City
				51 760	Richmond City
		VIRGINIA	6800		ROANOKE, VA MSA
8872		WASHINGTON-BALTIMORE, DC-MD-VA-WV CMSA		51 023	Botetourt
8840		WASHINGTON, DC-MD-VA-WV PMSA		51 161	Roanoke
	51 013	Arlington		51 770	Roanoke City
	51 043	Clarke		51 775	Salem City
	51 047	Culpeper			
	51 059	Fairfax			**WASHINGTON**
	51 061	Fauquier	6442		PORTLAND-SALEM, OR-WA CMSA
	51 099	King George	6440		PORTLAND-VANCOUVER, OR-WA PMSA
	51 107	Loudoun		53 011	Clark
	51 153	Prince William	7602		SEATTLE-TACOMA-BREMERTON, WA CMSA
	51 177	Spotsylvania	1150		BREMERTON, WA PMSA
	51 179	Stafford		53 035	Kitsap
	51 187	Warren	5910		OLYMPIA, WA PMSA
	51 510	Alexandria City		53 067	Thurston
	51 600	Fairfax City	7600		SEATTLE-BELLEVUE-EVERETT, WA PMSA
	51 610	Falls Church City		53 029	Island
	51 630	Fredericksburg City		53 033	King
	51 683	Manassas City		53 061	Snohomish
	51 685	Manassas Park City	8200		TACOMA, WA PMSA
1540		CHARLOTTESVILLE, VA MSA		53 053	Pierce
	51 003	Albemarle	0860		BELLINGHAM, WA MSA
	51 065	Fluvanna		53 073	Whatcom
	51 079	Greene	6740		RICHLAND-KENNEWICK-PASCO, WA MSA
	51 540	Charlottesville City		53 005	Benton
1950		DANVILLE, VA MSA		53 021	Franklin
	51 143	Pittsylvania	7840		SPOKANE, WA MSA
	51 590	Danville City		53 063	Spokane
3660		JOHNSON CITY-KINGSPORT-BRISTOL, TN-VA MSA	9260		YAKIMA, WA MSA
	51 169	Scott		53 077	Yakima
	51 191	Washington			
	51 520	Bristol City			**WEST VIRGINIA**
4640		LYNCHBURG, VA MSA	97		WASHINGTON-BALTIMORE, DC-MD-VA-WV CMSA
	51 009	Amherst	8840		WASHINGTON, DC-MD-VA-WV PMSA
	51 019	Bedford		54 003	Jefferson
	51 031	Campbell		54 037	Berkeley
	51 515	Bedford City	1480		CHARLESTON, WV MSA
	51 680	Lynchburg City		54 039	Kanawha
5720		NORFOLK-VIRGINIA BEACH-NEWPORT NEWS, VA-NC MSA		54 079	Putnam
			1900		CUMBERLAND, MD-WV MSA
	51 073	Gloucester		54 057	Mineral
	51 093	Isle of Wight	3400		HUNTINGTON-ASHLAND, WV-KY-OH MSA
	51 095	James City		54 011	Cabell
	51 115	Mathews		54 099	Wayne
	51 199	York	6020		PARKERSBURG-MARIETTA, WV-OH MSA
	51 550	Chesapeake City		54 107	Wood
	51 650	Hampton City	8080		STEUBENVILLE-WEIRTON, OH-WV MSA
	51 700	Newport News City		54 009	Brooke
	51 710	Norfolk City		54 029	Hancock
	51 735	Poquoson City			
	51 740	Portsmouth City			

(MSA = metropolitan statistical area; CMSA = consolidated MSA; PMSA = primary MSA; and
NECMA = New England county metropolitan area. For further information, see Appendix A.)

Geographic Codes MSA/CMSA/ PMSA/ NECMA	State and County	Title and Geographic Components	Geographic Codes MSA/CMSA/ PMSA/ NECMA	State and County	Title and Geographic Components
9000		WHEELING, WV-OH MSA	3080		GREEN BAY, WI MSA
	54 051	Marshall		55 009	Brown
	54 069	Ohio	3620		JANESVILLE-BELOIT, WI MSA
				55 105	Rock
		WISCONSIN	3870		LA CROSSE, WI-MN MSA
14		CHICAGO-GARY-KENOSHA, IL-IN-WI CMSA		55 063	La Crosse
3800		KENOSHA, WI PMSA	4720		MADISON, WI MSA
	55 059	Kenosha		55 025	Dane
5082		MILWAUKEE-RACINE, WI CMSA	5120		MINNEAPOLIS-ST. PAUL, MN-WI MSA
5080		MILWAUKEE-WAUKESHA, WI PMSA		55 093	Pierce
	55 079	Milwaukee		55 109	St. Croix
	55 089	Ozaukee	7620		SHEBOYGAN, WI MSA
	55 131	Washington		55 117	Sheboygan
	55 133	Waukesha	8940		WAUSAU, WI MSA
6600		RACINE, WI PMSA		55 073	Marathon
	55 101	Racine			
0460		APPLETON-OSHKOSH-NEENAH, WI MSA			**WYOMING**
	55 015	Calumet	1350		CASPER, WY MSA
	55 087	Outagamie		56 025	Natrona
	55 139	Winnebago	1580		CHEYENNE, WY MSA
2240		DULUTH-SUPERIOR, MN-WI MSA		56 021	Laramie
	55 031	Douglas			
2290		EAU CLAIRE, WI MSA			
	55 017	Chippewa			
	55 035	Eau Claire			

ALABAMA—Metropolitan Areas, Counties, and Central Cities

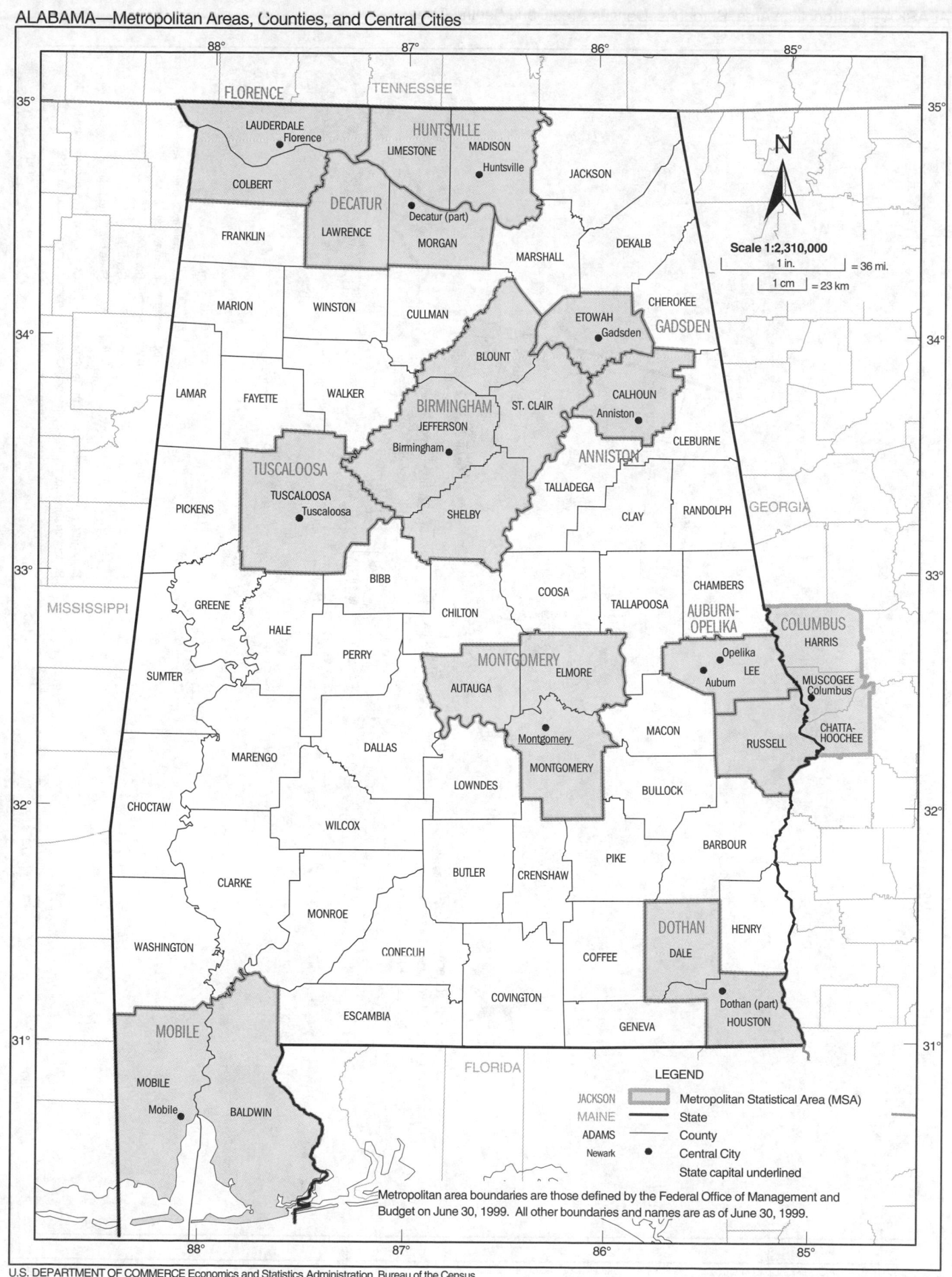

Scale 1:2,310,000

| 1 in. | = 36 mi. |
| 1 cm | = 23 km |

LEGEND

JACKSON		Metropolitan Statistical Area (MSA)
MAINE		State
ADAMS		County
Newark	●	Central City
		State capital underlined

Metropolitan area boundaries are those defined by the Federal Office of Management and Budget on June 30, 1999. All other boundaries and names are as of June 30, 1999.

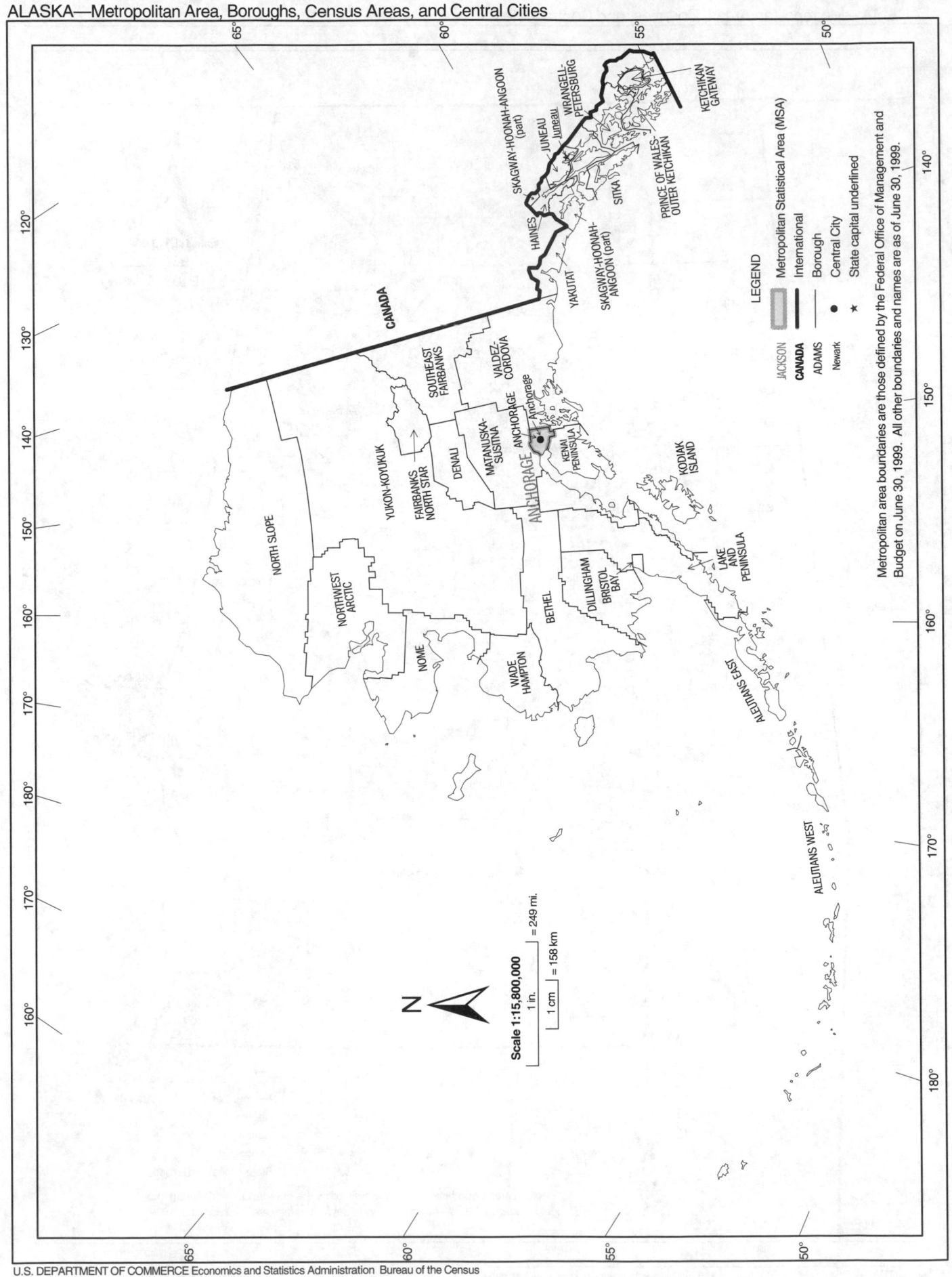

LEGEND

JACKSON	Metropolitan Statistical Area (MSA)
CANADA	International
ADAMS	Borough
● Newark	Central City
★	State capital underlined

Metropolitan area boundaries are those defined by the Federal Office of Management and Budget on June 30, 1999. All other boundaries and names are as of June 30, 1999.

Scale 1:15,800,000

1 in. ⌐ = 249 mi.

1 cm ⌐ = 158 km

N

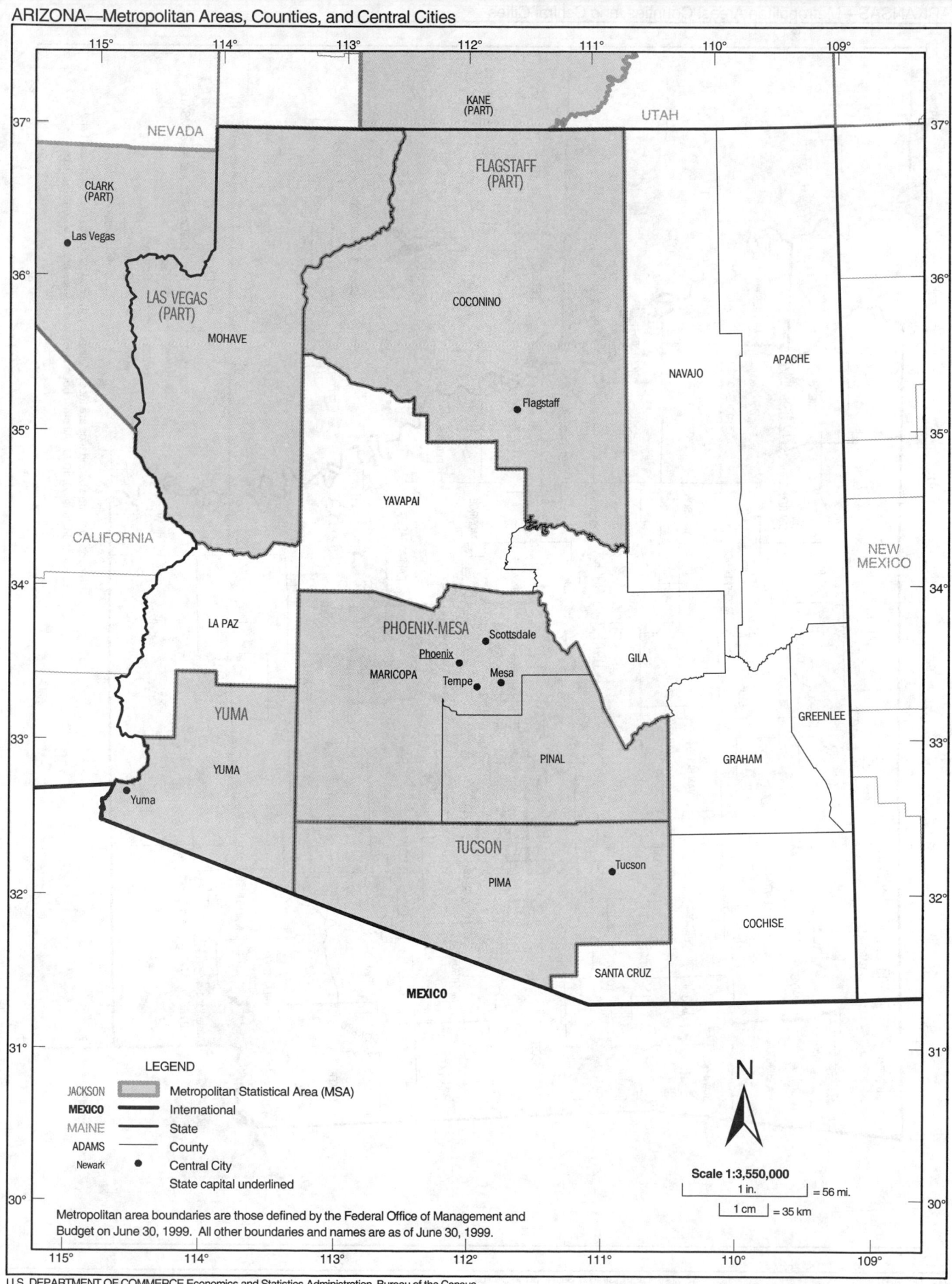

LEGEND

JACKSON	Metropolitan Statistical Area (MSA)
MEXICO	International
MAINE	State
ADAMS	County
Newark ●	Central City
	State capital underlined

Metropolitan area boundaries are those defined by the Federal Office of Management and Budget on June 30, 1999. All other boundaries and names are as of June 30, 1999.

Scale 1:3,550,000

1 in. = 56 mi.

1 cm = 35 km

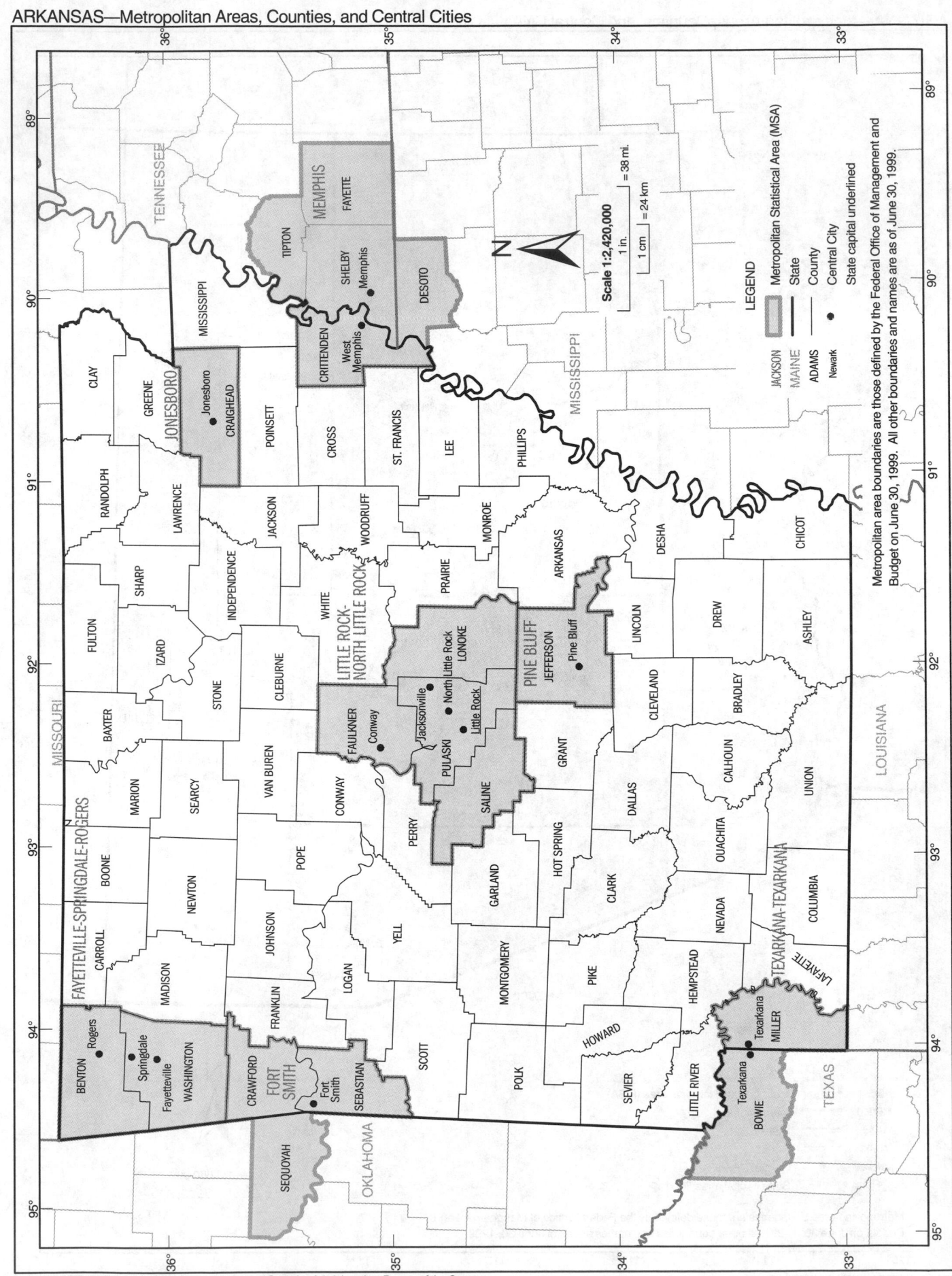

CALIFORNIA—Metropolitan Areas, Counties, and Central Cities

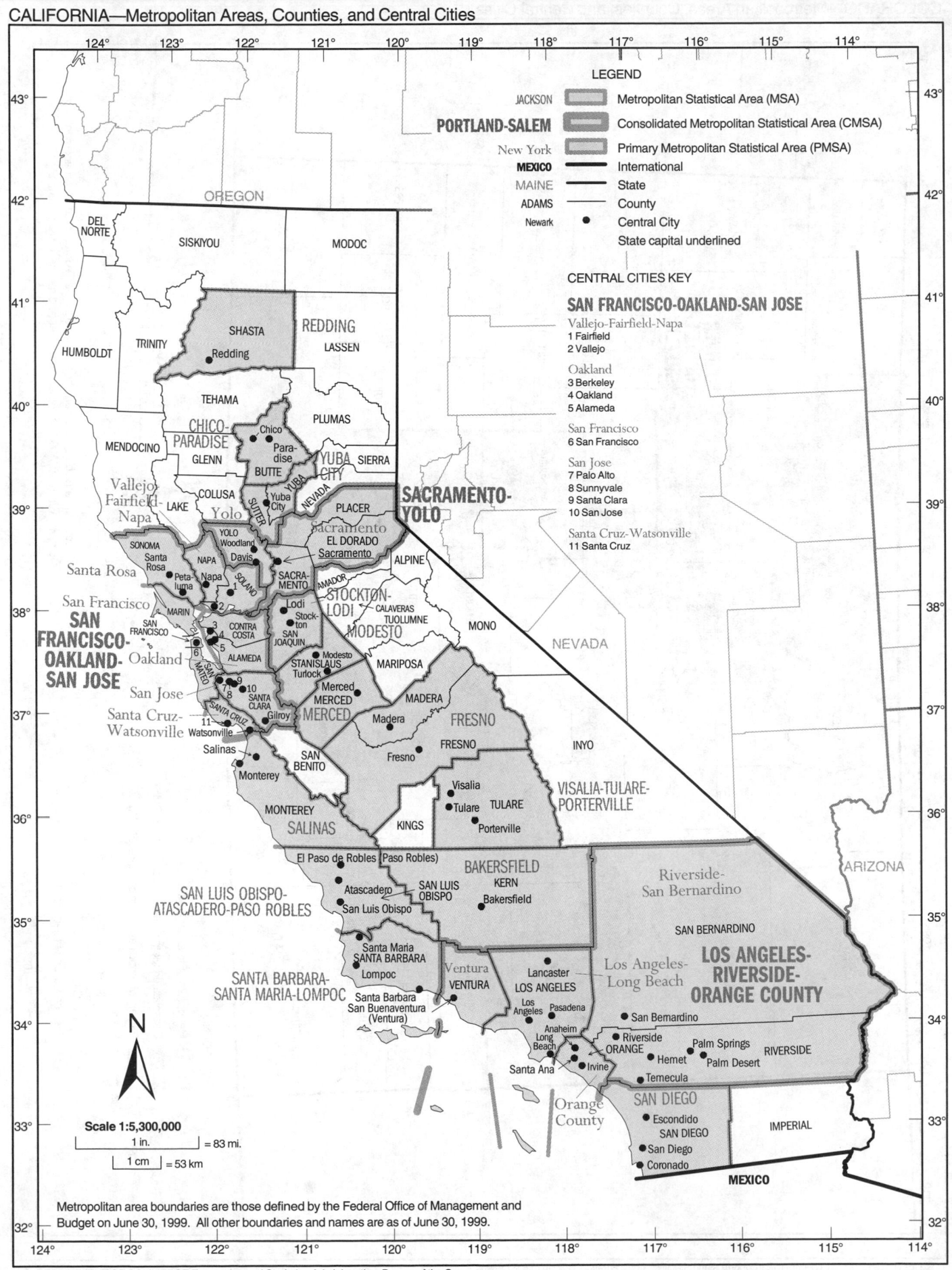

LEGEND

JACKSON	Metropolitan Statistical Area (MSA)
PORTLAND-SALEM	Consolidated Metropolitan Statistical Area (CMSA)
New York	Primary Metropolitan Statistical Area (PMSA)
MEXICO	International
MAINE	State
ADAMS	County
Newark ●	Central City
	State capital underlined

CENTRAL CITIES KEY

SAN FRANCISCO-OAKLAND-SAN JOSE

Vallejo-Fairfield-Napa
1 Fairfield
2 Vallejo

Oakland
3 Berkeley
4 Oakland
5 Alameda

San Francisco
6 San Francisco

San Jose
7 Palo Alto
8 Sunnyvale
9 Santa Clara
10 San Jose

Santa Cruz-Watsonville
11 Santa Cruz

Scale 1:5,300,000

1 in. = 83 mi.

1 cm = 53 km

Metropolitan area boundaries are those defined by the Federal Office of Management and Budget on June 30, 1999. All other boundaries and names are as of June 30, 1999.

U.S. DEPARTMENT OF COMMERCE Economics and Statistics Administration Bureau of the Census

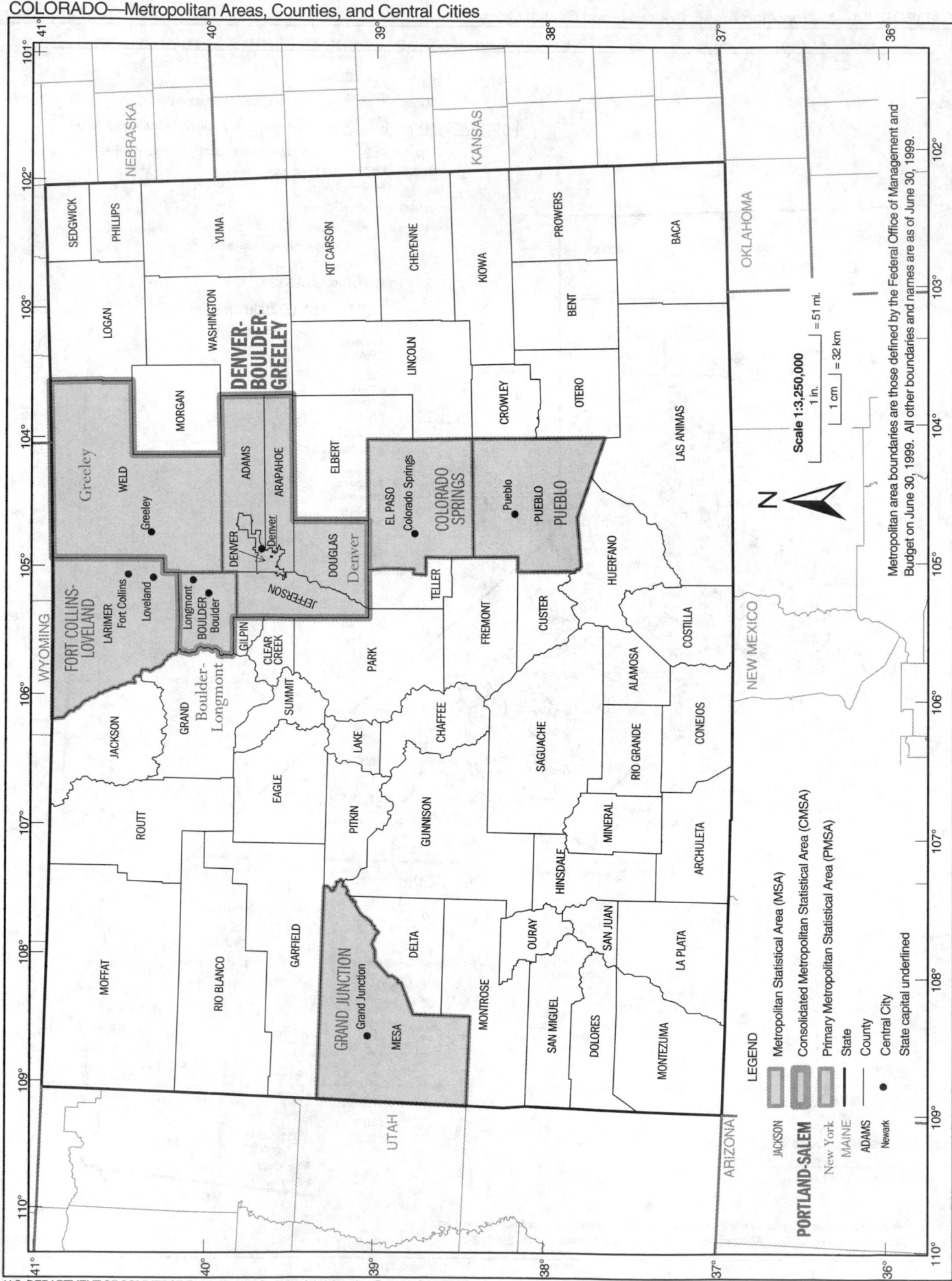

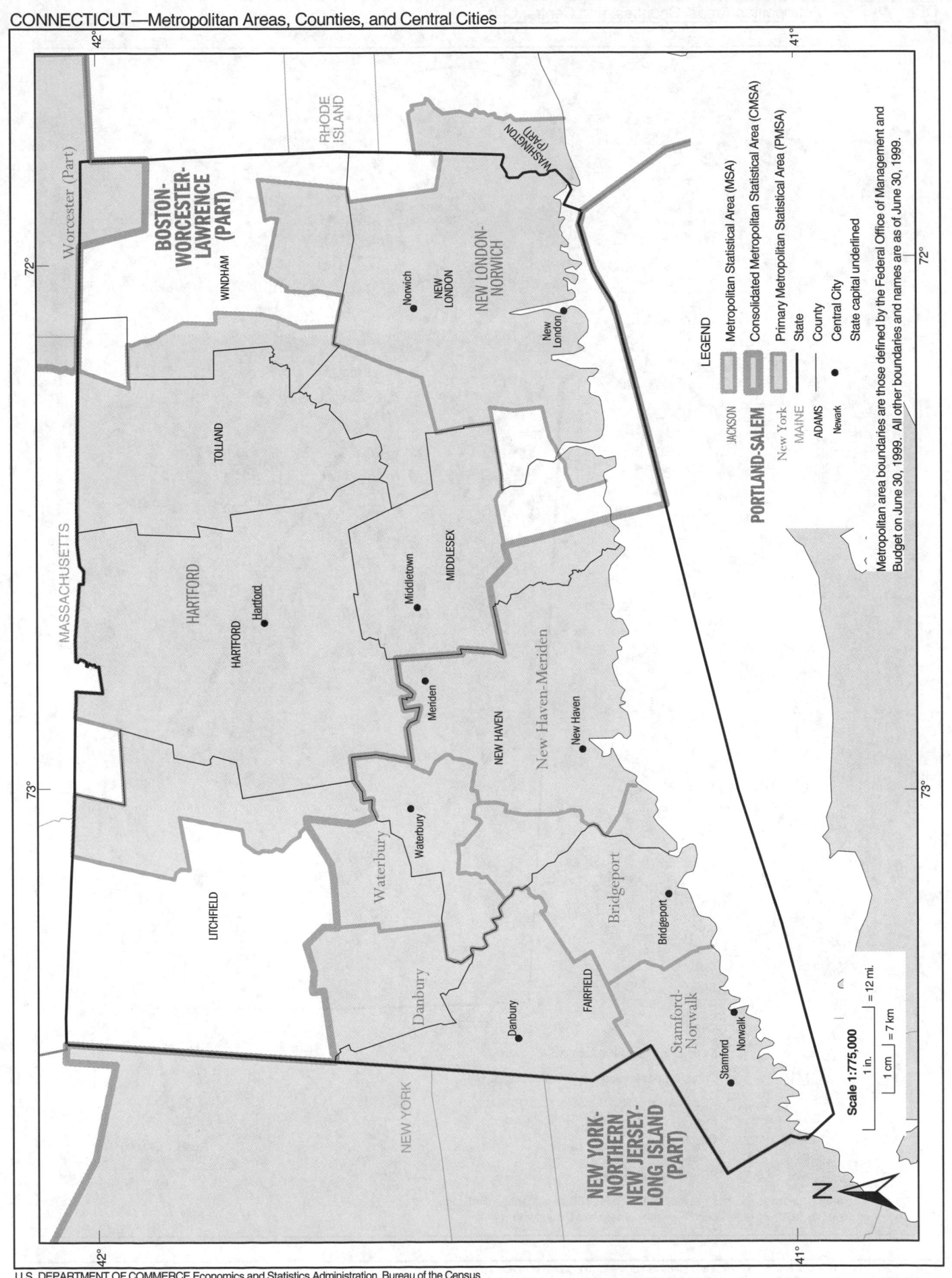

LEGEND

JACKSON	Metropolitan Statistical Area (MSA)
PORTLAND-SALEM	Consolidated Metropolitan Statistical Area (CMSA)
New York	Primary Metropolitan Statistical Area (PMSA)
MAINE	State
ADAMS	County
●	Central City
Newark	State capital underlined

Metropolitan area boundaries are those defined by the Federal Office of Management and Budget on June 30, 1999. All other boundaries and names are as of June 30, 1999.

Scale 1:775,000
1 in. = 12 mi.
1 cm = 7 km

N

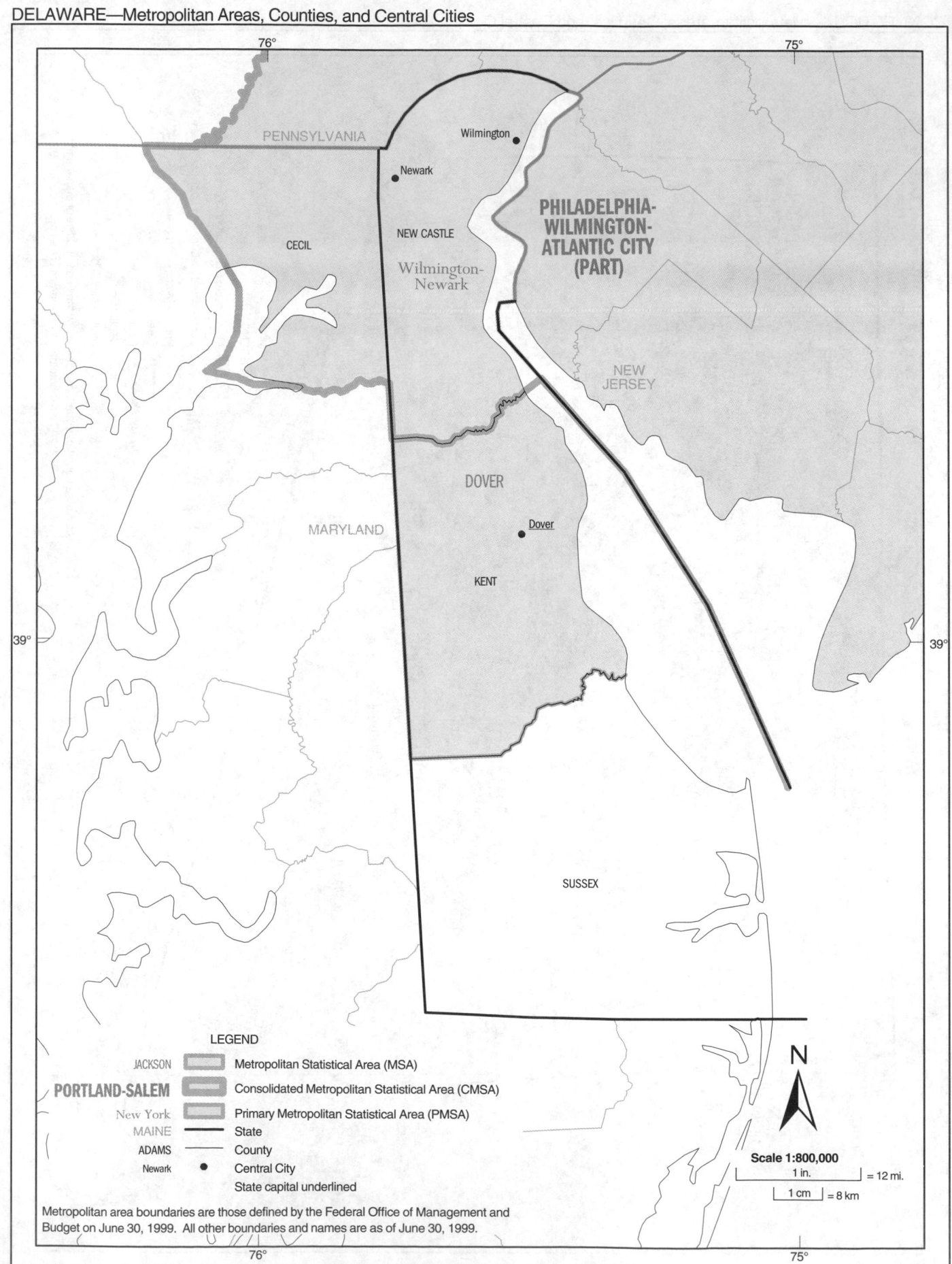

PENNSYLVANIA

Wilmington

Newark

CECIL

NEW CASTLE

Wilmington-
Newark

PHILADELPHIA-
WILMINGTON-
ATLANTIC CITY
(PART)

NEW
JERSEY

DOVER

Dover

MARYLAND

KENT

39°   39°

SUSSEX

N

LEGEND

JACKSON   Metropolitan Statistical Area (MSA)

PORTLAND-SALEM   Consolidated Metropolitan Statistical Area (CMSA)

New York   Primary Metropolitan Statistical Area (PMSA)

MAINE   State

ADAMS   County

Newark   ●   Central City
                 State capital underlined

Scale 1:800,000

| 1 in. | = 12 mi. |

| 1 cm | = 8 km |

Metropolitan area boundaries are those defined by the Federal Office of Management and
Budget on June 30, 1999. All other boundaries and names are as of June 30, 1999.

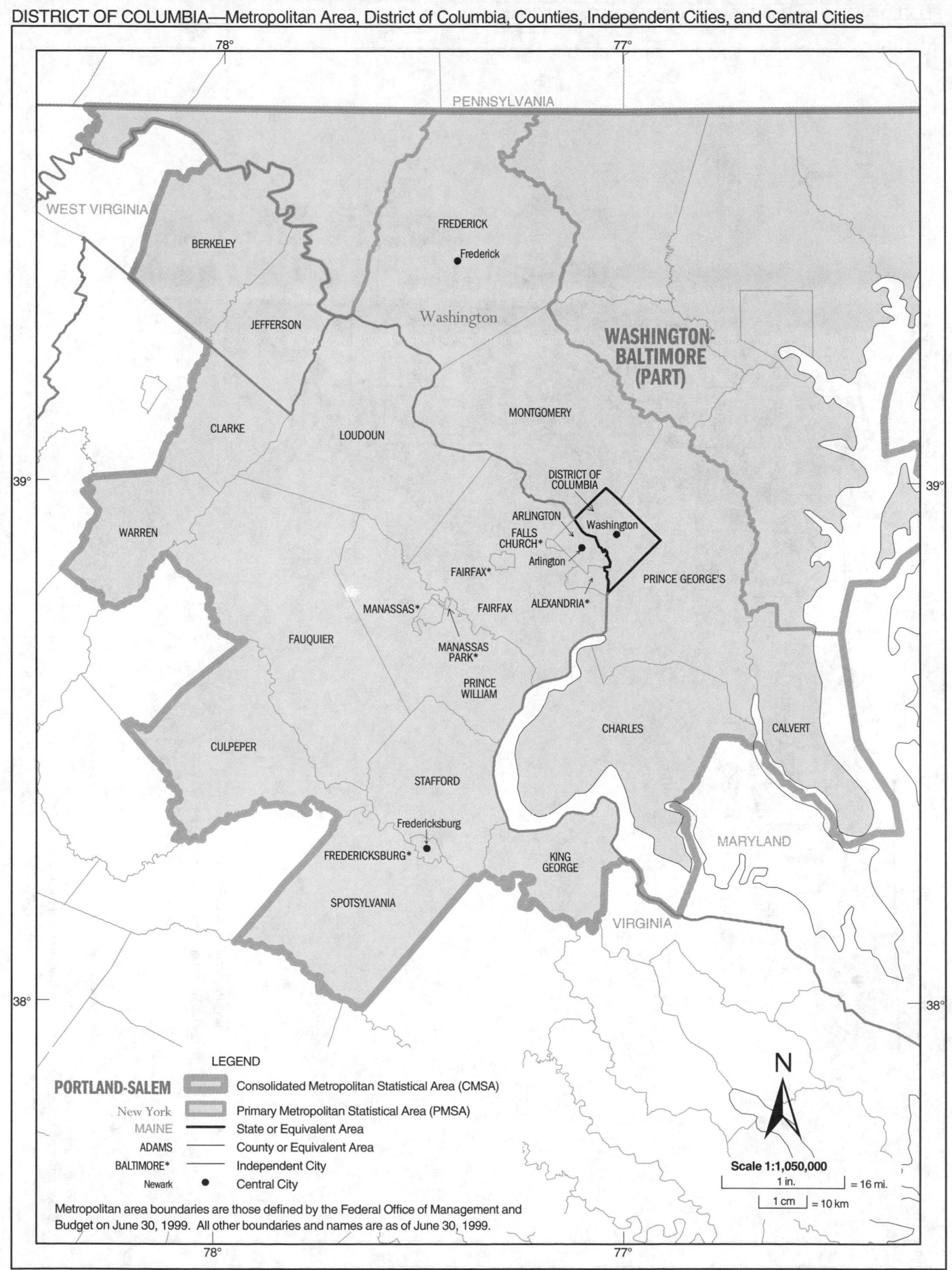

LEGEND

PORTLAND-SALEM — Consolidated Metropolitan Statistical Area (CMSA)

New York — Primary Metropolitan Statistical Area (PMSA)

MAINE — State or Equivalent Area

ADAMS — County or Equivalent Area

BALTIMORE* — Independent City

Newark ● — Central City

Metropolitan area boundaries are those defined by the Federal Office of Management and Budget on June 30, 1999. All other boundaries and names are as of June 30, 1999.

Scale 1:1,050,000
1 in. = 16 mi.
1 cm = 10 km

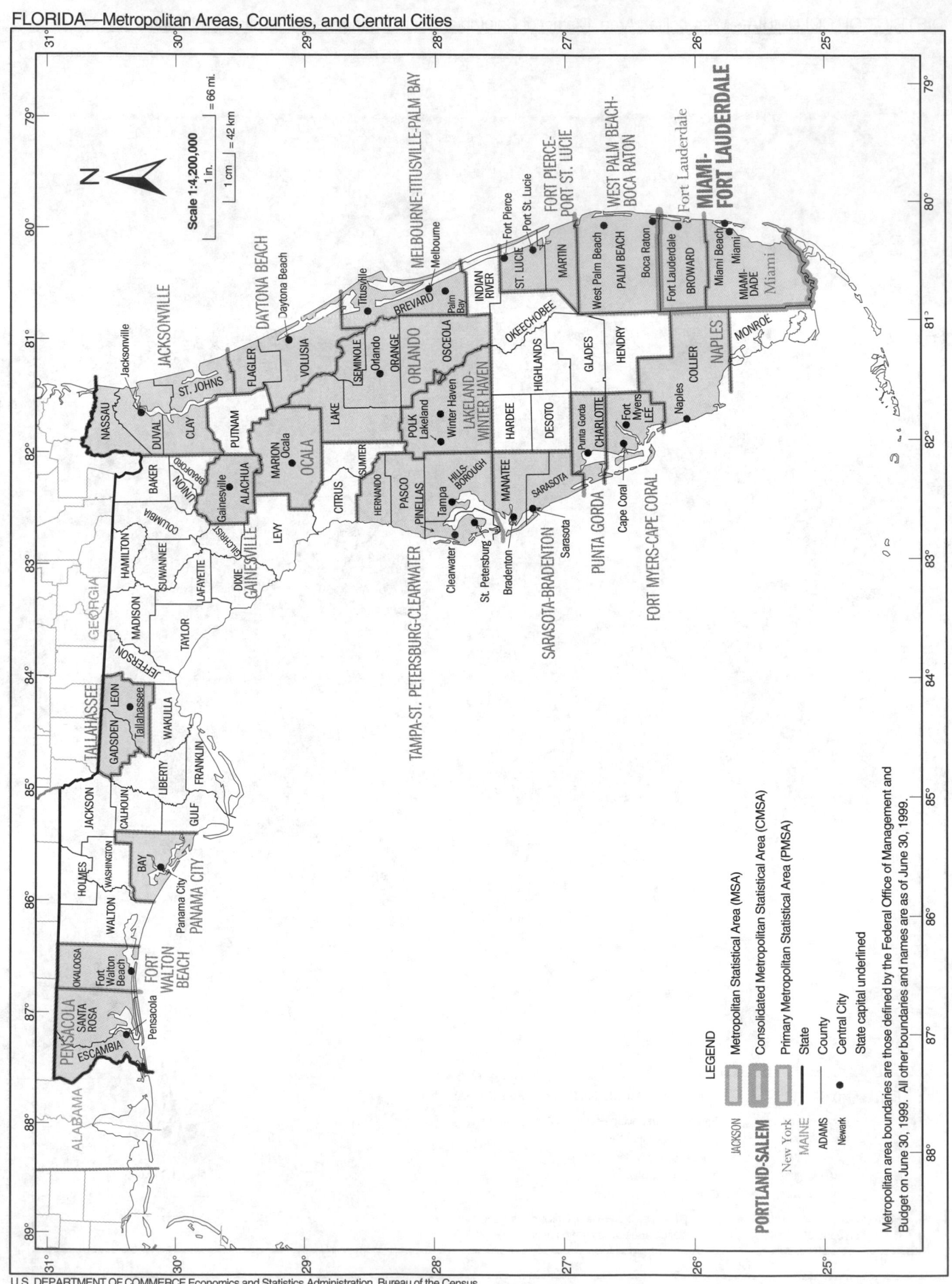

LEGEND

	Metropolitan Statistical Area (MSA)
	Consolidated Metropolitan Statistical Area (CMSA)
	Primary Metropolitan Statistical Area (PMSA)
JACKSON	State
PORTLAND-SALEM	County
New York / MAINE	
ADAMS	
Newark	Central City
	State capital underlined

• Central City

Metropolitan area boundaries are those defined by the Federal Office of Management and Budget on June 30, 1999. All other boundaries and names are as of June 30, 1999.

Scale 1:4,200,000

1 in. = 66 mi.

1 cm = 42 km

GEORGIA—Metropolitan Areas, Counties, and Central Cities

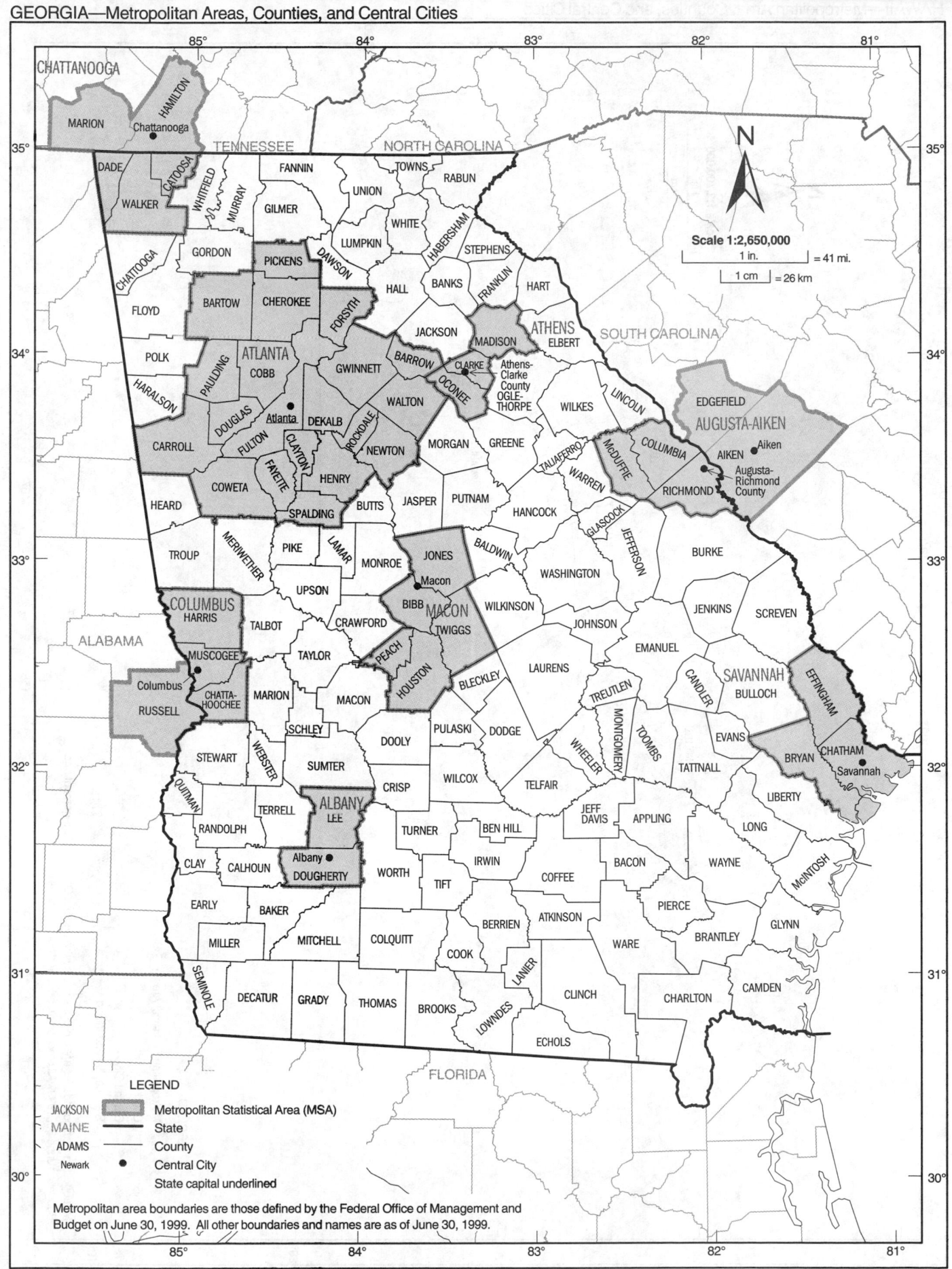

Scale 1:2,650,000

| 1 in. | = 41 mi. |
| 1 cm | = 26 km |

LEGEND

JACKSON	Metropolitan Statistical Area (MSA)
MAINE	State
ADAMS	County
Newark ●	Central City
	State capital underlined

Metropolitan area boundaries are those defined by the Federal Office of Management and Budget on June 30, 1999. All other boundaries and names are as of June 30, 1999.

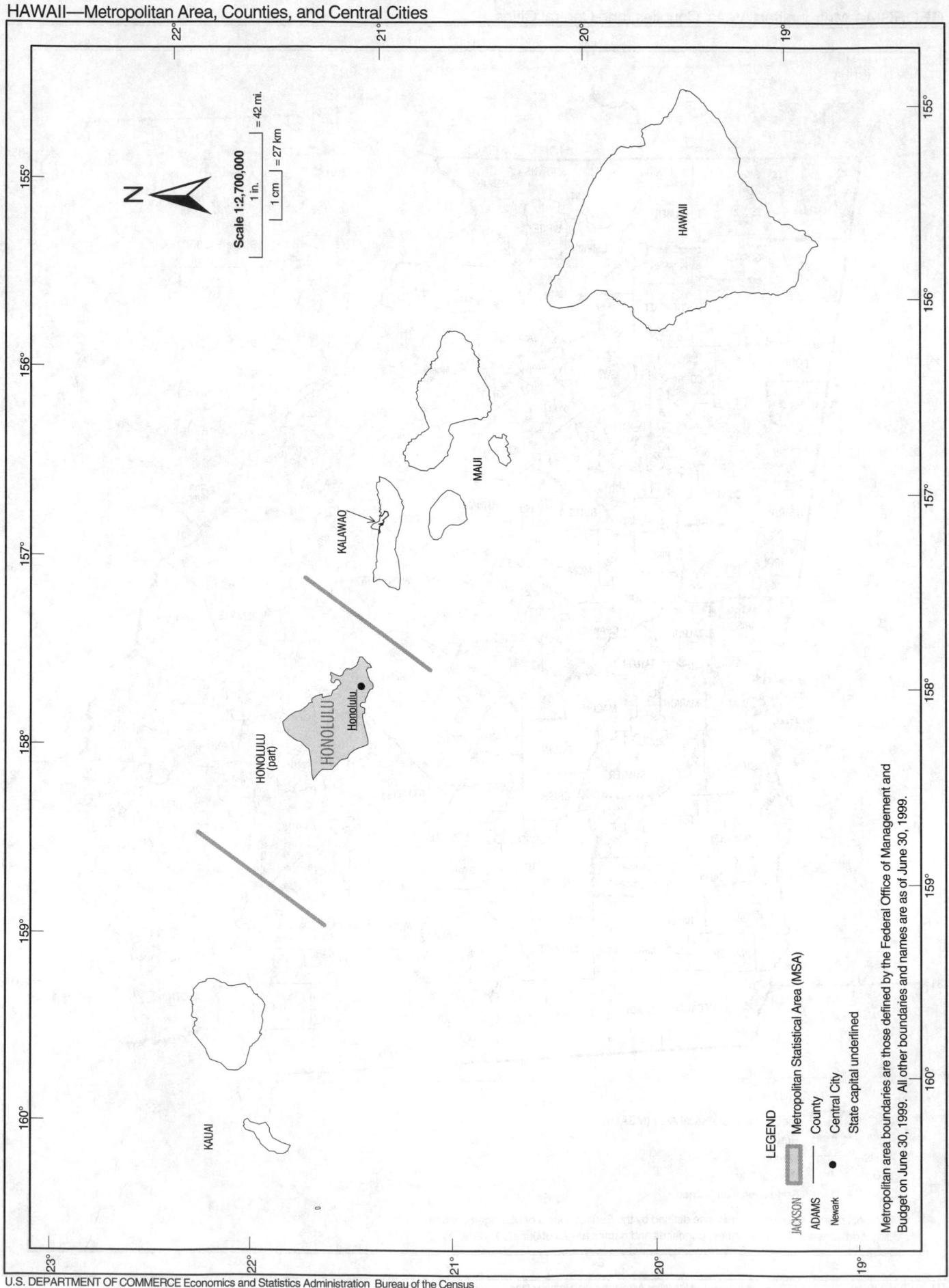

Scale 1:2,700,000

1 in. = 42 mi.

1 cm = 27 km

HAWAII

MAUI

KALAWAO

HONOLULU
(part)

HONOLULU

Honolulu

KAUAI

LEGEND

JACKSON   Metropolitan Statistical Area (MSA)

ADAMS   County

Newark • Central City

State capital underlined

Metropolitan area boundaries are those defined by the Federal Office of Management and
Budget on June 30, 1999. All other boundaries and names are as of June 30, 1999.

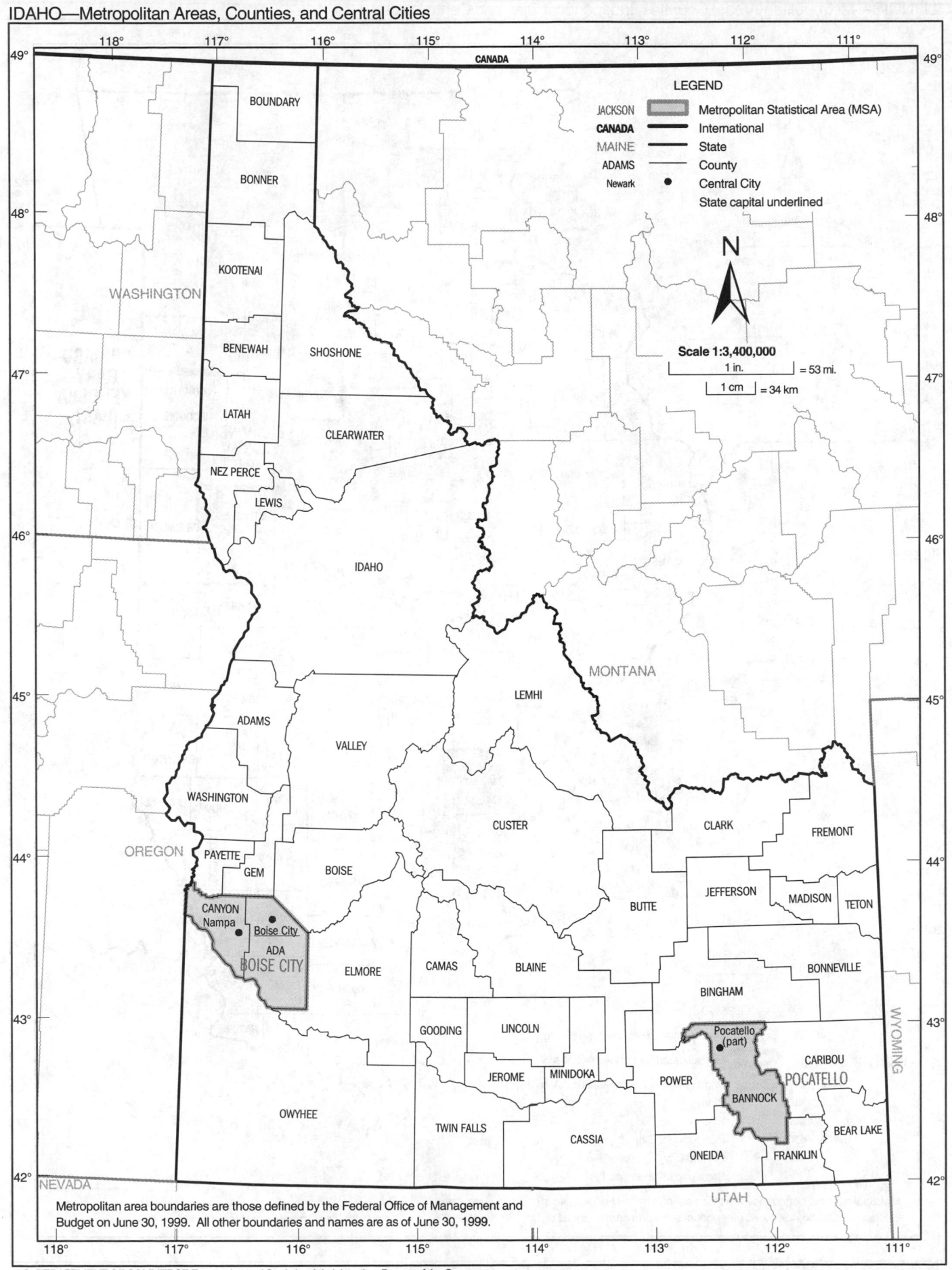

LEGEND

JACKSON	Metropolitan Statistical Area (MSA)
CANADA	International
MAINE	State
ADAMS	County
Newark ●	Central City
	State capital underlined

N

Scale 1:3,400,000

1 in. = 53 mi.

1 cm = 34 km

Metropolitan area boundaries are those defined by the Federal Office of Management and Budget on June 30, 1999. All other boundaries and names are as of June 30, 1999.

U.S. DEPARTMENT OF COMMERCE Economics and Statistics Administration Bureau of the Census

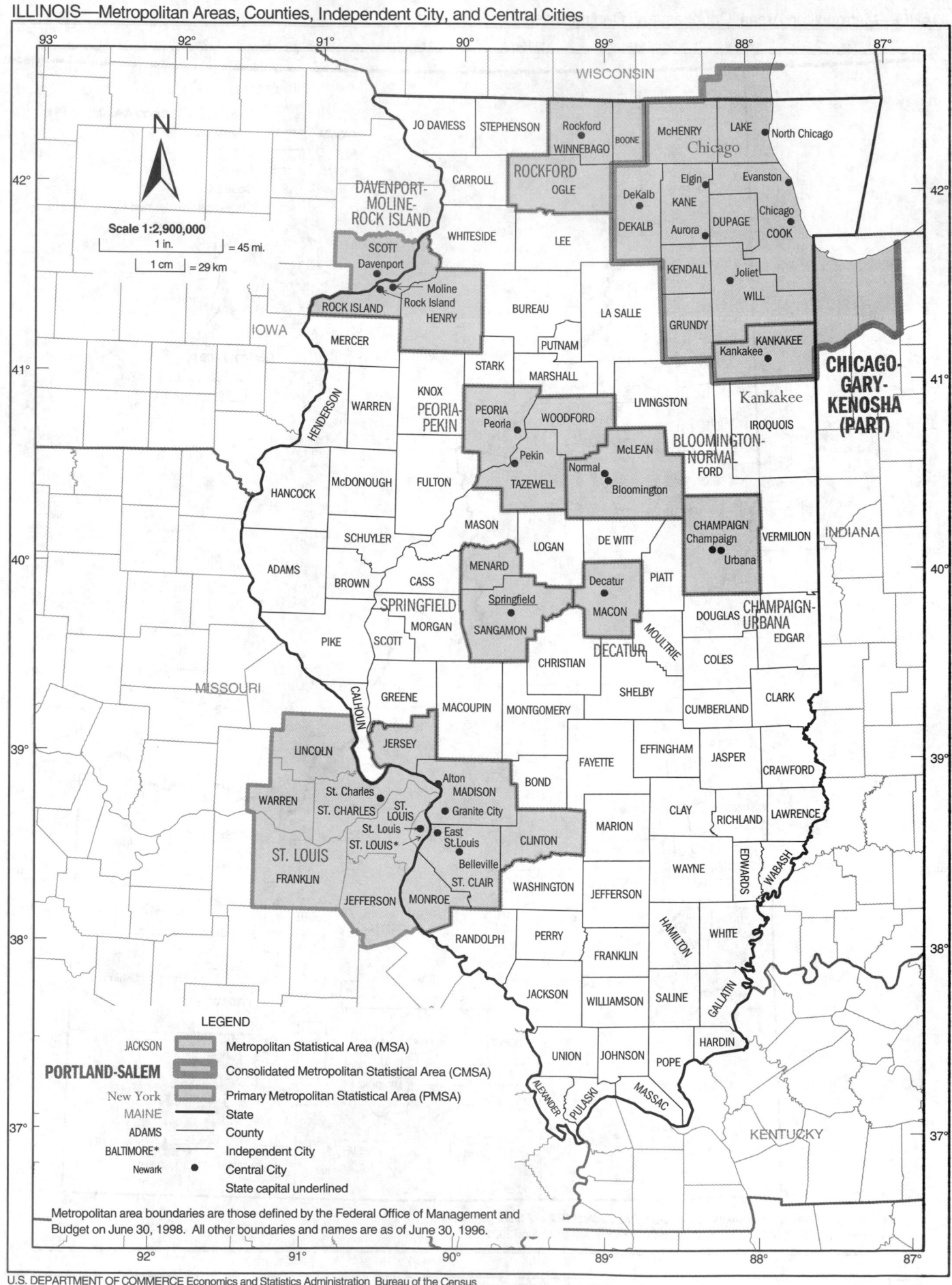

Scale 1:2,900,000

1 in. = 45 mi.

1 cm = 29 km

CHICAGO-GARY-KENOSHA (PART)

LEGEND

JACKSON	Metropolitan Statistical Area (MSA)
PORTLAND-SALEM	Consolidated Metropolitan Statistical Area (CMSA)
New York	Primary Metropolitan Statistical Area (PMSA)
MAINE	State
ADAMS	County
BALTIMORE*	Independent City
Newark ●	Central City
	State capital underlined

Metropolitan area boundaries are those defined by the Federal Office of Management and Budget on June 30, 1998. All other boundaries and names are as of June 30, 1996.

U.S. DEPARTMENT OF COMMERCE Economics and Statistics Administration Bureau of the Census

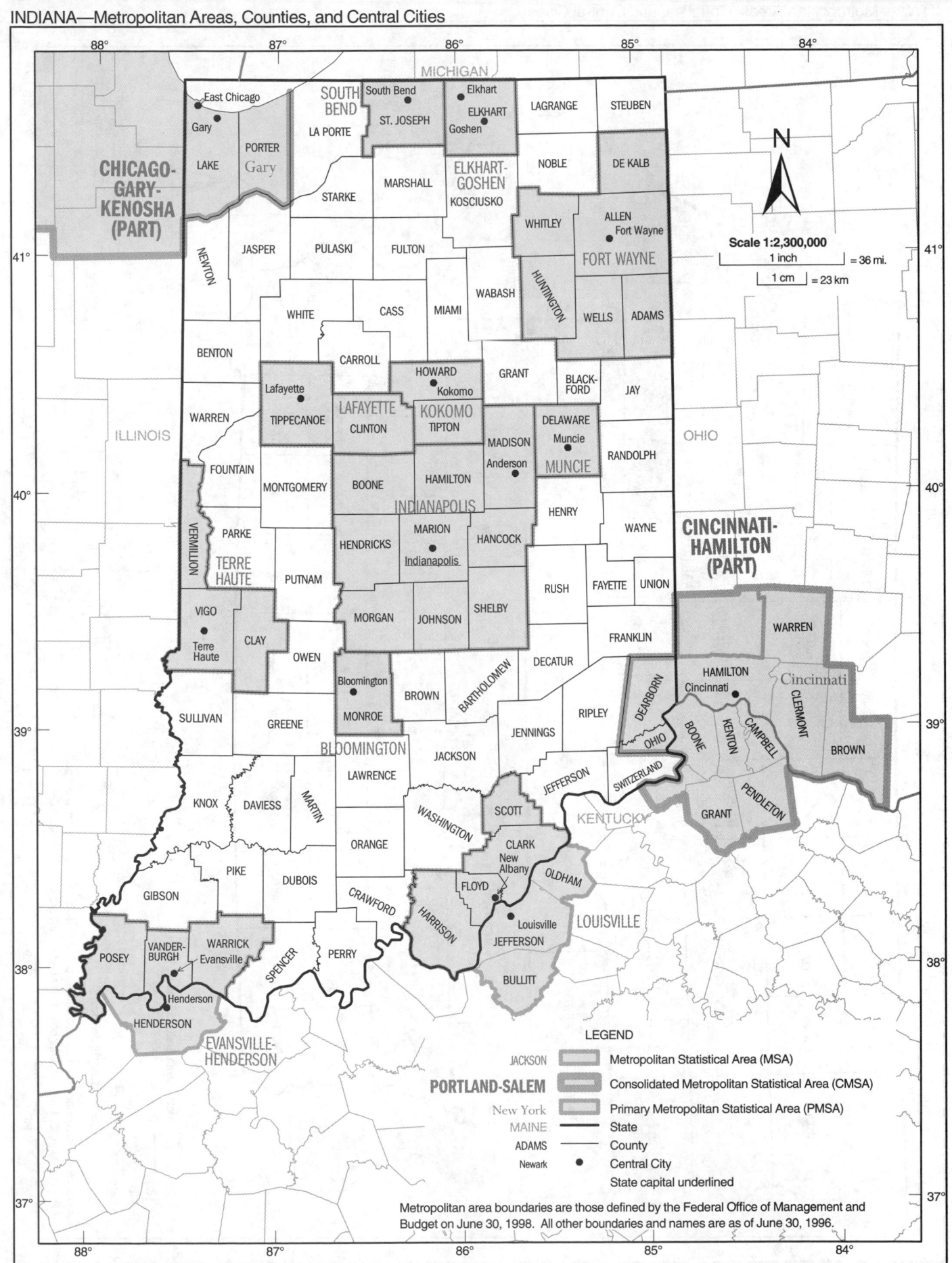

Scale 1:2,300,000

| 1 inch | = 36 mi. |
| 1 cm | = 23 km |

LEGEND

JACKSON	Metropolitan Statistical Area (MSA)
PORTLAND-SALEM	Consolidated Metropolitan Statistical Area (CMSA)
New York	Primary Metropolitan Statistical Area (PMSA)
MAINE	State
ADAMS	County
Newark ●	Central City
	State capital underlined

Metropolitan area boundaries are those defined by the Federal Office of Management and Budget on June 30, 1998. All other boundaries and names are as of June 30, 1996.

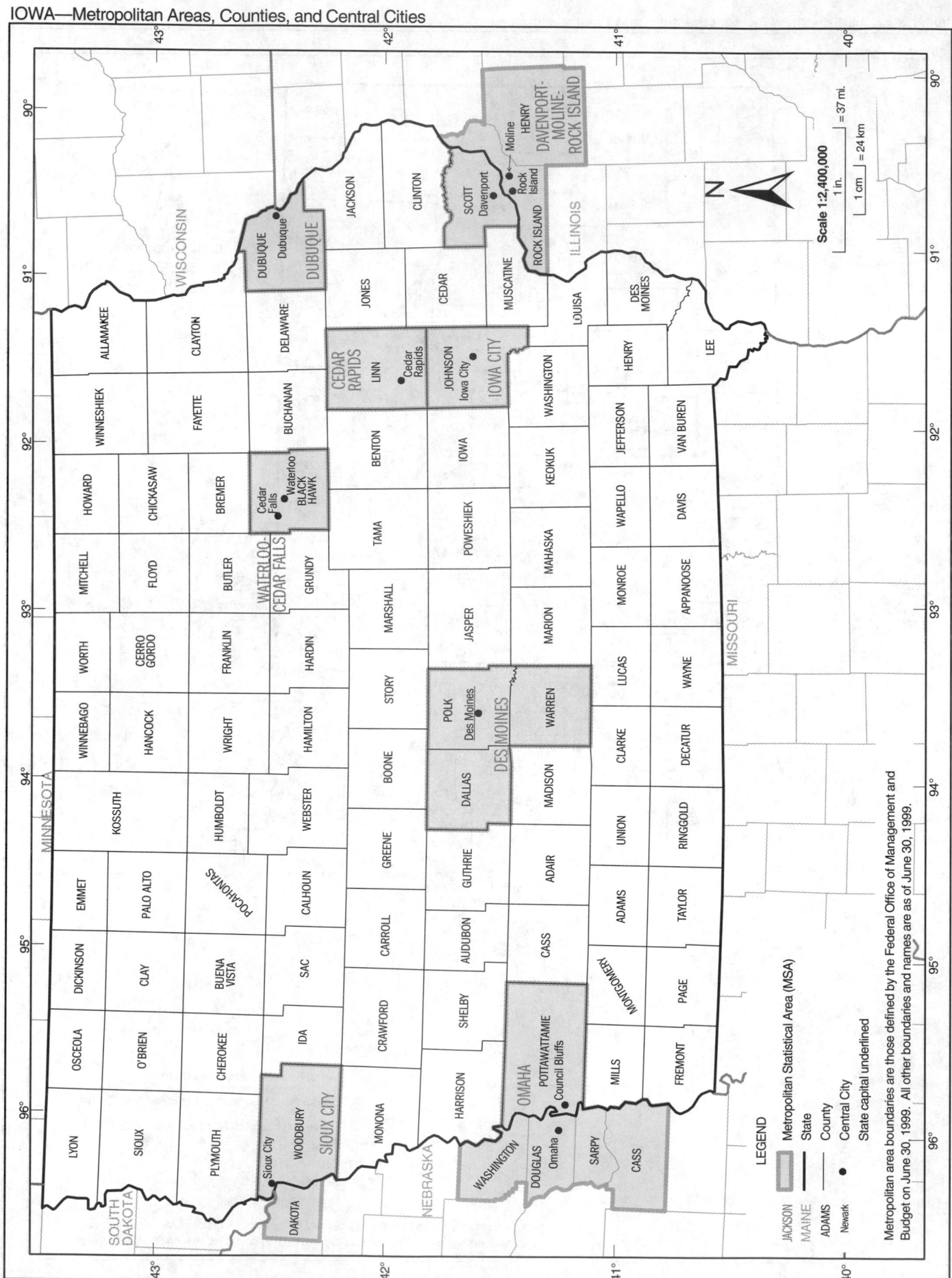

Scale 1:2,400,000

1 in. = 37 mi.

1 cm = 24 km

LEGEND

Metropolitan Statistical Area (MSA)

State

County

Central City

State capital underlined

JACKSON

MAINE

ADAMS

Newark

Metropolitan area boundaries are those defined by the Federal Office of Management and Budget on June 30, 1999. All other boundaries and names are as of June 30, 1999.

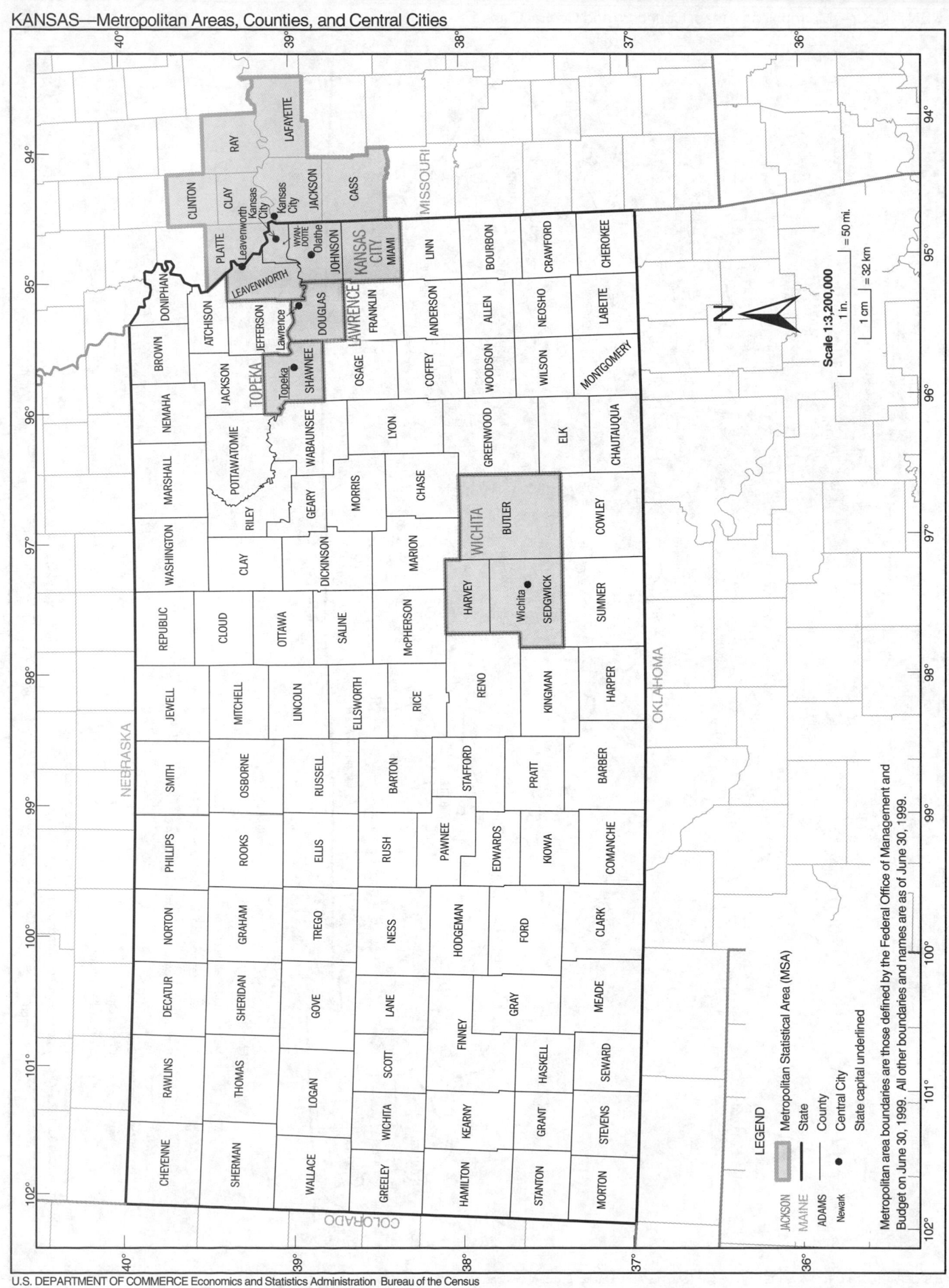

Scale 1:3,200,000

1 in.	= 50 mi.
1 cm	= 32 km

LEGEND

Metropolitan Statistical Area (MSA)
State
County
Central City
State capital underlined

Metropolitan area boundaries are those defined by the Federal Office of Management and Budget on June 30, 1999. All other boundaries and names are as of June 30, 1999.

JACKSON
MAINE
ADAMS
Newark

U.S. DEPARTMENT OF COMMERCE Economics and Statistics Administration Bureau of the Census

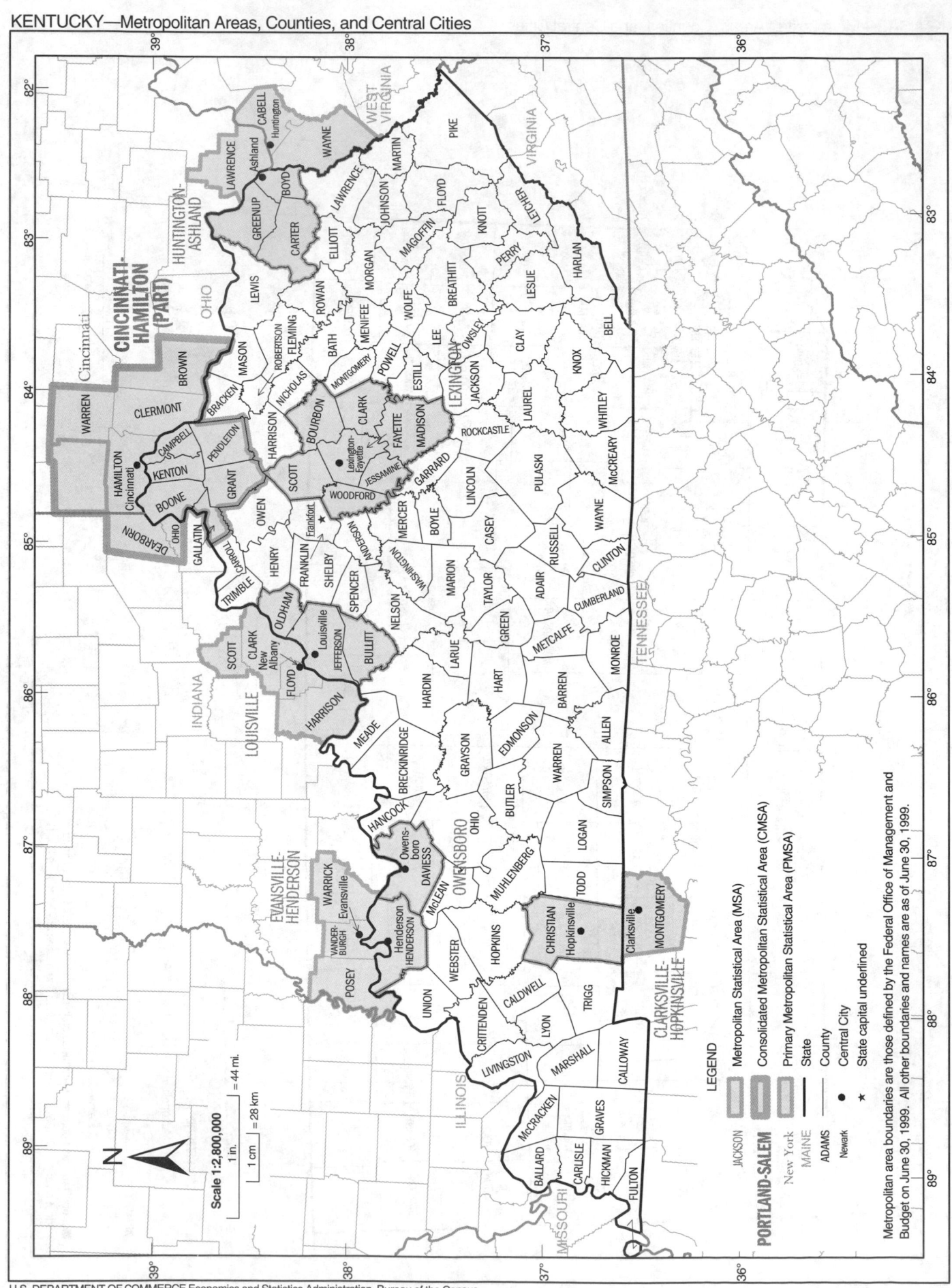

LEGEND

Metropolitan Statistical Area (MSA)

Consolidated Metropolitan Statistical Area (CMSA)

Primary Metropolitan Statistical Area (PMSA)

State

County

Central City ●

State capital underlined ★

Metropolitan area boundaries are those defined by the Federal Office of Management and Budget on June 30, 1999. All other boundaries and names are as of June 30, 1999.

JACKSON

ADAMS

Newark

PORTLAND-SALEM

New York

MAINE

Scale 1:2,800,000

1 in. = 44 mi.

1 cm = 28 km

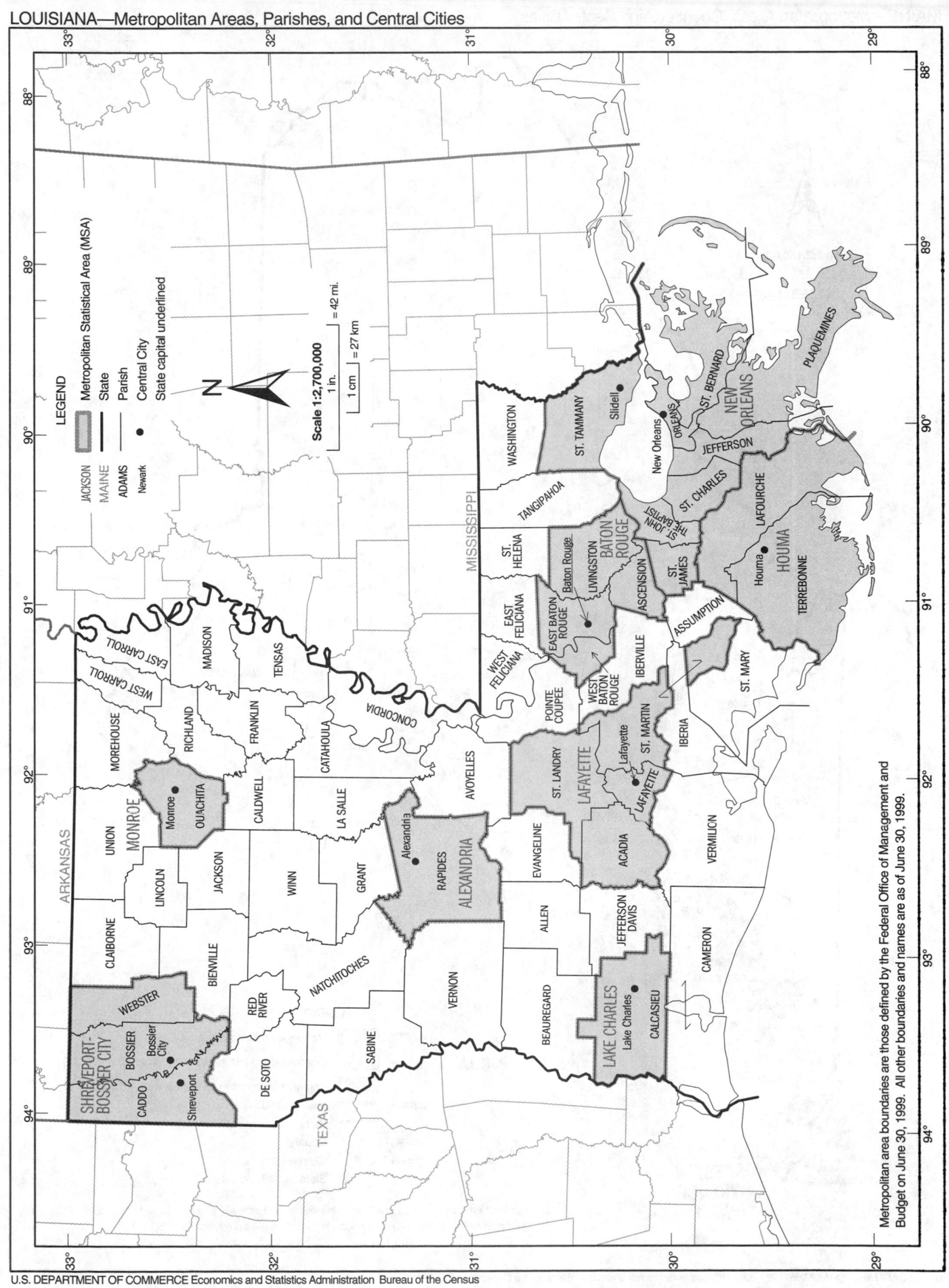

LEGEND

Metropolitan Statistical Area (MSA)
State
Parish
Central City
State capital underlined

JACKSON
MAINE
ADAMS
Newark

Scale 1:2,700,000

1 in. = 42 mi.
1 cm = 27 km

N

Metropolitan area boundaries are those defined by the Federal Office of Management and Budget on June 30, 1999. All other boundaries and names are as of June 30, 1999.

ARKANSAS

MISSISSIPPI

TEXAS

UNION
MOREHOUSE
CLAIBORNE
WEBSTER
BOSSIER
CADDO
LINCOLN
BIENVILLE
JACKSON
OUACHITA
RICHLAND
CALDWELL
WINN
LA SALLE
GRANT
NATCHITOCHES
RED RIVER
DE SOTO
SABINE
VERNON
RAPIDES
CATAHOULA
CONCORDIA
FRANKLIN
TENSAS
MADISON
EAST CARROLL
WEST CARROLL

SHREVEPORT-BOSSIER CITY
Bossier City
Shreveport

MONROE
Monroe

ALEXANDRIA
Alexandria

BEAUREGARD
ALLEN
EVANGELINE
AVOYELLES
ST. LANDRY
POINTE COUPEE
WEST FELICIANA
EAST FELICIANA

LAFAYETTE
Lafayette
ST. MARTIN
ACADIA
JEFFERSON DAVIS
CAMERON
VERMILION
IBERIA
ST. MARY

LAKE CHARLES
Lake Charles
CALCASIEU

IBERVILLE
WEST BATON ROUGE
BATON ROUGE
East Baton Rouge
LIVINGSTON
ASCENSION
ST. JAMES
ASSUMPTION
ST. HELENA
TANGIPAHOA
WASHINGTON
ST. TAMMANY
Slidell

HOUMA
Houma
TERREBONNE
LAFOURCHE

NEW ORLEANS
New Orleans
ORLEANS
JEFFERSON
ST. CHARLES
ST. JOHN THE BAPTIST
ST. BERNARD
PLAQUEMINES

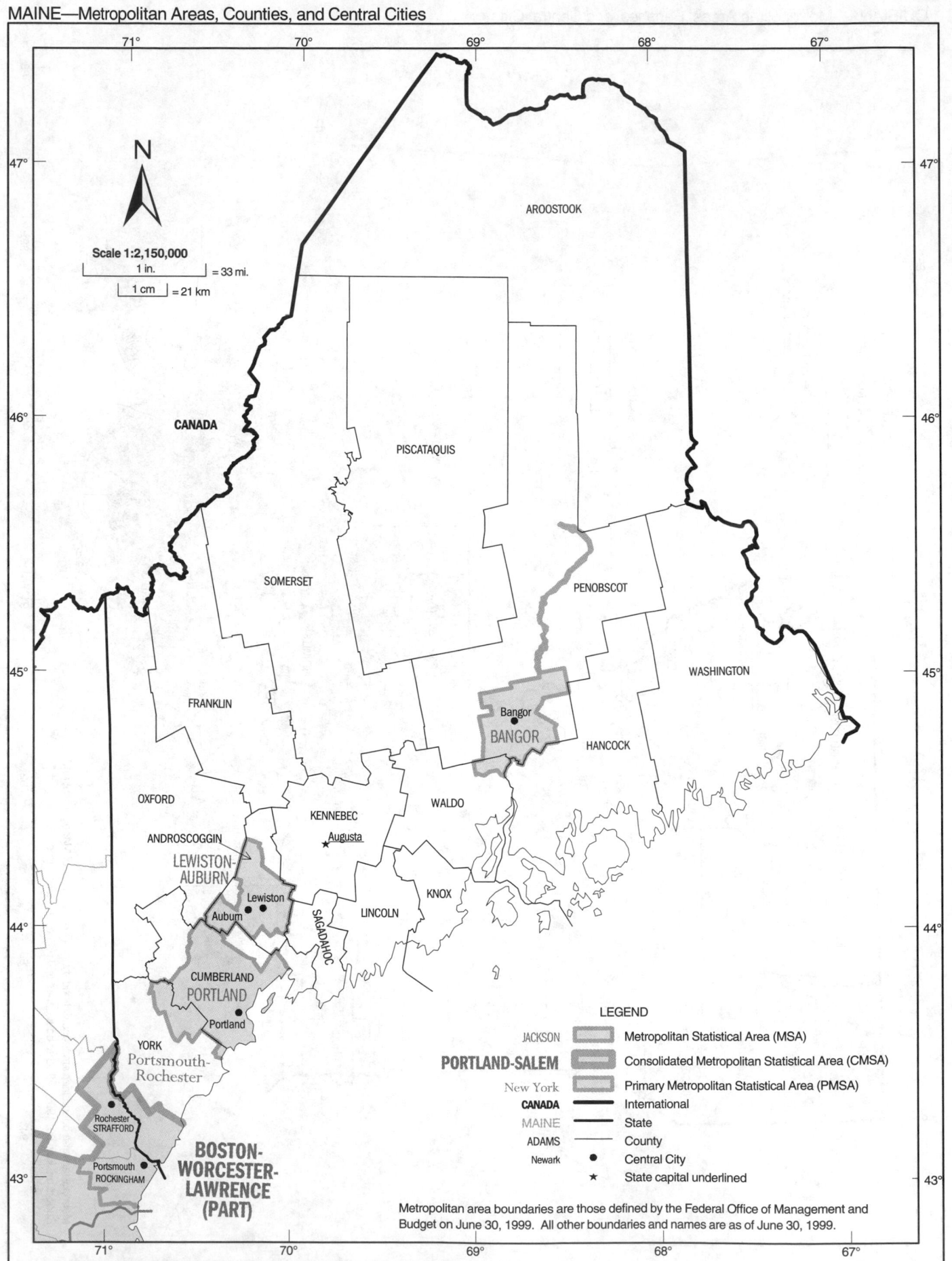

Scale 1:2,150,000

1 in. = 33 mi.

1 cm = 21 km

AROOSTOOK

CANADA

PISCATAQUIS

SOMERSET

PENOBSCOT

Bangor

BANGOR

WASHINGTON

FRANKLIN

HANCOCK

OXFORD

KENNEBEC

WALDO

ANDROSCOGGIN

Augusta

LEWISTON-AUBURN

Lewiston

Auburn

KNOX

LINCOLN

SAGADAHOC

CUMBERLAND

PORTLAND

Portland

YORK

Portsmouth-Rochester

Rochester
STRAFFORD

Portsmouth
ROCKINGHAM

BOSTON-WORCESTER-LAWRENCE (PART)

LEGEND

JACKSON	Metropolitan Statistical Area (MSA)
PORTLAND-SALEM	Consolidated Metropolitan Statistical Area (CMSA)
New York	Primary Metropolitan Statistical Area (PMSA)
CANADA	International
MAINE	State
ADAMS	County
Newark ●	Central City
★	State capital underlined

Metropolitan area boundaries are those defined by the Federal Office of Management and Budget on June 30, 1999. All other boundaries and names are as of June 30, 1999.

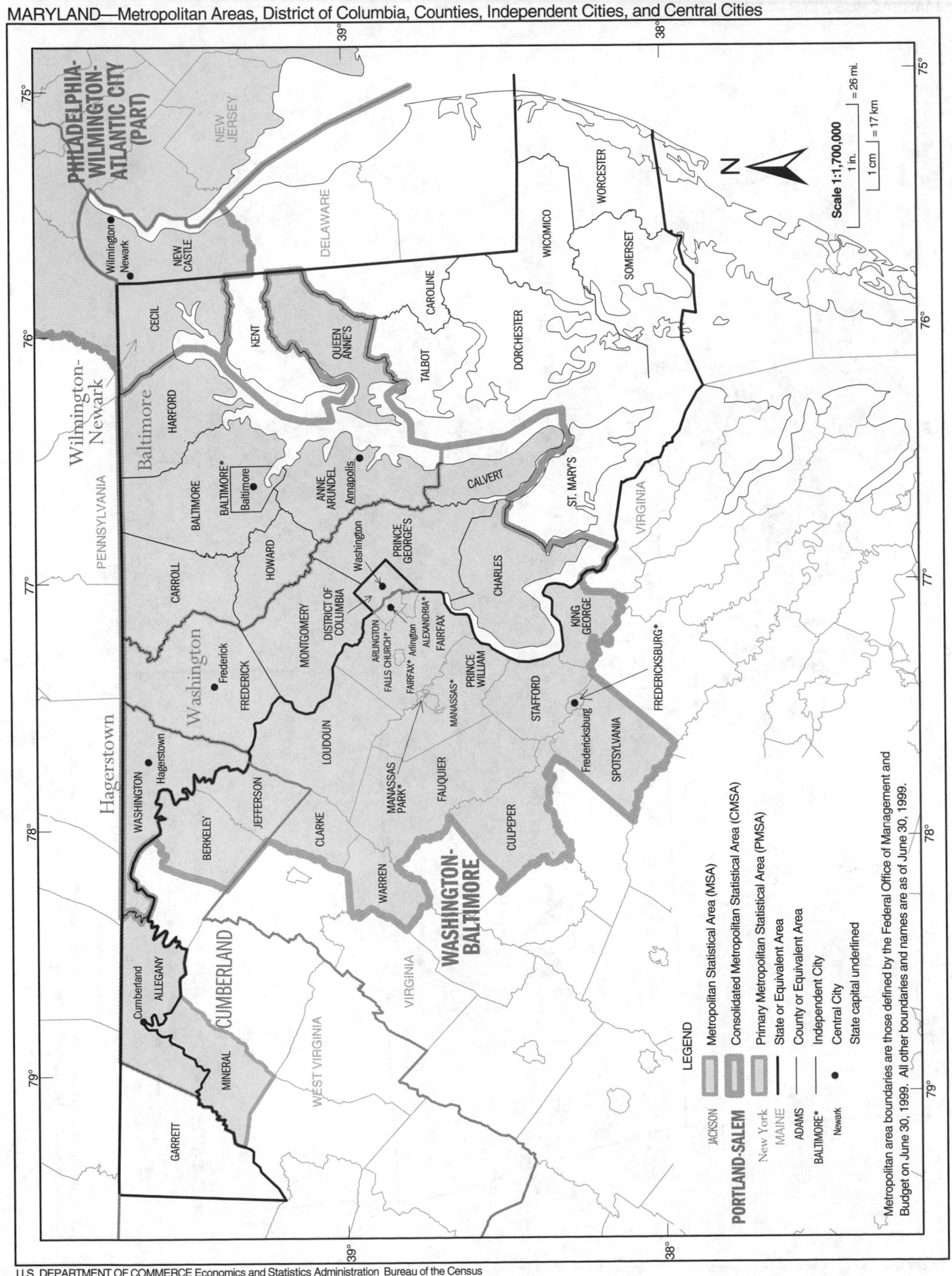

Scale 1:1,700,000

1 in. = 26 mi.

1 cm = 17 km

LEGEND

Metropolitan Statistical Area (MSA)

Consolidated Metropolitan Statistical Area (CMSA)

Primary Metropolitan Statistical Area (PMSA)

State or Equivalent Area

County or Equivalent Area

Independent City

Central City

State capital underlined

JACKSON

New York

MAINE

ADAMS

BALTIMORE*

PORTLAND-SALEM

Newark

Metropolitan area boundaries are those defined by the Federal Office of Management and Budget on June 30, 1999. All other boundaries and names are as of June 30, 1999.

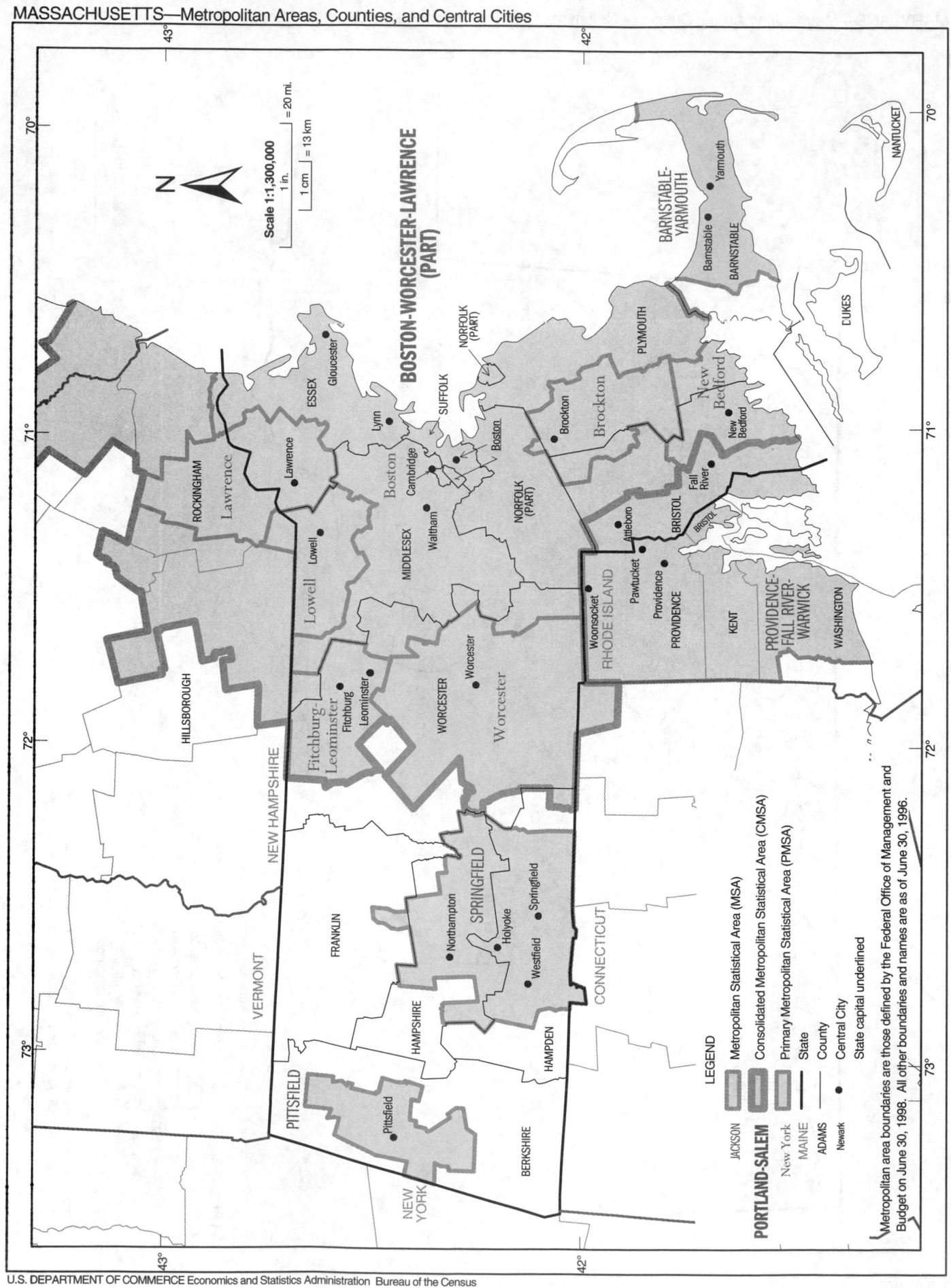

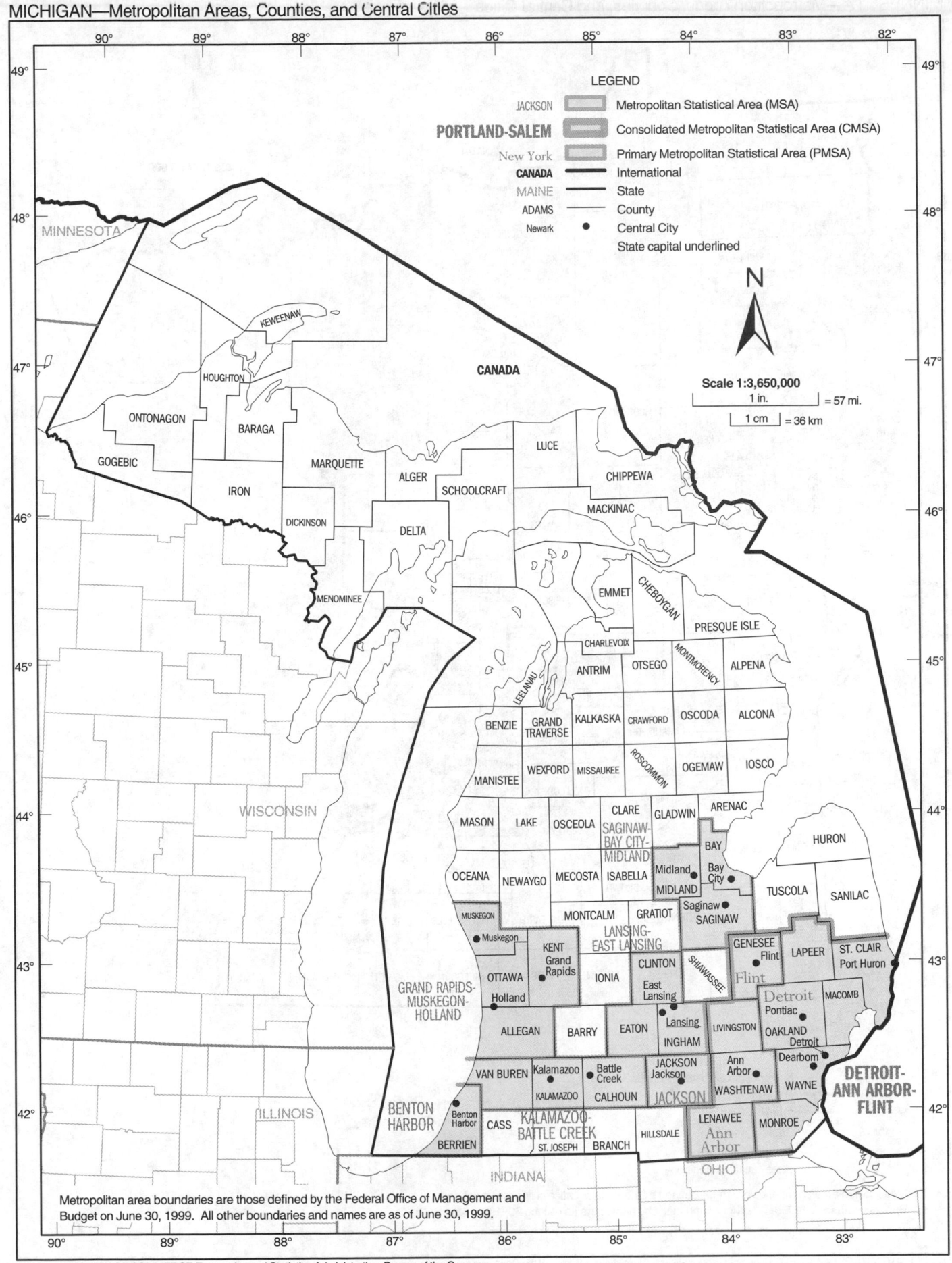

MICHIGAN—Metropolitan Areas, Counties, and Central Cities

LEGEND

JACKSON	Metropolitan Statistical Area (MSA)
PORTLAND-SALEM	Consolidated Metropolitan Statistical Area (CMSA)
New York	Primary Metropolitan Statistical Area (PMSA)
CANADA	International
MAINE	State
ADAMS	County
Newark ●	Central City
	State capital underlined

N

Scale 1:3,650,000
1 in. = 57 mi.
1 cm = 36 km

Metropolitan area boundaries are those defined by the Federal Office of Management and Budget on June 30, 1999. All other boundaries and names are as of June 30, 1999.

U.S. DEPARTMENT OF COMMERCE Economics and Statistics Administration Bureau of the Census

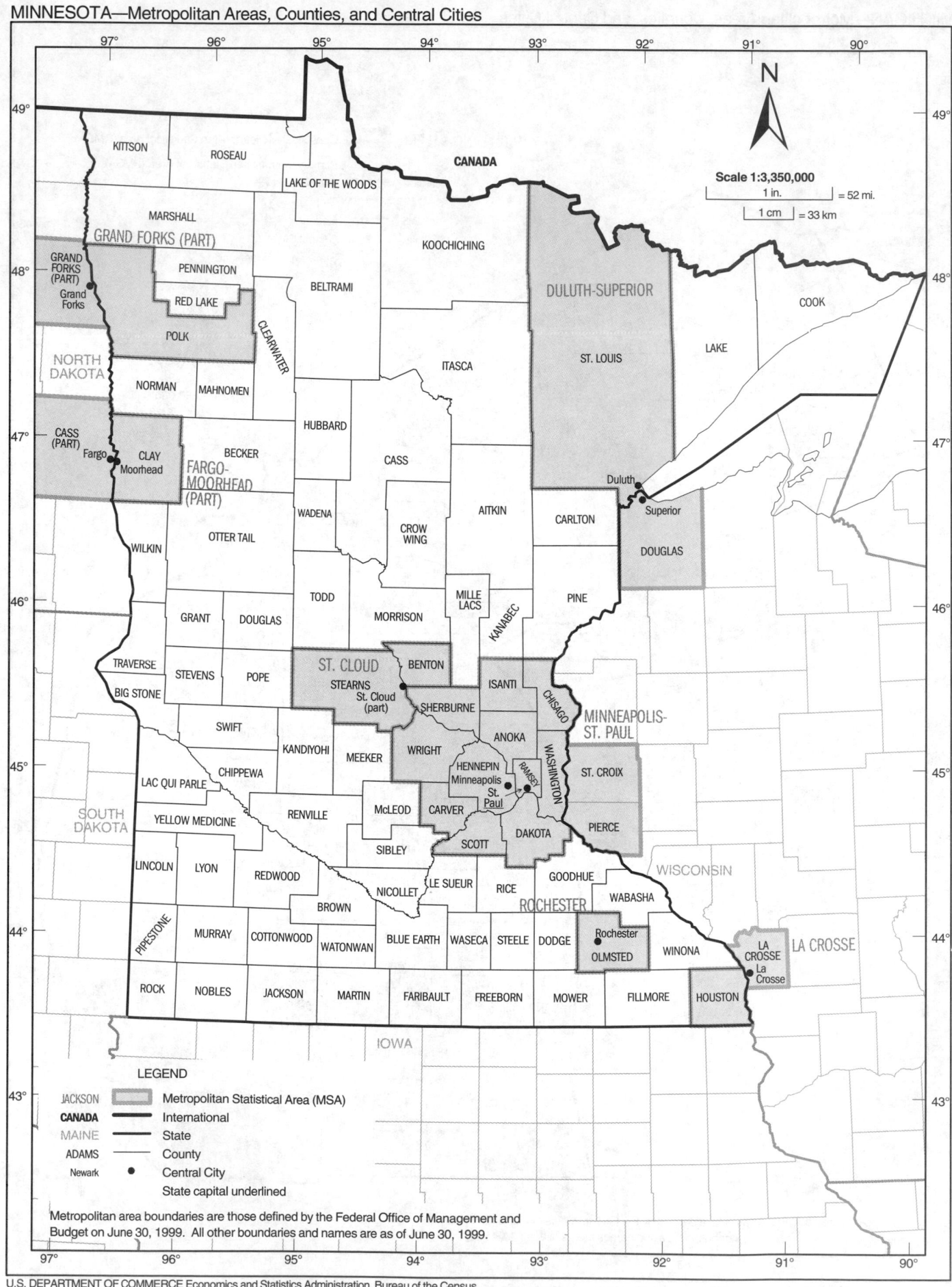

97° 96° 95° 94° 93° 92° 91° 90°

49°

N

KITTSON
ROSEAU
LAKE OF THE WOODS
CANADA

Scale 1:3,350,000
1 in. ___ = 52 mi.
1 cm ___ = 33 km

MARSHALL

GRAND FORKS (PART)

KOOCHICHING

48°

GRAND FORKS (PART)
Grand Forks

PENNINGTON
RED LAKE
POLK

BELTRAMI

DULUTH-SUPERIOR

COOK

CLEARWATER

NORTH DAKOTA

NORMAN
MAHNOMEN

ITASCA

ST. LOUIS

LAKE

47°

CASS (PART)
Fargo

CLAY
Moorhead

BECKER

HUBBARD

CASS

Duluth
Superior

DOUGLAS

FARGO-MOORHEAD (PART)

WADENA

CROW WING

AITKIN

CARLTON

WILKIN

OTTER TAIL

46°

TRAVERSE

GRANT
DOUGLAS

TODD

MORRISON

MILLE LACS

KANABEC

PINE

BIG STONE

STEVENS
POPE

ST. CLOUD
STEARNS
St. Cloud (part)

BENTON

SHERBURNE

ISANTI

CHISAGO

MINNEAPOLIS-ST. PAUL

SWIFT

KANDIYOHI
MEEKER

WRIGHT

ANOKA

WASHINGTON

ST. CROIX

45°

LAC QUI PARLE

CHIPPEWA

HENNEPIN
Minneapolis
St. Paul
RAMSEY

SOUTH DAKOTA

YELLOW MEDICINE

RENVILLE

McLEOD
CARVER

DAKOTA

PIERCE

LINCOLN
LYON

REDWOOD

SIBLEY

SCOTT

LE SUEUR
RICE

GOODHUE

WISCONSIN

NICOLLET

ROCHESTER

WABASHA

44°

PIPESTONE

MURRAY
COTTONWOOD

BROWN

WATONWAN

BLUE EARTH
WASECA
STEELE
DODGE

Rochester
OLMSTED

WINONA

LA CROSSE
La Crosse

LA CROSSE

ROCK
NOBLES
JACKSON
MARTIN
FARIBAULT
FREEBORN
MOWER
FILLMORE
HOUSTON

IOWA

43°

LEGEND

JACKSON [shaded] Metropolitan Statistical Area (MSA)
CANADA ——— International
MAINE ——— State
ADAMS ——— County
Newark ● Central City
State capital underlined

Metropolitan area boundaries are those defined by the Federal Office of Management and Budget on June 30, 1999. All other boundaries and names are as of June 30, 1999.

97° 96° 95° 94° 93° 92° 91° 90°

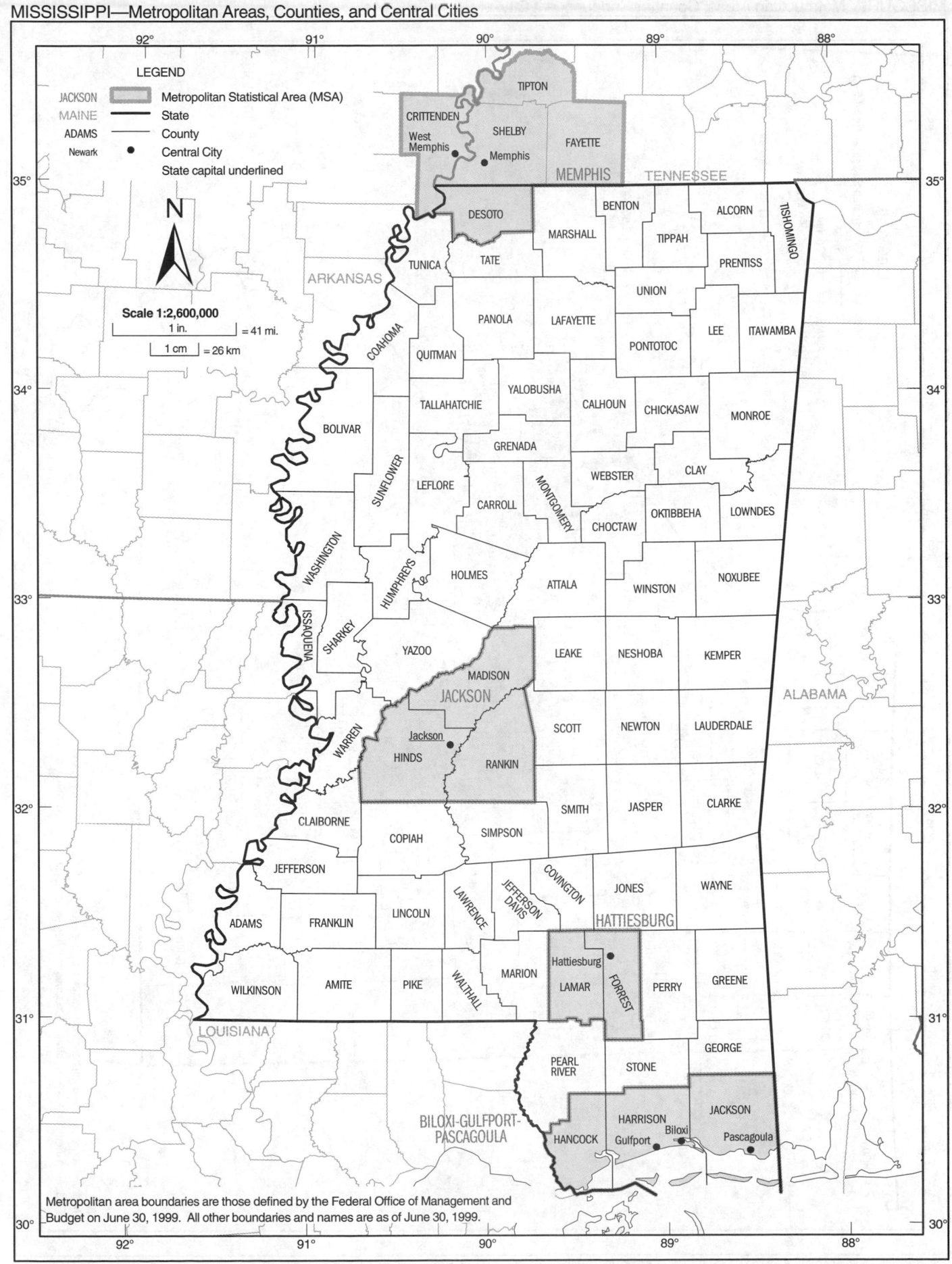

LEGEND

JACKSON   Metropolitan Statistical Area (MSA)

MAINE   State

ADAMS   County

Newark   ●   Central City

State capital underlined

N

Scale 1:2,600,000

1 in. = 41 mi.

1 cm = 26 km

Metropolitan area boundaries are those defined by the Federal Office of Management and Budget on June 30, 1999. All other boundaries and names are as of June 30, 1999.

MISSOURI—Metropolitan Areas, Counties, Independent City, and Central Cities

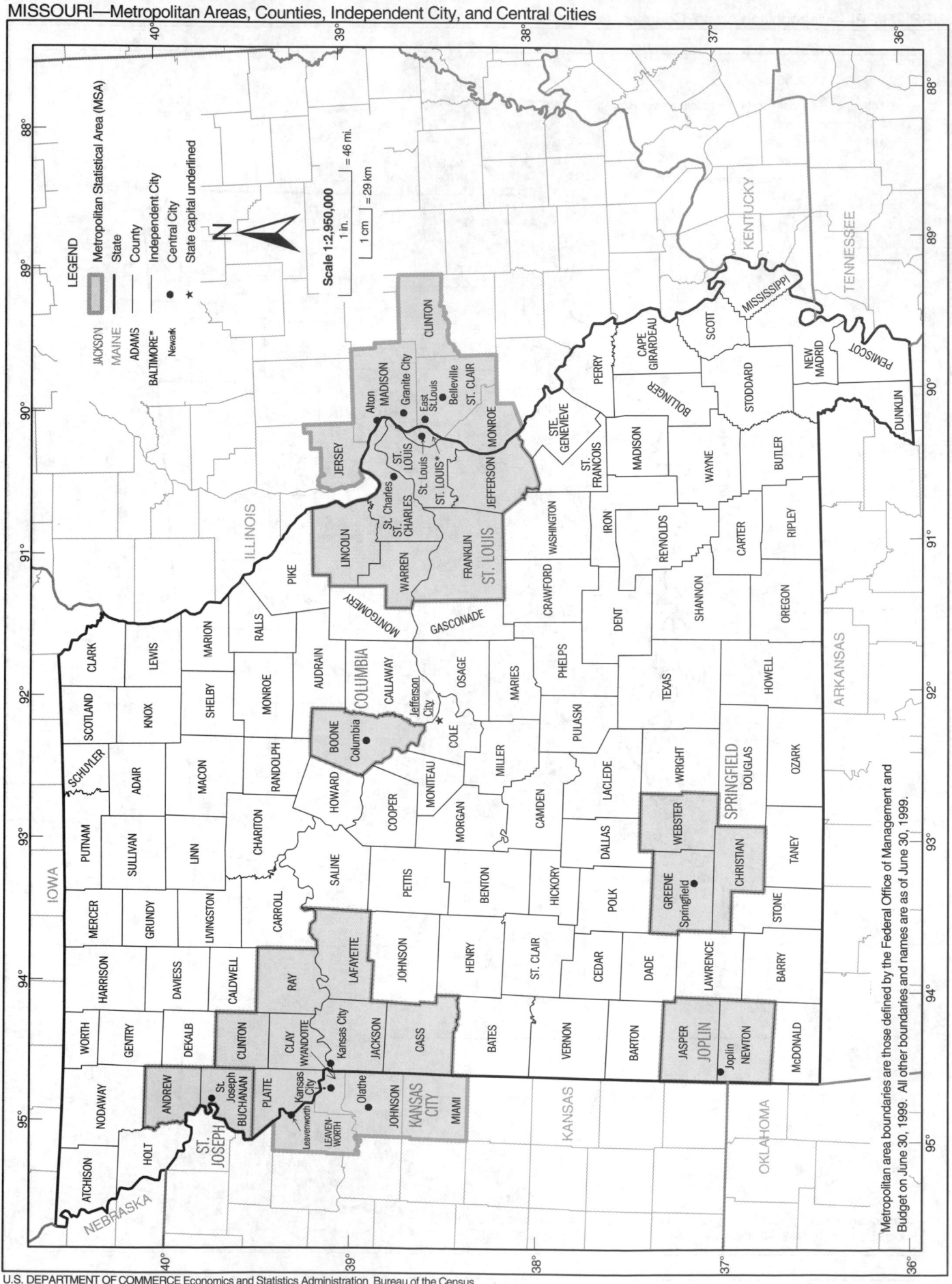

LEGEND

Metropolitan Statistical Area (MSA)
State
County
Independent City
Central City
State capital underlined

JACKSON
MAINE
ADAMS
BALTIMORE*
Newark

Scale 1:2,950,000
1 in. = 46 mi.
1 cm = 29 km

N

Metropolitan area boundaries are those defined by the Federal Office of Management and Budget on June 30, 1999. All other boundaries and names are as of June 30, 1999.

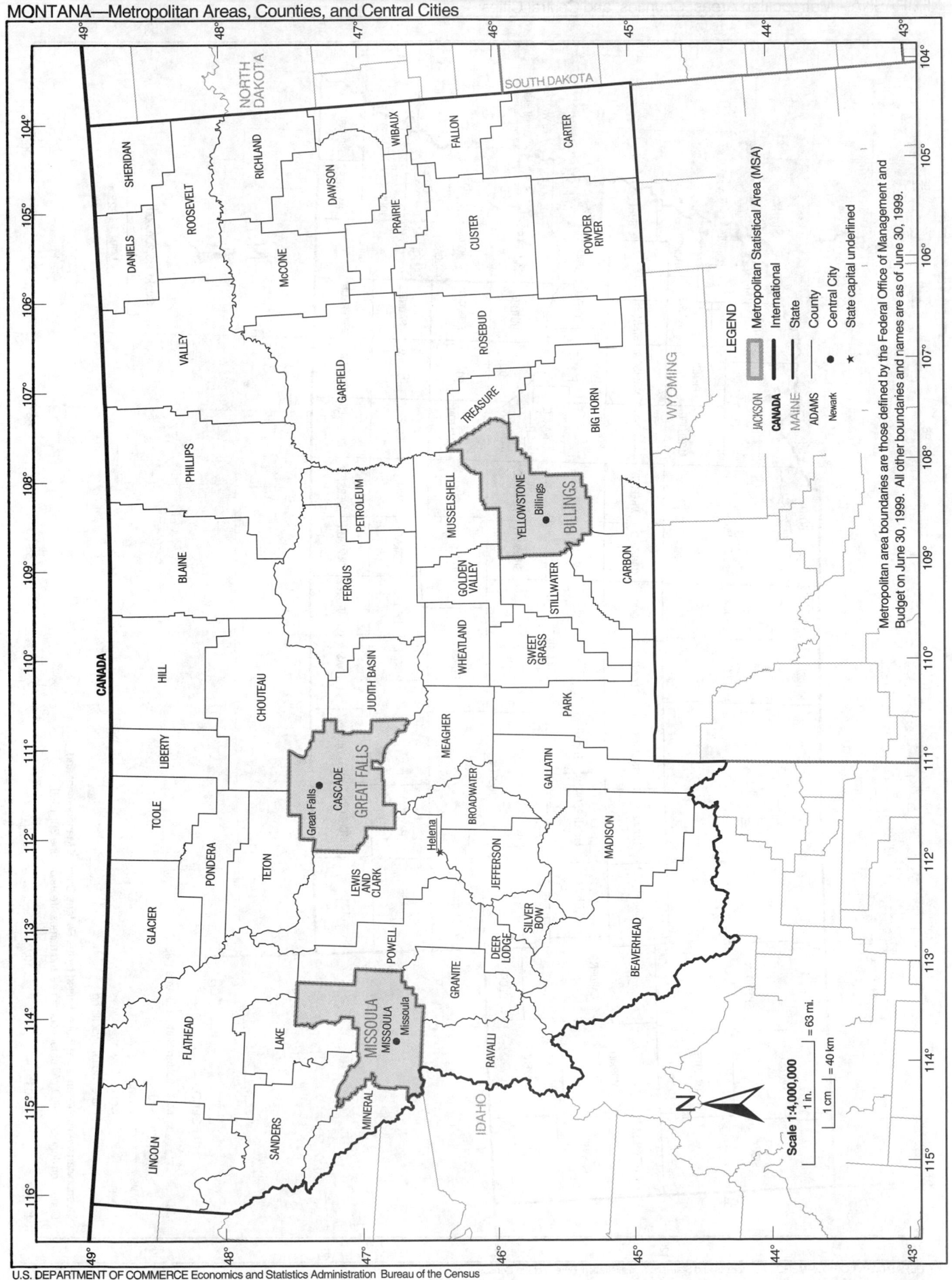

LEGEND

Metropolitan Statistical Area (MSA)

International
State
County
Central City ●
State capital underlined ★

JACKSON
CANADA
MAINE
ADAMS
Newark

Metropolitan area boundaries are those defined by the Federal Office of Management and Budget on June 30, 1999. All other boundaries and names are as of June 30, 1999.

Scale 1:4,000,000
1 in. = 63 mi.
1 cm = 40 km

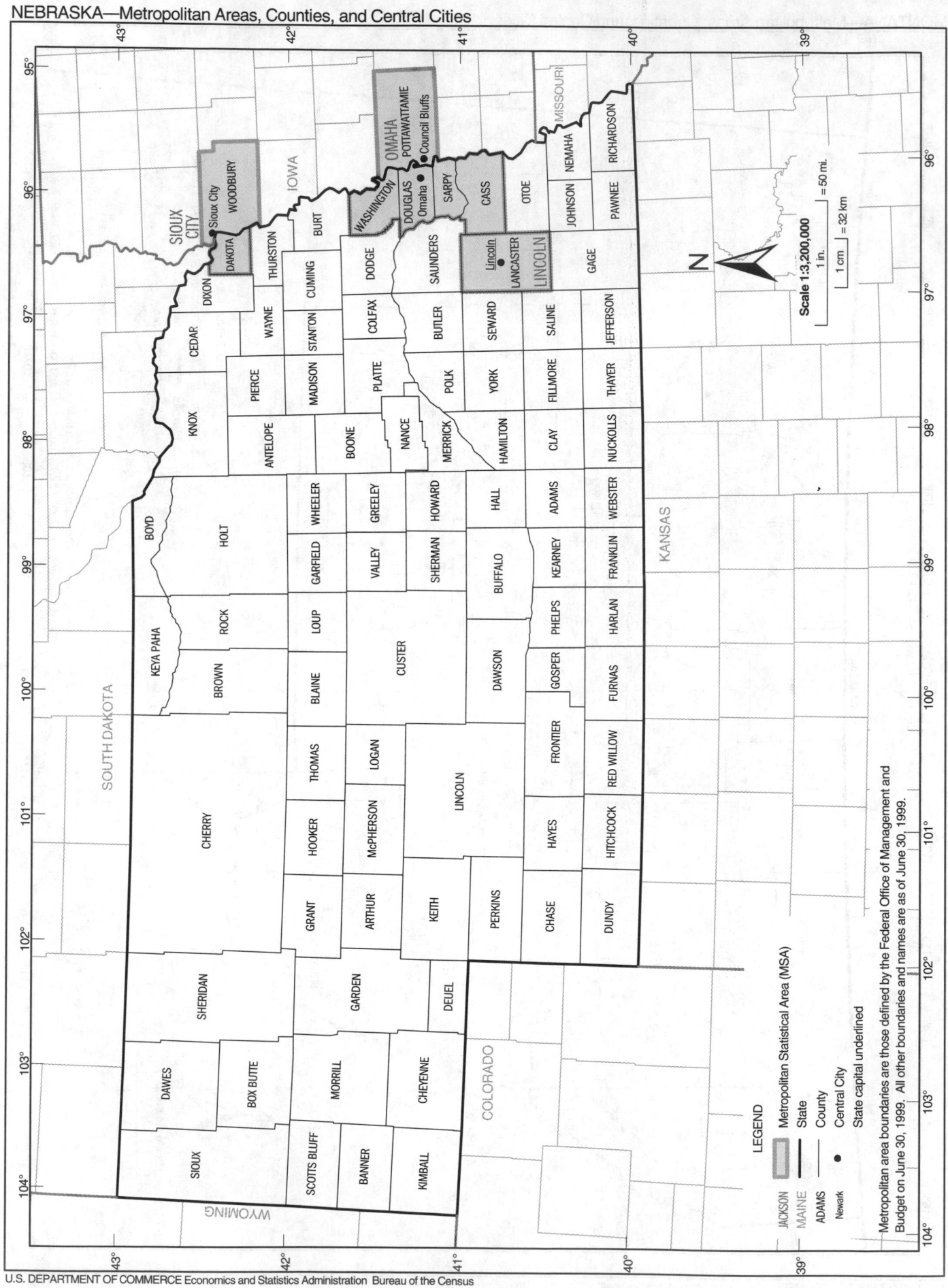

LEGEND

	Metropolitan Statistical Area (MSA)
	State
	County
●	Central City
	State capital underlined

JACKSON	
MAINE	
ADAMS	
Newark	

Metropolitan area boundaries are those defined by the Federal Office of Management and Budget on June 30, 1999. All other boundaries and names are as of June 30, 1999.

Scale 1:3,200,000

1 in. = 50 mi.
1 cm = 32 km

U.S. DEPARTMENT OF COMMERCE Economics and Statistics Administration Bureau of the Census

Appendix D

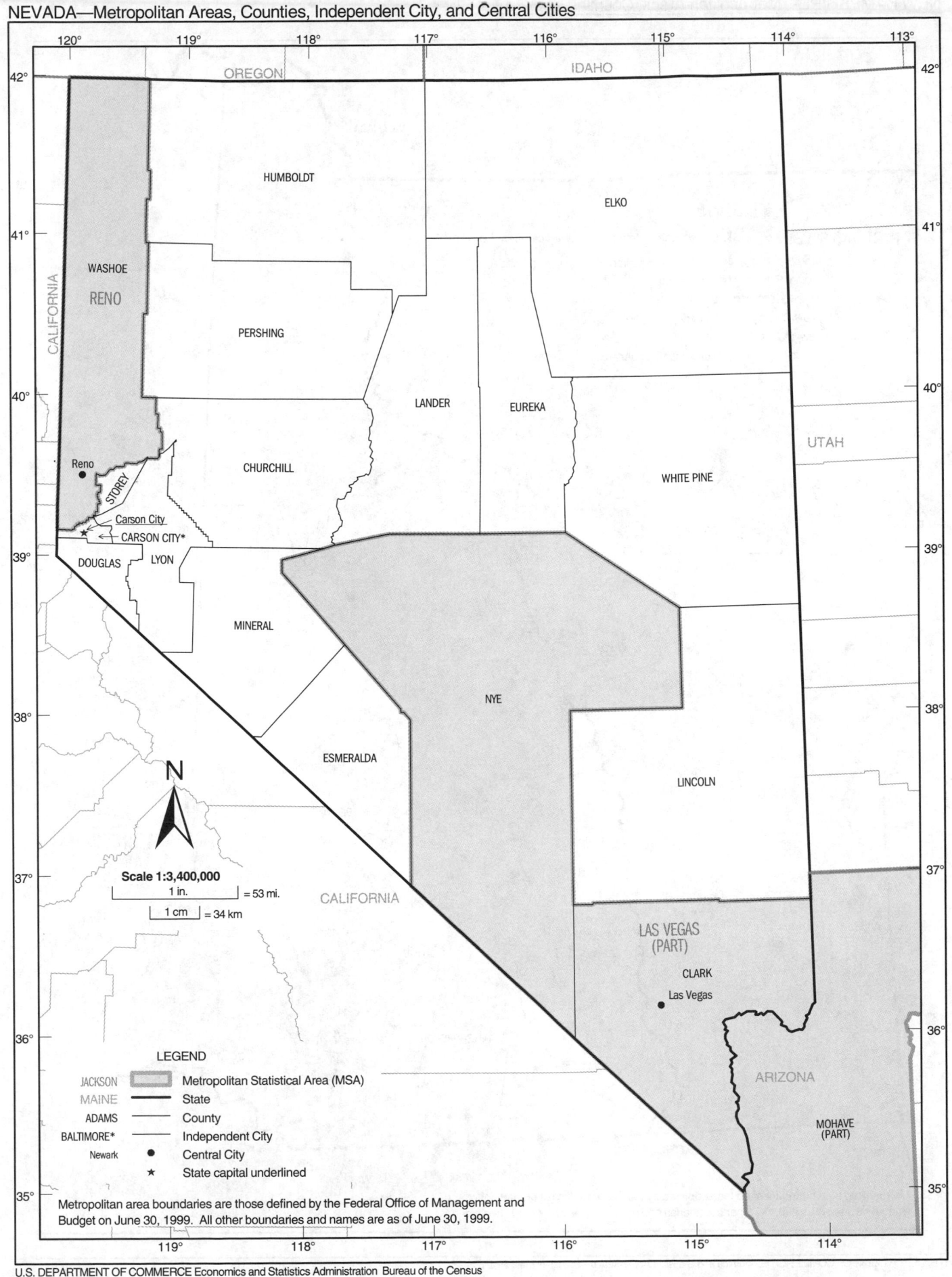

LEGEND

JACKSON	Metropolitan Statistical Area (MSA)
MAINE	State
ADAMS	County
BALTIMORE*	Independent City
Newark ●	Central City
★	State capital underlined

Metropolitan area boundaries are those defined by the Federal Office of Management and
Budget on June 30, 1999. All other boundaries and names are as of June 30, 1999.

Scale 1:3,400,000
1 in. = 53 mi.
1 cm = 34 km

N

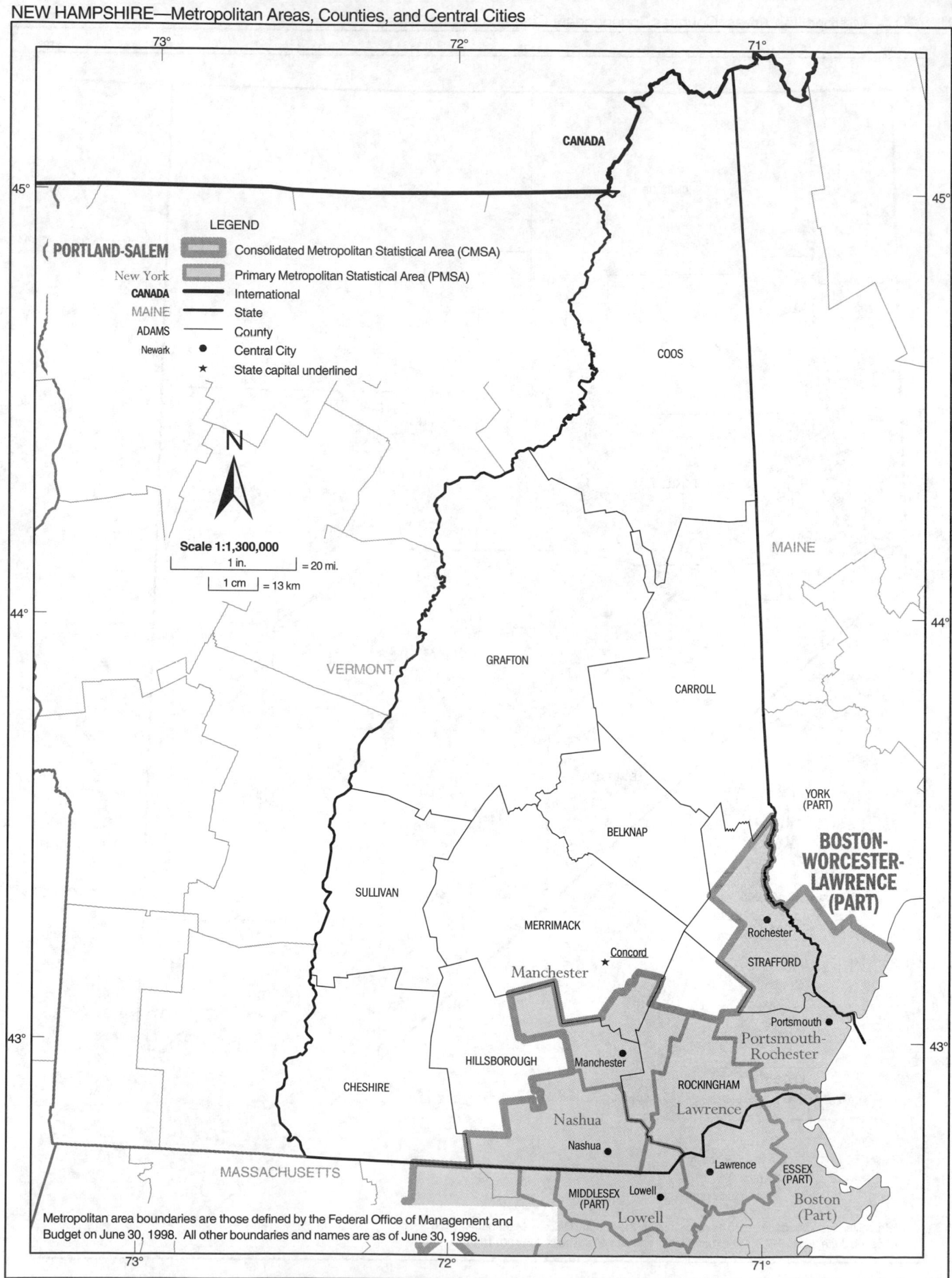

LEGEND

PORTLAND-SALEM	Consolidated Metropolitan Statistical Area (CMSA)
	Primary Metropolitan Statistical Area (PMSA)
CANADA	International
MAINE	State
ADAMS	County
Newark ●	Central City
★	State capital underlined

New York

N

Scale 1:1,300,000

1 in. = 20 mi.

1 cm = 13 km

CANADA

COOS

MAINE

VERMONT

GRAFTON

CARROLL

BELKNAP

YORK (PART)

BOSTON-WORCESTER-LAWRENCE (PART)

SULLIVAN

MERRIMACK

Rochester ●

STRAFFORD

Concord ★

Manchester

HILLSBOROUGH

Manchester ●

Portsmouth ●

Portsmouth-Rochester

CHESHIRE

ROCKINGHAM

Lawrence

Nashua

Nashua ●

Lawrence ●

ESSEX (PART)

MASSACHUSETTS

MIDDLESEX (PART)

Lowell ●

Boston (Part)

Lowell

Metropolitan area boundaries are those defined by the Federal Office of Management and
Budget on June 30, 1998. All other boundaries and names are as of June 30, 1996.

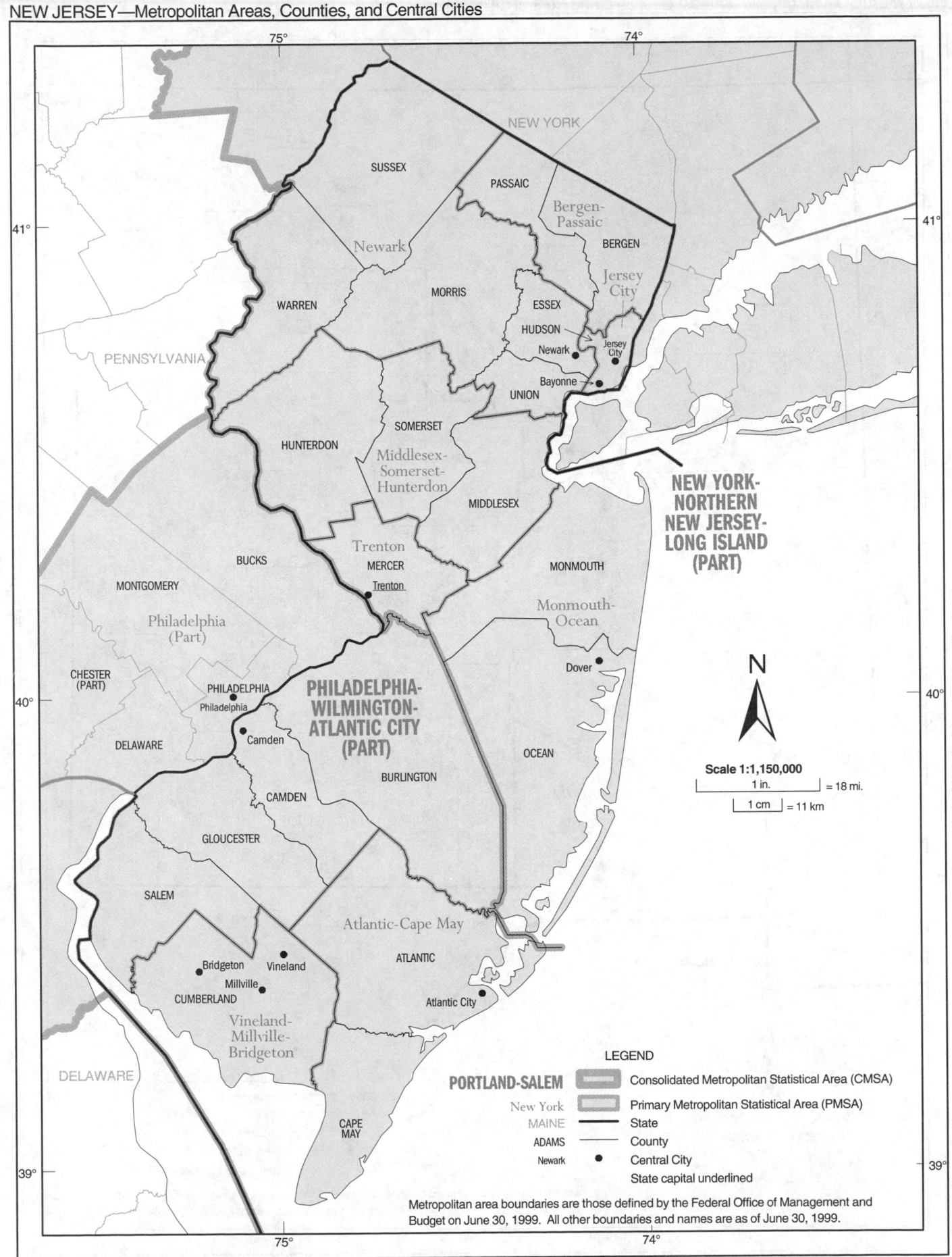

75°   74°

NEW YORK

SUSSEX

PASSAIC

Bergen-
Passaic

BERGEN

41°   41°

Newark

WARREN   MORRIS   ESSEX   Jersey
City

HUDSON

PENNSYLVANIA   Newark ●   ● Jersey
                                                                   City

                                                         Bayonne ●→

UNION

SOMERSET

HUNTERDON   Middlesex-
                  Somerset-
                  Hunterdon
                                    MIDDLESEX

                                                                NEW YORK-
                                                                NORTHERN
                                                                NEW JERSEY-
                                                                LONG ISLAND
                                                                (PART)

Trenton
                  MERCER   MONMOUTH
BUCKS   ● Trenton

MONTGOMERY   Monmouth-
                                   Ocean

Philadelphia
(Part)   Dover ●   N

CHESTER
(PART)   40°
40°
          PHILADELPHIA ●   PHILADELPHIA-
          Philadelphia   WILMINGTON-
DELAWARE   ATLANTIC CITY   OCEAN
                   ● Camden   (PART)   Scale 1:1,150,000
                                                                    ├─ 1 in. ─┤ = 18 mi.
          CAMDEN   BURLINGTON
                                                                    ├─ 1 cm ─┤ = 11 km
          CAMDEN

          GLOUCESTER

          SALEM

                  Atlantic-Cape May

          ● Bridgeton   ● Vineland   ATLANTIC

          ● Millville
CUMBERLAND   Atlantic City ●
          Vineland-
          Millville-   LEGEND
          Bridgeton
                                                 PORTLAND-SALEM ▭ Consolidated Metropolitan Statistical Area (CMSA)
DELAWARE
                                                 New York   ▭ Primary Metropolitan Statistical Area (PMSA)
          CAPE   MAINE   ── State
          MAY
                                                 ADAMS   ── County
39°   39°
                                                 Newark   ●   Central City
                                                                    State capital underlined

                            Metropolitan area boundaries are those defined by the Federal Office of Management and
                            Budget on June 30, 1999. All other boundaries and names are as of June 30, 1999.

75°   74°

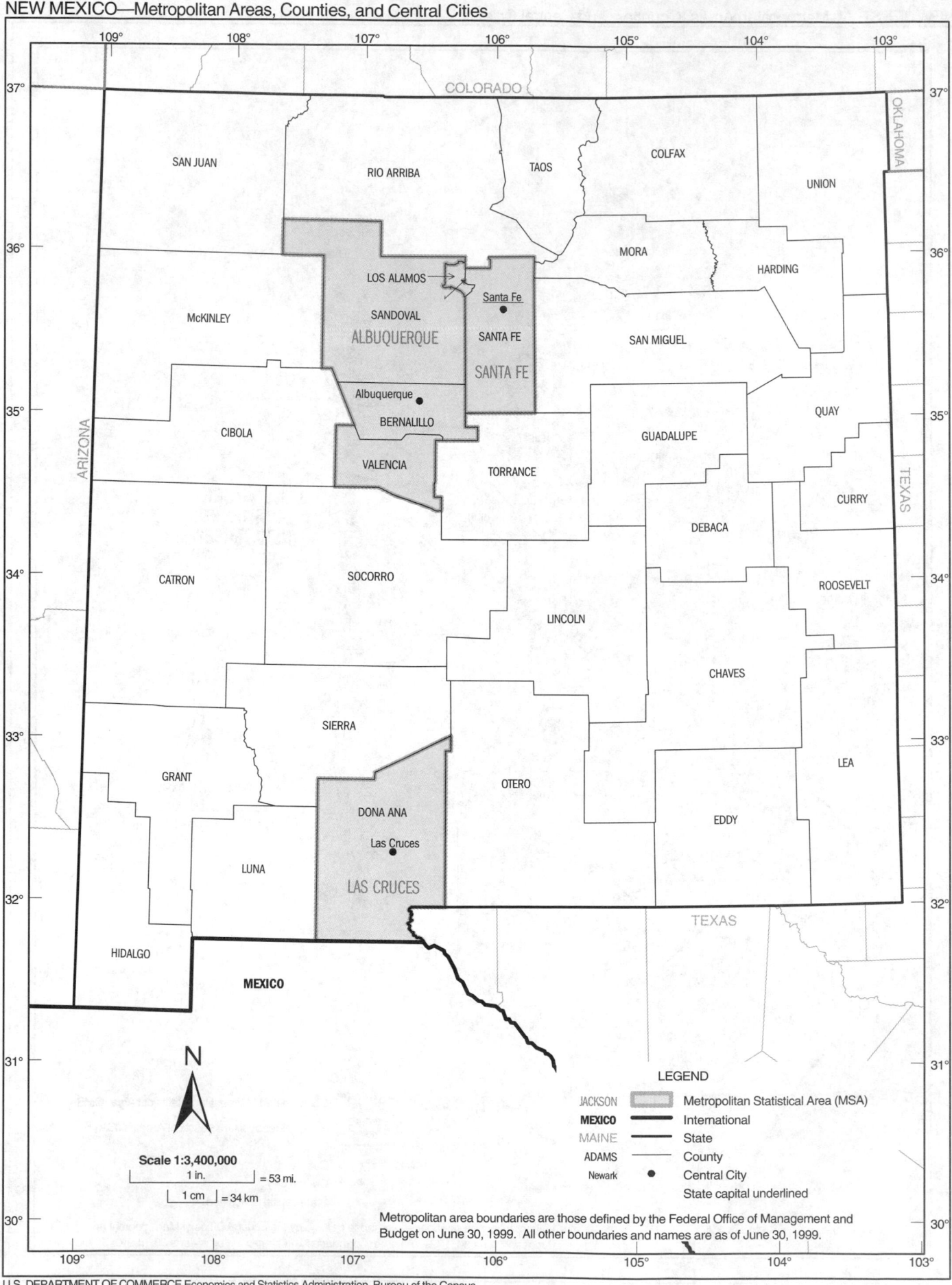

LEGEND

JACKSON	Metropolitan Statistical Area (MSA)
MEXICO	International
MAINE	State
ADAMS	County
Newark ●	Central City
	State capital underlined

Metropolitan area boundaries are those defined by the Federal Office of Management and Budget on June 30, 1999. All other boundaries and names are as of June 30, 1999.

Scale 1:3,400,000

1 in. = 53 mi.

1 cm = 34 km

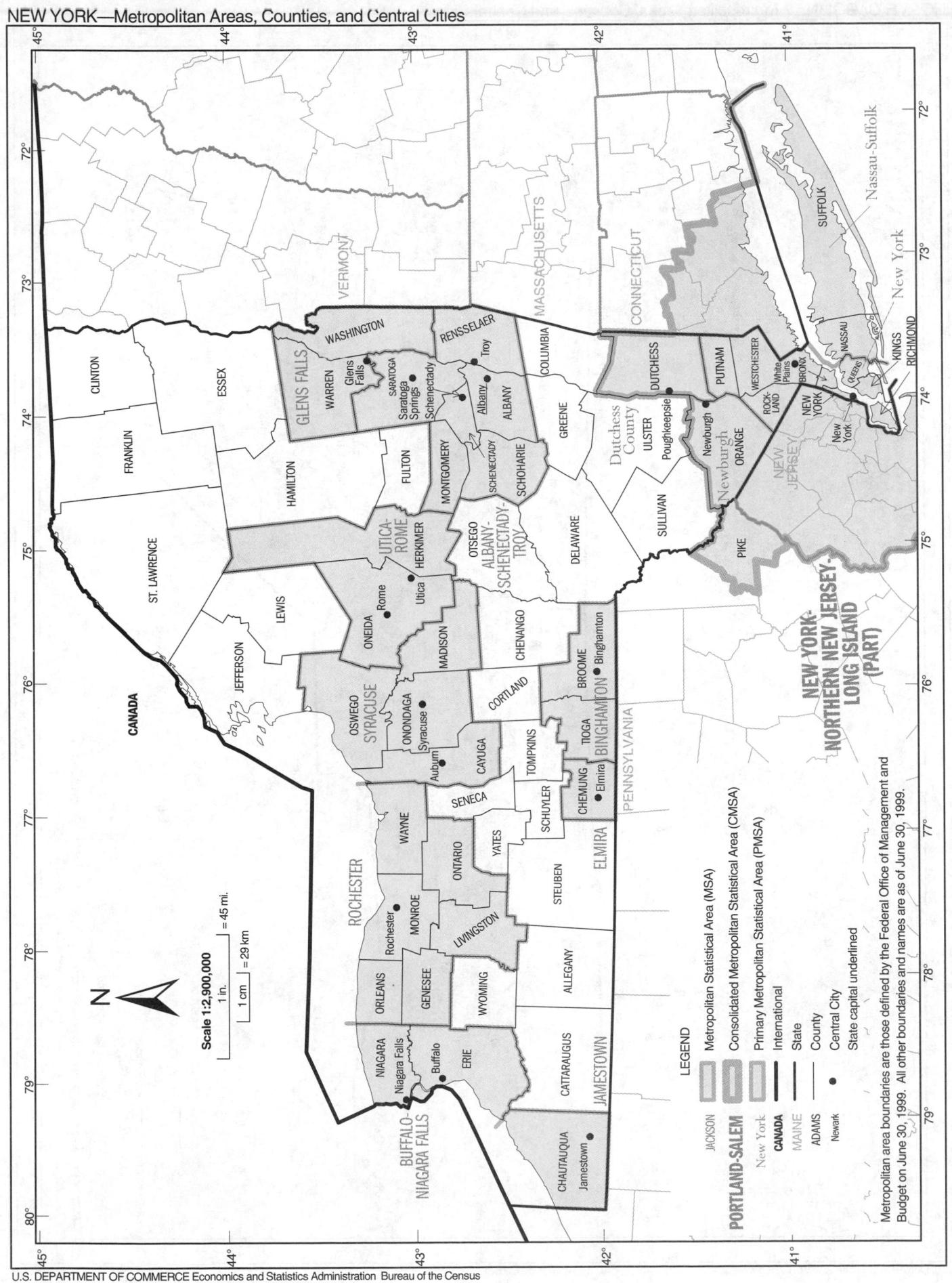

Scale 1:2,900,000
1 in. = 45 mi.
1 cm = 29 km

N

CANADA

LEGEND

JACKSON	Metropolitan Statistical Area (MSA)
	Consolidated Metropolitan Statistical Area (CMSA)
PORTLAND-SALEM	Primary Metropolitan Statistical Area (PMSA)
New York	International
CANADA	State
MAINE	County
ADAMS	Central City
Newark	State capital underlined

Metropolitan area boundaries are those defined by the Federal Office of Management and Budget on June 30, 1999. All other boundaries and names are as of June 30, 1999.

NEW YORK-NORTHERN NEW JERSEY-LONG ISLAND (PART)

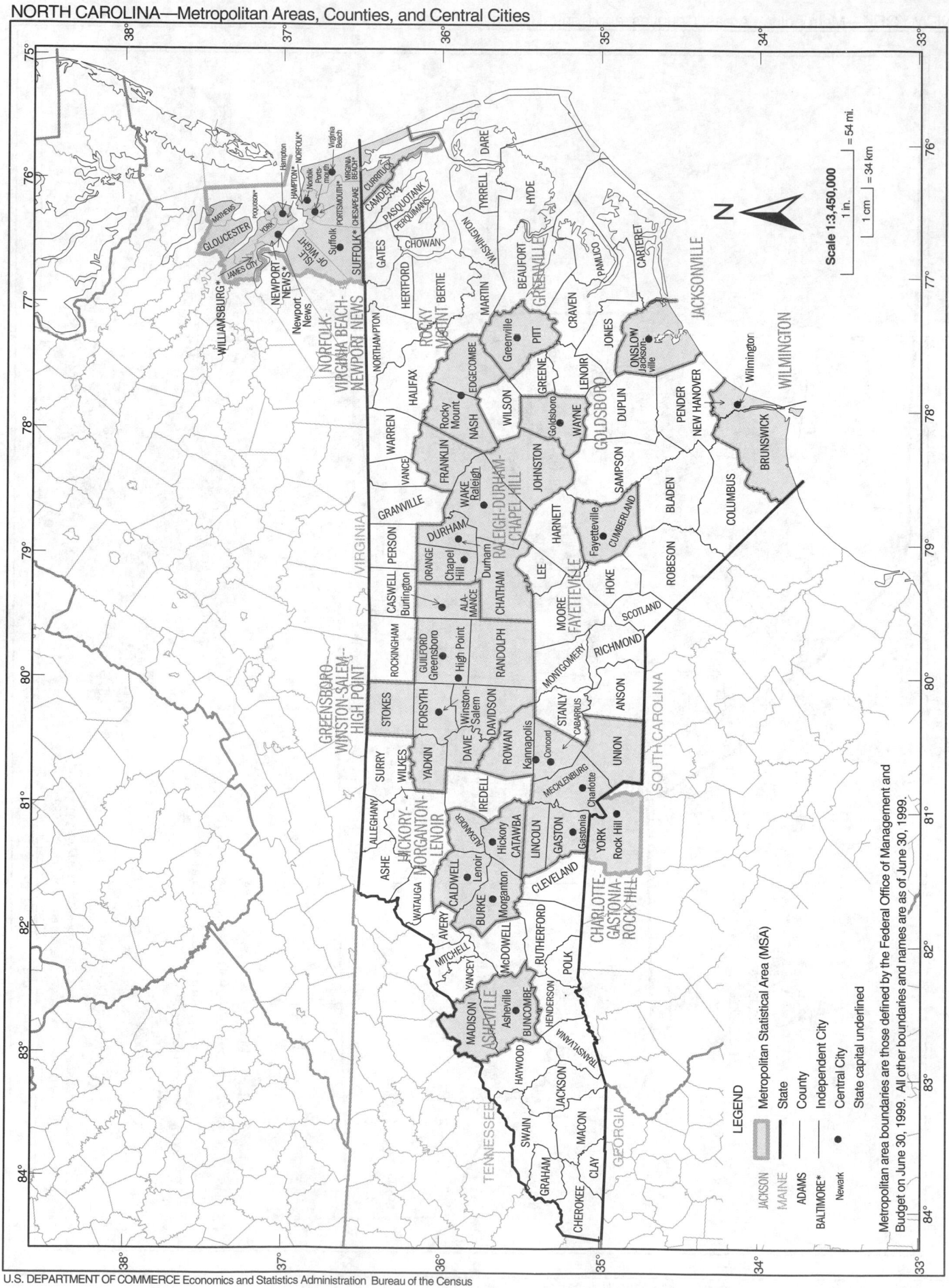

Scale 1:3,450,000

1 in. = 54 mi.

1 cm = 34 km

LEGEND

Metropolitan Statistical Area (MSA)

State

County

Independent City

Central City

State capital underlined

JACKSON
MAINE
ADAMS
BALTIMORE*
Newark

Metropolitan area boundaries are those defined by the Federal Office of Management and Budget on June 30, 1999. All other boundaries and names are as of June 30, 1999.

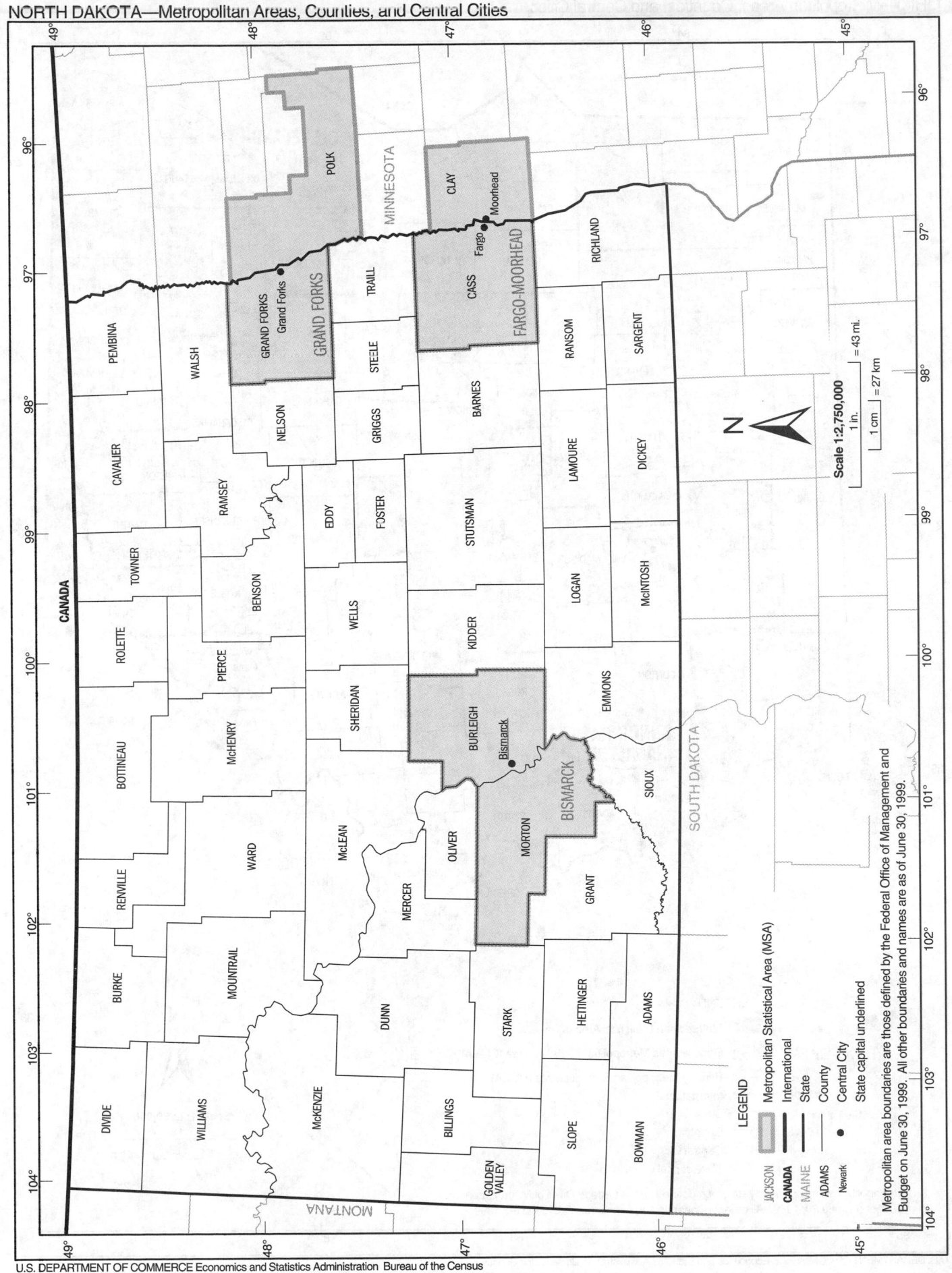

LEGEND

Metropolitan Statistical Area (MSA)

International

State

County

● Central City

State capital underlined

JACKSON
CANADA
MAINE
ADAMS
Newark

Metropolitan area boundaries are those defined by the Federal Office of Management and Budget on June 30, 1999. All other boundaries and names are as of June 30, 1999.

Scale 1:2,750,000

1 in. = 43 mi.

1 cm = 27 km

N

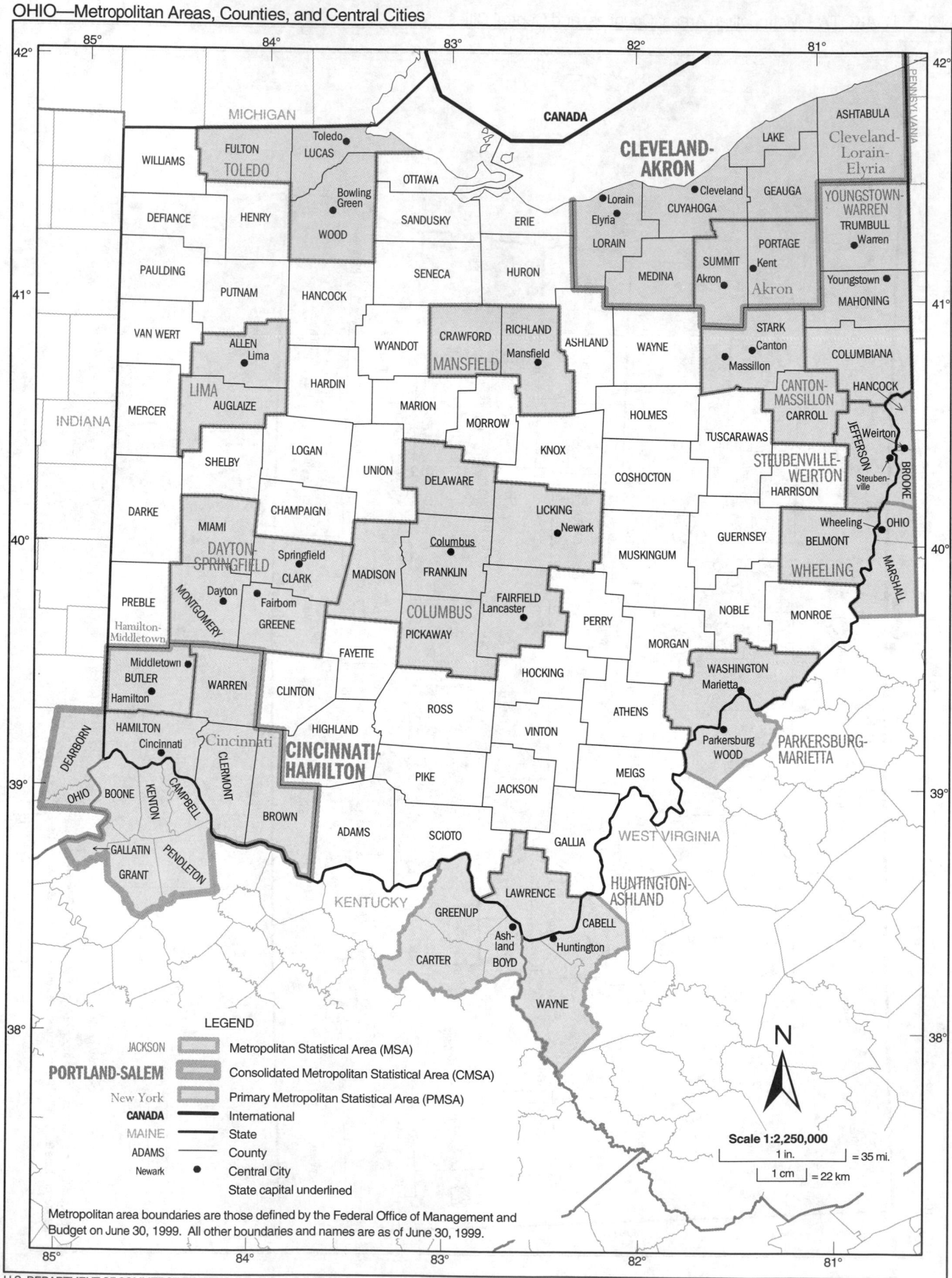

LEGEND

JACKSON	Metropolitan Statistical Area (MSA)
PORTLAND-SALEM	Consolidated Metropolitan Statistical Area (CMSA)
New York	Primary Metropolitan Statistical Area (PMSA)
CANADA	International
MAINE	State
ADAMS	County
Newark ●	Central City
	State capital underlined

Scale 1:2,250,000

1 in. = 35 mi.

1 cm = 22 km

N

Metropolitan area boundaries are those defined by the Federal Office of Management and Budget on June 30, 1999. All other boundaries and names are as of June 30, 1999.

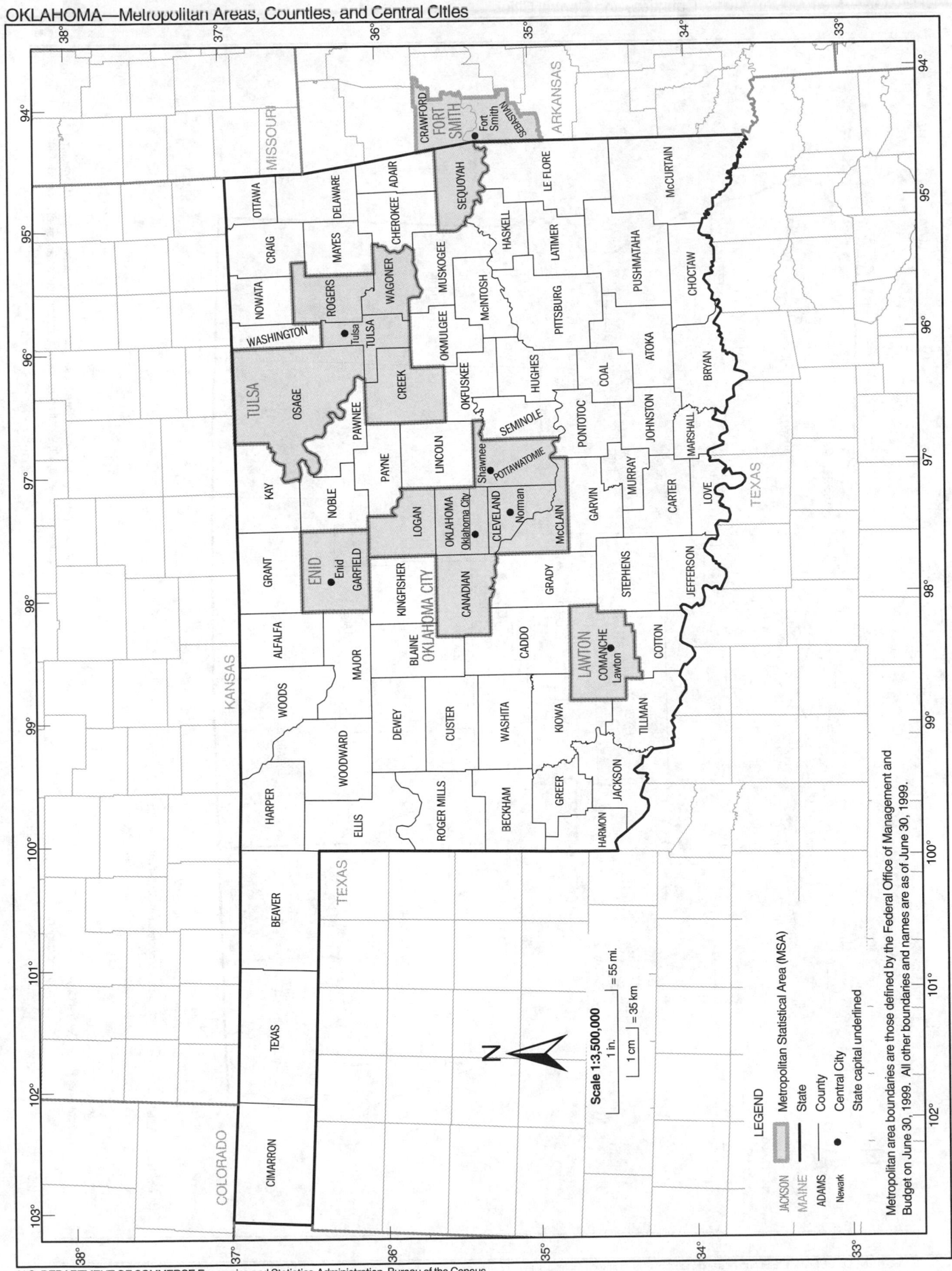

Scale 1:3,500,000

1 in. = 55 mi.

1 cm = 35 km

LEGEND

Metropolitan Statistical Area (MSA)

State

County

Central City

State capital underlined

JACKSON
MAINE
ADAMS
Newark

Metropolitan area boundaries are those defined by the Federal Office of Management and Budget on June 30, 1999. All other boundaries and names are as of June 30, 1999.

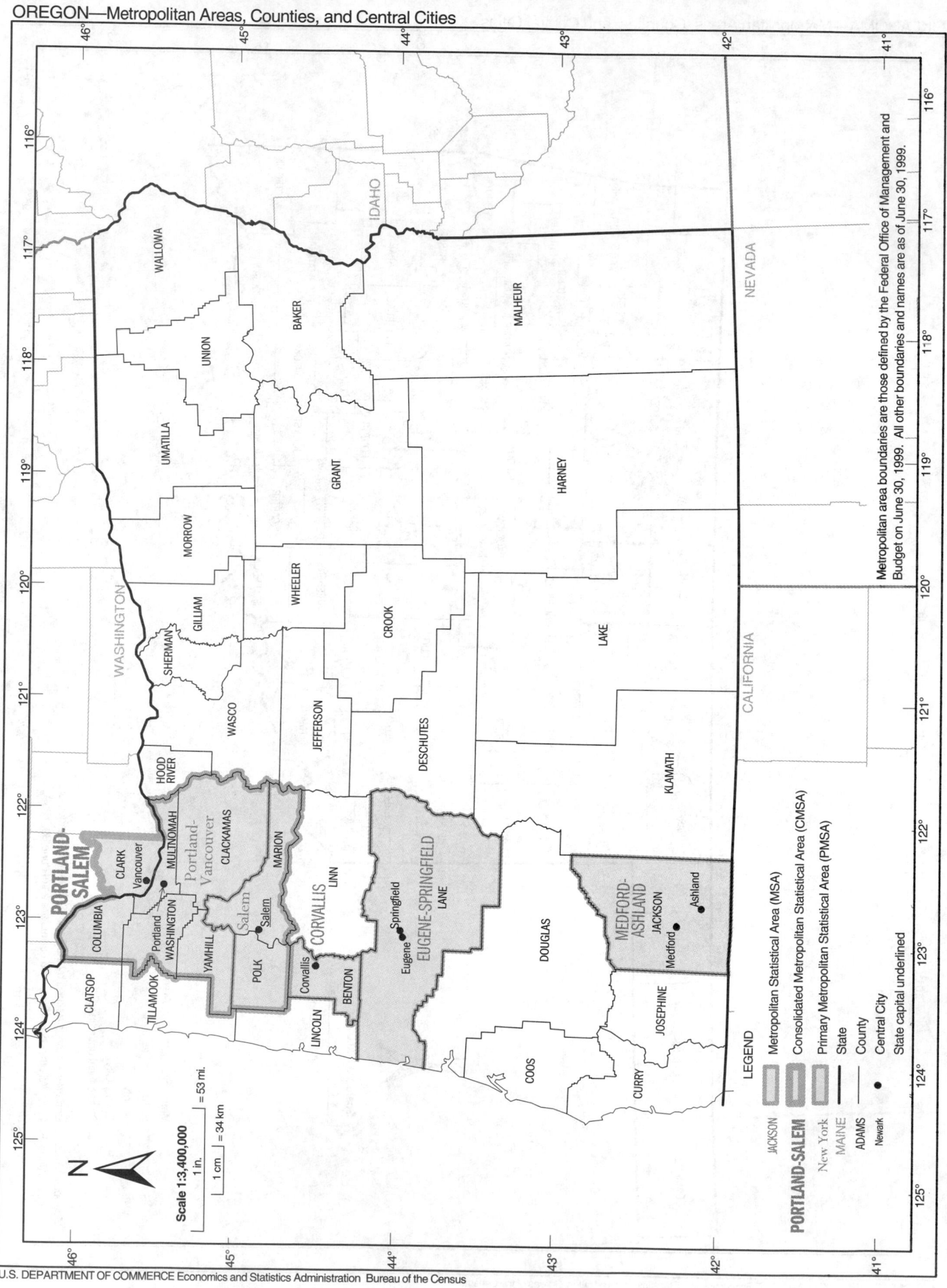

Metropolitan area boundaries are those defined by the Federal Office of Management and Budget on June 30, 1999. All other boundaries and names are as of June 30, 1999.

WASHINGTON

IDAHO

NEVADA

CALIFORNIA

WALLOWA

BAKER

MALHEUR

UNION

UMATILLA

GRANT

HARNEY

MORROW

WHEELER

GILLIAM

SHERMAN

CROOK

LAKE

WASCO

JEFFERSON

DESCHUTES

KLAMATH

HOOD RIVER

PORTLAND-SALEM

CLARK

Vancouver

MULTNOMAH

CLACKAMAS

Portland-Vancouver

MARION

LINN

COLUMBIA

Portland

WASHINGTON

Salem

Salem

CORVALLIS

EUGENE-SPRINGFIELD

LANE

Springfield

MEDFORD-ASHLAND

Ashland

JACKSON

YAMHILL

POLK

Corvallis

BENTON

Eugene

Medford

CLATSOP

TILLAMOOK

LINCOLN

DOUGLAS

JOSEPHINE

COOS

CURRY

LEGEND

Metropolitan Statistical Area (MSA)

Consolidated Metropolitan Statistical Area (CMSA)

Primary Metropolitan Statistical Area (PMSA)

State

County

Central City ●

State capital underlined

JACKSON — County

PORTLAND-SALEM

New York

MAINE — State

ADAMS

Newark ● — Central City

Scale 1:3,400,000

1 in. = 53 mi.

1 cm = 34 km

N

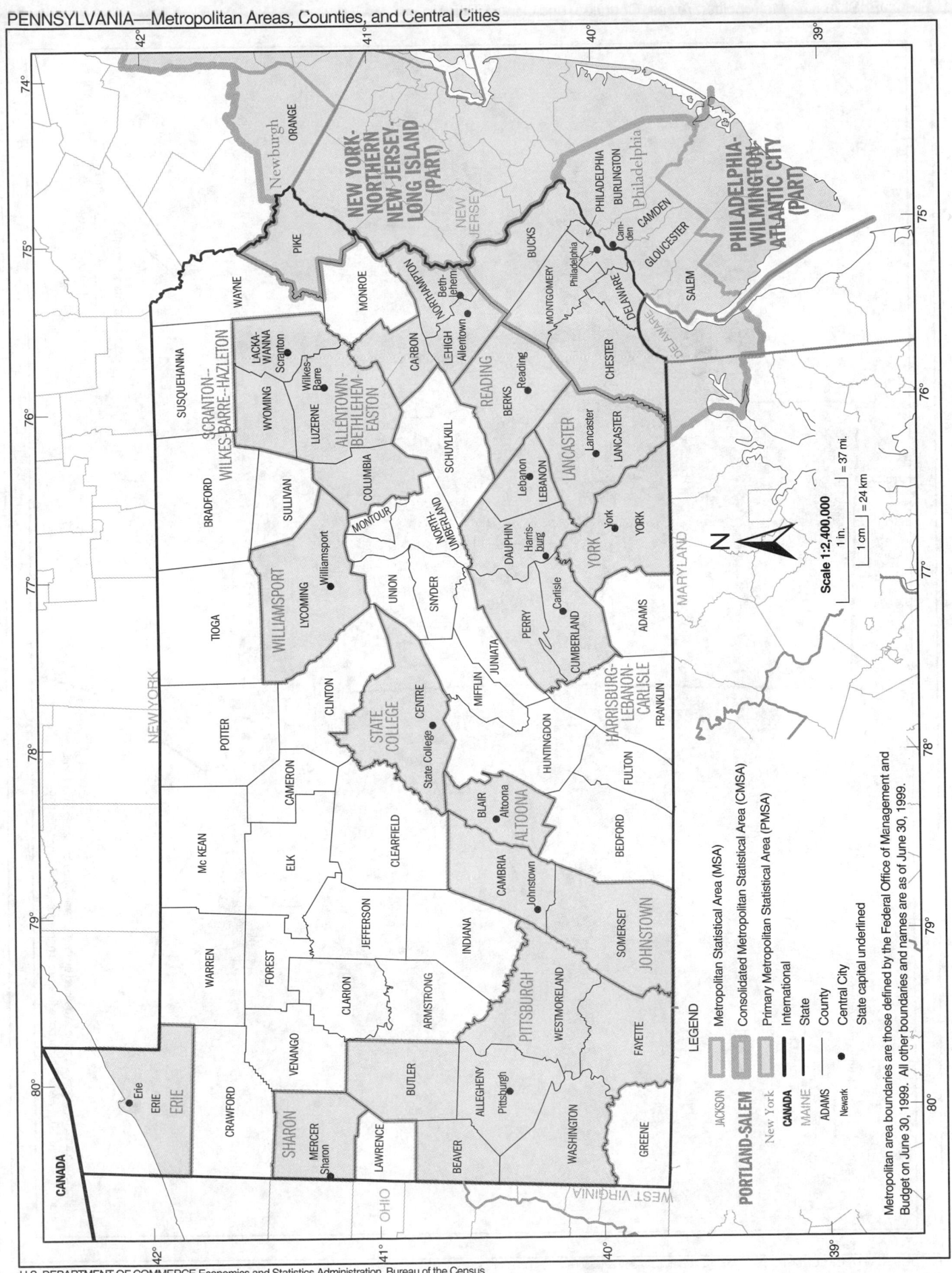

LEGEND

	Metropolitan Statistical Area (MSA)
	Consolidated Metropolitan Statistical Area (CMSA)
	Primary Metropolitan Statistical Area (PMSA)
	International
	State
	County
•	Central City
	State capital underlined

JACKSON

PORTLAND-SALEM

New York

CANADA

MAINE

ADAMS

Newark

Scale 1:2,400,000

1 in. = 37 mi.

1 cm = 24 km

N

Metropolitan area boundaries are those defined by the Federal Office of Management and Budget on June 30, 1999. All other boundaries and names are as of June 30, 1999.

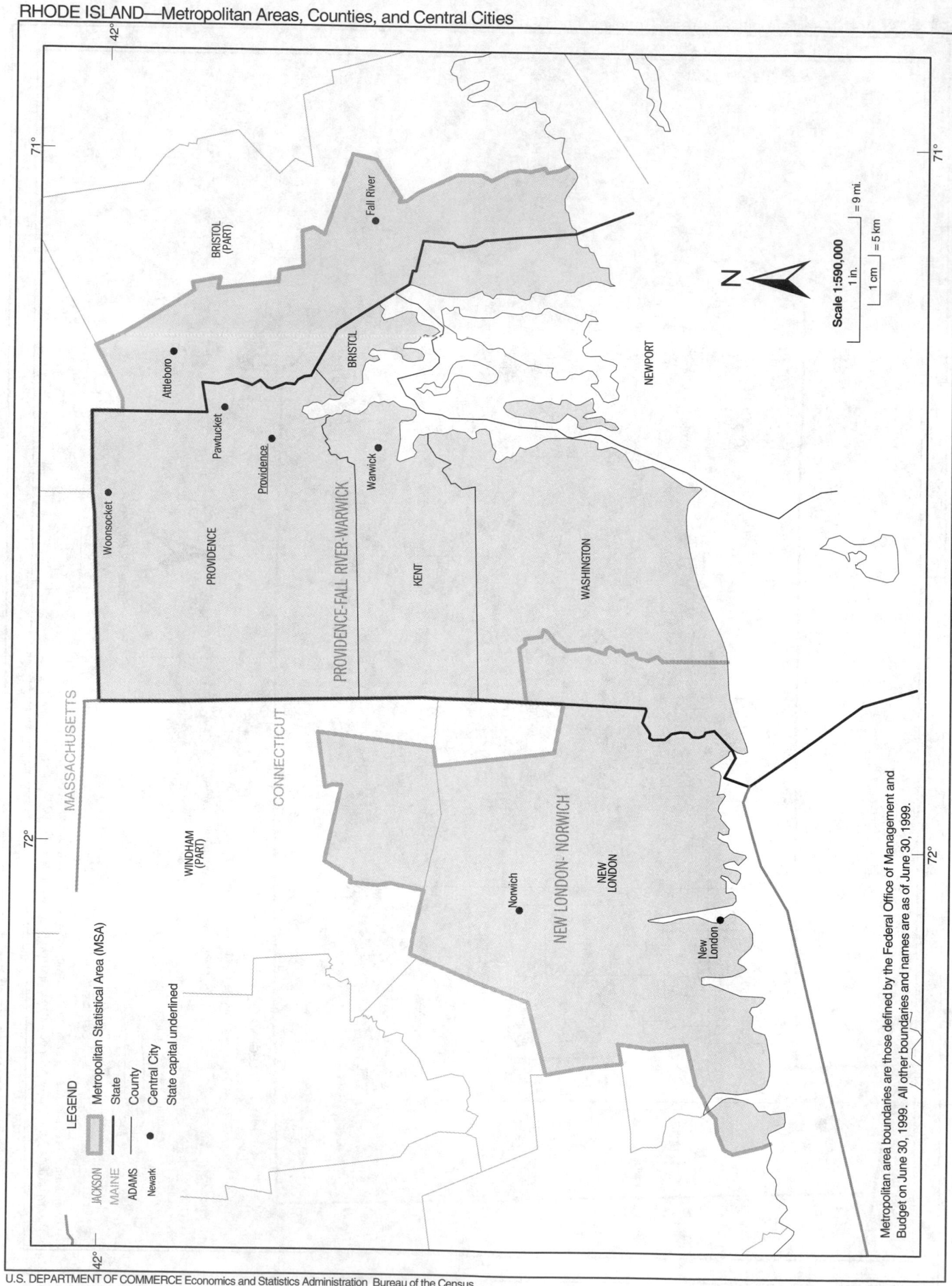

Scale 1:590,000

1 in. = 9 mi.

1 cm = 5 km

LEGEND

Metropolitan Statistical Area (MSA)

State

County

• Central City

State capital underlined

JACKSON

MAINE

ADAMS

Newark

Metropolitan area boundaries are those defined by the Federal Office of Management and Budget on June 30, 1999. All other boundaries and names are as of June 30, 1999.

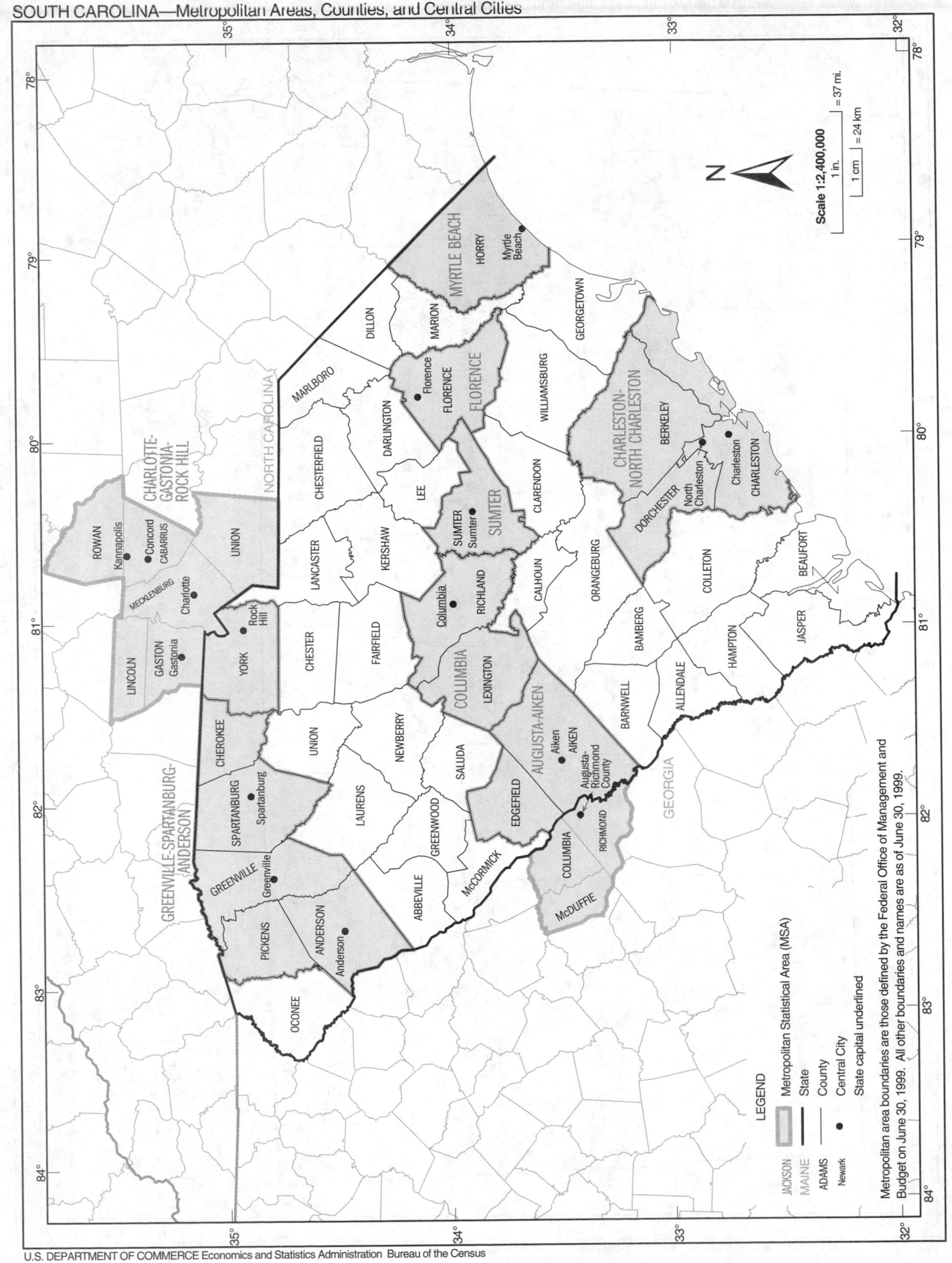

Scale 1:2,400,000
1 in. = 37 mi.
1 cm = 24 km

LEGEND

Metropolitan Statistical Area (MSA)
State
County
Central City
State capital underlined

JACKSON
MAINE
ADAMS
Newark

Metropolitan area boundaries are those defined by the Federal Office of Management and Budget on June 30, 1999. All other boundaries and names are as of June 30, 1999.

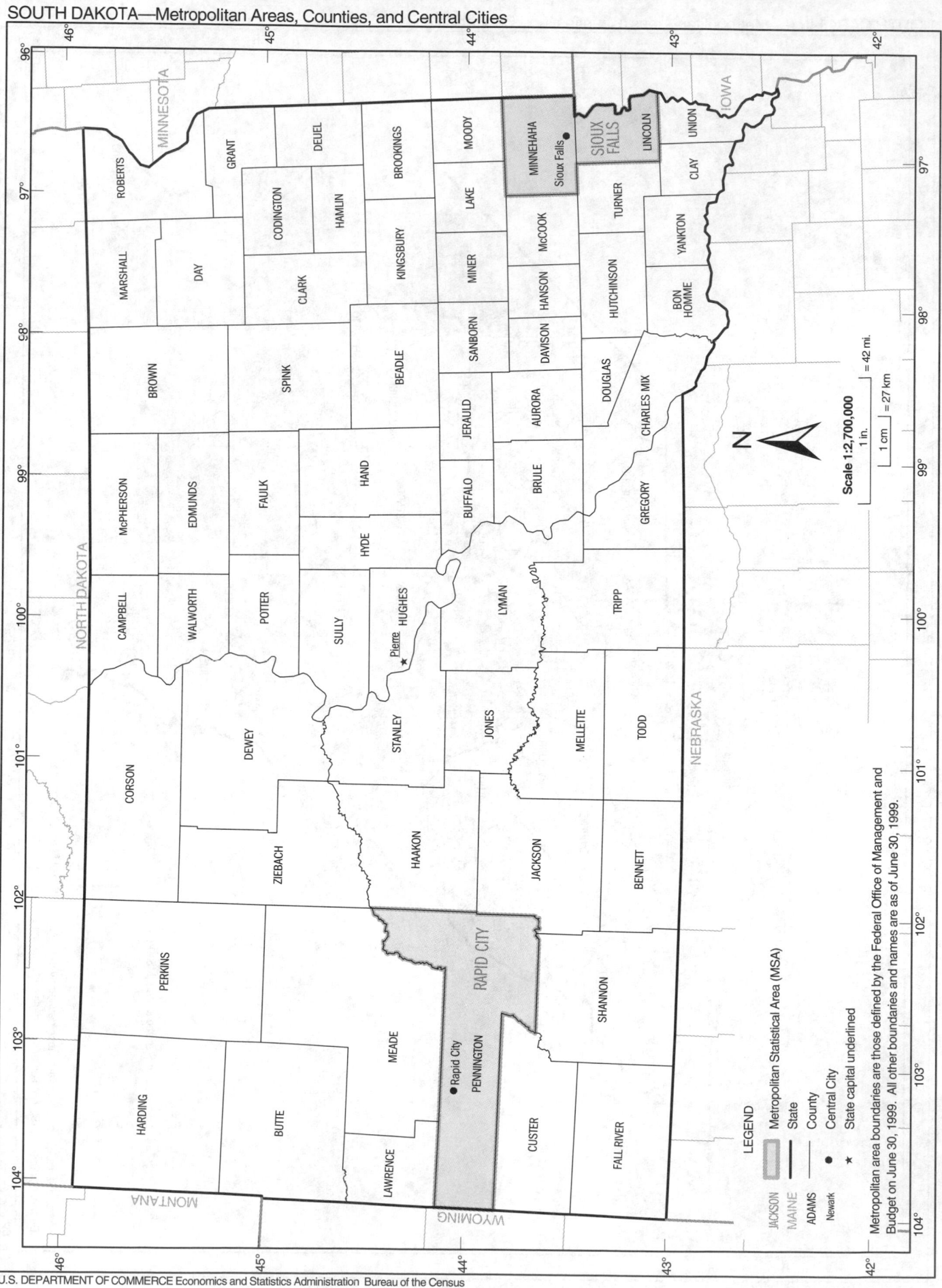

LEGEND

JACKSON	Metropolitan Statistical Area (MSA)
MAINE	State
ADAMS	County
Newark ●	Central City
★	State capital underlined

Metropolitan area boundaries are those defined by the Federal Office of Management and Budget on June 30, 1999. All other boundaries and names are as of June 30, 1999.

Scale 1:2,700,000

1 in. = 42 mi.
1 cm = 27 km

N

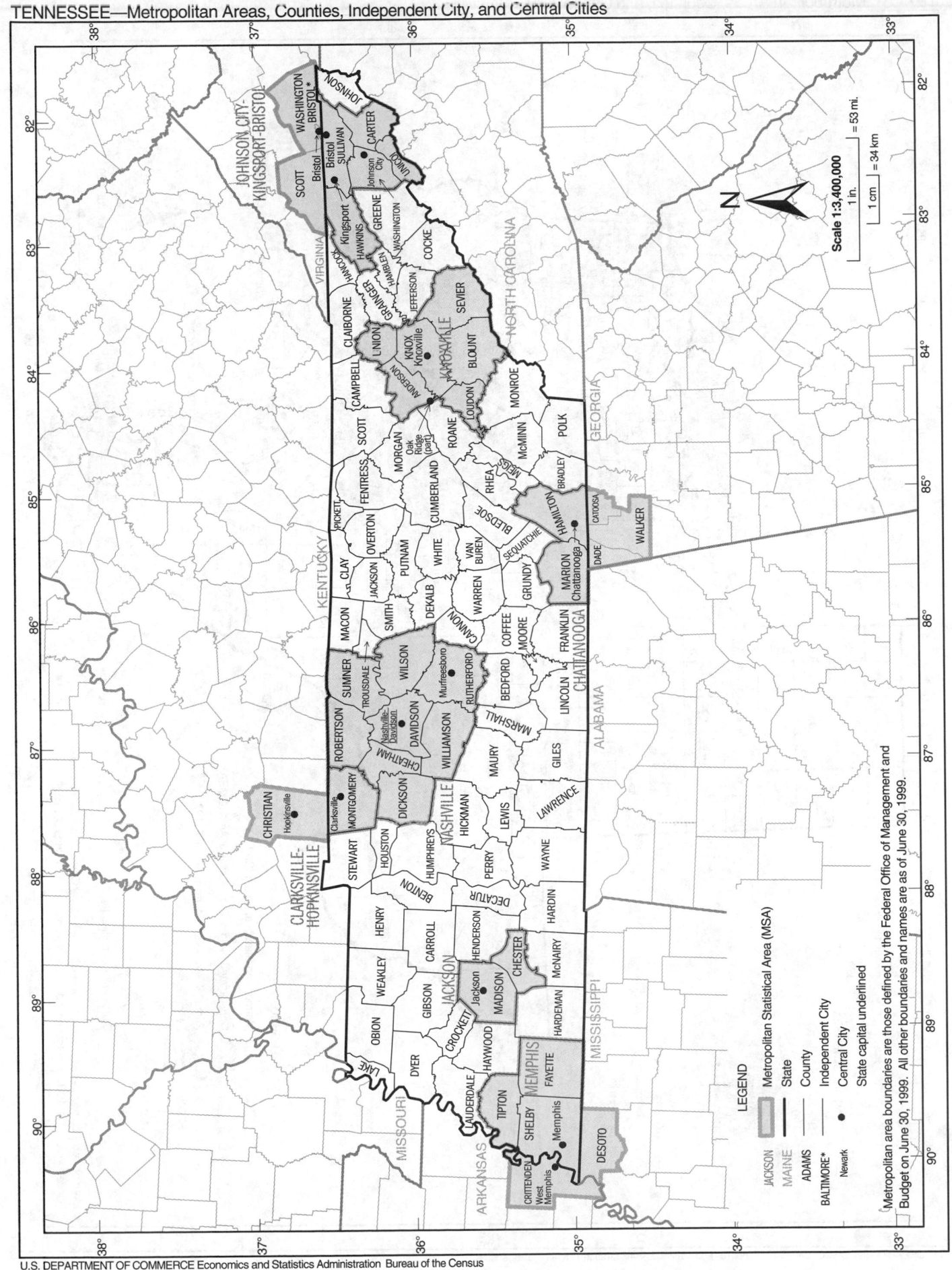

Scale 1:3,400,000

1 in. = 53 mi.

1 cm = 34 km

LEGEND

Metropolitan Statistical Area (MSA)
State
County
Independent City
Central City
State capital underlined

JACKSON
MAINE
ADAMS*
BALTIMORE*
Newark

Metropolitan area boundaries are those defined by the Federal Office of Management and Budget on June 30, 1999. All other boundaries and names are as of June 30, 1999.

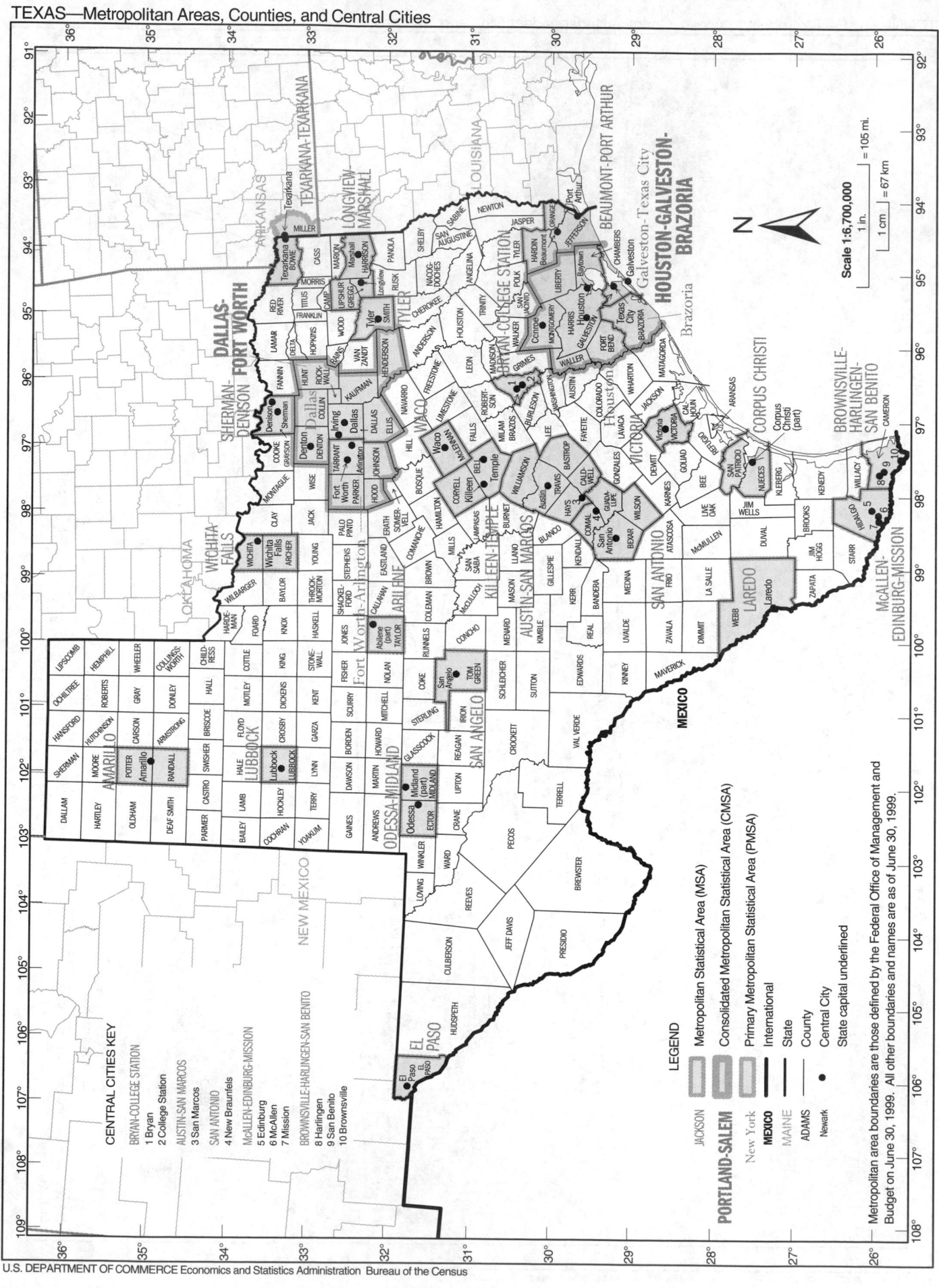

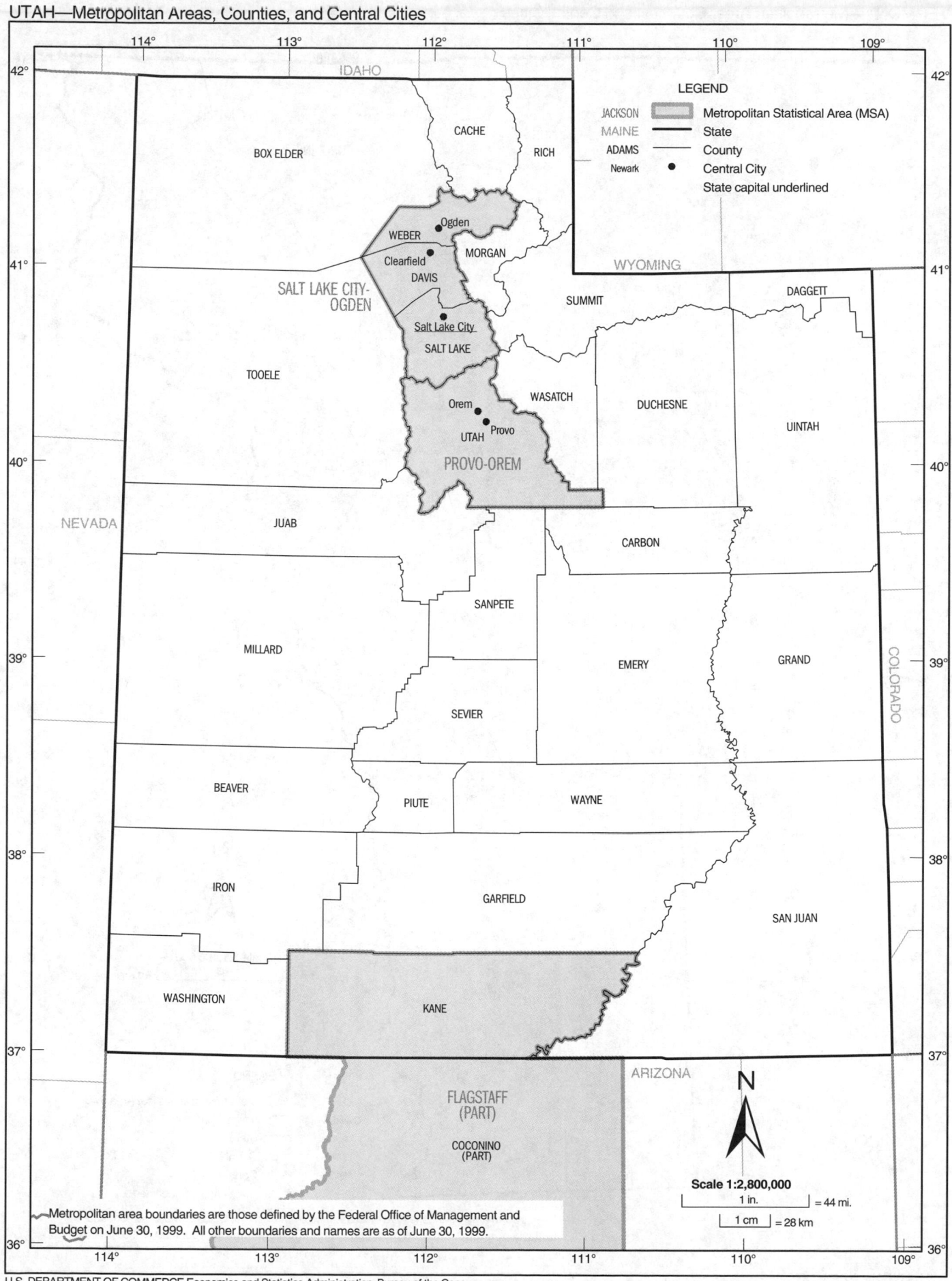

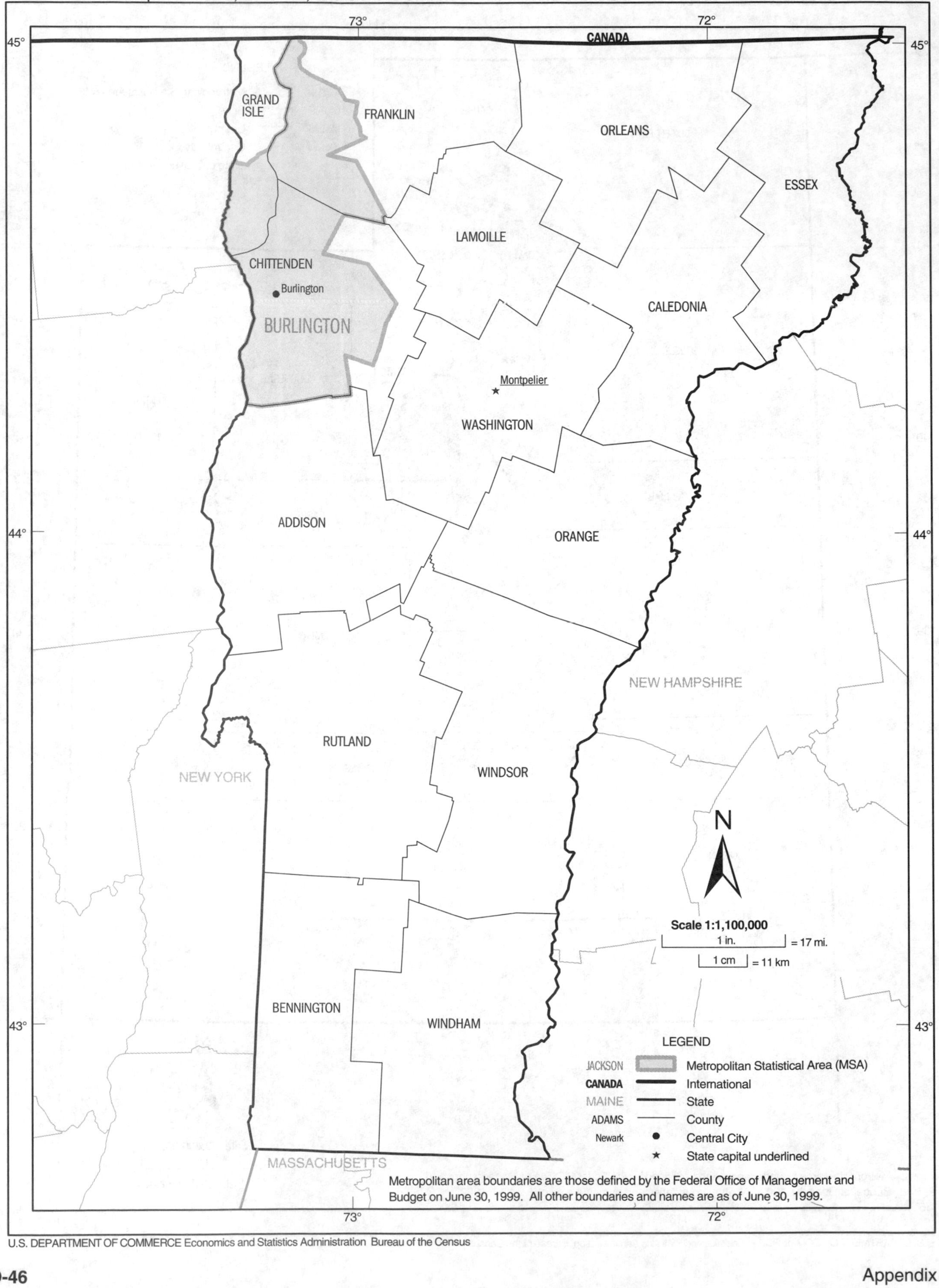

73°
72°
CANADA
45°
45°

GRAND
ISLE
FRANKLIN

ORLEANS

ESSEX

LAMOILLE

CHITTENDEN

• Burlington

CALEDONIA

BURLINGTON

Montpelier
★

WASHINGTON

44°
44°

ADDISON

ORANGE

NEW HAMPSHIRE

RUTLAND

NEW YORK

WINDSOR

N

Scale 1:1,100,000
1 in. ____ = 17 mi.
1 cm = 11 km

43°
43°

BENNINGTON

WINDHAM

LEGEND

JACKSON — Metropolitan Statistical Area (MSA)
CANADA — International
MAINE — State
ADAMS — County
Newark • Central City
★ State capital underlined

MASSACHUSETTS

Metropolitan area boundaries are those defined by the Federal Office of Management and
Budget on June 30, 1999. All other boundaries and names are as of June 30, 1999.

73°
72°

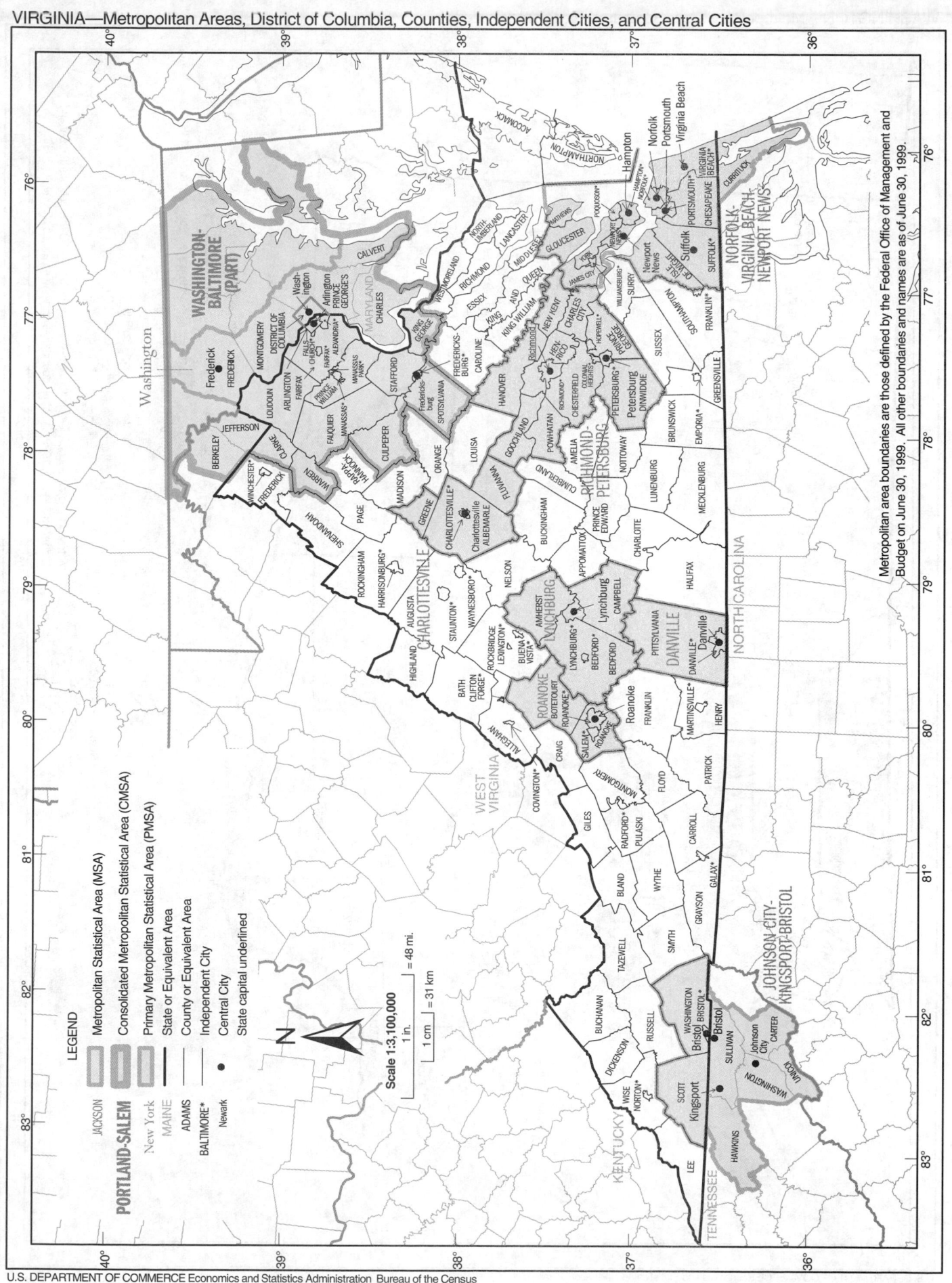

Metropolitan area boundaries are those defined by the Federal Office of Management and Budget on June 30, 1999. All other boundaries and names are as of June 30, 1999.

LEGEND

JACKSON	Metropolitan Statistical Area (MSA)
PORTLAND-SALEM	Consolidated Metropolitan Statistical Area (CMSA)
New York	Primary Metropolitan Statistical Area (PMSA)
MAINE	State or Equivalent Area
ADAMS	County or Equivalent Area
BALTIMORE*	Independent City
•	Central City
Newark	State capital underlined

Scale 1:3,100,000

1 in. = 48 mi.

1 cm = 31 km

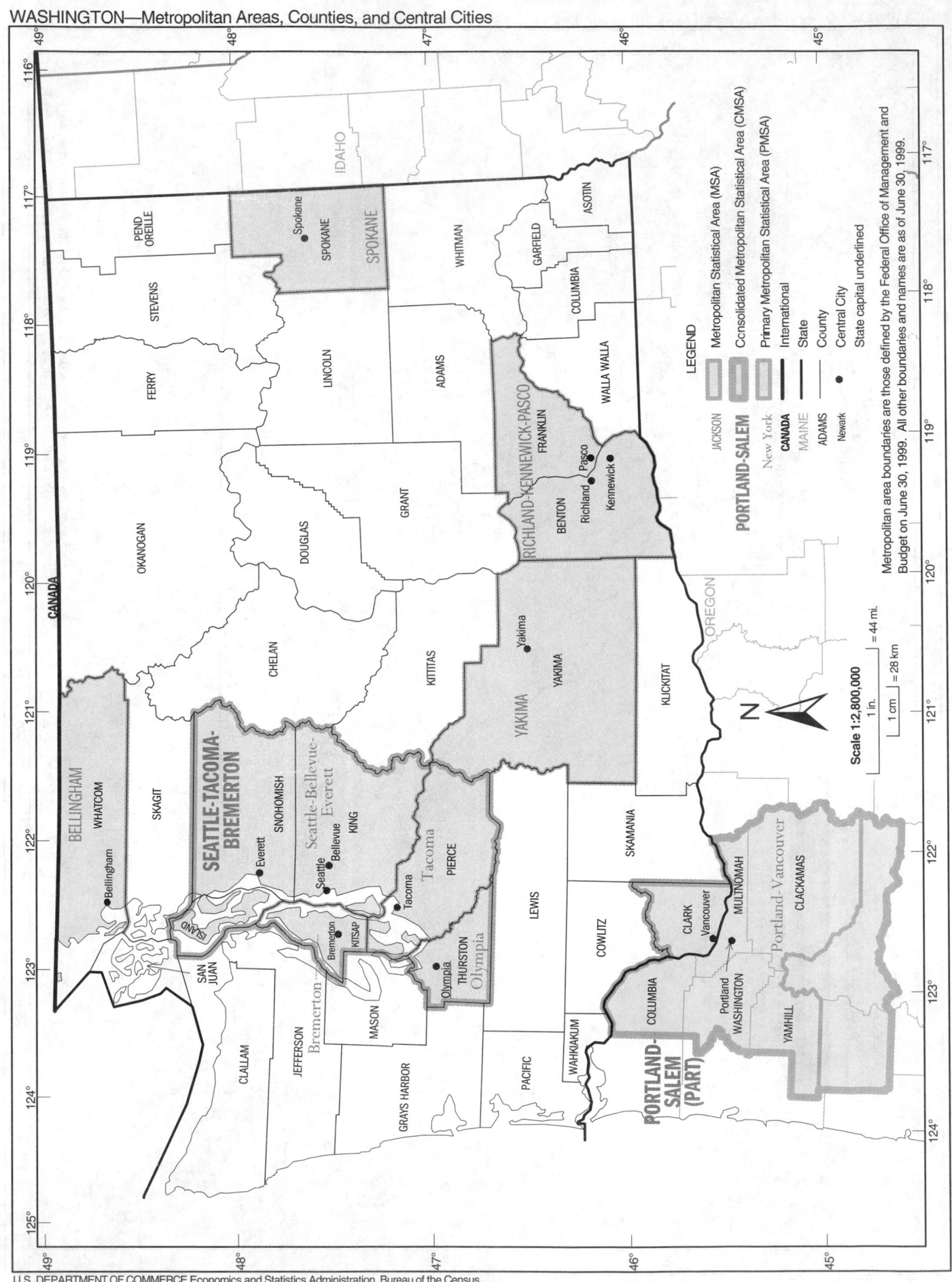

LEGEND

Metropolitan Statistical Area (MSA)

Consolidated Metropolitan Statistical Area (CMSA)

Primary Metropolitan Statistical Area (PMSA)

International

State

County

• Central City

State capital underlined

JACKSON   MSA
New York   CMSA
CANADA
MAINE
ADAMS
Newark   Central City

Metropolitan area boundaries are those defined by the Federal Office of Management and Budget on June 30, 1999. All other boundaries and names are as of June 30, 1999.

Scale 1:2,800,000

1 in. = 44 mi.

1 cm = 28 km

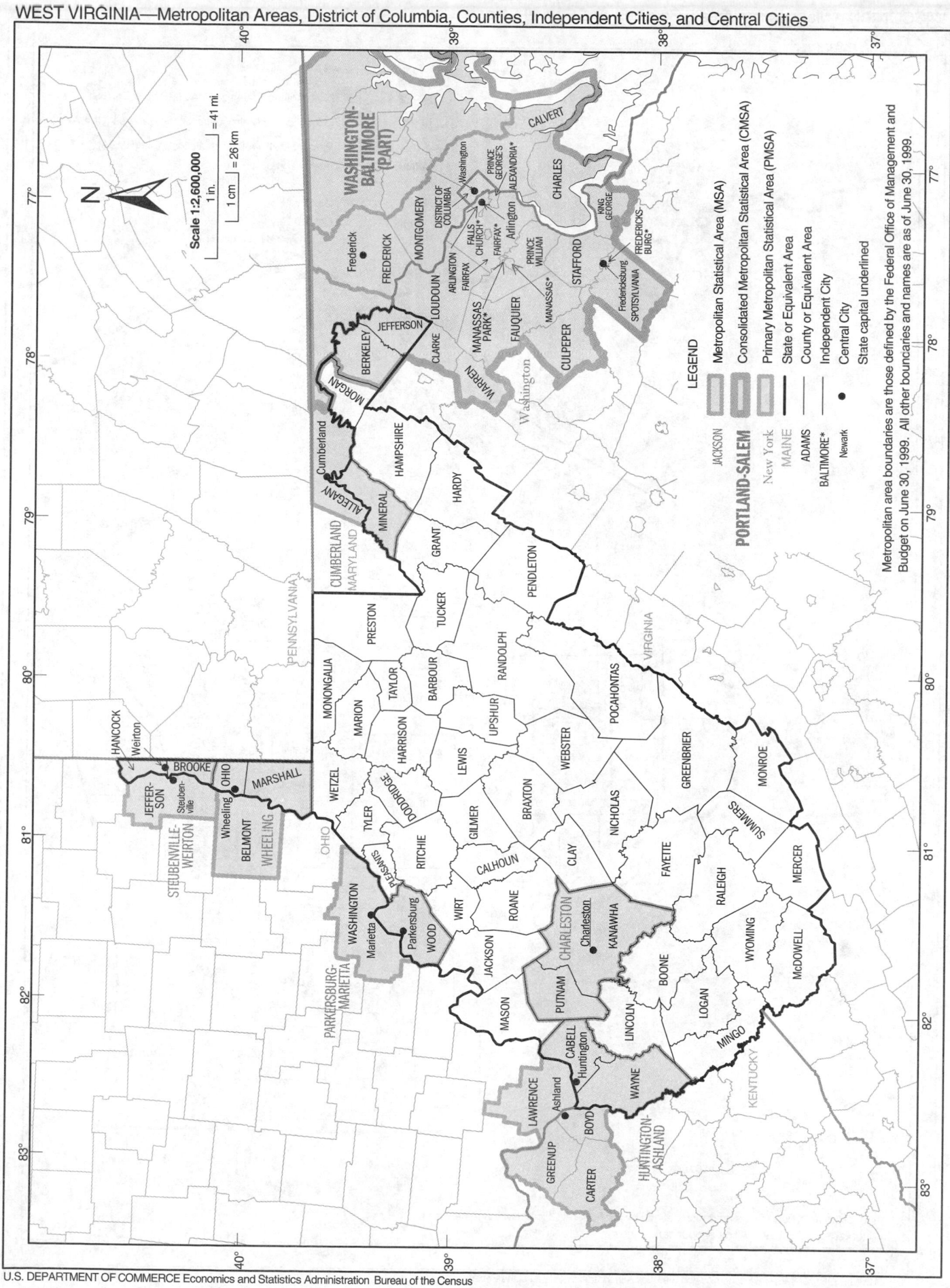

U.S. DEPARTMENT OF COMMERCE Economics and Statistics Administration Bureau of the Census

WISCONSIN—Metropolitan Areas, Counties, and Central Cities

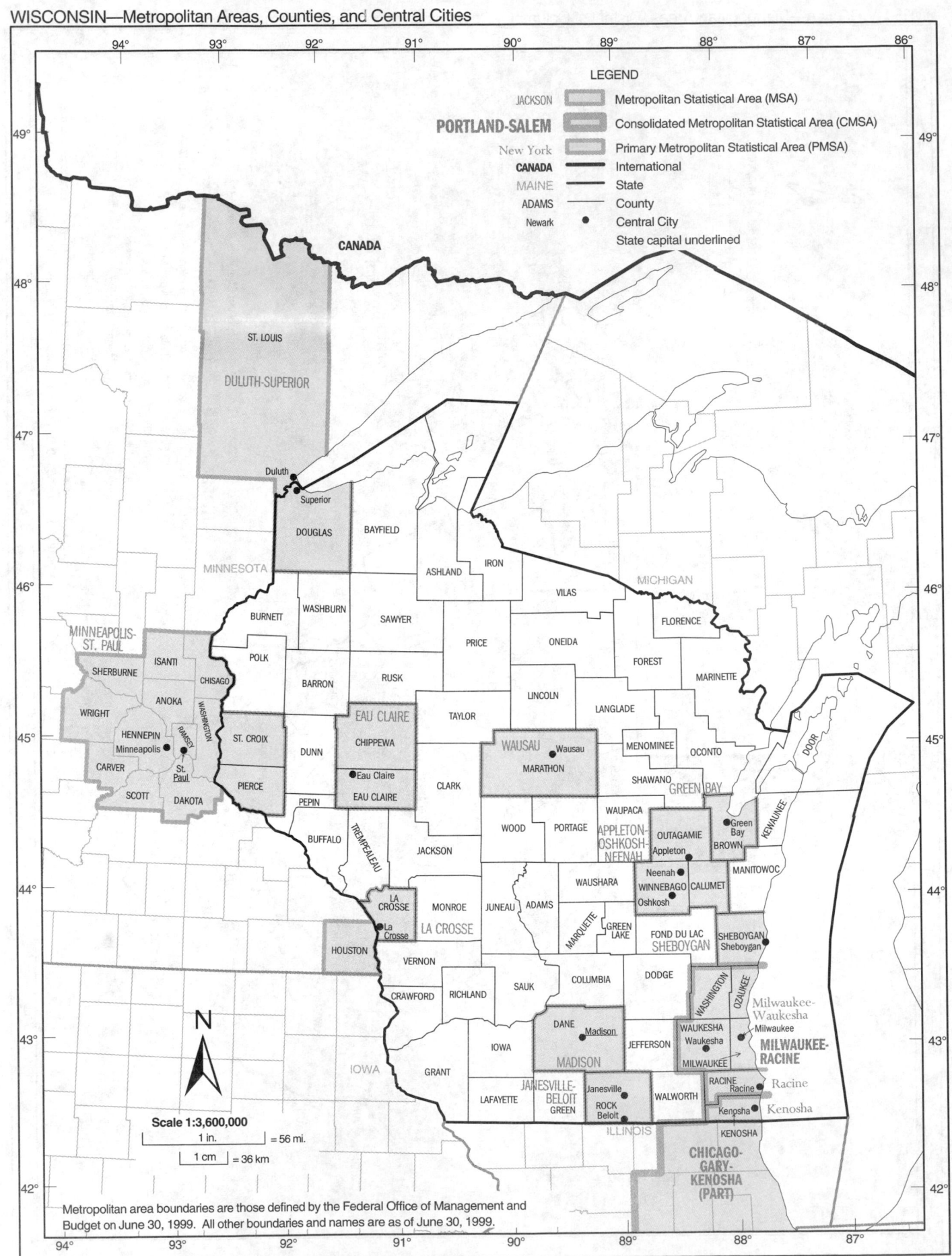

LEGEND

JACKSON	Metropolitan Statistical Area (MSA)
PORTLAND-SALEM	Consolidated Metropolitan Statistical Area (CMSA)
New York	Primary Metropolitan Statistical Area (PMSA)
CANADA	International
MAINE	State
ADAMS	County
Newark ●	Central City
	State capital underlined

CANADA

MINNESOTA

MICHIGAN

ST. LOUIS

DULUTH-SUPERIOR

Duluth

Superior

DOUGLAS

BAYFIELD

ASHLAND

IRON

VILAS

FLORENCE

BURNETT

WASHBURN

SAWYER

PRICE

ONEIDA

FOREST

MARINETTE

MINNEAPOLIS-ST. PAUL

SHERBURNE

ISANTI

CHISAGO

POLK

BARRON

RUSK

LINCOLN

LANGLADE

ANOKA

WASHINGTON

WRIGHT

HENNEPIN

RAMSEY

Minneapolis

St. Paul

ST. CROIX

DUNN

CHIPPEWA

EAU CLAIRE

Eau Claire

CLARK

TAYLOR

WAUSAU

Wausau

MARATHON

MENOMINEE

OCONTO

SHAWANO

GREEN BAY

CARVER

SCOTT

DAKOTA

PIERCE

PEPIN

EAU CLAIRE

BUFFALO

TREMPEALEAU

JACKSON

WOOD

PORTAGE

WAUPACA

APPLETON-OSHKOSH-NEENAH

OUTAGAMIE

Appleton

Green Bay

BROWN

KEWAUNEE

LA CROSSE

La Crosse

MONROE

JUNEAU

ADAMS

WAUSHARA

MARQUETTE

GREEN LAKE

WINNEBAGO

Neenah

Oshkosh

CALUMET

MANITOWOC

HOUSTON

VERNON

FOND DU LAC

SHEBOYGAN

Sheboygan

CRAWFORD

RICHLAND

SAUK

COLUMBIA

DODGE

WASHINGTON

OZAUKEE

DANE

Madison

MADISON

JEFFERSON

WAUKESHA

Waukesha

MILWAUKEE

Milwaukee-Waukesha

Milwaukee

MILWAUKEE-RACINE

IOWA

JANESVILLE-BELOIT

Janesville

ROCK

Beloit

WALWORTH

RACINE

Racine

Racine

LAFAYETTE

GREEN

Kenosha

Kenosha

KENOSHA

ILLINOIS

CHICAGO-GARY-KENOSHA (PART)

DOOR

N

Scale 1:3,600,000
1 in. = 56 mi.
1 cm = 36 km

Metropolitan area boundaries are those defined by the Federal Office of Management and Budget on June 30, 1999. All other boundaries and names are as of June 30, 1999.

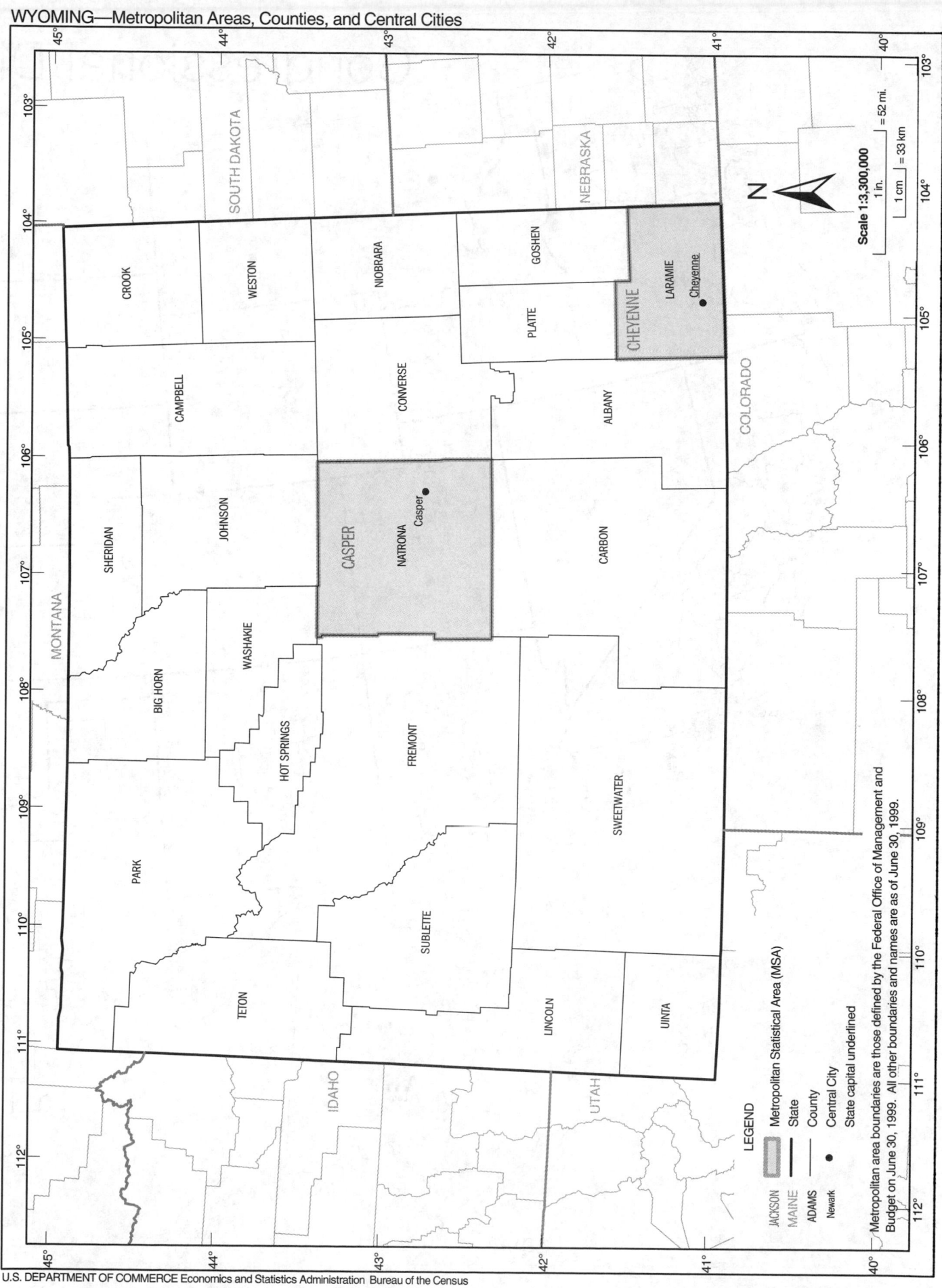

Scale 1:3,300,000

1 in. = 52 mi.

1 cm = 33 km

LEGEND

Metropolitan Statistical Area (MSA)

State

County

Central City

State capital underlined

JACKSON

MAINE

ADAMS

Newark

Metropolitan area boundaries are those defined by the Federal Office of Management and Budget on June 30, 1999. All other boundaries and names are as of June 30, 1999.

Congressional Dist

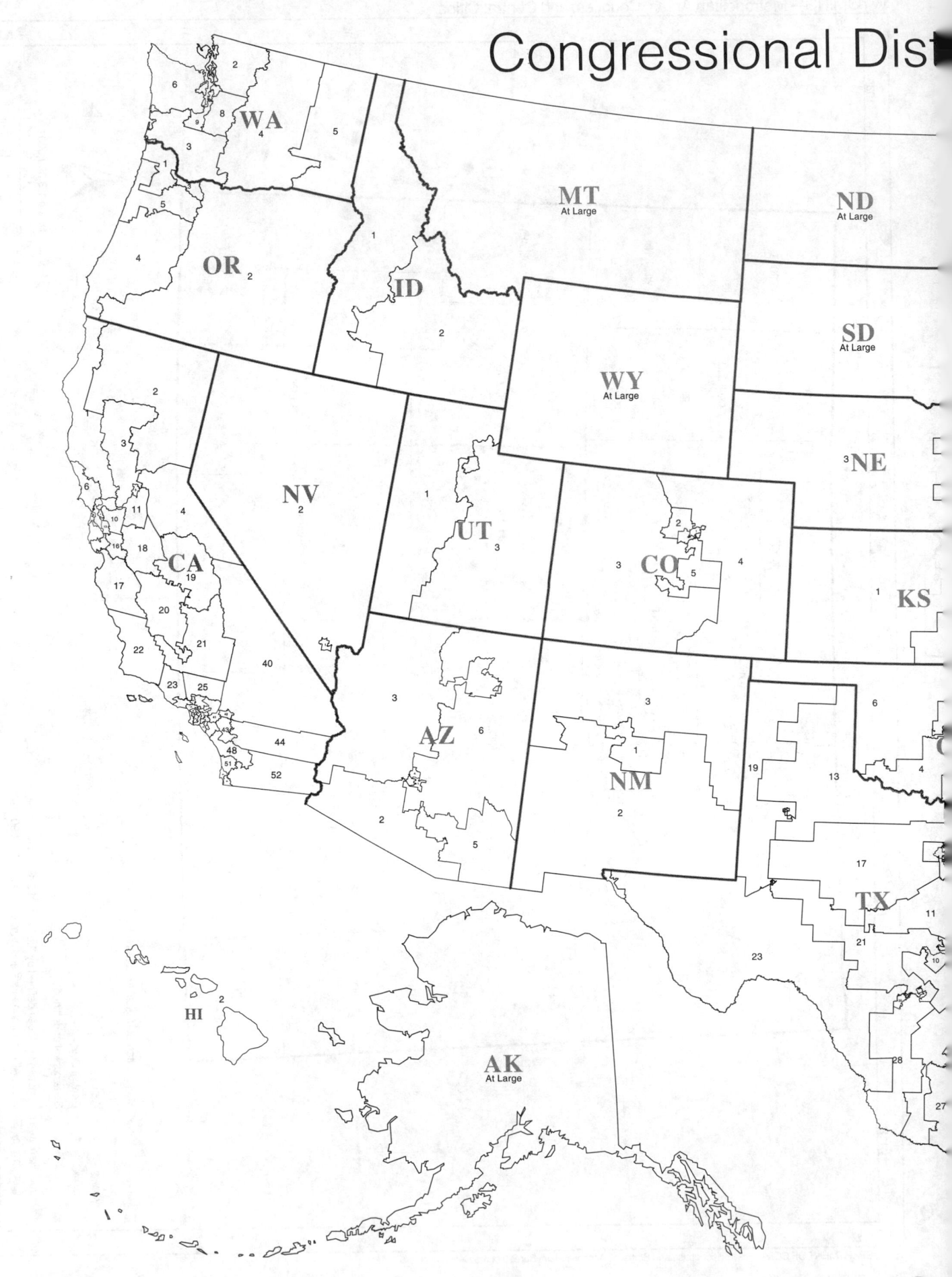

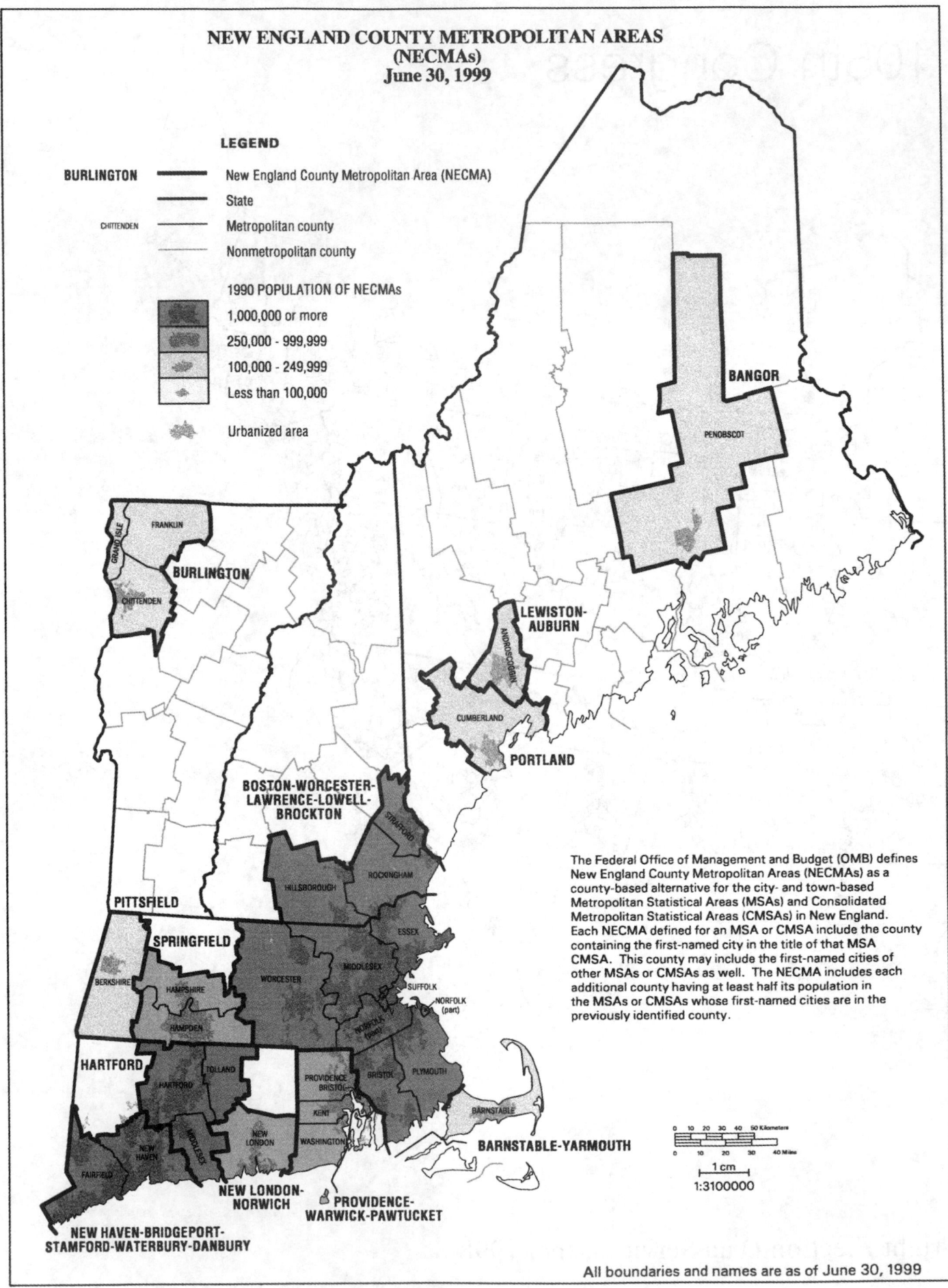

NEW ENGLAND COUNTY METROPOLITAN AREAS
(NECMAs)
June 30, 1999

LEGEND

BURLINGTON ——— New England County Metropolitan Area (NECMA)

——— State

CHITTENDEN ——— Metropolitan county

——— Nonmetropolitan county

1990 POPULATION OF NECMAs

1,000,000 or more

250,000 - 999,999

100,000 - 249,999

Less than 100,000

Urbanized area

BANGOR

PENOBSCOT

FRANKLIN

GRAND ISLE

BURLINGTON

CHITTENDEN

LEWISTON-AUBURN

ANDROSCOGGIN

CUMBERLAND

PORTLAND

BOSTON-WORCESTER-LAWRENCE-LOWELL-BROCKTON

STRAFFORD

ROCKINGHAM

HILLSBOROUGH

PITTSFIELD

ESSEX

SPRINGFIELD

BERKSHIRE

HAMPSHIRE

WORCESTER

MIDDLESEX

SUFFOLK

NORFOLK (part)

HAMPDEN

NORFOLK (part)

HARTFORD

TOLLAND

HARTFORD

PROVIDENCE BRISTOL

BRISTOL

PLYMOUTH

KENT

NEW LONDON

MIDDLESEX

NEW HAVEN

WASHINGTON

BARNSTABLE

FAIRFIELD

BARNSTABLE-YARMOUTH

NEW LONDON-NORWICH

PROVIDENCE-WARWICK-PAWTUCKET

NEW HAVEN-BRIDGEPORT-STAMFORD-WATERBURY-DANBURY

The Federal Office of Management and Budget (OMB) defines New England County Metropolitan Areas (NECMAs) as a county-based alternative for the city- and town-based Metropolitan Statistical Areas (MSAs) and Consolidated Metropolitan Statistical Areas (CMSAs) in New England. Each NECMA defined for an MSA or CMSA include the county containing the first-named city in the title of that MSA CMSA. This county may include the first-named cities of other MSAs or CMSAs as well. The NECMA includes each additional county having at least half its population in the MSAs or CMSAs whose first-named cities are in the previously identified county.

0 10 20 30 40 50 Kilometers

0 10 20 30 40 Miles

1 cm

1:3100000

All boundaries and names are as of June 30, 1999

APPENDIX E
CITIES BY COUNTY

The following table is arranged alphabetically by state. Under each state heading are listed all cities with a 2000 Census population over 25,000 along with their component counties and the population in each component.

State Code	Place Code	County Code	Geographic Area Name	2000 Population
01			**ALABAMA**	4 447 100
01	03076		Auburn city	42 987
01	03076	081	Lee County	42 987
01	05980		Bessemer city	29 672
01	05980	073	Jefferson County	29 672
01	07000		Birmingham city	242 820
01	07000	073	Jefferson County	242 307
01	07000	117	Shelby County	513
01	20104		Decatur city	53 929
01	20104	083	Limestone County	83
01	20104	103	Morgan County	53 846
01	21184		Dothan city	57 737
01	21184	045	Dale County	650
01	21184	067	Henry County	5
01	21184	069	Houston County	57 082
01	26896		Florence city	36 264
01	26896	077	Lauderdale County	36 264
01	28696		Gadsden city	38 978
01	28696	055	Etowah County	38 978
01	35800		Homewood city	25 043
01	35800	073	Jefferson County	25 043
01	35896		Hoover city	62 742
01	35896	073	Jefferson County	46 868
01	35896	117	Shelby County	15 874
01	37000		Huntsville city	158 216
01	37000	083	Limestone County	264
01	37000	089	Madison County	157 952
01	45784		Madison city	29 329
01	45784	083	Limestone County	139
01	45784	089	Madison County	29 190
01	50000		Mobile city	198 915
01	50000	097	Mobile County	198 915
01	51000		Montgomery city	201 568
01	51000	101	Montgomery County	201 568
01	59472		Phenix City city	28 265
01	59472	081	Lee County	1 980
01	59472	113	Russell County	26 285
01	62496		Prichard city	28 633
01	62496	097	Mobile County	28 633
01	77256		Tuscaloosa city	77 906
01	77256	125	Tuscaloosa County	77 906
02			**ALASKA**	626 932
02	03000		Anchorage municipality	260 283
02	03000	020	Anchorage Municipality	260 283
02	24230		Fairbanks city	30 224
02	24230	090	Fairbanks North Star Borough	30 224
02	36400		Juneau city and borough	30 711
02	36400	110	Juneau City and Borough	30 711
04			**ARIZONA**	5 130 632
04	02830		Apache Junction city	31 814
04	02830	013	Maricopa County	273
04	02830	021	Pinal County	31 541
04	04720		Avondale city	35 883
04	04720	013	Maricopa County	35 883
04	08220		Bullhead City city	33 769
04	08220	015	Mohave County	33 769
04	10530		Casa Grande city	25 224
04	10530	021	Pinal County	25 224
04	12000		Chandler city	176 581
04	12000	013	Maricopa County	176 581
04	23620		Flagstaff city	52 894
04	23620	005	Coconino County	52 894
04	27400		Gilbert town	109 697
04	27400	013	Maricopa County	109 697
04	27820		Glendale city	218 812
04	27820	013	Maricopa County	218 812
04	39370		Lake Havasu City city	41 938
04	39370	015	Mohave County	41 938
04	46000		Mesa city	396 375
04	46000	013	Maricopa County	396 375
04	51600		Oro Valley town	29 700
04	51600	019	Pima County	29 700
04	54050		Peoria city	108 364
04	54050	013	Maricopa County	108 363
04	54050	025	Yavapai County	1
04	55000		Phoenix city	1321 045
04	55000	013	Maricopa County	1321 045
04	57380		Prescott city	33 938
04	57380	025	Yavapai County	33 938
04	65000		Scottsdale city	202 705
04	65000	013	Maricopa County	202 705
04	66820		Sierra Vista city	37 775
04	66820	003	Cochise County	37 775
04	71510		Surprise city	30 848
04	71510	013	Maricopa County	30 848
04	73000		Tempe city	158 625
04	73000	013	Maricopa County	158 625
04	77000		Tucson city	486 699
04	77000	019	Pima County	486 699
04	85540		Yuma city	77 515
04	85540	027	Yuma County	77 515
05			**ARKANSAS**	2 673 400
05	15190		Conway city	43 167
05	15190	045	Faulkner County	43 167

State Code	Place Code	County Code	Geographic Area Name	2000 Population	State Code	Place Code	County Code	Geographic Area Name	2000 Population
05	23290		Fayetteville city.............................	58 047	06	04982		Bellflower city..............................	72 878
05	23290	143	Washington County	58 047	06	04982	037	Los Angeles County	72 878
05	24550		Fort Smith city..............................	80 268	06	04996		Bell Gardens city........................	44 054
05	24550	131	Sebastian County	80 268	06	04996	037	Los Angeles County	44 054
05	33400		Hot Springs city............................	35 750	06	05108		Belmont city................................	25 123
05	33400	051	Garland County	35 750	06	05108	081	San Mateo County	25 123
05	34750		Jacksonville city............................	29 916	06	05290		Benicia city.................................	26 865
05	34750	119	Pulaski County..........................	29 916	06	05290	095	Solano County	26 865
05	35710		Jonesboro city..............................	55 515	06	06000		Berkeley city...............................	102 743
05	35710	031	Craighead County......................	55 515	06	06000	001	Alameda County	102 743
05	41000		Little Rock city..............................	183 133	06	06308		Beverly Hills city.........................	33 784
05	41000	119	Pulaski County..........................	183 133	06	06308	037	Los Angeles County	33 784
05	50450		North Little Rock city....................	60 433	06	08100		Brea city.....................................	35 410
05	50450	119	Pulaski County..........................	60 433	06	08100	059	Orange County	35 410
05	55310		Pine Bluff city	55 085	06	08786		Buena Park city...........................	78 282
05	55310	069	Jefferson County......................	55 085	06	08786	059	Orange County	78 282
05	60410		Rogers city	38 829	06	08954		Burbank city................................	100 316
05	60410	007	Benton County	38 829	06	08954	037	Los Angeles County	100 316
05	66080		Springdale city.............................	45 798	06	09066		Burlingame city...........................	28 158
05	66080	007	Benton County	2 011	06	09066	081	San Mateo County....................	28 158
05	66080	143	Washington County	43 787	06	09710		Calexico city...............................	27 109
05	68810		Texarkana city..............................	26 448	06	09710	025	Imperial County........................	27 109
05	68810	091	Miller County............................	26 448	06	10046		Camarillo city..............................	57 077
05	74540		West Memphis city	27 666	06	10046	111	Ventura County........................	57 077
05	74540	035	Crittenden County.....................	27 666	06	10345		Campbell city..............................	38 138
06			**CALIFORNIA**..............................	33 871 648	06	10345	085	Santa Clara County	38 138
06	00562		Alameda city................................	72 259	06	11194		Carlsbad city...............................	78 247
06	00562	001	Alameda County	72 259	06	11194	073	San Diego County	78 247
06	00884		Alhambra city...............................	85 804	06	11530		Carson city	89 730
06	00884	037	Los Angeles County	85 804	06	11530	037	Los Angeles County	89 730
06	02000		Anaheim city................................	328 014	06	12048		Cathedral City city........................	42 647
06	02000	059	Orange County	328 014	06	12048	065	Riverside County	42 647
06	02252		Antioch city..................................	90 532	06	12524		Ceres city	34 609
06	02252	013	Contra Costa County	90 532	06	12524	099	Stanislaus County	34 609
06	02364		Apple Valley town.........................	54 239	06	12552		Cerritos city................................	51 488
06	02364	071	San Bernardino County	54 239	06	12552	037	Los Angeles County	51 488
06	02462		Arcadia city.................................	53 054	06	13014		Chico city....................................	59 954
06	02462	037	Los Angeles County	53 054	06	13014	007	Butte County	59 954
06	03064		Atascadero city............................	26 411	06	13210		Chino city....................................	67 168
06	03064	079	San Luis Obispo County..............	26 411	06	13210	071	San Bernardino County	67 168
06	03386		Azusa city...................................	44 712	06	13392		Chula Vista city...........................	173 556
06	03386	037	Los Angeles County	44 712	06	13392	073	San Diego County	173 556
06	03526		Bakersfield city	247 057	06	13756		Claremont city	33 998
06	03526	029	Kern County.............................	247 057	06	13756	037	Los Angeles County	33 998
06	03666		Baldwin Park city..........................	75 837	06	14218		Clovis city...................................	68 468
06	03666	037	Los Angeles County	75 837	06	14218	019	Fresno County	68 468
06	04870		Bell city......................................	36 664	06	14890		Colton city...................................	47 662
06	04870	037	Los Angeles County	36 664	06	14890	071	San Bernardino County	47 662

State Code	Place Code	County Code	Geographic Area Name	2000 Population	State Code	Place Code	County Code	Geographic Area Name	2000 Population
06	15044		Compton city	93 493	06	24638		Folsom city	51 884
06	15044	037	Los Angeles County	93 493	06	24638	067	Sacramento County	51 884
06	16000		Concord city	121 780	06	24680		Fontana city	128 929
06	16000	013	Contra Costa County	121 780	06	24680	071	San Bernardino County	128 929
06	16350		Corona city	124 966	06	25338		Foster City city	28 803
06	16350	065	Riverside County	124 966	06	25338	081	San Mateo County	28 803
06	16532		Costa Mesa city	108 724	06	25380		Fountain Valley city	54 978
06	16532	059	Orange County	108 724	06	25380	059	Orange County	54 978
06	16742		Covina city	46 837	06	26000		Fremont city	203 413
06	16742	037	Los Angeles County	46 837	06	26000	001	Alameda County	203 413
06	17568		Culver City city	38 816	06	27000		Fresno city	427 652
06	17568	037	Los Angeles County	38 816	06	27000	019	Fresno County	427 652
06	17610		Cupertino city	50 546	06	28000		Fullerton city	126 003
06	17610	085	Santa Clara County	50 546	06	28000	059	Orange County	126 003
06	17750		Cypress city	46 229	06	28168		Gardena city	57 746
06	17750	059	Orange County	46 229	06	28168	037	Los Angeles County	57 746
06	17918		Daly City city	103 621	06	29000		Garden Grove city	165 196
06	17918	081	San Mateo County	103 621	06	29000	059	Orange County	165 196
06	17946		Dana Point city	35 110	06	29504		Gilroy city	41 464
06	17946	059	Orange County	35 110	06	29504	085	Santa Clara County	41 464
06	17988		Danville town	41 715	06	30000		Glendale city	194 973
06	17988	013	Contra Costa County	41 715	06	30000	037	Los Angeles County	194 973
06	18100		Davis city	60 308	06	30014		Glendora city	49 415
06	18100	113	Yolo County	60 308	06	30014	037	Los Angeles County	49 415
06	18394		Delano city	38 824	06	31960		Hanford city	41 686
06	18394	029	Kern County	38 824	06	31960	031	Kings County	41 686
06	19192		Diamond Bar city	56 287	06	32548		Hawthorne city	84 112
06	19192	037	Los Angeles County	56 287	06	32548	037	Los Angeles County	84 112
06	19766		Downey city	107 323	06	33000		Hayward city	140 030
06	19766	037	Los Angeles County	107 323	06	33000	001	Alameda County	140 030
06	20018		Dublin city	29 973	06	33182		Hemet city	58 812
06	20018	001	Alameda County	29 973	06	33182	065	Riverside County	58 812
06	20956		East Palo Alto city	29 506	06	33434		Hesperia city	62 582
06	20956	081	San Mateo County	29 506	06	33434	071	San Bernardino County	62 582
06	21712		El Cajon city	94 869	06	33588		Highland city	44 605
06	21712	073	San Diego County	94 869	06	33588	071	San Bernardino County	44 605
06	21782		El Centro city	37 835	06	34120		Hollister city	34 413
06	21782	025	Imperial County	37 835	06	34120	069	San Benito County	34 413
06	22230		El Monte city	115 965	06	36000		Huntington Beach city	189 594
06	22230	037	Los Angeles County	115 965	06	36000	059	Orange County	189 594
06	22678		Encinitas city	58 014	06	36056		Huntington Park city	61 348
06	22678	073	San Diego County	58 014	06	36056	037	Los Angeles County	61 348
06	22804		Escondido city	133 559	06	36294		Imperial Beach city	26 992
06	22804	073	San Diego County	133 559	06	36294	073	San Diego County	26 992
06	23042		Eureka city	26 128	06	36448		Indio city	49 116
06	23042	023	Humboldt County	26 128	06	36448	065	Riverside County	49 116
06	23182		Fairfield city	96 178	06	36546		Inglewood city	112 580
06	23182	095	Solano County	96 178	06	36546	037	Los Angeles County	112 580

State Code	Place Code	County Code	Geographic Area Name	2000 Population	State Code	Place Code	County Code	Geographic Area Name	2000 Population
06	36770		Irvine city	143 072	06	45778		Marina city	25 101
06	36770	059	Orange County	143 072	06	45778	053	Monterey County	25 101
06	39248		Laguna Niguel city	61 891	06	46114		Martinez city	35 866
06	39248	059	Orange County	61 891	06	46114	013	Contra Costa County	35 866
06	39290		La Habra city	58 974	06	46492		Maywood city	28 083
06	39290	059	Orange County	58 974	06	46492	037	Los Angeles County	28 083
06	39486		Lake Elsinore city	28 928	06	46870		Menlo Park city	30 785
06	39486	065	Riverside County	28 928	06	46870	081	San Mateo County	30 785
06	39496		Lake Forest city	58 707	06	46898		Merced city	63 893
06	39496	059	Orange County	58 707	06	46898	047	Merced County	63 893
06	39892		Lakewood city	79 345	06	47766		Milpitas city	62 698
06	39892	037	Los Angeles County	79 345	06	47766	085	Santa Clara County	62 698
06	40004		La Mesa city	54 749	06	48256		Mission Viejo city	93 102
06	40004	073	San Diego County	54 749	06	48256	059	Orange County	93 102
06	40032		La Mirada city	46 783	06	48354		Modesto city	188 856
06	40032	037	Los Angeles County	46 783	06	48354	099	Stanislaus County	188 856
06	40130		Lancaster city	118 718	06	48648		Monrovia city	36 929
06	40130	037	Los Angeles County	118 718	06	48648	037	Los Angeles County	36 929
06	40340		La Puente city	41 063	06	48788		Montclair city	33 049
06	40340	037	Los Angeles County	41 063	06	48788	071	San Bernardino County	33 049
06	40830		La Verne city	31 638	06	48816		Montebello city	62 150
06	40830	037	Los Angeles County	31 638	06	48816	037	Los Angeles County	62 150
06	40886		Lawndale city	31 711	06	48872		Monterey city	29 674
06	40886	037	Los Angeles County	31 711	06	48872	053	Monterey County	29 674
06	41992		Livermore city	73 345	06	48914		Monterey Park city	60 051
06	41992	001	Alameda County	73 345	06	48914	037	Los Angeles County	60 051
06	42202		Lodi city	56 999	06	49138		Moorpark city	31 415
06	42202	077	San Joaquin County	56 999	06	49138	111	Ventura County	31 415
06	42524		Lompoc city	41 103	06	49270		Moreno Valley city	142 381
06	42524	083	Santa Barbara County	41 103	06	49270	065	Riverside County	142 381
06	43000		Long Beach city	461 522	06	49278		Morgan Hill city	33 556
06	43000	037	Los Angeles County	461 522	06	49278	085	Santa Clara County	33 556
06	43280		Los Altos city	27 693	06	49670		Mountain View city	70 708
06	43280	085	Santa Clara County	27 693	06	49670	085	Santa Clara County	70 708
06	44000		Los Angeles city	3694 820	06	50076		Murrieta city	44 282
06	44000	037	Los Angeles County	3694 820	06	50076	065	Riverside County	44 282
06	44028		Los Banos city	25 869	06	50258		Napa city	72 585
06	44028	047	Merced County	25 869	06	50258	055	Napa County	72 585
06	44112		Los Gatos town	28 592	06	50398		National City city	54 260
06	44112	085	Santa Clara County	28 592	06	50398	073	San Diego County	54 260
06	44574		Lynwood city	69 845	06	50916		Newark city	42 471
06	44574	037	Los Angeles County	69 845	06	50916	001	Alameda County	42 471
06	45022		Madera city	43 207	06	51182		Newport Beach city	70 032
06	45022	039	Madera County	43 207	06	51182	059	Orange County	70 032
06	45400		Manhattan Beach city	33 852	06	52526		Norwalk city	103 298
06	45400	037	Los Angeles County	33 852	06	52526	037	Los Angeles County	103 298
06	45484		Manteca city	49 258	06	52582		Novato city	47 630
06	45484	077	San Joaquin County	49 258	06	52582	041	Marin County	47 630

State Code	Place Code	County Code	Geographic Area Name	2000 Population	State Code	Place Code	County Code	Geographic Area Name	2000 Population
06	53000		Oakland city	399 484	06	59514		Rancho Palos Verdes city	41 145
06	53000	001	Alameda County	399 484	06	59514	037	Los Angeles County	41 145
06	53322		Oceanside city	161 029	06	59920		Redding city	80 865
06	53322	073	San Diego County	161 029	06	59920	089	Shasta County	80 865
06	53896		Ontario city	158 007	06	59962		Redlands city	63 591
06	53896	071	San Bernardino County	158 007	06	59962	071	San Bernardino County	63 591
06	53980		Orange city	128 821	06	60018		Redondo Beach city	63 261
06	53980	059	Orange County	128 821	06	60018	037	Los Angeles County	63 261
06	54652		Oxnard city	170 358	06	60102		Redwood City city	75 402
06	54652	111	Ventura County	170 358	06	60102	081	San Mateo County	75 402
06	54806		Pacifica city	38 390	06	60466		Rialto city	91 873
06	54806	081	San Mateo County	38 390	06	60466	071	San Bernardino County	91 873
06	55156		Palmdale city	116 670	06	60620		Richmond city	99 216
06	55156	037	Los Angeles County	116 670	06	60620	013	Contra Costa County	99 216
06	55184		Palm Desert city	41 155	06	62000		Riverside city	255 166
06	55184	065	Riverside County	41 155	06	62000	065	Riverside County	255 166
06	55254		Palm Springs city	42 807	06	62364		Rocklin city	36 330
06	55254	065	Riverside County	42 807	06	62364	061	Placer County	36 330
06	55282		Palo Alto city	58 598	06	62546		Rohnert Park city	42 236
06	55282	085	Santa Clara County	58 598	06	62546	097	Sonoma County	42 236
06	55520		Paradise town	26 408	06	62896		Rosemead city	53 505
06	55520	007	Butte County	26 408	06	62896	037	Los Angeles County	53 505
06	55618		Paramount city	55 266	06	62938		Roseville city	79 921
06	55618	037	Los Angeles County	55 266	06	62938	061	Placer County	79 921
06	56000		Pasadena city	133 936	06	64000		Sacramento city	407 018
06	56000	037	Los Angeles County	133 936	06	64000	067	Sacramento County	407 018
06	56700		Perris city	36 189	06	64224		Salinas city	151 060
06	56700	065	Riverside County	36 189	06	64224	053	Monterey County	151 060
06	56784		Petaluma city	54 548	06	65000		San Bernardino city	185 401
06	56784	097	Sonoma County	54 548	06	65000	071	San Bernardino County	185 401
06	56924		Pico Rivera city	63 428	06	65028		San Bruno city	40 165
06	56924	037	Los Angeles County	63 428	06	65028	081	San Mateo County	40 165
06	57456		Pittsburg city	56 769	06	65042		San Buenaventura (Ventura) city	100 916
06	57456	013	Contra Costa County	56 769	06	65042	111	Ventura County	100 916
06	57526		Placentia city	46 488	06	65070		San Carlos city	27 718
06	57526	059	Orange County	46 488	06	65070	081	San Mateo County	27 718
06	57764		Pleasant Hill city	32 837	06	65084		San Clemente city	49 936
06	57764	013	Contra Costa County	32 837	06	65084	059	Orange County	49 936
06	57792		Pleasanton city	63 654	06	66000		San Diego city	1223 400
06	57792	001	Alameda County	63 654	06	66000	073	San Diego County	1223 400
06	58072		Pomona city	149 473	06	66070		San Dimas city	34 980
06	58072	037	Los Angeles County	149 473	06	66070	037	Los Angeles County	34 980
06	58240		Porterville city	39 615	06	67000		San Francisco city	776 733
06	58240	107	Tulare County	39 615	06	67000	075	San Francisco County	776 733
06	58520		Poway city	48 044	06	67042		San Gabriel city	39 804
06	58520	073	San Diego County	48 044	06	67042	037	Los Angeles County	39 804
06	59451		Rancho Cucamonga city	127 743	06	68000		San Jose city	894 943
06	59451	071	San Bernardino County	127 743	06	68000	085	Santa Clara County	894 943

State Code	Place Code	County Code	Geographic Area Name	2000 Population	State Code	Place Code	County Code	Geographic Area Name	2000 Population
06	68028		San Juan Capistrano city	33 826	06	75000		Stockton city	243 771
06	68028	059	Orange County	33 826	06	75000	077	San Joaquin County	243 771
06	68084		San Leandro city	79 452	06	75630		Suisun City city	26 118
06	68084	001	Alameda County	79 452	06	75630	095	Solano County	26 118
06	68154		San Luis Obispo city	44 174	06	77000		Sunnyvale city	131 760
06	68154	079	San Luis Obispo County	44 174	06	77000	085	Santa Clara County	131 760
06	68196		San Marcos city	54 977	06	78120		Temecula city	57 716
06	68196	073	San Diego County	54 977	06	78120	065	Riverside County	57 716
06	68252		San Mateo city	92 482	06	78148		Temple City city	33 377
06	68252	081	San Mateo County	92 482	06	78148	037	Los Angeles County	33 377
06	68294		San Pablo city	30 215	06	78582		Thousand Oaks city	117 005
06	68294	013	Contra Costa County	30 215	06	78582	111	Ventura County	117 005
06	68364		San Rafael city	56 063	06	80000		Torrance city	137 946
06	68364	041	Marin County	56 063	06	80000	037	Los Angeles County	137 946
06	68378		San Ramon city	44 722	06	80238		Tracy city	56 929
06	68378	013	Contra Costa County	44 722	06	80238	077	San Joaquin County	56 929
06	69000		Santa Ana city	337 977	06	80644		Tulare city	43 994
06	69000	059	Orange County	337 977	06	80644	107	Tulare County	43 994
06	69070		Santa Barbara city	92 325	06	80812		Turlock city	55 810
06	69070	083	Santa Barbara County	92 325	06	80812	099	Stanislaus County	55 810
06	69084		Santa Clara city	102 361	06	80854		Tustin city	67 504
06	69084	085	Santa Clara County	102 361	06	80854	059	Orange County	67 504
06	69088		Santa Clarita city	151 088	06	81204		Union City city	66 869
06	69088	037	Los Angeles County	151 088	06	81204	001	Alameda County	66 869
06	69112		Santa Cruz city	54 593	06	81344		Upland city	68 393
06	69112	087	Santa Cruz County	54 593	06	81344	071	San Bernardino County	68 393
06	69196		Santa Maria city	77 423	06	81554		Vacaville city	88 625
06	69196	083	Santa Barbara County	77 423	06	81554	095	Solano County	88 625
06	70000		Santa Monica city	84 084	06	81666		Vallejo city	116 760
06	70000	037	Los Angeles County	84 084	06	81666	095	Solano County	116 760
06	70042		Santa Paula city	28 598	06	82590		Victorville city	64 029
06	70042	111	Ventura County	28 598	06	82590	071	San Bernardino County	64 029
06	70098		Santa Rosa city	147 595	06	82954		Visalia city	91 565
06	70098	097	Sonoma County	147 595	06	82954	107	Tulare County	91 565
06	70224		Santee city	52 975	06	82996		Vista city	89 857
06	70224	073	San Diego County	52 975	06	82996	073	San Diego County	89 857
06	70280		Saratoga city	29 843	06	83332		Walnut city	30 004
06	70280	085	Santa Clara County	29 843	06	83332	037	Los Angeles County	30 004
06	70742		Seaside city	31 696	06	83346		Walnut Creek city	64 296
06	70742	053	Monterey County	31 696	06	83346	013	Contra Costa County	64 296
06	72016		Simi Valley city	111 351	06	83668		Watsonville city	44 265
06	72016	111	Ventura County	111 351	06	83668	087	Santa Cruz County	44 265
06	73080		South Gate city	96 375	06	84200		West Covina city	105 080
06	73080	037	Los Angeles County	96 375	06	84200	037	Los Angeles County	105 080
06	73262		South San Francisco city	60 552	06	84410		West Hollywood city	35 716
06	73262	081	San Mateo County	60 552	06	84410	037	Los Angeles County	35 716
06	73962		Stanton city	37 403	06	84550		Westminster city	88 207
06	73962	059	Orange County	37 403	06	84550	059	Orange County	88 207

State Code	Place Code	County Code	Geographic Area Name	2000 Population
06	84816		West Sacramento city	31 615
06	84816	113	Yolo County	31 615
06	85292		Whittier city	83 680
06	85292	037	Los Angeles County	83 680
06	86328		Woodland city	49 151
06	86328	113	Yolo County	49 151
06	86832		Yorba Linda city	58 918
06	86832	059	Orange County	58 918
06	86972		Yuba City city	36 758
06	86972	101	Sutter County	36 758
06	87042		Yucaipa city	41 207
06	87042	071	San Bernardino County	41 207
08			**COLORADO**	4 301 261
08	03455		Arvada city	102 153
08	03455	001	Adams County	2 847
08	03455	059	Jefferson County	99 306
08	04000		Aurora city	276 393
08	04000	001	Adams County	40 249
08	04000	005	Arapahoe County	236 144
08	04000	035	Douglas County	0
08	07850		Boulder city	94 673
08	07850	013	Boulder County	94 673
08	09280		Broomfield city	38 272
08	09280	001	Adams County	15 239
08	09280	013	Boulder County	21 474
08	09280	059	Jefferson County	1 549
08	09280	123	Weld County	10
08	16000		Colorado Springs city	360 890
08	16000	041	El Paso County	360 890
08	20000		Denver city	554 636
08	20000	031	Denver County	554 636
08	24785		Englewood city	31 727
08	24785	005	Arapahoe County	31 727
08	27425		Fort Collins city	118 652
08	27425	069	Larimer County	118 652
08	31660		Grand Junction city	41 986
08	31660	077	Mesa County	41 986
08	32155		Greeley city	76 930
08	32155	123	Weld County	76 930
08	43000		Lakewood city	144 126
08	43000	059	Jefferson County	144 126
08	45255		Littleton city	40 340
08	45255	005	Arapahoe County	40 168
08	45255	035	Douglas County	63
08	45255	059	Jefferson County	109
08	45970		Longmont city	71 093
08	45970	013	Boulder County	71 069
08	45970	123	Weld County	24
08	46465		Loveland city	50 608
08	46465	069	Larimer County	50 608
08	54330		Northglenn city	31 575
08	54330	001	Adams County	31 563
08	54330	123	Weld County	12
08	62000		Pueblo city	102 121
08	62000	101	Pueblo County	102 121
08	77290		Thornton city	82 384
08	77290	001	Adams County	82 384
08	77290	123	Weld County	0
08	83835		Westminster city	100 940
08	83835	001	Adams County	57 419
08	83835	059	Jefferson County	43 521
08	84440		Wheat Ridge city	32 913
08	84440	059	Jefferson County	32 913
09			**CONNECTICUT**	3 405 565
09	08000		Bridgeport city	139 529
09	08000	001	Fairfield County	139 529
09	08420		Bristol city	60 062
09	08420	003	Hartford County	60 062
09	18430		Danbury city	74 848
09	18430	001	Fairfield County	74 848
09	37000		Hartford city	121 578
09	37000	003	Hartford County	121 578
09	46450		Meriden city	58 244
09	46450	009	New Haven County	58 244
09	47290		Middletown city	43 167
09	47290	007	Middlesex County	43 167
09	47500		Milford city	52 305
09	49880		Naugatuck borough	30 989
09	49880	009	New Haven County	30 989
09	50370		New Britain city	71 538
09	50370	003	Hartford County	71 538
09	52000		New Haven city	123 626
09	52000	009	New Haven County	123 626
09	52280		New London city	25 671
09	52280	011	New London County	25 671
09	55990		Norwalk city	82 951
09	55990	001	Fairfield County	82 951
09	56200		Norwich city	36 117
09	56200	011	New London County	36 117
09	68100		Shelton city	38 101
09	68100	001	Fairfield County	38 101
09	73000		Stamford city	117 083
09	73000	001	Fairfield County	117 083
09	76500		Torrington city	35 202
09	76500	005	Litchfield County	35 202
09	80000		Waterbury city	107 271
09	80000	009	New Haven County	107 271
09	82800		West Haven city	52 360
09	82800	009	New Haven County	52 360

Cities by County — Continued

State Code	Place Code	County Code	Geographic Area Name	2000 Population	State Code	Place Code	County Code	Geographic Area Name	2000 Population
10			**DELAWARE**	783 600	12	25175		Gainesville city	95 447
10	21200		Dover city	32 135	12	25175	001	Alachua County	95 447
10	21200	001	Kent County	32 135					
					12	27322		Greenacres city	27 569
10	50670		Newark city	28 547	12	27322	099	Palm Beach County	27 569
10	50670	003	New Castle County	28 547					
					12	28450		Hallandale city	34 282
10	77580		Wilmington city	72 664	12	28450	011	Broward County	34 282
10	77580	003	New Castle County	72 664					
					12	30000		Hialeah city	226 419
11			**DISTRICT OF COLUMBIA**	572 059	12	30000	086	Miami-Dade County	226 419
11	50000		Washington city	572 059					
11	50000	001	District of Columbia	572 059	12	32000		Hollywood city	139 357
					12	32000	011	Broward County	139 357
12			**FLORIDA**	15 982 378					
12	00950		Altamonte Springs city	41 200	12	32275		Homestead city	31 909
12	00950	117	Seminole County	41 200	12	32275	086	Miami-Dade County	31 909
12	01700		Apopka city	26 642	12	35000		Jacksonville city	735 617
12	01700	095	Orange County	26 642	12	35000	031	Duval County	735 617
12	07300		Boca Raton city	74 764	12	35875		Jupiter town	39 328
12	07300	099	Palm Beach County	74 764	12	35875	099	Palm Beach County	39 328
12	07875		Boynton Beach city	60 389	12	36550		Key West city	25 478
12	07875	099	Palm Beach County	60 389	12	36550	087	Monroe County	25 478
12	07950		Bradenton city	49 504	12	36950		Kissimmee city	47 814
12	07950	081	Manatee County	49 504	12	36950	097	Osceola County	47 814
12	10275		Cape Coral city	102 286	12	38250		Lakeland city	78 452
12	10275	071	Lee County	102 286	12	38250	105	Polk County	78 452
12	12875		Clearwater city	108 787	12	39075		Lake Worth city	35 133
12	12875	103	Pinellas County	108 787	12	39075	099	Palm Beach County	35 133
12	13275		Coconut Creek city	43 566	12	39425		Largo city	69 371
12	13275	011	Broward County	43 566	12	39425	103	Pinellas County	69 371
12	14125		Cooper City city	27 939	12	39525		Lauderdale Lakes city	31 705
12	14125	011	Broward County	27 939	12	39525	011	Broward County	31 705
12	14250		Coral Gables city	42 249	12	39550		Lauderhill city	57 585
12	14250	086	Miami-Dade County	42 249	12	39550	011	Broward County	57 585
12	14400		Coral Springs city	117 549	12	43125		Margate city	53 909
12	14400	011	Broward County	117 549	12	43125	011	Broward County	53 909
12	16475		Davie town	75 720	12	43975		Melbourne city	71 382
12	16475	011	Broward County	75 720	12	43975	009	Brevard County	71 382
12	16525		Daytona Beach city	64 112	12	45000		Miami city	362 470
12	16525	127	Volusia County	64 112	12	45000	086	Miami-Dade County	362 470
12	16725		Deerfield Beach city	64 583	12	45025		Miami Beach city	87 933
12	16725	011	Broward County	64 583	12	45025	086	Miami-Dade County	87 933
12	17100		Delray Beach city	60 020	12	45975		Miramar city	72 739
12	17100	099	Palm Beach County	60 020	12	45975	011	Broward County	72 739
12	18575		Dunedin city	35 691	12	49425		North Lauderdale city	32 264
12	18575	103	Pinellas County	35 691	12	49425	011	Broward County	32 264
12	24000		Fort Lauderdale city	152 397	12	49450		North Miami city	59 880
12	24000	011	Broward County	152 397	12	49450	086	Miami-Dade County	59 880
12	24125		Fort Myers city	48 208	12	49475		North Miami Beach city	40 786
12	24125	071	Lee County	48 208	12	49475	086	Miami-Dade County	40 786
12	24300		Fort Pierce city	37 516	12	50575		Oakland Park city	30 966
12	24300	111	St. Lucie County	37 516	12	50575	011	Broward County	30 966

State Code	Place Code	County Code	Geographic Area Name	2000 Population	State Code	Place Code	County Code	Geographic Area Name	2000 Population
12	50750		Ocala city	45 943	12	76582		Weston city	49 286
12	50750	083	Marion County	45 943	12	76582	011	Broward County	49 286
12	53000		Orlando city	185 951	12	76600		West Palm Beach city	82 103
12	53000	095	Orange County	185 951	12	76600	099	Palm Beach County	82 103
12	53150		Ormond Beach city	36 301	12	78275		Winter Haven city	26 487
12	53150	127	Volusia County	36 301	12	78275	105	Polk County	26 487
12	53575		Oviedo city	26 316	12	78325		Winter Springs city	31 666
12	53575	117	Seminole County	26 316	12	78325	117	Seminole County	31 666
12	54000		Palm Bay city	79 413	13			**GEORGIA**	8 186 453
12	54000	009	Brevard County	79 413	13	01052		Albany city	76 939
12	54075		Palm Beach Gardens city	35 058	13	01052	095	Dougherty County	76 939
12	54075	099	Palm Beach County	35 058	13	01696		Alpharetta city	34 854
12	54700		Panama City city	36 417	13	01696	121	Fulton County	34 854
12	54700	005	Bay County	36 417	13	03436		Athens-Clarke County	101 489
12	55775		Pembroke Pines city	137 427	13	04000		Atlanta city	416 474
12	55775	011	Broward County	137 427	13	04000	089	DeKalb County	29 775
					13	04000	121	Fulton County	386 699
12	55925		Pensacola city	56 255					
12	55925	033	Escambia County	56 255	13	04200		Augusta-Richmond County	199 775
12	56975		Pinellas Park city	45 658	13	19000		Columbus city	186 291
12	56975	103	Pinellas County	45 658					
					13	21380		Dalton city	27 912
12	57425		Plantation city	82 934	13	21380	313	Whitfield County	27 912
12	57425	011	Broward County	82 934					
					13	25720		East Point city	39 595
12	57550		Plant City city	29 915	13	25720	121	Fulton County	39 595
12	57550	057	Hillsborough County	29 915					
					13	31908		Gainesville city	25 578
12	58050		Pompano Beach city	78 191	13	31908	139	Hall County	25 578
12	58050	011	Broward County	78 191					
					13	38964		Hinesville city	30 392
12	58575		Port Orange city	45 823	13	38964	179	Liberty County	30 392
12	58575	127	Volusia County	45 823					
					13	44340		LaGrange city	25 998
12	58715		Port St. Lucie city	88 769	13	44340	285	Troup County	25 998
12	58715	111	St. Lucie County	88 769					
					13	49000		Macon city	97 255
12	60975		Riviera Beach city	29 884	13	49000	021	Bibb County	96 777
12	60975	099	Palm Beach County	29 884	13	49000	169	Jones County	478
12	63000		St. Petersburg city	248 232	13	49756		Marietta city	58 748
12	63000	103	Pinellas County	248 232	13	49756	067	Cobb County	58 748
12	63650		Sanford city	38 291	13	59724		Peachtree City city	31 580
12	63650	117	Seminole County	38 291	13	59724	113	Fayette County	31 580
12	64175		Sarasota city	52 715	13	66668		Rome city	34 980
12	64175	115	Sarasota County	52 715	13	66668	115	Floyd County	34 980
12	69700		Sunrise city	85 779	13	67284		Roswell city	79 334
12	69700	011	Broward County	85 779	13	67284	121	Fulton County	79 334
12	70600		Tallahassee city	150 624	13	69000		Savannah city	131 510
12	70600	073	Leon County	150 624	13	69000	051	Chatham County	131 510
12	70675		Tamarac city	55 588	13	71492		Smyrna city	40 999
12	70675	011	Broward County	55 588	13	71492	067	Cobb County	40 999
12	71000		Tampa city	303 447	13	78800		Valdosta city	43 724
12	71000	057	Hillsborough County	303 447	13	78800	185	Lowndes County	43 724
12	71900		Titusville city	40 670	13	80508		Warner Robins city	48 804
12	71900	009	Brevard County	40 670	13	80508	153	Houston County	48 787
					13	80508	225	Peach County	17

Cities by County — Continued

State Code	Place Code	County Code	Geographic Area Name	2000 Population
15			**HAWAII**	1 211 537
15	14650		Hilo CDP	40 759
15	14650	001	Hawaii County	40 759
15	17000		Honolulu CDP	371 657
15	17000	003	Honolulu County	371 657
15	23150		Kailua CDP	36 513
15	23150	003	Honolulu County	36 513
15	28250		Kaneohe CDP	34 970
15	28250	003	Honolulu County	34 970
15	51050		Mililani Town CDP	28 608
15	51050	003	Honolulu County	28 608
15	62600		Pearl City CDP	30 976
15	62600	003	Honolulu County	30 976
15	77750		Waimalu CDP	29 371
15	77750	003	Honolulu County	29 371
15	79700		Waipahu CDP	33 108
15	79700	003	Honolulu County	33 108
16			**IDAHO**	1 293 953
16	08830		Boise City city	185 787
16	08830	001	Ada County	185 787
16	12250		Caldwell city	25 967
16	12250	027	Canyon County	25 967
16	16750		Coeur d'Alene city	34 514
16	16750	055	Kootenai County	34 514
16	39700		Idaho Falls city	50 730
16	39700	019	Bonneville County	50 730
16	46540		Lewiston city	30 904
16	46540	069	Nez Perce County	30 904
16	52120		Meridian city	34 919
16	52120	001	Ada County	34 919
16	56260		Nampa city	51 867
16	56260	027	Canyon County	51 867
16	64090		Pocatello city	51 466
16	64090	005	Bannock County	51 442
16	64090	077	Power County	24
16	82810		Twin Falls city	34 469
16	82810	083	Twin Falls County	34 469
17			**ILLINOIS**	12 419 293
17	00243		Addison village	35 914
17	00243	043	DuPage County	35 914
17	01114		Alton city	30 496
17	01114	119	Madison County	30 496
17	02154		Arlington Heights village	76 031
17	02154	031	Cook County	76 031
17	02154	097	Lake County	0
17	03012		Aurora city	142 990
17	03012	043	DuPage County	38 905
17	03012	089	Kane County	100 290
17	03012	093	Kendall County	840
17	03012	197	Will County	2 955
17	04013		Bartlett village	36 706
17	04013	031	Cook County	12 196
17	04013	043	DuPage County	24 508
17	04013	089	Kane County	2
17	04845		Belleville city	41 410
17	04845	163	St. Clair County	41 410
17	05573		Berwyn city	54 016
17	05573	031	Cook County	54 016
17	06613		Bloomington city	64 808
17	06613	113	McLean County	64 808
17	07133		Bolingbrook village	56 321
17	07133	043	DuPage County	1 748
17	07133	197	Will County	54 573
17	09447		Buffalo Grove village	42 909
17	09447	031	Cook County	14 418
17	09447	097	Lake County	28 491
17	09642		Burbank city	27 902
17	09642	031	Cook County	27 902
17	10487		Calumet City city	39 071
17	10487	031	Cook County	39 071
17	11332		Carol Stream village	40 438
17	11332	043	DuPage County	40 438
17	11358		Carpentersville village	30 586
17	11358	089	Kane County	30 586
17	12385		Champaign city	67 518
17	12385	019	Champaign County	67 518
17	14000		Chicago city	2896 016
17	14000	031	Cook County	2896 014
17	14000	043	DuPage County	2
17	14026		Chicago Heights city	32 776
17	14026	031	Cook County	32 776
17	14351		Cicero town	85 616
17	14351	031	Cook County	85 616
17	17887		Crystal Lake city	38 000
17	17887	111	McHenry County	38 000
17	18563		Danville city	33 904
17	18563	183	Vermilion County	33 904
17	18823		Decatur city	81 860
17	18823	115	Macon County	81 860
17	19161		DeKalb city	39 018
17	19161	037	DeKalb County	39 018
17	19642		Des Plaines city	58 720
17	19642	031	Cook County	58 720
17	20292		Dolton village	25 614
17	20292	031	Cook County	25 614
17	20591		Downers Grove village	48 724
17	20591	043	DuPage County	48 724
17	22255		East St. Louis city	31 542
17	22255	163	St. Clair County	31 542

State Code	Place Code	County Code	Geographic Area Name	2000 Population	State Code	Place Code	County Code	Geographic Area Name	2000 Population
17	23074		Elgin city	94 487	17	51089		Mount Prospect village	56 265
17	23074	031	Cook County	20 474	17	51089	031	Cook County	56 265
17	23074	089	Kane County	74 013					
					17	51349		Mundelein village	30 935
17	23256		Elk Grove Village village	34 727	17	51349	097	Lake County	30 935
17	23256	031	Cook County	34 727					
17	23256	043	DuPage County	0	17	51622		Naperville city	128 358
					17	51622	043	DuPage County	90 984
17	23620		Elmhurst city	42 762	17	51622	197	Will County	37 374
17	23620	031	Cook County	0					
17	23620	043	DuPage County	42 762	17	53000		Niles village	30 068
					17	53000	031	Cook County	30 068
17	23724		Elmwood Park village	25 405					
17	23724	031	Cook County	25 405	17	53234		Normal town	45 386
					17	53234	113	McLean County	45 386
17	24582		Evanston city	74 239					
17	24582	031	Cook County	74 239	17	53481		Northbrook village	33 435
					17	53481	031	Cook County	33 435
17	27884		Freeport city	26 443					
17	27884	177	Stephenson County	26 443	17	53559		North Chicago city	35 918
					17	53559	097	Lake County	35 918
17	28326		Galesburg city	33 706					
17	28326	095	Knox County	33 706	17	54638		Oak Forest city	28 051
					17	54638	031	Cook County	28 051
17	29730		Glendale Heights village	31 765					
17	29730	043	DuPage County	31 765	17	54820		Oak Lawn village	55 245
					17	54820	031	Cook County	55 245
17	29756		Glen Ellyn village	26 999					
17	29756	043	DuPage County	26 999	17	54885		Oak Park village	52 524
					17	54885	031	Cook County	52 524
17	29938		Glenview village	41 847					
17	29938	031	Cook County	41 847	17	56640		Orland Park village	51 077
					17	56640	031	Cook County	51 071
17	30926		Granite City city	31 301	17	56640	197	Will County	6
17	30926	119	Madison County	31 301					
					17	57225		Palatine village	65 479
17	32018		Gurnee village	28 834	17	57225	031	Cook County	65 479
17	32018	097	Lake County	28 834					
					17	57875		Park Ridge city	37 775
17	32746		Hanover Park village	38 278	17	57875	031	Cook County	37 775
17	32746	031	Cook County	20 755					
17	32746	043	DuPage County	17 523	17	58447		Pekin city	33 857
					17	58447	143	Peoria County	0
17	33383		Harvey city	30 000	17	58447	179	Tazewell County	33 857
17	33383	031	Cook County	30 000					
					17	59000		Peoria city	112 936
17	34722		Highland Park city	31 365	17	59000	143	Peoria County	112 936
17	34722	097	Lake County	31 365					
					17	62367		Quincy city	40 366
17	35411		Hoffman Estates village	49 495	17	62367	001	Adams County	40 366
17	35411	031	Cook County	49 495					
17	35411	089	Kane County	0	17	65000		Rockford city	150 115
					17	65000	201	Winnebago County	150 115
17	38570		Joliet city	106 221					
17	38570	093	Kendall County	624	17	65078		Rock Island city	39 684
17	38570	197	Will County	105 597	17	65078	161	Rock Island County	39 684
17	38934		Kankakee city	27 491	17	66040		Round Lake Beach village	25 859
17	38934	091	Kankakee County	27 491	17	66040	097	Lake County	25 859
17	42028		Lansing village	28 332	17	66703		St. Charles city	27 896
17	42028	031	Cook County	28 332	17	66703	043	DuPage County	169
					17	66703	089	Kane County	27 727
17	44407		Lombard village	42 322					
17	44407	043	DuPage County	42 322	17	68003		Schaumburg village	75 386
					17	68003	031	Cook County	75 386
17	47774		Maywood village	26 987	17	68003	043	DuPage County	0
17	47774	031	Cook County	26 987					
					17	70122		Skokie village	63 348
17	49867		Moline city	43 768	17	70122	031	Cook County	63 348
17	49867	161	Rock Island County	43 768					

State Code	Place Code	County Code	Geographic Area Name	2000 Population	State Code	Place Code	County Code	Geographic Area Name	2000 Population
17	72000		Springfield city	111 454	18	34114		Hobart city	25 363
17	72000	167	Sangamon County	111 454	18	34114	089	Lake County	25 363
17	73157		Streamwood village	36 407	18	36000		Indianapolis city	791 926
17	73157	031	Cook County	36 407					
					18	38358		Jeffersonville city	27 362
17	75484		Tinley Park village	48 401	18	38358	019	Clark County	27 362
17	75484	031	Cook County	45 887					
17	75484	197	Will County	2 514	18	40392		Kokomo city	46 113
17	77005		Urbana city	36 395	18	40392	067	Howard County	46 113
17	77005	019	Champaign County	36 395	18	40788		Lafayette city	56 397
17	79293		Waukegan city	87 901	18	40788	157	Tippecanoe County	56 397
17	79293	097	Lake County	87 901					
					18	42426		Lawrence city	38 915
17	81048		Wheaton city	55 416	18	42426	097	Marion County	38 915
17	81048	043	DuPage County	55 416					
					18	46908		Marion city	31 320
17	81087		Wheeling village	34 496	18	46908	053	Grant County	31 320
17	81087	031	Cook County	34 496					
17	81087	097	Lake County	0	18	48528		Merrillville town	30 560
					18	48528	089	Lake County	30 560
17	82075		Wilmette village	27 651					
17	82075	031	Cook County	27 651	18	48798		Michigan City city	32 900
					18	48798	091	LaPorte County	32 900
17	83245		Woodridge village	30 934					
17	83245	031	Cook County	0	18	49932		Mishawaka city	46 557
17	83245	043	DuPage County	30 934	18	49932	141	St. Joseph County	46 557
17	83245	197	Will County	0					
					18	51876		Muncie city	67 430
18			**INDIANA**	6 080 485	18	51876	035	Delaware County	67 430
18	01468		Anderson city	59 734					
18	01468	095	Madison County	59 734	18	52326		New Albany city	37 603
					18	52326	043	Floyd County	37 603
18	05860		Bloomington city	69 291					
18	05860	105	Monroe County	69 291	18	54180		Noblesville city	28 590
					18	54180	057	Hamilton County	28 590
18	10342		Carmel city	37 733					
18	10342	057	Hamilton County	37 733	18	61092		Portage city	33 496
					18	61092	127	Porter County	33 496
18	14734		Columbus city	39 059					
18	14734	005	Bartholomew County	39 059	18	64260		Richmond city	39 124
					18	64260	177	Wayne County	39 124
18	19486		East Chicago city	32 414					
18	19486	089	Lake County	32 414	18	71000		South Bend city	107 789
					18	71000	141	St. Joseph County	107 789
18	20728		Elkhart city	51 874					
18	20728	039	Elkhart County	51 874	18	75428		Terre Haute city	59 614
					18	75428	167	Vigo County	59 614
18	22000		Evansville city	121 582					
18	22000	163	Vanderburgh County	121 582	18	78326		Valparaiso city	27 428
					18	78326	127	Porter County	27 428
18	23278		Fishers town	37 835					
18	23278	057	Hamilton County	37 835	18	82862		West Lafayette city	28 778
					18	82862	157	Tippecanoe County	28 778
18	25000		Fort Wayne city	205 727					
18	25000	003	Allen County	205 727	19			**IOWA**	2 926 324
					19	01855		Ames city	50 731
18	27000		Gary city	102 746	19	01855	169	Story County	50 731
18	27000	089	Lake County	102 746					
					19	02305		Ankeny city	27 117
18	28386		Goshen city	29 383	19	02305	153	Polk County	27 117
18	28386	039	Elkhart County	29 383					
					19	06355		Bettendorf city	31 275
18	29898		Greenwood city	36 037	19	06355	163	Scott County	31 275
18	29898	081	Johnson County	36 037					
					19	09550		Burlington city	26 839
18	31000		Hammond city	83 048	19	09550	057	Des Moines County	26 839
18	31000	089	Lake County	83 048					
					19	11755		Cedar Falls city	36 145
					19	11755	013	Black Hawk County	36 145

State Code	Place Code	County Code	Geographic Area Name	2000 Population	State Code	Place Code	County Code	Geographic Area Name	2000 Population
19	12000		Cedar Rapids city	120 758					
19	12000	113	Linn County	120 758	20	39350		Lenexa city	40 238
					20	39350	091	Johnson County	40 238
19	14430		Clinton city	27 772					
19	14430	045	Clinton County	27 772	20	44250		Manhattan city	44 831
					20	44250	149	Pottawatomie County	3
19	16860		Council Bluffs city	58 268	20	44250	161	Riley County	44 828
19	16860	155	Pottawattamie County	58 268					
					20	52575		Olathe city	92 962
19	19000		Davenport city	98 359	20	52575	091	Johnson County	92 962
19	19000	163	Scott County	98 359					
					20	53775		Overland Park city	149 080
19	21000		Des Moines city	198 682	20	53775	091	Johnson County	149 080
19	21000	153	Polk County	198 682					
					20	62700		Salina city	45 679
19	22395		Dubuque city	57 686	20	62700	169	Saline County	45 679
19	22395	061	Dubuque County	57 686					
					20	64500		Shawnee city	47 996
19	28515		Fort Dodge city	25 136	20	64500	091	Johnson County	47 996
19	28515	187	Webster County	25 136					
					20	71000		Topeka city	122 377
19	38595		Iowa City city	62 220	20	71000	177	Shawnee County	122 377
19	38595	103	Johnson County	62 220					
					20	79000		Wichita city	344 284
19	49485		Marion city	26 294	20	79000	173	Sedgwick County	344 284
19	49485	113	Linn County	26 294					
					21			**KENTUCKY**	4 041 769
19	49755		Marshalltown city	26 009	21	08902		Bowling Green city	49 296
19	49755	127	Marshall County	26 009	21	08902	227	Warren County	49 296
19	50160		Mason City city	29 172	21	17848		Covington city	43 370
19	50160	033	Cerro Gordo County	29 172	21	17848	117	Kenton County	43 370
19	73335		Sioux City city	85 013	21	28900		Frankfort city	27 741
19	73335	149	Plymouth County	0	21	28900	073	Franklin County	27 741
19	73335	193	Woodbury County	85 013					
					21	35866		Henderson city	27 373
19	79950		Urbandale city	29 072	21	35866	101	Henderson County	27 373
19	79950	049	Dallas County	327					
19	79950	153	Polk County	28 745	21	37918		Hopkinsville city	30 089
					21	37918	047	Christian County	30 089
19	82425		Waterloo city	68 747					
19	82425	013	Black Hawk County	68 747	21	40222		Jeffersontown city	26 633
					21	40222	111	Jefferson County	26 633
19	83910		West Des Moines city	46 403					
19	83910	049	Dallas County	3 878	21	46027		Lexington-Fayette	260 512
19	83910	153	Polk County	42 525	21	46027	067	Fayette County	260 512
20			**KANSAS**	2 688 418	21	48000		Louisville city	256 231
20	18250		Dodge City city	25 176	21	48000	111	Jefferson County	256 231
20	18250	057	Ford County	25 176					
					21	58620		Owensboro city	54 067
20	21275		Emporia city	26 760	21	58620	059	Daviess County	54 067
20	21275	111	Lyon County	26 760					
					21	58836		Paducah city	26 307
20	25325		Garden City city	28 451	21	58836	145	McCracken County	26 307
20	25325	055	Finney County	28 451					
					21	65226		Richmond city	27 152
20	33625		Hutchinson city	40 787	21	65226	151	Madison County	27 152
20	33625	155	Reno County	40 787					
					22			**LOUISIANA**	4 468 976
20	36000		Kansas City city	146 866	22	00975		Alexandria city	46 342
20	36000	209	Wyandotte County	146 866	22	00975	079	Rapides Parish	46 342
20	38900		Lawrence city	80 098	22	05000		Baton Rouge city	227 818
20	38900	045	Douglas County	80 098	22	05000	033	East Baton Rouge Parish	227 818
20	39000		Leavenworth city	35 420	22	08920		Bossier City city	56 461
20	39000	103	Leavenworth County	35 420	22	08920	015	Bossier Parish	56 461
20	39075		Leawood city	27 656	22	36255		Houma city	32 393
20	39075	091	Johnson County	27 656	22	36255	109	Terrebonne Parish	32 393

State Code	Place Code	County Code	Geographic Area Name	2000 Population	State Code	Place Code	County Code	Geographic Area Name	2000 Population
					25	07000		Boston city................................	589 141
22	39475		Kenner city....................................	70 517	25	07000	025	Suffolk County............................	589 141
22	39475	051	Jefferson Parish..........................	70 517					
					25	09000		Brockton city...............................	94 304
22	40735		Lafayette city................................	110 257	25	09000	023	Plymouth County	94 304
22	40735	055	Lafayette Parish...........................	110 257					
					25	11000		Cambridge city	101 355
22	41155		Lake Charles city.........................	71 757	25	11000	017	Middlesex County	101 355
22	41155	019	Calcasieu Parish.........................	71 757					
					25	13205		Chelsea city................................	35 080
22	51410		Monroe city..................................	53 107	25	13205	025	Suffolk County............................	35 080
22	51410	073	Ouachita Parish...........................	53 107					
					25	13660		Chicopee city..............................	54 653
22	54035		New Iberia city.............................	32 623	25	13660	013	Hampden County........................	54 653
22	54035	045	Iberia Parish................................	32 623					
					25	21990		Everett city..................................	38 037
22	55000		New Orleans city..........................	484 674	25	21990	017	Middlesex County	38 037
22	55000	071	Orleans Parish.............................	484 674					
					25	23000		Fall River city..............................	91 938
22	70000		Shreveport city	200 145	25	23000	005	Bristol County	91 938
22	70000	015	Bossier Parish..............................	734					
22	70000	017	Caddo Parish................................	199 411	25	23875		Fitchburg city..............................	39 102
					25	23875	027	Worcester County	39 102
22	70805		Slidell city	25 695					
22	70805	103	St. Tammany Parish..................	25 695	25	25100		Franklin city	29 560
23			**MAINE**................................	1 274 923	25	25100	021	Norfolk County............................	29 560
23	02795		Bangor city..................................	31 473					
23	02795	019	Penobscot County	31 473	25	26150		Gloucester city............................	30 273
					25	26150	009	Essex County.............................	30 273
23	38740		Lewiston city................................	35 690					
23	38740	001	Androscoggin County	35 690	25	29405		Haverhill city...............................	58 969
					25	29405	009	Essex County.............................	58 969
23	60545		Portland city................................	64 249					
23	60545	005	Cumberland County....................	64 249	25	30840		Holyoke city................................	39 838
					25	30840	013	Hampden County........................	39 838
24			**MARYLAND**............................	5 296 486	25	34550		Lawrence city	72 043
24	01600		Annapolis city	35 838	25	34550	009	Essex County.............................	72 043
24	01600	003	Anne Arundel County	35 838					
					25	35075		Leominster city	41 303
24	04000		Baltimore city..............................	651 154	25	35075	027	Worcester County	41 303
24	04000	510	Baltimore city	651 154					
					25	37000		Lowell city...................................	105 167
24	08775		Bowie city....................................	50 269	25	37000	017	Middlesex County	105 167
24	08775	033	Prince George's County	50 269					
					25	37490		Lynn city.....................................	89 050
24	30325		Frederick city	52 767	25	37490	009	Essex County.............................	89 050
24	30325	021	Frederick County	52 767					
					25	37875		Malden city.................................	56 340
24	31175		Gaithersburg city	52 613	25	37875	017	Middlesex County	56 340
24	31175	031	Montgomery County	52 613					
					25	38715		Marlborough city.........................	36 255
24	36075		Hagerstown city	36 687	25	38715	017	Middlesex County	36 255
24	36075	043	Washington County	36 687					
					25	39835		Medford city................................	55 765
24	67675		Rockville city...............................	47 388	25	39835	017	Middlesex County	55 765
24	67675	031	Montgomery County	47 388					
					25	40115		Melrose city................................	27 134
25			**MASSACHUSETTS**................	6 349 097	25	40115	017	Middlesex County	27 134
25	00765		Agawam city................................	28 144					
25	00765	013	Hampden County.....................	28 144	25	40710		Methuen city...............................	43 789
					25	40710	009	Essex County.............................	43 789
25	02690		Attleboro city...............................	42 068					
25	02690	005	Bristol County	42 068	25	45000		New Bedford city.........................	93 768
					25	45000	005	Bristol County	93 768
25	03600		Barnstable Town city...................	47 821					
25	03600	001	Barnstable County	47 821	25	45560		Newton city.................................	83 829
					25	45560	017	Middlesex County	83 829
25	05595		Beverly city.................................	39 862					
25	05595	009	Essex County.............................	39 862	25	46330		Northampton city	28 978
					25	46330	015	Hampshire County.....................	28 978

State Code	Place Code	County Code	Geographic Area Name	2000 Population	State Code	Place Code	County Code	Geographic Area Name	2000 Population
25	52490		Peabody city	48 129	26	29000		Flint city	124 943
25	52490	009	Essex County	48 129	26	29000	049	Genesee County	124 943
25	53960		Pittsfield city	45 793	26	31420		Garden City city	30 047
25	53960	003	Berkshire County	45 793	26	31420	163	Wayne County	30 047
25	55745		Quincy city	88 025	26	34000		Grand Rapids city	197 800
25	55745	021	Norfolk County	88 025	26	34000	081	Kent County	197 800
25	56585		Revere city	47 283	26	38640		Holland city	35 048
25	56585	025	Suffolk County	47 283	26	38640	005	Allegan County	7 202
					26	38640	139	Ottawa County	27 846
25	59105		Salem city	40 407					
25	59105	009	Essex County	40 407	26	40680		Inkster city	30 115
					26	40680	163	Wayne County	30 115
25	62535		Somerville city	77 478					
25	62535	017	Middlesex County	77 478	26	41420		Jackson city	36 316
					26	41420	075	Jackson County	36 316
25	67000		Springfield city	152 082					
25	67000	013	Hampden County	152 082	26	42160		Kalamazoo city	77 145
					26	42160	077	Kalamazoo County	77 145
25	69170		Taunton city	55 976					
25	69170	005	Bristol County	55 976	26	42820		Kentwood city	45 255
					26	42820	081	Kent County	45 255
25	72600		Waltham city	59 226					
25	72600	017	Middlesex County	59 226	26	46000		Lansing city	119 128
					26	46000	045	Eaton County	4 807
25	76030		Westfield city	40 072	26	46000	065	Ingham County	114 321
25	76030	013	Hampden County	40 072					
					26	47800		Lincoln Park city	40 008
25	81035		Woburn city	37 258	26	47800	163	Wayne County	40 008
25	81035	017	Middlesex County	37 258					
					26	49000		Livonia city	100 545
25	82000		Worcester city	172 648	26	49000	163	Wayne County	100 545
25	82000	027	Worcester County	172 648					
					26	50560		Madison Heights city	31 101
26			**MICHIGAN**	9 938 444	26	50560	125	Oakland County	31 101
26	01380		Allen Park city	29 376					
26	01380	163	Wayne County	29 376	26	53780		Midland city	41 685
					26	53780	017	Bay County	222
26	03000		Ann Arbor city	114 024	26	53780	111	Midland County	41 463
26	03000	161	Washtenaw County	114 024					
					26	56020		Mount Pleasant city	25 946
26	05920		Battle Creek city	53 364	26	56020	073	Isabella County	25 946
26	05920	025	Calhoun County	53 364					
					26	56320		Muskegon city	40 105
26	06020		Bay City city	36 817	26	56320	121	Muskegon County	40 105
26	06020	017	Bay County	36 817					
					26	59440		Novi city	47 386
26	12060		Burton city	30 308	26	59440	125	Oakland County	47 386
26	12060	049	Genesee County	30 308					
					26	59920		Oak Park city	29 793
26	21000		Dearborn city	97 775	26	59920	125	Oakland County	29 793
26	21000	163	Wayne County	97 775					
					26	65440		Pontiac city	66 337
26	21020		Dearborn Heights city	58 264	26	65440	125	Oakland County	66 337
26	21020	163	Wayne County	58 264					
					26	65560		Portage city	44 897
26	22000		Detroit city	951 270	26	65560	077	Kalamazoo County	44 897
26	22000	163	Wayne County	951 270					
					26	65820		Port Huron city	32 338
26	24120		East Lansing city	46 525	26	65820	147	St. Clair County	32 338
26	24120	037	Clinton County	34					
26	24120	065	Ingham County	46 491	26	69035		Rochester Hills city	68 825
					26	69035	125	Oakland County	68 825
26	24290		Eastpointe city	34 077					
26	24290	099	Macomb County	34 077	26	69800		Roseville city	48 129
					26	69800	099	Macomb County	48 129
26	27440		Farmington Hills city	82 111					
26	27440	125	Oakland County	82 111	26	70040		Royal Oak city	60 062
					26	70040	125	Oakland County	60 062

State Code	Place Code	County Code	Geographic Area Name	2000 Population	State Code	Place Code	County Code	Geographic Area Name	2000 Population
26	70520		Saginaw city	61 799	27	18188		Edina city	47 425
26	70520	145	Saginaw County	61 799	27	18188	053	Hennepin County	47 425
26	70760		St. Clair Shores city	63 096	27	22814		Fridley city	27 449
26	70760	099	Macomb County	63 096	27	22814	003	Anoka County	27 449
26	74900		Southfield city	78 296	27	31076		Inver Grove Heights city	29 751
26	74900	125	Oakland County	78 296	27	31076	037	Dakota County	29 751
26	74960		Southgate city	30 136	27	35180		Lakeville city	43 128
26	74960	163	Wayne County	30 136	27	35180	037	Dakota County	43 128
26	76460		Sterling Heights city	124 471	27	39878		Mankato city	32 427
26	76460	099	Macomb County	124 471	27	39878	013	Blue Earth County	32 427
					27	39878	079	Le Sueur County	0
26	79000		Taylor city	65 868	27	39878	103	Nicollet County	0
26	79000	163	Wayne County	65 868					
					27	40166		Maple Grove city	50 365
26	80700		Troy city	80 959	27	40166	053	Hennepin County	50 365
26	80700	125	Oakland County	80 959					
					27	40382		Maplewood city	34 947
26	84000		Warren city	138 247	27	40382	123	Ramsey County	34 947
26	84000	099	Macomb County	138 247					
					27	43000		Minneapolis city	382 618
26	86000		Westland city	86 602	27	43000	053	Hennepin County	382 618
26	86000	163	Wayne County	86 602					
					27	43252		Minnetonka city	51 301
26	88900		Wyandotte city	28 006	27	43252	053	Hennepin County	51 301
26	88900	163	Wayne County	28 006					
					27	43864		Moorhead city	32 177
26	88940		Wyoming city	69 368	27	43864	027	Clay County	32 177
26	88940	081	Kent County	69 368					
					27	47680		Oakdale city	26 653
27			**MINNESOTA**	4 919 479	27	47680	163	Washington County	26 653
27	01486		Andover city	26 588					
27	01486	003	Anoka County	26 588	27	51730		Plymouth city	65 894
					27	51730	053	Hennepin County	65 894
27	01900		Apple Valley city	45 527					
27	01900	037	Dakota County	45 527	27	54214		Richfield city	34 439
					27	54214	053	Hennepin County	34 439
27	06382		Blaine city	44 942					
27	06382	003	Anoka County	44 942	27	54880		Rochester city	85 806
27	06382	123	Ramsey County	0	27	54880	109	Olmsted County	85 806
27	06616		Bloomington city	85 172	27	55852		Roseville city	33 690
27	06616	053	Hennepin County	85 172	27	55852	123	Ramsey County	33 690
27	07948		Brooklyn Center city	29 172	27	56896		St. Cloud city	59 107
27	07948	053	Hennepin County	29 172	27	56896	009	Benton County	6 391
					27	56896	141	Sherburne County	5 982
27	07966		Brooklyn Park city	67 388	27	56896	145	Stearns County	46 734
27	07966	053	Hennepin County	67 388					
					27	57220		St. Louis Park city	44 126
27	08794		Burnsville city	60 220	27	57220	053	Hennepin County	44 126
27	08794	037	Dakota County	60 220					
					27	58000		St. Paul city	287 151
27	13114		Coon Rapids city	61 607	27	58000	123	Ramsey County	287 151
27	13114	003	Anoka County	61 607					
					27	59998		Shoreview city	25 924
27	13456		Cottage Grove city	30 582	27	59998	123	Ramsey County	25 924
27	13456	163	Washington County	30 582					
					27	71032		Winona city	27 069
27	17000		Duluth city	86 918	27	71032	169	Winona County	27 069
27	17000	137	St. Louis County	86 918					
					27	71428		Woodbury city	46 463
27	17288		Eagan city	63 557	27	71428	163	Washington County	46 463
27	17288	037	Dakota County	63 557					
					28			**MISSISSIPPI**	2 844 658
27	18116		Eden Prairie city	54 901	28	06220		Biloxi city	50 644
27	18116	053	Hennepin County	54 901	28	06220	047	Harrison County	50 644

Cities by County — Continued

State Code	Place Code	County Code	Geographic Area Name	2000 Population	State Code	Place Code	County Code	Geographic Area Name	2000 Population
28	15380		Columbus city	25 944	29	38000		Kansas City city	441 545
28	15380	087	Lowndes County	25 944	29	38000	037	Cass County	104
					29	38000	047	Clay County	84 009
28	29180		Greenville city	41 633	29	38000	095	Jackson County	322 806
28	29180	151	Washington County	41 633	29	38000	165	Platte County	34 626
28	29700		Gulfport city	71 127	29	39044		Kirkwood city	27 324
28	29700	047	Harrison County	71 127	29	39044	189	St. Louis County	27 324
28	31020		Hattiesburg city	44 779	29	41348		Lee's Summit city	70 700
28	31020	035	Forrest County	42 475	29	41348	037	Cass County	1 180
28	31020	073	Lamar County	2 304	29	41348	095	Jackson County	69 520
28	36000		Jackson city	184 256	29	42032		Liberty city	26 232
28	36000	049	Hinds County	183 723	29	42032	047	Clay County	26 232
28	36000	089	Madison County	533					
28	36000	121	Rankin County	0	29	46586		Maryland Heights city	25 756
					29	46586	189	St. Louis County	25 756
28	46640		Meridian city	39 968					
28	46640	075	Lauderdale County	39 968	29	54074		O'Fallon city	46 169
					29	54074	183	St. Charles County	46 169
28	55360		Pascagoula city	26 200					
28	55360	059	Jackson County	26 200	29	60788		Raytown city	30 388
					29	60788	095	Jackson County	30 388
28	69280		Southaven city	28 977					
28	69280	033	DeSoto County	28 977	29	64082		St. Charles city	60 321
					29	64082	183	St. Charles County	60 321
28	74840		Tupelo city	34 211					
28	74840	081	Lee County	34 211	29	64550		St. Joseph city	73 990
					29	64550	021	Buchanan County	73 990
28	76720		Vicksburg city	26 407					
28	76720	149	Warren County	26 407	29	65000		St. Louis city	348 189
					29	65000	510	St. Louis city	348 189
29			**MISSOURI**	5 595 211					
29	03160		Ballwin city	31 283	29	65126		St. Peters city	51 381
29	03160	189	St. Louis County	31 283	29	65126	183	St. Charles County	51 381
29	06652		Blue Springs city	48 080	29	70000		Springfield city	151 580
29	06652	095	Jackson County	48 080	29	70000	043	Christian County	4
					29	70000	077	Greene County	151 576
29	11242		Cape Girardeau city	35 349					
29	11242	031	Cape Girardeau County	35 349	29	75220		University City city	37 428
29	11242	201	Scott County	0	29	75220	189	St. Louis County	37 428
29	13600		Chesterfield city	46 802	29	79820		Wildwood city	32 884
29	13600	189	St. Louis County	46 802	29	79820	189	St. Louis County	32 884
29	15670		Columbia city	84 531	30			**MONTANA**	902 195
29	15670	019	Boone County	84 531	30	06550		Billings city	89 847
					30	06550	111	Yellowstone County	89 847
29	24778		Florissant city	50 497					
29	24778	189	St. Louis County	50 497	30	08950		Bozeman city	27 509
					30	08950	031	Gallatin County	27 509
29	27190		Gladstone city	26 365					
29	27190	047	Clay County	26 365	30	11390		Butte-Silver Bow	34 606
29	31276		Hazelwood city	26 206	30	32800		Great Falls city	56 690
29	31276	189	St. Louis County	26 206	30	32800	013	Cascade County	56 690
29	35000		Independence city	113 288	30	35600		Helena city	25 780
29	35000	047	Clay County	0	30	35600	049	Lewis and Clark County	25 780
29	35000	095	Jackson County	113 288					
					30	50200		Missoula city	57 053
29	37000		Jefferson City city	39 636	30	50200	063	Missoula County	57 053
29	37000	027	Callaway County	25					
29	37000	051	Cole County	39 611	31			**NEBRASKA**	1 711 263
					31			Bellevue city	44 382
29	37592		Joplin city	45 504	31	03950	153	Sarpy County	44 382
29	37592	097	Jasper County	40 433					
29	37592	145	Newton County	5 071	31	17670		Fremont city	25 174
					31	17670	053	Dodge County	25 174

Appendix E

E-17

State Code	Place Code	County Code	Geographic Area Name	2000 Population	State Code	Place Code	County Code	Geographic Area Name	2000 Population
31	19595		Grand Island city	42 940	34	22470		Fair Lawn borough	31 637
31	19595	079	Hall County	42 940	34	22470	003	Bergen County	31 637
31	25055		Kearney city	27 431	34	24420		Fort Lee borough	35 461
31	25055	019	Buffalo County	27 431	34	24420	003	Bergen County	35 461
31	28000		Lincoln city	225 581	34	25770		Garfield city	29 786
31	28000	109	Lancaster County	225 581	34	25770	003	Bergen County	29 786
31	37000		Omaha city	390 007	34	28680		Hackensack city	42 677
31	37000	055	Douglas County	390 007	34	28680	003	Bergen County	42 677
32			**NEVADA**	1 998 257	34	32250		Hoboken city	38 577
32	09700		Carson City	52 457	34	32250	017	Hudson County	38 577
32	09700	510	Carson City	52 457					
					34	36000		Jersey City city	240 055
32	31900		Henderson city	175 381	34	36000	017	Hudson County	240 055
32	31900	003	Clark County	175 381					
					34	36510		Kearny town	40 513
32	40000		Las Vegas city	478 434	34	36510	017	Hudson County	40 513
32	40000	003	Clark County	478 434					
					34	40350		Linden city	39 394
32	51800		North Las Vegas city	115 488	34	40350	039	Union County	39 394
32	51800	003	Clark County	115 488					
					34	41310		Long Branch city	31 340
32	60600		Reno city	180 480	34	41310	025	Monmouth County	31 340
32	60600	031	Washoe County	180 480					
					34	46680		Millville city	26 847
32	68400		Sparks city	66 346	34	46680	011	Cumberland County	26 847
32	68400	031	Washoe County	66 346					
					34	51000		Newark city	273 546
33			**NEW HAMPSHIRE**	1 235 786	34	51000	013	Essex County	273 546
33	14200		Concord city	40 687					
33	14200	013	Merrimack County	40 687	34	51210		New Brunswick city	48 573
					34	51210	023	Middlesex County	48 573
33	18820		Dover city	26 884					
33	18820	017	Strafford County	26 884	34	55950		Paramus borough	25 737
					34	55950	003	Bergen County	25 737
33	45140		Manchester city	107 006					
33	45140	011	Hillsborough County	107 006	34	56550		Passaic city	67 861
					34	56550	031	Passaic County	67 861
33	50260		Nashua city	86 605					
33	50260	011	Hillsborough County	86 605	34	57000		Paterson city	149 222
					34	57000	031	Passaic County	149 222
33	65140		Rochester city	28 461					
33	65140	017	Strafford County	28 461	34	58200		Perth Amboy city	47 303
					34	58200	023	Middlesex County	47 303
34			**NEW JERSEY**	8 414 350					
34	02080		Atlantic City city	40 517	34	59190		Plainfield city	47 829
34	02080	001	Atlantic County	40 517	34	59190	039	Union County	47 829
34	03580		Bayonne city	61 842	34	61530		Rahway city	26 500
34	03580	017	Hudson County	61 842	34	61530	039	Union County	26 500
34	05170		Bergenfield borough	26 247	34	65790		Sayreville borough	40 377
34	05170	003	Bergen County	26 247	34	65790	023	Middlesex County	40 377
34	10000		Camden city	79 904	34	74000		Trenton city	85 403
34	10000	007	Camden County	79 904	34	74000	021	Mercer County	85 403
34	13690		Clifton city	78 672	34	74630		Union City city	67 088
34	13690	031	Passaic County	78 672	34	74630	017	Hudson County	67 088
34	19390		East Orange city	69 824	34	76070		Vineland city	56 271
34	19390	013	Essex County	69 824	34	76070	011	Cumberland County	56 271
34	21000		Elizabeth city	120 568	34	79040		Westfield town	29 644
34	21000	039	Union County	120 568	34	79040	039	Union County	29 644
34	21480		Englewood city	26 203	34	79610		West New York town	45 768
34	21480	003	Bergen County	26 203	34	79610	017	Hudson County	45 768

Cities by County — Continued

State Code	Place Code	County Code	Geographic Area Name	2000 Population
35			**NEW MEXICO**	1 819 046
35	01780		Alamogordo city	35 582
35	01780	035	Otero County	35 582
35	02000		Albuquerque city	448 607
35	02000	001	Bernalillo County	448 607
35	12150		Carlsbad city	25 625
35	12150	015	Eddy County	25 625
35	16420		Clovis city	32 667
35	16420	009	Curry County	32 667
35	25800		Farmington city	37 844
35	25800	045	San Juan County	37 844
35	32520		Hobbs city	28 657
35	32520	025	Lea County	28 657
35	39380		Las Cruces city	74 267
35	39380	013	Dona Ana County	74 267
35	63460		Rio Rancho city	51 765
35	63460	001	Bernalillo County	0
35	63460	043	Sandoval County	51 765
35	64930		Roswell city	45 293
35	64930	005	Chaves County	45 293
35	70500		Santa Fe city	62 203
35	70500	049	Santa Fe County	62 203
36			**NEW YORK**	18 976 457
36	01000		Albany city	95 658
36	01000	001	Albany County	95 658
36	03078		Auburn city	28 574
36	03078	011	Cayuga County	28 574
36	06607		Binghamton city	47 380
36	06607	007	Broome County	47 380
36	11000		Buffalo city	292 648
36	11000	029	Erie County	292 648
36	24229		Elmira city	30 940
36	24229	015	Chemung County	30 940
36	27485		Freeport village	43 783
36	27485	059	Nassau County	43 783
36	29113		Glen Cove city	26 622
36	29113	059	Nassau County	26 622
36	33139		Hempstead village	56 554
36	33139	059	Nassau County	56 554
36	38077		Ithaca city	29 287
36	38077	109	Tompkins County	29 287
36	38264		Jamestown city	31 730
36	38264	013	Chautauqua County	31 730
36	42554		Lindenhurst village	27 819
36	42554	103	Suffolk County	27 819
36	43335		Long Beach city	35 462
36	43335	059	Nassau County	35 462
36	47042		Middletown city	25 388
36	47042	071	Orange County	25 388
36	49121		Mount Vernon city	68 381
36	49121	119	Westchester County	68 381
36	50034		Newburgh city	28 259
36	50034	071	Orange County	28 259
36	50617		New Rochelle city	72 182
36	50617	119	Westchester County	72 182
36	51000		New York city	8008 278
36	51000	005	Bronx County	1332 650
36	51000	047	Kings County	2465 326
36	51000	061	New York County	1537 195
36	51000	081	Queens County	2229 379
36	51000	085	Richmond County	443 728
36	51055		Niagara Falls city	55 593
36	51055	063	Niagara County	55 593
36	53682		North Tonawanda city	33 262
36	53682	063	Niagara County	33 262
36	59223		Port Chester village	27 867
36	59223	119	Westchester County	27 867
36	59641		Poughkeepsie city	29 871
36	59641	027	Dutchess County	29 871
36	63000		Rochester city	219 773
36	63000	055	Monroe County	219 773
36	63418		Rome city	34 950
36	63418	065	Oneida County	34 950
36	65255		Saratoga Springs city	26 186
36	65255	091	Saratoga County	26 186
36	65508		Schenectady city	61 821
36	65508	093	Schenectady County	61 821
36	70420		Spring Valley village	25 464
36	70420	087	Rockland County	25 464
36	73000		Syracuse city	147 306
36	73000	067	Onondaga County	147 306
36	75484		Troy city	49 170
36	75484	083	Rensselaer County	49 170
36	76540		Utica city	60 651
36	76540	065	Oneida County	60 651
36	76705		Valley Stream village	36 368
36	76705	059	Nassau County	36 368
36	78608		Watertown city	26 705
36	78608	045	Jefferson County	26 705
36	81677		White Plains city	53 077
36	81677	119	Westchester County	53 077
36	84000		Yonkers city	196 086
36	84000	119	Westchester County	196 086
37			**NORTH CAROLINA**	8 049 313
37	02140		Asheville city	68 889
37	02140	021	Buncombe County	68 889
37	09060		Burlington city	44 917
37	09060	001	Alamance County	44 917

State Code	Place Code	County Code	Geographic Area Name	2000 Population	State Code	Place Code	County Code	Geographic Area Name	2000 Population
37	10740		Cary town	94 536	37	75000		Winston-Salem city	185 776
37	10740	037	Chatham County	19	37	75000	067	Forsyth County	185 776
37	10740	183	Wake County	94 517	38			**NORTH DAKOTA**	642 200
37	11800		Chapel Hill town	48 715	38	07200		Bismarck city	55 532
37	11800	063	Durham County	1 917	38	07200	015	Burleigh County	55 532
37	11800	135	Orange County	46 798	38	25700		Fargo city	90 599
37	12000		Charlotte city	540 828	38	25700	017	Cass County	90 599
37	12000	119	Mecklenburg County	540 828	38	32060		Grand Forks city	49 321
37	14100		Concord city	55 977	38	32060	035	Grand Forks County	49 321
37	14100	025	Cabarrus County	55 977	38	53380		Minot city	36 567
37	19000		Durham city	187 035	38	53380	101	Ward County	36 567
37	19000	063	Durham County	186 996	39			**OHIO**	11 353 140
37	19000	135	Orange County	39	39	01000		Akron city	217 074
37	19000	183	Wake County	0	39	01000	153	Summit County	217 074
37	22920		Fayetteville city	121 015	39	03828		Barberton city	27 899
37	22920	051	Cumberland County	121 015	39	03828	153	Summit County	27 899
37	25580		Gastonia city	66 277	39	04720		Beavercreek city	37 984
37	25580	071	Gaston County	66 277	39	04720	057	Greene County	37 984
37	26880		Goldsboro city	39 043	39	07972		Bowling Green city	29 636
37	26880	191	Wayne County	39 043	39	07972	173	Wood County	29 636
37	28000		Greensboro city	223 891	39	09680		Brunswick city	33 388
37	28000	081	Guilford County	223 891	39	09680	103	Medina County	33 388
37	28080		Greenville city	60 476	39	12000		Canton city	80 806
37	28080	147	Pitt County	60 476	39	12000	151	Stark County	80 806
37	31060		Hickory city	37 222	39	15000		Cincinnati city	331 285
37	31060	023	Burke County	63	39	15000	061	Hamilton County	331 285
37	31060	027	Caldwell County	14	39	16000		Cleveland city	478 403
37	31060	035	Catawba County	37 145	39	16000	035	Cuyahoga County	478 403
37	31400		High Point city	85 839	39	16014		Cleveland Heights city	49 958
37	31400	057	Davidson County	1 163	39	16014	035	Cuyahoga County	49 958
37	31400	067	Forsyth County	6	39	18000		Columbus city	711 470
37	31400	081	Guilford County	84 656	39	18000	041	Delaware County	1 891
37	31400	151	Randolph County	14	39	18000	045	Fairfield County	7 447
37	34200		Jacksonville city	66 715	39	18000	049	Franklin County	702 132
37	34200	133	Onslow County	66 715	39	19778		Cuyahoga Falls city	49 374
37	35200		Kannapolis city	36 910	39	19778	153	Summit County	49 374
37	35200	025	Cabarrus County	27 890	39	21000		Dayton city	166 179
37	35200	159	Rowan County	9 020	39	21000	113	Montgomery County	166 179
37	43920		Monroe city	26 228	39	21434		Delaware city	25 243
37	43920	179	Union County	26 228	39	21434	041	Delaware County	25 243
37	55000		Raleigh city	276 093	39	22694		Dublin city	31 392
37	55000	063	Durham County	0	39	22694	041	Delaware County	4 283
37	55000	183	Wake County	276 093	39	22694	049	Franklin County	27 087
37	57500		Rocky Mount city	55 893	39	22694	159	Union County	22
37	57500	065	Edgecombe County	17 297	39	23380		East Cleveland city	27 217
37	57500	127	Nash County	38 596	39	23380	035	Cuyahoga County	27 217
37	58860		Salisbury city	26 462	39	25256		Elyria city	55 953
37	58860	159	Rowan County	26 462	39	25256	093	Lorain County	55 953
37	74440		Wilmington city	75 838	39	25704		Euclid city	52 717
37	74440	129	New Hanover County	75 838	39	25704	035	Cuyahoga County	52 717
37	74540		Wilson city	44 405					
37	74540	195	Wilson County	44 405					

State Code	Place Code	County Code	Geographic Area Name	2000 Population	State Code	Place Code	County Code	Geographic Area Name	2000 Population
39	25914		Fairborn city	32 052					
39	25914	057	Greene County	32 052	39	57008		North Royalton city	28 648
					39	57008	035	Cuyahoga County	28 648
39	25970		Fairfield city	42 097					
39	25970	017	Butler County	42 097	39	61000		Parma city	85 655
39	25970	061	Hamilton County	0	39	61000	035	Cuyahoga County	85 655
39	27048		Findlay city	38 967	39	66390		Reynoldsburg city	32 069
39	27048	063	Hancock County	38 967	39	66390	045	Fairfield County	0
					39	66390	049	Franklin County	26 388
39	29106		Gahanna city	32 636	39	66390	089	Licking County	5 681
39	29106	049	Franklin County	32 636					
					39	70380		Sandusky city	27 844
39	29428		Garfield Heights city	30 734	39	70380	043	Erie County	27 844
39	29428	035	Cuyahoga County	30 734					
					39	71682		Shaker Heights city	29 405
39	32592		Grove City city	27 075	39	71682	035	Cuyahoga County	29 405
39	32592	049	Franklin County	27 075					
					39	74118		Springfield city	65 358
39	33012		Hamilton city	60 690	39	74118	023	Clark County	65 358
39	33012	017	Butler County	60 690					
					39	74944		Stow city	32 139
39	36610		Huber Heights city	38 212	39	74944	153	Summit County	32 139
39	36610	109	Miami County	35					
39	36610	113	Montgomery County	38 177	39	75098		Strongsville city	43 858
					39	75098	035	Cuyahoga County	43 858
39	39872		Kent city	27 906					
39	39872	133	Portage County	27 906	39	77000		Toledo city	313 619
					39	77000	095	Lucas County	313 619
39	40040		Kettering city	57 502					
39	40040	057	Greene County	0	39	77504		Trotwood city	27 420
39	40040	113	Montgomery County	57 502	39	77504	113	Montgomery County	27 420
39	41664		Lakewood city	56 646	39	79002		Upper Arlington city	33 686
39	41664	035	Cuyahoga County	56 646	39	79002	049	Franklin County	33 686
39	41720		Lancaster city	35 335	39	80892		Warren city	46 832
39	41720	045	Fairfield County	35 335	39	80892	155	Trumbull County	46 832
39	43554		Lima city	40 081	39	83342		Westerville city	35 318
39	43554	003	Allen County	40 081	39	83342	041	Delaware County	5 900
					39	83342	049	Franklin County	29 418
39	44856		Lorain city	68 652					
39	44856	093	Lorain County	68 652	39	83622		Westlake city	31 719
					39	83622	035	Cuyahoga County	31 719
39	47138		Mansfield city	49 346					
39	47138	139	Richland County	49 346	39	88000		Youngstown city	82 026
					39	88000	099	Mahoning County	82 026
39	47306		Maple Heights city	26 156	39	88000	155	Trumbull County	0
39	47306	035	Cuyahoga County	26 156					
					39	88084		Zanesville city	25 586
39	47754		Marion city	35 318	39	88084	119	Muskingum County	25 586
39	47754	101	Marion County	35 318					
					40			**OKLAHOMA**	3 450 654
39	48244		Massillon city	31 325	40	04450		Bartlesville city	34 748
39	48244	151	Stark County	31 325	40	04450	113	Osage County	2
					40	04450	147	Washington County	34 746
39	48790		Medina city	25 139					
39	48790	103	Medina County	25 139	40	09050		Broken Arrow city	74 859
					40	09050	143	Tulsa County	67 791
39	49056		Mentor city	50 278	40	09050	145	Wagoner County	7 068
39	49056	085	Lake County	50 278					
					40	23200		Edmond city	68 315
39	49840		Middletown city	51 605	40	23200	109	Oklahoma County	68 315
39	49840	017	Butler County	49 574					
39	49840	165	Warren County	2 031	40	23950		Enid city	47 045
					40	23950	047	Garfield County	47 045
39	54040		Newark city	46 279					
39	54040	089	Licking County	46 279	40	41850		Lawton city	92 757
					40	41850	031	Comanche County	92 757
39	56882		North Olmsted city	34 113					
39	56882	035	Cuyahoga County	34 113					

State Code	Place Code	County Code	Geographic Area Name	2000 Population
40	48350		Midwest City city	54 088
40	48350	109	Oklahoma County	54 088
40	49200		Moore city	41 138
40	49200	027	Cleveland County	41 138
40	50050		Muskogee city	38 310
40	50050	101	Muskogee County	38 310
40	52500		Norman city	95 694
40	52500	027	Cleveland County	95 694
40	55000		Oklahoma City city	506 132
40	55000	017	Canadian County	26 311
40	55000	027	Cleveland County	47 271
40	55000	109	Oklahoma County	432 498
40	55000	125	Pottawatomie County	52
40	59850		Ponca City city	25 919
40	59850	071	Kay County	25 919
40	59850	113	Osage County	0
40	66800		Shawnee city	28 692
40	66800	125	Pottawatomie County	28 692
40	70300		Stillwater city	39 065
40	70300	119	Payne County	39 065
40	75000		Tulsa city	393 049
40	75000	113	Osage County	5 630
40	75000	131	Rogers County	0
40	75000	143	Tulsa County	387 419
41			**OREGON**	3 421 399
41	01000		Albany city	40 852
41	01000	003	Benton County	5 104
41	01000	043	Linn County	35 748
41	05350		Beaverton city	76 129
41	05350	067	Washington County	76 129
41	05800		Bend city	52 029
41	05800	017	Deschutes County	52 029
41	15800		Corvallis city	49 322
41	15800	003	Benton County	49 322
41	23850		Eugene city	137 893
41	23850	039	Lane County	137 893
41	31250		Gresham city	90 205
41	31250	051	Multnomah County	90 205
41	34100		Hillsboro city	70 186
41	34100	067	Washington County	70 186
41	38500		Keizer city	32 203
41	38500	047	Marion County	32 203
41	40550		Lake Oswego city	35 278
41	40550	005	Clackamas County	32 989
41	40550	051	Multnomah County	2 274
41	40550	067	Washington County	15
41	45000		McMinnville city	26 499
41	45000	071	Yamhill County	26 499
41	47000		Medford city	63 154
41	47000	029	Jackson County	63 154
41	55200		Oregon City city	25 754
41	55200	005	Clackamas County	25 754

State Code	Place Code	County Code	Geographic Area Name	2000 Population
41	59000		Portland city	529 121
41	59000	005	Clackamas County	747
41	59000	051	Multnomah County	526 986
41	59000	067	Washington County	1 388
41	64900		Salem city	136 924
41	64900	047	Marion County	119 040
41	64900	053	Polk County	17 884
41	69600		Springfield city	52 864
41	69600	039	Lane County	52 864
41	73650		Tigard city	41 223
41	73650	067	Washington County	41 223
42			**PENNSYLVANIA**	12 281 054
42	02000		Allentown city	106 632
42	02000	077	Lehigh County	106 632
42	02184		Altoona city	49 523
42	02184	013	Blair County	49 523
42	06064		Bethel Park borough	33 556
42	06064	003	Allegheny County	33 556
42	06088		Bethlehem city	71 329
42	06088	077	Lehigh County	19 029
42	06088	095	Northampton County	52 300
42	13208		Chester city	36 854
42	13208	045	Delaware County	36 854
42	21648		Easton city	26 263
42	21648	095	Northampton County	26 263
42	24000		Erie city	103 717
42	24000	049	Erie County	103 717
42	32800		Harrisburg city	48 950
42	32800	043	Dauphin County	48 950
42	41216		Lancaster city	56 348
42	41216	071	Lancaster County	56 348
42	52330		Municipality of Monroeville borough	29 349
42	52330	003	Allegheny County	29 349
42	53368		New Castle city	26 309
42	53368	073	Lawrence County	26 309
42	54656		Norristown borough	31 282
42	54656	091	Montgomery County	31 282
42	60000		Philadelphia city	1517 550
42	60000	101	Philadelphia County	1517 550
42	61000		Pittsburgh city	334 563
42	61000	003	Allegheny County	334 563
42	61536		Plum borough	26 940
42	61536	003	Allegheny County	26 940
42	63624		Reading city	81 207
42	63624	011	Berks County	81 207
42	69000		Scranton city	76 415
42	69000	069	Lackawanna County	76 415
42	73808		State College borough	38 420
42	73808	027	Centre County	38 420

State Code	Place Code	County Code	Geographic Area Name	2000 Population	State Code	Place Code	County Code	Geographic Area Name	2000 Population
42	85152		Wilkes-Barre city	43 123	45	70270		Summerville town	27 752
42	85152	079	Luzerne County	43 123	45	70270	015	Berkeley County	945
					45	70270	019	Charleston County	20
42	85312		Williamsport city	30 706	45	70270	035	Dorchester County	26 787
42	85312	081	Lycoming County	30 706					
					45	70405		Sumter city	39 643
42	87048		York city	40 862	45	70405	085	Sumter County	39 643
42	87048	133	York County	40 862					
					46			**SOUTH DAKOTA**	754 844
44			**RHODE ISLAND**	1 048 319	46	52980		Rapid City city	59 607
44	19180		Cranston city	79 269	46	52980	103	Pennington County	59 607
44	19180	007	Providence County	79 269					
					46	59020		Sioux Falls city	123 975
44	22960		East Providence city	48 688	46	59020	083	Lincoln County	6 620
44	22960	007	Providence County	48 688	46	59020	099	Minnehaha County	117 355
44	49960		Newport city	26 475	47			**TENNESSEE**	5 689 283
44	49960	005	Newport County	26 475	47	03440		Bartlett city	40 543
					47	03440	157	Shelby County	40 543
44	54640		Pawtucket city	72 958					
44	54640	007	Providence County	72 958	47	14000		Chattanooga city	155 554
					47	14000	065	Hamilton County	155 554
44	59000		Providence city	173 618	47	14000	115	Marion County	0
44	59000	007	Providence County	173 618					
					47	15160		Clarksville city	103 455
44	74300		Warwick city	85 808	47	15160	125	Montgomery County	103 455
44	74300	003	Kent County	85 808					
					47	15400		Cleveland city	37 192
44	80780		Woonsocket city	43 224	47	15400	011	Bradley County	37 192
44	80780	007	Providence County	43 224					
					47	16420		Collierville town	31 872
45			**SOUTH CAROLINA**	4 012 012	47	16420	157	Shelby County	31 872
45	00550		Aiken city	25 337					
45	00550	003	Aiken County	25 337	47	16540		Columbia city	33 055
					47	16540	119	Maury County	33 055
45	01360		Anderson city	25 514					
45	01360	007	Anderson County	25 514	47	27740		Franklin city	41 842
					47	27740	187	Williamson County	41 842
45	13330		Charleston city	96 650					
45	13330	015	Berkeley County	1 122	47	28960		Germantown city	37 348
45	13330	019	Charleston County	95 528	47	28960	157	Shelby County	37 348
45	16000		Columbia city	116 278	47	33280		Hendersonville city	40 620
45	16000	063	Lexington County	402	47	33280	165	Sumner County	40 620
45	16000	079	Richland County	115 876					
					47	37640		Jackson city	59 643
45	25810		Florence city	30 248	47	37640	113	Madison County	59 643
45	25810	041	Florence County	30 248					
					47	38320		Johnson City city	55 469
45	29815		Goose Creek city	29 208	47	38320	019	Carter County	1 138
45	29815	015	Berkeley County	29 208	47	38320	163	Sullivan County	240
45	29815	019	Charleston County	0	47	38320	179	Washington County	54 091
45	30850		Greenville city	56 002	47	39560		Kingsport city	44 905
45	30850	045	Greenville County	56 002	47	39560	073	Hawkins County	2 907
					47	39560	163	Sullivan County	41 998
45	34045		Hilton Head Island town	33 862					
45	34045	013	Beaufort County	33 862	47	40000		Knoxville city	173 890
					47	40000	093	Knox County	173 890
45	48535		Mount Pleasant town	47 609					
45	48535	019	Charleston County	47 609	47	48000		Memphis city	650 100
					47	48000	157	Shelby County	650 100
45	50875		North Charleston city	79 641					
45	50875	019	Charleston County	76 244	47	51560		Murfreesboro city	68 816
45	50875	035	Dorchester County	3 397	47	51560	149	Rutherford County	68 816
45	61405		Rock Hill city	49 765	47	52004		Nashville-Davidson	569 891
45	61405	091	York County	49 765					
					47	55120		Oak Ridge city	27 387
45	68290		Spartanburg city	39 673	47	55120	001	Anderson County	24 610
45	68290	083	Spartanburg County	39 673	47	55120	145	Roane County	2 777

State Code	Place Code	County Code	Geographic Area Name	2000 Population
47	69420		Smyrna town	25 569
47	69420	149	Rutherford County	25 569
48			**TEXAS**	20 851 820
48	01000		Abilene city	115 930
48	01000	253	Jones County	5 488
48	01000	441	Taylor County	110 442
48	01924		Allen city	43 554
48	01924	085	Collin County	43 554
48	03000		Amarillo city	173 627
48	03000	375	Potter County	99 833
48	03000	381	Randall County	73 794
48	04000		Arlington city	332 969
48	04000	439	Tarrant County	332 969
48	05000		Austin city	656 562
48	05000	453	Travis County	644 752
48	05000	491	Williamson County	11 810
48	06128		Baytown city	66 430
48	06128	071	Chambers County	3 081
48	06128	201	Harris County	63 349
48	07000		Beaumont city	113 866
48	07000	245	Jefferson County	113 866
48	07132		Bedford city	47 152
48	07132	439	Tarrant County	47 152
48	08236		Big Spring city	25 233
48	08236	227	Howard County	25 233
48	10768		Brownsville city	139 722
48	10768	061	Cameron County	139 722
48	10912		Bryan city	65 660
48	10912	041	Brazos County	65 660
48	13024		Carrollton city	109 576
48	13024	085	Collin County	0
48	13024	113	Dallas County	49 822
48	13024	121	Denton County	59 754
48	13492		Cedar Hill city	32 093
48	13492	113	Dallas County	32 044
48	13492	139	Ellis County	49
48	13552		Cedar Park city	26 049
48	13552	453	Travis County	541
48	13552	491	Williamson County	25 508
48	15364		Cleburne city	26 005
48	15364	251	Johnson County	26 005
48	15976		College Station city	67 890
48	15976	041	Brazos County	67 890
48	16432		Conroe city	36 811
48	16432	339	Montgomery County	36 811
48	16612		Coppell city	35 958
48	16612	113	Dallas County	35 734
48	16612	121	Denton County	224
48	16624		Copperas Cove city	29 592
48	16624	027	Bell County	0
48	16624	099	Coryell County	29 455
48	16624	281	Lampasas County	137
48	17000		Corpus Christi city	277 454
48	17000	273	Kleberg County	0
48	17000	355	Nueces County	277 450
48	17000	409	San Patricio County	4
48	19000		Dallas city	1 188 580
48	19000	085	Collin County	45 155
48	19000	113	Dallas County	1 121 131
48	19000	121	Denton County	22 273
48	19000	257	Kaufman County	0
48	19000	397	Rockwall County	21
48	19624		Deer Park city	28 520
48	19624	201	Harris County	28 520
48	19792		Del Rio city	33 867
48	19792	465	Val Verde County	33 867
48	19972		Denton city	80 537
48	19972	121	Denton County	80 537
48	20092		DeSoto city	37 646
48	20092	113	Dallas County	37 646
48	21628		Duncanville city	36 081
48	21628	113	Dallas County	36 081
48	22660		Edinburg city	48 465
48	22660	215	Hidalgo County	48 465
48	24000		El Paso city	563 662
48	24000	141	El Paso County	563 662
48	24768		Euless city	46 005
48	24768	439	Tarrant County	46 005
48	25452		Farmers Branch city	27 508
48	25452	113	Dallas County	27 508
48	26232		Flower Mound town	50 702
48	26232	121	Denton County	50 702
48	26232	439	Tarrant County	0
48	27000		Fort Worth city	534 694
48	27000	121	Denton County	44
48	27000	439	Tarrant County	534 650
48	27648		Friendswood city	29 037
48	27648	167	Galveston County	21 237
48	27648	201	Harris County	7 800
48	27684		Frisco city	33 714
48	27684	085	Collin County	30 312
48	27684	121	Denton County	3 402
48	28068		Galveston city	57 247
48	28068	167	Galveston County	57 247
48	29000		Garland city	215 768
48	29000	085	Collin County	0
48	29000	113	Dallas County	215 768
48	29000	397	Rockwall County	0
48	29336		Georgetown city	28 339
48	29336	491	Williamson County	28 339
48	30464		Grand Prairie city	127 427
48	30464	113	Dallas County	99 760
48	30464	139	Ellis County	46
48	30464	439	Tarrant County	27 621

State Code	Place Code	County Code	Geographic Area Name	2000 Population	State Code	Place Code	County Code	Geographic Area Name	2000 Population
48	30644		Grapevine city	42 059	48	46452	251	Johnson County................	622
48	30644	113	Dallas County	0	48	46452	439	Tarrant County................	27 280
48	30644	121	Denton County	2					
48	30644	439	Tarrant County	42 057	48	47892		Mesquite city	124 523
					48	47892	113	Dallas County	124 522
48	31928		Haltom City city	39 018	48	47892	257	Kaufman County	1
48	31928	439	Tarrant County	39 018					
					48	48072		Midland city	94 996
48	32372		Harlingen city	57 564	48	48072	317	Martin County	0
48	32372	061	Cameron County.....................	57 564	48	48072	329	Midland County	94 996
48	35000		Houston city	1953 631	48	48768		Mission city...........................	45 408
48	35000	157	Fort Bend County	33 384	48	48768	215	Hidalgo County	45 408
48	35000	201	Harris County	1919 789					
48	35000	339	Montgomery County	458	48	48804		Missouri City city	52 913
					48	48804	157	Fort Bend County	47 419
48	35528		Huntsville city	35 078	48	48804	201	Harris County	5 494
48	35528	471	Walker County	35 078					
					48	50256		Nacogdoches city...........................	29 914
48	35576		Hurst city	36 273	48	50256	347	Nacogdoches County	29 914
48	35576	439	Tarrant County...........................	36 273					
					48	50820		New Braunfels city	36 494
48	37000		Irving city	191 615	48	50820	091	Comal County	35 328
48	37000	113	Dallas County	191 615	48	50820	187	Guadalupe County.....................	1 166
48	38632		Keller city...........................	27 345	48	52356		North Richland Hills city	55 635
48	38632	439	Tarrant County	27 345	48	52356	439	Tarrant County	55 635
48	39148		Killeen city	86 911	48	53388		Odessa city...........................	90 943
48	39148	027	Bell County	86 911	48	53388	135	Ector County	89 901
					48	53388	329	Midland County	1 042
48	39352		Kingsville city...........................	25 575					
48	39352	273	Kleberg County	25 575	48	55080		Paris city...........................	25 898
					48	55080	277	Lamar County	25 898
48	40588		Lake Jackson city...........................	26 386					
48	40588	039	Brazoria County	26 386	48	56000		Pasadena city...........................	141 674
					48	56000	201	Harris County	141 674
48	41212		Lancaster city	25 894					
48	41212	113	Dallas County	25 894	48	56348		Pearland city...........................	37 640
					48	56348	039	Brazoria County.....................	35 696
48	41440		La Porte city	31 880	48	56348	157	Fort Bend County	0
48	41440	201	Harris County...........................	31 880	48	56348	201	Harris County	1 944
48	41464		Laredo city...........................	176 576	48	57200		Pharr city...........................	46 660
48	41464	479	Webb County	176 576	48	57200	215	Hidalgo County	46 660
48	41980		League City city...........................	45 444	48	58016		Plano city...........................	222 030
48	41980	167	Galveston County	45 306	48	58016	085	Collin County	219 890
48	41980	201	Harris County	138	48	58016	121	Denton County	2 140
48	42508		Lewisville city...........................	77 737	48	58820		Port Arthur city	57 755
48	42508	113	Dallas County	2	48	58820	245	Jefferson County.....................	57 755
48	42508	121	Denton County	77 735	48	58820	361	Orange County	0
48	43888		Longview city...........................	73 344	48	61796		Richardson city...........................	91 802
48	43888	183	Gregg County	71 746	48	61796	085	Collin County	20 873
48	43888	203	Harrison County.....................	1 598	48	61796	113	Dallas County	70 929
48	45000		Lubbock city	199 564	48	63500		Round Rock city	61 136
48	45000	303	Lubbock County.....................	199 564	48	63500	453	Travis County	1 076
					48	63500	491	Williamson County.....................	60 060
48	45072		Lufkin city	32 709					
48	45072	005	Angelina County	32 709	48	63572		Rowlett city...........................	44 503
					48	63572	113	Dallas County	37 462
48	45384		McAllen city	106 414	48	63572	397	Rockwall County	7 041
48	45384	215	Hidalgo County	106 414					
					48	64472		San Angelo city	88 439
48	45744		McKinney city	54 369	48	64472	451	Tom Green County................	88 439
48	45744	085	Collin County	54 369					
					48	65000		San Antonio city	1144 646
48	46452		Mansfield city...........................	28 031	48	65000	029	Bexar County	1144 646
48	46452	139	Ellis County................	129	48	65000	091	Comal County	0

State Code	Place Code	County Code	Geographic Area Name	2000 Population
48	65516		San Juan city	26 229
48	65516	215	Hidalgo County	26 229
48	65600		San Marcos city	34 733
48	65600	055	Caldwell County	0
48	65600	209	Hays County	34 733
48	67496		Sherman city	35 082
48	67496	181	Grayson County	35 082
48	68636		Socorro city	27 152
48	68636	141	El Paso County	27 152
48	70808		Sugar Land city	63 328
48	70808	157	Fort Bend County	63 328
48	72176		Temple city	54 514
48	72176	027	Bell County	54 514
48	72368		Texarkana city	34 782
48	72368	037	Bowie County	34 782
48	72392		Texas City city	41 521
48	72392	071	Chambers County	0
48	72392	167	Galveston County	41 521
48	72530		The Colony city	26 531
48	72530	121	Denton County	26 531
48	74144		Tyler city	83 650
48	74144	423	Smith County	83 650
48	75428		Victoria city	60 603
48	75428	469	Victoria County	60 603
48	76000		Waco city	113 726
48	76000	309	McLennan County	113 726
48	77272		Weslaco city	26 935
48	77272	215	Hidalgo County	26 935
48	79000		Wichita Falls city	104 197
48	79000	485	Wichita County	104 197
49			UTAH	2 233 169
49	07690		Bountiful city	41 301
49	07690	011	Davis County	41 301
49	13850		Clearfield city	25 974
49	13850	011	Davis County	25 974
49	20120		Draper city	25 220
49	20120	035	Salt Lake County	25 220
49	20120	049	Utah County	0
49	43660		Layton city	58 474
49	43660	011	Davis County	58 474
49	45860		Logan city	42 670
49	45860	005	Cache County	42 670
49	49710		Midvale city	27 029
49	49710	035	Salt Lake County	27 029
49	53230		Murray city	34 024
49	53230	035	Salt Lake County	34 024
49	55980		Ogden city	77 226
49	55980	057	Weber County	77 226
49	57300		Orem city	84 324
49	57300	049	Utah County	84 324
49	62470		Provo city	105 166
49	62470	049	Utah County	105 166
49	64340		Riverton city	25 011
49	64340	035	Salt Lake County	25 011
49	65110		Roy city	32 885
49	65110	057	Weber County	32 885
49	65330		St. George city	49 663
49	65330	053	Washington County	49 663
49	67000		Salt Lake City city	181 743
49	67000	035	Salt Lake County	181 743
49	67440		Sandy city	88 418
49	67440	035	Salt Lake County	88 418
49	70850		South Jordan city	29 437
49	70850	035	Salt Lake County	29 437
49	75360		Taylorsville city	57 439
49	75360	035	Salt Lake County	57 439
49	82950		West Jordan city	68 336
49	82950	035	Salt Lake County	68 336
49	83470		West Valley City city	108 896
49	83470	035	Salt Lake County	108 896
50			VERMONT	608 827
50	10675		Burlington city	38 889
50	10675	007	Chittenden County	38 889
51			VIRGINIA	7 078 515
51	01000		Alexandria city	128 283
51	01000	510	Alexandria city	128 283
51	07784		Blacksburg town	39 573
51	07784	121	Montgomery County	39 573
51	14968		Charlottesville city	45 049
51	14968	540	Charlottesville city	45 049
51	16000		Chesapeake city	199 184
51	16000	550	Chesapeake city	199 184
51	21344		Danville city	48 411
51	21344	590	Danville city	48 411
51	35000		Hampton city	146 437
51	35000	650	Hampton city	146 437
51	35624		Harrisonburg city	40 468
51	35624	660	Harrisonburg city	40 468
51	44984		Leesburg town	28 311
51	44984	107	Loudoun County	28 311
51	47672		Lynchburg city	65 269
51	47672	680	Lynchburg city	65 269
51	48952		Manassas city	35 135
51	48952	683	Manassas city	35 135
51	56000		Newport News city	180 150
51	56000	700	Newport News city	180 150

State Code	Place Code	County Code	Geographic Area Name	2000 Population
51	57000		Norfolk city	234 403
51	57000	710	Norfolk city	234 403
51	61832		Petersburg city	33 740
51	61832	730	Petersburg city	33 740
51	64000		Portsmouth city	100 565
51	64000	740	Portsmouth city	100 565
51	67000		Richmond city	197 790
51	67000	760	Richmond city	197 790
51	68000		Roanoke city	94 911
51	68000	770	Roanoke city	94 911
51	76432		Suffolk city	63 677
51	76432	800	Suffolk city	63 677
51	82000		Virginia Beach city	425 257
51	82000	810	Virginia Beach city	425 257
53			**WASHINGTON**	5 894 121
53	03180		Auburn city	40 314
53	03180	033	King County	40 168
53	03180	053	Pierce County	146
53	05210		Bellevue city	109 569
53	05210	033	King County	109 569
53	05280		Bellingham city	67 171
53	05280	073	Whatcom County	67 171
53	07380		Bothell city	30 150
53	07380	033	King County	16 185
53	07380	061	Snohomish County	13 965
53	07695		Bremerton city	37 259
53	07695	035	Kitsap County	37 259
53	17635		Des Moines city	29 267
53	17635	033	King County	29 267
53	20750		Edmonds city	39 515
53	20750	061	Snohomish County	39 515
53	22640		Everett city	91 488
53	22640	061	Snohomish County	91 488
53	35275		Kennewick city	54 693
53	35275	005	Benton County	54 693
53	35415		Kent city	79 524
53	35415	033	King County	79 524
53	35940		Kirkland city	45 054
53	35940	033	King County	45 054
53	36745		Lacey city	31 226
53	36745	067	Thurston County	31 226
53	40245		Longview city	34 660
53	40245	015	Cowlitz County	34 660
53	40840		Lynnwood city	33 847
53	40840	061	Snohomish County	33 847
53	43955		Marysville city	25 315
53	43955	061	Snohomish County	25 315
53	47560		Mount Vernon city	26 232
53	47560	057	Skagit County	26 232
53	51300		Olympia city	42 514
53	51300	067	Thurston County	42 514
53	53545		Pasco city	32 066
53	53545	021	Franklin County	32 066
53	56695		Puyallup city	33 011
53	56695	053	Pierce County	33 011
53	57535		Redmond city	45 256
53	57535	033	King County	45 256
53	57745		Renton city	50 052
53	57745	033	King County	50 052
53	58235		Richland city	38 708
53	58235	005	Benton County	38 708
53	61115		Sammamish city	34 104
53	61115	033	King County	34 104
53	63000		Seattle city	563 374
53	63000	033	King County	563 374
53	63960		Shoreline city	53 025
53	63960	033	King County	53 025
53	67000		Spokane city	195 629
53	67000	063	Spokane County	195 629
53	70000		Tacoma city	193 556
53	70000	053	Pierce County	193 556
53	74060		Vancouver city	143 560
53	74060	011	Clark County	143 560
53	75775		Walla Walla city	29 686
53	75775	071	Walla Walla County	29 686
53	77105		Wenatchee city	27 856
53	77105	007	Chelan County	27 856
53	80010		Yakima city	71 845
53	80010	077	Yakima County	71 845
54			**WEST VIRGINIA**	1 808 344
54	14600		Charleston city	53 421
54	14600	039	Kanawha County	53 421
54	39460		Huntington city	51 475
54	39460	011	Cabell County	47 341
54	39460	099	Wayne County	4 134
54	55756		Morgantown city	26 809
54	55756	061	Monongalia County	26 809
54	62140		Parkersburg city	33 099
54	62140	107	Wood County	33 099
54	86452		Wheeling city	31 419
54	86452	051	Marshall County	360
54	86452	069	Ohio County	31 059
55			**WISCONSIN**	5 363 675
55	02375		Appleton city	70 087
55	02375	015	Calumet County	10 974
55	02375	087	Outagamie County	58 301
55	02375	139	Winnebago County	812
55	06500		Beloit city	35 775
55	06500	105	Rock County	35 775

Cities by County — Continued

State Code	Place Code	County Code	Geographic Area Name	2000 Population	State Code	Place Code	County Code	Geographic Area Name	2000 Population
55	10025		Brookfield city	38 649	55	56375		New Berlin city	38 220
55	10025	133	Waukesha County	38 649	55	56375	133	Waukesha County	38 220
55	22300		Eau Claire city	61 704	55	58800		Oak Creek city	28 456
55	22300	017	Chippewa County	1 910	55	58800	079	Milwaukee County	28 456
55	22300	035	Eau Claire County	59 794	55	60500		Oshkosh city	62 916
55	26275		Fond du Lac city	42 203	55	60500	139	Winnebago County	62 916
55	26275	039	Fond du Lac County	42 203	55	66000		Racine city	81 855
55	27300		Franklin city	29 494	55	66000	101	Racine County	81 855
55	27300	079	Milwaukee County	29 494	55	72975		Sheboygan city	50 792
55	31000		Green Bay city	102 313	55	72975	117	Sheboygan County	50 792
55	31000	009	Brown County	102 313	55	78650		Superior city	27 368
55	31175		Greenfield city	35 476	55	78650	031	Douglas County	27 368
55	31175	079	Milwaukee County	35 476	55	84250		Waukesha city	64 825
55	37825		Janesville city	59 498	55	84250	133	Waukesha County	64 825
55	37825	105	Rock County	59 498	55	84475		Wausau city	38 426
55	39225		Kenosha city	90 352	55	84475	073	Marathon County	38 426
55	39225	059	Kenosha County	90 352	55	84675		Wauwatosa city	47 271
55	40775		La Crosse city	51 818	55	84675	079	Milwaukee County	47 271
55	40775	063	La Crosse County	51 818	55	85300		West Allis city	61 254
55	48000		Madison city	208 054	55	85300	079	Milwaukee County	61 254
55	48000	025	Dane County	208 054	55	85350		West Bend city	28 152
55	48500		Manitowoc city	34 053	55	85350	131	Washington County	28 152
55	48500	071	Manitowoc County	34 053	56			**WYOMING**	493 782
55	51000		Menomonee Falls village	32 647	56	13150		Casper city	49 644
55	51000	133	Waukesha County	32 647	56	13150	025	Natrona County	49 644
55	53000		Milwaukee city	596 974	56	13900		Cheyenne city	53 011
55	53000	079	Milwaukee County	596 974	56	13900	021	Laramie County	53 011
55	53000	131	Washington County	0	56	45050		Laramie city	27 204
55	53000	133	Waukesha County	0	56	45050	001	Albany County	27 204

APPENDIX F
DEFINITIONS

Tables A through F present 97 items for the United States as a whole, all states and the District of Columbia, all counties and county equivalents, all metropolitan areas, all cities with populations of 25,000 or more according to the 2000 Census, towns with populations or 25,000 or more in twelve states, and all congressional districts. Detailed descriptions and further information about the geographic concepts can be found in Appendix A.

All data in this volume are from the decennial censuses of 2000, 1990, and 1980. The 2000 Census data are from Summary File 1. The 1990 and 1980 data are from various published and electronic sources. Though every effort has been made to use updated, comparable data for 1980 and 1990, some of these items may not reflect corrections made throughout the decade. Furthermore, all changes in geographic entities may not be reflected in the data from prior censuses. Further information and additional details can be obtained at www.census.gov.

The following documentation is provided in the order in which the items appear in the tables.

LAND AREA, Items 1 and 5

Land area measurements are shown to the nearest square kilometer. Land area includes dry land and land temporarily or partially covered by water, such as marshlands, swamps, and river floodplains. Differences between the 1990 and 2000 measurements may be due to annexation or similar boundary changes, but some differences may be due to improved accuracy of digital measurement, or more precise exclusion of small bodies of water from the total land area.

POPULATION and POPULATION CHANGE, Items 2, 3, 6, 7, 49 through 53

The population data for 2000, 1990, and 1980 represent the resident population as of April 1 of the census year.

POPULATION PER SQUARE KILOMETER, Items 4 and 8

The population per square kilometer, or population density, is the total population of an area divided by its measurement in square kilometers.

RACE, Items 9 through 21; 23 through 26

The data on race were derived from answers to the question on race that was asked of all people. The concept of race, as used by the Census Bureau, reflects self-identification by people according to the race or races with which they most closely identify. These categories are socio-political constructs and should not be interpreted as being scientific or anthropological in nature.

Furthermore, the race categories include both racial and national-origin groups.

In the 2000 Census, respondents were offered the option of selecting one or more races. This was not the case in prior censuses, so comparisons should be made with caution. In this volume, columns 9 through 14 refer to individuals who identified with only one race, while columns 16 through 21 refer to individuals who identified with each racial category, either alone or in combination with other races. Columns 23 through 26 include racial categories from 1990 when each person indicated only one race.

The **White** population is defined as persons who indicated their race as white, as well as persons who did not classify themselves in one of the specific race categories listed on the questionnaire but entered a nationality such as Irish, German, Italian, Lebanese, Near Easterner, Arab, or Polish.

The **Black** population includes persons who indicated their race as "Black, African Am., or Negro", as well as persons who did not classify themselves in one of the specific race categories but reported entries such as African American, Afro American, Kenyan, Nigerian, or Haitian.

The **American Indian or Alaska Native** population includes persons who indicated their race as American Indian or Alaska Native, as well as persons who did not classify themselves in one of the specific race categories but reported entries such as Canadian Indian, French American Indian, Spanish-American Indian, Eskimo, Aleut, Alaska Indian, or any of the American Indian or Alaska Native tribes.

The **Asian** population includes persons who indicated their race as Asian Indian, Chinese, Filipino, Japanese, Korean, Vietnamese, or "Other Asian", as well as persons who provided write-in entries of such Asian groups as Cambodian, Laotian, Hmong, Pakistani, or Taiwanese. Also, persons who wrote in an entry indicating one of the specific categories were classified accordingly.

The **Native Hawaiian or Other Pacific Islander** population includes persons who indicated their race as "Native Hawaiian", "Guamanian or Chamorro", "Samoan" or "Other Pacific Islander", as well as persons who reported entries such as Part Hawaiian, American Samoan, Fijian, Melanesian, or Tahitian. Also, persons who wrote in an entry indicating one of the specific categories were classified accordingly.

In 1990, the **Asian** and **Native Hawaiian or Other Pacific Islander** categories were combined as **Asian and Pacific Islander**.

The population of **Some other race** includes all persons who indicated "Some other race" as well as persons who wrote in a category not included in the race categories described above, including entries such as multiracial, mixed, interracial, or a Hispanic/Latino group such as Mexican, Puerto Rican, or Cuban in the "Some other race" write-in space.

The **Two or More Races** population includes all persons who indicated more than one of the categories listed above.

Changes in specific listing of racial categories, the new practice of allowing more than one selection in 2000, and the order in which questions appeared on the questionnaire, could all affect comparability between the 2000 and 1990 censuses.

HISPANIC ORIGIN, Items 22 and 27

The Hispanic population is based on a complete-count question that asked respondents "Is this person Spanish/Hispanic/Latino?" Persons marking any one of the four Hispanic categories (i.e., Mexican, Puerto Rican, Cuban, or other Spanish) are collectively referred to as Hispanic.

In the 2000 Census, the Hispanic Origin question was placed before the race question and specific instructions indicated that both questions should be answered. These changes were designed to improve accuracy, and may affect comparability with 1990 data.

AGE, Items 28 through 37; 39 through 47

Age is defined as age at last birthday, as of April 1 of the census year. The 2000 Census also asked for the specific date of birth of the respondent, and 2000 census procedures used the birth date for deriving age data. For this reason, it is likely that the 2000 data have fewer problems than prior censuses, such as a tendency to round ages or report the person's age on the date the questionnaire was filled out rather than on April 1.

The median age divides the age distribution into two equal parts with one-half of the cases falling below the median value and one-half above the value. Median age is computed on the basis of a single year of age distribution.

PERCENT FEMALE, Items 38 and 48

The female population is shown as a percentage of the total population.

HOUSEHOLD RELATIONSHIP, Items 54 through 63

A household consists of persons occupying a single housing unit. A housing unit is a house, an apartment, a group of rooms, or a single room occupied as separate living quarters. The occupants may be a single family, one person living alone, two or more families living together, or any other group of related or unrelated persons who share a housing unit. The number of households is the same as the number of year-round occupied housing units.

A family household consists of two or more persons, including the householder, who are related by birth, marriage, or adoption and who live together as one household; all such persons are considered as members of one family. A married-couple family is one in which the householder and spouse are enumerated as members of the same household.

The data on relationship to householder were derived from the question "How is this person related to Person 1?" which was asked of Persons 2 and higher in all housing units. One person in each household is designated as the householder (Person 1).

In most cases, this is the person, or one of the people, in whose name the home is owned, being bought, or rented. If there is no such person in the household, any household member 15 years old or over could be designated as the householder and therefore referred to as Person 1.

The category Spouse (husband/wife) describes persons married to and living with householders, including people in formal marriages as well as people in common-law marriages.

The category Child includes sons or daughters by birth, stepchildren, and adopted children of the householder, regardless of the child's age or marital status. The category excludes sons-in-law, daughters-in-law, and foster children.

The category Own child under 18 years includes children under 18 years old who are sons or daughters by birth, marriage (stepchildren), or adoption.

Other relatives include any household members related to the householder by birth, marriage, or adoption, but not included specifically in another relationship category. This group includes grandchildren, brothers and sisters, parents, parents-in-law, sons- and daughters-in-law, and any other persons related by birth, marriage, or adoption.

Other relatives under 18 include all related people under 18 years of age who are not the children or spouse of the householder. Foster children are not included since they are not related to the householder.

The category Nonrelatives includes any household member who is not related to the householder by birth, marriage, or adoption, including foster children. Included in this category are roomers or boarders; housemates or roommates; unmarried partners and any other persons not related to the householder.

An Unmarried partner is a person who is not related to the householder, who shares living quarters, and who has a close personal relationship with the householder.

GROUP QUARTERS, Items 64 through 70

All people not living in housing units are classified by the Census Bureau as living in group quarters. There are two general categories of people in group quarters: institutionalized population and noninstitutionalized population.

Institutionalized population includes people under formally authorized, supervised care or custody in institutions at the time of enumeration.

Correctional institutions includes prisons, federal detention centers, military disciplinary barracks and jails, police lockups, halfway houses used for correctional purposes, local jails, and other confinement facilities, including work farms.

Nursing homes comprises a heterogeneous group of places providing continuous nursing and other services to patients. The majority of patients are elderly, although people who require nursing care because of chronic physical conditions may be found in these homes regardless of their age. Included in this category are skilled-nursing facilities, intermediate-care facilities, long-term care rooms in wards or buildings on the grounds of hospitals, or long-term care rooms/nursing wings in congregate housing facilities. Also included are nursing, convalescent, and rest homes, such as soldiers', sailors', veterans', and fraternal or religious homes for the aged, with nursing care.

Other institutions include mental (psychiatric) hospitals, hospitals or wards for the chronically ill, schools, hospitals, or wards for the mentally retarded, the physically handicapped, or for drug/alcohol abuse, wards in general or military hospitals for patients who have no usual home elsewhere, and juvenile institutions.

The **Noninstitutionalized population** includes people who live in group quarters other than institutions, including staff residing in military and nonmilitary group quarters on institutional grounds who provide formally authorized, supervised care or custody for the institutionalized population.

College dormitories include college students in dormitories (provided the dormitory is restricted to students who do not have their families living with them), fraternity and sorority houses, and on-campus residential quarters used exclusively for those in religious orders who are attending college. College dormitory housing includes university-owned, on-campus and off-campus housing for unmarried residents.

Military quarters includes military personnel living in barracks and dormitories on base, transient quarters on base for temporary residents (both civilian and military), and military ships. However, patients in military hospitals receiving treatment for chronic diseases or who had no usual home elsewhere, and people being held in military disciplinary barracks were included as part of the institutionalized population.

Other noninstitutionalized group quarters include community-based homes for the mentally ill, mentally retarded, and physically handicapped; drug/alcohol halfway houses not operated for correctional purposes; communes; and maternity homes for unwed mothers; religious residences such as monasteries, convents, and rectories; agriculture workers' dormitories; dormitories for other workers such as logging camps or construction workers' camps; dormitories for nurses and interns at hospitals; job corps and vocational training facilities; emergency and transitional shelters with sleeping facilities; shelters for children who are runaways, neglected, or without conventional housing; shelters for abused women; soup kitchens; regularly scheduled mobile food vans; and targeted nonsheltered outdoor locations; crews of maritime vessels; and other non-household living situations.

HOUSEHOLD TYPE, Items 71 through 86

A household consists of persons occupying a single housing unit. A housing unit is a house, an apartment, a group of rooms, or a single room occupied as separate living quarters. The occupants may be a single family, one person living alone, two or more families living together, or any other group of related or unrelated persons who share a housing unit. The number of households is the same as the number of year-round occupied housing units.

A **family household** consists of two or more persons, including the householder, who are related by birth, marriage, or adoption and who live together as one household; all such persons are considered as members of one family. A **married-couple family** is one in which the householder and spouse are enumerated as members of the same household. A **female householder family** is a family with a female householder and no spouse of the householder present.

Family households **with own children under 18** include households with children under 18 years old who are sons or daughters of the householder by birth, marriage (stepchildren), or adoption, regardless of the marital status of the child.

A **Nonfamily household** consists of a householder living alone or with nonrelatives only.

Average household size (a measure of persons per household) is obtained by dividing the number of persons in households by the number of households.

Average family size is obtained by dividing the number of persons in families by the total number of families.

HOUSING UNITS, Items 87-97

A **housing unit** is a house, apartment, mobile home or trailer, group of rooms, or single room occupied or, if vacant, intended for occupancy as separate living quarters. Separate living quarters are those in which the occupants live separately from any other individuals in the building and that have direct access from the outside of the building through a common hall. Both occupied and vacant housing units are included in the housing inventory, with the exception that recreational vehicles, tents, caves, boats, railroad cars, and the like are included only if they are occupied as a person's usual place of residence.

A housing unit is classified as an **occupied housing unit** if it is the usual place of residence of the person or group of persons living in it at the time of enumeration or if the occupants are only temporarily absent (e.g., away on vacation or business). The occupants of a housing unit may be a single family, one person living alone, or two or more families living together, or any other group of related or unrelated persons who share living quarters.

A housing unit is classified as a **vacant housing unit** if no one is living in it at the time of enumeration, unless its occupants are only temporarily absent. Units temporarily occupied at the time of enumeration entirely by people who have a usual residence elsewhere are classified as vacant.

Vacant housing units are considered f**or seasonal, recreational, or occasional use** if they are used or intended for use only in certain seasons, for weekends, or other occasional use throughout the year. Seasonal units include those used for summer or winter sports or recreation, such as beach cottages and hunting cabins. Seasonal units also may include quarters for such workers as herders and loggers. Interval ownership units, sometimes called shared-ownership or time-sharing condominiums, also are included in this category.

The **homeowner vacancy rate** is the proportion of the homeowner housing inventory that is vacant for sale. It is computed by dividing the number of vacant units for sale only by the sum of the owner-occupied units and vacant units that are for sale only.

The **rental vacancy rate** is the proportion of the rental inventory that is vacant for rent. It is computed by dividing the number of vacant units for rent by the sum of the renter-occupied units and the number of vacant units for rent.

A housing unit is **owner occupied** if the owner or co-owner lives in the unit even if it is mortgaged or not fully paid for. The owner or co-owner must live in the unit and usually is Person 1 on the census questionnaire.

All occupied housing units that are not owner occupied, whether they are rented for cash rent or occupied without payment of cash rent, are classified as **renter occupied**.

Average Household Size of Owner-Occupied Units is a measure obtained by dividing the number of people living in owner-occupied housing units by the number of owner-occupied housing units.

Average Household Size of Renter-Occupied Units is a measure obtained by dividing the number of people living in renter-occupied housing units by the number of renter-occupied housing units.